T0379801

The Statesman's Yearbook Companion

Palgrave Macmillan

The Statesman's Yearbook Companion

The Leaders, Events and Cities of the World

palgrave
macmillan

Palgrave Macmillan
Macmillan Publishers Ltd.
The Campus
London, UK

ISBN 978-1-349-95838-2   ISBN 978-1-349-95839-9 (eBook)
ISBN 978-1-349-95840-5 (print and electronic bundle)
https://doi.org/10.1057/978-1-349-95839-9

Library of Congress Control Number: 2019901218

This Palgrave Macmillan imprint is published by the registered company Springer Nature Limited.
The registered company address is: The Campus, 4 Crinan Street, London, N1 9XW, United Kingdom.

Reviews (Endorsements)

"... an invaluable tool for anyone who needs up-to-date, accurate and digestible accounts of the ever-changing world in which we live."

Dr Danny Rye, Liverpool Hope University

"For more than a century and a half *The Statesman's Yearbook* has provided scholars and practitioners with reliable and accurate political and economic information about the ever more complex world in which we live. Even in the age of the internet such a balanced and trustworthy resource remains essential."

Roger E. Kanet, University of Miami and University of Illinois at Urbana-Champaign (Retd)

"Precious source of solid and comprehensive information – an invaluable reminder that facts still matter."

Maria Lipman, Editor-in-Chief, *Counterpoint Journal*

"... an invaluable compendium for generations of researchers, writers and politicians to draw on."

Zak Cope, Academic Researcher

"This yearbook is an invaluable source of reliable and concise information in the world of international affairs where rapid change makes it almost impossible to keep track of who is who and who does what. The yearbook is sober and reliable, qualities that are all the more important when agendas shift with the current news in the media."

Professor Janne Haaland Matláry, Norwegian Military Staff College and the University of Oslo

"Over 1,000 pages of essential facts. Just as current but more reliable than the internet, I consult it almost daily."

Professor R.N. Lebow, King's College London

"This remains the preeminent and most comprehensive ready-reference source for current material about countries worldwide. Highly recommended."

Library Journal

"Perfect companion"

The Times

"This venerable reference work remains as indispensable as ever before. The information contained in this one volume is prodigious and if a researcher could only have one volume to hand, this would be it."

The Contemporary Review

"All you need to know about the population of various states and countries, officials, exports, constitutions, governments, diplomatic representatives, religion, finance, and basic histories."

The New York Times

"A masterpiece of pure quantification"

The Daily Telegraph, Victoria Glendinning's choice of Top Reference Book

"The book should be in every office which is concerned with world trade and indeed, in every school which produces the future traders. It is an essential tool of all global thinking."

Geographical Magazine

"*The Statesman's Yearbook* is the most convenient and reliable starting point for information on international affairs. Its coverage is unparalleled for a one-volume resource, and it has never let me down."

Senator George J. Mitchell

"A concise but comprehensive guide to world politics and economics. Reference at its best."

Simon Jenkins, *The Times*

"Over many years Macmillan has built up a deserved reputation for publishing reference books of the highest quality. *The Statesman's Yearbook* is one such example. Its pages are full of invaluable material about every country in the world. For someone like me who spends much of my time travelling, it is an invaluable treasure trove. I would warmly recommend it to other readers."

The Rt. Hon. Christopher F. Patten, CH, Chancellor of Oxford University

"In a volatile political world, this annual publication brings a sane voice to its presentation of the vital information every diplomat needs. And all in one volume. An essential purchase."

London Diplomat

"The SYB remains an indispensable, resource for reference librarians and others in need of quick, basic, accurate information."

American Reference Books Annual

"One of the top 20 best reference sources of the millennium."

Library Journal

"A must for any enquiring mind wishing to be well-informed on world facts and events." – review from user on www.amazon.com

Preface

In the middle of the nineteenth century, British Prime Minister Robert Peel initially put forward the idea of publishing "a handbook presenting in a compact shape a picture of the actual conditions, political and social, of the various states in the civilised world." The first edition of *The Statesman's Yearbook* was eventually published in 1864 and has appeared every year since then.

The Statesman's Yearbook Companion contains a wealth of information compiled since the turn of the century. We have profiles of more than 800 past presidents and prime ministers and over 400 profiles of major cities across the world. There are factsheets with key information on all of the countries, various chronologies, essays, and much more – filling a new volume as big as the Yearbook itself. Available in print for the first time, we believe it is a worthy companion to *The Statesman's Yearbook* family and an indispensable resource for researchers, students, and anyone with an interest in international affairs.

Enjoy exploring this invaluable new product!

Nicholas Heath-Brown
Publisher, *The Statesman's Yearbook*

About The Statesman's Yearbook

The first edition of *The Statesman's Yearbook* was inspired by the historian and essayist Thomas Carlyle. His proposal was enthusiastically supported by William Gladstone. Their vision for the book was an authoritative and accessible volume containing information essential for diplomats, politicians, and all those involved with international affairs. It quickly gained recognition as an indispensable reference tool and has been published annually since 1864. It was ranked by *Library Journal* as one of the top 20 best reference resources of the millennium.

Today, international affairs concern every one of us, and the scope of *The Statesman's Yearbook* has become correspondingly broader, with expanded coverage of history, politics, economics, trade, and infrastructure for each country, all thoroughly researched and verified by a dedicated editorial team.

In a world when opinion and propaganda can be overwhelming, *The Statesman's Yearbook* remains the first point of reference for reliable, concise information on any country in the world.

About the Editors

Frederick Martin (1864–1883)
Sir John Scott-Keltie (1883–1926)
Mortimer Epstein (1927–1946)
S. H. Steinberg (Sigfrid Henry Steinberg) (1946–1969)
John Paxton (1969–1990)
Brian Hunter (1990–1997)
Barry Turner (1997–2014)

Barry Turner was the seventh and final editor in the 154-year history of *The Statesman's Yearbook*. It is now maintained and updated by a dedicated editorial team in London.

Acknowledgments

Credits

Publisher: Nicholas Heath-Brown
Research Editor: Allan Cohen
Editorial Assistant: Eleanor Gaffney
Researchers: Daniel Smith, Richard German, Robert McGowan, Jill Fenner, Sara Hussain, Alexander Stilwell, Justine Foong, Ben Eastham, Thanh Tuan Chu, Noah Nzeribe, Victoria Nolte, Hanna Szymborska, Sharita Oomeer, James Wilson

The Statesman's Yearbook History

1849 In about 1849, Sir Robert Peel comments on the need for a good reference book on countries and states.

1855 Frederick Martin comes to England and is employed by Thomas Carlyle to work on his biography of Frederick the Great.

1860 It is believed that Carlyle and Gladstone, the then Chancellor of the Exchequer, introduce Martin to Alexander Macmillan. A proposal to publish a handbook of the "condition, political and social, of the various states of the civilised world" was accepted, and Martin began to work on it, possibly as early as 1860.

1862 A contract is signed between Alexander Macmillan and Frederick Martin at the office of Macmillan & Co. in Henrietta Street, London, for the publication of *The Statesman's Year-Book* (SYB).

1864 20th January, the first edition of the SYB is published. Priced at 8s 4d, it was 684 pages long.

1879 Alexander Macmillan secures an annual pension for Martin from Lord Beaconsfield (Disraeli), who was "struck by the usefulness" of the SYB.

1882 Frederick Martin signs an agreement with Macmillan, assigning the copyright in the SYB to the company.

1883 27th January, Frederick Martin dies, and the editorship passes to John Scott Keltie who had been working for Nature as a subeditor.

1890 John Scott Keltie reorganizes the SYB so that it starts with the British Empire.

1891 The first mention of electricity is made in the SYB.

1891 I. P. A. Renwick is taken on as the first assistant working on the SYB; his help is acknowledged in the 1892 edition.

1892 Richard Clay takes over the printing of the book from Eyre and Spottiswoode and continues to print it until 1993 (130th edition) – just over 100 years. Maps are introduced by J Scott Keltie for the first time, reflecting his interest in Geography. These include the density of population of the globe, the distribution of the British Empire, the partition of Africa, and the international frontiers on the Pamirs.

1906 The USA is given a section of its own.

1911 Mortimer Epstein is taken on as an assistant and is named from 1913 (50th edition).

1918 John Scott Keltie is knighted.

1919 The 56th edition is delayed in order to relate all the details of the peace terms following the end of the First World War.

1927 12th January, Scott Keltie dies. Although he held the editorship nominally until his death, his active involvement with the SYB had virtually ceased when he took on Mortimer Epstein. Epstein officially takes over as the third editor.

1943 During the war, it becomes difficult to obtain statistics from many countries, and yet the SYB continued to be published with as accurate information as possible.

1946 Sigfrid Henry Steinberg takes up the position of fourth editor of the SYB, following the death of Mortimer Epstein.

1947 The United Nations is introduced and given pride of place at the front of the book. The SYB sells out within a few weeks due to paper shortages following the war.

1962 The British Empire section becomes part of the Commonwealth of Nations, and the member countries are rearranged.

1964 John Paxton starts work for the SYB.

1965 Brian Hunter is taken on by S H Steinberg to contribute data to the SYB for all the communist countries except the USSR.

1969 John Paxton takes over as the fifth editor following the sudden death of S H Steinberg. New type face (Times New Roman) and page size are used.

1972 New features included a map of the Gulf States of the Middle East. Also, alterations to the Commonwealth section to read in alphabetical order rather than order of independence.

1975 Publication of the first *The Statesman's Year*-Book World Gazetteer edited by John Paxton as a companion to the SYB.

1978 Redesign and reorganization incorporating alphabetical listing of countries, reclassification of entries, and three special new maps for Belize and Guatemala, The Panama Canal, and World Desertification. The whole of the volume was reset, and photographic typesetting was used to produce characters in complete page form on film for conversion to printing plates – printed web-offset.

1990 John Paxton retires as editor, and Brian Hunter takes over from him as the sixth editor from the 128th edition.

1994 Small maps are introduced for each sovereign state to show its relative position and territorial extent within a continent, subcontinent, or ocean.

1995 Human Development Index (HDI) is added to the masthead of each country. This was the first edition to have the "Seagulls" logotype on the cover.

1996 The term "Historical" in the title is replaced by "Political and Economic," showing that the primary aim is to present a survey of the statistical, political, and economic date of the world. A topic finding list was also introduced.

1998 Barry Turner becomes the seventh editor of the SYB, following the retirement of Brian Hunter. Removal of the hyphen from the title, up to this date the title had been *The Statesman's Year-Book*. From now on, it becomes *The Statesman's Yearbook*. New features included six essays on topical issues written by leading political and academic figures. The International Organizations section was extended. A world map and flag illustration for the 192 countries of the world had been added. A database is introduced to facilitate the editorial processes and typesetting of the book.

2000 Millennium edition including internet usage figures for the first time. Publication of Centenary boxed set 1900 and 2000. SYB logo appears on the cover for the first time.

2000 Macmillan's new series, Statesman's Yearbook Country Profiles, appeared in the shops in January; these guides contain essential facts which addressed the needs of business travelers.

2006 The Statesman's Yearbook Online is launched, containing half a million more words than the printed book.

2007 Enlarged format to accommodate brief biographical profiles of all current leaders in the world, government histories, extended economic overviews, historical economic statistics, global economic overview, new half-page line maps for all 192 countries, and thematic essays on subjects of economic interest.

2009 The complete archive from 1864 is made available online as part of a site license at www.statesmansyearbook.com.

2011 Introduction of additional freely available material to website including Spotlight, Focus, City Profiles, and Essays.

2012 Comparison Tool is added to the website, making it possible to print content.

2013 *The Statesman's Yearbook 2014* (150th edition) is selected as a Core Collections Star Title in the USA.

2014 Barry Turner steps down as editor. The book is now managed, researched, and updated by a dedicated editorial team in London.

Contents

POLITICAL FIGUREHEADS' PROFILES

PALGRAVE TITLES PRESENTED BY THEIR AUTHORS

CHRONOLOGIES

TOPICAL ESSAYS (2007–16)

EDITED EXTRACTS OF PALGRAVE PUBLICATIONS

PALGRAVE TITLES PRESENTED BY THEIR AUTHORS

INFOGRAPHICS COMMEMORATING SIGNIFICANT HISTORICAL ANNIVERSARIES

INTERNATIONAL PAST LEADERS' PROFILES

Abacha, Sani (Nigeria)

Introduction

Abacha claimed the Nigerian presidency in Nov. 1993 following the army's refusal to acknowledge the results of the presidential election held earlier in the year. Though voicing a desire to reintroduce democracy to Nigeria, his tenure was marked by civil rights violations and the dismantling of democratic institutions. He died while in office.

Early Life

Sani Abacha was born on 20 Sep. 1943 in Kano. He entered the army at the age of 18 and received his military education in Nigeria, England and the United States. Having achieved the rank of brigadier, he was a leading figure in the military coup of 1983 led by Ibrahim Babangida that removed Alhaji Shehu Shagari from power. Babangida himself seized the presidency 2 years later and Abacha served as minister of defence in this government. Following the victory of the social democrat Moshood Abiola at the 1993 elections, the army declared the elections void and Abacha nominated himself president in Nov.

Career Peak

Abacha vowed to reintroduce civilian government by 1995 and provided economic aid to democratic organizations in Sierra Leone and Liberia. His domestic record was not impressive, however. He banned political gatherings and instigated media censorship. When Abiola reaffirmed his democratic claim to the presidency in June 1994 he was imprisoned. Members of the opposition National Democratic Coalition (NADECO) were arrested and in 1995 several environmental activists, including the writer Ken Saro-Wiwa, were executed for protests that resulted in the death of a pro-government chief.

Further civil rights violations followed. Having abolished several democratic institutions, Abacha postponed the elections scheduled for 1996. In 1997 the charging of Nobel Prize-winning exiled writer Wole Soyinka with treason was met with international outrage. Then Abacha promised elections for 1998, paving the way for his nomination as sole candidate for the presidency. He died suddenly in June 1998, reportedly of a heart attack.

Abbott, Tony (Australia)

Introduction

Tony Abbott became prime minister in Sept. 2013, leading his Liberal–National coalition to a decisive victory over the incumbent Labor government. A conservative on social issues, he won the election promising to strengthen the economy, limit the number of asylum seekers entering the country and revoke the recently introduced carbon tax.

Early Life

Anthony John 'Tony' Abbott was born in London, UK on 4 Nov. 1957 to Australian parents who returned to Sydney, Australia in 1960. He attended St Ignatius' College in the city's suburbs before reading economics and law at the University of Sydney and winning a Rhodes scholarship to study politics and philosophy at the University of Oxford in England. In 1984 he began training for the Catholic priesthood but left before ordination to become a journalist, writing for *The Bulletin* and *The Australian*, the biggest-selling national daily newspaper. He worked as press secretary to opposition leader Dr John Hewson from 1990–93 and was the first executive director of the anti-republican group, Australians for Constitutional Monarchy. In March 1994 he became Liberal MP for Warringah.

Following the election victory of the Liberal–National coalition in 1996, Abbott was appointed as a parliamentary secretary and in 1998 was promoted to minister of employment services, where he introduced the 'Work for the Dole' scheme to encourage job seekers to take voluntary placements in return for benefit entitlement. He set up the Australians for Honest Politics Trust in 1998, a fund to finance private lawsuits against the extreme right One Nation Party.

Abbott became employment minister and leader of the House of Representatives in 2001 prior to becoming minister for health and ageing in Oct. 2003. His controversial decision to block access to an abortion drug in 2006 resulted in parliament passing legislation to remove health ministers' power of veto in such matters.

After the Liberal–National defeat in the 2007 election, Abbott was touted as a likely successor to Howard but withdrew his candidature and entered Brendan Nelson's shadow cabinet as minister for families, community services and indigenous affairs. He continued to serve when the Liberal leadership passed to Malcolm Turnbull in Sept. 2008. In Nov. 2009 he resigned over Turnbull's support for the Rudd government's Emission Trading Scheme (ETS), which Abbott argued was financially unsound. A three-way leadership contest ensued between Abbott, Turnbull and Joe Hockey, with Abbott claiming a narrow victory over Turnbull and becoming leader on 1 Dec. 2009. On 3 Dec. the Liberal Party rejected the ETS bill in the Senate and in Feb. 2010 Abbott proposed a new policy that provided for a markedly less ambitious cut in emissions by 2020.

Other policy initiatives included extending parental leave and increasing corporate tax. After the Aug. 2010 general elections delivered a Labor minority government, Abbott was re-elected unopposed as leader of the Liberal Party. He opposed plans for a flood levy in the aftermath of the Queensland floods of 2010–11, proposed consultations on indigenous affairs in the Northern Territory and argued that the government had no mandate for its carbon tax policy. After campaigning on pledges to boost the economy, tighten border controls and abolish carbon tax, he led the Liberal–National coalition to a decisive victory in the Sept. 2013 general election, winning 88 seats in the House of Representatives to Labor's 57.

Career Peak

Abbott was sworn in on 18 Sept. 2013 and rapidly embarked on measures to repeal the carbon tax, as well as launching a controversial programme to turn back asylum seekers' boats to Indonesia. Facing the challenge of a slackening economy, he was expected to focus on boosting the private sector and reducing public spending and government regulation. He identified indigenous affairs as a priority while holding a conservative position on social issues, including same-sex marriage. Internationally, his tasks included easing tensions with Indonesia (further strained by revelations in Nov. 2013 that Australian intelligence services had tapped the telephone of Indonesia's president) and using Australia's 2014 presidency of the G20 group of major economies to achieve his stated aim of strengthening free trade.

His first year in office was marked by parliament's abolition of the carbon tax in July 2014, the strengthening of trade ties with Japan and South Korea, a free trade deal with China in the wake of the G20 summit hosted by Abbott in Brisbane in Nov. and Australia's military engagement in the US-led intervention in Iraq from mid-year against Islamic State jihadists. Meanwhile, tensions with Indonesia continued over his policy of turning back boats carrying asylum seekers.

© Springer Nature Limited 2019
Palgrave Macmillan (ed.), *The Statesman's Yearbook Companion*,
https://doi.org/10.1057/978-1-349-95839-9

Domestically, however, his unpopular first budget and reintroduction of knighthoods to Australia's honours system fuelled a plummeting voter approval rating. It also prompted a party rebellion in Feb. 2015 over his leadership, which he survived but with the support of only 60% of Liberal members of parliament.

On 14 Sept. 2015, Abbott lost a leadership spill motion proposed by the then minister of communications Malcolm Turnbull. Turnbull defeated Abbott in the subsequent ballot and took over first as leader of the Liberal Party and then as prime minister a day later after Abbott seceded the premiership.

Abdallah Abdereman, Ahmed (Comoros)

Introduction

Ahmed Abdallah Abdereman was head of the governing council in 1975 when he was overthrown in a coup, but returned to power as president from 1976–89. He viewed independence as a 'regrettable necessity'.

Early Life

Born on 12 June 1918, Abdallah was partly educated in Majunga, Madagascar. He held several posts in the Comoros' government from 1947 onwards. Following the Comoran declaration of independence in 1975, he was elected head of state by the national assembly.

Career Peak

The Abdallah government was overthrown by a coalition of six parties (the United National Front) on 3 Aug. 1975. Abdallah escaped to Nzwani, continuing his rule with a small armed contingent. In Sept., however, he was finally arrested. Three years later, the Soilihi government (established after the Aug. 1975 coup) was overturned by mercenary forces. Having helped to finance the coup Abdallah returned to Moroni from exile in Paris and was eventually named sole president.

Abdallah drafted a new constitution, giving each island limited self-rule but securing significant power for the presidency. It also provided for the restoration of Islam as the state religion. In 1982 all opposition political parties were banned, the culmination of several years of persecution of political opponents, especially those who had been in the Soilih camp.

The ongoing presence of the mercenary leader Bob Denard led to severe international criticism of the Abdallah regime. the Comoros' membership of the Organization of African Unity was suspended, diplomatic relations with Madagascar were severed and the UN threatened economic sanctions. However, Abdallah worked hard to maintain the diplomatic ties established by Soilih and there was a thawing in relations with France, particularly after he relaxed pressure over the question of Mahoré sovereignty and allowed French ships to use Comoran ports.

Grants from the European Economic Community and several Arab nations allowed for development of the Comoran infrastructure. However there was little significant upturn in the stagnant economy and funds that should have gone towards development went instead on staples such as rice. After a failed coup in 1981, opposition to Abdallah's rule was based predominantly abroad. With no rivals at home, he won over 99% of the vote in the 1984 presidential elections.

Protected by a Garde Presidentielle (PG, Presidential Guard) led by Denard and French and Belgian mercenaries, he ordered the arrest, killing and torture of dissidents. The regime was condemned by Amnesty International for human rights abuses and France threatened to cut off aid. The GP continued to wield its influence throughout the 1980s and Denard used his position for financial gain. Abdallah himself was criticized for his dominant role in Comoran business, often allowing personal interests to affect policy decisions.

Abdallah called a referendum in Nov. 1989, to approve constitutional amendments allowing him to stand for re-election in 1990. The polls were marked by violence and on the night of 26–27 Nov. Abdallah was shot dead. Two days later Denard and the GP seized control of the government.

Abdellahi, Sidi Mohamed Ould Cheikh (Mauritania)

Introduction

Sidi Abdellahi took office in April 2007 after winning the country's first fully-democratic multi-party elections. He stood as an independent candidate to replace the outgoing military junta. Abdellahi had previously served as minister of the economy from 1971–78. He was forced from office by a military coup in Aug. 2008.

Early Life

Abdellahi was born into an Arab marabout family in 1938 in Aleg, a town 250 km southeast of the capital, Nouakchott. After local schooling he completed his secondary education in Dakar, Senegal. He went on to study economics in Grenoble, France before returning to Mauritania in 1968.

Having worked as an economic strategy adviser to the government, Abdellahi joined Moktar Ould Daddah's administration in Sept. 1971. He held several posts including minister of state and minister of the economy, playing a key role in the nationalization of iron mining and creating a national currency. In 1974–75 he participated in negotiations for the Lomé Convention, a framework for co-operation between the African, Caribbean and Pacific Group of States and the EU.

Abdellahi was imprisoned in July 1978 following the overthrow of Ould Daddah. On his release in 1979, Abdellahi went to Kuwait to work as an adviser to the Kuwait Fund for Arab Economic Development from 1982–85. He returned to Mauritania in 1986 to serve in Ould Sid'Ahmed Taya's authoritarian government, first as minister of hydro-power and electricity and then as minister of fisheries. In 1987 Taya arrested him on allegations of corruption, prompting Abdellahi again to leave the country in 1989. This time he moved to Niger to advise the government on behalf of the Kuwait Fund until his return to Mauritania in 2003.

After a bloodless military coup ousted Taya in 2005, Abdellahi announced his intention to run for the presidency as an independent candidate. He defeated Ahmed Ould Daddah in a second round run-off on 25 March 2007 and took office on 19 April.

Career Peak

In April 2007 Mauritania regained a seat on the African Union and received an US$18 m. loan from the Islamic Development Bank. Abdellahi pledged to confront the country's ethnic inequalities, exacerbated by the unequal distribution of wealth from the discovery of oil off the Mauritanian coast in 2001.

In early 2008 rising food prices dented Abdallahi's popularity. He dismissed his cabinet and formed a new government that lacked broad support. In July 2008 the cabinet lost a parliamentary vote of no confidence, which was shortly followed by the resignation of 48 MPs from the ruling party. On 6 Aug. 2008 Abdallahi dismissed several prominent military figures. On the same day he was removed from his home by members of the Presidential Security wing and taken into army custody. The prime minister and interior ministry were also arrested. On 7 Aug. a High Council of State assumed executive power, with Gen. Abdel Aziz as its president. The new regime is expected to try Abdallahi on corruption charges. The coup received international condemnation.

Abdullah bin Abdulaziz Al-Saud (Saudi Arabia)

Introduction

King Abdullah administered Saudi Arabia on behalf of his half-brother, King Fahd bin Abdulaziz, between 1996 and Fahd's death on 1 Aug. 2005, following which he was named as successor. Abdullah maintained the strict Islamic code of governance associated with the Wahhabi Saudis while attempting to rein in the excesses of the princely class. He gained respect internationally for his efforts in the Middle East peace process but at times relations with the USA administration were strained. Abdullah died on 23 Jan. 2015.

Early Life

Prince Abdullah bin Abdulaziz was born in Riyadh in 1924, the only son of Fahda bint Asi bin Shurayim Shammar, the eighth wife of Abdulaziz bin Abdul Rahman Al-Saud, then Sultan of Nejd, who founded the Kingdom of Saudi Arabia in 1932. Abdulaziz, known as bin Saud by Europeans, reared his massive family in the Bedouin tradition, educating his sons at court and instilling them with Islamic and Arab virtues.

Abdullah's career began in 1952 when he was given the command of the Saudi National Guard by his half-brother, King Saud, the first son to succeed Abdulaziz. The National Guard comprised descendants of Abdulaziz's Bedouin warriors who took part in the expansion of Saudi power. On his accession in 1975, King Khalid bin Abdulaziz appointed Abdullah second deputy prime minister. In this post Abdullah became involved in foreign policy, visiting the USA in 1976 to meet President Gerald Ford. On the accession of King Fahd in 1982, Abdullah was designated crown prince and first deputy prime minister.

Career Peak

The succession in Saudi Arabia is decided by the Saudi princes, who number over 4,000 (some sources claim an estimated 8,000). A crown prince is traditionally selected by seniority and ability. Since the death of the kingdom's founder, Abdulaziz, in 1953, only his sons have been considered suitable for the succession. Abdullah, who had no full brothers, lacked a fraternal support base and relied on alliances forged with other factions within the family, most notably the sons of King Faisal, Prince Saud (foreign minister since 1975) and Prince Turki (head of Saudi intelligence).

Known as a devout Muslim, Abdullah had 14 sons and 20 daughters by six wives. His reputation for piety earned him support from religious leaders. Having assumed the position of regent in 1996, he was soon considered the *de facto* ruler of Saudi Arabia on account of King Fahd's recurrent illnesses and absences from the country. It was likely that Abdullah consulted and, to some extent, ruled with Fahd's Sudairi brothers, Sultan and Salman, the second deputy prime minister and the governor of Riyadh respectively.

Abdullah's foreign policy concentrated on improving relations within the Arab world and on encouraging the peace process in the Middle East (notably putting forward settlement proposals in 2002). He nevertheless showed support for militant Islamic groups such as Hizbollah and condemned Israeli military action in Lebanon and against the Palestinians. In March 2011 he sanctioned the deployment of Saudi troops to Bahrain in support of its fellow monarchy in response to Shia opposition demands for political reforms in the island kingdom.

Abdullah was less overtly pro-Western than King Fahd. The attacks on New York, USA, in Sept. 2001, although condemned, created serious tensions owing to the high proportion of Saudi nationals among the perpetrators. He had declined a visit to the USA on two occasions before the attacks, complaining that then President George W. Bush was 'uninformed' about the Middle East and the plight of the Palestinians. Nevertheless, he maintained that the USA would remain a firm ally, and Saudi Arabia has itself since become the target of several suspected al-Qaeda attacks.

In Dec. 2006 the UK government controversially suspended a fraud investigation into the 1980s al-Yamamah defence contract with Saudi Arabia, stating that diplomatic co-operation between the two countries was being put at risk (a decision subsequently confirmed as lawful by the British House of Lords in July 2008). In Nov. 2007 Pope Benedict XVI greeted Abdullah at the Vatican in the first such meeting between the head of the Roman Catholic Church and a Saudi monarch.

Internal liberalization was slow under Abdullah. He resisted Western calls for the abolition of Sharia law and the emancipation of women, stating that it is 'absurd to impose on an individual or a society rights that are alien to its beliefs or principles'. However, some key issues have been addressed. Female education, previously the preserve of the *ulema* (religious leaders), was placed under the jurisdiction of the ministry of education in 2002 and Abdullah supported the increase of female employment. The country's first ever elections in 2005, although with a limited franchise and

only for local councils, were a partial response to pressure for political change. A law to reform the judicial system was enacted in Oct. 2007 and provided for new specialized courts and the introduction of a supreme court as a final court of appeal. Plans were also announced to curb the powers of the religious police, which had come under increasing criticism over deaths in custody.

In Feb. 2009 Abdullah made extensive changes in government affecting top positions in the courts, the armed forces, the central bank, the health, education and information ministries, the religious police and the Consultative Council. He also appointed the country's first woman minister, Nora Al-Fayez, as deputy minister responsible for girls' education. In Sept. 2011 he announced that women would be eligible to stand and vote in local elections from 2015, and in Jan. 2013 he granted women seats on the Consultative Council for the first time. In 2011 he responded to political tensions generated by popular discontent across much of the Arab world by announcing a new welfare spending programme for the kingdom.

During Abdullah's latter years there was speculation about the issue of succession and internecine royal politics. In late 2006 he announced that a committee of senior princes would be formed to select the future crown prince and reduce the likelihood of family conflicts. The new committee would in theory have the power to remove a king if he was judged to be permanently incapacitated and would lead the country in a caretaker capacity until a successor was chosen. In Oct. 2011 the deputy prime minister and minister of interior, Prince Nayef bin Abdulaziz Al-Saud, was named as heir to the throne. However, he died in June 2012 and was succeeded by defence minister Prince Salman bin Abdulaziz Al-Saud.

In an unprecedented diplomatic step, the Saudi regime in Oct. 2013 renounced its right to a two-year term on the United Nations Security Council as a non-permanent member, citing the UN's failure to address the ongoing civil war in Syria or resolve the long-standing Israel–Palestine issue.

Abdullah, who had been suffering from poor health, died on 23 Jan. 2015. His half-brother, Salman bin Abdulaziz Al-Saud, was immediately sworn in as his successor.

Abdullah bin Hussein (Jordan)

Introduction

Abdullah I was the founder of the modern Hashemite Kingdom of Jordan. He assumed the throne of the Amirate of Transjordan in 1921 and took the title of King after his country achieved independence from Britain in 1946. Mentor to his grandson, Hussein bin Talal, Abdullah was assassinated in 1951.

Early Life

He was born in 1882, the second son of Hussein bin Ali (Amir of Makkah from 1908–16 and king of the Hejaz 1916–24). Under the Hashemite banner, Abdullah fought in the Arab revolt against Turkish occupation during the First World War. Following the collapse of the Ottoman Empire, Britain received a mandate over the Amirate of Transjordan (as well as the territory of Palestine and Kingdom of Iraq). Abdullah was made ruler (and his brother Faisal assumed the throne of Iraq).

Career Peak

Over the next 25 years he sought to develop centralized governmental authority over a mostly tribal and nomadic society. He promulgated the first constitution in 1928 and held elections for the first parliament in 1929. He also presided over a series of Anglo-Transjordanian treaties culminating in Britain's recognition of his country's full sovereign independence in March 1946. Transjordan became the Hashemite Kingdom of Jordan. The latter part of his reign witnessed the creation of the neighbouring Jewish State of Israel and the first Arab-Israeli War of 1948–49. Jordanian troops fought in the conflict in the defence of Jerusalem and parts of Palestine. After the war Abdullah concluded an armistice directly with Israel. On 20 July 1951 he was shot outside the Al-Aqsa Mosque in Jerusalem. The gunman was a Palestinian opposed to any dealings with Israel.

Abusahmain, Nouri (Libya)

Introduction

Nouri Abusahmain was elected Chairman of the General National Congress (GNC) on 25 June 2013, making him *de facto* head of state. His election came after Mohamed Magariaf resigned on 28 May 2013 following the ratification of a law prohibiting Gaddafi-era officials from holding office for 10 years after the law came into effect.

Early Life

Abusahmain was born in the western coastal town of Zuwarah into the Berber community, whose cultural identity was suppressed by the Gaddafi regime. He studied law and international relations in the UK in the 1970s and 1980s. He then worked in his home town's petrochemical industry. Following the Libyan uprising he was elected in 2012 to the GNC as the representative for Zuwarah.

In a vote for the GNC chairmanship by its 184 members on 25 June 2013, Abusahmain secured 96 votes against 80 for his opponent, Al-Sharif al-Wafi, with eight abstentions in a second round of polling. Although Abusahmain has maintained that he is independent, his success at the poll was widely accredited to the backing that he received from the Justice and Construction Party, the political arm of the Muslim Brotherhood.

Career Peak

Abusahmain's main tasks in office were to oversee the drafting and ratification of a new constitution and then to fix a date for a general election. A Constituent Assembly tasked with drafting the constitution was elected on 20 Feb. 2014. Abusahmain announced that general elections would be called as early as possible, with some commentators predicting polls as early as the end of 2014. However, with the Constituent Assembly needing to take account of an array of tribal, regional and ethnic fault lines, the transition to democracy was widely expected to take longer. Regional divisions within the country were further exacerbated in March by the dismissal of Ali Zeidan as prime minister by the GNC in a controversy over control of oil exports.

Elections were finally held on 25 June 2014, and Abusahmain subsequently stood down in his capacity as interim president when Aguila Salah Issa was elected president of the new House of Representatives and his successor by parliament on 5 Aug. 2014.

Adamkus, Valdas (Lithuania)

Introduction

At the age of 77 Valdas Adamkus was elected president of Lithuania for a second term in 2004, following the impeachment of Rolandas Paksas just 16 months after he took office. Once a blue-collar worker in a Chicago car plant, Adamkus returned to his native Lithuania in 1997 after 48 years in the USA and entered formal politics for the first time. Within a year he had become president.

Early Life

Valdas Adamkus was born in Kaunas on 3 Nov. 1926. His father, Ignas Adamkavičius, was a civil servant and served as a volunteer in battles for Lithuanian independence from Germany (achieved in Nov. 1918, although the capital, Vilnius, came under Polish control in 1920). Kaunas became the country's *de facto* capital in 1922. In the Second World War, when Lithuania was annexed by the USSR (July 1940), and then occupied by Nazi forces (July 1941), Adamkus joined a resistance movement and published an underground newspaper. When Lithuania was again invaded by the Red Army in 1944, he signed up to the National Defence Force and fought against Soviet rule at the battle of Seda in the west of the country. Subsequently Adamkus and his family were among around 60,000 Lithuanians who managed to flee to Germany, where they were liberated by the Western Allies. After graduation from a Lithuanian school in Germany, Adamkus entered the Faculty of Natural Science of the University of Munich. He also worked at the World YMCA organization where he focused on helping displaced Lithuanians. A keen sportsman, Adamkus competed at the Olympic Games of the Enslaved Nations in 1948 and won two gold medals.

Adamkus, along with his parents, brother and sister emigrated to the USA in 1949. He began work in a car factory and later took employment as a draughtsman for an engineering firm. In 1960 he graduated as a construction engineer from the Illinois Institute of Technology in Chicago. Throughout the 1950s and 1960s Adamkus organized demonstrations against the Soviet occupation of Lithuania and initiated numerous petitions. Between 1961–65 he was a member of the board of the Lithuanian Community in the USA. In the late 1960s he turned his attention to the environment, first heading a scientific research centre and later working as deputy administrator of the Environmental Protection Agency's mid-West office. His department's work on improving water quality and the environment in the Great Lakes was widely praised. From 1972 Adamkus became a regular visitor to Lithuania – he established links with Vilnius University and helped various Soviet institutions to build water purification facilities and set up environmental monitoring projects. When he resigned as administrator of the Environmental Protection Agency in June 1997 he received the agency's highest award for achievements in service and a letter of thanks from the US president, Bill Clinton.

Following the USSR's recognition of Lithuania's independence on 6 Sept. 1991, Adamkus became increasingly involved in Lithuanian politics. He spearheaded the electoral campaign of Stasys Lozoraitis (the ambassador to the USA) in the 1993 presidential elections, although Lozoraitis lost to the former communist Algirdas Brazauskas who had strong support in the poor, rural areas. Adamkus actively participated in the campaign leading up to the 1996 general election, helping to unite the centre-right Christian Democrats and the Homeland Union. They were guided to victory under Gediminas Vagnorius, who became prime minister. The following year Adamkus returned to Lithuania and was nominated by the Lithuanian Centre Union to represent the council of the northern city of Šiauliai. He stood in the presidential election as an independent candidate on 21 Dec. 1997, winning sufficient votes to contest a run-off with Artūras Paulauskas on 4 Jan. 1998.

Career Peak

Adamkus beat the former prosecutor general by a margin of less than 1% (14,256 votes), with his support coming mostly from the cities of Kaunas and Klaipėda and the west of the country. As president from 1998–2003 he laid the groundwork for Lithuania's membership of NATO and the European Union. Although popular with Lithuania's new middle class, he lost his 2003 bid for re-election to Rolandas Paksas by a narrow margin. However, the Paksas presidency was dogged by financial scandals and allegations of links with the Russian Mafia, resulting in his impeachment in April 2004 for divulging state secrets. In the presidential election of June 2004 Adamkus won a second term after narrowly defeating former prime minister Kazimiera Prunskienė in a run-off.

Most analysts predicted that Adamkus would continue to pursue a strongly pro-Western foreign policy with an emphasis on links with neighbouring Nordic states within the EU. In 2005 he declined the invitation to attend the Russian war anniversary celebrations in Moscow.

In May–June 2006 the coalition government led by the Social Democratic prime minister Algirdas Brazauskas collapsed. It was replaced by a new centre-left minority administration under Gediminas Kirkilas, who was approved by parliament as Adamkus' second nominee for the premiership in July. Following the Oct. 2008 parliamentary elections, Adamkus appointed Andrius Kubilius of the Homeland Union-Lithuanian Christian Democrats as prime minister of a new centre-right coalition government in Nov.

He chose not to stand again in the 2009 presidential elections and was succeeded by Dalia Grybauskaitė on 12 July 2009.

Adenauer, Konrad (Germany)

Introduction

Konrad Adenauer was the first Chancellor of the Federal Republic of Germany, holding the post from 1949–63. Mayor of Cologne before World

War II, he became Chancellor when he was 73. Having opposed the rise of Nazism, in the Cold War he turned his attention to the threat of Soviet expansion in Central Europe. A Christian Democrat, he saw the need for West Germany to align itself with the West and to this end pursued closer ties with the United States and worked to promote a united Europe. Though he was criticized for failing to promote the re-unification of the two Germanies, he succeeded in securing international recognition for West Germany, was integral to its economic success and assisted the nation in coming to terms with its recent past.

Early Life

Adenauer was born in Cologne on 5 Jan. 1876. He was the son of a civil servant and his family had a strong Catholic background. He graduated in Jurisprudence and Political Science, having studied at the Universities of Freiburg, Munich and Bonn. Active in Cologne's political life, he joined the Municipal Council in 1906, becoming Deputy Mayor 3 years later and Mayor in 1917. It was a position he held with distinction until 1933, when his opposition to Hitler led to his dismissal. He was also an active Centre Party member in the Provincial Diet and the Prussian State Council, of which he was President from 1920–33.

He was imprisoned by the Nazis in 1934 and again in 1944, when he was sent to a concentration camp. After World War II Adenauer was briefly restored to office in Cologne, only to be removed, this time by British officials. Adenauer was now able to devote all his energy to the formation of the new Christian Democratic Union, a political party established by Protestants and Catholics to oppose Nazism and promote economic growth in a devastated Germany. In 1946 Adenauer was elected CDU chairman in the British zone of occupation and soon after became its President.

Career Peak

After the Allies agreed a federal style government for West Germany, the CDU formed a coalition with the Christian Social Union (CSU) and won enough votes to form the government. In Sept. 1949 Adenauer was elected Chancellor by one parliamentary vote. He quickly set about the task of defining West Germany's role on the international scene and, though a pragmatist, his policies were guided by his Christian principles and a core belief in the freedoms and responsibilities of the individual.

In 1951 West Germany joined the Council of Europe and the European Coal and Steel Community (a precursor to the European Economic Community). Adenauer favoured a European Defence Community and when this project failed, West Germany joined NATO. The re-arming of the country put Germany in the front line of the Cold War but was opposed by those who still feared German aggression and by sections of the German population who were war-weary and guilt-ridden after World War II. In 1958 Adenauer made West Germany a founding member of the European Economic Community (EEC).

Adenauer's tenure as chancellor was the time of the German Economic Miracle, though responsibility for this lay more with Finance Minister and future Chancellor Ludwig Erhard than with Adenauer who concentrated on foreign affairs. Adenauer won convincing victories in the elections of 1953 and 1957 but, by this time in his 80s, he was aware that time was short. Erhard had become Vice Chancellor in 1957 but relations between the two men were uneasy, and there was conflict over the terms West Germany should accept to enter the EEC. Two years later Adenauer tried to block Erhard's path to the Chancellorship.

At the elections of 1961 Adenauer's popularity was at a low ebb. He was attacked for not having done more to oppose the building of the Berlin Wall, and there was growing concern about his age. He was forced to form a coalition government with the Free Democrat Party, who insisted that Adenauer must resign before the next general election. Beset by allegations of corruption, Adenauer lost a deal of credibility during the *Spiegel Affair* of 1962. The influential publication *Der Spiegel* had printed a number of articles criticising the government, including one which alleged that Minister of Defence, Franz Josef Strauss, had been drunk one night during the Cuban Missile Crisis. Soon afterwards the *Der Spiegel* offices were raided by the police. 11 people were arrested and the editor imprisoned for three and a half months on charges of endangering national security. Adenauer distanced himself but was later shown to have lied in parliament.

Adenauer's last major act as Chancellor was the culmination of his dream of closer relations with France. He met President de Gaulle in Paris in Jan. 1963 where they signed a Treaty of Friendship. A short while later he resigned.

Later Life

In retirement he wrote his biography and died on 20 April 1967, in Rhöndorf. Ludwig Erhard said of him, 'Germany's rebirth is indelibly linked with his name'.

Adulyadej, Bhumibol (Thailand)

Introduction

HM King Bhumibol Adulyadej (also known as Rama IX) enjoyed the longest reign of any Thai sovereign. He inherited a monarchy tarnished by the mysterious death of his predecessor and lacking a distinct role, having been forced to relinquish absolute power only 14 years previously. King Bhumibol re-established the monarchy as a central part of Thai society. He earned the respect of his people through his relative informality and by twice intervening in the political process to restore democracy.

Early Life

Prince Bhumibol Adulyadej was born on 5 Dec. 1927 at Cambridge, Massachusetts, where his father, Prince Mahidol, was at Harvard School of Public Health. The young prince was taken to Thailand for his primary schooling, but went to Switzerland for both secondary and university education. Bhumibol was accompanied by his elder brother, Ananda, who had succeeded to the throne in 1935 when he was a 10 year-old schoolboy. Ananda returned to Thailand in 1946 to take up his duties, but within weeks he was found shot dead in bed.

Career Peak

Bhumibol succeeded to the Thai throne on 9 July 1946 as result of his brother's violent and unexplained death. In the early years of his reign, the young sovereign had to define a new role as a constitutional monarch.

In 1950 Bhumibol married Sirikit, the daughter of Prince Chandaburi Suranath. The young couple tried to give the monarchy a more contemporary appeal, undertaking long programmes of public appearances and tours. Like so many Thai men, the King became a Buddhist monk for a short time. But he attracted publicity for his keen interest in jazz. Bhumibol founded his own jazz band and played on the public radio. He was an accomplished saxophonist, the composer of more than 40 pieces and played with Benny Goodman, Jack Teagarden and Stan Getz.

Bhumibol had won popularity by the time of his intervention in the political crisis of 1971–73. The imposition of military rule sparked student protests and later huge public demonstrations. Public dissent was ended only after a direct plea from the King, who was instrumental in forcing the leaders of the military government into exile. Bhumibol asked an academic to be interim premier to oversee the drafting of a democratic constitution.

The period of democracy was brief and Thailand, threatened by instability and the wars in neighbouring Indochina, suffered several coups. By 1988 a new modus vivendi had emerged: the military and parliament shared power with King Bhumibol acting as an intermediary between them. In 1992 popular unrest again brought the King into the political arena. King Bhumibol helped bring about the resignation of an unpopular army chief who was a leading member of the military junta. A new constitution restored civilian government.

The King's Golden Jubilee in 1996 was celebrated with genuine public affection, and on his 60th birthday he was proclaimed 'the Great' by the Prime Minister. In March and April 2010 the King received criticism for failing to speak out against the violent protests that erupted in central Bangkok between the government and pro-Thaksin red-shirt protesters. His silence was seen by some as an indication of the waning of his political influence and his increasing frailty after a 5 month period of hospitalization in late 2009.

On 22 May 2014 Bhumibol gave his approval to the military junta led by Prayuth Chan-ocha, who had overthrown the interim government installed following the impeachment of Prime Minister Yingluck Shinawatra.

Bhumibol died aged 88 in Oct. 2016. His son, the crown prince Vajiralongkorn, requested that his proclamation as king be delayed in order to prepare for the role. The president of the privy council, Prem Tinsulanonda, subsequently took over as interim regent, with Prince Vajiralongkorn eventually accepting the throne on 1 Dec. 2016.

Ahern, Bertie (Ireland)

Introduction

Bertie Ahern was Irish Prime Minister (*Taoiseach*) from 1997 to 2008, heading coalitions comprising his Fianna Fáil party, the Progressive Democrats and, following the 2007 elections, the Green Party. He was instrumental in brokering the 1998 Good Friday Agreement, the framework accord for peace in Northern Ireland. Staunchly pro-European, he has encouraged the expansion and closer unity of the EU. The second longest-serving *Taoiseach* since Ireland achieved independence, and the first since 1944 to be elected three times, Ahern oversaw a period of unprecedented prosperity and economic growth in Ireland. Forced out of office by investigations into his financial affairs, he remains an influential figure in Irish and European politics.

Early Life

Bartholomew Ahern was born on 12 Sept. 1951 in Dublin. After studying economics and computer science at University College Dublin and the London School of Economics, he entered the Irish parliament (the Dáil) in 1977 as the republican Fianna Fáil member for a Dublin seat. Two years later he joined the Dublin City Council, serving as lord mayor for a year in the late 1980s.

He first obtained government office in 1980 as a chief whip. Junior ministerial posts followed until 1987 when he was appointed minister for labour. In 1991 he took over the finance portfolio. In Nov. 1994, after 11 years as Fianna Fáil's deputy leader, Ahern was voted Albert Reynolds' successor. He led Fianna Fáil in opposition until 1997.

As Ireland's biggest party following the June 1997 elections, Ahern was prepared to form a coalition government with the Labour Party, but following last minute realignments he went into government with the Progressive Democrats.

Career Peak

Within a month of Ahern taking office the Irish Republican Army (IRA) renewed its ceasefire, and all-party peace talks resumed in Sept. These culminated in the Good Friday Agreement of April 1998. Amongst the agreement's key provisions were the creation of the Northern Irish assembly, North–South ministerial council and British–Irish Council. It also laid out guidelines for weapons decommissioning by paramilitary groups, although negotiations were to stall on several occasions over this issue. Ahern meanwhile acknowledged that ending paramilitary violence was only a first step in countering deep-rooted 'tribalism'.

Ahern's handling of the peace talks and Ireland's healthy economy maintained his popularity, although support fell in the Catholic community after his separation from his wife. Also, within a year of taking office, two of his long-term allies—former *Taoiseach* Charles Haughey and former minister Ray Burke—were involved in embarrassing funding scandals.

Ahern was a leading advocate for the EU. He oversaw the transition from the Irish pound to the euro in 2002 and expressed a wish that the UK would also adopt the new currency, thus facilitating commerce between the Republic of Ireland and the North. In Oct. 2002 he oversaw the endorsement via referendum of the Nice Treaty, allowing ten new countries to join the EU in 2004 (the treaty having been rejected in an earlier Irish referendum in 2001).

Ahern won another term of office when Fianna Fáil won the elections of May 2002. In Oct. 2002 the Northern Irish Assembly executive was suspended over allegations of IRA spying at the Northern Ireland Office. Direct rule from London was reimposed and shortly afterwards the IRA cut off its links with the international weapons decommissioning body. In May 2003 UK Prime Minister Blair postponed elections to the Northern Irish Assembly, claiming that Sinn Féin leader Gerry Adams' assurance that the IRA would not do anything to undermine the peace process did not provide a sufficient guarantee. Ahern refused to endorse Blair's position but restated his commitment to working with the UK government towards a lasting peace. Subsequently, in July 2005, the IRA declared formally that it was ending its armed campaign to pursue peaceful political dialogue—a move confirmed by the international decommissioning body in Sept. despite Unionist scepticism. In Oct. 2006 Ahern and Blair unveiled a new timetable for restoring government power-sharing in Northern Ireland between the Protestant and Catholic communities. The leaders of the Democratic Unionist Party and Sinn Féin subsequently reached an historic agreement to share power from 8 May 2007 in a devolved administration to replace direct rule by the British government.

In 2006 the Irish government became more unpopular as divisions emerged within the coalition and Ahern admitted to receiving several large loans from friends when he was finance minister in the 1990s. Nevertheless, Fianna Fáil remained the largest parliamentary party following elections in May 2007 (but without an overall majority) and in June Ahern formed a new coalition government with the Progressive Democrats and the Green Party. In Sept. 2007 Ahern narrowly survived a vote of no-confidence brought against him in the *Dáil* as the pressure on him owing to public investigations into his personal financial affairs intensified. In April 2008, in the wake of further revelations about financial irregularities, he announced that he would be standing down as prime minister and Fianna Fáil leader in May.

Later Life

In his resignation speech Ahern made explicit his intention to clear his name of the allegations of corruption that dogged his final years in office. He continues to represent his North Dublin constituency in the *Dáil*. In 2008 he was appointed to the World Economic Forum's Global Agenda Council on Negotiation and Conflict Resolution and became a board member for Co-operation Ireland, an anti-sectarian charity. He began writing a sports column in a national newspaper in Aug. 2009 and released his autobiography in Oct. 2009 but was criticized for claiming a tax break on his earnings.

Ahidjo, Ahmadou Babatoura (Cameroon)

Introduction

Ahmadou Babatoura Ahidjo was Cameroon's first president from 1960 until 1982.

Early Life

Ahmadou Babatoura Ahidjo was born on 24 Aug. 1924 in Garoua, northern Cameroon, to a Fulani village chief. From 1942–53 he worked as a radio operator in the French Colonial administration, and in 1947 was elected to the first territorial assembly. Re-elected in 1952, he became president of this consultative panel in 1957. From 1953–56 he also served in France as the Cameroon member of the French Union. In 1957 he was appointed vice premier and minister of the interior in Cameroon's government.

After the resignation in 1958 of the country's first premier, André-Marie Mbida, Ahidjo formed his own party, the Cameroonian Union (CNU), and was elected Mbida's successor. When French Cameroon won independence from France in 1960, he was sworn in as the nation's first president.

Career Peak

Following independence, Ahidjo oversaw unification with British Cameroon in 1961 to form the Federal Republic of Cameroon. In the following decade he faced rebellion from the Union of the Peoples of Cameroon, although by 1970 he had succeeded in quashing resistance. In 1972 he introduced an unpopular constitution that ended the independence of British Cameroon. In 1976 he banned all political parties other than the CNU. Although implementing authoritarian rule, Ahidjo established one of Africa's most stable countries, securing new terms in office in 1965, 1970, 1975 and 1980.

His economic policies brought about improvements in agriculture, education, healthcare and transport. In the 1970s the discovery of oil transformed the previously agrarian economy, paving the way for technological innovation and underpinning increased national savings.

On 6 Nov. 1982 Ahidjo resigned as president citing health reasons. He handed power to the prime minister, Paul Biya, though retained his position as president of the CNU.

Later Life

A growing rift between Ahidjo and Biya saw Ahidjo go into exile in France on 19 July 1983. In his absence, Biya accused Ahidjo of plotting a coup, sentencing him to death in Feb. 1984 (subsequently commuted to life imprisonment). Ahidjo never returned to Cameroon and died on 30 Nov. 1989 in Dakar, Senegal.

Ahmadinejad, Mahmoud (Iran)

Introduction

Mahmoud Ahmadinejad won the run-off in Iran's presidential election on 24 June 2005. The ultra-conservative former Revolutionary Guard and mayor of Tehran promised to tackle domestic poverty and corruption, and analysts expected an end to the fragile social reforms made under his predecessor, President Mohammad Khatami. In foreign policy he has hardened Iran's stance towards the West, particularly over its nuclear programme, and engaged in anti-Israeli rhetoric, which has heightened international tensions. Signs of internal dissension during his first term were reflected in his hotly disputed re-election in June 2009, which provoked waves of opposition protests and repressive government retaliation for the rest of the year and into 2010. He has since maintained his uncompromising position on Iran's nuclear development activities and sought to strengthen ties with left-leaning Latin American governments in Venezuela, Nicaragua, Cuba and Ecuador. However, in his second (and final term) of office he has overseen a further decline in the Iranian economy, aggravated by ongoing international sanctions, and has reportedly alienated Iran's Supreme Leader, Ayatollah Khamenei.

Early Life

The son of a blacksmith, Mahmoud Ahmadinejad was born in 1956 in the village of Aradan in northern Iran. The family moved to Tehran a year later. In 1976 he took up a place to study civil engineering at the Iran University of Science and Technology (IUST). As a conservative student, he was supportive of Ayatollah Khomeini's Islamic revolution in 1979. Some of the 52 Americans who were held hostage in the US embassy after the revolution allege that Ahmadinejad was among those who captured them, though he strongly denies the claim. He remained at the IUST until the late 1980s, taking a master's degree in civil engineering, followed by a PhD in traffic and transportation engineering and planning, and then winning a professorship.

Ahmadinejad was drawn into the long-running Iran–Iraq war in 1986, when he joined the Islamic Revolutionary Guards and fought on the Iraqi border near Kirkuk. When the war ended in 1988, he worked as an engineer in the local government offices of Maku and Khvoy in the province of West Azarbayejan. In 1993 he became governor of the northwestern province of Ardabil until he was ousted following the election of the reform-minded President Mohammad Khatami in 1997. Returning to Tehran, Ahmadinejad rejoined the IUST's civil engineering faculty, where he remained until May 2003.

Ahmadinejad was elected mayor of Tehran on 3 May 2003, and pursued conservative policies. He closed down some fast-food restaurants and banned an advertising campaign that featured a Western celebrity. His views were at odds with President Khatami, who barred him from attending cabinet meetings, a privilege normally accorded to mayors of the capital. With the backing of conservative groups, Ahmadinejad contested the June 2005 presidential elections. His campaign was aimed at the poor and disadvantaged, as well as religious hardliners. He emphasized his working-class upbringing and promised to redistribute the country's income from oil. In a run-off against the former president, Ali Akbar Hashemi Rafsanjani, on 24 June 2005, Ahmadinejad emerged victorious, with 63.4% of the vote, although there were complaints of voting irregularities.

Career Peak

On 3 Aug. Ahmadinejad received the formal approval of Ayatollah Khamenei, and he became president on 6 Aug. 2005. In his inaugural address, he called for unity and the building of a model state based on principles of 'modern, advanced, and strong Islamic government'. However, he quickly caused consternation both at home and abroad.

Within Iran, Ahmadinejad instituted a purge of various branches of government, state economic agencies and the diplomatic service, drawing accusations that he was exceeding his constitutional powers. By the end of 2006 there were signs of domestic opposition to his policies. In Dec. his supporters fared badly in elections to local councils and to the powerful Assembly of Experts. Iran's economic malaise under his management incurred parliamentary rebuke in Jan. 2007, reportedly supported by Khamenei, and in June 2007 his government introduced petrol rationing, provoking public protests. There was also increasing evidence in 2007 of an unpopular crackdown on civil liberties. However, in parliamentary elections in March–April 2008 (in which many pro-reform candidates were barred from standing) there was a strong showing by the president's supporters.

The June 2009 presidential election saw Ahmadinejad win 62.6% of the vote, ahead of his nearest rival Mir-Hossein Mousavi with 33.8%. However, the opposition challenged the official results and accused the government of election rigging, resulting in violent clashes between police and demonstrators. Opposition unrest continued over the following months and was met with a repressive backlash by security forces. The government, meanwhile, claimed that outside interference was responsible for fomenting the upheaval. In Dec. 2010 Ahmadinejad dismissed his foreign minister, Manouchehr Mottaki, considered a political rival within the Iranian leadership, and replaced him with Ali Akbar Salehi. However, his reported demand for the intelligence minister, Heidar Moslehi, to resign in April 2011 was overruled by Ayatollah Khamenei, fuelling speculation of a rift between them. In parliamentary elections in March–May 2012 to the Islamic Consultative Assembly, conservative candidates supporting Khamenei and opposing Ahmadinejad won the majority of seats.

On the international stage, Iran's resumption of uranium enrichment from Aug. 2005 intensified Western concerns over nuclear weapons proliferation. Ahmadinejad has maintained a belligerent stance on Iran's refusal to suspend enrichment, which has resulted in a series of punitive sanctions by the United Nations Security Council, the USA and the European Union. International suspicions were heightened in Sept. 2009 by the identification of a secret uranium enrichment plant (Fordo) near the city of Qom and by Iran's test-firing of missiles capable of reaching targets across the Middle East. Subsequent negotiations over the nuclear issue between Iran and the major Western powers have to date come to nothing as reports of an increasing enrichment capability at the Fordo facility have emanated from the International Atomic Energy Agency. Tensions were further exacerbated by US accusations in Oct. 2011 of Iranian complicity in an alleged plot to kill the Saudi ambassador to Washington and by the ransacking of the British embassy in Tehran by an Iranian crowd in Dec. that year, in response to which all Iranian diplomats were expelled from the UK. In Jan. 2012 Ahmadinejad's government threatened to block the shipping of oil exports through the Strait of Hormuz and warned its Arab Gulf neighbours not to back Western attempts to isolate Iran. Nevertheless, further punitive US and EU sanctions, targeting Iranian oil exports in particular, took effect in June and July that year.

Meanwhile, anti-Israeli speeches by Ahmadinejad and his denunciation of the Holocaust as a myth have continued to provoke international condemnation. In Sept. 2010, in his address to the UN General Assembly, he accused the US government of orchestrating the 11 Sept. 2001 suicide hijacking attacks to reverse its declining influence in the Middle East and to prop up Israel, prompting a walkout by Western diplomats. His remarks were labelled 'abhorrent and delusional'. In his UN address in Sept. 2012 he accused Israel of intimidating Iran with threats to attack its nuclear facilities.

Ahmadinejad was not eligible to stand again in presidential elections held in June 2013, which were won by Hassan Rouhani, a moderate cleric. On 3 Aug. 2013 Ahmadinejad stepped down as Rouhani took over the Iranian presidency. Ahmadinejad was subsequently appointed as a member of the Expediency Council, an advisory body for the Supreme Leader.

Later Life

In June 2016 it was reported that Ahmadinejad was planning to stand in the presidential election of May 2017. However, in Sept, 2016 Supreme Leader Ayatollah Ali Khamenei advised Ahmadinejad not to run for president. In April 2017 he registered to run but the *Guardian Council*, which vets candidates, rejected his nomination.

Ahmed, Abdullahi Yusuf (Somalia)

Introduction

Abdullahi Yusuf Ahmed was elected transitional president of Somalia in Oct. 2004. The transitional government began its return from exile in Kenya in June 2005, a step towards establishing the country's first functioning government since the overthrow of President Siad Barre in 1991. Following an Ethiopian-backed offensive by government forces against a rival Islamist administration at the end of 2006, he entered the capital, Mogadishu, for the first time as head of state in Jan. 2007. However, his authority over the country remained tenuous. Abdullahi resigned as president in Dec. 2008 following a bitter power struggle with Prime Minister Nur Hassan Hussein.

Early Life

Abdullahi Yusuf Ahmed was born on 15 Dec. 1934 in Galcacyo in the Mudug province of Italian Somalia. He studied in Italy and the Soviet Union and, following the country's independence in June 1960, joined the Somali National Army (SNA). He achieved the rank of colonel but refused to take part in the coup led by Siad Barre in Oct. 1969. Ahmed was jailed but released in the early 1970s and appointed manager of a state agency. He was reinstated as a commander in 1977 when the SNA attempted to 'liberate' the ethnically-Somali region of Ogaden in Ethiopia.

The following year, with the support of several members of his Majerteen clan, Ahmed staged an unsuccessful coup and fled to Kenya. Moving to Ethiopia in 1979, he formed the Somali Salvation Democratic Front (SSDF) to oppose Siad Barre. Ahmed became embroiled in arguments with the Ethiopian leader, Haile Mengistu, and was jailed, released only in 1991 when the dictator's regime fell.

Siad Barre was driven out of Mogadishu, the Somali capital, on 27 Jan. 1991 by the United Somali Congress militia. Somalia slid into anarchy, divided into a dozen regions controlled by warlords. Ahmed focused his political ambitions in Puntland and was elected president of the relatively peaceful province in July 1998. Having failed to extend his term of office, which expired on 1 July 2001, he fought for control of the country. In the election for the transitional presidency of Somalia, held in the Kenyan capital, Nairobi, on 10 Oct. 2004, he received 189 out of 268 votes.

Career Peak

Ahmed promised to rebuild his war-ravaged country and asked for international assistance. The transitional government began returning to Somalia in June 2005 but arguments broke out over its location, with Ahmed favouring Jowhar while other members supported a return to Mogadishu. The parliament met for the first time in Feb. 2006 at a compromise location, Baidoa in central Somalia.

The fragile authority of the transitional government was further undermined in mid-2006 by the rise of a rival Islamist administration whose militias seized control of Mogadishu and much of the south of the country from clan warlords who had held sway since the fall of Siad Barre. A political stand-off ensued between the Islamists and Ahmed's government, which turned to neighbouring Ethiopia to guarantee its security. In Dec. government troops backed by Ethiopian forces launched an offensive against the Islamist militias who retreated in Jan. 2007. Ahmed entered Mogadishu in late Dec. 2006 for the first time since taking office in 2004 to assume nominal authority over the country. However, despite the deployment of an African Union peacekeeping force from March 2007, fierce fighting between Islamist insurgents and Ethiopian-backed government forces ignited again throughout the year, particularly in Mogadishu, fuelling a refugee exodus and humanitarian crisis. Ahmed's strained relationship with Prime Minister Ali Muhammad Ghedi meanwhile resulted in the latter's resignation in Oct. 2007 and his replacement in Nov. by Nur Hassan Hussein. The president's relationship with the new prime minister was similarly turbulent and Ahmed resigned in Dec. 2008 after his attempt to sack Hussein was dismissed as unconstitutional by parliament.

Al Bakr, Ahmad (Iraq)

Introduction

Following the Arab Socialist Renaissance (Ba'ath) Party coup of 17 July 1968, Ahmad Al Bakr was the political leader of Iraq and commander-in-chief of the armed forces until his resignation in July 1979. He was also minister of defence from 1973–77.

Early Life

Al Bakr was born in Tikrit in 1914. He pursued a military career initially, serving in the army until 1958 when he was forced to retire for revolutionary activities as a member of the Ba'ath. Following the Feb. 1963 coup against Gen. Qassim, Al Bakr served briefly as Prime Minister and then Vice-President until Jan. 1964.

Career Peak

He took power as President, Prime Minister, and as Chairman of the newly-established Revolutionary Command Council following the Ba'ath coup in July 1968, thereafter governing in concert with his increasingly influential deputy, Saddam Hussein. In 1969 he was promoted to the military rank of Field Marshal. With a militant, nationalist background in the Ba'ath Party, he maintained total opposition while in office to any compromise with Israel in the Middle East conflict. Good relations with the Soviet Union were meanwhile reinforced by a 15-year friendship treaty in 1972. Al Bakr also oversaw a short-lived improvement in relations with Iran by agreeing a treaty in 1975 to settle the longstanding disputes over territorial sovereignty of the Shatt al-Arab waterway and Iranian aid to Kurdish rebels in Iraq. The later Iraqi abrogation of this agreement by Saddam Hussein sparked the Iran–Iraq war in Sept. 1980. On 16 July 1979 Al Bakr announced his retirement, reportedly because of declining health having earlier suffered a heart attack. Power was transferred peacefully to Saddam Hussein.

Later Life

Al Bakr died on 4 Oct. 1982 in Baghdad.

Al-Ahmed Al-Jaber Al-Sabah, Jabar (Kuwait)

Introduction

Shaikh Jaber succeeded Sabah al-Salim al-Sabah as Amir of Kuwait on the latter's death on 31 Dec. 1977. External events dominated his reign, in particular the Iran–Iraq War of 1980–88 and the Iraqi invasion and ensuing Gulf War in 1990–91. Despite the existence of a partially elected parliamentary assembly, Jabar maintained the absolute authority of the monarchy. He held the post of Amir until his death in Jan. 2006.

Early Life

Shaikh Jaber was born in 1928, the eldest son of Shaikh Ahmed al-Jaber al-Sabah, under whose regency oil had first been discovered in Kuwait in the 1930s. His mother was a royal cousin. He was educated in local private schools and by palace tutors before his first public appointment in 1949 as Chief of Public Security in the oilfields of Ahmadi governate. In 1959 he became head of the Department of Finance and Economy, which was renamed the Ministry of Finance in 1962 following Kuwaiti independence the previous year. He was appointed Crown Prince in May 1966, serving also as Prime Minister until his accession as Amir in 1977.

Career Peak

In 1980 Shaikh Jaber decreed the restoration of the National Assembly that his predecessor had dissolved in 1976, briefly raising expectations of greater democratization. Subsequently, his regime was damaged by the 1982 collapse of the Souk el-Manakh unofficial stock market and the political violence associated with the Iran-Iraq conflict that spilled over into the skaikhdom. Among the terrorist attacks by militant Shia Muslims was an assassination attempt on the Amir in May 1985. In July 1986 Jaber dissolved the National Assembly, imposed stricter press censorship, and declared that he would rule by decree. Pro-democracy pressure led to fresh elections for a new National Council in June 1990, but less than 2 months later the country was occupied by Iraqi forces. The invasion placed Kuwait under direct foreign rule for the first time in its history. Although sovereignty was restored in Feb. 1991, following the Gulf War, the Amir was criticised for spending the period of occupation abroad and delaying his return to Kuwait after the war ended. The National Assembly was reconstituted, again with limited suffrage, in Oct. 1992, but Shaikh Jaber and the royal family remained in control. The Amir reportedly suffered a brain haemorrhage in Sept. 2001.

In July 2003, following elections to the National Assembly, the Amir appointed his brother, the former foreign minister, Shaikh Sabah al-Ahmed al-Jaber al-Sabah as prime minister. This was the first time since independence that the premiership had not been held by the heir to the throne. In a further step towards democratization, and following on from the Amir's 1999 decree on women's suffrage, the National Assembly passed legislation in May 2005 granting women the right to vote and to run for office beginning in 2007.

Shaikh Jabar al-Ahmed al-Jabar al-Sabah died in Jan. 2006 after an extended period of ill health. Kuwait declared 40 days of mourning. Crown prince Shaikh Saad al-Abdullah al-Salim al-Sabah was appointed by the cabinet to succeed him. However, 9 days later Kuwaiti parliament voted 65–0 to oust the new Amir on health grounds. He was replaced by his cousin, prime minister Shaikh Sabah.

Al-Assad, Hafez (Syria)

Introduction

Hafez al-Assad, soldier and Ba'athist politician, came to power in Syria in 1970 after staging a successful coup while serving as defence minister. Having become Prime Minister, he was then sworn in as President in March 1971. He was reappointed for a fifth 7-year presidential term in 1999 but died in June 2000 when he was succeeded by his son Bashar. Assad is credited with bringing political stability to Syria, albeit through repression, and increasing his country's influence in the Arab world.

Early Life

Born on 6 Oct. 1930 in Qardaha, Lattakia district, Assad belonged to the minority Alawi Islamic sect. As a student activist, he was active against French colonial rule. Independence came in 1946, the year he joined the Arab Socialist Renaissance (Ba'ath) Party. In 1952 Assad entered the Military Academy at Homs, graduating in 1955 as a fighter pilot. His later military training included a period in the former Soviet Union, with which he was to maintain close political and military links. During Syria's brief federation with Egypt (as the United Arab Republic from 1958–61) Assad served in the air force in Cairo. He was transferred to a civilian post following Syria's secession from the federation after a new government took power in a coup in Sept. 1961. With other officers, he formed an underground military committee that plotted the Ba'athist takeover in March 1963. Factional conflict within the Ba'ath Party led to a further coup in Feb. 1966 by nationalist and military elements (including Assad) against the progressive, mainly civilian politicians. As minister of defence and air force commander, Assad was unable to prevent Syria's territorial loss of the Golan Heights during the Arab-Israeli Six-Day War of June 1967. Implacable hostility to Israel defined his political career from that time.

Career Peak

On 12 Nov. 1970 Assad took full control in the fifth coup attempt in Syria in a decade, arresting his chief rival (and the effective leader) Salah al-Jadid, and other members of the government. Once in power, he launched his 'corrective movement' aimed at stemming corruption in government and bringing Syria back into the Arab political mainstream. He became Prime Minister and then, following a referendum, President in March 1971. In Aug. 1971 the Syrian regional command of the Ba'ath Party elected Assad as secretary-general. A new constitution in 1973 confirmed the Ba'ath Party as 'the leading party in the state and society'. It also became the dominant force within the National Progressive Front, a broad umbrella grouping of the country's legal parties, formed in 1972.

With Soviet assistance, Assad sought to strengthen the Syrian military. He also courted wider domestic support by promoting economic development (under state control), land reform measures and the expansion of education. He would not, however, tolerate any challenge to his rule. Political and religious opposition, principally from within the Sunni Muslim majority population, was suppressed — most obviously in his military crackdown against a rebellion by the outlawed Muslim Brotherhood in Hama in 1982, which resulted in a shattered city and thousands of deaths.

In 1983 Assad suffered a heart attack. His brother and rival, Rifaat, used troops under his control to try to seize power in the early months of 1984, but Assad recovered sufficiently to regain control. Although stripped of any power base, Rifaat retained his nominal position as a vice president until his dismissal and exile in 1998.

Assad's foreign policy was founded on Arab nationalism, independence from foreign (particularly Western) influences, and opposition to Israel. His relations with other Middle Eastern states varied, periodic disputes erupting with Egypt, Iraq, Jordan, Lebanon and the more conservative Arab governments. A surprise Syrian-Egyptian offensive against Israel in Oct. 1973 (to recover territories lost in 1967 and in support of the Palestinian cause) proved unsuccessful despite initial military successes. In 1982, when Israel invaded and occupied Lebanon, Syrian forces were again repulsed. Although throughout his presidency Assad declared his readiness to conclude a peace agreement with Israel, he maintained his demand right up to his death that all occupied Syrian territory be returned. He also resented President Sadat of Egypt, Palestinian leader Yasser Arafat and King Hussein of Jordan for abandoning the common Arab nationalist front by signing their own bilateral peace agreements with Israel.

Assad's military intervention in the Lebanese civil war in 1976 led eventually to Syrian hegemony over its neighbour (despite further clashes with Israeli forces). He also established close links with Iran following the 1979 Islamic Revolution, a stance condemned by some Arab regimes during the war between Iraq and Iran in the 1980s. His alliance with Iran was partly for reasons of longstanding rivalry with the Iraqi wing of the Ba'ath Party and personal enmity towards Iraq's President Saddam Hussein. Assad contributed Syrian troops to the US-led coalition that drove Iraqi forces out of Kuwait following Saddam's invasion and occupation in Aug. 1990. This co-operation led to better relations with Western governments which had previously imposed diplomatic and other sanctions and accused Syria of sponsoring terrorism.

Re-elected overwhelmingly as President in Feb. 1999 (and similarly returned in 1978, 1985 and 1992), Assad died of a heart attack on 10 June 2000 in Damascus.

Alemán Lacayo, Arnoldo (Nicaragua)

Introduction

A former mayor of Managua, Arnoldo Alemán Lacayo was president of Nicaragua from 1996–2000, representing the right-wing Alianza Liberal (Liberal Alliance; AL) party. An opponent of the Sandinistas, Alemán defeated Ortega to become president of Nicaragua from 1996–2000. Known as El Gordo ('The Fat Man'. for his physical and financial appetite, he was convicted on corruption and theft charges in 2003.

Early Life

Born on 23 Jan. 1946, Alemán studied law at the Universidad Nacional Autónoma de Nicaragua in Managua, graduating in 1967. In 1986 while he was president of the National Association of Coffee Producers in Managua, he was imprisoned by the Sandinista government for counter-revolutionary activity. On his release he was banned from leaving the country for 3 years and put under surveillance.

Alemán was mayor of Managua between 1990–96 when he attempted to renovate the city using international aid, although results were limited. Much of the city centre destroyed in the 1972 earthquake had not been rebuilt. Alemán also ordered many of the murals depicting the revolution on public buildings to be painted over. During this time Alemán became involved with the conservative Partido Liberal Constitucionalista (Constitutional Liberal Party; PLC). In Dec. 1994 he formed the AL to support his 1996 presidential campaign. The party is an alliance of various liberal parties including the Partido Liberal Nacionalista, led by Alemán. On 20 Oct. 1996 he stood for election along with 25 other candidates. His main rival was the Frente Sandinista de Liberación Nacional (Sandinista National Liberation Front; FSLN) leader Daniel Ortega Saavedra. Alemán won with 51% of votes to Ortega's 38%.

Career Peak

On his election Alemán pledged to fight poverty and unemployment and promote economic growth, familiar promises in a country that is currently the poorest in the Western hemisphere. The main obstacle was Nicaragua's enormous debt. In 1995 Nicaragua's per capita GDP was US\$390, while per capita debt equalled US\$2100. High inflation, which at one time reached four figures, was also a problem. Alemán's other aims were to boost agriculture, encourage small producers, return to private ownership property appropriated by the Sandinista Marxist regime and reform the complex bureaucracy left over from the same era. A programme agreed with the IMF in Feb. 1998 underlined Alemán's aim to implement free market policies. By 1999 inflation had dropped to 12%, but unemployment was up to 70% in some areas. Any improvements made by the Alemán government were set back by Hurricane Mitch. In Oct. 1998 the hurricane devastated Central America and the Caribbean. In Nicaragua alone 2,447 people were killed and 20% of the population were left homeless. 80% of crops were destroyed and the total damage was estimated at US\$1bn. Alemán came under severe criticism for his handling of the crisis, including delays in distributing foreign aid and his refusal to accept the help of Cuban doctors, claiming it would cause more chaos.

Alemán came under pressure to explain a large increase in his bank account whilst Mayor of Managua. In Jan. 2000, Alemán and Ortega profited from their respective parties' majority in the assembly to arrange a pact limiting other parties' chances for the 2000 municipal elections and protecting Alemán's and Ortega's personal interests (Ortega himself faced charges of sexual abuse of his stepdaughter). As a consequence, public support plummeted and Nicaragua failed to qualify for debt relief under the Heavily Indebted Poor Countries Initiative. In the Nov. 2000 municipal elections the FSLN won many key seats, including Managua. Despite winning in over 90 towns, the AL lost the major city of Granada to the Partido Conservador de Nicaragua, among others, underlining the general swing away from Alemán's populist government. In a close fought election in Nov. 2001 Alemán's vice president, PLC representative Enrique Bolaños Geyer, beat the FSLN candidate Ortega by 56·3% of votes to 42·3%.

Later Life

The congressional immunity that Alemán had enjoyed since 2000 was revoked in Sept. 2002 following an historic vote by Nicaragua's parliament. This paved the way for him to face long-standing accusations of corruption when in office and in Dec. 2002 he was formally charged with the theft of US\$100m. of state funds. The charges were levelled by his successor and former vice-president, Bolaños, who vowed to fight corruption when he took office in 2001. Alemán denied the charges but his assets were frozen. After a period of house-arrest owing to ill-health, he was convicted of electoral crimes, money-laundering, fraud and embezzlement in Dec. 2003, sentenced to 20 years and fined US\$10m.

Alfonsín, Raúl (Argentina)

Introduction

Raúl Ricardo Alfonsín was president of Argentina between 1983–89 representing the centrist Unión Civica Radical (Radical Civic Union; UCR). He was democratically elected after 7 years of military rule. Despite reforming the military and promoting human rights, Alfonsín exacerbated the precarious economic situation he had inherited.

Early Life

Alfonsín was born on 13 March 1927 in Chascomús, Buenos Aires province. After a military academy schooling, he studied law at the Universidad Nacional de La Plata, graduating in 1950. Following 10 years of work in regional politics, Alfonsín was elected to UCR president Arturo Umberto Illia's parliament in 1963. In 1966 a military coup deposed Illia and his team. In 1973 Alfonsín stood as the UCR candidate in the presidential elections, but was defeated by the Peronist Frente Justicialista de Liberación candidate Héctor Cámpora.

During the 'Dirty War' (1976–83), Alfonsín was a vocal critic of the repressive military regime. He wrote his book *La cuestión Argentina* in response to human rights abuses and cofounded the Asamblea Permanente por los Derechos Humanos (Permanent Assembly for Human Rights).

Career Peak

In the democratic presidential elections of 1983, the UCR's main rival was the Peronist Partido Justicialista (Justicialist Party; PJ). Alfonsín's campaign was aided when the PJ candidate for Buenos Aires, Herminio Iglesias, burnt a coffin wrapped in the UCR flag. Alfonsín won with 52% of votes compared to Italo Lúdes' 40%.

On his election Alfonsín pledged to uphold democracy and stabilize Argentina after decades of coup and counter coup. He was faced with a dire economy left over from 8 years of military rule. High inflation and national debt were coupled with military discontent and labour disputes. After negotiations with the IMF, Alfonsín introduced his Plan Austral in 1985 with limited success. Despite failing to resolve Argentina's economic problems, Alfonsín was instrumental in reforming the military and appeasing human rights supporters. In addition to cuts in the military budget and staffing, trials in 1985–86 resulted in the imprisonment of key military leaders responsible for human rights abuses during the 'Dirty War'. But the military forced Alfonsín to abandon trying lower ranked military and police officers.

By 1989 the economy was in a disastrous state. Amid severe recession and hyperinflation Alfonsín was forced to give way to incoming president Carlos Menem 5 months early.

Later Life

Alfonsín died on 31 March 2009.

Al-Gaddafi, Muammar Abu Minyar (Libya)

Introduction

Muammar Gaddafi took power in a military coup against the monarchy in 1969, espousing radical Arab nationalism and Islamic socialist policies. His revolutionary fervour frequently brought him into conflict with the Western powers, which held him responsible for acts of international terrorism. However, in the first decade of the twenty-first century there were improvements in diplomatic and business relations after Gaddafi settled the Lockerbie bombing claims and agreed to stop developing weapons of mass destruction. Domestic opposition to his rule grew, however, and in early 2011 a popular movement emerged calling for him to step down. In Aug. 2011 insurgents seized control of the capital and installed an interim administration. Gaddafi remained in hiding until Oct. 2011 when he was captured by National Transitional Council forces and killed.

Early Life

Born into a Bedouin family near Sirte in June 1942, Gaddafi's education was strongly religious and he remains a devout and austere Muslim. He was also influenced in his early life by the Arab nationalist ideology of President Nasser and the Egyptian revolution. In 1965 Gaddafi graduated from the Royal Libyan Military Academy in Benghazi. As he and other officers of like mind rose through the ranks, their radicalism was fuelled by the humiliating defeat of Arab forces by Israel in the Six Day War of 1967. Gaddafi and others in a Revolutionary Command Council (RCC) deposed King Idris on 1 Sept. 1969 in a bloodless coup.

Career Peak

The RCC, with Gaddafi as chairman, instigated a programme of revolutionary reform. British and US military bases in Libya were closed in 1970, foreign-owned oil companies were nationalized and extended welfare provision was funded from oil export revenues. Assuming increasingly dictatorial powers, Gaddafi pursued wider Arab unity, initiating a series of unsuccessful schemes for merging Libya with other Arab countries (including Egypt, Syria, Tunisia, Chad, Morocco and Algeria), while maintaining implacable opposition to Israel. His Islamic socialist ideology was published in *The Green Book*, and in 1977 he promulgated a new constitution. This established the Great Socialist People's Libyan Arab Jamahiriya, which vested power in the masses through the General People's Congress (GPC). In 1979 Gaddafi relinquished his formal posts in the administration but remained Libya's undisputed leader.

With a reputation in international circles for erratic and unpredictable moves, Gaddafi mobilized Libya's oil wealth in support of revolutionary and terrorist groups around the world, intervening militarily in neighbouring states, particularly Chad. Accusing Gaddafi of sponsoring terrorism, the USA and UK bombed Tripoli and Benghazi in April 1986 in a reprisal air operation. In 1992 United Nations sanctions were imposed on Libya to force the extradition of two Libyan nationals implicated in an aircraft bombing atrocity over Lockerbie in Scotland in Dec. 1988. Gaddafi eventually relented and in 1999 surrendered the two principal suspects for trial in the Netherlands. One of the accused was convicted and sentenced in 2001. In 2003 Libya signed an agreement to compensate families of the Lockerbie bombing victims. Once the Libyan leader formally took responsibility for the atrocity, the UN Security Council voted to lift sanctions. In March 2004 the UK prime minister, Tony Blair, met with Gaddafi following the latter's promise to abandon programmes to develop weapons of mass destruction and to allow weapons inspectors into Libya. Diplomatic links with the USA were restored in May 2006.

In 2006 his unpredictable regime again came under international scrutiny as Libyan courts upheld death sentences on six foreign medical workers charged controversially with infecting hundreds of Libyan children with AIDS. However, the sentences were later commuted to imprisonment before the detainees were freed in July 2007 following diplomatic intervention by the European Union.

Libya's international rehabilitation progressed further in 2008 as the country took over the 1 month rotating presidency of the UN Security Council in Jan. and the US Secretary of State made the highest-level US visit to Libya since 1953 in Sept. In Feb. 2009 Gaddafi was elected to chair of the African Union for the year and in June made his first state visit to Italy.

In Aug. 2009 Abdelbaset Ali al-Megrahi, a Libyan national convicted in 2001 for the Lockerbie bombing, was released from prison in Scotland on compassionate grounds (he was suffering from a seemingly terminal illness). However, the decision was denounced by the US government and his triumphal return to Libya provoked outrage among the families of the victims of the atrocity.

In Feb.–March 2011 an eruption of popular opposition to autocratic governments across the Arab world led to an uprising against Gaddafi's long-standing regime, particularly in the east of the country. Gaddafi mobilized his supporters to resist the insurrection, not only incurring international condemnation over the level of violence but also prompting an exodus of foreign workers from the country as the threat of civil war grew. In March the UN, with Arab League backing, authorized a no-fly zone over Libya and permitted air strikes if deemed necessary to protect civilians. In May the International Criminal Court issued an arrest warrant for Gaddafi in respect of 'widespread and systematic attacks' on civilians. In Aug. rebel forces took Tripoli. The rebel-led National Transitional Council became the de facto government, although Gaddafi remained at large and refused to cede power. In Sept. a fresh assault on Gaddafi's hometown of Sirte was launched. Gaddafi was found hiding in a drainage pipe by National Transitional Council troops on 20 Oct. and killed. Acting Prime Minister Mahmoud Jibril, who announced the death, said he had been killed in a crossfire between Gaddafi loyalists and fighters from the transitional authorities, although the exact circumstances were unclear. He died aged 69, having ruled Libya for 42 years.

Al-Hariri, Rafiq (Lebanon)

Introduction

A Sunni Muslim and billionaire businessman, Rafiq al-Hariri took office as prime minister for a second time in Oct. 2000, having previously served as premier and minister of finance from 1992–98. He has been credited with the rebuilding of Beirut during the 1990s. He resigned in 2004.

Early Life

Al-Hariri was born in Sidon on 1 Nov. 1944. Having graduated from the Arab University of Beirut, he emigrated to Saudi Arabia in 1965, to work as a teacher. He then became a successful entrepreneur, particularly in engineering and construction, with an international reputation. Using his wealth, he set up the Hariri Foundation, a philanthropic organization supporting social and educational development projects. His political career started in 1983–84 when he took part in conferences in Lausanne and Geneva in Switzerland aiming to end the conflict in Lebanon. In 1989 he was involved in the successful negotiations leading to the Taif Accord for national conciliation, which was voted into the constitution of the Lebanese second republic the following year.

Career Peak

In Oct. 1992 al-Hariri became prime minister following the first elections to the National Assembly (adapted to reflect the sectarian balance) since 1972. He made the rehabilitation of the country's infrastructure, particularly in Beirut, a government priority, implementing a multi-billion dollar reconstruction programme but incurring a high level of public debt at the same time. He continued in office following parliamentary elections in 1996, but stood down in Dec.1998 amid differences with President Lahoud and allegations of government corruption. Voter dissatisfaction with the government of his successor was reflected in the National Assembly elections of Aug.–Sept. 2000, and Hariri was reappointed prime minister on 23 Oct. 2000. However, he resigned on 20 Oct. 2004 following differences over the extension to President Lahoud's period in office. Al-Hariri was killed in a car bomb attack in Beirut on 14 Feb. 2005.

Al-Hasi, Omar (Libya)

Introduction

On 25 Aug. 2014 the Islamist-dominated former General National Congress (GNC) appointed Omar al-Hasi as prime minister. This direct challenge to the elected House of Representatives left Libya with two rival governments, with al-Hasi's administration unrecognized by the wider international community but in control of large swathes of the country.

Early Life

Omar al-Hasi was a lecturer of political science at the University of Benghazi before he entered politics. A candidate for the premiership at the intended election of 29 April 2014, which was postponed when gunman stormed parliament, he was defeated by Ahmed Maiteeq in the rescheduled vote on 5 May.

In the ensuing political deadlock and amid fighting for control of the capital, Tripoli, the outgoing GNC reconvened with the attendance of 94 politicians, the minimum required for a recall of parliament. It appointed al-Hasi as premier and mandated him to form a 'salvation government'.

Career Peak

Against a backdrop of questions over its legitimacy, al-Hasi's administration has lacked widespread recognition by the international community, which has favoured the democratically-elected government based in Tobruk. In Nov. 2014 al-Hasi argued for new elections, insisting that an administration led by himself and the GNC could restore stability. He warned the Tobruk-based government that any attempt on its part to assert control over the oil industry would escalate the political conflict and could force the break-up of the country.

Alia, Ramiz (Albania)

Introduction

Ramiz Alia was President of Albania between 1982–92 but it was not until 1985, when his mentor Enver Hoxha died and he became leader of the Party of Labour, that he assumed full power. Though Hoxha's chosen successor, he was a more pragmatic leader and pursued closer links with the outside world in an effort to halt Albania's ever-worsening economic decline. He re-established links with the USA, USSR and China and relaxed some of the most unpopular social and political restrictions. It was too little, however, to satisfy the growing demands for reform from within Albania and in 1992 his party was defeated at the first democratic elections in decades.

Early Life

Alia was born on 18 Oct. 1925 in Shkodër, Albania to a Muslim family who were originally from Kosovo. He was educated at a French school in Tirana. He joined the Albanian Communist Party (which became the Party of Labour in 1948) during World War II, and was active in its associated Army of National Liberation. Following the war he worked with the Party's youth movement and in 1949 was elected to the Party's Central Committee. He spent a year in the Soviet Union to receive training during the mid-1950s and returned to Albania to hold the post of Minister of Education between 1955–58. During this period he also became an alternate member of the Politburo and was called onto the Party's Secretariat where he was put in charge of the Propaganda and Agitation Department.

Under Hoxha, Alia was heavily involved in criticizing Yugoslavia, the Soviet Union and China before the respective breaks with these countries and also played a leading role in enforcing Hoxha's will upon the Albanian people. Following Hoxha's political manoeuvring in 1981 and 1982, during which Prime Minister Mehmet Shehu and a number of his supporters died, he was made head of Parliament. Hoxha remained as the Party of Labour's First Secretary, but he gradually moved away from the political scene and died in 1985. Alia replaced him as head of the Party and was the country's undisputed leader.

Career Peak

No longer shackled by Hoxha's disastrous insistence on isolation, Alia began to re-establish ties with foreign partners. By the late 1980s there was contact between Albania and China, diplomatic relations with West Germany were re-instated in 1987, with the Soviet Union in 1990 (though the country had officially opposed Gorbachev's move towards reform) and with the USA the following year. Relations with Italy and Greece were also improved. International economic aid was slow in coming because Hoxha's 1976 constitution prohibited the acceptance of outside help. However, the country did benefit economically following its move away from isolationism.

Albania's industrial base was short on technology but began to improve under Alia via foreign expertise and resources. Nonetheless goods and services often had to be obtained by barter. Some free-market mechanisms were introduced along with social reforms including greater freedom of movement,

relaxation in restrictions of religious practice and a brake on the activities of the feared secret police.

Calls for reform continued to grow louder. In late 1990 the government was forced to permit other political parties. In a free election in March 1991 Alia's party won convincingly and, though Alia lost his own seat, he was re-appointed President. The government collapsed in June and renamed itself the Socialist Party. Popular protests continued, a general strike was threatened and new elections were called for March 1992 in which the Socialists were defeated by a Democrat-led opposition. Alia subsequently resigned as president.

Later Life

In Sept. 1992 Alia and a number of former allies were arrested on charges of corruption and in 1994 he was sentenced to 9 years imprisonment. He was released during an amnesty but was re-arrested on different charges before fleeing to Sweden in early 1997. Charges against him were dropped in Oct. 1997 and he returned to Albania the following Dec. Alia died of lung problems on 6 Oct. 2011 aged 85.

Aliyev, Heydar (Azerbaijan)

Introduction

Heydar Aliyev was head of the Soviet Republic of Azerbaijan from 1969–82 and deputy prime minister of the USSR from 1982–87. After a high-profile Soviet career he emerged as an Azeri nationalist and in 1993 became president of independent Azerbaijan. Confronted by the restructuring problems of a former Soviet state, his tenure was overshadowed by conflict with the separatist Nagorno-Karabakh region. Aliyev encouraged a cult of personality, and was reluctant to give free reign to opposition parties. His son, Ilham, succeeded him in dynastic fashion in 2003 shortly before his death.

Early Life

Heydar Alirza oglu Aliyev was born in the autonomous state of Nakhichevan on 10 May 1923. Leaving school at 16, he studied architecture at the Azerbaijan State University. After a period in the local government of Nakhichevan and study at the Soviet Ministry of State Security Academy in Leningrad, he joined the KGB, becoming a general in 1960 and serving as chairman from 1967–69. Closely connected to Soviet General Secretary Leonid Brezhnev, he became first secretary of the Azerbaijan Communist Party and leader of the Republic from 1969–82. He then returned to Moscow where he won full membership of the Politburo and served as first deputy prime minister of the USSR until 1987. An opponent of Mikhail Gorbachev and his foreign minister, Eduard Shevardnadze, he left office citing ill health and the death of his wife, Zarife. After initial restrictions on his movement, he returned to Azerbaijan and was elected to the Nakhichevan legislature in 1990, becoming its chairman and effective leader of the autonomous state.

Amid deteriorating Soviet–Azerbaijani relations, Aliyev vociferously denounced the Soviet suppression of a pro-independence rally in Baku in 1990. Independent Azerbaijan was initially led by Ayaz Mutalibov, whose brief tenure was dominated by defeat and atrocities in Nagorno-Karabakh. Abulfaz Elchibey, the leader of the dissident Popular Front, became Azerbaijan's democratically elected president in June 1992. The country was in economic chaos and the government fared badly in the war with Nagorno-Karabakh, the breakaway region with a large ethnic Armenian population. Amid increasing social tension Elchibey went into exile and Aliyev was invited to Baku to mediate. Utilizing his popular image as a nationalist, he assumed the presidency in June 1993.

Career Peak

Aliyev was confirmed as president in the elections of Oct. 1993. He appointed as prime minister Col. Suret Huseynov, the Karabakh commander who had instigated the uprising against Elchibey. Huseynov was ejected in Oct. 1994 on grounds of plotting to usurp Aliyev. Fleeing to Russia, he was extradited and sentenced to life imprisonment in 1999 for a range of crimes including treason and gun-running.

Aliyev secured re-election in Oct. 1998 in elections criticized by foreign and domestic observers. Faced with restructuring the country's weak economy, he set about attracting Western investment and oversaw several large deals with oil companies eager to exploit Azerbaijan's reserves. The economy, however, remained vulnerable.

Russia brokered a peace deal between Aliyev's government and Nagorno-Karabakh in 1994 after the territory was effectively lost to Azeri control but further fighting subsequently broke out. Aliyev's relations with Russia were turbulent. In 1998 he accused the Russian government of destabilizing the Caucasus and of fuelling the Karabakh conflict by providing Armenia with weapons including missile systems.

Close relations with the US were built on assistance in energy projects such as the oil pipeline to Ceyhan on the Turkish coast. Aliyev courted Turkey, emphasizing cultural affinities and economic ties, despite revelations that he had supported the Kurdish PKK while leading Azerbaijan in the 1970s. The pipeline was agreed with Turkish Prime Minister Bülent Ecevit in Dec. 1999.

In 1999 Aliyev underwent major heart surgery, focusing attention on the selection of a successor. In April 2003 questions over his health and re-election aspirations revived after Aliyev collapsed at a military ceremony broadcast live on television. His son, Ilham, the head of the national oil company and deputy leader of the New Azerbaijan Party, was approved as prime minister by parliament on 4 Aug. 2003, despite a boycott by the New Equality Party, one of the principal opposition parties. A constitutional amendment passed in 2002 allowed the prime minister to assume the powers of the president in case of incapacity—a scenario made increasingly likely in view of the president's absence for medical treatment abroad. In Oct. Heydar Aliyev withdrew his candidacy, allowing Ilham to win the presidential elections. Ilham Aliyev took office on 31 Oct. 2003.

Heydar Aliyev died of heart disease on 12 Dec. 2003 in Cleveland, USA.

Al-Jaafari, Ibrahim (Iraq)

Introduction

When he was sworn in as interim prime minister on 3 May 2005, Ibrahim al-Jaafari became Iraq's first democratically elected leader. A Shia Muslim and a long-time member of the conservative al-Dawa party, al-Jaafari was an exile in Iran and the UK for 23 years, and he became a powerful and vocal critic of Saddam Hussein's regime. He has argued for a new international 'Marshall Plan' for Iraq and the broader Middle East: 'Marshall repaired the decaying infrastructure of Germany after 6 years of war and 12 years of Nazi rule. In Iraq we have had nearly 40 years of fascist rule and have been at war for half that time'. In April 2006 al-Jaafari was succeeded by Nouri al-Maliki.

Early Life

Ibrahim al-Ashaiqir al-Jaafari was born in Karbala, south of Baghdad, in 1947. He studied medicine at the University of Mosul, where he joined al-Dawa, a conservative Shia Muslim group. After graduating in 1974, al-Jaafari practised medicine while becoming actively involved in al-Dawa and its opposition to the secular politics of the ruling Ba'ath party. In 1980, the year after Saddam Hussein took control of the Ba'ath party and began a violent crackdown on the al-Dawa group, al-Jaafari fled to Iran. He remained there until 1989, but has denied allegations that he was closely linked to Iran's ruling clerics. He studied Shia theology at the holy city of Qom, and subsequently organized resistance against Saddam.

In the early 1980s, al-Dawa carried out several suicide bombings in Baghdad and there was speculation that al-Jaafari was behind an attempted assassination of the then Iraqi-allied Kuwaiti amir. However, he has denied involvement. Having moved to London in 1990, al-Jaafari became the al-Dawa spokesperson in the UK and a key activist in the broader anti-Saddam movement. Al-Dawa claimed responsibility for an assassination attempt on Saddam's eldest son, Uday, in 1996.

Following the US-led invasion of Iraq in March 2003 and the fall of Saddam, al-Jaafari returned to his homeland. In July 2003 he was selected as a member of the US-backed Iraqi Governing Council and was the first to take the rotating chairmanship (and interim presidency) a month later.

In June 2004, after the USA handed over sovereignty of Iraq to an interim administration led by Dr Ayad al-Alawi, al-Jaafari was selected to be one of the government's two vice-presidents. He later brought al-Dawa into a coalition of Shia parties known as the United Iraqi Alliance (UIA). The coalition was endorsed by Iranian-born Grand Ayatollah Ali al-Sistani, Iraq's most influential Shia cleric, and it won a majority (140 of the parliament's 275 seats) in the Iraqi elections of 30 Jan. 2005. When Ahmed Chalabi dropped out of the race to become the prime minister, al-Jaafari became the UIA's undisputed candidate. On 7 April 2005 a presidential council of Iraq's new president, Jalal Talabani and his deputies, Ghazi al-Yawer and Adil Abdel-Mahdi, appointed al-Jaafari prime minister of Iraq.

Career Peak

As prime minister al-Jaafari was at the heart of negotiations to form Iraq's government. Finally, on 28 April 2005, after lengthy arguments against a backdrop of sustained violence, he secured parliamentary approval for his list of ministers. The majority of the 36 cabinet jobs went to Shias (who form about 60% of the population), although several key positions were also offered to Kurds and Sunni Arabs—the country's two largest minority groups. Initially, al-Jaafari also served as the defence minister, although the position was ceded to Saadoun al-Duleimi (a Sunni) in May 2005.

The new administration faced many daunting challenges, the most pressing being the continuing insurgency and the prevention of full-scale civil war. 'I think 2 years will be more than enough to establish security in our country,' al-Jaafari told a news conference, adding that building up Iraq's own security forces, controlling its borders and pushing ahead with the political process would all play a part. The administration drafted a new constitution, although there were deep divisions over fundamental matters such as the role of Islam in Iraqi law and the extent of federalism before its approval in a national referendum in Oct. 2005. Al-Jaafari told the press that Islam should be the official religion of Iraq 'and one of the main sources for legislation' but glossed over his party's official position, which calls for the Islamization of Iraqi society, including the implementation of Sharia law.

Following elections in 2005 that re-instated Jalal Talabani as president, al-Jaafari was replaced by Nouri al-Maliki in April 2006.

Allawi, Iyad (Iraq)

Introduction

The British-trained neurologist and former Ba'ath party member Iyad Allawi returned to Iraq after the fall of Saddam Hussein's regime in April 2003. He was chosen by the Iraqi Governing Council to be the prime minister of the US-backed Iraq interim government from 1 July 2004—from the United States' handover of sovereignty—until national elections, scheduled for early 2005.

Early Life

Iyad Allawi was born in Baghdad in 1945 to a prominent Shia merchant family; his grandfather helped to negotiate Iraq's independence from Britain, and his father was an MP. He studied medicine at the University of Baghdad in the mid to late 1960s, and it was there that he first met Saddam Hussein. At this time, Allawi joined the leftist, secular Ba'ath party whose members had dominated Iraq's governing council since 1963, following a military coup that was led by Colonel Abd al-Salam Aref. Allawi moved to Beirut in 1971, and then travelled to Britain, where he continued to study medicine, specializing in neurology at the University of London. He became president of the Iraqi Student Union in Europe, and it has been alleged that he continued to serve the Ba'ath party until he resigned in 1975. The regime in Iraq dealt harshly with dissenters, and Allawi came under pressure from Saddam, by then deputy to president Ahmad Al-Bakr, to rejoin the Ba'ath party. Saddam is believed to have been behind a brutal attack on Allawi at his home near London in Jan. 1978. Allawi survived, but he was badly injured and spent many months in hospital. His recovery in 1979 and subsequent graduation with a PhD in medicine coincided with Saddam's ascension to the presidency in Iraq. Throughout the 1980s, as war raged between Iraq and neighbouring Iran, Allawi built up an opposition network, with the aim of overthrowing

Saddam. He travelled extensively in the Middle East, holding clandestine meetings with other exiled Iraqis, and cultivating links with disaffected soldiers who remained in Iraq.

In Dec. 1990, in the aftermath of the first Gulf War and Saddam's retreat from Kuwait, Allawi and Salih Omar Ali Al-Tikriti launched the Iraqi National Accord (INA) with the backing of the US Central Intelligence Agency (CIA) and the British intelligence agency (MI6), as well as the administrations of Jordan, Saudi Arabia and Turkey. Both Allawi and Ahmed Chalabi (married to Allawi's sister) were recruited by the CIA and provided them with intelligence. The INA developed a plot to topple Saddam in a military coup in 1996, but it ended in failure, when the supposedly CIA-backed generals failed to lead their tanks against Saddam. Saddam took revenge by executing many of the coup plotters, and by seizing land owned for centuries by Allawi's family. The INA remained active, however, and gradually secured access to policymakers in Washington and London. In 2002 he channelled the report claiming that Iraq could deploy its supposed weapons of mass destruction 'within 45 min' to MI6, a claim that formed part of the British government's 'September Dossier' that argued for an invasion of Iraq. After the fall of Saddam in April 2003, Allawi returned to Baghdad and joined the US-appointed Iraqi Governing Council (IGC), holding the organization's rotating presidency during Oct. 2003. In April 2004 Allawi resigned as head of the IGC security committee over concerns about the US bombing of the city of Fallujah.

Career Peak

Chosen by the IGC to be Iraq's interim prime minister following the United States' handover of sovereignty on 28 June 2004, Allawi spelled out his determination to improve the country's security situation and prepare for national elections early in 2005. He swiftly reintroduced capital punishment, although gave assurances that he would not interfere with the forthcoming trial of Saddam. Allawi's links with the CIA, his long exile and his former membership of the Ba'ath party stoked resentment among Iraqis, and many regard him as an 'American candidate'. His decision to suspend Al-Jazeera, the Arabic TV news service, for a month in Aug. 2004 and his attempts to eliminate the radical cleric Moqtada al-Sadr did little to increase his popularity.

Despite daily news of violence, insecurity and vastly reduced oil production in Iraq, Allawi painted a positive picture of his country in an address to the US House of Representatives in Sept. 2004. Allawi said his government now commanded 100,000 trained soldiers, militiamen and police, and claimed that 15 of Iraq's 18 provinces were sufficiently peaceful for immediate elections. In the remaining three, he said, there were only small numbers of insurgents.

Allawi stood for the premiership at the elections of Jan. 2005. However, his Iraqi List won only 40 seats while the Shia-dominated United Iraqi Alliance won 140 seats. In Feb. 2005 Allawi announced he was forming a new coalition to challenge the Shia alliance and in April his party joined the interim government of his successor, Ibrahim al-Jaafari. Later in the month Allawi survived an attempt on his life. He was formally succeeded by al-Jaafari on 3 May 2005.

Later Life

Despite the Iraqi List's representation in the newly formed government of 2006, Allawi did not take up a cabinet position and withdrew from mainstream Iraqi politics (in spite of his continued leadership of the coalition). In 2009, however, he founded the al-Iraqiya List—an alliance of nationalist, anti-sectarian parties—and subsequently won parliamentary elections in 2010, defeating his main rival Nouri al-Maliki's 'state of Law' coalition. Nonetheless, after months of negotiations between the main parties, it was decided that al-Maliki would remain prime minister.

In Sept. 2014 Allawi returned to public office as vice president of Iraq under newly elected president Fuad Masum. However, his term as vice-president ended in Aug. 2015 when the post was abolished at the suggestion of the al-Abadi led government.

democratically transform Chile from capitalism to democratic socialism. His efforts led Chile into economic chaos, resulting in a military coup led by General Augusto Pinochet Ugarte in which Allende lost his life.

Early Life

Allende was born in Valparaíso on 26 July 1908. The son of a lawyer and a solicitor he studied medicine between 1926–32 at the Universidad de Chile in Santiago where he was an active Marxist. In 1930 he was vice-president of the Chilean students' union. A year after receiving his degree, Allende was instrumental in the founding of the PS, an amalgam of six left-wing parties dedicated to Marxist-Leninist principles. In 1936 Allende was elected to the chamber of deputies representing Valparaíso and Quillota. In Pedro Aguirre Cerda's administration, he served as health minister from 1939–42. Allende was nominated Secretary General of the PS in 1942. In 1945 he was elected Senator for the southern provinces of Valdivia, Llanquihue, Chiloé, Aysén and Magallanes. From 1948–57 the PS split into two factions, the Partido Socialista de Chile and the Partido Socialista Popular, the latter led by Allende.

Allende first stood in presidential elections in 1952, receiving 5% of votes. Six years later with the PS reunified, he stood again as the Frante de Accion Popular candidate, a combination of the PS and the Partido Comunista. This time he came a close second to the right-wing Jorge Alessandri Rodríguez. In his third attempt at presidency in 1964, Allende received 35% of votes, being beaten by Partido Demócratica Cristiana representative (Christian Democrats; PDC) Eduardo Frei Montalva.

Career Peak

Backed by the Unidad Popular—an alliance of Socialists, Radicals and Communists set up in 1969— Allende stood for his fourth presidential elections in 1970. His two main rivals were the right-wing representative Alessandri, who gained 34.9%, and the PDC candidate, Radomiro Tomic, who gained 28%. Allende led with 36% of votes. His victory was sealed with the backing of the PDC, despite strong right-wing opposition and little PDC enthusiasm. On his election, Allende set about changing Chile from a capitalist into a socialist state, albeit with a basis of democracy. Nationalization was the priority. Foreign control was removed from finance and mining. US-owned companies were expelled without compensation. Chile's primary export, copper, was the first industry nationalized. Banks and other businesses followed. Allende then enacted a series of land reforms based on collectivization, expropriating many farms. Aiming to promote equality of wealth, Allende agreed to large wage increases.

The reforms gained popularity, and the Unidad Popular increased its standing in the 1971 municipal elections, winning 50% of votes, and in the 1973 constitutional elections, 45% of votes with an increased parliamentary representation. Allende's reforms were less popular with the middle classes. Economic problems started when heavy industries were affected by international boycotts. Land reforms slowed production, inflation increased and exports decreased as did foreign investment. Food shortages coupled with an inflation rate of 1000% led to violent clashes between government supporters and opponents. Right-wing and centrist opposition parties united with anti-government factions of the military relied on financial backing from the US government.

On 11 Sept. 1973 a military coup led by Pinochet deposed Allende. Armed forces attacked the La Moneda presidential palace and with Allende still inside, military aircraft bombed the presidential palace. Over 3,000 people were killed during the coup. Allende died, although there is controversy over whether he was killed or committed suicide. In July 2011 a scientific autopsy confirmed that he did commit suicide. Replaced by a military junta, Chile, thus far the longest surviving Latin American democracy, entered 17 years of dictatorship.

Allende Gossens, Salvador (Chile)

Introduction

Salvador Allende Gossens was president of Chile from 1970–73, representing the Partido Socialista de Chile (PS). During his 3 year term, Allende tried to

---

Al-Maliki, Nouri (Iraq)

Introduction

Nouri al-Maliki was appointed Iraq's prime minister designate in April 2006. He succeeded his fellow member of the conservative Shia Muslim al-Dawa group, Ibrahim al-Jaafari, who had been unable to curb the violent insurgency or create alliances with Sunni and Kurdish factions since elections in Dec. 2005. Al-Maliki, who once commanded Shia forces against Saddam Hussein's regime from exile in Syria, promised an inclusive government. Although his first administration struggled to achieve a lasting political consensus, levels of violence did subside and in Nov. 2008 parliament approved an agreement with the USA that all US troops leave the country by the end of 2011. Al-Maliki's State of Law coalition came second at elections in March 2010 but he remained in office and sought to construct a workable coalition that was eventually approved by parliament at the end of that year. Sectarian and ethnic divisions and frequent associated violence have nevertheless continued to undermine political and social stability in Iraq.

Early Life

Nouri Kamel al-Maliki was born in Hindiyah, southern Iraq in 1950. While studying Arabic at Baghdad University in the early 1970s he joined al-Dawa, which was opposed to the secularism of the ruling Ba'ath party. In 1980 he was forced into exile, initially in Iran and from 1990 in Syria.

Following the US-led invasion of Iraq in March 2003, al-Maliki returned home. In July 2003 he was selected as a member of the US-backed Interim Governing Council, serving on a committee formed to purge Saddam's Ba'athist allies. However, many Sunni Muslims resented what they saw as a Shia plot to deny them a role in post-Saddam Iraq. As a senior member of al-Dawa, al-Maliki worked to forge a coalition of Shia parties, called the United Iraqi Alliance (UIA), which won a majority in the elections to a Transitional National Assembly in Jan. 2005. Al-Maliki was the senior Shia Assembly member charged with drafting the new constitution and he resisted efforts by Sunnis to reduce the autonomy given to Kurds in the north and Shias in the south.

Attempts by Prime Minister al-Jaafari to form a broad-based coalition government to reflect the results of the permanent Assembly elections on 15 Dec. 2005 became deadlocked and he stepped down on 21 April 2006. Al-Maliki emerged as the UIA's premiership candidate and was sworn in 20 May 2006.

Career Peak

Calling for an end to sectarian divisions, al-Maliki announced a national reconciliation plan in June 2006, including a conditional amnesty for insurgents and intra-communal dialogue between political leaders, clerics, armed militias and civil society representatives. However, sectarian violence continued and Sunni opinion was further inflamed by the widely criticized conduct of Saddam Hussein's execution for crimes against humanity at the end of Dec. 2006. In Jan. 2007 President Bush announced that he would send 21,000 extra US troops to Iraq to reassert the authority of al-Maliki's government. Meanwhile, al-Maliki struggled to find a political consensus on divisive issues, an impasse aggravated by the withdrawal from the national unity government of radical Shia members, secular-leaning Iraqis and the main Sunni coalition group (who rejoined in July 2008).

In Dec. 2007 the UK military contingent in Iraq handed control of Basra province to Iraqi forces, which in March 2008 launched a crackdown on the radical Shia Mahdi Army militia. Also in March, Iranian President Mahmoud Ahmadinejad made an unprecedented two day visit to Iraq for talks with al-Maliki, who returned the visit in June. In Nov. 2008 Iraq's parliament approved a security pact under which all US troops would leave the country by the end of 2011.

On 1 Jan. 2009 the Iraqi government took control of Baghdad's fortified Green Zone from US forces and assumed authority over foreign troops in the country. British troops formally ended their combat mission in Iraq in April 2009 and in June the Iraqi government declared a holiday to mark National Sovereign Day as US combat troops completed their withdrawal from towns and cities. In Oct. 2011 the US government confirmed that all remaining US troops would be out of Iraq by the end of the year.

In Oct. 2009 al-Maliki announced the formation of a multiconfessional nationalist State of Law grouping to contest the forthcoming general election after a split in the broad Shia coalition that won the 2005 polls. Unexpectedly, his alliance was narrowly defeated at elections in March 2010 by the Iraqi National Movement of former prime minister Iyad Allawi, although al-Maliki challenged the result. He remained in office during the drawn-out process of negotiating a coalition, which was eventually concluded in Dec. that year when, having been reappointed in Nov. as premier,

he named a new cabinet which was approved by parliament. Sectarian tensions in the government and parliament nevertheless continued through 2011 and 2012, prompting the arrest on terrorism charges and subsequent flight abroad of the Sunni vice president, Tariq al-Hashemi (who was convicted and sentenced to death *in absentia*), and fuelling further violence across the country.

At the same time Iraq was not isolated from the wave of popular disaffection that swept across much of the Arab world from early 2011, and there were also increasing tensions between the central government and the administration of autonomous Iraqi Kurdistan over oil contracts with foreign companies and the distribution of revenues. Continuing anti-government discontent in 2013 among the Sunni minority heralded the worst sectarian violence since 2007, with nearly 8,000 Iraqis killed during the year.

In Oct. 2013 it was announced that further parliamentary elections would be held at the end of April 2014, in which al-Maliki would run for a third term of office. However, despite his State of Law coalition's victory at the elections, al-Maliki stepped down as prime minister in Sept., after facing increased pressure from opposition groups to resign amid accusations that he had effectively monopolized power. He was also criticized for aggressively pursuing a pro-Shia agenda—allegations that had been steadily compounded by Iraq's descent into Sunni–Shia sectarian violence at the hands of the jihadist Islamic State.

Later Life

Al-Maliki became one of Iraq's three new vice-presidents in Sept. 2014 after stepping down as prime minister, joining Usama al-Nujayfi and longtime rival Iyad Allawi who were concurrently appointed to the executive. However, his term as vice-president ended in Aug. 2015 when the post was abolished at the suggestion of the al-Abadi led government.

Al-Salim Al-Sabah, Abdullah (Kuwait)

Introduction

Abdullah al-Salim al-Sabah ruled from 1950–65, succeeding his cousin Ahmed al-Jaber al-Sabah. During Abdullah's reign, Kuwait achieved full independence from Britain and was transformed into a wealthy, oil-producing shaikhdom. He also oversaw the introduction of a new constitution and the inauguration of the first Parliament.

Early Life

Born in 1895, he was from the Salim (rather than the Jaber) line of the al-Sabah dynasty which has ruled Kuwait since the 1750s.

Career Peak

In domestic affairs, Abdullah made two significant policy decisions following his accession. The first was to distribute the revenues from the expanding oil industry sector more widely among the population as a whole. He inaugurated a programme of public works and built up comprehensive and subsidized social services, particularly education and health care. The second was to broaden political participation, albeit on a limited basis, in the form of a National Assembly. Under a new constitution drafted in 1962, this Assembly of 50 members was elected and inaugurated in early 1963.

In foreign relations, Abdullah oversaw Kuwait's transformation into a formally independent state in June 1961. He signed new letters of friendship with representatives of the UK Government, terminating earlier agreements dating from 1899 under which Kuwait had become a British protectorate. Shaikh Abdullah then took the title of Amir. Shortly afterwards, he called for British military assistance as the new state was threatened by an Iraqi claim to sovereignty over its territory. Iraq agreed to recognize Kuwait's independence in 1963, although the issue continued to simmer (culminating in the events of 1990–91).

Abdullah died on 24 Nov. 1965 and was succeeded by his brother, Sabah al-Salim al-Sabah, whose reign, until 1977 proved to be largely a continuation and consolidation of Abdullah's policies.

Al-Sammad, Saleh Ali (Yemen)

Introduction

Saleh Ali al-Sammad was sworn in as president of Yemen's Supreme Political Council in Aug. 2016. He was the leader of the Iranian-backed Houthi movement that in Sept. 2014 wrested control of the capital Sana'a from President Abd Rabbo Mansour Hadi's government. The international community does not recognize the authority of the Supreme Political Council. On 19 April 2018 he was killed in a drone strike.

Early Life

Saleh al-Sammad was born in 1979 in Yemen's northern Saada governorate. The Shia Houthi movement to which he belongs is an offshoot of Ansar Allah, a theological group founded in the 1990s. In Sept. 2014 the Houthis seized control of Sana'a and agreed to a UN-brokered deal to take part in a unity government. However, in Jan. 2015 they rejected proposals to divide the country into six regions and forced the resignation of President Hadi (which he later retracted). A month later they replaced his government with a presidential council and announced that the council would form a transitional administration. In Aug. 2016, after tens of thousands of Yemenis took to the streets of Sana'a to declare their support for the Houthis, al-Sammad announced the establishment of a ten-member presidential council to govern the capital and other parts of the country under its control. The decree led to the breakdown of UN-sponsored peace talks.

Career Peak

With different Yemeni factions serving as proxies for other regional powers, Saleh al-Sammad faced a military campaign to regain Sana'a by the Saudi-led coalition backing Aden-based President Hadi. By the end of 2017 the conflict had inflicted devastation on what was already the poorest country in the Middle East, but with little prospect of peace in an apparent stalemate. Saleh al-Sammad was killed in a Saudi-led drone air strike on 19 April 2018 according to Houthi officials.

Altankhuyag, Norov (Mongolia)

Introduction

Norov Altankhuyag became prime minister in Aug. 2012 after securing 72% support from parliament. His appointment ended weeks of political uncertainty after the Democratic Party failed to win the required seats at the June 2012 elections to form their own government. He left office in Nov. 2014.

Early Life

Norov Altankhuyag was born on 20 Jan. 1958 in Ulaangom, Uvs Province. After graduating in physics from the National University of Mongolia, he took a teaching position in 1981 at the mathematics and physics department of his *alma mater*.

In 1990 he was involved in anti-Communist protests and helped to establish the Social Democratic Party, holding key posts including general secretary. He was elected to the *Great Hural* (the national parliament) in 1996, firstly for the Social Democratic Party and then the Democratic Party. He served as minister of agriculture and industry from 1998–99 and as minister of finance from 2004–06.

Altankhuyag was elected Democratic Party leader on 30 Aug. 2008 after Tsakhiagiin Elbegdorj stood down in the aftermath of disputed elections. Altankhuyag also became first deputy prime minister in a coalition government headed by the Mongolian People's Revolutionary Party (MPRP). He served as acting prime minister for 1 day on 28 Oct. 2009 after the incumbent, Sanj Bayar, resigned as a result of ill health. Sukhbaataryn Batbold was sworn in as premier the following day.

At a parliamentary election in June 2012 the Democratic Party won 31 seats. After weeks of negotiations, it formed a coalition with the Justice Coalition, which had come third in the election. On 10 Aug. 2012 Altankhuyag was confirmed as premier at a parliamentary session.

Career Peak

Altankhuyag's principal challenge was to manage the country's vast natural resources and secure the confidence of foreign investors while maintaining his fragile coalition between its pro-market Democratic members and the nationalist MPRP wing. He was also confronted with widespread corruption and a disparity in wealth between urban and rural communities.

Faced by decreased foreign investment and a mounting economic crisis exacerbated by collapsing commodity prices, Altankhuyag was ousted from the premiership on 5 Nov. 2014 following a successful parliamentary vote of no-confidence. He was replaced by his deputy Dendevyn Terbishdagva, who took over on an interim basis.

Al-Yawer, Ghazi (Iraq)

Introduction

Appointed interim president of the Iraqi transitional government on 2 June 2004, Sheikh Ghazi al-Yawer has been portrayed as a liberal leader who can unite the country as it edges towards national elections and full independence. A Sunni Arab and a member of one of the country's largest and most respected tribes, which comprises both Sunni and Shia Muslims, he enjoys good relations with Iraq's Kurds. Al-Yawer's business acumen and strong links with neighbouring countries are thought to make up for his lack of political experience.

Early Life

Sheikh Ghazi al-Yawer was born in Mosul, northern Iraq in 1958. A Sunni Muslim, his grandfather was chief of the powerful and influential al-Shamma tribe. Al-Yawer attended primary school in Mosul and secondary school in Baghdad, before returning to his tribal homelands near the Syrian border. In the late 1970s, as Iraq lurched towards war with Iran under Saddam Hussein, al-Yawer moved with his family to Saudi Arabia and studied engineering at the Petroleum and Mineral University in Dhahran. He went on to take a master's degree at Georgetown University in Washington, D.C. in 1984. Returning to Saudi Arabia, al-Yawer worked as a civil engineer and later established a telecommunications company with his maternal uncle, Sheikh Muhsin. Although vehemently opposed to Saddam's Ba'athist regime, al-Yawer shied away from involvement with political opposition groups—heeding family advice that as a high representative of a tribe, his priority was to retain his tribe's integrity.

Joining a band of returning exiles after the fall of Saddam, al-Yawer arrived in Baghdad in May 2003, although his wife and four children remained in Riyadh, Saudi Arabia. Events unfolded swiftly and he took over as head of the US-appointed interim governing council (ICG) after the assassination of the previous chief Abdel-Zahraa Othman, better known as Izzedin Salim. He soon demonstrated an independent spirit, denouncing the coalition forces for what he described as their inability to tackle the worsening security situation in Iraq. He also criticized the violent attacks by militants on US forces. In the weeks running up to the handover of sovereignty by US forces on 30 June 2004, the experienced Iraqi politician Adnan al-Pachachi, a Sunni Muslim, was invited to take on the post of president of Iraq. He turned down the offer and al-Yawer, who was endorsed by a large number of the ICG's members, became the first Iraqi president since the demise of the monarchy in 1958 to reach the position competitively, without bloodshed and without holding a military rank.

Career Peak

In his first interview as interim president, al-Yawer said that he will focus on 'a complete national reconciliation' and that he is 'determined to build our democratic experiment and liberate our country from the shackles of occupation.' He also said he would seek the support of Iraq's neighbours to establish a stable government that would be beneficial to all sides. Confirming his independent views and commitment to democracy, al-Yawer came out against an American order that would ban the radical cleric, Moqtada al-Sadr, from taking part in Iraq's first democratic elections in Jan. 2005. He argued that it is better to get radicals to join the political process than leave them outside the tent.

Amin, Idi (Uganda)

Introduction

Idi Amin Dada Oumee was an army officer who served as President of Uganda between 1971 and 1979. He came to power following a coup in which he had overthrown his one-time ally, Milton Obote. Physically large and personally charismatic, Amin was welcomed by the Ugandan people and the world at large but his mismanagement of the country, the ferocious cruelty of his dictatorial regime and his involvement in numerous international outrages ensured his popularity did not last. He fled Uganda following a Tanzanian invasion in 1979.

Early Life

Amin's year of birth is believed to be 1925. He was born in Koboko into the Kakwa tribe in northwest Uganda and was a Muslim. His education in missionary schools was patchy and during his leadership he was unable to write and was only slightly better at reading. In 1943 he joined the King's African Rifles, an African regiment of the British army, serving in Somalia, Uganda and Kenya. He was stationed in Kenya during the Mau Mau uprising, where Amin endeared himself to the British authorities by his skill and enthusiasm. He was Uganda's light heavyweight boxing champion between 1951 and 1960.

Uganda was led to independence in 1962 by Milton Obote, a close ally of Amin who by that time was one of only two African soldiers of officer rank in the KAR. In 1966 Obote appointed Amin commander of both the army and the air force but relations soured between the two men over the ensuing years. Fearful after an unsuccessful attempt on his life, Obote put Amin under house arrest in 1970. In Jan. 1971 Obote was on a visit to Singapore when Amin, galvanizing his support within the armed forces, staged a successful coup.

Career Peak

The Ugandan population, disillusioned by the corruption of the Obote regime, was generally welcoming, as was the West which had become nervous of Obote's far left political sympathies. It was hoped that Amin would keep his promise to restore civilian government.

However, Amin was quick to demonstrate his ruthlessness and set about purging the army of members of the Acholi and Lango ethnic groups, thus ridding Obote of his largest body of support as well as well as doing little to alleviate the country's already chronic tribal tensions. Following Obote's failed counter coup, launched from Tanzania in 1972, Amin forged ahead with his systematic ethnic persecution, victimizing civilians as well as military personnel.

In addition, in 1972 he ordered the expulsion of those resident Asians who had not taken Ugandan citizenship. Crucially, this section of society controlled much of the country's commercial sector and was instrumental in the efficient running of the civil service. While Amin tapped into a strong seam of resentment against the Asian population within the African population, his policy was economically disastrous. International isolation resulted and Amin left the running of many businesses, a lot of which he nationalized, to the military and to political allies who took what they could before allowing the businesses to fold.

Urban life became dominated by the black market, corruption and crime. Amin continued to terrorize his opponents through his State Research Bureau and the Public Safety Unit and it is estimated that his regime accounted for 100,000–300,000 victims. On the international stage, he alienated the USA and the UK by publicly condemning both countries. He also turned his back on a once strong relationship with Israel, instead forging ties with the Soviet Union, Libya and the Palestinian Liberation Organization. He was also suspected of direct involvement in a number of international terrorist exploits, including the hi-jacking of an Air France plane filled with Israelis which culminated in an Israeli rescue mission that saw deaths on both sides.

In Oct. 1978, in an attempt to generate some popular support, he set about an ill-advised invasion of Tanzania to claim the region of Kagera Salient. The Ugandan forces were not suitably prepared or motivated and proved no match for the Tanzanian forces who entered Uganda and made their way to the capital, Kampala. Amin fled, first to Libya and then to Jeddah in Saudi Arabia, and was replaced by a coalition of former exiles in April 1979.

Later Life

In March 1998 it was reported that Amin had been banished from Jeddah and isolated in Makkah (Mecca) following allegations of his involvement in an arms shipment to northern Uganda. He died on 16 Aug. 2003 of multiple organ failure. President Yoweri Museveni vetoed his return to Uganda for burial.

Andreotti, Giulio (Italy)

Introduction

Giulio Andreotti presided over seven governments in four terms as prime minister between 1972 and 1992. His political career lasted almost five decades and he occupied several of the most important posts in the country. His reputation as a skilful statesman who was indispensable to the country suffered when in the early 1990s he was accused of dealing with the Mafia.

Early Life

The youngest of three children, Andreotti was born in Rome on 14 Jan. 1919. He read law at the University of Rome where he was president of the Catholic student's federation. His political career began in 1942 when he met Alcide De Gaspari and heard of his plans to set up a Christian Democrat party after the fall of the fascist regime. Andreotti became a willing protégé. When De Gaspari was made prime minister a few years later Andreotti was appointed under-secretary to his cabinet. The following year he was elected to the Chamber of Deputies as a Christian Democrat and retained a seat there after every election from 1948–87. He joined the cabinet as minister of the interior and went on to hold dozens of ministerial appointments. His success was attributed to his skill as a political operator.

Career Peak

Andreotti was prime minister for the first time in 1972, when his government lasted 4 months. He soon regained power and formed a second cabinet that remained in office until June 1973. In 1976 he again became prime minister, on this occasion as head of a Christian Democrat government that had won its majority with the tacit endorsement of the Communist Party. Having instigated this uneasy alliance, he succeeded in stemming an economic crisis that threatened to engulf the country.

From 1983–89 he was minister of foreign affairs under a Socialist administration led by Bettino Craxi. He was then restored to the premiership for the last time. His tenure ended in April 1992 after disappointing election results attributed to a number of high profile corruption scandals, several of which involved Andreotti.

Later Life

In 1993 the Senate voted to remove Andreotti's immunity from prosecution in order for him to stand trial on charges of complicity with the Mafia, including in the murder of a journalist in 1979. He denied the charges but was indicted in 1995. He was acquitted in 1999, but 3 years later the verdict was overturned and Andreotti was sentenced to 24 years imprisonment. Andreotti appealed against the decision. In July 2003 The Palermo Appeals Court acquitted him of separate charges concerning relations with the Mafia. He died on 6 May 2013 at the age of 94.

Andropov, Yuri (Russia)

Introduction

Yuri Andropov was general secretary of the Soviet Communist Party, and thus *de facto* head of state and government, from 1982 until 1984. Former head of the KGB, he achieved little of long-term effect during his tenure. Despite a reputation as a conservative, he oversaw the development of several reformers, most notably Mikhail Gorbachev.

Early Life

Yuri Vladimirovic Andropov was born on 15 June 1914 (30 May by the Orthodox calendar) in Nagutskoye, Russia. His father was officially described as a railway worker although he is widely held to have been a white collar station master. Andropov left school at 16 and held a series of jobs including film operator, telegraph operator and ferryman. He later undertook studies at a technical college and at Petrozavodsk University.

He joined the Young Communist League (Komsomol), becoming an organizer for the Yaroslav branch. In 1939 he became a member of the Communist Party and the following year he took over the leadership of Komsomol in the Karelo-Finnish Autonomous Republic (which had been recently ceded from Finland). During World War II he was active in the Russian underground movement.

He remained in the Karelo party apparatus until being called to Moscow in 1951 to work on the communist secretariat staff. Strongly associated with the Stalinist movement, he lost popularity after Stalin's death in 1953 and was transferred to Budapest to work in the Soviet embassy. He was ambassador from 1954 until 1957, during which time he was instrumental in the 1956 Soviet invasion to suppress the Hungarian uprising.

In 1957 he returned to Moscow and headed the department of liaison between Moscow and the other Eastern Bloc regimes. Advocating a split with Chinese communism, in 1967 Andropov was named head of the KGB where he won a reputation for the ruthless suppression of political opposition, including the sectioning on mental health grounds and the enforced exile of critics. In 1973 he won full membership of the Politburo.

In 1982 Andropov resigned from the KGB and, with Leonid Brezhnev's health declining, emerged as a leading contender (along with Brezhnev's favourite Konstantin Chernenko) to become general secretary. Brezhnev died in Nov. 1982 and Andropov was selected to succeed him.

Career Peak

As well as party general secretary, Andropov became chairman of the Presidium of the Supreme Soviet in June 1983 but his tenure was dogged by ill health. He had promised to increase the economic efficiency of the USSR but achieved little of lasting impact. In foreign policy he continued the war in Afghanistan which had begun in 1979. Relations with the US continued on a downward spiral as he attempted to block the deployment of US missiles in West Germany. In Sept. 1983 a major international diplomatic incident occurred when the USSR shot down a South Korean civilian jet which had strayed into Soviet military airspace, killing 269 people. Andropov made his last public appearance in Aug. 1983 and died on 9 Feb. 1984 from kidney failure.

Ansip, Andrus (Estonia)

Introduction

When Andrus Ansip was sworn in as prime minister of Estonia on 13 April 2005, he took charge of the country's 12th government since its independence in 1991. A right-leaning former investment banker who was mayor of the second largest city, Tartu, for 6 years, Ansip pledged to implement policies that would attract investment and strengthen Estonia's position as a dynamic, post-industrial economy. His coalition government retained power in parliamentary elections in March 2007 and March 2011. He stood down in March 2014. In Nov. 2014 he took up a position in the European Commission under its new president Jean-Claude Juncker.

Early Life

Ansip was born in Tartu in the Soviet Republic of Estonia (ESSR) on 1 Oct. 1956. He attended local schools and graduated from the University of Tartu with a diploma in chemistry in 1979. He remained at the historic university to undertake further academic study, and later joined the municipal Committee of the Estonian Communist Party (ECP), which had been led, since 1978, by Karl Vaino, a Russian-born Estonian. The ESSR experienced increased Russification and 'sovietization' in the early 1980s, in accordance with the policy of the Soviet leader, Leonid Brezhnev. By 1988 however, there was growing opposition to the communist leadership and, against a backdrop of gradual economic liberalization, Ansip joined Estkompexim, a 'joint-venture' specializing in the import and export of foodstuffs. He was head of Estkompexim's Tartu office during 1991, when, following the collapse of the USSR, Estonia was internationally recognized as an independent nation. The following year Ansip attended a business management course at the University of York in Toronto, Canada.

On his return to Estonia in 1993, Ansip entered the rapidly evolving banking and investment sector, serving as a member of the board of directors of Rahvapank (the People's Bank) until 1995 and then chairman of the board of Livonia Privatization. In 1997 he was chief executive officer of the investment fund, Fondiinvesteeringu Maakler AS, as well as chairman of the board of Radio Tartu. The following year he was elected Mayor of Tartu as a candidate of the centre-right Estonian Reform Party (Reform), established in 1994 by Siim Kallas, a former governor of Estonia's central bank. A popular mayor, Ansip was credited with attracting investment to the country's second city and overseeing developments such as the Baltic Defence College and a new biomedical research institute which capitalized on Tartu's long-standing reputation as an academic centre.

On 13 Sept. 2004, shortly after Estonia joined the EU and NATO, Ansip was nominated to replace Meelis Atonen as the minister of economic affairs and communications. Two months later, he became chairman of Reform, which had formed part of the Res Publica-led coalition government under Juhan Parts since March 2003. His appointment followed the departure of Reform's leader (and former prime minister), Siim Kallas, to Brussels to become an EU commissioner. When, in March 2005, the *Riigikogu* (parliament) passed a vote of no confidence in the country's justice minister over proposed anti-corruption measures, Parts resigned as prime minister. On 31 March 2005 the president, Arnold Rüütel, asked Ansip to form a new government. He succeeded in forging a coalition with the Estonian Centre Party (Kesk) and the Estonian Peoples' Union (Rahvaliit). Ansip was backed by 53 out of 101 members of the *Riigikogu*, and was inaugurated as prime minister on 13 April 2005.

Career Peak

Ansip confirmed Estonia's aspiration to adopt the single European currency. However, he acknowledged that it would be tough to fulfil the criterion of holding inflation to no more than 1.5% points above that of the three lowest-inflation EU countries, given that Estonia's economy was growing at that time at around 7% a year and its exports had risen by 20% in its first 12 months in the EU. He pledged to maintain the previous government's tax-cutting agenda, as well as increasing social welfare measures to bridge the gap between the relatively wealthy, young urban population and poorer rural citizens. He retained the premiership following legislative elections in March 2007, forming a coalition with Union of Pro Patria and Res Publica (IRL) and the Social Democratic Party. However, in May 2009 the government lost its parliamentary majority as Ansip dismissed the three Social Democratic ministers in a dispute over economic policy, replacing them in June with IRL members and continuing on a minority basis.

Despite a sharp economic contraction in the wake of the global financial crisis, Estonia fared better than its Baltic neighbours in the ensuing downturn. The government acted quickly to implement spending cuts and adjustments to stem the rise in the budget deficit, while earlier prudent management of the public finances provided a buffer of fiscal reserves, with no requirement for support from the International Monetary Fund. Estonia became the 17th country to adopt the euro in Jan. 2011.

In foreign affairs, Ansip signed a border treaty agreement with Russia in May 2005. However, Russia subsequently withdrew from the agreement in response to a preamble to the text referring to the Soviet occupation that

Moscow deemed unacceptable. Relations with Russia soured further in early 2007 when the Estonian parliament passed legislation banning monuments glorifying Soviet rule and the government approved the removal of a Soviet war memorial in Tallinn.

Ansip secured another term in office when Reform won the March 2011 parliamentary election and resumed its coalition with the IRL.

In March 2014, Ansip resigned as premier in order to enable a successor to lead his Reform Party into elections scheduled for 2015. He was succeeded by Taavi Rõivas, who at the age of 34 became the youngest government leader in the European Union. At the time of his resignation, Ansip was the longest-serving premier in the EU.

Later Life

Ansip joined the new European Commission on 1 Nov. 2014 as the vice-president responsible for the digital single market.

Ántáll, József (Hungary)

Introduction

József Ántáll served as Prime Minister of Hungary between 1990–93, following the fall of the communist regime. He did not become active on the political scene until the late 1980s, when anti-communist reform movements grew throughout Central and Eastern Europe. Having become President of the fledgling Hungarian Democratic Forum in 1989, a year later he became the country's first democratically elected leader for over 40 years.

Early Life

Ántáll was born on 8 April 1932 in Budapest. His father, also called József, gained recognition for his work as a government commissioner for refugees during World War II, and was credited with ensuring the survival of large numbers of Jews. The son obtained a degree in Humanities and Political Science in Budapest, and then worked as a librarian, historian and teacher. At the time of the 1956 uprising he was the chairman of a revolutionary committee and the following year he was arrested for his political activities and banned from teaching or publishing any material for the following 6 years.

Ántáll played little part on the Hungarian political scene in the ensuing decades. However, by the 1980s the regime of János Kádár was in decline and a drive towards reform was underway. A new party, the Hungarian Democratic Forum (MDF), was established in 1988 and advocated a course of nationalist conservatism. Ántáll became Chairman of the MDF in 1989 and in March of the following year led them to a comprehensive election victory, taking 43% of the vote. They were, however, unable to form a majority government and so Ántáll led a coalition that also included the Christian Democratic Peoples' Party and the Independent Smallholders' Party.

Career Peak

The government was thus right of centre. Under Ántáll's guidance it set about developing the market economy and instigated a major privatization programme. The MDF's vocal far right nationalist wing soon alienated many voters and the party suffered heavy losses at local elections after a few months, The party's economic policies were also difficult, with inflation, unemployment (up from 1.5% to 12.0% in the period 1990–93) and crime all rising sharply in the early 1990s. The broader achievements of Ántáll's tenure concern the establishment of institutions and structures necessary for a functioning democracy. He also controversially re-established the teaching of Roman Catholicism into the national curriculum, oversaw the phased removal of Soviet troops from Hungarian territory and pursued closer relations with the West.

He was soon criticized for his domineering style of leadership and he had a difficult relationship with the President, Árpád Göncz, of the rival Alliance of Free Democrats. However, he retained his role as MDF chairman in early 1993. Ántáll had been diagnosed as suffering from cancer in 1990 and on 12 Dec. 1993, while he was in Budapest, it took his life. He was succeeded by Peter Boross.

Anthony, Kenny (St Lucia)

Introduction

Dr Kenny Anthony returned to office as prime minister on 30 Nov. 2011, having previously served two consecutive terms from 1997 to 2006. After electoral defeat in Dec. 2006, he remained leader of the Saint Lucia Labour Party (SLP) in opposition before returning to power.

Early Life

Kenny Davis Anthony was born on 8 Jan. 1951. He studied law at the University of the West Indies before studying for a PhD at Birmingham University in the United Kingdom.

He joined the SLP on his return to St Lucia, serving as minister of education from 1980–81. A former consultant to the United Nations on its development programmes, Anthony was also a member of the Caribbean Community secretariat from 1995–97 and served as chairman of the Organisation of Eastern Caribbean States. He became SLP leader in 1996 and was sworn in as prime minister for the first time in May 1997.

In his first term Anthony was at the centre of a dispute with the USA and World Trade Organization over alleged preferential treatment for former colonial banana suppliers to the European Union. In Sept. 2002 tropical storm Lili hit the island, devastating the banana crop and exacerbating economic problems. The government sought to diversify the economy, with a focus on increasing investment in tourism. Anthony also oversaw extensive domestic infrastructure development, while education spending rose significantly.

However, he was criticized for St Lucia's high levels of borrowing, with the debt-to-GDP ratio standing at around 63% in 2005. Meanwhile, the crime rate remained stubbornly high, despite the passage of a new criminal code. In July 2003 parliament amended the constitution to replace the oath of allegiance to the British monarch with a pledge of loyalty to the St Lucian people (although Queen Elizabeth II remained head of state).

At the general election of 11 Dec. 2006, the SLP won only six seats against 11 for the United Workers Party, headed by Sir John Compton. Anthony nonetheless retained his own constituency and continued as leader of the SLP. Compton died in Sept. 2007 and was succeeded as prime minister by Stephenson King. During his time in opposition, Anthony visited Cuba, where he thanked the Cuban administration for its aid to St Lucia and other Caribbean nations. In the general election held in Nov. 2011 the SLP were returned to power, taking 11 of the available 17 seats.

Career Peak

With the economy in need of urgent attention, Anthony warned the island's population that 'difficult times lie ahead'. He also faced a strained relationship with Taiwan following St Lucia's establishment of diplomatic ties with China during his previous tenure.

Legislation criminalizing gang membership came into force in June 2014 with the aim of countering a growing threat from gang-associated violence on the island.

Anthony's third term came to an end in June 2016 following the SLP's defeat at parliamentary elections that month.

Aquino III, Benigno (Philippines)

Introduction

Benigno Simeon Cojuangco Aquino III was sworn in as president in June 2010 after a landslide victory at the election in May. He campaigned on a platform of tackling corruption and eradicating poverty. He is due to leave office on 30 June 2016 following the elections of 9 May 2016 in which he was ineligible to stand.

Early Life

Aquino, popularly known as Noynoy, was born on 8 Feb. 1960 in Manila into the influential Aquino political family. His father, Benigno Simeon 'Ninoy' Aquino, Jr, was a prominent opposition leader who was assassinated by Ferdinand Marcos' regime. His mother, Corazón Aquino, led a non-violent people's revolution following her husband's death that brought about an end to the Marcos dictatorship and secured her the presidency. Benigno Aquino III graduated in economics from Ateneo de Manila University in 1981 before joining his family in exile in the USA. On his father's death in 1983, he returned to the Philippines.

From 1983–98 Aquino worked in business for companies including Nike, Intra-Strata Assurance Corp., Best Security Agency Corporation and Central Azucarera Tarlac, an organization owned by the Cojuangco clan. In 1989 in an attempted coup led by Gregorio Honasan against his mother's administration Aquino narrowly escaped assassination.

Joining the Liberal Party in 1998, he was elected to the House of Representatives to represent the 2nd District of Tarlac, a seat he held until 2007. He served as deputy speaker of the House from Nov. 2004–Feb. 2006, resigning when he joined other Liberal leaders in calling for the resignation of President Macapagal-Arroyo at the height of the 'Hello Garci' vote-rigging scandal. On 17 March 2006 Aquino was appointed vice chairman of the Liberal Party. Constitutionally unable to seek a fourth term in the House of Representatives, he won a Senate seat in the May 2007 elections.

After the death of his mother in Aug. 2009, there was a swell of public support for Aquino to stand for the presidency. Announcing his candidacy on 9 Sept. 2009 his subsequent campaign used the colour yellow to evoke his mother's 'people power' movement. The front runner leading up to the election, Aquino went on to win with 42% of the vote.

Career Peak

On assuming office, Aquino announced the creation of an independent commission to investigate the alleged corruption of the Arroyo administration (which led to the former president's arrest in Oct. 2012) and appointed a new justice secretary, Leila de Lima, the former head of the commission on human rights. In education, he pushed for the extension of the basic education system from a 10 year programme to 12 years. He also came out in support of a controversial family planning bill which, despite strong opposition from the Catholic Church, was eventually approved by parliament in Dec. 2012 and by the Supreme Court in April 2014. Critics have nevertheless questioned Aquino's ability to introduce reforms that act against the interests of the Philippines' powerful clans, from which he himself comes.

In Oct. 2012 Aquino signed a framework agreement on peace and autonomy between the government and the Moro Islamic Liberation Front, the Muslim separatist movement operating in the Mindanao region, with the aim of ending years of armed conflict. A power-sharing accord was signed in Dec. 2013 and a peace deal was concluded in March 2014. However, in Sept. 2013 there were violent clashes between a faction of another militant group, the Moro National Liberation Front, and government forces in the southern city of Zamboanga. Further conflict between Muslim rebels and security forces in Mindanao was also reported in Jan. 2015.

At the international level, there have been territorial tensions with China since mid-2012 over a disputed area of the South China Sea, while in May 2013 a diplomatic clash similarly arose with Taiwan following the killing of a Taiwanese fisherman by Filipino coastguards in an area of sea claimed by both countries.

In May 2013 pro-Aquino candidates won the majority of congressional seats in mid-term elections. However, in Nov. that year the Supreme Court ruled that a widely misused government fund for development projects, known as the DAP, was unconstitutional, which has tainted Aquino's anti-corruption image and undermined his ability to pursue economic reforms.

In Nov. 2013 the central provinces of the Philippines were devastated by Typhoon Haiyan, which killed thousands of people and displaced around 4 m. more.

As the constitution prohibits presidents from serving consecutive terms, Aquino was barred from running at the May 2016 elections. He was replaced by the winner, Rodrigo Duterte, the following month.

Aquino, Corazon (Philippines)

Introduction

Maria Corazon (Cory) Conjuangco Aquino is attributed with restoring democracy in the Philippines. She was the country's first female president (1986–92). The wife of murdered dissident Benigno Aquino, she defeated Ferdinand Marcos after disputed elections.

Early Life

Corazon Aquino was born on 25 Jan. 1933 in Tarlac province, Luzon. After studying in Manila, Aquino left the Philippines with her family for the United States where she finished her education at Mt Saint Vincent College in New York, graduating with a degree in French and mathematics.

After returning to the Philippines to resume her academic career she met and married the politician, Benigno Aquino Jr. in 1954. Benigno Aquino, a Liberal party opponent to Ferdinand Marcos and ardent critic of Marcos' 'Oplan Sagitarius'—a plan to declare martial law in the capital. He was arrested in 1972 and exiled in 1980. Upon Benigno Aquino's return to the Philippines in 1983 he was assassinated at Manila International Airport.

When, in 1986, President Marcos announced a surprise election the opposition to the Marcos regime unified behind Cory Aquino. Former Senator Salvador Laurel of the UNIDO Party stood down as presidential candidate to run as Aquino's vice-presidential candidate.

Career Peak

After a bitterly contested election Marcos and Aquino each claimed victory. Both were inaugurated by their respective supporters. Marcos, after his being inaugurated at Malacañang Palace fled the country, leaving Aquino to take power.

On 25 March 1986 Aquino proclaimed a provisional constitution (the Freedom Constitution) and then appointed a commission to write a new constitution. This was ratified by referendum in Feb. 1987 and included the provision that the head of state is directly elected for a non-renewable 6-year term. Despite attempts to address government corruption, including long-established commercial monopolies, Aquino failed to implement fundamental economic change. Corruption remained endemic, support from the military wavered and communist groups were a constant threat. She was replaced in 1992 by her defence minister, Fidel Ramos. She died of cardio-respiratory arrest on 1 Aug. 2009, aged 76.

Arafat, Yasser (Palestinian Territories, Israel)

Introduction

Yasser Arafat has been synonymous with the Palestinian campaign for independent statehood since the 1960s. Variously labelled a terrorist, resistance fighter and statesman, he remained the dominant personality in the Palestine Liberation Organization (PLO) and the figurehead with whom successive Israeli leaders had to deal. In the aftermath of the 1993 Oslo agreements, he was elected President of the Palestinian Authority in Jan. 1996. However, after the renewed Palestinian intifada from Sept. 2000 and the uncompromising military response of the Israeli government, he was sidelined internationally and his leadership called into question. In March 2003 he agreed to create the post of prime minister, a move demanded by Israel and the US before the peace process could resume. The following month an internationally-brokered 'roadmap to peace', allowing for the eventual establishment of a Palestinian state, was published.

Early Life

Arafat was born in Aug. 1929, although the exact date and place of his birth are disputed. He is believed to have spent his childhood in Cairo, except for a 4 year period living with relatives in Jerusalem. Active in Palestinian student politics while studying at Faud University, Cairo, he trained and worked as an engineer in Egypt and Kuwait until 1965. In the late 1950s he was a co-founder of Al-Fatah, an underground nationalist movement that became the core of the PLO in the 1960s. In 1964 Arafat left Kuwait for Jordan from where he led Fatah's revolutionary activity.

Career Peak

In 1969 Arafat became the acknowledged, though not universally popular, chairman of a fractious PLO. In the early 1970s his hostility towards any compromise with Israel and refusal to acknowledge its right to exist was reflected in international terrorism by the PLO, as well as violent conflict with King Hussein's Jordan, from where the PLO was expelled. He then adopted a strategy of militancy coupled with diplomacy. While maintaining his demand for Palestinian statehood, he gained recognition for the PLO at the United Nations in 1974. In 1982 the PLO was forced out of Lebanon by the Israeli invasion and Arafat's authority was weakened by disaffection. Despite the outbreak of the first Palestinian intifada in 1987, he implicitly accepted Israel's right to exist in 1988, based on an earlier UN Security Council land-for-peace principle.

Arafat's support for Iraqi President Saddam Hussein in the 1990–91 Gulf war damaged his standing with conservative Arab states and Western governments. Nevertheless, subsequent diplomatic efforts resulted in the Sept. 1993 Oslo agreements with Israel, providing for phased Palestinian autonomy on the West Bank and in Gaza. The following year he was jointly awarded the Nobel Peace Prize with Shimon Peres and Yitzhak Rabin. In Jan. 1996 Arafat was elected president of the Palestinian Authority. Frequent disruptions over political and security concerns, and the renewal of the Palestinian intifada in Sept. 2000, subsequently stalled the peace process.

In April 2002 tensions between Israelis and Palestinians increased as suicide bomb attacks on Israeli cities were countered with Israeli tanks occupying several Palestinian towns. As tanks surrounded the building housing Arafat, the Palestinian leader refused Sharon's offer of a safe exit in return for self-imposed exile. Later in the month Arafat was released after a 5 month barricade of his headquarters. Sharon refused to cooperate with a UN fact finding mission investigating Israel's military offensive in Jenin. Sharon's reluctance to negotiate with Arafat was reinforced by President Bush's outline for a settlement in June 2002. The proposals, which advocated the election of a new Palestinian leadership, caused international unease. Sharon later outlined a plan to grant Palestine around 40% of the West Bank, albeit demilitarized with Israeli control over all points of entry and exit and over airspace. Negotiations would not begin until Palestinian violence ended and Yasser Arafat was removed from power. The Palestinian authorities rejected the proposals.

In Sept. 2002, following a suicide bomb attack in Tel Aviv, Arafat was again put under siege in his Ramallah muqata'a. Ten days later, after the compound's destruction, widespread international condemnation and Palestinian protests, the Israeli army withdrew. In Jan. 2003 Sharon placed a travel ban on Palestinian officials, effectively barring them from attending peace talks in the UK. The UN, EU, Jordan, Egypt, Russia and Saudi Arabia were all due to attend the talks. The move came after a suicide bomb attack in Tel Aviv killed over 20 people.

In March 2003 the PLO's general secretary Mahmoud Abbas accepted Arafat's invitation to become the administration's first prime minister. Arafat had agreed to create the post to facilitate the resumption of an internationally mediated peace process. Under the terms of the premiership Abbas was responsible for the day-to-day running of the Palestinian Authority while Arafat retained control of defence and peace negotiations. Following disputes over several key appointments, Arafat and Abbas agreed on the composition of a cabinet in late-April 2003.

In April 2003 a 'roadmap to peace', a plan jointly produced by the UN, EU, US and Russia to secure a lasting peace, was published and delivered to Abbas. The document called for an immediate ceasefire, an end to the Israeli occupation of Palestinian towns, a clampdown on Palestinian militants and the dismantling of Israeli settlements built since 2001. It set out proposals for the establishment of an independent, democratic Palestinian state as early as 2005. The Palestinian Administration welcomed the development. In June 2003 Israel withdrew its troops from the main north-south highway in the Gaza Strip and from positions throughout northern Gaza. The move came after the three main Palestinian militant groups (Hamas, Islamic Jihad and Fatah) agreed to a ceasefire.

In July 2003 the Israeli government promised to release several hundred Palestinians, including members of militant organizations. In addition, Israeli checkpoints in Ramallah and Hebron were dismantled and 8000 workers from the Gaza Strip, Bethlehem and Tulkarem were allowed into Israel. However, the following month Sharon reiterated his commitment to building a 600 km-long 'security fence' around the West Bank, which he claimed was essential to prevent Palestinian suicide attacks.

Arafat alienated Abbas by retaining control of the Palestinian security forces, a jurisdiction promised to his prime minister. Abbas resigned in Sept. and Arafat appointed the speaker of the National Council, Ahmed Qureia, as his replacement. Following threats by the Israeli government against Arafat's life, the Palestinian president declared a state of emergency on 5 Oct. and announced an emergency government, headed by Qureia. This angered the members of the council, whose approval was required for the installation of the cabinet. After rumours of Arafat suffering a mild heart attack, Qureia reluctantly agreed to remain in his designated position until the approval of a prime minister by the council.

On 7 Oct. 2003 Arafat swore in the emergency cabinet, which included Qureia in the position of Prime Minister. Qureia had previously announced his commitment to the UN backed 'roadmap to peace' but stated he would not risk a civil war by using force against Palestinian militants. Days later Qureia threatened to resign owing to indignancy over Arafat's attempts to 'interfere' with security issues.

In Nov. 2003 Qureia agreed to retain his position and was asked by Arafat to form a new government. However, the formation was postponed after disputes between the leader and Qureia as to whom was to be appointed Interior Minister—a position which controls the Palestinian security forces. Eventually Arafat effectively retained control of the security apparatus by appointing the loyalist, Hakam Balawi.

In April 2004 Arafat stated that the Palestinian struggle would never end until there was an independent Palestinian state, with Jerusalem as its capital, but also added that any future peace agreement should preserve the Jewish character of the Israeli state and pledged to control Gaza if Israel withdrew. Nevertheless, following a series of kidnappings in Gaza, Arafat declared a state of emergency in July 2004 and suggested that the security forces be overhauled as Qureia again offered his resignation. Arafat rejected the offer and appointed Moussa Arafat—his nephew—as overall security chief. This appointment caused thousands of Palestinians to stage marches in Gaza in protest. These protests resulted in clashes between security forces and the al-Aqsa Martyrs Brigade—a military faction of Fatah—forcing Arafat to demote his nephew and re-appoint Abdel Razek al-Majeida as head of general security. Reluctantly Qureia agreed to remain Prime Minister as Fatah dissidents claimed their protests were not a challenge to Arafat's overall leadership, but to his methods of government. Arafat flew to Paris for medical care in Oct. 2004 but died in Nov. 2004.

After years of Palestinian claims that Israel poisoned Arafat his body was exhumed in Nov. 2012. Samples were retrieved from his remains and sent for tests that aim to finally determine his cause of death.

Arias Sánchez, Óscar (Costa Rica)

Introduction

Dr Óscar Arias became president of Costa Rica for the second time in May 2006, claiming victory over his rival, Otton Solís, after weeks of recounts. The centrist politician, best known for his economic reforms and his contribution to peace in Central America, previously held the presidency from 1986–90. His second term ended in May 2010.

Early Life

Óscar Rafael Arias Sánchez was born on 13 Sept. 1940 in Heredia, central Costa Rica. He was educated at St Francis College and the University of Costa

Rica, where he read law and economics. He received a doctorate from the University of Essex, Britain, before working for José Figueres, a National Liberation Party leader who had served as president from 1970–74. Appointed minister of planning and political economy in 1972, in 1979 Arias was named general secretary of the PLN, helping Luis Alberto Monge to victory in the elections of 1982. Arias himself was elected president on 8 May 1986, easily beating Rafael Calderón of the United Coalition.

Arias drafted a plan to promote peace and democracy in war-ravaged Central America, which led to the signing of the Esquipulas II Accords on 7 Aug. 1987 and for which he subsequently received the Nobel peace prize. He liberalized the Costa Rican economy, promoting tourism while reducing dependence on exports of bananas and coffee. Steady growth was maintained and unemployment fell to a regional low. After the end of his presidential term in May 1990, he served on the boards of various organizations including the International Crisis Group, Transparency International and the Stockholm International Peace Research Institute. Arias was widely recognized as a champion of democracy and demilitarization and became a prominent spokesman for the developing world.

Arias contested the 5 Feb. 2006 presidential election, promising a 'fresh start' for the country after a series of corruption scandals. However, his early lead in the opinion polls was eroded by a surge in support for Ottón Solís of the left-leaning Citizens' Action Party. The two candidates clashed regularly over the ratification of the controversial Central American Free-Trade Agreement (CAFTA), with Arias favouring approval. The election was followed by a manual recount and weeks of tension. On 7 March 2006 Arias was declared the victor with 40.9% of the vote and was sworn in on 8 May 2006.

Career Peak

Arias pledged to stamp out corruption and to implement economic reforms, although his narrow victory and weak parliamentary position suggested a struggle to win support for policies such as confirmation of CAFTA. However, in Oct. 2007 a national referendum narrowly decided in favour of ratifying the trade agreement and in Nov. 2008 the legislature voted to implement it. In June 2007 Arias announced that Costa Rica was withdrawing its diplomatic recognition of Taiwan in favour of new relations with China in order to attract Chinese investment. He was succeeded by Vice-President Laura Chinchilla on 8 May 2010.

Aristide, Jean-Bertrand (Haiti)

Introduction

Jean-Bertrand Aristide was elected president in 1990 but served only 7 months before being ousted in a military coup. Under threat of US invasion, the military junta stepped down in 1994 and Aristide saw out the rest of his term. Constitutionally barred from contesting the presidential election of 1996, he successfully stood for office again in 2000. A staunch opponent of the dictatorial regimes of Papa and Baby Doc, he was unable to resolve Haiti's economic and political crises. He was forced to flee the country in Feb. 2004 after a military insurrection.

Early Life

Aristide was born on 15 July 1953 in Port-Salut on Haiti but spent much of his youth in Port-au-Prince, the capital. He was educated in Roman Catholic schools and at the College Notre Dame in Cap-Haïtien before attending a seminary run by the Salesian Fathers in the Dominican Republic. He returned to the Grand Seminaire Notre Dame to undertake post-graduate philosophy studies and then to the State University of Haiti where he graduated in psychology in 1979. Aristide then studied theology in Rome and Israel.

In 1983 he returned to Haiti to be ordained and was named curate of St Joseph's church in Port-au-Prince. In 1985 Aristide completed his foreign studies and gained a master's degree from Canada's Montreal University. He returned to Port-au-Prince and the church of St Jean Bosco. Here he gained a reputation for his vociferous criticism of Jean-Claude Duvalier (Baby Doc) via his sermons and his broadcasts on a Catholic radio station and was warned by the Salesian order for his political activism.

In Feb. 1986 Baby Doc was forced from power and replaced by a military junta. Aristide won wide respect for heading a march to commemorate Duvalier's victims that was attacked by the army. In the same year he established the Lafanmi Selavi orphanage. In Sept. 1988 Aristide survived one of several attempts made on his life when St Jean Bosco's was attacked by a crowd of pro-government supporters as he preached. Several dozen worshippers died in the incident and the resultant public out-cry was regarded as key to the collapse of the military regime the following week. Aristide, however, was dismissed from the Salesian order for his political stance.

Aristide remained prominent in Haiti's fragile journey towards democracy through to the elections of 1990. Backed by the swelling support of the Lavalas (The Flood), a popular democratic movement, Aristide announced he would stand for the presidency and emerged victorious with 67% of the vote, although the election was beset by violence.

Career Peak

Aristide was sworn in on 7 Feb. 1991 and began a programme of democratization that won widespread support and brought much-needed international aid. However, in Sept. 1991 the military, led by Brigadier-General Raoul Cedras, staged a coup and Aristide went into exile in Venezuela and then Washington, D.C. as Haiti succumbed to a 3 year reign of terror that cost over 5,000 lives.

The US, UN and the OAS instigated sanctions against Haiti and, following the threat of a US invasion, Aristide was able to return to Haiti in Oct. 1994 to see out the remainder of his term. Faced with a devastated economy and a fractured political landscape, Aristide set about restructuring the armed forces and established a civilian police force. Elections were held in Feb. 1996 and Aristide, constitutionally prohibited from standing for a second consecutive term, was succeeded by Réné Préval in independent Haiti's first peaceful transition of power.

Whilst out of office Aristide established an eponymous foundation for democracy. In Nov. 1996 he founded the Fanmi Lavalas (Lavalas Family) Party. Haiti struggled to repair itself and Préval began rule by decree in 1999. Aristide announced his intention to stand for the presidency in elections in Nov. 2000. He won with 91.8% of the vote but several opposition groups alleged fraud and international aid was frozen. The political scene remained entrenched and in July 2001 Aristide accused several former army officers of attempting a coup. Thirty armed men attacked the National Palace in Dec. 2001 in a further challenge to the presidency. In July 2002 Aristide oversaw Haiti's entry into CARICOM despite fears of continuing human rights abuses within the country.

In July 2003 the Inter-American Development Bank granted loans worth US$220m. to fund improvements in transport, education and public health. However, Aristide's presidency was weakened by mass demonstrations in early 2004. Rebel forces seized the north of the country and Aristide fled abroad before the advancing militias.

Later Life

The chief justice, Boniface Alexandre, was sworn in as provisional president on 29 Feb. 2004. Aristide went first to the Central African Republic and then to Jamaica, from where he filed lawsuits against unspecified officials from the US and France, alleging he had been kidnapped and forced into exile.

Aristide returned to Haiti in March 2011.

Arthur, Owen (Barbados)

Introduction

Owen Arthur was Barbados' fifth prime minister and the leader of the Barbados Labour Party (BLP). He took office in 1994 and was re-elected in 1999 and 2003. Arthur ran for another term in office but suffered defeat at the 15 Jan. 2008 elections.

Early Life

Owen Seymour Arthur was born on 17 Oct. 1949 in Barbados. He studied in Jamaica at the University of the West Indies, graduating with a master's in economics. He worked in Jamaica for much of the 1970s, firstly as a researcher at the university's department of management, then at the national planning agency and later as director of economic research at the Jamaican bauxite institute.

In 1981 he joined the Barbados ministry of finance and planning as chief project analyst. He then became a research fellow at the University of the West Indies' institute of social and economic research. He also held positions on the boards of the Jamaican council for scientific research, the Barbados industrial development corporation and the central bank of Barbados. Between 1982–84 he was chairman of the Barbados agricultural development corporation.

Arthur began his political career in 1983 when he was appointed to the Barbados senate and the following year he was elected to the house of assembly. From 1993–94 he served as leader of the opposition. He led the BLP into the 1994 general election promising to develop a 'modern, technologically-dynamic economy'. The BLP won 19 of 28 available seats and Arthur was returned as prime minister.

Career Peak

Arthur has made economic development a main priority with emphasis on promotion of international trade and investment, incorporating an expansion of the tourism sector.

In the build-up to the 1999 election he vowed to make Barbados a republic, proposing that a ceremonial president replace the queen as head of state. There are plans for a referendum on the subject. Arthur's BLP won a landslide victory at the 1999 polls, claiming 26 of the 28 seats. In 2000 the OECD placed Barbados on a list of nations designated as uncooperative tax havens but was removed from the list 2 years later. Arthur's majority was slightly reduced at the election of 2003 when the BLP won 23 seats on a platform of reduced taxation and increased prosperity.

Arthur has been active in regional politics, taking a leading role in developing the Caribbean single market and economy. Additionally he was the chair of the Commonwealth ministerial group on small states, chair of the global conference on small states and a consultant to the OAS and CARICOM.

In 2004 relations with Trinidad and Tobago declined following a sea border disagreement when several Barbadian fishermen were arrested. The dispute was referred to the UN for adjudication. Ties between Barbados and Trinidad took a further knock in 2005 when Arthur suggested Tobago would be better off in a union with Barbados.

Arthur was minister of finance in addition to being prime minister.

Arthur sought a fourth consecutive term in office and in the run-up to the Jan. 2008 vote accused his rivals of taking donations from Taiwan, in return for promising to switch allegiance from China. The opposition, the Democratic Labour Party (DLP), had in turn suggested that Arthur had access to undeclared bank accounts. Arthur was defeated in the elections held on 15 Jan., but was re-elected to his own seat from St Peter constituency. On 19 Jan. 2008 Arthur stepped down as leader of the BLP, saying that he felt immediate leadership transition would be in the best interest of the party and Barbadian democracy.

Ásgrímsson, Halldór (Iceland)

Introduction

When Iceland's prime minister of 13 years, Davíð Oddsson, became ill in Aug. 2004, Halldór Ásgrímsson was chosen to replace him. The accountant-turned-politician, who had been minister for foreign affairs since 1995, took office on 15 Sept. 2004. He resigned in June 2006.

Early Life

Halldór Ásgrímsson was born in Vopnafjörður in eastern Iceland on 8th Sept. 1947. He attended the Co-operative College of Iceland in Reykjavík and graduated in 1965. He then specialized in finance and commerce and received a licence as a certified public accountant in 1970. The following year he undertook further studies abroad at the universities of Bergen and Copenhagen. Returning to Reykjavík in 1973, Ásgrímsson began working at the University of Iceland, lecturing at the faculty of economics and business

administration. A year later, in the general election that was brought about by a split in the ruling coalition over economic policies, Ásgrímsson was elected as a member of the *Alþingi* (Parliament) for the moderate Progressive Party (PP). In 1976 Ásgrímsson became a member of the board of the Central Bank of Iceland. He served as a member of the Icelandic delegation to the Copenhagen-based Nordic Council in 1977–78.

In 1980 he became vice-chairman of the PP, which had joined the People's Alliance (PA) in a coalition led by the former Independence Party (IP) leader Gunnar Thoroddsen. The presidential election of 1980 was won by Vigdís Finnbogadóttir, who became the world's first popularly elected female head of state. Ásgrímsson became the minister for fisheries in May 1983 following the general election which resulted in the PP leader Steingrímur Hermannsson becoming prime minister. Ásgrímsson later served as minister for Nordic co-operation (1985–87) and minister for justice and ecclesiastical affairs (1988–89). He took over as leader of the PP when Hermannsson stepped down in 1994. From 1995–2004 Ásgrímsson was minister for foreign affairs and external trade in a coalition government of the PP and the IP led by prime minister Davíð Oddsson. The period was broadly characterized by strong economic growth underpinned by fisheries and the production of aluminium. Oddsson emerged victorious in the May 2004 general election, but decided to make way for Ásgrímsson following a period of ill-health in Aug. Oddsson took the job of minister of foreign affairs until Sept. 2005.

Career Peak

According to an agreement between the two coalition parties (IP and PP), Ásgrímsson became prime minister of Iceland on 15 Sept. 2004. In his opening policy address he outlined his commitment to diversifying the Icelandic economy away from its dependence on fisheries by expanding the country's power-intensive industries and taking full advantage of abundant supplies of free geothermal energy. He also pledged to cut income tax over 3 years, raise child allowance and promised a review of the constitution. His government aimed to promote more active international co-operation following the announcement of Iceland's candidacy for a seat on the UN Security Council for the period 2009–10, with elections taking place in 2008.

Following a poor showing at the municipal elections of June 2006, Ásgrímsson announced that he was resigning as prime minister and would step down as leader of the Progressive Party before the end of 2006. He was succeeded by the chairman of the Independence Party, Geir Hilmar Haarde.

Ásgrímsson died on 18 May 2015 following a heart attack.

Aso, Taro (Japan)

Introduction

Taro Aso became prime minister in Sept. 2008 after the resignation of Yasuo Fukuda. With a reputation as a conservative and nationalist, he came to office promising to address Japan's economic problems. However, he faced a divided parliament, with the upper house controlled by the opposition, and severe challenges resulting from the global economic crisis.

Early Life

Taro Aso was born on 20 Sept. 1940 in Iizuka, Fukuoka. As owners of the Aso Cement Company, his family had a tradition of holding political office. After graduating in politics and economics at Gakushuin University, he studied at Stanford University in the USA and at the London School of Economics. In 1966 he joined the Aso Cement Company, for a period working in its Brazil offices, and was appointed company president in 1973. Aso also represented Japan at shooting at the 1976 Olympic Games.

In Oct. 1979 he was elected to the House of Representatives as a member of the ruling Liberal Democratic Party (LDP). He was appointed vice minister for education in 1988 and in 2003 joined Prime Minister Koizumi's cabinet as minister of internal affairs, posts and communications. In Oct. 2005 he was appointed minister for foreign affairs, a position he held for 3 years, during which time he supported sanctions against North Korea and criticized China's military spending, describing it as a threat to Japan and the region. In 2006 China was angered when he praised Taiwan (which China claims as an integral part of its territory) as a 'law-abiding country'. Aso's outspoken remarks nonetheless secured him popular support within Japan.

When Koizumi resigned in 2006, the LDP chose not to call a general election but to hold an internal contest for the leadership. Aso stood but was defeated by Shinzo Abe. He continued as foreign minister in Abe's government and when Abe resigned in Sept. 2007, announced his candidature to replace him. Opponents claimed the process was a return to old-style Japanese politics, in which leaders of the party factions pledged their support in advance of an open vote. Aso lost to the more moderate Yasuo Fukuda by 330 votes to 197.

Fukuda faced a split in parliament, with the upper house controlled by the opposition Democratic Party of Japan (DPJ). Aso declined offers of a ministerial portfolio and embarked on a political tour of the country. He changed his focus from foreign affairs and cultural issues to the economy and advocated a 'Japan Renewal Programme' based on regional decentralization, pension reforms and employment liberalization.

In Aug. 2008 Aso was appointed secretary-general of the LDP. On 1 Sept. 2008 Fukuda, unable to implement his policies, announced his resignation. Aso campaigned to replace him, identifying economic stability as his priority. On 22 Sept. 2008 he was elected president of the LDP with 351 of a possible 525 votes. However, the upper house voted for the DPJ candidate Ozawa ensuring Aso too faced a divided parliament.

Career Peak

Aso faced severe challenges as the global economic crisis worsened throughout 2008–09. He announced three economic stimulus plans (in Oct. and Dec. 2008 and Feb. 2009) but was criticized for delays in submitting detailed plans to parliament. There was concern at problems in the pension system among older voters, many of whom were angered when Aso criticized them for not taking better care of their health. By early 2009 there was widespread pressure for an early general election. In foreign relations, Aso moved to build bridges with China and met the Chinese premier for talks in Oct. 2008. In Feb. 2009 he visited President Obama, a meeting seen as a mutual confirmation of good relations between the two nations.

The Aug. 2009 elections to the House of Deputies saw the LDP lose to the Democratic Party of Japan, taking only 119 seats compared to their rivals' 308. On 16 Sept. Aso was succeeded as prime minister by Yukio Hatoyama.

Later Life

Aso joined Shinzo Abe's government in Dec. 2012 as deputy prime minister and minister of finance.

Atambayev, Almazbek (Kyrgyzstan)

Introduction

Almazbek Atambayev was sworn in as president on 1 Dec. 2011. His election represented the first peaceful handover of power since the country gained independence during the dissolution of the Soviet Union. He succeeded Roza Otunbayeva, who assumed the post on a temporary basis after the previous incumbent, Kurmanbek Bakiyev, was ousted in a violent uprising in April 2010. A successful entrepreneur, Atambayev has favoured closer ties with Russia.

Early Life

Atambayev was born on 17 Sept. 1956 in Chui, a northern region of what is now Kyrgyzstan. He studied at the Moscow Institute of Management, from where he graduated with a degree in economics. From 1983 until 1987, when the Kyrgyz Republic was still a constituent part of the Soviet Union, he served on the Supreme Council of the Republic.

In 1993, 2 years after the country had declared independence, Atambayev was one of the founders of the Social Democratic Party of Kyrgyzstan. Having established himself as a prosperous businessman in the post-Soviet era, he became chairman of the party in 1999. In 2000 he won 6% of the vote in a presidential election. In Dec. 2005 he was appointed minister of industry,

trade and tourism, but resigned 5 months later. In Nov. 2006 he was among the leaders of anti-government protests in the capital, Bishkek. He served as prime minister from March to Nov. 2007, and ran again for president in April 2009 but withdrew on the day of the ballot, citing electoral fraud.

Kurmanbek Bakiyev was overthrown in April 2010, prompting a wave of ethnic violence between Kyrgyz and Uzbek communities in the south of the country. A national referendum approved a new constitution that weakened the authority of the president and shifted power towards the legislature. Parliamentary elections followed and a coalition government was established for the first time in the country's history. Atambayev was appointed prime minister once more, a position he held until the presidential election in Oct. 2011.

Atambayev gained a comfortable victory at that election which, though criticized by some observers, was regarded as a significant democratic achievement.

Career Peak

Atambayev came to power in a country riven by ethnic division. He pledged to foster national unity and described Russia as the country's 'main strategic partner'. Soon after assuming office he said that he would look to close a US military base in the country when its lease expired. This policy was endorsed by parliament in June 2013, after which the base closed in June 2014.

In Sept. 2012 Atambayev appointed technocrat Zhantoro Satybaldiyev, a technocrat, as prime minister following the collapse of the coalition government in the wake of corruption allegations, a poor economic record and the resignation of former premier Omurbek Babanov. Further reports of corruption also prompted the fall of Satybaldiyev's administration in March 2014 and the subsequent appointment of Dzhoomart Otorbayev as the new premier, although with no changes to other key ministerial portfolios. He in turn resigned in April 2015 and was succeeded by Temir Sariyev. In parliamentary elections the following Oct. Atambayev's Social Democratic Party of Kyrgyzstan (SDPK) was returned as the largest party with 38 seats and another coalition government under Sariyev's premiership was formed.

In April 2016 Sooronbay Jeenbekov was sworn in as prime minister after Sariyev and his cabinet resigned having been accused of corruption by a parliamentary commission. Jeenbekov's government also resigned in Oct., but he was reappointed and nominated a largely unchanged new administration that was approved by parliament and by Atambayev the following month. In a national referendum in Dec. about 80% of voters endorsed proposed constitutional amendments that included increasing the powers of the prime minister and the SDPK-dominated government. However, critics believed that the amendments would strengthen the executive at the expense of parliament and the judiciary.

In accordance with the constitution, Atambayev was only eligible to serve one 6 year term. On 24 Nov. 2017 he was replaced by Sooronbay Jeenbekov, also from the SDPK, as president.

Attlee, Clement (United Kingdom of Great Britain and Northern Ireland)

Introduction

Clement Attlee was British Labour prime minister between 1945 and 1951. A social reformer, under his administration an advanced welfare state was created. On the world scene, he oversaw the initial stages of dismantling the British Empire and the difficult transition to a new international role for Britain.

Early Life

Born on 3 Jan. 1883 in Putney, southwest London, Clement Richard Attlee graduated from Oxford University with a law degree and subsequently qualified as a barrister. For 15 years until 1922 he lived in the East End of London and it was his exposure during this period to poor living standards that confirmed in him his belief in social reform. He served in the army during World War I, rising to the rank of Major.

Attlee's political life began in earnest when he joined the socialist Fabian Society in 1907 and the Independent Labour Party the following year. By 1919 he was mayor of Stepney in east London and by 1922 he had entered the House of Commons as the member for Limehouse. Limehouse was to remain his constituency until 1950 when he became MP for West Walthamstow. He held junior ministerial posts in Britain's first Labour governments, the 1924 and 1929–31 administrations of Ramsay MacDonald. However, unhappy at MacDonald's decision in 1931 to head the national coalition government which included Liberals and Conservatives, Attlee resigned. Later in the year he was appointed deputy to the new Labour leader, George Lansbury, and replaced him in 1935 with strong trade union backing.

In the lead up to World War II, Attlee voiced his opposition to the aggression of Europe's fascist powers but he was reluctant to support extensive rearmament or conscription. He refused to serve in Chamberlain's wartime cabinet but was a supporter of Churchill, serving as Lord Privy Seal, Secretary for the Dominions, Lord President of the Council and deputy prime minister during Churchill's premiership.

Career Peak

In the post-war election of July 1945, despite massive public affection for Churchill, Attlee's Labour Party won a landslide victory on the promise of social change. Attlee became the first Labour prime minister with a majority in the Commons. His term of office proved to be one of the most significant of the twentieth century, both domestically and internationally.

On the home front, Attlee's administration paved the way for the welfare state, as set out in W. H. Beveridge's *Social Insurance and Allied Services Report* of 1942, and also the National Health Service, principally installed by Minister of Health Aneurin Bevan. In addition, Attlee undertook a massive programme of nationalization. By the end of his tenure the Bank of England, telegraphs, railways, coal mining, gas, electricity, iron and steel had all been taken out of private hands. This equated to around one fifth of the British economy. Attlee also approved increased spending on education, and the school leaving age was raised to 16. However, these reforms were expensive, especially so in the aftermath of World War II, and Chancellor Stafford Cripps imposed severe economic constraints from 1947 onwards eventually leading to devaluation. Discontent spread throughout the party (Bevan himself eventually resigned in protest at cutbacks) with a consequent loss of popular support.

Foreign policy, under the control of Ernest Bevin for most of Attlee's administration, saw the repositioning of Britain's role on the world stage. His term of office found the British Empire in its death throes. Attlee had become convinced of the need for self-rule on the Indian sub-continent following a trip he had made there in 1927. Independence was granted in 1947 to India and the new state of Pakistan (under the guidance of Louis Mountbatten, the last Indian Viceroy), followed by Burma (now Myanmar), Ceylon (now Sri Lanka), and British withdrawal from Palestine (paving the way for the creation of Israel). This transitional phase was far from easy, and numerous unresolved questions led to problems evident still today, as epitomized by the disputes between India and Pakistan and between Israel and the Palestinians.

Meanwhile, closer ties with European neighbours were established with the signing of the Brussels Treaty in March 1948, forming an alliance between the UK, France, Luxembourg, the Netherlands and Belgium. The UK joined the Organization for European Economic Co-operation less than a month later and joined the Council of Europe in 1949 but there was strong resistance to joining the European Common Market. Closer relations also developed with the US in the face of the Soviet threat, much to the chagrin of many left-wingers within the Labour party. The US Marshall Plan of 1947 for European re-development was fully backed as was the creation in 1949 of the North Atlantic Treaty Organization (NATO). Attlee's government was also integral to the creation in 1950 of the Colombo Plan for Asian economic development.

Attlee won the general election of 1950, but as a result of the worsening economic climate his majority was slashed. In an attempt to improve this situation, he returned to the polls in Oct. 1951 but the gamble failed and the Conservatives, under Winston Churchill, came to power.

Later Life

Attlee remained leader of the opposition until Dec. 1955 when he retired and became 1st Earl Attlee, Viscount Prestwood. Hugh Gaitskill succeeded him as Labour leader and Attlee went on to pen his memoirs before he died, in Westminster, on 8 Oct. 1967. Though often perceived as a rather staid public figure, he was intelligent and witty and his time in office was one of the most difficult of any British prime minister.

Aung San (Myanmar)

Introduction

Aung San, the father of modern Myanmar, led the anti-colonial movement in the 1940s, securing independence for his country through post-war negotiations with the UK. A revolutionary student and Japanese-sponsored rebel, Aung San managed to unite the Burmans and the disparate ethic nationalities in a common struggle. Using both peaceful and military means, he forced the British administration to negotiate an organized transfer of power. His assassination the year before independence created a hero's cult. Aung San Sui Kyi, his third child with Daw Khin Kyi, has been associated with his achievements.

Early Life

Aung San was born on 13th Feb. 1915 at Natmauk in the central Burmese district of Magwe. His father, U Pha, a lawyer, and his mother, Daw Su, came from prosperous gentry families with a pedigree of resistance to colonial rule. He received his education in a monastic establishment and at the Vernacular High School in Natmauk and after at the National High School, Yenangyaung. In 1932 Aung San began studying English Literature, Modern History and Political Science at Rangoon University. He became involved in politics through the students' union and edited the union magazine. A university strike in 1938 forced the authorities to revoke his expulsion, ordered for a provocative article. He was elected president of the Students' Union while continuing his studies in law.

In Oct. 1938 Aung San joined the Dohbama Asi-ayone ("We-Burmese" Association), a nationalist and militant political organization, known ironically as the Thakins (*Thakin*, or 'master'. being the term of address used for the British). In 1939 Aung San became general secretary of the newly formed Freedom Bloc—a confederation of parties seeking independence from colonial rule.

The outbreak of the World War II precipitated negotiations with the British. Aung San attended the Indian National Congress assembly at Ramgrah in 1940 with the intention of seeking international support for Burmese independence. His anti-British activism in Rangoon provoked a warrant for his arrest, forcing him underground and subsequently to China (though the warrant was revoked). In Amoy, now Xiamen, Japanese agents offered Aung San assistance. On his return to Burma, he gathered a group of young nationalists, later known as the 'Thirty Comrades'. for military training in Japan. The Burma Independence Army (BIA) was formed in Bangkok in Dec. 1941 to assist the Japanese invasion of British-held Burma in 1942.

Career Peak

Rangoon was occupied on 8 March 1942 by Japanese forces and the BIA, commanded by Maj.-Gen. Aung San. The BIA grew in numbers during the takeover of the country and assumed the duties of local government under a Japanese administration. Aung San served as defence minister under the puppet regime of Ba Maw, relinquishing control of the BIA (transformed into the Burmese National Army) to Ne Win, the later dictator. Burma was declared sovereign on 1 Aug. 1943 but dissatisfaction with Japanese policies and treatment of the Burmese persuaded Aung San to approach the British in Nov. 1943. In 1944 he founded the Anti-Fascist Organization (AFO) in preparation for a general uprising against the Japanese on 27 March 1945. After the surrender of the Japanese in Aug. the AFO was reformed as the Anti-Fascist People's Freedom League (AFPFL), gaining widespread popular support. This convinced the British military commander, Lord Mountbatten, to defy the wishes of the returning colonial administration, which deemed Aung San a traitor, and re-appointed Sir Hubert Rance as governor. Rance's non-confrontational approach allowed for rapid negotiations with Aung San and the AFPFL.

In Sept. 1946 Aung San was appointed deputy chairman of the Executive Council of Burma. In this capacity, and as president of the AFPFL, he negotiated a schedule for Burmese independence with the British government in London. The Aung San-Attlee Agreement was signed on 27 Jan. 1947, securing total independence in a year's time. The issue of ethnic divisions was settled in Feb. when Aung San signed the Panglong Agreement with leaders of the nationalities, which supported the creation of a unified independent

Burma. Elections to the constitutional assembly were held in April 1947, giving the AFPFL 196 of the 202 seats.

On 19 July 1947 Aung San and six members of the Executive Council, including his brother, U Ba Win, were assassinated under the orders of U Saw, a former prime minister who opposed Aung San's compromises with the British. U Saw was subsequently tried and executed for the murders. Burma achieved independence from the UK on 4 Jan. 1948.

Auriol, Vincent (France)

Introduction

The first of the two presidents of the Fourth Republic, Auriol's 7 year term was blighted by post-war crises and the Indochina War. Friction with the communist party and the Gaullists, coupled with an alarming succession of prime ministers, rendered Auriol's period of rule unstable.

Early Life

The son of a baker, Vincent Auriol was born on 27 Aug. 1884 in Revel, near Toulouse. After studying law in Toulouse he joined the bar. At the time of his studies Auriol was already embracing socialism. He was involved with the Section Française de l'Internationale Ouvrière (International Workers Party; SFIO) later the Parti Socialiste, since its beginnings in 1905. In May 1914 he became Socialist deputy for Muret, Haute-Garonne, and was elected to the Chamber of Deputies. Between 1919–35 Auriol led the parliamentary body of the SFIO. From 1936–37, as finance minister in Léon Blum's Front Populaire government, he devalued the franc. From the following year Auriol was minister of justice under Camille Chautemps, who was prime minister from 1937–38, before rejoining Blum for his second term in 1938.

At the Fall of France, a vote was held on 10 July 1940 to determine whether Pétain should gain full control of the Vichy government. 80 members voted against, including Auriol. He was subsequently arrested and imprisoned. In 1943 he went first to London and then to Algiers. After the War, de Gaulle appointed him to the provisional government. Between 1945–46 he presided over two Constituent Assemblies and the National Assembly until Jan. 1947.

Career Peak

On 16 Jan. 1947 Auriol became the first president of the Fourth Republic. Despite having gained a reputation as a political mediator, he was unable to prevent friction in his coalition government. Both the communists and Gaullists proved incompatible and the tripartite coalition came to an end in May 1947 when the communist ministers were dismissed.

Instability was caused by a succession of prime ministers, who resigned or were replaced after short periods in office. During Auriol's presidency, there were eleven different prime ministers with sixteen changes of government. Their periods in office ranged from a maximum of a year to a minimum of 6 days. Between 16 Jan. 1947–16 Jan. 1954 the prime ministers were Paul Ramadier, Robert Schuman (twice), André Marie, Henri Queuille (three times), Jules Moch, René Mayer (twice), Georges Bidault, René Pleven (twice), Edgar Faure, Antoine Pinay and Joseph Laniel.

In the troubled post-war years, economic hardship provoked a culture of strikes and industrial action. Attempts at resolving problems were met with PCF obstruction and violent demonstrations. In Dec. 1947, after weeks of strikes, 16 people were killed when a sabotaged train was derailed. Communists had believed the train contained security forces on their way to break up the strikes. On the same day there were 15 other sabotages and six more derailments. An added difficulty was France's war with Indochina (1946–54), which drained the country's meagre resources. At the end of his term, Auriol declined to stand again. In the 1954 elections, René Coty was elected president.

Later Life

Auriol was a strong opponent of de Gaulle's Fifth Republic and in 1960 he retired from politics. He died on 1 Jan. 1966.

Ayrault, Jean-Marc (France)

Introduction

Jean-Marc Ayrault was appointed prime minister on 16 May 2012 by President François Hollande. Ayrault served as president of the cross-party Socialist group in the National Assembly from 1997 to 2012 and was mayor of Nantes between 1989 and 2012.

Early Life

Jean-Marc Ayrault was born on 25 Jan. 1950 in Maulévrier, Maine-et-Loire. In 1971 he graduated in German from Nantes University before gaining a teaching diploma and becoming a German teacher. He taught at Angevinière College in Saint-Herblain, a suburb of Nantes, from 1973 until 1986.

In 1971 Ayrault joined the Socialist Party (PS) and affiliated himself with Jean Poperen, who unsuccessfully challenged François Mitterrand for the party leadership that year. From 1976–82 he served as a regional councillor for Loire-Atlantique and in 1977 was elected mayor of Saint-Herblain, a post he held for 11 years. In 1979 he joined the PS national committee and in 1981 its executive committee. In 1986 he was elected to the National Assembly to represent Loire-Atlantique, a seat he held for the next six legislative elections.

In 1989 Ayrault became mayor of Nantes, winning re-election in 1995, 2001 and 2008. In 1997 he was elected president of the parliamentary Socialist group, the same year as he received a 6 month suspended prison sentence after the Nantes government awarded a newspaper contract without a public tender. He was a special adviser to François Hollande on his successful presidential campaign in 2012 and was subsequently appointed premier.

Career Peak

Ayrault's principal challenge was to rejuvenate the economy and improve the public finances. Together with Hollande, he pushed the European Commission to support the Greek economy. Domestically, he lowered the retirement age from 62 to 60 for some workers, cut ministerial salaries by up to 30% and announced plans to spend €2.5bn. by 2017 to help the poor. His government also introduced new capital gains and inheritance taxes, an exit tax for entrepreneurs, a temporary 75% tax on annual incomes over a €1m., an income tax hike from 41% to 45% on salaries over €150,000 and increased taxes on stock options, dividends and financial transactions.

Ayrault resigned as prime minister on 31 March 2014 after the Socialist Party suffered considerable losses in local elections. He was replaced a day later by the serving interior minister, Manuel Valls.

Later Life

Ayrault returned to government in Feb. 2016 when he was appointed minister of foreign affairs and international development, serving in the cabinet of Manuel Valls.

Ayub Khan, Muhammad (Pakistan)

Introduction

Muhammad Ayub Khan, Pakistan's president from 1958–68, was the first leader of Pakistan to impose direct military rule. His 'Great Decade'. which saw steady industrialization and an opening up of the economy to the West, but he lost support over the unsuccessful Indo-Pakistan war of 1965 and his monopolization of state power.

Early Life

Muhammad Ayub Khan was born on 14 May 1907 in Hazara in the northwest of Pakistan. He was born to Mir Dad Khan, a non-commissioned officer in the British Indian army. Educated at schools in Saria Saleh and Haripur, he went on to study at Alighar University in Uttar Pradesh, India. Before taking his exams he was selected for training at the Royal Military College at Sandhurst, England, where he spent 2 years (1926–28). In 1928 he was commissioned in the British Indian army. In the second world war Khan fought as second-in-command of a regiment in Burma and then as a battalion commander in India. When India gained independence in 1947 he joined the newly-formed Pakistani army, rising to become Maj.-Gen. in 1948 and the first Commander in Chief of Pakistan's armed forces in 1951.

In 1954 Ayub Khan was appointed defence minister in the government of Muhammad Ali Bogra, a post which he held until 1958. During this time he played a key role in Pakistan's involvement with a series of US-sponsored military alliances (CENTO and SEATO).

On 7 Oct. 1958 Iskander Mirza, aided by Khan, took power in a coup, declaring martial law. Mirza gained the presidency while Khan became Chief Martial Law Administrator. Relations between Mirza and Khan broke down following the coup and on 28 Oct. 1958 Khan dismissed Mirza and took power as Pakistan's president, retaining his role as Chief Martial Law Administrator while giving himself the title of Field Marshall.

Career Peak

Ayub Khan's presidential rule, which was confirmed by referendum in Feb. 1960, began promisingly. The public were generally welcoming towards him and regarded his take-over as a signal that political instability was at an end. Khan moved the capital from Karachi to Islamabad, where he constructed a modern, spacious city, and began a wide-ranging series of reforms in the agricultural, social and educational sectors. In the economic sphere he pursued a successful pro-market policy which encouraged foreign investment. His agricultural policies, however, came under fire for their bias towards the land-owning classes and powerful industrialists.

Realizing the need to lift the state of emergency and to normalize politics, he appointed a constitutional commission. Martial law was lifted on 8 June 1962. The new constitution introduced a system of 'Basic Democracy' which extended limited political power through a system of indirect election while maintaining military control over the judiciary and the civil service.

The US' even-handed support for India and Pakistan and the arming of India's military after the Indo-China border confrontation (1962) prompted Khan to develop closer ties with China, from whom Pakistan subsequently received military aid. At the same time, Pakistan's relations with India deteriorated as the situation in the contested region of Jammu and Kashmir worsened. In 1965 these tensions culminated in a brief war. After the UN called for a cease-fire, Ayub Khan agreed to the Tashkent declaration which established revised boundaries for Indian and Pakistani territory. This was viewed by Pakistanis as a capitulation on the gains made during the military conflict.

Ayub Khan retained power in the 1965 presidential elections. His main contender, Fatimah Jinnah (sister of Muhammad Ali Jinnah, the founding father of Pakistan) gained fewer votes than expected, prompting allegations of vote-rigging. The economic consequences of the war led to increasing dissatisfaction with Khan's rule. Zulfiqar Ali Bhutto, his right-hand man, turned against him and established the Pakistani People's Party (PPP) while in East Pakistan, the growing strength of the Awami League under Sheikh Mujibur Rahman increasingly undermined Khan. In spite of the unrest, in 1968 Khan chose to celebrate 10 years of power, or what he called the 'Great Decade'. This ill-judged celebration led to calls for strike action. In Jan. 1969 a Democratic Action Committee, an alliance of opposition parties, was formed with the single objective of ousting Khan. Khan initially declared that he would not seek re-election in 1970 yet the protest continued, forcing him to stand down. On 25 March 1969 martial law was re-introduced and Ayub Khan resigned, handing power to Yahya Khan, the Commander in Chief of the army.

Later Life

Having suffered poor health from 1968, Ayub Khan died in 1974.

Azarov, Mykola (Ukraine)

Introduction

Mykola Azarov was appointed prime minister on 11 March 2010. A close ally of President Viktor Yanukovych, his predecessor as leader of the Party of Regions, Azarov was regarded as a technocrat. Ethnically Russian, he was a veteran of the country's turbulent political system, having previously served as deputy prime minister, foreign minister and, on two occasions, acting prime minister.

Early Life

Mykola Azarov was born on 17 Dec. 1947 in the town of Kaluga, in what is now Russia. He studied geology at Moscow State University before working at a coal mine in the Russian city of Tula. In 1984 he moved to Donetsk to serve first as deputy director and later as director of the Ukrainian State Geological Institute. He became a member of Ukraine's parliament in 1994 and 2 years later was appointed head of the state tax authority.

During his 6 years there, Azarov had a reputation for authoritarianism and controversy. It was alleged that he promoted electoral fraud and the intimidation of journalists to secure the re-election of President Leonid Kuchma in 1999. Azarov staunchly denied the accusations, citing a plot against him by rivals.

In 2002 the European Choice parliamentary group, of which he was chairman, nominated Azarov for prime minister. He declined and stood aside for Yanukovych, who assumed both the leadership of the Party of Regions and the premiership. Yanukovych appointed Azarov as deputy prime minister and finance minister in his first cabinet, with Azarov serving until 2005 and then again in 2006–07. His most notable reform was to bring the variable tax rate on personal income down to a uniform flat rate.

During the political upheaval that accompanied the Orange Revolution over the winter of 2004–05, Azarov twice served briefly as acting prime minister. After masterminding Yanukovych's victorious presidential election campaign in 2010, he assumed the leadership of the Party of Regions and was confirmed as prime minister by parliament on 11 March 2010.

Career Peak

Azarov declared that his primary task was to restore the struggling economy. Admitting that 'the coffers are empty'. he pledged to push through a programme of budgetary restraints to encourage the IMF to resume funding suspended in 2009. However, in Nov. 2011 the IMF postponed loan instalment negotiations because of a lack of progress by the Azarov government on pension reform and the removal of domestic gas subsidies.

Criticized by opponents for his poor grasp of the Ukrainian language, Azarov promised that government affairs would be conducted in Ukrainian.

Following the Party of Regions' victory in parliamentary elections in Oct. 2012, President Yanukovych nominated Azarov in Dec. for a new term as prime minister of a reconstituted government. However, he resigned in Jan. 2014 amid widespread social unrest caused by the ongoing 'Euromaidan' protests with demonstrators demanding closer EU integration. Azarov had previously rejected conditions to joining the European Union (including the decriminalization of same sex marriage), whilst seeking to improve strained economic relations with Moscow.

Azikiwe, Nnamdi (Nigeria)

Introduction

Nnamdi Azikiwe, popularly known as 'Zik'. was the first governor-general of Nigeria between 1960–63. He served as president from 1963 to 1966, though the post held few significant powers.

Early Life

Benjamin Nnamdi Azikiwe was born on 16 Nov. 1904 in Zunguru, Northern Nigeria. His opposition to the colonial power was confirmed when his father lost his job as a civilian clerk in a British army regiment. He attended the Roman Catholic and Church Missionary Society's Anglican missions at Onitsha, after which he studied in Lagos and Calabar. He was fluent in the Ibo, Yoruba, and English languages besides his mother tongue, Hausa.

After working in the treasury department in Lagos from 1921–25 he headed for the United States where he obtained his MA in political science from Lincoln University in 1930. His first book, on international relations, was published in 1931. He graduated from the University of Pennsylvania in 1934 with an MSc in Anthropology.

For 3 years, he was editor of the *African Morning Post* in Sierra Leone. Back in Nigeria in 1937, he set up a number of newspapers and in his role as editor of the *West African Pilot*, he fought colonialism. He was the founder member and, after 1946, leader of the National Council for Nigeria and the Cameroons.

Career Peak

Azikiwe was premier of Eastern Nigeria until the 1959 pre-independence federal elections, after which his party formed a coalition with the Northern Peoples' Congress. On Nigerian independence in 1960 he became governor-general. He was made president in 1963 and was one of the founders of the University of Nigeria, Nsukka. He was deposed by a military coup in Jan. 1966, led by General Aguiyi-Ironsi.

After a second military counter-coup in June 1966 Azikiwe came out of retirement to support the Biafran cause in the civil war that followed the 1967 declaration of independence by the country's Eastern Region. However, in 1969 he changed his mind to argue for reunification and set about opposing the Biafran ruling party until its collapse in 1970.

Later Life

Having published his memoirs in 1970, Azikiwe became chancellor of the University of Lagos in 1972. In 1978 he founded the Nigerian People's Party to fight in the presidential elections of 1979 and 1983. Unsuccessful on both occasions he retired from politics and died on 11 May 1996 at his home in Nsukka.

Aznar, José María (Spain)

Introduction

José María Aznar López was elected prime minister in 1996, representing the right-wing Partido Popular (PP; formally the Francoist Alianza Popular). He ended a 14-year rule by the Partido Socialista Obrero Español (PSOE) led by Felipe González Márquez. Aznar's market-led economic policies and labour reforms brought increased prosperity, lower unemployment and successful entry into the single European currency, but he failed to resolve the ongoing dispute with the Basque nationalists, ETA. He has also faced public unease over his support of the USA's aggressive policy towards Iraq. Following terrorist attacks on Madrid shortly before the elections of March 2004, Aznar's PP were unexpectedly voted out of government.

Early Life

Aznar was born on 25 Feb. 1953 in Madrid. His father and grandfather both held government posts under General Franco. Aznar studied law at the Universidad Complutense de Madrid, after which he worked as a tax inspector in Valladolid. He became active in the Francoist Alianza Popular in the 1970s, becoming secretary-general of his local branch in 1979 and deputy of the Avila region in 1982. After a year as vice-president of the newly created PP, Aznar was elected party president in 1989. In 1995 Aznar survived a car bomb attack thought to be perpetrated by ETA.

Continued re-election of the PSOE at the expense of the Alianza Popular between 1982–96 was largely a consequence of the popular distrust of any party with Francoist connections. Aznar decided to reinvent the party. With a new name, he attracted a younger membership and pulled the PP to the centre of the political scale. His 1996 electoral campaign benefited from emerging PSOE corruption scandals even though the PSOE's campaign warned Aznar's leadership would threaten health, welfare and trade unions. The PP claimed 38.2% of votes, narrowly beating the PSOE. Without a majority, Aznar was forced to seek the backing of the Catalan nationalist Convergencia i Unio party (Convergence and Union) and the Partido Nacionalista Vasco, promising regional concessions.

Career Peak

On election Aznar pledged to reduce an unemployment rate of 23% and lower Spain's debt using market-based economic reforms. He implemented austerity measures to meet the economic criteria of the Maastricht Treaty. He continued the PSOE's privatization policy, selling the steel industry. He reformed employment laws, which had kept a third of Spaniards on short-term contracts, and reduced the top level income tax. Aznar's first term was economically successful. Unemployment was down to 15% by 2000, the economy grew by a fifth, Spain qualified for the single currency and its standing in the EU strengthened. Aznar appointed several independents to his government, including some from the left, thus easing Spaniards' fears of a return to right-wing dictatorship.

In 2000 elections Aznar won a second term and an absolute PP majority with 183 out of 350 parliamentary seats. His policy focused on encouraging small- and medium-sized businesses and continuing labour reforms. Companies were given financial incentives to employ 16–30-year-olds, women (especially those returning to work after childbirth) and the over-55s.

Despite economic success, the overwhelming issue was combating continued ETA violence, which had intensified over the 2000 election period. His initial hardline tactics appeared to be working when ETA announced a ceasefire in Sept. 1998 but this was revoked 14 months later. 2000 saw 33 people killed by ETA terrorism. A lower vote for Euskal Herritarrok, ETA's political coalition, in the May 2001 regional elections did not benefit the PP since nationalist sentiments remained high. Aznar rejected calls for multi-party peace talks on the recent Northern Ireland model and calls for a referendum on Basque separation. He went further in Aug. 2002, when a reconvened parliament voted 295 to 10 to ban ETA's political wing, Herri Batasuna, a move bolstered by a court ruling suspending party activities for 3 years.

On an international level, increasingly sour relations with Morocco came to a head in July 2002 when Moroccan troops landed on the uninhabited island of Perejil, 200 metres off the Moroccan coast. Spanish troops quickly retook the island, but the discord highlighted tensions over Spain's ownership of two enclaves on the Moroccan mainland, Ceuta and Melilla. Morocco had withdrawn its ambassador from Spain in Oct. 2001.

Aznar was criticized for his handling of the Prestige oil spillage off the coast of Galicia in Nov. 2002. During the preparations for war in Iraq in early 2003, he received further domestic criticism for his support of President Bush's policy towards Saddam Hussein. Aznar survived a secret parliamentary ballot by 184 votes to 164 but popular opinion remained largely anti-war. In May 2003 Spain co-sponsored a draft UN resolution with the US and UK on Iraq's post-war future. Having announced his intention to step down before the March 2004 general elections, his nominated successor and first deputy prime minister, Mariano Rajoy, was chosen as leader of the PP in Sept. 2003.

On 11 March 2004, Madrid's rail network was hit by a series of terrorist attacks that killed 191. Aznar's government blamed ETA in the aftermath but evidence soon pointed to a link with North Africa. At the general elections 3 days later, the PP suffered a backlash and were unexpectedly defeated by the PSOE. Aznar left office on 17 April 2004.

Bachelet, Michelle (Chile)

Introduction

Michelle Bachelet began her second term as president on 11 March 2014 following her electoral victory over centre-right opponent Evelyn Matthei in Dec. 2013. Leading the centre-left Nueva Mayoría (New Majority) coalition, Bachelet campaigned on a platform of addressing inequality through an ambitious programme of tax, educational and constitutional reforms.

Early Life

Verónica Michelle Bachelet Jeria was born on 29 Sept. 1951 in Santiago, the daughter of an air force general and an anthropologist. In 1962 the family moved to Washington, D.C., in the USA where her father was assigned to the Chilean embassy. Returning to Chile in 1964, Bachelet attended the Javiera Carrera Lyceum girls' school in Santiago. She then studied medicine at the University of Chile, where she joined the Socialist Youth Movement.

Following the 1973 coup against Salvador Allende's socialist government, her father was arrested for treason and later died in prison. Bachelet and her mother were arrested in Jan. 1975 and held at the notorious Villa Grimaldi in Santiago. Released later that month, they fled to Australia and then to East Germany, where Bachelet continued her medical studies at the Humboldt University in East Berlin.

Returning to Chile in 1979, Bachelet completed her medical degree at the University of Chile in 1983, specializing in paediatrics and public health. As a result of her family background, she found it hard to find employment but eventually gained work with various non-governmental organizations helping the children of the tortured and disappeared.

From the mid-1980s she became actively involved with the Socialist Party (PS). With the re-establishment of democracy in 1990 Bachelet began working for the health ministry and served as undersecretary of public health between March 1994 and July 1997. She attended the National Academy of Strategic and Political Studies in 1996 and the Inter-American Defense College in Washington, D.C., the following year. A member of the PS central committee from 1995, Bachelet joined the party's political committee in 1998 and worked on Ricardo Lagos' campaign for the presidency in 1999. He appointed her health minister in March 2000 and in Jan. 2002 she was given the defence portfolio.

On 15 Jan. 2006 Bachelet won a run-off against Sebastián Piñera with 53.5% of the vote to become the nation's first female president. Although her centre-left Concertación coalition was popular, it made only modest inroads into reducing inequality and faced accusations of incompetence, mismanagement of public funds and the slow handling of the aftermath of the Feb. 2010 earthquake that struck just 11 days before the end of Bachelet's term. Nonetheless, she left office with an 84% approval rating.

In April 2010 she established the Fundación Dialoga think tank and in Sept. 2010 was appointed to head the newly created UN Women, a body working for female empowerment. In March 2013 she announced her resignation, returning to Chile to seek a second presidential term. In the first round of polling on 17 Nov. 2013 she secured 47% of the vote, forcing a run-off against Evelyn Matthei. On 15 Dec. 2013 Bachelet received 62% of the vote and became the first leader since the end of military rule to attain two terms in office.

Career Peak

On returning to power Bachelet pledged to overhaul the country's educational, political and economic structures, many of which date back to Augusto Pinochet's administration. She promised free tuition for the poorest 70% of higher education students and was expected to reform the electoral system and introduce a new constitution to replace the one drawn up in 1980. During the first few months of her term, she pursued a range of proposals, particularly ambitious tax changes (including raising corporate tax rates) and a complex education reform, with the aim of promoting economic growth and fairness. However, her approval rating among voters has since dropped sharply in response to revelations of corruption scandals involving members of her family. Since the constitution prohibits presidents from serving consecutive terms, Bachelet was ineligible to stand in the 2018 presidential elections. On 11 March 2018 she was succeeded by Sebastián Piñera of Chile Vamos, who had previously been president in 2010–14.

Badawi, Abdullah (Malaysia)

Introduction

Tun Abdullah bin Haji Ahmad Badawi succeeded Mahathir Mohamad as prime minister in Oct. 2003. A less abrasive figure than Mahathir, he espoused moderate Islamic policies and social inclusion. He largely continued Mahathir's economic policies, making Malaysia's economy one of the most stable in the region, and sought to improve relations with Singapore after decades of fractiousness between the two countries. Badawi secured another term in March 2008 but with a much reduced majority. This weak showing led to his resignation in April 2009.

Early Life

Badawi was born on 26 Nov. 1939 on the island of Penang. In 1964 he graduated in Islamic studies from the University of Malaya. Badawi then entered the civil service, working in the department for public services until 1969 when he moved to the National Operation Council, which held executive powers after race riots that year. From 1971–73 he served as director general of the ministry of culture, Youth and Sports and in 1974 was made deputy secretary general of the department.

Badawi left the civil service in 1978 to pursue his political ambitions, having joined the United Malays National Organization (UMNO) in 1965. His father had been a co-founder of the party. He entered parliament as the member for Kepala Batas and was named parliamentary secretary to the Federal Territory ministry in the government of Mahathir Mohamad. In 1980 he was promoted to deputy minister for the department. From 1981–84 he was minister in the prime minister's department, then minister of education until 1986, minister of defence from 1986–87 and minister of foreign affairs from 1991–99. In 1999 he was made deputy prime minister with responsibility for home affairs, following the sacking and subsequent imprisonment of Mahathir's previous deputy, Anwar Ibrahim. Within UMNO, Badawi had become a member of the party's supreme council in 1981, and was then appointed party vice president 3 years later and party deputy president in 1999.

When Mahathir resigned after 22 years in power, at the end of Oct. 2003, Badawi assumed the premiership.

Career Peak

On taking office, Badawi was regarded as a less controversial figure than his predecessor. With a buoyant Malaysian economy, he announced few major policy changes. In addition to the premiership and home affairs portfolio (part of which he gave up in March 2004), Badawi also took control of the finance ministry.

Having no electoral mandate, Badawi called elections for March 2004. Though expected to win, many observers believed that the nation's growing Islamic fundamentalist parties (the Islamic Party of Malaysia, or PAS, being the largest) would gain support. The ruling National Front Coalition, of which UMNO is the main element, went on to win by a landslide, with the PAS losing power in one of two states it had previously controlled and only narrowly retaining power in the other. Opposition parties claimed electoral irregularities but failed to provide evidence. Armed with electoral success and a large parliamentary majority, Badawi continued to espouse moderate Islamic politics.

Badawi promised to crack down on the official corruption that blighted much of Mahathir's tenure. However, opponents were disappointed when many of Mahathir's key officials were retained in Badawi's first cabinet. Nevertheless, he deviated from some of the policies of the Mahathir era, for which he was criticized publicly by his predecessor. In March 2006 he introduced a new, multi-billion dollar plan with the goal of helping Malaysia to achieve developed-nation status by 2020. The new plan did not dismantle the longstanding positive-discrimination scheme for ethnic Malays, but did switch emphasis from grand infrastructure projects to tackling rural poverty and promoting education. In the international arena, he pursued closer ties with neighbouring Singapore, although in April 2006 he abandoned plans for a new bridge to the island state (a scheme that Mahathir had championed when in office).

In Nov. 2007, in the largest anti-government protests in almost a decade, thousands of demonstrators marched in Kuala Lumpur demanding reform of the electoral system. The elections of March 2008 were marred by allegations from Badawi's leading rivals of vote rigging. The National Front Coalition suffered its worst results since the 1960s. Its share of the parliamentary vote fell from two-thirds to a little over a half while at the state level it lost control of five assemblies. Badawi stood down as prime minister on 3 April 2009.

Bajnai, Gordon (Hungary)

Introduction

Gordon Bajnai took office as prime minister in April 2009, following the resignation of Prime Minister Ferenc Gyurcsány. A career banker, Bajnai had previously served in the ministry of economics and pledged to introduce a raft of economic reforms. He left office following Fidesz's landslide victory in the general election in April 2010.

Early Life

Born on 5 March 1968 in the southern Hungarian town of Szeged, György Gordon Bajnai was raised in Baja. He studied at the Budapest University of Economic Sciences (now Corvinus University), graduating from the international relations department in 1991. He entered the banking sector, working from 1991–93 at Creditum Financial Consulting Ltd. Following a 1993 internship at the European Bank for Reconstruction and Development in London, he joined Eurocorp International Finance Ltd (then under the directorship of Ferenc Gyurcsány).

From 1995–2000 Bajnai was managing director and then deputy chief executive officer of brokerage firm CA-IB Securities, where he oversaw the listing of several major companies on the stock exchange. From 2000–05 he was chief executive officer of Wallis ZRT, a trade and investment group with extensive holdings. During this period he served as a member of the board of directors of Graboplast, a flooring firm in which Wallis ZRT acquired a majority shareholding, and oversaw the liquidation of poultry-producing company Hajdu-Bet.

Bajnai became president of Budapest Airport Inc. in 2005, when he was also appointed to the supervisory committee of Zwack Inc. and became a member of the economic council of Corvinus University. On 1 July 2006 Prime Minister Gyurcsány appointed him head of the National Development Agency as part of a drive to prepare Hungary for eurozone membership. Bajnai became local government minister in 2007. In Oct. 2008, after the Alliance of Free Democrats (SzDSz) left the coalition government in protest at the slowing of economic reforms, Bajnai's department was renamed the ministry for national development and economy.

In March 2009, against a background of political deadlock, Bajnai announced that he would stand down and pass the premiership to the candidate with the greatest parliamentary support. On 30 March 2009 Bajnai won the backing of both the ruling Socialist Party (MSzP) and the SzDSz for his manifesto of economic reforms that combined cuts in welfare benefits with a stimulus package for business. Presenting himself as politically independent, Bajnai promised not to stand for re-election in polling scheduled for April 2010. On 14 April 2009 Gyurcsány initiated a constructive vote of no confidence and resigned in favour of Bajnai.

Career Peak

Bajnai was sworn in as prime minister on 14 April 2009 with 204 votes in favour and none against. He emphasized the severity of Hungary's economic crisis, predicting that the economy could shrink by up to 6% over the following year and advocating stringent austerity measures to reverse the decline. He identified his primary task as crisis management and announced that his new cabinet was selected on the basis of expertise rather than party allegiance. His early moves to cut state benefits, restructure taxes and invest in industry were well received by international markets. However, he faced severe challenges in winning public acceptance of his welfare reforms, especially changes to pension and benefit entitlement. He did not contest the general election of April 2010, having previously announced that he would not hold office for more than a year. He was succeeded by Viktor Orbán of Fidesz on 29 May 2010.

Bakili Muluzi, Elson (Malaŵi)

Introduction

Dr. Bakili Muluzi was president of Malaŵi from May 1994–May 2004. He succeeded Dr. Hastings Kamuzu Banda, who had ruled Malaŵi in an increasingly autocratic fashion since independence. A former protegé of Banda, Muluzi emerged as leader of the southern-dominated United Democratic Front in the country's first multi-party elections. Internationally respected for avoiding the dictatorial mistakes of his predecessor and many of his neighbours, Muluzi struggled to improve the living standards of one of Africa's poorest nations. Persuaded not to seek a constitutional amendment,

Muluzi stepped down after two terms on the election of his named successor, Bingu wa Mutharika.

A Muslim, Muluzi has two wives (one separated) and seven children.

Early Life

Elson Bakili Muluzi was born on 17 March 1943 in Machinga, Southern Province, the son of Chiutula Muluzi and Salile Abiti Sumani. Educated at Malosa Secondary School, Machinga District, Muluzi continued his education in Europe at the Bolton College of Education, England and the Thisted College of Further Education in Denmark. In 1973 he was appointed principal of Nasawa Technical College in Chiradzulu District, near Blantyre.

Entering politics in 1975, Muluzi was elected to the National Assembly as member for Machinga. The following year he joined the cabinet as junior minister for youth and culture, soon rising to education minister and minister without portfolio. Muluzi's influence was recognized when he became secretary-general of the sole legal party, the Malaŵi Congress Party (MCP). In 1981 he was abruptly demoted to minister of transport and communications by President Hastings Banda. Muluzi resigned from the government and left politics in 1982, turning his attention to business. His success brought him positions at the Road Transport Association and the Malaŵi Chamber of Commerce and Industry. Involvement with the underground political opposition led him to found the United Democratic Party in 1992. Calls, led by rights campaigner Chakufwa Chihana, for an end to the one-party state brought legalization of political parties in 1993 after a national referendum. In multi-party elections in May 1994 Muluzi's renamed United Democratic Front (UDF) took 85 out of 177 seats in the National Assembly. Banda's MCP won 56 seats and the Alliance for Democracy (AFORD) took 36 seats. Muluzi defeated Banda and two other opponents in presidential elections, gaining 47% of the vote.

Career Peak

Tortuous negotiations between the three elected parties resulted in a coalition between Muluzi's UDF and AFORD. Chihana accepted Muluzi's offer of a new position—second vice-president—despite objections in the National Assembly and the press to this disregard of the constitution. Muluzi gave Justin Malewezi, a Banda loyalist, the vice-presidency.

Ethnic, linguistic and social divisions dominated the 1994 and 1999 elections. Each of the major parties had clear geographic constituencies: the UDF's heartland was the populous Southern Region, where Muluzi held strong support from Muslims and the Yao, his ethnic group; AFORD represented the well-educated, less populated north while the MCP controlled the Chewa-dominated Central Region, Banda's birthplace.

Muluzi placed Banda under house arrest in 1995 on suspicion of organizing the murder of four ministers in 1993. A corruption case against the ex-president was cut short by his ill-health and death in 1997. Muluzi altered his attitude towards Banda, declaring a week of national mourning and giving him a state funeral.

Malaŵi's relations with her international creditors had been strained under Banda. In 1998 the International Monetary Fund (IMF) praised Muluzi's government for its economic reform programme and approved a US$27 m. loan. Concerns over corruption and fraud prompted criticism from the British government in Oct. 2000. Muluzi responded by sacking three senior ministers including Cassim Chilumpha, the education minister, after a damning report from the Public Accounts Committee. The report particularly condemned corrupt and wasteful contracts agreed by the education ministry.

The UDF narrowly missed an outright majority in the 1999 parliamentary elections, though Muluzi defeated Gwanda Chakuamba, the MCP/AFORD candidate. Violent opposition to the result focused on accusations of failure to register tens of thousands of voters in the MCP and AFORD heartlands in the centre and north, though international observers supported the result. Refusing to accept the result, Chakuamba had expected to win by running with the popular Chihana, whose reformist party lost seats through its alliance with the party of the old order. In 2000 Chakuamba was suspended for a year from the National Assembly for disrespect towards the president and for boycotting sittings.

In 2002 Malaŵi suffered its worse famine for 50 years; three-quarters of the population faced starvation. The government's reluctance to admit the scale of the problem delayed foreign aid. In July 2002 Italy and Germany announced debt relief measures totalling US$500,000 despite the IMF suspension of loans over allegations of corruption and bad management. In Dec. Muluzi negotiated a US$50 m. loan from the World Bank, pledging to cut costs and continue efforts to expunge corruption in government.

Fears that Muluzi would attempt to amend the constitution to allow him to seek a third term provoked violent clashes between opposition and UDF supporters in June 2002. Religious leaders, both Christian and Muslim, were particularly prominent in advising the president not to follow the path of his predecessor, who declared himself 'president for life' in 1972. In April 2003 he announced that he would step down as president and endorsed Bingu wa Mutharika, his economic planning minister. Support for Mutharika, who performed badly in the 1999 presidential election, was bolstered by a major cabinet reshuffle that excluded several opposition members, including Chihana.

The turn in Malaŵi's economic fortunes was marked by Muluzi's approval of the resumption of maize exports in July 2003. Economic improvements ended problems with the IMF, which agreed a US$9.2 m. loan and short-term assistance. The IMF decision encouraged European donors to resume aid programmes halted in 2001.

In Aug. 2003 several prominent UDF members split from the party, forming the National Democratic Alliance. However, the speaker of the National Assembly expelled the rebels, including former education minister Brown Mpinganjira, for quitting the party for which they had been elected. Vice-President Justin Malewezi defected to the People's Progressive Movement in Jan. 2004 but Muluzi was barred from sacking him without impeachment.

The run-up to elections in May 2004 was dominated by the opposition's failure to select a joint candidate. AIDS, previously a taboo subject, was an important campaign issue after Muluzi announced that his brother had died of an AIDS-related condition. Muluzi clashed with the EU election observers, threatening to deport them for bias and interference. The observers claimed serious flaws in the election that gave the UDF's Mutharika 35% of the vote, defeating John Tembo, with 27%, and Gwanda Chakuamba, with 26%. Both Tembo and Chakuamba rejected the result, demanding a recount. Nevertheless, Mutharika was installed as president on 24 May 2004.

Balaguer, Joaquín (Dominican Republic)

Introduction

A lawyer and writer, Joaquín Balaguer served as president from 1960–62, 1966–78 and 1986–96. Over seven terms, he outlasted all of his Latin American contemporaries with the exception of Fidel Castro.

Early Life

Joaquín Antonio Balaguer Ricardo was born on 1 Sept. 1906 in the northern town of Navarette. He studied law at the University of Santo Domingo, later gaining a PhD from the University of Paris. Following a short stint as a journalist, he moved into politics in 1930 when he was appointed Attorney General in the Court of Properties.

Balaguer held numerous posts during the dictatorship of Gen. Rafael Leonides Trujilio, including undersecretary of foreign relations (1937), secretary of education (1949–55) and secretary of state of foreign relations (1953–56). In 1957 he became vice-president and when Gen. Trujilio's brother, Héctor, resigned his nominal role as president in 1960, Balaguer was sworn in as his successor.

Career Peak

Initially, Balguer was the puppet of the dictator, lacking little power in his own right. However, following Rafael Trujilio's assassination in 1961, Belaguer adopted a more independent stance. His attempted reforms, though, met with opposition from both hard-line Trujillistas and liberal reformers, who deemed his proposals too weak. Balaguer held power until a military coup in 1962 forced him into exile in New York and then Puerto Rico.

US intervention in 1965 ended the Dominican Republic's brief civil war and the following year Balaguer returned to run in the presidential election against Juan Bosch. The US president, Lyndon B. Johnson, supported Balaguer as a champion against communism. Balaguer duly won at the polls, securing re-election in 1970 and 1974. In these elections, the

Dominican Revolutionary Party (PRD), the only viable opposition party, boycotted proceedings. Balaguer's 12 years in power from 1966 were marked by repression, though his tenure was considered less brutal than that of Trujilio.

Public work schemes, foreign investment, foreign borrowing and tourism all contributed to economic expansion. However, prosperity proved short lived. By the late 1970s growth had slowed and the country faced rising inflation and unemployment.

At the 1978 presidential election, Balaguer was defeated by Antonio Guzmán Fernández of the PRD and 4 years later he lost out to Salvador Jorge Blanco. However, Balaguer won a new term of office in 1986, aged 80. Blind, practically deaf and with his health in decline, his third presidency was marked by greater tolerance of opposition and an improved human rights record. He narrowly won re-election in 1990. Two years later, work was completed on his most visible legacy, the vast concrete Colombus Lighthouse to commemorate the landing of Columbus in Hispaniola in 1492. The controversial 10-storey edifice cost US$250m. at a time when the country faced 25% unemployment.

In 1994 Balaguer again won re-election amid charges of electoral fraud. Under international pressure, he agreed to stand down and schedule a new election in 1996.

Later Life

As a frail 92-year-old, he contested an eighth presidential term in 2000 but could secure only third place. On 14 July 2002 Balaguer died of heart failure in Santo Domingo.

Balkenende, Jan Peter (Netherlands)

Introduction

Jan Peter Balkenende, head of the Christian Democratic Appeal (CDA), succeeded Wim Kok as Dutch prime minister following the elections of May 2002. He briefly led a right-of-centre coalition which included the People's Party for Freedom and Democracy (VVD) and List Pim Fortuyn (LPF) until Oct. 2002, when LPF in-fighting forced the collapse of the government. Balkenende then led the CDA to victory at the elections of Jan. 2003 and formed a new coalition with the VVD and Democrats '66 (D66). Following the Nov. 2006 elections, in which the CDA was again returned as the largest party but lost ground, Balkenende remained prime minister as he formed a new coalition government. He was succeeded by Mark Rutte in Oct. 2010.

Early Life

Balkenende was born on 7 May 1956 in Kapelle. He graduated in history and law from the Amsterdam Free University. Between 1982 and 1984 he was a legal affairs policy officer for the Netherlands Universities Council before joining the policy institute of the CDA, where he stayed until 1998. Between 1993 and 2002 he held a professorship of Christian social thought on society and economics at the Amsterdam Free University. An alderman for Amstelveen, he won a parliamentary seat at the elections of 1998.

When Jaap de Hoop Scheffer resigned the party leadership in late 2001 there was a divisive contest to replace him. Balkenende came under fire for his lack of experience and perceived weak leadership skills, but eventually emerged victorious. In the build-up to the 2002 elections he refused to rule out a coalition with any party, including List Pim Fortuyn, although he distanced himself from some of its extremist policies.

Career Peak

Following the May 2002 elections Balkenende headed a coalition of the CDA, LPF and VVD. His cabinet was sworn in 9 weeks later. He pledged to tighten up immigration policy, reduce taxes and reduce the number of people receiving disability benefits. In addition, he sought a review of the Netherlands' liberal drugs and euthanasia legislation. However, his government was plagued by the instability of the LPF, whose leader, Mat Herben, resigned in Aug. 2002. LPF in-fighting was caused by a personality clash between two of its ministers, Eduard Bomhoff and Herman Heinsbroek, both of whom resigned in Oct. 2002. The CDA and VVD were unable to continue alone and the government resigned on 21 Oct. 2002. Balkenende agreed to remain in place in a caretaker capacity until new elections.

At elections to the Second Chamber in Jan. 2003, the CDA took 44 seats, two ahead of the Labour Party (PvdA). In May 2003, after months of negotiations, Balkenende was sworn in as head of a coalition government comprising the CDA, VVD and D66. His government's policies proved unpopular. In Oct. 2004 more than 200,000 people turned out in Amsterdam to protest against public spending cuts and welfare reform, and in June 2005 the electorate voted decisively against the proposed new European Union constitution in a national referendum.

In July 2006 Balkenende formed a temporary minority administration pending fresh elections. This resulted from the collapse of the previous coalition on the withdrawal of D66 in a row over immigration (a highly-charged issue in Dutch politics). The CDA lost support in the elections in Nov. 2006 but remained the largest parliamentary party with 41 seats. Balkenende eventually formed a new three-party centrist coalition in Feb. 2007. His government eased immigration legislation in 2007 and increased public spending on health care and education.

In Sept. 2008, as crisis in the credit system spread through continental Europe, the governments of the Netherlands, Belgium and Luxembourg partly nationalized Fortis, a large regional retail bank, amid uncertainty about its financial stability.

The CDA remained the largest Dutch party in the June 2009 polling for the European Parliament, taking five of 25 seats allocated to the Netherlands, but conceded electoral ground to the far-right Party for Freedom (PVV), which won four seats. However, Balkenende's preparations for the general election of June 2010 suffered a setback in Feb. 2010 when the PvdA left his coalition, causing the collapse of the cabinet. He remained in office as caretaker prime minister. After a disappointing result for the CDA in June's parliamentary elections Balkenende stood down as leader and renounced his seat. He remained in office until 14 Oct. when VVD leader Mark Rutte succeeded him.

Banda, Hastings (Malaŵi)

Introduction

Dr Hastings Kamuzu Banda was Malaŵi's (formerly Nyasaland's) leader from 1963 until 1994. Instrumental in Nyasaland's nationalist struggle, he became Prime Minister in 1963 following the collapse of the Federation of Rhodesia and Nyasaland. As President after 1965, he was known for his autocratic and often despotic rule, though his economic policies were conservative, and his willingness to work with white partners internationally made him unpopular with many fellow African leaders.

Early Life

Hastings Kamuzu Banda claimed to have been born on 14 May 1906 in Kasungu in Malaŵi (then the British Central Africa Protectorate). However, it is now generally accepted that he was born in 1899. His early education was in a Church of Scotland missionary school. In his early teens he travelled to South Africa, working as an interpreter for a Rand goldmining company and in 1923 he moved to the US. He took a degree in history and political science at the University of Chicago before studying medicine at an all-black university and moving to Edinburgh, Scotland in 1941 to continue his education. He remained in Britain throughout the 1940s and worked as a general practitioner until 1953, but he retained political links with Nyasaland.

The Federation of Rhodesia and Nyasaland which came into being in 1953 was regarded by Banda and his allies as an unacceptable extension of white dominance. In the same year he moved to Ghana but, after prompting from associates, he returned to Nyasaland to be met by around 12,000 supporters at the airport. He became President of the Nyasaland African Congress (which evolved into the Malaŵi Congress Party in 1960). In March the following year, with tensions rising and a state of emergency called, he was arrested by the British authorities and imprisoned in Southern Rhodesia after unsubstantiated charges were made linking him to a murder plot.

He was released in 1960 and negotiated with the colonial powers for constitutional amendments which increased African representation in the Nyasaland Legislative Assembly. Between 1961 and 1963 he served as Minister of Natural Resources and Local Government.

Career Peak

He then became prime minister and in 1964 Nyasaland was granted independence and changed its name to Malaŵi. An immediate conflict with the younger and more radical section of his party erupted and led to a number of sackings and ministerial resignations. A rebellion led by two former ministers was quashed the following year and in 1966 Malaŵi became a republic with Banda as its President. Six years later the office was made his for life.

The Malaŵi Banda inherited had certain severe disadvantages, including a scarcity of mineral resources, a failing agriculture system, large debts, weak infrastructure and an unevolved education system. His policies tended to be conservative and pragmatic in nature, and did bear fruit in the early years of his rule, with GDP growing consistently until the late 1970s. However, his autocratic style of rule was unpopular with many of his colleagues and he displayed some of the worst excesses of any of the African dictators. Malaŵi was a one-party state and though elections were ostensibly democratic, all candidates had to be approved by Banda. Political opponents were routinely dismissed from their positions or jailed, and torture and murder became an accepted part of the political agenda.

In terms of foreign policy, he was out of favour with many other African rulers, including Presidents Kaunda of Zambia and Nyerere of Tanzania. They felt that the economic progress he made was at the expense of the Africanization of social institutions within the country and there was considerable outrage at his willingness to improve ties with, and accept economic assistance from, the apartheid regime in South Africa and the Portuguese authorities in Mozambique. From 1977 onwards the economy also started to decline, principally due to the world-wide oil crisis and a succession of droughts.

In Oct. 1992 pro-democracy demonstrations led to the deaths of over 40 people and the West ceased to provide Banda with aid. Against this background he agreed to a referendum to decide if a multi-party system should be introduced. An overwhelming majority of the nation believed that it should and in 1994, in the first free elections since 1991, Banda and his party were ousted from power. A new president, Bakili Muluzi, was installed.

Later Life

The following year Banda was placed under house arrest in connection with the deaths of four ministers in 1983 who were discovered to have been clubbed to death by police. Banda was acquitted in 1996 before apologizing nationally for any atrocities that had occurred under his rule. He retired from politics in July 1997 and, after a corruption case against him was dismissed due to his failing health, he died on 25 Nov. 1997 in Johannesburg, South Africa. He was accompanied by his long time 'official hostess', Cecilia Kadzamira.

Banda, Joyce (Malaŵi)

Introduction

Joyce Banda was sworn in as president in April 2012 following the death of President Bingu wa Mutharika. A lifelong campaigner for women's rights, Banda was the first female president of Malaŵi and only the second female president of any African state. She is the leader of the People's Party, which she formed in 2011 after a dispute with Mutharika that saw her expelled from the Democratic Progressive Party (DPP).

Early Life

Joyce Banda was born in Malaŵi's Zomba District on 12 April 1950. In 1975 she left her abusive husband, who worked at Malaŵi's embassy in Nairobi, Kenya. Her decision, she said later, was inspired by a Kenyan women's movement.

Banda secured her financial independence by establishing a clothing manufacturing business, the first of several enterprises she set up. In 1990 she founded the National Association of Business Women, a non-governmental group aimed at improving the prospects of small, female-led businesses. In 1997 she set up the Joyce Banda Foundation, focusing on education.

She entered politics in 1999 as the member of parliament for the Zomba-Malosa constituency, serving under President Bakili Muluzi as minister of gender and community services. She was re-elected to parliament in 2004 but left the defeated United Democratic Front to join the DPP, the party of new president Bingu wa Mutharika. Banda was named foreign minister on 1 June 2006. During her time in the role she severed ties with Taiwan in favour of closer relations with the government in Beijing, paving the way for communist Chinese investment in Malaŵi's infrastructure.

In 2009 Mutharika selected Banda as his running mate in his bid for re-election, seeking to take advantage of her popularity in rural areas. However, once elected, Mutharika moved to isolate Banda, who had refused to support the planned succession to the presidency of Mutharika's brother. Having been ousted from the DPP, Banda established her own People's Party in 2011. She refused to relinquish the vice-presidency, and Mutharika lacked the constitutional powers to remove her.

Mutharika's sudden death from a heart attack on 5 April 2012 threatened a prolonged power struggle but after 2 days of political jockeying, constitutional procedure prevailed and Banda was sworn into office on 7 April.

Career Peak

Within days of becoming president Banda dismissed the chief of police, Peter Mukhito, who had been accused of mishandling anti-government riots in 2011 in which at least 19 people were killed. She replaced him with Lot Dzonzi, a human rights supporter. She also acted quickly to remove the minister of information, Patricia Kaliati, who had attempted to block Banda's accession after the death of Mutharika. In May 2012 she oversaw a currency devaluation to comply with International Monetary Fund conditions for a restoration of external funding. However, the move triggered steep increases in the prices of basic goods and in Jan. 2013 there were demonstrations against her government over rising inflation and economic austerity. In March 2013 several senior political figures were accused of having tried to prevent Banda's presidential succession following Mutharika's death and were charged with treason. Then, in Oct. Banda dissolved her cabinet amid allegations of high-level corruption in government and appointed a new administration.

A long-standing border dispute with Tanzania was exacerbated when Malaŵi awarded a licence for oil exploration in Lake Malaŵi. The dispute remained unresolved by early 2014.

Banda's term in office ended on 31 May 2014 after she lost presidential elections to DPP candidate Peter Mutharika. Despite initially alleging electoral fraud, Banda backtracked on her demands for a re-election and handed power to Mutharika.

Banda, Rupiah (Zambia)

Introduction

Rupiah Banda became president on 2 Nov. 2008 after winning the general election following the death of the incumbent Levy Mwanawasa. A career diplomat, the centrist Banda was a leading figure in Kenneth Kaunda's Marxist regime before joining the ruling Movement for Multi-Party Democracy in 2002.

Early Life

Rupiah Banda was born on 19 Feb. 1937 in Gwanda, then in British-ruled Southern Rhodesia, to parents originally from Northern Rhodesia. He was educated at Munali Secondary School in Lusaka from 1954–58, where he joined the youth wing of the United National Independence Party (UNIP), headed by Kenneth Kaunda. Banda studied economics at the University of Ethiopia in Addis Ababa and then at Sweden's Lund University from 1960. While there, he served as UNIP's representative in northern Europe,

organising scholarships for several other Africans who would later play a role in their countries' independence movements. Returning to Lusaka in newly independent Zambia in 1964, Banda enrolled at the National Institute for Public Affairs, which presaged a diplomatic career. Postings to Egypt (1965–67) and the USA (1967–69) followed.

Banda was a manager at the Rural Development Corporation and National Agricultural Marketing Board in the early 1970s. He also developed business interests, taking stakes in engineering firms linked to the copper mines that formed the backbone of the steadily growing economy. Returning to the international stage, Banda became Zambia's permanent representative to the United Nations in New York in 1974. He was chairman on the UN Council for Namibia, set up to steer South West Africa towards liberation from South Africa. The following year he was appointed the minister of foreign affairs in Kaunda's UNIP government (UNIP being the only legal party after Kaunda signed a constitutional amendment in Dec. 1972). Much of his work involved attempts to bring peace to Angola and to improve relations between the 'frontline states' (Angola, Botswana, Lesotho, Mozambique, Swaziland, Tanzania and Zambia) and South Africa.

Elected as an MP for the Munali constituency south of Lusaka in Dec. 1978, Banda's early parliamentary careers coincided with a collapse in copper prices that brought serious economic decline and growing opposition to Kaunda's regime. Banda lost his seat in the 1983 election and subsequently worked as a civil servant in Lusaka's civic authority, before being appointed minister of state for mines. Banda recaptured his parliamentary seat in 1988 but his party was beset by deteriorating economic conditions, corruption scandals and mismanagement. When multi-party democracy returned to Zambia following a referendum in Aug. 1991, the Movement for Multi-Party Democracy (MMD) brought an end to the Kaunda era. Having lost his seat to an MMD candidate, Ronald Penza, in the Oct. 1991 general election, Banda resumed his business interests.

He left the UNIP in 2000 and 2 years later joined the MMD, whose leader, Dr Mwanawasa, displayed an openness towards former opposition MPs. Banda helped galvanize support for the MMD in the east of the country and was rewarded with the position of vice president after the MMD victory in the Sept. 2006 general election. Following President Mwanawasa's death in Aug. 2008, Banda became acting president and stood as the MMD's candidate in the presidential election of 30 Oct. Initial results showed Banda's main challenger, Michael Sata of the Patriotic Front (PF), in the lead but as votes from rural areas were counted, Banda closed the gap. Final results on 2 Nov. 2008 showed Banda with 40% of the vote against 38% for Sata. The PF alleged vote rigging and refused to recognize Banda's victory, with Sata's supporters rioting in Lusaka and Kitwe.

Career Peak

Banda pledged to continue his predecessor's pro-business policies and anti-corruption efforts, as well as address the country's widespread poverty. He urged the opposition to set aside divisions after the closely fought election. He faced growing unrest in 2009 as the global economic downturn brought down the price of Zambia's main export commodities and led to job cuts. In presidential elections held in Sept. 2011 Banda lost to the opposition leader Michael Sata and he accordingly succeeded Banda as president.

Bandaranaike, Sirimavo (Sri Lanka)

Introduction

Sirimavo Bandaranaike served as prime minister of Sri Lanka between 1960–65, 1970–77 and 1994–2000. She was the world's first female prime minister. Her entry into politics followed the assassination of her husband, Prime Minister S. W. R. D. Bandaranaike in 1956, when she took control of the Sri Lankan Freedom Party. Bandaranaike's tenures were marked by controversy; despite a declared leaning towards a socialist agenda, her aggressive promotion of Sinhalese nationalism was criticized for exacerbating ethnic tensions between the majority Sinhalese and the minority Tamils.

Early Life

Sirimavo Ratwatte was born to a wealthy landowning family in British colonial Ceylon on 17 April 1916. Educated at St Bridget's, a Roman Catholic convent in Colombo, she married Solomon Bandaranaike in 1940. Her husband founded the Sri Lanka Freedom Party (SLFP) and both converted from Christianity to Buddhism, the dominant Sinhalese religion. As a Sinhalese Buddhist, Bandaranaike promised to put an end to the privileges the Tamils were seen to enjoy under British rule. Ceylon became an independent state in 1948.

In Sept. 1959, 3 years after he was elected prime minister, S. W. R. D. Bandaranaike was assassinated by a Buddhist monk. Threatened with the disintegration of the SLFP, Sirimavo Bandaranaike was called upon to succeed her husband as leader. In the 1960 elections 'the weeping widow' led the party to victory, while on 20 July Bandaranaike became the first woman to serve as prime minister.

Career Peak

Sirimavo Bandaranaike's policies aggravated the fundamental cultural and religious divisions between the Sinhalese and the Tamil population; the latter had already been alienated by her husband's decision to adopt Sinhalese as the official language. She continued the programme of commercial nationalization, instigated by her husband, and gave priority to the Sinhalese for places in universities, the government and the civil service. Tamils were replaced as heads of nationalized industries and Sinhalese were placed in control of the tea estates. Following the Tamil-based campaign of civil disobedience, in defiance of her husband's 'sinhala Only' strategy, Bandaranaike was forced to declare a state of emergency. She was supported by Felix Dias Bandaranaike, her nephew and minister of finance and justice, who famously called for 'a little bit of totalitarianism'. The Tamils responded with separatist demands.

By 1965 the coalition government formed to relieve the country's political and economic pressures had proved ineffective. Bandaranaike's first term ended with the victory of the opposition, the United National Party, in the March 1965 elections.

When Bandaranaike re-assumed power with a left-wing coalition (the United Front) in 1970, her measures to ensure stability were no less uncompromising. These measures and external factors led to mounting inflation, higher oil prices and unemployment, culminating in a student and activist-led rebellion that was brutally suppressed in 1971. Emergency law was reinstated, and remained until 1976.

1972 marked the creation of a new constitution. Ceylon became Sri Lanka and was declared a republic. The predominantly Hindu Tamil minority was further provoked when Buddhism was declared the state religion, and Sinhala the exclusive state language. Worsening economic conditions led to a general strike in 1976, again put down by the government; in the same year the Liberation Tigers of Tamil Eelam, a militant separatist movement, was formed. Defeated in the general elections of 1977, Bandaranaike was expelled from parliament 3 years later. Accused of abusing her rights as prime minister, she was denied her civil rights and banned from office for 6 years.

Later Life

Bandaranaike attempted to re-enter politics in the 1980s but her campaign for the presidency in 1988 was unsuccessful. In 1994 her daughter, Chandrika Bandaranaike Kumaratunga, was elected president and appointed her mother prime minister. The role of prime minister, however, had been rendered largely ceremonial by an amendment to the structure of government. Citing ill health, Bandaranaike stepped down in 2000. On the 10 Oct. 2000, hours after casting her vote in the country's general elections, Bandaranaike suffered a fatal heart attack. She was survived by three children, including President Kumaratunga and UNP opposition leader Anura Bandaranaike.

Banzer Suárez, Hugo (Bolivia)

Introduction

President between 1997–2001, Hugo Banzer Suárez represented the Acción Democrática Nacional (ADN), of which he was co-founder. From 1971–78 he led Bolivia as a military dictatorship before being ousted in a coup. During his last term, Banzer faced the challenge of remedying Bolivia's precarious economic situation and widespread poverty. He also attempted to eradicate the illegal, if traditional, production of coca, the basis of cocaine. In Aug. 2001 ill health forced him to hand over power to his vice president and fellow ADN member, Jorge Fernando Quiroga Ramírez.

Early Life

Banzer was born on 10 May 1926 in the eastern town of Concepción. He trained at the Colegio Militar de Ejérjito, before finishing his studies in Argentina as a Bolivian army representative. He pursued a successful army career rising to the post of general. Banzer's political career began in the education ministry in which he served from 1964–66 under the regime of Co-president Generals René Barrientos Ortuño and General Alfredo Ovando Candia.

Career Peak

The cycle of coup and counter coup in Bolivian politics was continued by Banzer when in 1971 he deposed the socialist army general, Juan Jose Torres, and established himself as leader of a right-wing military regime. He implemented successful economic policies, including public sector investment, which produced a strong economy with low inflation. The success was short lived and the consequent fall out in the early 1980s brought hyperinflation and large public debt. At the beginning of his rule, Banzer pledged to restore democracy with constitutional elections. However, following an attempted coup in 1974, he cancelled elections and banned all political activity. A strict regime was enforced in which many were imprisoned or pushed into exile. He neutralized the influence of the trade unions, which were powerful under the Marxist regime of Torres. In 1978 Banzer was, in turn, deposed by General Juan Pereda Asbún.

The following year Banzer reinvented himself in order to run for the presidency. He disassociated himself from his image as a military dictator, creating the ADN as a vehicle for election. The party pledged to lead Bolivia into democracy. In the 1979 elections Banzer came third with 14% of votes. In 1980 this increased to 16.9%. In 1981 Banzer was arrested for his part in plotting a coup. He returned to fight his third democratic election in 1985 receiving 28.6% of votes. Despite gaining the highest amount of votes, without a majority Banzer was pitted against the second place centre-left former president Victor Paz Estenssoro. Parliament chose the latter.

For his fourth attempt in 1989, the ADN joined forces with the Partido Demócrata Cristiano, choosing Banzer as the coalition's candidate. He came second behind his rival, the Movimiento Nacionalista Revolucionario (MNR) candidate Gonzalo Sánchez de Lozada. Fearing the latter would be chosen in a head-to-head, Banzer withdrew from the race. The coalition placed its support behind Jaime Paz Zamora, the third place candidate of the Movimiento Izquierda Revolucionaria (Movement of Revolutionary Left). Under Paz's presidency, Banzer was in charge of government policy as head of the Consejo del Gobierno de Unidad y Convergencia (Political Council of Convergence and National Unity). He also controlled senior appointments in the armed forces and the public sector.

Following an unsuccessful fifth attempt at the presidency in 1993, Banzer resigned as ADN leader, only to re-emerge in 1995. In 1997 he was finally preferred by parliament over the second place MNR candidate, Juan Carlos Durán Saucedo. On election Banzer promised better jobs and services and an end to the privatization schemes of his predecessor that had caused public discontent. The successful privatization of oil and gas companies had failed to provide increased employment or benefit the majority indigenous population living in poverty. Banzer had courted indigenous support by promising large investments. His major policy, though, was the US-supported eradication of coca production. A centuries-old crop traditionally cultivated for religious ceremonies and later to sustain workers in difficult conditions in the Andes, coca production increased dramatically in the 1970s to feed the booming illegal drug industry. At its height, around a third of Bolivians were financially dependent on its production and the trade generated millions of dollars for the black economy. Eradication programmes destroyed 40,000 ha in the Chapare region leaving many farmers destitute. Replacement schemes promoting banana and pineapple farming failed to provide enough jobs or revenue to compensate. Plans to cut into the 12,000 ha of legal coca crops in the Yungas highland caused protests. UN investment in alternative schemes has also failed owing to the near impossible farming terrain.

By 1999 Banzer's promises were still unfulfilled and the rate of economic growth had fallen. Anger with increased water charges (for a new reservoir), coupled with general economic misery, provoked widespread protests, strikes and roadblocks in April 2000. Violence ensued and Banzer announced a state of emergency. A police strike forced Banzer to grant wage increases to contain the protests. Social unrest continued over the following year. Farmers, coca growers, public sector workers and the unemployed united against rising unemployment and falling incomes brought on by falling economic growth. Meanwhile, Banzer's anti-poverty policy was languishing in congress awaiting authorization.

In July 2001 Banzer was diagnosed with cancer and in Aug. he resigned, appointing his vice president and fellow ADN member Quiroga to see out the rest of his term. Born on 5 May 1960 in Cochabamba, Quiroga studied industrial engineering and then business management in Texas. As well as working for various companies in the private sector, Quiroga built up a respectable political CV. He worked under Paz as finance minister among other positions. In 1993 he was the ADN's campaign manager before becoming its vice president. He was appointed Bolivia's vice president on Banzer's election.

Quiroga was left with a difficult economic and political situation. Yet, many saw his appointment as an opportunity for change. On his inauguration, Quiroga pledged to concentrate his efforts on fighting poverty and resolving the faltering economy by seeking foreign investment. But four earlier schemes to reactivate the economy while Quiroga was vice president failed. He also promised to eradicate corruption and nepotism in politics. But his year in power offered little time to make much impact.

Later Life

Banzer's illness persisted and in March 2002 he formally resigned as ADN leader. He died on 5 May 2002.

Barak, Ehud (Israel)

Introduction

Ehud Barak served as prime minister between 1999 and 2001, having held high rank in the army. His unsuccessful efforts to negotiate a truce with Palestine led to his resignation as premier but he remained head of the Labour Party until leaving to form his own party in 2011. Since 2007 he has served as minister of defence.

Early Life

Ehud Barak was born Ehud Brog in 1942 in Kibbutz Mishmar Hasharon in the former British mandate of Palestine. The eldest child of East European immigrant parents, he was drafted into the Israel Defence Forces (IDF) at the age of 17 and changed his name to Barak ('lightning' in Hebrew). A member of the elite, top-secret special forces unit, Sayeret Matkal, he took part in intelligence gathering and counter-terrorism operations and, by 1971, was unit commander. During his tenure he led several high-profile, hostage-freeing missions, including Operation Isotope in 1972 and Operation Entebbe in 1976, which were credited with leading to the break-up of the Palestinian militant group, Black September. However, Sayeret Matkal faced criticism for the assassinations of Palestine Liberation Organization (PLO) targets in a raid in Lebanon in 1973 led by Barak.

Alongside his military career, he graduated from the Hebrew University of Jerusalem in 1968 in physics and mathematics, before completing a master's in engineering and economics at Stanford, California in 1978. In 1982 he was appointed head of the planning branch of the IDF and a year later, head of the intelligence branch. By 1986 he was commander of IDF central command and in May 1987 was promoted to deputy chief-of staff. He assumed overall command of the IDF in April 1991 as chief of general staff, remaining in the position until 1995.

In July 1995 Barak entered politics as interior minister in the Labour government of Prime Minister Yitzhak Rabin. He subsequently served as foreign minister under Rabin's successor, Shimon Peres, until June 1996, when the latter was replaced by Likud's Binyamin Netanyahu. Despite Labour's defeat at the polls, Barak won his parliamentary seat and replaced Peres as party chairman in 1997. At the May 1999 elections, he defeated Netanyahu to become prime minister, heading his One Israel centre-left

coalition with the Meimad and Gesher parties. He was sworn in as prime minister and minister of defence on 6 July.

Career Peak

With One Israel having only won 26 of 120 seats in parliament, Barak was forced to extend the coalition into an unwieldy multi-party alliance that combined secular and religious parties. In May 2000 he withdrew Israeli troops from southern Lebanon and began peace talks with the PLO which culminated in the Middle East Peace Summit at Camp David in July 2000 with Yasser Arafat and Bill Clinton. However, attempts to negotiate a 'final status settlement' proved fruitless with both sides unwilling to compromise on key issues. The outbreak of the Second Intifada in Sept. 2000 and Israeli–Arab riots in Oct. further damaged Barak's credibility as leader. With his coalition destabilized by the withdrawal of several parties, he resigned in Feb. 2001 and lost prime ministerial elections to Likud leader Ariel Sharon.

Later Life

Having made a foray into business in 1995, Barak became a consultant in the USA for various security-related firms and established himself as a public speaker. In 2004, he re-entered politics to campaign for the Labour party leadership although when it emerged he lacked the support to win, he renounced his bid in favour of Shimon Peres. During his second attempt to regain the leadership in May 2007 he admitted that inexperience had caused him to make mistakes as prime minister. He won a second round run-off to defeat Ami Ayalon and shortly afterwards replaced previous Labour leader Amir Peretz as defence minister in Ehud Olmert's cabinet.

After Labour's poor performance at the 2009 elections in which they won only 13 seats, Barak faced opposition from his own party for entering into coalition with Likud but kept his position as defence minister in Binyamin Netanyahu's new administration.

In May 2010 Israel was widely criticized for an IDF attack on an international aid convoy to Gaza which resulted in nine civilian casualties. Facing an inquiry into the legality of the raid in Aug., Barak said he took full responsibility for the events and expressed regret for the deaths whilst defending the army's actions.

Following several months of infighting among Labour's MPs over the party's role in the Netanyahu government, Barak and four of his Labour colleagues left the party in Jan. 2011 to form a new party called Independence. Described by Barak as 'centrist, Zionist and democratic'. it remained part of the ruling coalition.

In Nov. 2012, in the wake of an 8 day conflict in Gaza, Barak announced his resignation from politics although he did remain defence minister until March 2013 when a new government was sworn in following parliamentary elections in Jan. of that year.

Barre, Raymond (France)

Introduction

Raymond Barre was a centrist economist who served as prime minister from 1976–81. With the economy struggling in the aftermath of the 1973 oil crisis, his government imposed unpopular austerity measures.

Early Life

Born on the French Indian Ocean island of Réunion on 12 April 1924 into a wealthy Roman Catholic family, Barre moved to Paris in 1946 to study law, economics and politics at the *Institut d'études politiques de Paris*. After graduating, he joined the economics faculty as a professor and in 1959 he accepted a senior position in the ministry of industry. From 1967–73 he served as a commissioner for economic and financial affairs within the institutional structure of the European Economic Community (forerunner of the EU), helping to draw up an influential proposal for European monetary co-operation.

Career Peak

Barre joined Prime Minister Jacques Chirac's cabinet as foreign trade minister in 1976. Although he had little public profile at the time, President Giscard d'Estaing appointed him premier and minister of economy and finance when Chirac resigned in Aug. 1976.

The international oil crisis of the early 1970s had brought to an end France's three decades of post-war prosperity. To tackle the new economic reality, Barre enforced tough anti-inflation policies, including reducing government spending and cutting thousands of jobs in loss-making industries such as steel and coal. Rising unemployment and declining living standards took a heavy toll on his popularity. He also angered the trade unions after calling on them 'to stop whingeing and start working'. He was succeeded as prime minister by Pierre Mauroy in May 1981 following the electoral victory of President François Mitterrand's Socialist Party.

Later Life

Barre contested the presidential elections of 1988, coming third with 16.5% of the first round vote, behind Mitterrand and Chirac. His last major political office was the mayorship of Lyon from 1995 until 2001. He retired from front-line politics the following year and died in Paris on 25 Aug. 2007.

Băsescu, Traian (Romania)

Introduction

Traian Băsescu, a former ship's captain and mayor of Bucharest, successfully fought the country's 2004 presidential elections on an anti-corruption platform. He took over from Ion Iliescu, who had served as president for much of the post-communist period. Băsescu was suspended from office in April 2007 but resumed his role a month later after a national referendum supported his reinstatement. He was narrowly re-elected in Dec. 2009.

Early Life

Băsescu was born in Basarabi near the port of Constanta on 4 Nov. 1951 and graduated from the Marine Institute in Constanta in 1976. He then joined the merchant navy, controlled in the communist era by NAVROM, winning promotion to captain in 1981 and to admiral of the merchant fleet in the mid-1980s. In 1987 he became head of NAVROM and in 1989 entered the political scene as general director of the State Inspectorate of Civic Navigation in the ministry of transport. After the dramatic collapse of the Ceauşescu regime in Dec. 1989, Băsescu was promoted to deputy minister of transport. He became minister of transport in 1991 in the government dominated by the National Salvation Front (FSN), which had received mass support in the first post-communist elections on 20 May 1990.

Following a split in the FSN in 1992, Băsescu joined Petre Roman in the new centre-left Democratic Party and, in 1996, he co-ordinated Roman's unsuccessful presidential campaign. Băsescu was re-elected as a Democratic Party MP in 1996 and served as minister of transport until 2000, when he stood as the Democratic Party candidate in the Bucharest mayoral election. He won and began co-ordinating the regeneration of large areas of the city, gaining praise for his direct approach to addressing problems—from cracking down on the notorious packs of stray dogs to improving traffic flow and municipal central heating systems.

Following disagreements with Petre Roman, Băsescu replaced him as leader of the (opposition) Democratic Party in 2001. Two years later, in Sept. 2003, Băsescu became a co-chairman of the centre-right Justice and Truth Alliance (DA), forged between his Democratic Party and the National Liberal Party (PNL). Băsescu's rule as mayor of Bucharest proved popular and he was re-elected in June 2004. He then decided to contest the 2004 presidential election as the DA candidate. Campaigning on an anti-corruption and pro-Western platform, he defeated the PSD candidate in the second round run-off in Dec.

Career Peak

Băsescu's first task as president was the formation of a new DA government, which became possible when the small Humanist Party (since renamed the

Conservative Party) pledged its support, in addition to the backing of the ethnic Hungarian Democratic Federation of Romania. Băsescu appointed the PNL leader and former minister of the economy Călin Popescu-Tăriceanu to the post of prime minister. In his inaugural address Băsescu said that fighting corruption would remain his priority and that he intended to steer Romania towards membership of the European Union. This was achieved on 1 Jan. 2007 as Romania and Bulgaria became the EU's 26th and 27th member states. He also stressed the need to strengthen strategic partnerships with the USA and the UK, as well as to improve relations with Russia and the former Soviet states.

Although allied within the ruling DA, Băsescu's relations with Popescu-Tăriceanu deteriorated to the point where, in April 2007, Popescu-Tăriceanu won a vote in parliament to suspend Băsescu for 'grave infringements of the constitution' and the Democratic Party was excluded from the government. Former prime minister Nicolae Văcăroiu was appointed interim president. However, Băsescu returned to office on 23 May 2007 after he was backed by 74.5% of voters in a referendum on his leadership. He then promised to campaign for electoral reform to increase MPs' accountability to the electorate and for a law that could be used to remove former senior officials of the Ceauşescu regime from their offices. In Dec. 2007 he called on Popescu-Tăriceanu to dismiss his justice minister because of corruption allegations. Also in Dec. 2007 the Democratic Party merged with the Liberal Democratic Party to form the Democratic Liberal Party (PD-L). Concerns over high-level corruption also prompted the EU in Feb. 2008 to threaten sanctions against Romania. In April 2008 Băsescu hosted a summit meeting of NATO leaders in Bucharest.

Following inconclusive parliamentary elections in Nov. 2008, Băsescu nominated Theodor Stolojan, an economist and former prime minister, to head a new government. Stolojan soon withdrew his acceptance and Băsescu then asked Emil Boc, the leader of the Democratic Liberal Party, to form the new administration, which was approved by parliament in Dec. 2008. However, in Oct. 2009 this government lost a confidence vote, although Boc carried on in a caretaker capacity until the pending presidential elections as Băsescu's subsequent nominees for prime minister-designate were not acceptable to parliament.

At the end of 2009 Băsescu stood for presidential re-election. His narrow win over Mircea Geoană of the PSD-PC alliance with 50.3% of the run-off vote was challenged by his opponent who claimed electoral fraud. Băsescu then turned again to Boc to form a new government, which was approved by parliament but which laboured with economic recession and austerity. With his government increasingly unpopular, Boc resigned in Feb. 2012. Mihai-Răzvan Ungureanu succeeded him as prime minister but his government also fell after only 2 months following a vote of no confidence in parliament. Victor Ponta of the Social Liberal Union then established an administration to govern until elections later in the year.

In July 2012 Băsescu faced a further challenge to his authority, this time from his new prime minister, and was suspended from office following a parliamentary vote pending efforts to impeach him. However, he survived an impeachment referendum as the majority vote to remove him failed to meet the required minimum turnout of the electorate and he resumed office in Aug. In the Dec. 2012 parliamentary elections Ponta's government won a clear majority against parties backed by Băsescu, after which the president and prime minister signed an agreement guaranteeing their institutional co-operation and respect for the constitution. However, in late 2013 Băsescu was reported to be reviewing the agreement after the deputy prime minister, Liviu Dragnea, was charged with attempting to influence the outcome of the impeachment referendum.

Having served the constitutional limit of two consecutive terms as head of state, Băsescu was ineligible to take part in the presidential elections of Nov. 2014. He was succeeded as president by Klaus Iohannis, who took office on 21 Dec. 2014.

Batbold, Sukhbaataryn (Mongolia)

Introduction

Sukhbaataryn Batbold became prime minister in Oct. 2009 after his predecessor, Sanj Bayar, resigned because of ill health. Batbold's appointment was approved with 62 of 66 votes cast in a plenary session of the Great Hural. His tenure lasted until parliamentary elections that were held in June 2012.

Early Life

Batbold was born in 1963 in Ulan Bator. He was educated at the University of Moscow, graduating from its School of International Relations in 1986. He joined the ministry of economic foreign relations and was appointed head of the Mongol Impex Cooperative in 1988. After returning to higher education, he graduated from the London School of Business in the UK in 1991. In 1992 he joined Altai Trading LLC as its director general, a post he held until 2000.

He was appointed deputy minister of foreign affairs after the return to power of the MPRP in 2000. From 2004–06 he served as minister of trade and industry and in 2008 was named minister of foreign affairs. During his tenure he hosted UN Secretary-General Ban Ki-moon's visit to Ulan Bator to discuss climate change in Mongolia and stood in for Bayar at a Council of Heads of State meeting of the Shanghai Cooperation Organisation.

On 26 Oct. 2009 parliament accepted Bayar's resignation and Batbold was nominated by the MPRP as his successor. His appointment was approved 3 days later.

Career Peak

Batbold's government undertook a review of strategies to take advantage of Mongolia's largely untapped natural resources without falling prey to 'Dutch Disease'. Where a sudden surge of wealth hampers long-term growth. He was also keen to loosen economic reliance on Russia and China by developing relationships with the USA and Canada, while at the same time ensuring Mongolia does not alienate its powerful neighbours. His first year in office was, however, overshadowed by the devastation of the country's livestock, and its effects on herder communities, by extreme bad weather. Batbold's MPP (former MPRP) lost its parliamentary majority to the Democratic Party (DP) at elections in June 2012. The chairman of the DP, Norov Altankhuyag, was nominated for the position of prime minister and was subsequently sworn in as the new prime minister of Mongolia in Aug. 2012, having received the approval of the president and the parliament.

Batista y Zaldívar, Fulgencio (Cuba)

Introduction

Fulgencio Batista twice ruled Cuba, from 1933–44 and 1952–59. He was supported by the USA, despite the increasing brutality of his regime and the civil unrest it eventually caused. In 1959 he was forced from office by a revolutionary group led by Fidel Castro and Che Guevara.

Early Life

Batista was born in Banes, Cuba, on 16 Jan. 1901 to poor farming parents of mixed race. A man of shrewdness and charm, he joined the army in 1921 as a private. He rose to the rank of sergeant, developing a large personal following among his peers. In 1933 he took a leading part in the 'Revolt of the Sergeants'. Which toppled the provisional presidency of Carlos Manuel de Céspedes, and installed the middle-class Ramón Grau San Martín as president. Batista appointed himself chief of staff and, with the blessing of the US, ruled Cuba through a succession of puppet leaders until he took over the presidency himself in 1940.

Career Peak

With the support of the armed forces and the civil service, Batista managed to govern strongly and effectively. Despite amassing a personal fortune, he also made vast improvements to education, public works and the economy.

In 1944 Batista lost power to his old rival Grau, and put himself into luxurious exile in Florida. During this time government corruption in Cuba worsened, and public services broke down.

Batista, by now a Cuban senator, returned to run for president again in 1952. On 10 March, 3 months before the elections, while trailing in the opinion polls, Batista seized power. On 27 March President Eisenhower formally recognised Batista's government.

Under his increasingly authoritarian rule, strikes were banned, constitutional guarantees suspended, and opposition crushed. Batista's secret police became notorious for political beatings, torture and murder while organized crime flourished.

On 26 July 1953 a young Fidel Castro led an attack on the Moncada army barracks in Santiago. He was sent to prison, but managed to stir the nation with his eloquent defence in court. To deflect the public unrest, Batista released Castro, who was exiled to Mexico. But student riots and anti-Batista demonstrations became more frequent. He tightened his control over the media, and refused calls for an immediate election.

In Dec. 1956 Castro launched an expedition from Mexico, retreating into the Sierra Maestra mountains to organize a guerrilla uprising. By 1958 it became clear that the regime was doomed. On New Year's Eve 1958, Batista resigned and fled to the Dominican Republic. He died in Spain on Aug. 6, 1973.

Batlle Ibañez, Jorge Luis (Uruguay)

Introduction

Jorge Luis Batlle Ibáñez was president of Uruguay from 1999 to 2005 and represented the Colorado party. Elected on his fifth attempt in 1999, he succeeded fellow Colorado president Julio Maria Sanguinetti. Batlle's preoccupation in office was to prevent the economy slipping into recession.

Early Life

Batlle was born on 25 Oct. 1927 into a Colorado family that had dominated a century of Uruguayan politics. He is the descendant of three former presidents—his grandfather Lorenzo (1868–72), his father Luis (1947–51, 1955–56) and his great uncle José (1899, 1903–07, 1911–15). After studying in London in 1947, he gained a doctorate in law and social sciences from the Universidad de la República. While studying he worked in radio and later for the *Diario Acción* newspaper until 1973 when the military dictatorship forced its closure. Strongly influenced by the family political legacy, he joined the PC in 1947. Batlle ascended the ranks from regional branch secretary to president of the party's executive committee. Between 1958–67 he was a PC deputy, standing for his first presidential elections in 1966. Between 1973–84 his political activities were hindered by imprisonment and a proscription handed out by the military leaders. In 1985 Batlle presided over the assembly as senator in the first post-dictatorship democratic government. The following year he represented Uruguay in the UN. In 1989 he fought his third election representing the PC faction, Batllismo Unido. He came second with 30% of votes. After again serving as senator between 1994–99, he stood for his fifth presidential election.

His main rival in the 1999 elections was Tabaré Vázquez, the left-wing Encuentro Progresista (Progressive Encounter) candidate and former mayor who led the first round of votes. The opposition Blanco candidate withdrew after coming third place. Batlle and Vázquez fought a run off. In his campaign, Vázquez offered economic stability and a change from over a century of political domination by the Colorados and the Blancos. To combat the strength of the left, the Colorado party persuaded the Blancos to back Batlle in exchange for jobs. Batlle claimed that Vázquez's proposed fiscal reforms would raise income tax. Batlle won by 54.1% to 45.9%. He formed a coalition government between the Colorados and the Blancos.

Career Peak

On election, Batlle pledged to cut public spending, limit bureaucracy and continue prudent fiscal policies. Five government jobs went to Blanco politicians. Despite inheriting a strong economy, Uruguay was already feeling the effects of the recession in neighbouring MERCOSUR countries. As Uruguay's chief trading partner, Brazil's economic problems spilled over. At the beginning of June 2000 the trade unions, PIT-CNT, organized a strike protesting against Batlle's austerity measures and rising unemployment, and demanding investment in health and education. Since the beginning of the twentieth century Uruguay's public-run services, especially a strong welfare state, had been strongly supported and Batlle debated over introducing unpopular privatization schemes. But he did manage to ease the state monopoly on natural gas.

In 2002 Uruguay suffered the effects of neighbour Argentina's economic instability. In Aug. the government closed the banks in an emergency measure to slow increased bank withdrawals. The move resulted in a general strike. A temporary US loan of US$1.5bn. allowed Uruguayan banks to reopen a week later and the country received a US$3.8bn. IMF loan. In Nov. the five Blanco ministers resigned complaining of being sidelined. Batlle retained an uneasy hold on government.

Human rights abuses committed under the military dictatorship (1973–85) remained an important issue. Batlle's plans for a cross-party commission to investigate the disappearance of people during the regime won widespread support. He became the first president to agree to meet the families involved and promised to question the military about its crimes. The inquiry found the government responsible for 26 of 39 deaths investigated.

Batlle was not eligible to stand for re-election in the presidential elections of Oct. 2004, but remained in office until his successor, Tabaré Vázquez, took office on 1 March 2005.

Later Life

Batlle remained active in Uruguayan politics during his later years and was a noted critic of president José Mujica. He died aged 88 on 24 Oct. 2016 after suffering a cerebral haemorrhage following a fall at a party.

Bayar, Celal (Turkey)

Introduction

In power between 1950–60, Celal Bayar was the third president of the Turkish Republic, and was twice re-elected. His decade in power saw the emergence of private enterprise in the country and the curbing of state authority.

Early Life

The son of a jurist, Bayar was born in Bursa in northwest Turkey on 15 May, 1883. He completed his education locally at a French school where he specialized in economics and finance. He then worked for the Bursa branch of a German bank and as an official in Gemlik judicial court.

Bayar's political career began in 1908 when he joined the Committee of Progress and Union which opposed the rule of Sultan Abdülhamid. He went on to become secretary for the Izmir (then Smyrna) branch of the committee. After the end of World War I, when the remnants of the Ottoman empire crumbled, Bayar enlisted in the nationalist movement led by Mustafa Kemal Atatürk. He helped to organize troops to fight the Allied occupation of Anatolia.

In 1920 Bayar was elected as the parliamentary deputy for Izmir, but the British suppressed the parliament and arrested many of the nationalist supporters. Bayar escaped, fleeing to Ankara where Atatürk had installed his provisional government, the Grand National Assembly. In 1921 Bayar was appointed economic minister, a post he held for a year before taking on the challenge of overseeing the reconstruction and settlement of the newly emancipated Turkish republic.

In 1924 Bayar was commissioned to establish Is Bank, and his financial acumen earned him the post of economics minister. At this stage in his career he favoured a state-run economy. In 1937 Atatürk appointed him prime minister of the 14th cabinet, but he resigned following the death of Atatürk in Jan. 1939. He was replaced by Refik Saydam.

Career Peak

In 1945 Bayar broke away from the Republican People's Party to form the opposing Democrat Party with support from Mehmed Fuad Köprülü, Adnan Menderes and Refik Koraltan. The new party advocated a policy of private enterprise and won 62 seats in the general election of 1946. Four years later, the party secured a convincing majority in parliament, and Bayar was elected President. He appointed Menderes as his prime minister and began to reduce the state's role in the economy to one of regulation and co-ordination. He was re-elected in 1954 and again in 1957.

Later Life

His political career was ended by a military coup in May 1960. Bayar was arrested and tried for treason. His trial lasted for 16 months, after which he and 15 other leading figures within the Democrat Party were sentenced to death. His sentence was commuted to life imprisonment and he was released in Nov. 1964 on grounds of ill health. He received an official pardon 2 years later, and wrote his memoirs entitled *I, Too, Have Written*. Bayar died on 22 Aug. 1986.

Bayar, Sanj (Mongolia)

Introduction

Sanj Bayar was elected prime minister by parliament on 22 Nov. 2007 following the resignation of Miyegombo Enkhbold. Bayar had replaced Enkhbold as MPRP chairman the previous month amid concerns within the party over Enkhbold's weak, minority government ahead of parliamentary elections scheduled for June 2008.

Early Life

Bayar was born in 1956 in Ulan Bator. He graduated in law from the Moscow State University in 1978 and went to work for the Ulan Bator city assembly. A year later he joined the general staff of the Mongolian armed forces. Leaving in 1983, he worked as a journalist, becoming chief editor of the Russian-language newspaper Novosti Mongolii and head of the state-run Montsame news agency.

In 1988 Bayar was appointed deputy chief officer of the state committee for Mongolian radio and television. He joined the MPRP in the same year. Between 1990–92 he was an elected member of the now defunct *Baga Hural* (*Small Hural*, the short-lived upper chamber) that drafted Mongolia's constitution. He also served as chairman of the standing committee on the state structure. In 1992 he was appointed director of the Strategic Research Center of Mongolia.

From 1997–2001 Bayar served as President Natsagiin Bagabandi's chief officer and in 2001 he became ambassador to Russia. He returned to Mongolia in 2005 and was elected secretary general of the MPRP. On 26 Oct. 2007 Bayar received over 60% of his party's votes to take over from Enkhbold as the MPRP's chairman.

Career Peak

Bayar promised to counter corruption, bring down the inflated prices of essential goods and cut bureaucracy in public services. In June 2008 the MPRP retained power in disputed parliamentary elections. On 26 Oct. 2009 Bayar announced his resignation owing to health reasons, with first deputy prime minister Norovyn Altankhuyag becoming acting prime minister. Foreign minister Sukhbaataryn Batbold was subsequently nominated and approved by parliament and took office as the new prime minister on 29 Oct.

Beckmann Geisel, Ernesto (Brazil)

Introduction

Ernesto Beckmann Geisel was president of Brazil from 1974 to 1979, the fourth of the five generals who ruled the country from 1964 to 1985. He played a central role in preparing the country for a return to democracy.

Early Life

Born in Bento Gonçalves on 3 Aug. 1908, Geisel was an army officer who participated in Getúlio Vargas' 1930 military coup. He served the government in various jobs until 1945 when he was instrumental in removing Vargas from power. He was subsequently deputy chief of the military staff of the presidency and sat on the national petroleum council.

In 1964 he participated in another military coup and took a senior military position in the government of Humberto Castelo Branco. Five years later he was appointed head of the national oil corporation. In March 1974 he assumed the national presidency.

Career Peak

Though dependent on the ruling military junta, Geisel promoted measures to reduce censorship and increase political freedom. He permitted free elections in 1974. His economic plan encouraged domestic industries, such as farming and mining, and expanded Brazil's transport infrastructure.

Geisel reverted to political oppression when electoral victory seemed doubtful. In April 1977 he dismissed congress when it failed to pass judicial reforms and used emergency powers to institute those reforms and other electoral and constitutional changes. He resigned from government in 1979, giving his backing to General João Baptista de Oliveira Figueiredo as his successor.

Later Life

Geisel died on 12 Sept. 1996.

Begin, Menachem (Israel)

Introduction

Having dominated the opposition in the Knesset to successive Labour administrations in the first three decades of Israel's existence, Menachem Begin became prime minister at the head of a right-wing Likud (Unity) government in June 1977. The outstanding achievement of his premiership, which lasted until Oct. 1983, was the Egyptian-Israeli peace treaty signed in 1979, for which he and President Sadat of Egypt were awarded the Nobel Peace Prize. However, world opinion turned against his government in the wake of atrocities during the 1982 Israeli invasion of Lebanon.

Early Life

Begin was born in Aug. 1913 in Brest-Litovsk, then in Poland and now in Belarus. A committed Zionist from an early age, he became the leader of the Betar Jewish youth movement in Poland after graduating with a law degree. When Nazi Germany invaded Poland in 1939, he fled to Soviet territory and was deported to Siberia until 1941. Released, he joined the Free Polish Army and went to Palestine in 1942 where he revitalized the Jewish Irgun Tzeva'I Le'umi (Etzel) underground organization. The increasing militancy of Etzel's operations against the British mandate brought Begin into conflict with the mainstream Zionist strategy of David Ben-Gurion. After the establishment of the Israeli state in 1948, Begin formed the Herut (Freedom) Party and served as opposition leader in the Knesset until 1967 when he joined the national unity government as minister without portfolio for almost 3 years. In 1973 he became chairman of the Likud coalition, which won the legislative elections in May 1977.

Career Peak

In Nov. 1977 Prime Minister Begin hosted Egyptian President Sadat's visit to Jerusalem. This inaugurated 2 years of negotiations leading to the US-brokered peace treaty in 1979 between the two countries (providing for Israel's phased withdrawal from the occupied Egyptian territory of Sinai) and to an agreement for ill-defined future Palestinian autonomy in Gaza and the West Bank. In 1981 Begin controversially ordered the Israeli air force to destroy Iraq's nuclear installation at Osirak near Baghdad. He incurred further international condemnation when Israel invaded Lebanon in June 1982, the second such incursion aimed at dislodging the PLO during his premiership. Israel's advance into Muslim west Beirut preceded a massacre of Palestinian refugees by Lebanese Christian militia groups. Begin left office in Oct. 1983 and died in March 1992.

Belaúnde Terry, Fernando (Peru)

Introduction

Fernando Belaúnde Terry was president of Peru between 1963–68 and 1980–85, representing the Accíon Popular (AC) party. Despite liberal and progressive socio-economic reforms, Belaúnde was a largely ineffectual president, blocked by opposition politicians, terrorist activity and an inability to resolve economic problems.

Early Life

Belaúnde was born in Lima on 7 Oct. 1912. From a wealthy family, his father, Rafael Belaúnde Diez Canseco, served as prime minister from 1945–46. Belaúnde studied architecture at the University of Texas and then in France. He practised in Mexico before continuing his career in Peru. He was elected to congress, serving as a deputy between 1945–48. In 1956 he stood for presidential election representing the AP, a right-wing party formed by Belaúnde to promote an alternative to military dictatorship or Marxist rule. Belaúnde promised economic modernization. The president and military dictator Manuel Odría, attempted to block Belaúnde's candidature. Following much protest and public support, Belaúnde was finally permitted to stand. In the 1956 elections he came second but the AP gained strong support.

Career Peak

In the 1963 elections, Belaúnde stood against Victor Raúl Haya de la Torre, the candidate for the centre left Partido Aprista Peruano—the Peruvian branch of the Alianja Popular Revolucionaria Americana (American Popular Revolutionary Alliance; APRA), founded by Haya de la Torre. With support from the Partido Demócrata Cristiano (Christian Democratic Party), Belaúnde won with 40% of the votes. Nevertheless, the opposition had a majority in Congress. Belaúnde's aim was to increase democracy, strengthen the economy and ameliorate conditions for Peru's rural poor. He outlined land and education reforms as well as industrial development. Large-scale construction of road networks was carried out to some of Peru's most rural and inaccessible areas, including the Andes. Belaúnde was pro-American in his outlook and supported the Alliance for Progress programme—the well-meaning but ineffectual international economic development programme begun in 1962 between the USA and 22 Latin American countries. Belaúnde was frustrated in his efforts by the opposition. Peru's inflation increased and there were protests against an American company, the International Petroleum Company, which had a monopoly of the development of oil fields in Northern Peru.

In 1968, amid increasing disillusionment with the government, Belaúnde was deposed in a military coup by General Juan Velasco. He fled to the USA where he pursued his career in architecture. He attempted to return to Peru in 1970, but was immediately deported.

In 1980, after 12 years of military dictatorship, Belaúnde was elected to a second term as president. He rescued projects from his first term, including the development of the Carretera Marginal de la Selva, a road running parallel to the Andes. He supported the idea of free-market economy. Yet, Belaúnde's second term was as ineffectual as his first. Inflation, foreign debt and unemployment increased and he proved powerless against the increasing threat of the Sendero Luminosa (Shining Path). The Maoist guerrilla group, formed by a small group of intellectuals in 1970, began extensive terrorist activity in 1980. Over 25,000 deaths are attributed to Sendero Luminosa. Corruption within the government became endemic. In 1985 Belaúnde was beaten convincingly by the APRA candidate, Alan García Pérez.

Later Life

Despite this heavy defeat, Belaúnde continued to play an active role in politics, remaining the leader of the AC party. In the 1990 elections, he actively supported Mario Vargas Llosa's presidential campaign. Belaúnde voiced strong opposition to President Alberto Fujimori's auto-coup in 1992. Belaúnde died on 4 June 2002.

Belka, Marek (Poland)

Introduction

Marek Belka became Poland's prime minister on 2 May 2004, the day after the nation's entry to the European Union. A professor of economics with a reputation for instigating harsh public-spending cuts while minister of finance in 2001–02, Belka continued to court unpopularity as he attempted to push through further financial and civil-service reforms.

Early Life

Marek Belka was born on 28 Jan. 1952 in Łódź. After attending a school in the city, he entered the Faculty of Economics and Sociology at Łódź University, and graduated with a master's degree in economics in 1972. He remained at the university, working as a research assistant and undertaking a PhD, graduating in 1978, the year in which Poland's communist-run economy is considered to have peaked. Post-1978 industrial and economic decline is now seen as a crucial factor in provoking the social discontent and political stalemate that afflicted Poland through much of the 1980s. In 1978 Belka went to the United States as a Fulbright Foundation fellow at Colombia University, where he met the neo-liberal economics professor, Milton Friedman.

He travelled again to the USA in 1985 under a scholarship from the American Council of Learned Societies at the University of Chicago. A year later, Belka joined the Institute of Economics at the Polish Academy of Sciences in Warsaw as Assistant Professor. After attending the London School of Economics in 1990 Belka returned to a country undergoing dramatic political and economic change. He became a consultant to the central planning office and at the Ministry of Finance. The policies of the finance minister Leszek Balcerowicz succeeded in stabilizing the currency in 1990, but the enormous budget deficit, rising inflation and spiralling unemployment led to political instability under the Bielecki (1991), Olszewski (1992) and Suchocka (1992–93) governments. Nevertheless, ministers and advisers including Belka managed to carry out complex reforms of the civil service and the state treasury, and by 1993 a capitalist infrastructure with a stock market and a modern banking system was established. Belka became professor at the Polish Institute of Sciences in 1994 and economic adviser to the president of Poland in 1997.

Belka was brought into the government for the first time in 1997 under prime minister Włodzimierz Cimoszewicz. He replaced Grzegorz Kolodko as finance minister and pressed ahead with unpopular reforms to pensions and welfare state provisions. In the same year the government was voted out of office. When, in 2001, the Democratic Left Alliance (SLD) party was once again voted into power (crushing the Solidarity government), the prime minister, Leszek Miller, reappointed Belka as finance minister. In an attempt to reduce the budget deficit and prepare for joining the European Union, Belka made harsh cuts to social welfare benefits. Faced with widespread hostility, the Miller government proposed a compromise on the welfare cuts and the cabinet drafted legislation restricting the powers of the central bank. Both measures were unacceptable to Belka and he resigned in July 2002.

From June 2003 Belka worked in the civil administration in occupied Iraq as economic adviser to Paul Bremer, head of the Coalition Provisional Authority. In Poland, the SLD government was faced by rocketing unemployment (almost 20% in late 2003), popular protests on the streets of Warsaw and allegations of ministerial corruption. In March 2004 a group of senators and deputies left the SLD to form a new party, forcing the resignation of Leszek Miller on 2 May, the day after Poland's entry to the European Union. The president, Aleksander Kwaśniewski, appointed Belka to replace Miller as prime minister.

Career Peak

Despite being rejected by the lower house of parliament (Sejm) in mid-May, Belka gained a vote of confidence to continue as prime minister of Poland on 24 June 2004. Belka also won another confidence vote on 15 Oct. He made it clear that he would continue the unpopular economic policies he espoused as finance minister. His austerity package included a borrowing cut of US\$13bn. in 4 years, which he argued was an essential precursor to joining the Eurozone. Belka advocated the continuing presence of Polish troops in Iraq.

In 2005 Belka unsuccessfully stood to be secretary general of the OECD. In May 2005 he proffered his resignation to Kwaśniewski when parliament rejected his attempt to bring forward elections so he could fulfil his promise that the caretaker government would stay in office for a maximum of a year. His resignation was rejected but he came under opposition pressure to step down in June 2005 amid allegations that he had co-operated with the secret police during Poland's communist era. His Alliance of the Democratic Left won only around 11% of the vote at the general elections of Sept. 2005 and Belka was replaced as prime minister by Kazimierz Marcinkiewicz.

Belka became director of the IMF's European Department in Nov. 2008 and was then named president of the National Bank of Poland in May 2010, serving a 6 year term from June 2010–June 2016.

Belkhadem, Abdelaziz (Algeria)

Introduction

Abdelaziz Belkhadem was prime minister of Algeria from May 2006 until June 2008. His appointment followed the resignation of Ahmed Ouyahia, who would return to succeed him as prime minister 2 years later. The leader of the ruling National Liberation Front (FLN) since 2005, Belkhadem was a close ally of Algeria's president, Abdelaziz Bouteflika.

Early Life

Abdelaziz Belkhadem was born on 8 Nov. 1945 in Aflou, Laghouat Province, French Algeria. Graduating with a diploma in administration and finance, he began work as a tax inspector in 1964, becoming a professor in 1968. He joined Algeria's administration in 1972, serving as deputy director of international relations in the Revolutionary Council led by Col. Houari Boumedienne (who became president in 1976).

In Feb. 1977 Belkhadem was elected to represent the FLN, the only legal party, in the national assembly. He was also deputy of the town of Sougueur, Tiaret from 1977 to 1992. In 1987 he was appointed director of the commission for education, training and scientific research and the following year he was elected vice president of the national assembly, becoming its president in 1990 after the departure of Rabah Bitat.

Between 1991 and 1997, when civil war was sparked by the military-backed government's decision to cancel multiparty elections that the Islamic Salvation Front had been poised to win, Belkhadem served in the political office of the FLN. Abdelaziz Bouteflika's victory in a controversial presidential election in April 1999 paved the way for a ceasefire and a period of relative stability. Belkhadem was appointed minister of foreign affairs in 2000, initially under Ali Benflis, the reformist prime minister and leader of the FLN. After almost a decade of civil war Algeria had become isolated internationally and Belkhadem was at the forefront of restoring relations with countries such as Morocco and France, notably via pan-African diplomacy.

The parliamentary elections in May 2002 saw large gains for the FLN, which claimed 199 out of 389 national assembly seats to become the dominant party in the ruling coalition. Tensions between the president and Ali Benflis were resolved in Feb. 2005 when Belkhadem, a Bouteflika loyalist, was elected secretary general at the party's congress. Following the resignation of the prime minister, Ahmed Ouyahia, on 24 May 2006, the president nominated Belkhadem to succeed him. Ouyahia's downfall followed his opposition to a general wage increase proposed by the unions and supported by the FLN.

Career Peak

Belkhadem prioritized a 'revision' of the constitution and increases in pay for public-sector workers. He also pledged to cut the unemployment and poverty afflicting millions of Algerians despite the country's hydrocarbon-fuelled economic upturn since 2004. In Nov. 2006 Belkhadem restated Algeria's aim to improve ties with France if the French government admits to having committed crimes during its 130 years as colonial ruler. In May 2007 Belkhadem retained the premiership as the FLN-led ruling coalition won parliamentary elections marked by a low voter turnout. His government briefly resigned in early June before his reappointment as premier. On 23 June 2008, in a move that surprised many observers, President Bouteflika named Ahmed Ouyahia prime minister. Belkhadem was appointed the president's 'personal representative'.

Ben Ali, Zine El Abidine (Tunisia)

Introduction

Appointed prime minister by Habib Bourguiba, Tunisia's leader from 1957, Zine El Abidine Ben Ali then became president after Bourguiba was deposed in 1987. Despite advocating moderate liberalization, his human rights record remained a source of international unease. He was scheduled to retire in 2004, but secured support in a referendum for changes to the constitution allowing him a further two terms in office. He was re-elected in Oct. 2009 but left office and fled to Saudi Arabia in the face of popular protests in Jan. 2011.

Early Life

Ben Ali was born in Hammam Sousse on 3 Sept. 1936. As a teenager he became involved in the nationalist movement, which culminated in Tunisia's independence from France in 1956. He resumed his studies abroad, training at the military academy at Saint-Cyr and at the artillery school of Châlons-sur-Marne in France, and later studying in the USA where he obtained a degree in electronic engineering.

Returning to Tunisia, he was appointed head of military security from 1964–74 and became a military attaché to the Tunisian embassy in Morocco. Upon his return, he was made head of national security and later served as ambassador to Poland. In 1986 he was appointed minister of the interior.

Ben Ali was active in fighting militant fundamentalist groups. In Oct. 1987 he was appointed prime minister by President Habib Bourguiba. Bourguiba was dogged by rumours of intermittent senility and in Nov. was declared unfit to rule by a committee of doctors and deposed in a bloodless coup. Ben Ali replaced him as president.

Career Peak

As leader of the Constitutional Democratic Rally (RCD), Ben Ali had been overwhelmingly re-elected in March 1994, Oct. 1999, Oct. 2004 and Oct. 2009. The cancellation of the 1992 election at a point when the opposition seemed likely to win prompted international criticism. Scheduled to retire in 2004, he initiated changes to the constitution in 2002 to allow him to govern for another two terms. In the Oct. 2004 elections the main opposition group, the Progressive Democratic Party, withdrew its candidates 2 days before polling, arguing that the vote would be worthless.

Ben Ali inherited an economically stable country and oversaw a reduction in the poverty rate and improving literacy levels. He expressed his commitment to furthering women's rights and authorized the release of some political prisoners, but human rights groups were critical of his regime. He maintained tight control of the media and the treatment of journalists and political opponents critical of his rule caused international concern.

Ben Ali was re-elected chairman of the RCD in July 2008 and president, with 90% of the vote, in Oct. 2009. Following weeks of violent protests driven by economic grievances and resentment over political repression, Ben Ali relinquished power in Jan. 2011 and fled to Saudi Arabia. Prime Minister Mohamed Ghannouchi agreed to act as interim president but was subsequently succeeded by Foued Mebazaa, the President of the Chamber of Deputies.

Later Life

In June 2011 Ben Ali and his wife were convicted in absentia of charges relating to arms, narcotics and the misappropriation of funds. Both were sentenced to 35 years in prison and fined US$65.5m. In June 2012 Ben Ali was given a life sentence by a military court, which found him guilty of 'inciting disorder, murder and looting'.

Ben Bella, Ahmed (Algeria)

Introduction

Ahmed Ben Bella became the first president of newly independent Algeria in Sept. 1963, serving until June 1965. A long-time opponent of French colonial rule, he endured several years of imprisonment and exile prior to independence.

Early Life

Ahmed Ben Bella was born in Maghnia on 25 Dec. 1918. He studied in Tlemcen but left school with no qualifications. He joined the French Army in 1936 and was posted to Marseille. During the Second World War he won a commendation for bravery at the 1944 battle of Monte Cassino.

Angry at France's brutal suppression of the anti-colonial movement in Algeria, Ben Bella refused an officer's commission and returned to his homeland entering politics. He became a municipal councillor in Maghnia and was a founding member of the anti-French, paramilitary Organisation Spéciale. After being arrested in 1951 for robbing a post office to raise funds for the group, he escaped and made his way to Cairo in Egypt, which was his base when the Algerian War of Independence broke out in 1954.

Ben Bella was one of nine members of a committee that led the Front de Libération Nationale/National Liberation Front (FLN) during the war and survived several assassination attempts. In 1956 he was arrested when the plane on which he was travelling was diverted by the French authorities to Algiers. While imprisoned in France he was elected vice-premier of the provisional government of Algeria, but was released in 1962 following the signing of a peace deal. Returning to Algeria, he was elected premier with the support of Col. Houari Boumedienne, chief of the Army of National Liberation, and in 1963 was voted president unopposed.

Career Peak

Ben Bella initiated a reform programme inspired by his anti-colonial and pro-Arab philosophy. He nationalized what was left of the colonial farming lands but his land reforms were largely unsuccessful and resulted in economic hardship. In education, meanwhile, he brought in large numbers of teachers from Egypt and Syria. He also fostered close economic ties with France, as well as negotiating aid from the USA and the USSR. However, with government reforms faltering and Ben Bella increasingly autocratic, Boumedienne headed a bloodless coup on 19 June 1965.

Later Life

Ben Bella was imprisoned or kept under house arrest for the next 14 years. Restrictions upon him were eased in 1979 and he was allowed to go into exile in Oct. 1980. In 1984 he launched the Movement for Democracy in Algeria and returned to the country in the 1990s, becoming a vocal critic of the country's destructive civil war. He died on 11 April 2012.

Benedict XVI (Vatican City State)

Introduction

Joseph Ratzinger was elected head of the Roman Catholic Church on 19 April 2005, becoming Pope Benedict XVI. His appointment followed the death of the popular and charismatic Pope John Paul II. A highly intellectual theologian from southern Germany, Benedict XVI has served in the Vatican as head of the department that defends Catholic orthodoxy since 1981. He has reinforced the broadly conservative policies of John Paul II, his friend and close ally, and opposed secularism and relativism, which he has described as 'letting oneself be tossed and swept by every wind of teaching'.

Early Life

Joseph Ratzinger was born in Marktl am Inn, southeastern Bavaria, Germany, on 16 April 1927, the third and youngest child of a police officer and his wife. In 1929 his father was posted to the town of Tittmoning on the Austrian border, where the family remained for 3 years, before moving to Aschau am Inn and then to Hufschlag, near Traunstein, when his father retired in 1937. Ratzinger attended the high school in Traunstein, and later opted to train for the priesthood, entering the town's seminary in 1939. At 14 years of age he joined the Hitler Youth—a legal requirement as part of the Nazis' efforts to convert the German population to the 'National Socialist spirit'. Two years later Ratzinger was drafted into the anti-aircraft artillery corps. His unit guarded facilities including an aircraft-engine plant near Munich. In late 1944 Ratzinger was drafted into the German army and served in and around Munich. Reportedly a reluctant soldier, he deserted weeks before Germany's surrender in 1945, and rejoined the seminary in Traunstein. After 2 years he took up a place at the Herzogliches Georgianum, a theological institute linked to the University of Munich. On 29 June 1951 he was ordained to the priesthood in the cathedral at Freising, near Munich.

Ratzinger continued with his study of theology at the University of Munich—his doctoral thesis focused on St Augustine and his view of Christianity in the fifth century. Having gained his doctorate in July 1953, he began post-doctoral research about St Bonaventure, a Franciscan theologian of the nineteenth century. In 1959 Ratzinger moved to Bonn to take up a professorship in fundamental theology at the city's university. He taught at the University of Münster for 3 years from 1963, before joining the University of Tübingen, near Stuttgart. When the wave of student uprisings swept across Europe in 1968, it brought Marxism to the Tübingen campus. Ratzinger was horrified by what he saw as a 'tyrannical, brutal and cruel' ideology that was undermining the Church. He accepted an offer of a teaching position at the new University of Regensburg a year later, and remained in the Bavarian city for the next 7 years. He began to take a more conservative approach to theology, and rose to become the dean and then vice-president of the university.

On 24 March 1977 Ratzinger was elected archbishop of Munich and Freising by Pope Paul VI. He was ordained to the episcopal order in May 1977 and a month later was elevated to cardinal priest. However, his work as an archbishop was to prove relatively short-lived. In Nov. 1981 he was called to Rome by Pope John Paul II (who had been elected in 1978) to take over the Congregation for the Doctrine of the Faith, the department in the Vatican responsible for defending and reinforcing Catholic orthodoxy (once known as the Inquisition). At the same time, he became president of the International Theological Commission and the Pontifical Biblical Commission. The Congregation for the Doctrine of the Faith courted controversy after publishing 'Dominus Jesus'. which described other Christian faiths and world religions as 'deficient or not quite real churches'.

Ratzinger was elevated to the position of cardinal bishop of the diocese of Velletri-Signi on 5 April 1993, and was elected vice-dean of the College of Cardinals in 1998. When he was appointed dean of the College in late 2002 (and cardinal bishop of the diocese of Ostia), Ratzinger had become one of the Vatican's most powerful and influential figures. He presided over the funeral of Pope John Paul II in St Peter's Basilica on 8 April 2005, and subsequently inaugurated the conclave for the election of the successor to St Peter in the Sistine chapel. On 19 April, after the fourth ballot of the conclave, the proto-deacon of the College of Cardinals, Jorge Estévez, announced to a crowd of tens of thousands in St Peter's Square: 'Dear brothers and sisters, we have a Pope. The most eminent and most reverend Lord, Lord Joseph, Cardinal of Holy Roman Church, Ratzinger, who has taken the name Benedict XVI'.

Career Peak

Pope Benedict XVI swiftly reappointed all former officers who had served under John Paul II. A hint of future Vatican policy came with the appointment of the US non-Cardinal William Joseph Levada to the post of prefect of the Congregation for the Doctrine of the Faith on 13 May 2005. The elevation of this deeply conservative prelate archbishop of the Archdiocese of San Francisco to one of the church's most powerful positions raised fears among reform-minded Catholics.

Controversy from another direction erupted in Sept. 2006 after the Pope delivered a lecture in Germany including a reference to a medieval text perceived as hostile to Islam. This provoked almost worldwide Muslim protest, forcing the Vatican to apologize for any unintentional offence. The incident threatened to derail a planned papal visit in Nov. to Turkey, a predominantly Muslim country, but the trip went ahead successfully, with Benedict advocating 'authentic dialogue' based on mutual respect between Christians and Muslims.

In 2007 the Pope met Russian president Vladimir Putin for the first time, and also King Abdullah of Saudi Arabia. It was the first such meeting between the head of the Roman Catholic Church and a Saudi monarch. In March 2009 he toured Africa and in May visited the Middle East where he appealed for peace and religious coexistence.

In Dec. 2008 Benedict again courted social controversy with a perceived attack on homosexuality that angered gay rights groups and activists. Then, in Jan. 2009, his controversial decision to readmit to the Church an ultra-conservative bishop who had denied the Holocaust angered Jews and many Catholics. Moreover, his assertion in Feb. 2010 that the effect of some equality legislation in Britain had been to impose unjust limitations on the freedom of religious communities to act in accordance with their beliefs was condemned by human rights campaigners.

In Oct. 2009 Benedict made an unprecedented offer to disaffected Anglicans to join the Catholic Church while still maintaining many of their own spiritual traditions. In early 2010 he was the subject of allegations that he failed to take timely action against paedophile priests while prefect of the Congregation for the Doctrine of the Faith (1981–2005), where he had responsibility for dealing with clerical abuse. The Vatican denied any wrongdoing but in Sept. 2010, while making the first papal visit to the United Kingdom since 1982, Benedict acknowledged that the paedophile scandal had undermined the moral credibility of the Church.

In Nov. 2010, in an apparent shift in traditional Vatican policy towards contraception, it was reported that the Pope was prepared to countenance the use of condoms to prevent the spread of HIV/AIDS.

Following a bomb attack on a Christian church in Alexandria, Egypt, Benedict called on Middle Eastern governments in Jan. 2011 to do more to protect religious minorities in their countries. This prompted the Egyptian government to recall its ambassador to the Vatican in protest at perceived interference in its internal affairs. He made a similar appeal for religious tolerance in Jan. 2012 following the bombing of a Christian church in Nigeria.

In July 2011 the Irish prime minister accused the Vatican of having tried to downplay the extent of sexual abuse of children by Catholic clergy in Ireland. In response, the Vatican recalled its envoy from Dublin.

In his traditional Christmas message from the Vatican in Dec. 2012, Benedict called for an end to hostilities in Syria and a resumption of Israeli-Palestinian negotiations. He also controversially denounced gay marriage as a 'manipulation of nature'.

In an unexpected move, Benedict announced his resignation from the papacy on 11 Feb. 2013, citing declining health and advanced age. The Pope stepped down on 28 Feb., being the first pope to resign since 1415.

Benediktsson, Bjarni (Iceland)

Introduction

Bjarni Benediktsson was sworn in as prime minister on 11 Jan. 2017, having previously been minister of finance and economic affairs in the outgoing coalition that was defeated in parliamentary elections in Oct. 2016. He is the chairman of the centre-right Independence Party (SSF), which traditionally dominated Icelandic politics from its formation in 1929 until it lost its uninterrupted status as the largest party in the wake of the 2008–09 financial crisis that bankrupted Iceland. Bjarni Benediktsson shares his name with an unrelated former prime minister of Iceland who served from 1963–70. He only held office for ten months, with Katrín Jakobsdóttir succeeding him as prime minister.

Early Life

Benediktsson was born in Reykjavík on 26 Jan. 1970. He studied law at the University of Iceland before furthering his education in Germany and the United States. After returning to his home country, he entered parliament as an SSF representative at the 2003 election. He subsequently served on committees overseeing the economy and taxation, health and social security, and industry, and was chairman of the foreign affairs committee from 2007 to 2009.

The SSF resigned from government in 2009 amid popular protests over the extent of Iceland's financial collapse. Benediktsson was appointed party chairman. In the ensuing parliamentary election it gained only 16 seats, an historic low for a party that had gained the largest share of the vote in every election since its establishment 80 years earlier. In the wake of the disastrous campaign, the SSF entered as a junior partner into government with the Social Democratic Alliance.

Benediktsson campaigned in the 2013 poll on a programme of restoring growth after a period of severe austerity. He pledged to lower taxes and take steps to reduce the heavy burden of debt on households. He offered to resign the chairmanship of the party only two weeks before the election following an attempted coup from within his own ranks, a move credited with boosting his appeal to the electorate. In the election, held on 27 April 2013, the SSF gained 19 (out of a total of 63) seats, against the same number for the Progressive Party (FSF) and nine for the Social Democratic Alliance. The SSF then joined a new coalition headed by Sigmundur Davíð Gunnlaugsson of the Progressive Party and Benediktsson took over the finance and economic affairs portfolio.

In April 2016 Gunnlaugsson stepped down after reports in the so-called *Panama Papers* of his secret offshore investments triggered mass public protests and demands for another election. The FSF deputy leader, Sigurður Ingi Jóhannsson, meanwhile became interim premier.

At the poll in Oct. 2016 the SSF emerged as the largest party with 21 parliamentary seats, but weeks of inter-party negotiations followed before Benediktsson could form a new SSF-led coalition with the centre-right Reform Party (Viðreisn) and centrist Bright Future in Jan. 2017.

Career Peak

Having taken office, Benediktsson was unable to draw a line under the political fall-out from the *Panama Papers*, as he declined a request by a parliamentary standing committee to answer questions about tax evasion by Icelanders amid international media reports that he had been similarly implicated. In Sept. 2017, following revelations of an alleged scandal involving Benediktsson's father, Bright Future announced that they would end their co-operation with the government only nine months after the swearing-in of the cabinet. After the subsequent Nov. 2017 snap parliamentary election, President Jóhannesson asked Katrín Jakobsdóttir of the Left-Green Movement (VG) to form a new government. She replaced Benediktsson as prime minister on 30 Nov. 2017.

Later Life

As had been agreed as part of the coalition agreement between the VG, the SSF and the FSF, Jakobsdóttir appointed Benediktsson as finance and economic affairs minister.

Ben-Gurion, David (Israel)

Introduction

Zionist leader and Labour statesman, David Ben-Gurion proclaimed the state of Israel on 14 May 1948. He was Israel's first and longest serving prime minister over two terms from 1948–53 and 1955–63. He died in Tel Aviv on 1 Dec. 1973.

Early Life

Ben-Gurion was born in Plonsk, in what is now Poland, in Oct. 1886. The son of an ardent Zionist, he migrated to Palestine in 1906. At the outbreak of the First World War he was expelled by the then ruling Ottoman authorities and went to the United States before returning to Palestine as a soldier in the Jewish Legion of the British Army. In the 1920s Ben-Gurion and others founded the Histadrut (General Federation of Jewish Labour). He served as its first secretary general until 1935, meanwhile assuming the leadership of the Mapai Party, formed from several labour factions. In 1935 he became head of the Jewish Agency, a government-in-waiting among the Jews of Palestine under the British mandate. At the end of the Second World War he orchestrated the Jewish campaign for statehood, becoming prime minister and minister of defence in 1948 of a territory under siege from hostile Arab neighbours.

Career Peak

Having secured the new state's military survival, Ben-Gurion sought to encourage and integrate waves of Jewish immigrants and to create a national, regular army—the Israel Defence Forces (IDF). In foreign affairs, he adopted a pro-Western policy, which set the stage for a closer strategic alliance with Britain and France. Having resigned from office in Dec. 1953, he resumed the premiership in Nov. 1955. In the 1956 Suez crisis, Israel colluded with Britain and France in an attack on Egypt in retaliation for Col. Nasser's nationalization of the Suez Canal. Israel, Britain and France were forced to withdraw under pressure from the United States and the United Nations.

Ben-Gurion resigned as prime minister in June 1963, probably as a result of division within the Mapai Party. He formed a new party (Rafi) in 1965 and retired from public life in 1970. He died in 1973.

Benkirane, Abdelilah (Morocco)

Introduction

Abdelilah Benkirane became prime minister in Nov. 2011 after his moderate, left-leaning Islamist party won a majority in legislative elections. Although reappointed in Oct. 2016 following further elections, he failed to form a new government and was dismissed in March 2017 by the King pending the installation of a successor. He nonetheless retained the premiership in a caretaker capacity.

Early Life

Benkirane was born in Rabat on 4 April 1954 and graduated in science and engineering in 1979. In 1983 he jointly founded a moderate, left-leaning Islamist group, Al Jamaa Al Islamiya, despite official resistance. In 1997 Benkirane and other moderate Islamists joined forces with the Popular Democratic and Constitutional Movement (MPDC) and in polling in Nov. he was elected to parliament. The following year the MPDC changed its name to the Party of Justice and Development (PJD).

In Sept. 2002 Benkirane was re-elected as the PJD took 42 parliamentary seats and in July 2008 he was elected party leader. Reformist protests in Feb. 2011, echoing unrest across the Arab world, led the King to amend the constitution in July to give new powers to a prime minister selected from the largest party in parliament. Following elections in Nov. 2011 the PJD formed a coalition with three parties that had been part of previous governments and Benkirane was appointed premier.

Career Peak

Benkirane aimed to achieve ambitious economic growth targets and to bring down unemployment by 2017. However, in May 2012 thousands rallied in Casablanca demanding jobs, accusing the government of failing to deliver on promised reforms.

Following the resignation of the Istiqlal Party from the government in mid-2013, Benkirane forged a power-sharing administration with the National Rally of Independents in Oct. that year. In Oct. 2016 the PJD again emerged as the largest party in elections and Benkirane was reappointed prime minister. However, his subsequent struggle to form a new coalition reflected a polarized political atmosphere and public anger over perceived abuses of state power and continuing unemployment. In March 2017 the king removed him from office, although Benkirane remained prime minister in a caretaker capacity ahead of the formal appointment of his successor.

Berger Perdomo, Óscar (Guatemala)

Introduction

President of Guatemala from Jan. 2004 to Jan. 2008, Óscar Berger Perdomo of the Grand National Alliance (GANA) was previously twice mayor of the capital, Guatemala City. On 14 Jan. 2008 Berger was succeeded by Álvaro Colom after Colom won the presidential elections in Nov. 2007.

Early Life

Born into a wealthy family on 11 Aug. 1946 in Guatemala City, Berger received a private education culminating in his graduation from the Jesuit Rafael Landívar University as a lawyer and notary. Having supported Álvaro Arzú, a classmate from university and later president of Guatemala, in his successful campaign in the mid-1980s to become mayor of Guatemala City, Berger then held this position himself from 1991–99. At the end of the 1980s, Berger and Arzú formed the National Advancement Party (PAN) to take advantage of what they saw as a gap in the political spectrum, hitherto dominated by conservative and far-right parties. Standing for the PAN in the Nov.–Dec. 1999 presidential elections, Berger lost to the FRG candidate, Alfonso Cabrera, in the second round of voting.

Career Peak

In late 2003 Berger stood again as a presidential election candidate, this time for the GANA, and won the second round run-off with 54.1% of the vote. He was sworn in on 14 Jan. 2004. Despite his personal victory, his GANA coalition failed to secure a congressional majority and he has faced political opposition to his government's programme. He has introduced improvements in education and health programmes and also initiated reductions in the armed forces. In Sept. 2006 some 3,000 troops and police stormed a prison controlled by inmates. In Oct. 2005 a state of emergency was declared following a devastating hurricane.

On 4 Nov. 2007 Álvaro Colom, leader of the social-democratic National Union of Hope (UNE), narrowly won the presidential election on a platform of economic development and fighting crime. Colom, who faced Berger in a run-off vote in Dec. 2003, was inaugurated on 14 Jan. 2008, succeeding Berger for a 4 year term.

Berisha, Sali (Albania)

Introduction

Former president Dr Sali Berisha returned as prime minister in Sept. 2005 after 8 years in opposition. He was a leading opponent of the communist regime in the late 1980s and served as Albania's first elected post-communist president from 1992–97. Breathing life into Albania's ailing economy, reforming its institutions and tackling corruption and organized crime have remained his policy priorities. Following parliamentary elections in June 2009, Berisha retained the premiership at the head of a new coalition formed in Sept. between his Democratic Party of Albania and its allies and the Socialist Movement for Integration.

Early Life

Sali Ram Berisha was born in Vuçidol in northern Albania on 15 Oct. 1944, the year in which the communist leader, Enver Hoxha, seized power and established a hard-line Stalinist regime. Berisha graduated in medicine from the University of Tirana in 1967, subsequently specializing in cardiology and publishing numerous textbooks and scientific papers. He joined the communist Party of Labour in 1971.

In the late 1980s Berisha was one of a group of intellectuals who called for democratic reforms. Following student protests at the University of Tirana in Dec. 1990, he founded the PD and was elected a member of parliament in the country's first multi-party elections on 31 March 1991. During the PD's first Congress in Sept. 1991 Berisha was voted chairman and led the party to victory in the general election of 22 March 1992. Elected president of Albania on 9 April 1992, he set out to open up the economy, promote foreign investment and reform the country's institutions. However, the administration was marred by corruption and Albania remained mired in poverty. Tens of thousands emigrated and Berisha faced growing opposition to his increasingly authoritarian rule, particularly in the south of the country.

Support for Berisha was further eroded by the collapse of various pyramid investment schemes in 1997. An uprising in the south threatened to spill over into civil war and tensions remained high when Berisha refused to step down after the electoral victory of a socialist-led coalition in June 1997. He eventually resigned under international pressure on 23 July 1997, to be replaced by the head of the Socialist Party, Rexhep Meidani. Fatos Nano, a fellow socialist and arch-rival of Berisha, became prime minister.

Tensions between the two main parties remained. Berisha accused Fatos Nano's administration of corruption and incompetence and withdrew from parliament between 1998 and early 2002. The arrival of hundreds of thousands of ethnic Albanian refugees from Kosovo in 1999 placed further strain on the faltering economy and infrastructure. Berisha fought the general election on 3 July 2005 on an anti-corruption platform and the PD claimed victory, although foreign monitors criticized the vote as falling short of international standards. Having formed a coalition with other centre-right groups to take control of 81 of the 140 seats in the legislature, Berisha was sworn in as prime minister on 11 Sept. 2005.

Career Peak

Berisha promised to build a 'social state' by streamlining the government and purging it of corrupt elements, reducing taxes and enabling private enterprise to flourish. He also declared his aim of eventual Albanian membership of NATO and the EU. In June 2006 his government signed a Stabilization and Association Agreement with the EU after 3 years of negotiations, and in April 2009 Albania joined NATO and applied for EU membership.

Berisha presided over an improvement in the economy, a revival of agriculture and the attraction of greater foreign investment. However, Albania's reputation for lawlessness has endured and criticisms of the country's ineffective judicial system remain. In March 2008 Berisha removed the defence minister, Fatmir Mediu, from office following a series of explosions at an ammunition depot near Tirana airport which killed 26 people and injured 250 more.

A new coalition government comprising the PD, the Republican Party of Albania, the Party for Justice and Integration and the Socialist Movement for Integration, with Berisha retaining the premiership, was sworn in on 17 Sept. 2009 following earlier parliamentary elections. However, the opposition Socialist Party maintained that the election result was fraudulent. The party's consequent campaign of demonstrations, civil disobedience and boycotting parliament resulted in political paralysis and prompted the EU's refusal in Nov. 2010 to grant Albania candidate membership status. The political climate deteriorated further in Jan. 2011 when an anti-government rally in the capital resulted in the killing of four protesters by security forces and led Berisha to accuse the opposition leader of trying to instigate a coup.

The parliamentary elections held in June 2013 were won by the opposition. Berisha publicly accepted the result and announced responsibility for the defeat. The following month he stepped down from the leadership of the PD. In Sept. 2013 Edi Rama succeeded Berisha as prime minister.

Berlusconi, Silvio (Italy)

Introduction

Silvio Berlusconi was Italy's longest-serving post-war prime minister, having served a total of three terms. His first government in 1994 lasted less than 8 months. He was returned to power as the head of Italy's government on 14 May 2001. His appointment was controversial, with many protesting that his position as the owner of the country's three main private television networks meant that he was able to unfairly influence the outcome of the election. Nevertheless, his centre-right coalition achieved a convincing majority in both the Senate and the lower house. In April 2005 the coalition collapsed, triggering a brief political crisis before another centre-right coalition under his premiership won a vote of confidence. His term ended in 2006 when his government lost parliamentary elections to Romano Prodi's Union coalition. However, after Prodi's own coalition collapsed in Feb. 2008, Berlusconi emerged victorious from the general election held in April. Berlusconi's third term was marred by scandals whilst he struggled to solve fiscal problems related to the European debt crisis. After losing his parliamentary majority he resigned in Nov. 2011.

Early Life

The son of a bank clerk, Silvio Berlusconi was born in Milan on 29 Sept. 1936. After graduating from the University of Milan he embarked on a career in property development, acquiring a large personal fortune by the early 1970s. In 1974 he founded a cable television company, *Telemilano*, which was later at the forefront of his campaign to end the state's monopoly on national television. By the end of the decade Berlusconi had established the country's first commercial television network, *Canale 5*. By this time he had also amassed stock in retail outlets, cinemas, AC Milan football club and publishing. These holdings were consolidated under a new umbrella organization that Berlusconi dubbed *Fininvest*. The conglomerate expanded throughout the 1980s and at its peak controlled over 150 separate businesses.

In Jan. 1994 a series of high profile corruption and bribery scandals engulfed the government and prompted demands for reforms. It was in this atmosphere that Berlusconi entered the political arena. He founded a new party, Forza Italia, which attracted floating voters disenchanted with politics after the demise of the Christian Democrats and Socialists. Forza Italia proclaimed its agenda as one of justice, economic liberalization and the reduction of bureaucracy and government intervention in commerce and industry. To secure power, the party allied itself with the right-wing Northern League and the neo-Fascist National Alliance. Called House of Freedoms (Casa delle Libertá), this coalition won a majority of seats in the Chamber of Deputies on 28 March 1994. Berlusconi, as the leader of the largest party in the alliance, was sworn in as prime minister in May.

Career Peak

Berlusconi's first term of office was short-lived. He immediately became entangled in a legal battle against political opponents who accused him of corruption and conflicts of interest. In Dec. 1994 an official investigation began into his past business dealings, prompting a no confidence vote. He resigned on 22 Dec. 1994. In the 1996 elections Berlusconi lost to Romano Prodi's centre-left Olive Tree coalition. Prodi left office in 1998 when he himself lost a no confidence vote.

Despite the popularity of the Olive Tree government, its leader in the 2001 elections, Francesco Rutelli, was unable to muster enough support to return the coalition to power. By this time Berlusconi's reputation had recovered. The centre-right won 368 seats in the Chamber of Deputies (a gain of 65 seats) compared to the Olive Tree's 242. In the Senate the centre-right coalition secured 177 of 315 seats, while the centre-left won just 125. This performance was enough to ensure Berlusconi the premiership.

Berlusconi pledged to cut taxes, raise pensions and create 1.5 m. new jobs. He also promised to form a stable government that would remain in power for the full five-year term. However, his term was marred by efforts to prosecute him for corruption and financial wrongdoing. Although his convictions for illegal party financing, false accounting and bribery were quashed, he stood trial in early 2003 for bribing the judiciary and business malpractice. However, in June 2003 parliament passed a law granting immunity from prosecution for leading government figures while they held office and Berlusconi's trial was dropped. Two of his smaller coalition partners threatened to leave government until the justice minister announced in Aug. 2003 that a judicial enquiry into Berlusconi's commercial affairs would still go ahead. Nevertheless, in Dec. 2004 he was cleared by the courts of a charge relating to his business affairs in the 1980s and another charge was dropped by virtue of the statute of limitations.

Meanwhile, in the aftermath of the attacks on the USA on 11 Sept. 2001, Berlusconi gave firm support to the US war on terror, backing military action in Afghanistan and Iraq, where Italian troops were deployed in the multinational forces.

On 20 April 2005 the centre-right coalition collapsed following a poor showing in regional elections. Berlusconi was forced to resign, but was reappointed a few days later by President Ciampi and formed a new coalition of all the parties in the previous administration. In April 2006 parliamentary elections were held, with House of Freedoms losing to Romano Prodi's centre-left coalition, Union. The results of the elections were close and disputed by Berlusconi, who claimed electoral fraud. He then called for a grand coalition government and for a House of Freedoms speaker in the Senate, where Union gained 158 seats to House of Freedoms' 156. He finally tendered his resignation on 2 May 2006, 3 weeks after his defeat. He remained in office as caretaker until Prodi was sworn in and formed the new government on 17 May 2006.

In Feb. 2008 Prodi's coalition collapsed and elections were called for April. Berlusconi announced he would stand for a third term, with the

intention of completing the reform programme started during his previous tenure. Attacking the left for 'bringing Italy to its knees'. he steered an alliance of centre-right parties to victory in the April elections and, in March 2009, oversaw the inaugural congress of the alliance (but excluding the independent Northern League) as a single People of Freedom (PdL) party.

Berlusconi's government was confronted by Italy's slide into economic recession under the shadow of its huge public debt and in the wake of the global financial crisis. In Oct. 2009 Italy's Constitutional Court overturned the law granting Berlusconi immunity from prosecution while in office. The ruling meant that he could face trial in two possible court actions. Also in 2009, the prime minister came under increasing media and opposition scrutiny over allegations about his conduct in his private life. On 13 Dec. 2009 he sustained facial injuries in an assault by a single assailant after addressing a rally in Milan.

Despite anti-government demonstrations backed by the opposition and the trade unions, Berlusconi's PdL made gains at the expense of the centre-left in regional elections in March 2010. However, in Aug. the government lost its parliamentary majority after more than 30 deputies broke away from the PdL, forming the Future and Freedom for Italy party (led by Gianfranco Fini, a former Berlusconi ally). The government subsequently survived several no-confidence votes up to Dec. but Berlusconi's political authority was further undermined as four ministers resigned in Nov. and claims about his personal life continued to surface. In Feb. 2011 he was indicted to stand trial by a judge on charges of paying a minor for sex and abuse of power.

On 8 Nov. 2011, amid growing fiscal problems related to the European debt crisis, Berlusconi lost his parliamentary majority. Berlusconi resigned on 13 Nov. after politicians approved an austerity package to protect the country and eurozone from financial collapse. His resignation was met with celebration outside the presidential palace.

Later Life

In Oct. 2012 a court in Milan convicted Berlusconi of tax fraud and sentenced him to 4 years in jail, although this was reduced to 1 year almost immediately. In May 2013 the appeals court upheld the 4-year sentence and reinstated a 5-year ban from public office that Berlusconi was given in Oct. Berlusconi was expelled from the Senate following his conviction and could face arrest over other criminal cases, having been stripped of immunity from prosecution.

In June 2013 he was found guilty of procuring an under-age dancer for sexual purposes and other related charges of abuse of power. He received a 7-year prison term and a lifelong ban from public office but in July 2014 an appeal court overturned his conviction.

Bērziņš, Andris (Latvia)

Introduction

Andris Bērziņš became president in June 2011 after an election dominated by rows over parliamentary links to business. A former banker, Bērziņš leads the Union of Greens and Farmers and advocates economic reforms and the consolidation of ties with the European Union (EU).

Early Life

Andris Bērziņš was born on 10 Dec. 1944 in Nītaure. After schooling in Nītaure and Sigulda, he studied radio engineering at the Riga Polytechnic Institute from 1966–71. He worked for R/A Elektrons from 1971–88, eventually as managing director. From 1987–88 he studied industrial planning at the University of Latvia, and from 1988–89 served as deputy minister of municipal services of the Latvian SSR. He was elected to the district council of the city of Valmiera in 1989, serving as its chairman until 1993. From 1990–93 he represented Valmiera on the Supreme Council of the Republic of Latvia, where he joined the Popular Front grouping. On 4 May 1990 he voted for Latvian independence from the USSR.

Between 1990 and 1992 Bērziņš served on the supervisory council of the Bank of Latvia, as the country began its conversion to a market economy. In 1993 he was appointed president of the newly founded commercial bank,

Latvijas Unibanka, overseeing its rapid growth until leaving the post in 2004. During this period he extended his own business interests into property.

In 2005 Bērziņš unsuccessfully stood for mayor of Riga, representing the Union of Greens and Farmers. He was president of the Latvian Chamber of Commerce and Industry from 2006 until 2010, and from 2007–09 was chairman of the supervisory council of the state-owned Latvenergo electricity company. In 2010 he entered parliament as a member of the Union of Greens and Farmers, which formed a coalition government with the Unity party.

From 2010 he served a year as chairman of the economic, agricultural, environmental and regional policy committee. In June 2011 he was elected president by parliament, beating the incumbent Valdis Zatlers in a second round of voting after Zatlers had accused MPs of being lax on corruption.

Career Peak

Bērziņš took office on 8 July 2011, promising to work independently of Latvia's oligarchs. He prioritized economic growth and the restoration of trust in the nation's democratic institutions. He also sought to consolidate Latvia's position in the EU, overseeing the country's adoption of the euro on 1 Jan. 2014. In the same month he appointed Laimdota Straujuma as Latvia's first female prime minister.

In April 2015, ahead of presidential elections scheduled for June, Bērziņš announced that he would not be seeking a second term. Raimonds Vējonis took over from Bērziņš on 8 July.

Bhattarai, Baburam (Nepal)

Introduction

Baburam Bhattarai became prime minister in Aug. 2011. His principal challenge was to draft a new constitution by the scheduled date of 28 May 2012 (exactly 4 years after Nepal became a republic). However, against an increasingly polarized political background, he failed to achieve this aim and was also unable to deliver fresh elections promised for Nov. after opposition parties refused to cooperate over electoral arrangements.

Early Life

Baburam Bhattarai was born on 18 June 1954 in Khoplang, Gorkha District. As a schoolboy he achieved among the nation's highest test results and graduated in architecture at the Chandigarh College of Architecture in 1977. He completed a master's degree in town and country planning from the School of Planning and Architecture, New Delhi in 1979 and received a doctorate in regional development planning from Jawaharlal Nehru University, New Delhi in 1986. While in India he founded the All India Nepalese Students' Association and in 1981 joined the Communist Party of Nepal (CPN). On his return to Nepal he became a Politburo Member of CPN (Unity Centre) and later of the Communist Party of Nepal (Maoist), which has in the meantime become the Unified Communist Party of Nepal (Maoist).

On 4 Feb. 1996 Bhattarai submitted a 40-point memorandum to the government on behalf of the United People's Front. Shortly afterwards he went into hiding when the Maoists launched their armed insurgency, emerging in 2003 as the Maoist party spokesman. He was a leading negotiator on the Nov. 2006 Comprehensive Peace Accord. In 2008 he was elected to parliament representing Gorkha constituency no. 2 and served as finance minister in Pushpa Kamal Dahal's short-lived government.

Parliament elected Bhattarai prime minister on 28 Aug. 2011 after the political parties failed to form a consensus government following Jhalanath Khanal's resignation. Bhattarai received 340 of the 575 votes cast. He was sworn in the following day.

Career Peak

Bhattarai's main challenge was to forge a cross-party consensus and draft a new constitution before 28 May 2012, at which point the Constituent Assembly was scheduled to be dissolved after a Nov. 2011 deadline was missed. However, the May 2012 deadline was also missed and Bhattarai then failed to hold promised new elections scheduled for Nov., which aggravated the political stalemate and heightened tensions between his government and President Yadav.

Meanwhile, in Nov. 2011 Bhattarai had secured the support of opposition parties and his own party hard-liners for a programme that would integrate into the army a third of the nation's 19,000 former Maoist fighters, while offering re-training and financial assistance to the rest. Securing the future of the fighters was seen as a major component of the peace process.

Later Life

In June 2016 Bhattarai founded Naya Shakti, a new party and alternative political force leaning towards economic development and the control of corruption.

Bhutto, Benazir (Pakistan)

Introduction

Benazir Bhutto served as Pakistan's prime minister between 1988–90 and 1993–96, becoming the first woman to head an Islamic state. She entered politics when her father, former prime minister Zulfiqar Ali Bhutto, was overthrown in a military coup. After his execution in 1979 she went on to lead the Pakistani People's Party (PPP) to electoral victory. Though absent from active politics and banned from contesting the premiership, Bhutto was the most vociferous critic of President Musharraf's leadership and maintained her role at head of the PPP. She returned to Pakistan from voluntary exile in late 2007 ahead of elections in 2008. On 27 Dec. 2007 she was assassinated as she left a political rally.

Early Life

Benazir Bhutto was born in Karachi on 21 June 1953 to the wealthy, land-holding family of Zulfiqar Ali Bhutto and Nusrat Bhutto. Her father was Pakistan's leader from 1971 until 1977 while her mother acted as deputy prime minister in his cabinet. Having received an early education in Pakistan, she studied at Harvard and then Oxford University, graduating in philosophy, politics and economics, before taking a further course in international law and diplomacy. In Jan. 1977 she was elected president of the Oxford student union.

She returned to Pakistan in June 1977 with the aim of joining the Pakistani foreign service, but the following month her father was removed from power in a coup led by Zia ul-Haq and she was placed under house arrest. As the campaign against her father intensified, Bhutto became strongly linked with the PPP. In 1979 Zulfiqar Ali Bhutto was hanged for conspiracy to murder. Benazir began a period of activism against Zia ul-Haq's government which lasted until 1985, during which she spent several years imprisoned (including ten months in solitary confinement) and 2 years living in exile in the UK. Despite political persecution, in 1981 she co-founded the Movement for the Restoration of Democracy.

In Nov. 1985 Zia lifted martial law and the following April Benazir Bhutto returned to Pakistan to a rapturous welcome. In May 1986 she was elected co-chairwoman of the PPP alongside her mother, backed by a growing tide of support for Zia's removal from power. Zia's death in 1988 led to national elections in which the PPP won the largest single bloc of seats (92 out of 207). An alliance with the Mohajir Qaumi Movement (MQM) gave them a majority and a government was formed with Bhutto at its head. She was sworn in as prime minister on 2 Dec., aged 35, becoming the youngest leader in Pakistan's history and the first woman to lead an Islamic government.

Career Peak

Bhutto's victory was warmly welcomed by Western governments, eager to see an end to Zia's military dictatorship and the inauguration of a more amenable democratic government. In power she showed herself keen to continue the socialist policies of her father, introducing a People's Program, designed to channel resources to the poor, introducing a monthly minimum wage, and lifting the ban on student and trade unions. Despite this, she proved herself unable to cope with a rising crime rate and the poor state of the economy. She also lacked the ability to ally Islamism and socialism in the same way that had marked her father's period in power. A narrowly won no-confidence motion in Nov. 1989 and the break-away of the MQM from its coalition with the PPP weakened Bhutto's government. Disputes with

President Ghulam Ishaq Khan over the appointment of military and judiciary officials led to a growing rift and on 6 Aug. 1990 Bhutto's government was dismissed on charges of 'economic mismanagement, corruption and decline in law and order'. Elections were held in Oct. 1990 but were lost to the Muslim League, headed by Nawaz Sharif, forcing the PPP into opposition.

The PPP was returned to power in 1993 at the head of another coalition with Bhutto as prime minister and Farooq Leghari replacing Ghulam Ishaq Khan as president. Although Bhutto demonstrated a more seasoned approach during her second tenure, establishing firm ties with the military, accusations of corruption continued to plague her. Her husband, appointed minister of investments in her cabinet, had been convicted on various charges of corruption in 1990 and was now accused of receiving kickbacks in government deals. Bhutto's government was dismissed in 1996 on the same grounds as in 1990.

Later Life

Bhutto was defeated in the national elections of 1997 and seemed a spent political force. In 1999 further charges of corruption and of involvement in the murder of Bhutto's brother, a political rival, forced her into exile in the UK and the UAE from where she appealed against the charges. In 2001 the Supreme Court of Pakistan ordered a retrial and set aside the charges of corruption. Under President Musharraf's government, however, the anti-corruption platform which served to support his military coup meant the continued ostracization of Bhutto.

In national elections held in Oct. 2002 the PPP came second to the pro-Musharraf Pakistan Muslim League (Quaid-e-Azam), despite winning a higher percentage of votes. Bhutto declined the opportunity to lead the party at the head of a national government. After 5 years apart, Bhutto and her husband were reunited in late 2004 but in 2006 the two were subject of an Interpol arrest warrant, instigated by Pakistan, on charges of corruption. Bhutto challenged its legal validity.

In 2007 she made a number of high-profile appearances in the West, meeting major political figures and appearing in the media. From mid-2007 the possibility emerged of Musharraf surrendering his military role but retaining the presidency, with Bhutto or a Bhutto-appointee coming in as prime minister. There was also speculation that the PPP might enter into a power-sharing agreement with the party of her historic political rival, Nawaz Sharif.

Ahead of the 2008 election and with the outstanding charges of corruption against her waived, she returned to Pakistan on 18 Oct. 2007. As she made her way to a rally in Karachi, a suicide bomber killed over 130 people and injured 450, though Bhutto was unscathed. At the beginning of Nov. Musharraf declared a state of emergency and Bhutto (along with other leading opposition figures) was temporarily placed under house arrest. When Musharraf was sworn in as a now civilian president at the end of the month, he pledged to lift the state of emergency by mid-Dec. Bhutto responded by launching her election manifesto, based around improving 'employment, education, energy, environment, equality'.

On 27 Dec. 2007 Bhutto was leaving a PPP rally in Rawalpindi when a suicide bomber attacked her car. She and 20 others died. The exact cause of death has been disputed but witnesses suggested shots were fired at her by a gunman. Her death was met with riots throughout the country. Al-Qaeda claimed responsibility for the killing.

Bhutto, Zulfiqar Ali (Pakistan)

Introduction

Zulfiqar Ali Bhutto was Pakistan's leader between 1971–77. His period in power was marked by an Islamization of Pakistan on socialist principles. He remains a controversial figure, at once acclaimed for his non-aligned foreign policy and supportive measures towards Pakistan's poor rural population yet equally criticised for his aggressively anti-Indian outlook and his drive towards turning Pakistan into a nuclear state.

Early Life

Zulfiqar Ali Bhutto was born on 5 Jan. 1928 in Larkana district to a wealthy, land-owning family. His father, Shahnawaz Khan Bhutto, had been a prominent figure in pre-independent Indian politics and had received a knighthood. Zulfiqar Ali Bhutto studied at Bombay Cathedral high school before joining the Berkley campus at the University of Southern California in 1949, going on to become the first Asian elected to Berkley student council. Graduating with honours in political science, he left to study law at Christ Church college, Oxford, in 1950. In 1951 he married Nusrat Ispahani with whom he had four children. In 1953 Bhutto was called to the bar at Lincoln's Inn, London, but left England to set up a legal practise in Karachi.

A charismatic orator, Bhutto's rise to political importance began through his successful leadership of several Pakistani delegations to the UN between 1957–65. In 1958, at the age of 30, he was appointed minister of commerce, becoming the youngest cabinet member in Ayub Khan's government. He took responsibility for several other portfolios, including information and national reconstruction (1959), fuel, power and natural resources (1960), and foreign Affairs (1963–66). In the last of these posts Bhutto was influential in directing Ayub Khan's foreign policy towards closer ties with China and an increasingly hostile stance towards India. Leading a delegation to the UN, Bhutto courted western disapproval by going against the US and voting for China's membership.

The 1965 war between Pakistan and India and the failure to gain control of Kashmir led to a growing divide between Bhutto and Khan. Bhutto, who felt that Khan had failed to represent Pakistan's interests in the Tashkent declaration which followed the war, remained vigorously opposed to the development of bilateral relations, famously declaring at a UN security council meeting that Pakistan would fight for Kashmir 'for a thousand years'. In June 1966 he resigned from the cabinet in protest to the Tashkent declaration.

In Nov. 1967 Bhutto founded the Islamic socialist Pakistani People's Party (PPP) with the slogan, 'Islam is our Faith, Democracy is our Policy, Socialism is our Economy, All Power to the People'. His party began agitation against Ayub Khan's government and Bhutto himself led a Mass Movement for the Restoration of Democracy in 1968 for which he was subsequently arrested.

In elections held on 7 Dec. 1970 the PPP gained a massive majority in West Pakistan while in East Pakistan the Awami League, under Sheikh Mujibur Rahman, was the biggest party. Yayha Khan, who had replaced Ayub Khan as president, was unable to stem the seccessionist movement in East Pakistan and after the 1971 war between East and West Pakistan (which led to the creation of Bangladesh) he resigned, leaving Bhutto in power. Bhutto subsequently became President and Chief Martial Law Administrator of Pakistan.

Career Peak

In 1972 martial law, which had been imposed under Yayha Khan's rule, was lifted. In April 1973 a new constitution, which designated Islam as the state religion, was unanimously accepted and in Aug. Bhutto was elected as prime minister.

Bhutto set about a range of reforms, including the nationalization of key industries, the setting of land ownership ceilings and tax reliefs for the rural poor. His government's withdrawal of Pakistan from a number of international groups such as SEATO and the British Commonwealth formed part of a wider foreign policy in which he sought to draw together the support of third world, Islamic countries and to move away from the ties to the western hemisphere which his predecessors had fostered. His desire to place Pakistan at the helm of these new international alliances came with nuclear aspirations. Despite warnings from US Secretary of State Henry Kissinger, in Nov. 1972 Pakistan's first nuclear power plant was established at Karachi.

Bhutto won popularity in 1972 with the signing of the Simla Agreement which saw 93,000 prisoners from the 1971 war returned to Pakistan. Over the following years he oversaw the establishment of the Pakistan Steel Mills, the Port Qasim Authority and the Quaid-e-Azam University. Yet his successes were marked by his repression of political dissent. In the run-up to national elections in 1977 nine opposition parties came together to form the Pakistan National Alliance (PNA). Though the elections were won by the PPP, there were accusations of vote rigging. The PNA subsequently withdrew from local elections and shortly afterwards fighting broke out. In an ill-advised attempt to quell the situation Bhutto had opposition politicians arrested and on 5 July 1977 Muhammad Zia ul-Haq staged a coup. Bhutto was imprisoned for a month.

Later Life

On his release Bhutto toured the country which was greeted with enthusiasm. Despite this, the new administration's determination to show the past leader as corrupt culminated with his arrest for alleged involvement in the murder of a political opponent in 1974. Bhutto protested innocence but was found guilty. The death sentence was approved by the Supreme Court and on 4 April 1979 Bhutto was hanged. His daughter, Benazir, followed Zia ul-Haq as president in 1988.

Biko, Stephen Bantu (South Africa)

Introduction

Steve Biko was a founding member of South Africa's Black Consciousness Movement. His death as a result of injuries inflicted whilst in police custody was powerfully symbolic of the political struggle of South African black nationalists against a repressive state and transformed Biko into an internationally renowned martyr to his cause.

Early Life

Biko was born in King Williams Town, Cape Province on 18 Dec. 1946. Having been expelled from school for political activism he enrolled at the more liberal St Francis College and went on to study medicine at Natal University Medical School where he became involved in the National Union of South African Students. The NUSAS was a multiracial organization working for racial equality in South Africa.

Career Peak

This view was in conflict with how Biko perceived the reality of NUSAS and in 1968 he and some colleagues established the exclusively black 'southern African Students' Organization'. Biko believed that political freedom could only be achieved if blacks stopped feeling inferior to whites, saying 'The most potent weapon of the oppressor is the mind of the oppressed.' SASO's aim was to raise black self-esteem and confidence. The movement spread widely throughout University campuses during the early '70s. In Feb. 1973 Biko and his colleagues were served with 'banning' orders. They were not allowed to communicate with each other and were restricted from attending social gatherings. Steve Biko responded by operating covertly and established the Zimele Trust Fund, a fund designed to help the families of political prisoners.

On 18 Aug. 1977 Steve Biko and a fellow activist were arrested and jailed in Port Elizabeth. The Truth & Reconciliation Commission Report states that:

> 'Stephen Bantu Biko died in police custody in Pretoria on 12 Sept. 1977. He was detained by the Security Branch in Port Elizabeth twenty-four days earlier, and was subjected to interrogation, during which he sustained serious brain injuries. He was examined by both a district surgeon and a medic. He was then transported naked in the back of a police van from Port Elizabeth to Pretoria. He died from brain damage in a prison cell shortly after his arrival in Pretoria...Minister Kruger... implied that Biko had died as a result of engaging in a hunger strike. At the inquest, the security police claimed that Biko had "become violent" during interrogation and had to be "subdued" by the interrogation team, in the course of which he hit his head against the wall.' An inquest at the time cleared the police of all allegations.

On 12 Sept. 1997 President Nelson Mandela called Steve Biko 'one of the greatest sons of our nation' and paid homage to him by unveiling a statue in East London.

Bin Hamad Al Thani, Khalifa (Qatar)

Introduction

Khalifa bin Hamad Al Thani deposed his cousin, Sheikh Ahmed bin Ali Al Thani, on 22 Feb. 1972 to become ruler of Qatar. After 23 years in power he was himself deposed by his son, Hamad bin Khalifa, in June 1995. This palace coup took place with the approval of the rest of the royal family and the armed forces.

Early Life

Sheikh Khalifa was born into the ruling Al Thani dynasty in 1932, the son of Sheikh Hamad bin Abdullah Al Thani, who was the Amir from 1940–48. Hamad was succeeded by Sheikh Ali bin Abdullah (1949–60) and Ahmed bin Ali (1960–72), neither of whom had any particular interest in supervising day-to-day government and administration. By default, these duties were assumed by Khalifa who was declared the heir apparent and deputy ruler in Oct. 1960. By 1970 he was prime minister, having already headed the ministries or departments of foreign affairs, finance and petroleum, education, and police and internal security.

Career Peak

It was Khalifa who declared Qatar's independence from Britain on 3 Sep. 1971, just a few months before becoming ruler. His assumption of power was portrayed as a simple succession in Qatar, but Western opinion viewed the event as an overthrow. Khalifa and other influential members of the Al Thani family were believed to be concerned by Sheikh Ahmed's financial profligacy. In the wake of the country's oil boom, Khalifa is credited with putting into effect a programme of economic development and modernization, which brought free health, education, and housing benefits to the broader population. Politically, there were no significant moves towards democracy.

From the early 1990s Khalifa left daily government to his sons, particularly Sheikh Hamad, the Crown Prince and defence minister. On 27 June 1995 Hamad took control of the country when his father was on a private visit to Switzerland. Khalifa was linked to an attempted counter-coup in Feb. 1996, before agreeing to release substantial state funds under his control in return for a peaceful retirement.

Later Life

Khalifa died on 23 Oct. 2016 at the age of 84.

Bin Khalifa Al Thani, Hamad (Qatar)

Introduction

Sheikh Hamad was the eighth member of the Al Thani family to rule Qatar, having seized power from his father, Sheikh Khalifa, on 27 June 1995. After 18 years in power he abdicated in favour of his son, Crown Prince Sheikh Tamim bin Hamad Al Thani, on 25 June 2013.

Early Life

Born in Doha in 1952, Hamad graduated from the Royal Military Academy, Sandhurst in 1971. He then joined the Qatari military with the rank of major. In 1975 he was promoted to major-general and commander-in-chief of the armed forces. On his appointment as Crown Prince and heir apparent in May 1977, he also became minister of defence.

Career Peak

Having ousted his father in 1995, Hamad appointed himself prime minister. However, in Oct. 1996 he relinquished the premiership to his younger brother, Sheikh Abdallah. The Amir is credited with initiating plans for an elected consultative council (through the new constitution which he approved in 2004 and which took effect in June 2005), giving women the right to vote in municipal elections (from 1999) and ending official media censorship. He has also encouraged foreign investment in Qatar's oil and natural gas industries.

In Aug. 2003 he named his fourth son as his heir apparent, and in April 2007 appointed his foreign minister and cousin, Sheikh Hamad bin Jasim bin Jabir Al Thani, prime minister. To pre-empt pressure for political liberalization in the wake of the discontent that spread across much of the Arab world from early 2011, Hamad announced in Nov. that year that elections to Qatar's Advisory Council would be held in 2013 although by April 2013 no fixed date had been set.

In foreign relations he has overseen the resolution of long-standing border disputes with Bahrain and Saudi Arabia. In 2011 Qatar was involved in international military operations against the Gaddafi regime in Libya, a fellow Arab state. The country's profile on the world stage was raised in Dec. 2010 when it successfully bid to host the football World Cup finals in 2022. In Sept. 2012 Hamad called on Arab nations to form a coalition to intervene in the Syrian conflict, and in Oct. he made the first visit to Gaza by a head of state since the Hamas government took control of the Palestinian territory.

Hamad abdicated in June 2013 in favour of his 33-year-old fourth son, Crown Prince Sheikh Tamim bin Hamad Al Thani. Hamad explained his decision by stating it was appropriate time for the new generation to take charge of the Gulf nation. Sheikh Hamad, aged 61, has been known to suffer from health problems in recent years, but official sources claim that his health did not influence the decision to abdicate.

Bin Rashid Al-Maktoum, Maktoum (United Arab Emirates)

Introduction

The ruler of Dubai emirate, Sheikh Maktoum became vice president and prime minister of the UAE federal government following the death of his father, Sheikh Rashid in 1990.

Early Life

Maktoum was born in 1941. The eldest of Rashid's four sons, he assumed the title of Crown Prince of Dubai. He served as the UAE's first federal prime minister of three cabinets before resigning in April 1979 in an effort to end discord among the seven member emirates. This had arisen because of rivalry among the rulers over the extent of federal government powers. Maktoum became one of two deputy prime ministers in a new government led by his father, Sheikh Rashid.

Career Peak

Following Rashid's death on 7 Oct. 1990, Maktoum became the ruler of Dubai and was sworn in the following month as federal prime minister (for a second time) and vice president. He served in both positions until 4 Jan. 2006, when he died after suffering a heart attack. He was succeeded by his brother, Sheikh Muhammad bin Rashid al-Maktoum.

Bin Said Al-Maktoum, Rashid (United Arab Emirates)

Introduction

The ruler of Dubai emirate from 1958–90, Sheikh Rashid was also vice president of the UAE from its formation in 1971, and prime minister of the federal government from 1979. His son, Sheikh Maktoum, succeeded on Rashid's death on 7 Oct. 1990. Sheikh Rashid is credited with Dubai's transformation into one of the most prosperous trading and commercial centres in the Middle East.

Early Life

Sheikh Rashid was born in 1912, the eldest son of Sheikh Maktoum bin Rashid al-Maktoum who ruled Dubai until his death in 1958. The al-Maktoum family are a branch of the Bani Yas tribe that includes the al-Nahyan, rulers of neighbouring Abu Dhabi. Rashid effectively ran the state as Prince Regent from about 1940, and so his direction of Dubai's economic evolution straddled both the pre- and post-oil eras. Before oil was discovered in the emirate, his administration had sought to modernize the

territory, borrowing from neighbouring states to develop the Dubai Creek and consolidating Dubai's position as the main trading hub for the then Trucial Coast.

Career Peak

In the late 1960s, oil was discovered in Dubai. Sheikh Rashid deployed export revenues for construction and infrastructure projects. However, aware of the risks of oil-dependency, he also promoted alternative industrial ventures—in particular, the creation of Jebel Ali port (the world's largest man-made harbour) and free trade zone, west of Dubai city. Upon the withdrawal of the British from the Gulf in 1971, Sheikh Rashid led Dubai into the new, independent UAE as the second largest constituent emirate after Abu Dhabi. He assumed the vice presidency and, in 1979, the federal premiership. He retained both posts until his death, but played a background role during in the 1980s when he was in failing health. His four sons continued his policies.

Bin Salman Al-Khalifa, Isa (Bahrain)

Introduction

Shaikh Isa succeeded to the throne on 2 Nov. 1961, and took the title of Amir on 16 Aug. 1971 following Bahrain's independence from Britain. His long reign ended on his death on 6 March 1999.

Early Life

Born in the village of Jasra on 3 July 1933, Shaikh Isa was educated in Bahrain by private tutors. From the age of 20 he assumed public administrative duties. Having been appointed a member, and subsequently deputy chairman, of the Administrative Council (later the Council of Ministers), he was named Crown Prince and heir-apparent by his father, Shaikh Salman bin Hamad, in July 1957.

Career Peak

Supported by oil revenues, Shaikh Isa presided over Bahrain's rapid economic and infrastructural development in the 1970s and 1980s. During his reign there was also diversification, particularly in the finance sector, making Bahrain the hub of the Gulf and the regional centre for offshore banking. Although a popularly-elected National Assembly was set up under a new constitution ratified in June 1973, the Amir dissolved it in Aug. 1975 and ruled by decree from then on. He did, however, agree the establishment of a Consultative Council in Dec. 1992. The last years of Shaikh Isa's reign, from the mid-1990s, were marked by unrest among the Shia Muslim majority community and violent agitation for political reform.

Bin Sultan Al-Nahyan, Zayed (United Arab Emirates)

Introduction

Ruler of Abu Dhabi, the largest of the seven emirates, Sheikh Zayed had been president of the UAE since it was established on 2 Dec. 1971 until he died in 2004.

Early Life

Zayed was born in 1918. He was governor of Abu Dhabi's eastern province based in Al-Ain from 1946 until 1966 when he deposed his brother Sheikh Shakhbut and became ruler of the sheikhdom. The Al-Nahyan family considered Shakhbut an obstacle to the investment of Abu Dhabi's new oil wealth (from 1962) in the development of the sheikhdom. As the United Kingdom ended its protectorate of the Trucial Coast, Zayed persuaded the other emirates (but not Bahrain or Qatar) to join in a federation. The UAE was formed in

Dec. 1971 (although Ras al-Khaimah did not accede until Feb.1972) and the rulers of the emirates elected Zayed to his first 5 year term as federal president.

Career Peak

Zayed had been re-elected president at 5 year intervals, overseeing rapid economic development, federal centralization and defence integration. This had taken place against a backdrop of stability in a traditionally volatile region. Abu Dhabi's, and Zayed's, image was dented in 1991 by the failure of the Bank of Credit and Commerce International. The institution had been founded in 1972 with Zayed's help and the Abu Dhabi government had bought the majority of shares in 1990. Zayed continued to rule until his death on 2 Nov. 2004.

Bin Sultan Bin Al-Nahyan, Shakhbut (United Arab Emirates)

Introduction

Sheikh Shakhbut was the ruler of Abu Dhabi within the then British-controlled Trucial Coast from 1928–66. At the end of his long reign he lost the support of other members of the al-Nahyan family and was replaced by his more progressive younger brother, Sheikh Zayed.

Early Life

Born in 1905, the eldest son of Sheikh Sultan, Shakhbut was selected by a family conclave as ruler of Abu Dhabi in 1928. At that time Abu Dhabi's fragile economy had been undermined by the collapse of the pearl market and the world economic depression. Shortly after the Second World War, the search for oil began in earnest as Sheikh Shakhbut granted exploration concessions. By 1958 the first oilfields were being exploited. The first oil was exported in 1962.

Career Peak

Throughout his reign Sheikh Shakhbut maintained friendly relations with the British. He resisted territorial incursions in a prolonged border dispute with Saudi Arabia over the oil-rich Buraimi oasis. The dispute was settled in 1974. Despite the emirate's new oil-based wealth, the Sheikh was reluctant to invest the earnings in development and infrastructure projects for the benefit of the state. On 6 Aug. 1966 he was replaced by his brother and went temporarily into exile. He died in Abu Dhabi in Feb. 1989.

Bin Taimur Al-Said, Said (Oman)

Introduction

Said bin Taimur Al-Said was Sultan of Oman (hereditary absolute monarch) from 1932–70. A reclusive and repressive ruler, his autocratic policies prompted popular unrest and armed revolt. In 1970 he was overthrown by his son Qaboos bin Said, the present Sultan, in a bloodless coup.

Early Life

Said bin Taimur succeeded his father, Taimur bin Faisal, in 1932. Said inherited a country virtually bankrupt and internally divided. The historical split between Oman's coastal areas, ruled by the Sultan, and the rest of the territory, had been recognised in the 1920 Treaty of As Sib (brokered by the British) under which Said's father conceded limited sovereignty to the tribes of the interior. The treaty was a de facto partition agreement, although the ruling Al-Said dynasty did not relinquish their claim to all of Oman.

Career Peak

In the early 1950s Said sought to extend his writ into the oil rich interior, which offered the means to alleviate the debt problems of his regime and reinforce his rule. However, the acquiescence of the interior tribal sheikhs was necessary for oil exploration. This was not forthcoming, and a rebellion broke out in 1954 under a new Imam (nominal head of the interior) who led a movement for independence. Britain intervened on the Sultan's behalf and by 1959 Said had fully re-established his authority.

Despite the potential of Oman's oil revenues, Said failed to modernize his country. While maintaining his military connection with the British, he opposed any social change, including popular educational. In 1958 he withdrew from Muscat to the coastal city of Salalah, the administrative capital of the Dhofar region in the southwest, where he remained except for periodic private visits to the United Kingdom.

Resistance to Said's conservative regime continued to simmer after the unrest of the 1950s. In 1964 another serious rebellion broke out, this time in Dhofar. The revolt, fuelled by the neighbouring Marxist state of Yemen, was to continue until 1975. On 23 July 1970 Said's Western-educated and more progressive son, Qaboos bin Said, took power in a palace coup with the tacit endorsement of the British. Said was forced to abdicate and withdrew to London, England, where he died in 1972.

Bird, Lester (Antigua and Barbuda)

Introduction

Lester Bird, the son of Vere Cornwall Bird (Antigua and Barbuda's first prime minister), served as the country's second prime minister from 1994 to 2004. His rule was marred by corruption scandals.

Early Life

Lester Bryant Bird was born in New York City on 21 Feb. 1938. A keen sportsman, he played cricket for the Leeward Islands and was an All-American long jumper at the University of Michigan, from where he graduated in 1962. He then completed his law studies in the UK and was called to the Bar in 1969. He returned to Antigua and Barbuda to work in private practice from 1969–76.

In 1971 Bird was appointed chairman of the Antigua Labour Party (ALP) and leader of the opposition in the Senate. After the 1976 election returned the ALP to power, Vere Bird named his son as deputy premier and put him in charge of the foreign affairs, tourism and energy portfolios.

In 1981 Lester Bird became minister for external affairs, and was named the first chairman of the Organization of Eastern Caribbean States in 1982 (a post he held again in 1989). In the late 1980s he became embroiled in a power battle with his brother, Vere Bird Jr, who was widely considered favourite to succeed their father. However, numerous scandals, including arms smuggling to the Colombian Medellín drug cartel, led to Vere Jr being dismissed as minister of public works by Vere Snr.

In 1992 V. C. Bird was caught misappropriating public funds and announced that he would step down ahead of the 1994 general election. Lester eventually defeated John St. Luce to win the ALP leadership in 1993. In 1994, at elections deemed neither fair nor free, the ALP won 11 of 17 seats and Lester Bird was sworn in as prime minister. Despite an inquiry recommending that Vere Jr never be allowed to hold ministerial office again, he was appointed to the cabinet by Lester as a special adviser.

Career Peak

As prime minister, Lester Bird also assumed the portfolios for external affairs, planning, social services and information. In a cabinet reshuffle in 1996, he added the communications, civil aviation, international transport and gaming portfolios. Further reshuffles saw him additionally in charge of the ministries of finance, legal affairs, justice and national security by 2002.

He implemented tax and tariff increases alongside sharp cuts in spending on health, education, and basic infrastructure, leading to a deterioration in services. The government nonetheless continued to borrow heavily in commercial markets, with foreign debt reaching US$466m. in 1997.

Bird secured victory at the 1999 election despite allegations from opposition parties of ALP bribery and intimidation. Although he promised the introduction of anti-corruption legislation, he continued to be dogged by scandal, including the arrest of his brother, Ivor, for trying to board a plane while in possession of 26 pounds of cocaine. His administration was also charged with diverting international relief aid and misusing funds and in 2004 Bird was accused of having a sexual affair with a minor.

The Bird family's domination of domestic politics that had lasted since the 1950s came to an end at the March 2004 election, when the United Progressive Party (UPP) defeated the ALP. Bird remained as the ALP's political leader but in 2012 was again involved in scandal when he was questioned by police over a multi-million dollar fraud case.

Bird, Vere Cornwall (Antigua and Barbuda)

Introduction

A dominant figure in Antiguan politics for more than 50 years, Sir Vere Cornwall Bird led his country to independence from Great Britain and was its first prime minister, holding office from 1981–94. He was credited with turning Antigua into one of the more prosperous of the Eastern Caribbean States, though his rule was marred by allegations of nepotism and corruption.

Early Life

Vere Cornwall Bird was born on 7 Dec. 1909 in the slums of the capital, St. John's. He had no formal post-primary education but enlisted in the Salvation Army when aged 18, serving for 2 years and attaining the rank of captain.

In 1939 Bird helped found the Antigua Trades and Labour Union (ATLU), the island's first union. In 1943 it won legal status and he became its president, a position he held until 1973. Bird worked to secure the rights of workers against oppressive and exploitative conditions, particularly in the sugar industry. He pressured plantation owners to turn over plots and homes to the sugar harvesters who had been their tenants, and fought to improve basic infrastructure. He oversaw improved conditions of work and pay, as well as the abolition of child labour.

Like other Caribbean contemporaries, Bird used union activism as a springboard to political office. After the formation of the Antigua Labor Party, Bird was elected to the colonial legislature in 1945. In 1946 he became a member of the executive council, securing universal adult suffrage in 1951. That same year, union representatives led by Bird won all eight elected seats on the local legislature, a feat repeated at each election until 1967.

Bird was a key figure at the 1947 Montego Bay Conference in Jamaica that led to the creation of the West Indian Federation (WIF). After the collapse of the WIF in 1962, Bird was instrumental (along with Errol Barrow of Barbados and Forbes Burnham of Guyana) in establishing the Caribbean Free Trade Association in 1965 (known as the Caribbean Community and Common Market from 1973).

Career Peak

On 11 Jan. 1960 Bird became first chief minister of Antigua and spearheaded attempts to diversify the economy away from its reliance on sugar. A deep water port and international airport (later renamed Vere Bird International) was built to boost tourism, while a construction boom was fuelled by hotel and resort development.

In 1966 Bird led a delegation to the United Kingdom to seek independence. Britain agreed to Associated Status, giving Antigua and Barbuda's government control of all internal affairs while defence and foreign affairs continued to be directed from London. In Feb. 1967 Bird was appointed the country's first premier.

Following elections in 1971, his government was succeeded by George Walter's Progressive Labour Movement administration. Despite allegations that he had orchestrated bombing campaigns to undermine the Walter government, Bird was re-elected to the premiership in 1976 and had Walter imprisoned for corruption. Bird secured another election victory in 1980,

with the nation winning full independence from London a year later and Bird taking the office of prime minister.

He hung on to power for another 10 years. Although he had overseen improvements in the education and telecommunications system and the introduction of free medical services, he was subject to allegations of corruption, nepotism, bribery and money laundering. The Bird family were linked to drug- and gun-running scandals from the late 1970s until the 1990s. In March 1994 Bird retired from politics and was succeeded by his son, Lester Bryant Bird.

Later Life

Upon retirement Bird was formally accorded the status of the country's first National Hero and in July 1998 was awarded the Order of the Caribbean Community in recognition of his role in the development of the region. He died on 28 June 1999.

Biyoghé Mba, Paul (Gabon)

Introduction

Paul Biyoghé Mba is a career civil servant who served as a minister under Gabon's autocratic president, Omar Bongo. In Oct. 2009 he was appointed prime minister by the late president's controversial successor, Ali Bongo.

Early Life

Biyoghé Mba was born on 18 April 1953 in Donguila, Estuaire province, in western Gabon. In the early 1970s he studied business administration at the University of Rennes, France, before returning to Gabon to work at the Banque Gabonaise de Développement. Biyoghé Mba served as the bank's deputy director from 1977–80, before joining the civil service, initially as an adviser to Omar Bongo on commercial, industrial and investment affairs (1980–83). This was when high international oil prices brought prosperity to Gabon and to the president personally.

Biyoghé Mba was deputy director to the presidential cabinet from 1984–89, when he helped secure US investment in a period of economic downturn. Disillusionment with Bongo's repressive policies brought demands for multi-party democracy. In 1990 Gabon held its first multi-party legislative elections for 22 years. Biyoghé Mba was elected for the Gabonese Democratic Party (PDG), which gained a majority in the National Assembly. He served as a deputy for 2 years until he was appointed minister of state control, parastatal reform and privatization.

Biyoghé Mba supported Bongo's re-election as president in 1993 but resigned from the government and the PDG the following year in protest at Bongo's authoritarian response to riots in Libreville and Port-Gentil. Returning to the National Assembly, he created a new party, the Communal Movement for Development (MCD), which eventually merged with the PDG in 2002. Elected to the newly established Senate in 1997, he was the minister responsible for small and medium-sized enterprises from 1999–2003. As Gabon's minister of trade and industrial development (2003–08) he was responsible for the New Partnership for Africa's Development (a programme of the African Union adopted in 2001). In Oct. 2008 he became minister for agriculture in Jean Eyeghe Ndong's government.

Career Peak

In the political upheaval that followed Bongo's death on 8 June 2009 (ending his 41-year rule), his son, Ali Bongo (then minister of defence) became the PDG's presidential candidate. Ndong resigned as prime minister to fight the election as an independent.

On 17 July 2009 the interim president, Rose Francine Rogombé, named Biyoghé Mba as interim prime minister. Ali-Ben Bongo Ondimba was sworn in as the new president on 16 Oct. 2009, nearly 2 months after his disputed election victory had triggered widespread civil unrest. On the same day, Bongo appointed Biyoghé Mba as prime minister, praising his managerial skills and experience. Biyoghé Mba named a government of 30 ministers (slimmed down from 44), which included 12 members from his previous cabinet. Following the victory of his party in the Dec. elections, Biyoghé Mba resigned on 13 Feb. 2012 as required by the constitution.

Blair, Tony (United Kingdom of Great Britain and Northern Ireland)

Introduction

Tony Blair, who led a rejuvenated Labour Party to a landslide victory in the 1997 general election, ending 18 years of Conservative rule, was returned to power in 2001 and 2005. Espousing 'Third Way' centrist policies, Blair instigated constitutional and public service reforms, pursued peace in Northern Ireland and sought closer integration with Europe. He was criticized on the left for his perceived attachment to Thatcherite economic policies, his centralized control over his party's and government's image, and his close alignment of UK foreign policy with that of the USA. After the 11 Sept. 2001 attacks on the USA, Blair was President George W. Bush's closest international ally in the 'war on terror' and fully supported US policy in Iraq, despite widespread opposition both domestically and from EU and UN partners. In Aug. 2003 Blair became the longest continuously-serving Labour prime minister and in May 2005 led the party to an unprecedented third consecutive term. In Sept. 2006 Blair delivered his final conference speech as Labour leader but declined to set a precise date for his departure from office. He eventually left office in June 2007.

Early Life

Anthony Charles Lynton Blair was born in Edinburgh on 6 May 1953. His mother was a teacher and his father a lawyer. Brought up in Durham and educated at Fettes College, Edinburgh, he graduated in law from St John's College, Oxford, in 1975 and was called to the bar a year later, joining the chambers of Derry Irvine (later to become Blair's Lord Chancellor).

Blair joined the Labour Party in 1976 and in 1982 unsuccessfully contested a by-election in Beaconsfield before winning the seat of Sedgefield at the 1983 general election. Under Neil Kinnock's party leadership, he became assistant spokesman on treasury affairs from 1984 and then deputy spokesman on trade and industry. He joined the shadow cabinet in Oct. 1988 as shadow secretary for energy, moving to employment in 1989. Following Labour's defeat at the 1992 elections, Kinnock was replaced by John Smith who made Blair shadow home secretary. When Smith suffered a fatal heart attack in 1994, Blair was elected to succeed him as leader. He continued his two predecessors' efforts to modernize the party, and in 1995 won a significant victory in abolishing Labour's longstanding commitment to public ownership of leading industries.

Promoting free-market economics, tough action on crime and a more positive European policy, Labour made major gains in the 1995 local elections. As John Major's Conservative government imploded, Blair's personal charisma and his skilled 'spin doctors' convinced voters previously fearful of Labour's left-wing heritage that the party was ready to govern. At the general election of May 1997 Labour inflicted a crushing national defeat on the Conservatives.

Career Peak

Once in office, Blair instigated major constitutional reforms. Following national referendums on devolution, Scotland gained its own parliament with tax-raising powers while Wales got an assembly with more limited authority. In the House of Lords the majority of hereditary peers were removed, while London was granted the right to elect its own mayor.

The economy generally prospered under Blair and Chancellor Gordon Brown, with steady growth and declining unemployment. In 1997 the Bank of England won independence, with a new Monetary Policy Committee having the power to set interest rates and maintain inflation within Treasury targets.

In foreign policy, Blair sought to preserve the close relationship with the USA while extending ties with the EU. Labour's victory in 1997, and Blair's commitment to sign up to the EU Social Chapter (rejected by the UK since the early 1990s), was welcomed by many EU governments. However, the UK remained outside the euro area.

After the 11 Sept. 2001 attacks on the USA, Blair was Bush's staunchest ally in the military campaigns in Afghanistan and Iraq. However, this commitment dented the prime minister's domestic and international standing. When in Sept. 2002 Bush challenged the UN to act on Iraq, Blair was the only other leader with the power of veto on the UN Security Council to unequivocally support the USA. As Bush pursued independent action, the Westminster parliament in March 2003 granted Blair permission to send UK forces to Iraq, although 139 Labour MPs voted against war—the strongest revolt by his own party since taking office in 1997. Several ministers resigned, including leader of the House of Commons and former foreign secretary Robin Cook.

US-led forces launched an invasion of Iraq in March 2003 and by early April Saddam Hussein's regime had collapsed. In May 2003 a UN resolution, co-sponsored by the USA, UK and Spain, endorsed co-operation between UN special representatives and the occupying forces in forming a new Iraqi government. Meanwhile, British media criticism over the failure to discover persuasive evidence of Iraqi weapons of mass destruction (WMD) raised doubts over the justification for war. This led in July 2003 to a public enquiry headed by Lord Hutton, who, in Jan. 2004, controversially exonerated the Blair government of exaggerating intelligence about Iraq's WMD. A further investigation, chaired by Lord Butler and delivered in July 2004, criticized the flawed quality of WMD intelligence but found no deliberate attempt to mislead. Despite efforts to introduce and sustain democratic government in Iraq, insurgent and sectarian violence escalated. As the situation deteriorated, British public opinion became increasingly hostile to Blair's stance and continuing UK military involvement.

In Northern Ireland, Blair continued the political initiatives started by the Major administration, and in 1998 secured the Good Friday Agreement. Establishing a power-sharing scheme centred on a Northern Ireland Assembly, it offered the first realistic chance of peace in the territory in 30 years. However, breakdowns in the peace process prompted the suspension of the devolved administration in Oct. 2002. Despite the suspension, fresh Assembly elections took place in Nov. 2003, with the hardline Democratic Unionist Party (DUP) and nationalist Sinn Féin making significant gains. There was no further progress until Oct. 2006 when Blair and his Irish counterpart outlined a new timetable back to power-sharing in the province. With conditional party support for the timetable, new Assembly elections were held in March 2007 in which the DUP and Sinn Féin were again predominant. Both parties came under pressure to compromise and on 26 March reached an historic agreement to share power from 8 May with a devolved Northern Ireland government replacing direct rule from London.

Within the EU, Blair championed a new constitution to reflect the enlargement of the Union from May 2004 but the project stalled following its rejection in French and Dutch referenda in 2005. He also supported accession negotiations with Turkey, which began tentatively in Oct. 2005. In Dec. 2005, as leaders of the 25 member states finally agreed a deal on the budget for the enlarged Union for 2007–13, Blair was forced to concede a reduction in the UK's annual budget rebate but failed to secure cuts in common agricultural spending.

In the public services, Blair put emphasis on improving the health and education systems, although progress in these areas is disputed. In April 2003 he established self-governing hospitals that would be financially rewarded for strong performance but suffered a significant Labour revolt amid fears that this could lead to a growing divide in service provision. Radical proposals for school reform (announced in late 2005) also drew opposition from some Labour MPs, while in Nov. 2005 Blair suffered his first parliamentary defeat since coming to power in a Labour rebellion over anti-terrorism legislation. In March 2007 he was forced to rely on Conservative Party support for parliamentary endorsement of his government's decision to build a new generation of the submarine-based Trident nuclear weapons system. 95 Labour MPs opposed the policy.

Blair's government was also criticized over the expensive failure of the Millennium Dome project, the mishandling of the foot-and-mouth agricultural crisis in 2001 and, more recently, the ballooning budget for the 2012 Olympic Games to be staged in London.

Meanwhile, Blair's aim to avoid allegations of sleaze that so damaged the previous Conservative government was undermined by the cabinet resignations of his close allies Peter Mandelson and David Blunkett, and by police investigations into the alleged sale of peerages and state honours.

After prolonged speculation, Blair announced on 10 May 2007 that he would leave office on 27 June. On 17 May Gordon Brown won the contest to succeed him. Blair resigned as an MP immediately after leaving his role as prime minister, and took a position representing the USA, EU, UN and Russia as envoy to the Middle East.

Later Life

Blair founded several organizations after leaving office including the Tony Blair Faith Foundation, the Tony Blair Sports Foundation and the Africa Governance Initiative, a charity to promote growth and development in countries such as Sierra Leone, Rwanda and Liberia. In addition he founded a consultancy firm called Tony Blair Associates and took consultancy posts at US bank JPMorgan Chase and the Swiss investment company Zurich Financial Services. In Jan. 2010 Blair testified at the UK's Iraq Inquiry where he defended the decision to go to war in 2003.

Boc, Emil (Romania)

Introduction

Emil Boc succeeded Călin Popescu-Tăriceanu as prime minister in Dec. 2008. The former mayor of Cluj-Napoca, Boc came from a centre-right background and was close to President Traian Băsescu. Following a closely fought general election in Nov. 2008 he headed a coalition charged with tackling a severe economic downturn. Following the collapse of this administration in Oct. 2009, Boc served in a caretaker capacity until Dec. that year when he formed a new centrist government endorsed by parliament. He resigned in Feb. 2012 amid protests over austerity measures and stagnant growth.

Early Life

Boc was born in the village of Rachitele, northwestern Romania on 6 Sept. 1966. After graduating in law from Babeş-Bolyai University in Cluj-Napoca in 1991, he taught history in a secondary school and later at the university, where he undertook further study in political science. During the mid- to late-1990s Boc combined teaching and legal practice in Cluj-Napoca and as a visiting scholar to the Universities of Virginia and Michigan in the USA and the Université Libre de Bruxelles, Belgium.

Boc was elected to parliament for the centre-right Democratic Party (PD) in the Nov. 2000 general election. Within 3 years he was party leader and successfully stood as the PD candidate for the mayoralty of Cluj-Napoca. He oversaw rapid economic growth in the city, winning praise from local and foreign investors before securing re-election in 2008 with 76% of the vote.

A breakdown in relations between President Băsescu and Prime Minister Popescu-Tăriceanu precipitated the collapse of the ruling Justice and Truth Alliance (forged between the PD and the National Liberal Party/PNL) in Jan. 2007. The prime minister formed a minority government consisting of the PNL and the Hungarian Democratic Federation of Romania. Boc remained at the helm of the PD and in Dec. 2007 orchestrated a merger with the Liberal Democratic Party, headed by former prime minister, Teodor Stolojan, to form the Democratic Liberal Party (PD-L). Boc led the new centre-right party to a narrow victory in the general election of 30 Nov. 2008.

Băsescu initially nominated Stolojan for the premiership but when Stolojan rejected the post, Boc was offered it. He was sworn in on 22 Dec. 2008, heading a grand coalition of the PD-L and the Social Democratic Party (PSD).

Career Peak

Boc had to confront a steep decline in Romania's economic fortunes amid the global slowdown. Priorities included tackling spiralling government and household debt, rising unemployment and a fast-devaluing currency. Tensions within the coalition soon emerged, with the PSD interior minister, Liviu Dragnea, resigning after 12 days. Sweeping cuts to public spending, including a policy reversal on recently-promised public-sector wage increases, proved unpopular but Boc was forced to announce further austerity measures as Romania had to accept IMF support in March 2009.

Bad feeling between the coalition partners came to a head in Sept. 2009 when Boc sacked interior minister Dan Nica of the PSD after Nica accused the PD-L of plotting to rig the voting in the forthcoming presidential election. Nica's dismissal prompted the remaining PSD cabinet ministers to resign in protest and a subsequent parliamentary vote of no-confidence passed by 254 votes to 176 on 13 Oct. resulted in the collapse of Boc's government. Subsequent nominees for the premiership failed to gain parliamentary

approval until Dec. when, following his re-election, President Băsescu reappointed Boc to head a new centrist coalition. This government was endorsed by parliament and quickly announced an austerity budget for 2010, promising tough and unpopular measures to meet IMF conditions. Thousands of public sector workers protested in the streets in May 2010 against planned cuts in pay and pension entitlements and in June, and again in Oct. 2010 and March 2011, the government narrowly survived no-confidence votes in parliament. Following further mass protests over austerity measures in early 2012, Boc resigned on 6 Feb. 2012.

Bokassa, Jean-Bedel (Central African Republic)

Introduction

Jean-Bedel Bokassa was head of state of the Central African Republic (CAR) from 1966 until 1979. He enjoyed close relations with the French government, particularly President Giscard d'Estaing, although his increasingly eccentric and brutal behaviour became a major embarrassment. Having crowned himself Emperor of the Central African Empire in 1977, his authorization of a massacre of protesting schoolchildren in 1979 prompted a French-backed coup d'état. After a period in exile, Bokassa was later convicted of murder.

Early Life

Jean-Bedel Bokassa was born on 22 Feb. 1921 in Bobangui in what was then the French colonial province of Oubangui-Chari. At the age of six his father was murdered by a colonial administrator and his mother committed suicide. He was educated at missionary schools and joined the French colonial army in 1939, serving in World War II and later in Indochina and Algeria.

David Dacko became president of the newly independent CAR in 1960, and Bokassa, an army captain, was appointed his Chief of Staff. Buoyed by public discontent at Dacko's rule, Bokassa deposed him in 1966 and declared himself president.

Career Peak

Bokassa soon established a dictatorial regime in which political opponents were routinely murdered. Corruption was rife and among the many charges levelled against him were cannibalism and the dropping of beggars from planes into the Oubangui River.

Despite his record of atrocities, he retained a level of domestic popularity as a result of public spending. The national road infrastructure was improved and university buildings and sports complexes constructed. Internationally, his reputation prompted disparate reactions. For many nations, his personal excesses, spontaneous violence and large entourage of wives and children marked him out as a cartoon-like African dictator though he managed to retain close ties with France. His gift of diamonds to French president Giscard d'Estaing and shared hunting holidays were indicative of the close personal relationship between the two men.

In 1972 Bokassa declared himself president for life. Five years later he re-named the country the Central African Empire and made himself emperor, placing the crown on his own head in the style of his hero Napoléon. His coronation ceremony in Dec. 1977, partly funded by France, cost between US$20m. and US$30m., conservatively estimated as equivalent to a third of the nation's entire GDP for the year.

However, his erratic behaviour (including a physical attack on the French ambassador) became increasingly embarrassing to the French. In 1979 Bokassa declared that all schoolchildren should wear a uniform which bore his likeness and was produced by a company in which he had a financial interest. There were widespread protests and he ordered several hundred demonstrating schoolchildren to be rounded up and imprisoned. In May 1979 Amnesty International reported 100 of the children had been clubbed to death. Following international outrage at the incident, French forces backed a coup led by former president Dacko while Bokassa was travelling in Libya in Sept.1979.

Later Life

Bokassa went into exile, living in a château in the Parisian suburbs. He returned to CAR in 1986 and was put on trial for murder and embezzlement. His trial included sensational evidence from a former chef who claimed he had murdered and eaten one of his political opponents. Bokassa was sentenced to death, later commuted to 20 years in prison. He was freed in 1993 and died in Bangui on 3 Nov. 1996 of a heart attack.

Bolaños, Enrique (Nicaragua)

Introduction

Enrique Bolaños, leader of the Constitutional Liberal Party, won the presidential elections of Nov. 2001. He assumed office in Jan. 2002, tasked with rejuvenating Nicaragua's ailing economy, but was hampered by congressional opposition. His term of office ended in Jan. 2007.

Early Life

Bolaños was born in 1928 near Managua. Having graduated from Saint Louis University in Missouri, USA, he embarked on a career in business. During the Sandinista revolution he was jailed for his criticism of the government, and his business interests were nationalized. In 1996 he was appointed vice-president in the corruption-tainted government of Arnoldo Aleman. With strong backing from the US government, and especially the governor of Florida, he stood successfully for the presidency at the elections of Nov. 2001, winning with 56.3% of the vote.

Career Peak

Among Bolaños' chief election promises was the elimination of government corruption, with offenders facing prison. Former president Aleman was subsequently convicted and jailed for fraud and money laundering. However, this move cost Bolaños the support of his party's Aleman loyalists who allied with the opposition Sandinistas to secure control of the National Assembly, leaving Bolaños politically isolated. In 2005 the Assembly sought to amend the constitution and weaken the president's powers, leading to court action and political stalemate.

Economically, advocating a free market with low unemployment and a redeveloped infrastructure, Bolaños negotiated with the World Bank, International Monetary Fund and Inter-American Development Bank in April 2002 to secure increased long-term financing of development projects, debt relief and structural support loans. In Jan. 2004 the World Bank agreed to cancel 80% of Nicaragua's debt, and later in that year Russia wrote off the country's debts incurred during the Soviet era. Bolaños also established a national development plan that sought to diversify the economy away from its traditional agricultural base.

Keen to develop relations with the USA, Bolaños vowed on election to combat drug smuggling and he supported the Bush regime in the aftermath of the 11 Sept. 2001 attacks. He subsequently signed trade agreements with the USA and other Central American countries, reducing tariffs on major exports.

With his tenure having been blighted by consistent opposition from congress, Bolaños was defeated by Daniel Ortega of the Sandinistas at the general election of 5 Nov. 2006. He was expected to play a prominent role in opposition. Instead, he retired from politics and established a foundation that aims to maintains a virtual library gathering documents on Nicaragua's history and politics.

Bolger, Jim (New Zealand)

Introduction

James Brendan Bolger, born on 31 May 1935 in Taranaki on North Island, was prime minister for 7 years from 1990. Formerly a sheep and cattle farmer, he led the National party for almost 12 years, subsequently becoming the country's ambassador to the United States. Surprised by his extremely narrow 1993 election win, Bolger famously remarked, 'Bugger the pollsters'.

Early Life

Bolger's politics developed in the 1960s when he joined National and was involved in farming organizations. In 1965, he set up a sheep and cattle farm in Te Kuiti, King Country, and was elected MP for King Country in 1972, the year of a landslide Labour victory. Bolger held this seat for nine terms. Following minor roles in the ministries of Maori affairs, agriculture and fisheries, and rural finance, he was appointed a parliamentary under-secretary after National's 1975 election win. Two years later, Bolger was named the country's first fisheries minister, and simultaneously became associate agriculture minister. He was involved in the establishment of a 200 mile exclusive economic zone for fishing. After the 1978 election Bolger was appointed minister of immigration until 1981 and of labour until 1984. In 1980 he led an unsuccessful coup with two other ministers to replace Prime Minister Robert Muldoon with his deputy Brain Talboys. Prior to National's electoral defeat in 1984, Bolger introduced legislation allowing weekend shopping and voluntary unionism, and served as president of the International Labour Organisation in 1983. Jim McLay, the next National leader, made Bolger his deputy in Nov. 1984. Bolger was elected leader of the opposition in March 1986. Four years later, he returned National to power with the largest parliamentary majority in New Zealand history.

Career Peak

Taking office as prime minister and minister for the security intelligence service on 2 Nov. 1990, Bolger revised the implementation of centre right fiscal policies that had led to recession and stock market crash under Labour 3 years earlier. He was appointed to the British Privy Council in the following year. Welfare benefits were cut and relations between unions and employers were deregulated. Bolger pursued an export-led economic strategy and outward-looking foreign policy, easing the country's defence relations with the United States which had been strained by Nuclear Free legislation. Between 1992–4, New Zealand was a member of the UN Security Council, chairing the Iraq sanctions committee. Bolger also represented the country at five APEC leaders' summits from 1993 onwards, and hosted the Commonwealth heads of government meeting in 1995. Following his dismissal of cabinet minister Winston Peters after disagreement over economic policy in 1991, Peters' centrist New Zealand First party reduced Bolger's support at the 1993 election. National remained in power with a majority of two, reporting 6% economic growth over the following year, and bringing the budget into surplus in 1994. By 1996 the country's economy was the third strongest in the OECD; when Bolger took office it had been one of the weakest. 1996 also marked Bolger's announcement of a uniquely New Zealand honours system structured around a five tier Order of Merit. The mixed member proportional representation election in 1996 led to Bolger's formation of a coalition government with New Zealand First, followed by a drop in National's popularity. While he attended a Commonwealth meeting in Edinburgh in 1997, a coup by Jenny Shipley provoked Bolger's resignation and his reappointment as minister of state and associate minister of foreign affairs and trade in Dec. of that year. In the new year's honours list he became a member of the Order of New Zealand, the country's highest honour.

Later Life

Bolger resigned from parliament on 6 April 1998. The former prime minister became his country's ambassador to the United States in June 1998, a position he held until 2001. Bolger also farms part time with Joan, his wife since 1965, and is a keen fisherman.

Bondevik, Kjell Magne (Norway)

Introduction

A Lutheran minister and leader of the Kristelig Folkeparti (Christian Democratic Party; KrF) party from 1983–95, Kjell Magne Bondevik was appointed prime minister for the second time in 2001. He retired from politics at the end of his term in 2005, having headed a centre right coalition of Høyre (Conservative), Venstre (Liberal Party) and the KrF. His first term as prime minister (1997–2000) was cut short when a disagreement over the construction of a power plant forced his resignation.

Early Life

Bondevik was born on 3 Sept. 1947 in Molde, eastern Norway. He graduated from the Free Faculty of Theology Norway in 1975, and 4 years later he was ordained a minister in the Church of Norway. Politically active from an early age, his political career took precedent over his religious duties. His uncle, Kjell Bondevik, had served as social security and education minister in the 1960s. By 1968 Kjell Magne Bondevik was vice president of the party's youth movement, being made its president 2 years later. In 1972 he joined the office of the prime minister and the following year became a member of the Storting (parliament) as a representative for his home county of Møre og Romsdal. In 1975 Bondevik was made KrF vice president under Kåre Kristiansen. In 1983 he succeeded as party leader. He served as education and religious affairs minister (1983–86) and foreign minister (1989–90). In 1995 he was succeeded as party leader by Valgerd Svarstad Gaugland.

Career Peak

In the 1997 elections, the Labour party won with 35% ahead of the KrF's 15.3%. But Labour leader Thorbjørn Jagland had promised to resign if his party polled less than 36.9% of votes. Despite his party coming second, Bondevik was made prime minister of a centrist coalition with Venstre and the Centre party.

In 1998 Bondevik, suffering from depression, took a month's leave. His openness on the matter with the public won him support. Nonetheless, the new prime minister became unpopular with the opposition when he suggested delaying the construction on environmental grounds of two new natural gas power stations. Despite arguing that the project should be delayed until the plant's potential for high carbon dioxide emissions could be reduced, the opposition called for immediate construction. A confidence vote was called which the government lost in March 2000 by 81 to 71. Bondevik was forced to resign and the opposition Labour leader Jens Stoltenberg saw out his term.

Bondevik led the party into the 2001 elections. The KrF came third with 26 of 165 seats behind the outgoing Labour party (43) and Høyre (38). Despite the KrF having six less seats, Bondevik managed to form a coalition with Høyre with himself as prime minister. They were joined by Venstre. Høyre's leader Jan Petersen was made finance minister.

On election, Bondevik pledged to invest in schools, hospitals and international aid, but also to cut taxes by 25bn. kroner. A year on, his 2003 budget outlined public sector spending but not the promise tax cuts. His government was opposed to EU membership.

Bondevik announced his retirement from frontline politics in 2005 and opted not to defend his parliamentary seat at the general elections. The elections were won by a Labour–Socialist Left–Centre Party coalition and Labour's Stoltenberg was appointed prime minister.

Later Life

In Jan. 2006 he established the Oslo Center for Peace and Human Rights, a foundation whose work is related to human rights, democracy, and inter-religious and intercultural dialogue.

Bongo, Omar (Gabon)

Introduction

El Hadj Omar Bongo Ondimba was Africa's longest serving head of state, ruling as president of Gabon from 1967 to 2009. After Fidel Castro of Cuba stood down in Feb. 2008 Bongo became the world's longest-serving president. His period in office was characterized by political stability, with Gabon having the highest per capita wealth in West Africa. Despite introducing multi-party democracy in the early 1990s, he was widely accused of corruption and a flawed electoral system gave concern to the international community.

Early Life

Bongo, given the name Albert-Bernard, was born in 1935 in what was then French Equatorial Africa. He was educated in Brazzaville (in present-day Republic of the Congo), went to Chad for military training and served in the French air force. He joined the civil service in 1958 and developed a close relationship with Leon M'ba, who became president following Gabon's independence in 1960. M'ba appointed Bongo director of the president's office in 1962.

The military attempted a coup in 1964 and held both M'ba and Bongo in custody until M'ba was returned to power with the support of French forces. Bongo was appointed minister of defence in 1965 and minister of information and tourism the following year. Bongo then became vice president and assumed the presidency following the death of M'ba in Nov. 1967.

Career Peak

Bongo declared Gabon a one-party state in 1968 and under this system was re-elected to the presidency in 1973, 1979 and 1986. In 1973 he converted to Islam and took the name Omar. In 1982 an opposition group, the Movement for National Renewal (MORENA), was founded and pushed for the return of a multi-party system. Gabon's economy had benefited greatly from oil revenues but was affected by declining world oil prices in the late 1980s. Popular dissatisfaction spilled over into violent protests in 1990, during which French forces entered the country to protect its nationals. With the democratic movement newly invigorated, Bongo agreed to a national conference which included opposition figures. Multi-party politics were formally reintroduced in 1991.

Bongo was again victorious at the presidential elections of 1993 but his leading rival, Father Paul M'ba Abessole, voiced widely-held suspicions of electoral irregularities. Serious civil unrest was narrowly averted when Bongo agreed a deal, known as the Paris agreement, which allowed for the establishment of an electoral commission and improved electoral processes. In 1997 a constitutional amendment extended the presidential tenure from 5 to 7 years, and Bongo's victory at the 1998 presidential polls was again widely questioned. An offer by Bongo to meet for talks with Pierre Mamboundou of the Gabonese People's Union (UPG) was rejected. The UPG called for a boycott of the 2001 parliamentary elections, which were dominated by Bongo's Gabonese Democratic Party (PDG). In an apparent gesture of reconciliation, the PDG invited opposition figures into the government.

A controversial constitutional amendment was then passed allowing the president to serve two consecutive 7 year terms, potentially granting power to Bongo until 2012. This was followed in June 2003 by further revisions permitting the president to contest the presidency as many times as he wished. In the following elections in Nov. 2005, Bongo was again re-elected with 79.2% of the popular vote, and in Dec. 2006 the PDG maintained its majority in polling for the National Assembly. In Jan. 2008 the government temporarily banned 20 non-governmental organizations for alleged interference in domestic politics.

In foreign policy, Bongo was involved in attempts to resolve regional conflicts, notably in Burundi, the Central African Republic, and in both the Republic of the Congo and Democratic Republic of the Congo. In March 2003 Cándido Muatetema Rivas, then prime minister of Equatorial Guinea, claimed Gabon's occupation of the oil-rich island of Mbagne was illegal. Both countries agreed in Feb. 2006 to start talks over the disputed territory. In April 2001 Bongo signed agreements with Russia on military and technical co-operation as well as trade and culture. Despite Gabon's relatively prosperous economy, boosted by oil sales and high levels of foreign investment, Bongo's lavish expenditure attracted international criticism.

Following a period of ill health, Bongo died from cancer on 8 June 2009.

Botha, P. W. (South Africa)

Introduction

P(ieter) W(illem) Botha served as South Africa's prime minister from 1978–84. In Sept. 1984 he became the country's first state president, a post he held until illness forced him from office in 1989. He was the last South

African leader to remain committed to white supremacy, although his tenure did witness some reforms of the apartheid system.

Early Life

Botha was born in Paul Roux in the Orange Free State on 12 Jan. 1912. In 1932 he began a law course at the University of Orange Free State in Bloemfontein, but left without taking his degree to pursue a full-time career in politics. He worked in administration for the National Party from the age of 20, and in 1948 he was elected as a Nationalist member of parliament. By the late 1950s he had risen to the rank of deputy minister for the interior, and went on to hold successive ministerial positions in the departments of commercial development, public works, defence and coloured affairs. Following the resignation of Vorster in 1978, Botha was appointed prime minister.

Career Peak

In his time as prime minister, the independence of several African states from white rule re-energized the opponents of segregation in South Africa. Student demonstrations and civil disobedience greatly increased.

In 1983 Botha re-wrote the country's constitution, making himself state president with extensive additional powers. The new constitution created three separate elected bodies for whites, Africans and Asians. The white body was larger than the other two combined. Two thirds of the white population approved of the constitution but the rest of the country was not given the chance to express a view and became increasingly alienated. Botha attempted to assuage black protesters and the international community by permitting independence to black homelands, and granting limited powers to the African and Asian population. These reforms were not enough to lift sanctions, while they were too much for the far right of the National Party which broke away to form the Conservative Party. Violent protest continued, and in 1985 Botha declared a state of emergency which remained in place until 1990. The media was censored and political dissidents were imprisoned without trial. Aside from African opposition to his policies, Botha was also threatened by the emergence of neo-Nazi paramilitary groups, the most notorious of which was the AWB led by Eugène Terre' Blanche.

The final years of Botha's leadership were marked by a failure to reconcile the many disparate factions involved in South African politics. In early 1989 Botha fell ill and resigned as party leader. He did not surrender the presidency until pressured by cabinet colleagues.

Later Life

After the 1994 elections Botha's conduct in power was investigated by the Truth and Reconciliation Commission. In 1998 his refusal to appear before the Commission brought him a fine and a suspended 5 year prison sentence. In July 1999 he was implicated in the 1985 murder of eight anti-apartheid activists. He died from a heart attack on 31 Oct. 2006.

Boumedienne, Houari (Algeria)

Introduction

Houari Boumedienne was leader of Algeria from 1965–78 (initially as chairman of a Revolutionary Council and, from 1976, as president). He died in office from a rare blood disorder.

Early Life

Boumedienne was born Mohammed Ben Brahim Boukharouba on 23 Aug. 1932 in Clauzel, eastern Algeria. He adopted his *nom de guerre*, Houari Boumedienne, in 1957. He had avoided conscription to the French colonial army in 1952 because he was studying at Al Azhar University in Cairo, Egypt.

A prominent member of the Algerian independence movement from 1955, he became chief of staff of the National Liberation Army in 1960. After Algeria gained independence in July 1962, Boumedienne served as defence minister and deputy to President Ahmed Ben Bella. However, he became increasingly dissatisfied with Ben Bella's rule and led a bloodless coup in June 1965.

Career Peak

Boumedienne initially headed a revolutionary council of 26 members, most of whom came from the military. He moved away from Ben Bella's agrarian-focused political programme in a bid to spur the nation's industrial development. While initially content to co-operate on equal terms with France-the former colonial power-relations soured when in 1971 Boumedienne nationalized the oil industry that had previously been two-thirds owned by French interests. He reinvested the resulting oil and gas wealth into his industrialization efforts. Meanwhile, on the international stage he fostered closer ties with the USA, and in 1974 the two nations exchanged ambassadors for the first time in 7 years.

Following a failed coup against him in 1967 and an assassination attempt the following year, Boumedienne took an increasingly hard line against his opponents, demoting potential enemies and regularly purging his political ranks. In 1976 a new constitution paved the way for a directly-elected president. In Dec. that year Boumedienne was duly elected to the post. However, his public appearances became infrequent. In Nov. 1978 he lapsed into a coma having contracted Waldenstrom's disease, an illness that attacks the blood and bone marrow. With rule effectively in the hands of the ministry of defence, he died on 22 Dec. 1978.

Bourguiba, Habib (Tunisia)

Introduction

Habib Ben Ali Bourguiba was the first president of post-independence Tunisia. Nicknamed the 'supreme Warrior'. he served from 1957–87 and is widely recognized as having been the driving force behind the country's liberation from French colonial rule.

Early Life

Bourguiba was born in Monastir on 3 Aug. 1903. In 1927 he graduated in law and political science from the University of Paris in France, and in 1932 set up a nationalist newspaper, *L'Action Tunisienne*. Two years later he founded the pro-independence Neo-Destour Party, serving as its secretary-general. As a result of his activism, Bourguiba was jailed and censured on numerous occasions by the French authorities. Shortly after Tunisia gained independence in 1956, he was elected prime minister and the following year he abolished the monarchy and became the president of a one-party state.

Career Peak

Bourguiba's main policy priorities as president were women's rights and education. He outlawed polygamy, legalized abortion, set up a free public education system and prohibited child labour. In the early years of his presidency per capita income and the literacy rate soared.

In foreign policy he maintained economic and trade connections with the West and sought closer ties with the USA. In 1962 he successfully negotiated the withdrawal of French troops from the country. He spent much of his presidential tenure fighting Islamic fundamentalism and supported recognition of Israel in defiance of broader Arab opinion. Despite boycotting the Arab League, he did offer Yasser Arafat and his Palestine Liberation Organization sanctuary in Tunisia when they were exiled from Lebanon in 1982.

In 1975 Bourguiba was elected president for life, but by the end of the decade and into the 1980s he was struggling both economically, against mass unemployment, and politically, with radical Islamist groups who violently opposed his style and direction of governance. In Nov. 1987 doctors declared him mentally unfit for office and and he was impeached by the then prime minister, Zine El Abidine Ben Ali, who subsequently held the presidency until 2011.

Later Life

Bourguiba was kept under house arrest in Monastir for the last 13 years of his life and died on 6 April 2000. He was nevertheless buried with national honours in a mausoleum engraved with the words 'Liberator of women, builder of modern Tunisia'.

Bozizé, François (Central African Republic)

Introduction

Gen. François Bozizé declared himself president of the Central African Republic following a military coup in March 2003, having been a prominent figure on the CAR's political scene during the regimes of Andre Kolingba and Ange-Félix Patassé. He was suspected of involvement in coup attempts in 1983, 2001 and 2002 before seizing control.

Early Life

Bozizé was born in 1946. He came to political prominence as a leading critic of Kolingba's military rule which began in 1981. Having led an unsuccessful coup in 1983, he was arrested and tortured by government forces before going into exile in Togo. There he met Patassé with whom he established strong ties. The two stood against each other at the free elections of 1993 and Bozizé lost. Nonetheless, he remained a Patassé ally, defending him against several uprisings during 1996 and 1997.

However, the relationship became increasingly strained. Bozizé accused Patassé's regime of mismanagement as popular discontent grew at government corruption and failure to pay salaries. In May 2001 Patassé used Libyan forces to put down a coup headed by former president Kolingba, who had been assisted by Bozizé. Bozizé was sacked as head of the army. In Nov. 2001 government troops attempted to arrest Bozizé, but fighting broke out with forces loyal to him. Bozizé held the north of Bangui for a period before taking around 300 troops into exile in Chad. In Oct. 2002 pro-Bozizé factions attempted to depose Patassé, but were defeated amid allegations that Bozizé had instigated the coup with support from Chad.

Career Peak

While Patassé was away in Niger in March 2003 Bozizé led around 1,000 troops into Bangui. They faced little opposition and secured vital strategic locations within a day. Patassé attempted to fly back into the city but was diverted to Cameroon. The Congolese rebels, on whose support Patassé had relied, meanwhile fled over the country.

Having seized power, Bozizé imposed a curfew, dissolved parliament, suspended the constitution and was named president amid promises of free elections. He announced plans to negotiate aid from the IMF and World Bank and promised to address government inefficiency and corruption, disunity in the armed forces and the growing AIDS threat.

Reaction to the coup was mixed. Opposition groups within the CAR welcomed the removal of Patassé, as did many central African nations. However, France, the former colonial power, described the coup as 'unacceptable' and the African Union threatened the CAR's expulsion. There was widespread looting and rioting in Bangui in the days following Bozizé's assumption of power and he appealed to the Economic Community of Central African States to restore order. He was also accused of using backing from Chad in the coup, a charge which provoked widespread unease throughout the country. There followed a period of transitional government until the 2005 presidential and parliamentary elections, in which Bozizé retained power with 43% of the vote.

The poverty-stricken country has, however, remained unstable owing to continuing violence spilling over from the conflict in Darfur in neighbouring Sudan and internal rebel violence in the northeast of the country. In Jan. 2008 civil servants and teachers began a series of strikes in protest at unpaid salaries over several months. At the same time, the prime minister, Élie Doté, resigned and was replaced by Faustin-Archange Touadéra, an academic with no previous political experience.

Following the adoption of an amnesty law, the government reached a peace accord with rebel forces in Dec. 2008 envisaging the formation of a unity government and fresh elections in March 2010. In Jan. 2009 Bozizé dissolved the government and reappointed Touadéra as prime minister of a reshuffled cabinet including representatives of rebel groups. However, sporadic clashes between government and rebel forces have since continued. The elections scheduled for March 2010 were postponed and Bozizé's term of office was extended, but eventually polling took place in Jan. 2011 with Bozizé securing a further term in office.

Fighting escalated in Dec. 2012 with the Séléka rebel coalition capturing several major towns. Although a ceasefire agreement was signed the following month that saw Bozizé appointing a prime minister chosen by his opponents, the peace broke down and the rebels renewed their offensive. Despite foreign troops safeguarding the capital the Séléka rebels seized control of Bangui in March 2013. Bozizé and his family fled abroad and sought political asylum in Benin.

Brandt, Willy (Germany)

Introduction

Willy Brandt was West German Chancellor from 1969–74 and leader of the Social Democratic Party (SPD) from 1964–87. He was Mayor of West Berlin (1957–66) and Vice Chancellor (1966–69). A pragmatist, he sought to improve ties with the Soviet Union and the rest of the Eastern Bloc, a policy which came to be known as *Ostpolitik*. He was criticized by some for what was perceived to be bowing towards the communist East, but Brandt believed that long term European peace and development would be most easily secured by recognition of a divided Germany. He resigned as Chancellor after a spying scandal in 1974, but remained a high-profiled and widely respected statesman for the next 18 years.

Early Life

Brandt was born Herbert Ernst Karl Frahm in Lübeck, Schleswig-Holstein on 18 Dec. 1913, the illegitimate son of a shop assistant. As a teenager he joined the German Social Democratic Party (SPD) before defecting to the more radical Socialist Workers' Party. He was in the early stages of his university career when the Nazis came to power and, because of his socialist leanings, was forced to flee the country. It was around this time that he adopted the name Willy Brandt. He went to Norway where he enrolled at the University of Oslo and began work as a journalist. He did administrative work for a Norwegian charity but following the German occupation fled to Sweden. He was active in the anti-German resistance movements throughout World War II. The Nazis repealed his German citizenship in 1938.

He returned to his native country in the aftermath of the war and was again involved with the SPD. In 1948 he married Rut, a Norwegian. He was elected Berlin's representative on the Social Democratic Party Executive Committee and entered parliament as the member for Berlin in 1949. In 1957 he became the Governor Mayor of West Berlin and in the troubled years that followed made his name on the international stage. The Soviets demanded the removal of Western troops from the city in 1958 and when this was refused relations between East and West deteriorated, leading to the building of the Berlin Wall in 1961. Brandt appeared to the world as a strong and reliable civic leader. He fought unsuccessfully for the Chancellorship in 1961, in 1964 became Chairman of the SPD, and lost elections for the Chancellorship again in 1965.

In the Christian Democrat/Social Democrat coalition government of 1996–69, under Kurt Georg Kiesinger, Brandt was Minister of Foreign Affairs and Kiesinger's Deputy. At the elections of 1969 he was elected Chancellor and headed a coalition of the SPD and Free Democrats.

Career Peak

Brandt worked hard to relax the tension between East and West Germany with his 'Ostpolitik' (Eastern Policy). He signed a nuclear non-proliferation treaty and also agreed non-aggression treaties with Poland and the Soviet Union in 1970. The latter gave recognition to the controversial Oder-Neisse line, confirming Poland's western border and signalling Germany's acceptance of the loss of its former territory. Many accused Brandt of surrendering to the communist East but Brandt himself believed that European relations would not improve unless the practicalities were accepted. He had previously made clear his commitment to West Germany's continuing alignment with the West, stating that West Germans would not be 'wanderers between two worlds'. This attitude was balanced by his belief, on which he was campaigning as early as 1965, that 'there will never be any real peace until we come to a settlement with our Eastern neighbours'.

In 1970 Brandt met the East German Premier, Willi Stoph, which led to a treaty of mutual recognition and co-operation between the two Germanies. The following year a treaty with Czechoslovakia was promulgated, and in 1973 East and West Germany both joined the United Nations. He also did much to promote the expansion of the European Economic Community. Brandt received the Nobel Peace Prize in 1971 for his efforts to bridge East and West, and his popularity was confirmed by unprecedented success for the SPD at the polls in 1972.

Disaster struck in May 1974 when Brandt was forced to resign as Chancellor after it was revealed that his colleague and aide, Günther Guillaume, was an East German agent.

Later Life

Brandt retained influence as an internationally respected statesman. He remained Chairman of the SPD until 1987, was president of Socialist International from 1976–92 and was also a member of the European Parliament from 1979–83. In the late 1970s he headed an international commission, which in 1980 published *North-South: A Programme for Survival*, calling for the prosperous nations to do more to help the development of poorer countries. He died on 8 Oct. 1992, some 3 years after the fall of the Berlin Wall and 2 years after German re-unification. Brandt summarized his political goals asserting that 'For centuries Germany was a bridge between East and West'. and adding, 'We are striving to build anew the shattered bridge, better, sturdier and more reliable'.

Bratušek, Alenka (Slovenia)

Introduction

Alenka Bratušek, leader of the Positive Slovenia party (PS), became prime minister in March 2013 after the previous government fell to a no confidence vote. Heading a four-party coalition covering a wide spectrum of political opinion, Bratušek pledged to balance austerity policies with measures to boost growth.

Early Life

Born on 31 March 1970 in Celje, Alenka Bratušek graduated from the faculty of natural sciences and technology at Ljubljana University in the early 1990s and earned a master's degree in management from the same institution in 2006. Entering public administration in 1995, she took a job at the ministry of the economy before moving to the ministry of finance in 1999. She became head of the ministry's budget directorate, responsible for administering the national budget, overseeing local government finances and drawing on European Union funding.

Bratušek stood unsuccessfully for parliament for the Zares party in 2008. Having joined the newly formed PS in 2011, she was elected to parliament in the election of Dec. that year when the PS unexpectedly claimed the largest share of the vote. However, the party was unable to form a government and went into opposition to Janez Janša's centre-right administration. In this period, Bratušek chaired the commission for public finance control and served on the committee for finance and monetary policy, as well as on the committee for justice, public administration and local self-government.

Following the publication of a report that alleged corruption against both Prime Minister Janša and PS leader Zoran Janković, Bratušek replaced Janković as acting party leader in Jan. 2013. When the government fell to a no confidence vote in Feb. 2013, Bratušek led all-party negotiations and emerged as leader of a broad coalition, uniting the centre-left PS and Social Democrats (SD) with the right-leaning Civic List (DL) and the Democratic Party of Pensioners of Slovenia (DeSUS).

Career Peak

Bratušek was voted in as prime minister on 20 March 2013 with the backing of 52 of 90 MPs. She took office with the country facing acute economic problems. She has sought to address the immediate financial crisis while implementing policies to secure long-term stability. In May she put forward a set of measures including an increase in value added tax, a major privatization programme and a restructuring of the troubled banking sector to arrest its

capital shortfall and avoid the need for an EU/IMF financial rescue package. In Nov. 2013 her government won a parliamentary vote of confidence.

Bratušek resigned as prime minister on 3 May 2014, after losing the leadership of the Positive Slovenia party to its founder Zoran Janković in a vote held a week earlier. She remained in her post in a caretaker capacity until 18 Sept. 2014, when Miro Cerar, who had won early parliamentary elections in July, was named premier.

Brazauskas, Algirdas (Lithuania)

Introduction

A former Communist Party first secretary and Lithuanian president (1992–98), Algirdas Mykolas Brazauskas became prime minister of Lithuania in July 2001, representing the A. Brazauskas Social Democratic Coalition. After his election he concentrated on leading Lithuania to European Union (EU) and NATO membership. He resigned from office in late May 2006 after his ruling coalition collapsed.

Early Life

Brazauskas was born on 22 Sept. 1932 in Rokiškis, northeast Lithuania. He studied engineering and economics at Kaunas Polytechnic, graduating in 1956. Over the next 10 years he worked in industry while becoming active in the Lithuanian Communist Party. In 1965 he joined the government of the Lithuanian Soviet Socialist Republic, serving first as construction materials minister and then as deputy chairman of the state planning committee 2 years later. By 1988 he was the first secretary of the Communist Party's central committee. As Communism weakened throughout the Eastern Bloc, Brazauskas was part of a group of pro-independence Communists who formed the Democratic Labour Party of Lithuania (LDDP), modelling the movement on social democratic lines. As deputy prime minister between 1990–91 he was involved in Lithuania's transition to independence. The Communist Party became illegal in 1991. A year later the LDDP successfully contested parliamentary elections.

Career Peak

In 1993 Brazauskas stood in Lithuania's first post-independence presidential elections against the independent candidate Stasys Lozoraitis. Winning the presidency with 60.1% of votes, Brazauskas stood down as leader of the LDDP in keeping with the impartiality of the largely ceremonial position. Over the next 5 years, despite slow progress, Lithuania moved towards a free market economy and forged links with Western governments, including an EU membership application in 1995 and involvement in NATO's Partnership for Peace programme from 1997. In 1994 a national currency, the litas, was introduced. Regionally, Lithuania strengthened its ties with Estonia and Latvia and signed a treaty to cement good relations first with Poland in 1994 and then Belarus the following year. In 1998 Brazauskas was succeeded as president by Valdas Adamkus.

Brazauskas returned to party politics heading the LDDP in opposition. The party joined forces with several other parties (including the Lithuanian Social Democratic Party—LSDP) as the A. Brazauskas Social Democratic Coalition, successfully contesting the 2000 parliamentary elections. The Lithuanian Liberal Union party's Rolandas Paksas became prime minister. The LDDP and the LSDP merged in 2001, and Brazauskas retained the party leadership.

When in June 2001 Paksas' coalition government collapsed over privatization disputes, President Adamkus nominated Brazauskas as Paksas' successor. The following month he was appointed with 84 votes to 45. As prime minister he continued his predecessor's reforms needed for EU membership. Lithuania joined in May 2004. Two months earlier Lithuania also joined NATO.

The Oct. 2004 elections left no party with a majority of seats in parliament, but Brazauskas agreed to form a broader power-sharing coalition (including the Labour Party which had won the most seats). He was nominated by the president to continue as prime minister and his appointment was approved by parliament in Dec. 2004.

Brazauskas' position came under pressure when one of his coalition partners, the New Union, withdrew in April 2006, and became untenable when another party, the Labour Party, left government after the president stated he did not trust two of their ministers following a party funding scandal. Brazauskas left office on 31 May 2006 and announced his retirement from politics. He died on 26 June 2010.

Brezhnev, Leonid Ilich (Russia)

Introduction

Leonid Brezhnev succeeded Nikita Khrushchev as Soviet leader in 1964 following a coup. He ruled until his death in 1982. Brezhnev devoted much of his tenure to military and foreign affairs. Less charismatic than his predecessor, under him the USSR strengthened its position as a superpower though at the expense of living standards for the average citizen.

Early Life

Leonid Brezhnev was born on 19 Dec. 1906 in Kamenskoye (later renamed Dneprodzerzhinsk) in Russified eastern Ukraine. His father was a steelworker and Brezhnev followed him into the industry at the age of 15. He graduated from a land management technical school in Kursk in 1927 and worked as a land surveyor in the region. Having joined the Communist Party in 1931, he rose steadily through the party ranks over the next decade. He was appointed propaganda secretary of the Dnepropetrovsk regional committee in 1939. During World War II, he served as a political commissar attached to the armed forces, becoming a major general in 1944.

After the war Brezhnev worked under Nikita Khrushchev in the Ukraine, later serving as communist party chief in Moldavia (1950–53) and Kazakhstan (1954–56). He was accepted on to the Communist Central Committee and as a candidate member of the Politburo in 1952. He lost these posts following the death of Stalin in 1953 but regained them 3 years later. In Feb. 1956 he was given control over the defence industry, space programme, heavy industry and capital construction. After supporting Kruschev during an unsuccessful attempt to remove him in 1957, Brezhnev won full membership of the Politburo. In 1960 he was elevated to chairman of the presidium.

Though the nominal head of state, Brezhnev resigned the chairmanship in 1964 to work as Khrushchev's number two on the central committee. In Oct. 1964 he led a coup against Khrushchev and replaced him as first secretary.

Career Peak

Supreme power was theoretically held jointly between Brezhnev and Aleksei Kosygin, chairmen of the council of ministers. However, it was soon clear that Brezhnev was the dominant partner and he often opposed Kosygin's economic reforms while protecting conservative, often corrupt bureaucrats.

Alexander Dubček's reformist regime in Czechoslovakia prompted Brezhnev to formulate a doctrine that was to be named after him. It asserted the right of the Warsaw Pact partners to intervene against 'anti-socialist degeneration' within the Soviet bloc. He ordered the invasion of Czechoslovakia after the Prague Spring in 1968, provoking international outrage, and his tenure also saw border clashes with China.

His foreign policy extended to assisting left-wing movements in Vietnam, the Middle East and the Third World. Throughout the 1970s he attempted to improve relations with West Germany and followed a policy of détente with the US. US–Soviet relations peaked in 1972 when Brezhnev and his opposite number Richard Nixon signed the SALT treaty that curbed the development of certain nuclear projects.

However, both sides remained deeply suspicious of the other. In 1979 the US congress failed to ratify SALT II and Brezhnev (by now titular head of state as well as party) ordered the invasion of Afghanistan to support its ailing leftist government. Relations between the two further soured when Brezhnev encouraged the suppression of the Polish Solidarity trade union movement in the early 1980s.

Brezhnev oversaw a rapid expansion of the Soviet military and industrial bases during the 1970s and agreed massive spending to ensure the USSR led the space race. The domestic price was great, with the agricultural and consumer-goods sectors failing badly and the standard of living declining. In addition, political oppression and persecution of dissidents was rife under his regime.

His last years in power were spent in senility. He suffered a mild stroke in March 1982 and died of a heart attack on 10 Nov.

Brooke, Basil (Northern Ireland, United Kingdom)

Introduction

Basil Brooke, who became 1st Viscount Brookeborough in 1952, was a British Ulster Unionist who served as Northern Ireland's prime minister from 1943 until 1963. A hard-line anti-Catholic, the later years of his tenure were dominated by a declining economy. He resigned the premiership on health grounds.

Early Life

Basil Stanlake Brooke was born on 9 June 1888, in Colebrooke Park, Brookeborough, County Fermanagh. His father was Sir Arthur Douglas Brooke, the 4th Baronet, and the family was raised on a 30,000-acre estate.

Basil was schooled for 5 years in Pau, in southwest France before attending Winchester College and then the Royal Military Academy at Sandhurst. He succeeded his father to become the 5th Baronet in 1907. In 1908 he joined the Royal Fusiliers and, 3 years later, the 10th Hussars. He served with distinction in the First World War before giving up military life for farming in 1920.

In 1921 he entered the Northern Ireland senate but served only a year before becoming commandant of the Ulster Special Constabulary, which was focussed on defeating the IRA. In 1929 he won the Lisnakea constituency in County Fermanagh and took his seat in Northern Ireland's parliament on behalf of the Ulster Unionist Party. He became minister of agriculture in 1933, urging landowners not to employ Catholics, whom he accused of being 'out to destroy Ulster'. He took over the commerce portfolio in 1941.

Career Peak

When John Andrews came under pressure to resign as prime minister in 1943, Brooke stepped in to replace him. He remained in parliament despite being made a Viscount in 1952 (which qualified him for a seat in the House of Lords). During his tenure, he sought to tighten links between the government and the Orange Order while distancing Catholics and trades unionists.

Northern Ireland's industrial base crumbled badly from the 1950s on. Popular support for Brooke fell away and his inability to reverse the economic decline prompted doubts over his leadership from within his own party. In 1963 he gave up the premiership because of poor health but remained in the Northern Irish parliament for another 5 years.

Later Life

From the back benches Brooke strongly opposed the conciliatory approach to Dublin taken by his successor, Terrence O'Neill. Away from politics, Brooke built up a large portfolio of business interests. He died at his family home on 18 Aug. 1973.

Brown, Gordon (United Kingdom of Great Britain and Northern Ireland)

Introduction

Gordon Brown became prime minister in June 2007, fulfilling the long-held expectation that he would succeed Tony Blair, his co-architect of New Labour in the 1990s. Before taking over the premiership, Brown was for 10 years chancellor of the exchequer, the longest serving holder of that office since the 1832 Reform Act. His tenure at the treasury coincided with a long period of economic growth but his premiership was progressively been overshadowed by the global banking and financial crisis that escalated from the autumn of 2008. With poor opinion poll ratings in the lead-up to the general election on 6 May 2010, Labour lost 91 seats and Brown failed to secure a fourth term in office. Subsequently he resigned as both prime minister and leader of the Labour party.

Early Life

James Gordon Brown was born on 20 Feb. 1951 in Glasgow, Scotland. His father was a Church of Scotland minister. Brown attended Kirkcaldy High School until, at 16, he went to Edinburgh University where he graduated with a first in history and undertook a PhD (*The Labour Party and Political Change in Scotland, 1918–29*). He joined the Labour Party in 1969 and between 1972–75 served as rector of Edinburgh University and chair of the University Court. From 1976–80 he was a lecturer at Edinburgh and Caledonian universities. In 1979 he ran an unsuccessful campaign to win the Edinburgh South seat at the general election. The following year he took a job with Scottish TV until 1983.

At the general elections of 1983 Brown was elected MP for Dunfermline East in Fife. He was appointed opposition spokesman on trade and industry before becoming shadow chief secretary to the treasury then shadow secretary of state for trade and industry. When John Smith, then shadow chancellor, suffered a heart attack in 1988, Brown took up Smith's position on an interim basis. His success in this role confirmed him as shadow chancellor in 1992. By then Smith had succeeded Neil Kinnock as party leader.

When Smith died in May 1994, Brown and Tony Blair were the two front-runners to take over. It is widely believed that they struck a deal allowing Blair a clear run for the party leadership and potentially the premiership, with Brown as heir apparent to Blair at a future date. This was to become a matter of personal contention.

Blair and Brown were the architects of New Labour in the mid-1990s. It was essentially a party rebranding that sought to banish memories of the high inflation, high unemployment and union unrest that marred Labour's last period in government in the 1970s. Espousing a political 'Third Way'. rooted between capitalism and liberal socialism, Brown used his time as shadow chancellor to convince the management and financial sector that he would be a safe pair of hands when in charge of the treasury.

The New Labour project came to fruition with a landslide victory over the Conservatives at the 1997 general election. Brown was duly appointed chancellor. Among Brown's first actions was to grant independence to the Bank of England in setting interest rates. This allayed fears that he would overly intervene in economic affairs. He also set out five economic tests for joining the European single currency (which remain unmet), including evidence of long-term convergence with other European economies. Under Brown the economy was to enjoy its longest ever period of sustained economic growth. Despite claims by opponents that he was reaping the rewards of careful management by his Conservative predecessors, he won a reputation as an 'Iron Chancellor' exercising responsible fiscal control.

It is generally accepted that relations between Brown and Blair deteriorated markedly from 2005. When Blair indicated that he would not fight a fourth election, pressure mounted on him to specify the date when he would leave office. The issue came to a head in Sept. 2006 when several Labour MPs spoke out, seemingly with tacit support from Brown, against Blair's silence. Blair announced that he would step down by Sept. 2007.

Brown's suitability to be prime minister was under scrutiny before he took office. Blairites accused him of hindering the 'Labour project'. with Alastair Campbell, Blair's chief spin doctor for many years, describing him as 'psychologically flawed'. While Brown's supporters considered him to be intellectually strong and highly principled, his critics objected to his over-reliance on a closed circle of confidantes.

Career Peak

On taking office on 27 June 2007 after winning the leadership of the Labour Party, Brown faced a resurgent Conservative party attempting to reclaim the political middle ground under the leadership of David Cameron. The threat from terrorism also remained, and the public finances were coming under greater strain than at any point during his term as chancellor. Nevertheless, early optimism about the Brown government's political prospects fuelled temporary speculation about a possible snap general election.

In Sept. 2007 a financial crisis (linked to a wider international credit contraction) at Northern Rock, the UK's fifth largest mortgage lender, led to emergency short-term support by the Bank of England and the first run on a British bank for 140 years. In Feb. 2008 the Brown government announced the bank's temporary nationalization. Further bad press from late 2007, relating to losses of computerized personal data held by public sector agencies on millions of citizens, also damaged the government's reputation. Renewed controversy over alleged covert and undeclared financial donations to the Labour Party prompted the first ministerial resignation from the Brown cabinet in Jan. 2008. By May, the fall in Labour's popularity was evident in its worst local election results in 40 years.

As the global financial crisis deepened and the threat of economic recession gathered pace in the autumn of 2008, the government part-nationalized three leading UK banks as part of a massive rescue package. A further major funding injection to support the domestic banking sector followed in Jan. 2009. Meanwhile, the Bank of England cut its base interest rate progressively to reach just 0.5%—the lowest level in its history—by March 2009. Nevertheless, unemployment continued to surge. Although Brown was praised in international forums such as the G20 for his leadership and decisive response to the global financial crisis, the UK's prolonged recession (with six consecutive quarters of contraction before slight growth was recorded in Oct.–Dec. 2009) had a negative effect on his poll ratings. Labour also fared poorly in elections to the European Parliament and the English local elections in June 2009, and there were rumblings of discontent within the party over Brown's leadership. A cabinet reshuffle in June 2009 followed damaging ministerial resignations, Labour lost a safe seat in a parliamentary by-election in Norwich in July, and in Jan. 2010 Brown survived a plot by backbench Labour MPs to dislodge him. Meanwhile, Parliament was undermined in the eyes of the public after a damaging scandal over members' expenses claims.

In foreign affairs, Brown maintained Britain's military commitments in Afghanistan and Iraq, although in Dec. 2008 he confirmed that British forces would end all combat operations in Iraq by the end of May 2009 and leave the country at the end of July. In Nov. 2009 he ordered a further 500 British soldiers to Afghanistan, despite mounting fatalities and dwindling public support for the war. Within the European Union, he endorsed the controversial new treaty on institutional and administrative reform, which was signed in Lisbon, Portugal in 2007 and eventually came into force in Dec. 2009. Despite early speculation that he would put some distance between UK and US foreign policy, Brown and President Barack Obama reaffirmed the special relationship between the two countries in March 2009 when the prime minister became the first European leader to meet his US counterpart in Washington.

In the run-up to the general election in May 2010, allegations were made about Brown's aggressive and bullying attitude to staff and colleagues, casting another shadow over Labour's prospects for victory. The Conservatives took 306 seats and 36.1% of the vote to Labour's 258 and 29.0%. Owing to the Conservatives' lack of an absolute majority Brown initially remained prime minister while coalition negotiations took place between the Conservatives and the Liberal Democrats. A 'rainbow' alliance between the Labour party, the Liberal Democrats and other minor parties was mooted but the Liberals eventually decided in favour of a Conservative coalition. Brown resigned on 11 May admitting that he held himself personally accountable for the Labour defeat and was succeeded by David Cameron as prime minister. Harriet Harman became acting Labour party leader.

Later Life

After leaving office Brown devoted time to helping more children have access to schooling around the world and boosting internet development, working for organizations such as the World Wide Web Foundation (as a board director) and the Global Campaign for Education. His book dealing with the global financial crisis, Beyond the Crash, was published in 2010. In April 2011 Brown was appointed to an unpaid advisory role at the World Economic Forum. He remained MP for Kirkcaldy and Cowdenbeath until 2015.

Brundtland, Gro Harlem (Norway)

Introduction

Doctor and politician, Gro Harlem Brundtland was three times prime minister of Norway between 1981–96 representing the Labour party. The first female Norwegian prime minister, she aimed to appoint an equal number of male and female ministers and set a minimum of 40% for the proportion of Labour party female candidates. Nationally, Brundtland implemented leftwing economic and social policies. Internationally, she championed global health and environment issues, her role leading to her appointment as Director-General of the World Health Organization (WHO) in 1998. Her international work raised Norway's profile within the international community.

Early Life

Born on 20 April 1939 in Baerum, Oslo, Brundtland's father was a doctor and an active member of the Labour party who served as defence minister. Brundtland herself was enrolled in the Labour party's junior section at the age of seven. Following her father's career to the US and later to Egypt, Brundtland developed an international outlook from an early age. She studied medicine at Oslo before winning a scholarship to the Harvard School of Public Health. In 1960 she married the leader of the opposition Conservative party, Arne Olav Brundtland. Gaining experience in public health from 1965 she worked for the health ministry, concentrating on children's health and in 1970 became director for the Oslo children's health service. In the 1970s her pro-abortion activism raised her public profile.

Brundtland's early politic activity was spent in local government, but her work for the health ministry led to her appointment as environment minister in 1974, a post she held for 5 years. Concurrently, she was raising her profile within the Labour party and between 1975–81 she was deputy leader. In 1979 she left her ministerial post to concentrate on modernizing the Labour party. In 1981 she ran for the party leadership and once secured, held the position for the next 11 years.

Career Peak

When in 1981 Prime Minister Nordli retired through ill health, Brundtland saw out his term, leading a minority Labour government. At 41 she was the youngest Norwegian leader and its first female prime minister. After 9 months, and with Labour's defeat by Kåre Willoch's Conservatives, she left national politics and concentrated on international issues concerning public health and the environment. In 1983 she was invited by the UN to found and lead the World Commission on Environment and Development, termed the Brundtland Commission, which promoted sustainable development. The commission produced the 1987 report *Our Common Future*, and its work was instrumental in bringing about the 1992 UN Rio Summit on environment. In 1985 she joined the board of the 'Better World Society' and also worked on the UN Commission for Disarmament and Security. Her international efforts for health, development and environment brought her recognition and in 1988 she was granted the Third World Foundation prize.

In 1986 Brundtland returned to national politics leading the Labour party to victory. In her second term her appointed cabinet comprised nine men and eight women, creating the most balanced female–male government in Western politics. She also created a 40% minimum rate of female candidature within the Labour party. On a domestic level, Brundtland implemented leftwing social and economic policies, but plummeting global oil prices led to the introduction of austerity measures. In the 1989 elections, Brundtland was defeated by a centre-right coalition led by Jan Peder. Its success was short lived and by the following year Brundtland was again appointed prime minister.

Three years later she was elected for a second consecutive term. She resigned as Labour leader in 1992 and was succeeded by Thorbjørn Jagland. Her international outlook put her in favour of EU membership and she led a strong campaign in the early 1990s. Despite these efforts, Norwegians voted against in a 1994 referendum. In 1996 she retired from national politics.

Later Life

Following her departure from Norwegian politics, Brundtland turned to international politics. Her dedication to the advancement of sustainable development led to her appointment in 1998 as Director-General of WHO, succeeding Hiroshi Nakayima. Her main initiatives were measures against malaria and tuberculosis. She retired in July 2003.

Bruton, John (Ireland)

Introduction

John Bruton was Irish Prime Minister (*Taoiseach*) from Dec. 1994–June 1997, heading a coalition government which included his Fine Gael party. He played a leading role in the Northern Irish Peace Process, arguing that a united Ireland would occur only if it received majority support in the North. His firm stance against the IRA and other paramilitary groups brought him into conflict with nationalists.

Early Life

John Gereard Bruton was born in Dublin on 18 May 1947. He studied economics at University College, Dublin before qualifying as a barrister from Kings Inn, Dublin at the age of 23. In 1969 he entered the Dáil as a member of Fine Gael. He worked in farming throughout his political career. During the 1970s he was the parliamentary secretary for the minister of education and later of industry and commerce.

In 1981, in Garret FitzGerald's coalition government, Bruton was appointed minister of finance, a post he held from mid-1981 to early 1982. He was minister at the time of the controversial budget clause imposing tax on childrens' shoes that precipitated the fall of the FitzGerald government. Between 1983 and 1986 Bruton was the minister for industry and trade, then finance minister and briefly minister for the public service.

In 1990 Bruton took over from Alan Dukes as leader of Fine Gael and led the party to a poor showing at the 1992 elections. However, the administration of Prime Minister Albert Reynolds was seriously undermined by internal party conflict and scandal. It collapsed in late 1994 and Bruton, without having to go to the polls, formed a coalition government. Known as the Rainbow Coalition, it comprised Fine Gael, Labour and the Democratic Left.

Career Peak

Bruton was criticized as a weak leader but his tenure coincided with an economic upsurge. He also won support for liberalizing divorce. As for Northern Ireland, he continued Reynold's work in establishing a framework with the British government for a negotiated peace. He positioned himself firmly against terrorist groups within the Republic and considered majority support in Ulster to be a pre-*requisite* for a re-unification. Shortly after he assumed office he launched a *Framework Document* with British Prime Minister John Major which set out the necessary conditions for a negotiated peace.

A *Joint Communique* followed in Nov. 1995 which invited parties to peace talks and established an international advisory group to investigate arms decommissioning. The subsequent report, known as the *Mitchell Report* after US senator George Mitchell and published in Jan. 1996, proposed discussions on a political formula and decommissioning proceeding in tandem. Talks, headed by Mitchell, began in June.

The IRA ended its ceasefire in 1996 but peace negotiations continued for the duration of Bruton's time in office. After losing the 1997 election he was replaced as prime minister by Bertie Ahern. The peace talks culminated in the *Good Friday Agreement* of 1998 which made provision for the devolution of government powers to a Northern Irish assembly.

Later Life

Bruton remained Fine Gael leader after the 1997 defeat. In 2000 the Northern Irish Assembly was suspended over the decommissioning of weapons. Bruton responded by urging an end to paramilitary attacks and by calling for paramilitary groups to sign up to the *Mitchell Principles* on which the

Good Friday Agreement was based. Bruton survived several party leadership challenges but in Jan. 2001 he lost a vote of confidence and resigned. He was succeeded by Michael Noonan.

Burnham, Forbes (Guyana)

Introduction

Forbes Burnham was the first prime minister of independent Guyana. He was in office for 21 years and was responsible for the formation of his country's political structure. Elected to government with the aid and approval of the USA in 1964 after a campaign of harassment against the previous government, Burnham proceeded to follow a pro–capitalist and moderate programme of reforms. His increasingly autocratic style at the end of the 1960s damaged the economy and quality of life deteriorated. His party was widely believed to have rigged the elections in 1968, 1973, 1978 and 1980 to maintain power. He was married twice, to Sheila Lataste in 1951 and to Viola Harper in 1967; he had five daughters.

Early Life

Linden Forbes Sampson Burnham was born in Kitty, East Demerara, British Guiana on the 20 Feb. 1923 to parents of African descent. He attended Queen's College in Georgetown, and in 1942 won the British Guiana Scholarship. He travelled to England in 1945 to study law at the University of London and gained his LLB in 1947.

In 1949 he returned to Guyana to enter politics, co–founding, with Cheddi Jagan, the People's Progressive Party in 1950. He was appointed chairman. Burnham was elected to Georgetown City Council in 1952, and to the Legislature a year later. He was made minister of education after the first general elections with universal suffrage. He challenged Jagan for the leadership of the party but was forced to back down. After 133 days the British, fearing the socialist direction of the new government, suspended the constitution on 9 Oct. 1953.

Encouraged by the British, on 13 Feb. 1955 Burnham led a split of the PPP. He proposed a more moderate party, less committed to socialism and acceptable to the British. The divide followed mainly racial lines, with Burnham leading the Afro–Guyanese section and Jagan heading the Indo–Guyanese faction. In the general election held under limited suffrage in Aug. 1957, Burnham's party performed worse than anticipated, winning only 3 out of 14 seats. Burnham was appointed leader of the opposition, merging with two other small parties to form the People's National Congress (PNC).

From 1957–64, Burnham continued to lead the opposition, with the PPP winning the 1961 election with 20 seats out of 35. The period of 1961–64 was characterized by strikes, riots and protests against the PPP and between the divided ethnic groups. The PNC combined with the United Front (UF) and was aided by CIA in attempts to destabilize the government. In May 1963 PNC headquarters were raided and ammunition and documents detailing assassination plans for PPP leaders were found.

The British government changed the voting system in 1964 in a response to pressure from the PNC as they believed it unfairly represented the East Indian community. The switch to proportional representation in the general election on 7 Dec. 1964 saw the vote split between the PPP (46%), the PNC (41%) and the UF (12%). At the invitation of the governor the PNC and the UF proceeded to form a coalition government and Burnham was elected prime minister.

Career Peak

In May 1966 Guyana became independent and Burnham was appointed prime minister. He enforced a moderate line, cutting ties with Cuba and encouraging local and foreign investment. He steered towards a non–aligned socialist state, but held to a pro–capitalist economic policy. He implemented a wider range of benefits especially in health (including the establishment of rural clinics) but also in education, housing, road and bridge building, agriculture and rural development. With these policies he attempted to attract members of the Afro–Guyanese middle class, differentiate himself from the PPP and attract international investment and aid. His tenure was disturbed by border disputes with Venezuela from Oct. 1966.

By the general election of 1968 the PNC, aided by defections from the PPP and the UF, held a majority in the National Assembly. The PNC won 30 seats, the PPP 19 and the UF 4; Burnham retained his position as prime minister though it was claimed by many that the elections were fraudulent.

Burnham's second term was marred in 1969 by a rebellion among ranchers in Rupununi region, which was put down by the military. Burnham started moving in a new political direction, proclaiming Guyana as a Cooperative Republic in 1970 and taking an increasingly socialist stance. His leadership also became increasingly autocratic. He re–established diplomatic relations with Cuba and the Soviet Union and between 1971–76 carried out a nationalization programme, reducing the private sector's share of the economy to 10% by seizing American and Canadian–owned mines and British sugar plantations and refineries.

In the general election of 10 July 1973 the PNC won a two third majority, though accusations of vote-rigging were again widespread. Burnham endeavoured to extend government control by amending the constitution and abolishing legal appeals to the Privy Council in London and politicizing the civil service. All mechanisms of state were considered part of the PNC and under its control. Burnham also sought a position of leadership among third world countries, becoming a force in the non–aligned movement. In 1972 he hosted the Conference of Foreign Ministers of Non–Aligned Countries.

In an attempt to consolidate his rule, Burnham cancelled the general election of 1978 in favour of a national referendum. Burnham claimed a 75% turnout and 97% approval for his government. In 1978 the mass suicide of 900 people of a religious cult called Jonestown, preceded by their assassination of a USA government official, put Burnham's government under intense foreign scrutiny.

Constitutional changes in 1980 gave Burnham even wider executive powers when he became president of Guyana. Elections later that year saw the PNC claim 77% of the vote. In the 1980s, Burnham held to his ambition to build a socialist society. The economy stagnated, the quality of life decreased and the country's infrastructure and public services deteriorated.

Burnham died in office on 6 Aug. 1985 whilst undergoing a throat operation.

Bush, George H. W. (United States of America)

Introduction

The 41st president of the United States, George Herbert Wallace Bush was vice-president of the United States under Ronald W. Reagan from 1991–89 and served one term as president from 1989–93. He is best remembered for establishing a multi-national military force which defeated Iraq during the 1991 Persian Gulf War and forced it to withdraw from Kuwait.

Early Life

Born on 12 June 1924 in Milton, Massachusetts, Bush's father was a senator and an investment banker. Bush grew up in Greenwich, Connecticut. After graduating from Phillips Academy in Andover he joined the U.S. Naval Reserve and during World War II served for 2 years as a torpedo bomber pilot in the Pacific. He flew 58 combat missions and won the Distinguished Flying Cross for his services. In 1945 Bush married Barbara Pierce with whom he would have six children, one of which died aged three of leukaemia. He attended Yale University and then moved with his family to Texas. In 1953 he co-founded the Zapata Petroleum Corporation and became president of the company's new subsidiary in 1954.

In 1964, Bush stood down as president of the Zapata Offshore Company to pursue a career in politics. He won the Republican nomination for a senate seat, although he lost to Democrat Ralph Yarborough. Bush was elected to the House of Representatives in 1966 and was re-elected 2 years later. He gave up his seat in 1970 to run for the senate but lost again this time to Democrat Lloyd Bentsen, Jr.

President Richard M. Nixon appointed Bush as the United States' ambassador to the United Nations and in 1973 he became chairman of the Republican National Committee. Bush initially supported Nixon during the Watergate crisis, but when it became clear that the president had been lying he wrote to him urging him to resign. Under President Gerald R. Ford, Bush served as the chief of the U.S. Liaison Office in Beijing for 2 years before becoming head of the Central Intelligence Agency in 1976. He resigned his post with the CIA in 1977 when James E. Carter became president and returned to Texas to work as the chairman of the First National Bank in Houston.

In 1979, Bush announced that he would seek the Republican presidential nomination. A more moderate candidate than his main rival Reagan, Bush was easily defeated but accepted Reagan's offer to be his running mate and helped him defeat Jimmy Carter his Democrat rival by a wide margin.

Career Peak

Bush was inaugurated as vice-president on 20 Jan. 1981 and 2 months later was forced to assume some presidential duties after Reagan was hospitalized by an assassination attempt. As vice-president, Bush visited more than 60 countries and headed task forces on terrorism and drugs. In 1984 Reagan and Bush were successfully re-nominated as Republican candidates and won a second term in office. Like Reagan, Bush denied direct involvement in the Iran-Contra affair claiming he was 'out of the loop'.

Bush published an autobiography in 1987 entitled Looking Forward and in Oct. announced that he would seek the Republican presidential nomination. After sweeping to success in the southern primaries, he was nominated by the Republican Convention in Aug. Choosing Dan Quayle as his running mate, he campaigned for a 'kinder, gentler nation'. famously announcing: 'Read my lips, no new taxes'. In the election, Bush defeated Democratic opponent Michael S. Dukakis by 54% to 46% to become the first vice-president to succeed directly to the presidency via election since 1836.

During his single presidential term, foreign affairs dominated Bush's agenda. In Dec. 1989 he authorized an invasion of Panama to topple General Manuel Antonio Noriega from power. In Nov. 1990, after the virtual collapse of communism in Eastern Europe, Bush signed a non-aggression pact with Soviet leader Mikhail Gorbachev which effectively ended the Cold War and went on to agree a mutual reduction of nuclear weapons.

In 1990–91 Bush assembled a coalition of European and Arab states to counter the Iraqi invasion of Kuwait. Around 500,000 US troops were stationed in the Persian Gulf and when trade embargoes and diplomacy failed to persuade Iraq to withdraw, Bush authorized a military offensive, beginning on 16 Jan. 1991. By the end of Feb. Kuwaiti independence had been restored. The same year Bush helped initiate peace talks between Israel and its Arab neighbours and withheld $10bn. in loan guarantees to Israel until it halted the building of new settlements in the occupied territories.

Domestically, Bush's hand was hampered by Democrat control of both houses of Congress. In 1990, Bush reneged on his pledge that there would be 'no new taxes'. a reversal that did much to damage his popularity. Bush was forced to draft a new budget proposal after his deficit-reduction plan was rejected and had to drop his plans to cut capital gains tax. Unemployment grew throughout 1991. Bush introduced new bills to supplement unemployment benefits and visited several countries in an attempt to increase exports and create new jobs.

In 1992, the uncertainties affecting the economy and his broken tax promise undermined Bush's campaign for re-election and he was defeated by William J. Clinton by 43% to 38% with third party candidate Ross Perot winning 19% of the vote

Later Life

After losing the 1992 election Bush returned to live in Houston and retired from political life. His son Jeb was elected governor of Florida in 1998 and his son George W. graduated from twice governor of Texas to the presidency by beating Al Gore in the 2000 presidential election—thereby rivalling the achievement of John Quincy Adams in 1824 by following his father into the White House.

Bush, George W. (United States of America)

Introduction

The 43rd president of the USA, George Walker Bush took office in 2001 after one of the most controversial presidential elections in history. He was the first

president since 1888 to reach the White House despite losing the popular vote. Within 9 months of taking office, Bush was plunged into one of the most challenging periods of any presidency after the USA was attacked by Islamic extremists on 11 Sept. 2001. There followed military action against the Taliban regime in Afghanistan. In Feb. 2003, against opposition in the UN, Bush authorized US-led forces to attack Iraq and remove Saddam Hussein from power. He was re-elected in Nov. 2004 for a second term with 51% of the popular vote and inaugurated in Jan. 2005. His approval ratings subsequently declined as public hostility to US military involvement in Iraq increased, culminating in defeat for his Republican Party in mid-term congressional elections in Nov. 2006. He left office on the completion of his second presidential term in Jan. 2009.

Early Life

Bush was born in New Haven, Connecticut on 6 July 1946 and grew up in Midland and Houston, Texas. He attended Phillips Academy, Yale University and the Harvard Business School, and was awarded a degree in history and an MBA. Bush served as a pilot in the Texas National Guard in the 1960s and set up his own oil and gas business in the mid-1970s.

Failing to get elected as a Republican Party candidate to the House of Representatives in 1978, he returned to his oil business until 1986 when he sold his interests to help his father George H. W. Bush in his successful campaign to become US president in the 1988 elections. In 1989 Bush headed a group of investors who bought the Texas Rangers baseball team and acted as managing general partner of the team for 5 years. In 1994 he successfully challenged Ann Richards, the Democratic governor of Texas, winning 53.5% of the vote.

Bush's tough stance on drugs and crime, allied with large tax cuts, a welfare reform programme and increased spending on education, proved popular and he was re-elected governor in 1998. In 1999 he announced that he would try for the Republican presidential nomination. His campaign fund raised $100 m., a figure that persuaded many of his opponents to withdraw from the race. Despite losing the New Hampshire primary, Bush recovered to secure the nomination and to pick former secretary of defense Richard Cheney as his running mate.

Bush's campaign focused on promises of tax cuts and 'compassionate conservative' social policies. Despite taking an early lead in the polls, the gap between Bush and his Democratic opponent Al Gore narrowed as the election approached. Bush lost the popular vote by 500,000 votes, but the outcome of the election ultimately hinged on Florida's 25 electoral college votes. Bush narrowly led Gore in Florida after machine counts, but Gore sought a manual recount of several counties and the final result of the election remained uncertain for 5 weeks as the courts debated legal challenges and counter-challenges. The Florida Supreme Court ordered a manual recount in two counties but the US Supreme Court reversed this decision, handing Bush the election by 271 electoral college votes to 266.

Career Peak

Bush was inaugurated as the 43rd president of the USA on 20 Jan. 2001, becoming only the second son of a former president to also reach the White House. With much controversy still surrounding his election he immediately struck a conciliatory stance, declaring: 'I was not elected to serve one party, but to serve one nation'.

In April 2001 Bush presented his first detailed budget proposals, including a $1.6 trn. tax cut. He was forced to trim this figure to $1.25 trn. in May after bowing to pressure from Congress. The same month, the Republicans lost control of the Senate for the first time in 7 years when Senator James Jeffords left the party to serve as an independent. Nevertheless, Bush still won approval from the House and the Senate for millions of tax refund cheques, reductions in most tax rates and tax relief measures for married couples and the parents of young children.

In March 2001, Bush refused to ratify the environmental measures recommended by the Kyoto Agreement on global warming and climate change, attracting criticism from European nations. In Aug. Congress approved his plan to stimulate energy production, involving billions of dollars in tax breaks and exploration incentives for energy producers.

Bush also initiated a highly controversial plan to replace the 1972 Anti-Ballistic Missile Treaty with a new accord so that he could introduce a US missile defence system. Having discussed this proposal with the Russian president Vladimir Putin, the two leaders agreed in May 2002 to reduce their respective strategic nuclear warheads by two-thirds over the next 10 years.

Bush's presidency and the US's relationship with the rest of the world were transformed by the events of 11 Sept. 2001 when two hijacked passenger airliners were crashed into the World Trade Center towers in New York City. Another hit the Pentagon in Washington, D.C., while a fourth came down in a Pennsylvania field before reaching its intended target, which may have been the White House. Both World Trade Center towers collapsed and part of the Pentagon was destroyed. The total number of people killed was around 3,000, including many rescue workers.

The attacks had international political and economic ramifications. Bush announced a war against terrorism. With evidence pointing to the involvement of Osama bin Laden and his al-Qaeda organization, the president threatened military action against Afghanistan's Taliban regime which had been sheltering the terrorist network. Bush sought to establish a global alliance to put pressure on Afghanistan, receiving support from Europe as well as co-operation from Pakistan and Uzbekistan and the acquiescence of Iran. In Oct. 2001 mainly US and British forces attacked Taliban and al-Qaeda forces in Afghanistan and the following month the Northern Alliance, an Afghan group opposed to the Taliban, retook the capital, Kabul. Meetings of various Afghan leaders were organized by the UN to produce a new interim government (headed by Hamid Karzai) and to ratify an agreement allowing a UN peacekeeping force to enter Afghanistan.

As well as maintaining his war on terror, Bush also sought to counter the economic effects of the Sept. 11 attacks as the USA entered recession. He announced an economic revitalization package, including an extra $18 bn. for emergency military spending, and sent the US budget into deficit for the first time in 5 years. Defence remained Bush's priority into 2002. In Nov. he announced the creation of a department of homeland security, an amalgamation of 22 agencies with a budget of $40 bn. He also set up a commission to investigate the failure of intelligence agencies to prevent the 11 Sept. 2001 attacks. In Jan. 2003 Bush announced a further stimulus for the US economy including tax cuts and extended unemployment aid.

In Jan. 2002, in his State of the Union address, Bush referred to North Korea, Iran and Iraq as 'an axis of evil'. From the following Sept. he began to focus on Saddam Hussein's regime in Iraq which he accused of stockpiling weapons of mass destruction (WMD). He successfully campaigned for a UN resolution demanding a renewal of weapons inspections. UN inspectors began their investigation in Nov. 2002 and were scheduled to make their final report in Jan. 2003. The resolution required Iraq's full co-operation, and in Dec. 2002 the government provided a dossier detailing Iraq's chemical, biological and nuclear capabilities. The document was sent to UN experts for analysis to decide if it complied with the resolution's demands. The USA increased its military presence in the Middle East throughout Dec. 2002 and Jan. 2003.

In his report to the Security Council on 27 Jan. 2003, the head of the UN weapons inspectors criticized Iraq's insufficient co-operation but concluded that the investigations neither proved nor disproved that Iraq had a nuclear weapons programme. Following talks with UK Prime Minister Tony Blair in early Feb. Bush agreed to work with the UN towards a further resolution sanctioning action against Iraq unless it disarmed. Deep divisions within the Security Council emerged, notably between the USA, UK and Spain in favour of a military threat and France, Germany, Russia and China opposing military intervention. With Bush emphasizing his right to act independently of the UN, attempts to draft a second resolution acceptable to all parties were abandoned.

US-led forces launched an invasion of Iraq in March 2003. By early April 2003 troops were in control of the country and Saddam Hussein's regime had collapsed. Bush also threatened Syria with sanctions after suggesting that the Syrian government was harbouring members of Saddam Hussein's regime and was developing chemical weapons. In May 2003 the UN ratified a resolution, co-sponsored by the USA, UK and Spain, on Iraq's future. Under its terms UN special representatives were to co-operate with the occupying forces to form a new government and the occupying forces were to remain until an internationally-acceptable government was in place. In July 2004 a critical US Senate report said that the USA and its allies had gone to war in Iraq on flawed intelligence.

While substantial US forces remained in Iraq helping to quell an Islamic insurgency, Bush supported moves to introduce representative government. National elections to a new parliament were held in Dec. 2005. However,

despite the formation of an Iraqi government of national unity, sectarian violence between the Shia and Sunni Muslim communities escalated during 2006. There was also much publicity surrounding the alleged abuse of Iraqi prisoners in US military custody (and similarly of terrorist suspects detained since the Afghanistan campaign at the US naval base at Guantánamo Bay in Cuba). Meanwhile, military involvement in Iraq was becoming increasingly unpopular with US voters. In Nov. 2006 Bush's authority was seriously undermined when the Republican Party lost control of both the House of Representatives and the Senate in mid-term congressional elections and his secretary of defense, Donald Rumsfeld, resigned. In Dec. 2006 a US bipartisan commission (known as the Iraq Study Group) suggested that the Bush administration could reduce the number of US troops in Iraq by the spring of 2008. Bush rejected the idea of troop withdrawal, choosing instead to deploy around a further 20,000 troops in 2007 to reinforce security in Baghdad.

Meanwhile, US policy towards Iran in particular remained hostile, based on alleged Iranian interference in Iraq and Lebanon and on Iran's continuing nuclear development programme in defiance of UN Security Council demands (in response to which the USA imposed further economic sanctions in Oct. 2007).

Attempts to settle the Israeli-Palestinian conflict led in April 2003 to the 'roadmap to peace'. jointly produced by the USA, UN, EU and Russia. This called for an immediate ceasefire to pave the way for a Palestinian state. Then in April 2004, in a major shift of US policy, Bush announced his endorsement of Israeli prime minister Ariel Sharon's plan to remove all Jewish settlements in Gaza (completed in summer 2005) while holding on to larger settlement blocs in the occupied West Bank, accepting that Israel would not make a full and complete return to its pre-1967 borders. Any prospects of peace in 2006 were undermined by a brief but destructive war in Lebanon in July–Aug. between Israel and the radical Lebanese Hizbollah Shia militia, for which Bush held Iranian and Syrian interference largely responsible. Meanwhile, the US administration sought to isolate the militant Islamist Hamas government which had come to power in Palestinian parliamentary elections in Jan. 2006. By mid-2007 factional hostility between Hamas and the mainstream Palestinian Fatah movement led by Palestinian President Mahmoud Abbas had escalated into civil war, resulting in Hamas taking control of Gaza and Fatah's ascendancy in the West Bank. In Nov. 2007 Bush hosted an international conference in Annapolis, Maryland, in an attempt to relaunch Israeli–Palestinian negotiations for peace. However, the early months of 2008 saw only an intensification of Israeli military action against the Palestinians in Gaza and Hamas rocket and suicide bombing attacks against Israel.

Relations with North Korea worsened from late 2002/early 2003 when Pyongyang reactivated a nuclear plant unused since a treaty was signed in 1994 while demanding the withdrawal of UN International Atomic Energy Agency (IAEA) inspectors. Kim Jong Il then withdrew from the nuclear Non-Proliferation Treaty, accusing the USA of posing a nuclear threat and planning to overthrow his government. Bush outlined a 'tailored containment' strategy, involving economic sanctions, but the proposals faced opposition from the South Korean government. There followed 2 years of inconclusive negotiations between North Korea and the USA, together with South Korea, Japan, China and Russia. During this period Kim's regime admitted publicly in Feb. 2005 that it had built nuclear weapons for self-defence before agreeing in principle in Sept. 2005 to give up its development programme in return for aid and security guarantees. However, that accord was almost immediately undermined when North Korea demanded the delivery of civil nuclear equipment. International tensions were then heightened in Oct. 2006 when North Korea announced that it had carried out its first nuclear weapon test. As the crisis threatened to escalate, Kim's regime signalled its willingness to rejoin multilateral negotiations and in Feb. 2007 agreed to shut down its nuclear facilities and readmit international inspectors in return for fuel aid. Bush gave the deal a guarded welcome but progress was slow, and by the end of 2007 North Korea had failed to deliver an inventory of its weapon development activities.

In Feb. 2008, in response to the threat of recession and a global financial downturn triggered by a bad debt crisis in the mortgage lending industry, Bush signed a major economic stimulus package worth $168 bn. His final year in office saw further economic decline and the highest number of job losses in a year since 1945, at 2.6 m.

Later Life

After leaving office, Bush retired to Dallas, Texas and has maintained a low public profile. His memoir, Decision Points, was published in Nov. 2010. Following the Haitian earthquake in Jan. 2010, he and Bill Clinton founded the Clinton Bush Haiti Fund to aid victims of the disaster.

Butkevičius, Algirdas (Lithuania)

Introduction

As leader of the Social Democratic Party of Lithuania (LSDP), Algirdas Butkevičius became prime minister in Dec. 2012 at the head of a coalition government. He remained in office until 2016.

Early Life

Born on 19 Nov. 1958 in Paežeriai in Radviliškis district, Butkevičius graduated in engineering economics from the Vilnius Civil Engineering Institute in 1984 and worked in the Vilkaviškis district for the industrial association žemūktechnika from 1982–85. From 1985–90 he was an architect and inspector for the state construction and architecture unit. In 1991 he gained a diploma in technical management from the Lithuanian Management Academy and in 1995 was awarded a master's degree in management from the Kaunas University of Technology.

After serving as deputy governor of Vilkaviškis district from 1991–95, Butkevičius spent a year as director of research and marketing for the private company, AB Vilkauta. He joined the LSDP in 1992 and was chairman of the party's Vilkaviškis branch from 1995–97. He sat on the Vilkaviškis municipal council from 1990–97 and again from 2000–02. Elected to parliament in 1996, he chaired its budget and finance committee from 2001–04. In 2004 he was appointed finance minister, serving for 5 months in the administration of Prime Minister Brazauskas. He resigned in April 2005 in protest at government proposals to introduce a corporate turnover tax. From 2006–08 he was minister for transport and communications under Prime Minister Kirkilas, overseeing Lithuania's participation in the 'east-west corridor' project to develop a transport network from Sweden to Vilnius.

After the LSDP lost power in 2008, Butkevičius was elected party chairman in March 2009 and unsuccessfully contested the presidency later that year. After 4 years of stringent austerity by the government of Andrius Kubilius, Butkevičius campaigned ahead of the 2012 parliamentary election on a platform of observing fiscal discipline and keeping the budget deficit under control while relaxing wage restraints to boost the economy. In Oct. 2012 the LSDP became the biggest party in parliament and entered negotiations to form a coalition government.

Career Peak

Butkevičius took office on 13 Dec. 2012 at the head of a four-party centre-left coalition after prolonged disagreement with President Grybauskaitė, who opposed the inclusion in the coalition of Labour Party members facing allegations of misconduct.

On the economic front Butkevičius had to combat high unemployment and low economic growth, while keeping to agreed borrowing targets.

In foreign affairs he initially signalled his intention to build better relations with Russia, although Moscow's perceived aggression towards Ukraine from 2014 raised concerns over the long-term security of the Baltic states and prompted the reinforcement of NATO's military presence in the region. Butkevičius also encouraged closer integration with the European Union. In July 2013 Lithuania took over the rotating 6 month EU presidency for the first time since its accession in 2004. Then, on 1 Jan. 2015, having earlier gained the agreement of his coalition partners to target accession to the eurozone, he oversaw Lithuania's adoption of the single currency. He left office after his party came only third in the general election of Nov. 2016.

Calderón, Felipe (Mexico)

Introduction

Felipe Calderón of the centre-right National Action Party (PAN) became president after winning the election of July 2006 by a margin of less than 1%. When his closest rival, López Obrador, disputed the result there were mass protests. Calderón pledged to reduce rising crime and to tackle poverty by creating incentives for foreign investment, but his anti-drugs strategy failed to stem a rising tide of related violence.

Early Life

Felipe de Jesús Calderón Hinojosa was born on 18 Aug. 1962 in Morelia, Michoacán. He studied law at the Escuela Libre de Derecho in Mexico City and economics at the Instituto Tecnológico Autónomo de México, before gaining a master's in public administration from Harvard University in the USA.

From a young age Calderón was a member of PAN, which his father had helped to found in 1939. Calderón became the organization's national youth leader in 1986 and served in the federal chamber of deputies from 1991–94. In 1993 he was elected the party's secretary-general when his mentor, Carlos Castillo Peraza, assumed the party presidency. Calderón succeeded Peraza in 1996 and during 3 years as leader maintained control of 14 state capitals.

However, Vicente Fox was selected to succeed him as party president in late 1999 and went on to contest the 2000 national elections. Fox forged a centre-right alliance (the Alliance for Change) with the Ecologist Green Party of Mexico and won elections to end 71 years of continuous rule by the Institutional Revolutionary Party (PRI).

Calderón was appointed parliamentary co-ordinator of PAN and president of the council of political co-ordination. He also served as a director of the state-owned development bank, Banco Nacional de Obras y Servicios Públicos (BANOBRAS), and in 2002 joined the cabinet as energy secretary. He resigned in 2004 in protest at Fox's support for Santiago Creel as PAN's presidential candidate. In a series of party primaries in late 2005, Calderón decisively defeated Creel and another contender, Alberto Cardenas.

During the election campaign he initially trailed Andrés Manuel López Obrador of the left-wing Party of the Democratic Revolution but closed the gap with promises of job creation and a clampdown on crime and corruption. In the election of 2 July 2006 both Calderón and López Obrador claimed victory before Calderón was declared victor by 0.56% 4 days later. López Obrador's claims of voting irregularities and electoral fraud resulted in large-scale public protests. A partial recount saw the result upheld but López Obrador continued to protest and formed a 'parallel administration'. Calderón was sworn in on 1 Dec. 2006 inside a barricaded parliament building.

Career Peak

During his first year in office Calderón introduced significant reforms to public sector pensions and the tax system, and launched an employment programme giving cash incentives to companies taking on new employees. He also agreed to an electoral reform law put forward by the opposition.

The economy was hit hard by the global downturn in 2008, forcing the government to respond with a package of emergency measures in Jan. 2009. Approval ratings for the president and the PAN slumped, and in mid-term congressional elections in July 2009 the opposition PRI made large gains to become the main force in the Chamber of Deputies.

Calderón's high-profile campaign against illegal drugs cartels has proved largely ineffective, despite the establishment of a new federal police force and the deployment of troops in an anti-trafficking drive. A US Justice Department report in Dec. 2008 stated that Mexican drug traffickers posed the largest organized crime threat to the USA. It was reported in Jan. 2011 that 34,600 people had died in drug-related killings since the presidential election, including 15,273 in 2010 (up from 9,616 the previous year). Thousands of people joined protests against drug crime during the summer of 2011 but acts of violence continued, including an attack in Aug. by armed gangsters on a casino in Monterrey. Fifty-two people died in the incident, which Calderón described as an abhorrent act.

Calderon's tenure came to an end on 30 Nov. 2012 and he left office as the Mexican constitution bans presidents from running for a second term. He subsequently became a fellow at the Kennedy School of Government of Harvard University in Cambridge, Massachusetts.

Callaghan, James (United Kingdom of Great Britain and Northern Ireland)

Introduction

James (Jim) Callaghan was British Labour prime minister from 1976–79 and one of the few politicians to hold all four great Offices of State—home secretary, foreign secretary, chancellor and prime minister. A moderate chosen as Labour leader in the hope that he might unify the fractured party, his premiership was characterized by a failing economy and crippling trade union action. In 1977 Callaghan embarked on a pact with the Liberal party to ensure his minority administration could continue. In 1979 his government became the first to lose a vote of confidence in the House of Commons for over 50 years.

Early Life

Leonard James Callaghan was born on 27 March 1912 in Portsmouth on the south coast of England, the son of a Chief Petty Officer in the Navy. He left school at the age of 14 and was a tax officer at 17, while heavily involved in trade union politics. He joined the Labour Party in 1931 and by 1937 was a full-time trade union official. During World War II he served with the Navy, becoming a Lieutenant in the Royal Naval Volunteer Reserve, and in 1945 he entered the House of Commons as the member for Cardiff South (later Cardiff Southeast), the constituency he would serve for the duration of his career.

He was briefly parliamentary private secretary to the under secretary of state for dominion affairs and then served for 3 years until 1950 as parliamentary secretary to the ministry of transport. During his time here he was active in implementing legislation to introduce zebra crossings and cats' eyes. He was then made parliamentary and private secretary to the treasury until the Conservative general election victory of 1951, before acting as opposition spokesman on successively transport, fuel and power and colonial affairs. He was appointed shadow chancellor in 1961, and became chancellor of the exchequer following Harold Wilson's Labour victory at the 1964 general election. As chancellor, Callaghan provoked controversy by introducing new corporation and capital-gains taxes. In addition, Callaghan spoke out strongly against devaluing sterling and when Wilson, faced with mounting economic pressure, gave permission for devaluation in Nov. 1967, Callaghan resigned.

He was subsequently appointed as home secretary, guiding the Race Relations Act through parliament in 1968 and sending troops into Northern Ireland in 1969. His firm defence of trade unions in the face of proposed reforms earned him the nickname 'Keeper of the Cloth Cap'. He served as home secretary until Edward Heath's Conservatives came to power in 1970 and was shadow home secretary until 1971 when he became opposition spokesman for employment. He was appointed shadow foreign secretary a year later. Wilson returned as prime minister in 1974, with Callaghan holding the office of secretary of state for foreign and Commonwealth affairs. In this post he played an integral part in re-negotiating British membership of the European Economic Community. Wilson announced his shock resignation in March 1976, leaving the party in disarray. With the economy in crisis and the party split, six candidates put themselves forward to succeed Wilson. Callaghan was regarded as the least divisive and after a third ballot he defeated his eventual successor Michael Foot to become prime minister and Labour leader.

Career Peak

Callaghan's premiership was plagued by difficulties. He had to turn to the IMF to resolve a sterling crisis but the IMF demanded reduced spending and pay constraints in return. The unions and left wing of the party were outraged and, at the subsequent Labour conference, supported increased government spending. In addition, the unpopular government lost numerous by-elections

and this combined with a succession of defections left Callaghan as head of a minority government. In March 1977 he struck up a deal with David Steel's Liberals, the Lib–Lab Pact, which ensured that the Liberals would back the government in the event of a confidence motion, but the deal ended in Aug. 1978.

Tensions in Northern Ireland were heightened during Callaghan's administration. Extra troops were sent to the province during 1976–77 and a year later the number of Northern Irish MPs was increased from 12 to 17. However, terrorism and sectarian violence did not abate and in March 1979 Airey Neave, Conservative spokesman on Northern Ireland, was murdered by the Irish Republican Army. In addition, Callaghan's relationship with the unions continued to deteriorate. As wage increase limits were imposed, the first ever national fire-fighters' strike took place in late 1977, and by the end of 1978 Britain was crippled by a succession of strikes that came to be known as 'the winter of discontent'. Ford workers, oil-tank drivers, grave diggers, water workers, sewerage staff, refuse collectors, ambulance and hospital workers, railway workers and large parts of the Civil Service all stopped work. On returning to the crisis from abroad, Callaghan commented that 'I don't think other people in the world would share the view that there is mounting chaos'. This was turned into a popular headline 'Crisis? What crisis?' and Callaghan came to be seen as out of touch. A vote of confidence was called in the Commons for 28 March 1979.

The Scottish National Party withdrew its support from the government over the issue of devolution and Callaghan lost the no confidence motion by one vote. On the same day he called a general election for 3 May. The Conservatives, under Margaret Thatcher, won with a majority of 43. Callaghan stayed as leader of the Labour party until Oct. 1980 and was then succeeded by the left-winger Michael Foot.

Later Life

Callaghan became a rather distant figure as the left-wing dominated the party for much of the 1980s and he left the Commons at the 1987 election. He was made a life peer shortly afterwards, becoming Lord Callaghan of Cardiff, and he remained active in the Lords for many years. He wrote numerous books, including his memoirs, and died on 26 March 2005.

Cameron, David (United Kingdom of Great Britain and Northern Ireland)

Introduction

David Cameron became prime minister of a coalition government with the Liberal Democrats on 11 May 2010, 5 days after the general election that returned the Conservatives to power following 13 years of Labour rule. On taking office he became the UK's youngest prime minister in nearly 200 years. In government he embraced broadly the same foreign policy as the previous Labour administration, aligning Britain with the USA and supporting British military involvement in Iraq and Afghanistan. However, he adopted a more sceptical stance on further integration with the European Union, pledging to negotiate a new relationship with the EU and to put the outcome to a national referendum. Regarding economic policy, he promised to reduce the large deficit in the public finances, while protecting key public services, but had to contend with the recurring threat of recession before signs of a recovery emerged by late 2013. His working relationship with the Liberal Democrats in his first term proved fractious but after his party attained an outright majority at the May 2015 polls he began his second premiership at the head of an all-Conservative government. However, only a year later and following his bruising and ultimately unsuccessful campaign to convince voters in the promised national referendum in June 2016 to maintain Britain's membership of the EU he resigned, with Theresa May succeeding him in July 2016.

Early Life

David William Duncan Cameron was born on 9 Oct. 1966 in London, the son of a stockbroker and a baronet's daughter. He grew up in Peasemore, Berkshire and was educated at Heatherdown Preparatory School and Eton College. From 1985–88 he studied politics, philosophy and economics at Brasenose

College, Oxford, after which he worked for the research department of the ruling Conservative party. He rose to lead the department's political section and in 1992 headed the economic section of the Conservatives' general election campaign team. Following their victory, he was appointed special adviser. He was working for the then Chancellor of the Exchequer, Norman Lamont, when the government was forced to withdraw sterling from the European Exchange Rate Mechanism on 'Black Wednesday'. 16 Sept. 1992.

In May 1993 he was appointed adviser to the Home Office where, under home secretary Michael Howard, he helped introduce criminal justice legislation and promoted initiatives for private companies to build and run prisons. Cameron left politics in 1994 to work in corporate affairs at media company Carlton Communications, where for 7 years he worked closely with chairman Michael Green, handling public relations and communications. At the 1997 general election he unsuccessfully contested Stafford for the Conservatives. In the June 2001 election, he was elected MP for Witney in Oxfordshire, increasing the Conservative share of the vote. In the subsequent Conservative leadership contest he initially supported modernizer Michael Portillo, before finally voting for Iain Duncan Smith, who was seen as an outsider candidate and a eurosceptic.

Cameron was appointed to the Home Affairs Select Committee, where he argued for a review of legislation on illegal drugs. He supported British participation in the 2003 Iraq war, in line with Conservative party policy, despite expressing doubts in the press. In June 2003 he was appointed shadow minister in the Privy Council office and in Nov. that year became deputy chairman of the Conservative party under newly elected leader Michael Howard. Cameron was named spokesman on local government finance in March 2004 and in June 2004, following poor local election results for the Conservatives, he was given responsibility for party policy co-ordination.

Cameron played a key role in developing the party's 2005 general election manifesto, which promised to cut taxes, increase numbers of police and prisons, and oppose the introduction of a European constitution. In May 2005 the Conservatives gained votes but failed to prevent a third successive Labour victory. Cameron was subsequently appointed shadow education secretary and when Howard resigned in Sept. that year he entered the contest for the party leadership. He positioned himself as a modernizer, able to appeal to a wide range of voters, while also winning the support of eurosceptics with a pledge to withdraw Conservative Members of the European Parliament (MEPs) from the European People's Party (EPP—the EU's main centre-right grouping) on the grounds that it was too federalist. After initially trailing his main rival, right-winger David Davis, he won support with his speech at the party conference in Oct. 2005. In the final ballot on 6 Dec. 2005 he defeated Davis, taking 67% of the vote.

In his acceptance speech he promised to address the under-representation of women among Conservative MPs, to reformulate the party's approach to the inner cities and to end 'Punch and Judy politics' by supporting government initiatives where they were in line with Conservative thinking. In July 2006 Cameron fulfilled his campaign promise and withdrew Conservative MEPs from the EPP, forming a new alliance with Czech and Polish MEPs, a move criticized by some as taking the party too far to the right. Identifying himself as a liberal conservative on social matters, he spoke in support of civil partnerships for gay couples at the 2006 party conference. During the same year he introduced the 'A-list' initiative, which required constituency parties to choose their parliamentary candidate from a centrally approved list. Intended to improve representation of women and ethnic minority candidates, this met resistance at local level.

In March 2007 Cameron launched a review into the quality of childhood in Britain and promised to promote marriage through taxation reforms. He repeatedly depicted Britain as a society in moral and economic decline, an interpretation summed up in his phrase 'broken Britain'. and declared his support for economic liberalism combined with the promotion of voluntary and charity work.

During 2007 he said that a Conservative government would aim for lower taxes, with priority given to reducing inheritance tax liability. These proposals were widely credited with prompting Labour government reforms to inheritance tax thresholds in Oct. 2007. Cameron also announced his intention to diversify provision of public services, in particular in education and the health service, proposing that funds could be diverted from state agencies to private enterprise or the voluntary sector.

In foreign policy Cameron continued to support British troop deployment in Iraq and Afghanistan. On domestic security issues, in June 2008 he opposed increasing the maximum period of detention without charge from 28 to 42 days, arguing that it threatened civil liberties. He advocated a new border protection service that would include armed police officers. In Feb. 2009 he pledged to repeal the Human Rights Act and replace it with a British

bill of rights, in response to public anxieties that the Act could be used to protect criminals. Cameron advocated increased prioritization of environmental policies, including proposals to expand nuclear energy, and he opposed plans—at that time—to build a third runway at Heathrow airport.

At the start of the international financial crisis in the autumn of 2008, he supported the Labour government's bank rescue package, though he strongly criticized its record of financial management, particularly the high level of the public finance deficit. The subsequent downturn forced him to reassess his party's policies. In 2009 he announced that tax cuts would be contingent on economic improvement and confirmed that this meant postponing further inheritance tax reforms. In Dec. 2009 ratification of the Lisbon Treaty on the European constitution obviated his previous pledge to hold a referendum on the issue. Instead he promised to introduce a sovereignty bill that would prevent any further transfer of power to the EU without a referendum. Cameron fought the 2010 general election on a platform of reduced government spending (with the exception of the NHS and overseas aid), fewer business regulations and increased choice in health and education services.

Career Peak

Cameron became prime minister on 11 May 2010. Although the Conservatives failed to secure an absolute majority in the election of 6 May they did win 306 seats compared to 258 for Labour and succeeded in forming a coalition (the UK's first since the Second World War) with the Liberal Democrats, who had won 57 seats.

Cameron's key challenges were to address the faltering economy and the growing gap between rich and poor. Following an initial austerity budget in June 2010, the coalition government went on to announce a raft of deep, and unpopular, public spending cuts aimed at reducing the UK's large budget deficit and also measures overhauling the state welfare system to be implemented over the course of the parliament.

On security issues Cameron pledged to maintain Britain's military commitment to, and offensive engagement in, Afghanistan until the anticipated withdrawal of NATO combat troops from the country in 2014. In 2011 Britain played a prominent military role in UN-sanctioned NATO intervention in Libya to protect civilians against the Gaddafi regime, which was overthrown in Oct. that year. In early 2013 the UK government provided logistical support for French military intervention in Mali to counter Islamist extremists controlling much of the north of the country. However, in response to the continuing civil war in Syria and the Assad regime's apparent use of banned chemical weapons, the rejection by the House of Commons in Aug. 2013 of any military intervention by UK forces in the conflict at that time proved a major setback for Cameron's political authority.

In June 2010 a long-running independent inquiry into 'Bloody Sunday'. in which unarmed Catholic civil rights demonstrators in Northern Ireland were shot dead by British troops in 1972, concluded that the killings were unjustified, prompting an apology by Cameron as prime minister on behalf of the British state.

In May 2011 voters in a national referendum rejected by a large margin a proposal to replace the first-past-the-post electoral system for the House of Commons with the alternative vote (AV) system. Cameron had strongly opposed the plan, placing considerable strain on his governing partnership with the Liberal Democrats, for whom such a change had been a central policy objective.

In Aug. 2011 the worst rioting and looting in decades erupted in London and other English major cities and was only contained by police after several days of disorder and mass arrests. The violence prompted Cameron to recall Parliament from its recess to debate appropriate responses.

The effects of the debt crisis in several eurozone countries further aggravated the UK's parlous financial situation in 2011 and 2012, and highlighted the political divisions within the Conservative Party towards the EU. In Oct. 2011 Cameron suffered a major revolt by Conservative MPs who, in defiance of government policy, supported a motion calling for a referendum on continued membership. The motion was only defeated with the support of Liberal Democrat and opposition Labour members. In Dec. 2011, aware of Conservative hostility to further European integration, Cameron vetoed an EU-wide treaty change proposing greater fiscal union on the grounds that it would undermine London's position as a leading international financial hub. Although popular with his own parliamentary eurosceptics, the move put Cameron's relationship with his pro-EU Liberal Democrat coalition partners under further pressure. This was exacerbated in Jan. 2013 when Cameron, acting after rising support for the anti-EU UK Independence Party in several parliamentary by-elections in 2012, promised a renegotiation of Britain's relationship with the EU and, more controversially, a referendum on continued membership after 2015. The following month Cameron claimed credit for spearheading successful intergovernmental negotiations to reduce the EU's 7-year budget for the first time in the Union's history.

The UK economy continued to struggle as official figures in Jan. 2012 indicated that net public sector debt (excluding bank bailouts) had risen above £1 trn. for the first time and the Chancellor of the Exchequer warned in Dec. that year of an extended period of austerity. There were, however, some signs of accelerating growth by the end of 2013, including a rise in employment figures and a more buoyant housing market. Discontent with the government's austerity measures had meanwhile been aggravated by public concerns over Cameron's championing of controversial reforms to the National Health Service and deep cuts in the level of social welfare provision.

In Jan. 2011 Cameron's director of communications, Andy Coulson, resigned amid allegations that he was aware of illegal telephone hacking by the national Sunday newspaper of which he was editor before his political appointment in 2007. The subsequent escalation of the controversy, which saw some commentators cast doubt on Cameron's personal judgment, led to an inquiry under Lord Justice Leveson that published its report in Nov. 2012 into the culture, practices and ethics of the newspaper industry. Cameron's rejection of Leveson's central recommendation of statutory press regulation again highlighted differences with his Liberal Democrat coalition partners. Tensions were aggravated further by the Conservatives' failure to fully embrace Liberal Democrat aspirations to reform the House of Lords and by the Liberal Democrat refusal to back Conservative efforts to update parliamentary constituency boundaries.

In addition to the coalition friction, Cameron courted further dissent within his own party in Jan. 2013 as government legislation to approve same-sex marriage failed to attract the support of over half of Conservative MPs and only passed with Liberal Democrat and opposition backing.

In Oct. 2012 Cameron and Alex Salmond, the First Minister of Scotland, agreed to stage a referendum in Sept. 2014 on Scottish independence from the rest of the United Kingdom. Cameron campaigned successfully against the breakaway, which was rejected by 55% of voters.

Throughout the parliament Cameron had faced increasing public pressure for government action on levels of immigration which, together with growing scepticism about continued EU membership, underpinned a surge in support in several by-elections in 2013 and 2014 for the UK Independence Party (UKIP). This was principally at the expense of the Conservative Party, which lost its Clacton constituency seat to a defector to UKIP. In July 2014, with the next general election on the political horizon, Cameron sought to revitalize his cabinet with an extensive reshuffle.

Despite polls suggesting a very close result, the Conservatives won an outright majority at the general election in May 2015 and Cameron formed an all-Conservative administration. In an early political setback, the new government announced its intention to impose swingeing cuts in welfare payments in continuance of its economic austerity strategy. However, proposed legislation limiting claimants' tax credits was controversially blocked by the House of Lords in Oct. and subsequently shelved in what was widely labelled a government climb-down. Cameron's authority was more persuasive in Dec. when the House of Commons voted overwhelmingly to extend British anti-jihadist military action from Iraq to Syria, reversing the earlier vote in Aug. 2013.

It was the contentious issue of EU membership that was nevertheless to define Cameron's ultimately brief second term of office. Against the background of Europe's worst refugee crisis in recent times and domestic opposition within the UK to further immigration, he sought a renegotiation of Britain's position within the EU. In Feb. 2016 he claimed to have secured a draft deal offering revised terms of membership, including an 'emergency brake' on EU migrants' entitlement to in-work benefits, a mechanism allowing national governments to block some EU legislation, prohibition of discrimination between EU currencies and a declaration that the UK would not be committed to further political integration into the EU. This proposed settlement failed to satisfy eurosceptic opinion, not least among some prominent members within Cameron's own Conservative Party who defied him and actively campaigned against continued membership in the national referendum held on 23 June. Following the narrow vote to leave the EU, Cameron announced that he would resign his office upon the election of a new Conservative leader. Theresa May subsequently took over as premier on 13 July 2016.

Later Life

In March 2017 Cameron became chairman of the LSE-Oxford Commission on State Fragility, Growth and Development, established under the auspices of the International Growth Centre (which is funded by the UK Department for International Development).

Campbell, Kim (Canada)

Introduction

The first woman to serve as prime minister of Canada, Kim Campbell held a brief tenure as leader from June to Oct. 1993 before her party suffered a crushing defeat at the general election.

Early Life

Born Avril Phaedra Campbell in March 1947, in Port Alberni, British Columbia, Campbell changed her name to Kim when she was 12, shortly after her mother had left the family. Campbell studied political science at the University of British Columbia, where she was elected president of the student's council, before attending the London School of Economics (1970–73) on a fellowship.

Returning to the University of British Columbia in 1980 to study law, she was elected a Vancouver school trustee in the same year and went on to gain a reputation for endorsing moderate fiscal policies.

After serving as a key policy adviser for Premier Bill Bennet, she won a seat in the Legislative Assembly in 1986 and ran for the leadership of the Social Credit Party the same year. Running against provincial leader Bill Vander Zalm, she made her mark by publicly opposing the premier's restrictive stance on abortion.

In 1988 she turned her attention to Federal politics and was elected to the House of Commons representing the Progressive Conservative Party for the British Columbia riding of Vancouver Centre.

Fostered as a successor to Prime Minister Brian Mulroney she became minister of state for Indian affairs and northern development (1989), minister of justice and attorney general of Canada (1990), and minister of defence and minister of veteran affairs (1993).

While justice minister she proved her political tenacity by introducing a bill amending the gun laws. In the wake of the 1989 Montreal massacre she had to satisfy both a public demanding more restrictive gun laws while a powerful gun-owning lobby within the Conservative support.

Career Peak

With the retirement of prime minister Brian Mulroney in 1993 Campbell was encouraged to run for the office, beating nearest rival Jean Charest in a close contest to become Canada's first female prime minister.

Articulate and photogenic, Conservatives hoped she would attract a new generation of voters, however, despite a brief surge in popularity she was unable to shake off the unhappy legacy of the party's long term in office. A sweeping tax on goods and services and the free trade agreement with the United States proved deeply unpopular, with Campbell herself proving to be an inexperienced and ineffective campaigner. In consequence, the Conservatives won only two Commons seats under her leadership, with Campbell herself losing her seat and resigning as leader in Jan. 1994.

Later Life

Retiring from politics Campbell accepted a fellowship from Harvard, before being appointed to the post of Consul General of Canada in Los Angeles.

Campbell, Menzies 'Ming' (United Kingdom of Great Britain and Northern Ireland)

Introduction

Ming Campbell succeeded Charles Kennedy as leader of the Liberal Democrat party in March 2006. Despite concerns about his age, he was hailed within the party as an astute intellect and a steadying influence. In Oct. 2007 Campbell resigned as leader of the party.

Early Life

Walter Menzies Campbell was born on 22 May 1941 in Glasgow, Scotland. He studied at the University of Glasgow and was elected as president of the University Union. He later undertook a scholarship at Stanford University in California.

In 1964 he competed as a sprinter at the Tokyo Olympics. His athletics career encompassed captaining Scotland at the Empire and Commonwealth Games in Jamaica in 1966, captaining the British squad in 1965 and 1966 and holding the British 100 m record between 1967 and 1974.

Having qualified as a lawyer, he was admitted to the Faculty of Advocates in 1968 and appointed a QC in 1982. Becoming chairman of the Scottish Liberals in 1975, he unsuccessfully stood for parliament three times before winning the North East Fife seat from the Conservatives in 1987. Five years later he was appointed party spokesman on defence issues and foreign affairs, becoming shadow foreign secretary in 1997.

Campbell decided not to contest the party leadership when Paddy Ashdown stepped down in 1999. In 2002 he was diagnosed with and made a full recovery from non-Hodgkins lymphona. The following year he succeeded Alan Beith as deputy leader of the party. In 2004 he received a knighthood for 'services to Parliament'. In late 2005 party leader Charles Kennedy was plagued by allegations of a drink problem and eventually stood down in Jan. 2006. Campbell faced Simon Hughes, a former London mayoral candidate, and the relatively unknown Chris Huhne for the leadership. Hughes fell after the first round of voting and Campbell went on to defeat Huhne in a second round.

Career Peak

Campbell spoke of the need for his party to raise its game in the face of the renaissance of the Conservatives under David Cameron. However, he oversaw a disappointing performance at local elections and came in for personal criticism for his performances at prime minister's question time. On 15 Oct. 2007 Campbell stepped down as leader of the Liberal Democrats. In his letter of resignation, addressed to party president Simon Hughes, he said questions about his leadership were 'getting in the way of further progress by the party'.

Carcasses Kalosil, Moana (Vanuatu)

Introduction

Moana Kalosil became prime minister in March 2013. A naturalized citizen, he was the first non-native-born head of government in the country's history.

Early Life

Kalosil was born on 27 Jan. 1963 in Taravoa, Tahiti, to a French father and a Tahitian mother. He joined the Green Confederation Party in 2000 and successfully stood as its candidate for the parliamentary seat in the capital, Port Vila, in 2002. From 2003–04 he served as foreign minister in the cabinet of Edward Natapei.

In July 2004 Kalosil became finance minister in Serge Vohor's government, staying in the post after Ham Lini became premier. Losing his cabinet seat when Lini resigned in 2005, Kalosil led the opposition at the 2008 general election and retained his Port Vila seat.

With Natapei forming the government, Kalosil was the opposition whip until joining the government in 2009 as minister of internal affairs and labour (despite having been threatened with suspension from parliament earlier in the year amid allegations of abetting a prison breakout, although the charges were subsequently dropped).

When Natapei left office in 2010 after a vote of no confidence, Kalosil joined the administration of Sato Kilman as minister of finance and economic management, positions he kept until Kilman was himself ousted by a no confidence vote in 2011.

Kalosil retained his seat at the 2012 election and sat as a backbencher to the reinstated Kilman government. In March 2013 he and eight other MPs defected to the opposition, forcing Kilman's resignation. Three days later, Kalosil was voted premier by parliamentary ballot, winning support from 34 of 52 MPs.

Career Peak

Only the world's second Green prime minister, Kalosil began his tenure by establishing a ministry of climate change. He was also expected to pursue closer ties with foreign partners including France, Australia and Vanuatu's Melanesian neighbours. He is a strong advocate of self-determination for the people of West Papua—a province of Indonesia in the island of New Guinea—and has opposed a decision made by the previous administration to grant Indonesia observer status at the intergovernmental Melanesian Spearhead Group.

In May 2014 Kalosil lost a parliamentary motion of no-confidence having survived three previous attempts to remove him from power. He had been accused of overspending on projects including the construction of a new international airport, whilst offsetting spiraling costs by selling diplomatic passports to foreign nationals. Joe Natuman was subsequently appointed to the premiership, replacing Kalosil on 15 May 2014.

Cardoso, Fernando Henrique (Brazil)

Introduction

Fernando Henrique Cardoso was president of Brazil from 1994–2002, becoming the first president to serve two consecutive 4 year terms. An academic, former finance minister and leader of the Partido da Social Democracia Brasileira (Social Democratic Party; PSDB), he oversaw a period of rapid economic development, albeit incurring a large public debt.

Early Life

Born in Rio de Janeiro on 18 June 1931, Cardoso was educated at the University of São Paulo and the University of Paris. An opponent of the military regime in power from 1964, he was stripped of his academic position. Having founded the Centre for Analysis and Research, a social science think tank, in late 1968, he was investigated by military intelligence and his institute was bombed by right-wing terrorists. He went into exile in the 1970s and 80s, working in Chile, the US and France and studying international relations.

In 1986 Cardoso was elected senator for São Paulo and a such campaigned for democratic reform. Two years later he helped found the Social Democratic party and was prominent in the re-drafting of the Brazilian constitution. In 1992 he resigned from the senate to become foreign minister in the government of Itamar Franco. Appointed finance minister in 1993, he introduced the Real Plan, a strategy to promote economic recovery and counter Brazil's rampant inflation which peaked at 10,000%. His success raised his public profile and he triumphed in the presidential election of 1994.

Career Peak

Cardoso's rule saw a period of economic growth and reform including the privatization of Brazil's state-run monopolies, the introduction of a new currency, a reduction in trade restrictions and increased spending on education and welfare. By the end of his term inflation was at 7%, infant mortality had fallen and unemployment remained steady.

A constitutional amendment in 1997 provided for consecutive presidential terms and the following year he won re-election. In Cardoso's second term a growing trade deficit led to reduced government spending, increased taxes and a slowing of the economy, in part affected by problems in neighbouring countries. Brazil had also accrued a public debt of US$260bn. In the 2002 presidential elections, Cardoso's successor José Serra was defeated by the leftwing leader Luiz Inácio Lula da Silva.

Later Life

Cardoso has been involved in a number of international initiatives and organizations since leaving the presidency. He was the president of the Club of Madrid from 2003–2006 and is also a member of 'the Elders'. An organization of elder statesmen describing themselves as 'independent global leaders working together for peace and human rights'.

Carmona, Anthony (Trinidad and Tobago)

Introduction

Anthony Carmona served as president from March 2013 until March 2018. Previously a high court judge, he had served on the International Criminal Tribunal for the former Yugoslavia (ICTY) and resigned from the International Criminal Court (ICC) following his election. He is regarded as a political independent.

Early Life

Carmona was born on 7 March 1953 in Fyzabad and educated at Presentation College, San Fernando. After studying English and political science at the University of the West Indies (UWI) in Jamaica, he studied law, first at the UWI in Barbados, then at the Sir Hugh Wooding Law School in Trinidad and Tobago, graduating in 1983. In this period he also taught in schools and at the UWI.

Carmona served as deputy director of public prosecutions from 1995–99, when he was appointed acting director. He was legal adviser to President A. N. R. Robinson on matters of criminal law relating to the establishment of the ICC, and was a member of the Trinidad and Tobago legislative review committee. He also advised the ministry of foreign affairs and the attorney general on international treaties and conventions.

From 2001–04 he served on the ICTY, dealing with the appeals of those convicted of war crimes, crimes against humanity and genocide. From 2004–13 he was a high court judge in Trinidad and Tobago. Elected one of six ICC judges in 2012, he was scheduled to take up his post in The Hague in March 2013. However, on 4 Feb. 2013 the then prime minister, Kamla Persad-Bissessar, nominated him for the presidency. Carmona was elected to the post by the Electoral College of parliament on 15 Feb. 2013, resigning from the ICC in order to take up the role.

Career Peak

Carmona took office on 18 March 2013. He pledged to champion a more open style of government. He was succeeded by Paula-Mae Weekes when his term finished in March 2018.

Carter, James Earl 'Jimmy' (United States of America)

Introduction

James Earl Carter, Jr was the 39th president of the United States, serving one term in office after defeating incumbent Republican president Gerald Ford in the 1976 election.

Early Life

Popularly known as 'Jimmy' Carter, he was born on 1 Oct. 1924 in Plains, Georgia to James Earl Carter and Lillian Gordy Carter, a staunch Baptist family. The young Carter attended Georgia Southwestern College and the Georgia Institute of Technology before graduating from the US Naval Academy at Annapolis in 1946. The same year he married Rosalynn Smith. After 2 years serving on battleships, Carter spent 5 years working on nuclear submarines before resigning his commission in 1953 after his father's death and returning to run the family's peanut farming and warehouse business in Georgia.

While transforming the family business Carter also embarked on a public career, serving as chairman of the Sumter county school board as well as the county hospital authority and acting as the president of the Plains Development Corporation and the Crop Improvement Association. He entered the political arena in 1962 when he won election as a Democrat to serve on the Georgia State Senate. Carter was successfully re-elected 2 years later with his terms in office characterized by a conservative approach to spending and a liberal view of social issues.

In 1966 Carter failed in a bid to become Governor of Georgia when he came third in a Democratic primary. This experience left him depressed and he became a born-again Baptist before launching another bid for Governor in 1970. This time he was successful, defeating Carl Sanders before attracting national attention by his vigorous opposition to racial discrimination—Carter ensured the state's offices were opened to blacks—and reorganizing the state government by condensing some 300 agencies and offices into 22 new, more streamlined units.

After the end of his term as governor in Jan. 1975, Carter immediately began to focus on winning the Democratic nomination for president. Campaigning as an anti-Washington candidate with no links to the Vietnam War or Watergate, Carter vowed to deliver honest, open government. His campaign gathered momentum and he saw off all his Democratic party challengers despite his low national profile and lack of major financial backers. He chose Walter F. Mondale as his running mate.

Career Peak

From the beginning of his presidential campaign against Republican rival Gerald D. Ford, Carter was the front-runner, a position that was bolstered by his well-received performances in three televised debates with the incumbent president. Despite a late charge from the Ford campaign Carter was elected president after winning 51% of the popular vote and gaining 297 electoral college votes to 240.

From his inauguration on 20 Jan. 1977 Carter made a conscious effort to project a more open, less formal style of presidency. But if Carter's image as a Washington outsider helped him gain election, it hamstrung his relations with Congress and the Senate. Despite Democratic majorities in both houses he failed to win support for many of his programmes. Proposals concerning tax, welfare reform, hospital costs and national health insurance all floundered. Like his predecessor Carter also struggled to contain inflation and unemployment. By 1980 inflation had risen to 12% from 4.8% in 1976 and unemployment was running at approximately 7.7%.

Carter had success with other domestic policies. The civil service was overhauled and he also initiated, with mixed success, a series of measures aimed at energy and environmental conservation. In 1979, with the dollar losing value in response to a petrol shortage, Carter successfully implemented many portions of a far-ranging energy programme that sought to limit wasteful uses of energy and introduce alternative sources such as solar power into the mainstream.

The centrepiece of Carter's foreign policy was his commitment to human rights. Carter also proved an effective diplomat, signing two treaties with Panama which guaranteed the neutrality of the Panama Canal, brokering an agreement between Egypt and Israel in 1978 (known as the Camp David accord) and establishing full diplomatic relations with China in 1979. Furthermore in 1979, Carter and Soviet Premier Leonid Brezhnev signed a strategic arms limitation treaty (SALT II) in Vienna, although approval from the Senate for the treaty was not forthcoming and it was put on ice after the Soviet invasion of Afghanistan in 1979—an invasion that also led to Carter insisting that the US team withdrew from the 1980 Olympics in Moscow.

The most severe problem Carter faced in office was the seizure of US hostages by radical Iranian students who stormed the US embassy in Tehran on 4 Nov. 1979. After trying for over a year to secure the hostages release, he oversaw the failure of a secret US military rescue mission. With the hostages still unreleased Carter was easily defeated in the 1980 presidential election by Republican rival Ronald W. Reagan, gaining just 49 electoral college votes to Reagan's 489. The hostages were finally released on 20 Jan. 1981, the day of Reagan's inauguration.

Later Life

After the end of his term Carter returned to his hometown of Plains. He has written several books and has continued to play an active role in foreign affairs, visiting Nicaragua, Panama, Ethiopia, North Korea, Haiti and Bosnia on peacekeeping and diplomatic missions. He has also established, with his wife Rosalynn, the Carter Presidential Centre in Atlanta. In 2002 he was awarded the Nobel Peace Prize.

Castro, Fidel (Cuba)

Introduction

Lawyer and revolutionary guerrilla, Fidel Alejandro Castro Ruz led Cuba for almost 50 years after he headed the 1959 revolution that overthrew the military dictatorship of Fulgencio Batista. Premier until 1976 when a new constitution created a presidency, Castro set up a socialist state, implemented agrarian reforms, nationalized industries and imposed single party rule. Full employment, free education and universal health care were promised, although all opposition was repressed and freedoms restricted. Strong Soviet links bolstered Cuba in the face of US hostility, but since the collapse of the USSR Castro became increasingly isolated. He transferred power provisionally to his brother after his health deteriorated seriously in July 2006. On 19 Feb. 2008 Castro announced in a letter published in the state-run newspaper Granma that he would be stepping down as president.

Early Life

Castro was born on 13 Aug. 1926 (his official birthday, although some sources dispute this date) in the Oriente province (now Santiago de Cuba) in eastern Cuba, the illegitimate son of a prosperous Spanish sugarcane farmer and his cook. From the age of six, Castro was educated at Jesuit schools in Santiago de Cuba, and in 1945 went to study law at the capital's Universidad de la Habana, where he became politically active. He was a supporter of Eduardo Chibas who formed the Ortodoxos party (Cuban People's Party) in 1947. After joining the party, Castro was involved with preparations for a coup to depose the Dominican Republic's leader Gen. Rafael Trujillo.

After graduating in 1950, Castro set up a law firm in Havana to help the poor and his political allies. He continued his involvement with Ortodoxos and was their candidate for Havana in the 1952 elections. Before they could take place former premier Batista deposed Prime Minister Carlos Prío Socarrás and set up a military dictatorship. Following unsuccessful legal challenges, Castro began recruiting for a revolutionary movement. After a failed raid on the Moncada army barracks on 26 July 1953, Castro was sentenced to 13 years imprisonment.

He was pardoned in 1955 following an amnesty and went to Mexico where he formed the revolutionary Movimiento 26 de Julio. There he met Ernesto 'Che' Guevara Lynch, who became the Movimiento's doctor. On 2 Dec. 1956 Castro and his followers attacked his native Oriente province. After losing nearly all of their number, the remaining few fighters took refuge in the Sierra Maestra mountains where Castro continued to recruit, gathering together as many as 800 volunteers. Following numerous battles, Batista was forced into exile on 1 Jan. 1959. Castro became commander-in-chief of the army while the premiership was taken by Manuel Urrutia. Forcing the latter out, in July 1959 Castro appointed himself premier, promising to restore civil and political liberties.

Career Peak

Despite promising moderate reforms, Castro's radicalism soon intensified, as did his affiliation to Marxism. Communists were favoured for governmental positions while enforced land distribution ended tenancy and private ownership. Foreign investors left and all industry and commerce was nationalized. By early 1960 Castro had established a favourable trade agreement with the USSR which provided Cuba with oil, weapons and loans while importing Cuban sugarcane at an advantageous price. In 1961 the Organizaciones Revolucionarias Integradas was created (the Cuban Communist Party—Partido Comunista de Cuba; PCC—from 1965), comprising Castro's Movimiento 26 de Julio, the Popular Socialist Party (Partido Socialista Popular) and the Revolutionary Directorate (Directorio Revolucionario). All opposition was outlawed. The immediate effect of Castro's reforms was the improvement of life for the poorest Cubans. Social services were made available, full employment was promised and illiteracy decreased. However, civil rights abuses led many middle class Cubans to flee the country.

In 1960 US suspicion of Castro and his links to communism led the USA to suspend trade agreements, impose an embargo and sever diplomatic relations. In April 1961 the US government supported and financed an attempted coup by 1,300 Cuban exiles. The unsuccessful invasion at the Bay of Pigs was soon contained by the Cuban army. The USA also mounted several assassination attempts. In 1962 Soviet ballistic missiles were secretly placed in Cuba in range of US cities. In retaliation the US navy surrounded Cuba. The world hovered on the brink of nuclear war until the Soviet leader Nikita Khrushchev agreed to remove the missiles in exchange for a removal of US missiles based in Turkey and a promise of an end to hostilities with Cuba.

In 1976 Castro created a new constitution and national assembly and appointed himself president. His brother Raúl was appointed minister of armed forces becoming de facto vice president. In 1980 Castro opened the northern port of Mariel for 5 months allowing thousands of Cubans to flee, including 125,000 who emigrated to the USA.

On an international level, Castro supported revolutionary activity in Bolivia, Venezuela and the Dominican Republic. Between 1975–89 the Cuban army aided communists in the Angolan civil war and helped Ethiopia combat Somalia's invasion in 1978. But Cuba's military expenditure was detrimental to its economic progress. Castro was unable to stimulate the country's industry or agriculture. In 1991 Cuba suffered heavily from the withdrawal of Soviet trade and rationing had to be imposed, leading to economic and social unrest in 1993. After public demonstrations, Castro agreed to relax restrictions on leaving the country. In 1994 the Cuban economy reached its nadir. Although Castro refused to change his regime after the fall of the USSR (free speech is still effectively banned), he was forced to adopt a pragmatic approach and to open up the economy and encourage a tourist industry. A two-tier financial system has meant plentiful supplies in tourist dollar shops but shortages for most Cubans.

At the end of the 1990s Castro formed an alliance with the Venezuelan premier Hugo Chávez and agreed a preferential trade arrangement exchanging Venezuelan oil for Cuban goods and services. Castro and Chávez also signed a co-operation agreement on agriculture and tourism. In Nov. 1999 relations with the USA were further strained by the Elián González affair, in which the two governments were involved in a custody battle over the fate of a 6-year old Cuban refugee.

Castro was re-elected for his sixth presidential term in 2003 with 100% of the 609 available parliamentary votes. In March 2003 relations with the USA deteriorated further when Castro arrested several dozen political dissidents who had met with the US envoy, James Cason. Castro accused Cason of subversion and restricted the movement of diplomats within the country in a tit-for-tat response after the USA imposed similar restrictions in Washington. The EU threatened sanctions in June 2003, but the following month promised to continue aid despite Castro attacking the EU as a 'Trojan horse' of the USA. Diplomatic contacts with the EU were restored in Jan. 2005. In May 2005 Castro unusually allowed a dissident group to hold a public meeting, although foreigners seeking to attend were turned away.

Concerns over Castro's declining health increased markedly from late July 2006 as he underwent intestinal surgery and, for the first time in 47 years, handed over power provisionally to his brother Raúl. Speculation about his condition heightened as he failed to attend Havana's May Day parade and the annual celebrations in July 2007 marking the anniversary of the revolution. However, he maintained that he was anticipating for a full recovery and in Sept. appeared in an hour-long interview on state television.

In Oct. 2007 President George W. Bush reaffirmed that the US trade embargo would be maintained while the Castro regime kept a 'monopoly' of power.

In Feb. 2008 Castro announced he would be resigning as president citing his 'critical condition'. He said that it would be a betrayal to his conscience to accept responsibility which required mobility and dedication that he was physically unable to offer. Castro added that retirement would not stop him from carrying on 'fighting like a soldier of ideas'. promising to continue writing essays entitled Reflections of Comrade Fidel. George W. Bush responded to the news by saying that the United States will 'help the people of Cuba realise the blessings of liberty'. Five days after Castro's announcement Cuba's National Assembly chose his younger brother Raúl to be the country's new president.

Later Life

In July 2010 Castro made his first appearance in public since the announcement of his illness in 2006. Photographs of the leader were tightly controlled by the state media although essays that he still wrote regularly published in state newspapers. He died at the age of 90 on 25 Nov. 2016 having been in bad health for several years.

Castro, Raúl (Cuba)

Introduction

Raúl Castro was elected president by the National Assembly of People's Power on 24 Feb. 2008. His first 5 year term began when he replaced his brother, Fidel, who had held office for 49 years. While less charismatic than his brother, he preserved the essence of Cuba's brand of socialism. He was re-elected in Feb. 2013.

Early Life

Raúl Castro was born on 3 June 1931 in Birán, in the Oriente province (now Santiago de Cuba). His father was a sugar plantation owner of Spanish origin and his mother a housemaid. After expulsion from his first school Raúl attended the Jesuit-run Colegio Dolores in Santiago and the Belén School in Havana, before graduating as a sergeant from military college. He attended the University of Havana until 1953, when his involvement in politics cut short his studies.

Raúl was a member of the Socialist Youth group, affiliated to the Moscow-orientated Popular Socialist Party. His travels to the Soviet bloc in 1953 prompted him to turn against the then president, Fulgencio Batista, culminating that year in the failed 26 July attack on the Moncada barracks alongside brother Fidel. Both were imprisoned but then exiled to Mexico 22 months later. Raúl subsequently helped organize the 26 July Revolutionary Movement and the failed coup attempt of 1956.

Raúl then took charge of the military campaign in the east of the country and victory was achieved in 1959 when Batista went into exile. Raúl secured his place as Fidel's right hand man, politically and militarily. He was appointed minister for the Revolutionary Armed Forces (FAR) and played a key role during the Bay of Pigs invasion of 1961 and in the Cuban missile crisis the following year.

In 1965 he was promoted to the Cuban Communist Party (PCC) Politburo and made second secretary of the central committee behind Fidel. In 1972 he became first vice-premier and 4 years later the new National Assembly of People's Power elected him vice-president. The Castro hierarchy was endorsed with total support at each of the congressional party sessions from 1975–97. As vice-president he was pivotal in the close relationship with the Eastern European communist bloc until the 1990s when he engineered the economic shift away from former Soviet dependency. From 2000–02 his public profile grew as he stood in for Fidel on diplomatic tours of China and South East Asia.

When Fidel underwent abdominal surgery in July 2006, Raúl became acting president. On 19 Feb. 2008 Fidel announced his formal resignation and Raúl was elected his successor by the National Assembly.

Career Peak

Raúl's key challenges have been economic. Early signs of greater market freedom included allowing Cubans to stay in tourist hotels and rent cars and the lifting of bans on ownership of consumer products such as mobile phones, computers and DVD players. However, such products have remained unaffordable to average citizens.

In mid-2008 the government relaxed restrictions on the amount of idle state-owned land available to private farmers and announced plans to abandon salary equality in a radical departure from Marxist principles. In the wake of two hurricanes in 2008 that devastated homes and crops in Cuba, a US offer of emergency aid was rejected by Raúl, who instead demanded a lifting of the long-standing US trade embargo.

In March 2009 and again in Jan. 2011 the Obama administration eased the US embargo, lifting restrictions on remittances and visits to Cuba by Cuban-Americans. Despite this slight thaw in relations, Raúl continued to crack down on political dissent. Nevertheless, in Sept. 2010 he unveiled limited plans to further liberalize the economy by laying off thousands of state employees while legalizing self-employment in many areas and allowing more private enterprise. In Nov. he also announced the convening of a long-overdue PCC congress to be held in April 2011 (the first since 1997) to approve the plans, at which he was elected first secretary of the party. The Organization of American States had meanwhile voted in June 2009 to end Cuba's diplomatic suspension dating back to 1962.

In Nov. 2011 legislation enabling individuals to buy and sell property for the first time since the revolution was passed. A subsequent papal visit to Cuba in March 2012 prompted a government amnesty for some 2,500 prisoners, including political detainees, and the restoration of recognition for a religious holiday. Then in Oct. the government abolished the requirement that most citizens, other than certain professionals, acquire exit visas to travel abroad.

Having been re-elected in Feb. 2013, Raúl announced that he would stand down at the end of his second term and in July that year he removed several senior figures from the PCC central committee in an apparent gradual transfer of power to a younger generation. In early 2014 parliament approved a new foreign investment law allowing Cubans living abroad to invest in certain enterprises for the first time, and the government also began talks with the European Union on restoring political relations and boosting economic ties.

In Dec. 2014 Castro and US president Barack Obama agreed a landmark deal, brokered in part by Pope Francis, to begin normalizing bilateral relations and in April 2015 they held the first leaders' summit in nearly 60 years. This was followed in July that year by the full restoration of diplomatic ties, and in March 2016 Obama became the first US president to visit Cuba since 1928. On 25 Nov. 2016 Castro announced the death of his brother Fidel at the age of 90.

First Vice-President Díaz-Canel was elected president by the National Assembly on 18 April 2018 and took office the next day, although Castro stayed on as head of the Communist Party.

Cavaco Silva, Aníbal (Portugal)

Introduction

Aníbal Cavaco Silva was elected president on 22 Jan. 2006, the first centre-right politician to fill the largely ceremonial post since the 1974 revolution. The free-market economist played a key role in preparing Portugal's entry in 1986 to the European Economic Community (EEC; later the European Union) and served as prime minister from 1985–95. He was re-elected president in Jan. 2011.

Early Life

Aníbal António Cavaco Silva was born in Boliqueime, Algarve on 15 July 1939. After graduating in finance in 1964, he worked at the Calouste Gulbenkian Foundation in Lisbon from 1967–71 before studying for a PhD in economics at the University of York in the UK.

Returning to Portugal in 1974—the year when the Caetano dictatorship was toppled—Cavaco Silva taught economics at the Catholic University of Portugal. He joined the new centre-right Popular Democratic Party, which became the Social Democratic Party (PSD) in 1976. From 1977 he headed the research and statistics department of the Bank of Portugal. Elected to parliament for the PSD in Oct. 1980, he served as minister of finance and planning.

An advocate of free-market economics, Cavaco Silva's reforms, combined with a constitutional reduction in presidential power, paved the way for Portugal's entry into the EEC in 1986. Elected head of the PSD in June 1985, he led the party to victory in elections the following Oct. He retained the position for 10 years, the longest tenure of any democratically elected prime minister in Portuguese history. The PSD won a clear majority of seats in legislative elections in both 1987 and 1991, with analysts attributing Cavaco Silva's success to economic liberalization, tax cuts and the flow of funds from the EEC.

Cavaco Silva stepped down as leader of the PSD prior to the 1995 elections, which were won by the Socialist Party (PS). He contested the 1996 presidential election but, after losing to the Socialist candidate, retired from politics to advise at the Bank of Portugal and teach economics at the Catholic University. In Oct. 2005 he returned to the political fray and announced his candidacy for the forthcoming presidential election. He received 50.5% of the votes cast and was sworn in on 9 March 2006.

Career Peak

Cavaco Silva's victory was a setback for the Socialist prime minister, Jóse Sócrates, who had presided over a period of economic stagnation. However, the result ushered in a new era of 'cohabitation' in politics, with analysts predicting that the two leaders would find common ground to implement economic reform. Although a Roman Catholic, Cavaco Silva endorsed legislation in April 2007 liberalizing abortion and aligning Portuguese law with that of most other European Union countries. In Oct. 2009, following parliamentary elections the previous month, he invited Sócrates to form a new PS government.

In Jan. 2011 Cavaco Silva's re-election as president coincided with a turbulent economic period. High debt levels and flat growth forced the negotiation in May that year of a financial rescue package with stringent deficit reduction conditions from the EU and IMF. Parliamentary elections in June 2011 saw the PS government replaced by a centre-right PSD/Democratic and Social Centre–People's Party coalition. Continuing austerity generated social and labour unrest and undermined the cohesion of the governing coalition—particularly in July 2013 when several senior ministers resigned over the handling of the economic situation—although the administration has survived.

Since Cavaco Silva was constitutionally barred from running for a third consecutive term, the winner of the Jan. 2016 presidential election, Marcelo Rebelo de Sousa, took over in March.

Ceaușescu, Nicolae (Romania)

Introduction

Nicolae Ceaușescu was the Communist leader of Romania from 1965 until 1989. An opponent of excessive intervention from the Soviet Union, he led a more independent foreign policy than many Eastern Bloc nations. However, disastrous domestic policies led to widespread poverty and starvation while Ceaușescu's regime, with the aid of the secret police, became ever more oppressive. He was executed following a revolution in Dec. 1989.

Early Life

Ceaușescu was born on 26 Jan. 1918 in Scornicești in Oltenia, southwest Romania. He was the third of 10 children and at the age of 11 he was employed as a shoemaker's apprentice in Bucharest. By the age of 14 he was a member of the Romanian Workers' Party and the illegal Union of Communist Youth and a year later he had joined the Romanian Communist Party. In 1933 he was arrested for the first time for his political activities and in 1935 he was exiled from Bucharest, though he remained in the city to continue undercover activities. In 1936 he was sentenced to 2 years in prison.

In 1939 Ceaușescu married Elena Petrescu, a fellow communist with whom he would have three children, but in 1940 he was again sent to prison, escaping 4 years later. During this period he shared a cell with Gheorghe Gheorghiu-Dej, who would become Romania's Communist leader in 1952. Following his escape Ceaușescu became Secretary of the Union of Communist Youth and, following the Communists' rise to power in 1947, served as Minister of Agriculture until 1950. He then spent 4 years as Deputy Minister of the Armed Forces before being elected on to the party's Central Committee.

Career Peak

When Gheorghiu-Dej died in March 1965, Ceaușescu was his natural successor as First Secretary of the party. 2 years later he became Chairman of the State Council and Supreme Commander of the Armed Forces. Effectively head of state, he would create the post of President for himself in 1974. Ceaușescu's independent foreign policy initially boosted his popularity. He was highly critical of the Soviet invasion of Czechoslovakia in 1968 and had little involvement in Warsaw Pact activities. In addition, he pursued trade with the West (with Romania enjoying most favoured nation trading status with the US for many years) and established diplomatic relations with West Germany. In later years he was critical of the Soviet invasion of Afghanistan and broke an Eastern Bloc boycott, allowing the Romanian team to attend the 1984 Olympic Games in Los Angeles.

However, his approach to home affairs was more hardline. He established the Securitate, a secret police force of around 60,000 loyal to Ceaușescu.

Opposition was put down ruthlessly and the media forced to endure severe constraints. In 1966 he pushed through a series of reforms outlawing abortion and contraception, making divorce more difficult and imposing punitive taxes on childless couples.

In the 1970s, influenced by meetings with China's Mao Zedong and North Korea's Kim Il-sung, Ceaușescu set about establishing a cult of the personality. He re-enforced this through nepotism, most notably by the promotion of his wife, Elena. In 1975, on the back of an almost entirely manufactured set of qualifications, she was made director of the Institute of Chemistry of the Romanian Academy. Cabinet positions followed and by the time of her death she was the second most powerful person in the country. Her brother was given influential roles in the trade union movement while Ceaușescu's brothers were placed in charge of the armed forces, the intelligence service and the Ministry of Agriculture. His son, Nicu, who was groomed as his successor, was made head of a county government in 1987.

Financial mismanagement during the 1970s led to a huge foreign debt which Ceaușescu set about clearing in the 1980s with disastrous results. Rates of agricultural and industrial production were increased but the results were sent *en masse* for export. Bread rationing was introduced in the early 1980s, followed by rationing of other basic food provisions and energy. The economy went into freefall, starvation became a genuine threat and many citizens died owing to the lack of medical provisions.

Against this background, the Ceaușescus continued with their own lavish lifestyles. Grandiose parties were given in their palaces and food was hoarded while the public starved. In 1984 Ceaușescu cleared 10,000 hectares of land near Bucharest to build Victory of Socialism Boulevard, which was planned to eclipse the Champs Elysees in Paris. He also devised an ill-conceived plan to destroy 7,000 out of around 13,000 villages and relocate the population to urban apartments in the 10 years following 1984. By the end of the 1980s Romania had one of Eastern Europe's lowest standards of living and one of its highest rates of infant mortality.

Riots broke out in the southwestern town of Timisoara on 16 Dec. 1989 and Ceaușescu responded by ordering the shooting and killing of dozens of protesters. The protests then spread to Bucharest. On 21 Dec., captured by television cameras, Ceaușescu was drowned out by calls for change as he tried to give a speech. The army turned against him and the following day he and Elena fled the city. They were captured by the army and there followed a 3 day long secret trial by a military court. Charged with genocide and other crimes against the people, the Ceaușescus refused to acknowledge the legality of the court. On 25 Dec. 1989 Nicolae and Elena Ceaușescu were convicted and executed by firing squad.

Chamoun, Camille (Lebanon)

Introduction

A Maronite (a member of the Christian sect which by political and religious convention holds the state presidency, while the prime minister must be a Sunni Muslim and the speaker of the National Assembly a Shia Muslim), Chamoun was president of Lebanon from 1952–58 and leader of the National Liberal Party (NLP) from 1958–86. He held various other government posts during a long political career that ended in 1987 when he died while still serving as minister of finance.

Early Life

Born on 3 April 1900, Chamoun qualified as a lawyer in 1924. He entered parliament in 1934 and was minister of finance in the pre-war French mandate regime. At independence he was minister of the interior, subsequently serving as a delegate to various United Nations conferences and committees and as Lebanese representative to London. By the late 1940s he was one of the most prominent members of a mainly Christian political faction known as the Constitutional Bloc. In Sept. 1952 a general strike forced the resignation of the then long-serving president Bishara al-Khuri and Chamoun was elected as his successor.

Career Peak

His 6 year presidential term, despite some early constitutional reforms, ended in political turmoil. In the Suez crisis of 1956 Muslim leaders demanded that Chamoun break off relations with Britain and France. His pro-Western alignment contributed to increasing resentment against his Christian-dominated government that erupted into a Muslim insurrection in May 1958. Chamoun appealed to the United States for military assistance and US marines landed near Beirut in July to re-establish government authority. He resisted demands for his resignation but did not seek re-election and left office in Sept. 1958.

Having founded the NPL in 1958, Chamoun retained an influential political role as a radical defender of Maronite Christian interests and was an uncompromising opponent of the Palestine Liberation Organization's presence in Lebanon when civil war broke out in 1975. At that time he rejoined the cabinet, holding several ministerial portfolios until Dec. 1976. He remained leader of the NPL until 1986, when his son Dany succeeded him. However, the party's ascendancy among Maronite Christians had by then been undermined by the rival right-wing Phalangist Party. In April 1984 he returned to government as minister of finance and died in office of a heart attack on 7 Aug. 1987.

Charles, Eugenia (Dominica)

Introduction

Dame Mary Eugenia Charles, nicknamed the 'Iron Lady of the Caribbean' was prime minister from 1980 to 1995.

Early Life

Mary Eugenia Charles was born on 15 May 1919 in the village of Pointe Michel in Dominica. She studied law at the University of Toronto in Canada and at the London School of Economics in the UK. After being called to the bar, she returned home to set up a practice specializing in property law, becoming Dominica's first female lawyer.

In the 1960s she campaigned against the ruling Labour Party, helping to found the Dominica Freedom Party (DFP) in 1968. She entered the House of Assembly in 1970 and became leader of the DFP 2 years later. Dominica gained formal independence in 1978 and, amid growing popular discontent with the government, the party won the country's first post-independence general election in June 1980. Charles thus became the Caribbean's first female prime minister.

Career Peak

She initiated reforms to the economy, education and health, as well as vowing to tackle government corruption. Corrupt officials were dismissed and the nation's 200-strong defence force was disbanded after military officials were found to have authorized an illegal arms deal. Charles also oversaw a reduction in spiralling inflation and cut the balance of trade deficit by a half. She secured aid to bolster the banana-dependent economy and improved transport infrastructure.

On the international stage, she served as the chair of the Organization of Eastern Caribbean States (OECS), appealing for US intervention following the execution of Grenada's prime minister, Maurice Bishop, in a coup in 1983. Having herself survived two attempted coups during her first term in office, she won renewed mandates in 1985 and 1990. However, against a backdrop of rising unemployment, she opted not to contest the 1995 election.

Later Life

After retiring from frontline politics, Charles lectured in international relations and forged close ties with the Carter Center, the human rights organization founded by the former US president, Jimmy Carter. Charles was made a Dame Commander of the British Empire in 1991 and died on 6 Sept. 2005.

Chávez, Hugo (Venezuela)

Introduction

Hugo Rafael Chávez Frías of the Movimiento V República (Movement for the Fifth Republic/MVR—which he founded in 1997) was elected president in Dec. 1998 as the candidate for the left-wing 'Patriotic Pole' coalition. Although re-elected in 2000, he was subsequently challenged by anti-government protests and a failed coup. He was nevertheless re-elected again at the end of 2006. In Dec. 2007 he suffered his first defeat in a popular vote when proposals to extend his powers and accelerate his socialist revolution were rejected in a referendum. His further re-election in Oct. 2012 was soon overshadowed by a serious relapse in his health, and his failure to attend his scheduled official inauguration in Jan. 2013 heightened concerns about his ability to resume his presidential duties.

Early Life

The son of teachers, Chávez was born on 28 July 1954 in Sabaneta, Barinas state. Embarking on a military career, he completed his higher education at the Academia Militar de Venezuela, graduating in 1975 with a degree in military science. After further military training, he took a master's degree in social science at the Universidad Simón Bolívar.

In 1982 Chávez co-founded the MBR-200, based on the ideals of the independence hero, Simón Bolívar. In Feb. 1992 Chávez led an abortive military coup attempting to overthrow the government of Carlos Andrés Pérez. He was captured and imprisoned until 1994 when he was pardoned by President Rafael Caldera. Having reformed the MBR-200 as the Movement for the Fifth Republic/MVR, he promised to fight social inequality in Venezuela, a country rich in natural resources but where the wealth benefited the minority elite. By 1998 over 90% of Venezuelans lived below the poverty line, social services had deteriorated to pre-1950s levels and inflation was high.

In Nov. 1998 Chávez's Patriotic Pole coalition won 34% of seats in legislative elections. The following month he ran for the presidency against the Proyecto Venezuela candidate, Henrique Salas Romer. With the highest majority for 40 years, Chávez won 56.5% of votes to 39.5%. His win ended the 40-year domination of Acción Democrática (Democratic Action) and the Partido Social Cristiano (Social Christian Party).

Career Peak

On election, Chávez pledged to modernize the government, root out corruption, implement radical reforms and revive the economy. In April 1999 he called a referendum in which 92% of voters called for a new constitution. In July elections to the constitutional assembly, Chávez supporters won 121 seats against ten for the opposition. A second referendum was called for Dec. in which 72% approved a new constitution, modelled on France's Fifth Republic. The two-tiered congress was combined into one National Assembly, the presidential term was extended from 5 to 6 years, presidential power over legislation and the budget was increased, and a second consecutive presidential term was permitted. Further changes included a reformed judiciary, an extension of universal economic and social rights, increased rights for indigenous Venezuelans, and more military involvement in policy implementation. Despite Chávez's popular support, members of the business community and the middle classes were wary of the power granted the president and US $4 bn. was transferred out of the country. Nonetheless, a rise in oil prices compensated for this financial loss and inflation fell, although the country suffered a recession following the 1998 economic crisis. Disastrous mudslides in Dec. 1999 in which tens of thousands of people died brought further financial strain for the government.

In the July 2000 presidential elections Chávez beat his former ally from the 1992 coup Lt.-Col. Francisco Arias Cárdenas with 59.8% of votes to 37.5%. His MVR party was equally successful in regional elections. Opposition candidates claimed the votes had been rigged and the military was called in to disperse protestors. On re-election Chávez pledged to fight unemployment with public spending, introduce a land rights bill to ease rural poverty, offer tax breaks for businesses, build new schools and encourage foreign investment. Though lacking a MVR majority in the assembly, Chávez was able to secure wide legislative powers. One of his first moves was to seek a union with the oil-producing Arab states which would reject Western pressure for increased output (and thus lower prices). In Sept. he made his international position clear by criticizing US involvement in Colombian military efforts to combat left-wing rebels (the Fuerzas Armadas Revolucionarias de Colombia or FARC), and by praising Cuban leader Fidel Castro's defiant rejection of US domination, as well as his economic and social policies. During a visit by Castro, Chávez agreed to sell oil to Cuba at a discounted price. In April 2001 Chávez hosted talks with Mexico and Colombia to pursue the implementation of a free trade zone, and to work towards extending free trade throughout the Americas. Despite international fears of a Castro reincarnate, he also visited the USA and Europe on numerous occasions.

As his 'Bolivarian Revolution' failed to produce the promised social and economic improvements, the country became increasingly divided between Chávez's supporters and opponents. In April 2002 anti-government protesters descended on the capital demanding his resignation. Taking advantage of the instability, a military coup was mounted with businessman Pedro Carmona Estanga at its head. Chávez was forced to resign and Carmona assumed the presidency. Western and Latin American governments (but not the USA) condemned the coup, refusing to acknowledge the new government, and protests by Chávez supporters quickly led to his reinstatement.

Nevertheless, Venezuelans remained polarized and more protests were staged in June and July. In Dec. 2002 a national strike was called by the opposition following a decision by the Supreme Court to overrule a referendum on Chávez's presidency called for Feb. 2003 by the Electoral Council. Protests focused on the state-owned petrol company Petróleos de Venezuela (PDVSA), the provider of around 40% of the country's revenues. Oil production plummeted and world prices increased, causing OPEC to increase production. The strike continued into 2003, threatening to destabilize the country's economy, but Chávez remained defiant. The strike abated in Feb. 2003, although workers at PDVSA continued to protest and the opposition petitioned for early elections.

In Aug. 2004 Chávez survived a national referendum on whether he should be allowed to serve the remainder of his term of office until 2006. Although credited with about 59% of the vote, opposition parties denounced the victory as electoral fraud. Then, in parliamentary elections in Dec. 2005 boycotted by the opposition, his MVR party won 114 of 167 National Assembly seats, with the remaining seats being won by his allies.

In Dec. 2006 Chávez won a third presidential term, defeating the main opposition candidate Manuel Rosales with 63% of the vote in the election. Pledging to maintain his socialist revolution, including widespread nationalization, he was granted sweeping powers by parliament at the end of Jan. 2007 to legislate by decree for an 18-month period. In the same month he announced that key energy and telecommunications utilities would be nationalized and in May the government took control of oil projects in the Orinoco Delta. Nationalizations continued into 2008, including in the banking, cement, steel and fuel sectors.

Popular discontent meanwhile surfaced over the closure in May 2007 of Radio Caracas Televisión (RCTV), the country's most popular-but anti-Chávez-television channel, which provoked large domestic demonstrations as well as international condemnation. Then in Dec. the president's proposal to reform the constitution and allow him to run for continuous re-election and to reinforce his socialist agenda was unexpectedly rejected by voters in a national referendum. Some disaffection with Chávez was also reflected in opposition gains in regional and mayoral elections in Nov. 2008. However, in a further constitutional referendum in Feb. 2009, there was a 54% majority in favour of abolishing presidential limits, clearing the way for Chávez to run for re-election in 2012.

In 2007 Colombia's president Uribe invited Chávez to try and broker a peace deal with the FARC. However, Uribe subsequently ended Chávez's involvement after a series of apparent diplomatic breaches. Relations between the two countries then deteriorated sharply in March 2008 after Colombian armed forces raided a FARC base in Ecuador, a Venezuelan ally. Chávez mobilized troops along Venezuelan-Colombian border and briefly threatened war before the crisis was defused diplomatically. Bilateral tensions resurfaced in late 2009 as US-Colombian plans for closer military ties in a drive against drug trafficking culminated in an agreement allowing US forces the use of Colombian bases, and escalated again in mid-2010 when diplomatic relations were temporarily severed.

As an oil-producing economy Venezuela suffered from the fall in the international price of oil that accompanied the global economic downturn from 2008. The economy continued to shrink in 2009 (by 5.8% in the last 3 months of the year alone) and in Jan. 2010 Chávez devalued the currency

against the US dollar (by up to 50% under a dual exchange rate) to boost revenue from oil exports. The downturn nevertheless persisted and in Jan. 2011 the government devalued the currency for the second time in a year while unifying the exchange rate.

Meanwhile, there were increasing signs of popular discontent with Chávez's rule. In Jan. 2010 the resignation of the vice president and defence minister, Ramón Carrizález, prompted speculation about tensions within the regime. Then, in congressional elections in Sept. 2010, the PSUV retained control but lost the two-thirds majority in parliament needed to carry out constitutional changes and make judicial appointments as the opposition made significant gains. However, Chávez was able to by-pass this setback as the outgoing congress approved measures at the end of the year allowing him to rule by decree again for 18 months and to appoint new Supreme Court judges. The opposition claimed that this amounted to a coup by the executive against the other branches of government.

In June-July 2011 Chávez underwent surgery for cancer in Cuba but on his return to Venezuela said that he would stand as his party's candidate in presidential elections scheduled for Oct. 2012. He had further treatment for his condition in Cuba in Feb. and April 2012 before his re-election for a fourth term in Oct. with 55% of the vote. However, in Nov. he was forced to return to Cuba for more cancer surgery and his inauguration ceremony was subsequently postponed. Vice-President and Minister of Foreign Affairs Nicolás Maduro, whom Chávez had named in Dec. 2012 as his preferred political successor, delivered the state-of-the-nation address to the National Assembly on the president's behalf in Jan. 2013.

Chávez's last public appearance was in Dec. shortly before he travelled to Cuba to undergo a fourth surgery. He returned home 2 months later but almost no information on his condition was revealed. Chávez was officially announced dead on 5 March. Seven days of mourning followed and elections were to be held in 30 days. Chávez had named vice president Nicolás Maduro as his successor, despite the constitution stating that in such cases the National Assembly President should assume temporary power.

Chehab, Fuad (Lebanon)

Introduction

Fuad Chehab, commander of the Lebanese army, succeeded Camille Chamoun as state president in Sept. 1958 in the wake of widespread sectarian conflict between Lebanon's Christian and Muslim communities. His term in office ended in 1964 and he was widely credited with restoring political stability and promoting economic and infrastructure development.

Early Life

Chehab was born in 1902 in Ghazir. Pursuing a military career, he served with French mandatory forces in Syria after World War I and by 1945 was commander of the Lebanese army.

Career Peak

Having adopted a non-partisan stance as military commander during the internal unrest at the end of Chamoun's term, Chehab enjoyed support from Christian and Muslim factions alike. He was elected by the National Assembly at the end of July 1958 and assumed presidential office on 23 Sept. While observing the terms of the 1943 national pact determining the allocation of political power between the main religious communities, he instituted some electoral reform and increased the membership of the National Assembly to encourage wider direct representation. In foreign affairs he effected the prompt withdrawal of the US troops deployed towards the end of his predecessor's presidency. Thereafter he followed a neutral foreign policy, with the aim of maintaining good relations with Arab as well as Western nations. Limited opposition to his regime was reflected in a coup attempt in 1961 by an extremist party advocating the creation of a greater Syria of several Arab states. Chehab rejected appeals that he should run for the presidency again, despite a parliamentary proposal for a constitutional amendment allowing him a second term. He left office in Sept. 1964 and died on 25 April 1973 in Beirut.

Chernenko, Konstantin (Russia)

Introduction

Konstantin Chernenko led the Soviet Union between 1984 and 1985. A favourite of Brezhnev, he was defeated in the 1982 contest to succeed him as general secretary by Yuri Andropov. Chernenko came to office after the death of Andropov in 1984 but was soon beset by ill-health and achieved little while in office.

Early Life

Konstantin Ustinovich Chernenko was born on 24 Sept. 1911 (11 Sept. by the Orthodox calendar) in Bolshaya Tes in the Yeniseysk region of Russia. In 1930 he served with the frontier guards on the Sino-Soviet border. The following year he joined the Communist Party, having joined Komsomol (the junior branch of the party) 5 years earlier.

He became a producer of propaganda for Stalin and in 1941 was named director of the Krasnoyarsk territorial party committee. He attended the higher school for party organizers from 1943 until 1945 and 8 years later completed his studies at the Kishinev pedagogical institute. Between 1948 and 1956 he was responsible for agitation and propaganda for Moldavia. In 1956, having gained the notice of Leonid Brezhnev, he took up an equivalent position in Moscow. When Brezhnev became general secretary in 1964 he appointed Chernenko chief-of-staff. Chernenko became a full member of the central committee 7 years later and in 1978 won full membership of the politburo.

As it became apparent during 1982 that Brezhnev's health was rapidly deteriorating, Chernenko began to rally support to succeed him. However, in Nov. 1982 he was defeated by Yuri Andropov, who was able to call on support from the KGB (which he had previously headed) and the emerging generation of reformers (including Mikhail Gorbachev). Andropov was immediately beset by ill health and when he died in Feb. 1984 Chernenko was selected to replace him as general secretary.

Career Peak

Chernenko also assumed the chairmanship of the Presidium of the Supreme Soviet in April 1984. Gorbachev, Andropov's favoured successor, was promoted to second in the party hierarchy. Chernenko was widely perceived as a conservative throwback to the stagnation of the later Brezhnev years. Domestically he achieved little and party privilege remained undiminished. In foreign policy he brokered trade agreements with China but relations with Ronald Reagan's US deteriorated, despite agreement in Jan. 1985 to a new round of arms talks. Chernenko suffered from poor health throughout his tenure and died in Moscow on 10 March 1985.

Chiang Kai-shek (Taiwan, China)

Introduction

Chiang Kai-shek (transliterated as Chiang Chieh-shih in the modern Wade-Giles romanisation) was leader of the Nationalist government of China from 1928 to 1949 and President from 1928 to 1931 and from 1943 to 1949. Defeated in the civil war against the Communists (1946–49), Chiang fled with the remains of his forces to Taiwan where he continued to style himself President of the Republic of China until his death in 1975.

Chiang was born on 31 Oct. 1887 in Zhejiang province into a prosperous commercial and farming family. He trained for a military career, first at a military academy in northern China (1906–07) and then in Japan (1907–11), where he met young Chinese who were conspiring against the Manchu imperial dynasty. Chiang became a convert to revolutionary ideas. When the 1911 uprising against the emperor broke out, Chiang returned home.

Early Life

Chiang took part in the fighting that overthrew the imperial system and was equally involved with the revolutionaries against the authoritarian president, Yuan Shih-kai, in 1913–16. In 1918 Chiang joined Sun Yat-sen's Nationalist Party and became Sun's close ally. Following the overthrow of Yuan, China disintegrated at the hands of local warlords. Sun reorganised the party on Soviet lines and sent Chiang to Moscow to study the Soviet system and Red Army in 1923. Returning to China, Chiang was placed in charge of a military academy at Huangpu, near Guangzhou, and built an effective army. At this stage the Nationalists were co-operating with the Communists to re-establish national unity, but rivalry between the two parties increased, particularly after the death of Sun in 1925.

As commander in chief of the Nationalist army from 1925, Chiang's power grew. In April 1927, he tried to suppress the Chinese Communist Party in a bloody campaign in which thousands of Communists were slaughtered. The remains of the party fled to the far western province of Jiangxi, beyond the reach of the Nationalists. In 1928 Chiang's army entered Beijing. With the greater part of the country reunited under Chiang's rule, he formed a government in Nanjing, which became the capital of China.

Career Peak

Chiang's power was illusory. The Communists controlled part of the southwest where they had established a Chinese Soviet Republic, the warlords could rebel again at any time and, in 1931, the Japanese invaded and occupied Manchuria. Chiang ignored the Japanese, concentrating on crushing the Communists. After a long campaign, the noose tightened round the Communist "statelet" but its leaders and a sizeable army escaped across China on the Long March (1934–35). Attempting to revive national unity, Chiang reinstated Confucianism as the state religion in 1934—although he was a Christian. In Dec. 1936 Chiang was kidnapped by military leaders who wanted to confront Japan rather than the Communists.

The full-scale invasion of China by the Japanese in 1937 obliged Chiang to call a truce with the Communists to face the common enemy. Compared with the Communists, Chiang's armies made little headway against the Japanese. In 1938 Chiang removed his capital to Chongqing, where he sat out the war. After the defeat of Japan following the use of nuclear weapons on Hiroshima and Nagasaki by the United States, Nationalists and Communists began negotiations concerning the future shape of China's government. But the talks broke down and civil war resumed in 1946. A crushing series of defeats led to the Communist victory. Chiang retreated to Taiwan with the remains of his forces.

Backed by the United States, Chiang insisted that he continued in office as President of the Republic of China. But his territory had been reduced to the island of Taiwan and a few small islands off the coast of China. Still technically at war with the Communists, Chiang maintained martial war and ruled as a dictator. American aid allowed Chiang to achieve remarkable economic development and soon Taiwan had a much higher standard of living than mainland China. Despite a defence pact with the USA in 1955, which guaranteed American assistance if the Communists should attack Taiwan, a rapprochement between Washington and Beijing troubled Chiang's final years. He died on 5 April 1975, 4 years before the United States severed its diplomatic ties with the Nationalists.

Chichester-Clark, James (Northern Ireland, United Kingdom)

Introduction

James Chichester-Clark was prime minister of Northern Ireland from April 1969–March 1971, a period of growing sectarian conflict. In 1969 he called in British troops to quell unrest, an act widely considered the start of 'the Troubles'. Chichester-Clark resigned in 1971 amid the polarization of Northern Ireland's politics.

Early Life

James Chichester-Clark was born on 12 Feb. 1923 in Moyola Park, Castledawson, Londonderry. His landowning family was prominent in Unionist politics and had regularly held the South Londonderry constituency. Educated at Eton College, Chichester-Clark joined the Irish Guards in 1942, serving in North Africa and Italy during the Second World War. In 1947 he was appointed Aide-de-camp to Lord Alexander of Tunis, then governor general of Canada. Following tours of duty in Germany and Egypt, he left the army in 1960 and succeeded his grandmother as Unionist MP for South Londonderry.

In 1963 he was appointed chief whip and in 1966 became leader of the Commons and a full cabinet member. From 1967–69 he served as minister of agriculture, offering qualified support to Prime Minister Terence O'Neill's policies of warmer relations with the Republic of Ireland and civil rights reform. In April 1969 Chichester-Clark resigned in protest at the introduction of 'one man one vote' in local government elections. This precipitated O'Neill's resignation on 28 Aug. Chichester-Clark won the leadership election against Brian Faulkner by 17–16, with O'Neill using his casting vote for Chichester-Clark.

Career Peak

He made an early effort to promote harmony by granting an amnesty for those charged with political offences since Oct. 1968. However, conflict escalated and Aug. 1969 saw riots in Londonderry and Belfast. The Royal Ulster Constabulary (RUC) and its auxiliary forces, particularly the B Specials, were accused of helping loyalists attack Catholic neighbourhoods. Over 1000 Catholic and 300 Protestant families fled their homes. On 14 Aug. Chichester-Clark called in British troops and the UK army took control of security operations in the province.

An uneasy calm soon prompted resentment among Catholics, who saw the troops as pro-Loyalist. By late 1969 paramilitary organizations, including the provisional IRA and the Protestant Ulster Volunteer Force (UVF), were carrying out attacks. Meanwhile, under pressure from the UK government, Chichester-Clark reorganized the police force and enacted reforms in housing and local government, angering many Unionists.

In 1970 breakaway Unionist parties campaigned against his leadership. In March 1971, after the IRA had killed three soldiers and the British government had turned down his request for draconian intervention, Chichester-Clark resigned.

Later Life

Given a life peerage as Baron Moyola of Castledawson, Chichester-Clark returned to Moyola Park and retired from public life. In 1998 he endorsed the Good Friday Agreement, which laid the foundations for power sharing. He died on 17 May 2002.

Chiluba, Frederick (Zambia)

Introduction

Frederick Chiluba, Zambia's first elected president following the return of multi-party democracy, held office from 1991–2002. Initially welcomed by the West, his tenure became mired in allegations of embezzlement and corruption.

Early Life

The son of a copper miner, Frederick Jacob Titus Chiluba was born on 30 April 1943 in Kitwe, in what was then Northern Rhodesia (now Zambia). After expulsion from secondary school for political activism, Chiluba worked as a sisal cutter, a bus driver, a city councillor and an accounts assistant. He joined the Zambia Congress of Trade Unions, eventually becoming its president. In 1981 Chiluba, along with several other opposition figures, was detained by President Kenneth Kaunda for calling a wildcat strike that paralyzed the economy. The detentions were declared unconstitutional by the judiciary and Chiluba was released after 3 months.

In 1990 he co-founded the Movement for Multiparty Democracy (MMC), a loose coalition of unions, civic and church groups and former government loyalists disillusioned with Kaunda's autocratic rule. In the first mulit-party elections since 1968, Chiluba won the presidency with 76% of the vote. Initially Chiluba was widely hailed for bringing an end to the country's one-party rule and was welcomed by the West for halting Kaunda's 27 years in power.

Career Peak

Once in office, Chiluba sought to rescue the failing economy and usher in a free market system. Import duties were slashed, currency controls abolished and copper mines privatized. However, these policies failed to deliver the hoped-for results and the majority of the population remained in poverty.

A charismatic speaker and born-again Christian, Chiluba originally positioned himself as a defender of civil liberties while deriding Kaunda's authoritarian approach. However, he adopted increasingly similar tactics against political opponents, jailing journalists and firing colleagues who dared to criticize him. In 1997 he imprisoned Kaunda for allegedly conspiring in a coup against him, before attempting to deport the former president and strip him of his citizenship.

In 1996 Chiluba was elected for a second 5 year term. His subsequent move to amend the constitution to allow for a third term failed to win support and sparked public protests. Consequently, Chiluba reluctantly left office at the end of his term in Jan. 2002. He was replaced by his vice president, Levy Mwanawasa.

Later Life

Mwanawasa proceeded to lift Chiluba's immunity from prosecution and targeted the former president in an anti-corruption drive. In Feb. 2003 Chiluba was charged, along with several other former ministers and senior officials, with embezzlement, amid claims he stole public funds to finance his extravagant lifestyle (he was accused of spending over US$500,000 on jewellery and clothing). After 6 years of drawn-out court proceedings, he was acquitted. However, in 2007 a UK civil court found him guilty of theft and money laundering through London and ordered him to repay US$58m.

Following the death of Mwanawasa in 2008, Rupiah Banda, a close friend of Chiluba, became president and the ruling, which Chiluba rejected on the basis of the court lacking jurisdiction, was never enforced. Nevertheless, others close to Chiluba, including his wife, were convicted on related charges. On 18 June 2011 Chiluba died of heart and kidney failure in Lusaka.

Chinchilla, Laura (Costa Rica)

Introduction

Laura Chinchilla was elected Costa Rica's first female president in Feb. 2010, continuing the centre-right National Liberation Party's (PLN) hold on government. A former justice minister, she has won praise for her attempts to tackle drug networks and improve public security.

Early Life

Laura Chinchilla Miranda was born on 28 March 1959 in Desamparados, a suburb of the capital, San José. She graduated in political science from the University of Costa Rica in 1981 and went on to earn a master's in public administration from Georgetown University in the USA. Returning to Costa Rica, she worked as a consultant to various international organizations including the US Agency for International Development, the UN Development Program and the Inter-American Development Bank, on issues such as public safety, border security, human rights and judicial reform.

Consultancy for the ministry of national planning and economic policy in the early 1990s led to Chinchilla being offered a senior role in government. In May 1994 she was appointed deputy minister of public security in the administration of José María Figueres Olsen, whose PLN had won the general election 3 months earlier. Chinchilla also led the national council of migration and foreign affairs and was a member of the board of the national drug council. She was promoted to minister for public security in 1996 and gained a reputation for her tough stance on criminal drugs activities.

Chinchilla was elected to the legislative assembly as a deputy for the province of San José in 2002 and served as vice-president under Oscar Arias of the PLN. Arias, who had served as president in the late 1980s and was awarded the Nobel Peace Prize for his contribution to democracy and peace in central America, enjoyed popular support and won a further term in Jan. 2006. Chinchilla served as both vice-president and justice minister until she left office in Oct. 2008 to mount a presidential campaign. She emerged victorious after the first round on 7 Feb. 2010, taking 47% of the vote, well ahead of nearest rival Ottón Solís of the left-leaning Citizens' Action Party on 25%.

Career Peak

Chinchilla was sworn in on 8 May 2010. She pledged to make Costa Rica the first developed country in Central America, confirmed her commitment to carbon neutrality by 2021 and promised to improve health care, safety and security.

In Nov. 2010 a dispute with neighbouring Nicaragua over a river border area led to the deployment of security forces by both countries. In March 2011 the International Court of Justice ruled that all troops should be withdrawn from the area in a judgment viewed as favouring Costa Rica.

Luis Guillermo Solís of the PAC succeeded Chinchilla as president after winning elections held in Feb. 2014. Since the constitution prohibits an incumbent president from serving successive terms, Chinchilla was not eligible to stand for re-election.

Chirac, Jacques (France)

Introduction

President Jacques René Chirac was elected president in 1995 on the ticket of the right-wing Gaullist party, Rassemblement pour la République (Rally for the Republic; RPR), of which he was the founder. He was prime minister under the right-wing Républicains Indépendants president Valéry Giscard d'Estaing between 1974–76 before resigning to form the RPR. Between 1986–88 he was again prime minister under Socialist Party (PS) president François Mitterrand. He was mayor of Paris between 1977–95. In the 2002 presidential elections he stood for re-election as the candidate of the UMP (Union pour la Majorité Presidentielle) right-wing coalition. Following the shock success of National Front candidate Jean-Marie Le Pen, popular opinion rallied around Chirac in the second round run-off, which he won with a landslide majority. He subsequently disbanded the RPR and formalized the UMP as the Union pour un Mouvement Populaire (Union for a Popular Movement). His opposition to US pressure for a war on Iraq in 2003 won him domestic popularity but led to a deterioration of relations with the USA and UK.

The French electorate's rejection in a referendum in May 2005 of the proposed EU constitution was a major political setback for Chirac, prompting his appointment of a new government. Later in the year, confronting the social devastation left by rioting during Oct.–Nov., Chirac asked parliament to extend a national state of emergency and pledged to fight unemployment and discrimination among disadvantaged sections of the population. However, unpopular labour legislation caused further unrest in spring 2006 and his political standing declined markedly through the year.

Early Life

Chirac was born in Paris on 29 Nov. 1932. The son of a banker, he was educated at the Institut d'Études Politiques de Paris before studying business at a Harvard University summer school. He was in Algeria for his national service between 1956–57. From 1957–59 he studied at the École Nationale d'Administration, the elite training institution for civil servants. As a young man Chirac was inclined to left-wing politics but his sympathies shifted right when he embarked on his career in the civil service. Chirac rose swiftly through the ranks of the civil service, becoming head of department and secretary of state. In 1967 he was elected parliamentary representative of his family's native Corrèze in Limousin, a post he held until he became president in 1995. Chirac was a close ally and protégé of former president Georges Pompidou, who supported Chirac's rise through the party and his election to the National Assembly in 1967. During Pompidou's premiership

under the presidency of Charles de Gaulle, Chirac aided Pompidou in resolving the May 1968 student-worker revolts.

Chirac's career advanced further after Pompidou became president. He served as minister for parliamentary relations (1971–72), agriculture minister (1972–74) and minister for the interior (1974). In the 1974 presidential elections Chirac refused to support the candidature of the official Gaullist candidate, Jacques Chaban-Delmas, choosing instead to support the successful right-wing Républicains Indépendants candidate, Valéry Giscard d'Estaing. The latter appointed Chirac prime minister in 1974 but he was soon at odds with the president and resigned in 1976. He then founded the RPR, based on de Gaulle's Rassemblement du Peuple Français (Rally of the French People) party. Between 1976–81 the RPR was well represented in the National Assembly.

In 1977 Chirac was elected Mayor of Paris, the first since the post was abolished in 1871. In 1981 Chirac stood in his first presidential election against François Mitterrand and Giscard d'Estaing. The right divided, Mitterrand won and Chirac came third. Between 1981–86 Chirac led the right-wing opposition in the Assembly. In 1986 the PS lost its majority and Chirac was appointed prime minister in the first *cohabitation* (power sharing). Over the next 2 years Chirac reversed Mitterrand's policy of nationalization, implementing widespread privatization schemes and abolishing the wealth tax. In 1988 he stood again for the presidency. In a run-off with Mitterrand, Chirac came second with 46% of votes. Over the next 7 years he remained mayor of Paris.

Career Peak

In 1995 Chirac stood for his third presidential election against the PS candidate Lionel Jospin and the prime minister and fellow RPR member Édouard Balladur. The latter had proved a popular prime minister and had the support of the right-wing Union pour la Démocratie Française (Union for the French Democracy). Chirac lost some right-wing support by defending the Maastricht Treaty which allowed for a closer European Union. But with strong campaigning, helped by a financial scandal involving Balladur, he came out ahead in the first round. In the second round run-off with Jospin, Chirac gained 52.6% of votes. Alain Juppé replaced Chirac as RPR president.

The first few months of Chirac's presidency were overshadowed by international condemnation of France for controversial nuclear tests in the Pacific Ocean. Reaction was such that Chile and New Zealand recalled their ambassadors and riots broke out in Tahiti. A poll showed 60% of French people against the testing and Chirac's popularity suffered. The timing of the testing was all the more controversial as it threatened the 1996 Comprehensive Nuclear Test-Ban Treaty.

Chirac went on to end conscription and to reform the military and the health service. To qualify for the European Monetary Union, the government needed to reduce budget deficits. He began a series of spending cuts including a reduction in welfare and a freezing of public-sector wages. Public discontent was coupled with rising unemployment which reached 12.6% by 1997. Chirac dissolved the Assembly and called early elections, hoping to gain support for his policies. The result was the loss of the parliamentary majority to a coalition of Socialists, Communists and Greens. Chirac was forced to appoint the Socialist Lionel Jospin prime minister in a second *cohabitation*.

The end of 2000 was difficult for Chirac. Allegations of corruption centred on the claim that when Chirac was mayor of Paris, bribes from building companies had been taken in exchange for construction and maintenance contracts. An estimated €95 m. was extorted, 70% of which went to the RPR, the rest being divided between the PS and the Parti Communiste Français (French Communist Party). In Sept. 2000 a posthumous confession from a former property developer and RPR official, Jean-Claude Méry, claimed the RPR had been bolstered by €5.5–6.5 m. a year. Although Chirac as the head of state is exempt from prosecution, his former aide, Michel Roussin, was investigated and imprisoned for refusing to answer questions.

Chirac's chairmanship of the 2000 EU summit in Nice was widely criticized. It was claimed that he was too much concerned with national interest, fighting hard to retain France's voting power against demands for votes to be allocated relative to population.

The 18 March 2001 municipal elections led to a shock left-wing victory in Paris, traditionally held by the right. The alleged corruption of the Chirac years was a major factor. In June 2001 an investigation began into how Chirac spent an alleged 2.4 m. francs on family air travel tickets while he was mayor in the early 1990s.

Chirac entered the first round presidential elections in April 2002 expecting to fight Jospin in the second round. But in a shock result, the

National Front leader Jean-Marie Le Pen came in second with 16.86% of votes to Chirac's 19.87%. Jospin, who came third with 16.17%, promptly resigned as prime minister and leader of the PS. The result caused a series of anti-Le Pen protest rallies across France and jolted voter apathy for the second round, for which the turnout was 79.7%. Socialist leaders urged their supporters to vote for Chirac and moderate voters, frightened by the prospect of a far-right government, rallied to the president. In a landslide victory, Chirac took 82.21% of votes. The success was consolidated in parliamentary elections the following month, giving Chirac control of policy for the first time in 5 years. He appointed Jean-Pierre Raffarin as his prime minister.

For his second presidential term, Chirac pledged to tackle crime and bolster national security—both issues which Le Pen had highlighted to his advantage—with increased prison capacity and a strengthened police force. He proposed a business-friendly fiscal policy and a more flexible integration of the 35-h working week, which had troubled many businesses. He also pledged to cut taxes by a third over his term. On the international stage, Chirac won domestic support but courted US anger for his refusal to support the US stance on Iraq. As one of the five countries in the UN with the power of veto, Chirac held the right to block UN-supported military action in Iraq. His position also found support in Algeria, which he visited in March 2003 on the first official visit by a French head of state since the end of the Franco–Algerian War in 1962. In May 2003 there were widespread strikes in protest at plans to increase pension contributions, raise the retirement age and to reduce benefits.

On Bastille Day 2002 Chirac survived an assassination attempt by a far-right extremist. In 2003 he came under the international spotlight again by threatening to veto any US-brokered UN resolution supporting an armed attack on Iraq. US-led troops invaded Iraq in March 2003 without a clear UN mandate and overthrew the Saddam Hussein regime the following month. France, Germany and Russia were among the most vociferous opponents of the war and the breakdown in relations between the USA and what it called 'Old Europe' led to renewed questions over the role of the UN, NATO and the EU in international politics. However, in May 2003 France voted to accept a UN resolution on Iraq's future which had been jointly proposed by the USA, UK and Spain. Chirac justified this acceptance as France's responsibility to the world, although he continued to emphasize the importance of the UN as an organization to prevent countries acting in isolation. In return for the immediate ending of sanctions, the UN was to co-operate with the occupying forces to form a new government. In addition France would be able to complete longstanding contracts with Iraq.

In July 2003 voters in a referendum in Corsica narrowly rejected plans to increase regional autonomy. Under the proposals, Corsica would have established a single regional assembly (streamlining three existing institutions) and would have won limited control over energy, transport and regional aid. Chirac had declared his support for the motion, but campaigning became dominated by the question of eventual full independence. In the same month Chirac caused consternation among several of the EU's smaller nations by calling for a relaxation of the stability and growth pact rules, under which the budget deficit of euro-zone countries is not to exceed 3% of GDP.

Despite the EU's emphasis on France reducing its deficit, the government endorsed €3.3 bn. worth of tax cuts in Sept. 2003. In March 2004 the governing party suffered local election defeats, resulting in the UMP holding on to only one of the 21 mainland regions. Despite the losses, Chirac urged ministers to press on with reforms aiming to boost economic growth, create more jobs and improve the healthcare system.

At the June 2004 European summit clashes occurred between France and the UK as Chirac and Prime Minister Tony Blair disagreed on the proposed new EU constitution and on candidates for the European Commission presidency. Also in June, Chirac rejected tentative US calls for NATO to become more involved in Iraq following the handover of power.

In May 2005 the French electorate voted against the new EU constitution in a referendum. Although it was a bitter defeat for Chirac, he resisted calls to stand down and responded by appointing a new government with Dominique de Villepin as the prime minister. Further discontent with his government was apparent during Oct.–Nov. in a 24-h national strike against the privatization programme and pension reform plans and in rioting across many French towns and cities. The riots started in the poorer suburbs of Paris before spreading more widely, leading to extensive destruction and the introduction of emergency security powers. Having been criticized for his silence during the riots, Chirac made his first formal speech on the subject as the disturbances subsided in mid-Nov. He confirmed that the government would extend the state of emergency by 3 months, but also pledged to improve life in the deprived suburbs. Acknowledging that the violence had highlighted a 'profound malaise' in France, he spoke of the need to recognise 'the diversity of French society'. There was further unrest in spring 2006 as new government proposals giving employers greater freedom to hire and fire young people triggered weeks of street demonstrations and strikes across the country, ultimately leading to the scrapping of the legislation.

In Sept. 2005 Chirac spent a few days in hospital after what officials called a vascular incident affecting his sight.

Later Life

On leaving office, Chirac was appointed a life-long member of the Constitutional Council of France. He also established the Jacques Chirac Foundation for Sustainable Development and Cultural Dialogue. Having lost his immunity from investigation, Chirac was questioned by police in connection with allegations that during his tenure as mayor of Paris the city authority was paying salaries to individuals not working for the city. On 7 March 2011 he was scheduled to stand trial on charges of embezzlement and breach of trust but hearings were suspended the next day following a legal challenge. He was the first current of former French head of state since the Second World War to stand trial. On 15 Dec. 2011 the Paris court declared Chirac guilty and gave him a 2-year suspended prison sentence for diverting public funds and abusing public confidence. Despite reiterating his innocence, the former French president announced that he would not seek appeal owing to ill health.

In Nov. 2009 the first volume of his memoirs was published to notable success.

Chissano, Joaquim (Mozambique)

Introduction

One of the founding members of the Mozambique Liberation Front (FRELIMO), Joaquim Chissano served as prime minister of the transitional government that led the country to independence in 1975, and was Mozambique's second president from 1986–2005. He was credited with transforming Mozambique from a war-torn state into one of Africa's more stable, modernising and democratic nations.

Early Life

Joaquim Alberto Chissano was born on 22 Oct. 1939 in the remote village of Malehice, Gaza Province, in the Portuguese colony of Mozambique. He was the first black student to enrol at the Liceu Salazar school in Lourenço Marque (later the capital city, Maputo). Chissano joined the African Secondary School Students' Organization in Mozambique (NESAM), later becoming the group's leader. He went on to study medicine at the University of Lisbon in Portugal, where he continued his involvement in politics. His opposition to Portuguese colonialism brought him to the attention of the Portuguese secret police and he was one of several students smuggled out of the country in June 1961.

While in France in 1961, Chissano, with the help of fellow activist Eduardo Mondlane, formed and headed the National Union of Mozambican Students (UNEMO). The following year other liberation groups united with UNEMO to form FRELIMO, the Mozambique independence movement led by Mondlane. Chissano fought with FRELIMO in the Mozambique War of Independence, attaining the rank of major-general. Following the assassination of Mondlane in 1969, Chissano was appointed FRELIMO's chief representative in Tanzania and played a key role in reconciling the group's hardline Marxists with its more moderate pragmatists.

He had a lead role in negotiating the 1974 Lusaka Agreement, which paved the way for Mozambique's independence on 25 June 1975. In Sept. 1974 he took office as prime minister of the transitional government. During his sole year as premier, he nationalised the medical and legal systems as well as agricultural estates, prompting many white professionals to leave the country.

In June 1975 Chissano was appointed foreign minister under Mozambique's first independent president, Samora Machel. Seeking aid from both capitalist and communist nations, the new government followed a policy of political non-alignment, which allowed for good relations with China, the USSR and many Western nations. Chissano continued to strengthen Mozambique's ties with the West and by 1984 the country had become the world's largest recipient of US food aid. In Oct. 1986 Machel died in an air crash and the following month Chissano succeeded him as national president, head of FRELIMO and chief of the armed forces.

Career Peak

Chissano's presidency coincided with a devastating civil war between FRELIMO, the conservative Mozambique National Resistance (RENAMO) and the national armed forces. At the same time, Chissano was faced with a collapsing economy. He established an economic recovery programme, devalued the currency and secured a major IMF loan. He continued to attract foreign investment and negotiated debt reductions to alleviate the strain of payments to international lenders. Although Mozambique remained one of the world's poorest countries, poverty levels fell during his tenure.

In Oct. 1992 Chissano and Afonso Dhlakama, RENAMO's leader, signed the Rome General Peace Accords to bring an end to the civil war. A UN peacekeeping force oversaw a 2 year transition to democracy.

After the war Chissano implemented a shift from Marxist-Leninist ideology to multiparty democracy and within 2 years had organised Mozambique's first multi-party elections. He became the country's first democratically elected president in 1994 and won a second term in 1999.

From July 2003–July 2004 he served as chairman of the African Union. Refusing to cling to domestic power, his favoured successor, Armando Guebuza, won the elections of 2004 and Chissano left office in Feb. 2005 with his reputation intact.

Later Life

After relinquishing power Chissano established the Joaquim Chissano Foundation, a private, non-profit organization dedicated to the promotion of peace, economic development and Mozambican culture. He also led several international peace initiatives, serving as special envoy of the UN secretary general to Guinea-Bissau, the Democratic Republic of the Congo, Northern Uganda and Southern Sudan.

In 2006 he was awarded the Chatham House Prize for his contribution to improving international relations and the following year won the Mo Ibrahim Foundation Prize for Achievement in African Leadership, an honour worth US$5m. He sits on the board of several companies including the Harmony Gold Mining Co., Teal Exploration & Mining inc. and the Bill and Melinda Gates Foundation.

Chrétien, Jean (Canada)

Introduction

Jean Chrétien served as prime minister from Nov. 1993 to Dec. 2003.

'Jean Chrétien in youth is small, skinny, deaf in one ear, deformed at the mouth, slightly dyslexic, poor of pocket and intellectually unadorned,' wrote biographer Lawrence Martin in the Globe and Mail before the 1997 Canadian election. However, from this inauspicious beginning, Jean Chrétien earned a reputation as an incisive and shrewd administrator and a man of the people, often receiving more public support than from his own party. He stepped down to allow his closest rival and one-time finance minister Paul Martin succeed him.

Early Life

Born on 11 Jan. 1934, the eighteenth of nineteen children in a working class family in Shawinigan, Quebec, Joseph-Jacques-Jean Chrétien inherited a passion for Liberal politics from his activist father and by the age of 15 was distributing pamphlets and attending rallies for the party. After attending the classical college in Trois-Rivières, Chrétien studied law at Laval University and, having married Aline Chaîné with whom he had three children, he was called to the bar in 1958.

By 1960 he was principal organizer for Jean Lesage, leader of the provincial Liberal party, standing for his first term in the House of Commons in 1963, representing the constituency of Saint-Maurice-Laflèche. He held several jobs in successive administrations including parliamentary secretary to the prime minister Lester Pearson in 1965, minister of state in 1967 and minister of national revenue in 1968.

After becoming minister of Indian affairs and northern development in 1968, one of his first tasks was to draft a policy paper on native issues. In 1972 he set up the Berger Commission to make recommendations on a proposed pipeline in the Mackenzie River Valley and later was the leading force behind the creation of ten new national parks. In 1977 he became the first French Canadian to become minister of finance, overseeing the removal of the wage and price controls that had been in effect since 1975.

As minister of justice and attorney general of Canada and minister for state for social development in 1980, he was responsible for supporting the 'no' campaign in the Quebec referendum on sovereignty. Despite popular support, in 1984 Chrétien narrowly lost to John Turner in a contest to succeed Pierre Trudeau as leader of the Liberal Party. Instead he became deputy prime minister and secretary of state for external affairs, before resigning his Commons seat in 1986.

After 4 years as a counsel with law firm Lang Michener Lawrence and Shaw, Chrétien returned to Parliament in 1990, defeating Paul Martin for the leadership of the party. He set about rebuilding the divided and demoralized Liberals and in Oct. 1993, with an electorate disillusioned by the Kim Campbell's governing Progressive Conservative Party, led the Liberals to a landslide victory.

Career Peak

His popularity remained high despite narrowly avoiding defeat in the 1995 referendum on Quebecois independence. As the champion of maintaining Canada's integrity he was criticized for not defeating the secessionists with a larger majority—50.1% rejected independence for Quebec. To secure further federal unity, Chrétien ensured the passage of the Clarity Act, that demands a 'clear majority' (considerably more than 50%) in support for Quebecois independence before the recognition from the federal government.

His credentials as a supporter of the welfare state were challenged after unpopular cuts in health and education transfer payments to the provinces. Winning a slim majority (with 155 out of 295 seats) in his second election in 1997 on the back of a booming economy, Chrétien oversaw the near total annihilation of the traditional Conservative opposition as a credible force. His government's ability to balance the budget gave Chrétien and his finance minister, Paul Martin, long-lasting fiscal credibility. Early elections were held in 2000, giving the Liberals an increased majority (a total of 170 seats), after pledges to increase spending after a series of austerity budgets.

Chrétien established a reputation in the international arena by renewing Canada's commitment to humanitarian intervention and the UN peacekeeping forces. His government made commitments to support development in Africa through humanitarian assistance, economic programmes and conflict management. In the aftermath of the 11 Sept. 2001 terrorist attacks on the US, the government explored new methods of intelligence sharing with the US authorities and agreed to cooperate on border control and immigration policies. Nevertheless, in Sept. 2002 Chrétien objected to unilateral US attacks on Iraq and urged cooperation with the UN Security Council. His refusal to support US President George W. Bush in the invasion of Iraq soured relations with the Bush administration. Despite popular support in Canada for his anti-war stance, Chrétien was criticized by the opposition for putting Canada's relationship with the USA in jeopardy.

Chrétien's position within the Liberal Party was less secure than in the country. His background and opinions were markedly different to the increasingly liberal and affluent party membership. His chief rival, Paul Martin, was popular as a successful businessman and for his record as finance minister. When Martin was dismissed from the government for launching an unsuccessful leadership challenge in June 2002, dissent within the party was halted but only temporarily. In Aug. 2002 Chrétien announced that he would not remain for another election, effectively paving the way for Martin to succeed him as prime minister. Martin was elected with 94% of the party vote in Nov. 2003 and became prime minister on the 12 Dec. 2003.

Christie, Perry (The Bahamas)

Introduction

Perry Christie was elected prime minister in May 2012. He had previously served as premier from 2002–07.

Early Life

Perry Gladstone Christie was born in Nassau on 21 Aug. 1943. He was schooled in New Providence before moving to the UK, where he graduated from Birmingham University in 1969 and was called to the Bar at London's Inner Temple. He represented The Bahamas in the triple jump at the 1962 Central American and Caribbean Games.

Christie was appointed to the Bahamian Senate in Nov. 1974 by Prime Minister Lynden Pindling. He became head of the national gaming board in Jan. 1977 and in the same year successfully stood in the general election as the Progressive Liberal Party (PLP) candidate for the Centreville constituency. He was subsequently named minister of health and national insurance and after the 1982 election took over the tourism portfolio. However, he left the government 2 years later amid allegations that several of his party colleagues had taken bribes. Reclaiming his parliamentary seat in 1987 as an independent, he rejoined the PLP in March 1990 and was appointed minister for agriculture, trade and industry.

At the general election of 1992 the PLP lost power for the first time since independence, giving way to the Free National Movement. In Jan. 1993 Christie was elected PLP deputy leader. He succeeded Pindling as leader in April 1997 and led the party to a landslide victory at the polls in May 2002.

In government the PLP was dogged by scandal, including the resignation of the immigration minister, Shane Gibson, over charges that he expedited the residency application of the actress and model Anna Nicole Smith. At parliamentary elections on 4 May 2007 the PLP was defeated by the Free National Movement but Christie remained at the head of the party. As leader of the opposition he proposed a referendum on the inauguration of a national lottery as a means of tackling mounting national debt.

He campaigned for the 2012 election on a platform of lowering the cost of electricity, helping struggling homeowners and championing national health insurance.

Career Peak

Sworn into office on 8 May 2012, Christie pledged to tackle unemployment (which had risen to 15%), address the escalating crime rate, and diversify the economy to reduce its dependency on tourism and the country's status as an offshore financial centre. He also appointed a constitutional commission to advise on possible amendments to the constitution, which has remained unchanged since the country gained independence in 1973.

In Jan. 2013 proposals to legalize gambling outside of casinos and to create a national lottery were rejected in a referendum.

Christie left office in May 2017 after the defeat of the PLP in the parliamentary elections. He was succeeded by Hubert Minnis.

Christofias, Dimitris (Cyprus)

Introduction

Dimitris Christofias became the European Union's only communist head of state when he was sworn in as president in Feb. 2008. Christofias, the leader of the far-left Progressive Party of the Working People (AKEL), was elected after two rounds of presidential elections. He vowed to pursue talks with the 'Turkish Republic of Northern Cyprus' ('TRNC'. to find a solution to the division of the island.

Early Life

Christofias was born on 29 Aug. 1946 in Kato Dikomo, Kyrenia province, which is now under Turkish control. His father was a member of the Pancyprian Federation of Labour (PEO), an umbrella organization of trade unions in Cyprus with close ties to the AKEL. Christofias attended the Nicosia Commercial Lyceum where he joined the Pancyprian United Student Organization (PEOM) at the age of 14. In 1969 he became a member of AKEL, PEO and the United Democratic Youth Organization (EDON; AKEL's youth wing). At the fifth congress of EDON held the same year, he was elected to the central council. From 1969–74 Christofias studied at the Institute of Social Sciences and the Academy of Social Sciences in Moscow, where he graduated with a doctorate in history.

On his return to Cyprus in 1974, Christofias was elected to the post of central organizing secretary of EDON. In 1976 he was elected member of the Nicosia-Kyrenia district committee of AKEL and the following year became general secretary of EDON. He was appointed to the AKEL central committee in 1982 and was elected a member of the political bureau in 1986. In 1987 he resigned as general secretary of EDON to take on his new post on the secretariat of the AKEL central committee and in April 1988 was made general secretary, a post he still holds.

In the 1991 parliamentary elections Christofias was voted into the House of Representatives, winning re-election in 1996 and 2001. On 7 June 2001 he became president of the House and retained the post in 2006. In his capacity as AKEL general secretary and president of the House, Christofias was a member of the national council, the advisory body to the president on the 'Cyprus problem'.

Ahead of the 2008 presidential election Christofias campaigned on finding a solution to reunite the divided island—despite backing the 2004 rejection of a UN reunification plan. In the first round of voting he came second with 33.3% of the vote, displacing the incumbent Tassos Papadopoulos of DIKO (Democratic Party). In the second round he received the support of DIKO and defeated right-winger Ioannis Kasoulidis, obtaining 53.4%.

Career Peak

Despite widespread reservations about his communist background, Christofias promised to preserve the country's market economy. He also quickly kick-started talks with Northern Cyprus, meeting Turkish Cypriot leader Mehmet Ali Talat in March 2008. Agreement was reached on reopening a key crossing in the divided capital, Nicosia, and they declared their intention to relaunch formal reunification talks. Meeting again in May, they acknowledged their differences but reaffirmed their commitment to 'a bi-zonal, bi-communal federation with political equality'. Following a further review in July, Christofias and Talat met again in Nicosia in Sept. to begin direct intensive negotiations.

Substantive progress was nevertheless slow, reflecting the underlying fragility of the peace process and the complexity of the issues of contention, such as governance and power-sharing, territorial adjustment, property ownership and security guarantees. In addition, parliamentary and presidential elections in the 'TRNC'. in April 2009 and April 2010 respectively, were won by the right-wing nationalist National Unity Party and its hardline leader Derviş Eroğlu, casting doubts on the prospects for further progress towards a reunification settlement.

Parliamentary elections for the House of Representatives in May 2011, which resulted in a narrow victory for the right-wing opposition DISI party, reduced Christofias' room for manoeuvre in negotiations. His political position was further undermined in Aug. when DIKO withdrew from the coalition government. At the same time, the already strained public finances came under increasing pressure in July following a munitions blast that knocked out the country's main power station, and in the same month Cyprus' international credit rating was downgraded.

The impasse in communal negotiations persisted in 2012. In April the UN acknowledged that progress to date was insufficient to warrant holding an international conference to finalize a durable settlement. Moreover, the prospects for any further political advance were complicated by the Cypriot assumption of the rotating presidency of the European Union from July and by Greek Cypriot presidential elections scheduled for Feb. 2013. In Nov. 2012 the Cypriot government agreed a financial bailout with the EU and International Monetary Fund in support of the flagging economy.

Christofias did not seek re-election at the presidential elections held in Feb. 2013.

Churchill, Winston (United Kingdom of Great Britain and Northern Ireland)

Introduction

Winston Churchill, politician, writer and orator, served two terms as British prime minister. His first term, 1940–45, was as head of the coalition government during World War II. During this testing time he was to display considerable personal skills and qualities that played a significant role in uniting the British people for the duration of the war and which were essential to Allied victory. His second term of office was between 1951 and 1955 as head of a Conservative administration. His contributions during World War II established him as one of the most highly regarded figures of British history.

Early Life

Winston Leonard Spencer Churchill was born on 30 Nov. 1874 at Blenheim Palace in Oxfordshire to Lord Randolph Churchill (descendant of the 1st Duke of Marlborough) and Jennie Jerome, who came from a wealthy American background. Winston was schooled at Harrow but was a lonely boy who failed to shine. After two unsuccessful applications, he was accepted into the Royal Military College at Sandhurst and in the late 1890s he saw active service in Cuba, India and South Africa. He also wrote dispatches from these areas for various newspapers. In 1899 he resigned his commission and returned to England to pursue his interests in writing and politics.

He became Conservative MP for Oldham in 1900 at the second attempt and, despite a speech impediment, began to make a name for himself as a talented speech-maker, though he was less successful as a debater. Unhappy at Conservative proposals for tariff reform, he defected to the Liberals in 1904. A close ally of future prime minister David Lloyd George, he was appointed President of the Board of Trade in 1908, the same year he married Clementine Hozier and won a seat in Dundee. In response to the House of Lords refusal of the budget in 1909, Churchill clashed with the upper house and, allied with his social reforms such as the introduction of labour exchanges, he became something of a working class hero for a short while. He was appointed Home Secretary in 1910 and First Lord of the Admiralty in 1911, where he began building up naval forces in response to German competition for dominance at sea.

World War I did not come as a surprise to him, but his involvement in the ill-fated Dardanelles and later Gallipoli campaigns led to his demotion under the coalition government of Herbert Asquith. In Nov. 1915 Churchill resigned from the government and saw active service in France before returning as an independent MP in June 1916. In July 1917 he was made minister for munitions, a largely administrative role, but returned to frontline government in Jan. 1919 when he was made Secretary of State for War. He moved to the Colonial Office in 1921 and in 1922, in the face of renewed Turkish aggression in the Dardanelles, he encouraged a firm response. However, he misjudged the mood of a war-weary public and, as the coalition crumbled, Churchill's reputation took a further knock.

He lost his seat at the 1922 elections but, after two unsuccessful campaigns elsewhere, he took Epping in Nov. 1924 as a 'Constitutionalist'. Stanley Baldwin, the Conservative prime minister, offered him the post of Chancellor, but his reintroduction of the gold standard led to an economic crisis and his handling of the 1926 general strike affected his popularity still further. He resigned from the cabinet in 1929 and was out of office for 10 years. Baldwin and Chamberlain both regarded him as too dangerous a maverick to include in government, a belief not unsupported by his championing of Edward VIII during the 1936 abdication crisis. He spent much of the decade writing, but he was also vociferous in his opposition to Nazi Germany and the policy of appeasement, even as Chamberlain was guaranteeing 'peace in our time'. When Britain declared war with Germany on 3 Sept. 1939 Churchill was again appointed First Lord of the Admiralty.

Career Peak

Chamberlain resigned following the German invasion of Norway in 1940, and despite high profile opposition from the Foreign Secretary, Lord Halifax, Churchill emerged as the choice to head an all-party coalition. Backed by a remarkably united cabinet and parliament, he determined to defeat Hitler at virtually any cost. To this end he maintained good relations with the US, whose involvement he realized would be essential to eventual victory. Throughout crisis after crisis (the Dunkirk evacuations, the fall of France, the Battle of Britain) Churchill's mastery of oratory and his unique leadership skills ensured that the war effort did not falter.

Though profoundly critical of Communism, the invasion of the USSR in 1941 led Churchill to seek out an alliance with Stalin, which was achieved in May 1942. A pact was also struck with American President Franklin D. Roosevelt following the Japanese attack on Pearl Harbor and the 'grand alliance' of the USA, USSR and UK came into being. The fortunes of the war continued to fluctuate. Germany secured North Africa in 1942 and took the war into Russia in 1943, but by the time of the allied D-Day landings in June 1944 the Soviet forces were also advancing and victory was in sight.

Relations had not always been easy with Roosevelt and Stalin and when the three leaders met at Yalta in 1945 to discuss the final stages of the war and the post-war zones of occupation, Churchill was aware of the problems that lay ahead. But he could do little to prevent the threat of Soviet expansion. Germany surrendered on 8 May 1945 and the war finished with Japan's surrender on 2 Sept.

Churchill lost the general election of July 1945 to the Labour party, who had captured the public mood with promises of social reform. In Oct. 1951 Churchill was re-elected Prime Minister. His second premiership was more concerned with foreign than with domestic issues. He approved the construction of a British atom bomb but before this could come to fruition he resigned as prime minister on 5 April 1955. Having rejected a peerage, he remained an MP until 1964.

Later Life

Churchill was made a Knight of the Garter in 1953 and also received the Nobel Prize for Literature. As a writer and historian, Churchill was responsible for many works including the monumental *The Second World War* and *A History of the English Speaking Peoples*. In 1963 he was given honorary American citizenship. He died in London on 24 Jan. 1965 and was honoured with a full state funeral. Churchill's skills and versatility led to a long and varied career that was not always harmonious and error-free. However, at the time of World War II, when the need for a strong, competent and charismatic leader was at its strongest, he proved himself unrivalled. At a memorial service on 29 Jan. 1965, American statesman Adlai Stevenson paid tribute to 'the voice that led nations, raised armies, inspired victories and blew fresh courage into the hearts of men'.

Ciampi, Carlo Azeglio (Italy)

Introduction

With no party affiliation, Carlo Azeglio Ciampi was brought into politics from his position as bank governor of the Bank of Italy, where he had worked for 47 years, to be prime minister of a caretaker government in 1993–94, a time of corruption scandals in Italy. He brought public expenditure under control and advanced the privatization of state assets. From 1996–99 he served as treasury minister, overseeing Italy's success in meeting the economic criteria for membership of the single European currency. In May 1999 he was elected president of the Italian Republic. His term ended on 15 May 2005.

Early Life

Ciampi was born in Livorno on 9 Dec. 1920. He obtained an arts degree and diploma before serving in the Italian army (and winning the Military Cross) in the Second World War. After the war he changed academic direction to study law, graduating from the University of Pisa in 1946. That year he joined the Bank of Italy and worked in a number of branch offices with administrative and supervisory functions. In 1960 he moved to the research department, of which he became director in 1970. Thereafter, Ciampi progressed to secretary-general of the Bank in 1973, deputy director-general in 1976, director-general in 1978, and then, in Oct. 1979, to Bank governor, a post he retained until 1993. He also served as chairman from 1979 of the Ufficio Italiano dei Cambi.

Career Peak

Ciampi agreed to be prime minister for 1 year from April 1993, overseeing a time of political and economic turbulence in Italy. In order to meet the economic criteria for economic and monetary union set out in the 1992 Maastricht treaty, his government pursued a vigorous programme of privatization. From 1994 he served as vice-president of the Bank for International Settlements, before returning to government as treasury minister in Romani Prodi's centre-left coalition following elections in April 1996. Widely respected in international banking circles, Ciampi was responsible for restructuring the public finances and enabling Italy to qualify for membership of the single European currency. When Massimo D'Alema replaced Prodi as prime minister in Oct. 1998, Ciampi was asked to continue in office. He was elected president in May 1999, securing over two-thirds of the electoral college votes in the first ballot. He advocated the need for Italy to move to a bipolar system of government, with stable majorities, and institutional and structural reforms to improve the performance of the Italian economy.

In May 2006 attempts were made by parliament to persuade Ciampi to stand for a second term as president. These were rejected by Ciampi and he tendered his resignation on 3 May. He was succeeded by Giorgio Napolitano on 15 May 2006.

Later Life

Ciampi died aged 95 in Sept. 2016.

Cioloş, Dacian (Romania)

Introduction

Dacian Cioloş became prime minister on 17 Nov. 2015. A former European Union commissioner, he was appointed after his predecessor, Victor Ponta, resigned in the wake of protests over the circumstances of a nightclub fire that left 63 dead. Cioloş, a political independent who specializes in agriculture, leads a technocrat government tasked with restoring public confidence in the state.

Early Life

Dacian Cioloş was born on 27 July 1969 in Zalău, in the northwest of Romania, and graduated in horticultural engineering from the University of Agricultural Sciences and Veterinary Medicine in Cluj-Napoca. He undertook postgraduate studies in France at the École Nationale Supérieure Agronomique in Rennes and later at the University of Montpellier, where he gained a doctorate.

Before entering politics, Cioloş worked as a consultant on several rural development projects as Romania transitioned to a market economy. In 2002 he was tasked with managing an agricultural programme designed by the European Commission to assist countries preparing to join the EU. In Jan. 2005 he was made an adviser to Romania's agriculture minister, and also served as the country's spokesman on the EU Council's special committee on agriculture. He was appointed minister of agriculture in Oct. 2007, after Decebal Traian Remeş resigned over a corruption scandal, serving in the post until the parliamentary elections of Dec. 2008.

In Feb. 2010 Cioloş was approved as the commissioner for agriculture under European Commission president José Manuel Barroso. In the course of his 4 year term he led a major reform of the Common Agricultural Policy, as well as negotiating a series of international trade agreements on behalf of the EU. In July 2015 he was named special adviser on food security to the new European Commission president, Jean-Claude Juncker.

The high death toll resulting from a fire at a Bucharest nightclub on 30 Oct. 2015 prompted thousands of people throughout Romania to protest against civic corruption. Prime Minister Victor Ponta, who was under investigation at the time for alleged corruption, was forced to step down. With public opinion ranged against the political classes, President Klaus Iohannis appointed Cioloş as his successor.

Career Peak

Although a political independent, Cioloş was often been aligned with the centre-right European People's Party, which first nominated him for a job at the European Commission. His appointment as prime minister was supported by both the ruling Social Democrats and opposition conservative parties, and his cabinet won parliamentary approval by 389 votes to 115 on 16 Nov. 2015.

Cioloş led a cabinet of 21 technocrats, which included experts on the EU and leaders from the private sector. He was charged with restoring public confidence in the government by implementing institutional reform and measures against corruption.

Following parliamentary elections in Dec. 2016 in which the Social Democratic Party won a convincing victory Cioloş was succeeded as prime minister by Sorin Grindeanu.

Clark, Helen (New Zealand)

Introduction

Formerly a university lecturer and the country's second successive female premier, Clark was elected leader of the centre-left Labour Party in Dec. 1993 and came to power as prime minister following the Nov. 1999 election. She won another two terms before Labour lost the general election of Nov. 2008 to the National Party.

Early Life

Born into a farming family in Hamilton on 26 Feb. 1950, Clark was educated at secondary level in Auckland before reading politics at the University of Auckland. Between 1973–75, while a junior lecturer at the university, she was also president of the Labour Party's Youth Council, and served on the Auckland Labour Regional Council. In 1975 she unsuccessfully contested the safe National Party seat of Piako, and in 1976 represented Labour at an international socialist congress. Clark returned to the University of Auckland to lecture in political studies from 1977–81, during which time she was secretary of the Labour Women's Council (1977). She joined the party's Executive in 1978 and became an MP at Labour's 1981 election victory.

In 1985 Clark represented New Zealand at the United Nations conference in Nairobi marking the close of the Decade for Women. As chair of the foreign affairs and defence select committee between 1984–87, and of 1984s ad hoc disarmament and arms control select committee, her promotion of international nuclear disarmament earned her the Danish Peace Foundation's 1986 peace prize. During this parliamentary term, Labour introduced 'nuclear free' legislation.

Following the party's re-election in 1987, Clark was appointed to the cabinet, initially as conservation minister (Aug. 1987–Jan. 1989) and housing minister (Aug. 1987–Aug. 1989), and then as health minister (Jan. 1989–Oct. 1990) and labour minister (Aug. 1989–Oct. 1990). Her responsibilities during this period included chairing the cabinet's social equity committee, and membership of its economic development and employment committee. As health minister, Clark promoted tobacco control legislation.

Aug. 1989 marked her appointment as deputy prime minister, and the following year she joined the Privy Council; she was the first New Zealand woman to hold these positions. Labour's defeat in the 1990 election placed Clark as deputy leader of the opposition. Until replacing Mike Moore as opposition leader on 1 Dec. 1993 she was additionally Labour's spokesperson for health and labour, and sat on the social services and labour select committees.

Career Peak

Clark was elected prime minister on 27 Nov. 1999, when Labour, in partnership with the Alliance Party and supported by the Green Party, won 39% of the vote. She also became minister for arts, culture and heritage, and assumed the ministerial services and security intelligence service portfolios. Advocating a democratic socialist 'third way'. her key policies included the allocation of NZ$142m. to the arts over a 4 year period; the Employment Relations Act 2000 (intended to foster 'good faith' employment); a 5 year NZ$187m. biodiversity conservation strategy; the establishment of an industrial apprenticeship scheme; financial support for Maori land claims; and the implementation in 2001 of a Disability Strategy and Positive Aging Strategy.

In 2002 Clark won a second term in office and formed a centre-left government with the Progressive Party. Then, at the following parliamentary elections in Sept. 2005, Labour was again returned to power, but by a narrow margin against a resurgent National Party under Don Brash's leadership. Clark formed a new minority coalition with the Progressive Party, with conditional support from the centrist United Future New Zealand, the populist New Zealand First Party and the Green Party.

In mid-2006 her government authorized the deployment of New Zealand troops in an intervention force to Timor-Leste to quell violent unrest. In Oct. 2007 police carried out anti-terrorist raids in North Island, citing a threat to public safety from Maori activists and a more specific threat to the prime minister.

At the general election of Nov. 2008 John Key replaced Clark as prime minister, having led the National Party to victory.

Later Life

In April 2009 Clark was appointed Administrator of the United Nations Development Programme, the first woman to hold the post. She also became Chair of the UN Development Group. In Feb. 2010 she was awarded the Order of New Zealand, the country's highest honour.

Clark, Joe (Canada)

Introduction

Charles Joseph Clark was prime minister of Canada from June 1979 to March 1980, the youngest ever to hold the post. Clark headed a minority Progressive Conservative government for 6 months before his government fell on a budget question and in the general elections that followed was defeated by Pierre Trudeau's Liberals.

Early Life

Born in High River, Alberta on 5 June 1939, Charles Joseph Clark was the son of a newspaper owner and editor. Raised and educated in Alberta, where he obtained degrees in history and political science before studying law at Dalhousie University, Clark worked as a journalist from 1964–66 before first becoming involved in mainstream politics as director of Peter Lougheed's campaign to become premier in Alberta and then as executive assistant to Robert L. Stanfield, the leader of the opposition in Ottawa from 1967–70.

Clark acquired a reputation as an expert political tactician and entered parliament as a Progressive Conservative MP for Rocky Mountain Riding in 1972.

He became party leader in 1976, beating political heavyweights such as Claude Wagner and Flora MacDonald, and set about reuniting the badly split party. Having overhauled the fundraising structure and introduced executive caucus meetings to concentrate attacks on government policy, Clark set about challenging the charismatic Pierre Trudeau's premiership.

Despite being lampooned in sections of the media as awkward and inept, Clark went on to defeat Trudeau at the May 1979 general election. Having won significant numbers of seats in Ontario and Western Canada, the Conservatives fell only six seats short of an overall majority, proceeding to govern as a minority.

Career Peak

Clark's period in office proved unpopular with a stringent budget of program cuts and tax increases fostering little parliamentary support outside the party, forcing a general election in Feb. 1980, which returned Trudeau's Liberals to power with a majority government. Clark's 272 day government turned out to be the shortest of any elected administration in Canada's history.

Clark remained as Conservative leader until 1983, when he was defeated at a leadership selection meeting by Brian Mulroney. Clark was re-elected as head of the Progressive Conservative party in 1998, the first Canadian leader to be directly elected by the grassroots members of a federal Party.

As one of the first leaders to recognize that Canada had to be prepared for the interdependent, global economy of the future, Joe Clark helped to initiate both the Canada-US Free Trade Agreement and the launch of the Uruguay Round/GATT negotiations. His other achievements as Minister of External Affairs included a new Asia-Pacific focus to foreign policy, a larger role for public input into the development of foreign policy, and Canada's entry into the Organisation of American States and La Francophonie, as well as the Canadian Freedom on Information Act, drafted when Clark was prime minister and kept by the incoming Liberal government.

Later Life

Despite the defeat, Clark continued to maintain a high profile political life with his reputation for integrity and competence enabling him to successfully hold the post of foreign minister from 1984–91 and Minister for Constitutional Affairs from 1991–93.

After 5 years out of politics, Joe Clark returned as leader of the Progressive Conservatives in Nov. 1998, returning to the House of Commons in Sept. 2000 after winning a by-election in the riding of Kings-Hants in Nova Scotia.

He was re-elected again 2 months later in the general federal election as the Member of Parliament for the riding of Calgary Centre in Alberta.

Clegg, Nick (United Kingdom of Great Britain and Northern Ireland)

Introduction

Nick Clegg succeeded Sir Menzies Campbell as leader of the Liberal Democrats in Dec. 2007. Clegg had served as an MEP for 5 years and as an MP for two, and was widely seen as representing a new generation. He identified his priorities as defending civil liberties, democratizing public services and safeguarding the environment. In the 2010 general election Clegg's public profile was raised in a series of televised leader debates in which he was credited with outperforming his rival candidates at times but this success failed to translate into increased parliamentary representation. With the absence of a majority for any of the parties, Clegg entered coalition negotiations with the Conservatives and on 11 May a joint government was announced with David Cameron as prime minister and Clegg as deputy prime minister.

Early Life

Nicholas William Peter Clegg was born on 7 Jan. 1967 in Chalfont St. Giles, Buckinghamshire, to a Dutch mother and half-Russian father. Brought up bilingually in Dutch and English, he attended Westminster School in London and from 1986–89 studied archaeology and anthropology at Robinson College, Cambridge University. After studying political philosophy at the University of Minnesota in 1989, he worked as an intern on *The Nation* magazine in New York. Clegg then moved to Brussels as an intern in the G24 Co-ordination Unit, administering aid to the countries of the former USSR. He obtained an MA in European Affairs from the College of Europe, Bruges in 1992.

After a brief period in journalism, Clegg worked for the European Commission from 1994–96, where he was again involved in developing aid projects to former Soviet Bloc countries. In 1996 he became policy adviser to EC vice president and trade commissioner Sir Leon Brittan and was closely involved in EC negotiations over Chinese and Russian accession to the World Trade Organization.

In 1999 Clegg was elected Liberal Democrat MEP for the East Midlands constituency. He served till 2004, gaining a reputation as a supporter of devolution and market liberalism within the EU. He was appointed trade and industry spokesman for the Alliance of Liberals and Democrats for Europe, co-founded a campaign for parliamentary reform, and was active in promoting legislation to open telephone networks to competition.

In May 2005 he was elected Liberal Democrat MP for Sheffield Hallam and was appointed spokesperson on Europe. Following Charles Kennedy's resignation in Jan. 2006, Clegg supported Menzies Campbell's successful leadership bid and was made home affairs spokesperson. He led the Liberal Democrats' campaign against compulsory identity cards and argued for decentralizing reform of the criminal justice system. In Oct. 2007 Campbell resigned the party leadership and on 18 Dec. 2007 Clegg was elected to succeed him, narrowly defeating rival Chris Huhne.

Career Peak

In March 2008 Clegg survived an early rebellion when 13 of his MPs defied his order to abstain on a Conservative proposal to force a referendum on the EU Lisbon Treaty. In June 2008 he led his party's campaign against the extension to 42 days of the UK limit of pre-charge detention for suspected terrorists. At the general election of May 2010 Clegg campaigned to raise the initial income tax threshold to £10,000 and introduce an electoral system based on proportional representation, as well as scrapping the Trident missile defence system. During the televised leader debates, his performances were widely acclaimed and opinion polls showed an increase in Liberal Democrat support. However, the party came third in the polls with 23.0% of the vote and lost five seats, bringing their total down to 57. Despite their poor electoral performance, the Liberal Democrats were instrumental in establishing a new government when coalition talks began in the absence of any party gaining a majority. Clegg was courted by both the Conservatives and the Labour Party but eventually agreed a deal with David Cameron to form a joint government. He was appointed deputy prime minister and four other Liberal Democrats were allocated ministerial posts in the cabinet.

Within the coalition Clegg pushed for electoral reform but in the nation-wide referendum on the voting system in May 2011 Britain rejected the Alternative Vote system. On the same day the Liberal Democrats suffered heavy defeats in English local elections and the Scottish parliamentary election. The coalition was put under strain in Dec. 2011 when Clegg criticized Cameron's decision to veto EU treaty changes. The government's controversial policies to tackle the UK's deficit contributed to further defeats for the Liberal Democrats in the May 2012 local elections.

The Liberal Democrats lost ten of 11 seats at the 2014 European Parliament elections, prompting sections of Clegg's party to call for his resignation. However, Clegg promised to continue in his position as leader.

Following the Liberal Democrats' crushing defeat at the 2015 general election, Clegg stepped down as party leader.

Clerides, Glafcos (Cyprus)

Introduction

Clerides has been the dominant figure in Cypriot politics since the country gained independence in 1960. A member of the House of Representatives from 1960–76 and from 1981–93, he was elected president of the Republic in Feb. 1993 (having assumed that role briefly in an acting capacity from July–Dec. 1974 during Archbishop Makarios' exile). He was also the founder and leader of the Democratic Rally, the main party in government from 1985–2001. Clerides was a staunch supporter of the UN formula for reuniting Cyprus as a bizonal and bicommunal federation and of Cyprus' application for membership of the European Union (EU). He was defeated in presidential elections in Feb. 2003, shortly before Cyprus was due to give its verdict on UN proposals for reunification.

Early Life

Born in Nicosia on 24 April 1919, Clerides was the son of an eminent Cypriot barrister. After his formal education at the Pancyprian Gymnasium, Nicosia, and in the UK, he volunteered for the British Royal Air Force in 1939. Shot down over Germany in 1942 during a bombing raid on Hamburg, he was captured and, despite several escape attempts, remained a prisoner until the end of the war. Having returned to the UK to study law at the University of London's King's College, he was awarded an LLB degree in 1948. Called to the Bar at Gray's Inn in 1951, he practiced law in Cyprus until 1960. He often represented Cypriots before the British colonial courts and was also responsible for drawing up documentation about alleged British breaches of human rights.

In 1959–60 he was a pivotal Greek Cypriot figure in the Zurich and London negotiations leading to independence and the adoption of a new power-sharing constitution. In the transitional period to independence he also served as minister of justice. Clerides backed Archbishop Makarios in 1959 for the presidency (despite his own father's proposed candidacy). In July 1960, representing the Patriotic Front for the Nicosia District, he was elected to the House of Representatives, which in turn elected him as its president the following month (a post he held until July 1976).

From 1968 Clerides represented the Greek Cypriot community in the UN-sponsored intercommunal talks with the Turkish Cypriots. However, policy differences with Archbishop Makarios led to his resignation in 1976, when he launched a new right-wing political party, the Democratic Rally Party (DISY). Under his leadership DISY was the largest parliamentary party by 1985. Clerides stood unsuccessfully in the next two presidential elections. In 1983 he was defeated in the first round (with 34% of the vote) by the incumbent President Kyprianou; and in 1988 he lost in the second round, winning 48.4% of the vote, against the independent candidate George Vassiliou.

Career Peak

Clerides defeated Vassiliou in the second round of voting in the Feb. 1993 presidential election. His victory (with 50.3% of the vote) was attributed

partly to the transfer of support from other parties opposed to a 1992 UN proposal for making Cyprus a federal state. Despite campaigning for reunification, Clerides distanced himself from the UN plan. After the election, the UN-sponsored negotiations with Turkish Cypriots to implement confidence-building measures resumed but failed to produce any positive results. Having been narrowly re-elected in the presidential run-off in Feb. 1998 (this time with 50.8% of the vote) Clerides formed an all-party national government to begin accession talks with the EU, describing membership as 'a catalyst for better or worse' in terms of ending the island's divisions. In 1998, responding to international pressure, Clerides agreed to shelve a controversial plan to deploy Russian anti-aircraft missiles.

In a potential diplomatic breakthrough, Clerides and the Turkish Cypriot leader, Rauf Denktaş, met face to face for the first time in 4 years in Jan. 2002, agreeing to continuing negotiations. The UN proposed a plan under which Cyprus would be run as a 'common' state with two 'component' states, along the lines of Switzerland and its cantons. Although resolutely opposed it, Clerides gave it a more favourable response. However in the presidential elections of Feb. 2003, Clerides lost to Tassos Papadopoulos of the Democratic Party after one round of voting. Papadopoulos took over negotiations with Denktaş and the UN but failed to reach an agreement by the 10 March deadline. He died at the age of 94 on 15 Nov. 2013.

Clinton, William J. 'Bill' (United States of America)

Introduction

The 42nd president of the United States, William Jefferson Clinton served for two terms from 1993–2001. Only the second president to be impeached, Clinton was charged with obstruction of justice and perjury over his attempted concealment of an extra-marital affair with White House intern Monica Lewinsky. He was acquitted by the senate in 1999. Despite media fixation with his private life, Clinton oversaw a period of economic prosperity, helped expand the concept of free trade and helped broker several peace agreements in Europe and the Middle East.

Early Life

Born William Jefferson Blythe IV on 19 Aug. 1946 in Hope, Arkansas, Clinton's father died in a car accident before his son's birth. His mother Virginia Dell Blythe remarried to Roger Clinton, who she would later divorce and then remarry. Clinton studied international affairs at Georgetown University, graduating in 1968, and worked as an intern for Senator William Fulbright of Arkansas. Clinton was firmly opposed to the Vietnam War and was able to defer being drafted after he won a Rhodes scholarship to study at Oxford University in England. After returning to the United States Clinton enrolled at Yale Law School. He graduated in 1973 and became a teacher at the University of Arkansas School of Law for the next 3 years. In 1975 Clinton married Hillary Rodham, a law student he had met at Yale.

Clinton failed in a bid to be elected to the House of Representatives in 1974 and campaigned for Democratic presidential hopefuls George McGovern (1972) and James E. Carter (1976). In 1976 he was elected attorney general of Arkansas. Two years later he became the United States' youngest governor after a successful campaign in Arkansas. However his policies (which included raising car tax) and abrasive style did not prove popular and he failed in his bid for re-election in 1980. The same year his wife gave birth to the couple's only child, Chelsea.

In 1982, Clinton regained the governor's office and would go on to serve a total of five successive terms in office. As governor Clinton helped raise the standard of education in Arkansas and by 1992 the state had the highest high school graduation rate of any southern state. He also oversaw a 61% increase in state income and several welfare reforms including job creation and training programmes and the introduction of school-based health clinics. In 1990, Clinton was elected chairman of the Democratic Leadership Council and began planning a bid for the presidency.

Clinton announced his candidacy for the White House towards the end of 1991 and was seen as the party's frontrunner. His campaign was nearly ruined by claims of marital infidelity made before the New Hampshire primary, but a television interview rallied Clinton's support, earning him the sobriquet the 'comeback kid'. He secured the Democratic nomination in June 1992 at the national party convention in New York City and selected Al Gore of Tennessee as his running mate.

Clinton fought an inspired and energetic campaign against incumbent president George H. W. Bush. Despite accusations of draft-dodging, further speculation about his private life and allegations of financial impropriety, Clinton defeated Bush and independent candidate Ross Perot, securing 43% of the popular vote and 370 electoral college votes to Bush's 168.

Career Peak

On his inauguration, Clinton inherited a Democrat-controlled Congress but found legislative success hard to come by in his first 2 years in office. His campaign promise to end discrimination against homosexuals in the military was opposed by Congress and criticised by prominent conservatives. A compromise policy was introduced which seemed to satisfy neither party. Clinton's proposed system of universal health insurance and a campaign finance reform initiative were also thwarted.

Economically Clinton enjoyed more success, securing the passage of the North American Free Trade Agreement, which created a free-trade zone between the United States, Canada and Mexico. In his first term Clinton cut the United States budget deficit by 50% and initiated important anti-crime measures, as well as the Family and Medical Leave Act. The Clinton administration was praised for promoting women and members of the ethnic minorities to important posts in his administration, including, in his second term, the appointment of Madeleine Albright as the first-ever female secretary of state.

In foreign affairs, Clinton enjoyed some notable successes. In 1993 he played host to Palestinian Liberation Organisation chairman Yasser Arafat and Israeli Prime Minister Yitzhak Rabin at the White House when they signed an accord granting a measure of Palestinian self-rule in Jericho and the Gaza Strip. Clinton sent peacekeeping troops to Bosnia-Herzegovina and Haiti. In 1995 the presidents of Serbia, Croatia and Bosnia-Herzegovina signed a peace pact at Wright-Patterson Air Force Base near Dayton, Ohio. Clinton normalised relations with Vietnam, ending a trade embargo against the Asian state, and improved relations and trade links with China after meeting President Jiang Zemin in New York in 1995. Clinton maintained the hard-line stance against Iraq formulated by his predecessor, sending forces to protect Kuwait in 1994. Two years later he ordered air strikes on Baghdad after Iraqi forces attacked the Kurdish city of Irbil.

In 1994 the Republicans gained control of both houses of Congress. The House of Representatives, led by Newt Gingrich, adopted a confrontational stance towards the Clinton presidency. A year later a congressional investigation began into the land deals made by the president and his wife in Arkansas in the 1980s in what became known as the 'Whitewater affair'. Nevertheless, continued economic growth served to galvanise support for the president and he was re-elected in 1996 after defeating Republican opponent Bob Dole by 379 electoral college votes to 159.

In his second term Clinton took advantage of the favourable economic climate to secure congressional approval for a tax cut, the first in the United States since 1981, and other measures intended to reduce the country's budget deficit. At the same time Clinton introduced a welfare reform bill, negotiated an increase in the minimum wage and oversaw a 30-year low in national unemployment figures. In 1998 the United States had a federal budget surplus of $70 bn., the first surplus since 1969.

Clinton continued to play an active role in foreign affairs during his second term in office. In 1996 and 1998 he ordered air strikes against Iraq for contravening the terms of the treaty that had ended the Persian Gulf War and for failing to cooperate with United Nations' weapons inspectors. Clinton authorised the firing of cruise missiles at targets in Sudan and Afghanistan in 1998 in response to intelligence reports linking the bombing of U.S. embassies in Tanzania and Kenya to a terrorist network controlled by Osama bin Laden. The president took an active interest in trying to bring peace to Northern Ireland, with American mediators helping broker the Good Friday agreement in 1998. In 1999, a Clinton-led NATO began a campaign of air strikes against Yugoslavia when the country's leaders refused to end a campaign of violence against ethnic Albanians in Kosovo. The air strikes ended when Yugoslav president Slobodan Milosevic agreed to withdraw his forces from Kosovo and allow an international peacekeeping force to be established there.

Despite his foreign policy and domestic economic successes Clinton's second term in office was overshadowed by revelations about his private life.

In 1998 he settled a 4-year long sexual harassment case brought against him by paying Arkansas State employee Paula Jones $850,000. Meanwhile from Jan. 1998 the Whitewater investigations expanded to focus on Clinton's alleged extramarital relationship with White House intern Monica Lewinsky. Clinton denied the accusation under oath but by Aug. the emergence of further evidence forced him to admit an 'inappropriate relationship'. This admission left Clinton open to charges of perjury and on 9 Sept. independent counsel Kenneth Starr delivered a report to the House of Representatives that led the House Judiciary Committee to begin impeachment proceedings against him. The Democrats proposed a motion censuring the president but on 19 Dec. Clinton was impeached for perjury and obstruction of justice. He was only the second US president ever to be impeached. On 6 Feb. the senate trial ended when neither motion gained a simple majority. In 2000 independent counsel Robert Ray closed the 6-year Whitewater affair by clearing Clinton and his wife of any criminal wrongdoing.

Clinton's final year in office was spent battling with the Republicans in Congress over health and gun control issues. Congress and the president did come together to normalise trade relations with China. Clinton supported his vice-president Al Gore's presidential campaign, only to see him defeated by George W. Bush.

Later Life

After leaving office, Clinton continued to travel widely giving talks and lectures and signed a publishing deal with Alfred A. Knopf, reportedly worth over $10 m., for his memoirs. He became increasingly active in philanthropy, setting up the William J. Clinton Foundation to tackle issues such as AIDS, poverty and childhood obesity. Between 2005 and 2007 he served as UN Special Envoy for Tsunami Recovery and worked with fellow former president George Bush Sr to establish a fund for the victims and for those of Hurricane Katrina. Clinton's reputation was dented by his perceived role in the failed campaign of his wife, Hillary, to gain the Democratic nomination for the presidential election in 2008. His state of health was cause for concern after he needed an emergency heart operation in Feb. 2010 having previously undergone a quadruple heart bypass in 2004.

Collor, Fernando (Brazil)

Introduction

Fernando Affonso Collor de Mello was president of Brazil from 1990 to 1992. He pursued a modernising programme but rising inflation and charges of corruption forced his resignation.

Early Life

Born in 1949, an economist by education, Collor entered politics as a Social Democrat. He soon rose to become mayor of Maceió, the capital of Alagôas state. He was subsequently appointed its governor and joined the National Congress in 1982, where he gained a reputation as a health and education reformer able to work within tight budgets. On assuming the presidency in 1990 as the National Reconstruction candidate, he became Brazil's youngest ever head of state.

Career Peak

As president, Collor set about radical economic reforms. He supported the free market and privatization and worked to reduce government intervention. He sought to lower Brazil's crippling national debt and entered into an economic affiliation with Argentina, Uruguay and Paraguay. But inflation remained a major problem. His concern for Brazil's environment led to his ending the country's nuclear programme and hosting the 1992 Earth Summit.

Allegations of corruption emerged in Oct. 1992 when Collor was suspended from the House of Congress. When impeachment proceedings began in Dec. 1992 he chose to resign in favour of Itamar Franco.

Later Life

Collor was barred from holding office until 2001 despite being found innocent of corruption charges in late 1994.

Colom Caballeros, Álvaro (Guatemala)

Introduction

Álvaro Colom was elected president on 4 Nov. 2007, the first social democrat to hold the office since 1954. Colom replaced Oscar Berger of the Gran Alianza Nacional and served until Jan. 2012.

Early Life

Colom was born into a politically active family in June 1951 in Guatemala City. He studied at the Liceo Guatemala, a private Catholic school, and then the state University of San Carlos (USAC). After graduating in 1974 as an industrial engineer, he entered the textile industry, becoming a leading representative in the 1980s.

In 1990 President Jorge Serrano Elias—a fellow alumnus of both Liceo Guatemala and USAC—appointed Colom vice minister for the economy and director of the Fund for Peace (FONAPAZ). After the 1997 peace accords ended decades of civil war, Colom worked in land conflict resolution and the promotion of reconciliation.

In 1999 he unsuccessfully ran for president for the centre-left ANN party. In 2003 he ran again, this time for the social democratic UNE, but was defeated by Oscar Berger in the second round. Nonetheless, it was the best left-wing showing in an election for almost 50 years though critics accused him of illegal campaign financing.

Career Peak

Colom's 2007 campaign centred on his 'Plan de la Esperanza', extending to 2032. As well as pledging to fight poverty and improve health, education and public security, he promised to create 700,000 new jobs, build 200,000 new homes and increase GDP growth to 6%. In May 2009 the government denied any complicity in the murder of a prominent lawyer who had claimed that Colom was seeking to kill him. Following presidential elections in 2011, Colom was succeeded by Otto Pérez Molina of the Partido Patriota in Jan. 2012.

Compaoré, Blaise (Burkina Faso)

Introduction

Blaise Compaoré came to power in 1987 after the assassination of Thomas Sankara, the president of the Conseil National de la Révolution (CNR; National Revolutionary Council). He was deposed in Oct. 2014. Compaoré attempted to deregulate the economy and improve relations with the West. Politically, however, his tenure was marked by strikes, unrest and political murders. His human rights record also attracted international condemnation.

Early Life

Born on 3 Feb. 1951 in Ouagadougou, Compaoré received his early education in Burkina Faso and became a secondary school teacher. In 1971 he joined the army and in 1975 went to Cameroon and France for military training. His friendship with Sankara began in Morocco in 1978 while he was serving as a parachute instructor. By 1981 Compaoré had achieved the rank of captain.

Although involved in the establishment in 1982 of the Conseil de Salut du Peuple (CSP; People's Salvation Council, led by Jean-Baptiste Ouédraogo), Compaoré and Sankara broke with the CSP in 1983 to form the more left-wing CNR. When Sankara was later arrested, Compaoré led an anti-government revolt that overthrew Ouédraogo and brought Sankara and the CNR to power. Compaoré was appointed vice-premier. However, growing dissatisfaction with Sankara's increasingly autocratic leadership led in 1987 to his assassination by soldiers loyal to Compaoré, who replaced his former ally as head of state.

Career Peak

Compaoré took office promising a continuation of the CNR's guiding principles, but with 'rectification'. He restored links with the business community, traditional chiefs and the army, and sought to reassure the West on whom he relied for aid. A new party—the Organization for Popular Democracy/Labour Movement (ODP/MT; Organisation pour la Démocratie Populaire/Mouvement du Travail)—was created in 1989 and provision made for the return of multi-party elections. However, political dissent was still treated heavy-handedly and the government virtually controlled the media. That year, two stalwarts of the Sankara era still holding senior office (Boukari Lingani and Henri Zongo) were accused of plotting a coup and executed. In 1991 an amnesty was called on all those guilty of 'political crimes' since 1960 and exiles were offered safe return.

Despite Compaoré's ostensible democratization of the election process and more moderate regime, the 1991 elections were boycotted by opposition groups. Compaoré, the sole candidate, won 90.4% of votes but less than 25% of the population participated. He was sworn in as president on 24 Dec. 1991. Amid high political tension, the assassination of opposition leader Clément Oumarou Ouédraogo and the postponement of legislative elections, Compaoré called a development forum of diverse political and social leaders. In the same year he agreed to a World Bank structural adjustment programme, although the resultant austerity measures led to strikes and protests by students.

The 1991 constitution was amended in 1997, allowing the president to stand for re-election more than once, and also restructuring parliament and provincial government. In addition the national anthem and the flag were modified to break with the revolutionary past. Compaoré was re-elected president in Nov. 1998 with more than 87% of votes (in a 56.1% turnout), although doubt was cast on the legitimacy of the electoral process. On 13 Dec. 1998 a journalist critical of Compaoré, Norbert Zongo, and three of his colleagues were murdered. There followed public protests and the arrest of opposition leaders.

A report of May 1999 suggested that the presidential bodyguard was behind the murders of Zongo and his colleagues. The conclusions led to student protests in the capital. Compaoré's human rights record fell under further scrutiny as more opposition leaders and independent journalists were arrested. Despite the offer of compensation to the victims' families and the release of several political prisoners, tensions remained high, and strikes and other protests persisted.

In parliamentary elections in May 2002, despite a stronger opposition performance, the pro-Compaoré Congress for Democracy and Progress (CDP) won 57 of the 111 National Assembly seats, and it took 73 of the 111 seats in the May 2007 elections. Meanwhile, although deemed unconstitutional by opposition politicians, Compaoré was re-elected for further presidential terms in Nov. 2005 and Nov. 2010, winning an overwhelming share of the vote on each occasion. In April 2009 the parliament adopted legislation requiring at least 30% of political party candidates in future elections to be women. A serious challenge to Compaoré's authority was posed in April 2011 by a military revolt over unpaid allowances, following popular protests over rising prices, which prompted his appointment of a new prime minister and cabinet. In Dec. 2012 legislative elections returned the CDP to power with an overall majority in an enlarged 127-member National Assembly.

Compaoré resigned as president on 31 Oct. 2014 and fled to Côte d'Ivoire following a popular uprising against the government. Hundreds of thousands of people had protested against his bid to extend his 27 year term of office as president, and violence had broken out near government buildings in the capital. The military subsequently installed Lieut.-Col Isaac Zida as interim president. Compaoré's regime was accused of corruption and alleged interference in civil wars in Liberia and Sierra Leone. The country also suffered from increased levels of unemployment during his final years as president.

Compton, John George Melvin (St Lucia)

Introduction

Sir John Compton led St Lucia to independence in 1979. Serving as its first prime minister until electoral defeat later that year, he returned as prime minister from 1982–96. He came out of retirement in 2005 to lead the United Workers' Party (UWP) back to power, winning 11 of the 17 seats in the House of Assembly and was sworn in for his third term as prime minister on 15 Dec. 2006. He died in office the following Sept.

Early Life

John George Melvin Compton was born on Canouan Island, St Vincent and the Grenadines in 1926. He studied economics and law at the London School of Economics before becoming a barrister in England. He moved back to the West Indies and established his own law practice on St Lucia in 1951. He formed the UWP in 1961 and was elected chief minister in 1964, serving as premier until St Lucia attained independence in 1979. He was then appointed prime minister.

Losing the elections in that same year, he returned as prime minister in 1982, remaining in office until he resigned in 1996. His tenures were marked by right-wing policies and fierce support for democracy and the rule of law. He was an ardent supporter of the US-led intervention in Grenada in Oct. 1983. Having retired he was knighted in 1997 but came back in 2005 to lead the party he founded.

Career Peak

Compton was elected on a platform of tackling crime and unemployment. He pledged to create new jobs in the construction industry through a programme of refurbishing public buildings and repairing roads, as well as focusing on tourism and the IT industry. In a bid to boost agriculture, a mission was sent to the UK to secure a larger market share for St Lucian bananas. Compton also raised the subject of foreign interference in domestic politics after two other Caribbean prime ministers visited St Lucia before the 2005 election to campaign for his opponent.

In 2007 much of the government's activity was centred on the country's role as co-host of the cricket world cup. In April 2007 St Lucia and Taiwan established diplomatic ties, despite protests from China and a split in Compton's cabinet. After several months of ill health, he died on 7 Sept.

Conté, Lansana (Guinea)

Introduction

Gen. Lansana Conté won a third term as president on 21 Dec. 2003. Many opposition parties boycotted the election claiming fraud and irregularities. He remained in control, despite reports of his declining health, until his death on 22 Dec. 2008.

Early Life

Lansana Conté was born in 1934 in Dubréka, Guinea. He was educated in Dubréka before completing his military training at preparatory schools in France and West Africa.

In 1955 he enlisted in the French army and was posted to Algeria during the war of independence. Guinea gained independence from France on 2 Oct. 1958, and when Conté returned home from military service he joined the new national army as a sergeant. In 1962 he attended the Camp Alpha Officer's School in Conakry, Guinea. He became a second lieutenant the following year before being promoted to lieutenant in 1965. In Nov. 1970 Guinean exiles invaded the country in an attempt to overthrow President Ahmed Sékou Touré. Conté was part of the military team that repelled the invasion and, in recognition of his contribution, was promoted to captain in 1971. Four years later he became assistant chief of staff of the army.

In 1977 Conté began his political career when he headed Guinea's delegation during negotiations to resolve a border dispute with Guinea-Bissau. In 1980 he was elected to the National Assembly. On 3 April 1984, following the death of President Touré, Conté led a bloodless coup to overthrow the interim government of Prime Minister Louis Lansana Beaogui. Conté created the Military Committee for National Recovery (CMRN), suspended the constitution and the National Assembly and banned all political activity. He denounced the Touré regime, released over 200 political prisoners and encouraged those Guineans exiled during Touré's rule to return to the country. He was proclaimed president 2 days later.

Career Peak

Conté's presidency was plagued by controversy. In July 1985 Prime Minister Diarra Traoré tried to seize power while Conté was attending an ECOWAS summit in Togo. Conté's troops prevented the coup and on his return 100 military personnel, including Traoré, were executed.

Conté assumed the rank of army general in 1990 and shortly afterwards the government introduced a new constitution which included provision for the establishment of civilian government. In June 1991 the CMRN was replaced by the Transitional Committee for National Recovery (CTRN).

In 1992 Conté legalized political parties in the build-up to presidential elections in Dec. 1993, the first multi-party election since independence. Conté's new party, the Party of Unity and Progress (PUP), was victorious but the elections were blighted by serious irregularities. In 1996 the government was subject to another unsuccessful coup attempt. Around a quarter of the Guinean army mutinied in protest over salaries and poor conditions and many died. A multi-party presidential election was held in 1998 and, despite a number of flaws and protests, Conté was confirmed as president.

In Nov. 2001 Conté's government approved constitutional amendments allowing the president to run for more than two consecutive terms. The referendum was boycotted by the opposition, who referred to the move as a 'constitutional coup' designed to ensure Conté's lifelong rule. Conté was confirmed for a third term in Dec. 2003 with all but one of the opposition parties boycotting elections. In Jan. 2005 he survived an assassination attempt and two general strikes were staged in Feb.–March and June 2006. In April 2006 Conté sacked the prime minister, Cellou Diallo, who was not replaced until Eugène Camara was appointed premier on 9 Feb. 2007. However, faced with a further general strike and growing violent protests against his regime, Conté dismissed Camara just over 2 weeks later, appointing Lansana Kouyaté in his place. In the midst of further unrest in 2008, Conté sacked Kouyaté in May and replaced him with Ahmed Tidiane Souaré, a former cabinet minister. Conté remained in office until his death on 22 Dec. 2008, after which the army seized control in a widely condemned coup.

Correa, Rafael (Ecuador)

Introduction

Rafael Correa started his 4 year presidential term in Jan. 2007. An economist educated in Europe and the USA, he has mostly enjoyed strong popular support and was re-elected in April 2009 and again in Feb. 2013.

Early Life

Correa was born in April 1963 in Ecuador's second city, Guayaquil. He graduated in economics from the Catholic University of Guayaquil and worked for a year in an indigenous community in the Cotopaxi region. He went on to postgraduate studies at the Catholic University of Leuven (Belgium) and the University of Illinois at Urbana-Champaign (USA).

Correa embarked on an academic career, rising to become dean of economics at the private University San Francisco de Quito. An economic analyst known for his anti-neoliberal and nationalist stance, he worked as a consultant for the UN Development Programme and the Japanese Development Bank among others. He was a notable opponent of Ecuadorian dollarization in 2000.

When popular revolts forced Lucio Gutiérrez to resign as president in April 2005, his successor Alfredo Palacio appointed Correa as finance minister. Correa held the position for 4 months, during which time he was critical of the World Bank and IMF and advocated poverty reduction and economic sovereignty schemes. When the World Bank withheld a loan in protest at various economic policies, Correa resigned his office. In 2006 he founded the Alianza PAIS movement, which allied itself with the Socialist Party in the run-up to general elections.

Career Peak

Correa campaigned for sustainable socio-economic revolution and Latin American integration. On taking office, he pledged a referendum on the establishment of a constitutional assembly to draft a new constitution, aimed at maintaining good relations with the USA (although his rejection of a free trade agreement, Ecuador's refusal to extend US use of the Manta military base in the Pacific and, in 2011, US allegations of corruption in the Ecuador police have strained ties) and promised that dollarization would remain in place during his tenure. He also guaranteed Ecuador's non-involvement in Colombia's internal conflict. Other policies included engagement with Colombia and Brazil in trade negotiations and talks with Argentina to renegotiate the terms of Ecuador's multi-billion dollar debt. In addition, Correa announced that he would renegotiate 'entrapping' oil contracts with transnational companies, consider Ecuador's re-entry into OPEC (which happened in Nov. 2007) and limit debt repayment in favour of social spending (although quick repayment of IMF debts would remain on the agenda).

In April 2007 he won referendum approval to set up a constituent assembly to rewrite the constitution. Elections to the assembly in Sept. resulted in a majority victory for Correa's allies over opposition parties that had dominated the Congress since the Oct. 2006 polls. In Nov. 2007 the assembly voted to dissolve the Congress and proceeded to act as a legislature. A new draft constitution increasing presidential powers and tenure, banning foreign military bases and enhancing state influence over the economy was approved by the assembly in July 2008 and endorsed in a national referendum on 28 Sept.

In March 2008 Ecuador's relations with Colombia were seriously undermined by a cross-border Colombian strike against a FARC guerrilla target in Ecuadorian territory, prompting Correa to cut diplomatic ties and send troops to the border. Relations worsened in July 2009 when a FARC military commander claimed that his organization had contributed funding to Correa's 2006 election campaign, and have remained strained.

Correa won an outright victory in the April 2009 presidential elections, avoiding the need for a second round run-off. His party won a legislative majority at the same time. However, in Sept. 2010 Correa was assaulted and then besieged in hospital by rebellious police officers protesting against pay cuts. The incident was denounced as a coup attempt by Correa and prompted the government to declare an indefinite state of emergency. In a further constitutional referendum in May 2011 voters approved a range of amendments, including extra presidential powers over the judiciary and media.

In June 2012 Julian Assange, the Australian founder of the WikiLeaks website that publicized secret US diplomatic documents, took refuge in Ecuador's embassy in London, England to evade extradition to Sweden on sexual assault charges. In Aug. Correa granted Assange diplomatic asylum, which has generated continuing tensions with the UK government.

Correa won a third term of office in Feb. 2013, winning over 50% of the vote against seven opponents. He promised 'another four years of revolution'. Although critics have accused him of autocratic tendencies. His economic policies have also generated increasing opposition from business interests and the middle class, which manifested itself in a series of organized protests in mid-2015.

Correa did not seek re-election in Feb. 2017. Lenín Moreno, who won a second round run-off 6 weeks later, took office as president on 24 May 2017.

Coty, René (France)

Introduction

René Coty was the second and final president of the Fourth Republic. Serving from 1954–59, his term embraced the Indochina War, the Suez Crisis and the Algerian War. The crisis point reached in 1958 forced the emergency reinstatement of Charles de Gaulle as prime minister and the end of the Fourth Republic.

Early Life

Coty was born in Le Havre on 20 March 1882. Coty took degrees in law and philosophy before becoming a solicitor at Le Havre in 1902. He was town councillor from 1907 and served in the 1914–18 War. In 1923 Coty was elected deputy of Seine-Maritime and, after a brief period as undersecretary of the interior in the Third Republic, became a senator in 1935. After the German invasion he voted to give Pétain full control of the Vichy government and then went into semi-retirement. He was minister of reconstruction between 1947–48 before returning to the Senate as its vice president.

Career Peak

In the 1954 elections Coty was nominated President on the 13th ballot, taking over from Auriol who declined to stand for re-election. He inherited an unstable government and a rocky economy, both of which continued to give trouble. While Coty was in office, eight prime ministers served—Joseph Laniel, Pierre Mendès France, Edgar Faure, Guy Mollet, Maurice Bourgès-Maunoury, Félix Gaillard, Pierre Pflimlin and finally Charles de Gaulle.

Throughout his term, Coty was forced by the constitution to leave much of the policy making to his prime ministers. But implementing policy was made near impossible by inter-party squabbling.

In 1954 there was disagreement over the European Defence Community (EDC), a plan originated by René Pleven, when prime minister under Auriol, and advanced by Robert Schuman. On 13 Aug. 1954 Gaullist ministers opposed to the EDC resigned with the result that the EDC was rejected by the Assembly. As one who supported the proposal, Coty was frustrated by political wrangling and favoured a strengthening of presidential authority.

Conflict dominated Coty's presidency. No sooner was peace achieved in Indochina in 1954 than violence broke out in Algeria. The Algerian Front de Libération Nationale (National Liberation Front; FLN) began their drive for independence. The FLN recruited other nationalist organizations to their cause and by 1956 they had set up their own provisional government. Open warfare in Algeria spilled over into France where terrorist activity caused more than 4,000 casualties. The Assembly was divided between those who were prepared to concede independence and those who believed Algeria was an integral part of France. In Jan. 1956 Jules Moch suggested splitting Algeria into two nations, part French, part Algerian Republic. Prime minister Mollet rejected the plan. Further fuel was added to the FLN's campaign when both Morocco and Tunisia gained independence on 3 and 20 of Jan. 1956 respectively.

To add to Coty's troubles, in July 1956 the Egyptian president, Gamal Abdel Nasser, responded to the withdrawal of American funding for the Aswan High Dam by announcing the nationalization of the Suez canal. Fearing the move would block oil supplies to Western Europe, France and Britain joined forces with Israel to oppose. On 29 Oct. Israeli forces invaded. Under the guise of a UN peace keeping force, France and Britain occupied the canal region a week later. Failing to gain support from the USA, the French and British forces withdrew on 22 Dec. The Israeli's followed 3 months later.

By 1958 France had reached crisis point in the Algerian War. On 13 May Coty threatened to resign if de Gaulle was not made prime minister. The then prime minister Pflimlin resigned and de Gaulle was instated on 1 June. The following day de Gaulle was given full power to end the Algerian War with extended authority over domestic affairs. On 8 Jan. 1959 the Fourth Republic gave way to the Fifth with the installation of de Gaulle as president.

Later Life

Coty retired to Le Havre and died of a heart attack on 22 Nov. 1962.

Cowen, Brian (Ireland)

Introduction

A member of the Dáil since 1984, Brian Cowen took over as Prime Minister (*Taoiseach*) in May 2008 following the resignation of Bertie Ahern. Strongly pro-European, he regarded close ties with the EU as vital for Ireland's economy. Having presided over increases in public spending as finance minister, he took office facing the challenges of an economic downturn that ultimately unseated his government.

Early Life

Brian Cowen was born on 10 Jan. 1960 in Clara, Co. Offaly, the son of Fianna Fáil politician Bernard Cowen. He was educated at Clara National School, Ard Scoil Naomh Chiaráin and the Cistercian College of Mount St Joseph. He then studied law at University College Dublin and the Incorporated Law Society of Ireland, qualifying as a solicitor. In 1984 he contested the Laois–Offaly by-election, caused by the death of his father, and succeeded him as the Fianna Fáil representative. Aged 24, he was the Dáil's youngest member. In the same year he was also elected to Offaly County Council.

Cowen served as a backbench MP for 7 years, gaining a reputation as a tough, outspoken politician. He opposed Fianna Fáil's decision to enter into a coalition government with the Progressive Democrats in 1989 and in Nov. 1991 he supported Albert Reynolds' campaign for the party leadership. Reynolds became *Taoiseach* the following year and in Feb. 1992 appointed Cowen minister for labour.

Following the inconclusive election of Nov. 1992, Cowen was active in negotiating a coalition between Fianna Fáil and the Labour Party. In Jan. 1993 he was appointed minister for transport, energy and communications. After Fianna Fáil was defeated in the 1994 general election, Cowen became opposition spokesman on agriculture, food and forestry under the new party leader, Bertie Ahern. In 1997 he was named spokesman for health. After the June 1997 general election he became minister for health and children in the governing Fianna Fáil–Progressive Democrat coalition. His handling of this newly expanded portfolio raised his profile and he was increasingly viewed as a possible successor to Ahern. In Jan. 2000 he was appointed minister for foreign affairs and his influence in the party was strengthened when he became its deputy leader in 2002.

As minister of foreign affairs, Cowen oversaw Ireland's term in 2002 as a non-permanent member of the United Nations Security Council and was closely involved in the Northern Ireland peace process. A firm supporter of the EU, he backed Ireland's conversion to the euro in 2002. During Ireland's presidency of the European Council in 2004, Cowen helped the EU prepare for expansion.

As minister for finance from 2004–08, he introduced tax reforms and directed funds to public services and welfare, introducing a new childcare package and increased pension allowances. In June 2007, following Fianna Fáil's success in the general election, Cowen became deputy prime minister as well as minister of finance. Ahern announced his resignation in April 2008 amid controversy over his personal financial affairs. Cowen was elected unopposed as leader of Fianna Fáil on 9 April 2008 and took office as *Taoiseach* on 7 May 2008.

Career Peak

Despite coming to office in a period of economic uncertainty, Cowen pledged to maintain public investment while controlling borrowing. He also signalled his continuing belief in the importance of the EU to Ireland's long-term prospects. Although voters in Ireland in a referendum in June 2008 rejected the Lisbon Treaty (signed in Dec. 2007) on EU institutional and administrative reform, this setback was reversed in a further referendum in Oct. 2009 after Cowen had secured assurances that Ireland would retain a permanent representative on the European Commission and that its strict anti-abortion laws and policy of neutrality would not be undermined.

Meanwhile, the economy deteriorated markedly into recession in the second half of 2008 in the wake of the global financial crisis, prompting a dramatic decline in public support for Cowen's government. Having announced plans in Feb. 2009 to rescue two of the country's largest banks, tough budgetary measures to address the widening deficit in the public finances and Ireland's declining credit rating status, including tax increases and public sector pay cuts, were introduced by the government in April 2009 and again in Dec.

The economy continued to deteriorate in 2010 and in Nov. Cowen agreed to an €85bn. EU–IMF bailout. To ensure coalition support for a new austerity budget outlining 4 years of spending cuts and tax rises, Cowen called a general election for Feb. 2011. Fianna Fáil were ravaged, coming third with 20 seats (down from 78 seats in 2007). Cowen, who had resigned as party leader on 22 Jan. but stayed on as *Taoiseach* until the election, left office with an approval rating of 8%.

Craxi, Benedetto (Italy)

Introduction

Bettino Craxi served as Italy's first Socialist prime minister from 1985–87. He led the Socialist Party from 1976–93 and made a profound impact on the Italian political landscape from the late 1970s onwards. His achievements in office, which included the radical reform of tax and pensions, have been overshadowed by allegations of corruption which were made towards the end of his tenure.

Early Life

Craxi was born in Milan on 24 Feb. 1934, the son of a local government official. He joined the Socialist Youth Movement and was president of the national student union. In the 1950s he worked as a journalist for the political review *Energie Nuove*. His political career began in 1960 when he won a seat on Milan's city council. Eight years later he was elected to the Italian Chamber of Deputies, and rapidly made his mark within his party and parliament. In 1976, after the Socialists had suffered their worst election results for years, Craxi was elected party secretary. He took the opportunity to move the party towards the centre, away from the Communist old guard. The elections of 1982 saw an increase in the Socialist vote, and in 1983 he was elected prime minister.

Career Peak

Craxi's first cabinet remained in power until June 1986, making it the longest continuous government since the war. In power Craxi oversaw an upturn in Italy's economic fortunes and declared war on corruption, tax evasion and Mafia activities. His anti-inflationary domestic policies and pro-American foreign policies were highly successful. Craxi formed a new coalition government in 1986 but was forced to resign in Apr. 1987.

Later Life

After an election campaign in 1992 which stressed Craxi's credentials as an honest politician, he was investigated for securing illegal funds for his party. Craxi argued that alternative funding was necessary because of the gross inefficiency of the existing system. This was to make him personally accountable for the scandal, and although parliament voted to grant him continued immunity from prosecution, there was public uproar and Craxi was forced to leave the country for Tunisia. His final years were marked by illness and increasingly desperate efforts to absolve himself from wrongdoing. In 1996 he was convicted in absentia, and sentenced to 5 years imprisonment. He was ordered to stand trial, but he managed to avoid doing so, despite receiving medical treatment in Italy. He died in Tunis on 19 Jan. 2000.

Crvenkovski, Branko (Macedonia)

Introduction

Branko Crvenkovski, a former prime minister of Macedonia, became president in 2004. He was the first to promote Albanian participation in Macedonian politics, and has made Macedonian membership of the European Union (EU) and North Atlantic Treaty Organization (NATO) key objectives. He chose not to stand for re-election in 2009 and left office in May.

Early Life

Crvenkovski was born 12 Oct. 1962 in Sarajevo. In 1986 he graduated with a degree in computer science and automation from the St Cyril and Methodius University in Skopje. His political career began on his election to the assembly of the Republic of Macedonia at the first multi-party elections in the former Yugoslavia in 1990. In 1991 he became the head of the SDSM despite having been a communist.

Career Peak

In Aug. 1992 Crvenkovski became Macedonia's first prime minister after its secession from Yugoslavia. At only 29 years of age, he was the youngest government leader in Europe. Re-elected in the Dec. 1994 elections, he retained the premiership until Nov. 1998. At the head of the SDSM, he implemented wide-ranging economic and social reforms, and guided the country out of the immediate post-Yugoslav era. He became prime minister again in 2002 after his SDSM party won elections. In April 2004 he won the presidential elections, defeating the centre-right candidate Saško Kedev, and took office on 12 May 2004, resigning as prime minister. In Dec. 2005 the EU agreed to make Macedonia a formal candidate member. However, NATO's invitation to Macedonia to join the alliance was blocked by Greece in April 2008.

Following the 2006 parliamentary elections, Crvenkovski's SDSM went into opposition as a new VMRO-DPMNE-led coalition government took office. The VMRO-DPMNE retained power in June 2008 as the largest party in early elections that were marred by violence.

In March 2009 Crvenkovski announced he would not run in the presidential elections later in the month. Gjorgje Ivanov claimed victory in the elections and Crvenkovski handed over power to him on 12 May.

Da Costa Gomes, Francisco (Portugal)

Introduction

Francisco da Costa Gomes was president between 1974–76. The successor to the short-lived president Gen. António Spínola, he was appointed by a revolutionary junta established after the April 1974 Carnation Revolution had ended 50 years of right-wing dictatorship of António da Oliveira Salazar. Costa Gomes presided over Portugal's turbulent transition from dictatorship to democracy, stabilized opposing left and right-wing radical forces while surviving several coups. He finally handed over to a democratically elected president in 1976.

Early Life

Costa Gomes was born on 30 June 1914 in the northern town of Chaves. The son of an army captain, he attended the Escola de Guerra national military academy in Lisbon before continuing his training at a cavalry school. After graduating with a maths degree from the University of Oporto, Costa Gomes forged a successful career in the Portuguese army from 1931 until he was appointed army chief of staff in 1972 by Salazar's successor, Marcello Caetano. He served in the colony of Macao in 1949 and was appointed undersecretary of the armed forces in Salazar's *Estado Nuevo* regime.

In 1961 Costa Gomes was implicated in a bungled coup against Salazar carried out by an army faction who objected to Portugal's contentious position in colonial Africa. Sacked, he took the opportunity to advance his studies at the Institute of Military Studies, where he also taught. He resumed his army career in 1964 and the following year served in Mozambique and then Angola where Portugal waged bloody wars with revolutionary guerrilla forces striving for independence. In 1974 Spínola, then Costa Gomes' second in command, wrote the controversial book *Portugal e o Futuro* describing his disaffection with Portugal's colonial wars. As a result, Caetano demanded Costa Gomes and Spínola pledge their support to his rule. On their refusal, both men were sacked in March 1974. The following month the Carnation Revolution led by the Movimento das Forças Armadas (Armed Forces Movement; MFA) ousted the dictatorship. A revolutionary junta appointed Spínola its president with Costa Gomes as his second in command.

Career Peak

The junta restored civil liberties to Portugal. Banned political parties were reinstated, freedom of speech and the press was allowed and Salazar's PVDE secret police (Polícia de Vigilância e Defesa do Estado) was abolished. In Sept. 1974 Costa Gomes succeeded Spínola as president, the latter proving too right wing for the junta. He inherited a chaotic situation. Portugal was struggling to reinvent itself while different factions pulled in opposite directions and wars in the colonies still raged. Strikes and demonstrations were commonplace. Costa Gomes' ability to avoid or survive the crises of the first 2 years of fragile transition led to his nickname 'the cork'. He acted as a conciliatory figure, neutralizing the extremist forces within the country and avoiding civil war. He negotiated with revolutionaries in Angola and Mozambique and helped set in motion their transition to independence. The Portuguese also quitted Timor-Leste.

Spínola's desire to create an extreme right-wing government led him to attempt a coup in 1975 which the president survived. The other end of the political scale, Costa Gomes prevented a coalition of MFA members and the Partido Comunista Portugués creating a Marxist state on a Soviet model. A constituent election for the provisional government on 25 April 1975, exactly a year after the revolution, was won by the moderate left, the Partido Socialista. Costa Gomes successfully installed a parliamentary democracy

and was able to hand over power to the first democratically elected president in 1976, the army chief General Antonio Ramalho Eanes.

Later Life

Costa Gomes did not stand for president in the first democratic elections due to lack of support and withdrew from Portuguese politics. After leaving government, he was involved in international causes related to peace and the environment. He died in Lisbon on 31 July 2001.

Dabwido, Sprent (Nauru)

Introduction

Sprent Dabwido became Nauru's third president in less than a week on 15 Nov. 2011, following the resignation of Marcus Stephen amid corruption allegations and the removal of Freddy Pitcher by a parliamentary vote of no confidence. In accordance with the constitution Dabwido became both head of government and head of state.

Early Life

Born on 16 Sept. 1972 Sprent Dabwido was elected to parliament at the 2004 general election when he won the seat of Meneng. He was re-elected in 2007 and 2008, and in 2009 he was appointed minister of telecommunications in Stephen's government. In this role Dabwido oversaw the introduction of a mobile telephone system to Nauru and retained his Meneng seat at the June 2010 general election.

On 15 Nov. 2011 Dabwido cut his ties with the ruling faction in parliament and joined the opposition in support of a motion of no confidence that brought down Pitcher. Dabwido was subsequently elected president by nine votes to eight in a parliamentary vote.

Career Peak

Dabwido represented the Pacific Small Island Developing States at the UN Climate Change Conference in Durban in Dec. 2011. He highlighted the problem of rising sea levels for Pacific island nations and called for a legally binding protocol to complement the existing Kyoto Protocol and Bali Action Plan.

In June 2012 he appointed a new cabinet, including opposition members, following an impasse over proposed constitutional reforms.

In Feb. 2013 the resignation and dismissal of several members of Dabwido's government produced a constitutional crisis. Parliament was dissolved in March and elections scheduled for April. However, the elections were postponed and set for 22 June. Dabwido declared a state of emergency and brought the elections forward to 8 June. Baron Waqa emerged victorious and was subsequently elected president. Dabwido did not contest the presidential election but won a seat and became an active member of the opposition. In June 2015 he was arrested and faced criminal charges amid protests against government corruption.

Dadis Camara, Moussa (Guinea)

Introduction

Capt. Moussa Dadis Camara claimed the presidency in Dec. 2008 as leader of the Conseil National de la Démocratie et du Développement/National Council for Democracy and Development (CNDD), after a coup d'état following the death of President Lansana Conté. Camara's stated aim was to restore order to a country crippled by corruption, inflation and high unemployment, and he vowed to hold free and fair elections.

Early Life

Moussa Dadis Camara was born in 1964 to a farming family in the south-eastern village of Koure, Lola Prefecture. He went to school in the regional capital of Nzérékoré before graduating in law and economics from Abdel Nasser University in Conakry. He later earned a master's degree in economics from the University of Conakry.

Camara joined the army in 1990 and was sent abroad on training courses, including 18 months in Germany from 2004–05. In May 2008 he was a prominent figure in a military revolt over unpaid bonuses and the release of military prisoners. In Nov. 2008 Camara became head of the army's fuel supply corps reporting to the defence minister.

Within hours of Conté's death on 23 Dec. 2008 Camara led the way in dissolving the government. Having suspended the constitution and all political and trade union activity, he set out the CNDD's plan to appoint a president from the military who, with a civilian prime minister, would head an ethnically balanced transitional government (to include 26 officers and six civilians). On 24 Dec. 2008 the appointment of Camara as leader of the CNDD and national president was announced.

Career Peak

Camara announced that the CNDD did not intend to stay in power indefinitely and promised 'credible and transparent' elections by the end of Dec. 2010. In Aug. 2009, under international pressure, he agreed to hold presidential elections at the end of Jan. 2010 and parliamentary elections in March, and he reiterated his promise not to stand.

Although members of the dissolved government had disputed the authority of the CNDD, most accepted Camara's leadership when ex-prime minister Ahmed Tidiane Souaré pledged to work with the junta. Camara declared zero tolerance on corruption, promised to renegotiate Guinea's numerous mining contracts and, in an apparent concession to the international community, called on the opposition, including the unions, to help choose a prime minister. However, his popular support waned amid reports of military abuse since the CNDD came to power. In particular, government troops in Sept. 2009 fired on pro-democracy protesters at an opposition rally in Conakry against the military junta, killing nearly 160 people and injuring over 1,000. In Oct. the European Union, African Union and USA imposed sanctions on Camara's regime.

On 3 Dec. 2009 Camara was wounded in an apparent assassination attempt by his military aide commanding the presidential guard and flown to Morocco for medical treatment. Sékouba Konaté was appointed acting president.

Dahal, Pushpa Kamal 'Prachanda' (Nepal)

Introduction

Pushpa Kamal Dahal was voted prime minister for the second time on 3 Aug. 2016 following the resignation of K. P. Oli. He previously held office from Aug. 2008 to May 2009 as head of a coalition government, following many years as leader of the military wing of the Communist Party of Nepal (Maoist), later renamed the Unified Communist Party of Nepal (Maoist) and now called the Communist Party of Nepal (Maoist-Centre). Known as Prachanda ('The fierce one'), he led a Maoist insurgency from Feb. 1996 until Nov. 2006.

Early Life

Prachanda was born on 11 Dec. 1954 in central Nepal to a poor farming family. In 1966 his family moved to Chitwan district, where he was introduced to communism. He graduated from the Institute of Agriculture and Animal Science in Rampur, Chitwan, in 1975. He briefly taught in a primary school before becoming active in the Communist Party of Nepal. The party underwent a series of splits, during which Prachanda joined the CPN (Mashal) wing. He became a member of the politburo, rising to the post of general secretary in 1989.

Following the popular uprising that forced King Birendra to relinquish absolute power and form a constitutional government in 1990, several radical parties merged to become the Communist Party of Nepal (Unity Centre), with Prachanda as general secretary. In 1995, following splits within the party, he renamed his wing the Communist Party of Nepal (Maoist)—known as CPN (M)—and developed the 'Prachanda Path'. A plan that combined the Maoist rural-based theory of revolution with the Marxist–Leninist urban-based approach. It proposed to establish a people's republic, to redistribute property and to dismantle existing patterns of capital and ownership, particularly those that gave economic control to Indian interests. Prachanda took command of the CPN (M)'s military wing, with the political wing headed by Dr Baburum Bhatterai.

In early 1996 Prachanda presented the government with a list of demands including the abolition of the monarchy and redistribution of land. When these were rejected he launched an insurgency, beginning a civil war that lasted for 10 years and resulted in 13,000 deaths. Prachanda spent the period in hiding, living in India for much of the time despite having identified it as an enemy of the Nepalese people. CPN (M) militia established control over many rural areas and in Nov. 2005, following King Gyanendra's resumption of absolute rule, Prachanda led the CPN (M) into an alliance with Nepal's mainstream political parties. After public unrest forced King Gyanendra to restore parliament in 2006, Prachanda entered negotiations with the government and signed a comprehensive peace agreement in Nov. of that year. His party won national elections in April 2008 but without an overall majority.

In Aug. 2008, 2 months after the monarchy was abolished, Prachanda was elected prime minister by an alliance consisting of the CPN (M) and several smaller groups, on a promise of radical reforms. However, his government struggled to tackle endemic poverty, rising food prices and fuel shortages, and was criticized for alleged human rights abuses and suppression of the press. In May 2009 Prachanda sought to dismiss the chief of the army over attempts to integrate former Maoist rebel fighters into the army but the dismissal was revoked by the president. Prachanda announced his resignation the following day.

In the 2013 parliamentary election, Prachanda was surprisingly defeated while defending his Kathmandu-10 constituency but won Siraha-5, the second constituency he was contesting, by a narrow margin. From 2013 he was heavily involved in the drawing up and promulgation of the new constitution that came into effect on 20 Sept. 2015. Following K. P. Oli's resignation in July 2016, Prachanda's candidacy for a second term as prime minister was announced with backing from the Nepali Congress and Madhesi Front coalition. On 3 Aug. Prachanda received 363 of the 573 votes cast in the 595-seat parliament. He was the only candidate.

Career Peak

Prachanda's main challenges were promoting economic development and bridging the ethnic divides brought about by the new constitution that redefined the boundaries of the country's provinces. He resigned in May 2017, with Sher Bahadur Deuba of the Nepali Congress assuming the premiership the following month in accordance with an agreement reached in 2016 between the two leaders.

Davutoğlu, Ahmet (Turkey)

Introduction

Ahmet Davutoğlu was sworn in as prime minister on 29 Aug. 2014 and also confirmed as leader of the ruling Justice and Development Party (AKP). He succeeded Recep Tayyip Erdoğan, the long-time party leader and prime minister, who became president of Turkey on the same date. A foreign policy specialist and proponent of pan-Islamic co-operation, Davutoğlu was instrumental in shaping Turkey's regional and international strategy after the AKP came to power in 2002.

Early Life

Davutoğlu was born on 26 Feb. 1959 in Taşkent. He graduated in economics and political science from Boğaziçi University, subsequently gaining a PhD in international relations from the same institution in 1983. He then embarked on an academic career, founding the political science department at the International Islamic University of Malaysia and becoming a professor at Marmara and Beykent Universities, both in İstanbul. In the mid-1990s he was a regular columnist for the conservative, Islamist newspaper *Yeni Safak*.

After the AKP swept to power in 2002 Davutoğlu was appointed ambassador-at-large and chief adviser to the prime minister. In May 2009 he was named foreign minister in Erdoğan's cabinet despite not being a member of parliament, although he successfully ran as an AKP candidate in the general election of June 2011. The architect of Turkish policy in the Middle East, Davutoğlu was among those to press for the removal of Syria's president, Bashar al-Assad, in the wake of the Syrian civil war, which began in 2011.

The election of Erdoğan as president in Aug. 2014 necessitated the election of a new leader of the AKP party, who would by extension become prime minister, and a meeting of the party's executive committee nominated Davutoğlu as the only candidate.

Career Peak

In his first cabinet Davutoğlu appointed Mevlüt Çavuşoglu as foreign minister but left other key posts unchanged, feeding speculation that Erdoğan would continue to control the political agenda despite the traditionally ceremonial role of Turkey's presidents.

In the first months of his tenure Davutoğlu was criticized for Turkey's failure to intervene against the rise of Islamic State jihadist insurgents in the Middle East. The passage of fighters through Turkey's borders incited tensions with the restive domestic Kurdish community and strained relations with international partners, but Davutoğlu said that Turkey would only become involved militarily if operations included action against President Assad's regime.

Davutoğlu's AKP party lost its parliamentary majority at the June 2015 elections, with the prime minister leading an interim government that was formed in order to preside over new elections. The party then regained its majority at the Nov. 2015 pollings and the prime minister was able to form a new government.

Davutoğlu resigned as prime minister in May 2016, reportedly over President Erdoğan's plans to increase his executive powers, thereby reducing the premier's mandate. He was replaced by Binali Yildirim, also of the AKP.

De Gasperi, Alcide (Italy)

Introduction

Alcide De Gasperi served as Italy's prime minister from 1945–53, leading eight successive coalition cabinets, all of which were dominated by his Christian Democrat Party. He is regarded as the architect of Italy's post-war recovery programme and was responsible for overseeing his country's entry into NATO.

Early Life

De Gasperi was born on 3 April 1881 in the village of Pieve Tesino in Trento province. At the time this region was annexed to the Austro-Hungarian empire, and from a young age De Gasperi was active in defending the cultural values of its Italian-speaking population. Voicing his opinions in the journal *Il Nuovo Trentino*, he became a member of the Christian Socialist movement in 1896. In 1905 he took a degree in philology from the University of Vienna. In 1921, after Trentino was incorporated into Italy, he helped found the Popular Party and was elected to the Italian Chamber of Deputies. Initially the party joined a coalition government with Mussolini, but De Gasperi soon came into conflict with the fascists and was imprisoned in Nov. 1926. When he was released 2 years later he took a job as a cataloguer in the Vatican library where he worked until July 1943 when the Fascist regime was toppled from power. During this period of political exile he wrote extensively about his ideas for the country's restoration, and drew up a manifesto for a new Christian Democrat party. He was able to put some of these ideas into practise, when after a brief term in office as foreign minister, he was elected Prime Minister in Dec. 1945.

Career Peak

In 1946 Italy voted to become a republic, and a year later De Gasperi signed a peace treaty with the Allied forces, thus ensuring Marshall Plan financial aid for Italy's reconstruction. De Gasperi then devised a new constitution which became law at the beginning of 1948. In April that year the Christian Democrats retained a majority in the parliamentary elections, a victory enabled De Gasperi's government to press for Italian membership of NATO. This was granted in 1949. In domestic politics, De Gasperi was responsible for a land reform programme in the impoverished southern and central areas of Italy.

Later Life

In the early 1950s, De Gasperi was active in organizing several European political bodies, including the Council of Europe and the European Coal and Steel Community. By this stage the left wing had grown increasingly intolerant of De Gasperi's centrist politics and although the party membership endorsed his leadership in 1952, his influence declined. In 1953 his government fell from power and he became general secretary and then president of his party, a post he held until his death in Aug. 1954.

De Gaulle, Charles (France)

Introduction

Charles André Joseph Marie de Gaulle, army general, statesman and writer, was the head of the Free French during World War II, the head of the Provisional French Government in 1944, president between 1959–69 and founder of the Fifth Republic. De Gaulle is considered by many to be the creator of modern France.

Early Life

Born in Lille on 22 Nov. 1890, de Gaulle, the son of a schoolteacher, was from a traditional, middle-class, Catholic family. He studied at the military academy in Saint-Cyr before serving under Maréchal Philippe Pétain in 1913. De Gaulle was captured in 1916 and spent the rest of the War as a prisoner despite attempts to escape. During the interwar years, he served in the Rhine (1927–29) and in the Middle East. In 1923 de Gaulle lectured at the Saint-Cyr academy before Pétain promoted de Gaulle to the Conseil Supérieur de la Guerre (Supreme War Council) in 1925. Later, he was a member of the Conseil Supérieur de la Défense Nationale (National Defence Council). Concurrently, de Gaulle wrote books on military tactics, including his most famous, *L'Armée du Métier* (1934). His outspoken views occasionally brought him trouble from traditionalists. His criticism of the Maginot Line incurred Pétain's wrath. Nevertheless, he commanded a tank brigade at the beginning of World War II and was brigadier general when he joined premier Paul Reynaud on 6 June 1940 as undersecretary of state for defence and war. Both de Gaulle and Reynaud supported French resistance to the German invasion.

With pressure from the rest of his cabinet to capitulate to the Germans, Reynaud gave way to his vice-premier Pétain on 16 June 1940. Equally opposed to Pétain's armistice, de Gaulle fled to London. On 18 June, de Gaulle broadcast an address to the French people calling on them to reject German occupation and to continue the war. This marked the beginning of the Free French movement. De Gaulle's relationship with the Free French was not always easy. He was at first treated with suspicion and it took political skill to assert himself as France's natural leader. On 2 Aug. 1940 de Gaulle was tried *in abstentia* by a French military court and sentenced to death.

Career Peak

De Gaulle's relationship with the British was never straightforward and in 1943 he moved to Algeria to head the Committee of National Liberation. It was only when de Gaulle returned to a liberated Paris in 1944 that he was considered a saviour and his reputation was established. The provisional government chose de Gaulle as their leader. Over the next 2 years he headed two provisional governments. Whilst the parties prepared their electoral campaigns for the election of a Constituent Assembly in Oct. 1945, De Gaulle remained passive, feeling perhaps he deserved automatic ascension to head of government. The leaders dominating the Assembly were not of this view and, in protest at a party coalition of the Fourth Republic, de Gaulle resigned in 1946. He strongly disapproved of a powerful Assembly, being in favour of presidential control.

In 1947 de Gaulle established his own party, Rassemblement du Peuple Français (Rally for the French People; RPF). The RPF had the sole aim of reinstating de Gaulle. Initially successful, the RPF received 120 seats in the Assembly in 1951 but, in 1953, when RPF members accepted ministerial posts, de Gaulle abandoned the party and retired to Colombey-les-Deux-Eglises to concentrate on his writing. In 1955 the RPF was dissolved. In 1958 de Gaulle returned to politics. The French government under René Coty was in crisis. Economic problems coupled with the Algerian War had made France unstable. On 13 May Coty threatened to resign if de Gaulle was not brought in as prime minister. The then prime minister, Pierre Pflimlin, resigned and de Gaulle was instated on 1 June 1958. He was granted full power to end the Algerian War as well as extended control over domestic matters. This move signalled the end of the Fourth Republic. De Gaulle decreed a new constitution that would restrict the influence of the National Assembly, while securing for the president overall control. The Fifth Republic was accepted on 28 Sept. 1958 and de Gaulle was elected its first president 7 weeks later.

In 1962 de Gaulle awarded Algeria its independence. This move was supported by the majority of French people except the far right and the *Pieds Noirs* (settlers). During the early 1960s de Gaulle led an economic recovery. He also sought to establish France as a power independent of the USA. In 1966 France withdrew from NATO. He refused to sign the Nuclear Test Ban Treaty, and he rejected Britain's entry into the EEC. His opposition to US involvement in the Vietnam War angered Americans, whilst his support for an independent Quebec riled the British.

The May 1968 riots signalled the end of de Gaulle's political career. Students, unhappy with the archaic authoritarian education system marched in Paris. Workers, demanding more pay and better working conditions, held widespread strikes. The government appeared vulnerable and de Gaulle called on the support of the military. With the necessary backing De Gaulle refused to allow the government to resign. In the elections of June 1968 the government retained its power with a large majority, although it was for the restoration of law and order not de Gaulle himself that the public voted. On 27 April 1969 de Gaulle was narrowly defeated in a referendum on constitutional and regional reform. He resigned and was succeeded by his prime minister of 8 years, Georges Pompidou.

Later Life

He retired to Colombey-les-Deux-Eglises where he died of a heart attack in 9 Nov. 1970. On 18 June 2000, 60 years after de Gaulle's London radio address appealing to the French to fight on, a museum named after de Gaulle was opened in Les Invalides, Paris, by Jacques Chirac.

De Klerk, F. W. (South Africa)

Introduction

F. W. de Klerk, served as the President of South Africa from 1989–94, and whilst in power was the joint architect of the end of apartheid and the introduction of universal suffrage.

Early Life

De Klerk was born in Johannesburg on 18 March 1936 the son of a prominent politician, Jan de Klerk, a cabinet minister and president of Southern Africa's Senate. De Klerk studied at Potchefstroom University and graduated with a law degree in 1958. He began his political life in 1972 when he was elected to parliament as a National Party representative for Vereeniging. In 1978 he joined the cabinet as minister of posts and telecommunications in the Vorster government. He went on to hold successive ministerial portfolios under the leadership of Pieter W. Botha, including environmental planning (1979–80), internal affairs (1982–5) and education (1984–9). In 1982 de Klerk was

named as the head of the National Party in Transvaal and was chosen as the party's leader in 1989. In the same year he became president of South Africa following the resignation of PW Botha.

Career Peak

De Klerk made it clear from the beginning of his tenure that he would attempt to dismantle the apparatus of apartheid. In 1990 he lifted a 30 year ban on the African National Congress and freed the ANC leader, Nelson Mandela, from Victor Verster Prison on Robben Island. De Klerk's government gradually began to introduce legislation that reduced segregation and discrimination. A referendum was held in 1992 in which almost 70% of the white population endorsed the programme of reforms. In 1993 de Klerk and Nelson Mandela agreed on a timetable for the implementation of majority rule. In the same year the two men were awarded the Nobel Peace Prize for 'their work for the peaceful termination of the apartheid regime, and for laying the foundations for a new democratic Southern Africa...' In the democratic elections that took place in 1994 de Klerk lost to Mandela but subsequently served as deputy president in the National-ANC coalition government.

Later Life

De Klerk retired from politics after resigning as leader of the National Party in 1997. In Jan. 1999 he published his autobiography *The Last Trek—A New Beginning*. He has since established the FW de Klerk Foundation which encourages the development of peaceful co-operation between conflicting ethnic, tribal and religious communities.

De la Madrid Hurtado, Miguel (Mexico)

Introduction

Miguel de la Madrid Hurtado was president of Mexico between 1982–8, representing the Partido Revolucionario Institucional (Institutional Revolutionary Party; PRI). During his presidency de la Madrid attempted to correct the country's economic crisis his predecessor had left behind. He sought to change the tradition of corruption within the party.

Early Life

Born in Colima on the Pacific coast on 12 Dec. 1934, Miguel de la Madrid moved to Mexico City at the age of two following the death of his father. In 1957 he graduated from the Universidad Autonoma del Estado de Mexico (National Autonomous University; UNAM) in the capital with a degree in law and subsequently studied at Harvard University. Graduating in 1965 with a master's in public administration, de la Madrid went to work as an advisor for the National Bank of Foreign Commerce and then for the Bank of Mexico. He also lectured in law at the UNAM; one of his pupils was his successor Carlos Salinas de Gortari.

De la Madrid's political career began in 1965 when he joined the ruling PRI party. He was soon called upon to use his economic knowledge in the Treasury. After working as Assistant Manager for Finance for the state owned oil company Petróleos Mexicanos (PEMEX), de la Madrid became Minister of Planning and Budget under José López Portillo. He was a key player in the governmental exploitation of PEMEX's discovery of large petroleum resources. The resulting economic problems would challenge de la Madrid throughout his presidency.

Career Peak

De la Madrid was elected president in 1982. He faced the worst economic situation of any post-revolutionary president. The enormous foreign debt accumulated during Echeverría's presidency was made worse by a fall in oil prices; a falling GNP; 100% inflation and a 40% loss in the value of the peso. These problems were exacerbated by one of the fastest growing birthrates in the world and an increasing public dissatisfaction with the PRI and particularly with one-party rule. De la Madrid adopted a policy of crisis management including new taxes, interest rate increases, price increases and federal budget cuts.

The measures did not go down well with the voters. Made cynical by the corruption surrounding the López Portillo presidency and conscious of the growing disparity between Mexico's rich and poor, the public was unwilling to suffer further for what they considered the governments' ineptitude.

During the early years of de la Madrid's presidency the hardline policies were largely ineffectual. On 19 Sept. 1985 an earthquake measuring 8.1 on the Richter scale decimated Mexico City. Destroying 100,000 housing units and many buildings and killing over 8,000 people, the earthquake was a huge set back to economic recovery. The government's tardy reaction served to fuel criticism. Local elections sparked off allegations of vote fraud. In March the body of the United States Drug Enforcement Administration special agent Enrique Camarena was found in the state of Michoacán. It appeared he had been brutally murdered by Mexican drug traffickers. Already nervous about Mexico's economic instability, relations with the USA were further hampered by Mexico's apparent reluctance to combat the drug trafficking problem highlighted by the murder. According to American sources, by the end of 1985 Mexico was the biggest trafficker of marijuana and heroin into the USA. In the elections of 1988 de la Madrid was succeeded by his fellow PRI candidate Carlos Salinas de Gortari.

Later Life

After leaving office, De la Madrid largely steered clear of political life. He died in Mexico City on 1 April 2012, aged 77.

De la Rúa, Fernando (Argentina)

Introduction

Fernando de la Rúa was president of Argentina between 1999–2001, replacing the Peronist Justicial president, Carlos Menem. A member of the Unión Civica Radical (UCR), de la Rúa represented the coalition Alianza para el Trabajo, la Justicia y la Educación (Alliance for Work, Justice and Education). His term in office was spent trying to stave off the country's deepening recession with a number of increasingly unpopular austerity measures. In Dec. 2001 following disastrous election results and amidst widespread anti-government demonstrations, de la Rúa resigned.

Early Life

De la Rúa was born on 15 Sept. 1937 in Córdoba. He studied law at the city's university. After graduation he joined the UCR and served as an advisor to the interior ministry between 1963–66 under President Arturo Illia. Having been elected senator for the Capital Federal region in 1973, de la Rúa was a legislator in the upper chamber until the military coup of 1976. Over the next few years he worked in universities in Mexico, USA and Venezuela. De la Rúa was re-elected the capital's senator in 1983 and again in 1989, when an agreement between the UCR and the PJ forced him to cede to a minority candidate. Three years later, he was restored to office. Traditionally appointed by the government, in 1996 de la Rúa became the first democratically elected mayor of Buenos Aires with 40% of votes.

In 1997 the UCR combined with the left-wing coalition Frepaso to form the Alianza as a challenge to the dominant PJ. Profiting from corruption charges surrounding Menem's government, the Alianza proved popular in the 1997 congressional elections, winning seats at the expense of the PJ. For the 1999 presidential elections, de la Rúa was chosen as the coalition's candidate. His main rival was the PJ candidate, Eduardo Duhalde. Du la Rúa's campaign to fight corruption and continue tight economic policies won him the presidency with 48% of votes. The victory was not enough for an Alianza majority and the PJ remained stronger by four seats, including the most important seat, Buenos Aires.

Career Peak

On election de la Rúa pledged to tackle corruption, unemployment, the widening gap between rich and poor and rampant tax evasion. In 1999 Argentina was suffering a recession and still had large debts, especially in the provinces. The economy was under pressure to perform well to meet IMF demands. In 1999 Argentina's fiscal deficit was at 3.8% of GDP compared to 2.2% in 1998. The IMF demanded a reduction to 1998 levels by 2000. De la

Rúa announced a continuation of key economic policies begun by Menem. He introduced large cuts in public spending, raised tax and set up an anti-corruption office. He outlined plans to streamline ministries, combining smaller ones to lower cost.

Despite the anti-corruption office, the end of 2000 saw corruption charges against several senators, mainly PJ members, accused of accepting bribes. In Oct. 2000 the vice president, Carlos Alberto Álvarez resigned rocking the Alianza coalition. In the same year, continued economic problems necessitated a US$39.7bn. IMF aid package.

By March 2001, the economy was in crisis as Argentina failed to meet IMF targets agreed in Dec. 2000. Argentina's 33 month recession continued and devaluation and default looked likely. Unemployment was up, the budget deficit was high and consumer spending had fallen sharply. The crisis was exacerbated by a fall in agricultural prices and the threat of foot and mouth disease, both affecting Argentina's lucrative beef exports. As an emergency measure, de la Rúa enlisted the aid of Domingo Cavallo, a successful finance minister in the early 1990s. Cavallo's austerity package included emergency spending cuts of US$1.5bn. in 2001 and US$4.3bn. in 2002 to cure the fiscal deficit. Cavallo was granted special powers to lower taxes, raise tariffs in order to attract investment and encourage production. He agreed a 'zero deficit' policy with the IMF allowing the government to spend only what it receives in tax. 13% pay cut for civil servants in Aug. increased the tension, as did the announcement that their salaries will be paid partly in bonds. Fearing a devaluation of the peso many Argentines removed their money from dollar bank accounts, further destabilizing the economy. In reaction, the government restricted offshore transfers and prevented Argentines from withdrawing more than US$1000 directly from their bank accounts In Dec. 2001 the IMF refused to grant US$1.3bn. in loans to the flailing economy. As unemployment passed 18%, a nationwide strike was called. Public discontent at austerity measures coupled with severe economic hardship led to mass anti-government protests. By 19 Dec. the government had declared a state of siege as rioting intensified and the country teetered on the brink of bankruptcy. Cavallo's special powers were revoked and he along with the entire cabinet, resigned soon after, followed on 20 Dec. by de la Rúa himself. He was forced to flee by helicopter from the rooftop of the presidential palace.

The crisis continued into the New Year as three acting or interim presidents resigned. On 1 Jan. 2002 Congress elected the PJ member Eduardo Duhalde as the country's new president to see out de la Rúa's term until 2003, and to attempt to stabilize both the country and the economy.

Later Life

In Aug. 2012 de la Rúa was put on trial, accused of bribing senators for votes during his presidency.

De Oliveira Salazar, António (Portugal)

Introduction

António de Oliveira Salazar was prime minister of Portugal between 1932–68. He created the Estado Novo (New State), an authoritarian constitution over which he maintained complete control.

Early Life

Salazar was born on 28 April 1889 at Santa Comba Dão, near Coimbra in central Portugal. The son of a farmer he was educated from 1900 at the Viseu seminary before studying economics at the Universidade de Coimbra. Graduating in 1914, Salazar began an academic career at the University becoming its professor of economics in 1918. The following year Salazar co-founded the Centro Academico para la Democracia Crista (Academic Centre for Christian Democracy) in opposition to anticlerical republican parties of the First Republic. In 1921 Salazar served a year in the national assembly before returning to academic life.

Following a military coup in 1926, Salazar was appointed finance minister. Disagreements over the amount of control granted to Salazar led him to resign after 5 days. Two years later he was reappointed by president General António Oscar de Fragoso Carmona with control over government spending. A respected economist, Salazar implemented hardline policies which stabilized the economy in under 2 years and created money for development. He was appointed minister for the colonies in 1930.

Career Peak

Salazar's success as finance minister led Carmona to appoint him prime minister in 1932. Given near total control the premier transformed the government, creating an authoritarian regime. He implemented a corporatist system along lines with undertones of Pope Leo XIII's 1891 encyclical *Rerum novarum* (Of New Things). Salazar appointed his own ministers, and his Estado Nuevo assembly was henceforth dominated by his supporters. Salazar led the only legal party, the União Nacional (Portuguese National Union). Opposition was outlawed and the PVDE secret police (Polícia de Vigilância e Defesa do Estado) was established in 1933 to enforce his rule. The PVDE set up its own prisons, the most notorious of which was the Tarrafal camp on the Cape Verde Islands, established in 1936. Propaganda and censorship were widespread. The Catholic Church, sidelined in 1910 with the establishment of the First Republic, regained political influence.

A supporter of Franco during the Spanish Civil War, Portugal remained neutral during World War II, although Salazar granted concessions to the British in the Azores. Portugal suffered shortages that led to industrial unrest in 1943–44. Underground opposition groups, boosted by popular discontent, tried to force elections in 1945. Salazar managed to suppress the opposition and survived several attempted coups in the late 1940s. In 1949 Portugal joined NATO, although it was not accepted into the UN until 1955.

Salazar kept tight control over economic matters, retaining the post of finance minister until 1940. His rule was economically successful and Portugal's economy strengthened further after World War II. Debt was reduced and annual economic growth from 1960 was consistently 5–7%. Industry, transport networks, energy and the military were developed. Investment in infrastructure was nonetheless to the detriment of education, health and welfare.

1961 brought the beginning of the colonial wars and a change in Salazar's fortunes. Rebellion in Angola and the Indian invasion of Goa and Damao Diu, was followed by revolutionary activity in Mozambique and Guinea-Bissau. Colonial wars were costly and domestic investment suffered. Portugal came under pressure from other European nations that had shed their colonies. But a wave of liberalism stimulated opposition including the student movement and the Portuguese Socialist Action, founded in 1964 and led by future president Mário Soares. Salazar reacted brutally. The Portuguese Writers' Society was closed and the left-wing General Humberto Delgado, defeated in presidential elections in 1958, was assassinated in Spain by the PVDE (renamed the PIDE).

In 1968 Salazar suffered a stroke, and was replaced by Marcel Caetano. He died on 27 July 1970 in Lisbon. Although effectively leaving office in 1968, Salazar's regime remained in place under Caetano until the Carnation Revolution of 25 April 1974 re-established democracy.

De Valera, Éamon (Ireland)

Introduction

Éamon de Valera was the dominant figure of twentieth century Irish politics. Determined to achieve a united independent Ireland, he served as President of the Provisional Government of Ireland (1919–21), Prime Minister of the Irish Free State (1932–48, 1951–54, 1957–59) and President of the Republic of Ireland from 1959–73. He emerged as a leader in the 1916 Easter Uprising and by the time of his death was a world-renowned statesman.

Early Life

De Valera, who was called Edward as a child, was born to an Irish mother and Spanish father in New York on 14 Oct. 1882. When his father died 2 years later, de Valera was sent to Co. Limerick where he was brought up my his mother's family. A talented mathematician, he graduated from Dublin's Royal University in 1904 and then held a series of teaching posts. In 1910 he married Sinead Flanagan, with whom he had seven children, and 3 years later he joined the Irish National Volunteers.

Operating within this organization, he led a battalion in the 1916 Easter Uprising and won recognition for his refusal to surrender until the last moment. The following year he was condemned to death but his sentence was commuted to life imprisonment, partly in recognition of his American birth. Meanwhile he was elected president of Sinn Féin (*We ourselves*), having become the MP for Clare. He was released from prison in a general amnesty but was re-arrested and sentenced in 1918, serving his time in Lincoln in England. He escaped the following year and fled to the USA where he solicited support for the nationalist cause and raised substantial finance.

While de Valera was in America, the Irish MP's formed an Irish Assembly (Dáil Éireann) and declared a republic under de Valera's presidency. In de Valera's absence, Arthur Griffith held the reins of power. The British government introduced the Government of Ireland Act in 1920, which allowed for most of Ulster to remain British while giving dominion status to the rest of Ireland. It failed to satisfy either side and Griffith (along with Michael Collins) negotiated a new Anglo-Irish Treaty (1921–22) with British Prime Minister David Lloyd George, which allowed for a slightly enlarged Irish state.

De Valera disapproved of the agreement because of the partition of Ireland, and he resigned his presidency of the Dáil and Sinn Féin. De Valera fought against the treaty in the ensuing civil war and served a spell in prison during 1923–24. In 1926 he formed a new party, Fianna Fáil (Soldiers of Destiny). He allowed his members to take the required oath of loyalty to the British sovereign but, as the main opposition, he campaigned for the removal of the oath, the end of partition and the termination of land purchase annuities to Britain.

Career Peak

After election success in 1932, de Valera became Prime Minister and in the same year became head of the Council of the League of Nations. The troubled relations with Britain resulted in economic hardship in Ireland, but Britain's 1936 abdication crisis strengthened de Valera's bargaining position. In 1937 he drafted the constitution that established Eire as a sovereign republic and removing many of the symbols of British domination. During World War II Ireland remained neutral and de Valera retained the premiership until 1948.

Ironically, it was the successor government of John Costello, that lasted until 1951, which withdrew Ireland from the British Commonwealth. de Valera had resisted such a move considering it detrimental to the chances of re-uniting the two Irelands. He re-gained power in 1951, was succeeded by Costello in 1954 and served a final spell as Prime Minister from 1957–59. His periods in government during the 1950s were overshadowed by mass emigration, declining industrial output and spiralling unemployment. de Valera's style of leadership was informed principally by his devout Catholicism and sense of social conservatism.

Later Life

By 1959 de Valera had failing eyesight and resigned as Prime Minister (a position known as *Taoiseach* since 1937). He successfully stood for election as President in June 1959 and won a consecutive term in 1966. He retired in 1973, moving into a nursing home near Dublin where he died on 29 Aug. 1975. He overshadowed virtually every other Irish politician of his age but, although he succeeded in creating an independent Irish state, Ireland remained divided.

De Villepin, Dominique (France)

Introduction

Dominique de Villepin, a flamboyant former diplomat and poet, was appointed prime minister of France by the president, Jacques Chirac, on 31 May 2005 following the electorate's dramatic rejection in a referendum of the European Union constitution that had been championed by the government. Villepin faced an uphill struggle to revive the French economy and reduce the high level of unemployment. Critics questioned his ability to unite the country, given that he was a member of the political elite who had never stood for election to public office and with little experience of domestic economic or social policy. Nevertheless, faced with the worst civil unrest in France since the troubles of 1968, he took tough emergency measures in Oct.–Nov. 2005 to deal with widespread rioting across the country. He courted further unpopularity in spring 2006 with controversial legislation on youth employment which was later withdrawn in the face of street demonstrations and strikes. In Dec. 2006 he became only the second serving prime minister to testify before judges over an alleged plot to discredit the interior minister, Nicolas Sarkozy, one of his political rivals.

Early Life

Dominique Marie François René Galouzeau de Villepin was born on 14 Nov. 1953 in Rabat, Morocco (then a French protectorate), the son of a senior civil servant and a businessman. The family moved from Morocco to Caracas, Venezuela, where Villepin attended the French lycée, and then New York, USA.

Villepin attended university in France, first studying literature in Toulouse in the early 1970s, followed by a law degree in Paris at the Institute of Political Studies. His military service included a spell as a naval officer on the aircraft carrier *Clemenceau*. In 1977 he joined the Rassemblement pour la République (RPR), which had been launched the year before by the former prime minister, Jacques Chirac. Villepin consolidated his place among France's governing elite by attending the prestigious École Nationale d'Administration (ENA) in Paris—graduating in May 1980 and being swiftly recruited by the ministry for foreign affairs. He spent 3 years as an adviser at the department for African and Malagasy affairs, before being posted to Washington, D.C. to work as press officer for the French embassy in 1984. He was responsible for dealing with enquiries on French policy in the Middle East at the time of 'Irangate' and the arms-for-hostages scandal. In 1987 Villepin was promoted to head of the press and information unit at the embassy.

Two years later he was transferred to the French embassy in New Delhi, India, serving as second councillor and then first councillor, before returning to Paris in 1992 to resume work at the ministry for foreign affairs. Villepin was assistant director in the department for African and Malagasy affairs in 1993, the year in which France offered support to the government of its former colony, Algeria, in its 'struggle against terrorism and religious fanaticism'. Later that year he became principal private secretary to Alain Juppé, the minister for foreign affairs. Following Jacques Chirac's victory in the presidential elections of May 1995, Villepin was appointed secretary-general of the presidency of the republic, a post he retained until May 2002. He became one of the president's closest confidants, and is thought to have advised Chirac to dissolve parliament in 1997, a year earlier than necessary, in an attempt to give the by then unpopular prime minister, Juppé, a mandate to see through an economic austerity package. However, Villepin and Chirac misjudged the mood of voters, who delivered an outright majority for the left and forced the appointment of Lionel Jospin as prime minister, heralding 5 years of *cohabitation* with the left.

When the centre-right regained control of the government in the 2002 legislative elections, Villepin was appointed minister for foreign affairs. He is credited with negotiating a peace settlement between the government and rebels in Côte d'Ivoire, which was enforced by 3,000 French troops. In early 2003, in the build-up to the US-led invasion of Iraq, Villepin became known internationally as one of the war's main opponents, particularly after his impassioned address to the United Nations on 14 Feb. 2003. Less well publicized, however, was his backing for French military intervention in the Central African Republic a few weeks later, following a coup in the former colony.

In a reshuffle in March 2004 Villepin succeeded Nicolas Sarkozy as minister for the interior, internal security and local freedoms. He built on Sarkozy's police service reforms and won plaudits for tightening visa regulations and cracking down on Islamic militancy. When, in a referendum on 29 May 2005, the French public voted against the ratification of the new EU constitution, the government, which had campaigned for the 'yes' vote, was forced to make changes. President Chirac accepted the resignation of his unpopular prime minister, Jean-Pierre Raffarin, on 30 May and immediately appointed Villepin as his successor.

Career Peak

Villepin formally took over from Raffarin in a brief handover ceremony at the prime minister's official residence on 31 May 2005. On 2 June the deputy secretary-general of the Elysée Palace unveiled the new cabinet of 31 ministers appointed by Villepin. In a television interview, Villepin gave himself 100 days to 'restore the confidence of the people'. and promised to make reducing France's high rate of unemployment his priority. In his general policy declaration to parliament on 8 June, Villepin restated his desire to 'win the battle for jobs'. He added that France, as 'a founding country, will occupy a full place in the European Union. It will respect its commitments. It will continue to pull the European adventure upwards... Europe has been built on the economy and pragmatism. People are now demanding more humanity and more protection: greater job security, increased attention to environmental issues, better defence of the values of respect and equal opportunities.' He continued: 'The meaning of Europe can be found in these values. It cannot be constructed through market forces alone'. Villepin's speech was followed by a vote of confidence from the National Assembly which he won by 363 votes to 178 (with 4 abstentions).

In Sept. 2005 Villepin announced his economic recovery plan. This included proposals for tax reform, financial incentives to encourage job seekers and to reduce the numbers of people receiving state benefits, and tighter controls on welfare payments. He also introduced new employment contracts with easier-dismissal rules for companies with fewer than 20 employees. Despite opposition from the trade unions, Villepin accelerated the privatization programme, selling a first government stake in Gaz de France. In Oct. there was a national strike in protest at new labour and welfare reforms. Later in the month rioting began in the largely immigrant suburbs of northeastern Paris. As the unrest escalated and the destruction spread across the country, Villepin declared a state of emergency, invoking a 1955 law that allowed local authorities to impose curfews and restrict movements in troubled areas. The government extended the state of emergency for 3 months as the country gradually calmed down after 3 weeks of unrest. Villepin acknowledged that the government had made mistakes in its treatment of its immigrants and promised to improve life in the suburbs for poorer communities with high levels of unemployment. In April 2006 his government was forced to scrap unpopular legislation on youth employment in response to widespread strikes and protests. Later in the year he was questioned about an attempt to smear his interior minister and political rival, Nicolas Sarkozy, over alleged secret payments and accounts relating to defence deals. Villepin tendered his resignation on 15 May 2007, the final day of Jacques Chirac's term.

Later Life

In Jan. 2010 Villepin was acquitted of attempting to smear Sarkozy. He also defeated a prosecution appeal against the verdict in Sept. 2011. The case strengthened Villepin's position as one of Sarkozy's leading right-wing opponents and in June 2010 he established a new centre-right party to challenge the UMP president. However, he failed to garner sufficient support to contest the presidency in 2012.

Demirel, Suleiman (Turkey)

Introduction

Demirel served seven terms as Turkey's prime minister, before becoming the country's ninth president in 1993. He retired from office in May 2000, and was replaced by Ahmet Necdet Sezer.

Early Life

Demirel was born on 6 Oct. 1924 in Islâmköy. He took a degree in engineering at İstanbul Technical University. In 1949 he started working for the Department of Electrical Works, and later went to the USA to work on a number of irrigation and electrification projects. He began his lengthy political career in 1961 when he was elected to parliament as a member of the Justice Party. He rose to be party leader 3 years later.

Career Peak

In Oct. 1965 Demirel was elected prime minister for the first time. In power he set out to strengthen Turkey's links with the West, and in particular the members of NATO. He also endeavoured to improve the lot of the Turkish peasantry by initiating a rural development programme.

Demirel went on to lead four successive coalition governments until 1971, when military opposition to his moderate policies forced his resignation. Demirel refused to capitulate to senior army officials who demanded an active political role in combating terrorism. He was restored to power in 1975 by a coalition of the Justice Party and a number of smaller, nationalist parties.

The major difficulties that dogged Demirel's ministry were inflation, a widening trade deficit, growing civil unrest and the terrorist activities of fundamentalist Islamic groups. In spite of these obstacles he continued to pursue a policy that aimed to generate economic growth, but was frustrated by the weak and fractured nature of his coalition governments. His fourth tenure in office ended in June 1977, but he returned to power intermittently until the end of the year when he became the leader of the opposition. His sixth term as prime minister began in Nov. 1979, and ended the following year, when the military again ousted him in the wake of further terrorist bloodshed. A ban was imposed on his participation in politics, and the Justice Party was barred from parliament. The ban was rescinded in 1987, and Demirel re-entered the political arena as the chairman of the new True Path Party (DYP). The electoral defeat of the Motherland Party returned him to prime ministerial office for a seventh time in Nov. 1991.

After the sudden death of Turgut Özal, Demirel was elected president. He retired from politics in May 2000.

Demirel died on 17 June 2015 aged 90.

Deng Xiaoping (China)

Introduction

Despite never having held any of the major state offices, Deng Xiaoping became one of the most influential leaders of modern China. His economic reforms rescued China from the chaos wrought by the Cultural Revolution of the 1960s and laid the foundations for his country's current economic progress.

Early Life

Deng was born on 22 Aug. 1922 in Sichuan province, into a prosperous family of landowners. Family money allowed him to study abroad between 1921–26, first in France, where he was first involved in the Communist movement, and then in the Soviet Union.

Returning to China after 1926, Deng made for the Chinese Soviet, established by the Communists in the south-west. He was soon involved in both political and military activities as the Communist 'statelet' was besieged by the Nationalist forces of Chiang Kai-shek (Chiang Chieh-shih). On the Long March (1934–35) Deng became a trusted colleague of the party leadership and was appointed political officer to the Communist Eighth Route Army in 1937.

Deng's career progress was slow. Although appointed to the Central Committee of the party in 1945 and to the leadership of the Second Field Army in 1948 during the civil war against the Nationalists, when the People's Republic of China was established on 1 Oct. 1949, Deng was not rewarded with a position in national government. Instead he was posted to the south-west as a regional party official. In 1952 Deng finally received the call to come to Beijing and became one of the deputy premiers. In 1955 he became a member of the Politburo.

As his reputation increased, Deng began to influence state policy, but he became a victim of the divisions within the party leadership. Mao Zedong placed emphasis on continuing revolution and equality. Deng, allied with the head of state, Liu Shaoqi, recognised that most individuals are motivated by personal economic rewards. Deng's pragmatism was out of tune with the revolutionary zeal of the Cultural Revolution and he was purged from high office in 1967. By 1969 Deng had vanished from public life. When the Cultural Revolution had been discredited, Deng's climb back was rapid. He was reappointed to a deputy premiership by Zhou Enlai in 1973, and by 1975 he was back in the Politburo and was deputy chairman of the Central Committee. As Zhou Enlai's health declined, his protégé, Deng, exercised more of the levers of power. But a second fall awaited him.

When Zhou died in Jan. 1976, the radical Gang of Four secured Deng's removal from government again. Nine months later, following Mao's death, the radicals in turn were purged and Deng's second return to power began.

Mao's successor Hua Guofeng lost the battle for the leadership of the party. In mid-1977 Deng was back in office in the Politburo and the Central Committee. In 1980 Hua was forced out of the premiership and in the following year had to resign the party leadership. Yet Deng did not take on either position.

Career Peak

From 1980–81 Deng Xiaoping was effectively the ruler of China, but he ruled through 'lieutenants'. Zhao Ziyang was appointed premier in 1980 and Hu Yaobang party leader in 1981. Deng and his allies were now free to implement reforms.

State-owned industries gained economic independence and managers were encouraged to make profits. Throughout the economy personal financial incentives were introduced. On the small scale, for example, peasants were allowed to determine their own production plans. On the macro-scale, free ports and development zones along the southern and eastern coasts were opened to foreign investment and enterprise. Many aspects of planning were decentralised. The result was strong economic growth and greatly increased agricultural production. Social reforms too were introduced, not all of them liberal. A rigid policy of family planning—including a legal requirement for families not to have more than one child—was introduced.

With his reform programme bringing success, Deng stepped further out of the limelight. He gave up his posts on the Politburo and Central Committee in 1987, but continued to govern the country through loyal colleagues. Yet one the biggest challenges to his plans was still to come. Economic reform increased public appetite for greater personal freedom and political reform—neither was forthcoming. Party leader Hu Yaobang gave some indication of sympathy towards these expectations and was subsequently removed as general secretary of the party in 1987. Hu's death in 1989 coincided with the death throes of Communism in eastern Europe, and his funeral was marked by large-scale student protests in favour of political freedoms. Students and workers occupied Tiananmen Square in central Beijing. In the face of this challenge to authority Deng momentarily wavered. But he came down in favour of the authoritarian old guard and the protests were crushed by force and loss of life.

After the Tiananmen Square massacre Jiang Zemin was appointed party leader, but Deng remained in charge of the country's economic development until his death on 19 Feb. 1997.

Denktaş, Rauf (Turkish Republic of Northern Cyprus, Cyprus)

Introduction

Turkish Cypriot leader and President of the Turkish Republic of Northern Cyprus (TRNC) since 1984, Rauf Denktaş was one of the key players in the proclamation of the breakaway Turkish Federated State of Cyprus in 1975. He sought international recognition for the sovereignty of the TRNC and maintained that Cyprus should be reunited as a confederation of two equal states. All attempts at peace talks between Denktaş and the Greek Cypriot government were unsuccessful. His fourth consecutive term as president ended in April 2005.

Early Life

Denktaş was born on 27 Jan. 1924 near Paphos. The son of a judge, he graduated from the Lefkosa British School in 1942, where he taught for a year before studying law in the UK. Admitted to the Bar from Lincoln's Inn in 1947, he returned to Cyprus to set up his own legal practice and from 1949–57 was a leading lawyer for the prosecution under the British colonial regime. When the Enosis issue created further tension in Cyprus after World War II, Denktaş served as the Turkish Affairs representative (in 1948–49) to the Constitutional Council established by the UK to consider constitutional reforms leading to Cypriot self-government.

In 1959–60 Denktaş led the Turkish delegation at the independence negotiations and the drafting of the new constitution. However, once the power-sharing agreement between the Turkish minority and Greek majority broke down in 1963 and sectarian violence escalated, Turkey demanded the partition of the island. In 1964 Denktaş was banned from returning to Cyprus from Ankara, the Turkish capital, and remained in exile until 1968. On his return, he assumed the vice-presidency and then from 1973 the presidency of the Turkish Cypriot Autonomous Administration. He was Turkish Cypriot spokesman at intermittent intercommunal talks until 1974 when Turkish forces invaded and effectively partitioned the island.

Career Peak

In 1975 Denktaş was declared president of the independent 'Turkish Federated State of Cyprus'. The following year he founded the conservative National Unity Party (UBP), which dominated the first Turkish Cypriot Assembly elections. He was re-elected in 1981 as the UBP candidate, but with a reduced majority (51.8% of the vote) as opposition groups, seeing their part of the island becoming poorer in contrast to the Greek Cypriot territory, advocated greater flexibility in the UN-sponsored talks.

In Nov. 1983, Denktaş proclaimed the Turkish Republic of Northern Cyprus (TRNC), which was condemned by the UN Security Council and recognised only by Turkey. However, he was returned in the June 1985 presidential election by an increased margin (70.5% of the vote). He began direct UN-sponsored negotiations with the newly-elected president of the Greek-Cypriot zone in 1988, but these were eventually abandoned in 1990 because Denktaş insisted on the right to self-determination for Turkish Cypriots.

In 1992 fresh talks based on a bicommunal approach for a settlement stalled over disagreements on the powers of the central government, demilitarization and the division of the territory. Denktaş was deemed responsible by the UN for the lack of progress. There was also conflict between Denktaş (who earlier had won the 1990 TRNC presidential election standing as an independent candidate) and the UBP Prime Minister Derviş Eroğlu (who advocated partition) over the handling of the talks. This divergence resulted in the setting up in July 1992 of the pro-Denktaş Democratic Party which included former UBP deputies. In the April 1995 and April 2000 elections Denktaş retained the presidency, defeating UBP leader Eroğlu on both occasions.

Despite further negotiations on a federal settlement, including in 2002 the first face-to-face meetings between Denktaş and the Greek Cypriot leader Glafcos Clerides in 4 years, little progress was made. In Dec. 2002, Reçep Tayyip Erdoğan, leader of Turkey's ruling Justice and Development Party, urged Denktaş to embark on new talks with the Greek Cypriot government, based on the UN's plans to create a demilitarized country divided into Swiss-style cantons. But by the March deadline, Denktaş and his new opposite number Tassos Papadopoulos had failed to accept the reunification proposals. Denktaş believed the agreement compromised too much land while Papadopoulos was unhappy with the number of Greek Cypriots allowed to return to the North.

As a result of the failure of the talks, it seemed likely that the Greek sector would accede alone to the EU in May 2004. Under increasing pressure from the Turkish Cypriot population, Denktaş made an unexpected gesture in April 2003 by opening the border in Nicosia to allow day-passage for members of both communities. The decision was welcomed by the Greek Cypriot government, which responded by lifting the trade ban and by offering the Turkish-Cypriot community healthcare and benefits.

Denktaş announced in May 2004 that he would not stand for president in the 2005 elections. He was succeeded by Mehmet Ali Talat on 25 April 2005. He died aged 87 on 13 Jan. 2012.

Deuba, Sher Bahadur (Nepal)

Introduction

Sher Bahadur Deuba has served four terms as prime minister of Nepal, most recently from June 2017–Feb. 2018.

Early Life

Sher Bahadur Deuba was born on 13 June 1946 in Dadeldhura. While at university, he was a founding member of the Nepal Students Union and was elected its president in 1971.

In 1994 he became the Nepali Congress parliamentary leader, and then prime minister in Sept. 1995. This term lasted until March 1997, and during this time he oversaw the Mahakali Treaty, signed with India, which regulated the development and use of the Mahakali River.

Deuba strengthened his position within his own party in 2001 after defeating Sushil Koirala in the election for parliamentary party leader. He began his second term as prime minister in July that year. However, he failed to bring Maoist rebels to any kind of agreement, which led to several states of emergency being announced, and King Gyanendra ended his premiership in Oct. 2002.

Deuba's third brief period as prime minister from June 2004–Feb. 2005 resulted once again in him being dismissed by the king, who was in the midst of establishing his own undisputed rule. Deuba was imprisoned under charges of corruption but released in Feb. 2006.

Disagreements in the party in 2002 led to the Nepali Congress splitting, with Deuba leading the Nepali Congress (Democratic) faction, although there was a reconciliation in 2007. Deuba successfully ran as the candidate for the Dadeldhura and Kanchanpur-4 constituencies for the Constituent Assembly elections of 10 April 2008. However, he lost his bid for the premiership in the Aug. elections of that year. In 2009 Ram Chandra Paul defeated Deuba in the race for parliamentary leader.

Career Peak

Pushpa Kamal Dahal of the Communist Party of Nepal (Maoist-Centre), who had been elected prime minister in Aug. 2016, resigned in May 2017, in what was an expected move. His coalition government with the Nepali Congress had scheduled such a power-sharing rotation, and he was replaced by Deuba, who had earlier become president of the Congress, on 7 June 2017.

Entering his fourth term as premier, Deuba promised to implement the new constitution of 2015, and pledged to hold the second phase of local elections in 2018.

However, he faced strong domestic opposition; he accused the Left alliance, comprising the Communist Party of Nepal (Unified Marxist-Leninist) and the Communist Party of Nepal (Maoist-Centre), of trying to derail democracy. Parliamentary elections in Dec. 2017 further undermined his position as the Left alliance won 174 seats against 63 for the Nepali Congress. Deuba resigned on 15 Feb. 2018 and was succeeded as prime minister by Khadga Prasad Oli.

Dewar, Donald (Scotland, United Kingdom)

Introduction

Donald Campbell Dewar was the Labour first minister (1999–2000) of Scotland's first parliament since the seventeenth century. A prominent Labour politician who had championed the cause of Scottish devolution since the late 1960s, he played a key role in Labour's general election success of 1997. However, his most important work came in establishing a Scottish parliament and serving as its first minister. He was plagued by ill health during its first year and died in office.

Early Life

Dewar was born on 21 Aug. 1937 in Glasgow, Scotland to Dr Alasdair Dewar, a consultant dermatologist, and Mary, who ran the Scottish Culture Society. His parents both suffered ill health and Dewar spent an unhappy spell at boarding school before attending the Glasgow Academy. He then studied law at Glasgow University, where he honed his debating skills as a member of the Labour Club and president of the University Union. He also became close friends with contemporaries including the future Labour leader John Smith and the future Liberal Democrat foreign affairs spokesman Menzies Campbell. He trained and practised as a solicitor and in 1964 he married Alison, whom he had met at university. They would have two children.

In the same year Dewar narrowly lost a parliamentary election in the seat of Aberdeen South but entered the house as the member for that constituency following the 1966 election. In Oct. 1967 he was appointed as parliamentary private secretary to Anthony Crossland, the president of the board of trade. The Scottish National Party were gaining in influence at this time and in response Dewar made a speech in support of Scottish devolution. Three years later Dewar narrowly lost his seat. In addition, he developed a back problem that would afflict him for the rest of his life and his wife left him for a former university friend, Derry Irvine, who would later become Lord Chancellor. It would be 8 years before Dewar returned to the Commons, winning the seat of Glasgow Garscadden in the face of strong Scottish Nationalist opposition. He served this constituency, which evolved into Glasgow Anniesland following boundary changes, until the end of his career.

Dewar campaigned with Conservative and Liberal representatives for devolution in the first referendum to be held on the subject in 1979. They won a small majority but less than the required 40% to proceed with the motion. In opposition he was chairman of the select committee on Scottish affairs, 1980–81, before becoming spokesman for Scottish affairs, a post held until 1992. He vociferously supported Scottish industry throughout the Conservative administration and spent much of the 1980s on the moderate wing of the Labour party in conflict with the far left. In 1984 he successfully defended a move by the left to deselect him from his parliamentary seat. In 1990 he played an instrumental part in the Scottish Constitutional Convention, which brought together Labour politicians, members of rival parties, trade union and church members to discuss a potential Scottish parliament. The blueprint would provide a foundation for his work in the years to come.

When John Smith became Labour leader in 1992 he named Dewar as shadow social services secretary, where he established a commission on social justice. Smith died suddenly in 1994 and his successor, Tony Blair, made Dewar the party's chief whip in 1996. Dewar became a privy counsellor in the same year and, as chief whip, ensured that there was a minimum of party dissension in the lead up to the May 1997 general election. Labour returned to power with a landslide victory and Dewar was rewarded with the post he most desired, secretary of state for Scotland. He immediately drew up plans for a Scottish Parliament and in the referendum on Scottish devolution held on 11 Sept. 1997, 74.3% voted for a parliament with 63.5% wanting it to have tax raising powers. He guided the relevant legislation through parliament and elections for the first Scottish parliament took place in May 1999.

Career Peak

Dewar was elected as first minister of an executive that included both Labour and Liberal Democrat members. The first year of the parliament was not to prove an easy one. There were divisive rows over university tuition fees and Section 28, a clause in the Local Government Act prohibiting the promotion of homosexuality as a 'pretended family relationship' by local authorities. There was also considerable controversy at the rising costs of the proposed Scottish parliament building. In May 2000 Dewar underwent major heart surgery at the Glasgow Royal Infirmary, before returning to work 3 months later. While retaining his enthusiasm for his work, his health had clearly suffered. In Oct. 2000 he had a fall outside his home in Edinburgh. His condition quickly deteriorated and it was found he had internal bleeding in the head. On 11 Oct. his children took the decision to switch off his life support machine. A politician respected across party boundaries for his intellect, wit and personal charm, his lasting monument was the establishment of the Scottish parliament.

Dhoinine, Ikililou (Comoros)

Introduction

Ikililou Dhoinine was sworn in as the president on 26 May 2011, assuming power five months after securing electoral victory. Dhoinine had previously served for 5 years as vice president to the departing head of state, Ahmed Abdallah Mohamed Sambi. The 2001 constitution demands that the presidency rotates every 4 years between representatives of the three islands of which the archipelago is composed. Dhoinine is the first president to hail from the federation's smallest island, Mohéli, and his appointment was only the second peaceful handover of power.

Early Life

Ikililou Dhoinine was born in Djoièzi, a village on Mohéli, on 14 Aug. 1962. Before entering government he qualified as a pharmacist. As vice president, he took responsibility for the budget and women's entrepreneurship. He also served for five days in March 2008 as provisional president of Anjouan (one of the Comorian islands) after a diplomatic crisis there resulted in an armed intervention by the federal government.

Following the second round of presidential elections on 26 Dec. 2010 the electoral commission announced that Dhoinine had won 61.1% of the popular vote. His closest rival, Mohamed Said Fazul, alleged electoral fraud but the election monitoring group concluded that any breaches of protocol had not been sufficient to alter the result. The opposition later complained that the five-month gap between polling and the new leader's inauguration amounted to an unconstitutional extension of office for the outgoing president. Sambi's tenure had exceeded its mandate by several months even before the election.

Career Peak

Dhoinine's peaceful assumption of the presidency suggested a degree of political stability that has hitherto eluded the country. He pledged to consolidate national unity while tackling the endemic corruption that has blighted the federation's governance since it gained independence. He campaigned specifically on a policy of much-needed infrastructure investment. An alleged plot against his government prompted several arrests in April 2013, and inter-island disputes and political rivalries have since persisted. Dhoinine left office in May 2016 and was succeeded by former coup leader and president Azali Assoumani, who won elections held in April.

Di Rupo, Elio (Belgium)

Introduction

Elio Di Rupo became prime minister in Dec. 2011 at the head of a six-party coalition, bringing to a conclusion talks that lasted 541 days. A French speaker from the Walloon region, Di Rupo is regarded as a pragmatist and a skilled negotiator.

Early Life

Born on 18 July 1951 in Morlanwelz to Italian migrant parents, Elio Di Rupo was awarded a PhD in chemistry from the University of Mons-Hainault (UMH). He taught at Leeds University in the UK from 1977 before returning to Belgium the following year to work at UMH and the Institute for Scientific Research in Industry and Agriculture.

He joined the Socialist Party (PS) and was elected a municipal councillor in Mons in 1982. In 1987 he entered parliament as MP for Mons-Borinage, serving until 1989 when he was elected a Member of the European Parliament. In 1991 he became a senator and from 1992–94 was minister of education for the French-speaking community, as well as minister for audiovisual policy from 1993–94. In 1994 Di Rupo was appointed deputy prime minister and minister for communications and public enterprises. He remained deputy prime minister following the 1995 parliamentary election but was named minister for the economy and telecommunications. In 1998 he was also put in charge of foreign trade.

After the 1999 election Di Rupo helped negotiate the 'rainbow coalition' of Liberals, Socialists and Greens. As minister-president of the Walloon region, he initiated a 10 year programme designed to lift the region out of economic decline. In Oct. 1999 he was elected president of the PS and resigned his minister-president post. He also became vice-president of the Socialist International group.

While serving as mayor of Mons from 2000–05, he was appointed minister of state, representing Belgium in talks on a European constitution. As president of the PS, Di Rupo oversaw a review to widen the party's appeal and, following its strong performance in the 2003 election, brought it into the 'Purple Coalition' of Liberals and Socialists. After updating his development plan for the Walloon region, he was reappointed its minister-president in Oct. 2005, holding the post until July 2007 when he again became mayor of Mons.

In the June 2010 general election the PS became the second largest party in parliament, one seat behind the nationalist New-Flemish Alliance (N-VA). Di Rupo participated in negotiations with N-VA to form a coalition government but differences over increased autonomy for the regions resulted in deadlock. In Oct. 2011 he instigated talks with five other parties to form a government. In Nov. 2011, after Belgium's credit status was downgraded, the parties agreed a package of budget cuts and constitutional reforms, including increased fiscal autonomy for the regions.

Career Peak

Di Rupo took office on 6 Dec. 2011 at the head of a coalition of Liberal, Socialist and Christian Democrat parties, promising to cut €11·3bn. from the national budget. In early 2012 his austerity measures provoked strikes and his centre-right coalition partners resisted planned tax increases. His principal task has been to maintain a coalition of diverse partners while addressing Belgium's economic difficulties. In addition, he faced opposition from Flemish nationalists, who favoured greater regional autonomy and who made major gains at local elections in Oct. 2012.

Di Rupo's stint as prime minister came to an end in Oct. 2014 when he was replaced by Charles Michel of the Reformist Movement, who had formed a new government in the aftermath of elections in May.

Díaz Ordaz, Gustavo (Mexico)

Introduction

Representing the dominant Partido Revolucionario Institucional (Institutional Revolutionary Party; PRI), Gustavo Díaz Ordaz was president of Mexico from 1964 to 1970. His presidency aimed to promote economic development for Mexico, but any achievements were clouded by civil unrest and discontentment, and especially by the 1968 student massacre in Mexico City.

Early Life

Díaz was born in Cuidad Serdánin in the state of Puebla on 12 March 1911. He was a relative of an associate of the nineteenth century Mexican president Benito Juárez (ruler between 1858–76), a Zapotec Indian from Oaxaca. A trained lawyer, Díaz's political career began as a Supreme Court president in Puebla and in 1946 he was elected to the Mexican senate, becoming interior minister in 1958. Díaz was elected president on 1 Dec. 1964, succeeding his fellow PRI colleague Adolfo López Mateo.

Career Peak

During his presidency, Díaz aimed to implement economic developments in Mexico, but his government did little to change the image of its party as conservative, restrictive and undemocratic. As in many countries across Europe, a wave of civil unrest began in 1966 with anti-government student demonstrations. These culminated in 1968 with the student protest in Mexico City that resulted in the Tlaelolco Massacre. The principle complaints about the government were its single party rule, restricted freedom of speech and excessive government spending. In 1968, as Mexico prepared to be the first 'third world' country to host the Olympic Games, there was much criticism of the amount of public money spent on the preparations and the consequent neglect of social programmes. On 2 Oct. 1968, 5,000 students and workers gathered in Mexico City's Plaza de las Tres Culturas to protest against the government. Their demands included the freeing of political prisoners and autonomy for the universities. The army surrounded the protesters and opened fire killing more than 250 people and injuring thousands, although the official death toll was much lower. The massacre led to a series of guerrilla movements that would disrupt Mexican society throughout the 1970s and blight the presidency of Díaz's successor Luis Echeverría Álvarez who took over the presidency from 1970.

Later Life

Díaz died in Mexico City on 15 July 1979.

Diefenbaker, John (Canada)

Introduction

John George Diefenbaker was the Progressive Conservative Prime Minister of Canada 1957–63. A social and economic reformer, he was a strong advocate of greater racial harmony within Canada and sought to reduce Canada's reliance on the United States. He was elected for a record 13 parliamentary terms, his last term starting just 3 months before his death.

Early Life

Diefenbaker was born in Neustadt, Ontario on 18 Sept. 1895. He was educated by his father and graduated from the University of Saskatchewan in 1916 with a degree in Political Science and Economics. He then served with the 105th Saskatoon Fusiliers in World War I, achieving the rank of lieutenant before being invalided home. In 1919 he qualified from the University of Saskatchewan with a degree in Law and was called to the Bar in that same year. He had a successful law practice and in 1930 he was created a King's Counsel.

In 1925 and 1926 Diefenbaker was unsuccessful in attempts to enter the House of Commons, and he also failed at the provincial elections of 1929, the mayoral elections for his adopted home of Prince Albert, Saskatchewan in 1933 and again at the provincial elections of 1938. Having become head of the Saskatchewan branch of the Conservatives in 1936, his party failed to gain any seats at the 1938 elections. However, in 1940 he was voted into the House of Commons as the member for Lake Centre, Saskatchewan. This would remain his constituency until 1953 when he became the member for Prince Albert, the area he would serve until his death.

Two years later he stood for the party leadership but was defeated. After the Conservatives changed their name to the Progressive Conservatives (PC) Diefenbaker again made an unsuccessful bid for the leadership. In 1956, at the third attempt, he won the battle to head his party, replacing George Drew.

Career Peak

In 1957 he led the Conservatives to election victory, ending 22 years of Liberal rule and replacing Louis St Laurent as Prime Minister on 11 June. The following year, PC made further election gains, claiming 208 out of 256 available seats, the Conservatives' largest ever majority.

As Canada's leader, Diefenbaker sought to improve ethnic relations within the country. 'In my party,' he said 'we have members of Italian, Dutch, German, Scandinavian, Chinese and Ukrainian origin–and they are all Canadians'. In 1958 he issued a Canadian Bill of Rights and made James Gladstone Canada's first aboriginal senator. In 1960 he extended the vote to all aboriginal groups. Diefenbaker supported the independence movements sweeping through many Commonwealth countries and he protested against South Africa's entry into the Commonwealth in 1961 on the grounds of its apartheid regime.

To reduce Canada's dependence on the United States he sought closer ties abroad, notably with Britain, though it was not a policy that was wholly successful. He introduced numerous social and economic reforms, including the Agricultural Rehabilitation and Development Act, which rejuvenated the industry and prompted vigorous trade with the Far East. He initiated schemes to boost the economy of Canada's northern area and to improve health and welfare.

In the debit side there was rising unemployment. The party also suffered when it cancelled the landmark Avro Arrow aircraft in 1959. Relations with America were variable as when Diefenbaker refused to support US intervention in Cuba in 1961. At the elections of 1962, the Conservatives were returned with a reduced majority, claiming only 116 seats. The following year saw a crisis over the proposed manufacture of nuclear weapons. On 5 Feb. 1963 Diefenbaker's government succumbed to two no-confidence motions. In the subsequent elections the Liberals won 129 seats against 95 for the PC.

Later Life

Diefenbaker retained the party leadership until 1967 when he was succeeded by Robert Stanfield. In 1969 he became Chancellor of the University of Saskatchewan, his *alma mater*. He died at his home in Ottawa on 16 Aug. 1979.

Diouf, Abdou (Senegal)

Introduction

Abdou Diouf was Senegal's first prime minister from 1970–80 and president from 1981–2000. A socialist, he was defeated in the elections of 2000 bringing to an end 40 years of socialist rule.

Early Life

Diouf was born on 7 Sept. 1935 in Louga, Senegal. Schooled in Saint-Louis, he attended the University of Dakar and in 1958 went to the Sorbonne in Paris to study law.

Diouf returned to Senegal in 1960 to take up a civil service post. He was appointed a regional governor the following year and became general secretary to the presidency in 1964. He was minister of planning and industry from 1968–70 when he was nominated prime minister in the government of President Senghor. When Senghor resigned the presidency in 1980, Diouf succeeded him, taking office on 1 Jan. 1981.

Career Peak

Continuing Senghor's policy of inter-African co-operation, Diouf was instrumental in the establishment of the Confederation of Senegal and Gambia in 1982, an affiliation that lasted for 7 years. He was re-elected president with more than 80% of votes in 1983. Diouf's international reputation grew particularly with involvement with the Organization of African Unity. He was its president in 1985–86, a post he held again 7 years later. He was also a prominent figure in the Economic Community of West African States, the Group of 15 (a summit group for emerging nations) and the Islamic Conference.

Despite his international stature, Diouf's tenure was often troubled. In the aftermath of the 1983 elections there were riots by separatists in the Casamance region of the country. Diouf's re-election in 1988 with more than 73% of votes were challenged by the opposition who accused him of fraud, which led to further rioting. Diouf responded by declaring a state of emergency, during which Abdoulaye Wade (later president and then in opposition) was arrested.

Tensions with neighbouring Mauritania seriously deteriorated in the late 1980s, resulting in an unofficial border war in 1990. Diplomatic relations between the two countries were restored in 1992. Diouf secured another term of office in 1993 but, despite significant international aid, the national economy was crippled and devaluation followed in 1994. In addition, a ceasefire agreed with Casamance separatists in 1993 fell apart 2 years later.

At the elections of March 2000 Diouf was defeated by Abdoulaye Wade, who became head of Senegal's first non-Socialist government.

Djibo, Salou (Niger)

Introduction

Salou Djibo came to power in Feb. 2010 after a military coup. An army squadron leader, he was one of a faction that objected to President Mamadou Tandja's law change allowing him to extend his term of office. Despite a low public profile, Djibo was named leader of the Supreme Council for the Restoration of Democracy by fellow coup members. He has pledged to prepare the country for democratic elections.

Early Life

Salou Djibo was born on 15 April 1965 in the village of Namaro in western Niger. He joined the army in 1987, serving in several divisions before training as an officer in Bouaké, Côte d'Ivoire. He rose through the ranks, becoming squadron leader by 2006. During this period he became a specialist in artillery warfare, participating in training programmes in China and Morocco. He served on two UN peacekeeping missions, in Côte d'Ivoire in 2004 and in

the Democratic Republic of the Congo in 2006, after which he returned to Niger to take command of a garrison in Niamey.

Following President Tandja's amendment of the constitution to extend his term of office, Djibo joined an army faction opposed to his actions in late 2009. Against a background of domestic protests and growing international pressure, during which Niger was suspended from the Economic Community of West African States, a group of senior officers including Djibo, planned a takeover. On 18 Feb. 2010 troops stormed the presidential palace and seized control of government, imprisoning Tandja. Djibo was named leader of the Supreme Council for the Restoration of Democracy and announced that he was forming a transitional government.

Career Peak

On taking power Djibo dissolved the constitution and put government business under the control of regional and ministerial leaders. On 24 Feb. 2010 he appointed Mahamadou Danda, a civilian and former spokesman of Niger's 1999 transitional government, as temporary prime minister. In March 2010 Djibo acknowledged that Niger would suffer famine later in the year. His government also announced a review of uranium contracts in a bid to ensure transparency. After enjoying initial widespread public support and cautious co-operation from the international community, Djibo insisted that the military-led government would work towards holding general elections and that no member of the junta would be allowed to stand in the presidential election (scheduled for Jan. 2011). In Oct. 2010 a new constitution designed to facilitate the restoration of civilian rule was approved in a national referendum. Djibo decided not to run in the 2011 presidential elections and was succeeded by Mahamadou Issoufou, who won the run-off on 12 March 2011.

Djohar, Saïd Mohamed (Comoros)

Introduction

Saïd Mohamed Djohar became interim head of state in Nov. 1989 after the death of Ahmed Abdallah Abdereman and the subsequent coup led by the mercenary, Bob Denard. Djohar was president from 1990–95.

Early Life

Djohar was born in the 1920s but little is known of his early life.

Career Peak

Following the death of Abdallah, Denard and the Garde Presidentielle (PG, Presidential Guard) installed Djohar as head of state. Djohar created a provisional government until elections of Feb. 1990, which were marred by accusations of fraud. In March 1990, Djohar was elected president with 55.3% of the votes. In Aug. 1991 the president of the Supreme Court announced the dismissal of Djohar on the grounds of negligence after which Djohar imposed a state of emergency.

International reaction was strong. France and South Africa (believed to have been the principal funders of the PG), cut off aid to the country and demanded Denard leave the country. He went to Pretoria, although a French commission ultimately exonerated him of blame in the death of Abdullah.

Djohar eventually formed a coalition government, including opposition parties that favoured the secession of Mwali, one of the four Comoran islands. In Nov. 1991, Udzima (Comoran Union for Progress), formerly supporters of Djohar, came out in opposition to his rule. New constitutional provisions were approved by 74% of voters in June 1992 and another government was formed.

In Oct. 1992, a demonstration by opposition parties demanding Djohar's resignation was forcibly suppressed. In Sept. 1992, there was another failed coup and the perpetrators were sentenced to death. Later that year, government forces attacked rebels in Mbenu (northeast of Moroni) and there was fighting on Nzwani. Dozens of people died in clashes between rebels and government forces. The Nov. 1992 elections were marked by violence and fraud. Strikes occurred on a regular basis, with the aim of forcing Djohar from power or as a protest at the non-payment of civil servants.

Djohar announced the formation of a new party, the Rassemblement pour la Démocratie et le Renouveau (RDRfor Democracy and Revival) in Oct. 1993. Elections in Dec. 1993 led to victory by the RDR but were marred by killings and accusations of corruption. In April 1994 after a violent suppression of strikes on Nzwani, pressure was exerted by the Comoran opposition and the French government for an amnesty on prisoners condemned to death. Djohar, however, refused to yield.

In Sept. 1995 Njazidja was invaded by mercenaries (led by Denard) and Comoran armed forces. Djohar was captured and removed from power.

Later Life

After French military intervention, Djohar was allowed to flee to Réunion. He returned to the Comoros in Jan. 1996 and died at his home outside Moroni on 23 Feb.

Djotodia, Michel Moana (Central African Republic)

Introduction

Michel Djotodia declared himself president of the Central African Republic (CAR) on 24 March 2013 after ousting François Bozizé, who himself came to power in 2003 on the back of a coup before winning two subsequent elections.

Early Life

Djotodia was born in 1949 in Vakaga, in the northeast of the CAR. He studied economics in the former Soviet Union, where he lived for 10 years. After returning to the CAR, he twice unsuccessfully attempted to win a seat in parliament in Vakaga Prefecture in the 1980s. He became a civil servant in the administration of Ange Félix-Patassé that began in 1993, working variously for the ministry of planning, the foreign ministry and as a diplomatic consul to Nyala in Sudan. When Félix-Patassé's government was overthrown by François Bozizé in 2003, Djotodia helped establish the rebel Union of Democratic Forces for Unity (UFDR).

In Oct. 2006 the UFDR captured the town of Birao in northern CAR. Djotodia, in Benin at the time, was subsequently arrested and imprisoned at Bozizé's request but was released in Feb. 2008 as part of a peace agreement between Bozizé and the rebels. Djotodia moved to South Sudan and reputedly cultivated links with Chadian and Sudanese fighters who would form the backbone of Séléka, a rebel coalition that included the UFDR. In Dec. 2012 Séléka came close to capturing the CAR capital, Bangui.

In Jan. 2013 a regionally-brokered peace treaty was signed, with Séléka forming a unity government alongside Bozizé to serve until elections in 2016. As part of the agreement Djotodia became first deputy minister for national defence. In March 2013 Séléka pulled out of the administration, accusing Bozizé of running a parallel administration and failing to release political prisoners. The group, boasting a force of 3,000, overran the capital a week later and Bozizé fled into exile. Djotodia declared himself president on 24 March 2013.

Career Peak

Djotodia established an interim government and pledged to hold elections in 2016, saying that he hoped 'to be the last rebel chief president of Central Africa'. A National Transitional Council confirmed his presidency on 13 April 2013. Nicolas Tiangaye, prime minister in the power-sharing government under Bozizé, was asked to remain in his post while 34 ministries were shared between former opposition figures and members of Séléka. Djotodia himself headed the ministry of defence and in Aug. he was officially sworn in as president.

His government incurred regional and international criticism owing to the country's descent into Christian–Muslim sectarian conflict. This prompted the deployment of additional African Union peacekeepers and further intervention by French military forces to arrest a spiralling

humanitarian crisis and threat of civil war. He resigned from the presidency in Jan. 2014 after failing to stop widespread inter-religious violence and was subsequently exiled to Benin at the request of regional leaders in the Central African Republic.

Dombrovskis, Valdis (Latvia)

Introduction

Valdis Dombrovskis became prime minister in March 2009 following the resignation of Ivars Godmanis. Before stepping down in Jan. 2014, the former finance minister's tenure was mainly focused on reversing the country's economic crisis. He became a European Commissioner in Nov. 2014.

Early Life

Dombrovskis was born on 5 Aug. 1971 in Riga, while Latvia was part of the USSR. He studied physics and economics at the University of Latvia in Riga and the Riga Technological University. He was employed at Germany's University of Mainz and at the University of Latvia's Institute of Solid-State Physics, and in 1998 became a research assistant at Maryland University in the USA.

Later that year he began working for the Bank of Latvia, leaving in 2002 after a year as chief economist. A member of the centre-right New Era party, he joined its governing board in 2002 and was also elected to parliament, serving until 2004 as finance minister in Einars Repše's government. From 2003–04 he was Latvia's observer at the Council of the European Union and became a member of the European Parliament (MEP) in 2004.

Against the backdrop of global economic turmoil, Latvia's economy crashed in 2008. The economy shrank by over 4%. Worse was to follow, with a contraction of 18% in 2009. In Dec. 2008, having nationalized the country's second biggest bank, Prime Minister Ivars Godmanis turned to the IMF, World Bank and European Union for a US$9.5bn. bail-out package. In return he was forced to accept public spending cuts and tax increases. After an anti-government riot in Riga in Jan. 2009, his coalition fell the following month. President Valdis Zatlers nominated Dombrovskis to form a new administration.

Career Peak

Having resigned as an MEP, Dombrovskis formed a six-party coalition and won parliamentary approval on 12 March 2009. In Aug. 2009 his government reached agreement with unions and employers on deep spending cuts and tax rises aimed at staving off bankruptcy and persuading the IMF and EU to release further tranches of loans. Subsequently, as a condition for these disbursements, the government committed to further cuts in fiscal expenditures to contain the budget deficit. Having lost his parliamentary majority in March 2010, Dombrovskis called an election in Oct. at which he was returned to power heading a Unity and Union of Greens and Farmers coalition. In further legislative elections in Sept. 2011, following a controversial dissolution of the *Saeima*, the pro-Russian Harmony Centre emerged as the largest party, but Dombrovskis retained the premiership at the head of a new coalition comprising Unity, Zatlers' Reform Party and the National Alliance, which together controlled 56 of the 100 parliamentary seats. In Feb. 2012 voters in a referendum rejected a proposal to make Russian an official language of Latvia.

He resigned as prime minister in Nov. 2013 after taking political responsibility for the collapse of a supermarket in the capital, Riga, that killed 54 people. His tenure was defined by Latvia's economic metamorphosis, with the country posting Europe's fastest GDP growth rates for two consecutive years (2011 and 2012). Dombrovskis also presided over Latvia's entry into the eurozone, which was completed in Jan. 2014.

Later Life

Dombrovskis became the European Commission's vice-president for the euro and social dialogue on 1 Nov. 2014. He joined three former prime ministers in the new Commission led by one of these, Jean-Claude Juncker.

Dos Santos, José Eduardo (Angola)

Introduction

José Eduardo dos Santos became president of Angola upon the death of the country's first post-colonial president Agostinho Neto in 1979. He is also head of the ruling Movimento Popular de Libertação de Angola (MPLA; Popular Movement for the Liberation of Angola) and was prime minister from 1999–2002.

Early Life

Dos Santos was born on 28 Aug. 1942 in Luanda and in 1961 he joined Neto's MPLA rebel movement. As his party standing increased, he founded the MPLA youth movement before being sent to Moscow to study telecommunications and petroleum engineering. He returned to fight for Angolan independence, which finally came in 1975. Under Neto's presidency, dos Santos served first as prime minister (1975–78) and then planning minister (1978–79). After Neto's death in Sept. 1979, dos Santos assumed the leadership.

Career Peak

During the first 10 years dos Santos upheld the MPLA's traditional Marxist doctrine and the government's single party rule while continuing the war against the UNITA rebels begun under his predecessor. The government received Cuban military help in the conflict and the Soviet Union supplied funds. The USA and South Africa meanwhile backed UNITA's leader Jonas Savimbi.

A rapprochement began in 1988 when both Cuba and South Africa withdrew their forces. In 1990, following the collapse of communism, dos Santos moved away from Marxism to adopt 'democratic socialism'. This allowed for the introduction of a free market economy and multi-party elections. The following year, a peace agreement signed in Lisbon culminated in Angola's first nationwide elections in 1992. In a turnout of 91% of registered voters, the MPLA won 54% compared to UNITA's 34%. In the presidential poll dos Santos secured 49.6%, while Savimbi polled 40.1%. Before a second round run-off, Savimbi rejected the election, claiming the first round results had been fraudulent. The civil war resumed and elections scheduled for 1997 were postponed indefinitely. In 1999 dos Santos assumed the role of prime minister and took over control of the armed forces. In Feb. 2002 Savimbi was killed by government soldiers and 2 months later a ceasefire was signed with the rebels. Since the end of hostilities, his government has committed substantial resources, financed by oil exports and diamonds, to reconstruction. Nevertheless, much of the population still lives in extreme poverty. Also, it was not until Aug. 2006 that a ceasefire agreement was achieved with separatists fighting for independence of the northern enclave of Cabinda, where much of Angola's oil wealth lies. The final stage of a United Nations refugee repatriation scheme, involving some 60,000 Angolans, began in Oct. 2006.

In Jan. 2007 dos Santos oversaw Angola's accession to the Organization of the Petroleum Exporting Countries (OPEC), and in Feb. he declared that parliamentary elections would be held in 2008 and presidential polls in 2009. The parliamentary polls took place in Sept. and resulted in a landslide victory for the ruling MPLA. Despite some criticisms of the poll by an observer mission from the European Union and the rejection of opposition demands for a rerun of voting in the capital Luanda, UNITA leader Isaias Samakuva accepted his party's defeat. In mid-2009 presidential elections scheduled for Sept. were postponed, reportedly to allow more time for the drafting of a new constitution that came into effect in Feb. 2010. Under the constitution the party with a parliamentary majority chooses the president, who is subject to a two-term limit, is responsible for judicial appointments and appoints a vice-president (replacing the post of prime minister). Parliamentary elections in Aug. 2012 resulted in another comfortable victory for the MPLA and so secured another presidential term for dos Santos.

In Feb. 2013 the Constitutional Court rejected an opposition claim that the president had exceeded his powers by creating a US$5bn. sovereign wealth fund, launched in Oct. 2012 to manage the country's oil wealth, without parliamentary approval. In May that year dos Santos replaced the finance and construction ministers in a government reshuffle and in a further change in

April 2014 he named a new defence minister. In May 2014 a national census was conducted for the first time since 1970.

In late 2014 human rights groups accused the government of using excessive force to deter political dissent and in May 2015 a prominent regime critic was given a suspended jail term sentence for linking senior army personnel to corruption and violence in the diamond mining industry.

Meanwhile, as Africa's second largest oil producer, Angola suffered from the collapse in world prices from mid-2014, which has impacted severely on economic growth and fuelled government unpopularity.

In Aug. 2016 dos Santos was re-elected leader of the MPLA. Earlier, in June, he had appointed his daughter to the prominent public position of head of the state-run oil firm, prompting speculation that he was intending to establish a dynasty. In Sept. he replaced the finance minister following the breakdown of government negotiations with the International Monetary Fund over emergency financing.

In Sept. 2017 the newly appointed chairman of the MPLA, João Lourenço, succeeded dos Santos as president after 38 years in office.

Douglas-Home, Alec (United Kingdom of Great Britain and Northern Ireland)

Introduction

Alec Douglas-Home was British Conservative prime minister from 1963 until 1964. He renounced his peerage in order to hold the post, succeeding Harold Macmillan as leader of a divided and scandal-hit administration. With a general election due, he had little opportunity to make a significant impact during his tenure, though defeat to Harold Wilson's Labour Party in 1964 was marginal. Douglas-Home was widely respected for his integrity and honesty and many of his finest achievements came during his two spells at the foreign office rather than in his time as prime minister.

Early Life

Alexander Frederick Douglas-Home was born on 2 July 1903 in London. He came from an aristocratic background, the son of Lord Dunglass (later the 13th Earl of Home) and Lady Lilian Lambton, whose father was the 4th Earl of Durham. When Douglas-Home's father took the title 13th Earl, Alexander in turn became Lord Dunglass. He was educated at Eton before reading History at Christ Church, Oxford. He played cricket for Middlesex on a few occasions, making him the only Prime Minister to have played the sport at first class level. He fought his first general election, unsuccessfully, in 1929 but entered the House of Commons 2 years later as the member for South Lanark.

In 1935 Douglas-Home was appointed by Neville Chamberlain as his parliamentary private secretary. A year later he married Elizabeth Arlington, with whom he had four children. Chamberlain became prime minister in 1937, with Douglas-Home accompanying him to Munich for talks with Adolf Hitler and Benito Mussolini a year later. Chamberlain's policy of appeasement proved to be ill-conceived and Douglas-Home's involvement, debatable as to its extent, was not to be forgotten. At the outbreak of World War II, Douglas-Home, a long-time Territorial Army officer, joined the Lanarkshire Yeomanry but he was invalided out and spent 2 years in a plaster cast as the result of a tubercular spinal virus.

Douglas-Home was a vehement critic of the 1945 Yalta Conference, and what he perceived to be the West's failure to protect Poland from Soviet expansionism. In Churchill's immediate post-war government, he was under secretary of state for foreign affairs, before losing his seat in the Labour landslide of July 1945. He returned as the member for South Lanark in 1950 but left the Commons for the Lords a year later as the 14th Earl of Home. He was appointed minister of state in the Scottish office by Churchill and became a Privy Counsellor in 1951, then served as secretary of state for Commonwealth relations 1955–60, also holding the posts of deputy leader and leader of the House of Lords during this period. Harold Macmillan appointed him foreign secretary in 1960. His time here coincided with an increase in Cold War tensions, the construction of the Berlin Wall, the Cuban Missile Crisis and the Bay of Pigs invasion. Douglas-Home thus played an important role in defusing these tensions and improving British relations with the USSR.

He also worked to establish an independent British nuclear deterrent and was instrumental in the creation of the Nuclear-Test Ban Treaty.

Macmillan resigned as prime minister in Oct. 1963. The Conservatives were divided and reeling from the Profumo scandal, during which secretary of state for war John Profumo was found to have had an affair with a woman linked to a Russian naval attaché. Deputy prime minister R. A. Butler and minister of science and technology Viscount Hailsham were among the favourites to take up the party leadership. Hailsham renounced his peerage by the terms of the new Peerage Act to make himself available, paving the way for Douglas-Home to follow suit. The contest between Hailsham and Butler was seen as potentially divisive by many party members, and the generally well-liked Douglas-Home was recommended by Macmillan as his successor. Having given up his peerage, Douglas-Home won a by-election in the Kinross constituency and returned to the Commons as prime minister.

Career Peak

However, Douglas-Home inherited a government with deep-rooted problems. It had already been in power for 13 years, the economy was failing, entry into the European Economic Community (EEC) had been refused and Labour was rejuvenated under Harold Wilson. In addition, Douglas-Home's appointment prompted the resignations of two prominent Conservatives and skilled politicians, Enoch Powell and Iain Macleod. The extent of Douglas-Home's problems were further evident in a speech from Jan. 1964 when he declared that 'there are two problems in my life. The political ones are insoluble and the economic ones are incomprehensible'. Though spoken in jest, he was not experienced in economic matters, a subject Wilson would use as the focus of numerous attacks. Similarly, Wilson, 'the common man'. made much of Douglas-Home's aristocratic background, mocking him as 'the 14th Earl of Home'. though Douglas-Home famously retorted that he assumed Mr. Wilson was 'the 14th Mr Wilson.' At the election of 15 Oct. 1964, Labour came to power with a majority of five. Shortly afterwards Douglas-Home resigned the Conservative leadership. He threw his support behind his successor, Edward Heath, and took on the post of shadow foreign secretary until Heath led the Conservatives to victory at the general election of June 1970.

Serving as foreign secretary in Heath's cabinet, Douglas-Home assisted Britain's entry into the EEC. In 1971 he expelled over 100 Soviet diplomats after spying allegations and, though criticized for the government's support of the Federalist government forces in the Nigerian civil war, he had an international reputation as a skilled and trusted statesman.

Later Life

Douglas-Home left the Commons before the general election of Oct. 1974, the second of the year following a Labour victory in March. He became Baron Home of the Hirsel of Coldstream in 1974 and supported Heath in his unsuccessful bid to retain the Conservative leadership against Margaret Thatcher the following year. Douglas-Home remained a prominent figure in the Lords until the end of his life. He published his autobiography in 1976 and two volumes of other writings and died on 9 Oct. 1995 at the Hirsel, Coldstream in Berwickshire, Scotland.

Drees, Willem (Netherlands)

Introduction

Willem Drees was the Prime Minister of the Netherlands for a decade (1948–58), and his four successive terms witnessed at least four major political developments including problematic decolonization, economic reconstruction, the augmentation of a comprehensive welfare state and the first step towards European integration in the formation of Benelux.

Early Life

Drees was born in Amsterdam on 5 July 1886. He was educated at Commercial School, Amsterdam and began his political career in 1907 as an official parliamentary stenographer, having become a member of the Social Democratic Party in 1904. He was elected to The Hague city council in 1913, and in 1919 he was appointed Alderman of the City of The Hague, an office which earned him considerable prestige and which he carried until 1933. In that same year Drees was elected to the Lower House of the Estates General, and in 1939 he rose to become the leader of his parliamentary party and one of the first two socialists to secure cabinet office in the Dutch Parliament.

In 1940 Drees was imprisoned for attempting to ferment opposition to the Nazi occupation of the Netherlands. He was released after a year, and returned to the resistance movement, acting on behalf of Dutch government which was in exile in London. He chaired the Fatherland Committee which prepared the country's course of action should German rule end.

Career Peak

When the Netherlands was liberated, Queen Wilhelmina invited Drees and Willem Schermerhorn to form the first post-war cabinet, and he was Minister of Social Affairs from 1945–8. In 1946 Drees and Schermerhorn founded the new Labour Party (Partij van den Arbeid). Drees was highly instrumental in the introduction of a temporary Old Age Pensions Act, and the legislation increased his popularity with the electorate, contributing to his appointment as Prime Minister on 6 Aug. 1948. He was to retain the office for four consecutive terms, and presided over a coalition of his own Labour Party and the Catholic People's Party.

The beginning of his tenure was marred by the outbreak of hostilities between the Dutch colonial authorities and Indonesians battling for independence. In 1949 Drees and his government partially capitulated to Indonesian demands, and recognized the United States of Indonesia as a partner in a federation. Indonesia finally dissolved this alliance in 1954. Whilst in power Drees ushered the Netherlands into NATO, the Western European Union and the European Economic Community. He also played a significant role in the creation of Benelux. His decade of leadership was brought to an end by a Cabinet dispute over tax proposals, and he reigned on 12 Dec. 1958.

Later Life

Following his official retirement from politics he was made an honorary Minister of State, and the Labour Party awarded him a permanent position on its Executive Council. Drees was unhappy with the new policy direction of the party he helped to create, and he renounced his membership as a result. In his later life he became an astute political commentator, publishing numerous books and articles until his death on 14 May 1988.

Drnovšek, Janez (Slovenia)

Introduction

Janez Drnovšek became Slovenia's president in Dec. 2002. He was independent Slovenia's first prime minister from 1992–2002, except for a brief period in opposition in 2000. Along with his presidential predecessor, Milan Kučan, he oversaw political and economic reforms resulting in entry into NATO and the European Union in 2004. Drnovšek decided not to stand for re-election, and on 23 Dec. 2007 formally handed over presidential duties to the newly-elected Danilo Türk.

Early Life

Drnovšek was born on 17 May 1950 in Celje. He studied monetary policy at the University of Maribor and worked in the banking sector before entering politics in the 1980s. Following Slovenia's democratic elections of 1989, Drnovšek was appointed Slovenian representative to the rotating presidency of Federal Yugoslavia. He was president of the collective presidency for a year until May 1990, during which time he headed the Non-Alignment Movement, which rejected association with either the USA or the USSR. He pressed for Yugoslav entry into the European Community (later the EU), economic reform, multi-party elections and the release of political prisoners held within federal Yugoslavia.

As Yugoslavia began to disintegrate, Drnovšek sought a diplomatic solution. A declaration of Slovenian independence won majority backing in a referendum during 1990 and the country announced its split with Yugoslavia in 1991. Yugoslav troops entered the country and a short war ensued. Drnovšek acted as a chief negotiator in the Brioni agreement that brought the conflict to an end. In April 1992 Slovenia held its first elections as an independent state, Drnovšek winning the premiership and Milan Kučan the presidency.

Career Peak

Drnovšek and Kučan retained their positions for 10 years, except for 7 months in 2000 when Drnovšek was out of office. Their long tenures provided Slovenia with political and economic stability that few other former Yugoslav states enjoyed. The two worked closely to ensure Slovenia's acceptance on the international stage and forged closer ties with the West. Slovenia joined the IMF in 1993 and became a member of NATO's Partnership for Peace Programme. In 1999 it granted airspace to NATO for its bombing raids on Kosovo and Serbia. In 1996 Slovenia signed an associate agreement with the EU and opened full membership talks the following year. In Oct. 2002 the EU included Slovenia in its plans for enlargement scheduled for 2004.

Domestically, Drnovšek oversaw the implementation of major economic reforms, including privatization programmes and restructuring of the banking and commercial sectors. Unable to rely on markets in the former Yugoslavia, increased trade was established with the USA and the EU. Slovenia was one of the founding members of the WTO.

Drnovšek was re-elected in 1996 but in 2000 his coalition was destabilized by party mergers among the centre-right. He called a vote of confidence in April 2000 but was defeated and replaced as prime minister by Andrej Bajuk of the Social Democrats. The new coalition split over plans to reform the electoral system and at the elections of Oct. 2000 Drnovšek was returned as prime minister, heading a government consisting of his centre-left Liberal Democrats, United List, the Slovene People's Party, the Slovene Young People's Party and the DeSUS party.

The Slovenian constitution barred Kučan from standing for a third term as president in Nov. 2002. Drnovšek ran against Barbara Brezigar, an independent backed by the centre-right, and won with 57% of the vote. As president, he oversaw Slovenia's integration into NATO and the EU in 2004 and the country's adoption of the European single currency in Jan. 2007.

On 21 Oct. 2007 Slovenia elected a new president to replace Drnovšek, who had decided not to seek another term. On 23 Dec. 2007 following a swearing-in ceremony in parliament, Danilo Türk formally took over duties from Drnovšek.

On 23 Feb. 2008 Drnovšek, who had been suffering from cancer, died at his home in Zaplana at the age of 57.

Duarte Frutos, Nicanor (Paraguay)

Introduction

Nicanor Duarte Frutos served as president of Paraguay from Aug. 2003 to Aug. 2008. His presidency extended the rule of the Republican National Alliance–Colorado Party (ANR), which had governed Paraguay continuously since 1947. Duarte represented the party's traditionalist faction.

Early Life

Óscar Nicanor Duarte Frutos was born on 11 Oct. 1956 and brought up in Coronel Oviedo, an agricultural town in Paraguay. He joined the Colorado Party at the age of 14, and went on to study law and political science before pursuing a career in journalism.

Having served as education minister in the 1990s, Duarte took 37% of the vote at the 2003 elections, defeating three other candidates. Elected in April, he took up his position as leader in Aug. that year.

Career Peak

Upon his election as president, Duarte announced plans to fight corruption, reinvigorate the economy and improve the nation's standing in the international community. He aimed to create jobs through public work programmes and, in a bid to improved efficiency in government, promised to reform the customs and internal revenue services. In 2004 he launched an overhaul of the tax system and introduced judicial reforms, particularly relating to Supreme Court appointments. The following year Duarte promised a crackdown on organized crime in the wake of a high-profile kidnapping and murder case, and in June 2006 his predecessor as president, Luis González Macchi, was sentenced to imprisonment for 6 years for illegal financial dealings.

In 2007 Duarte's government declared two states of emergency, firstly in response to an outbreak of dengue fever and then after fires destroyed huge

tracts of forest and agricultural land. Barred by the Constitution from standing for re-election, Duarte supported the candidacy of his education secretary, Blanca Ovelar. Her defeat by Fernando Lugo, of the Patriotic Alliance for Change (APC), brought to an end more than 60 years of continuous rule by the Republican National Alliance–Colorado Party (ANR).

Dubček, Alexander (Czech Republic)

Introduction

Alexander Dubček was First Secretary of the Czechoslovakian Communist Party in 1968–69 and was responsible for a period of social and political reform that came to be known as the Prague Spring. His programme aroused opposition in the Soviet Union and a number of other Eastern Bloc countries, and led to an invasion by Warsaw Pact Troops in Aug. 1968. Dubček was removed from power and most of his reforms overturned but, following the Velvet Revolution in 1989, he returned as Chairman of the Federal Assembly.

Early Life

Dubček was born on 27 Nov. 1921 in Uhrovec in what is now Slovakia. His father was a cabinet maker and both his parents were communists. They moved to the Soviet Union (to an area that is now part of Kyrgyzstan) when Dubček was 4 years old, returning to Slovakia in 1938. The following year Dubček joined the illegal Czechoslovakia Communist Party (KSC). During World War II he worked in an armaments factory and was active in the resistance movement, also taking part in the Slovak National Uprising in 1944. After the war Dubček worked in a yeast factory and in 1949 was appointed Secretary of the Trencin District Committee of the KSC.

By 1951 he was a member of the Slovak Communist Party Central Committee. Having taken a law degree at Comenius University in Bratislava, in 1955 he was sent to the Communist Party College in Moscow to study political science. He graduated 3 years later and a further 4 years after that he was a member of the Presidium of the Central Committee of the KSC. Throughout the 1960s the party was beset by problems, principally because of the faltering economy and of Slovakia's unease at the centralization of power in Prague. A reform movement gathered momentum, with Dubček at its forefront, which by late 1967 had forced the resignation of numerous leading party figures including First Secretary Antonín Novotný. Dubček took over as First Secretary on 5 Jan. 1968 with Oldrich Cherník installed as Premier.

Career Peak

In March 1968 Dubček spoke of his search for 'socialism with a human face' and in April the Central Committee published an Action Programme that would have a massive impact.

It proposed greater Slovakian authority, an independent judiciary, greater freedom of expression including press freedom, workers' reforms and the rehabilitation of citizens who had previously suffered civil rights infringements at the hands of the Party. It also proposed that the National Assembly should be the principal organ of government, rather than the party itself, that KSC posts should be filled by democratic processes and that opposition parties should be permitted to stand in elections. In late June a group of citizens, independent of Dubček, published an article that came to be known as *The 2,000 Words* and which proposed even more far-reaching reforms. An already nervous Moscow summoned Dubček to a meeting with Brezhnev and other Warsaw Pact leaders in Cierna, near Bratislava. After 4 days of negotiation, a joint announcement was made on 3 Aug. promising tighter media constraints.

However, on 20 Aug. a force comprising Soviet, Polish, Hungarian, Bulgarian and East German troops rolled into Prague. Dubček was one of six leaders arrested and taken to Moscow. He returned on 27 Aug. and in a famed radio broadcast in which he fought back tears, Dubček announced that the majority of his reforms would be reversed and that the Soviets would retain a military presence within the country. By the time dissident student Jan Palach had died by setting fire to himself in the middle of Prague's Wenceslas Square in Jan. 1969, the hard-liners within the KSC had begun to reassert their dominance. Dubček was removed from his post as First Secretary on 17 April 1969, becoming Ambassador to Turkey in Dec. He was forced out of the party in June 1970, resigned as an ambassador shortly afterwards and became a lowly forestry administration official.

Later Life

However, during the Velvet Revolution of Nov. 1989 he made speeches in Bratislava and later appeared with Václav Havel in Prague as events came to a victorious conclusion. 'socialism with a human face must function for a new generation,' he told the crowd in Wenceslas Square on 24 Nov. 'We have lived in the darkness for long enough'. He became Chairman of the National Assembly on 28 Aug. and was later elected leader of the Slovakian Social Democrats before he died on 7 Nov. 1992 from injuries sustained in a car crash some weeks earlier.

Duhalde, Eduardo (Argentina)

Introduction

Duhalde was elected president on the 1 Jan. 2002, Argentina's fifth president within a week. He completed the remaining term of Fernando de la Rua, who resigned in Dec. 2002 as a result of riots and protests among the population. Duhalde, a veteran within the Peronist party, was appointed president after the resignation of Eduardo Camaño who held office for just 1 day. Camaño acted as caretaker president following the resignation of Adolfo Rodruguez Saa who held office for a week. Previously, the constitutional successor Ramon Puerta, had held the presidency for less than 48 hours. Duhalde did not stand in the presidential elections of April 2003.

Early Life

Duhalde was born on 5 Oct. 1941 in Lomas de Zamore, outside Buenos Aires. He went to a local primary school, followed by secondary studies at Comercial 'Tomas Espora' in Temperley. He graduated in law from the University of Buenos Aires in 1970. He was appointed local councillor in Lomas de Zamora in 1971 and mayor in 1976. In 1986 he became regional president for the Justicialist Party (PJ-Peronist) and entered the Congress. He was elected governor of the biggest province, Buenos Aires, in 1995 and re-elected in 1999. His administration was accused of corruption and forcing the province into debt in order for him to win votes. Duhalde served as vice-president under Carlos Menem. In 1999 he ran for president but lost against Fernando de la Rua.

Career Peak

Duhalde lacked popular support. The country had suffered the world's biggest debt default, the collapse of a currency board with the peso pegged to the dollar and a freeze on bank savings. The economic situation did not rapidly improve and Duhalde failed to implement the programme demanded by the IMF. Aiming to protect local industry and to use public works projects to reduce unemployment, he blamed the crisis on economic liberalism. In Jan. 2002 he devalued the peso by 29% and floated the peso the following month. In April 2002 he appointed Roberto Lavagna, the country's ambassador to the European Union, as minister of economy, the sixth within 12 months. A major challenge for Duhalde and Lavagna was to persuade the IMF to resume its lending programme, which was cut off in Dec. 2001. Reforms included spending cuts and the abolition of an economic subversion law. In May 2002 Duhalde threatened to resign to encourage support for changes. In July 2002 Duhalde announced that he would bring forward the 2003 election by 6 months to March. Following a clash between protesters and the police in which two people were shot dead, pressure grew for his resignation. He did not stand for the presidency in April 2003.

Later Life

Duhalde contested the 2011 presidential elections, finishing third behind Ricardo Alfonsín and winner Cristina Fernández de Kirchner.

Dulles, John Foster (United States of America)

Introduction

John Foster Dulles was president Dwight D. Eisenhower's secretary of state from 1953 until 1959 when he resigned just a month before his death at the age of 71. He is remembered as a staunch opponent of communism whose opinions did much to shape US foreign policy during the Cold War.

Early Life

Born in Washington, D.C. on 25 Feb. 1888, Dulles was a grandson of John Watson Foster, secretary of state under President Benjamin Harrison. He graduated from Princeton University in 1908. After studying at the Sorbonne in Paris and George Washington University Law School he was admitted to the bar in 1911.

Dulles was counsel to the U.S. delegation to the Versailles Peace Conference in 1919 and built a reputation in the inter-war years as an authority on international law. In 1939 his book *War, Peace and Change* was published. Six years later, Dulles was appointed adviser to the US delegation at the San Francisco conference of the United Nations and for the following 4 years served as a delegate to the UN's general assembly.

In 1949, Dulles was given a seat in the senate in New York vacated by Robert Wagner but narrowly lost in his bid for re-election the following year. The following year his book *War or Peace* was published and in 1951 president Harry S. Truman gave him responsibility for concluding a peace treaty with Japan, signed on 8 Sept. 1951.

Career Peak

Dulles was appointed secretary of state by president Eisenhower in 1953. He advocated a hard-line approach against communist regimes in the Soviet Union and China, favouring the development of nuclear weapons so that, in the event of an attack, the United States could reply with 'massive retaliation'. Dulles also argued that the United States should be prepared to go to 'the brink' of war to achieve its objectives—a statement fiercely criticized by liberals.

Dulles was instrumental in establishing the European Defense Community and also instigated the Southeast Asia Treaty Organization (SEATO) in 1954 and the Baghdad Pact (1955), all of which were designed to contain Soviet and Chinese influence in Europe and Asia. On his secretary of state's advice, Eisenhower supported the South Vietnamese regime of Ngo Dinh Diem. The United States also offered financial and military assistance for Middle Eastern states, for example by supplying troops to Lebanon in 1958.

In 1958 Dulles was diagnosed with terminal cancer. He resigned from office in April and died in Bethesda, Maryland, on 24 May 1959.

Duncan Smith, Iain (United Kingdom of Great Britain and Northern Ireland)

Introduction

Iain Duncan Smith was elected leader of the Conservative Party in Sept. 2001, succeeding William Hague. Inheriting a party deeply divided and depressed by a second successive punishing election defeat, his support came chiefly from the Euro-sceptic right of the party. Considered to lack the charisma needed to galvanize the party, Duncan Smith was harassed by calls for another leader for much of his second year. Modest successes in local and regional elections in May 2003 failed to bolster his leadership. He was defeated in a parliamentary party vote in Oct. 2003. In May 2010 he became work and pensions secretary in the Conservative/Liberal Democrat coalition government.

Early Life

George Iain Duncan Smith was born on 9 April 1954 in Edinburgh. The son of a former fighter pilot, he was educated at HMS Conway (a school for children of military personnel) in Wales, Dunchurch College of Management, the Royal Military Academy at Sandhurst and a university in Perugia, Italy. As a member of the armed forces he served in Northern Ireland and Zimbabwe and in 1981, an admirer of Margaret Thatcher, he became a member of the Conservative Party. Around this time he also moved into corporate management in GEC-Marconi and, later, publishing. He is married to Betsy, with whom he has four children.

He stood unsuccessfully as Conservative candidate for Bradford West in the 1987 election. At the general election of 1992 he won the safe seat of Chingford (later Chingford and Woodford following boundary changes). A member of various select and backbench committees, he soon gained a reputation for right-wing opinions. He voted against the 1992 Maastricht Treaty that redefined the functions and influence of the EU and was prominent in debates on immigration.

In 1997 he was appointed shadow secretary of state for social security by William Hague and 2 years later took over the defence portfolio. Aside from his Euro-sceptic stance, Duncan Smith's views on domestic politics consolidated his position on the right. An advocate of corporal and capital punishment, he has also supported proposed cuts to child benefit and opposed the lowering of the homosexual age of consent and the banning of hunting with dogs.

Following the Conservatives' second heavy defeat in a general election, Hague resigned. In the subsequent battle for the leadership, Duncan Smith was an outsider until Michael Portillo was unexpectedly knocked out in the third round of voting. In the run-off with the former chancellor Kenneth Clarke, Duncan Smith gained over 60% of the 260,000 votes cast.

Career Peak

As leader of the opposition, Duncan Smith tried to shift his party's focus away from the European debate towards domestic issues, neglected during the Hague tenure. However, in May 2003, Duncan Smith called on the government for a referendum on joining the single European currency. This was followed in June with an attack on the 'European super-state'. again creating tensions within his party.

Hopes that his election would end divisive behaviour within the party lasted barely a year. The replacement of David Davis, while on holiday, as party chairman in July 2002 gave the Conservative Party its first female chairman, Theresa May, but angered Davis' supporters. The first major signs of dissent came in Dec. when ex-minister Michael Heseltine claimed that many Tory voters wanted to lose Duncan Smith. He was joined by Michael Portillo in Feb. 2003, who condemned the sacking of the party's chief executive, Mark MacGregor, and the policy director, Rick Nye—two key modernisers.

Despite gains in local council and Welsh Assembly elections in May 2003 resignations and attacks continued to undermine Duncan Smith's leadership. Trade spokesman Crispin Blunt resigned on the eve of the local elections, stating that the Conservatives would not win the general election under its current leader. MacGregor's replacement, Barry Legg, lasted just 3 months as chief executive.

Duncan Smith's image was ridiculed by the media. Describing himself as the 'quiet man' in the 2002 party conference, he responded to critics the following year by insisting that he was 'turning up the volume'. His 2003 conference speech aggressively attacked the government—'corrupt, mendacious, fraudulent, shameful, lying'—and those within the party looking to oust him—'get on board or get out of the way for we have got work to do.' Allegations concerning the employment of his wife as his diary secretary further undermined him but Duncan Smith refused to resign. However, a vote of no confidence in his leadership was carried on 29 Oct., forcing his resignation. Michael Howard, the former minister and shadow chancellor, was unanimously selected leader by the parliamentary party.

Later Life

After the Conservatives came to power in May 2010 Duncan Smith was appointed work and pensions secretary in David Cameron's first cabinet. He retained the work and pensions portfolio following the Conservatives' victory at the May 2015 general election.

Duncan Smith resigned as secretary of state for work and pensions in March 2016, opposing the chancellor's proposed cuts to disability benefits.

Durão Barroso, José Manuel (Portugal)

Introduction

The leader of the right-wing Partido Social Democrata (Social Democrats, PSD), José Manuel Durão Barroso was elected prime minister in March 2002, replacing the former Partido Socialista (Socialist Party, PSP) leader António Manuel de Oliveira Guterres.

Early Life

Born on 23 March 1956, Durão Barroso studied law at the Universidade de Lisboa. He gained a master's in political science from the Université de Genève before taking European studies. He lectured at universities in Geneva and the USA, as well as working for the department of international relations at Universidade Lusíada, Lisbon. He wrote for several science journals and founded a political science magazine.

In 1980 Durão Barroso joined the PSD. In 1985, 1995 and 1999 he was elected PSD deputy for Lisbon; in 1987 and 1991 for Viseu. He was president of the foreign office commission between 1995–96, then the interior ministry's deputy secretary before becoming foreign secretary. Between 1992–95 Durão Barroso was foreign minister under the PSD prime minister, Aníbal Cavaço Silva. On an international level, Durão Barroso led a delegation to Bosnia-Herzegovina in Sept. 1996, and was a UN peace officer in Tanzania in Oct. 1997. He was vice president of the European People's Party in 1999.

In 1999 he was elected party leader, replacing Marcelo Rebelo de Sousa. In the same year Durão Barroso stood for election against Guterres. Violent clashes during Timor-Leste's transition to independence from Indonesia in Aug. 1999 took the focus away from domestic politics and the election. Guterres' successful handling of the precarious situation helped his election campaign. The PSD attempted a coalition with the right-wing Partido Popular (PP) but the alliance was shortlived and both parties suffered from the fall out. Durão Barroso came second with 32.3% of votes to Guterres' 44.1%.

Two years later, with increasing criticism of the government's heavy public spending, the PSD recorded gains in local elections taking the key cities of Lisbon, Oporto and Coimbra. Guterres resigned and elections were brought forward from 2004 to March 2002. The PSD claimed a narrow victory with 40% of votes to 38% and 102 out of 230 seats, and Durão Barroso was appointed prime minister. To gain an assembly majority the party renewed its coalition with the PP fuelling concerns over the party's influence on government policy. The party has strong nationalist and anti-immigration policies and rejects further delegation of power to the EU.

Career Peak

On election Durão Barroso set about reviving the economy with strong economic measures. A reduction in public spending affected local authorities' budgets and civil service recruitment, while plans were made to streamline or dissolve numerous state bodies. He also planned to increase privatization, including the health service, and introduce labour reforms. Other proposals, such as a minimum annual pension scheme of €200, a 10% corporate tax reduction and a lowering of the top rate of income tax, were put on hold. In Nov. 2002 public sector workers held a 24 h strike, the first in 10 years, to protest at the austerity measures and proposed labour reforms. In response, Durão Barroso reaffirmed his determination to press ahead with his policies. To cut Portugal's deficit to 2.7%, the Barroso government imposed a wage freeze on employees earning more than €1,000, affecting half of Portugal's workforce.

In Jan. 2003 Durão Barroso was one of eight European leaders to issue a combined declaration of support for the United States in its efforts to disarm Iraq, while making it clear that Portugal would not take part in military action.

Following the agreement of the 25 EU ministers in June 2004 on the new European Union constitution, Portugal announced that it would hold a referendum on the issue. After dropping earlier reservations concerning the European Commission's next president, Spain and France joined the other members in June 2004 to invite Durão Barroso to succeed the incumbent president, Romano Prodi. Following his appointment, Barroso resigned as prime minister of Portugal and was replaced by Pedro Santana Lopes.

Later Life

Durão Barroso presided over the European Commission for almost 10 years, in which he oversaw the accession of Romania, Bulgaria and Croatia to the Union. His main challenges were to secure Ireland's signing of the Treaty of Lisbon (which made amendments to the EU constitution resulting in a more powerful European Parliament and European Council) and to guide the commission through an economic crisis. Durão Barroso was succeeded as European Commission president in Nov. 2014 by Luxembourg's former prime minister Jean-Claude Juncker. In July 2016 he was appointed non-executive chairman of Goldman Sachs International.

Dutra, Eurico Gaspar (Brazil)

Introduction

Eurico Gaspar Dutra was president of Brazil from 1945–50. His attempts to reverse the anti-democratic measures of President Vargas were hindered by a volatile economy.

Early Life

Born in 1885 in Cuiaba, Eurico Dutra's military career lasted from 1910 until 1932. Having opposed numerous attempted coups, he opposed the government of Getúlio Vargas that came to power in 1930. However, when Vargas himself was a victim of an attempted coup 2 years later, Dutra came to his defence. He was prominent in the subsequent reform of the Brazilian economy. In 1945 when Vargas attempted to block scheduled elections, Dutra led a Social Democrat-backed coup.

Career Peak

Dutra won popular support for a revival of the democratic institutions that had suffered under Vargas. He reversed Brazil's international isolation, seeking closer ties with the US and breaking off diplomatic relations with the USSR in 1947 while playing a prominent role in the Organization of American States. However, unable to cope with economic problems, he was replaced by Vargas after the 1951 presidential election. Dutra died on 11 June 1974.

Duvalier, François 'Papa Doc' (Haiti)

Introduction

François Duvalier, better known as Papa Doc, was Haiti's dictator between 1957 and 1971, an extraordinarily long term in Haiti's variable political climate. Espousing black nationalism and voodoo practices, he modelled himself as a spiritual, as well as political, leader. Supported by the Tonton Macoutes (*The Bogeymen*), a private militia, his reign was characterized by oppression, corruption and the violent removal of his opponents.

Early Life

François Duvalier was born in the Haitian capital, Port-au-Prince, on 14 April 1907 to Duval Duvalier, a teacher and journalist, and Uritia Abraham, who worked in a bakery. Raised as a Roman Catholic, Duvalier graduated in medicine from the University of Haiti and worked as a physician in a hospital. In 1939 he married Simone Ovide Faine, with whom he had four children. By 1943 he was heavily involved in a US-backed project to fight yaws (an aggressive skin disease) and 3 years later he was appointed Director General of the National Health Service by President Estimé. In 1948 he became Underminister of Labour and then Minister of Public Health and Labour, 1949–50.

Following Estimé's overthrow in 1950, Duvalier worked for the American Sanitary Mission and was prominent in the resistance to the military dictator, Paul E. Magloire. In 1954 Duvalier went underground and concentrated full-time on his resistance activities. Magloire stood down from power in the same year. In Dec. 1956. In Sept. of the following year, having campaigned on reform and black nationalist issues, Duvalier was elected President with a large majority.

Career Peak

Assisted by his close ally, Clément Barbot, Duvalier set about reducing army influence and replacing them with the Tonton Macoutes, a volunteer force devoted to Duvalier which facilitated his reign of terror among the population. Countless political opponents were hounded into exile or murdered, with their bodies often put on public display.

In addition, Duvalier undertook to create an image of himself as a demigod. Graffiti campaigns, thought to have been instigated by him, proclaimed that 'Duvalier is a god' early on in his reign. He dressed himself in a black top hat and coat in the style of a feared voodoo spirit, Baron Samedi. The Tonton Macoutes in turn wore blue denim and red neckties in the style of the voodoo spirit of agriculture and Duvalier appointed voodoo elders into various prominent positions. For a religious and superstitious populace, attracted by Duvalier's black nationalist policies anyway, it was a very powerful image.

By means of the Tonton Macoutes, Duvalier challenged the authority of the Catholic Church (who excommunicated him for his abuse of clergymen), the military powers and the influential mulatto business elite. The 1956 elections allowed him one unrenewable 6 year term, but he influenced the elections of 1961 so that he could stay on longer and in 1964 he proclaimed himself lifelong president. In 1963 Barbot, Duvalier's former right hand man, led an unsuccessful insurrection that resulted in his murder. By this stage, Duvalier had alienated virtually every government in the world, losing financial aid from the US and overseeing the worsening of relations with the Dominican Republic, Haiti's only land neighbour. During his reign the country's economy, already one of the weakest in the Americas, continued its decline and educational standards remained low so that illiteracy stood at around 90%.

Despite a number of insurrections and international isolation, Duvalier managed to retain power through his private army and the force of his personality. It is estimated that between 20,000–50,000 Haitians died and up to a fifth of the country went into exile. However, his long reign led to an element of national stability that saw the emergence of a black middle class, and he retained support from large swathes of the black population throughout. He died in Port-au-Prince on 21 April 1971, having decreed that his son, Jean-Claude (known as Baby Doc) would succeed him for life.

Duvalier, Jean-Claude 'Baby Doc' (Haiti)

Introduction

Jean-Claude Duvalier, known as Baby Doc, was Haiti's president from 1971 until 1986. Having been nominated for the post by his father, François (Papa Doc), he voiced support for mild social and political reforms following Papa Doc's despotic reign. However, there was little discernible change in the life of the country and, having been made president for life, Baby Doc went into exile in 1986 amid widespread social disaffection.

Early Life

Baby Doc was born on 3 July 1951 in Port-au-Prince, the only son of future president François Duvalier and Simone Ovide. François became president in 1957 but Baby Doc spent most of his childhood out of the public glare. However, he was the victim of an attempted kidnap in 1963. He began studying law in Port-au-Prince but failed to complete the course. Papa Doc died in April 1971, having arranged for his teenage son to succeed him.

Career Peak

Baby Doc inherited a country corrupt and internationally isolated. He set about improving relations with the US and the Dominican Republic, in a bid to secure foreign aid and thus kickstart the stagnant economy. He voiced support for an economic revolution, removed some of his father's cabinet stalwarts from power, freed some political prisoners and invited other political exiles back to the country, and relaxed media censorship laws.

In reality there was little action to back his words. Few exiles chose to return to Haiti and opposition to the president continued to be stamped out. Baby Doc's reliance on the Duvalierists who had swept his father to power made it virtually impossible to implement the required reforms, since it was the Duvalierist's authority that would be curbed. By the 1980s Baby Doc was taking an increasingly hard line against political rivals, continuing to exert authority through the secret police (Tonton Macoutes) established by his father. The arrest of several critical journalists ensured that the national media kept largely to the presidential line.

In 1980 Baby Doc married Michele Bennet, with whom he had one son and one daughter. Bennet, like Baby Doc's mother before her, became a major presence in the country's political life, but her bourgeois background alienated traditional Duvalierists. In addition, the manifest lack of social and economic reform and an ambiguous attitude in foreign policy eroded international support for the Baby Doc regime. With social tensions rising, Duvalier was forced from office on 7 Feb. 1986. He fled to France with his family and a fortune estimated at over US$100m.

Later Life

President at the age of 19, Baby Doc ran into financial difficulties after several years and in 1992 he parted from his wife. In 2000 he unsuccessfully bid for the presidency from his position in exile. In Jan. 2011 Baby Doc made an unexpected return to Haiti after 24 years in exile. Two days later he was taken into custody by Haitian authorities and charged with corruption and embezzlement during his 15 year rule. He was subsequently released but was subject to recall by the court.

Baby Doc died in Port-au-Prince on 4 Oct. 2014 following a heart attack. He had spent the last years of his life in Haiti living in relative obscurity, after charges brought against him in 2011 failed to gain support.

Dzurinda, Mikuláš (Slovakia)

Introduction

Mikuláš Dzurinda was appointed prime minister in 1998 as leader of the Slovak Democratic Coalition (SDK). Two years later he founded the Slovak Democratic and Christian Union (SDKÚ) and won a second term of office in 2002. He was credited with establishing good relations with NATO and the EU and for improving Slovakia's economic and political structure. He left office in 2006 following his party's defeat at general elections.

Early Life

Mikuláš Dzurinda was born on 4 Feb. 1955 in Spišský Štvrtok, a village in the east of Slovakia. He graduated from the University of Transport and Communication in Žilina in 1979 and went on to gain a Candidate of Sciences post-graduate degree in 1988. He worked as an economic analyst for the transport research institute and in the Bratislava division of Czechoslovak Railways before founding the Christian Democratic Movement (KDH).

The party was officially constituted in 1990 and Dzurinda became deputy minister of transportation and posts after the Czechoslovak elections of 1991. In 1992 he entered the Slovak national council, sitting on the committee for budget and finance. In 1993, after the establishment of the Slovak Republic, Dzurinda was appointed chairman of the KDH and in 1994 he became Slovak minister of transportation, posts and public works. Dzurinda returned to the opposition benches after the 1994 election. In 1997 he became spokesman for the SDK (comprising the KDH, the Democratic Party, the Democratic Union, the Social Democratic Party of Slovakia and the Green Party of Slovakia). The following year he was appointed its chairman. He led them to victory at that year's elections and was sworn in as prime minister on 30 Oct. 1998.

Career Peak

In Jan. 2000 Dzurinda founded the Slovak Democratic and Christian Union (SDKÚ), made up of the KDH, the Party of Hungarian Coalition (SMK) and the Alliance of the New Citizen. As leader of the coalition, he was elected prime minister again in Oct. 2002.

In Sept. 2000 Slovakia gained entry into the OECD. In Feb. 2001 Dzurinda approved changes to the constitution to facilitate Slovakia's entry into NATO and the EU. He de-centralized power while increasing the authority of the state audit office. There was greater recognition of minority rights, building on a law introduced in July 1999 to improve the status of minority languages. In Jan. 2002 eight regional parliaments were created in keeping with EU membership requirements. Accession talks were completed at the Copenhagen summit in Dec. 2002.

In May 2003 a referendum gave backing to accession and in May 2004 Slovakia was one of ten new countries to join the EU. Parliament ratified the EU constitution the following year. Slovakia was invited to join NATO in Nov. 2002 and admitted in March 2004. Dzurinda also worked hard to encourage foreign investment. During his first term the US steel industry pledged to invest around US$1bn. and Korea's Hyundai company were also significant investors. In 2003 Slovakia recorded a 4.5% growth rate, with growth predicted to continue steadily.

Domestically, Dzurinda overhauled the pensions and benefits system. There were cuts in benefits for those not actively seeking employment and healthcare costs rose. The tax system was simplified with the introduction of a 19% flat rate. However, while Dzurinda's economic overhaul of Slovakia was applauded by the international community, he faced some hostility at home. The average hourly wage remained low and there was little job security. In Feb. 2004 there were riots in eastern Slovakia in protest at benefits cuts. In 2005 several deputies quit in protest at Dzurinda's leadership and in Sept. 2005 the opposition boycotted parliament in an attempt to force early elections.

At general elections held in June 2006 Dzurinda's SDKÚ came second, winning 31 seats against 50 for Direction–Social Democracy (SMER). While retaining his seat in parliament, Dzurinda was replaced as prime minister on 4 July 2006 by Robert Fico, leader of SMER.

Later Life

Dzurinda served as foreign minister from July 2010–April 2012 under prime minister Iveta Radičová. Then in Dec. 2013 he was appointed chairman of the Wilfried Martens Centre for European Studies—the think tank of the European People's Party.

Ecevit, Bülent (Turkey)

Introduction

Bülent Ecevit served as Turkey's prime minister in 1974, 1977, 1978–79 and 1999–2002. He came to power for a fourth time following the collapse of Mesut Yilmaz's centre-right government. In order to secure his election he formed an uneasy alliance between his own Democratic Left Party (DLP) the centre-right Motherland Party and the far-right Nationalist Action Party. Towards the end of his tenure Turkey's increasing economic difficulties coupled with Ecevit's failing health led the opposition to demand early elections which brought the end to his premiership.

Early Life

The son of a professor of medicine and an artist, Ecevit was born on 28 May 1925 in İstanbul. He received a BA from Robert College, İstanbul and then read literature at the University of Ankara before studying languages and the history of art at London University. He then became a journalist, working for the Turkish press attaché in London. He began his political career in 1957 as a Republican People's Party (CHP) member for Ankara. As labour minister, Ecevit legalized strikes. He was elected secretary general of the CHP in 1966. During this time Ecevit also wrote poetry and translated a play by T.S. Eliot into Turkish. Throughout the 1960s he advocated 'democratic socialism' which he considered the best way to safeguard Turkey from communism. He also argued strongly against the intervention of the military in domestic politics, a stance that brought him into conflict with party leader Ismet Inönü. Ecevit became party chairman in 1972 and was elected prime minister for the first time in Jan. 1974.

Career Peak

When Ecevit came to power his most immediate problem was the diplomatic situation in Cyprus. Following the Greek overthrow of the Cypriot government, Ecevit, a committed patriot, ordered Turkish troops onto the island. The result was the division of Cyprus. This proved a divisive issue in domestic politics, and culminated in Ecevit's resignation following the loss of a vote of confidence in Sept. 1974.

He returned to power for under a month in 1977 and again in 1978 but economic difficulties ended his third tenure in Oct. the following year. Subsequently Ecevit suffered persecution for his left wing beliefs. Despite numerous prison sentences he managed to organize the clandestine Democratic Left Party (DLP, an offshoot of the banned CHP) through his wife Rahsan. His return from the political wilderness came in 1991 when he was elected to parliament.

Ecevit succeeded the beleaguered Mesut Yilmaz on a temporary basis in Jan. 1999, but elections in April that year confirmed his authority. He remained committed to a secular state and was vocal in his opposition to Islamic extremism. He was equally determined to maintain a military presence in Cyprus and in the Kurdish dominated southeast of the country. His policy towards Europe appeared less certain; he rejected preconditions for Turkish entry into the EU, such as the improvement of the country's human rights record and a resolution of the Kurdish and Cypriot problems. In Oct. 2002 Turkey was omitted from ten countries nominated to join the EU in 2004 as it was considered not in line with the Copenhagen Criteria.

Prompted by the prime minister's failing health, the government was on the brink of collapse in July 2002 as many key ministers resigned. Opposition parties called for the prime minister's resignation.

Ecevit attempted to halt the crisis by bringing forward elections from 2004 to Nov. 2002. The elections saw the defeat of Ecevit's coalition government by the new Justice and Development Party. His own DSP party took just 1.2% of votes. Ecevit tendered his resignation to President Sezer, and was replaced as prime minister by Abdullah Gül.

Having retired from active politics in 2004, Ecevit died on 18 May 2006 following a cerebral haemorrhage.

Echeverría Álvarez, Luis (Mexico)

Introduction

Representing the dominant Partido Revolucionario Institucional (Institutional Revolutionary Party; PRI), Echeverría Álvarez was president of Mexico from 1970 to 1976. His presidency abandoned the cautious fiscal policies of his predecessor Gustavo Díaz Ordaz in favour of a free-spending populist presidency. The result was that the external debt sextupled, the value of the Mexican currency was halved and real incomes fell by half.

Early Life

Echeverría was born in Mexico City in 1922. He trained as a lawyer and held a number of mid-level positions in the PRI and the government before being appointed interior minister in 1964. His career was decisively influenced by the massacre of student protesters in the Tlatelolco district of Mexico City in 1968. Although Echeverría has always denied responsibility for the massacre he was widely blamed for the deaths. Echeverría was elected president on 1 Dec. 1970, succeeding his fellow PRI colleague Gustavo Díaz Ordaz.

Career Peak

During his presidency, Echeverría responded to the unrest resulting from the 1968 student protests and the Tlatelolco massacre with a policy of 'democratic opening' designed to assimilate into the PRI regime the democratic forces unleashed by the events of 1968. He released the imprisoned leaders of the 1968 protests, increased the budget of the national university and cultivated intellectuals—notably the novelist Carlos Fuentes who was appointed as ambassador to France. Echeverría's rhetoric was populist—he spoke constantly in favour of peasants and workers and publicly took on big business. In accordance with PRI tradition, however, Echeverría combined increased democracy with selective repression of dissident groups. While he did much to cultivate the student movement, dissident students were violently

repressed, most notably in another massacre in Mexico City on Corpus Christi Thursday, 10 June 1971. In July 1976 he engineered the takeover of the outspoken newspaper, *Excélsior*. Echeverría adopted an equally populist economic policy designed to reduce the extreme levels of economic inequality in Mexico. He embraced the fashionable approaches of the Economic Commission for Latin America (CEPAL), which favoured state intervention in economic affairs, high tariff barriers and a closed economy. The result was a government spending spree. When the minister of the treasury, Hugo Margáin, told the president that Mexico's internal and external debts were at their limit and that spending had to be reined in, Echeverría forced his resignation and appointed him ambassador to Great Britain. The president replaced Margáin with his old friend José López Portillo and declared that from then on the Mexican economy would be run from his official residence, Los Pinos. The result was an economic crisis which would haunt his predecessor. The Mexican peso fell from 12.5 per US$ to 25, inflation rose from 13.7% to 27.2% and the external debt soared. Echeverría's successor, José López Portillo took over the presidency in 1976.

Later Life

After leaving office, Echeverría was appointed as Mexico's ambassador to UNESCO and subsequently to Australia.

Eden, Anthony (United Kingdom of Great Britain and Northern Ireland)

Introduction

Anthony Eden was the Conservative British prime minister from 1955 to 1957. He had previously served as foreign secretary, gaining an international reputation as a diplomat and skilled negotiator. However, his tenure as prime minister was dominated by the Suez Crisis and, in tandem with his ill health, led to his early downfall.

Early Life

Robert Anthony Eden was born in Bishop Auckland in the northeast of England on 12 June 1897 into an aristocratic family. He studied at Eton and then took Oriental Languages at Christ Church, Oxford. Twice rejected from Sandhurst on account of his poor vision, he served with the King's Royal Rifle Corps during World War I, achieving the rank of Major. In 1923 he entered the House of Commons as the member for Warwick and Leamington, the same year in which he married Beatrice Helen Beckett, with whom he had two sons.

Within 3 years he was appointed parliamentary private secretary at the foreign office by Prime Minister Stanley Baldwin. Under Ramsey MacDonald he became under secretary of state for foreign affairs in 1931, Lord Privy Seal with special responsibility for administrative duties in 1934 and the first minister of League of Nations affairs a year later. In Dec. 1935, with Stanley Baldwin again in power, he was made foreign secretary. Honing his skills as a negotiator, Eden hoped to bring his abilities to bear in his dealings with the Fascist powers. However, it was becoming apparent that appeasement was failing and when Prime Minister Neville Chamberlain opened up talks with his Italian counterpart Benito Mussolini in 1938, Eden resigned. Churchill would later comment on the resignation that 'there seemed one strong young figure standing up against. . .dismal tides of drift and surrender. Now he was gone'.

Eden re-entered Chamberlain's cabinet at the outbreak of the war as secretary of state for the dominions. When Churchill took office, he promoted him to secretary of state for war, in which capacity Eden instituted the Home Guard. In 1942 he was made leader of the Commons and Churchill groomed him as his natural successor. Labour took office following the general election of 1945 with Eden the deputy leader of the opposition, but when Churchill and the Conservatives returned to power in 1951, Eden resumed his post at the foreign office and also became deputy prime minister. It was during these years under Churchill that he would secure his reputation as a major international figure.

Eden was instrumental in diffusing the rising tensions developing in the Cold War, and in 1954 he negotiated with the Soviets for an interim peace in

Vietnam. He negotiated a conclusion to the Anglo-Iranian oil dispute, mediated during the Indochina War and between Italy and Yugoslavia in a dispute over Trieste, helped establish the Southeast Asia Treaty Organisation (SEATO) and assisted with Germany's entry into NATO. He was made a Knight of the Garter for his efforts but it was also during these years that his health started to fail. In 1953 he had his gall bladder removed but bile duct problems followed later in the year.

Career Peak

Churchill resigned the premiership on 5 April 1955 and Eden took over the following day. He remained influential in the foreign office, sometimes receiving criticism for the 'hands on' control he exerted. His efforts at easing Cold War tensions continued and he met Nikita Khrushchev shortly after entering No. 10. By the end of July 1956, though, the Suez Crisis was in the making.

Britain had already suffered from the economic fallout of the Anglo-Iranian dispute when the Egyptian President Gamal Abdel Nasser announced on 26 July that the Suez Canal would be nationalized. The canal was operated by a French and English run company, and nationalization was Nasser's response to the withdrawal of British and American funding for the Aswan High Dam. It was also thought that Nasser might use the state control of the canal to block oil supplies to western Europe. Britain and France decided to take action, alongside Egypt's long time enemy, Israel. Israeli forces invaded Egypt on 29 Oct. and British and French forces began occupation of the canal zone a week later, ostensibly as a peacekeeping force on behalf of the UN. The action met with Soviet condemnation and the US and UN made clear their disapproval. President Eisenhower spoke of the episode in the same breath as the Soviet's crushing of the Hungarian uprising that year, saying that 'we cannot subscribe to one law. . .for those opposing us, another for those allied with us'. Sterling was weak at the time and when Britain was threatened with the withdrawal of an International Monetary Fund loan, there was no choice but to terminate the operation. French and British troops left Egypt on 22 Dec. with the Israelis following in March 1957.

The incident severely damaged Britain's international standing and, with the return of his bile duct problem as well as a fever, Eden resigned as Prime Minister in Jan. 1957, leaving the Commons 2 days later.

Later Life

In 1961 Eden was made 1st Earl of Avon, Viscount Eden of Royal Leamington Spa and he released three autobiographical volumes during the 1960s. He fell ill while in America in early 1977 and died on 14 Jan. in Alvediston, Wiltshire in the southwest of England. His second wife Clarissa Churchill survived him.

Eisenhower, Dwight D. (United States of America)

Introduction

Dwight David Eisenhower, the 34th President of the United States was elected President in 1953 and again in 1957. He achieved military distinction as supreme allied commander of the invasion of Europe in 1944. As President, Eisenhower struggled to implement his policies against opposition from a Democrat controlled Congress.

Early Life

Born on 14 Oct. 1890 in Denison, Texas, Eisenhower's parents were members of a fundamentalist Christian group known as the River Brethren. After graduating from High School in 1909 Eisenhower entered the US Naval Academy at West Point, which he attended from 1911. A talented American football player, Eisenhower's sporting ambitions were curtailed by injury. After graduation from West Point in 1915 Eisenhower was made ND Lieutenant of Infantry. On 1 July 1916 he married Mamie Geneva Doud, with whom he would have two children, one of which died in infancy.

During World War I, Eisenhower earned a Distinguished Service Medal. In 1933 he was appointed assistant to chief of staff General Douglas MacArthur, and spent 4 years in the Philippines working on the islands'

defences. In 1940 Eisenhower was made a lieutenant colonel and in 1941 he was promoted to brigadier general and his chief of staff George Marshall gave him responsibility for the United States' War Plans division in the Far East. On 25 June 1942 Eisenhower was made commander of all the United States forces in Europe and head of the Operation Division a year later.

Eisenhower led the Allied invasion of North Africa in Nov. 1942. In July 1943, he led the Allies into Sicily, proclaiming the capture of Palermo as 'the first page in the story of the liberation of the European continent'. On 8 Sept. he announced that Italy had unconditionally surrendered. On 24 Dec. 1943 President Franklin D. Roosevelt appointed Eisenhower as supreme allied commander of the invasion of Western Europe, with Briton General Montgomery as his field commander.

On 6 June 1944 allied naval forces, supported by strong air forces, began landing Allied armies on the northern coast of France. Operation Overlord was the largest ever-combined land, sea and air military operation. By July German forces had been driven from Normandy and on 25 Aug. Allied forces retook Paris. The Germans attempted to hit back with an offensive in the Ardennes in Dec., but Eisenhower marshalled his troops and the Nazi counter-attack was over by the early part of 1945. The Germans eventually surrendered on 8 May 1945. Eisenhower remained in Europe for several months as head of the occupational forces until returning to America to become chief of staff.

After presiding over the demobilization of the American army Eisenhower was briefly the president of Columbia University before he was appointed supreme commander of the North Atlantic Treaty Organisation (NATO) in 1950. As a presidential candidate he was a popular choice of both Democrats and Republicans. In Jan. 1952 he threw his hat into the political ring, announcing that he would be prepared to run as a Republican. He won the Presidential nomination in July and resigned from the Army. One of his first acts was to select Senator Richard M. Nixon as his running mate.

Career Peak

In an election campaign that utilised the fast-developing medium of television, Eisenhower defeated Democratic opponent Adlai E. Stevenson by a majority of 6.45 m. votes. On 20 Jan. 1953 he was inaugurated as President.

One of his first acts on assuming control of the White House was to deal with the Korean war that he had inherited from Truman. A ceasefire followed soon after Eisenhower's inauguration. Domestically, Eisenhower's aim was to balance the federal budget. His other chief task was to try and limit the damage created by Senator Joseph McCarthy's investigations into undercover communism. In Aug. 1954, Eisenhower outlawed the Communist Party while distancing himself from McCarthy whose excesses earned him a congressional censure.

For the first 2 years of Eisenhower's Presidency, Republicans marginally controlled both Houses of Congress, but power shifted to the Democrats in 1954, forcing Eisenhower into a delicate balancing act as he sought to implement legislation. Mild civil rights proposals were defeated but Eisenhower did succeed in balancing the nation's budget in his first term.

In Sept. 1956 the assumption that Eisenhower would run for re-election was put in doubt after he suffered a heart attack. He recovered slowly but was sufficiently in command to intervene in the Suez crisis of 1956, by refusing to support the invasion of Egypt by British, French and Israeli forces.

On 6 Nov. Eisenhower defeated Adlai E. Stevenson for the second successive election, this time by more than 9 m. votes and 457 electoral votes to 73. Both at home and abroad, Eisenhower faced a difficult second term in office. Troublesome relationships with Congress continued and the Democrats increased their majorities in the Senate and Congress in 1958. Eisenhower's attempts to thaw the Cold War met with frustration. Anti-American feeling was particularly strong in Cuba, where Communist Fidel Castro had seized power. Just as a Big Four summit in Geneva in 1955 had ended in stalemate, so Eisenhower's attempt in 1960 to agree an accord with Soviet Premier Nikita Khrushchev was thwarted when the shooting down of an American U-2 plane over the USSR caused Khrushchev to boycott the meeting.

Eisenhower handed over the Republican presidential candidacy to his vice-president Richard Nixon—who would ultimately lose the 1960 election by a slim margin to John F. Kennedy.

Later Life

In retirement, Eisenhower was consulted by his successors Kennedy and Lyndon B. Johnson. In 1965, he suffered a major heart attack, and his health continued to deteriorate thereafter. After another heart attack in 1968 Eisenhower died in hospital in Washington, D.C. on 28 March 1969.

Elbegdorj, Tsakhiagiin (Mongolia)

Introduction

Tsakhiagiin Elbegdorj took office on 18 June 2009, the first president not to have been a member of the Mongolian People's Revolutionary Party (MPRP). Campaigning on a platform of change and anti-corruption that appealed to urban voters, he won the election with just over 51% of the vote on 24 May 2009, beating MPRP candidate and incumbent president Nambaryn Enkhbayar. He was re-elected in June 2013.

Early Life

Elbegdorj was born on 30 March 1963 in the district of Zereg. In 1988 he graduated from the Military Political Institute in Ukraine (then part of the USSR) and went on to attain a master's degree in public administration from Harvard University in the USA.

Elbegdorj was active in the fight against communism and in 1989 helped establish a recognized pro-democracy movement. The following year he founded Mongolia's first independent newspaper, *Democracy*. A few months later he was elected to government and was a key figure in drafting a new constitution, adopted in Jan. 1992. In 1996, as leader of the Democratic Party (DP), Elbegdorj led the Democratic Union Coalition to victory in parliamentary elections, paving the way for the country's first peaceful power transition.

Elbegdorj was elected prime minister in April 1998 but a banking scandal forced his resignation shortly afterwards. After the 2004 elections he was again appointed to the premiership, heading a fragile MPRP-DP coalition. During his tenure, he announced measures to boost tourism, reorganized domestic political structures, loosened control of the news media and oversaw the replacement of Russian by English as Mongolia's second language. In Jan. 2006 he was again forced to resign when the MPRP withdrew from the coalition, sparking public demonstrations in Ulaanbaatar.

At elections in May 2009 Elbegdorj won by only a narrow margin over the incumbent president. Nevertheless, the MPRP accepted the result, producing a peaceful outcome after fears of a repeat of the violence that followed the DP's claims of fraud at the 2008 parliamentary polling.

Career Peak

On taking office Elbegdorj faced the challenges of working with a parliament dominated at the time by the MPRP and tackling high levels of corruption and unemployment. He also aimed to spread the profits of Mongolia's mineral wealth more widely. On the foreign stage, he was expected to cultivate Western ties to counterbalance the influence of neighbouring Russia and China.

Following parliamentary elections in June 2012, Elbegdorj's DP was returned as the largest party but without an overall majority. This heralded the formation in Aug. of a DP-led government including the Justice Coalition. Elbegdorj secured his own re-election in June 2013, having again campaigned on an anti-corruption and liberalizing agenda. However, following the Mongolian People's Party's landslide victory over the DP in parliamentary elections in June 2016, Elbegdorj swore in Jargaltulgyn Erdenebat as prime minister at the head of a new MPP government.

Since the constitution does not permit three successive terms, Elbegdorj could not run for the presidential elections of June 2017. On 10 July he was succeeded by Khaltmaagiim Battulga (also of the Democratic Party).

Elchibey, Albufaz (Azerbaijan)

Introduction

Albufaz Elchibey became Azerbaijan's president in 1992. His tenure lasted only a year and was dominated by the war with Armenian forces over Nagorno-Karabakh. He went into exile in 1993.

Early Life

Albufaz Elchibey was born on 14 June 1938 in the village of Kalaki in Nakhichevan. He studied Arabic at the Baku State University and was later a professor there. He also worked as a translator in Egypt. A nationalist dissident, he was imprisoned in 1975 for anti-Soviet activities and banned from teaching. In 1989 he co-founded the Azerbaijan Popular Front Party (APF), serving as chairman until 2000.

Career Peak

Elchibey was elected president of Azerbaijan in June 1992, but served only 1 year of his 5 year term. He abolished the rouble in favour of the manat and replaced the Cyrillic alphabet with the Latin one. He supported calls for a unification of Turkic countries of which Azerbaijan is an ethnic member. His tenure was blighted by a painful phase of economic transition and by the war with Armenia over the break-away region of Nagorno-Karabakh. Heavy losses of troops and land and the creation of over 1 m. refugees ensured a steep decline in Elchibey's popularity. In June 1993, fearing a military coup, he fled Baku and went into exile. He died of prostate cancer in Ankara on 22 Aug. 2000.

English, Bill (New Zealand)

Introduction

Bill English took office as prime minister on 12 Dec. 2016 after winning the National Party's leadership contest unopposed. The election was triggered when John Key unexpectedly announced his resignation the previous week.

Early Life

Born on 30 Dec. 1961 in Lumsden, Simon William English graduated in economics from the University of Otago before reading English at Victoria University of Wellington. He joined the National Party in 1980 and was an analyst for the Treasury before returning to work for his family's farm in Dipton.

In 1990 he became the member of parliament for Wallace (now Clutha-Southland), a seat he held until 2014 when he became a list MP. He was elevated to the Cabinet in 1996 as minister for crown health enterprises and associate minister of education. He subsequently oversaw the health and education portfolios before becoming finance minister in 1999. However, he was in the post for only a few months before the National Party lost the general election that year.

English became leader of the National Party in 2001 but the party then suffered its worst-ever election defeat the following year, receiving just over 20% of votes. In Oct. 2003 he was replaced as leader by Don Brash. Following Brash's resignation in Nov. 2006, English became deputy leader under John Key. When the National Party won the general election in 2008, English was appointed deputy prime minister, minister of finance and minister of infrastructure. On 5 Dec. 2016 Key resigned as prime minister and National Party leader. He endorsed English as his successor, and English subsequently won the party leadership unopposed—a result that saw him automatically take over as premier.

Career Peak

A devout Roman Catholic known for his social conservatism, English entered office with a track record of opposing abortion, civil unions and gay marriage, euthanasia and the decriminalization of prostitution. He inherited a healthy economy and a budget surplus, but faces challenges including overseeing recovery from the 2016 Kaikoura earthquake, addressing the housing crisis and keeping the financial markets stable. In Oct. 2017, shortly after leading the National Party in obtaining a majority of seats at the parliamentary elections, he was replaced as premier by Jacinda Ardern, leader of the Labour Party, who formed a coalition with New Zealand First and the Greens.

Enkhbayar, Nambaryn (Mongolia)

Introduction

Nambaryn Enkhbayar, the candidate of the ruling MPRP, won presidential elections in May 2005, having been prime minister from 2000–04. He promised to modernize the country and tackle poverty and unemployment.

Early Life

Enkhbayar was born on 1 June 1958 in Ulan Bator. Having graduated from the Gorky Higher Institute of Literature in Moscow in 1980, he returned to Mongolia, working as a literary translator at the Mongolian Writer's Union and then as head of its foreign relations department. He also studied European literature at Leeds University in the UK in 1986. Enkhbayar's career in government began on the development committee for culture and art in 1990 as Mongolia embraced democratic reforms, legalized political parties and approved the transition to a market economy. Elected as an MPRP parliamentary representative in 1992, he served as minister of culture until 1996.

When the MPRP was ousted in the elections of June 1996, Enkhbayar replaced Budragchaagiyn Dash-Yondon as leader of the MPRP. He brought in sweeping party reforms, citing Tony Blair's modernization of the UK Labour Party as his inspiration. The MPRP stormed back to power on 2 July 2000, winning 72 out of 76 parliamentary seats, and Enkhbayar was appointed prime minister.

Career Peak

Enkhbayar launched initiatives such as the Millennium Road, a trans-Mongolian highway linking Russia and China, but progress on economic reforms was slow. When the MPRP's majority was slashed in the June 2004 elections, Enkhbayar ceded the premiership to Tsakhiagiin Elbegdorj. He then became parliamentary speaker and stood as the MPRP candidate in the 2005 presidential election. Having been proclaimed the victor, he was sworn in on 24 June. He vowed to unite the country after a year of instability and public protests and pledged to reduce unemployment and inflation and tackle corruption. However, following the MPRP's disputed victory in the June 2008 parliamentary elections, he declared a four-day state of emergency in response to rioting in the capital which left at least five people dead and hundreds injured.

At presidential elections on 24 May 2009 Enkhbayar lost to Tsakhiagiin Elbegdorj of the Democratic Party.

Later Life

In Aug. 2012 Enkhbayar was jailed for 4 years after having been convicted of corruption. He denied the charges, claiming that they were politically motivated. He was released in Aug. 2013 following a decree by then president Tsakhiagiin Elbegdorj.

Enkhbold, Miyegombo (Mongolia)

Introduction

Miyegombo Enkhbold succeeded Tsakhiagiin Elbegdorj as prime minister of Mongolia in Jan. 2006, ending two weeks of political crisis. A former mayor of the capital, Ulan Bator, he was also chairman of the Mongolian People's Revolutionary Party (MPRP). In Nov. 2007 Enkhbold lost his position as prime minister to Sanjaagiin Bayar.

Early Life

Miyegombo Enkhbold was born on 19 July 1964 in Ulan Bator. Graduating from the Mongolia State University with a degree in economics in 1987, he was employed as an economist in the capital's executive administration and in 1989 joined the staff of the ministry of communal economy and services.

In 1990 Mongolia embraced democratic reforms, legalizing political parties and approving the transition to a market economy. Enkhbold joined the ruling MPRP while it was being remoulded into a centre-left party. Having led the premises and services department of Ulan Bator's executive administration during 1991, Enkhbold was appointed deputy governor of the capital's Chingeltei district, a post he held for 4 years. In 1996 he attended a course in state administration and management with the Japanese government's international co-operation agency. The following year he became chairman of the MPRP's committee in Ulan Bator and a member of the party's *Little Hural* (the successor to the MPRP Central Committee from 1992).

Enkhbold became Ulan Bator's mayor in Jan. 1999 and was reappointed in Oct. 2000. He was elected a member of the MPRP's leadership council in March 2001. As mayor, Enkhbold oversaw the introduction of controversial land privatization laws in the capital, which came into force in 2003. In Aug. 2005, Enkhbold was elected to represent Ulan Bator's constituency #65 in the *Great Hural* (parliament) and became chairman of the MPRP.

Mongolia was gripped by crisis in Jan. 2006 when the MPRP withdrew from the governing coalition with the Democratic Party. Enkhbold blamed the Democratic Party prime minister, Tsakhiagiin Elbegdorj, who had overseen rising inflation and a slowdown in economic growth, although members of the Democratic Party claimed the walk-out was because alleged corruption by the MPRP was about to be discussed by parliament. The crisis triggered mass anti-corruption demonstrations, with protesters attempting to storm the MPRP's headquarters in Ulan Bator. Enkhbold's nomination to succeed Elbegdorj was approved by the president, Nambaryn Enkhbayar, and on 25 Jan. 2006 he won 85% support from parliament and duly became prime minister.

Career Peak

Enkhbold formed a 'government of national unity'. including several minor parties, which was approved by parliament on 27 Jan. 2006. The MPRP retained ten of the 17 cabinet seats and Enkhbold promised to focus on speeding up economic development and tackling poverty. In Oct. 2006 he survived a parliamentary vote of no confidence following allegations of government corruption and misconduct.

In Oct. 2007 Enkhbold was pressed to resign by party peers frustrated by a weak government and a general loss of confidence in the MPRP. He lost his position as chairman to former secretary general Sanjaagiin Bayar, who promised to reform the once-communist ruling MPRP and to eradicate corruption. The MPRP delegates also voted for the creation of a new government by Bayar and passed a resolution that the prime minister and the party chairman be the same person. Enkhbold submitted his resignation to parliament on 5 Nov. 2007 and left office when Bayar was elected on 22 Nov.

Life

Enkhbold served as deputy prime minister in the Bayar government from 2007–09.

Erdenebat, Jargaltulgyn (Mongolia)

Introduction

Jargaltulgyn Erdenebat, a former finance minister, was sworn in as prime minister in July 2016.

Early Life

Erdenebat was born on 17 June 1973 in the Mandal district of Selenge province, in northern Mongolia. He graduated from the Institute of Trade and Industry in 1995 before starting work as an accountant. He held several managerial roles in local government and was governor of Selenge from 2008–12. As a member of the Mongolian People's Party, he became a member of parliament at the 2012 election. From 2014–15 he served as minister of finance, in which post he oversaw the expansion of the country's mining operations.

He contested the 2016 general election on a platform of fiscal discipline and economic stabilization, against a backdrop of declining economic indicators. Direct foreign investment in Mongolia had fallen as a result of declining commodity prices for copper and coal, spiralling national debt and a weakening currency.

Career Peak

Erdenebat was sworn in as prime minister on 7 July after victory in the 2016 xelections. He was expected to strengthen economic ties with key diplomatic allies. In the month that he took office, he met with Chinese premier Li Keqiang to discuss a strategic partnership and increased investment from Chinese firms. However, a 4 day visit to Mongolia by the Dalai Lama angered Beijing, resulting in the postponement of bilateral meetings in Nov.

Erdenebat visited Japan in Oct. 2016, where Prime Minister Shinzo Abe indicated Japanese support for development of the Mongolian economy and also discussed potential regional security threats from North Korea. Erdenebat was replaced as prime minister by Ukhnaagiin Khurelsukh, the then vice prime minister, after parliament voted to remove him from office in Sept. 2017.

Erhard, Ludwig (Germany)

Introduction

Ludwig Erhard was West Germany's Chancellor between 1963–66 but is better remembered as Minister of Finance from 1949–63, when he masterminded Germany's 'economic miracle'. While Chancellor Adenauer concentrated on foreign affairs, Erhard was free to implement his 'social market' agenda. Freed from bureaucratic controls, the German economy was energized and industrial output spiralled.

Early Life

Erhard was born on 4 Feb. 1897 in Fürth, Germany. At 16 he left school to take up an apprenticeship. He went on to study economics and sociology at Nuremberg, qualifying in 1923 and gaining a doctorate from Frankfurt-am-Main in 1925. He worked for an economics research institute until removed from his post in 1942. He then set up his own institute and, as Germany's defeat became ever more likely, turned his mind to how Germany could rebuild itself in the aftermath.

Unsullied by Nazi activity, Erhard's career advanced rapidly after the allied victory. From 1945–46 he was Bavaria's Economic Minister. The following year he joined the Special Money and Credit Department in Frankfurt-am-Main and in 1948–49 was Director of the Bizonal Economic Council. In June 1948 he announced the immediate introduction of the deutschmark in place of the Reichsmark, a first step towards a strong stable currency. More controversially, he proposed an end to wage and price controls, against the advice of many Allied and German economists.

Adenauer persuaded Erhard to join his fledgling Christian Democratic Union (CDU), and in Sept. 1949 he became Minister of Finance. His reforms were already beginning to have an effect. Rationing had ended and commercial deregulation was well underway. It was Alfred Müller-Armack, Secretary of State at the Ministry of Economics, 1958–63, who termed Erhard's policies 'social market economics'. Production was left to the private sector and wages and prices were determined by market mechanisms, while the government was responsible for social equality and a reasonable distribution of wealth. In practical terms, the government undertook extensive programmes in farming, housing and social benefits.

Germany's economy benefited from grants obtained through the Marshall Plan, a US-inspired scheme to provide dollar aid for the rebuilding of war-torn Europe. Furthermore, West Germany had received well over 10 m. refugees in the aftermath of war and, while this influx put a strain on the social structure, it presented a plentiful and inexpensive supply of labour. The Korean War and its effects throughout the 1950s opened a wealth of new markets for West Germany. Within 2 years of Erhard's appointment, industrial production had increased three fold and by the end of the 1950s the country was one of the world's great economic powerhouses.

Adenauer's idealistic vision of a united Europe with Germany playing an integral part did not always rest easily with Erhard's cool economic pragmatism, and relations between the two became increasingly strained. Adenauer made attempts to halt Erhard's rise to power but, after significant losses by the CDU in the 1961 elections followed by a troubled few years of government, Erhard succeeded the ailing Adenauer. Erhard led a CDU-Christian Social Union coalition to convincing victory at general elections in 1965.

Career Peak

Erhard's period in office was blighted by difficult foreign relations and a large trade deficit. He also had difficulty reconciling several factions in government, particularly those who wished to move closer to the USA with opponents who saw the future with France. When a recession took hold in 1966 Erhard was forced to raise taxes, after which a number of his key supporters left the cabinet. His government lost the state election in Hesse in Nov. 1966 and on 1 Dec. he resigned as Chancellor.

Later Life

A year later Erhard was given the honorary role of Chairman of the CDU. He died in Bonn on 5 May 1967.

Erlander, Tage (Sweden)

Introduction

Tage Erlander served as Sweden's prime minister and party leader of the Social Democratic Party from 1946–69. After 23 years in office he was the longest serving prime minister in the western world. He was the chief architect of Sweden's welfare state, introducing higher old-age benefits, rent subsidies, and child allowances. He also extended compulsory education to 9 years.

Early Life

Erlander was born on 13 June 1901, the son of a teacher. He attended the University of Lund, graduating in political science and economics in 1928. Erlander was politically active throughout his student years. He began his career as an editor for the encyclopaedia Svensk Uppslagsbok from 1928 to 1938. In 1930 he joined the Social Democratic Labour Party and was elected to the Lund City Council. In 1932 he entered parliament as Social Democratic representative for the Malmö-Lund area. Erlander held several ministerial positions prior to 1946 and became an expert on education and social welfare. He served on key commissions of inquiry, including one on unemployment at the time of the recession. He was appointed Minister without Portfolio in 1944 and Minister for Education in 1945.

Career Peak

Following Prime Minister Per Albin Hansson's death in 1946, Erlander was elected leader of the Social Democratic Party and prime minister. Erlander's domestic policy called for extensions of the welfare state and the public sector, financed by taxation and underpinned by co-operation with both sides of industry. He coined the expression 'the strong society' arguing that as people's living standards improve, their demands on the society increase. In 1955 he introduced a national health service, and in 1959, a state pension scheme. During the cold war Erlander was sympathetic to the west, but preserved formal Swedish neutrality. In 1949 Denmark and Norway joined NATO (North Atlantic Treaty Organization), while Sweden kept firmly to its non-alliance policy. Erlander supported the United Nation's financial aid to the developing countries. In 1960 Sweden joined EFTA (European Free Trade Area), but stayed out of EEC (European Economic Community).

Later Life

After his retirement, Erlander wrote his memoirs. He died in 21 June 1985.

Eroğlu, Derviş (Turkish Republic of Northern Cyprus, Cyprus)

Introduction

Three times TRNC prime minister between 1985 and 2009, Eroğlu became president in 2010. Known for his hard line nationalist approach, his presidency cast doubts over the prospects for progress towards reunification.

Early Life

Derviş Eroğlu was born in Famagusta (also known as Gazimagusa), Cyprus in 1938. Having graduated in medicine from the University of İstanbul in 1963, he returned to Famgusta to practise. He later went back to Turkey to specialise in urology at Ankara's Numune Hospital, once again returning to Cyprus to work as a urology specialist from 1972 until 1976.

Eroğlu entered politics after the creation in 1975 of the Turkish Federated State of Cyprus (renamed the TRNC in 1983). From 1976–77 he served as the minister for education, culture, youth and sports in the assembly of the Republic of Northern Cyprus. He became head of the right wing nationalist National Unity Party (UBP) in Famagusta in 1977 and was elected leader of the party in 1983.

Eroğlu served his first term as prime minister from 1985–93 under President Rauf Denktaş (founder of the UBP). He returned to the post in Aug. 1996, heading several different coalitions until 2004. Intending to give way to 'fresh blood', Eroğlu resigned as leader of the UBP in 2005 but nonetheless became prime minister again in May 2009.

In presidential elections in April 2010 Eroğlu narrowly defeated the pro-settlement leader of the Turkish-Cypriots, Mehmet Ali Talat, with just over 50% of the vote. In contrast to Talat's pro-European approach, Eroğlu campaigned on a nationalist platform, favouring a two state solution. He was sworn in for a 5-year term on 23 April 2010.

Career Peak

Eroğlu began his tenure stating that he would not walk away from peace talks, although some have questioned his desire to achieve a settlement. Negotiations with Demetris Christofias, the Republic of Cyprus president, were slow, prompting United Nations secretary-general Ban Ki-moon to set a deadline of Oct. 2011 for reaching a comprehensive settlement. However, a series of summits ended without agreement on several key issues, with Ban Ki-Moon promising to broker new talks in 2012.

In Feb. 2014 Eroğlu signed a bill that decriminalized same-sex relations in the TRNC—the last territory in Europe where homosexuality was still outlawed. Arrests for gay sex had continued to take place as recently as 2011.

Eroğlu was defeated by Mustafa Akıncı at the April 2015 elections.

Eshkol, Levi (Israel)

Introduction

Levi Eshkol, Zionist and Labour politician, was prime minister from 1963–69. The high point of his premiership was the Israeli victory in the Six Day War with the Arab states in June 1967. He died in office from a heart attack on 26 Feb. 1969.

Early Life

Born in the Ukraine in 1895, Eshkol went to Palestine when he was 18. During the First World War he joined the Jewish Legion of the British Army. He was later among the founders of the Histadrut (General Federation of Jewish Labour), involved in the promotion of co-operative agriculture. He was director-general of the ministry of defence in 1950, minister of agriculture and development in 1951 and minister of finance from 1952–63. He was also treasurer of the Jewish Agency, responsible for raising development funds and overseeing the absorption of Jewish immigrants.

Career Peak

When Labour premier David Ben-Gurion retired from politics in June 1963, Eshkol succeeded him as prime minister and minister of defence. In 1964 he made the first state visit of an Israeli prime minister to the United States, laying the foundation of the close relationship that endures to this day. He also established diplomatic relations between Israel and the then Federal Republic of (West) Germany. In domestic politics he brought together rival factions to form the Labour Party, and set up a government of national unity, including opposition leader Menachem Begin, to secure victory in the Six Day War in 1967.

Essid, Habib (Tunisia)

Introduction

Habib Essid was nominated as prime minister on 5 Jan. 2015 and charged with forming a new government. An agricultural economist by profession, he had been a leading security official in the administration of deposed President Zine El Abidine Ben Ali.

Early Life

Habib Essid was born on 1 June 1949 in Sousse in the French Protectorate of Tunisia. He studied economics at the University of Tunis and graduated with a master's degree in agronomy from the University of Minnesota, USA in 1974. He became an irrigation specialist within Tunisia's ministry of agriculture, working in the Gafsa region for much of the 1980s.

In 1989 Essid was appointed chief of agricultural development for the northern city of Bizerte. He held senior positions in the government under President Ben Ali at the ministry of agriculture and, from 1997, the ministry of the interior. From 2001 he was secretary of state to the minister of agriculture, initially with responsibility for fisheries and subsequently for water resources. He also headed the Pipeline across the Sahara (TRAPSA) project from 2003–04. Between 2004 and 2010 he was director of the Madrid-based International Olive Oil Council.

Following the revolution that toppled Ben Ali in Jan. 2011 and sparked the Arab Spring, Essid was appointed interior minister in the interim government. After the Constituent Assembly elections on 23 Oct. 2011 he was named security adviser to Hamedi Jebali, the interim prime minister and leader of the moderate Islamist Ennahda movement. When Beji Caid Essebsi was elected president on 21 Dec. 2014, he appointed Essid as premier.

Career Peak

Essid was ostensibly chosen as prime minister for his considerable experience in economic affairs and security, as well as his reputation for independence and competence. However, his critics have pointed to his close ties to the autocratic Ben Ali administration, especially during his time in the interior ministry.

Having taken office, Essid attracted controversy by appointing a cabinet dominated by members of Nidaa Tounes (Call of Tunisia), a secular party founded by President Essebsi. He subsequently agreed to include members of other parties, including Ennahda and the leftist Popular Front, and on 5 Feb. 2015 his new cabinet won parliamentary approval.

Security was a major concern throughout 2015. In the wake of three major terror attacks by Islamist extremists in March, June and Nov.—on the country's leading museum, a tourist beach resort and the presidential guard respectively—Essid carried out a cabinet reshuffle in Jan. 2016 in an effort to improve government effectiveness. He replaced the interior and foreign ministers among a series of changes and also abolished a number of posts. Also in Jan. the government imposed a night-time curfew as violent protests against rising unemployment spread across the country.

In July 2016 Essid lost a parliamentary vote of no confidence by 118 votes to three. Youssef Chahed took over as prime minister in Aug.

Estrada, Joseph (Philippines)

Introduction

Joseph ('Erap' or 'Buddy') Estrada, a former film star, was the 13th president of the Philippines between 1998 and 2001. He was forced from power amid popular discontent, having been accused of corruption.

Early Life

Joseph Estrada was born Joseph Ejercito in Tondo, a ghetto area of Manila, on 19 April 1937. Estrada was educated at the Jesuit-run Ateneo de Manila University and the Mapua Institute of Technology. In the third year at Mapua Institute he decided on a career in the movies. Unhappy with his decision his parents forbade him to use the family name and forced him to adopt 'Estrada' (Spanish for 'street').

During his movie career Estrada played the lead role in over 100 films and had success as the producer of 70 more. Estrada's stock character was a Robin Hood-style champion of the poor, a role that was to add poignancy to his later career. In 1981 Estrada was elected to the Filipino Academy for Movie Arts and Sciences (FAMAS) hall of fame.

Career Peak

In 1968, buoyed by his popularity as a movie star, Estrada ran for the mayoralty of San Juan, winning by a narrow margin. In 1987 he was elected to the Philippine senate where he was a leading opponent of US military bases in the Philippines. In 1992 he ran for vice-president and won by a landslide. In this role he headed the newly created presidential anti-crime commission.

Estrada won the 1998 presidential elections convincingly, on a populist platform without the backing of President Fidel Ramos. He was the first president of the Philippines to be elected without endorsement from the USA. Excluded from Manila's political elite he was seen as a champion of the poor.

Estrada resigned in Jan. 2001 after members of his cabinet and military officials withdrew support. This was after an impeachment trial had collapsed and thousands of citizens had taken to the streets to protest. Estrada was accused of receiving US$8.9 m. in a gambling pay-off scheme and over US$2.8 m. from tobacco tax kickbacks. Accused of 'economic plunder'. a crime that commands the death penalty and allows no bail, Estrada was succeeded by his vice-president, Gloria Macapagal-Arroyo.

Later Life

In Sept. 2007 Estrada was found guilty of plunder and given a life sentence although he was freed after he received a presidential pardon. He ran for president again in 2010 but came second behind Benigno 'Noynoy' Aquino III. Then in May 2013 he was elected mayor of Manila, taking office the following month.

Eyadéma, Gnassingbé (Togo)

Introduction

Gnassingbé Eyadéma was until his death Africa's longest serving leader, having seized power in a coup in 1967. He allowed opposition parties to operate from the early-1990s but his regime had been accused of corruption and civil rights abuses. Relations with other African states had been strained over his alleged support for rebel forces in Angola.

Early Life

Eyadéma was born on 26 Dec. 1937 in Pya, in the French-controlled part of Togoland (now called Togo). Given the first name Etienne, he joined the French army in 1953 and served in Indochina, Dahomey, Niger and Algeria over the next 9 years.

In Jan. 1963 he took part in the coup that saw President Sylvanus Olympio killed and replaced by Nicolas Grunitzky. The Ewe tribe unsuccessfully attempted to depose Grunitzky in late 1966 and in the unrest that followed, the military, under the command of Eyadéma, seized control of the government in Jan. 1967. Eyadéma became president and minister of defence.

Career Peak

Eyadéma established the Togolese People's Assembly (RPT) in 1969, developing a one-party state and winning election to the presidency in 1979 and 1985. Despite maintaining close relations with France, the country's former colonial power, Eyadéma promoted Togo's African identity during the 1970s, changing his own name from Etienne to Gnassingbé.

Aiming to stabilize the national economy, he oversaw the nationalization of the phosphate industry in the mid-1970s but by the 1980s the economy was again struggling, amid allegations of state corruption and negligence. Amid rising popular discontent, in 1991 Eyadéma permitted an interim government to take control of national affairs in the build-up to new elections. With the pro-democracy movement gaining momentum, Eyadéma accepted a new democratic constitution in 1992, paving the way for the release of some political prisoners and the legalization of political opposition.

Eyadéma won the multi-party elections of 1993 and 1998, although the legitimacy of both votes was questioned. The EU suspended aid after the 1993 polls because of suspected vote rigging and in 2000 the UN and Organization of African Unity (now called the African Union) began an investigation into the suppression and murder of political opponents during the 1998 elections. The investigation commenced 2 months after Eyadéma had assumed the presidency of the OAU.

In the same year a UN report accused him and Blaise Compaore of Burkina Faso of assisting Angola's Unita rebel group in trading diamonds for weapons and fuel. Relations became strained with Angola and its allies, including Namibia and the Democratic Republic of Congo. Domestically, Eyadéma repeatedly suspended parliamentary elections scheduled for April 2000. Elections held in Oct. 2002 were boycotted by the main opposition parties. In Dec. 2002 the RPT-dominated national assembly amended the constitution to allow Eyadéma to stand for re-election in 2004.

Eyadéma died on 5 Feb. 2005 and was replaced hours later by his son Faure.

Eyeghe Ndong, Jean (Gabon)

Introduction

Jean Eyeghe Ndong was appointed prime minister in Jan. 2006. The French-educated civil servant and politician was a member of the ruling Gabonese Democratic Party (PDG) and an ally of the then president, Omar Bongo, who ruled the country between 1967 and 2009. Following Bongo's death, Ndong resigned in July 2009 to run in the presidential election scheduled for Aug.

Early Life

Jean Eyeghe Ndong was born on 12 Feb. 1946 in Libreville, Gabon, then part of the federation of French Equatorial Africa. A nephew of Leon M'ba, Gabon's first post-independence president, he was educated at l'École Mont-Fort, Libreville, followed by the Collège Saint-Gabriel de Mouila and the Collège Moderne d'Oyem. He studied for a diploma at the School of Social Sciences in Paris in the early 1960s and subsequently obtained a doctorate in political science from the University of Paris X-Nanterre.

Entering Gabon's public administration in 1980 as a civil servant, Ndong worked as director of administrative services and human resources in Libreville's city hall. Four years later he was promoted to director of pensions at the national office for social security, a post he occupied until he was made director of the national office of social insurance in 1990. That year saw widespread protests against the regime of President Bongo and subsequent constitutional amendments that restored the multi-party political system. Elections for a new National Assembly took place in Oct. 1990.

Following his election to the National Assembly in 1996 as a PDG representative, Ndong entered the government as secretary of state for finances, responsible for privatization. He was also elected to be a consultant to the municipal council of Libreville. President Bongo, who won a further 7 year term in Nov. 2005, appointed Ndong to replace Jean-François Ntoutoume-Emane as prime minister on 20 Jan. 2006.

Career Peak

On coming to power, Ndong stated that the government would work to promote economic development, social justice, public security, public health and education. 'It will be an open government, and it will work hard and earnestly to gain the people's trust.' In July 2009 Ali Bongo, the late president's son, was selected as the official candidate for the PDG in presidential elections scheduled for Aug. prompting Ndong to step down to run as an independent candidate against him.

Eyskens, Gaston (Belgium)

Introduction

Gaston Eyskens was elected Belgian prime minister three times (1949–50, 1958–61, 1968–73) and presided over some of the most momentous occasions in his country's history, including the ceding of independence to Congo, and the abdication crisis of Léopold III.

Early Life

Eyskens was born in Lier on 1 April 1905. His first appointment of interest was a professorship of economics at the Catholic University of Leuven in 1931, but his political career did not begin until 1939 when he was elected as a Catholic (now Christian Socialist) Party member for the Leuven district.

Career Peak

Having established himself in parliament, Eyskens rose to the position of Minister of Finance, an office he held from 1945–9 under the governments of Van Acker, Spaak and Harmel. He then became the leader of the Christian Socialist-Liberal coalition government, and served until the following year when the controversy ignited by plans to allow the exiled King Léopold III to return to Belgium. A poll in 1950 revealed widespread Catholic and Fleming support for the king's return, however, large proportions of Walloons, Liberals and Socialists opposed the idea. Léopold eventually renounced his sovereignty in favour of his son Baudouin in 1951. The crisis surrounding the so-called 'Royal Question' culminated in the withdrawal from the cabinet of several anti-Léopold Liberal ministers, and also in Eyskens' resignation.

Eyskens returned to head the government in 1958 for two consecutive, but incomplete, terms. Whilst in office he managed to resolve a long-standing dispute by enacting the Schools Pact which granted equal financial aid to public and parochial schools. Pressure was growing on the government to grant the Congo independence, since Belgium could no longer afford to maintain the colony, either politically or economically. Eyskens was instrumental in persuading parliament to relinquish the Congo. Having gained its independence the Congo was plunged into civil war, and the ensuing bloodbath coupled with Belgium's domestic economic difficulties led to the collapse of Eyskens' government. After a brief term as minister of finance, Eyskens embarked on his third and final tenure as prime minister. He was largely successful in concluding the revision of the constitution, however growing tensions between the Flemish and French language communities meant that Eyskens was unable to insert an article concerning regionalization into the document, with the result that in Nov. 1972 he again stepped down from power.

Later Life

Following his retirement from politics, Eyskens became the chairman of the Kredietbank NV in Brussels, and was made a viscount by King Baudouin. He died on 3 Jan. 1988.

Fahd bin Abdulaziz Al-Saud (Saudi Arabia)

Introduction

King Fahd succeeded to the throne on 13 June 1982 on the death of his half-brother, Khalid. A son of Abdulaziz Al-Saud, the founder of modern Saudi Arabia, he was the country's fifth king. Like his predecessors, he maintained absolute executive and legislative power, but broadened the process of political consultation and decision-making. He also encouraged the diversification of the economy away from reliance on oil, and oversaw the growth of the private sector's contribution to gross domestic product to more than a third. In international relations, he adopted a moderate stance on regional problems and allied the Kingdom closely with the western industrialised nations, particularly the United States.

Early Life

King Fahd was born in 1923. After his formal education in Riyadh he began his diplomatic career, initially as a member of the Saudi delegation to the signing in San Francisco in 1945 of the United Nations Charter. In 1953, during his father's reign, he was appointed as the first minister of education and is credited with helping to develop a nationwide school system. While continuing to represent the Kingdom in international diplomacy, he held the posts of interior minister from 1962–75 and, from 1967, second deputy prime minister. His first official visit to the United States in 1974 strengthened bilateral ties (at a tense time of rising oil prices) and resulted in the creation of a joint commission on economic co-operation.

In 1975, as Khalid was proclaimed King, Fahd was invested as Crown Prince and first deputy prime minister. In this role he backed the modernization of the country's infrastructure under the second and third 5 year development plans (1975–79 and 1980–84). In international affairs his increasingly active role was reflected in his eight-point peace plan to resolve the Arab-Israeli conflict. Proposed in 1981, it was accepted by Arab states (with some reservation and amendment) but rejected ultimately by Israel.

Career Peak

On Khalid's death in June 1982, Fahd assumed the crown. He continued the 5 year cycle of development programmes to expand the private sector and restructure the economy in favour of non-oil industrial sectors and social welfare. Politically, the King made significant changes within the confines of an absolute monarchy. In 1992 he introduced a new basic law defining the systems of central and municipal government. He also set up a Consultative Council (Majlis Al-Shura) of royal appointees in 1993, which has since been expanded to 90 members in 1997 and 120 in May 2001. As the Custodian of the Two Holy Mosques of Makkah and Madinah, the holiest of Islamic sites, Fahd continued the policy of his predecessors to extend facilities for the 2m. Muslim pilgrims from around the world who visit them each year.

King Fahd was a participant in successful diplomatic efforts to end the Iran-Iraq war in 1988 and in the 1989 Taif reconciliation accord bringing the 14 year Lebanese civil war to a close. His pro-western stance and co-operation in the 1990–91 Gulf crisis were crucial to the deployment and successful military operations of the US-led multinational force raised against Iraq following its invasion of Kuwait. He was later involved in international efforts to resolve crises in Bosnia, Afghanistan and Somalia, and supported the Middle East peace process launched in 1991.

After Fahd suffered a stroke in 1995, Crown Prince Abdullah Ibn Abdulaziz Al-Saud, his half-brother, assumed day-to-day administrative control. King Fahd died on 1 Aug. 2005.

Faisal bin Abdulaziz Al-Saud (Saudi Arabia)

Introduction

King Faisal assumed the throne on 2 Nov. 1964, having a few months earlier been named as regent. He effectively deposed his brother, Saud, who had ruled since the death of their father in 1953. Faisal's reign oversaw the beginnings of the Kingdom's dramatic economic restructuring based on oil revenues. It also witnessed the further deterioration of the Arab-Israeli dispute and the emergence of the 'oil weapon' in international diplomacy.

Early Life

Faisal was born in Riyadh in 1906, the son of the dynastic founder Abdulaziz Al-Saud. Influential in his father's military conquest of the Hejaz region in the mid-1920s, he became viceroy of the province in 1925. Upon the formal establishment of the Kingdom of Saudi Arabia, Faisal was appointed foreign minister in 1932. In 1953, when his brother Saud became king, he was declared Crown Prince and continued as foreign minister. He later served as prime minister from 1958–60 and from 1962 onwards. As an advocate of modernization and, to some extent, westernization, Faisal came into conflict with the more conservative Saud.

Career Peak

In Nov. 1964 Saud was forced to abdicate in Faisal's favour. As King and prime minister, Faisal instituted a programme of economic modernization, using the Kingdom's increasing oil production revenues. In 1970 he initiated the first of the 5 year economic development programmes. Over that same period, financial support was given to other Arab states in their conflict with Israel. The Oct. 1973 Arab-Israeli war heralded an oil crisis in which Arab producers, including Saudi Arabia, cut supplies to the United States and other western countries leading to a fourfold increase in oil prices. However, Faisal subsequently adopted a more conciliatory stance than more radical OPEC members and the close Saudi economic relationship with the US was preserved (and reinforced with a co-operation agreement in 1974). In March 1975 Faisal was assassinated by a nephew, who was reportedly mentally unstable, and his half-brother Khalid became king.

Falcam, Leo (Micronesia)

Introduction

Leo Falcam became president of the Federated States of Micronesia in July 1999. He aimed to revitalize the economy, protect Micronesian culture and develop international relations. He oversaw the renegotiation of the Compact of Free Association with the USA, which expired in 2001.

Early Life

Leo A. Falcam was born on 20 Nov. 1935 in Pohnpei State in the Federated States of Micronesia, then under Japanese jurisdiction. He graduated in sociology from the University of Hawaii in 1962. Returning home, he taught for a short while before joining the government of the US Trust Territory of the Pacific Islands (TTPI, established in 1947). In 1964 he was appointed assistant district administrator for Ponape District.

In 1965 Falcam studied public administration and international relations at the Woodrow Wilson School, Princeton University. The following year he rejoined the TTPI government, working for the high commissioner. In 1972 he was made the first native district administrator of the Ponape District. In 1975 he led the Pohnpei delegation at the convention to establish a Micronesian constitution. The following year he was put in charge of the Micronesia-US liaison office in Washington, which evolved into Micronesia's embassy.

Following the official establishment of the Federated States in May 1979, Falcam was named governor of Pohnpei State. In 1983 he chaired the State's constitutional convention. The following year he became postmaster general, holding the post until he was voted Pohnpei's senator in 1987. He also held senior positions with the Micronesian bank, the Pohnpei agriculture and trade school board of trustees and the PATS Peace foundation.

In May 1997 Falcam was elected vice president by congress. He won the presidency in May 1999.

Career Peak

In his inauguration speech Falcam outlined plans to kick-start the economy (which suffered from high levels of unemployment), protect Micronesian cultural values and establish closer international ties. Tourism was emphasized as a key economic sector, although the cost of developing infrastructure hampered the industry. Major reforms to the public sector were introduced.

The Micronesian economy received around US$100 m. a year between 1986 and 2001 from the US as part of the Compact of Free Association, which allowed US military bases in the region. The treaty was subject to re-negotiation but there was concern at the lack of accountability in Micronesia's expenditure programmes. Falcam's administration reached a compromise with Palau and the Marshall Islands over joint management of commercial fish stocks. In Jan. 2001 he was appointed chairman of the standing committee for the Pacific Islands leaders conference.

At elections in March 2003 Falcam lost his seat for the state of Pohnpei Micronesia to Resio Moses. Falcam remained in office until 11 May 2003 when Joseph Urusemal was elected president.

Faulkner, Brian (Northern Ireland, United Kingdom)

Introduction

Brian Faulkner, an Ulster Unionist, was prime minister of Northern Ireland from 1971–72. His tenure was marked by an increase in sectarian violence. He was responsible for the introduction of the controversial policy of internment (arrest without trial), an attempt to destroy the Irish Republican Army (IRA) which impacted almost exclusively on Roman Catholics. He and his government resigned, heralding the end of Northern Ireland's own parliament and the beginning of direct rule from Westminster.

Early Life

Arthur Brian Deane Faulkner was born on 18 Feb. 1921 in County Down and went on to study at Queen's University, Belfast. After several years as a businessman he entered the Northern Ireland parliament (Stormont) as the Unionist member for East Down. By 1956 he was chief whip and three years later he was appointed minister of home affairs. In 1963 he moved to the ministry of commerce, encouraging several multi-national companies to invest in the region.

In early 1969 Faulkner resigned in protest at the concessions and conciliatory gestures made by Prime Minister Terence O'Neill in response to the burgeoning Roman Catholic civil rights movement. Faulkner was widely expected to challenge for the premiership but O'Neill was instead replaced by James Chichester-Clarke, under whom Faulkner served as minister for development. Chichester-Clarke was unable to stem the growing tide of sectarian violence and in March 1971 Faulkner, by now espousing a more moderate line, succeeded him.

Career Peak

Once in office, Faulkner found that his moderate stance had lost him the support of hard-line Unionists while Nationalists remained cautious. Violence continued to increase and in Aug. 1971 he oversaw the introduction of internment. Several hundred people were rounded up, almost all of them Catholics, most of whom were freed without charge. The policy failed to identify a significant number of IRA members, caused widespread resentment among the Catholic population and ensured a groundswell in support for the IRA.

In Jan. 1972, on a day that came to be known as Bloody Sunday, a march was held in Londonderry (now Derry) against internment. The demonstration was illegal and British troops opened fire on the crowd, killing thirteen people and injuring many more. In late March, amid widespread anger at the events of Bloody Sunday, Faulkner met with British prime minister Edward Heath in London. Faulkner refused a power-sharing scheme and obstructed the transfer of security matters to London. Heath responded by dissolving Stormont on 24 March, forcing Faulkner and his government to resign, and imposing direct rule.

Though politically weakened, Faulkner took an active role in the 1973 Sunningdale talks that led to the creation of a power-sharing Northern Irish Assembly and a cross-border Council of Ireland. In Jan. 1974 he headed the power-sharing executive. However, the new assembly provoked resentment from many Unionists and in May 1974 the Protestant Ulster Workers' Council called a general strike that paralysed the region for a fortnight. Faulkner resigned, the assembly soon collapsed and direct rule was re-imposed.

Later Life

Faulkner founded the Protestant Unionist Party in Sept. 1974, leading it until Aug. 1976. In the same year he was created Baron Faulkner of Downpatrick. He died the following year in a riding accident.

Faymann, Werner (Austria)

Introduction

A career politician, Werner Faymann became leader of the Social Democratic Party (SPÖ) in June 2008. He led the party to narrow victories at the 2008 and 2013 general elections, serving as chancellor at the head of coalition governments on both occasions.

Early Life

Werner Faymann was born on 4 May 1960 in Vienna. He attended a grammar school in Vienna and studied law at the University of Vienna before joining the youth branch of the Vienna SPÖ. There he led campaigns and protests, becoming the group's chairman in 1985. From 1985–88 he also worked as a consultant at the Zentralsparkasse (now Bank of Austria). In 1985 he was elected to the Vienna state parliament and from 1988–94 led the board for tenants' rights. He was appointed councillor for housing and urban development in Vienna in 1995, serving until 2007 when Chancellor Gusenbauer appointed him federal minister for transport, technology and development.

In June 2008, with the 'grand coalition' between the SPÖ and the Austrian People's Party (ÖVP) under strain, the SPÖ separated the role of chancellor from that of party leader. Faymann was chosen to head the party. Faymann and Gusenbauer then published an open letter that reversed earlier SPÖ policy by promising to put all amendments to EU treaties affecting the national interest to a referendum. The ÖVP consequently abandoned the coalition, triggering a general election.

Faymann fought the election on a platform of social investment and populist scepticism about the EU. On 28 Sept. 2008 the SPÖ won the most seats, although with a reduced share of the vote (just under 30%). Refusing to consider a coalition with the right-wing Alliance for the Future of Austria or the anti-immigration Freedom Party, he entered into an agreement in Nov. with the ÖVP under its new leader Josef Pröll. On 2 Dec. 2008 Faymann was sworn in as chancellor.

Career Peak

Faymann initially faced challenges from the global economic crisis and in early 2009 introduced tax cuts to boost the economy. He has advocated EU aid to support struggling European economies, in part to safeguard large loans that Austria has made to Eastern European countries. In June 2013 his government withdrew its military participation in the United Nations monitoring force in the Israeli-occupied Golan Heights. Following the Sept. 2013 parliamentary elections, the SPÖ and ÖVP won sufficient support to form another coalition under Faymann's premiership, but both parties lost ground in the poll to right-wing and eurosceptic parties. In Aug. 2014 Michael Spindelegger resigned as vice chancellor and finance minister, citing disagreements within his ÖVP party over tax reform. He was replaced the following month by Reinhold Mitterlehner as vice chancellor and Hans Jörg Schelling as finance minister.

In June 2014 the government signed a controversial deal with Russia to complete the Austrian section of a gas pipeline for transporting Russian gas to Europe, despite the opposition of some EU member states and the European Commission in the wake of Russian intervention in Ukraine. However, the project was abandoned in Dec. 2014 as the EU imposed economic sanctions against Russia.

In Feb. 2015 the government approved a controversial legislative reform banning foreign funding for mosques and imams, partly aimed at tackling Islamist radicalism. Later in the year Faymann called for a unified response to Europe's deepening migrant crisis, prompted particularly by the civil war in Syria, and for an EU-wide quota to manage the huge flow of refugees and to prevent further transit deaths.

Faymann resigned in May 2016 after the SPÖ failed to progress a candidate to the second round run-off at presidential elections held in April.

Fernández de Kirchner, Cristina (Argentina)

Introduction

Cristina Fernández de Kirchner was sworn in as president on 10 Dec. 2007, representing the ruling Front for Victory party (FV). She succeeded her husband, Néstor Kirchner, and became the first elected female president of Argentina, though not the first female president. She was re-elected for a second term in Oct. 2011.

Early Life

Cristina Kirchner, also called Fernández, was born in 1953 in the La Plata region of Buenos Aires. Her father was a businessman and unionist of Spanish heritage. Her mother was a civil servant in the ministry for the economy and member of the Peronists of German decent. Fernández was educated at secondary level in Buenos Aires and at the Colegio Nuestra Señora de la Misericordia, a private college run by nuns.

During the 1970s she studied at La Plata National University, reading psychology before converting to law. In 1974 she met Néstor Kirchner, a law student, and they married after 6 months. Both were members of the Tendencia Revolucionaria faction of the Peronist Justicialista Party (PJ). In 1975, following Juan Perón's death, the Kirchners moved to Rio Gallegos, the capital of Santa Cruz. They set up a law practice and distanced themselves from politics while the military junta that had ended the Peronist government in 1976 with a coup d'état held power until 1983. Whether Fernández completed her law degree remains disputed.

Her political career began shortly after her husband's. In 1985 she became a member of the PJ and was elected provincial representative of Santa Cruz in 1989, 1993 and 1995. Her husband became mayor of Rio Gallegos in 1987 and governor of Santa Cruz in 1991. In 1995 Fernández resigned from provincial politics to represent Santa Cruz in the Senate, where she built her national profile. In 1997 and 2001 she was elected to represent Santa Cruz in the Chamber of Deputies. In 2003 she helped her husband win the presidential election and became first lady. Two years later she secured the senatorship for Buenos Aires, representing the FV. In 2007, despite good poll ratings, Néstor Kirchner decided not to run for re-election as president and Fernández was elected in his place.

Career Peak

Fernández pledged to further her husband's economic policies. However, in the early stages of her tenure she faced budget restrictions and other challenges, including an energy shortage, rising inflation, large public debt and dependency on GM soya exports. She also faced continuing accusations from the IMF that the national statistics institute manipulated official inflation figures. In July 2008, in a politically damaging defeat, Fernández cancelled tax increases on agricultural exports that had provoked months of protests by farmers. This was followed by another controversial government plan to nationalize private pension funds, ostensibly to protect pensioners' assets during the erupting global financial crisis, which was approved by parliament in Nov. As the economy deteriorated rapidly from late 2008 and her popularity slumped, Fernández brought forward partial congressional elections from Oct. 2009 to June. However, her party supporters still lost their absolute majorities in both parliamentary houses in the polling and her husband failed to gain election to the Chamber of Deputies.

In Oct. 2009 the government indicated its willingness to negotiate with holders of US$20bn. of bonds (on which Argentina had defaulted in 2001) in a debt restructuring initiative aimed at restoring the country's access to international credit. In April 2010 the government announced the terms of its offer to creditors, and by June about 90% of defaulted bonds had been exchanged. Earlier, in Jan. 2010, Fernández had secured the removal of the governor of the Central Bank, Martín Redrado, for opposing her proposal to use the Bank's hard-currency reserves to repay debt. In Nov. that year she announced that the Paris Club of creditor countries had agreed to negotiate Argentina's debt default repayment of about US$7.5bn. without any intervention from the IMF (whose policies were rejected by both Fernández and her predecessor). In May 2012 the government announced that it would nationalize a majority stake in the energy firm YFP, the former state oil company owned by Spain's Repsol. The move incurred trading retaliation by the Spanish government and a referral to the World Trade Organization by the European Union. The dispute was finally settled in Nov. 2013 when the government agreed to pay US$5bn. in compensation to Repsol.

Regarding social policy, in July 2010 Argentina became the first Latin American country to legalize same-sex marriage and give same-sex couples inheritance and adoption rights.

Internationally, Fernández has sought to raise Argentina's profile and has represented Argentina at the G20 forum of wealthy nations. Rancour with the UK over the disputed territory of the Falkland Islands has continued. In March 2013 the Falklands government held a referendum on the islands' political status in a bid to reaffirm UK sovereignty; 99.8% of votes cast were in favour of retaining the current status.

In Oct. 2010 Fernández was widowed as Néstor Kirchner died suddenly of a heart attack, depriving her not only of her husband but her principal political adviser.

Reflecting a revival in her popularity in the wake of stronger economic growth (but also rising inflation), Fernández won a second presidential term in elections in Oct. 2011 with 54% of the vote. However, in mid-term parliamentary elections in Oct. 2013 her party lost substantial support despite maintaining a narrow majority, diminishing her chances of revising the constitution and seeking re-election in 2015 for a third term. She was temporarily incapacitated from Aug. to Nov. 2013 by a head injury requiring cranial surgery.

In July 2014 Argentina entered into its second international debt default in 13 years after negotiations with US hedge fund investors suing for full repayment of bonds from the previous default broke down. In Sept. the National Congress approved controversial legislation to restructure the country's debt and circumvent an earlier US court ruling that Argentina could not pay other creditors until it settled with the hedge funds. In response, the US judge ruled that Argentina was in contempt of court.

Precluded from standing for re-election in 2015 for a third term without a constitutional change, Fernández entered the final year of her presidency in Oct. 2014. In Feb. 2015 she was formally accused by a prosecutor of trying to cover up the alleged involvement of Iranian officials in the bombing of a Jewish centre in Buenos Aires in 1994 that killed 85 people in the country's worst-ever terrorist attack.

The winner of the 2015 presidential elections, Maurcio Macri of the Republican Proposal party, took over from Fernández on 10 Dec. 2015.

Fernández, Leonel (Dominican Republic)

Introduction

Dr Leonel Fernández first became president in 1996 and won further 4 year terms in 2004 and 2008. He won plaudits for easing the country's economic crisis, but poverty, unemployment and corruption persist.

Early Life

Leonel Antonio Fernández Reyna was born on 26 Dec. 1953 in Santo Domingo, the capital city. In 1962 his family moved to New York, where he attended school before returning to Santo Domingo in 1971. He enrolled at the Independent University of Santo Domingo (UASD) to study law. In 1973 Fernández joined the leftist Dominican Liberation Party (PLD), the movement founded by his professor and mentor, the former president, Juan Bosch. Following his graduation with a doctorate in 1978, Fernández worked as a political journalist. He subsequently lectured at the UASD and the Latin American Faculty of Social Science in Santo Domingo. Elected to the PLD's central committee in 1985, he rose through the party's administrative ranks and stood as Bosch's running mate at the 1994 presidential election (won by Joaquín Balaguer). Balaguer was barred from running in the May 1996 elections and Fernández defeated José Francisco Peña Gómez in a run-off a month later.

Career Peak

Sworn in as president on 16 Aug. 1996, Fernández brought in sweeping economic and judicial reforms. However, despite increased foreign investment, economic growth and infrastructural improvements, he was displaced as president by Hipólito Mejía of the Dominican Revolutionary Party (PRD) in Aug. 2000 amid discontent over power cuts in the previously privatized electricity industry. Mejía presided over a deepening economic crisis and spiralling crime and unemployment. Fernández was re-elected president on 16 May 2004 and introduced austerity measures and succeeded in stabilizing inflation and the currency. However, attempts to tackle poverty and corruption and to resolve the energy crisis were less successful. A free trade agreement with the USA and the countries of Central America was ratified by the government in 2005. In parliamentary elections in May 2006 and in May 2010 the PLD and its allies secured a majority of congressional seats, while in May 2008 Fernández was again re-elected to the presidency.

In the 2012 presidential elections Leonel Fernández was constitutionally barred from seeking a third term. The elections were won by Danilo Medina (PLD) in a close vote (51% to 47%), with his opponent Hipolito Mejia accusing the ruling PLD of buying votes and other irregularities.

Fico, Robert (Slovakia)

Introduction

Robert Fico became prime minister for a second time after his Direction–Social Democracy (Smer–SD) party achieved outright victory in legislative elections held in March 2012 and he retained the premiership following further parliamentary polling in March2016. He sought to lead Slovakia into closer fiscal co-operation with the European Union. He resigned as prime minister in March 2018 and was succeeded by Peter Pellegrini.

Early Life

Robert Fico was born in Topol'čany, Czechoslovakia on 15 Sept. 1964. After studying law at Comenius University in Bratislava, he obtained a PhD in criminal law from the Slovak Academy of Sciences. On finishing military service in 1986 he worked for the law institute of the ministry of justice until 1995, holding the post of deputy director from 1992.

Career Peak

In 2013 Fico declared his candidacy for the presidential election scheduled for March 2014. Although he received the highest share of the vote in the first round, he was defeated in the run-off by Andrej Kiska.

Later in 2014 Fico implied that there were political reasons for reductions in Russian gas supplies to Slovakia amid broader EU-Russian tensions over the separatist conflict in eastern Ukraine.

In response to the escalating refugee influx into the EU in 2015, Fico expressed his strong opposition to proposed mandatory quotas for distributing asylum-seekers across member countries. In Nov. that year he pointed to Muslim migrants into Slovakia as a potential threat to national security and said that he was prepared to build border fences to protect Slovak citizens.

Smer–SD (as Smer is now known) won the parliamentary election of March 2016 but lost its overall majority. Fico was able to secure a further term as prime minister by forming a coalition with the Slovak National Party and two smaller parties, but opposition parties have continued to highlight corruption allegations surrounding senior government ministers.

In July 2016 Slovakia assumed the six-month presidency of the European Union. Earlier in the year Fico had undergone heart surgery. Fico resigned as prime minister in March 2018 with Peter Pellegrini, also of Smer–SD, succeeding him.

Figueiredo, João Baptista de Oliveira (Brazil)

Introduction

João Baptista de Oliveira Figueiredo was president of Brazil from 1979 to 1985, the last of five military officers to preside over the country's government following the 1964 coup. Figueiredo liberalized Brazil's military regime and slowly democratized the nation.

Early Life

Born on 15 Jan. 1918 in Rio de Janeiro, Figueiredo entered military school at age 10 and spent part of his youth in Argentina where his father had been exiled after an unsuccessful coup attempt in 1932. After the 1964 coup Figueiredo was promoted to colonel in charge of the national intelligence service bureau in Rio de Janeiro.

During the presidency of Gen. Emílio Médici, who took office in 1969, Figueiredo was appointed head of the military staff. In 1974, he became head of the intelligence service under Ernesto Geisel. He was then chosen by Geisel to assume the presidency in March 1979.

Career Peak

Figueiredo continued Geisel's policy of relaxing the military's hold on power and looked to move Brazil towards full democracy. Confronted with hyperinflation, he restored collective-bargaining rights, devalued the currency, and imposed a freeze on interest rates. However, conditions for the majority of the population failed to improve.

Having granted an amnesty to political dissidents, loosened controls on the media and allowed new parties to enter the political scene, he was met with hostility by right-wingers while attempts to ban the newly-established Workers' Party in the early 1980s led to widespread public discontent. By 1982, with the economy spiralling out of control and the country unable to meet its foreign debts, a series of bombings widely attributed to the right-wing military cemented popular opposition to the government.

In 1984 congress narrowly rejected a constitutional amendment providing for the direct election of the president. Figueiredo had opposed the amendment but the slender margin of victory indicated his weakening grip on power. In Jan. 1985 the electoral college approved the opposition candidate for the presidency and in the April, Figueiredo relinquished office, telling journalists to 'Forget me,' as he left.

Later Life

Figueiredo died on 29 Dec. 1999.

Fillon, François (France)

Introduction

François Fillon was appointed prime minister on 17 May 2007 by the recently-elected centre-right president, Nicolas Sarkozy. A former ally of Jacques Chirac, Fillon backed Sarkozy as the UMP presidential candidate and was a leading architect of his election campaign. Fillon held office for nearly 5 years, in the process becoming France's longest-serving prime minister since Georges Pompidou in the 1960s.

Early Life

François Fillon was born on 4 March 1954 in Le Mans, Sarthe. He took an MA in public law at the Université du Maine in Le Mans in 1976, before further study at the Université de Paris V: René Descartes. He subsequently received a DEA in political science from the Fondation Nationale des Sciences Politiques in Paris. From 1977 he was a parliamentary assistant to Joel le Theule, the deputy for Sarthe, continuing when Theule became minister of transport in 1978, then minister of defence in 1980.

Fillon's parliamentary career began in June 1981 when he was elected deputy of the 4th district of Sarthe, representing the conservative-Gaullist Rally for the Republic (RPR). He was also elected to serve on the council of Sable-sur-Sarthe, becoming town mayor in 1983, a position he would hold for 18 years. Fillon was appointed minister of higher education and research in 1993, serving under the RPR prime minister Édouard Balladur until 1995. Fillon then became minister for information technology and the post office. He regained his National Assembly seat at the 1997 elections, although Chirac's ruling centre-right grouping lost its parliamentary majority to a coalition of Socialists, Communists and Greens against a backdrop of rising unemployment and public discontent. That year Fillon was elected national secretary of the RPR and in 1998 he became president of the regional council of Pays de la Loire.

In the aftermath of Chirac's landslide re-election as president in April 2002, Fillon co-founded the UMP to fight in the forthcoming legislative elections. Formed from the merger of the RPR, Liberal Democracy (DL) and the Union for French Democracy (UDF), it won control of the government in the elections of June 2002. Fillon was named minister of social affairs in the administration of Jean-Pierre Raffarin, introducing controversial reforms to the 35 h working week and to the pensions system.

As minister for education and research from 2004–05, Fillon's proposals for sweeping reforms to the national curriculum met with mass student protests. Nevertheless, the 'Fillon law' was adopted in April 2005. He was not given a ministerial position in Prime Minister Dominique de Villepin's administration, formed in May 2005, and pledged his loyalty to Nicolas Sarkozy in the subsequent presidential election. Later in 2005 he was elected senator for the Sarthe département.

Fillon won plaudits for his management of Sarkozy's slick election campaign, which saw Sarkozy consistently polling ahead of rival Socialist candidate Ségolène Royal. Sarkozy emerged as president in the run-off on 6 May 2007 and on 17 May 2007 he appointed Fillon as prime minister.

Career Peak

Fillon took control of a slimmed-down government of 15 ministers, half its previous number. At the legislative elections of June 2007 the UMP won a majority, claiming 314 of 577 seats, down from 359. Fillon was expected to play a leading role in President Sarkozy's programme of employment and welfare reform, although these plans attracted a hostile response from public sector workers during the government's first months in office (and again in the autumn of 2010). In late 2008 Fillon threatened to nationalize banks unless they responded positively to the global credit crisis and lent more to French companies. Fillon won a parliamentary vote of confidence in March 2009, sparked by a debate over plans to rejoin NATO's military command, and retained the premiership in a cabinet reshuffle in June. He survived a further reshuffle in March 2010 following poor results for the UMP in regional elections and another in Nov. 2010 in the wake of social discontent over the government's pension reforms.

Fillon and his cabinet resigned in May 2012 following Sarkozy's loss in the presidential elections to Socialist François Hollande.

Later Life

In Nov. 2012 Fillon engaged in a bitter leadership battle with Jean-François Copé over the helm of the UMP by challenging the outcome of the contested party election that saw him lose to Copé. The disputed election has brought the UMP to the verge of splitting. The divisions within the UMP were further fuelled in May 2013 when Fillon announced that he would run in the 2017 presidential election. In Nov. 2016 he won the nomination to be the candidate for the Republicans (the successor of the UMP), defeating fellow former prime minister Alain Juppé in the second round of the party's primary. However, he was eliminated in the first round in April 2017 coming third behind Emmanuel Macron and Marine Le Pen.

Finnbogadóttir, Vigdís (Iceland)

Introduction

Vigdís Finnbogadóttir took office as president, a traditionally non-political position with primarily ceremonial duties, on 1 Aug. 1980, becoming the first woman in the world to be elected head of state in a parliamentary democracy. A popular incumbent, she was subsequently re-elected for a further three terms in 1984, 1988 and 1992 before standing down on 31 July 1996.

Early Life

Finnbogadóttir was born in Reykjavík on 15 April 1930, the daughter of a civil engineer and a senior nurse. After leaving Reykjavík College in 1949, she attended the University of Grenoble and the Sorbonne in France, University of Uppsala in Sweden and Copenhagen University in Denmark, studying French language and literature, drama and theatre history. She then graduated in English, French and education at the University of Iceland.

Having worked in experimental theatre and the performing arts, she served from 1972–80 as director of the Reykjavík Theatre Company. She also presented cultural programming on Icelandic state television and was a member of the Advisory Committee on Cultural Affairs in the Nordic Countries from 1976–80.

Although Finnbogadóttir had no previous formal involvement in politics, she was well regarded by leftist and feminist opinion in Iceland because of her prominent opposition in the 1960s and 1970s to the US military presence in the country and the North Atlantic Treaty Organization base at Keflavík. A divorced single mother, she was persuaded in 1980 to run for the state presidency with the support of the influential Icelandic women's movement.

Career Peak

Following a closely-contested election on 29 June 1980, Finnbogadóttir secured 33.6% of the votes cast to narrowly defeat three other male candidates. Despite her largely symbolic position, she took a leading role in promoting Iceland as a cultural ambassador, travelling extensively on the world stage, and was an active environmental campaigner. Reflecting her enhanced national standing, she was re-elected three times (twice unopposed) in 1984, 1988 and 1992.

After leaving office in 1996, she became founding chair of the Council of Women World Leaders at the John F. Kennedy School of Government at Harvard University in the USA. Then in 1998 she was designated United Nations Educational, Scientific and Cultural Organization Goodwill Ambassador and appointed president of the UNESCO World Commission on the Ethics of Scientific Knowledge and Technology.

Fischer, Heinz (Austria)

Introduction

Following his electoral victory on 25 April 2004 at the age of 65, Dr Heinz Fischer took office as Austria's first socialist federal president for 18 years on 8 July 2004. He was committed to maintaining the country's neutral foreign policy and the welfare state. Critics labelled him a *Berufspolitiker* ('professional politician'. who tended to avoid controversy and conflict.

Early Life

Heinz Fischer was born into a political family in Graz on 9 Oct. 1938. His father was state secretary in the ministry of trade from 1954–56. Fischer attended the Humanistisches Gymnasium in Vienna and went on to study law and political science at the University of Vienna, attaining a PhD in 1961. He entered politics 2 years later, becoming secretary to the Social Democratic Party (SPÖ) in the Austrian parliament, a position he held until 1975. Despite being elected as a member of parliament in 1971, Fischer continued his academic career. He was appointed associate professor of political science at the University of Innsbruck in 1978 and was made a full professor in 1994.

Fischer served as federal minister of science and research from 1983–86, under a coalition government headed by Fred Sinowatz of the SPÖ. In 1986 the SPÖ joined the Austrian People's Party (ÖVP) in a 'grand coalition' that retained control of the government through the 1990s. Fischer was elected president of the National Council in Nov. 1990, holding the office for 12 years until Dec. 2002. He also served as a member of the national security council and the foreign affairs council.

He was elected federal president on 25 April 2004 as the SPÖ candidate, polling 52·4% of the vote to defeat Benita Ferrero-Waldner, foreign minister in the ruling ÖVP-led conservative coalition.

Career Peak

On 8 July 2004 Fischer was sworn in for a 6 year term. Although a largely ceremonial post, the president is commander-in-chief of the military and has the constitutional power to reject nominations for cabinet ministers and to remove them from office. In his opening address, Fischer recalled how many Austrians had grown up 'sensitive to war and peace' and aware that 'peace and the politics to promote peace. . . must have a central role in our political efforts'. The consolidation of the basic values of democracy is another of his priorities: '. . .Consensus is very important to me. But consensus means to build bridges. Bridges between solid shores'.

Following the collapse of the governing coalition in July 2008, early parliamentary elections were held in Sept. Fischer subsequently asked SPÖ leader Werner Faymann, as head of the largest party, to form a new government. Faymann renewed the coalition with the ÖVP, excluding the resurgent far-right parties that had made gains in the elections, and his government took office in Dec. Fischer stressed that a stable and competent administration was in the national interest to deal with serious challenges confronting Austria, including the global financial crisis. In April 2010 Fischer was re-elected for a further 6 year presidential term, taking almost 80% of the vote.

He has written numerous books and publications on law and political science. He is also co-editor of the Austrian *Zeitschrift für Politikwissenschaft* (*Journal of Political Science*) and *Journal für Rechtspolitik* (*Journal of Law Policy*).

Fischer was not eligible to stand for re-election in April 2016 having served two terms. He left office after 12 years as president on 8 July 2016. with a council of three acting presidents taking over until the election of a new head of state.

Fischer, Jan (Czech Republic)

Introduction

Jan Fischer took over as prime minister on 8 May 2009. His appointment followed the collapse of Mirek Topolánek's government in March 2009. Fischer, the head of the Czech Statistical Office (ČSÚ), was approved for the role by the three centre-right governing coalition parties and the senior opposition, the Social Democrats.

Early Life

Fischer was born in Prague in Jan. 1951 into a family of professional mathematicians. Following his parents into statistical analysis, Fischer specialized in statistics and econometrics during his undergraduate study at Prague's University of Economics. He completed postgraduate studies in economic statistics at the same university in 1985. Fischer was a member of the Communist Party of Czechoslovakia from 1980–89. He has said that he became a member of the party only to ensure that he would not be obstructed in his career.

Having begun work at Czechoslovakia's central statistical office upon graduation, Fischer was appointed vice-president of the institution in 1990, a post he retained when the ČSÚ was created following the dissolution of Czechoslovakia in 1993. He was made head of the ČSÚ in April 2003 and was often required to attend cabinet meetings. As rival parliamentary parties sought a politically neutral figure with a good understanding of the political agenda to succeed Topolánek, Fischer was chosen as interim prime minister.

Career Peak

On assuming office Fischer said that he had no political ambitions. He aimed to focus on completing the Czech Republic's EU Presidency, leading the government until elections in May 2010, and then returning to his post at the statistical office. He duly resigned on 28 June 2010 and was succeeded by Petr Nečas of the Civic Democratic Party.

Later Life

Following the resignation of his government Fischer became the vice-president of the London-based European Bank for Reconstruction and Development. In July 2013 he returned to politics, taking up the post of finance minister and deputy prime minister in the caretaker administration of Jiří Rusnok.

Fitzgerald, Garret (Ireland)

Introduction

Garret FitzGerald was twice Prime Minister (*Taoiseach*), from 1981–82 and 1982–87, heading Fine Gael–Labour Party coalitions. He attempted, with limited success, to introduce several liberalizing reforms but his tenure is best remembered for the 1985 Anglo–Irish Agreement. An accord between the British and Irish governments, it allowed for Ireland to have more involvement in the affairs of the North and was regarded as a key stage in the peace process.

Early Life

FitzGerald was born in Dublin on 9 Feb. 1926. Although his mother was a Protestant from Ulster, his family were nationalists who had participated in the 1916 Easter Rising. His father had been minister of external affairs and defence during the era of the Irish Free State. FitzGerald was educated at University College, Dublin and King's Inns, Dublin. He then held a number of jobs in planning, journalism and lecturing.

In 1965 he entered Seanad Éireann (the Irish Senate). Election to the Dáil followed 4 years later as member for Dublin South East. In 1973, under the administration of Liam Cosgrave, FitzGerald was appointed foreign minister. In this capacity he was instrumental in formulating the Sunningdale Agreement, signed in Dec. 1973, which provided for limited power-sharing via a Council of Ireland. The deal, however, fell apart the following year after intense unionist opposition. He also did much to strengthen Ireland's standing within the European Community. FitzGerald remained foreign minister until 1977 when, as leader of Fine Gael, he set about modernizing and restructuring the party.

Career Peak

Prime Minister from June 1981, he admitted that the sectarianization of Irish society posed great problems for Northern Irish Protestants. FitzGerald's administration collapsed in Feb. 1982 when he lost support over new VAT charges. Charles Haughey replaced him as Prime Minister.

Haughey's tenure as Prime Minister was troubled and short-lived. FitzGerald returned as Prime Minister in Dec. 1982 to undertake a 'constitutional crusade' to improve relations between Catholics and Protestants through legislative reform. Up against sectarian intransigence, he was also defeated in attempts to liberalize laws on abortion (1983) and divorce (1986).

In May 1983 FitzGerald established the New Ireland Forum which advocated 'a united Ireland in the form of a sovereign independent state', although it proposed confederation or joint authority as alternatives. Though Margaret Thatcher's UK government rejected the findings out of hand, it provided a basis for the 1985 Anglo-Irish (Hillsborough) Agreement and gave impetus to the peace process. FitzGerald led Fine Gael to election defeat in 1987 and subsequently resigned as party leader.

Later Life

After publishing his biography in 1991 FitzGerald retired from the political scene. He has continued to write on Irish politics, for publications in Ireland and Britain, is a director of RTE (the Irish broadcaster) and is Chancellor of the National University of Ireland. In 1999 in the course of the Moriarty Tribunal (set up to investigate irregular payments to various Irish political figures) it emerged that FitzGerald had debts of £200,000 written off by two private banks after his retirement from politics. He strenuously denied any wrong-doing. He died aged 85 on 19 May 2011.

Flores Facussé, Carlos Roberto (Honduras)

Introduction

Carlos Roberto Flores Facussé was president of Honduras from 1998–2001. Representing the Partido Liberal de Honduras (PLH), he succeeded PLH president Carlos Roberto Reina. Disaster relief following Hurricane Mitch in 1998 dominated Flores' presidency while border conflict with Nicaragua was narrowly avoided. Falling coffee prices and high crime rates contributed to the PLH's defeat in the 2001 election.

Early Life

Flores was born on 10 March 1950 in the capital Tegucigalpa. He gained a degree in industrial engineering from Louisiana University before studying international economics. On his return to Honduras he worked in business and public finance, both for the national bank and the social security institute before running a media group. He became politically active with the PLH at the end of the 1970s. Regional leader between 1980–81, from 1982–94 he was deputy for the Francisco Morazán region. Between 1994–98 Flores was Reina's minister of the presidency.

In 1998 Flores stood for his second presidential elections, having campaigned unsuccessfully in 1990. Of four other candidates his main rival was Alba Nora Gúnera de Melgar, leader of the opposition Partido Nacional (PNH) and widow of the former military dictator Juan Alberto Melgar Castro. Flores won with 52.8% of votes.

Career Peak

On election Flores set out an economic strategy to reduce inflation and the deficit in public finances in accordance with IMF guidelines. But priorities were changed when Hurricane Mitch struck in Oct. 1998. Thousands were killed, many more displaced and whole villages wiped out. The banana harvest was destroyed, as was much of the country's infrastructure. Emergency relief was granted but much of it took 2 years or more to materialize. The government began a National Reconstruction and Transformation Plan to rebuild the country's infrastructure and economy helped by a 3 year moratorium on the country's foreign debt repayments. As the economy began to recover, a fire at the Cajón hydro-electricity plant which supplied 60% of the country's electricity caused more misery. In 2001 Flores was forced to call a national emergency as severe droughts destroyed crops, threatening widespread famine. Falling coffee prices and reduced trade with its main partner, the US, hampered recovery. The subsequent rise in crime, especially by *maras*, or street gangs, affected Flores' popularity.

With Honduras' history of military dictatorships, Flores was keen to reduce the military's civil power. In 1998 congress approved a plan to appoint a civilian defence minister. The military hierarchy attempted to block the reform. In July 1999 Flores sacked 26 military leaders amid rumours of an attempted coup.

On the international front, a long term border dispute with Nicaragua flared up in late Dec. 1999 when Honduras ratified a 1986 treaty agreed with Colombia which granted both countries rights over a maritime area claimed by Nicaragua. As relations between Honduras and Nicaragua deteriorated, Nicaraguan president Arnoldo Alemán hiked a 35% tax on Honduran goods, banned Honduras trawlers from the area and began a court challenge. The situation threatened to turn violent as both countries began mobilizing troops on the border. In March 2000 Foreign Minister Roberto Flores Bermúdez met his Nicaraguan counterpart in Miami and agreed to the creation of a military exclusion zone to resolve the crisis.

In 1999 relations with the US were strained when Foreign Minister Fernando Martinez criticized deaths caused by US air strikes on Iraq.

Claiming that his deputy had released the statement without his knowledge, he was nonetheless forced to resign. Honduras hosted a meeting of Central American leaders in 1999 and signed a free trade agreement with Mexico in 2000.

As presidents are ineligible to stand for a second term, for the 2001 election Congresss President Rafael Pineda was chosen as the PLH candidate to challenge the opposition PNH candidate Ricardo Maduro. With 53% of votes, Maduro replaced Flores as president in Nov. 2001.

Flores Pérez, Francisco Guillermo (El Salvador)

Introduction

Francisco Guillermo Flores Pérez was president of El Salvador from 1999–2004, representing the right-wing Alianza Republicana Nacionalista (Arena). Elected in 1999, he succeeded Armando Calderón Sol to become the third consecutive Arena president. Flores pledged to tackle poverty with market-led economic reforms, although privatization schemes were met with protests. Investigating war crimes from the country's 12 year civil war remained high in public concerns. Flores struggled to lead a recovery programme after two earthquakes in 2001 caused widespread destruction.

Early Life

Flores was born on 17 Oct. 1959 in Santa Ana, western El Salvador. He studied philosophy and economics in his homeland before taking a degree in political science in Boston's Amherst College. He studied at Harvard and Oxford before becoming a professor of philosophy. He joined Arena and in 1989 was elected vice minister of planning in President Alfredo Cristiani's cabinet. This was during the civil war which broke out in 1980 between the right wing government and a coalition of left-wing revolutionary groups, the Frente Farabundo Martí para la Liberación Nacional (FMLN). In 1992 international mediation brought an end to the conflict. As vice minister of the presidency Flores oversaw the enactment of the peace agreement. In 1994 he was a deputy in the assembly and Calderón's presidential information secretary before becoming assembly president in 1997.

The following year he was chosen as party candidate for the 1999 elections, party leaders believing his moderate stance would capture the votes of wavering Partido Demócrata Cristiano supporters alienated by the hardline radicals within Arena. Flores' main opponent was Facundo Guardado, a former FMLN commander, who represented the now legal political group. The strengthening FMLN had ended Arena's assembly majority in the 1997 parliamentary elections and Hector Silva had won the mayorship of the capital San Salvador. Flores took the presidency with 51.4% of votes to Guardado's 29%. A 35% turnout reflected the voters' disillusionment with politicians.

Career Peak

On election Flores outlined plans to improve health, education and housing to combat the country's endemic poverty. He promised to create jobs, encourage small and medium businesses, reduce the country's budget deficit and offer tax incentives to encourage foreign investors. Flores pledged to tackle crime with tighter laws, increased sentences and a strengthened police force. War crimes were a key issue. The murder in 1980 of Archbishop Romero, which had provoked the armed insurrection, was particularly poignant as the killers remained protected by an amnesty granted by Cristiani in 1993. There was outrage in 1998 when the convicted killers of three US nuns were released as part of a government policy to ease prison overcrowding. Despite calls to investigate war crimes perpetrated by Arena government forces, Flores distanced himself from his party's involvement, calling for the country to move on. Nonetheless, he ordered an inquiry into the murder in 1989 of six Jesuit priests by government troops. In Oct. 2000 the attorney general led a move to investigate the responsibility of high ranked officials, including Cristiani, the Arena party president.

After signing a free market agreement with Mexico, Honduras and Guatemala, El Salvador nonetheless experienced an economic slowdown, caused by low coffee prices. Attempting to revitalize the economy, in Nov. 2000 Flores introduced dollarization, which came into effect in Jan. 2001. He fixed the exchange rate at 8.75 *colones* to the US dollar and made it the only currency for economic and commercial transactions.

Flores' privatization of the telecommunications industry caused widespread protests a month before the March 2000 parliamentary election. As a result the opposition built on its earlier success by winning 8 of 14 regional capitals. Silva was re-elected mayor of San Salvador.

In Jan. and Feb. 2001 El Salvador was devastated by two earthquakes, killing 1,200, displacing 1 m. and causing massive infrastructural damage. Flores called on the international community to reconsider El Salvador's foreign debt, claiming that repayments were cancelling out disaster funds.

Barred by the constitution from re-election, Flores was succeeded by Antonio Saca, also of the Arena party, in 2004.

Flores died of a brain haemorrhage on 30 Jan. 2016.

Fogh Rasmussen, Anders (Denmark)

Introduction

Anders Fogh Rasmussen became Denmark's prime minister in Nov. 2001. His Liberal Party (Venstre or V) had the largest representation in parliament, but to form a government he had to forge a coalition with the Conservatives. Although espousing a centre-right line, his government was supported by the far-right Danish People's Party. Following the 2005 and 2007 general elections, he became the first Liberal leader to win a second, and then a third, consecutive term of office. On 4 April 2009 it was announced that Fogh Rasmussen would take over as Secretary General of NATO on 1 Aug. His successor, Lars Løkke Rasmussen, took office the next day.

Early Life

Fogh Rasmussen was born on 26 Jan. 1953 in Ginnerup, Jutland. He joined the Young Liberals (Venstres Ungdom) in 1970 and stood unsuccessfully as the Liberal parliamentary candidate for Viborg in Jan. 1973. The following year he was elected chairman of the Young Liberals, a post he held for 2 years. In 1978 Fogh Rasmussen graduated with a master's degree in economics from Aarhus University. In the same year he joined the Folketing as a replacement member for Viborg County.

From 1981–86 Fogh Rasmussen was vice chairman of the Folketing's housing committee, and in 1985 was appointed the Liberal Party's deputy chairman. After re-election at the 1987 general election, he became taxation minister, adding the role of finance minister in 1990. However, he was forced to resign 2 years later after a government commission concluded he had provided misleading information to parliament, although he denied the allegations.

In April 1998 he was elected Liberal chairman, having been its spokesman since 1992. Following the attacks on the USA in Sept. 2001, the incumbent Social Democrat prime minister, Poul Nyrup Rasmussen, called a snap election when his popularity ratings were high. The election campaign was fought largely on the issue of immigration, with Fogh Rasmussen gaining popular support for his proposed hard line. Having defeated the Social Democrats, he took office on 27 Nov. 2001.

Career Peak

Forming a minority coalition with the Conservatives, Fogh Rasmussen's key pledges for his first term in office were health reforms, better care provisions for the elderly, an increase in maternity leave, stiffer sentences for criminals and a ceiling on taxes. He also promised a tightening up of immigration laws. There were concerns, however, among Denmark's European neighbours about the parliamentary backing for (and potential influence on) his government from the far-right Danish People's Party (which had doubled its parliamentary representation in 2001). In foreign policy, Fogh Rasmussen was supportive of the US-led military campaign in Iraq in 2003. In Feb. 2005 he was re-elected as prime minister, again in coalition with the Conservatives with the parliamentary support of the Danish People's Party. He remained a strong advocate of the European Union (which, under Denmark's presidency from July–Dec. 2002, concluded negotiations for the accession to membership of ten new candidate countries).

In early 2006 the republication in western European newspapers of cartoon caricatures of the Prophet Muhammad, which first appeared in Denmark in Sept. 2005, sparked mass protests and unofficial boycotts of Danish exports across the Muslim world. While arguing that the issue was one of freedom of expression, Fogh Rasmussen's government sought, in the damaging aftermath of the affair, more effective engagement with Islamic opinion through conferences and other events to encourage understanding.

In Nov. 2007 Fogh Rasmussen won a third term as Liberal Party premier following early parliamentary elections and resumed his governing coalition with the Conservatives. He resigned shortly after his appointment as NATO Secretary General was announced on 4 April 2009. As deputy of the largest party in government Lars Løkke Rasmussen succeeded him.

Later Life

Rasmussen took over NATO Secretary General at a difficult time for the Alliance, with it suffering record casualties in the ongoing Afghanistan conflict to which he committed 7,000 new troops in Dec. 2009. The biggest challenge of his term as Secretary General was the 2011 Libyan civil war, with NATO forces intervening to end Muammar Gaddafi's rule over the country. Whilst head of NATO, Rasmussen promoted increased spending on defence by member states, stating that 'freedom does not come for free'.

His term as Secretary General had been scheduled to end in July 2013. However, it was extended twice until the end of Sept. 2014 so that he could prepare for and oversee the NATO summit to be held that month in the United Kingdom. Former prime minister of Norway Jens Stoltenberg took over as Secretary General on 1 Oct. 2014.

Ford, Gerald R. (United States of America)

Introduction

Gerald Rudolph Ford was the 38th President of the United States, and the first ever man to become vice-president and president without being elected, having succeeded Spiro T. Agnew and Richard M. Nixon after their resignations. Ford's tenure as president lasted from 1974–77. He is best remembered for granting his predecessor Nixon a 'full, free and absolute pardon' as well as for helping heal the wounds caused in America by the Watergate scandal.

Early Life

Born Leslie King Jr. on 14 July 1913 in Omaha, Nebraska, Ford later took the name of his stepfather after his mother divorced and remarried. After relocating to Grand Rapids, Michigan, Ford graduated from High School in 1931 and went to study economics and political science at the University of Michigan where he excelled on the football field. He then went to Yale where he worked as a football and boxing coach while studying for a law degree. He was admitted to the Michigan bar in 1941.

During World War II, Ford joined the navy and served in the South Pacific. When he was discharged he had reached the rank of lieutenant commander. After the war Ford returned to practicing law and, in 1948, married Elizabeth Bloomer, with whom he would have four children. The same year he entered the political arena, running successfully for Congress in the 5th district of Michigan. In 1963 he was elected chairman of the House Republican Conference and he served on the Warren Commission that investigated the assassination of President John F. Kennedy.

In 1965 he challenged the re-election of Republican Minority Leader Charles A. Halleck, defeating him by 73 votes to 67. On Oct. 10 1973 vice-president Spiro Agnew resigned after facing an income tax evasion charge and Nixon nominated Ford as his new vice-president, knowing that his affable reputation would carry the Democratic vote in Congress. Ford was sworn in as vice-president on 6 Dec. 1973.

Career Peak

The deepening Watergate scandal soon made it inevitable that Nixon would face criminal charges and, after he resigned from office, Ford was sworn in as president by Chief Justice Warren Burger on Aug. 9 1974. Seeking to re-establish public confidence in the presidency Ford nominated Nelson Rockefeller as his vice-president, and gradually replaced members of Nixon's cabinet. On 8 Sept. 1974 the new president controversially granted his predecessor a 'full, free and absolute pardon for all offences against the United States' committed whilst in office. Their decision was not well received by Congress or the general public, although Ford defended his action, arguing that it was necessary to end the national preoccupation with Watergate.

Ford inherited a high inflation economy which he attempted to slow down by reducing spending. The onset of a severe recession in 1974–75 and rising unemployment led Ford to push for $16bn. in tax cuts and to initiate the WIN programme ('Whip Inflation Now'). By the end of 1976 Ford had vetoed more than 50 congressional initiatives to increase spending.

Ford oversaw the end of the Vietnam War in 1975. After south Vietnamese forces withdrew from northern territories, American citizens were evacuated from the area and 100,000 Vietnamese refugees were resettled in the United States. Cambodia fell in April and Ford ordered the Marines into action after the new Cambodian government seized an American cargo vessel. 41 US lives were lost but the 39-member crew were saved. The end of American involvement in southeast Asia helped soothe relations with the Soviet Union.

In Sept. 1975 Ford survived two assassination attempts. By 1976 the recession had eased and unemployment had fallen. These factors helped Ford to win the Republican presidential nomination, albeit narrowly. After defeating Ronald Reagan he picked Senator Robert Dole of Kansas as his running mate. Democratic opponent Jimmy Carter led in the presidential race, benefitting from Ford's perceived ineptitude, dissatisfaction with the pardon he had granted Nixon and the slowing of the country's economic recovery. Ford failed to overhaul his opponent's early lead and was defeated in the Nov. 1976 election by a margin of 1.7 m. votes and 297 electoral college votes to 240.

Later Life

Ford was offered but refused a route back into politics in 1980 when Republican presidential candidate Ronald Reagan asked him to be his running mate. Instead he served as a director on the board of various companies.

On 13 Nov. 2006 Ford achieved the age of 93 years and 121 days, thus surpassing Ronald Reagan to become the longest-lived US president. He died at his home in Rancho Mirage, California on 26 Dec. 2006.

Foster, Arlene (Northern Ireland, United Kingdom)

Introduction

Arlene Foster is the first woman to have been both leader of the Democratic Unionist Party (DUP) and first minister of Northern Ireland. She took over from Peter Robinson in these roles and worked alongside the deputy first minister, Sinn Féin's Martin McGuinness.

Early Life

Arlene Isabel Foster was born on 3 July 1970 in County Fermanagh, Northern Ireland. She studied law at Queen's University, Belfast, where she joined the Queen's Unionist Association (part of the Ulster Unionist Party/UUP).

Foster remained an active member of the UUP following her graduation in 1993, becoming honorary secretary of the Ulster Unionist Council. In 2003 she was elected to the Northern Irish Assembly. However, she opted to resign from the UUP and joined the DUP in 2004. In 2005 she was selected as the DUP's candidate for the Fermanagh and South Tyrone constituency. She was minister for the environment from May 2007 until June 2008, subsequently becoming the minister of enterprise, trade and investment—a position she held until May 2015, as well as assuming the role of acting first minister on behalf of Peter Robinson in Jan. 2010 for a period of three weeks.

While minister for finance and personnel from May 2015, she once again took over the position of acting first minister in Sept., this time for ten days. On 17 Dec. 2015 she became leader of the DUP and was subsequently elected as Northern Ireland's first minister on 11 Jan. 2016.

Career Peak

In May 2016 the DUP emerged from the Northern Ireland Assembly elections with 38 of 108 seats, making it the largest party. Foster was subsequently re-elected as first minister, with Martin McGuinness reappointed as deputy first minister. During her campaign, Foster pledged to focus on healthcare, job creation, protecting family budgets, education and infrastructure investment. She also vowed to support victims of 'the Troubles'. On 9 Jan. 2017, over disagreements with Foster about the renewable heat incentive scheme, Martin McGuinness resigned from the government, forcing her to leave office in accordance with the power-sharing administration rules.

Fox, Vicente (Mexico)

Introduction

Representing the Partido Acción Nacional (PAN; National Action Party), Vicente Fox Quesada was elected president in July 2000 ending 71 years of hegemonic rule by the Partido Revolucionario Institucional (PRI; Institutional Revolutionary Party). He left office in Nov. 2006.

Early Life

Fox was born on 2 July 1942 in Mexico City to an Irish father and a Spanish mother, but grew up in the state of Guanajuato. From a wealthy agricultural family, he studied business at the Universidad Iberoamericana in Mexico City and then at Harvard University in the USA. In 1964 he was employed by Coca-Cola, climbing the ranks to become the company's youngest president for Mexico and Central America.

His political career began in 1987 when he was introduced to the PAN by presidential candidate Manuel J. Clouthier. The following year Fox was elected to congress where he concentrated on agricultural policy. Three years later, hoping to represent his home province of Guanajuato, he stood unsuccessfully in the regional elections, losing out to the PRI candidate, Ramón Aguirre, who claimed 51% of votes against Fox's 39%. Fox accused the government of fraud and protested until the government accepted the PAN victory. Ramón Aguirre was forced to stand down and a PAN representative took his place. Fox was elected at his second attempt in 1995.

Although short on political experience, Fox quickly climbed the ranks of the PAN, establishing a support network called 'Amigos de Fox' (Friends of Fox). In preparation for the 2000 presidential elections the Alianza por el Cambio (Alliance for Change) was formed, comprising the PAN and the small Partido Verde Ecologista de México (PVEM; Ecologist Green Party of Mexico). Fox was nominated as the coalition's presidential candidate for the 2000 election. His rival was the PRI candidate Francisco Labastida. Fox's manifesto was based on security, justice, ending corruption and promoting economic growth.

Career Peak

Fox won the 2000 presidential elections with 42.5% of votes against Labastida's 36.1%. His victory ended 71 years of continuous rule by the PRI, often maintained by questionable means, although it was the reforms of outgoing PRI president Ernesto Zedillo that created the environment for democratic elections. On election Fox outlined plans to promote a market-led economy, although he stopped short of privatizing the state oil company Pemex (Petróleos Mexicanos) claiming he was simply looking to attract foreign investment. He also pledged to solve the conflict with the rebel Ejército Zapatista de Liberación Nacional (EZLN; Zapatista Army of Liberation), formed to promote the rights of the indigenous population, especially in the southern Chiapas region. Peace talks under former president Ernesto Zedillo had stalled in 1996. Fox outlined a peace accord that would give the indigenous population more autonomy, and allow recognition of their culture, traditions and language. There were also moves to withdraw the army from the region and release imprisoned Zapatistas. In April 2001 Congress approved legislation granting indigenous communities the right to self-determination. However, despite these measures, the conflict is not yet fully resolved.

Other promised reforms in the policy agenda during Fox's tenure—such as fiscal and energy reform, tackling crime and corruption, and raising educational standards—failed to materialize. This reflected the president's lack of a congressional majority, the PAN having lost a quarter of its parliamentary seats in the July 2003 legislative elections. Economically, the slowdown in the early period of Fox's term—largely a consequence of economic difficulties suffered by the USA which takes about 90% of Mexican exports—improved in the latter half of his tenure. This was largely as a result of Mexico's standing as a major oil producer and high oil prices on the world market.

On an international level, Fox sought to promote relations with the USA. In Jan. 2001 he outlined plans to create a 'NAFTA Plus'. extending the current trade pact with North America to include more Latin American countries. He also pushed for talks with the US on illegal migration from Mexico to the US and made attempts to stimulate trade with Europe.

He was not eligible to stand for re-election in the presidential elections scheduled for July 2006 and officially left office on 30 Nov. 2006.

Fradkov, Mikhail (Russia)

Introduction

Mikhail Fradkov served as prime minister of Russia from March 2004 to Sept. 2007, working through the final years of Vladimir Putin's presidential administration. Fradkov entered into government as part of Russia's first reformist government following the fall of the Soviet Union, and he progressed through the ministerial ranks with a serenity made rare by the turbulent political climate of the 13 years preceding his appointment as prime minister. Fradkov's success under the regimes of both Yeltsin and Putin is attributed to his low-profile style and his perceived independence from warring factions in the Kremlin. His unexpected nomination by Putin to be prime minister, and his subsequent role as Director of the Foreign Intelligence Service, have led to speculation that he may have been involved in the Soviet Union's state security forces prior to his entry into government.

Early Life

Mikhail Yefimovich Fradkov was born on 1 Sept. 1950 in the village of Kurumoch, in the Kuibyshev region of southern Russia. He attended university in Moscow and graduated from the Machine-tool Building Institute in 1972 with a degree in mechanical engineering. From 1973–75 he worked as economic adviser to the Soviet ambassador in India. Some analysts have pointed to the gap between Fradkov's graduation and starting work at the Soviet embassy in New Delhi as evidence that he was recruited by intelligence talent scouts to attend the KGB Institute for Training in a new subject (economics and foreign trade) and to learn languages. In the 1970s the 'Indian sector' was considered important and getting an assignment there upon graduation was highly regarded. This interpretation makes Fradkov a 'hidden silovik'— he never formally worked for state security or intelligence agencies but he was rarely far away from them. After 2 years at the embassy in India, Fradkov returned to Moscow and served in the State Committee for Foreign Economic Relations (GKES). He graduated from the foreign trade academy in 1981 and held various positions at GKES until 1991.

Fradkov first joined the Russian government after the collapse of the Soviet Union in late 1991. He became senior counsellor of the Russian mission at the offices of the United Nations Organization in Geneva, as well as Russia's representative at the General Agreement on Tariffs and Trade (GATT). In Dec. 1992 he was appointed deputy foreign trade minister in the reformist government headed by Yegor Gaida. Fradkov's career took off in April 1997 when he was appointed minister of foreign economic relations and trade by president Yeltsin, but he was abruptly relieved of the post under a year later when the entire government was sacked. Fradkov responded by moving into the private sector, chairing the board of directors of an insurance company (Ingosstrakh), before becoming its general director in early 1999.

May 1999 saw the formation of a new government under Sergei Stepashin, and Fradkov was appointed as minister of trade. But the Stepashin cabinet was short-lived and was dismissed after less than 3 months by president Yeltsin (sacking Russia's government for the fourth time in 17 months). Vladimir Putin, head of the Federal Security Service (successor of the KGB), was approved as the new prime minister on 16 Aug. 1999 and swiftly reappointed Fradkov as trade minister. Putin's cabinet embarked on a hardline campaign to suppress rebels in Chechnya, which garnered much popular support.

Fradkov lost his job when Vladimir Putin won the presidential election in March 2000. But in a sign that the outgoing minister was not out of favour, he was nominated to Russia's influential security council, a narrowly circumscribed structure of tried and tested loyalists. Fradkov's most prominent post came in March 2001 when he was made head of the tax police. He is said to have helped put together the tax-evasion case against Yukos, an oil company that has been under scrutiny as part of Putin's plans to extract more revenues from the natural-resource firms. The tax police agency was disbanded during a government reshuffle in March 2003 and Fradkov was sent to Brussels to represent Russia in the European Commission.

Career Peak

Having been appointed prime minister in March 2004, Fradkov gave a hint at reforms to come by choosing Alexander Zhukov, an economist who heads parliament's budget committee and was seen as a liberal, as his deputy. However, widespread reforms were not forthcoming, and Fradkov maintained the low public profile which had characterized his political career. His reluctance to oppose the diktats of President Putin led to accusations that Fradkov was little more than a 'yes man' to the increasingly authoritarian head of state. Such allegations were not quelled by the award to Fradkov by Putin of the Order of Service to the Fatherland on his leaving office. Fradkov's premiership coincided with a period of stability and economic growth, but the market gave much of the credit for that to the fiscally prudent policies of Finance Minister Aleksey Kudrin.

Later Life

After tendering his resignation to President Putin in Sept. 2007 Fradkov assumed the role of Director of the Foreign Intelligence Service the following month. His appointment in this role has been perceived as an effort to buttress presidential power in the state intelligence services.

Franco, Federico (Paraguay)

Introduction

Federico Franco became president in June 2012 after the impeachment of his predecessor, Fernando Lugo. Franco had been vice-president since 2003.

Early Life

Luis Federico Franco Gómez was born in Asunción on 24 July 1962. The son of a physician active in the Liberal Party, he attended the San Jose Apostolic College before graduating in medicine from the National University of Asunción in 1986.

After postgraduate study in Cuba, he qualified as a surgeon and established a practice in Fernando de la Mora, a suburb of Asunción. A supporter of the centrist Authentic Radical Liberal Party (PLRA) since his student days, Franco was elected to represent them in the municipality of Fernando de la Mora in 1991 and became mayor in 1996.

In 2000 Franco's brother, Julio César, was elected PLRA party vice president. In the general election of April 2003, Franco was narrowly elected governor of the Central department but his brother lost the presidential race to Nicane Duarte Frutos of the Colorado Party. As governor of Central, Paraguay's most populous and prosperous department, Franco reformed its health services.

In Jan. 2008 Franco was elected leader of the PLRA, taking it into a new 12-party coalition, the Patriotic Alliance for Change (APC). The APC leader, Fernando Lugo, won the presidency on a platform of social reform, bringing an end to 61 years of Colorado Party rule. Franco became vice-president but policy differences with Lugo soon emerged, notably over land reform. Franco accused the president of failing to respect the law in his drive to push through measures to give land to poorer farmers.

Amid growing hostility from Congress and the armed forces, Lugo's authority was further undermined by paternity claims made against him by three women in 2009. In mid-2012 there were violent clashes between police and farmers occupying land that they claimed had been taken from them during the Stroessner dictatorship. Seven police and 11 farmers were killed. Parliament launched an impeachment of the president over his handling of the

crisis and a vote on 21 June ended his mandate. In accordance with the constitution, Franco took over as president until Aug. 2013.

Career Peak

Progress on Franco's promised land, tax and energy reforms has been undermined by weak support in Congress and a lack of recognition of his administration by regional neighbours. The governments of Venezuela and Ecuador were particularly critical, arguing that Lugo was not given sufficient time to present the case against his impeachment and that his removal was tantamount to a coup.

Franco did not contest the presidential and parliamentary elections in April 2013. On 15 Aug. 2013 he was succeeded as president by Horacio Cartes.

Franco, Francisco (Spain)

Introduction

A general in the Spanish army Francisco Franco instigated a military revolt against the Republican Government, the catalyst for the Spanish Civil War. Appointed leader of the Falange (Fascist) Party, he proclaimed himself ruler of Spain in 1939. He led the country until his death in 1975.

Early Life

Born in El Ferrol, Galicia on 4 Dec. 1892 to a naval paymaster, Franco's military career began in 1907 when he entered the Toledo Infantry Academy. Joining the army in 1910, he was posted to Morocco in 1912, where he served until 1927. In 1915 he became the youngest captain in the Spanish army. At the end of his time in Morocco he was appointed director of the Zaragoza Military Academy, becoming its Chief of General Staff in 1935, and was appointed Governor of the Canary Islands in 1936.

The years preceding the Civil War were politically turbulent with the government alternating between left and right. In the presidential elections of 1936 the left gained a clear majority and the leader of the Popular Front, Manuel Azaña, was elected president. Joining forces with General José Sarjurjo, on 18 July of that year General Franco launched a military revolt against the Republican Government. After the death of Sarjurjo, Franco became the leader of the uprising and, in 1937, of the Falange Party. This party, founded in 1933 by José António Primo de Rivera, son of the fascist leader who was in power up to 1930, was merged by Franco with other right-wing groups. Together they formed the only legal political party after the civil war, the Moviemento Nacional (National Movement). After 3 years of fighting, during which time Franco was supported by Germany and Italy, Franco claimed victory on 1 April 1939.

Career Peak

Pronouncing himself absolute leader, or *El Caudillo*, Franco became the head of state on 1 Oct. As a one party state, any political opposition to the regime was criminalized. In 1947 Franco reorganized the government reverting Spain to a monarchy, leaving open his choice of successor as head of state.

Franco's assumption of power coincided with the beginning of World War II. While sympathizing with the Axis powers, Franco remained neutral to concentrate on establishing the regime. After the fall of France he attempted to make a deal with Hitler. He would enter the war on the Axis side in return for control over France's North African territories at the end of the conflict. Hitler declined. When the Allies' victory seemed likely, Franco attempted to backtrack and in 1943 reaffirmed Spain as a neutral nation. But, distrusted by the Allies, Spain was excluded from the newly formed UN in 1945 and subsequently from NATO. Within Spain Franco turned ostracism to his advantage, heightening nationalist sentiment to validate his regime. International relations were restored in the early 1950s. With the outset of the Cold War, Spain was transformed from an ally of Nazi Germany to an opponent of Communism. In 1953 relations with the USA were tied with a 10-year military-assistance accord.

Spain was economically crippled by the Civil War. There was also considerable structural damage to the country. The 1940s were years of hardship, extreme food shortages and poverty—especially in rural areas—

worsened by an international trade boycott. The people remained divided between those who had supported Franco and those who had supported the Republic. Opposition was kept alive by the underground Partido Comunista de España (Communist Party). Franco resorted to brutal repression. A siege economy precluded all outside investment and centralized control quashed regional autonomy. The Galician, Catalan and Basque languages and cultures were banned. Education was controlled by the church. Opposition to the Franco regime was strongest in the provinces. The ETA (Euzkadi Ta Azkatsuna; Basque Homeland and Liberty) movement was formed in 1959 and targeted security force members. In Dec. 1973 a car bomb killed Admiral Luis Carrero Blanco who had served as vice premier between 1967–73 and as premier from June 1973.

To stave off economic crises, a Stabilization Plan was implemented in 1959 and the peseta devalued. From 1960 onwards Spain enjoyed an economic revival. Opened up to the global market. Spain saw an increase in international trade, foreign investment and tourism. The number of agricultural workers fell by half between 1960–76 as people sought better living standards in the towns. The migration was concentrated on Madrid, Barcelona, Seville, Valencia and Bilbao, spreading the cities' suburbs and shanty-towns. Despite Spain's apparent modernization, the Falange party continued to oppose change. The sole move away from absolute control came with the 1966 press law which gave the press greater freedom.

In 1969 Franco nominated Prince Juan Carlos, the grandson of Alfonso XIII, to be his successor. Franco expected the future king to continue all he had set up. Juan Carlos took provisional control 3 weeks before Franco's death on 20 Nov. 1975 and was crowned King the same day. Contrary to the dictator's wishes, the King proceeded to open up the government to democracy with devolution of power to the provinces. Each region has its own president, government and Supreme Court. The Catalan, Basque and Galician languages and cultures are no longer repressed.

Franco's posthumous reputation continues to dwindle. The memorial service for the 25th anniversary of his death attracted only a few thousands supporters.

Franco, Itamar (Brazil)

Introduction

Itamar Franco was president of Brazil from 1992 until 1994. He took over as provisional president when Fernando Collor resigned. He was unsuccessful in his efforts to revive the ailing economy.

Early Life

Born 28 July 1931, Itamar Augusto Cautiero Franco had early contact with politics in his home town of Juiz de Fora in the state of Minas Gerais. He was elected mayor in 1966 and 1972. He was senator for Minas Gerais from 1974–90. A founding member of the Brazilian Democratic Movement, he was appointed vice president in 1990.

Career Peak

Franco became acting president on 2 Oct. 1992 when Collor resigned in the face of impeachment charges. Franco and was sworn in as president on Dec. 29. An opponent of sweeping market reform, he soon clashed with the IMF and an early package of tax reforms were suspended when the Supreme Court questioned their constitutional validity. The hoped-for economic up-turn failed to materialize and inflation leapt towards 3,000%. Franco's apparent aloofness caused friction with other Latin American leaders and relations with the US were also delicate.

In Oct. 1993, when his approval rating had dropped below 15%, he offered his resignation if Congress would schedule early elections. After political manoeuvring among opposition parties, his resignation was declined. His fourth finance minister, Fernando Henrique Cardoso, was responsible for a successful economic plan which introduced a new currency and economic reforms. Buoyed by his popularity, Cardoso stood in the 1994 presidential election when Franco stepped down.

Later Life

After his spell as president Franco served as ambassador to Portugal and Brazil's representative to the Organization of American States in Washington, D.C. until 1998. He was governor of his home state of Minas Gerais from 1998–2003. Franco died on 2 July 2011. He was serving as a senator for Minas Gerais at the time of his death.

Franjieh, Suleiman (Lebanon)

Introduction

A Maronite Christian and state president from 1970–76, Franjieh was considered in large part responsible for Lebanon's descent in full-scale civil war in 1975. By that time his autocratic rule and alleged nepotism had alienated Shia and Sunni Muslims and rival Christian groups alike.

Early Life

Franjieh was born on 15 June 1910 in Zgharta in northern Lebanon. Having built a regional power base there, underpinned by clan allegiance and a private Maronite militia, he was elected to the National Assembly as an independent deputy in 1960. He held several ministerial posts in 1960–61, 1968 and 1969–70 before his narrow election by the National Assembly (by one vote on the third ballot) to the presidency in Aug. 1970.

Career Peak

He assumed office on 23 Sept. 1970. Early on in his troubled presidency there were frequent military exchanges between the increasing number of Palestinian guerrillas based in Lebanon (particularly after the PLO's expulsion from Jordan in 1970–71) and Israeli forces. In 1973 serious clashes erupted between the Palestinians and the Lebanese army. Coupled with the Palestinian problem, Christian and Muslim differences became more marked over the constitutional distribution of power. Violent sectarian incidents in April 1975 led to more persistent fighting across most of the country. Despite the PLO's official policy not to interfere in Lebanon's internal affairs, many Palestinian fighters joined the predominantly leftist Lebanese Muslim forces against the right-wing Christian militias. Franjieh's administration became increasingly ineffectual as the fighting continued and there were calls for his resignation in the National Assembly by March 1976. A successor was elected by the Assembly in May, but Franjieh refused to resign until the completion of his term of office in Sept. 1976, by which time Syrian forces had intervened to impose an uneasy peace.

Thereafter, Franjieh's pro-Syrian clan continued to wield regional power in the north of the country, provoking frequent intra-Christian friction with the rival Phalangists (who assassinated his son Tony in 1978) and National Liberal Party. In 1988 he announced his candidacy for the presidential elections, but was forced to withdraw in the face of opposition from other Maronite groups. He died in Beirut on 23 July 1992.

Fraser, Malcolm (Australia)

Introduction

Malcolm Fraser was Australia's Liberal Prime Minister from 1975–83; he was one of the longest serving premiers. He came to power following the controversial sacking of the Labor incumbent, Gough Whitlam. He cut public spending in an attempt to reverse the declining economic outlook following Whitlam's tenure, with limited success. He advocated increased Aboriginal rights and supported Australia's continuing role in the ANZUS Pact. He resigned following defeat by a rejuvenated Labor Party in 1983.

Early Life

John Malcolm Fraser was born on 21 May 1930 in Nareen, Victoria into a wealthy family. He graduated from Magdalene College, Oxford with a master's in politics, philosophy and economics. He entered parliament as the member for Wannon in Victoria in 1955, becoming the youngest member of parliament and a favourite of Robert Menzies. A year later he married Tamara Beggs, with whom he would have four children. In Jan. 1966, in the administration of Harold Holt, Fraser became minister for the Army, a post he held until made minister for Education and Science in Feb. 1968. In Nov. 1969 he was appointed defence minister but reverted back to Education and Science in March 1971. Fraser made two unsuccessful challenges for the Liberal leadership against Billy Snedden. He achieved victory at the third attempt on 24 March 1975. In 1975 Gough Whitlam's Labor government was reeling from the Loans Scandal, in which senior ministers were accused of acting unconstitutionally to secure foreign economic assistance. Whitlam's regime had been free spending in its quest to implement social change at a time when the Australian economy was not strong.

Career Peak

In Oct. 1975 when Whitlam put his budget before parliament, Fraser, in an unprecedented move, urged Liberals in the Senate to block it. In the ensuing impasse, Governor-General Sir John Kerr, gave him the option of calling an election and when Whitlam refused he was dismissed. A constitutional furore followed and Fraser took over as caretaker prime minister until elections in Dec. when he led the Liberals to a convincing victory. He formed a coalition with the National Country Party. Fraser's tenure was constrained by the difficult economic situation, exacerbated by Whitlam's high spending and characterized by spiralling inflation. He dramatically reduced government expenditure, provoking criticism for cutting back the advances made by the previous regime in social welfare. Other austerity measures included persuading trade unions not to demand large pay increases, with Fraser assuring the public that 'life is not meant to be easy'. It was a comment that was seized upon by his opponents as an example of his arrogance, especially regarding his own prosperous background. Fraser did much to advance Aboriginal opportunities and passed a far-reaching law concerning Northern Territory land rights. An advocate of multiculturalism, he broadened Australia's immigration policy. In terms of foreign policy, he continued support for the ANZUS Pact, a treaty of mutual security signed by the USA, Australia and New Zealand in 1951. He took a strong stance against South Africa's apartheid regime. Fraser led the Liberals to further election success in 1977 and 1980. However, his privileged upbringing, his air of aloofness (his nickname was 'The Freezer'. and the manner of his rise to the premiership in 1975 sat uneasily with large parts of the electorate. His continued success was in part due to the failings of the Labor Party. Fraser called an election in March 1983 hoping to catch Labor, under their new leader Bob Hawke, off guard. The plan backfired and the populist Hawke won the election. Fraser's downfall was later summarized by Hawke himself when he said that Fraser 'won the votes of the electorate but not their hearts.'.

Later Life

Fraser resigned the leadership and his parliamentary seat at the end of March 1983. He became a member of the Commonwealth Group of Eminent Persons that worked towards the end of apartheid in South Africa. He retained a presence on the political scene and continues to promote racial tolerance. Strongly critical of the Howard government's decision to support the USA in the Iraq War in 2003 and their policy on asylum seekers, he became increasingly disenchanted with the Liberal Party and in Dec. 2009 he resigned from the party saying that it was 'no longer a liberal party but a conservative party'.

On 20 March 2015, Fraser passed away aged 84.

Fujimori, Alberto (Peru)

Introduction

Alberto Keinya Fujimori was president of Peru between 1990–2000. Using hardline policies, Fujimori stabilized Peru's critical economy and restricted the influence of left-wing guerrillas. He was forced to resign amid charges of corruption, fraud and embezzlement.

Early Life

The son of Japanese immigrants and agricultural workers, Fujimori was born on 28 July 1938 in Lima. He was educated at the reputable La Molina University—the Agrarian National University—where he took a degree in agronomic engineering. After studying in Strasbourg and taking a master's in maths at the University of Wisconsin, he pursued a career in academic administration at La Molina. He was later hosted a television programme, in which he earned a reputation for political analysis.

Following years of military dictatorship and ineffectual governing, the democratically elected Alan García Pérez (1985–90) had left Peru in economic ruin. Corruption and guerrilla warfare were coupled with a low GNP, hyperinflation and massive foreign debt. In 1989 Fujimori created his Cambio 1990 party (Change 1990) to contest the presidential elections. His main opposition was the writer and politician, Mario Vargas Llosa, who represented the centre-right coalition, Fredemo (Frente Democrático; Democratic Front Movement). Vargas Llosa's proposal to resolve Peru's economic crisis with severe anti-inflation measures was unpopular with lower income groups. In contrast, Fujimori adopted a 'grass-roots' campaign, targeting the poor rural population. He gained support from black and Indian Peruvians when his opponents attempted to discredit his presidential challenge because he was an 'immigrant'.

Career Peak

After winning the 1990 elections Fujimori immediately set about implementing radical economic reforms. Reducing inflation, his aim was to promote a free market economy and encourage investment. Reforms included economic decentralization, transport deregularization, and lowering administrative costs, expenditure and tariffs.

His second objective was to combat the powerful guerrilla movements. The main group was the Maoist terrorist Sendero Luminosa (Shining Path; SL). The other was the Marxist-Leninist revolutionary Movimiento Revolución Tupac Amaru (MRTA). Hardline measures included arming the rural population. In 1992 the leader and founder of the SL, Abimael Guzmán, was arrested. Peru's economy began to stabilize. In the same year, claiming he was being blocked in his efforts to exercise control over dissidents and rebels, Fujimori performed an auto-coup. He dissolved the congress, sacked judges and government officials, and rewrote the constitution. He received vocal opposition of his dictatorial actions from other politicians. Fujimori rejected investment proffered by the USA, as it was dependent on Peru eradicating its coca production. Fujimori believed removing the livelihood of some of the poorest Peruvians would leave them open to the influence of terrorists.

In 1995, Fujimori entered the presidential elections against the Unión Por el Perú candidate, the fifth general-secretary of the UN (1982–91), Javier Pérez de Cuéllar. Fujimori won convincingly with 2/3 of votes. In Fujimori's second term, Peru experienced strong economic growth. In Dec. 1996 MRTA rebels broke into a party at the Japanese embassy and took 500 diplomats and businessmen hostage. The crisis continued into 1997 when government troops stormed the building containing. All 14 MRTA members were killed, including its leader, Nestor Cerpa. Fujimori's handling of the crisis increased his popularity.

In 1998 Fujimori announced his candidature for the 2000 presidential elections, despite the fact that the 1993 constitution written by Fujimori precluded a president standing for a third term. Several judges were dismissed by Fujimori when the court upheld his ineligibility. Fujimori's popularity declined as concerns mounted over the power of the military and the secret service and over abuses of human rights.

In 2000 Fujimori won a third consecutive presidential election despite claims of electoral fraud. It was then that his intelligence chief and closest political aide, Vladimiro Montesinos, was proved guilty of corruption. A videotape showed Montesinos bribing an opposition politician. Charges against Montesinos ranged from embezzlement to running death squads. Fujimori failed to abate the scandal or arrest Montesinos, who fled the country. The SIN (secret service) has since been closed down. While on presidential business in Japan in Nov. 2000, Fujimori announced his resignation.

In contrast to his earlier claims that he was born in Lima (and thus eligible to be president), Fujimori was now determined to prove his Japanese nationality. Japan upheld his claims and Fujimori currently resides in Japan where he is safe from prosecution. Although praising his actions at the time, in March 2001 Peruvian authorities charged Fujimori with the murder of the 14 MRTA rebels killed during the hostage crisis. Their bodies were exhumed to prove claims that they were executed by the military. A collection of 2,700 videos, accumulated over 10 years by Montesinos, has been seized. Many are said to incriminate Peru's leading politicians and professionals.

In Nov. 2000 Valentín Paniagua became the provisional president with Javier Pérez de Cuéllar as interim prime minister. He was succeeded in July 2001 by President Alejandro Toledo of the Perú Posible party.

Following self-imposed exile in Japan, Fujimori was detained in Chile in 2007 before being extradited to Peru to face charges of corruption. That year he was convicted and sentenced to 6 years in prison. In April 2009 he was found guilty of murder and kidnap and sentenced to a further 25 years. Three months later he was convicted on embezzlement charges and received an additional seven-and-a-half years on his sentence.

Later Life

In Dec. 2017 President Kuczynski granted Fujimori a humanitarian pardon on health grounds in a move that led to widespread protests. He was released from a Lima hospital in Jan. 2018.

Fukuda, Yasuo (Japan)

Introduction

Yasuo Fukuda became prime minister in Sept. 2007 following the resignation of Shinzo Abe. An experienced politician who had served as chief cabinet secretary in two administrations, he came with a reputation as a moderate with a strong base in the ruling party. Shifting away from the nationalistic rhetoric of his predecessors, he favoured stronger ties with Japan's Asian neighbours, notably China. At home he slowed the pace of economic reform in response to a hostile political climate. Lacking support in the upper house of parliament, he saw much of his proposed legislation blocked, prompting his resignation in Sept. 2008.

Early Life

Born on 16 July 1936 in Takasaki, Gunma, Yasuo Fukuda was the eldest son of Takeo Fukuda, a Liberal Democratic (LDP) politician who served as prime minister in the 1970s. After attending Asaba High School in Tokyo, Yasuo Fukuda studied economics at Wasada University. He graduated in 1959 and joined Maruzen Petroleum, where he stayed for the next 17 years. He was posted to the USA from 1962–64.

In 1976, when his father became prime minister, Fukuda became secretary to an LDP member of the Diet, and from 1977–78 worked as his father's political secretary. In Feb. 1990 Fukuda was elected to the Diet as LDP representative for Gunma 4th District. He served as director of the committee on foreign affairs from 1992–99 and as parliamentary vice-minister for foreign affairs between Aug. 1995–Jan. 1996. In Nov. 1995 he was appointed director of the LDP's foreign affairs division and became the party's deputy secretary general the following year.

Fukuda served as chief cabinet secretary and minister of state for gender equality from 2000–04 under the premiership of Yoshiro Mori, then Junichiro Koizumi. In the turbulence surrounding Koizumi's attempts to force through economic reforms—notably privatization of the postal and savings system—Fukuda gained a reputation as a moderate with the ability to build consensus. He emerged as a dove in foreign policy terms, distancing himself from Koizumi's nationalism and advocating closer ties with China. From 2005 he was involved in constitutional reform and continued his rise within the LDP, being elected to the party's general council in 2006. When Koizumi resigned in 2006, Fukuda was considered a potential successor but chose not to stand. Shinzo Abe became the new party leader and prime minister.

After heavy losses for the LDP in the elections of July 2007, Abe resigned and Fukuda stood against right-winger Taro Aso to replace him as party leader. The selection process was widely seen as a return to old-style Japanese politics, in which leaders of the party factions pledge their support in advance of the open vote. Fukuda campaigned on a platform of stabilizing the party and winning back the trust of the electorate which had been shaken by scandals and economic decline. He announced that he would not visit Tokyo's controversial Yasukuni shrine for the war dead, a statement intended as a conciliatory gesture to Japan's neighbours. Fukuda won the leadership race decisively but the vote in the Diet to elect a prime minister was split. The lower house elected Fukuda while the upper house, under the control of the opposition Democratic Party (Mt), chose Mt leader Ichiro Ozawa. Under Diet rules, the vote of the lower house prevailed and Fukuda took office on 26 Sept. 2007.

Career Peak

In a bid for stability, Fukuda kept many of his predecessor's ministers in the cabinet. However, with the Diet's upper house controlled by the Democrats, he faced difficulties in implementing his policies. In Nov. 2007, after failing in his attempt to extend Japan's naval mission in the Indian Ocean, he held secret talks with Ozawa on forming a coalition. However, plans were abandoned when they proved unpopular with voters. The ensuing stalemate saw the postponement of proposed tax and pension reforms. His choice for governor of the national bank was also overruled and plans for a new medical scheme for the elderly proved particularly unpopular. Internationally, he promoted stronger relations with regional neighbours and in Dec. 2007 made an official visit to China.

On 11 June 2008 the upper house passed a non-binding censure motion against Fukuda, which the lower house countered the following day. On 1 Sept. 2008 Fukuda resigned his office. He said that he hoped the shock move would end Japan's political deadlock.

Funes Cartagena, Carlos Mauricio (El Salvador)

Introduction

Mauricio Funes took office in June 2009 at the head of the left-wing Farabundo Martí National Liberation Front (FMLN) administration, ending 20 years of Nationalist Republican Alliance (ARENA) government.

Early Life

Funes was born on 18 Oct. 1959 in San Salvador. Schooled at the Colegio Centroamérica and the private Colegio Externado San José, he went in 1975 to study literature at the city's José Simón Cañas University.

In 1980 civil war broke out between the authoritarian government and leftist organizations, from which the FMLN was created. Mauricio's older brother was killed by police during a student demonstration. In 1986 Mauricio became a reporter for state television news. In 1997 he became head of news at Canal 12. However, after several run-ins—notably over criticism of the government after a 2001 earthquake—he left the station in 2005.

His public popularity paved the way for a move into politics, where he established a relationship with the FMLN. In Sept. 2007 the party chose him as its presidential candidate, a month before Funes' son was murdered in Paris. Funes is the first FMLN leader not to have fought as a guerrilla. At the presidential elections in March 2009 Funes defeated Rodrigo Ávila of ARENA, winning over 50% of the vote.

Career Peak

Amid claims that an FMLN victory would jeopardize US relations and turn the country into a satellite of Venezuela, Funes declared he would maintain a good relationship with Washington and that El Salvador would remain part of the Central American Free Trade Agreement, signed by ARENA in 2006. Meanwhile, he re-established ties with Cuba, cut off since 1961.

He offered ministerial portfolios to supporters from a range of political backgrounds. His primary challenges have been to address the troubled economy and reduce the large deficit (aided by loans from the IMF and development banks) and to cut crime, while maintaining the co-operation of a congress where the FMLN failed to secure an overall majority of seats at the elections in Jan. 2009 and March 2012. In Nov. 2009 he was also faced with the humanitarian consequences of a hurricane that left about 140 people dead and thousands homeless. In Sept. 2011 the ongoing problem of crime was highlighted as the US government added El Salvador to a blacklist of countries considered major producers of or transit routes for illegal drugs.

Funes left office at the end of his 5 year term on 1 June 2014 and was succeeded by Salvador Sánchez Cerén.

Galtieri, Leopoldo (Argentina)

Introduction

The commander in chief of the Argentine military at the beginning of the military dictatorship (1976–83), Galtieri headed the rightwing military junta between 1981–82. The instigator of the Falklands War in an attempt to deflect attention from economic crisis and popular protest, the disastrous campaign led to his resignation and subsequent imprisonment in 1986. Later pardoned, he was nonetheless arrested in 1998 and 2002 for murders committed during the Guerra Sucia (Dirty War).

Early Life

Born on 15 July 1926 in Casero, Buenos Aires, Galtieri joined the military in 1943. Graduating from the Escuela de las Américas military school, Panama, in 1949, he progressed to become commander in the Argentine army, a position he held when the 1976 coup replaced Isabelita Perón with a military junta led by Jorge Videla. The dictatorship imposed a repressive regime which included censorship, repression of trade unions and the closing of Congress. The junta implemented the 'Process of National Reorganization' now termed the Dirty War during which an estimated 9,000–30,000 people were killed or disappeared. Initially targeting leftwing activists, the repression was extended to journalists, intellectuals and those suspected of leftwing sympathies. When Videla retired in 1981 he was succeeded by Roberto Viola who, in turn, was replaced in Dec. 1981 by Galtieri as de facto president.

Career Peak

When Galtieri assumed the presidency, Argentina was suffering severe economic depression. Rising inflation and large national debt led to public discontent and popular protests. Despite repression, human rights groups protesting about the Desaparecidos ('disappeared') gained strength. Las Madres de Plaza de Mayo, a group of mothers of the Desaparecidos, set up a weekly vigil outside the presidential palace. To divert attention from domestic problems, in 1982 Galtieri ordered the invasion of the Falkland Islands (Islas Malvinas), a British territory since 1832 but long claimed by Argentina. Underestimating the reaction of the British government, the army was ill prepared and under equipped. It occupied the islands in April 1982, but within 3 months had been defeated. Galtieri was forced to resign as president in June 1982. His resignation saw an end to the military dictatorship and a return to civilian rule under the presidency of his successor, Reynaldo Bignone.

Later Life

Repeated attempts were made to bring Galtieri to court for his involvement in the Dirty War. In 1984 he was tried for human rights violations, but acquitted. In 1986 he was jailed for 12 years for his incompetence in the Falklands War, but President Carlos Menem pardoned Galtieri 3 years later, and immunities were extended. In renewed attempts to try those involved in the military dictatorship, Galtieri was arrested in 1998 for the murder of three people. In Nov. 2001 a court ruled the military's immunity granted by the Obediencia Debida law (1986) and the Punto Final law (1987) was unconstitutional. In July 2002 Galtieri was arrested in connection with the torture and death of 20 members of the Montanero leftwing group in 1980. The following day he was moved from jail to be put under house arrest. The arrest of 41 other police and military personnel was ordered. Former junta partner Jorge Videla was convicted of abducting the children of prisoners for adoption by military families.

Galtieri died on 12 Jan. 2003 while under house arrest.

Gamsakhurdia, Zviad (Georgia)

Introduction

In 1991 Zviad Gamsakhurdia became Georgia's first elected president after the collapse of the USSR and the declaration of Georgian independence. A renowned nationalist during the Soviet period, his tenure was marked by erratic behaviour and ardent nationalism, often at the expense of ethnic minorities. He lasted less than 9 months in office before being deposed. He led unsuccessful counter-coups and died in suspicious circumstances in 1993.

Early Life

Zviad Konstantinovich Gamsakhurdia was born in Tbilisi on 31 March 1939. His father, Konstantine, was an acclaimed academic and writer who escaped the Stalinist purges. Gamsakhurdia followed his father's interest in literature and the Georgian cause, establishing a nationalist youth organisation at the age of 16. His distribution of anti-communist writings detailing Soviet human rights abuses led to his arrest in 1956. He studied Western languages and literature at the Tbilisi State University, going on to become a lecturer from 1963–1977 and a professor from 1981–90.

In 1973 he formed the Human Rights Initiative Group with Merab Kostava to defend the rights of political prisoners and to promote the Georgian language and culture. He founded the underground press which published Alexander Solzhenitsyn's *Gulag Archipelago* and other dissident writing. Arrested in 1977 and exiled until 1979, he was a nominee for the Nobel peace prize in 1978. He was put under house arrest from 1982–83 during his campaign for the release of the dissident nationalist Merab Kostava. Freed from prison in 1987, Kostava joined forces with Gamsakhurdia in a new Georgian independence and human rights movement. They organised mass protests and were arrested again in 1989.

Career Peak

Following the collapse of the Soviet Union, Gamsakhurdia was among the dissidents who organised multiparty elections in 1990. He became leader of the electoral bloc Mrgvali Magida–Tavisupali Sakartvelo (Round Table–Free Georgia), winning a majority at the elections of Oct. 1990. In Nov. 1990 he was elected chairman of the supreme council of the Republic of Georgia, which appointed him president in March 1991. National elections in the following May confirmed him as Georgia's first democratically elected president.

Gamsakhurdia actively asserted Georgian independence, and refused to support the wish of Mikhail Gorbachev and, later, Boris Yeltsin that Georgia should join the Commonwealth of Independent States. Gamsakhurdia's fervent nationalism was further reflected in a hostile attitude towards non-ethnic Georgians. In Dec. 1991/Jan. 1992, amid allegations of corruption and civil rights abuses, he was forced from office in a bloody coup and went into exile. Eduard Shevardnadze, Gorbachev's former foreign minister, was named his successor. Gamsakhurdia returned to Georgia to lead an unsuccessful rebellion in 1993. He died on 30 Dec. 1993 in disputed circumstances. His wife, Manana Archvadze-Gamsakhurdia refused to yield his body up for an autopsy, and it has been variously alleged that he was murdered, committed suicide or died of cancer.

Gandhi, Indira (India)

Introduction

The daughter of India's first prime minister, Jawaharlal Nehru, Indira Gandhi served for three consecutive terms between 1966–77 and then again from 1980 until her assassination in 1984. She is remembered as a determined politician who imposed a State of Emergency (1975–77), to work through unpopular government policies such as compulsory sterilization and the imprisonment of political opponents.

Early Life

Born in Allahabad on 19 Nov. 1917, Indira was an only child. She received her education at Visva-Bharati University, West Bengal, and then Somerville College, Oxford. Her upbringing brought her into the company of the politicians and leaders of her time, including Mahatma Gandhi.

Her first active involvement in politics came in 1938 when she joined the Indian National Congress Party. In 1942, in defiance of her father, she married Feroze Gandhi who died in 1960. In the same year the British imprisoned her for 13 months. When Jawaharlal Nehru became the Prime Minister of India following independence, Indira Gandhi took on the role of confidante and official hostess to her father.

In 1955 she was elected to the Working Committee and Central Election Committee of the Congress Party, becoming the party's President in 1959. Continuing in her role as adviser to her father, she operated as Minister of Defense during the brief Indo-Chinese border war of 1962.

After the death of her father, the role of Prime Minister went to Lal Bahadur Shastri, who appointed Gandhi Minister for Information. With Shastri's death in 1966 rival factions in the Congress party joined to elect Gandhi as leader, assuming that she would be popular but also easily manipulated.

Career Peak

As prime minister Gandhi made it clear that she would follow her own agenda. Tensions within the party continued and a right-wing opposition was mounted under Moraji Desai, a former Finance Minister. Gandhi won a narrow victory in the fourth general election of 1967 when Desai was appointed deputy prime minister. Her socialistic stance won her popular appeal and in 1971 she won a landslide victory against a coalition of conservative parties. There followed the nationalization of banking and the abolition of pensions for former princely rulers.

Gandhi won a further majority in 1972. This was largely due to her success in the 1971 conflict between India and Pakistan over the territory of East Bengal. The Indian military repelled the invading Pakistani army, paving the way for the territory to become a democratic republic, now known as Bangladesh.

Increasing food shortages, parliamentary corruption and inflation led to civil unrest in the early 70's. In June 1975 she was accused of electoral fraud during the 1971 parliamentary elections. Facing a 6 year ban from political activity, Gandhi declared a state of national emergency on 26 June 1975. During the 21 months which followed tens of thousands were imprisoned and many civil rights were suspended. The compulsory sterilization of fathers with two or more children extended to 8 m. cases. Instituted by minister of health Karan Singh, sterilization targets were set for each region. Failure to meet targets was penalised by holding back on financial aid.

Opposition to this coercive policy found voice in Gandhi's defeat in a free election, called by Gandhi herself, in March 1977. Leading the Janata Party, Moraji Desai became Prime Minister.

In spite of being arrested in Nov. 1977 and briefly imprisoned in Dec. 1978 on charges of corruption, Gandhi's support within the Congress Party grew, creating a split which led to the formation of the Congress (I) Party. Problems within the Janata Party led to its dissolution on 22 Aug. 1979. The following year, Indira Gandhi returned to premiership at the head of her new party.

A rising Sikh secessionist movement in Punjab led to civil unrest and ultimately military action. Gandhi ordered the flushing out of terrorists who had established themselves within the Golden Temple at Amritsar. This resulted in some 400 deaths including that of the Sikh leader Jarnain Singh Bhindranwale.

Indira Gandhi was assassinated on 31 Oct. 1984 by two Sikh bodyguards, allegedly as an act of vengeance for the attack on their holy shrine. The outpouring of grief provided the impetus for her son, Rajiv to be elected as leader of the Congress (I) in Dec. the same year.

Gandhi, Mohandas 'Mahatma' (India)

Introduction

Mohandas Karamchand Gandhi, later to be known as Mahatma (Great Soul), was born on 2 Oct. 1869 in Porbandar, Gujarat in India. By the time of his death in 1948 he had become an international figurehead, leader of the Indian independence movement and the most successful exponent of non-violent protest.

Early Life

Born to Karamchand Gandhi, an uneducated but politically able administrator, and his religiously devout wife Putlibai, there was little in Gandhi's origins to suggest what lay ahead. Brought up in the culture of Vaishnavism and Jainism, he was imbued with beliefs in non-violence, mutual tolerance and fasting. He was a shy and largely unimpressive scholar who found himself married by the age of 13 and subsequently went through a phase of mild delinquency. Despite this unpromising start, he passed the entry exams for the University of Bombay and qualified as a barrister. He arrived in London in Sept. 1888 and became a member of the Inner Temple.

The next 3 years was to be a constructive period during which he became exposed to many new ideas and philosophies including socialism and humanitarianism. It was also around then that he became familiar with the Hindu text *Bhagavadgita*. The idea that material possessions are a burden and that work should be carried out without hope of success or fear of failure influenced him greatly.

Without work when he returned to India, Gandhi took a job with a legal firm in Natal, South Africa where he began his political activities. Having experienced various personal indignities inflicted on account of his race, he was driven to action when in June 1894 the Natal Legislative Assembly proposed to abolish Indian suffrage. Gandhi soon instituted the Natal Indian Congress and began to unite and organize disparate elements of the Indian community. In response to a proposed Indian registration scheme in 1906 he encouraged the community to ignore the ordinance. By 1913 large numbers of Indians had been imprisoned, flogged and shot but the South African government was eventually shamed into a compromise.

Career Peak

Gandhi returned to India in 1914. In 1919 the British tried to pass the Rowlatt Bills which provided for imprisonment without trial for anyone suspected of sedition. Gandhi's efforts for peaceful protest were soon overcome by violence, culminating in the Amritsar massacre when soldiers under British command killed almost 400 Indians. Gandhi called off his action but a lack of British remorse after the Amritsar incident allied with anger at the peace agreement struck with Muslim Turkey after World War I brought him swiftly back to the forefront.

1920 saw him restructuring and reforming the previously pedestrian Indian National Congress. He also embarked on a programme of non-violent non-cooperation during which British goods and British-run institutions were boycotted. Thousands of Indians endured subsequent imprisonment but spiralling violence once again disheartened Gandhi and he called the protest off. In 1922 he was himself imprisoned for sedition, serving 2 years of a 6 year sentence. His re-emergence on to the political scene in 1924 found the Congress Party undermined by internal conflict and Muslim–Hindu violence rife in society at large. He embarked on the first of his 14 hunger-strikes in an attempt to inspire non-violence.

Anglo–Indian relations remained strained over the following years and a lack of movement on the British side prompted Gandhi to appear at the 1928 Calcutta Conference to threaten a full-scale call for independence unless India was granted dominion status by the end of 1929. In 1930 he called another campaign of civil disobedience to protest against salt taxes. By the end of the year, he and 100,000 other Indians had been imprisoned.

After being freed in 1930, a truce was reached and he was encouraged by an invitation to the 2nd Round Table Conference to be held in London. However, the conference offered nationalists little hope. Meanwhile, Lord Willingdon had been appointed Viceroy of India. He set about the most aggressive oppression of the nationalist movement yet witnessed. Gandhi was in and out of prison during the next phase of the struggle and it was whilst in jail in Sept. 1932 that he began another hunger-strike. It was in response to new laws further segregating the *untouchables*, effectively the lowliest class in society characterized by their low caste and by certain professions and lifestyles. Gandhi struggled for many years for their emancipation and renamed them Harijans, or the Children of God.

By 1934 Gandhi's disillusionment with the political manoeuvring of the Congress Party led to his resignation. He set out on a scheme to boost rural areas, principally by improving education and encouraging small scale industry. His discontent with British rule continued and he called for immediate British withdrawal from India in 1942. The British response, influenced by the fluctuating circumstances of World War II, was prompt and harsh and included the imprisonment of the entire Congress Party leadership. Anglo-Indian relations thawed with the arrival of the Labour government in 1945 and in 1947 the Mountbatten Plan (formulated by Louis Mountbatten, 1st Earl Mountbatten of Burma, who was the last Viceroy and first Governor-General of India) was approved. Hindu and Muslim fighting provided a backdrop to the final stages of the constitutional negotiations but nonetheless the plan paved the way for the dominions of India and Pakistan to be created in Aug. 1947. For Gandhi, though, independence had come at a price; the Indian people were disunited.

Later Life

Gandhi had spent his life mediating between opposing forces: Indians and English, conservatives and radicals, rural and urban populations and members of different classes, castes and religions. The final months of his life were spent trying to heal the wounds between Hindus and Muslims. On 30 Jan. 1948 he was assassinated by Nathuram Godse, a Hindu fundamentalist. Gandhi himself once wrote that 'a life of sacrifice is the pinnacle of art, and is full of true joy'.

Gandhi, Rajiv (India)

Introduction

Rajiv Gandhi came to power following the assassination of his mother, Indira Gandhi, the preceding Prime Minister of India. Reluctantly drawn into the political sphere, the changes he made during his tenure did little to alleviate India's growing economic difficulties. The youngest Prime Minister to have ruled India, his initial appeal as a charming and ingenuous young man had changed, by the end of his government, into alienation towards an aloof political figure. Defeated in parliamentary elections in 1989, he set about revising his political agenda for a return to power. During the 1991 election campaign, however, he was killed in a bomb attack by Tamil Separatist sympathisers.

Early Life

The eldest of two sons, Rajiv was born on 20 Aug. 1944. He was educated at Doon School, Dehradun, before studying at Imperial College, London and then Trinity College, Cambridge. He failed to achieve a degree and returned to India to pursue a career as a commercial pilot, joining the Indian Airlines training course in Hyderabad in 1967.

Married in 1968 to Sonia Maino whom he had met at Cambridge, Gandhi had no interest in the political world. His brother, Sanjay, had followed their mother into politics, playing an important role during the State of Emergency (1975–77). Sanjay's death on 23 June 1980 deprived Indira Gandhi of her heir to the Nehru-Gandhi political dynasty and to the Congress Party leadership. More for filial than political reasons, Rajiv left his career as a pilot to pursue politics.

Rajiv Gandhi joined the Congress (I) Party on 11 May 1981. Winning a seat for his late brother's constituency in Amethi, Uttar Pradesh, he became a member of the Lok Sabha (House of the People) in Aug. of the same year. Rising within the party, on 3 Feb. 1983, Gandhi was appointed General Secretary of the All India Congress Committee (AICC). On 31 Oct. 1984, Indira Gandhi was assassinated by her own Sikh bodyguards. The following day, Rajiv was sworn in as Congress leader and Prime Minister. In parliamentary elections held in Dec., Indira Gandhi's martyrdom in the eyes of the nation supplied the impetus behind a landslide victory (401 out of 508) for the Congress Party.

Career Peak

In office, Gandhi immediately instituted a number of reforms, seeking to speed up administrative processes in all areas of government. He invested heavily in research and higher education, believing that expenditure in science and technology would lead to the development of successful strategies for dealing with poverty and illiteracy. These schemes were later lambasted as ineffective and out of touch.

On a grass roots level, he established various missions to increase adult literacy levels and primary school education. In line with this he revived the

Panchayati Raj. This scheme, which had lain dormant since the days of Jawaharlal Nehru, provided largely autonomous local government for rural areas, with a third of the seats reserved for women.

Gandhi's foreign policy was essentially one of co-operation and liberalised investment. On a global level, he advocated the total disarmament of nuclear weapons, presenting in 1988 an Action Plan before the UN General Assembly Special Session on Disarmament.

Problems closer to home proved more complex. Gandhi had arrived in power amidst secessionist unrest in the states of Punjab, Assam and Mizoram. He subsequently signed accords (1985–86) with leaders from each state to arrest insurgency with varying degrees of success (the Punjab accord resulted in the extremist assassination of Harachan Singh Longowal with whom Gandhi had signed the accord).

In spite of signing the Indo-Sri Lankan Peace Agreement in 1987 to resolve the Tamil-Sinhalese ethnic crisis, the deployment of Indian Peace Keeping Forces (IPKF) in 1987 led to armed conflict with the Liberation Tigers of Tamil Eelam (LTTE). Between 1987–89 the struggle resulted in the deaths of some 1500 Indian soldiers.

Gandhi took a direct approach to the Indo-Chinese border question, regarding it as integral to resolving tensions. His visit to China in 1988 was the first made by an Indian Prime Minister in over 20 years. A series of high-level talks throughout the 5 day visit produced the Joint Working Group (JWG), to find a resolution to the border dispute.

Corruption undermined electoral confidence in 1987, when Gandhi was accused of involvement in the US$1.3 bn. Bofors Swedish arms deal which saw millions of dollars paid in kickbacks to Indian government officials.

With the loss of public confidence in the Congress Party and its leader, Gandhi resigned his post as Prime Minister on 2 Dec. 1989.

Later Life

Retaining his role as Congress Leader and becoming the Leader of the Opposition against new Prime Minister, V. P. Singh and his National Front Party, Gandhi was assassinated in Sriperumbudur on 21 May 1991. In 1998, 26 people were convicted of conspiring his death, 3 of whom were sentenced to death. The act was seen as a revenge killing for Gandhi's handling of the Indo-Sri Lankan crisis and the violence which entailed with Tamil Separatist groups.

His wife, Sonia Gandhi, became leader of the Congress Party in March 1998.

García, Alan (Peru)

Introduction

Head of the Peruvian Aprista Party (PAP; formerly known as the American Popular Revolutionary Alliance/APRA), Alan García served two separate terms as Peru's president. His first term in office, from 1985–90, was marked by hyperinflation and a rising national debt as he tried to invigorate the economy through spending. After a period of exile García returned to Peru in 2001 and won the 2006 presidential election, promising to fight poverty whilst pursuing more orthodox economic policies.

Early Life

Born on 23 May 1949 in Lima, García was raised in a family with strong ties to the APRA party. His father, Carlos García Ronceros, served as party secretary and was imprisoned during García's childhood for political militancy. García was educated at the Colegio Nacional José María Eguren in Lima and the Pontificia Universidad Católica, before completing a law degree at the National University of San Marcos in 1971. He pursued further studies in Europe, obtaining a doctorate in political science from the Universidad Complutense in Madrid and a degree in sociology from the University of Paris. In 1978, when civilian government was restored in Peru after a 10 year period of military rule, García returned to build a political career with APRA.

García won the April 1985 presidential election on a platform of alleviating poverty and implementing social justice. After his inauguration on 28 July 1985, he launched ambitious public spending programmes to combat the poverty rate of 41.6%. His government printed money to finance the policies, resulting in soaring inflation. The unit of currency, the sol, was replaced by the inti in 1985 at a rate of 1,000 intis to 1 sol but inflation continued to rise, reaching a rate of more than 2 m. percent by 1991. García won some initial popularity at home by announcing that only 10% of Peru's export earnings would be devoted to debt repayments and by attempting to nationalize the banks in 1987. However, these policies alienated the IMF and international financial markets and added to the economic turmoil.

Insurgent groups, notably the Shining Path, carried out campaigns of political violence that were put down by government forces. The army was accused of human rights abuses, notably at Accomarco in Aug. 1985 and at Cayara in May 1988. By 1990 the numbers of people living in poverty had risen to 55%, per capita income had fallen to US$720 and the country had a deficit of US$900 m. After losing the 1990 election to Alberto Fujimori, García faced allegations of corruption and left Peru under the threat of criminal charges. He lived for the next 8 years in Colombia and France, returning in 2001 after Peru's Supreme Court ruled that any charges dating from his time in office had lapsed under the Statute of Limitations.

He fought the 2001 presidential election for APRA, losing narrowly to Alejandro Toledo of the Peru Possible party. From 2001–05 he was leader of the opposition. In the 2006 presidential election García fought a vigorous campaign, claiming that he had learned from past mistakes and would build international trade partnerships. He also exploited unease over the close connections between his main opponent, Ollanta Humala of the left-wing Union for Peru party, and Venezuelan president Hugo Chavéz. In the second round of voting on 4 June 2006 Humala conceded and García was voted in as president for the second time.

Career Peak

García signalled his willingness to work within prevailing economic orthodoxies by appointing a banker, Luis Carranza, as economic and finance minister, and renewing an aid package with the IMF. He accepted a free trade agreement with the USA and in Nov. 2006 signed 12 commercial agreements with Brazil. Also in late 2006 he allocated 968 m. nuevos soles (US$300 m.) to aid the poor. At the same time, he provoked protests from trade unions by announcing salary cuts for many state employees.

In April 2007 Congress agreed to give his government powers to legislate by decree in pursuit of its popular tough line against drug trafficking and organized crime. However, the failure of his economic policies to spread the benefits of growth more widely provoked violent demonstrations in July. In a speech marking the end of his first year in office, García asked Peruvians to show patience, promising that increased investment would reduce poverty before the end of his term. In 2008, despite an improvement in the economy and a high rate of growth, his popularity declined. By Oct., when he was obliged to replace members of the cabinet over a corruption scandal involving bribes for oil-exploration contracts, his approval rating among voters had fallen to only 20%.

His government was also criticized by environmental and human rights campaigners over plans to open up more Amazon forest territory to foreign energy companies. In June 2009 land ownership laws to this effect provoked violent demonstrations by indigenous groups in the area. Although the controversial decrees were subsequently repealed, this episode—along with a sharp decline in the economy in 2009–10 in the wake of the global downturn—contributed to a further steep fall in García's popularity. This was, however, of limited political significance since he was ineligible under the constitution to stand for a second consecutive term in the presidential elections on 10 April 2011 and was scheduled to leave office on 28 July. He was succeeded by Ollanta Moisés Humala Tasso.

In late 2009 relations with Chile were strained by Chilean military activity near the two countries' disputed border and by accusations against a Peruvian officer of spying for the Chilean military.

Garibashvili, Irakli (Georgia)

Introduction

Irakli Garibashvili took office as the prime minister on 20 Nov. 2013. A protégé of his predecessor, billionaire businessman Bidzina Ivanishvili, Garibashvili was the world's youngest elected leader at the time of his appointment.

Early Life

Born on 28 June 1982 in Tbilisi, Garibashvili earned a master's in international relations from Tbilisi State University in 2005. A year earlier he had begun working with Ivanishvili in several of the billionaire's organizations. Standing for the Georgian Dream–Democratic Georgia coalition (Georgian Dream having been launched by Ivanishvili in 2011), Garibashvili was elected to parliament in Oct. 2012 and was appointed interior minister in Ivanishvili's first cabinet. Ivanishvili stepped down after the Oct. 2013 presidential election, which saw a landslide victory for his party's candidate, Giorgi Margvelashvili. Ivanishvili's nomination of Garibashvili as his successor as premier was ratified by parliament in Nov. Garibashvili was also selected as Georgian Dream's leader.

Career Peak

Garibashvili rejected allegations that he was a pawn through which Ivanishvili would continue to exercise power. His first cabinet's composition was interpreted as a conciliatory gesture towards Russia, particularly with respect to the breakaway regions of Abkhazia and South Ossetia. However, his desire for better relations with Moscow sat uneasily with his aim of greater integration with the European Union. Although Georgia signed a trade partnership agreement with the EU in June 2014, Garibashvili dismissed the pro-Western defence minister Irakli Alasania in Nov. that year, which prompted a political crisis within the ruling coalition. In May 2015, following a series of ministerial resignations, Garibashvili nominated a new government. Most key posts were unchanged, although Tinatin Khidasheli, a pro-Western deputy, became the country's first female defence minister. Further changes in Aug.–Sept. saw the appointment of new interior and foreign ministers.

In March 2015 the government denounced an alliance and integration treaty between Russia and South Ossetia as a move by Moscow to annex Georgian territory.

Garibashvili resigned as prime minister in Dec. 2015 after polls suggested a steep decline in popularity for the coalition government and his Georgian Dream party. He was succeeded in the post by incumbent foreign affairs minister Giorgi Kvirikashvili.

Gašparovič, Ivan (Slovakia)

Introduction

Shortly before Slovakia became a member of the European Union on 1 May 2004, a respected lawyer, Ivan Gašparovič, was elected as the country's president. Instrumental in drawing up Slovakia's constitution prior to the dissolution of Czechoslovakia in 1993, he was also a close ally of the controversial nationalist former prime minister, Vladimír Mečiar, the man he beat in the second round of the presidential election. He was re-elected in April 2009.

Early Life

Ivan Gašparovič was born in Poltár, near Lučenec in southern Slovakia on 27 March 1941. His father, Vladimír Gašparovič, had migrated to the region from Rijeka, Croatia at the end of the First World War. The family moved to Bratislava, where Vladimír worked as a teacher in a secondary school. Having studied at the Law Faculty of the Komenský University in Bratislava from 1959–64, Ivan Gašparovič worked in the district prosecutor's office of Bratislava's Martin district (1965–66), and then became a prosecutor at the municipal prosecutor's office. In early 1968 he joined the Communist Party of Czechoslovakia and actively supported the reforms of Alexander Dubček, the party's Slovak first secretary. Under Dubček, in what became known as the Prague Spring, democratization went further than in any other Communist state—press censorship was reduced and Slovakia was granted political autonomy. However, opposition grew swiftly in the USSR and in other Warsaw Pact states which invaded Czechoslovakia on the night of 20 Aug. 1968. The following year Dubček was replaced by Gustáv Husák, who spearheaded a 'normalization' policy that turned Czechoslovakia into one of Central Europe's most repressive states.

Gašparovič left the Communist Party after the events of 1968 and began work as a teacher at the law faculty at the Komenský University. He remained there until 1990 when he became the vice chancellor in Feb. of that year, 2 months after the 'Velvet Revolution' had swept aside the Communists. Václav Havel, the playwright and former dissident who was elected federal president in Dec. 1989, nominated Gašparovič as prosecutor-general of Czechoslovakia. He moved to Prague and took up the post in July 1990, as the new government began to tackle the legacy of communism—a moribund economy, high unemployment and widespread social discontent. Under the 1968 constitution Czechoslovakia was a federal republic—each republic had a council and an assembly, but the federal government dealt with defence and foreign affairs. Arguments over the nature of the federation broke out and in 1991 Vladimír Mečiar formed the Movement for a Democratic Slovakia (HZDS). Gašparovič returned to Bratislava to teach at the Komenský University and joined the HZDS in 1992. Mečiar led the party to victory in the June 1992 elections, and Gašparovič became an HZDS member of the Slovak parliament. In late 1992 he was one of the authors of the constitution of Slovakia, which came into effect on 1 Jan. 1993 when the republic formally declared its independence.

Gašparovič was speaker of the Slovak parliament until Oct. 1998 and a close ally of Prime Minister Mečiar, whose controversial policies in the mid-1990s included stripping away the rights of the country's large Hungarian community and clamping down on the media. Slovakia became increasingly isolated from Western Europe until Mečiar's nationalist government was defeated in Sept. 1998 by an alliance of liberals, centrists, left-wingers and ethnic Hungarians. Mikuláš Dzurinda became prime minister and steered Slovakia through various reforms required for EU and NATO membership. From Oct. 1998–July 2002, when the HZDS was in opposition, Gašparovič was a member of the parliamentary committee for the supervision of the SIS (the Slovak equivalent of the US Central Intelligence Agency).

In July 2002 Gašparovič and others left the HZDS after being struck off the list of candidates for the parliamentary elections in Sept. The HZDS went on to poll only 3.3% of the vote, not enough to win any seats. Gašparovič returned to Komenský University, but also established a new political party called the Movement for Democracy (HZD). In April 2004 he ran for president against Mečiar, who was attempting to make a comeback after losing the 2002 legislative elections. Although Mečiar won more votes in the first round, he failed to win a majority. In the second round, Gašparovič secured nearly 60% of the vote with the support of the eliminated candidates.

Career Peak

Ivan Gašparovič succeeded Rudolf Schuster as president of the Slovak Republic on 15 June 2004 and began a 5 year term of office. Following elections to the National Council in June 2006, Gašparovič asked Robert Fico, the leader of the social democratic Direction Party, to form a new coalition government in place of Mikuláš Dzurinda's SDKÚ-led administration. Gašparovič secured a second term as president in April 2009, winning 55.5% of the vote in a second round run-off. Following further parliamentary elections in June 2010, the Direction Party remained the largest single party but Fico was unable to form a new coalition cabinet. Gašparovič instead turned to Iveta Radičová of the SDKÚ–DS, who took over as prime minister at the head of a four-party centre-right government in July.

In March 2010 Gašparovič vetoed a controversial nationalist law intended to instil patriotism by compulsory weekly national anthem-playing in state schools.

In Oct. 2011 the government was defeated in a parliamentary confidence vote but reappointed in a caretaker capacity. At elections in March 2012 the Direction–Social Democracy party won a majority and its leader, Robert Fico, became prime minister again.

Gašparovič was ineligible to stand again for the presidential elections in March 2014 and was succeeded by Andrej Kiska in June.

Gauck, Joachim (Germany)

Introduction

Joachim Gauck was elected president on 18 March 2012. His appointment alongside Chancellor Angela Merkel meant that the two most senior positions in government were held by East Germans for the first time since reunification. Gauck is best known as a pro-democracy activist who has exposed crimes committed by the secret police (the Stasi) in the former German Democratic Republic (GDR).

Early Life

Gauck was born on 24 Jan. 1940 in the town of Rostock. In 1951 his father was arrested by Soviet forces on charges of espionage and served 3 years in a Soviet prison, an event that moulded Joachim's political beliefs.

Gauck refused to join the communist Free German Youth movement and was denied the opportunity of becoming a journalist. Instead, he studied theology and became a Lutheran pastor, a position which brought him into conflict with the ruling communist regime and to the attention of the Stasi.

In 1989 Gauck became spokesman for the New Forum, a pro-democratic opposition movement, taking part in the series of peaceful demonstrations that led the way to the regime's collapse. After the dissolution of the GDR in Oct. 1990, the new federal government appointed him as a special representative to research the Stasi archives. In this role, which he held until 2000, he investigated crimes perpetrated by the secret police in the period of communist rule.

Gauck ran for the presidency in 2010 backed by the opposition Social Democratic Party (SPD) and the Greens. He was narrowly defeated by the governing coalition candidate, Christian Wulff, after three parliamentary ballots. When Wulff resigned in Feb. 2012 in the wake of a corruption scandal, Gauck was again put forward by the SPD and Greens and this time gained the support of Merkel's coalition. He faced one opponent, 'Nazi hunter' Beate Klarsfeld, who was proposed by the Left Party. In a vote by the Federal Assembly on 18 March, Gauck took 991 votes against 126 for Klarsfeld, with 108 abstentions.

Career Peak

A charismatic and popular figure, Gauck's election was seen by some commentators as threatening the authority of Chancellor Merkel, who had opposed his initial candidacy in 2010. He has controversially called for a more vigorous German approach to, and involvement in, international diplomacy.

In June 2016 Gauck announced that he would not seek a second mandate. In Feb. 2017 Frank-Walter Steinmeier was elected to succeed him. Gauck left office on 18 March 2017.

Gayoom, Maumoon Abdul (Maldives)

Introduction

In power as president of the Maldives from 1978–2008, Maumoon Abdul Gayoom was Asia's longest-serving leader. Gayoom had succeeded Ibrahim Nasir, who served from 1954 and was the premier when the Maldives became independent in 1965. He was re-elected by referendum for a sixth consecutive 5 year term in office in Oct. 2003 but lost out to Mohamed Nasheed in the presidential election of Oct. 2008. During Gayoom's tenure he developed industry, especially the main sectors of fishing and tourism, attracted investment and improved healthcare. But strict censorship and the suppression of opposition led to international concern.

Early Life

Gayoom was born on 29 Dec. 1937 in Malé where he received his early schooling. After studying in Sri Lanka and Cairo, Egypt, he completed a degree in Islamic studies at the Al-Azhar University, Cairo. He subsequently taught in Nigeria and Malé. He began working for the government in 1972 when he was employed in the shipping department. 2 years later he was appointed under-secretary in the prime minister's office before serving a year in Colombo as deputy ambassador to Sri Lanka. After representing the Maldives in the UN from 1976–77, he was made transport minister under Nasir's presidency. When Nasir resigned in 1978, Gayoom was chosen as president, a parliamentary decision ratified by a referendum in which 92.9% supported the appointment.

Career Peak

Gayoom invested in the nascent tourist industry which overtook fishing as the country's chief revenue earner (despite tourism being strictly controlled in an attempt to protect the Maldives' environment and to preserve its culture). As an archipelago of low-lying islands, the Maldives is threatened by the rising sea level caused by global warming. In 1989 Gayoom hosted an international environment conference.

The country's relative stability during Gayoom's rule was one factor in the attraction of foreign investment. He also invested in the country's health care and aimed to reduce the economic disparity between people living in the capital and those on the outer islands. However, Gayoom led an oligarchic government which maintained strict control, most notably through media censorship and intolerance of any criticism of the government. He survived attempted coups in 1980, 1983 and most notably in 1988 when help from Indian troops was needed to suppress a rising supported by Sri Lankan mercenaries.

On the international front, Gayoom tried to improve relations with India. He was a founder member of the South Asian Association for Regional Co-operation (SAARC) in 1985. In 1996 a Supreme Council for Islamic Affairs, under presidential control, was established to provide advice on matters related to Islam. In 1980 Gayoom established a Citizens' Majlis (Parliament) and, after 17 years of deliberation, it produced guidelines for a new constitution which became operational in Jan. 1998. It extended ministers' executive powers and increased the size of the Majlis. It also allowed self-nomination for presidency while stipulating that the candidate be a male Sunni Muslim over 35.

In Oct. 2003 Gayoom was re-elected for a sixth term with 90% of the vote in a referendum. In June 2005 the Majlis voted unanimously to introduce multiparty politics, and several opposition figures imprisoned for alleged criminal activities were subsequently pardoned and released. A national referendum in Aug. 2007 supported a proposal for a presidential rather than parliamentary system of government in a vote seen as an endorsement of Gayoom despite opposition claims of rigging. The following month 12 tourists were injured in Malé in the country's first bomb incident.

Oct. 2008 saw the Maldives' first free multi-party presidential election. Gayoom, standing for the Dhivehi Rayyithunge Party, was defeated by Ibrahim Nasir of the Maldivian Democratic Party. Nasir was sworn into office in early Nov. Gayoom remained the leader of his party.

Gbagbo, Laurent (Côte d'Ivoire)

Introduction

Laurent Gbagbo took over the presidency in Oct. 2000, succeeding Robert Guéï who had been forced into exile after claiming victory in a disputed presidential election. Gbagbo subsequently oversaw a long period of political and economic instability and fighting between the rebel, largely Muslim, north of the country and the government-controlled and mainly Christian south before a more enduring power-sharing agreement was concluded in March 2007. Following delayed presidential elections held in Oct.–Nov. 2010, Gbagbo refused to concede defeat to opposition leader Alassane Ouattara despite mounting international pressure. Following a short period of conflict, Gbagbo was arrested in April 2011. In Nov. he was extradited to the International Criminal Court to face charges of crimes against humanity.

Early Life

Gbagbo was born on 31 May 1945 in Gagnoa in the mid-west of the country. He graduated in history and was jailed in the early 1970s for subversive teaching. Increasingly involved in trade union politics, he was a critic of the regime of Félix Houphouët-Boigny who had been in power since 1960.

In the 1980s Gbagbo went into exile in France, from where he established the Ivorian Popular Front (FPI) and developed a nationalist agenda. Gbagbo returned to the country in 1988 and 2 years later Houphouët-Boigny agreed to multi-party elections. In 1993 Houphouët-Boigny was succeeded by Henri Konan Bédié, who remained in power until 1999, when he was deposed by Gen. Robert Guéï in a military coup.

Guéï announced new presidential elections in which he excluded anyone unable to prove 'pure' Ivorian heritage from running. This removed 15 candidates, including Ouattara of the Rally of the Republicans (RDR), which had widespread support in the Muslim north. Guéï claimed victory although Gbagbo was widely believed to have polled most votes. Popular protests forced Guéï to resign and Gbagbo assumed the presidency on 26 Oct. 2000.

Career Peak

Ouattara immediately urged Gbagbo to call new elections, but Gbagbo refused. Fighting broke out between Ouattara's Muslim supporters in the north and Gbagbo's Christian supporters in the south. In parliamentary elections held at the end of 2000, the FPI emerged as the largest party, although only one third of those eligible voted. In Jan. 2001 Gbagbo survived an attempted coup.

As well as increasing ethnic friction, he was confronted by an economy suffering from a decline in the global cocoa market (Côte d'Ivoire being the world's largest producer of cocoa). Also, his broad nationalist position led him to announce a ban on foreign ownership of property, causing unease among the country's immigrants making up around 30% of the population.

Gbagbo's human rights record received widespread criticism. Leading opposition politicians were arrested on disputed charges, and from 2001 the US embassy and Amnesty International voiced concerns over arbitrary detention and mistreatment. Alleged use of child slave labour further tarnished Gbagbo's regime. Côte d'Ivoire consequently suffered cuts in international aid, with the UN refusing to resume assistance until a domestic reconciliation process was in place.

In Sept. 2002 fighting erupted in Abidjan when 700 troops, believed to be loyal to Guéï, mutinied. Guéï was killed by government forces. ECOWAS agreed to broker negotiations between the government and the rebel factions and a short-lived ceasefire was signed in Oct. In Jan. 2003 the French authorities brokered another ceasefire and a power-sharing agreement to end the civil war (despite violent anti-French protests in Abidjan by pro-government supporters). Under the agreement Gbagbo would remain president, with a prime minister approved by consensus serving until elections scheduled for 2005. However, little progress was made in disarming militia forces or implementing political reform before a serious resurgence of conflict in Nov. 2004.

Following an attack by government forces across the ceasefire line against the rebels and on French peacekeeping troops, the French military retaliated by destroying the Ivorian air force, provoking more rioting by pro-government supporters in Abidjan. Further attempts at reconciliation, brokered by South Africa, resulted in a new agreement in April 2005 to revitalize power sharing, but it remained fragile and elections scheduled firstly for late 2005 and then for Oct. 2006 were postponed. In Nov. 2006 the UN Security Council extended Gbagbo's presidential mandate.

In March 2007 Gbagbo agreed a further power-sharing deal in an attempt to unify the country, under which the FN rebel leader, Guillaume Soro, became prime minister in a new administration. Nevertheless, the threat of further violence remained (Soro survived a rocket attack on his plane in June 2007) and presidential elections were postponed several times owing to security concerns and to problems over who is qualified to vote and the validity of identity cards. In Oct. 2008 the UN extended its arms embargo and sanctions on Côte d'Ivoire's diamond trade, but agreed to review the embargo once presidential elections had been held.

The elections were eventually staged over two rounds in Oct. and Nov. 2010 but only led to renewed turmoil. Gbagbo refused to cede power to Ouattara, the other main candidate, after the latter won the run-off with 54.1% of the vote according to the Election Commission. Instead, Gbagbo was declared the winner by the Constitutional Council which had rejected some results as fraudulent. Ouattara's victory was nevertheless endorsed by the United Nations, USA, European Union, African Union and ECOWAS.

After several months of conflict, Gbagbo was placed under house arrest by Ouattara's forces on 11 April 2011.

Later Life

In Oct. 2011 the International Criminal Court formally issued an arrest warrant for Gbagbo on four charges against humanity, including murder and rape, in the period 16 Dec. 2010–12 April 2011. He was subsequently transferred to the Netherlands and on 5 Dec. 2011 Gbagbo became the first present or former head of state to appear at the ICC in The Hague. The court was expected to announce in June 2012 whether the case will proceed to trial. However, the hearing was postponed indefinitely in Aug. 2012 following concerns over Gbagbo's health.

In Nov. 2012 the ICC stated that Gbagbo was fit to stand trial. He has denied responsibility for the violence. The trial is set to begin in Nov. 2015.

Gemayel, Amin (Lebanon)

Introduction

Amin Gemayel became state president on 23 Sept. 1982. His younger brother Bashir, the leader of the Christian Maronite Phalangist militia, had been elected unopposed by the National Assembly the previous month but was assassinated on 14 Sept. Although more moderate than his brother, and generally more acceptable to the Muslim population, Amin Gemayel proved no more successful than his predecessors in securing agreement between Lebanon's warring groups.

Early Life

He was born in Bikfaya, northeast of Beirut, on 22 Jan. 1942, the son of Pierre Gemayel who founded the Phalangist Party. He trained as a lawyer. More active in the political rather than the military sphere, he oversaw the Phalangist Party's business interests while his brother led the party militia. He also co-founded a right-wing French language newspaper, *Le Réveil*. Gemayel was elected to the National Assembly in 1970 and later fought in the 1975–76 civil war.

Career Peak

Following his brother's death in a bomb explosion, Gemayel was elected president by the Assembly. He received initial expressions of support from Sunni and Shia Muslim leaders, having maintained contacts with them in the period after the civil war, and from Arab leaders, notably the president of Syria. However, although Gemayel showed himself to be conciliatory towards the other religious groups, he was unable to assert any real authority over a country largely under Syrian and Israeli occupation, divided by sectarian and factional rivalries and terrorism, and in accelerating economic decline. Constitutionally, no progress was made in revising the 1943 power-sharing agreement to balance the Christian ascendancy with the Muslim numerical preponderance. Gemayel's 6 year-term of office ended on 23 Sept. 1988, with the National Assembly deadlocked over the election of a successor. His final act as president was the appointment of an interim military government headed by a Maronite Christian general, Michel Aoun. This was rejected by Lebanese Muslims and the Syrians. The country was essentially divided between a Christian government based in east Beirut and a Muslim administration in west Beirut, in turn leading to two further years of conflict. Having left office, Gemayel spent the next 12 years in France before returning to Lebanon in July 2000.

Gentiloni, Paolo (Italy)

Introduction

Paolo Gentiloni became prime minister on 12 Dec. 2016, following the resignation of Matteo Renzi (who had in turn succeeded Enrico Letta in Feb. 2014). A former journalist, Gentiloni entered national politics in 2001 and served in several subsequent centre-left coalitions. However, following elections in March 2018 that resulted in a hung parliament and advances by anti-establishment populist parties, Gentiloni assumed a caretaker role as premier.

Early Life

Paolo Gentiloni was born in Rome on 22 Nov. 1954. After graduating in political science from the Sapienza University of Rome, he worked in journalism, including as editor of an Italian environmental magazine. In 1993 he became a spokesman for the Federation of Greens.

Gentiloni entered parliament at the 2001 general election, representing the centre-left 'The Daisy' list. Then, as a founding member of Democracy is Freedom–The Daisy in 2002, he served as the party's communications spokesman for the next 5 years. Re-elected in 2006, he was part of the Olive Tree coalition led by Romano Prodi. He served as minister for communications for 2 years and was a founding committee member of the Democratic Party (PD), which was formed in 2007 from the merger of the Democrats of the Left and The Daisy.

Gentiloni retained his seat in the 2008 election and served in opposition to a centre-right coalition led by Silvio Berlusconi. Again re-elected in 2013, he was part of the 'Italy. Common Good' centre-left coalition. The new premier and leader of the PD, Matteo Renzi, appointed Gentiloni minister of foreign affairs in Oct. 2014.

Shortly after Renzi resigned in Dec. 2016, Gentiloni was asked by President Sergio Mattarella to form a new government and was sworn in as prime minister.

Career Peak

Gentiloni's challenges included stabilizing the banking sector against the backdrop of Italy's huge public debt level and countering illegal immigration from North Africa across the Mediterranean Sea. However, he also faced a growing electoral threat from populist movements that heralded the downfall of his government following the March 2018 legislative elections. After a 3 month political deadlock that followed the elections, the League and the Five Star Movement managed to form a coalition government under Giuseppe Conte. On 1 June 2018 Conte was confirmed by President Sergio Mattarella and replaced Gentiloni as prime minister.

Gheorghiu-Dej, Gheorghe (Romania)

Introduction

Gheorghe Gheorghiu-Dej led Romania, under various titles, from 1952–65. With Soviet backing, he was instrumental in removing the monarchy and establishing the communist People's Republic of Romania. Initially an ardent Stalinist, his relationship with the USSR deteriorated after Nikita Khrushchev came to power. Gheorghiu-Dej then pursued a more independent line and sought warmer relations with the West.

Early Life

Gheorghiu-Dej was born Gheorghe Gheorghiu on 8 Nov. 1901 in Bârlad, Romania. He became politically active after World War I, joining the outlawed Romanian Communist Party in 1930 while working on the tramways. He was involved in the 1933 Grivita rail strike and as a result was sentenced to 12 years imprisonment. He took the name Dej as this was the location of his jail. In 1936, though still in prison, he was elected to the party's Central Committee. He escaped in Aug. 1944, participated in the uprising that saw Romania join the Allies against Germany and became General Secretary of the Communist Party, which changed its name to the Romanian Workers' Party in 1948.

Assisted by the occupying Soviet forces, the communists dominated government and Gheorghiu-Dej held a succession of finance posts between 1946–52. He assisted in the establishment of the securitate, the widely feared secret police force. Leading a purge of political rivals in 1952, he became Prime Minister the same year. He resigned the premiership 3 years later but in 1961 became President of the Council of State.

Career Peak

During his early years Gheorghiu-Dej followed Stalinist doctrine and embarked on major programmes of industrialization and agricultural collectivization. He exerted almost complete control over education and culture and made Russian the country's second language. When Khrushchev came to power and positioned himself against Stalinist excesses, Gheorghiu-Dej was put on the defensive. Relations with the Soviet Union declined further when Moscow proposed that Romania should slow its industrial growth and serve as a feeder state, providing resources to other Eastern Bloc states.

Krushchev, believing he could rely on Gheorghiu-Dej's support, withdrew Soviet troops from Romania in 1958. From the early-1960s onwards, Gheorghiu-Dej asserted greater independence. In the face of Eastern Bloc opposition he hastened Romania's industrial growth and promoted the consumer goods sector. He lifted some restrictions on freedom of expression, released several thousand political prisoners and improved welfare provisions. Gheorghiu-Dej sought closer ties and increased trade with non-communist countries and pursued friendship with China, despite growing Soviet–Chinese conflict. Gheorghiu-Dej died of lung cancer in Bucharest on 19 March 1965 and was succeeded by Nicolae Ceauşescu.

Ghimpu, Mihai (Moldova)

Introduction

Mihai Ghimpu was appointed acting president in Sept. 2009 by the newly-installed pro-Western coalition government. A leading figure in the former Soviet Republic's independence movement, he once supported unification with Romania.

Early Life

Mihai Ghimpu was born in Coloniţa, Chişinău county, in the Moldavian SSR on 19 Nov. 1951. He attended secondary school in Chişinău, followed by military service in the Soviet army. He graduated in law in 1978 from Moldova State University and became a legal adviser to various state enterprises. In the era of *glasnost* ('openness') Ghimpu became a leading figure in the democratic movement. He co-founded the Popular Front of Moldova (FPM) in May 1989 with a manifesto calling for independence and for Moldovan (with a Romanized script) to be the official language.

In 1990 Ghimpu won a seat for the FPM in Moldova's Supreme Soviet. With 27% of elected members the party broke the Communist monopoly. Independence followed on 27 Aug. 1991. The FPM subsequently suffered from internal disputes and support for a proposed union with Romania dwindled. Ghimpu switched allegiance to the Congress of Intellectuals ahead of Moldova's first multiparty elections in Feb. 1994, winning a seat in parliament. However, he failed to be returned at the 1998 election, when he stood for the Party of Reform.

Ghimpu subsequently rebranded the Party of Reform as the Liberal Party (PL) and became its chairman. In 2007 he was elected to the Chişinău city council, where his nephew was mayor. He played a key role in opposing the ruling Party of Communists of the Republic of Moldova (PCRM) in the run-up to the April 2009 parliamentary election and was re-elected to parliament, where the Communists held a narrow majority. Accusations of electoral fraud led to clashes between demonstrators and police in Chişinău, leaving three dead and 300 injured. In a re-run election on 29 July 2009 a four-party pro-Western coalition (including the PL) won 53 of the 101 available seats. Ghimpu was elected speaker in Aug. 2009 and, following the resignation of the PCRM-backed President Voronin on 11 Sept., he was appointed as his acting successor.

Career Peak

Ghimpu's caretaker tenure stretched into 2010 following the governing coalition's failure to secure the three-fifths majority required to elect a successor to Voronin. In Oct. 2009 Ghimpu said that EU accession was a long-term goal but that his priority was to rescue the ailing economy. He blamed mismanagement and corruption by the Communist Party for the deficit of €500 m. A 'substantial assistance package' was promised by the European Commission once an agreement had been signed with the IMF.

Ghimpu called for new parliamentary elections in Nov. 2010 but when no party won sufficient support to elect a new president, he left office.

Gierek, Edward (Poland)

Introduction

Edward Gierek was First Secretary of the Polish Communist Party between 1970 and 1980. He replaced Władysław Gomułka following workers' protests, promising to enforce economic reforms and reverse declining standards of living. He attempted to adjust Soviet party line to suit the conditions of Poland and capitalized on improving East–West relations by securing international investments and loans. However, a fluctuating world economy allied with mismanagement of the Polish economy led to price rises in 1980. Strikes and demonstrations forced recognition of the Solidarity trade union movement and ultimately Gierek's demise.

Early Life

Gierek was born on 6 Jan. 1913 in Porabka, near Katowice, in what was then Austria-Hungary. His father was killed in a mining accident when Edward was 4 years old, and he and his mother subsequently moved to France. When he was 18 he became active in the French Communist Party. 6 years later he moved to Belgium, joining the Communist Party and serving in the Belgian Resistance during World War II. In 1946 he chaired the National Council of Poles in Belgium and in 1948 he returned to his homeland, taking a prominent role in the Upper Silesian branch of the Polish Communist Party.

In 1952 he was elected to parliament and 2 years later was given responsibility for heavy industry. He was appointed to the Politburo in 1956 and in the following year he became First Secretary of the party in the Katowice area, a post he held for 13 years. In late 1970 national first secretary Gomułka announced price rises and a wave of popular protests swept the country. Gierek, promoting himself as the most likely economic saviour, took control of the party when Gomułka fell from power.

Career Peak

He set out to reform the economy principally by looking to the West for financial support. This policy brought short term rewards but could not overcome the problems of a failing infrastructure, economic mismanagement of successive governments, and a faltering world economy following the Middle Eastern oil crises. Much of the capital inflow was spent in artificially boosting the consumer sector. Meanwhile Poland was accumulating vast foreign debts. Price rises similar to those that had toppled Gomułka became inevitable.

In 1976 there were protests and riots in a number of cities, notably Ursus and Radom where the authorities used strong arm tactics to maintain control. Some price increases were reversed and Gierek retained his hold on power, but Poland's economic problems did not improve. By 1980 another set of price rises was decreed and again there was civil unrest.

Following the events of 1976 a Workers' Defence Committee (KOR) was set up. Their demands were encompassed in a Charter of Workers' Rights. At the centre of the 1980 protests were the Gdansk shipyards, where Lech Wałęsa led a mass strike and co-ordinated similar actions across the country. The government was forced into talks and made far-reaching concessions including the recognition of free unions with the right to strike as well as a relaxation of laws on religion and political expression. The workers' movement was formally established as Solidarity in Sept. 1980.

Gierek's health declined during the period of turmoil and he suffered a heart attack. He resigned as First Secretary and was replaced by Stanisław Kania who in turn was replaced by Wojciech Jaruzelski.

Later Life

Jaruzelski's administration revealed the corruption of Gierek's regime and Gierek was subsequently removed from the Party before being interned for 12 months at the end of 1981. Gierek died on 29 July 2001.

Gillard, Julia (Australia)

Introduction

Julia Gillard became prime minister in June 2010 when she successfully challenged incumbent Kevin Rudd for the leadership of the ruling Australian Labor Party. Considered a left-of-centre consensus politician, she has chiefly focused on domestic issues. After Labor's weakened showing at elections in Aug. 2010, she agreed an alliance with Green and independent MPs to give herself a working majority of one seat.

Early Life

Julia Gillard was born in Barry, Wales on 29 Sept. 1961 and moved to Adelaide, Australia with her family in 1965. Educated at Mitcham Demonstration School and Unley High School, she went to Adelaide University in 1981 to study arts and law. While there she campaigned with the Labor Party against federal education budget cuts. She became vice president of the Australian Union of Students (AUS) in 1982, necessitating a move to Melbourne University where the AUS was based. In 1984 she was voted AUS president.

After graduating in 1986 she worked as a solicitor in Melbourne, specializing in industrial and employment law, and became a partner at the firm Slater & Gordon in 1990. From 1996–98 she was chief of staff to John Brumby, opposition leader in the state of Victoria. She was adopted as a parliamentary Labor candidate at her second attempt, successfully contesting the seat of Lalor at the 1998 election. From 1998–2001 she served on several committees, including the House of Representatives standing committee on employment, education and workplace relations.

Following Labor's defeat at the 2001 election, Gillard was appointed shadow minister for population and immigration, where she argued for a controlled and planned approach to immigration. In 2003 she was given the additional portfolio for reconciliation and indigenous affairs. From 2003–06 she was shadow minister for health, attracting notice for her combative challenges to her government opposite number, Tony Abbott. In Dec. 2006 she supported Kevin Rudd's bid for the Labor leadership, announcing herself as a candidate for the deputy leadership. Following Rudd's defeat of incumbent Kim Beazley, Gillard was elected unopposed as his deputy. She was named shadow minister for employment, industrial relations and social inclusion.

In Dec. 2007, following Labor's election victory, Gillard became deputy prime minister. She was given a wide-ranging portfolio, as minister for education, employment and workplace relations and social inclusion. She launched a programme of reforms including a $A16 bn. investment in schools infrastructure and measures to gauge academic performance in national tests. The Howard government's controversial industrial relations legislation was replaced by a collective bargaining framework, overseen by a single government body.

In the aftermath of the 2008 global financial crisis, when Prime Minister Rudd's popularity suffered, Gillard was viewed as a credible alternative leader of the Labor Party. Although she shared responsibility for some of the government's more unpopular moves, including delaying expenditure on schools and postponing the introduction of a long-promised emissions trading programme, she maintained her personal appeal. In June 2010, having won the backing of the Australian Workers' Union and many factions within her party, she challenged Rudd for the leadership. He stood aside without a vote and on 24 June 2010 Gillard was sworn in as Australia's first female prime minister.

Career Peak

Gillard declared her intention to manage Australia's natural resources boom so that revenues could be invested for future growth. She opened negotiations with the mining industry over a proposed profits tax which, despite industry resistance, was approved by parliament in March 2012. She also promised a planned approach to solving the shortage of skilled labour, introducing tax reforms to encourage retired and part-time workers into fuller participation. She also signalled her intention to seek sustainable and controlled immigration rather than the 'big Australia' vision of her predecessor. Her controversial proposal to process the rising numbers of asylum seekers through Malaysia was rejected in parliament in Oct. 2011 but in Sept. 2012 the government instead adopted an independent panel recommendation to re-establish holding centres in Nauru and Papua New Guinea. Other pressing challenges have included the environment, in particular rebuilding after the Queensland floods of early 2011, and devising controversial legislation on pricing carbon emissions, which completed its parliamentary passage in Nov. 2011 and came into force in July 2012. Gillard also promised to deliver a $A36 bn. national broadband system and to take over from individual states the majority of funding responsibility for public hospitals. In Feb. 2012 Rudd resigned as foreign minister and challenged Gillard's leadership. The prime minister won the backing of her Labor party colleagues in the leadership ballot, by 71 votes to 31. In April 2012 Gillard announced that the withdrawal of most Australian troops from Afghanistan would be completed in 2013. In early 2013 the aim was still to achieve this by the end of the year.

In June 2013 Gillard was defeated by Kevin Rudd in the Labor party leadership ballot. Rudd won the vote by 57 votes to 45, after which Gillard immediately resigned as prime minister. Keeping with her pledge given before the leadership vote, Gillard announced she would retire from politics.

Giscard d'Estaing, Valéry (France)

Introduction

Valéry Giscard d'Estaing was finance minister under presidents de Gaulle and Pompidou before becoming the third president of the Fifth Republic from 1974–81. He founded the right-wing political group, Républicains Indépendants (RI), in 1966. He implemented various progressive social policies, but his presidency was ineffectual against the rising tide of unemployment and gathering strength of left-wing parties.

Early Life

The son of a leading economist, Giscard d'Estaing was born on 2 Feb. 1926 in Koblenz, Germany. He studied at the Ecole Polytechnique, breaking his degree to serve in the French army between 1944–45. After studying at the Ecole Nationale d'Administration in Paris, Giscard d'Estaing entered the civil service in 1952 to work in the finance ministry. He was elected deputy of the Puy-de-Dôme department in 1956. A member of the conservative Centre National des Indépendants et Paysans (CNIP), he was one of the group that supported de Gaulle's move for an independent Algeria. Between 1959–62 he was secretary of state for finance. He was appointed finance minister by de Gaulle in 1962.

The promotion was not a success. In trying to move France away from American influence, he incurred mounting criticism from the business sector. He was dismissed in 1967 when he formed his own party, the RI. He regained his position as finance minister under Pompidou, when he devalued the franc as the foundation of a period of economic stability. When Pompidou died in 1974, Giscard d'Estaing fought for the presidency as the RI candidate. His rival, the Gaullist Jacques Chaban-Delmas, made little impact and the voters were not yet ready for a shift to the left as promised by François Mitterrand. Giscard d'Estaing became president in May 1974.

Career Peak

Giscard d'Estaing enacted various social reforms. Abortion was legalised, contraception was made easier to obtain and the vote was lowered to 18. Censorship in broadcasting and films was relaxed. Giscard d'Estaing was outward looking in his approach to international issues. In 1976 he began the G7 meetings of the seven leading industrial nations. He was more successful than Pompidou in his relations with Germany, working closely with Chancellor Helmut Schmidt on EC issues. Together they set up the European Monetary System in 1979. But Giscard d'Estaing's administration marked the end of France's *trente glorieuses*—a 30-year period of economic stability after World War II. Hardline economic measures proved unpopular.

Meanwhile, mayor of Paris, Jacques Chirac set about reviving the Gaullist party 'Rassemblement du Peuple Français'. In 1976 he formed the Rassemblement pour la République (RPR). In response, Giscard d'Estaing formed a centre-right coalition on 1 Feb. 1978, Union pour la Democratie Française (UDF). Battling against unfavourable economic trends, Giscard d'Estaing faced growing opposition from both the socialists led by Mitterrand and the RPR led by Chirac. In the 1981 presidential election, Giscard d'Estaing was defeated by François Mitterrand.

Later Life

Giscard d'Estaing was president of the UDF until 1996. He was a member of the European Parliament from 1989–93. In 2002 he was appointed by EC president Romano Prodi to head a special convention on the future of the EU. Draft proposals were published in May 2003, which strongly influenced the content of the European Constitution signed and approved by the European heads of state at Rome in 2004. Despite the rejection of the constitution by French and Dutch voters d'Estaing continued to lobby for greater European integration.

Gligorov, Kiro (Macedonia)

Introduction

Kiro Gligorov became president of the Republic of Macedonia following free elections after the collapse of Yugoslavia. From the end of World War II until the mid-1970s he held various finance posts in the Yugoslav administration when he was an advocate of free market principles. During the late 1970s and much of the 1980s he was in the political wilderness but gained popular support in Macedonia during the Yugoslav crisis of 1989–90 for his pro-democracy views. He survived an attempt on his life in 1995.

Early Life

Gligorov was born on 3 May 1917 in Shtip, now in the Republic of Macedonia. He attended Belgrade University and was active in student politics until his graduation in 1938. He then worked as a banker until World War II, during which time he devoted himself to various anti-fascist and pro-national liberation groups. Macedonia was briefly declared a republic in 1944 but was subsequently integrated into the Federal Republic of Yugoslavia.

Gligorov became a Macedonian representative in the Yugoslav parliament and held a number of positions within government over the following years. He was Assistant General Secretary to the Government between 1945–47, Assistant Minister of Finance between 1952–53, Deputy Director of the Federal Institute for Economic Planning between 1953–55, Secretary of the Federal Executive Council for Economic Issues between 1955–62, Federal Secretary of Finance between 1962–67 and Vice President of the Federal Executive Council from 1967 to 1969. Although his hopes for a free market were never realized under Tito, he was a prominent member of the Institute for International Politics and Economy and the Institute for Social Sciences.

During the 1970s Gligorov served as a member of the Yugoslav presidency and as President of the Yugoslav Parliament. His political career subsequently went into decline and he was largely absent from the political scene in the 1980s. However, he was in the government of Ante Marković in the late 1980s when he once again promoted his belief in free market principles. When the Yugoslavian crisis of 1989–90 erupted he called for multi-party elections.

Career Peak

In the election of Jan. 1991 he was elected president of the Republic of Macedonia. In a referendum to decide on independence from Yugoslavia on 8 Sept. 1991 about 75% of voters supported the proposal.

A new constitution was promulgated on 17 Nov. 1991 allowing Macedonia to leave the Yugoslav Federation peacefully. Gligorov succeeded in steering clear of the war between the Serbs and Croats while negotiating the withdrawal of Yugoslav troops from the country in early 1992. Macedonia was accepted into the United Nations on 13 April 1993 and UN troops entered the country shortly afterwards to monitor its troublesome border near Kosovo.

Relations with neighbouring Greece deteriorated when the Greek government opposed the use of the name Macedonia, arguing that it was offensive to the inhabitants of the Macedonia area within Greece. When the Republic of Macedonia established diplomatic ties with a number of EU countries in late 1993 and with the USA in early 1994, Greece responded by imposing an economic embargo. Macedonia agreed to revise its flag design and to talks over its name with the result that the embargo was lifted in Nov. 1995.

Meanwhile, following an election in Oct. 1994, Gligorov secured another term as President. This was despite sour relations with Greece, general unrest and a weak economy stretched to breaking point by an influx of hundreds of thousands of refugees fleeing the wars between former Yugoslav states. He also had to oversee controversial reforms that allowed for better representation for Macedonia's substantial Albanian minority. On 3 Oct. 1995 unknown assailants tried to assassinate Gligorov. A car bomb killed his chauffeur but Gligorov survived. Stojan Andov stood in for him as president until Jan. 1996.

Macedonia's economy suffered further setbacks when the UN declared sanctions against Serbia, thus weakening Macedonia's principal trade partner. As the Kosovo conflict escalated in 1999, the country received another huge wave of Albanian refugees, creating yet more economic, political and social problems. Parliamentary elections held in 1998 returned a coalition of right-wing parties and at the presidential elections of Nov. 1999 Gligorov lost to nationalist Boris Trajkovski.

Later Life

Gligorov withdrew from politics in 1999 but remained active during his retirement, publishing a number of books and establishing the Gligorov Foundation—a think tank concerned with the development of multi-ethnic societies. In 2005 he became the first recipient of the Order of the Republic of Macedonia.

Gligorov died peacefully on 1 Jan. 2012. In accordance with his request he was not given a state funeral.

Godmanis, Ivars (Latvia)

Introduction

Ivars Godmanis was elected prime minister by the 100-member parliament in Dec. 2007, claiming 54 votes. This followed the resignation of incumbent Aigars Kalvitis in response to opposition to his attempted dismissal of the head of the anti-corruption bureau. Godmanis, who had earlier served as Latvia's first post-Soviet premier, became head of the country's 14th government in 16 years.

Early Life

Ivars Godmanis was born in Riga on 27 Nov. 1957. After graduating from the University of Latvia in 1974, he joined the university's Institute of Solid-State Physics as a junior scientific assistant and rose to the post of senior lecturer by the time he left in 1988.

In that year Godmanis joined the Latvian Popular Front, becoming deputy chairman. After independence in 1990 he served as prime minister for a 3 year term that focused on economic transition. However, in the crisis that followed the freeing-up of prices he was forced out of office. For the next 5 years he worked in the private sector before returning as minister of finance from 1998–99. He then rejoined the private sector and in 2004 became a member of the Latvian Way Party. After elections in Nov. 2006, Godmanis joined the coalition government as minister of the interior. Following the resignation of Kalvitis, he was appointed prime minister by President Zatlers on 14 Dec. 2007.

Career Peak

Godmanis initially pledged to cut inflation, raise living standards to European levels within 10 years, and prepare for the introduction of the euro. However, Latvia's economy and national currency were undermined during 2008 by the global financial downturn, and by the end of the year his government was negotiating a rescue package with the International Monetary Fund and the Nordic countries. Meanwhile, Latvia's relations with Russia were aggravated in Jan. 2008 as each country expelled a diplomat for conduct 'incompatible with status' and in May the Latvian parliament approved the EU's Lisbon Treaty on institutional and administrative reform which had been signed in Dec. 2007.

In Feb. 2009 anti-government protests in Riga over the government's economic policy left 40 injured and resulted in over 100 arrests. Godmanis subsequently announced his resignation on losing the backing of the government's two main coalition partners. Valdis Dombrovskis was named his successor.

Goh Chok Tong (Singapore)

Introduction

Goh Chok Tong became prime minister of Singapore in Nov. 1990. Heading the People's Action Party, he succeeded Singapore's first prime minister, Lee

Kuan Yew. He remained in office until Aug. 2004 when he was succeeded by Lee Kuan Yew's elder son, Lee Hsien Loong.

Early Life

Goh Chok Tong was born in Singapore on 20 May 1941. He was educated at the Raffels Institution in Singapore and studied economics at the University of Singapore from 1961–64. He continued his studies at Williams College in the USA. He is married to Tan Choo Leng, with whom he has two children.

Goh Chok Tong was an administrative officer in the Singapore Administrative Service and entered parliament in 1976. Between 1969 and 1977 he worked for the Neptune Orient Lines, ending as managing director. He was appointed senior minister of state for finance in 1977. Between 1979 and 1990 he variously held the portfolios for trade and industry, health and defence, and in 1985 he was first deputy prime minister. A member of the People's Action Party central executive committee since 1979, he became secretary general in 1992.

Career Peak

Improving Singapore's economic success in the international arena has been his major objective. Despite a slowdown during the 1998 Asian crisis, Singapore has consolidated its position as one of the region's leading economies. Goh Chok Tong often cites China as an example for Singapore, with its low industrial and land costs. He has signed numerous trade agreements with foreign partners, although relations with the US were strained in the mid-1990s when he refused to apologise after a US citizen had been sentenced to a caning.

Goh Chok Tong retained tight control of the media. It is illegal to own a satellite dish, television and press censorship is widespread and internet access is restricted. He announced his resignation on 10 Aug. 2004, and was succeeded by Deputy Prime Minister Lee Hsien Loong. He stepped down from the cabinet in May 2011, becoming senior adviser to the Monetary Authority of Singapore.

Golding, Bruce (Jamaica)

Introduction

Bruce Golding was sworn in as prime minister on 11 Sept. 2007 after the Jamaica Labour Party (JLP) won polling earlier that month. Winning 33 of 60 parliamentary seats, the JLP came back to government after 18 years in opposition. After 4 years in power he resigned as head of the JLP and prime minister.

Early Life

Bruce Golding was born on 5 Dec. 1947. He graduated from the University of the West Indies in 1969 with a degree in economics and was elected to the central executive of the JLP immediately afterwards. In 1970 he co-founded Young Jamaica, the party's youth affiliate, before winning a seat in the 1972 general election.

In 1974 Golding was elected general secretary of the JLP but lost his constituency seat in 1976. A year later he was appointed to the senate and, when the JLP returned to power in 1980, was appointed minister of construction. In 1983 he won another seat and was elected JLP chairman in 1984. Following his party's failure at the 1989 polls, Golding became shadow minister of finance and chairman of the public accounts committee.

In the early 1990s Golding's attempts to change to the country's political practices met with resistance and he left the JLP to establish the National Democratic Movement (NDM) in 1995. However, he resigned from the NDM in 2001 and returned to the JLP in Sept. 2002 where he once again sat in the senate. He was given the post of shadow minister of foreign affairs and foreign trade. In Nov. 2003 Golding was elected unopposed as party chairman and in Feb. 2005 became its leader. In April 2005 he won the seat of West Kingston in a by-election and became leader of the opposition. He led the JLP to electoral victory in Sept. 2007, becoming the first JLP prime minister since 1989.

Career Peak

Golding promised to prioritize the tackling of crime, poverty and unemployment. He abolished tuition fees in secondary schools and established an independent body to investigate police corruption. However, his tenure was marred by allegations of inappropriate use of executive power, and crime remained a serious problem. Jamaica's murder rate is one of the highest in the world, in response to which parliament voted to retain the death penalty and Golding pledged to resume executions. In June 2010 security forces captured Christopher 'Dudus' Coke, a suspected drug trafficker, and extradited him to the USA, but only after violent resistance by Coke supporters in Kingston in which around 80 people died. In response to opposition criticism, in Oct. Golding announced the establishment of a commission of enquiry into the government's handling of the episode.

On 25 Sept. 2011 Golding made clear his intention not to seek re-election as leader of the JLP in Nov. 2011 and step down as prime minister once a new leader had been elected. Although this was rejected by the JLP's central executive, Golding's decision remained. He was succeeded by the minister of education Andrew Holness on 23 Oct. 2011.

Gomułka, Władysław (Poland)

Introduction

Władysław Gomułka was first secretary of the Polish Communist Party between 1956 and 1970. He became a member of the Politburo after World War II but was expelled from the party following a rift with Joseph Stalin. As discontent with Stalinism spread throughout Poland in 1956, he was re-instated and made First Secretary in the hope that he might appease a population that saw him as an enemy of Stalin and a liberal reformer. However, he failed to carry out the expected reforms and resigned his post following popular protests.

Early Life

Gomułka was born on 6 Feb. 1905 in Białbrzegi, near Krosno (then part of the Austro-Hungarian Empire and now part of Poland). His father, an oil-worker, was a fervent socialist. Gomułka left school at 12 to be employed as a locksmith's apprentice and joined a socialist youth organization by 1921. Five years later he was a member of the underground Polish Communist Party and was soon arrested. It was to be the first of many arrests and in 1932 he began a 2 year stint in jail following a strike of textile workers he had helped organize in his capacity as National Secretary of the Chemical Workers' Union.

Following his release in 1934 Gomułka went to Moscow to study at the International Lenin School. In 1936 he began a 7 year prison sentence back in Poland but was released at the outbreak of World War II. He was prominent in the Polish Resistance Movement throughout the war and in 1942 he joined the Central Committee of the Polish Workers' Party (PPR), becoming Secretary General in Nov. 1943. In the aftermath of World War II an interim government was established in Lublin, in which Gomułka served as Deputy Prime Minister and Minister for Territories Recovered from Germany.

He was also active in the merger of the PPR with the Polish Socialist Party to form a united communist party, and to this end he sought the elimination of the Polish Peasant Party which he saw as a potential obstacle. An independently minded politician, Gomułka entered into conflict with Stalin by opposing agricultural collectivization and by speaking out against the formation of Cominform (Communist Information Bureau) in 1947. As a result he was removed as Secretary General of the PPR in Sept. 1948 and, following the formation of the Polish United Workers Party in that Dec., his decline continued. Removed from the party altogether in late 1949, he was ultimately put under house arrest in July 1951.

He was released in 1954 and 2 years later, as part of Krushchev's campaign to repair some of the damage of Stalin's reign which had ended 2 years earlier, Gomułka was officially rehabilitated. With social unrest on the increase as food prices spiralled, Gomułka, the opponent of Stalinism, gained the stature of a folk hero. Events reached crisis point when a strike at a Poznań steel plant developed into riots during which the heavy-handed response of the authorities led to the death of 53 people. Gomułka, who had been allowed to re-join the party in Aug. 1956 and had been voted in as Secretary General of the Central Committee in Oct., was subsequently drafted into the Council of State (effectively a joint presidency).

Career Peak

Gomułka did cut the power of the secret police, halted agricultural collectivization and brought an end to attacks on the Catholic Church. In this he rectified some of the worse elements of Stalin's reign. However, his appointment to high office did not herald an end to the suppression of freedom of expression nor did he radically change economic policy. By the end of the decade there was little evident improvement in Poland's quality of living and his popular appeal faltered throughout the 1960s. Student riots sprang up around the country in March 1968 but Gomułka managed to retain his post as Secretary General.

In 1969 and 1970 he instigated a number of reformist policies. A treaty improving relations between Poland and West Germany was signed and some of the country's economic problems were confronted. It was too little too late, however, and a rise in food prices in Dec. 1970 led to workers' protests in numerous cities. On 20 Dec. 1970 he resigned as First Secretary and was replaced by Eduard Gierek. Though ostensibly a member of the Council of State until 1971 and Parliament until 1972, in practical terms it was the end of his politically active life.

Later Life

Gomułka died in Warsaw on 1 Sept. 1982.

González Macchi, Luis Angel (Paraguay)

Introduction

Angel González Macchi was president of Paraguay from 1999 until 2003, representing the Colorado party, which has dominated the country's politics for more than half a century. Unelected, González was appointed president to follow Raul Cubas Grau who was forced to resign when he was linked to the assassination of Vice President Luís Maria Argaña. González struggled to combat a worsening economic situation, high inflation and unemployment, coup attempts and public discontent. He survived many calls for his resignation.

Early Life

González was born on 13 Dec. 1947 in the capital Asunción. The son of a doctor, he studied law at the Universidad Nacional de Asunción before gaining a scholarship in 1970 to study in Madrid. A member of the ruling rightwing Asociación Nacional Republicana, or the Partido Colorado, he was president of the congress under Cubas' leadership. The latter's short term was ineffectual. When he refused to force his ally General Lino Oviedo to return to prison and see out a 10 year sentence incurred in 1996 for leading a failed coup, impeachment charges were brought. In 1999 Argaña was assassinated, allegedly under the command of Oviedo who feared Argaña was attempting to push out the president. Angry public demonstrators congregated outside the presidential palace to demand Cubas' resignation. Four protestors were shot by snipers. Both Cubas and Oviedo fled the country seeking immunity in Argentina and Brazil.

In the ensuing chaos the government formed an all-party coalition, attempting to create a united front to restore stability to a democracy only 11 years old. It represented an alternative to the half century rule by the Colorado party, including 34 years of dictatorship. In the absence of a vice president, González was chosen to lead the coalition and took up the presidency.

Career Peak

González's main challenges were to reignite the stagnant economy and give the people confidence in the government. Immediately González fell into dispute with his neighbouring MERCOSUR countries. There were calls for

the arrest of Cubas and Oviedo and both Argentina and Brazil refused to extradite them. Several of their allies implicated in the assassination were arrested. Further disputes arose internally and in Feb. 2000 the opposition Partido Liberal Radical Auténtico (PLRA) pulled out of the coalition. It claimed the dominant Colorado party was refusing to share power and blocking reforms, especially privatization schemes that were needed to boost the economy. This prompted the resignation of several ministers. González's standing was further threatened by continuing support for the exiled Oviedo, especially from the large rural poor who believe that Oviedo would solve their economic problems. Policies proposed by González provoked popular protest supported by the trade unions. In May 2000 the precarious democracy was further tested when rebels took over radio stations and attacked the presidential palace with tanks. The coup was contained and González announced a 30 day state of emergency in which 70 suspected Oviedo sympathisers were arrested.

In Aug. 2000 a close run vice presidential election was won by PLRA candidate Julio Cesar Franco who beat the Colorado candidate and former vice president's son Felix Argaña. Optimism was soon dampened by Franco's inability to achieve change and González's continued inability to reverse economic decline. A 4% fiscal deficit, high unemployment and a continued depreciation in GDP were not aided by stalled privatization. A loan by Taiwan in 1999 failed to ignite recovery. Internecine disputes led to more resignations.

In Aug. 2001 further pressure on González to resign followed claims that the president had been involved in bank fraud. He was further embarrassed when he was discovered driving a stolen car. While looking for an IMF loan in exchange for higher taxes and the long promised privatization, protesters gathered at the presidential palace in early Sept. 2001 calling once more for him to stand down, scenes which were repeated 12 months later. He narrowly escaped impeachment in Feb. 2003 by surviving a Senate vote to prosecute him for allegedly misspending 115.6 bn. guaranís ($17 m.) of government money. With voting 22 to 18 against him, the motion failed to attain the two thirds majority needed to oust him from power.

González did not stand for the presidency at the elections of 2003.

González Márquez, Felipe (Spain)

Introduction

Felipe González Márquez was prime minister of Spain from 1982–96, representing the Partido Socialista Obrero Español (Spanish Socialist Workers' Party; PSOE). He continued the Post-Franco transition towards democracy and opened Spain up internationally; Spain joined the EC (now the EU) in 1986.

Early Life

González was born in Seville on 5 Mar. 1942. The son of a strongly republican agricultural worker, he was the only child of six to attend higher education. He studied civil engineering at Seville University before changing to study law. His political career began during his student years. After activity in the Socialist Youth Movement, he joined the then-outlawed PSOE in 1964. He continued his studies in Leuven where he was influenced by Belgium's former prime minister, the Socialist Paul-Henri Spaak. In 1968 he set up a law firm in Seville. After climbing the ranks of the PSOE during the 1960s and early 70s, González became its secretary general in Oct. 1974 at the Suresnes Congress. González had moved away from the traditional leadership of the PSOE party. With his friend and colleague Alfonso Guerra, who became editor of *El Socialista*, he offered a new vision for the future, which proved popular.

Career Peak

When opposition parties were legalized in 1977, González was elected a deputy for Madrid. The elections of 1977 made the PSOE the leading opposition party. In 1982 the PSOE won an absolute majority and González became prime minister. He consolidated the democratic transition begun by Suárez. He dismantled much of the bureaucracy of the Franco regime and decentralized the government. To open up industrial relations and to encourage free trade, Spain joined NATO and the EC (EU), both in 1986. In the elections of 1986 the PSOE once again gained an absolute majority. Over the next few years Spain enjoyed strong economic growth. In 1989 Spain entered the European Monetary Union.

Conversely, the 1990s were years of recession and internal party struggles. The PSOE won the elections of 1989, but with a smaller majority. Economic growth fell and unemployment rose. Public spending increased, as did welfare costs. The subsequent years saw in-party squabbling over the succession to head the party. Despite decentralization, Basque terrorism reached record heights.

By the 1993 elections employment had reached over 20%, the highest of any country in the EU. Failing to gain an absolute majority, González formed an alliance with a coalition of Catalan politicians, including Jordi Pujol's Catalan Nationalists.

More problems were ahead. In 1994 the government was hit by a wave of scandals. It was revealed that between 1983–7 the government had ordered death squads to assassinate Basque terrorists residing in France. Similar acts during Franco's reign had brought international condemnation. The Catalonian politicians severed their alliance with the government. In the elections of 1996 the PSOE was defeated by the right-wing Partido Popular and González conceded the premiership to José María Aznar López.

Later Life

González has since worked for the OSCE (Organization for Security and Co-operation in Europe), leading the mission to Yugoslavia to persuade Milosevic to accept the 1996 local election results.

Gonzi, Lawrence (Malta)

Introduction

Appointed Malta's prime minister on 23 March 2004, Lawrence Gonzi oversaw the nation's accession to the EU six weeks later. Leading the right-of-centre Nationalist Party (NP), he advocated seizing the opportunities for trade and investment afforded by Malta's EU membership, including adoption of the single European currency. He was re-elected in 2008 but his government fell in Dec. 2012.

Early Life

Lawrence Gonzi was born on 1 July 1953 in Valletta, Malta. He attended St Joseph's school, St Aloysious College and The Archbishop's Seminary, and went on to study law at the University of Malta, graduating in 1975, the year after Malta became a fully independent republic (having achieved independence from Great Britain in 1964). Gonzi took up employment as a junior solicitor in a private firm and later worked as a company lawyer with the Mizzi Organization. From 1976 he was engaged in the voluntary sector, working with people with disabilities and mental health problems. He was also the general president of the Malta Catholic Action Movement between 1976 and 1986.

Gonzi entered politics in 1986, contesting the 1987 general election as a candidate for the Nationalist Party. Duly elected, he served in the government of the new Nationalist prime minister, Edward Fenech Adami. Gonzi was elected speaker of the House of Representatives on 10 Oct. 1988. The NP took up a pro-Western stance and argued for integration into the European Community. It also embarked on a programme to stimulate business, increase tourism and reduce the role of the government in the economy. The party held on to power in the 1992 general election, but lost the Oct. 1996 poll to a rejuvenated MLP, led by Alfred Sant.

Gonzi retained his parliamentary seat in the 1996 election and, a month later, was appointed opposition party whip, secretary to the parliamentary group and shadow minister for social policy. The following year he was elected secretary general of the Nationalist Party, subsequently playing a central role in achieving an NP electoral victory after just 22 months of the Labour administration. Gonzi was appointed minister for social policy and leader of the House of Representatives. The appointment of Prof. Guido de Marco as president of the republic on 2 May 1999 prompted Gonzi to contest the election for the deputy leadership of the NP. He was successful, and shortly afterwards was made deputy to Prime Minister Adami.

During his years at the social policy ministry, Gonzi is remembered for reforms to the industrial relations legislation, his zero-tolerance policy towards benefit fraud and for overseeing the restructuring of Malta's shipyards. In March 2003 Malta's population voted in favour of EU membership in a referendum, and the following month the NP was returned to power in a general election. Adami stepped down as NP leader in March 2004, and in the subsequent leadership contest, Gonzi emerged victorious. On 23 March 2004 he took office as prime minister (and minister of finance) of Malta.

Career Peak

In his first media briefing in April 2004, Prime Minister Gonzi announced his government's intention to adopt the euro 'when it is advantageous to Malta'. He also proposed to boost tourism (the nation's most important source of income), create favourable conditions for investment, restructure the public finances and improve Malta's competitiveness in the international market. In Nov. 2005 Gonzi hosted the Commonwealth Heads of Government Meeting (CHOGM). In Dec. 2007 his government signed the Lisbon treaty on streamlining the operation of the European Union and from 1 Jan. 2008 Malta adopted the single currency.

The NP won a third successive term by narrowly winning the popular vote in parliamentary elections in March 2008, with Gonzi being sworn in for a second prime ministerial term (but relinquishing the finance portfolio) on 11 March. In an address to the nation he said that his government would concentrate particularly on sustainable development, with an emphasis on the environment.

In April 2009 the Maltese government refused to accept 140 illegal African migrants aboard a cargo ship that had rescued them in rough waters near the island of Lampedusa, claiming that they were Italy's responsibility.

Entering the final year of his second term and in the wake of internal rifts within his Nationalist Party, Gonzi narrowly survived a parliamentary vote of confidence in June 2012. However, in Dec. his government was defeated on a budget vote and fell.

In Dec. 2012 Gonzi's government collapsed over negotiations on the following year's budget. In March 2013 the NP faced a crushing defeat at the general elections and Gonzi resigned from the party leadership.

Gorbachev, Mikhail (Russia)

Introduction

Mikhail Sergeyevich Gorbachev was leader of the Union of Soviet Socialist Republics from 1985–91. A reformer, he oversaw the democratization and modernization of the Soviet Union via his policies of *glasnost* ('openness') and *perestroika* ('restructuring'). His leadership led to the fall of communism throughout Eastern Europe and to the collapse of the Soviet Union in 1991.

Early Life

Gorbachev was born in Privolye in the Stravopol region of Russia on 2 March 1931. He became a member of the Young Communist League when he was 15 and worked as a machine operator before undertaking studies at Moscow State University. It was here in 1952 that he joined the Communist Party and 3 years later he earned a law degree. In 1956 he married Raisa Titorenko, whom he had met at the university.

In the coming years he held a number of party positions in Stavropol and in 1962 he began a 5 year correspondence course at the Stavropol Agricultural Institute. By 1970 he had been appointed 1st Secretary of the Stavropol Kraikom (the regional party committee) and a year later, at the 24th Party Congress, he was elected to the central committee of the Soviet Union. He progressed quickly within the party ranks during the 1970s and was a favourite of the influential Mikhail Suslov and Yuri Andropov.

Gorbachev was called to Moscow in 1978 and made secretary for agriculture. By Jan. 1979 he was officially 28th in the party hierarchy, by the end of the year he was a candidate member of the Politburo and by 1980 he had become a full member. Andropov was the party's general secretary between 1982 and 1984, with Gorbachev in close support. By the time Andropov's successor, Konstantin Chernenko, died in March 1985 it was little surprise that the upstart Gorbachev replaced him.

Career Peak

After initial economic and institutional reforms had failed to kickstart the Soviet economy, Gorbachev embarked on his policy of *glasnost*. As early as 1984 Gorbachev had spoken of *glasnost* as "a compulsory condition of socialist democracy and a norm for public life." Now it brought greatly extended cultural freedoms, including freedom of the press, and led to official rejection of Stalinist-style totalitarianism. *Glasnost* went hand in hand with *perestroika* and set in motion an overhaul of the political system, with electoral processes made more democratic and some free-market principles introduced into the economy.

Such reforms were bound to meet with hard-line opposition and Gorbachev set about changing communist party mechanisms in response. Between autumn 1988 and spring 1989, a new 2–house parliament (the Soviet Congress of People's Deputies) was established. It voted in a new Supreme Soviet that had more practical powers than previously and Gorbachev was installed at its head.

On the international scene great changes were afoot and Gorbachev was at the forefront. From the beginning of his leadership he had sought closer economic and political ties with both the East and West. He reduced military spending, embarked on mutual policies of nuclear disarmament with the US and withdrew troops from Afghanistan in 1989. Throughout 1989 and 1990 Gorbachev gave vocal support to the reforms sweeping through the Eastern bloc and as one communist regime after another began to fall he refused to intervene. As new governments came to power throughout the region he gave permission for the phased withdrawal of Soviet forces and in 1990 he agreed to the unification of the 2 Germanies. In that same year he received the Nobel Peace Prize.

During the same period there was increased unrest among the Soviet republics. Gorbachev left the military on alert while plans were made for the republics to withdraw peacefully and legally from the USSR. Political and constitutional reforms continued apace and in March 1991 Gorbachev was elected President of the USSR. He was the first and only man to hold the post. A short while later the law was changed so that opposition parties were permitted within the state. Over the coming months Gorbachev's refusal to sanction further economic reforms and his reluctance to move towards a privatization programme left the economy struggling. This in conjunction with the powerful enemies he had made through his reforms provided the circumstances for an attempted hard-line coup in Aug. 1991. Gorbachev was put under house arrest for 3 days and though the coup was ended, largely owing to Russian President Yeltsin's intervention, Gorbachev's leadership was existing on borrowed time. In quick succession Gorbachev resigned his party membership, dismantled the central committee and took KGB and military control away from the communists. On Christmas Day in 1991 he resigned as Soviet President and the Soviet Union itself was replaced by the Yeltsin-led Commonwealth of Independent States.

Later Life

Gorbachev has retained a presence on the international stage since his fall from power. His *Gorbachev Foundation* is an international institute specializing in socio-economic and political studies and he has also established *Green Cross International*, a non-governmental environmental organization. He has remained politically active with the *Civic Forum* movement and he ran for the Russian Presidency in 1996. Though he finished a distant 7th, Gorbachev's role in the cataclysmic years of the late 1980s and early 1990s has ensured his international standing.

Gottwald, Klement (Czech Republic)

Introduction

Klement Gottwald was the Communist President of Czechoslovakia from 1948 until his death in 1953, having previously held the positions of Prime Minister and Deputy Prime Minister. A hard-liner and staunch Stalinist, his rule was punctuated by purges of his enemies. His death preceded a short period of liberalization in Czechoslovakia but his rule ensured that his country remained a Soviet satellite state.

Early Life

Gottwald was born in Dedice, Moravia (then part of the Austro-Hungarian Empire and now located in the Czech Republic) on 23 Nov. 1896. He went to Vienna as a 12 year old to work as an apprentice to a carpenter before leaving to serve on the Eastern Front during World War I. Having deserted to Russia he returned to the recently established state of Czechoslovakia and was instrumental in setting up the Czechoslovakian Communist Party (KSC) 3 years later.

After a period of editing the party newspaper he was elected to the KSC Central Committee in 1925. From 1928 onwards he served on the executive committee of Comintern and in 1929 he became Secretary General of the KSC, immediately setting about putting the party at the disposal of Stalin. When in 1938 Germany began its occupation of Czechoslovakian territory, Gottwald fled to Moscow, once again editing a communist publication and retaining contact with the underground in his homeland. In late 1943 he met with Czechoslovakia's exiled President Edvard Beneš and returned to Prague in the aftermath of World War II to act as Deputy Prime Minister in Beneš's government.

Career Peak

In 1946 Gottwald was made Chairman of the KSC and, following general elections in which the Communists won 38% of the vote, he was installed as head of a coalition government. A falling out with Stalin occurred in 1947 after Gottwald accepted US aid via the Marshall Plan. By 1948 the KSC was not in an electorally strong position. Gottwald tried to force Beneš to accept a Communist-dominated parliament but Beneš, refusing to cave into the demands, instead resigned the presidency on 7 June 1948. A week later Gottwald took his place.

He embarked on the systematic Stalinization of the economy and society at large, until the Communist party came to dominate all elements of the country's life. From 1950 onwards he began purges of his enemies, the most notable of which was in Dec. 1952 when the Interior Minister, Rudolf Slansky, and 11 of his supporters were executed. In total around 180 executions, preceded by party show trials, were carried out during Gottwald's tenure. On 9 March 1953 Gottwald visited Moscow to attend the funeral of his mentor Stalin. Afflicted by the inclement weather, Gottwald developed pneumonia and died back in Prague on 14 March.

Gouled Aptidon, Hassan (Djibouti)

Introduction

Hassan Gouled Aptidon was Djibouti's first president, ruling the country from independence in 1977 until 1999. He was credited with reconciling rival clans to achieve regional stability.

Early Life

Hassan Gouled Aptidon was born on 15 Oct. 1916 to a family of Issa nomads in Garissa, in the Lughaya district of French Somaliland (now Djibouti). At the age of 14 he left home and worked as a street trader. He went on to serve in the French national assembly and the French senate, before returning home to become minister of education, a post he held from 1963–67. He served as prime minister from May–June 1977.

Gouled was a leading figurehead in the independence movement. After a split with France was rejected in a referendum in 1967, the result was reversed in a further referendum 10 years later and the independent Republic of Djibouti was inaugurated on 27 June 1977, with Gouled as president.

Career Peak

In 1981 Gouled made the Issa-dominated People's Rally for Progress (RPP) the country's only legal political party. He was elected to the presidency without opposition in June 1981 and returned again unopposed in elections in 1987. His authoritarian rule fuelled resentment among Djibouti's Afar community and in 1991 the country descended into civil war between the government and the Afar rebel group, the Front for the Restoration of Unity and Democracy (FRUD). Gouled negotiated a cease-fire. Multiparty elections, albeit with only four parties, were introduced in 1992.

He also served as a mediator between warring neighbours in the Horn of Africa and was instrumental in founding the Intergovernmental Authority on Drought and Development (IGADD) in 1985. As chairman of IGADD, he helped renew diplomatic relations between Ethiopia and Somalia.

In 1997 Gouled was elected for a fifth presidential term but in April 1999 ill health compelled him to step down. In elections that month, his nephew, Ismail Omar Guelleh, won 74% of the vote and was sworn in as his uncle's successor in May.

Gouled died in the capital city of Djibouti on 21 Nov. 2006.

Gowon, Yakubu (Nigeria)

Introduction

Yakubu Gowon became the leader of the Federal Military Government following a countercoup in June 1966. He played an important role in the ending of the Biafra civil war.

Early Life

Gowon was born on 19 Oct. 1934, the son of a missionary from a small Northern Region tribe, the Angas. After his schooling in Nigeria, he enrolled in the Nigerian Army and was sent to the Regular Officers' Special Training School in Ghana. He then received training at the Royal Military Academy Sandhurst in England between 1955–6. He served in the Congo twice and in 1963 he was appointed adjutant-general of the Nigerian army. Gowon did not play a major part in the countercoup of 1966 but was chosen as a compromise candidate to lead the government.

Career Peak

Promises of a return to civilian rule failed to come to fruition and in 1967 Gowon declared a state of emergency, restructuring Nigeria's four regions into 12 states. The Eastern Region responded by declaring independence as the state of Biafra. 3 years of civil war followed, after which Gowon pursued an enlightened policy of 'no victor, no vanquished'. Despite a growing international reputation, his government was tainted by corruption and economic mismanagement. He was overthrown in a bloodless military coup in July 1975 while attending a meeting in Uganda.

Later Life

Following his overthrow, Gowon went into exile in Great Britain.

Grímsson, Ólafur Ragnar (Iceland)

Introduction

Ólafur Ragnar Grímsson was leader of the People's Alliance until becoming president in 1996. Observers feared his background would politicize the presidency, which is traditionally a non-partisan, ceremonial post, but he enjoyed broad popular support and retained the office in 2000, 2004, 2008 and 2012.

Early Life

Grímsson was born on 14 May 1943 in Ísafjörður. He studied economics and political science at Manchester University in the UK, graduating with a doctorate in 1970. He took up a lecturing post at the University of Iceland and was appointed professor in 1973. From 1966 until 1973 he was on the board of the youth wing of the Progressive Party and between 1971 and 1973 he sat on the party's executive board.

He moved to the People's Alliance and was elected to the *Alþingi* (Parliament) in 1978 as a member for Reykjavík. From 1980 until 1983,

when he failed to win re-election to parliament, Grímsson led the People's Alliance in the *Alþingi*. During 1987–96 he was party chairman and between 1988–91 served as the minister of finance. Between 1984–90 he held senior posts with Parliamentarians for Global Action, an international organization with a membership of 1,800 throughout the world. Grímsson also held positions in the Council of Europe during the 1980s and 1990s.

In 1995 he led the People's Alliance to a poor showing at the polls, in which they secured less than 15% of the vote. Shortly afterwards Grímsson announced his candidacy for the presidency at the following year's elections. In June 1996 he was elected with 41% of the vote, defeating three other candidates.

Career Peak

The presidency is a largely ceremonial office and Grímsson's election prompted some observers to fear he would politicize the position. His relationship with the then prime minister, Davíð Oddsson, had been poor ever since the two had clashed as leaders of rival parties. Nevertheless, Grímsson was reappointed as president for a second term (without an election as there were no opposing candidates) and then re-elected by popular vote on 26 June 2004 with nearly 86% of the poll. During his presidency Grímsson has used his international profile to vigorously promote Iceland and its industrial potential, particularly in emerging sectors such as information technology. His reappointment in Aug. 2008 was unopposed.

In Dec. 2009 the *Alþingi* narrowly passed legislation to reimburse the UK and the Netherlands governments for bailing out British and Dutch depositors in Icesave, an Internet operation owned by the failed Icelandic bank Landsbanki. Grímsson, however, refused to sign the law and in a national referendum in March 2010 a majority rejected the measure and settlement negotiations continued. In Dec. 2010 new reimbursement legislation was proposed, including better repayment terms for Iceland, and was passed by the *Alþingi* in Feb. 2011. However, Grímsson again refused to sign the measure, leading to a further referendum and another voter rejection in April that year. In June 2012 he was elected for a record fifth presidential term.

In April 2016 Prime Minister Sigmundur Davíð Gunnlaugsson, who had been elected in 2013, was ensnared in revelations by investigative journalists about the secret offshore financial holdings of prominent international figures. Having unsuccessfully sought Grímsson's dissolution of the *Alþingi*, Gunnlaugsson resigned as premier and was replaced by Sigurður Ingi Jóhannsson, also of the Progressive Party.

Having announced that he would not run for a sixth term in office, Grímsson was replaced by the winner of the June 2016 presidential election Guðni Jóhannesson.

Grindeanu, Sorin (Romania)

Introduction

Sorin Grindeanu of the Social Democratic Party (PSD) was sworn in as prime minister on 4 Jan. 2017, at the head of a coalition with the Alliance of Liberals and Democrats.

Early Life

Grindeanu was born on 5 Dec. 1973 in Caransebeş and graduated from the mathematics and computer science faculty at the University of Timişoara West in 1997. He then undertook further studies in Germany, Portugal and the UK.

In Nov. 1996 he became a member of the PSD. He held several positions at the University of Timişoara West between 1998 and 2001, while also holding senior roles in the PSD youth organization in Timiş. From 2001–04 he was the director of the Timiş County youth and sports department and from 2005–08 he had senior management posts in two private companies.

Having sat on Timişoara's local council since 2004, in June 2008 Grindeanu became the city's deputy mayor and remained in office until Jan. 2013. After entering parliament in 2012, he was elected deputy secretary general of the PSD in 2013 and served as minister of communications and the information society from 2014–15. In June 2016 he was elected president of the Timiş County Council.

At the general election of Dec. 2016 the PSD won the most seats and initially nominated Sevil Shhaideh to be prime minister, but she was rejected by President Klaus Iohannis. Grindeanu was subsequently proposed as an alternative candidate by PSD leader Liviu Dragnea on 28 Dec., and Iohannis confirmed the selection two days later.

Career Peak

Grindeanu took office on the back of an electoral victory secured on promised increases in spending on healthcare, wages and pensions. In Feb. 2017 there were widespread protests—the largest since the fall of communism—when the government proposed decriminalizing most forms of official corruption. Grindeanu responded by attempting to reassure both the domestic and international community that his government took anti-corruption measures seriously.

On 15 June 2017 after the PSD withdrew its support of Grindeanu on grounds of disagreement on foreign policy matters, the ministers of his cabinet resigned. Grindeanu, however, refused to step down and remained in office until 21 June when the Parliament officially removed him with the vote of a motion of no-confidence. A week later he was replaced by Mihai Tudose.

Gromyko, Andrei Andreyevich (Russia)

Introduction

Soviet foreign minister from 1957–85, Andrei Gromyko served under the successive leaderships of Khrushchev, Brezhnev and Gorbachev before being made president of the Supreme Soviet. During his long tenure he was involved in many of the key events of Soviet history. A powerful negotiator and leading Soviet diplomat, he helped calm the Cuban Missile Crisis, implemented the policy of détente with the West and was significant in setting up the SALT treaties.

Early Life

Gromyko was born on 18 July 1909 in Starye Gromyki, Belarus (then part of the Tsarist Russian Empire). After studying agriculture at the Institute of Economics in Minsk, during which time he joined the Communist Party, he continued to work at the Institute from 1936–39. He began his diplomatic career in 1939 joining the Soviet Embassy in Washington, DC. In 1943 he became the Soviet ambassador to the US, attending the Tehran, Yalta and Potsdam conferences at the end of World War II.

In 1946 he was made deputy foreign minister and deputy of the Supreme Soviet. At the same time he became a UN representative, going on to use his power of veto 25 times. From 1952–53 he had a short spell as ambassador to Britain before being made Soviet foreign minister in 1957.

Career Peak

Over the next three decades Gromyko was involved in all aspects of Soviet diplomacy, representing the governments of Nikita Khrushchev, Leonid Brezhnev, Yuri Andropov, Konstantin Chernenko and Mikhail Gorbachev. Under Khrushchev he was a key negotiator in the 1962 Cuban Missile Crisis, offering assurance to US president Kennedy of the defensive nature of the Soviet missiles and securing Khrushchev's agreement to remove nuclear missiles in exchange for America's non-aggression towards Cuba. As part of Brezhnev's government he joined the Politburo in 1973. During the 1970s he pursued the policy of détente, facilitating a rapprochement with the West. This included a non-aggression pact with West Germany and the meeting between Brezhnev and Richard Nixon which resulted in the SALT I treaty that curbed the development of certain nuclear projects. Although US–Russian relations soured towards the end of the decade with the Soviet invasion of Afghanistan and the failure of either side to ratify SALT II.

Gromyko retained his position throughout the short tenures of Andropov and Chernenko and was made first deputy chairman of the council of ministers in 1983. When Gorbachev came to power in 1985, Gromyko was appointed to the largely ceremonial role of chairman of the presidium. He was replaced as foreign minister by Eduard Shevardnadze, later the president of Georgia.

Later Life

Gromyko was part of a dying breed of Soviet politicians. During his 3 years as chairman Gorbachev was implementing his policies of *glasnost* and *perestroika* paving the way for the break up of the Soviet Union. 3 years later Gromyko was a victim of Gorbachev's regime overhaul and ousted along with many old members. He was forced to tender his resignation and his Politburo seat. Gorbachev replaced him as chairman. The following year Gromyko was expelled from the Central Committee. He died on 2 July 1989 in Moscow.

Gross, Stanislav (Czech Republic)

Introduction

Completing a meteoric rise through the ranks of his party, Stanislav Gross was appointed Czech prime minister on 26 July 2004. The former railway technician and train driver became, at the age of 34, the youngest prime minister in Europe. Once described as the 'crown prince' of the Czech Social Democratic Party (ČSSD), Gross was expected to use his slick negotiating skills to rebuild the splintered leading coalition and pursue economic reforms to encourage businesses and cut unemployment. However, he was soon beset by allegations of financial impropriety and resigned his position in April 2005.

Early Life

Stanislav Gross was born in a working-class district of Prague on 30 Oct. 1969. After primary school, he attended a vocational secondary school that combined basic schooling with an apprenticeship as a train driver and mechanic at Prague's Vršovice railway depot. He then did 2 years' military service in the province of Olomouc, before joining the social democrats in 1989, the year of the collapse of the Communist party and the 'velvet revolution' that culminated in the election as president of the playwright and former dissident, Václav Havel. In 1990 Gross became leader of the ČSSD's youth wing, gaining a seat on the party executive in 1992. At this time, reforms to the Czechoslovak economy were leading to hardship, particularly in the east of the country. A strong separatist movement in Slovakia led eventually to the formal split of the Czech and Slovak republics into independent states on 1 Jan. 1993. Later in 1993, Gross joined the Czech Republic's new parliament in Prague. Václav Klaus headed the right-of-centre coalition government. Gross began a law degree at Prague's Charles University in 1993, combining study with his work as an MP, although questions over the veracity of the degree (awarded in 1999) rumble on.

Gross moved quickly through the party ranks, becoming chief whip in 1995 and deputy chairman of the parliament in 1998, the year in which Václav Havel was re-elected president. Miloš Zeman led the ČSSD to its first victory in the ensuing legislative elections, promising to prevent a repeat of the 1997 economic downturn and vowing to slow privatization and restore state control. On 4 April 2000 Gross was appointed minister of the interior, where he became known for his hard-line approach to law and order, organizing crackdowns on traffic violators and brothel owners. Gross reportedly employed many police officials who were graduates of the pre-1989 communist police schools. At the ČSSD party congress in 2001 Gross was elected vice-chairman. He was appointed deputy to prime minister Vladimír Špidla on 15 July 2002, following ČSSD's victory in the national elections with 30% of the vote. Špidla headed a three-party coalition that included the centrist Christian Democratic Union-Czechoslovak People's Party (KDU-ČSL) and the right-of-centre Freedom Union, but splits soon emerged, both in the coalition and within the ČSSD. Gross and other ČSSD 'pragmatists' became frustrated with what they saw as the slow pace of public finance reforms. Following a disastrous showing for ČSSD in the Czech Republic's first European Parliament elections, the coalition collapsed and Špidla resigned on 26 June 2004.

Career Peak

President Václav Klaus swiftly appointed Gross prime minister and charged him with forming a government. Living up to his reputation as a skilled negotiator, Gross succeeded in rebuilding the three-way coalition to recover its parliamentary majority. He appeared to have reconciled the Freedom

Union's desire for deeper and faster reforms to public spending and the welfare state with the more centrist and socially-oriented priorities of the KDU-ČSL and the leftist elements of his own party. Gross appeared regularly in the Czech and international media, but little detail about his vision for the country emerged, other than a promise that the government would be 'energetic' and would aim to boost economic growth, cut unemployment and tackle the budget deficit.

In 2005 Gross was the subject of allegations about his personal finances, particularly concerning the financing of an apartment he owned in Prague. In March 2005 the Christian Democrats left the ruling coalition, leaving Gross as head of a minority government. He survived a vote of no confidence after the Communists abstained but the scandal rolled on and he resigned on 25 April 2005.

Guebuza, Armando (Mozambique)

Introduction

Armando Guebuza, a veteran of Mozambique's fight for independence and one of the nation's wealthiest businessmen, was chosen as the ruling party's candidate for the 2004 presidential elections. Having won a large majority, he took office in Feb. 2005 and was re-elected for a second term in Oct. 2009, remaining in office until Jan. 2015.

Early Life

Armando Emílio Guebuza was born on 20 Jan. 1943 in Murrupula, in the northern province of Nampula. Politically active from an early age, he was elected in 1963 as president of the Mozambican Centre of African Students, a group created by Eduardo Mondlane, then the leader of Mozambique's fight for independence from Portugal. Later that year Guebuza joined the Liberation Front of Mozambique (FRELIMO) and in 1965 was elected to the organization's central and executive committees. Having undergone military training in Tanzania, Guebuza was involved in guerrilla fighting against the Portuguese administration in northern Mozambique. Following Mondlane's assassination in 1969, FRELIMO was led by Uria Simango and then Samora Machel. Under Machel it grew to include over 7,000 guerrillas and by the early 1970s had control over much of northern and central Mozambique. Guebuza became a general and was also an inspector of the schools run by FRELIMO.

When Marcello Caetano was overthrown in a military coup in Portugal on 25 April 1974, independence was assured for Mozambique. Following the signing of the Lusaka Agreements later in 1974, Guebuza was appointed to the transitional government that led the country to full independence in June 1975. He then served as minister of the interior in the single-party Marxist government led by President Machel. Guebuza was responsible for implementing the notorious '20–24' decree, which gave Portuguese settlers 24 h to leave the country, carrying a maximum of 20 kg of luggage. He went on to serve as vice minister of defence in 1980, against a backdrop of warfare with the Mozambican National Resistance (RENAMO), which was backed by the apartheid government in South Africa. While Guebuza was again minister of the interior (1983–85) he was heavily identified with the forcible resettlement of unemployed residents of Maputo and Beira to work-camps in the isolated northern province of Niassa.

Joaquim Chissano became president in 1986, following Machel's death in an aircraft crash, and Guebuza was appointed minister of transport. In 1990 he headed the FRELIMO government's delegation to negotiations with RENAMO, leading to the signing of the Rome Peace Agreement in Oct. 1992. Having formally renounced Marxism in 1989, the government set about developing a market-oriented economy with Guebuza spearheading many of the reforms. He developed business interests in many sectors, including brewing, investment banking and shipping. In the country's first multi-party elections in 1994, won by FRELIMO, Guebuza was elected head of its parliamentary group. He retained that position in the elections of 1999, when Joaquim Chissano again led FRELIMO to victory.

Chissano announced that he would stand down at the 2004 elections. During FRELIMO's national congress in 2002, Guebuza was elected the party's secretary-general and presidential candidate. His uncompromising nationalist stance and promise to continue the economic reforms of his predecessor won him a large majority in the presidential polling in Dec. 2004 (with 63.7% of the vote), although RENAMO alleged electoral fraud. In parliamentary elections at the same time FRELIMO retained its majority in the National Assembly.

Career Peak

Guebuza was sworn in as president on 2 Feb. 2005, pledging to fight poverty, tackle corruption and seek further foreign investment to build infrastructure. In mid-2005 a trade and investment agreement was signed with the USA, whose officials cited Mozambique as 'a positive model because of its impressive track record on democracy, political stability, economic growth, openness to foreign direct investment and expanding exports'. In July 2006 the World Bank cancelled most of the country's debt under a scheme backed by the major industrialized nations.

Guebuza and FRELIMO increased their respective vote shares in the presidential and parliamentary elections in Oct. 2009, although RENAMO again disputed the results. In Sept. 2010 there were riots in Maputo and other cities over food price rises and several people were killed as police fired on protesters.

In Sept. 2012 Guebuza was re-elected as head of FRELIMO. In a surprise cabinet reshuffle a month later, he dismissed Aires Ali as prime minister after only 9 months in the post and replaced him with Alberto Vaquina, previously a provincial governor.

Renewed military and political friction between the government and RENAMO through 2013 led to the latter's announcement in Oct. that it was abandoning the 1992 peace accord, prompting fears of a return to civil war.

Guebuza was succeeded as president by the winner of the Oct. 2014 elections, Felipe Nyusi (also of FRELIMO). Since the constitution does not permit three successive terms, Guebuza did not contest the election.

Guevara, Ernesto 'Che' (Cuba)

Introduction

Argentine-born Ernesto Guevara, commonly known as El Che or Che, was a key figure in the success of the Cuban Revolution in 1959 and subsequently a member of the government of Fidel Castro. His exploits in Cuba and engagement with revolutionary guerrilla movements across South America and Africa contributed to his status as a counter-cultural icon.

Early Life

Ernesto Guevara, the eldest of five children, was born on 14 June 1928 in Rosario, Argentina, to a middle-class family of Spanish and Irish descent. Exposed to politically-leftist thought from an early age by his father (who was an ardent supporter of the Republican side during the Spanish Civil War), the young Guevara developed an interest in Marxism. This was reinforced by his experiences travelling in South America as a student doctor, where he witnessed the extreme poverty faced by much of the population.

Convinced that armed struggle represented the only solution to the region's problems, he joined Cuba's revolutionary 26th of July Movement after meeting the organization's leader, Fidel Castro, while in Mexico in 1955.

Career Peak

Guevara played a key role in Castro's war against the Cuban dictator, Fulgencio Batista, both as a military leader and political ideologist, galvanizing Cuba's population against the US-backed regime. Following over 2 years of guerrilla warfare against the Cuban army and police, Batista was overthrown in Jan. 1959. Castro was elected prime minister the next month. Guevara was subsequently appointed president of the National Bank of Cuba and also served as minister of industries from 1961–65, during which time he championed nationalization, planned extensive land redistribution reforms and ran a nationwide literacy campaign. He also advocated allegiance to the Soviet Union—a move that caused the USA to freeze diplomatic relations with Cuba, which were only fully re-established in 2015. Cuba was also subjected to a longstanding US trade embargo that crippled its economy.

By 1964 Guevara had established himself on the world stage, travelling internationally as an ambassador for Cuba. His status as a revolutionary statesman was sealed with a speech to the United Nations in 1964, in which he criticized the apartheid structure in South Africa and the USA's treatment of its own black population. In 1965 Guevara resigned from his positions in the Cuban government and left the country to spread the revolutionary message to other parts of the developing world.

Later Life

Guevara travelled initially to the Congo, where he spent several months training rebel forces in guerrilla warfare and Marxist ideology. However, after becoming disillusioned with the rebel leadership, he secretly entered Bolivia in Nov. 1966 in order to lead a rebellion against President René Barrientos. Like Batista, Barrientos was supported by the USA and had risen to power following a CIA-backed coup in 1964. Guevara was, however, captured by the Bolivian army in Oct. 1967 and executed by firing squad shortly after.

His remains were discovered in 1997 and returned to Cuba where he was laid to rest in a purpose-built mausoleum in Santa Clara. Although Guevara's legacy continues to divide opinion, he is the enduring symbol of the quintessential revolutionary.

Gül, Abdullah (Turkey)

Introduction

Abdullah Gül was elected president on 28 Aug. 2007. His background in Islamist politics and membership of political parties banned under the country's secular constitution stoked widespread concern when he was nominated as a presidential candidate. A former prime minister and close ally of the incumbent premier, Recep Tayyip Erdoğan, Gül has taken a moderate line since 2001, advocating a pro-Western agenda and eventual EU membership.

Early Life

Abdullah Gül was born on 29 Oct. 1950 in Kayseri. He graduated in economics from İstanbul University in 1971 and began an academic career. From 1980–83 he taught economics at the Sakarya School of Engineering and Architecture. As a devout Muslim, and having received a PhD in 1983, he joined the Islamic Development Bank (in Jeddah, Saudi Arabia) as an economist.

Returning to Turkey in 1991, Gül entered politics. Campaigning for the Islamist Welfare Party, he was elected representative for Kayseri. He rose through the party ranks to become state minister and speaker for the government of Necmettin Erbakan in 1996. He was initially critical of Turkey's overtures towards the West and opposed EU membership. His ambitions were curtailed in 1997 by a military-backed campaign to oust the government. The following year a ban was imposed on the Welfare Party which was said to threaten the secular constitution. Gül joined the Virtue Party, contesting its leadership in 2000, but this party was also banned in June 2001.

In Aug. 2001 Gül joined Recep Tayyip Erdoğan's newly formed Justice and Development Party (AKP), which presented itself as pro-Western and democratic. In the 2002 parliamentary elections Erdoğan was barred from standing because he had a criminal conviction for reading an Islamic poem at a political rally. Nevertheless, the AKP attracted voters dissatisfied with the ruling government and won an outright victory to replace the three-party coalition. Two weeks after the election the party nominated Gül for the premiership.

Career Peak

As prime minister, Gül wanted to prove that Turkey could operate as both a Muslim and democratic state, and was committed to steering Turkey towards EU membership. He announced plans to reform the laws on the freedom of expression and human rights, supported further privatization and sought to achieve a modernized and efficient public administration.

In Dec. 2002 President Ahmet Necdet Sezer agreed to constitutional changes that would allow Erdoğan to stand for a parliamentary seat and thus become eligible for the premiership. Erdoğan returned to parliament in a by-election in March 2003 and was appointed prime minister. Gül became foreign minister, working to achieve an EU accession date, although this was thwarted by the continued impasse over the status of Cyprus.

Prime Minister Erdoğan announced in April 2007 that Gül would be the AKP candidate in the 2007 presidential election. This sparked Turkey's most serious political crisis in a decade, with mass protests in the big cities in support of secularism. The military also warned that it would defend secularism. The AKP was forced to call early elections for 22 July, which it won decisively. Gül was re-nominated as the AKP candidate and on 28 Aug. he was elected president in the third round of voting. The chief of the general staff absented himself from the swearing-in ceremony.

In his inauguration speech, Gül sought to dispel secularist fears of an AKP Islamist agenda. However, parliament's vote to remove the ban on women wearing headscarves at universities in Feb. 2008 was seized on by secularists as evidence that Gül was attempting to introduce Islamic rule. In June the Constitutional Court rejected the move in a ruling that was viewed as a setback for the AKP government.

In July 2009 Gül approved controversial government legislation allowing civilian courts to prosecute military personnel for offences against the state. Then in Aug. 2011, after Turkey's top military leadership had resigned en masse in a dispute over promotions, he moved quickly to appoint replacements and assert civilian control over the powerful and traditionally secular armed forces.

Gül continued to court controversy towards the twilight years of his mandate by supporting a number of laws that opposition groups regarded as unconstitutional. Increased restrictions on freedom of speech and the press led also to a spate of demonstrations and civil unrest around the country that eventually courted international attention during the Taksim Gezi Park sit-in of May–June 2013.

Gül's 7 year term as president came to an end on 28 Aug. 2014 when he was succeeded by prime minister Recep Tayyip Erdoğan—the first directly appointed president in Turkey's history.

Gunnlaugsson, Sigmundur Davíð (Iceland)

Introduction

Sigmundur Davíð Gunnlaugsson was sworn in as prime minister on 23 May 2013. Chairman of the liberal Progressive Party, he was 38 when elected to power, making him one of the world's youngest heads of government.

Early Life

Gunnlaugsson was born in Reykjavík on 12 March 1975. His father was a prominent businessman and chairman of Icelandair, the country's main airline. Gunnlaugsson graduated in business and economics from the University of Iceland before reading international relations and public administration at Copenhagen University. He earned his doctorate in economics and political science from the University of Oxford in England.

From 2000–07 he worked as a journalist at RUV, the Icelandic national broadcaster. He was elected to the Alþingi for the Reykjavík North constituency in April 2009, having become chairman of the Progressive Party earlier in the year. He was appointed to the parliamentary foreign affairs committee and in 2010 joined the EU–Iceland joint parliamentary committee.

His popular standing was boosted by the European Free Trade Association's ruling in Jan. 2013 that Iceland did not break European law by refusing to compensate foreign depositors after the collapse of the privately-owned Icelandic bank, Landsbanki, in 2008. The Progressive Party had opposed a negotiated settlement with the UK and the Netherlands in favour of taking the matter to court. Its stance was resoundingly supported in a national referendum. EFTA's decision saved the government hundreds of millions of euros.

In the general election of 27 April 2013 the Progressive Party gained 24.4% of the vote against 26.7% for the Independence Party, but both won 19 seats. Gunnlaugsson had campaigned on a promise to force foreign creditors of Iceland's collapsed banks to return a portion of the profits accruing from the credit, which would then be used to write down household mortgages.

In compliance with the preference of President Ólafur Ragnar Grímsson and following the Progressive Party's impressive gains in the general election—they had only won nine seats at the 2009 elections compared to 16 for the Independence Party—Gunnlaugsson was asked to form a government. He became prime minister of a centre-right coalition with the Independence Party leader, Bjarni Benediktsson, becoming minister of finance and economic affairs.

Career Peak

Eurosceptic in outlook, Gunnlaugsson's coalition government decided in Sept. 2013 to suspend indefinitely Iceland's negotiations, which had begun in 2010, to become a member of the European Union. Then in Feb. 2014 the government said that it would withdraw its membership application altogether, without holding a referendum on the issue. In March 2015 the government confirmed that it no longer regarded Iceland as an EU candidate country despite the protests of opposition parties. In June 2015 parliament approved measures to gradually dismantle the capital controls in place since the financial crisis in 2008.

Gunnlaugsson resigned as prime minister on 7 April following the release of the 'Panama Papers'—a set of leaked documents from Panamanian law firm Mossack Fonseca detailing client information for over 200,000 offshore companies—revealing that Gunnlaugsson's family had sheltered money in overseas accounts. Sigurður Ingi Jóhannsson, also of the Progressive Party, took over as prime minister.

Gusenbauer, Alfred (Austria)

Introduction

Alfred Gusenbauer became Austrian chancellor on 11 Jan. 2007. He was leader of the Social Democratic Party (SPÖ) and led an SPÖ–ÖVP (Austrian People's Party) coalition. The coalition collapsed in July 2008, a month after Gusenbauer was replaced as party leader. The SPÖ won the general election and another SPÖ–ÖVP coalition was formed, under the chancellorship of new SPÖ leader Werner Faymann.

Early Life

Alfred Gusenbauer was born on 8 Feb. 1960 in St Pölten, capital of the northern state of Lower Austria. After high school he studied science, philosophy and jurisprudence at the University of Vienna. In 1987 he obtained a doctorate in political science. Gusenbauer was politically active during university and joined the SPÖ's Young Socialists in support of the disarmament movement. From 1984–90 he was the group's federal leader, also serving as vice-president of Socialist Youth International from 1985–89. In 1989 he became Socialist International leader.

Gusenbauer was a senior research fellow in the economic policy department of the Lower Austria chamber of labour from 1990–99. In 1991 he was elected SPÖ chairman in Ybbs an der Donau and became Lower Austria's representative in the federal council (Bundesrat). In the same year he was a member of the Austrian delegation to the parliamentary meeting of the Council of Europe and from 1995–98 he served as chairman of the Council's social committee. He was chairman of the Bundesrat committee for development co-operation from 1996–99.

In 2000 the SPÖ elected Gusenbauer as its secretary-general. Under his leadership the SPÖ improved its vote in the 2002 elections but lost to Wolfgang Schüssel's ÖVP. In 2006 Gusenbauer and the SPÖ suffered public discredit for its links to the BAWAG scandal, in which directors of an Austrian bank owned by an SPÖ-linked trade union were accused of corruption, embezzlement and illicit speculation. In the run-up to the 2006 elections polls put the ÖVP ahead but the SPÖ emerged victorious, though unable to form a workable government. Gusenbauer thus negotiated an SPÖ–ÖVP 'grand coalition'.

Career Peak

Under the terms of the coalition, Gusenbauer was forced to abandon several high profile pre-election pledges including the scrapping of university tuition fees and the cancellation of a €2 bn. contract for 18 Eurofighter jets. Gusenbauer's term began amid student demonstrations and some dissent from within his own party.

Key government plans included lowering the voting age from 18 to 16 and extending future parliamentary tenures from 4 to 5 years. Gusenbauer pledged to increase spending by up to €1 bn. per year to 2010 on welfare, infrastructure, research and education, while aiming to reverse the budget deficit. He reiterated Austrian support for the European integration of the former Yugoslav countries but was sceptical towards Turkey's bid for full EU membership.

With the SPÖ beset by infighting over Gusenbauer's ability to lead the party, a leadership contest was held in June 2008. Gusenbauer was replaced as party leader by Werner Faymann. A month later the ÖVP resigned from the governing coalition, forcing Gusenbauer to call a snap election for Sept. The SPÖ emerged as the largest party but with weakened support. A new SPÖ–ÖVP took office in Dec. 2008, with Faymann as chancellor.

Gusmão, Xanana (Timor-Leste)

Introduction

Independent Timor-Leste's first president, Xanana Gusmão, having led the independence movement for over two decades, came to power in a landslide victory at elections in April 2002. He stood down in May 2007 but was subsequently appointed prime minister in Aug. that year.

Early Life

Xanana Gusmão was born José Alexandre Gusmão on 20 June 1946 in Laleia, Manatuto. After studying at a Jesuit seminary in Soibada and then at Dare, he became a civil servant.

He joined FRETILIN in 1974, becoming its leader in 1978. In 1981 he was elected commander-in-chief of its military wing and worked to integrate the various groups fighting for independence.

In Nov. 1992 he was captured by the Indonesian army and sentenced to life imprisonment on charges of subversion but remained the figurehead of the independence movement. Following an appeal from then UN Secretary-General Kofi Annan, Gusmão was released after the referendum of Sept. 1999 in which an overwhelming majority of Timorese voted for independence.

Timor-Leste gained independence on 20 May 2002 and Gusmão was inaugurated as president, having won a landslide victory in elections the previous month.

Career Peak

Gusmão appealed for reconciliation and an end of violence against those who opposed independence. The authority of the state and its institutions, however, remained fragile. In April 2006, 600 striking soldiers who had been sacked by Prime Minister Mari Alkatiri demonstrated in Dili. The protests turned into wider factional violence across the country and the government called in foreign troops led by Australia in May to restore law and order. At the same time, relations between president and prime minister broke down. In June Alkatiri stood down and was replaced by José Ramos-Horta. A UN peacekeeping mission was then set up in Aug. 2006.

Gusmão did not contest presidential elections held in April–May 2007, announcing his intention to run instead for prime minister as the leader of a new National Congress for Timorese Reconstruction (CNRT), having become disillusioned with FRETILIN. His close ally José Ramos-Horta succeeded him as president. Despite FRETILIN winning the largest number of seats in parliamentary elections in June 2007, Gusmão formed a coalition government and was sworn in as prime minister on 8 Aug. 2007.

Like then President Ramos-Horta, Gusmão was also targeted by rebel soldiers in Feb. 2008 in a separate attack, but was unhurt. He described the incident as a coup attempt and imposed a state of emergency.

In Oct. 2009 Gusmão's government survived an opposition vote of confidence in parliament over its controversial release of a pro-Indonesian militia leader accused of war crimes against Timorese citizens in 1999.

Acknowledging public concern over allegations of corruption against senior officials, in Feb. 2010 the government appointed the country's first anti-corruption commissioner.

In parliamentary elections in July 2012, the CNRT became the largest party with 30 seats, ahead of FRETILIN with 25.

In 2014 Timorese relations with Australia became increasingly fractious over spying allegations and a commercial dispute.

In Jan. 2014 Gusmão confirmed his intention to retire as premier in Sept. that year. However, he subsequently retracted his decision and was expected to remain in post until elections in 2017 when his term limit would have been reached but resigned as prime minister in Feb. 2015, with Rui Maria de Araújo taking over the premiership on 16 Feb. However, Gusmão remained in the government as minister of planning and strategic investment.

Guterres, António (Portugal)

Introduction

António Manuel de Oliveira Guterres was Portuguese prime minister between 1999–2002, representing the Partido Socialista (Socialist Party, PSP). On the centre-left, he was the first European leader to embrace 'new Socialism' at the end of the 1990s, an example followed by Tony Blair among others. A pro-European, Guterres led Portugal into the single currency in 1999. But heavy public spending with little evident reward cost the PSP heavily in local elections in Dec. 1999. Guterres resigned the premiership and his leadership of the PSP.

Early Life

Guterres was born on 30 April 1949 in Santos o Velho, Lisbon. Between 1966–72 he studied electronic engineering at the capital's Instituto Superior Técnico. A Catholic activist in the Juventude Universitária Católica (1968–72), Guterres took to politics during the revolution of 1974, when he joined the PSP. A participant in the post-revolution provisional governments, Guterres was elected to the Assembly in 1976 where he served in the ministry of economics and finance until 1979. A member of the Committee on European Integration, which negotiated Portugal's entry into the EU in 1986, he returned to domestic politics the following year, working to strengthen the PSP in opposition by adapting centrist policies. In 1992 he succeeded President Jorge Sampaio as leader of the PSP.

Career Peak

In the 1995 elections Guterres was elected prime minister with 43.9% of votes, ending 10 years of rule by the centre-right Partido Social Democrata (Social Democrats, PSD). Winning with a centrist manifesto, Guterres pledged to concentrate on social welfare, education and crime. He also planned a strict budgetary policy to prepare Portugal for the single currency. In his first term investment increased and public services and transport were improved. Unemployment fell to 5%. Portugal was accepted into the single currency in 1999.

In Oct. 1999 Guterres was re-elected prime minister with 44.1% of votes. The PSP's parliamentary seats increased from 112 to 115 but the party strength fell short of an absolute majority. Left-wing parties, including the Communists, also increased their representation. Following a 7 year term as vice president of the Socialist International, Guterres was elected chairman in Nov. of the same year, succeeding the former French prime minister, Pierre Mauroy. For his second term, Guterres maintained a tight budgetary policy, concentrating on health care, welfare, taxes and justice.

On an international level, the transition of Portugal's former colony Timor-Leste to self-government was hindered by attacks from Indonesian militia. A mass influx of refugees was coupled with anti-Indonesia demonstrations in Portugal. Guterres pledged a €264 m. aid package.

2000 was economically successful with a GDP increase of 3.5%. Unemployment was low as were interest rates, although inflation remained a worry. In 2000 a 10% increase in oil prices and concerns over rising crime levels led to public discontent. In Sept. the interior minister Fernando Gomes was sacked. Taking advantage of the government's weakness, the opposition mounted an unsuccessful no-confidence vote. Guterres refused early elections.

In the first half of 2000, Portugal took over the EU presidency. Guterres promoted the idea of labour mobility within the EU by setting minimum levels of academic competence in maths, foreign languages and technology. Plans for tax harmonization were discussed at a summit at Oporto in June. In 2001 Guterres called for more power for the European Commission and the European parliament.

Increased public spending caused economic problems. Opposition politicians criticized the €400 m. invested in the hosting of the Euro 2004 football tournament. In Dec. 2001 the PSD's success at the expense of the PSP led Guterres to resign as prime minister and to call early elections. In 2002 the PSD leader José Manuel Durão Barroso replaced him as prime minister.

Later Life

Guterres initially continued in his role as president of Socialist International but in June 2005 became the new High Commissioner for Refugees at the United Nations. In Oct. 2016 he was elected as Secretary-General of the United Nations, to take office at the beginning of 2017.

Gutiérrez, Lucío (Ecuador)

Introduction

A former army colonel and leader of a short lived coup in 2000, Lucío Edwin Gutiérrez Borbúa was elected president in Nov. 2002 on a leftwing populist agenda. Although politically inexperienced, his promises to tackle widespread poverty and corruption found favour with Ecuador's poor majority.

Early Life

Gutiérrez was born on 23 March 1957 in Quito. He spent his early years in Tena, Napo province, before joining the army at the age of 15. After graduating in 1977 from the Colegio Militar Eloy Alfaro (military college) in Quito, he studied civil engineering at the Escuela Politécnica del Ejército and later business administration. He rose to the rank of colonel.

Unknown to the public, Gutiérrez came onto the political scene in Jan. 2000 during popular protests against the government of President Jamil Mahuad. On 21 Jan. 2000 Gutiérrez joined forces with the Quechua leader Antonio Vargas Huatatoca to depose the president in a bloodless coup and form a junta government. Despite popular support for Vargas, and Gutiérrez's non-participation in the junta, international bodies were unhappy with the new government's military connection. Pressure from the UN, the OAS and neighbouring countries, forced Vargas to hand over power to a civilian leader just 5 h later. Mahuad's vice president Gustavo Noboa was chosen to see out the president's term.

Gutiérrez was subsequently imprisoned for 6 months for his role in the coup and dismissed from the army. On his release he began campaigning for presidential elections. He founded the Sociedad Patriótica 21 de Enero (21 Jan. Patriotic Society) which found support with the indigenous party, Pachacutik, and other leftwing groups. In his campaign he highlighted the institutionalized political corruption of established politics and his distance from traditional parties. As well as tackling corruption he pledged security, peace and employment.

In the first round of presidential elections in Oct. 2002, he gained 20.4% of votes, more than any other of the 11 candidates. His success caused some nervousness in the international financial community. During his second round of campaigning, he spent 3 days visiting investors and bankers in the US, promising to honour Ecuador's debt repayments and keep the recent dollarization. Initially campaigning in military fatigues he soon adopted civilian clothes. In a second round run-off with the businessman Alvaro Noboa (no relation), Ecuador's richest man, Gutiérrez took 54.3% of votes. But his supporters' standing in congress remained small, with the traditional parties holding the majority of seats.

Career Peak

Gutiérrez's election promises included tackling corruption, encouraging foreign investment and the growth of the tourism, agriculture and mining industries. He also aimed to balance budgets without lowering wages or imposing taxes while promising improved health care and cheaper housing for the poor. He sought to negotiate a standby loan with the IMF to ease the country's economic problems. In a drive to rid the political system of corruption, he proposed a reduction in the members of parliament and a reform of political appointments.

Gutiérrez introduced a programme of unpopular austerity measures as the country struggled to meet its financial commitments. An attempt by several leading parties to impeach him failed in Nov. 2004 and Gutiérrez responded by restructuring the Supreme Court in his favour. He was reliant on the support of the Roldosista Party, led by exiled ex-President Abdala Bucaram, to do this and, when corruption charges were subsequently dropped against Bucaram, there was widespread unease at the deal. When Gutiérrez proposed using violence to end the resulting popular protests, he was removed from power by a vote of Congress. Gutiérrez claimed the vote was unconstitutional.

Later Life

In April 2005 Gutiérrez was controversially permitted to leave the country and go into exile in Brazil.

Gyanendra Bir Bikram Shah Dev (Nepal)

Introduction

King Gyanendra, as he was formerly known, was the last head of the 239-year-old monarchy that reigned in Nepal before the establishment of a federal republic in 2008. Gyanendra came to the throne in June 2001 when his elder brother King Birendra was murdered by his heir, the Crown Prince Dipendra, who then committed suicide. Gyanendra advocated the continuation of the constitutional monarchy established in 1990 but in Feb. 2005, faced with the continuing Maoist insurgency, he dismissed Prime Minister Sher Bahadur Deuba's government (for a second time) and assumed direct control. However, in 2006 popular resistance to his direct rule forced him to relinquish powers to parliament. In Sept. 2007 Maoist representatives, demanding the abolition of the monarchy, temporarily withdrew from the coalition interim government. Parliament then voted in Dec. to replace the monarchy with a federal democratic republic following Constituent Assembly elections in April 2008. The victory of the Maoists in the Constituent Assembly elections sealed Gyanendra's fate, and he was stripped of his title.

Early Life

Gyanendra was born on 7 July 1947 in Kathmandu to King Mahendra Bir Bikram Shah and Crown Princess Indra Rajya Laxmi Devi Shah. He studied in Darjeeling in India, graduating in 1966, and 3 years later completed his studies at Kathmandu's Tribhuvan University. In addition to his business interests, he was involved in high-profile conservation work with the King Mahendra Trust for Nature Conservation and the World Wildlife Fund (now the World Wide Fund for Nature).

On 1 June 2001 Crown Prince Dipendra shot dead King Birendra, Queen Aishwarya and several other family members before turning the gun on himself. Dipendra was declared king, but died from his wounds three days later and Gyanendra succeeded him.

Career Peak

Early in Gyanendra's reign there was public unrest when an official report blamed Dipendra for the royal massacre, claiming that he was under the influence of alcohol and narcotics. However, Dipendra's sister, Ketaki, who was present at the massacre, confirmed the report's findings.

Birendra had ruled as absolute monarch until 1990, when he granted a multi-party democratic constitution. The ensuing years saw frequent changes of government and political instability. A month after Gyanendra came to the throne, Sher Bahadur Deuba became prime minister, amid growing violence by anti-monarchist Maoist rebels. Parliament was suspended in May 2002 in preparation for elections scheduled for Nov. 2002. However, in early Oct. 2002 Deuba, backed by the leading parliamentary parties, asked for the elections to be suspended and proposed an interim all-party government.

On 4 Oct. 2002 Gyanendra responded by dismissing Deuba and his cabinet. He appointed Lokendra Bahadur Chand of the monarchist RPP as prime minister, although opposition figures declared the move illegal. The King assumed the executive powers surrendered by the monarchy in 1990, postponed elections and announced that he would form a non-elected interim government. In a public broadcast he reaffirmed his commitment to the constitutional monarchy, but his actions were widely condemned.

In Jan. 2003 government forces and Maoist rebels agreed a ceasefire but this was short-lived. In May 2003 Chand resigned following pressure from opposition parties, which continued to refute the legitimacy of his appointment. When his replacement, Surya Bahadur Thapa, also resigned in May 2004, Sher Bahadu Deuba was reappointed the following month as prime minister. Meanwhile, the Maoist insurgency continued, with the rebels gaining control over much of the countryside.

In Feb. 2005 Gyanendra again dismissed Deuba and his government, taking power directly himself and imposing a state of emergency. Although he promised to restore multi-party democracy within 3 years, and the emergency was subsequently lifted in April 2005, his actions were criticized abroad, particularly by neighbouring India. In Sept. 2005 the Maoist rebels announced a unilateral ceasefire, but this was called off in early Jan. 2006 as explosions rocked the towns of Butwal, Pokhara and Bhairahawa. In April 2006, after prolonged strikes and demonstrations against his regime, Gyanendra announced the reinstatement of parliament and restoration of democracy.

An interim coalition government under Prime Minister Koirala subsequently began peace talks with the Maoist rebels as parliament voted to curtail the King's powers, including his command of the military. In Nov. 2006 the government and Maoists signed a peace deal and power-sharing agreement to end the 10 year civil war, and in Dec. a temporary constitution was agreed.

In April 2007 an interim government was formed that included Maoist ministers for the first time. However, in Sept. the Maoists withdrew, demanding the abolition of the monarchy ahead of elections to a new Constituent Assembly scheduled for Nov. The peace process was thrown into turmoil and the elections were postponed. However, to break the deadlock, Parliament voted into Dec. to abolish the monarchy and establish a republic after elections rearranged for April 2008. These elections resulted in victory for the Maoists who became the largest grouping in the new Assembly charged with writing a new constitution. The abolition of the monarchy was confirmed in the first session of the Assembly on 28 May 2008 with the foundation of the Federal Democratic Republic of Nepal. Gyanendra was provided with 2 weeks to vacate the Narayanhiti palace in Kathmandu, though he was not sent into exile abroad. Gyanendra's treatment by the new government was tempered by the high status the institution of the monarchy retains in Nepal, despite the deposed king's personal unpopularity.

Later Life

Despite the repossession of Narayanhiti palace and the crown jewels by the state, Gyanendra Shah (as he is now officially known) is rumoured to retain a substantial personal fortune, accumulated from his extensive tobacco, tea, hotel and property businesses. He resides in the relatively modest Nagarjung palace in northwestern Kathmandu.

Gyurcsány, Ferenc (Hungary)

Introduction

Multi-millionaire businessman Ferenc Gyurcsány became Hungary's prime minister on 29 Sept. 2004 after just 2 years in mainstream politics. His promotion came when his mentor and fellow Socialist Péter Medgyessy unexpectedly resigned. In the autumn of 2006 his premiership was undermined by violent anti-government protests in Budapest over revelations that he had misled voters at the April elections about the poor state of the public finances. His tarnished reputation declined further through 2008 as the global financial crisis highlighted the continuing poor performance and increasing vulnerability of the country's economy. He announced his intention to stand down as prime minister in March 2009 and left office in April.

Early Life

Gyurcsány was born in the town of Pápa in western Hungary on 4th June 1961. He entered the Janus Pannonius University in Pécs in 1980 and graduated with a teaching qualification in 1984. He remained at the university and studied economics for the next 6 years. During this time he was an active member of the Association of Young Communists (KISZ), becoming the president of its university wing in 1988. The forced resignation of Hungary's long-serving communist leader, János Kádár, in March 1988 led to the formation of a raft of opposition groups and political parties including the Hungarian Democratic Youth Association (DEMISZ), which Gyurcsány joined. He became its vice-president in 1989. Prime Minister Miklós Németh's decision to open Hungary's western border with Austria in Sept. 1989 precipitated the fall of the Iron Curtain and ushered in a new era. Gyurcsány graduated in economics in 1990 and worked as a financial consultant, establishing various companies and becoming Chief Executive Officer of ALTUS Investment and Assets Management Inc. in 1992, a post he held for the next 10 years.

Rumoured to be one of the wealthiest men in Hungary, Gyurcsány entered politics in 2002 as strategic adviser to the prime minister, Péter Medgyessy. Gyurcsány was promoted the following year to be the minister for sport and youth development. He was nominated as president of the Hungarian Socialist Party (MSzP) for the northwestern county of Győr-Moson-Sopron in Jan. 2004. Opinion polls suggested that public support for the MSzP was dwindling and, in Aug. 2004, tensions flared between the Socialists and their coalition partners, the Free Democrats, over a cabinet reshuffle. Medgyessy resigned and, a week later, Gyurcsány was nominated to succeed his mentor by members of the MSzP. He was formally approved as Hungary's prime minister on 29 Sept. 2004.

Career Peak

Gyurcsány pledged to boost Hungary's economic growth, cut the spiralling budget deficit and steer the country on a course for euro zone membership in 2010. Although hailing from the social democratic wing of the MSzP and advocating pro-market policies (not least the controversial privatization of the health service), Gyurcsány said that his party should be responsive to the poor in society. However, his critics from the political right frequently questioned the precise origin of his wealth and dubbed him a 'salon socialist'. He gained a further term in office when the Socialists won the elections of April 2006, thereby becoming the first Hungarian party to retain power at an election since the fall of socialism in 1989.

In Sept. 2006 a leaked tape revealed that Gyurcsány had lied about the state of the public finances in the run-up to the April parliamentary elections, sparking riots in the capital. He resisted demands that he should resign and further violent protests ensued in Oct. that overshadowed the 50th anniversary commemorations of the 1956 anti-Soviet uprising in Hungary. In Feb. 2007 a commission of enquiry report into the disturbances was critical of the government and the police.

In March 2008 the government was defeated in an opposition-sponsored referendum calling for the abolition of fees for health care and higher education that had been introduced as an austerity measure to reduce the country's budget deficit. The following month Gyurcsány had to reshuffle his cabinet in response to the withdrawal of the Free Democrats from the ruling coalition. The public finances continued to deteriorate in 2008 under the impact of the global credit crisis, and in Oct. the International Monetary Fund, EU and World Bank put together a US$25bn. loan rescue package for Hungary.

After Gyurcsány announced his resignation in March 2009, Gordon Bajnai was the only candidate to receive cross-party support. He took office after a constructive vote of no-confidence on 14 April.

Haarde, Geir (Iceland)

Introduction

Stepping down as prime minister in June 2006 following poor municipal election results, Halldór Ásgrímsson nominated Geir Haarde as his successor. An economist and former finance minister, Haarde has been the leader of the centre-right Independence Party (SSF) since 2005. He retained the premiership following parliamentary elections in May 2007, but his second term was largely overshadowed by economic contraction and a banking collapse. Following mass protests throughout late 2008 and early 2009 and the breakdown of talks with his coalition partner, the Social Democrats, Haarde announced the resignation of the government on 26 Jan. 2009.

Early Life

Geir Hilmar Haarde was born in Reykjavík on 8 April 1951. He attended university in the USA, initially as a Wien scholar at Brandeis University in Massachusetts, graduating in economics. He subsequently received masters degrees from Johns Hopkins University (1975) and the University of Minnesota (1977) before returning to Reykjavík to work as an economist in the central bank's international department. He also lectured in economics at the University of Iceland from 1979–83.

In 1983 he began working as an adviser to the finance minister, a position he held until the parliamentary elections of 1987, when he entered the Alþingi (Parliament) as a representative of the centre-right SSF. For years the country's largest party, the SSF had become embroiled in divisive leadership struggles in the mid-1980s and received only 27% of votes cast in the 1987 election.

Haarde became a member of the Nordic Council in 1991, the year in which the SSF, reunited under Davíð Oddsson, claimed almost 40% of the popular vote in parliamentary elections. Haarde served as a member of the foreign affairs committee (1991–98) and joined the executive committee of the Inter-Parliamentary Union (1994–98). From April 1998 to Sept. 2005 he served as minister of finance in an SSF–Progressive Party (PP) coalition, led by Oddsson. The government's free-market reforms stimulated strong economic growth, underpinned by the fisheries sector and aluminium production.

Appointed foreign minister in Sept. 2005, Haarde served under Halldór Ásgrímsson (of the PP), who had replaced Oddsson as prime minister a year earlier. Haarde was elected chairman of the SSF in an uncontested election following Oddsson's departure. When Ásgrímsson resigned the premiership in the wake of his party's poor showing in Reykjavík's municipal elections on 27 May 2006 he nominated Haarde as his successor as prime minister.

Career Peak

Haarde was inaugurated on 15 June 2006. He pledged to continue diversifying the economy away from its dependence on fisheries and welcomed the opening of a controversial aluminium smelter at Reyðarfjörður. He also promised to tackle the overheating economy and bring inflation down to around 2.5%. Haarde confirmed Iceland's contribution to international peacekeeping forces in Afghanistan and Sri Lanka. In Oct. 2006 the government lifted Iceland's longstanding moratorium on commercial whaling. Following legislative elections in May 2007, in which the SSF remained the largest party, the Progressive Party (FSF) withdrew from the ruling coalition and was replaced by the Social Democratic Alliance, giving Haarde a more secure governing majority.

However, by 2008 Iceland's economy was in serious difficulties owing to the huge amount of foreign debt incurred by its banks. This led in Oct. to a banking meltdown, described by the International Monetary Fund (IMF) as the largest collapse in banking history relative to the size of an economy. As the currency tumbled, Haarde's government took control of all three of the country's major banks in an effort to stabilize the financial system and in Nov. applied for emergency loan support from the IMF, which agreed a US$2·1bn. 2 year standby programme. Nordic countries also agreed to provide an extra US$2·5bn. The IMF meanwhile forecast that Iceland's economy would contract by about 10% in 2009.

Following demonstrations demanding that the government resign in the wake of the economic collapse, Haarde called a general election for 25 April, two years early. Nevertheless just days later, following the breakdown of relations with the Social Democrats, Haarde announced the resignation of his government. He was replaced by Jóhanna Sigurðardóttir of the Social Democrats, who became Iceland's first female prime minister.

Later Life

Haarde was appointed Iceland's ambassador to the United States in Feb. 2015.

Habré, Hissène (Chad)

Introduction

Hissène Habré served as president from 1982–90 after a brief period as prime minister from Aug. 1978–March 1979. His time inoffice was defined by violence and human rights abuses, and in May 2016 he was convicted of crimes against humanity by a court in Senegal and sentenced to life imprisonment.

Early Life

Born in 1942 in Faya-Largeau, northern Chad,into a family of shepherds, Habré secured a post in the French colonial administration and later won a scholarship to study at the prestigious Sciences-Po in Paris (an international research university).

On his return to Chad, Habré joined opposition forces and led a rebellion against the prevailing government from the desert region of Tibesti. He was named prime minister in Aug. 1978 in a power-sharing government established in a bid to bring about peace. However, the administration quickly broke down and Habré left office in March 1979.

Career Peak

After seizing power in a coup in 1982, Habré created a one-party regime in which power rested with his National Union for Independence and Revolution (UNIR). He also established a secret police force that propped up his rule while generating widespread fear. Despite accusations that his regime authorized the use of torture, extrajudicial killings and ethnic cleansing, Habré won Western (especially French and US) support. This was in part because he was regarded as a counterweight to the Libyan leader Col. Gaddafi, who led several interventions in Chad's civil conflict in the1970s and 1980s.

Habré remained in poweruntil 1990 when his purge of domestic opponents prompted his former chief ofstate, Idriss Déby, to break away and lead his own rebellion against theregime. After France withdrew its support of Habré'sincreasingly oppressive rule, Déby seized power and Habré fled to Senegal in Dec. 1990.

Later Life

Habré then lived in Senegal for 22 years despite numerous attempts to extradite him. In 2012, with intervention from the UN andthe African Union, he was put on trial in Senegal. In 30 May 2016 he was convicted of rape, sexual slavery, ordering the killing of 40,000 people andthe torture of some 200,000 more. He was sentenced to life imprisonment and ordered to pay compensation to each of his victims or their surviving relatives.

Habumuremyi, Pierre Damien (Rwanda)

Introduction

Pierre Damien Habumuremyi was sworn in as prime minister in Oct. 2011, succeeding Bernard Makuza. Makuza had served for 11 years, the longest serving head of government in Rwanda's post-genocide era, and was credited with bringing a degree of stability to the country. A technocrat, Habumuremyi was previously the minister of education.

Early Life

Habumuremyi was born in 1961 in Ruhondo, in Musanze District. He graduated in sociology from Lubumbashi University in the Democratic Republic of the Congo, before gaining postgraduate qualifications in education and political science.

He served from 2000–08 on the National Electoral Commission, including 5 years as executive secretary. In 2008 he was elected to represent the country at the East African Community Legislative Assembly.

In 2011 Habumuremyi was appointed Rwanda's minister of education, serving 5 months before being appointed prime minister. His promotion to the premiership surprised many commentators, given his relatively low profile and lack of government experience.

Career Peak

Habumuremyi pledged to rejuvenate the economy and develop its information and communications base. He also promised to fight corruption and has refuted suggestions that he is a puppet of the president. In Nov. 2013 he announced priority development targets to be addressed by the government in the 2013–14 fiscal year, notably the doubling of electricity generation and the expansion of water supply infrastructure.

Hubumuremyi's term as prime minister unexpectedly ended on 24 July 2014 when he was replaced by Anastase Murekezi, who had been nominated by President Paul Kagame.

Habyarimana, Juvénal (Rwanda)

Introduction

Juvénal Habyarimana became president of Rwanda in 1973 when he overthrew President Gregoire Kayibanda and the ruling Parmehtu Party. His tenure initially saw a move away from exclusively Hutu rule towards greater inclusion of the Tutsi minority in government and the professions. However, this rapprochement was short-lived and tensions between Tutsis and Hutus heightened during his period in office. On 6 April 1994 he was assassinated, precipitating civil war and genocide.

Early Life

Juvénal Habyarimana was born on 8 March 1937 in Gasiza, Gisenyi Province in what was then Ruanda-Urundi. A member of the Hutu majority ethnic group and raised a Roman Catholic, he studied mathematics at St Paul's College in Bukavu and medicine at the University of Lovanium in former Leopoldville, both in the former Belgian Congo. In 1960 he returned to Rwanda to train for the National Guard at the Officer's School in Kigali. He was chief of staff from 1963 to 1965 and as minister of defence and police chief of staff from 1965 to 1973. In April 1973 he was promoted to major-general.

Career Peak

On 5 July 1973 Habyarimana led a coup that ousted President Gregoire Kayibanda and the ruling Parmehtu Party. In 1975 he created the Mouvement Révolutionaire National Pour le Développement and established himself as sole ruler of a single-party state. Policies included quotas for Tutsis for jobs with universities and government services.

In 1978 a new constitution provided for a return to civilian rule and Habyarimana was elected president. He was re-elected in 1983 and again in 1988. In July 1990 he accepted some political reforms and in 1991 constitutional changes allowed for multi-party government. In Oct. 1990 a rebellion by the Tutsi-led Fronte Patriotique Rwandais (Rwandan Patriotic Front; RPF) exacerbated simmering ethnic tensions, with hundreds of Tutsi civilians killed by extremist Hutu militia, the Interahamwe.

On 4 Aug. 1993 Habyarimana signed a power-sharing agreement with the RPF in Arusha, Tanzania, arousing extremist opposition from within his own administration. In Jan. 1994 he was named president of a power-sharing transitional government based on the Arusha Accords.

On 6 April 1994 Habyarimana was returning from peace talks in his private jet with President Cyprien Ntaryamira, the Hutu leader of Burundi, when his plane was shot down over the grounds of the presidential palace. Responsibility for the attack was disputed, with Paul Kagame of the RPF (and later to become national president) held responsible by a French investigation concluded in 2006. Others, however, have pointed to the involvement ofHutu extremists. Following Habyarimana's death, the country descended into civil war, with the ensuing genocide claiming the lives of between 800,000 and 1 m. Tutsis and moderate Hutus.

Hague, William (United Kingdom of Great Britain and Northern Ireland)

Introduction

William Hague was leader of the Conservative party from 1997–2001. He took over from John Major following the party's defeat to Tony Blair's Labour party at the 1997 general election but resigned after overseeing a comparable loss 4 years later. Renowned as an orator and parliamentarian, he was nonetheless dogged by public relations mishaps and his anti-European stance led to allegations of xenophobia from the left of his own party. He returned to frontline politics in 2006 as shadow foreign secretary under the new Conservative leader, David Cameron and in May 2010 became foreign secretary in the Conservative/Liberal Democrat coalition government.

Early Life

William Jefferson Hague was born on 26 March 1961 in Richmond, Yorkshire. He first came to public attention when he addressed the Conservative party conference in 1977. He went on to study politics, philosophy and economics at Magdalen College, Oxford University and became president of the Oxford Union and the university Conservative association. He then studied for an MBA at the INSEAD Business School in France and worked for Shell UK and McKinsey and Co.

Hague unsuccessfully stood for the Wentworth seat at the elections of 1987 but entered parliament 2 years later following a byelection in Richmond. He joined the cabinet in 1995 as the secretary of state for Wales. Following Labour's victory at the 1997 elections, John Major resigned as leader of the party and was succeeded by Hague, who defeated Kenneth Clarke after three rounds of voting.

Career Peak

While leader of the opposition, Hague also became chairman of the International Democratic Union, an organization of which he remains deputy chairman. Hague won many plaudits for his consistent performances against Blair at prime minister's question time. However, he lost popular credibility after a series of publicity stunts misfired, including being pictured wearing a baseball cap and claiming to have drunk 'fourteen pints a day' in his youth. The Conservatives remained split over Europe and Hague's personal European scepticism drew criticism from influential Conservatives such as Michael Heseltine. When Hague oversaw only a single seat gain at the 2001 general elections, his resignation soon followed.

Later Life

While remaining an MP, Hague explored other business interests and became a regular face in the media. He also wrote a well-received biography of Pitt the Younger (to whom Margaret Thatcher had compared him in 1977). Hague's favoured successor, Iain Duncan Smith, took on the party leadership but oversaw the parties continuing stagnation and was succeeded by Michael Howard in 2003. After a third unsuccessful election, Howard gave way to David Cameron, who appointed Hague as shadow foreign secretary. Consequently, following the Conservatives' return to power in May 2010 he was made foreign secretary in Cameron's first cabinet. Shortly after his appointment, Hague outlined a foreign policy in which the UK would obtain 'greater reach and influence' in an increasingly fast-paced and 'networked' world.

The Arab Spring protests throughout the Middle East in 2011 presented Hague with his earliest and, arguably, most significant diplomatic challenge as foreign secretary. Whilst maintaining a critical stance towards the autocratic administrations of Libya's Muammar Gaddafi and Bashar al-Assad of Syria, he called for a peaceful resolution to the violent uprisings around the region. Nonetheless, Hague backed airstrikes co-ordinated by NATO against the Libyan regime and clarified the UK's recognition of the rebel Libyan council as the country's 'sole governmental authority' in July 2011. This trend in UK foreign policy would continue in Feb. 2012 when Hague announced his government's recognition of the Syrian National Council as the legitimate representative of Syria.

In July 2014 Hague's time as foreign secretary ended following the most extensive cabinet reshuffle of David Cameron's premiership. He remained within the cabinet, however, becoming leader of the House of Commons in the same month. Hague subsequently announced his intention to leave parliamentary politics following the general election in May 2015. He vacated the seat he held for 26 years as representative for Richmond, North Yorks in March 2015 and stood down as leader of the House of Commons and first secretary of state in May.

In Sept. 2015 Hague was appointed chairman of the security think tank, the Royal United Services Institute.

Haile Selassie I (Ethiopia)

Introduction

Haile Selassie was emperor of Ethiopia from 1930 until 1974, though exiled when Ethiopia fell under Italian rule between 1935 and 1941. An autocrat, he nonetheless did much to modernise Ethiopia's political and social infrastructures and raise the country's international standing. He was widely respected as a statesman, particularly for his conduct following the Italian invasion. However, as economic conditions deteriorated in the 1960s and 70s and reforms were slow in coming, opposition intensified. He was deposed by the military in 1974 and murdered the following year. Haile Selassie is a Rastafarian divine.

Early Life

Haile Selassie was born Tafari Makonnen near Harer in Ethiopia on 23 July 1892. The son of a chief adviser to Emperor Menilek II, he was made a provincial governor at the age of 14. In 1911 he married the emperor's granddaughter, Wayzaro Menen and became Ras (Prince) Tafari. On Menelik's death in 1913, his grandson Lij Yasu succeeded him but became unpopular with the ruling Christian elite when he embraced Islam. He was deposed in 1916 and when Menelik's daughter, Zauditu, became empress Tafari was named regent.

Career Peak

Tafari helped ensure Ethiopia's entry into the League of Nations in 1923, and oversaw the end of slavery. Educated and forward-thinking officials were moved into positions of authority. In 1928 Tafari became king of Ethiopia. Two years later Zauditu died in mysterious circumstances and Tafari was crowned emperor, adopting the name Haile Selassie (Might of the Trinity).

In 1931 he introduced a bicameral parliament while at the same time extending his own power. Heavy investment in the country's transport, communication and education systems was supported by revenues from the booming coffee trade.

In 1935, when Italy invaded Ethiopia, Haile Selassie led his troops into battle. Lacking equipment and organization they were soon defeated and the emperor forced into exile in Europe. He gained great respect for his eloquent appeal for help from the League of Nations in 1936 but failed to secure practical support. Only after Italy's entry into World War II in 1940 did Britain provide aid. Haile Selassie regained his throne in 1941.

He continued to implement social and institutional reforms, taking power away from regional elites. He also encouraged closer relations with the US as support from Britain diminished. In 1952 he secured the federation of Ethiopia and Eritrea. In 1955 a new constitution introduced universal suffrage but also reaffirmed Haile Selassie's autocratic power. Young radicals became increasingly disillusioned and there were revolts in Eritrea. In 1960 the imperial bodyguard led by Haile Selassie's son attempted a coup.

Despite its failure this stimulated discontent within the country. However, Haile Selassie's international stock continued to rise and in 1963 he played a major role in establishing the Organization of African Unity. He was adopted as a figurehead for the Rastafarian movement that believed he would deliver a black homeland in Africa.

At home inflation was out of control and corruption rife. In the early 1970s famine claimed several hundred thousand lives. In 1974 the military seized control of the government, nationalized Haile Selassie's estates and stripped him of his powers, formally deposing him on 12 Sept.

Later Life

The Provisional Military Administrative Council took Haile Selassie into custody in Sept. 1974 and he died on 26 Aug. 1975, almost certainly murdered. His body was exhumed in 1992 and reburied in Sept. 2000. Shortly before the ceremony the Ethiopian government condemned his reign as one characterized 'by brutality and extreme oppression.'

Hailemariam Desalegn (Ethiopia)

Introduction

Hailemariam Desalegn became prime minister, initially in an acting capacity after Meles Zenawi died of an undisclosed illness, in Aug. 2012. He had previously served as deputy prime minister under Meles and was minister of foreign affairs from 2010–12. He was the first premier from the Ethiopian Apostolic denomination.

Early Life

Hailemariam was born on 19 July 1965 in what is now the Southern Nations, Nationalities and Peoples Region (SNNPR) in the south of Ethiopia. At school, he joined a political youth group attached to the communist military junta of Mengistu Haile Mariam.

In 1988 Hailemariam graduated in civil engineering from Addis Ababa University, before taking up a post as a graduate assistant in the Arba Minch Water Technology Institute. In 1990 he won a scholarship to Tampere University of Technology in Finland to study for a masters' degree in sanitation engineering. Returning to Ethiopia, he worked in various academic and administrative positions for over a decade, during which time he earned a master's in organizational leadership from Azusa Pacific University in California.

Hailemariam served in senior management positions at the Hawassa and Wolayta Soddo Universities, the Addis Ababa Water Supply and Sewerage Authority, the Construction Design Share Company, the Ethiopian Maritime and Transit Service Enterprise, the Privatization and Public Enterprise Supervising Agency, and the Walta Information and Public Relations Center.

From the late 1990s he was increasingly involved in politics, joining Ethiopia's ruling party, the Ethiopian People's Revolutionary Democratic Front (EPRDF). A member of the SNNPR council between 1995 and 2008, he served as its vice-president from 2000–01 and as its president from 2001–06. He is also chairman of the Southern Ethiopian People's Democratic Movement and deputy chairman of the executive council of the EPRDF.

From 2006–08 Hailemariam was special adviser (with the rank of minister) to the prime minister on social affairs, civic organizations and partnership. From 2008–10 he was the government's chief whip in the House of People's Representatives. In Sept. 2010 Hailemariam was appointed deputy prime minister and minister of foreign affairs under the premiership of Meles Zenawi.

Career Peak

After Meles died in Aug. 2012, Hailemariam succeeded him as prime minister, serving in an interim capacity for a month. On 15 Sept. 2012 he was elected chairman of the EPRDF before being sworn in as the fully-mandated prime minister a week later. Increasingly repressive measures against journalists and opposition opinion were adopted by his government ahead of the general election in May 2015, in which the ruling party claimed a landslide victory. Despite impressive economic growth in 2015,there was increasing protest in 2016 against the authoritarianism of the EPRDF, prompting the government in Oct. that year to declare a state of emergency (although it was lifted by parliament in Aug. 2017). Additionally, there have been rising ethnic tensions and violence in 2017, particularly between Oromos and Somalis. In early 2018 anti-government demonstrations spread. Despite his attempts to quell the situation, Hailemariam resigned on 15 Feb. 2018 under pressure from opposition groups. However, he remained in office until Abiy Ahmed succeeded him as prime minister on 2 April 2018 after being elected by the parliament.

Halonen, Tarja (Finland)

Introduction

The first woman president in Finnish history, Tarja Kaarina Halonen served two presidential terms from 2000–12. A member of parliament from 1979 until her election to the presidency, she also served as a minister in three governments from 1987. From 1995–2000 she was the country's foreign minister.

Early Life

Tarja Halonen was born on 24 Dec. 1943. She was educated at the University of Helsinki where she received a degree in law. She was actively involved in student politics and served as the general secretary for the National Union of Finnish Students. From 1970–74 she was a lawyer with the central organization of Finnish Trade Unions. In 1974 she became the parliamentary secretary to prime minister Kalevi Sorsa, holding this position until Sorsa's term ended in 1975. Halonen was then elected to the Helsinki City council in 1977 (remaining a councillor until 1996) and 2 years later was elected a member of the Finnish parliament. She was chairman of the parliamentary social affairs committee (from 1984–87) before being appointed minister of social affairs and health. She went on to hold two further ministerial positions, serving as minister for Nordic co-operation (1989–91) and minister of justice (1990–91), before becoming the minister of foreign affairs in April 1995. In this role she oversaw Finland's assimilation into the European Union. In Jan. 2000 Halonen stood for election as the Social Democratic Party candidate for the presidency, campaigning on a liberal and feminist manifesto. She received 51.6% of the total votes cast in the second round of the presidential elections on 6 Feb. 2000, narrowly defeating the Centre Party's Esko Aho.

Career Peak

On the day of her inauguration, a new national constitution came into effect which reduced presidential powers and expanded and emphasized parliament as the most important body in the Finnish political system. The president was still granted a significant role in foreign policy, a fact which suited Halonen's diplomatic and linguistic skills. She continued her country's pro-European Union policies, although her position on NATO was less certain.

In Nov. 2005 the SDP nominated Halonen for re-election as its presidential candidate. Having failed to secure a majority in the first round of voting, she narrowly defeated the Conservative candidate, Sauli Niinistö, in a run-off in Jan. 2006.

In June 2010 Prime Minister Matti Vanhanen stood down as leader of the Centre Party and was succeeded by Mari Kiviniemi, who was sworn in by Halonen as the new premier.

Ineligible to run in the 2012 presidential elections owing to term limits, Halonen left office on 1 March 2012. She was succeeded by Sauli Niinistö.

Hammarskjöld, Dag (Sweden)

Introduction

Dag Hammarskjöld served as Secretary-General of the United Nations from 1953–61. He worked 31 years in finance, foreign relations, and global international affairs. He raised Sweden's profile within the international community and was awarded the Nobel Peace Prize in 1961.

Early Life

Dag Hammarskjöld was born on 29 July 1905. His father, Hjalmar Hammarskjöld was Sweden's prime minister during World War I, and also governor of the county of Uppland, member of the Hague Tribunal, and chairman of the Board of the Nobel Foundation. Dag Hammarskjöld studied linguistics, literature, and history at Uppsala University, graduating in 1925. He became a Bachelor of Laws in 1930. His doctoral thesis on

'Konjunkturspridningen' (The Spread of the Business Cycle) was followed by his appointment as assistant professor in political economy at the University of Stockholm. Though not a member of a political party, Hammarskjöld served in several Government posts. From 1936–45 he was undersecretary in the Ministry of Finance and from 1941–48 he was chairman of the Bank of Sweden. Hammarskjöld coined the term 'planned economy'. In 1945, he became adviser to the Cabinet on economic and financial problems. In 1949 he was Secretary-General of the foreign office, and later became deputy foreign minister. Hammarskjöld conducted a policy of international economic co-operation, representing Sweden in negotiations on the postwar reconstruction of Europe. He also led the Executive Committee of the OEEC (Organization for European Economic Co-operation). In 1954 he became a member of the Swedish Academy, the body that awards the Nobel Prize in Literature.

Career Peak

In 1953, Hammarskjöld was elected Secretary-General of the United Nations. In 1954 he negotiated the release of American soldiers captured by the Chinese in the Korean War. In 1955 he organized the international conference in Geneva on peaceful uses of atomic energy, and planned the UN conference (held in 1962) on the application of science and technology for the benefit of developing countries. Throughout his term in office, efforts were made to resolve the problems of Palestine. During the Suez Canal crisis of 1956, Hammarskjöld created the United Nations Emergency Force (UNEF). In 1958 he set up the UN Observation Group in Lebanon and the UN Office in Jordan, and persuaded the Americans and the British to withdraw their troops from the region. Hammarskjöld was involved in the problems of developing countries, chiefly in Africa. In 1960, during the Congo crisis, he set up and led a UN peace-keeping force. Hammarskjöld's peace mission in Congo ended on 17 Sept. 1961, when he was killed in a plane crash.

Harper, Stephen (Canada)

Introduction

Stephen Harper's victory in federal elections in Jan. 2006 represented a shift to the right after 12 years of Liberal government overshadowed by allegations of corruption. The free-market economist and leader of the Conservative Party cast himself as a moderate, progressive, centre-right politician, intent on tackling corruption, reducing taxes and leading a more efficient government. He retained power following the Conservative victory in further elections in Oct. 2008 and May 2011.

Early Life

Stephen Harper was born on 30 April 1959 in Toronto, Canada. He graduated from Richview Collegiate Institute in 1978 and moved to Edmonton, Alberta, where he worked as a computer programmer in the oil and gas industry. While studying economics at the University of Calgary in the early 1980s, Harper was influenced by the right-wing monetarist ideas espoused by Ronald Reagan in the USA and Margaret Thatcher in the UK. He graduated with a BA in economics in 1985 and began working for a Conservative member of parliament, Jim Hawkes.

Disillusioned with the Progressive Conservatives (PC) and the government of Brian Mulroney, Harper joined the newly established Reform Party of Canada in 1987, led by the economist Preston Manning. As chief policy officer, Harper helped draft the party's manifesto for the elections of 1988. He became legislative assistant to the Reform Party MP, Deborah Gray, after she won a by-election to represent Beaver River, Alberta in March 1989.

At the elections of Oct. 1993 Harper beat Jim Hawkes to win Calgary West for the Reform Party and became the party's spokesman on finance and national unity. In a run-up to a referendum in Oct. 1995 on the status of Quebec, Harper argued to maintain but decentralize the federation. Disagreements with Manning led to Harper's decision in late 1996 not to stand in the next election. He resigned his seat in Jan. 1997 and was appointed vice president of the conservative lobby group, the National Citizens Coalition. He also worked as a regular political commentator for the Canadian Broadcasting Corporation.

Harper rejected invitations to run for the PC leadership but returned to politics in March 2002 when he was elected to succeed Stockwell Day as leader of the Canadian Alliance party. He successfully contested a by-election for Calgary Southwest 2 months later and returned to the House of Commons as leader of the opposition. Following protracted negotiations, Harper reached agreement with the PC leader, Peter MacKay, on a merger between the two parties to form the Conservative Party of Canada in Dec. 2003.

Harper won the new party's leadership election in March 2004 and fought the Liberal prime minister, Paul Martin, in the 2004 election. After taking an early poll lead, the Conservatives lost ground with Harper criticized for supporting the US-led war on Iraq in March 2003. The election in June 2004 saw a victory for the Liberals, who took 135 seats against 99 for the Conservatives.

When the Liberals became mired in a corruption scandal in April 2005, Harper argued that the government had 'lost the moral authority to govern'. He introduced a motion of no confidence in Paul Martin's administration on 24 Nov. 2005, which was passed by 171–133. Parliament was dissolved and elections were scheduled for 23 Jan. 2006. Harper's campaign presented him as head of a modernizing centre-right party that would stimulate economic growth by lowering taxes. Having held a comfortable lead in the opinion polls, the Conservatives won the elections with 36% of the vote, though short of a parliamentary majority. Harper was sworn in as prime minister on 6 Feb. 2006.

Career Peak

Harper promised a smaller 'more focused and effective' government. Eager to pursue closer relations with the USA, he announced a settlement in April of Canada's long-running dispute over softwood timber exports to its neighbour. He also promised more respect for provincial autonomy, particularly in relation to French-speaking Quebec. In Nov. 2006 his proposal to recognize Quebec 'as a nation within a united Canada' was approved by the House of Commons. In foreign policy, he maintained the previous administration's position on Afghanistan, but brought Canadian combat involvement in the country to an end in July 2011. In June 2006 police arrested 17 Islamic extremists allegedly plotting to kill the prime minister.

Despite the shadow of global financial turmoil and opposition accusations of economic complacency, Harper sought a more secure mandate for his administration by calling an early general election for Oct. 2008 (although he had previously pushed through legislation fixing the normal life of a parliament at four years). The Conservatives improved their representation in the House of Commons but again failed to achieve a parliamentary majority. In Dec. the opposition parties sought to bring down the minority government over its response to the economic situation, but Harper asked the Governor-General to suspend parliament until Jan. 2009 thereby postponing a no-confidence vote. When parliament resumed in late Jan. the opposition alliance backed down and in Feb. the government secured approval of its 2009 budget, including a 2-year stimulus package for the economy, with conditional Liberal Party support that ensured Harper's political survival. However, in Oct. 2009 the Liberals tabled a no-confidence motion accusing the government of having lost control of the public finances. The motion was defeated by 144 votes to 117 with the help of the New Democratic Party and Bloc Québécois, and in Nov. the Conservatives gained two seats in four parliamentary by-elections, suggesting some improvement in the government's standing with the electorate.

At the end of Dec. 2009 Harper again successfully sought the prorogation of parliament until the beginning of March 2010, a move that attracted criticism from opposition leaders who accused him of seeking to avoid political debate. Nevertheless, at the general election in May 2011 Harper led the Conservatives to a decisive victory to head a majority government for the first time since taking office. A government proposal to reform the Senate from an appointed upper house of parliament to an elected chamber, first set out in 2006, has remained contentious, and a scandal over expenses involving three Conservative senators appointed by the prime minister prompted opposition attacks on his integrity in 2013.

In Dec. 2011 Canada became the first country to formally withdraw from the 1997 Kyoto Protocol on climate change, a decision which received widespread international criticism. Relations with Iran deteriorated from late 2011 as Canada supported a tightening of international sanctions over Tehran's nuclear development programme. In Sept. 2012 the Harper government broke off diplomatic relations, claiming Iran was a threat to world security. In Oct. 2013 he announced that an agreement on a long-awaited free trade deal between Canada and the European Union had been reached in principle. The following month he boycotted the Commonwealth heads of government meeting in Colombo, Sri Lanka, in response to claims of human rights violations by President Mahinda Rajapaksa's administration in that country against the Tamil minority. In Oct. 2014 Canada joined the US-led air campaign against Islamic State fundamentalists in Iraq, and in the same month suffered two suspected terror attacks in Ottawa and Quebec in which two soldiers were killed.

In June 2014 a Supreme Court landmark ruling granted title over an area of the western province of British Columbia to a First Nations group.

Harper's Conservative Party lost the Oct. 2015 parliamentary elections to the Justin Trudeau-led Liberal Party. Trudeau replaced Harper as prime minister in Nov.

Hatoyama, Yukio (Japan)

Introduction

Yukio Hatoyama became prime minister in Sept. 2009, leading the Democratic Party of Japan into government for the first time. A centre-left politician, Hatoyama moved to strengthen Japan's ties with other Asian countries, while signalling a more independent relationship with the United States. Domestically he favoured redirecting public money from large infrastructure projects into tax cuts, pensions and welfare.

Early Life

Yukio Hatoyama was born on 11 Feb. 1947 in Bunkyo, Tokyo. His grandfather had been prime minister and his father served as foreign minister, while his mother is heir to the founder of the Bridgestone Corporation tyre company. Brought up and educated in Tokyo, Hatoyama graduated from Tokyo University in 1969 with a degree in engineering and continued his studies at Stanford University, USA, where he was awarded a PhD in engineering in 1976. Returning to Japan, he worked at Senshu University, becoming an assistant professor in 1981. In 1983 he left academia to become private secretary to his father, Iichiro Hatoyama, in the House of Representatives.

In 1986 he was elected to the House of Representatives as a member of the ruling Liberal Democratic Party (LDP), representing his father's former seat in Hokkaido. In 1990 he became parliamentary vice minister of the Hokkaido Development Agency. In June 1993 he left the LDP and co-founded New Party Sakigake which, as part of a coalition, defeated the LDP in general elections that year. He served as deputy chief cabinet secretary under Prime Minister Morihiro Hosokawa until the government fell in 1994. In 1996 Hatoyama co-founded the centrist Democratic Party of Japan (DPJ) with his brother Kunio Hatoyama and, 2 years later, steered the party into a merger with three other opposition parties, becoming deputy secretary general of the enlarged DPJ in April 1998 and its president in 1999.

In 2002, following confusion arising from rumours that he was planning a merger with Ichiro Ozawa's Liberal Party, Hatoyama resigned from the leadership. The merger duly occurred in 2003. The DPJ campaigned for more open and accountable policy-making and advocated redirecting public money to improve welfare. It performed strongly in elections in 2003 and 2004, while Hatoyama served as shadow minister for internal affairs. In Sept. 2004 he became shadow minister for foreign affairs and secretary general of the DPJ. Having worked closely with Ozawa after the latter took over party leadership in 2006, Hatoyama regained the DPJ presidency in May 2009 when Ozawa resigned over financial scandals.

Hatoyama led the DPJ into the 2009 general election on a reformist platform. The party promised to address deepening economic problems by cutting funding for large infrastructure projects and boosting welfare provision. It advocated changing government procedures to shift policy-making powers from the civil service to ministers. It also argued for a more Asia-focused foreign policy and a re-evaluation of the relationship with the USA. In the general election of Aug. 2009 the DPJ decisively defeated the LDP, winning 308 seats to the LDP's 119, bringing to an end half a century of almost unbroken LDP rule.

Career Peak

Hatoyama took office on 16 Sept. 2009. He made early moves to strengthen Japan's relations with its Asian neighbours, initiating a series of visits. In Nov. 2009 he announced plans to boost the economy by developing a market in environmentally-friendly products and renewable power, and targeted 2020 for establishing a free trade zone in Asia. However, economic conditions hampered his attempts to introduce promised spending reforms. His popularity further suffered from rumours of financial impropriety surrounding his mother's donations to the DPJ.

In May 2010 a political crisis emerged after renegotiations with the USA over the future of its military bases on the island of Okinawa proved fruitless thus breaking one of Hatoyama's key electoral pledges. The SDP pulled out of the coalition government and on 1 June Hatoyama resigned. The deputy prime minister Naoto Kan was elected his successor by the Diet.

Haughey, Charles (Ireland)

Introduction

Charles Haughey was three times Prime Minister (*Taoiseach*) of the Republic of Ireland (1979–81, March–Dec. 1982 and 1987–92). As leader of Fianna Fáil, he was a fervent nationalist who voiced his opposition to the 1985 Anglo-Irish Treaty. However, he worked within its confines when in power. His career was underscored by allegations of corruption and dubious activities that led to his eventual resignation and criminal proceedings.

Early Life

Charles James Haughey was born in Castlebar, Country Mayo on 16 Sept. 1925 into a Catholic nationalist environment. He took a degree in law and accounting at University College Dublin before marrying the daughter of future Irish Prime Minister, Sean Lemass, in 1991. In 1957 he entered parliament (the Dáil) and 4 years later, under Lemass, he was appointed Minister of Justice. He later served as Minister in the Departments of Finance and Agriculture.

In 1970 he was sacked, along with fellow minister Neil Blaney, from government by Prime Minister Jack Lynch over alleged involvement in Irish Republican Army (IRA) arms shipments. In the criminal prosecution that followed both men were acquitted, but Haughey would be accused of involvement in several incidents of dubious legality throughout his career. Haughey returned to political life having ensured his financial security through a land deal that would later come under investigation. In 1973 he was returned to the Dáil, becoming Minister of Health and Social Welfare. Shortly afterwards he succeeded Jack Lynch as leader of Fianna Fáil.

Career Peak

In 1979 Haughey was elected Prime Minister but his government was faced with a mounting economic crisis. The agricultural sector was under extreme pressure and Ireland's trade deficit was poor. Anglo–Irish relations were at a low ebb and Fianna Fáil was rife with internal disputes, many of which centred on his style of leadership. In June 1981 Haughey lost power to a coalition headed by Garret FitzGerald but in elections held in Feb. 1982 Haughey returned as Prime Minister.

Haughey's second term lasted only until Dec. 1982 and ended ignominiously. Ireland's budget deficit was chronic and Haughey's government was hounded by allegations of phone tapping of journalists. A vote of no confidence led to new elections and FitzGerald formed another Fine Gael–Labour coalition. In Feb. 1983 Haughey only just staved off a no confidence motion from within his own party by 40 votes to 33.

In 1987 Haughey again won the premiership but in elections 2 years later he was forced to form a coalition (the first in his party's history) with the Progressive Democrats, a party which contained several former members of Fine Gael who had become disgruntled with Haughey. He had been a vociferous opponent of the 1985 Anglo–Irish Agreement, negotiated by FitzGerald and Margaret Thatcher, which allowed for the Republic to be consulted on various matters concerning Northern Ireland. However, once in power Haughey took a more pragmatic approach and worked within the terms of the treaty.

Haughey remained in office from 1987 until 1992. His tenure was again blighted by Ireland's weak economic situation and he was forced to implement austerity measures to combat the growing trade deficit. By the early 1990s Ireland had attracted major foreign investment and its economy was far more stable. However, the scandal concerning phone tapping of journalists in the early-1980s re-emerged. Sean Doherty, Minister of Justice at the time of the violations, confirmed that the allegations were true and Haughey had been aware of the practice. Despite his denials, Haughey was forced to resign the premiership and the party leadership in Feb. 1992.

Later Life

Haughey's retirement was dogged by further allegations of impropriety. In 1997 the Dáil established the Moriarty Tribunal, following the McCracken Tribunal that investigated payments to Haughey from supermarket magnate Ben Dunne. Haughey was accused of obstructing the McCracken Tribunal and faced trial proceedings that were later dropped. The Moriarty Tribunal investigated alleged illegal payments to several politicians including Haughey and assessed whether these payments may have affected Haughey's decision-making while in government. Haughey attempted to avoid giving evidence on medical grounds but his appeal was turned down.

Haughey died on 13 June 2006 after a long illness.

Havel, Václav (Czech Republic)

Introduction

Václav Havel served as Czechoslovak President from Dec. 1989 until July 1992, when he became President of the Czech Republic following the dissolution of the Czechoslovak state. He stood down from office in Feb. 2003. He was a poet, playwright and essayist and a leading dissident against Czechoslovakia's communist regime. As a founder of the Civic Forum movement, he was instrumental in the success of the 1989 Velvet Revolution which precipitated the end of the communist government.

Early Life

Havel was born on 5 Oct. 1936 in Prague, the son of a successful businessman. Much of the family's wealth was confiscated by the communist government in the late 1940s. As a result of his background, Havel was excluded from higher education. However, while working in a chemical laboratory he attended evening classes and in 1955 he began a degree in economics at Prague's Czech Technical University.

On completion of his military service, Havel worked in theatre as a stagehand. In 1960 he joined Prague's Theatre on the Balustrade, where he made his name as a writer, gaining an international reputation with *The Garden Party* in 1963. Havel was heavily influenced by Kafka and *absurdism*, and his plays challenged authoritarian society and its detrimental impact on the individual. In 1964 he married Olga Splichalova.

Havel promoted his liberal humanist ideology throughout the 1960s and was a key figure in the Prague Spring, suppressed by Soviet military intervention in 1968. Refusing to moderate his views, Havel suffered a backlash in the ensuing years as Moscow imposed a process of 'normalization'. His plays were banned, his passport confiscated and his activities closely monitored.

In 1975 Havel wrote an open letter to President Husák criticizing the government. Two years later he was a co-founder of Charter 77, a document signed by 250 intellectuals, artists and religious figures urging the government to conform to the Universal Declaration of Human Rights. He was subsequently placed under house arrest and in 1979 was sentenced to 4 years hard labour. Released in March 1983 he continued his condemnation of the communist regime through his writing.

Havel was again imprisoned for his underground activities in 1989 but, following his release, he became one of the leaders of the Civic Forum, a loose affiliation of liberal and democratic groups. As anti-communist protests spread throughout the Eastern Bloc, Prague became a centre of demonstrations in Nov. 1989.

Career Peak

Following the bloodless Velvet Revolution, the communists agreed to form a coalition with the Civic Forum in Dec. 1989. On 29 Dec. Havel was voted interim president, a job confirmed the following July for 2 years. Although the presidential office was essentially a ceremonial one, with day to day politics in the charge of the prime minister, Havel became one of Europe's most influential leaders.

As a non-partisan advocating liberal humanist ethics, he met with many of the world's leaders. He advocated expansion of NATO and the EU to include former Soviet satellites in a bid to bring stability and security to the region. However, when it became apparent in 1992 that Czechoslovakia was on the brink of splitting into its constituent states, Havel resigned. In July 1993 he was elected president of the Czech Republic. His country joined NATO in 1999 and the EU in 2004.

Václav Klaus was elected prime minister and Havel's moralistic approach to government clashed with Klaus' desire to implement freemarket reforms. Havel's wife died in Jan. 1996 and he himself suffered serious ill health during that year. His popularity was dented when he married the former actress Dagmar Veskrnova, 17 years his junior, in Jan. 1997.

Klaus' government was rocked by a series of personal and economic scandals during 1997. Havel made a speech to parliament in Dec. in which he promoted ethical standards in office and implicitly questioned the previously venerated reforms of Klaus. The Klaus regime subsequently collapsed and in 1998 Havel won narrow re-election to the presidency. Although dogged by ill-health and a lack of executive power, Havel remained one of the most respected figures on the international stage. He retired from the presidency on 2 Feb. 2003, although parliament failed to choose his successor until almost a month later.

Later Life

After leaving the presidency Havel returned to writing and published his memoirs in 2007. Havel also became Chair of the International Council of the Human Rights Foundation. He died on 18 Dec. 2011 aged 75, at his country home in Hrádeček.

Hawke, Robert (Australia)

Introduction

Robert James Lee (known as Bob) Hawke was leader of the Australian Labor Party (ALP) and Prime Minister of Australia, 1983–91. After many years as a trade union official, his conciliatory skills, down-to-earth manner and economic success made him a popular prime minister. Despite a generally weak global economy in the mid-1980s, he led the ALP to a record four consecutive election victories.

Early Life

Hawke was born on 9 Dec. 1929 in Bordertown in South Australia to Clement, a Congregational minister, and Ellie Lee, a teacher. Hawke's uncle, Albert, who became premier of Western Australia, was a formative influence on his nephew. Hawke graduated in Law and Economics from the University of Western Australia and was a Rhodes Scholar at Oxford University between 1953–55. During this time he also took the world record, 12 s, for the speediest drinking of a yard of ale. In 1956 he married Hazel Masterson, with whom he had three children. Having joined the ALP in 1947, he was offered a lectureship at Canberra University College in 1958 but instead joined the Australian Council of Trade Unions (ACTU) as a research officer. He gained a reputation as an excellent negotiator and became president of the Council in 1969, introducing trade unionism in the travel and retail sectors. On the National Executive of the ALP from 1971, Hawke served as president from 1973–78. In 1979 he was awarded the Companion of the Order of Australia and in 1980 he entered the House of Representatives as the member for Wills in Victoria. In Oct. 1980 he became opposition spokesman on industrial relations, employment and youth affairs. Two years later he stood for the leadership against Bill Hayden. He was defeated but made another bid early the next year. Malcolm Fraser, the Liberal prime minister, called a flash election, hoping to catch the ALP in disarray, but Hayden responded by resigning his post and Hawke took the leadership without a contest.

Career Peak

After heavy campaigning, Hawke's force of personality secured a landslide victory at the election of 11 March 1983. With treasurer Paul Keating, his eventual successor, he set about restoring economic prosperity. The Prices and Income Accord was an example of the consensus government favoured by Hawke, and its resulting price and wage restraints and improved industrial relations boosted the economy. The rate of inflation was halved by the end of 1984, and 3.7% annual economic growth was reported between 1983–85. Further economic reforms followed including the deregulation of financial services, the reduction of protectionist tariffs for manufacturing industry and the flotation of the Australian dollar. On the international scene, Hawke pursued closer ties with the US and the non-communist emerging economies of northeast Asia. Aided by Liberal disunity, Hawke was returned as prime minister at the elections of 1984 and 1987. However, his popularity started to wane in the late 1980s. The economy had suffered from the worldwide recession and his close ties with various Australian tycoons prompted criticism. Pensions means testing, health and education taxes and the introduction of a capital gains tax were also unpopular. He was again victorious in the 1990 election but his majority was slashed. Hawke was further weakened by a rift with Keating. A secret deal had been struck 2 years earlier by which Keating was to take over the premiership in 1990, but Hawke subsequently reneged. He defeated Keating in a leadership challenge in June 1991 but at a further ballot in Dec. he was beaten.

Later Life

Hawke resigned and left the political scene early in 1992, though he proved to be a vociferous critic of the Keating regime. His marriage to Hazel ended in divorce on account of his affair with his biographer, Blanche d'Alpuget; they married in 1995. Hawke was a keen supporter of Kim Beazley, who led the Labor Party from 1996–2001. The Hawke Institute at the University of South Australia currently supports work based on Hawke's career and ideology. He was made a life member of the Australian Labor Party in Aug. 2009.

Heath, Edward (United Kingdom of Great Britain and Northern Ireland)

Introduction

Edward Richard George Heath was the Conservative British prime minister between 1970 and 1974. A pro-European, his domestic policies were more interventionist than had been expected. His party came out ahead in two general elections but was unsuccessful in forming a government after the second.

Early Life

Heath was born on 9 July 1916 in Broadstairs, Kent in the southeast of England. His father was a carpenter and builder, an unusual background for a future Conservative leader in that era. He won an organ scholarship to Balliol College, Oxford where he studied Modern Greats (Politics, Philosophy and Economics). While there he held the positions of President of the University Conservative Association, Chairman of the Federation of University Conservative Associations and President of the Oxford Union, using his position in 1938 to condemn the government's policy of appeasing Germany. In the same year he won a legal scholarship to Grays Inn but joined the Royal Artillery at the outbreak of World War II, attaining the rank of Lieutenant Colonel and receiving an MBE (Military Division) in 1945.

After the war he was employed at the Ministry of Civil Aviation, then edited the *Church Times* 1948–49 before joining a merchant bank. He entered the House of Commons in 1950 as the member for Bexley (which would evolve into Old Bexley and Sidcup), the same year in which he and eight other Conservatives published *One Nation—A Conservative Approach to Social Problems*. He held a succession of posts in the Conservative governments of 1951–64, including assistant Chief Whip to the Lord Commissioner of the treasury, joint deputy Chief Whip, deputy Chief Whip, parliamentary secretary to the treasury and government Chief Whip. He was created a member of the Privy Counsel and took the post of minister of labour in 1959 before

becoming Lord Privy Seal the following year. He was also Conservative spokesman on foreign affairs in the Commons, in view of the fact that the foreign secretary, the Earl of Home, sat in the Lords at that stage. During this period Heath oversaw Britain's application to join the EEC, which was subsequently blocked by France.

In 1964 the Earl of Home, by then Prime Minister Alec Douglas-Home, made Heath secretary of state for industry, trade and regional affairs and president of the board of trade. When the Conservatives lost the general election of Oct. 1964 he became the opposition spokesman on economic affairs and when Douglas-Home resigned in July 1965 he was elected the party's new leader, defeating Reginald Maudling and Enoch Powell. He lost the general election of March 1966 to Harold Wilson's Labour Party but led the Conservatives to power in June 1970.

Career Peak

Heath's tenure was expected to see reduced taxation and public spending, but rising oil and commodity prices made this impossible. High inflation, rising unemployment and an unsatisfactory balance of payments posed major problems throughout his premiership. Government money was used to bail out failing businesses, and price and wage controls were imposed. Heath also attempted to take on the trade unions, putting forward an *Industrial Relations Act* in 1971. There were numerous strikes, the most serious of which was led by the miners, and in 1972 a 3 day working week was introduced as an energy saving measure. In the end, however, Heath was forced to give in to the miners' demands.

Meanwhile Northern Ireland's sectarian troubles continued to worsen, and in 1972 the Heath government imposed direct rule on the province. His greatest personal achievement on the international stage came in 1973 when he successfully negotiated Britain's entry into the EEC. However, it was not a wholly popular move with the nation at large. When Heath called a general election to strengthen his mandate in Feb. 1974, he failed to gain a majority and could not establish a coalition. Wilson did so and Labour won the year's second election in Oct. outright. In the ensuing Conservative party leadership election of 1975, Heath was ousted by Margaret Thatcher.

Later Life

Heath was member of Parliament for Old Bexley and Sidcup until he stood down in 2001 and was Father of the House (i.e. the longest serving member of the Commons) from 1992 until 2001. He has remained an active figure on the international scene, working with Willy Brandt in the 1970s and negotiating hostage releases with Saddam Hussein in the 1990s. Heath had a tempestuous relationship with Thatcher during her period in office and remained vocal on the pro-Europe wing of the party. He was made a Knight of the Garter in 1992. He is a keen sailor, having captained the British Admirals Cup-winning team in 1971. As a devotee of orchestral music, he helped found the European Community Youth Orchestra. He published his autobiography in 1998. He died in Salisbury, Wilts on 17 July 2005.

Hélou, Charles (Lebanon)

Introduction

Hélou's presidency from 1964–70 spanned the Arab-Israeli Six-day war of 1967 and its immediate aftermath. The most significant repercussion for Lebanon was the increased Palestinian encroachment on its territory as a base for guerrilla operations against Israel and the upsetting of the balance between Muslim and Christian Lebanese which led to civil war in 1975.

Early Life

Born on 25 Dec. 1912 and educated at the Christian Jesuit St. Joseph University in Beirut, Hélou began his working life as a lawyer and journalist. He was appointed Lebanese ambassador to the Vatican in 1947, elected to the Chamber of Deputies in 1951, and served as minister of justice and health in 1954–55 and of education in early 1964.

Career Peak

In Aug. 1964 Hélou was elected by the National Assembly to succeed Fuad Chehab as state president. Volatile regional politics overshadowed his 6 year term of office as he faced irreconcilable demands: from the guerrillas of the Palestinian refugee community in Lebanon; from Arab states and Lebanese Muslims keen to sponsor Palestinian resistance to Israel; from Lebanese Christians fearful for their continued independence and of Israeli military reprisals; from Israelis concerned about the security of their northern border; and from the Shia Muslim community increasingly displaced by instability in south of the country. Hélou sought to regulate the activities of Palestinian fighters through the 1969 Cairo agreement with PLO leader Yasser Arafat. However, this was to prove largely ineffective. He left office in Sept. 1970 and died on 7 Jan. 2001.

Hirohito (Japan)

Introduction

Emperor of Japan since 1926, Hirohito was known for his militaristic regime leading to World War II. After the atomic bomb attack on Hiroshima in 1945, he surrendered to General Douglas MacArthur. He was son of the crown prince, Yoshihito and as 124th emperor, was the longest reigning emperor in Japanese history.

Early Life

Hirohito was born in 1901. From the age of thirteen he attended a special school to prepare him for responsibilities as heir to the throne. He was the first Japanese emperor to travel extensively. He visited Britain and five European countries shortly after graduating in 1921. Upon his return to Japan, his father fell mentally ill and Hirohito ruled as regent until his father's death in Dec. 1926.

Career Peak

In 1924, Hirohito married Princess Nagako Kuni and 9 years later, Prince Akihito was born.

His approval of military expansion in the 1930's divided the country. Japan eventually entered World War II when Japanese bombers attacked Pearl Harbour. After Japan's surrender to SCAP (Supreme Command Allied Powers), Emperor Hirohito gave up his rights as sovereign ruler. Thereafter, his role was seen as purely symbolic. The Constitution of 1947 states that any interference by the Emperor in matters of state requires the approval of the Cabinet. There was a serious prospect of Hirohito being tried as a war criminal but MacArthur made use of the Emperor's authority to smooth the transition to a democratic Japan.

Later Life

Hirohito died on 7 Jan. 1989. His funeral was attended by more foreign dignitaries than any other funeral in world history.

Ho Chi Minh (Vietnam)

Introduction

Inspired by Lenin, Ho Chi Minh was nationalist leader, president of North Vietnam (1954–69) and founder of the Indo-Chinese Communist Party (1930). A strong opponent of French colonialism, he led the resistence to the French in the first Indochina War out of which the Democratic Republic of North Vietnam emerged. Founder of the Viet Cong guerrilla movement, he died during the Vietnam War.

Early Life

Ho Chi Minh was born on 19 May 1890 in Hoang Tru, central Vietnam. He attended school in Hue during his teenage years, worked as a schoolmaster in Phan Tiet, and went to a technical school in Saigon. In 1911, under the name Ba, he began work as a cook on a French steamer. This took him as far as Boston and New York. After 2 years in London (1915–17) he moved to Paris where he became an active socialist, using the name Nguyen Ai Quoc (Nguyen the Patriot) to organise a group of Vietnamese to protest against French colonial policy. In 1920 Ho Chi Minh participated in the founding of the French Communist Party.

Inspired by Lenin, Ho Chi Minh went to Moscow in 1923. There he participated in the fifth Congress of the Communist International, the world organisation of communist parties. In 1924 he was in Canton, a stronghold of China's communist revolutionaries. It was then that he recruited his first cadres of the Vietnamese Revolutionary Youth Association, the predecessor of the Communist Party of Vietnam (VNA). Chiang Kai-shek expelled the communists from Canton in 1927.

After the outbreak of World War II, Ho Chi Minh returned to Vietnam to organise the Vietnamese Independence Movement, the Viet Minh (League for the Independence of Vietnam) and a guerrilla army to resist Japanese colonisation. The Viet Minh liberated large parts of northern Vietnam and after the Japanese surrender to the allies the Viet Minh proclaimed, on 2 Sept. an independent Democratic Republic of Vietnam from Hanoi. In Oct. General Jacques Leclerc landed in Saigon with orders to regain control of Vietnam for the free French Government. A stalemate ensued with the Viet Minh in control of north Vietnam and the French in control of the south. On March 6, Vietnam was made a 'free state' within the French Union.

The agreement was short lived. A clash between French and Vietnamese troops, on 23 Nov. 1946 led to a French naval bombardment of Haiphong, killing nearly 6,000. The first Indochina War raged for 8 years until the French were defeated at Dien Bien Phu (1954) where 16,000 French troops surrendered.

Career Peak

The subsequent Geneva Conference divided Vietnam along the 17th parallel. Ho Chi Minh became the first president of the independent republic of North Vietnam. The accord also made provision for elections to be held in 1956 for the reunification of Vietnam. This was not accepted by the Bao Dai government in South Vietnam and by 1959, Hoh Chi Minh had begun a campaign of guerrilla insurgence in South Vietnam and established the National Liberation Front or Viet Cong. The same year he ceded his position as the Loa Dong (Workers' Party)'s secretary-general to Le Duan.

In Dec. 1961, South Vietnam's President Diem requested assistance from the USA. President Kennedy sent military advisers to South Vietnam and in July 1965 President Johnson committed up to 125,000 US troops. The Vietnam War outlived Ho Chi Minh, who died on 2 Sept. 1969, Vietnam's National Day.

Hollande, François (France)

Introduction

François Hollande was elected the 24th president of the French Republic in May 2012. A Socialist Party veteran, his election returned the Left to the Élysée Palace for the first time since his one-time mentor, François Mitterrand, departed office in 1995. Renowned for his understated manner and dry wit, Hollande led the Socialist Party from 1997–2008 but had never served in a ministerial role. His presidential tenure has focused heavily on economic issues in the wake of negative growth and continuing eurozone instability, which have prompted a sustained slide in his voter approval rating. More recently, however, radical Islamist threats to French domestic security have increasingly dominated the political agenda. Abroad, Hollande ordered French military intervention in the former African colony of Mali in Jan. 2013 in support of its government against Islamist rebels and in the Central African Republic in Dec. that year in response to sectarian violence. He left office in May 2017.

Early Life

François Hollande was born on 12 Aug. 1954 in Rouen, Normandy. The son of a social worker and a doctor, he attended the Paris Institute of Political Studies ('sciences Po'. before continuing his studies at the HEC Paris business school. In 1978 he won a place at the École Nationale d'Administration (ENA), the elite graduate school for those aspiring to high office.

On leaving the ENA in 1980, Hollande joined François Mitterrand's second presidential election campaign. When Mitterrand was sworn in the following year as France's first socialist president under the Fifth Republic, Hollande was appointed an economic adviser. During his time at the Élysée Palace he worked as chief of staff to the foreign minister, Roland Dumas, who would later give influential support to Hollande's run to become the Socialist Party's presidential candidate.

In 1988 Hollande was elected to the National Assembly as the representative for Corrèze, a rural department in south-central France. He served as mayor of the department's capital, Tulle, from 2001 until 2008. Corrèze was regarded as a power base for the then President Jacques Chirac, the nemesis of the French Left, and Hollande's ability to build popularity there was considered a significant achievement.

Chirac's decision to call a snap parliamentary election in 1997 saw Lionel Jospin installed as prime minister, with Hollande selected to succeed him as leader of the Socialist Party. Hollande's long-term partner, Ségolène Royal—with whom he has four children—was appointed minister of schools by Jospin. Despite not being a member of the cabinet, Hollande was a close adviser to the premier at the same time as overseeing a programme of modernization in the Socialist Party comparable to that undertaken by the British Labour Party and the German Social Democrats.

In 2002 Jospin ran for the presidency, only to be defeated in the first round by the far-right candidate, Jean-Marie Le Pen. A committed pro-European, Hollande went on to secure his party's support for a 'yes' vote in the 2005 referendum to ratify the European Constitutional Treaty, although the electorate rejected the treaty. In 2007 Ségolène Royal stood as the Socialist Party's presidential candidate but was defeated by Nicolas Sarkozy. Hollande and Royal announced the end of their relationship soon afterwards. In 2008 Hollande stepped down as secretary-general of the Socialist Party, to be succeeded by Martine Aubry.

In 2011 the Socialist Party held its first ever open primary to select a presidential candidate. Dominique Strauss-Kahn, previously the strong favourite for the nomination, elected not to stand following his arrest in New York on charges of sexual assault. Hollande, who used the primary campaign to declare his intention to be a 'président normal'. defeated Martine Aubry in a second round run-off on 16 Oct. 2011.

The contrast of his low-key approach with the belligerence of the presidential incumbent, Nicolas Sarkozy, was a cornerstone of Hollande's election campaign. In the first round of voting on 22 April 2012 Hollande took 28.6% of the vote, and in the second round on 6 May he defeated Sarkozy, taking 51.6% of the vote.

Career Peak

Hollande's electoral victory and his Socialist Party's subsequent success in parliamentary elections in June 2012 were quickly overshadowed by the ongoing debt crisis in the eurozone and growing concern over France's stalled economic growth and high unemployment. International ratings agencies downgraded France's credit status in 2012 and again in Nov. 2013, and the International Monetary Fund was critical of French labour costs and taxation levels. Hollande had meanwhile pledged to renegotiate the terms of the 2011 EU treaty setting strict limits on state deficits, arguing that the euro crisis was symptomatic of a wider 'failure of European governance'. The treaty was nevertheless ratified by the French parliament in Oct. 2012.

On the international stage, in Nov. 2012 France recognized the Syrian National Coalition for Revolutionary and Opposition Forces, representing the disparate anti-government groups seeking to topple the regime of President Bashar al-Assad. In Jan. 2013 Hollande sent French troops and aircraft to Mali to oust militant Islamist insurgents who had taken control of the north of the country during 2012 and threatened regional stability across West Africa. By early Feb. most of the main northern towns had been recaptured by French and Malian forces. Then in Dec. that year he deployed French peacekeeping forces to the Central African Republic to restore order against a background of spiralling sectarian conflict. In mid-2014 France became the first Western ally to join US-led military air strikes in Iraq against Islamic State jihadist insurgents and, from Sept. 2015, extended operations to Syria.

In social affairs, Hollande's government courted considerable domestic opposition over legislation to legalize gay marriage and adoption, which was passed in April 2013. In Jan. 2014 his image suffered further as press revelations surfaced about his marriage.

Following heavy Socialist losses at local elections in March 2014, Jean-Marc Ayrault resigned as premier. Hollande replaced him with Manuel Valls, a centre-left moderate and economic reformist. However, there was another electoral defeat in the European Parliament elections in May that year and in Sept. the Socialists and their allies also lost their parliamentary majority in the Senate. In Nov. Hollande disclosed that he would not seek re-election for a second term if he failed to cut the high rate of unemployment in France.

In Jan. 2015 Hollande faced a national crisis after 17 people were killed by Islamist gunmen in separate attacks in Paris. The majority died during an assault on the offices of the *Charlie Hebdo* satirical magazine, which had previously published cartoons of the prophet Mohammed. Despite the subsequent introduction of a range of new security measures, Islamist jihadists struck again in Nov. in co-ordinated terror attacks across public venues in Paris, killing 130 people and injuring over 300 more. In response, the government announced a state of emergency and stepped up air strikes on Islamic State targets in Syria. In the wake of the Paris attacks and the escalating foreign migrant crisis facing the EU, France's far-right, anti-immigration National Front attracted a significant number of new voters in regional elections in Dec.

Meanwhile, ahead of presidential elections in April and May 2017, Hollande continued to struggle with France's stuttering economy and rising joblessness, which prompted broad national strike action in Jan. 2016.

He did not stand for the presidency in 2017 and was succeeded by Emmanuel Macron on 8 May.

Holyoake, Keith (New Zealand)

Introduction

Keith Jacka Holyoake was born on 11 Feb. 1904 at Pahiatua on North Island. National party prime minister in 1957 and then from 1960–72, Holyoake was famous for his judicious diplomacy and skill at encouraging consensus. He later served as the country's governor-general for 3 years from 1977. At age 12, having left school after his father's death, Holyoake worked on the family farm while his mother continued his education at home. His school nickname, 'Kiwi Keith' which distinguished him from an Australian classmate, nevertheless remained with the statesman for life.

Early Life

Holyoake was active in local farming organizations during the 1930s and 40s and first stood for parliament in 1931. He unsuccessfully contested the Motueka seat for the United Party at the election of that year but won it in a 1932 by-election. The youngest member in the House, he held Motueka until 1938. He married Norma Ingram in 1935 and helped set up the National party in the following year after the United-Reform coalition collapsed. While out of parliament, Holyoake was named vice-president of the Farmers' Union. In 1943, he was re-elected as National member for Pahiatua, and 3 years later became the party's deputy leader. When National under Sidney Holland replaced the wartime Labour administration in 1949, Holyoake was appointed agriculture minister. Holding this post for 7 years, he introduced minimum wool prices and measures to curb New Zealand's rabbit population. 1949 also marked Holyoake's transition to deputy prime minister, a position to which he was the first to be formally appointed.

Career Peak

Holyoake became the country's longest serving prime minister. Sidney Holland's ill health led to his retirement and replacement by his deputy in 1957. Initially Holyoake was elected leader (13 Aug.) while Holland continued as prime minister. Closer to the election, Holland left politics and Holyoake formed his own cabinet (20 Sept.). The reorganized party's campaign was not successful, and Holyoake was voted into opposition for the next 3 years. However, Labour's stringent budgets, coupled with Holyoake's energetic self-promotion, including a 6 week Asian tour in 1960, laid the ground for

National's election victory in Dec. of that year. The party won a majority of 12 seats and went on to be re-elected in 1963, 1966, and 1969. Although maintaining Labour's socialist welfare policies, the Holyoake administration passed some 215 bills in its first term alone, revising legislation such as the liquor laws and the Crimes Act. Fiscal policy suffered from low export prices in the mid-1960s, leading to high national debt. To secure the currency, Holyoake borrowed US$62 m. from the IMF in Nov. 1965 and a further $A50 m. from the Australian government in the following year. Abroad, he actively supported the Commonwealth, sought to improve New Zealand's relations with South-East Asia and Australia, and was a prominent commentator on Britain's entry to the EEC. His decision to send troops to Vietnam, however, was contentious and provoked violence on the campaign trails in the latter half of the 1960s. Protests in 1966 gave way to brawls with police in 1969, when Holyoake too was mobbed. National nonetheless held its majority in an enlarged parliament of 84 seats. Holyoake was knighted in 1970.

Later Life

Holyoake stood down as prime minister on 7 Feb. 1972, and was replaced by his deputy since 1960, lawyer Jack Marshall. National lost the Dec. 1972 election but was returned to power under the leadership of Robert Muldoon 3 years later. Holyoake remained an MP and served as Muldoon's minister of state until 1977, when he retired from parliament to be governor-general. Holyoake was the first politician to hold this post, which he held for 3 years. He died in Dec. 1983.

Honecker, Erich (Germany)

Introduction

Erich Honecker was the Secretary General of the Socialist Unity Party of Germany (SED) from 1971–89, and held the post of Chairman of the Council of State from 1976–89. In these dual roles, he was head of both party and government in East Germany. A lifelong communist, he helped develop a closer relationship with West Germany with the country benefiting economically as a result. He was, however, a hard-liner who tried to stamp out criticism and encouraged a Stalinesque cult of the personality. His reluctance to adapt to the democratic reforms sweeping through the Eastern Bloc in the late 1980s led to his downfall in 1989, shortly before the collapse of the East German state.

Early Life

Honecker was born on 25 Aug. 1912 in Neunkirchen in Germany's Saar region. His father was a miner and communist. Honecker joined the Communist Youth Movement when he was in his early teens before joining the Communist party proper when he was 17. In 1930 he went to the International Lenin School in Moscow. A roofer by trade, his political activities soon took precedence and, after Hitler's rise to power in 1933, he was an organizer for the outlawed Communist Youth Movement. He was arrested 2 years later and in 1947 was sentenced to 10 years hard labour. With the arrival of the Red Army at the end of World War II in 1945 he was freed from prison in Brandenburg.

He helped prepare the Soviet-occupied zone of Germany for Communist government and in 1946 he established a new movement, Free German Youth, which he chaired until 1955. 1946 also saw the establishment of the SED, a party created by a merger between the German Communist Party and the Social Democrat Party. He travelled to Moscow in 1956–57 for further training, returning to East Germany the following year when he became a full member of the Politburo. He was given responsibility for security matters, and in this guise was responsible for the construction of the Berlin Wall in 1961.

East Germany's leader during this period was Walter Ulbricht, who had helped propel Honecker's career along since 1945. In 1967 Honecker was officially designated his successor. Their relationship, however, soured and in 1971 Honecker actively conspired with other Politburo members to have Ulbricht removed. Ulbricht resigned as First Secretary of the Party and Honecker was unanimously voted into the post, which was changed to

General Secretary 5 years later. Ulbricht died in 1973 and 3 years later Honecker became Chairman of the Council of State.

Career Peak

Honecker employed the feared Stasi (Secret Police) to retain order and eliminate opposition within the country. However, he did allow for a relaxation in the laws governing artistic expression. More radically, he pursued closer ties with capitalist West Germany. The rewards included extensive West German loans and grants, international recognition of East Germany, increasing world trade and a general upsurge in East Germany's economy. Guided by his Finance Minister Günter Mittag, East Germany enjoyed industrial modernization, improved social benefits and large-scale housing projects.

Détente with the West was not without its disadvantages, however, as the country became over reliant on Western money. As more people travelled to and from East Germany and Western media became more accessible, the lie that life in East Germany was incomparably better than elsewhere was hard to justify. This was even more so after Honecker positioned himself against the democratizing reforms, epitomised by Gorbachev's policy of *glasnost* ('openness'), that were sweeping through the Soviet sphere of influence.

In 1989 it was intended to hold celebrations throughout the country to mark the 40th anniversary of the East German state. However, in a climate of growing discontent, the celebrations turned into riots and calls for democratic elections. Honecker's resignation became inevitable when, on 9 Oct. 1989, his order to open fire on protesters in Leipzig was openly disobeyed. He was replaced briefly by Egon Krenz, but within a few weeks the Berlin Wall had fallen and communist rule came to an end.

Later Life

Honecker went first to a Soviet hospital in Berlin and then to Moscow. In Feb. 1990 treason and manslaughter were issued against him in Berlin. He went back to Germany in 1992 but, in consideration of his failing health, proceedings against him were dropped and he was allowed to go to Chile. On 29 May 1994 he died of liver cancer.

Houphouët-Boigny, Félix (Côte d'Ivoire)

Introduction

Felix Houphouët-Boigny served as president from 1960 until his death in 1993. Regarded as the father of the nation, when he died he was the third longest serving world leader, behind Kim Il-sung of North Korea and Fidel Castro of Cuba.

Early Life

Félix Houphouët-Boigny is thought to have been born on 18 Oct. 1905 in the town of Yamoussoukro. The son of a wealthy Baule tribe chief, he became a rural doctor as well as a wealthy planter. A Christian convert, he studied medicine in French Senegal and in 1944 co-founded the African Agricultural Syndicate to protect the interests of African planters against European settlers.

In 1945 he was the first African to be elected a deputy of the French National Assembly in the Côte d'Ivoire elections. In the same year he founded the Democratic Party of Côte d'Ivoire (PDCI), which was affiliated with the French Communist Party.

Career Peak

In 1958 President de Gaulle offered French territories a referendum on whether to join a French federal community or become independent. Houphouët-Boigny campaigned successfully for self-government within the French community. In 1959 he became prime minister and in 1960 president, going on to win five successive 5 year terms.

In 1963 Houphouët-Boigny survived a failed coup, after which many leading figures in Côte d'Ivoire were either detained or put under house arrest. There was also a student protest in 1970, after which universities were temporarily closed, followed by a pardon. Overall, however, Houphouët-Boigny's tenure was relatively stable compared to the post-independence experience of many of the country's neighbours. He instituted a strong national identity which helped to overcome the divisions among some 60 ethnic groups in the country.

Houphouët-Boigny pursued liberal free enterprise policies, developing the country into a major exporter of cocoa and palm oil and the world's third largest producer of coffee behind Brazil and Colombia. However, the 1973 oil crisis and a dramatic slump in world commodity prices hit the economy hard and external debt spiralled over the next two decades to around US$20 bn.

On the international stage, Houphouët-Boigny supported the unsuccessful Biafran war of secession from Nigeria, he was open to dialogue with apartheid South Africa and from 1973 he broke off relations with Israel.

Although there was a large measure of state control, Houphouët-Boigny preferred to assuage opposition through largesse rather than repression. However, he was branded a neo-colonialist due to the large number of roles given to French technical experts in government, banking and business. His personality cult fuelled ambitious projects such as the building of the world's largest Catholic cathedral in his home town, to where he achieved his dream of moving the country's capital from Abidjan. Despite criticism of his desire to retain power into old age, particularly from future president Laurent Gbagbo, Houphouët-Boigny won his final 5 year term in 1990, but died in office 3 years later.

Howard, John (Australia)

Introduction

Liberal Party member for Bennelong in northwest Sydney since 1974, John Howard became Australia's 25th prime minister in March 1996. Known as an economic rationalist, Howard is also a staunch monarchist who nevertheless organized the 1999 referendum on establishing a republic. His second and third terms were dominated by foreign policy initiatives, in the Asia-Pacific region and in support of the invasion of Iraq in 2003. Successes in Timor-Leste and the Solomon Islands boosted his support domestically but strained relations with several close neighbours, most notably Malaysia and Papua New Guinea. His fourth term of office began in Oct. 2004. Foreign affairs have again featured prominently as he announced further deployments of Australian forces to Afghanistan, Timor-Leste and the Solomon Islands in 2005 and 2006. Howard left office on 3 Dec. 2007 after being defeated by Kevin Rudd in the previous month's elections.

Early Life

John Winston Howard was born on 26 July 1939 in Earlwood, an industrial suburb of Sydney. After attending schools in the city he went on to graduate from Sydney University with a Bachelor of Laws in 1961. Howard joined the Young Liberal Movement at age 18, and in 1963 he became a member of the party's state executive. Practising as a solicitor in a Sydney firm until his election to parliament as member for Bennelong on 18 May 1974, Howard also served as Liberal vice-president for New South Wales during 1972–74. A year after his election, he was appointed minister for business and consumer affairs by Liberal prime minister Malcolm Fraser. In the months leading up to the 1977 election, Howard was made minister for special trade negotiations and minister assisting the prime minister. He was promoted to treasurer just prior to the Dec. election, at which Liberal victory secured Howard's position. He remained treasurer until Fraser lost to Labor in 1983, at which time he became deputy party leader and shadow treasurer. Howard led the party for 4 years from 5 Sept. 1985, eventually being replaced by his rival, former leader Andrew Peacock. Between 1989–94 he occupied a variety of shadow ministry positions, including industrial relations and industry, technology, and communications. He also served as chair of the Manpower and Labour Market Reform Group, and manager of opposition parliamentary business. Voted back as Liberal leader after Alexander Downer in Jan. 1995, Howard fought the next year's election campaign on the basis of economic reform. He became prime minister on 11 March 1996, ending 13 years of Labor government with a 44 seat Liberal-National coalition majority.

Career Peak

Upon gaining office, Howard pledged to slash government spending by $A8 bn. between 1996–99. This motivated the sale of numerous state-owned services, most controversially the telecommunications firm Telstra. Howard's bill for the sale of one third of Telstra was passed by the upper house in June 1999. Within the same week a set of bills was passed allowing a 'consumption' tax on goods and services (GST), the proposal of which had crippled Liberal support at the 1993 election. Howard described the success of the GST and Telstra legislation as personal achievements. Other important issues in his first term in office included a dispute over indigenous land rights following a 1996 court ruling against Aboriginal access to sites of cultural tradition owned by non-Aboriginals, and the contentious introduction of a 'work for the dole' scheme in 1998. The scheme became a new outlet for a longstanding disagreement over compulsory union membership between the trade unions and the Howard government. A bitter union dispute was also sparked in April of the same year when a major stevedoring company, acting with government support, replaced its 1,500 workforce with non-union staff overnight.

Howard survived a considerable swing to Labor, losing 11 seats, at the 3 Oct. 1998 election. In Nov. of the following year, he organized a referendum on the amendment of Australia's constitution to become a republic with a parliament-appointed president. This proposal was rejected. Howard's second term was characterized by criticism over immigration and foreign policy, particularly concerning Australia's military contributions to UN peacekeeping in Timor-Leste and NATO action against Serbia. In response to complaints that he was not providing for those displaced in the Serbian conflict, Howard welcomed Kosovar refugees in person at Sydney airport in May 1999. However, in July 2001 the refugee-laden Norwegian cargo ship Tampa was caught in a diplomatic gridlock between Australia, the UN, and Norway. The 'boat people' were eventually diverted to Papua New Guinea, with Howard taking a stern position against asylum seekers, to popular acclaim. His coalition government was re-elected at the 10 Nov. 2001 election with 82 seats. However, when Ansett, the country's second largest airline, stopped flying in Feb. 2002, Howard came under fire for failing to underwrite a last-minute sale. Owned by Air New Zealand but an Australian icon, the carrier had gone into administration in Sept. of the previous year.

In May 2003 Peter Hollingworth, Australia's governor-general, resigned. Hollingworth had been the subject of allegations of a rape in the 1960s (the charges were later dropped) and was censured for his failure to dismiss a paedophile member of the clergy when he was archbishop of Brisbane. Howard, who had recommended Hollingworth's appointment, accepted the resignation but confirmed his right to make future appointments without consultation.

Australian foreign policy in the Asia-Pacific region has become more aggressive under Howard's leadership. His interventionist approach was first tested in Timor-Leste in Sept. 1999 and deemed a success by the Australian public. The mission was strengthened by the confirmation of Timor-Leste's independence by the Indonesian parliament on 19 Oct. 1999, the same day a mass grave was unearthed. Australian involvement in the region was highlighted by the terrorist attack on a nightclub in Bali, Indonesia, on 16 Nov. 2002 when 88 Australians were killed. Despite the sympathy of Asian neighbours, Howard was criticized for declaring Australia's willingness to act pre-emptively if under threat. Malaysia's prime minister, Dr Mahathir Mohamad, accused Howard of arrogance in his approach to regional security, and the Thai government rejected suggestions that external assistance was necessary in controlling domestic terrorist threats.

In July 2003 Australia led a peacekeeping mission to the Solomon Islands at the request of the prime minister, Sir Allan Kemakeza. Although New Zealand, Papua New Guinea, the Fiji Islands and Tonga also contributed troops, Australia was seen to dominate the mission, causing unease among ex-colonies. Relations with the government of Papua New Guinea, led by Sir Michael Somare since Aug. 2002, became strained in mid-2003 over the issue of Australian involvement in Papua New Guinea's administration. Howard had enjoyed good relations with Somare's predecessor, Sir Mekere Morauta, and had declared him his country's last hope for political and economic revival. Howard insisted that Somare accepted Australian police and professionals for operational rather than observational involvement, threatening the withdrawal of Australia's crucial aid package.

Howard's support for the US-led invasion of Iraq in March 2003 attracted vociferous domestic opposition. The subsequent failure to demonstrate an Iraqi programme for weapons of mass destruction (WMD) provoked accusations of lying to justify the attack. However, opinion polls demonstrated strong support for Howard and involvement in the war. He was re-elected for a further term when the Liberal Party won the election of 9 Oct. 2004 taking 74 seats and 40.5% of the vote. In Dec. 2004 he became Australia's second longest-serving prime minister after Sir Robert Menzies.

In July 2005 Howard announced that Australian special forces were to be deployed to Afghanistan to deter rebel attacks and support the international coalition. Further deployments followed in 2006. Also in 2006 Australian troops spearheaded peacekeeping initiatives in the Solomon Islands and Timor-Leste after unrest in both countries during April–May. However, he ruled out Australian intervention in the Fiji Islands following a bloodless coup there in Dec. 2006.

An outbreak of unprecedented racial violence in Sydney in Dec. 2005 was condemned by Howard, but he denied that Australia was guilty of underlying racism despite widespread public hostility to asylum seekers. In Aug. 2006 he was forced to drop a controversial bill that would have tightened Australia's policy on refugees and asylum seekers in the face of defections within his government's ruling coalition. The proposed legislation would have extended the policy of sending many illegal entrants to be housed and processed in third countries.

Howard's coalition was defeated by Labor in the elections of 24 Nov. 2007. He remained in office until the formal swearing-in of Kevin Rudd's government on 3 Dec. Unlike Howard, Rudd was an ardent critic of the Iraq war.

Later Life

In March 2010 Howard was nominated for the presidency of the International Cricket Council by Australia and New Zealand to assume office in 2012. However, his appointment was opposed by South Africa, Zimbabwe and Sri Lanka who argued that he was not adequately qualified for the role. His autobiography *Lazarus Rising: a Personal and Political Autobiography* was published in Oct. 2010.

Howard, Michael (United Kingdom of Great Britain and Northern Ireland)

Introduction

Voted in as leader of Britain's Conservative Party in Nov. 2003 at the age of 62, Michael Howard's aim was to prevent a third successive term of office for Tony Blair's Labour. The former barrister served in Margaret Thatcher's cabinet as home secretary and is remembered for his tough, uncompromising approach to crime and disorder. A sharp and combative House of Commons performer, Mr. Howard pledged to fight for a 'British dream' that rewards people's own talents and efforts. He was opposed to Britain joining the single European currency and campaigned for a leaner, more efficient government. He stepped down as Conservative leader in Dec. 2005.

Early Life

Michael Howard was born into a Jewish family in Llanelli, South Wales on 7 July 1941. His father, Bernard, had left Romania in the early 1930s, establishing clothes shops in Llanelli and Carmarthen. Michael Howard attended Llanelli Grammar School, followed by the University of Cambridge, where he studied law. He was a member of the so-called 'Cambridge mafia' that was to play a leading role in the Conservative (Tory) governments of Margaret Thatcher and John Major.

Howard was called to the Bar in 1964 and was appointed a QC in 1982. He also nursed political ambitions, and, after two attempts, was elected the member of Parliament (Conservative Party) for Folkestone and Hythe in 1983, the year of Margaret Thatcher's landslide victory. He progressed rapidly, becoming a junior minister at the Department of Trade and Industry 2 years later. In 1987 he moved to the Department of the Environment, first as minister for local government and then as minister for water and planning.

In 1990 Howard entered the cabinet as secretary of state for employment, playing a key role in negotiating the UK's opt-out from the European Union's Social Chapter (of the Maastricht Treaty). His Eurosceptic views echoed those of Margaret Thatcher but other influential Conservative party figures took a much softer line on European integration. This split, combined with

fears over the growing public opposition to policies such as the poll tax, brought about a Conservative Party revolt that led to Thatcher's resignation in Nov. 1990. Her successor, John Major led the Conservatives to an unexpected victory in the 1992 general election and Howard was appointed secretary of state for the environment, in which capacity he is credited with helping to secure the participation of the USA at the Earth Summit in Rio. He was promoted again in May 1993, becoming home secretary and swiftly gaining a reputation for being tough and uncompromising. Howard's bold policies frequently inspired strong reactions among the party faithful and the Labour opposition. His expansion of the prison system came in for strong criticism, as did his plans to remove the right to silence for defendants. His proposed reforms of the police force drew fire from former Conservative Home Secretary Sir Willie Whitelaw, who said they would politicize the police. Official statistics suggested that during Howard's term of office crime fell by 15%. But falling crime figures were not enough to ensure a further term of office for the Conservatives—they lost heavily to Tony Blair's New Labour in the 1997 general election.

Michael Howard held onto his Folkestone and Hythe seat and made a bid for the party leadership that had been vacated by the defeated John Major. He lost out to William Hague but was appointed shadow foreign secretary and won plaudits for his energetic House of Commons debates with his opposite number Robin Cook. When he stepped down from the cabinet in 1999 it was assumed that any longer-term hopes of leadership were over. But following the Conservatives' poor performance at the polls in the June 2001 general election and William Hague's subsequent resignation, Howard rejoined the shadow cabinet as shadow chancellor. Under new party leader Iain Duncan-Smith, Howard boosted the morale of Tory Eurosceptics with a series of stinging critiques of Labour Chancellor Gordon Brown's plans for Britain's eventual passage into the single European currency.

Britain's sustained economic growth under Labour after their sizeable 2001 election victory spelt gloom for the Conservatives in the opinion polls. The Tories supported Labour in its decision to go to war in Iraq in March 2003 and were therefore unable to capitalize on the considerable anti-war sentiment among the public. After a lacklustre performance at the 2003 Conservative party conference, Iain Duncan-Smith failed to win sufficient backing in a confidence vote amongst Tory MPs and was forced to step down.

Career Peak

The experienced Michael Howard was voted party leader unopposed in Nov. 2003, becoming the first Welsh leader of the party. He championed a pared-down, efficient administration, criticizing what he described as Labour's 'wastage' and excessive spending on public services that are 'failing to deliver'. He appointed Oliver Letwin as shadow chancellor and David Davis as shadow home secretary. Howard apologized for the introduction of the poll tax in Scotland in 1989, admitting that it had been a mistake. He stated his intention to pull out of the Common Fisheries Policy, also implemented by Thatcher's government.

The Conservatives fared poorly in the European Parliament elections of June 2004, losing eight seats and taking 27.4% of votes cast (the lowest Tory share in a national election since 1832). The success of the UK Independence Party's (UKIP) Eurosceptic campaign was seen as a factor in the loss of Conservative seats.

After the publication of the Butler Report into weapons intelligence in July 2004, Howard attacked the government's judgement in trusting intelligence on weapons of mass destruction, declaring that he would not have supported the war in Iraq had the intelligence flaws and caveats been made public.

The Conservative Party failed to oust the Labour government in the elections of May 2005 but gained 33 seats, increasing their parliamentary representation to 197 seats. However, they faced some criticism over their election campaign, which focussed heavily on issues of immigration, asylum seekers and travellers. The day after the election Howard announced his plans to stand down as party leader, stating that he was 'too old' to lead the Conservatives into the next election. Despite this announcement Howard remained head of the party for a further 6 months, carrying out an extensive front bench reshuffle that would allow David Cameron to run for leader of the party after his departure. During this time the party contributed to Tony Blair's first parliamentary defeat, when they voted alongside the Liberal Democrats and a large number of Labour rebels against proposals to extend to 90 days the time that terror suspects can be held without charge. In his final Commons meeting in Nov. 2005 Howard called for Blair to join him in retirement. Howard stood down as leader of the Conservative Party in Dec. 2005.

Later Life

Michael Howard stood down as Conservative MP for Folkestone and Hythe at the 2010 general election. He was appointed a Conservative peer in the House of Lords in May 2010.

Hoxha, Enver (Albania)

Introduction

Enver Hoxha was Albania's head of state from 1946–85. A dedicated Stalinist, he revolutionized the essentially feudal Albanian economy by enforcing agricultural collectivization and the nationalization of industry. His rule was dictatorial and he often relied on terror to enforce his policies but while his effect on the economy was significant, poverty remained widespread. On the international stage he looked to Yugoslavia, the Soviet Union and China for support but fell out with each in turn. At his death Albania was almost entirely isolated.

Early Life

The son of a textile trader, Hoxha was born on 16 Oct. 1908 in Gjirokastër, Albania. His family was Muslim, though Hoxha became a determined atheist. He attended a French school in Korçë and then the American Technical School in Tirana. Between 1930 and 1936 he lived in France and Belgium, studying in Montpellier and then working at the Albanian Consulate in Brussels. Between 1936 and 1939 he took a teaching position back in Korçë but was removed from his job, following the Italian invasion of Albania and his refusal to join the Albanian Fascist Party.

Hoxha moved to Tirana to be a tobacconist, using his shop for subterfuge communist activities. In 1941 he received assistance from Yugoslav communists in establishing the Albanian Communist Party (re-named the Party of Labour in 1948), with Hoxha installed as its Secretary General. The following year he was prominent in the setting up of the Army of National Liberation, a resistance movement that fought the occupying fascist forces as well as two rival Albanian resistance movements. In late Nov. 1944, following the liberation of Albania, Hoxha and the Communists (including his close ally Mehmet Shehu) seized power.

Career Peak

Hoxha served as Prime Minister from 1944–54 and was also Foreign Minister from 1946–53. Albania changed its name to the People's Republic of Albania in 1946, the same year in which the USA broke off ties with the regime, an act that stalled Albania's entry into the UN until 1955. Between 1944–48 Hoxha had close ties with Yugoslavia but after 1948, when Tito and Stalin fell out, he became more reliant on the Soviet Union. Profoundly influenced by Stalin and his methods, Hoxha instigated a programme on agricultural collectivization and industrial nationalization. Like Stalin, he encouraged a cult of personality and dealt ruthlessly with any opposition. Purges were common and enemies and potential enemies were routinely removed from their jobs, persecuted, imprisoned and executed. Religious institutions were outlawed, private property confiscated and freedom of expression that went against the official line ruthlessly stamped out.

In 1954 Hoxha passed the premiership to Shehu, a position he would hold until his death in 1981, though Hoxha remained the effective leader of the country. Hoxha's relationship with the Soviet Union deteriorated after the death of Stalin. Hoxha perceived it as a move away from the true ideals of Marxist-Leninism that Krushchev should refuse to support the worst excesses of the Stalin regime. Removed from the Warsaw Pact and Comecon (Council for Mutual Economic Assistance) in 1961, Albania turned to China for international support. This relationship also became strained and broke down in 1978 after numerous ideological disputes and Hoxha's disgust at China's closer ties with the USA.

Hoxha opted now for international isolation, claiming that Albania was the world's only true remaining socialist country and that it would develop into the model socialist state. It was true that under Hoxha Albania had become more self-reliant, that basic education had improved and that there was an industrial sector where previously there had been virtually none. However, the price Albania paid for these developments was a wretched standard of living for most people, heavy-handed government and international isolation.

Later Life

The early-1980s witnessed another round of purges as Hoxha endeavoured to ensure his succession. Shehu had opposed the policy of isolation and was accused of being a Yugoslav spy shortly before it was reported that he had committed suicide. A number of Shehu's followers were removed from positions of power the following year and, as Hoxha gradually withdrew from the political life, Ramiz Alia (a favourite of Hoxha) was installed as his replacement. Made nominal head of government in 1982, he duly took over as head of the Party and the State when Hoxha died in Tirana on 11 April 1985, leaving his country financially destitute and politically friendless.

Hrawi, Elias (Lebanon)

Introduction

Elias Hrawi, a Maronite Christian, took office as president on 24 Nov. 1989. He replaced René Mouawad, who had been elected earlier in the month in the wake of the 1989 charter of national reconciliation (known as the Taif Accord) but assassinated on 22 Nov. Hrawi's term of office was extended in 1995 for a further 3 years by a constitutional amendment.

Early Life

Born in 1925 in Zahlé in the Bekaa Valley, Hrawi was a successful agricultural businessman before he was elected to the National Assembly as a Maronite deputy in 1972. He continued to serve as a parliamentary member until 1989 when he unsuccessfully challenged René Mouawad in the presidential election on 5 Nov. Mouawad was assassinated 17 days later, and on the 24 Nov. Hrawi was elected in his place. He was active in the negotiations on the Taif Accord and the amendments shifting considerable constitutional power from the (Maronite) president to the (Sunni Muslim) prime minister, maintaining good relations with Syria, the Maronite leadership and the Muslim community.

Career Peak

Gen. Michel Aoun, the Maronite army commander leading a transitional military government appointed by outgoing president Amin Gemayel in Sept. 1988, refused to recognise Mouawad's or Hrawi's election. Fighting between pro- and anti-Aoun Christian factions broke out and in 1990, at Hrawi's request, Syrian troops attacked Aoun's enclave. Aoun took refuge in the French embassy and later fled to France. In Sept. 1990 Hrawi established the second republic by signing the constitutional amendments negotiated under the Taif Accord. By the end of his presidency in 1998, neither Israeli nor Syrian forces had withdrawn from Lebanon and there were continuing clashes between Israeli troops and Palestinian and Shia Hizbollah guerrillas in the south of the country, particularly in April 1996. Nevertheless, the restoration of relative stability during his term in office allowed for the holding of National Assembly elections for the first time since 1972 and for the implementation of programmes to rebuild the country's shattered economy and infrastructure. Hrawi left office on 24 Nov. 1998. He died aged 79 on 7 July 2006.

Htin Kyaw (Myanmar)

Introduction

On 15 March 2016 parliament elected Htin Kyaw to serve as the first civilian president since 1962. A loyal supporter of long-time opposition figurehead Aung San Suu Kyi, he was expected to act as her proxy as she is constitutionally barred from holding the presidential office because her children are foreign nationals. He resigned in March 2018.

Early Life

Htin Kyaw was born on 20 July 1946 in Kungyangon. His father, Min Thu Wun, was well-known as a poet and National League for Democracy (NDL) politician. Htin Kyaw attended the English Methodist High School where Aung San Suu Kyi was a schoolmate. In 1968 he graduated in economics from the Rangoon Institute of Economics and from 1971–72 attended the Institute of Computer Science in London, England.

In the 1970s and 1980s Htin Kyaw held government positions in the ministries of industry and foreign affairs before resigning in 1992 when the ruling military junta took a more repressive line. In Sept. 2000 he was arrested for attempting to help Aung San Suu Kyi visit the then capital, Mandalay, and was imprisoned for 4 months. During Aung San Suu Kyi's years under house arrest, Htin Kyaw was one of the few people allowed to visit her, and he acted as her driver in her few brief periods of freedom. In 2012 he joined the Daw Khin Kyi Foundation—established by Aung San Suu Kyi and named in honour of her mother—as a senior executive. On 10 March 2016 he was announced as the NDL's presidential nominee, and on 15 March he received 360 of 652 parliamentary votes. He became president on 1 April.

Career Peak

Prior to the general election of Nov. 2015 that saw the NDL sweep to power, Aung San Suu Kyi had commented on the constitutional bar to her assuming the presidency: 'If the NLD wins the elections and we form a government, I am going to be the leader of that government whether or not I am the president.' Having taken office as president in April, Htin Kyaw duly appointed her State Counsellor (effectively making her the *de facto* head of government), as well as minister of the president's office and foreign affairs minister.

However, Htin Kyaw has failed to reconcile Aung San Suu Kyi's traditional support base with the still powerful military, who hold 25% of the parliamentary seats. Also, by the end of 2017 any optimism about the new government among Myanmar's minorities had given way to fear and disenchantment in the wake of a brutal army crackdown on the Rohingya Muslim minority in Rakhine state, which had forced an estimated 1 m. refugees to flee to neighbouring Bangladesh by Oct. and incurred widespread international condemnation of the government's inaction.

Htin Kyaw resigned in March 2018 as a result of ill health.

Hu Jintao (China)

Introduction

Hu Jintao was nominated general secretary of the Chinese Communist Party (CCP) in Nov. 2002, formally succeeding Jiang Zemin as head of state in March 2003 and as chairman of the Central Military Commission in Sept. 2004. Although widely perceived as a conservative—having supported the Tiananmen Square massacres in the late 1980s and cracked down on separatism in Tibet—he has continued Jiang's cautious reformist policies. He has maintained the drive for rapid industrial growth and also further developed China's international contacts, undertaking visits as state president to Latin America, Australia, Canada, Central Asia, the UK, USA and, in particular, Africa.

Early Life

Much of Hu's early history is disputed. He is believed to have been born in Dec. 1942 in Jixi, Anhui Province. His mother died when he was six and he was subsequently raised by an aunt. In 1959 he began engineering studies at Qinghua University and graduated in 1964, the same year in which he joined the CCP. He then held a variety of posts at the university and the ministry of water conservancy.

He is reported to have distanced himself from Mao's Cultural Revolution of the mid-1960s and was sentenced to 2 months of 'reform through labour'. Later, he worked on large-scale engineering projects in Gansu province. By the late 1970s Hu was a favourite of Deng Xiaoping, who became China's effective leader. He settled in Beijing in 1980, and within 2 years he was the youngest member of the party's central committee. Having risen through the ranks of the Communist Youth League, in 1985 he was appointed provincial

party secretary for Guizhou. In 1988 he became party secretary in charge of Tibet and authorized the killing of several independence protesters in March 1989. Shortly afterwards he declared martial law and oversaw the introduction of 100,000 troops into the region. Later in the year he was among the first of the provincial party secretaries to express his support for those who took part in the Tiananmen Square massacres.

In 1992 Hu was responsible for organizing Jiang's first party congress as leader, and soon after was designated a member of the Politburo Standing Committee. In 1998 he was named vice-president, from which point on he was Jiang's acknowledged successor. The following year he was prominent in protests at the US and British embassies in Beijing over the accidental bombing of the Chinese embassy in Belgrade during NATO military action against Serbia. He was also named deputy chairman of the Central Military Commission at that time.

Career Peak

At the CCP congress of Nov. 2002, Hu replaced Jiang as party general secretary and then succeeded him as state president in March 2003. Hu expressed his commitment to Jiang's *Theory of Three Representations* (treatise on Chinese political thought), suggesting a continuity of government style.

Hu has nevertheless pursued an active foreign policy, breaking from the Deng model which proscribed taking the lead in diplomatic negotiations. He has sought to resolve the issue of North Korea's nuclear ambitions through the ongoing six-nations talks between North and South Korea, China, Japan, Russia and the USA. He has also developed relations with neighbouring India and Pakistan, establishing military links with both countries in Nov. 2003. Earlier, in June 2003, Hu received the visiting Indian prime minister who conceded recognition of Tibet as an autonomous region of the People's Republic of China. As president, Hu has travelled widely, visiting Australia, Africa, Latin America, Canada and Central Asia in pursuit of closer economic and commercial links to supply the resources for China's industrial machine. In Nov. 2006 he hosted a Sino-African summit in Beijing attended by more than 40 African heads of state and government, and in 2007 undertook a tour of eight African countries to boost trade and investment. In July 2008 China and Russia finalized a treaty formally ending a 40-year-old border dispute that had provoked armed clashes during the Cold War.

Human rights, Taiwan, Tibet and trade have remained difficult issues in Sino-US relations. Perennial US accusations of 'backsliding' in human rights have been vigorously denied (although China reacted angrily to the award of the 2010 Nobel Peace Prize to imprisoned activist Liu Xiaobo), and Hu's government has pointed to US foreign policy as aggressive and harmful to the rights of civilians. Former President George W. Bush's less conciliatory attitude towards China over Taiwan led to a more turbulent relationship between the two countries, although Hu made a seemingly successful first presidential visit to the USA in April 2006. In Nov. 2009 US President Obama made his first visit to China, heralding declarations of bilateral co-operation on trade, climate change and other issues. At the CCP congress in Oct. 2007, Hu offered a peace agreement with Taiwan as long as the territory did not explicitly renounce its links with mainland China, and in June 2008 the first formal bilateral talks since 1999 took place. In July 2009 Hu exchanged direct messages with the president of Taiwan, the first such exchange between the national leaders in more than 60 years. Chinese–US tensions resurfaced in 2010 over the US decision to go ahead with arms sales to Taiwan, which prompted China's suspension in Jan. of high-level military exchanges with the USA, and over US claims that China was distorting trade because its currency is undervalued—a claim that China has denied.

In March 2008 the worst ethnic violence in two decades in Tibet against continuing Chinese rule prompted a security crackdown against separatist protesters and widespread international criticism of Hu's government ahead of the summer Olympic Games staged in Beijing in Aug. Further ethnic violence erupted in July 2009 in Urumqi, the capital of China's northwestern Xinjiang province, between indigenous Muslim Uighurs and Han Chinese settlers, which left around 200 people dead and 1700 injured.

In March 2011 the National People's Congress approved substantial additional expenditure on China's internal security apparatus, suggesting official concern over any contagion from the concurrent political disaffection spreading across much of the Arab world and also uncertainty over the potential for further ethnic unrest in the provinces. Disturbances erupted in Inner Mongolia in May 2011 and in Xinjiang in July–Aug., while anti-Chinese agitation continued in Tibet as a new head of the Tibetan government-in-exile took over in Aug. following the Dalai Lama's decision to relinquish his political role.

Hu's domestic agenda has focused on continuing China's rapid economic development—maintaining annual GDP growth of around 10% in 2010 and 2011, but with high inflation—and alleviating the poverty of the peasant population. An anti-corruption drive included the sacking and even execution of high-ranking state officials. Hu's government also championed increases in agricultural subsidies and the eventual termination of agricultural taxes—a programme interpreted as an attempt to create a larger middle class, committed to the CCP hegemony.

Hu was re-elected for a further term in March 2008. In Oct. 2009 he oversaw celebrations to mark the 60th anniversary of the Communist Party's assumption of power, and similarly marked the 90th anniversary of the party's founding in July 2011.

Hu was required to step down in March 2013 and was succeeded by Xi Jinping, who was elected general secretary of the CCP and as such president-designate in Nov. 2012.

Humala Tasso, Ollanta (Peru)

Introduction

Ollanta Humala became president in July 2011. Leader of the Peruvian Nationalist Party, he was elected after two rounds of voting, defeating Keiko Fujimori, daughter of former president Alberto Fujimori. Humala was backed by the Gana Perú coalition and succeeded Alan García. He is left office in July 2016 following elections in April in which he was ineligible to stand.

Early Life

Born in Lima in June 1962, Humala is the son of Isaac Humala who developed the ethno-nationalist ideology called 'ethnocacerism'. Ollanta Humala studied in Lima before joining the military. He trained initially as a paratrooper and amphibious combatant at the School of the Americas in Panama. In 1992, as head of a detachment in Tingo María, he was involved in operations against the rebel group Shining Path, for which he was later accused of human rights abuses. By 2000 he had been promoted to lieutenant-colonel.

Also in 2000, he led an uprising (along with his brother) in a bid to force out President Alberto Fujimori and leading military commanders. Following Fujimori's resignation the interim government pardoned Humala and awarded him the Peru Cross for Military Merit.

From 2000–04 Humala worked for the ministry of defence and in 2001 completed a master's degree in political sciences from the Pontifical Catholic University of Peru. He became the military attaché to the Peruvian embassy in Paris in 2003 and studied for a doctorate in international law at the Sorbonne. In 2004 he was posted to South Korea. While there his name was linked to an uprising in Peru against President Alejandro Toledo.

In 2005 Humala founded the Peruvian Nationalist Party (PNP). With support from the Union for Peru (UPP), he ran for the presidency in 2006 but lost support over questions about his past and his left-wing sympathies. From 2006–11 he fought off several legal cases related to previous coups. In 2011, backed by the Gana Perú coalition, he ran for the presidency again, defeating Keiko Fujimori.

Career Peak

In 2006 Humala had defined himself as 'anti-neoliberal' and 'anti-global capitalist' but in 2011 he adopted a more moderate profile. He distanced himself from associations with Venezuela's then president, Hugo Chávez, and stood on a platform of energy self-sufficiency, a more equitable distribution of wealth and increased taxes on mining. On coming to power, he chose a moderate cabinet, quelling worries in business circles and the Lima stock market. He announced social programmes including a non-contributory basic pension for the elderly, a public childcare programme and more scholarships to promote university education. The minimum wage was also increased.

Large-scale mining projects, such as the Conga copper and gold mine, offered potentially lucrative future revenue sources. However, popular opposition to mining schemes was widespread and protests led in Dec. 2011 to the resignation of Prime Minister Salomon Lerner, his replacement by Óscar Valdés and a major cabinet reshuffle. There were further violent anti-mining clashes in the southern Cusco region in May 2012 and in northern provinces in July, prompting the government to declare temporary states of emergency. Also in July that year, following the resignation of the unpopular Óscar Valdés and his administration in response to the unrest, Humala appointed Juan Jiménez Mayor as prime minister. However, in Sept. 2013, as thousands joined a general strike against the government's economic policies, he reshuffled the cabinet, swearing in César Villanueva Arévalo as the new premier in Oct. However, Villanueva resigned 4 months later following a conflict with the finance minister over an increase to the minimum wage. Housing, construction and sanitation minister René Cornejo was subsequently sworn in as premier, but he too resigned in July 2014, after which labour and employment promotion minister Ana Jara Velásquez was appointed. Having been censured by Congress over a spying scandal, she too was removed from office in April 2015. Her replacement, Pedro Cateriano, who had previously held the defence portfolio, became the seventh prime minister since Ollanta Humala took office as president in 2011.

A free trade agreement with the European Union came into effect in March 2013.

Humala was ineligible to run for a second term at the elections of April 2016 owing to constitutional term limits. Pedro Pablo Kuczynski succeeded him as president 3 months later.

Husák, Gustáv (Czech Republic)

Introduction

Gustáv Husák led the Czechoslovak Communist Party between 1969 and 1987 and was national President from 1975 until 1989. Though associated with the reforms of Alexander Dubček's Prague Spring, Husák quickly declared himself an opponent of liberalization and gained the favour of Moscow. He replaced Dubček as leader and oversaw 20 years of 'normalization'—the reversal of the 1968 reforms and the re-imposition of Soviet orthodoxy. By the late-1980s he was out of tune with the reformist climate and his fall coincided with the collapse of Communist rule in Czechoslovakia.

Early Life

Husák was born on 10 Jan. 1913 in Dúbravka, close to Bratislava in what is now Slovakia. In 1937 he graduated from Comenius University in Bratislava, having become active within the Slovakian Communist Party 4 years earlier. During World War II he was prominent in the Slovakian resistance, but was imprisoned from 1940–43. On his release he joined the party's Central Committee and was instrumental in the failed Slovakian national uprising of 1944.

In 1946 he was a deputy in the National Assembly and in the same year he took the chair of Slovakia's Board of Commissioners. Between 1948 and 1950 he was Gottwald's Minister of Agriculture but he fared badly in Stalin's 1950 purge of the Czechoslovakian Communist hierarchy and was again imprisoned between 1954–60. On his release he worked as a junior government official but by 1963 he had been rehabilitated and re-admitted to the Communist Party. He worked at the Academy of Sciences in Prague between 1963–68 and in April 1968 he was appointed Deputy Prime Minister to Dubček.

Dubček's Prague Spring ushered in a swathe of economic and social reforms and while Husák was at first apparently supportive of change, he began to preach a more conservative line as Muscovite displeasure increased. Becoming head of the Slovakian Communists in Aug. 1968, he demanded a reversal of the reforms already passed, thus endearing himself to the Soviet overlords. Further anti-Soviet protests throughout Czechoslovakia in March 1969 precipitated the fall of Dubček, who was then replaced by his former deputy.

Career Peak

Husák immediately set about purging reformers from the party, a process which carried on into 1970. Half of the Central Committee were removed and hundreds of thousands of party members who were excluded from or voluntarily left the party also lost their jobs. In Dec. 1970 Husák's government accepted the Soviet version of the events of 1968, which effectively stated that the Soviet invasion had been necessary to snuff out the threat of counter-revolutionaries. He tightened the oppressive censorship laws, made full use of the feared secret police and turned his back on the 1968 economic reforms, relying instead on an unaffordable level of consumerism. Recession resulted and inflation spiralled throughout the 1970s, whilst the nation's cultural life went into steep decline. He also promulgated a new constitution in 1969 that secured Slovakian autonomy.

By the mid-1980s Mikhail Gorbachev had come to power in the Soviet Union and was initiating his policies of *glasnost* ('openness') and *perestroika* ('restructuring'). Husák was not in step with the changing climate sweeping the communist regimes of the Eastern Bloc, and in 1987 he resigned the leadership of the Czechoslovakian Communist Party to be replaced by Miloš Jakeš. By Nov. 1989 the communist governments in Poland, Hungary and East Germany had all fallen. Pro-democracy protests by Czech students and intellectuals began in mid-Nov. and the authorities responded with strong arm tactics which succeeded only in increasing the reform movement's momentum.

The government agreed to negotiations with the hastily organized reform party Civic Forum, led by future-president Václav Havel, and the Communists resigned their posts en masse. Husák gave up the presidency within a month and was replaced by Havel.

Later Life

Husák died on 18 Nov. 1991 in Bratislava.

Hussein al-Tikriti, Saddam (Iraq)

Introduction

Saddam Hussein became president of the Republic, chairman of the Revolutionary Command Council (RCC) and secretary-general of the regional (Iraqi) command of the ruling Arab Socialist Renaissance (Ba'ath) Party after the resignation of Gen. Ahmad Al Bakr in July 1979. He took over the additional post of prime minister in May 1994. Despite the military reversals of the 1980–88 war with Iran and the 1990–91 Gulf War against an international coalition—both of which undermined his ambitions for Iraqi regional dominance—Hussein retained power as the pivotal figure in a highly centralized and authoritarian regime and was the focus of a pervasive personality cult. In 2002 his rule again became the focus of US foreign policy, with President George W. Bush advocating 'regime change'. US-led forces launched an attack on Iraq in March 2003 and by April 2003 Saddam Hussein had been removed from power. In Dec. 2003 he was captured by US special forces near to his home town of Tikrit. He was convicted of crimes against humanity and executed in Dec. 2006.

Early Life

Saddam Hussein, a Sunni Muslim, was born in Tikrit, north of Baghdad in Salah ad-Din governate, on 28 April 1937. He was educated in the Iraqi capital and in Cairo, Egypt. Encouraged by an uncle (an officer in the Iraqi army and proponent of Arab unity), he gravitated towards politics in his teenage years, becoming a pan-Arab nationalist. In 1956 he joined the Ba'ath Party. After the 1958 overthrow of the monarchy and establishment of the republic, Hussein conspired the following year to assassinate the military leader Gen. Abdul Karim Qassim. However, the plot was foiled and Hussein was wounded. He was forced to flee the country under sentence of death, first to Syria and then to Egypt. Returning to Iraq after Qassim's overthrow in Feb. 1963, he joined the regional (Iraqi) command of the Ba'ath Party. In 1964 he was arrested for allegedly plotting against the new president, Abdul Salam Aref. While serving a prison sentence he became assistant secretary-general of the Ba'ath in Iraq. Upon his release he played a major role in the July 1968 coup which brought Ahmad Al Bakr to power. The following year Hussein was appointed deputy chairman of the ruling RCC.

Hussein set out to strengthen the economy with a state-sponsored industrial modernization programme. Underpinned by the oil price rises of 1973

and 1979, the programme led to a more equitable distribution of wealth, increased access to education and health care, and to the redistribution of land. Success on the economic front spurred Hussein to pursue an ambitious foreign policy aimed at pushing Iraq to the forefront of the Arab world. Egypt's isolation in the region in the wake of the 1978 peace agreement with Israel also gave Iraq an opportunity for a more prominent role in Arab affairs.

Career Peak

Having become the power behind the ailing President Bakr during the 1970s, Hussein took formal control of the government on Bakr's resignation in July 1979. He was subsequently accused by the international community and by Iraqi exiles of ruling by terror—through arbitrary arrests and executions of suspected political opponents and potential rivals, the slaughter of rebellious Kurds in the north of the country by chemical weapons, and repression of Shia Muslims in the south, including the draining of their traditional homeland marshes. He harnessed Iraq's oil wealth to expand his armed forces in an attempt to achieve regional hegemony through military aggression, with ruinous consequences in the Iran–Iraq War and the invasion of Kuwait. Iraq remained subject to United Nations sanctions for refusal to comply with Security Council resolutions on the supervised elimination of suspected weapons of mass destruction. This defiance led to air attacks on Iraqi military and communication installations by US and UK warplanes which continued to patrol 'no-fly zones' over areas of the country in defence of the civilian population. Nevertheless, through family and tribal patronage and control of the military and the security police, Hussein maintained his grip on Iraq and its people.

On 15 Oct. 1995 a referendum was held to determine whether the President should remain in office for a further 7 years. Turnout was said to be 99.47% of the 8.4 m. eligible electors with 99.96% of the votes cast in favour. In a repeat referendum in Oct. 2002 all votes were cast in favour of Hussein. In celebration he announced an amnesty on Iraq's prisoners, pardoning all except murderers whose release would depend on their victims' families.

Following the 11 Sept. 2001 terrorist attacks on the US, President Bush branded Hussein's regime part of an 'axis of evil' supporting terrorism and advocated an end to Hussein's regime. Amid increasing tensions, Hussein made a public broadcast in which he vowed to stand firm against 'evil tyrants and oppressors'. but in Sept. 2002 he agreed to re-admit UN Security Council weapon inspectors. By the beginning of Oct. 2002, the US was pushing for a new UN resolution which would ensure joint military action in response to Iraqi non-compliance.

Led by Hans Blix, inspectors began their assessments in Nov. 2002. Under the terms of the UN resolution, Iraq was compelled to supply a dossier, which ran to 12,000 pages, detailing the country's chemical, biological and nuclear capabilities. The US, UK and Blix received the report with scepticism. In an address to the UN Security Council on 27 Jan. 2003, Blix said he had found no evidence of an illicit weapons programme in Iraq but added that 1,000 tonnes of chemical agents and 8,500 litres of anthrax remained unaccounted for. He criticized Iraq's lack of 'proactive cooperation' in, among other things, providing a full list of Iraqi scientists. Throughout Dec. 2002 and Jan. 2003 the US and the UK expanded their military presence in the region. Meanwhile, Saddam Hussein accused the UN's weapons inspecting team of undertaking 'pure intelligence work'.

In Feb. 2003 Iraq began destroying its al-Samoud II weapons in accordance with weapons inspectors' demands. While Hans Blix welcomed the development, the US and UK treated the move with scepticism. With splits evident within the UN security council over the appropriate course of action to take against the Iraqi regime, Bush and his closest ally, UK Prime Minister Tony Blair, abandoned attempts to push through a new resolution. Having previously emphasized his right to act independently of the UN, Bush authorized US-led forces to launch an invasion of Iraq in March 2003. By April 2003 American-led troops had secured control of the country.

Later Life

Saddam Hussein's regime effectively removed from power, speculation continued as to his whereabouts. In May 2003 the US government reported that he had authorized the withdrawal of over US$1 bn. from national reserves at the outbreak of hostilities. In July 2003 his sons, Uday and Qusay, were killed in a gun battle with US troops in Mosul.

Suicide bomb attacks and military ambushes continued to harrass occupying troops and international organizations for the rest of 2003. Although foreign mercenaries were blamed for many of the attacks, the survival of Saddam Hussein indicated that some of the attacks were organized by elements of the old regime. The failure to find the ex-president was a source of embarrassment for US forces until Operation Red Dawn located and captured him alive on 13 Dec. 2003. Hussein was hiding in al-Dawr, near to Tikrit. Film footage of his medical examination was broadcast around the world after DNA tests confirmed his identity.

Hussein and seven co-defendants went on trial before the Iraq Special Tribunal, charged with crimes against humanity. Specific charges related to Hussein's conduct in 1982 against the people of the city of Dujail (including 148 charges of murder and allegations of torture) after an unsuccessful assassination attempt against him. The trial was fraught with problems, including Hussein's questioning of the court's legitimacy, the murder of several lawyers working for the defence and the replacement of the chief judge amid allegations of bias. Hussein was found guilty on 5 Nov. 2006 and sentenced to death by hanging. His final appeal against the sentence failed on 26 Dec. and he was executed on 30 Dec. 2006. Footage of his final moments was shown around the world and there followed an upsurge in violence among parts of his Sunni support. He was buried in Al-Awja, his village of birth, near to Tikrit.

Hussein bin Talal (Jordan)

Introduction

King Hussein bin Talal ruled Jordan from 1953 until his death in 1999. By that time he was the world's longest serving executive head of state. Drawn from the Hashemite dynasty, he is believed by devout Muslims to have been the 42nd generation direct descendent of the Prophet Muhammad. Throughout his reign, in one of the most volatile and dangerous regions of the world, he managed to safeguard both his throne and the stability of his country.

Early Life

Hussein was born in Amman on 14 Nov. 1935 to Prince Talal bin Abdullah and Princess Zein al-Sharaf bint Jamil. At that time the intercommunal struggle between Arabs and Zionists for control of Palestine (then, with Transjordan, under the British Mandate) was approaching a decisive phase that was to lead to the creation of the Jewish state of Israel in May 1948. Following his elementary education in Amman, he studied at Victoria College in Alexandria, Egypt, and Harrow School in England. Later he received his military training at the Royal Military Academy Sandhurst, also in England.

The most traumatic moment of his early life was the assassination in July 1951 of his grandfather, King Abdullah, outside the Al-Aqsa Mosque in Jerusalem. The young prince witnessed the event and was fortunate to escape unharmed. The following year (on 11 Aug.), Hussein was proclaimed King and head of state. He replaced his father, who had succeeded briefly before abdicating owing to mental illness. A Regency Council was appointed until Hussein's formal accession on 2 May 1953. Having by then reached the age of 18, he assumed full constitutional powers. The new King was to strengthen and professionalize (with Western help) the Jordanian military establishment, asserting the authority of the crown.

Career Peak

Domestically, King Hussein is credited with developing Jordan's economic and industrial infrastructure, and with helping to raise living standards generally. But it was his political preoccupation with the Palestinian question, and relations with Israel, that defined his long reign. While keenly aware of Arab sensitivities towards Israeli regional domination and the Palestinian cause, he maintained a readiness to compromise and to accommodate his powerful neighbour. However, it was 1994 (in the wake of Israeli-Palestinian accords) before he agreed to a formal peace treaty. Jordan's alignment with the Western powers, meanwhile, often made the King the target of criticism by more radical Arab regimes.

In 1967 the already large, displaced Palestinian population in Jordan further increased following the Arab-Israeli Six-Day War. The Arab defeat resulted in the loss of the West Bank and East Jerusalem to Israel (territories that Jordan had annexed in 1950). After the conflict, Palestinian resistance

guerrillas based in Jordan grew in strength and threatened to destabilise Hussein's regime. In Sept. 1970, the King turned his army on the militant Palestine Liberation Organization. The PLO were expelled the following year.

Over the next two decades he continued to walk a fine diplomatic line—avoiding direct confrontation with Israel, fostering relations with the Palestinians and moderate Arab states, and maintaining links with the Western powers. In 1988 he disclaimed any ambition to restore Jordanian rule in the Israeli-occupied West Bank and endorsed the PLO as the sole representative of the Palestinian people. His subsequent neutrality—or perceived support for President Saddam Hussein of Iraq—during the 1990–91 Gulf crisis over Kuwait was less well received by Western and Gulf Arab states.

King Hussein died of cancer on 7 Feb. 1999. His funeral was attended by over 50 heads of state, including close allies, friends and some of his outspoken opponents (particularly the then President of Syria, Hafiz al-Assad). Several Arab countries declared a state of mourning. He was succeeded by his eldest son, Abdullah II, one of 12 children from his four marriages.

Hwang Kyo-ahn (South Korea)

Introduction

Hwang Kyo-ahn was named prime minister by President Park Geun-hye in May 2016. On 9 Dec. 2016 he became acting president after Park stepped aside to face impeachment proceedings. Hwang is a former justice minister who served as a public prosecutor for almost 30 years.

Early Life

Hwang Kyo-ahn was born on 15 April 1957. He graduated in 1981 from the College of Law at Sungkyunkwan University, earning his master's degree in law from the same institution in 2006.

Hwang began his career in 1983 as a public prosecutor in the Cheongju District Prosecutors' Office. He went on to serve in further public prosecution roles until 2011. He specialized in national security law, a focus that drew criticism from opposition and civil rights groups.

In 2011 he went into private practice with the firm Bae Kim & Lee, and also served as chairman of the Election Broadcast Deliberation Committee. In 2013 he was appointed minister of justice and was instrumental the following year in a government motion to outlaw the leftist Unified Progressive Party, which was accused of pro-North Korean views. In May 2015 Hwang was nominated as premier, a largely ceremonial role, by President Park and was sworn in the following month.

Career Peak

Despite having been the longest serving minister in Park's administration, Hwang was dismissed as prime minister in Nov. 2016 as the president sought to restore confidence in her administration in the face of a corruption scandal. Nonetheless, he remained in office as a replacement could not be agreed upon. In Dec. Park was suspended from office to face impeachment proceedings following a parliamentary vote and Hwang duly became acting president as well as prime minister.

After confirmation by the Constitutional Court of Park's impeachment in March 2017, presidential elections held on 9 May were won by Moon Jae-in. He succeeded Hwang as president the following day. On 11 May Yoo Il-ho became acting prime minister.

Ielemia, Apisai (Tuvalu)

Introduction

Apisai Ielemia took office in Aug. 2006, succeeding Maatia Toafa. He declared Tuvalu in immediate danger from rising sea levels and requested international assistance with evacuating and resettling residents. His other major priority was to address Tuvalu's economic difficulties. He left office in Sept. 2010.

Early Life

Born in Tuvalu on 19 Aug. 1955, Ielemia attended Hiram Bingham high school in Kiribati. In 1973 he entered the civil service and became island executive officer, based in Funafuti. From 1978–94 he was executive officer for the Tuvalu high commission and from 1994–98 was its first secretary.

From 1985–94 Ielemia was clerk to the Tuvalu parliament. In 1993 he graduated in management and political science from the University of the South Pacific in Suva in the Fiji Islands. In 1994 he became assistant secretary at the ministries of health and education and of foreign affairs and in 1998 was named permanent secretary at the ministry of tourism, trade and commerce.

In 2004 Ielemia became leader of the opposition. When parliamentary elections ousted most of the existing cabinet in Aug. 2006, he was appointed prime minister by a majority of one. He promised to lift restrictions on the media and improve economic administration, and also took responsibility for foreign affairs.

Career Peak

To combat rising sea levels Ielemia has requested help from Australia, New Zealand and the wider international community to evacuate and rehouse islanders. Almost a quarter of the population was evacuated; the largest exile community is in Auckland, New Zealand. In Dec. 2006 Ielemia visited Taiwan and secured increased financial aid and agreement on joint shipping and fishing ventures. He also took some controversial measures to improve the economy, such as restricting MPs' spending allowances. In Jan. 2009 Tuvalu applied for membership of the International Monetary Fund.

Ielemia retained his parliamentary seat in elections in Sept. 2010 but despite expressing a desire to form a coalition in the wake of the elections he did not receive enough nominations to run for office. He was succeeded as prime minister by Maatia Taofa on 29 Sept.

Iliescu, Ion (Romania)

Introduction

Ion Iliescu became Romanian President in Dec. 2000. From 1989 to 1996 he served as the first head of state after the revolution that removed Nicolae Ceauşescu and the communist regime. A former member of the Communist Party Central Committee and ally of Ceauşescu, Iliescu was removed from office in 1971 after criticising Ceauşescu. Iliescu's dissatisfaction with the incumbent regime subsequently increased and when popular discontent exploded in Dec. 1989 he was an obvious choice as leader.

Early Life

Iliescu was born on 3 March 1930 in Oltenita, south of Bucharest. Having joined the Communist Youth Union in 1944 and founded the Union of High School Students in 1948, he was educated at the Bucharest Polytechnic Institute and then at the Energy Institute, Moscow. He joined the Communist Party in 1953 and from 1955 was employed as a researcher at the Bucharest Institute of Energy Studies. In 1956 he founded the Union of Romanian Students' Associations. His wife Elena is an engineer.

As an ally of Ceauşescu Iliescu's stock rose when the latter became the communist's secretary general. In 1967 Iliescu was appointed minister of youth, remaining in the post for 4 years, and in 1968 became a full member of the central committee. Following ideological disputes between the two men, Iliescu lost much of his influence.

Between 1971 and 1979 Iliescu served as a regional party secretary, first in Timişoara and then in Iasi County. From 1979 until 1984 he was chairman of the National Waters Council before taking over as director of the National Publishing House for Technical Literature until 1989. Having been accused of 'intellectual deviation' by Ceauşescu, Iliescu was placed under intensive securitate (secret police) surveillance for several years.

In mid-Dec. 1989, as anti-communist feeling swept the Eastern Bloc, protests against the Ceauşescu regime broke out in Timişoara and quickly spread through Romania. On 22 Dec., with Ceauşescu deposed, Iliescu was asked to front the provisional government, the National Salvation Front Council. Free multi-party elections were held on 20 May 1990 and Iliescu was elected president with 85% of the vote.

Career Peak

Taking office at a time of post-communist euphoria, Iliescu was unable to deliver the radical reforms Romania needed. The economy continued to struggle and remained over-centralized. Despite this Iliescu was re-elected on 11 Oct. 1992, winning 61.5% of the vote. However, discontent with his rule grew. He was unable to rid state institutions of corruption and was criticized for his refusal to dismantle the state security framework.

Iliescu left the National Salvation Front in March 1992 to form the Democratic National Salvation Front. In the second round of presidential elections in Nov. 1996 Iliescu was defeated by the centre-right reformer Emil Constantinescu and his Democratic Convention. After elections in Dec. 2000 Iliescu was returned as president. Confronted with the challenge of kick-starting reform of Romania's social and economic institutions, his job was hindered by galloping inflation. His other priorities included reform of the military followed by NATO and EU membership. In 2002 Romania was given a target date of 2007 for entry into the EU and was one of seven countries invited to join NATO in 2004. Romania duly gained membership of the EU on 1 Jan. 2007. Iliescu stepped down on 20 Dec. 2004 after completing his maximum two terms in office.

Iloilo, Josefa (Fiji)

Introduction

Josefa Iloilo became acting president following the nationalist coup of 2000 and was given the job on a permanent basis in March 2001. He had to contend with a racially-divided, economically and politically unstable environment. He was deposed in a coup in Dec. 2006 when Commodore Frank Bainimarama assumed the presidential powers, but reinstated in Jan. 2007.

Early Life

Iloilo was born in 1920. He was Fiji's vice president when in May 2000 indigenous Fijian George Speight and his supporters took hostage the government of ethnic Indian prime minister, Mahendra Chaudhry. Chaudhry's administration was subsequently dismissed by decree of the Great Council of Chiefs. Speight, a bankrupt businessman, pronounced himself prime minister. The affair was the culmination of years of rising tensions between the ethnic Fijian population and Fiji's financially and politically powerful ethnic Indian minority. Fiji was suspended from the Commonwealth's councils in June 2000. The following month, with Chaudhry and his supporters having been released, Iloilo, father-in-law of Speight's brother, was chosen by the Council of Chiefs to be interim president. Speight was arrested in July 2000 by the military authorities under Commodore J. V. 'Frank' Bainimarama and Laisenia Qarase, an ethnic Fijian, was named interim prime minister.

Career Peak

In March 2001 Iloilo formally dismissed Chaudhry as prime minister. He then replaced Qarase, whose interim administration had been declared illegal by the Supreme Court, with Ratu Tevita Momoedonu, a tribal leader, for 24 h before reappointing Qarase and legitimizing the administration prior to fresh elections. Also in March 2001 the Council of Chiefs confirmed Iloilo as president.

As president, Iloilo was responsible for appointing the prime minister and was head of the armed forces. On taking office he committed himself to re-establishing national unity in the wake of the events of 2000. He sought to boost Fiji's two biggest industries, tourism and sugar production, which both went into decline after the coup attempt.

Elections were held in Aug.–Sept. 2001 in which Speight won a seat and Qarase's newly-formed Soqosoqo Duavata ni Lewenivanua party won most seats. In contravention of the constitution, Qarase failed to appoint any ethnic Indians from the Fiji Labour Party to his cabinet, and in Dec. 2001 Speight was suspended from parliament for failure to attend.

Iloilo oversaw Fiji's re-entry into the Commonwealth in Dec. 2001, although the domestic political environment remained unstable. In Jan. 2002 a constitutional court demanded the inclusion of Labour members in the cabinet and the following month Speight received a death sentence, later commuted by Iloilo to life imprisonment, for treason. In 2004 Iloilo's vice president, Ratu Jope Seniloli, was found guilty of treason for his involvement in the Speight coup. Seniloli had been named president by Speight during the 2000 crisis and was elected vice president by indigenous leaders after Speight's arrest. Iloilo was reappointed president for a further 5 year term in March 2006.

On 5 Dec. 2006 Commodore Frank Bainimarama, unhappy after the government's attempt to replace him, led a military coup, deposing both the prime minister and president. He took over the president's powers briefly himself before reinstating Iloilo on 4 Jan. 2007. The following day Iloilo swore in Bainimarama as interim prime minister. Iloilo retired at the age of 88 on 30 July 2009 and Vice President Ratu Epeli Nailatikau became acting president. He died on 6 Feb. 2011.

Ilves, Toomas Hendrik (Estonia)

Introduction

Toomas Hendrik Ilves began his first 5 year largely ceremonial term as president on 9 Oct. 2006, replacing Arnold Rüütel, and was re-elected in Aug. 2011.

Early Life

Ilves was born on 26 Dec. 1953 in Sweden, his parents having fled Estonia during the Soviet occupation in the 1940s. He studied psychology in the USA, first at Columbia University before completing his MA at Pennsylvania University. He then lectured in Vancouver on Estonian literature and linguistics before working as an analyst and researcher for Radio Free Europe.

He returned to Estonia in 1993, 2 years after the country regained independence. In the late 1990s he served as ambassador to the USA, Canada and Mexico. He also had two spells as minister for foreign affairs and was chairman of the North American Institute. From 2004–06 he was a member of the European Parliament, representing the Social Democratic Party.

Career Peak

Ilves' principal duty as president is to represent the country abroad. In Nov. 2006 George W. Bush became the first US president to visit Estonia. Ilves justified the participation of Estonian forces in Afghanistan as a necessary duty of NATO membership, and an increase in the Estonian deployment was approved by parliament in June 2009.

Ilves has sought greater integration of Estonia's large Russian-speaking minority. Relations between Estonia and Russia were tense during the early months of his tenure, particularly over the relocation by the Estonian government of a prominent Soviet war memorial out of the centre of Tallinn. However, in Feb. 2014 Estonia and Russia signed a new treaty ending a long-standing dispute over border formalization.

Ilves was re-elected for a second presidential term by parliament in Aug. 2011. Having served the maximum permitted two terms, he was succeeded by Kersti Kaljulaid in Oct. 2016.

Ingraham, Hubert (The Bahamas)

Introduction

Hubert Ingraham became prime minister for the second time on 4 May 2007, having secured a narrow victory for his Free National Movement (FNM) in the general election. The outgoing Progressive Liberal Party (PLP), led by Perry Christie, contested the result in several districts. Ingraham pledged to make government more accountable. Following the defeat of the FNM at the 2012 elections, Ingraham resigned as the party leader and Perry Christie returned for a second time as prime minister.

Early Life

Hubert Alexander Ingraham was born on 4 Aug. 1947 in Grand Bahama, then part of the British West Indies. He grew up in Cooper's Town on the island of Abaco and was educated in Nassau. After studying law, Ingraham was employed first by the Bahamas Telecommunications Corporation and then Chase Manhattan Bank. He was called to the Bahamas Bar in 1972 and worked in a private law practice.

Ingraham was elected to the national general council in the elections of 1977, representing the then ruling PLP. He served as a member of the standing committee on privilege and public accounts. Re-elected in 1982, he became minister of housing, national insurance and social service.

In 1984 Ingraham was dismissed from the Cabinet after an inquiry into drug-trafficking and alleged government corruption. He was expelled from the PLP in 1985, attributed in his official biography to his anti-corruption stance. Re-elected to parliament in 1987 as an independent, Ingraham joined the conservative FNM and became its leader in 1990. He led the party to an emphatic victory in the general election of Aug. 1992, ending Prime Minister Lynden Pindling's 25-year rule.

Career Peak

In 1993 Ingraham signed an agreement to establish an industrial park at Freeport for international high-tech companies. He led the FNM to victory in the March 1997 general election but was defeated by the PLP in May 2002. Ingraham nonetheless retained his North Abaco seat. During the party's Nov. 2005 convention, he was again elected FNM leader. In the run-up to the May 2007 parliamentary elections, he campaigned on issues of trust, criticizing the PLP for their involvement in a series of scandals. The FNM emerged victorious on 2 May 2007 with 23 of 41 available seats, although the PLP leader, Perry Christie, initially challenged the results. Ingraham pledged to improve the efficiency and transparency of government, to improve education and to tackle crime. In the general election held on 7 May 2012 the PLP won a majority of seats, defeating the FNM, and Christie once again succeeded Ingraham as prime minister. In the wake of the defeat Ingraham announced his resignation as FNM leader.

Jäätteenmäki, Anneli (Finland)

Introduction

Anneli Jäätteenmäki took office on 17 April 2003 as Finland's first female prime minister. A former lawyer and minister, Jäätteenmäki waged a controversial election campaign by criticizing the previous government's foreign policy, an area not traditionally debated in partisan terms in Finland. She resigned on 18 June 2003 stating that she had lost the confidence of her party over allegations of lying to MPs. The brevity of her tenure was a disappointment for feminist politicians, who had celebrated the concurrence of a female head of state and female head of government.

Early Life

Anneli Tuulikki Jäätteenmäki was born in Lapua, Western Finland on 11 Feb. 1955. She graduated from the University of Helsinki in law and practised in Lapua from 1982 until 1987, when she was elected as a member of parliament for the Centre Party. From 1987–94 Jäätteenmäki served on the Finnish Delegation to the Nordic Council. She became minister of justice in May 1994 under Prime Minister Esko Aho until the change of administration in 1995. In 2000 Jäätteenmäki became deputy leader of the Centre Party, and party leader in 2002.

The parliamentary elections on 16 March 2003 were won by Jäätteenmäki's Centre Party, which became the largest party with 55 seats in the 200-member parliament. Jäätteenmäki briefly took on the duties of speaker until her election in parliament as prime minister, in accordance with the constitution of 2000. Previous prime ministers were appointed by the president.

Career Peak

Jäätteenmäki's election campaign focused on the previous government's failure to halve unemployment, one of its key targets. She also criticised Paavo Lipponen's attitude towards the war in Iraq in 2003, which the ex-prime minister had not explicitly opposed.

As Finland's first female prime minister, Jäätteenmäki promoted female political contribution by appointing women to half of the ministerial positions. 37.5% of the new members of parliament were female. Her government was a coalition of the Centre Party and the Social Democratic Party, which both had eight ministers, and the Swedish People's Party, with two ministers.

Jäätteenmäki's first foreign visit as prime minister, in accordance with tradition, was to Sweden. She and her Swedish counterpart, Göran Persson, agreed to increase cooperation between their two countries, especially in European policy. Jäätteenmäki also showed a desire to develop relations with Estonia, which benefits from Finnish aid and investment. She emphasized the importance of environmental programmes for the Baltic Sea and the Gulf of Finland and the promotion of the Estonian language in Finland.

Her fall from office was caused by what was known as the 'Iraqgate' affair. Jäätteenmäki was accused of soliciting confidential documents concerning the policy of Paavo Lipponen, then prime minister, towards the USA before the Iraq war. Her use of this information for electioneering purposes and subsequent allegations of lying to MPs made her position untenable. Jäätteenmäki resigned on 18 June 2003, after just 2 months in office, the shortest tenure since 1944. She was succeeded by her defence minister, Matti Vanhanen, who re-appointed her cabinet. She resigned as head of the Centre Party on 24 June.

Later Life

Jäätteenmäki entered European politics shortly after her brief stint as prime minister, and has been a member of the European Parliament since July 2004. She was elected a vice president of the European Parliament in May 2015 following her compatriot Olli Rehn's resignation from his post.

Jagan, Cheddi (Guyana)

Introduction

Cheddi Jagan was a key figure in Guyanese politics from 1947 to 1997. He served as chief minister, prime minister, president, and leader of the opposition. The founder of the People's Progressive Party, he was the first democratically elected premier. His socialist beliefs and reforms in the 1950s and 60s attracted much attention because of the perceived threat of communism, but his moderate policies were beneficial to the country. Foreign interference saw his removal from power in 1964, until a political comeback in 1992 put him once again in office. The reforms he implemented were largely successful and led him to be regarded as a dedicated leader and international statesman. He died in office in 1997. Jagan was married to Janet Rosenberg and had two children.

Early Life

Cheddi Berret Jagan was born on 22 March 1918 in Port Mourant, Berbice, British Guiana and was the son of indentured sugar plantation workers who had immigrated from India. He was educated at Queen's College, Georgetown in 1933–35 before going to the USA to complete his further education. He attended Howard University, Washington, D.C. in 1936–38 for pre–med studies, and then Dental School at Northwestern University, Chicago in 1938–42 to achieve his DDS. He married Janet in 1943 and returned to Guyana to set up a dental practice.

Jagan became active in local trade union affairs whilst working as a dentist in Georgetown and established the Political Affairs Commission in 1946 to raise awareness of labour issues and represent their needs.

In 1947 he won the Central Demerara seat as an independent labour candidate in a general election with limited suffrage. Jagan believed in the need to form an organised political party to allow effective opposition to British colonial policy. This led to the formation in 1950 of the People's Progressive Party (PPP) with himself as leader, Forbes Burnham as chairman and Janet Jagan as secretary. The primary aim was to unite the

Afro–Guyanese and Indo–Guyanese factions of society against colonial rule and to form a 'just socialist society'.

Pressure forced Britain to introduce a new constitution in 1953, which allowed limited popular elections, a ministerial system and a bicameral elected legislature. The PPP won 18 seats out of 24 and Jagan was made chief minister and minister of agriculture.

Career Peak

Once in office, Jagan began a reformist socio–economic programme, repealing the Undesirable Publications Ordinance, implementing changes in the educational system and in agriculture and drawing up the Labour Relations Bill. Britain deemed these moves as threatening and moved to reassert power. The constitution was suspended on 9 Oct. 1953 after 133 days; troops were sent in and the movement of prominent PPP officials was restricted. In response, the PPP formulated a policy of civil disobedience, encouraging leading officials to resist British rule. Jagan, jailed in 1954 for ignoring restrictions on his movements, was detained for 6 months with hard labour.

In 1955 Jagan led the Indo–Guyanese faction of the PPP when it split along mainly racial lines. Britain, believing that this split would limit PPP power, allowed a general election under a limited constitution in Aug. 1957. The PPP won 9 of the 14 seats and Jagan became chief minister and minister of trade and industry. His attempts to improve agriculture included the Black Bush Polder and Tapakuma land development schemes. The Canadian–owned electricity company was nationalized. At the Constitutional Conference in London in 1960 he called for independence while Britain insisted on self–government with safeguards.

In the general election of Aug. 1961, the PPP won 20 seats out of 35; Jagan was appointed prime minister and minister for development and planning. He continued the drive for independence and a socialist economy. However, the People's National Congress (PNC, the breakaway faction of the PPP), and the UF (United Front) unified to try to remove the PPP from government. Assisted by the CIA, which was worried by a 'communist' government at the height of the Cold War, they mounted strikes, riots and racial disturbances. A large portion of the business district of Georgetown was burnt down in Feb. 1962, and during protests against the Labour Bill PPP supporters were attacked on the streets and government buildings were bombed.

In 1964 Britain instituted a proportional representation voting system, attempting to negate PPP influence and more accurately reflect the ethnic division. In the elections in Dec. 1964, the PPP received the highest proportion of the vote (46%) but Burnham's PNC (41%) joined with the UF (12%) to form a coalition government headed by Burnham. Guyana received independence in 1966. Jagan became leader of the opposition from 1964 and was general secretary of the PPP from 1970.

After Burnham's death in 1985, the reforms introduced under his successor Desmond Hoyte opened the way to internationally recognised free elections in 1992. The PPP/Civic won the elections with 54% of the vote and Jagan was inaugurated as president of Guyana on 9 Oct. 1992. Jagan's tenure was cut short by a heart attack while in office. He died on 6 March 1997.

Jagdeo, Bharrat (Guyana)

Introduction

Bharrat Jagdeo, representing the People's Progressive Party (PPP), took over from President Janet Jagan in 1999, when the latter retired on health grounds, and was re-elected in 2001 and 2006, serving until Dec. 2011. Jagdeo's main challenges were placating civil unrest caused by rivalry between supporters of the PPP and the opposition People's National Congress (PNC) and negotiating settlements of border disputes with Suriname and Venezuela.

Early Life

Jagdeo was born on 23 Jan. 1964. He studied economics before taking a master's degree at the Friendship University in Moscow, Russia. He had joined the PPP's youth group, the Progress Youth Organization, in 1977, becoming a full PPP member 3 years later. In 1990 he worked as an economist in the state planning secretariat. When the PPP came to power in 1992 he was appointed special adviser to the finance ministry from which he progressed to the post of junior finance minister the following year. He also served on various PPP committees. In 1995 he became finance minister (occasionally acting as prime minister), a position he kept when Janet Jagan came to power in 1997. In April 1999 Jagdeo negotiated with workers from the Guyana Public Service Union who went on strike for a 40% wage increase. The strike eventually ended after 8 weeks of suspended public services.

Career Peak

Favoured by Jagan as her successor, Jagdeo took over the presidency following her resignation in 1999. However, he inherited ongoing political and civil disputes between politicians and followers of the PPP and those of the PNC, despite both being socialist parties. The PNC claimed that the 1997 elections had been fixed and had never accepted Jagan, subsequently refusing to recognize the Jagdeo presidency. During negotiations in 1998 directed by CARICOM, the PPP agreed to shorten the presidential term by 2 years.

In 2001 the two parties and their followers were caught up in more widespread racial tensions that traditionally erupted around elections (the PPP representing the Indo-Guyanese population and the PNC the Afro-Guyanese community). For this reason the elections that year were closely monitored by international observers and a special commission. They passed off without too much trouble, and Jagdeo was elected with 53.1% of the vote against 41.7% for Desmond Hoyte of the PNC. Hoyte accused the PPP of fraud, claiming many voters had disappeared from the electoral role. Jagdeo admitted this, but said that both parties had been affected by the discrepancies. In Aug. 2006 he was again re-elected for a further 5 year term. Polling passed off peacefully despite the earlier murder in April of the agriculture minister.

On the international level, there were border disputes with Venezuela and Suriname. In June 2000 a Surinamese naval ship expelled a Canadian-owned oil rig which had been granted a licence for oil exploration by Guyana but was said to be in waters claimed by Suriname. Talks between Jagdeo and the then Surinamese president under the mediation of then Jamaican prime minister P. J. Patterson failed. At the same time, Jagdeo agreed the construction of a rocket launch site by a US company 40 km from the Venezuelan border. Claiming a large portion of Guyanese land up to the Essequibo River, Venezuela argued that the project could be used for military purposes. The PNC also voiced its opposition to the proposed site. In June 2004 the United Nations set up a tribunal to resolve Guyana's maritime border issues with Suriname, which was settled in Sept. 2007.

In Oct. 2008 Jagdeo signed up to a trade agreement between the European Union and a number of Caribbean countries, having earlier accused the EU of economic bullying in negotiations.

Having completed the second of two constitutionally allowed terms, Jagdeo stepped down in late 2011. His successor, Donald Ramotar, was sworn in on 4 Dec. 2011.

Jamali, Zafarullah Khan (Pakistan)

Introduction

Mir Zafarullah Khan Jamali was elected Pakistan's prime minister in Nov. 2002, the first premier from Balochistan. The appointment came after 3 years of military rule under President Pervez Musharraf. Jamali, regarded as a moderate, served in civilian and military regimes from the 1970s. He pursued an active foreign policy, most notably with improving relations with India and Afghanistan. Although he was expected to work in close co-operation with Musharraf, their relationship deteriorated in 2004. Jamali resigned in June 2004, nominating his party president to succeed him.

Early Life

Jamali was born in Rowjhan in the province of Balochistan in 1944, the son of Shah Nawaz Khan Jamali. His family was a key ally of Pakistan's architect, Muhammad Ali Jinnah, and was prominent in the Balochistan *Shahi Jirga* (tribal council), encouraging the Jirga to join Pakistan in 1947.

He was educated in Murree and Quetta, in Balochistan, and at Aitchison College, Lahore before gaining a history degree at Government College, Lahore and a history master's at Punjab University, completed in 1965. As well as working in the political arena, Jamali was a selector for the national hockey team.

In the 1970s he joined the Pakistan People's Party (PPP) and served in the government of Zulfiqar Ali Bhutto. He supported Bhutto's suppression of the Balochi revolt in the early 1970s. Following a coup in 1977 he left the PPP and served at the ministry of food under the military rule of Zia ul-Haq, representing Pakistan at the United Nations in 1980 and 1991. In 1985 Pakistan returned to civilian government under the premiership of Muhammad Khan Junejo, with Jamali holding the post of minister of water and power until 1988. In that year he was appointed chief minister for Balochistan but his administration collapsed within a few weeks. Voted into the national assembly in 1993 as a member of the Pakistan Muslim League (PML-N), he reclaimed the Balochistan premiership in 1996 when the government of Benazir Bhutto was dismissed.

In 1997 Jamali was elected senator for Islamabad. In 1999, when Musharraf deposed the PML-N President, Nawaz Sharif, in a bloodless coup, Jamali left the PML-N to join the breakaway Pakistan Muslim League-Quaid-e-Azam (PML-Q). The PML-Q maintained close relations with Musharraf and emerged as the largest party at the parliamentary elections of Oct. 2002, the first since the coup of 1999.

Musharraf amended the Legal Framework Order (LFO) to allow Jamali to stand as prime minister, since his two-term tenure as provincial governor would otherwise have disqualified him. In a parliamentary vote for the premiership on 21 Nov. 2002 Jamali won 172 of a possible 342 votes and relied on the support of several independents and 10 PPP members. Despite only narrowly achieving the absolute majority required, he significantly out-polled the candidates of the PPP and opposition Islamic groupings.

Career Peak

Jamali was sworn in on 23 Nov. 2002, ending 3 years of military rule. His cabinet included PPP defectors and unelected advisors as well as PML-Q members. Jamali affirmed his commitment to continuing the policies of Musharraf, especially co-operation in the war against terrorism. His good relations with the American diplomatic and intelligence community in South Asia reaffirmed Musharraf's foreign agenda.

Armed with only a slim majority, Jamali struggled to maintain his government. In addition, the constitutional changes introduced by Musharraf before the parliamentary elections—and Musharraf's controversial success in a referendum in April 2002 granting him the presidency until 2007—left Jamali accused of being a presidential puppet. As required by the constitution, Jamali's government submitted to a parliamentary vote of confidence, which he won comfortably on 30 Dec. 2002 having gained the support of smaller parties and PPP rebels.

Jamali travelled widely in the region, cementing relations with neighbours before and during the war in Iraq in March 2003. A joint statement with India on 12 March urged a non-military solution, highlighting domestic opinion opposed to an invasion. Economic relations were strengthened by a visit to Iran in Oct. 2003. Dialogue with India followed a ceasefire on Kashmir's Line of Control in Nov. 2003.

Jamali frequently asserted his government's independence from the military, rejecting PPP allegations that President Musharraf's powers to dismiss parliament and the government were unconstitutional.

Negotiations with India opened after an unofficial meeting in Lahore at the South Asian Association for Regional Co-operation (SAARC) summit in Jan. 2004. On a visit to Kabul later that month, Jamali promised action against militants on the Afghan-Pakistani border.

Jamali's relationship with Musharraf deteriorated in 2004. Although seen as an ally of the president, Jamali criticized Musharraf for wearing military uniform. His observation that no previous Pakistani government had been allowed to finish its term was received badly in military circles, prompting suggestions that Jamali would be forced from office. He resigned as prime minister on 26 June 2004, nominating as his successor Chaudhry Shujaat Hussain, the president of the united PML. Hussain was approved by the National Assembly and took office on 30 June. Many Pakistani newspapers criticized the departure of Jamali, describing the proceedings as a democratic sham and suggesting that he had been ousted by the president's circle. Hussain was widely tipped as an interim leader before Shaukut Aziz, the finance minister, could assume the premiership, once he had been elected to parliament.

Jammeh, Yahya (The Gambia)

Introduction

Former army colonel Yahya Jammeh came to power in a military coup in July 1994. Leading the APRC, he was elected to office in 1996 and re-elected in 2001, 2006 and 2011, amid allegations that he maintains his authority through patronage and repression.

Early Life

Yahya A. J. J. Jammeh was born in the Foni Kansala district on 25 May 1965. He joined the army in 1984, rising to captain by 1992, and on 22 July 1994 led a successful coup against Sir Dawda Jawara, the president since 1970.

Career Peak

In 1996 a new constitution was approved by referendum. Jammeh was confirmed as president that year and his Alliance for Patriotic Reorientation and Construction (APRC) secured a parliamentary majority in Jan. 1997. He was re-elected president in Oct. 2001. The 2002 parliamentary elections, in which the APRC won nearly all the seats, were boycotted by the main opposition party. Jammeh's re-election in Sept. 2006 was considered free and fair on the day by observers, but the Commonwealth Secretariat noted 'abuses of incumbency' before the vote.

Alleged coup attempts led to the imposition of death sentences on six military officials and two businessmen in July 2010 and of long prison terms on former army and navy chiefs in May 2011. Jammeh was overwhelmingly re-elected in Nov. 2011 and his APRC again won almost all seats at the March 2012 parliamentary elections, which the opposition once more boycotted.

In Jan. 2013 the government suspended political dialogue with the European Union in response to EU criticism of The Gambia's human rights record, and in Oct. that year the regime announced the country's withdrawal from membership of the Commonwealth.

In Dec. 2014, while Jammeh was out of the country and amid increasing signs of domestic opposition, a group of disaffected soldiers and expatriate Gambians launched a further unsuccessful attempt to overthrow him, prompting a wave of arrests into the following year.

In Dec. 2015 Jammeh declared The Gambia an Islamic republic. In Jan. 2017, however, the term 'Islamic' was removed from the country's official name by his successor, Adama Barrow.

In the 2016 presidential elections Jammeh lost to Adama Barrow, but rejected the results and attempted to cling to power. On 18 Jan. 2017 he forced parliament to extend his term, which was scheduled to end the next day. President-elect Barrow was sworn in at the Gambian embassy in Dakar on 19 Jan., and the Economic Community of West African States (ECOWAS) launched a military intervention on the Gambian territory in order to prepare for Barrow's return. In support of the intervention, several ministers resigned, forcing Jammeh to dissolve his cabinet on 20 Jan. On 21 Jan., under the pressure of the ECOWAS troops, Jammeh fled into exile in Equatorial Guinea where he was granted asylum.

Janša, Janez (Slovenia)

Introduction

A key figure in Slovenia's independence movement in the late 1980s, Janez Janša was elected prime minister for a second time on 28 Jan. 2012. He had previously served as premier from Nov. 2004 to Nov. 2008 and was twice defence minister.

Early Life

Janez Janša was born in Ljubljana on 17 Sept. 1958, when Slovenia was a constituent republic of Yugoslavia. In 1982 he graduated in defence studies from the University of Ljubljana. In the same year he was appointed president of a wing of the Alliance of the Socialist Youth of Slovenia.

In 1988 Janša was involved in the publication of a working paper on the constitution written by Slovene novelists, lawyers and sociologists. It was condemned by the Central Committee of the League of Communists and Janša was arrested and detained. He and three journalists were charged with betraying military secrets, with the trial of the 'Ljubljana Four' provoking mass demonstrations that became known as the Slovene Spring. Janša was found guilty and sentenced to 18 months' imprisonment.

On his release in 1989 Janša became editor of *Demokracija* magazine and co-founded the centre-right Slovene Democratic Alliance (SDZ). In Slovenia's first multi-party elections in April 1990, he was elected to parliament and became minister for defence in a coalition government. He managed the transformation of Slovenia's territorial defence force into the Slovene army which fought the Yugoslav People's Army in the 10-day war that followed Slovenia's declaration of independence on 25 June 1991.

In 1991 the Slovene Democratic Alliance fell apart and Janša joined the Social Democratic Party of Slovenia (SDS—which became the Slovenian Democratic Party in 2003). He was returned to parliament in 1992 and in May 1993 became president of the party. In March 1994 the National Assembly impeached Janša for 'transgression of the civilian sphere by the military' and removed him from office, prompting demonstrations against bureaucratic corruption. He was re-elected to the National Assembly in 1996 and served again as defence minister from June–Oct. 2000 in the short-lived government of Andrej Bajuk.

The SDS gained the largest share of the vote in parliamentary elections in Oct. 2004 and Janša was confirmed as prime minister on 9 Nov. He pursued a programme of privatization and oversaw Slovenia's entry into the eurozone in Jan. 2007. Slovenia assumed the 6-month rotating EU presidency in Jan. 2008. Janša's SDS narrowly lost the general election of Sept. 2008 and he was succeeded as prime minister by Borut Pahor.

Pahor's government fell after a parliamentary vote of no confidence in Sept. 2011. In a snap election on 4 Dec., a new centre-left party named Positive Slovenia gained an unexpected victory, taking 28 seats to the 26 won by the SDS. However, Positive Slovenia's leader, Zoran Janković, failed to build a viable coalition and in Jan. 2012 Janša was appointed as prime minister, having gained the support of four other centre-right parties.

The then president, Danilo Türk, stated that Janša lacked legitimacy given that he had recently been put on trial for bribery relating to a defence deal made by the government in 2006—the 'Patria Case'. However, parliament endorsed Janša's appointment on 28 Jan., with 51 votes in favour and 39 against.

Career Peak

Parliament approved Janša's first cabinet on 10 Feb. 2012, the slimmest since independence with only 12 ministers. He pledged to reduce public spending by 10% in his first year in office as part of sweeping efforts to tackle a budget deficit that had grown substantially under the previous government. His austerity programme met with widespread protests through the year.

The negative public sentiment with the government increased further in Jan. 2013 with the publication of an anti-corruption report that revealed Janša's repeated failure to report his assets. Janša's attempts to discredit the accusations rapidly escalated into a large-scale corruption scandal and the SDS was issued an ultimatum to find a replacement for Janša. The crisis culminated with the fall of Janša's government in Feb., following a vote of no confidence. The opposition leader Alenka Bratušek was tasked with forming a new government.

Later Life

In June 2013 Janša was sentenced to 2 years in prison by a Slovenian court after he and two accomplices were found guilty of soliciting €2 m. worth of bribes from a Finnish defence firm as part of a military supply contract in 2006. The ruling was later upheld in April 2014 by the High Court of Slovenia and his prison term began 2 months later.

Jaruzelski, Wojciech (Poland)

Introduction

Wojciech Witold Jaruzelski was Poland's leader from 1981–90, as premier and first secretary of the Polish United Workers' Party (PUWP), president of the Council of State and finally as president. Under intense pressure from his Soviet overlords, he introduced martial law in 1981 and oversaw the suppression of the Solidarity movement. By the late 1980s, hindered by a faltering economy, he was forced into negotiations with Solidarity that led to the collapse of the Polish communist regime.

Early Life

Jaruzelski was born on 6 July 1923 in Kurow, Poland into a middle-class background. When the Red Army invaded the country in 1940 his family were taken prisoner and he was taken to the Soviet Union where he was put in forced labour. During his imprisonment he was converted to communism. In 1944 he signed up with the Polish wing of the Red Army and returned to Poland to fight Germany.

Jaruzelski remained in the military after the war, studying at the Polish Higher Infantry School and graduating from the General Staff Academy. In 1947 he joined the Polish Communists (later to become the PUWP). By 1956 he was Chief of the General Staff and in 1968 he was appointed Minister of Defence. In this role he oversaw the involvement of Polish Troops in the Warsaw Pact invasion of the Czech Republic in the same year. Three years later he became a full member of the Politburo.

In 1976 the precursor to Solidarity, the Workers Defence Committee (KOR), emerged to promote workers rights. Following widespread strikes in 1980, and particularly in the shipyards of Gdańsk, KOR evolved into Solidarity under the leadership of Lech Wałęsa. By the following year its membership exceeded 10 m. people and its power was challenging the authority of the ruling communists. It was in this climate that Jaruzelski became premier on 11 Feb. 1981 and then party first secretary in Oct. 1981.

Career Peak

As defence minister during the nationwide strike of 1970 and 1976, Jaruzelski had resisted using the military to supress workers groups. However, with Soviet troops gathering around Poland's borders and under intense pressure from Moscow, Jaruzelski declared martial law in Dec. 1981. Several thousand dissidents were rounded up, including Wałęsa and most of the rest of the leadership of the outlawed Solidarity.

By the end of 1982 Solidarity had been removed from Poland's political scene. There are those who believe that he perpetuated Eastern Bloc communism for ten more years, while others hold that martial law was necessary to avoid a Soviet invasion of the country. Wałęsa was freed at the end of 1982 and martial law lifted in 1983, but Jaruzelski was the target of more popular discontent in 1984 following the murder by government agents of the dissident priest, Father Jerzy Popieluszko.

Poland's economic problems continued throughout the 1980s. Jaruzelski, having become President of the Council of State in 1985, proposed a new range of unpopular economic reforms in 1987. Support for the dormant Solidarity movement swelled again and there were country-wide strikes during 1988. Jaruzelski was forced to embark on negotiations with Wałęsa and the Catholic Church. Agreement was reached in April 1989 and Solidarity was given legal status and freedom to fight the up-coming elections, whilst the previously ceremonial post of Presidency was vested with new legislative powers. In return, Solidarity agreed to compete for only 35% of the seats in the Sejm.

At the July 1989 elections Solidarity won virtually all the seats they contested but because of the 35% rule Jaruzelski was voted in as president. However, the elections signalled the beginning of the end of Poland's communist regime. Solidarity refused to join the communists in a grand coalition and Jaruzelski had to appoint Tadeusz Mazowiecki, an official of Solidarity, to be Poland's first non-communist premier in over 40 years. Jaruzelski resigned his positions in the PUWP and in Nov. 1990 was succeeded as President by Wałęsa.

Later Life

In the mid-1990s charges were brought against Jaruzelski and several other high-ranking communists in connection with the murder of 44 workers during the 1970 food protests. In 1997 the Polish courts declared Jaruzelski unfit to stand trial. That decision was reversed in Nov. 1999 and Jaruzelski testified his innocence in Oct. 2001. In 2006 he faced further charges relating to abuses committed during his time in office. However, he avoided appearing before a court by citing ill health.

Jaruzelski died at the age of 90 on 25 May 2014.

Jawara, Dawda (The Gambia)

Introduction

Dawda Jawara was the nation's first prime minister from 1962 to 1970 and its first president from 1970 to 1994.

Early Life

Dawda Jawara was born on 16 May 1924 in the village of Baragally Tenda. He won a scholarship to Glasgow University, graduating in 1954 as a veterinary surgeon. As a student, Jawara was elected president of the African student association and became a member of the student labour movement. On his return to Gambia he joined the government veterinary service, working as chief veterinary officer from 1958–60.

In 1959 Jawara joined the Protectorate People's Party (later renamed the People's Progressive Party), becoming leader later that year. In 1960 he was elected to the House of Representatives and was appointed by the British as minister of education. Following the success of the People's Progressive Party at the 1962 election, Jawara was made premier. After Gambia gained independence on 18 Feb. 1965, he served as prime minister until 1970, before assuming the presidency of the republic of Gambia.

Career Peak

Jawara's primary challenge was to modernise a severely underdeveloped country. Gambia was reliant on colonial markets and boasted a single major export crop—groundnuts. Its infrastructure was poor, with decrepit health and education provision. In 1985 Jawara introduced an economic recovery program that saw the budget deficit reduced, foreign exchange supplies increased and debt slashed. Nonetheless, by the 1990s Gambia remained one of Africa's poorest countries.

In Dec. 1980 Jawara cut diplomatic ties with Libya after discovering that Tripoli had been recruiting Gambian men for guerrilla training. The following year Jawara uncovered a coup plot against him while he was travelling abroad and crushed it with the help of Senegalese troops. His reliance on foreign forces, however, severely undermined his authority at home, though his decision to give fair trials to the perpetrators won him international goodwill.

In April 1981, Jawara and President Diouf of Senegal formed the Senegambian Confederation. New transport and communication links quickly grew between the two countries but both leaders lacked domestic support for the alliance. Furthermore, in Gambia there was growing resentment over the use of Senegalese troops to provide protection to Jawara and key public buildings. In Aug. 1989 the confederation disintegrated.

In 1992 Jawara suggested that the country would benefit from a change in leadership, though his decision to stay in office over the short term created tension. On 22 July 1994 troops led by Yahal Jammeh overthrew Jawara in a bloodless coup. Jawara escaped to Senegal.

Jayaratne, Dissanayake Mudiyansalage (Sri Lanka)

Introduction

On 21 April 2010 D. M. Jayaratne was sworn in as prime minister, a largely ceremonial position. He also served as minister for Buddha Sasana and religious affairs. One of the country's longest serving politicians, he headed various government ministries and was a senior member of the Sri Lanka Freedom Party (SLFP). He left office in Jan. 2015.

Early Life

D. M. Jayaratne was born on 7 June 1931 in the Central Province hill town of Gampola. The fifth child of nine, he was schooled at Doluwa Maha Vidyalaya (Gampola), Zahira College (Kandy) and Mahatma Gandhi College (Kandy). In 1951 he became a teacher at Doluwa Maha Vidyalaya and from 1960–62 he was postmaster of Gampola.

By 1950 he was politically active, working in the grassroots community centre networks where he rose through the ranks, acting as secretary in the Kandy council and then chair of the island-wide network. In 1951 he joined the newly formed SLFP and in the 1970 general election he was elected to parliament as the representative for Gampola. In 1977 the SLFP suffered a landslide defeat and Jayaratne lost his seat. In 1989 he was elected MP for Kandy and appointed minister for agriculture, food and co-operatives.

Jayaratne was re-elected in 2000 and was reappointed to the agriculture, food and co-operatives portfolio. In 2004 he became minister of post and telecommunication and in 2007 took over at the ministry of plantation industries. He also served as chairman of the Asia-Pacific region of the Food and Agriculture Organization in 2001.

Career Peak

In April 2010 Jayaratne was appointed premier by President Mahinda Rajapaksa, heading up a seven-party United Popular Front coalition. With a coalition majority in parliament and backed by the popular president, Jayaratne began his tenure in a strong position. While his role is largely ceremonial, he is responsible for leading government business in parliament.

One of his key challenges was to oversee proposed constitutional reform, particularly the lifting of long-standing emergency powers and anti-terrorism laws. These, alongside reported human rights abuses and weak labour laws, have adversely affected the country's international trading relations, particularly with the European Union.

Jayaratne's mandate ended on 9 Jan. 2015 with the swearing in of a new government led by Ranil Wickremesinghe, who became prime minister for the third time.

Jebali, Hamadi (Tunisia)

Introduction

An engineer and journalist, Hamadi Jebali of the Islamist Ennahada Party served as prime minister from Dec. 2011 until March 2013 in the wake of the Arab Spring.

Early Life

Hamadi Jebali was born in Sousse on 12 Jan. 1949 and graduated from Tunis University in mechanical engineering. Specializing in solar and wind power, he set up his own practice in Sousse while pursuing a parallel career in journalism as editor-in-chief of *Al Fajr* (*Dawn*), the weekly newspaper of the Ennahada Party. In June 1990 he received a suspended sentence and a fine for an article criticizing the lack of democracy in Tunisia. In Nov. the same year, he was sentenced to 12 months in prison for publishing another article deemed inflammatory. In Aug. 1992 Jebali and 170 other members of Ennahada were charged with plotting a coup d'état. Despite protesting his innocence, Jebali was given a 16-year sentence.

Spending more than 10 years in solitary confinement, he engaged in several hunger strikes and was released in Feb. 2006 on the 50th anniversary of Tunisian independence. After the 'Arab Spring' civil unrest of Jan. 2011 that prompted President Ben Ali to flee into exile, Ennahada was legalized. An interim parliament was created in Oct. 2011 and Moncef Marzouki, head of the Congress for the Republic Party (CPR), was installed as president 2 months later. On 14 Dec. he appointed Jebali as prime minister.

Career Peak

With tourism weak in the wake of the 2011 uprising, Jebali took office faced with both political and economic instability and rampant unemployment. He was also confronted with building workable relations between Islamists and liberal secular forces in the wake of the collapse of the previous authoritarian government.

Implementation of a series of fiscal stimulus packages from June 2011 saw the economy embark on a slow and faltering recovery. However, hopes of improving the political climate were hit by the assassination of an opposition leader, Chokri Belaid, on 6 Feb. 2013. Jebali called for the creation of a new government of technocrats to see the country through the crisis but this was rejected by the Ennahada Party and Jebali resigned his premiership on 19 Feb. 2013.

Jiang Zemin (China)

Introduction

Jiang Zemin was appointed party leader (General Secretary) in the aftermath of the Tiananmen Square massacre in June 1989. In April 1993 he also became president. Jiang has overseen a period of economic liberalization but has maintained a conservative approach to social and political reform. China's human rights record under Jiang remains a source of international unease.

Early Life

Jiang Zemin was born on 17 Aug. 1926 in Gansu province. His family placed much importance on literature, both Chinese and foreign, but Jiang chose a career in technology. He was educated at Jiaoting University (an engineering institution) in Shanghai, where he took part in anti-Nationalist Party movements and, in 1946, joined the Chinese Communist Party. He graduated with a degree in electrical engineering in 1947. Jiang began work as an engineer in Shanghai and in 1955 was sent to the Soviet Union for training. On his return he received the first of several, increasingly prestigious, appointments as head of a technological institute.

Although he kept a low profile during the Cultural Revolution, Jiang's organizational abilities came to the notice of the authorities in Beijing and, in 1970, he was posted to Romania as a representative of the Ministry of Machine Building. In 1980 Jiang became deputy director of the State Import/Export Administration and the first administrator of the new special economic zone at Shenzhen, on the border with Hong Kong. Jiang held other government posts concurrently and in 1982 was appointed to the Central Committee of the Chinese Communist Party. In 1983 he became electronics minister.

In 1985 Jiang left Beijing when he was made mayor of Shanghai. In office, he attracted Western investment into the city, tackling its transport, pollution and communications problems and at the same time built up a network of contacts with like-minded economic reformists in the city, later to be known as the 'shanghai faction'. Jiang firmly handled unrest in the city during the pro-democracy demonstrations by students and workers in Beijing in 1989. At the beginning of the unrest he sacked the liberal editor of a Shanghai newspaper, a prominent figure in the city. Jiang's speedy reaction impressed Beijing and Deng Xiaoping brought Jiang back to the capital after the Tiananmen Square massacre. Jiang became a member of the Politburo and general secretary of the Central Committee of the Party in June 1989.

Career Peak

As party leader Jiang sought to increase economic development. But his first task was to purge the party of those who had sympathized with the Tiananmen Square protesters. Deng Xiaoping came to regard Jiang as his successor and as Deng's health deteriorated Jiang took on more of his day-to-day responsibilities. In 1990 Jiang became chairman of the Central Military Committee and in March 1993 was elected president. As head of state and party leader, his policy was interpreted by some observers as an attempt to stem the demand for human rights by offering economic prosperity.

Developing Deng's theory of a 'socialist market economy', Jiang was responsible for a privatization drive and increased foreign investment in the

1990s, which paved the way for China's entry into the WTO in 2001. He also successfully won backing from the military, not a natural source of support for Jiang, by initiating modernization following the 1991 Gulf Conflict.

His record in foreign affairs fluctuated. His economic reforms were well received in the West and in 1992 he re-established friendly relations with Russia. He was also instrumental in the establishment of the Shanghai Co-operation Organization (along with Russia, Kazakhstan, Kyrgyzstan, Tajikistan and Uzbekistan) to fight terrorism and promote national stability and economic growth in the region.

However, his international standing was coloured by his links to the Tiananmen Square massacre, frequent run-ins with Taiwan and a poor human rights record. Political corruption and oppression of opposition groups, such as the Fulan Gong religious movement, continued throughout his years in office. The return of Hong Kong (1997) and Macao (1999) to Chinese sovereignty put the nation's social and political infrastructures further under the international spotlight. There were several stand-offs with the US, notably after the US bombing of the Chinese embassy in Sarajevo in 1999 and the capture of a US spy plane in 2001. However, by 2002 the US and Chinese administrations were in frequent contact.

At the Communist Party congress of Nov. 2002 Jiang was succeeded as general secretary by Hu Jintao, who took over the presidency in early 2003. Jiang was expected to retain influence in Chinese government through his network of allies on the Politburo and by keeping control of the Central Military Committee. Many observers believed Hu would attempt to incorporate Jiang's *Theory of Three Representations* (his treatise on Chinese political thought) into the CCP charter.

Jinnah, Muhammad Ali (Pakistan)

Introduction

The founder of Pakistan, Muhammad Ali Jinnah, known in Islam as Quaid-e-Azam (the Great Leader), was responsible for advancing the case for the partition of India. He laid the constitution for a secular nation which would protect the interests of Indian Muslims, faced with the formation of an Hindu-biased government in post-Independence India. Though hailed by Gopal Krishna Gokhale (1866–1915) as the 'best ambassador of Hindu-Muslim unity'. Jinnah was not without political enemies. His wish for a separate Muslim home-land were opposed to the ideas of both the Indian National Congress and the British administration.

Early Life

Muhammad Ali Jinnah was born on 25 Dec. 1876 in Karachi, into the family of a wealthy merchant. His grandfather, a Gujarati Khoja Muslim, had been a Hindu before converting to Islam. Educated at Gokuldas Tejpal School, then Mission High School, Karachi, Jinnah passed the entrance examination for Bombay university at the age of sixteen. In 1893, following an arranged marriage to a child-bride, he was sent to England to join a trading company which did business with his father. Against parental wishes, he gave up his employment to train as a barrister. In 1895, at the age of 19, he was called to the bar, becoming the youngest Indian ever to qualify.

In England he was a frequent visitor to the House of Commons, coming under the influence of British Liberal prime minister, William Gladstone. In 1896 he returned to India to establish a legal career in Bombay.

In parallel to his rise to prominence as a lawyer (he became one of the most highly respected and highly paid lawyers of his time), Jinnah took a growing interest in Indian politics. In 1906 he attended the Calcutta session of the All-India Congress Party, presided over by Dadabhai Naoroji (the first Indian to be elected to the British parliament) for whom Jinnah acted as secretary. In the same year the All-India Muslim league was formed. Offering support to British rule, the party initially held no attraction to Jinnah.

On 25 Jan. 1910 Jinnah joined the Imperial Legislative Council as Bombay's Muslim representative. Three years later, while still a member of the Congress party, Jinnah joined an increasingly pro-independence Muslim League, helping to draft its constitution. Presiding over a Muslim League and Congress conference in 1916, Jinnah was instrumental in getting both parties to agree on a series of electoral reforms, resulting in 1916 in the Lucknow pact which proposed separate Muslim and Hindu electorates.

In 1918 Jinnah married Rattanbai Petit with whom he had a daughter, Dina (b. 1919). In 1919 the Rowlatt Acts (also known as the Black Acts) were instituted, giving powers to the viceroy to silence the press, detain political activists without trial and to make arrests without warrants. In protest, Jinnah resigned from the Imperial Legislative Council.

Taking a more stringent opposition to the Acts, Mohandas Gandhi (1869–1948) began the Satyagraha movement. Jinnah opposed the campaign as an incitement to violence. The Jallianwala Bagh massacre at Amritsar (1919), where 379 Indian protesters were killed by British forces, increased backing for the movement and for Gandhi. Jinnah resigned from the Home Rule League after Gandhi became its president, stating that the changes introduced were appeals to the 'the inexperienced youth, the ignorant and the illiterate'. Voicing his beliefs at a session of Congress in Nagpur in 1920, Jinnah was heckled off the stage.

Shortly afterwards he left for England where he attempted to win a seat in the British parliament. Unsuccessful in this and at the behest of several Muslim League members, he was persuaded to return to India and lead the Muslim League as their president (a role which he retained throughout the 1920s).

Leading the independent factions within the central legislative assembly, Jinnah signed a pact in 1924 with the Swaraj party, led by moderate politician, Motilal Nehru, to create an alternative to Gandhi's Congress party. Although this initially formed a powerful grouping, the pact subsequently broke down in 1925. Motilal Nehru, following appeals from Gandhi, shortly joined the non-cooperation movement. With relations between the Hindu and Muslim communities deteriorating (the abolition of the Muslim Khilafat movement in 1924 provoked rioting and a tide of anti-Hindu sentiment amongst Indian Muslims) Jinnah became politically isolated.

The Delhi Muslim proposals in March 1927, formulated by Jinnah, were an attempt to re-align Muslim and Hindu interests. A year later, the Nehru report, representing Congress proposals for the future constitution of an independent India, provided further blocks to unity with its rejection of separate electorates for Muslims and Hindus. In 1929 Jinnah drafted a fourteen point constitution in response, demanding one-third representation for Muslims in the central legislative assembly.

Witnessing the ever-increasing popularity of the Congress party, the movement towards independence and growing anti-British sentiment, Jinnah appealed to the British Labour prime minister, Ramsay Macdonald, to declare support for Indian dominion status. His hope was that such a declaration would pacify demands for complete independence. In the second of three Round Table Conferences (1930–32) Gandhi insisted that he alone should speak for India. With irreconcilable differences between Gandhi's Congress party and the representatives of Muslim, Christian and other minority groups, Jinnah withdrew from politics to continue his legal career in England.

In 1934 he returned to India to preside over a session of the Muslim League, an event which revived his interest in both the party and its role in Indian politics, and led him to re-adopt his role as party leader.

Career Peak

In 1935 the Government of India Act was passed, giving greater prominence to provincial elections. Two years later, the Congress party won a majority in 8 provinces while the Muslim League was in competition with other, smaller Muslim parties and failed to win a single province. Leading the Congress party, Jawaharlal Nehru claimed that India comprised of only two groups: the Congress party and the British, and urged that all other parties should 'line up'. an appeal rejected by Jinnah.

A few months later Jinnah changed tactics. With the specific aim of re-organizing the Muslim League to achieve a single political base for Muslim Indian interests, he focused on religion. In campaigning for a Muslim seat in a by-election to the Uttar Pradesh assembly, the Muslim League raised the cry of 'religion in danger'. whilst Jinnah's personal appeals were made in the name of 'Allah and the Holy Koran'. Jinnah accused the Congress party of being a Hindu organization that did not have the right to speak for other religious groups whilst proclaiming the exclusive right of the Muslim League to speak for Indian Muslims. At a session of the Muslim League in Lucknow in Oct. 1937 Jinnah argued that an over powerful Congress party would lead to 'class bitterness and communal war' and that 'justice or fair play at their hands' could not be expected. In April of the following year rioting broke out in Allahabad.

The advent of World War II in 1939 saw a growing rift between the British government and the Congress party. When talks between the two broke down, Jinnah called for Muslims to observe a Deliverance Day (22 Dec. 1939) from the 'tyranny, oppression and injustice' of the Congress ministries which had been formed 2 years previously. Three months later Jinnah made the first formal demand for separate 'autonomous and sovereign' Muslim states at a Muslim League session in Lahore. Later known as the Pakistan resolution, the demand was firmly opposed by Gandhi and Jawaharlal Nehru.

Gandhi's Quit India movement, launched in 1942, resulted in the imprisonment of major Congress party leaders. With the British administration seeing a new enemy in the Congress party, the Muslim League became a potential ally. In Muslim majority provinces, the Muslim League gained unprecedented support.

Dialogue between Jinnah and Gandhi in 1944 failed to produce a resolution. In spite of Gandhi's reluctant acceptance of partition as a concept, the two were unable to agree on its implementation. In 1946 negotiations opened, with a British Cabinet Mission. Jinnah demanded the accession of six provinces for autonomous Muslim rule in the northwest and east of India even though one of the provinces, Assam, in the east of the country, had only a 33% Muslim population. Jinnah was intransigent in his discussions with both the cabinet mission and the Congress party. His ultimate rejection of the Cabinet Mission Plan was accompanied by a reference to direct action. On 29 July 1946 Jinnah addressed the Muslim League council, stating 'this day we say good-bye to constitutional methods.' The Muslim League declared 16 Aug. as a day of direct action. Beginning in Calcutta, mass rioting spread across the country resulting in some 4,750 deaths and 15,000 injured. Jinnah argued that such violence was the inevitable consequence of a unified Muslim and Hindu country.

Although the Congress party had been given the role of leading the interim government during the process of British secession, Gandhi suggested that Jinnah and the Muslim League be invited to form India's first constitutional government as a final gesture to prevent partition. The suggestion was dismissed by Nehru.

Following the arrival of the last British Viceroy of India, Lord Louis Mountbatten, events moved quickly towards independence and partition. On 15 Aug. 1947 independence was granted with Jinnah sworn in as the first governor general of Pakistan and Nehru as the first prime minister of India. On 11 Aug. 1947 Jinnah gave an inaugural speech which called for a tolerant, secular state: 'You are free, free to go to your temples, you are free to go to your mosques or to any other places of worship in this State of Pakistan. You may belong to any religion or caste or creed—that has nothing to do with the business of the State.' Attempts were made to censor portions of the speech although the full transcript successfully went to press. In an official biography commissioned by the Pakistani government and published in 1954 whole sections of the speech were omitted.

Jinnah died on 11 Sept. 1948 in Karachi at the age of 71 from lung-related illnesses.

Jóhannsson, Sigurður Ingi (Iceland)

Introduction

Sigurður Ingi Jóhannsson became prime minister in April 2016 following the resignation of Sigmundur Davíð Gunnlaugsson.

Early Life

Born on 20 April 1962 in Selfoss, Sigurður Ingi Jóhannsson grew up on his family's farm. He studied veterinary medicine at the University of Copenhagen in Denmark and, after graduating, ran a farming and veterinary business. He joined the Progressive Party in 2001 and was elected to parliament in 2009. In the same year, he became deputy chairman of the Progressive Party's parliamentary group.

From 2009–10 he served on the parliamentary review committee on the Special Investigation Commission report into the country's banking collapse. He also sat on the fisheries and agriculture committee from 2009–11, and from 2009–13 was a member of the Icelandic delegation to the West Nordic council. Between 2011 and 2013 he served on the industrial affairs committee and as deputy speaker of parliament. Following the 2013 general election, when the Progressive Party entered a governing coalition with the Independence Party, Jóhannsson was appointed minister of fisheries and agriculture; from 2013–14 he also served as minister for the environment and natural resources.

The coalition government claimed success in negotiating a deal with the creditors of Iceland's failed banks and in taking steps to restore public trust in the banking system. However, in April 2016 the naming of Prime Minister Gunnlaugsson in reports of secret offshore investments triggered mass public demonstrations. Gunnlaugsson stepped down as prime minister, appointing Jóhannsson as his successor. Amid some initial confusion over the permanence of Gunnlaugsson's resignation, Jóhannsson was sworn in as prime minister on 7 April 2016.

Career Peak

Jóhannsson came to office promising to hold early general elections. Meanwhile he signalled that he would continue with the government's plans for a controlled exit from currency controls in a bid to restore Iceland's economic stability.

Jóhannsson resigned as prime minister on 30 Oct. 2016 following parliamentary elections held the previous day and left office in Jan. 2017 to be succeeded by Bjarni Benediktsson.

John Paul II (Vatican City State)

Introduction

Karol Józef Wojtyła, a Pole, was elected by the College of Cardinals to succeed Pope John Paul I in 1978. The 264th pope, he was the first from outside Italy since the Dutch Hadrian VI in 1523. Wojtyła played an important role in dismantling East European communism and had sought to build bridges with other major world religions, particularly Judaism. He had also sought closer relations with the Orthodox Eastern Church. Socially conservative, he re-enforced Vatican opposition to homosexual practices, abortion, contraception and the ordination of women. He also undertook many trips abroad, preaching to millions.

Early Life

Wojtyła was born in Wadowice, near Kraków, in Poland on 18 May 1920. His father served with the Polish army. His mother died when he was eight and his elder brother died 4 years later. Wojtyła enrolled at the Jagiellonian University in Kraków from 1938 but his studies were interrupted by the German invasion of Poland the following year. After a brief absence from the city, he returned to Kraków to continue his academic career.

Escaping deportation by virtue of his job in a chemical plant he became active in an underground actors company. His father died in early 1942 and late the following year he began attending a secret seminary group. He narrowly avoided a Nazi purge of Kraków in 1944 and spent the rest of the war hiding in the palace of the archbishop. Wojtyła was ordained in Nov. 1946 and left to study in Rome.

Returning to Poland in 1948, Wojtyła held junior clerical positions and academic posts at the Jagiellonian University and the Catholic University of Lublin. In Dec. 1963 he was appointed Archbishop of Kraków by Pope Paul VI. He took part in the Second Vatican Council (1963–65), working with the Commission for the Study of Problems of the Family, Population and Birth Rate and voicing support for better relations with Judaism.

Promoted to cardinal archbishop in June 1967, Wojtyła became skilled at serving the church within the officially atheistic communist setting. Though his time in Poland has not escaped criticism, notably his silence during the 1968 government-led pogrom, Wojtyła stood apart from the communist authorities.

Following the death of Paul VI in Aug. 1978, Albino Luciani was voted his successor but died just over a month after taking office. With the College of Cardinals facing a potential division over his replacement, Wojtyła was selected as a compromise candidate. He took the name John Paul II. On 22 Oct. he officially became bishop of Rome, vicar of Jesus Christ, successor of the prince of the apostles, supreme pontiff of the universal Church, patriarch of the West, primate of Italy, archbishop and metropolitan of the Roman province, sovereign of the state of Vatican City, and servant of the servants of God.

Career Peak

John Paul II made regular trips abroad, travelling further than all the previous popes combined. One of his earliest trips, in 1979, was to South America, during which he preached to a crowd of over 5 m. in Mexico. Among his most important expeditions were his 1979 trip to Turkey, where he met the head of the Eastern Orthodox church, and his visit back to Poland where his support for the Solidarity trade union movement contributed to the collapse of communism.

He escaped an attempted assassination in May 1981 by a Turkish assailant, Mehmet Ali Acga, widely believed to have been sponsored by the Soviet Union. John Paul was outspoken in criticizing dictatorial regimes, including those of João Baptista de Oliveira in Brazil, Ferdinand Marcos in the Philippines, Baby Doc in Haiti, Alfredo Stroessner in Paraguay, Augusto Pinochet in Chile and Chun Doo Hwan in South Korea. He was also critical of Western materialism.

John Paul made significant strides towards theological co-existence, though his stance caused controversy within the church. He made several symbolic gestures including preaching to Muslim audiences and entering Jewish synagogues. Also, the Vatican apologised for crimes against other religions and denominations. Having witnessed first hand the effects of the Holocaust in Poland, he discussed Pius XII's widely condemned silence throughout World War II, though without expressly apologising for his predecessor.

Though willing to accept the importance of science and empiricism, as epitomized by his assertion that parts of the Bible should be read not literally but symbolically, John Paul remained a conservative. He confirmed Vatican opposition to female ordination, pre-marital sex, abortion, euthanasia and homosexual acts. His continued denunciation of contraception attracted strong criticism with the spread of the AIDS epidemic, particularly in Africa. His autocratic leadership also attracted criticism. He stated that 'it is a mistake to apply American democratic principles to the faith and the truth' and backed conservative Catholic sects, notably Opus Dei.

John Paul's health deteriorated in the 1990s and in 2001 the Vatican confirmed that he was suffering from Parkinson's disease. Nonetheless, he continued to travel and make speeches. In 2002 he became the first pontiff to address the Italian parliament. He used his speech to encourage Italians to have more children (Italy had the second lowest birthrate in the world), and criticized Western consumerism. He also addressed political subjects, calling on parliament to reduce prison sentences to relieve overcrowding and to ease the financial burden on large families.

On 28 Sept. 2003 John Paul announced the appointment of 31 new cardinals, including six Italians, three from France and two from Spain. One was named *in pectore* to protect his identity. The college of cardinals was increased to 194, 135 of whom were under 80 years of age and therefore eligible to vote in the consistory for a new pope. After battling Parkinson's disease and other illnesses for many years John Paul II died on 2 April 2005. Over four million people went to view his body in what was probably the largest single Christian pilgrimage in history. On 1 May 2011 he was beatified, the last stage before being named a saint. He was declared a saint, along with Pope John XXIII, by Pope Francis on 27 April 2014.

Johnson, Lyndon B. (United States of America)

Introduction

As vice president to John F Kennedy, Lyndon Baines Johnson became the 36th president of the United States after Kennedy's assassination on 22 Nov. 1963. He was elected for a full term in office in 1964 and is credited with enacting civil rights legislation initiated by the Kennedy administration. Johnson is also remembered for escalating the war in Vietnam. He did not seek re-election in 1968.

Early Life

Born near Stonewall, Texas on 30 Aug. 1908, Johnson's parents were farmers. He was educated at Johnson City High School in 1924 and Southwest Texas State Teachers' College, graduating in 1930.

Campus politics led to him campaigning for Democratic congressman Richard M. Kleberg who appointed Johnson his secretary, a post he held for 4 years. In 1934 Johnson married Claudia Alta Taylor, with whom he would have two daughters.

In 1935 Johnson was made director of Texas' National Youth Administration. Two years later a congressional district in Texas became vacant and, campaigning on a pro-New Deal ticket, he was elected to the House of Representatives. He impressed President Franklin D. Roosevelt while serving on the Naval Affairs Committee and in 1940 was appointed head of the House Democratic Campaign Committee.

In 1941 Johnson lost the Democratic nomination for a senate seat to W. Lee O'Daniel despite having Roosevelt's support. In Dec. he joined the navy and was awarded the Silver Star Medal. He returned from active service to Washington in July 1942 to chair the Subcommittee on Naval Affairs and subsequently served on the Post-war Military Policy Committee. Johnson was elected to the senate in 1948. He became a member of the Armed Services Committee and supported President Truman's decision to intervene in Korea. In 1953 he was elected party leader of the Democratic minority.

A year later the Democrats regained control of the senate and Johnson was made majority leader. An effective deal-broker, he co-operated with Republican president Dwight D. Eisenhower to win congressional approval for measures of social reform, including, in 1957, a first civil rights bill. In 1960 Johnson hoped to win the Democratic nomination for president. However he was beaten by John F. Kennedy who then asked him to be his running mate, believing that Johnson could help 'deliver' the southern vote.

Sworn in as vice-president Johnson was appointed head of the National Aeronautics and Space Council (NASA). On a visit to southeast Asia in May 1961, he insisted that the United States would not back away from Vietnam. Later in his career, Johnson confessed that he 'detested every minute' of being vice-president.

Career Peak

On 22 Nov. 1963 Kennedy was assassinated and Johnson became president, taking the oath of office on the presidential plane Air Force One. 5 days later he addressed a joint session of Congress and signalled his immediate intention to push through legislation on taxes and civil rights that Kennedy had sought to implement but Congress had refused to pass.

Using the deal broking skills he had honed as senate leader, Johnson guided a Tax Reduction Bill through Congress in 1964. In May he outlined his concept of the Great Society—'a place where every child can find knowledge to enrich and enlarge his talent'. In July he persuaded Congress to pass the Civil Rights Act.

Buoyed by the whirlwind start to his presidency, Johnson selected Hubert H. Humphrey as his running mate and trounced Republican opponent Barry Goldwater in the 1964 presidential election, winning 43 million votes to 27 m., the largest winning margin in American history. He now had the support of a Congress controlled by liberal Democrats. Medicare, health insurance for the elderly, was set up while Johnson's commitment to civil rights was reinforced by a Voting Rights Act. New programmes to provide federal aid for education and housing in impoverished areas were also introduced.

Johnson's undoing was Vietnam. In 1964 he increased the number of American troops in South Vietnam from 16,000 to 25,000. By 1965, with a victory for the North Vietnamese in prospect, he gave another push to American involvement. By the end of the year there were 180,000 American troops in Vietnam, a figure that doubled in 1966. By the summer of 1967, nearly 80,000 Americans had been killed or wounded in the conflict. The public turned against involvement in southeast Asia, not least because increased military expenditure led to a delay in domestic reforms. In 1966 congressional elections saw the Republicans gain 47 seats in the house and three in the Senate.

Against the background of rising discontent, rioting occurred in the black neighbourhoods of several large American cities in the summer of 1967. At the same time significant anti-Vietnam war protests took place on university campuses across the country. By the beginning of 1968 there were 500,000 American troops in Vietnam but the Tet offensive in Jan. 1968 appeared to confirm that the war was unwinnable. Under increased political pressure after Robert Kennedy decided to seek the presidential nomination, Johnson announced on 31 March that there would be a pause in the US bombing of Vietnam and that he would not seek re-election. Johnson's preferred presidential candidate, Vice President Humphrey, won the Democratic nomination after Robert Kennedy was assassinated. However, Humphrey was defeated by Republican opponent Richard M. Nixon.

Later Life

After leaving office on 20 Jan. 1969, Johnson retired to the LBJ ranch near Johnson City, in Texas. He wrote and edited his memoirs and died of a heart attack at the age of 64 on 22 Jan. 1973.

Johnson-Sirleaf, Ellen (Liberia)

Introduction

Ellen Johnson-Sirleaf became Africa's first elected female president in Jan. 2006, having defeated the former footballer, George Weah, in a run-off. A US-educated economist, she returned from exile to attempt to resurrect Liberia's shattered economy after 14 years of civil war. She was re-elected in presidential polling held in Oct.–Nov. 2011, pledging to continue her reform and anti-corruption agenda.

Early Life

Ellen Johnson-Sirleaf was born in Monrovia, Liberia on 29 Oct. 1938. She was educated at the College of West Africa in Monrovia from 1948–55, before graduating in accountancy in 1964 from the University of Wisconsin in the USA. From 1967 she served as special assistant to the secretary of the treasury in Liberia before undertaking an MA in public administration at America's Harvard University from 1969–71. Returning to Liberia, Sirleaf became assistant minister of finance in the administration of William R. Tolbert, Jr. Following public criticisms of Tolbert's presidency she resigned and left the country, taking up a post as a loan officer for several Latin American countries at the World Bank. In 1977 she was invited to return home to become deputy minister of finance for fiscal and banking affairs. In Aug. 1979 she replaced James T. Philips as minister of finance.

Shortly after a coup d'état and Tolbert's assassination on 12 April 1980, the new military leader, Sgt Samuel Doe, appointed Sirleaf president of the Liberia Bank for Development and Investment. However, she resigned in Dec. 1980 and returned to the World Bank, before becoming vice-president of Citibank in Nairobi, Kenya in mid-1981. She stood in Liberia's general elections in Oct. 1985, at which Doe was controversially elected president. Sirleaf was elected senator but was sentenced to 10 years in jail as part of Doe's crackdown on 'opponents' following a failed coup in Nov. 1985. Pardoned and released in June 1986, she again left Liberia for the USA, where she worked for the Equator Bank in Washington, D.C., followed by the UN Development Programme (UNDP) in New York.

While in the USA, Sirleaf joined other Liberian exiles in criticizing Doe and helped raise funds for a fellow exile, Charles Taylor, to lead the National Patriotic Front of Liberia (NPFL) into Liberia from the Côte d'Ivoire in 1989. It triggered a devastating civil war that led to the deaths of over 200,000 people by the time a ceasefire was declared in Aug. 1996. Disillusioned with Taylor, Sirleaf resigned as director of the UNDP's Bureau for Africa (a post she held from July 1992) and stood against him on behalf of the Unity Party in presidential elections in 1997. She received only 10% of the vote (against 75% for Taylor) and was later charged with treason by him. Forced into exile again, she became active in various humanitarian projects, including investigations into the 1994 Rwandan genocide for the Organization for African Unity and serving on the board of the International Crisis Group and the Nelson Mandela Foundation. Liberia again descended into civil war but Sirleaf returned after Taylor was forced into exile in Aug. 2003 (to be later imprisoned in 2012 by the International Criminal Court for abetting war crimes in neighbouring Sierra Leone). She headed the governance reform commission until resigning in March 2005 to enter the presidential race.

During her campaign, Sirleaf criticized the transitional government's inability to fight corruption. She went through to a run-off against George Weah, a former World Footballer of the Year who was representing the Congress for Democratic Change, and on 11 Nov. the national elections commission declared Sirleaf the winner. Although Weah accused her of fraud, her victory was confirmed on 23 Nov. Independent observers declared the vote to be free, fair and transparent and her inauguration took place on 16 Jan. 2006.

Career Peak

In her inaugural speech, Sirleaf vowed to wage a war on corruption, promising that leading civil servants and ministers would have to declare their assets. She also pledged to work towards reconciliation by bringing former opponents into a government of national unity, and spoke of establishing peaceful relations with neighbouring West African states. She appointed a number of women to ministerial positions and controversially nominated a Nigerian soldier to head Liberia's army. While rebuilding the country's shattered economy—with a road network in ruins, no national telephone network, no national electricity grid and no piped water—has remained a major challenge, the World Bank and other international bodies have praised her government's efforts in office. A Truth and Reconciliation Commission was inaugurated with a mandate to investigate human rights abuses during the long civil war, and she has made progress in confronting poor governance and corrupt officialdom.

In Nov. 2010 Sirleaf appointed a 22-member acting cabinet after placing their predecessors on 'mass administrative leave'. Several ministers were subsequently reappointed to their posts. She retained the presidency in Nov. 2011 when she was re-elected in a second round of voting, but there was a low turnout after rival candidate William Tubman boycotted the process because of alleged electoral fraud.

In Oct. 2011 Sirleaf was jointly awarded the Nobel Peace Prize.

Her presidency from 2014 was dominated by efforts to contain the spread of an Ebola epidemic. The outbreak had killed nearly 5,000 Liberians by Jan. 2016 when the World Health Organization declared the whole of West Africa free of the disease. Furthermore, the crisis disrupted business and commerce and threatened to undermine the country's post-civil war economic revival.

In June 2016 UN peacekeeping troops handed responsibility for Liberia's security back to the country's military and police forces.

Owing to the constitutional term limit, Sirleaf was ineligible to stand for a third time in the presidential elections scheduled for 2017. During the campaign she refused to support Vice-President Joseph Boakai's candidacy and she was consequently expelled from the Unity Party. Rival candidate George Weah won a clear victory and succeeded Sirleaf as president on 22 Jan. 2018.

Jomaa, Mehdi (Tunisia)

Introduction

Mehdi Jomaa was appointed interim prime minister in Jan. 2014 after months of political paralysis. An engineer, he had no political affiliation and little political experience. His administration organised and oversaw the elections of Nov. and Dec. 2015.

Early Life

Mehdi Jomaa was born in Mahdia on 21 April 1962. He graduated from the National Engineering School of Tunis in 1989 and later received a postgraduate diploma in structural mechanics, design and modelling.

Having joined Hutchinson, part of the French conglomerate Total, in 1988, he spent the next 23 years working as a senior engineer and manager. Following the revolution that toppled the regime of President Zine El Abidine Ben Ali in Jan. 2011, Jomaa left the private sector to take a role in Tunisia's transition to democracy. He was invited to serve as an independent candidate in the Islamist (Ennahda)-led coalition government of Prime Minister Ali Larayedh, becoming minister of industry in March 2013.

The assassination of opposition politician Mohammed Brahmi in July 2013 triggered popular protests and a general strike, prompting the resignation of the government in Oct. After prolonged political deadlock, Ennahda and the mainly secular opposition agreed that Jomaa should lead an interim administration of independents ahead of fresh elections in 2014. He took office as interim prime minister on 29 Jan. 2014.

Career Peak

Despite having apparently garnered support from across the political spectrum, the task of organizing a free and fair general election by the end of 2014 is a significant challenge. In March Jomaa warned that Tunisia's economic woes were potentially 'catastrophic'. Faced with a US$2.5 bn. hole in the national budget, he announced plans for a bond issue while casting doubt on its ability to sufficiently boost the public coffers.

Jomaa's tenure as interim prime minister came to an end in Feb. 2015 following the appointment of Habib Essid to the premiership.

Jonathan, Goodluck Ebele (Nigeria)

Introduction

The National Assembly appointed Goodluck Jonathan as acting president in Feb. 2010, replacing President Umaru Yar'Adua. An academic and former governor of Bayelsa State, Jonathan had been vice-president since Nov. 2007. He became president in May 2010 on Yar'Adua's death and was then elected to the post in April 2011. His term in office became increasingly dominated by an escalating insurgency in the northeast of the country by Islamist militants aligned to the Boko Haram movement. Amid concerns over his government's inability to contain the security situation, he was defeated by Muhammadu Buhari at the polls in March 2015. He remained in office until handing over power in May.

Early Life

Goodluck Ebele Jonathan was born on 20 Nov. 1957 in Otueke, Bayelsa State, in the oil-rich Niger Delta. A member of the indigenous Ijaw people, he was raised as a Pentecostal Christian by his father, a canoe builder and fisherman. After attending local primary schools Jonathan went to Mater Dei High School in Imiringi. He graduated in zoology from Port Harcourt University in 1981.

After completing military service Jonathan pursued an academic career, gaining a master's degree in hydro-biology and fisheries in 1985 and a PhD in zoology 10 years later, both from Port Harcourt University. He worked as a lecturer, education inspector and environmental protection officer before entering politics in 1998 with the People's Democratic Party (PDP). He was appointed deputy governor of Bayelsa State in 1999 and again in 2003. When state governor Diepriye Alamieyeseigha was charged with corruption in the UK in 2005, Jonathan replaced him.

In Dec. 2006, months after his wife Patience Faka was accused of, but not charged with, money laundering, Jonathan was elected vice-presidential running mate to Yar'Adua for the 2007 elections. The pair won, although opponents questioned the legitimacy of the vote and Jonathan's house in Bayelsa was bombed shortly after.

Jonathan's knowledge of the Niger Delta region helped Yar'Adua secure a ceasefire and disarmament with Delta rebels, generally considered the biggest achievement of his time in office. In Nov. 2009 Yar'Adua left Nigeria for medical treatment in Saudi Arabia without designating an interim presidential replacement. Jonathan was granted presidential powers after much wrangling by a parliamentary resolution of 9 Feb. 2010, though its constitutional validity was questioned. Yar'Adua returned to Nigeria in Feb. 2010 but remained out of public view, fuelling speculation about his condition.

Career Peak

On becoming acting president, Jonathan made moves to secure his tenuous position. In a government reshuffle he replaced two-thirds of Yar'Adua's appointments, including the justice minister and the national security adviser. He selected a London-based Goldman Sachs banker as finance minister and named the first female oil minister.

Jonathan vowed to calm militancy in the Delta region and address electricity shortages. He met with major oil corporations in Feb. 2010 after one of the main rebel groups renewed its campaign against the oil infrastructure in Dec. 2009. In April 2010 he dismissed the head of the state-run Nigerian National Petroleum Corporation. After Yar'Adua died on 5 May 2010, Jonathan was sworn in as his successor the following day.

In Sept. 2010 Jonathan announced that he would contest presidential elections to be staged in 2011. The following month Nigeria marked 50 years of independence from Britain, although the celebrations were marred by a car bombing in Abuja in which at least 12 people were killed. The presidential poll took place in April 2011 and Jonathan was returned with almost 60% of the vote, although voting was divided along religious and ethnic lines.

In Feb. 2013 the main opposition parties merged to form the All Progressives Congress (APC), a new anti-PDP electoral alliance. At the same time, Jonathan faced serious divisions within his own party, as rival factions fought for influence ahead of the presidential poll scheduled initially for Feb. 2015. Having replaced several cabinet ministers in Sept. 2013, Jonathan then lost his majority in parliament in Dec. after 37 dissident PDP deputies defected to the APC. A powerful faction of state governors similarly crossed over to the APC, leaving the PDP with fewer governors than the opposition.

From 2011 Jonathan's administration was confronted with serious sectarian violence between the Christian and Muslim communities and an escalating insurgency, particularly in the northeast, orchestrated by the extremist Islamist Boko Haram sect. Most prominent among the continuing series of attacks and atrocities committed by Boko Haram, both in Nigeria and in neighbouring countries, was the abduction of more than 200 schoolgirls from a boarding school in Chibok in April 2014. The apparent inability of the security forces to obtain their release or contain the growing Islamist threat damaged Jonathan's domestic and international credibility. At elections postponed from Feb. 2015 until the following month, Jonathan was defeated by Muhammadu Buhari of the APC, who had been president in the 1980s. Jonathan remained in office until Buhari was sworn in on 29 May.

Josipović, Ivo (Croatia)

Introduction

Ivo Josipović was sworn in as president on 18 Feb. 2010 after winning the second round of elections on 10 Jan. 2010 on an anti-corruption platform. His term in the largely ceremonial role was for 5 years. He presided over Croatia's entry into the European Union in July 2013 and sought to improve relations with the country's ex-Yugoslav neighbours. He was defeated in the second round of the presidential election in Jan. 2015 and he was succeeded by Kolinda Grabar-Kitarović in Feb. 2015.

Early Life

Josipović was born on 28 Aug. 1957 in Zagreb. He studied law at the University of Zagreb, qualifying for the bar in 1980. He returned as a lecturer in 1984, specializing in criminal procedure and international crime. In 1985 he gained an MA in criminal law and in 1994 received his PhD in criminal sciences. Josipović also pursued musical interests, graduating from the composition department of the Zagreb Music Academy in 1983. From 1987–2004 he taught at the Academy and has written over 50 compositions and won several awards for his work.

He began his political career in 1980 when he joined the League of Communists of Croatia (SKH). The party rebranded its image in the early 1990s, with Josipović helping to write the first statutes of the new Social Democratic Party of Croatia (SDP). In 1994 he retired from politics to work as an international law specialist in cooperation with the International Criminal Tribunal for the former Yugoslavia in The Hague. He was a key author of Croatia's genocide case against Serbia before the International Court of Justice.

In 2003 Josipović returned to politics. Elected to parliament as an independent MP, he was selected as vice-president of the SDP Representatives' Group in parliament. In 2005 he became a representative in the City of Zagreb assembly and was re-elected to parliament in 2007, formally rejoining the SDP a year later. On 12 July 2009 he was selected as the SDP presidential candidate and on 27 Dec. 2009 won the first round of voting with 32% of the vote. He received 60% in the second round to secure the presidency.

Career Peak

Josipović's top priority was to fight corruption, a pre-requisite to Croatia's membership of the EU. He also faced the challenge of mending ties with ex-Yugoslav neighbours in the wake of the Balkan wars of the 1990s—most notably Serbia. In April 2010 Josipović went to the Bosnian parliament and expressed regret over Croatia's part in the Bosnian conflict. In July that year he also visited the Serbian capital of Belgrade, heralding an improvement in bilateral relations that was further encouraged by the Serbian president's visit in Nov. to the Croatian city of Vukovar, the site of wartime civilian killings by Serb forces.

Josipović's term as president ended on 15 Feb. 2015 following the swearing-in of Kolinda Grabar-Kitarović—Croatia's first female head of state. He had won the first round of elections held on 28 Dec. 2015, but lost in the 11 Jan. 2015 run-off against Grabar-Kitarović.

Jospin, Lionel (France)

Introduction

The former leader of the Parti Socialiste (PS), Lionel Jospin was prime minister of France between 1997–2002. Heading a coalition government of Socialist, Greens and Communists, Jospin formed a *cohabitation* (power sharing) with President Jacques Chirac who represented the right-wing Rassemblement pour la République (Rally for the Republic; RPR). Major reforms introduced by Jospin included a 35-h working week and limited autonomy for Corsica. A presidential candidate in the 1995 elections, Jospin stood again in the 2002 election. But when he was beaten by the Front National leader Jean-Marie Le Pen in the first round, Jospin fell out of the race. He immediately resigned as prime minister and leader of the PS.

Early Life

Jospin was born on 12 July 1937 in Meudon, Paris. The son of a teacher and a midwife, he is from a staunchly socialist family. In 1956 Jospin finished his studies at the Institute of Politics in Paris. Following 2 years national service, from 1965 he studied at the Ecole National d'Administration, the training ground for French politicians and senior civil servants. Two years later, Jospin joined the foreign ministry, becoming a secretary for foreign affairs. After studying in the USA, Jospin taught politics at the IUT University of Technology in Paris until 1981.

Jospin followed in the family political tradition and joined the PS in 1971. He became a protégé of François Mitterrand, serving as one of the group of experts around the party leader. Between 1975–79 Jospin was responsible for mediations between the PS and the Parti Communiste Français. In 1981 he supported Mitterrand's electoral campaign.

On Mitterrand's election, Jospin was voted party secretary of the PS, a post he held for 7 years. From 1988–92, he served as minister for education, youth and sport. Reforms included new classrooms nationwide and the building of seven new universities. He aroused opposition when he allowed Muslim girls to wear the hijab, or headscarf, at school. France's national education system had been strictly secular since reforms in 1882 disallowed any demonstration of religious allegiance. Internal disputes in the PS came to a head at a difficult party conference at Rennes in 1990. Unhappy with party wranglings, Jospin resigned from the PS committee in 1993, only returning to the PS when Michel Rocard took over its leadership. In 1995 Jospin was voted PS representative at the presidential elections with 65% of party votes. After leading the RPR candidates Balladur and Chirac in the first round, Jospin came second with 47% of votes to Chirac's 53% in a run-off election. He was voted Party Secretary for the second time with 94% of votes.

Career Peak

Chirac called an early election in 1997, a gamble that led to a socialist majority in the Assembly. Consequently, an opposition prime minister had to be instated. On election, Jospin promised lower unemployment, then running at 12.6%, and a reduction of the working week to 35 h. He also pledged to reverse unpopular right-wing economic policies, which had been introduced to meet qualification requirements for the single currency.

In his first 2 years, Jospin reversed the nationalization policies of Mitterrand and privatized £12 bn. of the public sector. By 2000 France's economy was in good shape. Unemployment was below 10%, and there was a 3% economic growth. Exports and foreign investments were aided by a weak euro. In Feb. 2000 the 35-h working week finally took effect. Economic prosperity in France allowed Jospin to cut taxes on income and profits. His failure to reduce fuel taxes led to angry demonstrations by fishermen, farmers and hauliers who blockaded ports and oil depots. Despite pressure from the Greens to remain firm on fuel tax, Jospin conceded a reduction. Following years of political tension and nationalist activism in Corsica, in Sept. 2000 Jospin controversially granted limited rights of autonomy and a promise of

devolved law making powers by 2004. Jean-Pierre Chevènement, the interior minister, resigned in protest.

Jospin's *cohabitation* with Chirac was not always easy. In defiance of the convention that the president should handle international affairs, in Feb. 2000 Jospin went on a controversial visit to Israel where he angered the Arab community by referring to Hizbollah activists as 'terrorists'. Despite falling unemployment, down to 8.7% in March 2001(the lowest since 1983), and healthy economic growth, large private sector redundancies led to public opposition. In the local elections of March 2001, the left lost ground. Strikes by railway workers and midwives added to Jospin's problems. By April 2001, tensions within the leftwing coalition were near breaking point.

Nonetheless, Jospin announced his candidature for the 2002 presidential election as the chief rival to Chirac. Despite sustained growth and lower unemployment under Jospin, and despite both candidates' awareness of the public's concern with crime, the inability of both prime minister and president to curb crime in the last 5 years led some voters to favour the extreme policies of Front National leader Jean-Marie Le Pen. In a shock first round result, Le Pen beat Jospin to second place with 16.86% of votes to 16.17%. Jospin resigned his premiership and stepped down from the leadership of the PS. In the June parliamentary elections the left lost their ruling majority to a rightwing coalition. Jospin's successor as Prime Minister was Jean-Pierre Raffarin.

Later Life

After leaving office, Jospin claimed he was retiring from active political life although in 2005 he published a book setting out his political vision which fuelled speculation that he was considering running for leadership of the PS. However, he ruled himself out in Sept. 2006 and campaigned on behalf of Ségolène Royal during the 2007 presidential election although he later revealed that he had voted for her rival Dominique Strauss-Kahn. He remains a leading figure within the PS and supported Martine Aubry for the leadership in 2008.

Juan Carlos (Spain)

Introduction

Juan Carlos Victor María de Borbón y Borbón became the King of Spain in 1975 after the death of General Francisco Franco ended a 36-year dictatorship. Considered by Franco as his natural successor to lead his right-wing Falangist party, Juan Carlos proved instead to be democratic. He encouraged the liberalization of Spanish society, paving the way for the election of a socialist government to lead the country between 1982–96. In 1981 an attempted coup by Francoists wanting to return Spain to autocratic rule was successfully aborted.

Early Life

Juan Carlos was born on 5 Jan. 1938 in Rome. His father was Juan Carlos Teresa Silverio Alfonso de Borbón y Battenburg, the third son and heir of the previous monarch, King Alfonso XIII. Alfonso had left Spain in 1931 when the country became a republic.

Juan Carlos was privately educated in Switzerland before being sent to continue his studies in Spain in 1947 where Franco set about moulding him as his successor. After his secondary education, the young prince was trained in the army, navy and air force in Zaragoza, Pontevedra and Murcia respectively. He studied international law and economics at Madrid's Complutense University. In 1962 he married Princess Sofia of Greece with whom he had three children, Princess Elena, Princess Christina and Crown Prince Felipe.

Career Peak

In 1969 Juan Carlos was designated Franco's successor. But he was not the upholder of right-wing ideology that Franco had hoped for. Instead, when he came to the throne after Franco's death in 1975, he restored multi-party government and cleared the way for the transition to democracy and liberalization. But Franco's supporters were still active. On 23 Feb. 1981 Civil Guards led by Lieutenant Colonel Antonio Tejero occupied parliament and General Milans del Bosch ordered his tanks onto the streets of Valencia. As head of the Spanish armed forces, Juan Carlos successfully resisted the coup.

In the elections of the following year, the Partido Socialista Obrero Español (Spanish Socialist Workers' Party) leader Felipe González Márquez came to power to begin his 14 year term in government. After the closed society of Franco, Spain opened up internationally joining NATO in 1981 and the EU in 1986. Subsequent to the 1982 elections, Juan Carlos served a largely ceremonial role in Spanish politics, acting almost exclusively on the advice of parliament. Indeed, for the majority of his reign, he was a relatively popular figure amongst the public, careful in appeasing both the left and right establishments of Spanish politics. His popularity waned considerably towards the end of his reign during Spain's economic crisis. This was compounded by the revelation that he had undertaken an elephant hunting trip to Botswana in 2012, for which he was widely criticized by both politicians and the media.

On 2 June 2014 Juan Carlos announced his abdication in favour of his son Prince Felipe of Asturias, who became King of Spain on 19 June. Upon relinquishing his title, he cited the need for a new, younger generation to respond to the economic challenges faced by Spain. Throughout his reign Juan Carlos received a number of international awards, including the Charlemagne Prize (1982) for his contribution to Europe, UNESCO's Bolivar Prize (1983) for representing the ideas of Venezuela's revolutionary hero Simón Bolívar and the Nansen Medal (1987).

Jugnauth, Anerood (Mauritius)

Introduction

One of the dominant figures of post-independence Mauritius, Sir Anerood Jugnauth has served as both president and prime minister. He was first elected premier in 1982 and his most recent tenure ended in Jan. 2017.

Early Life

Sir Anerood Jugnauth was born in Vacoas-Phoenix on 29 March 1930. He attended Regent College in Quatre Bornes before working as a teacher and a government clerk. He went on to study law in the UK, being called to the Bar in 1954.

In 1963 he became a member of the National Assembly (then the Legislative Assembly) for the first time as a member of the Independent Forward Bloc. He joined the Mauritian Militant Movement (MMM) in 1971 and soon rose to become head, serving as leader of the opposition from 1976–82 until assuming the premiership for the first time.

Shortly afterwards he left the MMM to found the Militant Socialist Movement (MSM). Jugnauth led his new party to victory at elections in 1983 and remained as prime minister for the next 12 years, winning two further mandates in that time. Under his tenure, the economy thrived amid a liberalization programme and a reduction in dependency on the sugarcane industry.

Jugnauth and the MSM suffered a resounding defeat at elections in 1995 but he returned as prime minister 5 years later on the back of a power-sharing deal with Paul Bérenger, leader of the MMM. During this tenure he encouraged the growth of technology industries in Mauritius and adopted a punitive policy towards drug offending. He resigned in 2003 to become president—a largely ceremonial role—as agreed in the deal with the MMM. He was re-elected president by parliament in 2008 and held the office until 2012.

In Dec. 2014 Jugnauth received his sixth mandate as prime minister, succeeding his political rival Navin Ramgoolam.

Career Peak

Jugnauth was sworn in on 17 Dec. 2014, vowing to bolster the economy. Early in his latest term he met with officials from the Seychelles to discuss a strengthening of ties in the interests of mutual maritime security. In March 2015 he hosted a visit by India's Prime Minister Narendra Modi, during which India offered Mauritius a US$500 m.-credit line for infrastructure development while also highlighting fears that a bilateral tax treaty was being abused by some Indian citizens for tax evasion purposes.

On 21 Jan. 2017 Jugnauth resigned from his position and handed power to his son, Pravind Kumar Jugnauth, the minister of finance and leader of the country's main political party. Two days later his resignation became effective and he was appointed minister mentor, minister of defence and minister for Rodrigues in the new cabinet.

Juncker, Jean-Claude (Luxembourg)

Introduction

Jean-Claude Juncker was appointed prime minister in Jan. 1995, replacing Jacques Santer who became president of the European Commission. Having been re-elected as prime minister in 1999, 2004 and 2009, Juncker was at the time of his resignation in July 2013 Europe's longest-serving head of government. Committed to European integration, he played an important role in the decisions leading up to the creation of the European Union's single currency (euro). In 2014 he became president of the European Commission.

Early Life

Juncker was born in Redange-sur-Attert on 9 Dec. 1954. He obtained his primary and secondary education in Luxembourg and Belgium. Having studied law at the University of Strasbourg, he was admitted to the Bar of Luxembourg in Feb. 1980. He was an active member of the CSV and chaired its youth organization from 1979–84. Juncker was appointed state secretary for employment and social affairs in 1982. In 1984 he was elected to Parliament for the first time as minister of labour, minister of social security and minister in charge of the budget. When Luxembourg held the presidency of the European Community in 1985, Juncker chaired the council of ministers for social affairs and the budget. In 1990 he was elected party leader of the CSV. As president of the EC Economic and Finance Council in 1991, Juncker was among the core co-authors of the Treaty of Maastricht. He was a governor of the World Bank from 1989–95, and since 1995 has been the country's governor of the European Investment Bank and the International Monetary Fund.

Career Peak

Juncker concurrently held the position of prime minister, minister of state and of the Treasury. In Oct. 2000 his government oversaw the abdication of the King, Grand Duke Jean, in favour of his son Prince Henri. In Feb. 2002 Juncker was awarded the Légion d'Honneur by French President Jacques Chirac. Following his re-election in mid-2004, he formed a new CSV coalition government with the Socialist Workers' Party. From Jan.–June 2005 he led Luxembourg's 6-month presidency of the European Union. In Dec. 2008 Luxembourg's parliament voted to amend the constitution so that bills no longer need the approval of Grand Duke Henri before passing into law following a controversy over proposed euthanasia legislation. In the June 2009 elections the CSV increased its vote share and its representation in the Chamber of Deputies and Juncker began his fourth term as prime minister at the head of the CSV–LSAP coalition.

On 11 July 2013 Juncker resigned as prime minister and called for quick elections following claims of several cases of misconduct by the country's security agency, which the prime minister oversees. He remained the head of a caretaker government until snap elections were held in Oct. and negotiations over the formation of a coalition government took place. In Dec. 2013 Xavier Bettel was sworn in as the new prime minister, bringing an end to Juncker's 18 years as the head of government.

Later Life

In June 2014 Juncker was named as the next president of the European Commission. He took office on 1 Nov. 2014.

Kabbah, Ahmad Tejan (Sierra Leone)

Introduction

Ahmad Tejan Kabbah, leader of the Sierra Leone People's Party, served as president from 1996–2007, though he was briefly ousted in a coup in 1997. He sought to build a lasting peace as the country emerged from a long civil war and took steps to strengthen a devastated economy.

Early Life

Kabbah was born in 1932 and was educated in Sierra Leone and the UK. He entered the civil service in 1959, becoming a permanent secretary in the late 1960s. He subsequently spent over 20 years working for the UN Development Programme, travelling throughout the world.

He returned to Sierra Leone in 1992, shortly after the military had seized power. They invited him to chair the National Advisory Council. He was elected president at elections in 1996.

Career Peak

In May 1997 Kabbah was removed in a military coup and fled to Guinea. However, with the support of a West African intervention force and the British military, Kabbah re-established his government 9 months later. Backed by the UN, he opened negotiations with the Revolutionary United Front (RUF) which resulted in several accords. By late 2001 the RUF acknowledged the legitimacy of the Kabbah government and in Jan. 2002 he declared the war at an end. In May 2002 he won re-election for a further 5-year term.

Despite lingering concerns in the international community over his authoritarian rule, he was promised significant international aid in a bid to rebuild the country. In July 2002 Kabbah inaugurated Sierra Leone's Truth and Reconciliation Commission, aiming to heal the rifts caused by the country's bloody conflicts. However, unlike the South African model, the commission did not have the power to grant an amnesty. Having heard around 9,000 testimonies, the Commission submitted its report in 2005.

Corruption remained a problem under Kabbah's government, deterring prospective donor and creditor countries, and the security situation necessitated the retention of UN peacekeeping forces until Dec. 2005. In Aug. 2006, although not eligible to stand for the presidency again, Kabbah called early general elections for July 2007 to demonstrate his commitment to good governance and democracy. In Dec. 2006 he announced that US$1.6 bn. of Sierra Leone's debt to international creditors had been written off. In accordance with the constitution, he stepped down from the presidency ahead of elections in Aug. 2007, postponed from July.

Kabbah died on 13 March 2014 at the age of 82 after a long battle with illness.

Lake Tanganyika where he created a mini-state based on Marxist-Socialist principles. Apart from a high-profile attempt to raise funds by kidnapping, the PRP attracted little international attention and, despite Sino-Soviet support, the movement was in serious decline by the 1980s.

After a spell as a gold dealer in Tanzania, Kabila returned to Zaïre in the 1990s and re-established the Alliance of Democratic Forces for the Liberation of Congo-Zaïre. Mobutu's pro-Hutu rule had resulted in large-scale civil discord between Hutus and Tutsis and in Oct. 1996 Kabila bolstered his movement with disaffected Tutsis, Rwandans and other anti-Mobutu factions and launched an offensive on Kinshasa, the capital, whilst Mobutu was out of the country. Mobutu went into exile in May 1997 and Kabila appointed himself president, renaming the country the Democratic Republic of the Congo.

Career Peak

Kabila's accession was well-received internationally, with US Secretary of State Madeleine Albright describing him as a 'beacon of hope'. His popularity soon diminished, however. He banned all rival political parties and welshed on his promise to hold free elections. He antagonized the international community by refusing to address US$14 bn. worth of debt and by obstructing UN investigations into allegations of massacres of Rwandan refugees during his rise to power. A national constituent and legislative assembly was established but Kabila became ever more ruthless in the suppression of his critics.

His failure to secure the shared borders with Uganda and Rwanda from rebel conflict led to a falling out with his former allies in Aug. 1998. The country was again overtaken by rebellion which reached the outskirts of Kinshasa. With the help of Angolan, Namibian and Zimbabwean forces he retained power but rebels controlled large areas in the east of the country.

In 1999 relations between the Ugandan-backed Congolese Liberation Movement (MLC) and the Rwandan-backed Rally for Congolese Democracy (RCD) deteriorated and the civil war intensified. Several internationally-brokered ceasefires were short-lived. On 18 Jan. 2001 Kabila was shot dead, apparently by one of his teenage bodyguards. His son Joseph Kabila succeeded him and took on the presidency of a country which had been crippled by war.

Kabila, Laurent (Democratic Republic of the Congo)

Introduction

Laurent Kabila was president of the Democratic Republic of Congo (DRC) between 1997–2001. He led the Alliance of Democratic Forces for the Liberation of Congo/Zaïre in the rebellion that overthrew President Mobutu Sésé Séko in May 1997. Kabila was unable to bring peace to his riven country and he was assassinated in 2001.

Early Life

Laurent Desiré Kabila was born in 1939 in Jadotville, in what was then called the Belgian Congo. He studied political philosophy in France and also attended the university of Dar es Salaam, Tanzania. Kabila's political career began when he became youth leader in the Mouvement National Congolais, an organization aligned with Patrice Lumumba, the Congo's first president after independence.

Lumumba was overthrown and later killed by military forces headed by a former favourite of Lumumba, Mobutu Sésé Séko, who became the nation's principal power-broker. Kabila rallied Lumumba supporters against the new regime and formed alliances with rebel networks in Uganda and Rwanda, as well as with South American revolutionary Che Guevara. Kabila launched a rebellion in 1964 as the head of Alliance of Democratic Forces for the Liberation of Congo/Zaïre (ADFL) but Mobutu suppressed the movement and seized power for himself in 1965. The country was renamed the Republic of Zaïre 6 years later.

In 1967 Kabila was one of 27 founder members of the People's Revolutionary Party (PRP). He based himself in the Kivu Province on the shores of

Kaczyński, Jarosław (Poland)

Introduction

Jarosław Kaczyński was sworn in as prime minister by the president, his identical twin brother, Lech Kaczyński, on 14 July 2006. Anti-communist activists in the 1970s and '80s, the brothers have garnered support for their right-wing Law and Justice Party by pledging to cut corruption and defend traditional Catholic values. In Oct. 2007 Kaczyński stepped down as prime minister after an electoral defeat.

Early Life

Jarosław Aleksander Kaczyński was born on 18 June 1949 in Warsaw. In 1971 he entered the University of Warsaw, where he studied law and administration to PhD level. He subsequently worked at the institute for science and higher educational policy in Warsaw University's branch in Białystok.

Involved in anti-communist opposition activities in the 1970s, he co-operated with the Workers' Defence Committee (Komitet Obrony Robotników) and, along with his brother Lech, he was a legal adviser to the Solidarność (Solidarity) movement. Lech, however, became more closely associated with Solidarity's leadership and moved to Gdańsk in 1980. From 1989 until the end of 1990 Jarosław Kaczyński was the editor-in-chief of Tygodnik Solidarność (Solidarity Weekly). In the multi-party elections of June 1989 he was elected a senator representing the Citizens' Parliamentary Caucus (OKP). He represented Solidarity in negotiations to form the government headed by Tadeusz Mazowiecki.

In May 1990 the Kaczyński brothers established the Centre Agreement Party (PC) to support the Solidarity leader, Lech Wałęsa, in his successful presidential campaign. Jarosław subsequently became minister of state for the chancellery in the presidential office but was ousted, along with Lech, in late

1991 by Wałęsa who blamed the brothers for the president's growing unpopularity. Jarosław remained chairman of the PC until 1997, but was unable to turn it into a major political party.

He was elected to the Sejm in 1997 representing the Solidarity Electoral Action (AWS) grouping of nationalist, conservative, centrist and Catholic parties. Despite performing well in the 1997 elections (gaining 201 seats in the Sejm and 34% of the vote) and forming the backbone of Jerzy Buzek's government, the AWS grouping became fragmented. In 2001, shortly before parliamentary elections in Sept., the Kaczyński brothers established the right-wing Law and Justice Party (PiS), which went on to win 44 seats in the Sejm. Jarosław became the head of the PiS parliamentary group and in 2003 he was elected the party's chairman, succeeding his brother who had been elected mayor of Warsaw.

Promising to fight crime and corruption Jarosław led the PiS to victory in the parliamentary elections of 25 Sept. 2005, taking 155 seats in the Sejm and ending 4 years of centre-left government. He appeared to be the front-runner to take the position of prime minister but instead backed the former physics teacher, Kazimierz Marcinkiewicz, who became premier in Oct. 2005. In the spring of 2006 the PiS reached a majority coalition agreement with the populist rural Self-Defence of the Polish Republic and the right-wing nationalist League of Polish Families. However, reports of disagreements over economic policy surfaced in mid-2006 and Marcinkiewicz resigned. The PiS political committee unanimously recommended Jarosław Kaczyński for the post of prime minister and on 14 July 2006 he was sworn in by the president.

Career Peak

On taking office, Kaczyński promised to stamp out corruption, reform public finances and build more roads and houses. The PiS fared reasonably well in local elections in Nov. 2006 but lost the battle for Warsaw when its candidate, Kazimierz Marcinkiewicz, was beaten by Hanna Gronkiewicz-Waltz, a former governor of the central bank. Holding together the fragile coalition, reforming public finances and curbing emigration are among the administration's key tasks. After the Oct. 2007 electoral defeat of the PiS, Kaczyński stepped down from the post of prime minister, becoming leader of the opposition. Power was handed over to Donald Tusk's Civic Platform party and its allies, a centre-right party which plans to repair relations with Europe and withdraw troops from Iraq.

Later Life

Kaczyński contested the Polish presidential election held in June 2010 after his twin brother Lech (and the president at the time) had died in a plane crash 2 months earlier. However, Kaczyński lost in the second round run-off to the then acting president Bronisław Komorowski. Kaczyński remains the chairman of the PiS.

Kaczyński, Lech (Poland)

Introduction

Lech Kaczyński beat Donald Tusk in a run-off for the presidency in Oct. 2005. The conservative former mayor of Warsaw campaigned on a nationalist platform and garnered most votes in the country's poorer eastern provinces. His victory confirmed Poland's shift to the political right—the parliamentary elections in Sept. 2005 were won by the conservative Law and Justice Party, led by Lech Kaczyński's identical twin brother, Jarosław, who subsequently became prime minister in July 2006. Jarosław's government collapsed in Aug. 2007, paving the way for early elections in Oct. which were won by Tusk's opposition Civic Platform. On 10 April 2010 President Kaczyński was killed in a plane crash while on his way to a commeration service for the Katyn massacre in Russia.

Early Life

Lech Aleksander Kaczyński was born on 18 June 1949 in Warsaw, the son of an engineer and a philologist. As a child, Lech Kaczyński and his brother, Jarosław, appeared in a popular film comedy, *The Two That Stole The Moon*. Lech studied law and administration at Warsaw University. Having received a

PhD from Gdańsk University in 1976, he embarked on an academic career, lecturing at both Gdańsk University and Cardinal Stefan Wyszynski University in Warsaw.

An activist in the democratic anti-communist movement, in Aug. 1980 Kaczyński became a legal adviser to the strike committee in the Gdańsk shipyard and the Solidarność (Solidarity) movement. However, Kaczyński was one of many Solidarity activists to be arrested and interned after Gen. Jaruzelski, the first secretary of the Polish United Workers' Party (PZPR), declared martial law in Dec. 1981. From the mid-1980s Kaczyński was an adviser to Solidarity's leader, Lech Wałęsa, and helped establish the Citizens' Parliamentary Caucus (OKP) in Dec. 1988. Kaczyński was present at the 'round table' negotiations that paved the way for multi-party elections in June 1989, at which he was elected a member of the Sejm.

In May 1990 Lech and his brother split the OKP and established the Centre Agreement Party (PC) to support Wałęsa's successful presidential campaign. Kaczyński was appointed minister of state for national security in the presidential office, but disagreements led to him leaving office in late 1991. Appointed chairman of the Supreme Control Chamber in Feb. 1992, Kaczyński became a leading critic of Wałęsa until the president was ousted by Aleksander Kwaśniewski in elections of Nov. 1995.

Kaczyński returned to the Sejm in 1997 as a representative of the Solidarity Electoral Action (AWS) grouping of nationalist, conservative, centrist and Catholic parties. He served as attorney general and minister of justice in Jerzy Buzek's government between June 2000 and July 2001, gaining popularity for his hard-line approach to law and order until dismissed by Buzek over a controversial criminal investigation. In 2001, shortly before parliamentary elections in Sept., the Kaczyński brothers established the right-wing Law and Justice Party (PiS). The Democratic Left Alliance (SLD) emerged victorious but the PiS took 44 seats in the 460-seat Sejm.

Lech Kaczyński was elected mayor of Warsaw in Nov. 2002 and supported the construction of the Museum of the Warsaw Rising. More controversially, he banned gay movement parades in 2004 and 2005. In March 2005 he declared his intention to run for president in the Oct. elections and campaigned on a nationalist platform, arguing the case for a Fourth Republic. He beat Donald Tusk of the Civic Platform with 54% of the vote in a run-off on 23 Oct. 2005.

Career Peak

Kaczyński said he would work to achieve a 'moral renewal' in Poland, campaigning for justice for victims of communist crimes, fighting corruption, providing economic security and combining modernization with tradition. He pledged to strengthen ties with the USA and improve relations with France, Ukraine and the Baltic States. However, relations with Russia and Germany have remained difficult.

In July 2006 Kazimierz Marcinkiewicz resigned as prime minister and was replaced by Lech's brother, Jarosław, at the head of the majority coalition government that had been formed in the spring between the PiS, the SRP and LPR, two small populist and eurosceptic parties. However, this populist and nationalist administration lasted only until Oct. 2007 when early elections resulted in the moderate Civil Platform gaining the largest share of the vote and forming a minority coalition government under Tusk's premiership.

The president has been criticized for gaffes in his conduct of foreign affairs, notably his withdrawal in July 2006 at short notice from a trilateral summit with France and Germany because of a satirical article in a German newspaper for which he demanded an apology.

In Oct. 2009 the eurosceptic Kaczyński finally signed the European Union's Lisbon Treaty on institutional and administrative reform, having stalled for months until the treaty was approved by Ireland following a second referendum. On 10 April 2010 he died in a plane crash along with 95 others including many of the country's most senior officials. The speaker of parliament, Bronisław Komorowski, was appointed acting president.

Kádár, János (Hungary)

Introduction

János Kádár had two terms as Hungary's Prime Minister (1956–58, 1961–65), and as First Secretary of the Hungarian Socialist Workers' Party

(1956–88) he was effectively his country's head of state. He was identified as an ally of Imre Nagy during the 1956 anti-Soviet uprising but shortly afterwards he altered his stance and was installed in power in the aftermath by Moscow. His unwillingness to adapt to the liberalizing reforms of the late 1980s led to his downfall.

Early Life

Kádár, who changed his surname from Czermanik, was born in Fiume in Hungary (now Rijeka in Croatia) on 26 May 1912. He did not know his natural parents and was brought up by foster parents in the village of Karpoly, where he went to the local school. Having trained as a mechanic, in 1931 he joined the Young Communist Workers' Federation and the then outlawed Communist Party. He was arrested on multiple occasions over the ensuing years for his activities and in 1942 he was called on to the Communist Central Committee. He was active within the Hungarian resistance movement throughout World War II, joined the Politburo in 1945 and became Assistant General Secretary of the Party a year later. In 1947, following disputed elections, the Communists came to power.

Kádár was appointed Minister of the Interior in 1948 but his view came to be regarded as anti-Stalinist. In 1950, under the Rákosi regime, he was removed from the party infrastructure and served a prison sentence from 1951 until 1954, when he was rehabilitated following Stalin's death in 1953. When the anti-Soviet Hungarian uprising of Oct. 1956 took place under the leadership of Imre Nagy, Kádár was regarded as one of Nagy's allies, publicly declaring it as 'our glorious revolution'.

Career Peak

Kádár was percieved as a 'national Communist'. one who believed that Communism within Hungary should be adapted to suit the particular conditions of Hungary and not imposed along strict lines set out by Moscow. He was, however, regarded as more friendly to the Soviet hierarchy than Nagy and became nervous about the pace and extent of reform. In the immediate aftermath of the uprising he formed a 'revolutionary peasant workers' government' with Soviet blessing and set about reversing many of Nagy's reforms. While promising a degree of internal reform and advocating negotiations for the removal of Warsaw Pact troops from Hungarian territory, he also now condemned the uprising as a 'counter-revolution' and re-acknowledged the authority of the Warsaw Pact.

In the years following the events of Oct. 1956, Kádár aggressively implemented Soviet authority, imprisoning and executing many of those who had been involved in the uprising. By the 1960s his regime was becoming more liberal. Surveillance of citizens was reduced, a large number of political prisoners were released in a 1963 amnesty and there was a relaxation in the suppression of freedom of expression. His approach to reform and to its opposition was encapsulated by his quote of the early 1960s that 'those who are not against us are for us'.

In economic terms, he encouraged partial decentralization and allowed certain market devices outlined in a new economic policy of 1968, as a result of which the economy boomed in relation to its Eastern Bloc neighbours. However, his foreign policy remained entwined with that of the Soviet Union, as when he allowed Hungarian troops to be used in the invasion of Czechoslovakia and the suppression of the burgeoning reform movement there in 1968.

From the mid-1970s onwards, Kádár's reformist tendencies once again withdrew and as a consequence the economy went into steady decline. By the late 1970s the growth rate had fallen from 6.0% to 1.6% and, without the technology to compete with foreign economies, unemployment and inflation both spiralled and Hungary had huge foreign debts. Kádár was unresponsive to the reforms that swept through the Eastern Bloc in the mid- and late 1980s following the rise to power of Mikhail Gorbachev in the Soviet Union. He was effectively removed from the political frontline when given the honorary post of party president in 1988 following political manoeuvering by Imre Pozsgay.

Later Life

Kádár remained party president until May of the following year when he was removed from the party structure altogether. He died on 6 July 1989 and by the end of the year the Communists had fallen from power in Hungary.

Kafando, Michel (Burkina Faso)

Introduction

Michel Kafando was sworn in as interim president on 18 Nov. 2014 to oversee a year-long transition to democratic elections. He was selected by a committee of the country's political, religious and military leaders after President Blaise Compaoré was ousted in the wake of mass protests. A former foreign minister and ambassador to the United Nations, Kafando also held the foreign affairs portfolio in the interim cabinet.

Early Life

Kafando was born in Ouagadougou, then the capital of the French-controlled Upper Volta, on 18 Aug. 1942. He studied law at France's University of Bordeaux, continuing his studies in Paris and Geneva. In 1990 he was awarded a doctorate in political science by the Sorbonne in Paris.

In 1982 he was appointed foreign minister, a post he retained through the 1982 coup led by Major Jean-Baptiste Ouédraogo. From 1998 until 2011 he served as the country's permanent representative to the United Nations, including a 1-year stint as president of the Security Council.

In Oct. 2014 protests broke out against President Compaoré's attempt to rewrite the constitution to make possible an extension to his 27-year rule. On 31 Oct., after violent demonstrations in the capital, Compaoré dissolved the government and fled the country. In the wake of Compaoré's resignation, Isaac Zida, a lieutenant colonel in the presidential guard, declared himself the new head of state. Facing protests from the opposition, and under threat of sanctions from the African Union and the United Nations, the army agreed to restore the constitution and return to civilian government. A 23-person panel was convened to select a candidate to lead the transition; Kafando was the army's preferred choice.

Career Peak

Kafando oversaw an interim government and operated with tight restrictions on his power stipulated by a Transition Charter. The conditions of his appointment meant that he was not allowed to stand in elections that took place in Nov. 2015.

In Sept. 2015 Kafando and prime minister Isaac Zida were arrested by members of the presidential guard loyal to ex-president Blaise Compaoré. However, a deal between the presidential guard and the regular army was agreed a week later and Kafando and Zida returned to power.

Kafando's term as interim president ended in Dec. 2015 following the election of Roch Marc Christian Kaboré to the post.

Kalam, Abdul (India)

Introduction

On 25 July 2002 Abdul Kalam succeeded K. R. Narayanan to become India's president. Credited with founding and developing the country's nuclear missile programme, Kalam promoted a plan for India's economic development by 2020. A Muslim brought up in impoverished circumstances, his desire for social unity drew criticism from Muslim leaders. His non-political background and concern for the people's social and economic welfare on the other hand made him a popular and respected public figure. Kalam chose not to contest presidential elections held in July 2007.

Early Life

Avul Pakir Jainulabdeen Abdul Kalam was born on 15 Oct. 1931 in the Rameswaram district of Tamil Nadu. He was educated at a missionary institute in Ramanathapuram and at St Joseph College in Tiruchirrapalli before going on to study aeronautical engineering at the Madras Institute of Technology.

Kalam's scientific career was involved principally with defence. He joined the Defence Research and Development Organisation (DRDO) in 1958 and the Indian Space Research Organization (ISRO) in 1963, when he was also invited to spend 4 months in the USA working for the National Aeronautics and Space Administration (NASA). Ten years after rejoining DRDO in 1982 Kalam became scientific adviser to the defence minister and secretary until 1999. From 1999 to 2001 he acted as principal scientific adviser to the government with the rank of cabinet minister.

In 1998, under Kalam's scientific direction, India detonated its first nuclear bomb. While this increased tension with neighbouring Pakistan and earned international condemnation and sanctions, many Indians have felt that this marked out India as an emerging world power.

Nominated by both Prime Minister Vajpayee's National Democratic Alliance and its primary opposition party, the Indian National Congress, Kalam was elected president on 18 July 2002. He defeated his chief rival, Lakshmi Sahgal, by a margin of over 800,000 votes.

Career Peak

While his powers of office were largely nominal and ceremonial, India's 'Missile Man' took advantage of his high profile to advocate the development and the promotion of science and technology. He upheld his pre-presidential vision of India as an economically developed country by 2020, largely through the exploitation of natural resources and education.

A practising Muslim, Kalam was said to be equally familiar with the Koran and the Bhagvad Gita. However, his endorsement of tolerance and pluralism met with disapproval by Muslim leaders, which led to accusations of affiliation with the Hindu militant group, Sangh Parivar. Although at first seen as an extension of India's military, Kalam's secular and humanitarian approach attracted wider support.

After losing the support of a number of political parties who had previously backed him, however, Kalam decided not to stand for a second term at presidential elections in July 2007. He was replaced by Pratibha Patil, India's first female president.

Later Life

In July 2015 Kalam suffered a heart attack while delivering a lecture at a university in Shillong and died aged 83.

Kallas, Siim (Estonia)

Introduction

Siim Kallas of the Reform Party was elected prime minister of Estonia in Jan. 2002 following the resignation of coalition partner Mart Laar. As head of the central bank in the post-communist period, he reintroduced the national currency. A proponent of a free market economy, he pushed for Estonia's membership of the EU and NATO. In March 2003 he led his party to third place in parliamentary elections.

Early Life

Kallas was born on 2 Oct. 1948 in Tallinn. In 1972 he gained an economics degree from Tartu University. After postgraduate studies, he joined the Estonian SSR's finance ministry in 1975, becoming director of the Estonian Savings Bank 4 years later, a post he held until 1986. A brief period as deputy editor of the state-owned Estonian language newspaper, *Rahva Hääl* (Peoples' Voice), was followed by chairmanship of the Trade Unions Association (1989–91). Between 1991–95 at the head of Estonia's National Bank he implemented a tight fiscal policy, lowering inflation and reintroducing the national currency, the kroon.

In 1994 he established the centre right Reform Party to contest the March 1995 parliamentary elections, winning 16.2% of the vote. Six months later the party joined a coalition government under Prime Minister Tiit Vähi. Kallas

became deputy premier and foreign minister, positions he held until the party left the coalition at the end of 1996. In 1999 he was made finance minister in Prime Minister Mart Laar's coalition government, comprising Laar's Pro Patria Party, the Reform Party and Mõõdukad.

Career Peak

At the beginning of 2002, disputes within the coalition forced Laar to step down. Kallas was chosen as Laar's successor and was appointed in Jan. 2002. Forming a coalition with the Centre Party, he pledged to continue to work towards EU and NATO membership. In 2002, Estonia was invited to join both organizations with effect from 2004.

In March 2003 the Reform Party came third in parliamentary elections with 19 seats, behind the Centre Party (28 seats) and Res Publica (27). Juhan Parts, the leader of the Res Publica party, was invited by the president to form a coalition government with the Reform Party and the People's Union.

Later Life

After leaving office, Kallas held a number of positions at the European Commission, serving as Commissioner for Economic and Monetary Affairs in 2004, and then as Commissioner for Administrative Affairs, Audit and Anti-Fraud from 2004–10. In Feb. 2010 Kallas was appointed to head the Commission for Transport. He also served as Vice-President of the European Commission from 2004–14 under President José Manuel Barroso.

Kalvītis, Aigars (Latvia)

Introduction

Aigars Kalvītis was prime minister from Dec. 2004–Dec. 2007. Prior to taking office, his ministerial responsibilities included 2 years as minister of economics and one as minister of agriculture. His centre-right coalition administration became Latvia's first government since independence to be returned to power in parliamentary elections in Oct. 2006. On 20 Dec. 2007 a new coalition government was approved after Kalvītis resigned amid widespread opposition.

Early Life

Born in Riga in 1966, Kalvītis is a former milkman and tractor driver. He first graduated in 1992 from the Latvian University of Agriculture with a degree in agricultural economics. This was supplemented by a master's degree in the same subject gained in 1995. In addition he was awarded a master's degree in food industry business administration from University College Cork in Ireland in 1993 and completed in-service training with the Holstein Association at the University of Wisconsin, USA. From 1992–98 he was the manager of a variety of agricultural businesses, and began his career in politics in 1997 as one of the founders of the People's Party. He was first elected to parliament in 1998. He served as the minister of agriculture from 1999–2000 and as minister of economics from 2000–02. Kalvītis was re-elected to parliament and became the leader of the parliamentary faction of the People's Party in 2002.

Career Peak

Kalvītis became prime minister on 2 Dec. 2004, leading a government consisting of his own People's Party, the New Era party, the Union of Greens and Farmers and Latvia's First Party (although the New Era party later withdrew in April 2006 in protest at alleged high-level corruption within the coalition). As prime minister, Kalvītis identified health issues and inflation as government priorities. In 2005 parliament ratified the proposed new EU constitution. Following the Oct. 2006 elections, in which the People's Party led the poll with 23 seats, Kalvītis re-established the ruling coalition with the Union of Greens and Farmers and Latvia's First Party and also included the Fatherland and Freedom Alliance/LNNK to bolster the government's majority in the legislature. He pledged to maintain policies designed to boost the free market. On 7 Nov. 2007 Kalvītis announced that he would step down on 5 Dec. 2007, after encountering widespread opposition, including two large street protests, following his dismissal of the head of the anti-corruption bureau. Latvian legislators approved a new coalition government headed by the new prime minister Ivars Godmanis.

Kan, Naoto (Japan)

Introduction

Naoto Kan became prime minister in June 2010 when he was voted leader of the Democratic Party of Japan (DPJ). This followed the resignation of the incumbent prime minister, Yukio Hatoyama. A populist figure who had spent much of his political career in opposition, Kan championed economic reforms, promising to cut bureaucracy and redirect investment to health and welfare. He had to govern without a majority in the upper house from July 2010. Following the devastating tsunami and subsequent nuclear accidents in March 2011, Kan's popularity suffered and he resigned in Aug. 2011.

Early Life

Born on 10 Oct. 1946 in Ube City, Yamaguchi Prefecture, Naoto Kan studied at the Tokyo Institute of Technology. After graduating in 1970, he worked in a patents office from 1971–74 and became active in politics, working for women's rights campaigner and MP Fusae Ichikawa and campaigning on environmental issues. He stood unsuccessfully for election to the Diet three times before being elected in 1980 as a representative of the small, centre-left Social Democratic Federation.

From Jan.–Nov. 1996 he was minister for health and welfare in the Liberal Democratic Party (LDP)-led coalition government of Ryutaro Hashimoto, winning praise for admitting the government's responsibility for distributing HIV-infected blood in the 1980s. In 1998 he joined Yukio Hatoyama in founding the DPJ, an amalgamation of four older parties, and was elected its president. As a vigorous critic of bureaucratic unaccountability, he identified himself as a grassroots politician from outside the ruling establishment.

In May 2004 he was forced to resign after accusations that he had failed to pay his full state pension contributions but he received widespread public support by making pilgrimages to Buddhist shrines and was subsequently exonerated. Following the DPJ's election victory in Sept. 2009, which overturned decades of LDP rule, he was appointed deputy prime minister under Hatoyama and given responsibility for science and technology, fiscal policy and national strategy. The last post included a brief to reassign power from bureaucrats to elected officials, a key DPJ policy.

From Jan.–June 2010 he served as finance minister, overseeing spending cuts and tax increases while warning against the unsustainability of the public deficit. In June 2010, following criticism over his failure to remove the US military base from Okinawa, Hatoyama resigned and his cabinet followed suit. Kan was elected leader of the DPJ and became premier on 8 June 2010.

Career Peak

Kan took office promising to cut the deficit and introduce stimulus measures to rebuild the economy but his proposal to increase sales tax from 5% to 10% failed in the face of strong resistance. At elections in July 2010, the DPJ lost its majority in the upper house of the Diet and in Sept. 2010 he survived a leadership challenge from former DPJ secretary general, Ichiro Ozawa. On 1 March 2011 the lower house passed Kan's 92.4trn. yen budget but he failed to obtain authorization from the upper house for government bonds to help fund it. Following the tsunami and nuclear accidents later in the month, Kan's approval ratings plummeted. In June Kan narrowly survived a parliamentary vote of no confidence. Facing mounting criticism and calls to step down, Kan agreed to resign but not until two pieces of legislation, the deficit financing bond bill and the new energy promotion bill, were passed. With the bills approved 2 months later, Kan resigned in Aug. 2011.

Karamanlis, Konstantinos (Greece)

Introduction

Konstantinos Karamanlis served as prime minister of Greece from Oct. 1955–Nov. 1963 and from July 1974–May 1980. He was the country's president from 1980–85 and again from 1990–95. He greatly assisted the restoration of democracy to Greece in 1974 after 7 years of military dictatorship. He was also a driving force behind Greece's assimilation into the EEC.

Early Life

Karamanlis was born on 23 Feb. 1907 in Proti, a village in the prefecture of Sérrai, northern Greece. He was the eldest son of a schoolmaster, and was educated with the assistance of local benefactors. He studied law at Athens University and received his degree in 1932. He went on to practise law in the capital, before entering the political arena in 1935 as a deputy for the Populist Party in the constituency of Sérrai. During the dictatorship of Metaxas and the Nazi occupation of Greece he withdrew from politics, returning in 1946 when he was appointed labour minister. He held numerous cabinet posts, but firmly established his administrative credentials as minister of social welfare. In this role he was to organize the repatriation of over half a million refugees who had fled their villages during the civil war. As minister of defence he again aided the rural poor by securing military help to rebuild many communities.

Career Peak

Karamanlis abandoned the ailing Populist Party in 1951 and joined the new right-wing Greek Rally, led by Field Marshal Alexander Papagos. He became minister of public works in 1952. When Papagos died in Oct. 1955, King Paul chose Karamanlis to be the new prime minister. This royal appointment caused his opponents to dismiss him as an illegitimate leader. Within 4 months of succeeding to power, he founded the National Radical Union (ERE) party, which won three successive elections in 1956, 1958 and 1961.

Under Karamanlis' first 8 year tenure Greece's economy and industrial infrastructure were strengthened to achieve a resilience and stability which had been hard to come by in the aftermath of the civil war. However, the left-wing and liberal alliance in the Greek parliament claimed that the 1961 election was rigged, and in the face of personal criticism after the assassination of the left-wing deputy Grigoris Lambrakis by right-wing hooligans in May 1963, Karamanlis resigned. In the elections that were held in Nov. that year, Giorgios Papandreou's Centre Union won a marginal victory, and the shocked Karamanlis handed the leadership of the ERE to his deputy, Panayotis Kanellopoulos. He went into voluntary exile in Paris for 11 years, during which time Greece was subject to military dictatorship.

Karamanlis returned to Greece in 1974 after Papadopoulos' junta had been deposed. He was invited to restore peace and order to the country in the wake of the military's disastrous attempt to annex Cyprus. He was sworn in as prime minister on 23 July, and quickly formed a government of national unity which managed to prevent war with Turkey, and brought the armed forces under government control. He established the New Democracy party, which was restored to power with a convincing majority in the elections of Nov. 1974. After the election he gave the people the chance to vote on whether they wanted Greece to be a republic or retain its monarchy. The outcome was two-to-one in favour of abandoning the monarchy. Karamanlis also legalized the Communist Party and was responsible for restoring Greek nationality to thousands of political refugees who had fled the country during the rule of the military junta. His most significant achievement was securing Greek membership of the EEC in May 1979.

In May 1980 he relinquished the leadership of the New Democracy party, and was elected as President of the Republic by a three-fifths majority. He resigned from this post in 1985 and went into retirement after the prime minister, Andreas Papandreou withdrew his support. When the 1990 presidential election resulted in stalemate, Karamanlis agreed to stand, and in May that year he was elected president once again. His advanced age and ill-health meant that he was less politically active than he had been during his first term, and eventually he resigned to make way for a middle-ground candidate, Costis Stephanopoulos. He died on 23 April 1998.

Karamanlis, Konstantinos 'Kostas' (Greece)

Introduction

Dr Konstantinos 'Kostas' Karamanlis became prime minister after leading the New Democracy (ND) to victory at the general election of March 2004, ending over 10 years rule by Pasok (the Panhellenic Socialist Movement). Karamanlis promised to streamline Greece's bureaucracy, fight corruption in government and reduce taxation while increasing social welfare spending. He retained the premiership as the ND narrowly won the Sept. 2007 general election, but his party lost to Pasok in the Oct. 2009 elections.

Early Life

Karamanlis was born on 14 Sept. 1956 in Athens. His uncle was Konstantinos Karamanlis, the founder of ND and three times prime minister of Greece. Karamanlis graduated from Athens University Law School, then undertook further study at the private Deree College before taking a doctorate in international relations and political science from the Fletcher School of Law and Diplomacy in the USA.

From 1974–79 Karamanlis served in ONNED, the youth arm of ND. Following his period of study in the USA, he practised as a lawyer from 1984–89. At the same time he was active within the infrastructures of ND and ONNED and was teaching politics at Deree College. In 1989 he entered parliament as the ND member for Thessaloniki, which he represented until 2004 when he became member for Larissa. Following electoral defeat in 1996, Karamanlis was chosen as party leader the following year. At the general election of 2000 Pasok defeated ND by less than one percentage point.

By early 2004 opinion polls were showing ND with an eight-point advantage over Pasok. The gap narrowed after Pasok's appointment of George Papandreou in Jan. 2004 and observers predicted a close-run election. At the polls on 7 March 2004, however, the ND won a sweeping victory and secured a large majority in parliament.

Career Peak

Although lacking ministerial experience, Karamanlis had been in frontline politics as leader of ND for 8 years when he took office. With preparations for the Athens Olympics in Aug. 2004 behind schedule and international concern over security arrangements, Karamanlis assumed control of the culture ministry, and thus responsibility for Olympics affairs. He announced his intention to reduce taxes, lower unemployment and increase spending on reforming the agricultural and education sectors. He also declared plans to privatize many of the larger state-owned industries and promised to encourage foreign investment. Despite pre-election pledges to reduce the size of government, his first cabinet comprised 47 members. In foreign affairs he was expected to continue to pursue a negotiated agreement with Turkey over the future of Cyprus, despite the rejection in April 2004 by the Greek Cypriot population of the UN-backed plan for the island's future.

Karamanlis' unpopular plans for pension and labour reforms, coupled with high unemployment and rising inflation, prompted industrial unrest in 2005 and 2006. His government also came under pressure from the European Commission to reduce Greece's budget deficit to the level permitted under the eurozone stability pact. Further criticism of the government in 2007 stemmed from a series of financial scandals and its handling of devastating summer forest fires. Karamanlis nevertheless called an early election in Sept. (6 months ahead of schedule), in which the ND secured a slender parliamentary majority.

Allegations of corruption within his government continued to undermine Karamanlis' approval ratings through 2008. In Oct. thousands of public-sector employees went on strike in protest over privatization, pay levels and pension reform. Then, in Dec., the shooting of a teenage boy by police in Athens sparked days of anti-government rioting and a general strike in the worst disturbances in the country since the end of military rule in 1974. There was further unrest in Jan. 2009 as farmers demanding more government subsidies paralysed much of the country by blocking main roads. Karamanlis was succeeded by Georgios Papandreou on 6 Oct. 2009 after ND lost to Pasok in the general election.

Karami, Rashid (Lebanon)

Introduction

A Sunni Muslim, Karami was the prime minister of Lebanon eight times between 1955 and 1987. He was killed on 1 June 1987 in a helicopter crash that was the result of sabotage.

Early Life

Born on 30 Dec. 1921 near Tripoli, Karami trained as a lawyer before entering politics in 1951 as an elected National Assembly deputy. After serving as minister of national economy, he became prime minister for the first time in Sept. 1955. However, his opposition to Maronite president Camille Chamoun led to his resignation in March 1956. Two years later he was reappointed as prime minister and served five terms under Presidents Chehab and Hélou by 1970 (from Sept. 1958–May 1960, Oct. 1961–Feb. 1964, July 1965–April 1966, Dec. 1966–Feb. 1968 and Jan. 1969–Sept. 1970).

Career Peak

Karami's seventh term as prime minister from July 1975–Dec. 1976, heading a government of national salvation, spanned the turbulent period of the civil war. He was reappointed prime minister under President Amin Gemayel for the last time in April 1984. However, his government wielded little authority over the divided country and made no headway in resolving constitutional or security issues by the time of his death in office in June 1987.

Karimov, Islam Abduganiyevich (Uzbekistan)

Introduction

Islam Karimov, a former Soviet official, was president from when Uzbekistan declared independence in 1990 through to Sept. 2016. His regime was characterized by the suppression of domestic political and religious opposition, and his electoral victories were questioned for their irregularities. Karimov sought to build ties with the West, and won US favour for co-operation in the war against terrorism in the aftermath of the 11 Sept. 2001 attacks. However, reports of torture and other human rights violations, culminating in an alleged massacre of Uzbek civilians in Andizhan in May 2005, provoked international criticism of his regime. In Dec. 2007 he retained the presidency in an election widely condemned as undemocratic and constitutionally illegal, and was returned again for a further term in March 2015. He died in Sept. 2016.

Early Life

Karimov was born on 30 Jan. 1938 in Samarkand. He qualified as a mechanical engineer at the Central Asian Polytechnical Institute and graduated in economics from the Tashkent Institute of National Economy. He then worked in Tashkent at farm machinery and aircraft plants. In 1966 he moved to the state planning committee of Uzbekistan, attaining the rank of vice-chairman.

In 1983 Karimov was appointed finance minister for Uzbekistan and 3 years later became deputy head of government, as well as chairman of the state planning committee. In 1989 he was named head of the Uzbek Communist Party. The following year Uzbekistan claimed sovereignty from the USSR and Karimov was chosen as president. Following the attempted coup against Mikhail Gorbachev in Moscow in 1991, Karimov declared full independence.

Career Peak

Against little organized opposition, Karimov dominated presidential elections and led Uzbekistan into the Commonwealth of Independent States. In 1992 he continued his campaign against domestic opposition, banning two leading parties—Birlik (Unity) and Erk (Freedom)—and imprisoning many members. In 1994 he agreed an economic integration treaty with Russia and signed a co-operation pact with Kazakhstan and Kyrgyzstan which was developed into a single economic community in 1996. In 1995 Karimov won a further 5 years in office by plebiscite.

In 1999 Tashkent was the scene of several car bombings which Karimov blamed on the Islamic Movement of Uzbekistan (IMU). Government and IMU forces clashed several times, the culmination of growing tensions between the two sides since the mid-1990s. In the same year Karimov withdrew Uzbekistan from the CIS agreement on collective security, increasing the nation's isolation among Central Asian nations predominantly loyal to Moscow.

Karimov was re-elected to the presidency in 2000 with over 90% of the vote, although the electoral process was severely criticized by the international community, notably the opposition candidate's assertion that he himself would vote for Karimov. Following the 11 Sept. attacks in New York and Washington, Karimov permitted the USA to use Uzbek air bases for the war in Afghanistan. In the same year he signed up to the Shanghai Co-operation Society (with China, Russia, Kazakhstan, Kyrgyzstan and Tajikistan), established to promote regional economic co-operation and fight religious and ethnic militancy.

In Jan. 2002 Karimov secured a constitutional change, accepted by referendum, extending the presidential term from 5 to 7 years. His assistance in the US campaign in Afghanistan was meanwhile rewarded by US$160 m. worth of aid from Washington. Also in 2002 a long-running border feud with Kazakhstan was settled.

In March 2004 a series of shootings and explosions in the Tashkent and Bukhara regions left dozens of people dead. Further bombings near the US and Israeli embassies and in the Prosecutor General's Office in Tashkent occurred in July. Karimov's government blamed Islamic militants. Then in May 2005 several hundred civilians, protesting against the trial of local businessmen accused of Islamic extremism, were reportedly killed by security forces in Andizhan. Unrest also spread to the towns of Paktabad and Kara Suu before troops reasserted government control. At the end of July, in a punitive response to international criticism of the massacre, Karimov gave the USA 6 months to close its military airbase in Uzbekistan. His relations with the European Union also became increasingly strained in the wake of the events in Andizhan and the subsequent convictions of those accused of instigating unrest. The EU imposed an arms embargo and a visa ban, and these sanctions were extended in 2006. Uzbekistan meanwhile sought to strengthen its military and economic co-operation with Russia.

In Dec. 2007 Karimov's re-election as president failed to meet democratic standards, according to international observers, and was condemned by opposition activists as a sham.

In late 2008 and early 2009 there was some improvement in relations with the West as Karimov allowed the USA and NATO to transport non-lethal supplies through Uzbekistan to their armed forces in Afghanistan and the EU eased sanctions despite continuing concerns about human rights. The EU's decision followed the release of some political prisoners and the abolition of the death penalty.

In mid-2009 two terrorist incidents in Andizhan and Khanabad were attributed to increasing Islamist militancy.

In Sept. 2012 Karimov warned of potential confrontations with neighbouring Tajikistan and Kyrgyzstan over their plans for large dam projects that he claimed would give the two countries unfair control of regional water resources.

In March 2013 the then 75-year-old Karimov was rumoured to have suffered a heart attack. This prompted speculation about potential successors, one of whom, his daughter Gulnara Karimova, was placed under house arrest and charged with corruption in 2014.

As in previous parliamentary elections, polling over two rounds in Dec. 2014 and Jan. 2015 returned only those political parties loyal to Karimov. At the presidential election of March 2015 he claimed over 90% of the vote to win a further term in office.

Karimov allegedly suffered a stroke in Aug. 2016, and died on 2 Sept. 2016. With no successor in place, chairman of the senate Nigmatilla Yuldashev took over the presidency on an interim basis.

Karmal, Babrak (Afghanistan)

Introduction

A Marxist, from 1979 until 1986 Babrak Karmal served as the third president of Afghanistan, in the period of the socialist Democratic Republic of Afghanistan (DRA).

Early Life

Babrak Karmal (roughly translated as 'little tiger'. was born on 6 Jan. 1929 in the village of Kamari, Afghanistan. His father, Maj. Gen. Mohammad Hussain, was a provincial governor and friend of the royal family, including Gen. Mohammad Daoud Khan, who served as prime minister from 1953–63 and president from 1973–78. Although born into a wealthy family, Karmal lived in hardship following the death of his mother.

Karmal graduated from Nejat High School in 1948. He was originally refused entry to Kabul University because of his leftist views but was accepted by the faculty of law and political science in 1951. His Marxist political activities led to his imprisonment in 1952. After his release in 1956, he worked in the ministry of education as a German and English translator. In 1957 he was conscripted for 2 years' military service, after which he resumed his university studies before entering the ministry of planning.

Karmal was one of the founders of the People's Democratic Party of Afghanistan (PDPA) in Jan. 1965. He served as its secretary and held posts in the National Assembly from 1965 until 1973. In 1967 the PDPA split into rival factions: the Khalq ('Masses'), consisting mainly of rural purists who emphasized the class struggle of classic Marxism, and the Parcham ('Banner'), a more middle-class, moderate faction sympathetic to the USSR. As leader of the Parcham, Karmal supported the government of Mohammad Daoud Khan that came to power in a coup in 1973. However, relations between Daoud and the political left soon soured. In 1977 the PDPA's factions reunited and the following year overthrew Daoud's government in a coup that culminated in the president's death.

Karmal was appointed first deputy prime minister in the new DRA. However, the PDPA split once again and the Khalq relieved most of the Parchamis of their government positions, exiling many to ambassadorial posts abroad. Karmal was sent to Prague as ambassador to Czechoslovakia from 1978–79. Khalq rule in Afghanistan grew increasingly unpopular, prompting a Soviet invasion in Dec. 1979. The Soviets assassinated the Khalq president, Hafizullah Amim, and installed Karmal as his replacement. Kharmal was also party secretary and head of the Revolutionary Council.

Career Peak

Following the Soviet invasion, Afghanistan descended into civil war between the PDPA–Communist-controlled regime and the Mujahideen. Many Afghans were reluctant to accept the legitimacy of a government widely viewed as a puppet administration of Moscow.

During his presidency Karmal proved little more than a figurehead, denied real power and unable to unite the country or win the trust of resistance fighters. After 7 years in office, he lost the support of the Kremlin and in May 1986 Mohammad Najibullah, former head of the secret police, replaced him as secretary-general of the PDPA. Six months later Karmal had little choice but to resign the presidency.

Later Life

Once relieved of all government and party posts, Karmal moved to Moscow purportedly to seek medical treatment. He returned to Afghanistan in 1991 but left once more and died of liver cancer in Moscow on 3 Dec. 1996. He was buried in Hayratan, Afghanistan.

Karzai, Hamid (Afghanistan)

Introduction

Hamid Karzai was sworn in as chairman of the interim government of Afghanistan in Dec. 2001 before taking the position permanently in June 2002. He was appointed by the United Nations in consultation with the Northern Alliance and the *Loya Jirga*, a group of elected tribal delegates. His main aim has been to bring stability to the country but resistance by the Taliban has continued, particularly in the south and east. His other major challenges have been tackling widespread corruption and drug-trafficking. He was controversially re-elected in autumn 2009 but was ineligible to stand again in the April 2014 presidential poll, after which he would remain in office until his successor was sworn in.

Early Life

Karzai was born on 24 Dec. 1957 into the powerful Popolzai tribe. His father, who was chief of the clan, was assassinated in 1999 in what was widely believed to be a Taliban attack.

Karzai first entered politics in the early 1980s during the Soviet occupation and organized the Pashtun Popolzai against Moscow. He spent time in Pakistan before returning to Afghanistan in 1992 and linking up with the leader of the Northern Alliance, Burhanuddin Rabbani. When Rabbani formed the first mujahideen government, Karzai served as the deputy foreign minister before leaving the government because of infighting.

Karzai initially supported the Taliban when it was created in 1994 but in 1995 he rejected a government post, disillusioned by increasing foreign interference. He left the country in 1996 but secretly re-entered in 2001 during the USA's post-11 Sept. air strikes to co-ordinate Pashtun resistance to the Taliban.

Career Peak

Since taking office, Karzai has enjoyed the support of a majority of the main tribal leaders. However, his military weakness has necessitated alliances with regional factions and his rule has remained tenuous outside the capital. Despite the precarious security situation, he won the country's first-ever democratic presidential election on 9 Oct. 2004 with 55.4% of votes cast.

In May–June 2006 Afghanistan experienced the worst insurgent violence and casualties since the US invasion and toppling of the Taliban in 2001. Having taken over the leadership of military operations in the south from July 2006, NATO then assumed responsibility for security across the whole of the country from Oct., taking command in the east from a US-led coalition force. NATO and Afghan forces have since sought to contain the Taliban resurgence, although Karzai has continually expressed his concern over the high and ongoing civilian casualty rate in military operations.

In 2009 US President Barack Obama announced a further substantial US troop deployment to Afghanistan, partly to train and support the Afghan army and police service. This reinforcement heralded the launch in Feb. 2010 in Helmand of the biggest coalition offensive in the country since the defeat of Taliban government in 2001.

Despite continuing violence in 2011, there were tentative moves towards opening channels of communication with the Taliban and in May 2012 NATO endorsed a planned withdrawal of foreign combat troops by the end of 2014, with Afghan forces progressively assuming increased security responsibilities.

Meanwhile, in Jan. 2011 Karzai had made the first official visit to Russia by an Afghan leader since the end of the Soviet occupation in 1989. In Oct. that year he signed a strategic partnership with India which further unsettled Afghanistan's already fragile relationship with Pakistan.

In 2009 Karzai had sought re-election as president in a campaign tainted by alleged widespread fraud. In the first round in Aug. he claimed to be ahead of rival candidate Abdullah Abdullah with 54% of the vote. In the face of domestic and international concern over the evidential scale of vote-rigging, he subsequently conceded that the elections should go to a second round that was scheduled for early Nov. However, Abdullah Abdullah then withdrew his candidacy and Karzai was declared the winner as the only remaining contender. The president subsequently struggled in Jan. and Feb.

2010 to form a new government as a hostile parliament rejected many of his nominees for cabinet posts.

In late Feb. 2010 Karzai provoked further criticism when he assumed exclusive power to appoint all five members of the independent Electoral Complaints Commission (three of whom had previously been UN nominees), which had earlier rejected his claims to a first-round victory in the 2009 presidential elections. Parliamentary elections were then held in Sept. that year, but reports of voting fraud again threatened to undermine the validity of the poll. Official results were not released until Nov. and indicated the disqualification of many candidates and votes cast owing to irregularities. The political influence of Karzai's majority ethnic Pashtun community was significantly reduced in the new parliament, which was inaugurated in Jan. 2011.

Against the background of continuing Taliban military action, the priority for Karzai's government in 2013 was building up the capacity of the security forces ahead of the scheduled NATO withdrawal in 2014. In June the Afghan army formally took over responsibility for all security operations from Western forces. However, agreement on a post-withdrawal mission to train and advise the Afghan army was hampered by Karzai's decision in Dec. not to sign a new security pact with the USA but to instead leave that responsibility to his successor following the April 2014 elections.

Ashraf Ghani Ahmadzai—also of Pashtun heritage and a former minister of finance—succeeded Karzai as president on 29 Sept. 2014. A new security pact with the USA allowing troops to remain in the country until 2016 was subsequently signed by Ghani's government.

Kasyanov, Mikhail (Russia)

Introduction

Mikhail Kasyanov was Russia's prime minister from May 2000–Feb. 2004. A technocratic market economist and a skilled negotiator, he was appointed by Vladimir Putin. While many observers had noted Putin's lack of economics experience, Kasyanov has little political experience outside the economics sector. He was regarded as a manager, overseeing economic reform and negotiations with the West, while Putin steered policy-making. He was dismissed before the 2004 presidential elections.

Early Life

Kasyanov was born in 1957 in Sointsevo, now an area of Moscow. He graduated in construction engineering from the Moscow Automotive and Road Engineering Institute and then worked within the state construction ministry. From 1989–90 he worked for the state planning committee's department of external economic ties. The following year he took a post at the economy ministry's department of external economic ties.

In 1993 he moved to the finance ministry, holding the ranks of deputy minister, first deputy minister and, from May 1999, minister. Having gained a reputation for skilful operations within the foreign credit and debts sector, he was appointed deputy prime minister by Putin in Jan. 2000. He was seen as independent of Russia's major financial oligarchies.

Career Peak

One of Kasyanov's most important tasks was the improvement of relations with the International Monetary Fund, which held back lending to Russia following the 1998 rouble crisis, and with major industrialized donor countries. In March 2001 he warned the West not to 'drive Russia into a corner' over debt repayments.

Kasyanov was criticized for lack of progress in restructuring debt repayments, and the Duma granted him only a small fraction of the budget required to fulfil repayment requirements. Despite a generally improving economy, in March 2001 he faced a motion of no confidence in the Duma, proposed by the Communist Party. However, with the Unity Party withdrawing their support from the Communists, he survived comfortably.

In Jan. 2001 Kasyanov authorized the destruction of the Mir space station, which had been in orbit for 10 years longer than its intended lifespan. In March 2001 he suggested that the proposed union with Belarus, signalled by a treaty between the two countries in 1999, had been made a distant prospect by

Belarus' weak economy. In Nov. 2001 he backed an Organization of Petroleum Exporting Countries' initiative to reduce oil production in an attempt to stabilize prices.

Seen as a survivor from the Yeltsin era and increasingly linked to the oligarch businessmen attacked by Putin, Kasyanov was sacked with the entire government in Feb. 2004—the only way the president could remove him constitutionally ahead of presidential elections. Deputy Prime Minister Viktor Khristenko became acting prime minister.

Katainen, Jyrki (Finland)

Introduction

Jyrki Katainen became prime minister in June 2011, heading a six-party coalition. He resigned as premier and leader of the centre-right National Coalition Party (KOK) in June 2014 in a bid to secure a top international post and the following month became a European Commissioner.

Early Life

Born on 14 Oct. 1971 in Siilinjärvi, Jyrki Katainen studied social sciences at Tampere University. In 1993 he was elected to the Siilinjärvi municipal council as a KOK member and served as the council's second vice-chair from 1997–98. In 1998 he obtained a master's degree in social sciences and spent the 1990s working as a supply teacher and at the National Education Association.

In 1997 he became a member of the regional council of Northern Savo, serving as its first vice-chair from 2001–04. In 1999 he was elected to parliament for the KOK. He was vice-president of the European People's Party (EPP) youth organization from 1998–2000 and in 2005 was elected vice-president of the EPP as a whole. During the same period he rose within the KOK to become its deputy chair in 2001, before successfully challenging Ville Itälä for the leadership in 2004.

He served on the foreign affairs committee from 2004–07 in the government of Matti Vanhanen. Following the KOK's entry into coalition government with the Centre Party in 2007, Katainen was appointed finance minister and deputy prime minister. In the aftermath of the 2008 global economic crisis, he won praise for controlling Finland's deficit and retaining its top-grade international credit rating. He continued to embrace fiscal discipline during recession in 2009. In 2010 he called for stronger IMF surveillance of financial systems. In April 2011 the KOK emerged from general elections as the largest party and, after complex negotiations, Katainen formed a coalition government with the centre-left Social Democratic Party and four smaller parties from across the political spectrum.

Career Peak

Katainen took office on 22 June 2011, pledging to rebuild the economy while limiting government borrowing. In late 2011 he signalled that Finland might require guarantees or stricter conditions before agreeing to further EU bailout measures. His chief challenges were economic uncertainty at home and abroad, which he attempted to confront whilst maintaining unity across his coalition in the face of strong opposition from the nationalist True Finns party. In 2013, Katainen invited representatives of political parties, research institutes and interest groups to the Heureka Forum—a conference exploring the future challenges faced by Finland's economy. However, despite attempts to revitalize the country's industry and finances, in particular by promoting entrepreneurship and start-up businesses, Katainen's government was met with widespread criticism from the public over its austerity programme.

In April 2014 Katainen announced his intention to vacate his chairmanship of the National Coalition Party and subsequently step down as prime minister of Finland in order to seek a European or international position. He was replaced as premier by newly appointed NCP leader Alexander Stubb.

Later Life

In July 2014 Katainen became European Commissioner for economic and monetary affairs and the euro under Commission president José Manuel Barroso. He was later confirmed as vice-president when Jean-Claude Juncker took over as president from Barroso, with responsibility for jobs, growth, investment and competitiveness.

Kaunda, Kenneth (Zambia)

Introduction

Kenneth Kaunda was Zambia's first president, remaining in office for 27 years. A respected leader of the independence movement, Kaunda lost popular and international support during his presidency for his one-party rule and his failed socialist economics. After losing dramatically in multiparty elections in 1991, Kaunda's reputation improved with his peaceful departure from office and his persecution at the hands of Frederick Chiluba's government. Known as 'Father of the Nation'. Kaunda has remained an influential figure in politics and in the anti-AIDS programme.

Early Life

Kenneth David Kaunda was born on 24 April 1924 at Lubwa Mission, near Chinsali in Northern Province, Northern Rhodesia. His parents, born in Nyasaland (Malawi), were teachers at the mission school where Kaunda received his primary education, before going on to the Munali Secondary School. He returned to Lubwa to teach, as headmaster from 1944–47. He married Betty Banda in 1946, with whom he had two daughters and seven sons (one adopted).

Kaunda became active in African welfare in the late 1940s, leading a farming association and serving as welfare officer at the Chingola Copper Mine. He returned to Lubwa where he founded a branch of the Northern Rhodesia National Congress, becoming its secretary-general in 1953 when it became the African National Congress (ANC). Kaunda gained political experience as an assistant to a member of the Legislative Council, Sir Stewart Gore-Browne. In Jan. 1954 Kaunda was arrested for possession of seditious material and was imprisoned for 2 months.

By the late 1950s he had built up a following within the ANC, a section of which, in 1958, supported his breakaway party, the Zambia African National Congress (ZANC). The ZANC was founded with Simon Kapwepwe, a childhood friend and radical anti-colonialist, to whom the country's independent name—Zambia—was attributed. The ZANC vociferously opposed Northern Rhodesia's inclusion in the Central African Federation with Southern Rhodesia and Nyasaland, instituted in 1953. Kaunda was imprisoned for promoting civil disobedience in 1959. Following his release in 1960 he became president of the United National Independence Party (UNIP), created in 1959 by Mainza Chona.

Kaunda and Kapwepwe attended negotiations held in London in Dec. 1960 on the future of Northern Rhodesia. The British government rejected the recommendations of the Moncton Commission, which had proposed a constitution giving Africans a legislative majority. Instead, a constitution was promulgated that aimed to guarantee protection for whites while appeasing African demands for representation. The ensuing elections gave no party a majority, though an African government was formed through a coalition of the UNIP and Harry Nkumbula's ANC. The federation with Southern Rhodesia and Nyasaland ended on 31 Dec. 1963, with independence promised by the colonial government.

An amended constitution was obtained by Kaunda, who convinced the British that an African government would not disregard the rights of white settlers. Elections with universal suffrage were achieved in 1964, giving Kaunda and his party decisive victories. He became president of the independent Zambia on 24 Oct. 1964.

Career Peak

Independent Zambia was faced with formidable challenges. The economy's dependence on copper mining exposed the lack of African industrial expertise. Kaunda focused investment on mining which provided income for welfare and communications schemes but left the economy vulnerable to world copper prices. The neglect of agricultural reform encouraged urban migration and necessitated food subsidies in the 1970s.

Kaunda's support for groups that opposed white supremacy in neighbouring states damaged the Zambian economy. Lusaka became the foreign headquarters for South Africa's ANC and was subject to raids by South African special forces. Zambia also hosted rebel forces fighting the Portuguese—the National Union for the Total Independence of Angola (UNITA)—and Ian Smith's government in Rhodesia—the Zimbabwe African People's Union (ZAPU). The closure of the border with Rhodesia in 1973 precipitated an energy and trade crisis, partly eased by Chinese investment in the rail link to Dar es Salaam.

Political divisions within the UNIP were exacerbated by the 'tribalism' of the Zambian polity and the absence of a common African language. Kaunda attempted to limit factionalism by responding to tribal pressures with frequent government changes. Relations with Kapwepwe, his foreign minister, were strained after 1967 when he replaced Kaunda's vice-president, Rueben Kamanga. As vice-president, Kapwepwe clashed with Kaunda on economic policy and raised tribal tensions. In 1971 Kapwepwe admitted to leading a rival party, the United Progressive Party (UPP), and resigned from the government.

The prohibition of the UPP in 1972 and the arrest of Kapwepwe and his followers signalled a crisis in Zambian politics. Kaunda decided to push through the abolition of all opposition parties in a bid to end tribal strife. He justified the legality of the UNIP as sole party on the grounds of its nationwide support. The 'second Republic' ('one-party participatory democracy'. was instituted on 1 Jan. 1973.

Kaunda cemented the hegemony of his party in the face of leadership challenges from Kapwepwe and Harry Nkumbula, the ex-ANC chief. Their last-minute disqualification demonstrated Kaunda's increasingly dictatorial style of leadership. Both withdrew from politics, denting Kaunda's reputation in the party and the state.

The oil crisis of 1973 and the drop in copper prices in 1975 spelled disaster for the Zambian economy. Heavy borrowing sustained ambitious spending schemes but the mismanagement of foreign aid discouraged foreign investment and, in 1987, lost the support of the International Monetary Fund.

Despite endorsements of his presidency in the one-candidate elections of 1983 and 1988, Kaunda faced increasing opposition in his final decade in power, beginning in Oct. 1980 with an attempted coup involving UNIP members. Popular grievances focused on government and administrative corruption and the one-party constitution. Kaunda's popularity waned after he banned strikes in public service sectors in 1985. Demonstrations continued in the late 80s, culminating in the riots in Lusaka in June 1990 caused by crippling price inflation, especially for maize, a staple food.

Political opposition crystallized in 1990 under the leadership of Frederick Chiluba, a trade unionist. Chiluba formed the Movement for Multiparty Democracy (MMD), bringing together a broad spectrum of politicians with the Zambian Congress of Trade Unions (ZTCU). After another attempted coup in July 1990, UNIP's national council bowed to public pressure and scheduled multiparty elections for Oct. 1991. Kaunda legalized opposition parties and agreed to foreign observers at the elections. Chiluba won 76% of the votes and took the MMD into government.

Later Life

Despite the peaceful transfer of power, Kaunda campaigned against the new president. After several years of popular dissatisfaction with Chiluba's government, Kaunda came out of semi-retirement to lead the UNIP as its president in June 1995. Attacking Chiluba's government on grounds of corruption and ethnic imbalance—his cabinets leant heavily on the Bemba ethnic group—he was arrested twice in 1995. The government outmanoeuvred Kaunda's attempt to challenge Chiluba in the 1996 presidential elections with a constitutional amendment prohibiting candidates whose parents were born abroad.

Following an attempted coup in Oct. 1997 and rumours of a foreign invasion to reinstate Kaunda as president, Kaunda was detained at Kamwala Prison as a security risk. Kaunda responded by going on hunger-strike. Popular disgust at his treatment and appeals from Nelson Mandela, Julius Nyerere and the British government forced Chiluba to release him. After 5 months of house arrest, Kaunda announced his retirement from politics.

Kaunda's security became a national issue after an assassination attempt in April 1999 and the murder of his son, Wezi Kaunda in Nov. 1999. Kaunda accused the government of persecuting him and his family (his daughter, Catherine, fled to South Africa in 1997) and claimed that Wezi's murder was politically motivated. Popular support for Kaunda increased in the face of attempts to end his pension and strip him of his Zambian citizenship in 2000.

Kaunda attacked Chiluba's attempts to amend the 1991 constitution, which barred the president from seeking a third term in office, and supported his son, Tilyenji Kaunda, in the 2001 presidential elections. Kaunda continued his bitter public feud with Chiluba during the presidency of Levy Mwanawasa, whose anti-corruption campaign stripped Chiluba of his immunity from prosecution. Kaunda welcomed Chiluba's arrest in Feb. 2003 on corruption and theft charges.

Keating, Paul (Australia)

Introduction

Paul Keating was Prime Minister of Australia and leader of the Australian Labor Party (ALP) between 1991 and 1996. He made his name as a combative and effective treasurer in the Bob Hawke administration, before ousting Hawke from the premiership. A republican, Keating embraced the Asia-Pacific region and pursued a reconciliation programme with the Aboriginal population.

Early Life

Keating was born in Sydney on 18 Jan. 1944. He left school at 15, joined the ALP and took a job with Sydney City Council before joining the New South Wales Electricity Commission. In 1968 he joined the Federated Municipal and Shire Council Employees' Union and a year later he entered the House of Representatives as the member for Blaxland, New South Wales. He was appointed minister for Northern Australia in 1975 for the last month of Gough Whitlam's government. In the same year he married Anna Johanna Maria Van Iersel (Annita), with whom he had four children. Between 1976–83 he served as opposition spokesman for agriculture, then for minerals and energy, before taking the post of shadow chancellor. Keating became chancellor following Hawke's victory at the election of 1983 and was instrumental in Australia's economic upturn. Under his guidance, the financial sector was deregulated, tax overhauled, the dollar floated and a wage and price agreement reached with the trade unions. In 1988 he struck a deal with Hawke by which Keating would become prime minister in 1990. However, when the time came, Hawke refused to resign. Keating broke away to launch two leadership bids in 1991. He lost the first in June but won the second in Dec. by 56 votes to 51. The once admired team, in which Hawke's 'man of the people' image was complemented by the sometimes aggressive style of Keating, was irredeemably split. Hawke became one of Keating's fiercest critics.

Career Peak

Australia's economy was deep in recession by the early 1990s. As prime minister, Keating launched his One Nation programme in Feb. 1992, setting out major tax cuts. He also introduced a superannuation scheme, deregulated the civil aviation and telecommunications sectors and established a National Electricity Grid Corporation. Although deemed an 'unwinnable' election, Keating led the ALP to victory with an increased majority in March 1993, against a John Hewson-led coalition.

The issue of Aboriginal land rights played a major role during his administration, following the High Court's Mabo decision of June 1992. The decision overturned a previous ruling that the Aboriginal title to land had not survived British settlement of the continent. Keating officially acknowledged the injustice done to the Aboriginal population and 'Native Title' legislation was passed in Dec. 1993. Keating's foreign policy hinged on a move away from Europe and America to the emerging Asian economies. He reached agreement on a security pact with Indonesia's President Suharto in Dec. 1995 and increased Australia's participation within the Asia-Pacific Economic Co-operation (APEC) group. Keating was also renowned as a republican and it was widely reported in the media when he laid a guiding hand upon the Queen's personage at an official function. He wanted to make Australia a republic by 2000, with the head of state chosen by parliament. However, before he could introduce the relevant legislation he was defeated at the election of 2 March 1996, losing to a coalition led by John Howard.

Later Life

Keating resigned from Parliament on 23 April 1996 and has subsequently taken various visiting professorships and worked as a business consultant. He and Annita separated in 1998. He retains a presence on the political scene and has been a prominent critic of Liberal Prime Minister John Howard. Keating claimed that Howard's intervention in Timor-Leste in 1999 was Australia's 'worst foreign policy disaster since the Vietnam War'.

Kekkonen, Urho (Finland)

Introduction

Urho Kekkonen served as Finland's prime minister on two occasions (1950–53, 1954–56) and as the president from 1956–81. His Soviet-oriented foreign policy aimed to win back Finnish territories occupied by the USSR, and neutralize the threat of further Soviet invasion. He was noted for his defence of the country's impoverished agricultural community. Kekkonen was acclaimed as one of the foremost statesmen of his age.

Early Life

Kekkonen was born on 3 Sept. 1900 in Kajana. He was the son of a forestry foreman, and was educated at the University of Helsinki, where he was awarded bachelor's and doctoral degrees in law. He began his career as a lawyer but from the 1920s onward he became increasingly interested in the agrarian movement. From 1927–32 he worked for a local government federation before transferring to the Ministry of Agriculture. He became a member of Parliament in 1936, representing the Agrarian Union. Initially he opposed Soviet incursions into Finnish territory, and favoured an alliance with Nazi Germany to prevent further occupation. However by 1943 it was clear that Germany would lose the war on the Eastern front and Kekkonen realized that if Finland wanted to retain its independence it had to conduct a foreign policy that leaned towards the Soviet Union without falling under its control.

Career Peak

In 1948 Kekkonen helped to negotiate the Treaty of Friendship, Co-operation and Mutual Assistance which guaranteed Finnish neutrality while upholding the principles of free democracy. After several ministerial and legislative roles (including Minister of Justice and Minister of the Interior) Kekkonen became prime minister in 1950 under the presidency of J.K. Paasikivi. In 1956 he succeeded Paasikivi and continued a cautious and tactful foreign policy which became known known as the Paasikivi-Kekkonen line. Kekkonen encouraged 'Finlandisation'. a guarded assertion of national identity, and a means of diplomatic survival in a difficult situation. Kekkonen was re-elected to the presidency on three successive occasions from 1962–78. In 1974 a majority of delegates from all parties voted to postpone the planned presidential elections, bypass the electorate and extend Kekkonen's tenure by 4 years. His position as president allowed him absolute control of foreign policy which he used to negotiate free trade agreements with EFTA and, later, the EC. This, combined with a thriving trade with the USSR, helped boost the Finnish economy.

Later Life

Kekkonen's later years were marred by illness which compelled him to resign from office in 1981. He died on 31 Aug. 1986.

Kemakeza, Allan (Solomon Islands)

Introduction

Sir Allan Kemakeza was elected prime minister of the Solomon Islands by parliament in Dec. 2001. He was confronted with a weak economy and a general breakdown in infrastructure and law and order, resulting from years of civil war, ethnic fighting and corruption. Earlier in 2001 Kemakeza had been forced to give up the vice-premiership after alleged financial irregularities, and his appointment as prime minister concerned many international aid donors. Following elections in April 2006, Kemakeza announced his resignation as prime minister and head of the People's Alliance Party.

Early Life

Kemakeza was born in 1951 and worked as a policeman before entering political life. He rose to be vice-premier in the government of Mannasseh Sogavare but was forced to resign when he was accused of diverting compensation for victims of the civil war (which ended in 2000) to his own family, friends and supporters. He denied any wrongdoing and stood for the premiership in Dec. 2001. He won 29 of the 50 available parliamentary votes and was sworn in on 17 Dec.

Career Peak

Although the war between the Isatabu Freedom Movement and the Malaita Eagle Force (MEF) was officially brought to an end in 2000 after 2 years during which Prime Minister Bartholomew Ulufa'alu was overthrown, fighting between the two groups continued to the detriment of national political and economic stability. Major export industries, including the timber trade, were badly hit and corruption in public life had depleted national reserves as well as dissuaded the international community from investing in national restructuring.

Kemakeza's involvement in the war compensation scandal in early 2001 saw his appointment receive a muted response from abroad. Australia and New Zealand, two potentially vital donor countries, set out requirements for further aid including the reformation of the police force, which contained many former militia accused of profiteering from their new positions.

In Jan. 2002 the government faced a strike by civil servants complaining about non-payment of wages. In the same month Australia promised to send government advisors to Honiara, the national capital, to assist in government reform. Nonetheless, law and order remained a major problem and the police force was accused of extorting money from the government. In Dec. 2002 Kemakeza defeated a confidence motion instigated by the opposition.

The Solomon Islands' fragile economy received a new setback in Dec. 2002 when Cyclone Zoe devastated two islands in the chain. Ethnic militancy escalated throughout 2003 and in June Kemakeza asked Australia and New Zealand for military assistance to restore order. In July 2003 a 2,225-strong Australian-led peacekeeping force landed, including troops from the Fiji Islands, New Zealand, Papua New Guinea and Tonga. The Malaita Eagle Force, among the country's most important rebel groups, announced it would surrender its arms to international peacekeeping forces on 15 Aug. 2003. The MEF had been in possession of the capital, Honiara, until the peacekeeping force arrived.

In Nov. 2003 a national economic recovery plan and budget was agreed by parliament and presented to donors. The World Bank and Asian Development Bank agreed to re-engage, and the European Union also announced the release of aid funds frozen since 2000.

In April 2006 parliamentary elections were held and the People's Alliance Party were defeated. Kemakeza tendered his resignation and parliament elected former deputy prime minister Snyder Rini to replace him on 18 April 2006.

Later Life

Kemakeza was appointed Minister of Forestry in Dec. 2007.

Kennedy, Charles (United Kingdom of Great Britain and Northern Ireland)

Introduction

Charles Kennedy succeeded Paddy Ashdown as leader of the Liberal Democrats (Lib Dems) in 1999. As head of what was then Britain's third party, after Labour and the Conservatives, Kennedy pursued broad co-operation with Blair's Labour government. He resigned in Jan. 2006.

Early Life

Charles Kennedy was born on 25 Nov. 1959 in Inverness, Scotland. Having joined the Labour Party when he was 15, he studied at Glasgow University, winning an MA in politics and philosophy and becoming president of the Union. In 1982 he was employed by BBC Highland before winning a Fulbright Scholarship at Indiana University in the USA, studying politics and communications.

Disillusioned by Labour's self-destructive dogmatism, Kennedy became an early member of the Social Democratic Party (SDP). In early 1983 he was selected as candidate for the SDP in the constituency of Ross, Cromarty and Skye. At the general election 6 weeks later he defeated a former Conservative minister and, at 23 years of age, became the youngest member of the House of Commons.

Kennedy variously served as a party spokesman on the welfare state, agriculture and rural affairs, Scotland, health and Europe. He was also an integral member of the all-party select committee that recommended televising parliament. In 1987 Kennedy was the first SDP member of parliament to support the proposed merger with the Liberal party. In 1990 he was appointed president of the Liberal Democrats, a post he held until 1994.

Kennedy's relationship with Ashdown faltered following Labour's landslide election victory in 1997 when Kennedy expressed reservations about making deals with the new government in return for promises of cabinet representation. However, when Ashdown retired from Westminster politics in 1999, Kennedy, a skilled media operator, defeated rival candidate Simon Hughes for the leadership.

Career Peak

Kennedy maintained close relations with Blair's government, while continuing to be critical of many aspects of government policy. His attitude to the Conservatives was less favourable and before the 2001 general election he observed that 'William Hague's Conservatives in government would be. . . an unmitigated disaster'.

Kennedy favoured co-operation with the government as the best chance of improving Britain's European relations and securing entry to the single currency, a major Lib Dem goal. This approach also ensured a Lib Dem ministerial presence in the Scottish parliament, where they were at the time the second party.

In Oct. 1999 Kennedy was appointed to the Privy Council. At the general election of June 2001 the Lib Dems increased their parliamentary representation from 47 to 52 seats. In the aftermath of the election he considered proposals to end the co-operation pact with the Labour government. The pact, agreed by Ashdown and Blair in 1997, established a joint consultative committee (JCC) to discuss Scottish and Welsh devolution and electoral reform. With the issue of devolution resolved, Lib Dem resentment grew at Blair's failure to hold a referendum on electoral reform. Kennedy's belief that the pact held his party back from 'effective opposition' led to a joint statement from the two leaders in Sept. 2001 formally disbanding the JCC.

In the general election of May 2005 the Lib Dems achieved a total of 62 seats (their highest number since 1923) and 22% of the overall vote. Despite this Kennedy attracted criticism within his party from those who felt that he had failed to take advantage of a weakened Conservative Party to push the Lib Dems forward. Donnachadh McCarthy, the former deputy chairman of the Federal Liberal Democrat Party, resigned claiming that the party was moving to the right in order to chase Conservative votes.

Kennedy came under fire again in Dec. 2005 when he handed out the ballot papers for the party leadership a week before the election was due to take place, leaving little preparation time for any potential challengers.

On 5 Jan. 2006 Kennedy announced that he had been receiving treatment for alcoholism. He acknowledged the damage that this had done to his relationship with his party and called a leadership contest to resolve the concerns surrounding his ability to continue as leader. Within days of his statement he received a letter signed by 25 Lib Dem frontbench speakers, calling for his resignation by 9 Jan. 2006. On 7 Jan. 2006 Charles Kennedy resigned as the leader of the Liberal Democrats.

Later Life

As well as remaining an active force within the party, in Feb. 2008 he was elected to serve a 3-year term as rector of the University of Glasgow. He kept his seat in the House of Commons as MP for Ross, Skye and Lochaber in the 2010 general election, winning over 50% of the vote, but lost it to the Scottish National Party in May 2015.

Kennedy died aged 55 at his home in Fort William, Scotland on 1 June 2015.

Kennedy, John F. (United States of America)

Introduction

John Fitzgerald Kennedy was the 35th President of the United States, taking office in Jan. 1961. His term was ended by his assassination on 22 Nov. 1963. The first Roman Catholic to become President, Kennedy had to deal with a volatile international situation but also managed to put in place several landmark domestic programmes that would come to full fruition after his death.

Early Life

Kennedy was born in Brookline, Massachusetts on 29 May 1917 to Joseph Patrick and Rose Kennedy (née Fitzgerald). The second of 9 children, Kennedy attended several private schools before spending the summer of 1935 in England at the London School of Economics. He then enrolled at Princeton University but had to leave after an attack of jaundice. In the autumn of 1936 he enrolled at Harvard University where he graduated in 1940. He spent several months studying at the Stanford University Graduate School of Business in California and was accepted into the Navy as a lieutenant in 1943 after being rejected by the Army because of a back problem.

After serving in World War II with distinction Kennedy was awarded the Purple Heart and the Navy and Marine Corps Medal. But recurring problems with his back and a bout of malaria, led to him being discharged from service in 1945. Meanwhile, his elder brother, Joseph, was killed in action. Kennedy returned to Boston in 1946 to enter politics, winning a democratic primary in June 1946. He was elected to the House of Representatives for the 11th Massachusetts Congressional District. Re-elected in 1948 and 1950, Kennedy entered the US Senate in Nov. 1952 after defeating Republican incumbent Henry Cabot Lodge, Jr.

After marrying Jacqueline Bouvier in Sept. 1953, he became seriously ill and had to undergo two spinal operations in 1954 and 1955. He returned to the senate in 1955 and was re-elected by a wide margin in 1958. In Jan. 1960 Kennedy announced that he would seek the Democratic Party's presidential nomination and after a hard fought campaign he defeated Hubert H. Humphrey Jr. in the primaries before seeing off the challenges of Lyndon B. Johnson and Adlai E. Stevenson to win the Democratic Party's nomination. In the presidential election he defeated his republican rival Richard M. Nixon by a little over 119,000 votes out of almost 69,000,000 cast and by 303 electoral college votes to 219.

Career Peak

Sworn in on 20 Jan. 1961 Kennedy made a famous inauguration speech urging the American people to struggle 'against the common enemies of man: tyranny, poverty, disease and war'. Young and charming, Kennedy and his family, including two children, Caroline and John Jr., born in 1957 and 1960, captured the public imagination. His early days in office were characterized by radical proposals on a whole gamut of issues from the reform of taxation to policies to spur economic growth. By 1962 $1.2 bn. had been pledged for social and housing programmes.

Domestic policies were overshadowed by a series of international crises. In April 1961 anti-Castro Cubans, trained and supported by the CIA, attempted and failed to invade the Bay of Pigs in Cuba. Kennedy took responsibility for the botched operation but was soon plunged into a battle of will with Soviet Premier Nikita Khrushchev. In Aug. 1961 the building of the Berlin Wall symbolized a hardening of the Cold War. Kennedy increased the American military presence in South Vietnam from 700 at the beginning of his term in office to 15,000 to counter the threat of communist domination.

The deterioration in US-Soviet relations culminated in the Cuban Missile Crisis of 1962 when, for a week, the US armed forces were on combat readiness after it was discovered that Soviet missile bases were being built in Cuba. After the Soviet Union backed down Kennedy was widely praised for his firmness and diplomatic skills. Thereafter relations between the two superpowers thawed to the point of negotiating the Nuclear Test Ban Treaty, which the USA, USSR and Great Britain signed in July 1963. This treaty saw the first halt in the expansion of nuclear arms since the beginning of the cold war.

Kennedy did not live to see many of his domestic reforms bear fruit. He boosted the USA's financial commitment to the space race and vowed to send an American into space by the end of the decade – a prediction that was fulfilled 6 years after his death. Similarly, significant civil rights legislation would only be introduced once his successor Lyndon Baines Johnson was in office.

At 12.30 pm on 22 Nov. 1963 Kennedy was assassinated while he drove through Dallas, Texas. Kennedy was pronounced dead at Parkland Memorial Hospital half an hour later. The same day Lee Harvey Oswald, an ex-Marine, was arrested for his murder, although he was himself shot dead 2 days later by nightclub owner Jack Ruby. Kennedy was buried on 25 Nov. in Arlington National Cemetery. A seven-member commission chaired by Chief Justice Earl Warren to investigate Kennedy's assassination concluded that Oswald had been a lone assassin, although conspiracy theories have abounded ever since.

Kennedy, Robert F. (United States of America)

Introduction

Robert Francis Kennedy (popularly known as 'Bobby'. served as US Attorney-General from 1961–64 while his brother John Fitzgerald Kennedy was president. After his brother's assassination he served as Senator for New York from 1965–68 and was campaigning to secure the Presidential nomination when he was assassinated in June 1968.

Early Life

Born in Brookline Massachusetts on 20 Nov. 1925 to Joseph Patrick and Rosemary Kennedy (née Fitzgerald), Robert Kennedy was one of nine children. During World War II he served in the US Navy. He then went to Harvard University where he gained a BA and the University of Virginia, where he was awarded an LLB.

Bobby served as campaign manager as his elder brother John ran for the Senate in 1952 and for president in 1960. He also came to national prominence for his work on the Senate Rackets Committee between 1957 and 1959.

Career Peak

After his brother was inaugurated as president, Bobby was appointed Attorney-General. His term was characterized by civil rights issues and attempts to crack down on organized crime. He also acted as his brother's confidante and advisor during the Cuban Missile Crisis of 1962. After John F. Kennedy's assassination on 22 Nov. 1963, Bobby continued to serve as Attorney-General under new president Lyndon Baines Johnson, but was rejected by the new president as a potential running mate in the 1964 election.

On 3 Sept. 1964 Kennedy resigned as Attorney-General to run for the Senate in New York. He was duly elected, as was his younger brother Edward who was elected Senator for Massachusetts. For the next 4 years Bobby supported Johnson on domestic matters, such as civil rights legislation, but grew increasingly critical of escalating American involvement in Vietnam.

Urged by many to challenge Johnson for the presidential nomination in 1968, Kennedy entered late, believing that Johnson was unbeatable. 15 days later the incumbent made the surprise announcement that he was withdrawing from the race. Kennedy was now the clear frontrunner to secure the Democratic nomination. However on 5 June, just before midnight, and only hours after defeating Senator Eugene McCarthy in a primary in California, Kennedy was shot and fatally wounded as he left the Ambassador Hotel in Los Angeles. His assassin was identified as Sirhan Sirhan, a Palestinian immigrant who was angered by Kennedy's support for the state of Israel. Surgeons fought to save Kennedy but he was pronounced dead on 6 June, 20 h after he had been shot.

Kenny, Enda (Ireland)

Introduction

Enda Kenny became prime minister (Taoiseach) on 9 March 2011. He was leader of the centrist Fine Gael from June 2002 to June 2017 and is currently Ireland's longest-serving member of parliament.

Early Life

Kenny was born in 1951 in Castlebar, Co. Mayo. He studied at the University of Galway and St Patrick's College of Education in Dublin and then worked as a primary school teacher for a year.

His father was the Fine Gael member of parliament for Mayo West and a parliamentary secretary. Enda regularly assisted with constituency matters and on his father's death in 1975 took over the Mayo West seat after winning a by-election. Over the next decade Kenny served as a backbencher but in 1986 was appointed junior minister for education and labour in the government of Garret FitzGerald.

After Fine Gael lost the 1987 election, Kenny served on the opposition front bench. He became party chief whip in 1993 and a year later, after the collapse of Albert Reynolds' Fianna Fáil government, helped negotiate a 'rainbow coalition' with the Labour Party and the Democratic Left. He served in that government as minister for tourism and trade and chaired the European Union Council of Trade Ministers during Ireland's 6 month presidency of the EU in 1996.

Fine Gael left government after the 1997 general election and Kenny ran unsuccessfully for party leader in 2001. In 2002, following the party's worst ever election performance, he was elected its new leader. In 2004 Fine Gael made significant gains at the European elections and out-polled Fianna Fáil, the first time Fianna Fáil had come second in elections across the country since 1927. In 2006 Kenny became vice-president of the European People's Party (EPP), the centre-right grouping in the European Parliament.

Kenny led Fine Gael to a strong showing at the 2007 general election despite coming second to Fianna Fáil. In 2010 he held off a leadership challenge before overseeing victory at the 2011 general election on the back of strong anti-Fianna Fáil sentiment in light of the country's economic collapse. With 76 of a possible 166 seats, Fine Gael was the largest single party for the first time in its history and Kenny formed a coalition government with the Labour Party.

Career Peak

Kenny's primary challenge was to spur a recovery in the financial system. Prior to the election he pledged to renegotiate the conditions of the €85 bn. EU–IMF bailout package agreed by the previous government. In July 2011 EU leaders agreed to cut the interest rate on the rescue deal and to extend the repayment period. Ireland's fiscal position improved under the austerity regime of tax rises and spending cuts but the economy has remained vulnerable. Continuing weak growth pushed the country back into recession in 2013, although in Dec. that year Ireland was able to formally exit the EU–IMF bailout programme.

In July 2011 Kenny courted diplomatic controversy with an attack on the Vatican, which he accused of having tried to cloud the extent of sexual abuse of children by Catholic clergy in Ireland. In response, the Vatican recalled its envoy from Dublin.

In July 2013 parliament passed a controversial law allowing limited abortion rights for the first time, despite strong Catholic opposition, while in May 2015 Ireland became the first country in the world to legalize same-sex marriage in a referendum with over 60% of the electorate voting in favour.

Kenny announced a series of ministerial changes, including five new appointments to the cabinet, in July 2014 during an address to parliament in which he said that the Irish economy was entering 'a new phase of recovery'.

However, in a snap general election in Feb. 2016 Fine Gael lost substantial ground, resulting in a hung parliament. In April Fine Gael secured opposition support to form a new minority government and in May Kenny became the first Fine Gael leader to be re-elected as prime minister by parliament.

In Aug. 2016 the European Commission ruled that long-standing taxation arrangements between US computer giant Apple Inc. and the Irish government constituted illegal state aid under European Union law and that the company should pay €13 bn. in corporate back taxes. Kenny said that the government would appeal the ruling as it would harm job creation and foreign investment in Ireland.

On 17 May 2017 Kenny announced his resignation as leader of Fine Gael but continued to carry on his duties as prime minister until Leo Varadkar was elected by Parliament to succeed him on 14 June 2017.

Kenyatta, Jomo (Kenya)

Introduction

Jomo Kenyatta was the first president of Kenya (1964–78). As a young African nationalist he was imprisoned during the Mau-Mau uprising. Later, as president he adopted a non-aligned policy. The stability that resulted from his tight control of the country attracted foreign investment. Many Africans saw Kenyatta as a role model. He wrote two books Facing Mount Kenya and Suffering Without Bitterness. He died in office and was succeeded by Daniel T. arap Moi. Kenyatta's image still looms large in Kenya today. His son was recently given one of parliament's reserved seats and is tipped as a possible successor to Moi.

Early Life

Jomo Kenyatta's exact date of birth is unknown, but is generally put between 1890 and 1893. He was educated in a Church of Scotland mission school outside Nairobi. In the 1920s he worked for Nairobi municipality, but soon joined the nationalist movements emerging in Nairobi. He became editor of the Kikuyu Central Association's magazine Muigwithania in 1923. The following year he went to Britain to give evidence to the Carter Land Commission on the injustice felt by the native African majority in Kenya. Kenyatta travelled around Europe between 1931–46. On his return to Kenya 15 years later he became leader of the newly formed Kenya African Union, the predecessor of the Kenya African National Union which governs Kenya today.

Kenyatta was imprisoned by the British in 1953 during the Mau-Mau uprising. Despite international attention an appeal for release was rejected and in 1959 he was sent to internal exile.

Career Peak

In 1960, while still in exile, Kenyatta was elected president of the newly founded Kenyan African National Union (KANU). In Aug. 1961 he was released and worked with the British to draft a new constitution for an independent Kenya. Kenyatta entered the Legislative council in 1962 and the following year became prime minister in the coalition government. When Kenya was granted independence in 1964 Kenyatta became its first president.

Although Kenyatta steered a successful economic policy and saw the national income double in the first 10 years of independence, political freedoms were lacking. In 1964 the main opposition party, Kenya Africa Democratic Party, dissolved and joined the coalition government.

Throughout the late 1960s key dissenting voices in and around government were silenced. There were several attempted coups. In 1969 opposition parties were outlawed and in 1974 a one-party state was established.

Kenyatta died on 22 Aug. 1978 while still in office.

Kérékou, Mathieu (Benin)

Introduction

Former army general Mathieu Kérékou was the dominant political figure in the Republic of Benin from the early 1970s. Following his military seizure of power in 1972, he ran Benin (then called Dahomey) as a Marxist state before renouncing the ideology in 1990 and restoring democracy. Having been defeated in the 1991 election by Nicéphore Soglo, he returned to power in

1996 and was re-elected in 2001. Kérékou's term ended in 2006. Kérékou died in Oct. 2015 aged 82.

Early Life

Born on 2 Sept. 1933 in Kouarfa, Kérékou was educated in Senegal and received his military training in France. During the rule of the first post-independence president, Hubert Maga (1960–63), he served as aide-de-camp in the national army. He became increasingly influential, both within the army and in politics. During the turbulent years of the 1960s he participated in several military coups. In 1970 a presidential commission, led by Maga, Justin Ahomadegbé-Tomêtin and Sourou Migan Apithy, took control in an attempt to restore stability. Kérékou held the post of minister of planning. When Maga handed over power to Ahomadegbé, Kérékou took the opportunity to seize control in a military coup on 26 Oct. 1972. The three-man council was dissolved and its leaders imprisoned.

Career Peak

Kérékou turned the country into a Marxist state, nationalizing the major economic sectors including banking. In 1975, using the name of a former African kingdom, he renamed the country Benin in an attempt to distance the state from its colonialist past. The new country nevertheless remained unstable, and Kérékou consequently imposed repressive state centralization and one-party rule. Throughout the 1970s and 1980s he sought aid from Communist states in eastern Europe and Asia. In Jan. 1987 he left the army to become a civilian head of state.

By the late 1980s Benin's economy had deteriorated. Faced with the loss of international support after the collapse of European Communism, and with increasing student and labour unrest at home, Kérékou was forced to accept political and institutional change. In 1989 he renounced Marxism, restored democracy and reintroduced multi-party politics. A transitional government was established after the Conférence Nationale des Forces Vives de la Nation (National Conference of the Active Forces of the Nation) in Feb. 1990. In presidential elections the following year, Kérékou was defeated by Nicéphore Soglo.

After a period of political inactivity he returned to contest the 1996 elections. His manifesto emphasized social reform, in contrast to Soglo's concentration on economic growth, and he won with 52.5% of votes in the run-off poll. During his second period of rule, Benin was divided into 12 administrative departments while the state monopoly on broadcasting was finally lifted in 1997. The new regime also sought to establish closer regional relations, by joint military exercises with Togo and Burkina Faso, and by contributing troops to the ECOWAS (Economic Community of West African States) Cease-fire Monitoring Group. In the 2001 presidential elections, Kérékou won the first round with 45.4% of the vote to Soglo's 27.1%. Soglo and the third place candidate, Adrien Houngbédji, then withdrew amid claims of polling irregularities. In the run-off with the fourth place candidate, Bruno Amoussou, Kérékou was returned to power with 84% of the vote. Parliamentary elections were held on 30 March 2003, in which the Presidential Movement supporting Kérékou took 52 of the 83 assembly seats.

Benin's constitution forbids a presidential candidate to be over the age of 70 and allows a president to stand for a maximum of two terms. Therefore, Kérékou was obliged to stand down in April 2006.

Later Life

Kérékou died on 14 Oct. 2015 of an undisclosed health issue.

Kern, Christian (Austria)

Introduction

Christian Kern, a social democrat, became chancellor at the head of the coalition government in May 2016.

Early Life

Christian Kern was born 4 Jan. 1966 in Vienna. He graduated in journalism and communication from the University of Vienna, then completed his postgraduate studies at the Management Zentrum St Gallen in Switzerland. In 1989 he began working as a business journalist. A member of the Social Democratic Party (SPÖ), he entered politics in the early 1990s as an assistant to the Federal Chancellery's undersecretary of state for the civil service.

In 1997 Kern joined Austria's largest electricity supplier, Verbund AG, and soon rose through the ranks to join its management board. In 2010 he was appointed CEO of Austria's federal railway operator. He won praise for improving industrial relations and strengthening the company finances. He was named chairman of the Community of European Railway and Infrastructure Companies in 2014, working to help shape European Union (EU) transport policy and the sector's regulatory practices. In 2015 he was also credited with assisting the smooth transportation of huge numbers of asylum seekers travelling to, and through, the country.

Career Peak

With a high public profile as a result of his role in the refugee crisis, Kern was chosen by the SPÖ to contest the chancellorship following the resignation of incumbent Werner Faymann in May 2016. Kern was appointed to the position on 17 May—8 days after Faymann's resignation—and became the SPÖ's party chairman on 25 June.

He heads a coalition with the Austrian People's Party and has ruled out any future deal with far-right parties such as the Freedom Party. As well as addressing Austria's faltering economy, he has called for reform of the EU although he has rejected holding a referendum on Austria's membership. Following the victory of the Austrian People's Party (ÖVP) in the parliamentary election of Oct. 2017, Sebastian Kurz replaced him as chancellor on 18 Dec.

Key, John (New Zealand)

Early Life

John Phillip Key was born on 9 Aug. 1961 in Auckland, where his British father and Austrian–Jewish mother ran a restaurant. When his father died in 1967 the family were left with large debts and lived in state housing in a suburb of Christchurch. After finishing at Burnside School, he graduated in accounting from the University of Canterbury. He then studied management at Harvard University in the USA.

In 1982 Key began working as an auditor, subsequently joining a clothing manufacturer as a project manager. In 1985 he started his career in foreign exchange (forex) trading just as the NZ dollar was floated on currency markets. In 1988 he was recruited by the Bankers Trust in Auckland as head of their forex dealing team, remaining there until 1995.

Key then joined Merrill Lynch as managing director of the Asia forex group in Singapore, subsequently becoming head of Merrill's global forex group in London. In 2001 he moved to Sydney as head of the institution's debt markets. In 2008 Key was listed in the National Business Review's rich list with an estimated wealth of NZ$50 m.

In 2001 he joined the National Party, winning the seat for Helensville, a newly created constituency in northwest Auckland. He won re-election in 2005, a year after joining the opposition front benches as finance spokesman, and again in 2008. In 2006 Key became party leader following the resignation of Don Brash. He led the party to victory at the general election of 8 Nov. 2008 and was sworn in as prime minister 11 days later.

Career Peak

Following the election, the National Party signed deals with ACT New Zealand, the Maori Party and United Future, which offered ministerial positions outside the cabinet. Key guaranteed the continuation of a number of Maori-specific parliamentary seats. He had a reputation as a pragmatic centrist and favoured privatization, but his first year in office was largely overshadowed by the longest economic recession in the country's history. In Feb. 2009 he launched an NZ$480 m. strategy to help small businesses, which included a 90-day probation period for workers, lowered provisional tax and relaxed tax penalties for businesses with incorrect tax returns. The plan also provided for short-term export credit and the fast-tracking of several government building projects.

In foreign affairs, there was a diplomatic rift over alleged interference by New Zealand in Fijian affairs that saw the mutual expulsion of high commissioners in 2009 before relations were restored in July 2012.

In Nov. 2010 Key declared a national state of mourning in response to a mining accident on the South Island in which 29 miners were killed. In Feb. 2011 Christchurch was struck by a 6.3-magnitude earthquake that killed at least 166 and caused damage put at US$12 bn.

In parliamentary elections in Nov. 2011 the National Party increased its share of the vote and Key won a second term in office, heading a new coalition with ACT New Zealand and United Future.

In April 2013 New Zealand became the first country in the Asia-Pacific region to legalize same-sex marriage. In Aug. parliament narrowly passed legislation which allowed its main intelligence agency to spy on residents and citizens in the interests of national security, despite strong opposition from domestic and international bodies. The following month an opinion poll showed that Key's popularity rating had fallen to its lowest level since he became prime minister. He nonetheless secured a third term in office as the National Party again emerged as the largest party in parliamentary elections in Sept. 2014.

In Oct. 2013 the government announced the resumption of bilateral military co-operation, after nearly three decades, with the USA to counter the growing regional influence of China.

On 5 Dec. 2016 Key handed in his resignation expressing a desire to spend more time with his family away from politics. He was succeeded as prime minister by Bill English.

Khalid bin Abdulaziz Al-Saud (Saudi Arabia)

Introduction

The fifth son of the founder of the Saudi dynasty, Khalid ascended to the throne on 25 March 1975 after the assassination of his brother Faisal. He was considered a reserved and unspectacular monarch, who nevertheless accelerated the economic development of the Kingdom and won respect in international circles. His caution and moderation served as a stabilising factor in the volatile politics of the Middle East. Under his leadership, the Gulf Co-operation Council (GCC) was established with five other Gulf states in 1981 against the backdrop of the outbreak of the Iran-Iraq war. Having been troubled for many years by bad health, he died of a heart attack on 13 June 1982.

Early Life

Born in 1913, Khalid had early experience of government as governor of the Hejaz region from 1932–34 and as interior minister from 1934. In 1964, on Faisal's accession to the throne, he was named as Crown Prince and deputy prime minister.

Career Peak

Khalid succeeded Faisal in March 1975, announcing that he would continue the late King's policies promoting Islamic solidarity and Arab unity in the wake of hostilities with Israel. In practice his moderate stance was in marked contrast to the militancy of many other Arab states, particularly over oil pricing by the Organization of Petroleum Exporting Countries and Egypt's 1978 peace treaty with Israel. Khalid was also involved in early efforts to stop the civil war in Lebanon, and inaugurated the GCC in 1981.

Domestically Khalid maintained the royal family's absolute political control and the conservative Islamic character of the country. However, some opposition to his regime was demonstrated in Nov. 1979 when Sunni Muslim extremists occupied the mosque at Makkah (Mecca). A 2 week siege ensued, with over 200 deaths. The second and third 5-year development plans (1975–79 and 1980–84), both launched by King Khalid, set in train the establishment of much of the country's current economic infrastructure. This in turn improved welfare services and the standard of living in general.

Owing to Khalid's poor health throughout his reign there were repeated rumours that he might abdicate. Much of his executive responsibility had already been assumed by Crown Prince Fahd before his death in 1982.

Khama, Ian (Botswana)

Introduction

Lieut.-Gen. (retd) Seretse Khama Ian Khama succeeded Festus Mogae as president in 2008. Formerly head of the army and a paramount chief of the Bamangwato people, he entered politics in 1998 and has been closely associated with government efforts to diversify the economy and promote transparency.

Early Life

Seretse Khama Ian Khama was born in the UK on 27 Feb. 1953, the son of Seretse Khama (who later became Botswana's first president) and his English wife. Following the family's return to Botswana in 1956, Khama grew up in Serowe and attended the local school. He pursued further studies in Zimbabwe (then Rhodesia), Swaziland and Switzerland, before enrolling at Sandhurst Military Academy in the UK. After graduating, he joined the Botswana Defence Force (BDF) and rose rapidly through the ranks. In 1977 he was promoted to brigadier and became deputy commander of the BDF under Lieut.-Gen. Mompati Merafhe.

In 1979 he was made paramount chief of the Bamangwato people, Botswana's largest tribal group. However, Khama devoted his time to the army and in 1989, when Merafhe retired to enter politics, became its commander. Under Khama the BDF developed into a professional force, participating in international peacekeeping, disaster relief and anti-poaching missions.

On 1 April 1998 Khama, newly retired from the army, was named vice-president by the incoming president Festus Mogae. The appointment was widely seen as an attempt to inject new blood into the ruling Botswana Democratic Party (BDP) and to tap into Khama's reputation and influence. Initially unable to take up his post because he did not hold a seat in the National Assembly, Khama was sworn in on 13 July 1998 after winning a by-election in Serowe North. He was put in charge of presidential administration and public affairs and became an arbiter of complaints against government ministers, which made him some political enemies.

Following the BDF's victory in the 1999 general election, Khama was controversially allowed a year's sabbatical to fulfil his duties as chief of the Bamangwato. On his return to the national scene he oversaw the implementation of the government's national development plan, which included privatization measures. Supporters praised him as forceful and efficient while critics accused him of authoritarianism. In 2000 he censured MPs for demanding a salary increase, winning support from the electorate but further alienating some colleagues.

In 2003 Khama became chairman of the BDP, fuelling speculation that he was Mogae's chosen successor. In March 2008 Mogae stood down and the National Assembly elected Khama to the presidency. He took office on 1 April 2008.

Career Peak

Khama was sworn in for his first full 5 year term on 20 Oct. 2009 following the BDP's success in parliamentary elections held on 16 Oct. in which they took 45 of the 57 available seats. In April 2010 a breakaway faction of disaffected BDP members formed the Botswana Movement for Democracy, a move criticized by Khama as misguided and self-interested. A damaging nationwide strike by public sector workers over pay in April–May 2011, reflecting deteriorating economic prospects, dented his administration's reputation for good governance and political stability. Nonetheless, the BDP retained power in parliamentary polling in Oct. 2014, albeit with a reduced majority, and Khama was re-elected as president and sworn in for a second term.

Having served for the maximum period allowed by the constitution, he stepped down on 1 April 2018, handing his duties over to his vice-president and fellow BDP member Mokgweetsi Masisi until the 2019 general election.

Khama, Seretse (Botswana)

Introduction

Leader of the Bechuanaland Democratic Party (BDP), Sir Seretse Khama was the founding president of Botswana from 1965 until his death in 1980. By exploiting Botswana's diamond resources to create a prosperous export-driven economy, Khama lifted his country from poverty and implemented welfare reforms. He also managed to uphold a liberal democracy in the face of tribal tensions to make his rule one of modern Africa's few success stories.

Early Life

Seretse Khama was born on 1 July 1921 in what was then known as Bechuanaland. He was the grandson of the famous chief, Khama III (c. 1835–1923), ruler of the Bangwato tribe. His father died when he was very young and he became chief, with his uncle Tshekedi acting as regent and later sole guardian. As a young nobleman he was sent to boarding school in South Africa and later went to Balliol College, Oxford to read law. Whilst studying there he met and married a young English typist called Ruth Williams. White supremacists in neighbouring South Africa pressured the British government to denounce Seretse's chieftainship and he was exiled from Botswana.

In 1956 the British government determined to distance itself from the racist institutions of South Africa and Seretse was able to return home. In 1961 he began to make a name for himself as a nationalist politician, becoming leader of the BDP, which won the first universal franchise elections in 1965. He was knighted a year later.

Career Peak

At this stage Botswana was still perceived to be a hostage nation, reliant on its wealthy neighbours for goods and support. However, its vast diamond wealth was soon uncovered and Khama took advantage of this good fortune to revamp Botswana's economy. He laid the foundations for an export-driven economy relying on the country's reserves of diamonds and copper and on its beef processing industry. On a domestic level he largely succeeded in fostering local democracy and the rule of law and dispensing with the traditional powers of the chiefs.

The result of these policies was the emergence of a country that was wealthy and yet upheld the tenets of liberal democracy in spite of the racial and tribal tensions evident in neighbouring states. Seretse Khama channelled the profits of the diamond and copper trade into providing educational, developmental and sanitary advances throughout Botswana. Internationally he continued to support the decolonization of other African nations, and was present during talks to liberate Rhodesia (modern day Zimbabwe).

Later Life

Khama was successively re-elected until his death on 13 July 1980.

Khanal, Jhalanath (Nepal)

Introduction

Jhalanath Khanal, leader of the Communist Party of Nepal-Unified Marxist Leninist (CPN-UML), was elected prime minister in Feb. 2011, ending months of political deadlock. A veteran left-winger, Khanal came to power with the support of Maoist Party MPs. However, after 6 months in office he resigned from the post, having failed to agree on a new constitution with the opposition and advance a peace process.

Early Life

Jhalanath Khanal was born on 20 May 1950 in Sakhejung in Ilam district, Mechi, Nepal. From 1965 he was an active pro-democracy campaigner and in

1967 served as president of the Mechi student union. After graduating in political science and history from Tribhuvan University in Kathmandu, he worked as a secondary school teacher from 1971–73. He was jailed for his political activism in 1969, from 1973–74 and again in 1975. On being released in 1975, he joined an underground revolutionary movement.

While serving a further jail term from 1976–79, Khanal became a founder member of the Communist Party of Nepal-Marxist Leninist (CPN-ML). Released during an amnesty for political prisoners, he spent the next 11 years masterminding underground political activities and served as general secretary of the CPN-ML from 1982–90. In 1990, after the monarchy relinquished absolute power, Khanal served in the government firstly as minister for agriculture, land reform and management, and then as minister for forest and environment. He was elected to parliament in 1991, representing the enlarged and renamed CPN-UML.

In 1997, after the Maoists had left parliament and begun an armed conflict aimed at ending the system of parliamentary monarchy, Khanal served as minister for information and communication in the coalition government of monarchist prime minister, Lokendra Bahadur Chand. After the end of the civil conflict in 2006 and the curtailment of the monarch's powers, Khanal was re-elected as CPN-UML representative for Ilam and, in 2008, succeeded Madhav Kumar Nepal as party general secretary, becoming chairman in Feb. 2009. In May 2009 the party left the Maoist-led coalition government, leading to its collapse.

The CPN-UML headed a replacement coalition, with Nepal briefly serving as prime minister. However, in June 2010 he resigned citing political deadlock. Following 16 inconclusive parliamentary ballots for the premiership in which Khanal repeatedly stood as the CPN-UML candidate, he was finally victorious in Feb. 2011 when the Maoists withdrew their candidate, Prachanda, and switched support to Khanal, giving him 368 of the 557 votes cast.

Career Peak

Khanal took office promising speedy progress on drafting a new constitution and reintegrating 19,000 former Maoist fighters. However, both issues led to problems in establishing a workable coalition. Having vowed to resign as premier if he could not make significant advances in the peace process, Khanal stepped down on 14 Aug. 2011.

Khatami, Hojatolislam Mohammad (Iran)

Introduction

Having served in post-revolution governments from 1982–92, Mohammad Khatami, a noted liberal, was elected President in May 1997. His first term of office signalled a shift away from Islamic extremism, his moderate policies provoking unease among conservatives within the governing establishment. He received a further mandate to pursue reform when he was re-elected in June 2001 with 77% of the popular vote and stood down before the elections of June 2005.

Early Life

Mohammad Khatami was born in 1943 in Ardakan in the central province of Yazd. The son of a respected Islamic clergyman, Khatami attended the theological colleges at Qom and Esfahan after his high school graduation in 1961. He obtained a BA degree in philosophy at Esfahan University in 1969 and then went to Tehran University in 1970 for a postgraduate MA course in education. Subsequently returning to Qom, he resumed his philosophical studies.

Khatami began his political activities within the Association of Muslim Students of Esfahan University. He also participated in the anti-Shah Islamic movement in Qom. Having headed the Islamic Centre in Hamburg, Germany, at the time of the 1979 revolution, he stood successfully for election to the Majlis in 1980.

Career Peak

In 1982 he joined the government as minister of Culture and Islamic Guidance, retaining that post until 1992, when he was appointed cultural adviser to the then President Rafsanjani and head of Iran's National Library. Appointed a member of the High Council for Cultural Revolution in 1996, he became its head on his election as the fifth president of the Islamic Republic on 23 May 1997. Despite opposition from the conservative Islamic establishment, his reformist approach proved a rallying point for a wide-ranging coalition of industrial interests, urban middle classes, university students and technocrats, and he secured an unexpected landslide electoral victory with almost 70% of the vote. Continuing support for his moves towards a more liberal society was confirmed by his re-election for a second term by an even larger margin on 8 June 2001.

In Jan. 2002 Khatami's government responded angrily to US President George W. Bush's assertion that Iran, along with Iraq and North Korea, formed an 'axis of evil'. In June 2003 the Atomic Energy Organization of Iran promised increased cooperation with the International Atomic Energy Agency (IAEA) but refused to allow inspections of the Kalaye Electric Company in Tehran, which it claims was not part of its nuclear programme. In the same month Tehran witnessed widespread popular protests against the ruling clerical regime. In July 2003 the EU threatened to review its relations with Tehran, indicating that any trade agreements will be dependent on Iran's co-operation on nuclear proliferation, terrorism, human rights and the Middle East peace process. Earlier in July 2003 Minister of Intelligence Ali Yunesi admitted for the first time that the Iranian government was holding members of the al-Qaeda terrorist network, including several leading figures.

Relations with the US improved in Oct. 2003 after Iran agreed to cooperate with the IAEA over its nuclear programme and delivered documentation to the agency. However, tensions remained between the two countries—the International Court of Justice delivered a verdict in Nov. concerning American attacks on Iranian oil platforms during the Iran-Iraq War. The Court refused compensation to either side but censured the US for the attacks. The European Union played an important part in preventing the deterioration of US–Iranian relations in the publication of the IAEA report, which set strict conditions for Iran but did not recommend sanctions.

The Iranian government's attitude towards the US-appointed administration in Iraq also improved in late 2003. The Iraqi Governing Council (IGC) announced the expulsion of the People's Mujahideen (Mujahideen-e-Khalq; MKO), an Iranian rebel organization supported by the Ba'athist regime, and the intention to provide reparations to Iran for the 1980 invasion.

A devastating earthquake hit Iran on 26 Dec. 2003, close to the ancient city of Bam, much of which was destroyed. Over 26,000 were killed and tens of thousands left homeless. International aid was swift, though Khatami's government rejected the American offer of a humanitarian delegation. Khatami, however, did improve relations with another long-running enemy—Egypt. In Dec. 2003 he met the Egyptian premier, Hosni Mubarak, in Geneva, paving the way for the restoration of full diplomatic ties. Tehran's city council removed one of the main stumbling blocks by changing the name of a street that remembered the assassin of Egyptian President Anwar Sadat.

A domestic crisis developed during preparations for parliamentary elections in Feb. 2004. The Council of Guardians disqualified over 2,000 candidates—mostly reformists—of a total of around 8,000. Khatami promised to fight for every candidate unfairly disqualified and threatened the resignation of his entire administration if hard-liners did not satisfy his demands. The largest student organization called for a boycott of elections and over 80 members of parliament, disqualified from contesting their seats, expressed their opposition with a sit-in at the Majlis. The intervention of Ayatollah Khamenei on national television in Jan. 2004 forced the Council of Guardians to compromise, restoring over 700 candidacies, including current politicians expressly supported by the spiritual leader. Nevertheless, over a third of the Majlis' deputies resigned on 1 Feb. in protest against the hard-line policy of the Council.

Khatami stood down from office at the 2005 presidential elections. He claimed that unnamed candidates had orchestrated 'dirty tricks' campaigns in the election build-up.

In 2009 he stood as a candidate in the presidential election initially against the incumbent, Mahmoud Ahmadinejad, but withdrew to back the campaign of Mir Hossein Mousavi. After Ahmadinejad won the disputed poll, Khatami continued to question the result's legitimacy.

Khomeini, Ruhollah (Iran)

Introduction

Returning to Iran from exile on the overthrow of the Shah's pro-Western regime in 1979, Ayatollah Khomeini assumed the role of head of state. Under his leadership a turbulent Islamic revolution restored fundamentalist Shia Muslim principles and traditions. His rule was marked by a protracted war with Iraq and the suppression of internal opposition. He died on 3 June 1989.

Early Life

Born Sayyed Ruhollah in Sept. 1902, Khomeini took his clerical name from his birthplace, Khomein, in central Iran. In the early 1920s he went to the holy city of Qom where he continued his theological studies and then taught in a seminary. By the 1950s he had emerged as a noted Islamic scholar and was designated an ayatollah. By the early 1960s he had received the title of grand ayatollah, thereby making him a supreme religious leader of the Shia Muslim community.

Khomeini first came to political prominence in 1962, when he led traditional religious opposition to the Shah's plans to reduce the clergy's property rights and to emancipate women. His arrest in 1963 provoked riots in Tehran and other cities. The following year he was ordered into exile by the Shah's secret police. After a brief period in Turkey, he settled in Iraq in the Shia holy city of Najaf in Oct. 1965. From there he called for the Shah's overthrow and the establishment of an Islamic republic.

In 1977–78, widespread demonstrations in support of Khomeini broke out across Iran. In Oct. 1978 he was forced to leave Iraq and moved to Paris, where he orchestrated the campaign against the Shah's rule. Intense civil unrest forced the departure of the Shah from Iran in Jan. 1979, and Khomeini returned to Tehran in Feb. to be acclaimed the religious leader of the revolution. On 1 April 1979, Khomeini proclaimed the establishment of the Islamic Republic of Iran. Under a new constitution, approved by referendum in Dec. 1979, he was designated the republic's spiritual leader (wali faqih) for life.

Career Peak

For the next decade Khomeini remained the centre of political power and the anchor of the Islamic regime, despite his increasing age and gradual withdrawal from day-to-day guidance of the revolution. Internal opposition was repressed and thousands of executions took place. Iran's foreign relations during his rule were dominated by the 1980–88 war with Iraq, and implacable hostility to the United States, relations with which reached a nadir in 1979–81 over the seizure of hostages in the US embassy in Tehran by Iranian students. Khomeini continued to denounce the US until his death in June 1989. Earlier that year, he caused further international controversy for exhorting devout Muslims to execute the British novelist Salman Rushdie and the publishers of his book *The Satanic Verses* for blasphemy.

An estimated 9 m. mourners attended his funeral in Tehran.

Khrushchev, Nikita Sergeyevich (Russia)

Introduction

Nikita Khrushchev succeeded Stalin as first secretary of the Soviet Communist Party, holding the post until his resignation in 1964. He was premier from 1958. In domestic policy, he allowed a modicum of liberalization and avoided the harsher excesses of Stalin's rule though his regime was characterized by oppressive cultural and intellectual policies. Relations with China deteriorated but he sought 'peaceful coexistence' with the West. However, during the 1962 Cuban missile crisis, the stand-off with the US threatened nuclear war.

Early Life

Khrushchev was born in Kalinovka on 17 April 1894 and trained as a mechanic in the Ukrainian coal mines where his father worked. He joined the Communist Party in 1918 and fought with the Red Army during the civil war. While working in the mines he was politically active as a local party secretary. He attended Moscow's Industrial Academy to study industrial administration. In 1931 he took a job with the district party committee in Moscow, becoming its first secretary 4 years later. In this appointment he was responsible for the construction of the Moscow underground. A rising star of the Stalin regime, he was involved with the political purges of the 1930s. In 1938 he was sent back to the Ukraine to become first secretary of the Republic's Communist Party and was appointed a full Politburo member the following year.

Khrushchev served in the Red Army during World War II, emerging with the rank of lieutenant general. During this period he was instrumental in suppressing burgeoning nationalist movements in Poland and the Ukraine. He also played prominent advisory roles in the battles of Stalingrad and Kursk.

In the aftermath of the war, Khrushchev had to deal with a debilitating famine in the Ukraine that was to influence his later views on agricultural policy. In 1949 he rejoined the Moscow party structure and became secretary of the Communist Central Committee. In an atmosphere of political intrigue intensified by Stalin's deteriorating health, Khrushchev's plan for restructuring the agricultural collectives was rejected in 1951.

Career Peak

Following Stalin's death in March 1953, Khrushchev won the power struggle to succeed him. He was instrumental in the execution of one of his chief rivals, Lavrenty Beria, and outmanoeuvred Georgi Malenkov to become first secretary of the party in Sept. 1953. Malenkov remained as prime minister for a further 2 years before Khrushchev supplanted him with Nikolai Bulganin.

Khrushchev's tenure saw a loosening of the political reigns Stalin had held so tightly. His speech at the 20th Party Congress in 1956 was groundbreaking in its denunciation not only of Stalin's tyranny and personality cult, but for the implicit criticism of the party itself. He followed this up with the release of political prisoners.

Khrushchev allowed expelled nationalities to return to their ethnic homelands within Russia (except for the Volga Germans and the Crimean Tatars), arguing that all Soviet nationalities would eventually meld with the Russians as the dominant group. He used his agricultural expertise to gain popular support, pioneering vast grain projects. When his plans met with opposition in Kazakhstan, he dismissed the republic's leaders and put future premier Leonid Brezhnev in charge.

Khrushchev's more liberal regime was, nonetheless, not free of tyrannical elements. Religious bodies suffered ruthless suppression and his attitude to dissident voices was inconsistent. For example, he was hard on Boris Pasternak (awarded the Nobel prize for literature in 1958) but more lenient to Aleksandr Solzhenitsyn, who documented life in Stalin's concentration camps. In addition, having survived an attempted coup in 1957, Khrushchev schemed to remove and discredit his opponents. Within a year he was prime minister as well as first secretary.

Khrushchev was a volatile figure on the international scene. Relations with the Soviet Union's great ideological ally, China, virtually collapsed over differences in interpretation of Marxist doctrine and Chinese opposition to Khrushchev's attempts at détente with the West (which came to be known as 'peaceful co-existence'. The Sino-Soviet arms aid agreement was abandoned in 1959.

Co-existence with the West came under severe strain on several occasions. The Soviet invasion of Hungary in 1956 to suppress the reforms of its liberal regime caused international uproar, although Khrushchev allowed greater autonomy in the Eastern Bloc states. A summit between President Eisenhower and Khrushchev in 1959 raised hopes of a thawing in US–Soviet relations. However, these were soon dashed by a spying scandal in 1960 in which a US U–2 reconnaissance aircraft was shot down and its pilot, Gary Powers, captured. Tensions were further raised by the building of the Berlin Wall in 1961, and by the unsuccessful Bay of Pigs invasion by US troops attempting to overthrow Fidel Castro's communist regime in Cuba.

Relations with the US reached their lowest point during the 1962 Cuban missile crisis. When it was feared that Khrushchev was planning to install nuclear weapons in Cuba, US President Kennedy imposed a naval blockade and the two powers came perilously close to nuclear war. After intense negotiations, Khrushchev agreed to remove the missiles in exchange for American assurances that Cuba would not be invaded. A nuclear test-ban treaty followed in 1963.

While Khrushchev was subsequently lauded for his role in averting disaster in 1962, his standing at home waned. The crisis was seen as a defeat for the Soviet Union and the collapse of relations with China as an added failure. His personal leadership style antagonized many senior party figures and, with his grand plans for agricultural expansion failing to reap rewards, his position was precarious. He was forced to resign on 14 Oct. 1964, following a coup led by his successor Leonid Brezhnev.

Later Life

Khrushchev in retirement took no further part in politics. His memoirs appeared in the West in 1970. He died on 11 Sept. 1971 but, unlike his predecessors, was not given a state burial at the Kremlin.

Kibaki, Mwai (Kenya)

Introduction

Economist and former vice president Mwai Kibaki was first elected president in Dec. 2002. Representing the National Rainbow Coalition (NARC) of opposition parties in a bid to oust the KANU party, in power since independence in 1963, he campaigned on an anti-corruption ticket to end Daniel arap Moi's 24 year-presidency. However, Kibaki's government itself became widely tainted by corruption scandals. His controversial re-election in Dec. 2007 was violently disputed by supporters of Raila Odinga, the leader of the opposition ODM, before a power-sharing agreement was negotiated in Feb. 2008.

Early Life

Kibaki was born on 15 Nov. 1931 in Othaya, Nyeri District. In 1950 he joined the youth section of the pro-independence Kenyan African Union. In 1954 he graduated in economics, history and political science at Makerere University, Uganda, before further studies at the London School of Economics in the UK (1956–59).

Along with the subsequent presidents Jomo Kenyatta and Daniel arap Moi, Kibaki campaigned for independence from British colonial rule, which was finally achieved in 1963. He contributed to a new constitution and was among the original members of the KANU party (Kenyan African National Union). He served as the party's chief executive officer from 1961–63 before being elected representative of Bahati, Nairobi in 1963. From 1963–66 he worked for the finance ministry, after which he was appointed commerce and industry minister. From 1970–81 he served as finance minister. Vice president under Kenyatta and then his successor Moi, he also served as home affairs minister (1982–88) and health minister (1988–91).

A one-party state from 1964, the ban on opposition parties was finally lifted in 1991. In 1992 Kibaki and other party members left KANU to form the Democratic Party, criticizing government corruption. In the country's first multi-party presidential elections that year, Kibaki took third place as Moi retained the presidency despite alleged irregularities. In 1997 he again stood against Moi, coming second with 30.9% of votes.

In 2002 he was chosen to head the opposition NARC. The ruling party was split when Moi announced his chosen successor to be Uhuru Kenyatta (son of Jomo Kenyatta), and several KANU members joined NARC. Kibaki's campaign focused on growing discontent with Moi's presidency. In the Dec. 2002 elections Kibaki won a landslide victory with 62.2% to Kenyatta's 31.3%, ending nearly 40 years of KANU rule.

Career Peak

On election, Kibaki prioritized the fight against corruption, which had deterred international aid donors and investors since 1997. All public figures were obliged to declare their wealth confidentially to the anti-corruption police. Kibaki also vowed to provide free education and outlined plans for a

new constitution, that was approved in a referendum by two-thirds of Kenyans in Aug. 2010 and promulgated later that month.

Kibaki was constitutionally barred from seeking re-election in the 2013 elections, already having served two terms. In April 2013 he was succeeded as president by Uhuru Kenyatta.

Kiesinger, Kurt Georg (Germany)

Introduction

Kurt Georg Kiesinger was West German Chancellor between 1966–69, heading the *Grand Coalition* of his own Christian Democratic Union (CDU) and the Social Democratic Party (SPD). He was the only Chancellor to have been a member of the Nazi Party, but after World War II was a conservative reformer who sought to improve West Germany's standing with the West, and to improve relations with East Germany.

Early Life

Kurt Georg Kiesinger was born in Ebingen, Germany on 6 April 1904. He studied at the universities in Tübingen and Berlin before practising as a lawyer. He joined the Nazi Party in 1933 and worked in the Propaganda Section of the Foreign Ministry throughout World War II. He was interned by Allied troops for 18 months after the war but was cleared of any illegal Nazi activities and released.

He became a member of Chancellor Adenauer's CDU, entered the *Bundestag* in 1949 and sat as chairman of the foreign policy committee. He advocated Germany's integration into international institutions and oversaw reform of the constitutional court. He left parliament in 1958 to take the post of Minister President (Prime Minister) of Baden-Württemberg and achieved success in rejuvenating the länder's economy. On a national level he pushed for reform of the higher education system. During 1962–63 he was president of the *Bundesrat* (the upper house of parliament).

Career Peak

When Ludwig Erhard resigned as Chancellor in Dec. 1966 Kiesinger replaced him. The *Grand Coalition* reformed the penal system, introduced changes to pensions and tax, and was successful in reversing the economic slump that marked the end of Erhard's tenure. Kiesinger also oversaw legislation that allowed more time for the prosecution of suspected Nazi war criminals. In foreign policy, he promoted closer relations with the USA and France. He believed in strengthening the European Economic Community and campaigned for the inclusion of the UK. While strongly opposed to the Soviet Union, he worked alongside Foreign Minister Willy Brandt to improve relations with East Germany and re-instituted diplomatic relations with Romania in 1967 and with Yugoslavia the following year. However, this early version of Ostpolitik (Eastern Policy) faltered after the Czechoslovakian crisis of 1968.

Kiesinger's links to the Nazis proved a major hurdle to his domestic popularity. A significant section of the electorate were immediately suspicious of his past, and when the right-wing National Democrat Party made gains in provincial elections he was in a weak position to condemn them. When student activism reached its zenith, Kiesinger was a popular target for the country's disaffected youth. Moreover, the Grand Coalition lacked parliamentary opposition. When it passed an Emergency Law, enabling an appointed council to take power in exceptional circumstances, Kiesinger was accused of moving towards authoritarianism.

By 1969 relations between the CDU and SPD were strained. Kiesinger's party did well at the elections of that year but the Coalition was dead and the SPD formed a government with the Free Democrats. Brandt succeeded Kiesinger as Chancellor on 21 Oct. 1969.

Later Life

Kiesinger remained President of the CDU until 1971 and left the *Bundestag* in 1976. He died on 9 March 1988 in Tübingen.

Kikwete, Jakaya (Tanzania)

Introduction

Jakaya Kikwete became president of Tanzania on 14 Dec. 2005, winning an overwhelming majority in national elections that were generally considered free and fair. A Muslim from the coastal district of Bagamoyo, Kikwete was a military leader in the 1970s and 1980s and served as foreign minister for 10 years from 1995. He was re-elected in Oct. 2010.

Early Life

Jakaya Mrisho Kikwete was born on 7 Oct. 1950 in Msoga, Bagamoyo District on the coast of Tanganyika. He attended schools in Msoga and Kibaha, before studying economics at the University of Dar es Salaam. In 1975, while at university, Kikwete joined the ruling Tanganyika African National Union, which later became the Chama Cha Mapinduzi (CCM, Revolutionary State Party). Following his graduation in 1978, Kikwete joined the Tanzania People's Defence Force (TPDF), where he served as a lieutenant from 1972–79 and subsequently as captain.

In 1984, having spent a year at the Monduli military officers college in Arusha, Kikwete became chief political instructor of the TPDF. In 1988 he was elected to represent Bagamoyo parliamentary constituency, a post he held for three consecutive terms. He was deputy minister of energy, water and minerals from 1988–90 before being promoted to minister and serving under President Ali Hassan Mwinyi for 4 years. Following constitutional reform that legalized opposition parties in 1992, Kikwete retired from the army.

In 1995, having served as finance minister for a year, Kikwete became one of 14 challengers for the CCM leadership. He lost to Benjamin Mkapa, who led the party to victory in national elections in Oct. 1995 amid widespread allegations of voting irregularities. Kikwete was appointed foreign minister, a post he held until 2005, winning praise for his mediation work in war-torn Burundi and the Democratic Republic of the Congo. His department was credited with advancing regional integration within the East African Community and in the Southern African Development Community. Kikwete won the right to lead his party into the 2005 national elections and emerged victorious from the poll on 14 Dec. He received 80% of the vote and replaced Mkapa as president. The CCM retained its overwhelming majority in parliament, with 206 out of 232 seats.

Career Peak

In his inauguration speech, Kikwete vowed to continue the free-market policies of Mkapa and prioritized the improvement of relations with the semi-autonomous islands of Zanzibar. He inherited a country in which poverty is widespread but whose economy had been growing at a rate of 6% a year. He sought to maintain political stability as the country benefited from rising gold production and donor-supported investment. In Aug. 2006, in recognition of the government's economic reform efforts, the African Development Bank cancelled US$645 m. of Tanzanian debt and also agreed a loan of US$74 m. for poverty reduction programmes.

In Feb. 2008 Prime Minister Edward Lowassa and two other ministers resigned in the wake of a corruption scandal involving an energy deal with a US-based electricity company, in response to which Kikwete dissolved the cabinet and appointed Mizengo Kayanza Peter Pinda as the new premier. Kikwete served as chairman of the African Union for 2008.

In Oct. 2010 Kikwete and the CCM were returned to power in presidential and parliamentary elections. Following allegations of ministerial misuse of public funds, Kikwete sacked six members of his cabinet in May 2012. In Dec. 2013 he sacked another four following accusations of abuses committed by security forces, prompting a further government reshuffle in Jan. 2014.

In Aug. 2012 the government confirmed that Iranian oil tankers had been operating under the Tanzanian flag to circumvent international sanctions on Iranian oil trading. The USA, in response, threatened possible action against Tanzania unless the practice was stopped.

There were increasing religious tensions between Christians and Muslims in the country in late 2012 and 2013, with attacks on churches and mosques.

Jakaya Kikwete's term as president ended in Nov. 2015 when he was succeeded by the winner of the Oct. elections, John Magufuli (also of the CCM). Kikwete was not eligible to stand for a third successive term owing to a constitutional limit on presidential mandates.

Kilman, Sato (Vanuatu)

Introduction

Sato Kilman, the leader of the People's Progress Party (part of the Alliance bloc), served a fourth term as prime minister from June 2015 to Feb. 2016. He came to office less than a fortnight after being sacked from his role as foreign minister by the incumbent prime minister, Joe Natuman. Kilman successfully moved a parliamentary vote of no confidence against Natuman before replacing him.

Early Life

Kilman grew up in Lakatoro, on Vanuatu's Malekula Island. He came to public attention in 2004 for his criticism of Prime Minister Serge Vohor's attempt to establish diplomatic relations with Taiwan. After moving the confidence motion that deposed Vohor, Kilman served as foreign minister from 2004–07 in the government of Ham Lini.

Kilman was dismissed in a cabinet reshuffle at the end of 2007 over allegations of misappropriating state funds. He and his Alliance bloc subsequently served in opposition until Nov. 2009, when Prime Minister Edward Natapei dismissed several of his coalition partners in favour of the Alliance. Kilman was appointed to succeed Lini as deputy prime minister.

Following a vote of no confidence in Natapei after he refused to hand over the rotating leadership of a regional trade forum to Fiji's interim prime minister, Kilman was appointed his successor by the parliamentary speaker on 2 Dec. 2010.

On 24 April 2011 Kilman was narrowly defeated in another vote of no confidence and replaced by Serge Vohor, who became prime minister for a fourth time. However, Vohor's election was declared invalid on 13 May 2011 because he could not claim an absolute majority. Kilman was reinstated, only to be ousted again after a court upheld the charge brought by Natapei that Kilman's initial appointment was unconstitutional because the speaker had failed to conduct a secret ballot. Kilman nevertheless returned to office on 26 June 2011 after gaining 29 parliamentary votes against Serge Vohor's 23, but resigned in March 2013 ahead of a no confidence motion. He was succeeded as prime minister by Moana Carcasses Kalosil, who was in office until May 2014 when Joe Natuman assumed the premiership.

On 4 June 2015 Kilman was sacked as foreign minister by Natuman for 'disloyalty'. However, after a motion of no confidence was passed against Natuman, Kilman defeated opposition MP Ham Lini in a parliamentary vote by 28 votes to 22, and again became prime minister.

Career Peak

Under Kilman's leadership in May 2011 Vanuatu became the fifth nation—after Nauru, Nicaragua, Russia and Venezuela—to recognize Abkhazia (in Georgia) as a sovereign nation. In May 2012 a diplomatic row with Australia erupted over an incident at Sydney airport involving alleged discourtesy to Kilman and the arrest of his private secretary on tax fraud charges. In response, a small Australian police contingent was expelled from Vanuatu.

Kilman's return to the premiership in June 2015 was widely interpreted as a blow to the hopes of West Papuan groups seeking membership of the Melanesian Spearhead Group (a move opposed by Indonesia, for whom Kilman made clear his support).

Domestically, corruption dogged Kilman's term, as 14 members of his government were convicted and imprisoned, and in Nov. President Baldwin Lonsdale dissolved parliament. Following snap elections in Jan. 2016, Charlot Salwai was elected unopposed by parliament the following month to succeed Kilman as premier.

Kim Dae-jung (South Korea)

Introduction

The election of Kim Dae-jung as President of South Korea on 18 Dec. 1997 completed a remarkable journey from persecuted dissident and opposition leader to head of state of a truly democratic nation. However, the success of the opposition in 2002 by-elections coupled with a corruption scandal surrounding Kim's family weakened his presidency. Under the terms of the constitution he was required to give up the presidency in 2003. The last months of his tenure were marked by increasing international tension over North Korea's nuclear activities.

Early Life

Kim was born to a farming family on 3 Dec. 1925. He came top of his school in his final examinations but poverty prevented him from having a university education. Kim took an office job with a Japanese-owned firm. When the Japanese occupation of Korea ended in 1945, Kim took over the firm. His business acumen helped the company prosper and he became a wealthy man.

As a successful businessman, Kim fell victim to the Communists during the Korean War (1950–53). Sentenced to death, he managed to escape capture. After the Korean War, he became one of the most eloquent voices of opposition in an increasingly authoritarian South Korea. He opposed the policies of President Rhee and then the military junta of General Park.

After several unsuccessful campaigns, Kim was eventually elected to the National Assembly in 1961. In 1970, Kim was elected leader of the opposition Korean Democratic Party. The following year he stood against Park for the presidency. In elections, generally regarded to be flawed, he still won more than 40% of the votes cast.

As President Park's rule became more dictatorial, opposition was increasingly risky. While he was in Japan, Kim was kidnapped and smuggled out of the country by the Korean secret service in 1973. The incident severely strained relations between Tokyo and Seoul. Kim's detention was brief.

In 1976 Kim's campaign for the restoration of democracy to South Korea led to his arrest. This time, he was detained for 3 years. Released just before Park was assassinated, Kim continued his fight for a democratic South Korea. However, he was arrested again by Park's successor, President Chun. Kim was sentenced to death but international protests, and pressure from the United States, led to the sentence being commuted to life imprisonment. This was later reduced to 20 years.

In 1982 Kim was allowed out of prison to receive medical treatment in the United States. He was not allowed back home until 1985 when he regained the leadership of the opposition. He ran for the presidency twice and lost in 1987 and 1992. In 1995 Kim founded a new political party, the National Congress for New Politics, now called the Millennium Democratic Party. By 1997 the political climate in South Korea had thawed but the system was also corrupt and inefficient. Kim won the 1997 presidential election, taking office in 1998.

Career Peak

In office Kim concentrated on ways to improve relations with the Communist North. His 'sunshine Policy' allowed South Korea to invest in the North. Also, a limited number of South Koreans are able to visit their relatives in the North. Kim held an unprecedented summit with Kim Jong-Il, the then leader of North Korea, in 2000. Both leaders agreed on reunification as a goal. Later that year Kim Dae-jung won the Nobel Peace Prize for his efforts to improve relations on the Korean peninsula.

However, relations deteriorated in late June 2002 after a naval battle in the Yellow Sea between North and South forces killed four South Korean and around 30 North Korean sailors. The North Korean president, Kim Jong, blamed the US and South Korea for the attack. Kim Dae-jung suspended rice shipments to the north and demanded an apology.

In by-elections 2 months later, the opposition Grand National Party gained a majority in the assembly when it took 11 of the 13 seats contested. At the same time, parliament rejected Kim's two nominees for the largely ceremonial role of prime minister, Chang Sang and Chang Dae-Whan. Furthermore, earlier in the year his family became embroiled in a corruption scandal for which he apologized in April 2002. Kim was constitutionally

barred from standing in the presidential elections of Dec. 2002 but the Millennium Democratic candidate, Roh Moo-hyun, secured victory. Roh Moo-hyun replaced Kim in Feb. 2003 and was expected to continue his predecessor's effort to find a diplomatic solution to the dispute over North Korea's nuclear weapons programme.

Kim died of heart failure on 19 Aug. 2009 after a long battle with pneumonia.

Kim Il-sung (North Korea)

Introduction

Kim Il-sung was the founder of the People's Democratic Republic of Korea (North Korea) and the originator of the Juche (self-help) philosophy. Routinely referred to in North Korea as the 'Great Leader'. he remains the centre of an unprecedented personality cult. Kim is addressed by many titles including 'The Greatest Genius the World has Known'. Every North Korean must wear a metal badge bearing a picture of the Great Leader and every home must display his portrait on the wall. Upon his death in 1994, Kim Il-sung was proclaimed Eternal President, and his son, and successor, Kim Jong-il left the presidency vacant.

Early Life

Kim was born of 15 April 1912 near Pyongyang. His original name was Kim Song-ju. In 1925, Kim's parents fled to neighbouring Manchuria to escape Japanese rule. During the 1930s, Kim joined a guerrilla group that fought the Japanese army of occupation in Korea. At this time, he adopted the name Kim Il-sung, the name of an earlier guerrilla leader who also fought the Japanese. His talents were spotted by his superiors who sent him to the Soviet Union for training.

During World War II (1939–45), Kim led a Korean brigade in the Soviet Army. When Japanese rule in Korea ended in 1945, and a Soviet zone of administration was established in the country, Kim returned to the peninsula with other Soviet-educated leaders. In Oct. 1945, they founded the (Communist) Korean Workers' Party. Kim became the first General Secretary of the Korean Workers' Party. Then, in Sept. 1948, a Communist government was established in Pyongyang, effectively partitioning Korea between a Communist North and a pro-Western South. North Korean sources give a different version of events, picturing Kim as the heroic leader of a guerrilla force based at Paekdusan, Korea's highest mountain, from where he drove the Japanese out in 1945.

Career Peak

Kim became the prime minister of the first government of the People's Democratic Republic of Korea in Sept. 1948. In office Kim initially achieved some success in raising living standards and in improving access to health and educational facilities. But, from the outset, his regime allowed no criticism. He attempted to reunite the partitioned country by invading the South in 1950. This action began the Korean War. Early military successes saw South Korea reduced to a rump around Pusan and other coastal cities, but US-led United Nations forces reversed the flow of the conflict. Only the intervention of Chinese forces supporting Kim prevented much of North Korea from being overrun.

The war ended in stalemate and partition confirmed. Kim set about tightening his grip on his country. He removed the last potential rivals to power and established an absolute dictatorship that soon became internationally known for its austerity. Into this militaristic society, Kim introduced his philosophy of Juche, by which the country was to develop without any help from outside. Industrialisation gathered pace in the later 1950s and the 1960s despite North Korea's international isolation. However, by the late 1970s North Korea had fallen far behind its southern neighbour and a period of stagnation began.

To strengthen his position, Kim introduced the personality cult that came to characterise his rule. This policy became more extreme after 1972 when he abandoned the premiership and assumed the presidency.

Kim maintained close relations with China and the Soviet Union, and maintained hostility towards the United States and South Korea. When the

Soviet Union collapsed in 1990–91 economic aid from Russia dried up. At the same time, the barter system that Pyongyang had negotiated with Moscow also ended. This coincided with an economic crisis that included a food shortage and widespread famine. Kim's policy of isolationism prevented news from outside from becoming public knowledge. North Koreans were unaware of how economically backward their country had become. They were told that famine was a world-wide problem and that their state was better off than most.

Kim Il-sung groomed his less charismatic son, Kim Jong-il, for the succession and created the first Communist dynasty. However, the elder Kim's death in office on 8 July 1994 left a vacuum at the centre of North Korean politics and society. Since his death, veneration of the Great Leader has intensified and has reached quasi-religious proportions.

Kim Jong-il (North Korea)

Introduction

Kim Jong-il was the second ruler of the world's only Communist dynasty. Groomed to succeed his father, Kim Il-Sung, the founder of the Democratic People's Republic of Korea (North Korea), Kim junior was commonly known to his countrymen as the 'Dear Leader'. North Korea's nuclear weapons programme caused international unease, particularly from Oct. 2006 when the country claimed to have carried out its first nuclear test. Multilateral talks with the USA, China, Russia, Japan and South Korea on disabling the North's nuclear facilities made stuttering progress and suspicions remained about the true ambitions of Kim's secretive regime.

Early Life

According to some accounts, Kim Jong-il was born on 16 Feb. 1941 on Paekdusan, the highest mountain in Korea, although it is probable he was born in the Siberian city of Khabarovsk, where his father was based at the time.

Kim Jong-il returned with his family to Korea after World War II, only to be sent to China for safety at the outbreak of the Korean War (1950–53). Thereafter, he grew up in North Korea, apart from a brief period in East Germany training to be a pilot. On his return he studied at the Kim Il-sung University in Pyongyang.

From the early 1960s Kim Jong-il was groomed to succeed his father and was named as his heir in 1980. During the 1970s and 1980s he was appointed to various high offices, beginning with election to the Korean Workers' Party (KWP) Politburo in 1974, and in Dec. 1991 he took over the country's armed forces.

Career Peak

Following Kim Il-sung's death in 1994, Kim Jong-il did not immediately assume any of his father's offices of state. He became general secretary of the KWP in 1997 and chairman of the National Defence Commission, a role that is effectively head of state. He maintained spending on the military, considered the base of his support, and encouraged the development of a missile programme. His regime was widely perceived to have nuclear ambitions and in Jan. 2002 US President George Bush labelled North Korea part of an 'axis of evil' with Iraq and Iran.

In 2000 he received the then South Korean president Kim Dae-jung on an unprecedented visit. Although the two leaders agreed that reunification was the eventual aim of both Koreas, relations deteriorated in June 2002 after a naval engagement in the Yellow Sea between North and South forces. In Sept. 2002 the then Japanese prime minister Junichiro Koizumi visited North Korea in a move to re-establish diplomatic relations, although Kim was forced to admit to, and apologize for, the kidnapping of 11 Japanese citizens in the 1970s and 1980s. In Oct. 2002 North Korea admitted to developing nuclear technology in contravention of an agreement signed with the USA in 1994. The crisis intensified in Dec. 2002 and Jan. 2003 when North Korea reactivated a nuclear plant and demanded the withdrawal of inspectors from the UN International Atomic Energy Agency (IAEA). North Korea then announced its withdrawal from the Nuclear Non-Proliferation Treaty.

President Bush responded with proposals for a 'tailored containment' strategy, potentially involving economic sanctions.

Relations with the international community deteriorated further in early 2003. The IAEA formally reported North Korea to the UN Security Council for failing to comply with nuclear non-proliferation accords. Pyongyang responded by asserting its capability to attack US interests throughout the world if provoked. Kim then withdrew from border liaison negotiations with US officials and the North Korean parliament increased its defence budget. Pyongyang had earlier claimed that joint military exercises between the USA and South Korea, which coincided with the invasion of Iraq, were a sign that the USA intended to launch strikes on the North's nuclear establishments. In April 2003 Chinese-brokered talks with the USA ended acrimoniously and the following month Pyongyang announced its withdrawal from a 1992 accord with South Korea guaranteeing the Korean peninsula as a nuclear weapon-free zone.

In July 2003 Pyongyang claimed to have produced enough plutonium to start making nuclear bombs. Over the next 3 years there were several rounds of inconclusive negotiations between North Korea and the USA, together with South Korea, Japan, China and Russia. Kim's regime admitted publicly in Feb. 2005 that it had built nuclear weapons for self-defence before agreeing in principle in Sept. 2005 to give up its development programme in return for aid and security guarantees. However, that accord was almost immediately undermined when North Korea then demanded the delivery of civil nuclear equipment. In July 2006 North Korea test-fired seven missiles in defiance of international warnings, and on 9 Oct. announced that it had carried out its first nuclear test. Reflecting worldwide condemnation, the UN Security Council voted to impose punitive sanctions, which Kim's regime called an act of war. However, as the crisis threatened to escalate further, Pyongyang announced at the end of Oct. that it would rejoin multilateral negotiations with the USA, China, Russia, Japan and South Korea, on dismantling its nuclear programme.

The talks resumed in Dec. 2006 and in Feb. 2007 North Korea agreed to shut its nuclear facilities at Yongbyon in return for fuel aid. Although implementation of the agreement was initially delayed, due to the freezing of North Korean funds under US-instigated international sanctions, inspectors were able to verify in July that Yongbyon had been shut down. There were further grounds for optimism in Oct. 2007 when Kim Jong-il met the South Korean president in Pyongyang for only the second-ever summit between the leaders of the divided peninsula since the Korean War. At the same time, at further multilateral talks in Beijing, North Korea agreed to declare all its nuclear development programmes by the end of 2007. However, Kim Jong-il failed to honour this commitment, giving no explanation for missing the deadline.

In June 2008 Pyongyang submitted its overdue declaration of nuclear assets, but fresh concerns over its intentions were triggered in Sept. by its threat to resume plutonium reprocessing. However, in Oct. the USA agreed to remove the North from its list of states that sponsor terrorism in return for full access for IAEA inspectors to nuclear sites. Meanwhile, Kim Jong-il's absence from public events fuelled speculation from mid-2008 over the state of his health.

International tensions increased again from late 2008 and in April 2009 North Korea walked out of negotiations on its nuclear activities. The following month a second underground nuclear weapon test was conducted, prompting worldwide condemnation, and the government declared that it would no longer be bound by the armistice that ended the Korean War in 1953. In response, the UN Security Council voted unanimously in June to impose new sanctions on the North. Some optimism was generated in Oct. when Pyongyang indicated that it might be willing to resume the international talks on the nuclear issue. However, in 2010 there was further serious friction between North and South Korea. In Jan. there were renewed military exchanges near their disputed maritime border. In March a South Korean naval vessel was sunk, killing 46 seamen, in an unexplained explosion for which the South blamed the North. Then, in Nov., North Korea launched an artillery attack on a small South Korean island close to the two countries' maritime border, which killed four people and prompted international condemnation. North-South contact eventually resumed in July 2011 as envoys from each side held their first nuclear talks since the collapse of negotiations in 2009.

In parliamentary elections in the North in March 2009, the 687 candidates nominated by the Democratic Front for the Reunification of the Fatherland (led by the Korean Workers' Party) were returned unopposed, and the following month the Supreme People's Assembly confirmed Kim Jong-il as Chairman of the National Defence Commission.

In a rare public apology to the people by the Pyongyang regime, in Feb. 2010 the prime minister acknowledged that a redenomination of the *won* in Nov. 2009 had led to a currency collapse, triggering steep price rises and threatening famine. In the same month lavish celebrations marked Kim Jong-il's birthday, although rumours of his declining health continued to circulate.

In Sept. 2010 Kim Jong-un, the youngest son of Kim Jong-il, was promoted to senior positions within the government and the KWP leading to strong speculation that he was to be named Kim Jong-il's successor. On 19 Dec. 2011 state-run television announced that Kim Jong-il had died 2 days earlier whilst on a train visiting an area outside Pyongyang. According to the official KCNA news agency, the 69-year-old suffered a heart attack owing to physical and mental over-work. His son, Kim Jong-un, was announced as Jong-il's heir and 'the great successor'.

King, Martin Luther, Jr (United States of America)

Introduction

Martin Luther King was an influential black Baptist minister who was a figurehead for the Civil Rights movement in the United States from the mid-1950s until his assassination in 1968. Through his non-violent tactics, King helped end the legal segregation of blacks in the southern states and was awarded the Nobel Peace Prize in 1964.

Early Life

King was born on 15 Jan. 1929 in Atlanta, Georgia, the son of the Reverend Martin Luther King, Sr. and Alberta Williams. His family were staunch Baptists and at the age of 15, King was accepted by Morehouse College before graduating high school under a special programme for exceptionally gifted children. King studied at Crozer Theological Seminary in Chester, Pennsylvania and was ordained as a minister in 1948 at the age of 19. At Crozer he studied the non-violent philosophies of Mohanda Gandhi and was awarded his bachelor of divinity in 1951 before going on to Boston University where he was awarded a PhD in 1955.

While studying in Boston, King met Corretta Scott, a student at the New England Conservatory of Music. The couple married in 1953 and went on to have four children. In 1954 King was made pastor of Dextor Avenue Baptist Church in Montgomery, Alabama. In 1955 King became leader of the Montgomery Improvement Association, a group formed to boycott the city's segregated bus system. Despite threats to his family and an attack on his home, King held firm and just over a year later the city's bus system was desegregated.

In 1957 King founded the Southern Christian Leadership Conference (SCLC) to press for further reforms and to bring the issue of civil rights to a wider audience. His involvement with the SCLC led him to resign his position at Dextor Avenue and move back to Atlanta in 1959 where he was appointed co-pastor with his father of Ebenezer Baptist Church. As head of the SCLC King lectured throughout the country and met a wide variety of political and religious figures.

Career Peak

From 1960 to 1965 King led a series of non-violent marches and sit-ins to bring about civil rights reform. In all he was arrested 30 times for his involvement in civil rights activities and was jailed in 1963 along with other demonstrators protesting against segregation. On 28 Aug. 1963 King helped organize the famous March on Washington when 200,000 people marched on the nation's capital to demand equal rights. After gathering by the Lincoln Memorial, King delivered a famous speech in which he outlined his 'dream' and belief that all men could live together as brothers, regardless of race.

The march helped swing public opinion behind the civil rights movement and in 1964 president Lyndon B. Johnson signed the Civil Rights Act, which ended segregation in public accommodation and facilities and outlawed discrimination of employment. At the end of the year King's contribution to the Civil Rights movement was recognized by the award of the Nobel Peace Prize.

Over the next 3 years, King's tactics were challenged by militant black groups who questioned his creed of non-violence. King's critics felt that the pace of civil rights reform was too slow, despite the introduction of the Voting Rights Act in 1965. However King remained committed to non-violence and in 1967 he led a rally condemning American military involvement in Vietnam.

In the early part of 1968, King was planning a Poor People's March to Washington when he visited Memphis, Tennessee to lend his support to a strike by sanitation workers. On 4 April he was shot and killed while standing on the balcony of his motel. James Earl Ray was arrested for his murder in London, England later that year and extradited back to the United States where he pleaded guilty to King's murder. He was convicted in 1969 and sentenced to 99 years in jail. Since 1986 the United States has observed a national holiday in King's honour on the third Monday of every Jan.

King, Stephenson (St Lucia)

Introduction

Stephenson King took office in Sept. 2007 to become St Lucia's ninth prime minister since independence in 1979. He succeeded Sir John Compton, who died in office, and served until Nov. 2011.

Early Life

King was born on 13 Nov. 1958. He entered parliament in 1987, representing the United Workers Party (UWP), and was appointed minister for community development, social affairs, youth and sport. He held a range of portfolios in the governments of Sir John Compton in the 1990s including health, local government, and information and broadcasting. From 1997–2006 the UWP was in opposition, with King serving in various capacities, including party general secretary. After winning the Castries North seat for the UWP in the Dec. 2006 general election, King was appointed minister for health and labour relations.

Career Peak

From May to Sept. 2007 King served as acting prime minister as Compton's health went into decline. Compton died on 7 Sept. Amid rumours that two UWP MPs were withholding support for King to succeed Compton unless they were given cabinet posts, all ten UWP representatives in the House of Assembly finally agreed on his appointment. King was sworn in as prime minister by Governor-General Dame Pearlette Louisy on 9 Sept.

In his first cabinet, King appointed himself minister of finance (including international financial services), external affairs, home affairs and national security. Tackling gang culture and the drugs trade was his first priority. He also sought US investment for the development of Castries into a major cruise ship and yachting destination. In late 2007, following wide-ranging price rises across the Caribbean, King announced price caps on certain food items. In Dec. 2007 the government launched a scheme to increase youth employment by providing private sector-driven training.

In Nov. 2007 a by-election candidate claimed that he was offered a position in the economics department if he suspended his campaign in favour of the daughter of the late Sir John Compton.

King suffered defeat in the general election held on 28 Nov. 2011, with his UWP receiving only six out of 17 seats in Parliament. He was succeeded by the opposition leader and former prime minister Kenny Anthony.

Kinnock, Neil (United Kingdom of Great Britain and Northern Ireland)

Introduction

Neil Kinnock was leader of the Labour Party from 1983–92 and, while never achieving electoral victory, was instrumental in reforming the party and paving the way for the Blairite era. On resigning the party leadership, Kinnock left the domestic political arena to become a UK commissioner at the European Commission before taking a seat in the House of Lords.

Early Life

Neil Gordon Kinnock was born on 28 March 1942 in Tredegar, South Wales. He studied industrial relations and history at Cardiff University before taking a postgraduate qualification in education.

In 1970 he entered the House of Commons as the member for Bedwellty (which became Islwyn in 1983), gaining a reputation as a leading light on the party's left wing. In 1975 he voted against Prime Minister Harold Wilson's spending cuts, designed to counter a currency crisis, and later refused junior office in the government of Jim Callaghan. Kinnock joined the shadow cabinet in 1980 as its education spokesman, winning prominence during the difficult years of Michael Foot's party leadership.

Career Peak

Kinnock was elected leader of the Labour party following the resignation of Foot, who had overseen the disastrous 1983 general election. The early phase of Kinnock's leadership was dominated by his conflict with the party's hard left Militant Tendency, a contributory factor in Labour's failure at the polls. The clash came to a head when Kinnock attacked Militant (and specifically its influence within Liverpool's council) at the 1985 party conference.

There followed a series of expulsions of Militant figures from the party as Kinnock, assisted by his director of communications, Peter Mandelson, began to renew Labour's image. The expulsions were generally well received, as was Kinnock's opposition to the hardline tactics of the miners' trade union leader, Arthur Scargill, during the long-running dispute with the Conservative government over pit closures. The party also adopted a new emblem, a red rose.

However, as Labour approached the 1987 election Kinnock was criticized for, among other things, his continued commitment to unilateral nuclear disarmament. Though avoiding the humiliation of being overtaken by the Social Democrats, Labour were unable to stop the Conservatives winning with a parliamentary majority of close to 200.

In 1988 Kinnock successfully defended his leadership against a challenge from the Left-wing Tony Benn, ushering in a period when the party re-established itself as a viable alternative to the Conservatives, as they were wrenched apart by disagreement over the poll tax and Europe, culminating in the removal from office of Prime Minister Margaret Thatcher in 1990. As the 1992 general elections neared, Labour was considered a likely winner. However, with much of the press lampooning Kinnock as a 'Welsh windbag' and after a number of public relations disasters (including a triumphalist party rally a week before the elections), Thatcher's successor, John Major, led the Conservatives to a fourth consecutive election victory. Clearly shocked by the defeat, Kinnock and his deputy, Roy Hattersley, resigned as leader and deputy leader of the party.

Later Life

Kinnock remained in parliament until 1995 and then served as a British commissioner in the European Commission from 1995–2004, taking an active role in reforming and streamlining the organization. In 2004 he became chairman of the British Council and also served as president of Cardiff University. Kinnock was made Baron Kinnock of Bedwellty in 2005.

Kirchner, Néstor (Argentina)

Introduction

Néstor Kirchner, a Peronist, was president of Argentina from May 2003 until Dec. 2007. Following the withdrawal of his opponent, Carlos Menem, from a run-off, Kirchner took office with only 22% support from a first round of voting. His tenure was largely focused on trying to restore Argentina's faltering economy. He did not stand for a further term in 2007 and was replaced as president by his wife, Cristina.

Early Life

Kirchner was born on 25 Feb. 1950 in Río Gallegos in the Santa Cruz province. In 1976 he graduated in law from La Universidad Nacional de La Plata and became active in the Justicialist Party and the Peronist youth movement.

In 1983 he took a job in the local government of Río Gallegos and in 1987 was elected mayor. He ran an efficient administration and in 1991 was elected governor of Santa Cruz. The province had one of the strongest economies in the country, benefiting from high oil revenues and a low population, and Kirchner won a reputation for his financial skills. However, he was criticized for depositing public money in Swiss and Luxembourgian banks and for unpopular spending cuts. He introduced changes to the regional constitution allowing him to keep the governorship for multiple terms and was re-elected in 1995 and 1999.

At the presidential elections of 2003 Kirchner represented Frente para la Victoria (Front for Victory), the Peronist grouping of incumbent president Eduardo Duhalde, against seven opponents. Kirchner won 22% of the vote in the first round while former president Carlos Menem, representing a rival Peronist group, polled 24%. Menem's opposition rallied behind Kirchner in the build-up to the run-off and, facing heavy defeat, Menem withdrew from the race. The move further splintered the already divided Peronists and left Kirchner without the clear mandate many observers considered essential to the rebuilding of the Argentinian economy. Kirchner was sworn in on 25 May 2003.

Career Peak

Kirchner sought to repair the economy which was in a fragile state after the crisis of Dec. 2001. Following his election, in a bid to win support from the commercial sector, he retained Roberto Lavagna, a Duhalde-appointment, as finance minister (Lavagna having been widely praised for restoring some economic stability in the aftermath of the 2001 crash). Once in office Kirchner set about persuading creditors to overlook defaulted debt repayments worth billions of dollars and instead accept repayments on the balance over several decades. He also undertook a purge of the national defence forces and the police.

In Aug. 2003 congress abolished amnesty laws that provided members of the repressive military regime of 1976–83 with immunity from prosecution for alleged human rights abuses. Kirchner, who had himself been briefly imprisoned by the military junta, had vowed to end this immunity, stating that 'a society without justice or memory does not have a destiny.'

Argentina failed to make a US$3 bn. debt repayment on 10 Sept. 2003, fuelling fears that Kirchner's government would fail in its attempt to turn the economy around. However, the following day an agreement was struck with the IMF for a 3-year aid plan. US$21 bn. of debt was refinanced in a bid to put Argentina back on the road to solvency. Kirchner has since taken much of the credit for a recovery that saw the economy grow by around 9% in both 2004 and 2005, although poverty and unemployment remained at high levels. In March 2005 he declared the restructuring of the country's sovereign debt to have been completed and in Jan. 2006 Argentina paid off its debts to the IMF in full.

In congressional elections on 23 Oct. 2005, Peronist supporters of Kirchner won 69 seats in the Chamber of Deputies. Despite facing a series of scandals, including the resignation of his economics minister when a bag containing US$60,000 was found in her office, Kirchner's popularity remained high. Ahead of elections in 2007, his poll rating was around 60%. However, in July 2007 he announced his intention not to stand for another term. Instead his wife, Cristina, ran for the presidency and comfortably won the election in Oct. 2007. Power was handed from husband to wife on 10 Dec.

Later Life

After leaving office, Kirchner continued to exert considerable political influence as head of the ruling Front for Victory party. However, he suffered a blow in the June 2009 legislative elections when they lost their majority in both houses and ceded the traditional Peronist stronghold of Buenos Aires Province district to the Republican Proposal. He was also subject to investigation over allegations that he authorized spying on political opponents during his time in office. In May 2010 he was unanimously elected to head the Union of South American Nations (UNASUR).

In 2010 Kirchner's health deteriorated. He underwent heart surgery in Feb. 2010 and again in Sept. 2010 following a heart attack. Strong rumours still circulated that he intended to run for president in 2011 but he died suddenly from heart failure on 27 Oct. He was granted a state funeral and the government declared 3 days of national mourning.

Kirkilas, Gediminas (Lithuania)

Introduction

Taking office as prime minister of Lithuania in July 2006, Gediminas Kirkilas headed the country's 14th government in 15 years. His appointment ended a political crisis that had started in May when Algirdas Brazauskas, leader of the centre-left Social Democrats, resigned as premier. Kirkilas' tenure ended in Oct. 2008 when his party was defeated at the general election.

Early Life

Gediminas Kirkilas was born on 30 Aug. 1951 in Vilnius, Lithuania, then a Soviet Socialist Republic. Having completed military service with the Navy in 1972 he worked at the monument restoration trust as an interior restorer. He studied Lithuanian language and literature at Vilnius' teacher training college and began working for the central committee of the Lithuanian Communist Party (LCP) in 1982. Promoted to the department of culture in 1986 he was the assistant to Algirdas Brazauskas, who became first secretary of the LCP in Oct. 1988.

As communism weakened, Kirkilas and Brazauskas were part of a group of pro-independence communists who formed the Democratic Labour Party of Lithuania (LDDP), modelling the movement on Western social democratic principles. As deputy chairman, Kirkilas helped guide the party to victory in parliamentary elections on 26 Oct. 1992, winning 75 out of 141 parliamentary seats. Brazauskas went on to win the presidential election of Feb. 1993.

Serving on the foreign affairs committee and as a delegate to the North Atlantic Assembly in the mid-1990s, Kirkilas developed closer ties with Baltic neighbours and Scandinavian states and took part in early negotiations to join NATO. He was re-elected to parliament (*Seimas*) in Oct. 1996, although the LDDP lost to the conservative Homeland Union amid corruption scandals and public resentment at continuing high levels of unemployment and poverty.

In Jan. 2001 the LDDP merged with the Lithuanian Social Democratic Party (LSDP) to form the Social Democratic Party of Lithuania (also known as LSDP), led by Brazauskas. In 2002 Kirkilas was appointed special representative to the president (Valdas Adamkus) on the thorny issue of transport routes through Lithuania between Russia and the Russian enclave of Kaliningrad. He also worked closely with Brazauskas (who had become prime minister in June 2001) to implement the reforms needed for EU membership. Lithuania joined the EU in May 2004.

Kirkilas was re-elected to the *Seimas* in the Oct. 2004 elections in which no party won overall control. Brazauskas agreed to form a broad power-sharing coalition (including the Labour Party, which had won the most seats). Having been nominated by the president in Dec. 2004 to continue as prime minister, Brazauskas appointed Kirkilas as defence minister. When a series of scandals forced the Labour Party to pull out of the ruling coalition in May 2006, Brazauskas found himself without a majority in parliament and resigned. The president nominated Kirkilas for the premiership, and after this was approved by parliament he was sworn in on 4 July 2006.

Career Peak

Kirkilas formed a four-party coalition government comprising the LSDP, the Lithuanian Peasant Popular Union (formerly the Peasants' and New Democratic Party Union), the Liberal and Centre Union, and Civil Democracy (a group which broke away from the Labour Party in May 2006). His priorities were Lithuanian membership of the Schengen area and the eurozone. He also pledged to promote education and access to health care

and promised to maintain the economy's robust growth by promoting high-tech industries and attracting investors to regional centres such as the port of Klaipėda.

At the general election of Oct. 2008 Kirkilas' Social Democrats came second to the Homeland Union party, which formed a new government.

Kissinger, Henry A. (United States of America)

Introduction

Henry Alfred Kissinger was US national security advisor from 1969–75 and secretary of state from 1973–77. A major force in shaping American foreign policy under Presidents Richard M. Nixon and Gerald R. Ford, Kissinger was jointly awarded the Nobel Peace Prize with North Vietnamese counterpart Le Duc Tho for his efforts in ending the Vietnam War.

Early Life

Born in Fürth, Germany on 27 May 1923, Kissinger and his family emigrated to the United States in 1943 to escape Nazi persecution. He was naturalized on 19 June 1943 and served in the US counter-intelligence corps from 1943–46. After the war, Kissinger studied at Harvard. After gaining a BA he went on to be awarded a PhD in 1954. From 1954 until 1971 Kissinger taught at Harvard in the department of government and the center for international affairs, also serving as director of the Defense Studies Program from 1959–69.

Throughout the 1950s and 60s he held numerous advisory posts which brought him into contact with the administrations of Dwight D. Eisenhower, John F. Kennedy and Lyndon B. Johnson. He was study director of nuclear weapons and foreign policy for the council of foreign relations from 1955–56 and director of the special studies project for the Rockefeller Brothers Fund from 1956–58.

Kissinger's 1957 book *Nuclear Weapons and Foreign Policy*, helped establish him as a leading authority on foreign and strategic policy. He proposed a policy of 'flexible response' in the event of a nuclear attack as opposed to Secretary of State John Foster Dulles' concept of 'massive retaliation'.

Career Peak

After Nixon was elected President in 1968, Kissinger was appointed assistant for national security affairs and became head of the national security council a year later. He worked for more cordial US–Soviet relations which led to the SALT I arms agreement of 1972. He also helped initiate a rapprochement with China. When Nixon was re-elected president in 1972 Kissinger was appointed the 56th US Secretary of State. He was sworn in on 22 Sept. 1973.

Advocating a hard-line policy towards North Vietnam, Kissinger helped plan the bombing of Cambodia in 1969–70. However by 1973, he was negotiating for the withdrawal of troops from South Vietnam. A cease-fire agreement and an outline for a permanent peace was announced on 23 Jan. 1973 for which Kissinger was later jointly awarded the Nobel Peace Prize, along with North Vietnamese negotiator Le Duc Tho. The same year, Kissinger played a major role in securing a truce that ended the Arab–Israeli War.

Later Life

After Nixon's resignation in 1974, Kissinger continued in office until 1977. He then formed his own company, Kissinger Associates, which advised on foreign investment and affairs. He also continued to write and lecture. In Nov. 2002 he was appointed by President George W. Bush to head a commission to investigate the failure of intelligence agencies to prevent the 11 Sept. 2001 attacks on New York and Washington. But shortly after he resigned from the post citing the conflict between his public role and his private business. Kissinger had been reluctant to make public details of Kissinger Associates.

Earlier in 2002, Kissinger was called as a witness by a Chilean judge investigating US involvement in the 1973 Chilean coup which overthrew the Socialist president Salvador Allende, and also by French and Spanish judges investigating the same period.

Kiviniemi, Mari (Finland)

Introduction

After Matti Vanhanen stood down, Mari Kiviniemi became prime minister in June 2010 as leader of the Centre Party, heading a centre-right coalition in power since 2003. Aiming to reduce the budget deficit through improvements in productivity, she led her party to fourth place at elections in April 2011. Her tenure continued as opposition parties sought to establish a coalition and she left office 2 months later.

Early Life

Born in Seinäjoki on 27 Sept. 1968 Kiviniemi was educated in Jalasjärvi before moving to the University of Helsinki to study economics in 1988. She became secretary general of the Centre Party student union and stood unsuccessfully for parliament in 1991. During this period she also became active in the Norden Association, a non-party political organization promoting co-operation between Nordic countries. From 1990–92 she was vice-chair of its Youth League in Finland and between 1998 and 2003 held a series of posts in the Pohjanmaa region.

In 1994 she completed a master's degree in social sciences. In 1995 she was elected to parliament for the Centre Party, representing a constituency in Etelä-Pohjanmaa. Over the next 12 years she served on the supervisory boards of various institutions, including Leonia Bank, the alcoholic beverage monopoly Alko, the food company Lännen Tehtaat Oyj and the Finnish National Fund for Research and Development. She was vice-chair on the parliamentary commerce committee in 1999 and again from 2000–03. She served on the parliamentary grand committee from 2003–07 and was twice vice-chair of the parliamentary foreign affairs committee (2003–04 and 2006–07).

In 2004, following the victory of the Centre Party's coalition in the previous year's general elections, Kiviniemi was appointed special adviser to Prime Minister Matti Vanhanen. From 2005–06 she served as minister for foreign trade and development, and minister at the prime minister's office. In 2007 she was appointed minister of public administration and local government, and minister at the ministry of the interior. She oversaw the merging of several municipalities, attracting criticism that the move would reduce the influence of Swedish-speaking Finns.

In Dec. 2009, with the Centre Party's support dropping in the face of economic problems and allegations of a funding scandal, Vanhanen announced his resignation. Kiviniemi bid to replace him in early 2010, arguing that Finland's economic problems could be addressed by improving productivity and introducing modest tax rises, while avoiding deep spending cuts. Appealing to the liberal urban electorate (and benefiting from being untainted by the funding allegations), she was elected with 57% of the vote. She took office as prime minister on 22 June 2010.

Career Peak

Kiviniemi's tenure began with the formulation of a national growth programme, which identified the green economy as an area of opportunity. In Aug. 2010 she called for closer co-operation between the EU and Russia. Attaching great importance to Russia, in Dec. 2010 she visited Prime Minister Putin to discuss developing trade relations. Her chief challenges included the budget deficit, the fallout of the global economic downturn and the strain placed on the economy by a rapidly ageing population.

Kiviniemi was succeeded by Jyrki Katainen, who formed a coalition after his National Coalition Party won the elections of April 2011.

Later Life

In June 2014 Kiviniemi was appointed a deputy secretary general of the Organisation for Economic Co-operation and Development (OECD).

Klaus, Václav (Czech Republic)

Introduction

Dr Václav Klaus was the first Czech minister of finance following the Velvet Revolution of 1989. He was elected prime minister in 1992 and oversaw the Republic's transition from a state-planned economy to a free market system, initially outstripping the economic growth of the other post-communist nations in the region. Having resigned in 1997 following a party financing scandal, he succeeded Václav Havel as president in March 2003 and was re-elected in Feb. 2008. A noted eurosceptic, Klaus was the last head of state to sign the European Union's Lisbon Treaty on institutional and administrative reform in Nov. 2009.

Early Life

Born on 19 April 1941 in Prague, Klaus graduated from the Prague School of Economics in 1963, continuing his education in Naples, Italy and at Cornell University in New York. He was then a researcher at the Institute of Economics of the Czechoslovak Academy of Sciences until 1970, during which time he came into contact with Václav Havel, the dissident writer and future Czech president.

From 1971 until 1987, Klaus held posts at the Czechoslovak State Bank before joining the Academy of Sciences' Economic Forecasting Institute. On 17 Nov. 1989, in the infancy of the Velvet Revolution, Klaus discovered that his son had escaped a beating from police in Prague. Two days later he joined the Civic Forum movement that would be instrumental in the overthrow of the communist regime. He was appointed finance minister in the first post-revolution government in Dec. 1989, implementing a range of reformist policies.

The Civic Forum, as a loose anti-communist alliance, began to splinter and Klaus joined the centre-right ODS, which aimed to restructure, deregulate and liberalize the market. He became party chairman in April 1991, deputy premier in Oct. and prime minister in June 1992 following the ODS electoral victory.

Career Peak

Following the split with Slovakia, the Czech Republic underwent rapid reform and privatization, and Klaus was acclaimed internationally as the architect of an economic miracle. However, the ODS faired less well than expected at the July 1996 elections and the governing coalition lost its majority in the House of Representatives. Klaus' authority within the ODS was further weakened that year by a public feud with his foreign minister, Josef Zieleniec. The economy was also beginning to suffer, and there followed a series of crisis budgets, austerity measures and ultimately devaluation in 1997. Further problems for Klaus included the resignation of Zieleniec, popular protests against the government and damaging corruption allegations concerning ODS party funding. The charges concerned improper donations in return for preferential treatment in relation to privatization and Zieleniec publicly declared that Klaus had been aware of certain key donations. President Havel called for the government to step down and Klaus resigned on 29 Nov. 1997, although he denied any wrongdoing. However, he retained significant influence as speaker of the Chamber of Deputies from 1998–2002. In Jan. 2003 he twice stood for election to the presidency in succession to Havel but, despite winning most votes on both occasions, failed to secure the requisite 50%. Havel resigned on 3 Feb. 2003 and Klaus was chosen to succeed him at the third attempt.

In June 2003 membership of the EU, scheduled for 2004, won 77% approval in a national referendum. Klaus, however, had described entry into the EU as a 'marriage of convenience rather than love'. Parliamentary elections in June 2006 resulted in a political stalemate until Sept., when a centre-right minority administration took office under Mirek Topolánek of the ODS. However, this government collapsed the following month. In Nov. Klaus again designated Topolánek as prime minister and a new coalition took office in Jan. 2007. Klaus was re-elected for a second term in Feb. 2008.

Topolánek resigned in March 2009 after his government lost a parliamentary vote of confidence and Klaus appointed Jan Fischer, an economist, as interim prime minister. Meanwhile, with the Czech Republic having assumed the 6-month presidency of the EU in Jan. 2009, Klaus made plain his distrust of the Union's Lisbon Treaty for national sovereignty reasons. However, having unsuccessfully sought a national opt-out from aspects of the treaty, Klaus eventually signed it in Nov. 2009 following a ruling by the Czech Constitutional Court on its legitimacy.

Following inconclusive parliamentary elections in May 2010, in which the Social Democrats (ČSSD) became the largest party but with insufficient support to form a government, Klaus asked Petr Nečas of the ODS, as the second largest party, to form a new centre-right coalition government that took office in July.

Shortly before completing his second term in office the Czech Senate charged Klaus with high treason over a highly controversial prisoner amnesty that he granted in Jan. 2013.

The Czech Republic's first direct presidential elections held in Jan. 2013 were won by Miloš Zeman. Term limits prevented Klaus from seeking re-election.

Klestil, Thomas (Austria)

Introduction

A former high-ranking career diplomat, Klestil won the presidential election as the Austrian People's Party (ÖVP) nominee in 1992. He was an effective emissary for Austrian interests in the European Union (EU) and beyond, helping to end Austria's international isolation after the presidency of Kurt Waldheim and to strengthen the country's ties with the emerging democracies in Central and Eastern Europe. In his second term from 1998 he was successful in limiting the international damage arising from the participation of right-wing Freedom Party (FPÖ) in the coalition government formed in early 2000. He died after a heart attack 2 days before the end of his second term.

Early Life

Thomas Klestil was born in Vienna on 4 Nov. 1932, the youngest of five children. His father, who died in 1941, came from Bohemia but had lived in Vienna since 1912. Klestil was educated in the capital, achieving a master's degree and doctorate in economics at the College of World Trade (now the University of Economics and Business Administration) in 1956–57. He then started a career in the civil service, joining the Department for Economic and Commercial Affairs in the Federal Chancellery. In 1959 he was assigned to the Austrian delegation to the Organization for European Cooperation and Development (OECD) in Paris and in 1962 was appointed economic attaché at the Austrian Embassy in Washington, D.C. Returning to Vienna in 1966, he served on the chancellor's personal staff advising on economic policy until his appointment as Austrian consul general in Los Angeles, USA, in 1969. From 1974 Klestil was director of the Foreign Ministry's Office for International Organisations. From 1978–82 he was Austria's permanent representative to the United Nations in New York (during Kurt Waldheim's second term as secretary-general), and then became Austrian ambassador to the USA and to the Organization of American States. Recalled from Washington in 1987, he served as secretary-general for foreign affairs in Vienna until his election as the presidential candidate of the Austrian People's Party (ÖVP) on 24 May 1992, receiving 56.9% of the vote in the second round.

Career Peak

Following his election Klestil made official visits to restore international links, particularly in Europe. He was a strong supporter of Austria's accession to the EU (approved by referendum in 1994 and achieved on 1 Jan. 1995) and of EU projects such as monetary union and enlargement to include former communist states. He also visited Israel where he expressed sympathy for the Jewish people in a speech before the Knesset. Klestil was a keen supporter of NATO. Austria joined the NATO Partnership for Peace programme following EU accession in 1995 but held back from applying for full membership. Public support for Austria's traditional neutrality was still strong but the accession of Eastern European states to NATO was believed to be crucial for Austrian support for joining the organization.

Although illness and publicity about marital difficulties overshadowed his first term, he was re-elected on 19 April 1998, defeating four contenders by a substantial majority with 63.4% of the vote. This time he stood as an independent candidate, with the backing of both the ÖVP and SPÖ. He also had the support of the FPÖ, paving the way for its incorporation into a coalition with the ÖVP in Feb.2000. Klestil married his political aide, Margot Löffler, shortly after his re-election.

The FPÖ, returned as the second strongest party in the 1999 elections, was critical to the formation in Feb. 2000 of the coalition government with the ÖVP. However, with its far-right credentials, its inclusion led to a storm of protest from the international community and Austria's EU partners. Klestil attempted to calm public agitation by declaring that the new government was constitutionally sound, despite personal hostility towards the FPÖ. Klestil also appealed to the EU against political sanctions. Addressing the European Parliament in April 2000, Klestil defended Austria's parliamentary democracy. After submitting to a human rights investigation, sanctions were lifted in Sept. 2000.

Relations with his own party and with the chancellor, Wolfgang Schüssel, deteriorated during his second term, especially after Klestil's opposition to the coalition with the FPÖ. However, when a new coalition was formed with the FPÖ in 2003, Klestil accepted it without criticism.

Klestil died on 6 July 2004 from multiple organ failure after a heart attack.

Kocharyan, Robert (Armenia)

Introduction

Robert Kocharyan served as president of Armenia from 1998 to 2008, having been appointed prime minister a year earlier. He had previously served as premier and president of Nagorno-Karabakh, the Armenian-dominated region at the centre of a dispute between Armenia and Azerbaijan since the collapse of the Soviet Union. Kocharyan's past as a leading independence fighter was a source of contention with Azerbaijan throughout his tenure.

Early Life

Kocharyan was born on 31 Aug. 1954 in Stepanakert in Nagorno-Karabakh, then an autonomous region within the Soviet Republic of Azerbaijan. From 1972–74 he served in the Red Army and in 1982 graduated in electrical engineering from the Polytechnic Institute in Yerevan. As a factory engineer in Stepanakert, he was active within Komsomol (the Soviet youth wing) and the communist party of Karabakh.

Calls for self-determination in Nagorno-Karabakh by the Armenian majority increased during the 1980s. Kocharyan was involved with the Groong movement, which promoted Armenian history and culture, and later founded Miatsum (Unification), which called for reunification with Armenia.

He was elected to the Supreme Council of Armenia in 1989 as the representative for Nagorno-Karabakh. In the same year fighting began in the enclave between Armenian nationalists and the Azeri minority, with Kocharyan a key figure in organizing armed nationalist forces. With the collapse of the Soviet Union in late 1991, Kocharyan was elected to the first Supreme Council of the Republic of Nagorno-Karabakh (RNK) and again took responsibility for military organization. Conflict escalated in Nagorno-Karabakh and the Azeri army occupied large areas of the region in 1992. Kocharyan was elected prime minister of the RNK and oversaw the expulsion of Azeri forces. In 1994 RNK and Azerbaijan agreed a ceasefire and a peace process began, brokered by the Organization for Security and Co-operation in Europe. Kocharyan was elected president of the RNK and set about rebuilding the ravaged economy.

In 1997 he was made prime minister of Armenia by President Levon Ter-Petrosyan, despite having only obtained citizenship a short time before. Ter-Petrosyan resigned over the Nagorno-Karabakh issue in Feb. 1998 and Kocharyan was approved by the electoral commission to stand for the presidency. He stood against Karen Demirchyan in a run-off in March 1998 and won with 59.7% of the vote.

Career Peak

Kocharyan's victory caused some international unease. The USA announced that it would not support any move by Armenia to annex Nagorno-Karabakh, while Azerbaijan viewed the appointment as a 'provocation'.

Faced with a depressed economy, Kocharyan authorized tax cuts in a bid to kick-start the industrial sector and reduce unemployment and attempted to bring in foreign investment. Significant funds were also directed to repairing infrastructure destroyed during an earthquake in 1988.

In Oct. 1999 Armenian Prime Minister Vazgen Sargsyan, the parliamentary speaker and six other officials were shot dead when a gang stormed Yerevan's parliament building. The assassins claimed they wanted to highlight Armenia's economic plight and government mismanagement and corruption. In late 2000 Armenia and Azerbaijan agreed to consolidate their ceasefire agreement and in Jan. 2001 jointly gained membership of the Council of Europe.

In presidential elections in Feb. 2003 Kocharyan won a further term, defeating Stepan Demirchyan in a run-off. The OSCE said that the election process 'fell short of international standards in several key respects'. In early 2004 there were sporadic demonstrations calling for his resignation and opposition parties began a boycott of parliament. A referendum on proposed constitutional amendments took place in Nov. 2005. The proposals aimed to enhance the role of parliament while placing some restrictions on presidential powers. Although voters favoured the changes, the opposition protested and claimed that the referendum had been rigged. In May 2006 the Country of Law Party left the pro-Kocharyan governing coalition and joined the opposition.

The issue of Nagorno-Karabakh was a feature of Kocharyan's time in office. Hopes of a breakthrough in negotiations were raised briefly in Feb. 2006 when he met Azerbaijan's President Aliyev in Paris, France, but the two sides failed to agree on a 'declaration of principles' on the disputed territory. In Dec. 2006 voters in the Armenian enclave opted overwhelmingly in a referendum for a constitution declaring their own sovereignty. However, Azerbaijan rejected any move towards independence.

In May 2007 pro-Kocharyan parties headed by the Republican Party of Armenia (HHK) retained power in parliamentary elections which European observers judged to have met international standards.

Later Life

Kocharyan was succeeded as president by his long-time ally Serzh Sargsyan, raising concerns that Kocharyan would continue to exert considerable influence over government policy-making and appointment beyond his official retirement. The 2008 presidential elections (in which Kocharyan did not stand but was the incumbent head of state) were marred by violent protests in their aftermath, in which several people died. Opposition leaders have since tried to pin the blame for the bloodshed on Kocharyan.

Kohl, Helmut (Germany)

Introduction

Helmut Kohl was Chancellor of West Germany between 1982–90 and then of re-unified Germany until 1998. His tenure will be best remembered for the German re-unification that he actively promoted and oversaw following the collapse of the Berlin Wall in 1989. Whilst the re-integration was inevitably painful at times, it was speedier and smoother than many observers had predicted. He was also one of the most significant driving forces behind European union and the single European currency. When Kohl fell from power after 16 years, his standing as an international statesman was high. However, his reputation was subsequently blighted by allegations of financial irregularities within his party, the Christian Democratic Union (CDU), during his time as leader.

Early Life

Kohl was born in Ludwigshafen-am-Rhein on 3 April 1930. His family were Catholic and conservative. He studied at the University of Frankfurt and received a Ph.D. in Political Science from the University of Heidelberg in 1958. Entering politics the next year, he was elected to the Rhineland-Palatinate state legislature, becoming CDU Deputy Chairman in 1961 and Chairman in 1963. He was Minister-President (Prime Minister) of the state in 1969 and joined the CDU's federal executive in 1966. Three years later he

became Deputy Chairman of the executive and in 1973 he was Chairman. In 1960 he had married Hannelore Renner, with whom he had two children.

Kohl served as Minister-President of Rhineland-Palatinate until 1976 when he was elected to the Bundestag, where he became Christian Democratic floor leader. Kohl lost his bid for the chancellorship in 1976 against Helmut Schmidt, but when Schmidt resigned following the collapse of his government in Oct. 1982 Kohl was voted in as his successor. His appointment was confirmed in general elections held on 6 March the following year when his CDU–Christian Social Union (CSU)–Free Democrats (FDP) coalition achieved a 53 seat majority.

Career Peak

Kohl's early years as Chancellor did not suggest that he would retire as one of the most respected politicians of his age. He was a poor public speaker and was thought to be more suited to domestic than international affairs. Following a conservative line, he reduced public spending on welfare and continued to emphasise West Germany's relationship with the USA and the rest of Western Europe. His party was returned at the general election of Jan. 1987 but with a reduced majority. His popularity fell again and the CDU made losses in the 1989 European and local elections.

Events in the Soviet Union and throughout the rest of the Eastern Bloc completely altered the political scene. When the Berlin Wall fell and the barrier between East and West Germany disappeared in Oct. 1989, many of the West's leaders were hesitant as to what to do next. But Kohl, in his own words, 'grabbed the mantle of history'. In late Nov. 1989 he announced firm proposals for the process of reunification and in Feb. 1990 set out plans to introduce a single German currency. There was anger abroad over his unilateral actions, but in elections held on 18 March 1990 he was shown to have the overwhelming support of the West German public. Reunification negotiations were concluded on 3 Oct. with the signing of the Two-plus-Four Treaty, by which the two states became one.

Pan-German elections were held in Dec. 1990 with Kohl and his party winning a handsome victory. The unification process hit many financial and social obstacles over the following decade, and the massive expenses incurred led to reductions in welfare spending and increases in taxation. Unemployment hovered around 18% among East Germans and the Far Right re-appeared in small clusters, capitalizing on animosity towards immigrants. Moreover, the strong economic growth enjoyed by West Germany since the 1950s began to slow.

The new Germany was quickly recognized internationally and continued to be a major player in world politics. Kohl had been an advocate of increased European unity throughout his political life and he continued with this policy after re-unification, attempting to allay fears of other member states fearful of Germany's increased power. He was instrumental in framing the Maastricht Treaty in the early 1990s, was among the driving forces behind European Monetary Union and was heavily involved in negotiations to provide aid to the former communist nations. Within NATO Germany played a major role in the conflicts in Iraq and in the Balkans during the 1990s.

In Nov. 1994 Kohl was elected to serve another term as Chancellor, albeit with the slimmest margin of his political career. He remained Chancellor until the elections of 27 Sept. 1998, when he was succeeded by Gerhard Schröder (Social Democratic Party/SPD). Kohl's refusal to resign earlier and hand over the leadership of the CDU to his appointed successor Wolfgang Schäuble was widely blamed for the defeat.

Later Life

In 1999 allegations were made regarding CDU funding during Kohl's era. Kohl refused to reveal the sources of several million dollars. In addition, a number of Swiss bank accounts were exposed and it was alleged that certain favoured politicians had received cash gifts from the Kohl regime. In Jan. 2000 Kohl was forced to resign as the party's honorary chairman and he was subject to a criminal investigation. These events marked a rapid decline in Kohl's reputation but his contribution towards German and European integration remains undiminished. His political ideology is epitomized by his comment at the time of re-unification that 'Germany is our fatherland, the united Europe our future'.

Kohl published *Mein Tagebuch* ('My Diary') in 2000. He talked about his life as a politician but does not provide more information about the sources of contribution. He subsequently released two volumes of memoirs in March 2004 and Nov. 2005. Following the suicide of his wife in July 2001, he remarried in April 2008. He died aged 87 on 16 June 2017.

Köhler, Horst (Germany)

Introduction

Horst Köhler took office as federal president of Germany on 1 July 2004, having previously served as the first German managing director of the International Monetary Fund (IMF) from 2000–04. Prior to the IMF, he was involved in German financial politics, particularly in regard to German reunification and the European Union Maastricht Treaty negotiations in 1991.

Early Life

Köhler was born on 22 Feb. 1943 in Skierbieszów, Poland. Following the Soviet invasion in the Second World War, his family fled to East Germany. In 1953 they moved into West Germany. He earned a doctorate in economics and politics from the University of Tübingen, where he was a scientific research assistant at the Institute for Applied Economic Research during 1969–76. Between 1976–89 he held various posts in Germany's ministries of economics and finance. He played an important role in the economic planning for Germany's reunification and assisted in providing aid to Russia after the collapse of the USSR. In 1991 Köhler was Germany's lead official in the negotiations that led to the Maastricht Treaty. From 1990–93 he served as Germany's deputy finance minister and from 1993–98 he was president of the German Savings Bank Association. In 1998 Köhler was appointed president of the European Bank for Reconstruction and Development (EBRD). He took part in focusing the EBRD's priorities on small businesses rather than large infrastructure projects. During his presidency the EBRD improved its finances, from having lost US$2,528 m. in 1998 to making a profit of US$41 m. in 1999. In addition he was deputy governor for Germany at the World Bank, and was the personal representative of the federal chancellor in the preparation of the Group of Seven (G7) economic summits from 1990–93.

On 23 March 2000 Köhler was elected managing director and chairman of the Executive Board of the IMF, the first German to hold the post. His appointment came after the then chancellor, Gerhard Schröder, had campaigned to persuade European nations to back him. In 2002 his plan to allow indebted countries to file for bankruptcy caused protests from international financial markets.

Career Peak

Relinquishing his position at the IMF, Köhler was elected federal president of Germany on 23 May 2004. In his inaugural speech he encouraged the government to persevere with its economic reform programme, despite the short-term hardships that it would present. Following inconclusive parliamentary elections in Sept. 2005, he formally appointed Angela Merkel of the CDU as the first female federal chancellor at the head of a new coalition government in Nov. 2005. In May 2008 Köhler announced his candidacy for a second term as president in elections scheduled for May 2009. He went on to win re-election, defeating two opponents. In May 2010 he unexpectedly resigned after being criticized for endorsing proactive military action as a means of protecting national finances during an interview in Afghanistan. Following his departure the president of the Bundesrat, Jens Böhrnsen, took over the presidency on an interim basis until fresh elections could be held.

Koirala, Sushil (Nepal)

Introduction

Sushil Koirala became prime minister in Feb. 2014, heading a coalition formed after 3 months of negotiations. The leader of the Nepali Congress party, he is related to three former prime ministers—Matrika Prasad Koirala, Bishweshwar Prasad Koirala and Girija Prasad Koirala. He resigned following the adoption of a new constitution in Sept. 2015.

Early Life

Koirala was born on 12 Aug. 1939 into a clan involved in political activities supporting India's struggle for independence. Having joined the Nepali Congress in 1954, he went into exile in India in 1960 after King Mahendra implemented the *panchayat* system of government that eschewed political parties.

While in India, Koirala raised support for Nepal's democracy movement and edited the Nepali Congress newspaper, *Tarun*. In 1974 he was involved in the hijacking of a Royal Nepal Airlines plane carrying cash and, after a period as a fugitive, served 3 years in Indian prisons. A member of the Nepali Congress central working party from 1979, he returned to Nepal after reforms extended the freedoms of political parties. In 1990 the Nepali Congress joined the People's Movement, a broad alliance of left-wing and communist parties that successfully agitated for parliamentary democracy and in Nov. that year drafted a new constitution.

Koirala became general secretary of the Nepali Congress in 1996, at which time the party was in government and struggling with the newly launched Maoist insurgency. In 1998 he became party vice president and in 2001 unsuccessfully challenged for leadership of the parliamentary party. In 2008, the year in which Nepal became a federal republic, he was appointed acting president of the party and in 2010 took over the leadership.

The Nepali Congress emerged as the largest single party in the Nov. 2013 constituent assembly elections. After months of negotiation, a deal was reached with the second largest party, the Communist Party of Nepal (Unified Marxist-Leninist), to back Koirala as the sole candidate for the premiership. In Feb. 2014 he won parliamentary approval by 405 votes to 148.

Career Peak

Koirala took office on 10 Feb. 2014 at the head of a coalition consisting of the two largest parties and an alliance of several smaller ones. His most pressing challenge was to draw up a new constitution, a task requiring him to achieve consensus across Nepal's disparate political spectrum. He was unable to oversee completion of a draft document by a deadline of 22 Jan. 2015, resulting in the continuation of political deadlock. However, a constitution was successfully promulgated on 20 Sept. 2015 after parliament voted in its favour by 507 votes to 25. It established Nepal as a federal and secular democratic republic.

Koirala subsequently resigned as prime minister following the adoption of the new constitution and was replaced by Khadga Prasad Oli.

Having been diagnosed with lung cancer in June 2014, Koirala succumbed to the disease on 9 Feb. 2016, passing away aged 78.

Koivisto, Mauno (Finland)

Introduction

Mauno Koivisto served as minister of finance (1966–67, 1972) before twice becoming prime minister (1968–70, 1979–80). In 1981 he was interim president, taking over from the ailing Urho Kekkonen. The following year he was elected president and served for two consecutive terms until 1994. He maintained his predecessor's foreign policy of friendly neutrality towards the USSR until the collapse of the Soviet Union at the end of the 1980s, when he moved Finland towards closer ties with Western Europe.

Early Life

Koivisto was born in 1923, the son of a ship's carpenter. After serving in the infantry in World War II, he began to take an active interest in politics. He joined the Finnish Social Democratic Party (SSDP) at university. After taking an initial degree in 1953, he wrote a doctoral thesis on social relations which was accepted 3 years later. He was the director of the Helsinki Workers' Savings Bank between 1959–68 and then governor of the Bank of Finland from 1968–82. In 1966 he was appointed minister of finance in the government of Rafael Paasio, where was regarded as shrewd and pragmatic. In 1968, increasing dissatisfaction with Paasio catapulted Koivisto into the front line of likely successors. After much dispute within the SSDP, he was chosen as the party candidate and elected prime minister later that year. Koivisto's first government came to an end in 1970.

Career Peak

In 1979, Koivisto was again elected prime minister, having built on his reputation for sound financial handling as governor of the Bank of Finland. In office he worked for a consensus with the left and the trade unions. When Kekkonen resigned because of failing health, Koivisto took the opportunity to launch a campaign for the presidency. He played a major role in dismantling the Treaty on Friendship, Cooperation and Mutual Assistance with the USSR which had been signed by a weakened Finland in1948. He also fostered relations with the EU, paving the way for the country to become a member.

In his last years as president, Koivisto was a key figure in three important developments. He was almost unique in appreciating the urgent need for external economic support from the Soviet Union, and sought to persuade the US and the International Monetary Fund to lend assistance. When the three Baltic republics emerged as independent states, they looked to nearby Finland as a role model and supportive ally, which caused difficulties given the tenuous balance of Finnish relations with Russia. Finally, the question of whether Finland should seek EU membership involved much national soul-searching as well as complex foreign negotiations which Koivisto handled with characteristic tact and delicacy.

Later Life

In retirement he wrote his political memoirs. He died on 12 May 2017 following a long battle with Alzheimer's disease.

Koizumi, Junichiro (Japan)

Introduction

Representing the Liberal Democratic Party (LDP), Koizumi became prime minister in 2001 following the resignation of Yoshiro Mori. Faced with a legacy of economic stagnation and a troubled banking system, he sought, with popular backing, a more radical approach to domestic reform. Internationally, he tried to effect a thawing of relations with North Korea, but courted wider regional hostility by his visits to Tokyo's Yasukuni shrine honouring Japan's war dead. He left office in Sept. 2006.

Early Life

Born on 8 Jan. 1942 in Yokosuka City in the Kanagawa Prefecture, Koizumi studied economics at Keio University. After graduating in 1967, he became involved in politics, working in 1970 as a secretary for the future prime minister Takeo Fukuda (1976–78). In 1972 he was elected to the Diet, where he served continuously until his premiership. He was appointed to his first cabinet post in Dec. 1988, with responsibility for health and welfare. He served in that capacity for several terms in subsequent governments through the 1990s, and also for a time as minister of posts and telecommunications. Within the LDP, he held senior posts from the early 1980s before being elected party president at his third attempt in 2001.

Following the resignation of Yoshiro Mori in April 2001, Koizumi stood against three other candidates to succeed him as LDP party leader and prime minister. Relatively unknown, and espousing radical proposals to counter Japan's economic problems, he defeated former prime minister Ryutaro Hashimoto (1996–98), whose own term had seen a period of economic decline.

Career Peak

On election, Koizumi attempted to reignite Japan's economy, signalling his intention to privatize the massive postal and savings system (the world's biggest financial institution). Nonetheless, recession continued. His perceived inaction on reform and an inability to stem deflation or the departure of businesses from Japan led the opposition to mount a confidence vote in July 2002. However, Koizumi survived with 280 votes to 185. In Sept. 2002 he reshuffled his cabinet, dismissing his financial services minister to force through a controversial reform to help the banking sector. For the first time,

the Bank of Japan allowed the government to use a 15trn. yen emergency fund to invest in commercial banks.

Improvements in the Japanese economy during 2003 eased pressure on Koizumi's leadership, and in the Nov. 2003 parliamentary elections the LDP won 237 seats in the 480-member Diet. Pursuing his policy of privatizing the postal and savings system in the face of broad parliamentary opposition, including from within his own party, Koizumi called a snap election in Aug. 2005. The LDP was returned with an increased mandate in Sept., vindicating his privatization plan and confirming his popular standing in the country.

At the international level, Koizumi sought to improve relations with North Korea, making two controversial visits to Pyongyang during his premiership. However, the issue of the disappearance of several Japanese citizens in the 1970s and 1980s, attributable to North Korea's intelligence services, remained unresolved to Japan's satisfaction. Koizumi also visited Seoul and offered an apology for the suffering that South Korea endured under Japanese colonial rule. Relations with China meanwhile deteriorated from April 2005 over Japan's textbook portrayal of its military history and Koizumi's visits to the Yasukuni shrine honouring Japan's war dead. On the wider stage, Koizumi's government launched Japan's application in Sept. 2004 for a permanent Japanese seat on the UN Security Council.

In April 2006 Koizumi became Japan's longest-serving prime minister since the early 1970s. However, in accordance with LDP rules, he resigned his office in Sept. 2006 ahead of a parliamentary vote to choose his successor. Shinzo Abe was selected on 20 Sept. 2006 and assumed office the following week.

Kok, Willem 'Wim' (Netherlands)

Introduction

Wim Kok served as prime minister between Aug. 1994 and April 2002. He was also president of the cabinet and minister of general affairs. His premiership attracted popular support for closer integration with the European Union. He resigned along with his entire administration after admitting that Dutch forces could have done more to prevent a war crime during the Bosnian conflict of the 1990s.

Early Life

Willem Kok was born in Bergambacht on 29 Sept. 1938. He graduated from the Nijenrode Business School and in 1961, after military service, he was appointed assistant international officer of the Netherlands Federation of Trade Unions, specialising in economic affairs. Throughout the 1970s Kok worked for various trade unions, eventually becoming chairman of the European Trade Union Confederation in 1979.

The first step of his political career came in 1986 when Kok was elected as a member of the Lower house for the Dutch Labour Party (PvdA). He was re-elected in 1989 and in the same year assumed the deputy chairmanship of the International Socialist Movement. In Nov. 1989 Kok was appointed Deputy Prime Minister and Minister of Finance in the third government of Ruud Lubbers. He held this post until 1994 when he was voted prime minister to succeed Lubbers.

Career Peak

In its first 4 years Kok's administration reduced the public-sector deficit from 4% to 1.5%, while the economy grew by an average 3.5% a year. Some 500,000 new jobs were created. Political commentators began to talk of a Dutch model for combining economic growth with a strong sense of social responsibility. Kok's government was also responsible for extending shopping hours and privatizing a number of state-owned utilities and companies. Income tax was lowered and savings were made by the reduction of the country's welfare provisions. Kok was returned to power in 1998. In his second term of office, he steered the Dutch economy into the first round of European Monetary Union. He also backed a controversial bill which exempted doctors from criminal liability if they assisted in the suicide of patients who had requested euthanasia.

Kok and his government resigned in April 2002, having admitted that Dutch peace keeping forces could have more strongly attempted to prevent the massacre of 8,000 Bosnian Muslims by Serb troops in Srebrenica in 1995.

Komorowski, Bronisław (Poland)

Introduction

Bronisław Komorowski was elected president in June 2010, having served as acting president following the death of incumbent Lech Kaczyński in an air crash in April 2010. A member of the governing Civic Platform (PO) party, he supports pro-market economic reforms and favours a more active role in the European Union.

Early Life

Bronisław Komorowski was born on 4 June 1952 in Oborniki Śląskie to an aristocratic family whose lands were confiscated by the Communist government. In 1977 he graduated in history from the University of Warsaw, where he had become politically active. He completed his master's degree the same year and from 1977–80 was editor of a Catholic journal. From 1980–81 he worked at the centre for social research of the trade union Solidarność (Solidarity), campaigning for democracy and against the existing communist regime.

After being interned for 4 months in 1981 when Poland came under martial law, he spent the next 8 years working as a teacher in Niepokalanów. Following the collapse of communism and the election of a Solidarity-led government in 1989, he was deputy minister for defence from 1990–93. At the 1991 general election he was elected as an MP for the Freedom Union party (UW), serving as its general secretary from 1993–95. In 1997 he co-founded a new party which allied itself with the Conservative People's Party to become part of the Solidarity Electoral Action (AWS) grouping.

Following the formation of an AWS–UW government in 1997, Komorowski was appointed head of the parliamentary national defence committee. As a member of Jerzy Buzek's government, he helped oversee Poland's entry into EU and NATO, and from 2000–01 served as defence minister. In 2001 Komorowski joined the new, reformist PO, led by Donald Tusk, and was elected to parliament at the 2001 general election, in which the AWS-UW lost power. Subsequently he served as deputy chairman of the parliamentary national defence committee and as a member of the parliamentary committee for foreign affairs.

In Oct. 2005 he was elected deputy speaker of the Sejm, becoming speaker in Nov. 2007. On 10 April 2010 President Lech Kaczyński died in an air crash. Under the constitution, Komorowski became acting president until presidential elections took place on 20 June 2010. Initially campaigning as a loyal supporter of Prime Minister Tusk's programme of economic reforms and public spending cuts, he promised not to use the presidential veto to block progress in these areas. However, during a closely fought contest he moderated his stance, softening his line on the need for reform of farmers' pensions and abandoning plans to raise the retirement age. Voting went to two rounds and in the run-off on 4 July 2010 he narrowly defeated the late president's twin brother, Jarosław Kaczyński, with 53.0% of the vote.

Career Peak

Komorowski sought to raise Poland's profile within the EU and to increase economic, defensive and diplomatic ties with key international partners, including the USA. However, in Aug. 2012 he accused US President Barack Obama of betraying Poland's national security over the 2009 cancellation of a controversial anti-ballistic missile system, and he called for Poland to build its own missile shield to ensure the country's defence.

Following the resignation of Prime Minister Tusk in Sept. 2014 to take up the EU position of president of the European Council, Komorowski asked Ewa Kopacz of the PO to form a new administration.

Komorowski's term as president came to an end in Aug. 2015 following his defeat to Andrzej Duda at elections held in May that year.

Kopacz, Ewa (Poland)

Introduction

Ewa Kopacz became prime minister on 22 Sept. 2014. She had previously acted as speaker of the Sejm, the first woman to hold that position.

Early Life

Born in Skaryszew on 3 Dec. 1956, Kopacz was raised in Radom. She graduated from the Medical University of Lublin in 1981, specializing in general practice and paediatrics. After working in several clinics, she headed the local health care facility in the town of Szydłowiec until 2001.

Kopacz joined the United People's Party in the 1980s and was later prominent in the Freedom Union Party in Radom. In 2001, having been elected as a parliamentary deputy, she joined the newly-established Civic Platform. In 2007 she was named minister of health when Civic Platform came to power and became the first female speaker of the Sejm in Nov. 2011.

Career Peak

Kopacz became Poland's second female prime minister in Sept. 2014 following the resignation of Donald Tusk to take up the EU position of president of the European Council. Her critics argued that she was chosen more for her loyalty to Tusk than for her competence and she has faced opposition from within her own party.

In her inaugural speech she called for 'one hundred days of cooperation' from her own party and the opposition. However, Civic Platform's position was weakened when it secured only a narrow electoral win over the Law and Justice Party in a contentious vote for provincial assemblies in Nov. 2014.

Outlining the government's plans in Jan. 2015, Kopacz designated significant funds for new crèches and kindergartens. She also aimed to oversee the extension of parental leave from 2016 and the introduction of other new parental benefits. In addition, she revealed plans to close four coalmines, leading to strikes involving some 3,000 miners the same month.

In foreign affairs, Kopacz said that she aimed to strengthen Poland's standing both within the EU and in central and eastern Europe. To this end, she made clear her intentions to veto UK Prime Minister David Cameron's plans to limit benefits paid to EU migrants in Britain and also sent humanitarian aid to Ukraine in response to the civil conflict in the country.

Kopacz's Civic Platform was defeated by the Law and Justice Party at the Oct. 2015 parliamentary elections. Kopacz's term as prime minister subsequently ended when she was replaced by Beata Szydło on 16 Nov. 2015.

Koroma, Ernest Bai (Sierra Leone)

Introduction

Ernest Bai Koroma became president in Sept. 2007 following victory in the second round of elections. He won re-election outright in the first round of voting in Nov. 2012. He had previously run unsuccessfully for the presidency in 2002.

Early Life

Koroma was born in 1953 in Bombali, northern Sierra Leone. Though the region is predominantly Muslim, Koroma is a Christian. After primary and secondary schooling, he graduated in 1976 from Fourah Bay College, part of the University of Sierra Leone, in Freetown. He then worked as a teacher before joining the National Insurance Company in 1978. In 1985 he moved to the Reliance Insurance Trust Corporation (Ritcorps), becoming managing director in 1988 and holding the post for 14 years.

A latecomer to politics, Koroma was chosen as the APC's presidential candidate in March 2002 but was beaten into second place by Ahmad Tejan Kabbah of the SLPP. Under Koroma's leadership the APC grew in popularity and won a landslide victory in the 2004 local government elections, winning almost all seats in the densely-populated Western Area (which includes Freetown). In June 2005 Koroma was briefly stripped of his party leadership after the Supreme Court found him guilty of illegally altering his party's constitution. However, he was unanimously re-elected leader in Sept. 2005. Having spent most of his life in Freetown, his support base was strongest in the north though he also made inroads in the south ahead of the 2007 presidential election. In a run-off in Sept. 2007 Koroma won against Solomon Berewa and was sworn in on 17 Sept.

Career Peak

Koroma took over an almost bankrupt country, at the time ranked last out of 177 in the Human Development Index world rankings. He had to maintain the peace process that followed 10 years of civil war that ended in 2001, and also faced major challenges to promote economic development and rejuvenate energy and public services. He pledged a zero tolerance approach to corruption and in Nov. 2007 his government published a report detailing inadequacies in tax collection, health care and security services, as well as suspect loans.

Also in Nov. 2007 Koroma signed a commercial investment deal to double the country's rutile (titanium ore) production capacity and secured China's cancellation of US$22 m. worth of debt. A large offshore oil discovery was reported in 2009 and in 2010 large iron ore extraction leases were granted to two British companies.

Koroma was re-elected president for a second term in Nov. 2012, with the APC securing a majority in parliamentary polling held at the same time. From 2014 his presidency was increasingly dominated by efforts to contain the spread of the Ebola virus epidemic in West Africa, which was classified by the World Health Organization (WHO) in Aug. that year as an international public health emergency. Sierra Leone was eventually declared free of the disease by the WHO in March 2016.

In March 2015 Koroma had dismissed Samuel Sam-Sumana as vice-president, accusing him of fomenting political violence and anti-APC activity, and replaced him with Victor Foh.

Having served the maximum permitted two terms, he was succeeded by Julius Maada Bio in April 2018.

Kosor, Jadranka (Croatia)

Introduction

Jadranka Kosor became Croatia's first female prime minister on 1 July 2009 following Ivo Sanader's resignation. Amid opposition calls for early elections, Kosor's premiership was endorsed with 83 votes from the 153-seat parliament on 6 July 2009.

Early Life

Kosor was born on 1 July 1953 in Pakrac. Having graduated in law from Zagreb University, in 1972 she became a print and radio journalist. From 1991–95, during Croatia's war of independence, she hosted a radio show for refugees on Croatian Radio.

Elected as an MP in 1995, Kosor became vice-president of the House of Representatives after Franjo Tuđman invited her to join the Croatian Democratic Union (HDZ), of which she was also vice-president from 1995–97 (and again from 2002–09). From 1998–2000 she headed the conservative HDZ Women's Association, named after Katarina Zrinski. Under her leadership the number of female candidates standing for the HDZ in the 2000 elections doubled from the previous election. In 2003 Kosor was appointed to Sanader's government as deputy prime minister and minister of family, veterans' affairs and intergenerational solidarity. She ran for the presidency in 2005 but was defeated in the run-off by the incumbent, Stjepan Mesić.

Recommended as a possible successor to the premiership by Sanader on his resignation in July 2009, Kosor was endorsed by parliament on 6 July 2009. On 4 July 2009 she was also named president of the HDZ.

Career Peak

Kosor pledged to continue the policies of her predecessor. Proposed budget cuts were an early test of her government's strength, with the prospect of an IMF bailout looming if they were rejected. Party in-fighting grew after the HDZ's poor showing at the first round of the presidential elections in Dec. 2009. On 4 Jan. 2010 Kosor took the decision to expel Sanader from the HDZ after alleged interference with her leadership.

Her key challenges included restarting talks on EU accession, which had been blocked by Slovenia until Nov. 2009 when Kosor met with her Slovenian counterpart in Stockholm to sign an agreement to bring their border dispute (over the bay of Piran on the Adriatic coast) to international arbitration.

In parliamentary elections held in Dec. 2011, Kosor and the HDZ were defeated by the Kukuriku coalition. Kosor was subsequently succeeded by the SDP leader Zoran Milanović on 23 Dec. 2011.

Koštunica, Vojislav (Serbia)

Introduction

Vojislav Koštunica served as prime minister of Serbia from March 2004 to July 2008. He had previously succeeded Slobodan Milošević as president of the Federal Republic of Yugoslavia in Oct. 2000 following disputed elections. After the first round of voting, Milošević claimed that Koštunica had failed to achieve the necessary absolute majority and pressed for a run-off. Public demonstrations led to the resignation of Milošević and the installation of Koštunica. A democratic nationalist, he pursued closer relations with the EU while distancing his regime from the USA. Following the break-up of Yugoslavia Koštunica became prime minister of Serbia in March 2004. He was re-elected to a second term in 2007, but could not keep the fragile coalition he had assembled to this purpose together and was forced to dissolve his government and call an election in May 2008. He was succeeded by Mirko Cvetković.

Early Life

Vojislav Koštunica was born on 24 March 1944 in Belgrade, into a family with a legal background. In 1966 he graduated from the Law School of the University of Belgrade, and completed a master's there 4 years later. Specializing in constitutional law, he lost his job at the University in 1974, following his criticism of the Tito government.

In 1976 Koštunica was awarded his doctorate. He speaks English, German and French and in 1981 published a Serbo-Croat translation of the Federalist Papers. Throughout his career he has advocated free speech. He never joined the communist party and when, in 1989, Milošević offered him a job at Belgrade University he refused.

In the same year Koštunica with Zoran Djindjić co-founded the Democratic Party. In 1990 he was elected to the federal parliament. He and Djindjić split in 1992 when Koštunica set-up the Democratic Party of Serbia. His opposition to Milošević throughout the 1990s was tempered by his own nationalist convictions and criticism of foreign intervention against Serbia. While he spoke out against ethnic cleansing and the worst excesses of Serbian paramilitary groups, he supported Serbian self-determination in Bosnia and opposed Kosovan independence. He condemned NATO's bombing of Serbia during the Kosovan conflict, not least for the galvanizing effect it had on Milošević's domestic popularity.

Though a relatively low profile figure in Yugoslav politics, Koštunica won the support of the opposition coalition to become Milošević's principal rival for the presidency. Untainted by any association with the old communist party or with Milošević himself, he rode a wave of popular enthusiasm. After the Milošević regime demanded a run-off, discontent erupted throughout the country and a crippling general strike was called on 4 Oct. The following day a crowd of several thousand gathered in Belgrade and surrounded parliament. Milošević, realizing that he could not rely on the support of the military and police, resigned. The following day Russia, having previously backed Milošević, recognized Koštunica as president.

Career Peak

The removal of Milošević and Koštunica's ascendancy were met by domestic and international euphoria. Koštunica, however, faced a massive task in restoring the fortunes of a financially impoverished, internationally isolated and much reduced Yugoslav state. His first major domestic challenge was Montenegrin independence. The government of Montenegro, one of the remaining Yugoslav constituent republics, boycotted the elections that brought Koštunica to power. Within a week of his presidency he announced that 'the will of the people will be respected... even if it means that Montenegro does not want to be part of a joint state.'.

Koštunica struck a power-sharing agreement with Milošević's former Socialist Party in Oct. 2000 before the Democratic Party won a convincing victory in the parliamentary elections of Dec. 2000. He assuaged foreign opinion by admitting Serbia's role in large-scale killings during the 1999 Kosovo conflict, although he refused immediate co-operation with a UN war crimes tribunal, insisting that Yugoslavia had more pressing problems of reconstruction. Despite this, Milošević was arrested by Yugoslav forces in April 2001 and handed over to the tribunal in the Hague.

Yugoslavia rejoined the UN on 1 Nov. 2000 and the OSCE on 8 Nov. On 14 March 2002 Serbia and Montenegro agreed to a new structure for the Yugoslav federation. Following European Union-brokered talks it was agreed that they would remain part of a single entity called Serbia and Montenegro, superseding the Yugoslavian state. On 9 April 2002 the parliaments of Serbia and Montenegro ratified the agreement, and on 31 May 2002 the Yugoslav federal parliament also adopted the agreement. A Constitutional Charter was drafted paving the way for the establishment of Serbia and Montenegro in Feb. 2003.

With the restructuring abolishing the post of Yugoslavian president, Koštunica unsuccessfully stood for the Serbian presidency in 2002, with two rounds of voting declared invalid owing to low turnout. Instead he became prime minister of Serbia in March 2004, heading a minority coalition government. In May 2006 Montenegro held a referendum which approved secession from the union with Serbia. Koštunica strongly opposed the planned split but was forced to accept the result. Montenegro declared independence in June 2006.

Koštunica continued to distance himself from the US administration and seek closer ties with the EU, beginning preliminary entry talks in Oct. 2005. However, discussions were suspended in May 2006 when Serbia missed a deadline to hand over the war crimes suspect Ratko Mladić. Koštunica made a direct appeal to Mladić to surrender himself to The Hague tribunal but to no effect.

In parliamentary elections held in Jan. 2007, the nationalist Serb Radical Party won the most seats with a manifesto promising to deny Kosovo independence. Koštunica managed to form a new coalition and retain power, but only after months of negotiations. This fragile coalition was rendered unworkable by the declared independence of Kosovo and continued disputes over membership of the European Union. Koštunica was forced to dissolve his government, and a parliamentary election was called for May 2008, won by the For a European Serbia Party.

Kravchuk, Leonid (Ukraine)

Introduction

The first popularly elected president of the Ukraine, Leonid Kravchuk served from 1991–94. Formally a prominent member of the Communist Party of the Ukraine SSR, he later advocated Ukraine's independence. But his economic reform programme failed and he was unable to secure a second term.

Early Life

Born on 10 Jan. 1934 in Velyky Zhytyn, west Ukraine, Kravchuk studied economics at the Kiev T.G. Shevchenko State University. In 1958 he joined the Communist Party, serving in the central committee and becoming the head of the ideology department in 1988. Two years later he was made chairman of Ukraine's Supreme Soviet. Opposed to independence, he took an ambiguous stance on the attempted coup of Russian leader Mikhail Gorbachev in 1991.

Career Peak

Changing his political stance, he left the Communist Party and in 1991, as a pro-independence nationalist, became the first democratically elected

Ukrainian president. With Boris Yeltsin and the Belorusian president Stanislau Shushkevich, he set up the CIS the same year.

But his term was marred by economic hardship as he failed to control the liberalization of the economy. Kravchuk had a difficult relationship with Russia, disagreeing over Russia's claim to the Crimean Peninsula, the division of the Black Sea Fleet and Yeltsin agreement with the US to reduce nuclear weapons. In 1993 Prime Minister Leonid Kuchma resigned and was replaced by Kravchuk. At the same time the economy collapsed, and the following year Kravchuk was succeeded as president by Kuchma on a pledge to cure the ailing economy and strengthen ties with Russia.

Later Life

Following his electoral defeat, Kravchuk continued his political career as a parliamentary deputy.

Kreisky, Bruno (Austria)

Introduction

Bruno Kreisky was chancellor of Austria from 1970 to 1983 and leader of the Social Democratic Party (SPÖ), 1967–83. Having been imprisoned for his socialist activities in the 1930s, he escaped to Sweden before the outbreak of World War II. After the war he served as a diplomat and later as the minister of foreign affairs. His tenure as chancellor was characterized by social reform, economic prosperity and the pursuance of peace on the international stage.

Early Life

Kreisky was born in Vienna on 22 Jan. 1911. His father Max was a successful Jewish businessman. Bruno joined the SPÖ in 1926 and in 1929 he enrolled at the University of Vienna to study Law and Economics. The SPÖ was made illegal in 1934 and in response Kreisky, along with his friend Roman Felleis, established the Revolutionary Socialist Youth movement. A year later he was arrested for his political activities and imprisoned. In 1936 he was released but was not allowed to return to his studies until 1938.

In March 1938, after Austria was occupied by German troops, Kreisky was arrested by the Gestapo and taken into 'protective custody'. He was released in Aug. on orders to leave the country and made preparations to go to Bolivia before political allies in Sweden urged him to go there instead. He worked for the Stockholm Consumer Co-operative Association throughout World War II, whilst writing for a number of newspapers and journals. On 23 April 1942 he married Vera Fürth, with whom he would have two children. In Oct. 1945, in the aftermath of the war, he was an important communication link between Austria and the Swedish relief agency.

In May 1946 he returned to Austria before being assigned to the Austrian legation in Stockholm in Feb. 1947. In Jan. 1951 he returned to Vienna, taking up a post as a secretary in the economics section of the foreign affairs department of the Austrian Chancellery. He entered the National Assembly following the elections of 1956 as the member for St Pölten in Lower Austria and quickly moved up the SPÖ ranks, becoming party deputy chairman in 1959. In July of the same year he was appointed foreign minister in Julius Raab's coalition government. In this role he succeeded in converting the department into a fully fledged cabinet ministry and was a major force in the establishment of the European Free Trade Association (EFTA).

In March 1963 he was re-appointed to the ministry despite opposition from Austrian People's Party partners in the coalition. When the SPÖ lost heavily in the elections of 1966 and left the government, Kreisky was prominent in reforming the party, becoming chairman in early 1967. Following a general election in April 1970 the SPÖ formed a minority government with Kreisky as chancellor. In Oct. 1970 they made a better showing at general elections and formed the first of three consecutive majority governments.

Career Peak

The Austrian economy boomed during Kreisky's tenure and unemployment was low, which ensured continued support from middle-class voters. The welfare state grew under his guidance, relations between employers and unions improved and the justice and higher education systems also underwent reform. In terms of foreign affairs, he pursued a policy of 'active neutrality' in which he sought closer ties with Eastern Bloc countries, including Czechoslovakia, Tito's Yugoslavia and other non-aligned neighbours. He hosted groundbreaking talks between Israeli officials and the Palestinian Liberation Organization.

His time in office, however, was not without its controversy and there were a number of political scandals, notably concerning links between the consultancy firm of Minister of Finance Hannes Androsch and contractors employed by the socialist government. Kreisky endured the indignity of having his proposals for a nuclear power plant defeated in 1978. By the time of the general elections of April 1983 there were various rumours concerning the state of Kreisky's health but he was nonetheless declared fit to stand for re-election. The SPÖ lost only five seats but it was enough to end the party's parliamentary majority. Kreisky, unwilling to lead a coalition government, resigned as chancellor and gave up the party chairmanship a few months later.

Later Life

In April 1984 Kreisky underwent a kidney transplant operation. On 29 July 1990 he died in Vienna and was given a state funeral on 7 Aug. He had published his memoirs 2 years earlier. The Bruno Kreisky Archives Foundation, the Bruno Kreisky Forum for International Dialogue and the Bruno Kreisky Foundation for Outstanding Achievements in Human Rights continue to document and promote work relating to his life's activities.

Krenz, Egon (Germany)

Introduction

Egon Krenz succeeded Erich Honecker as General Secretary of the East German Socialist Unity Party (SED) and as Head of State in Oct. 1989. By then the communist regimes in East Germany and throughout the rest of the Eastern Bloc were collapsing. He gave permission for restricted travel by East Germans to the West, paving the way for the collapse of the Berlin Wall. His fall from power thereafter was rapid and in 1997 he was convicted for involvement in the killing of German citizens at the Berlin Wall in the 1970s and 80s.

Early Life

Krenz was born on 19 March 1937 in Kolberg, Poland and moved to Damgarten in Germany when he was 7 years old. In 1953 he joined the Free German Youth movement (FDJ) and was apprenticed as a locksmith in Rostock. He then trained as a teacher in Putbus and around the same time became the secretary of the FDJ. He held a succession of different jobs in the FDJ before leaving for Moscow in 1964, where he studied until 1967.

He entered the *Volkskammer* (People's Chamber) in 1971 and 5 years later joined the Politburo with candidate status, becoming a full member in 1983. He was General Secretary of the FDJ from 1974 but relinquished his duties in 1983. At this time he was the Politburo's youngest member and was regarded as Honecker's natural successor. However he became concerned at the failing relationship between Honecker and Gorbachev's Soviet regime. When Honecker resigned on 18 Oct. 1989, Krenz replaced him as both Party Secretary and Head of State.

Career Peak

In a speech that same evening Krenz acknowledged the failure of the SED to anticipate developments and spoke vaguely of introducing change. On 24 Oct. he was elected by the Volkskammer as Chairman of the Council of State and Chairman of the National Defence Council, though for the first time in East German history it was not a unanimous decision. Almost immediately several thousand protesters gathered in East Berlin and demonstrations spread to other major cities.

On 8 Nov. the Politburo resigned but Krenz was re-confirmed as Secretary General of the SED. At the same time he opened the way for rival political parties, the most significant of which was Bärbel Bohley's New Forum. As

thousands of emigrants escaped to the West via the open borders with Poland, Czechoslovakia and Hungary, Krenz tried to save face by declaring that citizens could travel freely after obtaining official permission. This only served to add to the confusion. Border guards were powerless to stop the tens of thousands of citizens who gathered at the Berlin Wall and tore it down. On 28 Nov. Krenz denied that German reunification was a possibility but his power had all but disappeared and he resigned on 3 Dec.

Later Life

On 21 Jan. 1990 Krenz was expelled from the SED. Later, criminal charges were brought against him for his involvement in the killing of German citizens at the Wall between 1971 and 1989. He was convicted in 1997 and began a six and a half-year sentence in Jan. 2000 at the Hakenfelde Prison in Berlin. He appeared at the European Court of Human Rights in Nov. 2000 in a bid to overturn the conviction, arguing that he could not be held accountable under unified German law for crimes allegedly committed under East German law. In Feb. 2000 Krenz was relocated to an open prison and on 18 Dec. 2003 he was released early.

Kubilius, Andrius (Lithuania)

Introduction

Andrius Kubilius became prime minister for the second time after his nomination by President Valdas Adamkus was approved by parliament on 27 Nov. 2008. He had previously served as premier from 1999–2000. His centre-right coalition government had to confront a major economic crisis during the global downturn.

Early Life

Andrius Kubilius was born on 8 Dec. 1956 in Vilnius. In 1979 he graduated in physics from Vilnius University, where he remained for a further 11 years to pursue an academic career. In 1988 he became involved in the pro-independence movement and joined Sajūdis ('Unity'/Reform Movement of Lithuania). He was appointed executive secretary of its council in 1990, serving for 2 years until he was elected to the Seimas (parliament).

In 1993 Kubilius joined the newly-established conservative Homeland Union party and was re-elected to the Seimas in 1996, becoming its vice chairman. In Oct. 1999 he was named prime minister by President Valdas Adamkus following the resignation of Rolandas Paksas. Kubilius' appointment was approved by the Seimas by a vote of 82 to 20. His term lasted from Nov. 1999–Oct. 2000. Policy priorities included reform of the Soviet-era bureaucracy and economic liberalization.

In the Oct. 2000 general election Kubilius won re-election to the Seimas despite the Homeland Union suffering a heavy defeat. He served as the party's first deputy chairman from 2000 until 2003, when he became party leader. In Oct. 2006 he was appointed deputy speaker of the Seimas and chair of the parliamentary committee on European affairs.

After gaining a lead in the first round of voting at the Oct. 2008 general election, the Homeland Union-Lithuanian Christian Democrats (TS-LKD), which had formed in May 2008 following a merger between the two parties, won 44 of a possible 141 seats, providing a mandate to form a coalition government. The Homeland Union joined with three smaller centre-right parties, jointly controlling 79 seats.

Career Peak

Kubilius' principal challenge has been to tackle the country's worsening economic crisis. Hours after being sworn into office he won parliamentary approval for tax reforms, cuts to public spending and measures to support businesses. However, there was widespread public discontent at tax increases following election promises that they would be cut. He proposed adoption of the EU's single currency (euro) by 2011, but that target was missed in light of the economic downturn. Over the medium term, a return to growth depends on banks' ability to restart lending and on a recovery of external demand.

Kubilius' government oversaw the decommissioning of the Ignalina power plant at the end of 2009 as part of Lithuania's EU accession agreement. However, the closure of the plant has raised the spectre of dependency on Russian gas, a situation Kubilius is keen to avoid. An electricity bridge between Sweden and Lithuania that could solve the country's energy problem has yet to be built.

Kubilius' party, the Homeland Union-Lithuanian Christian Democrats, lost the Oct. 2012 parliamentary elections to Algirdas Butkevičius' Social Democrats. Butkevičius was appointed prime minister in Nov.

Kubitschek, Juscelino (Brazil)

Introduction

Juscelino Kubitschek De Oliveira was president of Brazil from 1956 to 1961. It was during his presidency that the costly building of the new capital, Brasilia, caused massive inflation.

Early Life

Born in Diamantina in 1902, Kubitschek studied medicine and practised as a surgeon. He entered the federal chamber of deputies in 1934, was mayor of Belo Horizonte from 1940 to 1945, returned to the federal chamber of deputies a year later and was governor of Minas Gerais from 1951–55, when he oversaw many large-scale public building and road construction schemes. Widely regarded as heir apparent to the former president Getulio Vargas, Kubitschek defeated two opponents for the presidency in 1956.

Career Peak

In office Kubitschek sought to increase industrial investment by offering tax incentives and instigating massive road-building programmes. Working to a 5-year plan, the economy suffered when coffee prices fell and industrial unrest became widespread.

In an attempt to accelerate the development of Brazil's interior, Kubitschek decided to move the national capital from Rio de Janiero to a new site, to be called Brasilia. However, the scale and ambition of the plan was costly, creating rapid inflation and leaving Brazil with a huge national debt. Accompanied by vast spending to assist the drought-hit northeast of the country, the economy ran into serious trouble. In 1961 Kubitschek was succeeded by Janio Quadros.

Kubitschek was elected to the national senate in 1962 and nominated for president again 2 years later by the Social Democratic Party. However, he was forced into exile by a military coup later in the year.

Later Life

Kubitschek returned to Brazil in 1967 and entered the banking profession. He died in a car crash on 22 Aug. 1976.

Kučan, Milan (Slovenia)

Introduction

Milan Kučan was president of Slovenia from the country's declaration of independence in 1991 until the elections of Nov. 2002. Previously he had led Slovenia within the federal structure of Yugoslavia. Widely regarded as a safe pair of political hands, Slovenia remained stable throughout his tenure.

Early Life

Kučan was born on 14 Jan. 1941 in Krizevci, in the Prekmurje region in eastern Slovenia. His father, a teacher who served in the resistance movement, died during World War II. Kučan graduated in law from Ljubljana University in 1964, joining the Slovenian youth association in the same year. He served

as the association's president from 1968–69. From 1969 until 1973 he sat on the central committee of Slovenia's League of Communists.

Between 1973 and 1978 he was secretary of the Socialist Alliance of Slovenia and was president of the Slovenian Assembly from 1978 until 1982. He was then the Slovenian representative on the presidency for the central committee of the Yugoslav League of Communists, leaving in 1986 to become president of the Slovenian branch of the central committee.

In 1989 the Slovenian parliament paved the way for secession from federal Yugoslavia. At the country's first multi-party elections the following year Kučan was elected president of the presidency, with Slovenia still part of the federal structure.

Career Peak

A declaration of independence won majority backing in a referendum during 1990 and Kučan announced the split with Yugoslavia in 1991. Armed conflict followed in which around a hundred people died. Yugoslav troops, under the terms of an EU-brokered agreement, withdrew from the country by the end of the year. In 1992 Slovenia held its first elections as an independent state. Kučan won the presidency with 64% of the vote. Janez Drnovšek of the Liberal Democrats won the premiership and the two held power until Nov. 2002, except for 7 months in 2000 when Drnovšek was out of office.

The long tenures of Kučan and Drnovšek provided Slovenia with political and economic stability that few other former Yugoslav states enjoyed. Slovenia joined the IMF in 1993 and became a member of NATO's Partnership for Peace Programme. In 1999 it granted airspace to NATO for its bombing raids on Kosovo and Serbia. In 1996 Slovenia signed an associate agreement with the EU and opened full membership talks the following year. In Oct. 2002 the EU included Slovenia in its plans for enlargement scheduled for 2004.

Kučan won re-election in 1997. In 2001 he entered negotiations with the Croatian president, Štipe Mesić, to improve relations between the two countries. They settled several border disputes, one of which granted Slovenian entry to the Adriatic, and agreed on joint management of the Slovenia-based Krsko nuclear power station.

The Slovenian constitution debarred Kučan from standing for a third term as president in Nov. 2002. He was succeeded by Drnovšek.

Kuchma, Leonid (Ukraine)

Introduction

Leonid Kuchma was elected Ukrainian president in 1994 and re-elected in 1999. He stood down in Nov. 2004. His free market reforms helped Ukraine broker the transition from communism to independence, but his alleged suppression of the media and involvement in the murder of an opposition journalist tarnished his leadership. Under Kuchma the Ukraine stalled on modernizing its administration and eradicating corruption.

Early Life

Kuchma was born on 9 Aug. 1938 in Chikino, Chernigov region. After studying engineering at the Dniepropetrovsk State University, between 1960–92 he worked at the world's largest space missile plant, Pivdenne design bureau, where his technological developments won him both the Lenin Prize and the Ukrainian State Prize. There he was Communist Party secretary between 1975–82. He also worked as a technical director at Baikonur space centre in Kazakhstan.

In 1990 he was elected to the Ukrainian parliament, and again 4 years later. Between 1992–93 he served as prime minister until a difference of opinion with President Leonid Kravchuk led Kuchma to resign his position.

Career Peak

In 1994 he stood for president against Kravchuk and five others. On election he proposed the implementation of free market reforms and closer relations with Russia. Privatization was begun that year and in Feb. 1998 a 10-year economic agreement was signed between Ukraine and Russia. But his reforms were slow, and much of the larger industrial sector enterprises remained state-owned. Ukraine also suffered the fall out of Russia's economic problems.

Kuchma did, however, reform the constitution, extending the president's powers in reform implementation and ministerial appointments. In 1999 he was elected for a second term with 56.3% of votes. He appointed Viktor Yushchenko as his prime minister who soon became popular not only within the Ukraine, where he was credited with kickstarting the economy, but also internationally. But in Dec. 2000 a journalist critical to Kuchma's leadership, Georgiy Gongadze, was murdered. Claims that Kuchma was involved in his disappearance, coupled with press freedom restrictions, led to public manifestations in Feb. 2001 and demands for his resignation from opposition politicians. The president defied these calls and denied accusations of his involvement. Two months later he sacked Yushchenko replacing him with Anatolii Kinakh, a member of Kuchma's own United Ukraine Party. Other allegations of the illegal sale of arms to Iraq further damaged his reputation.

Nonetheless, in 2000 the economy saw a 5.8% growth followed in 2001 by 9%. In March 2002 parliamentary elections, Yushchenko's Our Ukraine Party gained a narrow lead over Kuchma's United Ukraine Party, taking 112 seats to the latter's 102. With neither gaining a majority, Kuchma maintained influence over parliament.

As opponents accused him of employing increasingly authoritarian tactics, in Nov. 2002 Kuchma dissolved the government and replaced Kinakh as prime minister with Viktor Yanukovych, a close ally of the president. The previous month Kuchma had lost his presidential majority in parliament when five deputies withdrew support over an alleged police assault against one of their colleagues. Kuchma also faced a damaging miners strike over poor pay and working conditions.

A wave of popular protests in early 2003 forced Kuchma to agree to transfer some presidential powers to parliament, including the right to appoint the prime minister. However, his tenure continued to be dogged by scandal. A constitutional court ruled that Kuchma would be eligible to stand for a third term, claiming his first term did not count under the terms of the 1996 constitution. He was then forced to backtrack on a proposed constitutional amendment that would have seen future presidents selected by parliament rather than popular vote. In June 2004 there was widespread unease when Kuchma's son-in-law won a tender for the country's biggest steel plant.

Kuchma did not stand for a third term in Nov. 2004. Yanukovych, his chosen successor, narrowly lost the first round to the pro-Western Viktor Yushchenko. However, Yanukovych was declared winner of the run-off and a tense stand-off ensued as mass rallies took place in Kiev and throughout the country amid allegations of election fraud. The result was subsequently annulled by the Supreme Court. In new elections on 26 Dec. Yushchenko received 54.1% of the vote and Yanukovych 45.9%.

Later Life

In March 2005 Kuchma was questioned as part of the investigation into the murder of Georgiy Gongadze, shortly after Interior Minister Yuri Kravchenko apparently killed himself before he was due to give evidence. It was reported that Kravchenko left a note implying Kuchma's responsibility for Gongadze's death.

Kuczynski, Pedro Pablo (Peru)

Introduction

Pedro Pablo Kuczynski was sworn in as president on 28 July 2016. A former World Bank economist, he previously served as prime minister from 2005 to 2006. He resigned amid charges of corruption on 21 March 2018.

Early Life

Pedro Pablo Kuczynski, popularly known as PPK, was born in Lima on 3 Oct. 1938. His parents, a German-Jewish physician and Swiss-French teacher, had fled to the Peruvian capital in 1936 to escape Nazism in Europe. In 1953 Kuczynski was sent to boarding school in England and in 1956 won a scholarship to read politics, philosophy and economics at Exeter College, Oxford. On graduating, he moved to the USA to study at Princeton University.

Kuczynski began his career at the World Bank in 1961. In 1967 he moved back to Peru to become director of the Central Bank under President Fernando

Belaúnde Terry. When the president was ousted in a coup in 1968, Kuczynski accepted a new position at the World Bank but returned as minister of energy and mines when Belaúnde regained power in 1980. In 1982 he left government to pick up his career in international finance and private equity. Kuczynski served two stints as minister of economy and finance (2001–02 and 2004–05) under President Alejandro Toledo, and then served as prime minister from 2005–06. In 2007 he founded a non-governmental organization dedicated to delivering clean water to Peru's remote communities.

In the 2011 presidential elections Kuczynski stood as the candidate for a coalition of centrist parties but finished behind Keiko Fujimori and the eventual winner, Ollanta Humala. After coming second in the first round of the 2016 elections, his candidacy was boosted by the support of centrist and leftist parties opposed to Fujimori. In the run-off poll on 5 June, for which turnout was 80.1%, he won 50.1% of the vote against 49.9% for Fujimori.

Career Peak

Kuczynski's legislative plans for economic and judicial reform have been obstructed by parliament as his centre-right party, Peruvians for Change, had secured only 18 of the 130 seats against 73 for Keiko Fujimori's opposition Fuerza Popular following the April 2016 elections. Fuerza Popular has also sought to implicate Kuczynski in a major construction corruption scandal, although in Dec. 2017 he narrowly survived an impeachment vote in Congress as his opponents failed to muster the two-thirds majority needed to oust him. Later that month Kuczynski granted a humanitarian pardon to Keito Fujimori's father Alberto, a former president from 1990 to 2000 who had been sentenced to 25 years imprisonment in 2009 for human rights crimes. Earlier, in Sept. 2017, Congress had dismissed Prime Minister Fernando Zavala, who was replaced by Second Vice-President Mercedes Aráoz. He resigned in March 2018 and was succeeded by Martín Vizcarra.

Kufuor, John (Ghana)

Introduction

John Kufuor became president of Ghana in Jan. 2001. Leader of the New Patriotic Party, his principal aim was to revitalize the country's struggling economy. Kufuor stepped down in Dec. 2008 having served the maximum permitted two 4-year terms.

Early Life

John Agyekum Kufuor was born on 8 Dec. 1938 in Kumasi, Ghana. He was called to the Bar at Lincoln's Inn in England in 1961, and graduated in politics, philosophy and economics from the University of Oxford in 1964.

In 1967 he became Kumasi's chief legal officer and town clerk, and the following year sat in the constituent assembly which drafted a new constitution. He held a similar role when another constitution followed 10 years later. In 1969 he was appointed deputy foreign minister but left parliament following the 1972 military coup, returning in 1979. In 1982 he became local government minister in Jerry Rawlings' national government, laying the groundwork for the country's system of decentralized district assemblies. He resigned after 7 months to pursue business interests.

In 1996 Kufuor unsuccessfully challenged Rawlings for the presidency, standing as the NPP candidate. In Oct. 1998 he was selected as leader of the NPP and again stood for the presidency in Dec. 2000. When no candidate achieved the 50% threshold for victory after the first round, Kufuor went into a run-off against the National Democratic Congress' John Atta Mills. Kufuor won the support of the five candidates who dropped out after the first round and won the election with 57%.

Career Peak

Taking office in Jan. 2001, Kufuor aimed to lead Ghana into an economic 'golden age.' He faced inflation at over 40%, interest rates at over 50% and the collapse of the cedi, the national currency. By May 2002 inflation was down to 14%, interest rates down to 26% and the cedi had stabilized. However, the government's withdrawal of fuel subsidies saw petrol prices increase by 60% and the price of utilities also rocketed. In April 2001 Ghana received major debt relief under a World Bank/IMF scheme and in May 2002 the African Development Bank wrote off 80% of the country's debts. The relief was seen as a reward for Kufuor's handling of the economy.

His tenure was marked by continued tribal conflict, particularly in the north of the country, where a state of emergency was declared in April 2002. In May 2001 Kufuor declared a national day of mourning after 126 people died during a stampede at a soccer match, for which the police were heavily criticized. In June 2001 Accra experienced severe flooding which forced 100,000 people from their homes.

Kufuor did much to distance himself from the Jerry Rawlings era. In 2001 the government abandoned public holidays celebrating Rawlings' 1979 coup. In May 2002 he instituted a reconciliation committee to investigate allegations of human rights abuses during Rawlings' rule. He also attempted to improve relations with Ghana's West African neighbours.

In Dec. 2004 Kufuor was re-elected as president with 52.5% of the vote in the second round. The NPP meanwhile secured a majority of seats in parliamentary elections.

Kufuor was chairman of the African Union for a 1-year term of office in 2007. Ghana celebrated 50 years of independence from Britain in March 2007, and the discovery of a major offshore oilfield was announced in June of the same year. However, in Sept. 2007 the country experienced its worst flooding for more than 30 years.

Kufuor was succeeded in Dec. 2008 by John Atta Mills, who narrowly won a run-off vote against Nana Akufo-Addo of Kufuor's New Patriotic Party. Mills had been defeated by Kufuor in the two previous elections.

Kumaratunga, Chandrika Bandaranaike (Sri Lanka)

Introduction

Chandrika Bandaranaike Kumaratunga came to power in 1994. Both her parents served as prime ministers. Her mother, Sirimavo Bandaranaike, became the world's first female prime minister in 1961 while her father, Solomon West Ridgeway Dias Bandaranaike, served as prime minister from 1956 until his death in 1959. Kumaratunga frequently clashed with Ranil Wickremasinghe's United National Front (UNF) government (Dec. 2001–April 2004). A constitutionally empowered prime minister, Wickremasinghe forced a reluctant Kumaratunga to negotiate a peace settlement with Tamil rebels. Her party defeated the UNF in 2004 elections, allowing her to install the moderate Mahinda Rajapakse as prime minister. Rajapakse went on to succeed Kumaratunga as president in 2005. A widow by her husband's assassination in 1988, Chandrika Kumaratunga has a son and daughter.

Early Life

Chandrika Kumaratunga was born on 29 June 1945. After receiving a convent education at St Bridget's school, Colombo, she studied at Aquinas University College, Colombo, and then at the Institute of Political Studies, Paris. As a student she took part in and was influenced by the student riots of 1968. Graduating with a diploma in international relations, she began working towards a PhD in development economics. When her mother's government launched a land reform programme, Kumaratunga left France to serve as a director and then as principal director of the land reforms commission (1972–76), on behalf of the nationalist Sri Lanka Freedom Party (SLFP). Conflict between her socialist ideals and her mother's nationalist policies prompted her departure from the party along with her film-star/politician husband, Vijaya Kumaratunga, whom she married in 1978.

In 1986 she became president of the Sri Lanka Mahajana Party (SLMP), founded 2 years earlier by her husband. Following his assassination in 1988, Chandrika Kumaratunga became the leader of a four-party coalition, the United Socialist Alliance (USA). By the early 1990s, however, she had rejoined the SLFP which headed a coalition of left wing parties, the People's Alliance (PA). When provincial council elections were held in May 1993, Kumaratunga was returned for the Western province and appointed chief minister.

In Aug. 1994 she was prime ministerial candidate for the People's Alliance. The PA won the parliamentary elections and formed a government on 19 Aug. 1994 with Kumaratunga as prime minister. In the presidential elections of Nov. 1994, Kumaratunga was elected by an overwhelming majority to become the country's first female president. She appointed her mother as prime minister in a largely ceremonial role.

Career Peak

The PA toppled the United National Party (UNP), ending its 17 years of power. Although there was initial optimism regarding a settlement of the Tamil-Sinhalese ethnic conflict, this soon subsided. The Liberation Tigers of Tamil Eelam (LTTE) violated a 100-day truce while opposition groups in parliament stood against Kumaratunga's plans to devolve increased power to the northeastern region's Tamil population. An approach which at first coupled dialogue with the LTTE with their suppression by the Sri Lankan army gave way to all-out war. In Dec. 1995 Sri Lankan government forces captured the Jaffna peninsula. With violence continuing unabated Kumaratunga declared a state of emergency in April 1996. This was only partially successful and in 1999 Kumaratunga's government called for Norway to act as an independent mediator.

Presidential elections were held in Dec. 1999. In the run-up Kumaratunga was in a suicide bomb attack. 20 people were killed but Kumaratunga survived with minor injuries to her right eye. She capitalized on this by giving a television address to the nation wearing an eye patch. Winning by a narrow margin a second consecutive term as president, she lost out in the general election held in Dec. 2001 when her main political rival, Ranil Wickremasinghe, whom she had defeated in the earlier presidential elections, pledged to reduce presidential powers if his party, the United National Party (UNP), formed the government. The UNP won 109 seats against 77 for Kumaratunga's People's Alliance party. As prime minister, Wickremasinghe demanded freedom to appoint a cabinet of his choice. Kumaratunga was forced to give up control of the ministries of defence and finance, whilst retaining her title as commander-in-chief of the armed forces.

The elections, which placed in power a prime minister and president of opposing parties for the first time in 7 years, were viewed as an opportunity to move towards a peace-deal. A ceasefire was agreed in Dec. 2001 but Kumaratunga then criticized Wickremasinghe's confidence building measures with the LTTE. She also complained that the Norwegian mediators had overstepped their role by applying a demarcation line between government-controlled and LTTE-controlled areas and that this constituted an attack on Sri Lanka's sovereignty. Despite threats that she could, as commander-in-chief of the army, end the peace-deal whenever she wanted, Kumaratunga reluctantly followed Wickremasinghe's initiatives. In Sept. 2002, under pressure from the prime minister, she conceded to the lifting of the ban on the LTTE, a step which laid the ground for subsequent peace talks. In Dec. 2002 the government and LTTE signed a peace deal granting the Tamil population autonomy.

Kumaratunga created political turmoil in Nov. 2003 by removing three key portfolios from cabinet ministers and by proroguing parliament for two weeks. The defence, interior and information ministries were put under presidential control while the prime minister was meeting the US president, George W. Bush, in Washington, D.C. Citing national security interests for her actions, Kumaratunga declared a 10-day state of emergency on 6 Nov., condemned by the speaker of parliament, the prime minister, and the LTTE's Velupillai Prabhakaran. By the end of the month, Prabhakaran had threatened to resume the struggle for Tamil independence if the president and prime minister could not work together on the peace process.

On 13 Jan. 2004 Kumaratunga held a secret swearing-in ceremony to extend her term of office until the end of 2006. Heavily criticized by the prime minister, she defended the extra year by claiming it from her previous term, cut short by early elections in 1999. Kumaratunga furthered jeopardized the peace process by forging an alliance later that month with an extreme left-wing Sinhalese party, the People's United Liberation Front (JVP), which had voiced its opposition to Tamil autonomy. Prabhakaran condemned the alliance and a potential military agreement with India that would supply the Sri Lankan army. Dissolving parliament in Feb. 2004, Kumaratunga called early elections for 2 April. Her United People's Freedom Alliance took the most seats in parliament, defeating Prime Minister Wickremasinghe's party and forcing him to resign. She appointed Mahinda Rajapakse, her party's leader in parliament and a former fisheries minister, as prime minister. Rajapakse declared that he would seek constitutional reform to implement a parliamentary system and that he would cede the premiership to Kumaratunga.

The Supreme Court rejected Kumaratunga's claim to office until the end of 2006 and her term came to an end in Nov. 2005. on 18 Nov. 2005 she was succeeded as president by PM Rajapaske.

Kvirikashvili, Giorgi (Georgia)

Introduction

Giorgi Kvirikashvili became prime minister on 30th Dec. 2015 following Irakli Garibashvili's resignation the week before. He retained office following the Georgian Dream coalition's parliamentary election victory in Oct. 2016.

Early Life

Born in Tbilisi on 20 July 1967, Kvirikashvili graduated in medicine from the Tbilisi State Medical University in 1992. Three years later he received a degree in economics from the Tbilisi State University, followed by a master's degree in finance from the University of Illinois in the USA in 1998. From 1993–99 he also held executive positions at various banks.

In 1999, having won a parliamentary seat representing the New Rights party, Kvirikashvili joined the State Chancellery. However, following the 2003 'Rose Revolution' he returned to the banking sector. From 2006–11 he was chief executive of the Cartu Bank which was owned by business tycoon and future prime minister, Bidzina Ivanishvili. When the Georgian Dream coalition took power in Oct. 2012, Kvirikashvili was appointed minister of economy and sustainable development in Ivanishvili's cabinet. In July 2013 he also took the post of deputy prime minister, and in Sept. 2015 was named minister for foreign affairs. On 25 Dec. 2015 Georgian Dream named Kvirikashvili as Garibashvili's replacement as premier, and his candidature was confirmed in a parliamentary vote on 29 Dec.

Career Peak

Kvirikashvili was expected to continue implementing the policies pledged by Georgian Dream in 2012. These have included pursuing closer ties with the USA and the European Union, with a view to eventual EU and NATO membership. He also reiterated the need for a pragmatic approach to rebuilding relations with Russia. In economic terms, he is an advocate of privatization. His critics, however, have questioned his lack of front-line political experience and the extent of background influence Ivanishvili continues to yield over the government. The Georgian Dream coalition increased its representation in parliamentary elections in Oct. 2016, taking 115 of the 150 seats. In Oct. 2017 parliament approved constitutional changes promoting a more parliamentary system of government despite an earlier attempt to veto the legislation by President Margvelashvili. Kvirikashvili championed the amendments, claiming that they marked a major step forward in the democratic development of the country. He resigned on 13 June 2018 after relations with his own party deteriorated over his cabinet's economic policy.

Kwaśniewski, Aleksander (Poland)

Introduction

Aleksander Kwaśniewski became post-communist Poland's second president in 1995 and won a second term in 2000. His efforts to take Poland into the EU and NATO appeased leaders in Europe and the US who were worried about his communist past. As required by the constitution, he stood down from office at the end of his second term in Dec. 2005.

Early Life

Kwaśniewski was born on 15 Nov. 1954 in Bialogard in the northwest of Poland. He graduated in economics from Gdańsk University where he became active in communist politics. In 1977 he joined the Polish United Workers' Party and edited party publications in Warsaw until 1985. He then joined the council of ministers and 2 years later was appointed minister of youth affairs and physical culture. He married Jolanta Konty in 1979, with whom he has one child.

As communism lost its grip throughout Eastern Europe in the late 1980s, Kwaśniewski was part of the round table discussions (incorporating the church, Solidarity and other political groups) that paved the way for free elections. Following the dissolution of the United Workers' Party, he founded the Democratic Left Alliance which counted many former communists in its membership. It emerged as the largest party from the 1993 elections and Kwaśniewski formed a coalition with the Peasant Party, which itself had a large number of former communists.

At the presidential elections of 1995 Kwaśniewski stood against Lech Wałęsa, the Solidarity leader whose popularity had rapidly declined while in office. Kwaśniewski won and took office in Dec. 1995.

Career Peak

Kwaśniewski's communist heritage caused concern among many Western leaders but he confirmed his intention to press for EU and NATO membership. Market reforms and privatization continued apace. In 1999, at a joint ceremony with Czech president Vaclav Havel, Kwaśniewski signed Poland into NATO.

He consistently disassociated himself from his communist past and in 1998 promised to renew citizenship to Jews forced to flee during the pogrom of 1968. Also in 1998 Kwaśniewski formalized relations with the Vatican. However, he clashed with the church in 2000 when he refused to ratify an anti-pornography bill, claiming that sex education should be employed rather than censorship. Relations with the Vatican further deteriorated later in the year when a video was released of a close aid of Kwaśniewski mocking the pope.

In the build-up to the presidential elections of Oct. 2000 Kwaśniewski was accused of complicity with the secret police during the communist era but was subsequently cleared. He was re-elected to the presidency after one round of voting. In Oct. 2002 Poland was one of ten countries included in plans for EU expansion in 2004. Membership won 77% backing in a national referendum in June 2003.

Prime Minister Leszek Miller resigned on 2 May 2004, a day after accession to the EU. Kwaśniewski designated Finance Minister Marek Belka to succeed him. Belka was initially rejected by the Sejm but was confirmed as prime minister in June 2004. Kwaśniewski remained in office until his term ended on 23 Dec. 2005, when he handed power to his elected successor, Lech Kaczyński.

Later Life

Kwaśniewski is president of the board of Amicus Europae—an organization that he had founded in 2004 while still president of Poland to support European integration and to promote dialogue and reconciliation as a method of resolving political and regional conflicts.

In March 2006 he was appointed distinguished scholar in the practice of global leadership at Georgetown University. In Oct. 2008 he became chairman of the new European Council on Tolerance and Reconciliation, staying in the role until 2015 when he was succeeded by former British prime minister Tony Blair.

Between June 2012 and Nov. 2013 Kwaśniewski also co-led the European Parliament monitoring mission in Ukraine that aimed at monitoring criminal cases against former Ukrainian prime minister Yulia Tymoshenko, Yuriy Lutsenko and Valeriy Ivaschenko.

Lagos Escobar, Ricardo (Chile)

Introduction

Elected in 2000, Ricardo Lagos Escobar became the first Socialist president of Chile since Salvador Allende Gossens (1970–73), and the third consecutive Coalition of Parties for Democracy (CPD; Concertación de los Partidos por la Democracia) leader. On election Lagos had to cope with a severe recession and charges of corruption against outgoing president Eduardo Frei Ruíz-Tagle and his Christian Democrat Party (PDC; Partido Demócrata Cristiana), which forms part of the Coalition. He also faced the emotive issue of trying former dictator Gen. Augusto Pinochet Ugarte for human rights abuses.

Early Life

Lagos was born in the Chilean capital, Santiago, on 2 March 1938. The son of a farmer, he studied law at the Universidad de Chile before gaining a doctorate in economics from Duke University in North Carolina. In the 1960s Lagos became a member of the Socialist Party of Chile (PS; Partido Socialista de Chile). Between 1967–72 he continued his academic career at the Universidad de Chile, working as director of the economics school. In 1973 he was appointed by Allende's administration as Chile's ambassador to the Soviet Union.

Following the military coup led by Pinochet, Lagos lived in exile in the USA. After working at the University of North Carolina, he worked for the UN as an economist between 1978–84. On his return to Chile, he re-entered politics in opposition to Pinochet. He succeeded the PDC's Andrés Zaldívar Larraín as president of the opposition alliance known as the 'democratic opposition'. winning 71% of votes. In 1986 Lagos was imprisoned following an assassination attempt on Pinochet in which five of his bodyguards were killed. Lagos was held without charge, but was released after 19 days due to strong international pressure. As the PS was outlawed under the regime, in 1987 Lagos formed the Party for Democracy (PPD; Partido por la Democracia), a coalition of parties opposed to Pinochet.

In 1988 Lagos made a televised attack on Pinochet's rule. He called on people to overcome their fears and vote against Pinochet in the 1989 elections. At the end of 1988, the PPD joined the newly-formed CPD. The centrist coalition backed the candidature of the PDC leader Patricio Aylwin Azócar. Under Aylwin's administration, Lagos served as minister for education during which time he overturned a rule barring pregnant girls from education. From 1994–98 he served as minister for public works under Frei. Reforms included improved communication networks with Chile's neighbouring countries.

Career Peak

In the Dec. 1999 presidential elections, Lagos stood against the right-wing Independent Democratic Union (UDI; Unión Demócrata Independiente) representative, Joaquín Lavín Infante. Serving as an economist under Pinochet, Lavín was a long-time supporter of the regime. Even so, both campaigns promised similar policies, including job creation and the alleviation of rural poverty and street crime. Lagos received 47.96% of votes to Lavín's 47.52%, the strongest showing for the right since Pinochet's dictatorship. A run-off election was held on 16 Jan. 2000. The turnout was 7·3 m. voters out of a possible 8 m. Lagos took 51.3% of votes and Lavín conceded defeat with 48.7%.

On his election Lagos pledged to reform the labour code, increase the minimum wage, introduce unemployment insurance and provide better health care, education and housing. He also promised to abolish constitutional privileges, such as those extended to the 10 non-elected senators (including Pinochet) appointed by the military government, and announced performance targets for cabinet members. He made it clear that the prosecution of Pinochet was not a high priority, saying it was up to the courts to try him, not the government. Lagos meanwhile had to tackle the fall-out from the worst recession in Chile since the early 1980s, the result of a collapse in the price of copper.

Chile's economy improved during his first few months in power, although the second half of 2000 proved less optimistic. Despite a growth of 5.5% in GDP and a 20% increase in exports, unemployment increased to 10.7% from 8.4% in Jan. 2000. In the Oct. 2000 municipal elections, the CPD held an overall majority, although Santiago was won by the right-wing.

In March 2003 Lagos' government faced allegations of financial corruption after the executive vice president of Corfo, the state business development agency, was forced to resign and the head of Corfo's treasury department was charged with fraud. The scandal followed the criminal investigation in 2002 of several parliamentarians, including two former ministers, who had accepted bribes. Lagos refused the resignation of economics minister Jorge Rodriguez in March 2003, but investor confidence was nevertheless damaged.

In Aug. 2005 Lagos endorsed a bill embodying a series of constitutional reforms, effectively eliminating the remaining political influence of the military. The reforms cut the presidential term from 6 to 4 years, ended designated senators and senators for life, reduced the powers of the National Security Council, and restored power to the president to remove the armed forces' commanders.

In Jan. 2006, a month after the 2005 elections, Lagos was succeeded in office by Michelle Bachelet.

Later Life

In May 2007 Lagos was appointed as a United Nations Special Envoy on Climate Change.

Lahoud, Emile (Lebanon)

Introduction

Emile Lahoud was sworn in as president on 24 Nov. 1998. As commander of the armed forces, his election on 15 Oct. required a constitutional amendment as serving state officials were formerly prohibited from standing for the presidency. His mandate was extended for a further 3 years from Sept. 2004 under a constitutional amendment approved by parliament. On 23 Nov. 2007 Lahoud controversially declared a 'state of emergency'. handing over power to the army, leaving a political vacuum in Lebanon.

Early Life

Born in 1936 in Baabdat, Emile Lahoud was educated at Brumana High School before joining the Military Academy as a cadet officer in 1956. Between 1958–80 he attended courses at naval academies in the UK and USA as he progressed through the ranks to captain. By 1985 he was a rear-admiral and on 28 Nov. 1989 was promoted to general and commander of the armed forces at the start of Elias Haraoui's presidency.

Career Peak

Credited with rebuilding the Lebanese armed forces and restraining the warring militias that held sway in 1975–90, Lahoud was a respected public figure by the time of his election as president in Nov. 1998. He secured the votes of 118 deputies of the 128-member National Assembly, reflecting his wide acceptance across sectarian lines. The early part of his presidency saw the completion of Israel's military withdrawal from south Lebanon in May 2000. His term of office was originally set to end in late 2004, but was extended for a further 3 years when the parliament approved a controversial constitutional amendment (believed to have been influenced by Syria) in Sept. 2004. In Feb. 2005 the former prime minister Rafiq al-Hariri was killed by a massive car bomb in Beirut. The assassination caused a series of anti-Syrian rallies, which led to calls for Syria to withdraw its troops, and Lahoud came under pressure to resign. In April 2005 Syria claimed to have withdrawn all its military forces, as demanded by the United Nations.

In Nov. 2006 the pro-Syrian president indicated that he would not support a plan for an international tribunal to try suspects in the murder of al-Hariri (a United Nations inquiry having already implicated Syrian officials in the killing). Lahoud also claimed that Prime Minister Siniora's cabinet lacked sectarian balance following the resignation of a number of Shia Muslim ministers and called for a new government of national unity.

On 23 Nov. 2007 Lahoud declared a 'state of emergency'. deciding to hand power over to the army when his mandate expired after the government failed to elect a head of state. Rival leaders have agreed on Gen. Michel Suleiman as the consensus candidate to fill the presidency in the next vote. Under the Lebanese sectarian power-sharing system the president is elected by Parliament, not by popular vote, and must be a Maronite Christian.

Lavaka Ata 'Ulukalala (Tonga)

Introduction

After only a year's experience in government, Prince Lavaka Ata 'Ulukalala was appointed prime minister by his father, King Taufa'ahau Tupou IV, in Jan. 2000. He left office 6 years later amid pressure for less royal influence in government.

Early Life

Prince Lavaka ata 'Ulukalala was born on 12 July 1959 in Nuku'alofa, capital of what was then the British protectorate of Tonga. He is the youngest son of King Taufa'ahau Tupou IV and Queen Halaevalu Mata'aho. In 1981 Prince Lavaka joined the naval arm of the Tongan defence services, where he served for several years before enrolling at the US Naval War College in Newport, Rhode Island. He graduated with a diploma in strategic studies in 1988 and from 1991–95 he was commander of the Tongan navy.

Having gained an MA in defence studies from the University of New South Wales, Australia (1997) and an MA in international relations from Bond University, Queensland (1998), Prince Lavaka entered politics. He took over the portfolios for foreign affairs and defence from his brother, Crown Prince Tupouto'a, who resigned after 25 years in office to pursue business interests. Following the resignation of Prime Minister Baron Vaea on 3 Jan. 2000, the king (as both head of state and of government) appointed Prince Lavaka to succeed him.

Career Peak

By 2004 Prince Lavaka was also minister for agriculture and forestry, fisheries, marine and ports, civil aviation, communications, works and disaster relief activities. In March 2005, in the face of increasing public pressure, four additional ministers were appointed from the elected members of parliament. This step towards reform was well received. However, a series of pro-democracy protests demanding less royal involvement in government led to Prince Lavaka tendering his resignation on 11 Feb. 2006. He was succeeded by Feleti Sevele, Tonga's first non-noble prime minister.

Lee Kuan Yew (Singapore)

Introduction

Although he continued to hold the official title of Senior Minister until May 2011, Lee Kuan Yew was the first prime minister and architect of a modern and independent Singapore. Taking office in 1959, the multilingual Lee recreated Singapore as an economic powerhouse. However, Lee was criticized for repressive and authoritarian social and political policies. He was married to Kwa Geok Choo and had three children.

Early Life

Born on 16 Sept. 1923, Lee Kuan Yew was educated in Singapore at the Raffles Institution and Raffles College before moving to the UK to study at the London School of Economics and to read law at the University of Cambridge. Upon his return to Singapore in 1949 he began his career by practising law.

In Nov. 1954 he helped to found the socialist People's Action Party (PAP), of which he became secretary-general; he won a seat in the 1955 general elections. After Singapore had achieved full internal self-government in 1959, the PAP was elected the majority party in a new Legislative Assembly. On 5 June of that year Lee Kuan Yew was sworn in as Prime Minister of Singapore.

Career Peak

After Singapore left the Federation of Malaysia, 2 years after its inception in 1963, and the announcement of British withdrawal from its bases in 1968, he embarked on an ambitious economic programme that transformed Singapore from a trade distribution centre to a high-tech producer nation.

He raised the quantity and quality of the output by introducing new labour laws, improving education and exercising a high degree of control over the welfare state. The economic and social stability that followed supported foreign investor confidence, while both foreign and domestic enterprise was encouraged through subsidies and tax concessions. In the early 1970s, Singapore reached almost full employment.

While Lee did much to promote ethnic and cultural diversity with, for instance, the creation of the Constitutional Commission on Minority Rights in late 1965, Singapore's predominantly one-party state has come under severe criticism from those who advocate greater political freedom. Following Lee's voluntary resignation in 1990, the Singaporean government appointed him as senior minister; a largely symbolic post.

Later Life

Lee Kuan Yew's son, Lee Hsien Loong, became Singapore's third prime minister on 12 Aug. 2004. Lee Kuan Yew held the post of Minister Mentor in his son's administration until retiring from the cabinet in May 2011 at the age of 87.

Lee died aged 91 on 23 March 2015.

Lee Myung-bak (South Korea)

Introduction

Lee Myung-bak made his name by playing a key role in establishing Hyundai among the world's leading industrial firms. He was elected president in Dec. 2007, promising to revitalize the economy and resurrect close ties with the USA. However, his term in office proved difficult amid financial and currency turmoil and turbulent relations with North Korea.

Early Life

Lee Myung-bak was born on 19 Dec. 1941 near Osaka, Japan, where his Korean parents worked as farm labourers. The family moved to Pohang in the newly liberated southern Korea in 1946, with Lee attending Dongji Commercial High School. He studied business administration at Korea University in Seoul, financed in part by his work as a street cleaner.

A politically active student, Lee served a short prison term for demonstrating against the normalization of South Korea's diplomatic links with Japan. As a result, he struggled to find employment but was taken on by a then small manufacturing company, Hyundai Engineering. He became its youngest chief executive officer at the age of 35 and was chairman at 46. Known as 'the Bulldozer', Lee pushed through a range of large-scale construction projects that underpinned the country's transformation from a poor agricultural economy to a major industrial power. Hyundai became one of the region's most powerful conglomerates, with around 160,000 staff by the time Lee left in 1992. During the boom years of the 1970s and 1980s, Lee became a wealthy property owner.

Lee entered political life in the 1992 parliamentary elections with the then ruling conservative New Korea Party, the predecessor of the Grand National Party (GNP, formed in 1997). He contested the mayorship of Seoul in 1995 but lost to the former prime minister, Chung Wong-sik. Lee subsequently spent a year as a visiting professor at George Washington University in the USA.

On his return to South Korea, Lee established several companies specializing in internet-based financial services. In 2002 he returned to public life when he was elected mayor of Seoul. Over the next 5 years he earned plaudits for his campaigns to regenerate the city by investing in parks and open spaces and public transport. The restoration of the Cheonggye stream, which had been submerged by concrete in the 1970s, provoked protest but has become one of Seoul's most popular attractions. In 2007 he was named a 'hero of the environment' by *Time* magazine.

In May 2007 Lee declared his intention to run for the presidency of the right-leaning opposition GNP. Three months later he defeated Park Guen-hye in the party's primary. His campaign centred on economic issues, including the ambitious '747' plan aiming to achieve 7% annual GDP growth and to double average GDP per head to US\$40,000 to advance South Korea from the world's 11th to seventh largest economy over the next decade.

Lee's fondness for large-scale infrastructure projects was underlined by plans to build a canal between Seoul and the port of Busan, which he has claimed would create 300,000 jobs, improve and diversify the transport system and revitalize the country's interior. He also floated a plan to create a Korean high-tech version of Silicon Valley in the central region of Chungcheongnam. Much of his campaign was dogged by allegations of involvement in stock market price manipulation in 2001. He denied the charges and was formally cleared of fraud in Feb. 2008 after an investigation by an independent counsel. Lee won a landslide victory in the presidential election of 19 Dec. 2007, defeating Chung Dong-young of the United New Democratic Party.

Career Peak

Lee was sworn in as president on 25 Feb. 2008. He promised to slash economic regulations, initiate tax reforms, streamline government and attract foreign investment. He also pledged to strengthen ties with the USA and hinted at a tougher line than his predecessor, Roh Moo-hyun, in relations with North Korea. In April 2008 Lee's GNP won an overall parliamentary majority in elections to the National Assembly. However, his poll ratings then fell markedly in the wake of his unpopular agreement to resume US beef imports (suspended since 2003 on health grounds) and also the impact of the global credit crisis which led the government to announce a US$130bn. intervention package in Oct. 2008 to support the banking system and stabilize financial markets. In Feb. 2009 the central bank reduced interest rates to a record low as the economy faced its first contraction in over a decade, and in April the GNP suffered a crushing defeat in parliamentary by-elections. In Sept. 2009 Lee replaced his prime minister in a cabinet reshuffle and also removed the defence minister, with whom he had clashed over military spending. In June 2010 the GNP suffered a major defeat in local elections, heralding further senior cabinet changes including the prime minister in Aug.–Sept.

Meanwhile, relations with North Korea remained unpredictable and volatile. In Jan. 2009 the North announced that it was abandoning all military and political agreements signed with South Korea because of the latter's 'hostile intent'. Then in May the North conducted its second nuclear weapon test and declared that it was no longer bound by the armistice that ended the Korean War, heightening tensions further. However, later in the year Pyongyang made some conciliatory gestures towards Lee's government, including agreeing to resume a programme of family reunions suspended since 2008 and indicating a willingness to return to multilateral talks on its nuclear programme. But in 2010 hostilities again reignited as forces from both sides exchanged artillery fire near their disputed maritime border in Jan., a South Korean naval vessel was sunk allegedly by the North in March and the North launched an artillery attack on a small South Korean island close to the two countries' maritime border in Nov. North–South contacts eventually resumed in July 2011 as envoys from each side held their first nuclear talks since the collapse of negotiations in 2009.

In Aug. 2012 Japanese–South Korean relations deteriorated as a result of Lee's visit to the Liancourt Rocks, islets over which both countries claim sovereignty. He subsequently stated that the Japanese Emperor should not visit South Korea unless he apologized to the victims of Japan's past colonialism. Japan temporarily recalled its ambassador in Seoul.

Term limitations prevented Lee from seeking re-election at the Dec. 2012 presidential elections. Shortly before leaving office in Feb. 2013, Lee issued controversial pardons, triggering nationwide criticism.

Leterme, Yves (Belgium)

Introduction

Yves Camille Désiré Leterme first served as prime minister from March to Dec. 2008 and became premier for the second time in Nov. 2009, replacing Herman Van Rompuy who had resigned to become the first president of the European Council. The Flemish Leterme was leader of the Christian Democratic and Flemish Party (CD&V) and a former minister-president of Flanders. He served in a caretaker capacity since April 2010 when his fragile coalition government collapsed over a long-simmering linguistic dispute between Belgium's Flemish and French-speaking politicians, triggering early parliamentary elections. The elections proved inconclusive and negotiations over the formation of a new coalition remained deadlocked until King Albert II appointed a new prime minister in Dec. 2011.

Early Life

Yves Leterme was born in Wervik, West Flanders on 6 Oct. 1960. Brought up by his Dutch-speaking Flemish mother and French-speaking Walloon father, he is bilingual. He went to school in Ypres before graduating in law from the

Catholic University of Leuven in 1981. After obtaining a BSc in political sciences from Ghent University, he earned an LLB in law and then a master's in public administration. In 1984 he also completed a postgraduate course at the International Centre for European Training.

After becoming involved in local youth politics, the Christian People's Party (CVP) invited Leterme to join them and in 1983 he became the chairman of the Youth-CVP Ypres group. He worked closely with the CVP for the next decade, supporting two CVP regional parliamentarians, acting as Ypres district CVP secretary (1985–87) and then serving as national vice-secretary (1989–91) and national secretary (1991–92). He worked at the Court of Audits for 2 years (1987–89) and in 1992 became a civil servant at the European Commission, where he stayed for 5 years. During this period he remained politically active, becoming a municipal councillor in 1995 and an MP in 1997. In 2001 he became head of the CD&V (ex-CVP) faction in the Chamber of Representatives and in 2003 he was elected party leader.

In 2004 Leterme was appointed minister-president of the Flemish government. There he made significant strides in eliminating the government's debt and introducing public-private partnerships as a means of boosting investment. Following the CD&V success in the June 2007 elections, King Albert invited Leterme to negotiate a coalition while Guy Verhofstadt remained as caretaker prime minister. Negotiations faltered over constitutional reforms aimed at devolving powers to the Dutch-, French- and German-speaking communities, with Leterme twice threatening to resign before talks finally failed. From Dec. 2007–March 2008 he served as minister of budget, transport, institutional reform and the North Sea (focusing on environmental issues).

Career Peak

Leterme finally assumed the premiership in March 2008, serving for 9 months at the head of a five-party coalition. The central challenge he faced was pushing through reforms to allow greater independence for the separate language groups, most crucially in the Brussels-Halle-Vilvoorde region. His policy was widely rejected by the francophone community. Back in 2006 Leterme had angered parts of the Walloon community after a series of public relations blunders, including his comment that 'apparently the French speakers are intellectually not capable of learning Dutch'. He was subsequently caught out in an interview when he wrongly identified the francophone Belgian national anthem. Nonetheless, his personal popularity remained high.

Leterme's failure to achieve a consensus on language reforms prompted him to offer his resignation in July 2008, which was refused by King Albert. In Sept. 2008, amid the worsening global economic climate, Belgium (together with the Netherlands and Luxembourg) agreed to inject funds into the ailing Fortis regional retail bank and (with France and Luxembourg) to rescue Dexia Bank, the world's biggest lender to local governments. The following month saw a nationwide strike over rising prices. On 19 Dec. 2008 Leterme again offered his resignation as a crisis grew over the sale of Fortis Bank to BNP Paribas, with shareholders taking the government to court over lack of consultation. His resignation, and that of the entire government, was accepted on 22 Dec. He remained in office until 30 Dec. 2008 when he was succeeded by Herman Van Rompuy, also of the CD&V.

In a cabinet reshuffle in July 2009 Leterme was named foreign minister. In this post he established bilateral relations with Vietnam, making it the only Asian country with preferential trade agreements with Belgium. Leterme became prime minister for a second time in Nov. 2009 after Van Rompuy was elected the first president of the European Council. Though he maintained his commitment to institutional reform, Leterme's main challenges were economic. In Jan. 2010 Opel revealed it was closing one of its factories and InBev announced a 10% workforce cut.

In April 2010 the Open Vld party withdrew from the ruling coalition causing the collapse of the government. Leterme remained in office as caretaker prime minister. Early parliamentary elections were held in June but subsequent inter-party negotiations to construct a new coalition government proved unsuccessful. On 13 Sept. 2011 Leterme announced that he would leave the post of caretaker prime minister by the end of the year to become deputy secretary-general at the Organisation for Economic Co-operation and Development. After a record 541 days without a government, King Albert II named Elio Di Rupo as prime minister on 6 Dec. The following day Leterme was appointed to the honorary title of Minister of State.

Later Life

Following his departure from public office, Leterme became a deputy secretary general of the Organisation for Economic Co-operation and Development (OECD), serving from Dec. 2011–June 2014. In June 2014 he was appointed secretary general of the International Institute for Democracy and Electoral Assistance (IDEA).

Letta, Enrico (Italy)

Introduction

Enrico Letta was prime minister from April 2013–Feb. 2014, heading a grand coalition of his centre-left Democratic Party (PD) and Silvio Berlusconi's centre-right People of Freedom Party (PdL). Letta's appointment followed 2 months of post-electoral negotiation.

Early Life

Born on 20 Aug. 1966 in Pisa, Letta studied international law at the University of Pisa and completed a PhD in European Community law at the city's Sant'Anna School of Advanced Studies. Having joined Christian Democracy (DC), from 1991–95 he was president of the umbrella organization Youth of the European People's Party. He also worked for the Agency of Research and Legislation think tank, becoming its secretary general in 1993.

After the demise of the DC in 1994, Letta joined the successor Italian People's Party (PPI). In Nov. 1998 he was appointed minister of European affairs in the government of Massimo D'Alema before taking on the industry portfolio from 1999–2001. He was elected to parliament in 2001 representing Democracy is Freedom–The Daisy Party (DL), into which the PPI had merged. From 2001–04 he was the DL's shadow minister for economic policy.

From 2004–06 he sat in the European Parliament, serving on the committee for economic and monetary affairs. In 2006 he returned to national politics, joining Romano Prodi's centre-left coalition government. When the DL became part of the newly formed PD in 2007, Letta challenged for the leadership but secured only 11% of the vote. In 2008 he won a parliamentary seat and in 2009 became the PD's deputy leader under Pier Luigi Bersani. During the 2011–13 tenure of Prime Minister Mario Monti, Letta broadly supported the premier's programme of fiscal austerity.

In the inconclusive general election of Feb. 2013, the PD emerged as the largest party in the Chamber of Deputies. After 2 months of political deadlock and the rejection of successive presidential nominees, Bersani and the rest of the PD leadership resigned. In April 2013 President Giorgio Napolitano nominated Letta as prime minister at the head of a grand coalition of the PD and the PdL.

Career Peak

Letta was sworn in on 28 April 2013, having assembled a cabinet composed of figures from the left and right. He urged that policies to boost growth should run alongside existing fiscal austerity measures. As well as reviving the economy, he has faced the challenge of restoring public confidence in government while balancing the demands of his own party against those of the PdL. His task has been further complicated by Italy's reliance on economic support from the European Union and other international financial institutions.

In Oct. 2013, following the resignation of several of Berlusconi's centre-right ministers, Letta called for a confidence vote to keep the government alive. Berlusconi ultimately decided to support Letta and the government survived the confidence vote by 235 votes to 70. Berlusconi was subsequently expelled from the Senate following his earlier conviction for tax fraud.

Letta resigned as prime minister on 13 Feb. 2014 after the PD voted in favour of a new government. The party's secretary, Matteo Renzi, who had led criticism of Letta's failure to both push through bureaucratic reforms and improve the economy, was subsequently asked to form a government by president Giorgio Napolitano. He was sworn in as Letta's replacement on 22 Feb. 2014.

Later Life

In Sept. 2015 Letta became Dean of the Paris School of International Affairs at the Paris Institute of Political Studies (Sciences Po).

Leung Chun-ying (Hong Kong, China)

Introduction

Leung Chun-ying was sworn in as chief executive on 1 July 2012.

Early Life

Leung Chun-ying was born on 12 Aug. 1954 in Hong Kong and studied valuation and estate management at Bristol Polytechnic (now the University of the West of England) in the United Kingdom. In 1977 he returned to Hong Kong and worked for 5 years for the British real estate company, Jones Lang Wootton. In 1988 he was elected secretary-general of the Basic Law Consultative Committee, tasked with easing Hong Kong's transition to Chinese control in 1997.

In 1993 Leung established his own surveying company and was president of the Hong Kong Institute of Surveyors from 1995–96. He also served as an advisor to the governments of Shenzhen, Tianjian, Shanghai and Hebei province. In 1997 he became minister for housing before becoming leader of Hong Kong's Executive Council in 1999, a post he held until 2011. He was also a member of the Chinese People's Political Consultative Conference parliamentary body. He was chosen as chief executive of Hong Kong on 25 March 2012 with 689 of 1132 votes cast by the election committee.

Career Peak

Leung took office amid controversy over his alleged abuse of planning laws, something for which he had attacked a rival candidate. He advocates closer ties with mainland China but in Sept. 2012 withdrew plans to impose mandatory Chinese patriotism classes for schoolchildren after widespread public protest. He has pledged to build over 100,000 homes by 2018.

In Sept. 2014 protests organized by the Hong Kong Federation of Students and other opposition activist groups broke out following the proposal of electoral reforms by the government in Beijing. The reforms, which protesters alleged would restrict future chief executive appointments to candidates endorsed by the Chinese administration, were supported by Leung. His subsequent suggestion that open elections would negatively result in Hong Kong's impoverished population controlling politics further damaged his standing among the growing pro-democracy movement, which called for his resignation the following month. Beijing's proposals were subsequently rejected in a vote by the Hong Kong legislature in June 2015. In Dec. 2016 he announced that he would not be seeking re-election in 2017. He was succeeded by Carrie Lam on 1 July 2017.

Li Peng (China)

Introduction

Li Peng has been called the 'great survivor' of Communist China, adapting to the changing views of the prevailing Communist leadership until late in life. He has occupied a variety of state posts since 1979, and from 1988–98 was prime minister. During his premiership, Li oversaw great economic progress, but he will be remembered as the hard-liner who suppressed the Tiananmen Square demonstrations with great loss of life.

Early Life

Li was born in Oct. 1928 (the exact date is unknown) in Sichuan province. His father, the writer Li Shuoxin, was executed by the Kuomintang (Nationalist) authorities because of his Communist sympathies. The younger Li, an orphan, was adopted at the age of three by the future Communist premier Zhou Enlai, although after 1939 he was largely brought up by Zhou's wife Deng Yingchao. In 1948 Zhou sent his adopted son to Moscow to train as an engineer at the Moscow Power Institute. He did not return to China until 1955.

Li returned to a China that had been transformed. He had left a country wracked by civil war; he returned to a Communist state in which his foster father held high office. Li worked his way up the party hierarchy, but his energies were spent supervising major electrical power projects during the period 1955–79. The influence of Li's foster father eased a rapid career development.

From 1979 Li became more involved in politics. In 1982, he was appointed to the Central Committee of the Communist Party. He was elected to the Politburo in 1985 and to the standing committee of that body 2 years later. Li held only one ministerial post—education minister (1985–88)—before he was chosen by Deng Xiaoping to be prime minister in 1988.

Career Peak

In economic matters, Li was renowned for his caution. Nevertheless, he implemented the economic reforms of Deng Xiaoping. During his premiership an economic boom began, and the GDP grew by more than 10% per annum. Living standards rose but Li was concerned that with prosperity would come a growing demand for civil liberties.

In April 1989 Li strongly advocated the use of force against the student and worker demonstrators in Tiananmen Square, Beijing. Early in the crisis, he appeared on national television with student leader Wang Dan, who lectured him. Li never forgave this loss of face. He declared martial law and sent the military in to crush the demonstrations in June. Always perceived as austere, Li's unpopularity increased because of his part in the Tiananmen Square massacre.

Li remained uncompromising in the face of Western calls for respect for civil liberties in China and disregarded international criticism. He survived a heart attack in 1993 and had the satisfaction of seeing the Three Gorges power project, which he had advocated for many years, finally approved. He served two 5-year terms as prime minister (the limit set by the constitution).

Later Life

In 1998 Li was appointed chairman of the National People's Congress, the Chinese parliament. Although the legislature has limited power, Li was regarded as the leader of China's Communist hard-liners and second only to President Jiang Zemin in influence. At the Communist Party congress of Nov. 2002 he was among several high-profile figures to announce their retirement from the Politburo, effective in March 2003.

Lilo, Gordon Darcy (Solomon Islands)

Introduction

Gordon Darcy Lilo served as prime minister from Nov. 2011–Dec. 2014, taking over following the resignation of Danny Philip amid controversy over development funding. A finance minister in previous administrations, Lilo promised increased political transparency.

Early Life

Born on 28 Aug. 1965 in Ghatere on Kolombangara Island, Lilo studied economics at the University of Papua New Guinea. As a civil servant he was a permanent secretary at the ministries of environment and conservation and finance. He received a master's degree in development and administration from the Crawford School of Economics and Government at the Australian National University in 2001.

Having returned to the Solomon Islands, Lilo was elected to parliament as MP for Gizo/Kolombangara in Dec. 2001, serving as leader of the independent group in parliament from Dec. 2001 until April 2006. In May 2006 he was appointed finance minister by Prime Minister Sogavare. He then served as minister for environment and conservation under Prime Minister Sikua from Dec. 2007.

In Aug. 2010 Lilo was again appointed finance minister in the National Coalition for Rural Advancement (NCRA) government led by Danny Philip.

He subsequently oversaw development projects across a range of sectors including agriculture, forestry, education and infrastructure. In Nov. that year a scandal erupted over the alleged misuse of Taiwanese-provided development funds by Philip, forcing him to resign the premiership. In the ensuing parliamentary ballot Lilo was elected his successor by 29 votes to 20.

Career Peak

Taking office on 16 Nov. 2011, Lilo pledged to continue the main policies of the NCRA government. These included developing the Solomon Islands' agriculture sector and diversifying the economy away from logging. In response to criticism of cronyism in government, he proposed a stronger role for the audit office and increased public consultation.

In foreign affairs, closer relations were sought with Australia, New Zealand and Papua New Guinea.

Lilo's term as prime minister ended on 9 Dec. 2014 following his party's defeat at the general elections held in Nov. He was succeeded by former two-time premier Manasseh Sogavare, who returned to power almost 7 years after his last stint in office.

Lipponen, Paavo (Finland)

Introduction

Representing the 'rainbow coalition' which includes his own Finnish Social Democratic Party (SSDP), Paavo Lipponen has served as Finland's prime minister since 13 April 1995. Strongly pro-European, Lipponen administered Finland's entry into the EU in 1995 and promoted the adoption of the EMU in 1998. He led the SSDP to second place behind the Centre Party in the elections of March 2003 but has remained prime minister while a new government is formed.

Early Life

Born on 23 April 1941 in Turtola, Lipponen read political science at university where he was the editor of the student newspaper, *Ylioppilaslehti*. In 1965 he started working as a freelance reporter for the Finnish Broadcasting Company YLE. Two years later he became an active member of the SSDP, serving as the party's research and international affairs secretary and then as planning chief of the political section from 1967–79. In 1979 he became the political affairs adviser to the prime minister, a post he held until 1982. In 1983 he was elected a member of parliament and later became the Chairman of the SSDP in the Helsinki District. Whilst head of the Finnish Institute of International Affairs (1989–91), he was re-elected to parliament and appointed to the executive council of the SSDP. In 1993 he became the party chairman.

Career Peak

In response to the parliamentary elections of March 1995 when the ruling Finnish Centre Party suffered a heavy defeat, Lipponen formed the so-called 'rainbow coalition'. comprising the SSDP, the National Coalition Party, the Greens, the Left-Wing Alliance and the Swedish People's Party. Among the government's most notable achievements was securing favourable terms for Finland's entry to the European Union, boosting the domestic economy and reducing unemployment. In the 1999 elections the National Coalition Party and the Centre Party made substantial gains at the expense of the Social Democratic Party which nonetheless remained the biggest party in parliament. Lipponen formed his second rainbow coalition and the Centre Party again found itself in opposition. In July 1999 when Finland assumed the Presidency of the European Union, Lipponen made a strong effort to promote financial integration and monetary union in particular. In the same year Finland became one of the first wave of countries to adopt EMU. In the latter half of 2000 Lipponen embarked on a successful initiative to extend paternity leave in Finland.

In May 2002 the Greens left the government in protest at a vote authorizing the construction of a nuclear reactor, Europe's first in over a decade. The decision to build another reactor was an attempt to lessen Finland's dependence on Russia for energy.

The war in Iraq in 2003 caused difficulties for Lipponen's government. Amid popular opposition to the US-led war, Lipponen was criticised for his friendly relations with the American president. The official Finnish position demanded UN Security Council clearance for any military attack.

Later Life

At the elections of March 2003 the Centre Party won 55 of 200 seats (24.7% of the vote) while the SSDP won 53 seats (24.5%). The Centre Party leader, Anneli Jäätteenmäki, was elected prime minister by parliament on 17 April. She formed a coalition government with Lipponen's SSDP and the Swedish People's Party but Lipponen declined a ministerial position. He stated support for the new government and his intention to remain as his party's chairman until the end of his term in 2005. In April 2003 he was elected speaker of the Finnish parliament—a position he held until March 2007.

Lipponen contested the 2012 presidential election as the SSDP candidate but failed to progress beyond the first round of voting.

Liu Shaoqi (China)

Introduction

Liu Shaoqi was head of state of the People's Republic of China from 1959–68 and was considered, by many, to be Mao's heir. One of the outstanding leaders of Communist China, he fell from office in 1968 in circumstances that have still not been fully explained. His death, in 1969, was not made public until 11 years later.

Liu was born in Hunan province in 1889–the exact date of birth is not certain. By the time he was 30 was involved in politics, joining the Socialist Youth League.

Early Life

In 1920 Liu went to Moscow to study and joined the new Chinese Communist Party while he was learning about Communism firsthand in Russia. This time spent abroad made Liu one of the few Chinese leaders of his generation with any real experience of the outside world. Returning to China in 1922 he gained a party post in his native Hunan province and became active in labour leadership.

When the Nationalists turned on the Communists in 1927, Liu went underground. In the same year he was elected to the party's Central Committee. Joining Mao Zedong's forces in western China in the 1930s, Liu became a member of the Politburo, but he left the Long March to work in Beijing against the Japanese invaders. After being in charge of the (underground) party in North China and then in Central China, he returned to Mao's side. A series of lectures, *How to be a good Communist*, increased his influence and by the time China emerged from the Second World War, Liu was firmly established as one of the most powerful men in the Communist Party, of which he had become the official spokesman.

Career Peak

Upon the establishment of the People's Republic of China on 1 Oct. 1949, Liu was appointed deputy premier and a deputy leader of the party. His experience as a student in Moscow stood Liu in good stead as China's chief negotiator with the Soviet Union and his labour leadership made him an obvious choice to promote industrialisation. It fell to Liu to outline the Great Leap Forward that was intended to boost China's industries. By the mid-1950s Liu was clearly Mao's heir and in 1959 succeeded him as head of state (Chairman of the State Council).

As head of state Liu made many visits abroad. But in 1968, during the Cultural Revolution, he fell from power. It seems likely that Liu, the pragmatist, was opposed to the wilder excesses of the student Red Guards, the instruments of Mao's new revolution. What was perceived as the extravagant lifestyle of Liu's wife, Wang Guangmei, also attracted adverse comment. In Oct. 1968, Liu lost his post and party positions. At the same time his Politburo ally Deng Xiaoping was purged.

Later Life

Purged from the Communist Party, Liu Shaoqi disappeared from view. Rumours of his death spread in 1974 but the party did not announce that the former head of state had died on 12 Nov. 1969 in Henan province until 1980. In the same year, the party—led in fact if not in name by Deng Xiaoping—completely rehabilitated Liu, acknowledging the important part he played in the establishment of Communist China.

Lobo Sosa, Porfirio (Honduras)

Introduction

Porfirio Lobo Sosa was elected president on 29 Nov. 2009, ending months of political turmoil that followed the ousting of President Zelaya in a coup. The right-wing former agronomist has faced the challenge of uniting the country, re-establishing regional alliances and combating rising lawlessness and violence.

Early Life

Porfirio Lobo Sosa was born on 22 Dec. 1947 in Trujillo, Colón district, the son of a wealthy politician who served in Honduras' National Congress in the 1950s. Lobo grew up near Juticalpa, Olancho, attending a local Catholic school and then the San Francisco Institute of Tegucigalpa from 1961–65. He went to the University of Miami in 1966 to study business administration before returning to Honduras in 1970 to work in his family's agricultural business and to teach politics and economics at a college in Juticalpa. In the 1970s Lobo travelled to the Soviet Union and enrolled at Patrice Lumumba University in Moscow. He is reputed to have joined the Communist Party of Honduras on his return before making a political about-turn to join the right-wing National Party (PNH), becoming president of the party's Olancho branch in 1986.

In the general election of Nov. 1989 Lobo secured a seat in the National Congress for the PNH. He worked in the department for agriculture and economics under the new president, Rafael Leonardo Callejas, and headed the corporation for forestry development until 1994. Lobo was elected president of the PNH's central committee in June 1999 and served as president of congress from 2002–06. Selected as the PNH candidate to contest the presidential election of 27 Nov. 2005, he took a hard line on crime, promising the death penalty for convicted gang members. This contrasted with the approach of his rival, José Manuel Zelaya, of the centre-right Liberal Party (PLH) who pledged to introduce re-education programmes for criminals. Lobo was defeated with 46% of the vote to Zelaya's 50%.

Lobo took over as leader of the opposition PNH in Jan. 2006. He criticized Zelaya's lurch to the political left in 2007 and the president's alliance with the Venezuelan leader, Hugo Chávez, who persuaded Honduras to join regional leftist alliances. Zelaya's popularity was dented by his attempts in 2008 to hold a referendum to change the constitution that barred him from standing for re-election—a path taken by Chávez in Venezuela and President Morales in Bolivia. Zelaya pushed ahead with the referendum, despite opposition from the PNH, national legal bodies and much of the military.

On 28 June 2009, after the Supreme Court had ruled that the bid to change the constitution was illegal, the army launched a coup and forced Zelaya into exile in Costa Rica. A wave of international criticism (and suspension from the Organization of American States—OAS) ushered in 5 months of sometimes violent turmoil between Zelaya's supporters and backers of the interim president, Roberto Micheletti. In the presidential election of 29 Nov. 2009 (scheduled prior to the coup), Lobo secured 56% of the vote and was sworn in on 27 Jan. 2010.

Career Peak

Lobo promptly granted amnesty to those involved in the political crisis and paved the way for Zelaya to leave for exile in the Dominican Republic. The move was one of the conditions of an accord signed in Oct. 2009 after efforts by the OAS to broker a political settlement. Lobo promised to 're-establish channels of friendship with all nations' and to seek foreign investment to revive the economy. In 2010 Honduras was readmitted to the Central

American Integration System and in May 2011 an internationally-brokered agreement to allow Zelaya to return to the country prompted Honduras' resumption of participation in OAS proceedings in June. In Sept. 2011 Lobo replaced some members of his cabinet, including foreign minister Mario Canahuati and interior minister Óscar Álvarez, reportedly over political differences. Drug-related crime has meanwhile continued to increase, and Honduras has been ranked among the most violent countries in the world.

Lobo was succeeded as president by National Party candidate Juan Orlando Hernández on 27 Jan. 2014. Since the constitution of Honduras prohibits successive presidential terms, Sosa was not eligible to run for re-election.

Loeak, Christopher (Marshall Islands)

Introduction

Christopher Loeak was sworn into office on 10 Jan. 2012 following his appointment by the 33-member *Nitijela* (parliament) on 3 Jan. 2012.

Early Life

Christopher Loeak was born on 11 Nov. 1952 on Ailinglaplap Atoll to a family of tribal leaders. He was educated at Marshall Island High School before attending the Hawaii Pacific College. He completed his legal training at Gonzaga University, Washington in 1982.

Loeak then joined the Kwajalein Atoll Corporation as a lobbyist based in Hawaii. In 1983, whilst still in Hawaii, he unsuccessfully stood for the Ailinglaplap parliamentary seat. 2 years later he contested it again and won, serving in the cabinet of Amata Kabua as minister of justice from 1988–92. In 1992 he became minister of social services and in 1996 took on the education portfolio in Kunio Lemari's government, a post he retained after Imata Kabua (the younger cousin of Amata Kabua) took over as president.

Loeak was appointed minister for the Ralik Chain of islands in 1998 and a year later was also named minister in assistance to the president. Loeak was re-elected to the *Nitijela* in 2007 and in 2008 was reappointed as minister in assistance to President Litokwa Tomeing. He successfully defended his seat in the Nov. 2011 elections and on 2 Jan. 2012 was elected president when he won parliamentary backing by 21 votes to 11 against the incumbent president, Jurelang Zedkaia.

Career Peak

Loeak's main challenge has been to raise levels of education and to gain a measure of financial independence from the USA, on which the Marshall Islands have been heavily reliant for aid. In Sept. 2013 Loeak and other Pacific Islands Forum heads adopted the Majuro Declaration calling for urgent action to address climate change. In April 2014 the government began a legal action at the International Court of Justice against nine countries with nuclear weapons, arguing that they had violated their obligation to pursue disarmament.

Upon completion of his 4 year term, Loeak was replaced by Casten Nemra as president (although he was only in office for a week before in turn being replaced by Hilda Heine).

Lubbers, Ruud (Netherlands)

Introduction

Ruud Lubbers was the longest-serving Dutch Prime Minister, and he has continued to develop his political and especially his diplomatic expertise in the academic world following his retirement from domestic politics in 1994.

Early Life

Rudolphus Lubbers was born in Rotterdam on 7 May 1939. He graduated from the Netherlands School of Economics, and began his career working as a secretary of the board of Hollandia Machine factory, a family concern. He was an active member of several associations of Christian employers and became a member of the Catholic Party (KVP) in 1964. His entry into politics came later in 1970 when he was elected to Rotterdam's Rijnmond Council. Only 3 years later he joined the Den Uyl government as Minister for Economic Affairs, and in 1977 he became leader of the Lower House of the States-General. The following year Lubbers rose to the leadership of the new Christian Democratic Alliance.

Career Peak

In Nov. 1982 he was elected Prime Minister for the first time and went on to lead 3 consecutive Cabinets variously composed of Christian Democrats, Liberals and Social Democrats. During his first term he decided to take radical action to turn around the ailing Dutch economy, and he was successful to this end, consolidating the country's international economic performance. In doing so he was considered largely responsible for what came to be known as 'The Dutch Model'. Lubbers was also a notable problem-solver in other political arenas. He managed to resolve a conflict between anti-nuclear activists and NATO about the stationing of nuclear missiles in the Netherlands, and following this diplomatic triumph he became increasingly sought after as an international negotiator. The political furore that broke out at the 1991 Maastricht talks as a result of Dutch proposals for a more federal Europe was calmed to a considerable extent by Lubbers' personal intervention. His tact and diplomacy prevented the talks from concluding in acrimonious dispute, and ultimately secured the introduction of a revised Treaty of Maastricht under the Dutch EC presidency.

Later Life

Following his resignation in 1994 he was widely tipped for high international office, including the posts of Secretary-General of NATO and of chairman of the European Commission, he never achieved these titles, and instead retired to his family business. From 1995 to 2000 Lubbers was a professor of global international economic relations at the University of Tilburg. He served as the United Nations High Commissioner for Refugees from 2001 to 2005. He died on 14 Feb. 2018 aged 78.

Lugo Méndes, Fernando Armindo (Paraguay)

Introduction

Fernando Lugo was elected president in Aug. 2008 for a 5-year term. A former bishop of San Pedro, he was leader of the Christian Democratic Party and head of a 12-party coalition, the Patriotic Alliance for Change (APC). He was the first president from a party other than the National Republican Association (ANR, or Colorado Party) since 1947. In June 2012 Lugo was impeached by congress over a land dispute and removed from office.

Early Life

Fernando Lugo was born on 30 May 1951 in the San Pedro del Parana District of Itapúa. His parents were members of the ruling Colorado Party while Lugo's uncle, Epifanio Mendez Fleitas, was a Colorado Party dissident and the main rival of Gen. Alfredo Stroessner. During Stroessner's rule (1954–89), both Lugo's parents were arrested while his three brothers and uncle spent periods in exile.

In Oct. 1951 the Lugo family moved to Itapúa's capital, Encarnación, where Lugo completed his education and qualified as a teacher in 1969. He taught in the San Pedro department and in 1970 joined the Catholic Society of the Divine Word. In 1972 he took religious vows and in 1977 was ordained. He went as a missionary to Ecuador, where he spent five years and became influenced by liberation theology. Returning to Paraguay in 1982, the Church, under pressure from the Stroessner regime, sent Lugo to Rome to study at the Pontificia Università Gregoriana. In 1987 he graduated in sociology and returned to Paraguay. He taught at the Superior Institute of Theology in Asunción, set up national and regional Episcopal commissions and, after Stroessner's fall in 1989, pressed for land reform. In 1992 he became vice president of the Confederation of Religious Leaders and in 1994 was made bishop of the diocese of San Pedro.

As internal rifts weakened the Colorado Party, Lugo's public profile rose and he became a leading non-partisan critic of the government. In 2005 he resigned his bishopric and in Dec. 2006 applied to be laicized to allow him to run for president. In Oct. 2007 he joined the Christian Democratic Party in a 12-party coalition and won the presidential election of April 2008. The Pope accepted his laicism in July 2008.

Career Peak

Having campaigned on a platform of social reform, Lugo needed to confront the country's widespread poverty and social inequality and promised to enact land reform, prompting conservatives to label him a leftist ally of President Hugo Chávez of Venezuela. In 2009 he initiated modest reforms in education and health care and negotiated an agreement with neighbouring Brazil to increase Paraguay's revenue from their jointly-controlled Itaipu hydro-electric plant. However, he encountered increasing hostility and resistance within Congress and from the armed forces, and had his moral authority undermined by paternity claims made against him by three women. In Aug. 2010 he was diagnosed with cancer but said that he would continue in office. In an impeachment trial held on 22 June 2012 the Senate voted (39–4) to remove Lugo over a land dispute that resulted in the deaths of 17 people. Vice president Frederico Franco was sworn in to replace Lugo. His removal led to violent demonstrations by his supporters. Neighbouring countries denounced the proceedings, likening it to a coup d'état.

Lula da Silva, Luiz Inácio (Brazil)

Introduction

A former factory worker and trade union activist, Luiz Inácio Lula da Silva, better known as Lula, was elected president of Brazil in 2002 at his fourth attempt, representing the Workers' Party (PT; Partido dos Trabalhadores). The country's first elected socialist leader, he pledged to combat Brazil's widespread poverty while co-operating with the business sector and international community. He was re-elected in Oct. 2006.

Early Life

Lula was born on 27 Oct. 1945 in Garanhans in the northeastern state of Pernambuco, the seventh of eight surviving siblings. In 1952 his family moved to São Paulo state where his father worked as a docker. Living in Guarujá and Santos, Lula initially worked as a street vendor and shoe-shine boy and had little formal education. When his parents separated in 1956, he moved with his mother to the state capital. Following 2 years of odd jobs in the city's factories, he was employed from the age of 14 as a lathe operator in a São Paulo metalworks. He continued to work in the industry for the next 20 years.

In the late 1960s, when Brazil was under military rule, Lula became politically active in the metalworkers' trade union. Progressing through the union hierarchy, he was elected leader in 1975 with 92% support. He was re-elected just as emphatically 3 years later. In 1980 he founded the radical PT as a combination of trade unionists, left-wing groups and church activists. Contesting its first elections in 1982, the PT took only six seats, but increased its representation to nineteen 4 years later.

Lula first stood for the presidency in 1989 coming second to the National Reconstruction candidate Fernando Collor. Through the 1990s the party's rhetoric softened, although it continued its commitment to aiding the poor. Nonetheless, in the 1994 and 1998 presidential elections, Lula came second to the Social Democrat candidate Fernando Cardoso.

At the time of the Oct. 2002 elections, Brazil was suffering from the economic fall-out of a growing trade deficit, tax increases and reduced government spending. In the first round, Lula came first with 46.4% of votes. In the second round run-off with the Social Democrat candidate, José Serra, he took 61.3%. The PT also won the most seats in the Chamber of Deputies.

Career Peak

Lula took office in Jan. 2003, having pledged to reduce poverty and hunger by redistributing wealth, improving education and health, and implementing agrarian reform, with the creation of a new 'social emergency' ministry. Brazil's financial markets were nervous, and the *real* faltered at the prospect of a socialist revolution. However, Lula also promised to co-operate with the business and banking communities, to adhere to IMF guidelines, to repay foreign debt and to continue his predecessor's attempts to control inflation. His government pursued sound macroeconomic policies, taking credit for low inflation, significant job creation and strong annual growth in GDP.

From May 2005 the PT was undermined politically by financial corruption scandals, leading to the resignations of several senior party officials and Lula allies, which tarnished the government's claim to probity and threatened to jeopardize the president's hopes of re-election. However, in Oct. 2006 Lula secured a second term of office after two rounds of voting in the presidential elections. The PT lost ground marginally in the parliamentary poll to become the second largest party in the Chamber of Deputies. In 2007 corruption allegations continued to haunt Lula's administration as the Supreme Court indicted 40 people in Aug., including the president's former chief of staff and other senior PT politicians. Nevertheless, the president maintained his personal popularity, achieving a 78% approval rating in a poll in late 2008. He also drew political credit for the resilience of Brazil's economy which, although not immune to the global financial crisis that unfolded in the latter half of 2008, was quick to rebound through 2009, reflecting the sound financial system, robust domestic demand and diverse trading partnerships.

In foreign affairs, Lula sought increasing engagement with other emerging powers on the world stage, particularly India and China, and expanded Brazil's diplomatic representation in Africa. He also championed the country's candidacy for a permanent seat on the United Nations Security Council. Lula was closely involved in Rio de Janeiro's successful lobbying for selection to host the 2016 summer Olympic Games, which was confirmed in Oct. 2009. After two terms Lula left office on 1 Jan. 2011 with almost 90% approval ratings. He ceded his presidency to Dilma Rousseff, the first female president in Brazil's history. The following month, federal prosecutors in Brazil accused Lula of misusing public funds to finance a political campaign in 2004 and requested the freezing of his assets.

Later Life

Lula was diagnosed with throat cancer in Oct. 2011, but made a full recovery following chemotherapy treatment.

In July 2017 he was sentenced to nearly 9 years and 6 months in prison after being found guilty of corruption and money-laundering charges, although the judge ruled that he could remain free pending an appeal. In Sept. 2017 Brazil's chief federal prosecutor charged Lula, as well as his successor as president Dilma Rousseff, with forming a criminal organization to divert funds from Petrobras (the country's state oil company). An appeals court upheld the conviction ruling in Jan. 2018.

Lumumba, Patrice (Democratic Republic of the Congo)

Introduction

Founder of the Mouvement National Congolais (Congolese National Movement) and the first prime minister of independent Democratic Republic of Congo, Patrice Lumumba served only four months before being forced out of office and assassinated. Elected in 1960, the leftwing nationalist served in an uneasy alliance with Joseph Kasavubu, an opposition politician. Lumumba's death heralded 32 years of dictatorship under Mobutu Sésé Séko while securing his posthumous reputation as a freedom fighter and national hero.

Early Life

Lumumba was born on 2 July 1925 in Onalua, Kasai. After studying at a missionary school, he wrote for national journals before becoming a postal clerk in Kinshasa (then Léopoldville) and later a postal accountant in Kisangani (Stanleyville). He was involved in Congolese trade unionism and in the Belgian Liberal Party. After serving a year in prison for embezzlement, his political activism intensified. In 1958 he formed the MNC, which worked for the country's transition to independence from Belgium.

In 1959 an uprising resulted from an unpopular 5-year development plan. Although local elections were scheduled for Dec. 1959, nationalists were suspicious of Belgium's influence and refused to cooperate. When the Belgian authorities retaliated with force 30 people were killed in an uprising in which Lumumba was involved. He subsequently left the country but was imprisoned on his return. The MNC meanwhile entered the elections and took 90% of votes. In order to regain control, the Belgians held round table negotiations in Brussels. These were boycotted by the MNC until Lumumba was released from prison. The Belgian government capitulated and in early 1960 Lumumba joined the transitional negotiations. Independence was achieved in June 1960.

Career Peak

In the country's first elections in May 1960, the MNC won the most votes, taking 33 out of 137, but did not achieve a majority. With no party agreeing a coalition, the MNC compromised with the opposition Abako party (Alliance des Ba-Kongos), and Lumumba was appointed prime minister with the Abako leader Joseph Kasavubu becoming president. At his inauguration speech, attended by Belgian dignitaries, Lumumba riled his former colonists by attacking their treatment of the Congolese.

Before Lumumba could begin implementing any transitional reforms, the newly independent country fell into disarray. In July 1960 the army mutinied and the mineral rich Katanga region (now Shaba) declared its independence under Moise Tshombe (later reintegrated into the DRC in 1964). Belgium sent forces ostensibly to protect remaining Belgian nationals. Sacked by President Kasavubu on 5 Sept. 1960, Lumumba's attempts to reassert his premiership were unsuccessful. He called on the UN to intervene, and was rumoured to have requested assistance from the Soviet Union, which angered the West. Meanwhile, President Kasavubu and the army leader Joseph Mobutu (later Mobutu Sésé Séko) agreed a ruling partnership. The government was recognized by the UN but not by all African countries.

Lumumba was handed over to the Kasavubu district by the Belgian army and was killed in Jan. 1961 by Moise Tshombe's troops. Shot by firing squad, his body was dismembered and then dissolved in acid. It was over 40 years later that an independent Belgian investigation found the Belgian government complicit in Lumumba's murder. In 2002 Belgium apologized for its failure to protect the ousted prime minister.

Ma Ying-jeou (Taiwan, China)

Introduction

Ma Ying-Jeou of the Nationalist Party (Kuomintang or KMT) was elected president on 22 March 2008, ending 8 years of rule by the Democratic People's Party (DPP). The charismatic US-educated lawyer pledged to improve relations with mainland China after decades of impasse and to revive the economy.

Early Life

Ma Ying-Jeou was born on 13 July 1950 in Hong Kong, then a British overseas territory, to parents originally from Henan, China. His father, Ma Ho-ling, was a loyal supporter of China's Nationalist Party (Kuomintang, KMT), founded in 1894 to end Manchu rule and unify the country. When Ma was a year old, his family moved to Taipei, Taiwan, which had become the seat of government of the Republic of China in 1949.

Ma was schooled in Taipei and graduated in law from the National Taiwan University in 1972. Following a 2-year spell in Taiwan's Marine Corps and the Navy, he took up postgraduate studies at New York University's School of Law and then at the Harvard Law School. Ma subsequently worked as a legal consultant to the First National Bank of Boston and in 1981 was briefly employed by a Wall Street law firm.

Returning to Taiwan later that year, he began work as a civil servant in the presidential office, eventually serving as an English interpreter to President Chiang Ching-kuo. In 1984 Ma was appointed the KMT's deputy secretary-general for international affairs. Four years later he was promoted to the chair of the research, development and evaluation commission under the Executive Yuan (the government's executive branch). In 1991 he became deputy chairman and spokesman of the mainland affairs council. In the same year he was elected a KMT representative to the National Assembly. Having been appointed justice minister by President Lee Teng-hui in 1993, Ma sought to root out political corruption. This gained him plaudits from the public but made him enemies within the KMT and he was ousted in July 1996.

Maintaining his support for the KMT, Ma was briefly a minister without portfolio before resigning from government in 1997 in protest at continued corruption and public safety issues. Returning to academe, he took a position at the National Chengchi University Law School but less than a year later was persuaded to contest Taipei's mayoral election. He narrowly defeated the incumbent, Chen Shui-bian of the Democratic People's Party (DPP). Chen would go on to become Taiwan's president in 2000, defeating Lien Chan of the KMT.

Praised for his dynamism as mayor, Ma won a landslide re-election in Dec. 2002, receiving 64.1% of the vote. His second term was more difficult and Ma was criticized for failing to mobilize the Taipei city government sufficiently quickly to combat the threat of the SARS epidemic in early 2003. Nevertheless, he is credited with driving the regeneration of Taipei via a range of public infrastructure projects such as the M-Taipei Initiative (to create a city-wide wireless-internet network).

Ma was elected KMT chairman in 2005 and the party won local elections later that year. In 2006 he was at the centre of allegations that he had misused an expenses account while mayor. In Feb. 2007 he was indicted by the Taiwan High Prosecutors Office, forcing his resignation as KMT chairman. However, in mid-2007 he announced he would contest the presidency in 2008, promising to forge closer economic ties with Mainland China (via direct air and shipping links). He beat the DPP's Frank Hsieh in the election on 22 March 2008 with 58% of the vote. The following month he was cleared of all charges against him and on 20 May 2008 was sworn into office.

Career Peak

Ma has presided over thawing relations between Taiwan and Mainland China. The first direct weekend charter flights across the Taiwan Strait were launched in July 2008 and Taiwan was opened to tourists from mainland China. Ma has also eased restrictions on Taiwan investment on the mainland and approved measures allowing mainland investors to buy Taiwanese stocks. The moves were met by massive anti-China demonstrations in Taipei in Oct. 2008 with fears that Ma was compromising the independence of the state after the government failed to submit a request to become a United Nations member for the first time in 17 years. In 2010 further trade liberalization with China was expected after an Economic Co-operation Framework Agreement took effect in Sept. In May 2010 Taiwan was offered observer status at the World Health Organization, under the name Chinese Taipei. Ma was re-elected for a second term in Jan. 2012.

In April 2014 Ma's government came under pressure from mass demonstrations in Taipei protesting the Cross-Strait Service Trade Agreement—a treaty with mainland China intended to liberalize trade between the two economies.

Ma resigned as KMT chairman in Dec. 2014 following the party's crushing defeat at the Nov. local elections and was succeeded in Jan. 2015 by Eric Chu.

Ma's tenure as president ended in May 2016 following elections held in Jan. that year. He was ineligible to serve another term owing to constitutional limits, and Tsai Ing-wen of the Democratic Progressive Party took over as president.

Macapagal-Arroyo, Gloria (Philippines)

Introduction

Gloria Macapagal-Arroyo was swept to power in Jan. 2001 when her predecessor was forced from office by mass street protests. She is the daughter of

Diosdado Macapagal, the president of the Philippines from 1961–65. Returned to power in elections in 2004, she then survived two parliamentary attempts to impeach her over alleged corruption, human rights abuses and electoral fraud, and a failed coup attempt during the ensuing 6-year term.

Early Life

Gloria Macapagal was born on 5 April 1947 into a prominent Filipino political family. After education at a convent high school in the Philippines, she took a degree in commerce at Georgetown University in Washington, D.C., where the future US president Bill Clinton was one of her classmates. Returning to the Philippines, she studied for a master's degree and then spent time teaching, during which period she married, becoming Mrs. Arroyo, although in her subsequent political career she has used both her maiden and married names.

Prominent as an economist as well as a member of a political dynasty, Arroyo was appointed to the government of President Corazón Aquino in 1986 as assistant secretary of the department of trade and industry, rising to become under-secretary. She also held the post of executive director of the garments and textile export board. During her tenure the textile industry grew to become the country's top foreign-currency earner.

When Aquino's presidency ended in 1992, Arroyo stood for the Senate and was elected at her first attempt. Although she had held office in the outgoing government, Arroyo was still something of a political unknown, and her initial appeal to many voters was the memory of her popular father. However, when she stood for re-election in 1995 her own reputation won her nearly 16 m. votes, the greatest number ever received by an individual in Philippine elections.

In 1998, Arroyo stood as a candidate for the vice-presidency. The presidency was won by Joseph Estrada, a former cinema actor, but in her electoral race, Arroyo received more votes than Estrada—12.7 m., the most ever received by anyone in a Philippine presidential or vice-presidential contest.

President Estrada appointed her vice-president and secretary of social welfare and development. She resigned from the Cabinet in Oct. 2000, but retained her role as vice-president. By that time the Estrada government was in trouble, the president having been accused of cronyism and taking bribes from illegal gambling syndicates. Impeachment proceedings began. Arroyo led the calls for Estrada to resign. Mass street protests forced Estrada to flee the presidential palace and the Supreme Court declared the presidency to be vacant. On 20 Jan. 2001, Arroyo was sworn in as president.

Career Peak

The immediate challenge facing President Arroyo was reconciliation. Many supporters of Estrada initially refused to recognize the transfer of power. She took office at a difficult time for the country, politically and economically. Arroyo set economic recovery, including a privatization programme, and economic and social reform as her priorities. However, one of her main problems was Islamic terrorism and the continued guerrilla activity by separatists in the south of the country and by communist insurgents. In 2003 Arroyo negotiated a cessation of hostilities with the separatists pending formal peace talks, although clashes with government troops still took place. She meanwhile vowed to wipe out the Abu Sayyaf, an Islamic terrorist organization responsible for bombings and the kidnapping and murder of foreign tourists and others, which has been linked to al-Qaeda by the US government.

In July 2003 Ramon Cardenas, a former junior minister to ex-President Joseph Estrada, was arrested after leading a military uprising in Manila. Several hundred troops took possession of a shopping and residential complex but withdrew after accusing Arroyo's government of corruption. Standing for Lakas-Christian Muslim Democrats, Arroyo was returned to power in the presidential elections of May 2004, ahead of Fernando Poe, Jr. of the Coalition of United Filipinos. Despite coming under intense pressure to resign in July 2005 over allegations of electoral vote-rigging, she survived an opposition attempt to impeach her in Sept. Arroyo declared a week-long state of emergency in Feb. 2006 after the military reported a plot to oust her in a coup. In July–Aug. 2006 a second opposition attempt to impeach her was blocked by her majority supporters in the House of Representatives, but her attempt later in the year to change the constitution and abolish the more independent Senate was withdrawn in Dec. in the face of popular protest.

Parliamentary elections in May 2007 were marred by violence, voter intimidation and irregularities. The opposition won the majority of the Senate seats while Arroyo's support in the lower house was strengthened. In July Arroyo set out a new agenda, pledging to create jobs, improve education,

health and welfare, and bring peace to the troubled south. She also defended a controversial new anti-terrorism law. In Sept. former president Estrada was sentenced to life imprisonment for corruption, but was subsequently pardoned by Arroyo. In Nov. 2007 a coup attempt by renegade soldiers occupying a hotel in Manila was quashed by security forces.

In July 2008 the government reached an agreement with the Moro Islamic Liberation Front to extend self-government for the semi-autonomous Muslim region covering parts of Mindanao and nearby islands. However, the deal collapsed the following month after Christian communities raised objections and petitioned the Supreme Court, sparking renewed violence on Mindanao.

In Nov. 2009, 57 people were killed on the island of Mindanao in a massacre seemingly related to political rivalry between powerful local clans. Amid reports of her alleged links with the clan believed to be responsible, Arroyo quickly distanced herself from the outrage and its perpetrators and her government appointed an independent commission to oversee the disbanding of private armies in the country before the presidential, legislative and local elections that took place on 10 May 2010. Under the constitution Arroyo was not eligible to stand in the presidential poll and left office on 30 June.

Later Life

Arroyo was arrested in Nov. 2011 on charges of election fraud and banned from leaving the country. She had wanted to leave the Philippines to seek medical treatment, claiming she was suffering from a bone disease. She was detained in a military hospital but was released on bail in July 2012. However, she soon returned to custody at the military hospital after refusing to enter a plea on charges that she misappropriated state lottery funds during her time in office.

Arroyo was re-elected to the House of Representatives in May 2013 while still under detention. However, in July 2016 the Supreme Court acquitted her of the charges relating to the misuse of state lottery funds and she was subsequently released from the military hospital.

Macías Nguema, Francisco (Equatorial Guinea)

Introduction

Francisco Macías Nguema was, from 1968–79, the first post-colonial president of Equatorial Guinea. His 11 year reign of terror caused a third of the population to flee, the greatest refugee exodus by percentage of any country in modern history. He ordered the deaths of thousands of suspected opponents, closed down churches and presided over economic collapse. In 1979 he was overthrown by his nephew, and subsequently put on trial and sentenced to death.

Early Life

The son of a witch doctor, Francisco Macías Nguema was born on 1 Jan. 1924 in Oyen in the Woleu Nteu province of Gabon. He was raised in the village of Mongomo in what later became Equatorial Guinea. Despite failing the entrance exam on three occasions, Macías worked his way up the ranks of the civil service, becoming an assistant court translator in Mongomo in 1951. In 1963 he became mayor of Mongomo and the following year was appointed minister of public works in a transitional government.

In 1968 Spain granted independence to Equatorial Guinea and In Sept. Macías was elected president, having defeated incumbent Bonifacio Ondo Edu, president since 1964 under the Spanish administration, and Antanasio Ndong Miyone, the founder of Equatorial Guinea's original nationalist party. Ondu Edu subsequently fled to Gabon but was forced back to Equatorial Guinea where, along with his wife, he was murdered.

Career Peak

Under Macías, relations with Spain rapidly deteriorated and by March 1969 all but a few hundred Spaniards had fled the country. By July 1970 Macías had created a single party state under the Partido Unicao National de Trabajadores. From 1971–73 he ruled by decree, declaring himself 'president for life' on 14 July 1972.

Intellectuals across the country were targeted and, under his command, ten of the twelve members of his original cabinet were murdered, including his vice president, Bosio Dieo. Furthermore, he ordered the execution of the former lovers of his third wife and was known to have had killed the husbands of women he desired, along with members of his own family. By 1979 he was responsible for the murder of at least 20,000 citizens.

Meanwhile, the country's economy and infrastructure collapsed. Macías closed the central bank, executing the director and keeping the country's treasury in his own home. Newspapers, printing presses and libraries were all banned (as was the word 'intellectual'). Private education was deemed subversive and abolished in 1975. A militant atheist, he also banned the church.

In Aug. 1979, Macías' nephew, Teodoro Obiang Nguema Mbasogo, led a coup that forced his uncle to flee. When Macías was found in the jungle several weeks later, he was arrested and charged with genocide. Along with six co-defendants, he was sentenced to death by firing squad at Malabo's Blabich Prison. Fearing supernatural powers, the army refused to carry out the execution order which was undertaken by Moroccan soldiers on 29 Sept. 1979. Obiang Nguema assumed the presidency the following month.

Mackenzie King, William Lyon (Canada)

Introduction

William Lyon Mackenzie King was three times Liberal prime minister of Canada (1921–26, 1926–30 and 1935–48).

Early Life

King was born in Ontario in 1874. His maternal grandfather, William Lyon Mackenzie, had led the 1837 Rebellion in Upper Canada. A law graduate, King entered the civil service and in 1900 was appointed deputy minister of the department of labour. He was elected to the Commons in 1908 as a Liberal member and became labour minister the following year. King failed to win re-election in 1911 and 1917 but was made Liberal leader in 1919. Building on his popularity in Quebec, he was able to reunite the divided party and in 1921 the Liberals formed the government.

Career Peak

Dependent on the support of the farmers' groups during his first tenure, King reduced trade restrictions and tariffs. He was instrumental in creating Canada's welfare state, introducing a broad-based old-age pension scheme in 1926. However, in the same year the Liberals lost a vote of confidence. An election was called later in the year and King once more led his party to victory.

There followed a period of economic growth but in 1929 Canada was badly hit by the worldwide economic slump and the Wall Street Crash. The Liberals lost the elections of 1930 and King was opposition leader until winning a third term in 1935. With the worst of the economic downturn over, King led the country throughout World War II. As well as heading the war effort, he introduced unemployment insurance in 1940 and laid down the basis for health insurance. He retired from office in 1948.

Later Life

King died in 1950.

Macmillan, Harold (United Kingdom of Great Britain and Northern Ireland)

Introduction

Harold Macmillan succeeded Anthony Eden as Conservative British prime minister in 1957 and went on to secure another term in 1959 before resigning in 1963. In the earlier part of his administration, the economy was strong and prosperous but it experienced trouble in later years. In terms of foreign policy, Macmillan oversaw the granting of independence to numerous British colonies and also built closer ties with the US. His attempts to take Britain into the European Economic Community (EEC) were unsuccessful and the last months of his tenure were blighted by the Profumo affair.

Early Life

Maurice Harold Macmillan was born on 10 Feb. 1894 in London. He had American heritage on his maternal side and the Macmillan family were the owners of the London publishing house of the same name. He attended Eton and Balliol College, Oxford before serving with distinction in World War I with the Grenadier Guards. On his return he was employed in the family firm and in 1924 he entered the House of Commons as the Conservative member for Stockton-on-Tees in northeast England.

His constituency, a run-down industrial town, focused Macmillan's belief in the need for social reform and prompted him to join a leftist group within the Conservative party. He lost his seat in 1929 but regained it 2 years later and spent much of the 1930s expressing his disapproval of the government's economic policies and of German appeasement. Churchill gave Macmillan a junior ministerial position in 1940 and in 1942 he was appointed resident minister at Allied Forces HQ, Mediterranean Command, taking up his post in North Africa.

At the end of the war Macmillan lost his seat but soon returned as MP for Bromley. He was opposition spokesman for economic and industrial matters. When Churchill returned as prime minister in 1951 he made Macmillan minister for housing. He was moved to the ministry of defence 3 years later, then to the foreign office in 1955 before becoming chancellor of the exchequer later in the year.

Career Peak

Churchill's successor as prime minister, Anthony Eden, resigned in 1957 following the Suez Crisis. Macmillan was installed in his place having fought off a challenge from Rab Butler for the Conservative leadership. Despite his chancellor, Peter Thorneycroft, resigning in Jan. 1958 on the question of government spending, the economy was in a sound position, unemployment was falling and the government put into place various social reforms. By the time of the 1959 general election, the country's finances were so vibrant that Macmillan famously commented that 'most of our people have never had it so good'. Dubbed 'supermac' by the media, he won the election comfortably.

However, Macmillan's premiership after 1959 soon ran into problems. The economic boom was losing its momentum, despite the establishment of the National Economic Development Council (or Neddie) in 1962. In 1961 the government had implemented a pay freeze and the following year saw the 'night of the long knives' when Macmillan, faced with mounting public dissatisfaction, sacked six ministers in a single re-shuffle. On the international stage Macmillan courted America and met with both Presidents Eisenhower and Kennedy on a number of occasions. The Kennedy administration agreed to provide Britain with Polaris weapons in Dec. 1962 but this had a knock-on effect for Macmillan's other great aim, entry into the EEC. A displeased Charles de Gaulle, wary of American intervention in Europe, rejected Britain's application a month later.

In terms of colonial policy, Macmillan, a staunch supporter of the anti-apartheid movement, acknowledged the calls for African independence when he spoke of 'the wind of change…blowing through the continent' in 1960. During his tenure he ended the Federation of Rhodesia and Nyasaland (now Zambia and Zimbabwe) and granted independence to many other states. His international reputation was heightened in 1963 when he co-signed the Nuclear Test-Ban Treaty with the US and USSR. But domestic strife was taking a toll on his government's popularity at home.

The disastrous Profumo scandal broke in June 1963, marking the beginning of the end of Macmillan's time in office. John Profumo, secretary of state for war, was exposed as having shared a mistress with a Russian naval attaché. The mixture of vice, corruption and Cold War intrigue forced the resignation of Profumo and questions were raised over Macmillan's handling of the case. Macmillan was struck down by ill health and resigned as prime minister on 18 Oct. 1963.

Later Life

Macmillan resigned as an MP the following year to return to publishing and to write his memoirs. He also served as Chancellor of Oxford University. He initially rejected a peerage but entered the House of Lords in 1984 as 1st Earl of Stockton, Viscount Macmillan of Ovenden. He had retained his skills as a politician and was highly critical of the Thatcherite policy of privatization, likening it to selling the family silver. He died on 29 Dec. 1986 in Birch Grove, Sussex.

Mádl, Ferenc (Hungary)

Introduction

Ferenc Mádl was elected Hungary's non-partisan president in Aug. 2000. His role was largely ceremonial. He stood down in 2005.

Early Life

Mádl was born in 1931. Having graduated in law he became a professor, counting previous prime minister Viktor Orbán among his students. Between 1990–94, in Hungary's first post-communist government, Mádl held several ministerial posts. He unsuccessfully stood for the presidency as a centre-right candidate in 1995.

In 2000 the governing coalition of Viktor Orbán selected Mádl as its presidential candidate. He also won support from the opposition Socialist and Free Democrats, despite having called them a 'communist coalition' before the parliamentary elections of 1998. At the presidential election of 2000 Mádl convincingly defeated his one opponent, Istvan Csurka of the extreme right Hungarian Truth and Life Party.

Career Peak

The presidency inherited by Mádl had evolved under Goncz into a figurehead role with particular emphasis on social issues. Some opponents of Mádl suggested he was too closely associated with members of the government for such a role. He voiced support for ethnic minorities within Hungary while calling for equal rights for ethnic Hungarians abroad. In Oct. 2002 Hungary was invited to join the EU in 2004. Membership won 84% approval in a referendum held in April 2003. Mádl died aged 80 on 29 May 2011.

Maduro, Ricardo (Honduras)

Introduction

In Jan. 2002 Ricardo Maduro was sworn in as the sixth democratically elected president since the end of military rule in 1981. He stood down from office in Jan. 2006. A conservative economist fluent in English, Maduro sought to improve relations with the USA and other regional neighbours. His predecessor, Carlos Flores complicated Maduro's diplomatic programme by re-establishing diplomatic relations with Cuba just hours before Maduro's inauguration.

Early Life

Ricardo Maduro Joest was born on 20 April 1946 to a Panamanian father and a Honduran mother. His primary education took place in Tegucigalpa before he attended high school in Pennsylvania, USA. He graduated from Stanford University with a BA in Economics in 1969. Maduro's career began in business. He was general manager of Xerox in Honduras before becoming executive director of Inversiones La Paz, an investment holding company, in 1976.

His involvement in politics began as an activist for the Partido Nacional (PNH). He was a founder member of the 'Unity and Change' movement, which tried to reform the party. Maduro managed two presidential election campaigns for Rafael Leonardo Callejas in 1985 and 1989, the latter resulting in victory. He was rewarded with the chair of the Central Bank in 1991, where he remained until 1994, also serving as coordinator of the Economic Cabinet.

He played a major role in the restructuring of the Honduran economy, including the liberalization of the financial and foreign trade sectors and the renegotiation of debt repayment with the IMF.

In 1994 Maduro withdrew from public life. The murder of his son, Ricardo Ernesto, in a kidnapping attempt in 1997, focused national attention on violent crime, encouraging a hard line government policy. The Ricardo Ernesto Maduro Andreu Foundation (FEREMA) was set up in his memory. In 1999 Maduro decided to re-enter politics by running for the PNH presidential candidacy.

Career Peak

Maduro ran for office on an anti-crime platform. His 'zero-tolerance' policy towards violent crime and street gangs was part of a wider programme designed to clean up Honduran politics and governance. The suggestion of police involvement in serious crime and the murder of thousands of street children throughout the 1990s and into the millennium provoked outrage from Hondurans and the international community. Despite introducing harsher sentences for gang members and undertaking economic reforms in return for international aid, Honduras remained stricken by poverty and violent crime when he left office in Jan. 2006, with the PNH having lost the presidency to Manuel Zelaya of the Liberal Party of Honduras at the elections of Nov. 2005.

Maga, Hubert Coutoucou (Benin)

Introduction

Hubert Coutoucou Maga was instrumental in Benin's (previously called Dahomey to 1975) transition from French rule to independence and was the first president of Independent Benin from 1960–63. He served again between 1970–72 before, in an increasingly turbulent political climate, he was imprisoned and forced into exile.

Early Life

Born in Aug. 1916, in Parakou, Maga graduated from the Teachers Training College in Senegal. After teaching for 10 years, he became involved in politics. He was elected into the French parliament in 1951. He served as junior minister of labour in the French cabinet from 1957–58. A strong supporter of independence, Maga worked in the peaceful transition from colonial rule between 1958, when independence was proclaimed until his election as the first president of Independent Benin in 1960.

Career Peak

In celebration of the new country, Maga commissioned developmental schemes including the construction of the Presidential Palace, the Court of Justice and the Palace of Congress.

Despite the peaceful transition, Benin soon encountered economic difficulties and consequential political and public unrest. In 1963, in an attempt to stave off economic crisis, Maga cut public sector salaries by 10%. Strikes and demonstrations ensued, and the armed forces under the control of General Christophe Soglo took the opportunity to depose Maga in a coup. Benin then suffered a period of severe instability and several coups. In 1970, with presidential elections unworkable, a presidential council took control run by Maga, Justin Ahomadegbé-Tomêtin and Sourou Migan Apithy. He passed on the reins to Ahomadegbé in 1972, but that same year Mathieu Kérékou led another coup and the whole council was jailed. Maga was released in 1981 and sent to exile while Kérékou turned Benin into a Marxist state.

Later Life

After the Conférence Nationale des Forces Vives de la Nation (National Conference of Live Forces) in Feb. 1990, an amnesty was granted to all political exiles. On his return, Maga was able once again to involve himself in political life. He sat on the High Council of the Republic from 1990–93 and on the Constitutional Court from 1993–98. He died from a heart attack in office on the 7 May 2000.

Mahama, John Dramani (Ghana)

Introduction

John Dramani Mahama became president in July 2012 after the death of John Atta Mills. In line with the constitution, Mahama as vice-president succeeded Mills, also replacing him as leader of the National Democratic Congress (NDC).

Early Life

Mahama was born on 29 Nov. 1958, in Damongo, in the Northern region of Ghana. His father was the first member of parliament for the West Gonja constituency. Mahama graduated in history from the University of Ghana in 1981 and completed a postgraduate degree in communication studies 5 years later. He then undertook studies in social psychology at the Institute of Social Sciences in Moscow.

Mahama taught history at secondary school level before working in the information, culture and research office of the Japanese embassy in Accra from 1991 until 1995. From 1995–96 he was the international relations, sponsorship, communications and grants manager at the anti-poverty non-governmental organization, Plan International.

Mahama was elected to parliament in 1996 for the Bole/Bamboi constituency. In April 1997 he was appointed deputy minister of communications, becoming minister the following year. He held the position until 2001, when the NDC handed power to the New Patriotic Party. Mahama nonetheless twice retained his parliamentary seat.

From 2003–11 he was a member of the Pan-African Parliament based in Pretoria, South Africa, continuing a keen interest in international affairs. In 2005 he was appointed the minority spokesman for foreign affairs. The NDC regained power in 2008 but in 2009 he gave up his seat in parliament to become vice-president to John Atta Mills.

Career Peak

Following Atta Mills' death, Mahama broadly continued his predecessor's policies. Confronted by a large budget deficit and a tarnished global image, he championed a stimulus package to boost the economy and pledged his commitment to Atta Mills' Better Ghana Agenda, aimed at improving economic health, environmental, educational and employment provision.

Mahama has campaigned to counter the problem of plastic pollution in Africa. He keenly supports the use of information and communication technology to stimulate economic transformation and has sought to improve agricultural productivity and to encourage young people to see farming as a viable business. In the presidential election held on 7–8 Dec. 2012 Mahama secured a further term with 50.7% of the vote. He was sworn in on 7 Jan. 2013, although the main opposition New Patriotic Party appealed to the Supreme Court unsuccessfully to overturn the result, citing voting irregularities.

In July 2014 there were opposition protests against deteriorating living standards and alleged economic mismanagement. A month later the government sought IMF assistance in the face of a mounting budget deficit. A formal agreement with the Fund was reached in April 2015, although public resentment at the poor performance of the economy continued to simmer. Towards the end of the year the government suspended numerous members of the judiciary implicated in allegations of bribery.

Mahama participated in the 2016 presidential elections but failed to be re-elected. He conceded defeat to Nana Akufo-Addo, who succeeded him in Jan. 2017.

Major, John (United Kingdom of Great Britain and Northern Ireland)

Introduction

John Roy Major was the Conservative British prime minister between 1990 and 1997. From inauspicious beginnings he had a meteoric rise through the Conservative party ranks, but once he had succeeded Margaret Thatcher his tenure was fraught with difficulties and ended with the Labour Party returning to power for the first time in 18 years.

Early Life

Major was born on 29 March 1943 in Carshalton in southeast London to Gwen and Tom, whose employment included circus performer and gnome maker. Much of Major's childhood was spent in Brixton, a working-class and racially-mixed area of south London. He left school when he was 16 years of age and held a number of jobs before embarking on a successful career in banking when in his 20s. In 1968 he was voted on to Lambeth Borough Council and, after two unsuccessful attempts during 1974, he entered the House of Commons as the member for Huntingdonshire in 1979. Huntingdonshire was to evolve into the constituency of Huntingdon in 1983 and Major remained its MP until he retired from parliament.

From an early stage he was a favourite of Margaret Thatcher and between 1981 and 1987 he held various junior ministerial posts. In the summer of 1987 he was appointed chief secretary to the treasury and in the same year he also became a privy counsellor. In July of 1989 he was given the post of foreign secretary, one he did not relish at the time, but he was to be there for only 3 months before he became chancellor of the exchequer. He had been an enthusiastic supporter of Thatcher but her support within the party was waning, notably over her anti-European stance. In Nov. 1990 Michael Heseltine challenged her for the party leadership and though she won, it was by only a small margin. She tendered her resignation, paving the way for both Major and foreign secretary Douglas Hurd to enter the race. A second ballot was held on 27 Nov. with Major receiving 185 out of 372 votes. He duly became prime minister and, at 47 years of age, was the youngest person to hold the office in the twentieth century before Tony Blair.

Career Peak

Major's honeymoon period was short. He was lauded for his performance during the Gulf War and he abolished Thatcher's widely disliked poll tax, but from the outset he was lampooned by the media as a grey and weak figure constantly under the shadow of Thatcher. Britain was also deep in one of the century's worst recessions, from which it did not emerge until 1993. Ratification of the Maastricht Treaty in Feb. 1992 confirming closer European ties brought internal Tory conflict into focus. However, following a campaign characterized by his populist, soap box oratory, Major won what for many was a surprise victory against Neil Kinnock's Labour in the election of April 1992. There was to be little let up for Major, though. On 16 Sept. 1992, Black Wednesday, Chancellor Norman Lamont had to withdraw Britain from the European Exchange Rate Mechanism and sterling went into freefall, losing 15% of its value against the Deutschmark. As the City bet against the pound throughout the day, the country lost billions. Relations between Major and Lamont soured and the chancellor was sacked the following May. He fired a parting shot at the Major administration in a speech in the Commons, commenting that 'we give the impression of being in office but not in power'. Whether justified or not, it was an allegation that Major never truly overcame.

From the mid-1990s onwards there were definite signs of an economic recovery. Interest rates, inflation and unemployment were all falling while industrial production was increasing. In addition, Major was making more headway in his attempts to bring peace to Northern Ireland than any of his predecessors, with the IRA calling a ceasefire which paved the way for 1998's Good Friday Agreement. But the question of European Union and Britain's role within it provoked numerous rebellions within the party and undermined notions of Conservative unity. Angered by constant challenges to his leadership, Major took the unusual and risky step of resigning the Conservative leadership in June 1995, challenging his opponents to 'put up or shut up'. He entered into a leadership battle with the Welsh secretary, John Redwood, on the understanding that if Major lost he would resign and if he won he would resume the leadership unchallenged through to the next election. Major defeated Redwood by 218 votes to 89.

The question of Europe never went away and the last years of his term were also plagued by allegations of 'sleaze'. as the media exposed various sex and corruption scandals involving prominent figures like David Mellor, Neil Hamilton and Jonathan Aitken. Major's approval ratings were dipping below 20% at times and it was little surprise when the Labour Party, rejuvenated under John Smith and then Tony Blair, won a landslide victory in the election of 1 May 1997. Major resigned the party leadership immediately and was replaced by William Hague.

Later Life

Major remained an MP until the 2001 election and published his memoirs to wide acclaim in 1999. He won the *Spectator Parliamentarian of the Year Award* in 1999 before settling into retirement with his wife Norma. His resignation speech after the 1997 election defeat serves as a fitting tribute to his personal style when he asked the media throng to excuse him as he hoped 'Norma and I will be able, with the children, to get to the Oval in time for lunch and for some cricket this afternoon'. In 2002 Major's reputation was dented when it came to light that he had been conducting a 4 year extramarital affair with a fellow MP before he entered cabinet. He received a knighthood in 2005.

Makarios III (Cyprus)

Introduction

Archbishop Makarios was Patriarch of the Greek Orthodox Church from 1950 and first President of the independent Republic of Cyprus from Dec. 1959 until his death in 1977. Initially a leading figure in the movement for Enosis (the union of Cyprus with Greece), he was exiled by the British in 1956–57 for alleged involvement in a terrorist campaign by the guerrilla movement EOKA. Having returned to Cyprus in 1959, he was elected to the presidency later that year. Although deposed by a military coup in Aug. 1974, Makarios was reinstated the following year and continued in office until his death.

Early Life

Born on 13 Aug. 1913, Makarios was educated locally before attending the University of Athens and later the School of Theology at Boston University in the USA. He was ordained as a priest in 1946, elected Bishop of Kition in 1948 and was made Archbishop of the Orthodox Church in Cyprus in 1950. He became involved in politics as a supporter of Enosis, opposing British proposals for Cypriot independence within the Commonwealth and Turkish Cypriot demands for separation. Following a wave of terrorism and unrest in the mid-1950s, Makarios was arrested by the British on suspicion of collaboration with EOKA and exiled to the Seychelles until 1957, when he was permitted to move to Athens.

Career Peak

In March 1959 he was returned to Cyprus as the chief Greek-Cypriot Minister in a new Greek-Turkish provisional government to negotiate an agreement with the UK on power-sharing independence rather than union with Greece. On 13 Dec. he was elected president, and Cyprus became an independent republic on 16 Aug. 1960. Distancing himself from the extremes of the Enosis movement, Makarios attempted to make the power sharing agreement work with the Turkish Cypriot minority. However, serious problems arose over the interpretation and implementation of the constitution, including the formation of a national army, taxation issues and the system of separate municipalities. The Turkish Cypriots withdrew from the central government in Dec. 1963. In response to the subsequent outbreak of violence, the United Nations deployed a peacekeeping force from 1964. The Turkish Cypriot community meanwhile set up its own political structures.

Re-elected in 1968 (and again in 1973), Makarios came under increasing pressure from EOKA to accept greater Greek influence in Cypriot affairs. In July 1974, despite having tried to purge EOKA sympathisers from the police, civil service and armed forces, Makarios was deposed by a military coup, sponsored apparently by the ruling junta in Greece. After several months in exile, first in Malta and then in the UK, he returned to Cyprus in Dec. 1974 following the collapse of the Greek junta. However, he resumed the presidency of a truncated state. Turkey had occupied a third of the island in Aug. to prevent Greece imposing Enosis and had proclaimed a separate state in the north.

Makarios died of a heart attack on 3 Aug. 1977 and was buried on a hilltop tomb close to the Kykkos Monastery.

Makuza, Bernard (Rwanda)

Introduction

Bernard Makuza served as prime minister of Rwanda from March 2000 to Oct. 2011.

Early Life

Bernard Makuza was born in 1961 and served as an ambassador to Burundi and then Germany. In March 2000 Makuza returned to Rwanda to take up the post of prime minister, replacing Pierre-Celéstin Rwigema, who had resigned amidst corruption allegations. Makuza was a former head of the predominately Hutu Republican Democratic Movement (MDR) but ceased to be a member of a political party before his appointment as prime minister.

Career Peak

While the power of government resides with the president, the prime minister has a strong public image. In Jan. 2003 Makuza headed a national ceremony to mark the opening of rehabilitation centres for those who admitted taking part in the 1994 genocide. In Sept. 2004, alongside the then UN Secretary-General Kofi Annan and the Democratic Republic of the Congo's president, Joseph Kabila, Makuza was part of a UN-backed body created to resolve the civil unrest on the border between Rwanda and the DRC. In Oct. 2005 he opened the 6th African Congress on Savings and Credit Co-operatives; a 2 day conference held in Kigali, it discussed the reduction of poverty in Africa via the management of co-operatives. During his time in office Makuza aimed to improve political, economic and trade relations with foreign countries and forged a strong partnership with China.

He remained as the head of a new government named in March 2008 and, despite some speculation that he might be replaced, was reappointed to the post in Sept. 2010. However, in Oct. 2011 President Kagame appointed Pierre-Damien Habumuremyi as the new prime minister of Rwanda. After more than 10 years as premier, Makuza was appointed to the Senate in Oct. 2011.

Malan, Daniel François (South Africa)

Introduction

DF Malan served as South Africa's prime minister from 1948–54. His government is remembered as the instigator of the racial separation laws that came to be known as apartheid.

Early Life

Malan was born on 22 May 1874 near Riebeeck West. He was educated at Victoria College in Stellenbosch, and subsequently went to the Netherlands to study for a doctorate in divinity at the University of Utrecht. He graduated in 1905. He then returned to South Africa to pursue a career as a minister in the Dutch Reformed Church. After the outbreak of World War I he abandoned the pulpit in favour of editing a Cape Town based Afrikaner newspaper called *Die Burger* which supported J.B.M. Herzog's National Party. Malan was to remain committed to the cause of the Afrikaner population and their language for the rest of his life.

Malan's political career began in 1918 when he entered parliament as a National Party representative for Cape Province. He quickly developed a reputation as a gifted statesman and orator, and in 1924 he was appointed interior minister. He went on to hold successive ministerial portfolios in the departments of public health and education from 1924–33. During this era he secured official recognition of the Afrikaans language, as well as establishing a distinctive South African nationality. In 1934 Hertzog merged the National Party with the South African Party of Jan Smuts. Disillusioned, Malan led a splinter group which became the new Purified Nationalist Party.

Career Peak

Both Hertzog and Malan supported neutrality in World War II, a joint policy that restored their friendship and, in 1939, led to the reunification of the National Party. However, Malan and his followers rejected Hertzog's policy of equal rights for British South Africans and Afrikaners. As a result Hertzog retired from politics in 1940 and Malan became the new party leader. In the 1943 elections his party did moderately well, securing 43 seats in the House of Assembly. In 1948 the Nationalists achieved a slim majority after a campaign in which they appealed to the race-related concerns of the white population. Victory in 1948 meant that for the first time in the country's history, parliament was exclusively controlled by Afrikaners. This gave Malan the opportunity to enact segregationist legislation designed to enhance the power of white, Afrikaner citizens.

The Supreme Court questioned the legitimacy of his efforts to remove coloured people from official electoral rolls, thereby prohibiting them from voting. This constitutional crisis was short-lived, since Malan called fresh elections in 1953 which extended the National Party's majority, and hence allowed it to overrule the judiciary. Having overseen the first steps towards the implementation of the apartheid system, Malan retired from political life in 1954. He died 5 years later.

Malietoa Tanumafili II (Samoa)

Introduction

Malietoa Tanumafili II served as head of state from 1962–2007. At his death he was the third longest serving monarch in the world, after King Bhumibol Adulyade of Thailand and Queen Elizabeth II.

Early Life

Malietoa Tanumafili II was born on 4 Jan. 1913 and was educated in Samoa at the government-run Le ifi ifi School before studying in New Zealand at St. Stephen's College, Aukland, and Wesley College in Pukekohe. Upon the death of his father (Malietoa Tanumafili I) he succeeded to the title of Malietoa, one of Samoa's four paramount chiefs.

In 1940 Malietoa became a Fautua, or adviser to the New Zealand colonial administration, and represented Samoan interests at the UN in 1958. In 1959 he was appointed joint chairman of the working committee on independence and the constitutional convention, which helped pave Samoa's way to independence from New Zealand.

On Samoa gaining independence in 1962, Malietoa became joint O le Ao o le Malo (head of state) with Tupua Tamasese Meaole, a role they shared for 16 months. When Tupua died in 1963, Malietoa continued in the role alone.

Career Peak

Malietoa travelled widely, making state visits to China, South Korea, Japan and the UK, and was considered a stabilising influence on his country. He died on 11 May 2007, at 94 years old the then oldest head of state in the world. Under the constitution, his successor, Tuiatua Tupua Tamasese Efi, was elected by the legislative assembly for a 5 year term.

Early Life

Tandja Mamadou was born in 1938. A former lieutenant-colonel, he began his career in politics after taking part in a coup to overthrow Niger's first elected president, Diori Hamani. As minister of the interior, he was responsible for policing, national security and immigration.

In 1993 Mamadou ran for president but lost to Mahamane Ousmane. He ran again in 1996 but lost after a coup put Ibrahim Barré Maïnassara in power. In 1999 Maïnassara was assassinated, signalling a return to military government. Democracy was restored within the year and elections were held in Oct.–Nov. Mamadou was sworn in on 22 Dec. 1999, having defeated former prime minister Mahamadou Issoufou in the presidential poll.

Career Peak

When Mamadou took office Niger was heavily in debt, foreign aid having been cut following the Maïnassara coup. His priorities have since been to promote economic development, secure foreign investment and reduce government spending.

After drawing attention to environmental threats including soil erosion, deforestation and poaching, hunting was banned. In Oct. 2000 Mamadou gave support to the ECOWAS public health initiative aiming to immunize 70 m. children against polio. In 2001 students of the University of Niamey staged violent protests against reductions in their government grants. Aug. 2002 saw soldiers mutiny in protest at non-payment of wages and poor conditions.

In Jan. 2003 US President George W. Bush claimed to have documentary evidence that Iraq had attempted to buy uranium from Niger to use in the production of nuclear weapons. However, in March the IAEA (International Atomic Energy Agency) declared the documents forgeries and an apology was issued.

In Nov.–Dec. 2004 Mamadou again beat Issoufou for the presidency and his party won the largest number of parliamentary seats. Earlier in the year Niger held its first municipal elections, with parties backing the president winning the most seats.

Niger remains one of the poorest countries in the world, with high levels of unemployment and large foreign debt. Although Mamadou was praised for restoring stability, he faced internal hostility. This intensified in 2005 after the government cancelled a ceremony to release 7,000 slaves, claiming that slavery had ceased to exist since 2003. During 2005 there were widespread protests at tax increases, and in Aug. Mamadou was criticized for denying that the country was gripped by famine. In 2006 there was further agitation against his government in protest against the high cost of living, and aid agencies continued to warn of dwindling food supplies. A new rebel group, the Niger Movement for Justice (MNJ), based in the north of the country emerged in 2007. Demanding greater autonomy for the Tuareg people and a fairer share of the country's oil, uranium and gold wealth, the MNJ launched attacks on army targets and kidnapped dozens of soldiers. In response Mamadou dispatched 4,000 troops to the northern region of Agadez and declared a state of alert in Aug. 2007.

In elections in Oct. 2009, Mamadou's MNSD claimed 76 of the 113 National Assembly seats but the outcome was rejected by ECOWAS following a disputed referendum in Aug. to extend the president's term of office.

On 18 Feb. 2010 the government was deposed in a military coup launched by rebel soldiers. A group calling themselves the Supreme Council for the Restoration of Democracy led by Salou Djibo seized power.

Mamadou, Tandja (Niger)

Introduction

Both head of state and of government, Tandja Mamadou, became president in Dec. 1999 and was re-elected in Dec. 2004. He was leader of the National Movement for the Development Society (MNSD) from 1991 until his election. A referendum in Aug. 2009 approved the extension of his presidential term of office but he was overthrown following a military coup in Feb. 2010.

Mandela, Nelson (South Africa)

Introduction

Nelson Rolihlahla Mandela served as president of Southern Africa from 1994–99, having dedicated his early life to opposing apartheid. His commitment to multiracial democracy was at the cost of 27 years in prison, but eventually earned him world recognition and a Nobel Peace Prize. He remained a globally respected figure with a high international profile.

Early Life

Mandela was born on 18 July 1918 in the village of Mveso. He was the son of Chief Henry Mandela of the Xhosa speaking Tembu tribe. He was educated at a local mission school before being sent to Healdtown to attend a Wesleyan secondary school. Mandela attended the University College of Fort Hare where he studied for a BA, but was suspended for joining in student protests. He moved to Johannesburg where he qualified in Law in 1942. In the same year Mandela joined the African National Congress (ANC).

In Sept. 1944 Mandela helped set up the African National Congress Youth League (ANCYL). His commitment to the emancipation of black Southern Africans made a strong impression and in 1950 he was elected to the National Executive Committee.

As an active member of the ANCYL and as National Volunteer in Chief, Mandela attracted the attention of the white government and in 1952 he was convicted of contravening the Suppression of Communism Act. He received a suspended sentence and was denied participation in any form of political activity.

In 1952 Mandela was elected president of the ANCYL and the Transvaal region of the ANC. This secured for him the position of deputy president of the ANC. Throughout the 1950s he suffered many arrests and detentions. In 1960 the police opened fire on a rally at Sharpeville killing 69 demonstrators and wounding dozens more. The massacre provoked Mandela to abandon non-violent resistance to apartheid. Instead he formed Umkhonto we Sizwe (Spear of the Nation), the military wing of the ANC.

Returning from a tour of central and eastern African nations, Mandela was arrested and convicted of leaving the country unlawfully. While serving 5 years imprisonment he was charged, along with several others, with sabotage, treason and violent conspiracy. His closing statement in the Rivona Trial entered the history books as one of the great appeals for liberty.

'I have fought against white domination, and I have fought against black domination. I have cherished the ideal of a democratic and free society in which all persons live together in harmony and with equal opportunities. It is an ideal that I hope to live for and to achieve. But, if needs be, it is an ideal for which I am prepared to die'.

In 1964 Mandela was sentenced to life imprisonment and was taken to the maximum security Robben Island Prison, 7 km off the coast from Cape Town. In 1984 he was transferred to Pollsmoor Prison. 4 years later, when he was suffering from tuberculosis, he was moved again, this time to Victor Verster Prison.

Mandela's plight became an international cause célèbre. His release on 11 Feb. 1990 by the government of FW de Klerk was world news.

Mandela immediately resumed his campaign for 'freedom for all in our country'. He was elected to the presidency of the ANC at the first national conference of the newly legalized party whilst co-operating with the reformist president de Klerk. Together they established a programme that would ease South Africa into a new era of democracy.

Career Peak

In 1993 Mandela and de Klerk were jointly awarded the Nobel Peace Prize. In 1994 Mandela was voted president of the new democratic Republic of Southern Africa in the country's first free multiracial elections. The ANC won 252 of 400 seats in the national assembly. Mandela initially refused the presidency insisting that he was too old for the role but was persuaded to reconsider. Once elected president, the government of National Unity was formed, the Commonwealth restored South Africa's membership and international sanctions were lifted. South Africa was able to take part in the UN General Assembly, after an absence of 20 years and in 1995 South Africa hosted and won the rugby world cup.

Mandela's government consisted of many new and inexperienced ministers and on occasion he made unilateral decisions. Forceful in foreign policy, he pressed the Commonwealth to suspend Nigeria over the execution of opposition leader Ken Saro-Wiwa. In talks with President Clinton aimed at improving trade ties between South Africa and the US, Mandela refused to cut his country's links with Libya.

In 1998 Mandela's party was found by the Truth and Reconciliation Commission to have perpetrated human rights abuses during apartheid. His presidency also witnessed a steep rise in crime and unemployment. However, he achieved a measure of cohesion between disparate tribal, ethnic and religious interests. On 14 June 1999 Mandela was succeeded by his deputy Thabo Mbeki.

Later Life

In July 2002 Mandela's ex-wife Winnie Madikizela Mandela, who had been active in the ANC and had shared Mandela's high profile, was charged with 85 counts of fraud.

Since his resignation, Mandela has maintained a busy schedule of lectures and public appearances. In March 2001 he attended a meeting with South Korea's democratizing leader, Kim Dae-jung. Mandela has spoken out on the African Aids epidemic as well as the abuse of power by African leaders. He also headed negotiations between the warring factions in Burundi. In Sept. 2002 he condemned US President Bush's position on Iraq as a 'threat to world peace'. In 2004 Mandela announced he would be taking a less active public role owing to his declining health. Despite this, he founded 'The Elders' in 2007, a group of former political leaders including Kofi Annan, Jimmy Carter and Desmond Tutu to act as 'a fiercely independent and robust force for good'. He celebrated his 90th birthday on 18 July 2008 and in Nov. 2009 the UN declared the date would be annually celebrated as Mandela Day.

Mandela made his last public appearance in July 2010, at the football World Cup held in South Africa. After being plagued by a long illness, Mandela died in his home in the suburbs of Johannesburg on 5 Dec. 2013 aged 95. South Africans gathered across the country and globally to pay tribute to his life and work.

Manley, Michael (Jamaica)

Introduction

Michael Manley served three terms as Jamaican prime minister (1972–80 and 1989–92), and was the dominant figure in post-independence Caribbean politics, championing Third World issues and challenging US hegemony.

Early Life

Michel Norman Manley was born in Kingston on 10 Dec. 1924 to upper-class parents of mixed race. He was the son of Norman Manley, Jamaica's first Prime Minister, founder of the People's National Party (PNP), and a Jamaican National Hero. His mother was a noted sculptor.

After Jamaica College and service as a pilot in the Royal Canadian Air Force during World War II, Manley attended the London School of Economics, where he was influenced by his socialist professor, Harold Laski. Manley worked as a journalist in London (for the BBC and freelance), before returning to Jamaica in 1951 to write for the left-wing weekly *Public Opinion*. He became an active and senior trade-unionist, known for his skills as a negotiator and orator. In 1962 he was appointed to the Jamaican senate, and in 1967 the House of Representatives.

In 1969 Manley succeeded his father to the presidency of the PNP and, in 1972, he became prime minister.

Career Peak

Manley saw himself as a 'democratic socialist'. He tried to encourage economic self-reliance and became a champion of the less-developed nations. Once in office, he nationalized the country's bauxite mines, announced free tuition at secondary school and university level, and in 1973 helped found the Caribbean Community (CARICOM). He forged close ties with Cuba and eastern socialist countries, visiting Cuba in 1976 and receiving Fidel Castro the following year.

Although Manley was re-elected in 1976, partly thanks to Bob Marley's support, his economic strategy had failed disastrously. The 1973 rise in oil prices hit Jamaica hard, and Marley had his requests for financial aid turned down by the IMF. The rift caused by his anti-Americanism, his friendship with Fidel Castro, and his activism in the developing nations' Non-Aligned Movement did nothing to endear him to Washington, and the IMF was unwilling to discuss any long-term solution. Manley was initially defiant but was soon forced to return to the IMF to plead for help.

During this turbulent decade, the two main political parties (Manley's PNP and the Jamaica Labour Party) armed and supported their own street gangs to intimidate voters. It is believed that this was the beginning of the 'yardie' culture that still plagues the country. Matters came to a head in the 1980 election campaign, during which over 800 people were killed in the space of 2 weeks, most of them on election day itself. Manley lost the election to his bitter rival, the conservative Edward Seaga.

In 1989 Manley won back his premiership with a more moderate centrist programme, despite still claiming to be a socialist. This time he encouraged foreign investment and pursued free-market policies. In 1992 Marley was forced to resign owing to poor health. He died in Kingston on 6 March, 1997.

Manning, Patrick (Trinidad and Tobago)

Introduction

Patrick Augustus Mervyn Manning became prime minister for the second time in Dec. 2001, having previously held the post from 1991–95. The elections of Dec. 2001 returned a hung parliament but Manning's People's National Movement (PNM) gained a majority at elections held in Oct. 2002. He then retained the premiership as a result of the PNM's re-election in Nov. 2007. Manning sought to develop the country's oil, gas and tourism sectors, and achieved impressive economic growth rates on the back of new foreign investment and high energy prices. He left office in May 2010 after the PNM were defeated in snap parliamentary elections. Manning died in July 2016.

Early Life

Patrick Manning was born on 17 Aug. 1946 in San Fernando, Trinidad. He graduated from the town's Presentation College in 1965 and worked for a year as an oil refinery operator before studying geology at the University of the West Indies (Jamaica) from 1966–69. He was then employed as a geologist for the Texaco oil company until 1971.

In that year Manning joined parliament as the member for San Fernando East and was appointed parliamentary secretary at the ministry of petroleum and mines. Between 1973–78 he served as parliamentary secretary at the prime minister's office and at the ministries of planning and development, industry and commerce, and works, transport and communications. In 1978 he joined the finance ministry with responsibility for the maintenance portfolio and later the public service portfolio. He was then appointed minister of information in the prime minister's office. In 1981 he was named minister of information and minister of industry and commerce, and from 1981–86 served as minister of energy and natural resources.

In 1986 the PNM lost its first general election since independence in 1962. Manning succeeded George Chambers as party leader on an interim basis in Dec. 1986. He was confirmed in the job the following year and led the party to victory at the elections of Dec. 1991.

Career Peak

During his first tenure Manning set about making the economy more competitive. His government floated the Trinidad and Tobago dollar in a bid to encourage investment. In 1995 he attempted to dismiss the speaker of the House of Representatives, Occah Seapaul, over a scandal regarding testimony that Seapaul had given in a court trial. She refused to leave and suspended several government members. The PNM, already suffering a weakened majority after by-election losses the previous year, was thrown into crisis. Manning declared a state of emergency and put Seapaul under house arrest. He called early elections for Nov. 1995, hoping to take advantage of an improved economic outlook to bolster his government. However, the PNM lost to the United National Congress (UNC) and Manning was succeeded as prime minister by Basdeo Panday.

Panday won a second term in Dec. 2000 but at new elections 12 months later, following a split in the government, the UNC and PNM tied with 18 seats each. The two parties agreed a deal by which President Robinson would elect the prime minister. Panday withdrew from the pact when Manning was selected and demanded new elections. Without cross party co-operation Manning was unable to form a workable government. Parliament was suspended in April 2002, and at elections held in Oct. the PNM won a majority, claiming 20 of the 36 available seats.

To reform the economy, Manning proposed reductions in income and corporation tax. He also aimed to exploit the country's tourism sector while continuing to develop the oil and gas industries. In foreign policy, he sought a more prominent role for Trinidad and Tobago within CARICOM. In April 2005 the Caribbean Court of Justice, a final court of appeal intended to replace the British Privy Council, was inaugurated in Trinidad. Manning was, however, criticized for failing to bring the growing crime problem under control. In Oct. 2005 at least 10,000 people took part in a protest, named the Death March, against the level of violent crime, and in Jan. 2007 businesses and schools shut down in a mass demonstration against a spate of kidnappings. Also in Jan., the government announced that the country's long-established sugar industry could no longer be sustained because of cuts in European subsidies.

In Nov. 2007 Manning and the PNM retained power in elections, winning 26 of the 41 parliamentary seats. However, Manning's third term was marred by accusations of extravagant government spending after the nation hosted two international summits and the administration was criticized for neglecting healthcare provision and failing to curb rising crime rates. In April 2010 faced with a forthcoming parliamentary no-confidence vote, he called snap parliamentary elections which the PNM subsequently lost to the People's Partnership Coalition. Manning was succeeded as prime minister by Kamla Persad-Bissessar of the UNC on 26 May and also stood down as leader of the PNM.

Later Life

Manning died aged 69 on 2 July 2016, having been diagnosed with cancer 2 days earlier.

Mansour, Adly (Egypt)

Introduction

Adly Mansour became interim president in July 2013 following the ousting of President Morsi by the armed forces. A career lawyer and judge, Mansour announced in Nov. 2013 that he would not contest the presidential election, which were subsequently held on 26–28 May.

Early Life

Mansour was born in Cairo on 23 Dec. 1945 and graduated in law from Cairo University in 1967. He earned master's degrees in 1969 and 1970, in law and management science, respectively. He also studied at the École Nationale d'Administration in France, graduating in 1977.

He began his legal career as an assistant prosecutor in the state council, rising to become a judge in 1984. In this capacity he served in civil and state courts, and he also sat in religious courts where he ruled on Islamic observance. After working as a legal adviser to the Saudi Arabian ministry of trade from 1983–90, Mansour was appointed deputy chief justice of Egypt's Supreme Constitutional Court (SCC) in 1992.

In 2011, following the overthrow of President Mubarak, Mansour continued to serve on the SCC under newly-appointed chief justice, Maher el-Beheiry. The SCC ruled that the elections that brought Mohamed Morsi to power in June 2012 were flawed, a decision that opened the way for the armed forces to challenge Morsi's rule. From June 2012–July 2013 the SCC repeatedly came into conflict with Morsi's government. In May 2013 Mansour was appointed chief justice of the SCC by Morsi, taking office on 30 June. Two days later, when the armed forces deposed Morsi, Mansour was appointed interim president and was sworn in on 4 July.

Career Peak

In his early months in office Mansour faced widespread political unrest from Morsi supporters and the Muslim Brotherhood, with violent clashes resulting in a number of deaths. In Nov. 2013 his government introduced controversial restrictions on the right to demonstrate. Criticized by some for lack of progress in implementing human rights, he oversaw the drafting of a new constitution, which was approved by referendum in Jan. 2014. He faced the formidable challenge of managing the country's political and sectarian divisions while winning the confidence and economic support of international partners.

On 24 Feb. 2014 Prime Minister Hazem el-Beblawi and his government unexpectedly resigned to be replaced the following day by a new administration, headed by Ibrahim Mahlab, ahead of pending presidential elections. Army chief and deputy prime minister Field Marshal Abdel Fattah al-Sisi became the first candidate to present his credentials to the election committee.

Mansour was succeeded as president on 8 June 2014 by al-Sisi, who had won elections held in May.

Mao Zedong (China)

Introduction

Mao Zedong was the founder of Communist China: he proclaimed the People's Republic on 1 Oct. 1949. He was leader of the Chinese Communist Party (1935–76) and head of state (1949–59). Mao reworked Communism in his own image and his political theories were among the most influential of the twentieth century. But his radical Cultural Revolution proved destructive and set back China's development.

Mao was born on 26 Dec. 1893 in Hunan province. The son of a relatively prosperous farmer, Mao received only a basic education at the local village school before he was obliged to work on the family farm aged 13. Resenting the end of his education, Mao left home to continue studies at a local town and then attended a secondary school in Changsha. When military action reached Changsha, upon the overthrow of the imperial system in the revolution of 1911, Mao joined the revolutionary forces. In uniform for less than a year, Mao returned to his education which he did not complete until 1918.

Early Life

Mao's political career began in 1917 when he helped set up student organizations. In 1918 he went to Beijing where he briefly worked in the university library. There he met Li Dazhao and Chen Duxiu who were to lead the student protests in the radical May Fourth Movement. Chen and Li went on to found the Chinese Communist Party. Back in Changsha, Mao founded a revolutionary movement for students and workers, and by 1921 had become a Marxist and a teacher.

Mao was active in socialist politics in the early 1920s and, when other radicals joined the Nationalist Party, he too co-operated. A visit back to his home village led Mao to begin organizing political associations for peasants, but his political activities meant that he had to flee the authorities. Mao remained active in the Nationalist Party until Chiang Kai-shek (Chiang Chieh-shih) turned on the Communists in 1926–27. While Chiang's forces were massacring Communists in Shanghai, Mao was encouraging a peasant revolt in Hunan. When it became dangerous to remain, he led the survivors into the south-west of China.

For the next 4 years he led a guerrilla existence with the fledgling Communist People's Liberation Army (PLA) in the countryside. When a Chinese Soviet Republic was set up in Jiangxi province the Communists had a base to operate from. Between 1931–34 the Communist republic withstood attacks by Chiang's Nationalists. By Oct. 1934 the Communists were under threat and most of the PLA set off on the Long March to safety across China. During the Long March Mao became leader of the Communist Party. From 1936 to 1940 Mao wrote several important works on political philosophy as well as an account of his revolutionary struggles.

The 1937 invasion by Japan forced a reconciliation between Nationalists and Communists. Mao was initially pragmatic in his dealings with the Nationalists but, during the war, his anti-imperialist rhetoric strengthened. By 1938 Mao saw the necessity to adapt Soviet-style Marxism to Chinese conditions. This led to a power struggle with a pro-Soviet faction in the party. Mao's supporters won this Rectification campaign in 1943 and elements thought to be disloyal to Mao were purged. He now had control of the party. Soon he also had control of the country. When the Communists won the civil war against the Nationalists (1946–49), Mao proclaimed a new nation—the People's Republic of China—in Beijing on 1 Oct. 1949.

Career Peak

As the founding father of modern China, Mao exercised supreme power as head of state and leader of the Communist Party. Mao journeyed to Moscow to seal a pact with the Soviet Union, but, as a consequence, was soon dragged into the Korean War on the side of the Communist North (1950). Communist China initially depended upon Soviet assistance for economic development. A Soviet-style 5-year plan was put into action in 1953, but the relationship between Moscow was already showing signs of strain.

Mao introduced rapid collectivisation of farms in 1955. The countryside was to take the lead in implementing Communist economics. Mao's idea was not met with universal approval in the party but its implementation demonstrated his complete authority over the fortunes of the nation. He again ignored the opinions of senior colleagues when he launched the doctrine of letting a "hundred flowers bloom" in 1956—this freedom to express different views was a reaction to the legacy of Stalin's dictatorship in the Soviet Union. The new freedoms took a turn Mao did not expect and the role of the party was questioned by some intellectuals. Strict controls were reimposed and free-thinkers were sent to work in the countryside to be "re-educated".

In May 1958 Mao launched another ill-fated policy, the Great Leap Forward. To promote rapid industrialisation and socialism, the collectives were reorganized into larger units. Neither the resources nor trained personnel were available for this huge task. Backyard blast furnaces were set up to increase production of iron and steel. The results were predictably disappointing. When another member of the Central Committee, Peng Duhuai, criticised the Great Leap as poorly thought-out he was arrested and detained until his death. Peng was not alone in his beliefs in the leadership—others held their tongues.

By the early 1960s the Great Leap Forward was in trouble. Soviet advice against the project was ignored and a complete rift in relations with Moscow came in 1963 and Soviet assistance was withdrawn. Within China Mao was establishing an alternative power base in the PLA, under Defence Minister Lin Biao. Pragmatists, including Liu Shaoqi (who succeeded Mao as head of state in 1959) and Deng Xiaoping, wanted to reintroduce personal incentives and diminish the role of the collectives. Mao hesitated. These reforms might have been a way out of the economic chaos. But Mao had begun to believe in his own propaganda and placed the "class struggle" against the economic well-being of ordinary Chinese. He became the centre of a personality cult that almost took on the aura of a state religion. Mao's 'Thoughts' were published in the 'Little Red Book' and proclaimed to be invincible.

By 1964 Mao had determined that Liu and other pragmatists had to be purged. He set the Cultural Revolution in motion. Militant students were organized into groups of Red Guards to attack the existing party hierarchy. Anyone perceived to lack enthusiasm for Mao Zedong Thought was denounced. Thousands died as the students went out of control and the Army was eventually called in to restore order. Once again, Mao's enthusiasm for continuing revolution had ended in disaster.

Liu Shaoqi and other more moderate leaders had been purged. The skilled negotiator Zhou Enlai survived the storm and was able to engineer a temporary compromise between revolutionary rhetoric and economic necessity in 1971–72. Yet this cease-fire did not last long and the revolution continued to consume its own. In 1971 Mao's presumed heir, Lin Biao, vanished, apparently killed in an air crash while fleeing the country after an attempt to assassinate Mao. By 1976 Mao was again emphasizing dogma at the expense of order. Zhou's death early in 1976 seemed to open the way for further excesses, but Mao himself died on 9 Sept. in the same year. The radical Gang of Four, whose members included Mao's third wife—the former actress Jiang Qing—unsuccessfully attempted to seize power.

Mao's legacy was a superpower, Communist China, reunited—except for Taiwan where the Nationalists continued to rule—and largely freed from the corruption that had played such a major role in bringing pre-war China to its knees. Yet Mao's revolutionary enthusiasm had several times wrecked his country's economy and threatened public order. His political ideas were to prove an inspiration to a generation of left-wing radicals throughout the world. His memory is still officially revered in China, although Communist China's 'socialist market economy' pays little more than lip service to the Thoughts of Chairman Mao.

Marcinkiewicz, Kazimierz (Poland)

Introduction

Kazimierz Marcinkiewicz was elected Poland's prime minister in Oct. 2005. The teacher-turned-economist held conservative and nationalist views and was a close ally of President Lech Kaczyński. He resigned in July 2006 following a split with his party chairman.

Early Life

Kazimierz Marcinkiewicz was born on 20 Dec. 1959 in Gorzów Wielkopolski, northwest Poland. He graduated in physics from Wrocław University before completing a post-graduate course in administration at the Adam Mickiewicz University in Poznań. Returning to Gorzów Wielkopolski, he worked as a teacher and in 1983 he joined Solidarność (Solidarity), the self-governing trade union. He edited and published an independent educational periodical, *Pokolenie*, and the Catholic magazine, *Aspekty*. In Sept. 1989, amid the death throes of the ruling Polish United Workers' Party (PZPR) and the creation of a multi-party system, Marcinkiewicz became a founder-member of the Christian–National Union party (ZChN).

A conservative and nationalist party, ZChN performed well in the Oct. 1991 elections and its representative, Jan Olszewski, became prime minister. Marcinkiewicz, who had been head of the board of education in Gorzów Wielkopolski, was appointed deputy minister of national education in 1992 in the short-lived government of Hanna Suchoka. From 1994 he was a member of both the ZChN's main board and its regional administration in Gorzów Wielkopolski. The party was excluded from the Sejm from 1993–97 and was wracked by infighting but was nevertheless one of the key groupings within Solidarity Electoral Action (AWS). Marcinkiewicz served as deputy chairman of the Sejm education, science and youth commission and from 1999–2000 was head of the political cabinet under Prime Minister Jerzy Buzek (AWS). The AWS–UW (Freedom Union) coalition government was credited with implementing reforms to local government, health, pensions and education.

In Feb. 2001 Marcinkiewicz founded the Right-Wing Alliance party, which later became part of the Law and Justice party (PiS), founded by the twins Lech and Jarosław Kaczyński. He subsequently served as chairman of the Sejm state treasury commission and gained plaudits for his economic competence. Following the PiS' victory in the parliamentary elections of 25 Sept. 2005, Marcinkiewicz was nominated as their candidate for the premiership, with the blessing of PiS leader Jarosław Kaczyński. Marcinkiewicz was expected to form a coalition with the Citizen's Platform (PO), the pro-market party which came second in the elections, but talks collapsed and the PiS formed a minority government supported by the populist Samoobrona, the right-wing League of Polish Families (LPR) and the Polish Peasants' Party (PSL).

Career Peak

The PiS campaigned to defend traditionalist Catholic values by maintaining state benefits for the poor, cracking down on crime and corruption and overhauling security structures. Marcinkiewicz also pledged to tackle high unemployment, bring down the budget deficit and place the economy on a sounder footing.

Rumours abounded of a rift between Marcinkiewicz and Jarosław Kaczyński, the PiS chairman and twin brother of the president. Marcinkiewicz tendered his resignation on 7 July 2006 and was succeeded by Kaczyński a week later. Marcinkiewicz was subsequently appointed acting president (mayor) of Warsaw.

Marcos, Ferdinand Edralin (Philippines)

Introduction

Ferdinand Edralin Marcos was president of the Philippines between 1965 and 1986. Despite early economic success, he inspired opposition from students, communists and Muslim separatists. Accused of rigging the 1986 presidential elections, popular protest caused him to flee the country.

Early Life

Ferdiand Marcos was born in Sarrat, Ilocos Norte, on 11 Sept. 1917. He was the eldest son of Mariano Marcos (a teacher, lawyer and congressman for Ilocos Norte) and Josefa Quetelio Edralin, a teacher.

After graduating in law at the University of the Philippines, Marcos was tried and convicted in 1939 for the murder of Julio Nalundasan in 1933, a political opponent of his father. President Quezon offered the young Marcos an eleventh-hour pardon, which he declined. Marcos went to Laoag jail for 6 months where he spent much of his time writing an 800-page appeal. Marcos defended himself in an appeal in the supreme court and was acquitted of the crime in 1940.

After World War II, in which Marcos was an officer with the Philippine armed forces, President Manuel A. Roxas persuaded him to leave law and enter politics. He was duly elected as congressman of Ilocos Norte and served three consecutive terms. With his election, Marcos became the youngest member of the house of representatives. Between 1946–47 Marcos was technical assistant to President Roxas. He became a member of the senate in 1959 and served as senate president between 1963–65.

In 1964 Marcos left the Liberal party and won the Nacionalista party nomination for the presidential candidacy. In 1965, with the assistance of his former beauty queen wife, Imelda, and unofficial CIA sanctioning, Marcos was elected sixth president of the Third Republic of the Philippines, beating his Liberal party adversary and incumbent, Diosdado Macapagal.

Career Peak

Despite success with agricultural, education and economic policies, Marcos' leadership was dogged by student demonstrations and insurgent guerrilla activities by communists and Muslim separatists. On 21 Sept. 1972 Marcos declared martial law and suspended the 1938 constitution that would have denied him a third term. Marcos jailed many political opponents, including the influential and popular Senator Benigno Aquino Jnr. Aquino was allowed to leave the Philippines to undergo heart surgery in the USA in 1980. Marcos suspended martial law in Jan. 1981 but continued a dictatorial grip upon the country.

Returning from exile in 1983, Benigno Aquino was assassinated at Manila International Airport (Now known as Ninoy [Benigno] Aquino International Airport) as he left his aeroplane. Marcos was assumed to be responsible for the crime which led to widespread condemnation. To compound his problems the Philippine economy began to disintegrate and guerrilla activities intensified.

To reassert his authority Marcos called a snap election in 1986. Opposition united behind the assassinated Aquino's widow, Corazon Aquino.

After a much-disputed election, Marcos was heralded as the unlikely winner by the government led commission on elections. Inspired by the defection of the Philippine military and Corazon Aquino's call for a campaign of civil disobedience, over a million Filipinos gathered on the Epifanio de los Santos Avenue to stage their protest. This became known as the 'People Power' or 'EDSA' revolution.

Later Life

After his brief inauguration at Malacañang Palace, Ferdinand Marcos and his family were helicoptered, with US assistance, to Clark airbase and from there to Hawaii. Ferdinand and Imelda Marcos were indicted for embezzlement of US$270 m. but Ferdinand was considered too ill to leave Honolulu, having developed pneumonia. Ferdinand Marcos died of a heart attack in Hawaii on 28 Sept. 1989, aged 72.

Marović, Svetozar (Serbia)

Introduction

Svetozar Marović became the first president of the newly-constituted nation of Serbia and Montenegro in March 2003. A Montenegrin, he was deputy leader of the Democratic Party of Socialists (DPS) which advocated Montenegrin independence. On his election by the federal parliament, Marović pushed for increased integration into Europe and the European Union and promised greater co-operation with the UN War Crimes Tribunal in The Hague investigating atrocities in the Balkan wars of the 1990s. He supported Montenegrin independence in a referendum held in May 2006, when 55.5% came out in support of loosening ties with Serbia. Marović resigned from office in June 2006, bringing to an end the post of president of Serbia and Montenegro.

Early Life

Marović was born on 31 March 1955 in Kotor on Montenegro's Adriatic coast. He graduated in law from the University of Podgorica and entered Montenegro's parliament in 1990 as a representative of the DPS. He later became a member of the Montenegrin presidency, parliamentary speaker, chairman of the foreign policy and international relations committee and member of the federal parliament. He was voted DPS vice-president, deputy to Montenegro's Prime Minister Milo Djukanović. He was also the founder of Budva's annual summer theatre festival.

In March 2002 the parliaments of Yugoslavia, Serbia and Montenegro agreed to replace the federation of Yugoslavia with the more loosely affiliated Serbia and Montenegro. Vojislav Koštunica gave up his position as head of state to stand for the Serbian presidency. Serbia and Montenegro officially came into being in Feb. 2003. It was agreed that the new entity's first president would be from Montenegro and Marović was the only candidate. He was approved by parliament in March 2003.

Career Peak

Marović's term of office was scheduled to last at least 3 years, at which point either republic could call a referendum on full independence. He was expected to pursue closer ties with the EU and NATO and promised to work with the War Crimes Tribunal in The Hague. Towards this aim he stated his ambition to place the army and police under more transparent civilian control. Within days of Marović's selection by parliament, Serbia and Montenegro faced political unrest following the assassination of Serbian Prime Minister Zoran Djindjić.

Marović promised to improve living standards throughout the country. He also suggested that he could favour a change in the status of Kosovo—the Albanian-dominated province which saw some of the heaviest fighting during the break-up of Yugoslavia during the 1990s—paving the way for eventual Albanian self-determination but with safeguards for the rights of Serbian and other minorities in the province. In June 2003 the government agreed to talks with the authorities in Kosovo, the first since 1999, to discuss practical issues including infrastructure and communications.

In Oct. 2005 Serbia and Montenegro began talks on a Stabilization and Association Agreement with the EU. In May 2006 Montenegro held a referendum on independence, with a majority voting to dissolve the state union of Serbia and Montenegro. Marović resigned as head of the soon-to-be defunct country in early June 2006.

Martelly, Michel (Haiti)

Introduction

Michel Martelly was elected president of Haiti in March 2011. One of Haiti's most popular performers of Haitian dance music, he had strong support among younger voters. However, anti-government protests gained momentum during his tenure. He stood down upon the completion of his term in Feb. 2016 with no successor in place.

Early Life

Born on 12 Feb. 1961 in Port-au-Prince, Martelly is the son of an oil company executive. Educated at a Roman Catholic school in Port-au-Prince, he attended junior colleges in the USA but never graduated. After briefly working for a US construction company, Martelly enlisted at the Haitian Military Academy. In 1986 he embarked upon a musical career as a keyboardist and singer, playing Haitian *compas* dance music in Port-au-Prince. He was known by the stage name 'sweet Micky'.

Haiti's election of Nov. 2010 was its first since the devastating Jan. 2010 earthquake and was characterized by disorganization, voter intimidation and fraud according to foreign observers. Initially, Martelly was not included in the run-off poll but took his place when Jude Célestin, the candidate for the ruling Unity party, withdrew.

Despite his lack of a political background, voters bought into Martelly's vision of change for a country ravaged by poverty and political instability. He won 68% of the vote in the March run-off and was sworn into office on 14 May 2011.

Career Peak

Despite voter turnout of only 25%, his defeated opponent, the conservative former first lady Mirlande Manigat, did not challenge the result. The incumbent prime minister, Jean-Max Bellerive, resigned on 15 May 2011 to allow Martelly to choose his own premier. However, Martelly's first two nominations for premier, entrepreneur Daniel Rouzier and former justice minister Bernard Gousse, were rejected by parliament in June and Aug. 2011 respectively. Bellerive remained in a caretaker capacity until the appointment of Garry Conille as prime minister in Oct. 2011.

Martelly pledged to improve the faltering post-earthquake reconstruction programme. In Aug. 2011 he announced plans to reinstate the military, which had been disbanded by former president Jean-Bertrand Aristide. In Sept. 2011 he created an advisory board aimed at improving the economy and in Dec. 2011 he announced voting reforms.

Martelly has been criticized for his handling of the UN peacekeeping mission in Haiti. From Sept. 2010 there were popular anti-UN protests in the capital after a serious and prolonged outbreak of cholera was blamed on UN staff. The Senate in response passed a resolution for UN withdrawal, although the mission remains in operation.

Martelly's tenure hit further problems when Conille resigned on 24 Feb. 2012 after challenging Martelly's refusal to co-operate with an investigation into whether some government officials held dual nationality in contravention of the constitution. Martelly's nomination as Conille's successor was the foreign minister, Laurent Lamothe, who was confirmed in the post on 4 May 2012. In Sept. and Oct. that year protesters in Port-au-Prince called for the president's resignation, citing his failure to tackle poverty, the high cost of living and alleged corruption. Further anti-government protests in the capital in early 2014 amid anger over delayed elections and other issues prompted a major cabinet reshuffle in April, and there was more unrest in Dec. during which Lamothe and several other ministers resigned their posts.

From Sept. 2013 Haiti's relations with the Dominican Republic were severely strained after a ruling by the latter's constitutional court restricted citizenship rights and potentially rendered many residents of Haitian descent stateless. However, in May 2014 the Dominican president signed legislation overturning the court ruling and reinstated the citizenship of children born in the Republic to immigrant parents, which eased tensions with Haiti.

On 7 Feb. 2016 Martelly stepped down as president at the end of his term, leaving Haiti without a head of state. A presidential election run-off to appoint a successor has been postponed from Dec. 2015 to April 2016 amid allegations of fraud and fears of violence.

Martens, Wilfried (Belgium)

Introduction

Wilfried Martens served two terms as prime minister, from April 1979–April 1981 and again from Dec. 1981–March 1992. As Belgium's longest-serving premier since the Second World War, he led nine coalition governments. He later became president of the centre-right European People's Party grouping in the European Parliament. His two terms as Belgian premier were characterized by austere economic reforms and ongoing conflict between the country's French- and Flemish-speaking factions.

Early Life

Martens was born on 19 April 1936 in the East Flanders town of Sleidinge. He studied at the University of Leuven, attaining a doctorate of law and a degree in Thomistic philosophy. Having joined the Christian People's Party (CVP) in 1962, he quickly rose through its ranks and served as adviser to two prime ministers, Pierre Harmel and Paul Vanden Boeynants, from 1965–66. Martens became party chairman in 1972. He then won a seat in parliament in 1974 and, despite no ministerial experience, was invited in 1979 by King Baudouin to form a government following the resignation of Prime Minister Leo Tindemans.

Career Peak

At the beginning of the 1980s, the Belgian economy was in recession, undermined by high oil market prices and dwindling international demand for the country's traditional heavy industrial production. Martens' early years as prime minister were spent shepherding the country through this crisis via a controversial economic recovery plan, which involved devaluing the Belgian franc to increase export competitiveness. The economy steadily recovered, with unemployment rates receding and GDP growth peaking at 4.7% in 1988.

Martens also spearheaded reforms that led to Belgium's transformation into a fully federalized state in 1993. In 1980 the historically-distinct Flemish and French regions had become official Communities, with each assuming greater political autonomy. As part of further state reforms in 1989, his administration created a third region—the Brussels-Capital region.

Later Life

After leaving the national government in 1992, Martens focused on wider European Union politics, serving as chair (from 1990–2013) and leader (from 1994–99) of the European People's Party (which he had co-founded in 1976). He remained active in EU and Belgian political affairs up until his death in Oct. 2013.

Martin, Paul (Canada)

Introduction

Paul Martin succeeded his Liberal Party colleague, Jean Chrétien, as prime minister in Dec. 2003. He had previously served as finance minister between 1993 and 2002, during which time he recorded budget surpluses and reduced the national debt. As prime minister, his tenure has been undermined by the repercussions of a scandal involving the misuse by the previous Liberal government of public funds, although a judicial report on the affair published at the end of Oct. 2005 exonerated him personally of any blame. Martin's term as prime minister ended in Jan. 2006.

Early Life

Paul Martin was born in Windsor, Ontario on 28 Aug. 1938. His father, Paul Martin Sr, was a cabinet minister in four Liberal governments. Paul Jr studied philosophy and law at the University of Toronto and was called to the bar in Ontario in 1966. He subsequently took up senior positions with the Power Corporation of Canada and Canada Steamship Lines.

In 1988 Martin was elected to the House of Commons, representing the LaSalle-Emard riding in Quebec. Two years later he was defeated by Jean Chrétien in the race for the Liberal leadership. When the Liberals came to power in 1993, Martin was made minister of finance and was responsible for Quebec regional development (until 1996). As finance minister, he oversaw five consecutive budget surpluses, reduced public debt by $36 bn. CDN and granted large-scale tax cuts.

In June 2002 he left Chrétien's cabinet after the two fell out, ostensibly over Martin's campaigning for the party leadership. With Chrétien's decision to retire from the premiership, Martin was chosen as his successor as Liberal leader in Nov. 2003, winning 94% of the vote at a party convention. He was sworn in as prime minister on 12 Dec. 2003.

Career Peak

Martin announced plans to restructure government practices in a bid to combat perceived public apathy. A leading aspect of his foreign policy was expected to be improving ties with the USA. Relations became strained after Canada's refusal to support the US-led invasion of Iraq in 2003, but there were signs of a thaw in Jan. 2004 when President George W. Bush announced that Canadian businesses would be eligible to bid on Iraqi reconstruction projects.

In Feb. 2004 a report by the auditor-general criticized the misuse of $100 m. CDN of public funds. The money, part of a scheme to promote federal unity in Quebec following the province's narrow decision in the mid-1990s to remain within Canada, went to several public relations firms with ties to the Liberal Party. Martin ordered an enquiry amid confusion as to whether the allocation of finance had been decided by civil servants or members of the previous prime minister's office.

Although the Liberal term of office was not scheduled to finish for a further 2 years, Martin hoped to improve his position by calling elections for 28 June 2004. However, while the Liberals remained the largest party taking 135 of 308 seats, they lost their overall majority. Martin nevertheless formed a minority government and narrowly survived a parliamentary no-confidence vote in May 2005. Despite his earlier reputation for fiscal prudence, he has been accused of profligacy with the public finances since the elections by the Conservative opposition. In early Nov. 2005 the New Democratic Party withdrew support for Martin's minority government, increasing the likelihood of early elections.

In Jan. 2006 Martin called a general election which resulted in a Conservative Party victory. The day after the elections Martin announced his intention to resign as leader of the Liberal Party. On 6 Feb. 2006 he tendered his resignation and was succeeded by Stephen Harper.

Later Life

Martin stepped down as Liberal Party leader in March 2006 but remained in parliament. At the Oct. 2008 election he did not run for re-election.

Martinelli Berrocal, Ricardo (Panama)

Introduction

Businessman Ricardo Martinelli became president in May 2009. He led the Democratic Change party to a landslide victory, ending 40 years of bipartisan government.

Early Life

Ricardo Martinelli was born in March 1952 in Panama City to parents of Italian and Spanish descent. He was schooled in Panama City before attending Staunton Military Academy in Virginia, USA. In 1973 he graduated in business administration from Arkansas University and subsequently obtained a master's degree in the same subject from the Central American Institute of Business Administration in Costa Rica.

He returned to Panama to embark on a business career, first at Citibank before joining the retail company Almacen 99 in 1981. By 1985 he had set up the Super 99 supermarket chain and variously headed the Panamanian Chamber of Commerce, the Italian-Panamanian Chamber of Commerce and the governing association of retail companies. In 1991 he set up the Ricardo Martinelli Foundation, which grants scholarships to several thousand poor students each year. From 1993–96 Martinelli was involved with the Democratic Revolutionary Party (PRD) and was briefly head of the National Social Security Institute (CSS).

After 2 years out of the political spotlight, Martinelli established his own party in 1998, called Democratic Change (CD). In 1999 he allied himself with Mireya Moscoso in a conservative coalition against the PRD. When Moscoso went on to win the presidency, CD was rewarded with the ministry for the Panama Canal, just as management of the Canal was being handed over to Panama by the USA. Martinelli was a strong advocate for expansion of the Canal but progress was slow and in 2003 he resigned to stand for the presidency in 2004.

Although his 2004 campaign was unsuccessful, it positioned him in the public eye ahead of his second run in 2009. He stood as the candidate for the CD-led Alliance for Change coalition campaigning on a platform of change and fighting corruption. He won with over 60% of the vote.

Career Peak

Martinelli's election bucked the left-leaning trend in neighbouring El Salvador and Nicaragua. Among the policies he advocated were Panama's exit from the Central American Parliament (Parlacen), increased police wages, a monthly stipend of 100 balboas for the unpensioned elderly and the eradication of corruption. In 2009 he appointed the ex-military Gustavo Pérez as head of police and pledged to tackle the 'wild capitalism' of Panama. Martinelli also planned to reform the tax system and to overhaul Panama City's transport system with the construction of a metro network, which opened in 2014.

Panama maintained an impressive annual rate of economic growth during Martinelli's premiership. However, much of the country's wealth continued to stem from the nationally-administered Canal, ports and Colón free trade zone, while extreme poverty, although reduced, remains a problem. In Oct. 2011 Martinelli welcomed the ratification of a free trade agreement with the USA, which had been stalled since 2007.

Martinelli was criticized for political bullying and clashed with his vice-president, who accused him of corruption. He was ineligible to stand in the May 2014 presidential elections but stayed in office until Juan Carlos Varela was sworn into office as his successor in July.

Later Life

In Dec. 2015 Panama's supreme court ordered the arrest of Martinelli, who had been accused of using public funds to spy illegally on political opponents. Since May 2017 he has also been the subject of an Interpol warrant on the same charges.

Marzouki, Moncef (Tunisia)

Introduction

Moncef Marzouki was elected interim president in Dec. 2011, a year on from the start of the revolution that ignited the Arab Spring. A French-trained physician, human rights activist and leader of a secular, left-wing political party, he was a long-standing critic of the autocratic Ben Ali regime and spent many years in exile in France.

Early Life

Mohamed Moncef ben-Bedoui Marzouki was born in Grombalia in the northeast of the French Protectorate of Tunisia on 7 July 1945, the son of a magistrate. He attended Sadiki College in Tunis and then the Lycée Regnault in Tangier after his family moved to Morocco in 1956 amid the upheaval of Tunisia's independence.

In 1973 he graduated in medicine from Strasbourg University in France, specializing in neurology and practising in Alsace. Returning to Tunisia in 1979, he settled in Sousse and became a professor of community medicine at the city's university and a member of the Tunisian League for Human Rights (LTDH). Elected leader of the LTDH in 1989, he was an increasingly vocal critic of President Zine-Al Abidine Ben Ali, particularly in the wake of the government's violent crackdown on the Islamist Ennahda movement in 1991.

Marzouki failed in an attempt to contest the presidential election of March 1994, in which Ben Ali was the only official candidate. Marzouki was subsequently jailed and only released after an international outcry and the intervention of Nelson Mandela. In the 1990s he campaigned on behalf of Amnesty International and the Cairo-based Arab Organization for Human Rights.

In July 2001 he formed the Congress for the Republic (CPR), a centre-left, secular political party that was declared illegal. Having been forced out of the University of Sousse, Marzouki left Tunisia in 2002 for France, where he worked as a doctor in the suburbs of Paris. He published books and articles on community medicine, human rights and politics, cautioning against the 'Arab malaise' of societies caught 'between dictatorship and religious fundamentalism'.

Marzouki returned to Tunisia on 18 Jan. 2011 during a popular uprising fired by high unemployment, rising prices, corruption and lack of civil freedoms, which culminated in the overthrow of Ben Ali. The CPR came second behind the moderate Islamist Ennahda party in elections for the constituent assembly on 23 Oct. 2011. After the parties reached a coalition deal, Marzouki was elected interim president. He took office on 13 Dec. 2011.

Career Peak

Marzouki's mandate was to oversee the drafting of a new constitution and preparations for fresh elections. He was expected to direct foreign policy and to serve as commander in chief of the armed forces, although key decisions would require consultation with the prime minister.

Religious tensions sparked protests and some violence in 2012. Extreme Islamists staged a number of demonstrations demanding the incorporation of Sharia law into the new constitution, and in June 2012 the government imposed a curfew in some areas in response to riots. In Aug. that year there were also protests against constitutional provisions that some feared could limit sexual equality and women's rights.

In June 2012 the exiled former president, Ben Ali, received a life sentence *in absentia* for the deaths of demonstrators in the 2011 revolution.

In Feb. 2013 Prime Minister Hamadi Jebali resigned after failing to obtain backing from his Ennahda party to form a new coalition of technocrats. This was in response to the murder of a prominent left-wing anti-Islamist figure, Chokri Belaid, for which the secular opposition blamed Ennahda. Marzouki appointed the interior minister, Ali Larayedh, to replace him. Larayedh formed a coalition with the CPR, Ettakatol and independents.

The assassination of another opposition politician, Mohammed Brahmi, in July 2013 provoked more violence as protesters took to the streets to demand a non-partisan caretaker administration until a new constitution was approved and new elections held. Although radical Salafists were blamed for the killing, the opposition accused Ennahda of being too weak to deal with militant Islamists. In Oct. 2013 Ennahda agreed to step aside in favour of a caretaker government that would pave the way for fresh elections in 2014. In turn, Mehdi Jomaa, perceived as a politically neutral figure, was appointed by Marzouki as interim prime minister in early Jan. 2014 and asked to form a new cabinet. Later that month the Constituent Assembly approved a new constitution, marking a significant step to full democracy.

Marzouki's term as interim president came to an end on 31 Dec. 2014 when he was replaced by Beji Caid Essebsi, the winner of elections held in Nov. and Dec.

Masire, Quett (Botswana)

Introduction

Sir Quett Masire was Botswana's second president, holding office from 1980 until 1998. Leader of the Bechuanaland Democratic Party (BDP), he succeeded the nation's founding president, Sir Seretse Khama, upon Khama's death. Masire furthered the economic development and democratic reforms instigated by his predecessor, cementing Botswana's reputation as a model for stable African government.

Early Life

Sir Quett Ketumile Joni Masire was born on 23 July 1925 in Kanye, the capital of the Bangwaketse Reserve, in what was then known as Bechuanaland. His humble background was in contrast to that of his future political ally Seretse Khama, a nobleman educated at boarding school and Oxford University. Masire distinguished himself academically, graduating top of his class and winning a scholarship to Tiger Kloof Institute in South Africa.

In 1950 Masire co-founded Seepapitso Secondary School in the Bangwaketse Reserve, serving as teacher and headmaster until 1955. He subsequently established himself amongst the region's leading agriculturists. In both sectors Masire clashed with prominent figures in the colonial administration and gained a reputation for his eloquent criticism of the existing political system. After working in journalism and sitting on the Bangwaketse tribal council, Masire joined Seretse Khama in co-founding the Bechuanaland Democratic Party in 1962.

Masire served as the party's secretary-general and was its chief organizer and activist, as well as a foil to the party's charismatic leader. In 1965 the Bechuanaland Democratic Party won all but three of the Legislative Assembly's 31 seats. With the party's demand for the end of colonial rule thus strengthened, independence followed in 1966. Masire was named vice-president under Seretse Khama, a position he retained until Khama's death in 1980.

Career Peak

By the time he took over the presidency, Masire was recognized as a talented technocrat responsible for the nation's steady development since independence. His mandate was reinforced by overwhelming victories in the 1984 and 1989 general elections. Botswana's impressive post-independence economic growth continued throughout the 1980s, founded upon the country's extensive diamond reserves. Masire used diamond revenues to develop infrastructure and expand public services, though his free-market policies were unable to prevent the widening gap between the poor and the emergent middle-class.

Masire continued the policy of non-alignment practised by Khama, which led to some tensions with neighbouring South Africa in the apartheid era. Despite consistently advocated majority rule in South Africa, Botswana would not allow its territory to be used as a base for attacks against the country. Nonetheless, the 1980s were punctuated by acts of aggression against Botswana by South Africa.

Masire was re-elected for a final term in 1994, during which he faced the enduring challenges of combating hunger and improving social welfare. Evidence of economic stability was demonstrated by the withdrawal of the Agency for International Development in 1995. A rapprochement with South Africa was also achieved. Masire stepped down from power in 1998 to be replaced by his vice-president, Festus Mogae.

Later Life

Masire published an autobiography detailing his life in government and for many years continued to play an active role in Batswana and African public life. He died on 22 June 2017 at the age of 91.

Mbeki, Thabo (South Africa)

Introduction

A leading anti-apartheid campaigner and prominent member of the ANC, Thabo Mbeki was chosen in 1997 to replace Nelson Mandela as party leader. Two years later he led the ANC to electoral victory and succeeded Mandela as president. He was credited with improving South Africa's economy but was criticized for doubting the link between HIV and AIDS (which had reached epidemic proportions in South Africa) and for his ambivalence towards the extremist rule of Zimbabwe's Robert Mugabe. He resigned in Sept. 2008 under pressure from the ANC's National Executive.

Early Life

Thabo Mvuyelwa Mbeki was born in Idutywa, Transkei on 24 June 1942. Both his parents were teachers and anti-apartheid activists. Mbeki became politically active at the age of 14 when he enlisted in the ANC Youth League. Whilst studying for his A-levels he was elected secretary of the African Students' Association.

In 1962 his father was arrested and sentenced to life imprisonment. Mbeki went to the UK where he studied economics at Sussex University. He was employed in the ANC's London office by Oliver Tambo and in 1970 was sent to the USSR for military training. He then moved to Lusaka in Zambia where he was appointed assistant secretary of the Revolutionary Council. For the next 5 years Mbeki worked for the ANC in Swaziland, Botswana, Zambia and Nigeria. In 1978 he served as a political secretary to Tambo and subsequently became director of information and publicity. This role allowed him to increase international awareness of the plight of black South Africans and to enlist the support of many white South Africans who opposed apartheid. In 1989 Mbeki was chosen to head the ANC's department of international affairs, a position which involved him in the negotiations that ended apartheid. In 1993 he was appointed as the party's national chairman.

After the elections of April 1994 Mbeki was made deputy president of the government of national unity. He was chosen to succeed Mandela in Dec. 1997. In the June 1999 election his party won 66% votes and Mbeki replaced Mandela as president.

Career Peak

Mbeki's first months in office were dogged by speculation that he was introducing a more autocratic, less democratic style of government. This was largely brought on by his decision to replace several provincial premiers with nominees of his choosing. He made clear his intentions to change the segregated 'two nations' character of South Africa and in order to achieve this he acknowledged that his government would have to reduce crime, corruption and unemployment. His international reputation suffered when, despite overwhelming evidence, he refused to admit a link between the HIV virus and full-blown AIDS, claiming instead that the primary cause of the disease was poverty. This view attracted sharp criticism not just from his political opponents but from allies within the trade union movement, nurses, doctors, gay

rights groups and even Mandela himself. He was further criticized for failing to condemn the extremist rule of Zimbabwe's Robert Mugabe.

Within the party Mbeki's biggest problem was to secure agreement with ANC's leftwing partners—the Congress of South African Trade Unions (COSATU) and the Communist Party—on countering social and racial inequalities, while privatizing some state industries. A two-day strike was mounted by COSATU in Oct. 2002. In the same month white right-wing extremists began a terrorist bombing campaign in an attempt to overthrow the government. Nonetheless, Mbeki and the ANC retained a strong powerbase. At the 2002 ANC conference, as the sole candidate Mbeki was re-elected party chairman for a further 5 years, thus making him ANC candidate for the 2004 presidential elections.

Mbeki was one of the first leaders to respond to the USA's action against Iraq. Although he was not overtly critical, he made clear his wish for greater involvement by the United Nations.

Following the defection of two MPs in March 2003 the ANC gained control of the Western Cape province. South Africa's main opposition party, the Democratic Alliance, and the Inkatha Freedom Party formed a coalition in Nov. 2003 to strengthen their chances against the ANC in forthcoming elections.

The ANC were successful in the parliamentary elections of 14 April 2004, winning 279 of the 400 seats in the National Assembly with 69.7% of votes cast. The Democratic Alliance won 50 seats and Inkatha 28. Mbeki was unanimously voted president for another 5-year term. In June 2005 he sacked his vice-president, Jacob Zuma, after he was linked with a corruption scandal and replaced him with Phumzile Mlambo-Ngcuka, formerly the minister for minerals and energy. Corruption (and also rape) charges against Zuma were dismissed in 2006, boosting his chances of contesting the presidential elections scheduled for 2009. Under Mbeki's presidency, South Africa gained a non-permanent seat on the United Nations Security Council for the first time in Oct. 2006 and also became the first African country to legalize same-sex marriages the following month. In Dec. the government signalled a change of attitude towards the AIDS pandemic with the announcement of a new plan to fight the crisis.

In early 2007 demonstrators marched in some of the country's main cities in protest at the high levels of violent crime. Then, in June, thousands of public-sector workers took part in the biggest strike since the end of apartheid, lasting for four weeks and disrupting schools, hospitals and public transport. The action reflected trade union resistance to privatization, which was also opposed by the left wing of the ANC that viewed it as transferring state assets to the white and new 'black elite' business sector.

In Dec. 2007 Mbeki was defeated by Zuma in party elections for the ANC leadership, placing Zuma in prime position to become the next president. Subsequently, however, prosecutors brought new corruption charges against Zuma concerning a controversial arms deal.

In Jan. 2008 South Africa suffered a severe power crisis, with the government coming under fire for its failure to heed warnings of impending energy shortages. In May Mbeki called on the military to break up riots following attacks on immigrants fleeing the economic collapse of Zimbabwe. In Sept. 2008 Zuma was acquitted of all corruption charges amid allegations of political interference in the judicial process from, among others, Mbeki. The national executive of the ANC withdrew its support from Mbeki and on 21 Sept. he announced his resignation, effective from 25 Sept. Kgalema Mptlanthe, the party's deputy leader, succeeded him ahead of the 2009 presidential election.

McAleese, Mary (Ireland)

Introduction

Mary McAleese became Ireland's president in 1997, the first person from Northern Ireland to fill the post. A lawyer by profession, she is a devout Catholic with a conservative stance on social issues. Her campaign for the presidency was dogged by claims that she was a supporter of the nationalist Sinn Féin movement, allegations she strongly refuted. Having served the maximum two terms as president, McAleese stood down as president in Nov. 2011.

Early Life

Mary McAleese (*née* Leneghan) was born in Belfast on 27 June 1951. Her father was a pub landlord in Catholic West Belfast. The outbreak of sectarian violence in the late 1960s resulted in the family moving to County Down.

In 1973 she graduated in law from Queen's University, Belfast, and was called to the Bar the following year. In 1975 she took up a law professorship at Trinity College Dublin. She stayed in this position until 1987, although between 1979 and 1981 she worked as a television broadcaster and journalist.

In 1987 she unsuccessfully stood as a Fianna Fáil candidate for a Dublin seat at the general election. In 1994 she was appointed pro-vice chancellor of Queen's University, the first female to hold the post. Three years later she was selected by Fianna Fáil to stand in the presidential elections, defeating former prime minister Albert Reynolds for the candidacy. Unpopular with many unionists, she was accused of having links to Sinn Féin, the political arm of the paramilitary Irish Republican Army (IRA). Having denied the accusations, she presented herself as a 'builder of bridges' and won an overwhelming majority at the polls.

Career Peak

McAleese was inaugurated as president on 11 Nov. 1997. Her role was largely ceremonial and non-partisan. A practising Catholic, she opposed abortion and aligned herself with the Vatican on such issues as divorce and contraception. Nevertheless, she held liberal views regarding homosexuality and women priests. Describing the theme of her presidency as 'building bridges'. McAleese voiced support for peace-making in Northern Ireland and for continued cross-border co-operation. She was a regular visitor to Northern Ireland and, with the help of her husband, she publicly reached out to unionists who would traditionally have been hostile to Irish political figures. In Oct. 2004 she was appointed unopposed for a second presidential term. McAleese proved to be a popular figure and Queen Elizabeth II's visit in March 2011, the first state visit by a British monarch to the Republic of Ireland, was deemed one of the high points of her presidency. She left office on 10 Nov. 2011 and was succeeded by Michael D. Higgins.

Mebazaa, Foued (Tunisia)

Introduction

A career civil servant, diplomat and politician, Foued Mebazaa had been a senior figure in Tunisia's political firmament since independence. As leader of the lower house of parliament, he became interim president in mid-Jan. 2011 following a month-long popular uprising that led to the ousting of the incumbent, Zine El Abidine Ben Ali, and ignited revolutions across North Africa and the Middle East.

Early Life

Foued Mebazaa was born in on 15 June 1933 in Tunis. He attended the city's Sadiki College and studied law and economics in Paris. Having joined the Constitutional Youth political grouping in 1947, he was elected a member of the Aix-Marseille unit of the socialist Neo Destour (New Constitution) Party in 1954, which played a key role in securing Tunisian independence in 1957. A senior administrator of the General Union of Tunisian Students (UGET) from 1957–59, Mebazza entered mainstream politics under President Habib Bourguiba in 1961.

When the ruling Neo Destour evolved into the Parti Socialiste Destourien (PSD) in 1964 Mebazaa was elected to its central committee. He was the mayor of Tunis for 4 years from 1969–73, when he became a government minister. Between 1981 and 1986 he was Tunisia's permanent representative to the UN and then briefly ambassador in Morocco. He returned to government in 1987 as minister of youth and sport in the government of Gen. Zine El Abidine Ben Ali.

Mebazaa retained his position following a coup on 7 Nov. 1987 which resulted in Bourguiba being impeached and replaced by Ben Ali. The following year, amid sweeping economic reforms, the PSD was renamed the Rassemblement Constitutionel Démocratique (RCD) and Mebazaa was elected to its central committee. He served as mayor of Carthage for 3 years

from 1995 and in 1997 he was elected leader of the lower house of parliament, winning re-election in 2004 and 2009.

President Ben Ali proved unable to quell increasingly violent unrest over rising food prices, unemployment and corruption that began in the city of Sidi Bouzid on 17 Dec. 2010. He was forced to flee the country on 14 Jan. after 23 years of autocratic rule. The prime minister, Mohammed Ghannouchi, initially took over his duties but the constitutional council declared the president's departure permanent and gave Mebazaa, as leader of the house and as stipulated by the constitution, 60 days to organize new elections. He was sworn in as interim president on 15 Jan. 2011.

Career Peak

Despite Mebazaa's pledge to create a unity government including the long-ignored opposition, violent protests continued. Following the resignation of Ghannouchi and six other ministers in late Feb., Mebazaa appointed Béji Caïd Essebsi as premier. Sebsi unveiled a cabinet of technocrats, none of whom had served in previous governments under Ben Ali, to guide the country through to constituent assembly elections scheduled for 24 July 2011. Mebazaa said he would continue in office beyond his official 60-day term, arguing that the current constitution no longer had any credibility.

On 12 Dec. 2011 Moncef Marzouki was elected interim president by the constituent assembly and replaced Mebazaa in office the following day.

Mečiar, Vladimír (Slovakia)

Introduction

Vladimír Mečiar was three-times Prime Minister of Slovakia (June 1990–April 1991, June 1992–March 1994 and Dec. 1994–Oct. 1998). During his second period in office he oversaw the dissolution of Czechoslovakia and the establishment of the Slovak Republic. He was criticised for his authoritarian style, his treatment of ethnic minorities and his reluctance to instigate economic reform. Refused entry into NATO and the EU, he nonetheless remains an iconic figure to many Slovakians who support his strident nationalist sentiments.

Early Life

Mečiar was born on 26 July 1942 in Zvolen, Central Slovakia. He joined the Union of Czecho-Slovak Youth, a communist based organization. A talented amateur boxer, he held several administrative posts within the communist infrastructure. His support for the Dubček-led Prague Spring led to his sacking from the civil service and removal from the party in 1970. After working as a furnaceman, he studied law at Comenius University in Bratislava, qualified in 1974 and worked as a commercial lawyer.

In 1989, as the movement for reform gained pace throughout the Eastern Bloc, Mečiar was a leading figure in Slovakia's anti-communist Public Against Violence (PAV) movement. PAV advocated increased Slovakian autonomy and conservative reform of the economy. He was appointed Minister of the Interior in Czechoslovakia's first post-Velvet Revolution government and when PAV made a strong showing in the elections of June 1990, he became Slovakia's Prime Minister.

Career Peak

With Czech Prime Minister Vaclav Klaus promoting speedy and extensive economic reforms, relations between the two men were strained. Further damaged by allegations that he had collaborated with the communist secret police before the revolution of 1989, Mečiar lost the Slovak premiership in April 1991. He immediately broke with PAV and set up the Movement for a Democratic Slovakia (HZDS).

His opposition to the Prague-driven reforms and his belief in Slovak nationalism struck a chord with a Slovak electorate who felt like junior partners in the Czechoslovak federation. The HZDS made a strong showing at elections in June 1992 and Mečiar was re-elected Prime Minister. Having criticized the rapid pace of Klaus' reforms, the two prime ministers entered into negotiations for the dissolution of the federation. On 1 Jan. 1993 the two republics split and Slovakia became an independent sovereign state.

Tensions increased between Slovakians and the country's Hungarian and gypsy populations. In addition, the economy needed overhauling to reduce the dependence on heavy industry. Mečiar did little to encourage foreign investment, preferring to keep tight control over the economy, and unemployment spiralled. In March 1994 several of his cabinet resigned and Mečiar was forced out of office. He was replaced by Jozef Moravcik but following another strong election showing in Sept. Mečiar regained the premiership in Dec.

Mečiar's growing authoritarianism, manipulation of electoral law and domination of the Slovakian media, allied with allegations of government impropriety in business deals, blighted his reputation abroad. His relationship with Slovak President Michal Kovác, who advocated a more liberal regime, was strained and further weakened his position. In 1997 the EU rejected Slovakia's membership application, citing institutional corruption and ethnic problems as mitigating circumstances. NATO took a similar line. At elections in Sept. 1998 Mečiar's coalition was defeated and he resigned as prime minister the following month.

Later Life

In April 1999 he stood for the presidency, having held the position on an interim basis twice before, but was defeated in a run-off by Rudolf Schuster. In May 2000 Mečiar was arrested on charges of having made illegal payments to ministers between 1992–98, as well as for his alleged involvement in the 1995 kidnapping of President Kovác's son. Mečiar is married to Margita, with whom he has four children.

Medgyessy, Péter (Hungary)

Introduction

Péter Medgyessy became prime minister in May 2002, having led the Socialists to election victory. He headed a coalition with the Liberal Alliance of Free Democrats and took Hungary into the EU in May 2004.

Early Life

Medgyessy was born in Budapest in 1942 and graduated from the city's University of Economics. Joining the ministry of finance in 1966, he worked in the departments of economy, prices and international finance. He then headed the department of state budget and was deputy minister of finance before taking over the finance portfolio in 1987.

As deputy prime minister with responsibility for economics from 1988 until 1989 he laid the groundwork for the liberalization of the Hungarian economy. Chairman of Magyar Paribas from 1990 until 1994, he moved to the Hungarian Bank for Investment and Development where he stayed until 1996. He was then reappointed finance minister until 1998 when he took over as chairman of Inter-Europa Bank. A non-partisan, in June 2001 he was chosen by the Socialist party to stand for the premiership.

In the elections of April 2002, the Socialists won 178 seats to become the biggest party and Medgyessy formed a coalition with the Free Democrats.

Career Peak

Medgyessy's principle aim was to ensure Hungary's entry into the EU in 2004, with entry into the single currency 3 years later. In Oct. 2002 Hungary was confirmed as one of the ten nations scheduled to join the EU in 2004. Membership won 84% approval in a referendum held in April 2003.

He pledged financial support to low-income families and young couples, promised that the minimum wage would be untaxed and that key public sector workers would receive 50% pay increases. In June 2002 he came under pressure to resign after he admitted he had worked as a counter-intelligence agent for the communist regime. He defended himself, claiming his activities were solely to ensure Hungarian entry to the IMF. Having seen Hungary join the European Union in May 2004 he resigned in Aug. 2004 after the ruling Socialist Party withdrew its support.

Later Life

Medgyessy continued to serve as a member of parliament following his resignation, and was appointed 'travelling ambassador' by the then prime minister Ferenc Gyurcsány—a position he held until 2008.

Megawati Sukarnoputri (Indonesia)

Introduction

Megawati Sukarnoputri is the daughter of Sukarno, the country's first president following Indonesia's independence from the Dutch after World War II. (Sukarnoputri means 'daughter of Sukarno'). Megawati was elected president in July 2001. Since her family was removed from power in 1965 it had remained part of Jakarta's political and economic elite. Unlike Sukarno, she rarely gave interviews or spoke in public and there was much debate about her political positioning. During her time in power, she oversaw the partial stabilization of Indonesia's political scene but those who expected her to initiate major reforms were disappointed.

Early Life

Megawati was born on 23 Jan. 1947 in Jakarta. She studied agriculture and psychology at university but did not take a degree. In 1987 she was elected to the national parliament and in 1993 she became the opposition leader of the Indonesian Democratic Party (PDI), which originated as a nationalist party created by her father in the 1920s. In 1996 President Suharto tried to remove her as party leader. An attack on the PDI's headquarters led to the worst riots in 20 years. Megawati became a national heroine but was banned from contesting the May 1997 general election. Following Suharto's fall in 1998, Megawati formed her own party, the Indonesian Democratic Party of Struggle (PDIP). In the country's first free elections in 1999, the PDIP won 34% of the votes, the best return of any of the parties. However, Abdurrahman Wahid won the presidency, backed by an alliance of Muslim parties opposed to a female president. Megawati was elected vice president by the People's Consultative Assembly. In 2001 Wahid was removed from office and replaced by Megawati. The popularity of the Sukarno name and her resistance to Suharto's regime attracted popular support.

Career Peak

Megawati was criticized for lacking leadership skills and her father's charisma. Her quiet persona led to confusion about her politics. She won praise for defusing some of the political tension that had led to long-term instability, but failed to initiate fundamental reforms of political and economic life. Although committed to the IMF's plans for economic reform, she appeared unclear on restructuring the banking system and fighting corruption, while her approach to political and judicial reform was conservative. Her refusal to publicly support presidential elections scheduled for 2004 caused consternation among both her supporters and opponents.

Although Megawati earlier supported a hardline against the Aceh separatist guerrillas, the government and the Free Aceh Movement signed a peace deal in Dec. 2002 granting Aceh autonomy and self-government from 2004 in exchange for disarmament. However, fighting resumed in Aceh in May 2003 following the collapse of peace talks and Megawati declared martial law. In 2002 Megawati toured Asia, visiting China, India and North and South Korea. Following the Bali nightclub bombing in Oct. 2002, in which around 200 people died, Megawati authorized new anti-terrorist measures.

With unemployment rising and corruption still endemic, parliamentary elections were held in April 2004 and Megawati's PDIP was soundly beaten into second place. The first round of the country's first direct presidential elections were held in July 2004. In a run-off in Sept., Susilo Bambang Yudhoyono of the Democratic Party won 33.6% of the vote against 26.2% for Megawati. Megawati at first refused to concede defeat but Yudhoyono was sworn in as president on 20 Oct. 2004.

Meir, Golda (Israel)

Introduction

A leading figure in the Labour movement and a signatory of Israel's independence declaration in 1948, Golda Meir served as foreign minister from 1956–66 and prime minister from 1969 until her resignation in 1974. She died on 8 Dec. 1978.

Early Life

Golda Meir (née Mabovitch) was born in Kiev in Ukraine in May 1898. Her family emigrated to Milwaukee in the United States when she was 8 years old. Having married in 1917 and settled in Palestine in 1921, she took up social work and became active in the Histadrut (General Federation of Jewish Labour). A prominent advocate of the Zionist cause, she was appointed ambassador to the Soviet Union in 1948 after the proclamation of the state of Israel. The following year she was elected to the Knesset and appointed minister of labour and national insurance in Ben-Gurion's socialist government, a post she held until 1956. A supporter of unrestricted Jewish immigration to Israel, she was responsible for major housing and construction programmes.

Career Peak

Meir became foreign minister in 1956, the year of the Suez crisis, retaining that post until 1966. Subsequently, as secretary general of the Mapai Party, she helped forge a union with two smaller parties to establish the Labour Party in 1968. In March 1969 she succeeded Eshkol Levi as prime minister. Arab-Israeli relations polarised further during her premiership as Israel maintained its occupation of Arab territories overrun during the Six Day War of 1967. Arab resentment resulted in another war in Oct. 1973 as Egyptian and Syrian forces launched a surprise offensive on Yom Kippur, a Jewish holy day. The three-week campaign restored a degree of Arab military pride and had a profoundly disturbing effect on Israeli public opinion. Dissatisfaction with Meir's government over Israel's lack of readiness was reflected in the Dec. 1973 elections and she subsequently resigned. She was succeeded in June 1974 by Yitzhak Rabin.

Meles Zenawi (Ethiopia)

Introduction

Meles Zenawi headed Ethiopia's transitional government from 1991–95. He was then appointed prime minister, the most important executive position in the country. He had to cope with one of the world's weakest economies threatened by famine. His tenure witnessed a border war with Eritrea, which officially ended in 2000 but remains a source of contention. Relations with Sudan improved under Meles' guidance, but he remained troubled by separatist fighters in western Ethiopia. In late 2006 he launched a military offensive by Ethiopian forces to oust hostile Islamist militias that had taken control of much of neighbouring Somalia. Continuing insecurity prevented an early military withdrawal until late 2008 when, amid rising casualties and financial costs, Meles' government announced its decision to leave Somalia. He died while still in office in Aug. 2012.

Early Life

Meles Zenawi Asres was born in Adwa, in Ethiopia's Tigre region in 1955. He attended school in Adwa and Addis Ababa. In 1972 he began studying medicine at Addis Ababa University but left 2 years later to join the Tigre People's Liberation Front (TPLF) to fight against the Dirgue military government of Lieut. Col. Mengistu Haile Mariam. He served on the organization's central committee between 1979 and 1983 and sat on the executive council from 1983 until 1989. In 1989 he was elected chairman of the TPLF and of the Ethiopian People's Revolutionary Democratic Front (EPRDF), an alliance formed that year between the TPLF and the Ethiopian People's Democratic Movement.

Career Peak

Alongside his role as EPRDF chair, Meles was president of Ethiopia's transitional government, established after the overthrow of the Mengistu regime, from 1991 until 1995. During this period he oversaw the secession of Eritrea and the drafting of a new constitution which divided Ethiopia into ethnic regions. In 1995 the EPRDF-dominated elections were boycotted by the major opposition groups. In Aug. 1995 Meles was elected prime minister of the newly established Federal Democratic Republic of Ethiopia, while Negasso Gidada took the largely ceremonial role of president. Meles was also voted chairman of the Organization of African Unity (now the African Union) for 1995–96.

In 2000 the EPRDF again dominated parliamentary elections and Meles was confirmed as prime minister. Despite the liberalization of the media and a move away from the human rights abuses of the Mengistu years, there remained opposition to Meles' government, and in 2001 there were mass protests in the capital against police brutality and political and academic oppression. In May 2005 Meles won a third term of office in further elections that were bitterly contested. Following allegations of fraud, there were violent protests and elections were rerun in some constituencies in Aug. In Sept. the Election Board confirmed the final results giving the EPRDF and its affiliates a solid parliamentary majority. Meanwhile, however, opposition parties and demonstrators continued to contest the outcome, clashing in June with security forces in Addis Ababa where 36 people were killed. In Nov. at least 46 more protesters died during renewed violence. In May 2006 anti-Meles political parties and armed groups formed an opposition Alliance for Freedom and Democracy at a meeting in the Netherlands. In July 2007 Meles pardoned 38 opposition figures who had earlier been sentenced to life imprisonment on charges relating to the protests that followed the 2005 elections. In Jan. 2009 legislation was passed banning foreign agencies from work related to human rights or conflict resolution in Ethiopia in an apparent move to deter outside interference. The EPRDF won a further landslide victory in parliamentary elections in May 2010, handing Meles a fourth term as premier, but the poll was criticized by international observers and the results were again contested by the opposition.

On the economic front, Meles—formerly an advocate of Marxist-Leninism—adopted free market reforms that have generated considerable growth, although the country remains among the world's poorest. In 2002 an Economic Commission for Africa report highlighted excessive bureaucracy and the HIV/AIDS pandemic as major obstacles to sustained development.

In 1999 border fighting between Ethiopian and Eritrean forces escalated into a full-scale war, which cost 70,000 lives. A ceasefire was agreed in June 2000, with Ethiopia withdrawing its forces under UN supervision. A formal peace treaty was signed in Dec. 2000. Tensions remained, particularly concerning the control of the small border settlement of Badame. In May 2001 the countries agreed to abide by the decision of an international boundary commission. The commission awarded Badame to Eritrea, but Meles refused to accept the decision. Fears of a renewed conflict mounted in late 2005, after Eritrea expelled UN observers policing the militarized border region, and again in the autumn of 2006 as Eritrea moved troops into the buffer zone on the Ethiopian border in violation of the ceasefire. In Nov. 2007 Eritrea accepted a border demarcation proposal by an independent boundary commission but Ethiopia rejected it. In Jan. 2008 the UN Security Council extended the mandate of its peacekeeping mission on the border for a further 6 months (despite Eritrean opposition), but brought it to a close at the end of July. Relations deteriorated again in March–April 2011 as the Ethiopian government accused Eritrea of terrorist infiltration and then declared that it would support rebel forces aiming to overthrow Eritrea's President Afewerki.

Tensions with neighbouring Somalia took a new turn in Dec. 2006. Ethiopian troops launched an offensive in support of the weak, but internationally-recognized, transitional Somali administration (established in 2004) against Islamist militias that had seized control of the capital, Mogadishu, and much of the south of the country from clan warlords earlier in the year. Meles was determined not to allow an enemy Islamic state on Ethiopia's borders. The Islamist forces were initially defeated and dispersed by Jan. 2007, and nominal authority was restored to the transitional government. However, insecurity continued and in Nov. 2008, embroiled in a stalemate situation, the Ethiopian government announced that its troops would leave Somalia at the end of the year, raising the spectre of a renewed takeover of the country by Islamist groups. The troop withdrawal was completed in Jan. 2009, although the government disclosed in the middle of the year that it was maintaining reconnaissance operations in Somalia.

In 2011 Ethiopia was again threatened by mass hunger as the worst drought in several decades led the United Nations to declare a famine across the Horn of Africa and to appeal in July for emergency aid.

For several weeks in 2012 Meles was not seen in public and speculation about his health increased. He died at the age of 57 on 20 Aug. after contracting an infection.

Melo de Menezes, Fradique Bandeira (São Tomé and Príncipe)

Introduction

First elected president in Sept. 2001 and re-elected in July 2006, Fradique de Menezes weathered numerous political storms. During his two terms tensions mounted over the discovery of large offshore oil reserves.

Early Life

Fradique Bandeira Melo de Menezes was born in Madalena on the island of São Tomé in 1942, the son of a Portuguese father and a São Toméan mother. He attended school in both São Tomé and Portugal, before studying education and psychology at the Free University of Brussels, Belgium. De Menezes then completed postgraduate studies in international trade in the USA. In 1967 he took up work at Marconi Radio in Lisbon, before working for various US companies in Brussels.

He returned to São Tomé and Príncipe following the country's independence from Portugal in July 1975 and taught at the National High School. In the late 1970s he worked at the ministry of agriculture, under the Marxist-inspired Liberation Movement of São Tomé e Príncipe (MLSTP). De Menezes relocated to London in 1981, where he was director of São Tomé and Príncipe's Commercial Center. From 1983–86 he served as his country's ambassador to the European Community. When de Menezes returned to São Tomé in 1986 the MLSTP had begun to embrace economic and political reforms. He was appointed minister of foreign affairs but left politics to pursue business interests, establishing companies involved in shipping, agriculture (cocoa) and investment.

Following constitutional reform in 1990 and the country's first multi-party elections in Jan. 1991, de Menezes was elected to parliament. In the July 2001 presidential election, as the candidate of the centrist Independent Democratic Action (which had been founded in 1992), he ran against the former president, Manuel Pinto da Costa, and won in the first round with 56.3% of the vote. He was sworn in as president on 3 Sept. 2001.

Career Peak

Following his electoral success, de Menezes and his supporters set up a new party-the Force for Change Democratic Movement (MDFM). He promised to reverse the country's crippling economic crisis, but progress was slow. The discovery of substantial oil deposits offshore brought optimism but also raised the political temperature. While de Menezes was visiting Nigeria in July 2003 his government was toppled briefly in a military coup. International intervention led to an agreement with the coup leaders and he was reinstated on 23 July 2003. As political infighting continued, de Menezes dismissed the prime minister and appointed a new cabinet after a corruption scandal in Sept. 2004. There were further reshuffles in June 2005 and again in April 2006 following the resignation of the prime minister. Meanwhile, in Feb. 2005, São Tomé and Príncipe signed (jointly with Nigeria) its first offshore oil exploration and production-sharing agreement with international oil companies. In elections to the National Assembly in March 2006 the MDFM was returned as the largest party, and in July de Menezes was re-elected to the presidency as the MDFM representative.

Criticism of worsening economic conditions and the government's handling of dissent among police officers led de Menezes to replace several ministers in late 2007. In Feb. 2008 he appointed Patrice Trovoada of the ADI as prime minister. However, Trovoada's coalition government collapsed after only 3 months, having lost a parliamentary vote of confidence, and de Menezes turned in June to the MLSTP-PSD leader Rafael Branco to form a new administration. In Feb. 2009 it was reported that the authorities had foiled an attempted coup plot against Menezes and that over 30 people had been arrested. At the National Assembly elections in Aug. 2010, the opposition ADI won the most seats and de Menezes again nominated Patrice Trovoada as the new prime minister.

After two terms in power, de Menezes was obliged to step down. He was succeeded in Sept. 2011 by former president Manuel Pinto da Costa.

Menderes, Adnan (Turkey)

Introduction

Adnan Menderes served as the prime minister from 1950–60 under the presidency of Celal Bayar. Like Bayar he initially favoured a state-directed economy, but came to endorse private enterprise.

Early Life

Menderes was born in 1899 in Aydin, southwest Turkey. The son of a wealthy landowner, he was educated at an American College in Izmir (then Smyrna). He went on to study at the Faculty of Law in Ankara. His political career began in 1930 when he was elected to parliament as a member of Atatürk's Republican People's Party (RPP). At this time the RPP, as the sole parliamentary party, had instigated a state-run economy, a policy which Menderes and others began to question. As a result he was expelled from the party in 1945, and along with Bayar, Fuad Köprülü and Refik Koraltan he helped to establish the Democrat Party, the first legal opposition to the RPP.

Career Peak

In the 1950 elections the new party won a landslide victory, Bayar was elected president and chose Menderes to be his prime minister. Whilst in power Menderes continued to adopt the pro-Western foreign policy stance of the RPP, but he was more sensitive to the needs of the rural and traditional elements within Turkish society, and sought closer links with neighbouring Muslim countries.

He dispensed with the planned economy that had been installed by the RPP, and supported the development of private enterprise. In order to boost manufacturing and commerce, the government imported foreign goods and technology. These purchases improved the living standards of the average Turk, but they resulted in economic instability. Despite these fiscal difficulties the Democrat Party was re-elected twice, and Menderes retained his popularity with the rural poor.

Growing criticism caused Menderes to become increasingly intolerant of his opponents. He censored the press, authorized the arrests of numerous reporters and was said to have fixed a number of local elections. As a consequence, General Cemal Gürsel led a successful military *coup d'état* against the government in 1960. Menderes and many other leading figures within his party were arrested. He was later tried for violating the Turkish constitution and sentenced to death. Before his execution he attempted suicide, but failed. He was hanged on 17 Sept. 1961.

Menem, Carlos (Argentina)

Introduction

Carlos Raúl Menem was president of Argentina for two consecutive terms between 1989–99 representing the Peronist Partido Justicialista (Justicialist Party; PJ) of which he is still leader. During his presidency he implemented hardline economic policies to counteract recession, accelerated privatization and promoted a free market economy.

Early Life

Menem was born on 2 July 1930 in Anillaco in the northwestern region of La Rioja. The son of Syrian immigrant parents he studied law at the Universidad de Córdoba. It was at this time that Menem became politically active, having met President Juan Perón on a school visit to Buenos Aires in 1950. After graduating in 1955 Menem returned to La Rioja to defend political prisoners of the military government of General Juan José Valle. The following year he was imprisoned for political activism. In 1957 Menem formed the Juventud Peronista (Peronist Youth) party in La Rioja. At this time Menem did legal work for the Confederación General del Trabajo (trade unions) in the same region.

In 1962 Menem was elected congressman for the Castro Barros department in his home region. This tenure was cut short by another military coup. In March 1973 he was elected governor of La Rioja. Three years later he was again arrested, this time by the military that had overthrown Isabelita Perón's civilian government, and remained in prison for nearly 5 years. In 1983 he was re-elected governor of La Rioja and again in 1987. During this time Menem gained a reputation for encouraging business with favourable taxes.

Career Peak

In 1988 Menem was chosen as the PJ's candidate for the 1989 presidential elections. Following his successful campaign, Menem was inaugurated as president 5 months early when departing president Raúl Alfonsín was forced to stand down. With Argentina suffering from a severe recession and four-figured inflation, supported by Domingo Cavallo, Menem adopted radical reforms including a reduction in state employment, union power and the welfare system in favour of private pension schemes, and full convertibility between the peso and the dollar. The national oil company YPF was privatized in 1993. Free market policies included joining Mercosur (Mercado Común del Sur; Southern Common Market) with Brazil, Paraguay and Uruguay in 1991 (effective from 1995). The economy began to recover, but Menem came under criticism from his party who claimed he was departing from traditional Peronist principles. Towards the end of his first term, Menem amended the constitution to allow the president to stand for more than one term. He was re-elected in 1994 with 50% of votes.

Menem's second term also began with a recession. In 1995 unemployment rose to 18%. By 1997 the economy was in better shape and unemployment was down by 3%, but Menem's government was facing accusations of corruption. In 1997 the PJ was defeated in municipal elections by the centrist Unión Civica Radical (Radical Civic Union; UCR) and the left-wing Frepaso. In 1998 Menem was invited to London, the first Argentine leader to visit the UK since the Falklands War soured relations (1982).

Menem sought to stand again for election, arguing he had technically only served one term after 1994. His request was rejected by parliament. The PJ candidate in the 1999 elections, Eduardo Duhalde was beaten by the UCR's Fernando de la Rúa. Duhalde openly blamed Menem for his defeat claiming corruption charges against Menem's administration had affected his chances. In 2001 Menem was preparing for the 2003 presidential elections, but on 7 June he was placed under house arrest in Chile. A month later he was indicted over illegal arms sales. Along with three of his former cabinet ministers, he was accused of profiting from the illegal sales of weapons to Croatia and Ecuador when Argentina was bound under an international embargo. However, the arrest warrants were cancelled in 2004 and Menem returned to Argentina.

Menem stood again for the presidency in the elections of April 2003. He emerged from the first round as the leading candidate with 24% and was scheduled to meet Nestor Kirchner in a run-off in May 2003. However, opposition to Menem rallied behind Kirchner and, facing a landslide defeat, Menem withdrew from the race.

Later Life

In June 2013 Menem was sentenced to 7 years in prison following a renewed investigation into sales of weapons to Croatia and Ecuador between 1991 and 1995.

Menzies, Robert (Australia)

Introduction

Robert Gordon Menzies served as Australian Prime Minister between 1939–41—as leader of the United Australia Party—and between 1949–66—as leader of the Liberal Party. He was the longest continually-serving prime minister in Australian history and oversaw a period of Australian growth and economic boom. A fervent anti-Communist, he improved relations with the USA while maintaining the importance of Australia's role in the British Commonwealth.

Early Life

Menzies was born on 20 Dec. 1894 in Jeparit, Victoria to James Menzies, a store owner and later member of the Victorian parliament, and Kate Sampson. A gifted student, he studied law at the University of Melbourne before qualifying as a barrister in 1918. Two years later he married Pattie Maie Leckie, with whom he had three children. In 1929 he was made a King's Counsel, a year after he had entered the Upper House of the Victoria parliament as a Nationalist. By 1932 he was Victoria's deputy prime minister, railways minister and attorney general and 2 years later he entered federal government as the United Australia Party (UAP) member for Kooyong, Victoria. A UAP-Country Party coalition was in power under the UAP's Joe Lyons, with Menzies serving as attorney general and deputy leader of the party. He unsuccessfully challenged Lyons for the leadership in 1938, the year he earned the name 'Pig Iron Bob' for his part in selling pig iron to Japan, which many believed was being used to build armaments. When Lyons died suddenly the following year Menzies was chosen as his successor as both party leader and prime minister, taking office on 26 April. In Sept. 1939 Menzies announced Australia's entry into the Second World War, a decision taken without recourse to cabinet. It reflected his strong attachment to Britain as well as his sometimes autocratic style of leadership. A growing swell of dissatisfaction with his leadership from within his own party led to Menzies' resignation in 1941. In 1944 he became one of the co-founders of the Liberal party and, although he lost the election of 1946, he came to power once again 3 years later and would go on to win the elections of 1951, 1954, 1955, 1958, 1961 and 1963.

Career Peak

By 1949 Australia was entering upon a boom period as wool exports and mineral reserves boosted the economy. Menzies oversaw the introduction of protectionist policies for the farming and manufacturing sectors. He also embarked upon a crusade against communism, beginning in 1950 when he sent troops to support the Malayan government against communist rebels. In the same year he supplied troops to aid South Korea against the communist North and in 1951 he attempted to pass a bill outlawing the Australian Communist Party, an action which was deemed unconstitutional by the High Court. He pushed hard for Australian intervention in the Vietnam War and assisted Malaysia in the conflict with communist Indonesia during the 1960s. Domestically, Menzies' tenure came to be seen by many as a golden era for Australia. Throughout the 1950s there was virtually full employment, industry and foreign investment grew, incomes increased and a policy supporting immigration boosted population. In addition, there was an overhaul of the health and education systems, notably the higher education sector and support for the Commonwealth Scientific and Industrial Research Organisation (CSIRO). As national capital, Canberra was greatly developed. Though Menzies had to adopt stringent financial measures to control growing inflation in the early 1960s, he was still able to claim two further election victories against a divided Labor opposition. Menzies' allegiance to Britain (his support during the 1956 Suez Crisis was controversial) was balanced by a close relationship with the United States and the non-communist countries of Southeast Asia. He signed up to the Australia, New Zealand and United States (ANZUS) Security Alliance in 1951 and to the South East Asia Treaty Organisation (SEATO) 3 years later.

Later Life

Knighted in 1963 and succeeding Winston Churchill in the honorary role of Lord Warden of the Cinque Ports in 1965, Menzies resigned from political life in 1966. He was replaced as Liberal leader and prime minister on 26 Jan. by Harold Holt. Menzies went on to be chancellor of the University of Melbourne and in 1976 became the first to be awarded the honour of Knight of the Order of Australia. He died in Melbourne on 16 May 1978.

Meri, Lennart (Estonia)

Introduction

An ethnographer, writer and documentary film-maker, Lennart Meri was one of the leaders of Estonia's independence movement and the country's first post-Soviet president, serving from 1992 until 2001.

Early Life

Meri was born in Tallinn on 29 March 1929, the son of a diplomat. His father's postings took the family abroad and Lennart was educated in Berlin and Paris. At the time of the Soviet invasion in 1940 the Meris were in Tallinn. They were deported to Siberia and his father was sent to a labour camp while the 12-year-old Lennart undertook manual work to support the family. In 1946 they were reunited in Estonia and in 1953 Lennart graduated in history from Tartu University. Banned from working as an historian, he became a playwright for the theatre and radio.

While exiled in Siberia, Meri had developed a strong interest in Finno-Ugric language and ethnography, a theme he regularly explored in subsequent writings and documentary films (many of which were banned in the Soviet Union). In 1988 he founded the non-governmental Estonian Institute to promote cultural contact with the West. Its representations in Copenhagen, Stockholm, London, Bonn, Paris and Helsinki acted as *de facto* Estonian embassies until independence.

He was also an outspoken environmental campaigner, leading protests against Soviet plans to mine phosphate in Estonia. These protests evolved into a broader anti-Soviet movement that initially suffered violent suppression but helped achieve Estonian independence in 1991. Meri was initially appointed of the new nation and on 6 Oct. 1992 became its president.

Career Peak

Although the 1992 constitution granted the president limited powers, Meri was nonetheless highly influential in navigating the country through a volatile period of post-Soviet politics. He steered Estonia towards greater integration with Western Europe and sought membership of NATO. He also used his diplomatic skills to defuse tensions with Moscow over laws affecting the citizenship rights of Estonia's Russian community. In 1994 he negotiated the withdrawal of Russia's remaining troops from Estonian territory. He was elected president for a second term in 1996, serving until 2001 when he handed power to his long-time rival, Arnold Rüütel.

Later Life

Meri died on 14 March 2006 after a long period of failing health.

Mesić, Stipe (Croatia)

Introduction

Stipe Mesić became Croatian president in Feb. 2000, having previously been prime minister and the Croatian representative for the revolving Yugoslav presidency. Occupying the political centre, he advocated Croatian integration into NATO and the EU and received international support for his co-operation with the UN War Crimes Tribunal. He was re-elected in 2005.

Early Life

Mesić was born on 24 Dec. 1934 in Orahovica. He graduated in law from Zagreb University in 1961, where he was active in student politics. He entered the Croatian parliament in the early 1970s but served a year-long prison sentence for his role in the anti-Tito Croatian Spring of 1971.

As a member of the Croatian Democratic Union (HDZ), he served as Croatia's prime minister from 30 May–24 Aug. 1990 and was president of the collective Yugoslav presidency from July–Oct. 1991, resigning a few weeks before Croatia declared independence. From 1992–94 he was speaker of the Croatian parliament, but resigned his office and his membership of the HDZ in 1994. Unhappy with HDZ policy, especially concerning Bosnia and Herzegovina, he founded the Independent Croatian Democrats (HND). Three years later he moved to the Croatian People's Party (HNS), becoming its vice-president.

Following Franco Tudjman's death in Dec. 1999, he stood for the Croatian presidency and his progressive agenda and personal charisma proved popular with voters. In a run-off Mesić defeated Dražen Budiša of the Croatian Social Liberal Party and was sworn into office on 18 Feb. 2000.

Career Peak

Mesić resigned his party membership on assuming office. He promised to prune back presidential powers in a bid to avert the autocratic style epitomized by Tudjman, and vowed to clamp down on corruption. He also pressed the government to institute the necessary reforms to achieve membership of NATO and the EU. To this end he encouraged co-operation with the UN War Crimes Tribunal, although the decision to allow extradition met with considerable hostility, particularly from war veterans. In addition, Mesić made known his willingness to testify for the prosecution at the trial of Slobodan Milošević.

Mesić made headway in improving relations with neighbouring countries. After meetings with his then Serbian counterpart, Vojislav Koštunica, the two leaders agreed to improve diplomatic ties between their countries following the downgrading of relations during the 1999 Kosovo conflict. Mesić indicated that ethnic Serbs displaced during the 1990s would be accepted back into Croatia. Agreements to improve relations with Bosnia and Slovenia were also signed.

In Jan. 2005 Mesić was re-elected as president with 66% of the vote in a run-off poll against Jadranka Kosor of the HDZ. Following the inconclusive parliamentary elections in Nov. 2007, Mesić asked the incumbent prime minister Ivo Sanader to form a new coalition government which was subsequently approved by parliament in Jan. 2008.

Having served two successive terms, Mesić was not eligible to stand for re-election in Dec. 2009. He was succeeded by Ivo Josipović of the Social Democratic Party of Croatia on 18 Feb. 2010.

Michel, James (Seychelles)

Introduction

Former Vice-President James Michel came to power in April 2004, handpicked by then President France-Albert René to succeed to the presidency on René's retirement after 27 years in power. Michel had been vice-president since 1996 and had previously held a variety of ministerial positions. He was elected to the post in July 2006 and re-elected in May 2011 and Dec. 2015.

Early Life

James Alix Michel was born in the Seychelles on 18 Aug. 1944. He was a teacher before deciding to pursue a career in politics. His profile rose in the mid-1970s because of his involvement in the country's booming tourism industry.

In 1976, just before independence, he joined René's left-of-centre Seychelles People's United Party (SPUP)—renamed the Seychelles People's Progressive Front (SPPF) in 1978. He was a member of the SPUP's central committee when the party staged a bloodless coup in 1977, overthrowing the country's first president, James Mancham, and replacing him with René. There followed a 16-year one-party socialist dictatorship, during which time Michel held a series of important ruling party and ministerial positions. For several periods he was in charge of the highly-regulated Seychellois economy. On René's retirement in April 2004, Michel was sworn in as president.

Career Peak

Despite his allegiance to René, Michel was under pressure to speed up the country's democratization process, which had begun with multi-party elections in 1993. He also pledged to introduce more open political dialogue, particularly over matters concerning the Seychellois economy, and to develop the private sector. In Jan. 2005 Michel granted the Emirates Group the rights to operate non-stop flights three times a week between the Seychelles and Dubai in order to enhance the tourism industry and to increase trade for the business and cargo communities.

In March 2005 Michel detailed his foreign policy, underpinned by a desire to cement stronger regional ties in the Indian Ocean region—particularly in light of the Seychelles' exit in July 2004 from the Southern African Development Community, ostensibly because of high membership fees. He particularly focused on strengthening relations with Mauritius, working alongside the then Mauritian prime minister, Paul Bérenger, to strengthen the Indian Ocean Commission. Michel has favoured increased promotion of the Seychelles as a high-quality and safe tourist resort, and sought to make the country a leader in environmental issues.

In June 2005 Michel announced plans for a new national pension fund and a scheme to set-up a savings account of R1,000 for every Seychellois child, both of which came into effect in Jan. 2006.

After a close electoral contest in July 2006 he retained the presidency, defeating his Seychelles National Party rival. In the May 2007 parliamentary elections the SPPF retained its majority. Michel brought the poll forward after opposition MPs had boycotted parliamentary proceedings over moves to ban political parties (and also religious groups) from owning radio stations.

Confronted by a balance of payments and public debt crisis in 2008, Michel launched an economic reform programme with the help of the International Monetary Fund, which approved a 2-year US$26 m. support arrangement in Nov. As part of the programme, the government floated the currency and lifted foreign exchange controls. In Jan. 2009 he appealed for debt relief from international creditors as the Seychelles economy was hit by reduced tourist traffic and the effects of the global financial crisis. In Nov. that year the World Bank agreed a US$9 m. loan to help restore economic stability.

In response to the expansion of Somali piracy in the Indian Ocean, the Seychelles government entered into agreements with European Union countries and the USA to enhance naval and air patrol and surveillance to deter attacks on international shipping.

In Aug. 2010 the Seychelles ratified the statute establishing the International Criminal Court.

Michel was re-elected for a further term in May 2011 and his party won all 31 seats in parliamentary polling in Sept.–Oct. following an opposition boycott. He was re-elected again in Dec. 2015, with opposition figures claiming multiple irregularities in the polling.

Michel resigned in Sept. 2016 after his People's Party lost its parliamentary majority at elections held that same month. Incumbent vice-president Danny Faure was sworn in as the new president in Oct. 2016.

Mikati, Najib (Lebanon)

Introduction

Najib Mikati was sworn into office on 13 June 2011 having formed a government at the invitation of President Michel Suleiman following the collapse of Saad al-Hariri's government on 12 Jan. 2011. Mikati's centrist politics appealed to the country's major political groups, despite some critics labelling him pro-Syrian after he secured Hizbollah backing. However, his government resigned amid further political tensions in March 2013. He continued in office in a caretaker capacity until Feb. 2014 when Tammam Salam succeeded him as prime minister.

Early Life

Najib Azmi Mikati was born in Tripoli, Lebanon, on 24 Nov. 1955 to a Sunni family. He was educated at the American University of Beirut, earning a bachelor's degree and then an MBA. He also studied at the INSEAD business school in France and at Harvard University in the USA. While in education, Mikati co-founded a construction company, M1 Group, with his brother. In

1982, at the height of the civil war, the brothers saw the potential of the emerging telecommunications market and set up Investcom.

In 1998 Mikati was made minister of public works and transport, retaining both portfolios until 2004. He was elected to the National Assembly in 2000 but decided not to run against Rafiq al-Hariri for the premiership. Following al-Hariri's death in Feb. 2005, Mikati was invited to form a government. His assurances that he would remove the country's security commanders and oversee new elections won him the support of the anti-Syrian opposition. He subsequently stood down as prime minister after the June 2005 polls.

In June 2006 Investcom was sold to South Africa's MTN Group, although Mikati's M1 Group remained the second largest shareholder of MTN. Mikati was re-elected to parliament in June 2009 but did not join the government of Saad al-Hariri. After al-Hariri's coalition collapsed in Jan. 2011, Mikati was appointed prime minister designate after 68 parliamentarians approved his Hizbollah-backed nomination.

Career Peak

Mikati was sworn into office in June 2011 and, after months of negotiating, his government (with a pro-Hizbollah majority) won parliamentary approval in July. He was faced with forging a workable policy towards the disputed Special Tribunal for Lebanon investigating the 2005 assassination of Rafiq al-Hariri.

At the same time the conflict in neighbouring Syria and the subsequent refugee crisis threatened to destabilize Lebanon's fragile political and sectarian balance, particularly following the assassination in Beirut in Oct. 2012 of the head of police intelligence, a critic of Syria's President Assad.

Amid rising tensions and disagreements over the organization of parliamentary elections (scheduled in June 2013 but postponed until Nov. 2014), Mikati resigned on 22 March 2013. However, he remained in office until a new government was formed. During the transitional period there was a resurgence of sectarian violence in Lebanon fuelled by the continuing crisis in Syria. Car-bomb attacks on two mosques in Tripoli in Aug. killed about 50 people and two suicide bombings by suspected Sunni Muslims on the Iranian embassy compound in southern Beirut killed over 20 more. In Dec. a former Sunni Lebanese finance minister and critic of the Syrian regime was assassinated in central Beirut.

Mikati finally left office on 15 Feb. 2014 when a new government was formed by Tammam Salam.

Milanović, Zoran (Croatia)

Introduction

Zoran Milanović became prime minister in Dec. 2011. A lawyer and diplomat, he promised sweeping reforms after leading a centre-left bloc to a landslide victory in parliamentary elections. However, the economy remained in recession and in Jan. 2014 European Union finance ministers launched proceedings to force his government to reduce the budget deficit to within EU permitted limits.

Early Life

Zoran Milanović was born on 30 Oct. 1966 in Zagreb and graduated in law from Zagreb University in 1991. He trained in the city's commercial court for 2 years before joining independent Croatia's ministry of foreign affairs. He then served on a UN mission to the disputed former Soviet territory of Nagorno-Karabakh before moving to Brussels in 1996 to serve on Croatia's mission to the EU and NATO.

Returning to Croatia in 1999, which was then under a right-wing Croatian Democratic Union (HDZ) government, Milanović joined the opposition Social Democratic Party of Croatia (SDP). Following the party's victory (in coalition with the Croatian Social Liberal Party and four minor parties) at the Jan. 2000 election, Milanović worked in various diplomatic roles. After the ruling coalition lost at elections in Nov. 2003, he joined the SDP's executive in 2004.

When Ivica Račan resigned as SDP leader in early 2007, Milanović ran for the party leadership and unexpectedly won, defeating more experienced candidates. The closely fought parliamentary elections of Nov. 2007 eventually resulted in an HDZ-led coalition, with Milanović leading the opposition. He was re-elected president of the SDP at the party's convention in May 2008.

Milanović led a centre-left opposition bloc known as Kukuriku to victory in the legislative elections of 4 Dec. 2011, securing 81 seats in the 151-member parliament and ousting the HDZ, which had presided over a series of corruption scandals, a stagnating economy and soaring unemployment.

Career Peak

Milanović pursued minor reforms and public spending cuts to deter down-grading by international credit rating agencies ahead of Croatia's accession to the EU, which took place on 1 July 2013. The previous April, Croatia had elected its first members of the European Parliament in anticipation of entry. Milanović's SDP won five of the 12 seats while the HDZ secured six. Croatia's first months of EU membership were marred by a dispute over an extradition and arrest law that critics claimed could shield suspected war criminals. Under threat of financial sanctions, the government agreed in Oct. to amend the legislation. By the end of his term as prime minister, Milanović succeeded in lifting the economy out of recession.

The majority of voters in a constitutional referendum in Dec. 2013 supported the imposition of a ban on same-sex marriages.

Milanović's term as prime minister ended in Jan. 2016 following the elections of Nov. 2015 which were won by the HDZ. He was replaced by Tihomir Orešković, who led a HDZ– Most unity government.

Miliband, Ed (United Kingdom of Great Britain and Northern Ireland)

Introduction

Ed Miliband became leader of the Labour Party on 25 Sept. 2010 in the aftermath of its May 2010 general election defeat. He identified himself as part of a 'new generation' and distanced himself from specific policies of the previous administration, notably the decision to go to war in Iraq. Criticising the Conservative government's package of 25% cuts in public services over 4 years as damaging to growth, he promised to formulate a deficit reduction plan while protecting the 'squeezed middle' of society as well as the poorest sections. Miliband resigned as Labour Party leader following the party's defeat at the 2015 general election.

Early Life

Edward Samuel Miliband was born on 24 Dec. 1969 in London, the son of academics. He grew up in London and was educated at Haverstock School, Camden, and Corpus Christi College, Oxford, where he was active in student politics. In 1990 he graduated with a degree in politics, philosophy and economics, then gained an MSc in economics from the London School of Economics. After working briefly in television, he became researcher to Harriet Harman, shadow chief secretary to the Treasury, in 1993. In 1994 he was appointed speech writer and researcher to Gordon Brown, who was then shadow chancellor of the exchequer.

After Labour came to power in 1997 under Tony Blair, Miliband became Brown's special adviser at the Treasury. He worked closely with Brown throughout the first 8 years of the Labour administration and helped devise the Scottish Labour Party's strategy in advance of the 1999 Scottish Parliament elections. In 2002 he went to the USA to teach at Harvard University, returning in Jan. 2004 when he was appointed chairman of the Treasury's council of economic advisers, formulating long-term strategy. He entered parliament as the Labour MP for Doncaster North in 2005 and served as minister for the third sector (dealing with charities and volunteer work) in 2006–07. In June 2007, when Brown replaced Blair as Labour leader and prime minister, Miliband was appointed minister for the cabinet office, coordinating policy between departments.

From 2008–10 he served as secretary of state for energy and climate change, overseeing the passage of the Climate Change Act in 2008, which set annual targets for reductions in carbon emissions until 2050. In Dec. 2009 he earned praise from environmental campaigners for salvaging an agreement, albeit limited, at the Copenhagen climate change summit. Against the back-ground of the global economic crisis, he devised Labour's 2010 general election manifesto which promised to halve the public spending deficit over 4 years, introduce a bank levy and tighten controls on the financial conduct of MPs.

Following Labour's election defeat and Brown's resignation, Miliband stood as a candidate for the party leadership. Initially seen as an outside chance in the five-horse race, he long trailed his brother and former foreign secretary David Miliband but steadily gained support over the 5 month campaign. He argued that the party should acknowledge that it had lost touch with voters and needed to renew itself. In particular he distanced himself from the decision to go to war in Iraq, opening up a clear divide with his brother. He also signalled that he might soften the timetable on deficit reduction. On 25 Sept. 2010 he won the leadership by a narrow margin of 1.3% over David.

Career Peak

Miliband began his leadership by promising to consider when forming policy the well-being of middle earners, whom he called 'the squeezed middle'. He criticized the government's programme of deep funding cuts and advocated practical measures to support jobs and growth. With his brother David having chosen not to serve in the shadow cabinet, Miliband appointed Alan Johnson as shadow chancellor, Yvette Cooper as shadow foreign secretary and Ed Balls as shadow home secretary. However, following Johnson's resignation for personal reasons in 2011, Balls became shadow chancellor, Cooper shadow home secretary and Douglas Alexander shadow foreign secretary.

After mixed results in the 2011 local elections, Labour's 2012 campaign proved more successful. The Labour gains across England, Scotland and Wales strengthened Miliband's leadership. When in Jan. 2013 David Cameron proposed holding a referendum on EU membership after the next general election Miliband opposed the idea, insisting the UK's national interest lies in remaining in the EU and that holding a referendum in 2017 would result in 'four years of uncertainty' for British businesses.

Ahead of the 2014 Scottish independence referendum, he also argued that Scotland and the rest of the UK would be best served by Scotland remaining within the Union. At the vote in Sept. that year, 55% of participants rejected Scottish independence. Although Labour made further gains in local elections and retained its seats in several parliamentary by-elections in both 2013 and 2014, Miliband continued to register low personal approval and credibility ratings among voters.

Despite polls predicting a close race which would require the formation of another coalition government or a minority government, the Labour Party took only 30.4% of the vote and 232 seats in a landslide win for the Conservatives. A number of high-ranking members, including Shadow Chancellor Ed Balls, unexpectedly lost their seats, and incumbent Prime Minister David Cameron was able to form a majority government. Miliband resigned as leader of the Labour Party on 8 May 2015.

Miller, Leszek (Poland)

Introduction

Leszek Miller, leader of the Democratic Left Alliance (SLD), became Polish prime minister in Oct. 2001. A former communist, he remoulded himself as a social democrat. His key aim was to prepare Poland for entry into the EU and in late-2002 Poland was included in enlargement plans for 2004. Facing a deteriorating economy, he bid to cut the national debt by increases in taxation and spending cuts. His coalition lost its parliamentary majority in March 2003 when he dismissed the Peasant Party following a disagreement over government policy. Amid plummeting opinion poll ratings, Miller resigned on 2 May 2004, the day after EU accession.

Early Life

Miller was born on 3 July 1946 in Żyrardów. He graduated in political science and took a job in a linen factory, where he became involved in trade union politics. He joined the Polish United Workers' Party in 1969 and was secretary of its political bureau in the last years of the communist era. He played an instrumental role in organizing the Round Table talks of the late 1980s that paved the way for democratic elections.

He was a founding member of Social Democracy of the Republic of Poland in 1991, chairing the party from the end of 1997 until he became leader of the newly-constituted SLD in Dec. 1999. After the collapse of the communist regime he sat in the Sejm as the deputy for Łódź. He was minister of labour and social policy between 1993–96 and briefly held the post of minister-chief of the office of the council of ministers before taking up the interior portfolio in 1997.

With Poland's economy in crisis, Miller led the SLD to victory at the elections of Oct. 2001, forming a coalition with the Polish Peasants' Party and the Labour Union.

Career Peak

On being sworn in Miller pledged to stabilize the national economy and agreed to a budget cut of US$2 bn. He froze ministers' and central government workers' salaries. In June 2002 relations with Germany were strained when Miller refused to open a debate on re-admitting Germans expelled from Poland after the Second World War.

In Oct. 2002 Poland was one of ten countries included in plans for EU enlargement scheduled for 2004. Membership was a stated aim of Miller's coalition, although the Peasant Party was troubled by proposed EU curbs on agricultural subsidies. Membership won 77% backing in a national referendum in June 2003. In March 2003 Miller dismissed the Peasant Party from the coalition after it failed to back his plans for a tax levy to improve the country's road infrastructure. The government, comprising only the SLD and the Labour Union, lost its parliamentary majority but remained in power.

Miller stepped down as SLD leader in Feb. 2004. With opinion polls in early 2004 indicating less than 10% support for his party and the defection of 27 MPs from the SLD, he announced his intention to resign after Poland's accession to the EU. A string of corruption and fraud allegations severely damaged the government's popularity, including a media law bribery scandal—Miller was exonerated for this in April 2004. He resigned on 2 May.

Mills, John Atta (Ghana)

Introduction

John Atta Mills of the National Democratic Congress (NDC) became president after winning a tight run-off in Dec. 2008. The peaceful transfer of power was considered a triumph for Ghana's relatively stable democracy. Atta Mills had previously served as deputy to President Jerry Rawlings from 1997–2001.

Early Life

John Evans Atta Mills was born on 21 July 1944 in Tarkwa in the country's Western Region. In 1967 he graduated in Law from the University of Ghana, Legon, before continuing his studies at London's School of Oriental and African Studies and as a Fulbright scholar at the Stanford Law School in the USA. Having gained his PhD in 1971, he returned to Ghana to teach at the Law faculty of his alma mater. He continued to work in academia, publishing twelve scholarly titles.

In 1988 President Rawlings, leader of the NDC, appointed Atta Mills as commissioner of the internal revenue service. Nine years later Rawlings invited him to be his vice-president. In 2000 Rawlings, who had served the maximum two terms of office, nominated Atta Mills as the NDC candidate in the election of that year. Atta Mills lost the presidential race, and again in 2004, to John Kufuor of the New Patriotic Party (NPP).

Nonetheless, his party re-selected him, ahead of three rivals, to fight a third election in Dec. 2008. With Kufuor constitutionally banned from seeking another term, the NPP's Nana Akufo-Addo emerged from the first round of elections in the lead, though just short of the overall majority required to claim victory. The second round was dogged by claims of electoral malpractice on both sides but, after a re-run of voting in one rural constituency, Atta Mills received 50.2% of the vote, beating his opponent by less than 0.5%.

Career Peak

Atta Mills presented himself as a social democrat and vowed to work towards national unity. He attempted to distance himself from earlier pronouncements that as president he would consult with Rawlings, a highly divisive figure in Ghanaian politics. In July 2009 Ghana secured a US$600m. 3-year loan from the International Monetary Fund, and a further economic boost was anticipated from offshore oil production which began in Dec. 2010. In July 2011 Atta Mills was again selected as the NDC candidate for presidential elections scheduled to take place in late 2012, but in July 2012 he died suddenly. He had been suffering from throat cancer although his illness was never officially confirmed.

Milošević, Slobodan (Serbia)

Introduction

Slobodan Milošević was President of the Serbian League of Communists (1986–88), President of Serbia (1988–97) and President of the Federal Republic of Yugoslavia (1997–2000). He capitalized on the rapid growth in Serbian nationalism during the late 1980s, advocating policies that hastened the collapse of the Yugoslav state during the early 1990s. His ambition to create an enlarged Serbian state led to conflict throughout the Balkans and provoked military action by NATO. After attempting to keep a grasp on power following rigged elections, he resigned in late 2000.

Early Life

Milošević was born on 29 Aug. 1941 in Požarevac, near Belgrade. His parents both committed suicide, his father in 1962 and his mother in 1972. Milošević joined the Yugoslavian Communist Party (later the League of Communists of Yugoslavia/LCY) around 1959. He studied law at the University of Belgrade, where he met his wife-to-be and closest political ally, Mirjana Marković. Following university he went into business, rising to be director of a state gas company from 1973–78 and then president of Serbia's most important bank.

In 1983 he joined the Central Committee of the Communist League of Serbia (CLS), and a year later he succeeded his mentor, Ivan Stambolić, as head of the Belgrade communist organization. In 1986 he again replaced Stambolić, this time as President of the CLS. Until 1987 Milošević was not regarded as particularly radical. Instead he stood for moderate liberalizing of the economy and stronger federal government. However in 1987 he made a visit to Kosovo where he witnessed mass demonstrations by the province's Serbian minority complaining about conditions under the Albanian majority and protesting at heavy-handed treatment by Albanian police. Milošević told the crowd that 'no-one will ever beat you again'. and from then on became a nationalist hero for many Serbs.

Career Peak

As leader of the CLS, Milošević established new party regimes in Kosovo and Vojvodina and packed them with his supporters. The following year, after Stambolić had been ousted by Serbia's parliament, he became President of Serbia. In 1990 he pushed through a new constitution that strengthened Serbia's power at the expense of the other provinces. But demands for increased autonomy forced Milošević to agree to multi-party elections and he thus established the Socialist Party of Serbia. Non-communist governments came to power in Croatia and Slovenia in Dec. 1990 but in Serbia Milošević's Socialist Party was returned in a landslide. Two years later he was re-selected to the Serbian presidency.

In 1991 Slovenia, Croatia and Macedonia became independent states. Bosnia and Herzegovina voted to go the same way in 1992. Milošević responded by backing Serbian forces within Slovenia, Croatia and Bosnia-Herzegovina who were opposed to secession. The UN imposed crippling trade sanctions on Yugoslavia but the war continued for another 3 years and included 'ethnic cleansing'. in which the regions' Muslims were systematically forced into exile. However, by 1995 Croatian forces had gained the upper hand and Milošević was forced to agree to the Dayton Accord, a peace treaty brokered in the USA.

Milošević's popularity waned throughout 1996 and 1997 as the economy went into freefall and Serbs came to terms with the failure of these military campaigns. Widespread protests followed municipal elections in late 1996 when Milošević refused to accept defeat. He did eventually concede but retained his hold on power by repression and the abuse of the media. Constitutionally unable to serve a third term as Serbian President, he persuaded the federal parliament to appoint him as President of Yugoslavia on 23 July 1997.

Having imposed Serbian direct rule on Kosovo in 1988, relations between the Serbs and Kosovan Albanians worsened. The Kosovo Liberation Army (KLA) had long undertaken guerrilla campaigns but in 1999 the conflict descended into open warfare between the KLA and Serb forces. Again, Milošević pursued a policy of 'ethnic cleansing' in which some 850,000 Albanians were forced to flee to neighbouring countries. NATO responded with an aerial bombardment that lasted for 78 days while Milošević took the opportunity to re-mould himself as the Serbian hero struggling against the combined forces of the oppressor West. However, he was ultimately forced to agree to the withdrawal of his Serbian troops from Kosovo.

Serbia reeled from the combined effects of another military defeat, and the damage inflicted upon the national infrastructure by air strikes and continuing sanctions. In 1999 the UN International Court of Justice indicted Milošević on war crimes relating to events in Kosovo. He was the first head of state to face such charges since the end of World War II. Public discontent mounted and when presidential elections were held in Sept. 2000 Milošević was defeated by the nationalist democrat Vojislav Koštunica. Milošević at first claimed the result had been so close that a run-off was required but faced with popular protests in Belgrade and international pressure he resigned the presidency, to be replaced by Koštunica on 7 Oct. 2000.

Later Life

Despite Koštunica's initial reluctance to co-operate with the UN war crimes tribunal based in The Hague, Milošević was arrested by Yugoslav forces in April 2001 and handed over to the tribunal. He was charged with 60 counts of war crimes, genocide and crimes against humanity during the break-up of Yugoslavia in the 1990s. Milošević refused to acknowledge the legality of the court, choosing to conduct his own defence. He said he had 'no intention of appointing a counsel for a non-existant court'. His trial started in Feb. 2002 and in July 2002 there were re-newed concerns for his health. Milošević defended himself at the trial which saw 295 witnesses testify in the 466 days of hearings. He was found dead in his cell on 11 March 2006 having suffered a heart attack. The funeral was held in Milošević's home town of Požarevac, after tens of thousands of supporters attended a farewell ceremony in Belgrade.

Mintoff, Dom (Malta)

Introduction

Dom Mintoff was twice prime minister, between 1955–58 and 1971–84. With Malta having been granted independence in 1964, Mintoff pursued a strong nationalist agenda during his second tenure. He positioned Malta within the non-aligned movement and developed close relations with leading Communist states and Libya.

Early Life

Dominic Mintoff was born in Cospicua on 6 Aug. 1916. He graduated from the University of Malta in 1937 before taking up a Rhodes scholarship and graduating with a master's in engineering from the University of Oxford.

Mintoff was general secretary of the Malta Labour Party (MLP) from 1936–37 and in 1945 he was elected to the Council of Government and Executive Council. Standing for the MLP, he entered parliament in 1947 and was named deputy prime minister and minister for works and reconstruction until his resignation 2 years later.

Career Peak

In 1949 Mintoff became leader of the MLP and was prime minister between 1955–58. He gave up the premiership in order to head the Maltese Liberation Movement, which played a leading role in establishing Malta as an independent state within the Commonwealth in 1964. From 1962 Mintoff was leader of the opposition but became prime minister again in June 1971.

Among Mintoff's first acts during his second tenure was to seek talks with the UK about the dismantling of its Maltese military base. Difficult negotiations carried on into 1972 and a 7-year defence agreement was agreed with Britain and NATO on condition that the base would not be utilized against Arab nations. The Maltese government was given an annual payment for use of the base and also won several sympathetically-termed loans. Elsewhere, Mintoff signed a treaty of amicability and economic co-operation with China and forged close relations with Soviet bloc countries as well as Algeria and Libya, who had offered significant economic support to Mintoff during his dispute with the British. By 1973 he had positioned Malta in the non-aligned movement.

In 1974 Mintoff declared Malta a republic, though remaining within the Commonwealth, and set about vigorously asserting sovereignty. Large numbers of British businessmen and journalists were expelled and in 1979 the UK and NATO left their military positions on the island after Malta refused to renew the defence agreement. Mintoff then formally framed Malta's policy of non-aligned neutrality.

During the 1980s relations with Libya took a knock over a disagreement about the positioning of the continental shelf boundary. At the national elections of 1981 Mintoff's Labour Party lost the popular vote but retained a working majority. In Sept. 1983 he took responsibility for the interior ministry but resigned from government in Dec. 1984. He was employed as a consultant to the new government of Prime Minister Carmelo Mifsud Bonnici.

Later Life

During the 1990s the Labour party began moderating many of its policies to secure middle class appeal. On taking power in 1996 under Alfred Sant it introduced taxes and utility charges that proved unpopular with sections of the party including Mintoff, who had retained his parliamentary seat. In 1998 the government, which had a wafer-thin majority, proposed the controversial sale of harbour facilities to a US interest. Mintoff voted against the motion thus bringing down the government. He died at the age of 96 on 20 Aug. 2012.

Mitterrand, François (France)

Introduction

François Maurice Marie Mitterrand was French president for 14 years between 1981–95, representing the Parti Socialiste (Socialist party; PS), although he soon came to adopt more centrist policies. During his two terms he reduced France's traditional polarized political spectrum and advanced France's European stance, including orchestrating the Maastricht treaty.

Early Life

Mitterrand was born on 26 Oct. 1916 in Jarnac, Southwest France. The fifth of eight children, his father was a stationmaster before inheriting a vinegar distillery. From 1934 he was educated at the Paris University, gaining a degree in law and political science. At this time Mitterrand was involved in right-wing politics, a popular student trend at the time, and took part in marches and demonstrations. Conscripted into the army he was wounded and captured in 1940. Eighteen months later, and after two failed attempts, Mitterrand escaped and returned to France. He allied himself to the Vichy government and worked for Pétain in the intelligence service, being decorated with Vichy's Francisque medal in 1942. By 1943, however, he was working for the Resistance and met de Gaulle in Algiers where he was again decorated, this time for opposing Vichy.

After the War he was a member of de Gaulle's provisional government. In 1946 he was elected deputy for Nièvre representing the centrist party, the Union Démocratique et Socialiste de la Résistance. In 1947 he became a cabinet minister and served under ten successive governments over 11 years.

He was secretary of state for information from 1948–49, minister for overseas territories between 1950–51, minister of state from 1952–53, minister of the interior between 1954–55 and minister for justice from 1955–57.

In Oct. 1958, when he was out of office, Mitterrand survived an assassination attempt when shots were fired at his car. It was suggested that the attack had been staged by Mitterrand himself for publicity purposes, although this was strongly refuted. In 1959 he was elected mayor of Château-Chinon (Nièvre). His first attempt at the presidency was in 1965 representing the Fédération de la Gauche Démocrate et Socialiste (Democratic and Socialist Left; FGDS). His second attempt was during the May 1968 student-worker uprising. When it appeared strikes and protests would force out de Gaulle's government, Mitterrand offered to set up a provisional government to lead negotiations between strikers and the state. The offer was premature and de Gaulle's government survived the crisis. After de Gaulle resigned in 1969, Mitterrand did not stand for election.

Career Peak

Mitterrand was elected secretary of the PS in 1971. At this time the party was disorganized, extreme and unelectable. Mitterrand set about consolidating the differing factions and forming the PS into an electable party. Reorganization and co-operation with the Parti Communiste Français (Communist Party; PCF) made the PS the largest opposition party. In the general elections of 1974 Mitterrand gained 49.2% of the vote. In May 1981 Mitterrand defeated the president Valéry Giscard d'Estaing, gaining 51.7% of the vote and ending the Gaullist's dominance of the Fifth Republic. He dissolved the assembly and in the subsequent elections secured a majority for the left, allowing him to introduce radical reforms. He nationalized many financial institutions, including 36 banks, and some industries, increased the *smic* (minimum wage), paid out more in welfare benefits and imposed a wealth tax. The working week was reduced to 39 h, and retirement to 60. He also abolished the death penalty. The state's grip on radio and television was loosened.

But a year into his presidency, inflation had risen to 14%, unemployment was rising, as was the trade deficit. It took a devaluation of the franc to bring the economy back into line. Mitterrand moved away from left wing policies to pursue more conservative aims and in 1984 the PCF dissolved their alliance with the PS in protest. But the PCF's influence had waned and Mitterrand no longer needed their co-operation. In 1986 the PCF vote had fallen to 10%.

In 1986 the PS lost its majority in the Assembly and Mitterrand was forced to accept Jacques Chirac as a right-wing prime minister. In the presidential elections of 1988, Chirac, representing Rassemblement pour la République (Rally for the Republic; RPR), stood against Mitterrand. Mitterrand was elected with an 8% majority. Chirac was succeeded by the socialist Michel Rocard and then by Edith Cresson. The first female prime minister in France, Cresson's short term in office was unsuccessful. Ineffectual compared with Rocard, Cresson was also carelessly outspoken and Mitterrand was forced to replace her with the finance minister Pierre Bérégovoy. Rising unemployment coupled with party scandals deprived the PS of its Assembly majority and Mitterrand was forced into another *cohabitation* with a right wing prime minister, Edouard Balladur.

Mitterrand favoured a united Europe. He had a strong alliance with Helmut Kohl, the German chancellor and much of his term was spent promoting European integration. A lasting image was Mitterrand and Kohl holding hands at the 1984 memorial service for victims of both World Wars. In 1986 Mitterrand and Margaret Thatcher announced plans for the Channel tunnel. In 1987 he signed the Single European Act, and was instrumental in negotiating the Maastricht Treaty in 1992. The treaty prepared the way for a single European currency and the free movement of people and trade.

Among the grand cultural projects sponsored by Mitterrand were the Bastille Opera House, the Louvre pyramid, La Villette science complex and L'Arche at La Défence.

Towards the end of his period in office, there were revelations about Mitterrand's activities in the Vichy government. In 1994 it was revealed Mitterrand had housed a mistress and daughter at the Elysée at the taxpayers expense. The following year when he was 78, Mitterrand retired at the end of his second term. Scandals associated with the PSF coupled with over 4 m. unemployed led to a crushing defeat for the party in the 1995 elections. Jacques Chirac representing the RPR was elected president.

Mitterrand died from prostate cancer on 8 Jan. 1996.

Mkapa, Benjamin (Tanzania)

Introduction

Benjamin William Mkapa became president of Tanzania in 1995 and won re-election in 2000. He instituted large-scale free market and anti-corruption reforms which were welcomed by the international community and led to an increase in foreign aid and investment. The on-going question of Zanzibar's secession from Tanzania continued to attract attention throughout his presidency, as did the national AIDS epidemic.

Early Life

Mkapa was born on 12 Nov. 1938 in Ndanda, Masai in what was then Tanganyika. He graduated in English from Makerere University in Kampala, Uganda in 1962 before beginning work as a district administrator in Dodoma and Dar es Salaam. The following year he took a post with the foreign service and went on to take a master's degree at New York's Columbia University.

He joined the Tanganyika African National Union (TANU) and in 1966 became editor of the party newspaper. He went on to work on several other press titles before becoming President Nyerere's press secretary in 1974. Two years later he was named high commissioner to Nigeria and in 1977 he entered parliament and became minister for foreign affairs, a post he held until 1980 and again between 1984 and 1990. From 1980 until 1983 he was minister of information and culture and then became high commissioner to Canada and then ambassador to the US. From 1990 until 1992 he was minister of information and broadcasting, before taking over the science, technology and higher education portfolio until 1995.

He was elected to the national assembly in 1985 as the representative for Nanyumbu, Masai and in 1995 he was chosen as the presidential candidate for Chama Cha Mapinduzi (CCM), the party formed by Julius Nyerere. Mkapa contested the election of Oct. 1995, the country's first multi-party elections, with the blessing of Nyerere. However, the poll was blighted by claims of inefficiency and corruption. Several areas, including Dar es Salaam, were ordered to re-schedule voting, which was then boycotted by all opposition parties. Mkapa was victorious with 61.8% of the vote.

Career Peak

The dubious legitimacy of Mkapa's victory led to concern among Western nations upon whose aid and investment Tanzania relied. However, Mkapa continued the free market economic reforms begun by his predecessor, Ali Hassan Mwinyi, and won support from the IMF and World Bank. In 1997 he established a commission to investigate domestic corruption. 1,500 civil servants were dismissed within a few months. In 2000 Mkapa, who remained personally untainted by corruption charges levelled against his party, won re-election with increased support.

The question of Zanzibar's secession came increasingly under focus during his second term. There were widespread allegations of corruption in Zanzibar's 2000 elections, which saw the re-election of Sheikh Abeid Karume, who has received international condemnation for the brutality of his regime. However, Mkapa positioned himself against any move for more independent parliaments for Zanzibar and the mainland.

The exploitation of Tanzania's rich mineral reserves was key to Mkapa's long-term economic plans. Several large new gold mining operations were opened or commissioned during his tenure and Tanzania is now Africa's third largest gold producer. In Nov. 2001 Mkapa and his counterparts in Uganda and Kenya founded a regional parliament and court of justice based in Arusha to focus on issues including immigration and trade. In early 2001 Tanzania received over 100,000 refugees fleeing fighting in the Democratic Republic of Congo. In his first months in office Mkapa oversaw the final stages of repatriation of 500,000 refugees from Rwanda and Burundi who had entered Tanzania in late-1994/early-1995.

Mkapa worked with the US to find the 1998 bombers of the US embassy in Dar es Salaam, which was linked to Osama bin Laden and killed 260. In 2001 Mkapa appealed to pharmaceutical companies to support him in the fight against AIDS. Tanzania is estimated to have 3 m. sufferers, with treatment costing US$1 bn. per year. In Aug. 2002 he attracted criticism from opposition parties and the World Bank for commissioning a presidential jet costing US$20 m. Despite his personal reputation remaining intact, the government is dogged by allegations of corruption under his rule.

Benjamin Mkapa retired on 21 Dec. 2005, aged 67. He was succeeded by former foreign minister and ruling CCM candidate Jakaya Kikwete.

Mobutu Sese Seko (Democratic Republic of the Congo)

Introduction

Mobutu Sese Seko ruled the country he named Zaïre for 32 years. His ruthless autocratic style involved, amongst other things, bribing or executing political opponents, building a gigantic pink marble palace for himself in the heart of the jungle, and siphoning off an estimated £300 m. per year of his nation's mineral wealth to add to his personal fortune. His three decades in power were catastrophic for the country which had been considered one of the most promising post-colonial African states with huge reserves of copper and cobalt as well as gold, bauxite, diamonds and zinc.

Mobutu began his rule with the endorsement of the West after proclaiming his anti-Communist credentials. By the time his regime had crumbled, his country had become one of the poorest in the world, with a national debt conservatively estimated at US$8 bn.—a figure that corresponds to one estimate of Mobutu's personal fortune.

Early Life

He was born Joseph Désiré Mobutu on 14 Oct. 1930. The son of a Roman Catholic mission cook he was educated at a number of local Catholic schools in what was then called the Belgian Congo. He was expelled at school aged 20 for throwing ink at his teacher. As a punitive measure he was drafted into the army, but his slight physique meant that he spent his 7 years there as a military clerk. He also worked as a journalist and became editor of the weekly publication *Actualités Africanes*. Having earned a reputation there he was transferred to Brussels for further studies.

During this time he became involved in politics, joining Patrice Lumumba's *Mouvement National Congolais* (MNC), and eventually ascending, courtesy of Lumumba's patronage, to the rank of chief of staff. With characteristic acumen Mobutu seized the opportunity to turn this position of power to his advantage, amassing a considerable following within the armed forces. Mobutu resolved the parliamentary deadlock caused by the conflict between President Kasavubu and Prime Minister Lumumba by suspending all political institutions. He effectively took charge of the country and began to turn against his former patron—Lumumba's life ended violently in captivity. However, Mobutu was to endure another conflict between the new prime minister, Moise Tshombe, and President Kasavubu, before leading the *coup d'etat* that was to secure total control of the country for himself. He consolidated his position in 1966 by publicly hanging four of his political rivals.

Career Peak

Once installed in power he broke off all diplomatic ties with the USSR, encouraged US investment and was successful in requesting the Israelis to turn his personal military force into highly trained commandos. Despite growing rich on Western investment, Mobutu favoured what he termed 'a return to African authenticity'. He bought a prodigious quantity of leopard-skin hats from a Parisian furrier, and announced that he was henceforth to be known as Sese Seko Kuku Ngbendu wa za Banga, which translates as 'the all powerful warrior who by endurance and determination will go from conquest to conquest, leaving fire in his wake'. Mobutu's major achievement in power was to bind together, through a combination of guile, bribery and brute force, the many disparate elements within his nation. The state was composed of over 200 warring tribes, and it is to Mobutu's credit that civil war was avoided until it spilled over the borders from Rwanda in 1994.

Mobutu's regime was not without its opponents. He dealt ruthlessly with a series of insurgencies in the 1970s, but it finally began to collapse after ethnic conflicts between the Hutu and the Tutsi inhabitants within the region initiated some of the worst incidents of genocide in modern history. Mobutu allowed fleeing Hutu refugees to enter Zaïre and gave them control of refugee camps and arms. This provoked the formation of a rebel faction made up of Tutsi fighters and groups opposed to Mobutu's rule.

In Oct. 1996 the Alliance of Democratic Forces for the Liberation of Congo-Zaïre, under the command of Laurent-Désiré Kabila launched an offensive whilst Mobutu was out of the country undergoing surgery for prostate cancer. His absence was to prove a decisive factor in his deposition. On 15 May the following year the dictator was offered the choice of surrendering power or being deposed by force. He fled, initially to Gbadolite, his 'jungle Versailles' and later to Morocco having been refused asylum in Togo and France. To mark his succession to power, Kabila renamed the country the Democratic Republic of the Congo.

Later Life

Mobutu died in exile of cancer a few months later. He left a country in ruins, and a vast estate which included chateaux in Belgium and France and a Spanish palace. A French journalist whilst observing Mobutu in his heyday, cruising down the Congo in a dilapidated steamer and pausing only to lavish trinkets on bewildered villagers, was reminded of the trader Kurtz in Joseph Conrad's classic novel *The Heart of Darkness*, 'His intelligence was perfectly lucid, but his soul was mad'.

Mogae, Festus (Botswana)

Introduction

Mogae succeeded Sir Ketumile Masire as president in 1998 and served for the maximum period allowed by the constitution before stepping down in 2008. Mogae remains popular and well-respected in Botswana and abroad. His high-profile campaigning against the spread of HIV/AIDS is frequently contrasted with the attitude of contemporary South African President Thabo Mbeki, who has questioned the exclusivity of HIV as the cause of AIDS. Mogae also stands out for his criticism of Zimbabwe's President Robert Mugabe, with whom few leaders in Southern Africa have broken ranks.

Early Life

Gontebanye Mogae was born at Serowe, Central District, on 21 Aug. 1939. He was educated at Moeng College in Botswana. Mogae then studied economics at Northwest London Polytechnic and the University of Oxford and in 1970 gained an MA in development economics from the University of Sussex. In 1968 he returned to Botswana and joined the ministry of finance and development planning, becoming permanent secretary in 1975. During this period he was also involved with the IMF, African Development Bank and World Bank.

As permanent secretary to the president, he served on various parastatal boards, including the Housing Corporation and the Meat Commission. Mogae also held the position of director and later chairman of the Botswana Development Corporation and director of the De Beers Botswana Mining Company (diamond mining company). From 1978–80 he was executive director of the IMF for Anglophone Africa in Washington, D.C.

Mogae returned to Botswana in 1980 as governor of the Bank of Botswana before taking up the combined roles of permanent secretary to the president, secretary to the cabinet and supervisor of elections, which he held for most of the following decade. In 1989 he took up his first political position in government as minister of finance and development planning. President Ketumile Masire appointed him vice-president in 1992. From 1992–96 he held the chair of the Council of Ministers of the Southern African Development Community (SADC). In 1994 he was elected to the National Assembly for Palapye constituency. In Nov. 1997 Masire announced his retirement and designated Mogae as his successor until elections scheduled for 1999. Pressure had been mounting within the Botswana Democratic Party (BDP) for a change of leadership.

Career Peak

Mogae was sworn in as president of Botswana on 1 April 1998. His cabinet included as vice-president Lieut.-Gen. (retd) Ian Khama, the son of Botswana's first president, Sir Seretse Khama. Ian Khama, who had made his career in the army, was seen as a reluctant politician, included in the government to boost support for Mogae's BDP.

Foreign policy took a prominent position in Mogae's agenda from the start. Batswana troops were sent to Lesotho in Sept. 1998 as part of a SADC mission to restore order in the kingdom. Botswana, South Africa and Zimbabwe have guaranteed to protect democratic government in Lesotho and were responding to an uprising after the 1998 elections. Batswana troops finally left in May 1999. A dispute over water resources with Namibia in 1998 caused tense relations which further deteriorated in 1999 over Botswana's acceptance of refugees from the Caprivi Strip in northeast Namibia. The Caprivi separatist movement was suppressed by Namibian armed forces in Oct. 1998. Mogae encouraged voluntary repatriation but most were granted asylum.

Elections to the National Assembly on 16 Oct. 1999 were the eighth democratic and free elections in Botswana and the first to use written ballot papers. Mogae was criticized in the run-up for having to resort to a state of emergency to sort out a crisis in voter registration. The BDP won a landslide victory, securing 33 of the 40 elected seats and affirming Mogae's mandate as president. The opposition had fragmented, giving the ruling party a seat in the capital for the first time in 15 years. Mogae was inaugurated on 20 Oct. 1999. In Dec. he announced that his deputy, Khama, was to take a year-long sabbatical. No explanation was given.

The dominant theme of Mogae's presidency was the threat of HIV/AIDS. By 2002 Botswana had a prevalence rate of 36%, the highest in the world, according to the UN. This had a dramatic effect on life expectancy, which fell from 65 years in 1993 to 36 in 2003. Mogae led a vocal campaign for openness, discussion and education—uncommon among Southern African leaders—devoting approximately 13% of government expenditure in 2000 to the AIDS programme. While his efforts as president were praised by AIDS organizations, human rights groups have criticized what they see as potential infringements of privacy. His suggestion that AIDS represents a 'threat of annihilation' of the Batswana nation also received a mixed response.

Mogae's government, like that of his predecessor, was praised by international organizations for its transparency and moderation. In 2002 Transparency International, a Berlin-based anti-corruption organization of which Mogae was a member, placed Botswana as the 24th least corrupt nation in the world and the leader in transparency in Africa. However, in May 2001 the news director at Botswana's national television station resigned having accused the government of trying to control the content of broadcasting, after banning a documentary on the case of Mariette Bosch, a white South African executed in Botswana for murder.

Botswana's economy is heavily dependent on the export of diamonds. Mogae promoted Batswana diamonds as 'diamonds for development'. as opposed to 'conflict diamonds' used to finance civil wars in many parts of Africa. He also encouraged economic diversification, especially in manufacturing, tourism and services, and encouraged increased productivity in the agricultural sector (which accounts for less than 5% of GDP but involves 80% of the population).

Mogae viewed the land seizures in Zimbabwe more critically than most African leaders. In 2001 he stated that: 'the region cannot afford to have its second largest economy [Zimbabwe] sinking because of this situation. While we support land reform in Zimbabwe completely, we feel the implementation of the strategy is incorrect.' However, in 2002 he admitted that there was little he could do to arrest developments in Botswana's much more populous neighbour.

Social unrest within Botswana during Mogae's presidency focused on the rights of 'Bushmen'. or San. These indigenous inhabitants of the Kalahari Desert have resisted efforts to evict them from the Central Kalahari Game Reserve and took the government to court in March 2002. Although as few as 60 Bushmen still live in the area, the international media followed the progress of their legal battle closely and some accused the government of being motivated by diamond mining potential. In Dec. 2006 the Bushmen won their case for their ancestral rights.

The BDP won another landslide victory in parliamentary elections on 30 Oct. 2004, taking 44 of the 57 seats in the National Assembly. Limited by the constitution to 10 years in office, Mogae stepped down as president on 31 March 2008.

Later Life

Mogae's dignified retirement as president according to the terms of the constitution was widely lauded by the international community. The smooth

succession to vice-president Lieut.-Gen. (retd) Ian Khama stood in stark contrast to the political turbulence engulfing fellow African nations including Zimbabwe and Kenya. After leaving office Mogae announced plans for the formation of a pan-African Elder's Council in collaboration with prominent public figures including Archbishop Desmond Tutu and former president of Mozambique Joaquim Chissano. The Council proposes to work with regional leaders on the issue of HIV/AIDS.

Mohamud, Hassan Sheikh (Somalia)

Introduction

President from Sept. 2012 to Feb. 2017, Hassan Sheikh Mohamud was a relative newcomer to frontline politics but experienced in building civil institutions.

Early Life

Born on 29 Nov. 1955 in Jalalaqsi, Mohamud graduated in technology from Somalia National University in Mogadishu in 1981. From 1981–84 he worked as a secondary school teacher and from 1984–86 as a lecturer in teacher training. In 1988 he completed a master's degree in technical education at Bhopal University in India. Returning to Somalia the same year, he worked with UNESCO on a project to expand technical and vocational training.

Following the toppling of the Siyad Barre regime, Mohamud became an education officer for UNICEF in 1993, focusing on rebuilding educational services. From 1995–97 he worked with civic organizations to establish communication between rival factions and was subsequently key to negotiating the dismantling of the 'Green Line' that had divided Mogadishu since the outbreak of fighting in the early 1990s.

Mohamud co-founded the Somali Institute of Management and Administration Development in 1999 and worked for the Center for Research and Development from 2001, where he oversaw the establishment of the Somalia Civil Society Forum, an umbrella group of activists and organizations engaged in rebuilding civil society. From 2007 he was consultant to a number of international and local NGOs, working on projects to rebuild Somali society.

From 2007–09, in the period of Somalia's Transitional Federal Government (TFG), he was a consultant at the ministry of planning and international co-operation, overseeing aid management. In 2011 he co-founded the Peace and Development Party (PDP) and was elected its leader in April that year. In Sept. 2012 a presidential vote was held by parliament, with Mohamud achieving a surprise victory. He defeated the former president, Sharif Sheikh Ahmed, in a run-off, claiming 190 votes to 79.

Career Peak

Mohamud took office on 10 Sept. 2012 facing major challenges—a continuing insurgency, clan rivalries, widespread poverty and piracy. He pledged to tackle corruption and combat the radical Islamic al-Shabab militia, and also promised to develop education and provide jobs for young people. In Jan. 2013 the USA recognized the Mogadishu government for the first time in over 20 years and the EU agreed to negotiate a support agreement. In Sept. 2013 international donors pledged US$2.4 bn. in reconstruction aid.

In April 2013 the UN Security Council approved a partial lifting of its arms embargo, allowing the Somali government to strengthen its security forces against continuing al-Shabab attacks, particularly in Mogadishu. However, in Sept. that year al-Shabab claimed responsibility for a major assault on a shopping mall in neighbouring Kenya in apparent retaliation for Kenyan military assistance to the Somali government. Clan-based divisions and militant attacks on public targets, such as hotels, and on pro-government forces have since continued, reinforcing Somalia's unenviable reputation as a failed state.

In Dec. 2013 the prime minister, Abdi Farah Shirdon, who had been sworn in Oct. 2012, lost a confidence vote in parliament following disagreements with the president. He was replaced by Abdiweli Sheikh Ahmed, who announced his cabinet in Jan. 2014. However, he was similarly ousted by parliament in Dec. that year following a political power struggle with

Mohamud, who replaced him with Omar Abdirashid Ali Sharmarke, a former premier. In July 2015 Mohamud ruled out the possibility of holding national elections in 2016 because of the lack of security stemming from the al-Shabab insurgency. On 8 Feb. 2017, however, Mohamed Abdullahi Mohamed was sworn in as Somalia's president after being elected by the parliament.

Moi, Daniel T. Arap (Kenya)

Introduction

Daniel Toroitich arap Moi was president of Kenya from 1978–2002, succeeding Kenya's first post-independence president Jomo Kenyatta. He also took Kenyatta's role of leader of the Kenyan African National Union (KANU). His 24-year long rule ended when he was constitutionally obliged to stand down at the end of 2002. His chosen successor Uhuru Kenyatta was decisively defeated by Mwai Kibaki, the candidate for the opposition coalition National Rainbow Coalition (Narc). Moi's rule was tarnished by accusations of endemic corruption and economic difficulty, which eventually ended KANU's 39 years in power.

Early Life

Moi was born on 2 Sept. 1924 in Kuieng'wo village in the Baringo District of the North Rift Valley Province. His father died when Moi was young and he was raised by his mother. Educated in Missionary schools Moi joined the Teacher Training College in Kapsabet on leaving school in 1945. Between 1945 and 1955 Moi held numerous teaching posts before being promoted to assistant principal at Tambach Teacher Training College in Kabamet from 1950 to 1955.

In 1955 Moi went into politics. The same year he was elected member of the Legislative Council for the Rift Valley. In 1960, together with a number of other political activists, he established the Kenyan African Democratic Union (KADU) in opposition to Kenyatta's KANU to represent the minority tribes. Moi remained chairman of KADU until it was dissolved and merged with the KANU in 1963 following the general election.

Kenya gained independence from Britain in 1963 and Prime Minister Jomo Kenyatta became president the following year. In the period between 1961 and 1966 Moi held the following portfolios: education minister (1961), minister for local government (1962–64) and minister for home affairs (1964–67). In 1967 he became vice president of Kenya and went on to succeed Kenyatta when he died in 1978. Pledging to rule in Kenyatta's footsteps, Moi acquired the nickname Nyayo (footsteps).

Career Peak

In 1981 Moi was elected chairman of the Organization of African Unity (OAU). On the 1 Aug. 1982 a coup attempt by junior officers of the Kenya Air Force was quashed by the Kenyan Army. Moi's response to the coup was to turn Kenya into a de jure one-party state. In reaction the World Bank and the IMF froze aid to Kenya. In 1986 Moi's book *Kenyan African Nationalism* attempted to explain his Nyayo philosophy.

Throughout the early 1990s Kenyan civil society as well as the diplomatic community joined forces in pressuring Moi to opt for multiparty elections. In 1992 the first freely contested multiparty elections were held. Moi was re-elected president thanks to the opposition being split along tribal lines. Following the 1992 election there were accusations of vote rigging. Similar allegations accompanied his re-election in Dec. 1997. Opposition parties demanded changes to the electoral rules, freedom of speech and more civil liberties.

Moi's refusal to pass anti-corruption measures led to a freeze in international aid in 1997. In 2001 the IMF refused a US$40 m. loan to Kenya. The country was also accused of obstructing independent anti-corruption commissions. Kenya's economy declined towards the end of Moi's rule and the country entered its worst recession since independence as foreign investment was withdrawn.

There was much speculation as to whether Moi would stand down at the end of 2002, as constitutionally obliged, and in 2000 ministers began a campaign to extend his term. However, in July 2002 Moi named Uhuru Kenyatta, son of his predecessor, as his chosen successor. The announcement divided KANU and led some to openly criticize his choice. In response, Moi sacked his vice president George Saitoti, who defected to the opposition along with around 30 party members, including a junior minister, Peter Odoyo. As tension increased towards the Dec. 2002 elections, six ministers resigned. Much of the opposition united to form the National Rainbow Coalition with the former vice president Mwai Kibaki as its candidate. In a landslide win, Kibaki beat Kenyatta by 62.2% votes to 31.3% thus ending nearly 40 years of KANU rule. After 23 years as president Moi finally stood down.

Later Life

Since leaving office, Moi has concentrated on the administration of Kabarak University, which he chartered in 2002. He has also set up the Moi Foundation as a negotiating body for regional peace initiatives. In Sept. 2003 Moi stood down as chairman of KANU after a 24-year tenure. He surprised the party by failing to name Kenyatta, one of the vice-chairmen, as his successor.

Moisiu, Alfred (Albania)

Introduction

Alfred Moisiu was chosen as Albania's president by parliament in June 2002. A non-partisan, military professional, he won praise for his ability to find common ground among rival factions across the political spectrum. He was pro-Western and a prominent advocate of Albanian accession to NATO. Moisiu left office in July 2007.

Early Life

Moisiu was born on 1 Dec. 1929 in Shkodër, northern Albania. He went to school in Tirana and from 1943–45 was active in the war against the occupying German forces. In 1946 he began studying at the Military Engineering School in St Petersburg, Russia, leaving 2 years later and becoming a platoon commander at the Joint Officers' School in Tirana. Between 1949–51 he was an instructor at the Skanderbeg Military Academy in Tirana.

From 1952–58 he went to the Academy of Military Engineering in Moscow. Returning to Albania, he worked in the engineering directory of the ministry of defence until 1966. He then assumed command of the Pontoon Brigade at Kavajë until 1971, meanwhile undertaking a year-long course for senior general staff at Tirana's Defence Academy.

In 1971 he was appointed head of the office of engineering and fortifications at the ministry of defence. He held that post until 1981 (acquiring a PhD in military sciences in 1979) and then became vice minister of defence until Oct. 1982. After heading an engineering company in Burrel in the northwest of the country, he retired from 1985 until 1991 when he was appointed defence minister in Vilson Ahmeti's interim 'government of experts' that ruled from the collapse of communism until the democratic elections held in March 1992.

Moisiu worked as a defence adviser from 1992–94 before becoming vice minister of defence again in the government of Prime Minister Aleksander Meksi. In this role he advised on the reconstruction of the armed services and supported preparations for NATO membership. In 1994 he also became chairman of the Albanian Atlantic Association (a post he held until his election as state president). He left government office in 1997 following the electoral victory of the Socialist Party, but maintained a prominent role in international conferences concerned with regional defence and peace issues.

When Rexhep Meidani left the state presidency in 2002, Moisiu emerged as an acceptable candidate to both the Socialist and Democratic parties. Following a poll in the national assembly (in which he received 97 votes, with 19 against and 14 abstentions), he was sworn into office on 24 July 2002.

Career Peak

On assuming office, Moisiu pledged to keep his distance from party political issues. Nevertheless, he was critical of the then Socialist Prime Minister Fatos Nano for the slow pace of political reform. Following the parliamentary elections in July 2005, he asked Democratic Party leader Sali Berisha to form a government, which was sworn in on 11 Sept. 2005. Moisiu's foreign policy aims included working towards lasting peace in the Balkans and Albania's accession to NATO.

Moisiu's 5-year term ended in July 2007. Parliament elected Bamir Topi his successor after four rounds of voting.

Monti, Mario (Italy)

Introduction

Mario Monti became prime minister on 12 Nov. 2011 when he was invited by President Giorgio Napolitano to form a government following Silvio Berlusconi's resignation.

Early Life

Mario Monti was born in Varese, Lombardy on 19 March 1943. He graduated in economics from Bocconi University, Milan in 1965 before undertaking post-graduate studies at Yale University in the USA. He took up a teaching post at the University of Turin in 1970 and returned to Bocconi University in 1985, serving as rector from 1989–94. In 1994 he was appointed university president, a post he has held ever since.

That same year Monti was appointed to the Jacques Santer-led European Commission by the first Silvio Berlusconi cabinet. He worked in the office for the internal market and services and was nominated for a second term by Massimo D'Alema in 1999, with Monti becoming commissioner for competition. In this role he blocked a proposed merger between General Electric and Honeywell, battled Germany's powerful regional banks and launched an anti-trust case against Microsoft. He also oversaw reforms to the EU's anti-trust regulations and worked with the US authorities to create the International Competition Network. However, in 2004 the new Berlusconi administration refused to support Monti's seat on the Commission for a third term.

In 2005, shortly after leaving the Commission, Monti co-founded Bruegel, a Brussels-based think tank focusing on economic issues. He became a member of the Bilderberg Group and an international adviser to Goldman Sachs and Coca-Cola. From 2007–08 he was appointed by President Nicolas Sarkozy to the French government's Attali Commission, set up to stimulate economic growth.

Monti was key to brokering an electricity-sharing agreement between France and Spain in 2008 and in 2010 he was asked by the president of the EU Commission, Manuel Barroso, to draft proposals for the future of the EU's single market. The completed report made 12 recommendations intended to bring new stimulus to the European economy and was adopted by the EU on 13 April 2011.

On 9 Nov. 2011 Monti was made 'senator for life' by Napolitano against the backdrop of uncertainty over the future of the Berlusconi government. The appointment raised speculation that Napolitano was grooming Monti to succeed Berlusconi. Monti was formally asked to form a new government on 12 Nov. 2011 and was sworn into office 4 days later. His initial cabinet consisted mainly of former bankers and technocrats, with Monti himself heading the ministry of economy and finance.

Career Peak

On 4 Dec. 2011 Monti introduced a €30 bn. austerity package aimed at cutting spending, raising taxes and reforming pensions. Although challenged by the unions and the opposition, the package was approved by the lower house of parliament on 16 Dec. 2011 by 495 to 88 votes and by the upper house on 22 Dec. 2011 by 257 to 41 votes. The reforms were welcomed by the EU.

On 20 Jan. 2012 Monti's government introduced a second wave of measures to boost growth, including legislation to end restrictive practices and open up competition in various sectors of the economy. Within 4 months of taking office, Monti had overseen a fall in Italy's 10-year borrowing rate from 7% to 6%.

Monti fulfilled his promise to step down following the passage of the 2013 budget in Dec. 2012. He contested the Feb. 2013 election as the leader of the Civic Choice coalition, but failed to retain his position as prime minister.

Morgan, Rhodri (Wales, United Kingdom)

Introduction

Rhodri Morgan became first minister of the Welsh national assembly in Feb. 2000 and is leader of the Welsh group of Labour MP's. He was controversially defeated in elections for the premiership in the previous year by Alun Michael, widely recognized as the favoured candidate of Tony Blair.

Early Life

Morgan was born on 29 Sept. 1939 in Cardiff. He studied at St John's College, Oxford and Harvard before undertaking a career in the civil service. He sat on South Glamorgan County Council between 1974 and 1980 and headed the European Community office in Wales from 1980 until 1987, when he became the member of parliament for Cardiff West. In his parliamentary career he was opposition front bench spokesman on energy (1988–92) and Welsh affairs (1992–97). He married Julie Morgan (a fellow Labour MP) with whom he had three children.

In the Feb. 1999 election for the first minister of the assembly, Morgan was regarded as the 'grass roots' favourite. His chief opponent was Alun Michael, seen by Downing Street as the safer pair of hands. A tempestuous campaign followed in which Morgan accused the Michael camp of dirty tricks. Michael was elected to the post on the back of block union votes.

Michael was threatened with a vote of no confidence from Plaid Cymru members in Feb. 2000 and shortly before the vote was due he resigned. Morgan was appointed his successor in a caretaker capacity on 9 Feb. On 15 Feb. he was elected permanent successor unchallenged.

Career Peak

Among Morgan's first actions was a declaration of support for Tony Blair's leadership. In a cabinet reshuffle Morgan appointed himself secretary of economic development and entered a dialogue with Corus (formerly British Steel), one of the principle employers in the region, now engaged in major restructuring. In Nov. 2001 he urged that the National Assembly for Wales be given the more 'friendly' name of the Welsh Assembly Government.

In Feb. 2002 Morgan appointed Andrew Davies as his successor as economic development minister. In April 2002 Morgan identified NHS improvement as a major priority and later the same month he made an outspoken attack on the structural flaws of the Welsh rugby union. At assembly elections in May 2003, Labour won half of the seats, allowing the party to govern without the support of the Liberal Democrats. Morgan sought to encourage investment in the Welsh economy and tourist industry through a number of grants schemes, particularly focusing on aiding the recovery of the mining industry. In 2005 his government lost a vote on the introduction of 'top-up' university fees, subsequently agreeing to a deal that exempted Welsh students.

In the run-up to assembly elections in 2007 Morgan's failure to openly condemn the Iraq war was seized upon by the press and opposition parties. Labour suffered heavy losses in the elections and Morgan was controversially forced to enter a coalition with Plaid Cymru, the nationalist party, in July 2007. The deal was criticized by some Labour assembly members who fear that Plaid Cymru will push for a referendum on independence.

Morgan was hospitalized with heart problems later in July, with the deputy first minister Ieuan Wyn Jones standing in for him. On 8 Dec. 2009 Morgan resigned owing to his health problems. Carwyn Jones succeeded him. On 17 May 2017 he collapsed and died while cycling.

Mori, Emanuel (Micronesia)

Introduction

Emanuel 'Manny' Mori became the seventh president of the Federated States of Micronesia (FSM) on 11 May 2007. He was the second president to come from the state of Chuuk. The president, who is both head of state and of the unicameral government, serves for a 4-year term.

Early Life

Mori was born on 25 Dec. 1948 in Sapore on the island of Fefan, Chuuk. He spent his childhood in Fefan and attended the Xavier High School in Chuuk's capital, Weno. From 1969–73 he studied at the University of Guam, graduating in business management. He joined Citycorp Credit as a management intern, becoming assistant manager at the Saipan branch.

Mori returned to the FSM in 1976 and joined the Trust Territory social security office. In 1979 he became responsible for Chuuk's tax and revenue office. From 1981–83 he served as comptroller of the Development Bank of the FSM before being appointed its president and CEO. He held the post until Feb. 1997, when the bank's board ousted him in an attempt to encourage reform. He was subsequently named vice-president.

Mori's political career began in July 1999 when he was elected a Chuuk congressman. He held several positions including chair of the ways and means committee and vice-chair of the committee on judiciary and government operation. He also sat on the committees for resource and development and for health and social affairs. In 2003 he was elected senator-at-large for Chuuk for a 4-year term. In this capacity Mori served on the task force for national government restructuring and on the planning council of the College of Micronesia. He also served as a CEO of the Chuuk Public Utility Corporation and on the board of the Pacific Island Development Bank.

In May 2007 parliament selected Mori to replace Joseph Urusemal as president. Alik L. Alik was chosen as vice-president.

Career Peak

Under a Compact of Free Association Micronesia is guaranteed US aid until 2023. Chief among Mori's challenges has been to prepare for economic self-reliance and to reinvigorate the stagnant private sector. He was re-elected for a second term in May 2011.

Peter M. Christian was elected to succeed Mori as president on 11 May 2015.

Moro, Aldo (Italy)

Introduction

Aldo Moro was a lawyer and politician who served as Italy's prime minister on five occasions between 1963 and 1976. In office he was influential in uniting several of the disparate strands of Italian centre-left politics. However, his kidnapping and execution by left-wing extremists has left more of an impact on the national consciousness than his policies.

Early Life

Moro was active in Italian politics as a student at the University of Bari. He took a law degree and went on to become a professor of law. He also became president of the Federation of Italian University Catholics, and of the Movement of Catholic Graduates. Both these organizations had a political agenda. In 1946 Moro was elected to the Constituent Assembly and assisted in the drafting of a new Italian constitution. He also became a member of the legislature for the Christian Democrat Party. He was later appointed to a series of cabinet posts including under secretary of foreign affairs (Dec. 1947–May 1948). From 1953–55 he was the head of the Christian Democrats in the chamber of deputies. He was then made minister of justice, a post he held for 2 years before becoming the minister of public instruction. In 1959 he took on the role of party secretary at a time of conflict between the centrist and conservative wings of the Christian Democrats. Moro was centrist in inclination and formed an alliance with the Socialist party in order to oust the conservative Fernando Tambroni from power in July 1960.

Career Peak

Invited to form a government in Dec. 1963, Moro included several Socialists in his cabinet, thus granting the left-wing an influence it had not secured for over a decade. He resigned following the defeat of a budget proposal in July

the following year, but almost immediately returned to power with a barely altered cabinet. Moro strengthened Italy's links with NATO and the UN, but efforts at introducing a reformist programme at home were hampered by spiralling inflation. This failure angered his Socialist coalition partners who brought about Moro's defeat in Jan. 1966. He returned to power a month later but stepped down after the 1968 elections. He went on to be foreign minister (1970–72). Two years later he became premier once more, this time heading a coalition with the Republican party. This tenure ended in Jan. 1976, and Moro led the country for the last time from Feb–Apr. 1976.

Later Life

In Oct. 1976 Moro was elected president of the Christian Democrat Party, a job which enabled him to exert influence without holding public office. He was widely regarded as a president in the making but on 16 March 1978 he was kidnapped by activists of the Brigate Rosse (Red Brigades), an extremist left-wing terrorist organization. The terrorists demanded the release of several imprisoned members of their organization in exchange for Moro's life. After 2 months of negotiations, attempts to reach a settlement failed, and, despite international appeals and efforts, Moro was found executed on 9 May.

Morsi, Mohamed (Egypt)

Introduction

Mohamed Morsi became Egypt's first democratically elected president on 30 June 2012. He succeeded Hosni Mubarak, who resigned on 11 Feb. 2011 in the wake of a popular uprising. A Sunni Muslim, Morsi previously served as chairman of the Freedom and Justice Party, a nominally independent Islamist party with strong ties to the Muslim Brotherhood. However, he was ousted from power after only just over a year in power, and was later sentenced to death for his role in inciting violence during the 2011 revolution.

Early Life

Mohamed Morsi was born on 20 Aug. 1951 in the northern Sharkia governorate. He received a master's degree in engineering from Cairo University in 1978. 4 years later he completed a PhD at the University of Southern California, staying in the USA to work as a professor at the University of North Ridge, California. The eldest two of his five children were born in Los Angeles and hold American citizenship. Morsi returned to Egypt in 1985 to head the engineering faculty at Zagazig University, a post he held until 2010.

He was elected to the Egyptian People's Assembly in 2000. Although nominally an independent because the Muslim Brotherhood was barred from parliament under Mubarak, he was a member of the Brotherhood's executive office and spokesperson for the parliamentary bloc that aligned itself with the organization's Islamist policies. He failed to win re-election in 2005, a loss that the Muslim Brotherhood attributed to electoral fraud. Prominent in opposing state interference with the judiciary, Morsi spent 7 months in jail in 2006. He was detained again in Jan. 2011 as protests against Mubarak swept the country.

In the wake of this uprising, the Muslim Brotherhood founded the Freedom and Justice Party on 30 April 2011, with Morsi as chairman. He was nominated as the party's presidential candidate after its first choice, Khairat al-Shater, was disqualified by the electoral commission. In the second round of presidential elections on 16–17 June 2012, Morsi took 51.7% of the vote, defeating the former prime minister, Ahmed Shafik. Morsi immediately resigned from the Muslim Brotherhood and the Freedom and Justice Party to take up the presidency.

Career Peak

Previously an outspoken critic of Israel, Morsi helped mediate a ceasefire with Hamas after Israel's incursion into Gaza in Nov. 2012. In the same month his tenure came under the international spotlight when he issued a constitutional declaration that effectively granted him unlimited legislative power. After mass protests, Morsi annulled the decree on 8 Dec. 2012.

On 30 June 2013 mass protests took place across Egypt calling for Morsi's resignation. Morsi publicly rejected the Egyptian Army's 48 h ultimatum to meet the demands of the Egyptian people and on 3 July he was declared unseated and placed under house arrest. Mansour Adly, the Chief Justice of the Supreme Constitutional Court, was sworn in the following day as the interim leader. New elections were called, the constitution suspended and the parliament dissolved. Clashes between Morsi's opponents and loyalists demanding his reinstatement resulted in a wave of violence in major cities.

Later Life

Following his overthrow, Morsi faced charges relating to the 2011 Wadi el-Natrun prison breakout during the revolution and alleged conspiracy with foreign militant groups including Hamas. In May 2015 and after numerous delays, Egyptian prosecutors judged Morsi guilty of both charges, and he was handed the death penalty. Morsi repeatedly rejected the authority of the courts trying him and claimed still to be the rightful president of Egypt. The Court of Cassation reversed his death sentence in Nov. 2016 and ordered a retrial.

Moscoso Rodriguez, Mireya Elisa (Panama)

Introduction

Mireya Elisa Moscoso Rodriguez was president of Panama from 1999 to 2004, representing the Partido Arnulfista (PA), of which she is co-founder. Elected in 1999, her main challenges were to oversee the US handover of the Panama Canal and to stave off recession while keeping her promise of helping the poor with social security initiatives.

Early Life

Moscoso was born on 1 July 1946 in Panama City. The daughter of a poor schoolteacher, she spent her early years in the rural family home at Pedasí. Following secondary education, she worked as a secretary until she met her husband, the politician and thrice president Arnulfo Arias Madrid. She worked on his third successful electoral campaign. When Arias was deposed in a coup led by Omar Torrijos Herrera in 1968, the couple went into exile in Miami where Moscoso studied interior design. In 1969 at the age of 22 she married the 67-year-old Arias. During the 1980s Moscoso held various minor governmental posts.

In 1990 Moscoso co-founded the PA with a group of members from her (then late) husband's Partido Panameñista Auténtico. The following year she became party leader. For the 1994 elections she was chosen as the candidate for a coalition of the PA and the Alianza Democrática. She came second with 29% of votes, beaten by the Partido Revolucionario Democrático (PRD) leader Ernesto Pérez Balladares. In 1999, when Balladares was constitutionally prevented from standing for re-election, she stood against the PRD's candidate Martin Torrijos, son of Omar Torrijos. Moscoso campaigned on a populist manifesto, pledging to help the poor. Both candidates had similar policies, although Moscoso courted the populist vote, exploiting her poor rural background, while Torrijos concentrated on the business sector. Torrijos was the favourite to win until the PRD's chances were hampered by corruption charges. In the second democratic elections since the 1989 US military intervention overthrew the military regime led by Manuel Noriega, Moscoso won with 44.9% of votes to Torrijos' 38%, to become the first female leader of a Central American country.

Career Peak

Moscoso's biggest challenge was overseeing the handover of the Panama Canal 3 months into her presidency and providing a successful strategy of Panamanian management devoid of party politics. The handover was in accordance with a 1977 treaty signed between the US president Jimmy Carter and Torrijos. Moscoso called for a complete withdrawal of US military from the former US owned Panama Canal Zone.

There was scepticism about Moscoso's ability to govern successfully because of her lack of advanced education. Nevertheless, she outlined plans to tackle poverty, concentrating on the 14 neediest regions, including a social programme of improved health, primary education and housing. Agrarian policy included aid for small farmers and a stimulation of agricultural exports. She also announced plans to encourage technology, especially information

technology. Her populist policies were combined with a pledge to slow down the privatization begun by her predecessor whose neo-liberal economic policies had been popular with the International Development Bank but unpopular with the public. 1999 was the second successive year of economic slowdown and increasing fiscal deficit. Furthermore, Panamanian exports suffered when Colombia, its biggest customer, got into economic difficulties. By 2000 Panama had gained an IMF agreement which imposed welfare and tax reforms and a limit to government employment.

In 2000 Moscoso successfully hosted a summit of 19 Latin American countries, although she was criticized by human rights' organizations for welcoming former Peruvian intelligence chief, Vladimiro Montesinos, who was wanted on corruption charges. But despite US pressure, Montesinos' application for asylum was rejected.

Later Life

Since leaving office, Moscoso has been investigated on corruption charges along with members of her former cabinet.

Mosisili, Pakalitha Bethuel (Lesotho)

Introduction

Pakalitha Bethuel Mosisili, leader of the Democratic Congress (DC), began a new term as premier in March 2015, having previously served from May 1998 until June 2012. He succeeded Tom Thabane, who had replaced Mosisili in 2012. However, he lost a parliamentary vote of confidence in March 2017 prompting early elections scheduled for 3 June, during which time he continued in office in a caretaker capacity.

Early Life

Mosisili was born on 14 March 1945 in the Qacha's Nek District in Lesotho. He attended the University of Botswana, Lesotho and Swaziland (UBLS) from 1966–70, gaining a BA and a teaching qualification. He studied for an MA at the University of Wisconsin in the USA from 1975–76, before claiming a further BA from the University of South Africa (1977–78). In 1982 he gained a master's degree in education from the Simon Fraser University in Canada.

In 1967, whilst at UBLS, Mosisili joined the Basutoland Congress Party (BCP) and was an active member of its youth league. In 1970 he was detained under emergency regulations and sent to a maximum-security prison for 16 months.

Mosisili's political career began in 1993 when he was elected to parliament representing Qacha's Nek. He was appointed minister of education and training, sports, culture and youth affairs. In Feb. 1995 he became deputy prime minister following the death of Selometsi Baholo the previous year. He took responsibility for the home affairs and local government portfolios, roles he retained until the 1998 elections. In Feb. 1998 he succeeded Prime Minister Dr Ntsu Mokhehle as leader of the LCD.

Career Peak

The victory of the LCD at the elections of May 1998 led to opposition accusations of vote rigging. Mass rioting culminated in protesters seizing the palace grounds. Mosisili called on the Southern African Development Community (SADC) for military assistance to prevent a coup and troops remained in Lesotho until May 1999. In 2001 the government charged 33 protest leaders with treason. The SADC continued to provide military support and was again called in following more opposition allegations of electoral fraud after the LCD's re-election in 2002. In 2004 the first local elections since independence were held, but were boycotted by the opposition.

Mosisili pledged to tackle Lesotho's severe food shortages, high unemployment rates and rapidly escalating HIV/AIDS problem. However, poverty remained far-reaching and food output was affected by deaths of farmers from AIDS and by long periods of drought. In Feb. 2004 Mosisili declared a state of emergency and requested international food aid. In March 2004 the first phase of the Lesotho Highlands Water Project was opened, with the long-term aim of supplying water to large areas of southern Africa.

Mosisili aimed to address unemployment by encouraging foreign investment, emphasizing Lesotho's low corporate tax rates and eager workforce. However, thousands were left jobless when the textile industry collapsed after the World Trade Organization scrapped the global textile quota system in 2005. He also sought to diversify the economy, focusing on mining, electronics and industrial equipment manufactures. In 2005 his government opted to privatize the electricity system, having earlier done the same to telecommunications in 2000.

In Nov. 2006 Mosisili dissolved parliament following a split in the ruling LCD in which 18 parliamentary deputies left the party to form an opposition All Basotho Convention (ABC). The LCD won the election of Feb. 2007, although with a smaller majority than in 2002. In April 2009 he survived an apparent assassination attempt by gunmen in the capital, Maseru, for which seven suspected mercenaries were charged in April 2010. Prior to the parliamentary elections in May 2012 the LCD split again and Mosisili formed the new Democratic Congress, but he relinquished the premiership after the polls to Tom Thabane of the ABC.

Thabane's tenure was marred by internal security fears, especially after political divisions led to clashes between military and police personnel in 2014. Thabane fled the country, claiming the military was plotting a coup. Early elections were called in Feb. 2015, and although no outright winner emerged Mosisili was able to form a DC-led coalition. He was sworn in on 17 March, facing the challenge of restoring calm and stability to the nation. However, political instability persisted and the DC was undermined by increasing factionalism and ministerial dismissals and resignations over coalition differences. At the beginning of March 2017 Mosisili lost a confidence vote in parliament and a general election was called, 3 years ahead of schedule, for 3 June. He resisted opposition pressure to stand down in the intervening period but on 16 June 2017 he was replaced as prime minister by Tom Thabane, who had previously held the position between 2012 and 2015.

Mossadeq, Mohammad (Iran)

Introduction

Mohammad Mossadeq was prime minister from 1951 until his overthrow in a foreign-orchestrated coup in 1953. A symbol of Iranian nationalism, he was known internationally for his efforts to block overseas exploitation of Iranian oil reserves.

Early Life

Mohammed Mossadeq was born into a prominent family in Tehran on 16 June 1882. He studied in France before receiving a law doctorate from the University of Neuchâtel, Switzerland, in 1913.

On his return to Iran, he joined the ministry of finance but relocated to Switzerland in protest at the Anglo-Persian Treaty of 1919 that granted British rights to Iranian oil fields via the Anglo-Iranian Oil Company. The following year he returned to Iran and was appointed governor of the Fars province. He then served as minister of justice and minister of foreign affairs, as well as governor of the Azerbaijan province. Following the overthrow of the ruling Qajar dynasty in 1925, Mossadeq was a vocal critic of the new Shah, Reza Khan, before retreating from politics.

Mossadeq was imprisoned for several months in 1940 on the orders of the Shah but when the Shah was forced to abdicate in favour of his son, Mohammad Reza Shah, the following year, Mossadeq was released and returned to politics. Representing Tehran in the Majlis, he campaigned for an economically independent Iran, viewing oil as the country's 'life, hope, freedom.' He sought a renegotiation of terms with the Anglo-Iranian Oil Company, which hitherto saw Iran receive only 16% of oil earnings. He also opposed attempts to grant the Soviets oil rights and ultimately devised a plan to nationalize the oil industry. His proposals won widespread popular support and parliament elected him prime minister in April 1951, a month after his oil nationalization bill was passed.

Career Peak

Britain responded to the nationalization by imposing an economic blockade, withdrawing technical personnel and threatening possible military action.

Petroleum production came to a virtual standstill, causing significant hardship to the general population. The case was referred to the UN Security Council, which found in favour of Iran. Mossadeq's administration also introduced a swathe of social reforms including unemployment and sickness benefits and improved rights for peasants. However, he attracted the ire of the Shah and much of the ruling elite. After unsuccessfully attempting to depose Mossadeq in Aug. 1953, the Shah was briefly forced into exile but returned within a few days and, with support from Washington and London, engineered protests that forced Mossadeq from office on 20 Aug. 1953. He was succeeded as prime minister by Gen. Fazlollah Zahedi, who quickly signed accords with UK and US oil companies.

Later Life

Following the end of Mossadeq's tenure, many of his supporters were arrested and executed. Mossadeq himself was convicted of treason and spent 3 years in solitary confinement before being allowed to return to his home village. He remained under house arrest until his death on 5 March 1967.

Mubarak, Muhammad Hosni (Egypt)

Introduction

Following a career in the Air Force, Hosni Mubarak was appointed vice-president of Egypt in April 1975 and then became president in Oct. 1981 shortly after the assassination of Anwar Sadat by militant Islamic fundamentalists. He was re-elected as president on four occasions—in 1987, 1993, 1999 and 2005—and served as chairman of the National Democratic Party (NDP). Mubarak kept faith with most of his predecessor's policies, in particular reconciliation with the Western powers (after Gamal Abdel Nasser's pro-Soviet stance) and Egypt's controversial peace accord with Israel. However, he also sought to re-establish links with Arab states. He took a hard line with Muslim extremists and was the target of several assassination plots. In early 2011, after weeks of protests, he was forced to step down.

Early Life

Born in Kafr al Musailha on 4 May 1928, Mubarak attended high school and graduated from the military academy in Cairo before joining the Egyptian Air Force in 1950. He was promoted successively to squadron leader, base commander, director of the Air Force Academy (1967–69) and chief of staff (1969–72), before his appointment as commander of the Air Force and deputy minister for military affairs in 1972. In the 1973 war with Israel he was acclaimed for his command of Egyptian air operations. Two years later, in April 1975, Sadat made Mubarak his vice-president.

Career Peak

Following Sadat's assassination, Mubarak was inaugurated as president and prime minister on 14 Oct. 1981 (although he relinquished the latter post in Jan. 1982). Under his presidency, Egypt's isolation in the Arab world in the wake of Sadat's peace treaty with Israel came to an end. By the end of the 1980s the country had resumed a leading role in regional politics. Mubarak supported UN sanctions against Iraq after its occupation of Kuwait in 1990, and Egypt participated in the Gulf War of 1991 in support of the Western-led coalition against the Iraqi president Saddam Hussein. Thereafter, Egypt's foreign policy focused on a comprehensive settlement between Israel and other neighbouring Arab states, with particular emphasis on resolving Palestinian grievances. This policy, however, was undermined by the outbreak from Sept. 2000 of the Palestinian intifada in opposition to Israeli occupation.

Domestically Mubarak maintained the political status quo, albeit with a measure of liberalization. However, his economic reforms struggled to keep pace with inflation and rapid population growth, and he alienated poorer sections of society. There was a resurgence of violent Islamic fundamentalism in the 1990s, targeted in particular at foreign tourists, a major source of revenue. Mubarak narrowly survived an assassination attempt by Egyptian militants in Addis Ababa, Ethiopia, in June 1995. His NDP government responded with a security crackdown on activists. In 1997, 58 foreign tourists and four Egyptians were gunned down by extremists in Luxor.

Following the 11 Sept. 2001 attacks on the USA, Mubarak became a key supporter of the US campaign against terrorism. Mubarak hosted summits on the Middle East peace process in 2000–03, and worked with Israel and the Palestinian Authority during 2004–05 to facilitate stability following Israel's withdrawal from Gaza.

In early 2005 political reformers and opposition activists mounted a series of anti-government demonstrations. In Feb. Mubarak proposed amending the constitution to allow for the country's first multi-candidate presidential elections. That amendment was approved in a referendum in May, albeit with restrictions including a 5-year registration for parties wanting to nominate candidates. In July 2005 Islamist extremists bombed the resort city of Sharm el-Sheikh, killing 88 and injuring over 200. The previous year, 34 people had died when the towns of Taba Nuweiba were bombed.

As expected, Mubarak was re-elected for a fifth consecutive term in Sept. with 88.6% of the vote. However, only 23% of the eligible electorate turned out and there were allegations of vote buying and intimidation. In Dec. 2005 parliamentary elections ended with clashes between police and opposition supporters. Although the NDP retained its parliamentary majority, the Muslim Brotherhood won a record number of seats.

Following three bomb explosions in the resort town of Dahab on the Red Sea coast in April 2006, killing over 20 people, Mubarak extended controversial emergency legislation giving the security forces broad powers of arrest and detention. He had earlier promised to abolish the emergency regime during his campaign for re-election in 2005, but then claimed that it was necessary to combat Islamist terrorism. Despite opposition scepticism, he promised during an address to parliament in Nov. 2006 that he would introduce democratic and constitutional reform. A referendum was subsequently held in March 2007, in which amendments to the constitution, including controversial judicial and security provisions and a formal ban on religious parties, were approved by 76% of voters. Opponents of Mubarak's government, however, rejected the measures as a 'constitutional coup'.

Elections to the Shura Council (upper house of parliament) in June 2007 were dominated by the NDP as most Muslim Brotherhood candidates were barred from running and none won a seat. In April 2008, in the run-up to elections for local councils, the government imposed a further crackdown on the Brotherhood, sentencing 25 members to stiff prison terms and arresting about 800 others. In response, the Brotherhood boycotted the polls.

In April 2009 the Egyptian authorities accused Hizbollah—Lebanon's radical Shia militia aligned with Syria, Iran and the Palestinian Hamas Islamist movement in an anti-Israeli front—of espionage activities aimed against Mubarak's regime. Around 50 people were arrested in connection with the charges.

Speculation about Mubarak's prospective successors escalated as rumours of the ageing president's ill-health spread. Moreover, the return to Egypt in Feb. 2010 of Mohamed ElBaradei—a Nobel Peace Prize winner, former head of the International Atomic Energy Agency and a respected advocate of political change—provided a focus for opposition opinion ahead of presidential elections scheduled for 2011. Following popular protests in Tunisia that forced President Ben Ali into exile, Mubarak faced similar calls to stand down in Jan. and Feb. 2011. Amid growing tensions, he resigned and handed control to the Armed Forces Supreme Council on 11 Feb. 2011.

In Aug. 2011 Mubarak, along with his two sons Ala'a and Gamal, as well as former interior minister Habib el-Adly and six former police officials, stood trial for charges of profiteering, illegal business-dealing involving Israeli gas exports and the unlawful killing of protesters (a charge that carries the death penalty). Despite reportedly suffering from illness, Mubarak attended the trial in Cairo and pleaded not guilty.

On 2 June 2012, Mubarak was sentenced to life in prison by an Egyptian court for complicity in the killing of demonstrators. Shortly after, he suffered a series of health complications and fell into a coma. Mubarak was moved from prison to a military hospital. He appealed against the sentence and in April 2013 was ordered back to prison. He was retried on charges of killing protesters during the 2011 revolution in Aug. 2013, but was eventually found not guilty by an Egyptian court in Nov. 2014. Mubarak was, however, still serving a 3-year sentence on a separate embezzlement charge handed down in May 2014, and so remained incarcerated. He was released from a military hospital in March 2017 after he was cleared of the final murder charges against him.

Mugabe, Robert (Zimbabwe)

Introduction

Robert Mugabe came to power as newly independent Zimbabwe's (formerly Rhodesia) first prime minister in 1980, becoming president in 1987. Although initially hailed as a democratic reformer, his economic mismanagement of the country, violent electoral campaigns and controversial programme of land seizures have tarnished his image at home and abroad. He has defended his land reform programme as the conclusion of the process of decolonization, but his policies have been widely perceived as short-term political expediency for the maintenance of personal power. In the wake of the disputed presidential elections in 2008, Mugabe conceded to power-sharing with the opposition Movement for Democratic Change (MDC) after protracted negotiations. He nevertheless maintained his autocratic grip on the country and was re-elected in July 2013. He resigned the presidency in Nov. 2017.

Early Life

The son of a carpenter, Robert Gabriel Mugabe was born 21 Feb. 1924 at Kutama mission, northwest of Harare. After an early education at a Roman Catholic mission school, he studied at the University College of Fort Hare, South Africa, marking the beginning of an academic career boasting seven university degrees, three of which he completed during imprisonment. He worked as a primary school teacher in Ghana from 1956–60 when he returned to Rhodesia and joined Joshua Nkomo's Zimbabwe African People's Union (ZAPU). In 1963 he became a founding member of the breakaway Zimbabwe African National Union (ZANU) with Rev. Ndabaningi Sithole. A year later Mugabe was arrested for subversion and imprisoned, without trial, for 10 years. Despite imprisonment, he remained politically active and was able to orchestrate, in 1974, a coup against Sithole to become party leader. In 1975, freed from prison, Mugabe joined Nkomo as joint leader of the Patriotic Front of Zimbabwe which waged a guerrilla war against Ian Smith's white Rhodesian Front government. In 1980 independence was achieved and parliamentary elections took place in which Mugabe, at the head of ZANU, won a landslide victory to become prime minister.

Career Peak

In office Mugabe appeared set to usher in a bright new era for the country. Having built a coalition government with ZAPU, he adopted a conciliatory stance towards the white, landowning minority. He introduced higher wages, credit programmes and food subsidies for poor farmers, a better infrastructure and equal land rights for women. Reform in the education system saw primary school enrolment trebled and secondary school enrolment increased fivefold during the first 10 years of his rule (with Zimbabwe laying claim to the highest literacy rate of any African nation).

Troubles began in 1982 when ethnic turmoil between the Shona majority (represented by ZANU) and the Ndebele minority (represented by ZAPU) broke out after Mugabe dismissed Nkomo and ZAPU from government. The ensuing violence prompted much of the white population to emigrate, in turn creating an economic downturn. Centred in Matabeleland, the conflict drew international attention after the discovery of mass graves and alleged atrocities.

In 1987 Mugabe won the presidential elections and set about bringing ZAPU back into government. A unity agreement was signed and Nkomo became senior minister in a newly formed Zimbabwe African National Union-Patriotic Front (ZANU-PF) government. Mugabe was again re-elected in 1990 (in polling marred by violence) and 1996, but throughout the 1990s he adopted a series of unpopular policies. His military support for President Kabila's beleaguered government in the Democratic Republic of the Congo led to strikes within his own country. An announcement of pay increases for himself and his party officials in 1998 prompted rioting, coming as it did amidst a growing economic crisis. Plans to raise food and fuel prices and to introduce a tax to support war veterans from the 1970s were blocked by trades unions and further diminished his popularity.

In Feb. 2000 Mugabe lost a referendum in which he sought to increase his presidential powers. Blaming the white minority for the defeat, he then targeted the issue of land ownership. A programme of violent land seizure followed, with black settlers taking over white-owned farms. A court order to halt the seizures was ignored and Mugabe subsequently replaced high court judges with political allies. In June 2000 parliamentary elections were held. Mugabe won the elections, but only by a narrow margin and after a campaign of intimidation which led to more than 30 deaths.

Mugabe was re-elected president in March 2002. Final results gave him 56.2% of the vote against 42.0% for opposition rival, Morgan Tsvangirai, the leader of the MDC. However, the elections failed to meet international democratic standards. They were preceded by violence against opposition supporters, the passing of a law limiting press freedom, the withdrawal of the European Union monitoring team and the arrest of Mugabe's main political rival on charges of treason. As a result, Zimbabwe was suspended from the Commonwealth and a range of targeted sanctions from the UK, the USA and the EU were placed on Mugabe and his cabinet. In March 2003 the USA froze Zimbabwean assets and forbade US citizens from undertaking economic dealings with Mugabe and his government colleagues.

The state of political uncertainty and violence following the 2000 referendum damaged investor confidence, causing export prices to decline and unemployment and food shortages to rise. Coupled with this, severe drought in early 2002 raised the threat of mass starvation. In April 2002 Mugabe declared a state of disaster, allowing him the temporary use of 'extraordinary measures' to cope with the situation. Although little was done in practical terms to relieve the threat of famine, Mugabe pushed ahead with the land redistribution programme. In June 2002 he ordered almost 3,000 white farmers to leave their land within 45 days, or face imprisonment. In Sept. 2002 new legislation was passed allowing farmers only a week's notice after receiving an eviction order. In March 2003 Amnesty International reported that up to 500 people had been arrested following a general strike, with members of the MDC especially targeted. In the same month the Commonwealth extended Zimbabwe's suspension until at least Dec. 2003. In June 2003 police detained Tsvangirai, who had called for mass popular protests against Mugabe's government, and in Jan. 2004 he went on trial for treason. Although he was acquitted in Oct. 2004 of charges relating to an assassination plot against Mugabe, he still faced a separate treason charge. Meanwhile, relations with the international community worsened. In Dec. 2003 the Commonwealth (despite South African disapproval) again extended Zimbabwe's suspension, prompting Mugabe's withdrawal from the organization.

At the parliamentary elections in March 2005, ZANU-PF took 78 of 150 seats. The MDC claimed that there had been widespread vote rigging and intimidation. Then, in May, Mugabe's government launched a demolition of urban slum dwellings and illegal settlements, including business premises, around the country without compensation. The policy drew international condemnation as an estimated 700,000 people (according to the UN) lost their homes, or source of livelihood, or both. In Aug. 2005 parliament approved amendments to the constitution, including the reintroduction of the Senate, which had been abolished in 1990. Other changes provided for the government to confiscate passports of those deemed to pose a threat to national security and to strengthen control over land redistribution with no right of appeal. Also in Aug., the authorities dropped the remaining treason charge against Tsvangirai. ZANU-PF won the Nov. 2005 elections to the new Senate, securing an overwhelming majority of 66 seats amid low voter turnout and opposition calls for a boycott.

Repression of the MDC and wider opposition intensified from 2006, particularly in March 2007 when Tsvangirai was beaten by security forces and hospitalized after his arrest at a political rally. A meeting of regional leaders subsequently invited South Africa's president, Thabo Mbeki, to mediate in Zimbabwe's political and economic crisis. In Dec. 2007 Mugabe's presence at the EU–Africa summit in Lisbon provoked criticism of his regime's abuse of human rights.

Mugabe was endorsed as the ZANU-PF candidate for the March 2008 presidential (and parliamentary) elections. After a relatively peaceful campaign the MDC made a strong showing and ZANU-PF lost its legislative majority. Tsvangirai also claimed outright victory in the presidential race but Mugabe challenged the results. Despite international pressure, the electoral commission delayed the publication of results and a second round run-off was scheduled. There followed an orchestrated campaign of brutality against supporters of the opposition, which led to the withdrawal of Tsvangirai from the race in June. The international community was united in its condemnation of Mugabe's actions. The electoral crisis took place against a backdrop of economic meltdown.

Under international pressure, talks between Mugabe and Tsvangirai were brokered in Aug. 2008, which resulted in a deal the following month that saw Mugabe remain as president while Tsvangirai was to become executive prime minister. However, implementation of the agreement then stalled for several months over the allocation of cabinet posts between ZANU-PF and the MDC. The political deadlock was further exacerbated by the collapse of the economy and of basic services, which contributed to a serious outbreak of the disease cholera in Nov. 2008. In Jan. 2009, after months of acrimony and pressure from neighbouring states, Mugabe agreed to put power-sharing into effect and on 11 Feb. Tsvangirai was sworn in as prime minister. However, the failure of Mugabe's military and security service chiefs to attend the inauguration ceremony and the controversial detention of an MDC ministerial nominee did not represent an auspicious start for the new unity government.

In Sept. 2009 the EU sent its first high-level delegation to Zimbabwe for several years but refused to lift targeted sanctions. Donors were also cautious about releasing aid money to the government, fearing that it could be misused. In Oct. Mugabe called for improved relations with the West but added that the lifting of sanctions, which he blamed for ruining the country's economy, was an essential prerequisite. Mugabe's supporters had meanwhile continued to harass MDC activists, leading in Oct. to a stand-off between Mugabe and Tsvangirai in which the latter led an MDC boycott of cabinet meetings. The boycott was called off, however, after the intervention of the Southern African Development Community, which insisted that all 'outstanding issues' in the power-sharing pact be finally settled.

In Dec. 2009 Mugabe was re-elected as ZANU-PF leader for a further 5 years at a party congress in Harare. From 2010 he became increasingly outspoken about the shortcomings of the power-sharing agreement. He was again endorsed at the ZANU-PF congress in Dec. 2010 as the party's candidate for presidential elections that were scheduled to be held in 2013. In Feb. 2011, and again in Feb. 2012, the EU eased some sanctions on Zimbabwe but expressed concern at ZANU-PF's continuing failure to honour the unity government pact and at the reported rise in political violence and intimidation directed against the MDC.

In March 2013 a new constitution, which limited future presidents to two terms in office, was approved in a referendum, paving the way for elections at the end of July. Mugabe retained the presidency to extend his 33-year rule while ZANU-PF claimed an overwhelming majority of parliamentary seats, so ending the MDC's involvement in power-sharing. The results were denounced by Tsvangirai as fraudulent and a sham, and in Sept. the MDC boycotted the opening of the new parliament.

In Dec. 2014 Mugabe dismissed Joyce Mujuru as vice president and also sacked seven cabinet ministers, accusing them of corruption and plotting to kill him. Mujuru was replaced by justice minister Emmerson Mnangagwa.

In Jan. 2015 Mugabe was selected to serve as chairman for a year of the African Union. For the rest of that year speculation mounted in Zimbabwe and abroad about a likely successor to the ailing president. Nevertheless, while social and economic disaffection with the ruling elite became increasingly evident during 2016, Mugabe was again endorsed in Dec. as ZANU-PF's presidential candidate for elections scheduled for 2018.

Amid a power struggle for the leadership of the ZANU-PF between Emmerson Mnangagwa and First Lady Grace Mugabe, President Mugabe dismissed Mnangagwa from the vice presidency on 6 Nov. 2017. The army then seized power on 15 Nov. and 4 days later ZANU-PF officially removed Robert Mugabe as the party's head. On 21 Nov. the parliament started impeachment proceedings, leading Mugabe to resign the presidency after 37 years of ruling Zimbabwe. Legally vice President Phelekezela Mphoko became acting president (although he was not in Zimbabwe at the time) until Emmerson Mnangagwa was sworn in as the new president on 24 Nov. 2017.

Muhammad, Ali Nasser (Yemen)

Introduction

Ali Nasser Muhammad was one of the most influential politicians in the Marxist government of the People's Democratic Republic of Yemen in the 1970s and first half of the 1980s. Prime Minister from 1971, he was named by the central committee of the ruling Yemeni Socialist Party (YSP) as Chairman of the Presidium of the People's Supreme Assembly (and therefore head of state) and secretary-general of the party in April 1980. He retained the presidency until Jan. 1986, when mounting tensions between rival factions forced him into exile.

Early Life

Born in 1939, Muhammad was an active member of the National Liberation Front which took power in Southern Yemen in 1967 and declared independence after the withdrawal of the British. In 1968 he was placed at the head of the Second Governate and later that year became minister of local administration. In 1969 he was appointed minister of defence and, 2 years later, Prime Minister and a member of the Presidential Council.

Career Peak

Following the overthrow and killing in June 1978 of Salem Rubayyi Ali, the Chairman of the Presidential Council, Muhammad briefly assumed the chairmanship, making him head of state while retaining his duties as Prime Minister. However, in Dec. 1978 he was replaced as head of state by Abdul Fattah Ismail, a hard-line orthodox Marxist, who was elected chairman of the newly-created Presidium of the People's Supreme Assembly which superseded the Presidential Council. Muhammad remained Prime Minister and became the Deputy Chairman of the Presidium. Furthermore, he was a leading member of the ruling party, having in 1972 joined the political bureau of the National Front which in 1978 was reorganized to form the YSP.

On 21 April 1980 Ismail relinquished his responsibilities as Chairman of the Presidium and YSP secretary-general and was replaced by Muhammad. Western observers attributed Ismail's fall from office to a power struggle over policy differences. While maintaining South Yemen's close relations with the Soviet Union and its communist allies, Muhammad, unlike Ismail, favoured a reconciliation with moderate Arab states. In particular, he viewed improved relations with Saudi Arabia as necessary to further the proposed merger with the Yemen Arab Republic.

In Feb. 1985 Muhammad resigned his post as Prime Minister, but remained the head of state, YSP secretary-general and Presidium chairman. The rest of that year was marked by the re-emergence of former political rivalries, fuelled by the return from exile in Moscow of Abdul Fattah Ismail. This erupted into civil war in Jan. 1986. Muhammad tried to have his leading opponents killed in a pre-emptive strike. However, several of them survived and fierce factional fighting ensued. By the end of the month Muhammad had fled into exile in the Yemen Arab Republic.

Later Life

Muhammad was tried in absentia for treason, along with many of his senior supporters, by the new regime and sentenced to death in Dec. 1987.

Mujica, José (Uruguay)

Introduction

José Mujica took office on 1 March 2010 after winning a presidential run-off in Nov. 2009. A former leftist guerrilla, Mujica received 55% of the vote after campaigning on a platform of continued economic growth and policies to tackle crime and poverty.

Early Life

Mujica was born in Montevideo on 20 May 1935. He was a member of the centrist Partido Nacional (National Party) in his youth before joining the newly formed Movimiento de Liberación Nacional (popularly known as the Tupamaros) in the 1960s, an armed guerrilla movement inspired by the Cuban revolution.

In 1971 he was convicted by a military tribunal under the government of Jorge Pacheco Areco of killing a police officer. He escaped from Punta Carretas prison but was re-arrested in 1972. Following the 1973 military coup Mujica was transferred to a military prison where he was subjected to torture and solitary confinement. When the military dictatorship ended in 1985 he was freed under a general amnesty covering political crimes since 1962.

On his release and the restoration of democracy, Mujica steered the Tupamaros away from its guerrilla past and remodelled it into the Movimiento de Participación Popular (Movement of Popular Participation), a legitimate political party that later joined the left-wing Frente Amplio

(Broad Front) coalition. He was elected to the Chamber of Deputies in 1994 and in 1999 won a seat in the Senate, gaining re-election 5 years later.

On 1 March 2005 he resigned from the Senate when he was appointed minister of livestock, agriculture and fisheries by then president, Tabaré Vázquez. During his tenure Mujica intervened to keep down the price of beef, a staple of the Uruguayan people, winning popular acclaim. In 2008 he returned to the Senate after losing his cabinet post in a reshuffle.

On 28 June 2009 Mujica became Frente Amplio's presidential candidate after winning the coalition's primary election. He pledged to maintain the policies of outgoing President Vázquez, whose term of office had seen prolonged economic growth and strong social interventions by the government. In the first round of elections held in Oct. 2009 Mujica received 48% of the vote and on 30 Nov. 2009 he was declared winner of a run-off against Luis Alberto Lacalle of the National Party, with 55% of the vote.

Career Peak

Mujica was expected to improve Uruguay's often strained relations with its neighbours, and he expressed his support for MERCOSUR, the regional economic bloc. His other priorities included the improvement of educational standards and the maintenance of energy supplies.

Mujica opposed a parliamentary bid to annul legislation giving officers immunity from prosecution for crimes committed during the years of military rule and, despite support in the Senate, the bill was rejected by the Chamber of Deputies in May 2011. The legislation was subsequently revoked in a further congressional vote in Oct. that year.

In Oct. 2012 Mujica signed into law a controversial bill legalizing abortion for all women during the first 12 weeks of pregnancy, as Uruguay became only the second Latin American country after Cuba to decriminalize terminations. Further social legislation in April 2013 legalized same-sex marriage, while in Dec. Uruguay became the first country in the world to legalize and regulate the use and sale of marijuana. In the same month, Mujica appointed Central Bank governor Mario Bergara as economy and finance minister following the resignation of Fernando Lorenzo, amid corruption accusations.

In his Sept. 2013 speech to the UN General Assembly, Mujica highlighted environmental preservation and the need to limit economic fallout suffered by the poor as priorities for the international community.

Mujica was ineligible to stand for re-election in 2014 owing to the constitutional limit of 5 years for presidential terms. Tabaré Vázquez, also of the Broad Front and Mujica's immediate predecessor as president, won the elections of Oct. and Nov. 2014 and took office in March 2015.

Mukherjee, Pranab (India)

Introduction

A veteran politician with experience in previous administrations, Pranab Mukherjee was elected president in July 2012. He has a reputation as a skilled political broker with a track record in securing cross-party co-operation.

Early Life

Pranab Mukherjee was born on 11 Dec. 1935 in the village of Mirati in the Birbhum district of West Bengal. He studied law at Suri Vidyasagar College, affiliated to the University of Calcutta, where he also attained a master's degree in history and politics. He worked in teaching and journalism until 1969, when, with Indira Gandhi's support, he was elected to the upper house of parliament for the Indian National Congress party.

He rose rapidly, serving in a series of ministerial posts, covering industry (1973–74) and finance, revenue and banking (1975–77). He reached cabinet level in 1980 when he was appointed minister of commerce, steel and mines. Named finance minister in 1982, he resisted IMF pressure to implement austerity measures, instead pursuing a combination of tax reforms and government investment. His policies were claimed as a success when the economy recovered, allowing India to return part of an IMF loan.

Following Indira Gandhi's assassination in 1984, Mukherjee left government to head the West Bengal Pradesh Congress committee. In 1986 he formed the Rashtriya Samajwadi Congress (RSC) but after a lacklustre performance in the 1987 regional assembly elections, the RSC merged with the Congress Party of Rajiv Gandhi in 1989. 2 years later Mukherjee became deputy chairman of the planning commission in Narasimha Rao's government, a post he held until 1996. He re-entered cabinet in 1993 as minister of commerce and served as foreign minister from 1995–96.

Following the Congress' electoral defeat in 1996, Mukherjee supported Sonia Gandhi's successful bid for party presidency. He served as general secretary of the All India Congress Committee (AICC) from 1998–99 and as president of the West Bengal Pradesh Congress committee from 2000. He returned to government in 2004 in the Congress-led United Progressive Alliance (UPA), becoming leader of the lower house. He served as defence minister from 2004–06 and as foreign minister from 2006–09.

In 2009 he was appointed finance minister and faced the task of tightening fiscal discipline while maintaining inclusive growth strategies. Reforms proved difficult to implement, largely owing to political deadlock. While he won praise early in his tenure, he was later criticized for lack of progress on tax reforms, cutting subsidies and opening markets to foreign investment. He resigned in June 2012 to stand as the Congress' presidential nominee.

Career Peak

Mukherjee took office in July 2012, having gained 69% of the electoral college vote to defeat his nearest rival, P. A. Sangma. While the role is largely ceremonial, Mukherjee was viewed as well-placed to broker political agreements. In May 2014 he swore in Narendra Modi as the new prime minister following the BJP's landslide victory in parliamentary elections. Having announced that he would not run for a second term in office, Mukherjee was succeeded by the winner of the July 2017 presidential election Ram Nath Kovind.

Muldoon, Robert (New Zealand)

Introduction

Born in Auckland on 25 Sept. 1921, Robert David Muldoon served in World War II before training, in New Zealand and England, as a cost accountant. Known as 'Piggy Muldoon' reputedly because of both his distinctive laugh and association as finance minister with piggy banks, the National leader for 10 years was celebrated and attacked in equal measure for his uncompromising economic reforms.

Early Life

Muldoon joined the National Party in 1947, and became chairman of the Young Nationals 2 years later. He entered parliament as member for Tamaki in 1960 after unsuccessfully contesting Mount Albert in the 1954 and 1957 elections, and held the seat until retiring 31 years later. Under Keith Holyoake's administration, Muldoon's first parliamentary appointment was undersecretary to the finance minister from 1963–6. He took up the financial portfolio in 1967, a year in which he also served as tourism minister, and oversaw the country's change to decimal currency. He remained finance minister for 5 years until election defeat in 1972. Following a leadership change to Jack Marshall in Feb. of that year, Muldoon was also deputy prime minister. During the party's term in opposition, a parliamentary group known as the Young Turks set about replacing Marshall with Muldoon. He was elevated from deputy to leader of the opposition in 1974. Vigorous television campaigning and strong support from farmers and the elderly, dubbed 'Rob's Mob' saw National under Muldoon returned to power on 12 Dec. 1975.

Career Peak

Muldoon served, often controversially, as both minister of finance and prime minister throughout his 9 years in office. His economics were interventionist but resolutely anti-communist, his rhetoric famously truculent. After fixing the currency value and introducing permits and tariffs for all international trading, Muldoon later froze wages and prices in an attempt to cut inflation. His early 1980s 'Think Big' scheme saw the government investing borrowed money in immense industrial projects such as the Synfuel plant and Clyde dam. Other strategies were highly popular. Shoring up the rural economy and vote, he introduced loans and minimum prices for farmers, which led to the government buying surplus livestock and reselling it as fertilizer. In 1977,

Muldoon established universal pension provision without means testing. The year also marked Muldoon's selection as a Companion of Honour, following his appointment to the Privy Council in 1976. He chaired the World Bank governors and IMF from 1979–80, and led the OECD ministerial council 2 years later. In Oct. 1980, Muldoon's position was unsuccessfully challenged by colleagues, including Jim Bolger, who wanted to replace him with deputy Brain Talboys. Key issues during the Muldoon administration were the Falklands conflict, in which he backed Britain, and the South African rugby tour of New Zealand, which Muldoon also supported. Anti-apartheid protests peaked on 12 Sept. 1981, with 10,000 protestors disrupting the game at Eden Park stadium. Green issues came to the fore under Muldoon's leadership. Following the 1979 oil crisis, each car had to stay off the road at least 1 day a week. At the same time, the government invested in alternative energy sources though the 'Think Big' scheme. Muldoon held office for three terms until calling and losing a snap election on 26 July 1984, the year of his knighthood.

Later Life

After a brief period as opposition leader in 1984, Muldoon was succeeded by Jim McLay. After leading the party for less than 2 years, McLay lost his position to Bolger, who appointed Muldoon shadow foreign affairs minister from 1986–91. During National's time in opposition, the former prime minister served as president of the national football association (1986–8), and chair of the Global Economic Action Institute (1988–91). After retiring from politics in 1991, Muldoon hosted a radio talk programme, and appeared as a narrator in the Rocky Horror stage show. He died in Auckland on 6 Aug. 1992.

Mulroney, Brian (Canada)

Introduction

Prime Minister of Canada from 1984 to 1993, Brian Mulroney was the leader of the Progressive Conservative Party from 1983 to 1993.

Born the son of an electrician in Baie-Comeau, Quebec in 1939, Mulroney grew up bilingual in English and French. After studying at Saint Francis Xavier University in Nova Scotia, Mulroney studied law at Laval University, Quebec City. He began practising law in Montreal in 1965, specializing in Labour relations.

Early Life

He first came to prominence working on the Cliche Commission of Inquiry into the Quebec construction industry in 1974, which uncovered unprecedented corruption and violence in the industry.

He made his first bid for the leadership of the Conservatives in 1976 but having lost to Joe Clark on the third ballot, instead became president of the Iron Ore Company of Canada.

Mulroney finally won the party leadership in 1983 despite never having held public office, but as the only bilingual Quebec candidate, offered the Conservatives a wider electoral appeal. His leadership forged an alliance between Quebec nationalists and western conservatives, offering both national unity and recognition of Quebec's distinct status.

Career Peak

Leading the party to a landslide victory over the Liberals in 1984, the Conservatives won the greatest majority in Canadian history with 211 seats in the House of Commons. As Prime Minister, Mulroney sought closer co-operation with the United States on trade and environmental issues. The early period of his government saw strong economic growth and low inflation, with key industries deregulated and taxes reformed. He won a second term in 1988.

Trade was of primary importance for Mulroney, believing Canadian economic success could only be secured by maintaining access to foreign markets—in particular the United States. He oversaw two trade agreements with the United States with the 1988 Free Trade Agreement and later the North American Free Trade Agreement (NAFTA) with the United States and Mexico (signed in 1992).

Under his premiership, the Nunavut Agreement with the Inuit of the Eastern Arctic led to the creation of a third territory in Canada, and represented a major achievement in Aboriginal land settlement.

Endeavouring to achieve constitutional reform, Mulroney was one of the driving forces behind the Meech Lake accord, which attempted to end Quebec's boycott of the 1982 constitutional reform. However, the accord failed to become law when the Manitoba and Newfoundland legislatures refused to pass it. A second attempt with the Charlottetown accord of 1992 was defeated in a popular referendum.

Failing to heal the constitutional rift, Mulroney's popularity shrank and he announced his intention to retire from politics in 1993.

Later Life

Adverse criticism over arrangements made for some of his colleagues in the final months of his term of office led to Mulroney emerging from his retirement to bring a bitter libel suit.

Murekezi, Anastase (Rwanda)

Introduction

Anastase Murekezi, an ethnic Hutu and member of the Social Democratic Party, became prime minister on 24 July 2014. He was previously minister of public service and labour, and is an agricultural engineer by training.

Early Life

Born in 1952, Murekezi read agriculture at the Université Catholique de Louvain in Belgium. In 2004 he was appointed minister of state in charge of industry and investment. The following year he joined the cabinet as minister of agriculture, and from 2008–14 he held the civil service and labour portfolio. During his tenure he faced a parliamentary committee investigating irregularities in ministry-run departments. Nonetheless, President Paul Kagame appointed him premier in July 2014 after dismissing his predecessor in the post, Pierre Damien Habumuremyi, who had served since 2011.

Career Peak

While Kagame publicly gave no reason for sacking Habumuremyi, he appointed Murekezi after stating his desire to revitalize the cabinet. When Murekezi took office, he named five new cabinet ministers although the incumbents of key ministries including defence, foreign affairs, finance and internal security remained unchanged.

In Oct. 2014 Murekezi announced the launch of an Environment and Climate Change Fund (Fonerwa) to support sustainable development, backed by a number of international bilateral development agencies. Meanwhile, his opponents have exerted pressure on him to curb the government's increasingly hard-line approach to its critics. After the presidential election of Aug. 2017 Paul Kagame replaced him with Édoaurd Ngirente.

Musa, Said (Belize)

Introduction

Said Musa, leader of the People's United Party (PUP), became prime minister in 1998 and won a second term in March 2003. A leading figure in Belize's fight for independence, his tenure has been dominated by ongoing attempts to resolve territorial disputes with Guatemala. Musa was defeated in the elections on 7 Dec. 2007.

Early Life

Said Wilbert Musa was born on 19 March 1944 in San Ignacio in the Cayo District of what was then British Honduras. In 1966 he graduated in law from the University of Manchester in the UK and the following year was called to

the Bar at Gray's Inn. Musa returned to Belize and served as a circuit magistrate and a crown counsel for the office of public prosecutions. He was elected to the presidency of the public service union but in 1970 went into private legal practice. During this period he became involved with the United Black Association for Development and also co-founded the People's Action Committee and the Society for the Promotion of Education and Research.

He joined the PUP in 1974 but was defeated that year in his first bid for a parliamentary seat. Nonetheless, PUP Prime Minister George Price appointed him as a senator for a 5-year term of office. In 1979 Musa entered parliament as the representative for Fort George. In the new PUP government he served as Attorney General and education and sports minister, later adding the economic development portfolio.

Musa was a key figure in the negotiations with Britain and Guatemala which preceded full independence in 1981. He represented Belize at the UN, the Commonwealth and CARICOM, and played a leading role in the drafting of a national constitution. After independence Musa was named foreign minister and oversaw entry into the Organization of American States (OAS). He was in regular contact with the government of Guatemala, which claimed a large part of Belize's territory as its own, and helped smooth relations sufficiently that Guatemala recognized Belize's independent sovereignty in 1991.

In 1996 George Price, leader of Belize's independence movement since the 1950s, retired as leader of the PUP and was replaced by Musa. Musa led the PUP to a landslide victory at the elections of 1998 and was sworn in as prime minister.

Career Peak

Musa has had to contend with Guatemala's continuing claim on half of Belize's territory. In early 2000 the Guatemalan government announced its intention to work through the international courts. Following OAS-brokered talks the two sides reached a draft agreement in Sept. 2002 establishing a transition process, to be voted on in referenda in both countries. Musa's first term of office also saw Belize hit by two devastating hurricanes, Keith and Iris, in Oct. 2000 and Oct. 2001. In parliamentary elections on 5 March 2003 the PUP retained power with a slightly reduced majority. A new government was sworn in 2 days later. Countering the international illegal drugs trade and associated violent crime have continued to pose serious problems for the Musa government. In 2006 the US administration included Belize on a list of countries failing to do enough to tackle human trafficking.

Musa announced on the day of the Feb. 2008 presidential elections that it would be his last run in electoral politics. Less than a week later he announced that he would step down as party leader. Although he lost the presidential elections on 7 Feb. 2008 Musa won the Fort George seat in the general elections. Dean Barrow (United Democratic Party) succeeded Musa as prime minister on 8 Feb. 2008 ending his 10 years in office.

Musharraf, Pervez (Pakistan)

Introduction

Gen. Pervez Musharraf, president of Pakistan, took power in a bloodless coup in 1999, ousting the democratically-elected prime minister, Nawaz Sharif. It was the first time that a military leader had taken control of a nuclear power. Musharraf styled himself as a caretaker leader, responsible for safeguarding the country while corruption was dealt with, the economy revitalized and 'true' democratic elections held. His leadership was not recognized by the international community and drew sanctions from the USA. The war in neighbouring Afghanistan, however, allowed Musharraf to exploit Pakistan's strategic importance to the US military effort there and to re-establish political ties with Washington. He struggled to balance US pressure for action against Islamic extremism at home and a resurgent Taliban in Afghanistan with widespread anti-Western opinion within Pakistan. His personal popularity plummeted, particularly in the wake of opposition leader Benazir Bhutto's assassination in Dec. 2007. Under threat of impeachment from parliament, he resigned his office in Aug. 2008.

Early Life

Born in Delhi on 11 Aug. 1943, Pervez Musharraf's family migrated to newly-formed Pakistan in 1947. From the age of 6 to 13 he was brought up in Turkey where his father was a secretary of foreign affairs for the Pakistani government. He has frequently cited the Turkish leader Mustafa Kemal Atatürk, a secular modernizer who fought for Turkish independence, as his hero.

Following training in the command and staff college, Quetta, and in the UK, Musharraf was commissioned in the Pakistani artillery in 1964. He saw active service in the India-Pakistan war of 1965 when, as a Lieut.-Col., he had command of two artillery regiments. Following promotion to brigadier, he commanded an armoured division and an artillery and infantry brigade. In the second armed conflict with India he was in charge of a commando battalion of the Special Services Group. Further promotions in 1991 and 1995 took him to the ranks of Maj.-Gen. and Lieut.-Gen.

On 7 Oct. 1998 Nawaz Sharif, then prime minister of Pakistan, appointed Musharraf as Chief of Army Staff. At the time Musharraf was in command of the 1st Strike Corps based at Mangla, a key military element in Pakistani strategy in Kashmir. The appointment was widely interpreted as a move by Sharif to appoint a figure who would not pose a threat to his leadership. Musharraf's ethnic background (he was not a member of the Punjabi officer class) was seen as a block to his advancement.

In early 1999 the Joint Chief of Staff Committee (JCSC) was reorganized, giving it increased power in nuclear command and the promise that the chairman would always be from the military. Musharraf took on this additional role in April 1999, becoming the strategic commander of Pakistan's nuclear forces. During armed conflict in Kargil in 1999 between Indian and Pakistani forces, a growing gap between the increasingly powerful chief of army staff and the prime minister became obvious. As Sharif withdrew support, senior army officers became incensed at what they saw as a betrayal. Musharraf, meanwhile, raised his profile, frequently appearing on television to comment on the conflict.

The political crisis reached a climax on 12 Oct. 1999. While Musharraf was on a diplomatic trip to Sri Lanka, Sharif replaced him with Gen. Ziauddin. He then refused permission for Musharraf's plane to land at Karachi airport despite the plane being low on fuel. In a dramatic turn of events the army took power and placed Sharif under arrest. Musharraf declared himself Pakistan's Chief Executive.

Career Peak

The coup attracted international censure and led to sanctions from the USA. Within Pakistan itself, however, the response was ambivalent. To many, a determined military government appeared the last ditch solution to Pakistan's crippling economic and social problems.

Having announced a National Security Council to take over the administration of the country, Musharraf instituted a series of reforms. He created a juvenile justice ordinance protecting children's rights and a national commission on the status of women. His most highly publicized initiative was a National Accountability Bureau (NAB) to target defaulters on government loans. In its first few months repayments were estimated at US$152 m. (although this was only 6% of the total target revenue). While the measure won him popularity for combating corruption, he exempted the judiciary and the military from prosecutions relating to the NAB. The Bureau was given wide-ranging authority to investigate the legitimacy of private wealth when it went beyond 'visible means of income'. After the deadline was reached for the repayment of loans, a list of outstanding defaulters was published and 21 arrests made on charges of corruption. Both Nawaz Sharif and the husband of former prime minister Benazir Bhutto were included in the list.

Despite Musharraf's insistence that he would make efforts to restore democracy, Pakistan was suspended from the Commonwealth in mid-Nov. 1999. Later that month Nawaz Sharif was formally charged with hijacking, kidnapping and conspiracy to murder. He was sentenced to 14 years' imprisonment, subsequently leaving for exile in Saudi Arabia. Tough economic measures, avoided by Sharif's administration, were adopted by Musharraf. A 15% sales tax implemented in early 2000 provoked the longest strike in Pakistan's history.

On 12 May 2000 Pakistan's Supreme Court unanimously validated the Oct. 1999 coup and granted Musharraf executive and legislative authority for 3 years from the date of the coup. The security of his leadership was further strengthened in June 2001 when he unexpectedly declared himself president, dissolving the provisional and national assemblies and dismissing former head of state, Rafiq Tarar. Guaranteeing himself a future place in Pakistan's administration, regardless of the outcome of democratic elections, the move was also an attempt to strengthen the legitimacy of his leadership before the Agra summit with India, which took place 1 month later. This first meeting between Musharraf and the then Indian prime minister, Atal Bihari Vajpayee, was hailed as an important step for bilateral relations but failed to produce significant agreement, most notably over Kashmir. Musharraf's insistence on Kashmir as the core issue was met with an equal degree of insistence from India that Pakistani-funded cross-border terrorism was the central obstacle to improved relations.

The attacks of 11 Sept. 2001 in the USA brought Musharraf's leadership to greater prominence at the international level. As a neighbour of Afghanistan—home to al-Qaeda—and sharing strong political links with the Taliban (Afghanistan's de facto government), Pakistan became central to attempts to put diplomatic pressure on the regime to secure the surrender of chief suspect Osama bin Laden. Despite intense pressure from Muslims within his own country, Musharraf committed Pakistan to the international anti-terror coalition. Rioting in Quetta and Peshawar, on the Afghan border, followed the first US military strike on Afghanistan. Musharraf downplayed the public sentiment against the US campaign and gave his support for 'short… targeted' military action, stating that 'Pakistan [had taken] the decision of being part of the world community and a part of a coalition to fight terrorism'. Soon after, Musharraf ejected three senior ministers (all linked to the 1999 coup) who were seen to support hardline Islamic sentiment.

Meanwhile, Pakistan's relations with India remained fraught over terrorism in Kashmir. Musharraf denied giving financial backing to terrorists, admitting only to 'moral, diplomatic and political support' for the Kashmiri 'freedom-fighters'. However, a suicide attack on 1 Oct. 2001 in Srinagar (the administrative centre of Indian-controlled Kashmir) resulting in 38 deaths, and a further terrorist attack on the Indian parliament building in New Delhi on 13 Dec. 2001, forced the Pakistani president into action. Musharraf banned the two militant Islamic organizations linked to the attacks, the Jaish-e-Mohammed and the Lashkar-e-Taiba. Military tension across the Line of Control (the border between the Indian-occupied and Pakistani-occupied areas of Kashmir) increased throughout Dec. 2001 with a mass mobilization of troops on both sides. India produced a list of Pakistani terrorist suspects, demanding that they be handed over for trial. Although not meeting this demand, Musharraf ordered a series of arrests as part of a domestic clampdown and gave a ground-breaking address in Jan. 2002 denouncing extremism and condemning terrorist actions related to Kashmir. Well received by the USA, the speech made less impact in India. An attack on an Indian army base in Indian-controlled Kashmir in May, killing 31, undermined the confidence which Musharraf sought to build. Although Musharraf gave a second speech denouncing terrorism, he also went ahead with a series of missile tests between 25–28 May, provoking international criticism.

In a referendum held on 30 April 2002, 97.7% of the votes cast were in favour of extending Musharraf's presidential rule by 5 years. Following the referendum, Musharraf reconstituted a National Security Council giving him, as chairman, power to override prime ministerial decisions once a new, democratically-elected government had been installed. Following parliamentary elections held in Oct. 2002, the pro-Musharraf Pakistan Muslim League (Quaid-e-Azam) emerged as the largest party with 117 seats.

In March 2003 Pakistan and India both held tests of short-range nuclear-capable missiles. The tests followed soon after India had blamed Pakistan for a massacre of 24 Hindus in Kashmir. In the same month the USA granted US$250 m. of aid to Pakistan, ending the last of its sanctions against the country implemented after Musharraf's seizure of power in 1999. The aid was perceived as key to Pakistan's further co-operation in the US-led war against terrorism. Relations with India showed signs of improving from early May 2003. Indian Prime Minister Vajpayee declared his intention of restoring full diplomatic links which Musharraf welcomed and promised to reciprocate. By late 2003 relations had improved greatly; both sides declared a ceasefire across the Kashmir Line of Control, transport and sporting links were restored, and from Jan. 2004 direct flights were resumed. Pakistan hosted a meeting of the South Asian Association for Regional Co-operation (SAARC) in Jan. 2004, at which Musharraf met with Vajpayee and agreed to open direct talks on Kashmir. Musharraf's offer to drop demands for a Kashmiri referendum was welcomed by the international community and India. Following the election of a new Congress-led Indian government in May 2004, the two countries continued to engage in regular dialogue, and in April 2005 Musharraf visited New Delhi for informal talks with Prime Minister Manmohan Singh. Also in April, a bus service between Pakistani- and Indian-administered Kashmir (Muzaffarabad–Srinagar) began for the first time in nearly 60 years.

In Dec. 2003 Musharraf survived an assassination attempt in Islamabad, an attack he blamed on Islamic extremists. Despite internal opposition, he nevertheless consolidated his hold on political power during 2004. In April, parliament approved the new military-led National Security Council, thereby institutionalizing the role of the armed forces in civilian affairs. The following month, Pakistan was readmitted to the Commonwealth. Then in Dec. 2004, despite having promised to relinquish the role, Musharraf announced that he would continue as head of the Army.

In Oct. 2005, following a co-ordinated terrorist attack in the Indian capital of New Delhi by suspected Islamic militants, Musharraf condemned the atrocity and called for the demilitarization of Kashmir. In July 2006, terrorist bomb attacks on commuter trains and railway stations in Mumbai killed 200. The Indian government blamed Pakistan's intelligence services and diplomatic relations were frozen until a resumption of ministerial contacts in Jan. 2007.

Political opposition to Musharraf's regime intensified in 2007. In March the president suspended Pakistan's Chief Justice, Iftikhar Chaudhry, triggering widespread popular demonstrations and strikes. Then in July security forces stormed a mosque in Islamabad that was being occupied by radical anti-government students, resulting in around 100 deaths and fuelling Islamist anger across the country. Musharraf meanwhile continued to block the return of exiled opposition leaders Sharif and Bhutto (although he reportedly held secret negotiations with the latter in Abu Dhabi). In Oct. Musharraf was re-elected as president (although still head of the Army) by an electoral college comprising the national and provincial assemblies. Representatives of the Pakistan People's Party abstained in the election in response to Musharraf's agreement to grant an amnesty to PPP leader Bhutto. The following month Musharraf declared emergency rule, suspending the constitution and detaining opposition politicians and members of the judiciary. Pakistan was again suspended from the Commonwealth as a result. He then stood down as Army chief prior to his inauguration for a second presidential term and, in mid-Dec., lifted the state of emergency ahead of parliamentary elections scheduled for Jan. 2008.

Bhutto had meanwhile returned to Pakistan, but was assassinated on 27 Dec. in a suicide attack at an election rally in Rawalpindi, sparking violence among her supporters across the country. Government complicity in the attack was suspected, although Musharraf blamed Islamist extremism. In the subsequent parliamentary elections (postponed until 18 Feb.), the pro-Musharraf Pakistan Muslim League (Quaid-e-Azam) came third to the opposition PPP and Pakistan Muslim League (Nawaz Sharif). Sharif, who had previously returned from exile, and Asif Ali Zardari, husband of Bhutto and new PPP leader, reached an agreement in March to form a new coalition government.

In early Aug. 2008 Sahrif and Zardari formally appealed to Musharraf to leave office or face a parliament-led impeachment. On 16 Aug. the coalition leaders announced a 72-h deadline for him to stand down. Musharraf announced his resignation in a televised address to the nation on 18 Aug. 2008.

Later Life

His resignation was followed by a self-imposed exile in London. In Oct. 2010 Musharraf established a centre-right political party, the All Pakistan Muslim League (ALPM). Musharraf returned to Pakistan in March 2013 to seek the presidency in the election in July. However, the following month he was disqualified from running and since June 2013 has faced several charges in connection with the murder of Benazir Bhutto, for military operations conducted under his tenure and for treason.

In March 2014 Musharraf was charged with treason, having been accused of unlawfully suspending the constitution in 2007. He was permitted to leave the country in March 2016 to receive medical treatment but still faced the treason and Bhutto murder charges.

In Feb. 2017 Musharraf launched a new career as a political analyst on a television talk show.

Mwanawasa, Levy (Zambia)

Introduction

Representing the Movement for Multi-Party Democracy (MMD), Levy Patrick Mwanawasa assumed the presidency in 2002, the chosen successor of his predecessor Frederick Chiluba. Having won a disputed election in 2001 (legal challenges to which were not finally resolved until early 2005), his main challenges were tackling corruption and alleviating food shortages. He was re-elected for a second term in Sept. 2006 but died suddenly in Aug. 2008.

Early Life

Mwanawasa was born on 3 Sept. 1948 in Mufulira, the Copperbelt region, in what was Northern Rhodesia. He studied law at the University of Zambia, graduating in 1973. Politically active in student politics, he joined the protests against the remaining colonial powers in Southern Africa, becoming vice-president of his university student union. He set up his own law firm in 1978.

From 1982–83 he was vice-president of the Zambian law society. This led to his appointment as Zambian solicitor general in 1985, a position he held for a year. In 1989 he successfully defended several politicians accused of leading a coup against the then president Kenneth Kaunda. With an increased profile, he joined Chiluba's newly formed MMD opposition party, becoming party vice-chairman in 1991. In national elections of the same year, Chiluba took the presidency and Mwanawasa was appointed vice-president.

In Dec. 1991 he was involved in a car accident that saw him hospitalized for 3 months and left him with permanent side effects, including slurred speech. He remained vice-president, but citing rampant corruption within the government, resigned in 1994. 2 years later, he unsuccessfully challenged Chiluba for the party leadership, and subsequently left politics to continue his legal career.

Re-elected in 1996, President Chiluba attempted to change the constitution to allow him to stand for a third consecutive term. In protest, some MMD members left the party to form the Forum for Democracy and Development. When Chiluba failed in his bid to continue in office, the MMD was forced to look for a party candidate. Some were surprised when Mwanawasa, uninvolved in politics since his resignation in 1994, was chosen. Since Chiluba remained MMD leader, the opposition cast doubts on Mwanawasa's impartiality. In the elections of Dec. 2001 he secured the presidency but with only 28.8% of the vote.

Career Peak

The opposition claimed the election was rigged. All parties refused to attend Mwanawasa's inauguration and, although the High Court initially declined to investigate electoral fraud, three opposition parties mounted a legal challenge to the results. Revelations of corruption under Chiluba emerged in the trial. In an attempt to distance himself from Chiluba's legacy, Mwanawasa launched an anti-corruption campaign. In July 2002 parliament voted to remove the former president's immunity from prosecution. In Jan. 2003 Mwanawasa announced plans to appoint several opposition politicians to ministerial posts.

Following poor harvests in 2001, around 3 m. people needed food aid in Zambia, mirroring conditions across Southern Africa. In 2002 Mwanawasa appealed for international help, but became embroiled in a dispute over genetically-modified (GM) crops. In Oct. 2002 he rejected the use of GM crops as food aid, even if the grain was milled before use, as had been accepted in neighbouring countries. Despite growing criticism from his own people and the international community over delayed distribution, Mwanawasa requested a US$50 m. World Bank loan to buy organic maize.

In Aug. 2003 the president survived a motion in parliament to impeach him for corruption and other violations of the constitution. In the same month there was a general strike involving 120,000 public sector workers and civil servants over pay and allowances. In early 2005 the Supreme Court finally rejected opposition legal action against the 2001 election results. In July Mwanawasa defeated a challenge to his leadership of the MMD at the party's convention from the former vice-president Enoch Kavindele.

In 2005, while drought again forced the government to appeal for international food aid, the World Bank approved a debt relief package writing off more than 50% of Zambia's debt. The economy received a further boost in Oct. 2006 when Mwanawasa announced that oil reserves had been discovered in the west of the country, and in Feb. 2007 when the visiting president of China inaugurated a mining investment project in Zambia's copperbelt.

Despite suffering a minor stroke in April 2006, Mwanawasa recovered sufficiently to run successfully for re-election the following Sept. International observers commended the overall conduct of the poll, despite opposition protests. He won widespread praise from the international community when he became one of the first African leaders to condemn the regime of Robert Mugabe in Zimbabwe, describing its economy as 'a sinking Titanic'. He was expected to continue his criticism of the Zimbabwean government at a meeting of the African Union in Egypt in June 2008. However, he suffered a stroke a few hours before the summit began and died on 19 Aug. 2008.

Nagy, Imre (Hungary)

Introduction

Imre Nagy was the Communist leader of Hungary between 1953 and 1955 and for the duration of the Hungarian uprising against the Soviets in Oct.–Nov. 1956. A reformer who desired Hungarian independence from the Soviet Union, he was arrested in the aftermath of the Hungarian uprising and executed 2 years later.

Early Life

Nagy was born on 7 June 1896 in Kaposvár, then part of the Austro-Hungarian Empire. He laboured as a locksmith's apprentice until he fought for the Austro-Hungarian army in World War I. He was captured by Russian troops, became a Bolshevik and served in the Red Army, and was briefly a member of Béla Kun's post-war Bolshevik government in Hungary. Following the collapse of Kun's regime, Nagy fled the country but returned in 1921 to assist in the organization of the illegal Hungarian Communist Party. However, following his arrest, he fled to Moscow in 1929 and remained there until 1944.

During his Russian exile, Nagy attended the Moscow Institute to study agriculture. By the time he returned to Hungary the country was under Soviet occupation and he became an important figure in the setting up of the post-war government. He was Minister of Agriculture, 1945–46, and oversaw a number of reforms that empowered the peasants at the expense of large landowners. Later on he held the positions of Minister of the Interior and Parliamentary Speaker but when Mátyas Rakosi came to power he fell out of favour and was excluded from the party in 1949. He returned to the Politburo 2 years later but only after publicly renouncing his earlier criticisms.

Career Peak

During Rákosi's tenure, Nagy rose to become Deputy Premier and, following Stalin's death and the succession of Georgii Malenkov in the Soviet Union, he found himself once again in favour and became Premier in 1953. Nagy instigated liberal reforms, notably the easing of agricultural collectivization. He also permitted greater freedom of movement for workers, dispensed with labour camps, oversaw the increase in the availability of consumer goods and reduced the more extreme police powers. He was fiercely independent in the face of Soviet intervention and, whilst popular in Moscow in the immediate aftermath of Stalin's reign of tyranny, he fell foul of political manoeuvrings in Russia in 1955. He was forced to resign the premiership, was again ejected from the party and took up a teaching position.

1956 saw popular discontent grow in Hungary, boosted by events in Poland including the emergence of the liberal Wladyslaw Gomułka as leader. Student protests took place in Budapest in late Oct. and were violently suppressed by troops on 23 Oct. Nagy was installed as Premier on that evening in the hope that he could successfully mediate between Moscow and the protesters. Nagy went into action immediately, outlawing the one-party system and offering amnesty to the protesters. He also believed he had reached agreement for the withdrawal of Soviet forces from Hungarian soil but, when Moscow reneged on the deal, he withdrew his country from the Warsaw Pact and proclaimed Hungarian neutrality.

On 4 Nov. 1956 Soviet tanks rolled into Budapest. Nagy made a radio broadcast pleading for Western assistance, saying that 'the whole world will see how the Russian armed forces, contrary to all treaties and conventions, are crushing the resistance of the Hungarian people'. The West, itself operating in a climate of mistrust following the Suez Crisis earlier in the year, did nothing. Nagy sought refuge in the Yugoslav Embassy but, having been promised safe passage, was kidnapped along with a group of fellow resisters. They were taken to Romania and then later returned to Hungary, where they were pressurised to accept the regime of János Kádár. Nagy refused and, following a secret trial, was executed in Budapest on 16 June 1958.

Exactly 31 years to the day after his death, as the Hungarian communist regime was in its final throes, Nagy's life was publicly celebrated in Budapest's Heroes Square and he was given a martyr's burial. Since then a number of official Soviet documents have emerged that seem to confirm that Nagy acted as an agent for the KGB (the Soviet secret police) for a considerable part of his career though it has been argued that this was a far from unusual scenario among comparable figures in that era of Communism. He remains one of the great figures of the 1956 Hungarian uprising, admired for his liberalism and the challenge he presented to the Soviet authorities.

Nailatikau, Epeli (Fiji)

Introduction

Ratu Epeli Nailatikau was sworn into office on 5 Nov. 2009, having been acting president for the previous 3 months following the resignation of Ratu Josefa Iloilo on 30 July 2009.

Early Life

Nailatikau was born on 5 July 1941 to a family of politically powerful chieftains. After completing his education in Fiji, he joined the armed forces and was sent for training in New Zealand. In 1966 he was posted with the 1st Battalion, Royal New Zealand Infantry Regiment to Sarawak, Malaysia during the Indonesia–Malaysia confrontation. On his return to Fiji, he joined the Fiji Infantry Regiment, rising steadily through the ranks. By 1987 he was a Brigadier-General and Commander of the Royal Fiji Military Forces but was ousted in a military coup headed by Sitiveni Rabuka.

Pursuing a new career in the diplomatic service, Nailatikau completed the foreign service programme at the University of Oxford and was appointed High Commissioner to the United Kingdom, a portfolio that also included Denmark, Egypt, Germany, Israel and the Holy See. He went on to become Roving Ambassador and High Commissioner to the member states of the South Pacific Forum and, in 1999, was appointed permanent secretary for foreign affairs and external trade.

Following a coup in 2000, which he had strongly opposed, Nailatikau was nominated as prime minister in the subsequent interim military government of Commodore Frank Bainimarama. However, within 24 h Nailatikau had withdrawn in favour of Laisenia Qarase, instead taking the posts of deputy prime minister and minister for Fijian affairs. At the 2001 general election he put himself forward as speaker of the House of Representatives, a post he held until 2006. On 14 June 2005, Nailatikau was appointed the UNAIDS (The United Nations Joint Programme on HIV/AIDS) Special Representative for the Pacific. Outspoken in his campaign to tackle the AIDS crisis, he attracted controversy when he called for a public endorsement of safe sex.

In Jan. 2007 Nailatikau joined Bainimarama's interim government, formed in the wake of another coup d'état in Dec. 2006. He served as minister of foreign affairs, international co-operation and civil aviation. On 10 April 2007 he was nominated as vice-president by the newly reinstalled President Iloilo but his appointment was rejected by the Grand Council of Chiefs. Nailatikau took over the portfolio for provincial development and multi-ethnic affairs from Prime Minister Bainimarama in Oct. 2008, with his previous duties reassigned to the premier.

Nailatikau became vice-president on 17 April 2009 following a constitutional crisis in which the appeal court ruled that the military regime formed in 2006 was illegal, prompting Iloilo to repeal the constitution and sack the appeal court judges. With Bainimarama restored to the premiership, Nailatikau took over the presidency on 30 July 2009 in an acting capacity, until 5 Nov. 2009 when he was sworn in as Iloilo's successor.

Career Peak

Nailatikau's appointment, made behind closed doors, signalled that the military would continue to play a pivotal role in Fijian politics. On 29 Jan. 2010 he signed an extension of the public emergency regulation, in place since April 2009 to give power to the authorities to stop events they deemed a threat to national security. He was reappointed as president for a further 3 years in Nov. 2012. A new constitution was signed into law by Nailatikau in Sept. 2013.

Nailatikau's presidential term ended on 12 Nov. 2015 when Jioji Konousi Konrote was sworn in as president, having been elected by parliament in Oct.

Najib Razak (Malaysia)

Introduction

Dato' Sri Haji Mohd Najib bin Tun Haji Abdul Razak became prime minister on 3 April 2009, replacing Abdullah bin Haji Ahmad Badawi following the poor showing of the Barisan Nasional (National Front Coalition) at the general election of March 2008. Najib had replaced Badawi as head of the United Malays National Organization (UMNO), the senior party in the coalition, in March 2009. Although Najib won a further term in office in May 2013, the Barisan Nasional lost its majority at the following elections on 9 May 2018.

Early Life

Najib was born on 23 July 1953 in Kuala Lipis, Pahang, into a political family. His father was independent Malaysia's second prime minister and his uncle was its third. Najib was educated at St John's Institution, Kuala Lumpur, and at Malvern College in England before graduating from the University of Nottingham in 1974 with a bachelor's degree in industrial economics.

In 1976 he became Malaysia's youngest member of parliament when he stood uncontested for his late father's seat of Pekan. In his first year as an MP, Najib was appointed deputy minister of energy, telecommunications and posts. He was later appointed deputy minister of education and deputy minister of finance. In 1981 he joined UMNO's Supreme Council and the following year became the Menteri Besar (Chief Executive) of Pahang state.

Najib became vice president of UMNO Youth in 1982, a post he also held from 1987–93. Having lost his Pekan parliamentary seat, he regained it at the elections of 1986 and was appointed minister of culture, youth and sports. He went on to hold several other cabinet portfolios including defence and education. On 7 Jan. 2004 Najib was selected as Badawi's deputy and given the defence portfolio. In July 2004 he stood unopposed for the vice presidency of UMNO.

Although Barisan Nasional won the election of 2008, it was with a much reduced majority. Badawi named Najib as his likely successor and on 17 Sept. 2008 Najib was handed the finance portfolio as part of a gradual power transfer. On 26 March 2009 he stood unopposed for the UMNO presidency, ensuring him the post of prime minister when Badawi resigned on 2 April 2009.

Career Peak

In his first term Najib promised reform but was confronted with a severe economic downturn, a divided UMNO and the increasing unpopularity of a government accused by opponents of corruption and complacency. On the economic front he unveiled details in March 2010 of a new model intended to more than double per capita income by 2020, promote greater private-sector investment and revise a controversial ethnically-based affirmative action policy. However, he also generated controversies relating to allegations of an ongoing political conspiracy against former deputy prime minister Anwar Ibrahim (who was later jailed for 5 years in Feb. 2015), the murder of a Mongolian woman in which several associates (including his wife) were implicated, and problems with the national service programme that he devised and in which several conscripts died.

At the parliamentary election of 5 May 2013 Najib nonetheless led Barisan Nasional to victory again (but with less than 50% of the popular vote), winning 133 seats to the 89 of the People's Front coalition. He was sworn in for a second term as prime minister the following day.

Although Najib had promised in 2012 to repeal the long-standing Internal Security Act—legislation widely regarded as draconian—it remained in place, and in April and Dec. 2015 parliament approved further controversial anti-terrorism and arbitrary security measures.

Najib has also been implicated in a major financial scandal involving 1Malaysia Development Berhad, a state investment fund. In Jan. 2016 the attorney general controversially cleared him of any wrongdoing but he has continued to attract criticism both at home and abroad. In Nov. that year, undeterred by arrests of opposition activists and curbs on media sources, thousands of protesters marched in Kuala Lumpur demanding that Najib step down as prime minister.

Despite the growing hostility towards his government, which generated the formation of a new opposition coalition under the ageing former UMNO prime minister Mahathir Mohamad, Najib called an election for 9 May 2018. Barisan Nasional registered its worst-ever electoral performance, paving the way for Mahathir to assume the premiership on 10 May 2018.

Nano, Fatos (Albania)

Introduction

Fatos Nano was prime minister three times (1991, 1997–98, 2002–05). He was Socialist Party chairman from the party's creation in 1991. A liberal economist, he was a major force in post-communist Albanian politics. His career was marred by acrimonious relations with the founder of the Democratic Party, Sali Berisha.

Early Life

Nano was born in Tirana in 1952. He studied Political Economy at Tirana University where he remained as a professor for 10 years. In 1990 he was invited by the government to advise on the restructuring of the heavily centralized economy along free market lines. He was also involved in the transformation of the Labour Party, the only legal party from 1948 until 1990, which was renamed the Socialist Party of Albania (PSS). This new party, of which Nano was elected chairman in June 1991, declared its commitment to liberalization, allowing the opposition parties to contest the 1991 elections.

Career Peak

In Feb. 1991 President Ramiz Alia appointed Nano prime minister with the responsibility of preparing the first pluralist elections in March, which the PSS won. Nano's government embarked on a programme of privatization and political and economic reforms, most notably of the banking system. Diplomatic relations were established with the USA and the EC. However, change was too slow for public opinion and Nano's government was forced to resign in June amid widespread demonstrations and strikes. Elections were held in March 1992 and a landslide victory brought the Democratic Party (PDS) to power. The new president, Dr. Sali Berisha, accused Nano and the previous president, Ramiz Alia, of corruption and the 'appropriation of Italian aid'. Nano was sentenced to 13 years and imprisoned in March 1993.

The unrest resulting from the collapse of fraudulent pyramid investment schemes in 1997 forced the PDS government's resignation and Nano's release from prison. In June the PSS triumphed in elections, initiating Nano's second term in office. His attention turned abroad to the issue of ethnic Albanians in Kosovo and he met Yugoslav President Milošević at the Crete Summit in Nov. 1997, provoking criticism at home and from Kosovan leaders. Nano was also criticised by European leaders for allowing the transit of arms for Kosovan Albanians.

Widespread violence and disorder in early 1998, centred in the northern town of Shkodër, led to the PDS boycott of Parliament and claims of opposition involvement. The murder of Azem Hajdari, a prominent PDS politician and anti-Communist activist, on 12 Sept. 1998 sparked violent demonstrations in Tirana and an attempted coup. The PDS claimed that Nano directly ordered the assassination as revenge for Hajdari's part in the ousting of the first Nano administration in 1991. Nano's disappearance on the 13–14 Sept. and his failure to show decisive leadership weakened his popular support. Allegations of heavy drinking hastened his departure on 29 Sept., after he failed to form a new cabinet.

The factionalism that threatened the survival of the Socialist Party came to a head in Jan. 1999 with the resignation of Nano as chairman but he was re-elected by a tight margin at the PSS congress in Oct., forcing the resignation of Pandeli Majko, his successor as prime minister.

Iler Meta, Majko's successor, was ousted in Jan. 2002, largely because of Nano's refusal to confirm cabinet appointments. Meta claimed the chairman was using an anti-corruption platform to further his own aspirations for the presidency. Under pressure from EU leaders, Nano came to an unexpected agreement with his main rival, Berisha, whereby neither stood for the presidency. The election of Alfred Moisiu in June allowed Nano to return as prime minister in July, promising to crack down on crime and corruption and maintain the political consensus reached with the PDS leadership. Nano also managed to mend some of the divisions within his own party by appointing both previous prime ministers, Meta and Majko, as foreign and defence ministers respectively.

In Jan. 2003 Nano's government was rewarded with Stabilization and Association Agreement talks with the EU's Council of Foreign Ministers, seen as the first step towards EU membership.

Berisha attacked Nano's administration as corrupt and, with the economy struggling, Nano and his Socialists were defeated at the general elections of Sept. 2005.

Napolitano, Giorgio (Italy)

Introduction

In May 2006 Giorgio Napolitano became the first former communist to be elected president of Italy. Appointed senator for life by his predecessor, Carlo Azeglio Ciampi, in Oct. 2005, Napolitano was Italy's 11th post-war president and held office until Jan. 2015.

Early Life

Giorgio Napolitano was born in Naples on 29 June 1925. In 1942 he enrolled at the University of Naples Federico II to study law. Whilst there, he founded an anti-fascist communist group which took part in the Italian Resistance Movement in 1943. In 1945 Napolitano became a member of the Italian Communist Party (PCI). He graduated from university in 1947.

In 1953 Napolitano was elected to the Chamber of Deputies. He was later elected to the national committee of the PCI but the Hungarian Revolution in 1956 prompted a split in the PCI, with the party leadership branding the Hungarian rebels as counter-revolutionaries, while the Italian General Confederation of Labour, dominated by communists, defended the uprising. Napolitano gradually increased his influence within the party, becoming secretary of the federation in Naples in the early 1960s and co-ordinator of the secretary's office from 1966–69. He held a variety of posts during the 1970s and 1980s, and was variously responsible for economic policies and internal relations within the party.

When the PCI disbanded in 1991 Napolitano joined the social democratic party, Democrats of the Left. He went on to serve as president of the Chamber of Deputies from 1992–94 and minister of the interior from 1996–98. Subsequently, Napolitano was a member of the European Parliament from 1999–2004, and in Oct. 2005 was appointed senator for life by then president Carlo Azeglio Ciampi.

Career Peak

The centre-left experienced some hostility to its nomination of Napolitano for president, with former prime minister Silvio Berlusconi refusing to back him because of his communist past. Nonetheless, Napolitano was elected on 10 May 2006 after a fourth round of voting, taking 543 of a possible 1,009 votes. He was sworn in on 15 May 2006. In 2009 tensions arose between Napolitano and prime minister Berlusconi over the case of a coma patient whose family had obtained a court ruling to allow her life support to be removed after 17 years. Napolitano blocked an emergency decree issued by Berlusconi to prevent the alleged euthanasia from taking place claiming it would be unconstitutional to overrule the court's decision.

Napolitano was re-elected president on 20 April 2013, winning 738 votes to Stefano Rodotà's 217. In the process he became Italy's first ever second-term president. Faced with continued economic hardship and rising unemployment rates, Napolitano immediately began consultations with Italy's largest political parties and both parliamentary chambers in order to forge a government equipped to tackle these issues. Napolitano subsequently asked Enrico Letta of the Democratic Party to form a government, which was sworn in on 28 April 2013.

With Italy's economy recovering at slower than expected pace, Letta resigned in Feb. 2014 having faced criticism from within his own party—in particular from party secretary Matteo Renzi. Napolitano accepted Letta's resignation and swore in a new government led by Renzi on 22 Feb. 2014.

Napolitano stepped down as president on 14 Jan. 2015, citing old age. At his resignation, he was Italy's longest-serving head of state. Pietro Grasso became acting president, with Sergio Mattarella taking over from him on a permanent basis in Feb. 2015.

Narasimha Rao, P. V. (India)

Introduction

Pamulaparti Venkata (P. V.) Narasimha Rao was the leader of the Congress (I) Party and prime minister of India between 1991 and 1996. He introduced a series of reforms to pull the country from its economic decline and open it up to a free global market. Although these measures were effective, his period in office was dogged by rising nationalist and fundamentalist sentiment as well as accusations of corruption. He resigned as leader of the Congress (I) Party in Dec. 1996, following their electoral defeat in May, amidst allegations of bribery.

Early Life

Narasimha Rao was born in Karimnagar (Andhra Pradesh region) on 28 June 1921, to wealthy agrarian parents. Unlike many of his contemporaries and predecessors (including Mahatma Gandhi, Jawaharlal Nehru, Rajiv and Indira Gandhi), Rao received his education exclusively within India, studying at Osmania University in Hyderabad as well as universities in Pune and Nagpur.

Enthused by Mahatma Gandhi's teachings, he was an activist for the Indian National Congress Party in its struggle to gain independence. In 1951 he became a member of the All India Congress Committee (to which he was appointed General Secretary in 1975–76) later joining the Legislative Assembly for the Andhra Pradesh region in 1957. Appointed to the regional state government in 1962, he was successively Minister for Law and Endowments, Law and Information, Health and Medicine, and Education. He became Chief Minister for the state between 1971–73, during which time he was elected to the Indian Parliament (1972).

He held ministerial positions under the reigns of both Indira and Rajiv Gandhi though he later admitted to feeling resentment at his "subservience" during this period. As well as occupying the posts of Minister for Home Affairs, Minister for Defense and Minister for Human Resource Development, Rao was Minister for External Affairs between 1980–84, and again between 1988–89.

India's role as chair to the Non Aligned Movement increased Rao's importance and in 1983 he led the Special Non Aligned Mission in its attempt to resolve the Palestinian liberation conflict.

Following the assassination of Rajiv Gandhi on 21 May 1991, Rao was unanimously elected to the leadership of the Congress (I) Party.

Career Peak

The Congress (I) Party formed a minority government in 1991. Rao continued the Nehruvian tradition of secular and democratic government though he undertook a more radical economic policy.

Rao inherited a weak economy, with India's foreign exchange reserves so low that the repayment of international loans was impossible. Under the instigation of the then Minister of Finance, Manmohan Singh, Rao engineered the privatisation of many state-run industries, abolished regulations which had inhibited foreign trade and investment, and set about encouraging joint foreign ventures.

The New Industrial Policy of 24 July 1991 allowed western companies to invest and set up branches within India without restrictions. Technological joint ventures were also encouraged by the policy changes, harnessing the highly educated elite of India's working force. Other initiatives included the development of Assam, the disinvestment of holdings in the public sector and attempts to create employment opportunities within the state of Jammu and Kashmir.

Nevertheless, the Party was severely undermined during its reign by opposition from nationalist groups. Facing a motion of no confidence on 28 July 1993, Rao's government survived by 265 votes to 251. In Jan. 1996 Ravinder Kumar, president of the Rashtriya Mukti Morcha Party, claimed that opposition members had been bribed to vote against the no confidence motion. Following investigations, charges were brought against members of the Jharkhand Mukti Morcha Party and the Janta Dal Party, as well as Rao himself and cabinet colleague, Buta Singh.

The elections in April and May 1996 brought an end to both Rao's tenure as prime minister and the reign of the Congress (I) Party. Later in the year he was accused for his involvement in cheating an expatriate businessman of US$100,000.

Rao (allegedly at the suggestion of Congress president, Sitaram Kesri) gave up his post on 20 Dec. 1996.

Later Life

After his resignation, Rao set about refuting the accusations made against him. On 12 Oct. 2000 he was sentenced to 3 years imprisonment with an accompanying fine of US$2,150 following a conviction for criminal conspiracy, bribery and corruption. Along with Buta Singh (who received a similar sentence), Rao was granted bail and did not serve time in prison. A renowned intellectual (and chairman of the Telugu Academy from 1968–74) Rao also published two politically-based novels. He died in Dec. 2004.

Nasheed, Mohamed (Maldives)

Introduction

Mohamed Nasheed, popularly known as 'Anni' became the Maldives' first democratically elected president in Oct. 2008. Anni, a former political prisoner, defeated incumbent Maumoon Abdul Gayoom, who had held office for 30 years, on a reform platform. After 3 years in office he was forced to resign in Feb. 2012 amid protests.

Early Life

Mohamed Nasheed was born on 17 July 1967 in Malé. He went to school in Sri Lanka and England before graduating from Liverpool John Moores University with a degree in maritime studies in 1989.

In 1990 Anni became a journalist in the Maldives with a current affairs magazine, *Sandhaanu*, where he earned a reputation for anti-government commentaries at a time when such criticism was rare. *Sandhaanu* was banned the following year and Anni was arrested, the first of 13 detentions for his opposition to Gayoom's administration. Amnesty International declared him a prisoner of conscience.

He was elected to the Citizens' Majlis (Parliament) in 2000 as the member for Malé, which was to become his central power base. In 2001, 6 months after his election, he was arrested and sentenced to two-and-a-half-years imprisonment for the theft of unspecified 'government property'. His supporters claimed the charge was politically motivated. After his release in 2003 Anni went into exile, firstly in Sri Lanka and then in Britain where, in Nov. 2003, he formed the Maldivian Democratic Party (MDP) with Mohamed Latheef. Anni was granted political asylum by the British government in 2004 but returned to Malé in April 2005.

On 12 Aug. 2005 he was arrested during a protest to mark the first anniversary of Black Friday (when anti-government protests ended in violent conflict with security forces). Anni was charged under the Terrorism Act but released in Sept. 2006 without trial following a British-brokered deal between the government and the MDP. Anni had been named chairperson of the MDP in absentia on 20 Dec. 2005.

He resigned as chairperson in Feb. 2008 to make a successful run for the MDP presidential candidature in the party's primary elections. In the first round of the presidential election on 8 Oct. 2008 Anni was placed second behind Gayoom, with 25% of the vote. With the support of the four defeated candidates in the run-off on 28 Oct. 2008, he received 54% of the vote and was sworn into office on 11 Nov. 2008.

Career Peak

On taking office Anni committed US$350 m. to improve the quality of life for Maldivians and to create a 'sovereign wealth fund' to buy a new homeland should the country disappear as sea levels rise. Anni's challenges have included maintaining the lucrative tourist trade, ensuring a fairer distribution of wealth and tackling the youth drugs culture.

In multi-party elections in May 2009, Anni's MDP narrowly came second to the opposition DRP, taking 26 of 77 parliamentary seats. Subsequent alleged attempts by the opposition-controlled parliament to disrupt government business led to serious political and legal upheaval in the latter half of 2010, prompting claims that the parliament was hijacking executive powers and preventing Anni's cabinet from performing its legal obligations.

On 16 Jan. 2012 Anni ordered the military to arrest Abdulla Mohamed, the Chief Justice of the Criminal Court. The arrest sparked a series of protests led by supporters of the former president Maumoon Abdul Gayoom. Faced with the prospect of escalating violence, Anni resigned on 7 Feb. The president stated that he was forced to resign 'at gunpoint' by police and army officers in a coup. Vice president Mohamed Waheed Hassan Manik was sworn in as the new president on the same day but Anni urged Hassan to stand down and called for immediate elections.

After his resignation Anni faced charges of abuse of power. He was subsequently arrested for ignoring a court summons and a travel ban, but released shortly afterwards. In Feb. 2013, fearing arrest again over his non-appearance in a local court, he sought refuge in the Indian High Commission in Malé. After reports of a deal brokered by India, Nasheed left the Indian mission 10 days later.

Later Life

In March 2015 Nasheed was sentenced to 13 years' imprisonment after being found guilty on terrorism charges stemming from the imprisonment of a state judge during his tenure as president. However, he received support from his party and retained the presidency of the MDP—a position that he had held since Aug. 2014. Institutions including Amnesty International and the United States Department of State expressed conviction over his conviction, which is widely regarded as being politically motivated.

Nasser, Gamal Abdel (Egypt)

Introduction

Col. Gamal Abdel Nasser was Prime Minister and then President of Egypt from 1954–70. A radical Arab nationalist and socialist, he was the power behind an army coup in 1952 that heralded the end of the Egyptian monarchy. His nationalization of the Suez Canal led to Israeli and Anglo-French military action against Egypt in 1956, while his ambitions for an Egyptian-led union of Arab states added to the regional tensions leading up to the Six-Day War with Israel in 1967. The Arab defeat led briefly to Nasser's resignation, but he resumed the presidency until his sudden death in 1970.

Early Life

Nasser was born on 15 Jan. 1918 to southern Egyptian parents in the Bacos suburb of Alexandria. After his secondary schooling, he attended a law college for a few months and then entered the military academy in Cairo. Having graduated in 1938, he joined the Egyptian army. Together with a group of colleagues (including Muhammad Anwar Sadat, who was to succeed him as president of the republic in 1970), he formed a secretive revolutionary (and anti-British) organization called the Free Officers. The bitter experience of Egyptian defeat in the first Arab-Israeli War of 1948–49, and dissatisfaction with the corruption of King Farouk's regime, led the Free Officers to stage an almost bloodless coup in July 1952. Although the coup was led nominally by Gen. Muhammad Neguib, a respected senior officer and figurehead, Nasser controlled the Revolutionary Command Council that took power.

Career Peak

In 1953 Egypt was declared a republic, with Neguib as its first president. However, increasing tension and suspicion between Nasser and Neguib culminated in Nasser's assumption of the premiership in April 1954 and of presidential powers in Nov. 1954 when Neguib was finally deposed. In Oct. of that year Nasser survived an assassination attempt in Alexandria by a member of the extremist Muslim Brotherhood. The organization was outlawed and its members imprisoned.

In Jan. 1956 a new constitution proclaimed Egypt a socialist Arab state under a one-party political system, with Islam as the official religion. On 23 June 1956 Nasser was officially elected president of the republic. In the same month the last British troops were withdrawn from Egypt in accordance with a bilateral agreement in 1954. This recognized the international importance of the Suez Canal and expressed the determination of both parties to uphold the 1888 Constantinople Convention on free and open access. Nasser's next move—the expropriation of the Canal—led in Oct. 1956 to Israeli military action against Egypt, with British and French collusion and subsequent participation. However, the strength of opposition in the international community allowed Nasser to turn a military failure into a political victory. Britain, France and Israel withdrew, and he emerged from the Suez crisis with enhanced prestige throughout the Arab world.

In 1958 Egypt and Syria formed the United Arab Republic, which in turn entered into a loose association with Yemen. However, this was as far as Nasser's wider ambitions for pan-Arab unity progressed. Syria withdrew from the UAR (and Yemen's association was dissolved) in 1961. Meanwhile, Nasser's implacable opposition to Israel, his criticism of the Western powers, and his strengthening of ties with the Soviet Union further added to the volatility of Middle East politics. For Egypt, the Arab defeat in the Six-Day War of 1967 resulted principally in its loss of the Sinai Peninsula to Israeli occupation. The career of an Arab leader of lesser stature than Nasser would have been destroyed by such a disastrous outcome. He did indeed try to resign, but popular opinion demanded that he remain in power.

On the wider international stage, Nasser was a leading figure in the Non-Aligned Movement in the 1950s and 1960s, along with India's Jawaharlal Nehru, Indonesia's Sukarno and Yugoslavia's Josip Broz Tito. The movement's advocacy of positive neutrality gave Nasser the opportunity to be a power broker in the politics of the post-colonial, developing world.

In domestic affairs, he pursued a socialist agenda. This included agrarian reform and land redistribution in favour of the peasant majority, and the establishment of educational programmes and health services. He was also responsible for the construction of the Aswan High Dam (built with Soviet aid), enhancing Egypt's agricultural and industrial development potential. However, his rule was also marked by authoritarianism, political repression, media censorship and bureaucratic inefficiency.

His death on 28 Sept. 1970 from a heart attack had a major impact throughout the Arab world. Millions of Egyptian citizens followed his funeral procession through Cairo—a testament to the regard in which he was held by the nation.

Nastase, Adrian (Romania)

Introduction

As the centrist prime minister of Romania, Adrian Nastase took office in Dec. 2000. He spent his entire political career in the post-communist era. His main challenges were tackling a faltering economy and combating a growth in nationalism in order to fulfil his aim of gaining entry to the EU.

Early Life

Nastase was born on 22 June 1950 in Bucharest. A student of the University of Bucharest, he graduated in law in 1973, was awarded a master's in sociology in 1978 and a PhD in international law in 1987. From 1973 until 1990 he worked as a researcher at the Institute for Law Research at the Romanian Academy, Bucharest.

In June 1990 Nastase was made foreign minister in the post-communist government of President Iliescu. He remained in the post until Oct. 1992 when he became president of the chamber of deputies, remaining there until the end of Iliescu's presidency in late 1996. Nastase then became vice president of the chamber. In 1994 he had been appointed associate professor of public international law at the Sorbonne in Paris and between 1993 and 1997 he was executive president of the executive board of the Romanian Social Democratic Party. Iliescu returned as president in Dec. 2000 and

Nastase was made prime minister. On 19 Jan. 2001 he was voted president of the Social Democratic Party.

Career Peak

Nastase was opposed by the extreme right wing Greater Romania Party, which advocates anti-Gypsy, anti-Jewish and anti-ethnic Hungarian policies. Forced to rely on the cooperation of weaker centrist groups in parliament, Nastase faced severe obstacles in forcing through much needed social and economic reforms. His relationship with the president was uneasy and he was also under increasing international pressure to accelerate reform. Both Iliescu and Nastase were united in pushing for a greater role in the international community, and particularly membership of the EU. In 2002 Romania was given a target date of 2007 for entry into the EU and was one of seven European countries invited to join NATO in 2004. Nastase was defeated in elections in Dec. 2004 by opposition leader Traian Băsescu.

Later Life

In Jan. 2012 Romania's highest court found Nastase guilty of corruption and sentenced the former prime minister to 2 years in prison. Nastase was the highest-ranking former official to face prison for graft. In June 2012 Nastase shot himself in the neck when police came to his home to take him to jail to begin a 2-year sentence for corruption. He underwent surgery at a Bucharest hospital.

Natuman, Joe (Vanuatu)

Introduction

Joe Natuman was appointed prime minister on 15 May 2014 after his predecessor, Moana Carcasses Kalosil, lost a parliamentary confidence vote. A member of the Party of Our Land (Vanua'aka Pati), Natuman was the third person to hold the office since the general election of 2012.

Early Life

Natuman was born on 24 Nov. 1952 on the island of Tanna. He graduated from the University of the South Pacific in the Fiji Islands in 1978. He then entered the civil service, working his way through the ranks to serve as first secretary to the prime minister's office from 1987 until 1991. On leaving the service, Natuman returned to the University of the South Pacific to work as a registrar.

In 1995 he successfully stood as the Vanua'aka candidate for Tanna, a constituency he has served ever since. He subsequently held several senior positions in government, including two stints as minister of education (in 1998 and 2004). In 2010 he became minister for foreign affairs, external trade and communications in the government of Edward Natapei, before returning to the opposition benches when Sato Kilman came to power in June 2011.

In May 2014 a surprise vote of no-confidence was brought by the opposition against Prime Minister Moana Carcasses Kalosil. It was carried by 35 votes against 11 abstentions. In the subsequent vote to determine Kalosil's successor, Natuman—who was at that time serving as leader of government business—was the only nominee. He was endorsed by 40 of 52 votes cast.

Career Peak

In an address to the United Nations General Assembly on 29 Sept. 2014, Natuman said that Vanuatu faced an 'existential threat' and urged the international community to unite to address the issue of climate change.

He appointed a diverse cabinet on coming to power, including two former prime ministers. Among them was Sato Kilman, who took the foreign affairs portfolio. Kilman and Natuman have previously disagreed over the prominent local issue of West Papuan independence, with the latter supporting the population's right to self-determination.

Natuman was ousted in June 2015 after losing a parliamentary vote of no confidence by 27 votes to 25. Sato Kilman took office for a fourth time on 11 June.

Natuman returned to government in Feb. 2016 as deputy prime minister following the election of Charlot Salwai to the premiership.

Ndayizeye, Domitien (Burundi)

Introduction

Domitien Ndayizeye, a Hutu, took over the presidency in April 2003 as part of the Tutsi-Hutu power-sharing agreement brokered by Nelson Mandela at Arusha in 2001. Tensions between Tutsis and Hutus remained high, with 5% of the population having died in ethnic fighting since 1993, and Ndayizeye's aim of national unity was frustrated by the refusal of the Palipehutu-FNL, a Hutu rebel group, to recognize the power-sharing agreement. He was succeeded by Pierre Nkurunziza in Aug. 2005.

Early Life

Ndayizeye was born on 2 May 1953 in Murago, Kayannza in the north of the country. He was studying at the Kamenge technical school in Bujumbura in 1972 when a wave of Tutsi-led massacres forced him into exile in Belgium. In 1981, while still in exile, he graduated in electronic engineering. During this period he joined the Hutu Diaspora Movement (HDM).

In 1981 he went to Rwanda, remaining active within the HDM until returning to Burundi in 1993. The HDM evolved into the Hutu Front for Democracy in Burundi (Frodebu) and because of his political activities Ndayizeye was imprisoned in 1995 and again the following year. In 1996 Pierre Buyoya, a Tutsi, seized power in a coup. He deposed Sylvestre Ntibantunganya, Burundi's third Hutu prime minister since Melchior Ndadaye became its first in 1993.

Buyoya agreed to engage Frodebu in peace talks, brokered firstly by Tanzania's former president, Julius Nyerere and later South Africa's former president, Nelson Mandela. Negotiations made little progress until 2001 when Mandela proposed a power-sharing 3 year long interim government. Buyoya would hold the presidency for the first 18 months with a Hutu as his vice-president. Power would then transfer to the vice-president, who in turn would appoint a Tutsi deputy, until democratic elections 18 months later.

Ndayizeye was named Buyoya's vice-president. As his tenure approached its end Buyoya pressed for a parliamentary debate to secure a further term but on 31 April 2003 power was handed peacefully to Ndayizeye.

Career Peak

The peaceful transfer of power confounded the expectations of many observers. However, the power-share was seriously undermined by the refusal of the two main Hutu rebel groups—the Conseil National pour la Défense de la Democratie-Forces pour la Défense de la Democratie (CNDD-FDD), the largest Hutu group, and the Parti pour la Libération du Peuple Hutu (Palipehutu) and its military wing, the Forces Nationales de Libération (FNL)—to recognize the government's legitimacy. In the days immediately after Ndayizeye's inauguration there was fighting between the army and rebels around Bujumbura. In July 2003 violence had spread across the country and the FNL attacked Bujumbura, prompting calls by Ugandan President Yoweri Museveni for a UN peacekeeping force to support the already operational African Union (AU) force.

Ndayizeye met with the CNDD-FDD, negotiating a settlement in Dar es Salaam in Nov. 2003. However, the FNL's leader, Pasteur Habimana, refused to negotiate with the Hutu president, suggesting that power still lay with the Tutsi-dominated army. The CNDD-FDD leader, Pierre Nkurunziza, and three of his associates were invited to join the government and on 8 Jan. 2004 Ndayizeye established a 33-member joint military command, which included 13 CNDD-FDD representatives. Later that month the FNL agreed to meet Ndayizeye in Amsterdam during the president's European fund-raising tour, which amounted to a multilateral pledge of US\$1.03 bn. for reconstruction.

In May 2004 the government's request for an extension to the transitional period was rejected by the foreign mediation team, which insisted on keeping to the deadline of 1 Nov. The UN Operation in Burundi (ONUB) finally assumed responsibility for peacekeeping in early June, succeeding the AU's mandate. Palipehutu-FNL's refusal to negotiate and continuing attacks on the capital led to condemnation and sanctions from the leaders of the Great Lakes, who issued a 3-month ultimatum on 9 June.

In early 2005 Ndayizeye attracted opposition criticism as he sought an extension to his tenure, delaying elections scheduled for April in which he was forbidden to stand. He was eventually granted an extra 4 months, with elections to be held by 19 Aug. A new power-sharing constitution won popular backing in a referendum in March 2005. In April 2005 the FDD temporarily withdrew from the government following a dispute with Ndayizeye over the appointment of a new interior minister. Pierre Nkurunziza of the FDD was elected president by both houses of parliament in Aug. 2005.

Ndong Sima, Raymond (Gabon)

Introduction

Raymond Ndong Sima, a former minister of agriculture, was prime minister from 2012–14. He was appointed by President Ali-Ben Bongo in Feb. 2012 following the victory of the ruling Gabonese Democratic Party (PDG) in parliamentary elections. Ndong Sima had combined careers in politics and private enterprise and was regarded as a key figure in Bongo's plan to diversify the economy. He was the first person from Gabon's less developed northern region to become prime minister.

Early Life

Ndong Sima was born on 23 Jan. 1955 in Oyem in the province of Woleu-Ntem in the north of Gabon. He was educated in Oyem, at Bessieux College in Libreville and in Algeria. In 1981 he received a master's degree in economics from the University of Paris IX-Dauphine in France. Returning to Gabon later that year, he worked as a researcher for the department of the economy.

In 1986, during an economic crisis, Ndong Sima joined the cabinet as minister for economy and planning. From 1992–94 he served as director general of the economy, managing Gabon's negotiations with the IMF and the World Bank. He was director of Hévégab, the state-owned rubber company, from 1994–98 and in the late 1990s was made director of Gabon's state railway operator, CECFT, serving until 2001. In 2003 he founded a private bus company.

In 2009, following the victory of Ali-Ben Bongo in presidential elections after the death of his father, Ndong Sima was appointed minister of agriculture, livestock, fisheries and rural development. He oversaw the introduction of a US\$1.3 m. agricultural development programme, backed by the European Union and the UN Food and Agriculture Organization. In Dec. 2011 he won a seat in parliament for the ruling PDG, representing the constituency of Kye in Woleu-Ntem province.

With the PDG retaining power at the legislative election, the incumbent prime minister, Paul Biyoghé Mba, stepped down. President Bongo appointed Ndong Sima as his successor on 27 Feb. 2012, citing Ndong Sima's combination of business expertise and administrative experience as key to the appointment.

Career Peak

On becoming prime minister Ndong Sima made substantial changes to the administration, bringing 14 newcomers into ministerial and deputy ministerial posts. One of his principal tasks was to implement Bongo's 'Emerging Gabon' project to diversify the economy away from oil and to build up the services, industrial and environmental sectors.

However, towards the end of his tenure as prime minister his position within the administration had been weakened by the government's failure to stop a national teachers' strike. Following regional elections in Dec. 2013, president Ali Bongo Ondimba replaced Ndong Sima as new prime minister with Daniel Ona Ondo.

Ne Win (Myanmar)

Introduction

Ne Win twice led Burma (now Myanmar), seizing power each time in military coups. He headed a ruling military council from 1958–60 and in 1962 deposed President U Nu, first heading a revolutionary council and then formally assuming the presidency. He created a one-party state, ruthlessly suppressed opposition and pursued a disastrous national socialist economic agenda. His eccentric authoritarianism and record of human rights abuses had resulted in Burma's international isolation by the time he resigned from office in 1988.

Early Life

Ne Win was born as Shu Maung on 24 May 1911 in Paungdale in what was then the British colony of Burma (now Myanmar). In 1929 he began studying medicine at the University of Rangoon (Yangon) but failed to complete his course and instead became a postal clerk. He became active in the pro-democracy movement during the 1930s and, after Japan invaded the colony in 1941, he was one of the Thirty Comrades who received specialist military training in Japan.

Having taken on the name of Ne Win (*Brilliant as the Sun*) during this period, he became commander of the Burma National Army (BNA), a puppet organization of the Japanese. Soon tiring of Japanese interference, he led the BNA in a guerrilla war against the invading power from late-1944, culminating in the return of British authority by Aug. 1945.

Ne Win co-operated with the British powers until Burma won independence in 1948. Under the government of U Nu, the new nation lacked stability and ethnic fighting divided the country. In Feb. 1945 Ne Win was appointed chief-of-staff of the army to restore discipline in the armed forces. From 1948 he was home defence minister. U Nu's government failed to resolve Burma's problems and in 1958 Ne Win headed an interim military administration. Having called elections in 1960, he stood down to be replaced by U Nu's re-elected parliamentary government. Ethnic violence again dominated political life and in 1962 Ne Win deposed U Nu in a military coup.

Career Peak

Ne Win promised a new form of government based on 'political and economic mysticism'. firstly under his Revolutionary Council of the Union of Burma and, from 1964, under the Burmese Socialist Program Party (BSPP). The army-led BSPP was the only permitted political party and Ne Win adopted an authoritarian style, in which opposition forces risked torture and murder.

The one-party state was formalized in a constitution promulgated in 1973 and the following year Ne Win assumed the presidency. His 'Burmese road to socialism' was based on the expulsion of foreign investors and the nationalization of private enterprise. Having been among the world's most important rice exporters when Ne Win seized power, Burma's economy went into freefall and the black market thrived. There were numerous uprisings and coup attempts throughout the 1970s and 1980s.

In 1981 he gave up the post of president but, as chairman of the BSPP, remained the *de facto* head of state. While the economy continued its decline, Ne Win's belief in numerology resulted in several eccentric policy decisions. He twice withdrew the currency and re-introduced notes in denominations of 45 and 90 *kyats* because they were divisible by his favoured number, 9. In 1987 food shortages resulted in protests. In July 1988 Ne Win resigned and the BSPP remodelled itself as the State Law and Order Restoration Council (SLORC).

Later Life

Despite stepping down from office, many observers considered Ne Win to be a major force behind SLORC, and the pro-democracy movement which gained momentum following his resignation was brutally suppressed a few months later. However, his influence waned during the 1990s.

He suffered a heart attack in Sept. 2001, while living with his daughter, Sander Win. In early 2002 Sander Win, her husband and their three children were arrested on charges of plotting a military coup. The husband and children each received death sentences. Ne Win, though not formally implicated with the charges, was put under house arrest along with his daughter. He died on 5 Dec. 2002.

Nečas, Petr (Czech Republic)

Introduction

Petr Nečas, leader of the Civic Democratic Party, was sworn in as prime minister on 13 July 2010 at the head of a coalition government. He had previously served as deputy minister for defence and deputy prime minister.

Early Life

Nečas was born in Nov. 1964 in Uherské Hradiště in the southeast of the country, near the current Slovak border. From 1983 he studied physics at the University of Brno, undertaking post-graduate studies in natural sciences. In 1988 he became an engineering researcher for Tesla Rožnov, an electronics manufacturer.

In 1992 he joined Václav Klaus' recently formed Civic Democratic Party (ODS), serving on committees for defence, intelligence and foreign/EU relations. His first government post came in 1995 when Klaus appointed him deputy minister of defence. In 2006, after a series of electoral defeats for the party, Mirek Topolánek defeated Nečas in the race to succeed Klaus as ODS leader. Topolánek formed a minority government in which Nečas served as his deputy prime minister.

Topolánek's government collapsed after a confidence vote in 2009. He resigned as ODS chairman in 2010 and Nečas was elected in his place. Despite the ODS suffering a 15% drop in support at the May 2010 elections, Nečas was able to negotiate a centre-right conservative coalition with the Public Affairs party (VV) and TOP 09 to form a government in July 2010.

Career Peak

Having campaigned on a platform of reforming social benefit and fighting corruption, Nečas aimed for fiscal consolidation to reduce the public deficit and fulfil the criteria necessary to join the eurozone. He undertook a programme of austerity measures, including cutting public salaries by 10% and reducing expenditure on the health sector and pensions, and sought to save money by streamlining defence procurement procedures. In Dec. 2010 he also joined in criticism, led by the UK, of EU plans to raise its own budget. The coalition has since become more fractious, undermined by a corruption scandal that led to a split in Public Affairs (VV) and by popular discontent over the austerity measures. Nevertheless, Nečas' government narrowly survived a parliamentary no-confidence vote in April 2012 and formed a new coalition with TOP 09 and LIDEM–Liberal Democrats, which was founded in May 2012 by former members of VV.

In June 2013 the government became embroiled in yet another scandal involving allegations of corruption and abuse of power. Nečas opted to resign as it had became clear that the coalition would not survive a parliamentary no-confidence vote. He stayed on as the caretaker prime minister until Jiří Rusnok succeeded him.

Nehru, Jawaharlal (India)

Introduction

The first prime minister of independent India, Jawaharlal Nehru laid the foundations for the modern countrys infrastructure, economy and government. Imprisoned for his activities within the Indian National Congress during the fight for independence, Jawaharlal was a close friend of Mohandas (Mahatma) Gandhi (1869–1948), sharing many of the latter's ideals. He saw the future success of India as dependent on the maintenance of a secular, pluralistic democracy, with a foreign policy that would keep India free from external influences, founding, along with leaders from 28 other developing countries, the Non-Aligned Movement. His daughter, Indira, became prime minister after his death.

Early Life

Jawaharlal Nehru was born in Allahabad on 14 Nov. 1889 into the family of Motilal Nehru, a prosperous and politically influential Brahman lawyer. Educated in England, the young Nehru studied at Trinity College, Cambridge before joining the Inner Temple, London. He returned to India in 1912 and joined the Allahabad High Court Bar.

In 1916 Nehru married Kamala Kaul and in the following year Indira was born. After meeting Mahatma Gandhi in Lucknow at the 1916 session of Congress, Nehru joined Gandhi's Satyagraha Sabha (non-violent movement).

In 1920 he was appointed to the Allahabad municipal assembly. His importance within Congress grew and between 1924–25 he was appointed General Secretary of the AICC. A year in Europe in 1926 shaped his socialist ideals.

In 1929 Nehru was elected President of the AICC. In 1942 he took over from Gandhi as the leader of the Congress Party. In the same year he was arrested for his participation in the Quit India Movement. As the British withdrew, Nehru became Prime Minister of an interim government and acted as chief negotiator of the Congress for the transfer of power. When India was granted independence on 15 Aug. 1947, he was sworn in as the country's first prime minister.

Career Peak

Jawaharlal Nehru's intention was to create a pluralistic and secular democracy that would incorporate the nation's many languages and religious minorities.

With independence came the dispute over the contested region of Jammu and Kashmir, and subsequently the first of many conflicts between India and the newly formed Pakistan. But Nehru succeeded in absorbing the many regal states although in the case of Hyderabad this required military force.

Following the pattern of Soviet government, he introduced a series of 5 year plans, beginning a process of industrialisation and investment in the public sector. Somewhat neglecting the advancement of agriculture (the premise of Gandhi's vision), Nehru had to fall back on food aid from the US.

Realising the dangers posed by the Cold War, Nehru co-founded, with leaders Nasser and Tito, the Non-Aligned Movement. By this means India was able to receive aid from the Russian and American power blocs, whilst remaining free from creating military alliances.

In 1961 Nehru oversaw the acquisition of Goa from the Portuguese. The following year saw the eruption of further territorial disputes in the Indo-Chinese War. Border incursions by Chinese troops in the region of Arunachal Pradesh provoked a series of skirmishes in Sept. 1962. Announcing a ceasefire on 21 Nov., the Chinese drew back their forces, but only after the death of around 1000 Indian soldiers. Nehru was blamed for this disaster. It was said that his impetuosity in ordering the Chinese to "be thrown out" prompted pre-emptive measures by the neighbouring country. The 2 years between the Indo-Chinese War and Jawaharlal's death on 27 May 1964, saw the extensive re-building of India's armed forces.

Nehru was succeeded by Lal Bahadur Shastri, who was able, following the military revisions made in the last stage of Nehru's leadership, to successfully combat the Pakistanis in the second Indo-Pakistani War of 1965.

India's first Prime Minister has come under heavy criticism since his death, perhaps most obviously for the rigid trade restrictions which held up foreign investment. He was, however, a popular leader, voted in successively by large majorities.

Nepal, Madhav Kumar (Nepal)

Introduction

Madhav Kumar Nepal became prime minister on 25 May 2009 when he was elected by parliament to replace Pushpa Kamal Dahal, who had resigned. The former general secretary of the Communist Party of Nepal/Unified Marxist-Leninist, Madhav Nepal headed a 22-party coalition.

Early Life

Madhav Nepal was born on 6 March 1953 in the southern Nepalese district of Rautahat. He studied at Sitamarhi in Bihar and graduated in commerce from Tribhuvan University in 1973. He joined the underground Marxist Leninist

communist movement in 1969, and in 1971 became a district committee member of the Nepal Revolutionary Coordinating Committee (Marxist Leninist), otherwise known as the ANCRCC (ML). He pursued a career in banking and then in the civil service before taking up politics full-time.

In 1978 the ANCRCC (ML) legitimized itself as the Communist Party of Nepal/Unified Marxist-Leninist (CPN-UML), with Madhav Nepal elected to its politburo. From 1991–99 he was the CPN-UML leader of the opposition and served as deputy prime minister in the CPN-UML minority government of 1994–95. He argued against mobilizing the army during the civil war and in 2005 he campaigned against the king's usurpation of executive powers. At the 2008 election Madhav Nepal lost the Kathmandu seat and his home town seat of Rautahat to Maoist candidates, prompting him to resign as party general secretary.

In May 2009 the Maoist premier, Pushpa Kamal Dahal, resigned in protest at the president's refusal to accept his dismissal of the army chief. Madhav Nepal was chosen by parliament to replace Dahal in an unopposed poll, boycotted by the opposition.

Career Peak

After becoming prime minister, he all but officially revoked the previous government's dismissal of the army chief. Attempts to pass the budget were obstructed by opposition parties unhappy with Madhav Nepal's lack of commitment to spending on agriculture and infrastructure. Meanwhile, he agreed to negotiations towards some level of independence for the Madhesi region in the south of the country. The premier succeeded in clearing Kathmandu of much of its street rubbish problem and he instigated plans to erect a monument to the republic.

He faced three key challenges: to establish a new constitution; to reintegrate and resettle ex-Maoist combatants (19,000 of whom were in UN-monitored cantonments in early 2010); and to ensure adherence to the comprehensive peace accord. In March 2010 the Maoist opposition showed signs that it would not co-operate with the government and there was speculation that a motion of no confidence was under preparation. Madhav Nepal tendered his resignation on 30 June saying he hoped it would 'pave the way for a political resolution and consensus that will complete the peace process and the new constitution'.

Neto, Agostinho (Angola)

Introduction

Doctor, poet and vociferous opponent of Portuguese colonial rule, Agostinho Neto was president of Movimento Popular de Libertação de Angola (MPLA). He led the fight for independence during the 1960s and 70s and was the first president of independent Angola in 1975, but he failed to resolve the subsequent civil war before his death in 1979.

Early Life

Born the son of a Methodist minister in Bengo, Angola, Neto trained as a doctor in Portugal. He first emerged on the political scene as a result of the publication of a volume of poems which vehemently opposed the colonial rule of the Portuguese and celebrated indigenous Angolan culture. He was imprisoned from 1955–57 in Portugal, and upon his release returned to Angola and began to practise as a doctor. Because of his increasingly militant opposition to Portuguese rule he was arrested again in 1960. On this occasion Neto's patients protested in support of him, with the result that his captors opened fire on them, killing several and wounding 200.

Neto was confined to prisons in Portugal and Cape Verde for a further 2 years, but managed to escape to Morocco where he enlisted in the Angolan liberation movement.

Career Peak

By the end of 1962 Neto was voted president of the MPLA, a party he was to head until his death. The MPLA was one of several groups to fight against Portuguese occupation throughout the 1960s and early 1970s, winning independence in 1975. However the various factions began to turn against each other and civil war broke out. With the aid of Cuba and the USSR, Neto was able to gain control of the central part of the country which included Luanda the capital. He was proclaimed the official President of Angola, but he was unable to bring an end to the conflict, and died in Moscow on 10 Sept. 1979 as war continued to blight his country.

Nguyen Minh Triet (Vietnam)

Introduction

Nguyen Minh Triet was elected president in 2006 and served until 2011.

Early Life

Nguyen Minh Triet was born on 8 Oct. 1942 into a farming family of the Phu An commune, Ben Cat district in the province of Binh Duong. He graduated in mathematics and political science before teaching mathematics in Saigon. Active in the leftist student movement Triet was admitted to the Communist Party in March 1965, becoming a full party member a year later.

He was appointed party chief of southern Song Be province in 1992, focusing on the economic development of the largely agricultural province. Ascending to the Politburo in 1997, Triet was appointed party head of Ho Chi Minh City in 2000. In this role he launched a crackdown against organized crime and corruption, overseeing the high-profile arrest and execution of underworld kingpin Truong Van Cam (also known as Nam Cam). Triet was elected national president by the National Assembly on 27 June 2006.

Career Peak

Triet's presidency focused on economic growth and development, and he did much to attract foreign investors. Under Triet, the USA, the country's historic enemy, was its single largest trading partner with bilateral trade valued at US$7.8 bn. in 2005. George Bush made a state visit in 2006, reciprocated by Triet's visit to the USA in 2007, with both leaders keen to nurture future investment. While Vietnam's executive power predominantly resides with the party's general secretary, Triet's ceremonial duties were supplemented by his role as head of a judicial reform committee, seen as key to Vietnam's continuing development.

In July 2011, Triet's term expired and the National Assembly elected Senior Politburo member Truong Tan Sang as his successor.

Nguyen Tan Dung (Vietnam)

Introduction

Nguyen Tan Dung was appointed prime minister in June 2006. Seen as part of the new generation aspiring to leadership of Vietnam's single-party government, he has been a proponent of economic reform and liberalization. He was reappointed for a second term in Jan. 2011, but in Jan. 2016 he failed to secure a seat on the new central committee at the Communist Party's five-yearly congress, forcing him out of government on the expiry of his prime ministerial term in April that year.

Early Life

Nguyen Tan Dung was born in Ca Mau in the south of Vietnam on 17 Nov. 1949. While serving in the army he joined the Communist Party in 1967, and then enrolled in the elite Nguyen Ai Quoc Party School in 1981 to study political theory.

Dung advanced rapidly within the party, serving on influential committees and supporting Vietnam's 'doi moi' programme of economic reform to move the country towards a market economy. In Jan. 1995 he became deputy minister for home affairs and in May the following year he became the youngest person ever to be appointed to the politburo. Tipped as a future party leader, he was appointed deputy prime minister and also director of the central committee's economic commission in charge of the party's finances in 1997. The following year he took over as governor of the state bank.

From 1998–2006 Dung was groomed for leadership by the then prime minister Phan Van Khai, a fellow modernizer. Appointed to a range of key party posts during that time, he oversaw the continuing liberalization of Vietnam's economy. Dung expanded foreign trade relations and prepared Vietnam's accession to the World Trade Organization (WTO). He was also given responsibility for tackling domestic corruption and organized crime. When Khai resigned the premiership, Dung was confirmed as prime minister by the National Assembly on 27 June 2006.

Career Peak

Dung reiterated his intention to proceed with economic and social reform. His first action was to replace several government figures who had been implicated in corruption. He sought to strengthen commercial links internationally, notably with the European Union. In Nov. 2006 Vietnam was approved for membership of the WTO and also hosted the annual Asia-Pacific Economic Co-operation meeting.

However, the economy remained in a malaise. In Nov. 2009 the government devalued the Vietnamese currency (for the third time since June 2008) by about 5% against the US dollar, at the same time increasing interest rates in a bid to dampen rising inflation. Vietnam also experienced a sharp decline in exports in 2009 and in Dec. that year the World Bank approved a loan worth US$500 m. By 2011 the country was facing further increases in inflation, a weakening currency (devalued twice in 2010) and uncertainty over the country's financing that resulted in a credit rating downgrade in 2010.

During an official visit to Moscow in Dec. 2009, Dung announced multi-billion dollar contracts to buy submarines, fighter jets and other military hardware from Russia, as well as agreements on co-operation relating to oil and gas, mining and financial services.

Dung had been closely associated with the communist regime's strategy of building up large state-run conglomerates and he faced criticism in the National Assembly in 2010 over the financial collapse of Vinashin, the giant state-owned shipbuilder. Dung conceded that his administration was partly responsible for the inadequate supervision of the company's management. Despite speculation that his opponents would use the failure as a way of removing him from office, in Jan. 2011 the Communist Party congress gave him a second term as prime minister. However, against a background of continuing scandals in state-owned enterprises, the Communist Party secretary general's acknowledgment in Oct. 2012 that the government had failed to address corruption in its top ranks was widely viewed as an indictment of Dung's premiership.

In 2013 the government came under international scrutiny after issuing a decree banning internet users from discussing current affairs. In Oct. 2014 the USA partially eased its long-standing embargo on arms sales to Vietnam, reflecting the gradual improvement in bilateral ties since the mid-1990s.

At the Communist Party congress in Jan. 2016, Dung was unsuccessful in his attempt to replace Nguyen Phu Trong as secretary general, heralding an end to his political career on the expiry of his premiership in April.

Nikolić, Tomislav (Serbia)

Introduction

Tomislav Nikolić was elected president in May 2012. Once an ultra-nationalist, he reinvented himself as a moderate supporting Serbian EU membership while maintaining Serbian claims over Kosovo. He was due to leave office in late May 2017 following the election in April of Prime Minister Aleksandar Vučić to be his successor.

Early Life

Born on 15 Dec. 1952 in Kragujevac, Nikolić was educated there and in Novi Sad. He worked in building construction from 1971–78 before taking up an investment and management role with a company in Kragujevac.

A member of the National Radical Party, in Feb. 1991 he oversaw its merger with the Serb National Renewal Party to form the ultra-nationalist Serb Radical Party (SRS). In the same year he became party vice-president under the leadership of Vojislav Šešelj and was elected to the National Assembly.

The SRS formed periodic alliances with the governments of Slobodan Milošević in the 1990s, endorsing military action in Bosnia and Kosovo and advocating the formation of a 'Greater Serbia'. Nikolić served as deputy prime minister of Serbia from March 1998–Nov. 1999 and deputy premier of the Federal Republic of Yugoslavia from 1999–2000. In 2000, 2003 and 2004 he launched unsuccessful bids for the national presidency, each time unsuccessfully.

In Feb. 2003 Nikolić took over the leadership of the SRS after Šešelj was indicted for war crimes by the International Criminal Tribunal for the Former Yugoslavia (ICTY). In 2007 he was briefly speaker of the National Assembly and in 2008 again stood for the presidency, losing narrowly to the incumbent Boris Tadić. In Sept. 2008 Nikolić broke with the SRS and formed the Serbian Progressive Party (SNS) following Šešelj's accusations that he had betrayed SRS ideology by expressing support for EU accession rather than looking towards Russia as Šešelj advocated. Nonetheless, Nikolić did not abandon the nationalist agenda, arguing that Kosovo remained an integral part of Serbia and rejecting its declaration of independence in Feb. 2008.

In April 2011 Nikolić led an unsuccessful bid to bring about early elections amid growing public frustration at rampant corruption and the country's grave economic situation. He contested his fifth presidential election in 2012 and won despite controversy over his political and educational track records. He defeated Tadić in a second round of voting on 20 May 2012 and resigned the leadership of the SNS.

Career Peak

Nikolić was sworn into office on 31 May 2012 and had to contend with a struggling economy and high unemployment. He also faced opposition to Serbia's EU membership application, notably over the refusal to recognize Kosovo's independence. However, in April 2013 an EU-brokered agreement was reached whereby Serbia recognized Kosovan government authority over the province in return for a measure of autonomy for Serbs living in the territory. Consequently, formal talks on Serbia's EU accession bid were able to begin in Brussels in Jan. 2014. In April that year, following parliamentary elections, Nikolić designated SNS leader Aleksandar Vučić as the new prime minister. Following the April 2017 presidential election, Vučić succeeded him as president the following month.

Nishani, Bujar (Albania)

Introduction

Bujar Nishani was elected president by the Albanian parliament in June 2012, although the then main opposition Socialist Party (PS) boycotted the vote. He had previously served as a justice and interior minister in the Democratic Party of Albania (PD)-led coalition government under prime minister Sali Berisha.

Early Life

Bujar Nishani was born in Durrës on 29 Sept. 1966. He attended the Skënderbej Military Academy in Tirana, taking a teaching post there in 1988. In 1991 he joined the newly established centre-right PD, headed by Sali Berisha, who led his party to victory in the country's first free parliamentary election in March 1992.

The following year Nishani served as director of foreign affairs in the ministry of defence. While the PD made progress in opening up the economy, reforming institutions and promoting foreign investment, the administration became embroiled in allegations of corruption while much of the country remained in poverty. The collapse of government pyramid investment schemes in 1997 led to violent protests, almost sparking civil war in the south. The government resigned and a snap election was won comfortably by a Socialist-led coalition.

Nishani took a law degree at Tirana University before turning to municipal politics. In 2001 he was elected secretary of the PD's Tirana branch and 2 years later he was elected to the capital's municipal council. At the 2005 parliamentary election, he won a seat in Tirana as the PD returned to power.

Appointed interior minister in March 2007, he sought to modernize the country's institutions and championed an electronic ID card scheme. As justice minister from Sept. 2009, after the PD had secured re-election in July that year, he attempted to tackle corruption in the justice system against a political backdrop of discontent fuelled by allegations of electoral fraud.

In April 2011 Nishani was reappointed minister of the interior, a post he kept until June 2012 when he was elected to replace Bamir Topi as president. Nishani was the only candidate put forward by the ruling coalition led by Berisha, with the Socialists boycotting the vote after several failures to agree an opposition candidate.

Career Peak

On taking office, Nishani prioritized reforming the justice system, public administration and the functioning of parliament as prerequisites for attaining EU candidate member status for Albania, which was subsequently granted in June 2014.

Following a majority victory at parliamentary elections in June 2013 by the leftist Alliance for a European Albania, headed by the Socialists, Nishani asked PS leader Edi Rama to form a coalition government that took office in Sept. that year.

On 24 July 2017 Ilir Meta succeeded him as president following the election 3 months earlier.

Nixon, Richard M. (United States of America)

Introduction

Richard Milhous Nixon was the 37th President of the United States. He served from Jan. 1969 until Aug. 1974. Nixon remains best known for his part in the Watergate scandal and is the only US president ever to resign. However, he also ended American involvement in the Vietnam War.

Early Life

Nixon was born on 9 Jan. 1913 in Yorba Linda, California to Francis A. and Hannah Milhous Nixon. Raised as a Quaker, Nixon won a scholarship to Duke University Law School in Durham, North Carolina after graduating from Whittier College in 1934. He then returned to Whittier and joined the town's oldest legal firm. Through his hobby of amateur dramatics he met a local schoolteacher, Thelma Patricia Ryan, whom he married in 1940.

In World War II, Nixon worked in a tire-rationing section before joining the navy. After the end of the war he was endorsed by the Republican Party as a candidate for Congress. He was elected in 1946, defeating his Democratic rival Jerry Voorhis.

Nixon served in the House for 4 years, sitting on the Committee on Education and Labor as well as a special committee that visited Europe to examine the effects of war on economy. He also served on the House Committee investigating Un-American Activities. In 1950 he won the Republican nomination to run for the Senate in California. Labelling his opponent, Congresswoman Helen Gahagan Douglas, the 'pink lady' Nixon claimed the choice for the electorate was 'between freedom and state socialism'. Many disapproved of his campaign tactics, but Nixon won the election and became a senator in Dec. 1950.

Nixon quickly won a reputation as a fine orator and caught the attention of former Presidential candidate Thomas E. Dewey, who was helping run Gen. Dwight D. Eisenhower's presidential campaign. It was Dewey who advised Eisenhower to make Nixon his running mate. Eisenhower and Nixon easily defeated the Democratic team of Adlai E. Stevenson and John J. Sparkman and in 1953 the 39-year-old Nixon was sworn in as the second youngest vice-president in history. He won re-election to the post, running alongside Eisenhower once again, in the 1956 presidential election.

During his two terms as vice-president, Nixon assumed some of Eisenhower's executive and ceremonial duties when the President suffered a heart attack in 1955, an operation in 1956 and a stroke in 1957. He also made trips abroad, visiting 56 countries in total. Nixon was the overwhelming choice for the Republican presidential nomination in 1960, but his bid to win office was thwarted by John F. Kennedy who defeated him by just over 100,000 votes and by 303 electoral college votes to 219. Nixon withdrew from politics for 2 years before returning in a bid to secure the governorship of California in 1962. However he was defeated by Governor Edmund G. Brown and seemed to have renounced any future political ambitions when he famously remarked to the press that 'you won't have Nixon to kick around anymore'.

Career Peak

Nixon returned to practicing law and soon reconsidered his decision to step out of politics. He campaigned for Barry Goldwater in 1964 and then won the Republican nomination for himself in 1968. In the presidential election Nixon narrowly defeated Hubert H. Humphrey in the popular vote by 43.4% to 42.7% but overwhelmingly won the electoral college vote by 301 to 191.

Nixon's first term in office was dominated by foreign affairs. Disengagement was the centrepiece of his policy. The number of US troops stationed in Vietnam fell from 555,000 in 1969 to around 30,000 by 1972. Nixon also authorized military operations in North Vietnam, Laos and Cambodia in the hope of forcing North Vietnam to the negotiating table, although some saw it as a dangerous expansion of hostilities.

Nixon managed to improve the USA's relations with the Soviet Union and China. From 1969, the United States and the Soviet Union opened talks on limiting strategic weapons. Nixon's visit to Moscow in May 1972 coincided with the successful conclusion of the talks and the two countries signed the Strategic Arms Limitation Treaty (SALT) and a deal to sell American grain to the Soviets. Nixon relaxed trade restrictions against China and was received by Chairman Mao Zedong in Feb. 1972. Talks between the leaders led to the opening of a semi-formal relationship between the two countries.

Domestically, Nixon's first term in office was characterized by the fight against inflation and unemployment. In 1971 he introduced a temporary wage freeze, announced that the US would no longer convert foreign-held dollars into gold and cut federal spending. American goods became cheaper abroad and unemployment fell, although some prices continued to rise sharply. More federal funds were made available to municipalities and states. However he frequently came into conflict with Congress. He vetoed several measures that would have increased spending and in reply Congress blocked two of his appointments to the Supreme Court. Frustrated, Nixon created a Domestic Council in an attempt to limit Congress' influence.

In the 1972 presidential election Nixon easily overcame his Democratic rival George McGovern, polling 47 m. votes to 29 m. and losing just two states. He was re-inaugurated on 20 Jan. 1973 along with vice-president Spiro T. Agnew. Days later Nixon was able to announce a ceasefire in the conflict with North Vietnam and a framework for American withdrawal from South Vietnam. Part of the terms of the agreement, which Nixon called 'peace with honour' led to the release of nearly 600 American prisoners of war.

Nine months later vice-president Agnew resigned after charges of income tax evasion. The incident foreshadowed Nixon's own fall from power. In the summer of 1972 a break-in had occurred at the Democratic Party headquarters in the Watergate complex, Washington, D.C. Rumours of White House involvement grew steadily throughout 1973 and one of the two men who was convicted of the break-in claimed that advisors in the White House had prior knowledge of the incident. On 5 Aug. 1974 the White House released taped transcripts in which Nixon was implicated in authorizing a cover-up of the affair. After realising that he did not have enough support in Congress to avoid impeachment Nixon announced his resignation on 8 Aug. in a televised address to the nation. His resignation took effect the next day when vice-president Gerald R. Ford was sworn in.

Later Life

One of Ford's first acts as president was to grant his predecessor a full pardon. Nixon retired from politics to write his memoirs and several other books. He died in New York on 22 April 1994.

Niyazov, Saparmurad (Turkmenistan)

Introduction

Saparmurad Niyazov was chairman of the Turkmenistan Supreme Soviet and became effective head of state when Turkmenistan claimed sovereignty in 1990. He oversaw the nation's declaration of independence in 1991 and was head of state and government until his death in Dec. 2006. Styling himself 'Turkmenbashi'. he was constitutionally promised his position for life. His autocratic rule was characterized by eccentric lawmaking and overspending on public projects. He was also severely criticized internationally for human rights abuses and the absence of an organized political opposition.

Early Life

Saparmurad Niyazov was born on 18 Feb. 1940 in Ashgabat. According to official biographies, his father died during World War II and the rest of his family perished in the 1948 Ashgabat earthquake. In 1962 Niyazov joined the Communist Party and 4 years later graduated in engineering from the Leningrad Polytechnical Institute. He worked in the mining and energy industries and rose through the Communist ranks. In 1985 he was appointed president of the Council of Ministers of the Soviet Socialist Republic of Turkmenistan and, later, first secretary of the central committee of the Communist Party of Turkmenistan.

In early 1990 he became chairman of the Republic's Supreme Soviet. In Oct. 1990 the Supreme Soviet proclaimed its political and economic sovereignty, Niyazov therefore becoming its effective head of state. He supported the unsuccessful coup attempt against the president of the USSR, Mikhail Gorbachev, in 1991. Shortly before the collapse of the USSR at the end of that year, he declared Turkmenistan's independence and took the country into the Russian-led Commonwealth of Independent States.

Career Peak

In 1992 Niyazov was elected unopposed as president, heading a new Democratic Party (DP) the policies of which did not differ greatly from those of the Communist Party he had earlier banned. Also in 1992 a new constitution was promulgated, enhancing Niyazov's position as both head of state and government, as well as supreme commander of the armed forces.

In a referendum in Jan. 1994 his period of office was extended to 2002, and in Dec. 1999 the parliament, made up exclusively of DP members, proclaimed him head of state for life. In 2001 he announced he would step down by 2010. His time in office was dominated by the construction of a personality cult. Modelling himself as 'Turkmenbashi' (leader of all Turkmen), his drive for the 'complete and universal' introduction of the national language in public life compelled officials to speak Turkmen or lose their positions, while foreign languages were removed from the school curriculum. He also introduced a development programme which was to produce a fully democratic society by 2010 but which would require the continuation of the one-party state in the interim.

In Aug. 2002 Niyazov revised the calendar, naming the months after himself, his mother and Rukhname, a spiritual guide written by him which was added to the school curriculum in Sept. 2002. He also redefined the ages of man, stating that adolescence lasts until 25 years of age and old age begins at 85. He had earlier banned smoking in public as a result of himself suffering a smoking-related heart complaint. Niyazov's government exercised firm control over the Turkmen media, and in 2000 Niyazov launched a television station named 'The Epoch of Turkmenbashi'.

His attempts to boost the economy included the legalization of private landownership and the encouragement of foreign investment, particularly in the country's oil- and gas-rich regions. However, he received international criticism for his lavish spending on projects such as the Palace of Congress and a fountain complex in Ashgabat while poverty remained widespread. In 2000 he set out plans for a 2,000 km^2 man-made lake in the Karakum desert to ensure year-round availability of water, but environmentalists believe any such construction would devastate the region's ecosystem. In 2004 he ordered the construction of a giant ice palace in the Turkmen desert. Nonetheless, Turkmenistan's large oil and gas reserves ensured him a degree of leverage on the global stage. In late 2004 he met with Jean Chrétien, Canada's prime minister, to discuss a major oil contract. In 2006, having agreed to a 'human rights dialogue' with the EU, Turkmenistan was awarded most favoured trading status with the EU.

In mid-2002 an opposition alliance-in-exile, the Turkmen Democratic Opposition, was formed in Vienna, consisting of members of banned parties and social movements. In Nov. 2002 there was a coup attempt against Niyazov. He blamed exiled opponents who in turn accused him of fabricating the attempt in order to crack down further on domestic opposition. A new wave of repression and imprisonment followed the incident, including the detention of a former foreign minister Boris Shikhmuradov who was considered to be the leader of the exiled activists. Surveillance cameras were installed on main streets in Ashgabat after the failed coup. Parliamentary elections in Dec. 2004 and Jan. 2005 returned presidential supporters to all seats.

Under Niyazov, Turkmenistan has an uneasy relationship with its neighbours, preferring to avoid regional co-operation. In 2003 Niyazov issued a decree cancelling the 1993 dual citizenship agreement with Russia. Those holding dual citizenship were given 2 months in which to decide which passport to retain, causing a diplomatic row with Moscow. Russians were reported to fear being trapped in a country widely criticized for human rights abuses and with severe restrictions on foreign travel for its citizens. Relations with Uzbekistan worsened after Niyazov's government accused the Uzbek government in 2002 of shielding opposition leaders. However, the two presidents later signed a friendship declaration and an agreement on water resources in 2004.

Niyazov died of heart failure on 21 Dec. 2006. In the immediate aftermath of his death there were fears of a power vacuum. Kurbanguly Berdymukhamedov, the deputy prime minister, was named interim head of state until a meeting of the country's highest representative body appointed a permanent successor.

Nkrumah, Kwame (Ghana)

Introduction

Kwame Nkrumah led Ghana (formerly the Gold Coast) to independence in 1957 and won an international reputation for his vision of Pan-African unity. Serving as prime minister and then president from 1957 until 1966, his rule became increasingly authoritarian and, after an initial period of growth, led to the collapse of the Ghanaian economy. He was removed from power in a coup and forced into exile.

Early Life

Nkrumah was born in Sept. 1909 in Nkroful, in the Gold Coast. Raised a Roman Catholic, he became a primary school teacher. In 1935 he moved to the USA and studied at Lincoln University and Pennsylvania University, before studying law in London. During this period he took a senior position in the West African Students' Union and organized the Fifth Pan-African Congress in Manchester.

Returning to the Gold Coast in 1947, Nkrumah was appointed general secretary of the United Gold Coast Convention (UGCC), which was pushing for self-government. Nkrumah encouraged a campaign of peaceful 'positive action' but he was arrested by the British following riots in 1948. He resigned from the UGCC in 1949 and established the Convention People's Party. With Nkrumah again arrested for his political activities in 1950, the CPP coasted to victory at its first elections the following year. Nkrumah was subsequently released. He was named leader of government business, becoming the Gold Coast's de facto prime minister and officially assuming that title the following year.

Career Peak

The Gold Coast and British Togoland achieved independence within the Commonwealth in March 1957, taking the name Ghana. Nkrumah was elected prime minister. The early years of his tenure were marked by popular spending programmes, improving the country's health, education and travel infrastructures. He adopted an autocratic stance from the outset, and in 1958 a law was passed allowing individuals identified as national security risks to be imprisoned without trial.

1960 saw Nkrumah become president of the newly constituted Republic of Ghana. The economy went into rapid decline, prompted by the collapse of world cocoa prices. Foreign debt and unemployment spiralled out of control and popular discontent led to a general strike in late 1961. Nkrumah spent more time abroad, advocating his vision of pan-African unity and developing relations with communist states.

Nkrumah survived an assassination attempt in Aug. 1962 and several other attacks in the following years. In 1964 he banned political opposition and named himself head of state and the CPP for life. He was increasingly absent from public life in Ghana, and developed and encouraged a cult to grow around his self-styled alter-ego, Osagyefo (The Redeemer).

Ghana's economic climate continued to deteriorate and there were food shortages in some areas. Nkrumah raised taxes and imprisoned political enemies. He pushed through legislation reducing the power of traditional chiefs. In Jan. 1966 he made one of his last public appearances at the opening of the vast Volta Dam. He travelled on to Burma and China and on 24 Feb. 1966, in his absence, the army and police seized power in Accra.

Later Life

Exiled, Nkrumah sought refuge in Guinea, where President Sekou Toure named him 'co-president.' He continued to find a large audience for his vision of a 'United States of Africa' until his death from cancer in Bucharest on 27 April 1972.

Noboa Bejarano, Gustavo (Ecuador)

Introduction

Gustavo Noboa Bejarano became president of Ecuador in Jan. 2000 after a bloodless coup deposed President Jamil Mahuad Witt. The interim junta ruled for just 5 h before ceding power to Noboa, Mahuad's vice president. During his short presidency, Noboa, who represented no political party, sought to resolve economic crises, pacify the indigenous Ecuadorians (both catalysts in the coup) and stabilize a country which had seen six presidents in 4 years.

Early Life

Noboa was born on 21 Aug. 1937 in Ecuador's second city, Guayaquil. He studied political and social science at the Universidad Católica de Guayaquil before completing a doctorate in law there in 1965. He pursued a successful academic career before his appointment as head of a private industrial agricultural company. He then began working for the government in an advisory role and represented Ecuador in negotiations with Brazil and Peru over contentious border disputes. Independent of all political parties, he was nonetheless politically active and became an independent governor for his native Guayas state in 1983.

Under the presidency of Sixto Durán Ballén (1992–96) Noboa rejected offers to become a minister or vice president. Instead in 1995 he ran an education commission evaluating the country's higher education system and worked within the foreign ministry. Despite his apolitical stance, in 1998 Noboa accepted the role of vice president under the presidency of the centrist Democracia Popular member, Mahuad. The president's inability to stop recession and hyperinflation coupled with his proposal to introduce dollarization at the expense of the sucre caused widespread discontent. In Jan. 2000 protesters marched on the capital and surrounded the presidential palace calling for Mahuad's resignation. Demonstrations spread to Guayaquil and Porto Viejo and the president was soon deposed.

The junta comprised the army leader Colonel Lucio Gutiérrez and the Quechua leader and president of the Confederación de Nacionalidades Indígenas de Ecuador (CONAIE), Antonio Vargas Huatatoca. On 21 Jan. 2000 the junta established themselves as the country's leaders. Vargas' presence gained widespread support for the junta, but international bodies were unhappy with military rule. In protest the US threatened to stop aid and block investment. Additional pressure from the UN, the OAS and neighbouring countries, including a joint statement from MERCOSUR, forced the junta to hand over power to a civilian leader. Thus, with the backing of the military and parliament, Noboa was chosen to replace Mahuad 5 h after he had been deposed, and to see out his term until 2003.

Career Peak

On his appointment, Noboa promised to restore stability and implement measures to combat the recession. A surprise television address by Mahuad pledged his support to Noboa, although he took the opportunity to condemn the coup. The CONAIE members and other indigenous supporters were angry at Noboa's appointment, seeing it as a betrayal. Noboa implemented a modified version of Mahuad's dollarization policy, pegging the sucre to the dollar.

By Aug. 2000 foreign exchange had stabilized, although inflation remained high. Attracted by the high price of oil, foreign investment increased. Noboa managed to renegotiate Ecuador's foreign debt and IMF targets were met. Despite the improvements, disagreements with congress over the appointment of a speaker split the politicians into rival camps. Public discontent continued. At the beginning of 2001 Noboa's proposed austerity measures including a 100% increase in domestic fuel and a 75% increase in transport costs provoked mass protests. After imposing a state of emergency, the protesters were dispersed. In Aug. 2001 Noboa proposed a 2% tax increase to help meet IMF targets, but was forced to back down when it was rejected by the constitutional tribunal. Noboa's struggles to save Ecuador's precarious economy continued until the end of his term.

He was defeated in presidential elections by Gutiérrez in Nov. 2002.

Later Life

In July 2003 Noboa applied for political asylum in the Dominican Republic having been prevented from flying to Miami, Florida. He claimed that political persecution had made remaining in Ecuador impossible. Investigations into Noboa's management of Ecuador's foreign debt repayments were instigated after he left office by ex-president Febres Cordero.

Noda, Yoshihiko (Japan)

Introduction

Yoshihiko Noda became prime minister in Sept. 2011, following the resignation of Naoto Kan. Regarded as a fiscal conservative and a reformer, he favoured raising taxes and reining in public spending. As well as addressing Japan's deficit, he faced the challenges of reconstruction after the devastation caused by the March 2011 earthquake and tsunami.

Early Life

Yoshihiko Noda was born on 20 May 1957 in Funabashi, Chiba Prefecture. The son of a paratrooper, he graduated from the school of political science and economics at Waseda University in 1980. After postgraduate studies at the Matsushita School of Government and Management, he entered local politics and in 1987 was elected to the assembly of the Chiba Prefecture.

He was a founder member of the centre-left Japan New Party (JNP) in 1992 and the following year he was elected to the Diet. In 1999 he joined the newly formed Democratic Party of Japan (DPJ), serving as shadow minister for administrative and regulatory reform in 2001 and as shadow finance minister in 2004. Following the DPJ's victory in the Sept. 2009 general election, Noda became senior vice finance minister until June 2010, when he succeeded newly elected prime minister Naoto Kan as finance minister.

He argued for fiscal discipline to control Japan's mounting public debt and called for ministries to cut their budgets by 10% in 2011–12. Although the government budget was passed, its implementation was impeded by opposition control of the upper house. Sovereign debt crises overseas caused the yen to rise, threatening Japan's ability to export, and in Jan. 2011 Noda made the first of several interventions in international finance markets in a bid to stabilize the currency.

In March 2011 an earthquake and tsunami struck eastern Japan, causing the Fukushima nuclear plant disaster and confronting the government with an estimated 20–25trn. yen of reconstruction costs, as well as producing a humanitarian crisis and energy shortages. Noda backed Kan's proposals to continue cutting the deficit while rebuilding but when concerted opposition forced Kan's resignation, Noda successfully contested the DPJ leadership, winning in the second round by 215 votes to 177. He took office on 2 Sept. 2011.

Career Peak

Noda argued for sustained fiscal tightening and proposed an increase in consumption tax to pay for social security and reconstruction. This provoked opposition within the DPJ and in Jan. 2012 nine MPs left to form the Kizuna Party. In response, Noda reshuffled his cabinet and called for cross-party discussions on implementing reforms. Besides having to win opposition

support in the upper house, he continued to be hampered by divisions within the DPJ and a financial scandal involving a veteran former minister.

Internationally, Noda emphasized the importance of Japan's relationship with the USA, while maintaining co-operation with China. Relations with China remained sensitive, especially over issues of national identity. In Nov. 2011 Noda committed Japan to negotiations on joining the Trans-Pacific Partnership, a regional free trade agreement. This had popular support but was opposed by most opposition parties and by some within the DPJ because of its potential impact on Japan's rice farmers.

Later Life

Following the DPJ's loss in the Dec. 2012 general election Noda resigned as the leader of the Democratic Party of Japan.

Nong Duc Manh (Vietnam)

Introduction

Nong Duc Manh was elected secretary general of the ruling Communist Party in 2001 and so became Vietnam's effective centre of power. Regarded as a modernizer, he set out to accelerate industrialization and encourage foreign investment, which enabled Vietnam to join the World Trade Organization as its 150th member in Jan. 2007.

Early Life

Nong Duc Manh was born on 11 Sept. 1940 into the Tay ethnic group in Hung Cuong commune, Na Ri district in the then-province of Bach Thai. From 1958–65 he worked as an engineer with the provincial forestry service and during this period joined the Communist Party. In 1966 he was appointed to the board of the forestry service. From the mid-1970s he ascended the party structure, sitting as a member of the Bach Thai executive committee. In 1986 he was made an alternate member of the Communist central committee and was elected to full membership 3 years later. In the same year he became deputy chairman of the National Assembly. He was chosen as chairman in Sept. 1992 and re-elected to the post in 1997. He was elected secretary general of the Communist Party in April 2001.

Career Peak

Manh set out his plans to modernize Vietnam's political and legal systems, reducing corruption and streamlining bureaucracy. However, Vietnam has remained a one-party state with tight Communist control over the media, and critics suggest political suppression is widespread. He continued the economic liberalization that began in the 1980s and under Manh growth rates were strong as foreign investment and aid increased. Nevertheless, there remained a large gap in wealth between the richer urban and struggling rural populations. Manh's crackdown on organized crime was exemplified by the trial in 2003 of over 150 gangsters, particularly Nam Cam (a Ho Chi Minh City criminal), who was executed in 2004.

On the international stage, Manh pursued closer relations with the USA. Trade relations were normalized in Dec. 2001 and the USA became Vietnam's chief export destination. Commercial flights from the USA resumed in 2004 for the first time since the end of the Vietnam war. In June 2005 the then prime minister, Phan Van Khai, travelled to the USA for a meeting with President George W. Bush, the first post-war meeting between leaders from the two countries. In May 2002 Russia relinquished control of the Cam Ranh Bay naval base, previously the biggest Soviet-operated base outside of the Warsaw Pact countries.

Manh was reappointed for a further 5-year term in April 2006, although 2 months later the prime minister, president and National Assembly chairman were replaced by younger political leaders. In 2007 there were several high-profile arrests and trials of political activists. This refocused international attention on Vietnam's human rights record, particularly in June during President Nguyen Minh Triet's first visit by a Vietnamese head of state to the USA since the end of the Vietnam War.

Despite a broad amnesty in Jan. 2009 in which more than 15,000 prisoners were granted early release, there had been no easing of policy towards political dissent, particularly with regard to the media and the internet. In Jan.

2009 two pro-reform newspaper editors were convicted for their reporting of a high-level corruption trial, in Sept. the government restricted the right to conduct research on the Communist Party, in Dec. another dissident was jailed for allegedly posting pro-democracy articles on the internet and in Jan. 2010 four activists, including a human rights lawyer and an internet entrepreneur, were jailed for advocating multi-party democracy.

After 10 years as secretary general Manh decided to retire. Nguyen Phu Trong was appointed his successor in Jan. 2011.

Noriega, Manuel (Panama)

Introduction

As head of the armed forces, Gen. Noriega was Panama's *de facto* head of state between 1983 and 1989. From the 1960s he worked closely with US intelligence services, providing contact with and intelligence from Central and South America. However, evidence of involvement in illegal arms and drugs dealing and suspicions that he was selling on US intelligence led to a collapse in the relationship with the US. American forces invaded Panama in 1989 and arrested him. He was sentenced to 30 years in prison by an American court.

Early Life

Manuel Antonio Noriega Morena was born into a poor background in Panama City in 1934. After finishing school he won a scholarship to Peru's Chorrillos military school. Back in Panama he joined the army as a sub-lieutenant and began a rapid rise through the ranks. In 1968 he was promoted to first lieutenant and supported captain Omar Torrijos, who deposed the civilian government of Arnulfo Arias. After Noriega defeated a counter-coup he won promotion to lieutenant colonel and was given command of military intelligence.

Noriega developed a reputation for the brutal treatment of political enemies via his role with the intelligence services. He also established a profitable relationship with the US, to whom he provided intelligence and assistance in dealing with several regimes including Castro's Cuba. In 1981 Torrijos was killed in a plane crash and was succeeded by General Paredes, head of the national guard. When Paredes relinquished his military post in order to stand in the presidential elections of Aug. 1983, Noriega took control of the military. Noriega undermined Paredes' candidature by refusing to publicly back him and Paredes left the race the following month. Noriega then restructured the national guard into the Panama Defence Forces (PDF), with the president as its nominal head but with Noriega holding executive power.

Career Peak

Able to rely on the support of the military, Noriega became Panama's most effective powerbroker. The presidential elections of May 1984 were beset by accusations of vote rigging and procedural irregularity. Ardito Barletta, a candidate favourable to Noriega at the time, was declared victor by a narrow majority after several days of violence. In 1985 Dr. Hugo Spadafora, one of Noriega's most outspoken critics, was murdered after claiming to have evidence of the General's involvement in arms and drugs dealing. Shortly after Barletta announced an investigation into the murder, Noriega came out in opposition to him, accusing Barletta's government of incompetence. Barletta resigned shortly afterwards.

By the mid-1980s tensions between the US and Panama were high as the two administrations negotiated the future of the Panama Canal. The cumulative effect of the Spadafora murder, Barletta's subsequent demise, increasing evidence of Noriega's role in laundering arms and drugs money and accusations that he was selling US intelligence to hostile regimes caused the relationship to deteriorate further. In 1988 the US indicted Noriega on drugs charges and imposed economic sanctions but he maintained his grip on power.

In 1989 Noriega cancelled scheduled presidential elections and made himself head of state. In Oct. of that year a US-backed coup attempt failed and on 15 Dec. 1989 Gen. Noriega declared a 'state of war' with the USA. On 20 Dec., on the orders of President George Bush, the USA invaded. After a short siege in Panama City, Noriega surrendered to the US on 3 Jan. 1990. He was replaced by Guillermo Endara.

Later Life

In 1992 Noriega was convicted in Miami on eight charges linked to racketeering, drug smuggling and money laundering. He was sentenced to 40 years in jail, reduced to 30 years on appeal. In 1999 he was convicted in France *in absentia* to 10 years for laundering drugs money. He was extradited to France in April 2010 where he was sentenced to 7 years in jail. Noriega died on 29 May 2017 aged 83 following brain surgery in March.

Ntoutoume-Emane, Jean-François (Gabon)

Introduction

Jean-François Ntoutoume-Emane was prime minister from 1999–2006. The French-educated politician is a member of the ruling Gabonese Democratic Party (PDG) and was a close ally of the president, Omar Bongo, who ruled the country from 1967 until his death in 2009.

Early Life

Jean-François Ntoutoume-Emane was born on 6 Oct. 1939 in Libreville, Gabon, then part of the federation of French Equatorial Africa. He attended the city's Ecole Montfort and College Bessieux, graduating in 1960, the year of Gabon's independence. He subsequently studied law, economics and history at the universities of Rennes and Paris during the early to mid 1960s, completing a doctorate in political science in 1968. Returning to Gabon, Ntoutoume-Emane entered the civil service, working in the departments of finance, banking and transportation. He also lectured in law, sociology and political science at the National University of Gabon. From 1972 Ntoutoume-Emane edited *Dialogue*, the newspaper of the ruling PDG, the country's sole political party from 1968 to 1990.

In 1975 he became advisor to President Bongo and from 1976–87 held ministerial posts in economic and financial affairs, against a backdrop of rapidly growing prosperity, principally from the export of oil. He served as minister of commerce from 1987–89. Following the restoration of multi-party politics and Bongo's resignation as head of the PDG, elections for the national assembly were held in Sept. 1990. Ntoutoume-Emane was elected as the PDG representative for Estuary province. He served as minister of planning and housing from 1997 and organised Bongo's successful presidential election campaign in Dec. 1998. When Prime Minister Obame-Nguema resigned, Ntoutoume-Emane was appointed to the post and took office on 23 Jan. 1999.

Career Peak

Ntoutoume-Emane led a PDG-dominated government, although power remained effectively in the hands of President Bongo, who was re-elected for a further 7 year term in Nov. 2005. Ntoutoume-Emane's administration promised to distribute the country's oil wealth more equitably and to diversify the economy but progress was slow. When Omar Bongo was sworn in again on 20 Jan. 2006, Ntoutoume-Emane was replaced as prime minister by fellow PDG member Jean Eyeghe Ndong.

Nujoma, Sam (Namibia)

Introduction

Sam Nujoma became Namibia's first post-independence president in 1990. Since 1960 he was leader of the South West African People's Organization

(SWAPO), which won UN recognition as the only legitimate representative body of the Namibian people in 1973. A moderate reformer, he was accused of authoritarianism.

Early Life

Samuel Shafiihuma Nujoma was born on 12 May 1929 in the Owamboland region of South West Africa (now Namibia) into a rural family. He received his early education from missionaries and courses at night school. He began working on the railways when he was 16, where he unsuccessfully tried to establish a trade union. He was later employed as a shop worker and in administrative posts.

Married in 1956, he became increasingly involved in nationalist politics and in 1959 was elected leader of the Owambo People's Organization, which evolved into SWAPO. SWAPO regularly made appeals to the UN demanding the removal of South African forces from Namibia. Nujoma was forced into exile in 1960 but returned briefly in 1966 and led the People's Liberation Army of Namibia (PLAN) in an armed campaign. The war prompted renewed international attention and in 1973 SWAPO was recognized by the UN as the only truly representative voice of the Namibian people. Nujoma led SWAPO at UN-hosted talks in 1977 and the following year plans for Namibia's independence were proposed. However, it was 10 years before a ceasefire was called and the resolution implemented.

Nujoma returned from exile in Sept. 1989 and led SWAPO to victory in Namibia's first democratic elections 2 months later. On 21 March 1990 Namibia achieved independence and Nujoma was appointed president.

Career Peak

Having dropped his support of a Marxist single party state, the early years of Nujoma's tenure were marked by moderate social democratic reforms. He won re-election in 1994, and in 1998 the constitution was changed to allow him to stand for a third term.

In 1998 the government cracked down on a seperatist movement in the Caprivi Strip, causing hundreds to flee to Botswana. A state of emergency was declared the following year after an upsurge in separatist activities. Elsewhere, Nujoma sent troops to the Democratic Republic of Congo in support of the regime of Laurent Kabila. In 2001 it was revealed that several members of Nujoma's government profited from diamond mining under the Kabila regime, although the president denied any personal interest. In 1999 the World Court ruled against Namibia in its dispute with Botswana over the island of Sedudu in the Chobe River. In late 1999 Nujoma secured his third term of office.

Nujoma had been accused of becoming increasingly autocratic. In 2001 he forbade government departments to purchase *The Namibian*, a national newspaper critical of his leadership. In Aug. 2002 he sacked his prime minister of 12 years, Hage Geingob, replacing him with foreign minister Theo-Ben Gurirab. At the sustainable development summit in Johannesburg, he defended President Mugabe's regime in Zimbabwe. Nujoma attacked Western interference in African affairs and pledged to continue his policy of 'willing seller–willing buyer'. whereby the government has first refusal on farmland offered for sale by white farmers which it then redistributes among the landless population. In addition, he outlined plans to confiscate 192 farms belonging to foreign absentee landlords. Nujoma was unable to run for a fourth term in Nov. 2004 and was replaced by Hifikepunye Pohamba as the SWAPO candidate for the presidency. Pohamba was sworn in as president on 21 March 2005.

Nyerere, Julius (Tanzania)

Introduction

Julius Nyerere was Tanzania's president from its creation in 1964 until his resignation in 1985. He had previously been prime minister and president of newly-independent Tanganyika. Despite the failure of his socialist economic reforms, he was internationally respected for overseeing Tanzania's peaceful transition to independence. A leading figure in the pan-African movement, he co-founded the Organization of African Unity (OAU). He was the first post-independence African leader to voluntarily relinquish power.

Early Life

Julius Kambarage Nyerere was born on 13 April 1922 in Butiama in the northwest of what was then Tanganyika, governed by the UK under League of Nations mandate. The son of a Zanaki tribal leader, Nyerere received schooling from Roman Catholic priests and converted to Roman Catholicism. He qualified as a teacher from the Makerere College in Kampala, Uganda and taught at several Catholic schools before graduating with a master's degree in history and economics from Edinburgh University in 1952.

He returned to Tanganyika to resume teaching and became active in politics. Tanganyika was now under a UN trusteeship and a pro-independence movement was gaining momentum. Nyerere joined the Tanganyika African Association, winning its presidency in 1953. Over the following year the Association was reformed into the Tanganyika African National Union (TANU). Aiming for a peaceful transition to independence, Nyerere addressed the UN in 1955 and began preliminary negotiations with the British government. He entered the Tanganyika legislative council but resigned in 1957 when he felt negotiations were stalling. In 1958 he led TANU to significant gains in the council and by 1960 TANU held all but one of the 71 seats.

After successful negotiations with the British governor, Sir Richard Turnbull, Tanganyika was granted self-government in Sept. 1960, with Nyerere as chief minister. In May of the following year he became prime minister and by the end of 1961 Tanganyika had won full independence. In 1962 it became a republic with Nyerere elected its first president.

Career Peak

In 1963 Nyerere was one of the key figures in the founding of the OAU (now called the African Union). The following year he oversaw the union of Tanganyika with Zanzibar to form the new state of Tanzania and in 1965 he won re-election to the presidency, despite a mutiny by the Tanganyikam army in 1964. The union with Zanzibar meant Nyerere was forced into a close relationship with Zanzibar's president, Sheikh Abeid Karume, who was internationally condemned for the brutality of his regime.

Nyerere's 1967 Arusha declaration set out his domestic agenda, outlining his vision of a socialist state for Africa, which was to be based on *ujamaa* (familyhood). He introduced programmes of universal education and a greatly improved health service. However, the corner stone of his plans, collectivized agriculture, caused widespread resentment and was an economic failure. Industrial growth lacked the necessary infrastructures. Nervous of any political instability, he developed Tanzania as a one-party state, in which only his own Chama Cha Mapinduzi was tolerated.

Nyerere's greater success came as an international figurehead of the Pan-African movement. As well as his leading role in the OAU, he was chief among those campaigning for majority rule throughout the continent, and notably in South Africa, Rhodesia (later Zimbabwe), South West Africa (later Namibia), Angola, Botswana, Mozambique and Zambia. Relations with the UK were strained when Nyerere criticized the UK government for failing to act against Ian Smith after he made a unilateral declaration of independence in Rhodesia in 1965. Tanzania's relationship with the US also deteriorated as Nyerere pursued closer ties with communist China. He was critical of the despotic rule of Idi Amin in neighbouring Uganda and in 1979 authorized the use of Tanzanian troops in the coup that saw Amin replaced by Milton Obote.

Whilst Nyerere retained international respect as a moderate who campaigned for an African identity unblighted by ethnic in-fighting, the failure of his domestic economic strategies were apparent by the 1980s. The inefficiencies of agricultural collectivization resulted in over-reliance on foreign aid and the nation's transport and industrial infrastructures were inadequate. Nonetheless, he secured a level of political stability which compared well with the rest of post-colonial Africa and his education reforms ensured Tanzania had one of the continent's highest literacy rates.

Later Life

Despite resigning the presidency Nyerere remained head of the Chama Cha Mapinduzi until 1990. He remained politically active, notably in international affairs. He was chair of the Intergovernmental South Centre which sought to reduce the gap between living standards in the Northern and Southern hemispheres. In 1996 he was chief mediator in the ultimately unsuccessful talks to end the Burundi conflict. He died of leukaemia in London on 14 Oct. 1999.

O'Neil, Terence (Northern Ireland, United Kingdom)

Introduction

Terence O'Neill, leader of the Ulster Unionists, served as prime minister from 1963–69. He attempted to reduce sectarianism by promoting closer relations with the Republic of Ireland and introducing civil rights reforms. A controversial figure in his own party, he resigned amid rising sectarian violence but his reforms helped pave the way for eventual power-sharing.

Early Life

Terence Marne O'Neill was born in London on 10 Sept. 1914 to an aristocratic Anglo-Irish family with roots in Randalstown, Northern Ireland. He was educated at Eton College and the Royal Military Academy, Sandhurst, before serving with the Irish Guards during the Second World War. In 1945 he moved with his family to County Antrim and in 1946 entered the Stormont as Ulster Unionist MP for the Bannside constituency.

O'Neill served as parliamentary secretary in the ministry of health and local government from Feb. 1948–Nov. 1953. He then became chairman of ways and means and deputy speaker of the House of Commons. In April 1956 he was appointed minister of home affairs and in Oct. 1956 became minister for finance. During a period of industrial decline, he gained a reputation as a modernizer and in March 1963 succeeded Lord Brookeborough as prime minister.

Career Peak

O'Neill promoted cooperation between Protestants and Catholics as a means of developing the economy. In 1965 he held trade relations talks with the Republic's Taioseach and in 1966 declared the paramilitary Ulster Volunteer Force (UVF) illegal. He was vigorously opposed by some Ulster Unionists, including Ian Paisley who formed the breakaway Protestant Unionist Party.

In 1967 the Northern Ireland Civil Rights Association (NICRA) started campaigning to end anti-Catholic discrimination in housing, employment and voting practices. O'Neill was in favour of making concessions but was opposed by leading figures within his party. In Oct. 1968, after violent police action against NICRA marches prompted international protests, O'Neill sacked his hardline home affairs minister, William Craig, and agreed a five point reform programme. Its concessions infuriated many Protestants while falling short of meeting Catholic demands for 'one man-one vote'. Further violence against marchers in Jan. 1969 led to riots and O'Neill's deputy resigned in protest at his decision to hold an enquiry. O'Neill called a surprise election in Feb. 1969 in a bid to re-establish his authority but won only a narrow victory. He remained in office for 3 months, reforming the local council franchise to 'one man one vote' before resigning as prime minister and leader of the Ulster Unionists on 28 April 1969.

Later Life

In 1969 O'Neill published a book, *Ulster at the Crossroads*. In 1970 he resigned his seat at Stormont and was made a life peer as Baron O'Neill of the Maine, of Ahoghill in the County of Antrim. He took up his seat in the House of Lords as a crossbencher and published his autobiography in 1972. He died on 12 June 1990.

Obama, Barack (United States of America)

Introduction

Barack Obama became the 44th president of the USA in Jan. 2009 and the first African American to hold the office. Having secured the Democratic candidacy, he contested the presidential election in Nov. 2008 against a background of deepening economic crisis. Viewed as on the centre-liberal wing of his party, Obama's principal electoral pledges included the introduction of a national health insurance plan and a scaling down of the US troop presence in Iraq. He also sought to counter the economic crisis with stimulus measures, while his Republican opponent advocated a curb on spending. On foreign policy, Obama confirmed the USA's military commitment to the campaign against terrorism, while seeking to promote compliance with international law and the adoption of democratic values across the world political stage. He was re-elected for a second and final term on 6 Nov. 2012 and was inaugurated in Jan. 2013. In his final annual state-of-the-union address in Jan. 2016, he defended his domestic record but lamented the congressional partisan divisions that increasingly hampered the progress of his presidency and its legacy.

Early Life

Barack Hussein Obama was born on 4 Aug. 1961 in Honolulu, Hawaii, to a Kenyan father and white American mother. His parents divorced and, following his mother's remarriage in 1967, the family moved to Indonesia, where Obama was educated until the age of 10. He attended Punahou School in Honolulu and Occidental College, Los Angeles, before graduating from Columbia University, New York, in 1983 with a BA in political science. From 1983–85 he worked at Business International Corporation and at the New York Public Interest Research Group, then moved to Chicago to become director of the church-based Developing Communities Project (DCP). From 1985–88 he led the DCP, expanding its staff and budget and establishing new projects. He attended Harvard Law School from 1988–91 and was elected president of the *Harvard Law Review* in 1990.

Following his graduation Obama took up a fellowship with the University of Chicago Law School, where he taught constitutional law from 1992–2004. In 1992 he directed 'Illinois Project Vote!'. a campaign to register African Americans to vote, and from 1992–2002 he served on the boards of various community organizations and foundations, including the Joyce Foundation and Public Allies. In 1993 he joined law firm Davis, Miner, Barnhill & Galland, practising first as an associate then as a counsel. In 1995 he published a memoir, *Dreams from My Father: A Story of Race and Inheritance*.

In 1996 Obama was elected senator for the 13th District of Illinois, subsequently winning re-election in 1998 and 2002. As senator he supported health care and welfare reforms, sponsored a law to increase tax credits for low paid workers and promoted tighter regulation of the mortgage industry. In 2003, in co-operation with Republican senators, he led legislation to monitor police procedures in the state of Illinois, requiring police to profile the ethnicity of motorists they stopped and making it compulsory to videotape interrogations of homicide suspects.

After an unsuccessful run for the House of Representatives in 2000, Obama mounted a campaign for the 2004 US Senate elections. He attracted national attention at that year's National Democratic Convention when he gave a keynote speech, 'The Audacity of Hope'. in which he spoke of the shared aspirations and efforts of American citizens and set out government's obligations towards them. In Nov. 2004 Obama was elected to the US Senate with 70% of the vote, the largest winning margin in Illinois state history. In office he supported legislation to reduce carbon emissions, voted for robust border controls and immigration reform, and campaigned for controls on political financing, in particular gifts and funding provided by lobbyists.

Having opposed military action against Iraq in 2003, he continued to criticize the conduct of the war. As a member of the Senate's foreign relations committee, he explored ways of reducing the threat from conventional weapons and, with Republican Senator Richard G. Lugar, co-authored a law extending US co-operation in identifying and disposing of stockpiled weapons. He supported successive bills calling for international intervention in Sudan and in 2006 voted for a no-fly zone over Darfur. Obama also served on the health, education, labour and pensions committees, the committee on veterans' affairs and the committee on homeland security and governmental affairs. In these areas he supported moves to expand early years schooling, to increase financial help for low-income high school and college students and to provide funding for veterans to attend college.

In Feb. 2007 Obama announced his candidacy for the Democratic presidential nomination. Campaigning on the themes of change and unity, he promised to address the key issues of Iraq, health care and the USA's dependence on oil. Obama fought a vigorous contest with main rival Hillary Clinton throughout 2007 and early 2008, gaining praise for his oratory while defending himself against charges of inexperience. In May 2007 he pledged a national health insurance plan open to all. Criticized by environmentalists for supporting liquefied coal, he subsequently modified his position. On the Iraq War, he argued for the phased redeployment of US forces and the withdrawal of combat troops, as proposed in his Iraq War De-Escalation Act of 2007.

By June 2008 Obama had secured the support of a majority of Democratic Party delegates and was confirmed at the Democratic National Convention of Aug. 2008. He selected Joe Biden, the long-serving senator of Delaware, as his running mate. During the early weeks of campaigning, polls showed a close contest between Obama and Republican candidate John McCain, with Obama being seen as inexperienced in foreign affairs. However, the failure of key US financial institutions in late 2008 focused attention on the economy, prompting a spike in Obama's support as he called for regulatory reforms and a bipartisan approach to tackling the crisis. Obama won the election on 4 Nov. 2008 with 53% of the vote to McCain's 46% and by 365 electoral college votes to 173.

In the transition between his election and inauguration, Obama appointed Rahm Emanuel as chief of staff and former election rival, Hillary Clinton, as secretary of state. Both appointments were seen as an indication that he would tap the experience of long-serving politicians and officials and retain much of the previous administration's foreign policy. He also gathered an economic team and began preparing a stimulus plan to aid economic recovery through investment.

Career Peak

Obama was inaugurated on 20 Jan. 2009. Because of a minor misreading of the oath of office on the part of Chief Justice John Roberts, which caused Obama to make a similar error, he took the oath for a second time on 21 Jan. 2009. Among his first presidential aims was the fulfilment of an election pledge that the administration would run down and eventually close the detention facility for terrorist suspects at the US naval base in Guantanamo Bay. However, this aspiration proved elusive throughout his terms of office. Other early measures included tightening restrictions on lobbyists joining the administration, introducing stricter curbs on fuel emissions, enacting equal pay legislation and expanding children's health care.

Obama sought bipartisan support for a $825 bn. stimulus package, which aimed to boost economic recovery through sustained investment programmes. However, most Republicans opposed the package, arguing for less direct government spending and for tax reductions. After Republicans forced substantial amendments, the American Recovery and Reinvestment Act was passed on 13 Feb. 2009, relying almost exclusively on Democrat support. Worth a slightly reduced $787 bn., it detailed plans for unprecedented levels of investment in education, healthcare, infrastructure, the environment, employment and tax reduction.

On foreign policy, Obama's early months saw a move away from the hawkish tone of the previous administration. In Feb. 2009 he announced that most US troops would be withdrawn from Iraq by 31 Aug. 2010, with residual forces leaving by the end of 2011. He also signalled a change of approach on Afghanistan, indicating that, although troop numbers would initially be increased in an echo of the 'surge' tactics employed in Iraq, he was reviewing strategy and did not believe the region could be stabilized by military means alone. Obama also changed the tone of the USA's dealings with the Middle East, sending envoys to Syria in March 2009 and expressing a willingness to talk to Iran's leaders, subject to their compliance with UN directives on nuclear development. He was similarly cautious on the Israeli–Palestinian conflict, reaffirming the USA's commitment to pursuing a two-state solution while maintaining the previous administration's stance of refusing to talk to the militant Hamas leadership in Gaza. He gave moderate encouragement to the idea of closer dialogue between the USA and China and opened up the possibility of negotiations between the USA and Russia on cutting nuclear stockpiles and on curbing the development of new weapons.

However, 1 year on from his inauguration Obama had yet to secure any major policy objectives and his personal approval rating among voters had slipped markedly according to opinion polls. Despite the significant injections of borrowed money to stimulate demand and boost the economy, job creation proved slow and unemployment rose to 10% in 2009. Economic weakness in turn further undermined the country's fiscal position.

Obama's radical health care reform plan to extend insurance cover to all Americans proved particularly contentious. Legislation was passed in March 2010, by 56–43 votes in the Senate and by 220–207 in the House of Representatives, and it was hoped that under its terms coverage would extend to a further 32 m. Americans. However, it was the subject of fierce congressional division and continued to be widely challenged as unconstitutional

before its validity was upheld by a majority vote of the Supreme Court in June 2012. Implementation of the system, from 1 Oct. 2013, was also plagued by operational shortcomings and remained a focus of public discontent.

In Sept. 2009 Obama eased friction with Russia as he announced the abandonment of a missile defence deployment in the Czech Republic and Poland. In March 2010 the two countries agreed a treaty to replace the START Treaty on nuclear arms reduction. Obama was awarded the Nobel Peace Prize in Oct. 2009 for his efforts to create 'a new international atmosphere'. Relations with China, however, worsened over trade and currency policy, US weapons sales to Taiwan and, in Feb. 2010, the president's meeting with the Dalai Lama of Tibet.

In April 2010 an explosion in the Gulf of Mexico led to the biggest oil spill in US history, causing huge damage to local communities and the economy. The political fallout, together with the rise in support for the conservative libertarian Tea Party movement, again hit Obama's approval ratings. In mid-term congressional elections in Nov. that year, the Republicans made sweeping gains to regain control of the House of Representatives, heralding a legislative gridlock with the Democratic majority in the Senate.

Obama's pressure on the Israeli government to stop settlement building on Palestinian land in the Middle East was (and would continue to be) resisted by Prime Minister Netanyahu, undermining US efforts to broker further talks between the Israeli and Palestinian authorities. Although critical of Israeli policy, the US government did, however, oppose the UN General Assembly's recognition in Nov. 2012 of Palestine's enhanced status as a non-member observer state. After some progress in improving relations with Syria, with a US ambassador appointed in Feb. 2010 after a 5-year gap, President Assad's violent response to domestic dissent and the country's subsequent descent into civil war from 2011 ruptured US–Syrian ties and led to threats of US military intervention. In March 2011 Obama committed the USA to join the NATO military intervention in Libya to protect civilians against the Gaddafi regime, stating that Americans could not brush aside 'responsibilities to our fellow human beings'. Meanwhile, there was a potential thaw in long-standing US–Iranian enmity from the second half of 2013. In Sept. a telephone conversation between Obama and new Iranian president Hassan Rouhani marked the first direct communication between leaders of the two countries since 1979, and in July 2015 Iran reached a historic agreement with the major Western countries, Russia and China to limit its controversial nuclear development programme in return for an easing of economic sanctions.

In Afghanistan Obama initially intensified the war, announcing further troop deployments during 2009 to fight the Taliban insurgency. There was a subsequent scaling down of foreign involvement in the country and NATO combat forces (including US troops) were finally withdrawn by the end of 2014, apart from residual personnel to help train and advise the Afghan army. However, in March 2015 Obama announced that the US withdrawal would be postponed and in Oct. he proposed to keep some 5,000 US troops in the country to help with counter-terrorism operations.

In May 2011 US special forces killed Osama bin Laden, having traced him to a compound in Abbottabad in northwestern Pakistan. Bin Laden, the leader of the al-Qaeda movement responsible for the 11 Sept. attacks on New York and Washington, D.C. in 2001, had been in hiding for almost 10 years. Obama commented that 'his demise should be welcomed by all who believe in peace and human dignity'. The operation strained already uneasy relations between the USA and Pakistan.

Following his re-election on 6 Nov. 2012 Obama was again embroiled in congressional discord over US debt and federal expenditure. Earlier, in 2011, the government had reached its legal federal debt ceiling, heralding several months of political wrangling before a last-minute cross-party debt-reduction agreement in Aug. to raise the ceiling and stave off the risk of a default. At the same time, Standard & Poor's international rating agency downgraded the USA's triple-A credit rating for the first time. In Oct. 2013 the federal government shut down non-essential operations for over 2 weeks after Congress failed to approve a spending bill for the next financial year. A damaging default was avoided when Democrats and Republicans reached another cross-party deal to end the stand-off. In Feb. 2014 Congress passed legislation to raise the debt ceiling for another year and in Dec. reached a $1 trn. budget agreement to fund the federal government until Sept. 2015. The following month Obama and the outgoing Republican Speaker of the House of Representatives—to the surprise of many commentators—reached a new agreement to suspend the debt ceiling and settle spending for 2016 and 2017. Earlier, in Oct. 2014 the Federal Reserve Board had announced that it was ending its quantitative easing programme launched 6 years previously to support the US economy through the global financial crisis.

US diplomatic integrity was seriously compromised in 2013 by leaked revelations about the worldwide covert electronic surveillance activities of its National Security Agency, including the monitoring of close allies. In response, Obama proposed reforms in Jan. 2014 to include curbs on warrantless intrusion and the retention of data. US-Russian relations deteriorated sharply from March 2014 as Russia annexed the Ukrainian territory of Crimea in response to a separatist rebellion in the east of that country, and the US government imposed punitive sanctions on the Kremlin. Meanwhile, the rapid rise that year of the militant Islamic State (IS) jihadist movement across swathes of Iraq and Syria prompted ongoing US-led military air strikes against IS targets, with support from some Arab and Western nations, from Sept. However, Russia's subsequent large-scale intervention in the Syrian civil war from Sept. 2015, with air operations in support of President Assad's government forces, led to accusations that Obama had surrendered the military initiative in the region to Moscow. On a more positive note, in Dec. 2014 Obama and Cuba's president, Raúl Castro, reached an historic agreement to normalize relations between their countries after decades of enmity. In July 2015 Cuban and US embassies reopened in the respective capitals of Washington, D.C. and Havana.

In Nov. 2014, reflecting continuing voter dissatisfaction with Obama and the Democrats, the Republican Party won its biggest majority in the House of Representatives in over 60 years and also regained control of the Senate at the mid-term congressional elections. In the same month, Obama courted controversy when he said that he would use his executive powers to allow millions of illegal immigrants to apply for work permits and avoid the threat of deportation, further straining congressional bipartisan co-operation. Meanwhile, reacting to the catalogue of fatal shooting incidents and mass casualties including children during his presidency, Obama also sought to introduce limited gun control in the USA, but his attempts were resisted by the influential National Rifle Association lobby group. In Jan. 2016, against the background of continuing friction between the White House and Congress, Obama called on the American people in his last state-of-the-union address to 'fix our politics' and break through the rancour of partisan differences. However, by Nov. the depth of voter disaffection with the political status quo manifested itself in the surprise election of Donald Trump, a populist and controversial Republican businessman with no government experience, as president.

In Sept. 2016, as his tenure was drawing to a close, Obama ratified—jointly with the Chinese president—a landmark international climate change agreement that had been reached in Dec. 2015 at a United Nations summit in Paris, France, and later took executive environmental action to protect coastal waters off Alaska and parts of the Atlantic seaboard from future oil and gas exploration. A nadir in his relationship with the Israeli and Russian leaders was then reached in Dec. by his administration's unprecedented refusal to veto a UN Security Council resolution demanding an end to Israeli settlement building in the Palestinian West Bank and by his expulsion of 35 Russian diplomats in response to Moscow's alleged cyber hacking interference in the US presidential election campaign.

He relinquished the presidency on 20 Jan. 2017.

Obasanjo, Olusegun (Nigeria)

Introduction

Olusegun Obasanjo became president again in 1999, having previously held the office from 1976–79. During his first tenure he guided the country through the transition from military dictatorship to civilian government. In May 2006 the Senate rejected proposed constitutional changes permitting him to seek election in 2007 for another presidential term.

Early Life

Olusegun Obasanjo was born on 5 March 1937 in Abeokuta, in southwest Nigeria. He joined the army in 1958 and received military training both in Nigeria and abroad. During his military career, he served with UN peacekeeping forces and led an army commando division in the 1967–70 Biafran civil war. Obasanjo became chief of staff to Gen. Muhammed who led a military coup in June 1975, deposing Yakubu Gowon and promising to return Nigeria to civilian rule by Oct. 1979.

Career Peak

When Muhammed was assassinated in 1976, Obasanjo took over as head of state, paving the way for democratic elections and civilian rule, as well as tightening links with the USA.

During Obasanjo's first presidential term Abuja was made the new capital. A new constitution, published in 1978, lifted the ban on political activity and the formation of political parties. In line with his determination to return to civilian government, elections were held in 1979. Obasanjo, who chose not to stand, handed power to Alhaji Shehu Shagari, a northerner from the National Party of Nigeria (NPN).

In Oct. 2002 Obasanjo was at the centre of a territorial dispute when the International Court of Justice (ICJ) awarded Cameroon ownership of the Bakassi Peninsula in the Gulf of Guinea and ordered Nigeria to withdraw from the oil-rich area. The decision was based on a 1917 agreement between Britain and Germany, then the colonial powers. Obasanjo denied the validity of territorial treaties made before independence but was later reported to have accepted the court's decision.

The build-up to the presidential elections of April 2003, when 19 candidates stood, was marked by rising tensions. Obasanjo claimed victory with 62% of the vote, with Muhammadu Buhari, candidate for the All Nigeria People's Party (ANPP), winning 32%. However, Buhari rejected the result and international monitors reported major voting irregularities. Nevertheless, Obasanjo received international recognition. Despite the region's oil wealth, poverty and high unemployment among the indigenous population remain high, which provoked increasing attacks in 2006 by militants on the operations of foreign oil companies and the kidnapping of foreign workers.

Obasanjo was not eligible to stand for re-election in the presidential elections held in April 2007. However, his supporters proposed an amendment to the constitution which would allow him to run for a third term in office. Following widespread debate the amendment was defeated and Obasanjo stepped down as president after the elections, which were won by his chosen successor Umaru Yar'Adua.

Later Life

In 2008 then United Nations secretary-general Ban Ki-moon appointed Obasanjo special envoy on the Great Lakes region in the wake of the ongoing conflict in North Kivu.

Obote, Milton (Uganda)

Introduction

Apollo Milton Obote led Uganda to independence in 1962 but was removed from power in a coup by Idi Amin in 1971. Obote returned as president from 1980 to 1985. Both his tenures were overshadowed by ethnic fighting, economic failure and authoritarian rule.

Early Life

Obote was born on 28 Dec. 1925 in the village of Akoroko, in the Lango region of Uganda, then under British sovereignty. He began studies at Kampala's Makerere College in 1948 but was expelled the following year for his anti-colonial activities and forbidden from taking up offers of international scholarships. He went to Kenya in 1950, holding a succession of temporary jobs while becoming active in the pro-independence Kenyan African Union.

Returning to Uganda in 1957, he joined the Uganda National Congress Party (UNCP) and the following year entered the national legislative council. He took an anti-colonialist line and, following the collapse of the UNCP, formed the Uganda People's Congress (UPC). Political life was based on regional differences, with the UPC broadly representing the northern groups (including Obote's own Lango people and the Acholi) against the Kebaka Yeka party (KYP) representing Mutesa II's Buganda kingdom in the south.

Uganda achieved independence in 1962, shortly after Obote had been elected prime minister.

Career Peak

In 1962 a new constitution gave federal status to five kingdoms, including that of Mutesa, who was appointed president in 1963. Relations between prime minister and president, and between their respective peoples, remained tense. In 1964 Obote fended off an attempted coup by the military. In 1966 he was accused, along with his army and air force chief Idi Amin, of supporting rebels in Congo in return for gold and ivory. Before an official investigation could get underway Obote purged the government of his accusers. Mutesa responded by demanding that national government personnel leave Buganda. Obote ordered a military attack on Mutesa, who fled the country. Obote withdrew the federal status of the kingdoms and appointed himself president.

In 1969 Obote instigated socialist economic reforms known as the 'Move to the Left'. Businesses were nationalized and foreign investment drained out of the country. The middle class was alienated and dissatisfaction with the one-party state grew. Increasingly reliant on police and military enforcement of his rule, Obote allowed Idi Amin's power to grow unchecked as relations between the two deteriorated. In 1970 Obote put Amin under house arrest but in Jan. 1971, when Obote was on a visit to Singapore, Amin staged a coup.

Obote went into exile in Tanzania and led an unsuccessful counter-coup the following year. He remained in Tanzania and nurtured an army of exiles which he put under the command of Tito Okello. Sponsored by the Tanzanian authorities the army invaded and deposed Amin in 1979. Obote returned to Uganda the following year to successfully contest the presidential elections, although many observers questioned the legitimacy of his victory. With the country ravaged by Amin's rule, Obote looked to kickstart the economy with foreign money. However, ethnic fighting continued, with the army itself responsible for a number of atrocities in the south and in Amin's homeland in the northwest. Corruption, economic decline and human rights abuses caused domestic and international unrest. Yoweri Museveni headed the National Resistance Army and waged an efficient guerrilla war against Obote. In 1985 Okello staged a coup in which he removed Obote and appointed himself head of a ruling military council.

Later Life

Obote went into exile in Zambia. In 1999 Museveni, by now president of Uganda, said Obote would not be prevented from returning to Uganda. He died on 10 Oct. 2005.

Oddsson, Davíð (Iceland)

Introduction

Davíð Oddsson served as prime minister of Iceland between 1991 and 2004, having made his name in Reykjavik's municipal government. As leader of the Independence Party, his tenure was marked by a commitment to increasing Iceland's image as an independent sovereign state.

Early Life

Oddsson was born on 17 Jan. 1948 in Reykjavik. He studied at Reykjavik College and in 1976 graduated in law from the University of Iceland. Between 1970 and 1972 he worked for the theatre of Reykjavik. From 1973 until 1976 he worked in journalism and publishing and then took a post with the Reykjavik health insurance fund. He became its managing director and also chaired the executive committee of the city's arts festival from 1976 until 1978. In 1982 he was made mayor of the capital, a post he held for 9 years.

Oddsson was a director of the youth wing of the Independence Party during the 1970s and sat on the executive committee of the full party from 1979. In 1991 he was named party chairman and in April of that year he was elected to parliament and assumed the premiership.

Career Peak

Oddsson has headed coalitions with the Social Democratic Party and, latterly, the Progressive Party. Oddsson is regarded as a conservative and has tended to support Iceland's sovereignty above increasing integration into Europe. He had several high-profile run-ins with Ólafur Ragnar Grímsson when Grímsson was leader of the People's Alliance and their relationship has remained strained since Grimsson became president in 1996. In 2001 Oddsson announced plans for Iceland to resume commercial whaling, a decision which received intense international scrutiny. He stood down in Sept. 2004 after being defeated in an attempt to restrict private media ownership and following a period of ill health.

Later Life

After stepping down from the post of prime minister Oddsson served briefly as Iceland's foreign minister and was chairman of the board of governors of the Central Bank of Iceland from 2005–09.

In Sept. 2009 Oddsson was announced as the new editor of the national daily newspaper *Morgunblaðið*, a move that reportedly prompted a third of its subscribers to cancel their subscriptions.

Oddsson contested the June 2016 presidential election, but came fourth of nine candidates.

Odumegwu Ojukwu, Chukwuemeka (Nigeria)

Introduction

Chukwuemeka Odumegwu Ojukwu was military governor of Nigeria's Eastern Region and head of the state of Biafra from 1967–70.

Early Life

Born on 4 Nov. 1933, Ojukwu was the son of a wealthy businessman. He graduated from Oxford University in 1955, after school in Lagos. He joined the army in 1957 and was soon promoted to the rank of major. He then served in the Congo under a UN peacekeeping programme.

Career Peak

When the Igbo secessionist movement seized power in 1966, Ojukwu became leader of the Eastern Region. After General Gowon was named Nigeria's president following a counter-coup, Ojukwu managed to retain his position. However, with the Igbos increasingly isolated, he declared independence for the Eastern Region, re-naming it the 'Republic of Biafra' in May 1967. Civil war broke out, ending in defeat for the Biafran government and Ojukwu's exile to the Ivory Coast.

Later Life

Returning to Nigeria in 1982 he joined the National Party of Nigeria (NPN) in Jan. 1983. His attempts to re-enter politics as a presidential candidate failed when the elections of 1983 ended in violence. Ojukwu died in the United Kingdom on 26 Nov. 2011.

Olmert, Ehud (Israel)

Introduction

Ehud Olmert was thrust into the political limelight in Jan. 2006 when the prime minister, Ariel Sharon, suffered a severe stroke. Olmert, a lawyer and close aide to Sharon, was appointed acting prime minister and led the newly established Kadima party to a narrow victory in the Knesset elections of March 2006. He officially replaced Sharon as prime minister in April 2006. Following a leadership challenge in July 2008, Olmert announced he would resign as soon as a new government could be formed. Binyamin Netanyahu eventually achieved this and Olmert stood down on 31 March 2009.

Early Life

Ehud Olmert was born on 30 Sept. 1945 near Binyamina in the British Mandate of Palestine. His parents were Zionists who joined the right-wing Herut Party after Israel's independence in 1948. A member of the Betar Youth Organisation, Ehud Olmert studied philosophy, psychology and law at the Hebrew University of Jerusalem and later served in the Israeli Defense Forces (IDF) as a combat infantry unit officer and a military correspondent.

In 1973 Olmert was elected to the Knesset as a member of Gahal, the parliamentary bloc of Herut and the Liberals led by Menachem Begin, which later became the Likud bloc in opposition to the governing Labour Alignment. Olmert served on the law and justice committee, campaigning against corruption in public life. From 1974 he built a successful legal practice, despite facing allegations of corruption himself in the 1980s.

Begin led Likud to victory in the 1977 elections but Olmert opposed his stance on withdrawal from land captured from Egypt in the Six Day War and voted against the 1978 Camp David Peace Accords. However, he was to become a staunch supporter of the pullout of Israeli settlers from Gaza in 2005. From 1981–88 Olmert was a member of the foreign affairs and security committee. Under Prime Minister Yitzhak Shamir, he served as minister without portfolio (responsible for minority affairs) from 1988–90 and then as minister of health until 1992.

In Nov. 1993 Olmert became mayor of Jerusalem, on a platform of unifying the city. He initiated projects to improve the road and rail infrastructure as well as reforming the education system. However, on resigning in Jan. 2003 to run for the Knesset his critics pointed to the gulf between the level of services in Palestinian East Jerusalem and those in wealthier Jewish areas.

In Jan. 2003 Ariel Sharon, the Likud leader, won a landslide re-election to the premiership, doubling his party's parliamentary representation. Olmert became minister of trade and industry and deputy prime minister. By Dec. 2003 Olmert had abandoned the dream of a Greater Israel including Gaza and the West Bank. Working with Sharon, he formulated plans for Israeli settlers to leave Gaza. After Binyamin Netanyahu resigned in Aug. 2005 in protest at 'disengagement'. Olmert became finance minister. In Nov. 2005 Olmert followed Sharon from Likud to form the Kadima Party ahead of elections in March 2006. On 4 Jan. 2006 Sharon suffered a severe haemorrhagic stroke and Olmert assumed the powers of acting prime minister, holding a cabinet meeting on 5 Jan. to signal the transfer of power.

Career Peak

Olmert was elected acting chairman of Kadima on 16 Jan. 2006. In a speech on 24 Jan. 2006 he backed the creation of a Palestinian State, arguing that Israel would have to relinquish control of parts of the West Bank to maintain its Jewish majority. In elections on 28 March Kadima won most votes, taking 29 of 120 seats, but lacked an outright majority with turnout at a record low. With Sharon declared 'permanently incapacitated'. Olmert took over as prime minister outright on 14 April 2006 and formed a four-party coalition cabinet which took office on 4 May 2006.

Olmert declared that he would attempt to settle the final borders of Israel in an agreement with the Palestinians. However, analysts saw little hope of progress towards a negotiated two-state solution, given that the Palestinians' Hamas government continued to reject Israel's right to exist. Selling Kadima's plans to potential coalition partners, none of whom stood for unilateral withdrawals before the election, also posed a serious challenge to Olmert's tenure. The first major test of his leadership erupted in July 2006 as an attack by Hizbollah, a Lebanese Shia militia, on Israeli forces on the Israel-Lebanon border led to full-scale hostilities between the Israeli military and Hizbollah guerrillas, resulting in many civilian casualties and a Lebanese refugee crisis. Following a month of conflict, a ceasefire came into effect in Aug. with United Nations backing. However, the Israeli military offensive had proved inconclusive, prompting ongoing criticism of Olmert's handling of the war and, in Jan. 2007, the resignation of the head of the Israeli armed forces. In other political setbacks, he had to accept the ministerial inclusion of a member of the right-wing Yisrael Beytenu party in Oct. 2006 to shore up his government's parliamentary position, and in unguarded public comments in Dec. he seemingly confirmed his country's nuclear weapon capability.

In the course of 2007 Olmert sought to forge closer contacts with Palestinian president Mahmoud Abbas, particularly in the wake of the confrontation between the latter's Fatah party and the Islamist Hamas faction in the Gaza Strip. This culminated in a US-hosted conference at Annapolis, Maryland, in late Nov. to relaunch Israeli-Palestinian peace negotiations, which was attended by Olmert and Abbas as well as representatives of the Egyptian, Jordanian, Saudi Arabian and Syrian governments.

In Oct. 2007 Olmert disclosed that he had been diagnosed with prostate cancer but that he could continue in office as premier. In July 2008 Olmert announced that he would not stand for re-election as head of Kadima after he faced a leadership challenge from Tzipi Livni and promised to step down as prime minister as soon as a new government was formed. Livni won the subsequent leadership contest but was unsuccessful in uniting the parties needed for a coalition. Instead elections were held in Feb. 2009 in which Kadima narrowly defeated Likud. Nevertheless President Shimon Peres appointed Binyamin Netanyahu of Likud prime minister. He took office on 31 March.

Later Life

In Aug. 2009, Olmert faced charges of fraud, breach of trust, tax evasion and falsification of corporate documents. He was subsequently convicted of bribery and breach of trust and sentenced to 6 years imprisonment to begin in Sept. 2014. However, the Supreme Court ruled that Olmert could stay out of jail pending appeal. In May 2015 a court in Jerusalem found him guilty of fraud and breach of trust and he was again sentenced to a jail term, this time for 8 months. Olmert began a 19-month jail sentence in Feb. 2016 relating to the original bribery charges levelled against him in 2009.

Ona Ondo, Daniel (Gabon)

Introduction

Daniel Ona Ondo was appointed prime minister by President Ali-Ben Bongo Ondimba in Jan. 2014, replacing Raymond Ndong Sima.

Early Life

Ona Ondo was born on 10 July 1945 in Oyem in Woleu-Ntem province. He attended the Lycée National Léon Mba in Libreville before enrolling at the Université de Picardie, France. In 1980 he graduated with a doctorate in economics from the Université Paris 1 Panthéon-Sorbonne and joined the faculty of law and economics at the Université Omar Bongo in Libreville. In 1990 he became rector of the university and was made a trade and industry adviser to then President Omar Bongo.

In Dec. 1996 Ona Ondo won a seat in the National Assembly and the following year was appointed minister delegate to the minister of health. From 1999–2002 he served as minister of arts and culture before taking over the education portfolio. He was re-elected to the Assembly in May 2002 as a Gabonese Democratic Party (PDG) member representing Woleu Department. In 2005 he became minister of posts and telecommunications and, following further re-election in Dec. 2006, was appointed first vice-president of the Assembly. On 27 Jan. 2014 he was sworn in as prime minister.

Career Peak

Ona Ondo's main task was to implement the Strategic Plan for Emerging Gabon, an initiative designed to position Gabon as an emerging economy by 2025. Challenges also included the inadequate education and healthcare systems, as well as addressing high levels of youth unemployment and a significant wealth gap between the urban elite and rural poor.

In Sept. 2016 Ona Ondo was replaced as prime minister by Emmanuel Issoze-Ngondet following the presidential election held in Aug.

Oresharski, Plamen (Bulgaria)

Introduction

Plamen Oresharski took office in May 2013. A former faculty dean of Sofia's University of National and World Economy (UNWE), he has been a member of the National Assembly since 2009 and was minister of finance from 2005–09.

Early Life

Oresharski was born in Feb. 1960 in Dupnitsa, Bulgaria. He graduated from UNWE, Sofia in 1985 and obtained a doctorate in investment and investment analysis in 1992. He subsequently undertook further studies in banking, capital markets and sovereign debt in the USA and the UK.

From 1992–93 Oresharski was vice-dean of UNWE's finance department and in 1993 became director of the state treasury and debt division of the ministry of finance. He served on the governing council of the Bulgarian Stock Exchange (1995–97), on the board of UniCredit Bulbank (1997–2000) and in 1997 was appointed deputy minister of finance in Prime Minister Ivan Kostov's Union of Democratic Forces administration. He returned to UNWE as dean of the finance and accounting faculty and deputy rector between 2003 and 2005.

In 2005 Oresharski became finance minister in the government of Sergey Stanishev of the Bulgarian Socialist Party (BSP), introducing a 10% flat tax rate. A parliamentary deputy on a BSP ticket from 2009, he was confirmed as the new prime minister of a Socialist-led technocrat government following elections in May 2013.

Career Peak

The formation of the Oresharski administration followed the early resignation of Boyko Borisov's GERB government in response to widespread protests over energy price hikes and the failing economy. On taking office Oresharski said that 'Bulgaria is in a deep institutional crisis, continuing economic depression and worsening disintegration of society'. He pledged to maintain close co-operation with the EU, boost growth, restore fiscal stability, review energy prices, increase social benefits and speed payments to business.

His government faced a series of popular protests from the outset, with opponents claiming that it had inappropriate ties to business figures, and Oresharski has since striven to remove the taint of corruption. He has also attempted to directly influence energy prices. In Jan. 2014 he ratified a contract with the European Bank for Reconstruction and Development for an electronic public procurement system.

Oresharski and his government resigned on 23 July 2014. The outgoing administration had suffered widespread opposition throughout its 16-month tenure, in particular with regard to its financial reforms and perceived failure in dealing with deadly floods that hit Bulgaria in June 2014. A caretaker government led by Georgi Bliznashki took office on 6 Aug. 2014.

Orešković, Tihomir (Croatia)

Introduction

Tihomir Orešković, who holds dual Croatian and Canadian citizenship, became prime minister in Jan. 2016. A relative political novice, his appointment followed close national elections in Nov. 2015 and his surprise nomination by a conservative coalition. He was Croatia's first non-partisan premier.

Early Life

Tihomir (Tim) Orešković was born in Zagreb on 1 Jan. 1966. His family moved to Hamilton, Canada when he was a child and he graduated in chemistry from McMaster University in 1989. In 1991 he earned his master's degree in finance and information systems from the same institution.

In 1992 he joined the US pharmaceutical company Eli Lilly, where he held various finance roles before becoming an associate vice-president overseeing relations with the government of Ottawa in Toronto. In 2005 he left the company to take up a post with generic drugs manufacturer Teva Novopharm, relocating to Zagreb in 2009 to serve as the firm's chief financial officer for Eastern Europe and Africa. In 2014 he moved with the company again, this time to Amsterdam in the Netherlands.

At the Croatian elections of Nov. 2015, support was split almost equally between the Croatian Democratic Union (HDZ)-led coalition and the Social Democratic Party of Croatia (SDP)-led coalition of outgoing premier Zoran Milanović. After 76 days of political manoeuvring, Tomislav Karamarko's

HDZ and Most, a smaller conservative party led by Bozo Petrov, nominated Orešković as its prime ministerial candidate and secured sufficient backing to form a government.

Career Peak

Orešković's key aim was to revive the economy, 2015 having recorded the first growth since 2009. Other principal targets included cutting public debt to below 80% of GDP by 2020, trimming the budget deficit to within the European Union's 3% of GDP ceiling (from around 5%) and reducing unemployment. The new government also promised to invest in energy and infrastructure while reducing business red tape. It also had to confront the challenges posed by Europe's migrant and refugee crisis.

In June 2016 Orešković lost a parliamentary vote of no confidence by 125 votes to 15. He was subsequently replaced as prime minister by Andrej Plenković of the HDZ in Oct.

Otunbayeva, Roza (Kyrgyzstan)

Introduction

Roza Otunbayeva became the head of an interim government established on 8 April 2010 following anti-government protests that forced incumbent president, Kurmanbek Bakiyev, to flee the capital. A former ally of the ousted president, Otunbayeva was a veteran opposition politician who had served as foreign minister and ambassador to the UK and the USA. She was confirmed as president on 19 May and sworn in on 3 July.

Early Life

Otunbayeva was born on 23 Aug. 1950 in Osh, in the south of what was then the Kyrgyz Soviet Socialist Republic. Graduating from the faculty of philosophy at Moscow State University in 1972, she completed a postgraduate course at the same institution 3 years later, then went on to spend 6 years as head of the philosophy department of the Kyrgyz State National University.

Otunbayeva entered politics in 1981 as second secretary of the Lenin Regional Council of Frunze (now Bishkek). She later served as vice-chairman of the Republic's council of ministers and in 1992 became the recently independent Kyrgyzstan's first ambassador to the USA and Canada. After 2 years she was appointed the country's first and thus far only female foreign minister, before requesting a posting to the UK in 1997 to become Kyrgyzstan's first post-Soviet ambassador in London.

Between 2002 and 2004 Otunbayeva was the deputy special representative of the UN secretary-general on the Georgian-Abkhazian settlement. She was present during the 'Rose Revolution' of 2003 that deposed President Eduard Shevardnadze. In Dec. 2004, on returning from Georgia, Otunbayeva founded an opposition movement, Ata-Szhurt (Fatherland), to contest forthcoming parliamentary elections. In Jan. 2005 her candidate registration was rejected on the grounds that she had not been resident in Kyrgyzstan for all of the preceding 5 years.

Otunbayeva was one of the senior opposition figures during the 'Tulip Revolution' of March 2005. In the aftermath of President Askar Akayev's deposition, she was named acting foreign minister under the interim administration of Kurmanbek Bakiyev. However, when Bakiyev became president Otunbayeva failed to secure parliamentary backing to win the post on a permanent basis. In Dec. 2007 she was elected to the Kyrgyz parliament as a representative of the Social Democratic Party and became party leader in Oct. 2009.

On 8 April 2010, after violent protests had driven the incumbent president from Bishkek, the Kyrgyz opposition elected Otunbayeva to head an interim 'government of people's trust'.

Career Peak

On coming to power Otunbayeva announced that her temporary government would put together a new constitution to establish a parliamentary democracy. She promised that elections would be held within 6 months but in May 2010, amidst continuing political unrest, it was announced that elections would be postponed until 2011. Having acted as interim leader, she was officially sworn in as president in July.

Simmering ethnic conflict erupted in June 2010 into violent clashes between the Kyrgyz and minority Uzbek communities, which left up to 2,000 people dead and hundreds of thousands displaced. The new government nevertheless went ahead with a constitutional referendum in which voters endorsed devolving power from the presidency to parliament. Parliamentary elections were held in Oct. 2010 but produced no outright winner. Otunbayeva's Ata-Zhurt emerged as the largest party but still with only 28 of the 120 seats.

Ineligible to run in the presidential elections on Oct. 2011, Otunbayeva was succeeded by the former prime minister Almazbek Atambayev on 1 Dec. 2011.

Ould Taya, Maaouya (Mauritania)

Introduction

Maaouya Ould Sid'Ahmed Taya ruled the Islamic Republic of Mauritania from 1984 until he was deposed in Aug. 2005. He came to power as head of a military junta and from 1992 he was the elected president of a civilian government. With Ould Taya out of the country in Aug. 2005, Col. Ely Ould Mohamed Vall seized power but has failed to gain international recognition.

Early Life

Born in Atâr in 1941, Ould Taya was a pupil at the city's Franco-Arabic Coranic School from 1949–55, and attended secondary school in Rosso, southern Mauritania. Graduating with officer status from military school in France, he continued his military training until 1975. Returning to Mauritania, he served as head of the defence ministry in 1978 and chief of police in 1980, before heading the army in 1981. Ould Taya rose to power in a military coup in 1984.

Career Peak

Ethnic tension and a reduction in foreign development and defence aid led to violence. Under increasing pressure, Ould Taya promulgated a new constitution in July 1991. A civilian government replaced the ruling military junta, and Ould Taya won elections in 1992 and 1997.

While Ould Tata claimed Mauritania was now a multi-party democracy, critics and opponents questioned the legitimacy of both these elections. Human rights groups frequently criticized Ould Taya's regime. However, an attempted coup in June 2003 received little popular support. In what was the first serious challenge to his leadership, rebels opposed to Ould Taya's ties with Israel and the West attempted to seize power but were crushed by loyalist forces. A second coup was quelled in Aug. 2004.

Ould Taya has overseen a period of economic regeneration, with official figures suggesting that inflation has fallen by half. The UN Development Programme estimates a reduction from 56% to 46% of the population living below the poverty line during the period 1990–2000. The African Development Bank reported economic growth of 4% per year for Mauritania over the same period. However, drought (particularly in agricultural regions) and widespread poverty remain a blight and the government has fallen under increasing pressure from foreign creditors demanding reassurances that funds are being used for development and social services.

In Aug. 2005, while Ould Taya was attending the funeral of King Fahd of Saudi Arabia, troops took control of several government buildings. Led by Ely Ould Mohamed Vall, who had been regarded as an Ould Taya ally, a group of officers announced that Ould Taya had been removed from power and been replaced by a 'military council for justice and democracy'. Ould Vall's administration was initially condemned as illegitimate by the African Union, EU, UN, South Africa and the USA. Ould Vall has promised to oversee new elections after 2 years.

Ould Taya left the country firstly for Niger before moving on to Gambia and Qatar.

Özal, Turgut (Turkey)

Introduction

Turgut Özal dominated Turkish politics for over a decade, first as prime minister (1983–9) and then as president from 1989 until his death in 1993. His tenure in office witnessed the increased liberalization of trade and a foreign policy programme that sought to strengthen Turkey's ties with the west.

Early Life

Özal was born in Malatya in the south of the country on 13 Oct. 1927. He was educated at İstanbul Technical University where he studied electrical engineering, and in the USA, where he read economics for a year. In İstanbul he made friends Süleyman Demirel, a relationship that was to gain him political influence when Demirel became prime minister. Özal played a prominent role in his country's electrification programme, overseeing the construction of power stations, and serving as a technical consultant to the ministry of defence. In 1967 he was appointed an under-secretary to the State Planning Organization (SPO).

Career Peak

In 1971 when Demirel was overthrown by a military *coup d'état*, Özal went to the USA to work as an economist for the World Bank. Demirel was restored to power in 1975, and Özal resumed his role as a government advisor. In 1980, after a second coup ousted Demirel, Özal was made deputy prime minister. He embarked on a programme of economic reforms, but resigned in 1983 in the wake of a financial scandal. In the same year he founded the right-wing Motherland Party (ANAP) which won a comfortable majority in the 1983 general election. Once in power, he continued to pursue free-market economics, increased Turkey's commitment to NATO, and made an unsuccessful effort to join the European Community. He was re-elected in 1987, but grew less popular towards the end of his second term as inflation and unemployment soared. He was elected president by parliament in 1989. Özal supported the rights of the Kurdish minority within Turkey, and in 1990 he played an important role in opposing the Iraqi invasion of Kuwait. He died of a heart attack in 1993 while still in office.

Pacheco de la Espriella, Abel (Costa Rica)

Introduction

Abel Pacheco was sworn in as president of Costa Rica in May 2002, heading the conservative Social Christian Unity Party (PUSC; Partido de Unidad Social Cristiana) in its second governing term. A supporter of free market reforms, he pledged to reduce poverty and corruption, and to control public finances and indebtedness. His term ended in May 2006.

Early Life

Abel Pacheco was born in San José on 22 Dec. 1933. Brought up in the province of Limón, he trained as a doctor in Mexico, becoming a hospital director. He moved into television, producing documentaries, and in the mid-1980s became a businessman. Married twice, he has six children.

Pacheco was a parliamentary deputy for the San José Province between 1998 and 2002, before standing successfully for the presidency.

Career Peak

Pacheco promised to form an inclusive government, consisting of the 'best men and women regardless of their party political leanings'. His term in office was relatively uneventful, although he had to contend with a faltering economy, hit by declining coffee prices, and with labour unrest which prompted some ministerial resignations in 2003 and 2004. Corruption scandals involving senior political and public figures continued to taint the government and Pacheco's privatization and tax reform plans met with strong opposition. Nevertheless, Costa Rica has maintained a higher standard of living and greater social cohesion than many of its neighbours.

Pacheco did not stand in the 2006 presidential election. His term ended on 8 May 2006.

Paisley, Ian (Northern Ireland, United Kingdom)

Introduction

A leading opponent of a united Ireland, Dr Ian Paisley had been one of the leading Unionist figures in Northern Ireland for over 50 years before he became the Northern Irish assembly's first minister in May 2007, with Sinn Féin's Martin McGuinness as his deputy. Renowned for his firm stance against co-operating with Sinn Féin, such a partnership was thought highly improbable until shortly before the appointments. However, during his brief time in office Paisley developed a working and apparently amicable relationship with his deputy that surprised many who had traced his political career.

Early Life

Ian Richard Kyle Paisley was born on 6 April 1926 in Armagh, Northern Ireland to an Independent Baptist pastor father and a Scottish evangelical mother. He attended the Model School in Ballymena, County Antrim before working on a farm in County Tyrone. He later studied at the theological Barry School of Evangelism (Wales) and at the Reformed Presbyterian Theological Hall in Belfast. He was awarded an Honorary Doctorate from the Bob Jones University (South Carolina) in 1966.

Paisley was ordained in 1946. In the early 1950s he was refused permission to use a Presbyterian church in County Down as a gospel mission, prompting him to co-establish the Free Presbyterian Church of Ulster, based at Crossgar, County Down. He was appointed the church's second moderator, a position he has retained. Avowedly anti-Catholic and anti-republican, he campaigned with the Ulster Protestant Action throughout the 1950s and '60s to secure the safety and rights of Belfast's protestant unionist community. He was a major figure in protests against Northern Irish prime minister Terrence O'Neill's attempts to improve relations with the Irish Republic in the 1960s. Paisley's demand that a Republic tricolour flag be removed from the Belfast base of Sinn Féin in 1964 led to widespread rioting. Five years later he served a prison sentence for organizing an illegal demonstration against a Northern Ireland Civil Rights Association march.

In 1971 Paisley co-founded the DUP with Desmond Boal, a year after Paisley had been elected as the MP for North Antrim. In 1973 he was a vocal opponent of the Sunningdale Agreement to set up a Northern Irish power-sharing executive and a cross border Council of Ireland. Paisley was instrumental in a crippling strike by the Ulster Workers Council which saw the agreement collapse. In 1979 he became one of Northern Ireland's three MEPs and thus concurrently sat as an MP at Westminster, an MEP and as a member of the Northern Ireland legislative assembly (MLA).

In 1985 Paisley was at the forefront of opposition to the Anglo-Irish agreement, which allowed Dublin an advisory role in Northern Ireland's governance. He and his fellow Unionist MPs (both Ulster Unionists and DUP members) resigned their seats in protest and all but one were re-elected in a show of support. After an initial role in talks towards the 1998 Good Friday Agreement, Paisley withdrew his party when Sinn Féin was allowed to participate following the IRA's declaration of a ceasefire. The Agreement provided for a power-sharing Northern Irish Assembly and a North-South Ministerial Council to deal with cross-border issues. Under its terms the constitutional future of Northern Ireland was to be determined by majority vote of its citizens, the Republic would give up its *de jure* claim to the whole island and paramilitary weapons would be decommissioned. Despite the DUP opposition, when referenda were held the Agreement won 70% support in Northern Ireland and 90% in the Republic.

The DUP contested the subsequent Assembly elections, claiming two seats on the executive while refusing to attend executive meetings. Tensions over decommissioning and allegations of an IRA spy-ring led to the suspension of the Assembly in Oct. 2002. Campaigning for a renegotiated treaty, the DUP performed well in elections in 2003, emerging as the leading party. When the DUP took nine Westminster seats at the general election of 2005 (as against one for the Ulster Unionists led by David Trimble), Paisley and the DUP were unarguably the dominant unionist force in Northern Irish politics.

With the IRA's decommissioning programme completed by Sept. 2005, the UK government moved towards the re-establishment of the Assembly as the alternative to direct rule from London. Paisley maintained his antipathy towards Sinn Féin, announcing in July 2006 that 'IRA/Sinn Féin' would only serve in a power-sharing government 'over our dead bodies'. However, there were signs of a thaw, epitomised by his meeting with Ireland's Catholic Primate in Oct. 2006 (despite having previously described the pope as the 'whore of Babylon'). Later in the month Paisley gave assurances in the St Andrew's Agreement that he would support a joint executive if the republicans 'complete the transition to democracy and the rule of law'. When Sinn Féin agreed to accept the powers of the Police Service of Northern Ireland, the future of the Assembly was secured.

The UK government set a deadline of 26 March 2007 for its re-establishment. Paisley met Gerry Adams of Sinn Féin and the two sides agreed to re-establish the Assembly on 8 May.

Career Peak

On that day power was devolved from London. Paisley, as leader of Northern Ireland's largest party in the 2007 elections to the Northern Irish assembly, was formally elected first minister, with Martin McGuinness of Sinn Féin as his deputy. During his time in office Paisley developed an amicable relationship with his previously sworn enemy, at least in public, that did much to improve relations between Northern Ireland's religious factions. His retirement as first minister in May 2008 was attributed by some commentators to pressure from those in his own party who wanted a tougher stance against Sinn Féin and Irish republicanism. Paisley's conciliatory attitude in office led to speculation that, had he been more flexible earlier in his political career, he might have contributed more to the stability of Northern Ireland. Instead he acquired an enduring reputation as a 'no' man, a blocker of reform and an opponent of measures likely to bring an earlier peace to the province.

Later Life

Following his retirement Paisley continued to hold the North Antrim seat he had retained since his election in 1970 but in March 2010 he announced that he would not contest the next general election. His son Ian Paisley Jr, also of the DUP, won the North Antrim constituency. In May 2010 Paisley was made a life peer in the House of Lords.

Ian Paisley died aged 88 on 12 Sept. 2014. A private funeral service took place at his home in Belfast, with assembly business suspended as a mark of respect to the late former DUP leader.

Palacio, Alfredo (Ecuador)

Introduction

Dr Alfredo Palacio, a cardiologist with little ministerial experience, was elected by the national congress to be the country's president on 20 April 2005. His appointment came amid a week of mass protests that resulted in the sacking of Lucio Gutiérrez as president. Palacio was faced with the task of introducing economic reforms, fighting poverty and quelling unrest in the oil-producing east of the country. He left office in Jan. 2007 when his term of office ended and was replaced by Rafael Correa, who had won the presidential elections of Nov. 2006.

Early Life

Luis Alfredo Palacio González was born on 22 Jan. 1939 in the port-city of Guayaquil. He attended the Abdón Calderón primary school and the Colegio San José La Salle, before graduating in medicine from the Guayaquil University in 1967. He moved to Cleveland, Ohio in June 1969 to work as an intern specializing in cardiology at the city's Mount Sinai hospital. Two years later he relocated to Missouri, first working at the state's Veteran's

Administration hospital and, from July 1972, at Barnes Hospital, Washington University in St Louis. Returning to Ecuador in 1979, Palacio practised at the National Institute of Cardiology. He maintained an academic career, lecturing in cardiology and public health at Guayaquil University's faculty of medicine and publishing numerous papers and books. By 1989 he was the faculty's principal professor in cardiology.

Although not a member of a political party, Palacio became minister for public health in 1994, in the government of the moderate-conservative Sixto Durán-Ballén, who had won the presidential election of July 1992. Durán's government ushered in a new economic programme, which included cutting state subsidies, joining the World Trade Organization and encouraging foreign investment. However, interest rates remained high and a resumption of the border war with Peru in early 1995 left the country with a crippling debt. When Durán was ousted in the presidential election of July 1996, Palacio left the political stage to continue his academic work and cardiology practice. The late 1990s saw an economic downturn and increasing political instability, which culminated in a bloodless military coup in Jan. 2000, led by Lucio Gutiérrez (although Gustavo Noboa became the president). Dollarization of the currency and an IMF structural-adjustment programme followed, as did widespread emigration. Palacio re-entered the political scene in late 2002, as the running mate for Gutiérrez in the Nov. presidential elections. They campaigned on a left-wing, populist platform, promising to tackle poverty, social problems and corruption. When Gutiérrez won the run-off, Palacio took up the post of vice-president.

Gutiérrez attempted to reduce Ecuador's debt by cutting subsidies on food and cooking gas, leading to widespread resentment. The president's popularity plunged and, though he survived an attempt to impeach him in Nov. 2004, he lost further support when he was accused of intervening in the affairs of the Supreme Court. By mid-April 2005 the country was gripped by mass protest. When the presidential palace in the capital, Quito, was engulfed by over 100,000 protestors on 20 April 2005, congress sacked Gutiérrez and named Alfredo Palacio as the new president.

Career Peak

Palacio was critical of Gutiérrez during the final months of his presidency, and Palacio's lack of an affinity with a political party was seen by many in congress as a strength, although analysts observed that many of the ministers he chose hailed from the Izquierda Democratia (Democratic Left). Palacio promised to fight poverty and implement reform programmes, including amendments to the country's 1998 constitution. Unrest continued, however, particularly in the oil-producing areas in the east of the country. Protesters sabotaged drilling equipment and blocked roads, demanding that foreign oil companies provide money and jobs for local people. In Aug. 2005 Palacio declared a state of emergency in the provinces of Sucumbíos and Orellana and granted some concessions to protesters.

Palacio was a candidate for the post of director general of the WHO following the death of Dr. Lee Jong-wook in 2006. However, Palacio removed himself from the running in order to concentrate on his presidency until his term ended in Jan. 2007. After two rounds of voting in the presidential elections of Nov. 2006, in which Palacio did not stand, Rafael Correa emerged victorious and succeeded Palacio.

Palme, Olof (Sweden)

Introduction

Olof Palme was leader of the Swedish Social Democratic Party from 1969–86 and was Prime Minister from 1969–76 and 1982–86. An advocate of social equality and an active government role in social welfare, he was also an opponent of colonialism and nuclear arms. His outspoken attacks on USA involvement in the Vietnam war left relations between Sweden and the US strained. He was murdered in 1986 by an unknown assailant.

Early Life

Sven Olof Joachim Palme was born on 30 Jan. 1927 in Stockholm into a wealthy family. His father died when he was 6 years old and Olof suffered with ill health for much of his childhood. He matriculated from school at the unusually early age of 17, undertook national service and then enrolled at the University of Stockholm. He graduated in political science in 1948, having spent a year at Kenyon College, Ohio, USA, and then studied law, completing his degree in 1951. He joined the Social Democratic Party and served as Chairman of the National Union of Students, then spent a period travelling and working on the Defence Staff.

He was appointed Personal Secretary to Prime Minister Tage Erlander in 1953. Two years later he was also Director of Studies for the Social Democratic Youth League, a position he held for 6 years. In 1956 he married Lisbet Beck-Friis. Palme entered parliament in 1958 as the member for the county of Jönköping. After a spell during the early 1960s with the Swedish Agency for International Assistance he entered the cabinet as Minister without Portfolio in 1963, while remaining an advisor to Erlander. Two years later Palme was moved to the Ministry of Transport and Communications, where he oversaw the conversion to driving on the right. In 1967 he transferred to the Ministry of Education and Cultural Affairs. His special interest was higher education. He opened up admission processes and advocated more adult and vocational education.

From 1965 onwards, Palme was making public criticisms of US involvement in Vietnam. In 1968 he was photographed alongside a North Vietnamese ambassador on a protest march in the Swedish capital and, while Swedish public opinion was largely behind him, it caused considerable friction with America.

Career Peak

When Erlander resigned from frontline political life in Oct. 1969, Palme was elected as party leader and took office as Prime Minister on 14 Oct. He continued his attacks on American activity in Vietnam, likening the bombing of Hanoi in 1972 to actions of fascist and communist regimes. He provoked further US indignation by accepting military deserters into Sweden.

In 1971 Palme was key to the rejection of a Swedish bid for European Community membership, arguing that it went against the national policy of neutrality that forbade peacetime alliances. He also advocated increased trade union influence in Sweden and proposed a controversial wage-earner funds scheme in which employees had majority control. In addition, he spoke out against the nuclear arms race and the system of apartheid in South Africa, and in support of Cuba's Fidel Castro and of the Palestinian Liberation Organization. Palme was returned with diminishing support at the elections of 1970 and 1973. In 1976 the Social Democrats were removed from power for the first time in 44 years, to be replaced by a non-socialist coalition.

While in opposition he served on the Brandt Commission, which dealt with world economy issues, and then headed the Independent Commission on Disarmament and Security Issues. He also had a term as President of the Nordic Council and was used as a special envoy during the Iran–Iraq war by the UN. By 1982 the non-socialist coalition, struggling with the economy, was near collapse and Palme was re-elected Prime Minister. He began to re-assert socialist economic principle as the economy started to recover, and continued to express his views on European security issues. During this time he also spoke out against international 'neo-liberal' economic policies which he saw as responsible for widening the gap between the rich and poor.

On the night of 28 Feb. 1986 Palme was walking home from a cinema in Stockholm with his wife when he was gunned down. A man was convicted of his murder in 1989 but subsequently freed on appeal. Conspiracy theories have abounded since his death but there is still no satisfactory explanation for the events of that night. Palme achieved a higher international profile than any other Swedish politician of the twentieth century.

Papademos, Lucas (Greece)

Introduction

Lucas Papademos became prime minister in Nov. 2011 following the resignation of George Papandreou over his handling of the EU bailout. A career economist, Papademos took office at the head of an interim coalition committed to implementing austerity measures. After heading a 5-month debt rescue, Papademos submitted his resignation after the parliamentary election of May 2012 failed to produce a working government.

Early Life

Born on 11 Oct. 1947 in Athens, Lucas Papademos was educated at Athens College before obtaining a degree in physics from the Massachusetts Institute of Technology in 1970. He went on to earn a master's degree in electrical engineering in 1972 and a PhD in economics in 1978. He taught economics at Columbia University from 1975–84 and served as a senior economist at the Federal Reserve Bank of Boston in 1980.

Having returned to Greece, he served as chief economist at the Bank of Greece from 1985–93, also teaching economics at the University of Athens from 1988–93. In 1993 he was appointed deputy governor of the Bank of Greece, taking over as governor the following year. During his tenure, which lasted until 2002, he strongly advocated Greece's adoption of the single European currency and used a mix of monetary policies (including devaluation of the drachma and the maintenance of high interest rates) to facilitate Greece's entry into the eurozone in 2001. From 2002–10 Papademos was vice-president of the European Central Bank, a post he left to become adviser to Prime Minister Papandreou.

Having taken office during Greece's worsening sovereign debt crisis, in April 2011 Papandreou entered negotiations with the 'troika' of the EU, IMF and ECB to activate the EU support mechanism for the Greek economy. Amid widespread popular protests at spending cuts, a financial bailout was agreed in Oct. 2011, conditional on further austerity measures. In Nov. 2011 Papandreou proposed to put the plan to a public vote, prompting anger among Greece's EU partners. After intensive negotiations, Papandreou agreed to resign and an interim coalition government under Papademos was formed, incorporating Papandreou's Panhellenic Socialist Movement (Pasok), the conservative New Democracy and the far-right Popular Orthodox Rally (LAOS).

Career Peak

Papademos was sworn in on 11 Nov. 2011, pledging to implement the spending cuts and structural reforms laid out in the terms of the bailout. In early 2012 he oversaw an agreement with Greece's private creditors to write down Greek debt. In Feb. 2012 his government survived the defection of LAOS, which refused to back his austerity measures.

At the general election on 6 May 2012 Antonis Samaras' New Democracy emerged as the largest party in parliament with 108 of 300 seats, but Samaras was unable to establish a workable coalition. Alexis Tsipras of the far-left Syriza group, which came second at the polls, was then given an opportunity to form a government, but his coalition talks also failed. International markets responded nervously and Greece's already perilous economic situation worsened. With negotiations unable to produce a government, further elections were scheduled for 17 June 2012. Papademos stood down after the announcement of the new poll and was replaced by Panagiotis Pikrammenos.

Papadopoulos, Giorgios (Greece)

Introduction

Giorgios Papadopoulos led the infamous "Colonels' Revolt" that seized power in Greece in 1967. He spent most of his life on a patriotic crusade against communism, and in doing so denied his countrymen democratic rule from 1967–73.

Early Life

Papadopoulos was born on 5 May 1919 at Eleochorion in the northern Peloponnese. He was the eldest of a village schoolmaster's sons. Unable to afford sending their son to university, Papadopoulos' parents enrolled him in military academy instead. He graduated as a second lieutenant in the artillery division a few months before the Italian invasion of Oct. 1940. He was decorated three times during the war. His official biography states that he joined the Greek resistance movement that opposed Nazi occupation.

After the liberation of Greece in Nov. 1944 civil war broke out. Papadopoulos became a battery commander in the army, and suppressed several communist guerrilla insurgencies in the mountains. The fighting stopped in 1949, but he remained in the military to receive extensive staff training. He was eventually recruited by the anti-communist Greek Central

Intelligence, and was promoted to colonel in 1960. Papadopoulos first appeared on the political scene in 1964 when he claimed to have uncovered a communist conspiracy in the army. Fearing a coup, the centrist government made a series of illegal arrests in an attempt to quell dissent. It became quickly apparent that their fears were groundless, and Papadopoulos spent 2 years in disgrace before being promoted to deputy chief of operations at Army General Staff. In Dec. 1966 Constantine dismissed Georgios Papandreou from power and installed a caretaker government to prepare for elections the following May. The election was expected to sweep the left wing into power, and Papadopoulos conspired with several senior figures in the military to prevent this by force. They launched a 3 h *Coup d'état*, and Papadopoulos justified the junta's actions by stating, 'If things had been allowed to go on as they were, it is mathematically certain that Greece would have ended up behind the Iron Curtain.'.

Career Peak

The seizure of power led to the arrest of thousands, and the imposition of restrictions on freedom of speech and trade union activity. King Constantine initially co-operated with the junta, but became increasingly convinced that their stentorian measures (which included the banning of long hair for men and mini-skirts for women) were dragging Greece into international disrepute. In Dec. 1967 he broadcast an appeal for assistance in deposing the regime of the Colonels. As a result of this appeal the junta deprived him of his sovereignty. Constantine fled to Rome, and the junta drew up a new constitution proclaiming a Greek republic. Papadopoulos was sworn in as prime minister. Martial law was instigated.

In 1969 Papadopoulos withdrew Greece from the Council of Europe, and by 1972 he had taken on the roles of prime minister, defence minister, foreign minister and self-styled Regent of Greece. However, opposition to his rule had begun to ferment throughout the country. A naval mutiny in 1973 was followed by student riots in Athens protesting against his leadership. In the end it was a right-wing coup, led by Brigadier Dimitris Ioannidis, that ousted Papadopoulos from power. The new regime did not last long, and in July 1974 democracy was finally restored.

Later Life

Papadopoulos was convicted of treason and sentenced to death but the sentence was later commuted to one of life imprisonment. He spent his final 3 years in hospital under armed guard. He died on 27 June 1999.

Papadopoulos, Tassos (Cyprus)

Introduction

Tassos Papadopoulos, Greek Cypriot nationalist leader of the centre-right Democratic Party (DIKO; Dimokratiko Komma), was elected president in Feb. 2003 after defeating incumbent Glafcos Clerides. He is considered more hardline than his predecessor on the issue of Cypriot reunification. In 2004 he oversaw Cyprus' entry into the EU. Papadopoulos was eliminated in the first round of the presidential elections held on 17 Feb. 2008.

Early Life

Papadopoulos was born on 7 Jan. 1934 in Nicosia. He graduated in law from King's College, London, England, and was called to the Bar as a member of Gray's Inn. Between 1955 and 1959 he was an important figure in the EOKA national liberation movement. In 1960 he opposed the Zurich-London agreements which established an independent Cypriot state, but went on to play a prominent role in drafting the constitution. He held several ministerial portfolios including internal affairs (1959–60), labour and social insurance (1960–70), agriculture and natural resources (1964–67) and health (1967–70).

In 1970 he entered parliament as the Eniaion (Unified) Party representative for Nicosia. He was re-elected in 1976 as a non-partisan and acted as the intercommunal negotiator on behalf of President Clerides in talks over Cyprus' future following the establishment of the 'Turkish Republic of Northern Cyprus' ('TRNC') 2 years earlier. In 1991 he was elected to parliament for the Democratic Party (DIKO) and was the party spokesman in parliament until 2001. He also represented Cyprus in several international organizations, including the UN general assembly and the ILO, and helped negotiate the country's passage to EU membership.

In 2000 Papadopoulos was elected chairman of DIKO, and in Feb. 2003 defeated Clerides for the state presidency with 51.5% of the vote in the first round in a high turnout.

Career Peak

Among Papadopoulos' first tasks was to oversee continuing negotiations to reunify the 'TRNC' with the rest of the country, having been critical of the soft negotiating line previously adopted by Clerides. In March 2004 the UN Secretary-General proposed a revised plan for Cypriot reunification based on a federation of two largely autonomous states. A referendum on the plan was held the following month, in which Papadopoulos urged the Greek Cypriot community to vote no, insisting that the provisions for their return to their former homes in the north were not good enough. Although the Turkish Cypriot community endorsed the UN plan, Greek Cypriots rejected it by a large majority. Consequently, Cyprus joined the EU in May 2004 as a partitioned state. Hopes of progress on reunification were rekindled in July 2006 when Papadopoulos and the Turkish Cypriot leader agreed at UN-sponsored talks on a new series of confidence-building measures and contacts between the two communities. In early 2007 both communities demolished parts of the barrier dividing the old city of Nicosia, paving the way for a buffer zone pedestrian crossing point in the capital. Meanwhile, Turkey continued to block Greek Cypriot shipping and air traffic from its territory while the trade embargo on northern Cyprus remained in force.

On 17 Feb. 2008 Papadopoulos was eliminated in the first round in the presidential elections. The new president Dimitris Christofias called for speedy negotiations on the issue of reunification. Christofias made an alliance with the party of the defeated Papadopoulos.

Following a lengthy period of illness, Papadopoulos died from lung cancer on 12 Dec. 2008 aged 74.

Papandreou, Georgios (Greece)

Introduction

Georgios Papandreou assumed office as prime minister on 6 Oct. 2009 after leading his party, the Panhellenic Socialist Movement (Pasok), to victory over the conservative New Democracy party in snap legislative elections. Having previously served as foreign minister from 1999–2004, Papandreou was also president of Socialist International, a worldwide collective of socialist parties. He was the third generation of his family to serve as prime minister of Greece, following his grandfather (also Georgios) and father (Andreas). Papandreou resigned amid financial and political turmoil in Nov. 2011.

Early Life

Papandreou was born in June 1952 in St Paul, Minnesota, USA, where his father held a teaching post. He read sociology at the University of Massachusetts, Amherst, and gained a master's degree in the same subject from the London School of Economics in the UK. He also studied in Stockholm, Sweden, and in 1992 he was made a fellow at Harvard's Centre for International Affairs.

Papandreou returned to Greece after the fall of the military junta in 1974, when his father established the centre-left Pasok. In 1981, the year that his father became prime minister, he was elected MP for Achaia. He served as minister of education and religious affairs and deputy foreign minister before becoming foreign minister in Feb. 1999. During his 5 years in the post Papandreou sought closer relations with Greece's neighbours, particularly Albania and Bulgaria. He was praised for achieving a partial rapprochement with Turkey, resulting in the accession of the Republic of Cyprus to the EU.

He replaced the former prime minister, Kostas Simitis, as leader of Pasok in 2004, before losing a general election in the same year. He held on to the party leadership and in 2009 secured an absolute majority against an incumbent government made unpopular by allegations of corruption.

Career Peak

Papandreou pledged to restore the struggling economy, but the prospects for a speedy recovery were undermined by the acknowledgment that the financial situation was considerably worse than had been reported by the preceding administration. In order to slash the large budget deficit and avoid a default on Greece's sovereign debt, Papandreou imposed a series of wide-ranging and stringent austerity measures in Dec. 2009 and in Jan., March and April 2010. He likened the crisis to a 'wartime situation' prompting a wave of social and labour unrest. In May Greece's partner countries in the eurozone, together with the International Monetary Fund, approved a €110 bn. rescue package, although Germany was initially hostile to the arrangement. Despite public discontent over the economy, voters in Greek local elections in Nov. broadly backed Papandreou's Pasok ahead of the opposition New Democracy. As Greece's sovereign debt crisis in worsened in 2011, support for Papandreou's government waned. Although a fresh eurozone bailout deal had been agreed in Oct., Papandreou announced his government's intentions to hold a referendum on it's terms. The proposal was dropped but sparked a deeper financial and political crisis. Despite narrowly winning a confidence vote on 5 Nov., the prime minister faced continuing pressure to resign amid chaos over the debt crisis. Papandreou agreed to step down as part of a deal to form a national unity government to push through the EU deal. Former European Central Bank vice-president Lucas Papademos was subsequently chosen as Greece's interim prime minister.

Papandreou, Georgios A. (Greece)

Introduction

Georgios Papandreou served three terms as the prime minister of Greece (1944–45, 1946–52 and 1964–65), and his Centre Union government achieved a number of important and far-reaching reforms, most notably the release of all political prisoners.

Early Life

Papandreou was born in Kaléntzi on 13 Feb. 1888. He was educated at the University of Athens and in Germany. The first notable appointment of his political career came when he was made governor of the Aegean islands, a post he held for 3 years. In 1929 he was minister of education in the government of Eleftherios Venizelos. In 1935 he left the Liberal Party to found the Democratic Socialist Party, but was forced into exile by the Metaxas regime.

Career Peak

In 1942 Papandreou was arrested by the Nazis, and was imprisoned until 1944 when he escaped. He led a Greek coalition government in exile until the withdrawal of German forces in Oct. 1944. He remained in power until Jan. 1945. By this time the country was embroiled in a civil war. In 1946 Papandreou returned to ministerial office. In 1952 electoral defeat forced him into opposition, and during this period he was largely responsible for the merger of the Liberal Party with his own Democratic Socialist Party. By 1961 a new centre-left coalition, the Centre Union, had emerged, and 2 years later it secured a slim majority in the general election. Papandreou was made prime minister but resigned from the post in an effort to achieve a more convincing majority. He did so in 1964 and used his support to instigate a programme of social reforms and to remove what he regarded as the pernicious influence of the USA on Greece.

Papandreou's policies aroused the suspicion of the military, and right wing factions opposed to his government began to appear. In an attempt to regain control of the army, Papandreou tried to take on the job of minister of defence, a move that failed to gain the approval of King Constantine. Greece was plunged into constitutional crisis. Papandreou resigned in disgust in 1965. In 1967 Constantine called fresh elections but when it became obvious the Centre Union was heading for another electoral victory, a military junta seized control and brought an end to Papandreou's hopes of further reform. He died on 1 Nov. 1968.

Papoulias, Karolos (Greece)

Introduction

Karolos Papoulias was sworn in as president of Greece on 12 March 2005, having been elected by an unprecedented parliamentary majority of 279 out of the 300 available votes. A founding member of the Panhellenic Socialist Movement (Pasok) and foreign minister throughout the 1980s and 1990s, Papoulias succeeded Kostis Stephanopoulos in this largely ceremonial role and was re-elected in Feb. 2010.

Early Life

Born on 4 June 1929 in the city of Ioannina, Papoulias studied law at the Universities of Athens and of Milan in Italy, followed by a doctorate in private international law at Cologne in Germany.

In 1967, while he was in Cologne and following a coup that saw the right-wing Greek government replaced by a military dictatorship, Papoulias founded the Overseas Socialist Democratic Union, which mobilized exiled Greeks against the regime until 1974. With the fall of the dictatorship and the establishment of the democratic Third Hellenic Republic that year, Papoulias returned to Greece, where, with fellow returnee Andreas Papandreou, he helped to found Pasok. With its principles of 'National Independence, Popular Sovereignty, Social Emancipation and Democratic Process'. Pasok dominated Greek political life throughout the 1980s and 1990s.

At the Nov. 1974 elections Pasok won 13.5% of the vote, coming third behind the Liberal Party and the conservative New Democracy party. By Nov. 1977, however, Pasok had doubled its percentage of the votes and become the official opposition. In the elections of Oct. 1981 Pasok won a resounding 48% of the vote and, with Papoulias' long-time associate Andreas Papandreou as prime minister, formed the first socialist government in the history of Greece. Papoulias served as secretary of Pasok's International Relations Committee from 1975–85, and from 1976–80 he was also a member of the party's Co-ordinating Council. In 1977 he entered parliament for the first time, representing Ioannina as a Pasok member. He was to be re-elected eight times, serving a total of 27 years continuously until 2004. In Oct. 1981 he gave up his law practice to take up a full-time post as deputy foreign minister in the Pasok government. He held his post until 1984, becoming foreign minister from 1985–90, and again from 1993–96.

Under the leadership of Papoulias, Pasok foreign policy in the Balkan states contributed significantly to the stability of at least some parts of this historically volatile area. Inter-Balkan conferences in 1976, 1979 and 1982, initiated by the Greek government, led in 1984 to talks on the denuclearization of the Balkan region. Also, despite the two countries having been officially at war since 1940, Greco-Albanian relations improved dramatically during the mid-1980s and, in 1985, the Greco-Albanian border was reopened for the first time in 45 years, with full normalization of relations in 1987.

Following the death of Andreas Papandreou in June 1996 and a general election in Sept., Papoulias left the cabinet to become the Greek representative at the Organization for Security and Co-operation in Europe (OSCE).

On 12 Dec. 2004 Prime Minister Karamanlis (New Democracy) and leader of the opposition George Papandreou (Pasok) named Papoulias as the only presidential candidate in the Feb. 2005 election. Gaining 279 out of 300 votes Papoulias was elected by a huge majority of MPs representing all the parliamentary parties.

Career Peak

The appointment of Papoulias ended months of speculation that Pasok MPs might withhold the votes required for the endorsement of a new president, forcing early elections just 1 year after the centre-right New Democracy party had come to power. Papoulias, who enjoyed popularity across the political spectrum, spoke of his desire to see a united Cyprus and expressed hope that Turkey's EU membership aspirations would trigger progress on the issue.

Following defeat in a snap general election in Oct. 2009, Prime Minister Karamanlis resigned and Papoulias asked Pasok leader George Papandreou to form a new government. Papoulias was subsequently re-elected for a second presidential term unopposed in Feb. 2010. The Pasok government struggled to address Greece's deteriorating economy and burgeoning sovereign debt crisis, and in Nov. 2011 Papandreou submitted his resignation to Papoulias who subsequently swore in Lucas Papademos, a respected economist and banker, as interim prime minister of a national unity administration. Elections in May 2012 failed to produce a working government but, following a further election a month later, a New Democracy-led coalition was formed under Antonis Samaras.

Papoulias' term as president came to an end in March 2015 when he was succeeded by Prokopis Pavlopoulos of the New Democracy party.

Park Chung-hee (South Korea)

Introduction

Park Chung-hee was the military ruler of South Korea for 16 years. His period in office gave his country stability and economic development but his dictatorship stifled human rights.

Early Life

Park was born into rural poverty on 14 Nov. 1917. He received an elementary education and showed great promise as a pupil. Park became a primary school teacher but left teaching for a military career, joining the army of the Japanese occupiers of Korea. Park's potential was quickly recognized and he was sent to a military academy in Japan. During World War II (1939–45) he served as an officer in the Japanese Imperial Army and joined the infant Korean forces after the Japanese occupation of his country ended in 1945.

Rapid promotion followed. He served with some distinction in the Korean War (1950–53) and became a brigadier-general in 1953. Promotion to general came in 1961. As one of the most senior army officers in the country Park led the military coup in May 1961 and made himself head of the military junta that ruled the country for the next 2 years.

Career Peak

A new constitution restored civilian rule, in theory, in 1963. Park was elected President in the same year and held office until his death on 26 Oct. 1979. In office, Park restricted opposition parties, controlled the media, expanded the secret service and curtailed civil liberties, citing the need to fight Communism as justification. In 1972 he introduced a more authoritarian constitution and declared martial law.

While the country was cowed into acceptance of Park's near-dictatorship, US investment boosted industry and raised living standards. In Oct. 1979 Park threw a popular opposition figure out of parliament. Riots paralyzed Seoul and other major cities. Park refused to give way and was consequently assassinated by a former close colleague, Kim Jae-gyu.

Park Geun-hye (South Korea)

Introduction

Park Geun-hye became the country's first female president on 25 Feb. 2013 at the head of one of the world's most male-dominated governments. She had to contend with the legacy of her late father, Park Chung-hee, a former president both revered as the driving force behind South Korea's economic miracle and condemned for his suppression of opposition.

Early Life

Park Geun-hye was born on 2 Feb. 1952 in Jung-gu, Daegu. She graduated in electronic engineering from Seoul's Sogang University in 1974. She then studied at the University of Grenoble, France, before returning to Seoul following the death of her mother on 15 Aug. 1974 in a botched assassination attempt on Park Chung-hee. Park stepped into the role of first lady until 26 Oct. 1979 when her father was assassinated by his intelligence chief.

Following her father's death, Park retreated from politics and served on the boards of various charities and educational institutions. In 1997 she joined the Grand National Party (GNP) and won a seat in the National Assembly after winning a by-election for Dalseong, Daegu in 1998. In the run-up to the 2004 general election the GNP, beleaguered by scandals, appointed Park as leader. Despite its lacklustre performance at the election, under Park's leadership the GNP recovered in the following years by winning all the by-elections it contested.

In 2006 Park stepped down from the party leadership in a bid to become the GNP candidate at the following year's presidential election. She was narrowly defeated at the party primaries by Lee Myung-bak, who went on to become president. In Dec. 2011 Park was chosen to chair the GNP's emergency committee, overseeing the party's name change to Saenuri (New Frontier) to signal a fresh start in the face of growing voter dissatisfaction. Stepping back from the party in May 2012 to run for the presidency, she won the election on 19 Dec. 2012 with 51.6% of the vote.

Career Peak

Park's centrist agenda aimed to continue economic growth, close the wealth gap, increase spending on social welfare and reduce unemployment, especially among the young. Although she has favoured improved relations with North Korea, her tenure has been marked by military provocations, both conventional and nuclear, and threatening rhetoric by the North. In 2014 and the first half of 2015 North Korea continued to conduct missile tests, including, it was claimed, from a submarine for the first time. Tensions escalated further from Aug. 2015 following an artillery confrontation along the border over the South's propaganda broadcasts across the demilitarized zone. Then in Jan. 2016 the North claimed that it had conducted its fourth nuclear weapon test since 2006, prompting international condemnation and threats of further sanctions.

In April 2014 Park accepted the resignation of Prime Minister Chung Hong-won, who took responsibility for the government's heavily criticized response to the MV *Sewol* ferry disaster that left more than 300 of the 476 people on board (mostly schoolchildren) dead or missing. Chung remained in office until Feb. 2015 when he was replaced by Lee Wan-koo. Two other candidates for the premiership had earlier failed to secure sufficient parliamentary backing. However, following a bribery scandal he too submitted his resignation just 2 months later, which Park also accepted, and was replaced in May by Hwang Kyo-ahn. In the wake of protests in Seoul against the government's economic policy, Park announced a cabinet reshuffle in Dec. and named new finance and interior ministers.

Also in Dec. 2015 Japan agreed to settle a long-standing dispute with the South Korean government over the sexual abuse of Korean women in the Second World War by the Japanese military.

On 9 Dec. 2016 the National Assembly voted to impeach her over corruption allegations. On 10 March 2017 South Korea's Constitutional Court upheld that decision, definitively removing Park from power. During her impeachment trial and before the presidential election scheduled to be held in May 2017, Prime Minister Hwang Kyo-ahn assumed the presidential powers.

Paroubek, Jiří (Czech Republic)

Introduction

The Czech Republic's third prime minister in 9 months, Jiří Paroubek's appointment on 25 April 2005 followed the resignation of his controversial party colleague, Stanislav Gross. Paroubek is an economist who worked for various state-owned industries under communist rule and became a consultant following the sweeping reforms and upheavals of the early 1990s. Although he worked as the deputy mayor of Prague for 6 years, Paroubek had little ministerial experience. He was faced with the task of holding together the fractious centre-left coalition government. He led his party to electoral defeat in 2006.

Early Life

Jiří Paroubek was born in Olomouc, central Czechoslovakia on 21 Aug. 1952. He attended the School of Economics in the capital, Prague, from 1970–76 and in 1970 joined the 'revived National Front' although it had no influence

while the country was ruled by the Communist Party of Czechoslovakia (CPCz). Having graduated in 1976, Paroubek worked as an economist at several state-owned organizations including Prefa Malešice, Obuv Praha (a shoe company) and Jídelny a Restaurace (restaurants and food facilities), where he was head of the planning and financial department.

Following the dramatic 'Velvet Revolution' in Nov. 1989 that culminated in the playwright and former dissident Václav Havel being elected president, Paroubek joined the newly reborn Czech Social Democratic Party (ČSSD). In 1990 he was elected as central secretary of the ČSSD and contributed to establishing its organizational structure and financial base. In the same year he was also elected as a member of the municipal assembly of Prague's city hall. In 1991 Paroubek established EPC, an economic consultancy that advised small businesses. At this time, sweeping reforms to the Czechoslovak economy were leading to serious hardship, particularly in the east of the country. A separatist movement in Slovakia led eventually to a formal split into independent states on 1 Jan. 1993.

Paroubek was elected the deputy mayor of Prague in 1998, the year in which Václav Havel was re-elected president. Miloš Zeman led the ČSSD to its first victory in the ensuing legislative elections, promising to prevent a repeat of the 1997 economic downturn and vowing to slow privatization and restore more control to the state. As deputy mayor, responsible for financial policy, Paroubek organized the funding for the renovation of Prague's Congress Centre and secured loans and bonds to improve the city's infrastructure. However, he was criticized for his decision to have bonds worth €170 m. issued in euros rather than Czech koruny, which allegedly caused heavy losses for the city in interest-rate speculation. He was also accused of selling off the city's stake in the water utility, Praské Vodovody a Kanalizace (PVK), to the French company, Vivendi Water, for less than the market rate. Paroubek countered that the funds from the sale were required to repair buildings and roads that were ruined in the floods of Aug. 2002.

In Aug. 2004 he was appointed minister for regional development in Gross' new ČSSD-led coalition. Despite his reputation for deal-making and his energetic approach, Gross came under fire just 6 months into his term of office when it was revealed that in 1999 he had bought a luxury apartment costing far more than his government salary. Gross' attempts to explain the purchase, combined with controversy over his wife's business dealings, led to his resignation. On 25 April 2005 the president, Václav Klaus, named Paroubek prime minister of the Czech Republic. On 13 May 2005 the government (which remained the coalition of the ČSSD and Koalice) passed a motion of confidence in Paroubek.

Career Peak

Paroubek was generally seen as politically to the left of his predecessor but he did not initiate any major policy changes. A strong advocate for the European Constitution, he accepted that it was 'impossible at present' to continue with plans for a referendum to ratify the constitution in the light of its rejection by voters in France and the Netherlands. Paroubek also pledged to bring in tax cuts for the poor and deregulate state-owned property.

He received criticism in 2005 when opposition figures accused his government of heavy-handedness after a music festival was broken up by 1,000 riot police. He came under further media scrutiny later in the year over the appointment of David Rath as health minister at the same time as he was serving as president of the Czech Medical Chamber. Nonetheless, Paroubek received overwhelming backing from his party to lead them into the elections of June 2006. The ČSSD came second to the Civic Democrats at the polls and Paroubek left office on 16 Aug. 2006.

Parts, Juhan (Estonia)

Introduction

Juhan Parts became the youngest prime minister in Europe when he took office in April 2003. He led Estonia towards European Union accession in 2004. Parts campaigned on a transparency platform and his government was designed to represent a change from the old order.

Early Life

Parts was born on 27 Aug. 1966 in Tallinn. He graduated in 1991 from the University of Tartu with a law degree and became deputy secretary general of the ministry of justice in 1992. In 1998, at the age of 31, he was appointed auditor general by President Lennart Meri. As auditor general he was a prominent critic of the Centre Party-Reform Party coalition, especially concerning state appointments and financial management. In 2002 he entered politics by becoming president of the newly formed Res Publica Party (RESP).

Career Peak

The parliamentary elections held in March 2003 produced no clear winner. As a result of post-election negotiations Parts was invited to form a coalition government with the Reform Party and the People's Union. He rejected on moral grounds any power-sharing agreement with the Centre Party, led by Edgar Savisaar, the former interior minister. Savisaar was forced to resign in 1995 as a result of allegations of covertly recording his political rivals.

In addition to his anti-corruption agenda, Parts pledged to reduce the tax burden and introduce direct presidential elections by 2006. In March 2005 parliament passed a vote of no confidence in Justice Minister Ken-Marti Vaher over his administering of proposed anti-corruption legislation. In response, Parts dissolved his government. His term as prime minister officially ended the following month.

Later Life

In 2007 Parts was appointed minister of economic affairs and communications in the government of Andrus Ansip and held the position until March 2014 when the prime minister resigned. Parts has since remained in public office and was re-elected as a member of parliament at the March 2015 elections.

Parvanov, Georgi (Bulgaria)

Introduction

Georgi Parvanov, leader of the Socialist party, was elected president of Bulgaria in Nov. 2001, defeating his predecessor, Petar Stoyanov. He was sworn into office in Jan. 2002. Re-elected in Oct. 2006, he became the first Bulgarian president to retain office through a democratic mandate, albeit in a very low turnout.

Early Life

Georgi Sedefchov Parvanov was born in Sirishtchnik, Bulgaria on 28 June 1957. He graduated from Mathematics High School in Pernik in 1975 then studied for an MA and a PhD in history at Sofia University St Kliment Ohridski.

Parvanov joined the Bulgarian Communist Party (BCP) in 1981 as a researcher in its institute of history. By 1989 he held the post of senior research associate. In 1990 the BCP changed its name to the Bulgarian Socialist Party (BSP), a year after dethroning their chairman Todor Zhivkov, and in 1991 Parvanov was elected to a party post for the first time. He began a steady climb up the party ladder, becoming deputy chairman in 1994 and in 1996 replacing Zhan Videnov as the elected chairman of the BSP supreme council. He won the post again in 2000.

As an MP from 1994–2001, Parvanov held several posts, including chairman of the parliamentary group for friendship with Greece (1994–97), chairman of the parliamentary group of the Democratic Left (1997–2001) and chairman of the parliamentary group of the Coalition for Bulgaria (1997–2001). In 1999, during NATO's air bombing campaign of Yugoslavia, Parvanov led his parliamentary group in a vote against granting NATO access to Bulgarian air space. However, a year later he announced his party's support for Bulgaria's admission to NATO and the European Union.

Career Peak

Georgi Parvanov became the first former communist to win a presidential election in post-communist Bulgaria. His priorities included stabilizing the country's economy, modernizing the Bulgarian army and fighting crime and corruption. He sought a stronger role for the state in national life and supported closer ties with former allies such as Russia and Ukraine. In Dec. 2001 parliament agreed to the destruction of Soviet-made missiles.

In Nov. 2002 Bulgaria was invited to join NATO and in March 2004 was granted admission. In April 2005 it signed the EU accession treaty and became a full member on 1 Jan. 2007. Parvanov was re-elected as president over two rounds of voting in Oct. 2006. Following parliamentary elections in July 2009, Parvanov asked Boyko Borisov, the leader of the populist centre-right Citizens for the European Development of Bulgaria which emerged as the largest party, to form a new government in place of the outgoing Socialist Party administration.

In Jan. 2012, after two terms in office, Parvanov was succeeded by Rosen Plevneliev, who had won the presidential elections held in Oct. 2011.

Passos Coelho, Pedro (Portugal)

Introduction

Pedro Passos Coelho became prime minister in June 2011 when Portugal was suffering a severe sovereign debt crisis. A centre-right politician, he advocated cutting government expenditure and privatizing many of Portugal's state-owned businesses to improve efficiency and to restore the confidence of international investors.

Early Life

Born in Coimbra on 24 July 1964, Pedro Passos Coelho was educated in Silva Porto, Portugal and Luanda, Angola, where his family lived from 1969–74. He joined the Social Democratic Party (PSD) and served on the national council of its junior wing from 1980–82.

In 1982 he began studying mathematics at Lisbon University but left before graduating to work in private enterprise and to pursue his political career. Leader of the junior PSD from 1990–95, he was elected to parliament in 1991. He served as vice-chairman of the PSD parliamentary group from 1996–99 and, after standing unsuccessfully for mayor of Amadora in 1997, served as a municipal councillor from 1997–2001.

He left parliament in 1999 following the PSD general election defeat and studied economics at Lusíada University, Lisbon, graduating in 2001. After working in consultancy firms, he joined the Fomentinvest investment holding company in 2004 and became finance director. He also served as vice president of the PSD from 2005–06, gaining a business-friendly and pragmatic reputation.

In 2008 he unsuccessfully contested the party leadership, and also established a think tank to develop policies based on economic liberalization and partial privatization. In May 2010 he again contested the leadership and won with 61% of the vote.

As leader of the opposition, Passos Coelho helped vote down the government budget in March 2011, arguing it relied too heavily on tax increases rather than spending cuts. The government collapsed and a caretaker administration then agreed a €78 bn. IMF–EU bailout, with stringent austerity conditions attached.

Passos Coelho campaigned at the June 2011 parliamentary election on a platform of economic reform. The PSD won the most votes and formed a coalition with the centre-right Democratic and Social Centre–People's Party.

Career Peak

In its early months Passos Coelho's government increased taxes, cut state spending and announced a privatization programme. However, after discovering further debt, he announced the transfer of €6 bn. of banks' pension funds to the state in order to reduce the short-term deficit and boost liquidity. To comply with the bailout terms, the government was required to implement labour law reform but its proposals and austerity measures provoked strike action and street protests in 2012. Passos Coelho's government was granted an additional year by the IMF and EU to meet deficit targets. However, in April 2013 the Constitutional Court invalidated certain measures in the 2013 budget and Passos Coelho had to seek other deficit reduction avenues. In July that year his government suffered a political crisis when several senior ministers resigned in the wake of widespread public resistance to further austerity. The reshuffled coalition survived a no confidence motion in parliament but its subsequent deficit reduction policies were again derailed by Constitutional Court rulings during the year. Nevertheless, the government did launch a €3.25 bn. bond sale in Jan. 2014 and in May Portugal exited the international bailout programme, without a precautionary credit line, as the country returned to economic growth.

In Nov. 2014 Miguel Macedo was replaced as interior minister following his resignation over a corruption inquiry.

Passos Coelho was reappointed prime minister on 22 Oct. 2015 following the victory of the centre-right Portugal Ahead alliance at elections held earlier in the month. However, 11 days later his new government lost a parliamentary vote of no-confidence by 123 votes to 107. Passos Coelho subsequently called for snap elections to take place before April 2016 but his government was replaced in Nov. 2015 by a leftist administration led by António Costa of the Socialist Party.

Pastrana Arango, Andrés (Colombia)

Introduction

Andrés Pastrana Arango was president of Colombia between 1998–2002, representing the conservative Partido Social Conservador (PSC). During his presidency he concentrated on resolving the conflict between left-wing guerrillas and right-wing paramilitaries. His efforts were hindered by recession. The continued violence, especially surrounding the 2002 elections, formed a platform for his successor Alvaro Uribe to promote hardline military force.

Early Life

Pastrana was born on 17 Aug. 1954, the son of the former president Misael Pastrana Borrero (1970–74). He read law at the Colegio Mayor de Nuestra Señora del Rosario in Bogotá, later studying at Harvard. In the late 1970s he had a career in journalism, founding the magazine *Guión* in 1978 and the news programme *Noticiero TV hoy* in 1979. Politically active during his student career, Pastrana was later twice elected as town councillor for Bogotá, and became the city's first elected mayor in 1988. In 1990 Pastrana formed his own political party, La Nueva Fuerza Democrática, which supported him in his campaign to be elected to the Senate.

In the 1994 presidential election Pastrana stood against Ernesto Samper losing by 48.64% to 50.37% in one of the closest fought elections in Colombian history. Allegations about Samper's involvement with the Cali drug barons forced Pastrana into exile for 2 years. In 1998 Pastrana stood again for presidency against the Liberal Horacio Serpa and the outsider Noemi Sanin. In the second round, Pastrana won with 50.5% of votes in a record turnout of over 12 m.

Career Peak

On his election, Pastrana pledged to end the conflict between the left-wing guerrillas FARC and ELN, the government and the paramilitaries. Up to then, 30,000 people had died, 1 m. had been displaced. As president-elect, Pastrana met the FARC for secret talks. On 7 Jan. 1999 Pastrana officially met with FARC's leader Manuel Marulanda Veléz in San Vincente del Caguan, becoming the first president to do so. In response to the government initiative, the AUC paramilitaries (Autodefensas Unidas de Colombia; United Self-Defence Forces of Colombia) renewed violence. Despite demilitarizing 40,000 km^2 of the southeastern region of Caquetá in the Amazonia region in Nov. 1998, where the FARC has its stronghold, the group later renewed offensives. In one attack three American human rights workers were assassinated on the Venezuelan border. There were calls for stronger government action. Continued offensives on the guerrillas by right-wing paramilitaries, including the AUC, slowed the peace effort.

On 25 Jan. 1999 Colombia suffered an earthquake which left 2,000 people dead. At the same time, the country slipped into recession. Although inflation was stable at 15%, unemployment rose to 20%. Strikes closed schools and hospitals and Pastrana was forced to concede 15% pay rises. Pastrana faced the challenge of fighting the economy, the guerrillas, the paramilitaries and international hostility.

The year 2000 showed a slight improvement in the economy, although peace was no nearer. An emerging corruption scandal revealed payments of US$3 m. for political favours. Pastrana's popularity slumped. In 1998 Pastrana visited Washington, becoming the first Colombian president to do so in 20 years. FARC's demands were at odds with Pastrana's conservative, free-market government. The left was willing to pull out of the drug trade only in return for wealth distribution and political, military and agrarian reform. Controversial measures supported by the American government, called Plan Colombia, aimed to destroy poppy and coca crops. This was part of a US$1.3 bn. aid package from the USA in military aid to combat the guerrillas, announced in June 2000. But legal harvests were destroyed in the process. On 5 Jan. 2001 a humanitarian accord was signed between the government and FARC allowing for the exchange of sick prisoners. Reacting to internal and international pressure, on 14 Feb. 2001 FARC yielded 62 children between 13 and 16 and promised to let 500 others go free.

Pastrana and Marulanda met again in Feb. 2001 in an attempt to restart peace talks, but Pastrana's pledge to solve the decades-long civil war failed to halt the violence. In the build up to the 2002 presidential elections (for which Pastrana was constitutionally banned from running) rebel action intensified. Highlighting Pastrana's inability to resolve the conflict, his successor, the rightwing independent Alvaro Uribe, campaigned on combating FARC activities.

Later Life

In Oct. 2005 Pastrana was appointed ambassador to the United States by president Álvaro Uribe Vélez and held the post until his resignation in July 2006.

Patil, Pratibha (India)

Introduction

Pratibha Patil was sworn in as India's first female president in July 2007. Backed by the ruling United Progressive Alliance (UPA) and the Left Front, she won nearly two-thirds of the votes cast in state assemblies and in India's parliament.

Early Life

Pratibha Patil was born on 19 Dec.1934 in Nadgaon, Maharashtra. She graduated with a master's degree in political science and economics from Mooljee Jaitha College, Jalgaon and then studied at the Government Law College in Mumbai. She worked at the Jalgaon District Court before entering politics in 1962 when she successfully contested a seat in the Maharashtra State Assembly, representing the Indian National Congress (INC) party. Following re-election in 1967 she was appointed deputy minister working in the offices of public health, prohibition, tourism, housing and parliamentary affairs. From 1972–77 she held several cabinet portfolios including social welfare, public health and prohibition, rehabilitation and cultural affairs.

When the INC split in 1977 after Indira Gandhi's electoral defeat in the wake of the Indian Emergency, Patil remained loyal to Gandhi. She protested the arrest of Gandhi in Dec. 1977 and was herself arrested and imprisoned for ten days. Patil was appointed minister for education in 1978 and became leader of the opposition in the state assembly in July 1979 when Congress (Urs), a breakaway faction of the INC, came to power. The INC returned to power in 1980 and Patil was a frontrunner for the post of chief minister of Maharashtra but ultimately lost out to A. R. Antulay. She returned to the Maharashtra state assembly where she was minister for urban development and housing from 1982–83, then minister for civil supplies and social welfare from 1983–85.

In 1985 Patil was elected as an INC representative to the Rajya Sabha, parliament's upper house. Between 1986–88 she was variously deputy chairperson of the house, a member of the business advisory committee and chairman of the committee of privileges. Following a rift with Prabha Rau, president of the Maharashtra Pradesh Congress Committee (MPCC), Patil was chosen by Rajiv Gandhi as Rau's replacement in 1988, holding the post until 1990. In the elections of 1991 Patil was elected to the 10th Lok Sabha, the lower house of parliament, where she was chairperson of the House Committee. Having completed her term in April 1996 she did not stand for re-election.

In Nov. 2004 Patil became the first female governor of Rajasthan. In this capacity she refused to sign the contentious Rajasthan Freedom of Religion Bill in 2006, which had been introduced by the Bharatiya Janata Party-led state government and sought to ban forced religious conversion. Patil held that clauses in the bill infringed fundamental rights, including freedom of speech and freedom to practise and propagate religion.

Patil was announced as the United Progressive Alliance (UPA)–Left Front presidential candidate on 14 June 2007, the result of a last-minute compromise between the UPA and Left Front. Her campaign was marred by a series of allegations against her, including claims of a murder cover-up and financial irregularities. However, the allegations were not substantiated and she became president on 21 July 2007.

Career Peak

Though chiefly a ceremonial role, as president Patil had to navigate and reconcile the frequently bitter divides of party politics. A keen supporter of rights for women and the poor, she championed the spread of education to all Indian children—in April 2010 legislation guaranteeing free schooling for children aged 6–14 came into effect—and pledged to tackle abuses such as female infanticide. She retired from office in July 2012 and was succeeded by Pranab Mukherjee.

Patterson, P. J. (Jamaica)

Introduction

P. J. Patterson became Jamaica's prime minister in 1992, and won a record third term in 2002. Originally a socialist, he came to adopt free market policies. Whilst he did much to stabilize Jamaica's economy, his tenure was marked by violent crime and political infighting.

Early Life

Percival James Patterson was born in 1935 in St Andrew, Jamaica. He graduated in English from the University of the West Indies in 1959. He then studied law at the London School of Economics in England and was called to the Bar. In 1967, while running a private legal practice, he entered the Senate as a member of the socialist-leaning People's National Party (PNP).

He became party vice president and was responsible for the election campaigns of Michael Manley in 1972, 1976 and 1989. During Manley's tenures of the 1970s, Patterson played a leading role in forging ties with Cuba. Between 1972 and Manley's defeat by Edward Seaga of the Jamaica Labour Party (JLP) in 1980, Patterson was minister for industry and tourism and, later, foreign affairs. He was deputy prime minister from 1978–80.

When Manley returned to power in 1989 Patterson was regarded as his most likely successor. As deputy prime minister and minister of finance, Patterson set about rejuvenating the economy and devalued the Jamaican dollar. Devaluation adversely affected much of the population and this, combined with a scandal concerning tax incentives to oil companies, forced Patterson's resignation. However, when Manley retired because of bad health in 1992 Patterson succeeded him as party leader and prime minister.

Career Peak

Patterson led the PNP to victory at the 1993 elections, having remodelled himself as an advocate of the free market. The PNP won 54 of the 60 seats in the House of Representatives. Patterson has enforced tight monetary and fiscal restraints and overseen a programme of privatization. Despite the unpopularity of many of these measures, he secured re-election in 1997.

A collapse in the world price of bauxite in the late 1990s weakened the economy, while increasing crime rates damaged tourism. An increase in oil prices then prompted violent protests in Kingston, with troops being drafted in to restore order in July 1999. Drug crime and politically-motivated violence continued to escalate, and by 2005 the number of murders had reached 1674.

On the international scene, relations with the USA became strained in 1998 when Patterson criticized the American trade embargo on Cuba. In 2002 he criticized the British Privy Council for blocking judicial executions on several Caribbean islands including Jamaica. He in turn was criticized for his refusal to reform anti-homosexual legislation which breached international human rights. Also in 2002 Jamaica and Honduras clashed when Jamaica seized several hundred Hondurans said to be fishing illegally in Jamaican waters.

In the build-up to the elections of Oct. 2002 there was further political violence, with up to 60 people dying in the weeks leading to the opening of the polls. Patterson and his JLP rival, Seaga, made a joint statement calling for calm. Patterson and the PNP won with 34 of the 60 available seats.

Patterson caused controversy in 2004 when he declared that Jamaica would not acknowledge the government of new Haitian president Gérard Latortue, after former president Jean-Bertrand Aristide was ousted.

In April 2006 Patterson was succeeded as leader of the PNP and prime minister by Portia Simson-Miller following a party vote.

Paz Estenssoro, Víctor (Bolivia)

Introduction

Víctor Paz Estenssoro was four times president of Bolivia (1952–56, 1960–64, 1964, 1985–89) representing the Movimiento Nacionalista Revolucionario (MNR), of which he was co-founder. In his radical first term he nationalized the tin mines, granted universal suffrage and expropriated land for redistribution. In his final term he reversed many of his original policies, introducing privatization and encouraging foreign investment. He was the most important Bolivian politician of the 20th century.

Early Life

Paz was born on 2 Oct. 1907 in Tarija, southern Bolivia to a land owning family, part of the country's elite. He studied economics and law at the Universidad Mayor de San Andrés at La Paz, opening a law firm there in 1927. He also taught law and worked as a civil servant in the statistics department of the ministry of finance. From 1932–35 he fought in the Chaco War with Paraguay. It was during the disastrous war that Paz, with other educated Bolivians, was for the first time involved with Bolivia's indigenous population, an experience that shaped his political beliefs. The war provoked a wave of malcontent among both peasants and intellectuals who were ready to fight for change from the oligarchic two-party government.

In 1938 Paz became deputy for Tarija and then 2 years later vice-president of the lower house in congress. In 1942 Paz co-founded the MNR with a group of journalists and lecturers. The party joined forces with a wave of dissatisfied militaries and supported the 1943 military coup in which MNR representative Major Gualberto Villarroel became president. From 1943–46 Paz served as finance minister. When a military coup deposed and lynched the president in 1946, Paz went into exile in Argentina.

Career Peak

Paz remained politically active in exile and in 1951 fought the election from Argentina, promising democratic reforms. He won the election, but a military coup prevented him assuming power, causing an armed revolt by miners, MNR and the police. This April Revolution brought Paz to power in 1952. Paz nationalized the country's main industry, the foreign-owned tin mines, upon which the country's economy was largely reliant. He expropriated land, of which over 80% was owned by three families and established co-operatives. Paz introduced universal suffrage and free education, empowering the impoverished indigenous majority, for whom little had changed since independence in 1825. Paz's reforms transformed the political environment and from then on the indigenous population and tin miners' unions became important political forces.

Between 1956–59 Paz lived in London as the Bolivian ambassador to the UK. The presidency passed to Paz's vice president, Hernán Siles Zuazo, although the former retained his influence over the government. In 1959 he returned to Bolivia to contest the presidential elections. Receiving a large majority, in 1960 he began a second less radical presidential term. His reforms alienated miners and the indigenous population. Falling tin prices pushed Paz into seeking US aid. Nevertheless, Paz began a third term in 1964, having passed an amendment allowing him to stand for a second consecutive term.

Three months into his term, Paz was forced to flee to Peru following a military coup by his vice-president General Rene Barrientos Ortuno. He taught developmental economics in Lima and then wrote on his return to Bolivia in 1971. Three years later a third forced exile took Paz to the USA.

After standing unsuccessfully in the 1979 election, Paz was elected for a fourth term in 1985. He replaced his former vice president Siles Zuazo, whose presidency (1982–85) had left Bolivia's economy in crisis. Inflation was at 25,000% and 2 m. pesos were worth US$1. Bolivia had a huge external debt and the tin mining industry had collapsed. Austerity measures included cuts in government spending and floating the currency. Reversing his original reforms, Paz closed many mines and sold the rest. 25,000 miners lost their jobs and were forced into the booming, but illegal, coca trade. Paz's hardline policies benefited the economy, lowering inflation within a year. Yet the free-market policies, praised by IMF and the World Bank, did not benefit the poorest Bolivians and there were violent protests. In 1989 Paz handed over the presidency to his nephew Jaime Paz Zamora.

Later Life

Paz retired to his hometown in 1989. He died on 7 June 2001.

Pearson, Lester (Canada)

Introduction

Lester Bowles Pearson was the Liberal Prime Minister of Canada between 1963 and 1968. Best known as a diplomat and peace-maker, he was a forceful advocate for the United Nations (UN), the North Atlantic Treaty Organization (NATO) and the Food and Agricultural Organization (FAO).

Early Life

Pearson, the son of a Methodist minister, was born on 23 April 1897 in Newtonbrook (now an area of Toronto), Ontario. His studies at the University of Toronto were interrupted by World War I, during which he served as a medical orderly in Salonika before joining the Royal Air Force. He was invalided home following a road accident in London and finished his degree in 1919. He had a spell working in a meat processing factory before going to Oxford University, where he gained an MA in Modern History in 1925. He was an accomplished athlete, playing semi-professional baseball, gaining a half blue in lacrosse and appearing for the British ice hockey team at the 1922 Winter Olympics.

In 1925 Pearson began teaching History at the University of Toronto, the same year he married Maryon Moody with whom he would have two children. In 1928 he joined the department of External Affairs and was made First Secretary. In 1935 he moved to the Canadian High Commission in London, remaining there until he became Assistant Under-secretary of State for External Affairs in May 1941. In June of the following year he moved to Washington to the Canadian Embassy and in 1945 he became Canadian Ambassador to the US. Another promotion came in 1946 when he was made Under-secretary of State for External Affairs.

Pearson's intellect and diplomatic skills came to the fore during his 20 years with the Department of External Affairs. In the 1930s he was secretary to Canadian commissions on wheat futures and commodity prices. He attended numerous major international gatherings including the 1930 Hague Conference on the Codification of International Law, the 1933–34 Geneva World Disarmament Conference and various meetings of the League of Nations. In 1943 he assisted in the establishment of the United Nations Relief and Rehabilitation Administration (UNNRA) which sought to assist areas devastated by World War II. He was key to the establishment of the FAO, set in motion at a conference in Hot Springs, Virginia following which Pearson took the chairmanship of the Interim Commission.

Having played a leading role in setting up the United Nations, Pearson headed the Canadian delegation from 1946 until 1956. He was President of the General Assembly in 1952–53, a term dominated by the Korean conflict. In 1948 he entered parliament as the member for Algoma East, Ontario, the constituency he served until his retirement. In the government of Louis St Lawrence, who had been Minister of External Affairs when Pearson had been Deputy, Pearson was given charge of the Ministry himself, remaining there

for 9 years. He drafted St Laurent's speech in which the establishment of NATO was proposed and signed the enabling treaty in 1949. He headed the Canadian delegation until 1957 and was chairman of the NATO Council, 1951–52.

Pearson's finest hour came in 1956 with the Suez Crisis, when British, French and Israeli troops invaded Egypt to prevent Egypt's nationalization of the Suez Canal. Recognizing a threat to world security, Pearson suggested a UN peacekeeping force led by Canadian troops, to supervise the withdrawal of the invading forces. Later in the year his proposal for UN intervention in the Hungarian Revolution was rejected but in 1957 he was rewarded for his efforts with the Nobel Peace Prize.

Career Peak

Pearson was elected St Laurent's successor to the Liberal leadership in 1958, but his election record proved patchy. Having led the party to heavy defeat, he managed to form a minority government in 1963. His time as Prime Minister was dogged by scandal and corruption allegations. However, his Medicare Plan made a free national health service possible and he made significant reforms to the pensions and family assistance programmes. A Royal Commission on Bilingualism and Biculturalism brought the issue of French separatism into focus and paved the way for eventual bilingualism. He also introduced the Canadian maple leaf flag, though in the face of strong Conservative opposition. In terms of foreign policy he sought to assert Canadian independence, a position that led to a sometimes tempestuous relationship with the US.

Later Life

Pearson retired from politics in April 1968 to be succeeded by Pierre Trudeau. In that year Pearson headed an International Bank for Reconstruction and Development review on economic aid to developing nations. He later taught foreign affairs, was Chancellor at Ottawa's Carleton University and published a volume of memoirs. He died in Ottawa on 27 Dec. 1972. The Lester B. Pearson Canadian International Peacekeeping Training Centre is in Nova Scotia.

Pereira, Aristides (Cabo Verde)

Introduction

A guerrilla fighter against the Portuguese colonial administration, Aristides Pereira became Cabo Verde's first post-independence president in 1975. His tenure lasted until the country's first multi-party elections in 1991.

Early Life

Aristedes Maria Pereira was born on 17 Nov. 1923 in Fundo Figueiras, in the north of the island of Boa Vista. He trained as a radio-telegraph technician at the Lycee de Cap-Vert. Extreme drought in Cape Verde prompted him to emigrate to Guinea-Bissau (then Portuguese Guinea) in 1947. There he began working as a telegraph operator and rose to head the country's telecommunications services.

In 1951, after meeting the prominent nationalist Amílcar Cabral, Pereira became involved in the anti-colonial movement. In 1956, along with Cabral and four others, he co-founded the Partido Africano da Independcia da Guiné e Cabo Verde (PAIGC). He was the party's assistant secretary-general between 1964 and 1973.

The PAIGC, with the support of the Soviet Union and Cuba, launched guerilla campaigns in the early 1960s to end Portuguese rule. Following Cabral's assassination by the Portuguese secret police, Pereira was elected as the PAIGC's general secretary in 1973. Portuguese Guinea declared independence that year and Cabral's brother, Luis, was made president of the newly independent nation of Guinea-Bissau.

In the aftermath of the April 1974 revolution in Portugal, the PAIGC became an active political movement in Cape Verde. On 5 July 1975 the country declared its independence and Pereira was named president, with Pedro Pires as prime minister.

Career Peak

Pereira's primary challenge was to secure the new nation's economic survival. With Cape Verde susceptible to drought and famine, the government instituted resource-management and agrarian reforms. Although the PAIGC instituted one-party rule, Pereira pursued a foreign policy of non-alignment, winning support from both the USA and the USSR, along with other Western nations including Sweden. With international assistance, the government created a viable infrastructure and a national health service.

Despite the initial intention of uniting the two countries, relations between Guinea-Bissau and Cape Verde were strained and in 1981 the Cape Verdean PAIGC changed its name to the African Party for the Independence of Cape Verde (PAICV). Pereira was re-elected in 1981 and 1986 but the PAICV faced growing pressure for pluralistic democracy. In 1990 an emergency congress led to the end of one-party rule.

In the first multi-party elections held in 1991, Pereira was defeated by the Movement for Democracy (MPD) candidate, Antonio Mascarenhas Monteiro, and subsequently retired from political life. The elections marked the first time in sub-Saharan Africa that a single-party government was voted out of office.

In July 2007 Pereira was hospitalized in France after suffering from heart problems and diabetes. He died in Coimbra, Portugal, in Sept. 2011. A state funeral was held in Cape Verde's capital, Cidade da Praia, and Boa Vista's Rabil Airport was renamed as Aristides Pereira International Airport in Nov. 2011.

Peres, Shimon (Israel)

Introduction

A veteran Labour politician, Shimon Peres has served as prime minister on three occasions since 1977 and held the deputy premiership and foreign affairs portfolio in Ariel Sharon's Likud/Labour-led coalition. He was instrumental in the negotiations leading to the Sept. 1993 peace accord with the PLO and the 1994 treaty with Jordan. In 2007 he succeeded Moshe Katsav as president of Israel. Peres was the oldest head of state when his term as president came to an end in 2014. He died aged 93 in Sept. 2016.

Early Life

Born in Poland in Aug. 1923, Peres emigrated to Palestine with his family in 1934 and was educated at the Ben Shemen Agricultural High School. In 1943 he was elected secretary of the Labour-Zionist youth movement. During and after the 1948–49 war with the Arabs he served as head of naval services, and from 1953–59 was director-general of the ministry of defence. Elected to the Knesset in 1959, Peres became deputy minister of defence until 1965 when he left the factious Mapai Party with David Ben-Gurion. He returned to the reconstituted Labour Party in 1968, holding various ministerial responsibilities until mid-1977 when his three-month tenure as acting prime minister in succession to Yitzhak Rabin ended in electoral defeat by Likud. After the election Peres assumed the Labour chairmanship, holding it until 1992.

Career Peak

From Sept. 1984–Oct. 1986 Peres served as prime minister in a national unity government based on a rotation arrangement with the then Likud leader Yitzhak Shamir. Deputy prime minister from 1986–90, he then led the opposition in the Knesset from 1990–92. After Labour's return to power under Yitzhak Rabin in 1992, Peres was appointed foreign minister. He played an integral part in the negotiations leading to the Oslo agreements with the PLO in Sept. 1993, for which he shared the Nobel Peace Prize. A further term as prime minister followed Rabin's assassination in Nov. 1995. However, he lost narrowly in the May 1996 elections to Binyamin Netanyahu. Having surrendered the Labour chairmanship to Ehud Barak in June 1997, he then served in Barak's administration as minister of regional co-operation from July 1999 until Feb. 2001 when Ariel Sharon was directly elected as prime minister. In 2000 Peres was defeated in presidential elections by Moshe Katsav. He was subsequently appointed deputy prime minister and foreign minister in Sharon's coalition government.

In 2007 Katsav, whose term had been marred by allegations of criminal offences, stood down as president. The Knesset elected Peres his successor, defeating Reuven Rivlin of Likud and Colette Avital of Labour. Although the role is largely ceremonial, Peres pledged to rise above party politics and unify Israeli society. He left the Knesset after 48 years to take up the position of president.

On the resignation of the prime minister, Ehud Olmert, in Sept. 2008, Peres asked Tzipi Livni, the foreign minister and new leader of the Kadima Party, to try and form a new government. However, the following month Livni announced her failure to negotiate another coalition, heralding an early general election scheduled for Feb. 2009 following which Binyamin Netanyahu of Likud became prime minister for a second time.

In April 2013 Peres announced that he would not seek re-election, which was to end on 27 July 2014. Aged 90, he was the world's oldest head of state upon leaving office. Reuven Rivlin of the Likud party was chosen by the Knesset to succeed Peres as head of state.

Later Life

Peres suffered from a stroke in Sept. 2016 and was hospitalized in Tel Aviv. He died 2 weeks later.

Pérez Molina, Otto (Guatemala)

Introduction

Otto Pérez Molina took office as president in Jan. 2012. A former director of military intelligence, he has adopted a hardline policy towards tackling crime.

Early Life

Born in Guatemala City on 1 Dec. 1950, Pérez Molina graduated from the country's military academy in 1973. He rose through the army ranks, serving in counterinsurgency campaigns during the 1980s, particularly in the Quiché region. Allegations of atrocities committed under his command have persisted but have never been proven.

In 1983 he backed the coup that removed President Ríos Montt. In the late 1980s he studied at the Army School of the Americas and the Inter-American Defense College, both in the USA, after which he worked in military intelligence, serving as director from 1992–93. After helping to force the resignation of President Serrano in 1993, he served from 1993–95 as chief of staff to President de León Carpio.

Appointed inspector general of the army in 1996, he represented the military in negotiations with guerrilla forces that resulted in a peace treaty ending 36 years of civil war. He was also Guatemala's delegate on the Inter-American Defense Board from 1998–2000. In Feb. 2001 Pérez Molina founded the conservative Patriotic Party (PP), guiding it into the Grand National Alliance (GANA) 2 years later.

Elected to parliament in Nov. 2003, he subsequently withdrew the PP from GANA while serving as commissioner for defence and security. In 2007 he unsuccessfully contested the presidential election as the PP candidate, but stood again and won in 2011 promising tough policing and increased social spending.

Career Peak

Pérez Molina took office on 14 Jan. 2012. He asked for international help in combating the drugs trade and has introduced a system of checkpoints aimed at curtailing violent crime. His other challenges have included reducing poverty and unemployment, as well as managing the conflict between the mining industry and indigenous groups defending their land rights. This led the government to declare a state of emergency in southeastern areas of the country in May 2013.

Pérez Molina resigned on 2 Sept. 2015 amid allegations of his involvement with a customs fraud ring. He was arrested a day later and put in prison, with vice-president Alejandro Maldonado Aguirre taking over on an interim basis.

Perón, Juan (Argentina)

Introduction

Lieutenant-General Juan Domingo Perón Sosa was three times president of Argentina twice between 1946 and 55 and from 1973 until his death. Leader of the *Peronista* movement inspired by Italian fascism, Perón heavily influenced the current Partido Justicialista. During his first term Perón's policy of industrialization and social reform won him mass populist support. His following was boosted by his politically active wife Eva Perón. His second term was less successful and led to a military coup and exile. His final term in office was characterized by political instability.

Early Life

Perón was born on 1895 in Lobos, Buenos Aires province. The son of a small rancher, he was educated at military school. He rose to the rank of lieutenant, becoming an instructor in the war academy and teacher of military history. In 1936 he served in Chile as a military attaché before travelling to Europe. On visits to Spain, Germany and Italy in the late 1930s and early 40s he formed the basis of his own political ideology, founded on fascism. On his return to Argentina, Perón joined the fascist-style Grupo de Oficiales Unidos (Group of United Officers; GOU). When in 1943 Perón was part of a GOU coup that deposed the civilian government, he became secretary for labour and social welfare in the military junta. Over the next 2 years he gradually increased his power base gaining popularity with the workers and the military. He became minister of war and then in 1945 vice-president.

Career Peak

Fearful of his power, the military government forced Perón to resign and in 1945 he was imprisoned. His partner Eva Duarte along with several of Perón's allies rallied a workers protest forcing his release. The same day Perón's address from the balcony of the presidential palace was heard by more than 300,000 supporters in Buenos Aires. The following year he was elected president with 56% of votes on a populist manifesto.

Perón played on populist and nationalistic sentiment implementing a 'third way' of politics known as *justicialismo*. This involved widespread industrialization and social reform, including increased wages and benefits. Social security and education were available to all, and improved housing and leisure facilities were created. He nationalized the railways and invested in the shipbuilding and iron and steel industries. Perón's political strength was reinforced by support for his wife Eva Perón known popularly as Evita who acted as de facto minister of health and labour.

In 1951 Perón was re-elected president. His second term was marred by the death of Evita in 1952 and less than successful economic policy. Resources were exhausted, inflation was increasing and there was growing discontent in the armed forces as Perón's rule became increasingly autocratic and dictatorial. Perón was also at odds with the Catholic Church. In 1955 the military deposed Perón and forced him into exile.

Later Life

Perón eventually settled in Madrid. During his years in exile he maintained a strong base in Argentina. One of his supporters was the future Argentine president Carlos Menem, who founded the Juventud Peronista (Peronist Youth) movement. The ban on Peronists holding office was lifted when General Alejandro Lanusse came to power in 1971. He announced free elections for 1973 in which all political parties could participate. Perón was able to return to Argentina for the 1973 election when the Peronists represented by Héctor J Cámpora won an outright victory. Cámpora then stood down and another election was called in Oct. 1973. Having retained working class support Perón was victorious, but his final term in office was politically and economically unstable. Having retained working class support throughout his exile, once in power Perón turned to the military and right wing groups. He appointed his third wife, Maria Estela Martínez (known as Isabelita) as vice-president despite her unpopularity. Perón died in office in Buenos Aires on 1 July 1974. On Perón's death Isabelita Perón took over his presidency to become the hemisphere's first woman president. She was deposed in a military coup in 1976.

Persad-Bissessar, Kamla (Trinidad and Tobago)

Introduction

Kamla Persad-Bissessar was sworn in as the country's first female prime minister in May 2010.

Early Life

Persad-Bissessar was born on 22 April 1952 in Siparia, southern Trinidad. She studied at the University of the West Indies, the Hugh Wooding Law School in Trinidad and Tobago, Norwood Technical College in England and the Arthur Lok Jack Graduate School of Business, Trinidad.

While in England, Persad-Bissessar was a social worker with the Church of England Children's Society of London. She then worked as a teacher in Jamaica. She later taught at the St Augustine campus of the University of the West Indies in Trinidad. She also lectured at the Jamaica College of Insurance. After 6 years in education, Persad-Bissessar became a full-time attorney-at-law.

From 1987 to 1991 she served as an alderman for St Patrick County Council. She joined the Senate in 1994 representing the United National Congress (UNC). From 1995 she was the MP for Siparia. She twice served as attorney general, in 1995 and in 2001. In Dec. 2000 she became minister of education. The UNC returned to the opposition benches in 2002, with Persad-Bissessar elected leader of the parliamentary opposition in April 2006.

Career Peak

On 24 Jan. 2010 Persad-Bissessar was elected party leader of the UNC. After a landslide victory for the People's Partnership coalition (of which the UNC is a part) at a snap general election on 24 May 2010, she replaced Patrick Manning as prime minister, promising increased transparency in government.

In March 2012 she defeated a no confidence motion in parliament brought by the opposition leader, who accused her government of not properly managing the economic, political and social issues facing the country.

Persad-Bissessar's term as prime minister ended in Sept. 2015 after the People's Partnership was defeated at parliamentary elections held that month. She was succeeded by Keith Rowley of the People's National Movement.

Persson, Göran (Sweden)

Introduction

Göran Persson was elected leader of the Swedish Social Democratic Labour Party (SAP) in 1996 following Ingvar Carlsson's retirement. The general election held in spring that year returned the Social Democrats to government, and Persson became prime minister on 21 March. He was re-elected, albeit on a reduced share of the vote, on 21 Sept. 1998. He led the SAP to re-election in Sept. 2002 to form a minority government reliant on the support of either the Greens or the Left Party. In Sept. 2006 he led the SAP to electoral defeat against the centre-right 'Alliance for Sweden' coalition.

Early Life

Persson was born in Vingåker on 29 Jan. 1949. He was educated at the University College of Örebro and began his political career in 1971 as a secretary for the Swedish Social Democratic Youth League. He became a board member of the League the following year. From 1974–76 he was the secretary of the Worker's Educational Association in Sörmland. For a decade Persson pursued a career in finance as the vice-chairman of the board of Oppunda Savings Bank, but continued to participate in municipal politics and was elected as a member of parliament in 1979. During the 1980s he continued to balance his political career with participation in various local and private projects. In 1984 he abandoned his parliamentary seat, and the following year he became a municipal commissioner for Katrineholm. In

1989 Persson received his first ministerial portfolio, that of a minister in the department of education. He was re-elected to parliament in 1991, and in the same year became the chairman of the standing committee on policy. In 1992 he became a party spokesman on industrial policy. In 1993 he was chosen as a deputy member of the SAP executive committee, and in 1994 he was appointed minister of finance. This latter role groomed Persson for the party leadership, which he was awarded in 1996. In March that year he became prime minister.

Career Peak

In his first term Persson was preoccupied with Sweden's entry into the EU and its political and economic consequences. On the domestic front he remained committed to imposing a high level tax on top earners to finance the welfare state. A gradual disenchantment with social democratic policies meant that in 1998 Persson led the SAP to their worst general election performance in 40 years. As a result he rapidly came under pressure to cut taxes, liberalize Sweden's labour market and shift the welfare budget from direct transfers to spending on health care and education. A growing mood of scepticism about Sweden's role in the EU in the wake of the Danish rejection of monetary union also hindered the pro-Europe Persson. In 2001 Persson was further immersed in European politics as the union presidency passed to Sweden. During this period he argued tirelessly for the enlargement of the EU to take in Central European applicants.

Persson again led the SAP at the Sept. 2002 elections, winning almost 40% of the vote. Unable to form a majority government, he survived a vote of confidence in early Oct. when he secured the support of the Green Party. His minority administration relied on the backing of the Greens or the Left Party to stay in office. In return for Green support, Persson agreed to implement a green tax, cut defence expenditure and reduce greenhouse gas emissions by 2010. In Sept. 2003 Swedish voters rejected a proposal to adopt the EU single currency by 56–42% in a referendum, despite the ruling SAP's support for the euro. Although the Swedish economy remained robust compared with most other European countries, Persson's government lost popular support over continuing high levels of unemployment.

At elections on 17 Sept. 2006 Persson led the SAP to their worst showing in 92 years, winning just over 35% of votes cast. They lost power to the 'Alliance for Sweden' coalition, consisting of the Moderate Party, the Centre Party, the Christian Democratic Party and the Liberal Party. Persson stepped down as party leader in March 2007 to be succeeded by Mona Stahlin.

Phan Van Khai (Vietnam)

Introduction

Phan Van Khai was head of government from 1997 to 2006. He was seen as a reformer and was unusual among the rulers of modern Vietnam in that his roots and political career were in the south. Before Khai, Vietnam's Communist leadership has been largely Hanoi-dominated. His historic visit to the USA in June 2005 was seen as a boost to Vietnam's economic status.

Early Life

Phan Van Khai was born on 25 Dec. 1933 in a village suburb of Saigon, then part of French Indochina. As a child of 14 he joined a movement opposed to French rule and advocating socialism. By 1954 Khai was an experienced resistance soldier, having fought in the civil war for the Communists against the Western-sponsored southern forces. When Vietnam was partitioned in 1954, he settled in Communist North Vietnam. There, he attended the Foreign Languages College in Hanoi, before being sent to Moscow to study economics at the Plekhanov Institute. It was during his 5 years in Moscow that he joined the Vietnamese Communist Party.

Returning to North Vietnam, Khai held a variety of party posts, eventually working for the State Planning Committee. Reunification of Vietnam in 1976 gave him the opportunity to return to Ho Chi Minh City (as Saigon was renamed), and he was appointed deputy director, and later director, of the city's planning department.

In 1978 Khai gained his first important Communist Party office when he became a deputy mayor of Ho Chi Minh City. In the following year, he was appointed a member of the party committee for the city. Khai was elected to the (national) central committee of the party as an alternate member in 1982, and as a full member in 1984. He was appointed mayor of Ho Chi Minh City in 1985 and remained in that post until he was brought back to Hanoi as chairman of the State Planning Committee in 1989. Two years later he became a member of the Vietnamese cabinet and of the party's Politburo. In 1992 he was made deputy prime minister.

Career Peak

In Sept. 1997 Phan Van Khai succeeded Vo Van Kiet as prime minister of Vietnam. Although he oversaw the normalization of trade relations with the USA and the progress of Vietnam's bid for WTO membership, Khai was not prepared to sanction political reforms to match economic liberalization. Following the elections in 2002 which returned the ruling Communist Party unopposed, the National Assembly reappointed him as prime minister. In June 2005 he made the first visit to the USA by a Vietnamese leader since the end of the Vietnam War. However, the visit provoked some protests in the USA over Vietnam's human rights record.

He resigned on 24 June 2006, along with President Tran Duc Luong and Assembly Speaker Nguyen Van An. The three left, unable to guarantee re-election to the politburo, claiming they were making way for a new generation of politicians in line with party policy. He died aged 84 on 17 April 2018.

Philip, Danny (Solomon Islands)

Introduction

Danny Philip was named prime minister on 24 Aug. 2010 after nearly 3 weeks of negotiations following a general election. Despite leading a minority party, he won the premiership with a narrow majority in parliament.

Early Life

Danny Philip was born on 5 Aug. 1953. Prior to his career in politics, he was an English teacher. In 1984 he was elected to the National Parliament representing the Vona Vona, Rendova and Tetepare constituency, for whom he served two terms. From 1993–2001, following boundary changes to the constituency, Philip held the seat of South New Georgia, Rendova and Tetepare. He served as foreign minister from 1995–96 and was appointed leader of the People's Progressive Party in 1997, a post he kept for 3 years. In June 2000 he was reappointed as foreign minister but lost the portfolio in a cabinet reshuffle in July 2001.

On 18 April 2010 Philip launched the Reform and Democratic Party of the Solomon Islands (RDP-SI), naming himself as party president. Having established the party to contest the general election, he regained the old seat of South New Georgia, Rendova and Tetepare on 4 Aug. 2010. With no party winning more than 14 of the 50 available seats, a period of intense horse trading began. The RDP-SI won only two seats but, nonetheless, Philip won a run-off for the premiership on 25 Aug, defeating Steve Abana of the Democratic Party by 26 votes to 23 in the parliamentary vote.

Career Peak

Philip campaigned on a platform of introducing a new federal constitution. His government's key challenges included improving law and order, finding investment for health and education, and strengthening diplomatic ties with international neighbours. Philip also pledged to work with RAMSI, the Australian-led Regional Assistance Mission to the Solomon Islands, arguing that the force had a pivotal role to play in assisting the Solomon Islands in meeting its development goals. Following the defection of five ministers and seven backbenchers to the opposition, Philip stood down on 11 Nov. 2011 to avoid a no confidence vote. He was succeeded by finance minister Gordon Darcy Lilo.

Later Life

Philip joined the newly appointed government led by Manasseh Sogavare in Dec. 2014 as minister of national development planning and aid co-ordination, but resigned in Oct. 2017.

Pindling, Lynden (The Bahamas)

Introduction

Lynden Oscar Pindling was prime minister of the Bahamas from 1967–92. He ended the centuries-long domination by the white minority and brought independence and democracy to his country. But his term was overshadowed by allegations of corruption and government involvement in drug-trafficking.

Early Life

Pindling was born in Nassau on 22 March 1930 of a Bahamian mother and a Jamaican father. The son of a policeman, Pindling was educated at the Government High School before studying Law in London between 1948–52. He was called to the Bahamian Bar in 1953. Soon after he joined the newly formed Progressive Liberal Party (PLP), which had been set up to challenge the white-dominated government. Politics was still rooted in the 18th century, with the white Bahamian 'Bay Street Boys' (named after the main business centre in Nassau) as an automatically re-elected oligarchy.

Pindling was elected to the Assembly in 1956 as the junior member for the southern district of New Providence. Pindling became the leader of the PLP in the election year, 1956 when the party gained six seats. In response the white leaders formed their own party, the United Bahamian Party (UBP). Pindling led the PLP into the 1962 elections. He had strong support from the working classes and black population. Nevertheless, the UBP won, mainly due to secure votes in the family islands (those islands other than New Providence and Grand Bahama).

Initially disconcerted, the PLP soon focused on rousing popular support for the next election. Universal suffrage, granted in 1964, helped its cause. The following year, the rejection of a commission report on government boundaries fuelled a public demonstration led by Pindling. The result was the introduction of new boundaries. The 1967 general election was fraught and intense. Despite a large UBP campaign budget, the elections resulted in a tie. Two independent parties, including an ex-PLP minister Randol Fawkes, sided with Pindling and the Bahamas' first black prime minister was elected.

Career Peak

On his ascension to power, Pindling put his energies into the fight for Bahamian independence from Britain. He dissolved the Assembly and in the ensuing general election of 1968 called for a mandate for change. The PLP won 28 of the 38 seats. Pindling's policies were based on the advancement of the black majority. Freeport, long controlled by the powerful Port Authority, was brought under government control. Industry developed and the government cracked down on immigration—especially the large number of illegal Haitians—in order to provide more jobs for Bahamians. The UBP fell apart and the PLP dominated future elections. Opposition eventually came from dissident PLP members. Disagreeing with Pindling's style of government, and claiming it to be dictatorial, Cecil Wallace-Whitfield left the PLP to form the Free-PLP. This party became the Free National Movement (FNM), which attracted floating UBP members and developed into the major opposition party. The 1972 elections were dominated by the issue of independence. The PLP strove for immediate independence, while the FNM was prepared to delay it. The PLP was successful, winning 29 seats. On 10 July 1973 the Bahamas gained independence.

In 1974 the College of the Bahamas was opened, offering tertiary education. In the same year, the Central Bank opened extending the profitable finance industry. Despite rising wages, unemployment was still a major problem in the Bahamas, especially among the young. Further problems arose from the trade in drugs. From the late 1960s, the Bahamas provided the ideal stop-off point on the route between South America and the USA. Money laundering, which reached a height in the mid-1970s, was a further problem. There were accusations of government involvement in both illegal trades. In 1983 Pindling sued the American television channel NBC for

defamation and set up a royal commission to investigate the charges. It found no evidence to link Pindling directly to the traffic, although several of his ministers were inculpated. Nevertheless, the commission found that Pindling had received large sums of money as 'gifts' and 'loans'. and that his income was far inferior to his expenditure.

In the 1987 elections the FNM inferred government involvement in drug-trafficking. In return, Pindling highlighted national and race issues and attached the FNM's relations with the USA. Pindling held onto power for a fifth consecutive term.

Later Life

In the early 1990s, the Bahamas went into recession. Unemployment and crime rose as prosperity fell. A scandal involving the state-owned Bahamasair erupted. In the 1992 elections, the PLP's domination was ended with an FNM victory. Hubert Ingraham succeeded Pindling who had been prime minister for 25 years. Pindling's offer to resign as leader of the PLP was rejected. He continued his political career in opposition until he resigned from the Assembly in 1997. He died on 26 Aug. 2000. Pindling was knighted in 1983.

Pinochet Ugarte, Augusto (Chile)

Introduction

General Augusto Pinochet Ugarte was president of Chile from 1973 to 1990 having led a military coup which overthrew the socialist government of Salvador Allende Gossens. Pinochet implemented free-market policies and widespread privatization. He achieved economic growth but led a hardline repressive regime. He died in Dec. 2006, having spent many years under threat of trial for human rights abuses.

Early Life

Pinochet was born on 26 Nov. 1915 in the coastal city of Valparaíso. The son of a customs official, he was educated at the Military Academy of Santiago. Having climbed the ranks of the officers' corps, in the early 1950s he was associated with the suppression of the Chilean Communist Party. In 1968 he became sub-director of the War Academy. During the presidency of the Partido Socialista de Chile leader, Allende, he gained the rank of general. In 1973 he was promoted to commander-in-chief of the Chilean army.

Chile was experiencing an economic crisis. Allende's nationalization and land collectivization policies had led to high inflation, a shortage of consumer goods and civil unrest. In the military, there was an emerging opposition faction linked to Pinochet who organized and led the military coup on 23 Sept. 1973, 18 days after Allende appointed him as commander-in-chief. A military junta representing all branches of the Chilean armed forces was established with Pinochet as head of state.

Career Peak

Pinochet set about reversing Allende's socialist policies. He implemented privatization schemes and free-market policies. By the end of the 1970s Chile was enjoying an economic boom but Pinochet's policies polarized Chile's rich and poor. He closed down parliament and elected himself absolute ruler. He outlawed opposition politicians and trade unions. In Oct. 1973 over 70 political prisoners fell victim to the notorious 'caravan of death'. An execution squad which toured the country hunting out Allende's supporters. In 1974 Pinochet elected himself president demoting the rest of the junta to an advisory role. Previous plans to rotate the presidency were abandoned. Many left-wing politicians and liberal minded citizens were forced into exile, tortured or killed. It is estimated that over 3,000 of Allende's supporters lost their lives, over 30,000 were forced into exile and more than 130,000 were arrested over a 3 year period.

In 1978 a plebiscite showed 75% of voters supported Pinochet, albeit in a political climate in which opposition was barely tolerated. In 1980 a constitutional amendment created ten senator-for-life places, four for army leaders and one for Pinochet. A plebiscite held the same year extended Pinochet's rule for 10 years. From the mid-1980s, exiled opposition politicians returned to set up a 'democratic opposition' alliance. In 1986 Pinochet survived an assassination attempt. In the fallout, Pinochet imprisoned opposition politicians, including future president Ricardo Lagos Escobar. Widespread international condemnation forced their release. With growing confidence the opposition united under the Comando por el No group which rallied voters to reject Pinochet in the Oct. 1988 referendum. Fifty-five percent voted against, while only 43% voted for the President. Pinochet stepped down although he remained commander-in-chief of the army, thereby preventing any move to prosecute him for human rights abuses.

Later Life

In 1998 Pinochet retired as head of the army. On a trip to Britain in Oct. of the same year, Pinochet was arrested, pending extradition to Spain where a warrant had been issued for his arrest to stand trial for human rights abuses and murder charges. Following prolonged legal arguments Pinochet's extradition was blocked despite opposition from the governments of Spain, France, Belgium and Switzerland. A 2-year legal battle culminated with Pinochet, now suffering heart problems, being released on compassionate grounds. On 3 March 2000 Pinochet arrived back in Chile where he was stripped of his immunity to face trial in his native country. However, his failing health ensured he was never tried and he died on 10 Dec. 2006. The government announced that he would not receive a state funeral and there were clashes in Santiago between his supporters and critics.

Pinto da Costa, Manuel (São Tomé and Príncipe)

Introduction

Manuel Pinto da Costa, a Marxist, came out of retirement to win the presidency in Aug. 2011. He promised to tackle corruption and poverty but opponents warned of a return to authoritarian rule.

Early Life

Manuel Pinto da Costa was born in São Tomé on 5th Aug. 1937. The son of a plantation official, he was educated in São Tomé, Angola and Portugal. He graduated from the University of Lisbon and was a founder of the Committee for the Liberation of São Tomé e Príncipe in 1960. Da Costa spent time in France and Cuba in the early part of the decade before completing a doctorate in economics at Humboldt University in East Berlin.

Elected secretary-general of the new Movement for the Liberation of São Tomé and Príncipe (MLSTP) in 1972, da Costa developed links with other independence groups in Angola, Guinea-Bissau and Mozambique. When Portugal's fascist government was overthrown in April 1974, he spearheaded negotiations that led to independence in July 1975.

As leader of the MLSTP, the sole legal party, da Costa was blamed for the economic hardships that accompanied the nationalization of plantations and the departure of skilled workers to Portugal. After an attempted coup by foreign-based mercenaries in 1978 and amid rising political tensions the following year, da Costa called upon Angolan troops to maintain the peace in a deeply unpopular move.

During the early 1980s he became increasingly authoritarian, but a new constitution ended one-party rule in 1990 and he announced that he would not contest the 1991 multi-party elections. Miguel Trovoada became president, elected unopposed as an independent candidate, and da Costa moved to Angola.

He nonetheless returned to contest the 1996 presidential election, narrowly losing to Trovoada. Re-elected leader of the MLSTP in 1998, he also contested the 2001 presidential election, this time losing to Fradique de Menezes. He remained party leader until retiring in Feb. 2004. However, he returned again to run as an independent candidate for the presidency in July 2011, promising to overcome instability, poverty and corruption. He received sufficient support to force a run-off against the parliamentary speaker, Evaristo Carvalho, and emerged victorious with 52.9% of the vote. He was sworn in on 3 Sept. 2011.

Career Peak

Pinto da Costa's priority was to revitalize the struggling economy by developing tourism, the nascent oil industry and coffee exports, while working in conjunction with Patrice Trovoada, whose Independent Democratic Action (ADI) party had won legislative elections in 2010. In Nov. 2012 Trovoada lost a no-confidence vote in the National Assembly and da Costa dismissed his government the following month, appointing Gabriel Arcanjo da Costa as premier. However, the ADI won an outright majority of seats in further elections in Oct. 2014 and Trovoada was reappointed as prime minister.

Pinto da Costa's term as president ended in Sept. 2016, having lost elections held in July and Aug. to ADI candidate Evaristo Carvalho. Da Costa, who had lost by a significant margin in the first round of voting, boycotted the second round, alleging fraud, resulting with Carvalho's automatic election.

Plevneliev, Rosen (Bulgaria)

Introduction

Rosen Plevneliev was sworn in as president on 22 Jan. 2012, having been elected in Oct. 2011 with the support of the centre-right Citizens for the European Development of Bulgaria (GERB). He succeeded the Socialist Georgi Parvanov, who had held the presidency for the maximum two terms. Prior to the election Plevneliev had never run for public office, having worked as a non-partisan member of the cabinet.

Early Life

Rosen Plevneliev was born in Gotse Delchev, southern Bulgaria in 1964. Having graduated in engineering from the Sofia Technical University in 1989, he founded a building firm, Iris International. From 1991 he worked in Germany as the co-owner of a construction firm subcontracting for the German conglomerate Lindner. In 1998 he returned to Bulgaria to head the Lindner Bulgaria group.

Plevneliev entered politics in June 2009 as part of the GERB economic policy team. The following month he was appointed minister of regional development and public works in Boyko Borisov's cabinet, delivering several long-delayed, large-scale infrastructure projects.

On 4 Sept. 2011 he was nominated as GERB's candidate for the presidency. In a second round of polling, Plevneliev and his vice presidential candidate, former justice minister Margarita Popova, gained 52.6% of the vote to defeat the Socialist candidate, Ivailo Kalfin, and his running mate.

Career Peak

Plevneliev, a pro-European, pledged to oversee the reduction of the budget deficit and implement further austerity measures. He was expected to push for the development of regional and international trade. The diversification of energy supplies was among his most pressing challenges, although a referendum on controversial plans to expand Bulgaria's nuclear generating capacity was invalidated in Jan. 2013 by a low turnout.

In Feb. 2013, in the face of violent protests against economic austerity, Prime Minister Boyko Borisov and his government resigned and Plevneliev appointed a caretaker administration pending fresh parliamentary elections that took place in May. An inconclusive outcome, with no majority party, resulted in the establishment of a Socialist-led government headed by Plamen Oresharski. However, continued political and economic instability, and a banking crisis, led to the resignation of Oresharski and his fragile administration in July 2014, prompting a further election in Oct. This produced another divided parliament, including eight different parties. Plevneliev asked Borisov, as head of the largest party, to form a GERB-led coalition government and his new cabinet was endorsed by parliament in early Nov.

In May 2016 Plevneliev announced that he would not be standing for re-election at the presidential election scheduled for Oct. of that year, citing personal reasons. He left office in Jan. 2017 when he was succeeded by the pro-Russia independent candidate Rumen Radev.

Pohamba, Hifikepunye (Namibia)

Introduction

Lucas Hifikepunye Pohamba, representing the ruling South West Africa People's Organization (SWAPO), won a landslide victory at presidential elections in Nov. 2004 and took office in March 2005. He succeeded Namibia's 'founding father' and former president, Sam Nujoma, and has continued with the same broad political programme. He was re-elected in Nov. 2009.

Early Life

Pohamba was born on 18 Aug. 1935 at Okanghudi in South West Africa (modern Namibia) and educated at the Holy Cross Mission School at Onamunama. He worked in the Tsumeb copper mines and joined SWAPO in April 1959. He joined Nujoma in exile in Dar es Salaam (Tanzania) and became a leading figure in SWAPO, representing it in Zambia and Algeria and raising funds. In 1969 he was appointed to SWAPO's central committee and in 1975 became secretary for finance and administration. From 1979 until the late 1980s he was based in Luanda, Angola.

Following Nujoma's victory in the country's first presidential elections on 7 Nov. 1989, Pohamba was appointed as minister of home affairs. In 1995 he became minister for fisheries and marine resources until 2001, when he took responsibility for lands, resettlement and rehabilitation. As such, he pushed ahead with Namibia's controversial 'land reform' scheme, involving the compulsory purchase of land owned by white farmers for distribution to black citizens.

Career Peak

Since his inauguration on 21 March 2005 Pohamba has pursued established policies, including development of education, the rural water supply and the infrastructure network. He has also continued the controversial compulsory land purchases scheme. In elections in Nov. 2009, Pohamba was returned to the presidency with about 75% of the vote and SWAPO retained its majority of parliamentary seats with a similar vote share. A legal challenge launched in 2010 by opposition parties against the election results was dismissed by the High Court in Feb. 2011 for lack of evidence.

In Dec. 2012 Pohamba carried out a cabinet reshuffle and appointed SWAPO vice-president and former trade minister, Hage Geingob, as prime minister. In 2013 Pohamba launched several major public infrastructure projects, including the National Mass Housing Development Programme, the deepening of Walvis Bay harbour and the construction of the Neckartal Dam in !Karas region.

Pohamba was unable to stand for re-election at the Nov. 2014 elections due to constitutional limits. He was succeeded as president by incumbent prime minister Hage Geingob.

Pol Pot (Cambodia)

Introduction

Pol Pot, supported by the nationalist communist Khmer Rouge, ruled Cambodia between 1975 and 1979. Believing in the supremacy of the Cambodian race and preaching the destruction of urbanism and intellectualism, he led a totalitarian regime that resulted in the deaths of between 1,000,000 and 2,500,000 people. Though overthrown in 1979, he retained a significant influence in the Khmer Rouge until just before his death when internal splits led to his arrest.

Early Life

Pol Pot, originally called Saloth Sar, was born on 19 May 1925 in Kompong Province. His father was a land-owning farmer and Pol Pot was educated at a number of French-speaking schools in Phnom Penh. He spent some 6 years in a Buddhist Monastery and it is believed was himself a monk for 2 years. He went on to study carpentry for a year and was a member of the anti-French resistance in the late 1940s. In 1949 he moved to Paris to study radio electronics, becoming an activist in the Communist party, but had to return to Phnom Penh 4 years later when his scholarship was withdrawn.

Married in 1956, he became a school teacher but gave most of his time to strengthening the Cambodian Communist Party. Bent on the overthrow of the government of Prince Norodon Sihanouk, he turned to Vietnam for protection but by 1965 the Vietnamese Communist hierarchy was less interested in Cambodia than in defeating the US. Pol Pot went to China, then in the midst of Mao Zedong's Cultural Revolution, where he planned his takeover of Cambodia.

1970 saw Sihanouk replaced by General Lon Nol's US-backed military regime. Pol Pot and the Khmer Rouge, backed by the Vietnamese Communists, began a guerrilla war. In April 1975 Lon Nol was removed from power and Pol Pot headed a new Khmer Rouge government, renaming the country Democratic Kampuchea.

Career Peak

Almost at once the 2 m. residents of Phnom Penh, who had received Pol Pot's invaders in the hope that the fighting would end, were forcibly moved into rural communes. The media, organized education, markets, religion and private property, all came under sustained attack.

In 1976 Pol Pot devised a 4-Year Plan which set out largely unrealistic targets for the country's agricultural growth. The problem of failing harvests and chronic overwork were exacerbated by grain restrictions imposed by Khmer Rouge officials and the absence of a medical infrastructure, leading to the deaths of hundreds of thousands of civilians. Officially sanctioned torture and executions accounted for many more lives. By 1978 tensions with Vietnam had turned in to full-blown war and the Khmer Rouge, having been refused Chinese assistance, were overpowered. On 25 Dec. 1978 over 100,000 Vietnamese troops entered Cambodia and Pol Pot fled to Thailand on 7 Jan. 1979.

Hiding out in the Thai and north Cambodian forests, he led the Khmer Rouge in further attacks on Vietnamese-backed Phnom Penh. In 1982 the Khmer Rouge was the dominant partner in the Coalition Government of Democratic Kampuchea (CGDK) which held Cambodia's UN seat and gained Western recognition. Pol Pot resigned as leader in 1985 but remained a powerful figure.

Later Life

The Khmer Rouge was part of a UN-backed coalition in 1991 but declined to participate in democratic elections and reverted to guerrilla tactics 2 years later, reputedly under the guidance of Pol Pot.

A rift seems to have riven the Khmer Rouge in the mid-1990s. Pol Pot's former foreign minister and brother-in-law, Leng Sary, was one of many defectors from the party and in 1996–97 Pol Pot led a purge of the party moderates. Following an internal power struggle he was arrested on the orders of one of the party elders, Ta Mok, who was rumoured to be preparing to hand him over to the Americans. The Khmer Rouge carried out their own show trial, sentencing Pol Pot to life imprisonment. On the evening of 15 April 1998, Pol Pot was found dead, supposedly of heart failure. His body was destroyed by Khmer Rouge officials before an autopsy could be held. Despite being responsible for the death of around a quarter of the country's population, he told a journalist in Oct. 1997 that 'my conscience is clear'.

Pompidou, Georges (France)

Introduction

Georges Jean Raymond Pompidou was prime minister between 1962–68, and president from 1969 until his death in 1974. As prime minister he had key roles in the resolution of the Algerian War and of the May 1968 student uprising. As president he promoted France's economic and industrial advance.

Early Life

Pompidou was born in Montboudif, Auvergne on 5 July 1911 and educated at the École Normale Supérieure in Paris. After gaining a diploma in administration, he taught in Marseilles until his conscription in 1939. After the Fall of France in June 1940, he taught at the Lycée Henri IV in Paris until 1944. After meeting Charles de Gaulle who was leading the Free French from exile in London, Pompidou was appointed his adviser. When France was liberated in 1944, Pompidou was in de Gaulle's cabinet in the provisional government, later holding the position of maître des requêtes in the Conseil d'Etat from 1946. Concurrently, he was assistant to the general commissioner for tourism. He resigned in 1953 and went to work for the Rothschild Bank, becoming its director general in 1959.

De Gaulle had resigned on 20 Jan. 1946, but returned to power in May 1958 to end the Algerian War (1954–62). Pompidou, who had worked on de Gaulle's *Rassemblement pour la France* campaign in the late 1940s and early 50s, was asked to assist in drafting the constitution of the Fifth Republic. At the same time, Pompidou worked on plans for France's economic recovery. When, in 1959, de Gaulle was elected first president of the Fifth Republic, Pompidou rejoined the private sector.

In 1961 Pompidou returned to politics to orchestrate secret negotiations with the Algerian revolutionaries, the Front de Libération Nationale. His intervention led to a ceasefire and the signing of the Evian Agreements.

Career Peak

In 1962 Pompidou replaced prime minister Michel Debré. Pompidou was prime minister for four consecutive terms—April–Sept. 1962, Dec. 1962–Jan.1966, Jan. 1966–March 1967, and April 1967–July 1968. In May 1968 Pompidou was faced with the student-worker riots. Workers demanded more pay and better conditions, but both groups were unhappy with de Gaulle's authoritarian leadership. Pompidou, aided by Jacques Chirac, mediated between the government and the strikers and persuaded the president to offer concessions. Revolution was averted but de Gaulle felt let down.

Pompidou was relieved of the premiership by de Gaulle in July 1968. It has been suggested this was to allow Pompidou to inherit the presidency. Others argue that he resigned over criticism of his handling of the May '68 crisis. Pompidou maintained links with the government and when de Gaulle resigned in 1969 and retreated to his home in Colombey-les-Deux-Eglises, Pompidou campaigned for the presidency. He was elected on 15 June 1969 with 58% of the votes.

Pompidou was dedicated to modernization. He gave the go-ahead to the pioneering rail network, the TGV (train à grande vitesse; high-speed train), that would create electrically-powered trains with a top speed of 370 km/ph. He also invested in the roads and telephone networks. On an international level, Pompidou kept good relations and economic ties with Arab counties, although he failed to improve relations with either Germany or the USA. He facilitated the UK's entry into the European Economic Community (EU) in 1973, a move that had been blocked by de Gaulle. Throughout his presidency, Pompidou maintained economic stability in France, although war in the Middle East in 1973 led to an oil crisis and a rise in unemployment. He managed to regain the presidency in 1973, despite a strengthening of the Socialist and Communist parties.

The victim of a rare form of blood cancer, Pompidou died in office on 2 April 1974. A centre for arts and culture, the Centre Pompidou was completed after his death and opened on 31 Jan. 1977.

Early Life

Ponta was born on 20 Sept. 1972 in Bucharest. He graduated in law from the University of Bucharest in 1995 and worked as a prosecutor specializing in corruption cases. Employed in the Supreme Court of Justice from 1998–2001, he was also an assistant professor in public law at the Romanian-American University (RAU) in the capital. He received his master's degree from Italy's University of Catania in 2000 and graduated from the National Defence College in 2002. The same year he began lecturing at the RAU, receiving his PhD from the University of Bucharest in 2003 and becoming an associate professor at RAU in 2007.

A youth wing member of the Social Democratic Party (PSD), Ponta joined the party's national council and was chairman of Social Democratic Youth from 2002–06. In 2004 he entered the Chamber of Deputies, securing re-election 4 years later. In Dec. 2006 he was elected PSD vice-president and became party president in 2010.

In 2008 Ponta was named minister responsible for liaison with parliament in the coalition of Emil Boc of the Democratic Liberal Party but he and his PSD colleagues resigned from the cabinet in Oct. 2009 in protest at the sacking of the interior minister, Dan Nica.

The government collapsed, but Boc formed a new coalition that brought in austerity measures to meet IMF conditions. In 2011 Ponta led the PSD into an alliance with the National Liberal Party (PNL), forming the USL. Amid growing popular discontent, Boc resigned from office in Feb. 2012 and Mihai-Răzvan Ungureanu replaced him. However, that government fell 2 months later when it lost a confidence vote. President Băsescu then invited Ponta to form a new administration.

Career Peak

On 1 May 2012 Ponta announced his cabinet, with the USL's constituent parties sharing portfolios equally. His initial mandate lasted only until elections scheduled for late 2012. He pledged to create jobs and to 'right the social injustices' caused by his predecessors' austerity measures. As his relationship with Băsescu deteriorated, Ponta launched an unsuccessful attempt to impeach the president in July that year. Their mutual hostility persisted until Ponta's USL won a comfortable victory in parliamentary elections the following Dec., after which they signed an agreement to set aside their differences to end the political turmoil. However, in Oct. 2013 state prosecutors charged Ponta's deputy prime minister, Liviu Dragnea, with fraudulently trying to sway the outcome of the impeachment referendum that had failed to oust President Băsescu.

In March 2014 the PNL ministers left the government and Ponta formed a new coalition administration. Then in Nov. he contested the presidential election. Despite being the frontrunner in the first round, he nonetheless lost in the run-off to Klaus Iohannis of the PNL.

Ponta's government survived a parliamentary vote of no confidence in June 2015 with the motion receiving only 194 of a required 278 votes. The prime minister had faced accusations of corruption and money laundering, and parliament had previously voted to grant Ponta immunity with regards to any charges brought before him.

Ponta survived another vote of no confidence in Sept. 2015, 1 week after going on trial for corruption charges. He became the first Romanian prime minister to go on trial while still in office. However, following widespread public dissent and protests triggered by a deadly fire in a Bucharest nightclub, Ponta and his government resigned. Sorin Cîmpeanu took over as prime minister on an interim basis.

Popescu-Tăriceanu, Călin (Romania)

Ponta, Victor (Romania)

Introduction

Victor Ponta became prime minister in May 2012 following the collapse of the short-lived government led by Mihai-Răzvan Ungureanu. Ponta's Social Liberal Union administration (USL) secured a parliamentary mandate following elections in Dec. 2012. In Nov. 2014 he made an unsuccessful electoral bid for the presidency. Ponta resigned in Nov. 2015 following allegations of corruption.

Introduction

Călin Popescu-Tăriceanu entered Romanian politics in early 1990 following the collapse of Nicolae Ceauşescu's Communist regime. He was appointed prime minister in Dec. 2004 by President Traian Băsescu, his fellow member of the then centre-right Justice and Truth Alliance, although their relationship subsequently deteriorated. In April 2007 Popescu-Tăriceanu formed a new minority government without the president's Democratic Party and went on to survive a parliamentary confidence vote in Oct. 2007. Following inconclusive general elections in Nov. 2008 President Băsescu asked economist and former Prime Minister Theodor Stolojan to form a new government.

Early Life

Born in Bucharest on 14 Jan. 1952, Popescu-Tăriceanu was educated at the Sf. Sava High School and then at the Hydro-engineering faculty of the Bucharest Construction Institute. A master's degree in science, research methods and mathematics followed at Bucharest University. In 1976 Popescu-Tăriceanu served as an engineer at the National Water Administration in Argeş county division and at a construction company in Bucharest. Returning to the Bucharest Construction Institute in 1980, he worked as a tutor in hydro-engineering, a position he held for the next 10 years. Following the collapse of Nicolae Ceauşescu's regime in Dec. 1989, Popescu-Tăriceanu entered politics, helping to re-establish the National Liberal Party (PNL). He was a member of the provisional Council of National Unity, an unelected parliament that governed Romania in the spring of 1990. After the first post-Communist elections on 20 May 1990, Popescu-Tăriceanu represented the PNL in a government that was dominated by the National Salvation Front (FSN). At this time he also founded Romania's first private radio station. In Dec. 1990 the PNL, together with other right-of-centre opposition groups, formed the Democratic Convention of Romania (CDR), which served in the government of Theodor Stolojan from Oct. 1991. After withdrawing from the Democratic Convention in April 1992, the PNL suffered a disastrous defeat in the elections held on 27 Sept. 1992. This led to serious splits in the party, and Popescu-Tăriceanu concentrated on his business interests, becoming Director General of Radio Contact Romania and establishing the Association of Automobile Producers and Importers (APIA).

Popescu-Tăriceanu returned to parliament in 1996 when he was elected as a deputy representing the CDR. He served in the cabinet headed by Prime Minister Victor Ciorbea and held the portfolio of trade and industry in 1996–97, where he became unpopular with trade unions for his decision to close unprofitable mines. He also led attempts to restructure Romania's oil sector and the National Electric Company. Following the crushing defeat of the CDR by the Social Democratic Party (PSD), led by Ion Iliescu, in the Nov. 2000 general election, Popescu-Tăriceanu and others led the PNL out of the CDR, and later (in early 2002) joined forces with the reformist Democratic Party to form the Justice and Truth Alliance (DA). It was intended to be a vehicle for co-ordinating opposition efforts against the ruling, and allegedly corrupt, PSD.

In March 2004 Popescu-Tăriceanu was made manager of the DA's campaign for the local elections in June. In late Oct. 2004 the alliance endorsed Popescu-Tăriceanu as its prime ministerial candidate in the Romanian legislative elections, which took place alongside the presidential election on 28 Nov. Both Popescu-Tăriceanu and the DA's presidential candidate, Traian Băsescu, campaigned on fighting corruption, creating jobs, alleviating poverty and establishing a non-political judiciary. The DA performed strongly at the polls, coming within a few percentage points of the PSD and eliminating the government's majority. When Băsescu triumphed over Adrian Năstase in the presidential run-off on 12 Dec., he invited Popescu-Tăriceanu to form the next government. Alliances were forged with both the Hungarian Democratic Federation of Romania and the Humanist Party (renamed the Conservative Party in May 2005) in a centre-right coalition that was approved by parliament on 28 Dec. The following day, Popescu-Tăriceanu was sworn in as Romania's prime minister.

Career Peak

Presenting his government's programme to parliament, Popescu-Tăriceanu pledged to fight corruption and poverty and carry out reforms needed for his country's entry into the European Union in 2007. His first step was to lower income and corporate profit taxes to a 16% flat rate, in a bid to reduce the size of the country's black market economy and encourage foreign investment. In Sept. 2006, despite continuing reservations about levels of crime and corruption, the European Commission confirmed Romania's eligibility to join the EU. On 1 Jan. 2007 Romania, with neighbouring Bulgaria, became the EU's 26th and 27th member states.

Subsequent tensions within the government and a breakdown of relations with President Băsescu led Popescu-Tăriceanu to formally end the alliance with the Democratic Party in April 2007 when he formed a minority government consisting of the PNL and the Hungarian Democratic Federation of Romania. The parliament then voted in favour of a motion to suspend President Băsescu from office because of alleged abuse of his constitutional powers, although he was returned to power in May following a national referendum. In Oct., after further months of feuding, Popescu-Tăriceanu survived a parliamentary no-confidence vote tabled by the opposition Social Democratic Party, which had accused the government of inefficiency.

In Nov. 2007 the PNL suffered a heavy defeat in Romania's first elections to the European Parliament, coming third with only six seats. The EU had earlier urged the government to do more to combat corruption and in Dec. the justice minister resigned having been accused of abusing his position. The EU also threatened to withhold farm aid if Romania did not reform its agricultural payments system.

Following the inconclusive general election of Nov. 2008, Popescu-Tăriceanu was stripped of his position. President Băsescu asked the former Prime Minister Theodor Stolojan to form a new government. However, Stolojan turned down his nomination and the position was instead taken by Emil Boc, the leader of the Democratic Liberal Party.

Portillo Cabrera, Alfonso Antonio (Guatemala)

Introduction

Alfonso Antonio Portillo Cabrera was president of Guatemala representing the rightwing Frente Republicano Guatemalteco (FRG) party. Elected in 1999 in the first democratic elections after the end of the 36-year civil war, Portillo took over from Álvaro Arzú Irigoyen, leader of the Partido de Avanzade Nacional (PAN). Inheriting a precarious economy, Portillo's challenges were to uphold democracy and to implement the peace agreement.

Early Life

Portillo was born in the Zacapa department on 24 Sept. 1951. He studied law at the Universidad Autónoma de Guerrero (Mexico) before taking a doctorate in economics at Mexico's national Universidad Autónoma. At the end of the 1970s he became involved with left-wing guerrilla groups. He worked with the Ejérjito Guerillero de los Pobres, one of four groups comprising the Unidad Revolucionaria Nacional Guatemalteca, which fought against the suppression of indigenous culture. In 1982 Portillo killed two rival law professors in Mexico. He fled the region to escape trial. On his return to Guatemala in 1989 he joined the Partido Socialista Democrática, at that time the only legal left-wing political party. His political views shifted to the right and he joined the leading Democracia Cristiano Guatemalteca (DCG). In 1993 he became deputy leader of the party, presiding over several ministries including finance and foreign trade. Concurrently, he directed the Instituto Guatemalteco de Estudios Sociales y Políticos, and wrote for the *Siglo Veintiuno* daily newspaper.

In 1995, with corruption scandals surrounding the DCG, Portillo left the party to join the FRG, led by the right-wing former dictator Ríos Montt. When a Supreme Court ruling prevented Montt from standing in the 1995 elections, Portillo replaced him as FRG candidate. Gaining 22% of votes, he forced a run-off with Partido de Avanzada Nacional candidate, Alvaro Arzú Yrigoyen, who narrowly won with 51.2%. Following this success, Portillo replaced Montt as party leader and prepared his candidacy for the 1999 elections, the first democratic elections after the 1996 peace accord. His main rival was PAN candidate and former mayor of Guatemala City, Óscar Berger Perdomo. During the election campaign, Portillo was haunted by the 1982 murders and tarnished by his affiliation to Montt who had been accused of allowing paramilitary atrocities. Nonetheless, Portillo's courting of the popular vote, his promise to combat rising crime and his exploitation of discontent with the failures of the current leadership outweighed the accusation that he was Montt's puppet. He won the first round of voting with 48% and in a landslide run-off gained 68%.

Career Peak

On election Portillo called for unity in an attempt to stabilize and strengthen the precarious, nascent democracy. He outlined plans to combat crime, improve the situation of the poorest Guatemalans and reduce the disparity between rich and poor. He acknowledged that the economy was on the brink of collapse. In accordance with the peace treaty, he also promised to dismantle the military security force, the *Estado Mayor* (EMP), and create a civilian force.

Portillo's term was soon marred by violent rioting. In April 2000 there were protests against increased bus fares, followed in Aug. by a protest against tax increases, and a spate of public lynchings in rural areas. He was more successful on an international level. In Sept. 2001 he hosted a meeting of Central American governments in Guatemala City that concentrated on resolving low coffee prices on the international market. The meeting produced a non aggression pact with neighbouring countries aimed at border disputes.

In Aug. 2000 Portillo admitted the culpability of past governments in crimes against humanity. The death of 100,000 people and the disappearance of 50,000 since 1961, the majority civilian, had hitherto been blamed on guerrillas. An investigation was set up. He also announced an investigation into the 1998 killing of Juan Gerardi, a Catholic bishop who had headed the church's human rights office. Portillo pledged to solve the murder within 6 months, although it was not until June 2001 that the former head of military intelligence, Desrail Lima, two other soldiers and a priest were sentenced to 30 years imprisonment. Despite this, the EMP has still not been disbanded. Further conditions of the peace accord not implemented include tax and human rights reforms and the reduction of the army's powers. The deadline for those reforms has been postponed from 2000 to 2004.

In Sept. 2001 severe drought brought food shortages and the threat of famine. Emergency taxes highlighted Guatemala's lack of economic progress.

Portillo was barred from standing for re-election in 2003 and was succeeded by his 1999 opponent, Óscar Berger, on 14 Jan. 2004.

Later Life

After leaving office Portillo fled to Mexico. But in 2008 he was extradited to Guatemala to stand trial on charges that he stole US$15 m. from the military in 2001. He was cleared of those charges in 2011. Then in May 2013 he was extradited to the USA to face charges of laundering US$70 m. through US banks during his time in office, a charge that he refuted. In May 2014, Portillo was found guilty of these charges and sentenced to 5 years and 10 months imprisonment. He was released in Feb. 2015 and returned to Guatemala.

Portillo y Pacheco, José López (Mexico)

Introduction

José López Portillo was president of Mexico between 1976 and 1982, representing the Partido Revolucionario Institucional (Institutional Revolutionary Party; PRI). During his presidency Portillo served as a mediator in Pan-American disputes and encouraged industrial development by the creation of non-agricultural jobs and the exploitation of Mexico's natural resources. He continued the programme implemented by his predecessor Echeverría to promote population control. However, any successes he had during his presidency were overshadowed by charges of corruption within his administration and by the economic crisis brought on by excessive spending and borrowing.

Early Life

Portillo was born in Mexico City on 16 June 1920. He became a lawyer and university professor who wrote both novels and essays on political theory. He studied at the Universidad Nacional Autónoma de México and the University of Chile before becoming a professor. He joined the PRI in 1954 and subsequently worked in the governments of both Gustavo Díaz Ordaz and Luis Echeverría, serving as finance minister under the latter when he modernized tax-collection procedures and reduced public spending.

Career Peak

At the beginning of his term Portillo's aim was to promote economic stability. Originally there were hopes of radical economic and social change. He set out to achieve this by nationalizing the country's banks. The major key in Portillo's presidency was the discovery of oil by the state-owned Petróleos Méxicanos in the Tobasco and Veracruz regions, a discovery he exploited to the full. But instead of implementing tax reforms, he borrowed heavily on the strength of the oil reserves. The money raised was used for public spending to

create employment and improve education and living conditions of the poorest Mexicans. However, when oil prices plummeted at the beginning of the 1980s, the Mexican government was left with massive debts. The resulting economic problems included a rise in inflation and unemployment and a large migration of rural Mexicans to the larger towns and to the USA.

The Portillo government was beset by accusations of corruption. There were claims that revenue from the country's oil production, instead of going to repay the international debt, was being filtered off by the government. Controversy also surrounded the appointment of his personal security chief and childhood friend, Arturo Durazo Moreno, or 'El Negro Durazo'. as commander of the Mexico City Police. During 6 years in the job there was a high level of police corruption, especially in drug trafficking and bribe taking. The División de Investigación para la Prevención de la Delincuencia (Crime Prevention Investigation Division), founded by Durazo, may have kept the streets safe but only by acts of brutality, including torture, which provoked the concern of human rights activists. Portillo's links to such a figure led many PRI colleagues to disassociate themselves. In the elections of 1982, the PRI candidate Miguel de la Madrid Hurtado was elected as Portillo's successor. Portillo died on 17 Feb. 2004.

Prabhakaran, Velupillai (Sri Lanka)

Introduction

Velupillai Prabhakaran was the leader of the Liberation Tigers of Tamil Eelam (LTTE)—also known as the Tamil Tigers—a separatist militant group claiming to represent the Tamil population of Sri Lanka. A skilled military strategist, Prabhakaran had no experience of civilian government. He was killed on 18 May 2009 after the Sri Lankan army launched a military campaign to eradicate the rebel forces.

Early Life

Velupillai Prabhakaran was born on 26 Nov. 1954 in Velvettithurai, a coastal town on the northern Jaffna peninsula, into a lower caste family. The son of a civil servant and youngest of four children, Prabhakaran became active early on in the Tamil separatist movement, joining the Tamil Youth Front in 1973. Facing police arrest, that same year he fled to Madras (capital of the southern Indian state of Tamil Nadu), where he underwent military training. In 1975 he returned to Jaffna and joined the New Tamil Tigers (NTT) becoming its head within a year. On 27 July 1975, in the first of many political assassinations, Prabhakaran and two other members of the NTT shot Jaffna's Mayor, Alfred Duraiappa. In 1976 the NTT reformed as LTTE with Prabhakaran remaining at its head.

Career Peak

When in 1983, the Sri Lankan government called for the main Tamil parliamentary presence, the Tamil United Liberation Front, to renounce its wishes for a separate state, Prabhakaran took part in an ambush on a Sri Lankan army convoy killing 13 soldiers. A wave of retaliatory Sinhalese aggression throughout the island gave a pretext for Prabhakaran to declare an all-out guerrilla war against the Sri Lankan state.

Retreating to the northern stronghold of Jaffna, the LTTE expanded rapidly and by the end of 1984 commanded over 10,000 cadres. Over the next few years Prabhakaran began a process of assimilating, or more frequently, eradicating the many rival Tamil guerrilla groups. During this period intra-Tamil violence reached a high-point, over-shadowing violence between the Tamil groups and the Sinhalese government.

In 1989 Prabhakaran created a political wing to the LTTE, the People's Front of Liberation Tigers, for which he appointed his deputy, Kopalaswamy Mahendrarajah, as leader. Through this medium Prabhakaran began consultation with Sri Lankan President Ranasinghe Premadasa's government over the issue of ejecting the Indian Peace Keeping Force, brought in following the Indo–Sri Lanka accord in 1987 to resolve the ethnic conflict. In 1990 talks between the two broke down. Indian Prime Minister Rajiv Gandhi and Sri Lankan President Premadasa were assassinated, in 1991 and 1993 respectively, in suicide bomb attacks linked to the LTTE. Prabhakaran also imprisoned and executed Kopalaswamy Mahendrarajah, apprehensive of the latter's ties with Premadasa.

In Jan. 1995 a ceasefire was established between the LTTE and the Sri Lankan government. Despite offers from the latter to lift economic embargoes on LTTE-held areas (which were subsequently carried through), Prabhakaran broke the ceasefire, citing delays in this process, and fighting again broke out.

Movement towards a permanent settlement of the conflict gained ground with the signing of a month-long ceasefire in Dec. 2001, followed by an internationally-monitored ceasefire in Feb. 2002. In the wake of the terrorist attacks in the US on 11 Sept. 2001 and the international consensus on combatting terrorism, many of the LTTE's financial assets were frozen. Eager to throw off the LTTE's adverse image, Prabhakaran made his first public appearance in 12 years on 10 April 2002, declaring an end to the 'Black Tiger' suicide bombings for which the LTTE had become famous. In return, Prabhakaran demanded that the ban on the LTTE should be lifted prior to peace talks, a step which was taken on 4 Sept. 2002. On 31 Oct. 2002, a Sri Lankan court passed a 200-year jail sentence on Prabhakaran for his alleged involvement in the bombing of Sri Lanka's central bank in 1996. Despite this, peace talks moved towards a compromise agreement between the government and the LTTE. Prabhakaran reduced his demands for a separate Tamil state after a peace deal was signed in Dec. 2002 granting Tamil autonomy.

The LTTE pulled out of talks in 2003 and violence recommenced the following year. New peace talks failed in Oct. 2006 in Geneva and by Jan. 2008 the government had pulled out of the 2002 ceasefire agreement. In May 2009 the government launched a campaign to eradicate the last Tamil stronghold in the northeast of the island and reported that Prabhakaran had been killed on 18 May. Despite initial denials, the LTTE confirmed his death a week later and conceded defeat.

Préval, René (Haiti)

Introduction

René Préval won a controversial election in Feb. 2006 to become president of Haiti for the second time. However, the already difficult task of restoring hope to the poorest nation in the western hemisphere was undermined by political instability and the devastating consequences of natural disasters. Following further presidential elections in Nov. 2010 with a second round in March 2011, in which he could not stand, Préval left office in May 2011.

Early Life

René Garcia Préval was born on 17 Jan. 1943 in Port-au-Prince. His family was forced into exile in 1963 by the dictator, François 'Papa Doc' Duvalier. He studied agronomy at the College of Gembloux, Belgium, before moving to New York, USA in 1970, where he lived for 5 years. Having returned to Haiti, he became active in politics and charity work following the fall of Jean-Claude 'Baby Doc' Duvalier in Feb. 1986. He grew close to the radical slum preacher, Jean-Bertrand Aristide, who in Dec. 1990 was elected president. Préval was appointed prime minister in Feb. 1991 but was forced to flee the country shortly after a military coup led by Gen. Raoul Cedras in Sept. 1991.

Joining the exiled constitutional government in the USA in 1992, Préval held the prime minister's portfolio. Aristide was reinstated as president in Oct. 1994 but was constitutionally barred from running in the Dec. 1995 election. Préval won with 88% of the vote and took office on 7 Feb. 1996, inheriting a country with a devastated economy. In Jan. 1999, following a series of disagreements with legislators, Préval began to rule by decree. Following Aristide's return to power after a controversial presidential election in Nov. 2000, Préval, whose relationship with Aristide had deteriorated from the mid-1990s, retreated from politics.

Poverty and unemployment, together with Aristide's increasingly authoritarian rule, led to violent protests which forced the president into exile in Feb. 2004. His successor, former chief justice Boniface Alexandre, worked with a US-led international force to stabilize the country and prepare for fresh elections. Préval unexpectedly returned to the fray, running as the candidate for Lespwa. Following repeated delays, the presidential election was held on 7 Feb. 2006 and Préval was subsequently declared the outright winner, with 51.2% of the vote.

Career Peak

Préval pledged to create 'cohesion' in Haiti's fractured society and restore peace in an effort to revive the ailing economy and provide employment. However, political in-fighting, economic vulnerability, organized crime and natural disasters continued to undermine the stability of the country. Jacques-Edouard Alexis and Michèle Pierre-Louis were both dismissed as prime minister before Préval named Jean-Max Bellerive as the new premier in Oct. 2009. Meanwhile, in Aug. and Sept. 2008 tropical storms caused extensive flooding across the country, and in Jan. 2010 Port-au-Prince and the surrounding region were hit by an earthquake that left over 200,000 dead and further weakened the fragile economy.

Préval's preferred successor, Jude Célestin, contested the first round of presidential elections in Nov. 2010 but was subsequently disqualified from standing in the delayed run-off poll in March 2011. Préval's mandate was extended until 14 May 2011 when he was succeeded by Michel Martelly. He died in Port-au-Prince on 3 March 2017 at the age of 74.

Price, Cadle (Belize)

Introduction

George Price was the first prime minister of Belize—formerly British Honduras—from 1981–84 and served a second term from 1989–93. Regarded as the 'father of the nation'. he played a key role in negotiating independence from British rule.

Early Life

The third of eleven children, George Cadle Price was born on 15 Jan. 1919 in Belize City. Raised a devout Catholic, he attended St. John's College, a prominent Jesuit-run secondary school, and decided to train for the priesthood, studying at seminaries in Mississippi and Guatemala City. However, the Second World War prevented him from studying in Rome. He returned to Belize to attend his ailing father.

Price entered politics in 1944 to contest, unsuccessfully, the Belize Town Board elections. Three years later he won a seat on the Belize City council. Angered by the colonial authority's decision to devalue the British Honduran dollar in 1949, he co-founded the People's Committee in Sept. 1950, which evolved into the pro-independence People's United Party (PUP). Three of the PUP's founders were found guilty of sedition but Price escaped imprisonment. Starting as party secretary, he became its leader in 1956, a position he held for 40 years.

Price served as mayor of Belize City from 1956–62. In 1961, under a revised constitution, he was elected first minister. In 1964 Belize became self-governing except in matters of defence, internal security and external affairs. All the governor's powers were handed to an Executive Council headed by Price.

Career Peak

Guatemala's long-standing claim to Belize proved an obstacle to independence. As premier of British Honduras, Price rejected calls for Belize to become an 'associated state' of Guatemala, instead orienting external relations towards North and Central America and building on established links with the English-speaking Caribbean. Price secured the support of near neighbours including Cuba, Mexico, Panama and Nicaragua. In Nov. 1980 the United Nations supported Belize's independence. The country formally gained independence on 21 Sept. 1981, with Price serving as both prime minister and foreign minister.

In the first post-independence elections, held in 1984, the PUP lost to the United Democratic Party (UDP) of Manuel Esquivel. However, Price returned to power in 1989 before again giving way to the UDP and Esquivel in 1993. Price was replaced by Said Musa as leader of the PUP in 1996 but he remained a prominent figure in the party and was a senior minister in Musa's government until his retirement from active politics in 2003.

Later Life

In Sept. 2000 Price received Belize's highest honour, the Order of National Hero, for his part in winning independence. On 19 Sept. 2011, 2 days before the 30th anniversary of Belize's independence, he died. Prime Minister Dean Barrow declared a week of mourning and the country's first premier received a state funeral.

Privert, Jocelerme (Haiti)

Introduction

Jocelerme Privert was elected interim president on 14 Feb. 2016 by parliament after the second round of national polling to replace the outgoing Michel Martelly had been postponed amid fears of violence. Privert was scheduled to serve a term of up to 120 days and to oversee fresh elections initially rescheduled for April 2016 but then delayed owing to the continuing political stalemate.

Early Life

Jocelerme Privert was born on 1 Feb. 1953 in Petit-Trou-de-Nippes. Having graduated in accounting from Centre Universitaire Maurice Laroche, Port-au-Prince, he enrolled in 1978 at l'École Nationale d'Administration Financière (ENAF) and a year later joined the Directorate of General Taxation. In 1995 he became its director general and in 2001 was named secretary of state for finance under President Jean-Bertrand Aristide. In 2002 he was appointed interior minister.

Privert was arrested in April 2004 on suspicion of orchestrating the killings of several people presumed to be opponents of Aristide in the town of Saint Marc. He spent 26 months in jail without trial and was released in June 2006 after he went on hunger strike. From 2008–10 he served as an adviser to President René Préval, and in 2010 was elected to the Senate. On 14 Jan. 2016 Privert became president of the Senate, a role he held for a month before resigning to become interim state president. He received 77 votes after two rounds of parliamentary polling (against a combined 35 for his two opponents) to assume the office.

Career Peak

Although his indirect election was immediately denounced by his opponents, it was hoped Privert's reputation as a pragmatic bureaucrat would bring respite from the political chaos and violent demonstrations that marred the presidential elections. He was charged with overseeing the formation of a provisional electoral council to complete rescheduled legislative, municipal and presidential elections and with forming a workable government for the interim period. They were initially scheduled for 24 April 2016 but were postponed yet again. Privert stated that it might not be held until late Oct. The elections eventually took place on 20 Nov. 2016, when Jovenel Moïse was elected in the first round. Prevert left office on 7 Feb. 2017 when Moïse was sworn in as president.

Prodi, Romano (Italy)

Introduction

In April 2006 Romano Prodi was elected prime minister for the second time, defeating his arch-rival Silvio Berlusconi by a slim majority. Leading a diverse leftist coalition, Prodi initially struggled to maintain his government in power and briefly resigned in Feb. 2007. He was previously prime minister from 1996–98 and was credited with steering the Italian economy towards European Monetary Union (EMU). As president of the European Commission between 1999–2004 he was instrumental in working towards the expansion of the European Union and closer unity between the member states.

Early Life

Romano Prodi was born on 9 Aug. 1939 in Scandiano, Reggio Emilia. On completion of his schooling in Reggio Emilia, he studied law at the Catholic University of Milan before undertaking postgraduate studies at the London School of Economics in the UK. He went on to hold the post of professor of industrial organization and policy at the University of Bologna for over 25 years. He was also a visiting professor at Harvard University and had a long association with the Stanford Research Institute, both in the USA. In 1978 he commenced his political career, holding an array of posts including minister for industry (in the government of Giulio Andreotti) and chairman of the institute for industrial reconstruction (a government holding company). While in the latter position, he was subject to allegations of conflict of interest in relation to his private business concerns, but was acquitted of any wrongdoing.

In 1995 Prodi became chairman of the *Ulivo* (Olive Tree) centre-left coalition and stood in the 1996 elections against the then prime minister, media millionaire and owner of AC Milan football club, Silvio Berlusconi. *Ulivo* won the election with a narrow majority and in May 1996 Prodi was appointed prime minister. During his 28-month premiership he introduced a swathe of financial reforms and reduced the public sector deficit. He also introduced changes in the areas of public administration, fiscal planning and corporate governance law. On 9 Oct. 1998 Prodi lost a vote of no confidence, initiated by the leader of the Communist Refoundation party, Fausto Bertinotti.

Prodi was elected president of the European Commission in May 1999. In this role he promoted increased powers for the European Union (EU) and common foreign and immigration policies. He also oversaw increased EU involvement in national economic policies. When his tenure expired in Nov. 2004, he was replaced as president of the European Commission by José Manuel Durão Barroso.

Following the end of his European Commission presidency Prodi returned to the national political arena, leading the opposition against Silvio Berlusconi's ruling right-wing coalition, *Forza Italia*. In Oct. 2004 the centre-left opposition coalition, formerly known as *Ulivo*, was refounded and renamed the Great Democratic Alliance (GAD). Key to this restructuring was the inclusion of the far-left Communist Refoundation party led by Fausto Bertinotti. On 6 Oct. 2005, 4 m. people voted in primary elections to choose the opposition candidate to stand against Berlusconi in general elections planned for April 2006. Prodi claimed a landslide victory, winning 73.5% of the vote, while Bertinotti polled 15.4%.

A general election took place on 10 April 2006. Following a record-breaking electoral turnout of 83%, the result was a knife-edge victory for Prodi and his Union coalition. Recent changes to the electoral system provided the winner of the lower house with a working majority, 348 seats against 281 for *Forza Italia*. Less comfortably, the Union coalition won only 158 seats in the upper house against 156 for *Forza Italia*. With both houses holding equal power, the government was vulnerable.

Career Peak

Berlusconi contested the results of the election, demanding a recount in several areas. However, Prodi's victory was confirmed by the judiciary on 22 April 2006. There were further delays before Prodi was able to take office. The new government had to wait until Giorgio Napolitano, the newly-elected president, had formally replaced outgoing president Carlo Azeglio Ciampi on 15 May. Chosen after four rounds of voting, 80-year-old Napolitano was Prodi's favoured candidate. The speakers of both houses of parliament were also elected following several rounds of close voting, with the position in the lower house going to Fausto Bertinotti and in the upper house to moderate trade union leader Franco Marini. In both cases the speakers were Prodi's chosen candidates.

By the time of the election, with a public debt that had ballooned to 106.5% of gross domestic product and a budget deficit that had exceeded European Union limits for the previous 2 years, Italians chose a prime minister who promised to improve tax collection, slim down the country's overweight bureaucracy, increase competition and gradually reduce the budget deficit. However, his rainbow coalition of parties ranging from communists to Catholic centrists was fragile, with widely differing views on issues such as privatization and the war in Iraq (against which Prodi has long been an outspoken opponent). And with a majority in the upper house so small that the absence of a single senator could change the outcome of a vote, the ability of the government to implement the reforms necessary for the long-term revitalization of the Italian economy was questionable. Nevertheless, Prodi made several significant policy changes during his first year in office, including rejecting devolution reforms proposed by the Berlusconi government and pledging to withdraw Italian troops from Iraq. He also introduced a range of deregulatory measures and initiated a clampdown on tax evasion.

The government's precarious parliamentary position was demonstrated in Feb. 2007 when it was defeated in the Senate over foreign policy issues. However, President Napolitano rejected Prodi's resignation and called on the prime minister to return to parliament for a confidence vote. At the end of the month Prodi won a narrow 162–157 majority in the upper house and then secured a more comfortable victory in the Chamber of Deputies by 342–253 votes in early March.

Qarase, Laisenia (Fiji)

Introduction

Laisenia Qarase was appointed prime minister of an interim government following the collapse of Mahendra Chaudhry's government in a coup in May 2000. Qarase formed a new party, Soqosoqo Duavata ni Lewenivanua, and won the elections of Aug.–Sept. 2001. An ethnic Fijian, he ruled out a return to the pre-coup situation of government by the Indian minority. His major challenges were to return Fiji to political stability and revitalize the economy. He was deposed in late 2006 in a military coup led by Commodore Frank Bainimarama, who had been instrumental in his rise to power in 2000.

Early Life

Qarase was born in 1941 in Mavana on the eastern Lau islands. He was schooled in Suva and graduated in commerce from the University of Auckland in New Zealand. He returned to Fiji and took a job with the Fijian Affairs Board. He then became deputy secretary of the finance department, permanent secretary for commerce and industry, and secretary of the Public Service Commission. Between 1983 and 1998 he headed the Fiji Development Bank and in 1998 moved into the private sector to take charge of a merchant bank.

In 1999 he was appointed to the Senate, where he gained a reputation for his vociferous criticism of the regime of Mahendra Chaudhry, Fiji's first ethnic Indian prime minister. In May 2000 George Speight, an indigenous Fijian, stormed parliament with his supporters and took the government hostage. Chaudhry's administration was dismissed by decree of the Great Council of Chiefs and Speight, a bankrupt businessman, pronounced himself prime minister. Qarase was named prime minister of an interim government in July 2000 as part of the deal which saw the release of Chaudhry and his colleagues. The affair was the culmination of years of rising tensions between the ethnic Fijian population and the Fiji's financially and politically powerful ethnic Indian minority.

Career Peak

During Qarase's first month in office the hostages were freed and Speight was arrested. Fiji had been suspended from the Commonwealth's councils the previous month and was subject to sanctions by Australia, New Zealand, France and the USA. Qarase was charged with restoring stability to the political scene. He was to pave the way for new elections, prepare a new constitution and revive the badly-hit economy.

In March 2001 the Supreme Court declared the interim government illegal. President Iloilo, who had come to power after the coup, formally dismissed Chaudhry (who had been effectively excluded from political life since the coup) and replaced Qarase with Ratu Tevita Momoedonu, a tribal leader, for 24 h. He then reappointed Qarase, thus legitimizing the new administration, despite Chaudhry's protests that his sacking was unconstitutional.

In the build-up to the elections of Aug.–Sept. 2001 Qarase formed a new nationalist party, Soqosoqo Duavata ni Lewenivanua (SDL). He announced that a new constitution would not be of the multi-racial nature of the 1997 document which allowed for the appointment of Chaudhry. Instead Qarase stated that 'there must be better guarantees for indigenous Fijians to be in control of their political destiny'. The SDL won 32 out of 71 seats, against 27 for Chaudhry's Fiji Labour Party.

Qarase was constitutionally required to invite Chaudhry into the new government but actively encouraged his opponent not to accept any posts, claiming a joint government would be unworkable. Chaudhry announced plans to establish an opposition group within the government. In his first 18-man cabinet Qarase failed to appoint any Labour members but did include two allies of Speight, whose Matanitu Vanua had won six seats. Chaudhry claimed his party was entitled to six cabinet posts, a view upheld by an appeal court in Feb. 2002 and by the Supreme Court in July 2003.

Qarase oversaw Fiji's re-entry into the Commonwealth in Dec. 2001, although the domestic political environment remained unstable. In Jan. 2002 a gang was arrested for plotting Qarase's kidnapping in order to secure the freedom of Speight who in Feb. 2002 received a death sentence, later commuted by life imprisonment, for treason. In June 2002 Qarase came under investigation for vote-buying at the previous year's elections. The political fall-out from the Speight-led coup was again evident in 2004 when the vice president, Ratu Jope Seniloli, was found guilty of treason for his involvement.

Meanwhile, negotiation had not resolved the problem of the number of cabinet posts to which the Labour Party was entitled. In 2004 Chaudhry declined any seats and took the position of leader of the opposition. In 2005 Qarase's government introduced the Promotion of Reconciliation, Tolerance and Unity Bill. This generated considerable opposition from many sections of society towards the proposed amnesty for those who were involved in the 2000 coup, and led to friction between the government and the military.

This friction came to a head when the government tried to replace Commodore Frank Bainimarama in 2006. Bainimarama, who had been a prominent figure in the 2000 coup, led a bloodless coup on 5 Dec. 2006. He assumed the president's powers and removed Qarase, whom he accused of corruption. Jona Senilagakali was named Qarase's successor and charged with overseeing an eventual return to democracy. Fiji was suspended from the Commonwealth on 9 Dec.

Qassim, Abdul Karim (Iraq)

Introduction

Gen. Qassim was the main architect of the overthrow the Hashemite monarchy of Iraq on the 14 July 1958 and became prime minister in the new republic's government. Although an Arab nationalist with left-wing sympathies, he rejected the pan-Arab cause advocated by Egypt's President Nasser. Faced with increasing political opposition and rebellion among the Kurdish population, his power deteriorated steadily. On 8 Feb. 1963 he was overthrown and executed by nationalist army officers and civilian members of the Arab Socialist Renaissance (Ba'ath) Party.

Early Life

Qassim was born in Baghdad in 1914. After graduating from the Iraqi Military Academy in 1934, he attended the Army Staff College. Following distinguished service in campaigns against the Kurds and in the Palestinian war of 1948, he had become a high-ranking officer by 1955. Like many Iraqis, Qassim was hostile to the conservative and pro-Western policies of the monarchy. He became active in the opposition movement that spread within the army officer corps, and in 1958 instigated the coup that ushered in the new republic.

Career Peak

Almost immediately Qassim clashed with his deputy premier, Col. Abdul Salem Aref. Aref was associated with elements of the Ba'ath Party and favoured union between Iraq and the then United Arab Republic (of Egypt and Syria). Qassim sought internal Iraqi stability ahead of pan-Arab federation and dismissed Aref from office in Sept. 1958. In 1959 Qassim survived an assassination attempt by young Ba'ath activists (including Saddam Hussein). In the same year he announced the withdrawal of Iraq from the international Baghdad Pact. His rule became increasingly repressive and, from 1961, he faced a serious Kurdish rebellion. An alliance of nationalist army officers and the Ba'ath Party seized power in Feb. 1963. Qassim was captured and shot.

Qureia, Ahmed (Palestinian Territories, Israel)

Introduction

Following the resignation of Mahmoud Abbas on 6 Sept. 2003, Jerusalem-born Ahmed Qureia was nominated as prime minister by Palestinian leader Yasser Arafat. Recognised as one of the leading Palestinian representatives of the 1993 Oslo Agreement, the first Palestinian-Israeli peace accord, Qureia's pragmatism and negotiating experience were anticipated to bring a measure of stability to the peace process despite his loyalty to Yasser Arafat (who died in Nov. 2004) and restrictions in his power of office. Qureia's term ended with his resignation in Jan. 2006.

Early Life

Ahmed Ali Sulieman Qureia was born to a wealthy family in the village of Abu Dis in Jerusalem in 1937. In 1968 Qureia left a banking career to pursue politics, joining the Fatah wing of the Palestine Liberation Organisation (PLO). His background in business helped his rise to prominence in the mid-1970s when he took control of Fatah's extensive enterprises in Lebanon. Following the PLO's expulsion from Lebanon by Israeli troops in 1982, Qureia joined Fatah leader Arafat in Tunis. The following year he became head of the PLO's executive committee's economic department. Qureia's influence increased as the number of PLO leaders diminished, and in 1989 he was elected member of the Fatah central committee.

Qureia first came to international attention as a key negotiator in the secret talks between Israel and Palestine in Norway in 1993. The interim peace agreement that followed led to an autonomous Palestinian administration in the West Bank and Gaza Strip, and marked the beginning of his participation in peace talks involving Israel and the USA. These included talks in Camp David in July 2000 and in Taba, Egypt, in Jan. 2001.

In 1993 Qureia drafted a Palestinian development plan, presented at a World Bank conference on aid that year. He helped develop the Palestinian Economic Council for Development and Reconstruction (PECDAR), and assumed the role of secretary-general. He also served as minister of economy and trade and minister of industry for the Palestinian Authority between 1994 and 1996, when he was elected a member of the Palestinian Legislative Council and subsequently its speaker.

After the resignation of Mahmoud Abbas on 6 Sept. 2003, 4 months after taking office, Qureia was appointed prime minister with the support of Fatah and the Palestine Liberation Army.

Career Peak

Prior to the creation of the office of prime minister, Qureia served as Arafat's second in command as speaker for the Palestinian Legislative Council. His position of prime minister was fragile, given Arafat's reluctance to relinquish power. The days succeeding Qureia's appointment were dominated by retaliative acts of aggression from both Israel and Palestine, and Arafat's decision to install Qureia as head of an emergency government on 5 Oct. 2003 angered representatives in the National Council, bypassed by presidential decree. Nasser Yousef, named as interior minister and thus head of the Palestinian security forces, refused to be sworn into office on 7 Oct., stating that he needed the approval of the Council. Persuaded not to resign, Qureia agreed to remain for the 3 weeks of emergency government allowed by the Palestinian charter. Arafat's reluctance to relinquish control of the security forces undermined Qureia as it did his predecessor.

On completion of his term as head of the emergency government, Arafat requested that Qureia remain in power and form a new government. He accepted and in Nov. 2003 stated his aims: a ceasefire with Israel, an international peace conference, an Israeli withdrawal from certain territories to allow elections to take place and an end to the violence of Palestinian militant groups. In Dec. 2003 Qureia reaffirmed his commitment to the 'road map to peace' while expressing that any unilateral action by Israel would be disastrous. In Feb. 2004 he called for immediate action to deal with the Israeli security fence being built in the West Bank, claiming that it was threatening the peaceful creation of a separate Palestinian state. On his first tour outside the Middle East since coming to office, Qureia campaigned against the construction of the wall and

openly criticized the USA for not doing enough to help the peace process. In May, however, after a meeting between Qureia and US Secretary of State Colin Powell, the US administration stressed its commitment to a future Palestinian state and asserted that the Israeli withdrawal from Gaza (announced by Prime Minister Sharon in Feb. 2004) should be seen as a chance for peace.

As the violence continued, and after an unpopular reform of the security services by Arafat resulting in reappointments of key officials and mass protests, Qureia threatened to resign in July 2004. As a result Arafat conceded some security powers to his prime minister. In Nov. 2004 Arafat died and in Jan. 2005 Mahmoud Abbas was elected president. Qureia retained the premiership and formed a new cabinet of technocrats in Feb. 2005. Qureia resigned briefly in Dec. 2005 to run for parliament. Nine days later he changed his mind and resumed his position as prime minister.

On 26 Jan. 2006 Qureia resigned for the final time when Fatah was defeated in legislative elections by Palestinian Islamist group Hamas. At the request of Mahmoud Abbas, he remained as caretaker prime minister until Hamas formed the government and appointed a successor.

Rabbani, Burhanuddin (Afghanistan)

Introduction

A religious scholar and founding father of the Afghan mujahideen, Burhanuddin Rabbani played a key role in ending the Soviet occupation of Afghanistan in 1988–89. He served as president from 1992–96 and again in 2001. As head of the High Peace Council, Rabbani attempted to bring Taliban leaders into the reconciliation process. He was killed in a suicide bomb attack in 2011.

Early Life

Burhanuddin Rabbani was born in 1940 in the northern province of Badakhshan. He attended Abu-Hanifa, a religious school in Kabul, and graduated in Islamic law and theology from Kabul University in 1963. He then taught at the University and later gained a master's degree in Islamic philosophy from Al-Azhar University in Cairo.

Returning to Kabul University's faculty of Islamic law in 1968, he was increasingly inspired by the revivalist pan-Islamism of the Egyptian Muslim Brotherhood. In 1972 he became head of the activist Jamiat-e Islami (Islamic Society of Afghanistan). Under threat of arrest for his pro-Islamic stance, Rabbani fled the country in 1973 and settled in Pakistan. In 1979 Soviet forces invaded Afghanistan and Rabbani became a leading figure in the mujahideen, offering religious inspiration to fighters including military leader Ahmed Shah Massoud who later served as Afghanistan's minister of defence during Rabbani's presidency.

Career Peak

After the Soviet withdrawal in 1989 and the collapse of the pro-Moscow government of Mohammed Najibullah in 1992, Jamiat-e Islami fighters were the first to enter Kabul. Rabbani was appointed president under an agreement designed to ensure the annual rotation of the presidency. However, he refused to relinquish power and stayed in office for a further 4 years.

As the mujahideen failed to bring peace to Afghanistan, Taliban forces gained in strength and took over Kabul in 1996. Forced to leave the city, Rabbani retreated to his home town of Faisabad. During the Taliban rule he established himself as leader of the United National and Islamic Front for the Salvation of Afghanistan, commonly known as the Northern Alliance—the main armed opposition to the Taliban.

Following the US invasion and fall of the Taliban regime at the end of 2001, Rabbani returned to Kabul and served as president in a temporary capacity from Nov. to Dec. of that year. Marginalized as an ethnic Tajik, he reluctantly handed power to the Pashtun tribal leader Hamid Karzai, who was backed by the UN-backed Bonn conference.

For the next decade Rabbani remained leader of the Jamiat-e Islami. In Oct. 2010 Karzai appointed him head of Afghanistan's 68-member High Peace Council (HPC) to negotiate with the Taliban and other insurgent groups. On 20 Sept. 2011 he was killed in a suicide bomb attack at his home. Afghan officials blamed the Quetta Shura, a group of insurgents operating out of Quetta in Pakistan.

Rabin, Yitzhak (Israel)

Introduction

A career soldier until the late 1960s, Rabin was ambassador to the United States until he entered politics as a leading figure in the Labour Party. He served as prime minister (the first native-born premier) from 1974–77 and again from 1992 until his assassination by a fellow Jew in Nov. 1995. The crowning achievement of his second premiership was the peace accord between Israel and the Palestine Liberation Organization (PLO) in Sept. 1993.

Early Life

Rabin was born in Jerusalem in March 1922 into a Zionist family. He was educated at the Kadoorie Agricultural High School and then served in the Palmach, an elite force of the Jewish Haganah underground defence organization, during the 1940s. Upon the establishment of the state of Israel in 1948, Rabin joined the Israel Defence Forces (IDF), achieving the rank of lieutenant-general by 1962 when he was appointed chief of the general staff. The architect of the Israeli victory in the Six Day War of 1967, he retired from the IDF in 1968 and became Israel's ambassador to the United States. He promoted strategic bilateral co-operation with the US and secured massive military aid for Israel.

Having returned to Israel, Rabin was elected to the Knesset as a Labour deputy in Dec. 1973. Following the resignation of Golda Meir, he successfully contested the Labour leadership and became prime minister in June 1974. In the aftermath of the Yom Kippur war of Oct. 1973, Rabin's government negotiated the 1974–75 military disengagement agreements with Egypt and Syria. In 1977 a scandal involving his wife Leah's breach of foreign currency regulations forced his resignation as Labour leader prior to elections which swept opposition leader Menachem Begin into office. Rabin remained a member of the Knesset and served as minister of defence from 1984–90 in national unity governments.

Career Peak

In Feb. 1992 he unseated his long-time rival Shimon Peres as Labour leader and, after the party's election victory in June that year, began his second tenure as prime minister. Following months of secret negotiations, Rabin signed an accord with the PLO in Sept. 1993 (the Oslo agreements) providing for the phased handover of the Gaza Strip and Jericho to Palestinian authority and a lesser degree of autonomy in the rest of the West Bank (an achievement for which he shared the Nobel Peace Prize). In Oct. 1994 a peace treaty was also signed with the kingdom of Jordan. However, Rabin's policies were not universally popular, particularly among Jewish settlers in the occupied territories. On 4 Nov. 1995 he was shot dead by a right-wing Jewish extremist.

Radičová, Iveta (Slovakia)

Introduction

Radičová became Slovakia's first female prime minister in July 2010 at the head of a centre-right coalition. She promised to tackle Slovakia's economic crisis by cutting public debt and floated a renegotiation of Slovakia's commitments to EU funding. Having lost a vote of confidence in Oct. 2011, early elections were held in March 2012 and the following month Radičová was succeeded by former prime minister Robert Fico.

Early Life

Born in Bratislava on 7 Dec. 1956 to Polish–Slovak parents, Iveta Radičová grew up in Bratislava and studied sociology at Comenius University. After graduating, she was a researcher in family policy at the Slovak Academy of Sciences from 1979–89, during which time she gained a PhD. She entered politics in 1990, joining the Public Against Violence organization, speaking on their behalf until 1992. After completing postdoctoral studies at Oxford University in 1991, she returned to Slovakia and founded the Center for Analysis of Social Policy. From 1991–2005 she served as its executive director and lectured in sociology, political science and social work at Comenius University, where she was appointed professor of sociology in 2005.

That year she joined the centre-right government of Mikuláš Dzurinda as minister of labour, social affairs and family. She served until the general election of 2006, when Dzurinda's Slovak Democratic and Christian Union–Democratic Party (SDKÚ–DS) lost power to the centre-left Direction–Social Democracy (Smer–SD). In the same election, Radičová was elected to parliament for the SDKÚ–DS and became deputy chair of the party and deputy chair of the parliamentary committee on social affairs and housing. She contested the 2009 presidential election as the SDKÚ–DS candidate, with the endorsement of the conservative Christian Democratic Movement (KDH) and the Party of the Hungarian coalition (SMK–MKP), losing to the incumbent President Gašparovič in the second round. On 23 April 2009 she resigned her seat in parliament after a controversy involving a violation of parliamentary voting rules.

In Feb. 2010 Radičová successfully contested the leadership of the SDKÚ–DS, succeeding former finance minister Ivan Mikloš. The party lost heavily in the June 2010 general elections, polling just 15% of the vote to the ruling Smer–SD's 35%. However, Smer–SD was unable to renew its coalition owing to the poor performance of its coalition partners and on 23 June 2010, as leader of the largest opposition party, Radičová was asked to form a government. The SDKÚ–DS formed a coalition with the KDH, the socially progressive, fiscally conservative Freedom and Solidarity party (SaS) and the Most–Híd party, which promotes Slovak–Hungarian co-operation. Radičová took office on 8 July 2010.

Career Peak

Radičová came to power promising to cut government spending and tackle corruption. In late 2010 she drew up a plan to reduce expenditure by 7%. Identifying long-term unemployment as a key challenge, she announced that pension reform and education were priorities. Aside from the ailing economy, her main challenges included instability in the euro zone, tensions between Slovakia and Hungary, and lack of transparency in Slovakian financial affairs. However, her administration collapsed in Oct. 2011 as the SaS, one of the coalition parties, abstained in a parliamentary vote of confidence in her government over the issue of ratifying an enlarged euro zone bail-out facility. An early election was held in March 2012 but the opposition Direction–Social Democracy won and former prime minister Robert Fico returned to power the following month.

Raffarin, Jean-Pierre (France)

Introduction

Jean-Pierre Raffarin was made French prime minister in 2002. A relatively unknown politician but with experience in regional government, Raffarin was appointed by President Jacques Chirac on the resignation of Lionel Jospin. A senator of the Démocratie Libérale party (DL; originally an offshoot of the Union pour la Démocratie Française, UDF, and now part of the centre right ruling coalition), Raffarin was committed to working in close cooperation with Chirac.

Early Life

Raffarin was born in Poitiers on 3 Aug. 1948. He studied law and finance in Paris before working in corporate marketing. His first political role was employment ministry advisor from 1976. The following year he was elected councillor for Poitiers, a position he held until 1995; in 1988 he also became the leader of the Poitou-Charentes local council. A senator for Vienne between 1995–97, his party representation included UDF leader in 1995 and DL vice president from 1997. He served as minister of commerce, craft and small and medium businesses, a subsection of the industry and finance ministry, under the government of Alain Juppé.

Career Peak

Following the surprise defeat of prime minister and Parti Socialiste leader Lionel Jospin in the first round of the May 2002 presidential elections, Jospin resigned the premiership. President Jacques Chirac appointed the relatively unknown Raffarin as interim prime minister in the run up to the June 2002 parliamentary elections. His position was consolidated with a centre right victory.

In Raffarin's first speech to parliament he reiterated Chirac's policies, including investment in law and order (a subject central to the election), increased decentralization and tax cuts. €3.5 bn. was allocated to the justice ministry while €5.6 bn. was put into an increased police force, increased prison capacity, an extension of civil offences (such as aggressive begging) and a proposed civil volunteer force. The plan to reduce income tax by a third over 5 years raised concerns from other EU countries that France would not keep to its promise to balance its budget by 2004. Raffarin announced increased autonomy for Corsica, as a front for decentralization, including €2 bn. for development, a policy initiated by Jospin but previously rejected by Chirac.

Raffarin's budget for 2003 proposed an overhaul of the culture, tertiary education and housing ministries, though he admitted that as a result of the global downturn and the war in Iraq, the economy would grow at a much slower pace than was earlier predicted.

Local election defeats for the governing party in March 2004 appeared to threaten Raffarin's position but Chirac immediately reappointed him. The European elections that took place in June 2004 were also disappointing for the Raffarin government. The UMP party won only 16.4% of the vote, leading to calls for the resignation of the government.

Set against the backdrop of a faltering economy, Raffarin's approval rating fell to 24%. France held a referendum on whether or not to accept the proposed EU constitution on 29 May 2005 and the poll was widely seen as an opportunity to express dissatisfaction with Raffarin, a champion of the 'Yes' vote, and his government. The constitution was rejected and Raffarin resigned from office.

Later Life

After standing down, Raffarin was re-elected UMP senator for Vienne in Sept. 2005. Following Nicolas Sarkozy's election to the French presidency, Raffarin was named UMP vice-president. He launched an unsuccessful bid to become Senate president in Sept. 2008, losing in the primary to Gerard Lárcher. In Feb. 2010 Raffarin turned down the office of French ambassador to China.

Rafsanjani, Hashemi Ali Akbar (Iran)

Introduction

In a smooth transfer of political power following the death of Ayatollah Khomeini, Hashemi Rafsanjani was elected the fourth President of the Islamic Republic on 28 July 1989, replacing Seyed Ali Khamenei who became Iran's new spiritual leader. Pragmatic and relatively moderate, Rafsanjani sought to revive the war-damaged economy, improve relations with the West, and re-establish Iran as a regional power. He retained the presidency for two terms until 1997.

Early Life

Born in 1934, Rafsanjani was a theology student under Ayatollah Khomeini in Qom in the early 1950s, remaining a close associate thereafter. After Khomeini was ordered into exile in 1964, Rafsanjani remained in Iran to organize his mentor's opposition to the Shah and was imprisoned several times in the 1960s and 1970s for his political activities. Following the Islamic revolution in 1979, he was appointed to the ruling Revolutionary Council and was a co-founder of the Islamic Republican Party (which was dissolved in 1987). Having been elected to the Majlis in early 1980, he built his power base as the Assembly's Speaker from July of that year until 1989. From 1988–89 he was also acting commander-in-chief of the armed forces, and strongly advocated the Iranian acceptance in July 1988 of the ceasefire resolution bringing the war with Iraq to a close.

Career Peak

With the support of almost all the country's political, religious and military groups, Rafsanjani was elected President in July 1989, attracting 94% of the votes cast. In a referendum held at the same time, voters approved constitutional amendments strengthening the presidency. The position of Prime Minister was abolished, thereby bestowing exclusive executive power on Rafsanjani, who was also empowered to appoint ministers with the approval of the Majlis and to take direct control of the economy. Legislative elections held in April/May 1992 strengthened the position of supporters of Rafsanjani's reformist policies of economic liberalization and openness in foreign relations (although Iran's relations with Western countries remained tense). Returned for a second successive 4-year presidential term on 11 June 1993, albeit by a much reduced 63% of the vote, he was barred constitutionally from seeking a third term in the 1997 elections. However, he retained considerable influence through his chairmanship of the Council of Expediency, established in 1989 to arbitrate in the event of a dispute between the Majlis and the Council of Constitutional Guardians.

Later Life

Once out of presidential office, Rafsanjani retained considerable influence in public life through his chairmanship of the Council of Expediency, established in 1989 to arbitrate in the event of a dispute between the Majlis and the Council of Guardians. From 2007–11 he was chairman of the Assembly of Experts, charged with supervising the activities of the Supreme Leader. In May 2013 he registered to contest the presidential election but the electoral watchdog subsequently disbarred him. He died at the age of 82 on 8 Jan. 2017.

Rainier III (Monaco)

Introduction

Prince Rainier III belonged to the Grimaldi family, which has ruled Monaco since 1297 and is one of Europe's oldest royal families. He succeeded to the throne on 9 May 1949 and reigned until his death in April 2005. Since 1911, the prince acts as chief of state and shares power (under the 1962 constitution) with the National Council. Legal power is invested in the prince which he delegates to the courts, to dispense justice in his name.

Early Life

Rainer-Louis-Henri-Maxence-Bertrand De Grimaldi, Monaco's 31st ruler, was born on 31 May 1923 in Monaco. His father, who died on 10 Nov. 1964, Prince Pierre-Marie-Xavier-Antoine-Melchoir, Count of Polignac, was named Grimaldi by Order in Council on 18 March 1920. His mother, Princess Charlotte Louise Juliette, Duchess of Valentinois, died on 16 Nov. 1977. Rainier III studied in England, Switzerland and France (University of Montpellier). In 1944 he joined the French army as a foreign serviceman. Following World War II, he continued his studies at the University of Paris. His mother having renounced the throne in 1944, Rainier succeeded his grandfather, Prince Louis II, in 1949. On 18 April 1956 the prince married the American actress Grace Patricia Kelly, who was in Monaco filming the Hitchcock film 'To Catch A Thief'. Princess Grace was killed in a car crash in 1982. The couple had three children, Princess Caroline Louise Marguerite (born on 23 Jan. 1957), Prince Albert Alexandre Louise Pierre, heir to the throne and Marquis of Baux (born on 14 March 1958) and Princess Stéphanie Marie Elisabeth (born on 1 Feb. 1965).

Career Peak

Rainier III reigned for almost 56 years, one of the longest reigns in Monaco's history. He aimed to attract business to the country, relying less on income from tourism and the casino. In 1954 he opened the Monte Carlo television station and in 1961 he founded the International Television Festival. Through land reclamation, he increased the size of Monaco from 150 ha to 195 ha. The prince had a friendly relationship with France, though in Oct. 2000 he announced that Monaco wanted to regain full sovereignty. During his reign Monaco was granted Embassy status. Within the arts, Rainier III established an award for musical composition and a literary award to French authors. The prince's family had a high profile in Europe and attention often turned to the private lives of his daughters, Caroline and Stephanie.

Rainier's health deteriorated sharply in March 2005 and, after a period of hospitalization, he died on 6 April 2005. He was succeeded by his son, Albert.

Rajapaksa, Mahinda (Sri Lanka)

Introduction

Mahinda Rajapaksa succeeded Chandrika Kumaratunga as the executive president of Sri Lanka in Nov. 2005. A human rights lawyer and former prime minister, he rejected outright the demands of the Liberation Tigers of Tamil Eelam (LTTE) for an ethnic homeland and sought to crush the Tamil rebellion through military force. He achieved this objective by May 2009 and was re-elected president in Jan. 2010. However, his rule was criticized for its authoritarianism and human rights abuses. Rajapaksa lost presidential elections and resigned as chairman of the Sri Lanka Freedom Party (SLEP) in Jan. 2015.

Early Life

Mahinda Rajapaksa was born on 18 Nov. 1945 in Weeraketiya in the southern district of Hambantota. He was educated at Richmond College, Galle, followed by Nalanda and Thurston Colleges in Colombo. While studying law at Vidyodaya University he joined the centre-left Sri Lanka Freedom Party (SLFP) and in 1970 was elected as the party's parliamentary representative for Beliatta, Hambantota (a seat held by his father for the SLFP from 1948–65). Having graduated in 1974, Rajapaksa practised as a lawyer specializing in labour law and human rights and received plaudits for his work on behalf of the underprivileged.

Rajapaksa lost his parliamentary seat in the landslide defeat of the SLFP to the United National Party (UNP) in the general election of 1977. The UNP administration liberalized the economy and reduced unemployment but was unable to stem violence. The parliamentary elections in Feb. 1989 (in which Rajapaksa regained his seat) were preceded by terror campaigns by both the LTTE and the banned People's Liberation Front (JVP) in the south. Rajapaksa joined Mangala Samaraweera's 'Mother's Front'. a group representing the mothers of those who 'disappeared' in the violence of 1988–89. He served on the central committee of the SLFP from the early 1990s and became an increasingly vocal critic of President Ranasinghe Premadasa's UNP government.

Following narrow victory for the SLFP (as part of the People's Alliance coalition) in the parliamentary elections of 1994, Rajapaksa was appointed minister for labour by President Chandrika Kumaratunga. His attempts to reform labour laws and introduce a workers' charter met with resistance. He was moved to the fisheries ministry, establishing a coast guard service and a university of oceanography. Following defeat for the People's Alliance in elections in Dec. 2001, Rajapaksa became leader of the parliamentary opposition. He forged alliances including, controversially, with the Sinhala-nationalist JVP to form the United People's Freedom Alliance (UPFA). The Alliance won the parliamentary elections that followed Kumaratunga's sacking of the UNP government in Feb. 2004. Kumaratunga then appointed Rajapaksa as prime minister and he was sworn in on 6 April 2004.

Career Peak

Without a commanding parliamentary majority, Rajapaksa's UPFA government struggled to implement its promises to halt privatization, increase wages and create new jobs. It was also criticized for its handling of the aftermath of the Indian Ocean tsunami in Dec. 2004, which killed 31,000 Sri Lankans and displaced nearly half a million.

Rajapaksa was chosen as the SLFP's presidential candidate for the election of Nov. 2005 and narrowly defeated the UNP's Ranil Wickremesinghe. He vowed a tougher approach to dealings with the LTTE, arguing that the 2002 ceasefire agreement had not brought peace, and appointed Ratnasiri Wickremanayake as prime minister. The security situation deteriorated seriously in 2006, and Rajapaksa reiterated his determination to defeat rebel violence as he revived draconian anti-terrorism legislation that had been suspended in 2002. Further escalation in 2007 of LTTE attacks and retaliatory offensives by state forces on LTTE positions in the north and east culminated in the government's formal abrogation of the 2002 ceasefire in Jan. 2008.

Rajapaksa intensified the military campaign against strategic LTTE positions through 2008, making significant territorial advances. In Jan. 2009 government troops captured Kilinochchi, the rebels' administrative headquarters, and also Elephant Pass linking the Jaffna peninsula with the mainland. Despite international concern over the safety of Tamil civilians trapped in the remaining LTTE-controlled enclave, government forces maintained their offensive (reportedly entering the last rebel-held town in Feb.) until Rajapaksa delivered a victory speech to parliament in May.

Meanwhile, the global financial crisis had a significant negative impact on the economy and in July 2009 the IMF approved a stand-by arrangement equivalent to US\$2.6bn. to support recovery and help rebuild after the civil war.

A bitter breakdown in the relationship between Rajapaksa and his army chief Sarath Fonseka led the latter to resign and challenge the president in the elections in Jan. 2010. Capitalizing on his post-war popularity among the Sinhalese majority population, Rajapaksa was re-elected with almost 58% of the vote. The result was contested by Fonseka, but he was subsequently court-martialled, jailed and politically sidelined following his release in May 2012. In Sept. 2010 parliament endorsed a constitutional amendment allowing Rajapaksa to stand for an unlimited number of presidential terms.

In April 2011 Rajapaksa rejected as biased a United Nations report accusing both sides in the civil war of human rights abuses against civilians, although he did agree in Aug. to allow the expiry of long-standing and contentious state of emergency legislation. The UN Human Rights Council has since pressed the Sri Lankan government to investigate alleged serious violations committed during the final stages of the conflict. Continuing international concerns over the rule of law in Sri Lanka and the Rajapaksa government's response to dissent led India and Canada to boycott the biennial Commonwealth heads of government meeting in Colombo in Nov. 2013.

In Nov. 2014, Rajapaksa called for early elections, which were held in Jan. 2015. He lost to Maithripala Sirisena of the New Democratic Front amid allegations he had misused state funds and resources during the campaign. Sirisena was sworn in on 9 Jan. 2015 following an election mired in violence and controversy. On 15 Jan, Rajapaksa resigned as chairman of the SLEP.

Rajoelina, Andry (Madagascar)

Introduction

Andry Rajoelina assumed the presidency on 21 March 2009. He was installed by the military after the former president, Marc Ravalomanana, ceded power following 3 months of political turmoil. On assuming office Rajoelina suspended parliament and set up a transitional authority to run the country. His mandate was not universally recognized by the international community.

Early Life

Rajoelina was born on 30 May 1974 into the wealthy family of a colonel in the Malagasy army. He rose to prominence as a disc jockey in Antananarivo, before setting up a TV and radio station and running an advertising company. Rajoelina's brash personality earned him the nickname TGV, after the French high-speed train. The initials went on to serve as the acronym for his political movement, Tanora malaGasy Vonona (Young Malagasies Determined). He harnessed his public profile to win the Antananarivo mayoral election in Dec. 2007.

In Dec. 2008 and Jan. 2009 Rajoelina's radio and TV networks were shut down by the government, which accused them of 'inciting civil disobedience'. Rajoelina called a general strike, resulting in widespread disorder. On 17 March Ravalomanana stepped down under pressure from military chiefs who immediately installed Rajoelina as his successor. The African Union (AU) denounced the change of government as a coup and suspended Madagascar's membership. Rajoelina's ascent to power was also condemned by the European Union and the USA.

Career Peak

Aged 34, Rajoelina was the youngest president in Madagascar's history, although the prevailing constitution stipulated that presidential candidates must be at least 40 years of age. At that time he promised a new constitution and elections within 2 years.

On 17 April 2009 Rajoelina issued a warrant for the arrest of Ravalomanana, who was then tried *in absentia* (having fled to South Africa) and sentenced in June to 4 years in prison for abuse of office. In Aug. 2009 a power-sharing agreement, sponsored by international mediators, was signed between the rival Rajoelina and Ravalomanana political camps with the aim of establishing a transitional unity government. However, continued disputes prevented its effective implementation and in Dec. 2009 Rajoelina announced that he was abandoning the agreement. This prompted the AU to impose targeted sanctions against his administration in March 2010. Then, in Aug., a court sentenced Ravalomanana *in absentia* to life imprisonment for conspiracy to commit murder.

A referendum on a new constitution took place in Nov. 2010. The referendum was boycotted by the main opposition parties, which regarded the revision as an illegal attempt to consolidate Rajoelina's hold on power by lowering the age requirement for the presidency from 40 to 35. 74% of participants voted in favour. At the same time, an attempted coup against Rajoelina failed as loyal troops arrested a group of dissident army officers.

In Nov. 2011 a transitional cross-party administration took office pending fresh elections. Despite promising not to run for election as part of an agreement between the transitional government and ousted president Marc Ravalomanana, Rajoelina announced his candidacy for president in May 2013. However, in light of pressure from the African Union and the suspension of electoral funding from the European Union, neither Rajoelina nor Marc Ravalonmana ultimately contested the presidency in elections held in Oct. and Dec. 2013.

On 25 Jan. 2014 Rajoelina was replaced as head of state by former minister of finance, Hery Rajaonarimampianina, who had won the presidential run-off a month earlier.

Rajoy, Mariano (Spain)

Introduction

A veteran of the conservative Popular Party (PP), Mariano Rajoy became prime minister in 2011 during a period of financial crisis. He implemented sweeping economic reforms and committed his government to accepting austere deficit reduction targets set by the European Union. In Oct. 2016, following two inconclusive parliamentary elections, he was reconfirmed as prime minister at the head of a new minority coalition government.

Early Life

Mariano Rajoy was born on 27 March 1955 in Santiago de Compostela, Galicia. In 1978 he graduated in law from Santiago de Compostela University before working in the civil service as a property registrar from 1979–81. His political career began in 1981 when he won a seat in the newly inaugurated Galician parliament, representing the conservative People's Alliance (AP).

He served as regional minister of institutional relations from 1982–86 and as president of Pontevedra council from 1986–91. He was elected to Spain's national parliament in June 1986, serving briefly as a deputy before resigning to return to the Galician parliament in Nov. 1986, where he served as vice-president until Sept. 1987. In 1989 the AP merged with other parties to form the PP, with Rajoy appointed to its national executive committee.

He won re-election to parliament in 1993 and was minister of public administration in José María Aznar's government from 1996–99, before serving as minister of culture until 2000. After the PP retained power at the 2000 election, Rajoy was appointed deputy prime minister. From 2001–02 he served as minister of the interior and in 2004 fought the general election as party leader-designate. However, the PP unexpectedly lost to the Spanish Socialist Workers' Party (PSOE) in the aftermath of the train bombings in Madrid that the PP government had wrongly blamed on the Basque separatist group ETA.

Rajoy took over as party leader in Oct. 2004 and fought the 2008 election on a platform of liberal economic policies and social conservatism, including restrictions on immigration and opposition to further regional devolution. Although the DP gained seats, it narrowly failed to secure a majority.

As Spain struggled with recession and high unemployment, Rajoy adopted more moderate positions on social and cultural matters while calling for budget cuts. In the 2011 election campaign he committed his party to the ambitious deficit reduction targets set by the EU, balanced against promises to boost growth. In Nov. 2011 the PP won a decisive election victory, claiming 45% of the vote and 186 of 350 parliamentary seats.

Career Peak

Rajoy took office on 21 Dec. 2011 and in an effort to meet deficit reduction targets applied swingeing spending cuts, along with increases in income and property taxes and tax breaks for companies hiring staff. While his parliamentary majority allowed him to pass his reforms, maintaining public support for austerity proved a major challenge. In June 2012 his administration had to seek approval from its eurozone partners to access emergency financial assistance in order to bail out the ailing banking sector, while a number of heavily-indebted regional governments applied for rescue funds from the central government. However, Spain emerged from recession in the third quarter of 2013 amid signs of returning investor confidence.

Despite winning the Dec. 2015 election Rajoy's PP fell far short of securing a parliamentary majority. After lengthy attempts by all the main parties failed to render a workable coalition, King Felipe formally acknowledged that the negotiating process was deadlocked by April 2016. Rajoy consequently remained in office in a caretaker capacity, with new elections scheduled for 26 June 2016. Again, no party was able to secure a majority and Rajoy continued as acting prime minister. He was eventually confirmed as prime minister on 29 Oct. 2016 with parliament voting in favour of his new coalition government by 170 votes to 111. The PSOE elected to abstain from the vote in order to avoid a third election.

In addition to simmering diplomatic friction with the United Kingdom over the issue of sovereignty over Gibraltar, Rajoy has had to contend with sustained pressure from Catalan separatists that has generated a constitutional crisis. In Nov. 2014 the Madrid government had refused to acknowledge a majority referendum vote in Catalonia in favour of secession. Then in Oct. 2017, following another unauthorized referendum, Catalonia's parliament approved a unilateral declaration of independence, in response to which Rajoy imposed direct rule by Madrid and called a regional election for Dec. Pro-independence parties won a majority of seats in the poll, further aggravating the secession issue.

Meanwhile, in Nov. 2012 Rajoy's government had rejected an offer from the Basque separatist group ETA to enter talks with Spain and France on a definitive end to its operations, stating that it would not negotiate with a terrorist organization. Nevertheless, in April 2017 ETA effectively ended its 50-year campaign as it surrendered its arms caches to the French authorities.

In Aug. 2017, two Islamist terror attacks in Barcelona and the nearby town of Cambrils killed 14 people and injured more than 100.

After several PP members were convicted of corruption in May 2018, Rajoy lost a motion of no confidence supported by PSOE leader Pedro Sánchez. In accordance with the constitution Sánchez replaced him as prime minister and was sworn in on 2 June 2018.

Rákosi, Mátyás (Hungary)

Introduction

Mátyás Rákosi was leader of the Hungarian Communists between 1945 and 1956, serving two terms as prime minister (1952–53, 1955–56). A staunch Stalinist, his reign relied on inducing terror and systematically plotting against his ideological enemies. His policies of forced agricultural collectivization and industrialization made little concession to the practical needs of the country and proved economically disastrous. Following the death of Stalin his support within Moscow dwindled and he was ultimately removed from power as a conciliatory gesture by the Soviet Union towards Yugoslavia's General Tito, with whom he had had a number of disputes.

Early Life

Rákosi (whose surname at birth was Rosenkrantz) was born on 14 March 1892 in Ada, Serbia into a well-to-do Jewish family. The family moved to Hungary when Rákosi was still young and he proved a notable student while being schooled in Budapest, learning 8 languages. Politically, he leaned towards a Social Democratic ideology and in the years before the outbreak of World War I he moved to Britain and worked in London as a banker.

In 1914 he was called into the Austro-Hungarian Army and while fighting on the Eastern Front he was captured by the Russians. He was released in 1918, by which time he had become an adherent of communist ideology. In 1919 Béla Kun established himself as head of the short-lived and ill-fated Soviet Republic of Hungary. Rákosi served in the Kun government as Commissar for Socialist Production, before the regime fell after defeat by Romanian troops.

Rákosi fled to Moscow and worked for Comintern before returning to Hungary in 1924 to assist in the expansion of the Hungarian communist movement. He was imprisoned in 1925 for his activities, freed in 1934 but immediately re-arrested and imprisoned for life. In 1940 he was given permission to leave the country in a deal that saw the Soviet Union return a number of nineteenth century Hungarian flags, and he went once again to Moscow. Four years later he re-entered Hungary and, with the support of Soviet troops, became Secretary of the Communist Hungarian Workers' Party.

After general elections in 1947 which were widely believed to have been fraudulent, Rákosi set about consolidating power. By 1949 Hungary was a 1-party state and a new constitution was promulgated establishing the Hungarian People's Republic. Rákosi exercised ruthlessness in his rule, assisted by the feared Secret Police (AVO), and executed or imprisoned large numbers of his opponents, including the nationalist László Rajk. Both religious and secular institutions were purged of potential dissenters, industries were nationalized, agricultural collectivization enforced and freedom of expression severely curbed. In 1949 the country also joined the Moscow-oriented Council for Mutual Economic Assistance.

Career Peak

While to all intents and purposes he was Hungarian leader in his capacity as Party Secretary, he became Prime Minister in 1952. By this time the economy was in severe trouble and when Stalin died the following year, Rákosi came under intense criticism from the new regime in Moscow, notably from Prime Minister Georgy Malenkov. He was replaced by Imre Nagy, who set about reversing many of Rákosi's reforms as well as relaxing restrictions on civil liberties.

Rákosi, however, had retained his position as Party Secretary and, with the Soviet Union becoming ever more concerned at the pace of Nagy's reforms, he was perfectly placed to move against Nagy. Malenkov fell from power in Feb. 1955 and Nagy was forced to resign his position, with Rákosi once again taking the reins of power. He embarked on another programme of Stalinist policies but in July 1956, in a Soviet attempt to appease the non-conformist General Tito in Yugoslavia with whom Rákosi had an on-going dispute, Rákoski was again removed from power at the instigation of Moscow. He was replaced by his deputy, Erno Gero.

Later Life

Under Gero, dissent grew throughout Hungary and culminated in the uprising of Oct. 1956, during which Nagy returned to power. Rákosi fled to the Soviet Union, ostensibly for health reasons, and was officially removed from the Hungarian party in 1962. He never ventured back to Hungary and he died on 5 Feb. 1971 at Gorky in the Soviet Union.

Ramgoolam, Navin (Mauritius)

Introduction

Navin Ramgoolam served two terms as prime minister from Dec. 1995 to Sept. 2000, and July 2005 to Dec. 2014.

Early Life

Navin Ramgoolam was born in Mauritius on 14 July 1947, the son of Seewoosagur Ramgoolam, the country's first president following independence in 1968. The younger Ramgoolam studied sciences at the Royal College at Curepipe in Mauritius before moving to Dublin, Ireland to train as a doctor at the Royal College of Surgeons in 1968. He gained full registration with the UK General Medical Council in 1977. Over the next 10 years he worked as a senior medical officer and as a general practitioner in Mauritius, also holding the post of resident medical officer at the Yorkshire Clinic in the UK.

In 1987 Ramgoolam abandoned medicine to study for a master's degree in law at the London School of Economics. However, he subsequently abandoned a legal career in favour of politics, becoming leader of the Mauritius Labour Party in 1991. He went on to succeed Sir Anerood Jugnauth as prime minister in 1995.

Career Peak

In 2000, towards the end of Ramgoolam's first period in office, Mauritius secured a temporary seat on the United Nations Security Council. Having lost the premiership to his predecessor, Jugnauth, at elections later that year, he then formed the Social Alliance, a coalition led by the Mauritian Labour Party and including the Mauritian Party of Xavier-Luc Duval, the Mauritian Social Democrat Party, the Greens, the Republican Movement and the Militant Socialist Movement (MSM).

At the election of July 2005 the Social Alliance won 42 of a possible 70 seats, giving Ramgoolam a further term as prime minister. On coming to power he announced plans to tackle rising inflation and high levels of unemployment, and sought trade agreements to protect Mauritian exports, particularly sugar and textiles. By 2008 he had overseen a reduction in both unemployment and the budget deficit and the attraction of increasing levels of foreign investment. However, as Mauritius imports most of its food and energy, rising world prices for these commodities then pushed up inflation while recession in the developed world has posed a threat to the country's tourism industry and export potential. Nevertheless, Ramgoolam's ruling coalition won the May 2010 parliamentary election, maintaining a secure majority until Aug. 2011 when the MSM withdrew, citing disagreements with the Mauritius Labour Party. In March 2012 the state president, Sir Anerood Jugnauth of the MSM, similarly resigned from office, being replaced following elections in July by Rajkeswur Purryag.

In Nov. 2013 Ramgoolam boycotted the Commonwealth heads of government meeting in Colombo, Sri Lanka, in response to claims of human rights violations by President Mahinda Rajapaksa's administration against the Tamil minority population in that country.

The Alliance of Unity and Modernity led by Ramgoolam was soundly beaten by the Alliance Lepep at the Dec. 2014 general elections. After losing his own seat in the National Assembly, Ramgoolam conceded defeat and was succeeded by veteran politician Sir Anerood Jugnauth, who had served as prime minister twice before.

Ramgoolam, Seewoosagur (Mauritius)

Introduction

Doctor and politician, Seewoosagur Ramgoolam was instrumental in securing Mauritian independence. Premier from 1964–82 representing the Parti Travailliste (Labour Party; PT), he administered his country's transition to independence in 1968. During his premiership he implemented labour, education, health and welfare reforms.

Early Life

Seewoosagur Ramgoolam was born on the 18 Sept. 1900 at Belle Rive Village, Flacq District, to an immigrant Indian labourer. His early education concentrated on Indian culture and philosophy and the Hindi language. After studying with English tutors at the Royal College, Curepipe, and 3 months in the civil service, in 1921 he went to study medicine at University College Hospital, London. Politically aware as a student, he formed pro-independence ideas. He worked with the Indian National Congress' London office, becoming its president in 1924. The shaping of his political ideas was influenced by mixing with London based Fabian socialists. After the completion of his studies in the 1930s, he went back to Mauritius to set up a medical practice in Port-Louis. Ramgoolam was involved with the PT from its establishment in 1936.

In 1940 he founded the newspaper *Advance* to campaign for independence and social reform. Nominated for the Legislative Council in 1948, he won concessions on self-rule. Ramgoolam became the head of the PT in 1956. Generally considered a Hindu party by the Franco-Mauritian and Creole communities, Ramgoolam attempted to widen the party's support network throughout all Mauritian society. Two years later he was made mayor of Port-Louis.

The first elections under universal suffrage were held in 1959. The PT won a majority of seats and Ramgoolam became the leader of the house and finance minister. In 1961 he became chief minister in the first phase of self-government.

Career Peak

In the 1963 general elections were successful for the PT and Ramgoolam became premier the following year. For the next few years he fought for complete independence from Britain. In 1967 independence was supported by 54% of the electorate and was granted on 12 March 1968. Ramgoolam became the first prime minister of independent Mauritius representing a PT-led coalition government.

Ramgoolam strived to promote democracy and economic growth and fought to relieve ethnic tensions within Mauritian politics. His reforms included lowing the age of suffrage to 18 and granting free education on all levels.

In 1975 Mauritius was devastated by a cyclone, badly affecting the sugar plantations upon which the economy was reliant. Thereafter the government embarked on a policy of agricultural diversification. He was awarded the UN Human Rights Award in 1973 and served as OAU chairman between 1976–77, the first non-African to do so.

Throughout the 1970s a new branch of militant socialism was being fostered by a group of young politicians who had formed the Mauritian Militant Movement (MMM) in 1969. Strongly influenced by the Marxist revolutionary feeling sweeping the world in 1968, they recruited the support of the trade unions. Several strikes occurred over the next decade as the MMM gained ground. The government reacted by imposing a state of emergency in 1971, only reprieved in 1978. In 1982 elections, the PT was overwhelmingly defeated by the MMM and Ramgoolam was replaced by Aneerood Jugnauth.

Later Life

In 1983 Ramgoolam took the largely ceremonial position of governor-general. He died at the age of 85 in Dec. 1985.

Ramos, Fidel (Philippines)

Introduction

Fidel (Steady Eddie) Valdez Ramos was president of the Philippines between 1992 and 1998. A relative of Ferdinand Marcos, he had prominent roles in the Marcos administrations before offering his support to Corazon Aquino after the disputed 1986 elections.

Early Life

Fidel Ramos was born in Lingayen, Pangasinan on 18 March 1928. His father was Narciso Ramos (a lawyer, journalist and secretary of foreign affairs under Marcos) and Angela Marcos Valdez. He was second cousin to Ferdinand Marcos. Educated in Lingayen, Manila and then at the US Military Academy, West Point, Ramos went to the University of Illinois where he graduated in civil engineering in 1951.

After joining the Philippine army Ramos served in Korea with the Philippine expeditionary force and in Vietnam where he rose from chief of staff of the Philippine civic action group to presidential assistant on military affairs. In 1972 Ramos became chief of the Philippine constabulary. As chief of staff Ramos was responsible for detaining many opposition leaders in during the years of martial law.

After the fraudulent re-election of Ferdinand Marcos in 1986 Ramos and the defence secretary, Juan Ponce Enrile, stood firmly behind Corazon Aquino, widow of the assassinated Benigno Aquino Jr. This action did much to inspire the EDSA revolution that overthrew the Marcos regime. Ramos remained secretary of national defence in the Aquino cabinet.

Career Peak

In May 1992 Ramos was elected 8th president of the Third Republic of the Philippines, succeeding Corazon Aquino, as her nominated choice, in a seven-candidate race.

Ramos implemented several radical reforms during his tenure. He confronted police corruption, removing large numbers of officers, and improved relations with leading communist and Muslim dissident groups. He also advocated use of contraceptives in a bid to halt the country's spiralling population growth. Economically, he promoted deregulation and campaigned against several monopolies and corrupt business practices. The economy grew rapidly throughout the mid-1990s and suffered less than many of its counterparts during the Asian economic downturn of 1998. In March 1997 the Supreme Court rejected calls to allow Ramos to amend the post-Marcos constitution to give him an extended presidential term.

Ramos-Horta, José (Timor-Leste)

Introduction

José Ramos-Horta, a key figure in Timor-Leste's struggle for independence for over 30 years, became president after a landslide victory in the second round of presidential elections in May 2007 but was defeated at the presidential poll of 2012.

Early Life

Ramos-Horta was born on 26 Dec. 1949 in Dili to a Timorese mother and a Portuguese father who was a political exile. In 1969 he became a journalist but was exiled to Mozambique from 1970–71 for his political activities. As Portugal began pulling out of Timor-Leste in 1975, Ramos-Horta, a member of FRETILIN, emerged as a key figure in the nationalist leadership. On 28 Nov. 1975 FRETILIN proclaimed independence and appointed him foreign minister. Three days before Indonesia's invasion on 7 Dec. 1975 he pleaded the Timorese case before the United Nations in New York.

Stranded in exile, he was nevertheless FRETILIN's permanent representative at the UN from 1977–85. He also studied at The Hague Academy of International Law, the International Institute of Human Rights in Strasbourg and Antioch University in Ohio. In 1996 Ramos-Horta and Carlos Filipe Ximines Belo jointly won the Nobel Peace Prize for their commitment to the East Timorese struggle for independence.

Following Indonesia's agreement to a referendum on Timor-Leste's status, Ramos-Horta returned home in Dec. 1999. After independence in May 2002 he served as foreign minister (to July 2006) and then prime minister before winning the presidency in May 2007.

Career Peak

The presidential role is largely ceremonial, but Ramos-Horta pledged to work on reform and national reconciliation with the National Congress for Timorese Reconstruction-led government. He was seriously wounded in an attack by rebel soldiers in Feb. 2008 but, following treatment in Australia, returned to Dili 2 months later to resume his presidency. In the first round of the presidential election on 17 March 2012, Ramos-Horta came third and was eliminated. Following the run-off on 16 April he was succeeded as president by Taur Matan Ruak on 20 May.

Later Life

From Jan. 2013–July 2014 Ramos-Horta served as then UN Secretary-General Ban Ki-moon's special representative to Guinea-Bissau. He was named as counsellor for national security in Timor-Leste's new government that took office in Sept. 2017.

Ramotar, Donald (Guyana)

Introduction

Donald Ramotar became president in Dec. 2011, succeeding Bharrat Jagdeo. An economist, Ramotar has spent most of his career working within the socialist People's Progressive Party/Civic (PPP/C), whose support base is the Indo-Guyanese community. The party had been in power since 1992 but lost its overall parliamentary majority for the first time at the Nov. 2011 elections. Ramotar then lost the May 2015 presidential election to David Granger.

Early Life

Donald Rabindranauth Ramotar was born on 22 Oct. 1950 in Guyana's Essequibo-West Demerera province. He was at school in Georgetown and graduated in economics from the University of Guyana before taking a master's degree at the Patrice Lumumba Peoples' Friendship University in Moscow.

Returning to Guyana, he worked in the timber industry and, from 1966, the Guyana Import-Export Company, a commercial venture under the opposition PPP/C. Between 1975 and 1983 Ramotar was the manager of Freedom House, the Georgetown headquarters of the PPP/C, before becoming the editor of a journal, *Problems of Peace and Socialism*.

He served as international secretary of the Guyana Agricultural Workers' Union (GAWU) between 1988 and 1993, when he assumed the role of PPP/C executive secretary. The party had been restored to power in Oct. 1992 under Cheddi Jagan. Following President Jagan's death in March 1997, Ramotar replaced him as party general secretary, a post he still holds. Janet Jagan led the PPP/C to victory in the Dec. 1997 elections although she was forced to retire through ill-health in 1999 and was succeeded by Bharrat Jagdeo.

Ramotar has served on the Africa Caribbean Pacific (ACP)-EU Joint Parliamentary Assembly and on several corporate boards. In April 2011 he was selected as the PPP/C's presidential candidate. Later that month he was appointed political adviser to President Jagdeo, a move criticized by the opposition A Partnership for National Unity (APNU).

Ramotar emerged victorious in the election on 28 Nov. 2011 and his PPP/C took 32 seats in parliament (compared with 26 for APNU) to form a minority administration, the first since independence in 1966.

Career Peak

Ramotar was sworn in as president on 3 Dec. 2011. He pledged to build on the achievements of the previous administration, developing the country's infrastructure and raising competitiveness while reducing poverty within a programme agreed with international financial institutions. While Ramotar called for unity, Guyana's politics remained divided on ethnic lines and relations between the two main parties were frequently hostile. In Nov. 2014 he discontinued the National Assembly session to avert a no-confidence vote that the opposition majority in the legislature likened to a constitutional coup and a denial of democracy.

At the May 2015 general election, Ramotar was defeated by David Granger of the National Unity and Alliance for Change (APNU+AFC) coalition. Granger was sworn in as president on 16 May.

Rasizade, Artur (Azerbaijan)

Introduction

Artur Rasizade, an oil engineer-turned-politician, has been prime minister since 1996. He was appointed by President Heidar Aliyev and has served under his son, Ilham Aliyev, since Oct. 2003.

Early Life

Artur Tahir oglu Rasizade was born on 26 Feb. 1935 in Gandja in the Transcaucasian Soviet Federated Socialist Republic. Educated at the Azerbaijan Institute of Industry in Baku, Azerbaijan Soviet Socialist Republic, Rasizade began work as an engineer at the Institute of Oil Machine Construction in 1957. He served as chief engineer at Trust Soyuzneftemash from 1973–77, before taking the post of deputy head of the Azerbaijan state planning committee.

In 1986, after 5 years as bureau chief of the central committee of the Communist Party of Azerbaijan, Rasizade became first deputy prime minister under Kamran Baghirov, who had been widely blamed for the Republic's economic stagnation and the escalating tension with Armenia over Nagorno-Karabakh (now Artsakh).

Following the break-up of the Soviet Union and Azerbaijan's declaration of independence in Aug. 1991, Rasizade became an adviser to the foundation for economic reforms. He served as an assistant to President Heidar Aliyev in early 1996 and was then appointed first deputy prime minister. He was appointed prime minister when Fuad Kuliev resigned following accusations by Aliyev of economic mismanagement. The National Assembly endorsed Rasizade's appointment and he took office on 26 Dec. 1996.

Career Peak

Heidar Aliyev won the presidential election in Oct. 1998 and retained Rasizade (a fellow member of the New Azerbaijan Party) as prime minister until 4 Aug. 2003, when the premier unexpectedly resigned. Rasizade's departure, ostensibly for health reasons, paved the way for Ilham Aliyev to assume office. Ilham Aliyev contested the presidential election of 15 Oct. 2003 and emerged victorious, although the opposition staged mass protests, alleging intimidation and fraud. On 4 Nov. 2003 Rasizade was formally reinstated as prime minister. He was reappointed in Oct. 2008, following Aliyev's first re-election as president, and again in Oct. 2013. He was replaced as prime minister by Novruz Mammadov in April 2018.

Rasmussen, Poul Nyrup (Denmark)

Introduction

Poul Nyrup Rasmussen served as the leader of the Social Democratic Party from 1992–2002 and was Denmark's prime minister between 1993–2001. He tried to convince the Danish electorate of the value of European integration, and in particular the need for entry into the single currency.

Early Life

Poul Nyrup Rasmussen was born in Esbjerg on 15 June, 1943. He read economics at the University of Copenhagen and received his degree in 1971. From 1971–80 he worked as an economist for the Danish Trade Union Council. In 1980 he became the Council's chief economist and held this post until 1986 when he was appointed as the managing director of the Employees' Capital Pension Fund and chairman of Lalandia Investment. The following year he began his political career as the deputy chairman of the Social Democrats. Rasmussen was first elected as a member of parliament in 1988 and was chosen to chair the parliamentary committee on commerce, industry and shipping. He served on this committee until 1991 when he became a member of the parliamentary Labour Market Committee and the Political-Economic Committee. In 1992 he was elected as the chairman of the Social Democrats. In late 1992 the Ministry of Justice was implicated in preventing a group of Tamil refugees from Sri Lanka entering the country. This scandal toppled the conservative Schlüter government on 14 Jan. 1993 and triggered a general election. Rasmussen campaigned for increased expenditure on welfare provisions and for the ratification of the Maastricht Treaty. An SDP and Radical Liberal (RV) coalition won a slim majority and Rasmussen became prime minister.

Career Peak

Rasmussen's first major duty as prime minister was to convince the electorate, and many members of his own party to adopt the Maastricht Treaty on

European integration. In 1993 the treaty had been rejected in a referendum, but voters overwhelmingly approved a revised version which included exemptions for Denmark.

In the 1998 elections the SDP-RV coalition retained office by the narrowest of margins and Rasmussen was forced to compromise with his opponents in his efforts to promote the single currency and a liberal immigration policy. He was assisted by the performance of the Danish economy under his premiership: from 1993 GDP grew by an average 3% a year, and unemployment fell from 12.4% in 1993 to about 7.4% in 1998. The government budget went into surplus for the first time in 10 years.

In spite of the SDP's vigorous 'Best for Denmark' campaign to persuade Danes to adopt the single currency the electorate rejected the euro, by 53% to 47% in Sept. 2000. This was a critical blow for Rasmussen. However, following the events of 11 Sept. 2001 his popularity rating increased. He called snap elections for Nov. 2001 but in a campaign dominated by immigration, a popular anti-immigration stance by Venstre shifted the balance in favour of the opposition. Rasmussen was defeated by Venstre party leader Anders Fogh Rasmussen.

Ratsiraka, Didier (Madagascar)

Introduction

Ratsiraka was president of Madagascar representing AREMA (The Pillar and Structure for the Salvation of Madagascar Party) between 1997 and 2002. He was previously leader between 1975–93, coming to power following the assassination of his predecessor, Colonel Richard Ratsimandrava, during a period of military rule and political instability. In his autocratic and repressive leadership, he implemented a scheme of leftist policies including nationalization while furthering ties with Communist countries until economic crisis forced him to adopt free market policies. Defeated in 1993, he returned to power in 1997 but was forced out of power in 2002 after disputed elections.

Early Life

A *côtier* (from the coast), Didier Ratsiraka was born on the 4 Nov. 1936 in the province of Tamatave. After his secondary schooling in Tananarive, he studied mathematics. He embarked on a military career as lieutenant commander in the Malagasy navy following training at the Brest naval academy. He was military attaché to the Malagasy embassy in Paris and later became minister of foreign affairs.

Career Peak

Following the assassination of Colonial Ratsimandrava after 6 days in control, Ratsiraka took power of the revolutionary council amid a climate of violent political instability which had forced martial law, press censorship and the suspension of political parties. After a referendum held in Dec. 1975 he was confirmed president of the newly established Democratic Republic of Madagascar as leader of the military Conseil Suprême de la Révolution (Supreme Revolutionary Council; CSR).

He continued the leftist reforms instigated by Ratsimandrava's predecessor, General Gabriel Ramanantsoa. A programme of nationalization included shipping and petroleum industries, mineral resources and the financial sector. He advocated the demilitarization of the Indian Ocean and adopted a foreign policy of non-alignment. He was re-elected in the Nov. 1983 presidential election with 80% of votes. Economic crisis forced Ratsiraka to adopt IMF austerity measures and eventually to implement a free market economy. He was re-elected for a third consecutive term in 1989 with 62%. However these results were contested and riots followed. In March 1990 the government formally assented to the resumption of multi-party politics and ended press censorship and the state monopoly of the media.

Despite these advances, the new climate allowed Ratsiraka's political opponents to gain ground. An alliance of opposition factions united the same year under the Forces Vives (Live Forces; FV). They were soon calling for Ratsiraka's resignation. In July 1991, he declared a state of emergency, and soon after dissolved his government. Following shootings during a peaceful protest at his residence, he resigned and was offered asylum by the French

government. In Oct. 1991 the constitution was suspended and Ratsiraka relinquished all executive powers, although he remained politically active.

A new constitution was approved in Aug. 1992 to pave the way for elections the following year. Having returned from exile, Ratsiraka contested the election against the Union Nationale pour le Développement et la Démocratie leader Albert Zafy. The latter took the presidency, but Ratsiraka returned to power 3 years later, albeit with less than 25% of votes (remaining votes being spoilt or counted as abstentions). He went to Washington, Paris and Brussels to strengthen relations and secure aid. In the 1998 national assembly elections, he was again re-elected and his government won a majority. However, at the presidential elections of May 2002 his opponent, Marc Ravalomanana, was declared president. Ratsiraka rejected the result but several regions under his control were taken by troops loyal to the new president. In June 2002 Ratsiraka fled to the Seychelles.

Later Life

In Aug. 2003 Ratsiraka was sentenced *in absentia* to 10 years hard labour on charges of stealing US$8 m. of public money before going into exile. He was also declared unfit for public office.

Rau, Johannes (Germany)

Introduction

Johannes Rau was president of Germany from July 1999 to June 2004. Best-known as the moderate Social Democrat premier of North-Rhine Westphalia from 1978–98, he stood unsuccessfully for the chancellorship in 1987 and the presidency in 1994. His duties as president were largely ceremonial.

Early Life

Johannes Rau was born on 16 Jan. 1931 in Wuppertal-Barmen. His father was a Protestant preacher. Rau left school in 1949 and undertook a career in publishing and journalism, specializing in publishing Protestant literature. In 1952 he joined the All-German People's Party. In 1957 the party disbanded and he joined the Social Democratic Party (SPD). During this period he developed a close working relationship with Gustav Heinemann who served as German president (1969–74). Heinemann's granddaughter, Christine Delius, became Rau's wife in 1982.

In 1958 Rau was appointed president chairman of the Young Socialists in Wuppertal and gained a seat in the North-Rhine Westphalia parliament. He joined the Wuppertal SPD executive board the following year, became a city councillor in 1964 and mayor of Wuppertal from 1969–70. In 1970 he was made minister of science and education for North-Rhine Westphalia, in which post he opened several new higher education institutions.

In 1977 he won the chairmanship of his regional party and the following year successfully stood for the premiership of North-Rhine Westphalia. He oversaw victory at the 1980 regional elections, the first time the SPD had achieved an absolute majority in the *Länd*. Further election victories followed in 1985, 1990 and 1995.

In 1982 he became deputy chairman of the federal SPD and in 1987 ran for the chancellorship, although he was heavily defeated by Helmut Kohl. In elections for the 1994 presidency he lost to Roman Herzog. On 23 May 1999 Rau was selected as Herzog's successor, and took his oath of office in Bonn on 1 July.

Career Peak

After almost 50 years of active political life, Rau was recognized as an important figurehead. He was renowned for his highly personalized style of oratory. He was strongly associated with his motto 'to reconcile, not divide' and he worked to achieve reconciliation with the Jewish community. In 2000 Rau became the first German head of state since the holocaust to address the Israeli parliament in German. The controversial move won praise from the Israeli president, who applauded Rau for trying to bridge the gap between the two countries.

Rau left office in June 2004 and was succeeded as president by Horst Köhler on 1 July 2004.

Later Life

After leaving politics Rau divided his time between family homes in Berlin and Wuppertal. He had a long history of heart disease and after an extended period of illness, he died on 27 Jan. 2006, aged 75. He is survived by his wife and their three children.

Ravalomanana, Marc (Madagascar)

Introduction

Marc Ravalomanana became president in May 2002 following disputed presidential elections held in Dec. 2001. Having accused incumbent Didier Ratsiraka of rigging the vote that saw neither man achieve the necessary majority to take office, there followed several months of political and social unrest before Ratsiraka went into exile. Having secured international recognition, Ravalomanana's principal task was to lead an economic recovery. He won a second 5-year presidential term in elections in Dec. 2006 but was forced out of office in 2009. He resigned on 17 March.

Early Life

Ravalomanana was born on 12 Dec. 1949 as a member of the Merina ethnic group in Imerikasina, a village outside the capital city, Antananarivo. He was educated at a protestant school in Sweden but finished his academic pursuits in his early twenties to set up a yoghurt manufacturing operation in Antananarivo. Having secured World Bank funding for expansion, his company grew to claim a monopoly of Madagascar's dairy and oil products and to become the biggest locally-owned company in the country.

In 1999 Ravalomanana was elected mayor of Antananarivo and set about a programme of urban redevelopment. Recognized for his dynamism, several of his schemes were also controversial, such as when he ordered the destruction of a hundred habitations on aesthetic grounds. When the first round of presidential elections were held in Dec. 2001, neither Ravalomanana nor incumbent President Didier Ratsiraka gained the required 50% plus one vote needed to take office.

Career Peak

A run-off was set to take place in late Feb. 2002 but Ravalomanana accused his opponent of electoral corruption and claimed that he had won 52% of the vote outright. Ravalomanana's supporters took part in mass protests and declared a general strike. In response, Ratsiraka's supporters blockaded the capital. It was estimated that the strike was costing the already impoverished nation US$14 m. per day. An international mediation team, including the secretary of the Organization of African Unity (as was), brokered a deal that saw the run-off postponed. However, on 22 Feb. Ravalomanana declared himself president. Ratsiraka set up a rival government in Tamatave, a port city on the east coast. There followed a suspension from the Organization of African Unity, which claimed the transfer of power from Ratsiraka to Ravalomanana was unconstitutional.

On 29 April the High Constitutional Court ruled that Ravalomanana had indeed won the election and he formally took office on 6 May 2002. Fighting continued between the two camps throughout the country, resulting in extensive casualties. Ravalomanana gradually gained the upper hand and secured international recognition, first from the USA and later from France, the former colonial power and chief trading partner. Having lost control of what had been his provincial heartlands, Ratsiraka went into exile in July 2002. In Feb. 2003 a former head of the armed services was charged with an attempted coup. Six months later Ratsiraka was sentenced in absentia to 10 years hard labour for embezzlement. In Dec. 2003 former prime minister Tantely Adrianarivo was given 12 years for corruption.

The months of instability following the election had severely weakened what was already a failing economy. Parliamentary elections were held in Dec. 2002 and the strong showing of Ravalomanana's I Love Madagascar party was seen as a reassertion of popular support for the president, who continued to implement free market reforms, provide free primary education for all and oversee improvements in the medical and transport infrastructures. The economy was further hit when two cyclones wreaked havoc and left many thousands homeless in Feb. and March 2004, but received a boost in

Oct. 2004 when the World Bank and IMF announced that US$2 bn. of Madagascar's debt was to be written off. In March 2005 Madagascar became one of the first beneficiaries of a new US development aid scheme designed to reward nations promoting democratic and free market principles.

A coup attempt by a dissident military officer in Nov. 2006 was suppressed, and in Dec. Ravalomanana was re-elected president with 55% of the vote. For his second term in office he introduced an action plan to reduce poverty and promote development. In April 2007 constitutional reforms increasing his presidential powers were endorsed in a national referendum, and in Sept. his party won an overwhelming majority of seats in parliamentary elections, albeit in a low voter turnout.

In Feb. 2008 the government was confronted by the devastating effects of one of the largest tropical cyclones to strike Madagascar. Nearly 100 people were killed and over 300,000 made homeless.

Violent protests erupted in Jan. 2009 following the closure of opposition radio and television stations and again in Feb. when Ravalomanana sacked opposition leader Andry Rajoelina as mayor of Antananarivo. Ravalomanana resigned on 17 March after he lost the support of the military and went into exile in South Africa. In June he was sentenced to a four-year jail term in absentia on corruption charges and fined US$70 m. to make amends for having purchased a jet for US$60 m. in Dec. 2008. He signed a power-sharing agreement with Rajoelina and other party leaders in Nov. 2009 but attempts to found a transitional coalition government have yet to be successful.

Rawlings, Jerry John (Ghana)

Introduction

Jerry John Rawlings held power for three and a half months in 1979 and from Dec. 1981 to Dec. 2000. On both occasions he seized power in a military coup. From 1992 he held the position of elected president. Credited with some free market reforms and overseeing a period of relative internal peace, his human rights record is less impressive.

Early Life

Jerry John Rawlings was born on 22 June 1947 in Accra, Ghana. His father was a pharmacist from Scotland and his mother was Ghanaian. Having graduated from the military academy at Teshie, he joined the air force in 1969, reaching the rank of flight-lieutenant. In May 1979 he was charged with leading a mutiny but, having outlined the social injustices which he claimed inspired the mutiny, he escaped custody during a court appearance in June. With large-scale support from the armed forces, he overthrew the ruling supreme military council and headed a new ruling armed forces revolutionary council.

In office for 112 days, he set about removing officials he considered corrupt, executing eight people and imprisoning many more. Elections were held in July 1979 and Rawlings handed power over to the victor, Hilla Limann, in Sept. 1979. Shortly afterwards Limann retired Rawlings from the military. Limann's government was unsuccessful in combating Ghana's hyper-inflation and large foreign debts. In Dec. 1981 Rawlings removed Limann in a coup, naming himself head of the provisional national defence council.

Career Peak

Initially basing government on his Marxist ideology, Rawlings set up workers' councils to supervise industry and established localized workers' defence committees. When these measures failed to make any significant impact on the economy he adopted a more pragmatic approach. He authorized the devaluation of the currency, cut public spending, subsidies and price controls, and privatized several industries, including the coffee and cocoa sectors. Having earlier looked to the USSR for support, Rawlings' free market initiatives won praise from the IMF and significant aid and foreign investment. By the early-1990s, after Rawlings had survived several attempted coups, the economy was more stable.

Rawlings was a charismatic populist, once declaring that 'I don't know any law and I don't understand economics, but I know when my stomach is empty.' He was accused of civil rights abuses, including the illegal imprisonment and murder of political opponents. In 1992 he established the National Democratic Congress (NDC) and ran for the presidency, winning 58% of the vote. He won re-election in 1996 despite claims from the opposition New Patriotic Party that the election was flawed. During the 1990s he imposed curfews in the north of the country in a bid to curb ethnic violence.

In foreign policy Rawlings retained the favour of many early allies including Libya and Nigeria while meeting with Western leaders. Constitutionally prohibited from standing for re-election in 2000, he supported NDC vice president John Atta Mills, who was defeated by John Kufuor in a run-off.

Later Life

In May 2002 Kufuor initiated a reconciliation committee to investigate civil rights abuses during the Rawlings period. 120 petitions were received on the first day. In Aug. 2002 Rawlings criticized the Kufuor government's record and called for 'positive defiance'. The speech was widely condemned as incitement and he was held briefly for questioning.

Razak, Abdul (Malaysia)

Introduction

Abdul Razak was the second prime minister of Malaysia. Although he held office for 5 years, Abdul Razak's main achievements were as minister for rural development.

Early Life

Abdul Razak was born into a noble family in the Malay state of Pahang. His father had the title Dato, held by local chieftains. Razak trained as a lawyer but did not practise for many years. In 1950 he joined the colonial civil service and was soon drawn to the Malay nationalist cause. He entered politics in 1955 and attracted the attention of Tunku Abdul Rahman Putra, the leader of the independence movement.

When Malaya gained independence in 1957, Abdul Razak was appointed deputy premier and minister of defence, an important role given the guerrilla uprising by ethnic Chinese Communists in the north of the country. As a cabinet member of the newly named Malaysia (1963), he continued in both posts until 1970. However, it was as minister of rural development that he made his major contribution. He was responsible for improving life in the villages and for encouraging industries into rural communities. Abdul Razak held this portfolio from 1959 until 1969. In 1959 he was awarded a high order, which gave him the title Tun (lord).

In the late 1960s, ethnic violence between Malays and Chinese broke out in the cities of Malaysia. Abdul Razak was appointed chair of the National Operations Council with a brief to contain the violence. When the ethnic riots ended, the premier, Tunku Abdul Rahman Putra, resigned, opening the way for his deputy to succeed.

Career Peak

As Prime Minister, Abdul Razak was able to ease the racial tension. He pursued a non-aligned stance in foreign policy. He died in office on 14 Jan. 1976, while visiting London.

Reagan, Ronald W. (United States of America)

Introduction

The 40th president of the United States, Ronald Wilson Reagan served two successive terms from 1981–89. Best remembered for his anti-communism and his genial style, Reagan's economic policies, which became known as 'Reaganomics' helped define the 1980s.

Early Life

Reagan was born in Tampico, Illinois on 6 Feb. 1911 to shoe salesman John Edward Reagan, an Irish-born Roman Catholic, and Nelle Wilson Reagan, who was of Scottish-English ancestry. In 1920 his family moved to Dixon, Illinois and Reagan entered Eureka College, from where he graduated in 1932 with a degree in economics and sociology. After working as an announcer for radio stations WOC and WHO, a trip to California led to a successful screen test with Warner Brothers. Reagan went on to play a variety of roles in more than 50 movies over the next 27 years. In 1940 he married actress Jane Wyman, who he had met on set in 1938, although they divorced in 1948. During the Second World War he entered the US Army, working for an army film unit for 3 years in Los Angeles from 1942–45.

After being discharged from the army Reagan turned increasingly to politics. In 1947 he was elected president of the screen actors' guild, a position that he would retain for a further 5 years. Reagan was initially a 'New Deal' Democrat and he campaigned for Harry S. Truman in the 1948 presidential election. However his belief that communist sympathies were eroding American institutions increasingly led him to the political right. He testified to the Un-American Activities Committee and assisted with the blacklisting of actors, directors and screenwriters who were suspected of having left-wing sympathies.

In 1950 Reagan campaigned on behalf of Republican senatorial candidate Richard M. Nixon. Two years later he married Nancy Davis. Increasingly politics took the place of acting in Reagan's life and in 1964 he made an impact with a televised address on behalf of Republican presidential candidate Barry Goldwater. This speech helped him win support when he announced his candidacy for the governorship of California in 1966. He won the Republican nomination with 64.7% of the vote and then defeated Democratic incumbent Edmund G. Brown Sr. by almost one million votes.

Reagan served for 8 years as California governor (1966–74), winning a second term when he defeated Democrat rival Jesse Unrah in 1970. Reagan's gubernatorial style was to concentrate on the broader picture and leave day-to-day policy matters to department heads and assistants. Reagan's main achievement was large-scale reform of California's welfare system, which saw the number of recipients drop dramatically, while those who still received benefits saw their payments increase by 40%. Reagan also oversaw an increase in the state budget from $4.6 bn. to $10.2 bn. and took a hard-line view of student demonstrations, cutting university spending by 27% in his first 2 years in office and urging the University of California at Berkeley to fire president Clark Kerr. After the student demonstration movement had faded Reagan increased spending on higher education, more than doubling it by 1974.

The high profile of his role as governor saw Reagan begin to focus on a presidential bid. A last-minute attempt to secure the Republican nomination in 1968 saw him finish third behind Richard M. Nixon and Nelson Rockefeller. In 1974 Reagan decided not to seek re-election in California and to concentrate his efforts on a presidential bid in 1976. However Nixon's subsequent resignation and the succession of Gerald R. Ford to the presidency made success unlikely. He challenged Ford for the Republican nomination but was defeated by 60 votes.

Career Peak

In 1980 Reagan won the Republican nomination with ease, choosing one of his defeated opponents, George Bush, as his running mate. High inflation and the failure of incumbent president Jimmy Carter to solve the Iran hostage crisis as well as Reagan's considerable charm, helped him win the election by 51% to Carter's 42% and 483 electoral college votes to 49. On the day of his inauguration Reagan announced the release of the remaining American hostages in Iran. On 30 March 1981 Reagan survived an assassination attempt by John W. Hinckley, Jr. in Washington, D.C. during which a bullet punctured a lung and only just missed his heart.

Reagan's first year in office was dominated by economic reforms. A 25% tax cut for individuals and corporations was introduced in an effort to stimulate the economy. Welfare expenditure was cut but military expenditure was increased by $1.5 trn. over a 5-year period. Through his policy of 'new federalism' Reagan sought to delegate many federal programmes to state and local levels. A severe recession in 1982 saw bankruptcies hit record levels and unemployment rise to nearly 11%. Reagan was forced to support a large tax increase and by 1983 inflation and unemployment had fallen. However the long-term effect of the recession saw the country's trade deficit increase to $111 bn. by 1984 (up from $25 bn. in 1980). Socially, Reagan endorsed many fundamentalist policies, such as anti-abortion, but failed to win Congress' support for such measures.

In his foreign policy, Reagan sought to reassert the United States' military pre-eminence. He was unstinting in his criticism of the Soviet Union, denouncing it as 'the focus of evil in the modern world'. The shooting down of a South Korean airliner containing American citizens in 1983 and the increased US deployment of missiles in Western Europe both worsened relations between the two countries as did Reagan's announcement of the intended development of the Strategic Defense Initiative (SDI). This proposal aimed to introduce a missile defence system in space and was dubbed 'Star Wars' by the media.

In 1983 Reagan ordered an invasion of Grenada after a coup in order to limit Soviet–Cuban influence in the Caribbean. In 1984 Reagan and Bush were re-nominated by the Republican party and swept to victory against Democratic opponents Walter Mondale and Geraldine Ferraro, winning every state expect Minnesota and the District of Columbia and gaining 525 electoral college votes, the highest ever by a presidential candidate. In his second term Reagan continued his tax reforms. In 1986 he reduced the number of tax rates, abolishing tax altogether for many low-income earners.

On 19 Oct. 1987 the economy suffered its biggest crisis under Reagan when the stock market collapsed. The Dow Jones index fell by over a third in just 2 months. Reagan's critics blamed his economic policies for encouraging a culture of boom and bust. By the end of his second term the United States' national debt had more than tripled to $2.5 trn.

Relations with the Soviet Union improved during Reagan's second term after he met Soviet leader Mikhail Gorbachev in 1985. Two years later the two leaders signed a treaty in Washington, D.C. agreeing to destroy a wide array of intermediate-range nuclear weapons and in 1988 Reagan visited Moscow. Reagan continued to use military force when he thought American interests were under threat. In 1986, after suspected Libyan involvement in the bombing of a nightclub in West Berlin which killed two American servicemen, Reagan authorized American planes to bomb Tripoli.

In 1987 the Reagan administration was involved in what became known as the Iran-Contra affair. The United States had been secretly selling arms to Iran, using profits from the sales to assist anti-communist guerrillas in Nicaragua. Investigations into the affair cleared Reagan of any direct involvement but criticized his 'personal management style' which had allowed the affair to develop. The scandal dented Reagan's popularity but was never a serious threat to his presidency.

Later Life

Reagan campaigned on behalf of George Bush in the 1988 presidential election, helping his former vice-president reach the White House, and then retired from politics. His autobiography, entitled *An American Life*, was published in 1990. Four years later, in a public letter, Reagan announced that he had been diagnosed with Alzheimer's Disease. He died on 5 June 2004 and was honoured with a state presidential funeral and a day of national mourning.

Regmi, Khil Raj (Nepal)

Introduction

Khil Raj Regmi, the chief justice of the Supreme Court of Nepal, was sworn in as prime minister on 14 March 2013, heading an interim government charged with supervising elections initially scheduled for June 2013 but which were delayed until Nov. He succeeded Maoist leader Baburam Bhattarai, who stepped down amid the political stalemate that had left the nascent republic without a functioning parliament since May 2012.

Early Life

Khil Raj Regmi was born on 31 May 1949 in Pokharathok in the Lumbini Zone of southern Nepal. He studied arts at Tribhuvan University in Kathmandu before completing a master's degree in law at the same institution. He became a district judge in 1974, rising through the judicial ranks to become chief justice of the Supreme Court on 6 May 2011.

Regmi's appointment as prime minister in March 2013 was the result of a compromise deal between the four main political parties (the United Democratic Madhesi Front, the Nepali Congress, the Communist Party of Nepal

[Unified Marxist-Leninist] and the United Communist Party of Nepal [Maoists]). They had been unable to agree on a suitable candidate since May 2012 when a special assembly was dissolved having failed to draft a new constitution.

Regmi was regarded as a political independent with the bureaucratic skills to lead an interim administration. Though his appointment was well received by the international community, domestic opponents criticized it for blurring the separation between executive and judicial power.

Career Peak

Regmi announced an 11-member cabinet on 19 March 2013, made up entirely of ex-civil servants in accordance with the cross-party agreement that brought him to power. He was charged with overseeing elections to select a constituent assembly to finish drafting the country's first constitution since the monarchy was abolished in 2008. In those elections, which were staged in Nov., the Nepali Congress emerged as the largest party ahead of the Communist Party of Nepal and the Maoists. The latter, who had earlier questioned the validity of Regmi's appointment as head of government, claimed that the elections were rigged but agreed in Dec. to join the new assembly.

His premiership ended in Feb. 2014, following defeat by Nepali Congress candidate Sushil Koirala in constituent assembly elections in 2013. As prime minister, Regmi faced difficult economic conditions as the nation, dependent on foreign aid and tourism, struggled to rebuild after the 10-year civil war that ended in 2006.

Reinfeldt, Fredrik (Sweden)

Introduction

Fredrik Reinfeldt led a centre-right alliance to victory in the legislative elections of Sept. 2006, ousting the Social Democrats (SAP) from over a decade in power. After taking over the leadership of the Moderate Party in 2003, Reinfeldt rebranded it as a centrist party advocating entrepreneurship and job creation coupled with reform of Sweden's cherished welfare system. He retained the premiership following the Sept. 2010 elections.

Early Life

John Fredrik Reinfeldt was born in Stockholm on 4 Aug. 1965. He joined the youth wing of the conservative Moderate Party in 1983. Having completed military service, in 1990 he graduated in business and economics from Stockholm University, where he was active in student politics. He embarked on a political career, becoming chairman of the Moderate Youth League and standing in the legislative elections of Sept. 1991. He won a seat in parliament as the Moderate Party emerged as the leading non-socialist party. The SAP remained the largest single party, but without an overall majority, and Moderate leader Carl Bildt became the first Conservative prime minister since 1930, heading a four-party coalition. The government attempted to tackle the economic crisis that gripped Sweden in 1992 by introducing market reforms, imposing spending cuts and privatizing publicly-owned enterprises. It also sought accession to the European Union.

In the Sept. 1994 elections the Moderates held on to the 80 seats they had won in 1991, but some of their centre-right coalition partners fared badly and the Social Democrats were returned to power. After Bo Lundgren succeeded Bildt as Moderate leader in 1999, Reinfeldt was promoted to chairman of the parliamentary justice committee in 2001–02.

The Moderate Party's poor performance in the 2002 elections was compounded by a scandal in 2003 in which some members were accused of racism. Lundgren was forced to resign as leader in Oct. 2003 and Reinfeldt was elected unanimously to succeed him. Reinfeldt rebranded the party as the New Moderates and shifted the focus to the centre ground. In the run-up to the Sept. 2006 legislative elections, he formed the Alliance for Sweden, aiming to unite a four-party centre-right coalition (New Moderates plus the Centre Party, Liberal Party and Christian Democrats). Presenting a joint manifesto, the alliance narrowly beat the SAP. The New Moderates took 26.1% of the vote, a record for the party, and Reinfeldt was nominated prime minister on 5 Oct. 2006.

Career Peak

On taking office, Reinfeldt initiated a programme of reforms aimed at strengthening incentives to work, reducing welfare dependency and streamlining the state's role in the economy. However, in the wake of the global financial crisis, Sweden slipped into recession in 2008, and in Dec. Reinfeldt proposed a stimulus package to boost the economy. The downturn nevertheless had a significant impact on Sweden's trade-oriented economy in 2009 as exports declined and job losses mounted.

Reinfeldt's own party has favoured joining the single European currency and, in principle, supports membership of NATO. In 2008 the Alliance, supported by the SAP, ratified the Lisbon Treaty (signed in Dec. 2007) on EU institutional and administrative reform. From July–Dec. 2009 Sweden held the rotating EU presidency and oversaw the treaty's implementation. The Swedish presidency also pressed the EU to take the lead in fighting climate change. In Feb. 2009 Reinfeldt's government announced its intention to lift a 30-year-old ban on building new nuclear energy capacity.

In the Sept. 2010 legislative elections the Alliance fell narrowly short of a parliamentary majority but Reinfeldt formed a new minority government the following month with no changes in key ministerial portfolios.

In May 2013 Stockholm suffered several nights of rioting in mainly inter-ethnic suburbs, prompting leftist criticism of Reinfeldt for social spending cuts and right-wing attacks for his immigration and asylum policies.

Reinfeldt's term as prime minister came to an end when his New Moderates lost the 2014 general election to the Social Democrats. At the time of his departure from office he was the longest-serving conservative premier in Sweden's history. He subsequently announced his resignation from the party and was succeeded as leader by Anna Kinberg Batra in Jan. 2015. Stefan Löfven of the SAP took over as prime minister on 3 Oct. 2014.

René, France Albert (Seychelles)

Introduction

France Albert René was president of the Seychelles from 1977–2004, representing the Seychelles People's Progressive Front (SPPF; called the Seychelles People's United Party until 1978). A socialist and campaigner for independence from British rule, he came to power in 1977 when he deposed the then president, Seychelles Democratic Party (SDP) leader James Mancham. He implemented wide social reforms, but imposed one party rule and strict censorship. After relaxing political restrictions, he was returned to the presidency in 1993 in the first multiparty elections and again in 1998 and 2001.

Early Life

René was born on the island of Mahé on 16 Nov. 1935. He was educated in Switzerland and Britain before completing a law degree in London in 1957. He was politically active during his student years, becoming involved with the British Labour Party. Returning to work in the Seychelles, he continued his political activity, founding the island's first trade union. This formed the basis for the SPPF, which René created in 1964. The party campaigned against British rule, opposing Mancham who wanted membership of the Commonwealth. Between 1967–70 René served in the islands' administration.

In 1975 the SPPF and the SDP formed a coalition government, and the following year the Seychelles became an independent republic. Mancham was appointed president and René was chosen as his prime minister.

Career Peak

While Mancham was in London at a Commonwealth conference in 1977, René took the opportunity to lead a bloodless coup and establish himself as president. As leader, he implemented policies of social reform to improve education, housing and employment and increased social security including establishing a minimum wage. Increased investment in agriculture and fishing improved the economy, while efforts were made to encourage tourism. René classified much of the islands as protected sites to preserve the Seychelles' natural beauty, a major tourist attraction.

Yet, despite these reforms, a new constitution was adopted in 1979 creating a one-party state with the SPPF as the only legal party. Strict censorship and government control of the media were imposed. He maintained close links with Tanzania, from whom he received military support, and was allied with the USSR, Cuba and China. Political opponents, including Mancham, were forced into exile. In total around 10,000 islanders fled. Several attempts were made to depose René, including a failed operation in 1981 by South African mercenaries. The president imposed a state of emergency that was not lifted until 1992. In 1987, the government embarked on a campaign to acquire land owned by dissident Seychellois living abroad. The president was re-elected in 1984 and 1989.

Following increased international pressure and the fall of European communist states, René restored multi-party democracy in 1991. Opposition politicians returned and were involved in establishing a new constitution which separated legislative, judicial and executive powers. In 1993 it was approved by 73.9% of votes. Presidential elections were held in the same year, in which René was returned to power with 60% of votes to Mancham's 37%. In 1998 he won a fifth term in office with 66.7% to the Seychelles National Party candidate Wavel Ramkalawan's 19.5%. A sixth term followed in 2001 when he defeated Wavel Ramkalawan (Seychelles National Party) and Philippe Boullé, claiming 54% of the vote.

In the last years of his presidency, René moved away from traditional socialist policies by encouraging a free-market economy. On 14 April 2004 he stepped down as president and was succeeded by his vice-president, James Michel. René remained the leader of the SPPF.

Renner, Karl (Austria)

Introduction

Karl Renner was Austrian chancellor twice (from 1918–20 and in 1945) and the country's first President from 1945–50. Before World War II he was a supporter of the *Anschluss*, by which Germany annexed Austria, but his political involvement decreased as the war progressed. He co-operated with Soviet officials after the war to re-constitute an independent government. He assisted in Austria's re-integration into the international community and developed a policy of neutrality.

Early Life

Renner was born on 14 Dec. 1870 in Unter-Tannowitz in Bohemia (then part of the Austro-Hungarian Empire and now part of the Czech Republic), the tenth son of a poor farming family. He studied at the University of Vienna, achieving his degree in law in 1896. Around this time he joined the Social Democratic Party and married. His wife, Luise, remained an influential figure till her death.

He entered parliament in 1907 and when Emperor Charles I abdicated in 1918, Renner became Chancellor of the new republic.

Career Peak

Renner held the post until July 1920, during which time Austria lost territory to Italy, Czechoslovakia and Yugoslavia in post-World War I settlements. In addition, Austria agreed to a permanent ban on union with Germany. Renner was President of the Parliament from 1931–33, but Austria's international status had collapsed, its economy was weak and its prospects bleak.

By the late-1930s Renner was pursuing union with Germany. He advocated Germany's annexation of the country in 1938, commenting that 'Austria has no future'. Austria's democratic framework was dismantled by the Nazi regime and Renner left his home in Vienna to move to Lower Austria. Victorious Soviet troops entered the city in April 1945 and Renner quickly opened negotiations with them. Within 4 weeks he was Chancellor of a new provisional government that comprised Social Democrats, Communists, Conservatives and non-partisans.

Independence was declared, the *Anschlus* officially dissolved and by Oct. the government had the support of the other Allied countries. A free general election was held in Nov. 1945. The following month parliament appointed Renner as President for a 6-year term. He campaigned for the re-integration of South Tyrol into Austria and was critical of the Allied system of occupation zones. Controversially, he suggested that post-war Austria would not welcome migrating East European Jews when unemployment was rife among the country's existing population. He distanced himself from the idea of German unification and voiced support for the United Nations, to the disappointment of the Soviet Union. By 1949 the Communists were effectively killed off as a major force within Austrian politics. He died while in office on 31 Dec. 1950 in Doebling, Austria. The Renner Institute in Vienna is the Social Democrat's affiliated political academy.

Renzi, Matteo (Italy)

Early Life

Matteo Renzi was born on 11 Jan. 1975 in Florence and graduated in law from the city's university. In 1996 he joined the centrist Italian People's Party (which in 2002 integrated with the Democratic Party; PD) and within 3 years was appointed its regional secretary. In June 2004 he was elected president of the province of Florence.

After 5 years in the post, Renzi announced his candidacy for Florence's mayoral election. He won 48% of the vote on 9 June 2009, comfortably defeating his nearest rival, Giovanni Galli, and used his time in office to pedestrianize the city centre and cultivate his political persona.

He suffered the first significant setback of his political career in Dec. 2012 when he was defeated by the veteran Pier Luigi Bersani in the race for the PD-led centre-left coalition's endorsement as a prime ministerial candidate. However, Bersani's inability to build a workable governing coalition in the wake of the election of Feb. 2013 forced his resignation. PD deputy leader Enrico Letta subsequently established a coalition and was sworn in as prime minister.

In Dec. 2013 Renzi was elected PD leader and declared his intention to sweep away the party old guard—an ambition that brought him into conflict with Letta. In Feb. 2014 tensions came to a head and Renzi formally asked Letta to resign the premiership. When he did so, then President Giorgio Napolitano invited Renzi to form a new government.

Career Peak

Renzi came to power in the midst of Italy's worst economic crisis since the end of the Second World War, with two consecutive years of recession compounding a sovereign debt level in excess of annual GDP. He pledged major reforms, including constitutional changes and a new electoral law and a restructuring of the labour market and tax system. In April 2014 he outlined the government's framework economic policy, envisaging a reduction in income tax for lower earners and cuts in public spending, and in Sept. set out a controversial programme to reform restrictive employment rules, which was approved by parliament in Nov. Meanwhile, his plan to reduce the size and powers of the Senate was accepted by the upper house in Aug. 2014, while in May 2015 parliament approved an electoral reform giving the largest political party an automatic majority of seats. However, the credibility and reputation of Renzi's government was undermined in mid-2015 by a series of political scandals, resulting in a fall in public support. Following his defeat in a referendum held on 4 Dec. 2016, Renzi handed in his resignation to the president. He was succeeded as prime minister by Paolo Gentiloni.

Reynolds, Albert (Ireland)

Introduction

Albert Reynolds was Irish Prime Minister (*Taoiseach*) from 1992–95. Leader of Fianna Fáil, he made peace in Northern Ireland his main objective. After talks with British Prime Minister John Major, he was party to the 1993 Joint (Downing Street) Declaration that set out criteria for a lasting resolution to the Irish problem. He was forced to resign after his coalition broke up but his Declaration was to have a lasting impact on Irish politics.

Early Life

Reynolds was born on 3 Nov. 1932 in Rooskey, County Roscommon. He attended Summerhill College in County Sligo before starting a career in commerce. He worked for a shipping firm, became a local newspaper proprietor and made a fortune from a dog food business. In 1977 he entered the Dáil as the Fianna Fáil member for Longford.

In 1979 he was made minister for transport, posts and telegraphs. Three years later he moved to the Department of Energy and from 1987–88 he was minister of industry and commerce. He was appointed minister of finance in 1988 but left the post in 1991 after unsuccessfully challenging prime minister Charles Haughey for the party leadership. He succeeded Haughey the following year.

Career Peak

Emphasizing his commitment to the Northern Irish peace process, Reynolds was perceived as a pragmatist who was unburdened by previous involvement in Northern Irish issues. He embarked on negotiations with the UK government to establish a framework for peace talks. He and John Major issued their Joint Declaration on Peace on 15 Dec. 1993.

The Agreement stressed that Northern Ireland's status would be decided by the will of the majority and that peace negotiations would involve all groups who renounced violence. The agreement led to the first Irish Republican Army (IRA) ceasefire in 1994.

Despite this breakthrough, Reynolds' premiership was dogged by internal party conflicts and opposition from those who distrusted his pragmatic approach. There was further controversy over a deal he had made to secure meat exports when minister of finance. In Dec. 1994 he resigned the premiership, remaining in office until his successor, John Bruton, was installed in early 1995.

Later Life

An investigation into Reynolds' business affairs published in the British newspaper *The Sunday Times* led to a drawn-out libel trial which found in favour of Reynolds but awarded him only one penny damages and left him with large costs. Having been given leave to appeal the size of the award, he came to an out-of-court settlement with the newspaper. The Joint Declaration was an important step on the road to Northern Irish peace, leading directly to the 1998 Good Friday Agreement.

Reynolds died on 21 Aug. 2014 following a long battle with Alzheimer's disease. He was buried at Shanganagh Cemetery in Dublin with full military honours.

Reza Pahlavi, Mohammad (Iran)

Introduction

Mohammad Reza Pahlavi was the Shah (monarch) of Iran from 1941–79, before being deposed in an Islamic revolution. His reign, although repressive, was marked by attempts at reform and modernization. However, during the 1970s Iran's economy deteriorated, social inequalities widened, and discontent grew among religious fundamentalists over perceived decadent Western influences. Opposition to the monarchy culminated in the Shah's flight abroad in Jan. 1979. He died in Egypt on 27 July 1980.

Early Life

Born on 26 Oct. 1919 in Tehran, Mohammad Reza was educated in Switzerland before returning to Iran in 1935 to attend military academy. He came to the throne in Sept. 1941 after British and Soviet forces had occupied Iran and forced his father Reza Shah, a Nazi sympathiser, to abdicate. The new Shah proclaimed an end to absolute rule, granting political powers to the Cabinet and Assembly (Majlis). In 1949, after narrowly escaping assassination, he banned the pro-Soviet Tudeh Party.

During the late 1940s public discontent grew in Iran over British ownership of the Anglo-Iranian Oil Company which controlled a large part of the country's oil assets. In 1951 the Prime Minister, Mohammad Mossadeq, nationalized the oil industry, incurring British sanctions. The economy declined, giving rise to internal unrest. In Aug. 1953 army officers loyal to the Shah tried to overthrow the Prime Minister and his supporters. The Shah was forced briefly into exile before his reinstatement in a coup, widely believed to have involved the British and United States security services. Over the following years he sought to consolidate his personal authority over Iran.

Career Peak

In pursuit of his aim of turning Iran into an industrial nation based on Western rather than traditional values and culture, the Shah received extensive financial and military backing from the United States. In the early 1960s he launched a reform programme—his so-called 'white revolution'—which included land redistribution, the promotion of literacy, the emancipation of women and extensive construction. However, in the process of the breaking up the old feudal structures, the peasantry and urban poor became increasingly isolated from the oil-based wealth of a minority of Iranians. The Shah's pro-Western stance also provoked criticism from the Muslim clergy.

As popular discontent became more evident in the early 1970s, the Shah grew more repressive. Opposition was dealt with harshly by his national intelligence and security agency, SAVAK. Despite the oil price rise in 1973–74, wealth inequalities persisted. A survey in 1976 revealed that only 3% of Iranians shared 90% of the nation's wealth. Protests and riots worsened during 1977–78, and the opposition movement threw its support behind the exiled religious leader, Ayatollah Khomeini.

On 16 Jan. 1979, the Shah fled the country and Khomeini returned to Iran to direct the Islamic revolution. After brief periods of exile in Egypt, Morocco, the Bahamas, Mexico, the US and Panama, he returned to Egypt in May 1980. His death 2 months later in Cairo was attributed to complications induced by treatment for cancer.

Richards, George Maxwell (Trinidad and Tobago)

Introduction

George Maxwell Richards became president in March 2003. A chemical engineer by training, he is non-partisan and, with his mixed-race background, has sought to offset ethnic tensions in the country's political life. He was re-elected for a second term in Feb. 2008.

Early Life

Richards was born in San Fernando, Trinidad in 1931. He graduated from the Queen's Royal College in Port of Spain in 1955 and took a master's degree in chemical engineering at Manchester University in England. In 1963 he obtained his PhD from Cambridge University.

From 1957–65 he worked for Shell Trinidad before taking a lectureship in chemical engineering at the University of the West Indies. Five years later he became professor of chemical engineering and in 1985 was promoted to principal of the university, a post he held until late 1986. Richards was also active on the boards of several commercial companies and chaired the government salaries review commission from 1977–2003.

Following tied parliamentary elections in 2001, Arthur Robinson, then president, was forced to choose between Patrick Manning and Basdeo Panday for the premiership. When Robinson selected Manning he was accused of bias and the non-partisan nature of the presidency came under scrutiny. When Manning nominated Richards for the presidency, he cited Richards' lack of a party political background as a key reason. In a secret ballot in Feb. 2003 parliament elected Richards by 43 votes to 25.

Career Peak

The presidency is primarily a ceremonial role and, following the controversy after the 2001 elections, Richards emphasized on assuming office that he was 'completely apolitical'. With his mixed race (including black, Chinese and white) roots, he aimed to diffuse some of the tension arising from the racially divided political structure and in Feb. 2008 was re-elected by parliament as the sole presidential candidate. In May 2010 he swore in Kamla Persad-Bissessar as the country's first female prime minister.

Richards' presidency came to an end in March 2013; Anthony Carmona was subsequently sworn in as the fifth president of Trinidad and Tobago.

Later Life

Richards died in Port of Spain on 8 Jan. 2018 at the age of 86 following a heart attack.

Robinson, Mary (Ireland)

Introduction

Mary Robinson was Ireland's first female President, holding office from 1990–97. A barrister, she served in the Seanad Éireann (the Irish Senate) from 1969–89. Her unexpected victory in the 1990 presidential election ended 45 years of Fianna Fáil domination of the presidency. Robinson raised the profile of the presidency, a largely ceremonial post, and used her office to boost Ireland's international image and to highlight global human rights issues. She ended her tenure early to become the UN High Commissioner for Human Rights.

Early Life

Robinson was born Mary Bourke on 21 May 1944 in Ballina, County Mayo. Her family background was Roman Catholic but she studied at the traditionally Protestant Trinity College, Dublin, gaining a master's degree in 1970. She went on to get a Law degree from King's Inn, Dublin before continuing her legal studies at Harvard University. In 1969 she became Reid Professor of Law at Trinity College where she specialized in constitutional and human rights issues.

In 1969 she joined the Senate as representative of the University and a year later she married a Protestant, Nicholas Robinson, with whom she would have three children. She joined the Labour Party in 1976 and fought two unsuccessful campaigns for election to the Dáil, in 1977 and 1981. From 1979–83 she was a member of Dublin City Council. In 1985 she resigned from the party in protest at the signing of the Anglo–Irish Treaty, which she believed was slanted unfairly against Unionists.

In 1988 she and her husband founded the Irish Centre for European Law. Robinson remained its director until 1990. In 1989 she was approached by Labour leader Dick Spring to stand as an independent candidate against Fianna Fáil's Brian Lenihan in the presidential elections. Her campaign centred around policies that reflected her human rights interests, including liberalization of laws on divorce, contraception, abortion and homosexuality. Boosted by a large female turnout, she won a narrow victory commenting that Ireland's women 'instead of rocking the cradle had rocked the system'.

Career Peak

The symbolic nature of the Irish presidency enabled Robinson to rise above the minutiae of day to day politics. Her tenure coincided with a period of economic stability and growth which combined with her natural charm and eloquence ensured her popularity with the Irish public. The presidency gained prestige on the international scene. She campaigned on behalf of the oppressed and weak throughout the world, drawing parallels between Third World poverty and unrest and Ireland's own turbulent history. While remaining non-partisan, she worked to encourage peace in Northern Ireland and in a landmark gesture shook hands with the Sinn Fein leader, Gerry Adams.

In 1997 the UN General Secretary invited Robinson to become High Commissioner on Human Rights. Despite the approaching presidential election which she was likely to win, Robinson resigned a few months early to take up the UN post. In her new capacity she highlighted human rights abuses in Timor-Leste, Sierra Leone and Kosovo. In March 2001 Robinson confirmed she would not seek a second term, claiming that she could achieve more outside the 'constraints' of the UN.

Robinson, Peter (Northern Ireland, United Kingdom)

Introduction

A member of the Democratic Unionist Party (DUP) since its foundation, Peter Robinson served as deputy leader of the party for 28 years, almost without interruption, before being elected unopposed to the leadership following the resignation of Ian Paisley in May 2008. He was sworn in as first minister of Northern Ireland the following month.

Early Life

Peter David Robinson was born in Belfast on 29 Dec. 1948. He attended Castlereagh College before becoming an estate agent. The death of an old school friend in an IRA bombing at the Northern Ireland Electricity headquarters in 1971 prompted Robinson to begin a political career. In the same year he joined the DUP, recently founded by Ian Paisley and Desmond Boal. Quickly winning renown for his managerial skills, Robinson rose through the party ranks. He was made an executive member in 1973 and was appointed party secretary-general in 1975. In 1980 Robinson became deputy leader.

Standing for the DUP in the constituency of Belfast East, Robinson was elected to parliament in May 1979. Having overturned (by 64 votes) an Ulster Unionist majority of 17,000, Robinson has successfully defended the seat six times. He is the longest serving member of parliament for any Belfast constituency since the Act of Union. Robinson's wife Iris (neé Collins) is also an MP.

In common with all Unionist MPs (both DUP and Ulster Unionist), Robinson resigned his seat in 1985 in protest at the implementation of the Anglo-Irish Agreement that allowed Dublin an advisory role in the governance of Northern Ireland. He was returned in the subsequent by-election. Motivated by his staunch opposition to the settlement, on 7 Aug. 1986 Robinson was among 500 loyalists to descend upon the village of Clontribet, County Monaghan, in the Republic of Ireland. Robinson was arrested and pleaded guilty to unlawful assembly. He resigned his position as deputy leader of the DUP, though he was reinstated within months.

The DUP withdrew from talks leading to the 1998 Good Friday Agreement in protest at the participation of Sinn Féin following the declaration of an IRA ceasefire. The Agreement was approved by referenda on both sides of the Irish border, despite the opposition of the DUP. This allowed for the establishment of the power-sharing Northern Irish Assembly. Although refusing to attend Stormont Executive meetings, in 1999 Robinson took office as minister for regional development and won further plaudits for his efficient management and organizational skills. Responsible for the introduction of free public transport for older people, he was also a key architect of the St Andrews Agreement which preceded the restoration of power to the Northern Irish Assembly in 2007. Robinson negotiated the inclusion of a power of veto, which his party has since used on several occasions.

The expansion of the DUP's appeal—historically limited to the white protestant working classes—is often attributed to Robinson, who is seen as representing the urban, secular wing of Unionism. The DUP won the largest share of votes of any party at the Northern Ireland Assembly elections in March 2007. This victory entitled the party to nominate its leader for the position of first minister. Following Ian Paisley's resignation as leader of the DUP on 31 May 2008, Robinson was elected unopposed to the party leadership. He was subsequently confirmed as first minister by the Assembly.

Career Peak

In partnership with a Sinn Féin representative, Robinson heads an administration of ten ministers and two junior ministers drawn from the DUP, Sinn Féin, the Ulster Unionists and the nationalist Social Democratic and Labour Party. The strikingly amicable relationship between Robinson's predecessor, Ian Paisley, and the deputy minister, Sinn Féin's Martin McGuinness, was a cause of dissatisfaction among much of the DUP's core membership. Robinson is expected to distance himself from any close personal relationship while striving to maintain a pragmatic working relationship with the deputy first minister. Widely regarded as a technocrat and lacking Paisley's force of personality, Robinson's challenge is to maintain unity in his own party while working in tandem with his partners in government.

In Jan. 2010 it came to light that Peter Robinson's wife and DUP MP for Strangford, Iris Robinson, had been involved in illegal property dealings and that her husband had been aware of her actions. Robinson claimed he had not acted improperly but stood down temporarily while an inquiry into his conduct could be carried out. Arlene Foster, the minister for enterprise, became acting first minister. Robinson resumed his duties on 3 Feb. In the May general election he lost his parliamentary seat in Belfast East which he had held for 31 years to Alliance Party rival Naomi Long but stayed on as DUP leader and First Minister.

In May 2015 Robinson suffered a suspected heart attack, but made a full recovery.

Robinson temporarily stood aside as first minister on 10 Sept. 2015 after parties rejected a proposal to adjourn power-sharing institutions in Northern Ireland in the wake of allegations that the IRA had been involved in a recent murder in Belfast. Robinson stated that the continued existence of IRA structures 'pushed devolution to the brink' following Sinn Féin's denial that the IRA still existed. He appointed Arlene Foster to serve again as acting first minister.

Robinson resigned as first minister on 11 Jan. 2016, with Arlene Foster taking over on an official basis.

Rodríguez Echeverría, Miguel Ángel (Costa Rica)

Introduction

Miguel Angel Rodríguez Echeverría was president of Costa Rica between 1998–2002, representing the conservative Partido Unidad Social Cristiana (PUSC). When he replaced the centre-left Partido Liberación Nacional (PLN) leader José María Figueres Olsen, he inherited a growing economy, which was further boosted by his success in attracting foreign investment. His major challenges were settling border disputes with Nicaragua and placating opposition to the reform and privatization of the national electricity company.

Early Life

Rodríguez was born on 9 Jan. 1940 in San José. He studied law and economics at the Universidad de Costa Rica before finishing his higher education at Berkeley University in 1966. He wrote a column for La Nación newspaper at the end of the 1960s. Between 1970–90 he was economics professor at the national university, writing books on political and social economics. A successful businessman, he worked for agroindustrial companies. Rodríguez began his government career in 1966 as planning minister under the presidency of José Joaquín Trejos while simultaneously managing the Costa Rican national bank. He joined the PUSC's ruling body and in 1990 became deputy for San José. He served as a deputy in the legislative assembly between 1990–93, acting as president of the assembly between 1991–92. In the 1986 presidential election he fought party colleague and future president Rafael Angel Calderón. In 1994 he was the PUSC's presidential candidate, but lost to Figueres.

Career Peak

Austerity measures brought on by an economic slump in the mid-1990s led to public discontent with Figueres' government and his party. Before the 1998 presidential elections Rodríguez was far ahead in the opinion polls but in the end a slim margin of votes separated him from the PLN candidate, José Corrales, the latter receiving 44.4% to Rodríguez's 46.9%.

On election Rodríguez pledged to improve opportunities for women, the young and the poor. He continued Figueres' economic policies, including the unpopular austerity measures. He planned to cut government spending, implement market reforms, including limited privatization, and encourage foreign investment in order to lower the country's fiscal deficit from 3.7% of GDP to 1.7% by the end of 1999 and to reduce Costa Rica's US\$4 bn. national debt. The first and most significant foreign investment led in 1998 to the setting up of production centres in San José for two leading American computer chip companies. The following year the country experienced its first trade surplus for 15 years. By 2000 government investment in high-tech companies had improved GDP, further boosting a general economic recovery with reduced inflation and lower unemployment.

Attempts to reform and privatize the state owned electricity and telecommunications company, ICE, led to a strike by public sector workers and protests in early 2000. Rodríguez planned to split the company into two parts—energy and telecommunications—to attract the maximum foreign investment. Despite support from opposition parties, strikers rejected the proposal believing it would mean job losses. Rodríguez agreed to delay legislation while a bipartisan committee reviewed the bill, but a ruling by the Supreme Court making it unconstitutional stopped it going further.

Rodríguez renewed ties with the US, travelling to Washington, D.C. to promote trade relations. In 1999 a long-standing border dispute with Nicaragua flared up, increasing tension between the two governments. Nonetheless, following the devastation of hurricane Mitch, Rodríguez granted an amnesty for illegal immigrants in Costa Rica, according all 150,000 mainly Nicaraguan applicants permanent residency status with full access to the welfare state. Nicaraguans make up 10% of Costa Rica's inhabitants.

Rodríguez was replaced as president by fellow PUSC member Abel Pacheco de la Espriella.

Later Life

In 2004 Rodríguez was briefly Secretary General of the Organization of American States. In April 2011 he was sentenced to 5 years in prison for accepting bribes from the French telecommunications company Alcatel.

Rodríguez, Eduardo (Bolivia)

Introduction

Eduardo Rodríguez was named Bolivia's interim president on 10 June 2005, after mass protests in the crisis-hit country led to the resignation of President Carlos Mesa. The lawyer and former head of the Supreme Court, who was considered untainted by political life, faced the task of leading one of Latin America's poorest and most divided countries into the elections of Dec. 2005.

Early Life

Eduardo Rodríguez Veltzé was born on 2 March 1956 in Cochabamba. He attended the San Agustín High School in the city and went on to read law at the Universidad Mayor de San Simon, also in Cochabamba. After graduating in 1981, Rodríguez began work as a solicitor. He travelled to the US in 1988 to take a master's degree in public administration at Harvard University. On his return to Bolivia he joined the civil service, taking up the post of deputy of legal services in the treasury and in the ministry of foreign affairs, serving in the government of President Jaime Paz Zamora of the Movement of the Revolutionary Left (Movimiento de la Izquierda Revolucionaria). Rodríguez subsequently worked as co-ordinator of the department for the prevention of crime and the treatment of delinquency at the United Nations' Institute of Latin America. He also practised as a legal consultant on a number of international projects.

From the mid-1990s Rodríguez taught law at the Universidad Católica Boliviana, the Universidad Andina Simón Bolívar and the Universidad Mayor de San Andrés in La Paz. He was nominated as one of 12 justices of the Supreme Court, confirmed by the national congress in March 1999. Rodríguez was closely involved in a drive to improve the country's court system, particularly the implementation of the code of criminal procedures in May 2002, which attempted to root-out corruption and protect human rights. In March 2004 Rodríguez was elected chief justice of the Supreme Court.

After the arrival of a new president, Carlos Mesa, in Oct. 2003, Bolivia was gripped by social unrest, caused by the poverty of the majority indigenous community coupled with the desire of wealthier provinces for autonomy. By April 2005 there were mass protests on the streets of La Paz, with demonstrators calling for the nationalization of the energy sector. A blockade led to shortages of food and fuel in La Paz and when clashes erupted between the police and protesters, Mesa was forced to flee under an armed escort. He resigned shortly afterwards. After Hormando Vaca Diez and Mario Cossio,

presidents of the senate and chamber of deputies respectively, both declined the post of interim president, it was accepted by Rodríguez, who, as head of the judiciary, was considered to be above party politics.

Career Peak

Rodríguez was sworn in as interim president on 10 June 2005. Emphasizing his neutrality, he urged Bolivians to unite in the spirit of national solidarity. Shortly afterwards, Rodríguez announced that fresh elections would be held in Dec. 2005, to ensure that a 'fairer and more equitable democracy emerged'. And that a referendum on regional autonomy would take place in July 2006. True to his word, presidential elections were held on 18 Dec. 2005. Socialist leader Evo Morales was declared the winner and was sworn in as premier on 22 Jan. 2006.

Roh Moo-hyun (South Korea)

Introduction

Roh Moo-hyun won the presidential elections of Dec. 2002 and succeeded incumbent Kim Dae-jung in Feb. 2003. A member of Kim's Millennium Democratic Party (MDP) until Sept. 2003, Roh has continued Kim's policy of promoting closer ties with North Korea. He has commanded most support among young voters who favour a close relationship with the North, although his stance has strained relations with the US leadership, which has taken a hardline against Pyongyang over its nuclear development activities. Lee Myung-bak replaced Roh as South Korea's president in Feb. 2008 after Roh's 5-year term came to an end.

Early Life

Roh was born on 6 Aug. 1946 in Gimhae in the Gyeongsangbuk region. In 1966 he graduated from Busan Commercial High School and undertook various low-paid jobs while teaching himself law. He passed his state bar exams in 1975. In 1977 he was appointed a district court judge in the city of Daejeon, and the following year he opened his own law office. In 1981, after representing a student prosecuted for owning outlawed literature, he committed himself to human rights cases and became a prominent pro-democracy campaigner. In 1987 Roh was imprisoned for three weeks for assisting striking workers.

The following year he entered parliament as part of a grouping led by future president, Kim Young-sam. In the same year he won recognition as a member of a parliamentary committee which investigated the 1980 massacres of protesters during the rule of Chun Doo-hwan. Having lost his parliamentary seat in 1992, Roh re-entered parliament in 1998 after winning a seat in Seoul.

In 2000 he joined the supreme council of the MDP. Between Aug. 2000–March 2001 he was minister for fisheries and maritime affairs. With President Kim Dae-jung constitutionally barred from standing for re-election in 2002, Roh was selected as the MDP's candidate. The election campaign was fought in the shadow of rising tensions between the USA and North Korea over the North's nuclear programmes. Roh and the MDP continued to espouse Kim's 'sunshine policy' of engagement with Pyongyang. Lee Hoi-chang of the Grand National Party (GNP), Roh's chief opponent, favoured the freezing of talks until the North ended all nuclear activities and was thus regarded as Washington's favoured candidate.

Roh's close ties with the MDP and Kim Dae-jung cost him support as several corruption scandals came to light. Roh's campaign was further weakened shortly before polls opened when his running-mate, Chung Moon-jung, pulled out. Chung had a popular following based on the successful staging of the 2002 football World Cup finals but he withdrew from the elections following Roh's perceived anti-US comment that 'if the US and North Korea start a fight, we should dissuade them.' Nonetheless, Roh won large-scale support from young voters and claimed victory at the elections of Dec. 2002 with 49% of the vote against Lee's 46.6%.

Career Peak

Roh was sworn into office in Feb. 2003. He appointed former mayor of Seoul, Goh Kun, as prime minister. Goh Kun had previously held the office in

1997–98. Roh's first major challenge was to establish a policy on North Korea acceptable both domestically and to the USA. Although a vocal supporter of Kim's 'sunshine policy'. Roh had to demonstrate a more conciliatory approach towards Washington. In May 2002 he sought to heal rifts with the USA by supporting the continued presence of US forces in the region, having previously called for the removal of 30,000 troops stationed in South Korea. The more aggressive policy of US President George W. Bush towards North Korea—threatening the North by placing it in the 'Axis of Evil' declaration—made the continuation of peaceful engagement with Pyongyang more difficult, especially so since the North's first test of a nuclear device in Oct. 2006 and the subsequent imposition of punitive sanctions by the United Nations Security Council.

In the domestic sphere, Roh sought on his election to repair the cultural and commercial split between South Korea's south-eastern and south-western regions. Large-scale business and the media were both expected to be subject to major reforms and the president promised to prevent the further rise in property prices, which grew 16% in 2002 despite economic stagnation. Decentralization and autonomy were central to Roh's domestic agenda. To relieve population pressure in the Seoul area, Roh outlined a national development programme, including the construction of a new administrative capital in the central region of Chungcheong, scheduled to begin during 2007.

Negotiations for free trade areas with Singapore and Japan made a promising start. Economic relations with North Korea, although strained by tensions with the USA, continued to expand. Inter-Korean ministerial talks in Oct. 2003 focused on the construction of the Kaesong Industrial Complex in North Korea, one of three large-scale economic projects agreed by the Kim Dae-jung government. In Feb. 2006 South Korea and the USA began negotiations on a major bilateral free trade agreement.

Roh's determination to distance himself from the corruption scandals of the previous presidency led him to leave the MDP in Sept. 2003. His decision was anticipated after the departure of parliamentary allies who formed a new party—the Uri Party—with a reformist agenda. In March 2004 Roh was suspended from office following a vote in the National Assembly to impeach him for allegedly trying to influence unfairly the outcome of parliamentary elections due in April 2004. Prime Minister Goh Kun took over as acting president. The pro-Roh Uri Party gained a slim overall majority in the April elections, winning 152 seats in the 299-member Assembly, and the following month Roh was reinstated after the Constitutional Court overturned his impeachment. Goh Kun meanwhile resigned as prime minister and was replaced in June 2004 by Lee Hai-chan. In his new year message at the start of 2005 Roh promised to make revitalizing the flagging South Korean economy his policy priority. Nevertheless, his government's popularity continued to wane. In April 2006 Han Myeong-sook became the country's first female prime minister in place of Lee Hai-chan, but the following month Roh's Uri party suffered a heavy defeat in local elections. Han Myeong-sook resigned as premier in March 2007 and Han Duck-soo was appointed her successor.

In Feb. 2007 Roh announced that he would leave his Uri Party, acknowledging that he had become a political liability in advance of the Dec. 2007 presidential election. Unable to run for re-election under the constitution, Roh's 5-year term ended in Feb. 2008, putting an end to liberal rule which critics say hindered economic growth and showered unconditional aid on North Korea with little to show for it. Roh died on 23 May 2009 after falling from a mountain near his home. His death was later confirmed as suicide.

Rõivas, Taavi (Estonia)

Introduction

Taavi Rõivas became prime minister in March 2014 following the resignation of Andrus Ansip. A former minister of social affairs, he leads a coalition comprising the Estonian Reform Party (Reform) and the centre-left Social Democratic Party (SDE). Retaining the premiership after Reform emerged as the biggest single party at elections in March 2015, he headed up another coalition administration with the SDE and also the Pro Patria and Res Publica Union (IRL).

Early Life

Born on 26 Sept. 1979 in Tallinn, Rõivas studied international economics and marketing at the University of Tartu. He began his political career while still a student, joining Reform in 1998 and becoming adviser to the minister of justice, Märt Rask, in 1999. After graduating, he worked for the AS IT Grupp and became adviser/officer manager for the minister of population affairs, Paul-Eerik Rummo, in 2003.

From 2004–05 he was mayor of the Haabersti City District in Tallinn. He advised Prime Minister Andrus Ansip from 2005–07 and was elected to parliament in 2007. He served on its social affairs committee from 2007–09 and was chairman of the finance committee from 2009–11. From 2011–12 he chaired the European Union affairs committee while continuing to serve on the finance committee. In Dec. 2012 he was appointed minister of social affairs, where he had a key role in delivering government austerity measures.

After Ansip resigned as premier on 4 March 2014 and Reform's founder Siim Kallas withdrew as a potential successor, President Toomas Hendrik Ilves appointed Rõivas as prime minister.

Career Peak

Rõivas took office on 26 March 2014 when parliament narrowly voted (by 52 votes out of 101) to back a new coalition of Reform and the SDE. He was elected leader of Reform 11 days later. Rõivas pledged to focus on security issues in the aftermath of Russia's intervention in Ukraine, and in Oct. his government announced that Estonia would bolster its troop presence and monitoring of its border after Russia's alleged abduction of an Estonian security officer. Domestically, he promised to increase public spending from 2015, with plans to lower labour taxes, increase child benefit, bring forward pension increases and raise salaries for teachers and the police. At the general election in March 2015 Reform won the most seats of any party (30 of 101), securing Rõivas a further term as premier. His main challenges included addressing faltering economic growth and managing differences within his coalition government.

On 9 Nov. 2016 Taavi resigned after a vote of no confidence was supported by 63 votes to 28. He was replaced as prime minister by Jüri Ratas.

Rojas Pinilla, Gustavo (Colombia)

Introduction

Gustavo Rojas Pinilla was president of Colombia between 1953–57, originally at the head of a military government and later as leader of the left-wing Alianza Nacional Popular (ANAPO). His presidency was blighted by widespread guerrilla violence which largely thwarted attempts at social and economic reform.

Early Life

Rojas Pinilla was born on 12 March 1900 in Tunja, Colombia. He attended the Colombian Military Academy until 1920, and studied civil engineering in the United States until 1927. In the 1930s he worked on several large-scale highways projects and was also employed as a military engineer. He was appointed commander of the First Brigade at the end of 1946. Rojas Pinilla played a significant role in suppressing the rioting that ensued after the assassination of the left-wing leader Jorge Eliécer Gaitán in April 1948 and was promoted to lieutenant general. He was appointed to the Inter-American Defense Board in 1951 and was named commander-in-chief of the armed forces at the end of 1952.

Career Peak

Rojas Pinilla took power in military coup on 13 June 1953, bringing to an end the 4-year regime of President Laureano Gómez. Rojas Pinilla espoused the ideology of the revolutionary, Simón Bolívar, and promised social justice and freedom. However, his rule by decree and the utilization of media censorship and the secret police against political opponents soon aroused popular discontent. Accusations of siphoning government monies for personal use and an aggressive policy against the Protestant church increased his unpopularity.

Rojas Pinilla granted an amnesty on rural guerrillas in June 1953 but continued violence led to a military offensive 2 years later, known as the War of Villarica. He enjoyed partial success in forcing a guerrilla retreat to the Andean foothills but by 1957 he was confronted by student strikes and unified protests by conservative and liberal forces which forced him into exile in the United States. A military junta came to power in his place.

Later Life

When Rojas Pinilla returned to Colombia in Oct. 1958 he was impeached and in April 1959 he was stripped of his civil liberties. In the same year, the conservative and liberal elites created the National Front to end the civil war which had claimed 250–300,000 victims since 1948. The failure of the National Front and the left-wing Liberal Party helped revive Rojas Pinilla's appeal and he achieved a small share of the vote at the presidential elections of 1962. He founded the Alianza Nacional Popular (ANAPO), which claimed widespread support among the poor working class, and in 1966 had his civil rights legally re-established. He came a close second at the 1970 presidential polls and claimed that winner Misael Pastrana Borrero had stolen victory. His supporters were responsible for violent protests that led to a declaration of martial law. Rojas Pinilla's health deteriorated and he retired from political life in 1973. He died from a heart attack on 17 Jan. 1975, a year after his daughter had unsuccessfully stood as the ANAPO candidate for the presidency.

Roosevelt, Franklin D. (United States of America)

Introduction

Franklin Delano Roosevelt was the 32nd President of the United States, serving from March 1933 until April 1945 when he died in office just weeks before Germany's surrender in World War II. He is remembered best for leading the United States into World War II, as well as for social and economic reforms which pulled a demoralized nation out of the Great Depression.

Early Life

Born on 30 Jan. 1882 on his aristocratic family's estate in Hyde Park in the state of New York, Roosevelt was educated at home by tutors until his early teens. He then attended Groton School in Massachusetts between 1896 and 1900, a school whose emphasis on teaching a sense of public responsibility did much to form his political opinions. However the future president's academic record was unimpressive, as it was at Harvard University, which he attended from 1900 until 1904. In 1905 Franklin married Eleanor Roosevelt, a distant cousin, and the couple had five children in the next 11 years.

Roosevelt drifted between law school and Wall Street without conspicuous success until he entered politics in 1910 when he was elected to the New York State senate for the Democratic Party, securing re-election in 1912. His fledgling political career suffered a setback in 1914 when he was defeated in his attempt to become a senator. Nevertheless, in 1921, Roosevelt, who had acquired a reputation as a charismatic political performer, secured the Democratic Party's vice-presidential nomination. However he and James M. Fox were beaten by Warren Harding and Calvin Coolidge.

Having contracted polio in 1921 Roosevelt found himself paralysed in both legs and largely wheelchair-bound, although he would later be able to walk for several steps at a time with the aid of leg braces. He retreated from the limelight for several years before returning to the political stage in 1928 when he became governor of New York. His sureness of touch while handling the early days of the depression saw him re-elected in 1930 by the largest margin in the state's history. During this period Roosevelt also set up an influential think-tank to devise new political ideas to combat the Great Depression.

Career Peak

Roosevelt won the Democratic nomination to run for the presidency in 1932 with John Nance Garner as his running mate. Founding his campaign on the promise of 'a New Deal for the American people' Roosevelt defeated President Herbert Hoover by 472 electoral college votes to 59. Three months after his election victory Roosevelt survived an assassination attempt when he was fired upon by an unemployed bricklayer in an incident that saw four other men injured and one killed.

When Roosevelt was inaugurated in March 1933, the United States was in crisis with unemployment running at around 14 m. The new president embarked on an energetic period in which he initiated a whirlwind of legislation through an emergency 99-day session of Congress. This period came to be known as Roosevelt's '100 days'.

The USA deserted the gold standard and the Emergency Banking Relief Act gave Roosevelt greater powers to control the economy. Meanwhile the National Industry Recovery Act gave Roosevelt's government far-reaching powers to control industry. Farmers were given considerable subsidies while the Public Works Administration created more jobs in the construction industry.

Unemployment fell rapidly as a consequence of Roosevelt's policies, although the effectiveness of many of his programmes was far from total. However, the new president's charisma succeeded in re-motivating America—a mood he enhanced further by repealing the prohibition laws with the words 'I think this would be a good time for a beer'.

In 1935, Roosevelt initiated 3 major pieces of legislation including the Works Progress Administration bill, which would eventually see $11bn. of works relief distributed, and the Wagner Act, which gave workers the right to bargain on equal terms with their employers. The Social Security Act of the same year saw the United States gain the bare bones of a welfare state by offering relief to the elderly, unemployed and the disabled.

Some of Roosevelt's measures, such as the National Industrial Recovery Act and the Agricultural Adjustment Act, were later ruled unconstitutional by the Supreme Court. Nevertheless, in 1936, he was re-elected president by a landslide margin over Republican opponent Alfred M. Landon, carrying every state bar 2 and winning the popular vote by 28 m. votes to 17 m. Roosevelt's domestic programme suffered a setback soon afterwards when a bill he introduced giving him the power to appoint a new justice for every justice already over the age of 70 was rejected. The incident soured his relations with Congress and the Republicans made significant gains in the congressional elections of 1938, which put an end to any further development of his New Deal programme.

Disturbing developments abroad, particularly in Germany, Italy and Japan now absorbed Roosevelt's time. Congress passed a Neutrality Act in 1937 and Roosevelt maintained guarded neutrality to appease the many anti-interventionalists in Congress and safeguard his domestic legislative programme. However he came to realise that war was inevitable. He also surmised that increased spending on defence would help pull the United States out of recession.

After Germany invaded Poland in 1939, Roosevelt asked Congress to lift an arms embargo, they refused and the president acted unilaterally in supplying 50 American destroyers to the British and introducing a peacetime draft. In 1940 Roosevelt secured re-election for an unprecedented third term when he defeated Wendell Willkie, although his margin of victory, 27 m. votes to 22 m., showed a marked decline. He continued to aid the Allies without entering the war by seizing Axis ships in US ports after a German submarine sunk an American destroyer and stationing forces in Iceland and Greenland.

The United States finally entered World War II after being attacked by Japan in Pearl Harbour, Hawaii on 7 Dec. 1941 which Roosevelt dubbed 'a day that will live in infamy'. During the war Roosevelt's military policies caused some controversy – particularly his insistence on unconditional surrender as well as his refusal to fight on a second front against Germany until 1944.

In his diplomatic efforts Roosevelt was also criticized for an over-reliance on personal charm, rather than more accepted diplomatic protocol. Nevertheless, he succeeded in maintaining alliances with Great Britain and the Soviet Union in trying circumstances and successfully guided the Allies' broad strategy while delegating responsibility for specific military plans to his generals.

By 1944, Roosevelt was drained by the efforts of war and was suffering from heart disease. He was re-elected for a fourth term in office in 1944, with Harry Truman as his vice-president, when he defeated Republican Thomas E. Dewey. Three months later, with Allied victory looking inevitable, he met British Prime Minister Winston Churchill and Soviet leader Joseph Stalin at Yalta to begin planning the post-war European map. On 12 April 1945, Roosevelt died of a cerebral haemorrhage and Truman was sworn in as president in his place. The German surrender came just weeks later on 7 May.

Rousseff, Dilma (Brazil)

Introduction

Dilma Rousseff became Brazil's first female president on 1 Jan. 2011. A left-winger from the Workers' Party, she succeeded Luiz Inácio Lula da Silva, whom she had served as chief of staff for 5 years and with whose policies she had been closely associated. She was narrowly re-elected in Oct. 2014. Rousseff was impeached and removed from office in Aug. 2016.

Early Life

Rousseff was born on 14 Dec. 1947 in Belo Horizonte, the state capital of Minas Gerais, to a Bulgarian émigré and his teacher wife. Her father had fled Europe in the 1920s, fearing persecution because of his involvement with the Bulgarian Communist Party. In Brazil he became a successful businessman.

Rousseff was schooled first at a francophone nunnery and then at Central State High School. In 1967 she joined the Worker's Politics faction of the Brazilian Socialist Party. Committed to armed struggle as the best means of achieving socialism's aims, Rousseff became involved in the militant Colina ('National Liberation Command') She was also editor of a Marxist newspaper, *The Piquet*, and married fellow militant, Cláudio Galeno Linhares, in 1968. Fearing arrest, Rousseff abandoned her studies at the Minas Gerais Federal University School of Economics and moved to Rio de Janeiro in 1969. Her first marriage failed when she began an affair with another militant, Carlos Araújo, whom she later married.

Rousseff became a leading member of the VAR Palmares (Palmares Armed Revolutionary Vanguard), a military-political organization. In 1970 she was arrested in São Paulo and subsequently claimed that she suffered torture for 22 days. Following her release from jail at the end of 1972 she moved to Porto Alegre, the state capital of Rio Grande do Sul. She graduated with a degree in economics from its Federal University.

In the late 1970s she co-founded the Democratic Labour Party (PDT) of Rio Grande do Sul and was involved in the Direct Elections Now movement, credited with helping bring an end to Brazil's military regime. Having made the transition to mainstream politics, Rousseff was appointed municipal secretary of treasury in Porto Alegre in 1986. She later led the national economics and statistics foundation as well as serving as secretary of energy and communications for Rio Grande do Sul. In the latter role she oversaw a major increase in power production and distribution that ensured the state avoided the power cuts that routinely blighted much of the rest of Brazil.

In 2001 Rousseff joined the Workers' Party led by Luiz Inácio Lula da Silva. In 2002 she was named minister of mines and energy by the newly elected president. The following year she became director of the Brazilian state-controlled oil conglomerate Petrobras. On 21 June 2005 she was appointed Lula's chief of staff following the resignation of José Dirceu in the wake of the Mensalão scandal that rocked the Lula administration. In April 2010 she resigned her position at Petrobras. In June 2010 she announced she was standing for the presidency. Promising to continue the populist policies of Lula, she claimed 56% of the vote in a run-off against her centre-right opponent, José Serra.

Career Peak

Never before elected to public office, Rousseff campaigned on a broad commitment to continue the left-leaning policies of her predecessor. She was also expected to forge close ties with other leftist South American leaders. As a former head of Petrobras, Rousseff has supported state involvement in key areas of the economy including banking, the oil industry and energy.

Growth figures released in March 2011 indicated that Brazil had overtaken Italy to become the world's seventh largest economy, but Rousseff's government had to introduce unpopular measures to forestall economic overheating and reduce inflation. She was also weakened politically in 2011 by the resignations of her chief of staff and the ministers of transport, agricultural and sports, together with her dismissal of the defence minister, over corruption allegations that would continue to cast a shadow over her administration. Despite antipathy towards privatization, she announced plans in Aug. 2012 to encourage private involvement in the building and running of new and essential national infrastructure, while resisting the pay demands of

public sector workers. Against a background of stagnating economic growth, a wave of street demonstrations erupted in cities across the country in June 2013, protesting against high prices, poor public services and the cost of hosting the 2014 World Cup football finals.

In May 2012 Rousseff established a truth commission to investigate the abuses committed during the military dictatorship between 1964 and 1985. In Sept. 2013 she reacted angrily to reports suggesting that the US National Security Agency had been monitoring her personal communications and those of other senior government and public officials. She cancelled a planned state visit to Washington in protest.

Rousseff was re-elected as president following her victory in a run-off against Aécio Neves of the Brazilian Social Democracy Party in the elections of Oct. 2014. However, the first year of her second term was blighted by a major corruption scandal involving politicians and former executives of Petrobras while Rousseff was chair of the company. Public indignation over the scandal and the ailing economy led to massive protests across the country, and from late 2015 opposition calls for her impeachment. The lower house of Congress moved to impeach Rousseff in April 2016, with the Senate due to decide its position in May. Rousseff could only have been impeached with the support of both houses.

In May 2016 the Senate successfully voted to suspend Rousseff's presidential powers for 6 months while it reached a verdict on whether to formally impeach her. Vice president Michel Temer took over the presidency on an interim basis. She was formally impeached by the Senate in Aug. 2016, and Temer fully took over for the rest of her term.

Later Life

In Sept. 2017 Brazil's chief federal prosecutor charged Rousseff, as well her predecessor as president Luiz Inacio Lula da Silva ('Lula'), with forming a criminal organization to divert funds from Petrobras (the country's state oil company).

Rudd, Kevin (Australia)

Introduction

Having defeated Kim Beazley to become leader of the Australian Labor Party (ALP) in Dec. 2006, Kevin Rudd maintained his political momentum into the Nov. 2007 general election in which he ousted Prime Minister John Howard's centre-right government from power. He sought to modernize the ALP—out of power for more than a decade—but faced opposition from trade unions (over proposed changes to industrial relations laws) and from within the party. Although his fiscal policy plans were deflected by the effects of the global financial crisis, he maintained a high voter approval rating as a capable leader and economic manager through to 2010 when he stood down in June following a challenge from his deputy prime minister, Julia Gillard. He became prime minister for a second time in June 2013. Following the ALP's defeat in the general election of Sept. 2013, Rudd resigned from parliament.

Early Life

Kevin Rudd was born on 21 Sept. 1957 in Queensland, the son of a dairy farmer who died after a car accident when Kevin was just 11. At 15 Rudd joined the Labor Party. In 1981 he graduated in Chinese language and history from Australian National University. His fluency in Mandarin led to a role as a diplomat, working at embassies in Beijing and Stockholm before moving to the Department of Foreign Affairs and Trade's Policy Planning Bureau.

In 1988 Rudd moved into state politics, becoming chief of staff to the then Queensland opposition leader Wayne Goss. The ALP came to power the following year after 32 years in opposition. Rudd was appointed director general of the Office of the Cabinet in Goss' government, during which time he earned a reputation for overseeing public service cutbacks. In 1996 Rudd stood for election to the federal House of Representatives. However, the ALP suffered heavy losses at both state and federal levels and he was unsuccessful. He left politics immediately after, becoming a business consultant and adjunct professor of Asian languages at the University of Queensland.

In 1998 Rudd secured election to the federal parliamentary seat of Griffith, Brisbane, although the ALP failed to dislodge the ruling Liberal-National coalition from power. He was promoted to opposition spokesman on foreign affairs, trade and national security and led criticism of Howard's handling of the 2003 Iraq war, calling for an inquiry into intelligence failures. His political rise was nevertheless controversial; he was accused of self-promotion in 2003 when he greeted Hu Jintao, the Chinese president, in Mandarin and was attacked ferociously by a former ALP leader, Mark Latham, in his autobiography.

In Nov. 2006 Rudd declared that he would challenge Kim Beazley for the leadership of the ALP, pledging a new style of politics. He won by 49 votes to 39 and was officially announced as leader on 4 Dec. 2006.

Career Peak

Following the ALP's election victory, Rudd was sworn in on 3 Dec. 2007. He promised the staged withdrawal of Australian combat troops from Iraq (achieved by mid-2008) and a 'three pillars' approach to foreign policy through closer engagement with the UN, Asia and the US-led coalition. He also pledged substantial extra investment in health and education, despite some concerns over a faltering economy. On taking office he immediately reversed the Howard government's refusal to ratify the Kyoto protocol on climate change and its decision to sell uranium to India (which is not a signatory of the Nuclear Non-Proliferation Treaty).

In Feb. 2008 Rudd made a formal apology in parliament for past injustices by the state against the indigenous population, and in July he reversed the long-standing policy of detaining all asylum seekers upon arrival until their cases are heard. Meanwhile, on his return from an overseas tour of the USA, Europe and China, he announced the appointment in April of human rights lawyer Quentin Bryce as Australia's first female Governor-General.

His government's first budget, presented in May 2008, sought to address rising inflation while earmarking anticipated budget surplus funds for infrastructure, education and health service investment. However, in response to the effects of the worsening global financial crisis, Rudd announced in Oct. a \$A10.4 bn. stimulus package to boost the economy, support families and households, and create jobs. Further government funding to help the ailing Australian motor industry followed in Nov. The next budget, delivered in May 2009, revealed a deficit of nearly 5% of GDP (one of the largest ever), underlining the economy's fragility. Rudd nevertheless used the budget to invest further in infrastructure and clean energy projects while cutting forms of middle class tax breaks. Also in May 2009, the government published a defence White Paper envisaging weapons modernization and procurement costing about US\$70 bn.

In Nov. 2009 Rudd offered a formal apology to surviving British children who had been forcibly shipped to Australian orphanages and other institutions and suffered abuse and neglect between 1930 and 1970.

His popularity waned severely in the first half of 2010 following a series of badly received policy decisions including the scrapping of an emissions trading scheme, a key part of the government's climate change strategy which was scheduled to take effect in 2011. He also announced the introduction of a supplementary tax on the mining industry which proved a divisive issue amongst voters. When rumours emerged that the deputy prime minister Julia Gillard was mounting a leadership challenge against him, Rudd initially sought to defend his position. However, when it became clear that he had insufficient support within the party he bowed out of the contest. Gillard stood unopposed at a leadership ballot on 24 June and was sworn in on the same day.

In Sept. 2010 Rudd was appointed foreign minister in Gillard's second cabinet. However, in Feb. 2012 he resigned as foreign minister and challenged Gillard's leadership. The prime minister won the backing of her Labor party colleagues in the leadership ballot, by 71 votes to 31.

By June 2013 Labor's popularity had significantly slumped in the polls and a landslide defeat in the upcoming elections was predicted. On 26 June Rudd challenged Gillard's leadership and emerged victorious in the ballot by 57 votes to 45. He was sworn in as prime minister for the second time on 27 June, 3 years after being ousted by Gillard.

During his second term as prime minister, Rudd was seen to have performed a reversal on a number of key policies and issues of his first tenure as premier. Rudd became the first Australian premier to publicly support same-sex marriage, having previously opposed it in 2007. He also backtracked on his stance against offshore asylum seeker processing, and signed an agreement with Nauru which allowed asylum seekers arriving by

boat to be detained on the island. The deal also permitted legitimate political refugees to be resettled on Nauru.

On 4 Aug. 2013, Rudd announced that general elections would take place in Sept., after parliament was dissolved by the Governor General at his request. He was subsequently defeated by Tony Abbott of the Liberal Party at the elections, and stood down from parliament shortly after.

Rüütel, Arnold (Estonia)

Introduction

Arnold Rüütel was the president of Estonia between 2001–06.

Early Life

Arnold Rüütel was born in Saaremaa, Estonia on 10 May 1928. He graduated from agricultural college in 1949 and from 1949–57 worked in agronomics and as a teacher of agriculture. In 1957 he became director and livestock expert of an experimental farm owned by the Estonian livestock breeding and veterinary institute. In 1963 he was appointed director of the Tartu Model Sovkhoz state farm. He was also studying during this period and graduated from the Estonian academy of agriculture in 1964. In 1969 he was appointed rector of the academy, a position he held for 8 years. He continued his studies into the 1990s, being awarded his doctorate in agriculture in 1991.

Rüütel's political career began in 1977 when he took the first of a series of posts in the communist institutions of the Estonian Soviet Socialist Republic (ESSR). In 1983 he was selected as chairman of the presidium of the supreme council of the ESSR (effectively head of state). He held the position until 1990 and was key in the preparation of the Estonian declaration of sovereignty adopted on 16 Nov. 1988.

Estonia declared independence on 20 Aug. 1991. Rüütel was a member of the constitutional assembly from 1991–92 and was instrumental in drafting the new Republic's constitution. In 1992 Rüütel stood for the presidency but lost to Lennart Meri. In 1995 he was elected to parliament as vice-speaker. From 1994–2000 he was party chairman of the People's Union of Estonia.

Career Peak

When Rüütel came to power in 2001 Estonia was aiming to join NATO and the EU. To this end and to benefit the third of Estonians who are native Russian speakers Rüütel ratified a law in Dec. 2001 opening public office to non-Estonian speakers. In Nov. 2002 NATO invited Estonia to join the alliance, with the EU issuing a similar invitation a month later. In Sept. 2003 EU membership won overwhelming backing in a referendum and Estonia was one of ten new states to join the EU in May 2004. Full NATO membership was granted in March 2004.

Although the presidency is largely ceremonial, the president has been much involved with a ruling coalition subject to inter-party hostility. In 2002, Prime Minister Mart Laar resigned after parliamentary confusion threatened entry into NATO and the EU. In April 2003 Rüütel invited Juhan Parts, leader of the conservative Res Publica party, to be prime minister in a coalition with the Reform Party and the People's Union. In Feb. 2005 he sacked foreign minister Kristina Ojuland after secret files, mostly concerned with Estonia's position at EU summits, had disappeared from her ministry. Parts submitted the government's resignation after a vote of no confidence in the justice minister over a tough anti-corruption programme. Rüütel invited Reform Party leader Andrus Ansip to take over the premiership.

In March 2005 Rüütel declined an invitation to attend Moscow's celebrations to mark the anniversary of the end of the Second World War as a protest against the suffering and loss experienced by Estonia during the Soviet occupation.

Rüütel found himself at the centre of controversy in Jan. 2006 when it was reported that his underage grandchildren had hosted a party on presidential grounds which included alcohol. Amid speculation that he would not stand for office again, in June 2006 he announced he would contest a further presidential term. After two failed attempts to select a president, parliament met for a third time on 23 Sept. Rüütel received 162 votes to 174 for Toomas Hendrik Ilves and Ilves duly succeeded Rüütel on 9 Oct. 2006.

Saakashvili, Mikheil (Georgia)

Introduction

Mikheil Saakashvili was first elected president on 4 Jan. 2004. A former protégé of President Eduard Shevardnadze, he led opposition to the rigged parliamentary elections of Nov. 2003 and forced the president to resign. Saakashvili's peaceful management of the 'rose revolution' earned him respect at home and abroad and even the support of the ousted Shevardnadze. However, he faced increasing domestic opposition. He secured re-election as president in Jan. 2008, but with a much reduced majority, and was further undermined as he entered the final year of his second presidential term when an opposition coalition won control of parliament in elections in Oct. 2012. Relations with Russia, which were shattered in Aug. 2008 when Georgian military action against the separatist enclave of South Ossetia provoked a retaliatory invasion by Russian forces, have remained fraught. Sakashvili renounced his Georgian citizenship in 2015 in order to become a Ukrainian national.

Early Life

Mikheil (Mikhail in Russian) Saakashvili was born on 21 Dec. 1967 in Tbilisi. He received law degrees from Kyiv University, Ukraine in 1992 and Columbia University, New York in 1994 and completed a doctorate in juridical science at George Washington University, Washington, D.C. He pursued further studies in Florence and Strasbourg.

While working for a New York law firm, Saakashvili was approached by Zurab Zhvania, speaker of the Georgian parliament. The Georgian leader, Eduard Shevardnadze, was seeking potential parliamentary candidates, unconnected to the Soviet system. Saakashvili returned home and was elected to parliament in Dec. 1995. As a member of Shevardnadze's Citizens' Union and a trained jurist, his political career developed rapidly. He served as chairman of the parliamentary committee on electoral reform and contributed to the drafting of the 1995 constitution. He led the Citizens' Union in parliament from 1998–99 and was appointed vice-president of the Council of Europe's parliamentary assembly in Jan. 2000.

Appointed justice minister in Oct. 2000, Saakashvili attempted an over-haul of the judicial system, condemned by international observers as highly corrupt. He also tried to reform the prison system and proposed a bill on illegal property confiscation, which was blocked by Shevardnadze. His programme was cut short when he openly accused the ministers for economics and state security and Tbilisi's head of police of corruption and profiteering. Shevardnadze, then president, refused to act on these charges, forcing Saakashvili to resign in Sept. 2001.

Having left the government, he continued his anti-corruption programme by forming a party, the United National Movement (UNM), to represent Georgia's reformist elements. Coalition partners included the small ideological Republican Party and the Union of National Forces. Support was widened by alliances with Zurab Zhvania's United Democrats and the Burjanadze-Democrats, led by Nino Burjanadze, Zhvania's replacement as speaker. Saakashvili was elected chairman of the Tbilisi Assembly in June 2002.

Saakashvili campaigned for the Nov. 2003 parliamentary elections on an anti-Shevardnadze platform, drawing large crowds with his energetic rhetoric, especially in Adjara, in the southwest, and Kvemo Kartli, a province in the southeast with a large Azeri minority. Despite OSCE sponsorship, the elections on 2 Nov. were chaotic and heavily rigged by the ruling Citizens' Union. The delayed announcement of provisional results provoked accusations of electoral fraud. Burjanadze and Zhvania agreed to form a coalition with Saakashvili—the United Opposition Front—and massive demonstrations were organized night after night in Tbilisi. After the results were announced, putting Saakashvili's UNM in third place, a boycott of parliament was declared by the coalition. Shevardnadze refused to compromise and opened parliament on 22 Nov. Saakashvili responded by summoning his national supporters to Tbilisi and demanded the president's resignation. During Shevardnadze's opening address Saakashvili burst into the assembly, brandishing a rose, the symbol of the peaceful demonstrations. His supporters occupied the chancellery, causing the president to declare a state of emergency.

Bereft of support from abroad and in his own government, Shevardnadze finally resigned on 23 Nov. His avoidance of a military solution was praised internationally and by the opposition leaders. In the wake of his resignation, Saakashvili, Burjanadze and Zhvania agreed to present a united front in immediate presidential elections, the former gaining the support from the other two in exchange for senior government positions. On 4 Jan. 2004 Saakashvili won the presidential election with just over 96% of the votes. His electoral promises were broad and ambitious: the abolition of taxes on small businesses, doubling of pensions and public sector salaries and swift punishment for the worst abuses of the previous regime. His campaign was strengthened by the co-operation of Shevardnadze, who voted for his successor.

Career Peak

Saakashvili declared his priorities in office as maintaining the territorial integrity of Georgia and his anti-corruption programme. He consolidated his political position in March 2004 when the National Movement–Democrats bloc won the parliamentary elections with a substantial majority of seats. Tension increased with Adjara's president, Aslan Abashidze, who declared a state of emergency in his jurisdiction and rejected the new central government's authority. Saakashvili reasserted direct control over Adjara in May 2004 after popular demonstrations in Batumi forced Abashidze to step down. Elsewhere, Saakashvili proposed giving greater autonomy—but not full independence—to the separatist regions of South Ossetia and Abkhazia.

Despite friction with Russia over its links with these regions, its military bases in Georgia and the conflict in Chechnya (where Russia has accused Georgia of aiding Chechen fighters), Saakashvili initially sought to improve relations between the two countries. Nevertheless, bilateral tensions resurfaced in 2006 as energy supplies from Russia were disrupted in Jan., Russia suspended imports of Georgian wine and mineral water on health grounds in March–May, and Georgia briefly detained and then expelled four Russian army officers on spying charges in Sept.–Oct. (in retaliation for which Russia imposed a transport blockade and adopted punitive measures against ethnic Georgians living in Russia). In Dec. 2006 the Georgian government accepted a doubling of the price of Russian natural gas supplies, but accused its powerful neighbour of political blackmail.

Tension continued through 2007, as Georgia accused Russia of violations of its airspace in Aug. and of orchestrating mass opposition demonstrations in Tbilisi against Saakashvili's government which in Nov. led to a police crackdown and temporary state of emergency. The protests were sparked particularly by allegations of corruption and murder against Saakashvili made by a former defence minister in Sept. Despite his apparent unpopularity and opposition claims of fraud and vote rigging, Saakashvili was re-elected as president in polling in Jan. 2008, and in May the ruling UNM won a landslide victory in parliamentary elections.

Meanwhile, suspicious of Georgia's aspirations to join NATO, Russia stated in April 2008 that it would strengthen its links with South Ossetia and Abkhazia. This prompted the Georgian government to accuse Russia of planning military intervention and annexation of the regions. In Aug. continuing tensions escalated into outright military conflict after Georgian troops had mounted an attack of separatist forces in South Ossetia. Russian forces occupied the enclaves and advanced deep into Georgian territory, destroying strategic targets, before agreeing a French-brokered ceasefire following diplomatic intervention by the European Union. Later in the month, Russia unilaterally recognized the independence of Abkhazia and South Ossetia, a move rejected by Saakashvili and the Western nations. In Sept. Russia announced that it would keep troops in Abkhazia and South Ossetia but completed the withdrawal from the rest of Georgia in Oct.

Also in Oct. 2008, Saakashvili's former ally, Nino Burjanadze, announced the creation of a new opposition group, claiming that the government was not capable of protecting the country and should face fresh elections. Opposition agitation against the president and his powers continued in 2009 and in May the authorities quelled a military mutiny. In May 2011 riot police violently broke up a rally in Tbilisi by opposition protesters calling on Saakashvili to resign, and in May 2012 a massive anti-government demonstration took place in the capital. In elections in Oct. 2012, the opposition Georgian Dream coalition led by Bidzina Ivanishvili won a parliamentary majority to oust the ruling pro-Saakashvili UNM administration.

Georgia's relations with Russia thawed in the first few months of 2010 as direct air traffic resumed in Jan. and a border crossing closed since 2006 was reopened in March. However, in Aug. Russia announced that it was deploying air defence systems in Abkhazia and South Ossetia in defiance of Georgian sovereignty.

In the lead-up to the Oct. 2013 presidential elections public support for Saakashvili plummeted, reflecting the general disillusionment with his rule in recent years, as the president was increasingly criticized for extensive authoritarianism. Saakashvili was forbidden from contesting the elections owing to term limits and Giorgi Margvelashvili, an ally of Prime Minister Bidzina Ivanishvili, was elected president, while UNM's candidate obtained only a fifth of the vote. Saakashvili stepped down as president in Nov. and faces questioning over the 2008 war and for his alleged role in the 2005 death of Zurab Zhvania, the prime minister at the time.

Later Life

Saakashvili left Georgia shortly after the 2013 election, moving to the United States to take up a teaching position at Tufts University in Massachusetts. During his period abroad he voiced support for the 2014 Ukrainian revolution, and in Feb. 2015 was appointed by Ukrainian president Petro Poroshenko to lead an advisory body working to implement reforms in the country.

In June 2015 Saakashvili became a Ukrainian citizen (renouncing his Georgian citizenship) and was appointed governor of Odesa province. He resigned in Nov. 2016, citing corruption in the Ukrainian government, and in July 2017 he was stripped of Ukrainian citizenship.

Saca, Elías Antonio (El Salvador)

Introduction

Antonio Saca, a sports broadcaster and media mogul with limited political experience, was elected president in March 2004. His conservative administration strengthened ties with the USA through a free-trade agreement. Saca left office on 1 June 2009 at the end of his term in office.

Early Life

Elías Antonio Saca González was born on 9 March 1965 in Usulután, the son of Palestinian immigrants. Educated at the San Agustin school in Usulután and the Cervantes Institute in the capital, San Salvador, Saca began working in the media, initially for Radio Vanguardia. From 1980, against the backdrop of civil war, Saca specialized in sports commentary for radio while studying journalism at the University of El Salvador. In 1983 he became head of sports coverage at El Salvador's Channel 4 television station, a position he held for 10 years. By the mid-1990s he was a well-known national figure, as well as the owner of several radio stations. In 1997 he became president of the Salvadorean Association of Radio Broadcasters (ASDER) and was later elected to the presidency of the Association of Private Businessmen.

Saca contested the presidential election of March 2004 as candidate for the conservative Nationalist Republican Alliance (ARENA). Despite his lack of political experience, he easily defeated the National Liberation Front candidate, Schafik Hándal. Opponents were critical of Saca's influence over the media.

Career Peak

Sworn in as president on 1 June 2004, Saca built on the conservative, pro-US policies of his predecessor, Francisco Flores. Saca pledged to fight poverty and unemployment and attract inward investment. In March 2006 the government implemented the Central America-Dominican Republic-United States Free Trade Agreement (CAFTA-DR) along with the USA, the Dominican Republic, Guatemala, Honduras and Nicaragua. In the same month Saca's ARENA party emerged as the largest party in parliamentary elections, although in those of Jan. 2009 ARENA was defeated by the left-wing Farabundo Martí National Liberation Front (FMLN). Saca left office on 1 June 2009 at the conclusion of his 5 year term. He was succeeded by Mauricio Funes of the FMLN, who became the first leftist president of El Salvador for 20 years.

Later Life

In 2014 Saca contested the presidential election held in Feb. but failed to progress beyond the first round, gaining just 11.4% of the vote.

In March 2016 the supreme court ordered that Saca should stand trial on charges of illegal enrichment during his time in office. He was arrested in Oct. 2016, along with several other suspects accused of diverting US$246 m. of public funds.

Sadat, Muhammad Anwar (Egypt)

Introduction

Muhammad Anwar Sadat became President of Egypt in 1970, at a time when the country was preoccupied with neighbouring Israel. Having emerged a hero from the fourth Arab-Israeli War of 1973, his most controversial political move came in 1977 when he travelled to Jerusalem with overtures of peace. This initiative won Sadat the 1978 Nobel Peace Prize (together with Israeli Prime Minister Menachem Begin). But the consequent Camp David accords (in Sept. 1978) and bilateral peace treaty (signed in March 1979), which were brokered by United States President Jimmy Carter, earned Sadat the enmity of the rest of the Arab world. He was assassinated, while still in office, by Muslim extremists in 1981.

Early Life

Sadat was born into a family of 13 children on 25 Dec. 1918. He grew up in the town of Mit Abu al-Kom, north of Cairo. Like his contemporary, Gamal Abdel Nasser, he went to the military academy in Cairo and graduated in 1938. He was then commissioned in the Egyptian army. An ardent nationalist, Sadat was imprisoned in 1942 during the Second World War for plotting with the Germans against the British-backed Egyptian establishment. Later he joined Nasser's Free Officers revolutionary organization. Having taken part in the successful coup against the monarchy in 1952, he supported Nasser's election to the presidency in 1956. Under the Nasser regime, Sadat held various high offices, serving as vice president between 1964–7 and 1969–70. On Nasser's death, although largely unknown and untested, he became acting president and was then elected to the post in a plebiscite on 15 Oct. 1970.

Career Peak

Sadat's enduring presidential legacy was his redirection of Egyptian foreign policy and his impact on international diplomacy generally. He made bold moves. In 1972 he expelled thousands of Russian technicians and advisers from the country in the wake of deterioration in the Egyptian-Soviet relationship fostered by his predecessor. He launched, with the Syrians, a joint surprise attack on Israel heralding the 'Yom Kippur' war of Oct. 1973. This campaign restored a degree of Arab military pride and prestige. It undermined the image of Israeli invincibility and gave Sadat greater credibility and respect both at home and abroad. But his most dramatic initiative was his historic personal address to the Israeli Parliament in the cause of peace in Nov. 1977 during the first official visit by an Arab head of state to Israel since its foundation. In his address to the Knesset, Sadat explicitly accepted (with conditions) the existence of Israel as a Middle East state. This led to a series of diplomatic contacts culminating in the Camp David accords of Sept. 1978—which provided for the staged Israeli withdrawal from Sinai and moves towards the establishment of Palestinian autonomy and a self-governing authority in the occupied territories of Gaza and the West Bank.

However, his peace initiative isolated Egypt from the rest of the Arab world. The Arab League relocated its headquarters from Cairo to Tunis and many Arab countries broke off diplomatic and trading relations. At home, hostility to negotiation with Israel, ongoing economic hardship, the growth of Islamic fundamentalism, and government repression further undermined Sadat's standing.

On 6 Oct. 1981 Sadat was assassinated at a military parade in Cairo. In contrast to the public grief displayed at the death of his predecessor, Sadat's funeral elicited little reaction from his people.

Saikhanbileg, Chimed (Mongolia)

Introduction

Chimed Saikhanbileg became prime minister on 21 Nov. 2014 after his predecessor, Norov Altankhuyag, was ousted after a parliamentary vote of no confidence on 5 Nov. Saikhanbileg had previously been minister of the Cabinet Office and was a former minister for education.

Early Life

Saikhanbileg was born in 1969 in Dornod. He was schooled in the capital, Ulaanbaatar, before graduating in history from Russia's Moscow State University for the Humanities in 1991. He later received a law degree from the National University of Mongolia in 1995 and a master's degree in the same subject from George Washington University in Washington, D.C., USA in 2002.

An aspiring career politician, in 1991 Saikhanbileg became an officer in the Mongolian Youth Federation (MYF) and acted as its secretary in Ulaanbaatar until 1997. In 1996 he was elected to parliament for the DP, serving until 2000 and re-entering parliament in 2008. From 1997–2002 he served as national president of the MYF, and was minister for education from 1998–2000. Between 2000 and 2008 he worked in private legal practice and as a government press officer. In 2008 he was re-elected to parliament, becoming leader of the DP caucus. From 2012–14 he was minister of the Cabinet Office.

Career Peak

Saikhanbileg was elected to the premiership in Nov. 2014 by parliament, claiming 44 of 46 available votes. However, the poll was boycotted by 32 members of the opposition Mongolian People's Party (MPP), who claimed that Saikhanbileg was equally culpable in the Altankhuyag government's failure to tackle the slowing economy, attract foreign investment and monetize rich mineral resources. The MPP nonetheless joined the new coalition government comprising Saikhanbileg's DP and the Justice Coalition.

Needing to rejuvenate the mining sector, which has been affected by disputes and delays to projects, Saikhanbileg promptly began negotiating with the International Monetary Fund to secure financial support. He also signed a trade deal with Japan, including a US$308 m. loan to finance a new international airport in Ulaanbaatar.

Ahead of elections scheduled for June 2016, Saikhanbileg dismissed the six MPP ministers in his coalition cabinet in Aug. 2015—a move endorsed by the DP-controlled parliament but opposed by President Elbegdorj—and replaced them in Sept. with new appointments.

Saikhanbileg left office in July 2016 having failed to secure re-election as a member of parliament in June.

Sakskoburggotski, Simeon (Bulgaria)

Introduction

Simeon II was Bulgaria's prime minister from 2001–05 and its former monarch, having been deposed and exiled by the communists in 1946. He formed the National Movement for Simeon the Second (Nacionalno Dviženie Simeon Tvori/NDST) 2 months before general elections in 2001 when he claimed half of the parliamentary seats. He formed a coalition with the Movement for Rights and Freedoms (Dviženie za Pravata i Svobodie/DPS), representing the Turkish minority. Opponents initially feared he would attempt to reinstitute the monarchy but no such move was ever made. Simeon sought to implement market reforms to kickstart the economy and supported membership of the EU and NATO.

Early Life

Simeon Borisov Sakskoburggotski was born on 16 June 1937 in Sofia, the son of King Boris III. His father died in Aug. 1943, widely believed to have been murdered, and the 6-year old Simeon succeeded him, though day-to-day rule was in the hands of a council of regency. Soviet forces invaded the country in Sept. 1944 and 2 years later oversaw a referendum that abolished the monarchy. Shortly afterwards Simeon fled the country, though without officially abdicating.

Settling first in Egypt, where he studied at Victoria College in Alexandria until 1951, he then moved to Spain and attended the French School there. On his 18th birthday he issued a proclamation challenging the legality of the Soviet takeover and reasserting his constitutional rights. After finishing his schooling, he attended at the Valley Forge Military Academy, Pennsylvania before studying business administration and law.

In 1962 he married Margarita Gómez-Acebo y Cejuela, with whom he had five children. Fluent in six languages, Simeon then embarked on a career in commerce. He made his return to Bulgaria in 1996, 7 years after the collapse of the communist regime, and received widespread public support. His former estates were returned to him in 1998. He was considering standing in the presidential elections of Oct. 2001 but was ineligible on residency grounds. Having declared that his aim was 'to work for Bulgaria, not for one party'. he established the NDST to fight the parliamentary elections.

In April 2001 a Sofia court ruled than his party did not meet several criteria necessary to be registered for the June elections. This ruling was subsequently overturned and the party, which included politicians from across the political spectrum, won 42.7% of the vote and 120 seats. Having reached agreement for a coalition with the DPS, Simeon was asked to form a government by President Stoyanov in July 2001.

Career Peak

Simeon's government set out an optimistic agenda that included the eradication of corruption and the 'substantial improvement' of living standards within 800 days of taking office. Among his proposed economic reforms were wholesale privatization, tax cuts and business deregulation. It was also hoped that an overhaul of the country's economy would hasten acceptance into the EU and NATO. In Oct. 2002 Bulgaria was refused entry into the EU during the planned expansion of 2004 but was given a target date for membership of 2007. The country was invited to join NATO in 2004 and, as planned, became a member of the EU on 1 Jan. 2007.

Among the considerable problems his administration faced were unemployment (officially running at 18%, though other observers have suggested a base rate closer to 28%), poverty affecting 65% of the population, rampant inflation and the long-term impact of emigration (10% of the population having left the country since the collapse of communism in 1989).

At the elections Simeon's party claimed 20% of the vote, behind the Socialists who, under Sergei Stanishev, went on to form the government after a month of political wrangling. Having initially refused to join the ruling coalition, Simeon joined Stanishev's administration in 2005.

Salad Hassan, Abdiqasim (Somalia)

Introduction

Following the removal from office of the Somali dictator Siyad Barre in 1991 by a coalition of clan leaders, Somalia sank into anarchy. There was no central government, the infrastructure of the country was destroyed and two breakaway states in the north—Somaliland (the former British Somaliland) and Puntland—effectively seceded. In Aug. 2000, a Somali peace conference, boycotted by some factions, elected Abdiqassim Salad Hassan as president of a transitional government, the authority of which is limited to less than one quarter of the country. He served as interim president from 2000 through to 2004.

Early Life

Abdiqassim Salad Hassan was born in 1942 into the powerful Hawiye clan in Mogadishu, the capital of Somalia. He was too young to have been involved in the Somali struggle for independence from Italian rule. However, he became politically active during the presidency of Adan Abdullah Osman, the first president of Somalia, who held office until 1967. When Siyad Barre seized power in 1969, Salad Hassan was already an established political figure. Initially sympathetic to the aims of Barre, Salad Hassan was appointed interior minister in 1971 and later became deputy prime minister.

When Barre was overthrown, Salad Hassan fled to Egypt. He and his family established themselves in Cairo while Somalia disintegrated into warring factions controlled by local warlords. Leaving his family in Egypt to campaign for a peace conference to set up a national government, Salad Hassan spent all but 17 months of the period 1991–2000 in Somalia. From 1997 he was based in Mogadishu. The conference, held in Djibouti in 2000, established a framework for a transitional government to run for 3 years. On 27 Aug. 2000, Abdiqasim Salad Hassan was elected by the conference to head the government.

Career Peak

Most Western governments withheld recognition from Salad Hassan. The four strong southern warlords, including one of the most powerful of Somalia's faction leaders, Xusen (Hussein) Mohammed Aydeed, also refused recognition.

Salad Hassan eventually returned to Mogadishu, a city in ruins, without electricity or running water, in Oct. 2000. He began to form a national army and a police force, and appointed a 25-member government, in part from the Somali diaspora in Europe and North America. However, his progress was hampered by the continuing secession of Puntland and Somaliland and the transitional authority's inability to control more than a fraction of the national territory. Since March 2001, Salad Hassan has faced opposition from the five-person Somali Reconciliation and Restoration Council, whose members rotate monthly the nominal role of chairman. This Council is the meeting place for the principal warlords outside the control of the transitional government.

Rumours of possible links between al-Qaeda and an Islamic organization in Somalia called al Itihaad surfaced in 2001. Salad Hassan has denied these links.

In Oct. 2002 peace talks between the Somali government and rebel groups were held in Eldoret, Kenya. Representatives of other East African nations, the African Union and the Arab League also attended. After 2 weeks of negotiations a ceasefire was signed.

In the presidential elections held in Oct. 2004 Salad Hassan was eliminated in the second round of voting.

Salam, Tammam (Lebanon)

Introduction

Tammam Salam was nominated as prime minister-designate in April 2013 by President Michel Suleiman following Najib Mikati's resignation 2 weeks earlier. Considered a centrist, Salam received support for his premiership from parties across the political spectrum, including Hizbollah. However, the process of forming a cabinet with broad political appeal took until Feb. 2014. He was acting president from May 2014 to Oct. 2016.

Early Life

Salam was born in Beirut on 13 May 1945 to a prominent Sunni Muslim family. His father, Saeb, was prime minister on four separate occasions between 1952 and 1973 and his grandfather, Salim Ali Salam, was an official in the Ottoman Empire and later in the French colonial mandate. Salam was educated at Brummana High School and Haigazian University in Beirut. He later graduated with a degree in economics and management after studying in the United Kingdom.

In 1974 Salam founded Ruwwad Al Islah in Beirut, a movement advocating political reform, but disbanded it at the start of the civil war as he distanced himself from militant activities. In 1978 he joined the board of Makassed, an Islamic philanthropic organization with strong ties to the Salam family, and in 1982 took over its presidency from his father. He stayed in the role until 2000.

He first stood for election to parliament in 1992 but withdrew his candidacy in protest at Syrian dominance of Lebanese politics. He stood again in 1996 with the support of Prime Minister Rafiq al-Hariri and was elected to represent a Beirut constituency. By 2000 the alliance between al-Hariri and Salam had collapsed and Salam failed to win re-election. On 11 July 2008 Salam was appointed minister of culture in Fouad Siniora's government and returned to parliament at the 2009 election.

Following Mikati's resignation as premier on 23 March 2013, the 14 March Alliance nominated Salam to replace him. He won 124 of a possible 128 votes from parliament and on 6 April 2013 President Suleiman tasked him with forming a government. However, it was not until 15 Feb. 2014 that he was sworn into office.

Career Peak

Having spent almost a year negotiating the composition of his government, Salam's main task was to organize legislative elections that were initially scheduled for Nov. 2014. However, parliament's term was subsequently extended to 2017, given its deadlock over electing a new state president, in whose place Salam had assumed acting responsibilities on 25 May 2014. Salam was subsequently confronted by political rivalries, serious sectarian tensions, economic problems and a refugee crisis caused by the continuing conflict in neighbouring Syria. Inconclusive efforts to elect a new president continued for a record period extended into 2016 when parliament finally elected Michel Aoun. Shortly after, Aoun named Saad al-Hariri prime minister, a position he had already held from Sept. 2009 to June 2011. Aoun was succeeded as prime minister by al-Hariri in Dec. 2016.

Saleh, Ali Abdullah (Yemen)

Introduction

Ali Abdullah Saleh came to power at the age of 36 in July 1978 as president and commander-in-chief of the armed forces of the Yemen Arab Republic (YAR). On the YAR's unification with the People's Democratic Republic (South Yemen) in May 1990, he assumed the presidency of the new Republic of Yemen. In 1994 his regime crushed an attempted secession by southern forces in a brief civil war. Secure in power, Saleh was re-elected president in 1999 and 2006. After months of protests, Saleh signed an agreement that transferred his powers to the Vice President, Abdo Rabu Mansour al-Hadi, who was sworn in as president in Feb. 2012. Saleh was Yemen's longest-serving president and the fourth Arab leader to fall since the beginning of the Arab Spring revolutions.

Early Life

Saleh was born in 1942 in Bait Al Ahmar in Sana'a governorate and joined the armed forces at the age of 16. In Sept. 1962 Imam Muhammad al-Badr (king and spiritual leader) was deposed in a military revolution and an eight-year civil war ensued, in which Saleh fought for the new Yemen Arab Republic government, aided by Egypt, against the royalist forces supported by Saudi Arabia. The YAR regime retained power and secured international recognition, but remained unstable throughout the 1970s, partly owing to tensions with the Marxist regime in southern Yemen. Saleh meanwhile gained military promotions, and reportedly played a role in a coup that brought Ibrahim al-Hamadi to power in 1974. When President Ahmad al-Ghashmi (in power from Oct. 1977) was assassinated in June 1978, Saleh was military commander of Ta'iz governorate. After the assassination (blamed on the regime in Aden), the Constituent Assembly formed a provisional Presidential Council, including Saleh. On 17 July the Assembly elected him president of the YAR.

Career Peak

Saleh's early months in power were turbulent. In Sept.–Oct. 1978 he survived an assassination attempt and a coup plot, both thought to have external backing. In Feb.–March 1979 further sporadic conflict with South Yemen escalated into full-scale war. Arab League mediation brought the fighting to an end and subsequent protracted negotiations resulted in reunification as the Republic of Yemen on 22 May 1990. Saleh had previously been re-elected as

YAR president by the Constituent Assembly in May 1983 and again in July 1988 by a new Consultative Council. On unification and political liberalization in May 1990, a five-member Presidential Council assumed power and Saleh was chosen as president of the new republic for a transitional period. A rebellion by disaffected southern forces was suppressed in 1994. In Oct. of that year Saleh was elected president of the republic by parliament. His position was further reinforced in Sept. 1999 when he was directly elected by the people as president for the first time (albeit on a low turnout). An extension of his presidential term from five to 7 years was approved in a referendum in Feb. 2001 and he continued to head the General People's Congress, which won decisively the most recent parliamentary elections in April 2003. In Sept. 2006 Saleh was re-elected for a further presidential term with 77% of the popular vote. Despite opposition protests, the parliament voted in Jan. 2011 in favour of constitutional amendments that could have seen the president in power for life. Subsequently, however, there were increasing demonstrations against his 32-year rule, fuelled by anti-government sentiment across the Arab world, and in Feb. he announced that he would not stand for re-election again.

Saleh imposed a crackdown against Islamic terrorism following al-Qaeda attacks on a US warship in Aden in Oct. 2000 and on a French supertanker off the Yemeni coast in Oct. 2002. However, the country has since remained vulnerable to anti-Western terrorist violence, with bomb attacks on diplomatic, business, transport and tourist targets. In 2010 government forces stepped up their campaign to counter the growing and destabilizing presence of the al-Qaeda terrorist network in Yemen. In particular, al-Qaeda claimed responsibility for the failed attack on a US passenger airliner in Dec. 2009 and for planting explosive packages that were intercepted aboard commercial cargo planes flying from Yemen to the USA in Oct. 2010.

Since 2004 there has been frequent fighting between government forces and rebellious tribesmen demanding regional autonomy. These clashes have also provoked military confrontation with Saudi Arabia along the two countries' common border.

On 3 June 2011 Saleh was injured in an attack on his presidential compound. After 9 months of mass protests calling for his resignation, Saleh signed the Gulf Cooperation Council (GCC) plan on 23 Nov. 2011, which agreed to transfer the office and powers of the presidency to his deputy, Vice President Abdo Rabu Mansour al-Hadi. Al-Hadi was sworn in as the new president on 25 Feb. 2012, bringing an end to Saleh's 33 years in power.

Later Life

The Houthis, an Islamic rebel movement that took part in the 2011 protests, disagreed with the terms of the GCC plan and used this as a pretext to expand the territories they already controlled in North and West Yemen. Allegedly supported by Iran, by 2014 they had reached Sana'a. In Jan. 2015 they seized the presidential palace, forcing President al-Hadi to flee to Saudi Arabia. In response, a Saudi-led military coalition aimed at re-establishing him as president. In the conflict, Ali Abdullah Saleh—who had kept some political influence—surprisingly approved the Houthi rebels, but on 2 Dec. 2017 he changed his mind and urged the population to come forward and fight them. As he was trying to escape Sana'a 2 days later he was shot dead in a clash with the Houthis.

Salinas de Gortari, Carlos (Mexico)

Introduction

Economist and government official for the dominant PRI party, Carlos Salinas de Gortari was president of Mexico from 1988 to 1994. He aimed to lead Mexico onto a more capitalist track, privatizing many state owned corporations and opening up the economy to foreign investment. His major achievements included taking Mexico into the North American Free Trade Agreement (NAFTA) with the USA and Canada in 1992. However, the successes of Salinas' reforms were in some cases short lived and his reputation has been clouded by the Zapatista uprising of 1994 and its aftermath, as well as claims of corruption and scandal.

Early Life

Salinas was born in Mexico City on 3 April 1948, the son of a Mexican senator. He studied economics at the Universidad Autonoma del Estado de México (National Autonomous University), where his professors included his political predecessor Miguel de la Madrid, the Mexican president between 1982 and 1988. Subsequently, Salinas studied at Harvard University. His political career began at the age of 18 when he joined the Partido Revolucionario Institucional (Institutional Revolutionary Party; PRI) and progressed from 1971 as he held increasingly important economic roles in the government. His political career was advanced further by the election of de la Madrid in whose cabinet he was minister of planning and budget. In 1987, de la Madrid nominated Salinas to be his successor as the PRI candidate in the 1988 presidential elections. His rival was the Fronte Democratico Nacional (National Democratic Front; FDN) candidate Cuauhtemo Cárdenas, the son of the former president Lazaro Cárdenas. The long domination of the PRI appeared to be threatened as Cárdenas gained a majority of the votes and prepared to be the next president. However, a mid-election computer crash resulted in a recount that installed Salinas de Gortari as de la Madrid's successor with 50.4% of the votes.

Career Peak

Despite accusations of electoral fraud, de Gortari was considered more successful than his immediate predecessors. He instigated a series of economic reforms that resulted in the reduction of Mexico's foreign debt and a lowering of inflation. He reduced public spending, devalued the peso, reformed the tax system, removed import controls and tariff reductions and renegotiated Mexico's US$100 m. debt. Salinas continued de la Madrid's privatization policies, selling off many state-owned corporations so that by early 1992 approximately 85% had become privately owned. Privatized companies included the Banco Nacional de Mexico and the Banco de Comercio as well as the telephone company Telefonos de Mexico. By 1993 Salinas' policies had resulted in a 10% lowering of inflation and a US$25 bn. reduction of foreign debt. These reforms were widely praised internationally and laid the groundwork for the implementation of NAFTA with the USA and Canada, which served to reduce tariffs between these 3 countries. This agreement was signed on 7 Oct. 1992 and came into effect on 1 Jan. 1994. One industrial benefit of the treaty has been a large increase in car production.

The increasing trend towards capitalism under Salinas' government resulted in a slackening of anticlericalism which led to a re-establishment of diplomatic relations with the Vatican, an authorization of religious schools and the right to vote for nuns and priests.

As a result of increased privatization, Salinas reduced the power of the trade unions, a measure that resulted in a mud-slinging campaign by the hitherto powerful leader of the oil union, Joaquín Hernández Galicia. He distributed defamatory leaflets about Salinas, an act that led to his subsequent arrest and imprisonment. Living standards fell sharply for many poorer Mexicans as wealth inequality widened. The abolition of the *ejidos* system of agricultural co-operatives led to financial problems for the poorest farmers who could not afford to buy the privatized land. These reforms were a catalyst for the revolt in early 1994, commencing with an armed insurrection in the southern state of Chiapas where *campesinos*, or peasant farmers, took over the state capital San Cristóbal de las Casas, under the command of the guerrilla leader Subcomandante Marcos. Fighting under the name of the revolutionary hero Emiliano Zapata, the Ejército Zapatista de Liberación Nacional (Zapatista Army of National Liberation; EZLN) fought for land reform policies and social and economic equality. Despite a forceful army reaction to the uprising, in which more than 145 people died, EZLN continued to defy government control and to gain support. After failed attempts to suppress the insurrection, President Salinas opened negotiations with the Zapatistas. A direct consequence of the Zapatista insurrection was a virtual collapse of the Mexican currency in 1994, sending the economy into chaos.

In March 1994 the popular PRI candidate, Luis Donaldo Colosio, who was due to succeed Salinas, was assassinated in Tijuana. Consequently, it was Ernesto Zedillo who led the PRI into the next election and succeeded Salinas as president. Colosio had shortly before promoted controversial changes for the PRI, and there were rumours of government involvement in his assassination.

Salmond, Alexander (Scotland, United Kingdom)

Introduction

Leader of the Scottish National Party (SNP), Alex Salmond became Scotland's first minister on 16 May 2007 and headed a minority Scottish Government from 2007–11. Following a historic victory by the SNP in the 2011 Scottish Parliament election Salmond now heads a majority government. As one of the foremost proponents of Scottish independence, Salmond and the SNP supported the campaign for secession from the United Kingdom leading to the Sept. 2014 referendum on whether Scotland should become an independent country. He subsequently resigned as leader of the SNP and first minister after Scotland voted to stay in the union.

Early Life

Alexander Elliot Anderson Salmond was born on 31 Dec. 1954 in Linlithgow. He was educated at Linlithgow Academy and the University of St Andrews, where he gained an MA in economics and history. He became active in the SNP when he joined the Federation of Student Nationalists at St Andrews in 1973, later becoming its president. In 1978 Salmond joined the department of agriculture and fisheries for Scotland as an assistant economist. He was recruited to the Royal Bank of Scotland in 1980.

As a young activist, Salmond was a committed left-winger and a leading member of the 79 Group, a socialist republican organization within the SNP. He was expelled from the party in 1982 for his hard-line views but readmitted a year later. In 1987 he won the parliamentary seat of Banff and Buchan, which he has held ever since. In 1990 he was elected the leader of the SNP. Under Salmond's leadership the SNP emerged as the second largest party in Scotland, developing its image as socially democratic, pro-European and with a gradualist approach toward independence.

In 1999 Salmond was elected to the Scottish parliament but unexpectedly stood down as leader of the SNP in 2000 and left the Scottish parliament a year later to concentrate his efforts in Westminster. In 2004 Salmond had a change of heart and decided to run again for the SNP leadership, which he won with an overwhelming majority. On 3 May 2007 he was re-elected to the Scottish parliament when he won the constituency of Gordon.

Career Peak

From 2007–11 Salmond's minority government faced tough opposition to its more radical policies, including a referendum on Scottish independence. In the general election of May 2010 the SNP retained its six seats but failed to reach Salmond's ambitious target of 20, a result Salmond blamed on the exclusion of minor parties from the televised leader debates. However, in the May 2011 Scottish Parliament election the SNP won 69 seats, delivering the first majority government since the opening of the Scottish Parliament in 1999. There was now sufficient support in the Scottish Parliament for a referendum on Scottish independence. In Jan. 2012 Salmond announced his intention to hold the referendum in the autumn of 2014.

In March 2013 the Scottish government announced that the referendum would be held on 18 Sept. 2014. Arrangements for the referendum set out in the Scottish Independence Referendum Bill were subsequently ratified by the Scottish parliament and given royal assent. According to an ICM poll held in July 2014, 34% of Scots were in favour of independence.

A 670-page document outlining the case for Scottish independence was published by the Scottish government in Nov. 2013. Titled *Scotland's Future*, it addressed key issues regarding a potential independent Scotland, including the retention of the British monarch as head of state, new employment legislation, renationalization of the Royal Mail and the removal of Trident nuclear weapons. The paper was described by Salmond as 'the most comprehensive blueprint for an independent country ever published'.

In the referendum on Scottish independence from the United Kingdom held on 18 Sept. 2014 voters decided to remain in the union, with 44.7% of votes in favour of independence and 55.3% against. The next day Salmond announced his resignation as leader of the SNP and first minister of Scotland. He continued as leader of the SNP until the party conference held in Nov., and stood down as first minister of Scotland less than a week later. Nicola Sturgeon, who had been deputy leader of the SNP since 2004, took over both offices.

Samaras, Antonis (Greece)

Introduction

Antonis Samaras was sworn in as prime minister on 20 June 2012. His appointment ended a 7-week stalemate in which successive parties had failed to form a workable coalition. He was faced with rebuilding an economy damaged by the global financial crisis. He remained in office until Jan. 2015 when he was succeeded by Alexis Tsipras of the radical left Syriza party.

Early Life

Samaras was born in Athens on 23 May 1951 and educated at the elite Athens College. In his youth he was a close friend of his future political rival, the socialist prime minister, Georgios Papandreou.

Samaras graduated in economics from Amherst College, a private liberal arts college in the USA, and completed an MBA at Harvard Business School. He was elected to parliament in 1977 as the New Democracy representative for Messenia and was appointed finance minister in 1989. He was named minister of foreign affairs in the cabinet of Konstantinos Mitsotakis 3 years later.

Samaras led hard-line opposition to the former Yugoslav Republic of Macedonia using that name as a newly independent state on the grounds that it is also the name of a bordering Greek province. It was a stance that led to his expulsion from the Greek government. He responded by establishing his own political party, Political Spring, creating a schism on the Greek right that prompted the demise of Mitsotakis' government in 1993.

Political Spring remained a fringe party until its dissolution in 2004, when Samaras rejoined New Democracy. He was elected to the European Parliament that year, resigning in 2007 after winning a seat in the Greek parliament. In 2009 he defeated Dora Bakogiannis, the daughter of Konstantinos Mitsotakis, for the party leadership.

Although New Democracy emerged as the largest party in the inconclusive May 2012 elections, Samaras was unable to mediate a coalition. The stalemate forced a second election in June, with New Democracy claiming 129 of the 300 available seats (an increase of 21 on the May result). Samaras forged a coalition with the centre-left Pasok and the small Democratic Left party.

Career Peak

Aiming to secure Greece's future inside the eurozone, Samaras' first task was to implement further austerity measures demanded by the European Union, IMF and European Central Bank in return for continued bailout instalments. A programme meeting the terms of the loan aid met with widespread public hostility and the coalition suffered a number of defections before the measures gained parliamentary approval in late 2012. Samaras also encountered rising domestic extremism and strong anti-immigrant sentiment as the economy continued to contract and unemployment soared. Further austerity provisions were agreed with the EU and IMF in April 2013 and in July parliament approved extensive reductions in the public sector workforce. The previous month the government had announced the closure of the state broadcaster ERT—an unpopular move that prompted the Democratic Left to leave the coalition.

Early parliamentary elections were automatically triggered following parliament's failure to appoint a new president on 29 Dec. 2014. Samaras lost the elections held on 25 Jan. 2015 to Alexis Tsipras and his Syriza party. His term as premier ended a day later when Tsipras was sworn in as Greece's new prime minister.

Samba-Panza, Catherine (Central African Republic)

Introduction

Catherine Samba-Panza became the country's first female head of state when she was elected interim president by the National Transitional Council (CNT) on 20 Jan. 2014. Her election took place 10 days after the resignation of Michel Djotodia, the former leader of Séléka (founded as a predominantly Muslim rebel organization), who had come under international pressure for not reining in sectarian conflict between the Christian majority and Muslim minority populations. Samba-Panza, a Christian, is regarded as non-partisan and is scheduled to hold the post until elections, in which she will not be allowed to stand, can be held in a less volatile security environment.

Early Life

Samba-Panza was born on 26 June 1954 in Fort-Lamy, Chad, to a Cameroonian father and a mother from the Central African Republic (CAR). She studied law at the Panthéon-Assas University in Paris, France, before settling in the CAR in the 1990s. Working as a corporate lawyer and in insurance, she experienced at first hand the difficulties in doing business in, and attracting investment to, a country suffering long-term instability. She worked closely with various non-governmental organizations, most notably l'Association des Femmes Juristes de Centrafrique, with whom she campaigned for greater inclusion of women in government positions and for the rights of victims of violence, especially survivors of sexual violence.

Samba-Panza entered politics in 2003 when she co-chaired the National Dialogue Table, a forum aimed at addressing national reconciliation and socio-economic recovery. She was later chosen to lead the committee monitoring the forum's recommendations. In May 2013, shortly after Djotodia's coup, Samba-Panza was selected as mayor of Bangui by the CNT, an appointment welcomed by both Séléka and the 'anti-balaka' ('anti-machete'). Christian militias, as well as by France. Following Djotodia's resignation on 10 Jan. 2014, Samba-Panza was chosen to succeed him by the CNT on 20 Jan. after two rounds of voting. She was sworn in 3 days later.

Career Peak

Nicknamed 'Mother Courage' by her supporters, Samba-Panza's main task has been to try to open up dialogue with Christian and Muslim armed groups in order to restore security and ensure a functioning state. A programme of disarmament, demobilization and reintegration will be required, although she is expected to avoid the much-criticized previous strategy of incorporating former rebel fighters into newly formed police and military units.

As per the terms of her mandate as interim president, Samba-Panza was not permitted to stand in the presidential elections held in Dec. 2015 and Feb. 2016. The winner of the elections, Faustin-Archange Touadéra, was sworn in as president in March 2016.

Sambi, Ahmed Abdallah Mohamed (Comoros)

Introduction

Known as the 'Ayatollah' after studying in Iran, Ahmed Abdallah Sambi was elected president in May 2006, marking the country's first peaceful handover of power. A moderate Islamist, he defeated two other candidates from the island of Anjouan, in accordance with the federal power-rotation agreement between the three islands. Following further presidential elections in Nov.–Dec. 2010, in which he did not stand, Sambi left office on 26 May 2011 with Ikililou Dhoinine—one of two Vice Presidents—succeeding him.

Early Life

Ahmed Abdallah Mohamed Sambi was born on 5 June 1958 at Mutsamadu on the Comorian island of Anjouan (Nzwani), where he attended primary and secondary school. He later studied in Saudi Arabia, Sudan and Iran. In 1980 he launched the first Comorian periodical, *Retour à la Source*. His preaching took him to Madagascar in 1982 and Mauritius in 1984 before he returned to the Comoros in 1986. On Anjouan he founded a girls' school and organized evening lectures which were banned by the police and led to his arrest.

In 1990 Sambi entered politics, helping to form the Front National pour la Justice, which supported Mohamed Taki Abdoulkarim (who later became president). In 1993 he was active in raising money for Bosnian Muslims and the following year opposed the establishment of diplomatic relations with Israel. He was elected to the then Federal Assembly in Dec. 1996 and was appointed president of the Law Commission. Sambi opposed the central government's crackdown on Anjouan in Aug. 1997 and was forced to resign his seat in the Assembly. Despite urging Anjouan's separatists to negotiate, he fled to Madagascar in Jan. 1999 amid accusations of separatist sympathies. In May 2005 he announced his candidacy for the presidency and came first in the April 2006 primary, held only on Anjouan.

Career Peak

Supervised by South African peacekeepers, Sambi defeated two secular candidates, Deputy Speaker Mohamed Djaanfari and the veteran politician Ibrahim Halidi, in a national vote in May 2006, although his rivals alleged fraud. Sambi voiced support for the reinstitution of an Islamic state in the Comoros, sparking fears of Islamic radicalization and restrictions on women's freedoms. Doubts were also raised concerning the authority of an Anjouanais over the central government bureaucracy, which is dominated by Grande Comorians. In mid-2007 Anjouan's regional president Mohamed Bacar, who had refused to step down after his five-year term, held an illegal election in defiance of Sambi and the federal government and claimed a landslide victory. Negotiations failed to resolve the impasse and in March 2008 Comorian and African Union troops invaded Anjouan to oust Bacar who fled to the French island of Réunion.

In May 2009 voters in a referendum approved constitutional changes to streamline the complex decentralized governance system and to extend the president's term of office by 12 months, allowing Sambi to serve until 2011. He left office on 26 May following elections in late 2010.

Sampaio, Jorge (Portugal)

Introduction

Jorge Fernando Branco de Sampaio was first elected president in 1996 and won a second term in 2001. A student activist and protester against the Salazar dictatorship, Sampaio was secretary-general of the Partido Socialista Portugués (PSP) between 1989–91 and mayor of Lisbon from 1989–95. His second presidential term ended in Jan. 2006.

Early Life

Sampaio was born in Lisbon on 18 Sept. 1939. The son of a doctor and a teacher, he spent part of his early life in London and the USA. He studied law at the Universidade de Lisboa, graduating in 1961. Sampaio's political activism began during his university career. He was the law school's student union president from 1960–61 and the following year was secretary-general of the Federation of Students Associations. He was involved in the student uprising in 1962 and the continuing battles between students and Salazar's government that helped end the dictatorship. Concurrently, Sampaio practised as a lawyer defending political prisoners.

Sampaio was active in the Comisión Democrática Electoral (Democratic Electoral Commission; CDE), the left-wing opposition party and front organization of the outlawed Partido Comunista Portugués. In 1968 he was elected to the national assembly as a CDE representative. In 1974 he co-founded the Movimento de Esquerda Socialista, but left soon after owing to policy disagreements. In 1975 he joined the fourth post-revolution provisional government as deputy minister for external co-operation.

Sampaio joined the PSP in 1978 and was elected to parliament the following year as a PSP representative. He was re-elected in four consecutive elections. Between 1979–84 he sat on the European Human Rights Commission of the Council of Europe. Following several senior positions in the PSP, Sampaio was made secretary-general in 1989. In the same year he was elected mayor of Lisbon, a position he retained in the 1993 municipal elections.

Career Peak

Having given up the leadership of the PSP to Antonio Guterres in 1991, Sampaio decided to run in the 1996 presidential elections, replacing outgoing president Mário Soares as PSP candidate. Sampaio's main competitor for the largely ceremonial post was the Partido Social Democrata (PSD) candidate Aníbal Cavaco Silva. Sampaio was elected with 53.8% of votes to Cavaco Silva's 46.2%.

After a successful first term, Sampaio ran for re-election in 2001. With three quarters of votes counted, he claimed 55.5%. His PSD opponent, Joaquim Ferreira do Amaral, conceded with 34.85%.

In 2004 Sampaio met with strong resistance from left wing parties when he refused to hold early elections following the resignation of prime minister José Manuel Durão Barroso. Sampaio elected Pedro Santana Lopes to the post but after four difficult months dissolved parliament and called elections for Feb. 2005, which resulted in José Sócrates taking office as prime minister.

At the presidential elections of Jan. 2006 Sampaio was succeeded by Aníbal Cavaco Silva, who was prime minister from 1985–95.

Samper Pizano, Ernesto (Colombia)

Introduction

Ernesto Samper Pizano was president of Colombia between 1994–98, representing the Partido Liberal (PL). His presidency was dominated by the struggle to control the drug cartels and concurrently defending himself from investigations into the cartels' support of his presidential campaign. The continuing activity of left-wing guerrillas and right-wing paramilitaries further hindered Samper's attempts to implement social policies, leaving an unstable economy.

Early Life

Samper was born on 3 Aug. 1950 in Bogotá. He studied economics and law at the capital's Universidad Javeriana until 1973. Samper's political career began as a councillor in Bogotá. He was then elected to the Senate. During Alfonso López Michelsen's 1982 campaign, Samper served as campaign treasurer and co-ordinator. On 3 March 1989 he survived an assassination attempt in which the leader of the Unión Patriótica, José Antequera, was killed by right-wing paramilitaries. The following year he became the leader of the PL and unsuccessfully stood in the presidential elections. Under the leadership of his PL colleague, Virgilio Barco Vargas, Samper served as minister for economic development.

Career Peak

In 1994 he stood in his second presidential elections, this time against Partido Social Conservador candidate, Andres Pastrana Arango. In a close run race, Samper won with 50.4% of votes. On his election, Samper pledged to tackle social inequality and poverty through public sector spending, especially on health, education and sanitation and to attract foreign investment. Yet, these promises were soon overtaken by accusations of the PL's involvement with the drug cartels. Tapes were released incriminating Samper's presidential campaign treasurer, Santiago Medina. One year into his presidency, the attorney general, Alfonso Valdivieso, began an investigation into the charges that £4 m. donation by the Cali drug cartels had boosted Samper's presidential campaign. Those indicted included Samper's campaign manager, and then defence minister, Fernando Botero. Foreign investment and aid came to an end. Samper was forced to issue compulsory war bonds to finance combating guerrillas.

Throughout his presidency Samper struggled to control left-wing guerrilla activities, the two principal groups being FARC (Fuerzas Armadas Revolucionarias de Colombia; Colombia Revolutionary Forces) and ELN

(Ejército de Liberación Nacional; National Liberation Army). The country was further destabilized by right-wing paramilitaries.

Samper's other problem was curtailing the influence of the powerful narcotraffickers, who controlled a substantial illegal economy. In June 1991, under the administration of César Gaviria Trujillo, a promise not to enforce extradition to America led to the surrender of the drug baron, Pablo Escobar, leader of the dominant Medellin cartel. By 1995 many of the key players in the Cali cartel had been imprisoned. Critics claimed the imprisonments in La Picota jail were as farcical as the personalized, luxurious million dollar 'imprisonment' of Escobar when the Medellin cartels were tackled. In 1996 Samper passed a law allowing the state to confiscate around £1.4 bn. of Escobar's property. During Samper's term over 200 tonnes of cocaine were seized and 1,500 km^2 of coca and poppy crops were destroyed through aerial spraying. In 1997 Samper reversed Trujillo's promise and introduced non-retrospective extradition for captured narcotraffickers. Despite Samper's efforts to eliminate the Cali cartels, the Clinton administration 'decertified' Colombia as an anti-drugs ally. Samper claimed this treatment hindered his efforts. Embarrassingly, in 1996 when travelling to present an anti-drugs speech to the UN, 3.7 kg of heroin were found on Samper's plane. The USA refused Samper a visa.

In June 1997 the Chamber of Deputies acquitted Samper of knowingly receiving drug traffickers' funding. Financially, Samper's presidency left Colombia unstable. In 1996 exports were affected by a rise in the peso while a US$4 bn budget deficit was a result of insufficient tax collection and large public spending. In 1997 a state of economic emergency was declared. Banana and coffee markets suffered. By 1998 unemployment had reached 15.8% in the cities, twice the rate on Samper's arrival. Inflation was at 18%, interest rates over 40%. In the 1998 elections Samper was replaced by Pastrana.

Later Life

In Sept. 2014 Samper was appointed secretary general of the Union of South American Nations (UNASUR) and promised to tackle poverty on the continent as his main priority.

Sanader, Ivo (Croatia)

Introduction

Ivo Sanader was elected prime minister in Dec. 2003. A member of President Tudjman's right-wing administration throughout the 1990s, the former literary agent campaigned to steer the country to eventual EU membership. Following parliamentary elections in Nov. 2007 he retained the premiership and formed a new coalition government.

Early Life

Ivo Sanader was born on 8 June 1953 in Split, Yugoslavia. He studied comparative literature and Romansch languages at Innsbruck University in Austria, graduating with a PhD in 1982. Returning to Split, he began work as a literary agent for the *Logo* publishing house, becoming editor-in-chief in 1988. In 1991, following a 3-year spell as a freelance writer and publisher in Innsbruck, Sanader was appointed general manager of the Croatian National Theatre. In Aug. 1992, having been elected to represent the right-wing Croatian Democratic Union (HDZ) in the Republic of Croatia's new parliament, Sanader became minister of science and technology. Appointed deputy foreign minister in early 1993, he participated in the bilateral talks which led to the establishment of the Croat–Muslim Federation of Bosnia and Herzegovina.

Following the signing of the Dayton Peace Accord in Nov. 1995, Sanader was named chief of staff to President Tudjman, then leader of the HDZ. Sanader was appointed to the defence and national security council, serving as deputy foreign minister from 1996 until the parliamentary elections of Jan. 2000, when the ruling HDZ was defeated by a coalition of the Social Democratic Party and the Croatian Social-Liberal Party. Subsequently elected leader of the HDZ, Sanader brought in sweeping reforms, attempting to root out corruption and draw a line under its authoritarian past. He was re-elected president of the HDZ at the party's congress in April 2002 and led the party to victory in the Nov. 2003 parliamentary elections (winning 66 seats of 152). President Mesić named Sanader prime minister designate on 9 Dec. 2003 and, following parliamentary consent, he was sworn in 2 weeks later.

Career Peak

Sanader pledged his commitment to democracy, the rule of law and free market economics. He also promised to cut taxes, fight corruption and prepare Croatia for membership of NATO and the EU. However, constrained by a coalition administration, his economic reforms were slower than expected. In the Nov. 2007 elections the HDZ maintained its position as the largest parliamentary party, but Sanader again had to negotiate a coalition—this time backed by the Croatian Social Liberal Party, the Croatian Peasant Party and the Independent Democratic Serbian Party—which took office in Jan. 2008. After a series of delays, EU accession talks began in Oct. 2005. Membership could be possible by 2011, but the European Commission president advised Sanader in Sept. 2008 of the need for more action on judicial and competition reforms and tackling organized crime and corruption. In April 2008 Croatia was formally invited by NATO to begin negotiations on accession to the alliance and in April 2009 it became a full member.

Contrary to rumours that he intended to step down early to run for president in 2010, Sanader announced on 1 July 2009 that he was quitting politics for good citing personal reasons. His suggested successor, vice prime minister Jadranka Kosor, took office on his departure on 6 July having gained parliamentary approval. Sanader also resigned as leader of the HDZ.

Later Life

Wanted in connection with a corruption investigation, Sanader fled Croatia in Dec. 2010 but was arrested the following day in Austria. In May 2011 an Austrian court ruled that he could be extradited back to Croatia to face charges.

In Nov. 2012 Ivo Sanader was sentenced to 10 years in prison on war profiteering and corruption charges in a case closely watched by the European Union. Sanader, the highest Croatian official to have been convicted for corruption, was found guilty of taking millions of dollars of bribes from a Hungarian energy company and an Austrian bank. The court has also ordered him to pay back 41.1 m. kuna (€5.4 m.).

Ivo Sanader was handed a further 9 years in prison by a Croatian court in March 2014, after he and the HDZ were found guilty of illegally siphoning funds from state-run firms during his terms in office between 2003 and 2009. Sanader was ordered to pay back €2.0 m. and the HDZ €3.8 m. Three former HDZ party officials were also sentenced to prison terms.

Sánchez de Lozada, Gonzalo (Bolivia)

Introduction

Gonzalo Sánchez de Lozada was president of Bolivia from Aug. 1993–Aug. 1997 and Aug. 2002–Oct. 2003. He represented the right wing Movimiento Nacionalista Revolucionara (Nationalist Revolutionary Movement, MNR). Following a close run first round, Sánchez was appointed by Congress in 2002 ahead of Evo Morales of the Movimiento al Socialismo (Movement to Socialism party). Sánchez advocated free market policies, pledging to counter unemployment by investing heavily in public works, though attempts to impose tax rises led to violent protests. Opposition to proposals to export natural gas to the USA spiralled out of control. Sánchez failed to demonstrate the benefits to the economy and was forced to relinquish office to his vice-president.

Early Life

Sánchez was born in La Paz on 1 June 1930. The son of a diplomat, he was educated in Ohio before taking an English literature and philosophy degree in Chicago. A businessman and millionaire, he was involved in the running of the Andean Geo Services mine (1957–62) and the Compañía Minera del Sur (Southern Mining Company, 1962–79).

His political career began in 1979 when he was elected deputy of Cochabamba, a position to which he was re-elected in 1982. Between 1986–88 he served as planning minister in Víctor Paz Estenssoro's government, during

which time he managed to combat hyperinflation which had peaked at 25,000%. The following year, despite winning the most votes in presidential elections, he lost out to Jaime Paz Zamora who had support from the opposition Acción Democrática Nacional (National Democratic Action, ADN) party.

Career Peak

In 1990 Sánchez replaced Paz Estenssoro as MNR leader. He stood successfully for election in 1993, beating ADN candidate Hugo Banzer Suárez. In his first term in office he implemented free market reforms and encouraged foreign investment, although the privatization of oil and gas companies failed to provide increased employment or benefit the majority indigenous population living in poverty. In 1997 he was replaced by Banzer, who implemented a controversial US-backed coca eradication programme. A centuries-old crop traditionally cultivated for religious ceremonies and later to sustain workers in difficult conditions in the Andes, coca production increased dramatically in the 1970s to feed the booming illegal drug industry. At its height, around a third of Bolivians were financially dependent on its production and the trade generated millions of dollars for the black economy. Eradication programmes destroyed 40,000 ha in the Chapare region leaving many farmers destitute.

When Sánchez stood for re-election in 2002, his main rival was Morales, an indigenous Andean representative of coca farmers who attacked the programme. Sánchez again campaigned on free market policies. The narrow margin in the first round results, with Sánchez taking 22.5% of votes to Morales' 21%, forced congress to decide between the two. Sánchez was chosen with 84 votes to 43.

On election he outlined his plans to reduce unemployment by investing US$1 bn. (or US$5 bn. over 5 years) in public works developments. He was also faced with the need to cut Bolivia's fiscal deficit in order to quality for IMF aid. Police strikes in Feb. 2003 over pay led to violent demonstrations and looting of government buildings in La Paz. Trade unions and the political opposition joined farmers in protesting against Sánchez's austerity measures. His attempt to raise income tax to 12.5% was abandoned after the deaths of 33 people, mainly policemen. Consequently, the cabinet resigned and Sánchez cut five ministries to reduce costs.

Sánchez came under US pressure to continue Banzer's coca eradication programme. The US threatened to scupper a deal for Bolivia to export natural gas to California if the eradication programme did not continue. But after continued protests from coca farmers, Sánchez announced plans to investigate the possibility of extending the legal coca farming capacity of 12,000 ha to allow the government more control over illegal trafficking, despite the threat of losing both US and IMF aid.

Having promised public consultation over the export of natural gas to the US, Sánchez provoked further demonstrations in Sept. and Oct. 2003 by pressing on with negotiations. Demands were made for the heavily subsidized sale of gas supplies in Bolivia before any gas was exported. Sánchez accused the opposition Socialist Movement of fomenting violence by trying to 'govern from the streets'. Demonstrators also demanded land reform, investment in education and healthcare, and the withdrawal of Bolivia from Mercosur, the South American free trade area.

Demonstrations continued for over 4 weeks across the country with violent confrontations between protesters and the armed forces protecting Sánchez in the presidential palace at La Paz. On 13 Oct. Sánchez agreed to end immediate negotiations to sell gas but opposition leader Evo Morales refused to accept the compromise, demanding Sánchez's resignation. Over 70 people died in fighting with the police and armed forces, forcing Sánchez to resign on 17 Oct., handing power to his vice-president, Carlos Mesa Gilbert. Morales called for the prosecution of the ex-president for the deaths of protestors after Sánchez left the country for Miami, Florida.

Sanhá, Malam Bacaï (Guinea-Bissau)

Introduction

Malam Bacaï Sanhá was sworn in as president in Sept. 2009 after elections praised by the international community for their orderly running and served until his death in Jan. 2012. He was a member of the African Party for the Independence of Guinea and Cape Verde (PAIGC).

Early Life

Sanhá was born on 5 May 1947 in Dar Salam in the Quinara region. He worked as an aide to Amílcar Cabral, the founder of the PAIGC, and served as governor of the Gabú and Biombo regions. From 1994–99 he was president of the National People's Assembly and from 14 May 1999 to 17 Feb. 2000 he was acting head of state, having been appointed by the military following the ousting of João Bernardo Vieira in the 1998–99 civil war.

Sanhá, a vociferous critic of Vieira, finished second to Kumba Ialá in the presidential elections that straddled 1999 and 2000 and again in 2005 (a result Sanhá challenged). In 2008 he unsuccessfully challenged Carlos Gomes Júnior for the PAIGC leadership.

In March 2009 President Vieira was assassinated and presidential elections were scheduled for June. Sanhá led the polls after the first round of voting and defeated Mohamed Ialá Embaló in a second round in July. He was sworn into office on 8 Sept.

Career Peak

In his inaugural speech Sanhá promised to investigate the March 2009 killings of Vieira and army chief of staff Batista Tagme Na Waie. He also prioritized the fight against crime, particularly drug trafficking and corruption. In Sept. 2009 China pledged US$1.5 m. to help feed the army, and in Dec. 2009 the European Union promised US$37 m. to help pay Guinea-Bissau's domestic debt and government workers' salaries. In April 2010 soldiers mutinied, briefly invading the prime minister's residence and forcing the replacement of the army chief of staff.

A diabetic, Sanhá suffered numerous bouts of ill health and died on 9 Jan. 2012 in Paris. Raimundo Pereira, the President of the National People's Assembly, had been serving as interim president during Sanhá's illness and was sworn in as acting president following the president's death.

Sankara, Thomas (Burkina Faso)

Introduction

The leader of a radical leftwing military regime, Thomas Sankara was president of Burkina Faso between 1983 until his assassination in 1987. Deposing President Jean-Baptiste Ouedraogo, Sankara came to power in 1983 as a leader of a breakaway faction of the original Conseil de Salut du Peuple (People's Salvation Council; CSP) military revolutionary group which itself had deposed President Sayé Zerbo in 1982. Throughout his tenure he implemented progressive social reforms and changed the country's colonial name from Upper Volta to Burkina Faso. But his tough control became unpopular and leftwing elements within the ruling council felt he had betrayed their original revolutionary Marxist-Leninist principles. He was overthrown by his second in command and longtime ally, current president Blaise Compaoré.

Early Life

Sankara was born on 21 Dec. 1949 in Yako, Upper Volta, and completed his secondary education in the capital Ouagadougou. The son of a World War II combatant, upon leaving school Sankara joined the military. He was soon posted to the military academy in Antsirabé, Madagascar where he attained the grade of officer. He formed his revolutionary ideas when he participated in the overthrow of the Malagasy neo-colonial regime. He then trained with a parachute regiment in Pau, France, before working in Rabat, Morocco, where he met Blaise Compaoré.

Returning to Upper Volta, he became involved in government, serving as information secretary under President Zerbo. This was a time of political instability in Upper Volta, as coups were followed by counter coups. Himself having attained power by force in 1980, 2 years later Zerbo was overthrown by army officials who set up a 120-member military junta, the CSP, with Ouedraogo at its head. Sankara worked under Ouedraogo, becoming prime minister in Jan. 1983. But he was involved in an increasingly factionalized leftwing element within the CSP who broke away to create the Conseil National de la Révolution (CNR), with Thomas Sankara at its head. In May 1983 Sankara was imprisoned by Ouedraogo on charges of treason.

Anti-government revolts ensued, led by Campaoré, and the president was ousted. The CNR seized power with the freed Sankara as president.

Career Peak

Sankara's leadership was based on Marxist-Leninist ideology. He pledged to eradicate rural poverty and all traces of neo-colonialism beginning with a series of progressive social and economic reforms including investment in education, housing and agriculture. Health policies included a widespread vaccination programme to combat the country's high infant mortality rate. He also campaigned for women's rights, banning female circumcision and appointing five female ministers to his government. Top civil servants received pay cuts, including the president himself. Living conditions improved and food production increased. In 1984 he replaced the country's colonial name with Burkina Faso, a combination of two native languages meaning 'Land of the Upright People'. Civilian Revolutionary Committees were established throughout the country to implement government policy while Revolutionary People's tribunals were installed to try former public officials charged with corruption.

On an international front, Sankara allied Burkina Faso with Cuba, North Korea and Libya. He developed close relations with Ghana, even talking of merging the two countries. A brief war with Mali over the Agaeher Strip in 1985 was settled by the International Court of Justice. Opposed to any forms of neo-colonialism, he rejected the conditions of World Bank loans.

Despite progressive reforms, Sankara was intolerant of opposition. He provoked the ire of rural Mossi chiefs by pledging to eradicate patriarchy and feudalism, and his contempt for the 'bourgeoisie' alienated prospective investors and forced entrepreneurs to leave the country. He also lost the support of trade unions and of the far left in the CNR. Towards the end of his tenure, Sankara had improved relations with France and the US and this was seen as an abandonment of his original revolutionary principles. In an attempt to mollify his critics, in 1987 he proposed a cooperative one party state which was refused. Along with several allies, Sankara was assassinated on 15 Oct. 1987 by soldiers loyal to Compaoré. Compaoré was installed as president, a position he still holds.

Santana Lopes, Pedro (Portugal)

Introduction

Plucked from his position as mayor of Lisbon during a period of political upheaval, Pedro Santana Lopes succeeded José Manuel Durão Barroso as Portugal's prime minister on 19 July 2004. The leader of the centre-right Social Democratic Party (PSD) and former Culture Secretary pledged to continue the structural and economic reforms of his predecessor. Santana Lopes' detractors accused him of being 'Portugal's answer to (Italian Prime Minister) Silvio Berlusconi' because of his tendency to mix media, football and politics. However, he only held office for 8 months, resigning after President Sampáio had called early elections.

Early Life

Pedro Miguel Santana Lopes was born in Lisbon on 29 June 1956. He attended the Padre António Vieira secondary school from 1966 and went on to read law at Lisbon University in 1974, teaching at night and selling books to help pay for his studies. While at university he led the Independent Law Movement and joined the centre-right Social Democratic Party (PSD), one of four political parties to have emerged in the aftermath of Portugal's 1974 revolution. Santana Lopes graduated in 1978 and won a scholarship from the German government to study Political Science and European Studies. After completing this course he entered the team of Prime Minister Sá Carneiro (founder of the PSD) as his legal adviser. In 1980, at 24 years of age, he was elected a member of parliament. The PSD-led coalition government advocated strong free-enterprise measures and succeeded in implementing a process of constitutional revision which reduced presidential power and paved the way for Portugal's entry into the European Community in 1986.

Prime Minister Cavaco Silva (elected in Oct. 1985) appointed Santana Lopes as Secretary of State of the Presidency of the Council of Ministers, a job which was interrupted in 1987 when he spent 2 years as a member of the

European Parliament. In Jan. 1990 Santana Lopes became Secretary of State for Culture, orchestrating the restoration of buildings and the opening of libraries, cinemas and theatres. Economic progress and relative stability were key factors behind the PSD's victory by a clear majority in the general legislative elections of July 1991. The following year Santana Lopes presided over the European Council of Ministers of Culture. After his party's defeat to the Socialist Party (PSP), led by António Guterres, in the 1995 general election Santana Lopes left politics and became president of the soccer club Sporting Lisbon. In 1997 he was elected mayor of Figueira da Foz, a small town north of Lisbon. Four years later he won the race for Lisbon's mayor and began an ambitious programme to improve the traffic movement in the city and to upgrade urban spaces, although he was accused by some of adopting cosmetic solutions rather than long-term strategies. While mayor of Lisbon, Santana Lopes became a high-profile public figure, making regular TV appearances as a political commentator and writing a football column in the press.

Santana Lopes was thrust back into the political limelight in June 2004 when the prime minister and leader of the PSD, José Manuel Durão Barroso, resigned to accept the nomination to become the next president of the European Commission. Portugal's president, Jorge Sampaio, resisted pressure from the opposition Socialist Party (PSP) to call a fresh election, and instead let the PSD form a new government. Pedro Santana Lopes was elected leader of the PSD and appointed prime minister by Sampaio.

Career Peak

Santana Lopes was regarded as a populist, slightly to the right of Barroso. In his inauguration speech, Santana Lopes vowed to continue the work of his predecessor, including reducing the national deficit. However, in Dec. 2004 he announced his resignation after President Sampāio called early elections for Feb. 2005.

Santer, Jacques (Luxembourg)

Introduction

Jacques Santer was prime minister of Luxembourg from 1984–95, winning re-election twice in that period. He became president of the European Commission in 1995 but resigned along with the entire commission in 1999 following allegations of fraud, corruption and mismanagement.

Early Life

Santer was born on 18 May 1937 in Wasserbillig, Luxembourg. He graduated in law from the University of Strasbourg in France and received a master's degree in political sciences from the Paris Institute of Political Studies before embarking on a career as a solicitor. He entered Luxembourg politics in 1966 and became president of the Christian Social People's Party 8 years later. In 1979 he was appointed finance minister, a position he kept for the next decade. He was also a member of the European Parliament from 1975–79, acting as its vice-president for 2 years.

Career Peak

Santer became prime minister of Luxembourg in 1984 and was a key figure in drafting the 1986 Single European Act—the first major revision of the 1957 Treaty of Rome? that aimed to create a single European market by 1992.

In the contest to become president of the European Commission in 1994, Santer was not the first choice of any member state. However, he was widely considered a viable compromise candidate and was duly elected to the post in Jan. 1995. His 4-year tenure saw the implementation of the Schengen Agreement in 1995 and the introduction of the single European currency in 1999.

However, his presidency was overshadowed by the mass resignation of the Commission after an independent investigatory committee found a lack of political control. Santer was cited for giving evidence to the committee which was considered evasive to the point of being misleading. Lacking the power to dismiss individuals accused of fraud and corruption, Santer called an emergency meeting before announcing the Commission's collective resignation on 15 March 1999.

Later Life

Santer remained a member of the European Parliament until 2004. As an honorary minister of state for Luxembourg he has held various positions, including president of the Academy for European Law and president of the European Union of Federalists group. In 2012 he became head of the Special Purpose Investment Vehicle (SPIV)—part of the European Financial Stability Facility—and in May 2013 was made an honorary member of SME Europe (Small and Medium Entrepreneurs Europe).

Sargsyan, Serzh (Armenia)

Introduction

Serzh Sargsyan was sworn into office on 9 April 2008, nearly 2 months after he was declared the winner of the disputed presidential election. Although said to be fair by international observers, the election sparked violent clashes between protesters and police. A 20-day state of emergency was declared by the government before Sargsyan took office. He nevertheless won re-election in Feb. 2013.

Early Life

Sargsyan was born on 30 June 1954 in Stepanakert, in the Nagorno-Karabakh region. He enrolled at Yerevan State University in 1971 but served in the Soviet armed forces from 1972–74. He then worked as a metal turner from 1975–79 before graduating from the philological department of Yerevan State University in 1979. In the same year he became the divisional head of the Young Communist Union for Stepanakert.

Rising through the ranks of the Communist Party, Sargsyan was the leader of the Nagorno-Karabakh Republic self-defence forces committee during the Nagorno-Karabakh conflict of 1989–93. From 1993–95 he served as minister of defence and was later promoted to minister of national security. In 1996 he took over the ministry of interior portfolio when it merged with the national security ministry. When the offices separated in 1999, Sargsyan retained responsibility for national security. In the same year he joined the president's office as chief of staff and was selected as secretary of Armenia's national security council. In 2000 he returned to the defence ministry, where he served until 2007.

Sargsyan joined the conservative Republican Party of Armenia (HHK) in 2006 and became party chairman in Nov. 2007. In April 2007 President Robert Kocharyan appointed Sargsyan prime minister and in Feb. 2008 he went on to win the presidential election by a landslide.

Career Peak

Responding to the violent protests that followed his election victory, Sargsyan called for unity and co-operation among all political factions.

In addition to promoting economic growth, he sought to improve international relations, especially with Armenia's neighbours. Turkey's rejection of charges of genocide in Armenia during the First World War has posed a stumbling block to bilateral reconciliation. In Oct. 2009 the two governments agreed on a framework to normalize relations, but in April 2010 Armenia suspended the ratification process accusing Turkey of imposing preconditions, including a resolution of Armenia's territorial dispute with Azerbaijan. Azerbaijan has meanwhile refused to concede its claim on Nagorno-Karabakh despite several Russian-brokered meetings between Sargsyan and the Azeri president and tensions have continued to fuel periodic clashes between Armenian and Azeri troops, most recently in Feb. 2017.

In parliamentary elections in May 2012, boycotted by the opposition, the governing pro-Sargsyan HHK retained its majority in the National Assembly, while in Feb. 2013 Sargsyan was re-elected president, winning almost 59% of the vote. In a referendum in Dec. 2015 around 66% of voters were in favour of constitutional amendments championed by Sargsyan that envisaged Armenia's transition to a parliamentary system of government. The amendments enhanced the powers of the prime minister and cabinet appointed from the majority parliamentary party and demoted the president (henceforth to be elected by an electoral college) to a largely ceremonial role. Opponents accused Sargsyan of aiming to perpetuate his political influence after his second and final presidential term ends in 2018. In April 2017 Sargsyan's

HHK again secured parliamentary control in legislative elections that were criticized by European observers and the opposition for alleged voting irregularities.

In Oct. 2014 Sargsyan shunned closer ties with the European Union as he signed a treaty with the leaders of Russia, Kazakhstan and Belarus incorporating Armenia into the Eurasian Economic Union, a free trade zone superseding the former Eurasian Economic Community from 1 Jan. 2015. Armen Sarkissian was chosen by the National Assembly to succeed him as president and Sargsyan left office on 9 April 2018.

Sarkis, Elias (Lebanon)

Introduction

Lawyer, banker and Maronite Christian politician, Sarkis served as state president from 1976–82. His presidency was dominated by continuing civil strife between opposing militia groups and by foreign military intervention.

Early Life

Sarkis was born on 24 July 1924 and was educated at the St. Joseph University in Beirut. Having worked in law and banking, he became director-general of the president's office under President Chehab in 1962. From 1967–76 he was the governor of the Banque du Liban (central bank). He lost by a single vote to Suleiman Franjieh in the 1970 presidential election, but stood again successfully in 1976 during the civil war.

Career Peak

Sarkis took office in Sept. 1976. Despite the deployment of the Syrian-dominated Arab Deterrent Force (ADF), large areas of the country remained outside government control, including Muslim West Beirut. Frequent sectarian conflict was exacerbated by an Israeli invasion of southern Lebanon in 1978. This was followed by the installation of Israeli-controlled Christian Lebanese militia forces in border areas to deter Palestinian attacks. Sarkis' administration tried to formulate a national accord but remained unable to exert its authority. As the end of his presidential term approached, Israel launched a second invasion in June 1982 which led to the expulsion of PLO forces from Lebanon by Sept.

Sarkis died in Paris, France, on 27 June 1985.

Sarkozy, Nicolas (France)

Introduction

Nicolas Sarkozy became president in May 2007, succeeding Jacques Chirac. Having been minister of the interior and the economy, he defeated the Socialist Ségolène Royal and ten other candidates for the presidency. Despite his electoral mandate to introduce modernizing reforms and his commitment to reinvigorating the economy and reducing unemployment, he encountered widespread labour opposition to some of his policies and was confronted by the impact of the global credit crisis and ensuing economic downturn. He nevertheless pursued an active and influential role on the world diplomatic stage. Sarkozy was defeated in the 2012 election by François Hollande and after leaving office announced his retirement from politics.

Early Life

Nicolas Sarkozy de Nagy-Bosca was born in Paris on 28 Jan. 1955, the son of a Hungarian aristocrat and a French-Jewish mother. Educated at a private Catholic school, he graduated in political science and law and undertook further studies at the Institut d'études politiques de Paris, although he did not graduate. He entered the legal profession as a barrister specializing in business law and began his political life in 1977 as a councillor for Neuilly-sur-Seine. He became a national youth delegate for the newly founded neo-Gaullist Rally for the Republic (RPR) a year later. In 1979 Sarkozy was elected president of the RPR's youth wing under the party's leader Jacques Chirac, who subsequently lost the 1981 presidential campaign to the Socialist, François Mitterrand.

In 1983 Sarkozy was elected mayor of Neuilly-sur-Seine. A member of the Île-de-France Regional Council from 1983–88, he was elected as a parliamentary deputy for the département of Hauts-de-Seine in June 1988 following Mitterrand's re-election as president. Sarkozy was re-elected to the National Assembly at the 1993 elections, in which the RPR made significant progress and the Socialists were reduced to their weakest position since 1958. Sarkozy was appointed minister for the budget before becoming spokesman for the executive in the cabinet of Prime Minister Édouard Balladur.

His decision to back Balladur rather than his mentor, Chirac, in the presidential election of 1995 led to a prolonged rift. Sarkozy retreated into the RPR's internal politics, becoming the party's secretary general in 1998 and its interim president a year later. He also sat as an MEP in 1999.

When Chirac won a landslide victory in the 2002 presidential election he appointed Jean-Pierre Raffarin as prime minister and made Sarkozy minister of the interior. Sarkozy's 'tough on crime' policies divided opinion with his critics claiming his measures infringed civil rights.

As minister for the economy, finance and industry from 2002–04 Sarkozy introduced market-led reforms, including the reduction of the government's stake in France Télécom. However, he also backed a partial renationalization of the troubled manufacturing company, Alstom. In Nov. 2004 Sarkozy was elected to succeed Alain Juppé as leader of the Union for a Popular Movement (UMP, which grew out of a merger of the RPR and Liberal Democracy in 2002). Reappointed minister of the interior in the government of Dominique de Villepin in June 2005, Sarkozy responded to rioting in some suburbs of Paris by promising to toughen justice measures for delinquents and to counter illegal immigration.

Having been endorsed by the UMP as its candidate in the 2007 presidential election, Sarkozy pledged his support for reducing bureaucracy to help create jobs and to nurture an entrepreneurial culture.

Career Peak

Having defeated Ségolène Royal in a second round of voting held on 6 May 2007, Sarkozy outlined plans for a more dynamic economy with France playing a more prominent global role. He announced his cabinet on 18 May 2007, including François Fillon as prime minister. In June 2007 the UMP won the parliamentary elections, but with a reduced majority. Also in June, Sarkozy enjoyed a successful diplomatic debut at the European Union summit of heads of government, where a new draft treaty on the Union's institutional structure and decision-making process was agreed (and which eventually came into force in Dec. 2009). Later in 2007 his plans for public sector pension benefits provoked paralysing strike action in Nov. by civil servants and workers in the transport and energy sectors. Also in Nov. he was confronted with a renewed, although brief, eruption of rioting in poor immigrant suburbs in Paris and Toulouse.

Public attention in early 2008 focused largely on Sarkozy's private life and remarriage before his UMP party fared badly against the Socialists in municipal elections in March. However, after France assumed the rotating EU presidency in July, he took a prominent role in calling for reform of the world's financial system in response to the global credit crisis and, acting in the name of the EU, helped to secure a ceasefire in the violent conflict that erupted in Aug. between Russia and Georgia. Also in July, a new Union for the Mediterranean was launched at a summit of regional heads of state and government hosted by Sarkozy in Paris.

In early 2009 the government faced strikes and protests in response to the economic downturn. However, France unexpectedly pulled out of recession with a return to growth in the second quarter of the year and Sarkozy's UMP party topped the polls in French elections to the European Parliament in June.

In March 2009, in a significant foreign policy move, Sarkozy confirmed that France would rejoin NATO's integrated military command, reversing its withdrawal of 43 years earlier. The following May he opened France's first military base in the Persian Gulf area with the stationing of forces in the United Arab Emirates. Then in Nov. 2010 he and the UK prime minister signed a 50-year Anglo–French defence and security co-operation agreement.

Sarkozy's political fortunes declined markedly in 2010. In March the UMP endured heavy losses in regional elections, and in June the government announced deep public spending cuts, including unpopular pension reforms, to reduce the high level of public debt. Then in July prosecutors started an inquiry into alleged illegal financial donations by Liliane Bettencourt, heiress to the L'Oreal cosmetics business empire, to Sarkozy's presidential election campaign. Meanwhile, the deportation from France of illegal Roma immigrants back to Romania and Bulgaria, which began in Aug., attracted international media coverage and was strongly criticized by the EU justice commissioner. Attention in Sept. and Oct. was focused on trade union-led action against the government's pension reforms. However, despite several waves of disruptive strikes and street protests, the French parliament gave its final approval to legislation raising the retirement age from 60 to 62 at the end of Oct. In Nov. Sarkozy carried out a minor reshuffle of his cabinet, retaining Prime Minister François Fillon but replacing Bernard Kouchner as foreign minister.

Sarkozy was one of ten candidates who participated in the first round of voting in the 2012 presidential elections. Coming second, he faced the Socialist Party candidate François Hollande in the run-off but failed to be re-elected for a second term. Conceding to Hollande, Sarkozy announced that he would retire from politics.

Later Life

Despite being charged with corruption and abuses of power by a French court in July 2014, Sarkozy announced his intention to return to politics and run as a candidate for the UMP leadership at party elections held in Nov. He subsequently took 65.4% of the vote against two other candidates and assumed the presidency of the centre-right party for the second time later the same month. The case against his alleged influencing of public officials and misreporting of campaign funds had been suspended the previous month.

In Aug. 2016 Sarkozy announced his candidacy for the French presidential race in 2017. However, 3 months later he lost in the first round of the primary of the Republicans—which was founded in May 2015 as the successor to the UMP.

Sarney, José (Brazil)

Introduction

José Sarney was president of Brazil from 1985 to 1990. His attempts to consolidate pro-democracy reforms were hampered by crippling economic and social problems.

Early Life

Born in 1930 in Maranhão state, José Sarney entered politics as a federal representative in 1955. He became Maranhão state governor in 1965 and then president of the Social Democratic Party in 1970. Failing to secure the approval of the military government, his attempts to return to the governorship of Maranhão in 1974 and 1978 were vetoed.

He became vice president following the 1985 elections, which saw the end of 21 years of military rule. On the death of president-elect Tancredo Neves in April 1985, Sarney was sworn in as president.

Career Peak

Sarney was confronted by massive economic problems, a hangover from the years of military rule. Foreign debt, inflation and unemployment were all at unmanageable levels. Price and wage freezes set out in the Cruzado Plan succeeded briefly in bringing down inflation, but during his period in office Sarney had to implement four austerity programmes. In the presidential run-off of Dec. 1989 voters backed the two candidates who had vociferously criticized the Sarney presidency, Fernando Collor and Luís Inácio Lula da Silva.

Later Life

Sarney remained a senator until Feb. 2015, serving as president of the federal senate on three occasions.

Sata, Michael Chilufya (Zambia)

Introduction

Michael Sata was head of state between Sept. 2011 and Oct. 2014 when he passed away whilst still in office. He presided over a buoyant economy but was criticized for his alleged political bullying and imperious style.

Early Life

Born in 1937, Sata was raised in Mpika in the Northern Province of what was then Northern Rhodesia. Before entering politics he worked as a policeman, railwayman and trade unionist. After Zambia won independence in 1964 he became a member of the ruling United National Independence Party until joining the Movement for Multi-Party Democracy (MMD) in 1991. In the 1990s he variously served as minister for local government, health and labour, as well as minister without portfolio.

When Levy Mwanawasa was chosen as the MMD's 2001 presidential candidate, Sata left to form the Patriotic Front. However, he made little impact at the polls and in parliamentary elections his new party won only a single seat. He stood for the presidency in 2006, finishing second behind Mwanawasa who secured a second term. Sata was arrested for making a false declaration of his assets when registering for the campaign but the charge was dropped. In 2007 he was deported on arrival in neighbouring Malaŵi on allegations that he was plotting a coup. Later the same year his passport was withdrawn by the Zambian authorities, who accused him of bypassing regulations.

After an apparent reconciliation with President Mwanawasa in May 2008, Sata suffered a heart attack. When Mwanawasa died in Aug. that year, Sata was banned from attending the funeral. On 30 Aug. 2008 he was unanimously chosen as the Patriotic Front's presidential candidate but lost to Rupiah Banda of the MMD.

At the presidential poll on 23 Sept. 2011, Sata gained 42% of the vote against Banda's 35% after a campaign marred by violence. Sata was sworn in to office in Lusaka within hours of the results being declared. His victory ended two decades of MMD rule.

Career Peak

Sata campaigned on promises to help the nation's poor and fight corruption, and pledged to reinstate a 25% windfall tax on mining revenues abolished by the MMD in 2009. He has also encouraged foreign investment while demanding improved working conditions, having criticized the employment practices of companies from China, a heavy investor in Zambia's mining industries.

Having previously expressed his admiration for Zimbabwe's President Robert Mugabe, Sata (known as 'King Cobra' for his fiery rhetoric) has been accused of political authoritarianism and intimidation.

Sata died somewhat unexpectedly in the United Kingdom on 28 Oct. 2014. His public appearances had decreased dramatically since June, and he had been receiving treatment at a hospital in London for an undisclosed medical condition. His vice-president Guy Scott was sworn in as acting president the following day.

Sato, Eisaku (Japan)

Introduction

Eisaku Sato was Japan's longest serving prime minister (1964–72). He was a prime mover in Japan's development as a leading economic and political power.

Early Life

Sato was born in 1901. He graduated in law at Tokyo Imperial University in 1924. Elected as a member of the Diet in 1945–74, he was leader of the Liberal Democrat Party from 1950. He was Minister of Construction 1952–53; Finance minister 1957–60 and Minister of Nuclear Science, energy and technology, 1960–64.

Career Peak

During his premiership, Sato stabilized South Korean–Japanese relations and in 1972 regained from the US sovereign rights over Okinawa and the Ryuku Islands. Discontent over permission for US forces to remain on the islands resulted in Sato's resignation.

Later Lifer

In 1974, Sato received the Nobel Peace Prize for his contribution to limiting the spread of nuclear weapons. Sato died in Tokyo on 3 June 1975.

Savimbi, Jonas (Angola)

Introduction

Jonas Savimbi led the rebel National Union for the Total Independence of Angola (UNITA) group, in opposition to the post-independence government of Angola. During this time the group conducted guerrilla insurgencies against the ruling Popular Movement for the Liberation of Angola (MPLA), which met with a mix of international support and condemnation. A mysterious and unpredictable figure in political life, Savimbi was instrumental in both restoring peace and provoking war.

Early Life

Savimbi was born on 3 Aug. 1934. The son of a railroad stationmaster, he was educated at mission schools, winning a scholarship to study abroad. He studied medicine at the University of Lisbon, and then later travelled to Lausanne in Switzerland where he studied political science. In 1965 Savimbi and 11 other pro-independence militants left for China where they were trained in guerrilla warfare. On Mao Zedong's advice they decided to conduct a guerrilla campaign to secure Angola's liberation from Portugal. In March 1966 Savimbi formed the UNITA after entering the country in secret. He was briefly detained by Zambian authorities the following year and sent into exile in Cairo. On his return in 1968 he installed himself and his followers deep within the jungle and began to wage war against the colonial rulers. He was the only leader of a nationalist movement to remain in Angola throughout the conflict with Portugal.

Savimbi was present at the Mombasa Conference in 1975 when he agreed with the other two Angolan nationalist leaders, Agostinho Neto and Holden Roberto, to create an independent democratic Angola. Only 12 days later on 15 Jan. 1975, the Portuguese president, Costa Gomes, and the three nationalist leaders signed the Alvor accords which granted Angola independence.

Career Peak

Almost immediately the three factions began to squabble for power, and by June 1975 the stability of the country was at risk. There were massacres in Luanda. Following the failure of talks to resolve the escalating conflict, Savimbi and his followers abandoned the city of Huambo and returned to the bush. UNITA based its headquarters in the southeast of Angola, relying on the Ovimbundu, the largest tribal group in the country, for support.

Savimbi made several visits abroad to canvas international support for UNITA, at various times obtaining backing from South Africa, China and the USA to oppose the Marxist MPLA regime. He was recognized as a freedom fighter by President Ronald Reagan in 1986.

In 1991 Savimbi signed a peace agreement with the MPLA that ended the violence and culminated in Angola's first nationwide elections in 1992. After a turnout of 91% of registered voters, UNITA won 34% compared to the MPLA's 54%. In the presidential poll the results were closer still. Dos Santos of the MPLA secured 49.6%, while Savimbi polled 40.7%. The narrow defeat prompted Savimbi to reject the UN monitored election, claiming the results

were fraudulent. The civil war resumed and though a tenuous peace was established in 1994, by 1998 the fighting had escalated once again. On this occasion the conflict was initiated by the government in response to what it regarded as UNITA's wilful failure to adhere to the UN peace agreement.

The MPLA denounced UNITA as a treacherous and unreliable adversary, but conceded that the future of peace in Angola depended upon gaining support from Savimbi. Styling itself as the champion of the disenfranchised rural peasantry, support for UNITA was made all too clear in the 1992 election. Having recognized this the government made some peaceful overtures towards Savimbi, offering an amnesty to him and a pardon to his troops. Savimbi continued with UNITA's offensive and was killed by government forces on 22 Feb. 2002. Hopes that Savimba's demise would prompt renewed efforts for peace were rewarded when a ceasefire was signed in April 2002.

Sayasone, Choummaly (Laos)

Introduction

Choummaly Sayasone was elected president in June 2006, succeeding his long-time mentor, Khamtay Siphandone. Part of the Lao ruling elite for decades, Sayasone had previously served as vice president and minister of national defence. He was re-elected by the National Assembly in June 2011.

Early Life

Born on 6 March 1936 into a farming family in Vat Neua village, Attopeu province, Sayasone took up arms with the revolutionary Pathet Lao guerrilla forces in 1954. While fighting in Houaphan province in 1955, he joined the People's Revolutionary Party. A successful soldier, Sayasone became deputy head of a regiment of Pathet Lao forces in 1959. He also held a variety of posts within the party hierarchy and was appointed head of the military department in 1972.

When the Pathet Lao took over government in 1975, he worked as a close ally of Khamtay Siphandone, minister of national defence and deputy prime minister. Sayasone became Siphandone's deputy at the defence ministry in 1982 and was promoted to minister of national defence in 1991. Sayasone became vice president in 2001 and on 21 March 2006 he was elected secretary general of the People's Revolutionary Party of Laos. On Siphandone's retirement as president, the National Assembly chose Sayasone as his successor in June 2006.

Career Peak

Sayasone has continued his predecessor's policies, including the banning of rival political parties and tight control of the media. Some economic liberalization has nevertheless been under way since Laos joined ASEAN in 1997, including the opening of a stock market in Vientiane in Jan. 2011. Sayasone was re-elected for a further 5-year term in June 2011. In July 2012 Hillary Clinton made the first visit to Laos by a US secretary of state since the 1950s.

Sayasone did not seek re-election at the 10th LPRP Congress in Jan. 2016 and retired from public life.

Schmidt, Helmut (Germany)

Introduction

Helmut Schmidt was Chancellor of West Germany between 1974–82 and Vice Chairman of the Social Democratic Party (SPD) from 1968–83. He oversaw the continued strength of the West German economy throughout the 1970s both as Minister of Finance and then Chancellor. In retirement he remained influential on the international political scene and edited the respected political review *Die Zeit* (The Times).

Early Life

Schmidt was born on 23 Dec. 1918 in Hamburg. During World War II he served on both the Eastern and Western Fronts and towards the war's end he was captured by British troops and detained in Belgium. After the war he studied Economics at the University of Hamburg and became involved in the Social Democrat movement, becoming Chairman of the Socialist Students' League in 1947.

In 1949 he was employed in the Department of Transport Management for Hamburg. In 1953 he left municipal government to enter parliament (*Bundestag*), serving for 8 years before losing his seat and returning to Hamburg's state administration in the Ministry of the Interior. Within a few months of taking this post he had to deal with the effects of extensive flooding in the area, which did much to revive his political profile. In 1965 he won re-election to the *Bundestag*. He took the job of Vice Chairman of the SPD in 1968 and, in the coalition of Chancellor Brandt, was appointed Defence Minister. In 1972 he was moved to the Ministry of Finance before succeeding Willy Brandt, who had resigned following a spy scandal, on 16 May 1974.

Career Peak

As both Finance Minister and Chancellor, Schmidt had to contend with a worldwide downturn in the economy, caused chiefly by the Middle Eastern oil crises of 1973 and 1979. Inflation increased, public welfare suffered and unemployment tripled during his tenure, yet he managed re-election in 1976 and 1980. By the early 1980s inflation was under control with resumed economic growth.

Schmidt's period in office was troubled by terrorist activity, particularly by the Baader-Meinhof Gang, a group with vague humanitarian aims. While it had generated support during the early 1970s, it soon descended into calculated acts of terrorism that resulted in numerous deaths. Several leaders were imprisoned but terrorist activity continued throughout the decade, culminating with the hi-jacking of a Lufthansa jet in late 1977 by Palestinian militants who demanded the release of their Baader-Meinhof allies. The aircraft was taken to Mogadishu in Somalia, and Schmidt, facing a highly sensitive issue, sent in a specially trained police squad. Three hi-jackers were killed but all the hostages emerged unharmed. As the news broke, three of the imprisoned Baader-Meinhof gang committed suicide.

Schmidt continued Brandt's efforts to promote relations with East Germany and the Soviet Union. He also attempted to heal old wounds between France and Germany, promoting economic co-operation among the Western European nations and between West Germany and the USA. As early as 1978 he was advocating European Monetary Union. In 1979 he attended a major summit with US President Jimmy Carter, French President Giscard d'Estaing and British Prime Minister James Callaghan. Discussions were held on the Strategic Arms Limitation Treaty and what NATO's response should be to Soviet plans to deploy missiles aimed at Western targets. China and its changing world role was also an important topic.

Energy and the environment became major concerns on Germany's domestic scene throughout the 1970s and early 1980s. The Green Party emerged in the late-1970s. By 1980 it was making gains in *Länder* elections and threatening to impact on federal elections. A number of the SPD's left wing members subsequently defected to the new party. The German economy experienced a downturn in the 1980s, as did most other Western economies, but Schmidt refused to sanction cuts in the welfare budget as many economists were demanding. In response the Free Democratic Party left Schmidt's coalition government, leaving the Chancellor without a workable majority. Following a vote of no confidence by the Bundestag on 1 Oct. 1982, Schmidt resigned, to be replaced by Helmut Kohl who went on to win the federal elections of 1983.

Later Life

Schmidt remained in the *Bundestag* until his retirement in Sept. 1986. Between 1983–89 he was publisher of *Die Zeit*, a respected weekly political newspaper. A multi-linguist, he continued to write for other publications and also wrote several political works. He has remained an influential and respected voice on the international political scene. He died aged 96 on 10 Nov. 2015.

Schmitt, Pál (Hungary)

Introduction

Pál Schmitt was sworn in as president on 6 Aug. 2010. Schmitt first achieved fame as a sportsman, winning Olympic gold in fencing. He entered politics in the 1980s. Seen as a less interventionist president than his predecessor, he declared that he would not use the largely ceremonial role to obstruct government business. After being stripped of his doctorate over plagiarism, Schmitt resigned in April 2012.

Early Life

Schmitt was born in Budapest on 13 May 1942 and graduated from the city's university as a student of economics. Having started fencing competitively in his early teens, Schmitt went on to win the team épée gold medals at the 1968 and 1972 Olympic Games. He also won team and individual world championships before retiring from fencing in 1977. As a sports administrator, he was appointed the government's undersecretary of sports in 1981, a position he held until 1990, when he became president of the Hungarian Olympic Committee. He subsequently held a succession of posts with the International Olympic Committee.

In 1993 Schmitt was named the ambassador to Spain, later becoming ambassador to Switzerland. In 2002 he unsuccessfully ran for the mayorship of Budapest. Although an independent, his candidacy was supported by the centre-right Fidesz party. The following year, he was named deputy president of the party. In 2004 Schmitt was elected to the European Parliament at the head of the Fidesz list, and in July 2009 was confirmed as one of the parliament's 14 vice presidents.

In the aftermath of Hungary's parliamentary election in April 2010, Schmitt became speaker. He was then selected as the joint presidential nominee of Fidesz-MPSz and its Christian Democratic partners. In the presidential election, held among members of the national assembly, he defeated András Balogh of the Socialist Party by 263 votes to 59.

Career Peak

László Sólyom, Schmitt's predecessor as president, clashed with parties on both sides of the political divide by regularly sending laws back to parliament for reconsideration. Schmitt distanced himself from such an interpretation of the presidential role, stating that he did not want to impede policies approved by parliament. He pledged to work to promote public health, sports, education, the Hungarian language and civil solidarity.

Hungary assumed the European Union rotating presidency on 1 Jan. 2011, at a time when the EU was struggling to come to terms with the sovereign debt crises in several member states. The passage of a controversial media law in Hungary, entitling the government to force journalists to reveal sources under certain circumstances, drew questions about the country's suitability to head the EU. The government responded by amending the legislation to meet EU concerns.

In April 2011 Schmitt signed a revised Hungarian constitution into law. The following year Semmelweis University stripped Schmitt of his doctorate after it found that large parts of his thesis were plagiarized. Facing calls to stand down, Schmitt announced his resignation on 2 April 2012.

Later Life

In Jan. 2016 Schmitt was appointed chairman of Budapest's bid for the 2024 Summer Olympic Games.

Schröder, Gerhard (Germany)

Introduction

Schröder became Germany's chancellor in Oct. 1998, ending 16 years of Christian Democrat rule under Helmut Kohl. Schröder, claiming the political centre, was seen as a leading exponent of 'third way' politics, along with Tony Blair in the UK and Bill Clinton in the US. His government declined in popularity during its first year as the economy contracted. In addition, he caused unease among several of his European partners by his proposals for a 'European Federation'. He was re-elected chancellor in 2002, narrowly defeating Christian Democratic Union/Christian Social Union (CDU/CSU) candidate Edmund Stoiber. He left office in Nov. 2005 having been narrowly defeated for the chancellorship by the CDU's Angela Merkel.

Early Life

Schröder was born on 7 April 1944 in Mossenburg, Lower Saxony. His father was killed during World War II and his mother worked as a cleaner while raising five children. Schröder left school at 14 to find employment. He obtained his school certificates by attending evening classes, and in 1976 he graduated from Goettingen University with a degree in law. From 1978–90 he had a private practice in Hanover.

Having become active within the Social Democratic Party (SPD) following his studies, Schröder was appointed to lead the Young Socialists in 1978. Two years later, regarded as on the far-left of the party, he won a seat in the German parliament. In 1986 he was appointed to the national executive body of the SPD, and in 1990 became prime minister of Lower Saxony.

During the course of the 1980s and 1990s, he moved from the political left to the centre, establishing links within the German business community. In 1996 he married his fourth wife. In April 1998, following his success in regional elections, Schröder was nominated as the SPD's candidate for the chancellorship in the Sept. elections. Youthfully vibrant in comparison with Helmut Kohl, Schröder promised to upkeep Germany's expansive welfare provisions while improving conditions for business. The SPD emerged from the elections as the biggest party, and Schröder was elected chancellor by parliament on 27 Oct. 1998.

Career Peak

In Oct. 1998 Schröder agreed a coalition with the Greens, which entitled the junior partner to fill certain key government posts including foreign affairs and the environment. His centrist stance soon brought him into conflict with senior colleagues on the left, most notably the finance minister, Oskar Lafontaine, the candidate for the chancellorship at the 1990 elections and SPD national chairman since 1995. Their disputes ultimately led to Lafontaine's resignation in March 1999, with Schröder replacing him as party leader.

Lafontaine was replaced by Hans Eichel, who oversaw a rapid series of market reforms, of the type traditionally associated with the CDU. However, the coalition failed in their chief aim of reducing unemployment and consequently they suffered a decline in popularity, with losses in European, state and local elections.

On the international scene, Schröder caused disquiet among European partners including France and the UK in 2001 when he set out his vision of a European Federation. Among his proposals was the conversion of the European Council into the European parliament's 'upper house'. Further delineation of policy areas to be decided centrally, nationally and regionally; joint financing of agricultural subsidies by the EU and relevant states. In the aftermath of the 11 Sept. terrorist attacks, he offered broad support to US initiatives, sending troops to Afghanistan as part of the international peacekeeping force. At the end of 2001 Bonn hosted UN brokered talks on the future of Afghanistan. However, he refused to support proposals for a US-led attack on Iraq, stating in Aug. 2002 that 'under my leadership Germany will not be available for adventures.' Relations with both the UK and US deteriorated further in 2003 when, along with France, Russia and China, Germany was among the most critical opponents of the US-led invasion that saw Saddam Hussein's regime deposed in April. The split between Washington and what it regarded as 'Old Europe' posed long-term questions over the role of the UN, NATO and the EU on the international stage. However, in May 2003 Germany voted to accept a UN resolution on Iraq's future jointly proposed by the US, UK and Spain. In return for the immediate ending of sanctions, the UN was to co-operate with the occupying forces to form a new government.

In the build up to the 2002 elections, Schröder had to contend with a poor economic climate and high unemployment. His party was hit by scandal in July 2002 when his defence minister, Rudolf Sharping, resigned over allegations of financial irregularity. In Aug. 2002 Schröder announced that tax cuts scheduled for Jan. 2003 would be postponed as a result of extensive flooding estimated to have caused €10 bn. of damage. However, Schröder retained significant public support. His proposals for a modernization of Germany's

immigration policy, partly in response to the growing need to expand the country's worker base in order to support an aging population, was well received. In addition, his market reforms were viewed favourably by the business community although his failure to reduce unemployment was widely attacked. In June 2003 Schröder won support from his party for a series of social and economic reforms, including a cut in pension and health care spending, lower unemployment benefits for those under 55 and greater employer freedom to dismiss staff. In the same month he announced income tax cuts intended to encourage consumer spending to kickstart the economy. It was hoped the cuts would increase the income of average earners by 10% per year.

At the elections of Sept. 2002, Schröder's SPD finished neck and neck with the CDU/CSU, the party of his chief opponent for the chancellorship, Edmund Stoiber. Both parties achieved a 38.5% share of the vote, with the SPD gaining 3 seats more than its rival. The strong showing of the Greens, Schröder's coalition allies, secured him a further term in office. In Oct. 2002 Schröder appointed Wolfgang Clement, the Social Democrat leader of North Rhine-Westphalia, as leader of the new labour and economics 'superministry'. He replaced the former economy and labour ministers. The new ministry's main task was to combat unemployment and reform the labour market.

In state elections in Feb. 2003 the SPD lost ground in Schröder's traditional strongholds of Lower Saxony and Hessen, while the CDU increased its standing in the *Bundesrat*. The results were considered a reaction to his unpopular economic measures and lack of success in revitalizing the economy and labour market.

During the Iraq war in 2003 Schröder opposed the US-led military invasion, leading to arguably the lowest point in post-war German-US relations. He regarded the war as untenable without a specific UN Security Council resolution. Schröder's relationship with Bush was strained but subsequently improved.

In Feb. 2004 Schröder resigned as chairman of his party as a result of criticism of his economic reform agenda. That same month Schröder, Tony Blair and Jacques Chirac met in Berlin to talk about economic challenges in Europe. They called for a EU economic reform 'tsar' to make Europe more globally competitive. Other European countries regarded the meeting as elitist, excluding other members from decision-making.

In Aug. and Sept. 2004 there were large popular protests in the east of the country against planned cuts in welfare benefits and labour reforms. In May 2005, during which parliament ratified the EU constitution, the SPD performed badly in regional elections in North Rhein-Westphalia. Schröder called for general elections to be brought forward to Sept. 2005. In a close-fought contest neither Schröder or Angela Merkel of the CDU would concede defeat in their fight for the chancellorship. Several weeks of talks followed as both tried to form a workable coalition. In early Oct. Schröder announced that Merkel would head a grand coalition including both parties and that he would leave politics.

Later Life

In Dec. 2005 Schröder announced he was joining the advisory board of a company overseeing construction of a Euro–Baltic Sea gas pipeline worth several billion euros. Schröder had signed Germany up to the project while chancellor, leading to allegations of conflict of interest. He also joined the media firm Ringier AG as an adviser for international political affairs. In Sept. 2017 he became chairman of Rosneft, Russia's biggest oil producer.

Schüssel, Wolfgang (Austria)

Introduction

A former lawyer, Schüssel came through the ranks of the Austrian People's Party (ÖVP) to become, on 4 Feb. 2000, Austria's first centre-right chancellor in 30 years. He achieved this in a controversial alliance with Jörg Haider's far-right Freedom Party (FPÖ). A pro-European moderate, his resistance to EU diplomatic sanctions (imposed in response to the FPÖ presence in government) in his first few months of office transformed him into a dominant political figure. His coalition collapsed in Sept. 2002 when the FPÖ succumbed to internal wranglings. In new elections in Nov. 2002 he led the

ÖVP to sweeping gains but revived the coalition with the FPÖ. After electoral defeat in 2006 he left office in Jan. 2007.

Early Life

Schüssel was born 7 June 1945 in Vienna and educated at Schottengymnasium until 1963. Having gained a PhD in law from Vienna University in 1968, he was secretary to the ÖVP parliamentary group until 1975 and then secretary-general of the Austrian Economic Federation (a post he retained until 1991). He was elected a member of the National Council in 1979, serving as leader of the Group of Economic Federation parliamentary delegates, deputy chairman of the parliamentary ÖVP and deputy chairman of the parliamentary finance committee before his appointment as minister of economic affairs in April 1989. In April 1995 he was elected party leader (following the slide in his party's popularity in the 1994 elections) and assumed the federal posts of vice chancellor and foreign minister in the SPÖ-ÖVP coalition government.

Career Peak

Schüssel first announced that he would take the ÖVP into opposition after it was beaten into third place (albeit by a few hundred votes) by the right-wing FPÖ in the Oct. 1999 elections. However, in Feb. 2000 he made a controversial strategic move to include the FPÖ in a coalition government, although it was emphasized that the ÖVP did not embrace that party's more extreme policies. As a result Austria was boycotted diplomatically by its European Union partners. Schüssel did not relent and in Sept. 2000 the EU lifted its sanctions, by which time Haider had resigned as official FPÖ leader and Schüssel's political standing in Europe had been strengthened.

Schüssel's government initiated tough policy measures to reform the public sector (notably the *proporz* system under which public-sector appointments were shared between party supporters), to reduce the budget deficit and to accelerate privatization. However, he was vulnerable to tensions with his coalition partners on issues such as EU enlargement and immigration.

In Sept. 2002 two FPÖ ministers resigned their government posts and the coalition government collapsed. Schüssel declared his readiness to form a new administration with any of the three main opposition parties, but the Social Democrats (the second biggest party) ruled out an agreement. He therefore called new elections, which were held on 24 Nov. 2002 and won by the ÖVP, and revived the ruling alliance with the FPÖ. However, the coalition's stability was again undermined in April 2005 as Jörg Haider and his supporters left the FPÖ to form a new political party.

At the elections of Oct. 2006 the SPÖ defeated the ÖVP and the two parties set about forming a coalition under the leadership of Alfred Gusenbauer (head of the SPÖ), who took office as chancellor in Jan. 2007. When the interior minister Liese Prokop died suddenly on 21 Dec. 2006, Schüssel was sworn in as her interim replacement on 2 Jan. until a new government was formed 9 days later.

Schuster, Rudolf (Slovakia)

Introduction

In June 1999 Rudolf Schuster assumed the post of president, which had been vacant since the resignation of Michal Kovác in March 1998. Schuster was Slovakia's first directly elected president and has strongly supported entry into the EU and NATO. He held office for nearly 5 years, being defeated in the presidential election of April 2004.

Early Life

Schuster was born on 4 Jan. 1934 in Košice, then part of Czechoslovakia. In 1959 he graduated in civil engineering from the Slovak Technical University in Bratislava. The following year he became a designer at the Regional Institute for Agricultural Projects in Bratislava and was an assistant at the Institute of Hydrology and Hydraulics of the Slovak Academy of Sciences in Bratislava.

In 1962 Schuster began working for the East Slovakian Iron and Steel Works. In 1964 he joined the Czechoslovakian Communist Party (KSČ), remaining a member until the party's demise in 1990. In 1974 he was

appointed vice chairman of the national committee of Košice with responsibility for services. Five years later he took over the local economy portfolio, and in 1983 he became the city mayor, a position he held until 1986.

From 1986 until 1989 he was chairman of the East Slovak regional national committee before taking the chairmanship of the Slovak national council, a post he held for a year. Serving as an ambassador in Canada between 1990–92, the following year he became foreign affairs minister. In 1994 he returned as mayor of Košice.

When incumbent president Mikhal Kovac stood down in March 1998 no candidate was able to secure the necessary 60% support from parliament to succeed him. Constitutional changes were promulgated allowing for the direct election of the president. Having resigned his mayorship, Schuster stood in the elections of May 1999, defeating Prime Minister Vladimír Mečiar after a rancorous campaign. He was sworn in on 15 June 1999.

Career Peak

The presidency is principally a ceremonial post and Schuster has repeatedly stressed that he is non-partisan. He is a strong advocate for entry into the EU and NATO and has encouraged the necessary reforms to facilitate admission. In 2002 Slovakia was invited to join both organizations in 2004.

In May 2001 Schuster gave a speech to parliament in which he condemned the government, a wide coalition beset by in-fighting, for its failure to undertake economic reform. In June 2001 he underwent bowel surgery in Austria and took several months to recuperate. He was defeated in the 2004 presidential election, coming fourth of six candidates.

Scotty, Ludwig (Nauru)

Introduction

Scotty was president of Nauru, the world's smallest republic, from June 2004 until Dec. 2007, having previously held the post for part of 2003. He attempted to push through financial and legislative reforms necessary to stave off bankruptcy and build the foundations of a sustainable economy. He left his post after losing a vote of confidence.

Early Life

Ludwig Derangadage Scotty was born on 20 June 1948 in Anabar, in the north of Nauru, then a UN Trust Territory under Australian administration. He completed his secondary education in 1964 and studied law at the University of the South Pacific, Suva, Fiji Islands. Returning to Nauru, which gained independence on 31 Jan. 1968, he held several prominent positions including chairman of the Bank of Nauru and member of the executive committee of Air Nauru. The 1970s saw political stability under president Hammer DeRoburt and unprecedented prosperity from the export of the island's valuable phosphorous deposits.

Scotty was elected as one of 18 members of parliament on 15 March 1983, representing the Anabar constituency. He served as parliamentary speaker from the late 1990s and briefly held the ministerial portfolio for health in 2003. During the caretaker administration of Derog Gioura, Scotty was elected president by ten parliamentary votes to seven, defeating the former president, Kinza Clodamur. He was sworn in on 28 May 2003.

Career Peak

With the national phosphate reserves exhausted, Scotty introduced sweeping reforms and unpopular austerity measures to stave off bankruptcy. Following a vote of no confidence on 8 Aug. 2003, he was ousted and replaced by René Harris. Harris himself then lost a vote of confidence and Scotty regained the presidency in June 2004. When the government failed to pass a reform budget by a designated deadline, Scotty dissolved parliament and called a general election for 23 Oct. 2004 and was re-elected unopposed. The reform-minded parliament subsequently cut government spending and tightened regulations in Nauru's offshore banking industry. Longer-term goals included rehabilitating the devastated environment and developing alternative sources of revenue.

In May 2005 his administration agreed to restore diplomatic ties with Taiwan in a move which angered the People's Republic of China. In Nov.

2007 Scotty narrowly survived a vote of no confidence, raised against him for his continued support of the foreign minister, David Adeang, who had been accused of misconduct. A second confidence motion was brought a month later which Scotty failed to defeat and he was subsequently ousted.

Later Life

In Nov. 2010 Scotty was elected Speaker of Parliament for the second time. He resigned in April 2013 amid increasing parliamentary deadlock only to be elected for a third time following elections in June of that year. He lost his parliamentary seat in the elections of July 2016.

Sellal, Abdelmalek (Algeria)

Introduction

Abdelmalek Sellal became prime minister in Sept. 2012. He was appointed by President Abdelaziz Bouteflika following the resignation of Ahmed Ouyahia.

Early Life

Sellal was born in Aug. 1948 in Constantine, Algeria. He finished his secondary education at the National College of Administration and became an adviser to the prefect of Guelma province. He then took a post at the ministry of education and subsequently served as prefect of several Algerian provinces.

Sellal was Algeria's ambassador to Hungary when, in 1998, he was named minister of the interior. In 1999 he was moved to the ministry of youth and sports, then to the ministry of public works in 2001, the ministry of transport in 2002 and the ministry of water in 2004 where he stayed until 2012.

Sellal guided Bouteflika's presidential re-election campaigns in 2004 and 2009. Following the resignation of Prime Minister Ahmed Ouyahia in 2012 after 4 years in office, Bouteflika appointed Sellal to the premiership.

Career Peak

Seen as a technocrat, Sellal does not belong to any political party. On taking office in 2012 he maintained much of his predecessor's cabinet and pledged to continue the reform programme laid out by President Bouteflika. In March 2014 Sellal resigned from the premiership in order to run Bouteflika's campaign for re-election. He was replaced by the then energy and mines minister, Youcef Yousfi, who became acting prime minister. However, Sellal returned to the post after Bouteflika was successfully elected to a fourth term as president in April 2014. As a long-standing presidential stalwart, as expected Sellal kept his prime ministerial position in a major cabinet reshuffle carried out by Bouteflika in May 2015. Following the victory of the National Liberation Front in the parliamentary election of May 2017, Abdelmadjdjid Tebboune took office as prime minister on 25 May.

Senghor, Léopold Sédar (Senegal)

Introduction

A poet and writer, Léopold Sédar Senghor was the first president of independent Senegal from 1960–80. He was a leading advocate of the concept of negritude, which acknowledged and celebrated the contributions, achievements and aspirations of black Africa. Conscious of the risk of creating a splintered and weak Africa in the post-colonial era, he favoured African federalism and fought for continuing ties with France after Senegalese independence. Espousing broadly socialist principals adapted for African culture, he resigned mid-way through his fifth term in office as a widely respected figure on the international stage.

Early Life

Senghor was born on 9 Oct. 1906 in Joal, a coastal town, the son of a successful trader. His father was from the Serer tribe. After schooling in Senegal, Senghor continued his studies in Paris. He was a French teacher in France in the years leading up to World War II. His association with the Martinican poet Aimé Césaire led to the development of their *negritude* philosophy.

Having obtained French nationality Senghor joined the French army in 1939, was captured in 1940 and spent 2 years in German concentration camps. These experiences heavily influenced his first collection of poems (*Chants d'ombre/Songs of Shadows*), published in 1945.

In the same year he was elected to the French constituent assembly and in 1946 became one of Senegal's two deputies at the French national assembly. Originally a member of the Parti Socialiste Français (French Socialist Party), in 1948 he left to found the Bloc Démocratique Sénégalais (Senegalese Democratic Bloc/BDS) and was also leader of the Indépendants d'Outremer faction (Independents from Overseas) in the French assembly. The BDS achieved election success in Senegal in 1951 and 1952, while Senghor served in the governments of Edgar Faure and De Gaulle.

When France granted several African nations self-rule during the mid-1950s, Senghor helped to promote African federalism. This led to the creation of the Mali Federation in 1959, which included the modern states of Senegal, Mali, Benin and Burkina Faso until its collapse the following year. In 1960 Senghor was appointed president of independent Senegal.

Career Peak

As President, Senghor looked to implement democratic socialist principals adapted to the African experience. He introduced rural reform, established multi-party politics and fought corruption. He survived an attempted coup by his former ally Mamadou Dia in 1962.

In foreign policy he favoured a continuing relationship with France and closer ties with other independent African nations. Dakar hosted the World Festival of Negro Arts in 1966. He made primary education compulsory and free. Though French was the official medium in schools, he incorporated the ethnic languages of Wolof, Sérère, Diola, Peul, Mandingue and Sarakholé into the curriculum.

Senghor was the Christian leader of a largely Muslim nation and though Senegal did not suffer the same intertribal conflict as many of its neighbours, racial tensions were a growing problem throughout the 1970s. He resigned in Dec. 1980, having been re-elected for a fifth term, and was succeeded by his prime minister Abdou Diouf.

Later Life

Senghor was first married in 1948, to Ginette Eboué with whom he had two children. After they divorced, he married Collette Hubert, with whom he spent his retirement. He became a member of the L'Académie Française (The French Academy) in 1983, the first black man to do so. He died on 20 Dec. 2001.

Sevele, Fred (Tonga)

Introduction

Fred Sevele was appointed Tonga's first 'citizen' prime minister in March 2006 by King Taufa'ahau Tupou IV. With a background in business, Sevele aimed to boost the economy by developing the fishing and tourism sectors. Although an advocate of greater democracy, his early tenure was marked by civil disorder and the imposition of a state of emergency. His second term began in 2008 with plans to create a parliament with elected members and a cabinet drawn from the Legislative Assembly.

Early Life

Feleti 'Fred' Vaka'uta Sevele was born in 1945 in the Kingdom of Tonga and educated at Apifo'ou College, Tonga, followed by St John's College on Ovalau, Fiji Islands and the Marist Brothers High School on Suva, Fiji Islands. He later studied economic geography at the University of Canterbury,

New Zealand, receiving his PhD in 1972. He went on to establish numerous businesses in Tonga, becoming one of the archipelago's most successful entrepreneurs. By the late 1990s he was a prominent supporter of the pro-democracy movement.

In March 1999 Sevele was elected as one of nine people's representatives to the Legislative Assembly, winning re-election in 2002 and 2005. In March 2005 King Taufa'ahau Tupou IV named Sevele as minister of labour, commerce and industries, in line with new guidelines requiring four cabinet ministers to be appointed from the elected members. Sevele won plaudits for negotiating Tonga's entry into the World Trade Organization.

When the prime minister, HRH Prince 'Ulukalala Lavaka Ata, unexpectedly resigned on 11 Feb. 2006 after 6 years in the post, the king appointed Sevele as acting prime minister. No official reason was given for 'Ulukalala's departure but it followed 3 years of political upheaval that saw the collapse of Royal Tongan Airlines, a strike by civil servants and budgetary shortfalls. On 30 March 2006 the king announced that Sevele had been appointed Tonga's first non-aristocratic prime minister.

Career Peak

Sevele stated his determination to make better use of local resources and rely less on overseas aid and assistance programmes. He was also expected to push for greater democracy, particularly in the wake of the death in Sept. 2006 of King Taufa'ahau Tupou IV and the succession of his eldest son as King Tupou V. However, impatience at the pace of reform led in Nov. 2006 to rioting in the capital, resulting in eight deaths, extensive commercial damage and the declaration of a state of emergency. In mid-2007 a tripartite committee of nobles, ministers and people's representatives was established to find a consensus on political reform and to make recommendations to parliament.

In polling for the nine elected seats in the 33-member Legislative Assembly in April 2008, pro-democracy candidates were returned in the majority of them, indicating growing popular support for faster political reform. The government proposed increasing the number of directly elected parliamentarians from 2010 and diluting the power of the monarchy, recommendations upheld by a constitutional review committee in Nov. 2009. In 2010 Sevele decided not to seek re-election and stood down following the Nov. elections. He was succeeded by Lord Tu'ivakano.

Sezer, Ahmet Necdet (Turkey)

Introduction

In April 2000 the Turkish Grand National Assembly rejected a constitutional amendment allowing Süleyman Demirel a second term of office as president. Sezer, at the time the president of the Constitutional Court, was sworn in as the tenth president of the republic on 16 May 2000. A staunch secularist and supporter of freedom of expression, he was the first president in modern Turkish history to have been neither an active politician nor a military commander. Sezer left office in Aug. 2007 when Abdullah Gül was eventually appointed to succeed him.

Early Life

Ahmet Necdet Sezer was born in Afyon on 13 Sept. 1941. He attended Afyon High School and read law at the University of Ankara. After completion of military service he returned to his legal career and became a supervisory judge at the court of appeals in Ankara. In 1978 he received a master's degree in civil law. Five years later he was elected to the High Court. His political influence increased in 1988 when President Kenan Evren appointed him to the Constitutional Court. Sezer became Chief Justice of the Constitutional Court in Jan. 1998. He won the presidential election after a third ballot in May 2000.

Career Peak

Despite winning Bülent Ecevit's backing for the presidency, Sezer came into conflict with the prime minister after he vetoed two bills, one allowing for the dismissal of public employees deemed to have been subversive and the second privatizing several state-owned banks. His first official foreign engagement came on 23 June 2000 when he made a controversial visit to

the Turkish Republic of Northern Cyprus (recognized only by Turkey), underlining Turkey's support for the Turkish Cypriots. During his first few months in office, Sezer also made clear his commitment to maintaining the country's secular status and ensuring Turkish entry to the EU. However, the failure in March 2003 of the leaders of the Greek and Turkish sectors of Cyprus to agree on UN proposals for the island's reunification put Turkey's own ambitions to join the EU at risk, since it would not be able to recognize one of the member states (Greek Cyprus).

Turkey underwent a constitutional crisis in 2002 when the Justice and Development Party (AKP) won the Nov. general elections but its leader, Recep Tayyip Erdoğan, was ineligible for a parliamentary seat (and therefore the premiership) because of a conviction received under a defunct religious law. The AKP's deputy leader, Abdullah Gül, was named prime minister. In Dec. 2002, after pressure to call a referendum which he was likely to lose, Sezer agreed to constitutional changes which would allow Erdoğan to stand for a parliamentary seat and so become eligible for the premiership. Erdoğan returned to parliament in a by-election in March 2003 and was subsequently appointed prime minister.

In March 2003 Turkey authorized limited assistance to the USA during the war with Iraq and was rewarded with substantial aid. However, Turkey's deployment of troops in Kurdish-held northern Iraq to block any attempts to establish a Kurdish separatist state caused international unease. In April 2005 Sezer made an official visit to Syria, despite objections from the US government regarding the presence of Syrian troops in Lebanon. He stated that the purpose of the visit was to strengthen bilateral ties and contribute to peace and stability in the region.

In mid-2005 Sezer came into conflict with parliament by blocking amendments to a new penal code which eased restrictions on Islamic teaching. His presidential veto was subsequently overturned. In May 2006 he denounced the assassination of a prominent judge by an Islamist gunman as an attack on the secular republic.

Sezer's term of office was scheduled to expire in May 2007. Abdullah Gül, the foreign minister, was proposed as his presidential successor in April 2007. However, Gül was unable to gain the required number of votes in parliament and his candidacy was opposed by the army who saw his Muslim background as a threat to the country's secular status. Sezer's term was extended until after parliamentary elections held in July 2007. Gül was eventually elected and sworn in on 28 Aug.

Shamir, Yitzhak (Israel)

Introduction

Yitzhak Shamir was twice prime minister, from 1983–84 and 1986–92, so becoming Israel's second longest serving prime minister after David Ben-Gurion.

Early Life

Yitzhak Shamir was born Icchak Jazernicki on 22 Oct. 1915 in Ruzhany, Poland, and was educated in a Hebrew secondary school in Białystok. A Zionist, he emigrated to Palestine in 1935, while members of his family who remained in Poland were killed in the Holocaust.

He took the Hebrew name 'shamir' after emigrating and joined the Zionist militia Lehi (also known as the Stern Gang), eventually becoming one of its leaders. He was implicated in plots to assassinate both Lord Moyne, the British minister for Middle East affairs, and the UN negotiator, Count Folke Bernadotte. Shamir twice escaped after being captured by the authorities, the second time avoiding internment in Eritrea and taking refuge in France. He returned to the newly independent Israel in 1948, working for Mossad (the secret service) between 1955 and 1965.

In 1970 he joined the Herut Party (which later became Likud) and won a seat in the Knesset in 1973, rising rapidly through the party ranks to become chairman of the Herut executive. In 1977, after Likud had won power, Shamir was appointed speaker of the Knesset and became foreign minister in 1980. After Menachem Begin's sudden retirement in Oct. 1983, he succeeded him as prime minister.

Career Peak

Shamir held the post until Sept. 1984 and then entered into a rotation agreement that saw Avoda's leader, Shimon Peres, take office for the first half of a new 4-year term after an inconclusive election. Shamir took over prime minister in 1986 and continued in the role after winning the election of 1988.

An advocate of assertive Zionism, Shamir oversaw expansive settlement in the West Bank and Gaza Strip. The Jewish population in the Occupied Territories increased by nearly 30% while he was in office. He deployed thousands of troops to quell the Palestinian *intifada* (uprising) that began in Dec. 1987, though violence dragged on until 1991 against a backdrop of mounting global concern.

In 1991 Shamir secured the good will of Washington when he did not retaliate against Iraq after Saddam Hussein fired missiles on Tel Aviv. Meanwhile, Shamir campaigned in favour of *aliya* (immigration of Jews to Israel), particularly from former Soviet territories. 350,000 immigrants arrived during 1990–91 alone, with Operation Solomon airlifting 14,000 Ethiopian Jews overnight following a change of regime in Ethiopia.

Later Life

After Likud lost the 1992 election to Yitzhak Rabin's Labour, Shamir resigned the party leadership. However, he remained in the Knesset until 1996, becoming a vocal critic of his Likud successor, Binyamin Netanyahu. He died on 30 June 2012.

Sharif Sheikh Ahmed (Somalia)

Introduction

In Jan. 2009 Sheikh Sharif Sheikh Ahmed was elected president of Somalia at the head of a Transitional Federal Government (TFG).

Early Life

Ahmed was born in 1964 in the Mahaday district, northeast of Mogadishu. He comes from a section of the Abgaal clan of Hawiye, which dominates central-southern Somalia. He studied at a school attached to the local mosque before attending the Egyptian-run Sheikh Sufi Institute, associated with Cairo's Al Azhar University, in Mogadishu. In the 1990s Ahmed studied in Sudan and at the Open University in Libya, graduating in Islamic Sharia and Law in 1998 before returning to Somalia.

He became head of an Islamic court in Jowhar in 2002 but fled to Mogadishu in 2003 after forces led by the warlord Mohammed Dheere (a future mayor of Jowhar and a TFG ally) attacked the region. In Mogadishu Ahmed taught at Jubba Secondary School and became a central organizer of the Islamic Courts Union (ICU). In mid-2006 the ICU took control of the capital and Ahmed emerged as ICU chairman, working alongside Hassan Dahir Aweys. For 6 months the ICU controlled large swathes of southern and central Somalia, establishing varying degrees of Sharia law, reopening Mogadishu's sea- and airports and quelling piracy along the coast. In Dec. 2006, backed by Ethiopian forces, the TFG expelled the ICU and Ahmed fled to Kenya.

In Eritrea in 2007, Ahmed, Aweys and anti-TFG elements formed the Alliance for the Re-Liberation of Somalia (ARS). However, in 2008 Ahmed entered UN-brokered talks with the TFG in Djibouti and split from ARS hardliners including Aweys. Ahmed's supporters joined with the TFG to form a parliament that elected him president of Somalia in Jan. 2009.

Career Peak

Throughout Ahmed's term in office Somalia has remained in turmoil from civil war, with thousands of civilians fleeing the capital and several million dependent on food aid. In June 2009 he declared a state of emergency as the Islamist insurgency intensified. In Sept. that year the Shahab Islamist group, controlling most of the south of the country, proclaimed its allegiance to Osama bin Laden, the leader of al-Qaeda. Shahab rebel action against the TFG continued in 2010, but in 2011 government and African Union forces made significant military gains and Shabab troops pulled out of their positions

in Mogadishu in Aug. Shabab militants nevertheless continued to attack TFG targets in Somalia and also made incursions into Kenya to abduct foreign nationals. In response, Kenya launched a cross-border military offensive against the Shabab in Oct. 2011.

Another major problem for the TFG was the increasing incidence and range of piracy in the seas off Somalia. Many foreign navies were deployed to patrol the area to deter Somali pirates but recorded hijackings continued to rise.

In Oct. 2010 Ahmed appointed Mohamed Abdulahi Mohamed as prime minister in place of Omar Abdirashid Ali Sharmarke. Mohamed was in turn replaced by Abdiweli Mohamed Ali in June 2011 as a condition of the Kampala Accord signed between Ahmed and the speaker of the transitional parliament to end months of political infighting between them. The Accord extended their respective terms in office for a further year, deferring elections for a state president and parliamentary speaker until Aug. 2012.

Meanwhile, in mid-2011 the United Nations formally declared a famine across five areas of Somalia.

Ahmed was beaten in the Sept. 2012 presidential run-off by Hassan Sheikh Mohamud by 190 votes to 70 in parliament. He conceded defeat during a live broadcast, stating that he was 'satisfied' with his time in power and glad to be witnessing the first fair election in Mogadishu in 42 years.

Sharif, Nawaz (Pakistan)

Introduction

Nawaz Sharif became prime minister in June 2013. A wealthy industrialist, he has been a key political figure in the country for over 30 years. Head of the Pakistan Muslim League (PML-N), he was previously prime minister from 1990–93 and 1997–99.

Early Life

Sharif was born on 25 Dec. 1949 in Lahore, Punjab, where his father Muhammad Sharif had founded the Ittefaq Group/Sharif Group conglomerate. Sharif studied at the Government University College (Lahore) before graduating from Punjab University Law College. He then joined the Ittefaq Group.

He entered provincial politics in the 1970s and joined the PML around the time that the Ittefaq steel business was nationalized by Zulfiqar Ali Bhutto. In 1981, during the rule of Gen. Zia ul-Haq who returned the steel business to the family, Sharif joined the Punjab Advisory Council, serving as finance minister and, from 1985, chief minister. As leader of the PML, the largest party in the Islamic Democratic Alliance, he unsuccessfully ran against Benazir Bhutto in the 1988 general election.

In 1990 Bhutto was dismissed by President Ghulam Ishaq Khan for alleged corruption. Sharif was subsequently elected prime minister and pursued a privatization programme. He also drew international attention to the Kashmir conflict, announced a nuclear development programme and introduced a number of Islamic laws.

In 1993 Ishaq Khan dismissed Sharif and Bhutto returned, only to be dismissed again in 1996.

Sharif was re-elected premier in a landslide victory. During his second tenure he brought in constitutional amendments curbing the president's power. After he attempted to block the appointment of five Supreme Court judges, a constitutional crisis ensued that ended in the resignation of the president, Farooq Leghari, and the suspension of the Chief Justice.

In 1998 Sharif ordered nuclear tests that prompted sanctions from the West, pushing the country close to bankruptcy. In 1999 he signed the Lahore Declaration with India in a bid to avert a nuclear arms race. His second premiership ended in a bloodless military coup led by Gen. Pervez Musharraf. Sharif was subsequently convicted of hijacking, terrorism and corruption. Facing the death sentence, he agreed to go into exile for 10 years and retreat from political life after the Saudi Arabian authorities helped negotiate a deal.

In 2007 Sharif returned to Pakistan and a year later contested the 2008 elections, during which Benazir Bhutto was assassinated. The Pakistan People's Party, led by Bhutto's widower Asif Ali Zardari, triumphed at the polls, and Zardari and Sharif together impeached Musharraf in Aug. 2008. Sharif successfully reinstated several judges and the courts overturned his previous convictions. He led the PML-N to victory at the 2013 general election.

Career Peak

Sharif campaigned on pledges to stem electricity shortages, improve infrastructure, rebuild the economy, nurture better relations with India and fight corruption. Other major challenges have included attempting to rein in the stifling political influence of the Pakistani military and countering insurgent Taliban operations.

In Sept. 2013 Sharif accepted a US$6.7 bn. IMF loan in return for economic reforms, including further privatization. In early 2014 he launched several power generation projects. Also in early 2014 peace talks were initiated with the Taliban despite ongoing violence. However, these talks collapsed in June following a terrorist assault on Karachi international airport, after which the army launched a new offensive in the tribal region of North Waziristan. Retaliatory action by the Taliban included an attack on a military-run school in Peshawar in Dec. 2014 that killed 145 people, mainly children, and an assault on a Shia mosque in Shikarpur in Jan. 2015 claiming over 60 lives. More attacks in 2016, particularly in Peshawar, Lahore and Quetta that resulted in scores of deaths, underlined Pakistan's continued vulnerability to Islamist extremism.

Relations with India remained frigid in the wake of the election as prime minister in May 2014 of Narendra Modi, a Hindu nationalist, and sporadic military clashes have continued over the disputed state of Kashmir.

In July 2017 the Supreme Court of Pakistan disqualified Sharif from public office over corruption allegations. Before leaving office he nominated Shahid Abbasi, also of the PML-N, as interim prime minister. On 1 Aug. Abbasi was confirmed by lawmakers with 221 of 339 votes.

Sharon, Ariel (Israel)

Introduction

Former soldier, conservative politician and prominent 'hawk' in the Likud Party until Nov. 2005, Ariel Sharon was elected prime minister on 6 Feb. 2001 as Israeli voters moved sharply to the right under the impact of the renewed Palestinian uprising. Retaining power in the elections of 2003, he continued to take an uncompromising line towards Israeli security. However, at the same time he pursued his plan for Israeli disengagement from the Gaza Strip and some of the West Bank, completed in Sept. 2005, and sought to negotiate with the more moderate mainstream Palestinian leadership following the death of Yasser Arafat in Nov. 2004. In Nov. 2005, facing continuing discontent from within Likud over his policies towards the occupied territories and with his government fractured by the new Labour leader's refusal to continue in the coalition, Sharon formed a new centrist party called Kadima to fight early elections scheduled for March 2006. However, after suffering a stroke in Jan. 2006 he was declared temporarily unable to rule. Deputy prime minister Ehud Olmert was confirmed as acting prime minister on 4 Jan. 2006.

Early Life

Sharon was born in 1928 to Russian parents who emigrated to Palestine at the end of the First World War. As a young man he joined the Jewish Haganah underground defence organization and fought in the 1948–49 war following the creation of the Jewish state. Pursuing a military career, he rose to the rank of brigadier-general before retiring from military service after the 1973 Yom Kippur war.

Career Peak

Sharon served as a security adviser to Prime Minister Rabin before joining Menachem Begin's Likud government which came to power in 1977. From 1977–81 he was minister of agriculture. In June 1982, as minister of defence, he masterminded Israel's invasion of Lebanon and advance to Beirut, a strike which ended in the expulsion of Yasser Arafat's Palestine Liberation Organisation (PLO). In Sept. 1982 about 2,000 Palestinians in the refugee camps of Chatilla and Sabra near Beirut were massacred by Lebanese Christian Phalangist, an atrocity for which Sharon was held indirectly responsible by

an Israeli investigating commission. He relinquished the defence ministry in Feb. 1983 but remained in Begin's cabinet as a minister without portfolio.

From 1984–90 he was minister of trade and industry, and then minister of housing from 1990–92 promoting Jewish settlement building in the occupied territories. In the 1996–99 Likud government he served as minister of national infrastructure and later as minister of foreign affairs. Sharon succeeded Binyamin Netanyahu as Likud leader after the party's electoral defeat in May 1999. In Sept. 2000 he visited Temple Mount in East Jerusalem in a provocative demonstration of Israeli sovereignty over Muslim holy sites. This action triggered a renewed Palestinian uprising, in turn reigniting deep-seated Israeli fears over security. In Feb. 2001, campaigning against further territorial or political concessions and promising reprisals against Palestinian disorder, Sharon became prime minister in a landslide electoral victory.

His early premiership saw no end to the cycle of violence and no progress in the peace process. Tensions between Israelis and Palestinians increased as suicide bomb attacks on Israeli cities were countered with Israeli military reprisals against Palestinian targets. Sharon's reluctance to negotiate with Yasser Arafat, the Palestinian leader, was reinforced by President Bush's outline for a settlement in June 2002, which advocated a change of Palestinian leadership. In Jan. 2003 Sharon placed a travel ban on Palestinian officials, effectively barring them from attending peace talks in the UK. The UN, EU, Jordan, Egypt, Russia and Saudi Arabia were all due to attend the talks. Sharon had previously outlined a plan to grant Palestine around 40% of the West Bank, albeit demilitarized with Israeli control over all points of entry and exit and over airspace. Negotiations would not begin until Palestinian violence ended and Arafat was removed from power. The Palestinian authorities rejected the proposals.

In Oct. 2002 the government's main coalition partner, the Labour Party, resigned following disputes over budget proposals. Sharon's attempts to form a new coalition with far right nationalist parties failed, and despite surviving a confidence vote on 4 Nov., he called early elections for Jan. 2003. In addition to a leadership challenge by Netanyahu, Sharon's standing was affected by accusations of financial impropriety involving his 1999 campaign funds. However, campaigning on security and defence, Likud increased its Knesset representation from 19 to 37 seats, while the opposition Labour Party fell from 23 to 19. With Labour's leader Amram Mitzna having refused to join a government, Sharon struggled to form a broad-based coalition administration. However, in Feb. 2003 he secured the support of the Shinui Party and the National Religious Party to provide him with a parliamentary majority.

In April 2003 the 'Roadmap to Peace'. produced by the UN, EU, USA and Russia, was published. The document called for an immediate ceasefire, an end to the Israeli occupation of Palestinian towns, a clampdown on Palestinian militants and the dismantling of Israeli settlements built since 2001. It set out proposals for the establishment of an independent, democratic Palestinian state as early as 2005. The following month the Israeli cabinet accepted the 'road map' (albeit with 14 'reservations') Sharon sparked criticism from sections of Likud when he said that the Israeli 'occupation' of the Palestinian-administered territories was 'the worst thing for Israel, for the Palestinians and the Israeli economy'. It represented a rare acknowledgement that the Israeli presence in the West Bank and Gaza Strip was an occupation.

In July 2003, following a ceasefire with three main Palestinian militant groups (Hamas, Islamic Jihad and Fatah), Sharon's government agreed to the release of 540 Palestinians. Israeli checkpoints in Ramallah and Hebron were dismantled and 8,000 workers from the Gaza Strip, Bethlehem and Tulkarem were admitted into Israel. However, the following month the USA threatened to withdraw loan guarantees worth US$10 bn. in response to Sharon's refusal to stop building a 600 km-long 'security fence' around the West Bank, which he claimed was essential to prevent Palestinian suicide attacks. The approval of 600 more settlement homes in the West Bank, announced in Oct. 2003, further antagonized the Palestinian leadership and the USA and was criticized by the liberal Israeli media.

Sharon and his government faced the possibility of UN censure after authorizing an attack on 'terrorist camps' in Syria in Oct. 2003 in retaliation for a suicide bombing in Haifa. But Syria's attempts to draw up a UN Security Council resolution condemning the attack failed. The USA, though opposed to Israel's actions, refused to support Syria, which it has threatened with sanctions. Syria responded by threatening an offensive against Israel (the two states are still officially at war) if its territory is again attacked.

Against the background of continuing violence, Sharon announced his plan in Feb. 2004 for an Israeli withdrawal from the Gaza Strip (where approximately 8,500 Jews were settled) and northern areas of the West Bank. President Bush gave his support in April to the Israeli disengagement plan, but in May 2004 59.5% of the ruling Likud party voted against Sharon's proposals. Despite continuing opposition from within his Likud party and his government, Sharon won the approval of the Knesset in Oct. 2004 for disengagement, and in Dec. persuaded Likud to endorse his formation of a new coalition including the Labour Party. Yasser Arafat's death in Nov. 2004 meanwhile resulted in the accession to power of a more moderate mainstream Palestinian leadership under Mahmoud Abbas, who was elected president of the Palestinian Authority in Jan. 2005. Guarded optimism about a revival of the peace process followed a declaration in Feb. by Sharon and Abbas of a cessation of hostilities.

From late June 2005 clashes between Jewish settlers and Israeli security forces erupted ahead of the Gaza/West Bank evacuation, and the fragile ceasefire with the Palestinians was undermined by a suicide bombing in the Israeli town of Netanya in July. Nevertheless, the disengagement was completed in Sept., prompting the resignation from Sharon's government of Binyamin Netanyahu who vowed to challenge the prime minister for the Likud leadership. There was also a resurgence of fighting from Sept. between Palestinian militants and Israeli forces in the occupied territories.

A new Labour leader, Amir Peretz, was elected in early Nov. and declared his intention to withdraw the party from Sharon's coalition government, triggering an early election to be held in March 2006. Later in Nov., in a major shift in Israel's political landscape, Sharon quit the Likud party to contest the elections at the head of a new centrist party called Kadima (meaning Forward).

On 4 Jan. 2006 Sharon suffered a massive haemorrhagic stroke and fell into a coma. He remained unconscious for the next 8 years. Despite his absence, Kadima, led by acting prime minister Ehud Olmert, won the largest number of seats in the Knesset at elections held on 28 March 2006. He died at the age of 85 on 11 Jan. 2014.

Shevardnadze, Eduard (Georgia)

Introduction

Eduard Amvrosievich Shevardnadze became Georgia's head of state in 1992 and was elected president in 1995 and 2000. Soviet foreign minister during the Gorbachev era, his tenure as Georgian leader was marked by hostilities in the breakaway province of Abkhazia.

Early Life

Shevardnadze was born on 25 Jan. 1928 in Mamati, a village in the Lanchkuti region of Georgia. He joined the Soviet Communist Party in 1946 and was prominent in the Communist Youth League, serving as first secretary of the Georgian branch between 1957 and 1961. He graduated in history from the Kutaisi Pedagogical Institute in 1959 and had a successful career in the civilian police, becoming chief of police in 1965.

He left the post in 1972 when he was appointed first secretary of the Georgian Communists. From 1976 he sat on the central committee of the Soviet Communist party, becoming a full member of the Politburo and Soviet foreign minister in 1985. Alongside former Russian president Mikhail Gorbachev he gained Western trust and an international profile. He played prominent roles in the Soviet withdrawal from Afghanistan and arms negotiations with the US and did not stand in the way of the dismantling of East European communism. Domestically, he believed in Gorbachev's programmes of reform and when he sensed a slowdown in the pace of change in late 1990, he resigned his post and his party membership.

In 1991 he returned to lead the Soviet foreign ministry, having distanced himself from Gorbachev during the attempted hard-line Moscow coup earlier in the year. He sought to preserve the Soviet Union as a collection of sovereign states, but as its end became inevitable he turned his attention to Georgia. Along with other reformers, he established the Democratic Reform Movement. With President Zviad Gamsakhurdia ousted in 1992, Shevardnadze, chairman of the state council, was elected parliamentary speaker and became the effective head of state in Oct. 1992.

Career Peak

Shevardnadze's international standing won him recognition from Western leaders and Georgia became a member of the Organization for Security and Co-operation in Europe (OSCE), the IMF and the UN. Shevardnadze was set on Georgia joining NATO and eventually the European Union. In compliance with OSCE demands, he proposed the abolition of the death penalty, passed by parliament in 1997.

Secessionist movements dominated Shevardnadze's leadership. South Ossetia (Tskhinvali), which refused to acknowledge the authority of Tbilisi, agreed in June 1992 to a ceasefire and joint peacekeeping. Shevardnadze deplored the actions of his predecessor, stating that the abolition of Ossetian autonomy was a serious mistake. Calls for secession in the province of Abkhazia developed into civil war. In 1993 Russian-backed troops were sent in to the breakaway territory, obliging Georgia to join the Commonwealth of Independent States. Shevardnadze conceded a ceasefire in July 1993, despite domestic opposition. However, the ceasefire was broken in Sept. by Abkhaz forces (probably supported by the Russian military), who expelled the over two thirds of the population, comprising Georgians, Armenians, Russians and Greeks. Shevardnadze left the constitutional future of South Ossetia, Abkhazia and Adjara unspecified in Georgia's 1995 constitution. 1997 negotiations with the Ossetian leader, Lyudvig Chibirov, failed to break the stalemate. In March 2001 Georgia and Abkhazia signed a peace accord but fighting erupted again in Oct. 2001.

In 1993 Gamsakhurdia was killed attempting to oust Shevardnadze, against whom assassination attempts were made in Aug. 1995 and Feb. 1998. He was elected president of Georgia in Nov. 1995 and re-elected in the presidential elections of April 2000, campaigning on an anti-corruption ticket. In April 2000 Shevardnadze attempted to foster reconciliation by granting an amnesty to over 200 prisoners, including supporters of Gamsakhurdia.

Shevardnadze's relationship with the Russian leadership was complicated by his role in the dismantling of the Soviet Union. He repeatedly accused Russia of destabilizing the Caucasus region by encouraging the self-determination of minority groups. In Feb. 1999 he threatened to withdraw from the Commonwealth of Independent States (CIS) security pact. Refusing to patrol the Pankissi Gorge area, close to the border with Chechnya, the Russians accused him of harbouring rebel fighters. Russian President Vladimir Putin threatened military action in Sept. 2002 if Georgia refused to act against Chechen rebels. A month later the two leaders met in Moldova and agreed to joint patrols on the shared border.

Adjara, the autonomous republic in Georgia's southwest, was a frequent headache for Shevardnadze, especially the Adjaran leader, Aslan Abashidze, who led the main opposition party, the Union for Georgian Revival. Adjara's constitutional reform in July 2001, without the consultation of Tbilisi, sparked fears of secessionist intentions. Later that year Abashidze further provoked the central government by organizing local elections in Adjara. Tbilisi was forced to follow suit to prevent the fragmentation of the electoral system.

In Nov. 2001 popular protests broke out against Shevardnadze over a raid by security forces on the Rustavi-2 television station, renowned for its criticism of his regime. Looking for allies, Shevardnadze visited Abashidze, previously his main opponent, in the Adjaran capital, Batumi. A deal was struck and Abashidze drummed up support for the president abroad, most notably from Russia. Nevertheless, Shevardnadze subsequently sacked his government and appointed a new cabinet. Nino Burdzhanadze, a former protégée of the president, was elected speaker of parliament—the second highest office in Georgia—demonstrating the increasing unity of the opposition. Shevardnadze's position was threatened after the rigged parliamentary elections of Nov. 2003. Peaceful demonstrations in Tbilisi, led by the opposition leader Mikhail Saakashvili, began on 4 Nov. Again Shevardnadze looked for support from Abashidze, known to despise Saakashvili and his associates. The president's choice of ally further alienated the opposition; Saakashvili accused him of striking a deal with Abashidze and Putin to protect his leadership with force. Protests continued daily until Shevardnadze's resignation on 23 Nov. Burdzhanadze, as speaker, became acting president and offered protection to the ousted president and his family.

Later Life

Following his departure from politics in 2003, Shevardnadze spent the remainder of his life in quiet retirement. Despite continuing to receive journalists and guests at his home in Tbilisi, he eventually withdrew from public life owing to failing health. He died on 7 July 2014.

Shinawatra, Thaksin (Thailand)

Introduction

Thaksin Shinawatra took office as prime minister of Thailand in Feb. 2001, having previously been a senior police officer and the founder of a telecommunications and computing corporation. In Feb. 2005, reflecting his wide popular appeal, he became the country's first democratically-elected premier to complete a 4-year term and win re-election. However, his popularity declined amid allegations of corruption and his troubled government was deposed by the military in Sept. 2006.

Early Life

Thaksin Shinawatra was born on 26 July 1949 in the northern Thai city of Chiang Mai. His family had a silk, bus and cinema business. He entered the Police Cadet School, from which he emerged as the top graduate in 1973. Winning a scholarship to continue his education in the USA, he gained a master's degree and PhD in criminal justice studies. Returning to Thailand, he continued his career in the police force.

In 1982 Thaksin began a computer dealership business with his wife, supplying the police with computer software. Five years later he resigned from the police to concentrate on his business interests. His Shinawatra Company eventually became the Shin Corporation, the leading player in telecommunications in Thailand, with a majority stake in the country's biggest mobile phone operator and its own communications satellites. In 1990 Thaksin became the wealthiest businessman in Thailand.

During the early 1990s Thaksin spoke of the need to clean up the political system. Although not an elected politician, he was nominated in Nov. 1994 to serve in the coalition government led by Chuan Leekpai of the Democrat Party (PP). Thaksin became foreign minister, resigning all his business positions to prove that he had 'clean hands'. Thaksin held office until Feb. 1995. In May 1995 he became leader of the Democrat Party, and in July returned to government as deputy prime minister, before resigning in Aug. 1996. From Aug.–Nov. 1997 he was deputy prime minister in another short-lived coalition. In 1998 Thaksin founded his own populist party, the Thai Rak Thai (TRT), which won 248 out of 500 seats in parliamentary elections in Jan. 2001, then the biggest margin of victory in Thai political history.

Career Peak

Thaksin took office as prime minister on 9 Feb. 2001, pledging to run the country as efficiently as his own business. However, he remained a controversial figure. He faced charges of falsely declaring his assets. His credibility was also shaken by his support for the claims of four men who announced they had discovered a mystery treasure trove of US bonds—the men were later charged with attempting to trade fake US bonds with a face value of US$24.7 bn. and Thaksin's government had to admit it had been taken in by the hoax.

Thaksin promised economic reform and clean government, introducing decentralized decision-making and encouraging Thai companies to use Thai, rather than multinational, agencies. He launched a programme of populist policies, including debt relief for farmers and subsidized healthcare schemes. However, economic recovery was slow and Thaksin was accused by his critics of being less than totally committed to the democratic process. A government crackdown on the Thai drugs trade which saw between 1,000 and 2,000 people killed in early 2003 prompted concern from the UN. Thaksin's hard-line policy in 2004 towards violence in the southern and largely Muslim provinces was also criticized by human rights groups. He nevertheless won support for his handling of the relief effort in the wake of the Indian Ocean tsunami in Dec. 2004, which devastated communities on the western coast of southern Thailand, and for his promise to eradicate poverty in the country if he was re-elected. His party was re-elected in Feb. 2005 with a landslide majority of 375 parliamentary seats, although it lost all seats in the three main southern provinces to the opposition.

However, allegations of corruption and abuse of power continued to grow. In Feb. 2006 anti-Thaksin street rallies began after it emerged that the Shinawatra family had sold its share of the Shin Corporation to Temasek Holdings, a Singaporean company. Protesters accused him of exploiting tax regulations and of selling an important national asset to foreign investors.

Following two impeachment attempts, Thaksin called a snap election for 2 April 2006. The main opposition parties boycotted the polls and a large number of voters registered a 'no vote'. When Thaksin appeared on television to announce a TRT victory, protests escalated.

On 4 April 2006 Thaksin announced that he would step down as prime minister and called for national unity. He handed power over to his deputy, Chidchai Vanasatidya, but returned as premier in May following judicial nullification of the April election results. On 19 Sept. 2006, while Thaksin was on a visit to New York, the military overthrew his government in a bloodless coup and established a Council for Democratic Reform under the leadership of Sonthi Boonyaratkalin, promising an orderly return to civilian rule.

Later Life

Thaksin and his family took up residency in the United Kingdom in the aftermath of the coup, where he took over ownership of Manchester City Football Club. In 2007 Thailand's constitutional court banned Shinawatra from political office for 5 years when it was discovered that the TRT had violated electoral regulations. However, the election to power of Thaksin's close ally Samak Sundaravej in Jan. 2008 demonstrated that the former prime minister retains a considerable influence over Thai politics. In Sept. 2008 his brother-in-law, Somchai Wongsawat, became prime minister. The following month the high court in Bangkok sentenced Thaksin to 2 years imprisonment *in absentia* for a 2003 property deal involving his then wife prompting the British authorities to revoke his visa.

Thaksin's supporters formed the anti-government United Front for Democracy Against Dictatorship (UDD) following the 2006 coup. Known as 'red shirts' they have received financial support from the former prime minister and are responsible for instigating numerous attempts to topple the government. In April 2009 a state of emergency was declared owing to UDD protests against prime minister Abhisit Vejjajiva.

In Feb. 2010 Thaksin was stripped of US$1.4 bn. assets after he was found guilty on five accounts of corruption by the Thai Supreme Court sparking more red shirt protests. Peaceful demonstrations began in March but escalated into violence until they were eventually broken up in mid-May in a government crackdown. An arrest warrant was issued for Thaksin on terrorist charges on 25 May after he was accused of stoking anti-government violence.

Shinawatra, Yingluck (Thailand)

Introduction

Yingluck Shinawatra became prime minister in Aug. 2011 after leading the Pheu Thai Party (PTP) to a landslide victory. The younger sister of former prime minister Thaksin Shinawatra, she was the country's first female premier.

Early Life

Yingluck was born in June 1967 in the northern province of Chiang Mai, the youngest of nine children. Her father, Lert Shinawatra, was a businessman and MP while her mother, Yindi Ramingwong, was the daughter of Princess Jantip Na Chiang Mai. In 1988 Yingluck graduated in public administration from Chiang Mai University and in 1991 completed a master's degree at Kentucky State University in the USA.

She joined Shinawatra Directories Co. in 1993, one of a number of businesses run by her brother, Thaksin. In 1994 she worked with Rainbow Media before returning to the family business as general productions manager and, from 1997, vice-president.

In 1999 Thaksin's businesses were brought together under Shin Corporation and in 2002 Yingluck became CEO of the group's flagship company and Thailand's biggest mobile phone enterprise, AIS (Advance Info Service). She resigned in 2006 when Shin Corporation was sold to Temasek Holdings and took over as executive president of the family-owned property development company, SC Asset. She also served on the committee of the Thaicom Foundation, which provides educational opportunities for underprivileged children.

Thaksin was elected prime minister in 2001 but was ousted in a military coup in Sept. 2006. His party was dissolved by the constitutional court in 2007 and he has subsequently spent much of his time in exile. However, his followers established the Pheu Thai Party (PTP) in 2008 and convinced Yingluck, a political newcomer, to run in the July 2011 elections. The PTP won a majority in parliament and elected Yingluck prime minister the following month.

Career Peak

Expected to continue the economic liberalization pursued by her brother, Yingluck surrounded herself with a team of long-established political operators. Among her key challenges was addressing the country's long-standing political instability, which had resulted in violent social clashes in April 2009 and April–May 2010. She pledged to support an Independent Truth and Reconciliation Commission, although work on reconciliation legislation and a proposed amnesty provoked opposition through 2012 from urban protesters fearful that it would pave the way for Thaksin's return to power. She also promised to eliminate poverty by 2020, cut corporate tax and raise the minimum wage. In addition, she backed proposals for free public Wi-Fi access and a computer for every school child.

In Nov. 2012 she survived a parliamentary no-confidence motion in the wake of a major anti-government demonstration in Bangkok. Political discontent nevertheless continued through 2013, aggravated by a cut in rice subsidies. In response to further violent street protests at the end of the year, Yingluck called for early elections on 2 Feb. 2014. Opposition parties boycotted and disrupted the polling, resulting in incomplete and disputed results that were invalidated by the Constitutional Court in March.

In early May 2014 Yingluck appeared before Thailand's Constitutional Court facing corruption charges relating to abuses of power—specifically the illegal transfer of the chief of national security to another post in 2011. She was found guilty and was subsequently removed from power. The National Anti-Corruption Commission had also begun an investigation into allegations that millions of farmers had not been compensated under a government rice-pledging scheme. If found guilty, Yingluck could face a sentence of 10 years imprisonment. In Jan. 2015 she was banned from politics for 5 years by the ruling military junta. The following month she was formally charged by a state-appointed prosecutor over corruption surrounding the rice-pledging scheme.

Shipley, Jenny (New Zealand)

Introduction

Liberal in her social policy and right-wing in her economics, Shipley was New Zealand's first woman prime minister between Dec. 1997–Dec. 1999. Having organized a coup against National leader Jim Bolger, she unsuccessfully steered a minority government into the 1999 election. Famously pragmatic and often controversial, she has been compared to Margaret Thatcher.

Early Life

Born at Gore on South Island on 4 Feb. 1952, Shipley was educated in Blenheim and Christchurch, where she qualified as a primary school teacher in 1971. She worked in local schools until 1976, and later tutored at Lincoln College from 1983–87. Having joined the National Party in 1975, the same year as her marriage, Shipley's political interests developed through her experience as a young mother in rural Ashburton. She served on the executive of the local Plunkett centre for community nursing and child care (1979–84), joined educational and agricultural committees, and was president of the playcentre movement between 1980–82. From 1983 until 1987, Shipley served as a Malvern county councillor, while holding various local and regional positions within the National Party. In the 1987 election, she stood successfully for parliament, increasing National's majority in Ashburton from 500 to 5,000. Shipley continues to hold this constituency, now renamed Rakaia. Her first term, during which she was opposition spokesperson on social welfare, was uneventful; 3 years later, when Labour lost power, Shipley was swiftly appointed to Jim Bolger's new cabinet.

As social welfare minister between 1990–93, Shipley curbed state benefits, particularly for parents, in an attempt to reduce the NZ$50 bn. national debt. As Minister of Health from 1993–96, she provoked further controversy by setting up an internal market in the health service and increasing patient costs. At the same time, as Minister of Women's Affairs between 1990–96, she cut prescription charges for contraceptive pills. She campaigned against domestic violence. In the year following National's 1996 re-election, she exchanged her women's affairs portfolio for state services, transport, state-owned enterprises, Radio New Zealand and accident rehabilitation and compensation insurance. Returning to women's affairs in 1997, she aspired to the party leadership, considering Bolger's methods too cautious. While he attended the Commonwealth heads of government conference at Edinburgh, Scotland, in Nov. 1997, Shipley mustered party support to force his resignation.

Career Peak

As prime minister from 8 Dec. 1997–5 Dec. 1999, Shipley oversaw economic growth despite the 1998 Asian crisis and break up of the coalition government. In Jan. 1999 she attracted government ministers from 20 countries to a high profile 'ministerial on ice' in Antarctica to promote the continent's conservation. However, National's support slumped at the Nov. election, 3 days after Shipley had fired her immigration minister, Tuariki John Delamere. Delamere had illegally granted residency to Chinese investors. National was voted into opposition, with Shipley continuing to lead despite a minor heart attack in June 2000. Shipley was replaced as leader of the National Party, and consequently as leader of the opposition, by Bill English in Oct. 2001.

Shushkevich, Stanislau Stanislavavich (Belarus)

Introduction

The chairman of the Supreme Soviet between 1990–94, Stanislau Shushkevich was Belarus' first post-Soviet leader. At the head of a communist-dominated parliament mainly appointed before independence, Shushkevich's moves towards a free-market economy were rejected and he was forced to resign.

Early Life

Shushkevich was born on 15 Dec. 1934 in Minsk. The son of a poet killed in the Stalinist purges, he studied physics and embarked on an academic career, becoming the vice-chancellor of the Belarus State University. He joined the Communist party but only became actively involved in politics after the Chernobyl disaster of 1986.

Career Peak

In 1990 he was elected to the Supreme Soviet, becoming first deputy chairman. His nationalist tendencies, such as promoting the Belarusian language, gained him support. However, as one of the original signatories of the Commonwealth of Independent States, he garnered the opposition of the pro-Russian parliament by refusing to sign the security treaty which would have jeopardized Belarus' sovereignty and neutrality. He strongly disagreed with his prime minister Vyacheslau Kebich over policy. His wish to implement a free-market economy lacked support, and in Jan. 1994 an anti-corruption committee was set up, headed by Alyaksandr Lukashenka, which targeted Shushkevich. A vote of no confidence held in the same month was supported by 209 votes to 36, and he was forced to resign. Two months later, parliament held its first presidential elections in which Shushkevich stood against Kebich and Lukashenka. Taking just 10% of the vote, Shushkevich was succeeded by Lukashenka.

Later Life

Opposed to his successor and his increasingly autocratic tendencies, Shushkevich rejected Lukashenka's 1996 referendum which gave the leader increased power. Shushkevich was a key member of the Charter 97 pro-democracy movement and in 1998 became leader of the Belarusian Social Democratic Assembly. In 1999 he called on Russia to stop supporting the government of Lukashenka.

Sigurðardóttir, Jóhanna (Iceland)

Introduction

Jóhanna Sigurðardóttir became prime minister in Jan. 2009 following economic crisis and the collapse of Geir Haarde's administration. Heading a coalition including her centre-left Social Democratic Alliance (SF) along with the Left-Green Movement (VG), she became the country's first female leader. She announced in Sept. 2012 that she would retire from politics at the end of her term of office in 2013. After the election of April 2013 she remained prime minister until the two main opposition parties established a coalition.

Early Life

Sigurðardóttir was born on 4 Oct. 1942 in Reykjavík. After studying business at Iceland's Commercial College, she undertook a varied career that included flight attendant, trade union organizer and office administrator. In 1978 she entered *Alþingi* (Parliament) as the Social Democratic Party representative for the Reykjavík constituency. Subsequent boundary changes saw her become the MP for Reykjavík South and then for the North. In 1979 and from 1983–84 she was the speaker of the *Alþingi* and from 1987–94 she was minister of social affairs but resigned and made an unsuccessful run for her party's leadership.

She subsequently left the Social Democrats to form a new party, the National Movement, which won four seats at the 1995 general election. It merged 5 years later with her old party and two others to form the SF in a bid to end the dominance of the Independence Party (SSF). In 2007 the Alliance joined the Independence Party in a coalition headed by Haarde. Sigurðardóttir was reappointed to the social affairs portfolio. Working on behalf of the elderly, disabled and disadvantaged, she retained high personal approval ratings even in the depths of the national financial crisis in 2008.

When the country's independent banking system collapsed in late 2008, Haarde and his cabinet came under pressure to resign. On 23 Jan. 2009 Haarde called elections for early May but within 3 days the coalition had fallen apart. Talks between the SF and the SSF to form a new coalition failed and Alliance turned instead to the Left-Green Movement. With SF leader Ingibjorg Gisladóttir suffering ill health, Sigurðardóttir was proposed for prime minister. By the end of the month VG had agreed to form a coalition ahead of a general election scheduled for 25 April.

Career Peak

Sigurðardóttir's appointment received international media coverage as she became not only the first woman premier of Iceland but also the world's first openly gay head of government. She led her party to victory at the April 2009 general election, receiving 29.8% of the vote.

Her major challenge was to restore economic stability. In Feb. 2009 she engineered the removal of the central bank head, former prime minister Davíð Oddsson, who was widely blamed for the banking collapse. In July 2009 her government applied for EU membership, with negotiations beginning a year later despite an ongoing dispute with the UK and the Netherlands over compensation relating to the banking collapse. When a proposal to solve the issue was rejected by referendum in April 2011, the opposition Independence Party tabled a no-confidence motion against Sigurðardóttir and her government, which she narrowly survived. The dispute was subsequently referred to the European Free Trade Association Surveillance Authority.

Meanwhile, in April and May 2010 ash clouds from an Icelandic volcano led to unprecedented bans on flights and airport closures across Europe, causing disruption and heavy financial losses.

In the wake of the 2008 financial collapse, voters in a consultative referendum in Oct. 2012 supported a new draft constitution prepared by a council of 25 ordinary citizens. It advocated more direct democracy and greater control of the country's natural resources, such as fish and geothermal energy.

Sigurðardóttir was succeeded by Sigmundur Davíð Gunnlaugsson of the Progressive Party, who formed a coalition with the Independence Party 4 weeks after the election of April 2013.

Sihanouk, Norodom (Cambodia)

Introduction

HM Preah Bat Samdech Preah Norodom Sihanouk Varman was the king of Cambodia from 1941 to 1955 and 1993 to 2004. First coming to the throne in 1941, he won autonomy for his country within the French Union 8 years later. Full independence followed in 1953. Deposed in a US-backed coup in 1970, he returned to power in 1975 at the behest of the Khmer Rouge but was imprisoned a year later. He led a coalition government in exile during the 1980s and in 1993, following free elections, was re-crowned king for life.

Early Life

Norodom Sihanouk was born in Phnom Penh on 31 Oct. 1922 and educated in Saigon and Paris. He was crowned king, at the age of 19, on 26 April 1941 by the governor-general of French Indochina after the death of King Sisowath Monivong.

Career Peak

Later that year the Japanese invaded South-East Asia including all of French Indochina. The Japanese supported Sihanouk's claim to the throne and allowed French representatives to administrate Vietnam, Cambodia and Laos. Simultaneously they supported the Khmer Issarak (Free Khmer) partisans and anti-French Cambodian guerrillas. In 1945, recognising that they would lose control over Indochina, the Japanese ordered Sihanouk to declare Cambodia's independence from France.

After the war Sihanouk (1949) achieved autonomy within the French Union. The country's first elections were held in 1950 but Sihanouk dissolved the assembly and ruled by decree. The following year he became Prime Minister and appointed a cabinet consisting largely, of royal family nominees. He then campaigned for complete independence, which was granted in 1953.

During the Vietnam War Sihanouk attempted to follow a neutral course but broke off diplomatic relations with the USA after Cambodians were killed in United States and South Vietnamese incursions. In 1970 his policy of neutrality ended abruptly when he was deposed in a US supported coup led by Gen. Lon Nol. He established a government in exile in Beijing and appealed to Cambodian forces to drive out the Americans. One of the first groups to answer this appeal was the Khmer Rouge, a radical communist guerrilla movement. Sihanouk returned as Head of State when, in 1975, the Khmer Rouge, led by Pol Pot, won control of the country, but was placed under house arrest in 1976. In Jan. 1979, with the Khmer losing power, Sihanouk was released. After denouncing the recent Vietnamese invasion of Cambodia he moved swiftly to distance himself from the Khmer Rouge.

In 1982 Sihanouk became president of a coalition government-in-exile comprising his Neutralist party, the Khmer Rouge and the anticommunist Khmer People's National Liberation Front (FUNCINPEC). In 1991 he was elected president of Cambodia's Supreme National Council.

In May 1993 the United Nations Transitional Authority in Cambodia (UNTAC) presided over the country's first free elections in which 90% of registered voters went to the polls. FUNCINPEC candidates won 58 of the available 120 assembly seats. A coalition government with Prince Norodom Ranariddh (Sihanouk's son) and Hun Sen as joint premiers was established. In Sept. 1993 Sihanouk was again crowned king of Cambodia and head of State for life.

On 24 Sept. 1995 Sihanouk promulgated a new constitution including his own authority to that of constitutional monarch. He abdicated in Oct. 2004, despite there being no provision for this in the constitution, on grounds of health.

Later Life

Following his abdication Sihanouk assumed the title of 'king-father' a position in which he retains much of his power. He died on 15 Oct. 2012 at the age of 89, having been in poor health for several years.

Sikua, Derek (Solomon Islands)

Introduction

Derek Sikua took office in Dec. 2007 to become the Solomon Islands' 13th prime minister since independence in 1978. He defeated the foreign minister, Patteson Oti, in the parliamentary poll.

Early Life

Derek Sikua was born on 10 Sept. 1959 in Ngalitavethi Village, East Tasiboko, Guadalcanal Province. He worked as a teacher and deputy principal from 1982–86 and graduated in education from the University of Southern Queensland (Australia) in 1985. He then took a master's degree in educational policy and administration at Monash University (Australia) and a PhD in educational decentralization at the University of Waikato (New Zealand).

Between 1993 and 1997 Sikua worked at the ministry of education and human resources development, devising and implementing educational policy in the Solomon Islands. From 1997–98 he was permanent secretary in the ministry of forests, environment and conservation. From 2003–05 he returned to the ministry of education and human resources development as permanent secretary, and from 2006 also served as chairman of the Solomon Islands national commission for UNESCO.

Career Peak

Sikua entered parliament on 5 April 2006, representing the North East Guadalcanal constituency in the government of Prime Minister Manasseh Sogavare. On 4 May 2006 he was appointed minister for education and human resources, a post he held until Nov. 2007. On 13 Dec. 2007 Sikua led a parliamentary motion of no confidence against Sogavare. Supported by seven other cabinet ministers and one backbencher, Sikua defected from the government.

The events leading to the no-confidence vote sparked the formation of the Coalition for National Unity and Rural Advancement under Sikua's leadership. On 20 Dec. he defeated Patteson Oti, the foreign affairs minister, by 32 votes to 15 to be elected prime minister. Sikua pledged to work towards economic reform (particularly rural development), to regulate the logging industry and to hold consultations on a new federal constitution. In Aug. 2008 he defeated a no-confidence motion brought by opposition members.

In April 2009 the government announced austerity measures as the effects of the global economic crisis depressed demand for commodity exports and reduced revenues.

Despite Sikua retaining his seat in the Aug. 2010 parliamentary election, he was not nominated to contest the premiership. He was succeeded by Danny Philip on 25 Aug. following the latter's victory in the leadership contest.

Later Life

Sikua returned to public office in Dec. 2014 when he was named education and human resource development minister by newly appointed prime minister Manasseh Sogavare, who was also making a return to government having served two previous terms as premier. However, Sikua resigned in Oct. 2015 alongside six other ministers amid concerns over Sogavare's leadership style.

Simitis, Konstantinos (Greece)

Introduction

Konstantinos Simitis became prime minister for the first time in Jan. 1996. The success of his party, the Panhellenic Socialist Movement (PASOK), in the general election of April 2000 returned him to office for a second term. He promised further integration within the European Union and was a keen advocate of monetary union. He resigned from office before the general elections of March 2004.

Early Life

Simitis was born in Athens on 23 June 1936. His father was a lawyer and left-wing politician. He studied law at the University of Marburg in Germany, and later received a doctorate in jurisprudence. At the start of the 1960s he read economics and political science at the London School of Economics and embarked on an academic career. When, in 1967, a right-wing military dictatorship headed by Giorgios Papadopoulos seized power in Greece, Simitis chose to remain in Germany to avoid persecution. In exile he was an active member of several clandestine political organizations and wrote articles protesting against the junta. In 1974 he returned to Greece in the aftermath of the coup that ended Papadopoulos' regime. Having helped to establish PASOK as a legitimate political party, albeit with limited appeal, Simitis continued his academic career. In 1981 his party came to power for the first time and Simitis was elected to represent Piraeus. He went on to hold various ministerial portfolios, including those of education and religious affairs, agriculture and energy, industry, technology and commerce. He occupied the latter post until 1995 when the incumbent prime minister, Andreas Papandreou, fell ill and retired from politics. In Jan. 1996 his fellow MPs chose Simitis to succeed Papandreou.

Career Peak

In his first term of office Simitis steered PASOK towards the political centre, seeking to distance the party from its traditional socialist roots. To prepare the Greek economy for European monetary union, he supported gradual privatization and a moderate foreign policy. His slow but steady political style and fondness for statistics earned him the nickname of 'the book-keeper'. However, despite the absence of the political dynamism that characterized his predecessor, Simitis was largely successful in his efforts to improve the economy. He was re-elected for a second term, albeit on a reduced majority, in April 2000.

International relations with the UK and Dutch governments were strained in April 2002 when 14 British and Dutch plane spotters were sentenced to 1–3 years imprisonment for recording information about Greek military planes while on holiday, although they were later released. Later Simitis played a leading role in UN-brokered peace talks for Cyprus but failed to reach an agreement on the island's future with his Turkish and Northern Cypriot counterparts.

In Jan. 2004, with PASOK behind in opinion polls, Simitis called elections for March but announced that he would not be seeking re-election. PASOK was defeated, winning 117 seats to New Democracy's 165. Simitis left office on 10 March.

Simpson-Miller, Portia (Jamaica)

Introduction

Portia Simpson-Miller was sworn in as prime minister for a second time on 5 Jan. 2012 after the People's National Party defeated the Jamaica Labour Party in elections held on 29 Dec. 2011. She previously served in the post from 30 March 2006 to 11 Sept. 2007. A member of the Council of Women World Leaders, Simpson-Miller was her country's first democratically elected female leader on taking office in 2006.

Early Life

Portia Simpson-Miller was born on 12 Dec. 1945 in Wood Hall, St Catherine's Parish, Jamaica. She was educated at St Martin's High School and the Union Institute, Miami, USA, where she graduated with a degree in public administration. She entered politics as a councillor for the left-leaning PNP in 1974, winning the inner-city seat of Trench Town West in the Kingston & St Andrew Corporation.

In 1977 she was appointed parliamentary secretary in the ministry of local government and the following year was elected vice-president of the PNP, a post she held for the next 27 years. Despite the PNP's crushing defeat in the 1980 general election, she retained her councillor's seat and from 1983–89 served as the party spokesperson on women's affairs and pensions, social security and consumer affairs.

In the 1989 general election, when Michael Manley returned the PNP to power, Simpson-Miller was elected MP for South West St Andrew and was appointed minister of labour, social security and sport. Following Manley's resignation in 1992 she unsuccessfully challenged P. J. Patterson for the premiership. Promoted to minister for tourism and sport in 2000, Simpson-Miller won plaudits for her work to rebuild the tourism sector in the wake of the 11 Sept. 2001 attacks on the USA.

Following the general election of Oct. 2002 she regained the local government portfolio in an expanded ministry of local government, community development and sport. On 25 Feb. 2006 she narrowly defeated Peter Phillips to succeed Patterson as head of the PNP and become prime minister-elect. She was sworn into office on 30 March 2006. During her 18 months as premier Simpson-Miller sought to tackle poverty and crime. However, with unemployment running at 9% and crime still endemic, Simpson-Miller's PNP was narrowly defeated by the Labour Party in the parliamentary elections of Sept. 2007, ending 18 years of PNP rule. The following year, Simpson-Miller's leadership of the PNP was challenged by Peter Phillips but she defeated her rival and continued to lead the party in opposition.

Simpson-Miller performed strongly on the 2011 election campaign trail, with her charismatic populism widely credited with swinging public opinion in favour of the PNP. In what had been predicted to be a tight election, she led her party to a landslide win, taking 42 of 63 available seats and ensuring the two-thirds majority necessary to alter the constitution.

Career Peak

Simpson-Miller's priorities were to slash the rising rate of unemployment and tackle the massive debt-to-GDP ratio. She said that she would consider reviewing Jamaica's controversial criminalization of homosexuality, while in June 2014 her government announced plans to decriminalize the possession of marijuana and its use for medicinal purposes (which was subsequently approved by parliament in Feb. 2015). An avowed republican, she has stated her intention to move towards the severance of ties with the UK, although any such decision must be ratified by popular referendum. Simpson-Miller assumed the defence portfolio upon taking office as prime minister.

Simpson-Miller's term as prime minister ended in March 2016 following her party's defeat at elections held the previous month.

Singh, Manmohan (India)

Introduction

After three decades as a civil servant, the former academic and economist was sworn in as India's first Sikh prime minister on 22 May 2004. His appointment followed the general election victory of the Indian National Congress (INC) over the Bharatiya Janata Party (BJP; Indian People's Party) and Sonia Gandhi's unexpected rejection of the top job. A low-profile technocrat and adviser throughout the 1970s and 1980s, Singh came to the fore in 1991 when he was appointed finance minister in the cabinet of P. V. Narasimha Rao. India was in severe financial crisis and Singh was credited with bringing about a recovery, becoming known as the 'architect of India's economic reform'. His coalition won an emphatic victory at the 2009 elections, coming close to securing an absolute majority in parliament. In Jan. 2014 he announced that he would step down after nearly 10 years in office following the parliamentary elections scheduled for April–May 2014.

Early Life

Manmohan Singh was born in Gah, West Punjab (now in Pakistan), on 26 Sept. 1932, the son of a shopkeeper. He was educated at Punjab University in Chandigarh and also attended the universities of Cambridge and Oxford in England on scholarships, winning Cambridge's prestigious Adam Smith Prize in 1956. Returning to India as an economics lecturer, he remained at Punjab University before being made professor in 1963. Three years later he joined UNCTAD (the UN Conference on Trade and Development) at the United Nations Secretariat in New York, as economic affairs officer. In 1969 Singh returned to India to the University of Delhi as professor of international trade.

Cutting short his academic career in 1971, Singh joined Indira Gandhi's New Congress Party-led government to serve as an economic adviser to the ministry of foreign trade and, from 1972–76, as chief economic adviser in the finance ministry. Stronger ties with the USSR, which influenced Indian economic policy and brought in new aid agreements, marked this period. In 1976 Singh became director of the Reserve Bank of India, a post he held for 4 years. From 1982–85 he was its governor and then deputy chairman of the Planning Commission from 1985–87, undertaking various assignments at the International Monetary Fund and the Asian Development Bank. He was first selected for the Rajya Sabha (the upper house of parliament) in 1991, representing the Congress.

In 1991, with India in financial crisis, Singh was appointed finance minister in P. V. Narasimha Rao's cabinet. Foreign exchange reserves were nearly exhausted and the country was close to defaulting on its international debt. Singh brought in an ambitious and unprecedented economic reform programme. He slashed red tape, simplified the tax system and ended the 'license Raj' regulations that forced businesses to get government approval for most decisions. He also devalued the rupee, cut subsidies for domestically produced goods, and privatized some state-run companies. Singh spoke of wanting to 'release the innovative, entrepreneurial spirit which was always there in India in such a manner that our economy would grow at a much faster pace, sooner than most people believed.' The programme worked; industry picked up, inflation was checked, and growth rates remained consistently high through the 1990s (his policies were broadly continued by the BJP-led coalition after they were elected in 1996).

Career Peak

When Singh was sworn in as prime minister on 22 May 2004, he took on a healthy economy. GDP growth was at 7%, foreign exchange reserves were comfortable at US$118 bn. and inflation stood at just 4%. However, hundreds of millions of Indians were still living in poverty and Singh faced a tough task in bringing about improvements in living standards, while balancing the demands of leftist and communist parties in the coalition. His first address as prime minister called for 'economic reforms with a human face' stressing the need to achieve friendly relations with neighbouring countries, especially Pakistan. Although Singh has a reputation for honesty and even-handedness, there were some questions about his lack of election-winning political experience—he had failed to win a seat in the Lok Sabha (Lower House) elections for South Delhi in 1999.

While India's economy continued to perform strongly, Singh's early premiership had to contend with the devastating effects of a number of severe natural disasters, including the tsunami across the Indian Ocean in Dec. 2004 which hit coastal communities in the south of the country and the Andaman and Nicobar Islands, floods and landslides in Maharashtra in July 2005 and an earthquake in Kashmir in Oct. 2005.

Terrorism has remained a serious problem for the government. Bomb attacks on commuter trains and railway stations in Mumbai in July 2006 killed about 200 people. This atrocity, blamed by India on Pakistan's intelligence services, threatened to undermine previous improvements in the volatile relations between the two nuclear-armed neighbours. A further terrorist bomb attack in Feb. 2007 on a train travelling from New Delhi to Lahore in Pakistan killed about 70 people. Terrorist incidents continued in 2008, particularly in Nov. when suspected Islamic extremists launched a co-ordinated series of attacks on prominent landmarks in India's commercial capital, Mumbai, killing civilians with grenades and machine guns and taking foreign hostages before being overcome by the security forces. The slaughter, in which some 190 people died, led to the resignation of the home affairs minister. India blamed militants from Pakistan for the atrocity, leading Singh's government to lodge a formal protest. Bilateral talks between the two countries resumed following Singh's positive meeting with his Pakistani counterpart in April 2010 at a summit meeting of the South Asian Association for Regional Co-operation in Bhutan and, despite further terrorist attacks in Mumbai and Delhi in July and Sept. 2011, the two leaders met again in Nov. pledging to open a fresh chapter in bilateral relations. Singh has nevertheless continued to insist that Pakistan do more to dismantle terror organizations operating from its territory.

Although India is not party to the Nuclear Non-Proliferation Treaty, Singh signed a controversial agreement with the USA in March 2006 giving India access to civilian nuclear energy technology in return for having its nuclear sites inspected. The deal was approved by the US Congress in Dec. 2006 but was stalled by political opposition within the Indian parliament. In July 2008 left-wing parties withdrew their parliamentary support for Singh's government, but it survived a no-confidence vote that cleared the way for it to try and finalize the agreement. In the USA the deal was signed into law in Oct. In the same month, Singh signed a security co-operation agreement with Japan.

Following the victory at the general election in April and May 2009 of the United Progressive Alliance (of which the INC won nearly 80% of the vote), Singh became only the second Indian prime minister after Indira Gandhi to hold office for two consecutive terms. Since then, although the economy has continued to prosper, Singh has faced considerable domestic criticism for his handling of a series of high-profile corruption scandals, for the poor organization that plagued the preparations for the Commonwealth Games staged in New Delhi in Oct. 2010, and for controversial retail sector reform plans (which were approved by parliament in Dec. 2012). There have also been protests in Andhra Pradesh both for and against the government's proposal to create a separate state called Telangana (which was approved in Feb. 2014), as well as disquiet over a high court ruling that one of the most bitterly contested religious sites in India at Ayodhya should be divided between Muslims and Hindus.

In 2012 the INC suffered several poor results in state elections. Deteriorating relations with some coalition allies prompted Singh to conduct an extensive cabinet reshuffle in Oct. that saw Salman Khurshid appointed foreign minister, only the third Muslim to hold the position in India's history. Meanwhile Pranab Mukherjee, a senior INC figure and former finance minister, was elected in July 2012 as the new national president by the federal and state assemblies. The INC endured heavy defeats by the BJP in four state elections in Dec. 2013 and in Jan. 2014 Singh announced his decision to stand down at the pending general election. He was succeeded as prime minister by Narendra Modi, who successfully led the BJP to a parliamentary majority in elections held in April–May 2014.

Siniora, Fouad (Lebanon)

Introduction

Fouad Siniora became prime minister of a Western-backed government in July 2005, shortly after the assassination of his predecessor, Rafiq al-Hariri, and the withdrawal of Syrian forces from Lebanese territory.

Early Life

Born into a Sunni Muslim family in Sidon in 1943, Siniora studied business before a career in international finance. In 1982 he went to work for Rafiq al-Hariri, a successful businessman and the future prime minister. He would later be finance minister in al-Hariri's five cabinets.

Al-Hariri's assassination (with suspected Syrian involvement) in Feb. 2005 led to political unrest, the resignation of Omar Karame's Lebanese government and Syria's troop withdrawal from Lebanon. Subsequent parliamentary elections were dominated by the anti-Syrian opposition bloc led by Saad al-Hariri (son of Rafiq), resulting in Siniora becoming prime minister. Sworn into office in July 2005, his coalition government included a representative of the militant anti-Israeli Hizbollah movement for the first time.

Career Peak

Siniora aimed to improve relations with Syria, restore domestic security and implement electoral and economic reform. Despite large public debt, signs of an economic upturn followed the relatively smooth transition of power though bombings aimed at political and civilian targets continued throughout 2005. He struggled to maintain authority in 2006 amid hostilities between Hizbollah and Israeli forces that caused many Lebanese civilian casualties, a refugee crisis and extensive infrastructure damage before a ceasefire was declared in Aug. In Nov. Hizbollah and the Shia Amal movement withdrew their ministers from the cabinet after their call for more representation was rejected. Sectarian tensions were heightened by the assassination of Pierre Gemayel, an anti-Syrian government minister. Siniora refused to resign despite mass demonstrations by Christian and Shia Muslim opposition protesters in Dec. seeking a more representative national unity government.

Political paralysis persisted through 2007, aggravated by fighting during May–Sept. between the Lebanese army and Palestinian militants in the Nahr al-Bared refugee camp and by the assassinations of two anti-Syrian MPs. In Nov. 2007, in the absence of a parliamentary vote to elect a successor to President Emile Lahoud, Siniora's cabinet assumed the powers of the presidency until Gen. Michel Suleiman took office in May 2008 in the wake of serious clashes between Hizbollah and pro-government factions. At the end of that month Siniora was reappointed as prime minister and in July formed a new unity government. In Oct. Lebanon and Syria signed an accord formalizing diplomatic ties for the first time since both countries achieved independence.

Following the ruling 14 March Alliance's victory in the June 2009 parliamentary elections, its leader Saad Hariri, son of the assassinated former prime minister Rafiq al-Hariri, was named prime minister designate and given the task of composing a unity government. In Sept. Hariri stepped down after his initial cabinet line-up was rejected by the Hizbollah-led opposition but was subsequently renominated prime minister by Siniora. On 9 Nov. Siniora stood down and Hariri and his cabinet took office.

Siphandone, Khamtay (Laos)

Introduction

Having served as prime minister from 1991–98, army general Khamtay Siphandone then served two terms as president, being re-elected in March 2001 before resigning in 2006.

Early Life

Born on 8 Feb. 1924 in Champassak province, Siphandone joined the Lao revolutionary movement in 1947. In 1952 he became a member of the central committee of the Lao Issara (Free Laos) movement, and between 1952–54 was chairman of the committee of the Central Region. His membership of the People's Revolutionary Party of Laos began in 1956, whilst serving as chief of staff of the Pathet Lao forces. He was soon a member of the central party committee and rapidly became head of its office. In 1960 he took charge of military affairs of the central party committee and became commander-in-chief of the Pathet Lao forces. When the Pathet Lao took over the government in 1975 he was appointed deputy prime minister, minister of national defence and commander-in-chief of the Lao People's Army. He served in all three positions concurrently until the early 1990s. On 15 Aug. 1991 he was elected prime minister. Seven years later he was voted president by the National Assembly.

Career Peak

After becoming president, Siphandone did little to further democracy in the country. He kept tight restrictions on the media, although some opening of the economy and society followed Laos' entry into the Association of South East Asian Nations (ASEAN) in 1997. Laos' hosting of the 2004 ASEAN summit received strong support from the president.

In March 2006 Siphandone was replaced as leader of the People's Revolutionary Party of Laos by Vice President Choummali Saignason. As expected Siphandone also gave up the presidency, formally leaving office on 8 June 2006, after assembly election held at the end of April.

Smith, Ian (Zimbabwe)

Introduction

Ian Smith became prime minister of Southern Rhodesia (now Zimbabwe) in 1964 and declared independence from Britain the following year. His refusal to negotiate a transition to black majority rule resulted in the country's international isolation and a devastating civil war with black nationalists. He lost office in 1979 shortly before Robert Mugabe took control of the newly-established Zimbabwe, but he has remained a vocal critic of the Mugabe regime.

Early Life

Ian Douglas Smith, whose father was a butcher, was born on 8 April 1919 in Selukwe, Rhodesia (now Shurugwi, Zimbabwe). He attended Rhodes University in South Africa but his studies in commerce were interrupted by World War II, during which he served in the Royal Air Force and was shot down over Italy. Having completed his degree he entered the Southern Rhodesia Assembly in 1948 as the member for Selukwe and 5 years later he went to the federal parliament as the United Federal Party member for Midlands. Within 2 years he had been appointed Chief Whip but Smith fell out with the party as it moved towards increased black representation.

Career Peak

In response Smith helped found the Rhodesian Front in 1961, which achieved election victory the following year by espousing policies of white supremacy and national independence. Smith was deputy to Prime Minister Winston Field but succeeded him as Prime Minister of Southern Rhodesia (which had once again become a self-governing British colony following the break up of the federation with Northern Rhodesia and Nyasaland in 1963) in April 1964. Early in his tenure the arrest of a group of black nationalists led to civil unrest which was forcefully put down by the authorities.

He continued to oppose proposed constitutional changes that would ultimately allow for a black-dominated government, refusing to budge at a Commonwealth Conference in 1964. Despite international pressure to reconsider, on 11 Nov. 1965 he made a Unilateral Declaration of Independence (UDI) on behalf of Rhodesia, later claiming it was a course of action he had not wanted to take. Britain imposed retaliatory sanctions and persuaded the UN to do likewise. Smith in turn withdrew Rhodesia from the Commonwealth and declared a republic on 2 March 1970.

There followed a bloody civil war, characterized by guerrilla tactics which cost thousands of lives. One of the principal rebel groups was the Patriotic Front, headed by Joshua Nkomo and Robert Mugabe, the future president of Zimbabwe. As the violence continued unabated, the economy went into steep decline, suffering from the sanctions, increased government expenditure on military resources and the exodus of large numbers of whites.

In 1977, with conditions in the country worsening, Smith agreed to talks with Bishop Muzorewa, leader of the United African Council and more moderate than Mugabe and Nkomo. Negotiations led the following year to proposals for a transitional government and black enfranchisement in return for certain guarantees concerning white property and rights. Smith was to be a part of the Transitional Executive Council and served as Prime Minister until May 1979. He continued as a minister until the end of the year, remaining leader of the Republican Front until 1987 and leaving government only in 1988.

Later Life

In May 2000 it was reported that Smith's farm had been seized by blacks during a Mugabe-sponsored programme of land reclamation by war veterans. Smith countered by suggesting that he would consider standing for government if he 'could be of some use to my country'. He died on 20 Nov. 2007.

Soares, Mário (Portugal)

Introduction

Mário Alberto Nobre Lopes Soares was twice prime minister (1976–78; 1983–85) and twice president (1985–96), representing the Partido Socialista Portugués (PSP). He was the first democratically elected leader since 1926. A political activist and opponent of the Salazar dictatorship, he is, along with Salazar, one of the two most influential political figures of twentieth century Portugal. He refounded the PSP, twice resolved economic crises resulting from years of dictatorship and provisional governments and led Portugal into the EU.

Early Life

Soares was born on 7 Dec. 1924 in Lisbon. He was the son of João Soares, a liberal republican and minister in the First Republic (1910–26), who was a strong opponent of the Salazar dictatorship. His father's political views strongly influenced Soares. In 1943 he joined the communist dominated Movimento de Unidade Nacional Anti-Fascista (National Anti-Fascist Movement). He took a first degree in philosophy at the Universidade de Lisboa, where he became politically active. Because of his political views, Soares was unable to get teaching work and so took a second degree in law. After graduating in 1957 he worked to defend political dissidents.

Soares supported the unsuccessful opposition candidate General Humberto Delgado in the 1958 presidential elections. After being involved in several opposition movements, Soares became leader of the Acção Socialista Portuguesa (Portuguese Socialist Action), of which he was co-founder in 1964. Soares continued to defend political opponents. In 1968 he represented the Delgado family following the General's assassination by the PVDE secret police (Polícia de Vigilância e Defesa do Estado) in Spain in 1965. Consequently, Soares was immediately imprisoned without trial in the infamous camp for political prisoners on São Tomé. It was the 13th time he had been arrested by the PVDE.

Following his imprisonment, Soares went to France where he tried to re-establish the PSP. Founded in 1875, the party had been dissolved in 1933 by Salazar. After several failed attempts, the PSP, with the aid of the Socialists International and the German Social Democrats, re-emerged in 1973 at a Socialist conference in West Germany. Uniting with the Communists, the PSP fought to bring down the Portuguese dictatorship. After the 1974 Carnation Revolution, Soares returned to Portugal. His first role was a diplomatic European tour to promote external relations with the newly democratic Portugal. He served as minister of foreign affairs for the first three military-led provisional governments, beginning decolonization talks with Mozambique and Cape Verde, and was a minister without portfolio in the fourth. In 1975 Soares resigned from the fourth government in protest over growing totalitarianism.

Career Peak

In 1976 Soares was elected prime minister in the first post-revolution constitutional government, although the PSP did not win an absolute majority in the assembly. In the same year he was elected vice-president of the Socialist International at the Geneva Conference. Portugal was in serious economic difficulty following years of instability. Near bankruptcy necessitated a large IMF loan. Concurrently, a new constitution was established, including a new civil code and agrarian reforms. In 1977 Soares opened negotiations on Portuguese entry to the EU.

Between 1978–83 Soares was opposition leader. In 1980 he resumed the leadership of the PSP. In 1983 he was elected prime minister as the representative of a coalition between the PSP and the PSD (Partido Social Democrata). During his second term, Soares steered Portugal out of a second economic crisis. He also led Portugal into the EU, signing the Treaty of Ascension in 1985. Portugal officially became a member the following year. In 1985 the PSP/PSD coalition broke down and the PSP lost its assembly majority.

In 1986 Soares was elected to the largely ceremonial position of president with 51.3% of votes, becoming the first Portuguese civilian president to be democratically elected in 60 years. In 1991 he was re-elected with 70.4% of votes.

Later Life

At the end of his second term, Soares turned to international politics. In 1997 he became president of the European Movement. In 1999 he was elected deputy of the European Parliament representing the PSP. He was also president of the Mário Soares Foundation, which sponsors events connected with human rights and international relations. He died at the age of 92 on 7 Jan. 2017.

Sobotka, Bohuslav (Czech Republic)

Introduction

Bohuslav Sobotka took office as prime minister on 29 Jan. 2014. A representative of the centre-left Czech Social Democratic Party (ČSSD), he is a career politician.

Early Life

Sobotka was born on 23 Oct. 1971 in Telnice near Brno, in what was then the Socialist Republic of Czechoslovakia. He joined the ČSSD in Dec. 1989, at the climax of the Velvet Revolution that ended communist rule in Czechoslovakia, and the following year co-founded the party's youth wing. He graduated from the law faculty of Brno's Masaryk University in 1995.

He entered parliament in 1996 as the ČSSD candidate for the South Bohemian Region, which he has continued to represent. Following the ČSSD's victory in the 2002 parliamentary elections, he was appointed minister of finance by Vladimír Špidla, overseeing solid economic growth in his 4 years in the post and also serving terms as a deputy prime minister. He returned to opposition when the ČSSD coalition was defeated in the 2006 elections.

Despite winning the most seats of any party at the 2010 elections, the ČSSD's inability to form a workable coalition led to the resignation of its leader, Jiří Paroubek. Sobotka succeeded him on an interim basis until he was officially elected party chairman in March 2011. He was soon confronted by a leadership challenge, his handling of which is credited with increasing his popularity among the wider electorate.

Sobotka's reputation as an uncharismatic but reliable figure left him well placed to capitalize on a spying, sex and corruption scandal that engulfed Prime Minister Petr Nečas, triggering a snap parliamentary election in Oct. 2013 from which the ČSSD again emerged as the largest party. Sobotka negotiated a coalition with the recently formed pro-business, populist ANO party, led by billionaire Andrej Babiš, and the Christian Democrats, giving him a majority of 111 seats in the 200-strong Chamber of Deputies.

Career Peak

On coming to power, Sobotka stated that his government's priorities were to stimulate economic growth and employment, as well as 'restoring people's trust in politics'. He also had to navigate a strained relationship with President Miloš Zeman, dating back to Sobotka's refusal to support Zeman's failed 2003 presidential bid. The stability of his coalition has since been bolstered by a recovery of the economy, although the government faced an unsuccessful parliamentary no-confidence motion tabled in May 2015 by opposition parties over alleged conflicts of interest surrounding Andrej Babiš's role as finance minister. Sobotka meanwhile maintained that mandatory migrant quotas would not help to resolve the causes of the European Union's escalating foreign refugee crisis. Following elections to the Senate in Oct. 2016, the ČSSD lost ground but remained the largest party with 25 seats. Following the victory of ANO 2011 in the parliamentary election of Oct. 2017, Andrej Babiš took office as prime minister on 6 Dec.

Sócrates, José (Portugal)

Introduction

José Sócrates was swept into power as Portugal's prime minister following a resounding victory for his Socialist Party (PS) in a snap parliamentary election on 20 Feb. 2005. The former civil engineer is a modernizer who has described himself as a 'market-oriented socialist'. Previously an environment minister, he was committed to sustainable development and championed educational reform and the development of high-tech industries as a way of reviving the country's flagging economy. His economic reforms nevertheless proved controversial, provoking public protests. He retained the premiership following parliamentary elections in Sept. 2009 but resigned in 2011 after parliament rejected his government's austerity measures. In Nov. 2014 Sócrates was arrested following an investigation into alleged corruption, money laundering and tax fraud.

Early Life

José Sócrates Carvalho Pinto de Sousa was born in Vilar de Macada, Alijó, near the northern city of Porto, on 6 Sept. 1957. He attended secondary school in Covilhã in the district of Castelo Branco and went on to study at the Institute of Engineering in Coimbra, before completing a master's degree in medical engineering at the National School of Public Health. Sócrates then worked as a medical engineer for Castelo Branco's municipal authority. He

joined the PS in 1981 and was first elected as a member of the Portuguese assembly in 1987, the year after the government—a Social Democratic Party (PSD)-led coalition—had taken the country into the European Community. In 1991 Sócrates became a member of the National Secretariat of the PS, and was spokesman for the environment.

Following the victory of the Socialists over the centre-right PSD in the 1995 general election, Sócrates held a range of portfolios under Prime Minister António Guterres. He served as secretary of state in the ministry of the environment and territorial planning for 2 years from 1995, before being made deputy minister to Guterres. In Oct. 1999, after Guterres had led the PS to another election win, Sócrates was promoted to minister for the environment, a post he held until the parliamentary elections of March 2002. He gained a reputation for boldness and determination, and is widely regarded as the man who brought the Euro 2004 football tournament to Portugal.

When the Socialists lost power to the PSD, led by José Manuel Durão Barroso, in March 2002, Sócrates remained in the spotlight by taking part in a weekly television debate against Pedro Santana Lopes, then the Social Democratic mayor of Lisbon. Following the resignation of Ferro Rodrigues as leader of the PS in 2004, Sócrates bid for the post of secretary-general, and won the vote of almost 80% of party members in Sept. 2004. Sócrates was again in direct opposition to Santana Lopes, who had taken over as prime minister and leader of the PSD in July 2004 when Barroso resigned to become head of the European Commission. Already unpopular at the time of Barroso's resignation, the PSD-led coalition struggled to improve Portugal's moribund economy. There was also a month-long delay to the start of the school year and disunity over Santana Lopes' plan to introduce tax cuts and public-sector pay rises. By Nov. loss of confidence in Santana Lopes' administration had reached the point where the president, Jorge Sampaio, felt obliged to dissolve parliament and call a snap general election, 2 years ahead of schedule.

Sócrates focused the PS' campaign on the promise to provide disciplined and transparent leadership and pledged to reform the country's education system, alleviate poverty and boost employment. The strategy proved successful—the PS gained 45% of the vote in the elections on 20 Feb. 2005, up from 38% in 2002. With 121 seats in Portugal's 230-seat parliament, it was the first time since the end of the Salazar-Caetano dictatorship in 1974 that the PS had received an outright majority. On 24 Feb. Sócrates was called on by President Sampaio to form a new government, which took office on 12 March 2005.

Career Peak

In his inaugural address as Portugal's prime minister, Sócrates pledged to restore confidence in the country and its institutions. He also vowed to increase the economy's competitiveness while cutting the budget deficit and fulfilling the requirements of the eurozone's stability and growth pact. Sócrates said his model for the country was a 'Nordic social democracy'—a society combining efficient capitalist enterprise with generous social services. Critics nevertheless described Sócrates' vision as unobtainable, pointing out that his economic reforms would lead to further job losses and suggesting that improvements to the education system to provide a labour force adapted to high-tech industries would take many years.

To comply with EU fiscal requirements, the 2006 budget included reforms to pension schemes and public administration wage structures. However, the government continued to struggle with the budget deficit in 2007 and in March there were mass demonstrations and industrial action against Sócrates' economic policies.

Portugal's 6-month presidency of the European Union, which began in July 2007, culminated in the signature in Dec. by the heads of government of the Lisbon Treaty streamlining the institutional structure and operation of the enlarged EU. Parliament then ratified the treaty in April 2008.

Parliamentary elections in Sept. 2009 were contested against a background of economic contraction and uncertainty in the wake of the global financial crisis. The PS was returned as the largest single party but lost its overall majority in the National Assembly. Sócrates continued as prime minister for a second term, but at the head of a minority government which was sworn in on 26 Oct. Portugal's economy and strained public finances caused mounting concern through 2010, along with other vulnerable economies in the eurozone which came under pressure over their sovereign debt levels and budget deficits. Several leading international credit agencies downgraded Portugal's government debt, forcing the Sócrates administration to introduce an unpopular austerity budget in Nov. that prompted trade union calls for a general strike.

On 23 March 2011 Sócrates submitted his resignation to the president after his government's latest austerity package was rejected in parliament. Sócrates remained in office as caretaker prime minister until June when legislative elections took place. After losing the election he resigned as Secretary-General of the Socialist Party.

Sócrates was arrested and charged with corruption, money laundering and tax fraud by a Portuguese court in Nov. 2014. Investigators had questioned a number of suspicious financial transactions made 'without known justification or legal admissibility'. and an additional three individuals including Sócrates' personal driver were charged alongside Portugal's former prime minister. His arrest came days after the resignation of incumbent interior minister Miguel Macedo over separate and unrelated corruption allegations.

Sogavare, Manasseh (Solomon Islands)

Introduction

Manasseh Sogavare's first premiership (2000–01) began in the wake of a coup and ended after a controversial attempt to postpone elections. He took office for the second time in May 2006 after the brief tenure of Snyder Rini, when the capital, Honiara, suffered rioting with attacks on the Chinese community. However, Sogavare was ousted again in a parliamentary vote of no confidence on 13 Dec. 2007. He was elected to a third term as prime minister in Nov. 2014 and sworn in the following month.

Early Life

Manasseh Damukana Sogavare was born in 1955 at Gauraisa, northern Papua New Guinea, the son of missionaries from the island of Choiseul in the western Solomons. He was initially educated in Madang Province (PNG) before moving to Honiara in 1965, where he attended high school. He later graduated from the University of the South Pacific at Suva and from New Zealand's Waikato University.

Sogavare pursued a civil service career, becoming chief tax collector. In 1997 he became MP for East Choiseul. Prime Minister Bartholomew Ulufa'alu appointed him finance minister after the Aug. election that year but dismissed him in July 1998. Tensions grew in 1998 between the indigenous peoples of Guadalcanal island (site of the capital) and long-term residents from Malaita island, who were seen to dominate the civil service. In 2000 Sogavare became leader of the People's Progressive Party (PPP). Ulufa'alu resigned after Malaitan militias seized parliament and Sogavare was chosen to succeed him by MPs.

Sogavare took office on 30 June 2000, forming the Coalition for National Unity, Reconciliation and Peace. Snyder Rini, leader of the Association of Independents, was finance minister. In Oct. 2000 a peace treaty was signed with the militias, followed by a further treaty in Feb. 2001. Parliament was dissolved in Aug. 2001 ahead of scheduled elections but the government attempted to push through a constitutional amendment to extend its mandate by another year. Amid corruption allegations, widespread unrest and trade union pressure for a general strike, Sogavare called elections for 5 Dec. 2001. The PPP won only three seats and Sogavare was succeeded by Sir Allan Kemakeza.

The Social Credit Party, a new party led by Sogavare, ran in the elections of 5 April 2006 on a platform of monetary and financial reform (based on New Zealand's Social Credit Party). Sogavare and his allies attempted to oust Kemakeza's successor, Rini, on 18 April 2006 but, having come third in a parliamentary vote for premier, he switched his allegiance to Rini, in exchange for control of the commerce ministry. Rioting broke out in Honiara in protest at perceived Taiwanese and local Chinese political interference, and much of the city's Chinatown area was destroyed. Following a no-confidence motion, Rini resigned on 26 April and Sogavare was elected prime minister on 4 May. On 5 May he appointed a five-party unity cabinet.

In Oct. 2006 Sogavare survived a parliamentary no-confidence vote following a serious diplomatic dispute with Australia. This related to his claims about the role of Australian security personnel in the April rioting

and to Australia's efforts to effect the extradition of Sogavare's controversial attorney-general for an alleged criminal offence. Government leaders attending a meeting of the Pacific Islands Forum in Fiji in Oct. agreed to an independent review of the Australian-led regional peacekeeping force in the Solomon Islands.

On 13 Dec. 2007 Sogavare was defeated in a parliamentary vote after facing criticism for his abrasive style and accusations of damaging the nation's international image. He remained in office in a caretaker capacity until 20 Dec. In 2010, together with other opposition representatives, he launched Our Party, which contested the general elections that year but won only four seats, including his own East Choiseul constituency.

Career Peak

Sogavare was elected to a third term as prime minister in a secret ballot of MPs following a general election held in Nov. 2014 in which the majority of the elected MPs were returned as independents and the then prime minister, Gordon Darcy Lilo, who had taken office in Nov. 2011, unexpectedly lost his seat. Sogavare pledged to rebuild the country's economy with increased foreign investment, to improve public services and to tackle corruption.

In Oct. 2015 seven of Sogavare's senior ministers resigned citing issues with the prime minister's style of leadership and his position as premier has remained insecure amid fluid political allegiances. On 6 Nov. 2017 Sogavare succumbed to a no-confidence vote. The parliament subsequently elected Rick Hou prime minister although Sogavare remained in the government as minister of finance and treasury.

Soilih, Ali (Comoros)

Introduction

Ali Soilih was head of state from 1976–78. His rule was marked by continued hostility between France and the Comoros. His radical attempts to reform the country against a backdrop of economic instability led to diminishing support among the Comoran populace. He was ousted from power in a coup.

Early Life

Soilih was born in Jan. 1937 and studied in Madagascar. Shortly after the Comoros' declaration of independence, Soilih was a third of the triumvirate that supplanted Ahmed Abdullah as head of state on 3 Aug. 1975. Though the motives for the coup remain unclear, it was believed that with Abdullah out of power there was an increased chance of France surrendering control of Mahoré (which had voted to remain a French dependency).

Career Peak

Soilih attempted a break with many traditional Comoran customs and remnants of French colonialism in a bid to modernize the country. This policy included banning the *grand mariage* (an expensive celebration to achieve social and political status), expensive funerals and the wearing of veils. French government archives were destroyed in 1976.

Advocating a secular state, Soilih called for restrictions on the powers of the muftis (Muslim jurists in Islamic Law) and there were frequent raids on mosques and attacks on village elders. Realizing the need to win the support of young people, he lowered the voting age to 14 and founded a revolutionary militia of young people (the Moissy) to implement change.

In foreign policy, relations with France fast deteriorated, particularly over the question of Mahoré sovereignty. Regarding the Chinese cultural revolution as a model for his reform movement, Soilih sought closer ties with China as well as Tanzania (who shared military expertise), Nigeria, North Korea and Saudi Arabia.

International aid followed food crises in 1976–77 but, with the economy weak, there were many public protests. One demonstration, by fishermen in March 1978, led to a massacre. On 12 May 1978 a mercenary force, backed by Abdullah, overthrew Soilih. He died on 29 May, reputedly while trying to escape.

Solís, Luis Guillermo (Costa Rica)

Introduction

Luis Guillermo Solís became president in May 2014. An academic and diplomat, he led the centre-left Citizens' Action Party (PAC) to electoral victory on a platform of combating corruption, developing the national infrastructure and boosting the economy.

Early Life

Born in San José on 25 April 1958, Solís graduated in history from the University of Costa Rica and received a master's degree from Tulane University in New Orleans, USA. He embarked on an academic career, holding research and teaching posts at institutions including the University of Costa Rica and Florida International University.

Having joined the National Liberation Party (PLN), he worked as chief of staff in the foreign ministry from 1986–90 in the government of Óscar Arias. In this post he was involved in regional negotiations to bring peace to Central America. He was director of the Arias Foundation's Center for Peace and Reconciliation from 1992–94 and served as ambassador for Central American affairs from 1994–96. Between 1996 and 1998 he was director general for policy at the foreign ministry.

He held a succession of senior party posts, serving as the PLN's general secretary from 2002–03. However, in 2005 he resigned from the PLN after reporting electoral irregularities and returned to academia. In 2009 he joined the PAC and in 2012 became its presidential candidate, campaigning on promises to fight corruption, invest in infrastructure, improve the provision of health care and social services, and boost the economy. After achieving a surprise victory by 0.9% in the first round of voting in Feb. 2014, he promised to postpone tax increases for 2 years, proposing instead to trim government spending. In April 2014 he won a second round run-off with 77.8% of the vote against Johnny Araya, whose name remained on the ballot paper despite his withdrawal from active campaigning in the weeks leading up to the poll.

Career Peak

Solís took office on 8 May 2014 promising to rebuild confidence in the economy and institutions of governance. His chief challenges were to reduce a widening fiscal deficit and increasing debt stock, and to contain a volatile labour market while contending with a fractious and divided parliament. However, in early 2017 Moody's international credit rating agency downgraded Costa Rica's financial standing, particularly citing the still rising fiscal deficit and government debt payment burden and also the lack of political consensus to implement corrective measures.

In Dec. 2015 the International Court of Justice ruled in Costa Rica's favour in a sovereignty dispute with Nicaragua over a small border area known as Isla Portillo. In May 2018, following the presidential elections run-off that took place in April of the same year, Solís was succeeded as president by his fellow PAC member Carlos Alvarado Quesada.

Sólyom, László (Hungary)

Introduction

As a professor of law and an environmental activist, László Sólyom was closely involved in the negotiations between opposition civic groups and the Communist regime that led to the fall of the Iron Curtain. For most of the 1990s Sólyom was chief justice in Hungary's newly-established constitutional court, overseeing sweeping reforms to the country's legal system. He became president on 5 Aug. 2005.

Early Life

László Sólyom was born in the southern Hungarian city of Pécs on 3 Jan. 1942. In 1965 he graduated in law from the University of Pécs. Later that year he qualified as a librarian at the National Széchenyi Library in Budapest. Between 1966 and 1969 he studied for a doctorate and worked as assistant lecturer at the institute of civil law at the Friedrich Schiller University in Jena in East Germany, an institution known as a dissident stronghold. Returning to Budapest in 1969, Sólyom became a fellow of the institute of political and legal sciences at the Hungarian Academy of Sciences (MTA). He also worked as a librarian at the library of parliament. In 1978 Sólyom joined the Eötvös Loránd University in Budapest as an assistant professor in the department of civil law. Five years later he became a professor at the university. He specialized in the field of the right to privacy, and was largely responsible for the introduction of data protection legislation in Hungary. Sólyom also worked as a legal adviser to some of the country's new and radical civil and environmental organizations during the 1980s, and helped to prevent the construction of the controversial Nagymaros dam on the river Danube.

Sólyom was one of a group of dissident intellectuals that met at the town of Lakitelek in Sept. 1987 and formed the Hungarian Democratic Forum (MDF), which became a fully-fledged political party 6 months later. As a member of the MDF's executive committee, Sólyom participated in roundtable negotiations that precipitated the end of Hungary's Communist regime and the dismantling of the Iron Curtain between Hungary and Austria in May 1989. Sólyom was elected onto the newly-established constitutional court of Hungary on 24 Nov. 1989, and was made the court's chief justice shortly afterwards. He remained in this post for 9 years, playing a key role in strengthening democracy in Hungary. Highly activist, with the power to review and invalidate parliamentary acts, the court did much to promote freedom of opinion and the removal of capital punishment.

When his mandate expired in 1998 Sólyom continued his academic career, lecturing at universities throughout Hungary and internationally, including the University of Cologne (Köln), Germany, where he was visiting professor in 1999 and 2000. He joined numerous boards and committees, including the Council of Europe's Commission for Democracy through Law, the Hungarian Accreditation Commission and the Geneva-based International Commission of Jurists. He became a member of the Védegylet (an environmental and civil-society organization) when it was founded in early 2000 and it was this group which nominated him to replace Ferenc Mádl as the country's president in 2005. Backed by the right-leaning opposition MDF and Fidesz, Sólyom went head-to-head with Katalin Szili, the parliamentary speaker and candidate of the Socialist-led coalition government. In a third-round run-off on 7 June 2005, Sólyom emerged victorious with 185 votes to Szili's 182.

Career Peak

Sólyom was inaugurated as president on 5 Aug. 2005. He was critical of some politicians, accusing them of spending their time attacking each other instead of dealing with the key issues at hand. He was succeeded by Pál Schmitt in Aug. 2010.

Somoza Debayle, Anastasio (Nicaragua)

Introduction

Anastasio Somoza Debayle was the last of the Somoza dynasty to hold power in Nicaragua. He was *de facto* leader from 1967 until 1979, when he fled the country following the Sandinista uprising. He held the office of president from 1967 to 1971 and from 1974 until 1979. His rule was charaterized by corruption and ruthless political oppression.

Early Life

Somoza Debayle was born on 5 Dec. 1925 in Léon, Nicaragua, the second son of Anastasio Somoza García, head of the national guard and, from 1936, Nicaragua's president. He was schooled in Florida and studied at New York's La Salle military academy. On his return to Nicaragua in 1946 he joined the national guard and 9 years later became its commander.

Somoza García was assassinated in 1956, having established vast personal wealth and political influence for his family. Somoza Debayle's elder brother, Luis, assumed the presidency, winning an elected term in 1957. He declined to stand for another term in 1963 and instead installed a ruling committee of political allies. Anastasio Somoza Debayle successfully ran for the presidency in the elections of 1967.

Career Peak

Somoza Debayle adopted an aggressive leadership style more reminiscent of his father than his brother. He vigorously suppressed political opposition and oversaw a period of increasing corruption and nepotism. He allowed the military considerable freedom and largely overlooked civil abuses committed by the national guard, thus securing its continued support. With the economy in decline, Somoza Debayle's popular standing declined quickly. The situation was exacerbated in 1970 when he amended the constitution to permit him a further year in government. In 1971 he was persuaded to resign the presidency and install a ruling committee to oversee the drafting of a new constitution. Despite relinquishing his official position, Somoza Debayle remained the *de facto* head of state and government.

In 1972, Managua, the capital, suffered an earthquake that killed 10,000 and displaced 50,000 families. In the aftermath the national guard was accused of looting the city while Somoza Debayle was accused of filtering off several million dollars worth of international aid. Amid an atmosphere of rising tensions martial law was declared and Somoza Debayle was named the government's chief executive. In Sept. 1974 he won the presidency in a disputed election and, under the terms of a new constitution, began a tenure scheduled to last for 7 years.

Somoza Debayle's second period in office was marked by increasingly organized opposition, particularly from the militant Sandinista National Liberation Front (FSLN). The FSLN kidnapped several leading Somoza Debayle associates in late 1974 and successfully negotiated a US$1 m. ransom, the release of 14 FSLN prisoners and an escape route to Cuba. Somoza Debayle responded by increasing press censorship, authorizing the ruthless suppression of rival political movements and allowing the national guard to terrorize the civilian population. Nonetheless, the rebel movement was invigorated. The US, fearing the country would fall to communism, had been long-time supporters of the Somoza dynasty but when Jimmy Carter became president in 1977 he demanded an improvement in Somoza Debayle's human rights record. When it failed to materialize Carter withdrew military assistance, forcing Somoza Debayle to find new sources for arms procurement, paying prices which the failing economy could not afford.

At home the Broad Opposition Front (FAO), including a group of high-profile business and academic figures known as Los Doce (The Group of 12), was pushing Somoza Debayle for a negotiated settlement. The FSLN, having forged ties with the FAO, orchestrated a national strike in Jan. 1978 when Pedro Chamorro, editor of the leading anti-government newspaper, was murdered. The FSLN then seized the national palace in Aug. 1978 and held over 2,000 officials hostage for 2 days. The FSLN won another large ransom, safe passage out of the country for the kidnappers and the distribution of an FSLN statement through the national media. At the end of 1978 the UN condemned the Somoza Debayle regime for human rights abuses.

During 1978 and 1979 the FSLN seized several individual cities but was each time defeated by concentrated national guard opposition. In May, boosted by weapons from Venezuela, Cuba and Panama, the FSLN launched a nationwide operation and by the end of June had seized control of all major cities except Managua. International opinion decisively turned against Somoza Debayle at this time when the murder by the national guard of an American Broadcasting Company news reporter, Bill Stewart, was caught on camera. With total defeat imminent and the national infrastructure and economy ravaged by the civil war, Somoza Debayle resigned the presidency on 17 July 1979 and went into exile in Florida. The FSLN leader Daniel Ortega succeeded him as president.

Later Life

From Miami, Somoza Debayle went to Paraguay, having smuggled out large sums of money from Nicaragua in the preceding months. In Sept. 1980 he was assassinated in Asunción in what was believed to be a rocket attack by a communist organization.

Spaak, Paul-Henri (Belgium)

Introduction

Twice Belgian prime minister (1938–39, 1947–49), Paul-Henri Spaak was a founder of Benelux, the economic union of Belgium, the Netherlands and Luxembourg, and a key player in the establishment of the Common Market. His chairmanship of the European Economic Community (1948–50) and the European Coal and Steel Community (1952–54) earned him the nickname 'Mr Europe'.

Early Life

Spaak was born on 25 Jan. 1899 in Schaerbeek, Belgium. His mother was the first female senator in the country's parliament, and he inherited his interest in socialist politics from her. After World War I he studied law in Brussels and continued to practice as a lawyer for 10 years after taking his degree.

Spaak was elected as a Socialist member of the Chamber of Deputies in 1932. He held the post of minister of transport, posts and telegraphs from 1935–36, before becoming foreign minister in 1936. Whilst in the latter position, he secured British and French approval for Belgium's independent foreign policy.

Career Peak

In 1938 he was elected as Belgium's first Socialist prime minister, but resigned from the post the following year. Spaak resumed his role as foreign minister in Hubert Pierlot's government. Which was forced into exile in London when Nazi Germany occupied Belgium. Whilst in London Spaak helped to formulate a plan for a Benelux customs union. He also played a significant role in the drafting of the United Nations Charter in 1945, and was elected to serve as the first president of the United Nations General Assembly in 1946.

In 1947 he was elected prime minister of the coalition government again. During this tenure he brought the Benelux customs union into existence. He also presided over the introduction of female suffrage, and the state's acquisition of the National Bank. In 1948 he signed the Brussels Treaty, enabling the existence of a regional defence alliance between Britain, France and the Benelux nations which was to culminate in the formation of NATO in 1949.

Spaak's socialist and republican sympathies led him to advise Léopold III to abandon his throne in the face of political upheaval. His counsel proved influential and Léopold abdicated in 1951. Having previously been nationalist in inclination, Spaak became increasingly committed to the cause of a unified Europe. In the 1950s he chaired a number of organizations which promoted European political and economic co-operation, including the European Coal and Steel Community, a forerunner of the Common Market. His experience and interest in European integration meant that he played a major role in the 1957 negotiation of the Treaty of Rome, which was to inaugurate the Common Market.

In the same year Spaak became secretary general of NATO, having served as a foreign minister for the previous 3 years. He held this post until 1961 and then resumed political office in Belgium as deputy premier and foreign minister under the leadership of Théo Lefevre.

Later Life

Spaak finally retired from politics in 1966 and for the last 6 years of his life worked in private business, dying in Brussels on 31 July 1972. He continues to be remembered as a founding father of the political, social and economic institutions of the EU.

Spencer, Baldwin (Antigua and Barbuda)

Introduction

Baldwin Spencer is leader of the United Progressive Party (UPP) and took office as prime minister in March 2004, defeating the Antigua Labour Party (ALP), which had held power continuously since 1976.

Early Life

Baldwin Spencer was born on 8 Oct. 1948 in Grays Green, Antigua. After secondary school, he studied social leadership at St Francis Xavier University's Coady International Institute in Nova Scotia. He also obtained a diploma in labour and economic studies from Ruskin College (at Oxford in the UK) and in labour and industrial relations from Oslo University.

In the 1970s Spencer worked as a trade unionist, serving as vice-president and, later, assistant general secretary of the Antigua and Barbuda Workers' Union (AWU). He also served as president of the Caribbean Maritime and Aviation Council.

In 1989 Spencer entered parliament as the United Democratic Party (UNDP) representative for St John's Rural West constituency. In 1991 he became leader of the UNDP and, as leader of the opposition in parliament, formed an alliance with the two other main opposition parties, the Antigua Caribbean Liberation Movement and the Progressive Labour Movement. They merged in 1992 to form the UPP.

During the 1990s Spencer regularly accused Prime Minister Vere Bird, Sr and his ALP of corruption. The campaign helped exploit rifts within the government and Bird's own son, Lester Bird, called for his father's resignation. Lester Bird took over as prime minister shortly before the general election of March 2004. Spencer led the UPP into the election promising more transparent government, and the party won 12 of 17 seats.

Career Peak

Spencer vowed to combat corruption, develop tourism and foster economic co-operation with other countries. In the first year he introduced legislation to improve government accountability and took steps to de-politicize the government-owned media. However, corruption investigations were hampered by the loss of government files and in 2005 Spencer set up a taskforce to tackle organized crime and corruption among officials.

In Oct. 2004 an IMF report concluded that Antigua and Barbuda's economy suffered from high levels of public debt and over-reliance on the government for jobs (accounting for 40% of total employment). Spencer responded in 2005 by launching a drive to expand the tourism industry, taking measures to cut the public service salary bill, and reintroducing income tax. The tourism drive was undermined, however, in July 2008 by the murder of a visiting British couple. Spencer's UPP won a second term by taking 9 of the 17 seats in the parliamentary elections of March 2009.

He pursued closer ties with Brazil, China, India, Russia and neighbouring Caribbean countries (serving as chair of CARICOM in 2004) but was locked in a trade dispute with the USA over intellectual property rights. However, the WTO eventually ruled that Antigua could suspend these rights. This would permit online gambling companies access to the US market.

Spencer's UPP party was defeated at parliamentary elections held on 12 June 2014, and he was subsequently replaced as premier by ABLP leader Gaston Browne.

Špidla, Vladimír (Czech Republic)

Introduction

Following electoral victory for the Social Democratic Party (ČSSD), Vladimír Špidla became prime minister on 12 July 2002. He had replaced incumbent Miloš Zeman as party leader in April 2001. Špidla heads a coalition with a narrow majority, although he has broad cross-party support in preparing the Czech Republic for entry into the EU. He resigned the premiership on 1 July 2004.

Early Life

Špidla was born on 22 April 1951 in Prague. He graduated in history from the Charles University in Prague. After several manual jobs in a factory, a dairy and backstage of a theatre, he took an administrative role with the cultural department of the Jindrichuv Hradec District national committee and was later an archaeologist with the district museum.

In 1990 he was appointed vice chairman of the Jindrichuv Hradec District national committee with special responsibility for education, health and social issues. In the same year he became a founding member of the ČSSD. From 1991–96 he was director of the local labour office. In 1996 he was made ČSSD spokesman on social and labour affairs and became chairman of the South Bohemian wing of the party, as well as a vice president of the national party.

In April 2001 the prime minister, Miloš Zeman, resigned the party leadership and announced that he would stand down as premier before the elections of 2002. Špidla was elected his successor as chairman of the ČSSD. He led the party to victory at the June 2002 elections, when they won 30.2% of the vote.

Career Peak

A coalition with the centrist Christian Democrats and the Freedom Union gave Špidla 101 of the 200 parliamentary seats. He pledged to prepare the country for entry into the EU and in Oct. 2002 it was confirmed that the Czech Republic could join in 2004. He also promised high levels of welfare spending, ruling out Czech Republic entry into the single currency until 2010 at the earliest. His spending promises risk confrontation with the Freedom Union. Relations with Germany and Austria deteriorated over the Czech parliament's refusal to repeal the Beneš decree, which allowed for the expulsion of 2.5 m. ethnic Germans after the Second World War.

In Aug. 2002 the Czech Republic suffered massive flooding, causing damage estimated at more than US$2 bn. As a result Špidla was expected to authorize increased borrowing, as parliament rejected a tax increase to help victims. The defence ministry cancelled an order for jet fighters worth US$2 bn. which were to have brought the country's air defences up to NATO standards. In June 2003 membership of the EU won 77% approval in a national referendum.

Špidla's domestic agenda has focused on EU compliance, specifically the Maastricht criteria for accession to the euro. Špidla aims to reduce the budget deficit to 4% of GDP by 2006. A package of reforms, on which the government had staked its future, was passed by the Chamber of Deputies in Sept. 2003. The reforms included raising the pension age, increasing consumer tax and cutting benefits for illness. However, tensions within the government have developed over the deficit reduction programme. Finance Minister Bohuslav Sobotka opposed wage increases for a raft of public sector employees, including customs officers and firemen, sponsored by Špidla and Interior Minister Stanislav Gross. The reform programme is opposed by trade unions, who see it as unnecessarily severe, and economists, who point to the need for fundamental reform of the social welfare system and for significant reductions in corporate income tax to encourage foreign investment.

Relations with Špidla's predecessor, Miloš Zeman, and his supporters deteriorated after the 2002 parliamentary elections. Špidla opposed Zeman's bid for the presidency, which he lost in the first round. However, Špidla survived an attempt to dislodge him at the party's caucus in 2003. He announced his resignation on 26 June 2004 in the wake of his party's defeat in the June 2004 European Parliament elections and officially resigned on 1 July.

Stalin, Joseph (Russia)

Introduction

As secretary-general of the Communist party, Joseph Stalin was effectively the Soviet Union's head-of-state from 1924–53. He was premier from 1941.

An advocate of Leninism, he rapidly industrialized the economy and enforced agricultural collectivization. He led the Soviet Union to ultimate victory during World War II and was overlord of the communist Eastern Bloc in the aftermath. He encouraged a personality cult and his totalitarian regime relied on terror as its chief weapon of enforcement. The persecution of perceived political enemies, allied to the disastrous effects of agricultural collectivization and the limited benefits of industrialization resulted in the deaths of tens of millions of Soviet citizens. His animosity towards the West propelled the world into the Cold War, the impact of his reign continuing long after his death.

Early Life

Stalin was born as Iosef Vissaryonovich Dzhugashvili on 21 Dec. 1879 in Gori (Georgia), the son of a cobbler and a washerwoman. He trained to be a priest but engaged in underground political activities from 1900, joining the Bolshevik Party 3 years later. In 1904 he married Ekaterina Svanidze, who had one son before dying in 1907.

Frequently arrested for his revolutionary activities, Stalin attended party congresses abroad and worked in the Georgian party press. In 1912, having adopted the name Stalin (derived from the Russian word for *steel*), he went to St Petersburg and was elected to the party's central committee. In 1913 he was sent into Siberian exile for 4 years. He became editor of *Pravda*, and when the Bolsheviks took power in Nov. 1917, he became the people's commissar of nationalities and a state inspector. Succeeding to the job of party secretary in 1922, he was in the strongest position to take over from Lenin as party leader, ahead of his chief rivals Leon Trotsky, Lev Kamenev and Grigory Zinoviev. The last two ruled briefly with Stalin in a three-pronged leadership following Lenin's death.

Career Peak

Between 1924 and 1929 Stalin forced out other leading Bolsheviks. Trotsky was exiled from the Soviet Union in 1929. Stalin's command economy led to agricultural collectivization and industrialization at all costs. Working with the credo that the end justifies the means, millions died of starvation between 1932 and 1934. His 5 year plans (first applied in1928) were implemented ruthlessly. Political repression and terror reached their height in the 1930s. In public trials, a large number of prominent politicians including Nikolai Bukharin (a leading policy adviser who assisted in drafting the 1936 constitution), Kamenev, Zinoviev and Marshall Mikhail Tukhachevsky (a leading military figure), were charged with conspiring to overthrow the regime and executed. Others who opposed Stalin's methods met a similar fate or were sent to concentration camps where up to 10 m. peasants are believed to have died. Stalin's second wife, Nadezhda Alliluyeva, with whom he had two children, committed suicide in 1932.

Stalin's foreign policy in the 1930s focused initially on alliances with Britain and France against Nazi Germany but culminated in the Molotov-Ribbentrop non-aggression pact with Germany in 1939. He then made several incursions into Eastern Europe in a bid to strengthen his Western borders. The German invasion of the Soviet Union in 1941, however, brought an abrupt end to the policy of appeasement. Stalin took charge of the counter offensives, directing the gruelling battles of Stalingrad in 1942 and Kursk in 1943, eventually forcing the Germans to capitulate.

At the Tehran and Yalta Conferences, in talks with the US President Roosevelt and the British Prime Minister Winston Churchill, Stalin managed to gain Western recognition of a Soviet sphere of influence in Eastern Europe. The Baltic States and large tracts of land from neighbouring countries were annexed into the Soviet Union, while Poland, Czechoslovakia, eastern Germany, Hungary, Bulgaria, Yugoslavia and Romania all fell under indirect rule from Moscow. In 1949 the Soviet Union exploded a nuclear bomb, a precursor to the intensification of East-West mistrust and fear over the next 40 years.

Stalin's final years were marked by increasing paranoia. His command over the Eastern Bloc was brought into question, particularly by the independent action of General Tito's Yugoslavia. There followed a period of terror reminiscent of the 1930s. Show trials were again common, while Andrei Zhdanov was the chief henchman responsible for controlling the cultural and philosophical climate of Soviet life.

Stalin died suddenly on 5 March 1953. His body was placed next to Lenin's in the Red Square mausoleum but was later removed. His successor Nikita Khrushchev took the unprecedented action of denouncing the worst excesses of Stalin's reign at the 1956 party congress.

Stanishev, Sergey (Bulgaria)

Introduction

Sergey Stanishev, leader of the Bulgarian Socialist Party (BSP), emerged as prime minister of Bulgaria in Aug. 2005 after a closely-fought general election and weeks of negotiations. The Soviet-educated son of a high-ranking official from the communist era, Stanishev spearheaded sweeping reforms to the BSP. He was committed to liberalizing the economy and succeeded in steering the country into the EU in 2007. His chief challenges were to hold together the three-party Coalition for Bulgaria while creating jobs and tackling poverty and crime.

Early Life

Sergey Dimitrievich Stanishev was born on 5 May 1966 in Kherson in the Soviet Republic of Ukraine to a Russian mother and a Bulgarian father, a high-ranking official in the Bulgarian Communist Party (BCP). While studying history at Moscow State University (MGU) in the mid- to late-1980s, he was the Moscow correspondent of *Krugozor*, then Bulgaria's main dissident newspaper. Stanishev remained at MGU after his graduation in 1989 to study for a PhD in late-19th century Russian politics. On his return to Bulgaria in 1994 he worked as a freelance journalist specializing in foreign-policy issues. A year later, under the BSP-led government of Zhan Videnov, he was appointed senior analyst at the department of foreign policy and international affairs within the BSP's supreme council. In 1996, against a backdrop of economic crisis and severe food shortages which culminated in the resignation of Videnov's cabinet, Stanishev was promoted to director of the BSP's department for foreign policy and international affairs, a position he held for 4 years. He continued his studies at the School of Political Studies in Moscow in 1998 and later specialized in international relations at the London School of Economics (1999–2000).

Under the guidance of Georgi Parvanov, the reformist leader of the BSP, Stanishev became more closely involved in the party's organization. Elected to its supreme council in May 2000, he stood in the legislative elections of June 2001 and, despite a generally poor showing by the BSP, went on to represent the town of Rousse in parliament. Following the election of Parvanov as president in Nov. 2001, Stanishev was voted chairman of the BSP and chairman of the parliamentary group of the BSP-led Coalition for Bulgaria. Although inexperienced, he was credited with reforming the structure of the party and updating its image, attracting younger members. Having been re-elected BSP chairman in June 2002, he forged alliances with other European socialist parties, and the BSP became a member of Socialist International in Oct. 2003.

In the run-up to the general election of 25 June 2005, Stanishev criticized Simeon II's ruling National Movement (NMS) for failing to improve living standards. Parvanov promised to boost wages and pensions by 20%, spend more on health and social services and create more than 200,000 new jobs. He won the seat of the port city of Bourgas but the BSP-led coalition claimed an insufficient cut of the overall vote to rule alone and political deadlock ensued. On 27 July parliament chose Stanishev as prime minister in a coalition with the NMS but voted against his proposed cabinet, leading to further wrangling. Under pressure from the EU, a coalition of the BSP, the NMS and the ethnic-Turkish Movement for Rights and Freedoms (MRF) was formed. On 16 Aug. Stanishev received 168 parliamentary votes (against 67) and was sworn in as prime minister the same day.

Career Peak

As well as ensuring Bulgaria's accession to the EU, which took place on 1 Jan. 2007, Stanishev's priorities as prime minister included sustaining economic growth, reforming the judiciary and introducing measures against crime and corruption. However, gangland shootings continued and anti-corruption drives did not produce convincing results, prompting censure by the European Commission and the suspension in July 2008 of EU aid payments.

At parliamentary elections on 5 July 2009 the coalition led by the Bulgarian Socialist Party won only 40 seats compared to the 116 taken by Citizens for the European Development of Bulgaria. The mayor of Sofia, Boyko Borisov, was named prime minister delegate and succeeded Stanishev on 27 July.

Later Life

Stanishev has remained active in European politics following his term as prime minister and is currently president of the Party of European Socialists European political party—a position he has held since Nov. 2011.

Stephanopoulos, Constantinos Dimitriou (Greece)

Introduction

A veteran, centre-right politician, Stephanopoulos was elected by parliament to the mainly ceremonial office of president of the Hellenic Republic in 1995 and again in 2000. He was the first president to have been elected to two consecutive terms since the fall of the military dictatorship in 1974.

Early Life

Stephanopoulos was born on 15 Aug. 1926 in Patras. Following his graduation from the University of Athens, he practised as a lawyer in Patras from 1954–74, often representing opponents of the military junta. He first entered parliament for the constituency of Achaia in 1964 as a National Radical Union candidate. However, in 1974 he joined the New Democracy (ND) party founded by Constantine Karamanlis. After election to the party's central committee, he held several ministerial positions (with responsibility successively for commerce, interior affairs, social affairs, and as secretary of state to the prime minister) in the post-dictatorship governments from 1974–81. After losing two party leadership contests—in 1981 following the ND's general election defeat and in 1984 following the party's poor performance in the European Parliament elections—Stephanopoulos resigned in Sept. 1985 to form a right-wing splinter grouping, the Democratic Renewal Party, with other dissident ND members. He retreated into semi retirement after dissolving the party in 1994 when it failed to win representation in the elections to the European Parliament. However, he remained a respected public figure.

Career Peak

Nominated as a presidential candidate by the rightwing, populist Political Spring movement, but also backed by the ruling Pan-Hellenic Socialist Movement (PASOK), Stephanopoulos was elected president by the Chamber of Deputies on 8 March 1995. He was re-elected on 8 Feb. 2000 with a sweeping majority, receiving 269 of the 300 parliamentary votes, the largest margin of victory in a presidential poll since the military dictatorship. Stephanopoulos was replaced with Karolos Papoulias after his second 5-year term ended on 11 March 2005.

Later Life

Stephanopoulos died on 20 Nov. 2016 at the age of 90 after a short illness.

Stephen, Marcus (Nauru)

Introduction

Marcus Stephen became president in Dec. 2007 after a vote of no confidence against the previous incumbent, Ludwig Scotty. Stephen had served as education and finance minister from 2003–04 and represented Nauru on the International Whaling Commission (IWC) from 2005. He was re-elected by parliament in Nov. 2010. In Nov. 2011 Stephen resigned following corruption claims from opposition members of parliament.

Early Life

Born in Nauru on 1 Oct. 1969, Marcus Stephen attended secondary school and university in Australia. After completing his education, he returned to Nauru and played Australian rules football before switching to weightlifting. His success in the sport led to the establishment of the Nauru Weightlifting Federation in 1989. Stephen subsequently represented Nauru in the 1996 and 2000 Olympics, won a series of gold and silver medals in four successive Commonwealth Games and was a runner-up in the 1999 World Championship. He was appointed treasurer of the Nauru Olympic Committee in 1997. On 3 May 2003 he was elected to parliament, representing the constituency of Ewa and Anetan.

Stephen served as education and finance minister in the government of René Harris from Aug. 2003–June 2004. He was re-elected to parliament in Oct. 2004, when he served under President Ludwig Scotty. When Nauru joined the IWC in June 2005, Stephen was nominated as a delegate for Nauru. Following parliamentary elections in Aug. 2007, he stood as a presidential candidate but lost out to Scotty. Allegations of corruption within the Scotty government led to a vote of no confidence in Nov. 2007, supported by Stephen. Scotty survived the vote but on 19 Dec. 2007 a second vote forced his resignation, paving the way for Stephen to become president.

Career Peak

Stephen took office promising transparency in public affairs. Dr. Kieren Keke, who had been instrumental in bringing the votes of no confidence against Scotty, was appointed foreign minister. Early indications suggested Stephen was likely to maintain the financial reform programme and tighter banking regulations brought in by Scotty. The beginning of 2008 saw a deterioration in the economic climate when a controversial Australian immigrants' detention centre was closed. The island had hosted the centre, which generated 20% of GDP, for 7 years. Replacing this income source was an urgent priority. Longer term challenges included a fundamental rebuilding of the economy and reparation of the environment.

In April 2008 a snap parliamentary election called by Stephen resulted in a win for his supporters, and at the parliament's first sitting he was re-elected as president. Further inconclusive parliamentary elections in April and June 2010 resulted in a political impasse, with the government continuing in a caretaker capacity until Nov. when Stephen was finally confirmed as president by parliament for another 3-year term. However, his second term proved short-lived. The opposition accused the president of seeking to illegally profit from a phosphate deal and on 10 Nov. 2011 Stephen announced his resignation.

Later Life

Stephen returned to the cabinet in June 2012 when he was appointed minister for commerce, industry and the environment.

Stevenson, Adlai E. (United States of America)

Introduction

Adlai Ewing Stevenson was Governor of Illinois from 1949–53 and an unsuccessful Democratic Presidential candidate in 1952 and 1956 (on both occasions losing to Republican Dwight D. Eisenhower). From 1961–65 he served as the US ambassador to the United Nations, playing an important role in helping defuse the Cuban Missile Crisis.

Early Life

Born in Los Angeles on 5 Feb. 1900, Stevenson had politics in his blood—his grandfather having served as Vice-President from 1893–97. After studying at Princeton and Northwestern University, Stevenson began practicing law in Chicago in 1926.

In 1932 President Roosevelt appointed Stevenson special counsel to the Agricultural Adjustment Agency. Throughout the 1930s Stevenson, an anti-isolationist, was also chairman of the Chicago chapter of the Committee to

Defend America by Aiding the Allies and head of the Civil Rights Committee of the Chicago Bar Association. From 1941 until 1944, Stevenson was special assistant to Frank Knox, the secretary of the Navy. In 1945 he was appointed senior advisor of the American delegation that met in San Francisco and then London to found the United Nations.

Career Peak

In 1948 Stevenson was elected governor of Illinois by the then largest majority in the state's history. He increased state aid for schools, improved the state highway system and attacked organized gambling. Persuaded to accept a draft nomination as Democratic presidential candidate in 1952, Stevenson fought an energetic campaign but was easily defeated by war hero Dwight D. Eisenhower by 442 electoral college votes to 89.

Maintaining his interest in foreign affairs, Stevenson secured the Democratic nomination for the 1956 election on the first ballot at the Democratic National Convention. However he once again lost to Eisenhower, this time by an even greater margin. His emphasis on foreign affairs and his proposal to end H-bomb testing contributed to the scale of his defeat.

Later Life

After John F. Kennedy was elected president in 1960, Stevenson was appointed US ambassador to the United Nations. His influence on the Kennedy and Johnson administrations led to the Nuclear Test Ban Treaty of 1963, and he played an active role in the Cuban Missile Crisis, when he persuaded many UN member countries to support America's stance or remain neutral. Stevenson died in London of a heart attack on 14 July 1965.

Stoltenberg, Jens (Norway)

Introduction

Jens Stoltenberg became prime minister of Norway for a second time on 17 Oct. 2005, following the victory of his centre-left coalition in parliamentary elections, having previously held the office from 2000–01. He was returned to power again in elections in Sept. 2009 and served a 4-year term before his Labour Party and its coalition allies lost power in the elections of Sept. 2013.

Early Life

Jens Stoltenberg was born in Oslo on 16 March 1959, the son of politicians. He studied economics at Oslo University, where he joined the Norwegian Labour Party (Det Norske Arbeiderpartiet, DNA). In 1985 he was appointed leader of the Labour Youth League and from 1985–89 was vice president of the International Union of Socialist Youth. He also worked briefly at the National Statistics Office and was an economics lecturer at Oslo University before serving for 2 years as leader of the Oslo Labour Party (1990–92). He was also a state secretary at the department of the environment at this time.

Elected a member of the Storting (parliament) for Oslo in the Sept. 1993 general election, Stoltenberg served as minister of trade and energy from 1993–96 and oversaw Norway's accession to the European Economic Area in 1994. In Oct. 1996 he was made minister of finance, a post he held for a year until the DNA lost power to the conservative Christian People's Party, led by Kjell Magne Bondevik. Bondevik, who attempted to govern with a coalition which held a slim majority, resigned in March 2000 and Stoltenberg (by now deputy leader of the DNA) was asked to form a government as the youngest prime minister in Norway's history.

Career Peak

Stoltenberg controversially ushered in reforms to the welfare state that included the part-privatization of several state-owned services. In the parliamentary elections of Sept. 2001 the party suffered a heavy defeat and Bondevik returned as prime minister of a centre-right coalition. A DNA party leadership battle between Stoltenberg and Jagland (leader since 1992) ensued with Stoltenberg emerging victorious.

Thanks to burgeoning oil and gas exports and high international prices, the economy prospered under Bondevik but the DNA's campaign in the run-up to the Sept. 2005 parliamentary elections centred on increased funding for education, health and care of the elderly. In partnership with the Socialist Left Party and the Centre Party, the DNA took 87 of 169 seats. Stoltenberg was sworn in to office on 17 Oct. 2005.

Stoltenberg vowed to reform the welfare system while creating conditions for Norway to develop as a knowledge-based economy. He also pledged sustainable management of the country's fish and energy resources. In 2006 his administration approved the expansion of oil exploration in the Barents Sea and also the merger of Norway's two largest energy companies, Statoil and Norsk Hydro (with the government having a controlling stake in the combined group). Stoltenberg withdrew the small contingent of Norwegian troops from Iraq, but promised to increase the country's participation in United Nations peacekeeping missions elsewhere in the world.

In Sept. 2009 his centre-left coalition was returned to power in parliamentary elections, with the DNA (renamed the Labour Party/AP in April 2011) marginally increasing its share of the vote.

In July 2011 the government was confronted with an unprecedented act of violence in Norway as a right-wing extremist set off a bomb in central Oslo, killing eight people, before going on a shooting rampage at a political youth camp run by Stoltenberg's AP near the capital and murdering another 69 victims. The perpetrator was sentenced to the maximum allowable prison term in Aug. 2012.

In Sept. 2012 Stoltenberg carried out an extensive cabinet reshuffle as he entered the final year of his term before elections scheduled for Sept. 2013. The changes included the appointment to the culture portfolio of Hadia Tajik, who became Norway's youngest-ever cabinet member and first Muslim minister.

Stoltenberg sought re-election at the 2013 elections, but his Red–Green coalition failed to secure a majority, despite the Labour Party winning most seats and the highest share of the vote. He was succeeded as prime minister on 16 Oct. 2013 by Erna Solberg.

Later Life

In March 2014 Stoltenberg was named as the next Secretary General of NATO. He took over from Anders Fogh Rasmussen of Denmark on 1 Oct. 2014.

Straujuma, Laimdota (Latvia)

Introduction

On 6 Jan. 2014 Laimdota Straujuma was appointed as Latvia's first female prime minister by President Andris Bērziņš following the resignation of Valdis Dombrovskis in Nov. 2013. She is an economist and civil servant who was previously minister for agriculture.

Early Life

Straujuma was born on 24 Feb. 1951. She read mathematics and physics at the University of Latvia from 1968–73 and undertook post-graduate studies in agricultural economics at the Institute of Economics of the Latvian Academy of Sciences in 1987. In 1992 she completed her doctorate and in 1996 studied business management at the University of Central Lancashire in England.

After working with the Latvian Agricultural Consulting and Educational Support Centre in the 1990s, Straujuma entered government in 1999 as deputy secretary of state in the ministry for agriculture. From 2000–06 she served as its secretary of state and was also a member of the council of the Mortgage and Land Bank of Latvia from 2002–07. She was secretary of state of the ministry for regional development and local government from 2006 until 2010, then spent a year as deputy state secretary of the ministry of environmental protection and regional development. Between Oct. 2011 and Jan. 2014 she was minister for agriculture.

In Nov. 2013 Dombrovskis resigned as premier after the collapse of a supermarket roof in Riga. Straujuma was nominated by the Unity-led coalition as his replacement.

Career Peak

Straujuma stated that her centre-right government would continue the tight fiscal policies of the previous administration—which had seen Latvia become one of the fastest-growing economies in the eurozone—in the run-up to the general election scheduled for Oct. 2014. In March 2014 she condemned Russia's intervention in Ukrainian territory, which also heightened Latvian concerns over Russian intentions towards the Balkan states. At the Oct. poll her pro-European stance contributed to the coalition's re-election with a clear parliamentary majority. In Jan. 2015 Latvia assumed the rotating 6-month presidency of the European Union.

Amid infighting within the government, Straujuma announced her resignation in Dec. 2015, citing a need for 'new ideas, a new contribution and a new energy'. However, she remained in the position until Māris Kučinskis of the Union of Greens and Farmers was sworn in as her replacement in Feb. 2016.

Stroessner, Alfredo (Paraguay)

Introduction

Alfredo Stroessner ruled Paraguay for 35 years as a military dictator. He seized power in a coup in 1954 and led the country until he in turn was deposed in Feb. 1989. During his dictatorship he suppressed all opposition and was implicated in numerous human rights abuses and even genocide.

Early Life

The son of a German immigrant, Alfredo Stroessner was born on 3 Nov. 1912, in Encarnación, Paraguay. He attended the Military College in Asunción, and was granted a commission into the Paraguayan army in 1932. He fought in the Chaco War against Bolivia (1932–35), winning two medals during the conflict and gaining the respect of his troops through his courage and leadership. He rose through the ranks to general and in 1951 became the commander-in-chief of the armed forces.

Career Peak

Through his position in the armed forces, Stroessner orchestrated a coup d'état against President Federico Chávez in May 1954, forcing his resignation. Once elected candidate for the Colorado Party, he assumed the presidency later that year after an election in which only he was eligible.

His regime achieved some success through modernization: the main roads were paved, there was a significant increase in the number of schools and colleges, the Catholic University of Asunción was founded, the Itaipú Dam hydro-electric power plant (the world's largest) was built and many remote areas were colonized and populated. He stabilized the currency and reduced inflation but also spent a high proportion of the national budget on the military to maintain his authority.

New constitutions were passed in 1967 and 1977 to legitimize his eight successive election victories. Opposition was repressed nationally and in the government: Stroessner's control of the armed forces and use of secret police meant that detractors faced possible torture, exile and death.

In the early morning of 3 Feb. 1989 General Andrés Rodríguez led a coup against the 76-year-old dictator in a bid to take the country towards democracy and allowed Stroessner (his father-in-law) 12 h to leave. He was accepted into Brazil where he lives in exile.

Later Life

In Dec. 1992, Dr. Martin Almeda, a Paraguayan lawyer and human rights activist, stumbled upon a mass of documents relating to one of the most controversial aspects of Stroessner's reign: his involvement of Paraguay in Operation Condor. This was a reciprocal agreement between the dictators of South America's Southern Cone countries (Brazil, Argentina, Uruguay, Chile and Paraguay) to work together in the elimination or suppression of perceived leftist activity in the area during the 1970s and 80s. The files document thousands of human rights abuses and illegal arrests and extraditions conducted under Stroessner.

Despite repeated extradition requests, and the discovery of yet more files in Feb. 2002, Stroessner remained in political asylum in Brazil. He died on 16 Aug. 2006 after a long period of ill health.

Stuart, Freundel (Barbados)

Introduction

Freundel Stuart was sworn into office in Oct. 2010 after the death of David Thompson, having served as acting prime minister since May that year when Thompson took a leave of absence. In Feb. 2013 he led his Democratic Labour Party to electoral victory.

Early Life

Freundel Jerome Stuart was born on 27 April 1951 in the parish of St Philip. He was educated at Christ Church Boys' Foundation School. He later taught history and Spanish at the Princess Margaret Secondary School in St Philip. In 1970 he joined the Democratic Labour Party (DLP) but did not stand for election until the 1990s.

Stuart graduated in history and political science from the University of the West Indies at Cave Hill in 1975. He gained further degrees in law and was called to the Barbados Bar in 1984. Beginning in criminal law, he later switched to the civil code.

In 1994 Stuart won the seat of St Philip South which he subsequently lost at the 1999 election. From 2003–07 he served in the Senate but in 2008 returned to the lower house after winning the constituency of St Michael South. He was also admitted to the Inner Bar and appointed Queen's Counsel. Stuart joined the Thompson administration as minister of home affairs and was later appointed attorney general and deputy prime minister.

In May 2010 Stuart was named acting prime minister when Thompson took leave because of ill health. On 23 Oct. 2010, after Thompson's death from cancer, Stuart was selected by the DLP as his successor.

Career Peak

Upon taking office, Stuart made few changes to the cabinet except for the appointment of Adriel Brathwaite as attorney general and minister of home affairs. Stuart has largely followed his predecessor's programme, which aims to tackle poverty, unemployment and housing shortages. On 20 Jan. 2011 the government was boosted when Mara Thompson, David Thompson's widow, won the by-election for her late husband's St John seat by an overwhelming majority.

At the general election of 21 Feb. 2013 the DLP won 16 of the 30 parliamentary seats, securing Stuart a mandate for a full term in office. Polls prior to the election had suggested the DLP were running behind the opposition Barbados Labour Party, which took 14 seats. After the opposition Barbados Labour Party won all 30 House of Assembly seats at the May 2018 general election Stuart was replaced as prime minister by Mia Mottley, who became the country's first female prime minister.

Stubb, Alexander (Finland)

Introduction

Alexander Stubb became prime minister in June 2014, when he took over as leader of the ruling right-of-centre National Coalition Party at the head of a coalition government. In April 2015 his party was defeated in parliamentary elections, after which his tenure continued in a caretaker capacity until a new coalition took office nearly 6 weeks later.

Early Life

Stubb was born on 1 April 1968 in Helsinki. After finishing his military service, he graduated in 1993 in political science from Furman University,

South Carolina, USA. He then undertook graduate studies in French and European Affairs at, respectively, the Sorbonne in Paris, France and the College of Europe in Belgium, before completing a doctorate in 1999 on integration in the EU at the London School of Economics in England.

He then worked as a researcher at the Finnish ministry of foreign affairs and at the Academy of Finland. From 1999–2001 he was a member of the Finnish team negotiating the EU Treaty of Nice, which paved the way for the Union's eastward expansion. From 2001 he was an adviser to the president of the European Commission, and in 2003–04 served as a delegate on intergovernmental negotiations on the European Convention (on the Future of Europe). Between 2004 and 2008 he was a member of the European Parliament for the National Coalition Party, serving as vice-president of the committee on the internal market and consumer protection. In 2006 he produced a report on the cost of translation services to the EU.

In April 2008 Stubb was appointed Finland's foreign minister, in which role he chaired the Organization for Security and Co-operation in Europe (OSCE) during its monitoring role in the 2008 conflict in Georgia. Elected to the Finnish parliament for the first time in 2011, he was appointed minister for European affairs and foreign trade, consolidating his reputation as a champion of liberal economics. In April 2014, following Prime Minister Jyrki Katainen's decision to resign, he entered the contest for his party's leadership, winning after a second round by 500 votes to 349. He then set about forming a five-party coalition and was appointed premier by President Sauli Niinistö on 24 June 2014.

Career Peak

On assuming office, Stubb was faced with maintaining economic stability in the face of significant pressures and managing delicate relations with neighbouring Russia. He pledged to implement reforms and tax cuts to reinvigorate the economy, while strongly advocating Finland's accession to NATO.

He succeeded by Juha Sipilä, who formed a coalition after his Centre Party won the elections of April 2015 in which the National Coalition Party came third. Stubb joined Sipilä's government as finance minister.

Stubb was ousted as leader of the National Coalition Party in June 2016 following a vote at the party congress. Petteri Orpo took over as leader of the party and replaced Stubb as finance minister.

Suárez González, Adolfo (Spain)

Introduction

Adolfo Suárez González was prime minister of Spain between 1976–81. Originally representing the Movimiento Nacional (National Movement), he won the 1977 elections as head of the Unión Centro Democrático (Union of the Democratic Centre Party; UCD). He was instrumental in Spain's transition from the Franco regime to democracy.

Early Life

González was born on 25 Sept. 1932 in Cebreros, Avila. The son of a civil servant, Suárez studied law at the University of Salamanca and later at the University of Madrid. He held various posts within the Movimiento Nacional before entering a career in national television and radio. He was director-general of the national broadcasting network from 1965 to 1973. He held key positions in the Movimiento Nacional as civil governor and then as head of the party in Segovia. In 1975 he became the party's secretary-general and in Dec. of that year achieved cabinet rank.

Career Peak

Between 1975–6, directly after Franco's death, the head of government was Arias Navarro. Unable to guide Spain's transition to democracy, and amid public demonstrations of discontent, Navarro resigned in July 1976. King Juan Carlos appointed Suárez as his successor. The King's choice provoked some surprise. At this time Suárez was relatively unknown, having worked mainly in provincial politics. The scepticism surrounding Suárez's appointment derived from his history with Franco's Movimiento Nacional and his close connections to the Catholic group Opus Dei, an organization with close ties to the Franco regime. But Suárez took every opportunity to prove his democratic credentials.

In 1976 the government implemented a law to allow workers to organize their own unions. The following year, Suárez revoked the Law of Association, which had outlawed opposition parties. Ten political parties were acknowledged including the UCD, The Partido Comunista de España (Spanish Communist Party; PCE) and the Partido Socialista Obrero Español (Spanish Socialist Workers' Party; PSOE). The first democratic elections in Spain for over 40 years took place in June 1977 and were won by Suárez representing the UCD. This party, set up by Suárez, was a coalition of centre groups. In 1978 Spain was established as a democratic parliamentary monarchy.

Suárez's government moved even further away from Franco's regime by acknowledging the Basque and Catalonian regions. In 1978 both regions were given provisional autonomy which was confirmed in 1980. Nevertheless, several regions demanded further autonomy. Basque terrorism became a serious problem and the death toll in 1980 ran to one political assassination every 3 days. Meanwhile, the PSOE was gaining support. In the 1979 elections, Suárez lost overall majority.

The introduction of the new constitution was the highpoint of Suárez's premiership. After they had achieved this goal, the constituent groups within the UCD became increasingly factious. Suárez found his time taken up with trying to resolve these squabbles. His popularity was further affected when he appeased the Andalucian Socialist party by promising the region's autonomy. Finally the in-party squabbling became too destructive and Suárez resigned as prime minister in Jan. 1981. He was replaced by Leopoldo Calvo Sotelo.

Over the 4 years as Spain's premier Suárez effected a remarkable transition towards democracy. Yet, at the time of his resignation Spanish democracy was still vulnerable. The following month saw the last resistance of Francoist sympathizers who tried to stage a coup. Civil Guards led by Lieutenant Colonel Antonio Tejero invaded parliament on 23 Feb. and General Milans del Bosch ordered his tanks onto the streets of Valencia. The coup was quickly put down. In the elections of 1982 the UCD lost power to the PSOE led by Felipe González.

Later Life

After his resignation Suárez founded the Democratic and Social Centre. Over the next few years he vacillated between left and rightwing politics. In 1992 he retired from politics. He died on 23 March 2014 following a long battle with Alzheimer's disease. Spain subsequently renamed Madrid-Barajas airport 'Adolfo Suárez Madrid-Barajas Airport' in honour of him.

Suharto, Mohamed (Indonesia)

Introduction

Mohamed (Thojib N. *also* Raden) Suharto was a military commander and Indonesian president from 1967 until 1998. He presided over the rapid growth of the country's economy while maintaining a dictatorial and often corrupt grip on government.

Early Life

Suharto was born at Kemsu (Kemuju) Argamulija, Java on 8 June 1921. He was trained at the Dutch colonial military school in Gombong (Java), fought as commander of a Japanese-sponsored local army (1943–45) and was instrumental in the struggle for independence (1945–49) against Dutch colonial rule. In 1965 he became Indonesia's chief of army staff. The same year, Suharto repressed a communist coup led by Lt. Col Untung. On 11 March 1967 Suharto forced President Sukarno to sign an executive order, handing him supreme authority. The next day Sukarno was stripped of all political power and Suharto was installed as acting president.

Career Peak

Suharto's first move was to end territorial disputes with Malaysia and re-establish links with the United Nations. Suharto was influential in establishing the Association of South East Asian Nations (ASEAN). His economic policies resulted in a stabilisation of the rupiah, the expansion of manufacturing and the encouragement of foreign investment. The collapse of the oil boom in the mid 1980s destabilised the growing economy and led to inflation. Corruption and cronyism, which typified Suharto's rule, led to social unrest. Riots erupted on 12 May 1998 throughout the archipelago, resulting in the deaths of more than 500 people and the widespread destruction of property. On 21 May, after the Indonesian parliament threatened impeachment proceedings, Suharto resigned ending 32 years of autocratic rule. The 61-year-old Vice President, Bacharuddin Jusuf Habibie took over the presidency.

Later Life

In Aug. 2000 Suharto was charged with corruption and stealing more than US$500 m. from the state. The charges coincided with Forbes Magazine's naming of Suharto as the sixth wealthiest man in the world. By Dec. 2001 his ailing health led to a period of hospitalization and in 2006 judges ruled he was too ill to stand trial. He died on 27 Jan. 2008.

Sukarno, Achmad (Indonesia)

Introduction

Achmad Sukarno (Soekarno) was the founding member of the Partai Nasional Indonesia (PNI; Indonesian National Party) and independent Indonesia's first president from 1949 until 1966. He was instrumental in the struggle for Indonesian independence and became popularly known as Bung (brother or comrade) Karno.

Early Life

Achmad Sukarno was born on 6 June 1901 in Surabaya, East Java. His interest in politics was kindled whilst studying at Hogere Burger School in Surabaya and lodging at the home of Omar Said Tjokroaminoto, a prominent social and religious leader and founding member of Sarekat Islam (Islamic Association). Sukarno exhibited a natural flair for languages which would become instrumental in his rise to power, mastering Javanese, Sundanese, Balinese, Arabic, Dutch, German, French, English and, later, Japanese.

In 1927, after graduating with a degree in civil engineering Sukarno, and colleagues from the nationalist 'General Study Club'. founded the Indonesian Nationalist Association that was to become the PNI. The success of this new movement was to hinge on its bipartisan approach to the struggle for independence and its move away from the call to establish an exclusively communist or Islamic state. The PNI adopted a militant policy of non-co-operation with the Dutch East Indies Government. The movement's initial success was short lived with Sukarno, now Chairman, being arrested, tried and convicted to 4 years' imprisonment for public order offences. Sukarno was released from prison in 1931 to find that the struggle for independence had lost momentum. The PNI disbanded and reformed as Partindo. In 1933 Sukarno was arrested again and exiled to Flores and later at Bengkulu (Benkulan or Bencoolen) in Southern Sumatra.

World War II, the Japanese invasion of the Dutch East Indies and the surrender of the colonial forces in March 1942 changed the backdrop against which the struggle for independence was played. Sukarno welcomed the Japanese as liberators who, in turn, made him their chief advisor. It soon became apparent to many that the Japanese, far from instigating the plan of 'Great East Asia Co-prosperity' as promised, had merely replaced one form of subjugation with their own brand of colonialism. With their supply lines in disarray and increased Indonesian nationalist insurgence the Japanese placed the civil administration of the country in Sukarno's hands. On 17 Aug. 1945, only 2 days after Japan's surrender, Sukarno declared Indonesia's independence.

Career Peak

Sukarno became the first president and chief executive of the new Republic. Mohammad Hatta was his vice-president On 5 Sept. 1945 the first cabinet was formed and Sukarno instated Indonesia's first constitution. A national philosophical ideology, it was called Pancasila and consisted of five guiding principles: belief in one supreme; just and civilised humanitarianism; Indonesian unity; popular sovereignty governed by wise policies arrived at through deliberation and representation; social justice for all Indonesian people. It has subsequently become part of the standard curriculum, and all organisations in Indonesia are required to adopt Pancasila as their guiding ideology.

The fledgling republic soon came under threat from their erstwhile Dutch overlords. Fighting with Dutch forces lasted until 1949 until the Dutch agreed to pass sovereignty to the Federal Republic of Indonesia on 27 Dec. The triumphant Sukarno arrived in Jakarta on 28 Dec. and established his government in the palace of the Dutch governor-general.

Many could only stand and watch as Sukarno indulged himself in a whirlwind round of parties, dances and receptions. The economy faltered. Sukarno disposed of parliamentary democracy with its 60 political parties. In 1959, with popular and military support, he instituted the so-called 'Guided Democracy' and 'Guided Economy'. An executive-dominated electoral system with all parties reorganised into 11 groupings. In 1963 Sukarno declared himself president for life. On 20 Jan. 1965 Sukarno officially withdrew Indonesia from the United Nations in protest of the UN's support for the British-sponsored Federation of Malaysia, calling it 'an imperialist plot of encirclement.'

An attempted communist coup d'etat of Oct. 1965, led by Lt. Col Untung, was brutally quashed by Sukarno's commander of the army, Lt. Col. Mohamed Suharto. Sukarno was forced to sign an executive order on 11 March 1967 handing supreme authority to Suharto. The next day Sukarno was stripped of all political power and Suharto was installed as acting president.

Later Life

Sukarno died on 21 June 1970, under house arrest and with a kidney ailment. More than 500,000 people turned out to pay their last respects in Jakarta. He was buried next to his mother at Biltar, East Java.

Suleiman, Michel (Lebanon)

Introduction

Gen. Michel Suleiman was sworn into office on 25 May 2008, filling a vacuum created when Emile Lahoud's term ended in Nov. 2007. Suleiman was appointed as a 'compromise candidate' after negotiations between the Siniora Western-backed government at that time and the Hizbollah-led opposition.

Early Life

Michel Suleiman was born in Amsheet on 21 Nov. 1948 to a prominent Maronite Christian family. He joined the armed forces in 1967 and graduated from Lebanon's Military Academy in 1970. He went on to complete a degree in political and administrative sciences at the Lebanese University.

Suleiman rose rapidly through the ranks of the armed forces at a time when Syria played a dominant role in Lebanon's military. On 21 Dec. 1998 he was appointed commander of the armed forces when Emile Lahoud left the post to take over the presidency. During his tenure Suleiman managed to maintain the military's non-partisan status and built good relationships with all sides. Following the Feb. 2005 assassination of Rafiq al-Hariri, Suleiman refused to crack down on anti-Syrian demonstrations or sanction military intervention. His stance was credited with paving the way to Syria's withdrawal from Lebanon. Suleiman also ensured that the military stood back when Hizbollah and Israel fought a 34-day war in 2006 and oversaw a successful operation against Fatah al-Islam militants at the Nahr el-Bared refugee camp in 2007.

On 25 May 2008 Suleiman won the presidency with 118 of 127 parliamentary votes after Qatari-brokered talks on Lebanon's political future. His appointment ended 6 months of political deadlock, with the government and opposition agreeing to a power-sharing deal.

Career Peak

Suleiman reappointed pro-Western Fouad Siniora as prime minister on 28 May 2008 and invited him to form a national unity cabinet. In Oct. 2008 Lebanon and Syria established diplomatic ties. However, Suleiman still faced formidable challenges, including the implementation of the UN Security Council resolution calling for all militias in Lebanon to be disarmed. Following general elections in June 2009 in which the pro-Western 14 March Alliance won a majority of seats in the National Assembly, Suleiman designated Alliance leader Saad al-Hariri as the new prime minister. Al-Hariri eventually succeeded in forming a national unity government in Nov. that year but it collapsed in Jan. 2011 after Hizbollah withdrew support and Najib Mikati was appointed prime minister-designate by Suleiman.

Only after 5 months was Mikati able to successfully negotiate the composition of a new administration, for which he relied on Hizbollah's backing. Mikati's government resigned in March 2013 amid disagreements over the organization of parliamentary elections that were scheduled for June. Polling was then postponed at the end of May until Nov. 2014, in view of concerns over the deteriorating security situation in neighbouring Syria. Suleiman nominated Tamman Salam as prime minister-designate in April, but his attempts to form a new government proved unsuccessful until Feb. 2014, during which time Mikati and his ministers remained in office in a caretaker capacity.

Suleiman's constitutionally mandated 6-year term in office ended on 25 May 2014. Since the constitution also prohibits successive presidential terms, the Lebanese parliament was forced to convene to appoint a successor. Suleiman's powers were ultimately transferred to incumbent prime minister Tammam Salam on an interim basis after parliament failed to elect a new president by that date.

Syngman Rhee (South Korea)

Introduction

Syngman Rhee was the first President of Korea. Much of his life was spent in the USA, and his western education and Christianity are often at odds with his Korean nationalism and ever-increasing authoritarianism as President.

Early Life

Rhee was born to a prosperous family on 26 March 1875. A gifted pupil, he received a traditional Confucian education before he was enrolled at a Methodist college. As a student he became a nationalist and converted to Christianity. But his anti-monarchical views, as a member of the Independence Club, attracted the attention of the government. Rhee was arrested in 1898 and imprisoned for 6 years.

After his release, Rhee went to the United States to continue his studies. Eventually he enrolled at Princeton and became the first Korean to graduate from that institution with a PhD. In 1910 he returned to Korea just as the Japanese occupation was beginning. As a nationalist, his activities again fell foul of the authorities and Rhee went back to the United States in 1912.

Rhee remained in America until the end of World War II, leading the Korean campaign for independence. In 1919 a provisional Korean government in exile was formed, with Rhee as its President. He retained the leadership of the independence movement until 1939 when younger exiles in China took over the provisional government. However, Rhee based in Washington, D.C. had the ear of the U.S. government and, when the Japanese occupation of Korea ended in 1945, the Americans installed him as head of the provisional government in Seoul.

Career Peak

In office Rhee showed the ruthlessness that characterized his rule. He founded a political movement that won the first elections in the south of the newly partitioned Korea in 1948. The murder of his rivals, in which he was not directly implicated, cleared the way to Rhee's election as first President of (South) Korea in 1948. He soon banned the opposition party and had its leader tried and executed. Rhee assumed near-dictatorial powers.

When the Korean War broke out in 1950 Rhee sought international assistance to repel the Communist invasion from the north. A US-led UN force was deployed in Korea, but Rhee pursued his own ends when he realised it would not reconquer North Korea. Rhee broke the agreement that had been negotiated with the North but a renewed attack by Communist forces brought him back to the negotiating table in 1953.

Rhee was re-elected in 1952 during the Korean War, in circumstances that prevented a free and universal poll. He was again returned to power in 1956. In 1960 when it was announced that he had won 90% of the poll, students took to the streets. Their protests were put down with heavy casualties, but Rhee's hold on power lost all legitimacy. He went into exile in Hawaii where he died on 19 July 1965.

Szydło, Beata (Poland)

Introduction

Beata Szydło took office as prime minister on 16 Nov. 2015 following the success of her Law and Justice Party (PiS) at parliamentary elections a month earlier. A protégé of often controversial PiS leader Jarosław Kaczyński, Szydło's main challenge was to emerge from his shadow to present a more moderate governing style. However, 1 year on from the election, popular discontent with PiS policies had escalated markedly.

Early Life

Szydło was born on 15 April 1963 in Oświęcim, the daughter of a miner. In 1987 she graduated in ethnography from the Jagiellonian University in Kraków. From 1987–95 she worked as ethnographer at the Historical Museum of Kraków, before going on to establish the Libiaskiego Cultural Centre in 1995. In 1997 she became director of the Brzeszczach Cultural Centre, and in 1998 was appointed mayor of Brzeszcze. In her 7-year tenure she served on various regional councils, and in 2004 she participated in an international leadership programme organised by the US Department of State.

In 2005 Szydło joined the PiS, winning election to the Sejm in Sept. that year. She was re-elected to parliament in 2007, 2011 and 2015. On 24 July 2010 she was appointed PiS vice-president, and in Sept. 2014 became party treasurer. She was a leading figure in her party's 2015 presidential and parliamentary election bids, being credited for the management of Andrzej Duda's successful presidential campaign in May. On 20 June 2015 Kaczyński nominated Szydło as the party's prime ministerial candidate and on 9 Nov. her appointment was confirmed. She replaced Ewa Kopacz on 16 Nov.

Career Peak

Szydło was expected to pursue her party's conservative, nationalistic, anti-Russian and eurosceptic line and to introduce legislation to increase family-focused welfare spending, curb immigration, reduce the retirement age and raise the minimum wage. She indicated that her government would break ranks with the EU by refusing to take an EU quota of migrant refugees agreed by the previous administration, citing security concerns in light of the 2015 Paris Islamist terror attacks.

A perceived drift towards government authoritarianism in 2016 then bred an increasing wave of public dissent that included mass protests against plans to limit the powers of the Constitutional Court and to tighten anti-abortion legislation, as well as a parliamentary sit-in by opposition members in Dec. over PiS moves to restrict freedom of assembly and the rights of the press. Despite winning a no-confidence vote on 7 Dec. 2017 her party asked her to resign and chose finance minister Mateusz Morawiecki to replace her as prime minister. He was sworn in 4 days later, with Szydło remaining in the government as deputy prime minister.

Tadić, Boris (Serbia)

Introduction

Boris Tadić became president of Serbia and Montenegro on 11 July 2004, having narrowly defeated the right-wing nationalist, Tomislav Nikolić, in a run-off. The pro-Western, reform-minded politician had been an anti-communist activist and was central to the opposition campaign to bring down Slobodan Milošević in the late 1990s. Advocating integration in the European Union and free market reforms, he was re-elected in Feb. 2008, again defeating Nikolić but only by a slim margin. He resigned in April 2012 in order to stand in the presidential election a month later but was defeated by Nikolić in a run-off.

Early Life

Boris Tadić was born in Sarajevo on 15 Jan. 1958, the son of the philosopher and dissident, Ljubomir Tadić. He attended school in Belgrade and graduated in psychology from the University of Belgrade. During his student years Tadić was convicted for anti-communist political activities. After further study and research in psychology at the University, he became a clinical psychologist in the army.

In 1990, amid the collapse of communism, Yugoslavia was in deep economic recession and nationalism was growing among the constituent republics. Tadić joined the centrist Democratic Party (DS), becoming secretary of the general committee and party vice-president. He was a close ally of Zoran Đinđić, who became president of the party in 1993. In the winter of 1996–97 Tadić and Đinđić helped organize the mass street demonstrations against the attempts by Milošević to annul the victory of the Zajedno (Together) bloc in municipal elections across Serbia.

In 2002 Tadić became telecommunications minister in the Democratic Opposition of Serbia ruling coalition of the Federal Republic of Yugoslavia, led by Đinđić who had become prime minister in Dec. 2000 after Milošević's fall. Tadić was then appointed minister of defence in the newly-declared Serbia and Montenegro in March 2003 (days before Đinđić's assassination).

He took over the presidency of the DS in Feb. 2004 and stood in the first round of the presidential election, winning 27.6% of the vote. In his campaign he stood on a democratic, pro-European and reform-minded platform. He narrowly defeated Nikolić in the second round with 53.7% of the vote and was sworn in on 11 July 2004.

Career Peak

At his inauguration Tadić expressed his hopes of leading the country into the EU, urging the Union to begin negotiations on a stabilization and association agreement (SAA). He pledged to co-operate with the UN war crimes tribunal and said he was committed to the idea of a democratic solution for the province of Kosovo, based on UN Security Council resolution 1244. This resolution of 1999 recognized Kosovo as an autonomous constituent of Yugoslavia (as it then was) while acknowledging its status as a UN protectorate.

Talks on an SAA with the EU finally began in Oct. 2005 but were suspended in May 2006 after the country's repeated failures to hand over Ratko Mladić, the Bosnian Serb commander wanted on genocide charges for the 1995 massacre of 8,000 Muslims in Srebrenica. NATO, however, did admit Serbia to its Partnership for Peace programme in Dec. of that year.

Following Montenegro's declaration of independence on 4 June 2006, the government declared Serbia the legal successor to the union of Serbia and Montenegro. Shortly afterwards Tadić expressed his desire for mutual co-operation and friendship between the two countries.

Tadić's re-election as president in Feb. 2008 was welcomed by the EU, which pledged more support for his bid to join the Union. However, judgment of his second term was likely to rest on a lasting settlement of the status of Kosovo. In Feb. 2008 the province unilaterally declared itself an independent state, but this move was denounced by Serb opinion and was not universally recognized abroad. (The International Court of Justice subsequently ruled in July 2010 that Kosovo's declaration had not been illegal despite Serbia's assertion that its territorial integrity was violated.) Disagreements within the Serbian coalition government over policy towards the EU in the wake of Kosovo's declaration led Tadić in March 2008 to accept calls for fresh parliamentary elections. After a bitter campaign, no party won an outright advantage in the elections in May. Tadić asked Mirko Cvetković, a pro-European independent, to try to form a government and in July his new coalition was approved by parliament and sworn in.

Also in July 2008, the former Bosnian Serb leader Radovan Karadžić, who had been sought for war crimes for almost 13 years, was arrested in Belgrade and transferred to The Hague to stand trial.

In April 2008 the EU eventually signed an SAA with Serbia as a first step towards eventual membership, but implementation was hindered by a Dutch veto because of the continuing failure to arrest Mladić. In Dec. 2009 this veto was lifted (although the lack of further progress in detaining war criminals remained contentious), at which time Serbia submitted a formal application to join the Union. In Oct. 2010 EU foreign ministers agreed to progress the application to the European Commission.

Serbia's economy contracted sharply in the first half of 2009 in the wake of the global financial crisis. In response, the International Monetary Fund approved a stand-by arrangement in May worth almost €3 bn. (covering more than 2 years), and in Oct. 2009 Russia granted a €1 bn. loan to help cover Serbia's budget deficit.

In March 2010 Serbia's parliament passed a resolution formally apologizing for the 1995 Srebrenica massacre. Then, in July, the Croatian president visited Belgrade, heralding an improvement in bilateral relations that was further encouraged by Tadić's visit in Nov. to the Croatian city of Vukovar, the site of wartime civilian killings by Serb forces.

Significant developments in 2011 included the eventual arrest of Mladić in May and of Goran Hadzić, a Croatian war crimes suspect, in July. On 1 March 2012 Serbia was granted formal EU candidate status. To secure approval, Serbia made several concessions in the preceding months towards Kosovo, which had declared independence from Serbia in 2008. However, Belgrade refused to acknowledge Kosovo as a sovereign state and ongoing conflict over Kosovo's status is expected to prove an obstacle to Serbia's full accession to the EU.

Tadić resigned the presidency on 5 April 2012 to stand for a third term in office at elections brought forward to 6 May to coincide with parliamentary elections. The constitution allows for only two consecutive presidential terms. Tadić led after the first round of voting but came second in the run-off with Tomislav Nikolić on 20 May 2012.

Taki Abdoulkarim, Mohamed (Comoros)

Introduction

Mohamed Taki Abdoulkarim was elected president of the Comoros in 1996.

Early Life

Born in 1936, Taki was educated in Madagascar and France. With his engineering qualification, he was made minister of public utilities under the renowned pre-independence leader Said Mohamed Cheikh. In 1970 he became minister of development.

Taki was arrested in April 1977 in connection with the coup against Soilih but was released in May 1978. Under Ahmed Abdallah Abdereman, he was secretary general with responsibility for pushing through one-party legislation. In 1984, he broke with Abdallah and fled to France.

After the assassination of Abdallah in 1989, Taki returned to the Comoros to run in the presidential elections of Feb./March 1990. As leader of the Union Nationale pour la Démocratie aux Comores (UNDC/National Union for Democracy in Comoros), Taki obtained 44.7% of votes but was defeated by Saïd Mohamed Dhojar. In Nov. 1991, Taki agreed to form a government with Djohar. In Jan. 1992 the new transitional government was formed under the leadership of Taki but 6 months later he was dismissed and returned to France.

Career Peak

In the March 1996 presidential elections, Taki won 64% of the vote after several ballots. In April 1996 he dissolved the national assembly and appointed a new governor for each island, all from the UNDC. In June 1996, Taki received the backing of French President Chirac to develop Comoran education and public finance, as well as the judicial and health systems.

Taki pushed for a new constitution to extend the jurisdiction of the presidency, to introduce a new national flag to reinforce Islam and to reintroduce Islamic Sharia's Law (including public executions). It was approved by a constitutional committee in Oct. 1996, though boycotted by some opposition parties.

Legislative elections of late 1996 were tainted by allegations of fraud. The RND (Rassemblement National pour le Développement/National Union for Development, including UNDC and other pro-government parties) won a majority of seats.

Secessionist movements gathered strength on the islands of Nzwani and Mwali, while opposition to Taki's attempts to centralize power mounted. Both islands declared their independence in Aug. 1997 and appointed their own administrations. Taki ordered the invasion of Nzwani in Sept. 1997 but after battles in which more than 100 people were killed, the rebel government remained in place. Subsequent attempts at reconciliation, guided by the Organisation of Africa Unity, failed. With the question of the islands' sovereignty still unresolved, Taki died on 6 Nov. 1998, reportedly from a heart attack. He was succeeded by Tadjidine Ben Said Massounde.

Talabani, Jalal (Iraq)

Introduction

Jalal Talabani, an experienced Iraqi Kurdish politician, was named state president of Iraq on 6 April 2005 by the Iraqi National Assembly. He was elected by parliament to a second term in April 2006 and re-elected in Nov. 2010. He was previously the founder and secretary general of the Patriotic Union of Kurdistan (PUK), and later a prominent member of the Iraqi Governing Council which was established following the US-led invasion of Iraq in 2003.

Early Life

Jalal Talabani was born in Kelkan, Irbil province in Iraqi Kurdistan in 1933. He attended the Law College in Baghdad from 1952–55 before being forced to leave because of his political activities as a young member of the Kurdistan Democratic Party (KDP). Following the Iraqi revolution in 1958 and the overthrow of the monarchy, Talabani rejoined the college, and graduated in 1959. He subsequently served in the Iraqi army before working as a journalist.

When the Kurdish north launched an armed uprising against the Iraqi government in Sept. 1961, Talabani joined the forces led by Mulla Mustafa al-Barzani (the *peshmerga*) and fought in the Kirkuk and As-Sulaymaniyah areas. He also led Kurdish diplomatic delegations to Europe and the Middle East and negotiated with the secular Ba'ath party, whose members dominated Iraq's governing council following a coup led by Abdul Salam Aref in Feb. 1963.

By 1964, when profound disagreements were emerging within the KDP, Talabani established a more secular, urban and left-leaning faction, criticizing al-Barzani for 'conservative and tribal' politics. Factional divisions throughout the late 1960s and early 1970s occasionally erupted into armed confrontations. Although deals that secured some autonomy for the Kurds were struck between the KDP and the ruling Ba'ath party, arguments broke out over access to the region's oil supplies and whether Kurds could maintain an army. When the Kurdish revolt collapsed in 1975 (partly as a result of Iran withdrawing its support), Talabani formed a new party, the Patriotic Union of Kurdistan (PUK).

The PUK opposed the Ba'ath party's enforced resettlement of Kurds to Arab areas of Iraq in the late 1970s, and there were also numerous armed confrontations with the KDP. In the aftermath of Iraqi leader Saddam Hussein's chemical weapons attack that killed around 5,000 Kurds at Halabja in 1988 and the subsequent military action that led to more than 100,000 Kurds fleeing to Turkey, Talabani made efforts to bring unity to Kurdish politics. He improved relations between the PUK and the KDP (then led by Mas'ud al-Barzani) and later formed the Iraqi Kurdistan Front, seeking international support for Kurdish autonomy.

Following elections in the haven created for Kurds by the Western alliance after the first Gulf War, a PUK-KDP joint administration was formed in 1992. However, tensions resurfaced and led to serious confrontations between the two groups in 1994. Both parties signed a peace deal in Washington, D.C. in 1998 and the accord was cemented in Oct. 2002 when the regional parliament reconvened in a session attended by both parties' MPs.

Following the US-led invasion of Iraq and the fall of Saddam in April 2003, Talabani joined the US-appointed Iraqi Governing Council (IGC), distancing himself from the movement for Kurdish independence and pledging to support Iraqi federalism. In the Iraqi elections on 30 Jan. 2005, a Shia alliance won a slim majority in parliament and the Kurdish coalition came second in the polls. For over 2 months, with the country under sustained attacks from insurgents, both groups argued about the formation of the new government before electing Talabani as the president (a largely ceremonial role) on 6 April 2005.

Career Peak

A presidential council of Talabani and two vice-presidents appointed Ibrahim al-Jaafari, a conservative from the majority Shia community, as prime

minister on 7 April 2005. Talabani promised as president to represent all the country's ethnic and religious groups and to reach out to Iraq's Arab and Islamic neighbours.

Against a backdrop of continuing violence in Iraq, many analysts questioned the strength of the Shia-Kurdish alliance, given that the two groups had little previous common ground beyond resistance against Saddam Hussein. In Oct. 2005 a new Iraqi constitution was approved narrowly in a national referendum, heralding fresh parliamentary elections on 15 Dec. 2005. After months of political deadlock, Iraq's parliament convened on 22 April 2006 to fill the top leadership posts and Talabani was elected by parliament to a second presidential term. On the same day he appointed the Shia politician Nouri al-Maliki as prime minister designate after the latter was nominated by his Shia coalition, the United Iraqi Alliance (UIA).

Following the restoration of Iraqi-Syrian diplomatic ties in Nov. 2006, Talabani became the first Iraqi head of state to visit Damascus for 30 years in Jan. 2007.

In Nov. 2010 Talabani was again re-elected as president by the National Assembly on the second ballot. He then tasked Prime Minister al-Maliki with forming a new coalition government and bringing to an end the political stalemate prevailing since inconclusive parliamentary elections the previous March.

In Dec. 2012 Talabani underwent medical treatment and rehabilitation in Germany after suffering a stroke. He returned to Iraq in July 2014, but did not contest the indirect presidential election that took place that month. With large swathes of Iraqi territory under control of the jihadist group the Islamic State and the country in a state of political crisis, Talabani's term as president ended on 24 July 2014 when he was replaced by Fuad Masum. He died in Berlin of a brain hemorrhage on 3 Oct. 2017 aged 83.

Tantawi, Mohamed Hussein (Egypt)

Introduction

Mohamed Hussein Tantawi became the de facto leader of Egypt on 11 Feb. 2011 after Hosni Mubarak resigned as president following mass demonstrations calling for him to step down. He served as Chairman of the Supreme Council of the Armed Forces until a new president was elected and took office in June 2012.

Early Life

Mohamed Hussein Tantawi Soliman was born on 31 Oct. 1935 to a Nubian family. He joined the army as an infantryman and received his officer's commission in 1956 after completing a master's degree in military science at the High War College at Nasser High Military Academy.

Tantawi served in the Sinai War of 1956, the 6-Day War of 1967 and the Yom Kippur War of 1973. Rising through the ranks, he was assigned as a military attaché to Pakistan and Afghanistan. In 1991, following the Iraqi invasion of Kuwait, Tantawi served as head of the Armed Forces Operation Room, a part of the Gulf War coalition forces. For his service, he received Kuwait Liberation medals from Egypt, Kuwait and Saudi Arabia. In 1991 he was appointed minister of defence and military production, and in 1993 was made field marshal. Two years later he became commander-in-chief of the Egyptian armed forces. Known as a traditionalist, Tantawi was a Mubarak supporter.

On 31 Jan. 2011, following Mubarak's sacking of the entire cabinet in the face of popular protests, Tantawi was named deputy prime minister while retaining the defence and military production portfolios. On 11 Feb. 2011 Mubarak resigned as president and handed authority over to the Supreme Council of the Armed Forces, headed by Tantawi. Although seen as part of the old regime, Tantawi was largely untarnished by the human rights abuses committed by the intelligence and police agencies. The military council was to govern the country alongside the supreme constitutional court until the election of a new parliament and president.

Career Peak

Following a referendum on 19 March 2011 that saw a 77% vote in favour of amendments to the 1971 constitution, Tantawi was mandated to oversee the preparation and conduct of fresh parliamentary and presidential elections. Ahead of the elections, his aim was to reassure Egypt's allies that it remained committed to pre-existing alliances and treaties, notably with the USA and Israel. As the year progressed, however, Tantawi and the military faced growing discontent among pro-democracy activists demanding the immediate transfer of political power to a civilian administration. Despite renewed violent clashes in Cairo and other cities between demonstrators and security forces, the military council pressed ahead with its schedule for national parliamentary elections in stages from Nov. 2011 to Jan. 2012.

Moderate Islamists aligned to the Muslim Brotherhood's Freedom and Justice Party emerged as the strongest political force in the elections and were predominant in the new parliament that held its inaugural session on 23 Jan. Tantawi and the military council relinquished power following the election of Mohamed Morsy as new state president in June 2012.

Taylor, Charles (Liberia)

Introduction

Charles Taylor became president after an election landslide in 1997. Having founded the National Patriotic Front of Liberia (NPFL) while in exile, he overthrew the government of Samuel Doe in 1990. There followed a long and bloody civil war; fighting between government and rebel forces dominated Taylor's presidency. Having been indicted for war crimes in Sierra Leone, Taylor eventually agreed to relinquish power to a transitional government and an ECOWAS peacekeeping force on 11 Aug. 2003.

Early Life

Charles McArthur Ghankay Taylor was born on 28 Jan. 1948 in Arthington, Liberia to a Liberian mother and American father. He travelled to the US in 1972 and graduated in economics from Bentley College in Watham, Massachusetts in 1977. During this period he became active in the Union of Liberian Associations and went on to serve as the national president.

Liberian President William Tolbert met Taylor during a visit to the US in 1979 when Taylor co-ordinated protests against the president. Tolbert nonetheless invited Taylor to talks in Liberia the following year. Taylor arrived in early 1980 and in April Tolbert was killed during an army coup led by Samuel K. Doe. Doe appointed himself president and adopted emergency powers. The presidency had traditionally gone to members of Liberia's ruling Americo-Liberian class, descended from black slaves who settled in Liberia from the US in the nineteenth century. Doe was the country's first president from indigenous stock. Many Americo-Liberians fled but, despite his own Americo-Liberian background, Taylor became a prominent figure in Doe's administration, heading the state purchasing agency.

In 1983 Taylor fled to the US, having been accused of embezzling government funds. Twelve months later he was arrested by the US authorities and imprisoned pending extradition. However, in March 1985 he escaped and left the country. Taylor found refuge in Libya, where he formed the NPFL. With a force estimated at less than 500 Taylor launched an invasion into Liberia from neighbouring Sierra Leone on 24 Dec. 1989. Having secured the support of large sections of the rural population, NPFL troops made incursions into the capital, Monrovia, in July 1990 and Doe was executed. However, the NPFL began to fragment, with General Prince Johnson leading a breakaway faction.

A long civil war ensued, characterized by atrocities on both sides against civilians. 200,000 people died and over 1 m. others were displaced in the fighting which spilled over the border into Sierra Leone. ECOWAS troops were brought in to establish a peace while former US President Jimmy Carter brokered a ceasefire and worked towards a long-term settlement, establishing a six-man ruling council in a bid to return Liberia to democracy.

National elections were scheduled for 1997. Armed with significant financial reserves as well as control of the state radio, Taylor was accused by opponents of bribing the electorate in the build-up to the election. Nonetheless, international observers declared the elections free and Taylor became president with 75.3% of the vote.

Career Peak

Taylor had to contend with a collapsed infrastructure and an economy ravaged by years of war. In addition, thousands of disaffected war veterans, unemployed and without access to essential health care, were becoming an increasingly important political voice. In the early weeks of his tenure Taylor won international support by establishing a national reconciliation policy and by offering senior government positions to non-NPFL members.

However, unresolved domestic and regional conflicts soon re-emerged. In Jan. 1999 Nigeria and Ghana accused Taylor of providing backing to rebels in Sierra Leone. In April rebel forces from Guinea made incursions into the country. Guerrilla fighting with rebels in Liberia's north escalated while at the same time the UK and USA threatened to cut aid unless Taylor withdrew support for Sierra Leone's Revolutionary United Front. In late 2000 Taylor accused Guinea of launching attacks on Liberian villages in the border region and supporting Liberian rebel groups.

In May 2001 the UN imposed an arms embargo in response to Liberia's weapons for diamonds trade with rebels in Sierra Leone. Diamond exports were forbidden and movement of senior government figures restricted. The government launched renewed attacks on rebels in the north and in Feb. 2002 Taylor declared a state of emergency. In Sept. 2002 the state of emergency was lifted and Taylor permitted political gatherings. Several leading opposition factions undertook talks with the aim of forming a united alliance to fight Taylor at elections scheduled for 2003.

By March 2003 the situation had rapidly deteriorated and the army was involved in fighting with rebels within 10 miles of Monrovia and at locations throughout the country. Taylor told the UN that as a result he had been forced to contravene its embargo by recommencing weapons imports. As well as large numbers of fatalities, the renewed fighting created tens of thousands more refugees.

In April 2003 Taylor and Côte d'Ivoire's President Laurent Gbagbo agreed to greater co-ordination of military patrols on their shared border in a bid to counter rebel incursions. The two presidents had previously accused one another of providing backing to rebel movements.

In June 2003 Taylor was indicted for war crimes because of his alleged support for Sierra Leone's rebel movement. Later in the same month Liberians United for Reconciliation and Democracy (Lurd), Liberia's largest rebel group, attempted a coup against Taylor. Several days of fierce fighting in Monrovia, the capital, left 300 civilians dead, 1,000 injured and 250,000 displaced before a ceasefire was called. UN Secretary-General Kofi Annan called for an international peacekeeping force while US President George W. Bush urged Taylor to relinquish power. In July 2003 Taylor accepted an offer of asylum from Nigeria but insisted he would not leave the country until he could guarantee an orderly handover of power.

In Aug. 2003 the UN adopted a resolution drafted by the US calling for the immediate deployment of an ECOWAS peacekeeping force, to be replaced by a full UN force on 1 Oct. The first of 1,500 Nigerian troops began arriving on 4 Aug. 2003, with 2,000 troops from other ECOWAS states to follow. Taylor relinquished office on 11 Aug. 2003. He left Liberia for exile in Nigeria.

Later Life

In April 2012 Taylor was found guilty of aiding and abetting rebels in Sierra Leone during the 1991–2002 civil war and was convicted on 11 charges of 11 war crimes and crimes against humanity. Taylor was sentenced to 50 years in jail by a UN-backed war crimes court the following month.

Telavi, Willy (Tuvalu)

Introduction

Tuvalu's long-standing police commissioner, Willy Telavi, was first elected to parliament in 2006 and served as minister for home affairs. He was elected prime minister in Dec. 2010 following a vote of no confidence in the previous incumbent, Maatia Toafa.

Early Life

Willy Telavi was born on Nanumea, the north-westernmost of Tuvalu's nine islands. He completed a diploma in legal studies at the University of the South Pacific in 1999 and received a master's degree in international management from the University of the Northern Territory (now Charles Darwin University), Australia, in 2000.

Between 1993 and 2009 he served as Tuvalu's police commissioner and in 2006 he was elected to the 15-member parliament as one of two representatives of Nanumea. He was appointed minister of home affairs in the government of Apisai Ielemia, a position he retained following the general election of Sept. 2010 when Maatia Toafa became prime minister.

Toafa's premiership soon came under pressure amid widespread concerns that the government could no longer cover the full costs of medical treatment for patients needing to go abroad. When a motion of no confidence in Toafa was tabled in Dec. 2010 Telavi, along with two other MPs, withdrew his support from the prime minister and joined the opposition, enabling the motion to be carried and parliament to be dissolved. Willy Telavi was elected premier on 24 Dec. 2010.

Career Peak

Telavi's administration came under pressure in early Jan. 2011 when protesters from the island of Nukufetau peacefully demanded the resignation of Lotoala Metia, the finance and economic development minister, after he allegedly snubbed a meeting with island elders. On 13 Jan., following a protest on the main island of Funafuti that was supported by five members of the opposition and appeared to be linked to a campaign for another change in government, Telavi declared a state of emergency—the first in the nation's history—and imposed a 14-day ban on public gatherings. Metia was placed under police guard and the country's naval patrol boat was deployed to guard the coastline near Telavi's home and those of other government ministers.

In Aug. 2012 Telavi agreed to stop letting ships owned by Iran operate under its national flag, having been accused by the USA of breaking international sanctions on Iranian oil trading.

In June 2013 the government lost its parliamentary majority in a by-election. Despite Telavi's attempts to stay in power by avoiding a no-confidence vote, the Governor-General removed him from office on 1 Aug. Enele Sopoaga succeeded Telavi as caretaker leader the same day and was sworn in as prime minister on 5 Aug. following a parliamentary ballot.

Ter-Petrosyan, Levon (Armenia)

Introduction

Armenia's first democratically-elected president, Levon Ter-Petrosyan resigned after 6 years in power when conflict over the issue of disputed territory in Nagorno-Karabakh reached crisis point.

Early Life

Ter-Petrosyan was born in 1945 in Syria, where his father was involved in establishing the Syrian and Lebanese Communist parties. Ter-Petrosyan learned several languages, including Russian, Arabic and French, before completing a degree in history at Yerevan State University in Armenia. He later received a doctorate in Oriental Studies in Leningrad (now St Petersburg). Serving in the Soviet Red Army, Ter-Petrosyan reached the rank of lieutenant.

In 1988 he was arrested for involvement with the Karabakh Committee, an informal organisation aimed at the unification of the Nagorno-Karabakh region, a disputed territory located between Armenia and Azerbaijan. Later the Committee became the Armenian Nationalist Movement and Ter-Petrosyan its leader.

In 1990 he was elected chairman of the Armenian Supreme Soviet and in 1991 became president.

Career Peak

In spite of early moves towards a more democratic system, Ter-Petrosyan caused controversy by placing restrictions on the press and, in Dec. 1994, by banning the Armenian Revolutionary Federation on the grounds that it harboured a clandestine terrorist group and that its structure contradicted Armenian law. The elections of 1996 were blighted by the military suppression of popular demonstrations following allegations of ballot-rigging and voting irregularities.

From Armenia's declaration of independence in 1991, Ter-Petrosyan's time in power was dogged by increasingly violent conflict over Nagorno-Karabakh, a region with an ethnic Armenian majority. The Azeri army occupied large areas of the region in 1992 but fierce fighting led up to a 1994 ceasefire between Azerbaijan and the forces of the self-proclaimed Republic of Nagorno-Karabakh (RNK). A peace process began, brokered by the Organization for Security and Cooperation in Europe, and in 1997 President Levon Ter-Petrosyan appointed Robert Kocharyan, the former president of the RNK, prime minister despite Kocharyan only having recently obtained citizenship. With the country split on an appropriate course of action regarding Nagorno-Karabakh, Ter-Petrosyan resigned in Feb. 1998 and was succeeded by Robert Kocharyan.

Later Life

Ter-Petrosyan rarely appeared in public following his resignation, but returned to politics in 2008 when he contested that year's presidential election, finishing second. He founded the Armenian National Congress coalition later that year which he led through the 2012 parliamentary elections.

Than Shwe (Myanmar)

Introduction

Than Shwe became head of state and government in 1992. Political oppression under his military regime attracted international condemnation while the economy was blighted by corruption and bad management. Than Shwe did not stand for president following parliamentary elections in Nov. 2010.

Early Life

Than Shwe was born on 2 Feb. 1933 in Kyaukse. After working initially as a postman he had a decorated army career before succeeding Saw Maung in 1992 as chairman of the State Law and Order Restoration Council (SLORC), prime minister and minister of defence.

Career Peak

Than Shwe's political legitimacy was challenged by Aung San Suu Kyi, who had led the National League for Democracy (NLD) to victory in free elections of 1990. The military refused to recognize the result and instead continued to oppress the NLD, including imposing repeated terms of house arrest on Aung San Suu Kyi. She received the Nobel Peace Prize in 1991. In 1997 the SLORC reconstituted itself as the State Peace and Development Council (SPDC).

In foreign policy, the oppressive nature of Than Shwe's dictatorship saw Myanmar increasingly isolated, although the country was accepted into ASEAN in 1997 and closer relations with Bangladesh were fostered from 2002. Also in 2002 the international community expressed concern at Than Shwe's deal with Russia to develop nuclear facilities. The USA, EU, China and IAEA all raised doubts over Myanmar's ability to ensure the safety of such enterprises, while the NLD suggested that it could lead to the development of nuclear arms.

The renewed detention of Aung San Suu Kyi in May 2003 provoked further hostility from the international community and unprecedented public criticism from ASEAN. Fresh sanctions were imposed by the USA and the EU.

From May–July 2004 a national convention was reconvened for the first time since 1996 to draw up a new constitution. It met again intermittently between Feb. 2005 and Jan. 2006, with a further session beginning in Oct. 2006. However, without the participation of the main opposition and ethnic minority groups, independent observers questioned the validity of the process. UN concern about the junta's policies prompted the preparation of a critical Security Council resolution but this was vetoed by China and Russia in Jan. 2007.

In Sept. 2007 the government declared that constitutional talks were complete and closed the national convention. Buddhist monks then led a series of pro-democracy demonstrations in Yangon and other cities that provoked a violent response from the authorities and mass detentions. The UN Security Council condemned the military crackdown and the EU adopted tighter sanctions. In April 2008 the government published the proposed new constitution, which reserved 25% of parliamentary seats for the military and banned Aung San Suu Kyi from holding office. In a subsequent national referendum in May, the government claimed that 93% of voters endorsed the constitution.

The referendum took place amid a humanitarian crisis, following a cyclone that hit the south of the country. By the end of May 2008 about 145,000 people were thought to have died, with thousands more made homeless. The effects of the disaster were exacerbated by restrictions imposed on international relief efforts by Than Shwe's regime, which played down the scale of the devastation.

In Aug. 2009 tougher sanctions were imposed on Myanmar by the international community after Aung San Suu Kyi's detention was extended. In Oct., however, she met with a minister from the military government in the first such contact for 2 years and was also allowed to meet Western diplomats.

In March 2010 the government announced new party registration laws in preparation for national and state elections. However, the NLD considered them too restrictive. The elections took place in Nov., resulting in an overwhelming victory for the military-backed Union Solidarity and Development Party, although opposition groups claimed widespread fraud and international observers condemned the poll. A week later, Aung San Suu Kyi was once more released from house arrest, having been prevented from taking any part in the electoral process.

In Feb. 2011 the new parliament named Thein Sein, previously the prime minister, as the new state president. In March 2011 the SPDC was dissolved and a month later he retired from the military. Although it was believed that Than Shwe would continue to pull strings after his proclaimed retirement he seems to have completely retired from politics.

Thapa, Surya Bahadur (Nepal)

Introduction

Veteran politician Surya Bahadur Thapa was prime minister of Nepal five times: 1963–64, 1965–69, 1979–83, 1997–98 and June 2003–June 2004. He took up the role for the fifth time following the forced departure of King Gyanendra's leader of choice, Lokendra Bahadur Chand, in June 2003. Thapa stepped in amidst widespread unrest, as demonstrators accused the king of unconstitutionally dismissing the government and appointing Chand. Despite promising elections, Thapa failed to appease the opposition, who demanded the recall of parliament, and was abandoned by his own party.

Early Life

Born on the 21 March 1928, Surya Bahadur Thapa became involved in politics while at Allahabad University. Starting his career in 1958 as chairman of the advisory council, he became minister of agriculture, forest and industry in 1960 before his first appointment as prime minister in 1963. Filling this post three times under the executive monarchy that held power for 30 years, Thapa was also elected prime minister at the head of a coalition in 1997, following the return of democratic elections in 1990.

Thapa's 2003 appointment came at a time of political tension. King Gyanendra succeeded his brother Birendra in 2001, following the massacre of Birendra and several other members of the royal family by Crown Prince Dipendra. Gyanendra dismissed his coalition government in Oct. 2002 to replace it with one headed by Lokendra Bhadur Chand. Chand was forced to resign following popular outcry. Gyanendra held talks with the leaders of a number of parties who had been critical of the Chand appointment but overruled their recommendation to appoint Thapa. Critics claimed Thapa's

appointment would further delay elections and thus bolster the power of left-wing parties eager for the dissolution of the monarchy.

Career Peak

Thapa, like his predecessor Chand, was a member of the conservative Rashtriya Prahatantra Party (RPP) and advocated a broad-based alliance between the palace and parliamentary parties. His primary concern was to return stability to the political system and oversee peace talks between the government and Maoist rebels, whose campaign of violence began in the mid-1990s.

Following his appointment as prime minister, Thapa stated his intention to form an all-party government but appointed a cabinet made up entirely of RPP members. He retained several key portfolios himself including home, defence, and foreign affairs. Months of demonstrations were organized by an implacable opposition, which demanded that parliament be recalled. Thapa's failure to do this or to create a broad-based coalition led to the RPP central committee demanding his resignation in Nov. 2003. Thanks to royal support, Thapa remained in office but by early 2004 his position had become untenable. He resigned on 2 June 2004 and was replaced with Sher Bahadur Deuba, who had led the 2002 coalition government.

Later Life

Thapa died from respiratory failure on 15 April 2015 at the age of 87.

Thatcher, Margaret (United Kingdom of Great Britain and Northern Ireland)

Introduction

Margaret Hilda Thatcher (*née* Roberts) was the Conservative British Prime Minister from 1979 until 1990. Britain's first female Prime Minister and the longest serving of the twentieth century, her political philosophy and personalized style of leadership came to be known as Thatcherism.

Early Life

Thatcher was born on 13 Oct. 1925 in Grantham, Lincolnshire in the east Midlands of England. Her father was a grocer and influential figure in local politics, holding the office of Mayor of Grantham. Margaret left local grammar school to study Chemistry at Somerville College, Oxford. She became President of the University Conservative Association and worked as a research chemist from 1947–51. In 1950 and 1951 she failed in attempts to enter the House of Commons, was then called to the Bar in 1953 and worked as a barrister specializing in tax law until 1959. Meanwhile, she had married a wealthy business man, Dennis Thatcher, in 1951 and had given birth to twins in 1953.

1959 saw her become Member of Parliament for Finchley in north London. Harold Macmillan appointed her joint parliamentary secretary for the ministry of pensions and national insurance in 1961, a post she held until Labour came to power 3 years later. She then became opposition spokesman for education and when Edward Heath's Conservatives returned to government in 1970, she was made secretary of state for education and science, during which time she received the nickname 'Ma Thatcher, Milk Snatcher' after withdrawing the right to free school milk.

Following the Conservatives' loss at the 1974 general election, Thatcher challenged Heath for the party leadership on 4 Feb. 1975. Defeating him and one other opponent by taking 130 of 265 votes, she went into a second ballot a week later against four new opponents, claiming victory with 110 from 228 votes. On 3 May 1979, following the 'winter of discontent' when Britain was paralysed by union-led mass strike action, she won a convincing victory at the general election. Ten years earlier she had stated that 'no woman in my time will be prime minister'. From the outset of her tenure, Thatcher ruled her cabinet and party strictly, modelling herself as 'the Iron Lady' and leading a backlash against the 'wets' the Conservatives' more liberal wing.

Career Peak

Thatcher's political ideology was underpinned by the ideas that the government's role in society should be tightly restricted and that emphasis should be placed on individual responsibility. In economic terms, she believed in monetarist theories, controlling the flow of money and imposing high interest rates as the cure for high inflation. Public spending and taxation were cut and certain market mechanisms were introduced into the public education and health systems. Thatcher also undertook a sweeping programme of privatization, which saw numerous industries removed from public hands, including gas, steel, civil aviation and telecommunications. Trade Union powers were reduced and local government (including the Greater London Council) had their authority cut. Later, the policy of allowing tenants to purchase their council homes was put into place.

On the international stage Thatcher encouraged the close relationship between Britain and the US and had good personal relationships with both Ronald Reagan and Mikhail Gorbachev. She voiced the necessity for Britain to retain its own nuclear deterrent, and with regard to the Irish question she believed that for Britain to relinquish any power in the region would be a threat to British sovereignty. The IRA bombing of the Grand Hotel in Brighton during the Conservative party conference of 1984, which almost killed her and her cabinet, only strengthened her conviction. She also took a firm stance against the Argentinian invasion of the British-held Falkland Islands in 1982, sending over armed forces who reclaimed the islands to much popular acclaim. However, Thatcher's attitude towards the European Union, which always reflected her considerable mistrust of the institution, was highly controversial and would ultimately be instrumental in her downfall.

By the general election of 1983, the Conservative economic policy was yet to reap its rewards. Unemployment was around the 3 m. mark, up from just over 1 m. in 1979, and social unrest had been illustrated by violent inner-city riots, notably during 1981 at Brixton in London and Toxteth in Liverpool. However, faced with Michael Foot's Labour Party in utter disarray, and in the midst of post-Falklands euphoria, she won the election of 1983 with ease. During her second term the City and service industries boomed and the economy flourished from 1985 onwards, although manufacturing industries had been severely depleted and many regions felt few of the benefits evident in London and the southeast. Her conflict with the trade unions came to a head with the year long miners' strike of 1984, from which she eventually emerged victorious. She claimed a third term at the general election of 1987 against Neil Kinnock's Labour, a term during which the European question would dominate.

While the country was in a mid-economic boom at the start of the third term, by 1990 it was about to experience severe recession. In addition, Thatcher had lost her long-time chancellor, Nigel Lawson, in 1989 in a dispute over her reliance on her economic adviser, Sir Alan Walters. She had also taken the highly unpopular decision to replace local rates with a new community charge, commonly known as the poll tax. On 31 March 1990 fierce rioting took place around Trafalgar Square in the heart of London. Thatcher, famed for her quote of 1980 that 'the lady's not for turning' was not prepared to backtrack and her support within the party was further strained. However, it was her open hostility to the European Union that set in train the events leading to her downfall.

Her European-friendly foreign secretary, Geoffrey Howe, resigned his post in Oct. 1990. In his resignation speech, he condemned her autocratic leadership and European stance. His speech led the way for a leadership challenge, which Michael Heseltine duly took up. Though she defeated him in the first ballot of 20 Nov. 1990 by 204 votes to 152, it was not enough to avoid a second ballot. She was persuaded to resign and back John Major, who won the second ballot a week later.

Later Life

Thatcher became Baroness Thatcher of Kesteven in 1992, taking her seat in the House of Lords, and she remained a considerable background presence throughout John Major's period in office. After her resignation she established the Thatcher Foundation, which aims to promote her political ideology, and wrote two volumes of memoirs. Her strong-willed style of leadership was summed up by her own assertion that 'I'm extraordinarily patient provided I get my own way in the end.' She had a number of small strokes in 2002 and subsequently suffered from dementia. She died on 8 April 2013 at the age of 87 following a stroke.

Thinley, Jigme (Bhutan)

Introduction

Jigme Thinley, a civil servant and former government minister, became Bhutan's first ever democratically elected prime minister on 24 March 2008.

Early Life

Jigme Yoser Thinley was born in 1952 in Bumthang, northern Bhutan and educated at Dr. Graham's Homes in Kalimpong, northeastern India. He graduated from St Stephen's College at the University of Delhi and subsequently earned a master's degree in public administration from Penn State University in the USA. He later studied manpower planning and management at Manchester University in the UK.

Having joined Bhutan's civil service in 1974 as a trainee officer in the ministry of home affairs, Thinley went on to hold a range of posts including, in 1990, administrator of Bhutan's six eastern districts. He became a secretary in the ministry of home affairs in 1992 and was promoted to deputy minister in 1994. In the same year he was appointed as Bhutan's permanent representative to the UN and other international organizations.

Career Peak

From July 1998 to July 1999 and again from Aug. 2003 to Aug. 2004, Thinley was the royal appointee as prime minister. He also served as minister of foreign affairs between 1998 and 2003. In March 2008, in the run-up to Bhutan's first multi-party elections, Thinley stood as leader of the new DPT. The party won 45 of the 47 seats in the National Assembly, making Thinley the country's first democratically elected premier. He took office on 9 April 2008, promising to make democracy a success and to provide a transparent and corruption-free government.

The DPT lost the parliamentary election in 2013 to the People's Democratic Party and Tshering Tobgay succeeded Thinley as prime minister on 27 July. Subsequently, Thinley also resigned from the parliament.

Thomas, Tillman (Grenada)

Introduction

Tillman Thomas was appointed prime minister on 9 July 2008, ending 13 years of rule by Keith Mitchell and his New National Party. As leader of the National Democratic Congress (NDC), Thomas gained advantage from the reaction against Mitchell's increasingly autocratic rule. A veteran legislator and one-time political prisoner, Thomas promised to fashion a more open and inclusive government.

Early Life

Thomas was born in 1945 in Hermitage in St Patrick, Grenada's northernmost parish. A graduate of the University of West Indies and Trinidad's Hugh Wooding Law School, he began his career as an attorney. He was imprisoned on political grounds in 1981 during the Marxist and Cuba-aligned regime of Maurice Bishop, who had come to power following a coup. Thomas was released in 1983 following a military invasion by US and Caribbean troops.

In 1984 Thomas was elected to the House of Representatives as the New National Party member for St Patrick East. In 1987 he was one of the founding members of the NDC, serving for 6 years as its assistant general secretary. Despite losing his seat at the 1990 general election, Thomas was appointed minister of works, communications and public utilities in 1991. He subsequently served as minister of finance and as minister of tourism, culture, civil aviation and sports.

Following the NDC's failure to gain a single seat in the 1999 general election, Thomas was appointed party leader. The NDC came close to gaining power in 2003, winning seven of the 15 available seats, with Thomas reclaiming St Patrick East. As leader of the opposition, he accused Mitchell of mismanagement and played upon voter frustration with rising prices and a tourist-based economy struggling to recover from the devastation wreaked by Hurricane Ivan in 2004.

Career Peak

The NDC won a resounding victory at the 2008 general election, taking 11 of the 15 seats. One of Thomas' first actions was to repeal the national reconstruction levy, a tax of 3% on income over EC$1,000 per month imposed in the aftermath of Hurricane Ivan. Thomas has also promised free school books for all primary and secondary schools. He vowed to create a more participatory government focusing on improving the economy and lowering the cost of living for Grenada's poorest families.

The NDC suffered a historic defeat and lost all of its seats in the House of Representatives at the general election held in Feb. 2013. Thomas continued as the party leader.

Thompson, David (Barbados)

Introduction

David Thompson, the leader of the Democratic Labour Party (DLP), became prime minister in Jan. 2008 after leading his party to victory in a general election. Claiming 20 out of 30 available seats, the DLP returned to power after 14 years in opposition.

Early Life

David John Howard Thompson was born on 25 Dec. 1961 in London to Barbadian parents. He was educated at Combermere School before graduating in law from the University of the West Indies in 1984. While a student Thompson was active within the Young Democrats, the youth wing of the DLP, serving as its president from 1980–82. Thompson went on to the Hugh Wooding Law School at the University of the West Indies in Trinidad, obtaining his Legal Education Certificate. In 1986 he joined Trident Chambers, the chambers of Errol Barrow, Barbados' first prime minister. Between 1986 and 1988 Thompson was a part-time tutor at the University of the West Indies.

Following Barrow's death in 1987, Thompson won the by-election for Barrow's constituency of St John, which he has represented ever since. He was also selected as general secretary of the DLP, a position he retained until 1994. In 1991 he joined the cabinet of Prime Minister Lloyd Sandiford, in charge of the community development and culture portfolios. He moved to the ministry of finance in 1992 as minister of state. From 1993–94 he was minister of finance and oversaw the implementation of IMF structural reforms, and an overhaul of the sugar industry and offshore sector.

In 1994 Thompson became leader of the DLP after Sandiford lost a motion of no confidence. Thompson saw his party defeated in the general elections of 1994 and 1999 before he resigned as party head in Sept. 2001. He returned to his legal practice where he specialized in corporate, insurance, international business and property law. In Jan. 2006 he took up the DLP leadership again following the defection from the DLP of Clyde Mascoll, a former party leader. Thompson was widely lauded for his efforts to restore public confidence in the party. On 15 Jan. 2008 he was re-elected to his St John constituency with 84% of the vote and led his party to electoral victory.

Career Peak

In addition to the premiership, Thompson took over the portfolios of finance, economic affairs and development (which he later relinquished), labour, civil service and energy. He had campaigned on a platform of improving health care and transport infrastructure while fighting the rising cost of living. Although the collapse of a major Caribbean insurance conglomerate in early 2009 precipitated a financial crisis in Barbados, Thompson survived a consequent parliamentary motion of no confidence in March over his handling of the emergency.

Having suffered bouts of illness since March 2010, Thompson appointed his deputy Freundal Stuart acting prime minister in May while he underwent medical tests. He reassumed his post in Aug. but in Sept. revealed that he had been diagnosed with pancreatic cancer. On 23 Oct. he died from his illness at the age of 48. Stuart succeeded him as prime minister.

Thorn, Gaston (Luxembourg)

Introduction

Leader of the Social Democratic Party, Gaston Thorn became prime minister in Jan. 1974 and headed a Liberal-Socialist coalition until 1979. He succeeded Pierre Warner who had been premier for 15 years.

Early Life

Gaston Egmond Thorn was born in Luxembourg City on 3 Sept. 1928. During the Second World War he was arrested for his resistance activities and spent several months in a concentration camp. He subsequently studied law at universities in France and Switzerland and was admitted to the Bar of Luxembourg. He became president of both the National Union of Students of Luxembourg and the International Student Conference.

Thorn served as deputy mayor of Luxembourg City from 1951 to 1963. In 1959 he was elected to the national legislature and also took a seat in the European parliament, which he held for 10 years. In 1961 he became chairman of the Liberal Democratic Party and 8 years later was appointed foreign minister and foreign trade minister, portfolios he held until 1980.

Career Peak

From 1974 to 1979 Thorn served as prime minister, leading a Liberal-Socialist coalition that ended 75 years of rule by the Christian Social Party. An advocate of European integration, in 1975–76 he also held the presidency of the United Nations General Assembly.

Later Life

After losing the 1979 national election, Thorn served as deputy prime minister in the Christian Social-Democratic coalition of Pierre Warner. He was also given the foreign affairs, foreign trade, economic affairs and justice portfolios. He then served 4 years as head of the Commission of the European Economic Community from 1981. Leaving front-line politics in 1985 to focus on business, he became chairman of Luxembourg's biggest media company and president of the Banque Internationale de Luxembourg. He remained politically active as president of the and the, while also sitting on the (which seeks to foster closer ties between Western Europe, Japan and North America) and the pro-European Committee.

Thorn died on 26 Aug. 2007.

Thorning-Schmidt, Helle (Denmark)

Introduction

Helle Thorning-Schmidt took office on 3 Oct. 2011, heading a Social Democrat-led coalition. She was the country's first female prime minister.

Early Life

Born on 14 Dec. 1966 in Rødovre, Helle Thorning-Schmidt completed her early education at Ishøj Gymnasium, Copenhagen. From 1987–94 she studied political science at the University of Copenhagen. In 1992 she was selected by the ministry of foreign affairs to attend the College of Europe in Bruges, Belgium, where she obtained a master's degree in European studies, specialising in policy and public administration. While in Belgium she became involved with the Social Democrats there and joined the Danish Social Democrats in 1993.

From 1994–97 Thorning-Schmidt headed the party's secretariat in the European Parliament. She then joined the Danish Confederation of Trade Unions as a consultant before being elected to the European Parliament as a member of the Party of European Socialists in 1999. She subsequently sat on the employment and social committee and co-founded the Campaign for Parliament Reform (CPR).

In Feb. 2005 Thorning-Schmidt won a seat in the Folketing. On 12 April 2005 she was elected leader of the Social Democrats following Mogens Lykketoft's resignation. At the 2007 general election Thorning-Schmidt campaigned on relaxing immigration regulations, increasing welfare spending and ensuring that 45% of Denmark's energy requirements are met by renewable sources by 2025.

Despite electoral defeat, Thorning-Schmidt kept her post and the Social Democrats remained the largest opposition party. In 2011 she campaigned to raise taxes for high earners, increase public spending and liberalize immigration policies. Her centre-left coalition secured a narrow victory at the general election.

Career Peak

Thorning-Schmidt's primary aim on taking office was to revitalize the economy by creating jobs via education, green energy and infrastructure projects. However, building consensus within her coalition has been a challenge. Attempts to review aspects of the welfare state, including a tax reform package agreed with the centre-right opposition, led to a slump in public support for the Social Democrats in the first year of her premiership. Nevertheless, the party fared better than expected in local elections in Nov. 2013, retaining control of Copenhagen and other larger cities with the highest share of the vote. Denmark's 6-month presidency of the European Union from Jan.–June 2012 was dominated by the debt crisis in the eurozone, of which Denmark is not a member.

Frequent reports of ministerial sleaze or incompetence, as well as ongoing tensions between the coalition partners, prompted Thorning-Schmidt to carry out cabinet reshuffles in Aug. and Dec. 2013 before the Socialist People's Party withdrew from the government in Jan. 2014 in a dispute over planned private investment in a state-owned energy company.

Thorning-Schmidt led her Social Democrats to the largest share of seats at the June 2015 general elections. However, she resigned as prime minister and party leader following the opposition Blue bloc's overall victory and was replaced by her predecessor, Lars Løkke Rasmussen, who returned to power 4 years after his defeat at the previous election.

Later Life

In Jan. 2016 Thorning-Schmidt was appointed as Chief Executive of Save the Children International.

Timofti, Nicolae (Moldova)

Introduction

Nicolae Timofti was sworn in as president on 23 March 2012 after the Constitutional Court confirmed the results of the previous week's parliamentary poll. He secured his appointment with 62 votes in the 101-seat parliament—one vote more than the minimum required—ending nearly 3 years of political deadlock. He left office in Dec. 2016.

Early Life

Nicolae Timofti was born on 22 Dec. 1948 in Ciutuleşti, north-eastern Moldova. Graduating in law from Moldova State University, Chişinău, in 1972, he completed 2 years national service in the Soviet Army. Having then pursued a legal career, in 2003 he was appointed to the Chişinău court of appeal and 2 years later was posted to the supreme court of justice. In 2011 he became president of the supreme council of magistrates.

In 1996 he joined the court of appeal and later became its president. In 2003 he was appointed to the Chişinău court of appeal and was made a member of the supreme council of magistrates. Two years later he was posted to the supreme court of justice and in 2011 became president of the supreme council of magistrates.

Timofti was nominated for the presidency in early 2012 by the pro-European ruling Alliance for European Integration coalition. On 16 March 2012 he was elected into office by parliament, though the vote was boycotted by the opposition Communist Party. He was the first permanently-appointed president since the end of Vladimir Voronin's tenure in 2009.

Career Peak

Timofti, considered by many as a neutral figure in Moldovan politics, pledged to fight corruption and support democratic and free-market reforms. Nonetheless, some critics accuse him of failing to overhaul the notoriously corrupt judiciary while holding senior judicial positions.

Timofti has supported Moldova's application for EU membership (progress towards which saw the signature of an Association Agreement in June 2014) and has sought to maintain relations with Russia, despite the latter's hostility to closer Moldovan-EU ties and concerns over Russian territorial designs on the breakaway region of Transnistria.

In March 2013 the prime minister, Vladimir Filat, resigned after his government lost a confidence vote. The foreign minister, Iurie Leancă, was then sworn in as acting prime minister in April 2013 before parliamentary elections in Nov. 2014 returned a majority for pro-EU parties, although the pro-Russian Party of Socialists of the Republic of Moldova emerged as the largest single group. In Feb. 2015 Timofti designated a new prime minister, Chiril Gaburici of the Liberal Democratic Party. He subsequently resigned in June and was replaced the following month by Valeriu Streleţ, also a Liberal Democrat. However, in Oct. parliament dismissed his government in a no-confidence vote and Gheorghe Brega of the Liberal Party briefly took over as acting prime minister before Timofti nominated Ion Sturza, a former premier, in his place in Dec. However, in Jan. 2016 Sturza withdrew his candidacy, as did his successor Ion Paduraru, before Timofti's next nominee, Pavel Filip, and his government were confirmed in office.

Timofti did not contest the presidential election of Nov. 2016—the first direct presidential election for 20 years—and left office on 23 Dec. that year.

Tindemans, Leo (Belgium)

Introduction

Leo Tindemans was involved in Belgian and European politics for nearly 40 years from 1961, serving as Belgium's prime minister, minister of foreign affairs and minister of state as well has holding the presidency of the European People's Party and the co-presidency of the ACP-EC Joint Assembly.

Early Life

Leo Tindemans was born on 16 April 1922 and was educated at the State University of Ghent and the Catholic University of Louvain. He took a master's degree in Business and Consular Sciences, as well as in Politics and Social Sciences.

Tindemans was elected as a CVP member of the Chamber of Deputies in 1961. From 1965–73 he was the secretary general of the European Union of Christian Democrats, and during this time he also held various ministerial positions within the Belgian government–he was to be the minister of community affairs from 1968–71, minister of agriculture and the self-employed from 1972–73 and deputy prime minister (1973–74).

Career Peak

Tindemans was elected prime minister in 1974. He completed one term of office and commenced another before a dispute broke out with members of his coalition on restructuring Belgium into a federal state with separate assemblies for its different language communities. Unable to reach agreement, Tindemans tendered his resignation on 10 Oct. 1979.

Later Life

Tindemans attached great importance to securing international peace, promoting human rights and furthering European integration; his recent career reflects these passions. He was the president of the European People's Party (or EPP, a pan-European alliance of Christian Democrat politicians) from 1976–85, during which time he also served as Belgium's foreign minister. Upon finishing his tenure as a minister in 1989, he became a member of the European Parliament and co-president of the ACP-EC Joint Assembly, a role he continued in until 1992 when he was named president of the EPP Group. He found time to devote himself to several EU commissions, including ones for foreign affairs, social and defence policy and a subcommission dealing with security and nuclear disarmament. He was also the author credited with the 1997 Report of the International Commission on the Balkans which made recommendations on human rights, the conduct of war and the role that the European Union could play in bringing peace to the troubled region.

Tindemans died on 26 Dec. 2014 aged 92. He was widely regarded as one of Europe's most accomplished and experienced statesmen.

Tito, Josip Broz (Serbia)

Introduction

Josip Broz was leader of Yugoslavia (Serbia, Montenegro, Bosnia-Herzegovina, Croatia, Macedonia and Slovenia) from the end of World War II until 1980, becoming President in 1953 and remaining in the post until his death. He pursued domestic policies independent of the Soviet Union and in terms of foreign policy he promoted a policy of active non-alignment, a system in which he strove to avoid traditional East or West alliances. He introduced federalist government to Yugoslavia which he was able to hold together by the force of his personality but which would ultimately lead to the collapse of the Yugoslavian state after his death.

Early Life

Josip Broz was born on 7 May 1892 in Kumrovec, near Zagreb (part of Croatia and then also part of the Austro-Hungarian empire). His father was Croat while his mother was from Slovenia. Broz trained as a locksmith and became involved with the Social Democratic Party of Croatia-Slavonia when he was 18. He served with the Austro-Hungarian army when World War I began but was captured by Russian forces on the Eastern Front in 1915. During spells in military hospitals and prisoner of war camps he was exposed to Bolshevik ideology and went on to fight for the Red Army during the Russian Revolution. He also married a Russian woman during this period.

He returned to Croatia around 1920, finding employment as a metalworker and was active in the Yugoslav Communist Party (YCP). Throughout the 1920s he acted as a trade union leader and political agitator and in 1928 he was arrested after a number of bombs had been found in his possession. He presented a spirited defence of communism at his trial but he was nonetheless imprisoned, being released in March 1934. His years of incarceration had seen a clampdown on the YCP by Alexander I and his authorities but Milan Gorkič, the party's exiled leader, drafted Broz into the Politburo. It was around this time that Broz took on the underground name of Tito.

Tito went to Moscow in 1935 to work for the Comintern but was back in Yugoslavia by 1937. Stalin purged the YCP shortly afterwards, with Gorkič one of a number of high-profile casualties. Tito was installed as Secretary General, with Muscovite blessing, in 1939 supported by a new hierarchy of political allies. The Axis powers invaded Yugoslavia in 1941 and Tito responded by mobilizing a guerrilla resistance movement, becoming Marshall in 1943.

A rival resistance movement was also in operation, the Serb-based Chetniks headed by Dragoljub Mihailovič, who were loyal to the exiled royal government. By Sept. 1943 Tito's army had overpowered them and in Nov. 1943 he announced the creation of the Federal People's Republic of Yugoslavia, with himself as head of a provisional government. Western governments gave him recognition, the exiled royal government was forced to co-operate with Tito and following elections of dubious legality in Nov. 1945 the monarchy was abolished and Tito was installed as Prime Minister and Foreign Minister of a communist-dominated government.

Career Peak

In the aftermath of the war Tito instigated a number of Stalinist-style purges, carried out by a secret police force headed by his ally Alexander Rankovič, and organized numerous show trials of opponents. However, Tito was conscious that his power base, unlike that of the other Eastern Bloc leaders, had not relied on Soviet might to install it and as such he aimed to pursue policies

independent of Moscow. He nationalized industry and initiated a centrally planned economy but, while requiring large contributions from farmers, he did not attempt wholesale agricultural collectivization. By 1948, insisting on an independent line, Tito had come into open conflict with Stalin and, after a failed bid to purge the YCP leadership, Stalin expelled Yugoslavia from the Cominform. In 1953 Tito introduced a new constitution, the provisions of which included his installation as President of Yugoslavia (a post which would be conferred upon him for life by the terms of the 1974 constitution).

Economic and military support was granted to Yugoslavia by the West, who were aware of the potential advantages of establishing closer ties with a disenchanted and independently-minded Eastern Bloc country. By the early 1950s, assisted by Vice President Edvard Kardelj and Minister of Propaganda Milovan Djilas, Tito was developing a form of self-government for workers that relied less on the centralized authorities of the Soviet model of socialism. He also moved much power away from the Yugoslav federal authorities and towards the constituent republics.

Tito's Yugoslavia followed an independent foreign policy that would ultimately develop into the policy of non-alignment. Having grown closer to the West during the late Stalin years, Krushchev's arrival paved the way for a potential reconciliation with the Soviet Union. However, the Hungarian uprising and its subsequent repression in 1956 by Soviet forces brought Tito into conflict with Moscow once again and relations were frequently cool over the coming years. Negotiations began with India and Egypt to establish a network of nations not only neutral but 'actively non-aligned'.

The decentralization of power within Yugoslavia resulted in heightened domestic tension throughout the 1960s and 1970s as old nationalist rivalries surfaced. The most dramatic incarnation of the problem was the Croatian Spring of 1971 when Tito responded to dangerously increasing nationalist sentiments by purging the region's leadership. In 1974 he promulgated a new constitution (one of many during his time in power) which sought to equalize the standing of the 6 republics (Serbia, Croatia, Bosnia, Slovenia, Macedonia and Montenegro) and 2 autonomous provinces (Kosovo and Vojvodina) by measures such as a rotating presidency to come into force after his death.

By the 1970s Yugoslavia's economy was suffering from the combined effects of external debt, inflation and faltering productivity. The constitutional reforms had also displaced Croatia and Serbia, who felt their power as the largest republics was being whittled away to the benefit of smaller neighbours. Nationalism remained a problem with the result that Tito increased restrictions on freedom of expression, when once the nation's cultural liberalism had set it apart from many other communist states. He died in Ljubljana (then in Yugoslavia and now in Slovenia) on 4 May 1980. Without his strength of leadership the problems of nationalism escalated and Yugoslavia went on to tear itself apart within 12 years of his death.

Toafa, Maatia (Tuvalu)

Introduction

Maatia Toafa became prime minister in 2004, succeeding Saufatu Sopanga. The threat posed by global warming to low-lying Tuvalu was among the most pressing issues he faced. He left office in Aug. 2006 but became prime minister again in Sept. 2010.

Early Life

Toafa was born on 1 May 1954. He was schooled in Kiribati and in 1978 graduated in business studies from the Co-operative Education Centre based at Suva in the Fiji Islands. He later studied at the International Co-operative College at Loughborough in the UK and gained an MBA in 1997 from Suva's University of the South Pacific.

From 1976–96 he worked for the Tuvalu Co-operative Society, eventually holding the post of general manager. In 1997 he became a project officer with the Pacific Islands forum secretariat, based in the Fiji Islands, a post he held for 5 years.

In Aug. 2003 he was named deputy prime minister with responsibility for works, communications and transport. In Aug. 2004 the government of Prime Minister Saufatu Sopanga lost a parliamentary vote of confidence and Toafa was appointed acting prime minister. The appointment was confirmed by parliamentary vote and he was sworn in on 11 Oct. 2004. As prime minister, he automatically assumed responsibility for the foreign relations portfolio.

Career Peak

Climate change was of ongoing concern for Toafa's administration. At only four metres above sea level at its highest point, his government faced fears that Tuvalu could become the first nation state to be submerged by rising sea levels caused by global warming. In Oct. 2005 Toafa voiced his support for a UN proposal to designate those fleeing environmental catastrophes as refugees. In June 2005 Toafa protested that Australia and New Zealand should not pressurize Tuvalu into ending its support of sustainable whale hunting.

Toafa oversaw an extensive review of the constitution which some commentators believed could eventually lead to a referendum on Queen Elizabeth II's continuing role as head of state.

At elections held in Aug. 2006, Toafa was the only member of his cabinet to retain a parliamentary seat and he was succeeded as prime minister on 14 Aug. by Apisai Ielemia.

In Sept. 2010 he beat Kausea Natano by one vote to regain the premiership. However, on 21 Dec. 2010, after only 3 months in power, Toafa and his government were ousted in a vote of no confidence by eight votes to seven. The motion was reportedly initiated owing to MPs' concerns over the budget and a debt Toafa owed to the government for machinery hire. Willy Telavi, the former home affairs minister who had crossed the floor in the vote of no confidence, was elected prime minister 3 days later.

Toledo, Alejandro (Peru)

Introduction

A former economist for the World Bank, President Alejandro Toledo represented the Possible Peru (Perú Posible) party. Elected in July 2001, Toledo took over from interim president Valentín Paniagua, following the resignation of former president Alberto Fujimori in Nov. 2000 amid corruption allegations. The first elected president of indigenous origin, Toledo pledged to combat widespread poverty, invigorate the economy and eradicate government corruption.

Early Life

Toledo was born on 28 March 1946 in Cabana, a small Andean village. From a large, poor family, he grew up in the coastal town of Chimbote where his parents had moved to find work in the fishing business. The young Toledo worked at odd jobs including shoeshining. While studying in San Pedro, he took to politics while writing for *La Prensa* newspaper. On winning a scholarship, he studied economics at San Francisco University and completed a doctorate in human resources at Stanford University in the USA. He then worked as an economics advisor for international organizations including the UN, the World Bank and the International Labour Organization in Geneva.

On his return to Peru, he became actively involved in politics. Representing Peru Possible, a mix of left and centre politicians, he fought his first presidential campaign in 1995 when he received 4% of the vote. In his second attempt in 2000 he competed against Fujimori, who was running for a third consecutive term. Gaining only 23% of votes, Toledo withdrew from the presidential race accusing the Fujimori camp of vote rigging. Fujimori's third term was short-lived and the autocratic leader resigned a few months later. Having gone into exile in Japan, he was subsequently charged in Peru with treason.

Toledo fought his third election against the former president, Alan García, who represented the American Popular Revolutionary Alliance. During Toledo's electoral campaign he exploited his indigenous roots, aiming to attract those Peruvians who had suffered discrimination by the European elite. Toledo's wife, the Belgian anthropologist Elaine Karp, delivered campaign speeches in Quechua (the main indigenous language). Toledo claimed that during García's 1985–90 rule Peruvians had been subjected to food rationing caused by hyperinflation, corruption, terrorism and army brutality and that human rights had suffered. García fought back accusing Toledo of financing his campaign with laundered money. Videotapes collected by Fujimori's former spy chief Vladimiro Montesinos, imprisoned from 2002 for abuse of power, reveal that corruption, bribery and blackmail were endemic in the previous government.

After the first round of voting in April 2001, Toledo was ahead of García, but without a clear majority. In the run-off García conceded to Toledo. International observers agreed the election had been free and democratic.

Career Peak

Following his inauguration, Toledo attended a religious ceremony in his honour at the ancient Inca citadel Machu Picchu. He pledged to combat the country's endemic poverty by boosting industry and agriculture and kick-starting the flagging economy. He aimed to continue the free-market policies of Fujimori in order to attract foreign investors, and hoped to create 1 m. jobs over 5 years. Owing to Lima's overwhelming economic and political domination, Toledo also promised decentralization. During his presidency, his government achieved sustained growth in the economy, but his efforts to reduce poverty did not make a significant impact and he encountered difficulties in implementing institutional reforms. Corruption and other scandals dampened Toledo's personal popularity, and in Jan. 2005 a former army officer, Ollanta Humala, and his nationalist followers staged a brief but unsuccessful rebellion in the south of the country, calling on Toledo to resign. In May 2005 a commission found the president guilty of electoral fraud, although Congress later voted not to impeach him.

In 2005–06 Toledo's reputation was further damaged through professional and personal scandal. In Aug. 2005 his approval fell to just 7% and in Feb. 2006 his nephew was given a suspended prison sentence after being found guilty of rape. Toledo subsequently decided not to run in the 2006 presidential elections. He was succeeded on 28 July 2006 by former president Alan García.

Later Life

Toledo then returned to the United States and joined the Brookings Institution as a non-resident senior fellow in 2009. In Dec. 2010 he announced his candidacy for the 2011 presidential election, but only won 15.6% of votes cast. In Feb. 2017 a Peruvian court issued an international arrest warrant for Toledo, who was accused of accepting US$20 m. in bribes from a Brazilian construction firm.

Tomeing, Litokwa (Marshall Islands)

Introduction

Litokwa Tomeing was elected president by a parliamentary vote on 7 Jan. 2008, beating Kessai Note by 18 votes to 15. On 14 Jan. Tomeing and his cabinet of ten ministers were sworn in.

Early Life

Tomeing was born on 14 Oct. 1937 on Wotje Atoll in the Ratak Chain of the Marshall Islands, where he is a traditional chief. In 1999 he was elected as speaker of the *Nitijela*, the lower house of the legislature, where he served for 8 years.

Initially a member of the United Democratic Party, in Nov. 2007 Tomeing defected to the opposition United People's Party–Aelon Kein Ad (UPP/AKA) coalition. The election of Nov. 2007 was won narrowly by the UPP although the poll was widely criticized for chaotic organization. The results were tested in the courts and several recounts held. When parliament met to select the president in Jan. 2008, Tomeing defeated the incumbent Kessai Note.

Career Peak

Tomeing emphasized the need to promote *Mantin Majol* (a system of traditional customs) in everyday life. He pledged to reform the electoral system and in Feb. 2008 set up a commission to investigate the events of Nov. 2007. He also secured a multi-million dollar grant to re-establish the national airline.

Tomeing had claimed to favour closer links with China so it was thought his election may have signalled a departure from the Marshall Islands' pro-Taiwan policy. However, his choice as foreign minister was the since-dismissed Tony deBrum, who had held the same post when the Marshall

Islands first recognized Taiwan in 1998. On 29 Jan. Tomeing reaffirmed diplomatic ties at a meeting with the then Taiwanese Vice President, Annette Lu, during her visit to the Marshall Islands. Tomeing's relationship with the USA, the Islands' biggest aid donor, was expected to come under strain over American use of a long-range missile testing base on Kwajalein Atoll.

In Feb. 2009 cabinet ministers objected to Tomeing's sacking of Tony de Brum (UPP) as foreign minister. Relations within the government were further strained when he replaced other UPP ministers by UDP ones in a reshuffle. At the instigation of his rival former president Kessai Note (UDP), a parliamentary vote of no-confidence was held on 21 Oct. 2009, the third he faced in 1 year. Tomeing lost by 17 votes to 15. He was succeeded by Ruben Zackhras who took the office on a temporary basis until a presidential election was held on 26 Oct. The speaker Jurelang Zedkaia was elected after receiving 17 votes against 15 for Kessai Note.

Topi, Bamir (Albania)

Introduction

Bamir Myrteza Topi was sworn in as president in July 2007 after four rounds of voting, succeeding the Socialist Party's Alfred Moisiu. A former minister of agriculture and chairman of the Democratic Party of Albania (PD) parliamentary group, Topi is no longer formally linked to any political party.

Early Life

Topi was born in April 1957 in Tirana. After graduating in veterinary medicine at the Tirana Agricultural University, he moved to the neighbouring town of Petrela to continue studies in toxicology and pharmacology. In 1984 he took up a position as a researcher at the Institute of Veterinary Studies. From 1987–90 he left the Institute for Italy, where he completed a doctorate in molecular biology. His return to Albania coincided with the first large scale anti-communist protests. Topi became the Veterinary Institute's director, lecturing in toxicology and pharmacology until 1995 when he was conferred a professorship.

Topi entered professional politics in 1996, winning an Assembly seat as a PD candidate before being appointed minister of food and agriculture. In 1997 accusations of fraud and civil unrest briefly forced the PD, led by Sali Berisha, out of power. Topi remained loyal to Berisha and in July 2001 was elected PD candidate for Tirana and appointed to lead the PD caucus in parliament. In Dec. he was appointed party vice president.

In March 2007 Topi was announced as the PD candidate for the presidential election later in the year. While attracting support from the Christian Democrat and Republican parties, he faced fierce opposition from the Socialists. After failing to achieve the required three-fifths majority in three successive polls, the Assembly elected Topi president on 20 July 2007 in the penultimate round of scheduled voting. Topi resigned his party affiliation before being sworn in on 24 July.

Career Peak

Chief among Topi's objectives as president was driving forward Albania's campaign to join the European Union and NATO. In 2006 the government had signed a Stabilization and Association Agreement with the EU, and Topi subsequently negotiated a relaxation of the EU's visa conditions for Albania from Jan. 2008. Albania secured an invitation to membership of NATO in April 2008 and became a member in April 2009. In the same month Albania's application to join the EU was submitted. The issue of the independence of predominantly Albanian Kosovo has also taken centre stage, with Topi maintaining a supportive stance for the province's unilateral declaration of separation from Serbia in Feb. 2008.

At the domestic level, with the EU pushing for a tougher line on corruption, Topi was confronted in Oct. 2007 with a corruption scandal when several ministers were arrested on charges of embezzlement.

Topi decided not to stand for a second term and was succeeded as president by Bujar Nishani in July 2012.

Topolánek, Mirek (Czech Republic)

Introduction

Mirek Topolánek succeeded Jiří Paroubek as prime minister in Aug. 2006 following inconclusive elections held in June. After his minority centre-right Civic Democrat (ODS) government failed to win a vote of confidence, Topolánek was forced to negotiate with other parties. His coalition took office in Jan. 2007, comprising three parties holding half of parliament's 200 seats. He and his government were forced to resign after losing a parliamentary vote of confidence in March 2009.

Early Life

Mirek Topolánek was born on 15 May 1956 in Vsetín. He studied engineering at the University of Technology in Brno before undertaking corporate management training at the Management Centre in Čelákovice. He worked as a designer for a mining company, OKD Ostrava, from 1980–87 and then as a design management specialist for Eneroprojekt Prague until 1991. He was a member of the city council of Ostrava-Poruba from 1990–94 and became a senator in the Czech parliament in 1995. He served as deputy chairman of the Senate committee for economy, agriculture and transport, and then as deputy chairman of the Senate from 2002–04.

Topolánek ran for election in 2006 on a platform of reforming public finances and the welfare system and cutting bureaucracy. The election held in June saw the ODS emerge as the biggest party but with insufficient seats to form a workable government. After 2 months of political wrangling, Topolánek took office in Aug. but lost a vote of confidence. He returned in Jan. 2007 as head of a coalition of the ODS, the centrist Christian Democrats and the Green Party.

Career Peak

Topolánek's advocacy of EU reform, especially the deregulation of internal markets and the importance of equality for all member states in a revised EU constitution, took on added weight as the Czech Republic assumed the 6-month presidency of the Union in Jan. 2009.

In July 2008 Topolánek's government signed an agreement allowing the USA to base components of its planned missile defence system in the Czech Republic, despite widespread public opposition. Topolánek has argued that the facility will increase the security of the Republic and Europe as a whole, but his stance has provoked Russian hostility.

On 8 May 2009 Topolánek stood down as prime minister.

Torrijos Espino, Martín Erasto (Panama)

Introduction

Martín Torrijos became president in Sept. 2004, his election campaign having focused heavily on the legacy of his father, the former military dictator Omar Torrijos. Martín Torrijos promised to overhaul the social security system and fight corruption, and in 2006 launched a project to expand the Panama Canal, creating thousands of new jobs. He chose not to stand for re-election in May 2009 and left office on 1 July.

Early Life

Torrijos was born on 18 July 1963 in Panama City, the son of Omar Torrijos, who came to power in a military coup and served as *de facto* president from 1968–81. Omar Torrijos won popularity by negotiating a deal with US President Jimmy Carter in 1977 to transfer control of the Panama Canal to Panama in 1999.

In 1977 Martín Torrijos attended the St John's Military Academy in Wisconsin, USA. During the summer of 1979 he participated in the anti-Somoza movement in Nicaragua. Graduating in economics and political science from the Texas A&M University in 1988, on returning to Panama he became heavily involved in the Democratic Revolutionary Party (PRD).

A successful businessman, in 1994 he was appointed deputy minister for justice and the interior in Ernesto Pérez Balladares' cabinet. At the 1999 presidential election Torrijos stood as the PRD candidate, but was defeated by the Arnulfist Party candidate Mireya Moscoso, the wife of Arnulfo Arias who had been deposed by Omar Torrijos in 1968. Moscoso's government was accused of corruption and ineptitude and soon lost public backing.

Meanwhile, Torrijos was acting as economic adviser to numerous international companies while overseeing a restructuring of the PRD. As the PRD candidate at the 2004 elections he pledged to fight corruption and unemployment while improving the social security system, and regularly evoked the memory of his father, popularly regarded as the liberator of the Panama Canal. Martín Torrijos was elected to the presidency with 47.5% of the vote on 2 May 2004 and was sworn in on 1 Sept.

Career Peak

In the weeks before Torrijos took office, Moscoso pardoned four Cuban exiles who had been accused of attempting to assassinate Cuban president Fidel Castro. Havana immediately cut diplomatic ties, as did Venezuela. On taking office Torrijos set about normalizing relations and ties were restored in Nov. 2004.

In May 2005 Torrijos began his social security reforms by announcing plans to raise pension contributions and increase the retirement age. Several weeks of popular protest ensued. He also promised that proposals to modernize the Panama Canal, including a US$5 bn. canal-widening project, would be put to popular referendum. In a bid to distance himself from the excesses of his father's rule, he promised an investigation into alleged human rights abuses during Omar Torrijos' time in office.

As promised, the referendum on expansion of the Panama Canal took place in Oct. 2006 and was approved by nearly 80% of voters. The US$5.25 bn. project, expected to be completed by 2014, will widen and deepen the waterway to double shipping capacity. In Dec. 2006 Panama and the USA reached agreement on a free trade deal.

Torrijos handed over power to Ricardo Martinelli of the Alliance for Change on 1 July 2009.

Touré, Amadou Toumani (Mali)

Introduction

In 2002 Amadou Toumani Touré won Mali's election to become the country's second democratically-elected president. He had previously acted as head of state in 1991 when, as an army general, he overthrew military leader Moussa Traoré. He was re-elected in April 2007. Following a coup in March 2012, Touré was ousted from power and went into hiding.

Early Life

Amadou Toumani Touré was born on 4 Nov. 1948 in Mopti. From 1966–69 he studied at Badalabougou Standard Secondary School in Bamako with the intention of becoming a teacher. However, he abandoned teaching in favour of military training and joined the army, enrolling at the Kita-Inter Military College. He then trained in the former USSR and France before joining the parachute corps as a commander in 1984.

Touré led a coup in 1991 against Moussa Traoré after the latter's security forces killed more than a hundred pro-democracy demonstrators. In 1992 Touré handed power back to the newly-elected president Alpha Oumar Konaré, ending 23 years of military dictatorship and earning himself the nickname 'soldier of Democracy'.

Having retired from the army in Sept. 2001, he decided to return to politics as an independent presidential candidate in 2002, beating Soumaïla Cissé in the second round of elections.

Career Peak

Touré took office with the support of 22 minor parties and a number of other groups. He pledged to promote education and youth employment and created a children's foundation. He also pledged to ease poverty and improve the

health system. In Aug. 2005 he launched a food security website, developed in conjunction with the Malian food security commission and designed to monitor and improve the country's food distribution capacity. Touré was returned for a second term in April 2007 and the ruling pro-president Alliance for Democracy and Progress coalition won parliamentary elections in July that year.

In June 2006 his government signed an Algerian-brokered peace agreement with Tuareg rebels seeking greater autonomy for the north of the country. Despite these peace overtures, however, attacks involving suspected Tuareg insurgents continued until early 2009 when the government claimed to have taken control of Tuareg bases and some 700 rebels surrendered their weapons.

Following the resignation of Prime Minister Modibo Sidibé, Touré appointed Cissé Mariam Sidibe Kaïdama his successor in April 2011. In June 2011 Touré announced that he would not stand in the 2012 presidential election. However, in March 2012, a few months before his scheduled departure from office, a military coup forced him into hiding. The coup leader, Capt. Amadou Haya Sanogo, proclaimed himself chairman of the National Committee for the Restoration of Democracy and State.

Trajkovski, Boris (Macedonia)

Introduction

A lawyer and former deputy foreign minister, Trajkovski was elected Macedonia's president in 1999. He represented the centre-right nationalist Internal Macedonian Revolutionary Organization-Democratic Party for Macedonian National Unity (VMRO-DPMNE), and sought to steer Macedonia towards EU and NATO membership. His main challenge was resolving the conflict between ethnic Albanian rebel groups and Macedonian forces that threatened to escalate into civil war.

Early Life

Trajkovski was born on 25 June 1956 in Strumica, southeastern Macedonia. After studying law at university in the capital Skopje, he read theology at a Protestant college in the US. He then made a career in commercial law, working until 1997 for a construction company in Skopje. He joined the VMRO-DPMNE in 1992 and in Jan. 1999 was appointed deputy foreign minister in Ljubcho Georgievski's government. At this time, regional tensions escalated with the war in Kosovo. Thousands of Kosovan ethnic Albanian refugees attempted to cross a closed border to find protection in Macedonia. Trajkovski favoured opening the border, despite the threat of exacerbating tensions between the majority ethnic Slav population and the large minority ethnic Albanian population. The refugees were allowed entry, although most left at the end of the crisis (June 1999).

Career Peak

In the presidential election held between 31 Oct. and 5 Dec. 1999 Trajkovski stood as the VMRO-DPMNE candidate. Despite trailing the Social Democrat candidate Tito Petkovski after the first round, Trajkovski's moderate stance on ethnic Albanians gained him 52.9% of votes in the run-off. He succeeded Kiro Gligorov to become the second president of independent Macedonia, with his fellow party member Ljubèo Georgievski as prime minister.

As president he attempted to raise the international profile of Macedonia, calling for more Western support in return for Macedonia's cooperation during the Kosovan crisis. Border tensions continued throughout 2000. In March 2001 there were a series of clashes between government forces and ethnic Albanian separatists near the border between Macedonia and Kosovo. As violence escalated Macedonia found itself on the brink of civil war. In May 2001 the government gave ethnic Albanian rebels a 'final warning' to end their uprising. A number of Macedonian soldiers were killed in clashes with the rebels, and following reverses in the military campaign the commander of the Macedonian army, Jovan Andrevski, resigned in June 2001. As the crisis worsened, a stand-off within the government between the Macedonian and the ethnic Albanian parties was only resolved after mediation between Trajkovski and Javier Solana, the EU's foreign and security policy chief. In Aug. 2001 a peace accord was negotiated giving more constitutional rights to ethnic Albanians (Albanian was made an official language June 2002) in return for guerrilla disarmament. Despite a cessation of violence, NATO continued its presence in the region. Tensions surfaced once more during parliamentary elections in Sept. 2002 in which Trajkovski's VMRO-DPMNE was defeated. Prime Minister Georgievski stood down and in Nov. 2002 the representative of the 'Together for Macedonia' coalition—and leader of the Social Democratic League of Macedonia—Branko Crvenkovski was made prime minister.

Keen to secure Macedonia's eventual membership of the EU and NATO, in Feb. 2004 Trajkovski signed a formal application for EU membership. A few days later, on 26 Feb. 2004, he was killed in a plane crash in Bosnia-Herzegovina. An international investigation concluded the crash was accidental, caused by pilot error.

Tran Duc Luong (Vietnam)

Introduction

The presidency of Vietnam is the least powerful of the three great offices of state. The Prime Minister and the Secretary General of the Communist Party hold effective power. Tran Duc Luong held this largely ceremonial post from 1997–2006.

Early Life

Tran Duc Luong was born in central coastal region of Vietnam on 5 May 1937. Too young to have taken part in the struggle against the country's French colonial rulers, Luong was nevertheless politically conscious and opted for North Vietnam when the country was divided into a Communist North and a pro-Western South by the Geneva Agreement of 1954.

Luong became a geology technician, and in 1970 he was appointed deputy director of geological map department at the (national) Mining and Geology College. Promoted to become General Director, he was responsible for the 1:200,000 geological map project of Vietnam. In 1981, he was sent to the Soviet Union to study economic management.

Luong joined the Communist Party in 1959 and helped run a number of youth groups. In 1964, he became cell secretary for his geology group and then was active for the party in various roles. Having completed a training course for senior Party officials in 1976, it was only a matter of time before he was selected for election to the (single-party) National Assembly. As a National Assembly member from 1981, Luong held a series of governmental scientific posts, including Deputy Chairman and, later Chairman, of the National Assembly Science and Technology Commission. In 1987, Luong was appointed Deputy Prime Minister and in 1996 he was elected to the Party Central Committee and to the Politburo.

Career Peak

In Sept. 1997, Luong was elected President. His ability to speak French, English and Russian were considered useful tools in his efforts to represent his country's interests in the world context. On 24 June 2006 he resigned, along with Prime Minister Phan Van Khai and Assembly Speaker Nguyen Van An. The three left, unable to guarentee re-election to the politburo, claiming they were making way for a new generation of politicians in line with party policy.

Traoré, Dioncounda (Mali)

Introduction

Dioncounda Traoré was sworn in as interim president on 8 April 2012, ending a brief period of military rule after the removal of the former president, Amadou Toumani Touré, in a coup on 21 March. As parliamentary speaker, Traoré was next in the constitutional succession after Touré's enforced resignation.

Early Life

Dioncounda Traoré was born in Kati on 23 Feb. 1942, the son of army colonel Sékou Traoré. He read mathematics in Moscow from 1963 to 1965 before continuing his studies at the University of Algiers. He was later awarded a doctorate from the University of Nice. He started work as a teacher at the Ecole Normale Supérieure in Bamako in 1977 but was jailed in 1980 for his trade union activities.

A militant trade unionist and pro-democracy activist throughout the 1980s, Traoré was a founding member of the Alliance for Democracy in Mali (ADEMA), a coalition of opponents to the dictatorship of Moussa Traoré. After Moussa Traoré was overthrown in 1991, ADEMA evolved into ADEMA-PASJ (African Party for Solidarity and Justice), with Dioncounda Traoré elected the party's second vice-president.

After Mali's first democratic elections, Traoré was appointed to the council of ministers by President Alpha Oumar Konaré in June 1992. He variously held the portfolios for public works, defence and foreign affairs before resigning from the council in 1997 to take his place in the National Assembly as the representative for Nara.

In 2000 Ibrahim Boubacar Kéïta resigned as prime minister and leader of ADEMA-PASJ, with Traoré elected to succeed him in the party post. In 2007 Traoré became president of the National Assembly but fled Mali during the 2012 coup. He returned when the junta, led by Capt. Amadou Haya Sanogo, agreed to an Economic Community of West African States (ECOWAS)-brokered handover to an interim administration. The junta nevertheless retained considerable power and influence.

Career Peak

In the period between the military coup and Traoré's installation as interim president, Tuareg and militant Islamist insurgents made significant gains in the country's north, culminating in a declaration of independence in April 2012. While the claim went unrecognized internationally, Traoré entered office under pressure to prevent the spread of insurgency to neighbouring regions. Preparations for military action against the rebel groups in the north, with the aid of ECOWAS forces and with United Nations and African Union backing, proceeded slowly over the following months. However, tensions between the civilian government and junta, which led in Dec. to Prime Minister Cheick Modibo Diarra's forced resignation by the junta and the appointment of Diango Cissoko as premier by Traoré, threatened to undermine plans for intervention and prompted international demands for a restoration of constitutional rule.

Ibrahim Kéïta won the presidential elections held in the summer of 2013 and succeeded Traoré as president in Sept.

Trimble, David (Northern Ireland, United Kingdom)

Introduction

David Trimble, first minister of the Northern Ireland Assembly from 1998 until June 2001 and again from Nov. 2001 until Oct. 2002, was leader of the Ulster Unionist Party (UUP) from 1995 to 2005. He was a member of the British parliament from 1990 to 2005. On his election to the party leadership it was believed that Trimble would peddle a Unionist hardline but he soon proved himself a pragmatic negotiator in search of peace. His role in brokering the 1998 Good Friday Agreement earned him a share of the Nobel Peace Prize. However, opposition increased within his own party, notably over IRA arms decommissioning. Trimble resigned as party leader following his party's poor showing at the general election of 2005.

Early Life

Trimble was born on 15 Oct. 1944 in Bangor, County Down. He studied law at Queen's University, Belfast. As a non-practising barrister, he became a law lecturer at Queen's and was known for his strong Unionist tendencies. A prominent member of the Vanguard Unionist Progressive Party (VUPP) during the 1970s, he became party deputy leader. In 1977 he joined the Ulster Unionist Party (UUP). In 1990 he was elected the UUP MP for Upper Bann.

When James Molyneaux's rule of the party ended in 1995, Trimble stood for the leadership against John Taylor. Trimble was regarded as intransigent by many observers and was noted for his close alliance with the hardline leader of the Ulster Democratic Unionist Party, Ian Paisley, and for his commitment to ensuring the controversial marching rights of the Protestant Orange Order. Upsetting the odds, Trimble was elected UUP leader.

Career Peak

In late 1997 Trimble was present at groundbreaking peace talks that included members of Sinn Féin, the IRA's political arm. Trimble, proving more flexible than widely predicted, was instrumental in concluding the Good Friday Agreement in April 1998. The agreement laid plans for a Northern Ireland Assembly and several cross-border power-sharing institutions. Trimble lost support from large parts of his party and relations with Paisley, who saw the agreement as a sell-out to republicanism, soured. However, the agreement gained widespread support in referenda in both the North and the Republic.

Elections were soon held for the Northern Irish Assembly and the UUP became the biggest party, with Trimble as first minister. The Good Friday Agreement soon came under strain and with it Trimble's authority. On 15 Aug. 1998 the Real IRA, a nationalist paramilitary group, planted a bomb in the town of Omagh, murdering 29 people and injuring several hundred more. In addition, the issue of IRA weapons decommissioning became a major bone of contention. Despite these potential pitfalls, Trimble was awarded the 1998 Nobel Peace Prize in partnership with the nationalist politician John Hume.

The row over IRA decommissioning rumbled on into the summer of 1999 when Trimble and his party refused to sit with Sinn Féin members on the executive. Under the mediating guidance of US Senator George Mitchell, Trimble persuaded his party that the executive could be set up prior to decommissioning. Trimble staked much of his reputation and the goodwill of his party to do this, and when decommissioning was still no closer 3 months later, the UUP pulled out and Peter Mandelson (then the British government's Northern Ireland Minister) suspended the assembly. In March 2000 Trimble survived a challenge to his UUP leadership by the Rev. Martin Smyth, previously leader of the Orange Order. But the party's ruling council put new curbs on Trimble's power to negotiate.

After several months of wrangling, the assembly was reconvened in June 2000, with Trimble back as first minister. A programme of decommissioning was yet to be agreed and tensions increased following the publication in Nov. 2000 of Chris Patten's report into the reform of the Royal Ulster Constabulary (RUC). Many unionists believed it to be a further diminution of British sovereignty for little visible return. Various dissident terrorist groups, unionist and nationalist, remained active and Trimble's own party was divided and his hold on power delicate.

In May 2001 Trimble announced his intention to resign as first minister at the end of June if the decommissioning issue was still unresolved. When no progress was made he carried out his threat and by so doing also put deputy first minister Seamus Mallon (of the Social Democratic and Labour Party) out of office. Trimble nominated trade minister Sir Reg Empey (UUP) to take over his administrative duties, though he did leave the door open for his return as first minister if the pace of negotiations accelerated. Trimble was re-elected first minister in Nov. 2001.

In Oct. 2002 the Northern Irish Assembly executive and the office of first minister was again suspended following allegations of IRA spying at the Northern Ireland Office. Direct rule from London was re-imposed and shortly afterwards the IRA cut off its links with the weapons de-commissioning body. Trimble criticized the suspension, arguing that exclusion of Sinn Féin members would have secured the Assembly's survival.

Later Life

In May 2003 Tony Blair postponed elections to the Northern Irish Assembly. He defended the move on the grounds that Sinn Féin leader Gerry Adams' assurance that the IRA would not do anything to undermine the peace process did not provide a specific guarantee. Trimble pronounced his support for Blair's stance, stating that the 'underlying problem that caused the suspension' remained unresolved.

With the issue of IRA arms decommissioning still unresolved, the UUP made a disastrous showing at the 2005 general election. Trimble lost his seat and the party retained only one Westminster seat, while the Democratic Unionist Party of hardliner Rev. Ian Paisley became the biggest Unionist party with nine seats. Trimble resigned as party leader, to be succeeded by Sir

Reg Empey. At the end of July 2005 the IRA announced the end of its armed campaign and ordered its units to dump its arms.

In June 2006 he was made Baron Trimble of Lisnagarvey and gained a seat in the House of Lords. In April 2007 he announced that he was leaving the UUP to join the Conservative Party.

Trudeau, Pierre (Canada)

Introduction

Pierre Elliot Trudeau was the Liberal Prime Minister of Canada from 1968 until 1979 and from 1980 until 1984. A charismatic and flamboyant man, he believed in a federal Canada which embraced ethnic equality and bilingualism. Trained as a lawyer and specializing in civil and labour relations law, he also introduced a number of important constitutional reforms. His years in office were dogged by fluctuating economic fortunes but he became one of the longest serving Western leaders of the second half of the twentieth century.

Early Life

Trudeau was born on 18 Oct. 1919 in the suburbs of Montreal in Quebec to a mother of Scottish descent and a French Canadian father who had made a fortune through his business activities. Trudeau had a Jesuit education before qualifying in Law from the University of Montreal in 1943 and undertaking further studies at Harvard in the USA, the London School of Economics and the Sorbonne in Paris. He then travelled widely before becoming an advisor to the Privy Council in 1949. A year later he set up *Cité Libre*, a critical magazine, with a group of like-minded intellectuals and in 1951 he began in legal practice.

In 1961 he took a law professorship at the University of Montreal while working at the *Institut de recherches en droit public* (Institute of Public Law Research). He left both posts in 1965 upon entering the House of Commons as the Liberal member for Mount Royal, Quebec, the constituency he would serve until his retirement in 1984. He was made Parliamentary Secretary by Prime Minister Lester Pearson in 1966 and Minister of Justice the following year. In this office he oversaw the implementation of a number of liberalizing reforms, notably concerning gun control, divorce, abortion, homosexuality and public lotteries. Pearson resigned the Liberal leadership in 1968 and Trudeau took his place on 6 April following 4 ballots. Within a fortnight, carried along on the tide of "Trudeaumania" that swept the country, he was elected prime minister with a strong majority.

Career Peak

Early in his tenure Trudeau introduced the Official Languages Bill which promoted bilingualism and made it a civil service requirement. However, the question of independence for Quebec remained a thorny issue with matters coming to a head during the October Crisis of 1970. The Front de Libération de Québec (The Quebec Liberation Front) kidnapped a British diplomat, and Trudeau, in co-operation with the Quebec Prime Minister, imposed the controversial War Measures Act, which allowed for sweeping arrests without charges. The diplomat was freed but some 450 people were placed under arrest. Pierre Laporte, a cabinet minister for Quebec, was murdered.

Trudeau already had a reputation for a lively private life when in 1971 he married Margaret Sinclair, who was 30 years his junior. The couple had 3 children but split in 1977 and divorced 7 years later. By the time of the general elections in 1972, Canada was experiencing high unemployment and Trudeau's Liberals only just sneaked victory, relying on the support of the New Democratic Party to form a government. The world oil crisis struck the next year and with public spending remaining high, inflation and unemployment continued to spiral so that in 1975 the government, returned the previous year, had to introduce wage and price controls.

The economy failed to pick up and at the general elections of May 1979 the Liberals were defeated by the Conservatives under Joseph Clarke. Trudeau announced his retirement but was persuaded into a re-think and was victorious again at the elections of 3 May 1980. On 20 May a referendum was held in Quebec to decide the issue of French separatism but, with the help of

Trudeau, the notion was soundly defeated. He then set about constitutional reforms, the most important of which were the Canadian Charter of Rights and independence from the British parliament. The proposed constitution won a large majority in the Commons and was passed on 2 Dec. 1981, with Queen Elizabeth II assenting to it on 4 April 1982. In addition, in 1984 Canada became officially bilingual.

On the international stage, Trudeau had normalized relations with China early in his first spell as Prime Minister. He also sought to reduce involvement with Nato, improve ties with the European Economic Community (despite the increase in its offshore fishing jurisdiction antagonizing Spain), become more active within the UN and the Commonwealth and pursue a détente with the Soviet Union. His relationship with the USA was variable. He was aware of the necessity for co-operation but did not want Canada to be dependent on its powerful neighbour. In the last years of his time in office, Trudeau espoused the need for dialogue between wealthy and developing nations, and also campaigned for an international reduction in nuclear weapons and a thawing in the Cold War.

Later Life

Trudeau retired from government on 29 Feb. 1984 to be replaced by John Turner. He returned to legal practice, received the Companion of the Order of Canada in 1985 and in 1993 he published his memoirs. He died in Montreal on 28 Sept. 2000.

Truman, Harry S. (United States of America)

Introduction

Harry S. Truman was the 33rd President of the United States, taking office in April 1945 on the death of Franklin D. Roosevelt and serving one full term after winning the 1948 election before he decided not to run for presidential office again. Remembered for taking the decision to drop atom bombs on Hiroshima and Nagasaki, Truman also led the United States through the early years of the Cold War and into combat in Korea.

Early Life

Born in Lamar, Montana on 8 May 1884 Truman's family was too poor to send him to college. In his late teens and early twenties he did jobs on the railroads and then for a bank before working on the family farm with his father for 11 years.

During this time Truman became involved in the local Democratic Party. In World War I his leadership qualities began to take shape when he served in France as a captain in the American Expeditionary Forces. Truman returned to the United States in 1919 and married Elizabeth Wallace. The couple based themselves in Kansas City and started a clothes shop, which went bust during the Great Depression, leaving Truman penniless. Truman turned to politics and won election as a judge in the Jackson county court in 1922. By 1934 he was a presiding judge and in 1936 he ran for a seat in the US Senate.

Truman was an unswerving advocate of Franklin D. Roosevelt's 'New Deal' policies, which helped him win this election. Re-election to the senate followed in 1940 and Truman made a name for himself through his work as Head of the Special Committee to investigate the National Defense Program. He also continued to support Roosevelt's domestic and foreign policies. This brought him to the president's attention and, in the lead up to the 1944 election, Truman was persuaded to run against Henry Wallace, who had been a relatively unpopular deputy to Roosevelt, for the vice-presidential nomination. Truman duly defeated Wallace and helped Roosevelt win an unprecedented fourth presidential election victory.

Career Peak

A few months later, on 12 April 1945, Truman found himself catapulted into the position of President after Roosevelt's death. Germany's unconditional surrender in World War II came several weeks later and Truman was plunged into a crucial decision as to how to bring about Japanese surrender. Threatening 'a rain of ruin from the air, the like of which has never been seen on this earth'. the new President authorized dropping atomic bombs on the Japanese cities of Hiroshima and Nagasaki on 6 and 9 Aug. 1945.

Truman reasoned that it would hasten the end of war and save lives, although some commentators speculated that he was also intending to send a message to the Soviet Union as he sought to assert the United States' status in a post-war world order. Unconditional Japanese surrender from Emperor Hirohito duly arrived on 14 Aug. with Truman declaring: 'This is the day we have been waiting for since Pearl Harbor'.

Over the next few years Truman became heavily involved with international affairs as he sought to help map out the international political map in a way that would limit Soviet influence in Europe. Truman favoured a 'get-tough' policy towards the Soviet Union. In March 1947 he introduced the Truman doctrine, a $400 m. aid package for the Turkish and Greek governments which signalled his determination to shake off the last vestiges of US isolationism. In June he denounced the communist coup in Hungary as 'an outrage'. Meanwhile, the Marshall Plan, also introduced that year, sought to offer economic aid to areas of Europe impoverished by the war. Several countries, such as Czechoslovakia, Poland and Finland, elected to remain in the Soviet sphere of influence by not taking part in the scheme.

At home Truman continued Roosevelt's new deal policies, which he re-branded the 'fair deal'. However many of his proposals were obstructed by Congress and Truman succeeded in winning few significant domestic victories. As a consequence, he was given little chance of winning the 1948 presidential election against Republican opponent Thomas E. Dewey. Truman campaigned vigorously and tirelessly, stressing that the Republican dominated Congress of 1947–48 had been a 'do-nothing' body that had blocked his attempts at legislation and reform in the areas of civil rights and labour management.

Exit polls predicted a landslide Dewey victory and the Chicago Tribune even went to press on the day after the election with a first edition headlined 'Dewey defeats Truman'. However, Truman pulled off a shock victory, defeating his opponent by a margin of around 1.2 m. votes and 303 electoral college votes to 189.

In his first full term in office, Truman's domestic policy was hampered by tactical coalitions between southern-based Democrats and conservative Republicans, although he did secure the passage of the important 1949 Housing Act. Foreign policy continued to define Truman's presidency. In March 1949, he took the United States into the North Atlantic Treaty Organisation (NATO), an alliance of 8 Western countries intended to act as a deterrent against possible acts of military aggression. From 25 June 1950, Truman became even more involved in foreign affairs after Communist North Korea invaded South Korea. A day later the president offered immediate American air and naval support to the South, a decision that was ratified by the United Nations Security Council at a meeting that was boycotted by the Soviet Union.

However difficulties soon arose between Truman and his commander in the war, General Douglas MacArthur. Initially, MacArthur's men drove the North Koreans out of South Korea after landing at Inchon in Sept. 1950. However, when the Chinese entered the conflict on 16 Sept. the situation became more complicated.

Truman was determined not to allow the conflict to escalate into World War III, while MacArthur, with considerable support from many Republicans, argued that combat should be widened through direct attacks on China. Truman repeatedly warned MacArthur not to make any public political statements, however eventually, on 1 April 1951, he felt compelled to fire the general, arguing that US policy in the Far East should be dictated by the aim of preventing further conflict.

Truman's authority was severely weakened by the episode. After clashes with Senator Joseph R. McCarthy over his 'witch-hunt' of American communists, Truman decided not to stand for re-election in the 1952 presidential election. Democratic candidate Adlai E. Stevenson subsequently lost the White House to his Republican opponent Dwight D. Eisenhower, a popular military hero who had been appointed supreme commander of NATO by Truman in 1950.

Later Life

In political retirement, Truman travelled widely and published two volumes of memoirs in 1955 and 1956. He died on 6 Dec. 1972 in Kansas City, Montana.

Truong Tan Sang (Vietnam)

Introduction

Truong Tan Sang was elected to the largely ceremonial post of president in July 2011 at the Communist Party's 11th national congress, replacing Nguyen Minh Triet. Truong tan Sang is a former head of the party secretariat and party secretary for Ho Chi Minh City.

Early Life

Truong Tan Sang was born in My Hanh in the Duc Hoa district of Long An province, on 21 Jan. 1949. Between 1966 and 1968 he was leader of the youth student movement P.K.2, and from 1969 until 1971, while a party committee member, was youth union secretary and managed a secret armed group in Duc Hoa town.

In 1971 he was captured by the South Vietnamese and was detained in Bien Hoa prison in the Phu Quoc island district. He was released in 1973 under the terms of the Paris Peace Accords. Between April 1975 and Oct. 1978 he worked at the Gia Dinh Trade Union, serving as deputy head of the Ho Chi Minh City new economic zone development department and as secretary of the Ho Chi Minh Communist Youth Union (with responsibility for the city plantations and new economic zones).

Between 1978 and 1983 he held posts including director of the Van Hai Farm and alternate member of the Ho Chi Minh City party committee. From 1983 to 1986 he headed the Ho Chi Minh forestry department and the new economic zone development department. He was also Ho Chi Minh's party committee member in charge of youth volunteer forces and was promoted to the standing board of the city's party committee. In 1992 he became party chairman for Ho Chi Minh and in 1996 joined the Politburo as its 14th-ranked member.

Between 1999 and 2000 he was party secretary for Ho Chi Minh and in April 2001 was promoted to 10th position in the national party and head of its economic commission. In April 2006 he rose to fifth position and headed the party's secretariat. In Oct. 2009 he was named second in the party hierarchy and in July 2011 the National Assembly overwhelmingly elected him national president.

Career Peak

On taking office, against the backdrop of the ongoing dispute with China over the Spratly Islands, Sang pledged to defend Vietnam's independence and territorial integrity. Despite clashes between Chinese naval boats and Vietnamese oil exploration vessels resulting in the Vietnamese navy conducting live-fire exercises, Sang vowed to resolve the dispute peacefully. In Oct. 2011 he travelled to India to solicit diplomatic support, strengthen economic ties and seek military assistance.

Faced by a weakening economy, with Asia's highest inflation rate in 2011 at over 20%, Sang underlined his support for the 5-year socio-economic reform agenda agreed at the 11th National Congress in Jan. 2011. Despite ongoing reports of human rights abuses, including the imprisonment of religious activists, Sang's government forged ties with both India and the USA.

Following the completion of his 5 year term as president in 2016, Sang was replaced by Tran Dai Quang.

Tsang, Donald (Hong Kong, China)

Introduction

Donald Tsang became Chief Executive of the Hong Kong Special Administrative Region following the resignation of Tung Chee-Hwa in early 2005. During a long career as a civil servant, Tsang specialized in economic issues and was finance secretary after the transfer to Chinese sovereignty in 1997. After 45 years in government and 7 years as Chief Executive, Tsang stood down in 2012.

Early Life

Donald Yam-Kuen Tsang was born in Hong Kong on 7 Oct. 1944, the son of an officer in the Royal Hong Kong police force. Having completed his secondary education at the Roman Catholic Wah Yan College, Tsang worked as a sales representative for a US pharmaceutical firm, Pfizer Corporation, before entering the civil service in 1967. He served in various departments, including a 3-year stint from 1974 in the finance branch. He later spent a year at the Asian Development Bank in Manila working on water supply and railway development projects in the Philippines and Bangladesh. In 1981 he left for the USA to take a master's degree in public administration at Harvard University's Kennedy School of Government.

As deputy secretary of the general duties department from 1985–89, Tsang was responsible for implementing the Sino-British Joint Declaration, signed in Dec. 1984, which paved the way for Hong Kong's absorption into the People's Republic of China (PRC). The agreement stipulated that Hong Kong's economic, legal and social systems would be preserved for 50 years. Tsang became the director-general of trade in 1991, responsible for all aspects of trade negotiation and administration, and 2 years later was promoted to secretary for the treasury, with responsibility for taxation and resource allocation.

In 1995 Tsang was appointed financial secretary, the first ethnic Chinese person to hold the position in 150 years of British rule. Following Hong Kong's transition to its Special Administrative Region status on 1 July 1997, he retained the position in the administration of Chief Executive Tung Che Hwa. Tsang won plaudits for his role in steering Hong Kong through the Asian financial crisis of 1998, notably a bold stock market intervention to ward off attacks on the currency by international speculators.

Tsang's relative popularity contrasted with the growing dissatisfaction at Tung's leadership, both in Hong Kong and Beijing. Particularly damaging was a national security bill that prompted mass protests in mid-2003 and demands for Tung's resignation. Later that year Tsang proposed a system of greater popular representation in Hong Kong but the reforms were rejected by the legislature, which believed they did not go far enough. When Tung resigned on health grounds in March 2005, Tsang took over as acting chief executive. He was declared the permanent chief executive without contest and took office on 24 June 2005.

Career Peak

Although Tsang faced widespread criticism for the failure of his democratic reforms, he won praise for his stewardship of the economy with unemployment falling to a 7-year low in 2007. On 25 March 2007 Tsang overwhelmingly defeated Alan Leong to retain his position as chief executive for a new 5-year term. Under Tsang, Hong Kong weathered the global financial crisis relatively well. Although Tsang's introduction of a minimum wage bill and a bill to ban anticompetitive practices were heralded as significant achievements, he was criticized for failing to address the city's widening wealth gap. Unable by law to seek a third term, he was succeeded by Leung Chun-ying on 1 July 2012. Tsang's final months in office were marred by scandal, including accepting hospitality from local tycoons.

Later Life

In Feb. 2017 Tsang was sentenced to 20 months' imprisonment for misconduct in public office.

Tsiranana, Philibert (Madagascar)

Introduction

A leading figure in Madagascar's move to independence, Philibert Tsiranana was president from 1960–72 representing the Parti Social Démocrate de Madagascar (PSD). Insurrections and violence at the end of his term forced him to hand over power to General Gabriel Ramanantsoa.

Early Life

Tsiranana was born on the 18 Oct. 1910 in the northwestern town of Ambarikorano. After his primary and secondary education, he attended the

Tananarive Teacher Training College, graduating in 1930. In 1946 he went to study in Montpellier. He was one of the founders of the Parti des Déshérités de Madagascar (PDM; the Disinherited of Madagascar Party). He came back to Madagascar in 1952 and eventually sided with moderate nationalists who were in favour of independence.

Career Peak

In 1956 he founded the PSD. He was elected deputy and represented his country in the French national assembly. When the autonomous Malagasy Republic was proclaimed in Oct. 1958, he headed the provisional government. Standing against Assembly President Norbert Zafimahova in the 1959 election, Tsiranana was elected president. Full independence was granted on 26 June 1960. He retained close economic and political ties with the French government.

Over the next 12 years the PSD, led by Tsiranana, retained control of Madagascar and dominated government. The regime strongly favoured the *côtiers*, or people from the coast, over inland peoples such as the Merina. Tsiranana was re-elected in 1965, and then as sole candidate in the presidential elections of Jan. 1972, he was re-elected with 99.9% of votes. In May 1972, following a resurgence of violent anti-government protest, he relinquished power to General Gabriel Ramanantsoa, the Merina head of Madagascar's armed forces, who became prime minister. Tsiranana resigned as president in Oct. 1972.

Later Life

In 1975 Tsiranana's proposal for a 'Council of Wise Men' under his presidency was rejected. Following his refusal to support incoming president Didier Ratsiraka, the PSM was dissolved and Tsiranana's political career ended. He died in April 1978.

Tsvangirai, Morgan (Zimbabwe)

Introduction

Morgan Tsvangirai is leader of the Movement for Democratic Change (MDC), the only significant opposition to President Robert Mugabe's regime since independence was established in 1980. Tsvangirai became an increasingly credible alternative to Mugabe as dissatisfaction with the ever more authoritarian regime and its vast mishandling of the national economy grew. This electoral viability made Tsvangirai and his supporters a target for violence and intimidation, culminating in the nationwide bloodshed that followed the disputed 2008 presidential elections. Subsequently, however, the implementation of a power-sharing agreement brokered with Mugabe under international pressure led to Tsvangirai's inauguration as executive prime minister of a unity government in Feb. 2009. Despite some progress in Zimbabwe's economic fortunes, political instability has nevertheless persisted and Tsvangirai's ability to carry out his executive functions has been impeded.

Early Life

Tsvangirai was born in 1952 in Buhera, then part of Southern Rhodesia. He left school at 16 and took a job in a textile factory and then at a nickel mine in Bindura, eventually becoming general foreman and branch chairman of the Associated Mineworkers' Union (AMU). A strong supporter of Mugabe's ZANU-PF, Tsvangirai was brought into the first post-independence government. However, Tsvangirai's lack of direct involvement in the guerrilla war that led to the end of minority white rule in 1980 has been used against him by Mugabe's supporters.

In 1985 Tsvangirai left to become vice president of the AMU, having been voted onto the national executive 2 years earlier. In 1987 he was named secretary-general of the Southern Africa Miners' Federation. After a period studying in the UK, Tsvangirai was named general secretary of the Zimbabwe Congress of Trade Unions (ZCTU) in 1988. Six years later he became secretary general of the Southern African Trade Union co-ordinating council.

Under his leadership the ZCTU began to dissent from the ZANU-PF line. In the late-1980s and early-1990s Tsvangirai and Mugabe repeatedly clashed, notably over a programme of structural reform adopted by Mugabe. Though

in line with IMF demands, Tsvangirai condemned the programme as an attack on workers' rights. He led several mass protests against the proposals, which forced Mugabe to back down. Tsvangirai was later jailed on unproven charges of being a South African spy.

Over the course of the 1990s the ZCTU became the focus of opposition to Mugabe's government. In Sept. 1999 Tsvangirai formed the MDC to formally challenge the dominance of ZANU-PF. In Feb. 2000 the MDC co-ordinated the defeat in a referendum of a government-championed constitutional amendment that would have extended Mugabe's personal power. It represented Mugabe's first significant defeat in a public vote since taking office. In Sept. 2000 Tsvangirai was charged with treason for comments made against Mugabe but the charges were later judged to be unconstitutional.

At the parliamentary elections of June 2000 the MDC won 57 of 150 seats, only five behind ZANU-PF. Mugabe's pre-election campaign received widespread international condemnation as white-owned farms were illegally seized and opposition supporters intimidated. Tsvangirai was defeated at the presidential elections of March 2002, winning 42.1% against Mugabe's 56.1%. However, observers claimed the elections failed to meet international standards and it was widely believed that Tsvangirai would have triumphed in a free vote.

Shortly before the election a video tape was exhibited allegedly showing Tsvangirai discussing an assassination attempt against Mugabe. Tsvangirai was charged with treason, carrying a possible death sentence, and his trial began in Feb. 2003. In June 2003 he called for mass action against Mugabe via a general strike and anti-government rallies. The MDC was targeted by government forces in the preceding weeks and Tsvangirai was arrested and subjected to new treason charges. He was acquitted of all charges in 2004.

Mugabe's regime met with international condemnation in March 2007 when Tsvangirai suffered serious head injuries whilst in police custody. More than 50 opposition leaders were arrested during a prayer meeting although no-one was charged. In June Tsvangirai toured Western Europe with rival opposition leader Arthur Mutambara, calling on European politicians to support their struggle for democracy.

In the general election of 29 March 2008 the MDC gained a majority in the House of Assembly, removing ZANU-PF from overall parliamentary control for the first time since Zimbabwe gained independence. Tsvangirai claimed the largest number of votes in the presidential election of the same date, winning 47.9% of the ballot against 43.2% for President Mugabe (according to the Zimbabwe Electoral Commission). However, the margin of victory was disputed, with the MDC claiming that Tsvangirai had gained the absolute majority required to avoid a second round run-off against the incumbent. These claims were rejected by the government and a run-off was scheduled for 27 June. There followed a sustained campaign of intimidation and violence against supporters of Tsvangirai. The MDC reported the death of 85 and the displacement of 200,000 of its followers over the following weeks. Five days before the ballot, having been forced to take refuge in the Dutch embassy, Tsvangirai withdrew from the race, professing that he could no longer force the Zimbabwean people to 'suffer this torture'. Over the following days he appealed to the international community, contending that 'the words of indignation from global leaders [must] be backed by the moral rectitude of military force'. Nevertheless, he subsequently entered into talks with Mugabe in Aug. 2008, which resulted in a deal the following month that provided for Mugabe to remain as president with Tsvangirai taking the premiership.

Career Peak

Implementation of the power-sharing deal was hampered by disagreements over the allocation of ministerial portfolios in a unity government until the end of Jan. 2009 when Tsvangirai accepted an arrangement giving the Movement for Democratic Change-Tsvangirai/MDC-T and the Movement for Democratic Change-Mutambara/MDC-M 16 and four posts respectively in a 35-member cabinet. On 11 Feb. Tsvangirai was sworn in as prime minister. However, there remained deep-seated domestic and international reservations about the viability of the new government, given the animosity between prime minister and president, Mugabe's autocratic track record and the conspicuous absence of the pro-Mugabe leaders of the security forces from Tsvangirai's inauguration ceremony.

With the finance portfolio under MDC control, the use of foreign currency was authorized, effectively replacing the worthless Zimbabwean dollar by the US dollar and South African rand and helping to bring about an end to years of hyperinflation. During a tour of the USA and Europe in June 2009, Tsvangirai successfully lobbied Western donors and the IMF to restore aid for essential services, although they refused to lift sanctions or release more substantive aid until the new administration had undertaken political and other reforms.

However, progress towards a new constitution was hindered by further political wrangling and in Oct. 2009 Tsvangirai temporarily boycotted meetings of the cabinet in protest at Mugabe's failure to honour agreements. The MDC meanwhile continued to face violence and intimidation from ZANU-PF supporters.

In Jan. 2010 Tsvangirai again urged the easing of targeted international sanctions in recognition of the unity government's economic record. The EU made some concessions in 2011 and 2012 but continued to express concern at political intimidation in Zimbabwe. Meanwhile, relations between Tsvangirai and Mugabe deteriorated further as the latter sought to sideline the prime minister and maintain control over executive decision-making. In Oct. 2012, against a background of rising violence directed against the MDC and its supporters in the approach to elections expected before the end of 2013, Tsvangirai once more threatened to withdraw from the unity government. On 6 March 2009 Tsvangirai survived a car crash in which his wife, Susan, died.

In July 2013 Tsvangirai lost a presidential election to Mugabe and the MDC also suffered a heavy defeat in the legislative elections. Mugabe appointed a new cabinet consisting only of ZANU-PF ministers—the post of prime minister was abolished altogether. Tsvangirai died from cancer on 14 Feb. 2018 aged 65.

Tu'ivakano (Tonga)

Introduction

Lord Tu'ivakano became prime minister in Dec. 2010 after winning a majority in the Legislative Assembly. His victory came as a blow to pro-democracy hopes that recent reforms would reduce the influence of the traditional power brokers.

Early Life

Lord Tu'ivakano was born Siale 'Ataongo Kaho on 15 Jan. 1952 in Niutoua, in the Western District of Tongatapu. He was educated in New Zealand at Three Kings School, Auckland, and at Wesley College, Paerata. In 1974 he graduated with a diploma in teaching from Ardmore Teachers' College, Auckland.

On his return to Tonga in 1975, Tu'ivakano joined the staff at of Tonga High School before moving to the physical education department of the ministry of education. In 1980 he was appointed head of the youth, sports and culture division, where he developed a physical health curriculum for primary schools.

On his father's death in Jan. 1986 he became the 17th Lord Tu'ivakano and inherited four estates in Tongatapu. In 1991 he graduated in political science from Flinders University in South Australia. The following year he returned to the ministry of education as senior education officer for youth, sport and culture but resigned in 1996 when he entered parliament as a Nobles' Representative for the island of Tongatapu.

From 2002–04 Tu'ivakano served as speaker of the Legislative Assembly and in March 2005 joined the cabinet as minister for works. Following a reshuffle in May 2006 he was given the portfolio of training, employment, youth and sport. In the Nov. 2010 elections he was re-elected as representative for Tongatapu and, following constitutional reforms, became the first prime minister elected by parliament, winning 14 of the 26 votes cast in a secret ballot. He was sworn into office on 22 Dec. 2010.

Career Peak

Tu'ivakano's election was regarded as a victory for traditionalists over the pro-democracy movement. He was expected to put the revitalization of the agriculture and tourism sectors at the heart of his premiership and to spur manufacturing growth. However, in Oct. 2012 he narrowly survived a parliamentary no confidence motion after the opposition accused his government of misappropriating funds. In Jan. 2014 he dismissed Lisiate 'Akolo as finance minister over disagreements on the budget and replaced him with 'Aisake Valu Eke.

Tu'ivakano's term ended on 30 Dec. 2014 after parliament elected? Akilisi Pōhiva to the premiership.

Tudjman, Franjo (Croatia)

Introduction

Franjo Tudjman was Croatia's President from 1990–99. A nationalist, he helped found the Croatian Democratic Communist Party (later the Croatian Democratic Union/HDZ) in 1989 and declared Croatia's independence from Yugoslavia in 1991. A vicious war with Yugoslavia ensued but Tudjman succeeded in gaining international recognition for his new country and ultimately re-claimed all territory that had been lost to Slobodan Milošević's regime. Tudjman's authoritarian regime and civil rights violations encountered much foreign opposition.

Early Life

Tudjman was born on 14 May 1922 in Veliko Trgovisce, Croatia. During World War II he fought with Tito's partisan anti-Fascist army and after the war he was employed by the Yugoslav army's Political Section. Between 1955–57 he was stationed in Belgrade, studying at the Higher Military Academy. By 1960 he was a major general. However, his passion for political and military history led to his resignation the following year to head the Institute of the History of the Workers' Movement. In 1963 he was employed at the University of Zagreb, where he taught political history and gained his doctorate in 1965.

In the same year he entered Croatia's parliament where he advocated Croatian nationalism. Two years later he antagonized Tito and the communist hierarchy by claiming that the Yugoslav communists had fabricated statistics concerning the number of deaths at the hands of the region's Nazi collaborators (the Ustasha) in World War II. He was expelled from the Communist Party and lost his political positions. He then played an active role in the 'Croatian Spring' of 1969–71, which sought cultural reform and nationalist expression. For this he was imprisoned by Tito, serving 1 year.

He was sentenced to a further 3 years in jail in the early 1980s for his criticism of the government following Tito's death, and was designated a 'Prisoner of Conscience' by Amnesty International. He had other civil liberties removed, including his right to travel abroad, and suffered a number of heart attacks. In Feb. 1989, as the movement for reform took hold throughout the Eastern Bloc, Tudjman established the HDZ and called for a looser confederal Yugoslavia. The party received legal recognition and won a landslide at Croatia's elections of April 1990, with Tudjman becoming President.

Career Peak

As his hopes for the confederation died, Tudjman unilaterally declared independence on 25 June 1991. When fighting broke out between Serbs and Croats within Croatia, Milošević sent in an army that claimed around one third of the new nation's territory. The international community recognized Croatia and sent in UN troops to secure peace. Lightening strikes by Tudjman's troops in July and Aug. 1995 reclaimed most of the lost land and expelled swathes of the Serb population.

Tudjman's regime came under UN criticism for its conduct in the war in Bosnia in 1993, and for its refusal to accept displaced Serbs back into Croatia. Moreover, while the elections of 1992, 1995 and 1997 that confirmed him as president were deemed free and legal by international observers, his control of the national media was considered to give him an unfair advantage. The Croatian economy struggled during Tudjman's tenure, partly because of war and regional instability but also because of mismanagement. He oversaw the transition from a central to a market economy but the standard of living remained low.

His authoritarian style of leadership, his treatment of the Serb minority and his refusal to co-operate with war crimes tribunals provoked international wrath on a number of occasions. Croatia was banned from several UN and NATO projects as well as the EU PHARE Programme, providing aid in Central and Eastern Europe, while the World Bank withheld financial assistance. Some observers claimed that Tudjman was a dangerous maverick who wished to establish a Greater Croatia in the Balkan region, but others regarded his regime as a counterweight to Milošević in Yugoslavia. Tudjman died on 10 Dec. 1999 in Zagreb from stomach cancer. He left a wife, Anika Zumbar, and three children.

Tudose, Mihai (Romania)

Introduction

Mihai Tudose was appointed prime minister on 26 June 2017. He replaced his Social Democratic Party (PSD) colleague Sorin Grindeanu, who was ousted through a vote of no confidence in parliament after 6 months in office.

Early Life

Tudose was born on 6 March 1967 in the southeastern port city of Brăila on the River Danube. He read law at the Dimitrie Cantemir Christian University in Bucharest (1991–95) and became a member of the PSDR (later rebranded the PSD in 2001) in 1992. From 1992–96 he served as a technical adviser to the PSD's parliamentary group and rose through the party ranks.

In 1999 Tudose was appointed as a local councillor for Brăila; he also took on work as a commercial lawyer for a company in the city. In 2000 he was elected member of parliament for Brăila, serving consecutive terms ever since. While an MP he furthered his academic credentials with multiple postgraduate studies, including a doctorate from the National Academy of Intelligence Mihai Viteazul in 2010 that he rescinded in 2016 following allegations of plagiarism.

From 2014–15 Tudose served as minister of the economy under Victor Ponta. He lost the post in a reshuffle after Ponta's resignation but stayed on as PSD vice-president alongside new leader Liviu Dragnea. In 2015 he won a fifth term as MP for Brăila. After the PSD's victory in the Dec. 2016 elections, Tudose was reinstated as minister of the economy, working alongside Grindeanu. However, when Grindeanu was ousted at the instigation of his own party, Tudose was appointed premier.

Career Peak

Tudose took office in the heat of political turmoil and public hostility towards official tolerance of corruption (Grindeanu's downfall having followed what was perceived as a failed attempt to weaken anti-corruption laws). He oversaw a major tax code overhaul promised by the PSD and in Jan. 2018 income tax was cut from 16% to 10%, while social tax and VAT contributions were also reformed. However, he was forced to resign on 15 Jan. 2018 when his party retracted support in the wake of his inflammatory comments about the autonomy aspirations of the Székely (Hungarian) ethnic community in Romania. He was succeeded by Viorica Dăncilă.

Tung Chee-hwa (Hong Kong, China)

Introduction

On 1 July 1997 Shanghai-born Tung Chee-hwa became the first chief executive of the post-colonial Hong Kong SAR (Special Administrative Region). Appointed by China to uphold the official policy of 'one country, two systems', his objective of keeping Hong Kong prosperous and stable was made more difficult by a series of financial crises. As a conduit between British and Chinese sovereignty and in a government of limited democracy, he came under criticism for his perceived pro-Beijing stance and approach to human rights.

Early Life

Born in Shanghai on 29 May 1937, Tung Chee-hwa's family left for Hong Kong in 1947 where he completed secondary school. Having received a BSc in marine engineering from the University of Liverpool in 1960, Tung's career began in business and he worked for General Electric in the United States until 1969.

In 1979, 10 years after his return to Hong Kong, Tung took over the chairmanship of the family-owned Orient Overseas Container Line (OOCL). In 1985 he was invited by Beijing to join the Basic Law Consultative Committee, which was to outline Hong Kong's constitution. After the death of his father, C.Y. Tung, in 1986, the OOCL faced bankruptcy and it has been alleged that it was the Chinese government that paid off its debts.

1992 marked the start of Tung's political career. He joined governor Chris Patten's Executive Council, where he remained until 1996. A member of the Preparatory Committee, which was designed to facilitate the transition of power, he resigned in 1995, stating a conflict of interest. On 16 Dec. 1996 Tung was formally appointed chief executive designate by the Central People's Government; a position which he assumed on 1 July 1997.

Career Peak

Tung's early leadership was dominated by the 1997 Asian economic crisis. The crash of the Hang Seng Index, the Hong Kong stock exchange, in Oct. 1997 led to an unprecedented level of direct government intervention in the country's free-market economy. Two years later, the territory met its first constitutional test when, at the Hong Kong government's request, Beijing reinterpreted a decision made by the Court of Final Appeal over the right of abode.

In the midst of a global downturn, Tung was reappointed to a second 5-year term in Feb. 2002. Worries over increased state control and diminished levels of human rights amplified in June 2002 with the trial of 12 members of the Falun Gong, the banned Chinese spiritual movement, and the introduction of a civil service governed by ministers appointed by Tung. The outbreak of the SARS virus in 2003 aggravated an already battered economy; its alleged mishandling and protest over the proposed anti-subversion bill led to calls for Tung's resignation. As a result, Tung vowed to increase his accountability through improved communication with political parties, community leaders and the media. In Sept. 2003 he announced that the anti-subversion bill would be shelved and promised public consultation in framing future bills concerning security. However, on 10 March 2005 he announced his resignation and cited poor health for his decision.

Tunku Abdul Rahman (Malaysia)

Introduction

Tunku Abdul Rahman Putra was the first, and only, prime minister of independent Malaya and, in many ways, the creator of the federation of Malaysia, of which he was also the first premier. He is an honoured figure in the history of his country, and the new administrative capital of Malaysia, Putrajaya, is named after him.

Early Life

Tunku (Prince) Abdul Rahman Putra was born on 8 Feb. 1903, in Kedah state. He was the 20th child of Sultan Abdul-Hamid of Kedah, who reigned from 1881 to 1943. Educated in Malaya and in Thailand, he was sent to England in 1920 to complete his education. He won a place at St Catherine's College, Cambridge, but the racial prejudice he encountered in England determined him to win independence for the Malays from British rule.

Abdul Rahman graduated in 1925, and went to study law in the Inner Temple. He founded an association for Malay students in Britain but before completing his legal studies, returned to Malaya in 1930 to join the civil service. In 1935 he was given administrative responsibility for a district of Kedah. When the Japanese invaded in 1941, they ceded Kedah to Thailand. The Thais appointed the Tunku as Supervisor of Education for Kedah, a post he held until British rule was restored in 1945. Determined to complete his legal studies, he returned to the Inns of Court in London in 1947 and qualified in 1949.

Abdul Rahman went back to Malaya to work in the Malay federal legal department. At the same time, he became chairman of the United Malays National Organisation (UMNO) in his home state of Kedah. When the national chairman resigned in 1951, Abdul Rahman gave up his legal career and was appointed leader of the party. In this capacity, he sought to unite the various peoples of Malaya and in 1953 incorporated the Malayan Chinese

Association (MCA) into a new political alliance. In 1955, he was also instrumental in persuading the Malayan Indian Congress into the alliance. In July 1955, in Malaya's first general election, he led the alliance to victory in 51 of the 52 seats contested. He was subsequently appointed chief minister and home minister.

Career Peak

In Sept. 1955, the new chief minister of Malaya held talks to end the insurgency by Communist guerrillas that had begun in the late 1940s. The talks failed, but Abdul Rahman continued in his efforts to accommodate the guerrillas who were finally crushed by military in 1960. His government strove to weld together the different states and peoples of the federation and to create a sense of national unity.

On 31 Aug. 1957 he led Malaya to independence and became both prime minister and foreign minister. In 1960 he proposed an enlarged federation, including Singapore, Brunei, British North Borneo (Sabah) and Sarawak. In July 1963, the new federation, Malaysia, was formed, but Brunei stayed out and Singapore withdrew in Aug. 1965. The inclusion of Sabah and Sarawak was opposed by the Philippines and Indonesia and a period of confrontation with Indonesia followed in Borneo.

By 1969 Malaysia's neighbours had become reconciled to the enlarged federation, but underlying tensions between the principal ethnic groups in Malaysia surfaced in riots between ethnic Chinese and Malays. In Sept. 1970, when the violence had ended Abdul Rahman resigned.

Later Life

In retirement, Abdul Rahman continued to emphasize national unity, tolerance and co-operation between the various ethnic groups of Malaysia. He published books and articles. In 1988 he accused premier Mahathir Mohamed of authoritarianism. He died on 6 Dec. 1990.

Turchynov, Oleksandr (Ukraine)

Introduction

Oleksandr Turchynov became acting president in Feb. 2014 after his predecessor, Viktor Yanukovych, fled the country following mass demonstrations. An established member of Ukraine's political elite, he is not recognized by Russia, which annexed the Crimean peninsula soon after his appointment.

Early Life

Turchynov was born in the eastern city of Dnipropetrovsk on 31 March 1964. He graduated from the city's Metallurgical Institute in 1986 before entering politics as a member of Komsomol, the Soviet Communist Party's youth organization.

It was as a leader of the party's liberalizing wing, the Democratic Platform, that he first met Leonid Kuchma, the future prime minister and president but then head of a missile manufacturer based in Dnipropetrovsk. As premier, Kuchma appointed Turchynov as his economics aide in 1993. In the same year Turchynov and Pavlo Lazarenko, a business associate of the oligarch Yuliya Tymoshenko, founded the Hromada Party. Turchynov was elected to parliament in 1998 but Hromada collapsed the following year when Lazarenko fled amid an investigation into embezzlement during his prime ministerial tenure from 1996–97.

Turchynov and Tymoshenko reacted by creating the Fatherland party that opposed Kuchma—by then president—and his designated successor, Viktor Yanukovych. In the lead-up to the 2004 presidential election, Turchynov worked as campaign co-ordinator for Viktor Yushchenko, whose defeat by Yanukovych prompted allegations of vote-rigging that triggered the Orange Revolution. With Tymoshenko installed as prime minister under Yushchenko, Turchynov was appointed head of the Ukraine Security Service in Feb. 2005. In 2007 he became deputy prime minister.

He stood for the mayoralty of Kyiv in May 2008 but came a distant second to the incumbent, Leonid Chernovetskyi. In 2010 Turchynov briefly served as interim prime minister after Tymoshenko's defeat in the presidential election. With Tymoshenko in jail following conviction for abuse of power, Turchynov was prominent in the demonstrations against Viktor Yanukovych that erupted

in Nov. 2013. For his role, he was placed under investigation by the security services but in the wake of Yanukovych's flight from the country he was elected parliamentary speaker on 22 Feb. 2014 and interim president the following day.

Career Peak

Turchynov angered many who had protested for root and branch reform when he told crowds gathered in Kyiv's Maidan (one of the main squares) that they had achieved their aims with the defeat of Yanukovych.

Within days of his taking office, Russia had wrestled control of the Crimean peninsula. Speaking with UN Secretary-General Ban Ki-moon on 21 March 2014, Turchynov said that Ukraine would never accept the seizure of its territory. On 26 March 2014 he submitted a bill to parliament to allow foreign forces access to Ukrainian territory for military exercises.

On 7 June 2014 he was succeeded as president by Petro Poroshenko, who had won early elections held on 25 May.

Later Life

On 16 Dec. 2014 Turchynov was appointed secretary of the National Security and Defense Council.

Türk, Danilo (Slovenia)

Introduction

Danilo Türk was sworn in as president in Dec. 2007 after winning 68% of votes cast in the second round of the presidential election. Backed by the centre-left opposition, Türk assumed office just 10 days before the country took over the revolving 6-month presidency of the European Union (the first former communist state to do so).

Early Life

Türk was born on 19 Feb. 1952 in Maribor. He graduated in law from the University of Ljubljana in 1975 and started working as the secretary of the commission for minorities and migrants of the Socialist Alliance of the Working People of Slovenia (SZDL). He also became involved with Amnesty International, acting as an adviser on human rights cases in the former Yugoslavia. In 1978 he obtained his master's degree in law from the University of Belgrade and returned to the University of Ljubljana as an academic assistant, teaching international law. Returning to his work for the SZDL, he served as its chairman until 1981. Türk was elected vice-chairman of the UN working group on the right to development in 1981 and held the post until 1984.

He obtained his law doctorate from the University of Ljubljana in 1982 and became assistant professor at the university's faculty of law in Dec. that year. From 1983–92 he headed the university's institute of international law and international relations. From 1984–92 he was a member of the UN subcommission on prevention of discrimination and protection of minorities, becoming its chairman in 1991. In 1987 Türk helped establish the Human Rights Council in Slovenia, later becoming the vice-president. He was also promoted to the post of associate professor in 1987.

Following Slovenia's declaration of independence, Türk served in the Slovenian delegation at the Conference of Yugoslavia from July 1991–Aug. 1992. From 11 Sept. 1992 he represented Slovenia at the United Nations. During his ambassadorship Slovenia was elected to a non-permanent seat on the Security Council for the period of 1998–99 and held the presidency on two occasions (Aug. 1998 and Nov. 1999). He left his post as ambassador on 31 Jan. 2000 to become assistant secretary-general for political affairs at the United Nations. For the next 5 years Türk was closely involved in trying to solve crises in the Balkans, Afghanistan, Iraq and Haiti.

Türk returned to teaching international law at the University of Ljubljana in 2005 and in May 2006 was appointed vice-dean of the faculty of law. He formalized his candidacy for the presidency in June 2007 and was placed second in the first round of voting on 21 Oct. 2007, claiming 24.5% of the vote. In the run-off on 11 Nov. 2007 Türk beat his opponent, the centre-right candidate Lojze Peterle, in a landslide victory. He was sworn in on 22 Dec.

Career Peak

Although the role of the president is largely ceremonial, Türk had influence over defence and foreign policy. His long diplomatic experience assisted the smooth running of Slovenia's EU presidency from Jan.–June 2008. In domestic politics, he pledged 'constructive, co-ordinated and balanced co-operation with the government and parliament'. In Sept. 2011 the Social Democrat-led coalition government collapsed after losing a parliamentary confidence vote, prompting Türk to call early elections in Dec. in which the centre-left Positive Slovenia, led by Zoran Janković, emerged as the largest grouping. However, Janković's candidacy for the premiership was rejected by parliament, with former prime minister Janez Janša of the Slovenian Democratic Party taking the position instead in Feb. 2012.

Türk stood for re-election in the 2012 presidential elections but lost to Borut Pahor in the second round.

Turner, John Napier (Canada)

Introduction

John Napier Turner was the leader of the Liberal Party of Canada from 1984 to 1989 and Canadian Prime Minister for 3 months in 1984.

Early Life

Born in Richmond, London of an English father and Canadian mother, Turner's family emigrated to Canada in 1932 with the death of his father. Settling first in Rossland, British Columbia, Turner received his early education in Ottawa after his mother was offered a job with the Tariff Board.

When Turner's mother married a wealthy Vancouver businessman, Frank Mackenzie Ross, the family moved West, and Turner enrolled at the University of British Columbia.

Graduating in political science he went on to study in Paris and as a Rhodes scholar at Oxford, earning a law degree in 1952 and a master's in 1957.

He made his first political steps in 1957 after Liberal cabinet minister CD Howe asked him to help in the election campaign. His involvement with the party continued until he was persuaded to seek the nomination for the riding of St-Laurent-St-Georges in 1962—a seat he won at the June election.

Despite joining a vocal group of young Liberals, dubbed 'the Young Turks' advocating reforms in party policy, Turner's rise continued unabated with his appointment to his first cabinet post in 1965 as minister without portfolio.

Having worked for several corporations, he won election to the House of Commons as a Liberal in 1962 and was given his first cabinet post in 1965.

After losing in his bid for the leadership of the Liberal Party in 1968 to Pierre Trudeau, Turner served as justice minister and then in 1972 as minister of finance.

As finance minister in a minority government, his budgets had to be acceptable to one or other of the opposition parties, a task he failed in 1974, leading to a general election.

Although continuing as finance minister he became increasingly disillusioned with the position and seeing no alternatives in the cabinet, he abruptly resigned from his ministerial position in Sept. 1975, and parliament itself in Feb. 1976. He returned to corporate law for the next 8 years, working for the Toronto firm McMillan Binch.

Career Peak

Turner stood for leadership of the party again in 1984 after Trudeau announced he would not be seeking re-election. Despite winning the leadership vote, with strong support in the party, he inherited serious problems and having gambled on an early election to take advantage of his new popularity as leader, his brief tenure as Prime Minister was ended by the party's routing at the hands of the Conservatives in the 1984 elections.

Whilst in opposition, Turner fought hard against the free trade agreements being negotiated by the government, but failed to convince the electorate, narrowly losing the 1988 general election.

Later Life

Resigning from politics in 1989, Turner returned to his legal career.

Tusk, Donald (Poland)

Introduction

Donald Tusk became prime minister on 9 Nov. 2007 following his party's resounding victory in parliamentary elections. The former Solidarity activist has taken a pro-business stance and has been keen to establish closer relations with EU neighbours. He began a second term following elections in Oct. 2011.

Early Life

Donald Franciszek Tusk was born on 22 April 1957 in Gdańsk. His family is part of the city's long-established minority Kashubian community. Following his secondary education he attended the University of Gdańsk where he studied history. A long-time critic of the communist administration, Tusk helped to establish the student committee of the Solidarity movement, which grew out of the nationwide industrial unrest centred on the Gdańsk shipyard during the summer of 1980. He subsequently co-founded the Independent Polish Students' Association (NZS). Following the authorities' crackdown on Solidarity in 1981, Tusk and other activists were forced into the shadows. He earned a living as a builder, an experience subsequently presented as evidence of his empathy with 'ordinary people'.

In the late 1980s Tusk left Solidarity to join the nascent liberal movement and in 1991 joined the Liberal Democratic Congress (KLD), which contested the first multi-party elections in Oct. 1991 on a free-market platform calling for privatization, freedom of movement and accession to the EU. Tusk took one of the KLD's 37 seats in the Sejm. Although he was re-elected as a deputy in the 1993 elections, the KLD fared poorly and in March 1994 merged with the Democratic Union to form a new centre-right party, Freedom Union (UW). The party secured 13.4% of the vote in the 1997 elections, becoming the junior partner in Jerzy Buzek's coalition government. Tusk was elected to the Senate, where from 1998–2001 he served as vice-speaker.

Having failed to win the chairmanship of the UW in 2000, Tusk resigned from the party. He joined Andrzej Olechowski (who had performed creditably in the 2000 presidential contest) and Maciej Płażyński in establishing the secular, liberal Civic Platform (PO) in early 2001, with Płażyński at the helm. The PO performed strongly in the 2001 elections, taking 65 seats in the Sejm and becoming the largest opposition party to Leszek Miller's government. In June 2003 Tusk became the PO's chairman. He was a vocal critic of the left-leaning SLD government, particularly its economic policies. His standing improved as the SLD became mired in corruption scandals but he failed in his 2005 bid for the presidency, losing to Lech Kaczyński of the socially conservative, nationalist Law and Justice Party. Later in 2005 the PO suffered further electoral defeat to Law and Justice, led by Jarosław Kaczyński (Lech's twin brother), who became prime minister.

Tusk remained leader of the PO and took a more aggressive approach in the run-up to the early election called for Oct. 2007. The election followed the collapse of the Law and Justice-led coalition amid allegations of corruption. Tusk accused Kaczyński of incompetence on international relations—notably deteriorating relations with Germany—and of failing to prevent the mass movement of Poles to Britain and Ireland in search of work. Tusk campaigned on a platform to speed up privatization, lower taxes and reduce business bureaucracy to encourage investors.

In parliamentary elections on 21 Oct. 2007 the PO emerged victorious, taking around 41% of the vote against 32% for Law and Justice. Tusk took office as prime minister on 16 Nov. and his cabinet won a confidence vote in the Sejm on 24 Nov. 2007.

Career Peak

Tusk pledged to create jobs and promote economic development by cutting bureaucracy and regulation. However, the global financial downturn in 2008 undermined Poland's growth prospects, prompting the government to launch an economic stimulus programme in Dec. that year and to negotiate a one-year US$20.6 bn. credit line with the International Monetary Fund which was approved in May 2009. In July 2010 Tusk's political position was strengthened by the election of the PO's candidate, Bronisław Komorowski, as state president in place of Lech Kaczyński, who had been killed in an air crash the previous April.

On the international stage, Tusk oversaw the withdrawal in Oct. 2008 of Poland's last troops stationed in Iraq, fulfilling a key electoral pledge. However, plans agreed in 2008 for Poland to host a controversial missile defence shield for the USA were effectively abandoned in Sept. 2009 when the US president announced the scrapping of key elements of the system. Despite the Polish government's disappointment at the decision, Tusk insisted that the USA and Poland would remain close allies. In July 2011 Poland assumed the EU's 6-month rotating presidency for the first time since the country's accession to the organization in 2004.

In Oct. 2011 Tusk's PO was returned to power as the largest party in national parliamentary elections. However, having introduced unpopular fiscal measures in May 2012—including increasing the retirement age—his administration lost ground in opinion polls to the opposition Law and Justice Party. In Oct. that year the government narrowly won a parliamentary vote of confidence after pledging US$95 bn. in infrastructure and other investments to boost growth. In 2013 Tusk's administration survived further parliamentary confidence votes but anti-government sentiment continued over unpopular fiscal measures, particularly reform of the pension system. In Nov. Tusk reshuffled his cabinet, including replacing the finance minister, in an effort to revive his political standing.

Tusk was appointed the next president of the European Council in Aug. 2014 and took office on 1 Dec. 2014, succeeding Herman Van Rompuy. He resigned as prime minister on 9 Sept. 2014, and was subsequently succeeded by Ewa Kopacz (also of the PO) who was sworn in as premier on 22 Sept.

Tutu, Desmond (South Africa)

Introduction

A leader of the South African religious community, Desmond Mpilo Tutu used his position to campaign against apartheid. Internationally respected, he was awarded the Nobel Peace Prize in 1984 for his advocacy of non-violent protest. After the abolition of apartheid, he was appointed president of the South African Truth and Reconciliation Commission in 1995.

Early Life

Desmond Mpilo Tutu was born in Klerksdorp, Transvaal in 1931. His father was a teacher. In 1954 he graduated from the University of South Africa and became a schoolteacher. After 3 years of teaching he began to study theology. He was ordained an Anglican priest in 1960, and lectured at a seminary in Johannesburg. During the years 1962–66 Tutu studied theology at Kings College, London where he obtained a master's degree. From 1972–5 he served as an assistant director for the World Council of Churches.

Career Peak

In 1975 he was made dean of St Mary's Cathedral in Johannesburg. Tutu was the first black person to hold such a position. In 1978 he was appointed general secretary of the South African Council of Churches to speak on behalf of the black South African majority. Unlike many other anti-apartheid campaigners, Tutu always advocated victory by non-violent means, and to this end he favoured the imposition of economic sanctions on South Africa.

In 1984 Tutu was awarded the Nobel Peace Prize. The following year he became Johannesburg's first black bishop and in 1986 he was elected the first black archbishop of Cape Town. This made Tutu the primate of the Anglican Church in South Africa. Following the collapse of apartheid Tutu became Chairman of the South African Truth and Reconciliation Commission (created in 1995), a body that called upon South Africans of all races to confess their past in the racial turmoil of the apartheid era. The fact that Tutu did not excuse outrages committed in the cause of liberation brought him into dispute with the ruling ANC.

Later Life

Tutu retired from the primacy of the Anglican church in South Africa in 1996. He has published a collection of his lectures (*The Divine Intention*) and a separate collection of his sermons entitled *Hope and Suffering*.

Tymoshenko, Yuliya (Ukraine)

Introduction

Yuliya Tymoshenko, Ukraine's first female prime minister, took office for the second time in Dec. 2007. She was first appointed in Jan. 2005 by President Viktor Yushchenko after campaigning for him in the 'Orange Revolution'. However, she was sacked in Sept. 2005 amid allegations of financial irregularities. She returned to office in 2007 as part of a coalition with Yushchenko's party. A popular but controversial figure, Tymoshenko promoted Ukrainian entry into the EU and pledged to fight corruption in business and public life. She was forced out of office on 3 March 2010 after losing a parliamentary vote of no confidence.

Early Life

Yuliya Volodymyrivna Grigyan was born on 27 Nov. 1960 in Dnipropetrovsk, in the east of the Soviet Socialist Republic of Ukraine. After marrying Oleksandr Tymoshenko in 1979 and studying economics at Dnipropetrovsk State University, she worked from 1984–89 as an engineer and economist at the Vladimir Iliych Lenin machinery plant. After economic liberalization began in 1989, she established a successful chain of video-rental stores. Following Ukrainian independence in 1991, Tymoshenko ran several energy companies in which her family had major interests. From 1995–97 she was president of United Energy Systems of Ukraine (UESU), the country's main importer of natural gas from Russia.

Tymoshenko was elected to represent Kirovohradska province in central Ukraine in 1996, and was re-elected in 1998, when she was also appointed chair of the parliamentary budget committee. From 1999–2001 she served as vice prime minister with responsibility for energy in Viktor Yushchenko's government. Tymoshenko built a reputation as a reformer, ending corrupt practices in the energy sector, and was closely involved with negotiations to pay off Ukraine's debts to Russia. In 2001 she was sacked by President Kuchma and accused of smuggling, forgery and tax evasion offences during her presidency of UESU, all of which she denied.

Following a vote of no confidence in Prime Minister Yushchenko, Tymoshenko united four opposition parties—the Batkivshchyna (Motherland) party, Sobor, the Ukrainian Republican Party (URP) and the Ukrainian Social Democratic Party (USDP)—into the Yuliya Tymoshenko Election Bloc. The bloc won 7.2% of the vote in parliamentary elections in March 2002. Tymoshenko backed Yushchenko in the 2004 presidential election and played a leading role in the 'Orange Revolution' when tens of thousands of protesters swept into Kyiv and other Ukrainian cities on 21 Nov. 2004 after Viktor Yanukovych was controversially declared to have beaten Yushchenko in a run-off. Amid allegations of vote-rigging, the Supreme Court forced a re-run which Yushchenko won in Jan. 2005. He nominated Tymoshenko as his acting prime minister; she was confirmed in the post on 4 Feb. 2005.

Tymoshenko supported Yushchenko's ambitions for Ukraine to join the EU, and introduced some economic and political reforms. However, political infighting and attacks on her integrity culminated in her sacking, along with the rest of the cabinet, in Sept. 2005. She was vocal in opposition and in 2006 her party took second place in the parliamentary elections, behind Yanukovych's Party of Regions. After prolonged negotiations, and a power struggle between Yushchenko and newly appointed prime minister Yanukovych, snap elections were called for Sept. 2007. A coalition between Tymoshenko's party and Yushchenko's Our Ukraine emerged as narrow winners. Tymoshenko was eventually elected prime minister by a margin of one vote in the parliament.

Career Peak

After taking office on 18 Dec. 2007, Tymoshenko supported moves to combat corruption and implement financial reforms. Her other challenges included upgrading the country's gas transport system, maintaining good relations with Russia and building links with the EU. However, continuing political rivalry with Yushchenko undermined the government, which collapsed in Sept. 2008 amid policy differences towards Russia and Ukraine's economic deterioration. A further parliamentary election was averted when Tymoshenko re-formed the coalition in Dec., although her soured relationship with the president remained an obstacle to effective administration. In Jan. 2009 she and Prime Minister Putin of Russia signed a formal agreement in Moscow ending a damaging dispute over gas prices and sales that had also disrupted onward supplies to Europe. In Feb. 2009 she and her cabinet survived a no-confidence motion in parliament.

Tymoshenko ran for president in the 2010 elections but was defeated by a narrow margin in the second round by Viktor Yanukovych. She challenged the results resulting in their suspension on 17 Feb. pending a full electoral inquiry. However, claiming insurmountable judicial prejudice in favour of her opponent, she dropped the case a few days later. Consequently, Yanukovych was sworn in as president in 25 Feb. although Tymoshenko refused to recognize his authority and vowed not to stand down as prime minister. But on 3 March parliament passed a vote of no confidence in her administration with 243 of 450 votes in favour. She was succeeded by Oleksandr Turchynov who was appointed in an acting capacity by President Yanukovych until the formation of a new government could be finalized.

Later Life

Tymoshenko was arrested in Aug. 2011 on charges of abuse of power over the natural gas contract signed with Russia in 2009. She was jailed for contempt of court for her behaviour during the trial and in Oct. 2011 the former premier was sentenced to seven years in prison. Tymoshenko was ordered to repay the state gas company, Naftogaz, approximately US$190 m. The EU condemned the verdict as politically motivated.

In April 2012 she went on hunger strike after accusing staff at the prison of beating her during an attempt to move her to a hospital where she would be treated by Ukrainian doctors. She ended the hunger strike 3 weeks later after being moved to a hospital to be treated by a German doctor. She went on hunger strike again in Oct. 2012 to protest against alleged vote-rigging in the parliamentary elections the previous day, but also ended that after meeting with a team of German doctors.

Following Viktor Yanyukovych's impeachment in Feb. 2014, Tymoshenko was released from prison. She is eligible to run for office after parliament decriminalized the procedure under which she was convicted.

Ulbricht, Walter (Germany)

Introduction

Walter Ulbricht was one of the leading founders of communist East Germany at the end of World War II. He was First Secretary of the Socialist Unity Party from 1950 until 1971 and Head of State from 1960 until his death in 1973. A hard-liner who kept faith with Leninist and Stalinist principles, Ulbricht imposed a highly centralized economy with heavy restrictions on civil liberties. He was responsible for the building of the Berlin Wall in 1961.

Early Life

The son of a tailor, Ulbricht was born on 30 June 1893 in Leipzig. Starting as a carpenter's apprentice, by the age of 13 he was active in the Socialist Youth Movement. At 17 he enrolled in the Union of Woodworkers and in 1912 he joined the Socialist Party, aligning himself with the radical wing. With the onset of World War I he fought on the Eastern Front but deserted twice. In the aftermath of war he was instrumental in setting up the German Communist Party (KPD).

After a period of training in the Soviet Union he was elected to the Reichstag in 1928 to represent South Westphalia. The previous year had seen him appointed to the KPD's Central Committee. When the Nazis came to power Ulbricht was forced into exile, returning to the USSR. He retained his links with the KPD and also worked for Comintern as a single-minded promoter of Stalinist orthodoxy. Between 1936–38 he fought in the Spanish Civil War. After the German invasion of the USSR in 1941 he was once again

in Moscow but returned to Germany in 1945 to take a leading role in the government of the Soviet zone. In 1946, the KPD merged with the Socialist Party to form the Socialist Unity Party (SED).

In Oct. 1949 the German Democratic Republic (GDR) was established and Ulbricht was made Deputy Prime Minister. In 1950 he became General Secretary (a post which was later changed to First Secretary) of the SED. He embarked on a programme of nationalization and agricultural collectivization. In June 1953 there was a strike in East Berlin in protest against plans for increased industrial output. When the protest spread Soviet troops were brought in to establish order. Over 20 people were killed and many more injured. The following year the GDR was recognized as a sovereign state by the Soviet Union and joined the Warsaw Pact in 1955.

Career Peak

There followed a degree of relaxation in communist rule within the GDR but from 1958 Ulbricht returned to the hardline. When President Wilhelm Pieck died in 1960 he was not replaced. Ulbricht became Chairman of the Council of State and, as effective head of state, increased his already formidable power base to impose ever-stricter rule. As disenchanted East Germans fled to West Berlin (some 3 m. crossed the border in the 16 years after the war) Ulbricht decided on a barrier between East and West, the Berlin Wall. On 13 Aug. 1961 a barbed wire fence was put up, later to be replaced by a 3 m-high concrete barrier. The wall became the most potent symbol of the ideological divide between the communist East and the capitalist West.

Despite Ulbricht's close ties with Moscow, his relationship with Leonid Brezhnev was not always easy. Ulbricht resigned as SED Chairman in May 1971, ostensibly because of failing health but almost certainly as a result of political manoeuvring within the Soviet Union.

Later Life

Ulbricht remained Chairman of the State Council until his death, but with his power strongly reduced. He died in East Berlin on 1 Aug. 1973.

Ulmanis, Guntis (Latvia)

Introduction

Guntis Ulmanis was Latvian president from 1993–99. The first post-independence leader, Ulmanis strove to make Latvia eligible for EU and NATO membership.

Early Life

Born in Riga on 13 Sept. 1939, Ulmanis was a nephew of Karlis Ulmanis, the last pre-Soviet president. Two years later, his family was deported to Krasnoyarsk, Siberia where they were held for 5 years. The family then settled in northwestern Latvia. After studying economics at the Latvian State University, Ulmanis served 2 years in the Soviet army from 1963–65. On leaving the service, he joined the communist party and worked as an economist in Riga's local administration. In 1989 he left the communist party and 3 years later joined the board of the Bank of Latvia. At the same time he was made honorary president of the centre-right Farmers' Union Party.

Career Peak

Elected to parliament in June 1993, a month later Ulmanis was elected president with 53 votes to 35, replacing the head of the Supreme Council (1990–93) Anatolijs Gorbunovs. He was re-elected in 1996 with 53 votes to 44. As the first elected president of independent Latvia, Ulmanis was keen to promote Latvia's language and culture and to make the country eligible for EU and NATO membership. As a first step, Latvia joined NATO's Partnership for Peace Programme in 1994 and in 1996 imposed a moratorium on the death penalty, which was abolished for ordinary crimes in 1999. Ulmanis also had to weather difficult relations with Russia. In 1994 he and Boris Yeltsin agreed to the withdrawal of Russian troops from Latvia, which helped ease tensions. But disputes continued regarding the large Russian-speaking minority living in Latvia and the country's strict citizen laws. In the face of increasing criticism from Russia (who threatened to impose sanctions) and the OSCE,

Ulmanis was forced to review the law forcing Russian speakers to pass a Latvian language test before becoming eligible for citizenship. In a referendum in 1998, 53% voted to relax the law. Constitutionally barred from standing for a third term, in 1999 he was replaced by Vaira Vike-Freiberga.

Later Life

Ulmanis worked in party politics as honorary president of the Farmers' Union Party until 2001 when he joined the new right-wing party New Era, created by the president of the Bank of Latvia, Einars Repse.

Ungureanu, Mihai-Răzvan (Romania)

Introduction

Mihai-Răzvan Ungureanu, a former head of Romania's intelligence agency, became prime minister on 9 Feb. 2012, the youngest premier in the country's history. His appointment followed the resignation of Emil Boc after weeks of violent protests against government austerity measures. Ungureanu's priorities were to boost the economy while implementing conditions demanded by the IMF's bail-out package. In May 2012, Ungureanu was replaced by Victor Ponta after his government lost a no-confidence vote.

Early Life

Ungureanu was born on 22 Sept. 1968 in Iaşi, Romania. He graduated in history and philosophy from Iaşi's Alexandru Ioan Cuza University in 1992 and took a master's degree in Hebrew Studies at St Cross College, Oxford University in the UK the following year. He then returned to Iaşi University to lecture and write his doctorate on Romanian social history.

Ungureanu joined Romania's diplomatic service in 1998 and, from 2001, was the country's special envoy at the Stability Pact for South Eastern Europe in Vienna. From 2003–04 he was a co-ordinator at the Vienna-based South-East European Co-operative Initiative.

A member of the centre-right National Liberal Party (PNL) that became part of the Justice and Truth Alliance, Ungureanu was appointed minister of foreign affairs in Dec. 2004 by President Traian Băsescu (whose bid for the presidency had been supported by the PNL). Ungureanu was key to negotiations securing Romania's membership of the European Union on 1 Jan. 2007. A month later he was asked by the prime minister, Călin Popescu-Tăriceanu, to resign following a row over Romanian workers detained by coalition forces in Iraq.

After a brief spell in the political wilderness, in Nov. 2007 MPs voted for Ungureanu to lead the Foreign Intelligence Service (SIE). When the prime minister, Emil Boc, resigned in early Feb. 2012 amid violent protests over cuts in public spending, the president turned to Ungureanu, whose proposed government was approved by MPs on 9 Feb. 2012.

Career Peak

Ungureanu pledged to continue the austerity drive that secured an IMF bail-out in 2010, although he hinted that the government may increase pensions and wages should the economy pick up. However, after less than 3 months in office, opposition parties seized on widespread discontent over austerity measures and the government lost a no-confidence vote. Ungureanu was replaced by the left-wing opposition leader Victor Ponta on 7 May 2012.

Uribe Vélez, Álvaro (Colombia)

Introduction

Álvaro Uribe Vélez was elected president of Colombia in May 2002 in an outright first-round victory. An independent candidate, his hardline mandate of combating left-wing guerrillas and right-wing paramilitaries found popularity with the electorate after attempts at peace talks by his predecessor Andrés Pastrana had failed. He was re-elected in May 2006.

Early Life

Uribe was born on 4 July 1952 in Medellín. After completing a law degree at the Universidad de Antioquia, he studied management at Harvard University in the USA and worked as an associate professor at Oxford University in England.

At the age of 24 he began working for Medellín Public Works, following which he was secretary general of the labour ministry (1977–78), worked for the civil aeronautics department (1980–82) and was then mayor of Medellín. He was a member of the Senate from 1986–94. His career in his native region continued between 1995–97 when he served as governor of the Antioquia region. As such he streamlined the local government department and increased spending on education, health and road infrastructure. He set up the 'Convivirs' security networks which diminished the presence of the left-wing guerrilla Fuerzas Armadas Revolucionarias de Colombia (FARC; Colombian Revolutionary Armed Forces) in Antioquia. But he was criticized for allowing the right-wing paramilitary Autodefensas Unidas de Colombia (AUC; United Self-Defence Forces of Colombia) to take advantage of the reduced FARC profile.

Uribe's hardline view on guerrilla activity in part stemmed from his father's assassination in 1983 by FARC members during a bungled kidnapping attempt. Combatting terrorism was made the central issue of his 2002 presidential campaign. Peace talks between incumbent president Pastrana and FARC leaders had failed to stem violence and kidnappings, and Uribe's pledge to forcefully oppose terrorist activity was well received among voters. Violence increased in the lead-up to the polls, including numerous assassination attempts on Uribe and the kidnapping of the independent candidate Ingrid Betancourt. The election itself passed relatively peacefully and, with a turnout of 47%, Uribe beat the Colombian Liberal Party candidate Horacio Serpa by 53% of votes to 32%. Despite a military presence of 20,000, Uribe's inauguration in Aug. 2002 was marred by explosions around Bogotá which killed 20 people and injured 60.

Career Peak

On election Uribe planned to double the size of the army and create a 1 m-strong civil militia. He also sought to amend the constitution to allow for martial law and states of siege. His plans received a positive response from the USA, with the possibility of increased military aid, although FARC promised to resist the government forces. Unlike his predecessor, Uribe demanded a full FARC ceasefire and halt in kidnappings before any peace talks could be brokered. FARC demanded control of two southern provinces, Caquetá and Putumayo, in return. Although Uribe also targeted terrorism by the smaller left-wing Ejército de Liberación Nacional (ELN; National Liberation Army) and the AUC, the latter responded positively to the president's election and formal peace talks began in mid-2003, leading to an AUC commitment to demobilize in exchange for amnesty.

In July 2005 the 'justice and peace' law won congressional approval, making generous concessions to illegal fighters in return for laying down their arms. Human rights groups have been critical of the law, however, viewing it as a charter of impunity for war criminals. The government announced in April 2006 that the demobilization of the AUC had been completed.

In 2007 Uribe offered to free guerrilla prisoners and start peace talks with FARC in exchange for the release of hostages, and invited President Hugo Chávez of Venezuela to try and broker a deal. However, Uribe ended Chávez's involvement in Nov. after a series of apparent diplomatic breaches. In 2008 the release of several high-profile FARC hostages was secured and there were signs of reconciliation between Uribe and Chávez, but links with Ecuador were seriously undermined by a cross-border Colombian strike against a FARC target in Ecuadorian territory. Relations with Venezuela were again strained in 2009 by Uribe's agreement to allow US armed forces to use Colombian military bases for joint operations against drug trafficking and guerrillas and by Venezuela's alleged supply of arms to FARC.

In Oct. 2005 the Constitutional Court had upheld an amendment to the constitution allowing presidential re-election and the following month set out conditions under which an incumbent could stand, so allowing Uribe to campaign for a second term in elections which he won in May 2006. He was formally inaugurated in Aug. that year. Then, in Sept. 2009, the House of Representatives approved the final text of a law to call a referendum on changing the constitution to allow Uribe to run for an unprecedented third consecutive term in presidential elections scheduled for May 2010. However, the Constitutional Court blocked the plans after ruling that they were unconstitutional.

Uribe's other aims during his presidency included tackling corruption, targeting crime and drug trafficking and, on his Antioquia model, reducing expenditure on public administration. The drug trade has been closely linked to guerrilla and paramilitary activities, and in May 2008 the government extradited 14 paramilitary leaders to the USA to stand trial on trafficking charges.

In July 2010 Uribe accused Venezuela of harbouring and protecting FARC and ELN guerrillas, prompting a diplomatic rift between the countries. However, on 7 Aug. Uribe was succeeded by Juan Manuel Santos of the Social National Unity Party who swiftly negotiated a reconciliation with Chávez.

Later Life

Uribe was re-elected to the Senate at the July 2014 elections, 20 years after he had last been a member.

Uribe strongly opposed the peace negotiations with the FARC guerrilla group that began in 2012, refusing to meet with President Juan Manuel Santos and FARC leader Rodrigo 'Timochenko' Londoño during the talks.

Urusemal, Joseph (Micronesia)

Introduction

Elected the sixth president of the Federated States of Micronesia on 11 May 2003, Joseph Urusemal has pledged to tackle poverty and unemployment and reduce the nation's dependence on foreign aid. He has endeavoured to raise international awareness of the threat posed to Micronesia by global climate change, exemplified by the increasing frequency and intensity of storms in the Pacific. Urusemal left office in 2007.

Early Life

Joseph J. Urusemal was born on 19 March 1952, on Woleai, one of the Yap islands in the US-administered Trust Territory of the Pacific Islands (TPPI). He attended Xavier High School in the Truk islands and graduated from Rockhurst College, Kansas City, Missouri, USA with a BA in administration of justice in 1973. Urusemal then worked for the government of Jackson County for 6 years. In 1982 he returned to Yap, which in 1979 had become part of the Federated States of Micronesia (FSM), and worked as a teacher at the Outer Islands High School. He also served on the education steering committee.

In 1987 Urusemal was elected Yap States' representative to the FSM Congress. In 1991 he was promoted to floor leader in the congress and held membership of the standing committees for health, education and social affairs, resources and development, transportation and communication and judiciary and government operations. He was elected president by congress on 11 May 2003, succeeding Leo Falcam, who had held office since 1999.

Career Peak

Seven months after Urusemal took office a renewed Compact of Free Association with the USA was signed into law. Its terms ensured the survival of US military bases in the FSM in return for financial assistance worth around US$3.5 bn. to the FSM and the Marshall Islands. Urusemal, who highlighted the need to lessen the FSM's dependency on foreign aid, focused on developing tourism and improving commercial links with Japan and Australia. He pledged to oversee the reform and increased accountability of the Chuuk State (formerly Truk) administration, noted for financial and administrative crises for several years.

Urusemal's term as president ended on 11 May 2007 when congress selected Immanuel 'Manny' Mori, the senator for Chuuk, as his replacement.

Văcăroiu, Nicolae (Romania)

Introduction

Nicolae Văcăroiu was appointed interim president on 20 April 2007, following the suspension of President Traian Băsescu. Văcăroiu had full presidential powers except the authority to dissolve or address parliament or organize a referendum. He left office on 20 May after the reinstatement of Băsescu.

Early Life

Văcăroiu was born outside present-day Romania on 5 Dec. 1943 in Bolhrad, in the Soviet-controlled region of Bessarabia, now in Ukraine. In 1969 he graduated from the Academy of Economic Studies (ASE) in Bucharest. From 1969–72 he worked as an economist with the Design and Planning Institute of Ilfov County, rising to become director of the Economic-Financial Synthesis Directorate of the State Planning Committee. He was director until 1989, when revolution ended communist rule. At this time he was listed as an associate professor with the sociology faculties of Bucharest University and ASE.

Văcăroiu joined Romania's first democratic government and in 1990 was appointed deputy minister of the new ministry of national economics. Subsequently, he was head of the finance ministry's pricing department and finally head of its rates and taxes department, working on the strategy for Romania's transition to a market economy. With experience as chairman of the inter-ministerial committee on foreign trade credit guarantees, he was a key figure in negotiations between Romania, the International Monetary Fund and other international financial bodies.

In 1992 President Ion Iliescu appointed the relatively unknown Văcăroiu prime minister. He represented the minority Democratic National Salvation Front, which evolved into the Social Democratic Party. In a period of political and economic instability, his administration was criticized for its failure to institute reform and to prevent the spread of corruption. However, it did grant the National Bank of Romania a degree of independence and contained inflation. In the 1996 elections, discontent over corruption and slow reform brought defeat for the Social Democratic Party.

Văcăroiu served as senator for Argeș from 1996–2000, as well as chairman of the senate committee on privatizations (1996–99) and deputy chairman of the senate standing bureau (1999–2000). In Nov. 2000 he was re-elected senator of Argeș and appointed co-chair of the Bucharest–Chişinău inter-parliamentary commission. In Dec. 2000 he became senate chairman and was elected deputy chairman of the Social Democratic Party 6 months later. Re-elected chairman of the senate in 2004, he held the post until his appointment as interim president in April 2007.

Career Peak

Văcăroiu took office after accusations of corruption against President Băsescu and Prime Minister Popescu-Tăriceanu. On 19 April 2007 parliament voted to suspend Băsescu for violating the constitution. The constitutional court upheld the decision the following day and, in accordance with Romanian law, appointed Văcăroiu interim president. With the European Union, which Romania joined in 2007, demanding a quick solution, a referendum was scheduled for 19 May to decide whether or not to impeach Băsescu. A majority vote with more than 50% attendance was required for the result to stand.

On taking office, Văcăroiu met Băsescu's aids and heads of government departments. He pledged to meet the supreme defence council to negotiate a series of national security laws. With European Union backing, he also pushed for legislation to establish a national agency for integrity to act as an anti-corruption check on high officials.

Văcăroiu's term of office ended when Băsescu was reinstated on 23 May 2007 after voters rejected attempts to impeach him. Văcăroiu subsequently returned to his position as senate chairman.

Vajpayee, Atal Bihari (India)

Introduction

Previously regarded as an elder statesman whose best days were behind him, Atal Bihari Vajpayee came to power in 1996 when the Bharatiya Janata Party (BJP) formed its first coalition government. A former BJP president, his role in Indian politics, at the forefront of the Congress Party's main opposition, often led the party away from its nationalist background towards a more moderate stance. With coalition government emerging as the most viable form of political rule in India, Vajpayee was the first Indian prime minister to manage such a coalition through successive periods in office. His time in office was dominated by fluctuating relations with Pakistan, the future of Kashmir and violent communal unrest. The 2004 elections saw the defeat of Vajpayee's National Democratic Alliance (NDA) and the return of a Congress-led government. However, Vajpayee's third period in office was the first full-term non-Congress government since independence.

A renowned poet, Vajpayee had several books published. A bachelor, he has a foster son, Ranjan Bhattacharya, who is politically influential.

Early Life

Atal Bihari Vajpayee was born into an upper caste family in Gwalior (now part of Madhya Pradesh) on 25 Dec. 1924. Educated at Victoria College, Gwalior then D. V. A. College, Kanpur, he took to journalism. In 1947 he became joint editor of *Rashtra Dharma*, a monthly publication tied to right-wing Hindu nationalist party, the Rashtriya Swayamsevak Sangh (RSS).

In 1951 he was a founder member of the RSS-linked Bharatiya Jana Sangh party (BJS). In 1950 he made his first attempt to gain a seat in parliament. Defeated in the Lucknow constituency, he became the parliamentary leader of the BJS in 1957 after his successful election to the Lok Sabha where he remained until his appointment in 1962 to the Rajya Sabha. Following the death of Deendayal Upadhyaya in 1968, Vajpayee took over the role of BJS party president.

Under his leadership, the BJS supported the ruling Congress party in the movement towards the secession of East Pakistan (1970–72). Indira Gandhi's declaration of a state of Emergency from June 1975 to April 1977 saw thousands of her political opponents imprisoned, including Vajpayee. Between 1977–79 Vajpayee served as cabinet minister for external affairs becoming the first non-Congress Party foreign minister. During his tenure he was instrumental in establishing closer ties with Pakistan.

In 1980 he became founding president of the Bharatiya Janata Party. Resulting from the failure of the dual-membership concept integral to the Bharatiya Jana Sangh party (sharing membership with the RSS), the newly formed BJP attempted to steer a more liberal path. Poor electoral results—the BJP gained only two parliamentary seats—saw Vajpayee replaced, in 1984, by L. K. Advani, the party's former general secretary. His re-election to the Rajya Sabha indicated an apparent withdrawal from the political limelight.

On 6 Dec. 1992 the razing of the Babri Masjid mosque in Ayodhya by a group of Hindu extremists with links to the BJP raised issues over the party's direction. Although Vajpayee went against the tide of implicit support for the act from within the party by condemning the action, the event and the issues surrounding it continue to create political tension for the BJP.

In 1996, after his successful handling of internal dissent within the Gujarat constituency, Vajpayee was called upon to lead the party to an electoral victory as part of a coalition government.

Career Peak

Vajpayee's first period as prime minister and minister of external affairs lasted only 13 days. He returned to office on 19 March 1998, naming L. K. Advani as minister for home affairs. On 11 and 13 May 1998 India carried out a series of five nuclear tests in Pokharan in the desert region of Rajasthan. The tests invoked sanctions from the US and Japan, whilst bolstering public support for Vajpayee. In spite of fears of an arms race between India and Pakistan, Vajpayee's symbolic Lahore bus trip in Feb. 1999 (a journey from Delhi, India, to Lahore, Pakistan, where Vajpayee met former Pakistani prime minister Nawaz Sharif) was widely viewed as the first positive move towards closer bilateral relations.

A vote of no-confidence passed in April 1999 ousted Vajpayee by a single vote. Indian President, K. R. Narayanan, requested Vajpayee to remain as caretaker prime minister until parliamentary elections were held. The armed conflict in Kargil between Pakistani-backed militants, Pakistani soldiers and Indian troops refreshed support for the BJP, heightening Vajpayee's popularity. Elections in Sept. and Oct. 1999 brought the BJP into government at the head of a 24-party coalition—the National Democratic Alliance (NDA)—and began Vajpayee's third period in office as prime minister (sworn in 13 Oct. 1999). Vajpayee's electoral campaign was a personality contest with his main rival, Congress Leader Sonia Gandhi. Following dissent in her own party over the issue of her Italian descent, the BJP adopted a populist rhetoric which pointed up differences between foreign and 'home-grown' interests and politics. Pledging further economic liberalization and reform, Vajpayee attracted large support from the middle and upper classes.

His government was hit by scandal in March 2001 when journalists from the Tehelka news agency, posing as arms dealers, offered financial gifts to senior politicians and officials as part of a fake arms deal. The scandal brought the first charges of corruption against Vajpayee's government and prompted the resignation of BJP Leader Bangaru Laxman and Defence Minister George Fernandes. The NDA survived the scandal though this was in no small part thanks to an electorate weary of political instability.

The Agra summit, held 14–16 June 2001 with Pakistan's leader, Gen. Pervez Musharraf, was the first of its kind. Though seen as a serious attempt to normalize relations, the talks were marred by Musharraf's insistence on focusing almost exclusively on the Kashmir issue whilst Vajpayee, displaying a similar tenacity, attempted to draw the Pakistani leader into a dialogue over the issue of cross-border terrorism. Shortly after the summit an invitation was extended to Vajpayee to continue talks in Islamabad. The peace process was interrupted by the events of 11 Sept. 2001 when hijacked planes crashed into New York's World Trade Centre buildings.

Vajpayee was the first leader in South Asia to offer military support to the US. The expectation that the US would in turn offer support to India against terrorism in Kashmir was complicated by US military reliance on Pakistan as a doorway for attacks on Afghanistan. A suicide attack on the state assembly building in Kashmir's summer capital, by Pakistani militant group Jaish-e-Mohammad, killing 38 people, prompted condemnation from western powers. Vajpayee sought to draw parallels between the anti-terrorism coalition mounted by the US and his own country's problems in Kashmir.

Further terrorist attacks, including an attack on the Indian parliament buildings in Delhi in Dec. 2001, led to the collapse of relations between India and Pakistan and military tension along the border continued to mount. Vajpayee took a firm stance throughout the crisis (which reached its high-point in May 2002) yet contributed to easing tensions by making a proposal for joint patrols along the border.

In 2002 Vajpayee faced his most challenging domestic crisis since coming to power when communal violence flared up in the northeastern state of Gujarat. Escalating political tension over the scheduled construction of the temple at Ayodhya led to an arson attack on 27 Feb. killing 58 members of hardline Hindu organization, the Vishwa Hindu Parishad (VHP). The attack provoked widespread rioting and attacks against Muslims, in which over 900 people were killed. Vajpayee was criticized for not acting quickly enough to deal with the situation.

Allegations of funding for separatists in Kashmir in Feb. 2003 led to tit-for-tat expulsions of the acting high commissioners from Islamabad and Delhi. In March 2003 India and Pakistan held contemporaneous tests of short-range, nuclear-capable missiles. The tests followed shortly after India had blamed Pakistan for a recent massacre of 24 Hindus in Kashmir. In early May 2003 Vajpayee made another attempt to normalize relations with Pakistan by announcing his intention to appoint a high commissioner to Islamabad. This was welcomed by Pakistan, which promised to reciprocate.

In June 2003, during a bridge-building visit to China, Vajpayee conceded recognition of Tibet as an autonomous region of the People's Republic of China and promised to prevent 'anti-China political activities in India' by Tibetans.

Negotiations with Pakistan accelerated during the second half of 2003. By Oct. both governments had agreed to resume transport links and the highly symbolic sporting ties, notably cricket. Vajpayee announced that his government would meet the Kashmiri separatist alliance for the first time and suggested direct road links between the two Kashmirs. Direct flights between Delhi and Lahore were restored in Jan. 2004 after a 2-year suspension. At a meeting of the South Asian Association for Regional Cooperation (SAARC) in Lahore in Jan., Vajpayee agreed with Musharraf to hold direct talks on a settlement for Kashmir in Feb. The SAARC meeting also produced an agreement to set up a free trade area from Jan. 2006.

While campaigning in March 2004 for upcoming early elections, Vajpayee declared the end of military conflict with Pakistan and promised increased trade and communication between the two countries. However, the NDA's 22-party coalition was decisively defeated by the Congress party's alliance. Regional BJP allies—in Andhra Pradesh and Tamil Nadu—fared badly, as did the BJP in India's poorer states—Bihar and Uttar Pradesh—where the BJP's 'India Shining' slogan failed to win support. Vajpayee left office on 22 May 2004 and was succeeded by Congress' Manmohan Singh, after Sonia Gandhi turned down the premiership. He returned to the Lok Sabha on 2 June as the member for Lucknow. Elected chairman of the BJP parliamentary party, he relinquished the party leadership to L. K. Advani.

Vall, Ely Ould Mohammed (Mauritania)

Introduction

Col. Ely Ould Mohammed Vall deposed Mauritania's President Taya in a bloodless coup in Aug. 2005 and promised to pave the way for genuine multi-party elections within 2 years.

Early Life

Ely Ould Mohammed Vall was born in 1953 in Nouakchott, Mauritania, then part of the Federation of French West Africa. He was educated in Nouakchott and in the French cities of Aix-en-Provence and Le Mans and in 1973 he joined the Meknès military academy in Morocco. While developing his military career, he also studied law. On his return to Mauritania, Vall served in the war against Western Sahara's pro-independence Polisario Front, commanding military posts at Bir-Mogreïn, Ouadane and Aïn-Benteli. From 1979–81 he commanded the Compagnie du Quartier Général before becoming head of the military district of Rosso.

In 1984, while commander of the military district of Nouakchott, Vall played a key role in the coup led by his ally and fellow military commander, Col. Maaouya Ould Sid'Ahmed Taya. In Nov. 1985 Vall was appointed director of national security. President Taya legalized opposition parties in 1991 but subsequent multi-party presidential elections were nonetheless criticized for irregularities. Taya's regime became increasingly unpopular and reportedly survived three attempted coups during 2003–04.

With the president attending King Fahd's funeral in Saudi Arabia, Vall led a coup against Taya on 3 Aug. 2005 and appeared to have broad domestic backing. However, Vall came under fire from the exiled opposition amid allegations that he had sanctioned torture in jails under his command.

Career Peak

Vall declared that his governing military council would remain in power for up to 2 years while it created conditions for genuine democratic institutions. The African Union, EU, UN, South Africa and the USA initially denounced Vall's administration as illegitimate. However, in the meantime the international community engaged with the regime in expectation of democratic parliamentary elections, which took place in Nov.–Dec. 2006. There nevertheless remains some scepticism as to whether power will be ceded to civilian rulers, not least because Mauritania is expected to benefit from substantial wealth from its oil and gas reserves in the near future. He died of a heart attack at the age of 64 on 5 May 2017.

Valls, Manuel (France)

Introduction

Manuel Valls was prime minister from April 2014 until Dec. 2016, when he launched an unsuccessful campaign for the presidency. A member of the Socialist Party, he had gained a reputation for toughness as minister of the interior before becoming prime minister in April 2014. Following François Hollande's decision in Dec. 2016 not to run for re-election, Valls declared himself a candidate for the presidency and resigned as premier.

Early Life

Manuel Carlos Valls was born on 13 Aug. 1962 in Barcelona, to a Spanish father and Swiss mother. He moved to France as a teenager, joined the Socialist Party and studied history at the University of Paris 1, where he was active in the student union movement.

Valls was elected to the regional council for the Île-de-France in 1986, becoming its vice-president in 1998 having served as deputy mayor of Argenteuil-Bezons in 1988. He was elected mayor of Évry in 2001.

In June 2009 Valls announced that he would contest the Socialist candidacy for the 2012 presidential election. Defeated in the first round after winning only 6% of the vote, he immediately endorsed the victor, François Hollande, and served as communications director for his successful presidential campaign.

As minister of the interior from May 2012, Valls adopted tough stances on immigration and crime that alienated wings of his own party but proved popular with the public. After the Socialist Party suffered losses in municipal elections, the incumbent premier, Jean-Marc Ayrault, announced his resignation on 31 March 2014. Hollande appointed Valls as Ayrault's successor the following day.

Career Peak

In his first speech to the National Assembly, Valls announced sweeping tax cuts and labour reforms, as well as swingeing reductions in public expenditure, with the aim of promoting growth and cutting the budget deficit. His economic and social policies were unpopular among many on the left of his party and in Aug. 2014 he overhauled the cabinet in response to three ministerial resignations over government austerity measures. Nonetheless, he survived two parliamentary votes of confidence in his first 6 months in office.

In June 2015 the government survived another confidence vote, which took place after Valls utilized a rarely used constitutional device to force through economic reforms.

In the wake of co-ordinated terrorist attacks across Paris on 13 Nov. 2015 by Islamist extremists, Valls spearheaded the government's security response and the nationwide state of emergency. Following a further devastating attack in Nice in July 2016, for which the Islamic State jihadist movement claimed responsibility, Valls was criticized for claiming that France would forthwith 'have to live with terrorism'.

On 6 Dec. Valls resigned as prime minister to launch his bid for the presidency, and was replaced by Bernard Cazeneuve, the former interior minister. In the Socialist Party presidential primary election held in Jan. 2017, he lost to Benoît Hamon who later received only 6.4% of the total votes cast in the first round of the presidential election.

At the June 2017 parliamentary elections, although he first expressed his willingness to join Emmanuel Macron's party La République en Marche!, he ran for the Socialist Party and won a seat in Évry.

Van Rompuy, Herman (Belgium)

Introduction

Herman Van Rompuy was prime minister from Dec. 2008–Nov. 2009. The leader of the Christian Democratic & Flemish Party (CD&V), Van Rompuy was asked by King Albert II to form a government after the previous administration resigned in the wake of the break-up of Fortis bank.

Early Life

Van Rompuy was born in Oct. 1947 in Etterbeek, in the Brussels-Capital Region. He graduated in philosophy from the University of Leuven in 1968 before studying for a master's degree in economic science.

Beginning his political career as vice-president of the Young Christian People's Party, he graduated in 1978 to become a member of the national bureau of the Christian People's Party. By the end of the 1970s he was serving in the cabinet of Léo Tindemans and in 1980 was appointed director of the

CVP Study Centre. In 1988 he was elected to the Senate and became president of the CVP, serving until his promotion to minister for the budget and deputy prime minister in 1993.

In his 6-year tenure as budget minister Van Rompuy significantly reduced the national debt, which had stood at 130% of GDP when he took office. He criticized the previous government's plans to increase the budget deficit and spend its way out of recession. In 1995 he left the Senate to take up a seat in the Chamber of Representatives.

The heavy defeat of the CVP at the 1999 election, which followed a scandal concerning the contamination of feedstock with dioxins, precipitated a crisis in the party that saw it renamed as the CD&V. After 8 years out of power, the 2007 general election returned the CD&V to government, with Van Rompuy serving as speaker of the Chamber.

On 19 Dec. 2008 Belgium's Supreme Court announced 'strong indications' that the incumbent government had attempted to influence a court decision on the break-up of the financial group Fortis. Albert II accepted the resignation of Prime Minister Yves Leterme's administration and on 28 Dec. asked Van Rompuy to form a government. Van Rompuy was reportedly reluctant to assume the premiership but bowed to pressure from party members eager to prevent the return of ex-prime minister Guy Verhofstadt.

Career Peak

Through most of 2009 Van Rompuy sought to rebuild confidence in the political system, while confronting Belgium's financial crisis and also attempting to diffuse tensions between the Dutch- and French-speaking communities. Then, in Nov., he was selected, with effect from 1 Jan. 2010, for the post of president of the European Council.

Later Life

Van Rompuy's tenure as president of the European Council was dominated by the fallout from the global financial crisis and the pressing need for EU governments to devise mechanisms to deal with sovereign debt problems in a number of eurozone member states.

In Dec. 2012 Van Rompuy, together with the presidents of the European Commission and European Parliament, accepted the Nobel Peace Prize on behalf of the European Union, which had received the annual award for its advancement of peace and reconciliation, democracy and human rights in Europe. In March 2013 he announced that the expiry of his EU mandate at the end of Nov. 2014 would mark the end of his political career. The former prime minister of Poland Donald Tusk subsequently took over from Van Rompuy as president of the European Council.

Vanhanen, Matti (Finland)

Introduction

Matti Vanhanen took over as Finland's prime minister in June 2003 when the 3-month tenure of Anneli Jäätteenmäki ended amid political scandal. A member of the Centre Party like his predecessor, Vanhanen is widely regarded as a cautious and reliable politician. He retained the premiership following parliamentary elections in March 2007.

Early Life

Matti Taneli Vanhanen was born 4 Nov. 1955 in Jyväskylä, Finland. From 1980–83 he was chairman of the Centre Party's youth organization, and in 1989 completed a university degree in political science. His early career as a journalist, working as editor-in-chief of *Kehäsanomat* from 1988–91, won him a reputation as an expert on the European Union. In 1991 he was elected to the Finnish parliament, where he became vice-president of the party and, later, defence minister.

On 18 June 2003 Jäätteenmäki resigned from both her role as prime minister and as leader of the Centre Party, following allegations over her use of information concerning her predecessor, Paavo Lipponen, in the build-up to the elections of March 2003. Jäätteenmäki was in office for just 63 days.

Career Peak

Observers viewed the appointment of Vanhanen as an attempt to restore calm to Finnish national politics and one of his principal tasks was to win back public trust. He initially headed a coalition comprising the Centre Party, the Social Democrats and the Swedish People's Party, and was expected to pursue a similar economic programme to that of Jäätteenmäki. He spoke out against plans for a proposed EU common defence policy, was a leading advocate of ecological and environmental issues, and voiced his opposition to plans to build a fifth nuclear reactor in Finland.

In 2005 a 7-week industrial dispute in the paper mill industry over pay and conditions caused nationwide strikes before being settled by mediation. Losses in export earnings were expected to reach €5 bn. and Vanhanen's government faced considerable losses in tax revenue.

In Oct. 2005 Vanhanen was nominated as the presidential candidate of the Centre Party for the Jan. 2006 election but came third with just under 19% of the vote. During Finland's 6-month presidency of the EU from July–Dec. 2006, he sought to build a wider consensus among Europe's leaders on reviving the stalled EU constitution and on conditions for future membership expansion, particularly in relation to Turkey.

He was re-elected as prime minister by parliament in April 2007, following the Centre's Party's narrow victory in parliamentary polls in March, and formed a new centre-right coalition government with the Swedish People's Party, the National Rally Party and the Green League.

In Sept. 2008 he called for stricter firearms controls after a gunman killed nine students and a teacher at a college in the town of Kauhajoki before taking his own life.

In Oct. 2009 alleged election financing irregularities by the Centre Party led to the tabling of a parliamentary no-confidence motion in Vanhanen's coalition by opposition left-wing parties in Oct. 2009, but this was defeated by 117–27 votes with 56 abstentions. Vanhanen resigned in June 2010 having announced in Dec. 2009 that he would step down as Centre Party leader before its next congress and also as prime minister owing to a forthcoming leg operation. He was succeeded in both positions by Mari Kiviniemi who served as minister for local government and public administration in his cabinet.

Later Life

Shortly after leaving office Vanhanen was appointed managing director of the Finnish Family Firms Association. However, in Nov. 2014 he announced his resignation from the organization and returned as a member of parliament following the April 2015 elections.

Vargas, Getúlio Dornelles (Brazil)

Introduction

Getúlio Dornelles Vargas was twice president of Brazil, from 1930 to 1945 and then from 1951 to 1954. A social and economic reformer, his rule was increasingly authoritarian.

Early Life

Born in 1883 in São Borja, in the state of Rio Grande do Sul, Vargas was raised on local politics. Having completed a brief stint in the military, he graduated in law in 1908 and entered politics. He served in the national congress from 1922–26 before being appointed finance minister under President de Souza. Two years later he became governor of Rio Grande do Sul. Failing to win the presidency in 1930, he had a prominent role in the revolution of Oct. 1930 which overthrew the republic.

Career Peak

Vargas relied on the support of the military for most of his first period in office. Between 1930 and July 1934 he held the title of provisional president. He was then elected president by the constituent assembly but in Nov. 1937 he dismissed the constitutional government and created the Estado Novo (New State) based on the Portuguese totalitarian model.

With his opponents, notably the communists, removed, Vargas was free to institute radical reforms. Central government was strengthened to reduce the power of the large landowners. A wider suffrage, including women, expanded the electorate fourfold. Social reforms included the introduction of a minimum wage. Vargas attempted to keep big business on side by promoting rapid industrialization, while his anti-Nazi stance ensured development funding from the US.

Despite popular support, his reforms were only partially successful. Opposition to censorship and a faltering economy led to his overthrow in Oct. 1945. He was elected senator for Rio Grande do Sul later that year but his political profile remained low until he stood as the Labour candidate in the presidential election of 1950. Having regained office, he was unable to hold support for a programme of economic austerity. His government was beset by allegations of corruption and by July 1954 the military was demanding his dismissal. Vargas shot himself on 24 Aug. 1954.

Vejjajiva, Abhisit (Thailand)

Introduction

Abhisit Vejjajiva served as prime minister from Dec. 2008–Aug. 2011. His election, which took place 2 weeks after the constitutional court banned three parties from the previous coalition government, was marked by party defections and allegations of vote rigging. Abhisit vowed to restore the economy and rebuild political confidence.

Early Life

Abhisit Vejjajiva was born in Newcastle-upon-Tyne, England to a family of wealthy Thai-Chinese physicians on 3 Aug. 1964. He attended Eton College before graduating from St John's College, Oxford with a degree in philosophy, politics and economics. After a brief teaching stint at Chulachomklao Royal Military Academy in Thailand, Abhisit returned to Oxford where he gained a master's degree in economics. Returning to Thailand, he taught economics at Thammasat University before graduating in law from Ramkhamhaeng University in 1990.

In 1992 Abhisit joined the Democrat Party and became the MP for Bangkok. Rising through the party ranks, he became deputy party leader in 1999 and leader in 2005. In 2006 he led a boycott against snap elections called by the incumbent prime minister, Thaksin Shinawatra, claiming they lacked legitimacy.

In April 2007 Abhisit campaigned for the premier's office with the slogan 'Putting People First' and an agenda filled with populist policies. Criticized over his muted condemnation of the Sept. 2006 military coup, Abhisit backed the junta's draft constitution as the 'lesser of two evils'. In 2007 and 2008 he lost two parliamentary votes for the premiership before finally winning on 15 Dec. 2008.

Career Peak

Lacking a popular mandate to lead, Abhisit came under intense pressure after taking office. He was accused of deal-brokering in cabinet appointments and faced allegations of corruption before defeating a vote of no confidence on 21 March 2009. Thaksin supporters continued to demand new elections and on 26 March stepped up their protests by surrounding Abhisit's office and calling for his resignation. Anti-government demonstrators also stormed the venue of an ASEAN summit meeting in Pattaya in April (Thailand having begun an 18-month term as chair of the organization in July 2008), forcing its abandonment. Abhisit declared a state of emergency in response and brought in troops in a crackdown on opposition.

In June 2009 parliament approved the government's US$23 bn. fiscal stimulus plan to boost the economy in the wake of the global financial crisis. In Nov. 2009 a diplomatic row broke out between Thailand and Cambodia over Thaksin's appointment as an economic adviser to the Cambodian government and the rejection of a Thai request for his extradition. However, in Aug. 2010 it was reported that Thaksin had relinquished his role and that the two governments had normalized their relations.

In Feb. 2010 the Supreme Court stripped the Thaksin family of half its estimated US$1.4 bn. fortune, claiming it was gained through corruption. Thaksin supporters responded the following month by surrounding the prime minister's office and again demanding his resignation. The demonstrations in Bangkok continued into April, leading to violent clashes between protesters

and the military, but ended in May following decisive intervention by the army in which about 90 people were killed and over 2,000 injured. In Dec. 2010 the government lifted the state of emergency in Bangkok and surrounding areas. Also in late 2010 the Constitutional Court dismissed accusations of electoral misconduct that could have resulted in the dissolution of Abhisit's ruling Democrat Party.

In elections held in July 2011, Abhisit's Democrat Party lost to the Pheu Thai Party (PTP) and the Thai parliament subsequently elected Yingluck Shinawatra as Abhisit's successor. Fulfilling an earlier promise made during the election campaign Abhisit stood down as the party leader, but was then re-elected at a party assembly.

Velasco Alvarado, Juan (Peru)

Introduction

General Juan Velasco Alvarado headed a military junta between 1968–75. A socialist, he implemented key socio-economic reforms before failing health ended his rule.

Early Life

Velasco was born in Piura, in North Peru, on 16 June 1910. He trained at the Chorrillos military academy at Lima. After a successful military career, Velasco achieved the rank of general. At this time there was a wave of military discontent. Economic reforms under President Fernando Belaúnde had failed causing growing disillusionment and Belaúnde's pro-USA stance was unpopular. There was a major dispute over the La Brea and Pariña's oilfields in the north of Peru. The people, and the military, were unhappy with the monopoly of the American company, the International Petroleum Co., and its influence over the surrounding regions. Velasco led a bloodless coup and established himself as the head of an all-military government.

Career Peak

Unlike other military dictatorships, Velasco's government was reformist and populist. He set about implementing social and economic reforms aimed at improving the economy and reducing the disparity between the rich and Peru's majority poor by raising levels of education and social security. He also implemented a nationalization programme of transport, electricity, oil, mining and communications. In extensive agrarian reforms, co-operatives were established on formerly private farms. Price controls were imposed and Velasco promoted workers involvement in decision making. To support the large indigenous population, many of whom represented Peru's most poor, he made Quechua Peru's official second language. But he also restricted the freedom of the press.

Velasco reversed Belaúnde's policy of encouraging US influence. He took the disputed oil fields back under Peruvian control, leaving the American owners uncompensated. He banned American fishermen from Peruvian waters, sought a Latin American alliance against the USA and was unmoved when the USA suspended arms sales. Velasco strongly opposed American sanctions of Cuba.

Velasco's first 5 years in power were judged but in 1973 his health failed and his power waned. He continued to run the government for a further 2 years before, amid strikes, he was deposed by his prime minister, General Francisco Morales Bermúndez. The latter continued the military dictatorship, but reversed all of Velasco's reforms. Velasco died on 24 Dec. 1977 and his funeral procession through the streets of Lima was accompanied by a large anti-government protest.

Velasco Ibarra, José María (Ecuador)

Introduction

José María Velasco Ibarra was a major political figure in Ecuador from the 1930s to the 1970s and served as president five times. A noted orator, he was also a distinguished lawyer and author, writing seven books on political discourse and statecraft. He seemed able to win any election, such was his popularity with the masses, but his terms in office were marked by sudden reversals in policy, contradictory economic programmes, temporary suspensions of civil liberties and military interventions. Despite his five presidencies, in which he governed both as constitutional president and dictator, he only managed to serve one full term and spent more time in exile than as president, governing for 12 years and 10 months in total.

Early Life

Velasco was born on 19 March 1893 into a wealthy family in Quito. He was educated at home until the age of 10 before attending the Seminario Menor de San Luis and Colegio San Gabriel. From 1911 he studied Law at the Universidad Central de Ecuador, where he founded and presided over a number of political associations for students and obtained a doctorate in 1922. Following his studies he became a columnist for newspaper El Comercio de Quito and a professor of Law. In 1933 Velasco was appointed as the Conservative party's election candidate and in Sept. 1934 he assumed the presidency, the first of five terms in office.

Career Peak

Velasco's economic proposals included the division of large landed estates, which failed to win the support of Congress. He responded by assuming dictatorial powers, imprisoning opposition leaders and censoring the press. In Aug. 1935 he was deposed by army leaders after 11 months in office and went into exile in Colombia.

In 1944 Velasco returned to Ecuador at the head of the Democratic Alliance, a multi-party coalition of Ecuadorian politicians dedicated to replacing current president Carlos Arroyo. On 28 May 1944 there was an uprising which saw the military and civilian supporters of the alliance pitted against Arroyo's police. The president resigned the following day and the military handed power to the Democratic Alliance who in turn named Velasco as president. The exiled leader returned triumphantly from Colombia and during a 3-day journey to Quito was greeted by enthusiasts who believed they were witnessing the birth of a popular revolution. As president, Velasco imprisoned and exiled Arroyo's supporters and baited the business community and the right wing. The Constituent Assembly, which was dominated by the Democratic Alliance, convened to write a new constitution. However, the leftist elements of this alliance were destined to be disappointed as the new president imposed a series of repressive policies. As hostilities grew, Velasco condemned the new constitution and dismissed the Assembly. He aggravated the nation's economic problems by failing to reduce the high level of inflation; living standards continued to fall. When in Aug. 1947 he was ousted by his minister of defence and again forced into exile, he enjoyed little support and was replaced by Carlos Mancheno.

In June 1952 Velasco triumphed in the elections, taking 43% of the vote, and in Sept. he commenced his third and only full 4-year term. Ecuador was enjoying a period of economic stability and although Velasco continued to spend as before—building bridges and schools and implementing salary increases for members of Congress—in contrast to his previous terms in office there were now sufficient funds to pay for his spending programmes. Camilo Ponce Enríquez won the 1956 elections and Velasco indicated that he would be retiring from political life. For the first time Velasco was not obliged to flee the country at the end of his presidency.

However, following widespread riots in 1960, Velasco felt a 'duty to the Ecuadorian people' to stand for the presidency for the fourth time and came to power with 49% of the votes, his widest margin of victory. Velasco's populism continued into his inaugural address when he renounced the Rio Protocol of 1942, a treaty which ended Peru's occupation of Ecuador by ceding some 200,000 square kilometres of land to Peru. He thus assumed the presidency with the support of the masses, but saddled himself with expensive commitments to the poor at a time when the budget deficit was approaching a critical level. He announced a programme of economic reform but soon became unpopular as a result of austerity measures, sparking a series of strikes and demonstrations in several major cities. Velasco ordered the arrest of his vice-president, a move which left him open to charges of violating the constitution and in Nov. 1961 he was forced by an army junta to resign.

In the June 1968 presidential elections the 75-year old Velasco was voted in for the fifth time, 34 years after his initial victory. However, Velasco won barely one third of the votes, foreshadowing the political difficulties that plagued him during his final term. He was faced by a hostile Congress, overwhelming economic problems and increasing political chaos. After rioting by thousands of university students he disbanded Congress and the Supreme Court and, with the backing of the army, assumed dictatorial powers in June 1970. Velasco subsequently decreed a number of necessary, though extremely unpopular economic measures. In 1971 he lost his most important ally, Gen. Jorge Acosta Velasco, his nephew and minister of defence, who had continually reshuffled the high command in order to keep supporters of Velasco in key posts. In Feb. 1972, after Velasco insisted upon holding elections in which populist leader Assad Bucaram seemed certain to win, military leaders overthrew Velasco and replaced him with a junta headed by Gen. Guillermo Rodriguez Lara.

Later Life

Following his fifth administration, Velasco was exiled to Argentina. He retired from politics becoming a professor of Law at the University of Buenos Aires. In Feb. 1979 his wife was killed in a bus accident and Velasco accompanied her body to Quito where he remained until his death on 30 March 1979 at the age of 86.

Venetiaan, Runaldo Ronald (Suriname)

Introduction

Runaldo Ronald Venetiaan was president of Suriname from 2000 to 2010, having previously held the office between 1991 and 1996. Dedicated to free market principles, he implemented a series of measures to bring the struggling economy that he inherited under control. His first term in office was also characterized by a programme of austerity measures.

Early Life

Venetiaan was born on 18 June 1936 in Paramaribo. He later moved to the Netherlands, where he studied mathematics and physics at Leiden University. Returning to Suriname, he undertook a teaching career before being appointed minister of education in 1973 in the government of Henck Arron, holding office until a military coup in 1980. After civilian government was re-established, Venetiaan resumed his role in the education ministry in 1988. In 1991 the New Front for Democracy won parliamentary elections and elected Venetiaan to the presidency.

Career Peak

In 1992 Venetiaan signed a peace accord with the rebel Surinamese Liberation Army, which had been operational since the mid-1980s. A primary aim of his first term was to secure economic stability after the years of coups and counter-coups. Despite stabilizing the currency and achieving a budget surplus, his austerity measures were widely unpopular and he lost the 1996 election to Jules Wijdenbosch, an ally of former military dictator Desi Bouterse, who instigated increased public spending.

With Wijdenbosch increasingly under attack for economic mismanagement, elections were called for May 2000 and Venetiaan led the New Front to victory. He again took over a faltering economy burdened by bureaucracy, high inflation, a devalued currency, overwhelming international debt and a collapsing healthcare system. In response, he cut public spending, replaced the guilder (in Jan. 2004) with the Suriname dollar and restructured the economically significant banana industry. Foreign relations were meanwhile dominated by a longstanding disagreement with Guyana over maritime boundaries. The UN established a tribunal to mediate in 2004 and in Sept. 2007 it awarded two-thirds of the disputed area to Guyana.

At the parliamentary elections of May 2005 Venetiaan's New Front for Democracy coalition returned the largest number of MPs, with the National Democratic Party of Bouterse second. However, the New Front failed to obtain the two-thirds majority required to elect the president. In Aug. 2005 Venetiaan won a second term of office when he polled 560 votes against 315 for his opponent, Rabin Parmessar, in a vote by the United People's Conference, consisting of MPs and elected local and district representatives.

He did not stand for re-election in 2010 and was succeeded by Dési Bouterse on 12 Aug.

Verhofstadt, Guy (Belgium)

Introduction

Verhofstadt was prime minister of Belgium for a period spanning almost 9 years, including two full terms and an emergency, interim appointment after his defeat at the polls in 2007. The election of his Flemish Liberals and Democrats (VLD; Vlaamse Liberalen en Demokraten) party in June 1999 ended decades of dominance by the Christian Democrats. He is the president of the Alliance of Liberals and Democrats for Europe group at the European Parliament and continues to be an important figure in pan-European politics.

Early Life

Verhofstadt was born on 11 April 1953 in Dendermonde, one of three children of a trade union lawyer. He attended secondary school in Ghent and went on to study law at the city's university. Having graduated in 1975, he became involved in local politics the following year. His first major step in national politics came 4 years later when he was elected chairman of the Young Liberals, introducing a new radical manifesto to attract younger voters. In 1982 he was appointed chairman of the Flemish Liberal Party (PVV) and in 1985 was elected to the Belgian parliament, subsequently holding senior ministerial portfolios in the coalition government. Forced into opposition in 1988, Verhofstadt planned a radical overhaul of the party, which in Nov. 1992 adopted the new name of the Flemish Liberals and Democrats (VLD). In the 1995 general election the VLD failed to oust the Christian Democrats from power and in the summer of that year Verhofstadt resigned as party chairman. He returned to the political arena in May the following year with a revised citizen's manifesto appealing to the middle ground. In 1997 he resumed the VLD leadership. The party made significant gains in the June 1999 parliamentary elections and Verhofstadt became the country's first Liberal prime minister for 60 years.

Career Peak

In the immediate aftermath of the 1999 election Verhofstadt was successful in resolving the dioxin crisis that had hit Belgian agriculture and resulted in the downfall of his predecessor. Then, presiding over a 'rainbow coalition' of Liberals, Socialists and Greens (representing Belgium's two main linguistic communities), he pledged in his first term to achieve a balanced budget, reduce taxation and promulgate an amnesty for asylum seekers. This latter policy led to conflict with an increasingly vocal far-right anti-immigration lobby. Verhofstadt meanwhile maintained his strong support for European integration.

In parliamentary elections on 18 May 2003 the VLD won the largest vote share with 15.4% and 25 seats in the 150-member Chamber of Representatives (two more seats than in 1999). Verhofstadt reconstituted his coalition government (but without environmentalist representation) and he was inaugurated for his second term as prime minister on 12 July 2003. The previous month he announced plans to reform war crimes legislation which, under existing terms, allowed for charges to be brought against foreign nationals accused of abuses committed outside Belgian jurisdiction. This issue had attracted US hostility, particularly in the light of Belgium's opposition to the 2003 invasion of Iraq.

Heavy losses for Verhofstadt's VLD party in the local elections of Oct. 2006 proved a prelude to a poor performance in the parliamentary elections in June 2007. On the evening of election day Verhofstadt conceded defeat and announced his resignation as leader of the VLD, calling for a new generation of politicians to further the party's cause. However, the inability of the opposition coalition to form an effective government threatened to become a crisis as important policy matters went unresolved. As a stopgap measure the King asked Verhofstadt to form an interim government to address the most pressing issues. This arrangement was approved by parliament on 23 Dec. 2007, and the government was provided with a 3-month term. The programme of the government was largely restricted to the achievement of two urgent goals: drawing up a budget for 2008 and achieving a consensus for the renewal of the Belgian state, the unity of which had been strained by the political crisis. On 25 Feb. 2008 the government approved a two stage framework for the reform of the state, focusing on the decentralization of policy-making powers in the first stage and in the second on more fundamental 'major state reform'. It was announced on 26 Feb. 2008 that the 2008 budget had been agreed. On 20 March 2008 the interim government was succeeded by a coalition led by the CD&V's Yves Leterme.

Later Life

Verhofstadt opted to take a 1-year sabbatical following his retirement from office. In July 2009 he was elected to the European parliament and also became president of the Alliance of Liberals and Democrats for Europe group. Verhofstadt was re-elected as a European MP following the elections of May 2014, and ran unsuccessfully as ALDE's candidate for the European Commission presidency that same year. In Sept. 2016 he was chosen to lead the European parliament's negotiations with the UK over its exit from the EU.

Verwoerd, Hendrik Frensch (South Africa)

Introduction

Hendrik Frensch Verwoerd was an academic and politician who became one of the chief architects of the apartheid system. He served as prime minister from 1958–66.

Early Life

Verwoerd was born in Amsterdam on 8 Sept. 1901. He was still an infant when his family emigrated to South Africa. He went on to pursue an academic career as a professor of applied psychology at the University of Stellenbosch. In 1933 Verwoerd was appointed chair of psychology and social work. His entrance into the political arena came in 1937 when he took up the post of editor for the Nationalist newspaper *Die Transvaler*. When the Nationalists won the election of 1948 he abandoned journalism to become a senator in the South African parliament.

Career Peak

Verwoerd quickly achieved senior rank as minister of native affairs, and from 1950 onwards was the instigator of a programme of legislative segregation that was dubbed apartheid. In 1958 the Nationalists chose Verwoerd as leader. Once in power Verwoerd's dream of a segregated state became a reality, and Africans, Asians and cape coloureds were gradually driven into separate townships on the periphery of major cities.

In 1959 Verwoerd ensured that the Promotion of Bantu Self-Government Act became law. The act laid out plans for the compulsory resettlement of the black population into eight distinct homelands. Verwoerd's rigorous commitment to segregationist politics sparked demonstrations, including, in March 1960, one at Sharpeville during which the police fired on the crowd, killing 69 demonstrators. The African National Congress and Pan African Congress were subsequently banned and the police were granted powers to detain indefinitely without trial.

In April 1960 Verwoerd was the victim of a failed assassination attempt. He was convinced that his survival was a sign of God's approval of his policies. Confronted by growing international disgust in the wake of the Sharpeville massacre, he offered the white population the chance to decide in a referendum whether South Africa should leave the Commonwealth. By a slim majority the country became a republic on 31 May 1961. It was during Verwoerd's tenure in office that Nelson Mandela was sentenced to life imprisonment.

On 6 Sept. 1966 Verwoerd was stabbed to death by a parliamentary employee of mixed race, whose motives were never clearly established.

Videla, Jorge Rafaél (Argentina)

Introduction

Jorge Videla ruled Argentina from March 1976 until March 1981, the former army general having led a coup against Isabel Perón to establish himself as de facto president. Considered the architect of a 'dirty' war to eliminate left-wing guerillas and their supporters, he was later sentenced to life imprisonment.

Early Life

Jorge Rafaél Videla was born on 2 Aug. 1925 in the city of Mercedes in the San Luis province of Argentina. The son of a military officer, Videla entered the National Military College at the age of 16 and graduated in 1944 with the rank of second lieutenant. After attending the Escuela Superior de Guerra between 1952 and 1954, he served at the ministry of defence and thereafter directed the Military Academy until 1962. Ha became chief of the army's general staff in 1973 and, 2 years later, Isabel Perón appointed him commander-in-chief of the army.

Unhappy with Perón's leadership, particularly in the face of terrorist attacks from the Marxist ERP and the Montoneros, in March 1976 Videla and his supporters seized power in a bloodless coup. It was the sixth time the army had seized power since 1930. Two days later Videla assumed the presidency.

Career Peak

He headed a three-man military junta that included Gen. Orlando Ramón Agosti and Adm. Eduardo Emilio Massera. Once in power, Videla dissolved congress, appointed loyal officers to key government positions, banned trade unions and imposed military control. Terming his administration the 'National Reorganization Process'. Videla ruled by terror. Although he had pledged to stay in power for only 3 years, in May 1978 the leaders of the junta installed him for a second term.

Under his regime left-wing figures (or 'subversives'. were subject to jail, torture and extra-judicial killing. Political arrests and executions extended to journalists and intellectuals, while it was also alleged that children of government opponents were kidnapped and illegally adopted by members of the military. Estimates of the number of people killed or 'disappeared' range from 9,000 to 30,000 and his campaign against the left elicited international condemnation.

Videla appointed José Alfredo Martínez de Hoz as minister of economy, charged with economic stabilization and the privatization of state-owned companies. A free market policy was adopted to curb inflation but, despite some early success, foreign debt increased fourfold.

Videla escaped three assassination attempts by Marxist groups. In 1981 he relinquished power to Gen. Roberto Viola, a former junta member.

Later Life

With the return of representative democratic government, Videla was sentenced to life imprisonment in 1985. After 5 years in prison he was pardoned as part of a decree by President Carlos Menem. In 1998 Videla was re-arrested on kidnapping charges relating to his time in power. He briefly returned to prison but was transferred to house arrest following concerns over his health. After the election of Néstor Kirchner in 2003 the government no longer recognized Videla as one time legal president. In April 2010 the Supreme Court overturned Menem's pardon. Videla was subsequently re-tried for murder, kidnapping and torture and was convicted of 31 killings. He was sentenced to life imprisonment in Dec. 2010. Videla died in prison in May 2013.

Vieira, João Bernardo (Guinea-Bissau)

Introduction

After leading a military coup in 1980 João Vieira held the presidency until 1999, when he was ousted by the army. After 6 years in exile he returned to contest the 2005 presidential elections, modelling himself as a 'soldier of peace'. He narrowly won the second round in July and took office in Oct. Following clashes between the government and the army, Vieira was assassinated on 2 March 2009.

Early Life

João Bernardo (Nino) Vieira was born on 27 April 1939 in Bissau, then part of Portuguese Guinea. He joined the African Party for the Independence of Guinea and Cape Verde (PAIGC) in 1960, was the party's political commissioner in the Catio region from 1961, and was a commander (rising to head of military operations in the War Council) in the war of independence from 1964. Following independence in Sept. 1974, he became commander in chief of the armed forces under President Luis Cabral. On 14 Nov. 1980 Vieira overthrew Cabral and appointed himself president, chair of the revolutionary council and, from 1981, secretary general of the PAIGC.

Career Peak

Vieira led the country for the next 18 years, latterly introducing a market economy and multi-party system. In 1994 he retired from the army and stood as the PAIGC candidate in the country's first free presidential elections, narrowly defeating Kumba Ialá of the Party for Social Renewal. Criticized for his increasingly autocratic leadership, Vieira alienated sections of the army, whose unsuccessful attempt to oust him in 1998 triggered a short civil war. In May 1999 he was finally forced into exile in Portugal. Following a further coup in Sept. 2003, the caretaker government of Carlos Gomes, Jr. tabled fresh presidential elections for 2005. Vieira returned from exile to stand as a candidate and won with 52% of the vote.

On 1 Nov. 2005 he sacked the government and appointed a long-term ally, Aristides Gomes, as prime minister. In April 2007 Aristides Gomes was succeeded by Martinho Ndafa Kabi, who served until Aug. 2008 when Vieira dissolved parliament and appointed Carlos Correia to head the government in the run-up to fresh elections in Nov., which were won by the PAIGC. During the campaign, Ialá accused Vieira of being the leading illicit drug trafficker in the country. A week after the poll, rebellious soldiers attacked Vieira's presidential residence but were repulsed by security forces.

Vieira's alleged involvement in the slaying of the army's chief of staff in a car bomb on 1 March 2009 led to his own assassination the next day. He was succeeded by Raimundo Pereira as acting president.

Vīķe-Freiberga, Vaira (Latvia)

Introduction

A university professor who lived for much of her life in Canada, Vaira Vīķe-Freiberga was politically unknown when elected Latvian president by the *Saeima* (parliament) in 1999. Throughout her presidential career she promoted Latvian membership to the European Union and NATO. Vīķe-Freiberga's term of office ended in 2007.

Early Life

Vīķe-Freiberga was born in Riga on 1 Dec. 1937. Towards the end of World War II, with the arrival of Russian troops, she and her family left Latvia and went as refugees to Lübeck, Germany. In 1949 the family moved to Morocco. Five years later they emigrated to Canada where they lived in a Latvian community in Toronto. There she studied psychology and linguistics before pursuing a career in academia. A professor of psychology at the University of Montreal, she was also involved in the study and promotion of the Latvian language and culture. After Latvia's independence, Vīķe-Freiberga returned to Latvia and between 1998–99 headed the Latvian Institute in Riga.

Career Peak

In 1999, although recently returned to Latvia, Vīķe-Freiberga stood as an independent candidate in the presidential elections. In the seventh round of voting, she took 53 votes to beat the foreign minister Valdis Birkavs and the finance minister Ingrīda Ūdre. She replaced Guntis Ulmanis.

After being elected, Vīķe-Freiberga worked to promote Latvia to the West and encourage the country's entry into the EU and NATO. After criticism from the EU, the OSCE and Russia, in Dec. 1999 she amended a proposed language law which would have made the Latvian language mandatory in public life and the workplace. The proposals were seen as discriminating against the Russian-speaking population, which constitutes about a third of Latvian inhabitants. In June 2003 she was re-elected president by parliament, receiving 88 votes out of 96. In 2004 Latvia joined both the EU and NATO. Despite protests from Latvian war veterans, Vīķe-Freiberga attended Russia's war anniversary celebrations in Moscow in 2005 (the only Baltic state president to do so).

Vīķe-Freiberga was unable to stand for re-election in May 2007 having served two full terms. She was succeeded by Valdis Zatlers.

Voronin, Vladimir (Moldova)

Introduction

Vladimir Voronin was chosen by parliament as Moldova's president following the victory of the Party of Communists of the Republic of Moldova (PCRM) in the Feb. 2001 parliamentary elections. The former Soviet Communist Party bureaucrat sought initially to forge closer ties with Russia, but when relations cooled from 2003 over the issue of Transnistria he looked increasingly to integration with the European Union.

Early Life

Vladimir Nicolae Voronin was born on 25 May 1941 in the village of Corjova, Chişinău county. He attended the technical co-operatist secondary school in Chişinău and graduated from the USSR's extramural institute of food industry in 1971, having worked as the director of the bread factory in Dubosari from 1966–71. For the next decade, he worked in the regional committee of the PCRM, heading the town councils of Dubosari and Ungheni. Promotion to the central committee of the party came in 1983. In 1985, the year in which Mikhail Gorbachev became leader of the USSR, Voronin was elected as a member of the supreme council of the Moldovan Soviet Socialist Republic (MSSR). Gorbachev's reform programme reversed the suppression of national characteristics within the USSR and by the late 1980s the Romanian language was in common and official use in Moldova. In 1990, when Voronin served as the minister of internal affairs of the MSSR, Moldova achieved *de facto* independence. Full independence followed the dramatic collapse of the USSR in Aug. 1991.

In late 1991 an ex-communist reformer, Mircea Snegur, won an election for the presidency. Four months later Moldova achieved formal recognition as an independent state at the United Nations. But independence brought a guerrilla war to the Transnistria region in the north and east of the country, populated by many ethnic Russians and Ukrainians who feared a Moldovan merger with Romania. A ceasefire in 1992 brought limited autonomy to the region, and Russian 'peacekeeping' troops were stationed there.

Voronin rose through the ranks of the PCRM, becoming first secretary to the central committee in 1994, the year of Moldova's first parliamentary election. Snegur's Agrarian Democratic Party (ADP) won a majority but was subsequently wracked by infighting. In Dec. 1995 residents of Transnistria overwhelmingly voted for independence from Moldova, although the referendum was considered illegal by the central government. Voronin contested a presidential run-off election against Snegur in Dec. 1996 but the eventual victor was Petru Lucinschi, a former communist running as an independent.

In May 1997 Moldova and Transnistria signed an agreement to keep Moldova a single state. During the March 1998 legislative elections the PCRM received the biggest share of the vote but was unable to form a government, leading to a series of short-lived, non-affiliated governments. In 2000 parliament failed to elect a successor to President Lucinschi, leading to early general elections in Feb. 2001. The PCRM won over 50% of the vote and parliament elected Voronin as president on 4 April.

Career Peak

Voronin used his inaugural address to criticize his predecessors, saying they had reduced Moldova to humanitarian catastrophe and dire poverty. He promised major reform in three areas: modernization of the country's ancient administrative structures, liberalization of the economy and the creation of a 'civil society' by strengthening institutions and organizations operating outside state control. Voronin was initially broadly pro-Russian (Russian language lessons having being reintroduced as compulsory in Moldovan schools), but his government later made a fundamental policy change and adopted a pro-European Union position. At the March 2005 parliamentary elections the PCRM was returned to power but with a reduced majority and Voronin was re-elected as president the following month.

In an attempt to resolve the thorny Transnistria issue, a federal system was proposed in 2002 under which Transnistria and the Turkic enclave of Gagauz Yeri would enjoy constitutional autonomy. However, in the face of violent popular protest, the Moldovan government backed down in Nov. 2003. Then, in a referendum in the breakaway province in Sept. 2006, voters overwhelmingly backed independence and ultimately union with Russia. However, the poll was not recognized by the Moldovan government or the international community. Meanwhile, despite Voronin's repeated calls for their departure, Russian military forces remained in Transnistria. Relations with Russia were further soured by Russian demands in 2006 for large rises in prices of natural gas supplies to Moldova and the suspension of imports of Moldovan wine, reportedly on health grounds. Moldova continued to face economic problems in the agriculture sector because of harvest failure and drought and from the widening trade deficit with Russia.

In March 2008, following Prime Minister Vasile Tarlev's resignation, Voronin nominated Zinaida Greceanîi, also from the PCRM, as the country's first female premier.

Voronin was not eligible to stand for a third term in office but retained the presidency on an acting basis following disputed elections in April 2009. The results prompted outbreaks of civil unrest across the country with claims that the elections were fraudulent. The PCRM won the majority of the vote but did not gain enough seats to elect a president of their choosing. In May Voronin was elected speaker of parliament but was forced to dissolve parliament over the presidential issue and schedule more elections for July. The PCRM again received the most votes of any single party but were beaten into second place after the opposition formed a coalition in Aug. Although a new parliamentary speaker was elected to replace Voronin, the coalition lacked enough seats to appoint their own presidential candidate. However, conceding defeat, Voronin stood down on 11 Sept. and the new speaker of parliament, Mihai Ghimpu, took over in an acting capacity.

Vranitzky, Franz (Austria)

Introduction

Franz Vranitzky was chancellor of Austria and leader of the Social Democratic Party (SPÖ) from 1986–97. He oversaw Austria's accession to the European Union from 1995, and helped to restore the country's international image after the presidency of Kurt Waldheim. His earlier banking career led the media to label him 'the pin-striped socialist'.

Early Life

Vranitzky was born on 4 Oct. 1937 in Vienna and educated in the capital, graduating from the University of Commerce in 1960. Following a brief period in industry, he joined the Austrian National Bank in 1961. From 1970–76 he served as a policy adviser to the federal minister of finance, and from 1976–81 as deputy chairman of the board of directors of Creditanstalt-Bankverein. He then became the head of the Österreichische Landerbank (then the second largest Austrian bank) until his appointment in 1984 as federal minister of finance.

Career Peak

Having become federal chancellor on 16 June 1986, Vranitzky presided over a series of SPÖ coalitions with the conservative People's Party (ÖVP) during his decade in office. He was credited in his first 4 years with an upswing in the national economy, and then campaigned successfully for Austria's accession to the EU. This was approved by a two-thirds majority in a national referendum in June 1994 and formalized on 1 Jan. 1995. However, economic conditions subsequently worsened as the government wrestled with a large budget deficit. Despite better than expected federal election results for the SPÖ in Dec. 1995, the party slumped in the first direct elections to the European Parliament in Oct. 1996. Vranitzky resigned as chancellor in Jan. 1997 and was succeeded by Viktor Klima, who also took over the SPÖ chairmanship the following April.

Vujanović, Filip (Montenegro)

Introduction

Filip Vujanović became Montenegro's president following independence in June 2006. He had served as president of Montenegro within the confederation of Serbia and Montenegro for the previous 3 years. Economic and structural reforms have included a programme of privatization, while closer links have been pursued with the European Union including an official application for EU membership. During his presidency, Montenegro also joined the North Atlantic Treaty Organization (NATO). Vujanović left office in May 2018.

Early Life

Born on 1 Sept. 1954 in Belgrade, then the capital of Yugoslavia, Vujanović was educated in Nikšić and studied law at the University of Belgrade. After graduating in 1978 he worked as a court official in Belgrade before moving south to Podgorica in 1981.

Following a period at the Podgorica district court, Vujanović worked as an attorney from 1981–93. After the break-up of the Yugoslav Federation, Serbia and Montenegro formed the Federal Republic of Yugoslavia in 1992. In March 1993 the Montenegrin Prime Minister Đukanović appointed Vujanović as minister for justice. He served for 2 years as a close ally of Đukanović, adopting a pro-independence and pro-European stance, and in May 1995 he took over as minister of the interior. When the ruling Democratic Party of Socialists of Montenegro (DPS CG) split into two factions in 1996, Vujanović backed Đukanović against his rival Momir Bulatović, a former ally of Serbian leader Slobodan Milošević.

In 1997 Đukanović was elected president of Montenegro and in Feb. 1998 Vujanović took up the premiership. While supporting Montenegro's independence campaign, he maintained good relations with Serbia. He offered his resignation in April 2002 during a constitutional crisis over ratification of a looser federation between Serbia and Montenegro.

Following legislative elections in Oct. 2002 Vujanović was appointed parliamentary speaker and stood as the DPS CG candidate for Montenegro's presidency. He won both rounds in Dec. 2002 and Feb. 2003 convincingly, but the result was declared invalid as less than 50% of the electorate voted. Parliament subsequently abolished the minimum turnout rule and Vujanović became president in March 2003 with 63% of the vote.

Career Peak

Vujanović identified Montenegro's integration into Western political and military structures through accession to the EU and entry into NATO's Partnership for Peace programme as priorities. He oversaw the privatization of key parts of the economy, including the banking sector and Kombinat Aluminijuma Podgorica (the country's largest industrial company), introduced social and judicial reforms and made a start in combating organized crime. He also opened cross-border talks on joint commercial ventures with Croatia, Slovenia and Serbia.

On 3 June 2006, following a referendum, Montenegro declared independence and on 28 June 2006 became a member of the United Nations. The country has since joined the World Bank and International Monetary Fund, and in Dec. 2008 submitted a formal application to join the EU (achieving candidate status in Dec. 2010). Its decision in Jan. 2010 to establish diplomatic relations with Kosovo, which had unilaterally declared itself independent from Serbia in 2008, has aggravated tensions with the Serbian government.

Vujanović was re-elected for a further 5-year term in April 2008. In Dec. 2010 he nominated Igor Lukšić as prime minister following the resignation of Đukanović, but following parliamentary elections in Oct. 2012 Đukanović resumed the premiership at the head of a centre-left coalition. Vujanović narrowly secured a third term at the presidential election held in April 2013, defeating Miodrag Lekić of the Democratic Front.

Although the DPS CG again won the most seats in parliamentary elections in Oct. 2016, Đukanović shortly afterwards announced his resignation as prime minister. Vujanović named Duško Marković, previously a deputy premier, as prime minister-designate and his new government was approved by parliament at the end of Nov. that year.

In June 2017 Montenegro became the 29th full member of the NATO alliance.

Vujanović served as president for 16 years and was the longest-serving president of Montenegro since the country's independence. He was succeeded in May 2018 by Milo Đjukanović.

Wa Mutharika, Bingu (Malaŵi)

Introduction

Dr. Bingu wa Mutharika became president of Malaŵi following elections in May 2004, having been nominated by former president (and his former political foe), Bakili Muluzi, who retired after two consecutive terms in office. He was re-elected in May 2009. Mutharika died of a heart attack whilst in office in April 2012.

Early Life

Bingu wa Mutharika was born in Thyolo, Malaŵi on 24 Feb. 1934. The son of a Catholic primary school teacher, he gained a master's degree in economics from the University of Delhi, India, before studying for a PhD in development economics at Pacific Western University in Los Angeles, USA. He then went to work for the Malaŵian civil service and later for the Zambian government.

In 1978 Mutharika joined the UN, motivated by his opposition to the regime of Hastings Banda, Malaŵi's self-declared 'President for Life'. He was given the post of director for trade and development finance for Africa. In 1991 he became secretary-general of the Common Market for Eastern and Southern Africa (COMESA).

Mutharika was a founding member of the United Democratic Front (UDF), the party led by Muluzi that went on to win Malaŵi's first multiparty elections in 1994. The two became adversaries when Mutharika opposed Muluzi's economic policies. Mutharika left the UDF to form the United Party (UP) in 1997. However, after unsuccessfully contesting the presidency in 1999, he disbanded the UP and returned to the UDF, where he was made minister of economic planning and development in 2002.

Career Peak

In Feb. 2005, following a series of clashes with Muluzi and an alleged assassination attempt in Jan. by UDF members, Mutharika again resigned from the party, subsequently forming the Democratic Progressive Party (DPP). In June 2005 he survived an impeachment motion backed by the UDF. In April 2006 Vice President Chilumpha was charged with treason and in July Muluzi was arrested on corruption charges. In May 2008 several opposition figures were arrested after Mutharika accused Muluzi of plotting to overthrow him. Mutharika retained power following elections in May 2009 in which he received 66% of the vote in the presidential poll and his DPP secured 114 of the 193 seats in the National Assembly. However, external electoral observers were critical of the government's use of state-controlled radio and television to obtain unfair advantage, and in May 2011 the British High Commissioner was expelled from Malaŵi after he criticized Mutharika as increasingly dictatorial in a leaked diplomatic cable.

Mutharika's principal economic challenges in office have remained the reduction of poverty and regeneration by encouraging foreign investment. He has also pursued a high-profile anti-corruption campaign. In May 2010 he granted a presidential pardon to two homosexual men whose earlier conviction for gross indecency had provoked international condemnation.

Internationally, in Jan. 2008 he ended diplomatic ties with Taiwan and switched Malawi's allegiance to communist China.

On 5 April 2012 Mutharika suffered a heart attack and died in hospital 2 days later, aged 78. In line with the constitution, vice president Joyce Banda was sworn in as his successor.

Wade, Abdoulaye (Senegal)

Introduction

A barrister, writer and newspaper editor, Abdoulaye Wade spent nearly 40 years in opposition before becoming president at his fifth attempt in 2000. His election marked the end of Senegal's socialist era. He was re-elected in Feb. 2007 but his controversial bid for a third term proved unsuccessful, losing to former prime minister Macky Sall in a run-off in March 2012.

Early Life

Wade was born on 29 May 1926, in Kébémer. He was educated in Senegal and at the Sorbonne in Paris, France, where he studied law and economics. After practising as a barrister in France for some years, he returned to Senegal to take up an academic post at the University of Dakar.

In 1974 he created the liberal Parti Démocratique Sénégalais (PDS; Senegalese Democratic Party), one of the three parties allowed under the 1976 constitution. He unsuccessfully stood as a presidential candidate in the 1978 elections against Léopold Sédar Senghor. In the same year he entered the National Assembly.

He lost the 1988 presidential race against Abdou Diouf. The latter accused Wade of inflaming riots with his claims of election fraud and Wade was arrested. He spent several months in prison while Diouf declared a state of emergency. However, following his release Wade was appointed a minister in Diouf's government in 1991. He resigned the following year and in 1993 once more stood unsuccessfully for the presidency. He joined Diouf's government again in March 1995, resigning 3 years later.

By 2000 public dissatisfaction with Diouf's leadership was running high, yet he emerged with most votes after the first round of a presidential poll against Wade and six other candidates. Diouf and Wade went into a run-off, and Wade, benefiting from the absence of the other candidates (particularly Moustapha Niasse), won 58.5% of the vote. He was sworn in as the new president on 1 April 2000 and formed a coalition government with Niasse as prime minister.

Career Peak

Wade's election promises included boosting the economy and confronting growing poverty, while raising literacy and health levels. However, attempts to implement necessary reforms were hampered by Senegal's crippling levels of international debt. In addition, Wade's popular standing was diminished by the resignation of Niasse in 2001, on whom he had relied for electoral victory. Nevertheless, his coalition won almost 75% of National Assembly seats in the 2001 elections. In Nov. 2002 Wade dismissed Prime Minister Madior Boye (who on her appointment was Africa's only female leader) and her entire cabinet, replacing her with Idrissa Seck. He in turn was replaced in April 2004 by Macky Sall of the PDS (and subsequently detained from July 2005 until Feb. 2006 on charges of fraud and sedition). In April 2005, 14 PDS deputies in the National Assembly defected, protesting an increasing lack of democracy and transparency.

Negotiations between the government and the Casamance movement culminated in a ceasefire in 2004 and the signing of a peace agreement in 2005.

Wade was closely involved in the launch of the New Partnership for Africa's Development (NEPAD), an African-led strategy (endorsed by the then Organization of African Unity in July 2001) for economic recovery, good governance and sustainable growth.

He was elected to a further term in the presidential election of Feb. 2007 and his ruling coalition increased its majority in legislative elections the following June, with Cheikh Hadjibou Soumaré replacing Macky Sall as prime minister. However, the parliamentary poll was boycotted by the main opposition parties. In local elections in March 2009 opposition parties made substantial gains, prompting the resignation of Soumaré as prime minister and his replacement by Souleymane Ndéné Ndiaye in April. In April 2010 Senegal marked 50 years of independence from France.

Wade's acceptance of his party's nomination to seek a third term in the Feb. 2012 presidential elections provoked violent opposition protests as the constitution does not allow for a president to serve more than two terms. However, a court ruling found in favour of Wade running for re-election on the grounds that the constitution was promulgated in 2001, a year after his first term began. Wade failed to win a majority in the first round of the elections and subsequently lost to the opposition candidate Macky Sall in a run-off in March 2012. Sall succeeded Wade on 2 April 2012.

Waheed Hassan, Mohammed (Maldives)

Introduction

Mohammed Waheed Hassan took office as president in Feb. 2012 after incumbent Mohamed Nasheed's resignation following public protests over the arrest of a senior judge. Waheed, formerly Nasheed's deputy, was defeated in the second round of the Nov. 2013 presidential election although he had won the most votes in the re-run first round.

Early Life

Mohammed Waheed Hassan was born on 3 Jan. 1953 in the capital, Malé. He graduated in English Language and gained a diploma in teaching from the American University of Beirut in 1976, before returning to Malé to teach. In 1978 he became the first anchor on Maldivian television with TVM (Television Maldives).

Waheed won a scholarship to Stanford University, California, where he completed a master's degree in education planning in 1979. He joined the Maldivian ministry of education and in 1980 was appointed by President Gayoom as an adviser to a special session of the Majlis (parliament) tasked with reviewing the constitution.

In 1982 Waheed returned to Stanford to study political science. In 1987 he was awarded his PhD in international development education. In 1988 he was appointed director of educational services at the ministry of education and in 1989 won the seat of Malé in the general election. Having resigned over the poor human rights record of Gayoom's government, he left the Maldives in 1991 to work as a freelance consultant with the UN on educational development programmes.

In 2008 he set up the Gaumee Itthihaad party, which formed the 'MDP Itthihaad' with the Maldivian Democratic Party (MDP) to contest the 2008 elections. The coalition emerged victorious and on 11 Nov. 2008 Nasheed—a co-founder of the MDP in 2003—and Waheed were sworn into office as president and vice-president respectively. On 7 Feb. 2012 Nasheed resigned amid growing public unrest following his arrest of the chief justice, Abdullah Mohamed. Waheed was sworn in as president later that day, leading an administration consisting largely of technocrats and Gayoom appointees.

Career Peak

Waheed's first task was to rebut Nasheed's claim that his successor helped organize his removal from office. Waheed denied the charge but Nasheed's supporters have continued to protest and demand early elections. Waheed appealed to the international community for support and in Aug. 2012 a Commonwealth-backed commission dismissed Nasheed's assertion that he had been ousted in a coup and confirmed the constitutional legitimacy of the transfer of power. In Oct. Nasheed was arrested for defying a summons to stand trial for the arrest of the chief justice, which had triggered the crisis in Feb.

In the presidential elections held in Nov. 2013 (after an annulled election 2 months earlier) Waheed was defeated in the run-off by Abdulla Yameen of the Progressive Party of Maldives. Yameen succeeded Waheed as president on 17 Nov. 2013.

Waldheim, Kurt (Austria)

Introduction

Kurt Waldheim was secretary general of the United Nations between 1972 and 1981 and president of Austria, 1986–92. Renowned as a diplomat, he gained notoriety during the 1986 presidential election when allegations were made about his involvement in Nazi war atrocities. He was cleared by an international commission and won the presidency, but the allegations blighted his tenure and he did not run again in 1992.

Early Life

Waldheim was born in Sankt Andrä-Wörden in Lower Austria on 21 Dec. 1918, the son of a Catholic Czech civil servant. In 1937–38 he was in the Austrian army before undertaking studies at the Vienna Consular Academy. He then began studying for a degree in jurisprudence at the University of Vienna but his studies were interrupted when he was drafted into the German army. Fighting on the Russian front in 1941, he was wounded and it was the subsequent period of his life that was at the centre of later allegations against him.

He eventually finished his legal studies at the University of Vienna. In 1945, with Austria regarded as an unwilling partner to Germany's actions, Waldheim entered the Diplomatic Service. For 2 years he served with the Austrian delegation to the Austrian State Treaty negotiations. He was first secretary of the Austrian delegation in Paris between 1948 and 1951 and followed this with a period as chief of the department of personnel at the ministry of foreign affairs in Vienna until 1955. In 1955–56 he was Austria's permanent observer to the UN, then minister plenipotentiary to Canada (based in Ottawa) for 2 years and ambassador to Canada for a further two.

From 1960–64 he worked again at the ministry of foreign affairs, as chief of the political department (West) until 1962 and then as director-general for political affairs. He was Austria's ambassador to the UN, 1964–68, when he worked on the exploration and peaceful uses of outer space. Between Jan. 1968 and April 1970 he was minister of foreign affairs in the government of Josef Klaus, but left the post following the collapse of Klaus' administration. In April of the following year he stood for the national presidency on behalf of the conservative People's Party but was defeated.

In 1972 he was appointed UN secretary-general, a post he held for over 9 years. His tenure saw humanitarian projects in Bangladesh, Guatemala and Nicaragua. He actively pursued Middle East peace, making visits to Israel, Egypt, Jordan, Syria and Lebanon. He oversaw peacekeeping operations in Cyprus, visiting the country three times, and in Guinea, Yemen and Angola. His re-election in 1976 was opposed by a number of Third World nations but he secured re-appointment. He was defeated in 1981 by a Chinese veto. The following year he took up a professorship at Georgetown University in Washington, D.C.

In 1986 he once again stood as the People's Party's candidate for the Austrian presidency. During the election campaign the opposition made claims about Waldheim's war record. His history after his wounding in 1941 up until the end of the war had been hazy and his opponents produced documentation that suggested he had known of and been involved in Nazi war atrocities. As a counter-intelligence officer for General Alexander Löhr until the latter stages of the war, it was alleged that Waldheim had taken part in vicious reprisals against dissidents in Yugoslavia and had then participated in the mass deportation to concentration camps of Jews from Thessaloniki in Greece. This contrasted with Waldheim's version that he had returned to his studies in Austria following his discharge from the Eastern Front. An international commission judged in his favour but was critical of his lack of candidness about this period of his life.

Career Peak

Waldheim subsequently became Austria's first non-Socialist president since the war. However, Austria found it difficult to assert influence in the international arena with Waldheim as its head of government. He served out his 6-year term but did not stand for re-election in 1992. He died aged 88 on 14 June 2007.

Wałęsa, Lech (Poland)

Introduction

Lech Wałęsa led the Solidarity movement in Poland which precipitated the collapse of the country's communist regime. He served as president from 1990 until 1995. A Gdańsk electrician, he fought for workers rights during the 1970s and early 1980s. Solidarity, a nationwide workers' alliance, came into being in 1980 and, despite government attempts to supress it, its membership grew to 10 m. Wałęsa's role in the downfall of Polish communism is regarded as key to the subsequent collapse of communism in the rest of the Eastern Bloc.

Early Life

Wałęsa was born on 29 Sept. 1943 in Popowo, Poland into a poor farming background. His father was held in a concentration camp during World War II and died shortly after his liberation in 1945. Wałęsa attended vocational school and became a farm machinary mechanic until entering the military in 1961. He left the army in 1967 and moved to Gdańsk, where he became an electrician in the Lenin Shipyard.

Wałęsa had his first taste of political life during the 1970 Gdańsk riots when workers protested at rises in food prices. Gdańsk witnessed more anti-government strikes in 1976. As one of the leaders Wałęsa was arrested and sacked from his job. More protests broke out in 1980 with workers barracading themselves in the Lenin Shipyard. Wałęsa climbed the yard's fences to join his former colleagues who designated him their leader.

Taking their cue from the Workers' Defence Committee (KOR), founded during the 1976 strikes, the 17,000 Gdańsk strikers presented the government with a Charter of Workers' Rights in Aug. 1980. The government granted the right to strike and loosened restrictions on the freedom of expression. A meeting in Gdańsk of regional trade union leaders led to the founding of Solidarity (*Solidarność*) on 22 Sept. By early 1981, under the leadership of Wałęsa, Solidarity boasted a membership of over 10 m.

As Solidarity's strength grew there were calls for free elections and trade union rights. Facing extreme pressure from Moscow, President Jaruzelski imposed martial law in Dec. 1981. Solidarity lost its legal status and its leadership, including Wałęsa, was arrested and imprisoned. Solidarity was severely weakened as a political force over the following year. However, it was revitalized in 1983 when Wałęsa was awarded the Nobel Peace Prize, to the anger of the Polish government.

Career Peak

Wałęsa led Solidarity as an underground movement for much of the 1980s. However, in 1988 President Jaruzelski's attempts to impose economic reforms precipitated an increase in labour unrest. The government agreed to negotiations with Wałęsa and the Solidarity leadership as well as the influential Catholic Church, in what became known as the Round Table talks. Solidarity was once more guaranteed legal status and the government agreed to free elections, with the proviso that the opposition contest only a minority of seats.

In the elections of June 1989 Solidarity won a convincing victory, taking virtually all the seats to which it was entitled. The communists attempted to form a coalition with Solidarity but Wałęsa refused and Jaruzelski had little option but to appoint Wałęsa's associate, Tadeusz Mazowiecki, as Prime Minister. Wałęsa stood against Mazowiecki in the presidential elections of 1990 and won by a landslide.

Wałęsa set about reforming the Polish economy and oversaw the transition to a free market economy, a job made more difficult by a succession of weak and short-lived parliaments. Despite severe struggles during most of Wałęsa's period in office, the Polish economy prospered. However, Wałęsa's popular appeal diminished as his tenure progressed. His skills as Solidarity's leader revolved around his ability to speak for the common people, but in government his tone was often regarded as aggressive and his style of leadership autocratic. His critics also accused him of jingoism and he lost further popularity when, as a devout Catholic, he tightened up laws on abortion. At the presidential elections of 1995 Wałęsa narrowly lost to

Aleksander Kwaśniewski, leader of the Democratic Left Alliance, a grouping of reconstituted communists.

Later Life

Following his presidential defeat, Wałęsa was reluctant to withdraw from the political scene. In Aug. 2000 he faced a Polish court charged with cooperating with the secret police during the communist era. He was acquitted on all charges, paving the way for him to stand at the elections of Oct. 2000. Kwaśniewski was re-elected by a majority with Wałęsa coming in a distant sixth with 1% of the vote. Wałęsa subsequently announced his retirement from political life.

In May 2004 Gdańsk International Airport was officially renamed Gdańsk Lech Wałęsa Airport. Wałęsa left the Solidarity movement in Aug. 2006 owing to his disapproval of the party's leadership under the Kaczyński brothers. He launched a libel suit against Lech Kaczyński after the latter repeated allegations that Wałęsa had worked as a communist spy.

Wangchuk, Jigme Singye (Bhutan)

Introduction

Jigme Singye Wangchuk became king of Bhutan in 1972, ruling as an absolute monarch until his abdication in Dec. 2006. He partially opened up the country to foreign influence, but strove at the same time to preserve traditional Bhutanese ways of life. In 1998 he devolved some of his powers to the National Assembly and a ministerial cabinet. A draft constitution, published in March 2005, proposed to make the country a parliamentary democracy with a constitutional monarchy, though practical power was to remain with the throne. Jigme Singye's reign was accompanied by international unease about the treatment of the nation's ethnic Nepalese minority.

Early Life

Jigme Singye was born on 11 Nov. 1955, the son of King Jigme Dorji Wangchuck. He was educated in the UK and India before attending the Ugyen Wangchuck Academy in Paro. Jigme Dorji died in July 1972 and Jigme Singye succeeded him, although his formal coronation did not take place until 2 June 1974.

Career Peak

Taking the title of Druk Gyalpo (Dragon King), Jigme Singye continued the cautious modernization of Bhutan begun by his father. This included the admission of foreign tourists for the first time in 1974, although tourist numbers remain restricted. This gradual opening-up was accompanied by a determination to maintain Bhutanese customs, as epitomized by the legal requirement that citizens wear traditional dress. In 1979, the year in which Jigme Singye married four sisters as queens, the government declared that refugees must take Bhutanese citizenship or face repatriation. The move marked the beginning of a steady decline in relations between the government and ethnic minorities.

In 1986 new legislation laid down terms for citizenship on the basis of length of residency. A national census in 1988 declared thousands of people, mostly ethnic Nepalese who had been resident for up to 20 years, to be illegal immigrants. The following year Nepali ceased to be a standard language of tuition in schools. Ethnic tensions spilled into violence in the south of the country in the early 1990s, and thousands of ethnic Nepalese crossed the border into eastern Nepal where they remain in refugee camps, their fate still unresolved. Bhutan demanded the repatriation of anyone proven to be a Bhutanese national but denied that to be the case for most of those in the camps. Refugee leaders, however, claimed that Jigme Singye's regime forcibly removed the majority of the displaced people.

In 1998 the King ceded some of his power, theoretically allowing the National Assembly to dethrone him with a two-thirds majority. The following year he permitted television and Internet access for the first time.

In early 2005 proposals were published for the adoption of a parliamentary democracy with a constitutional monarchy by 2008. In Sept. 2006 plans were announced for a two-phase election. There was to be no restriction on those allowed to vote and any number of candidates were to be permitted in the first round of voting, although only the two leading parties would contest the second round. It was expected that the King would abdicate in favour of his son, Jigme Khesar Namgyel Wangchuk, at the time of the elections but on 14 Dec. 2006 Jigme Singye transferred power to his son with immediate effect.

Jigme Singye oversaw Bhutan's entry into numerous international organizations including the IMF, the FAO, the WHO, UNESCO, UNIDO and ECOSOC.

Wen Jiabao (China)

Introduction

Wen Jiabao was confirmed as China's Premier of the State Council (prime minister) in March 2003. Although relatively low-profile, he has established a reputation for reliability and durability. A leading figure in the liberalization of China's economic and environmental policies in the 1990s, he has promoted the development of the traditionally poorer and less urban west of the country.

Early Life

Wen Jiabao was born in Tianjin in the east of China in Sept. 1942. In 1965 he obtained a degree from the Beijing Institute of Geology and joined the Chinese Communist Party (CCP). In 1968 he received his master's degree and began working with the geomechanics survey team at the Gansu provincial geological bureau (until 1982).

Wen then moved to Beijing to work at the ministry of geology and mineral resources. After heading the policy and research section he was appointed vice-minister. In 1985 he was made deputy director of the general office of the CCP central committee, working closely with the party chairman, Hu Yaobang. Wen emerged unscathed after Hu's 1987 purge and took over as director of the general office as well as becoming an alternate member of the Politburo of the CCP central committee and secretary of the central committee's work committee of departments.

In 1989 Wen was in attendance when General Secretary Zhao Ziyang visited Tiananmen Square during the student protests. Zhao was subsequently purged, but again Wen's position remained secure. In 1992 he took on additional roles within the CCP central committee. Having led the team responsible for drafting the national 5-year plan in 1995, Wen won full membership of the Politburo of the central committee 2 years later.

Throughout the 1990s Wen was a prominent figure in the formation of the party's economic policy. He was involved in banking reform and the restructuring of the finance ministry. By the late 1990s he was increasingly involved in environmental and rural affairs. In March 2003 Wen was confirmed as Zhu Rhongji's successor to the premiership with 99.3% support from the National People's Congress.

Career Peak

Although perceived as less charismatic than Zhu, Wen has won respect within the Chinese political establishment for his longevity and experience. His management style has traditionally been based on seeking consensus.

When he was in Gansu, Wen became one of the few leading Chinese politicians to work for an extended period in the economically less prosperous west of the country. He stated that his aim is to narrow the prosperity gap between the east and west of China. In addition, many observers hoped that he could confront the problems of China's economically weak agricultural sector. Under Jiang, Wen did much to promote the land rights of the rural peasant population. In addition, he has pushed for a reduction in the tax burden on rural communities and promoted freedom for farmers to sell their holdings.

Despite his contribution to banking reform in the 1990s, Wen was not expected to champion radical reforms to counter the crippling problem of bad debts. In 2002 he called for a 'gradual approach' to further deregulation and in 2003 he stated that China would not be pressured by the international community into a revaluation of the yuan (*renminbi*). Nevertheless, in July

2005 China did revalue the currency, abandoning its 11-year peg to the US dollar and linking it to a basket of currencies. In March 2010 Wen again resisted international pressure on China for further revaluation, branding it a form of 'trade protectionism'.

Wen's programme for assisting the rural poor took shape at the opening of the National People's Congress in March 2004. Stressing the importance of social development in poorer regions, he highlighted the damaging disparity in wealth between the rich, industrial coastal provinces and the poorer rural provinces of the interior. He promised investment in agriculture, emphasizing the need to increase overall grain production capability. His programme also included the recognition of private property, requiring an amendment to the constitution, designed to prevent the unlawful requisition of property by officials.

However, the government's slow reaction to SARS, originating in Guangdong in 2002 and 2003, was criticized by the international community as nearly 350 people died from the virus, despite quarantines and travel bans. Then the government was criticized for its attitude towards HIV/AIDS, prompting the health minister in 2004 to announce plans to combat the epidemic. Furthermore, in Sept. 2008 a scandal over tainted milk supplies, which caused around 50,000 children to fall ill, prompted a public apology by Wen.

In April 2007 Wen visited Japan and became the first Chinese premier to make a formal address to the Japanese legislature, in which he urged friendship and reconciliation after their countries' difficult shared history. Relations deteriorated, however, in Sept. and Oct. 2010 as Chinese fishermen were arrested off Japanese-controlled, but disputed, islands in the East China Sea.

Wen was re-elected for a further term in March 2008. In Nov. he disclosed that the effects of the global financial crisis on China were worse than had been expected, prompting the government to announce a US$586 bn. spending stimulus to boost the economy. Nevertheless, by the second quarter of 2010 official figures suggested that China had overtaken Japan as the world's second largest economy. Earlier, in March 2009, China's central bank called for a new global reserve currency run by the International Monetary Fund to replace the US dollar and Wen, while voicing his confidence in the Chinese economy, expressed concern over China's significant holdings of US government bonds.

In June 2011 Wen travelled to Hungary, the UK and Germany to sign trade and investment agreements, and said that China would lend investment support to countries in the eurozone struggling with sovereign debt.

Wen, like President Hu Jintao, stepped down in March 2013 and was succeeded by Li Keqiang.

Werner, Pierre (Luxembourg)

Introduction

Pierre Werner was prime minister for more than 20 years, serving from 1959–74 and again from 1979–84. The first politician to propose the introduction of a European single currency, he is known as 'the father of the euro'.

Early Life

Pierre Werner was born on 29 Dec. 1913 at Saint-André, near the Northern French town of Lille. He studied law in Luxembourg and at the University of Paris, and was awarded a diploma in economics and finance from the École Libre des Sciences Politiques. He achieved his PhD in law in 1938, beginning his career as a lawyer but working for the Banque Generale du Luxembourg during the Nazi occupation.

After the Second World War, Werner joined the ministry of finance as a civil servant. In 1945 he was appointed commissioner for banking control, with responsibility for banking regulation, the credit market and international financial collaboration. A member of the centre-right Christian Social People's Party (CSV), he was appointed minister of finance and minister of defence in 1953 and became the leader of the CSV in 1954. He succeeded Pierre Friedon as prime minister in March 1959 after leading the party to electoral victory.

Career Peak

Werner was a leading advocate for a common currency, believing that the economic problems of the 1920s and 1930s were the root cause of the Second World War and arguing that economic union was a way to prevent further conflict. Although the Treaty of Rome in 1957 had made reference to a single currency, it was Werner in a speech at Strasbourg in 1960 who called for the early adoption of a common currency, the 'Euror'.

In 1970 Werner was appointed chairman of the European Economic Community (EEC) and was tasked with reducing currency exchange rate volatility. The Werner Report, published later that year, proposed a three-stage process towards economic and monetary union and a single currency, to be completed by 1980. However, political disagreements, the collapse of the Bretton Woods fixed exchange rate system and the global oil crisis frustrated plans for a shared currency.

Werner was re-elected as premier in 1964, taking on the additional portfolios of foreign affairs and the treasury, and won a third term in 1969. However, in 1974 the CSV was defeated at the polls for the first time since its birth 30 years earlier and Werner was succeeded as premier by Gaston Thorn, who headed a Liberal–Socialist coalition. Werner led his party to electoral victory once again in June 1979, securing his fourth term as prime minister. The CSV was the biggest party at the 1984 elections but Werner chose the moment to retire from politics and was succeeded to the premiership by Jacques Santer.

Later Life

Werner subsequently pursued his business interests, serving as chairman of the Compagnie Luxembourgeoise de Télédiffusion (CLT) and of Société Européenne des Satellites, Europe's first private satellite operator.

As well as his pivotal role in the creation of the euro, Werner was also credited with helping transform Luxembourg into one of Western Europe's richest nations. As the steel industry declined in the late 1960s and 1970s, he was instrumental in developing the country as a leading international financial centre. He died on 24 June 2002, 6 months after the euro was launched. In 2003 the Pierre Werner Institute was created in Luxembourg to stimulate intellectual exchanges and promote research between European countries.

Whitlam, Gough (Australia)

Introduction

Gough Whitlam was Australia's Labor Prime Minister from 1972–75. He introduced major reforms in the welfare system, immigration and foreign policy but his tenure was blighted by scandals within his cabinet and in 1975 the Opposition failed to approve his finance bill. Faced with this impasse, he refused to call a general election. He was controversially sacked by Australia's Governor-General, an act unprecedented in Australian history.

Early Life

Edward Gough Whitlam was born on 11 July 1916 in Melbourne. His mother was Martha Maddocks and his father was Frederick Ernest Whitlam, a solicitor who was active in the drafting of the Universal Declaration of Human Rights. Whitlam graduated from the University of Sydney with a BA in 1938. He then served in the Royal Australian Air Force during the Second World War before completing a law degree from Sydney in 1946. In 1942 he married Margaret Dovey, with whom he had four children. Whitlam joined the Labor Party in 1945 and started practising as a barrister in New South Wales in 1947. He was defeated in state elections in 1950 but entered parliament as the representative for Werriwa 2 years later. In 1960 he became deputy leader of the party, a position he held until 1967. In that year he replaced Arthur Calwell as leader. Whitlam led Labor to defeat at elections for the House of Representatives in 1969 and for the Senate a year later. In 1972 he was victorious at House of Representative elections, becoming prime minister and ending Labor's 23 years in opposition.

Career Peak

Whitlam immediately embarked on a batch of radical reforms. Forming a two-man government for 2 weeks with his deputy, Lance Barnard, he withdrew Australia from Vietnam and ended conscription. With a cabinet elected by the parliamentary party, Whitlam abolished university fees, set up a Schools Commission, improved welfare provisions for single parents and the homeless, abolished the death penalty and lowered the voting age to 18. In addition, he increased funding for culture and public transport, made improvements to the universal health insurance scheme, promoted equal pay for women and men, relaxed restrictions on immigration from Asia and Africa and extended Aboriginal rights—thus eradicating the 'White Australia' policy. His foreign policy was similarly dynamic. He withdrew Australia's troops from Vietnam. Papua New Guinea was granted self government, then independence in Sept. 1975. The government hardened its line against the apartheid regime in South Africa. Meanwhile, Whitlam pursued closer relations with China, sought to lessen Australia's reliance on the USA and loosened ties with Britain. However, his attitude towards Indonesia and Portuguese Timor has been heavily criticized, especially since the release of confidential foreign affairs department papers in 2000. Having deemed Timor-Leste 'too small' for self-determination, it is alleged that Whitlam encouraged Indonesia's *Operasi Comodo* (an undercover destabilization operation). President Suharto ordered an invasion after the former colony declared its independence in Nov. 1975.

Whitlam's government was beset by rising unemployment and inflation and the effects of the world oil crises. In 1974 he called elections for both houses and won a majority in the House of Representatives but not the Senate. A high profile loans scandal broke in 1975 when it was revealed that Rex Connor and Dr. Jim Cairns, senior members of the government, had unconstitutionally attempted to secure $A2 bn. in foreign loans to assist the government's work. A further scandal concerning Cairns and his secretary soon followed. Lacking the support of the Senate, Whitlam was unable to gain parliamentary approval for his finance bill. The stalemate in Oct. 1975 resulted in a complex constitutional problem that was still unresolved when Whitlam met Governor-General Sir John Kerr, the titular head of state, who had been nominated for the position by Whitlam. Kerr encouraged Whitlam to break the deadlock by calling a general election but Whitlam refused. Kerr dismissed him from his post and appointed Liberal Malcolm Fraser as his interim successor. That an unelected head of state should be able to remove a democratically elected prime minister caused a constitutional crisis.

Later Life

Whitlam remained Labor leader but the party lost the election in Dec. 1975 and again in 1977. He resigned from politics in July 1978. He has held various academic positions and maintained a presence on the international political scene. In 1983 he was appointed by Bob Hawke as Australia's Ambassador to UNESCO and between 1986–91 sat on the Australia–China Council. He has published several books including a memoir of his time in government.

Whitlam died on 21 Oct. 2014 at an aged-care facility aged 98. At the time of his death, he ranked as Australia's longest-living former prime minister ever.

elected at the July 1960 legislative elections to represent the Kalutara district, Horana for the People's United Front alliance. Sirimavo Bandaranaike led the SLFP to victory at that time and became the world's first female prime minister.

Wickremanayake joined the SLFP in 1962 and became deputy minister for justice following the parliamentary elections of May 1970. The government increased state involvement in the economy, but anger at the slow pace of reforms triggered an armed rebellion by the Marxist People's Liberation Front (JVP) in April 1971. The uprising was crushed but spiralling inflation (partly caused by rapidly rising oil prices), high unemployment and a growing trade deficit followed, and the SLFP suffered a humiliating defeat to the United National Party (UNP) in the elections of July 1977.

Wickremanayake was promoted to general secretary of the SLFP in 1977, although Bandaranaike remained party leader. The SLFP was returned to power in Aug. 1994 as the principal party of the People's Alliance (PA) and Wickremanayake was appointed minister of public administration, home affairs and plantation industries. He also served as leader of the house in the cabinet of the new president, Chandrika Kumaratunga, the daughter of Bandaranaike. The government attempted to broker peace with the LTTE but the war intensified after April 1995.

Wickremanayake became prime minister in Aug. 2000 after the resignation of Bandaranaike and headed a minority SLFP government supported by the JVP until Oct. 2001, when it became apparent that the government was about to lose a no-confidence motion. While prime minister, Wickremanayake spurned suggestions of compromise with the LTTE. He was then leader of the opposition until he made way for Mahinda Rajapaksa in April 2002. Following the victory of the United People's Freedom Alliance (UPFA—which included the SLFP and the JVP) in elections that followed Kumaratunga's sacking of the UNP government in Feb. 2004, Wickremanayake was appointed minister of Buddhist affairs, public security, and law and order, and deputy minister for defence. He held these posts until the new president (and former prime minister), Rajapaksa, appointed him prime minister in 2005.

Career Peak

Wickremanayake's appointment reinforced President Rajapaksa's hardline stance on any future peace negotiations with the LTTE. There followed an intensification of violence between the Tamils and government forces despite token adherence to the 2002 ceasefire. By the end of 2006 the government had reintroduced sweeping anti-terrorism measures and in Jan. 2008 it formally annulled the ceasefire. Government military action against the LTTE escalated in 2008 and registered increasing territorial gains, leading Wickremanayake to state in Feb. 2009 that the government had entered 'the final phase of eradicating terrorism'. Following the defeat of the LTTE in May, he pledged to root out any remnants of rebel militancy. Following parliamentary elections in April 2010 in which the United People's Freedom Alliance again secured a strong majority, President Mahinda Rajapaksa appointed D. M. Jayaratne prime minister. Wickremanayake left office on 21 April. He died aged 83 on 27 Dec. 2016.

Wickremanayake, Ratnasiri (Sri Lanka)

Introduction

Ratnasiri Wickremanayake, from the leftist Sri Lanka Freedom Party (SLFP), was unexpectedly returned to the largely ceremonial office of prime minister in Nov. 2005 by the new executive president, Mahinda Rajapaksa. Known as a hardliner, he advocated that the Liberation Tigers of Tamil Eelam (LTTE), who had waged a separatist ethnic insurgency from 1972, should be militarily defeated, an objective that was finally achieved in May 2009. He was succeeded in April 2010 by D. M. Jayaratne.

Early Life

Ratnasiri Wickremanayake was born in southern Ceylon on 5 May 1933. He was educated at Ananda College, Colombo and studied law in London during the 1950s before entering politics. Following his return to Sri Lanka, he was

Wilson, Harold (United Kingdom of Great Britain and Northern Ireland)

Introduction

James Harold Wilson was British Labour prime minister from 1964–70 and 1974–76. A wily political manipulator, he managed to govern with wafer thin majorities. His terms of office were plagued by economic problems and serious divisions within the ranks of the Labour Party. His most significant achievement was ensuring the Labour Party remained unified while under his leadership.

Early Life

He was born on 11 March 1916 in Huddersfield, Yorkshire in the north of England. His father was an industrial chemist and his mother a schoolteacher.

Wilson was educated at Wirral Grammar School (he would become the first British prime minister educated at state school) before gaining a First in Politics, Philosophy and Economics from Jesus College, Oxford. While at Oxford he was a member of the Liberal Club (but not the Labour Club) and, unusually for a prime minister in the making, he played no role in the Oxford Union. By 1938 he had become a Fellow of University College, Oxford and went on to work with Sir William Beveridge on the report that would lay the foundations for the welfare reforms of Clement Attlee's premiership.

Wilson joined the civil service during World War II and became director of economics and statistics for the ministry of fuel and power, his *New Deal for Coal* report paving the way for the post-war nationalization of mining. In 1940 he had married Mary Baldwin, with whom he had two children. He was awarded an OBE in 1945, briefly returning to academe before entering the House of Commons as the member for Ormskirk, an area of Merseyside. Electoral changes meant his constituency evolved into Huyton, the area he served until his retirement from the Commons. In 1947, at 31 years of age, he was appointed president of the board of trade, the youngest cabinet minister since the eighteenth century. However, disappointed at proposed welfare cuts and increased defence spending, he resigned in 1951.

During 1955–59 he was opposition spokesman on economic affairs and in 1960 he unsuccessfully challenged Hugh Gaitskill for the party leadership. He failed too in his bid for the deputy leadership. A year later he was shadow spokesman for foreign affairs and in 1963 he again challenged for the leadership, following the sudden death of Gaitskill. His opponents were deputy leader George Brown and future prime minister James Callaghan. Callaghan was knocked out in the first ballot and Wilson won the second by a narrow margin. He led Labour to victory in the general election of 1964, though with a majority of just five.

Career Peak

Hopes were high that Wilson's tenure would see a dramatic change in the social and economic landscape. He had told the 1963 Labour Conference that 'we are redefining…our socialism in terms of the scientific revolution…the Britain that is going to be forged in the white heat of this revolution will be no place for restrictive practices or outdated methods on either side of industry'. Wilson returned to the polls in 1966 and won an increased majority but the 'revolution' was already faltering. The *National Plan*, devised by the new Department of Economic Affairs, did not have the expected impact and in 1966 the economy was further hit by a seamen's strike, against which Wilson stood firm leading to charges of betrayal by the Labour left. He then took the unpopular step of enforcing a general wage freeze to be followed by wage controls, and on 18 Nov. 1967 he reluctantly gave permission for the devaluation of sterling.

1969 saw his government backtrack on proposed Lords' reform, and similarly Barbara Castle's *In Place of Strife* trade union reforms were not followed through. The economy struggled, unemployment rose and strike action increased, resulting in a Conservative victory at the general election of 18 June 1970. At the next election in Feb. 1974 the Conservatives won the largest number of seats of any party but failed to secure an absolute majority. When the Liberals rejected a Liberal-Conservative coalition, Wilson stepped in to hold power until a second election in Oct. of the same year saw him establish a majority of three.

Though Wilson's governments were not as reformist as supporters had hoped, there were a number of significant pieces of legislation passed during his terms in office. The Open University and comprehensive schools were established, the voting age was reduced to 18, the death penalty abolished and laws governing divorce, homosexuality and abortion reformed. In terms of foreign policy, he believed Britain still had a crucial role on the world stage. In his first term, without committing British forces, he supported US action in Vietnam, a stance unpopular with many on the Labour left, and his support for the Nigerian government during the Nigerian civil war was to further dilute his popularity among some Labour members. In 1965 he was faced with Ian Smith's illegal declaration of independence in the British colony of Rhodesia (now Zimbabwe). Wilson imposed economic sanctions, rather than military force, but they were ineffective and a negotiated settlement was not achieved until the 1980s. In addition, sectarian violence in Northern Ireland had been on the increase throughout the 1960s and 1970s. Direct British rule had been imposed by Heath's government in 1972 between Wilson's two tenures, but neither the Conservatives nor Labour made any discernible progress in pursuit of peace. The question of Britain's role within the European Economic Community also proved a considerable problem for Wilson, dangerously splitting his own party. However, in a bid to prove public support for Britain's

membership, and thus stave off its critics at least in the short term, Wilson authorized Britain's first ever referendum in June 1975 in which membership received majority support.

Domestically, Wilson's second period of government was blighted by economic strife, industrial action and growing rifts between the various wings of the Labour party. To general shock he resigned in March 1976 and was replaced by James Callaghan. There was some controversy surrounding his last honours list, known as the 'lavender list' which rewarded close friends and allies, including the manufacturer of his famous raincoats who would later be convicted of fraud.

Later Life

Wilson was created a Knight of the Garter in 1976 and, following his departure from the Commons in 1983, he was made a life peer, Baron Wilson of Rievaulx. He wrote his memoirs and several other volumes in retirement, but his health failed badly in later years and he died in London on 24 May 1985.

Wilson is often seen as a politician's politician, a man best remembered for his adept political manoeuvring, although a number of his reforms remain influential today. The first man since the nineteenth century prime minister William Gladstone to win four general elections, he would later comment that 'I wish I could have been prime minister in happier and easier times'. His oft-repeated sentiment that 'a week is a long time in politics' however, gives an indication of the short-term expediency that was to govern so much of his time in office.

Wulff, Christian (Germany)

Introduction

Christian Wulff was sworn in as the youngest ever president of Germany on 2 July 2010. He was elected by the Federal Assembly after his predecessor, Horst Köhler, resigned after comments about the overseas deployment of the German military that were considered to have overstepped the role of the federal president. The deputy leader of Angela Merkel's Christian Democratic Union (CDU) at the time of his appointment, Wulff became the first Catholic to serve as president in over 40 years. Wulff resigned in Feb. 2012 after allegations of corruption relating to his time as prime minister of Lower Saxony.

Early Life

Wulff was born on 19 June 1959 in Osnabrück, Lower Saxony. Raised a Roman Catholic by his mother after his father left the family, he studied law and economics at the University of Osnabrück. He joined the CDU in 1975 and was chairman of the School Students Union of Germany from 1978–1980. Having worked for several years as part of the Junge Union (the joint youth wing of the conservative CDU and Christian Social Union of Bavaria), he was elected to the CDU's executive board in Lower Saxony in 1984.

Wulff continued to live in Osnabrück and was elected to the city council in 1986, remaining a member for 15 years. He qualified as a solicitor in 1990 but discontinued his professional practice in 1994 on being elected to the Landtag of Lower Saxony, representing the constituency of Osnabrück-West. He retained the seat until his appointment to the presidency. Over the years Wulff cemented his position as a senior member of the CDU, serving as one of four deputy chairmen of the party in 1998 and as minister-president of Lower Saxony from 4 Mar 2003 until he became federal president.

Career Peak

In the wake of the controversy surrounding the resignation of Köhler, Wulff was considered a safe pair of hands. A conciliatory figure who, it was hoped, could overcome differences in the fragile coalition, he pledged to 'build bridges' in a society divided by immigration, the reintegration of East and West, and unemployment. Nevertheless, in Aug. 2011 he made a controversial intervention on financial developments in the European Union when he questioned the legality of the European Central Bank's bond-buying in support of Germany's heavily-indebted southern euro zone partners. On 17 Feb. 2012 Wulff resigned as president owing to allegations of misconduct during his tenure as leader of Lower Saxony.

Yadav, Ram Baran (Nepal)

Introduction

Ram Baran Yadav became president in July 2008 after winning a comfortable majority in the first presidential elections since the country became a federal democratic republic. Yadav's role was largely ceremonial, including the performance of traditional Hindu duties previously carried out by the abolished monarchy.

Early Life

Ram Baran Yadav was born on 4 Feb. 1948 to an ethnic Madhesi family in the village of Sapahi, in the Dhanusha District. He studied medicine at the School of Tropical Medicine (Kolkata) and the Calcutta Medical College. He obtained his postgraduate degree from the Institute of Medical Education and Research in Chandigarh, India. Upon returning to Nepal, Yadav ran his own medical practice in Janakpur.

While in India, Yadav had become involved in the Nepali pro-democracy movement and in 1980 he joined the Nepali Congress (NC) party. He participated in the 1990 Jana Andolan (People's Movement) but was arrested and jailed for 3 months until the implementation of a democratic constitution. Yadav was elected to parliament as an NC candidate in 1991 and served as minister of health for 3 years in the administration of Girija Prasad Koirala.

At the 1999 general election Yadav was re-elected and continued as health minister, establishing a healthcare system in rural Nepal. He then became general secretary of the NC. He won the seat of Dhanusa-5 at elections for the constituent assembly in April 2008.

Yadav contested the presidential election of July 2008 on an NC ticket but fell four votes short of the 298 needed to win a simple majority. In a second round of voting he won 308 of 590 votes cast. Yadav's victory came as an upset to the Communist Party of Nepal (Maoist) (CPN-M) who were seeking to form the government after their win in the April 2008 Constituent Assembly election. Yadav was sworn into office on 23 July 2008.

Career Peak

Yadav prioritized the drafting of a new democratic constitution in a bid to end Nepal's long track record of political violence, and has been keen to maintain friendly ties with both India and China. However, he faced opposition from the CPN-M whose leader, Pushpa Kamal Dahal (Prachanda), led a coalition government from Aug. 2008 until May 2009 when he resigned in protest at Yadav's blocking of his controversial attempt to dismiss the country's army head. Madhav Kumar Nepal of the Communist Party (Unified Marxist-Leninist) was sworn in as the prime minister of a new coalition, excluding the CPN-M, later in the month. The CPN-M demanded a return to power, claiming that Yadav had acted unconstitutionally, and kept up prolonged political pressure on Madhav Kumar Nepal until he resigned as prime minister in June 2010.

The previous month the coalition government and Maoist opposition had agreed to extend a deadline for drafting a new constitution until May 2011. Repeated efforts to elect a new premier were unsuccessful until Feb. 2011 when, following the withdrawal of Pushpa Kamal Dahal and then Ram Chandra Poudel of the NC as candidates, Jhalanath Khanal of the Communist Party of Nepal (Unified Marxist-Leninist) was approved by parliament and sworn in by Yadav. In a further premiership change in Aug. 2011 Khanal resigned after the government and opposition had failed to meet the May deadline for agreeing a new constitution and was replaced by Baburam Bhattarai of the Unified Communist Party of Nepal (Maoist). Bhattarai similarly missed a constitutional deadline of May 2012 and also failed to hold elections promised for Nov., prolonging the political stalemate and generating increasing friction with Yadav, who called the Maoist government's legitimacy into question.

In March 2013 Yadav swore in Khil Raj Regmi, the chief justice, as prime minister of an interim government pending elections that took place in Nov. for a constituent assembly to complete the drafting of a new constitution. Following these elections, Yadav in turn swore in Sushil Koirala of the NC as prime minister in Feb. 2014.

Yadav's term as president ended in Oct. 2015 following Bidhya Devi Bhandari's election to the post. Yadav was ineligible to stand due to a constitutional limit on successive terms.

Yaméogo, Maurice (Burkina Faso)

Introduction

Maurice Yaméogo was the first elected president of newly independent Upper Volta (now Burkina Faso). Elected to the colonial executive council in 1958, he administered the country's transition from semi-autonomy to independence, despite being pessimistic as to Burkina Faso's ability to survive without French backing. An autocratic leader, he was overthrown in a 1966 military coup led by Colonel Sangoulé Lamizana.

Early Life

Yaméogo was born in 1921 in Koudougou, Upper Volta. He studied at Pabret and qualified as a teacher. He soon became involved in politics. Shortly after its creation, Yaméogo became involved with the Parti de Regroupement Africain (African Union Party). In the French colonial administration he served successively as minister for agriculture, the interior, information and justice. In 1957 a law was passed allowing an executive council to be appointed and the following year, the French African colonies voted for autonomy. Burkina Faso voted overwhelmingly for semi-autonomy. Conversely, Yaméogo was against the idea of independence believing the country's extreme poverty and its lack of trade or reserves rendered it too weak to survive economically at that time without colonial support.

Career Peak

In 1958 Yaméogo was elected president of Upper Volta's government council. The following year the country joined a union of former French colonies together with Niger, the Côte d'Ivoire, Dahomey (Benin) and Togo. A trade accord with the Côte d'Ivoire underlined Burkina Faso's subordinate economic position. Nonetheless, in 1960 Burkina Faso achieved full independence and Yaméogo was democratically elected the country's first independent president, representing the Union Democratique Voltique (UDV). This party was the Burkina arm of the radical Rassemblement Démocratique Africain (African Democratic Union) founded by the Ivorian and later president, Félix Houphouët-Boigny.

An autocratic leader, Yaméogo imposed a one-party government, outlawing all opposition to his UDV. Continuing economic difficulties provoked dissatisfaction within the country. He was re-elected in 1965, but his second term was short lived. In 1966 his attempts to cut civil servants' wages led to widespread strikes. In this unstable atmosphere, Colonel Sangoulé Lamizana took the opportunity to depose Yaméogo in a military coup. Lamizana led the country for the next 14 years.

Later Life

Yaméogo died on 15 Sept. 1993.

Yanukovych, Viktor (Ukraine)

Introduction

Having served as prime minister under President Kuchma from 2002–05, Viktor Yanukovych was briefly declared president after the bitterly contested 2004 election. When the result was annulled he lost the re-run and resigned as prime minister. In March 2006 his Party of Regions won the largest number of seats in parliament and in Aug. 2006 he became prime minister in a coalition government. His power base is in eastern Ukraine, where he has strong links with industrialists, and he favours close ties between Ukraine and Russia.

On 18 Dec. 2007 Yanukovych was formally dismissed by parliament. In 2010 he fought a bitterly contested presidential election against Yuliya Tymoshenko, narrowly defeating her in the second round of voting. Tymoshenko contested the results, claiming electoral misconduct, but Yanukovych was sworn in as president on 25 Feb.

Early Life

Viktor Yanukovych was born on 9 July 1950 in Yenakiyeve, Donetsk Oblast, in Russian-speaking eastern Ukraine. His mother, an ethnic Ukrainian nurse, died when he was two, and his father, an ethnic Belarusian train driver, died when he was in his teens, leaving him in the care of his grandmother. He served a prison sentence in 1967 for robbery and another in 1970 for bodily injury, although he claims to have been later cleared of both crimes. In 1972 he began working in the Donetsk coal industry and completed his education, graduating in mechanical engineering from Donetsk Polytechnic Institute, in 1980. He joined the Communist Party and rose rapidly as a manager in Donetsk regional transport.

He entered politics in Aug. 1996 as deputy head of Donetsk Oblast administration and was appointed head in May 1997. From May 1999–May 2001 he was head of the Donetsk Oblast regional council and became closely associated with a group of business and political figures known as the 'Clan of Donetsk', led by the coal and steel oligarch Rinat Akhmetov. His lobbying for them brought him strong political and financial support but also fuelled rumours of links to organized crime. In Nov. 2002 he was appointed prime minister by President Leonid Kuchma.

Yanukovych oversaw the continuing liberalization of the economy, cutting higher rates of income tax and encouraging land privatization. He often favoured the interests of Ukrainian industrialists over international investors, helping to power the domestic economy but leading to allegations of corruption. He maintained strong links with Russia and spoke against Ukraine joining the European Union and NATO. In 2003 his government signed an agreement to take Ukraine into a free trade zone and customs alliance with Russia, Belarus and Kazakhstan, although negotiations subsequently stalled. Kuchma chose not to fight the 2004 presidential election and Yanukovych stood as his successor, openly supported by Russia's President Putin.

Yanukovych lost the first round to Viktor Yushchenko of the pro-west, liberal Our Ukraine party but won the second round on 21 Nov. 2004. The result was challenged and Yushchenko's supporters staged huge street protests dubbed the 'Orange Revolution'. The Supreme Court annulled the result and a re-run of the second round saw Yushchenko triumph. Following a parliamentary vote of no confidence in his government, Yanukovych resigned as prime minister in Jan. 2005.

Yanukovych spent 2005 building on his grassroots support in eastern Ukraine. He profited from disillusionment with Yushchenko's government, which was divided and indecisive. Yanukovych's Party of Regions emerged as the largest party at the March 2006 parliamentary elections with 186 seats out of 450, ahead of the Tymoshenko Bloc and Our Ukraine. However, with no overall parliamentary majority, months of wrangling over a new government ensued before Yushchenko was forced to nominate Yanukovych as prime minister in Aug. 2006. Yanukovych agreed a coalition deal with Yushchenko's party, but the working relationship was uneasy from the outset. In Dec. 2007, following further elections in Sept., he was replaced by Tymoshenko as prime minister of a new coalition between her supporters and Yushchenko's Our Ukraine.

Career Peak

Yanukovych regained the presidency in Feb. 2010 after comprehensively defeating Yushchenko in the first round of elections and then prime minister Tymoshenko in the second, winning by a 3.5% margin. Tymoshenko accused him of vote-rigging and mounted a legal challenge against the results. However, she subsequently dropped her action stating that she would not receive a fair hearing. She and her party nevertheless refused to recognize Yanukovych's election and boycotted the inauguration ceremony. In March Yanukovych appointed a longstanding ally, Mykola Azarov, to succeed Tymoshenko as prime minister.

In Oct. 2010 Yanukovych forced through constitutional changes overturning limits on presidential power that had been introduced in 2004. At the end of the year Tymoshenko and former interior minister Yuriy Lutsenko were charged with abuse of state funds while in office. Both rejected the accusation as a politically motivated manoeuvre by the Yanukovych

government, but in Oct. 2011 Tymoshenko was found guilty and jailed for 7 years. Her conviction prompted international condemnation, particularly from the European Union whose high representative for foreign policy warned of 'profound implications' for EU–Ukraine relations, including for Ukraine's hope of concluding a trade and association agreement.

In Oct. 2012 the Party of Regions retained power after a decisive win in parliamentary elections, although international monitors criticized the conduct of the poll. In Dec. Yanukovych appointed a reconstituted but largely unchanged government under Prime Minister Azarov.

Under Yanukovych's presidency, Ukraine gradually improved its relations with neighbouring Russia, ending years of hostility between the two countries. In April 2010 he signed an agreement with Russian president Dmitry Medvedev, which extended the lease of the Russian Black Sea naval base in Crimea for 25 years in exchange for accords on cheaper gas supplies. A month later, parliament voted to abandon Ukraine's NATO membership aspirations, conforming to Russia's opposition to any Ukrainian involvement with the organization.

However, on 22 Feb. 2014 following popular opposition in Ukraine to closer ties with Russia (culminating in the 'Euromaidan' demonstrations of 2013–14), Yanukovych was impeached by parliament and removed from the presidency. He was subsequently disowned by his party, the Party of Regions, and fled the capital amid escalating violence between Euromaidan protesters and state authorities.

On 25 Feb. 2014 the provisional Ukrainian parliament voted in favour of sending Yanukovych to The Hague to face trial for the violence that resulted in the deaths of at least 82 protesters during the final days of his presidency. He fled to Russia, where he has since maintained that he remains Ukraine's sole legitimate leader.

Yar'adua, Umaru Musa (Nigeria)

Introduction

Umaru Yar'Adua was sworn into office on 29 May 2007 after a landslide victory in disputed presidential elections. Selected candidate for the governing People's Democratic Party (PDP), he succeeded outgoing president, Olusegun Obasanjo. Yar'Adua's electoral success marked the first time in Nigeria that an elected civilian head was replaced by another civil leader.

Early Life

Umaru Musa Yar'Adua was born on 9 July 1951 in Katsina to a politically active family. His father served as a minister in the First Republic and his older brother, Shehu Musa Yar'Adua, was vice president in Olusegun Obasanjo's military government. Yar'Adua graduated from Ahmadu Bello University with a degree in chemistry in 1975. After graduation he undertook a mandatory year in the National Youth Service Corps (NYSC), teaching at the Holy Child College in Lagos. He then moved to the Katsina College of Arts, Science and Technology, remaining there until 1979. In 1980 Yar'Adua earned an MSc in analytical chemistry from Ahmadu Bello University and continued teaching at Katsina Polytechnic until 1983, when he moved to the private sector.

In the early 1980s Yar'Adua entered party politics, becoming an active member of the People's Redemption Party (PRP). He later became a founding member of the People's Front, which was subsumed into the Social Democratic Party (SDP) in 1988. In the same year he became a member of the SDP's constituent assembly, a member of its national caucus and, subsequently, the SDP state secretary for Katsina State. Away from politics Yar'Adua was thriving in the private sector, holding directorships of several companies including Hamada Holdings and Habib Nigeria Bank Ltd.

In 1998, at the start of Gen. Abdulsalam Abubakar's transition rule, Yar'Adua established the K34 political association, which would become part of the PDP. He was returned as governor of Katsina State in 1999, winning re-election in 2003. During his 8-year tenure he proved himself a prudent and transparent leader while Katsina State underwent unprecedented growth, especially in the health and education sectors. On 17 Dec. 2006 he was selected by the PDP as its presidential candidate for the April 2007 elections after parliament denied Olusegun Obasanjo the opportunity to run for a third term. He was announced winner of the election, although the results were challenged before a special election tribunal that upheld them in Feb. 2008.

Career Peak

Yar'Adua pledged that the rule of law, the constitutional separation of powers, non-interference and economic growth would be the guiding principles of his presidency. However, his first cabinet was criticized for containing too many ministers linked to the Obasanjo era and, despite making reconciliatory noises to the opposition, Yar'Adua appointed only two opposition members as assistant ministers.

He pledged to ease the volatile situation in the oil-producing Niger Delta and entered into talks with rebel militias. However, attacks on oil installations by militants continued through 2008 and into 2009, reducing output sharply. In Nov. 2008 the government was also confronted by violent sectarian clashes between Christian and Muslims in Plateau state in central Nigeria that killed an estimated 400 people. Further violence by Boka Haram, an Islamic fundamentalist sect, in the north-east of the country in July 2009 provoked clashes with the security forces leading to several hundred more deaths.

Speculation about Yar'Adua's state of health created a mood of political uncertainty, heightened in Nov. 2009 when he left the country to receive medical treatment abroad. His absence prompted the senate to transfer presidential power to vice president Goodluck Jonathan in Feb. as an interim measure. Although Yar'Adua returned at the end of the month he was thought to be too ill to take up his duties and Jonathan remained acting president. Yar'Adua died on 5 May 2010.

Yasuhiro, Nakasone (Japan)

Introduction

A member of the conservative Liberal Democratic Party (LDP), Yasuhiro Nakasone was prime minister of Japan from 1982–87. During his premiership he encouraged Japan's participation in international affairs and promoted closer links with the United States, forging a special relationship with the then US president Ronald Reagan. He was forced to resign from the LDP in 1989 following a share purchase scandal, but rejoined in 1991.

Early Life

Nakasone was born into a wealthy family on 27 May 1917 in Takasaki. In 1941 he graduated from Tokyo Imperial University and then served in the navy during the Second World War. In 1947 he was elected to the lower house of parliament, retaining his seat in successive elections. He was appointed director-general of the Science and Technology Agency and chairman of the Atomic Agency Commission in 1959–60 and held ministerial posts from 1967, including for transport (1967–68), defence (1970–71) and international trade and industry (1972–74). He also served as LDP secretary-general in 1974–76 and chairman of the party's executive council in 1971–72 and 1977–80.

Career Peak

In Oct. 1982 Suzuki Zenko resigned as LDP president and as prime minister of Japan. Having built up a strong factional backing within the LDP, Nakasone stood successfully for election to the party presidency. By virtue of the LDP's parliamentary dominance, he was also elected prime minister by the legislature in Nov. 1982. In Dec. 1983 the LDP lost its absolute majority in an electoral backlash following the conviction for corruption of Kakuei Tanaka, an influential faction leader and former prime minister. However, Nakasone remained as prime minister of a coalition administration with a small conservative party. In Oct. 1984 he was reaffirmed as LDP president for a further 2 years. Capitalizing on his personal popularity, he led the party to a convincing victory in parliamentary elections in July 1986. Later that year his tenure as LDP president was extended for a further 12 months. Under Nakasone's premiership, which ended in Nov. 1987, Japan's economy began to rival that of the United States and the country became the world's

largest creditor nation. He also raised Japan's political profile significantly in the international community and controversially increased its defence spending. Nakasone retained considerable influence within the factional rivalries of the LDP until he was forced to resign from the party for 2 years in May 1989 in response to a financial scandal.

Yatsenyuk, Arseniy (Ukraine)

Introduction

Arseniy Yatsenyuk became acting prime minister in Feb. 2014 following the impeachment of the former president, Viktor Yanukovych. Yatsenyuk was approved for the post in a parliamentary poll, winning 371 votes from the 450-member assembly, and was reappointed in Nov. He resigned in April 2016.

Early Life

Arseniy Petrovych Yatsenyuk was born on 22 May 1974 in Chernivtsi to a family of Jewish ancestry, although opponents have accused him of downplaying this aspect of his heritage to win favour with ethnic Ukrainian voters in the west of the country. In 1996 he graduated in law from the Chernivtsi National University, where his parents were academics, before joining Raiffeisen Bank Aval. In 2001 he earned a degree in accounting from the Chernivtsi Trade and Economics Institute.

In Sept. 2001 Yatsenyuk joined the Crimean ministry of economy, working against a backdrop of distrust towards Kyiv from the region's largely ethnic Russian population. He joined the National Bank of Ukraine in 2003 as vice-president and later became its acting head. During the 2004 Orange Revolution he advocated limiting cash withdrawals, a move subsequently recognized as key to saving the country's banking system.

He was named minister of economy in Sept. 2005 and oversaw talks on Ukraine's prospective membership of the World Trade Organization and the European Union (EU). In Sept. 2006 he became first deputy head of the secretariat of the president and served as the president's representative to the cabinet. In March 2007 he was voted by parliament to be foreign minister in Viktor Yushchenko's government, and in elections in Sept. 2007 he won a parliamentary seat. In Dec. that year he was named chairman of the house but was dismissed from the post in Nov. 2008.

At the 2010 presidential election Yatsenyuk stood as the candidate for his own Front for Change party, but won less than 7% support in the first round. After Yuliya Tymoshenko was imprisoned on embezzlement charges in 2011, he took the helm of her Fatherland party, with Front for Change formally merging into it in June 2013. At the height of the protests against Yanukovych's government in Jan. 2014, Yatsenyuk was offered but rejected the premiership. However, following Yanukovych's departure for Russia, Yatsenyuk was elected acting prime minister on 27 Feb. 2014.

Career Peak

Yatsenyuk quickly secured recognition for his government from the EU, United Nations and USA. His most pressing security challenge has been to contend with the continuing conflict between the Kyiv government and pro-Russian separatists in the east of the country and Russia's military threat following its annexation of Crimea in March 2014. He has also needed to address endemic corruption and a deep economic recession. He has stated his belief that the country's future lies in the EU (with which an association accord was signed in June 2014 and a free trade deal came into force in Jan. 2016) while trying to improve relations with Russia.

Following parliamentary elections in Oct. 2014, in which his pro-Western People's Front attracted the largest share of the overall vote with about 22%, Yatsenyuk was reappointed prime minister on 27 Nov. 2014, securing 341 of 450 parliamentary votes.

Yatsenyuk's government survived a parliamentary vote of no confidence in Feb. 2016 following allegations of corruption and criticism over the slow pace of reforms. President Petro Poroshenko had called for Yatsenyuk's resignation prior to the vote, claiming that the prime minister had lost the support of the governing coalition. Yatsenyuk eventually resigned on 14 April 2016.

Yekhanurov, Yuriy (Ukraine)

Introduction

Yuriy Yekhanurov, an experienced technocrat, economist and long-time ally of President Yushchenko, was appointed as Ukraine's prime minister in Sept. 2005. Ahead of the March 2006 parliamentary elections, he was charged with stabilizing government and the economy after the first post-'.range Revolution' administration had become mired in infighting and allegations of corruption. He left office in Aug. 2006.

Early Life

Yuriy Ivanovich Yekhanurov was born on 23 Aug. 1948 in Belkachi, Yakutia, in Soviet Russia. He was at school in Bichursk, Buryatia (Siberia) until 1963. When his family moved to Kyiv in the Ukrainian Soviet Socialist Republic, he attended the Technical School for Construction. Having begun work as an apprentice in a concrete manufacturing plant in 1967, Yekhanurov rose to become the complex's executive director in 1978, a position he held for 7 years. During this period he undertook advanced studies in economics at the Kyiv Institute of Economics, graduating in 1983 with a 'candidate degree' (equivalent to a PhD). In Aug. 1988 he was nominated deputy director of Glavkievstroy (the municipal department for construction).

Following the break-up of the USSR and Ukraine's declaration of independence in Aug. 1991, Yekhanurov was involved in economic policy as an advocate of sweeping liberalization and privatization. In 1992 he joined the department for economic reform in Kyiv's municipal administration and a year later entered the government as deputy minister of the economy. Between 1994 and early 1997 he oversaw the initial stage of privatization in Ukraine as head of the State Property Fund. Subsequently he served as minister of the economy in the government of Pavlo Lazarenko, before being nominated as head of the state committee for business development. He became a member of the Popular Democratic Party in 1998 (providing political support to President Leonid Kuchma) and was elected as the parliamentary member for Zhytomyr district. In Dec. 1999 he was appointed first vice-prime minister of Ukraine in the new government of Viktor Yushchenko, the former head of the National Bank of Ukraine.

After the government was ousted by President Leonid Kuchma in May 2001, Yekhanurov became first deputy head of the presidential administration, working on issues of administrative reform. He joined Yushchenko's 'Our Ukraine' centre-right opposition and represented the bloc in parliament in 2002. He then served as chairman of the committee for industrial policy and entrepreneurship and took up a professorship at the Taras Shevchenko National University. On 3 April 2005, following the 'Orange Revolution'. the newly-elected President Yushchenko appointed Yekhanurov as governor of the city of Dnipropetrovsk.

Career Peak

On 8 Sept. 2005 Yekhanurov was appointed acting prime minister by Yushchenko. The president's action came in the wake of his decision to sack his entire cabinet, including Prime Minister Tymoshenko, because of infighting and allegations of corruption. Parliamentary approval for Yekhanurov's appointment required two rounds of voting and on 22 Sept. 2005 he secured the support of 289 out of 339 deputies. Yekhanurov set out his plans to improve the country's business climate by lifting state controls and to achieve Ukraine's membership of the World Trade Organization. In Jan. 2006, following an agreement with Russia ending a dispute over Russian gas prices, Ukraine's parliament dismissed Yekhanurov's government. However, President Yushchenko questioned the legal basis of the action ahead of the March 2006 parliamentary elections. Yekhanurov continued to perform his duties but in an acting capacity.

The elections of March 2006 were won by Viktor Yanukovych's party, with the parties of Yuliya Tymoshenko and President Yushchenko in second and third places respectively. However, with Yanukovych unable to form a majority government, it appeared that power would go to a coalition made up of the parties of Tymoshenko and Yushchenko plus the Socialists. When this deal collapsed, Yanukovych's Party of Regions sought an alliance with the Socialists and Communists. In July the president decided to accept Yanukovych's proposed coalition rather than call fresh elections. Yekhanurov left office on 4 Aug. 2006.

Yeltsin, Boris Nikolayevich (Russia)

Introduction

Boris Yeltsin was elected president of Russia (then within the USSR) by the Russian parliament in 1990. The following year he was elected president in popular elections, Russia's first leader to so secure office. He was at the forefront of the dissolution of the Soviet Union and the establishment of the Commonwealth of Independent States in 1991. Despite ailing health, economic difficulties and the war in Chechnya, he won re-election in 1996. His second term was marked by erratic policy making and frequent changes of government personnel. He unexpectedly resigned in late 1999 and handed power to Vladimir Putin.

Early Life

Yeltsin was born in the village of Butka in the region of Sverdlovsk on 1 Feb. 1931. In 1955 he graduated from the Ural Kirov Technical College with a degree in engineering. Two years later he married Naina Girina, with whom he had two children. He joined the Communist Party in 1961 and became head of the construction department under the Sverdlovsk regional party committee. In 1975 he became secretary of the Sverdlovsk CPSU regional committee in charge of industrial regional developments, and the following year was named first secretary of the Sverdlovsk CPSU regional committee, a position he held until 1985. During that time he also served on the USSR supreme council (1978–89) and as Moscow's mayor from 1985–87. In 1981 he was elected a member of the CPSU central committee, a position he occupied until 1990.

In Dec. 1985 Boris Yeltsin was named first secretary of the Moscow Communist Party by Mikhail Gorbachev, with a specific brief to rid the party of corruption. He was promoted to the Politburo the following year. However, he was ousted on 11 Nov. 1987 after delivering a speech criticising the party leadership. His next post was a step down to first deputy-chairman of the USSR state construction committee, where he stayed from Nov. 1987 to early 1989.

In March 1989 Yeltsin made a political comeback, winning 90% of the vote to join the Congress of People's Deputies. In a major political rebuff to Gorbachev, Yeltsin was elected Chairman of the Russian Supreme Council by the legislature on 29 May 1990. He left the Communist Party in July, and became Russia's first popularly elected president on 12 June 1991.

Gorbachev came under increasing pressure from conservatives, fearful of the reform movement that had swept Eastern Europe since 1989. In Aug. they attempted a coup. Yeltsin, based in Moscow, was at the forefront of resistance to them and was widely credited with their defeat. Gorbachev remained in power but was increasingly reliant upon Yeltsin. On 8 Dec. 1991 Yeltsin signed a treaty dissolving the Soviet Union and forming the Commonwealth of Independent States along with ten other former Soviet republics. Gorbachev's declining power was highlighted when he found out about the agreement after George Bush, the American president. Gorbachev resigned on 25 Dec. from his positions in the defunct USSR and Yeltsin held the reigns of the CIS government.

Career Peak

Yeltsin quickly set about reforming the economy, encouraging a free market. He ended state interference in the funding and pricing of many food and consumer goods, but his policies met opposition in parliament. In 1993 the Duma introduced reforms to reduce presidential powers, but a national referendum in April supported Yeltsin.

On 21 Sept. 1993 Yeltsin disbanded parliament and ordered new elections. When vice president Alexander Rutskoi declared himself the new leader and was sworn in by parliament, Yeltsin successfully besieged the building. Dec. 1993 saw widespread voter support for Yeltsin's proposed constitution, but the elections also gave nationalists a strong voice in parliament. In Dec. 1994 Yeltsin sent Russian troops into the breakaway region of Chechnya. The war proved long, bloody and inconclusive.

Presidential elections were held on 4 July 1996. Yeltsin's economic reforms had seemingly borne little fruit by this time and the issue of Chechnya was thorny. In addition, he suffered a heart attack while on the campaign trail in the month before the elections and it was widely expected that he would struggle at the polls. However, he defeated his Communist challenger, Gennady Zyuganov, after two rounds. He underwent a heart bypass operation in Nov., having been virtually absent from the political scene in the preceding months.

In 1997 Yeltsin established a precarious peace with the rebel Chechnyan forces. On 23 March 1998 Yeltsin dismissed his entire government, blaming the failure of economic reforms. In June Russia's stock market fell sharply, fuelling investors' fears of a collapse of the rouble and pressurising the government to devalue the rouble. In mid-1999, the peace with Chechnya broke after rebels invaded Dagestan and were blamed for several bomb attacks within Russia. Yeltsin staved off attempts by parliament to impeach him, while concerns over his health and prodigious drinking grew. Yeltsin resigned on 31 Dec. 1999 and Vladimir Putin, the seventh prime minister of Yeltsin's tenure, succeeded him as president.

Later Life

Yeltsin retired to the country where he wrote his memoirs. President Putin controversially granted him immunity from any future prosecution. On 23 April 2007 Yeltsin died at the age of 76.

Yudhoyono, Susilo Bambang (Indonesia)

Introduction

Retired general Susilo Bambang Yudhoyono, known widely by his acronym SBY, succeeded Megawati Sukarnoputri as president of Indonesia on 20 Oct. 2004. In the country's first direct presidential election he polled 61% of an estimated 125 m. votes and he became the first incumbent to be re-elected in July 2009. He left office on the completion of his second presidential term in Oct. 2014.

Early Life

Susilo Bambang Yudhoyono was born on 9 Sept. 1949 in the small town of Pacitan, in the east of the Indonesian island of Java. His family were observant Muslims and he attended a traditional *pesantren* (Muslim boarding school). He graduated from Indonesia's military academy in 1973 and joined the army, which was then, with Gen. Suharto as president, the country's dominant authority. He served as a senior officer in Indonesia's 1975 invasion of Timor-Leste, then a Portuguese colony. Gen. Suharto's 'New Order' political system was characterized by a strongly anti-communist foreign policy and relatively good relations with the USA. Yudhoyono travelled to the USA in 1976 and 1982, attending military training programmes at Fort Benning, Georgia. He later took a master's degree in business management from Webster University in Missouri and has since described the USA as his 'second home'. Between 1984 and 1987 Yudhoyono returned to Timor-Leste and commanded Battalion 744 in the city of Dili. By the mid-1990s he had risen through the ranks to become chief-of-staff in the Jakarta command. Questions have been asked about his knowledge of a raid by security forces on the Jakarta offices of the Indonesian Democratic Party (PDI) on 27 July 1996 (then chaired by Megawati Sukarnoputri), which left five dead and 23 missing.

In 1996 Yudhoyono served as chief military observer with the United Nations force in Bosnia. Two years later, with Indonesia in turmoil following the ousting of President Suharto in March 1998, he left the army and was appointed the minister for mining and energy in the administration of Abdurrahman Wahid. When the Muslim cleric was succeeded as president in 2001 by Mrs Megawati, daughter of former president Sukarno, Yudhoyono joined her cabinet as chief security minister. He was praised for the way he handled the aftermath of the Oct. 2002 Bali bombing that killed 202 people. He subsequently helped draft Indonesia's first counter-terrorist law and attempted to broker a peace agreement with separatist rebels in the historically troubled province of Aceh in Sumatra in 2003, which collapsed in May of that year. In March 2004 Yudhoyono resigned from Megawati's increasingly unpopular cabinet to establish the Democratic Party (PD). In the first round of elections in April (for choosing the members of parliament and three tiers of local officials) the PD had a strong showing. On 5 July, when Yudhoyono, along with his running mate Jusuf Kalla—a business tycoon with ties to many of the country's Islamic clerics—fought in the country's first direct presidential elections, no candidate won more than 50% of the vote. This forced a run-off election between Yudhoyono and Megawati on 20 Sept. which Yudhoyono won with 60.9% of the vote. He was officially sworn in as president on 20 Oct. 2004.

Career Peak

Yudhoyono vowed to fight terrorism, eradicate corruption, restore Indonesian institutions and the rule of law, and rebuild the economy. The president set himself the goal of creating jobs for 50 m. unemployed Indonesians. He also pledged to repair the often fractious relationship with Australia. In the aftermath of the Indian Ocean tsunami of 26 Dec. 2004, which is estimated to have killed some 166,000 people on the Indonesian island of Sumatra, Yudhoyono was quick to accept aid and expertise from the international community. Handling relief and reconstruction was an opportunity for him to be a more decisive and approachable leader than his predecessor. It was also an opportunity for him to improve relations between Jakarta and Aceh—the region worst-affected by the tsunami—and in Aug. 2005 his government signed a peace agreement with separatist leaders granting greater political autonomy to the province. Elections for a provincial governor and district officials in Aceh took place in Dec. 2006.

Yudhoyono's government was confronted by renewed terrorism, as suicide bombers again targeted the tourist resort of Bali in Oct. 2005 killing 19 people, and by further natural disasters. In Nov. 2008 three Islamic terrorists convicted for their part in the Bali bombing in 2002 were executed by firing squad. However, extremist activity continued, notably the launching of suicide bomb attacks in July 2009 on two luxury hotels in Jakarta which killed nine people and injured at least 50 more. In the first half of 2010 a number of suspected Islamist militants were arrested in a series of anti-terrorist raids by security forces. Meanwhile, an earthquake in May 2006 and another tsunami in July killed around 6,500 people on Java, floods in Jakarta in Feb. 2007 left an estimated 340,000 people homeless, another earthquake in Sumatra the following month killed more than 50 and, in Sept. 2009, an earthquake off the coast of Sumatra left more than 1,000 dead. Further extensive casualties followed another earthquake off the western coast of Sumatra and the volcanic eruption of Mount Merapi in Oct. 2010.

By 2008 Yudhoyono's political popularity was being undermined by continuing unemployment, rising prices and a cut in fuel subsidies, despite increased spending on anti-poverty programmes and significant progress in his anti-corruption drive. Nevertheless, in parliamentary elections in April 2009 his Democratic Party emerged as the largest party and in July he was returned to office with 60.8% of the vote in the presidential poll.

Following a final report in July 2008 by a joint investigative commission that blamed Indonesia for human rights violations in the run-up to Timor-Leste's independence in 2002, Yudhoyono expressed the Indonesian government's deep regret but did not apologize.

Towards the end of his term in office, Yudhoyono was criticized for a failure to counter corruption or combat increasing incidents of religious intolerance and sectarian violence by hardline Islamic groups. Indonesia's brittle relations with Australia were strained by revelations in Nov. 2013 that Australian intelligence services had tapped the telephones of Yudhoyono and his close confidantes, prompting the recall of Indonesia's ambassador.

Since the constitution prohibits presidents from serving more than two terms, Yudhoyono was ineligible to stand for a third term in the presidential elections scheduled of 2014. On 20 Oct. 2014 he was succeeded by Joko Widodo of the Indonesian Democratic Party–Struggle.

Yushchenko, Viktor (Ukraine)

Introduction

After a drawn-out and bitter contest for the presidency of Ukraine, the pro-EU and reformist former banker, Viktor Yushchenko, emerged as the winner in Jan. 2005. Following allegations of vote-rigging in the Nov. 2004 election, tens of thousands of Yushchenko's orange-clad supporters protested and forced a rerun. However, his presidency was undermined by political rivalries, dissension within the government and parliamentary opposition. Having performed badly in the first round of presidential elections in early 2010, he was succeeded by Victor Yanukovych on 25 Feb. 2010.

Early Life

Viktor Andriyovich Yushchenko was born on 23 Feb. 1954 in Khoruzhivka, Sumy Oblast. He attended the Finance and Economics Institute in Ternopil and graduated in 1975. Returning to Sumy in 1976 after service in the Soviet army, Yushchenko worked as an economist and department chief at the Ulyanivka branch of the USSR's central bank. In 1984 he obtained a post-graduate degree in finance and credit. Shortly afterwards he moved to Kyiv, taking up appointments as Deputy Director for Agricultural Credit at the Ukrainian office of the USSR's central bank, then Department Director at the Kyiv office of the USSR's Agro-Industrial bank, and, in 1991, Deputy Chairman of the Agro-Industrial bank's Board of Directors.

He was a key figure in the establishment of the National Bank of Ukraine, becoming its governor in 1993. He oversaw the introduction of Ukraine's new currency, the hryvnia, in 1996 and was credited with policies that diminished the impact of the Russian rouble crash on Ukraine's economy in 1997. Yushchenko then survived a corruption scandal that engulfed the central bank before being appointed prime minister in Dec. 1999 by President Leonid Kuchma. His free-market approach, his decision to pay off Ukraine's debts to Russia and his promotion of foreign and domestic investment brought some improvement to the economy. However, his government came into conflict with oligarchs from eastern Ukraine, who controlled the oil and gas sectors and were linked to Kuchma (and Moscow), and was ousted in 2001 by a no-confidence vote.

Yushchenko began talks with liberal and nationalist opposition forces and, in Jan. 2002, created 'Our Ukraine'—a coalition of centre-right groups. In the parliamentary elections in March 2002 Our Ukraine reduced the Communist Party's dominance in parliament, but failed to secure the majority needed to form a new government. Instead, pro-Kuchma forces, led by the For United Ukraine party, received enough support to hold the balance of power.

When Kuchma's term ended in 2004, Yushchenko ran against the prime minister, Viktor Yanukovych (backed by the powerful clans in eastern Ukraine and Moscow), for the presidency. During an acrimonious campaign, Yushchenko became ill with a condition that left his face disfigured, prompting accusations of poisoning by the intelligence agencies. After neither candidate reached the 50% margin required for victory in the first round, a run-off vote showed a victory for Yanukovych, which contrasted sharply with exit polls. International observers reported electoral irregularities and there were huge public protests in Kyiv and elsewhere, which led to the invalidation of the results by the Supreme Court and the re-running of the election in Dec. Yushchenko was declared the winner, although this time Yanukovych claimed to have been the victim of electoral fraud. Despite resigning as prime minister, Yanukovych continued to protest about the conduct of the election until the electoral commission reaffirmed Yushchenko as the official winner with 54.1% of the vote and the Supreme Court rejected Yanukovych's final appeal in Jan. 2005.

Career Peak

Addressing a crowd estimated at more than 100,000 in Kyiv, Yushchenko described his inauguration as president on 23 Jan. as a victory of freedom over tyranny. He promised to create new jobs, fight corruption, enforce taxes and make business transparent, adding: 'My goal is Ukraine in a united Europe'.

On 4 Feb. 2005 the Ukrainian parliament approved Yushchenko's nomination of Yuliya Tymoshenko as the new prime minister. She was one of his key supporters, but a controversial figure—Russian authorities having accused her of bribery when she ran a Ukrainian gas trading company in the mid-1990s. However, the optimism that followed the 'Orange Revolution' soon faded and, following public disagreements within the government and further corruption allegations, Yushchenko sacked his entire cabinet on 8 Sept. 2005, including Tymoshenko who subsequently became a political rival. He appointed Yuriy Yekhanurov, an economist and technocrat, as the new prime minister.

In Jan. 2006, after the signing of an agreement with Russia ending a damaging dispute over prices for Russian gas supplies, the Ukrainian parliament passed a vote of no confidence in the Yekhanurov government, although Yushchenko questioned the legal validity of the move ahead of the March 2006 parliamentary elections.

The elections returned the Party of Regions of Ukraine, supporting the pro-Russian former prime minister Yanukovych, as the largest party but without an overall majority. Tymoshenko's Election Bloc meanwhile pushed Yushchenko's Our Ukraine into third place. After several months of political stalemate, Yushchenko was forced to nominate Yanukovych as prime minister in an attempt to resolve the impasse. However, Yushchenko's relations with a largely hostile legislature continued to deteriorate, and in Jan. 2007 the parliament voted controversially to curtail the president's constitutional powers. Political tensions were exacerbated further in April by a disputed presidential decree dissolving parliament before Yushchenko and Yanukovych reached a compromise agreement in May to hold fresh elections at the end of Sept. The elections left no grouping with an outright majority but after weeks of negotiations Yushchenko again nominated Tymoshenko as prime minister of a pro-Western coalition government comprising their respective supporters. Tymoshenko's appointment was narrowly approved by parliament in Dec. 2007.

Damaging rivalry between Yushchenko and Tymoshenko nevertheless continued through 2008. In May the prime minister's party prevented the president from making his annual address to parliament in protest at his interference in government economic policies. Then in Sept., amid increasing concerns over Russia's hostility towards Ukraine's aspirations to join NATO and Russian military intervention in Georgia, the coalition government collapsed. Yushchenko dissolved parliament and called an election (although this was postponed owing to the financial crisis). Meanwhile, Ukraine's economy suffered a downturn in the wake of the global financial crisis, necessitating the arrangement of a US$16.5 bn. loan support package from the International Monetary Fund in Oct. In Dec. Tymoshenko managed to form another coalition government with backing from some of the president's supporters, but it was viewed by some commentators as weak and unstable.

In a further dispute over gas prices and unpaid bills, Russia shut off gas exports to Ukraine (also disrupting onward pipeline flows to much of Europe) for 3 weeks in Jan. 2009 before a resolution was reached.

Presidential elections on 17 Jan. 2010 saw Yushcenhko win a mere 5.5% of the vote thus excluding him from the second round run-off in which his old opponent Viktor Yanukovych narrowly defeated Yuliya Tymoshenko. Yushcenhko was succeeded by Yanukovych on 25 Feb. 2010.

Zafy, Albert (Madagascar)

Introduction

A medical professor and politician, Albert Zafy created the Union Nationale pour le Développement et la Démocratie (The National Union for Development and Democracy; UNDD) and was president from 1993–96. He was one of the leading figures in non-violent mass protests against Didier Ratsiraka's autocratic Conseil Suprême de la Révolution (CSR) government, which helped topple his predecessor in 1992. His own term ended when impeachment charges were brought against him.

Early Life

Zafy was born on 1 May 1927 into a Catholic family in Betsiaka, Antseranana province. After completing his secondary education in the Malagasan capital, he obtained his medical qualifications in Montpellier. In 1964 he returned to Madagascar to work in the Antananarivo public hospital. After a further 4 years in France, he became the head of surgery in the Malagasy capital. He also taught at the University of Madagascar (now the University of Antananarivo).

He was health minister between 1972–75, first under Philibert Tsiranana and then under the subsequent military rule, but left the government when Ratsiraka came to power in 1975. Returning to his non-political career, he helped set up La Clinique des Frères Francisquains (Clinic of Franciscan Brothers) at Ambanja, becoming its director in 1987. With fellow professionals he founded the KMZ, a committee for the defence of human rights. In 1990 he returned to the political scene, creating the UNDD which formed part of an opposition coalition, the Forces Vives (Live Forces; FV) of which Zafy was made president. The alliance put pressure on Ratsiraka to resign, creating a provisional government in July 1991 with Zafy at its head. In 1991, Ratsiraka finally conceded defeat and stepped down. Zafy headed a transitional government, the 31-member Haute Autorité de l'Etat (High State Authority), replacing the CSR. In 1992 he survived assassination attempts and the following year contested free elections against Ratsiraka whom he defeated with 67% of votes, most other candidates having transferred their support to him to defeat Ratsiraka.

Career Peak

Zafy changed the constitution to allow the president to appoint the prime minister instead of the national assembly. The bill was passed following a referendum. In 1996 economic hardship led to a series of strikes and protests. In Sept. the national assembly impeached Zafy for abusing his constitutional powers. He stepped down in Oct. although he stood for the elections in Dec. 1996. He was defeated by Ratsiraka.

Later Life

Zafy has remained politically active as an opposition leader since leaving office. He played an active role in discussions to end the 2009 political crisis caused by the coup d'état led by Andry Rajoelina, and was a staunch critic of the transitional government in place until 2014. He suffered a stroke on 11 Oct. 2017 and was hospitalized in La Réunion. He died 2 days later aged 90.

Zapatero, José Luis Rodríguez (Spain)

Introduction

José Luis Rodríguez Zapatero, leader of the Spanish Socialist Workers' Party (PSOE; Partido Socialista Obrero Español), became prime minister in March 2004 when his party unexpectedly defeated the Popular Party (PP) in the aftermath of the terrorist attack that month on Madrid. After taking office, he announced the withdrawal of Spanish troops from Iraq and called for greater international co-operation against terrorism. However, his judgment was called into question over his policy towards Basque separatism. Zapatero secured a second term after the PSOE won the March 2008 elections and he was re-elected in April.

Early Life

Rodríguez Zapatero (known as Zapatero) was born on 4 Aug. 1960 in Valladolid. He studied law at the Universidad de León before embarking on a career in politics. From a traditionally left-wing family, Zapatero was strongly inspired by his grandfather, a republican captain executed by nationalists in 1936 at the beginning of the Spanish Civil War. In 1977, before the first post-Franco democratic elections, Zapatero attended a socialist political rally in Gijón. He was inspired by former PSOE leader Felipe González Márquez and in 1978 he joined the PSOE as a youth member. Four years later he became the PSOE youth leader in his home region of León. In 1986 he was elected to parliament representing León, becoming the youngest member of the *Cortes* at that time. His party standing was further enhanced in 1988 when he became the regional leader of the León PSOE.

In 1996 the PSOE's 14-year domination ended with the election of José María Aznar. The following year González resigned as PSOE leader amid corruption charges and the revelation of his government's brutal treatment of captured Basque terrorists, for which two of his former ministers were imprisoned. During the following 3 years the party floundered under the leadership of Joaquín Almunia, who resigned in March 2000 following a humiliating election defeat. Zapatero then became one of four candidates for the party leadership, along with the better-known members José Bono, Matilde Fernández and Rosa Diez. At the 35th PSOE party conference, Zapatero won a surprise victory with 41.8%, narrowly defeating Bono's 40.8%.

On election Zapatero set out his plans for the rejuvenation of the flagging PSOE. He changed the party's executive committee, installing many young politicians in a bid to revitalize the party's image. Zapatero's ambition was to create an effective opposition to Aznar and present himself as a strong candidate for prime minister. His *Nueva Vía* (New Way) represented a shift from the traditions of socialism to more centrist politics, with echoes of Tony Blair's New Labour ideology in British politics. This move reduced the ideological distance between the ruling and opposition leaders, Aznar having abandoned traditional right-wing politics for a more moderate, centrist stance.

On 11 March 2004 Madrid's rail network was hit by terrorist bombings that killed 191 people. Aznar's government blamed ETA in the immediate aftermath, but evidence soon pointed to a link with North Africa. At the general election three days later, the PP suffered a backlash of voter hostility and were unexpectedly defeated by the PSOE. Zapatero was sworn in as prime minister on 17 April 2004.

Career Peak

Although lacking an absolute majority, Zapatero declined to form a coalition, saying that he would govern through consensus with other groups. Reiterating his opposition to the war in Iraq and criticizing the failure of US-led forces to install a workable post-war structure, he announced that Spanish troops would be withdrawn from Iraq by the end of May 2004. At the same time, he increased Spain's military commitment to the UN-led force in Afghanistan and called for more international co-operation to counter terrorism. His domestic agenda included an expected increase in welfare spending and promised reform of the tax system. Observers believed he would be more sympathetic than his predecessor to regions with large nationalist movements.

In Feb. 2005 a car bomb exploded in Madrid, injuring about 40 people. Although ETA was thought to be responsible, the Zapatero government offered peace talks the following May if the organization would disarm. Also in Feb. the Spanish electorate endorsed the European Union's proposed new constitution treaty in a referendum. In June 2005 parliament defied the Roman Catholic Church by legalizing gay marriage and granting homosexual couples adoption and inheritance rights.

In March 2006 ETA declared a permanent ceasefire, marking a supposed end to four decades of separatist violence. However, Zapatero's willingness to negotiate with the organization was criticized severely when ETA broke the truce with a bomb attack on Madrid airport in Dec. that year which killed two people. In a subsequent parliamentary debate he apologized to the nation for having 'made a mistake' about ETA. Zapatero meanwhile gave his government's support to a new charter giving greater autonomy to Catalonia which was approved by 74% of voters in a referendum in the region in June 2006. Andalusia voted in favour of similar reforms in Feb. 2007.

After the ETA attack at Madrid airport Zapatero adopted a harder line against the group, suspending all peace moves. In response, ETA withdrew its ceasefire in June 2007. In Oct. several people were convicted and imprisoned for the Madrid train bombings in 2004.

In Nov. 2007 the Spanish parliament passed a bill formally denouncing the Franco dictatorship and ordering the removal of all related statues and symbols from streets and buildings.

The PSOE won the elections of March 2008, taking 169 of the 350 seats. Zapatero was subsequently re-elected prime minister by parliament in April 2008. His new cabinet for the first time included more women than men.

In response to sharply rising unemployment in the wake of the global financial crisis, Zapatero unveiled an €11 bn. plan in Nov. 2008 to boost the economy through investment in public works and infrastructure. Spain nevertheless went into recession in Jan. 2009 and unemployment continued to rise through the year. In June the PSOE came second to the opposition Popular Party in the elections to the European Parliament.

Meanwhile, in July 2009, a Spanish government minister visited British Gibraltar for the first time in 300 years but insisted that Spain would not relinquish its claim to the territory. In Jan. 2010 Spain took over the rotating six-month presidency of the European Union.

The impact of the economic downturn cast a long shadow over the political landscape in 2010. Government austerity measures to reduce Spain's budget deficit, unpopular labour reform and rising unemployment (reaching 20%) prompted widespread unrest and strikes by workers as Zapatero's approval ratings among voters plummeted. Meanwhile, ETA's announcement in Jan. 2011 that a further ceasefire announced four months earlier was 'permanent' was dismissed by the government.

On 2 April 2011 Zapatero announced he would not stand for re-election in the 2011 parliamentary election. Following the defeat his party suffered in the Nov. elections, Zapatero left office on 21 Dec. 2011.

Zardari, Asif Ali (Pakistan)

Introduction

Asif Ali Zardari became Pakistan's president in Sept. 2008 following the resignation of Pervez Musharraf. He has been co-chairman of the Pakistan's People's Party (PPP), the largest grouping in the National Assembly, since the assassination of his wife, Benazir Bhutto, in Dec. 2007. A controversial figure, he has struggled to maintain a stable coalition government.

Early Life

Born on 26 July 1955 in Nawabshah, Zardari was brought up and educated in Karachi. He established a career in business and property and in 1983 unsuccessfully contested local elections in Nawabshah. In 1987 Zardari married Benazir Bhutto, then leader-in-exile of the PPP in London. The following year Bhutto became prime minister when the PPP won the general election.

During Bhutto's first term of office Zardari prospered amid rumours of corruption. In 1990 Bhutto was ousted by President Ghulam Ishaq Khan, and Zardari was arrested and jailed on corruption and blackmail charges although never brought to trial. He claimed the action was politically motivated. While in prison Zardari was elected to the National Assembly and in 1993, when Bhutto won a second term as prime minister, the charges against him were dropped. He then served as minister for the environment from 1993–96 and as minister for investment from 1995–96.

In 1996 Bhutto was again removed from office and Zardari was arrested on charges of murder and corruption. He was detained for 8 years, during which time he and Bhutto appealed against a Swiss court conviction for money laundering. With Bhutto in exile in Dubai, Zardari continued to deny all charges and claimed political persecution. In 2004 he was freed and the charges against him in Pakistan were dropped. From 2004–07 he lived primarily in the USA, where he received medical treatment for several conditions.

In Nov. 2007 President Musharraf introduced a measure to cancel criminal charges against National Assembly members, clearing the way for Zardari and Bhutto to return to Pakistan. Following Bhutto's assassination during a PPP rally on 27 Dec. 2007, Zardari assumed joint chairmanship of the party with his 19-year-old son, Bilawal. In Feb. 2008 the PPP won the general election in coalition with the Pakistan Muslim League-Nawaz Sharif (PML-N). Zardari and Sharif sought to establish a coalition government and made preparations to impeach Musharraf, who was refusing to relinquish power. Musharraf finally resigned on 18 Aug. 2008 and four days later the PPP nominated Zardari as their presidential candidate. However, on 25 Aug. Sharif took his party out of the coalition, protesting at the concentration of executive power in Zardari's hands and claiming that he had reneged on a promise to reinstate 60 Supreme Court judges. Zardari was elected president on 6 Sept. 2008.

Career Peak

Zardari's tenure has been marked by political tensions, both domestic and with neighbouring states. In March 2009 he defused mounting friction with the Pakistani judiciary and the PML-N by announcing the reinstatement of former chief justice Iftikhar Chaudhry—sacked by Musharraf in 2007 and since championed by Sharif—in response to widespread popular protests. Zardari also pledged to reduce some of the powers invested in the presidency (under constitutional changes which were later approved by parliament in April 2010), and in Nov. 2009 relinquished control of the country's nuclear weapons to the prime minister in an apparent effort to deflect growing opposition. This gesture, however, was overshadowed the following month as the Supreme Court quashed an earlier legal amnesty protecting Zardari and several political allies from corruption charges. Zardari's opponents renewed calls for his resignation. Prime Minister Gilani's failure to pursue further investigations into Zardari prompted the Court to charge the premier with contempt in Feb. 2012. In June it disqualified Gilani from holding office and he was succeeded by Raja Pervez Ashraf.

Zardari's attempts to improve relations with India have been hampered by allegations of Pakistani involvement in the major terrorist attack in Mumbai in 2008 and further attacks in Mumbai and Delhi in July and Sept. 2011. Furthermore, longstanding tensions over the disputed territory of Kashmir led to border clashes in Jan. 2013. Zardari has also faced an increasing domestic security threat from Islamic extremists, especially in the volatile northwest region of the country. In response to a series of attacks, government forces launched major military offensives against Taliban militants from April 2009 in the Swat valley and from Oct. 2009 in the tribal area of South Waziristan. However, suicide bombings by militants continued unabated in many of Pakistan's major cities, further undermining Zardari's authority.

In July–Aug. 2010 Zardari was criticized for his government's response to a humanitarian crisis following flooding that devastated large areas of the country. More than 1,600 people were killed and 20 m. displaced by the deluge.

Relations with the USA became increasingly strained in 2010 and 2011. Cross-border US air strikes in anti-Taliban operations led Pakistan to temporarily suspend NATO's supply routes into Afghanistan in Sept. 2010 and again in Nov. 2011. Meanwhile, Osama bin Laden, founder of the al-Qaeda militant network, was killed by US special forces in Abbottabad in Pakistan in May 2011. The Pakistani security establishment's apparent ignorance about Bin Laden's presence in the city, and the US government's failure to notify the Pakistani authorities about its military intentions, caused further friction between the two uneasy allies.

Concurrently, there were increasing tensions between the Zardari government and Pakistan's powerful military leadership. In Dec. 2011 Zardari underwent hospital treatment in Dubai, triggering rumours of his resignation under coercion from the army, and in Jan. 2012 a scandal over a leaked memo alleging that senior government officials had sought US aid against a possible military coup further soured the political atmosphere.

In March 2013 parliament dissolved itself ahead of elections scheduled for 11 May. In so doing, it became the first parliament in Pakistan's history to complete a full 5-year term. Zardari stepped down as president in Sept. 2013, handing his duties over to a democratically elected successor, Mamnoon Hussain. Although no longer protected by presidential immunity against charges of money laundering and bribery, Zardari has vowed to stay on in Pakistan to oversee reforms to the PPP.

Zatlers, Valdis (Latvia)

Introduction

Valdis Zatlers was elected president by Latvia's parliament, the *Saeima*, in May 2007. He began his 4-year term in July, taking over from Vaira Vīķe-Freiberga. The president's role is principally ceremonial with limited legislative powers.

Early Life

Zatlers was born on 22 March 1955 in Riga. He attended secondary school before going on to the Riga Institute of Medicine in 1973 to train as a surgeon. He graduated in 1979 in orthopaedic and trauma surgery and began working at Riga Hospital No. 2. From 1985–94 he was head of the hospital's traumatology unit. His initial foray into politics saw him join the Popular Front of Latvia in 1988, shortly before the first significant protests against Soviet rule. In 1990–91 Zatlers completed 6 months of medical training at the universities of Yale and Syracuse in the USA, returning to Latvia as it won its independence.

From 1994–98 he was director of the State Orthopaedic and Traumatology Hospital, during which time he worked with patients suffering the effects of the 1996 Chernobyl disaster. He left the hospital in 2007, having been accused of malpractice over the purchasing of medical supplies and of accepting undeclared payments from patients, but was cleared of wrongdoing in both cases. Though a signatory of the People's Party's 1998 founding manifesto, Zatlers was not affiliated to any party before his election to the presidency on 31 May 2007, when he defeated Aivars Endzinš.

Career Peak

Zatlers' election by the ruling coalition was viewed as a compromise deal by the major parties. As president he sought to strengthen Latvia's bilateral economic relations through state visits and by raising the country's profile in the United Nations.

After anti-government demonstrations in Oct. and Nov. 2007 forced the resignation of Prime Minister Aigars Kalvītis, Zatlers appointed the interior minister, Ivars Godmanis, as premier. In Dec. 2007 the Schengen Treaty, abolishing border controls between certain EU member states, came into force in Latvia. With the country under increasing economic pressure, Godmanis' administration collapsed in Feb. 2009. Zatlers nominated Valdis Dombrovskis as premier of a new government that was approved the following month.

Although widely expected to win the vote, Zatlers was defeated by Andris Bērziņš in the presidential election held on 2 June 2011. The following month Zatlers formed the centre-right Zatlers' Reform Party.

Zedillo Ponce de León, Ernesto (Mexico)

Introduction

Representing the Partido Revolucionario Institucional (Institutional Revolutionary Party; PRI), Ernesto Zedillo Ponce de León was president of Mexico from 1 Dec. 1994 to 30 Nov. 2000. Zedillo's steady recovery of the Mexican economy and negotiations of the Zapatista problem, both inherited from his predecessor, will be less well remembered than changes he made to the system that promoted a more democratic government and eventually made it possible to end the 71-year dominance of the PRI in Mexican politics.

Early Life

Zedillo was born in Mexico City on 27 Dec. 1951. The son of an electrician, he spent his childhood in the northern town of Mexicali. An economist, he studied at the Instituto Politécnico Nacional in Mexico, then at Bradford, England and finally at Yale University where in 1981 he earned his PhD in a study of the issue of public indebtedness in Mexico and its links to future growth of petroleum exports. Zedillo worked in the central bank of Mexico from 1978–88, engaging in economic research and analysis. During this time he gained wide recognition as one of the main proponents of economic modernization policies, establishing the Exchange Risk Coverage Trust Fund (FICORCA), the agency that made it possible to restructure the debt of many Mexican companies in the early 1980s. Zedillo joined the dominant PRI in 1971. His first political roles as Undersecretary and then Secretary of Planning and Budget Control from 1987–92, continued his successful economic career by reducing the rate of inflation from 160% to approximately 8%. He was Secretary of Education from 1992–94, during which time he was campaign manager for Luis Donaldo Colosio. However, on 23 March 1993 Colosio was assassinated in Tijuana and Zedillo was named as his replacement.

Career Peak

Contrary to the Mexicans' love of personality, Zedillo was considered uncharismatic. The incoming president himself claimed to be surprised at his election in Aug. 1994 when he came to power with only 48.8% of votes, the lowest majority of any PRI candidate since their rise to power in 1929. Even so, Zedillo set out on a programme that would move away from the traditional PRI way of governing as he sought to promote a more democratic parliament, even appointing a member of an opposition party to his cabinet. By spending more on health and education, Zedillo's aims were to promote a more egalitarian society by combating poverty. He also vowed to eradicate corruption. He did this by ordering a public investigation into the assassination of the PRI secretary general, José Francisco Ruiz Massieu, eventually arresting the brother of his predecessor Carlos Salinas, Raul. Despite good intentions, Zedillo's goals were undermined by an economic crisis that occurred immediately after his arrival as president, a crisis brought on by his predecessor Salinas. By the end of 1994 the peso had been devalued by

over 40%. This recession had the knock-on effect of increasing crime, especially drug related offences, and causing a large number of Mexicans, driven out by unemployment, to emigrate illegally to the USA. Although Zedillo managed to bring the economy back to the level at which it had been when he took over, by the end of his term there were still approximately 40 m. people in Mexico living in poverty.

Equal in complexity and as challenging a problem as the recession was the conflict with the Ejército Zapatista de Liberación Nacional (Zapatista Army of Liberation; EZLN). The conflict began with an uprising in Chiapas on 1 Jan. 1994 and continued throughout Zedillo's presidency. Zedillo originally managed to handle the problem successfully by putting down the uprising without bloodshed, even capturing the rebels' headquarters in 1995. The following year Zedillo's government signed the San Andreas Accord on Rights and Indigenous Cultures, an act taken as a sign that the government was sensitive to the problems faced by the indigenous population. An investigation into the Chiapas state where the rebels were based revealed that 90% of inhabitants were living in poverty, with 75% in extreme poverty. Even so, the problem of the paramilitaries, who had a tacit link to the government, soured any attempts to resolve the crisis. Reports of brutality culminated in the massacre of 45 displaced Tzotil Indians in a village church in Chiapas in 1997. Claims that the government backtracked on the San Andreas Accord and supported the anti-Zapatista paramilitary groups had derailed peace talks. Opposition parties, such as the Partido Acción Nacional (National Action Party; PAN), took the opportunity to exploit anti-PRI sentiment and civil discontent brought on by the recession.

Despite these problems, Zedillo's most important move was to create a more democratic political system, which allowed an end to the continual domination of the PRI. Changes made to the electoral system meant the congressional elections of 1997 left the PRI without an overall majority. For the first time in its history, Mexico City elected a mayor who was not a PRI candidate, Cuauhtemoc Cárdenas. This paved the way for the 2000 elections, which saw the election of the PAN candidate Vicente Fox Quesada end the 71-year domination of the PRI party.

Later Life

Since leaving office Zedillo has had several jobs as an economic consultant. He is currently the director of the Yale Center for the Study of Globalization at Yale University in the USA.

Zedkaia, Jurelang (Marshall Islands)

Introduction

Jurelang Zedkaia was elected president in Oct. 2009. Having represented the capital, Majuro, in parliament for 19 years, he vowed to unite the nation after 2 years of political tumult.

Early Life

Iroji Jurelang Zedkaia was born on 13 July 1950 on Majuro Atoll, the administrative centre of the Marshall Islands, then part of the US-controlled Trust Territory of the Pacific Islands. He attended local schools and the Calvary Bible Institute (1967–69) before employment in the health service.

In the mid-1980s Zedkaia joined the Majuro Atoll's local authority, looking after the health, education and social affairs portfolios. First elected to represent Majuro in the *Nitijela* (lower house of the legislature) in 1991, he held his seat in 1994 and was elected vice speaker for the *Nitijela* in 1997. He was returned as Majuro's representative for the Aelon Kein Ad (Our Islands) Party in the 2000 general election and again in Nov. 2007, when the United People's Party (UPP) eventually emerged as victors. After the results were challenged in the courts, the new president, Litokwa Tomeing, appointed Zedkaia as speaker in Jan. 2008.

The controversy surrounding the Nov. 2007 general election ushered in a power struggle between Tomeing and the defeated former president, Kessai Note. Against a backdrop of the global financial crisis, numerous party defections and new alliances, Tomeing weathered two motions of no confidence. However, in a third vote held on 21 Oct. 2009 a majority voted to oust him, triggering a presidential election. Zedkaia narrowly defeated Note by 17 votes to 15 and he was sworn into office on 2 Nov. 2009.

Career Peak

In his inaugural address, Zedkaia called for the country to put aside political divisions. He prioritized improvements to health care, the education system and conditions for outer islanders, as well as forming closer relations with other countries. He attended the UN summit on climate change in Copenhagen, Denmark in Dec. 2009 and pledged to support the resulting accord while pushing for a legally-binding treaty to protect island nations vulnerable to rising seas. Following the general election in Nov. 2011, parliament elected Christopher Loeak as the new president in Jan. 2012.

Later Life

Zedkaia passed away on 7 Oct. 2015 aged 65 from a suspected heart attack.

Zeidan, Ali (Libya)

Introduction

Ali Zeidan became prime minister in Oct. 2012. Having spent 30 years in exile opposing Muammar Gaddafi, Zeidan was a key figure in securing Western support for the rebellion that overthrew the former dictator in 2011.

Early Life

Ali Zeidan was born on 15 Dec. 1950 and grew up in the town of Waddan in central Libya. In the 1970s he served in the Libyan embassy in India before defecting from Libya in 1980 and joining the opposition National Front for the Salvation of Libya. Zeidan spent the next three decades in exile, working as a lawyer in Geneva and campaigning for human rights in his homeland.

During the 2011 Libyan uprising, Zeidan served as European envoy for the National Transitional Council (the rebel movement's chief political arm). He was widely credited with convincing Western leaders, including France's President Nicolas Sarkozy, to support the insurgency.

In Libya's first ever democratic elections in July 2012, Zeidan was elected as an independent for Al Jufrah. He stood for the premiership after a no-confidence vote was carried against the interim leader, Abdurrahim al-Keib. In a vote in the 200-seat General National Congress on 14 Oct. 2012, he secured the support of a liberal coalition led by the National Forces Alliance, gaining 93 votes against 85 for the only other candidate, local government minister Mohammed al-Hrari (who had been the choice of the Justice and Construction Party founded by the Muslim Brotherhood).

Career Peak

Parliament approved Zeidan's cabinet on 31 Oct. 2012. His primary task was to unite a country riven by political and regional affiliations. At his swearing-in, he pledged that 'this government will give its utmost best to the nation based on the rule of law, human rights, democracy, rights, and the belief in God, his Prophet and a state based on Islam'. He prioritized the recruitment and training of a professional army and police force to confront an environment awash with arms and militias in the wake of the revolution. In Oct. 2013 Zeidan was briefly kidnapped in Tripoli, apparently by militia gunmen. He was released unharmed and denounced the abduction as a failed coup attempt, which nonetheless raised international concerns over Libya's political stability.

Zeidan was ousted from the premiership in a parliamentary vote of no confidence on 11 March 2014, following a prolonged port blockade by militias in eastern parts of the country that had caused a dramatic downturn in the country's oil output. It had also emerged that a North Korean-flagged tanker had illegally loaded oil from a rebel controlled port in Libya, and subsequently escaped into international waters. Defence minister Abdullah al-Thanay was named interim prime minister by congress the same day.

Zelaya, Manuel (Honduras)

Introduction

Manuel Zelaya was sworn in as president in Jan. 2006 after a bitterly contested election. A wealthy landowner and member of the Liberal Party (PLH), he had to confront high levels of unemployment, widespread poverty and a serious crime wave.

Early Life

José Manuel Zelaya Rosales was born on 20 Sept. 1952 in Catacamas in the Olancho department of Honduras and studied civil engineering at the National University of Honduras in the capital, Tegucigalpa. He inherited land in Olancho and worked there as a rancher during the 1970s, when Honduras was under military rule. In 1980 he began working as a co-ordinator for the PLH, which won the 1981 presidential election with its candidate, Roberto Suazo Cordova. Zelaya was elected a deputy in the national congress at the elections of Nov. 1985, a position he held until 1998. From 1987–94 he was on the board of the national council for private enterprise and was president of the industrial association of Medera.

Following the victory of Carlos Roberto Reina (PLH) in the presidential election of Nov. 1993, Zelaya was appointed minister for investment in charge of the social investment fund. From late 1997, under the PLH-led government of Carlos Roberto Flores, Zelaya introduced a programme to return power to local communities. Selected as the PLH candidate to contest the presidential election of 27 Nov. 2005, Zelaya campaigned on a platform of tackling crime by doubling police numbers and introducing re-education programmes for criminals. This contrasted with the approach of his National Party rival, Porfirio Lobo Sosa, who promised the death penalty for convicted gang members. Results were delayed for a week but Zelaya emerged victorious with 49.9% of the vote to Lobo Sosa's 46.2%. He was sworn in as president in Tegucigalpa on 27 Jan. 2006.

Career Peak

In addition to his vow to fight gang violence and drug trafficking, Zelaya pledged more job training, reforms to the education system and cuts in red tape. He also laid out plans for 'civil assemblies' to monitor government, and guaranteed food for the poor and the creation of 400,000 new jobs. The success of his programme rested largely on expanded trade under the US-Central America free trade agreement (which came into effect in April 2006) and on debt relief under the World Bank's Heavily Indebted Poor Countries (HIPC) initiative.

In Oct. 2007 the Nicaraguan and Honduran governments accepted an International Court of Justice ruling settling a long-running territorial dispute and Zelaya made the first official visit to Cuba by a Honduran leader for 46 years. In Aug. 2008 Honduras—traditionally an ally of the USA—joined the Bolivarian Alternative for the Americas, an alliance of leftist countries in Latin America headed by Venezuela's anti-US President Hugo Chávez. Zelaya cited a lack of international support to tackle poverty as the motive for the move.

In 2009 tensions mounted over the president's desire to amend the constitution in order to run for a second term in office. The changes were to be put to a referendum on 28 June but a Supreme Court ruling declared the ballot illegal. The military staged a coup before voting could commence, ousting Zelaya from power and placing him in exile initially in Costa Rica and later in the Dominican Republic. President of the National Congress, Roberto Micheletti, was sworn in as interim president declaring his intention to remain in office until scheduled presidential elections could be held in Nov.

Later Life

In May 2011 an appeal court judgment resulted in all corruption charges levelled against Zelaya being dropped, paving the way for his return from exile and Honduras' readmittance into the Organization of American States.

Zhivkov, Todor (Bulgaria)

Introduction

Todor Zhivkov was First Secretary of the Bulgarian Communist Party from 1954–89 and was President from 1971–89. He was instrumental in deposing the monarchy in favour of a communist regime and became the Eastern Bloc's longest serving leader. Opposed to the reforms sweeping through the Soviet Union and Eastern Europe during the Gorbachev years, he was forced from power by members of his own party.

Early Life

Zhivkov was born on 7 Sept. 1911 in Bravets, Bulgaria but soon moved to Sofia. He joined the youth wing of the outlawed Communist Party when he was in his late teens and enrolled in the party proper in 1932, moving up its ranks until 1937. He led a partisan resistance movement during World War II and was active in the removal of the monarchy and the suppression of anti-communists in the war's aftermath.

With the Communists installed in power, Zhivkov advanced rapidly in the party hierarchy, joining the Politburo in 1951. In March 1954 he replaced Vulko Chervenkov, who fell out of favour in Moscow after the death of Stalin, to become First Secretary of the Communist Party. He cultivated close ties with Nikita Khrushchev and consolidated his support at home, becoming Prime Minister in 1962. 9 years later he was made Chairman of the Council of State, a post equivalent to President.

Career Peak

Though he had criticized Chervenkov for the Stalinesque cult of personality, Zhivkov created an even stronger cult around himself. He proceeded with agricultural collectivization and did much to improve the country's industrial base. However, to achieve these results he executed his power ruthlessly. In the 1950s and 1960s he imprisoned thousands of his rivals and often resorted to the feared State Security forces, who set up the murder of the noted dissident Georgi Markov in London in 1978.

Zhivkov bound his country to the USSR more tightly than any of his East European neighbours. He improved ties with the Balkan states but relations with Yugoslavia were strained, particularly over the issue of Macedonian nationality. Relations with Bulgaria's significant Turkish minority declined during the 1980s when Zhivkov, concerned with the falling birth rate and increases in foreign debts, attempted to assimilate them. In practice, this policy involved the suppression of Turkish heritage and culture, leading to around 300,000 Turks leaving the country.

This added to the country's economic troubles and by 1989, having positioned himself against the liberalizing reforms of Gorbachev, opposition to his rule was growing. On 10 Nov. 1989 he was forced to resign and was replaced by Petur Mladenov.

Later Life

In the following month Zhivkov was expelled by the party. In 1992 he was convicted on charges of corruption and sentenced to house arrest, although the verdict was overturned in 1996. Two years later he was accepted into the Socialist Party, which had been established after the dissolution of the Communists, but his health was poor and he died on 5 Aug. 1998 in Sofia.

Zhou Enlai (China)

Introduction

Zhou Enlai was Prime Minister of the People's Republic of China between 1949 and 1976, and had been one of the leading players in the Chinese Communist Party since its foundation.

Zhou was born in Gansu province in 1898—the exact date is unknown. His family's relative wealth enabled Zhou to receive a good education in Tianjin before he was sent to Japan as a student in 1917. Returning to Beijing 2 years later he became involved in radical student politics and was arrested in 1920. Released the same year, his family's money allowed him to travel to France to study.

Early Life

As a student in France, Zhou embraced Communism and became the organizer of the Chinese Communist Party in Europe, after the party's foundation in 1921. Returning to China in 1924, Zhou was active in Sun Yat-sen's revolution of 1925 and the seizure of Shanghai by workers in 1927. By the time the Nationalists turned on the Communists in 1927, Zhou was in charge of the military division of the Communist Party and a member of the Politburo. During the Nationalists' military campaign against the Communists, he worked underground for the party in Shanghai until 1931.

When Communist activity in the cities became increasingly difficult Zhou retreated to the west where the Chinese Soviet Republic had been established. On the Long March (1934–35) he became Mao's close ally. After the all-out Japanese invasion of China, Zhou was the Communists' negotiator with the Nationalists as they attempted to form a common front against the Japanese. He remained in Chongqing through most of the war as the Communists' representative to the Nationalists. Later, Zhou led the Communist delegation in post-war negotiations, which proved fruitless and civil war between the two sides recommenced in 1946.

Career Peak

When the People's Republic of China was established on 1 Oct. 1949, Zhou became the new Communist state's first prime minister and (until 1958) the foreign minister. He travelled widely, promoted the alliance with the Soviet Union (which collapsed in the mid-1960s) and was influential in setting up the historic meeting between US President Richard Nixon and Mao Zedong in 1971. Perhaps his greatest contribution to modern China was as foreign minister and through his involvement in international affairs long after he relinquished the foreign affairs portfolio. He was an effective representative of his country as well as a survivor in the internal wars in the Chinese Communist Party. Zhou's negotiating skills, and personal charm, were important during the squabbles within the Central Committee and Politburo during the Cultural Revolution. Zhou was a moderating influence and, after the excesses of the Red Guards had discredited the Cultural Revolution, Zhou worked to bring moderates, including Deng Xiaoping, back into the leadership. He died in harness on 8 Jan. 1976, shortly before Mao.

Zhu Rongji (China)

Introduction

A keen economic reformer, Zhu Rongji held office as prime minister of the People's Republic of China from March 1998 until March 2003. Zhu made his name running the municipal government of Shanghai, China's largest city, and had had only a short ministerial career in national government when he was chosen as premier.

Early Life

Zhu Rongji was born on 1 Oct. 1928 in Henan province. He was educated at Tsinghua University in Beijing where he received a degree in electrical engineering in 1951. Two years before graduation he had joined the Chinese Communist Party, a necessary step for a successful career. The young graduate gained an appointment in the State Planning Commission. However, his career did not progress smoothly. A pragmatist, Zhu did not approve of the more radical economic decisions taken by Mao Zedong. His discrete opposition earned him demotion and internal exile, but also brought him to the notice of the future reformist leader, Deng Xiaoping.

When Deng became effective ruler of China, Zhu's career took off. In 1998 he became deputy leader of the party in Shanghai and then, in the same year, mayor. Able to put his liberal economic ideas into practice, Zhu opened up the great port-city to foreign investors. Business in Shanghai flourished and standards of living improved. In 1993 Deng Xiaoping rewarded Shanghai's reforming mayor with one of the country's deputy prime ministerial posts. Zhu immersed himself in economic matters and got himself appointed head of the national bank (the People's Bank of China). He took measures to help boost the economy and cut inflation.

Career Peak

Zhu implemented wide-ranging reforms, not only economic. A major concern was the reform of the country's antiquated banking system. He also did not shy away from tackling the bad debts that many large state-run corporations had run up. Zhu introduced many elements of a market economy, for example allowing local authorities to charge economic rents for public housing, and his economic reforms have, in part, made possible China's membership of the World Trade Organization (WTO). He attempted to reform the military, reducing the number in arms by more than 900,000. But one of his biggest challenges was reshaping government: the administration had grown unwieldy with too many departments and deputy ministers. Zhu was partially successful in creating a leaner, more efficient system.

At the Communist Party congress of Nov. 2002 he was among several high-profile figures to announce their retirement from senior office, effective in March 2003.

Zia ul-Haq, Muhammad (Pakistan)

Introduction

Muhammad Zia ul-Haq was president of Pakistan between 1978–88 and the third head of state to enforce martial law.

Early Life

Zia ul-Haq was born in Jalundhar on 12 Aug. 1924. He was educated at the Government High School, Simla, then at St. Stephen's College, Delhi, before gaining a commission in the British army in 1943. With the end of the Second World War he remained in the armed forces and, with the partition of the subcontinent in 1947, became a member of the Pakistani army.

Having taken a training course in the US (1963–64) Zia acted as assistant quarter master of the 101 infantry division during the 1965 war with India. After the war he went on to teach at a military camp in Jordan until his appointment as Core Commander of Multan in 1975.

A year later, Zia superseded five senior colleagues to become Chief of Army Staff. His appointment, by President Zulfiqar Ali Bhutto, was seen as a calculated move to appoint a supporter of Bhutto's leadership. The choice proved ill-fated and on 5 July 1977 the political opposition which had been mounted against Bhutto culminated in a bloodless coup, led by Zia. With Bhutto imprisoned, Zia placed the country under martial law and took control as Chief Martial Law Administrator.

Career Peak

Zia-ul-Haq reneged on his promise to return the country to civilian rule within 90 days and instead, in Oct. 1977, announced his intention to bring corrupt past leaders to account. The Disqualification Tribunal subsequently excluded many former cabinet members from active politics for 7 years. Amongst those accused by the tribunal was former president, Zulfiqar Ali Bhutto. Bhutto was executed in 1979 for his alleged involvement in the murder of a political opponent.

Zia took office as president on 16 Sept. 1978, establishing an advisory body, the Majlis-i-Shura. The Shura, which carried no real political weight, comprised 284 professionals, journalists, clerics and intellectuals, all hand-picked by Zia.

Zia pursued a policy geared towards the Islamization of all social institutions. In 1979 he ordered the introduction of shariat courts to exercise Islamic law and took steps towards the Islamization of the economy.

In response to increasing pressure to hand over to a democratically elected government, Zia agreed to elections in March 1985. But a national referendum signalled 98% approval for Zia's process of Islamization. Zia took this as a vote of confidence and extended his tenure by a further 5 years. The

elections, which were boycotted by opposition parties, saw Muhammad Khan Junejo appointed as prime minister. Zia lifted the state of emergency but amended the constitution to increase his presidential powers.

A growing divide between Zia and his premier came to a head in May 1988 when Zia dissolved the national assembly and removed Junejo from his post.

Elections were again promised within 90 days, but with opposition from the Muslim League and threatened by the popularity of Benazir Bhutto, Zia once more looked set to postpone them. Before this could happen, however, on 17 Aug. 1988 Zia was killed in an air crash which also claimed the lives of many of Pakistan's top-ranking military. Sabotage was claimed though no-one was ever brought to trial. Zia's remains were buried at Faisal Mosque, Islamabad.

Zia, Khaleda (Bangladesh)

Introduction

Bangladesh's first female prime minister (1991–96) and widow of Ziaur Rahman, the country's president between 1977–81, Khaleda Zia returned to office in Oct. 2001 at the head of the Bangladesh Jatiyatabadi Dal (Bangladesh Nationalist Party; BJD). Her re-election took place amidst social and political unrest over the treatment of Bangladesh's Hindu, Buddhist and Christian minorities, with both her and her main political rival, former premier and leader of the Awami League, Sheikh Hasina Wahed, accused of fomenting communal violence. Her term of office ended in Oct. 2006.

Early Life

Khaleda Zia was born on 15 Aug. 1945 in the Dinajpur district of what was then East Bengal to a businessman father, Iskander Majumder.

In 1960 she married Ziaur Rahman. A hero of the 1971 secessionist war against Pakistan, Rahman became president of Bangladesh in 1977, forming the centre-right BJD. Following his assassination in 1981 as part of a failed military coup, leadership went to Rahman's vice-president, Abdus Sattar, who ruled until a second coup, a year later, which put the country under the dictatorial sway of Gen. H. M. Ershad. Ershad proclaimed martial law on 24 March 1982, abolishing all political parties and suspending the constitution. Having remained in the shadows during her husband's presidency, after his death Zia joined the BJD. In 1983 she was made a vice-chairman, going on to be elected leader of the party the following year. In 1983 the BJD formed a seven-party alliance. By 1990 the growing popularity of Zia's alliance and the eight-party alliance formed by Sheikh Hasina Wajed, the daughter of Bangladesh's first prime minister, Sheikh Mujibur Rahman, forced the resignation of Gen. Ershad. During the 8 years of Ershad's rule, Zia had been imprisoned seven times. Although Zia's BJD failed to win an overall majority in parliament, it received sufficient support from several smaller parties to gain power. On 20 March 1991 Zia was sworn in as prime minister.

Career Peak

Zia's first months in office were beset with catastrophe as Bangladesh experienced one of its worst cyclones in recent years, causing 131,000 deaths and damage at US$2 bn. Although Zia appealed for international assistance, relief efforts were hindered by flooding and storms. Her leadership subsequently came under fire for her failure to deal effectively with the crisis.

In Aug. 1991 she was successful in reinstating a parliamentary system of government and in Sept. she became head of government after new elections. She tried to revitalize the agricultural industry and undertook reforms in education including the introduction of compulsory free primary education and measures to increase female enrolment.

In 1992 the destruction of the Babri Masjid Mosque in neighbouring India and the ensuing violence provoked fundamentalist sentiment and attacks against Hindus which Zia failed to quash. At this time, Zia's government intelligence unit shared links with Pakistan's Inter-Services Intelligence (ISI), an agency which has since been denounced for its involvement with militant Islamic fundamentalism and terrorist activities.

Although Zia won the election held on 15 Feb. 1996 giving her a second consecutive term in power, the election was boycotted by all major opposition parties. Handing over power to a caretaker administration, Zia was then forced into opposition by the Awami League, headed by Sheikh Hasina Wajed.

In 1999 she formed a four-party alliance with the Jatiya Party, the Jamaat-e-Islami and the Islami Oikya Jote, both linked to violence against Bangladesh's Hindu minority. In the 2001 election she accused the Awami League of failing to protect Hindus, though the Awami League, traditionally seen as tolerant towards minorities, put the blame for the violence on the BJD. In the 2001 election, held on 1 Oct., the BJD achieved a two-thirds majority and Zia was returned as prime minister. Balloting was chaotic and the next month saw a spate of violence against Hindus by supporters of the BJD alliance.

Among the dominant issues which Zia's government faced was the export of natural gas to India. A liberalization of trade in this area had long been pushed by the Indian government, the USA and the World Bank, yet Zia held back, citing doubts as to the extent of natural gas reserves and future domestic demands. Illegal emigration to India was another long-running source of contention. Talks between the two countries in April 2003 aimed to alleviate tensions over their joint border.

The poor state of the economy played second place to political rivalry and the issue of communal violence. A third of the country's clothing factories closed following the attacks on New York and Washington of 11 Sept. 2001 and the subsequent war in Afghanistan. Roughly 74% of the country's export revenue comes from this industry. Coupled with fallen foreign exchange reserves, the onus rested on Zia to revitalize the economy.

In Dec. 2002 Zia held break-through talks with Senior Gen. Than Shwe, leader of neighbouring Myanmar, on closer economic co-operation and improved road and shipping links. Ties between the two governments had been strained since the early 1990s, when up to 250,000 Muslim Rohingya refugees entered Bangladesh from Myanmar. The situation had been aggravated by Myanmar's plans for a controversial dam on the shared Naf River, until Than Shwe abandoned the project in 2001. The first authorized sea route between the two countries was opened in Feb. 2003. In March 2003 Zia made the first official visit to Myanmar by a Bangladeshi prime minister.

In May 2004 Zia's government approved a constitutional amendment providing for 45 seats to be reserved for female MPs. The opposition orchestrated a series of general strikes throughout 2004 aimed at destabilizing the government. Zia responded to international criticism over her government's treatment of opposition groups, the country's weak human rights record and the growth in influence of radical Islamic groups by warning that foreign countries and international aid organizations had no business interfering in the nation's domestic politics. Over several months in 2004 serious flooding killed several hundred and left several million homeless and in need of food. In Aug. 2005 a banned Islamic militant group claimed responsibility for a series of minor explosions throughout the country.

When Zia's term of office ended on 27 Oct. 2006, Dhaka descended into rioting amid uncertainty as to who would succeed her.

Later Life

In Sept. 2007 Zia was indicted for corruption while in office and jailed ahead of a trial. She was released on bail in Sept. 2008 ahead of elections aimed at restoring multi-party democracy.

Zia was arrested again in Feb. 2015 following further allegations of corruption. In Aug. 2015 the High Court stated that her trial must begin by Oct. 2015. In Feb. 2018 she was convicted of embezzling money meant for an orphanage and sentenced to 8 years in prison.

Zuma, Jacob (South Africa)

Introduction

Jacob Zuma became president of the ANC on 18 Dec. 2007 after defeating incumbent Thabo Mbeki in a leadership election. He was elected national president after the ANC won the general election of 22 April 2009 and was re-elected for a second term in May 2014.

Early Life

Zuma was born in what is now the KwaZulu-Natal Province on 12 April 1942. Influenced by his family's trade unionist background, he became involved in politics at the age of 17.

Zuma joined the ANC in 1959. With the party banned by the apartheid government the following year, by 1962 he was an active member of Umkhonto we Sizwe (the military wing of the ANC), which was subsequently classified as a terrorist organization. In 1963 Zuma was arrested and convicted of conspiring to overthrow the government. He was jailed for 10 years, serving part of the sentence on Robben Island alongside Nelson Mandela.

After his release Zuma helped re-establish the ANC as an underground movement in Natal. In 1975 he left South Africa, living in Swaziland and then Mozambique. He was then appointed to the ANC national executive committee in 1977 and served as its deputy chief representative in Mozambique until the signing of the Nkomati Accord between South Africa and Mozambique in 1984, when he became chief representative. Forced to leave Mozambique in 1987, Zuma was appointed head of underground structures and chief of the intelligence department, serving on the ANC's political and military council.

When the ban on the ANC was lifted in 1990 Zuma returned to South Africa and was elected ANC chairperson for the Southern Natal region. In 1991 he was elected the party's deputy secretary general, and at the 1994 general election he agreed to Thabo Mbeki running unopposed for the deputy presidency. Zuma was appointed to the executive committee of economic affairs and tourism for the ANC in the KwaZulu-Natal provincial government. In 1997 he became the ANC's deputy president and 2 years later was chosen as South Africa's executive deputy president.

In 2005, following the conviction of Zuma's financial adviser Schabir Shaik on charges of corruption and fraud, Zuma was dismissed as deputy president by Mbeki. However, in Dec. 2007 he was elected ANC party president standing against Mbeki. His rhetoric found favour with many disadvantaged South Africans who felt marginalized by Mbeki's business-friendly policies. Zuma was thus clear favourite to become the next president of South Africa.

Career Peak

Mbeki resigned as president of South Africa on 21 Sept. 2008 after losing the support of the ANC over claims that he had interfered in the case against Zuma and in April 2009 the National Prosecuting Authority dismissed all charges. The ANC triumphed at the general election on 22 April 2009 and Zuma was elected president by parliament. He was sworn into office on 9 May 2009, succeeding Kgalema Motlanthe, who stepped aside after having replaced Mbeki.

Also in May 2009, the South African economy officially went into recession following a sharp downturn in the manufacturing and mining sectors. Unemployment accelerated and strikes and violent protests in July–Aug. were roundly condemned by Zuma. In a speech to the ANC in Jan. 2010 he warned that recovery from the economic crisis would be slow and that there would be a lag in job creation. A national strike by public sector workers over pay, which began in Aug. that year and paralysed hospitals, education and other services for 3 weeks before the action was suspended, undermined relations between the ANC and the Congress of South African Trade Unions.

In Oct. 2010 Zuma announced major changes to the composition of his cabinet, appointing a host of new ministers and deputy ministers. However, allegations of high-level corruption continued to blight his administration and in Oct. 2011 he sacked two senior ministers and suspended the chief of police. Local elections earlier in May had maintained the ANC's political dominance, but the opposition Democratic Alliance increased its vote share to about 24%. In Nov. the ANC suspended Julius Malema, its militant youth wing leader and a prominent Zuma critic, for 5 years for bringing the party into disrepute.

In Jan. 2012 Zuma addressed a rally in Bloemfontein in celebration of the ANC's 100th anniversary. In Aug. 2012, 34 platinum miners in the town of Marikana were killed and around 80 more were wounded by police during an industrial dispute over wages. Public condemnation of the treatment of the miners prompted Zuma to establish a judicial commission of inquiry in Oct.

In Dec. 2012 Zuma was re-elected leader of the ANC at the party's 5-yearly conference and in July 2013 he carried out the fourth cabinet reshuffle of his term, dismissing three ministers. The rest of the year was dominated by the declining health and ultimate death in Dec. of Nelson Mandela, the revered anti-apartheid campaigner and South Africa's first majority democratically elected president. Zuma's waning popularity was apparent at the subsequent memorial service for Mandela in Johannesburg, when he was barracked by many in the attending crowd, and also by the decision of the National Union of Metalworkers in the same month to withdraw its support for the ANC ahead of pending parliamentary elections. These took place in May 2014 and were comfortably won by the ANC, guaranteeing Zuma a second term in office.

In Feb. 2015 Zuma announced land reform proposals, long promised by the ANC, to redistribute farmland to black farmers and to ban foreign ownership. Later in the year, however, he attracted increasing criticism over further allegations of corruption, particularly in relation to South Africa's successful bid to host the 2010 football World Cup, and also for allowing Sudan's President Bashir to visit South Africa in defiance of his International Criminal Court arrest warrant on charges of genocide and war crimes. Zuma's controversial appointments to the post of finance minister in Dec. 2015 also incurred negative reaction from the currency markets and from within his own party.

Mounting corruption allegations and a weak economic outlook fuelled speculation that Zuma might resign ahead of being constitutionally obliged to step down in 2019. He nevertheless survived two parliamentary votes of no confidence in March and Nov. 2016, as well as an impeachment motion against him in parliament in April that year. However, Zuma resigned in Feb. 2018 after facing criticism from within his own party over new corruption allegations. Deputy President Cyril Ramaphosa, who took over as the ANC leader in Dec. 2017, was sworn in as his successor as president on 15 Feb. 2018.

POLITICAL FIGUREHEADS' PROFILES

Abbas, Mahmoud
(Palestinian Territories, Israel)

Position

President

Introduction

Mahmoud Abbas, also known as Abu Mazen, succeeded Yasser Arafat as president of the Palestinian Administrative Authority following elections held in Jan. 2005. Abbas held the post of prime minister in 2003. He was offered the premiership after Israel and the US refused to deal with Arafat but Arafat's reluctance to delegate powers to his new prime minister weakened Abbas' position, leading to his resignation in Sept. 2003.

Early Life

Mahmoud Abbas was born in 1935 in Saffad, near Galilee in northern Palestine, then under a British mandate. Following the creation of the state of Israel, Abbas and his family emigrated to Syria in 1948. He worked as a teacher before graduating in law from the University of Damascus and gaining a PhD in history from Moscow's Oriental College. He took a job in Qatar's civil service where he became involved in organizing Palestinian groups.

Abbas was a co-founder of the Palestinian National Liberation Movement (Fatah), which became the driving force of the PLO and a key group in the 1965 Palestinian independence revolution. He subsequently went into exile with Arafat in Jordan, Lebanon and Tunisia. In 1968 Abbas joined the Palestinian National Council (PNC) and the executive committee of the PLO. He entered into talks with several Jewish movements during the 1970s and was a pivotal figure in talks with the Israeli general, Matityahu Peled, which culminated in the 1977 'principle of peace,' calling for a two-state solution to the Israeli-Palestinian conflict.

In 1980 Abbas became the PLO's head of national and international relations and in 1988 was put in charge of the Occupied Territories portfolio. He was a leading figure in the secret talks that led to the 1993 Oslo accords which reignited the peace process. In 1995 he was the PLO's signatory on the interim peace agreement with Israel. Abbas returned from exile to the Occupied Territories in the same year.

In 1996 he was elected general secretary of the PLO executive committee. In the same year he headed the Palestinian legislative council's central election commission and won a seat as the representative for Qalqilya. In 2000 came the publication of 'Framework for the Conclusion of a Final Status Agreement between Israel and the PLO', a controversial plan he had devised with his Israeli colleague, Yossi Beilin, in the mid-1990s.

Since the beginning of the second Intifada in Sept. 2000 Abbas has been a vociferous advocate of a non-violent solution. He has pressed for an end to Palestinian attacks on Israeli targets, believing that Israel will then be unable to attack legitimately the existing autonomous structures of the Palestinian-Administered Territories. By early-2003 Israel and the US refused to engage with an Arafat-dominated administration. Under pressure to share power with a prime minister, Arafat nominated Abbas for the post and his appointment was ratified by the legislative council in March 2003. Abbas was to be responsible for the day-to-day running of the Palestinian Authority while Arafat retained control of defence and peace negotiations.

Following disputes over several key appointments, Arafat and Abbas agreed on the composition of a cabinet in late-April 2003. Later in the month the 'roadmap to peace', a plan jointly produced by the UN, EU, US and Russia to secure a lasting peace, was published and delivered to Abbas. The document called for an immediate ceasefire, an end to the Israeli occupation of Palestinian towns, a clampdown on Palestinian militants and the dismantling of Israeli settlements built since 2001. It set out proposals for the establishment of an independent, democratic Palestinian state as early as 2005. The Palestinian Administration welcomed the development. Abbas met Sharon in late-May 2003 and called for the loosening of restrictions on Arafat. In June 2003 Israel withdrew its troops from the main north-south highway in the Gaza Strip and from positions throughout northern Gaza. The move came after the three main Palestinian militant groups (Hamas, Islamic Jihad and Fatah) agreed to a ceasefire. In July 2003 the Israeli government promised to release several hundred Palestinians, including members of militant organizations. In addition, Israeli checkpoints in Ramallah and Hebron were dismantled and 8,000 workers from the Gaza Strip, Bethlehem and Tulkarem were allowed into Israel. However, the following month Sharon reiterated his commitment to building a 600 km-long 'security fence' around the West Bank, which he claimed was essential to prevent Palestinian suicide attacks.

Abbas' continuing struggle with Arafat over control of key Authority portfolios and of Palestinian security forces hampered the prime minister's attempts to control Palestinian militants. After numerous calls for support from the leadership, Abbas tendered his resignation in Sept. 2003. Arafat nominated another moderate, Ahmed Qureia, as his successor. Abbas' departure was seen as the death blow to the 'roadmap to peace,' which had been effectively abandoned after the resumption of hostilities between Palestinian militants and the Israeli army.

Career in Office

Following Yasser Arafat's death in Nov. 2004, Abbas was appointed chairman of the PLO. Subsequently, Fatah's Revolutionary Council announced its endorsement of Abbas as its preferred presidential candidate. Elections were scheduled for 9 Jan. 2006. Seven candidates were listed but after his main contender, Marwan Bargouti, stood down, Abbas took 62% of the total vote. Abbas was sworn in on 15 Jan. 2006, calling for Palestinian groups to cease violence against the Israelis.

However, attacks by military groups continued throughout Jan. On 12 Jan. Islamic Jihad launched an assault on Gaza, followed on the 13 Jan. by a suicide attack on the Karni crossing by Palestinians from Fatah's al-Aqsa Martyrs' Brigades, Hamas and the Popular Resistance Committees that left six Israelis dead. Israel retaliated by shutting down the cargo terminal and breaking relations with Abbas and the Palestinian Authority.

On 23 Jan. 2005 it was reported that Abbas had negotiated a 30-day ceasefire with Hamas and Islamic Jihad. Abbas then met with Ariel Sharon at a summit in Egypt and a joint ceasefire was declared on 8 Feb. However, on 12 Feb. a group of Palestinians attacked Israeli settlements. Abbas reacted by firing a number of security officers. In the same month he travelled to Gaza for talks to persuade militants to agree a ceasefire with the Israelis. Attacks continued on both sides.

In early April 2005 Abbas accused Israeli forces of deliberately violating the ceasefire after three young Palestinian boys were shot dead in Southern Gaza while playing football near the border fence. The Israeli troops claimed they were attempting to smuggle weapons. Abbas demanded demonstrative action by Israel to affirm its commitment to the truce. Towards the end of April a series of attacks by Palestinian militants, firing homemade rockets from the Gaza strip, led to Sharon refusing to release Palestinian prisoners as part of the truce deal. He called on Abbas to act more vigorously to tackle the continuing violence.

In May 2005 Abbas met with George W. Bush. The USA pledged US$50m. in support of its pledge for a free Palestinian state. Subsequently, Canadian prime minister Paul Martin pledged a further $9·5m. in support of judicial reform, housing projects and border management.

In June 2005 Abbas again met with Sharon to discuss a ceasefire and Israeli withdrawal from the Gaza strip. He also reinstated the death penalty in an attempt to curb lawlessness. Militant assaults continued despite pleas from Abbas for both sides to uphold the ceasefire. In July 2005 he announced his intention to move his office to Gaza until the Israeli settlement withdrawal

© Springer Nature Limited 2019
Palgrave Macmillan (ed.), *The Statesman's Yearbook Companion*,
https://doi.org/10.1057/978-1-349-95839-9

was complete. He also cancelled elections scheduled for 17 July until Jan. 2006, despite unrest in Gaza.

At the beginning of Jan. 2006 Abbas stated that he would not run for office when his current term ends. Legislative council elections were held on 25 Jan. 2006, with Change and Reform (Hamas) winning 74 seats and the Fatah Movement, 45.

In 2007 Abbas reformed the electoral system to allow all seats to be decided through proportional representation in an attempt to lessen the influence of Hamas who declared the changes illegal. Abbas' term in office was set to expire in Jan. 2009 but he extended it by 1 year to allow for simultaneous presidential and parliamentary elections to be held. Hamas criticized the move but following reconciliation talks in March 2009 elections were scheduled for 24 Jan. 2010. Intra-Palestinian political disputes between Fatah and Hamas further delayed presidential and parliamentary elections. They were intended to be held within a year from 4 May 2011 but have been postponed on several occasions. Abbas has ruled himself out from standing for re-election.

On 2 June 2014 Abbas swore in a new unity government led by Rami Hamdallah, which was backed by rival factions Fatah and Hamas. The new administration was tasked with organizing general elections to be held 'within six months'.

Abbas signed Palestine into the International Criminal Court on 31 Dec. 2014, risking increased tension with Israel and the USA who described the move as 'escalatory' and 'deeply troubling'. Palestine's entry into the ICC provides the court a mandate from which to pursue convictions for crimes committed on Palestinian territory backdated to June 2014.

In Aug. 2015 Abbas announced his resignation as leader of the PLO, with the party citing a need to 'inject new blood' into the organization. However, he continues to serve at the head of the Palastinian National Authority.

Akihito (Japan)

Position

Emperor of Japan

Introduction

Akihito succeeded his father, Hirohito, as Emperor in 1989. Regarded as the 125th direct descendant of Japan's first Emperor, Jimmu, his accession ushered in a new Heisei ('Achieving Peace') era. As Crown Prince, in 1952, he became the first of his imperial line (the oldest in the world) to marry a commoner. He assumed a throne stripped of its political power after the Second World War, but the Emperor remains a symbol of the unity of the Japanese people.

Early Life

Akihito was born on 23 Dec. 1933 in Tokyo, the fifth child and eldest son of Emperor Hirohito and Empress Nagako. He was educated at Gakushuin elementary, junior and senior high schools until 1952 when he came of age and was invested as heir to the Japanese throne.

His early traditional imperial education was broadened in the post-war climate to include instruction in English and other aspects of Western culture. In 1953 he made a six-month tour of the USA and Western Europe, including a visit to London as a Japanese representative at the coronation of the British Queen Elizabeth II, before returning to continue his studies in politics and economics at Gakushuin University. In April 1959, breaking centuries of tradition, he married a commoner, Michiko Shoda, the daughter of an industrialist. They have had three children—Crown Prince Naruhito (Hironomiya), Prince Fumihito (Akishinomiya) and Princess Sayako (Norinomiya).

Career in Office

Akihito became de facto regent after his father fell ill in Sept. 1988 and emperor on 7 Jan.1989 on his father's death. He was formally enthroned on 12 Nov. 1990, declaring his support for the constitution which prohibits his involvement in government. In 1993 he permitted the Crown Prince to marry a commoner, Masako Owada. The Emperor ended years of speculation at his 68th birthday press conference by acknowledging Korean blood in the imperial line—the mother of Emperor Kammu who reigned from AD 781–806 was of the line of King Muryong of Paekche, the ruler of the Korean Paekche Kingdom from AD 501–23. The birth in Dec. 2001 of Akihito's granddaughter and the Crown Prince's first child prompted political speculation about changes to the law to permit female succession to the imperial throne. In Nov. 2005 Akihito's only daughter, Sayako, married a commoner, Yoshiki Kuroda, therefore relinquishing her privileged status as a member of the royal family.

Akihito is an acknowledged authority on ichthyology (study of fish) and has published numerous academic papers on the subject.

In Aug. 2016 Akihito made a rare televised address in which he acknowledged his failing health and advanced age. The announcement was regarded by many to have been an admission of his will to abdicate. Then in May 2017 the government approved a bill allowing him to abdicate. He is expected to do so in April 2019, when he will be 85.

Akıncı, Mustafa (Turkish Republic of Northern Cyprus, Cyprus)

Position

President

Introduction

Mustafa Akıncı is the fourth president of the Turkish Republic of Northern Cyprus. He took office in April 2015 for a 5-year term.

Early Life

Akıncı was born in Limassol, Cyprus, on 28 Dec. 1947. He studied architecture at the Middle East Technical University in Turkey and returned to Cyprus in 1973. In 1976 he became the first elected mayor of the Nicosia Turkish Municipality, holding this position until 1990. During his 14–year tenure he worked closely with Lellos Demetriades, the mayor of Greek Cypriot Nicosia, on large infrastructure projects. Meanwhile, Akıncı became influential within the Communal Liberation Party (TKP), becoming secretary general and then leader in 1987. He also served as a member of parliament between 1993 and 2009 and as deputy prime minister and minister of state between 1999 and 2001.

Akıncı ran for the TRNC presidency at the April 2000 elections as the TKP candidate. Receiving 11.7% of the vote, he finished third behind independent Rauf Denktaş and Derviş Eroğlu of the National Unity Party. He retained his ministerial position until June 2001, when the government collapsed. In 2003 he established the social democratic Peace and Democracy Movement, the main aims of which were the promotion of Cypriot reunification, based on the proposed Annan Plan, and subsequent EU accession for Cyprus.

Akıncı was elected president in April 2015, winning 60.5% of the vote in the run-off poll, and was sworn at the end of that month.

Career in Office

As a long-standing advocate of reintegration, Akıncı expressed a desire throughout his election campaign to hold discussions on the reunification of Cyprus and the reopening of Varosha, the abandoned former tourist quarter of Famagusta. He has also opposed Turkey's increasing influence in Northern Cyprus, saying prior to the election: 'I want a more brotherly relationship [with Turkey], rather than a mother–daughter relationship. I want to see Turkish Cypriots standing on their own feet firmly.'

Aung San Suu Kyi (Myanmar)

Position

President of the National League for Democracy.

Introduction

Daw Aung San Suu Kyi led the pro-democracy movement in Myanmar on her return to the country in 1988. Her party, the National League for Democracy (NLD), won a landslide victory in democratic elections held in 1990 but was prevented from taking office by the military. She was then subjected to prolonged house arrests that provoked condemnation from the United Nations. Known as 'the Lady' by her supporters, she won the Nobel Peace Prize in 1991 for her campaign against the repressive regime. She assumed the de facto leadership of the NLD government that came to power after fresh parliamentary elections in Nov. 2015, but her reputation was severely undermined by her failure to condemn alleged human rights abuses by the still powerful military against Myanmar's Rohingya Muslim minority, some 1m. of whom were forced to flee as refugees to neighbouring Bangladesh.

Early Life

Daw Aung San Suu Kyi was born on 19 June 1945 in the Burmese capital, Yangon (Rangoon). Her father, nationalist leader Gen. Aung San, was assassinated under the orders of a political rival, U Saw, in July 1947. She received her primary schooling in Yangon before leaving for Delhi in 1960, where her mother was ambassador. Aung San Suu Kyi studied philosophy, politics and economics at St Hugh's College, Oxford, England, graduating in 1967.

Her career began at the United Nations in New York as assistant secretary on the Advisory Committee on Administrative and Budgetary Questions. She took up a research position at the Bhutanese foreign ministry in 1972, the same year she married Dr. Michael Aris, the tutor to Bhutan's royal children and later a professor of Tibetan Studies at the University of Oxford. She returned to the UK in 1973 where she gave birth to her two sons. Family life and postgraduate study in Oxford occupied her until 1985 when she became a visiting scholar at the Centre of Southeast Asian Studies at Kyoto University. Aung San Suu Kyi studied Japanese for research into her father's relations with Japan during the Second World War. She continued her studies at the Indian Institute of Advanced Studies in Simla in 1987.

In March 1988 she returned to Burma to be with her mother, who was seriously ill. She arrived during student demonstrations on an unprecedented scale that forced the resignation of Gen. Ne Win as chairman of the Burma Socialist Programme Party (BSPP) in July. The 8 Aug. marked the beginning of a nationwide insurgency, now known as the 8/8/88 uprising, that was bloodily repressed by the army, headed by a military junta which took power in Sept. as the State Law and Order Restoration Council (SLORC). Between 3000 and 10,000 civilians were killed. Aung San Suu Kyi became involved with the democracy movement, advocating peaceful protest, and the military authorities began to target her when she became secretary general of the newly-formed NLD in Sept. 1988.

Career in Office

The SLORC embarked on a campaign of slander through the state-controlled media in an attempt to discredit her. Burmese society traditionally scorned inter-racial marriage. The media paid particular attention to her marriage to a British man, in view of her position as daughter of the anti-colonial founder of modern Burma. Gen. Saw Muang had promised democratic elections, already scheduled by the BSPP but in reality a nervous reaction to the suspension of US economic and military aid. This was followed by the suspension of trade benefits by the USA in April 1989.

The slander campaign was largely ineffective, as evinced by the support shown at the funeral of Aung San Suu Kyi's mother, Daw Khin Kyi, in Dec. 1988. Aung San Suu Kyi encouraged the democracy movement outside the capital by touring the provinces. While campaigning in the Irrawaddy Delta in April 1989, she narrowly avoided an assassination attempt by an army unit thanks to the intervention of an army major. Tensions between the NLD and the SLORC escalated until the detention of Aung San Suu Kyi on 20 July 1989 for 'nurturing public hatred for the military'. House arrest disqualified her and the NLD's vice-chairman U Tin Oo from standing for the multi-party elections in May 1990, the first in 30 years.

Despite restrictions on campaigning, the free elections gave the NLD a landslide victory. The SLORC, whose party—the National Unity Party (NUP)—won only eight seats, refused to acknowledge the results, withholding the declarations of four remote constituencies. Excluding these, the NLD secured 397 seats, amounting to 82% of the seats in the anticipated People's Assembly. The United Nationalities League, claiming a similar pro-democracy programme, won 62 seats. Despite professed commitments to a handover to elected civilian rule, the SLORC refused to allow the convocation of the Assembly before a new constitution had been drawn up and approved by referendum. Having abolished the 1974 constitution, martial law was maintained, with total control of the media and the judicial system. Universities, the seat of the pro-democracy movement, were closed in the wake of the 1988 uprisings.

Foreign attention to human rights abuses and the collapse of the democratic process in Myanmar (as it became in 1989) became focused on Aung San Suu Kyi. She was awarded the Sakharov Prize for Freedom of Thought from the European Parliament and the Nobel Peace Prize in 1991 in recognition of her actions. However, international opinion was divided as how to address Myanmar's political problems. The USA persuaded many key donors, such as Japan, to end direct assistance and impose trade sanctions. Other countries and bodies adopted a more conciliatory approach, especially when the SLORC made constructive gestures, such as releasing Aung San Suu Kyi from detention in July 1995. South Korea offered a US$16·8 m. government loan in Oct. 1995 and the Association of South East Asian Nations (ASEAN) encouraged the SLORC application for membership in 1996.

During her 6-year house arrest, the NLD had been systematically persecuted by the military authorities, which imprisoned most of its leaders and imposed draconian conditions on rights to speech and assembly. A national constitutional convention organized in 1993 by the SLORC excluded most of those elected in 1990. In Oct. 1995 Aung San Suu Kyi was reappointed secretary general of the party and the NLD withdrew its delegates in Nov., claiming the convention was insincere and fundamentally flawed. Despite her release, the detention of other political opponents continued. Public speeches were banned in 1997 and attempts to convene an NLD congress were thwarted.

International attention was drawn in 1998 to Aung San Suu Kyi's clashes with the State Peace and Development Council (SPDC, as SLORC had been renamed in 1997). The NLD leadership had resumed campaigning outside Yangon until forcibly prevented in July and Aug. 1998, although protests by Aung San Suu Kyi and her colleagues were criticized by U Win Naing of the League for Democracy and Peace for distracting from constructive dialogue with the SPDC. She was also criticized for setting up the Committee Representing People's Parliament (CRPP) as a rival authority.

In 1999 Aung San Suu Kyi rejected the government's offer for her to visit her dying husband in the UK for fear of being refused re-entry to Myanmar. In March 2000 Senior Gen. Than Shwe, who had replaced Saw Maung as leader of the military junta in 1992, called for the elimination of forces undermining the stability of the regime. Aung San Suu Kyi was again prevented from travelling to regional offices and her house was raided, leading to the arrest of several party members. In Sept. 2000 she and other NLD leaders were again placed under house arrest.

The United Nations urged the SPDC to engage directly with the NLD. The UN Special Representative, Razali Ismail, persuaded Khin Nyunt, the first secretary, to negotiate with Aung San Suu Kyi, who was awarded the Presidential Medal of Freedom by US President Bill Clinton in Dec. 2000. Other senior NLD members were released, including vice-chairman U Tin Oo, and Aung Shwe, the chairman of the CRPP. In 2001, attacks on Aung San Suu Kyi in the media were terminated and the NLD was permitted to reopen its headquarters and many regional offices. However, Aung San Suu Kyi was not released until 6 May 2002 after 19 months of confinement and prolonged shuttle diplomacy by Razali Ismail. The government promised political freedom but talks with the NLD failed later in the year.

Aung San Suu Kyi's negotiations with the government collapsed entirely in April 2003 when she made a public attack on the regime's unwillingness to make formal concessions to democracy. A perceived split within the SPDC leadership over how to deal with the opposition led to a hardening of the government line and to the 'protective custody' of Aung San Suu Kyi on

30 May 2003 after attacks on her entourage. The EU and USA reacted with sanctions, although China, which consistently supported the military regime, warned against confrontation. Elsewhere in Asia, criticism of Aung San Suu Kyi's detention was most vocal from Malaysia's then prime minister, Mahathir Mohamad, who suggested in July 2003 that Myanmar be expelled from ASEAN if the government failed to release her.

In Nov. 2005 the NLD announced that Aung San Suu Kyi's detention would continue for another year. Hopes for a 2006 release were raised when, on 20 May 2006, she met with UN Undersecretary-General for Political Affairs Ibrahim Gambari (her first meeting with a foreign official since 2004), but the government nonetheless extended her house arrest at the end of May 2006 and then again in May 2007. The USA, backed by Britain, sought a UN resolution in Jan. 2007 condemning Myanmar and demanding the release of all political prisoners. However, despite not disputing Myanmar's human rights abuses, the resolution was vetoed by China and Russia. India also continued to financially underpin the regime, investing in the Shwe gas project, expected to become the government's largest source of revenue.

It had been hoped that the international pressure on the country's military regime as a consequence of its dismissive reaction to the devastation caused by Cyclone Nargis in May 2008 might force a political concession. Such hopes were dashed by the ratification of a new constitution tightening the military's grip on power and the announcement that month that Aung San Suu Kyi's detention without charge would be extended for a further 12 months. A year later Suu Kyi was charged with violating the terms of her detention and in Aug. 2009 was sentenced to another 18 months' house arrest.

In March 2010 the military junta introduced the Political Parties Registration Law preventing anyone carrying a court conviction from joining a political party or voting, effectively excluding Aung San Suu Kyi and other senior members of the NLD from participating in the general election scheduled for 7 Nov. 2010. Her calls for pro-democracy parties to boycott the elections went unheeded by many and there were suggestions that her political influence had waned. However, widespread reports of rigged ballots emerged in the wake of the vote. She was released from house arrest on 13 Nov. In by-elections held in April 2012 she was elected to the Pyithu Hluttaw, the lower house of the parliament, as the NLD secured all 37 seats that were being contested. The international community greeted her election as a step towards democracy.

In July 2013 she stated her desire to run for president. However, with two British sons, she was ineligible for election under the constitution prohibiting persons with children holding foreign citizenship from standing. Nevertheless, her NLD party won a convincing majority at the Nov. 2015 parliamentary elections and she was appointed to the cabinet in March 2016, taking on the foreign affairs and president's office portfolios. Despite initial optimism over her assumption of power, the new government struggled to reconcile the country's entrenched ethnic and religious divisions or to assert political control over the military, which in 2017 launched violent operations in Rakhine state against alleged Rohingya Muslim militants. Aung San Suu Kyi's inaction and seeming indifference to the perceived persecution of the Rohingyas led some critics to call for her Nobel Peace prize to be revoked.

Carl XVI Gustaf (Sweden)

Position

King

Introduction

Carl XVI Gustaf belongs to the Bernadotte dynasty which has ruled in Sweden since 1818. He came to the throne in 1973. The king's duties are chiefly ceremonial. He is the senior representative of the Swedish defence establishment, and the country's principal international representative.

Early Life

Carl Gustaf Folke Hubertus was born on 30 April 1946, at Haga Palace in Stockholm. His father, King Gustaf Adolf, was killed in an air crash in 1947, and his mother, Princess Sibylla of Sachsen-Coburn-Gotha, died in 1972.

Following the death of King Gustaf VI Adolf in 1973, Crown Prince Carl Gustaf became Sweden's head of state at the age of 27. The king was taught privately at the Royal Palace of Stockholm, followed by studies at Broms School and Sigtuna Boarding School. He then completed two and a half years training in the Army, Navy, and Air Force. The king's academic studies included history, sociology, political science and law at the University of Uppsala and economics at the University of Stockholm. In addition, the king took part in the work of The Permanent Mission of Sweden to the United Nations in New York and with SIDA (Swedish International Development Co-operation Agency) in Africa.

In 1976, Carl XVI Gustaf married Silvia Sommerlath (daughter of German Walther Sommerlath and Brazilian Alice de Toledo). Carl Gustaf and Queen Silvia have three children, Crown Princess Victoria (born on 14 July 1977), Prince Carl Philip (born on 13 May 1979), and Princess Madeleine (born on 10 June 1982). In 1980, an amendment to the Swedish constitution made the firstborn of the royal children, whether male or female, to follow in succession.

Career in Office

The king opens the annual session of the Riksdag (parliament), and chairs the special council when there is a change of government. He also leads the meetings of the Advisory Council on Foreign Affairs. He holds supreme rank in all of Sweden's defence forces. In 1988, Carl XVI Gustaf became Chairman of the Swedish branch of the World Wide Fund for Nature (WWF). The king is patron of the Royal Swedish Academies and of several organizations, associations and societies. He is particularly involved in the proceedings of the Royal Swedish Academy of Agriculture and Forestry, the Royal Swedish Academy of Sciences (KVA), and the Royal Swedish Academy of Engineering Sciences (IVA). He is the honorary chairman of the World Scout Foundation.

Corbyn, Jeremy (United Kingdom)

Position

Leader of the Opposition

Introduction

Jeremy Corbyn became leader of the Labour Party, and consequently leader of the official opposition to David Cameron's Conservative government, in Sept. 2015. He has been the member of parliament (MP) for the London constituency of Islington North since 1983. Although widely criticized across the political spectrum and by the media during his first 2 years as party leader, he nevertheless led an effective campaign in the snap general election in June 2017, in which the Labour Party increased its parliamentary representation sufficiently to deny the ruling Conservatives their overall majority in the House of Commons.

Early Life

Corbyn was born on 26 May 1949 in Chippenham, Wiltshire. After completing his secondary education at Adam's Grammar School, he undertook 2 years of voluntary work in Jamaica. Following his return to the UK he worked for two trade unions, the National Union of Public Employees and the Amalgamated Engineering and Electrical Union. He was elected as a councillor in the London Borough of Haringey in 1974, a position he held until 1983 when he became an MP.

He soon won a reputation as a campaigning backbencher. He was a vociferous opponent of the apartheid regime in South Africa and in 1984 was arrested for breaching a ban on protesting outside the South African embassy in London. He also joined the Socialist Campaign Group and sat on the Parliamentary London Regional Select Committee until 1987. In addition, he maintained strong links with a number of trade unions, was (and continues to be) a prominent opponent of the UK's nuclear deterrent and courted controversy by calling for an open dialogue with Sinn Féin, the Northern Irish political party with links to the militant Irish Republican Army, even inviting its leader Gerry Adams to the Westminster parliament in 1984.

Within parliament, Corbyn variously sat on the social security select committee (1992–97) and the justice select committee (2010–15). At the height of the parliamentary expenses scandal in 2009, he was revealed to have the smallest expense claims of any sitting MP, a fact he attributed to his being 'parsimonious'. Meanwhile, Hansard recorded him as the most rebellious Labour MP during the period of Labour government from 1997 until 2010, most notably when exercising his opposition to the Iraq War in 2003.

Career in Office

Following the resignation of Labour leader Ed Miliband after the party's defeat at the May 2015 general election, Corbyn put himself forward as a candidate to succeed him. Regarded as a rank outsider, Corbyn garnered sufficient nominations to run in the election with only a few minutes to spare. However, riding a wave of support among the party grassroots (and despite lacking corresponding support from most of the parliamentary party), on 12 Sept. 2015 he was elected Labour leader with a landslide 59.5% of votes.

Corbyn's tenure in opposition has been characterized to date by his criticism of the incumbent government's 'austerity politics'. His other defining policy positions have included the renationalization of key public services, increased taxation for higher earners and the abolition of university tuition fees. He has also opposed renewing the UK's Trident nuclear weapons system, although that stance is not official Labour policy.

In Dec. 2015 he voted against military intervention in Syria alongside the majority of his party, having earlier stated that Labour MPs would be given a free vote on the issue. The parliamentary vote was nevertheless approved by 397 to 223 and air strikes against Islamic State targets took place hours later.

Although a long-standing critic of aspects of European Union policy and its supranational powers, Corbyn pledged that the Labour Party would back retention of Britain's membership of the EU in the UK's national referendum on 23 June 2016. However, his low profile and alleged inaction during the referendum campaign, together with the eventual narrow vote to withdraw, highlighted deep scepticism about his wider electoral appeal among his parliamentary party. Nevertheless, with growing rank and file membership support, Corbyn rebuffed a leadership challenge by Owen Smith, a sitting MP, in Sept. 2016 and continued to pursue a left-wing policy agenda.

Seemingly aiming to exploit Labour's divisions, the ruling Conservatives called a general election in June 2017. However, Corbyn oversaw an unexpectedly effective campaign, increasing the party's parliamentary representation with a significant rise in the vote share, and prompting him to declare Labour a government-in-waiting.

Dhondrub, Lhamo 'Dalai Lama' (China)

Position

Leader of the Tibetan Government-in-Exile

Introduction

The Dalai Lama was the spiritual leader and both head of state and of government of Tibet from the beginning of the 15th century until 1959. Each succeeding holder of this office was regarded as a reincarnation of the first Dalai Lama and a manifestation of the Buddha of Compassion. In the early 18th century the 8th Dalai Lama was obliged to recognise Chinese overlordship, but the 13th Dalai Lama took advantage of the Chinese revolution that overthrew the Manchu dynasty to re-establish Tibet as a sovereign state in 1912. The title in Tibetan is Dalai Lama Rgyalba Rinpoche, which means Great Precious Conqueror, but he is routinely referred to as Kundun, which means The Presence.

Early Life

Lhamo Dhondrub, the child who was to become the 14th Dalai Lama, was born on 6 July 1935 to a poor peasant family in northeastern Tibet. Some reports state he was born in China to Tibetan parents. Lhamo Dhondrub, also later known as Tenzing Gyatso, was recognised as a reincarnation of his predecessor, the 13th Dalai Lama, in 1937.

The child was taken to the Tibetan capital, Lhasa, where he was enthroned on 22 Feb. 1940. His education began when he was six. The Dalai Lama took examinations at all three monastic universities in Tibet and gained a doctorate in Buddhist philosophy when he was 25. But, by then, he had assumed his role as temporal ruler of his country.

Career in Office

In Nov. 1950 the 14th Dalai Lama assumed full temporal powers when Chinese troops invaded Tibet. This invasion ended the period of sovereignty that Tibet had enjoyed since 1912, although China had never recognised Tibetan independence. In 1954 the Dalai Lama was made a member of the Consultative Conference of the People's Republic of China and in 1954 he attended the National Congress in Beijing. While there, he had talks with Mao Zedong and other Chinese leaders in an attempt to resolve the position of Tibet. The talks were inconclusive and in 1956 (a reduced) Tibet was made an autonomous region of the People's Republic of China. China's oppressive rule in Tibet sparked a revolt in the east of the country in March 1959. The uprising spread to Lhasa, but was quickly put down with great loss of life. The Dalai Lama was forced to flee to India and was followed by some 80,000 refugees.

In exile in India, the Dalai Lama established a Tibetan government-in-exile in 1960 at Dharmsala, in Himachal Pradesh state. He appealed to the United Nations and was influential in securing three resolutions of the General Assembly, in 1959, 1961 and 1965, calling on China to respect Tibet's rights to self determination. Since then, the Dalai Lama has concentrated his efforts on preserving Tibetan culture and society among the community in exile. In 1973 he granted a constitution under which a Tibetan assembly and government are directly elected by the Tibetan refugee community in India. He stated that, if restored, he would be a spiritual ruler only. He was awarded the 1989 Nobel Peace Prize for his advocacy of non-violence in his campaign to end the Chinese occupation of Tibet.

The Dalai Lama remains a Buddhist monk, but has a high international profile, visiting many world leaders. He has regularly voiced a desire for world leaders to take collective action on climate change and to deal with the discord over major religions.

In 2008 the Dalai Lama was accused of orchestrating the violence that broke out in Tibet. Following the riots the Dalai Lama's representatives met with the government of China. Although no nearer to regaining independence or halting the influx of ethnic Chinese, which could result in a Tibetan minority, this was the first time since 1993 that formal contact was re-established.

In March 2011 the Dalai Lama took the unprecedented step of resigning his role as a temporal leader, delegating his duties to a newly elected prime minister of the government-in-exile. He nonetheless maintained his role as spiritual leader

Since retiring from his political duties the Dalai Lama has questioned the future of the tradition of the Dalai Lama, citing a need for there to be consultations with relevant parties on whether a successor is necessary. The Chinese government responded by stating that only Beijing had the authority to approve any future Dalai Lama.

Elizabeth II (United Kingdom)

Position

Queen

Introduction

The Queen is the head of state, of the Commonwealth and of the Church of England. As a constitutional monarch she is responsible for opening and dissolving parliament, appointing prime ministers and signing of acts of parliament, but she does not actively form or influence government policy. Elizabeth succeeded her father George VI in 1952. In her early years she continued the work of her father in consolidating the popularity of the monarchy following rocky years after the 1936 abdication crisis. Although generally positive in the early years, media scrutiny of the royal family has intensified over the course of Elizabeth's reign. Despite family discord, the Queen's personal popularity remains high. The Queen celebrates two birthdays each year—her actual birthday, on 21 April, and her official birthday, on a Saturday in June (marked by the Trooping the Colour ceremony).

Early Life

Elizabeth Alexandra Mary was born in London on 21 April 1926, to the Duke and Duchess of York. Elizabeth had no expectation of ascending to the throne until Edward VIII abdicated in 1936 in order to marry a divorcee, and Elizabeth's father became George VI. Receiving most of her education from private tutors, Elizabeth joined the Auxiliary Territorial Service during the last months of World War II.

On 20 Nov. 1947 Elizabeth married Philip Mountbatten, a distant cousin and member of the Greek royal family. The first of their four children, and the heir to the throne, Prince Charles was born on 14 Nov. 1948. By the early 1950s the health of George VI was waning and on 6 Feb. 1952, while Elizabeth and Philip were in Africa *en route* to a state visit of Australasia, he died. Elizabeth succeeded him and was crowned in Westminster Abbey on 2 June 1953.

Career in Office

In the 1960s the media was openly questioning the relevance of the royal family. The queen responded by allowing new levels of media access, as epitomized by the 1969 television documentary *Royal Family* which sought to present the family as close knit and 'normal'. The Queen's Silver Jubilee in 1977 and the marriage of Prince Charles to Lady Diana Spencer in 1981 boosted the Queen's popular standing.

By 1990 the monarchy was again under attack. Talk of marital problems between Charles and Diana was widespread and questions over the 'purpose' of the royal family continued. In the early 1990s the Queen appeased some of her opposition by agreeing to a series of constitutional reforms. For the first time the monarchy had to pay income tax and the civil list was reduced. In another conciliatory gesture, she agreed to give up the royal yacht.

In Nov. 1992 a fire broke out at Windsor Castle, causing extensive damage which took 5 years to repair. The 1990s also witnessed the divorces of the Queen's three oldest children, Charles, Anne and Andrew. In particular, public sympathy for Diana roused unprecedented levels of animosity towards the royal family.

In the aftermath of Princess Diana's death in a car accident in Paris in 1997, the Queen and royal family encountered widespread public hostility. Mishandling of public relations, including a failure to cut short a holiday and a delay in flying the flag at Buckingham Palace at half-mast, were perceived as insults to Diana. An abrasive eulogy by her brother, Earl Spencer, at her funeral increased pressure on the monarchy. Prince Charles ongoing relationship with Camilla Parker-Bowles has been the subject of much popular debate, though criticism has lessened since the couple married in 2005.

Despite these threats to the stability of the monarchy as an institution, the Queen has been praised for her handling of her role and for her sense of duty. Her international standing and popular appeal abroad remain impressive. With the enduring popularity of other prominent royals (including the eventual heir to the throne, Prince William), high levels of public sympathy following the deaths of Princess Margaret and the Queen Mother and the success of the Queen's Golden Jubilee celebrations in 2002 and her Diamond Jubilee celebrations in 2012, it seems likely that Elizabeth's reign has secured the future of the British monarchy, though further reforms are likely. On 12 May 2011 Elizabeth became the second-longest serving monarch in British history. On 17 May 2011 Elizabeth became the first British monarch to visit the Republic of Ireland in a visit hailed as a diplomatic triumph. In 2012 and in particular from 2–5 June the United Kingdom and the Commonwealth celebrated the Queen's Diamond Jubilee, marking the 60th anniversary of her accession to the throne. In Sept. 2015 she surpassed Queen Victoria, who reigned for 63 years 7 months and 2 days, as the longest reigning British monarch.

Felipe VI (Spain)

Position

King

Introduction

Felipe Juan Pablo Alfonso de Todos los Santos de Borbón y Grecia became king on 19 June 2014 following the abdication of his father, Juan Carlos.

Early Life

Felipe was born on 30 Jan. 1968 in Madrid, Spain, the third child and only son of Juan Carlos–who at that time, owing to Franco's dictatorship, had yet to ascend to the throne–and Sofia of Greece and Denmark. On his 18th birthday, Felipe formally swore allegiance to the constitution and the king of Spain, thereby accepting his role as his father's successor.

In 1999 he completed 4 years of military service, during which he trained as a helicopter pilot. In 1992 he represented Spain in sailing at the summer Olympics in Barcelona, claiming sixth place in the Soling class competition. He graduated from the Autonomous University of Madrid the following year with a degree in law. In 1995 he earned a master's degree in foreign relations from Georgetown University in the USA.

In May 2004 Felipe married Letizia Ortiz Rocasolano, a Spanish journalist. They have two daughters: Leonor (born 31 Oct. 2005) and Sofia (born 29 April 2007).

Career in Office

Felipe ascended to the throne in June 2014. Amidst a backdrop of national economic hardship and growing domestic opposition to the monarchy—exacerbated by a number of royal scandals and the perceived extravagance of the ruling family—he pledged to modernize the institution. 'Now more than ever,' he said, 'citizens of Spain are rightly demanding fundamental ethical principles should govern our public life'.

Following inconclusive elections in Dec. 2015 in which no party was able to gain a parliamentary majority, Felipe announced in May 2016 that new elections would take place in June.

Harald V (Norway)

Position

King

Introduction

Harald V became king of Norway in 1991. As a constitutional monarch, most of his duties are ceremonial. He was at the centre of a constitutional debate when he chose to marry a commoner in 1968, but emerged with both parliamentary and popular support. A gifted sportsman, he has represented Norway at the Olympic Games.

Early Life

Harald was born on 21 Feb. 1937 in Skaugum, Norway, the son of Crown Princess Märtha and Crown Prince Olaf (later King Olaf V). In April 1940 Norway was invaded by German forces and the royal family went into exile. Harald lived with his parents and siblings near Washington, D.C. until Norway was liberated in 1945.

In 1955 he undertook studies in science at the University of Oslo before completing military training 4 years later. He then attended Balliol College at the University of Oxford in England. In 1957 he was made crown prince and took his place on the Council of State.

There was a minor constitutional crisis when Harald announced his intention to marry his commoner friend of several years, Sonja Haraldsen, in 1968. Olaf consulted leading political figures before giving his blessing to the marriage, news of which was received warmly by the public. Their first child, Märtha Louise, was born in Sept. 1971 and Haakon Magnus, Norway's crown prince, was born in July 1973.

Following the death of Olaf V, Harald acceded to the throne on 21 Jan. 1991 and was consecrated at Nidaros Cathedral Trondheim on 23 June.

Career in Office

The duties of the Norwegian monarch are principally ceremonial. Harald, a talented sportsman who had previously represented Norway at sailing in the Olympic Games, was actively involved in preparations for the 1994 Winter Olympics held in Lillehammer. Relations with Russia became strained in early 1998 following a series of tit-for-tat diplomatic expulsions, but the royal couple visited that country later in the year. This was the first visit by a

Norwegian monarch since 1905, and Harald was credited with helping to normalize relations between the two nations.

However, the monarchy and its long-term future came into question during 2000–01 following a series of stories concerning Prince Haakon. He was associated with a pop festival where drug offences had taken place, and it was then announced that he was to marry a commoner who had a son from a previous marriage. In newspaper polls, over 50% of the population were in favour of a referendum concerning the monarchy, although abolition of the institution garnered little support. Following Haakon's marriage in Aug. 2001 the popularity of the royal family revived.

Haakon has twice served as regent while Harald recovered from ill health, firstly from 25 Nov. 2003–12 April 2004 and then from 29 March–7 June 2005.

Jigme Khesar Namgyel Wangchuck (Bhutan)

Position

King

Introduction

Jigme Khesar Namgyel succeeded his father, Jigme Singye Wangchuck, who abdicated in his favour on 14 Dec. 2006. He became the nation's fifth hereditary Druk Gyalpo (Dragon King). Jigme Khesar's accession came as a surprise following Jigme Singye's announcement in Dec. 2005 that he would remain in office until 2008, when Bhutan held its first democratic elections. He later explained that his early abdication was to ensure that Jigme Khesar gained the necessary experience in office before elections took place.

Early Life

Jigme Khesar Namgyel was born on 21 Feb. 1980. He received his early education in Bhutan before attending Cushing Academy and Wheaton College in Massachusetts, USA. He went on to gain an MPhil. degree in politics from Magdalen College, Oxford in 2003.

On 22 Oct. 2004 Jigme Khesar was formally appointed the Chhoetse Penlop (heir) to the 'Golden Throne'. His appointment as the 16th Chhoetse Penlop ensured the continuity of the monarchy as the country transfers from a system of absolute monarchy to that of a parliamentary democracy.

Career in Office

Jigme Khesar has continued his father's modernization programme to achieve 'National Happiness', but is facing the challenges of growing levels of alcohol and drug abuse. Resolving the future of the Bhutanese refugees residing in Nepal (mostly in UNHCR-camps) will be a further test as Bhutan attempts to improve its human rights record.

Jones, Carwyn (Wales, United Kingdom)

Position

First Minister

Introduction

After succeeding Rhodri Morgan as leader of the Welsh Labour Party, Carwyn Jones became Wales' third first minister on 9 Dec. 2009. He heads the 'One Wales' coalition with Plaid Cymru.

Early Life

Carwyn Howell Jones was born in Swansea in 1967. A fluent Welsh speaker, he attended Brynteg Comprehensive School in Bridgend before reading law at the University of Wales in Aberystwyth, where he joined the Welsh Labour Party. After training as a barrister in London, he worked for 10 years for a Swansea chambers specializing in criminal, family and personal injury law.

In May 1999 he was elected to the Welsh Assembly and held a range of posts within Morgan's government. Starting as deputy minister for local government, finance and land in Feb. 2000, he became minister for rural affairs in July that year and added the open government portfolio in June 2002. In May 2003 he was appointed minister for environment, planning and the countryside, a post he held until 2007. He then briefly served as education minister prior to being made counsel general and leader of the house.

In Sept. 2009 Morgan announced his intention to resign. Jones made a bid for the leadership against fellow Labour assembly members Edwina Hart and Huw Lewis. Favourite from the outset, Jones campaigned to protect education spending and won over 50% of the vote. He was sworn in as party leader and first minister on 1 Dec. and 9 Dec. respectively.

Career in Office

Since taking office Jones has sought to maintain One Wales' previous commitments, announcing in March 2010 that key policies including free prescriptions and free school breakfasts would be unaffected by budget cuts. A referendum on increased Welsh autonomy deemed crucial to the future of the Plaid Cymru–Labour coalition was held on 3 March 2011. The referendum, which asked if the National Assembly should be able to create laws on subject areas it already has powers for (without referring to the UK parliament for approval), was approved with 63.5% of votes cast in favour.

Jones has faced a struggle over financial restrictions imposed by Westminster. In June 2010 he criticized emergency budget cuts as 'disproportionately' affecting Wales. In the same month he launched a project to transform Anglesey into an 'energy island' that will house tidal, wind and biomass energy generation plants and is expected to deliver 5000 new jobs to the region.

Following the May 2011 elections, in which Labour won 30 of the Assembly's 60 seats, Jones was reappointed unopposed as first minister. He subsequently vigorously opposed government spending cuts, especially in the health sector and education.

In Dec. 2013 Jones stated that he opposed Scottish independence as laid out by the referendum planned for 18 Sept. 2014, claiming that the secession of Scotland from the United Kingdom would negatively affect Wales and Northern Ireland. Addressing fears that Scottish independence would result in an overbalance of power in Westminster to the detriment of political devolution in Wales, he reiterated his preference for a federal Britain including Scotland.

The Labour Party was two seats short of a majority following elections to the Assembly in May 2016 and Jones was required to negotiate with opposition parties to retain his post as first minister. After he tied with Plaid Cymru's Leanne Wood in a leadership election and following further negotiations with Plaid Cymru, Jones was re-elected first minister unopposed in a further round of voting.

Lam, Carrie (Hong Kong, China)

Position

Chief Executive

Introduction

Carrie Lam became Hong Kong's first female chief executive on 1 July 2017.

Early Life

Carrie Lam Cheng Yuet-ngor was born on 13 May 1957 and graduated in social sciences from Hong Kong University in 1980. She subsequently worked for the civil service, including 7 years in the financial services and treasury bureau where she acted as deputy director from 1996 to 2000.

She then served as director of the social welfare department until 2003, before stints at the house and planning bureau, the economic and trade office, and the civil affairs bureau.

In 2007 Lam became director of the development bureau before being appointed chief secretary for administration by Hong Kong's then chief executive, Leung Chun-ying. Lam opposed the demands of the 2014 pro-democracy protests (prompted by Beijing's attempts to alter the electoral process) that the 2017 candidates for the chief executive role be chosen by the public.

Career in Office

Facing two rivals for the position, Lam won 777 of the 1194 election committee votes before taking office as chief executive on 1 July 2017. Her critics portrayed her as Beijing's preferred candidate who was expected to preserve the political *status quo*. They pointed to her declaration in June 2017 that she would defer to mainland China on the issue of five Hong Kong booksellers allegedly kidnapped by Beijing agents in 2015.

Lam has vowed to oversee major infrastructure programmes, increased spending in education, research and technology, along with business tax reforms. She has also spearheaded a drive to involve more young people (aged 18–35) in policy advisory boards.

Margrethe (Denmark)

Position

Queen

Introduction

Margrethe became Denmark's first queen in a thousand years when she succeeded her father, Federik IX, in 1972. Her role is largely ceremonial and she is expected to remain unpartisan. A highly respected artist, her popularity among the Danish people is high.

Early Life

Margrethe Alexandrine Thorhildur Ingrid was born on 16 April 1940 in Copenhagen, the daughter of Frederick IX and Queen Ingrid. In the week before her birth Nazi forces invaded the country.

Her higher education included studies in constitutional law and philosophy at the University of Copenhagen, archaeology at the University of Cambridge, Danish affairs at the University of Aarhus and sociology at the London School of Economics. A constitutional change was implemented in 1953 that allowed for a female to ascend the Danish throne, and Margrethe took the title 'throne heiress'. On achieving adulthood she became active in the council of state.

In 1967 she married a French diplomat, Count Henri de Labourde de Monpezat, who assumed the title Prince Henrik. They have two children. Crown Prince Frederik was born in May 1968 and Prince Joachim in June of the following year. Frederik IX, Margrethe's father died on 14 Jan. 1972.

Career in Office

Margrethe's style is accessible and informal, as epitomised by several unguarded interviews she has given and by her new years' speeches. Her wide-ranging education has been evident in her regular briefings with political leaders.

In addition, she is a respected artist in her own right. She is particularly famed for her 1977 illustrated version of Lord of the Rings, as well as a translation (in partnership with Henrik) of Simone de Beauvoir's All Men are Mortal. She has had several exhibitions and has worked on set designs for the Royal Theatre.

Margrethe's reign experienced rare turmoil in Jan. 2002 amid rumours that Henrik had returned to France to consider his role. It was reported that he felt his position was becoming subsumed by that of Frederik.

In 2012 Denmark celebrated Margrethe's ruby jubilee, marking 40 years on the throne.

Norodom Sihamoni (Cambodia)

Position

King

Introduction

A former ballet dancer and choreographer, and long-term resident of Paris, Norodom Sihamoni was crowned King of Cambodia on 29 Oct. 2004, 2 weeks after the unexpected abdication of his father, Norodom Sihanouk.

Early Life

Norodom Sihamoni was born on 14 May 1953 in Phnom Penh, Cambodia, the year the country achieved independence from France. He is the son of Norodom Sihanouk, former King of Cambodia, and his sixth wife, Monique Izzi (Queen Norodom Monineath Sihanouk). Norodom Sihamoni attended primary school in Phnom Penh and was taken to Prague, in the then Czechoslovakia in 1962 for secondary education. Czechoslovakia was one of many Communist countries with which King Norodom Sihanouk maintained cordial relations during the mid-1960s. After graduating from the Prague Lycee in 1967 Norodom Sihamoni studied dance, music and theatre at Prague's Conservatorium, gaining the first prize in classical dance in 1971. He then joined Prague's Academy of Musical Art. Having completed his thesis on Cambodian Fine Arts in 1975 Norodom Sihamoni moved to Pyongyang, North Korea, where he studied cinematography.

Returning to Cambodia in 1976 he rejoined his father who had emerged from exile in Sept. 1975 (having been deposed as head of state in a right-wing coup led by Lon Nol in 1970). Some analysts allege Norodom Sihamoni was duped into leaving North Korea when he received a letter falsely bearing his father's signature. The new premier, Pol Pot, whose Khmer Rouge had toppled Lon Nol in 1975, never allowed Norodom Sihanouk to wield any power. The royal family was kept under house arrest until Pol Pot's genocidal regime was forced from Phnom Penh by the Vietnamese army in Jan. 1979. Later that year Norodom Sihamoni served his father as his private secretary in exile abroad, first in Beijing, then in Pyongyang where the family were guests of Kim Il Sung.

In 1981 Norodom Sihamoni left Cambodia for France where he taught as professor of classical dance and artistic pedagogy at the Marius Petipa conservatory, the Gabriel Fauré conservatory and the W. A. Mozart conservatory in Paris. He established his own troupe, the Ballet Deva, and set up the film production company Khemara Pictures in 1990. From Feb. 1992 until Nov. 1993 he was the permanent representative of the Supreme National Council at the United Nations, after which he was appointed Cambodian ambassador to the UN Educational, Scientific and Cultural Organization (UNESCO). He served as ambassador until early 2004 when he moved to Beijing, where his father was receiving medical treatment. The first indication that Norodom Sihamoni might succeed to the Cambodian throne came at an Independence Day ceremony in 2002 when he deputized for his father. It was confirmed on 14 Oct. 2004 when Norodom Sihanouk abdicated and the members of the throne council unanimously voted for Norodom Sihamoni to become king. He was crowned in a traditional ceremony on 29 Oct. 2004.

Career in Office

Having spent most of his adult life outside Cambodia, Norodom Sihamoni had a low personal profile among Cambodians and was much less known than his half-brother Prince Ranariddh who headed the royalist political party: the United National Front for an Independent, Neutral, Peaceful and Co-operative Cambodia (FUNCINPEC). The king of Cambodia is nevertheless a largely ceremonial role and power has remained in the hands of the prime minister, Hun Sen, who has dominated Cambodian politics for over three decades.

Pence, Mike (United States of America)

Position

Vice-President

Introduction

Michael Richard Pence is the vice-president of the USA. He was named as Donald Trump's running-mate on the Republican ticket in July 2016. Pence previously served in the House of Representatives from 2001–13 and was governor of Indiana between 2013 and 2017.

Early Life

Mike Pence was born on 7 June 1959 and brought up in Columbus, Indiana. Initially a Democrat, he voted for Jimmy Carter in the 1980 presidential election although his views began to change during Ronald Reagan's presidency. After graduating in history from Hanover College in 1981, he then earned a degree from the Indiana University School of Law in Indianapolis. Before entering politics, he worked as an attorney in private practice, presided over a conservative think-tank and hosted a political talk-radio show. He ran unsuccessfully for Congress in 1988 and 1990 before winning a seat in the US House of Representatives elections in 2000.

As representative for Indiana in the House from 2001–13, he became chairman of the Republican Conference in Jan. 2009. A member of the Tea Party Caucus, he championed a range of socially conservative causes. He opposed President Obama's federal stimulus package, health care reforms and tobacco regulations, and also voted against measures to raise the federal minimum wage and ban workplace discrimination on the basis of sexual orientation.

As governor of Indiana, Pence supported policies that limited gun control and clean energy but which extended restrictions on abortion. He also vowed to cut federal resettlement funding to bar Syrian refugees from Indiana, a move that was later deemed unconstitutional. During his tenure, he enacted the highest tax cuts in the state's history.

In March 2015 Pence signed the Religious Freedom Restoration Act, which allowed individuals and businesses to cite the free exercise of religion as a legal defence. The law proved controversial due to fears that it would lead to discrimination on grounds of sexual orientation. The act was amended following a national backlash—which included state-wide boycotts by corporations, sports leagues and government agencies.

Career in Office

Pence was appointed chairman of Trump's transition team following the Republican election victory in Nov. 2016, a role that included advising the then president-elect on political appointments. He was sworn in as vice-president on 20 Jan. 2017. As the *ex officio* president of the Senate, Pence has twice invoked the power to cast tie-breaking votes—once to confirm Betsy DeVos as secretary of education and once to advance a bill to de-fund Planned Parenthood, an organization providing reproductive health care and advice.

In April 2017 Pence toured South Korea and Japan, pledging to defend US allies in the region against nuclear threats from North Korea.

Philippe (Belgium)

Position

King

Introduction

Philippe, of the House of Saxe-Coburg and Gotha, succeeded to the throne in July 2013 on the abdication of his father, Albert II. Although the monarch plays a largely ceremonial role, he is the commander of the armed forces and has a duty to intervene in constitutional crises.

Early Life

Philippe, the eldest child of Albert II and Queen Paola, was born on 15 April 1960. After completing his schooling, he spent 3 years at the Belgian Royal Military Academy before studying in the UK at Trinity College, Oxford, and earning an MA in political studies from Stanford University in the USA. On returning to Belgium, Philippe resumed his military career, becoming a lieutenant-general and vice admiral. In 1993 he succeeded his father as honorary chairman of the Belgian Foreign Trade Board, heading more than 60 high-level trade missions worldwide.

In 1999 he married Mathilde d'Udekem d'Acoz, daughter of a Walloon count and a descendant of Polish nobility. The couple have four children, Princess Elisabeth (born 25 Oct. 2001), Prince Gabriel (born 20 Aug. 2003), Prince Emmanuel (born 4 Oct. 2005) and Princess Eléonore (born 16 April 2008). Princess Elisabeth is the first in line to the throne following a constitutional amendment allowing the first born to become heir, regardless of gender.

Career in Office

On 21 July 2013 Philippe became Belgium's seventh king since it gained independence. He must attempt to unify the country at a time of faltering relations between Dutch-speaking Flanders in the north and the French-speaking Walloon Region in the south. With Flemish separatist parties expected to make a good showing at the 2014 elections, Philippe will hope to be able to help fend off a crisis of the type that saw Belgium without a government for over 500 days after the elections of 2010.

Scheer, Andrew (Canada)

Position

Opposition Leader

Introduction

Andrew Scheer became leader of the Conservative Party of Canada—and consequently leader of the official opposition to Justin Trudeau's Liberal government—in May 2017.

Early Life

Scheer was born on 20 May 1979 in Ottawa, Ontario. He studied history and politics at the University of Ottawa before graduating from the University of Regina after he moved to Saskatchewan. He then began working as an insurance broker, but soon left to join the constituency office of Canadian Alliance MP Larry Spencer. In 2004 Scheer was elected to the House of Commons as the Conservative member for the district of Regina-Qu'Appelle. He defeated Lorne Nystrom of the New Democratic Party who was at the time the longest-serving member of the House.

After the Conservative Party won a parliamentary majority in 2011, Scheer was elected as the House's youngest-ever Speaker. He remained in the post until Dec. 2015. Two months earlier, the Conservative Party had been defeated at a general election by Justin Trudeau's Liberal Party. Nonetheless, Scheer was re-elected in his constituency and was appointed Leader of the Opposition in parliament by Rona Ambrose, then interim leader of the Conservative Party. Scheer stepped down 10 months later in order to prepare for the Conservative leadership election.

Career in Office

Scheer was elected leader in May 2017, ending Ambrose's interim stint as head of the party. His narrow victory over Maxime Bernier was due largely to support from the socially conservative wing of the party. In anticipation of the 2019 federal elections, and as a long-time pro-life and pro-family activist, Scheer promised he would create tax breaks for parents, intro-duce liberal reforms to the economy, protect freedom of speech in universities and balance the federal budget within 2 years. He would not, however, introduce legislation re-opening debates related to abortion or same-sex marriage.

Shaikh Khalifa (Bahrain)

Position

Prime Minister

Introduction

Uncle of the present Amir (and brother to his father), Shaikh Khalifa has been prime minister of Bahrain since 1971, making him the longest-serving PM of any sovereign country.

Early Life

Born in 1936, he attended primary and secondary school in Bahrain before going on to higher education in England. Returning home, he was appointed president of the Education Council in 1957, head of Government Finance in 1960, and chairman of the Administrative Council in 1966. The Administrative Council became the State Council and then, in 1971, the Council of Ministers, with Shaikh Khalifa as Prime Minister.

Career in Office

Shaikh Khalifa is identified with the hawkish faction within the royal family and has cracked down on political dissent. This was evident during the 2011 opposition uprising in Bahrain, when police used lethal force in response to demonstrations. Considered a hardliner in Bahraini politics, his stance towards the opposition has often contrasted with that of Crown Prince Salman bin Hamad bin Isa Al-Khalifa, who has demonstrated a comparatively moderate approach.

In addition to his prime ministerial responsibilities, Shaikh Khalifa is also head of the Supreme Defence Council and various other public bodies.

Shorten, Bill (Australia)

Position

Leader of the Opposition

Introduction

Bill Shorten succeeded Kevin Rudd as leader of the Australian Labor Party (ALP) on 13 Oct. 2013. Since 2007 he has been the member of parliament for Maribyrnong. As a senior member of the Rudd and Gillard Labor governments, Shorten helped launch the National Disability Insurance Scheme and oversaw an increase in universal pension payments.

Early Life

William Richard Shorten was born on 12 May 1967 in Melbourne, Victoria. He joined the ALP in 1984 and graduated from Monash University with an arts degree in 1989 and a law degree in 1992. While a student, he worked for Labor ministers Neil Pope, Gareth Evans and Bill Landeryou. After graduating he began a career as a lawyer specializing in social justice and compensation.

From the mid-1990s he rose through the ranks of the Australian Workers' Union, holding the position of secretary of its Victorian branch from 1997–2006 and then national secretary from 2001–07. In that year he became parliamentary secretary for disabilities and children's services in the Rudd government, having entered the House of Representatives as the member for Maribyrnong. He was promoted to the Cabinet as minister for financial services and superannuation in Sept. 2010. In 2011 he was named minister for workplace relations.

He served as minister of education from June 2013, when Rudd briefly replaced Gillard as party leader and premier. However, when Rudd was defeated at the federal elections in Sept. that year, Shorten resigned his post. Shorten succeeded Rudd as ALP leader on 13 Oct. 2013, defeating Anthony Albanese with 52% of the combined vote of the federal caucus and rank and file members.

Career in Office

Shorten pledged to unite the ALP, improve education and health care and campaign for the rights of small businesses and farmers. In May 2015 he delivered Labor's budget reply speech, at the centre of which was the party's 'Futuresmart' policy, which aims for computer coding to be taught in every primary and secondary school by 2020. He also vowed to cancel the debts of up to 100,000 university students studying for science, technology, engineering and mathematics degrees if the ALP is elected in 2017. In addition, he has proposed a tax rate reduction for small businesses.

Shorten led the ALP into the 2016 federal elections, when the Liberal/National Coalition only just managed to achieve a majority—winning 76 of the 150 seats.

Sturgeon, Nicola (Scotland, United Kingdom)

Position

First Minister

Introduction

Nicola Sturgeon is the first woman to hold either of the offices of leader of the Scottish National Party and First Minister of Scotland. Taking over from Alex Salmond in both roles in Nov. 2014, she consolidated a surge in SNP support by leading the party to a gain of 50 seats at the 2015 UK general election. However, while remaining the largest party in Scotland at the subsequent June 2017 UK election, the SNP lost more than a third of its Westminster seats, possibly reflecting declining support for Sturgeon's continued pursuit of future Scottish independence despite the 2014 referendum outcome.

Early Life

Nicola Ferguson Sturgeon was born on 19 July 1970 in Irvine, Scotland, and was raised in Prestwick and Dreghorn. She graduated in law from the University of Glasgow in 1993, before working as a solicitor in Glasgow.

Formerly a member of the Campaign for Nuclear Disarmament, Sturgeon joined the SNP in 1986 and quickly rose through the party ranks, working as the party's vice convener for youth affairs and publicity. In 1992 she was the youngest Scottish candidate to contest a seat at the UK general election, but failed to displace the Labour Party in the Glasgow Shettleston constituency. She also ran in the 1997 general election but again failed to overturn a Labour stronghold, this time in the since abolished Glasgow Govan constituency.

In 1999 Sturgeon became a member of the Scottish Parliament (MSP) after winning the regional list vote for the city of Glasgow in the first ever election to the newly-established legislature at Holyrood. As an MSP, she served in the shadow cabinets of Alex Salmond and John Swinney, winning re-election in 2003.

In June 2004, following the departure of John Swinney, Sturgeon announced her candidacy for the party leadership but stood down once Salmond announced his intention to run. She subsequently became his running mate and then deputy leader of the party upon his victory in Sept. With Salmond also sitting in the House of Commons at Westminster, Sturgeon led the party at Holyrood until Salmond was elected an MSP and became First Minister of Scotland in 2007.

Sturgeon's standing in Scottish politics rose during her tenure as Salmond's deputy, as did the party's influence in Holyrood. Following the

SNP's majority victory at the 2011 Scottish parliamentary election, the party followed through on one of its key manifesto commitments—a referendum on independence. Over the next 3 years Sturgeon oversaw the SNP's campaign for independence, as well as holding a number of cabinet positions.

In Sept. 2014 Salmond announced his resignation as SNP leader and First Minister following defeat at the independence referendum. Sturgeon was appointed his successor as party leader and was then elected First Minister by the Scottish parliament. She was sworn into office on 19 Nov. 2014.

Career in Office

Sturgeon continued to pursue devolution from the United Kingdom, and identified the removal of the UK's Trident nuclear deterrent system from Scotland as a 'red-line issue' for the SNP. Amid surging popularity, she led the party to a landslide victory at the 2015 general election, in which the SNP won 56 of Scotland's Westminster 59 seats to become the UK's third largest party. She was then re-elected as Scotland's first minister by MSPs in May 2016 following elections to the Scottish Parliament, in which the SNP remained the largest party but failed to retain its overall majority.

Sturgeon continued to advocate future Scottish independence and also vociferously opposed the Westminster Conservative government's policy and negotiating stance on British withdrawal from the European Union. However, despite remaining the largest party in Scotland following the snap UK general election in June 2017, the SNP lost 21 of its previous 56 seats, particularly to a rejuvenated Scottish Conservative Party.

Thaçi, Hashim (Kosovo, Serbia)

Position

President

Introduction

Hashim Thaçi was elected president in Feb. 2016. He had led the paramilitary Kosovo Liberation Army (KLA) during the armed conflict with Yugoslav forces in 1998–99 and served as prime minister of the territory from 1999–2000 and from 2008–14.

Early Life

Thaçi was born on 24 April 1968 in Srbica, Yugoslavia (now part of Kosovo). He studied philosophy and history at the University of Pristina, and by 1993 was living in Switzerland where he enrolled as a postgraduate student at the University of Zurich.

Thaçi's involvement with the KLA ethnic Albanian independence group began in 1993. Nicknamed 'Gjarpëri' (the Snake), he was allegedly responsible for securing finance and arms for the KLA, while overseeing the training of recruits in Albania to be dispatched to the resistance in Kosovo. By 1999 Thaçi had become leader of the KLA, which was by then known for engaging in criminal activities including drug trafficking, extortion and intimidation of political rivals.

In March 1999 Thaçi took part in the NATO-endorsed peace negotiations between Kosovo and Yugoslavia as the leader of the Kosovar Albanian team. Thaçi was perceived by the West as a relatively moderate voice within the KLA owing to his willingness to compromise on autonomy for Kosovo within Serbia, in opposition to the majority of the paramilitaries who demanded full independence.

Following the breakdown of negotiations, Thaçi consolidated his power within the KLA and utilized his influence with Western powers to transform himself from rebel fighter to head of the Democratic Party of Kosovo (PDK). He named himself prime minister of the provisional government in Kosovo in April 1999 and served in the role until Feb. 2000. He became prime minister again in 2008 after the PDK won the Nov. 2007 parliamentary elections, and in Feb. 2008 Kosovo declared its independence. Thaçi remained as prime minister until 2014.

Career in Office

During the parliamentary elections of June 2014, Thaçi and the leader of the Democratic League of Kosovo, Isa Mustafa, reached a power-sharing agreement. Mustafa became prime minister in Dec. 2014, with Thaçi serving in his cabinet as deputy prime minister and foreign minister. They agreed that Thaçi would assume the presidency at the conclusion of Atifete Jahjaga's term in April 2016.

Tsai Ing-wen (Taiwan, China)

Position

President

Introduction

In May 2016 Tsai Ing-wen became the first female president of Taiwan.

Early Life

Tsai Ing-wen was born on 31 Aug. 1956 and grew up in the southern village of Fenggang. In 1978 she graduated in law from the National Taiwan University. She went on to further studies at Cornell University Law School in the USA (earning a master's degree in law in 1980) and the London School of Economics in the UK, receiving her PhD in 1984. She then returned to Taipei to teach law.

In the 1990s she became a government adviser on trade policy and was involved in Taiwan's entry into the World Trade Organization. She also drafted foreign policy briefings for the then president, Lee Teng-hui. In 2000 Tsai was named chair of the Mainland Affairs Council. Four years later she entered parliament as a Democratic Progressive Party (DPP) member, retaining the seat until 2006 when she was appointed vice-premier.

She became mired in controversy when she was accused of giving preferential treatment to a biotechnology company of which she was the chair, but was cleared of all allegations. After the DPP's defeat in the 2008 general election, Tsai became party chair and worked to reform its image after corruption scandals surrounding its former leader, Chen Shui-bian, and herself. She ran for the mayoralty of Taipei in 2010 but lost to Eric Chu.

In 2011 Tsai became the country's first female presidential candidate when she opposed the incumbent Ma Ying-jeou. She was highly critical of the free trade agreement signed between Beijing and Taipei, which she argued would open Taiwan up to cheap Chinese imports. When she was defeated at the polls, she resigned as chairman of the DPP but resumed the position in 2014.

Career in Office

Tsai ran for the presidency again and won the election on 16 Jan. 2016. Her campaign focused on the economic record of the incumbent administration and Taiwan's growing ties with China. She was sworn in as president on 20 May 2016.

Tsai has also been a vocal advocate for lesbian, gay, bisexual, and transgender rights, having endorsed same-sex marriage. As of Nov. 2016, three bills supporting marriage equality were in progress. Following the election of Donald Trump as US president in the same month, Tsai reiterated her commitment to strengthening trade and economic cooperation between their two countries.

Vajiralongkorn (Thailand)

Position

King

Introduction

Following the death of King Bhumibol Adulyadej on 13 Oct. 2016, his son, the Crown Prince, was formally invited by parliament on 29 Nov. to become King Maha Vajiralongkorn Bodindradebayavarangkun. He accepted in a televised statement on 12 Jan. 2017.

Early Life

King Vajiralongkorn was born on 28 July 1952 in Bangkok, the only son of King Bhumibol and Queen Sirikit. Initially educated in Thailand, he went to boarding school in the United Kingdom and then studied at the Royal Military College in Canberra, Australia. He subsequently served in the Royal Thai Army as a pilot, although his role in the military became increasingly ceremonial. He was named Crown Prince by his father in 1972.

Although it is illegal to openly express criticism of the Thai royal family, Vajiralongkorn has long been a controversial figure in his homeland. Branded the 'playboy prince' by the international press, he has been accused of having dubious business connections and is well-known for a turbulent personal life that has included three marriages.

Career in Office

Although Thailand has a constitutional monarchy, the royal family still exerts significant influence on the nation's often tumultuous political landscape. King Bhumibol in particular was regarded as a pillar of stability for the Thai people. Yet, despite having been Crown Prince, Vajiralongkorn has had limited experience engaging in royal duties amid persistent debate over his fitness to succeed his father. Nonetheless, commentators have stressed the importance of the monarchy in bringing together a country that experienced a divisive military coup as recently as 2014.

Willem-Alexander (Netherlands)

Position

King

Introduction

Willem-Alexander was crowned King on 30 April 2013 after the abdication of his mother, Queen Beatrix.

Early Life

Willem-Alexander was born on 27 April 1967 in Utrecht, Netherlands, the eldest child of Queen Beatrix and her German diplomat husband, Claus von Amsberg. On turning 18, he became a member of the Council of State of the Netherlands.

After completing two years military service with the navy in 1987, Willem-Alexander studied history at Leiden University. In 2005 he was promoted to the rank of commodore in the naval reserve, brigadier general in the army, and air commodore in the air force. He flew humanitarian relief missions in Kenya in 1989 and 1991. In 1998 he joined the International Olympic Committee and in 2006 was named chairman of the UN Secretary General's advisory board on water and sanitation.

In Feb. 2002 Willem-Alexander married Máxima Cerruti, an Argentinian economist. Their relationship initially sparked controversy as her father was a minister in the Argentinian military dictatorship of the 1970s. The couple have three daughters: Princess Catharina-Amalia (born 7 Dec. 2003), Princess Alexia Juliana Marcela Laurentien (born 26 June 2005) and Princess Ariane Wilhelmina Máxima Inés (born 10 April 2007).

Career in Office

The first male to ascend the Dutch throne since 1890, Willem-Alexander has pledged to modernize the monarchy to meet the challenges of the twenty-first century.

PROFILES OF MAJOR CITIES AROUND THE WORLD

Aarhus, Denmark

Introduction

Aarhus is Denmark's second largest city and capital of the Aarhus administrative region in eastern Jutland. With a history of more than a 1,000 years, it emerged as a major industrial centre during the late-nineteenth and early-twentieth centuries.

History

Aarhus was founded by Vikings and became a bishopric in the mid-tenth century. There followed a period of growth during which several notable churches, still standing today, were constructed. The town's importance diminished with the Reformation in the sixteenth century.

In the latter part of the nineteenth century expansion of the city's industrial base and port facilities, and its integration into the Danish rail network, led to an influx of rural immigrants. Rapid population growth continued throughout the twentieth century.

Modern City

Besides the port and related activities, the city's most important industries include engineering, metalwork, chemicals, food processing and textiles. Aarhus has an international airport 40 km outside the city. A major railway hub, there are two stations, one for passengers and the other for freight. It is on several major motorway routes, while transport within the city is provided by buses. There is a university.

Places of Interest

The Old Town is a large open air museum, featuring historically-important buildings transferred from around Denmark. Among the city's most important churches are the Church of Our Lady (with the eleventh century St Nicholas' crypt) and the thirteenth century gothic cathedral of St Clement. Twentieth century Danish architecture is represented by the town hall and university buildings.

There are several art museums as well as museums of pre-history and natural history, city history, the Vikings, and women. In addition, there are tropical glasshouses open to the public, as well as the Ole Rømer Observatory. The annual Aarhus festival hosts around 300 cultural events each Sept. while the concert hall and theatre put on productions all year round.

Aarhus was chosen by the EU to be one of the European Capitals for Culture for 2017, alongside Paphos in Cyprus.

Abidjan, Côte d'Ivoire

Introduction

The largest city, seat of government and chief port, Abidjan lies on the Ébrié Lagoon and is separated from the Gulf of Guinea and the Atlantic by the Vridi Plage sandbar.

History

Portuguese explorers reached the coast in the fifteenth century and began trading in slaves and ivory. Abidjan was one of the many trading ports set up by the Europeans in the nineteenth century. The Côte d'Ivoire was made a

French protectorate in 1889 and a colony in 1893. Divided by a lagoon the first European settlement in the area, Abidjan-Plateau, was set up to the north in 1903 and Treichville, the first large African settlement, was to the south. A rail terminus was set up in 1904 and in 1934 Abidjan succeeded Bingerville as capital of the French colony. With the opening of the Vridi Canal in 1950 the city soon became a major shipping and financial centre. The first of two bridges linking the mainland to Petit-Bassam Island was built in 1958.

In 1958 Côte d'Ivoire was proclaimed a republic within the French Community and in 1960 achieved full independence. Abidjan remained the capital until 1983 when Yamoussoukro was named the administrative capital. The 1960s and 70s saw a period of economic growth and political stability despite challenges from the military and students at the University of Abidjan in 1982. In 1999 the president Henri Konan Bédié was ousted following a military coup by the country's military chief, General Robert Guéï. Thereafter Abidjan, along with the rest of the country, experienced violence and ethnic tensions. Ethnic rioting in 2001 left dozens dead in Abidjan. Outsiders are not welcome.

Modern City

Exports include cocoa beans, timber, tinned tuna, bananas, pineapples and cotton. The main export markets are France and Germany. Imports include petroleum products and non-electrical machinery. Le Plateau is the high-rise, commercial area with the industrial area located south at Petit-Bassam. Mineral and petroleum docks spread along the Vridi Canal. Here too are the districts of Treichville (the site of a large market), Marcory and Koumassi where the poor live. Squatters have developed the area to the west at Youpougon-Attié and Abobo. The presidential tower mansion and the most expensive residential area lies to the east in Cocody. There is an international airport at Abidjan Port-Bouet 16 km to the southeast of the city centre. A metre-gauge railway runs to Leraba, Ouagadougou and Kaya all in Burkina Faso. Buses run to Accra (Ghana), Ouagadougou, Bamako (Mali) and the capital Yamoussoukro. The National University of Côte d'Ivoire opened in 1958 and there are several technical colleges and libraries.

Places of Interest

The National Museum has collections of Ivorian art. The Branco National Park is an area of tropical rainforest located to the north of the city. The Hôtel Ivoire, in Cocody, is a major attraction offering an ice rink, a casino, a bowling alley, a swimming pool and a cinema.

Abu Dhabi City, United Arab Emirates

Introduction

Capital of the emirate of Abu Dhabi, federal capital of the UAE, and one of the most modern cities in the world. Abu Dhabi City is the seat of government, and a financial, transportation and communications centre of the oil-rich confederation. The headquarters of the main oil operating companies and most foreign embassies are based in the city.

History

Archaeological research shows evidence of a trading culture in the early 3rd millennium BC along the northern coast of the present UAE. The small enclaves that emerged along the Gulf coast were later absorbed by Persian dynasties. Trade with India and China expanded in the early Islamic period, from the early seventh century AD. European intervention in the Gulf area began in the early sixteenth century with the Portuguese, who established a commercial monopoly. Their ascendancy was later challenged by the Dutch and then by the British who, as they consolidated their supremacy over India, became predominant in the eighteenth century.

The settlement of Abu Dhabi, with its fertile oases of Liwa and Al-Ain, was founded in the 1760s. In 1793 it became the seat of government of the rulers of the surrounding emirate. Piracy, largely operating from Ras al-Khaimah, was rife until the early nineteenth century when it was suppressed by British naval expeditions. Treaties against piracy and the slave trade were subsequently signed between the British and the sheikhs of the Trucial Coast (as the area became known from the 1850s). Britain undertook to protect them from external attack. This close relationship was maintained until 1971 when British forces were withdrawn and the UK's defence responsibilities came to an end. Abu Dhabi and other Trucial States formed the independent United Arab Emirates. Abu Dhabi City was designated the provisional capital of the newly formed state became the permanent capital in 1990s.

Modern City

Abu Dhabi City's importance increased significantly with the discovery of vast oil reserves in the region in the 1950s and early 1960s. Since then it has undergone major development, reflecting its oil-based wealth. A modern infrastructure of air and sea ports, roads and highways, and telecommunications, together with elaborate architectural projects and town planning, have contributed to its present commercial and international standing.

Places of Interest

Places of interest in the city include the main thoroughfare, the 7-km-long Corniche (a landscaped, seafront boulevard); the Cultural Foundation, housing the national archives and library; the White Fort (or Old Fort), the oldest building in Abu Dhabi (and now a document and research centre); Louvre Abu Dhabi (an art and civilization museum), opened in 2017; a government-run Women's Craft Centre; and the Dhow Wharf at the eastern end of the Corniche. There is also a large sports centre.

Abuja, Nigeria

Introduction

Abuja is Nigeria's capital and its first planned city. Conceived in 1975, it is 500 km northeast of Lagos. It was chosen for its central location, cooler climate and lower population density than the former capital city, Lagos. That transfer dislodged the indigenous Gwari inhabitants from their land, a move that remains a source of contention. It is envisaged that the city will have a population of 3 m. once completed.

History

The Abuja federal capital territory came into existence in 1976, with the city located on the Chukuku hills. In 1982 Abuja was designated as successor to Lagos as the national capital. A university was founded in 1988 and central government re-located there in Dec. 1991.

Modern City

Abuja is the first Nigerian city not to have a dominant tribe or religion. The centre of Abuja houses the presidency, the headquarters of all federal ministries and many other government bodies. An international airport and a network of highways link Abuja to other major cities.

Development plans include allocation of land to agriculture, fisheries and livestock rearing. Minerals are another potential source of income. A metro line was introduced to tackle the city's shortage of public transport.

Places of Interest

The city is subdivided into two major zones; one for housing and commerce and the other for government and culture. Many of the major national cultural institutions have relocated or are relocating to the capital.

Accra, Ghana

Introduction

Accra is the capital, largest city, commercial and communications centre of Ghana. It is situated on the Gulf of Guinea in West Africa. Since 1962 its port has been located at Tema, 27 km to the east. Accra is derived from a word meaning black ants, which are abundant in the area.

History

When the Portuguese arrived on the south coast of Ghana in 1482, the area now known as Accra was occupied by the Ga tribes. Its vast gold reserves gave the name to the Gold Coast. The British, Dutch and Danish arrived in the seventeenth century to build trading posts but in the nineteenth century the British bought the Dutch and Danish rights and in 1874 the Gold Coast became a British colony. The three main trading posts gradually merged to form Accra which was declared the capital in 1877. In 1879 a municipal council was created to improve the town. It 1901 it became a British protectorate. Much of the city layout was planned in the 1920s and its growth since has been rapid. In 1960 Accra became capital of the independent Republic of Ghana. The seat of government, Osu Castle, one of Accra's most historic structures, is closed to the public.

Modern City

Ghana is seen by the World Bank as the Gateway to West Africa with the World Trade Center Accra set up to facilitate international trade. The stock exchange opened in 1990. Main exports in 2000 were minerals (gold, diamonds and manganese), cocoa and timber. Main export markets are Togo, the UK and Italy. Major imports were plant machinery, petroleum and raw materials from Nigeria, the UK and the Ivory Coast. Accra has well paved roads, a good municipal bus service and is connected by rail to Kumasi in the interior as well as to Tema which has taken over the city's port function. Kotoka is an international airport 9 km north of the city served by Ghana Airways with flights to almost every country in West Africa as well as New York and London. There are also a number of western carriers including British Airways. Makola Market offers glass beadware and batik and Kaneshie Market, on the western side, sells food and spices. The Arts Centre is the best craft market in the country. The University of Ghana, founded in 1948, is located to the north at Legon.

Places of Interest

In addition to the forts, Accra has buildings of modern, colonial and African architecture. The seventeenth century Christianborg Castle is now the residence of the chief of state. Churches include the Holy Spirit (Roman Catholic), the Holy Trinity (Anglican) and a number of Methodist cathedrals. Independence Arch in Black Star Square is used for ceremonial parades. The beaches are a big attraction but most are located a few kilometres out of town and require private transport.

Addis Ababa, Ethiopia

Introduction

Addis Ababa is Ethiopia's capital, situated in the Shewa province highlands at an altitude of 2,400 metres. Founded in 1887, it is home to several major international organizations. Despite being the country's political, commercial and cultural nucleus, it suffers from mass unemployment, lack of housing and a poor sanitation infrastructure.

History

Addis Ababa was founded by Emperor Menelik II in 1887. Looking for a base from which he could unite the northern and southern populations of his empire he initially established a camp high on the foothills of the Entotto

Mountains. It was his wife who, reputedly attracted by the area's hot springs, relocated the encampment lower down.

Addis Ababa was Shewa's provincial capital until 1889 when, after Menelik was crowned emperor of Ethiopia (then called Abyssinia), it replaced Intotto as the national capital. Menelik rapidly built up the city and in 1917 a rail link to Djibouti was completed, ensuring vital trade outlets. In 1936 Mussolini's Italy invaded and the city was taken in May. Aside from improvements to the infrastructures, Addis Ababa suffered greatly at the hands of the fascist regime. Mussolini removed many statues and monuments in an attempt to de-Ethiopianize the area and Italian settlers moved into clearly defined neighbourhoods (the modern day commercial and residential zones), enacting racial segregation.

The Italian forces were driven out by Haile Selassie in 1941. Between the mid-1960s and mid-1970s the population swelled as a result of mass migration from rural areas. Inflation spiraled and unemployment was rife, leading to popular protests that led to Haile Selassie's overthrow. It was at this time that much of the land owned by the imperial family and the Orthodox church was nationalized.

The population again surged during the 1980s and 1990s as a result of an influx of refugees following widespread famine and the intensifying war with the former Ethiopian province of Eritrea.

Modern City

Addis Ababa has an old quarter that houses many of the most popular tourist attractions. It is connected to the lower quarter, the commercial district, by the main thoroughfare, Churchill Avenue. The city boundaries are constantly expanding to cope with the overspill of people, with ethnic groups tending to live in defined neighbourhoods. Official unemployment stands at around 30% and over 80% of the population live in slums, the largest of which is Erri be Kentu (*To cry for no help*). The lack of adequate sanitation causes major health problems.

The city is at the centre of Ethiopia's road network while a railway links directly to Djibouti. The main international airport is Bole, around 8 km from the city centre. A system of mini-vans, known as *Wee Euts*, operates in the city, picking up passengers along scheduled routes.

Addis Ababa is home to the headquarters of the Organization of African Unity (established in 1963) and the UN Economic Commission for Africa. Among the leading industries are cement, tobacco and textiles. Addis Ababa is also the centre for the Ethiopian trade in coffee, the country's most important export.

Places of Interest

Among the city's leading attractions are Jubilee Palace, built for Haile Selassie's silver jubilee, and the Menelik Mausoleum, which houses the bodies of Menelik II and Haile Selassie. There are two cathedrals, St George's Cathedral (built in 1896 by Menelik II to celebrate the victory over the Italians) and Trinity Cathedral (built to commemorate the 1941 liberation from the Italians). The Merkato is the main market and there is a National Museum and an Addis Ababa Museum. The city is home to the national theatre and university (which houses ethnographic and zoological museums).

Adelaide, Australia

Introduction

Capital of South Australia and home to two thirds of the state's population, Adelaide occupies 2,000 km^2 around the Torrens River between Gulf St Vincent and the Mount Lofty Ranges. Once dubbed the 'city of churches', Adelaide is known for its clement weather and elegant stone buildings, dating from its foundation in 1837.

History

The land occupied by Adelaide was home to some 300 Kaurna Aborigines until European ships arrived in 1836. The original European settlement, on the site of present day Gleneg, began the colonization of South Australia, which was not a penal colony unlike other Australian settlements.

Named after Queen Adelaide, wife of William IV, the city's location was chosen on 31 Dec. 1836 by Englishman Colonel William Light (1786–1839), the state's first Surveyor-General. He planned Adelaide on a grid according to garden city principles of formal squares, wide streets, and parklands around the city centre. The next building boom occurred in the 1870s and '80s when the wheat trade flourished. Wine production and mining (in particular opal) became significant industries and remain important today.

Satellite villages began to proliferate almost as soon as the centre was constructed; there were 30 by the early 1840s. Adelaide's reputation as an oasis of civil and religious freedom attracted Europeans fleeing persecution, in particular Prussian Lutherans. The high proportion of 'wowsers' (puritans) led to an equally disproportionate number of churches. The population climbed from 6,500 to 14,500 in the 1840s. By the time of national Federation in 1901, the city's population had increased almost sevenfold.

The city expanded further during the First World War and the 1920s. The 1930s saw an industrialization programme by the state government, bringing 80% of South Australia's factory jobs to Adelaide by the end of the following decade. A surge of European immigrants, especially from Italy, characterized the post-Second World War years. South Australia was notable in the 1970s for its radical legislation against racial and sexual discrimination, including the formal recognition of Aboriginal land rights.

Modern City

Adelaide is served by interstate trains and buses, and an international airport situated 7 km west of the CBD. The city has two major centres: North Adelaide and Adelaide Central. Major shopping destinations include Rundle Mall, the country's first street mall opened in 1976 and now home to 600 retail outlets. The Central Market, established in 1869, is the largest of its kind in the southern hemisphere.

Unemployment was 7.4% in Dec. 2000. Key industries include sheep and fish farming, and beverage production. The South Australian wine industry, centred upon the Barossa Valley to the north of Adelaide, accounts for 50% of Australian wines and 65% of national wine exports. Nearby McLaren Vale has 40 wineries. The city is home to the Australian Wine Research Institute, set up in 1955, and a National Wine Centre, which opened in 2001. Tasting Australia, the national food and wine festival, has been held biennially in Adelaide since Oct. 1997.

Adelaide is home to a major biennial multi-arts festival, staged at a cost of A\$12 m., and a simultaneous fringe festival; both are held during Feb.–March in even numbered years. 400 other regular festivals and events include celebrations of cabaret, roses, ideas, and gay and lesbian culture. Since 1991, WOMAD (World of Music, Arts and Dance) has staged the Womadelaide festival biennially in Feb.

There are three universities in the city, with a total student population of 50,500: the University of Adelaide, established in 1874, Flinders University, set up in 1966 and named after British navigator and South Australia surveyor Matthew Flinders (1774–1814), and the University of South Australia, established in 1991 but dating from the 1856 opening of the state art school.

The National Cricket Academy and Cycling Institute are located in the city. Other popular recreations are football, netball, and water sports.

Places of Interest

The Botanical Gardens, opened in 1855, contain the largest glasshouse in the southern hemisphere. The city's zoo was established in the Gardens 28 years later. Popular walking trails wind around Mount Loft Summit (727 m). Also near Adelaide are the Belair and Onkaparinga national parks, the Black Hill, Cleland, Horsnell Gully, and Morialta conservation parks, and Warrawong Sanctuary. Belair is the state's oldest national park.

Cultural institutions are clustered along North Terrace. The state gallery was opened in 1881; its collection of 22 Rodin sculptures is the southern hemisphere's largest. Internationally renowned batsman Sir Donald Bradman's (1908–2001) collection of cricket memorabilia has been on view to the public since 1997 at the State Library Institute. Tandanya, the National Aboriginal Cultural Institute, takes its name from the Kaurna word for Adelaide. It is the country's only multidisciplinary facility for Aboriginal art and performance. The Jam Factory Craft and Design Centre presents work by contemporary Australian artists of all ethnic backgrounds.

Major museums include the South Australian Museum and museums dedicated to migration, theatre, and maritime history. Adelaide is also home to the National Motor Museum. The 1839 treasury building, 1851 police barracks, and 1855 parliament house have been converted into museums. Other historical sites are Hahndorf, a German Lutheran settlement dating from 1839, and the gum tree at Glenelg where South Australia was proclaimed a colony by Governor Hindmarsh in 1836. It is now surrounded by a modern seaside resort.

Popular entertainment venues include Her Majesty's Theatre, built in 1913, and the Adelaide Entertainment Centre, opened in 1991, incorporating the Amphitheatre, Festival Theatre, Playhouse, and the Space, as well as a 12,000-capacity arena.

Aden, Yemen

Introduction

Located on the north coast of the Gulf of Aden near the southern entrance to the Red Sea, Aden is the chief port of Yemen. It consists of two peninsulas, Aden and Little Aden, and an intervening stretch of the mainland. The bay between the peninsulas forms a natural harbour.

History

Aden's natural port, on an old volcanic site, was a coveted strategic and commercial location on the trading routes from India from ancient times. It was ruled by the pre-Islamic Aswan and Sabaean kingdoms before coming under Muslim Arab control from the seventh to the sixteenth centuries AD. The Portuguese failed in an attempt to capture it in 1513, but in 1538 it fell to the Ottoman Turks, although their hold on Yemen was to prove tenuous. At the end of the eighteenth century, Aden's importance as a strategic post grew as a result of British policy to contain the French threat to communications with British India following Napoléon's conquest of Egypt. With the coming of the steamship, Britain's need for a military and refuelling base in the region became more pressing. In 1839 the British captured Aden from the sultan of Lahej and it was attached administratively to India. In the 1850s the Perim, Kamaran, and Kuria Muria islands were made part of Aden, which became a free port. Britain also purchased areas on the mainland from local rulers and entered into protectionist agreements with them. The opening of the Suez Canal in 1869 further enhanced Aden's commercial and strategic significance.

Aden was formally made a British crown colony in 1937, and the surrounding region became known as the Aden protectorate. In 1962 the Aden colony became partially self-governing, and the following year was incorporated in the Federation of South Arabia (with the protectorate territories). Subsequently a power struggle for political control took place between rival nationalist groups. This resulted after the British withdrawal in 1967 in the creation of the independent Marxist state, with Aden as the capital, renamed the People's Democratic Republic of Yemen (PDRY) in 1970. Mistrust between the two Yemeni states characterized the next decade. In Jan.–Feb. 1986 Aden witnessed some of the heaviest fighting in the brief civil war between rival factions in the government and ruling hierarchies.

At the unification of the PDRY and the Yemen Arab Republic in 1990, Aden was declared the commercial capital of the new Republic of Yemen and a free trade zone. It suffered considerable damage in the brief civil war that erupted in mid-1994 between southern secessionists and the Sana'a-based government.

Modern City

Aden peninsula contains most of the city's population and is divided into three districts—Crater (the oldest quarter), Ma'allah and At-Tawahi. Little Aden is the centre of industry and site of a large oil refinery. Madinat ash-Sha'b, on the mainland, is the administrative hub of the city. Two suburbs, Khormaksar and Sheikh Othman, lie to the north of the port city, with an international airport between them. The city's economy remains largely based on its status as a port and regional commercial centre and as a refuelling stop for shipping. Aden suffered severe flooding in 1993.

Places of Interest

The Tanks of Aden are man-made cisterns dating from the first century AD (probably built by the Himyarites), which can store up to 45 m. litres of water. Partly cut out of rock, they are situated above the oldest part of the city on the volcanic slopes. The National Museum of Antiquities, Military Museum,

Ethnographic Museum, Al-Aidrus Mosque (dating from the fourteenth century) and Aden Minaret are all in Crater.

Aleppo, Syria

Introduction

Aleppo is Syria's second largest city. It is an historical commercial centre located in the northwest of the country. Like Damascus, it is claimed to be one of the oldest inhabited settlements in the world. It has been devastated in the civil war that has ravaged the country since 2011.

History

The earliest mentions of the city are recorded in texts dating from the end of the 3rd millennium BC. From that time onwards it became the capital of a succession of city-states under the Amorites, the Hittites, the Assyrians, the Persians, the Greeks (from 333 BC in the form of Seleucid dynasty founded by one of Alexander the Great's Macedonian generals), and the Romans (from 64 BC). A major trading centre between Asia and the Mediterranean, it remained under Roman control within the Byzantine Empire until AD 637 when it was conquered by the Muslim Arabs. In the tenth century Aleppo was briefly an independent principality under the Hamdanid dynasty until it was retaken by the Byzantines in AD 962. Having later become a centre of Islamic resistance to the Crusaders, Aleppo was taken over by Saladin and the Ayyubid dynasty in the second half of the twelfth century. The Ayyubids were succeeded by the Mameluks in the mid thirteenth century, around which time Aleppo was sacked by the invading Mongols (who were to devastate the city again in 1400–01). Mameluk rule gave way to incorporation into the Turkish Ottoman Empire from 1516. Having been an important staging post on the overland Silk Road throughout the Middle Ages, Aleppo lost some of its influence as a trading centre from the sixteenth century as Europe redirected its trade with India and China through sea routes. Ottoman control endured until the early twentieth century when the Empire disintegrated in the First World War. After the war France was granted a League of Nations mandate for the whole of Syria and Lebanon. Aleppo accordingly came under French rule until Syria's independence in 1946.

In 2012 Aleppo became a theatre for fierce fighting between anti-government armed forces and the Ba'athist regime led by Bashar al-Assad. Much of the city's infrastructure was laid to ruin following heavy mortar and air bombardment and ground-based firefights, while many sections of the old city have also been destroyed. The Sunni Islamist group Islamic State (IS), kept a presence of fluctuating strength in Aleppo from 2012 before being expelled by Assad's forces in late 2016.

Modern City

Before the civil war of 2011, Aleppo was a cosmopolitan city, hosting a range of nationalities and cultures, including a large Christian community chiefly consisting of Armenian refugees from Turkey. It had retained its commercial and trading heritage, with silk weaving, cotton printing, leather and food processing becoming important. It was home to a university, institute of music and several Muslim theological schools (madrasas).

It has an international airport that ceased handling civilian flights in Dec. 2012 owing to the civil war. However, it reopened in Jan. 2014 to allow international journalists access to the city.

IS forces imposed their brand of sharia law on the civilian population, who were also forced to endure internecine fighting among the rebel forces, a severely compromised infrastructure, disease and food shortages. In 2016 conditions declined further when Assad's forces imposed a blockade, depriving Aleppo's citizens of vital supplies. Russian-backed air strikes throughout 2016 weakened the rebels' grip on the city and government forces reclaimed it in Dec. 2016, amid evidence of large-scale devastation and a humanitarian crisis.

Places of Interest

Many of Aleppo's historical landmarks have been destroyed or severely damaged during the civil war, including the eighth century Umayyad-era mosque, whose minaret was demolished as a result of the conflict.

The Aleppo Citadel, surrounded by a moat, is traditionally the city's dominant landmark but was also significantly damaged in the civil war, during which time it was used as a base by government forces. The site became a fortress during the Seleucid dynasty, with later additions, particularly its large, fortified gate in the twelfth century. The Great Mosque (named after Zacharias, father of John the Baptist) was erected in the early Islamic period and largely rebuilt in the twelfth and thirteenth centuries (although its detached, freestanding minaret dates from 1090).

Surrounding Aleppo are numerous late-Roman and Byzantine sites, collectively called the Dead Cities. The most famous is Qala'at Samaan, where stands the Church of St Simeon (built in the fifth century AD and the largest Christian building at that time). However, these sites have been under threat from IS, who are ideologically opposed to the reverence of holy sites, both Christian and Muslim.

Alexandria, Egypt

Introduction

Alexandria is Egypt's chief seaport and second largest city, with an estimated population in 1998 of 3.3m. It is situated in the north of the country, on the Mediterranean coast at the western edge of the Nile Delta. Once the greatest city of the ancient world, it is now an industrial and commercial centre, linked by canal with the River Nile. It is also Egypt's main holiday resort.

History

In 332 BC Alexander the Great, having occupied Egypt, founded Alexandria, intending it as the capital of his new dominion and as a strategic seaport and naval base. On his death in 323 BC and the partition of his empire, control of the city was assumed by Ptolemy (one of Alexander's Macedonian generals) who founded the Egyptian dynasty that took his name. Populated chiefly by Greeks, Jews and Egyptians, Alexandria quickly became a major trading centre and a focal point of learning and scholarship in the Mediterranean world. Under the early Ptolemies, the Alexandrian Library and Museum were founded, and schools of philosophy, religion and other branches of learning were established. By the early third century BC, the Library was reputed to hold 0.5m. books, the largest collection in the ancient world. It was Ptolemy I who ordered the construction of the Pharos of Alexandria, one of the seven wonders of the ancient world. Completed in about 280 BC, this lighthouse tower stood until the fourteenth century when it was destroyed by an earthquake.

The rise of imperial Rome in the second and first centuries BC mirrored the decline of the Ptolemy dynasty. After the defeat of Queen Cleopatra (the last of the Ptolemies) at Actium in 31 BC by Octavian (later the Roman emperor Augustus), Egypt formally came under Roman rule. The Jewish and Christian communities of Alexandria suffered periodic persecution by their Roman overlords. In AD 116 a large part of the city was destroyed in the suppression of a Jewish revolt. The Roman emperor Caracalla ordered a massacre of its male inhabitants in 215, and in 284 (according to the history of the Coptic Church) nearly 150,000 Christians were killed.

From the fourth century Alexandria's influence began to wane, particularly so after the mid-seventh century when it was conquered by the Muslim Arabs for whom Cairo was of more strategic importance. Alexandria continued as a trading centre and as a naval base under the Fatimid and Mameluk dynasties. However, its position as an important seaport for trade between Europe and Asia (particularly the spice trade) was weakened by the discovery of the direct sea route to India in 1498. Its fortunes declined further under Ottoman rule from 1517. By the time of Napoléon's occupation from 1798–1801, Alexandria was a small fishing town of about 5,000 inhabitants. The completion of the Mahmudiyah Canal in 1820, reopening Alexandria's access to the Nile, revived the city's economy and its population began to recover. It also prospered from a booming Egyptian cotton trade in the nineteenth century, and from the heavy increase in sea traffic in the eastern Mediterranean following the opening of the Suez Canal in 1869. Under British occupation from 1882–1922, the city continued to expand and to attract a growing foreign community (which by the late 1940s accounted for 10% of its population). Following the military coup in 1952, Alexandria's expatriate population declined markedly. British and French citizens were expelled from Egypt after the Suez crisis of 1956.

Modern City

Modern Alexandria's economy relies principally on industry (particularly textile manufacturing), shipping and warehousing, and banking. An estimated 80% of Egypt's imports and exports pass through its two harbours. The city has road, rail and international air links, and a tramway network.

Places of Interest

Alexandria's cultural attractions include the Greco-Roman Museum (with some 40,000 artefacts), the Roman amphitheatre (Kom al-Dikka, discovered in 1964), the catacombs of Kom ash-Shuqqafa (dating back to the second century AD), Fort Qaitbey (built in the fifteenth century on the ruins of the Pharos of Alexandria), and the Al-Muntazah Palace (once the summer residence of the royal family). There are also botanic gardens and popular Mediterranean beach resorts.

Algiers (Al-Jaza'ir), Algeria

Introduction

Algeria's capital city sprawls along the Bay of Algiers on the Mediterranean coast and is set against the tree-lined Sahel Hills. The core of the town is divided into two sections with the modern French section down below and the old, labyrinthine, whitewashed Kasbah above it.

History

The Phoenicians established a port in the bay around 1200 BC and by 146 BC, Algiers (then known as Icosium) had been integrated into the Roman Empire. The city was then to undergo a series of conquests by various invading forces. The Vandals all but destroyed the city during the fifth century, it became part of the Byzantine empire in the sixth century and by 650 it had fallen under Arab influence. The roots of modern Algiers may be traced to 950 when the Berber leader Bologhin Ibn Ziri revived the city as a commercial centre and gave it its modern Arabic name.

Between the thirteenth and fifteenth centuries, the Hasfid and Mermid dynasties wrestled each other for control of Algiers, but by 1514 the biggest threat to Algiers was posed by Spanish forces who had fortified the island of Peñon in the Bay of Algiers. In response, the city turned to the Turkish Khayr ad-Din Pasha, or Barbarossa, to drive the Spanish from the area. Barbarossa had succeeded in removing them by 1529, and placed Algiers under Ottoman rule. It signalled the start of 300 years when Algiers acted as base for the Barbary pirates. Numerous attempts by the Holy Roman Empire and British, Dutch and American forces failed to remove the pirate threat over the coming centuries and it was only with the French capture of the city in 1830 that piracy was extinguished.

French colonial rule remained in place until Algerian independence was declared. During World War II, Algiers acted as headquarters for both the North African Allied Forces and the French provisional government under the leadership of Charles de Gaulle. By the 1950s Algiers had become the focal point of the violent struggle for independence against France. After this was achieved in 1962, Algiers looked to become a modern socialist capital, and in the years that followed many of the Europeans resident in the city departed. The city's population problems were also alleviated by the construction of many new suburbs to the south.

Modern City

Today, Algiers remains a vital transport link and trade centre. A metro system is scheduled to open in the course of 2011. Major imports include raw materials and industrial goods, while principal exports include wine, fruit, vegetables and iron ore. Other important industries are oil refining, metallurgy, chemicals, engineering and consumer goods.

Places of Interest

For tourists, the architectural and cultural mix of old and new and east and west is intriguing. The French section is spacious and open with a cathedral and university and the museums, galleries, theatres and eating places to be expected in a modern cultured city. The Kasbah, however, while it retains its romantic reputation, contains some of the worst slums in northern Africa.

Almaty, Kazakhstan

Introduction

Almaty, in the foothills of the Trans-Ili Alatau at the confluence of the rivers Bolshaya and Malaya Almaatinka in the southeast of the country, is Kazakhstan's biggest city and was its capital until 1997.

History

A city on the site of Almaty first appears in written sources in the mid-thirteenth century. Destroyed by Mongols, the modern city grew out of the Zailiyskoye fortress built by Russia in 1854. It was renamed Verney the following year and the area was populated by Cossacks, Tartars and others connected with the oil and mineral markets. In 1867 Almaty was recognized as a town and was made capital of a province of Turkistan. Twenty years later it suffered its first major earthquake, in which over 300 people died and 95% of buildings were destroyed. There was another serious earthquake in 1911.

In 1918 the city fell under Soviet rule. Renamed Alma-Ata in 1921 (the same year as it endured a calamitous mud slide), in 1929 it was chosen as capital of Kazakhstan. Benefitting from the construction of the Turkstan-Siberian railway, it underwent a period of rapid expansion. Between the mid-1920s and the start of World War II the population grew fivefold to 220,000. Light and heavy industries were developed, particularly during World War II. In 1996 a dam was built by controlled explosions in a bid to reduce the risk of further landslides. Seven years later the dam held out against a large mountain torrent that threatened the city for 19 days.

In 1986 Alma-Ata was the scene of serious ethnic rioting. Kazakh youths were angered by the replacement of Dinmukhamed Kunayev, the first secretary of the Kazakh Communist Party (CPKZ), by Gennady Kolbin, an ethnic Chuvash from Russia. Kunayev had been in office for over 20 years and was one of few ethnic Kazakhs to hold a key political position. The violence lasted for 2 days and caused over 200 deaths. In 1991,when Kazakhstan won independence from the USSR, Alma-Ata reverted to its Kazakh name, Almaty, derived from the word for apple in recognition of the fertile apple-growing region that surrounds the city.

Concerns about the city's vulnerability to natural disaster contributed to Astana's selection as the new capital in 1994. The transfer happened in 1997. Almaty remains the country's commercial, cultural and transport centre.

Modern City

Most commercial, governmental and municipal buildings are located in Novaya Ploshad, also one of the most densely populated parts of the city. There are good road, rail and air connections.

Food processing is the principle employer. Other major industries include tobacco processing, machine building and repair and various light industries. There is a university and several institutes of higher education.

Places of Interest

The wooden Zenkov cathedral, surrounded by the Panfilov Park, was built in Tsarist times and is among the most recognizable of Almaty's tourist sites. The city is home to the national museum and gallery as well as a museum of folk instruments and the Central State museum with a replica of the Golden Man, an ornate set of armour made in gold. Other attractions include the state circus, botanical gardens, the Arasan baths and a zoo. There are several theatres and an opera house.

Amman, Jordan

Introduction

Amman is Jordan's capital and by far its largest city. With an estimated population of about 1.2 m., it is located in the northwest of the country. It was originally built on a group of seven hills, but is now spread over a wider area of upland terrain. The main parts of the city (such as Jebel Amman and Jebel al-Hussein) gain their names from the hills on whose slopes they lie.

History

Inhabited since at least 3000 BC, Amman was known as Rabbath Ammon in biblical times. During the Iron Age, it was the chief city of the Ammonites, a semitic people. In the third century BC, it was captured by the Egyptians and renamed Philadelphia. It was thus styled throughout the eras of the Roman and Byzantine empires. The city was lost to the Byzantines at the rise of Islam and subsequently conquered by the Arabs in AD 635. Despite its strategic position and location on important trade routes, it had fallen into decline by about 1300.

In 1878 the Ottoman Turks resettled the site with a group of Circassian emigrants from Russia. Many of their descendents still reside in Amman. Having been an Ottoman base during the First World War, it was taken from the Turks by British forces in 1918. Following Turkey's defeat, the Amirate of Transjordan was established in the area east of the River Jordan as a state under the British Mandate. Amman became the hub of this new entity. As the Mandate neared its end, Transjordan became a sovereign independent country in 1946 (subsequently renamed the Hashemite Kingdom of Jordan), with Amman as its capital.

In the wake of the Arab-Israeli War of 1948–49, Amman absorbed large numbers of Palestinian refugees from the new Jewish state. A further influx followed the Six-Day War in 1967 when Jordan lost control to Israel of its territories west of the River Jordan occupied by Palestinians. Political conflict between the Jordanian Government and the militant Palestine Liberation Organization led to civil war in 1970. The city suffered heavy damage during the fighting.

Modern City

Amman remains the commercial, industrial and administrative centre of Jordan. Its principal industries include food processing, textiles, leather goods, electrical batteries and cement. Phosphate extraction and oil refining are also important. The city is at the centre of Jordan's transport network, straddling the main north-south highway, and has international rail and air links.

Places of Interest

Jordan's principal museums and artistic attractions are to be found in Amman. Historical sites of interest include the preserved Roman amphitheatre, the Odeon, the Nymphaeum (the main fountain), and the Citadel. The second century amphitheatre, with room for 6,000 people, is the most obvious remnant of ancient Philadelphia. The Citadel is the site of Amman's earliest fortifications. Mostly in ruins, but displaying evidence of Roman, Byzantine and Islamic construction, it is situated on its own hill at the heart of the city. Jordan's capital is also home to a number of grand mosques—the King Abdullah Mosque (built in the 1980s), the King Hussein Mosque, and the Abu Darwish Mosque with its distinctive black and white chequered patterns. The Hussein Sports City complex is the main site housing sports, cultural events and national festivities. Overlooking this complex is the Royal Cultural Centre.

Amsterdam, Netherlands

Introduction

The city is located on the south side of the mouth of the IJ, an inland arm of the IJsselmeer. It is connected to the North Sea via a canal, and is divided in two by the canalized Amstel River. The ancient medieval section of the city, the area around the major railway terminus at Centraal Station, is contained within a ring of buildings dating from the seventeenth century. Dam Square, the heart of Amsterdam is situated just south of the old city.

History

As far as can be ascertained, Amsterdam came into being as a small fishing village in the thirteenth century AD. The incipient city came under the authority of the counts of Flanders, and was granted a toll charter in 1275, though the full city charter was not to appear for a further 30 years. Amsterdam grew rapidly during the fourteenth century, emerging as a centre for trade between the North and Baltic Seas and southern Europe.

By the sixteenth century the city's increasing mercantile wealth led to it becoming a focal point for Protestant dissent against the rule of the Catholic Spanish, and whereas Antwerp was recaptured in 1585 by Philip II's troops, Amsterdam retained its autonomy. The result was an influx of Protestant immigrants fleeing from persecution in the southern lowlands. The city became renowned for its religious tolerance and Jews expelled from Portugal arrived soon afterwards. This flood of refugees served to treble the population between 1565 and 1618. These new arrivals extended Amsterdam's cultural, intellectual and above all commercial influence, and when the 80 Years' War with Spain finally drew to an end in 1648, the city had become the major trading centre of the world, dominating Europe with its financial prosperity.

The eighteenth century witnessed the start of the city's decline from power. London and Hamburg gradually superseded it as a commercial centre, although Amsterdam remained the financial heart of Europe. French occupation in 1795 culminated in the collapse of the city's trade, since the French placed an embargo on trade with Britain, and the British blockaded Amsterdam in return.

The city began to recover by cultivating its industrial potential, which it achieved through steel production. However, the harbour's appalling condition meant that rehabilitation did not really become a reality until a canal connecting Amsterdam to the North Sea was constructed from 1865–76. Following this the population again increased, reaching half a million by 1900. The revenues generated by the Dutch East India Company brought Amsterdam back some of its former glories, but the German occupation during World War II proved catastrophic. Many of its industrial facilities were bombed into extinction and worse still, its considerable Jewish population was virtually eradicated by the Nazis—only 1 in 16 Amsterdam Jews survived the war. The city was liberated in May 1945, and began the arduous process of rebuilding and recovering itself.

Modern City

Modern Amsterdam is thriving with tourism providing a significant contribution to the local economy. The new media, transport and distribution, banking, finance and diamond processing are also particularly strong sectors. Transport within the city is very good—at Centraal Station tram, bus and metro networks converge and provide travellers with regular services to all locations inside and outside Amsterdam. Trams are recommended for inner city travel, whereas the bus and metro cater for destinations further afield. Driving in the city is actively discouraged, there is no free parking within the Canal Zone, and heavy fines or clamps are imposed on those without parking vouchers. Cycling is also a very popular means of getting around, and there are over 500,000 bicycles in Amsterdam. Schiphol, one of Europe's busiest international airports, is located 18 km (11 miles) to the south of the city.

Places of Interest

Amsterdam has many sites of artistic significance and interest. The famous Rijksmuseum houses a celebrated collection of work by the Flemish Masters, as well as thousands of other objects of art. It was reopened in April 2013 after 10 years of renovation. The Stedelijk Museum is a major international centre for modern art and contains paintings by Picasso, Matisse and Chagall as well as works by artists with Dutch origins such as Karel Appel and Willem de Kooning. The Van Gogh Museum pays tribute to one of Holland's greatest painters, and accommodates work by Vincent Van Gogh and his contemporaries. The canal tours, Anne Frank's house and the city zoo are also popular with visitors to the city.

Andorra-la-Vella (Andorre-la-Vieille; Andorra-la-Vieja), Andorra

Introduction

Andorra's capital and largest town is situated 1,000 m above sea level in the Pyrenees on the River Valira and is one of the 7 parishes that make up Andorra. The country had historically been under the shared sovereignty of Spain and France before independence in 1993, and both Spanish and French influences are evident in the town's culture.

History

Andorra-la-Vella can trace its roots back to around the 800s but it was still little more than a tiny, rustic mountain village at the beginning of the twentieth century. A number of roads were built during the 1930s and its population began to increase after World War II as the tourist industry prospered. By the 1970s it had become a commercial centre, well positioned to take advantage of the growing winter sports market and becoming a major duty free shopping area.

Modern City

Today, Andorra-la-Vella's economy remains reliant on tourism and shopping and it is the country's commercial, political and cultural centre. Though well served by roads, it has no local rail or air links.

Places of Interest

The Barri Antic (Old Quarter) is the traditional core of Andorra-la-Vella and it retains its narrow, cobblestoned charm. It is also the location of Plaça la Poble (The People's Square) and Casa de la Vall (House of the Valley) which was built in 1580 and has served as the parliament building since 1702. Also in the Barri Antic is the Sala de la Justicia (the country's only courtroom) and a number of churches, including the church of Santa Coloma which dates back to the ninth century.

Ankara, Turkey

Introduction

Ankara is in the northwest about 200 km south of the Black Sea. It is situated on a hill above the Anatolian plateau. It is the capital of Turkey.

History

Evidence of settlement dates back to the Stone Age, and by the end of the second millennium BC a thriving town existed, serving as an important transport hub for a caravan route. Ankara was captured by Rome in 25 BC, and remained significant within the Byzantine Empire after the Roman Empire fragmented, although it was constantly under threat from Persian and Arab invasion. The Seljuq Turks finally seized control of the city in the late eleventh century, but with the expansion of the Seljuq empire it began to decline, and it was not restored to its former prosperity until the sultan Orhan defeated the Seljuq rulers to claim Ankara for the Ottoman dynasty.

The city began to recover its commercial powers after it was officially incorporated into the Ottoman empire in 1403. It remained a trading centre of some significance throughout the following centuries, but did not develop from being a sleepy provincial town until the twentieth century. After World War I, Kemal Ataürk chose Ankara as the centre for a resistance movement which sought to overthrow the Ottoman sultanate and defend the country from Greek invasion. This decision was to have immense impact on the city's status, after the Greeks were defeated and the Ottoman regime was toppled. In 1923 Atatürk proclaimed Ankara the capital of Turkey.

Modern City

The modern city's architecture traces its history from an outpost of the Roman Empire through the Ottoman period until Atatürk's rule. The area most frequented by tourists is the Hisar, a Byzantine citadel on a hill to the east of the old city. Old Ankara retains its fifteenth century market, as well as a bazaar from the same era. Most of the cities hotels are in this area which is only a kilometre away from the main station. To the south of the old city, sprawls modern Ankara, which contains Atatürk's mausoleum and the presidential mansion.

The city is home to all government offices, three universities, the national library and the state theatre. It is also second only to Istanbul as a centre for industry, producing alcoholic drinks, sugar, cement and other construction materials, mosaic paving, milk and flour. The service industry continues to grow as an increasing number of tourists visit the city. Ankara is an important transport hub, served by road, rail and air with Esenboga International airport lying to the northeast.

Places of Interest

The Museum of Anatolian Civilization houses a world-renowned collection of antiquities and artefacts from Turkey's pre-Ottoman past. The Ethnographic museum features notable collections of woodwork and calligraphy.

Antananarivo, Madagascar

Introduction

Spread over 12 sacred foothills in the centre of the island, Antananarivo is Madagascar's capital and largest city. Until 1975 it was known as Tananarive.

History

Antananarivo was established as a walled citadel in the Ikopa valley on the central plateau at the beginning of the seventeenth century. It came under the control of the Merina Kingdom, who made Antananarivo its capital. They ruled the surrounding area from their hilltop castle until the end of the nineteenth century. Under Merina King Radama I (1810–28), Antananarivo became the capital of all Madagascar.

Tana, as the city is known, was the centre of power for successive empires and colonial powers, including Arabs, Portuguese, English and French settlers. Combined with the migration from surrounding countries throughout the island's history, Antananarivo has a diverse ethnic make up. In recent times, pressure on the city's infrastructure and housing has increased with the influx of rural migrants.

Modern City

The political and administrative capital, it is the seat of the presidential palace and government ministries, as well as major businesses. Founded in 1961, the national university is in the capital. Industries include food processing and leather goods. The city is surrounded by paddy fields. Antananarivo is connected by air to Madagascar's major cities and international locations.

Places of Interest

There are remnants of the seventeenth century palace, the Rova, of Merina king Andrianjaka which was destroyed by fire in 1995. Islam was introduced before the fifteenth century and there are mosques throughout Antananarivo. Exhibitions are held in the National Library to promote Malagasy culture. Markets include le Zoma and Antohomadinika. Artists of the Malagasy opera, the Mpira Gasy, perform weekly. The Antananarivo museum houses collections of skeletons of extinct animals, including the elephant bird and giant lemurs. Other museums include the municipal theatre of Isotry.

There is a botanical garden and a local zoo at Tsimbasasa. The Mazorevo Farm and Croc-Farm are also open to visitors. Traditional crafts are displayed in the National Centre of Malagasy Crafts.

Antwerp, Belgium

Introduction

Antwerp is situated on the Scheldt River in the north of the country, some 88 km (55 miles) from the North Sea, and 40 km (25 miles) from Brussels. It is the second-largest port in Europe, and forms a crucial part of a vast harbour complex.

History

The site is thought to have been inhabited as early as the second century AD. Antwerp almost certainly developed from 2 separate settlements: to the south, Chanelaus-Caloes-Callo, and to the north, a younger northern community clustered around the ninth century Steen Castle.

Christianity arrived in the seventh century and in 1124 the religious centre of the region shifted to the northern community at Steen castle, and modern Antwerp began to emerge. By the beginning of the fourteenth century it had become a major trading post for English, Venetian and Genoese merchants, and was established as the capital of the Duchy of Brabant. In the fifteenth century the city had replaced Brugge as the commercial hub of western Europe, prospering from early colonial trade and the fabulous New World wealth discovered by the Spanish and Portuguese. As the population grew, new industries such as bleaching, brewing and malting appeared, and, taking into account the economic contribution made by Antwerp's lucrative cloth trade, they combined to make the city a formidable industrial and financial power. A stock exchange was inaugurated in 1531. Antwerp suffered a setback during the Dutch Revolt when many of its citizens were butchered and buildings burned. Following the revolt Amsterdam replaced it as the commercial centre of the region, but the city remained the economic heart of the Spanish Netherlands. The nineteenth century expansion of Antwerp's port facilities continued throughout the twentieth, hindered only by the world wars. After German bombardment towards the end of World War II, the city was left damaged but with its infrastructure intact.

Modern City

Present day Antwerp is divided into the old city within the sixteenth century walls; the nineteenth century city which envelops the old centre, and the post-1945 section, largely consisting of dockyards, warehouses and harbour developments. The largest part of Antwerp is the seaport complex to the north, which is mainly non-residential.

Major industries include chemical and sugar refining and car manufacturing. The city is famous as a producer of cut diamonds and photographic and electronic equipment. Served by a dense network of railway lines and roads, Antwerp is also an important destination for Europe's inland waterways.

Places of Interest

The city's proud artistic heritage is in evidence in the Royal Museum of Fine Arts, the Cathedral of Our Lady and in the preserved residences of the famous painter Peter Paul Rubens and the sixteenth century humanist printer, Christophe Plantin. The ancient Steen Castle now houses the National Maritime Museum and the Antwerp zoo is one of the oldest and best maintained in Europe. Antwerp is also home to the Royal Flemish Opera House and the Royal Dutch Theatre.

Apia, Samoa

Introduction

Apia, on the northern edge of Upolu Island, is Samoa's capital and chief port.

History

The western end of Samoa's harbour, called Mulinu'u, was capital of an old Samoan kingdom. Several Western companies established themselves in

Apia in the 1850s, making it one of the most important trading centres in the Pacific region. In the nineteenth century Germany, the UK and the US vied for power in Samoa. When, in 1889, a typhoon destroyed three German and three American vessels, the disaster played a part in the signing of the Treaty of Berlin which acknowledged the local monarch but left Apia under the joint control of the three Western powers.

After more jostling for influence, Samoa became a German protectorate. In Aug. 1914 Apia was taken by New Zealand forces supported by Australian and French troops, thus becoming the first German territory to fall in World War I. In Nov. 1914 a New Zealand ship docked in Apia and brought with it Spanish influenza in an epidemic lasting 2 weeks. Over 7,500 Islanders died in the world's worst known outbreak.

US marines based in Apia during World War II did much to improve the island's transport links. Calls for Samoan independence grew after World War II. In 1959 a draft constitution for self-government was drafted and a government established in Apia. In Jan. 1962 Apia became capital of independent Western Samoa (later re-named Samoa). In July 1999 Apia was at the centre of an attempted coup, during which a cabinet minister was assassinated.

Modern City

Apia is Samoa's only major port. There is a good road infrastructure (with Beach Road at its heart) and a bus station. Fagali'I airport is a few kilometre outside the city centre. The local economy relies on the port and related industries and tourism. Major exports are cocoa, copra, bananas and root crops. Other industries include electrical engineering and diverse manufacturing.

Places of Interest

The residence of the head of state, Vailima, used to be the home of the writer Robert Louis Stevenson who lived on the island in the year leading up to his death. The clocktower in the town centre is a memorial to those killed during World War II. There is a popular flea market and the city's famous Aggie Grey Hotel has welcomed many movie stars over the years.

Arequipa, Peru

Introduction

Located on the Chili River in a fertile plain at the base of the Andes, Arequipa is the capital of the region of the same name. It is the second largest city in the country and is the commercial and political focus of Southern Peru. The volcanic mountain of El Mistri dominates the skyline.

History

Archaeological findings reveal the presence of hunter gatherers in the Arequipa region between 8000–1000 BC. Arequipa was settled by Aymara Indians during the Early Horizon era (around 1000–300 BC). After a period of isolation between 800–1200 AD the Lupaca came to the region. In the fourteenth century the town was an important link in the Inca trade route from Cuzco in the Andean Mountains to the coast. The city was part of Kuntisuyo, one of the four regions of the Inca Empire. On 15 Aug. 1540 the town was founded by Conquistadors, under the command of Francisco Pizarro, as Nuestra Señora de la Asunción del Valle Hermoso.

Arequipa was built on a site prone to earthquakes and consequently none of the original colonial buildings remain. There are buildings in the colonial style, constructed using the local *sillar*, a white porous volcanic stone, many dating from the eighteenth century. *Sillar* was used in much of Arequipa's architecture, including the late sixteenth-century bridge traversing the Chili River, the Puente Bolognasi. It was for its white stone that Arequipa became known as 'The White City'. The University of San Agustín was built in 1828 and the Catholic University of Santa María was founded in 1961. Arequipa's cathedral dates from 1612.

Recent constructions have incorporated traditional architectural styles, as evidenced by buildings from the 1950s, for example the Teatro Municipal. Expansion and development encouraged migration from the surrounding rural areas from the 1970s onwards, causing rapid growth of the suburbs and the emergence of large shanty towns.

Modern City

Arequipa is the centre of Peru's wool-processing industry and manufactures textiles and soap. Other industries include flour milling and tanning. Rail and road connect the city with the port of Mollendo, 88 km to the Southwest. A week long annual festival around 15 Aug. commemorates the founding of the city.

Places of Interest

In 1576 the Santa Catalina convent was founded by María de Guzmán. Over an area of 2.5 hectares, the convent is a virtual citadel containing squares and houses. It has been destroyed and restored on numerous occasions. The convent was closed to visitors until 1970, when the addition of electricity and running water led the Nuns to open the place to tourists. La Recoleta monastery contains a library of around 20,000 books, the oldest of which dates from fifteenth century. It also houses a museum containing Inca artefacts. The Museo Histórico Municipal exhibits paintings and artefacts documenting the city's history. The University at Arequipa has the remains of an Inca girl, used as human sacrifice 500 years ago.

Ashgabat, Turkmenistan

Introduction

Ashgabat, the capital of Turkmenistan, lies between the Kara Kum Desert and the Kopet Dag mountains. It was virtually rebuilt following a devastating earthquake in 1948.

History

There is evidence of human habitation in the Parthian period. Nisa, the ancient capital of the Parthians, is located around 20 km from Ashgabat. The name Ashgabat is believed to derive from the Arabic for 'the city built on love'.

Russian troops arrived in Krasnovodsk (now Turkmenbashi) in 1869 and built a fortress at Ashgabat in 1881. The Russian takeover was famously disputed at the siege of Geoktepe, where 15,000 people died. The defeat is commemorated annually and a mosque has been built in memory of the victims.

In 1885 the Trans-Caspian Railway linked Ashgabat, then capital of the Transcaspian oblast, to Russia and started an economic boom. Soviet rule was established in Ashgabat in 1917 and the following year the city was renamed Poltorask after a local Commissar for Labour. In 1924 Poltorask was designated capital of the Turkmen Soviet Socialist Republic, reverting to the name Ashgabat in 1927.

In the 1920s the textile, metal and construction industries brought wealth to the city but in 1948 it was devastated by an earthquake which killed up to 30% of the population. Rebuilt to reflect its earlier design, Ashgabat suffered water shortages until it was connected to the Kara Kum Canal in 1962. It became capital of independent Turkmenistan in 1991.

Modern City

The country's commercial and administrative centre, Ashgabat is an important transport hub, with rail and road connections and an airport. The canal forms a lake outside the city, providing transportation, irrigation, hydroelectric energy and recreation. Buses run within the city. Among the most important industries are carpet-making (Ashgabat is home to the famed Bukhara rugs), fabric production, glass and metalworking. The city is often used by film makers. There is a university and several institutes of higher education.

Since independence, a major building programme has included a national museum and a presidential palace.

Places of Interest

Turkmen carpets, which adorn every public institution, can be bought at the huge Tolkuchka bazaar. The city's Sunday market is among the largest in Central Asia. There is also a carpet factory and museum. Other attractions include the state history museum, the museum of fine arts and the opera house. Close by is Nisa, the ancient capital of the Parthian state.

Asmara, Eritrea

Introduction

Asmara, in Eritrea's central highlands, is the national capital.

History

Originally a small village belonging to the Tigre people, Italians occupied the town in 1890 and made it capital of the colony of Eritrea 10 years later. It was rapidly developed during the 1930s when the Italians used it as the base to invade Ethiopia in 1935. Seized by British forces in 1941, as part of Eritrea it entered into federation with Ethiopia in 1952. An Eritrean Liberation Front soon emerged seeking independence and Asmara was of vital strategic importance during the ensuing civil war. In 1977 the US telecommunications base at Kagnew closed after 35 years. In 1993 Asmara became capital of the newly independent Eritrea.

Modern City

Asmara's architecture is influenced by its Italian colonial period. It is planned around wide boulevards, with Liberation Avenue forming the main artery. It is well served by road and rail links which connect it to the nearby Red Sea port at Massawa. Asmara's airport was of importance during the civil war.

Major industries include meat processing, brewing and distilling, textiles, leather-tanning and ceramics. It is also a trading centre for local agricultural produce. There is a university.

Places of Interest

The city's Romanesque cathedral dates from 1922 and the Grand Mosque from 1937 while St Mary's is one of the largest Ethiopian Orthodox churches in the region. Other major landmarks include the former governor's palace (now a government residential building), the parliament building, the municipal complex, the Romanesque opera house and the Cinema Impero. The National Museum has archaeological and ethnographic collections. Also popular are the municipal park, the main market and the Tank Cemetery, the resting place of large numbers of decommissioned military vehicles.

Astana, Kazakhstan

Introduction

Astana, on the River Ishim in the centre of the country, has been the national capital since 1997.

History

Established by the Russians as the Akmola fortress in 1824, Astana's location on the steppe rendered it a traditional contact point between various ethnic groups. The Great Steppe route mentioned by Greek historian Herodotus ran across this territory, which subsequently became part of the Silk Road.

An important administrative seat by the late 1860s, it was designated capital of its oblast in 1939. It was a busy trading centre and mining town until the 1950s, when it became the centre of Kruschev's Virgin Lands scheme. A quarter of a million square kilometres of steppe were turned into wheatfields and Astana was the central point of the project, being renamed Tselinograd (Virgin Fields City) in 1961.

Between 1960 and 1965 it served as capital of a region comprising five oblasts within the Kazakh Soviet Socialist Republic. The period was characterised by rapid urban expansion. Following Kazakh independence in 1991 Tselinograd was renamed Aqmola (White Grave). Three years later there were plans to move the national capital to the centrally located and seismatically less sensitive city. The transfer occurred in 1997 and in 1998 Aqmola was again renamed, this time as Astana, meaning 'Capital City'. Astana hosted Expo 2017.

Modern City

Astana's road, rail and air links have improved since it became capital. Buses run within the city. Important industries include machinery and consumer goods, food processing and textiles. A fifth of the country's grain is produced here.

Places of Interest

Astana is a major staging post on the Trans-Kazakhstan and South Siberian railways.

Asunción, Paraguay

Introduction

In the southeast of Paraguay near the Argentine boarder, Asunción is on the eastern bank of the Paraguay River near the confluence with the Pilcomayo River. The capital of Paraguay and its only large city, it is the country's economic, social and cultural centre.

History

The surrounding area was originally inhabited by the semi-nomadic Guaraní. The city was founded in 1537 by the conquistadors Juan de Salazar and Gonzalo de Mendoza as Nuesta Señora de la Asunción. Soon after, Domingo Martínez de Irala established the first *cabildo* (council) in the New World at Asunción which he governed until the late 1550s. The Guaraní accepted the colonialists and the two communities intermarried, the Spaniards adopting the Guaraní language and customs although remaining politically dominant. When the inhabitants of nearby Buenos Aires were forced out by a Pampa uprising in 1541, Asunción became their refuge. Over the next half a century the town was the centre of Spanish expansion across the south of the continent until Buenos Aires was reclaimed. Many returned and Asunción's importance declined. In 1588 Jesuit missionaries arrived and set up religious communities, although they were expelled by 1767.

One of the earliest nationalist movements arose in Asunción and by 1811 Paraguay had gained independence from both Spain and Argentina. The ruling López dynasty led Paraguay into war against Brazil, Uruguay and Argentina between 1864–70. The war proved costly to Paraguay in both lives and territory and between 1868–76 Asunción was under the control of Brazil. Around this time an influx of Argentine and European immigrants added to the capital's population. The city was slow to develop in comparison to other South American cities (many streets remained unpaved into the twentieth century) and progress was further hampered by the Chaco War with Bolivia between 1932–35. In the second half of the twentieth century, the city developed and expanded.

Modern City

Asunción is Paraguay's seat of government and the cultural and economic centre. Industries include the processing of agricultural produce from the surrounding area such as cotton, sugarcane and cattle. The city also has meatpacking and flour milling industries as well as textile and footwear production. Most of Paraguay's business is conducted in the city. Among several academic institutions are the Universidad Nacional founded in 1890 and the Universidad Católica opened in 1960. Asunción is linked with Buenos Aires by rail, and the city has an international airport.

Places of Interest

As one of the continent's oldest cities, Asunción still retains its colonial feel. The oldest building in Asunción, the Casa de la Independencia, was the site of the signing of independence in 1811. Pre-Colombian artefacts are displayed in the Museo Etnográfica Andrés Barbero while modern art can be seen in the Museo del Barro. The Panteón Nacional is a memorial to Paraguayan war heroes.

Athens, Greece

Introduction

Athens is in southeastern Greece surrounded by mountains and divided north to south by a line of hills. The city is about 8 km from the Bay of Phaleron, where its port, Piraeus, opens into the Aegean Sea. It is the country's capital.

History

There is evidence that the site was inhabited from the Neolithic period onwards, but the first notable settlement was a fortified village known as Kekropia that dates back to 3000 BC. The sixth century BC witnessed the first major expansion of Athens under the rule of Peisistratus. He enhanced the naval and military capabilities of the city state and extended its geographical boundaries and political influence. In 530 BC the original temple to Athena Polis was constructed on the Acropolis, and around the same time a new agora was built in the lower city.

In 480 BC the invasion by the Persian army resulted in the destruction of many important buildings. Once the Persians had been driven out, long walls were constructed to protect the city from further assault and to connect the city with Piraeus. Peace with Persia was finally made some 30 years later. Under the guidance of Pericles the Acropolis was rebuilt and work on the Parthenon was begun, and Athens entered its golden age. The zenith of Athenian cultural and political influence was short-lived, and the outbreak of the Peloponnesian war with Sparta in 432 BC signified the beginning of the city's decline. During a temporary cessation of hostilities, the building of the Erectheum was begun. Whilst damaging to Athens politically, the war inspired the great philosophers such as Socrates and Plato in their examination of human reason.

Sparta gradually seized the advantage and in 404 BC the war ended with the defeat of Athens. The elaborate civic building programme was stopped, and the city lay weak and exposed to foreign invasion. In 338 BC Athens, and the other city-states of Greece, were occupied by Philip II of Macedon, father of Alexander the Great. Alexander himself favoured Athens for its cultural significance, and in his time the Theatre of Dionysus was rebuilt and enlarged.

The Roman invasion of Athens in 86 BC concluded with the razing of the city and the slaughter of its people, although once occupied the city was at first treated with respect. The emperor Hadrian graced it with several monumental buildings including the temple of Olympian Zeus. Athens embraced Christianity after the visit of the apostle Paul, and was a part of the Byzantine Empire for centuries. The city finally sank into obscurity when Justinian I closed its schools of philosophy in AD 529. By this time its influence and power had been superseded by Constantinople.

The Ottoman Turks occupied the city in 1458. During the Turkish rule the Parthenon was converted into a mosque and the Erectheum became a harem. Athens remained under Ottoman control until a series of insurgencies in the 1820s secured the city's independence. In 1833 it was chosen as the capital of the new kingdom of Greece.

Modern City

After occupation by Nazi Germany during World War II, the city embarked on a programme of rapid construction and industrialisation, and its character and layout today is largely a product of this era of expansion and population growth. Athens came under the international spotlight when it hosted the Olympic Games in 2004. The city's major streets centre around Syntagma (Constitution) Square. To the south lies the old Turkish quarter of Plaka, which is sheltered by the Acropolis and popular with tourists seeking accommodation. To the west is the market district of Monastiraki. To the east lies the chic residential area of Kolonaki. Due north of Syntagma is the more downmarket district of Omonia, an important transport hub for the city, in spite of the proliferation of brothels and crime in its streets.

Athens has two major intercity bus stations and two major railway stations—Larissa serving northern Greece, Evia and Europe, and Peloponnese, from which trains depart for the Peloponnese. The city is also served by Eleftherios Venizelos International, which lies 21 km to the east of central Athens. The metropolitan transport system consists of an electric rail network (which runs underground in the city centre), buses and trams.

Athens has been the industrial and commercial hub of the country since the end of World War I. It manufactures and exports wine, olive oil, tomatoes, cement, bauxite and textiles. Its industrial region includes petrochemical works, breweries, distilleries, cotton mills, soap and carpet factories. Industrialisation has led to a high level of pollution.

Places of Interest

In addition to the ancient buildings on and around the Acropolis, popular sites of cultural interest include the National Archaeological Museum which houses a world-renowned collection of Mycenean artefacts and Minoan frescoes, and the Goulandris museum of Cycladic and Ancient Greek art which has a notable collection of sculptures.

Atlanta, United States of America

Introduction

Located on the Piedmont Plateau on the eastern slope of the Appalachian mountains, Atlanta is the capital city of Georgia and the seat of Fulton county. The city of Atlanta is relatively small (around 134 sq. miles or 347 km^2) but it occupies part of a far larger metropolitan area. The city is the major centre for distribution of services and goods as well as the most significant financial and business centre in the southeastern United States.

History

Cherokee and Creek people lived in the area now occupied by modern-day Atlanta before they were forcibly removed to make way for extended railroads in the 1830s. A town named Terminus was built to the east of the Chattahoochee River. Terminus grew steadily and changed its name to Marthasville and then Atlanta in 1845, in recognition of the Western and Atlantic railroad terminating there. Two years later Atlanta was incorporated as a city. A crucial transportation and supply centre for the Confederate states during the Civil War, Atlanta was captured by Union General William T. Sherman in 1864 and much of the city was burned.

Atlanta became the permanent state capital of Georgia in 1877 and by the turn of the century was the largest city in the state. Rigidly segregated, Atlanta came to symbolise many of the racial tensions of the American south. At one stage it was the headquarters for the Ku Klux Klan and in 1906 there were serious race riots. However, in the second half of the 20th century, segregation laws were gradually eroded and racial tensions soothed. In 1973, Atlanta became the first southern city to elect a black mayor. In 1996, the city hosted the summer Olympic Games.

Modern City

Many American corporations have their headquarters in Atlanta, including Delta Air Lines, Coca-Cola and the United Parcel Service. Eighty percent of the United States' largest companies have branch offices in the city. The leading industries are paper products, clothing, chemicals, aircraft and motor vehicles. Atlanta is also one of the leading convention centres in the country.

Atlanta's transportation system received a $2 bn. boost as a result of hosting the 1996 Olympics. The city is served by Hartsfield International Airport, the busiest airport in the United States. The Atlanta Airport Shuttle links Hartsfield to the city. The Metropolitan Area Rapid Transit Authority (MARTA) runs extensive bus and subway services and there is an Amtrak station and a Greyhound bus terminal.

Places of Interest

Atlanta was the birthplace of Martin Luther King Jr., who is remembered in a National Historic Site in the east of the city encompassing his birthplace, the church where he preached and his grave.

Downtown Atlanta was revamped in time for the 1996 Olympics and contains Underground Atlanta, a huge subterranean shopping complex, and Centennial Park. Other places of interest include the Atlanta Public Library, which has a room devoted to Margaret Mitchell, the locally born author of *Gone With the Wind*, the Atlanta Historical Center, the Fernbank Science Center and the Atlanta Museum.

The Fox Theater, an Art Deco building, hosts regular theatrical performances while the Woodruff Arts Center contains the High Museum of Art—a gallery of contemporary and African art. Grant Park, located to the south of downtown Atlanta, contains the Atlanta Zoo and the Cyclorama, a large (50 ft. by 900 ft) circular painting which depicts the Battle of Atlanta during the American Civil War.

The Olympic stadium has been renamed Turner Field and houses the Atlanta Braves baseball team. The city's American football team the Atlanta Falcons is based at the Georgia Dome and the Philips Arena hosts basketball and ice hockey matches.

Auckland, New Zealand

Introduction

With one in four households owning a boat, Auckland is known as the 'City of Sails'. The largest city in New Zealand, and the sixth largest city in Oceania, Auckland lies across an isthmus near the northern tip of North Island. Auckland surrounds Mount Eden (200 metres), an extinct volcano, with the Hauraki Gulf to its east, and the Tasman Sea to its west. It enjoys a temperate climate with westerly winds. Some 10% of New Zealand's population live in Auckland, which provides more than 50% of the jobs in the Greater Auckland region. The other centres in the region are Franklin, Manukau, North Shore, Papakura, Rodney, and Waitakere. In the year to March 1999, Auckland accounted for 17% of the national GDP.

History

Before 1840, New Zealand's capital was Russell, in the Bay of Islands. After the Treaty of Waitangi, British governor William Hobson selected Commercial Bay as his new administrative centre. Hobson acquired 3,000 acres of land around Waitemata Harbour (Maori for 'sea of sparkling waters') from the local Ngati Whatua iwi, and renamed it Auckland, in honour of his patron George Eden, Lord Auckland, who was First Lord of the Admiralty.

The early years of the settlement were dogged by incompetent administration and poor sanitation; today's main shopping area, Queen Street, was once an open sewer. The first council was set up in 1854, but it was not until 1871, when Auckland became a city, that an effective council was inaugurated. However, by this time, the seat of government had moved to Wellington, a central location from which to co-ordinate the 1860s gold rush.

Historically, Auckland's position on the isthmus, 11 km at its widest point, has made urban expansion complicated. Water (1866), electricity (1908), and waste disposal utilities (1905) had to be established outside the city after considerable trial and error, as did a cemetery (1886) and abattoir (1877). A professional fire brigade was established in the 1860s. As recently as the 1990s, there was a citywide severe water shortage, and a power supply crisis in the central business district (1994 and 1998, respectively). Traffic has been difficult to manage almost since the first vehicle was registered in 1904; today, Auckland is the only New Zealand city with a traffic problem. However, the council's 1938 town planning scheme was the first of its kind in the country, and the city is now predominantly clean and green, overlooked by Auckland Domain, a 340 acre park on the slopes of Mount Eden. It has grown beyond Hobson's initial 3,000 acre plot to cover some 15,200 hectares.

The city and nation were shaken in July 1985 when the Greenpeace protest ship, Rainbow Warrior, was sabotaged at Auckland's Marsden Wharf by order of the French Secret Service.

Four notable projects in the city's history are the public library, established in 1887 in a building shared with the art gallery and council offices; the town hall, completed in 1911, and renovated from 1988–97 at a cost of NZ$40 m.; the harbour bridge of 1959 that links Auckland to Northcote and beyond; and 1990s Aotea centre. The completion of the Aotea, meaning cultural, centre and auditorium, originally conceived in 1910, coincided with the city's 150th birthday and its hosting of the Commonwealth Games.

Modern City

Auckland's GDP in the year to March 1999 was NZ$16,954 m. The key economic sectors during this period were business and financial services

(25% of GDP); trade and hospitality (15%); and manufacturing (15%). Around 24% of the city's population work in finance, real estate, information technology and public relations. The population is comparatively young. After Europeans the next largest ethnic group are Asians (around 22% of the population).

The University of Auckland is the largest university in New Zealand, with 26,000 students. Other tertiary institutions include the Auckland University of Technology and the Manukau Institute of Technology. Nineteen percent of the population hold a degree, while 23% of Aucklanders possess no formal qualifications. Auckland's unemployment rate (5–7%) exceeds that of its surrounding region, and New Zealand as a whole, by just over 1%. In the year to July 2000, around 12% of all reported crimes in New Zealand took place in Auckland.

Thirteen percent of Auckland is zoned for business use, and 50% for residential properties. Rented apartments have become popular in recent years. Commercial and industrial construction in the year to Dec. 1999 was valued at NZ$411 m.

There are over 9,000 vessels in Auckland's marinas and harbours; the city's port, which is the largest in the country, handles around 50% of all New Zealand containers. It is also a destination for cruise liners during the summer months. In 2000, when Team New Zealand successfully defended the America's Cup yachting trophy against Italy, over 4 m. people visited the Cup Village at Viaduct Harbour. Auckland is the home of New Zealand's Police Maritime Unit. The Unit originated in 1903 and covers over 3,400 km^2 of water.

Places of Interest

The Sky Tower—a casino, shopping centre, and hotel with a revolving restaurant—was opened in 1997. Overlooking the harbour from 328 metres, it is New Zealand's tallest building and one of the tallest freestanding structures in the southern hemisphere.

Notable historic buildings in Auckland include Alberton, an elaborate Indian-style mansion dating from 1863. Celebrated museums within the city are the War Memorial Museum in the 138-hectare Auckland Domain; the Museum of Transport, Technology, and Social History; and the Maritime Museum. The latter is situated at Hobson's Wharf, a popular waterfront complex of shops and cafés. Auckland is home to a zoo, between 200–300 parks and reserves, and an underwater aquarium.

Attractions of cultural interest include the 1888 City Art Gallery, and Kelly Tarlton's Antarctic Encounter. The Antarctic Encounter, opened in 1994, features real snow and penguins, and also an exact replica of Robert Scott's Antarctic hut.

Baghdad, Iraq

Introduction

The foremost city in ancient Mesopotamia, Baghdad is the capital and largest city of modern Iraq. Situated on the eastern side of the country, about 530 km northwest of the Persian Gulf, it stands on both banks of the River Tigris. The district of Rusafah lies on the east side of the river and the Karkh district is on the west. Baghdad is the seat of national government, and also a provincial capital. It has a population of about 4.7 m.

History

The city was founded in AD 762 by the second caliph of the Abbasid dynasty. Originally known as the City of Peace (Madinat as-Salam), it was built on the western bank of the Tigris, enclosed by a circular wall with five gates. The centre comprised the caliph's palace and the grand mosque. Gradually the city expanded beyond its walls to the eastern bank of the river. In the 8th and 9th centuries, Baghdad enjoyed great commercial prosperity, based on its location at important trade route crossroads between east and west, with a reputation as a centre of intellectual eminence. From the later 9th century, the authority of the Abbasid caliphate declined. It was undermined initially by civil war, and then destroyed in the Mongol invasions of the 13th century. Baghdad was part of the Ottoman Empire from 1534–1918, during which time it fell into relative obscurity and neglect. The subsequent British occupation of the Kingdom of Iraq under a post-First World War League of Nations mandate came to an end in 1932, with Baghdad as the capital of the new independent state.

In 2014, Baghdad's western flank came under threat from the Sunni Islamist group known as Islamic State (IS). The militant group had begun to occupy sections of the neighbouring city of Fallujah, located approximately 69 km from the capital.

Modern City

The oil boom of the 1970s brought increased wealth to Baghdad, underpinning the construction of transport links, water and sewerage systems and other development projects. However, such improvements were curtailed by the war with Iran in the 1980s and the Gulf crisis of 1990–91. Since then, periodic bombing raids on military and other installations in and around the city by US and UK warplanes have led to further infrastructure damage.

Non-oil industries include financial services, textiles and leather goods, tobacco, processed foods, wood products, cement, chemicals and electrical equipment. Baghdad is the hub of the national transport system. There is an international airport, although there were no flights after the Gulf War until 2000 when air links were re-established with Egypt, Jordan and Syria. The major lines of the state-owned railway system meet in Baghdad, which is also the centre of the regional road network.

Baghdad suffered widespread damage during the invasion of Iraq in March–April 2003 by US and UK forces. The 'shock and awe' bombing campaign of major military targets destroyed much of Saddam Hussein's legacy, such as the massive palaces and government offices along the west bank of the Tigris. Looting and destruction of ministries and monuments by civilians after the withdrawal and surrender of Iraqi troops left Baghdad a greatly diminished city, though little of the historic city was destroyed.

Places of Interest

Much of the old city has disappeared as modernisation has changed the physical character of Baghdad, but some significant historic buildings and many traditional souks (markets) survive. There are several museums and galleries, in particular the National Museum of Iraq (sometimes called the Iraq Museum), which was closed during the coalition invasion in 2003 but reopened in Feb. 2015. The Kadhimain Mosque, with its gold-capped domes and minarets, is the most important in Iraq after those at Karbala and An-Najaf. Dating from the 16th century, it was built on the site of the shrines of two imams (Musa al-Kadhim and Muhammad al-Jawad) said to be descendents of the Prophet. Architectural attractions include the Abbasid Palace and the Mustansiriyah School, both built in the 13th century in the reigns of the late caliphs of the Abbasid dynasty, and the Khan Murjan, designed in the 14th century as an inn and dwelling place for university scholars.

Bairiki (Tarawa), Kiribati

Introduction

Tarawa is made up of several islets surrounded by a coral atoll, including Bairiki which serves as the seat of the Kiribati government.

History

As part of the British-protectorate of the Gilbert and Ellice Islands, Tarawa was captured by Japanese forces in 1941. Considered of high strategic importance by the Allies, American troops recovered it in 1943 after a fierce battle in which 1,000 US troops and 4,000 Japanese troops perished. It developed as a commercial centre after the war and became capital of independent Kiribati in 1979.

Modern City

Bairiki is home to all the government and most other official buildings and a branch of the South Pacific University. The southern islets are connected by a causeway. The other islets are navigable by boat. There is an international airport on Bonriki in the southeast. Major exports include copra, phosphates and pearl shell.

Places of Interest

There are many unspoiled beaches and the waters are rich in wildlife and World War II wrecks. Fishing and diving are popular pastimes.

Baku (Baki), Azerbaijan

Introduction

Azerbaijan's capital is situated on the western coast of the Caspian Sea, built on the Abseron Peninsula as it slopes down into the Bay of Baku. Once an important trading town and a dynastic capital, it came to prominence again in the 19th century as the main city of one of the world's most important oil regions. Oil remains crucial to Baku's future prosperity.

History

There is archaeological evidence of Bronze Age habitation in Baku, and reference to the city by the Greeks and Romans. By the 11th century AD, Baku was in the possession of the Shirvan Shahs (from the southeastern part of the Caucasus), who made it their capital the following century, constructing two sets of perimeter walls. This period also saw the construction of the mosque to Mohammed and of the Maiden Tower, still to be seen today and so called because of a legend in which a love-lorn young maiden threw herself to her death from the building. The Mongols made a number of attacks during the 13th and 14th centuries, occupying the city in 1258, but the Shirvan Shahs regained control and began construction of the magnificent Shirvan-Shah Palace in the 15th century. The extent of the city at this time equates to Ichari Sahar, the Old Town area of the modern city.

During the Middle Ages, Baku's economy prospered as a result of its position on the trade routes of the camel chains. The Persians took control of the city between the 16th and 18th centuries, but in July 1823 Russian forces under Peter the Great occupied. There followed a series of conflicts between the Persians and Russians, during which the Persians re-took the city in 1735 before Russia secured it in 1806.

The 19th century was to see the dramatic expansion of Baku on the back of the oil industry. It had been known for around 1,000 years that the area possessed oil and surface wells had been in place since the 15th century. The first oil refinery appeared in 1859 and serious commercial activity began during the 1870s. By 1900 there were over 1,700 oil wells in the city and surrounding region and by 1910 around 50% of the world's oil industry production emanated from Baku. Where there had been a population of 8,000 in 1800, by 1913 there were 400,000 citizens, and the city had grown and developed accordingly. However, Baku became part of the Soviet regime in 1918, and by the 1940s much of its reserves had been used.

Modern City

Modern Baku's economy is still reliant on oil and related industries, generally found in the east and southwest parts of the city, although it is no longer the "Black Gold Capital" it was once known as. It is also important as a port and a centre for shipbuilding, chemical processing and textile manufacturing. There is public transport in the city, though it does get crowded and the deaths of 300 people in a fire on the underground system in 1995 have raised concern about safety. Taxis are a cheap and plentiful alternative.

Places of Interest

The Old Town is the city's tourist hub and there are many galleries, museums (notably to Baku's famed textile and carpet traditions) and theatres. Famous ex-residents include the Nobel Prize-winning physicist Lev Landau, the cellist Mstislav Rostropovich and the world chess champion Gary Kasparov.

Bamako, Mali

Introduction

Bamako, on the River Niger in the southwest of the country, is national capital and capital of the Bamako region. It is the country's most important transport hub.

History

As part of the Mali Empire (11th–15th centuries), Bamako was an important centre of Muslim learning. However, it went into decline and was a minor village by the time it was occupied by French forces in the 1880s. In 1908, shortly after the railway was introduced, it was designated capital of French Sudan, prompting a period of rapid expansion. In 1946 the influential Rassemblement Démocratique Africain was founded in the city. Bamoko became capital of independent Mali in 1960. In the 1960s and 1970s there was a population explosion of immigrants from the surrounding agricultural region, devastated by drought.

Modern City

Among the most important commodities traded via Bamoko are nuts and related products, kapok, cotton, cattle, cement and petroleum. Other industries include textiles, food processing, metal and plastic goods manufacturing and fishing.

As well as road links, Bamoko is on the Dakar–Niger railway and uses the River Niger for transportation. There is also an airport.

Places of Interest

The national museum is renowned for its ethnographic collections. Also popular are the botanical gardens and zoo. The famous Grand Marché Market burned down in the early 1990s and has yet to be re-built. Many of the former stallholders set up in the city centre, near to where the market used to be.

Bandar Seri Begawan, Brunei

Introduction

Known as Brunei Town until 1970, Bandar Seri Begawan is the capital, home of the Sultan, an agricultural centre, a river port and the largest city located on the Brunei River about 15 km from its mouth on Brunei Bay, an inlet of the South China Sea. About two thirds of the country's population live here.

History

The site was first inhabited in the 7th century. At that time it was a water village, not dissimilar to the existing old part of the city, Kampong Ayer, a group of houses built on stilts in Brunei River. It became a wealthy settlement from the 14th to 16th centuries when Brunei controlled nearly all of Borneo and part of the Philippines. A treaty with Britain led to the country becoming a British protectorate in 1888. By 1920 Bandar had become the capital of the country. In 1929 oil was discovered which did much to help Brunei's economy. However during WWII the country was occupied by the Japanese from and Bandar suffered extensive damage.

In 1959 Brunei achieved self-government with Bandar its capital. In 1970 the city was given its current name. Brunei became fully independent in 1984 when an Islamic sultanate was proclaimed.

Modern City

After WWII, many new buildings appeared including a royal palace, a sports stadium and the Sultan Omar Ali Saifuddin Mosque, one of the largest in the Far East. A deep-water port was opened in Muara at the mouth of the Brunei River in 1973. Tourism is encouraged, although since 1991 alcohol cannot be sold or drunk in public places. The National Day of Brunei is celebrated every year on 23 Feb. The month of Ramadan in Nov. is strictly observed. The Royal Brunei Airline operates from the international airport 8 km from the capital. The University of Brunei Darussalam opened in 1987 and the Malay Technology Museum in 1988. Regular shipping services operate from Singapore, Hong Kong, Sarawak and Sabah to the capital and a daily passenger ferry runs between BSB and Labuan Island. Local bus services are cheap but inefficient and crowded.

Places of Interest

Built in 1958, the Omar Ali Saifuddin Mosque stands on an artificial lagoon in the centre of the city. It features a giant golden dome and Italian marble walls. The area of Kampong Ayer, where 28 water villages, built on stilts in the Brunei River, house over 30,000 inhabitants, attracts visitors. Exhibits on water village architecture and technology can be seen in the Malay Technology Museum. The Sultan's palace, Istana Nurul Iman, is open to the public at the end of Ramadan. The Royal Regalia Museum was built in 1992 to commemorate the Silver Jubilee of the present Sultan's accession to the throne. The Brunei History Centre opened in 1982 to research into the history and genealogy of the royal family. Brunei Museum has exhibits on the heritage and culture of the country.

Bandung, Indonesia

Introduction

Bandung is the capital city of West Java, Indonesia.

History

The first reference to Bandung dates from 1488 at the time of the Hindu Pajajaran kingdom. The city's earliest inhabitants, the Sundanese, were farmers who exploited the fertile area surrounding Bandung.

European interest in the area led to construction of a main road in 1786 connecting Jakarta, Bogor, Cianjur and Bandung. The 19th century saw a period of development under Bupati Wiranatakusmah II with the building of the Grand Mosque, the palace and the city square. The city and the surrounding region began to prosper as quinine, tea and coffee were farmed.

In 1880 rail connections with Jakarta were established. As a result, light industry flourished and a process of urbanization began. Chinese labourers, brought in to work in the new industries, established a community within the city and Bandung's Chinatown was built.

In the early 20th century Bandung became known as the Paris of Java after European architects and planners, brought in by the Dutch administrators, changed the face of the city.

Although the city escaped damage during the Second World War, the prospect of a return to Dutch colonial rule prompted the burning of parts of the city in what became known as Bandung Lautan Api (Bandung Ocean of Fire).

Following Indonesian independence in 1949, Bandung's population soared from 230,000 to 1 m. The 1990s saw further economic and demographic growth. A suburban area developed to cater for the city's burgeoning middle class.

Modern City

An important commercial and administrative centre, Bandung is also home to 25 schools of higher learning including the Padjadjaran and Parahyangan universities. It is the most important centre for textile production in the country. Main industries include textiles, coffee and tea.

Places of Interest

Alongside its older buildings and attractions, the city boasts fine examples of Art Deco architecture dating from the early 20th century. The city is home to a number of galleries and parks.

Bangalore, India

Introduction

Known as the Garden City of India, Bangalore has been the capital of the region of Karnataka since 1830.

History

The settlement first grew around a fort built in 1537 by a local chief called Kempe Gowda. It has supported some of the great dynasties of southern India such as the Kadambas, the Holysalas and Vijayanagar emperors. The British made it an administrative centre between 1831–81, making Bangalore the largest military settlement in Southern India. Though the Raja was restored in 1881, Britain maintained a military presence in the region until the partition of 1947. Main languages spoken in the city include Kannada (31%), Tamil (27%), Telugu (17%) and Hindustani/Urdu (15%).

Bangalore has also become renowned for its scientific community. It is home to the Indian Institute of Science (1909), the Raman Research Institute (1943), the National Aeronautical Research Laboratory (1960), the University of Agricultural Sciences (1964) and Bangalore University (1964), originally part of Mysore University (1916). It was at Bangalore University that Sir C. V. Raman, after whom the Raman Research Institute was named, announced the discovery of the Raman Effect. He was the first Asian to be awarded the Nobel Prize for Physics. Bangalore University is now the largest institution of its kind in India with 375 colleges and over 70 Post Graduate Departments.

Modern City

Main industries include printing and publishing. The city also manufactures aircraft, heavy machinery, cars and generators. But by far the most important commercial enterprise is the city's software sector. Having played an important role in the Indian software boom, Bangalore is known as India's *Silicon Valley*. The industry has grown from 13 software units in 1992 to nearly 300 in 1999. Export growth has seen the industry expand from Rs. 15 m. in 1992 to Rs. 32 bn. in 1999. Bangalore accounts for 32% of India's IT software production and the IT sector in Bangalore is expanding by around 58% a year. IT growth has been attributed to the large pool of skilled workers trained in Bangalore and progressive government policy. IBM, Compaq and Infosys are among many IT giants to have set up software units in the city.

Bangalore has strong transport links with the other main cities of India. Indian Airlines as well as private airlines operate services from Bangalore airport, situated 8 km. to the east of the city. International flights from Singapore, London, Hong Kong and Saudi Arabia also land at Bangalore. The rail network connects Bangalore with other major cities with daily express trains to Delhi, Chennai, Kolkata and Hyderabad. Bangalore is directly connected with Mumbai by National Highway 4, and Hyderabad by Highway 7.

Places of Interest

The city boasts several tourist attractions. Lal Bagh is one of the most famous of the many gardens in the city. Founded by the rulers of Mysore in 1760, the garden stretches across 240 acres and houses exotic tropical and subtropical plants and flowers. The Lal Bagh rock formation is believed to be 3,000 m. years old, making it the oldest formation on earth. Cubbon Park, located in the centre, was founded by Lord Cubbon in 1864, and stretches over 300 acres. Other places of interest include the state legislature building, Vidhana Saudha, built in 1956 in the Dravidian style, and the Visveswaraya Industrial and Technical Museum, named after M. Visveswaraya, the Dewan Mysore from 1912–18.

Bangkok (Krungthep), Thailand

Introduction

With a population at around 6 m. Bangkok is the largest city in Thailand. As well as being its capital and principal port it is the cultural, educational, political and economic centre of Thailand. The word Bangkok is derived from two primitive Thai words Bang (village) and Kok (Olive).

History

Bangkok's origins were by no means as grand as the city is today, having been a collection of small fishing villages on the banks of the great Chao Phya River delta.

Bangkok, then called Phra Buddha Yodfa Chulaloke, was founded in 1782 by King Rama I, the founder of the Chakkri dynasty, after the fall of the former and ancient royal capital Krung Sri Ayutthaya at the hands of the Burmese in 1767. After the sacking of Ayutthaya and the assassination of the royal family a popular and daring general, Phraya Thaksin founded a new capital Thonburi, on the western bank of the Chao Phya River. Thanksin was ousted in a coup and replaced by Chao Phraya Chakri (Rama I). The new king soon realised that the western bank of the river afforded little room for expansion and so relocated the capital at the site of modern Bangkok.

Under Rama I and his successors Bangkok grew and flourished as a trading centre and many of the Wats and shrines that typify Thai culture were built during this period of prosperity.

Rama IV (Mongkut) 1804–68 presided over a period of particular stability for Thailand courtesy of his diplomatic prowess and his ability to negotiate treaties with foreign powers. This prevented the colonisation of Thailand and assisted in securing further overseas trade. This period of stability extended until 1910 and the death of Rama V.

In 1912 a group of disgruntled soldiers led an unsuccessful coup against Rama VI. The bloodless coup of 1932 instigated by civil servants and western-educated students ended Thailand's absolute Monarchy replacing it with a constitutional model. Two years later Rama VII abdicated placing the 10-year-old Rama VIII in power. The reins of power were taken up my Field Marshall Phibun, the first of Thailand's many military dictators. Phibun allied Thailand with the Japanese during World War II thereby ensuring the safety of the city. Thailand's current King, Bhumibol (Rama XI) was crowned in 1946.

Modern City

In 1973 student demonstrations led to the ousting of the military dictator, Gen. Thanom, who subsequently went into exile. The civilian government that ensued lasted until 1976 when General Thanom returned despite further student protest. In 1980 General Prem Tinsulanonda, the man credited with guiding Thailand out of the post war depression and confusion caused by the perceived spectre of Asian communism came to power. Since then Bangkok has been the scene of two further military coups and massive demonstrations during the 1997 Asian Economic crisis. From March to May 2010 a series of prolonged political protests against the Democrat Party-led government resulted in the deaths of over 80 civilians and six soldiers.

Modern Bangkok is a mixture of urban squalor and affluence, where ancient temples exist, cheek-by-jowl with skyscrapers looking down onto shantytowns.

For many years agriculture was the main source of income in Bangkok, but over the last two decades industrial activity has shifted to the manufacture of textiles, computers and electronics. Since the economic downturn of 1997 the industrial sectors that have lifted production sharply are electronics and electrical products, steel and related products, automobiles and jewellery, even though all of them rely on imported raw materials. Tourism has become a main source of revenue, with increasing numbers of visitors visiting and passing through Bangkok en-route to rural and coastal Thailand.

Places of Interest

The Grand Palace is one of the most famous attractions in all of Thailand. Originally built for King Rama I in the late 18th century it has developed and grown into a huge complex which houses Wat Phra Kaew, the temple of the Emerald Buddha. This magnificent temple, built in 1780, houses the 75 cm-tall jade carving of the Buddha as well as many other culturally important and interesting statues, carvings and murals.

Wat Traimit, Temple of the Golden Buddha, is famous for its five-and-a-half-ton solid gold image, designed in the Sukhothai style. This image was 'discovered' in the 1950s under a plaster exterior when it fell from a crane while being relocated. The plaster was probably added to disguise the image from thieves during the Sukhothai and later Ayutthaya periods.

The Democracy Monument, located on Ratchadamnoen Klang Avenue, was conceived and constructed during the administration of Field Marshal Plaek Phibulsongkhram to commemorate the peaceful changeover from absolute monarchy to constitutional monarchy on 24 June 1932. The monument, in the centre of a busy roundabout, sports four seven-metre high wings.

In 1968 a U.S. citizen, accredited with revitalising Thailand's silk trade, Jim Thompson, mysteriously vanished in Malaysia. Since then his house, a fine example of traditional Thai architecture and filled with rare antiques has become a popular tourist destination.

The National Museum, on Na Prathat Road, houses the largest collection of Thai art and artefacts dating from neolithic times to the present.

No trip to Bangkok is complete without a trip to a floating market (talaat naam). All floating markets are typified by canals (klongs) filled with small boats laden with fruit, flowers, vegetables and other produce from nearby orchards and communities.

Far from being merely a tourist attraction these are very important commercial centres for Thais living on the banks of the many klongs. Bang Khu Wiang Floating Market can be reached by boat from Tha Chang Pier near the Grand Palace. The market operates from 4.00 a.m. until late morning but the best time to visit is around sunrise.

Bangui, Central African Republic

Introduction

The commercial and administrative centre of the country, Bangui is situated on the western bank of the Ubangi River. The city is linked by river and rail to the ports of Pointe-Noire and Brazzaville.

History

The French founded the city in 1889, naming it after the rough waters of the Ubangi River in the region. Towards the end of the 19th century the French leased the town, along with many of their central African territories, to private companies who forced the natives to harvest rubber and hunt elephants for ivory. After several anti-colonial uprisings France granted Central Africans limited self-government. In 1960 the CAR was granted independence and the city became the national capital.

Modern City

Five km from the city centre, the area known as K-Cinq, is the location of most of the city's markets, bars and clubs. The centre is largely administrative and houses government buildings and the Central Market. To the north-east is the presidential palace, and to the west is the main commercial street, Avenue Boganda. Local industries include brewing and the manufacture of soap.

In recent years life there has been sporadic violence between the government and rebel military and civilian groups over pay, living conditions, and lack of political representation. The fighting has led to a general state of lawlessness in the city, with bandits targeting foreign visitors.

Places of Interest

The Boganda museum contains a collection of musical instruments and pygmy tools. The Emperor Bokassa's palace, with its lion cages and crocodile pits, provides an insight into his tyrannical regime.

Banjul, The Gambia

Introduction

Banjul, formerly Bathurst, capital of The Gambia, is on Banjul Island, formerly St Mary's Island, at the mouth of the Gambia River where it meets the Atlantic Ocean. It is the principal port, commercial centre and seat of government. One of the smallest capitals in Africa, it is the second largest city in the country.

History

Tools, pottery and stone circles found near Banjul suggest early occupation around the 8th century. In the 14th century numerous ethnic groups entered the area including the Mandingo, Wolof and Fulani peoples. The Portuguese established trading stations along the coast in the 15th century but did not settle. The next two centuries saw the arrival of the British, French and Dutch who also established trading posts. In 1816 Captain Alexander Grant was sent to establish a base from which the navy could control the slave trade. Banjul Island, which was renamed St Mary's Island, was bought from the King of Kombo. Here Grant established the town of Bathurst, named after the Secretary of State for the Colonies. Administered from the British Colony of Sierra Leone from 1807–43, it was part of a separate colony with its own ruler until control returned to Sierra Leone in 1889. Bathurst became the capital of the crown colony and a British protectorate in 1894. After 1947 it was governed by a town council. When The Gambia gained independence in 1965 the town was granted city status and became the national capital. In 1970 The Gambia became a republic within the Commonwealth. The capital's name was changed from Bathurst to Banjul in 1973.

Modern City

There are several peanut decorticating plants and oil mills. Major exports include peanuts, peanut oil, palm kernels, fish preparations, hides and skins. In 1994 the major export markets were Belgium and Luxembourg. Following the coup in 1994 tourist numbers dropped but revived after 1996 and tourism is now a major source of foreign exchange. Albert Market sells local handicrafts including wood carvings, filigree jewellery and batik. Banjul International Airport, at Yundum, 30 km to the southwest, opened in 1997. It is served by Gambia Airways and a number of other carriers. There are no railways. A new ferry service, L'Express du Senegal, is in operation between the capital and Dakar and Ziguinchor. Most roads leading from the capital to major towns are tarred. Buses and bush taxis are available as are cars and bicycles for hire. The largest schools, institutes, hospitals and public library are located here, although there is no university.

Places of Interest

The Gambia National Museum has exhibits and archaeology on the African peoples and the colonial period. The tallest building at 35 metres is the Arch 22 built to celebrate the military coup in 1994. It provides excellent views of the city and coast. The Abuko Nature Reserve lies on the road between Banjul and the airport. There are over 200 species of birds as well as antelope, crocodiles, monkeys and baboons.

Barcelona, Spain

Introduction

The second largest city in Spain, Barcelona is the capital of the northeastern region of Catalonia. Located on the Mediterranean coast, the city is situated on a plain surrounded by the Besós and Llobregat rivers and the 192 metre-hill to the southwest, Montjuich.

History

Barcelona is believed to have been founded as Barcino by the Carthaginian leader, and father of Hannibal, Hamilcar Barca around 230 BC. Under the Romans it became prosperous but remained small. It was the capital of Layetania, a district of the Roman territory of Hispania Tarraconensis. Around 15 BC it was named Colonia Faventia Julia Augusta Pia Barcino. The town was destroyed by the Franks in 263 AD, but the Romans eventually recaptured it. It was named Barcinona by the Visigoths, who controlled the town for 3 centuries, and was made their capital in 415 by Ataulf. The city was subsequently captured by the Moors in 713. Charlemagne took the city under his rule in 801.

The Counts of Barcelona ruled the principality of Catalonia from the 9th century, although the city was sacked in 985 by the Moorish commander Almanzor. Around this period Barcelona's wealth came mainly from farming, although by the end of the 11th century it had become increasingly important as a centre of maritime trade. In 1137 Catalonia was joined with Aragón.

Barcelona continued to develop in stature and importance between the 13th–15th centuries, becoming the capital of the joined territory in 1442.

Barcelona declined from the 15th century. With the discovery of the New World, Seville became the centre of maritime trade. Even so, a monument to Columbus built in the 1880s stands near the harbour at the end of La Rambla, Barcelona's famous tree-lined esplanade. The city was the site of Columbus' announcement of the discovery of America.

Barcelona was the first industrialized city in Spain and retains its cultural pre-eminence. It developed an important trade in textiles in the 18th century making Catalonia Spain's wealthiest region. Revenue generated from this trade allowed the city to develop industrially, especially in machinery and metallurgy. In 1854 the medieval city walls were destroyed to make way for expansion. The *Eixample* (extension) with planned open spaces was built from 1859. But pressure of population led eventually to overcrowding. Barcelona's wealth and industrialization attracted many immigrants. The disparity between rich and poor coupled with the high-density industry led to revolutionary politics. Class conflict combined with anti-clericalism and in 1835 numerous churches were burned. Uprisings throughout the 19th century culminated in the *Setmana Tràgica* (tragic week) of 1909. Between 1917–23 approximately 1,000 people died including 100 anarchists who were shot by the government.

During the Civil War, Barcelona was a Republican stronghold. When the city fell to Franco, he took away the region's autonomy and the Catalan language was outlawed. After Franco's death, Catalonia was granted a certain amount of autonomy and the *Generalitat* was restored in 1977.

Modern City

The largest seaport in Spain, Barcelona is a highly industrial city specializing in textiles, vehicles, electrical equipment and petrochemicals. Barcelona is the capital of the province of Barcelona, which, combined with Gerona, Tarragona and Lérida, makes up Catalonia. The region is a mixture of coastal towns and inland farms. Agricultural produce is mainly wine, olive oil and almonds for export and potatoes and corn for domestic use.

Barcelona is linked nationally and internationally by air, sea, rail and road. International flights go to all European capitals, while rail services connect the city to Paris, Berne, Milan and Zurich. The city has a metro service.

Places of Interest

Barcelona's extensive range of museums includes a modern art museum and the Medieval, Renaissance and Baroque collections of the Museu Monsestir de Pedralbes. The Joan Miró Foundation charts the development of this native artist, while the Museu Picasso specializes in the artist's early works. Spanish artist, Pablo Picasso (1881–1973), lived in Barcelona at the end of the 19th century where he attended La Lonja (Esquella de Bellas Artes) and frequented the Els Quatre Gats bar, which served as a meeting place for the Catalan modernist movement. The bar is situated to the west of the Barri Gòtic, at the heart of the medieval town.

The maritime museum is based in the shipyards which originated in the 14th century. The distinctive works of another local, Antoni Gaudi (1852–1926), one of the most famous Spanish architects, can be seen throughout the city. Born in the small Catalonian coastal town of Reus, he spent much of his working life in Barcelona. Originally interested in Catalonia's medieval history and architecture, he was one of the principal artists of Catalonian *modernisme*, a style related to Art Nouveau. His most famous project is the still-unfinished Sagrada Familia (1882–1926), which dominated much of his career. The church is in the northeast of the *Eixample*.

For the Olympic games in 1992, the city underwent much restoration. The old docks were reconstructed and the gloomy Barri Xines was transformed. In 1999 the Royal Institute of British Architects awarded Barcelona the Royal Gold Medal.

Basle, Switzerland

Introduction

Basle is situated in the north on the River Rhine, where the French, German and Swiss borders meet. It is the second largest city in the country, and is the centre of the Swiss pharmaceutical industry.

History

In 374 AD there was a Roman fort called Basilia, although evidence of settlement by Celtic tribes dates back to the 1st century AD. In the early 5th century it became a bishopric. Despite attacks by the Huns which left its Carolingian cathedral in ruins, Basle was a major town by the 13th century, primarily because it was a crossing point on the Rhine. In 1460 Pope Pius II founded its university, Switzerland's oldest. By the end of the 15th century the town had emerged as an important centre for the humanist movement. The philosopher Erasmus who taught at the university for many years, is buried in the cathedral. During the 16th and 17th centuries the city's population and industry was boosted by an influx of Protestant refugees fleeing Catholic prosecution. Basle became an increasingly prosperous commercial city, and political control of the canton shifted from the church and nobles to the trade guilds. The increased power wielded by the city's oligarchs led to a revolt by the rural poor in 1831, and the subsequent separation of the canton into the urban Basel-Stadt and the rural Basel-Land remains in effect today.

Modern City

Rapid industrialization during the 19th century culminated in the construction of port facilities which account for over 30% of total Swiss customs revenue. The port and the major industries are located to the north of the river. Also to the north is the multicultural residential area of Kleinbasel. Grossbasel, the city's well-preserved historic centre, is on the south bank, and is notable for the imposing cathedral and the late Gothic Rathaus (town hall). Basle is renowned as the headquarters of several of the largest pharmaceutical companies. Its industry is led by chemical production. The city is also home to the Bank of International Settlements while banking, silk manufacture, publishing and electrical engineering are significant sources of revenue. Basle is still a significant river port and has an international airport at Saint-Louis, 13 km to the northwest.

Places of Interest

Cultural attractions include the two old town squares, numerous medieval churches and the cathedral itself. The Kunstmuseum is world-famous and houses impressive collections of 20th century and medieval art. Basle has more than 30 museums.

Basra, Iraq

Introduction

Basra is Iraq's principal seaport and second largest city. It is in the southeast of the country, about 100 km north of the Persian Gulf, on the western bank of the Shatt al-Arab waterway (formed by the confluence of the Rivers Euphrates and Tigris).

History

Basra was founded in AD 637 by the second caliph, Omar. Originally a military settlement, given its proximity to the Gulf and access to the Euphrates and Tigris waterways, it grew rapidly into a major city and a centre of learning and culture. However, its early history was also marked by political upheaval between competing religious factions of Islam and by social insurrection. From the 10th century, the city declined in importance in the shadow of Baghdad, the Abbasid capital, and was later sacked by the Mongols in the 13th century. By the 16th century it had become an important departure point for Arab trading ships sailing to the Far East. From 1668 it was taken over by the Turks. The city remained under nominal Turkish sovereignty (despite frequent clashes with the indigenous Arabs of the southern marshes and the Persians) until the collapse of the Ottoman Empire in the First World War. Thereafter, it was under the control of the British until their League of Nations mandate gave way to Iraqi independence in 1932.

Modern City

With the development of Iraq's oil industry after the Second World War, Basra became a major refining and exporting centre. However, its oil facilities and surrounding agricultural land were damaged badly during the Iran-Iraq War and the Shia rebellion against Saddam Hussein's rule following the Gulf War in early 1991. The modern city is made up of three main areas: the old commercial centre of Ashar; the Margil area, which includes the port and a modern residential district; and the old residential sector of the town, which has some unique architecture.

Basra's strategic importance made it the main focus for British troops in the US-led invasion of Iraq in 2003. Occupying forces entered the city on 6 April and remained in the city for over 4 years. Popular looting, insurgency groups and the threat of a cholera epidemic created difficulties for the British military who were resented by many of the Shia inhabitants for failing to support their rebellion against Saddam Hussein's regime in 1991. British troops handed over control of the city to the Iraqi authorities in 2007.

Places of Interest

The Basra Museum, Floating Navy Museum, Museum for Martyrs of the Persian Aggression and the bazaar in the Ashar district are the city's main attractions. However, Basra is perhaps better known to Westerners as the port from which Sinbad is reputed to have set sail on his legendary voyages.

Basseterre, St Kitts and Nevis

Introduction

The capital of St Kitts and Nevis, Basseterre is on the southwestern coast of the northern St Kitts Island.

History

Originally inhabited by Carib Indians, Basseterre was founded by French colonists in 1627 as their first Caribbean colonial capital, although the islands were shared British and French colonies between 1625–1713. The British eventually took possession of Basseterre in 1783 when it replaced Old Road as the island's capital. In 1867 a fire caused widespread destruction and much of the city had to be rebuilt. In 1983 Basseterre became capital of Independent St Kitts and Nevis. It suffered severe structural damage during Hurricane Georges in Sept. 1998.

Modern City

The county's chief port, around half the population of St Kitts and Nevis live in the capital. Principal industries are salt extraction and sugar refining, while exports include molasses and cotton. An airport links the capital with the rest of the Caribbean while the deep water port is capable of receiving cruise ships.

Places of Interest

Once the site of the slave market, Independence Square is now a park. Originally built in 1670 as Notre Dame, St George's Church was rebuilt several times following fires and an earthquake. Other religious buildings include the Immaculate Conception Cathedral built in 1927. St Christopher Heritage Society has a museum tracking the city's history.

Batumi, Georgia

Introduction

Batumi is the capital of the autonomous republic of Adjaria. An industrial town and popular seaside resort, it lies on the Black Sea in southwest Georgia.

History

Formerly part of the ancient Greek region of Batis, Batumi was under Georgian jurisdiction in the Middle Ages. In the 15th century, after the collapse of the Georgian state, it was a part of Guria, ruled by Prince Gurieli.

Occupied by the Turks in 1547, it was acquired by the Russians in 1878. Under the Russians it was developed as a major oil-exporting port. In 1936 the communists destroyed the church built to celebrate Tsar Alexander III's visit, the largest church in the Caucasus.

Modern City

Major industries include ship-building and port-related activities, oil refining (petroleum is received directly from Baku), food processing, tourism and a variety of light industries. Tea and citrus fruits are grown in the surrounding area.

The port offers cargo and passenger services, there are good road connections and the city is on the Trans-Caucasian railway. There is a domestic airport. Buses and trolley buses run within the city.

Places of Interest

There is a mosque and Orthodox church dating from the 19th century and several lavish modern marble constructions built by the son of President Abashidze. Primorsky Boulevard is the main street through the green city centre. There is a theatre, several museums and a dolphinarium. Beyond the city centre is Gonio, an ancient Roman-Byzantine fortress. There are botanical gardens at Mtsvane Konskhi (Green Cape).

Beijing, China

Introduction

The capital of the People's Republic of China, Beijing, is sometimes referred to by its former English name Peking. The city has been the seat of China's administration and its cultural centre for most of the past 750 years. Although not on a river, Beijing is a natural route centre given its position at the convergence point of routes between the North China Plain and ranges of hills and ridges to the north. The city has a rectangular street pattern. Beijing has grown dramatically in the last six decades, but the built-up area occupies only 15% of the municipality: the remainder is countryside and villages and 42% of the population is rural.

History

The site of Beijing has been occupied since prehistoric times: the remains of 'Peking man', who lived about 500,000 years ago, were found at a village 50 km from the city centre. An important military and trading post was established on the north-eastern frontier of China, where Beijing now stands, more than 2,400 years ago. This centre became the city of Chi, capital of the kingdom of Yen. Chi was destroyed in the 3rd century BC and its successor, Yen, remained a provincial town, at times falling under the control of northern nomads.

In the 13th century all of China was conquered by the Mongol hordes under Kublai Khan, who built a new city on the present site of Beijing in 1267–72. He named the city Ta-tu and established it as the administrative centre of his Yüan (Mongol) dynasty. The first emperors of the Ming dynasty transferred the capital to Nanjing (meaning 'Southern Capital') in 1344 but the third Ming emperor moved the imperial seat back in 1421 to what became known as Beijing ('Northern Capital'). In the 15th and 16th centuries Beijing was rebuilt with inner (northern) and outer walls (the latter enclosing more than 50 square kilometres), and many temples and palaces were constructed.

The city was not damaged when overrun by the Manchus in the 17th century, but the original Summer Palace was destroyed by British and French troops in 1860. The legation quarter for foreign embassies, established in the middle of the 19th century, was besieged for months by nationalist Boxer rebels in 1900.

Beijing was the centre of the 1911 revolution when the imperial system was swept away. But, in 1928, the ruling Nationalists removed the seat of government to Nanjing. In 1937 Japanese forces occupying Manchuria entered Beijing, which remained under Japanese control until 1945. The Nationalists took control of Beijing in 1945 but the city was taken by the Communists during the subsequent civil war. In 1949 the People's Republic of China was proclaimed in Beijing.

In 1989 growing pressures for liberalisation and political change culminated in the occupation of Tiananmen Square by up to one million workers and students. After a stand-off, troops entered the square killing more than 1,500 and arresting many.

Modern City

Beijing is the principal cultural and political centre of China and, after Shanghai, the main industrial centre. The city has China's main international airport and is a hub of road and rail routes. The new West Station is the largest in Asia. Beijing houses many foreign financial institutions and more than 400 scientific research institutes. Industries include metallurgy, chemicals and petro-chemicals, engineering, electronics, textiles and clothing, and food processing. Broad highways and tower blocks have recently replaced much of the older quarter and many of the remaining historic alleys and courtyard houses are being swept away, a process accelerated by the regeneration of the city that accompanied the run-up to the 2008 Olympic Games. In the last decade, tourism has become a major foreign-currency earner.

In 2003 Beijing was at the centre of an outbreak of severe acute respiratory syndrome (SARS), during which over 15,000 people were quarantined.

Places of Interest

The heart of Beijing is the monumental Tiananmen Square, where parades are held. The mausoleum of Mao Zedong is in the square, in whose south-west corner rises the imposing Great Hall of the People in which the National People's Congress holds its infrequent meetings in the grand auditorium. The Museum of Chinese History, which includes the Museum of the Chinese Revolution, is also in the square.

North of Tiananmen Square is the Forbidden City whose Imperial Palaces are surrounded by a moat and walls. With their throne rooms, courtyards, golden roofs and marble columns and bridges, the palaces are a major visitor attraction. The Palace of Heavenly Purity was the seat of state occasions and imperial audiences, while the other two palaces were residences of the imperial family. All three palaces now form the Palace Museum, the home of mainland China's greatest art treasures.

The Temple of Heaven is generally recognised as the greatest example of traditional Chinese architecture. Constructed between 1420 and 1749, the temple comprises three buildings approached by a magnificent avenue of cypress trees. The Temple of the Imperial Ancestors, now the Working People's Cultural Palace, is built round a huge courtyard, whose verandas can seat nearly 10,000 people. The halls of this palace stage many important exhibitions.

Beijing's open spaces include Ching-shan Park, from whose artificial hill the best view of the city can be obtained. Most tourists to Beijing also visit the Great Wall of China, which at its nearest to the city is about 50 km (30 miles) to the north.

Beirut, Lebanon

Introduction

Lying along the coast of the eastern Mediterranean, Beirut is Lebanon's capital, main port and largest city. It suffered severely during the years of sectarian conflict and foreign incursions from 1975–90, but has since undergone extensive reconstruction. It is one of the Middle East's most cosmopolitan cities.

History

Beirut was a port from the end of the second millennium BC in Phoenician times. Having been occupied by the Romans from 64 BC, it was named Colonia Julia Augusta Felix Berytus in 14 BC and acquired the rights of a Roman city state. It subsequently became famous for its school of law, which existed for over 300 years. Roman rule ended abruptly in AD 551 as the city was devastated by earthquakes, fire and a tidal wave. In AD 635 Beirut came under the control of the Muslim Arabs, who dominated until the Christian crusaders captured it in 1110. They were succeeded by the Mameluks (a Muslim dynasty of Egypt and Syria) at the end of the 13th century. Although the city was nominally under Ottoman rule from 1516, the Turks

granted local leaders autonomy over the next 3 centuries and powerful Druze (a Muslim sub-sect) and Maronite Christian chieftains emerged. In 1860, at the end of a civil war that culminated in a massacre of Maronites by the Druze, Britain and France intervened and pressured the Ottoman Turks into establishing a new Christian-dominated administration for the territory which lasted until the First World War. Beirut became the capital of Lebanon under the French mandate from 1920–43, during which time the city absorbed many Western customs and influences, particularly affecting the Christian Lebanese.

Following Lebanon's independence, Beirut developed as a major trade, financial, educational and tourist centre of the Middle East. However, Muslim dissatisfaction with the sectarian power-sharing arrangement of 1943 and the gradual suction of the country into the Arab-Israeli conflict led ultimately to the outbreak of the civil war in 1975. The city's division into Christian-east and Muslim-west Beirut (by the symbolic Green Line) was compounded by factionalism, with Sunni, Shia, Druze, Palestinian, Maronite and other groups exercising control over pockets of territory. By 1990 this conflict, coupled with Syrian and Israeli military intervention, had reduced large areas of Beirut to ruins.

Modern City

Beirut is the seat of national government. Relative political stability since the 1989 Taif Accord has allowed for the reconstruction of the capital's infrastructure. The city has re-established itself as a commercial and financial centre and its port remains central to Lebanon's economy. With its international airport, it is also the hub of the country's transport system. Major highways run north and south of Beirut along the coastline and east towards Damascus in Syria. The city hosts the long-established American University of Beirut (founded in 1866), Beirut Arab University and St. Joseph University.

Places of Interest

Whole areas of Beirut, including the old city centre, were destroyed in 1975–90 and are under reconstruction. Attractions include the National Museum, Sursock Museum, Grand Mosque, Roman Baths (unearthed during renovation work), Corniche (coastal promenade along the western and northern shores) and the landmark Pigeon Rocks.

Belfast (Béal Feirste), United Kingdom of Great Britain and Northern Ireland

Introduction

Belfast, the capital city of Northern Ireland, lies at the mouth of the River Lagan. A village until the 17th century, it became the provincial capital following the 1920 partition of Ireland. Though blighted by sectarian violence in the latter decades of the 20th century, it is now at the centre of continuing peace negotiations.

History

There is evidence to suggest that Belfast was the site of Stone and Bronze Age settlements. John de Courci, the Norman conqueror of the Ulster region, built a castle at Belfast in the last quarter of the 12th century. In 1611 Baron Arthur Chichester built a castle and did much to encourage the growth of the town. As the English Lord Deputy of Ireland from 1604 to 1614 Chichester developed a plan for colonizing Ulster with English and Scottish settlers. The economy of the town, largely based on the production of rope, net and sailcloth, grew quickly.

By the end of the 17th century, following the introduction of machines for spinning and weaving and an influx of skilled Huguenot refugees, Belfast was one of the largest linen centres in the world. Belfast itself grew from a town of 20,000 inhabitants in 1800 to over 100,000 in 1850, gaining city status in 1888. For many years a leading ship building port, Belfast still has the world's largest dry dock.

After the division of Ireland, Belfast's economy went into steady decline and unemployment was rife. The city's modern history has been fraught with trouble. In 1968 a Roman Catholic civil rights campaign began and the following year Belfast was the scene of much rioting. British troops were dispatched to suppress the Protestant–Catholic fighting. The violence escalated, including a marked increase in the use of bombs and modern firearms, and extremists from both sides committed atrocities.

Modern City

The Peace Process has consistently faltered but Stormont Castle, the seat of the government of Northern Ireland, has remained at the centre of negotiations for an autonomous Northern Ireland Government and the cessation of paramilitary violence. Modern Belfast still suffers economic hardship but peace hopes and favourable tax rates have encouraged investment. Some heavy industry still exists, though shipbuilding is no longer prominent. Linen, tobacco and agricultural products are major exports and Belfast is Northern Ireland's main centre for commerce and service industries.

Places of Interest

Among the city's leading tourist attractions are:

St. Anne's Anglican Cathedral, built in a Romanesque style and completed in 1904. The only person to be buried inside the cathedral is Edward Carson, a major figure in the Anglo–Irish troubles;
the City Hall, built in 1903 in the grand Classical Renaissance style and located at the heart of the main shopping area;
the Queen's University of Belfast, Northern Ireland's most prestigious university, designed along the lines of Magdalen College in Oxford and completed in 1849;
Ulster Museum and Botanic Gardens, home to exhibitions of antiquities, ethnography, fine and applied arts, botany, zoology, geology, local history and archaeology;
Ormeau Baths Gallery, which hosts collections of contemporary art;
Linen Hall Library, opened in the late-18th century and containing notable collections of Irish writing and a Robert Burns archive;
Belfast Zoo, located in the raised Bellevue Gardens;
Belfast Port and Harbour, including the dock where *RMS Titanic* was built.

Belgrade (Beograd), Serbia

Introduction

Belgrade is the capital of Serbia and was formerly the capital of Yugoslavia. Situated where the River Danube and River Sava converge, it is a focal point on the trade routes between Central and Western Europe and the Balkan region. It was the scene of conflict between Turks and Serbs from the 16th until the 19th century and was badly damaged in World War I and II. In 1999 it suffered extensive damage after NATO airstrikes against the regime of Slobodan Milošević.

History

There is evidence of pre-historic habitation in the region around Belgrade and of a Celtic settlement in the 4th century BC. Under the jurisdiction of the Roman Empire, the area was known as Singidunum. In the 5th century AD, Huns razed it to the ground before the settlement passed to the Sarmatians, then the Goths and finally the Gepidae, all Germanic tribes. The city fell under Byzantine control but changed hands between the Byzantines and Goths until the mid-6th century when the Byzantine Emperor Justinian renovated it and built new walls. By the 9th century the city was known as Belgrade.

Over the next 3 centuries Belgrade fell under the control of the Bulgars, Hungarians and Byzantines. The Hungarians destroyed the city in 1127 and retained control, with Byzantine and Serbian interludes, until 1521. By the middle of the 15th century the Ottomans were making inroads and in 1521 Belgrade fell to Suleiman the Magnificent. The city remained at the centre of conflicts between the Turks and Hungarians over the ensuing centuries but

benefited economically by catering for the military. It was also a major trade hub for the Ottoman Empire.

The Austrian Hapsburgs seized control of Belgrade in 1688–90, 1717–39 and 1789–91. The Serbians then re-asserted their claims, making it their capital in 1807, when Belgrade came under the fractious dual-rule of Serbian and Turkish authorities. Ottoman power was gradually whittled away until Turkish troops left in 1867. Belgrade prospered (it had a network of electric street lighting before either London or Paris) and, despite the Balkan Wars of 1912–13, was thriving at the outbreak of World War I.

Belgrade came under siege for 15 months between 1914–15 when German forces destroyed the city before occupying it for 3 years. After the German defeat planners set about constructing new government buildings, cultural and educational institutes and a zoo. In 1929 Belgrade became the capital of the newly founded Kingdom of Yugoslavia. In April 1941 Belgrade again fell to German attack and was occupied until Oct. 1944. Its infrastructure was badly damaged by heavy bombardment at the beginning and end of the occupation.

Modern City

Post-World War II witnessed rapid industrialization under Tito and Belgrade's population swelled as migrants moved in from rural areas. By 1990–91 the Yugoslav state was collapsing and at the end of the 20th century the city was the capital only of Serbia and Montenegro. It went into steep economic decline throughout the 1990s as a result of economic sanctions imposed by the UN. In 1999, following Milošević's refusal to withdraw troops from Kosovo, NATO began 2 months of aerial bombardment, flattening many key buildings.

Since the fall of Milošević in late 2000, Belgrade has recovered somewhat but damage will take many years to repair. Industries include vehicle production, chemicals, textiles, heavy machinery, oil refining and metal work. It is on the route of three major railways, and had a well-developed road and river transport infrastructure until the recent conflicts. There is an airport at nearby Surcin.

Places of Interest

While the events of the 1990s all but destroyed the tourist industry, major sites include the ancient Kalemegdan Fortress, the National Museum and an Ethnographic Museum. Kneza Mihaila is the city's main pedestrianized boulevard.

Belize City, Belize

Introduction

On Belize's eastern Caribbean coast, Belize City is at the mouth of Belize River. The city is split by the Haulover Creek. Once the capital, the city's susceptibility to hurricanes led the government to move to the new central and protected city of Belmopan. Nonetheless, Belize City remains the country's largest city, with nearly a quarter of the country's population, its chief port and the commercial and cultural centre.

History

Belize River was a central focus of Mayan trade, and archaeological evidence suggests the area now Belize City originated as a Mayan fishing camp. The coastal area was settled in the seventeenth century by British explorers whose main industry was harvesting logwood and mahogany. By the eighteenth century a permanent settlement known as Belize Town had been established. The settlement was attacked by the Spanish in 1798. Formerly under Spanish rule, the country became the British Crown Colony of British Honduras in 1862 and Belize City was made its capital 30 years later.

The low lying capital was susceptible to hurricanes and tidal waves throughout the 19th and 20th centuries and suffered repeated damage. In 1931 around 10% of the population perished. Following the particularly destructive Hurricane Hattie in 1961 in which 300 people died, the government decided to create a new capital in the centre of the country. In 1970 capital status was transferred from Belize City to Belmopan. Eight years later another devastating hurricane left Belize City badly damaged. In 1980 work started on deepening the port to accommodate large vessels while some renovations to the city's infrastructure were carried out.

Modern City

Belize City is the country's main port and its commercial and transport centre. Exports include timber, maize, citrus fruits and coconuts. Industries include agriculture, fishing and the manufacture of wood items, while the surrounding area is populated with mangrove swamps. Belize City is linked by road to Belmopan and Guatemala, while an international airport is 16 km to the northwest of the city.

Places of Interest

The Government House Museum focusses on the British colonial heritage while the Image Factory Art Foundation displays the work of local artists. St John's Cathedral was the first Anglican church built in Central America. Fifty kilometres outside Belize City is the excavated Mayan settlement of Altun Ha. Belize City is the country's main transport centre and as such the starting point for Suriname's nature reserves and offshore cays.

Belmopan, Belize

Introduction

Belize's capital is one of the world's newer and smaller capitals, having only been built from the mid-1960s onwards. Situated on the Belize River in the Cayo District in the centre of the country, it is protected from the region's potentially devastating hurricanes.

History

Belmopan's predecessor as the capital was Belize City, but in 1961 it was ravaged by Hurricane Hattie. When the British granted the country self-government in 1964, it was decided to relocate the capital. Belmopan was chosen as the site and building began, largely financed by a UK grant, in 1966. Government buildings and diplomatic mission were established in 1970, many in the style of Mayan architecture. The principal government buildings are to be found on the central Independence Plazza, next to the city's commercial hub, Market Square. Construction continued throughout the 1970s. In 1981 British Honduras officially became independent Belize, with Belmopan the designated capital.

Modern City

The political and administrative centre, the Belizian capital is nonetheless limited to that function. Most of the small population consists of government employees and their families. Buses link Belmopan to the larger Belize City.

Places of Interest

Among Belmopan's chief attractions are the National Archives and the Department of Archaeology, which has many examples of Mayan relics. Within easy reach of the city are the Guanacaste National Park and the Maya Mountains.

Bergen, Norway

Introduction

Norway's former capital and now the country's second city after Olso, Bergen is capital of the county of Hordaland in the southwest of the country. A major commercial centre for the oil and fishing industries, it provides a jumping off point for tourists exploring the Norwegian fjords.

History

In 1070 King Olaf III (Olaf Kyrre) established a city called Bjørgvin that would evolve into Bergen. Thirty years later a castle was constructed near Vågen harbour. Its location ensured the city's strategic importance as a trade centre, particularly for fish and animal products, and by the 12th century Bergen was the capital city. It remained so for much of the 13th century and during the 14th century it became a vital centre for the Hanseatic League, a position it held until the 18th century. In 1665 the city's harbour witnessed the routing of the English fleet, which had been chasing the Dutch merchant fleet.

In 1702 the city was ravaged by fire and in 1916 it again fell victim to a fire in which 3,000 people were made homeless. In the early 20th century the Bergen School, a team of meteorologists influential in the study of weather fronts, was active in the city. The discovery of North Sea oil deposits kickstarted the local economy in the 1980s.

Modern City

Bergen's economy relies on oil, fishing, shipbuilding and engineering. Other important industries include food processing and the manufacture of paper, rope, pottery and furniture.

As well as its harbour (which offers ferry services), Bergen is well served by road links, lies on the Oslo–Bergen railway and has the Flesland international airport not far from the city centre. Buses run within the city. There is a university as well as several institutes of higher education.

Places of Interest

St Mary's church, dating from the 12th century, is the oldest building in the city. The Bergenhus fortress includes the 12th century Håkonshallen ceremonial hall and the defensive Rosenkrantz Tower (predominantly 16th century but incorporating part of a 13th century keep). The harbour is a bustling centre of activity, with the tall ship *Statsraad Lehmkuhl* among Bergen's leading attractions, as are the fish market, aquarium and natural history museum.

Bergen hosts an annual jazz festival and the Grieg Hall, named after the native composer, was opened in 1978. The main theatre is Norway's oldest permanent theatre. Many visitors use Bergen as a base for visiting the surrounding fjord country. The biggest local peak, Ulriken, is accessible by cablecar and a funicular runs to the top of Mount Fløien.

Berlin, Germany

Introduction

Berlin is the capital of reunified Germany and is situated in the east of Germany on the Spree and Havel rivers. It is within, but administratively not a part of, Brandenburg. It was under the rule of the Hohenzollern family from the mid-14th century until 1918 and served as Germany's capital from 1871 until 1945, when the country split in two. It became capital after the collapse of the Berlin Wall in 1989.

History

Berlin was formed by the merging of two villages in the 13th century and became a leading member of the Hanseatic League (an association of German towns and traders), emerging as one of Central Europe's leading trade and communications hubs. Falling under the Hohenzollern rule of Elector Friedrich II of Brandenburg in the 1440s, his son made it his capital. It suffered extensive damage during the 30 Years' War (1618–48) but underwent a renaissance during the reign of Friedrich Wilhelm (the Great Elector).

Berlin was the capital of Prussia from the early-18th century and expanded throughout the century, particularly during the rule of Friedrich II who was responsible for several major architectural schemes. Growth was sustained into the 19th century, despite the Napoleonic occupation of 1806–08 and popular uprisings in the 1830s and 1840s. Its economy was boosted in the second half of the century by the Industrial Revolution and in 1871 Berlin became the capital of the newly constituted German Empire.

Following the defeat of Germany in World War I, Germany became a republic with Berlin remaining the capital. When Hitler became Chancellor in 1933 Berlin was the focus of world attention. It was the burning of the city's Reichstag building in 1933 that allowed Hitler to assume absolute control and eliminate his opposition. In the same year Berlin was the scene of mass book burnings against authors deemed enemies of the state and 3 years later it hosted the Olympic Games, an event hijacked by Hitler to demonstrate the grandeur of Nazi Germany. In 1938 the city witnessed Reichskristallnacht (Night of Broken Glass), during which Nazi stormtroopers unleashed the organized persecution of the Jewish population.

During World War II Berlin was badly damaged by Allied bombing and Soviet artillery attack. In 1945 it was divided into occupation zones (The British, American and French eventually becoming West Berlin and the Soviet zone becoming East Berlin). Berlin's political status became a major bone of contention between East and West and in 1948–49 the Western powers undertook a large-scale airlift to supply West Berlin with provisions during a Soviet blockade. In 1949 East Berlin became the capital of the German Democratic Republic and in 1950 West Berlin became a *Land* but Bonn was made capital of the Federal Republic of Germany.

Relations between East and West continued to deteriorate and, in a bid to stem the exodus of Germans from East Berlin, the East German authorities erected the Berlin Wall along the line of partition in Aug. 1961. The Wall was broken down in Nov. 1989 and the East German communist regime collapsed soon afterwards. German reunification occurred in Oct. 1990 and the amalgamated Berlin became capital. In 1991 Parliament voted to move the federal government to Berlin.

Modern City

The city's major manufactures include electrical equipment, chemicals and clothing. It is also a major international finance centre. Berlin has three international airports: Flughafen Tegel (Otto Lilienthal Airport), Flughafen Tempelhof and Flughafen Schönefeld. The main railway station is Berlin Hauptbahnhof (main station), which was opened in May 2006 and is located in the city centre. Prior to its inauguration the main stations were Zoologischer Garten in the west of Berlin and Ostbahnhof, formerly Hauptbahnhof, in the east. Berlin is on several major road links and has one of the most efficient public transportation systems in the world, consisting of surface rail (S-Bahn), tram (Straßenbahn), bus and underground (U-Bahn).

Places of Interest

Berlin has a thriving tourist sector and contains many important galleries, museums and cultural institutions. Among the most popular attractions are the gallery of the Charlottenburg Palace (with a major collection of Rembrandts), the Pergamon Museum (with collections of classical art), Tiergarten-Kulturforum (which houses the Kunstbibliothek and the Kupferstichkabinett, a collection of lithographs and drawings by old masters from the 14th–18th centuries), the Neue Nationalgalerie, Kunstgewerbemuseum (Museum of Applied Arts) and the Alte Nationalgalerie. Museumsinsel (Museum Island) comprises four separate museums while the Dahlem Museums includes a museum of ethnology, an art gallery, sculpture collection and museums of Indian, Islamic and Oriental art.

The Reichstag was renovated after the reunification on the designs of British architect, Norman Foster, and now has a glass dome to represent parliament's transparency. The nearby Brandenburg Gate, designed by Karl Gotthard Langhans in 1791, formed part of the Berlin Wall and symbolised the boundary between the east and west sectors of the city. Schloß Charlottenburg is the 17th century summer residence built for Queen Sophie-Charlotte. A further major landmark is Potsdamer Platz, the busiest junction in Europe before World War I but a no-man's land after the Berlin Wall went up. It is now the site of a huge building project aimed at re-establishing it as the focal point of the city with shopping centres, cinemas, hotels, embassies, restaurants, offices and apartments. Alexanderplatz is a square dominated by communist-era concrete buildings and a statue of Karl Marx and is also home to the Fernsehturm (TV tower), Berlin's tallest structure and the fifth tallest freestanding structure in Europe. The Berlin Philharmonic Orchestra plays at the Philharmonie and world class opera can be seen at both the Staatsoper and Deutsche Oper.

Berne, Switzerland

Introduction

Berne is located in the west along a bend of the Aare River. It is the country's capital and home of the Swiss parliament, but despite this political significance it is geographically small.

History

The city was founded at the end of the 12th century by Berthold V, duke of Zähringen. It was originally used as a military post, but following the decline of the dynasty it became a free imperial city. Berne gradually expanded and prospered, partly due to its proximity to the wealthy kingdom of Burgundy. After defeating the nobility of Burgundy at the battle of Laupen in 1339, Berne asserted its independent statehood by joining the Swiss Confederation in 1353. It soon began to dominate the confederation.

In 1405 much of the old city was devastated by fire, and Berne was rebuilt with sandstone rather than timber, although several buildings from the era before the fire still survive in the city centre. In 1528 a civil disputation between Catholic and Protestant factions culminated in the state's acceptance of Protestant doctrine. In the 16th and 17th centuries Berne increased its patrician powers over the surrounding territories. The city's grandees suppressed several revolts, and maintained considerable political control, but the rule of the nobles was ended by the invasion of France in 1798. The 1814 Congress of Vienna compelled Berne to surrender its lands to the east and west. This created the cantons of Aargau and Vaud. In spite of this loss, Berne remained prestigious enough to be chosen as the capital of the revived Swiss Confederation in 1848. During the 20th century the city continued to grow, and new bridges were constructed to connect newly built districts to the centre.

Modern City

Old Berne is on the left bank of the Aare and is linked by several bridges to the modern city on the right bank. To the south lies the planned suburb of Kirchenfeld; it is an upmarket residential area. To the west lies the more multicultural district of Bümpliz which accommodates much of the city's immigrant population. The large railway station is located to the west of the old town, and Berne is well served by road and rail connections. The city also has a small airport 9 km to the southeast, but it does not operate many services during the winter.

Berne's industries are noted for manufacturing chocolate, electrical equipment, machinery, chemicals, textiles and pharmaceuticals. The city is an important market for agricultural goods and the headquarters of the country's government offices and national library as well as its postal, telegraph, copyright and railway unions.

Places of Interest

The Kunstmuseum houses the world's largest collection of works by the Swiss artist Paul Klee as well as numerous other notable exhibits.

Bilbao (Bilbo), Spain

Introduction

The capital of the province of Biscay (Spanish: Vizcaya; *Euskara*: Bizkaia) in the Basque country, Bilbao is situated near the North Atlantic coast 11 km from the Bay of Biscay. The Basque country (País Vasco) is made up of three provinces in Spain—Guipúzcoa, Biscay and Álava—as well as parts of the neighbouring Navarra region and parts of south-western France.

History

Known collectively as Euskadi, the Basques have their own language and culture. The language *Euskara* is one of the most ancient languages of Europe, pre-dating the Indo-European languages evolved from migrants and settlers from the east. However, *Euskara* was solely an oral language until the 16th century. The mountainous landscape of the Basque country discouraged invaders and settlers and, thus, unlike the rest of Spain, it has had little contact with migrants.

Bilbao was originally a settlement of mariners and ironworkers around the River Nervión. It was founded in 1300 by the Lord of Biscay, Diego López de Haro. From the Middle Ages onwards Bilbao's inhabitants profited from the trade in iron ore and its by-products, for example swords. The old English words bilbo (cutlass) and bilboes (iron fetters) attest to the importance of this trade. A key port, Bilbao was an important exporter of wool from Castille. Bilbao profited from the discovery of the New World, and trade with the Americas in the 18th century brought great prosperity to the town.

Bilbao's founder granted the town the right to self-government. A commercial tribunal with the power to make its own laws was founded in 1511. One such law of 1737 was the basis of the original commercial code in Spain, set up in 1829. The Basque Country had autonomy from Madrid in the guise of *fueros*—independent rights of self-government.

From its beginning in 1300 to the 19th century Bilbao's history was relatively uneventful. Its troubles began with the Peninsular War (1808–16) when the French sacked the city in 1808. During the subsequent Carlist wars Bilbao was besieged four times and suffered from fire and bombardment. The Basque country had supported the Carlists and their defeat in 1876 saw the removal of the *fueros*. During the Civil War Bilbao was a Republican stronghold—the Biscay and Guipúzcoa provinces supported the Republicans, whilst Navarra and Álava backed Franco—but was taken by the Nationalist on 19 June 1937. Bilbao and the surrounding Basque country suffered under Franco, who took away any remaining autonomy. The culture was suppressed and the language was outlawed. Since the death of Franco and the advent of democracy, Bilbao has become an autonomous region.

From the mid-19th century, Bilbao became increasingly industrialized. In 1896 a dry dock was constructed which led to the revival of shipbuilding and a golden age that lasted until the 1920s. Today, much of Bilbao's industry has gone and the steel works are now a building site, although its shipbuilding industry survives.

Modern City

The largest city in the Basque country, the city's major industries are metallurgy, especially iron, and shipbuilding. Situated on the navigable River Nervión, Bilbao is an important port and traditionally the centre of the Spanish wool trade for Castile. Bilbao now exports lead, iron ore and wine.

The city is important commercially and as a centre of finance and education. Bilbao and its surrounding suburbs are home to four fifths of the Basque population. Even so, the presence of the Basque separatist group ETA (Euzkadi Ta Azkatasuna; Basque Homeland and Liberty) could threaten the city's future investment.

Bilbao is accessible by road, rail and air. The redevelopment programme at the end of the 20th century produced a new subway system. Opened in 1995, it was designed by the British architect Sir Norman Foster.

Places of Interest

The nucleus of the medieval town is Las Siete Calles (seven streets), which contains the Gothic Catedral de Santiago as well as the Teatro Arriaga. Six bridges across the River Nervión link the old city to the new commercial centre. The town boasts two universities and the Museo Guggenheim de Arte Contemporáneo opened on 19 Oct. 1997. Set on the waterfront, at 24,000 sq.metres the museum is the largest gallery in the world. Designed by the American architect and designer Frank Gehry, the immense titanium covered structure is devoted to 20th-century art, including Basque and Spanish artists. The original Museo de Bellas Artes, situated in the north of the town, exhibits the native Basque sculptor, Eduardo Chillida. The award-winning artist famously used the local iron for his sculptures.

Birmingham, United Kingdom of Great Britain and Northern Ireland

Introduction

Birmingham is the second largest city in the United Kingdom and an important regional centre for industry and culture. It established its prosperity during the industrial revolution, when it was able to take advantage of its geographical location and its manufacturing capabilities, although the modern economy is broad-based.

History

The city owes much of its prominence to its geographical location at the heart of the country. In 1086 the Domesday Book recorded Birmingham as a hamlet worth 20 shillings. Its rise came under the the de Birmingham family, Lords of Birmingham for 400 years.

In 1156 Peter de Birmingham was granted a market charter from Henry II and the small town began to grow. Within Birmingham many iron workers plied their trade and during the English civil war (1642–51) the town supplied armory to the Parliamentarian forces fighting against the supporters of King Charles I. This helped to establish the town as a metal working area. However its position in central England, with no easy coastal access, impeded its growth until the industrial revolution in the mid-18th century. By then Birmingham had a reputation as a manufacturing city and was well placed to take advantage of the improvements in transportation, especially that offered by canals. Birmingham boasts more canals than Venice.

Birmingham became the epicentre of the Industrial Revolution in Britain. Its leading industrial sons included James Watt, the Scottish inventor who developed the steam engine; John Baskerville, the pioneering printer and font designer; and Joseph Priestley, one of the discoverers of oxygen and a political theorist. It was also in Birmingham that the steam engine was developed for industrial purposes as well as for transportation. Birmingham received its city status in 1889.

As an important arms manufacturing city, Birmingham fared badly in the bombing raids of World War II. The post-war era was characterized by extensive rebuilding but the brutalist architecture of the 1950s was widely criticized and recently Birmingham has re-discovered its Victorian heartland with the restoration of many fine buildings.

Modern City

Birmingham has an international airport and is a major centre on the national road and rail networks. In 1999 the Midland Metro (a light rail system) was opened, linking Birmingham with Wolverhampton and in 2010 Birmingham Moor Street station was reopened. The city's main railway station, Birmingham New Street, has undergone a £700 m. refurbishment that was completed in 2015.

Among the city's chief industries are motor vehicle manufacturing, chemicals, plastics and chocolate making. Birmingham is home to five universities: Aston University, Birmingham City University, University of Birmingham, University College Birmingham and Newman University.

Despite the recent economic downturn there has been a continued emphasis on cultural heritage heralding the recent development of the Repertory Theatre, the opening of the new Birmingham Central Library in 2013 and the development of the 'Eastside City Park'.

Places of Interest

Among the city's attractions are the Town Hall, which was graced by the likes of Charles Dickens, Elgar and the Beatles before reopening in 2007 with its 6,000 pipe organ restored, St Philip's Church, consecrated in 1715, and the city's cathedral. Just outside Birmingham is the NEC (National Exhibition Centre), which is one of the UK's most prestigious venues for exhibitions and events. Birmingham is also home to Aston Hall, a 17th century Jacobean mansion and scene of a Civil War siege, Soho House, home of industrialist Matthew Boulton from 1766–1809 and Weoley Castle, which had been inhabited from the 12th century. The Birmingham 'Think Tank' specializes in science and technology while the Birmingham Museum and Art Gallery concentrates on fine art and world and local history—it boasts the Stafford-shire Hoard and one of the largest collections of Pre-Raphaelite works in the world. Symphony Hall is the home of the city's Symphony Orchestra, the CBSO.

Bishkek, Kyrgyzstan

Introduction

Bishkek, on the rivers Alaarcha and Alamedin in the Chu River valley near the Kyrgyz mountains, is the national capital.

History

Founded in 1825 by the Kokand khanate, Russia seized the town in 1862 and called it Pipshek. Designated the administrative centre of the Kyrgyz auton-omous oblast in 1924, it became capital of the Kirghiz Autonomous Republic in 1926, then of the Kirghiz Soviet Socialist Republic in 1936. In Soviet times it was named Frunze after a local Red Army hero. Heavy industries were developed during World War II. In 1991, after the country had gained independence, the city was renamed Bishkek. The word describes a wooden churn used to make fermented mare's milk, a popular drink in Kyrgyzstan.

Modern City

A modern city, Bishkek has wide boulevards and large green spaces. It has many factories producing textiles, leather and agricultural machinery. There is a university and several institutes of higher education.

Bishkek is well served by road and rail links and Manas international airport is close by. The Great Chuysky Canal runs through the city.

Places of Interest

Many of Bishkek's monuments pay homage to the national history. The Victory monument is based on the structure of a yurt (a sort of nomadic tent) and there are statues to the nationally important poet, Manas. The monument to the martyrs of the revolution was completed in 1978.

The city acts as a hopping-off point to the surrounding mountain and lake regions. The Ala-Archa Canyon nature park is 40 km south of the city.

Bissau, Guinea-Bissau

Introduction

Bissau is the capital and chief port of Guinea-Bissau. It is in the central west of the country near the mouth of the Canal do Gêba.

History

Founded in 1687, the city developed as a slave trading centre for the Portu-guese. It became a free port in 1869, prospering from European trade, and replaced Bolama as the administrative capital in 1941.

In 1959, 50 striking dockworkers were shot dead in what became known as the Pidjiguiti massacre. The struggle which followed led to Guinea-Bissau's declaration of independence in 1973. With the first domestic gov-ernment in place, half the country's resources were allocated to the capital, a decision which left rural areas badly under-developed and failed to alleviate the country's debt problems and poor infrastructure.

The failed coup attempt by Gen. Ansumane Mane in 1998 and the resulting civil war saw fighting within the capital between President Vieira's government, backed by Senegal and Guinea, and rebel forces. Many of the city's population fled. By the time Vieira's government fell in 1999 large parts of the city had been badly damaged.

Modern City

The city's port has been improved, including the enlargement of the harbour. It handles the country's main export products: cashew nuts and frozen fish.

The city has an international airport and road connections with major towns.

Places of Interest

There is a national museum containing local art and artifacts.

Bloemfontein, South Africa

Introduction

Bloemfontein is the provincial capital of the Free State and the judicial capital of South Africa. The city is on a plateau 1,390 m. above sea level. The 'fountain of flowers' was named after the farm of the Voortrekker Johannes Nicolaas Brits. Bloemfontein is known to the Tswana people as Mangawung or 'the place of the cheetahs', a reminder of the wilderness that existed before farmers tamed the high velds.

History

Bloemfontein was founded in 1846 by Major H. Douglas Warden. Originally a fort it became the seat of British jurisdiction in the Orange River Sover-eignty in the mid-19th century. It was then to become a Boer settlement at the heart of the newly named Orange Free State, formed in 1854 at the Bloem-fontein Convention.

By the mid-19th century Bloemfontein was still a small village but had already shown that it had legislative and judicial flair. The latter half of the 19th century saw the town transform from a small backwater into a thriving capital. In the 20th century it became the centre of South Africa's transport industry and expanded rapidly after gold was struck in the Free State Gold-fields, about 160 km to the north of the city.

Modern City

Bloemfontein Airport is 10 km from the centre on the Maseru road. Bloem-fontein is linked by bus to Cape Town, Durban, East London, Johannesburg, Pretoria and Port Elizabeth. The main railway station is on Harvey Street and serves Durban, Cape Town, Johannesburg, East London, Port Elizabeth, Kimberley and Pretoria. Taxis are plentiful. Minibus taxis depart from the vicinity of the main railway station.

Places of Interest

Bloemfontein Zoo, in King's Park, boasts an animal known as a 'liger' which is a hybrid cross between a lion and a tiger. The Botanical Gardens, 45 square ha, cultivates a wide variety of plants in their natural habitats. Bloemfontein's National Museum houses one of the best public entomology collections in the country. The Military Museum of the Boer Republics, recalling the days of the Anglo-Boer war, is situated south of the city centre on Monument Road. The Johannes Stegmann Art Gallery, at the University of the Orange Free State, showcases work of local and native artists as well as the work of students. Sand du Plessis Theatre presents drama, ballet and opera.

The Soetdoring Nature Reserve is about 37 km to the northwest of the city. This valley is home to many beautiful birds including secretary birds. Maria Moroka National Park is nearly 200 km along the N8 from Bloemfon-tein towards the border with Lesotho.

Bobo-Dioulasso, Burkina Faso

Introduction

In the southwest of Burkina Faso, Bobo-Dioulasso is the country's second largest city.

History

Bobo-Dioulasso was founded in the 14th century and was inhabited by the indigenous Bobo people. It developed into an important market town. In 1885 the town was taken by French colonialists. Improved communications and the arrival of rail allowed an expansion of Bobo-Dioulasso in the mid-20th century.

Modern City

As the country's second city, Bobo-Dioulasso is economically and culturally important. Its first train station was built in 1934, and since 1954 the town has been linked by rail to Ouagadougou. There is also an airport. The town hosts the Semaine Nationale de la Culture every 2 years which celebrates music, dance and theatre.

Places of Interest

A focal point is the Sudanese-style Grande Mosquée. Built out of clay in the late 19th century, it has distinctive cylindrical minarets. Traditional regional art, African art, sculpture and batiks are displayed in the Musée Provincial du Houët while most artisans are based in the Kibidwé district. French culture is promoted by the Centre Culturel Français Henri Matisse. The old quarter contains the 14th century 'maison mère', *Konsa*, the house of the founder of Bobo-Dioulasso.

Bogotá (Santa Fé de Bogotá; Bogotá, Distrito Capital), Colombia

Introduction

The capital of Colombia, Bogotá is located in the heart of the country in the district of Cundinamarca. The city is on the Sabana plateau in the Cordillera Oriental of the Andes. Flanked to the east by two mountains, Monserrate and Guadalupe, Bogotá is the commercial, financial, social and academic centre of Colombia.

History

At the time of the Conquest, the high valleys surrounding Bogotá were inhabited by the Muisca people, part of the Chibcha linguistic family. Comprising around 500,000 people, the Chibcha were the most organized and advanced people in the New World after the Incas. Living in hierarchical groups, they were skilled weavers and goldsmiths. Their mainstay was agriculture and commerce with El Caribe people, another ethnolinguistic group living in Cundinamarca, who exchanged their gold for the Muisca's cotton.

In 1537 the Conquistadors, under Gonzalo Jiménez de Quesada, conquered the indigenous peoples, appropriating their wealth and treasures. El Caribe resisted the Spanish, but were eventually overcome. The following year, Jiménez de Quesada founded Santa Fé de Bacatá, naming it after his birthplace in Spain and the indigenous name of a Muisca centre nearby. What later became Bogotá spread out from the central district of La Candelaria around the Plaza Real, now known as the Plaza de Bolívar. It was designed in a grid-like plan typical of Spanish colonial cities in South America.

In 1717 Bogotá became the capital of the Vice Royalty of New Granada, encompassing Colombia, Panama, Venezuela and Ecuador, and as such was the centre of colonial power in South America. Rebelling against Spanish rule, the country was liberated by Simon Bolívar in 1819 following the Battle of Boyacá. After Independence, Bogotá became the capital of the renamed Gran Colombia. Gran Colombia was dissolved as the surrounding countries gained their independence, and in 1830 Bogotá became the capital of New Granada, eventually renamed the Republic of Colombia.

During subsequent years Bogotá, along with the rest of the country, was embroiled in La Violencia, a bitter dispute between Liberals and Conservatives which climaxed in the 1940s. In 1948 the assassination of Jorge Eliécer Gaitán, leader of the Liberals, led to the *bogotazo*—widespread violence and riots in which a fire destroyed many of Bogotá's buildings.

A mass influx from the 1940s onwards led to the first high rise accommodation. Even so, shantytowns and marginal *barrios* developed around the city.

In the 20th century air travel improved communications with other major industrial centres. The first commercial airline established in South America, Avianca (Aerovías Nacionales de Colombia) is based in Bogotá. Modern day Bogotá suffers from a high level of poverty with a large percentage of *Bogotanos* living in shantytowns. The city continues to swell as the displaced inhabitants of rural areas flee violence and conflict between left-wing guerrillas and right-wing paramilitaries, creating housing and social problems. In 1985 the Palacio de Justicia in central Bogotá was taken by 35 M-19 guerrillas. In the ensuing conflict between the army and the guerrillas more than 100 people died including 11 supreme court judges. A human rights lawyer, Eduardo Umana Mendoza, claimed the figure was as high as 150 and that 60 people were buried in mass graves. In 1998 a court order permitted an exhumation, but on 18 April Mendoza was assassinated.

Modern City

The international airport of Eldorado is 13 km northwest of Bogotá. The Universidad Santo Tomás was founded in 1580, and the Pontificia Universidad Javeriana in 1622. Many banks and businesses have their headquarters in the capital. Industries include textiles, engineering, pharmaceuticals, vehicles, printing and publishing. The surrounding district produces coffee, sugar cane, potatoes and corn.

Places of Interest

At the heart of the old town and in the centre of the city is the Plaza de Bolívar, dominated by a bronze statue of the liberator of Colombia. The square is lined with public buildings in varying architectural styles, from colonial structures to modern housing. The Capitolio Nacional, once the Viceroy's palace and now the seat of Congress, was designed by the British architect Thomas Reed in 1847. The Neo-classical Catedral Primada is based on the original site of the first mass celebrated in Bogotá. Built in 1823, it was designed by the Spanish architect and Capuchin monk, Domingo de Petrés. The Iglesia de Santa Clara, home of the Clarissa Nuns was built between 1619–30. In 1968 it became the museum of religious art and a concert hall. The Museo del Oro boasts the largest collection of pre-Hispanic gold objects in Latin America, with over 33,000 items from all cultures.

Bonn, Germany

Introduction

Bonn, an important university town, is located in the region of North Rhine-Westphalia, on the River Rhine. Bonn was the capital of West Germany from 1949. In 1991 the German parliament voted to move the federal government back to Berlin. Government departments began to leave Bonn in 1999, though many government offices remain and many of the embassies will take some years to complete the move.

History

Bonn was settled by the Romans and celebrated its 2000th anniversary in 1989. From the sixteenth to the eighteenth century, Bonn was the residence of the prince-electors and archbishops of Cologne and was the capital city of the see of Cologne. Some of the fine baroque architecture from this period has survived, despite heavy bombing in World War II.

Modern City

Bonn has been designated the federal city for science and communication and is home to Deutsche Telekom and the Centre for Advanced European Studies and Research (CAESAR). Manufactures include ceramic and metal goods, chemicals and pharmaceuticals as well as Haribo's money-spinning Gummi-Bears (Gummibärchen).

Bonn shares its airport, Köln-Bonn Flughafen, with Cologne. The city is linked to Cologne and other Rhine cities by the VRS (Verkehrsverbund Rhein-Sieg) S-Bahn, U-Bahn and Bundesbahn network. This system also serves as the public transport system within the city. Bonn is at the hub of several major Autobahnen (motorways). The main station is the Hauptbahnhof.

Places of Interest

Among Bonn's most famous landmarks is the Poppelsdorfer Schloß, an eighteenth century building with a French style façade and Italian courtyard, designed by the French architect Robert de Cotte. It is linked with Bonn's other great castle, Kurfürstliches Schloß (now the centre of the Friedrich-Wilhelms-Universität), by a carriageway bordered by rows of chestnut trees. To the rear of the palace are the university's botanical gardens. Münster Basilika (Collegiate Church) is a leading example of late Rhineland Romanesque architecture (constructed after the fire of 1239 on the site of a Roman necropolis).

Bonn has several notable galleries and museums. Beethoven Geburtshaus is the house where Beethoven was born. At the first Beethoven festival here, Franz Liszt fought with Hector Berlioz while King Ludwig's mistress, Lola Montez, danced on the tables. Haus der Geschichte der Bundesrepublik Deutschland is the first museum in Germany devoted to contemporary history. Exhibits include antique Volkswagen cars, Konrad Adenuaer's official Mercedes, the rough wooden seats that Mikhail Gorbachev and Helmut Kohl sat on during the 1990 summit in Kaukasus Platz and a moving scroll of holocaust victims.

Deutsche Museum Bonn is an offshoot of the museum of science and technology in Munich and has as its theme 'Research and Technology in Germany since 1945'. Kunstmuseum Bonn (Bonn Museum of Art) houses a large and impressive collection of expressionists and modern German painting in a building designed by Axel Schulter.

Bordeaux, France

Introduction

An inland port situated on the Garonne River, Bordeaux is the capital of the Gironde department in Southwest France. A commercial centre, the surrounding region is renowned for its fine wines.

History

Bordeaux was founded by the Celtic tribe, Bituriges Vivisci. Named Burdigala, the town was linked to the tin trade. When settled by the Romans in 56 BC, Bordeaux flourished as a port and city, serving as the capital of Aquitania. The tin trade was succeeded by wine production centred on the plains of Médoc.

After several centuries of unrest, Bordeaux stabilized and prospered during the eleventh century under the rule of the dukes of Aquitaine. Bordeaux came under Capician rule with the alliance of Eleanor of Aquitaine and the future King Louis VII in 1137. Her subsequent marriage to Henry Plantagenet allied the city with England, and Bordeaux came under English rule in 1154 with Henry II's ascension.

From 1360 Bordeaux served as a base for the Black Prince Edward during his campaigns against French-held possessions in the Southwest, and it was there his son, Richard II, was born in 1367. The revenue from the export of Bordeaux wine to England from the châteaux along the banks of the Garonne and Dordogne Rivers allowed for expansion of the port. The trade continued throughout the Hundred Years War (fourteenth–fifteenth century) and Bordeaux's merchants prospered. In 1453 the Battle of Castillon returned Bordeaux to French rule.

During the eighteenth century Bordeaux prospered by the slave trade. The population increased threefold and Bordeaux became the third most important French city after Paris and Lyons. Medieval Bordeaux was converted into a modern city with wide avenues and classical buildings through the work of Intendants, or Royal representatives. This prosperity was damaged by the Revolution (1789), when there was feuding between a group of Bordeaux deputies known as the Girondins and the opposing group of radical deputies, the Montagnards.

A post-Revolution slump was reversed in the nineteenth century with increased trade with South America and West Africa. Bordeaux was the temporary seat of the French government in 1870 during the Franco-Prussian

War, and again in 1914 and 1940 during World Wars I and II. The city suffered bombardment during World War II.

From 1960 Bordeaux expanded and in 1966 became the capital of Aquitaine. Since the 1970s the French mint, Etablissement Monétaire, has been housed in Bordeaux.

Modern City

Bordeaux has shipbuilding and oil-refining industries as well as engineering and the manufacture of chemicals. The surrounding region produces wine in the districts of Graves, Médoc, St Emilion, Pomerol and Sauternes. The University was founded in 1441. A regional transport centre, Bordeaux is connected by road and rail to Paris, the Atlantic Coast and the Southeast. The Airport de Bordeaux Merignac is 10 km west of the city.

Places of Interest

Many of the city's historic monuments have been restored. These include the Classical Grand Théatre. Built between 1773–1802 by Victor Louis, it is considered one of France's finest. The Gothic Catédrale St André, built between eleventh–sixteenth centuries, was extensively renovated in the nineteenth century. Bordeaux's museums include the Musée d'Aquitaine and the Musée des Beaux-Arts, which was originally intended to house Napoléon's war spoils. The eighteenth century old town behind the quayside, the quartier des chartons, was originally the centre of the wine trade and ship chandlers.

Boston, United States of America

Introduction

The capital of the state of Massachusetts and the seat of Suffolk county, Boston is located on the northeastern coast of the United States on a peninsula on the state's Atlantic Ocean coastline. The city occupies an area of 90 sq. miles (232 km^2) and is about 198 miles (320 km) northeast of New York City.

History

Native Americans lived in the area now known as Boston as long ago as 6000 BC. However the first explorations along the New England coast made by Europeans were in 1524 by Giovanni da Verrazzano and 1605 and 1606 by Samuel de Champlain. English captain John Smith explored Massachusetts Bay in 1614 and, along with other Europeans, brought diseases to the area which devastated the Native American population. Boston was first settled by Europeans in 1624 by Englishman William Blackstone and the area soon became the heart of Puritan culture and life in New England.

In 1629 the British crown granted a charter to the Massachusetts Bay Company and a year later John Winthrop arrived with 700 Puritans to establish the colony of Massachusetts Bay. Originally called Trimountain, after the three hills that make up its geography, the settlers renamed the area Boston, after a town in Lincolnshire, England.

Initially trade in Boston consisted of providing services and foodstuffs for the large number of immigrants arriving from Britain.

In the mid-seventeenth century sea trade flourished and by 1700 Boston had become the most important port in New England and the third busiest in the British Empire. England tried to gain more control over Boston by annulling the Massachusetts Bay Colony's charter and, in 1686, Sir Edmund Andros arrived in the city to become the first royal governor of the Province of Massachusetts Bay.

By the mid-eighteenth century Boston was the centre of the growing movement for American independence. The Stamp Act of 1765 considered by Bostonians to be a form of 'taxation without representation' created tensions, which were exasperated by the appearance of royal soldiers in Massachusetts in Oct. 1768. In 1773 a tax protest led to shiploads of tea being thrown into the harbour in an incident known as the Boston Tea Party. The British responded by closing the harbour in 1774 and sending troops to Boston. In April 1775 the first exchanges of the American War of Independence were fought near Boston at Concord, Massachusetts. Boston's role in the war eventually ended on 17 March 1776 when rebels gained control of the harbour and the British troops departed.

After the end of the war, Boston suffered economic hardship as access to other ports in the British Empire was blocked. From then on, the influence of shipping and shipbuilding in the city waned while investment in railways and manufacturing rapidly increased. Textiles became Boston's main source of income and the city's innovations in manufacturing techniques and distribution methods helped spearhead the American industrial revolution. By 1865 Boston was the USA's fourth largest manufacturing city.

The nineteenth century saw Boston fall on harder times. The development of cheap labour markets in the south and the economic expansions in New York, Chicago, and the western states affected the city's prosperity. The city's ethnic profile was dramatically altered after the potato famine in Ireland, which drove thousands of immigrants to the city. Boston's economy rallied during World War II but declined steadily thereafter. The post-war period was characterized by major urban renewal projects, which saw a migration of the middle-classes to the suburbs.

Modern City

Boston has retained many of the ideals of its Puritan founders and is home to one of the leading Irish-American communities in the USA. By 1980, however, Afro-Americans had become the largest ethnic group in the city. Boston has remained an important port and is at the hub of the USA's further education sector. Harvard University and the Massachusetts Institute of Technology (MIT) are located in nearby Cambridge and there are major scientific and computer research facilities, along with more than two dozen colleges and universities.

Clothes manufacturing, publishing and food processing are Boston's biggest industries. Only one-fifth of the city's population lives in the metropolitan area of the city and there is a large commuter population in the suburbs. In the 1980s the financial district underwent rapid expansion and several large financial institutions, such as Fidelity and Credit Swiss First Boston now have their headquarters in the city.

Boston is served by Logan International Airport (BOS) and is linked to Rowes Wharf by a water shuttle. The main bus station is near the financial district. The city is also on the Amtrak network. The Boston subway, which opened in 1895, is the USA's oldest. There are several ferry services.

Boston is home to several of the only major league sports teams in the New England region, including the Boston Red Sox (baseball), the Boston Celtics (basketball), and the Boston Bruins (ice hockey).

In April 2013, three people died and an estimated 264 were left injured when the Boston Marathon was targeted by two jihadists who set off bombs near the finish line. Sections of the city were controversially locked down in the ensuing manhunt for the suspects.

Places of Interest

There are resident ballet, opera and theatre companies. The Boston Symphony Orchestra, which was founded in 1881, performs in Symphony Hall while in the summer major concerts are held in the Hatch Memorial Shell. Major architectural attractions include the Government Center, the John Hancock Tower and the John F. Kennedy Memorial Library.

The Massachusetts State House, built in 1798 in the downtown neighbourhood of Beacon Hill, is still used by the state legislature. The Old Granary Burying Ground contains the graves of John Hancock and Samuel Adams. Also located on Beacon Hill are the Old State House, where Bostonians first read the declaration of Independence, and the Old South Meeting House where the movement that developed into the Boston Tea Party can be traced. The Bunker Hill Monument and Monument Square are both found in the Charlestown neighbourhood.

Brasília, Brazil

Introduction

Brasília was purpose built as the administrative capital to open up central Brazil and encourage people away from the densely populated coastal areas. Inaugurated on 21 April 1960, the Brazilian capital is one of the best known twentieth century planned cities and is a landmark in contemporary town planning and modern architecture. Despite its huge expense and questionable benefits, Brasília is symbolized by its Modernist architecture, designed by Brazilian architect Oscar Niemeyer. As part of the Distrito Federal, Brasília is in an area ceded by the state of Goiás in west central Brazil. It is bordered by the Rivers Preto to the east and Descoberto to the west, covering an area of 5,822 sq. km.

History

Although the creation of an inland capital had been considered since the eighteenth century, it was not until 1956 that 'Brasília', a name suggested by Jose Bonifácio in 1823, began to take shape. Moving the nation's capital from Rio was long and drawn out. In 1891 Article 3 of the Republic of Brazil's first written constitution outlined the creation of a new capital. In 1892 the Comissão Exploradora do Planalto Central (known as the Cruls Mission after its head, the Brazilian astronomer Luis Cruls) was appointed. Two years later it earmarked an area of 14,400 sq. km for the new capital. In 1922 the foundation stone of the future capital was laid near the city of Planaltina, on the outskirts of the present day Federal District.

In 1956, having won an election on the promise of instituting Article 3 of the constitution, President Juscelino Kubitschek established the construction company NOVACAP (Nova Capital) to build the new capital in an area chosen the previous year. Centrally located, it was 1,015 km from São Paulo, 1,148 km from Rio de Janeiro and 2,120 km from Belém. The nearest railway line was 125 km away, the nearest paved road over 600 km and the nearest airport some 190 km from the planned location. Transport connections were built to connect the interior to the major cities. Despite the infrastructural and geographical obstacles Brasília was operational as a capital city in just 4 years.

The competition to design the master plan for the city was won by the Brazilian architect and urban planner, Lúcio Costa. His design was submitted on five medium sized cards with no technical drawings. The government buildings were designed by the Brazilian architect chosen to head NOVACAP, Oscar Niemeyer, in a modern style, and the landscape designer Roberto Burl Marx chose the plant varieties and layout of the open spaces.

Brasília was officially inaugurated on 21 April 1960 when the government and officials moved in. The construction of the city has continued ever since with the University of Brasília inaugurated in 1962, the TV Tower that dominates the city's skyline completed in 1967, the cathedral opening in 1970, the city park in 1978 and the central bank building in 1981. In 1987 UNESCO declared Brasília a world heritage site.

Modern City

Brasília was based on the Modernist ideas of Le Corbusier who recommended separate residential, professional, governmental and recreational areas as well as an extensive road infrastructure. The construction left a debt of over R$5bn. and caused considerable damage to the surrounding rainforest.

Brasília is the administrative, political and communications centre of the country but has little industry compared to other leading cities. There are road, rail and air links to the rest of Brazil. The international airport is 12 km to the south of the city. Brasília's metro system was opened in 2001.

Places of Interest

The Praça dos Três Poderes, the city's main square houses the Congress building, the Palacio do Planalto (president's office), Palacio da Justica and the Panteão Tancredo Neves. 19 ministry buildings line the Esplanada dos Ministérios, west of the Praça, which culminates in two towers, linked by a walkway to form the letter 'H', representing 'humanity'.

Brasília's centrepiece cathedral, the Catedral Metropolitana was designed in circular form by Oscar Niemeyer to represent the crown of thorns. Inside are three aluminium angels designed by the sculptor Alfredo Scesciatte suspended from the domed, stained-glass ceiling.

Begun in 1965, the Television Tower has a 75 m-high viewing gallery. Designed by Lucio Costa, it is one of the few buildings in the city not attributable to Oscar Niemeyer.

A memorial to the man who conceived and built Brasília, the Juscelino Kubitschek Memorial was designed by Oscar Niemeyer. Inside the monument are Kubitschek's tomb, an exhibition on his life and the construction of Brasília. Among Brasília's museums are an art museum displaying paintings, prints and sculptures by native artists, a history museum charting the city's development and a museum of northeastern arts and traditions.

Bratislava, Slovakia

Introduction

Bratislava is the capital of Slovakia and the administrative region of Bratislava, lying close to the couture's western border with Austria and Hungary. It was a key location for the Roman and Austro-Hungarian empires and, after Prague, was the second most important city in Czechoslovakia. It became capital of the newly independent Republic of Slovakia in 1993.

History

The site of Bratislava was inhabited around 5,000 years ago. It fell under the rule of the Roman Empire in the first century AD, with Slav tribes first appearing in the area during the fifth and sixth centuries. The Slavs established the Great Moravian Empire during the ninth century. A castle built 10 km north of what is now Bratislava's old town served as the royal seat. Bratislava itself first appeared in historical records in the following century.

In the eleventh century the Great Moravian Empire was subsumed by Hungary and Bratislava's Germanic population swelled under King Stephen I. During the fifteenth century, the city was a centre for trade and Renaissance culture. In the 1460s, during the reign of Mathias Corvinus, the Universitas Istropolitana was established. When Turkish forces seized Buda in 1526 the Hungarian capital was moved to Bratislava (then known as Poszony by Hungary and Pressburg by Austria).

The 1491 treaty of Pressburg secured Austrian Habsburg succession to the Austrian throne. Turks besieged the city during the seventeenth century but were ousted after a long and bloody conflict. Relations between the city and its Habsburg rulers worsened over the century, as religious and social freedoms were restricted. However, Empress Maria Theresa (1717–80) favoured Bratislava and her rule coincided with its *golden age* as commerce and the arts thrived.

The Habsburgs reinstated Bude as the capital of the Hungarian Kingdom in 1783. By the early nineteenth century Napoléon was making incursions into the region. In 1809 he gained large parts of Central Europe and the Balkans at the expense of the Habsburgs. Two years later, the castle, which had been neglected for several years, burnt down. As the nineteenth century progressed Bratislava became a centre of rising nationalist sentiment, while increased industrialization led to an influx of Slovak, German and Hungarian migrants.

Austria lost control of Bratislava at the end of World War I and in 1919 the city was incorporated into the new Czechoslovakian State. In the same year the Comenius University was established. Following the invasion by Nazi forces in 1938–39, the city became the base for the puppet government under Monsignor Tiso that administered the newly-created 'Bohemian Protectorate' until Soviet liberation in 1945. After World War II Czechoslovakia was re-instituted with Prague as its capital. The Slovak National Council, based in Bratislava, retained authority within Slovak territory until the communists seized control in 1948 and centralized power.

Much of Bratislava's cultural heritage was neglected in the subsequent decades, and the communists instigated massive and unsightly building projects. Much of the Old Town and Jewish Quarter were demolished in 1968 to make way for the New Bridge. The city was the setting for popular protests in 1989, echoed throughout the country, which resulted in the collapse of the communist regime. This *Velvet Revolution* was followed in 1993 by the *Velvet Divorce*, in which Czechoslovakia broke up into its constituent states. Bratislava became capital of the newly independent Slovak Republic.

Modern City

In the immediate aftermath of the *Velvet Divorce* Bratislava had to battle against its image as the poor relation to Prague. The establishment of a legitimate business community was stifled by a large mafia presence, although the situation improved in the latter part of the 1990s and the local economy has since prospered. Many new restaurant and hotel complexes were constructed following the opening of negotiations in 2000 for Slovakia to join the EU.

Among the most important industries are chemicals, oil, rubber, textiles, electrics and engineering manufactures. Bratislava is on major road and rail networks and the M. R. Stefanik International Airport is 9 km from the city centre. Public transport within the city includes buses, trams and trolley buses.

Places of Interest

The castle, originally built by the Romans but extensively rebuilt in the second half of the twentieth century, dominates the city. Among the leading museums (mostly located in the Old Town) are the national museum, national theatre and national gallery, the municipal museum, and museums devoted to winemaking and folk music. Also popular is the Primates Palace and the Mirbach Palace, an example of Rococo architecture.

Brazzaville, Republic of the Congo

Introduction

The administrative and commercial hub of the country, Brazzaville is on the northern bank of the Congo River. Brazzaville connects to Pointe-Noire, the republic's major seaport, by rail and river.

History

Prior to colonization, Brazzaville, known as Nkuma, was a small settlement of the Téké people. In 1883 the French bought the settlement and its surrounding lands. They named it after the explorer Pierre Savorgnan de Brazza, and used the new town as a point of access to the interior of the Congo basin. Gradually Brazzaville increased in importance and became the capital of French Equatorial Africa in 1903. In the 1930s a railway was built to connect the city with the coast. This led to expansion and increased prosperity.

Further growth followed the decision to make Brazzaville the capital of Free France in sub-Saharan Africa during World War II. After the war, Brazzaville was a focal point for the burgeoning nationalist movement and, in 1960, the city became the capital of the newly independent Congo. This resulted in mass rural migration. In the 1980s unemployment escalated to 50%, and demonstrations, civil unrest and industrial action became common.

Modern City

The port is the terminus of a transport system running from the coast. There are steamer services to the upper Congo river. Brazzaville is linked by ferry to Kinshasa across the 24-km-wide river. Food processing is a major industry, but Brazzaville is primarily an administrative centre.

Brazzaville used to be celebrated for its wide, picturesque boulevards but many of its residential neighbourhoods have been destroyed in conflicts between rival militias. In spite of this devastation Brazzaville remains the commercial and political centre of the country. The Congo-Ocean railway line began operation again in Aug. 2000 after 2 years of suspended service.

Places of Interest

The Poto-Poto School of African Art holds exhibitions of native arts and crafts. Many notable buildings have been destroyed during the civil wars.

Bremen, Germany

Introduction

Bremen is the capital of the Land of Bremen, situated in the northwest of Germany on the River Weser. Long an important trading centre, by the twentieth century it was among Germany's leading industrial and commercial powerhouses.

History

In the eighth century, the, sent troops to convert local tribes to Christianity. In 787 the area was officially recognized as a diocesan town and became the base for Christianization in northern Europe. It was made an archbishopric in 845 and in 888 King Arnulf of East Francia granted the town the right to hold its own market, mint coins and make local laws.

In 1358 Bremen joined the Hanseatic League, an alliance of Northern European trading towns that operated until the seventeenth century. Its location near the point where the Weser flows into the North Sea made it a natural hub for trade. In 1646 it was declared a Free Imperial City. Napoleon invaded in 1811, with French troops occupying until 1813.

Bremen joined the North German Confederation in 1867 and 4 years later became a federal state within the German empire. Allied bombing in the Second World War damaged the city, though many key historical landmarks remain and others were restored or rebuilt. Post-war, Bremen was in the American occupation zone until 1947, when it came under the jurisdiction of the West German government in Bonn.

Modern City

Bremen is a commercial and industrial centre producing ships, cars, steel, machinery, electrical equipment and textiles. It is also one of Europe's most important aerospace hubs and home to major food producing companies including Kellogg's and Kraft. Cotton, wool, tobacco and copper are traded through its thriving river port.

There is a major railway station and an international airport (Flughafen Bremen) lies 3.5 km south of the city. Local transport is provided by the S-Bahn, U-Bahn, buses and Straßenbahn (trams).

Places of Interest

Many of the city's major landmarks are in the Old Town. Around the Marktplatz (Market Square) is the Gothic town hall, a fifteenth century statue of the city's protector Bremen Roland, a twentieth-century bronze sculpture of town musicians based on a Brothers Grimm fairy tale, a Romanesque and gothic cathedral and the eleventh-century Liebfrauenkirche church. Böttcherstrasse, a street linking the Marktplatz and the River Weser, is renowned for its mix of art deco and gothic architecture.

Among the most popular museums are the oyster-shaped Universum Science Center, the Kunsthalle Bremen that houses a collection of nineteenth- and twentieth-century French and German paintings including works by Monet, Manet and Cézanne, and the Bremen Ethnological Museum.

Brest, Belarus

Introduction

On the River Boog, Brest is Belarussia's second city and an important transport and trade hub.

History

Brest first appears in 1019 as Bierascie in the Duchy of Turau. It served as a customs point between Poland, the Baltics and Western Europe. Its pivotal position made it a frequent battleground for Polish and Kievan dukes. It belonged to the Kievan Duchy in 1044, and in the twelfth century became part of the Galich-Valyn Duchy, passing into Lithuanian hands. Slavonic dukes built fortifications, some of which remain today.

The Bierascie Land was invaded by the Mongols in 1240 but returned to the Grand Duchy of Lithuania in the fourteenth century. Teutonic crusaders invaded the city in 1379, after which it became a centre of trade and crafts. Immigration grew, swelling the Jewish population. Bierascie was granted the Magdeburg right of self-government in 1390, which extended into the seventeenth century. During this time Muscovites, Swedes and Poles all invaded.

Brest was annexed as part of the Russian empire in 1795. A widescale Russification process began with the Russians building a fortress (finished in 1842) which was incorporated into the city's coat of arms. From the early eighteenth to the early twentieth centuries, the city was called Brest-Litowsk. In 1863 Kastus Kalinousky led an uprising against the Russian occupation. Brest continued to be a major industrial centre, and by 1890 was an important railway hub between Moscow, Warsaw and other cities of the region. When World War I broke out, it became a centre of military operations. The city was taken by the Germans in 1915 and remained under their control until 1918.

A year later the city was captured by the Poles as they fought against Soviet Russia. The 1921 Treaty of Riga allocated Western Belarus and Ukraine to Polish rule, and the Polish constitution was adopted. Belarusian nationalism was quashed under the Poles as it had been under the Russians.

With the outbreak of World War II the city once again fell captive to Germany. The Jewish population was decimated while Stalinist terror also claimed many lives and much of the city's infrastructure was destroyed.

Modern City

As part of the Soviet Union, Belarus had a leading role in manufacturing and assembly, but much of the industry collapsed along with the USSR. Its importance as a river port remains, and there is much light industry.

Places of Interest

Brest Fortress, which held out against the Nazis for a month in 1941, is among the most visited sights, along with Nikolaivsky church and the St Simon Orthodox Cathedral. There is an archaeological museum with excavations of thirteenth century log cabins. North of the city is Belovezhskaya Pushcha nature reserve, where the documents confirming the dissolution of the USSR in 1991 were signed.

Bridgetown, Barbados

Introduction

The capital of Barbados, Bridgetown nestles on the arc of Carlisle Bay in the southwest of the island. Built on former swampland, it is now an important trade centre and popular tourist destination.

History

The town was founded in 1628 by an Englishman, Charles Wolverstone, sent by the Earl of Carlisle who was then in charge of the Bahamas. The settlement was called Indian Bridge after the bridge already present on the site but was known as St. Michael's Town for a period before receiving its current name around the mid-1650s when a new bridge was constructed.

The city has been subject to a number of natural disasters over the years. In 1667 it was devastated by a major fire and hurricane, and a cycle of drought and excessive rain impacted in the following years. The city suffered numerous other major fires and In 1854 an outbreak of cholera was responsible for 20,000 deaths.

In 1937 the city was the scene of protests over falling sugar prices, during which a local man, Clement Payne, proposed the introduction of trade unions. He was deported prompting the Bajans, the citizens of Barbados, to protest. Rioting lasted for 3 days and inspired the emergence of a nationalist movement, leading ultimately to Bridgetown becoming the capital of an independent Barbados in 1966. Also in the 1960s, the remainder of the swamp was filled in and a deepwater harbour was built.

Modern City

As well as being an active port, Bridgetown's economy is reliant upon tourism, sugar, molasses and rum distilling. The island has international sea and air connections as well as links to nearby islands. Among Bridgetown's most notable inhabitants are Edward Kamau Brathwaite, a writer and historian, Sir Frank Worrell, the first black to captain the West Indies cricket team long term, and Sir Garfield Sobers, who was rated the second greatest cricketer of the twentieth century by Wisden Cricketers' Almanack.

Places of Interest

Bridgetown's main thoroughfare is Broadstreet, which leads on to the islands Parliament Buildings and Trafalgar Square (renamed Heroes Square in 1999). Complete with a statue of Lord Nelson erected in 1813 it pre-dates London's own Trafalgar Square. 1870 saw the construction of St. Michael's Anglican Cathedral, funded by a lottery to replace a cathedral that had been destroyed in a hurricane 90 years earlier.

Brisbane, Australia

Introduction

Brisbane is the capital of Queensland and Australia's third most populous city after Sydney and Melbourne. Lying on the River Brisbane in the southeast of the state, it serves as a major port. Originally established as a penal colony, it is now a popular tourist base attracting visitors to its tropical climate.

History

There is evidence of aboriginal habitation in the region dating back 40,000 years. The British explorer, John Oxley, came to the area in 1823 in search of suitable new locations for settlements. A penal settlement, Moreton Bay, was founded in 1824 in nearby Redcliffe and moved to the site of Brisbane, then part of New South Wales, the following year. Its ready water supply but otherwise inhospitable location made it a natural choice for holding prisoners, and in its early years free settlers were forbidden to come within 50 miles of the site. Originally called Edenglassie, its name was changed to commemorate the former state governor, Sir Thomas Brisbane.

Brisbane received town status in 1834 and in 1842 its role as a detention centre ended and free settlers arrived in large numbers. By the mid-1850s it was the most important port town in the area and, when Queensland was constituted a state in 1859, Brisbane became the capital. By the late 1880s the town had modern and grand buildings to replace the convict-built constructions.

The economy declined in the 1890s and Brisbane endured several major floods but in 1902 it was recognized as a city and prospered again. In the 1920s the City of Greater Brisbane came into being. During the Second World War the city served as the base for the American Gen. Douglas MacArthur, and it was from there that he controlled US operations in the Southwest Pacific Theatre. The city continued to grow, although a flood which struck in Jan. 1974 caused widespread damage and saw 14,000 homes evacuated. Brisbane hosted the 1982 Commonwealth Games and Expo88.

Modern City

The city is an important transport hub and is at the centre of several major road and rail routes. There is an international airport. The economy still relies on the port and related activities, with wool, agricultural products, sugar and foods among the leading exports. Other major industries include shipbuilding, food processing, engineering, oil refineries, rubber, cement and vehicles.

Places of Interest

Brisbane's principal tourist attractions are its outdoor facilities and its proximity to the Gold Coast and Sunshine Coast. Other attractions within the city include Australia's biggest koala sanctuary, the Queensland Art Gallery and the Observatory, originally built by convicts in 1829.

Bristol, United Kingdom of Great Britain and Northern Ireland

Introduction

Bristol is a metropolitan city at the confluence of the rivers Avon and Frome to the east of where the Avon meets the River Severn. Bristol is the largest city in the southwest of England and has a rich maritime history.

History

There is evidence of habitation around Bristol as early as 4000 BC. During Anglo-Saxon times a settlement called Brigstow (the meeting place by the bridge) was established at a fording point across the Frome and Avon Rivers. After the Norman Conquest Bristol traded with ports in south Wales and Ireland. William the Conqueror put Geoffrey of Mowbray in command of the town. But it was the Earl of Gloucester who developed it as a power base.

As Bristol's trading activity increased, the existing port was no longer able to satisfy the city's needs. In 1239 a cut was excavated to divert the course of the Frome. By the fourteenth century the city was trading with Spain, Portugal, the Mediterranean and Iceland. The Hundred Years' War led to the blocking of French trade and the beginning of the trade in Spanish and Portuguese wines. Bristol became England's second port after London and was made a county in 1373.

In 1497 John Cabot, an Italian adventurer financed by Bristol merchants, set sail in *Matthew* to find a passage to the Spice Islands. He actually discovered Newfoundland in Canada, paving the way for Britain's future claim on the region. In 1603 Martin Pring sailed from Bristol to America, discovering the bay that would become Plymouth Harbour. During the English Civil War Bristol was a Royalist stronghold but was captured by Parliamentarian troops in 1645. Bristol was also a hotbed of religious non-conformism and became a major centre for Quakers. In the early-eighteenth century the city was prominent in the rise of John Wesley's Methodist movement.

During the eighteenth century Bristol was heavily involved in the slave trade and, as a result, ships returned to Bristol laden with goods from the New World, including cane sugar, tobacco, rum and cocoa. Bristol grew wealthy from the trade with Britain's western colonies and it was during this period that wealthy merchants built large houses in the suburb of Clifton, away from the docks.

By the nineteenth century the rise of the Lancashire cotton industry, coupled with the shipping limitations of the River Avon, had led to a transfer of maritime trade to Liverpool. However, the shipping industry remained key and during the nineteenth century the city was home to Samuel Plimsoll, inventor of the plimsoll mark which assisted ship loading, and to Isambard Kingdom Brunel, an engineering genius who anticipated the days of the great ocean going liners by designing *SS Great Britain*, *SS Great Western* and *SS Great Eastern*. He was also responsible for the nearby Clifton Suspension Bridge that spans the Avon Gorge. New docks built at the mouth of the Avon and the introduction of the railway system revitalized Bristol's trade in the middle of the nineteenth century, although its greatest days had already passed.

Modern City

The city suffered large-scale damage during World War II bombing raids and has subsequently been rebuilt on modern lines. Bristol's port activities remain integral to the local economy. Other important industries include engineering (especially aircraft), food and drink processing and ceramics. It is a large commercial and tourist centre and a major centre for media industries.

Places of Interest

Among the city's most popular tourist attractions are:

Brunel's *SS Great Britain*, the world's first iron hulled propellered ship, built in Bristol in 1843;
Brunel's Clifton Suspension Bridge, spanning over 240 ft. and finished in 1864;
Bristol Cathedral, founded in 1140 by Robert Fitzhardinge as an Augustinian Abbey;
the Georgian House, built in the late seventeenth century by John Pinney, a successful sugar merchant, and preserved to give an insight into a middle-class household;
the Exploratory, a 'hands on' science museum;
the City Museum and Art Gallery, housing exhibitions of Egyptology, geology, fine art, archaeology, natural history and oriental art.

Brno, Czech Republic

Introduction

Brno is the Czech Republic's second city behind Prague, and the most important in Moravia. It lies on the junction of the Svratka and Svitava Rivers in the southeast of the country, between the Drakanska Highlands to the north and the South Moravian Lowlands to the south. The modern city was founded around AD 1000 and its history has been punctuated by attacks and invasions, though today it is a centre of commerce and education.

History

Archaeological digs have revealed evidence of human habitation in the region around the city dating back 400,000 years, and Celts and Slavs were present in the area from the fifth and sixth centuries AD onwards. The settlement known as Staré Brno (Old Brno), which formed the basis of the current city, was established at the end of the first millennium. Germans took control of the area early in the thirteenth century and in 1243 it became an incorporated city. During this century the imposing Špilberk Castle was rebuilt along Gothic lines and by the fourteenth century the city was under the control of the Moravian Margraves. The heavily fortified city survived sieges by Hussite invaders in both 1428 and 1430 and endured the effects of civil war in 1464 when King Jiří of Poděbrady and Matthias Corvinus (whom Brno supported) clashed for power.

In the sixteenth century the city came under Capuchin and Jesuit influence as the Catholic church attempted to reverse the trend towards Protestantism within the city. In 1643 and 1645 it repelled the attacks of the Swedish forces of Lennart Torstenson during the Thirty Years' War, and was subsequently equipped with new fortifications. Prussia attempted and failed to invade the city in 1742 during the Silesian War of the Austrian Succession, and 35 years later Brno was established as a bishopric. Napoléon did manage an occupation in 1805, and it was just southeast of the city that he masterminded his victory over a united Austro-Russian force at the battle of Austerlitz.

Špilberk Castle was converted into a political prison by the Austrian Habsburgs shortly afterwards and was renowned for its harsh conditions. Brno itself developed as an industrial centre throughout the eighteenth and nineteenth centuries, with the city boundaries expanding to cope with a growing population of engineering and textile workers. However, as the twentieth century approached the friction between Czechs and Germans in the city worsened, culminating with the end of a German majority in the city authorities in 1919. During World War II Brno was badly damaged by Nazi forces and a large number of the German population were removed from the city in the aftermath of the war. It went into economic and cultural stagnation under the subsequent communist regime, the effects of which it is still suffering.

Modern City

Brno is well served by rail links, has an international airport and is connected to Prague, Vienna, Bratislava and Ostrava by road. Commercially, the textile and armaments industries remain vital (the Bren gun originated here), and the manufacture of engineering goods, furniture and soap are also important. It is a major centre for trade fairs, hosting a particularly large annual machinery fair, and is home to six universities including Masaryk University, founded in 1919.

Places of Interest

The heart of the old city is a network of narrow, intertwined streets, surrounded by an area of wide boulevards and open space which leads on to more modern suburban developments. Among the city's most notable past inhabitants are Johann Gregor Mendel (the nineteenth century father of modern genetics), Leoš Janáček (the composer who died in 1928), Bohuslav Fuchs (an influential architect) and Tomáš Masaryk (Czechoslovakia's first president, who studied in Brno in 1865–66).

Brugge (Bruges), Belgium

Introduction

Brugge (Bruges) is located in the northwest of Belgium, some 16 km (10 miles) south of its seaport Zebrugge.

History

The city started life as a landing place on the Zwijn estuary (indeed its name is thought to stem from the Old Norse word for landing stage) and was mentioned in historical records as early as the seventh century. Following the evangelical mission to the city by St Eligius, the city was fortified against the threat of Viking raiders. It was to become the most important fortification in the region.

By the thirteenth century Brugge had secured a monopoly on English wool which allowed it to profit from the production of Flemish cloth, a high quality woollen material that was highly prized in medieval Europe. In 1384 control of Brugge passed to the Duke of Burgundy, and the city emerged as the most important trading centre in northern Europe. Following the death of Mari of Burgundy in 1482, the citizens rebelled against her husband. International traders, like the Burgundian court, began to abandon the city. The sixteenth century witnessed some recovery, but Antwerp had replaced Brugge as the region's principal centre of commerce, and the Dutch Revolt was to culminate in the city losing all its former wealth and becoming a poverty-stricken backwater. The French novelist Georges Rodenbach was to describe Brugge as decaying but mysterious in his famous novel *Bruges La Morte*.

The city's revival did not come about until the inauguration of the port of Zebrugge in 1907. Following the liberation from Nazi occupation in 1944, Brugge began to re-establish itself as a place of commercial and cultural importance. By the end of the twentieth century it had transformed itself into a prosperous city.

Modern City

Brugge today is served by a number of major roads, railways and canals. It depends largely on tourism for its income, but there is a growing industrial section to the north which manufactures ships, industrial glass, electronic goods, dies and yeast. Spinning, lace making and weaving, the traditional handcrafts of Brugge, still continue but the products are mainly sold as souvenirs. Brugge was made one of the European Capitals of Culture for 2002.

Places of Interest

Brugge was designated cultural capital of Europe for 2002. The ancient medieval centre with its Gothic spires and cobbled marketplace are perfectly suited to cultural pageantry, a famous example of which is found in the Procession of Holy Blood, held every year on Ascension Day. Amongst Brugge's numerous chapels and churches is The Chapel of the Holy Blood (so called because it contains a casket said to hold a few drops of Christ's blood) and the twelfth century Cathedral of St. Salvator. The city is also enriched by Flemish architecture—notably the béguinage and the fifteenth century Gruuthuse mansion. The Memling Museum and the Groeninge museum both house fine collections of Flemish art.

Brussels, Belgium

Introduction

Belgium's capital lies on the River Siene in the centre of the country. Having once been among the most important capitals in the Habsburg Empire, Brussels is today one of Europe's most cosmopolitan and politically influential cities. Occupied twice by hostile German forces during the twentieth century, it now houses the headquarters of NATO and numerous important EU institutions. It is officially a bilingual city with both French and Flemish co-existing, though French is more common.

History

Brussels grew out of a Gallic-Roman settlement around the seventh century and its location on trade routes between Ghent, Bruges and various German towns ensured its growth throughout the early Middle Ages. Charles of France settled in the area in 977 AD and began the construction of a fortress on the site 2 years later. 979 is thus seen as the city's foundation year. The city would prosper over the ensuing centuries, its economy based on the manufacture of fine quality textiles. The city came under the rule of the dukes of

Brabant during the fourteenth century, and was named capital of the Duchy in 1383. The Duchy of Burgundy swallowed up Brabant in the following years and it was under Burgundian influence that the city gained a reputation as a centre of culture and a seat of learning. In 1421 a workers' revolt led to the workers' guilds obtaining some political influence in the city's administration but by 1477 Brussels was about to embark upon a long period under Habsburg control.

The guilds had their political power withdrawn in 1528 and 2 years later Brussels was made the capital of the Netherlands (comprising the modern Netherlands and Belgium). By the middle of the century the Spanish Habsburgs dominated the city, though Calvinists briefly took control between 1577–85. It subsequently fell under the control of the Austrian Habsburgs before the French attacked in 1695. Unsuccessful in this attempt, they would seize Brussels and cause massive damage in the process under Napoléon in 1793. It remained in French hands until the end of the Napoleonic Wars in 1815. Brussels became central to Belgium's growing nationalist movement and following a revolution in 1830 it was named capital of the new state of Belgium the following year. The remainder of the century witnessed the rapid expansion of the city, both in terms of buildings (the old city walls were knocked down, waterways covered, sewers constructed) and population. Brussels was occupied by Germany throughout World War I and, after a period of regeneration during the 1930s, fell to Nazi forces in May 1940 until Sept. 1944.

Modern City

Reforms between 1970–93 provided Belgium with a federal structure with Brussels at its heart. In addition, its roles as NATO headquarters and EU capital have ensured rapid city growth and one of the most culturally mixed populations in Europe. Immigrants and foreign workers account for around 25% of the population. NATO and the EU provide much of the city's employment but other important industries include steel, chemicals, electronics, textiles, brewing and food processing (Brussels has an international reputation for its beer, frites and chocolate). Brussels serves as a major railway junction and has an international airport as well as buses, trams and an overground/undergound metro hybrid within the city.

Places of Interest

The Old Town houses many of the most popular tourist sites, including the fine medieval square Grand Place, the Gothic Town Hall, Manneken-Pis (a statue of a urinating child) and numerous galleries and museums. Among the most celebrated cultural figures to have emerged from Brussels are the artists Rogier van der Weyden and Pieter Brueghel, the architects Henri van de Velde and Victor Horta, and the cartoonist who created TinTin, Hergé. The Lower Town is home to many commercial institutions, including countless banks and a stock exchange, while the Upper Town is the location for most of the government buildings. The Bruxellois now inhabit a confident, vibrant and international city that has succeeded in integrating its modern role with its long and varied history.

Bucharest (Bucuresti), Romania

Introduction

Bucharest is Romania's capital and is located on the banks of the River Dambovita in the southeast of the country. Its history goes back to the fourteenth century when it rose to prominence as a city on the trade routes between Turkey and the rest of Europe. Romania's major political, cultural and commercial centre, it was re-designed and expanded during the communist era, particularly under Nicolae Ceauşescu. It received worldwide media attention in 1989 as the Ceauşescu regime collapsed.

History

There is evidence of prehistoric habitation in the region around Bucharest. In the fifteenth century it was the location of a fortress built by Vlad III (Vlad the Impaler) to protect the lands of Walachia against Turkish attack. The Ottomans ultimately took control of the region and in 1659 Bucharest became capital of Walachia. The city thrived commercially and many professional guilds were established.

The 1812 Treaty of Bucharest left Walachia and Moldavia under Turkish dominion but the city became a hotbed of discontent. The unpopular reign of the Phanariotes (a section of Constantinople's ruling class) was ended by a rebellion in 1821 and in 1859 Walachia and Moldavia were unified. Three years later Bucharest was proclaimed capital of the newly conceived Romania. It gained international recognition at the end of the Russo-Turkish war in 1878 and then grew rapidly.

Bucharest was occupied by troops of the Central Powers during World War I but Romania benefitted from subsequent peace treaties and the city's power and influence increased. Romania allied with Germany in World War II but by the end of the war it was under Soviet control and in 1948 Bucharest became capital of the communist People's Republic of Romania. Huge building projects were undertaken by successive communist regimes and the city has been criticized for its brutal, if grand, buildings.

Under Ceauşescu the construction of monumental buildings and boulevards continued, even though it put an unbearable strain on Bucharest's economy, which like the rest of the country was weak from mismanagement. His greatest folly was the People's Palace, started in 1984 and still incomplete at the time of his death in 1989. The location selected for the Palace was an area of the city untouched by the 1977 earthquake and some 10,000 hectares was flattened to make space for it. 700 architects and over 20,000 labourers worked on the building, with plans regularly altered to serve the whim of the Ceauşescu family. The Palace sapped the city's finances and a nationwide embargo was placed on the export of the marble, crystal and wood required for decoration. With 1,100 rooms, it is the world's second largest building and is widely disliked by the city's population who regard it as a monument to Ceauşescu excess.

In 1989 popular discontent led to the overthrow and execution of Nicolae Ceauşescu and his wife, but not before troops had killed several dozen protesters. It was only after his death that the low standard of living in Bucharest and the country at large came to light.

Modern City

The city's economy is still struggling to grow and its most important industries include oil refining, chemical, clothing, food processing and engineering. It is on major road and rail routes and has a local and an international airport while a three-line metro system is in operation within the city. Tourism is important, although Bucharest retains a façade of austerity.

Places of Interest

Bucharest's most popular attraction is the People's Palace (now called Parliamentary Palace) while the old Museum of the Communist Party is now the Peasant Museum (1996 winner of the Council of Europe's European Museum of the Year award). The Village Museum is one of the earliest examples of an ethnographic museum and the Csimigiu Gardens are popular in summer. There are numerous galleries, museums and churches. The city's main thoroughfare is Calea Victoriei (Victory Street).

Budapest, Hungary

Introduction

Hungary's capital and seat of government came into being in 1873 when the three towns of Buda, Pest and Obuda were amalgamated. Lying on the banks of the River Danube in the north of Hungary, Buda, on the hilly west bank, is the site of the historical castle and many tourist attractions, whereas Pest, on the flat east bank, is the cultural, administrative and commercial centre and home to the national Parliament. A number of bridges and an underground connect the two sides.

History

There is evidence of neolithic habitation in the region, and the Celts established a settlement nearby. The Romans then founded a town, Aquincum, the ruins of which may still be seen. When Rome's authority ended in the fifth century the town came under the control of Huns, Visigoths, Longobards and Avars. Hungarian Magyars settled around the ninth century.

After the Mongol invasion in the mid-thirteenth century saw Pest ravaged, King Béla IV built a walled town and a royal palace on the site of the present castle in Buda. The town's fortunes boomed under the rule of Matthias I, who came to power in 1458 but a decline followed his death in 1490. After the battle of Mohács in 1541, Buda was taken by Turks who settled there. They were driven out in the late seventeenth century by troops of the Holy Roman Empire, but by then Buda had no more than 1,000 inhabitants.

In 1703 Emperor Leopold I designated Buda and Pest as royal free towns. The population was boosted by an influx of Serbs, Germans and Slovaks and the first bridge to be built across the Danube linking Buda and Pest, the Chain Bridge commissioned by Count Széchenyi, was constructed. Maria Theresa built a new royal palace around 1760 and the two towns prospered under the Hapsburgs, becoming the national centres for administration, law and education.

Despite their combined power, Buda and Pest remained distinct entities, and their differences became more evident as the nineteenth century progressed. While Buda clung to its aristocratic, Germanic heritage, Pest was key to the growth of the national consciousness. Rebellion broke out in Pest in 1848 and Buda was besieged the following year. The dual Austro-Hungarian monarchy inflicted a harsh rule but after the Compromise of 1867, industrialization took hold and led to a flourishing of trade. Five years later the city of Buda-Pest came into being. The city built Europe's first underground system in 1896.

After World War I, Béla Kun led an ill-fated communist regime for 4 months before he was overthrown. The city set about rebuilding itself but was ravaged again at the end of World War II in fighting between German and Soviet troops. A quarter of the city was destroyed. Budapest was rebuilt and expanded during the 1950s and was the focus of world attention in 1956 when it was the scene of an uprising against the nation's communist regime. Soviet troops crushed the rebellion, killing many protesters and causing still more structural damage.

Modern City

Hungary remained one of the Eastern Bloc's more economically liberal states and Budapest was commercially more successful than many other communist cities. When the movement for reform swept through Eastern Europe during the late 1980s, Budapest was once more at the forefront for change. Protests centred on the city during 1989 led to the fall of the communist regime. Economic expansion was gaining pace as the twentieth century came to an end.

Major industries include engineering, chemicals, clothing, food processing and metallurgy. Hungary's road and rail networks centre on Budapest and it is the location of the country's major airport. A free port lies in the suburb of Csepel and trams and an efficient and cheap metro system operate within Budapest. Tourism has grown in recent years.

Places of Interest

Divided into 23 districts, the city's most popular attractions are in the Castle District, incorporating the medieval Old Town and the Royal Palace. Many museums and galleries, including the National Gallery, are housed in this area. Andrássy utca, an opulent boulevard, is the location of the Opera House and the Museum of Fine Arts. Also popular are the public thermal baths, many of which were built by the Turks.

Buenos Aires, Argentina

Introduction

On the south bank of the River Plate 240 km inland from the Atlantic Ocean, Buenos Aires is the largest city in Argentina and the largest city in South America outside Brazil. The economic, cultural, academic and industrial centre of Argentina, Buenos Aires has one of the world's largest ports.

History

The area was originally inhabited by the Querandí, a nomadic people. In 1536 the first settlement, Nuestra Señora del Buen Ayre, was established by Pedro de Mendoza, the first governor of the Río de la Plata region. It lasted 5 years before Querandí resistance forced its abandonment. The city was refounded by Juan de Garay in 1580. He constructed the Plaza del Fuerte, now the Plaza de Mayo. The original foundations were developed in a grid pattern, in the style of most Latin America colonial cities. In its early years its economy relied on ranching and illegal trade with the English and Portuguese, in defiance of Spanish mercantile restrictions. For the first two centuries of its existence, Buenos Aires was inferior to Córdoba. Nonetheless, its position as a port facilitated steady growth. At the beginning of the eighteenth century, there was a flourishing illegal export of cereals and leather to Brazil and the Caribbean. In 1776 when Buenos Aires had 24,000 inhabitants it was made capital of the Viceroyalty of River Plate.

Buenos Aires resisted British incursions in 1806 and 1807. In May 1810 the first Junta was established following revolts against colonial rule. Independence was achieved in 1816. Buenos Aires was made capital of the United Provinces of the Río de la Plata, encompassing modern day Argentina, Bolivia, Paraguay and Uruguay. Continued war with Spain sent Buenos Aires into decline in the middle part of the nineteenth century, coinciding with the removal of the city's capital status. Following years of civil war between *porteños* (Buenos Aires' inhabitants) and inland provinces, Buenos Aires was reinstated as capital in 1862. At the end of the nineteenth century Argentina's agricultural potential began to be exploited while immigration soon tripled to make Buenos Aires the largest city in Latin America. Most immigrants arrived from Spain and Italy but there were significant numbers from Eastern Europe, Germany and Britain. The influx contributed to the strong European influence still present in modern Buenos Aires. From the 1930s onwards European migration was replaced by people from the rural north of the country, Bolivia, Paraguay and Uruguay. These contributed to a large unskilled and unemployed population who inhabited the outlying *villas miserias*, or shanty towns.

Modern City

Buenos Aires comprises over 50 barrios. The city is Argentina's economic heartland. Eight kilometres in length, the port handles a third of Argentina's maritime activity. Buenos Aires is the home of banking and finance and has its own stock market. Industries include chemicals, oils, metallurgy and the processing of beef and grains. Meat packing plants are situated by the docks. Buenos Aires' main exports are beef and wool. The principal university is the Universidad de Buenos Aires, founded in 1821. The city is well served by sea, air, rail and road. Rail connections link Buenos Aires to the Pampas, Chile and Bolivia. Colectivos, or microbuses, facilitate innercity movement. The Aeropuerto Internacional Ezeiza in Matanza is 35 km south of the city while Don Torcuato Airport in Tigre caters for international flights. Both are linked with the city by expressways. To the north is the Aeroparque Jorge Newbery, for domestic flights. Buenos Aires' underground system, built in 1913, serves part of the city.

Places of Interest

The *Microcentro* is the site of the original settlement with the Plaza de Mayo is at its heart. Situated on the Plaza is the Cathedral. Originally dating from 1593, it was rebuilt in 1689–1791 and designed by the Italian architect Antonio Masella. Fellow Italian architects Andrea Bianchi and Giovanni Battista Primoli created the cathedral's façade, and the former designed other churches in the city such as Nuestra Señora del Pilar in 1732. The cathedral contains the tomb of Argentina's liberator, José de San Martín. Also in the Plaza are the eighteenth century Cabildo (Town Hall) and the Casa Rosada (Government House). Neo-classical in style and known for its perfect acoustics, the famous opera house, Teatro Colón, was designed by Italian architect Vittorio Meano, completed by Belgian architect Jules Formal and opened in 1908. Of Argentina's many museums, the Museo Nacional de Bellas Artes contains works by nineteenth and twentieth century Argentine artists as well as Renoir, Monet and Van Gogh. Other museums include the Museo Nacional de Arte Decorativo, the Museo Histórico Nacional and the Casa Nacional del Bicentenario.

Bujumbura, Burundi

Introduction

Bujumbura is the capital of Burundi and of Bujum province. It is Burundi's largest city and its main administrative and commercial centre.

History

Once a small village known as Usumbura, in 1899 Bujumbura became a military outpost for the German army. In 1923 it was made the administrative centre for the Belgian League of Nations mandate of Ruanda-Urundi. On gaining independence in 1962, Burundi changed the name of its capital city to Bujumbura.

In the decades following independence Bujumbura became a scene of conflict between the country's two main ethnic groups, with fighting taking place between the Tutsi-dominated army and Hutu rebels. Attacks in July 2003 by rebel soldiers of the Hutu-dominated Forces Nationales de Libération (FNL) led to calls for a UN peacekeeping force to support existing AU forces.

Modern City

Main industries include: cement, textiles, chemicals and food products. Bujumbura is also the trade centre for the region's agricultural produce.

The city is connected by road and rail to the Congo and Rwanda and acts as Burundi's main port. There is an international airport located 10 km from the city.

Places of Interest

The city is home to the University of Burundi (founded 1960).

Bukhara, Uzbekistan

Introduction

Capital of the Bukhara region, Bukhara (meaning 'monastery' in Sanskrit) is in the Zeravshan River valley. One of the oldest trade centres in the Central Asian region, it has a rich architectural heritage.

History

Established in the fifth century BC and conquered by Alexander the Great, Bukhara was later under the rule of the Kushan empire. Taken by Arab conquerors in the early eighth century, by which time it was a thriving trading town, in the ninth century it was designated capital of the Samanid lands. During the following century it attracted many great poets and scientists.

Bukhara was subsequently ruled by the Qarakhanids and the Karakitais, fell to the Mongols under Genghis Khan in the early thirteenth century and to Timur (heading a Turkish-Mongol force) around 1370. Taken by the Shaybanids at the start of the sixteenth century, it was designated capital of the khanate of Bukhara. The city reached its zenith under Shaybanid rule at the end of the sixteenth century. In 1868 it was ceded, along with the rest of the khanate, to Russia, although the emir still reigned.

Soviets deposed the emir in 1920 and Bukhara became part of the Bukharan People's Soviet Republic before it joined the Uzbek Soviet Socialist Republic 4 years later. The discovery of natural gas sparked an economic boom in the 1950s. In 1991, after the collapse of the USSR, Bukhara became part of independent Uzbekistan.

Modern City

Light industries, such as textile manufacture (particularly from fleeces), dominate the economy. Bukhara rugs, however, actually originate in Ashgabat in Turkmenistan. Also important are food processing and cottage industries such as gold embroidery. The city's location on a natural gas field is also exploited.

The city is served by road, rail and air links.

Places of Interest

Bukhara has over 140 listed buildings. The mausoleum of Ismail Samani dates from the tenth century, while the Kalan Minaret from 1127 was once Asia's tallest. Also impressive is the seventeenth century Labi-hauz, a plaza built around a pool, and there are several enclosed bazaars. The Ark is the ancient city fortress, believed to date from the first century AD but rebuilt in the sixteenth, while the Ulugh Beg, Mir-e 'Arab, Kukeldash Kukeldash and Abdul al-Aziz Khan madrasahs span the fifteenth to seventeenth centuries.

Bulawayo, Zimbabwe

Introduction

The second largest city and principal industrial centre, Bulawayo lies along the Matsheumlope River in the southwest of the country. It is a national distribution point and rail centre. The name means 'place of slaughter'.

History

In 1834 the Ndebele, or Matabele, tribes attacked the Rozwi and made Gubulawayo their kraal (headquarters) under King Lobengula. Cecil Rhodes founded the British South Africa Company and Lobengula signed an agreement allowing Rhodes and the British to set up a mining settlement. However the British gradually encroached on more land than was agreed and when Lobengula and his people protested in 1893 he was defeated and killed whilst fleeing the area. In 1894 the village was moved 5 km (3 miles) south to its current location, declared a town and became known as Bulawayo. In 1897 it became a municipality and in 1943, a city. The streets were built in a grid pattern, wide enough to allow a team of sixteen oxen to make a full turn. A rail link was added in 1897. It was the first city to embark on a water supply programme, the first to provide educational facilities and the first to introduce low-cost housing.

Modern City

Major products include cars, tyres, concrete and building materials, radios, furniture and food. Industries include printing, publishing and brewing. As headquarters of the Zimbabwe railways, it is the major centre for goods moving to and from South Africa. However a number of factories have closed following the economic disaster of the 2000s, and many industries remain in crisis. Several companies have relocated to South Africa, particularly in the food sector. The Bulawayo Technical College was founded in 1927.

Places of Interest

The Natural History Museum in Centenary Park has a mammal collection of over 75,000 specimens. Also located here are artifacts from the Khami Ruins National Monument, designated a World Heritage Site in 1986. The Railway Museum depicts the history of the country's railways and features the Pullman car that brought Cecil Rhodes' body from Cape Town to his burial in the nearby Matobos National Park. The Mzilikazi Arts and Crafts Centre, established in 1963, is located on the outskirts of the town.

Busan, South Korea

Introduction

The second city of South Korea, Pusan, is rarely referred to in the West by its Korean name Busan. The city is South Korea's principal commercial port and is also a ferry terminus for Japan and Jeju Island. Although Pusan escaped occupation by Communist forces in the Korean War (1950–53), it has few ancient buildings. The city's principal attraction is its fine coastal location, backed by mountains.

History

Pusan lacks the history of other large Korean cities. There was settlement in this region, on the extreme south-eastern tip of the Korean peninsula, more than 4,000 years ago, but no city emerged where Pusan now stands. By the seventh century AD the port had grown important enough to acquire a large temple complex.

A city gradually developed over the next 400 years and gained fortifications. Pusan became an important port and the entry point to Korea from Japan. In 1592–93, a Japanese invasion destroyed much of Pusan. At the beginning of the eighteenth century, major fortifications were built on Geumjeongsan mountain just outside the city. This stronghold took 100 years to complete, but by the nineteenth century it had become obsolete.

Korea's hermit-like existence was shattered in the nineteenth century when foreign traders and missionaries were able to penetrate the country. In 1876, Pusan was open to trade with Japan. Seven years later, shipping from other nations was also allowed into Pusan's harbour. Pusan was the main gateway to Korea for Japanese forces when Japan's occupation of Korea began in 1910. Under Japanese rule, Pusan grew rapidly. It became a modern commercial and ferry port and an industrial centre. At the end of World War II Pusan's population was swollen by returning Koreans repatriated from Japan.

The city's population grew again during the Korean War (1950–53) when 4 m. refugees flooded into Pusan from further north, attempting to escape the advance of the Communist armies. The Korean government took refuge in the city, which became the temporary capital of Korea after the Communists gained Seoul in 1950. Pusan, the headquarters of the U.S.-led UN forces that embarked in Korea, was besieged by Communist forces in Aug. and Sept. 1950. The battle along the defensive lines north of the city had a greater number of casualties than any other in the Korean War.

Modern City

Pusan is a bustling port and centre of commerce. The port is divided into two by an island: the smaller western section is Korea's largest fishing port; the eastern basin is a ferry port and the fifth largest container port in the world. The city's industries include electrical and electronic engineering, vehicles, shipbuilding, chemicals and paper. Pusan has a subway system, an international airport (Kimhae) and is a road and rail route centre. The city has two principal universities, several other tertiary colleges and is the venue of an annual international film festival.

Places of Interest

Pusan is the main seaside resort in Korea: Haeundae Beach, 14 km from the city centre, can be reached by subway and is often crowded.

The main tourist sight near the city centre is the Beomeosa temple complex, the largest in Korea. An oasis of tranquillity, Beomeosa dates from the seventh century, but most of the temple was rebuilt in the seventeenth century. The main gateway, hall and belfry are among the finest examples of Buddhist architecture in Korea.

Busan's tallest building is Tower A of the Haeundae Doosan We've the Zenith, a complex of three residential towers completed in 2011. The tallest of the three has 80 storeys and is 300 m high. Geumjeongsanseong fortress, 790 m above the city, offers a panoramic view. The largest fortress in Korea, eighteenth-century Geumjeongsanseong has impressive walls and gates. The fort is reached by cable car from a park, which houses the city's zoo, aquarium and botanical gardens.

Cairo, Egypt

Introduction

Egypt's capital and the largest city in Africa and the Middle East, Cairo lies on the River Nile's east bank, south of the Nile Delta. Among the world's most important Islamic centres, it has been granted World Heritage Site status by UNESCO. Its sprawling landscape reflects the vicissitudes of Egyptian history since the city's conception over 1,000 years ago. The city's official Arabic name refers to the Fatimid conquest and translates as 'The Conqueror' or 'The Victorious', though it is more popularly known among Cairenes as Masr, which refers to the city but also to the Egyptian homeland itself.

History

Although Cairo's roots lie with the Fatimid invasion of Egypt in AD 969, there had been a city (Memphis) not far from the site of Cairo from around 3100 BC and the Romans had established the city of Babylon (now part of Cairo) in the first century AD. Babylon's fortress tower may still be seen. In AD 641 a new military camp, named al-Fusat, was soon a thriving port that was to expand greatly over the coming centuries. Jawhar, the Fatimid general, established another settlement a little to the north in 969. Known as al-Qahirah, it became the Fatimid dynasty's capital in 973. During the Crusades of the latter half of the twelfth century, al-Fusat was abandoned by Cairo's Islamic defenders, led by Salah el-Din (better known as Saladin).

Saladin established the Ayyubid dynasty, during which time Cairo became an imperial capital. New buildings and city walls were constructed, some using stone from the Pyramids, and building commenced on the Citadel, a raised fortress that still exists. By 1260 the Ayyubids had given way to the Mameluks, a class of influential slaves and former slaves. During this dynasty, Cairo established itself as one of the great world cities. The course of the Nile actually moved further west around this time, freeing up land for further expansion. By 1340 the city had half a million inhabitants, the economy boomed on the back of the spice trade and al-Azhar University was the world's most important centre of Islamic study. However, the spice trade was to diminish, natural disaster, including the plague, struck and in 1516 the Mameluks fell to the Ottomans.

The Ottomans ruled a massive empire, of which Cairo was a minor part. The Mameluks stayed in power as the local authority, but the city became neglected and the economy struggled. That said, a new merchant class emerged and prospered, which led to some significant building work. In 1796 the Cairenes rebelled against the Ottomans. Napoléon arrived a year later, bringing some of the benefits of European scholarliness (it was during this time that the Rosetta Stone was deciphered) but also the mistreatment of the Islamic people. He left in 1799 and the Ottomans and French jockeyed for power over the next few years until the British invasion of 1807.

An Ottoman officer, the Albanian Mohamed Ali, generated enough support to defeat the British forces and in 1811 he massacred over 500 Mameluk leaders, leaving him in sole charge of the country. During his reign, new quarters sprang up in Cairo, influenced by Parisian city planning, and various infrastructures, including barrages, were set in place. As a tribute to himself, the grand Mosque of Mohamed Ali was built and the city remained prosperous under his successor, Abbas. Under the reign of Ismail (1863–79) the building continued, the Suez Canal was inaugurated and the arts given hefty patronage. However, crippling debts forced him to abdicate and heralded the British occupation of 1882. Under the British, new infrastructures, including electricity, were established and more suburbs built, but Arab nationalism was on the rise. Cairene protests in the aftermath of the First World War over the enforced exile of the nationalist Said Zaghloul led to a British u-turn. The Arab League was formed in the city in 1945 and threatened civil action a year later which forced British troops to leave the city. Further violent protests in 1952 paved the way for the complete British withdrawal from Egypt.

Modern City

Since the British withdrawal, more suburbs and satellite towns have appeared, though the housing problem remains acute. The death of over 500 people in an earthquake in 1992 highlighted the poor condition of many buildings. Unemployment is also rife and pollution represents a genuine threat to public health. The economy relies on its position as the country's centre of government, finance, trade and manufacturing. It remains a vital port and major industries include textiles, steel, consumer products and fruit and vegetable processing. Cairo has road, rail, sea and air links and in the city there are trams, buses and an underground system.

Places of Interest

Despite a number of Islamic fundamentalist attacks on Western visitors in recent years, tourism is still a major earner. Among the numerous attractions are the Great Pyramids of Giza and the Sphinx (to the southwest of the city), the treasure-laden National Museum, the Museum of Islamic Art and the Coptic Museum, the National Library, Zoological Gardens, the Citadel, many mosques including those of Ibn Tulun and Mohamed Ali, the bustling bazaars and the macabre City of the Dead (an area of elaborate tombs and cemeteries inhabited by thousands of squatters).

Calgary, Canada

Introduction

Calgary is situated on the edge of the Great Plains, at the confluence of the Bow and Elbow rivers. Originally home to the Blackfoot, Sarcee and Stoney Indians, modern Calgary is one of the youngest major cities in Canada.

History

Founded in 1875 as the North West Mounted Police post Fort Brisebois, the lands were first explored by fur traders working for the Hudsons Bay Company and the Northwest Company (which were later to merge). The first settler and rancher in Calgary was Sam Livingston who settled in the early 1870s after returning from the California Gold Rush of 1849.

Whiskey traders arrived in the area around this time, selling their wares to native Indians and white settlers, a trade which inevitably led to trouble.

To solve the problem the first North West Mounted police stockade in the West was established, changing its name to Fort Calgary in 1876.

The town first began to take off with the arrival of the Canadian Pacific Railway in 1883, which quickly attracted British farmers and ranchers as well as US ranchers, whose own lands had become overgrazed.

In 1896 the transcontinental railroad began carrying passengers and freight to the Pacific Ocean, and the city began to grow quickly being a jumping off point for new settlers in the area. The city became a major commercial centre as agricultural goods were sold for eastern consumption, and the farmers bought manufactured goods, brought from the east by the railroad.

Fires had destroyed much of the town by 1886 leading to an edict stating any new building must be constructed of sandstone. By 1895 the city was awarded city status.

The town's main purpose was as an agricultural processing and distribution centre.

The city's economic expansion was largely due to the rich oil and gas deposits in the nearby Turner Valley in 1914 and Leduc in 1947. The city's first refinery was opened in 1923 and by 1950 its population had doubled.

Modern City

The oil crisis of the 1970s stimulated the city's growth further, becoming a world energy centre and the headquarters for some four hundred oil industry and service businesses.

The city's population grew from 325,000 in 1974 to 650,000 by the early 1980s.

The boom also led to the building of much of the city's downtown skyscrapers, which dominate the city centre.

The boom largely ended in 1981 with the 'National Energy Program' (NEP) legislation created by Finance Minister Jean Chrétien (who also later served as Canada's prime minister), unfairly sucking over $100 billion in oil industry profits from the West. The recession the NEP caused forced Albertans to diversify their economy away from oil and gas, and is responsible for recent booms in the forestry, tourism and technology sectors of the economy.

The city is now the second largest city in Alberta with its location near the Trans-Canada Highway and two transcontinental railways ensuring continuing growth.

Calgary's development was consolidated in 1988 when it hosted the Winter Olympic Games.

Places of Interest

Calgary's premier attraction is the Glenbow Museum, the most renowned of a number of special interest museums. The Calgary Tower, opposite the Glenbow, gives the best view of the city and its hinterland. In addition, a number of attractions lie outside the city centre, including Fort Calgary, Heritage Park and the Calgary Zoo.

Canberra, Australia

Introduction

On a plain on the banks of the Molonglo River in southeast Australia, Canberra was selected as a compromise capital to appease rival factions in Sydney and Melbourne. The Australian Capital Territory (ACT) of 2,356 sq. metres, around 40% of which now constitutes Namadgi National Park, was established on 1 Jan. 1911. Canberra and its suburbs account for 2% of Australia's GDP and 2% of the country's population.

History

Aborigines have lived on the land occupied by Canberra since 12,000 BC. The first Europeans arrived in 1824 when Joshua John Moore established a settlement in the shadow of Black Mountain. He reputedly coined the name Canberry after hearing Aboriginals refer to the area as Corroboree, which means a meeting of rivers or tribes. The name had evolved into Canberra by 1836 but it was not until 1913 that it was formally adopted.

After the area of Yass-Canberra was chosen as the site for the capital in the early part of the twentieth century, a competition for city designs was won by Chicagoan Walter Burley Griffin, assisted by his wife Marion Mahony, the world's first female licensed architect. Influenced by Frank Lloyd Wright, with whom Walter had worked, they proposed designs based on the City Beautiful and Garden City movements, incorporating spacious buildings and avenues and designated green areas. The Griffins proposed a city that would provide for 25,000 people with potential for a further 50,000; the current population is closer to 380,000.

On 12 March 1913 Canberra's foundation stone was laid. 14 years later the federal parliament re-located from its Melbourne home. The building of the city was interrupted by the onset of the First World War and then by lack of finances and opposition to the Griffins' plans. Government departments were still dispersed between Canberra, Melbourne and Sydney during the Second World War. In 1957 the National Capital Development Commission (NCDC) was established to take matters in hand and work gathered momentum. Griffin's plans were revisited in the construction of a 'parliamentary triangle' of avenues and bridges around Capital Hill and the creation of Lake Burley Griffin by damming the Molonglo in 1964. An influx of public service personnel throughout the 1960s brought housing issues to a head and, over the following years, the satellite towns of Woden (1964), Belconnen (1967), Weston Creek (1969), Tuggeranong (1973) and Gungahlin (1975) were built.

Modern City

A new parliament house was opened after 10 years of construction in May 1988 by Queen Elizabeth II. At the apex of the Parliamentary Triangle, the House's 81 metre four-legged flagpole is one of the largest steel structures in the world.

The government employs some 45% of Canberra's residents and accounts for 26% of the city's economy. Other key industries are retail, property, and business (13% of Gross State Product) and construction (12%). The chamber of commerce, established in 1932, has 1,300 members. Biotechnology is a notable growth area.

At Dec. 2000, 73% of ACT residents aged 15–69 were in employment, with 28% of the workforce possessing a degree or higher qualification. There are four higher education institutions in the city. The Australian National University, with 7,600 students, was founded in 1946. The University of Canberra was established as a university in 1989 and has 9,000 students. The Australian Defence Force Academy, formed in 1986 as part of the University of New South Wales, has a student population of 1,700. The Australian Catholic University, set up in 1991, also has a campus in Canberra. Other tertiary institutions include an Institute of Technology with 19,000 students.

The Australian Institute of Sport was opened in 1981. Around half of the Australian medallists at the 2000 Olympics and Paralympics were trained at the Institute. Bruce Stadium, built in 1977 with an 11,500 capacity, hosted the Olympic football. There are nine public golf courses around the city and parts of the capital are used for motor rallies such as the GMC 400. Canberrans are keen rugby fans, and the state invested $A17m. in sport during 2001–02.

The capital is home to the National Archives and the sound and screen archive, ScreenSound Australia. At the National Botanic Gardens, opened in

1933, 90,000 native plants from 5,500 species are cultivated and catalogued. In 2001–02, the Canberran government spent $A22.8 m. on the environment and heritage. Key civic institutions include the Royal Mint, National Library, National Gallery, and the architecturally contentious High Court, dubbed 'Gar's Mahal' after Sir Garfield Barwick, Chief Justice during its 1980 opening.

While the capital has yet to catch the collective imagination in the manner of Melbourne or Sydney, it has a symphony orchestra, festivals celebrating science, music, flowers, and multiculturalism, and over 300 restaurants. A water jet commemorating James Cook's discovery of Australia fires 250 litres of Lake Burley Griffin to a height of 147 metres every second. The lake is popular for water sports and steamboat trips and provides spectacular scenery for hot air ballooning. The annual Balloon Fiesta, held over nine days in March, sees 60 balloons drift over the lake. The Deep Space Communication Complex at Tidbinbilla is now home to DSS 46, the antenna that relayed to the world Neil Armstrong's first steps on the moon.

In Jan. 2003 Canberra was threatened by bushfires which raged out of control for several days. Four people were killed and several thousand were forced to leave their homes. The cost of property damage was estimated at several hundred million dollars.

Places of Interest

The city's museum and gallery opened in 1998. Important heritage sites include the Australian War Memorial, at the head of ANZAC Parade. Mugga Mugga, a shepherd's cottage dating from 1830, St. John's Schoolhouse, Canberra's first school which opened in 1845, and Blundell's Cottage, built in 1860, are among the city's oldest buildings. The new National Museum of Australia opened in March 2001 at a cost of $A152m., drawing 27,000 visitors on its first day.

Art collections of international significance are held at the National Gallery, opened in 1982 and home to 95,000 works including Jackson Pollock's *Blue Poles*, and the National Portrait Gallery in Old Parliament House, opened in 1998 and one of only four such galleries in the world. There are also 30 commercial art and craft galleries.

The Telstra Tower, a telecommunications facility rising 195 metres from the summit of Black Mountain, provides 360-degree views of Canberra from its public gallery. Canberra is also home to the country's reptile centre, zoo and aquarium, science and technology centre, and dinosaur museum.

Cape Town, South Africa

Introduction

The capital of Western Cape Province, sea port and legislative capital of South Africa, Cape Town is often referred to as the country's 'mother city' since it is the site of the first European settlement in South Africa.

History

The first European to drop anchor at Table Bay was António de Saldanha, although the Cape of Good Hope or 'Cabo da Boa Esperança' had been named many years earlier by the Portuguese navigator Bartholomeu Dias. In 1647 Dutch sailors shipwrecked at Table Bay gave such enthusiastic reports as to encourage the Dutch East India Company to establish a supply station. Jan van Reibeeck came ashore on 7 April 1652 to build a fort and establish trading links with the local Khoikhoi tribe. By 1657 many of those who had landed with Reibeeck were setting up as burghers or farmers in the fertile region.

During the Napoleonic Wars, the Cape was successfully defended against a British fleet by a mixed Franco-Dutch force. After Britain defeated the Dutch at Bloubergstrand in 1806 it took control of Cape Town and the surrounding areas, which were incorporated into the British Empire in 1814. When Britain abolished the slave trade many Afrikaners embarked on the Great Trek (1834–40) to create their own homelands. In 1854 the first parliament was established. This was a multiracial parliament and began the long tradition of tolerance in the Western Cape Province. During the last century there were no racial bars in Cape Town, where any race could vote and hold office.

In 1989 over 40,000 people took to the streets of Cape Town to promote their belief that all people regardless of ethnicity and colour have the right to elect their leaders and stand for election. This demonstration gave courage to many like-minded communities and did much to instigate the release of Nelson Mandela and the end of apartheid in South Africa.

Modern City

Cape Town's port handles around 5m. tonnes of cargo each year. The city also has an international airport with frequent flights to Europe and America. The main railway station is the terminus for services across South Africa and Zimbabwe. Industries include ship repair and maintenance as well as the manufacture of petrochemicals, fertilizers, cars, plastics, clothing, leather goods and cement. Fish distribution, food processing and fruit exportation are also important. Since the collapse of apartheid, tourism has become a major revenue earner.

Places of Interest

Table Mountain is the most famous landmark. The Castle of Good Hope stands near the site of Jan van Riebeeck's original fort. It was built between 1666 and 1697 making it one of the oldest European structures in South Africa. The Kirstenbosch Botanical Gardens, established by Cecil Rhodes in 1895 overlook False Bay and Cape Flats.

The South African Museum, established in 1825, is the oldest museum in sub-Saharan Africa. Its vast collections from fossils to clothing combine natural and cultural history; exhibitions include a life-size blue whale skeleton and the African dinosaur display. The Bertram House Museum is part of the South African Cultural History Museum; exhibits include porcelain, furniture, silver and glass. The Bo-Kaap Museum in the centre of Bo-Kaap, the Malay quarter, is furnished as a nineteenth century Muslim home and gives an insight into the lives of non-white settlers to the South African colony. The National Gallery displays native and international art, including photographs of black township life many of which appeared in Drum magazine in the 1950s.

Caracas, Venezuela

Introduction

The capital of Venezuela and of the Distrito Federal region, Caracas is near the northern Caribbean coast. At an altitude of 900 m, the city is flanked to the north by the Andean Avila mountain range, and is located on a high plain.

History

The surrounding region was originally the hunting ground of the indigenous Caracas Indians. Although the first colonial settlement in the area was in 1557, Santiago de León de Caracas was founded 10 years later by the Spanish Conquistador, Diego de Losada. The town developed on a grid-plan around a central Plaza, laid out by Diego de Henares. The surrounding areas were made up of *haciendas* controlling sugar and coffee plantations. These became the foundation for the districts of modern Caracas. The increasing importance and influence of the town's *cabildo* (town council) led to its appointment in 1577 as provincial capital. Under colonial rule the development of Caracas was interrupted by earthquakes and epidemics. Much of the indigenous population was wiped out in a smallpox epidemic. English buccaneers sacked Caracas in 1595. In mid-seventeenth century, Caracas' civic and religious importance overtook that of Coro, the first capital of the Province of Venezuela. In the eighteenth century Caracas' prosperity increased with the development of the cacao trade. Exports were controlled from La Guaira, now Caracas' coastal port. Earthquakes in 1641, 1755 and 1812 caused severe damage.

In 1806, the revolutionary hero, Francisco de Miranda, attempted to free Caracas from colonial rule. He was betrayed to the Spanish and died in jail in Cadíz. A native of the city, Simón Bolívar took over the fight for independence. From an important Venezuelan family, Bolívar left Caracas for

Colombia where he recruited revolutionary fighters. In Aug. 1813 Bolívar took Caracas and was named El Libertador (Liberator). When Venezuela became an independent nation in 1830, Caracas remained its capital. Under the rule of the Caudillo (military dictator) Antonio Guzmán Blanco (1870–89), Caracas underwent substantial urban development. Spanish colonial architectural style was abandoned in favour of French Neo-classical. Guzmán commissioned the construction of grand buildings, including the Panteón Nacional. The Plaza Mayor was renamed Plaza Bolívar.

Although the discovery of oil in the 1910s brought great wealth to Venezuela, it was closely controlled by the dictator General Juan Vincent Gómez and the majority of people did not benefit. When he died in 1935, people rioted on the streets of Caracas in protest against the social inequality Gómez's rule had produced. From 1936 oil money led to rapid growth in the capital's population. The face of Caracas changed dramatically in the second half of the twentieth century. From 1951–57 the dictator Marcos Pérez Jiménez initiated a grand modernization scheme. Much of the old city was replaced by ultra modern architecture and colonial architecture was eradicated. The new city included designs by Venezuelan architect Carlos Raul Villanueva and the Italian architect Gio Ponti and the French artist Fernand Leger. Transport links were improved with the coast and the interior. The presence of the Andes around Caracas prevented the city's expansion northwards. Despite this, the city has continued to develop and now sprawls for 20 km from east to west. High rise blocks of glass and chrome are contrasted with barrios (shantytowns) on the city's extremities and on the mountainsides. In Dec. 1999 Caracas suffered severe floods and mudslides in which thousands of people died.

Modern City

20% of Venezuela's industries are located in the capital and Caracas employs 30% of the industrial workforce. The city is the centre of Venezuela's oil companies and oil refining is among its main industries. Other commercial activities include textiles, food processing, automobile production and chemical manufacturing. The headquarters of Venezuela's major businesses and banks are based in Caracas. The city is linked by road to its port, La Guaira, and the international Simón Bolívar airport. After 1953 the 34 km road around the mountains between Caracas and the coast was replaced by an 18 km road with tunnels through the mountain range. Caracas also has two smaller airports, Francisco de Miranda and La Carlota airport. The city has a subway system, opened in 1983.

Places of Interest

One the few remaining colonial buildings, the Catedral de Caracas was constructed between 1665–1713 to replace the original, which had collapsed in the 1641 earthquake. Simón Bolívar's birthplace, the Casa Natal del Liberator, where he was born on 24 July 1783, has been made a museum. Tito Salas, a twentieth century realist painter from Caracas, was commissioned to decorate the Casa with scenes from Bolívar's life. Similar murals decorate the Panteón Nacional. Commissioned by Guzmán Blanco, this building contains 163 tombs of eminent Venezuelans and is dedicated to Bolívar, himself entombed in a bronze sarcophagus. The national hero's funeral was conducted in the Iglesias de San Francisco. It was also the setting for Bolívar's christening as El Libertador in 1813. Museums include the Museo de Arte Contemporáneo, which displays works of native and international artists, including 100 engravings by Picasso. Caracas also has a Museo de Arte Colonial and the Museo Sacro de Caracas which shows religious art.

Cardiff (Caerdydd), United Kingdom of Great Britain and Northern Ireland

Introduction

Cardiff is the capital city of Wales, the district seat of South and Mid Glamorgan and the seat of the Welsh Assembly. It is at the mouth of the Rivers Taff, Ely and Rhymney on the Bristol Channel and from the sixteenth century became an increasingly significant port. Its importance as a government and administrative centre has grown following the establishment of the Welsh Assembly in 1999.

History

There is evidence of human habitation in the area around Cardiff dating back to 4000 BC. In the first century AD Cardiff was the site of a Roman fort which was subsequently defended and strengthened to combat Irish raids further up the River Taff. After the Romans left the region the fortress came under the jurisdiction of local kings and was employed in the ninth century to repel Viking incursions. During the eleventh century Robert Fitzhamon, an ally of William the Conqueror, rebuilt and improved the castle.

In 1126 the castle was used to imprison Robert of Normandy, the uncle of King Henry I. A town gradually grew outside the castle walls and trade with other parts of Wales was brisk. In the fifteenth century Cardiff was burnt and plundered by Owain Glendwr but by the late sixteenth century it was a major commercial hub and a prosperous port, also used as a base for pirating in the Bristol Channel.

In 1642, during the Civil War, the castle became a royal stronghold but in 1645 Charles I was refused refuge there. In the decades that followed Cardiff went into decline and its population fell steeply. However, the castle, which had come under royal jurisdiction during the fifteenth century, passed to the first Marquis of Bute in 1796. The Marquis and his descendants became closely linked to the growth and success of Cardiff and later bequeathed land to the city for a civic centre and parkland. The second Marquis of Bute, although in increasing debt, financed the building of the city's first docks in 1839 and in 1868 the third Marquis instructed the architect William Burgess to redesign the castle in the neo-Gothic fashion.

By the beginning of the nineteenth century Cardiff had grown to a city holding just over 1,000 people and the next century was to see rapid growth. The development of rail connections into the rich coalfields of south Wales brought money and employment. In 1905 Cardiff received official city status from Edward VII. The system of docks, which were not completed until 1907, meant that by 1913 Cardiff had become the largest coal-exporting city in the world. Coal mining went into terminal decline following World War I and Cardiff transformed itself into an industrial centre for food processing, engineering and other light industries as well as a major tourist destination. Since 1955 Cardiff has been the capital city of Wales.

Modern City

Since 1987 the Cardiff Bay Development Corporation has been regenerating 2,700 acres of decrepit docklands. A number of the area's original buildings were preserved and new offices, leisure facilities, housing and a man-made lake developed. Following a referendum in Sept. 1997 a new Welsh Assembly was constituted, and opened officially in May 1999 in a building located in the Bay.

Cardiff's city centre is the focus of Wales' political, administrative, commercial and cultural life. There is a main railway station in the middle of the city and a nearby international airport. An efficient bus service runs within the city, though the centre is compact and easy to walk around.

Places of Interest

The Civic Centre (Cathay's Park) comprises buildings of white Portland stone and was built between 1905 and the late 1980s. Among the institutions based in the Park are the City Hall, the National Museum and Gallery, the law courts, the national war memorial and Cardiff University. National Museum and Gallery has collections of fine art (including extensive Impressionist works) as well as exhibitions of natural sciences, archaeology and geology.

Other attractions for visitors include the castle and grounds, Llandaff Cathedral (just outside the centre of Cardiff and home to a controversial aluminium sculpture of Christ by Sir Jacob Epstein), the Museum of Welsh Life (located at nearby St Fagans and housing re-erected buildings from all over Wales as well as exhibitions of cultural and social history), and Castle Coch (another elaborate creation of William Burgess). The city is the home of the Welsh rugby team and the Millennium Stadium (formerly Cardiff Arms Park), regarded among the world's finest stadia.

Casablanca, Morocco

Introduction

Situated on the Atlantic Coast of NW Africa, Casablanca is the country's largest city, main port and chief business, industrial and commercial centre. It is a mix of old Muslim quarter, modern European city and outlying shanty-town. The Hassan II Mosque, completed in 1993, is the largest in the world.

History

A Berber village called Anfa, now a suburb, stood here in the twelfth century. It was destroyed by the Portuguese in 1468 in reprisal for piracy. In 1515 the Portuguese returned and built a new town called Casa Branca (White House), but this was abandoned in 1755 following an earthquake. Rebuilt in the eighteenth century by Sidi Mohammed ben Abdullah it was renamed Dar Al Beida which the Spanish merchants translated as Casablanca and the French called, Maison Blanche. In the nineteenth century French influence grew, the harbour was developed and commercial relations with Europe strengthened. Following an attack on French workmen in 1907, a force was sent to occupy the city. In 1912 it came under the French protectorate with General Lyautey appointed Resident-General. The harbour was completed and the city grew to be the major metropolitan centre. Independence in 1956 and the withdrawal of the French led to economic hardship but increased industry and a thriving tourist trade have restored prosperity. During WWII Casablanca was one of the key landing places for the invasion of North Africa by Allied forces and the scene of the 1943 Casablanca Conference, a summit meeting between Franklin D. Roosevelt and Sir Winston Churchill.

In May 2003 approximately 40 people died in terrorist attacks on western targets in the city. Suicide bombers hit a Spanish restaurant, a hotel, a Jewish centre and the Belgian consulate. The perpetrators were Moroccans from Casablanca's shanty-towns. However, the sophistication of the attacks led to accusations of Al-Qaeda support and planning.

Modern City

Casablanca has one of the world's largest manmade harbours which handles most of the country's trade. Fishing and fishcanning are the major industries and the chief export is phosphate. Other important industries include textiles, electronics, chemicals, cement, food processing and tourism. Mohammad V Square, also known as United Nations Square, is the business and administrative centre. To the south are parks and the white Cathedral of Sacre Coeur. To the west is the residential area with large numbers of poor living in outlying shantytowns. Mohammed V International Airport is located 30 km south of the city. Buses are the principal means of public transport but there are rail links to Algeria and Tunisia. Hassan II University was founded in 1976 and there are Arab and French schools including a number of institutes such as the Goethe-Institut.

Places of Interest

The old quarter in Anfa has narrow cobbled streets with mosques and hammams (Turkish baths). One of the largest and most spectacular mosques, Hassan II Mosque (1993) can accommodate over 25,000 worshippers and the piazza another 80,000. It mixes Moroccan traditions with state of the art technology and features the world's tallest minaret. In Mohammed V Square there are fine examples of Mauresque architecture. One of the main centres for recreation, Casablanca has beaches and promenades along the seafront, lined with tourist shops.

Castries, St Lucia

Introduction

Castries, the capital and commercial centre of St Lucia, is one of the chief ports in the Caribbean. The landlocked deepwater harbour's position at the centre of the Eastern Caribbean is ideal for shipping. The city was named in 1758 after Marechal de Castries, a Minister of the French Navy and the Colonies.

History

The region was first settled by Arawaks between 1000 and 500 BC. In 800 AD the Carib Indians, having conquered the Arawaks, established permanent settlements. In 1650 the French, having fought the British over the island, claimed St Lucia for the French West India Company. The French established the town Castries and developed sugar plantations. The British invaded in 1778 and gained control over St Lucia in 1814. The city suffered fires three times in 1785–1812 and again in 1948. In 1979 the island was independent, as a member of the British Commonwealth with Castries remaining as capital.

Modern City

Castries is the political and administrative centre of St Lucia. The majority of the population are of African descent, although the French influence is still strong in language, religion and street names. Since independence tourism has boomed. Exports include bananas, sugarcane, rum, cacao, coconuts, tropical fruits and vegetables. There is an international airport (Hewanorra) outside the capital. Most convenient forms of transport are taxis and water taxis. Rental cars are available, but require a temporary St Lucia driver's licence (available at the airport or police station).

Places of Interest

The volcanic crater is one of the main tourist attractions. Many of the city's historical buildings have been destroyed by fire. At the centre of the old town is the Columbus Square with the Cathedral of the Immaculate Conception, built in 1897 with colonial style architecture. The Derek Walcott Square is surrounded by nineteenth century wooden buildings, including a Victorian library. The Carnival in July is celebrated with calypso music, costumed parades and band competitions. There is also a Jazz Festival every year in May. Independence Day celebrations in Feb. include a craft exhibition. Overlooking Castries is a fortress on Mount Fortune.

Cebu, Philippines

Introduction

Cebu (Sugbu) City, Cebu Island, is the regional capital of the Visayas in the centre of the Philippine archipelago. It is one of the country's largest cities and a bustling port and a major tourist destination.

History

Cebu is one of the oldest settlement in the Philippines. It was a prosperous settlement before Ferdinand Magellan arrived in 1521, maintaining trade relations across Southeast Asia and China. Magellan converted the local ruler Rajah Humabon and 800 other islanders to Christianity but was killed by Chief Lapu-lapu, of neighbouring Macatan Island, shortly afterwards.

On 8 May 1565, Miguel Lopez de Lagaspi and an Augustinian friar, Andrés de Urdaneta, founded the present city changing its name from Villa de San Miguel to La Villa del Sanissimo Nombre de Jesus. Cebu was the Spanish colonial capital for 6 years until Legaspi's move to Manila and remained the principal Spanish bastion in the central and southern part of the archipelago.

Cebu was opened to foreign trade in 1860 and received a city charter in 1936.

Modern City

With many Manila-based companies maintaining branches here, Cebu is a collection and export centre for surrounding islands. Exports include textiles, fruit, ratan-ware, vegetable oil and chemicals.

The City is home to the University of San Carlos, University of the Visayas, University of the Southern Philippines, Southwestern University and Cebu Institute of Technology. The harbour of Cebu City is an international port and home to many inter-island shipping companies.

Places of Interest

Magellan's Cross, housed in an octagonal shrine with paintings depicting events from Magellan's visit to the Philippines, marks the spot where Rajah Humabon, Queen Juana and 800 natives were baptised in 1521. It is the original wooden cross that Magellan brought with him to the islands.

The Basilica Minore del Santo Niño is the oldest church in the Philippines; the only basilica in the Far East. It contains the image of the child Jesus given by Magellan to Rajah Humabon.

Fort San Pedro is a small tri-bastion fort that served as the staging post for the initial Spanish colonisation of the Philippines.

Chennai (Madras), India

Introduction

The capital of the Tamil Nadu region, Chennai is India's fourth largest city and third largest seaport. It is popularly known as the 'gateway to south India'.

History

Officially named Chennai from 1996, Madras was a group of fishing villages until the British arrived and developed the area into a major sea port. The East India Company built a trading post in the village of Madraspatnam in 1639 to establish and protect the local cotton weaving industry. The land was ceded by the Raja of Chandragiri, a member of the Vijayanager Kingdom of Hampi. In 1644, the Company built Fort St. George which lead to an expansion of the settlement commencing in 1668. The British and the French fought over the growing city and though the French briefly occupied it, they were unable to take full control. By 1801 British domination of southern India had helped strengthen Chennai's position as a commercial capital.

The city was the seat of the Madras presidency, one of the four divisions of Imperial India, throughout the nineteenth century and though it lost much of its power and influence when the British relocated their operations to the north of the country, it remained the most important city in the South.

Modern City

Industry in Chennai includes car, rubber, and fertiliser production with the main exports being leather, iron, ore and cotton textiles. The city has several major national and international travel links. Anna International Airport and the Kamaraj National Terminal are situated just outside the city at Trisulam, and are served by Air India for both international and domestic flights. The main headquarters of the Southern Railway are situated in Chennai and its rail links stretch across India.

The population of Chennai comprises Muslims, Hindus, Jews, Christians, Buddhists, and Zoroastrians. Despite this cosmopolitan mix, Chennai is conservative relative to cities such as Delhi and Mumbai with native music and old Indian traditions playing a great part in everyday life. The city's pollution levels are low in relation to India's other main cities though it is still approaching dangerous levels. Chennai's proximity to the sea makes the air humid. The climate is tropical with little temperature variation between winter and summer.

Places of Interest

Though relatively young (about 360 years old) the city is steeped in history with evidence of Indo-Sarcenic architecture in every region. There are seven Dravidian temples, including Gandhi Mandapam and Vallur Kottam, in the areas of Gearge Town, Triplicane and Mylapore. The Deccan Muslim constructions of the British period include the High Court and the University of Madras. Moghul architecture is exemplified by the Chepauk Palace. Within Fort St. George lies the oldest Anglican church in India. St. Mary's Church was built in 1680 and was the place of worship for early empire builders such as Elihu Yale, governor of the fort 1667–92, and Thomas Pitt, a one time governor.

The University of Madras, an example of Victorian architecture, was one of the three universities to be established in India by the British in 1857. Now spread over four campuses, the university has 70 departments and 185 affiliated colleges offering undergraduate and post-graduate courses. There are also state medical colleges, the College of Carnatic Music, the College of Art and Crafts, and colleges of technology, engineering, and teacher training.

The city's Government museum boasts a world famous collection of over 2000 south Indian bronzes. These include large statues of Indian deities such as Shiva, the destroyer god of Trimurti (the term applied to the three main Hindu gods), Vishnu, the preserver god of the Trimurti, and Parvati, a benevolent form of the universal goddess, Devi, as well as other smaller figurines.

Chiang Mai, Thailand

Introduction

In northwest Thailand on the Ping River near the Myanmar border, Chiang Mai is northern Thailand's principal city.

History

Chiang Mai originated as a royal residence of King Mengrai in 1292 before a village was created 4 years later. It became the capital of Lanna Thai ('kingdom of a million rice fields') until it was incorporated into Myanmar between 1558–1775. Thereafter the capital of an autonomous region, the city came under Thai rule at the end of the nineteenth century.

Modern City

Thailand's fourth largest city, Chiang Mai is the cultural, religious, economic and transportation centre in the North. It has a large Lao population. The city is a distribution centre for local handicrafts, such as pottery, silk weaving, wood carving and silverwork, while tourism is increasingly important. Chiang Mai is linked to Bangkok by rail and road and has an international airport. Educational institutions include Chiang Mai University, opened in 1964, the Northern Technical Institute, founded in 1957, and the Tribal Research Centre.

Places of Interest

Chiang Mai has several thirteenth and fourteenth century temples, such as Wat Chiang Man (c. 1296), located in the old walled area of the city. In the surrounding area The Wat Phra That Doi Suthep temple overlooks the city from the top of Suthep Mountain, which is encompassed by the 16,000-hectare Pui National Park. The Chiang Mai National Museum displays images of Buddha and medieval artwork.

Chicago, United States of America

Introduction

Chicago is the third most populous city and metropolitan area in the United States. Located in the northeast of the state of Illinois on the Chicago and Calumet rivers, the city stretches along the southwestern shore of Lake Michigan and covers an area of 234 sq. miles (606 km^2). In the 17th century French explorers were thought to be the first Europeans to travel through the area, while the first settlements were established by Haitian trader Jean Baptiste Point du Sable in the 1700s.

History

Chicago's rapid development in the early 1800s owed much to its strategic position at the lakeside interior of a rapidly expanding country and it soon became a nexus for goods transport via newly established canals and railways. Initially the city thrived as a port but it soon developed into a railroad manufacturing centre. Attracted by the city's burgeoning economy and its status as the major city of the Midwest, the arrival of huge numbers of Eastern European and Irish immigrants swelled the city's population. Disaster struck in 1871 with the Great Fire of Chicago, which lasted from Oct. 8–10 and destroyed much of central Chicago, leaving 90,000 people homeless.

The city was soon rebuilt and the population continued to grow apace, reaching around 2 m. in 1900 (compared to 4,000 just 63 years earlier). With its large number of industrial workers, Chicago was the birthplace of American trade unionism. After the formation of the American Federation of Labor, improved working conditions were won at the cost of violent clashes between workers and police in 1886 and 1894. During the Prohibition era of 1919–33, criminal syndicates led by the likes of Al Capone, 'Bugs' Moran and John Dillinger battled for supremacy of the bootleg alcohol market. The population of the city peaked at around 3.6 m. in 1950 but has dropped since.

Modern City

Chicago has retained its status as the financial, industrial and cultural centre of middle America. There are significant food, printing, electronics, chemical, steel and machinery industries and the city also houses the Chicago Board of Trade and the Chicago Mercantile Exchange (commodities markets which between them buy and sell around one third of the world's industrial and agricultural stocks).

Architecturally the city is an arresting site, boasting many skyscrapers, including the USA's second tallest and world's 11th tallest, the 108-storey Willis Tower (formerly the Sears Tower). The world's first skyscraper was built in the city in 1885 and many others followed, designed by renowned figures such as Frank Lloyd Wright. Chicago has also maintained its position as an important transport centre. O'Hare International Airport sees more take-offs and landings each year than any other airport in the world. Chicago is also at the heart of the vast Amtrak rail network.

Despite being the very epitome of a modern American city, Chicago's occasionally turbulent past still bubbles to the surface. Political leadership has often been held by controversial figures. In 1968 anti-Vietnam war protestors were aggressively handled by police on the orders of then Mayor Richard J. Daley, who remained in office from 1955–76.

Places of Interest

The city's colourful past, along with its abundance of areas of cultural interest continue to make the city a powerful draw for visitors. The Art Institute of Chicago is a showcase for major paintings and sculpture from Europe and the United States. Other attractions include the John G. Shedd Aquarium, the Field Museum of Natural History and the Adler Planetarium. The Smart Museum has a 7,000-object art collection spanning five millennia and including works by Rembrandt, Rodin and Matisse. Other museums include the Mexican Fine Arts Center Museum, the DuSable Museum of African American History and the Museum of Contemporary Photography.

Chicago has two zoos, Brookfield and Lincoln Park, and the Sears Tower and the John Hancock building both have observatories offering striking views of the city. The city boasts one of the biggest theatrical communities in the country with dozens of theatres including the world-famous Steppenwolf Theatre Company.

Chişinău (Kishinev), Moldova

Introduction

The capital of Moldova, Chişinău is on the Byk River in the centre of the country. Originally under the Moldavian monarchy, Chişinău has spent much of its history under Turkish, Romanian or Russian rule. In 1991 the city became the capital of the Republic of Moldova.

History

Although archaeological evidence points to settlements in the area from Palaeolithic times, the first known record of Chişinău is a mid-15th century land grant of the Moldavian prince Stefan III. After his death the Ottoman Turks took control of the city. The Russo-Turkish wars of 1739 and 1788 caused much destruction.

Chişinău was absorbed into the Russian empire in 1812, after which it was known by the Russian name of Kishinev. Industry grew in the 19th century, aided by the arrival of the railway in 1871, and the population expanded rapidly. After World War I control transferred to Romania and the city's name reverted to Chişinău. In 1940 the city was incorporated into the Soviet Union as the capital of the Moldavian SSR. As a front line city it suffered severe damage in the World War II, with two thirds of its housing destroyed. Rapid reconstruction and industrial development in the postwar period led to a population boom. With the collapse of the Soviet Union, in 1991 Chişinău became the capital of the Republic of Moldova. Soon after the republic replaced the Cyrillic alphabet with Latin.

Modern City

Although a small capital, Chişinău is Moldova's industrial, economic and cultural centre. Industries include light engineering, food and leather processing and furniture manufacturing. Educational institutions include a scientific research academy and a university. Fifteen kilometres southwest of the centre, Chişinău's international airport was opened in 1960.

Places of Interest

Sights include the Orthodox cathedral and the Arc de Triomphe. The baroque Museum of Art is one of the city's more attractive buildings, while elements of Byzantine, Roman and Gothic architecture can still be found. There are various parks and a lake suitable for bathing and boating. The main street, Boulevard Stefan cel Mare, is named after the nationalist medieval warlord. A great many of the city's monuments are war memorials.

Chongqing, China

Introduction

An important river port on the Chang Jiang (Yangtze), Chongqing, known as the Mountain City, lies 2,250 km (1,400 miles) inland. Like Beijing, Shanghai and Tianjin, the municipality of Chongqing now has provincial status. The municipality is China's largest in area (a little larger than the US state of Kansas) and in population (similar in size to that of California), yet the city itself accounts for only one-fifth of that population.

History

In the 11th century BC, Chongqing became the centre of a small state known as Pa. The city grew where the Chang Jiang is met by a large tributary, the Qian. Major fortifications were built in the 3rd century BC. For 2,000 years, the region was sometimes independent, sometimes ruled by the empire based in northern China and at other times subject to states in central China. Chongqing did not finally become part of the Chinese state until the 14th century.

A rebellion in the 1630s led to the destruction of much of the city, but its 8 km of walls were repaired. Chongqing prospered as a river port in 18th and 19th centuries and, by a treaty in 1890, was opened up to British ships for trade. Yet only sailing boats could reach the port as the Chang Jiang was initially impassable to larger steam vessels. In 1895 Japan forced China to open up the Chang Jiang to its ships and a Japanese concession was established on the southern bank of the river opposite the old city. Chongqing grew as both British and Japanese traders flourished.

After the 1911 revolution, the central government lost control over the region for nearly two decades. War with Japan broke out in 1937 and, the following year, the Nationalist government moved its capital from Nanjing to Chongqing. The city boomed when administrators, refugees and diplomatic missions fled to the city, which remained beyond Japanese control throughout the war. In 1946, the Nationalists moved their capital back to Nanjing, although Chongqing was once again briefly capital of China in 1949 after most other major cities had fallen to the Communists during the civil war. Damage caused by heavy Japanese bombing and during the civil war was severe, but the city was soon rebuilt.

Modern City

Chongqing urban area has experienced very rapid growth. The city, now one of the largest in China, has been modernised but it has fallen behind the cities of the eastern and southern coasts in the prosperity stakes. The port channels trade from the upper basin of the Chang Jiang and imports oil. The city is the hub of communications in south-western China. Heavy industry is dominated by one of China's largest iron and steel complexes. Other major industries include agricultural engineering, vehicle manufacture, chemicals, textiles and clothing. Industrial pollution is a major problem and the view of the surrounding mountains is often obscured.

Places of Interest

War damage in the 1940s destroyed many of Chongqing's historic monuments. Of those remaining, the ancient temple of the Empress Yu is most celebrated. Many traditional houses remain on the steeper slopes in the outskirts of the city. The Nan-wen-chaun gardens feature hot springs, pagodas and lakes. The city is near the Three Gorges, site of the world's biggest hydroelectric power scheme under construction and the surrounding region is known for its fine scenery.

Christchurch, New Zealand

Introduction

5,300 hectares of parkland, an annual festival of flowers, and top prize in 1997s international Nations in Bloom competition have made Christchurch the country's 'garden city'. The second largest city after Auckland, Christchurch is home to 8.5% of New Zealanders. It has the mild, temperate climate of the Canterbury Plains. Occupying 46,000 hectares on the east coast of South Island, in which it is the largest urban centre, Christchurch is the hub of the Canterbury region, which also includes Ashburton, Banks Peninsula, Hurunui, Kaikoura, Mackenzie, Selwyn, Timaru, Waimakariri, Waimate, and Waitaki. Mt Cook, the highest peak in New Zealand at 3764 metres, is situated nearby within the Mackenzie district; Christchurch's Port Lyttelton is an extinct volcano. Two rivers run through the city: the Avon and the Heathcote. The Canterbury region accounts for some 15% of the national economy, and 65% of its residents live in Christchurch.

History

Maori lived in the Canterbury region from about AD 1000. In the seventeenth century, the area was particularly important for Maori jade traders; also during this period, the Ngai Tahu iwi settled on the banks of the Otakaro. Today, the Otakaro is Christchurch's River Avon, popular for punting. The Maori settlement was named Otautahi, after its first chief, Tautahi; Port Lyttelton was known in Maori as the harbour of bulrush reeds. European settlers arrived in 1840, but their settlement lasted only a year. It was the 1848 inception of the Canterbury Association, with its mission to found a Church of England Colony, that led to the founding of a city. Two years later on 16 Dec., the first Association ships sailed into port. John Godley, a key member of the Association, attended Christchurch College at Oxford University; hence, Otautahi acquired its European name.

Christchurch became New Zealand's first city, on 31 July 1856. The Victorian cycle craze was such that when Mark Twain visited in 1895, he described Christchurch as a town where half the people ride bicycles and the other half are kept busy dodging them.

Notable cultural milestones in the city's history include New Zealand's first rugby game, played by pupils of Christ's College, in 1853; the election of New Zealand's first female member of parliament, Mrs. McCombs, in 1933; and the 1975 inauguration of the New Zealand games. In 1864, the council formed a 'committee on swans', which failed to persuade its imported birds to trim watercress on the Avon.

Christchurch was the site of the first ever railway tunnel drilled through a volcano rim—at the time, the longest railway tunnel in the world—in 1867. The city was the location for New Zealand's first airport in 1917, and also for

its first international and jet airports, in 1950 and 1965 respectively. Christchurch became the country's first Antarctic aviation portal in 1955. The first broadcast in New Zealand came from Christchurch in 1894; it was transmitted by Nobel prize-winning physicist Ernest Rutherford from the basement of Canterbury University. The country's earliest television signal was also transmitted from the university, 58 years later, in May 1952.

As part of Turning Point 2000, the city's portfolio of 150th anniversary community projects, the Canterbury Association was revived in London by descendents of the original settlers.

Modern City

There are some 23,600 businesses in Christchurch, of which the largest sectors are business and property services (28% of all businesses in 1999), retail (15%), and construction (11%). 4.9% of the city is zoned for commercial and industrial use, of which floor space in the central business district accounts for 1.6 m. sq. metres.

The proportion of Maori is around half that of New Zealand as a whole. Europeans comprised 84% of the population in 1996, and the city is famous for its picturesque English ambiance. However, the Ngai Tahu iwi are still active in Christchurch and Canterbury, successfully managing several businesses including forestry, property investment, and tourism operations. The city has a 92.5% employment rate. The major employers (followed by employees in 1999) are: manufacturing (28,718), retail (21,370), property and business services (19,740), and health and community services (17,635).

40% of Christchurch residents over the age of 15 possess a tertiary qualification, of whom some 22% hold a degree. 26,000 students are enrolled at the tertiary institutions, including an institute of technology and two universities. The University of Canterbury was founded in 1873, and two of its alumni, Baron Rutherford and the first Maori graduate Apirana Ngata, appear on New Zealand bank notes.

Port Lyttelton, 12 km from the city centre, is one of New Zealand's two deep water ports; the other is Wellington's Port Nicholson. In 1996, Lyttelton accounted for 8% of the country's overseas cargo trade. The cruise industry contributes around NZ$6 m. p.a. to the local economy.

Christchurch is served by air, rail, and bus connections. The train line runs the length of South Island's east coast. There are also scenic railway routes through the Southern Alps. The international airport recorded its highest ever international passenger figures in Jan. 2001—some 53,500 departures. The more modest city tram runs along a 2.5 km circuit with 9 stops across the central area.

The council spent NZ$12.2 m. on sporting and cultural events in 2000. The convention centre seats 2,500, and is linked to the town hall—the main performing arts venue. Outside the central city, the WestPac Trust Centre can seat 8,500. Christchurch observes more than a dozen festivals each year, including a buskers festival in Jan., a festival of romance in Feb., and a heritage week in May–June. February's Festival of Flowers, together with the Blossoms Festival in Sept.–Oct., celebrate the city's 665 parks. High profile projects in the city included the construction of the Christchurch Art Gallery which cost NZ$47.5 m. and opened on 10 May 2003.

In Feb. 2011 Christchurch was struck by a 6.3 magnitude earthquake, resulting in widespread damage and the deaths of 181 people.

Places of Interest

Christchurch's oldest European building, dating from 1843, is Deans Cottage at Riccarton. Some 600 historic objects and buildings are registered on the city plan. The rare timeball mechanism of the harbour clock, constructed as a mock castle in 1876, is still in working order. The old University of Canterbury buildings in the city centre now house an arts centre, with restaurants and a theatre. The arts centre is adjacent to the cathedral, botanic gardens, Canterbury Museum, and the 1932 Robert McDougall Gallery. Also in downtown Christchurch is the Centre of Contemporary Art, established in 1880 and composed of five galleries.

The tallest building in Christchurch, at 86 metres, is the Pacific Tower. The city has an aquarium, an aviation museum, a casino, and 26 golf courses. It is home to the national Marae (meeting house), Nga Hau E Wha. This is the country's largest Marae. The waters north of Christchurch are home to one of the highest concentrations of sperm whales on earth, where penguin and whale watchers can also swim with the diminutive hector dolphins, the rarest in the world.

Coimbra, Portugal

Introduction

Situated in central Portugal, Coimbra is on the hill of Acáçova on the north bank of the Mondego River. A one time capital of Portugal, Coimbra is the centre of Portuguese academic life.

History

Coimbra was originally the Roman town of Aeminium. It became an episcopal see in the 7th century. Coimbra was under Moorish rule from the 8th century until 872 when it was claimed by King Alfonso III of Asturias and Leon. In 987 the Moorish leader Almanzor sacked the city restoring Moorish control until Fernando I of Castile reclaimed it in 1064 with the help of the Castilian military leader, El Cid. At this time, Aeminium was a small town under the influence of the larger Conímbriga. When the citizens of Conímbriga abandoned the city for safety reasons they moved to Aeminium. The two towns merged and Aeminium became Coimbra. In 1139 Coimbra was made the Portuguese capital, replacing Guimarãos to become focal point for the reconquest of the rest of Portugal. The birthplace of six medieval kings from Sancho I (1185) to Ferdinand I (1367), the first *cortes* (parliament) of the newly established Portugal was held in Coimbra in 1211.

After the transfer of the capital to Lisbon in 1260, Coimbra lost much of its influence. In 1290 the first university in Portugal, and one of the oldest in the world, was founded in Lisbon. The Universidade de Coimbra oscillated between Lisbon and Coimbra before settling in the latter in 1537, a move that made Coimbra the academic centre of Portugal. Churches, colleges and convents sprung up, the population increased and the city became one of Portugal's principal cities. Coimbra was a centre of polyphonic music in the 16th century, and developed a school of sculptors in the latter part of the century, including João de Ruão. In 1808 Coimbra was occupied by the French who were expelled by the combined British and Portuguese forces 2 years later. Urban expansion commissioned by prime minister Antonio de Oliveira Salazar in the 1940s replaced some of the city's most celebrated buildings in the alta district with modern architecture.

Modern City

Coimbra's industries include pottery, beer, wine, textiles, olives and grain. Agriculture and fishing are the mainstays of the surrounding region. Coimbra is renowned as a cultural centre. Coimbra is served by rail and coach. The city has three railway stations and an international bus service to Spain, France and Germany.

Places of Interest

The Romanesque Sé Velha (Old Cathedral) is one of the city's oldest buildings. Unaltered since its construction in the 12th century, the cathedral influenced the architects of the cathedral in Santiago de Compostela. A Sé Nova (new cathedral) was built for the Jesuits in the 17th century. Museums include the 16th century Museu Machado de Castro, formally the bishop's palace. The Baroque library is the most famous building in Coimbra. Dating from the early 17th century, it contains over 1 m. books and several thousand manuscripts. Eighteenth century Botanical gardens covering over 20 hectares are south of the city centre. Sixteen kilometre southwest of Coimbra is the ancient city of Conímbriga, the most important Roman site in Portugal and at one time an important post between Olisipo (Lisbon) and Bracara Augusta (Braga).

Cologne (Köln), Germany

Introduction

Cologne is on the River Rhine in North Rhine-Westphalia, in the west of Germany. Long an important trade centre, by the 20th century it was among Germany's leading industrial and commercial powerhouses.

History

Founded in the 1st century BC by the Romans (hence the name Köln – 'colony'), Cologne flourished from the 4th–13th centuries under powerful archbishops. Throughout the Middle Ages, Cologne's position at the crossroads of many international trade routes made it a thriving centre for commerce and the arts. With 40,000 people living within the walls of Cologne, it was the biggest and most densely populated city in the country.

By the beginning of the 14th century, Cologne had become a centre for religious, intellectual and artistic life, attracting many eminent scholars. This led to the creation of Cologne University in 1338. In 1475 Cologne became a free imperial city (having been essentially self-governing since 1288) and in the 15th century, a member of the Hanseatic League (an alliance of German trading towns in operation between the 13th and 17th centuries).

French Revolution forces took the city without bloodshed in 1794, but in 1815 Cologne fell under Prussian jurisdiction. Steady expansion continued until, in the late 19th century and early 20th century, industrialization accelerated growth. From 1917–33, Konrad Adenauer (West Germany's Chancellor following World War II) was lord mayor. The city was badly damaged in World War II, although many fine buildings, such as the great Gothic cathedral, survived and have been restored.

Modern City

Cologne is a thriving river port and an industrial centre producing electronic equipment, chemicals and luxury goods, including the famous Eau de Cologne perfume. The media centre of Germany, Cologne has eight television stations, five radio stations, numerous publishing houses, a media park and an Academy of Media Arts. The city is also the centre of the German Roman Catholic Church.

Cologne shares an airport, Köln-Bonn Flughafen, with Bonn. The main railway station is Hauptbahnhof and main line and S-Bahn trains link Cologne with Bonn. The city is also accessible by several Autobahnen (motorways). Inner-city transport is provided by buses, S-Bahn and U-Bahn trains and trams.

Places of Interest

Among Cologne's most easily recognisable sites is the Kölner Dom (Cathedral), dedicated to St Peter and St Mary, begun in 1248 but not completed until 1880. The largest and most perfect example of high Gothic of its kind in the world, it rises to almost 157 metres. St Peter's Bell is the world's largest swinging bell (at 24 tons) and is known as der große Peter. In the shadow of the cathedral, the Hohenzollern Brücke crosses the Rhine and opens out into a promenade guarded by equestrian statues of the royal family.

The Rathaus (Town Hall) is surmounted by a Gothic tower, and the 1570 Renaissance arcade and loggia (the only section that survived the war) is decorated with flights of Baroque cherubs. Nearby, the Romanische Praetorium und Kanal recall Cologne's Roman past and the excavated ruins of a former Roman governor's palace can be seen as well as a Roman sewer. Cologne also has several fine Romanesque Churches built in a period of prosperity between 1150 and 1250. Among the most impressive are Groß St Martin, St Maria im Kapitol and St Gereon on Christophstr., which has a four storey decagonal dome.

Among Germany's finest galleries is the Wallraf-Richartz Museum, which contains works from the Cologne Masters from the 14th to 16th century. There are also works by Rembrandt, Rubens, Dürer, Lorenzetti, Titian, Tintoretto, Caspar David Friedrich, Lovis Corinth, Renoir, Monet, Sisley, Cézanne, Van Gogh, Gauguin, Degas and Rodin. Museum Ludwig displays modern and contemporary art of the 20th century, with works by Kandinsky, Kokoschka, Max Ernst, Modigliani and Delauney. Agfa-Foto-Historama is compiled from the archives of the Agfa company and the Stengler Collection, as well as other private collections, and chronicles the advances made in photography over the last 150 years.

The Römische-Germanisches Museum contains an extensive collection of Roman artefacts found in the Rhine region. Built on the site of a Roman Villa, it includes the Mausoleum of Poblicius (30–40 AD) and the Dionysius Mosaic. Heinrich-Böll-Platz is a complex of three museums in a spectacular modern building. Also popular is the Beatles Museum paying homage to the band, who spent the early part of their career in the city.

Colombo, Sri Lanka

Introduction

Colombo is the commercial capital of Sri Lanka and its largest city. It lies on the west coast of the country, some 5 miles (8 km) northwest of Kotte. The capital of Sri Lanka during British rule, its political importance declined following independence in 1948, although it remained the country's main trade centre. Colombo port, one of the world's largest artificial harbours, handles the bulk of Sri Lanka's overseas trade.

History

Although references to a settlement go back to the 5th century, it was not until the 8th century, when Arab traders settled near the port, that the city gained importance as a trade centre. When the Portuguese captain Lourenço de Almeida landed in Colombo in 1505, the warm welcome he received from the king of Kotte encouraged him to establish formal ties to permit commercial use of the port. A succession of Sinhalese leaders in need of military support from the Portuguese led to the almost complete annexation of the island in 1597. Before this, however, their presence in Colombo had been asserted through their development of the port and the construction of Franciscan churches and missionary orders.

Aided by the Dutch, the Kandyan king, Râjasinha II (1629–87), sought to expel the Portuguese from Colombo and to regain control of the coast. Despite promises from the Dutch that Colombo would be returned to his control, the Dutch forces conquered the city in 1656 and then shut out the Sinhalese king's army. With his withdrawal, Râjasinha laid waste to the area surrounding the city.

Like the Portuguese, the Dutch left behind an architectural legacy. It includes the Wolvendahl church and the Cinnamon Gardens, south of the Beira Lake. Cultivation of the spice, which had been monopolised by the Portuguese, was further developed by the Dutch. The gardens now form a major tourist attraction.

The arrival of the British in 1796 led to a further period of development to both port and city. In 1815 it was made capital. Though Colombo prospered during this period, the latter half of the 20th century witnessed its diminishing importance as an administrative and political centre as rapid expansion, coupled with a shortage of buildings and building space, prompted migration towards nearby Kotte. Colombo's main administrative and governmental buildings have since been moved to Kotte which in the early 1980s replaced Colombo as Sri Lanka's legislative and administrative capital.

Modern City

Industries include motor vehicles, machinery, processed food and tobacco. The central bank, which suffered a bomb attack in 1996, is located in the Fort district.

Colombo is the transport hub of the island. There are train services to major cities in the country and an international airport located some 35 km north at Katunayake. A second airport at Ratmalana handles inbound flights. In Aug. 2001 the international airport was bombed by Tamil Tiger rebels. Although no civilians were killed in the attack, several countries including the UK warned against visiting the country and tourist arrivals have dropped sharply.

Places of Interest

The oldest parts of the city are the Fort and the Pettah, dating from the Portuguese period, both located to the north. The Pettah developed as an area just outside the confines of the Fort and is nowadays a busy commercial district. The national zoological gardens are at nearby Dehiwala. The city is home to the National Museum (Sri Lanka's first public museum, established 1877) as well as several art galleries.

Conakry, Guinea

Introduction

The capital of Guinea, Conakry is a major West African port and the country's largest city. It is located jointly on Tombo Island and the Kaloum peninsula.

History

The city was founded by the French in 1884 on the site of an earlier village. It served as the capital in Guinea's period as a French protectorate, a French colony and then as a constituent territory of French West Africa. It remained the capital in 1958 when Guinea achieved independence.

The city developed in the 1950s with the successes of iron mining on the Kaloum peninsula and after the exploitation of Guinea's bauxite deposits (the country lays claim to 25% of the world's reserves).

Modern City

Conakry's deepwater harbour is located on Tombo island. Its main exports include bauxite, alumina, gold and coffee. An international airport is located 15 km northeast.

There is a national university and several vocational colleges.

Places of Interest

The city is home to a botanical garden and a national museum. There are regular boat trips to the Los islands, some 10 km southwest.

Constanţa, Romania

Introduction

Constanţa is Romania's largest coastal port and one of the Black Sea's principal trade destinations.

History

The first settlement on the site of modern Constanţa dates back to 600 BC, when Greeks from Miletus, Anatolia founded the city of Tomis. Tomis began to prosper as Greek colonists traded with the native Thraco-Getians. In the 1st century BC Tomis became part of the Roman Empire. The location's geography was exploited and the city again experienced a period of growth. During this period, the mix of Roman, indigenous Thracian and Greek inhabitants produced a Latinate tongue now believed to be the root of the modern Romanian language. Much of the city's history from this time derives from the writings of Ovid who was exiled to Tomis between AD 9–17.

The Romans' departure from Tomis in AD 271 exposed the settlement to the invading forces which had long been harassing it. Shortly after this evacuation, Tomis was made once more, albeit briefly, a site of Roman control, as Constantine the Great reconstructed the city and renamed it Constantiana. Migrations of Visigoths, Huns, Ostrogoths, Gepids, and Lombards continued throughout the following centuries as these peoples sought richer lands further west and south. In the 6th and 7th centuries AD, the Avars and then the Slavs invaded, the latter significantly contributing to the developing Romanian language.

The Turkish invasion in the early 15th century led to a decline in Constanţa's status. This continued until the 19th century and the Independence War of 1877–78, when Constanţa returned to Romanian control. As capital of the region (also named Constanţa), the harbour was remodelled and civic modernization began.

The two world wars had devastating effects on Constanţa, each entailing major reconstruction. Since the end of World War II however, the city has gained importance as a European trade hub.

Modern City

Perhaps the most contentious of recent issues involving Constanța has been the planned construction of the Constanța–Trieste pipeline. Vigorous EU opposition to the pipeline's bypassing Serbia has subsided and construction of the massive conduit should soon be underway. In 1984 work started on building a canal linking the port with the Danube, thus connecting with ports on the North sea and other Central European countries. It was the culmination of ambitions stretching back to the city's Roman occupation.

Constanța's port processes an annual 85 m. tons. Industries include pre-fabricated concrete and processed food.

Places of Interest

Constanța has numerous museums, theatres and galleries. The tourist harbour, casino, and nearby beach resort of Mamaia are popular destinations.

Constantine, Algeria

Introduction

At 650 metres above sea level, the historic city of Constantine is Algeria's third largest city. In the mountainous northeast of Algeria surrounded by the Rhumel River, the city is connected by several bridges.

History

Archaeological evidence points to prehistoric habitation. Founded by the Carthaginians as Sarim Batim, by the 3rd century BC Constantine had developed into the important Numidian city of Cirta (the city). As Numidia was swallowed up into the Roman Empire, Cirta was destroyed in battles in 311. Two years later the Emperor Constantine (274–337) rebuilt the city, naming it after himself. The city flourished under Roman rule producing much of its wealth as a grain distribution point. From the 8th century, Constantine was ruled by a succession of Arab dynasties until it came under Ottoman rule in the 16th century. The rule of Salah Bey (1770–92) produced many of the city's religious buildings. Constantine was one of the last cities in the region to resist French invasion but finally succumbed in 1837. Between 1942–43, the city was a key Allied base. Since its independence from French rule in 1962, Constantine has remained an important city in independent Algeria.

Modern City

A centre of grain distribution, Constantine is also involved in the production of textiles and leather goods. The sale of local handicrafts is also important. The University of Constantine dates from 1969.

Places of Interest

Constantine's long history is evident in the ruins of the Roman city of Tiddis and the Casbah. Monuments include the Palace of Ahmed Bey, the Djamma el-Kebir Mosque and the Soumma Mausoleum. The Gustave Mercier Museum displays ancient and modern art.

Copenhagen, Denmark

Introduction

Copenhagen is in the east on the islands of Zealand and Amager. It is the country's capital and its largest city. It is also the main commercial and industrial centre, and an important sea harbour.

History

There was a small settlement on the island of Slotsholmen in the 10th century. In 1167 the Bishop of Roskilde ordered the construction of a fortress to protect the region from German marauders. This led to the expansion of the original harbourside village. Increasing prosperity prompted its inhabitants to name it Kømandshavn (meaning 'merchant's port', eventually abbreviated to København.) When the fortress was razed in a German attack in the mid 14th century, better defences were built, including Copenhagen castle. King Eric of Pomerania transfered his court to the city in 1416. From this time Copenhagen served as the de facto capital, and was officially recognised as such in 1445. Trade revenues increased steadily throughout the 16th century and as a result the city grew in size and population. It was during this period that many of Copenhagen's Grand Renaissance buildings such as the Børsen (exchange), the Homens Church and the Rundetårn (round tower) were constructed. Plague wiped out much of its population at the turn of the 18th century and many of Copenhagen's oldest buildings were destroyed during the war with Sweden (1658–60) and in the fires of 1728 and 1795. The city also suffered bombardment by the British fleet in 1807. Following this disastrous phase the civic authorities decided to modernize Copenhagen. In the mid 19th century the ancient ramparts were removed to allow for the development of suburbs and satellite towns. With these improvements came a burgeoning of the city's intellectual life. Nineteenth century Copenhagen's artistic golden age was dominated by such as the writer Hans Christian Andersen, the artist Christoffer Eckersberg and the philosopher Søren Kierkegaard.

The twentieth century saw the continuing economic development of Copenhagen interrupted by Nazi occupation in World War II. After 1945 another era of modernization and expansion began, and Copenhagen established itself as a prominent financial, commercial and cultural centre within the European Union.

Modern City

Copenhagen is centred around the Town Hall Square (Raadhuspladsen) although the historic centre lies to the northeast near the royal palaces of Thott and Charlottenborg. To the south is the harbour where most of the city's industry is located. Major industries include shipbuilding, brewing and machine production. Copenhagen is the home of several important educational establishments including the Technical University of Denmark, the national Engineering Academy and the Royal Danish Academy of Music. Transport within the city is provided by electric rail and bus. The capital is linked by road and rail to other cities in Denmark and continental Europe. In 2000 Copenhagen was connected to the Swedish city of Malmö across the Sound by the Oresund fixed link. There is an international airport to the south at Kastrup.

Places of Interest

The 150-year old Tivoli amusement park is one of the most famous in Europe. Besides the usual rides and rollercoasters the park also has theatres, concert halls, restaurants and garden walks. The Nationalmuseet (National Museum) is in the Prinsens palace and has a large collection of Danish historical artefacts, including the 3,500 year-old Sun Chariot. The Ny Carlsberg Glypotek houses ancient Egyptian and Etruscan relics and has a modern wing notable for its impressionist works. The 17th century Thott and Charlottenborg palaces are located in the centre of Copenhagen, the latter now houses the Royal Academy of Fine Arts.

Córdoba, Argentina

Introduction

On a central valley at the foothills of the Sierra de Córdoba, Córdoba is Argentina's second largest city and capital of the Córdoba Province. To the north of the Pampas, the city is traversed by the Primero River.

History

The surrounding area was originally inhabited by the Comechingones. Farmers and hunters, the Comechingones lived in semi-subterranean stone houses, bred llamas and grew maize, beans and pumpkin. The Comechingones temporarily resisted colonial invasion but in June 1573 the Conquistador Jerónimo Luis de Cabrera founded Córdoba de la Nueva Andalucía (Córdoba of the new Andalusia). The settlement was established on a trade route between Chile, Buenos Aires and the Viceroyalty of Peru, a prime position which guaranteed its prosperity and development. By the end of the 17th century Córdoba was established as one of the most important cities south of Peru.

With Jesuit, Franciscan and Dominican orders, Córdoba developed into a cultural and educational centre. The Jesuits in particular had a strong influence on the city and surrounding area. The village of Alta Gracia, 35 km southwest of Córdoba supplied the Jesuit community with provisions until 1767. Established in 1613, the Universidad Nacional de Córdoba was the first university in the country. After Independence from colonial rule, Córdoba's economic importance suffered. The newly formed Viceroyalty of Río de Plata, encompassing modern-day Argentina, Southern Bolivia, Uruguay and Paraguay, established its capital in Buenos Aires. Tension between the two cities, which occasionally erupted into violence, lasted until the 1860s.

In 1866 the San Roque Dam was built on the Primero River. In 1869 a railway connected Córdoba with the east. The city expanded and many communities were settled in the surrounding region. Despite the city's conservative tradition, Córdoba's expanding workforce in the 20th century gave rise to labour activism and radicalism. In 1955 Córdoba was instrumental in the demise of President Juan Perón, which began when General Eduardo Lonardi captured the city. In the late 1960s Córdoba experienced a period of civil unrest culminating in May 1969 when workers and students united in revolt against the economic policies of Adalbert Krieger Vasena's military government.

Modern City

The Sam Roque Dam provides Córdoba with hydro-electricity. Industries include textiles, automobiles, leather and glass. The dam provides Córdoba's water and also irrigates the surrounding agriculture. The Córdoba province specializes in cattle, wheat and maize. There are major tourist resorts in the region and Córdoba is an important rail terminus. The Aeropuerto Pajas Blancas is 15 km north of Córdoba.

Places of Interest

Córdoba has a rich colonial history and many of the original buildings survive. The cathedral is in the Plaza San Martín, Córdoba's main square and centre of the city. The Cabildo (town hall) is also in the square. Just south of the plaza, Calle Obispo Trejos contains many examples of colonial architecture. The University was built on the site of a plot given to Jesuits in the 16th century and ruins can still be seen of the Jesuit hermitage. The Obispo Mercadillo House was constructed at the beginning of the 18th century. Museums include the Museo Histórico Provincia Marqués de Sobremonte; a selection of religious art is housed in the Convento de las Teresas.

Cork, Ireland

Introduction

Located on the River Lee, Cork is Ireland's second city and the capital of Cork County. Key to the Irish uprising against British rule in 1921, it is now a major centre for food and drink processing and offshore oil exploration.

History

St Finbarr founded a monastery on the site in 606 AD. Over the centuries the settlement fell victim to fire and foreign invasion, principally from Scandinavia. By the 12th century Cork was under the control of the MacCarthy clan and several Danish overlords. However, in 1172 the English king, Henry II, seized control and established a garrison. It marked the beginning of centuries of English occupation.

In the late 15th century Cork supported the pretender Perkin Warbeck, who impersonated Richard, Duke of York in a bid to claim the English throne from Henry VII. John Waters, twice mayor of Cork, and one of his chief allies was convicted of treason and executed.

Early in the 17th century the city suffered major floods and fires. In 1649 Cork again was in opposition to the English throne, supporting Oliver Cromwell against Charles II in the English civil war. After the restoration, Cork supported the Catholic King James II against his Protestant daughter, Mary, and her husband, William of Orange. As a result the city was besieged by the Earl of Marlborough in 1688, falling in 1690. The military garrison subsequently went into decline, while Cork thrived as a centre of commerce.

Cork, like much of the rest of Ireland, endured famine in the mid-19th century, an experience that attracted support for the nationalist movement. In the uprising in 1919–20, one lord mayor died in clashes with the British forces and his replacement died as a result of a hunger strike while being held on the mainland. Several key buildings were destroyed by fire. Further damage occurred when Cork fell under the control of republicans opposed to the 1921 Anglo–Irish treaty.

Modern City

The modern city is a major focus of commerce for southern Ireland. Cork's harbour serves as a base for offshore oil exploration. Other major industries include vehicle engineering, fishing and textiles. It is also a central trading point for agriculture and is home to various light industries.

Cork has an international airport and ferries run regularly to Swansea in Wales and Roscoff in France. There are bus routes to Limerick, Galway and Ballina. Intercity trains link Cork with destinations throughout Ireland. The city was the European Capital of Culture in 2005.

Places of Interest

The Protestant St Finn Barre's Cathedral, on the site of the original monastic settlement, is a French gothic building completed in the late 19th century. There is also a Catholic cathedral, St Mary's, completed in the early part of the 19th century. The city's harbour is popular for water sports.

Other landmarks include the City Hall (set on the river bank), the imposing Shandon Steeple, the opera house, the University College building, the Grand Parade with its Berwick fountain, and the statue to Father Theobald Matthew (a 19th century Apostle of Temperance) on Patrick Street.

Other attractions include the English Market, a covered fresh produce market that dates from the 17th century, the Cork Heritage Park, the Beamish and Crawford brewery, the old gaol, the Cork Vision Centre, Cork museum and several galleries. Not far from the city is Blarney castle, home to the blarney stone.

Cotonou, Benin

Introduction

The largest city and port, Cotonou is in southern Benin. It is the country's economic and administrative centre.

History

At the beginning of the 19th century, Cotonou was the farming centre of the country's main export, palm oil. King Ghézo's (1818–58) commercial representatives were based in the city. This continued under his successor, King Gièlè's, whose representatives lived in the nearby Gbégamey forest. From there they ran their trade with Europeans. France took possession of Cotonou when a treaty of transfer was signed in 1868. Over the 20th century, Cotonou's economy developed, making it Benin's leading commercial city.

Modern City

Although Porto-Novo is officially the capital, Cotonou is the political capital of Benin, housing the presidential residence and most government ministries. Economic activity includes fishing, palm products, cotton, cacao, coffee, peanuts, textiles and cements. Cotonou houses the international market of Dantokpa, the National University of Benin and the large banks of West

Africa. The construction of the Benin–Niger railway was started under French occupation. Never completed, it terminates at Parakou.

Places of Interest

Attractions include a large market, the Grand Marché de Dantokpa, and the nearby town of Ganvié. North of Cotonou, this village on stilts is out on Lake Nokoué.

Daegu, South Korea

Introduction

The third city of South Korea, Taegu is sometimes known in the West by its Korean name, Daegu. The city lacks tourist attractions and history, but is a major regional centre for south-eastern Korea and an important stepping-off point for historical sites.

History

The site of Taegu, at the confluence of two rivers in a fertile valley, has been settled for several thousand years. By 1000 B.C. Taegu, known then as Dalguwha, was an important city and a provincial capital by the 14th century.

At the end of the 18th century, the city's name was changed to Taegu, which means 'big town'. A century later, Taegu lost its administrative role when the provincial boundaries of Korea were redrawn but by then it was a major centre of commerce. Under Japanese rule (1910–45), Taegu became an industrial centre. In 1907 a nationalist movement began in Taegu and the city was one of the hotbeds of anti-Japanese activities during the occupation of Korea.

The dramatic growth of Taegu into the nation's third city did not occur until the 1950s. The Korean War (1950–53) made many refugees. People fled from the north and centre of Korea before the advancing Communist armies, many settling in Taegu.

This influx gave Taegu a ready workforce when industry developed after the war. During the 1950s and 1960s the population of the city grew tenfold as new factories were built and the city expanded.

Modern City

Taegu is a modern city. Rebuilt and greatly expanded after the Korean War, it has a largely rectangular grid pattern and recently-constructed buildings. It is a road and rail route centre. The city has a subway system and an airport with domestic flights and a limited number of flights to Japan. Industries include textiles, clothing, textile machinery, machine building and metal working. Food processing is also important: the region is a major fruit-growing area and its apples are exported throughout the Far East. Taegu has five universities and other tertiary colleges.

Places of Interest

In Taegu there are very few old buildings. The main tourist attraction in the city is Talsong Fort. Apsan Park, reached by cable car, offers a panoramic view over the city. Palgongsan mountain, 20 km north, is a popular outing. But the main attraction is the Haeinasa temple complex, a World Heritage site.

Dakar, Senegal

Introduction

Dakar, a major port, is the capital of Senegal. It lies at the tip of the Cape Verde peninsula and was founded in the mid-19th century.

History

Traders and fishermen (mostly of the Lebus tribe) were increasingly active in the region from the 1830s onwards, when it was under French jurisdiction. A fort was constructed in 1857 and a planned town sprang up 5 years later. The construction of the port of Dakar was completed in 1866.

Dakar was one of three major settlements in the area, the others being Gorée and Rufisque. The construction of a railway between Dakar and Saint-Louis in 1885 and the burgeoning trade in peanut products prompted an economic boom. Having eclipsed its neighbours, Dakar became the capital of French West Africa in 1904 and was a vital port during World War I.

Railway links with French Sudan (now Mali) brought growth in the inter-war period, although expansion all but ceased during the period of the French Vichy government in the early 1940s. Urbanization took hold after World War II and in 1959 Dakar was made capital of the ill-fated Mali Federation. The following year it was designated capital of the newly independent Senegal.

Modern City

Dakar is the home of Senegalese government, with most public buildings in the southern quarter. Among its most important industries, alongside its role as a port, are food and drink processing (with peanuts still vital to the local economy) and petroleum. The commercial district is centred on the heavily build up northern area of the city.

Yoff is the international airport and Dakar is well served by road, rail and sea links. The annual Paris-Dakar Rally is among the world's most famous motor races,

Places of Interest

Among the leading museums is the Institut Fondamental d'Afrique Noir-Cheikh Anta Diop (IFAN-CAD), home to major collections of masks, statues and musical instruments from West Africa. The Galerie Antenna houses Venetian pearls, masks and terracotta from Central and West Africa while the Galerie Wéwé exhibits pottery and textiles. There are also several galleries of contemporary art including the National Gallery of Contemporary Art, Thiossane, Lézard and Wiitef Vema. Outside the city centre is the impressive Grand Mosquée (built in 1964). Though not open to non-Muslims, its surrounding medina (native quarter) is. There is a cathedral and a university. Dakar has two major markets, Marché Kermel and Marché Sandaga, while the Presidential Palace and its grounds are popular with visitors.

Dallas, United States of America

Introduction

Dallas is located where three junctions of the Trinity River meet in northern Texas. The seat of Dallas county, the city is 33 miles east of Fort Worth and is surrounded by hills and prairie land. The second largest city in the state, it is at the heart of an urban sprawl that also includes seven other smaller cities. Dallas is the banking and financial hub of the southwestern United States as well as a major distribution centre for manufactured goods.

History

The area now known as Dallas was originally inhabited by Anadrako Indians who traded with French settlers in the 18th century. John Neely Bryan, a lawyer from Tennessee, founded a prairie trading post in the area in 1841 and 5 years later a small village was built and named Dallas, probably in honour of George M. Dallas, who was vice-president of the United States from 1845–49. French and Swiss settlers from a failed 'utopian' colony at La Réunion arrived in 1858 and the establishment of railroads in the following decades helped the city grow rapidly.

Cotton was at first Dallas' most important product and the Dallas Cotton Exchange was founded in 1907. By the 1920s the area around the city was producing 40% of the United States' cotton crop. In 1930 a major oil field was discovered in East Texas and Dallas became an important centre of the petroleum and fuel industries.

After World War II, Dallas thrived, thanks to the presence of many oil companies, insurance firms and aircraft and automobile manufacturing plants.

In 1963 the city suffered a major blow to its image when president John F. Kennedy was assassinated. A resurgence in the city's economy in the 1970s and early 80s, as well as the worldwide fame engendered by the popular TV drama 'Dallas' helped the city get back on its feet. Although a high crime rate and rising unemployment figures had taken their toll by the beginning of the 1990s, the city remains, along with Houston, the most important in Texas.

Modern City

Dallas is a commercial and financial centre and the most important city for banking in the southwestern United States. Major industries include the manufacture of transportation equipment, food processing and clothes. Over 100 insurance companies are based in the city along with the headquarters of many oil and petroleum companies. Publishing, advertising and computer sciences are also important to the city's economy.

The city is served by two major airports. Dallas/Fort Worth is located midway between the two Texan cities and is the world's second-busiest airport. Love Field airport is 9 miles northwest of Dallas. The city is on the Amtrak network and has a Greyhound bus terminal. The Dallas Area Rapid Transit System (DART) operates extensive bus services and a light railway network that connects downtown Dallas with the west of the city.

The city contains several higher education institutions including Southern Methodist University, the University of Dallas, the University of Texas at Dallas and Dallas Baptist University. Its status as a centre for medical research and education is enhanced by the presence of the University of Texas Southwestern Medical Center at Dallas, Baylor College of Dentistry and the headquarters of the American Heart Association.

Places of Interest

The city has several cultural attractions including the Dallas Museum of Art. The Dallas Museum of Natural History, the African-American Museum and the Dallas Aquarium are all located in Fair Park, a large Art Deco plaza. The Dallas Theater Centre is the only theatre designed by Frank Lloyd Wright. The city hosts ballets, operas and concerts, many of the latter being performed at the Morton H. Meyerson Symphony Center.

On the site where John Neely Bryan established the modern day city's roots is a restored log cabin. Dealey Plaza, where John F. Kennedy was assassinated, has become a historical site. The Dallas Historical Plaza houses a memorial to Kennedy and a Conspiracy Museum.

Damascus, Syria

Introduction

Capital of Syria, Damascus is among the world's oldest (if not the oldest) continuously inhabited cities. It lies in the southwest of the country, at the Ghouta oasis which is fed by the Barada River. Bordered to the west by the Anti-Lebanon mountain range and the desert to the east, Damascus has long been an important administrative and commercial centre.

History

Archaeological excavations suggest urban settlement near Damascus from prehistoric times. Pottery from the 3rd millennium BC has been found in the old city (a World Heritage Site). The first written reference to the city is in Egyptian inscriptions dating from during the 2nd millennium BC. Later biblical sources describe it as the capital of the Aramean Kingdom. It was then conquered successively from the 8th century BC by the Assyrians, Babylonians, Persians (under Alexander the Great in 333 BC) and, in the 1st century BC, by the Romans. Having become a provincial outpost of the Byzantines following the division of the Roman Empire at the end of the 4th century AD, Damascus fell to Muslim Arab forces in 635. From 661 the city was the base of the caliphs of the Umayyid dynasty and the administrative centre of Islam. However, it declined in importance following the transfer of the Muslim capital to Baghdad in 750 (upon the accession of the Abbasid dynasty).

Having been seized by the Seljuk Turks in 1076, Damascus then came under the rule of Saladin and the Ayyubid dynasty in the later 12th century. By around 1250 the Ayyubids had given way to the Egyptian Mameluks, during

whose rule Damascus was sacked by the Mongols under Tamerlane (in 1401). In 1516 the city was wrested from Mameluk control by the Ottoman Turks, who maintained their sovereignty (except for a short period in the 1830s) until the disintegration of their empire in the First World War. During this time a massacre of Jews in 1840 was followed in 1860 by the destruction of the Christian quarter of the city. In 1920 the French, having been granted a League of Nations mandate over Syria, occupied Damascus. Subsequent revolts by the Druze, a religious sect, in the mid-1920s resulted in heavy French bombardment and destruction of the city. In 1941, during the Second World War, a combined Allied force attacked Syria and took Damascus (then under a pro-German Vichy French colonial regime). In 1946, at the end of the war, Syria gained its independence from France and Damascus became the capital of the new state.

The city came under threat during the civil war that began in 2011. A major battle took place from July–Aug. 2012. Damascus continues to act as the primary base of Syria's administration and the government drove back the bulk of opposition fighters in 2012. Nonetheless, bombings and guerilla-style attacks are frequently perpetrated by the militant groups.

Modern City

Damascus is the seat of government and administration in Syria. It is also the economic centre of the country, where banks and other leading commercial and industrial companies have their head offices. Industries include handicrafts (particularly silk weaving and leather goods), food processing, clothing manufacture and printing and publishing. In addition, the city is an important cultural, tourist and educational base. Syria's principal international airport is at Damascus.

Places of Interest

Major attractions include the old city, surrounded by what was once a Roman wall (much rebuilt since then); the Souk al-Hamaidiye (main market); remains of the western gate of the Roman Temple of Jupiter; the Umayyad Mosque, dating from AD 705—an adaptation of an earlier Christian church (and legendary burial site of the head of John the Baptist), which was itself built on the site of a Roman temple; the mausoleum of Saladin; the Takiyeh al-Suleimaniyeh mosque, built in 1554 by the Ottoman architect Sinan; the National Museum; the Azem Palace (housing the Museum of the Arts and Popular Traditions); and the Via Recta ('Street called Straight'), on which the Apostle St Paul is said to have lived.

Dar es Salaam, Tanzania

Introduction

Dar es Salaam, meaning 'Haven of Peace', is Tanzania's main port and largest city. It served as the country's capital before 1974, before it was moved to Dodoma.

History

In 1866 the sultan of Zanzibar established a city on the site of an earlier village and began constructing a palace built from blocks of coral from the island of Changuu. The city was far from completion when it became part of German East Africa. The building of a rail terminus in 1887 increased its importance. In 1891 it was made capital of German East Africa, remaining so until 1916. It became capital of Tanganyika in 1961 and then of independent Tanzania in 1964. The Tanzanian government decided to move the capital to Dodoma in 1974 but the move was delayed by financial difficulties. The city saw rapid growth after the Second World War and has retained its importance as Tanzania's main educational and industrial centre.

In 1998 the US embassy in Dar es Salaam was bombed in an attack attributed to Osama Bin Laden's Al-Qaeda organization, killing 11 people and injuring many more.

Modern City

Dar es Salaam is the main outlet for Tanzania's export trade. Products include cigarettes, textiles, soap, metal goods and processed food.

The port is linked by rail with Mwanza on Lake Victoria, Kigoma on Lake Tanganyika and to Zambia.

The city is home to various educational institutions including the University of Dar es Salaam, Kivukoni college and a college for business education.

Places of Interest

Tanzania's national museum, national library and national archives are all within the city.

Darwin, Australia

Introduction

Darwin is the capital of the Northern Territory. The city lies on a peninsula above Port Darwin, adjoined to the Clarence strait and the state's most important port. Settled in 1869, Darwin has been razed three times, twice by cyclones and once by bombs. The last and most devastating tornado struck in the mid-1970s.

History

In 1839 John Lort Stokes named Port Darwin after the naturalist Charles Darwin, with whom he had sailed aboard HMS Beagle. However, it was not until 1869 that the city was established. It fell under the jurisdiction of the South Australia authorities, who were keen to develop it as a trade centre. The settlement was named Palmerston (after the former British Prime Minister), reverting to Darwin in 1911.

When the Overland Telegraph System came to Darwin between 1870–72, telegraph workers discovered gold 200 km away from the city. A gold rush ensued and Darwin's population was swelled by Chinese immigrants. Economic depression followed the rush and in 1897 Darwin was devastated by a cyclone. Jurisdiction for the Northern Territory transferred from South Australia to the Commonwealth of Australia in 1911 and Darwin became an administrative centre for the region.

During the 1930s the town developed as an air base and, although damaged again by a cyclone in 1937, it was used by the military during the Second World War. In Feb. 1942 it was targeted by Japanese bombers and suffered extensive damage. On 1 day alone 243 people died and around 300 were injured. The city was rebuilt and an improved transport network with other areas of Australia established. Darwin became a city in 1959 and enjoyed a period of prosperity until the 1970s.

During Christmas 1974, Cyclone Tracy devastated the city. Over 60 people died, thousands more were hurt and over 30,000 people were airlifted away from the danger zone. Much of the city, including the port, was flattened and there followed an intensive rebuilding programme that has left Darwin with a hi-tech modern appearance. The population today includes large numbers of British, Greek and Filipinos. In Feb. 2004 the Ghan railway was extended from Alice Springs to Darwin, linking Darwin to the national rail network.

Modern City

Major industries include mining (Darwin is a large exporter of uranium ore), food processing, saw-milling and agriculture. The port and related activities are essential to the city's economic wellbeing. Darwin is on major road, rail and shipping routes and has an international airport. An efficient bus system operates within the city. The climate is tropical all year round and tourism is a significant income earner.

Places of Interest

Among the chief attractions are the numerous outdoor markets, the Parliament House, the Second World War oil storage tunnels and the Chinese temple. Nearby there is a crocodile farm and several national parks, notably Lichfield and Kakadu (which featured in the film *Crocodile Dundee*). The Darwin Cup is a popular annual horse race.

Daugavpils, Latvia

Introduction

Daugavpils, on the River Daugava in the southeast of the country, is Latvia's second city.

History

Founded in 1275 by knights of the Livonian Order, Daugavpils (then called Dünaburg) was razed several times during dynastic conflicts. Rebuilt by Ivan IV (The Terrible) in the 1570s, it was granted town status in 1582. Under Polish rule, when it was called Dvinsk, it was the administrative seat of the Latgalia province but during the First Polish Partition in 1772, it was ceded to Russia. The Russians renamed it Borisoglebsk and built a fortress in the town in 1810, which was taken by Napoléon a year later.

There was rapid urban growth in the 19th century, particularly after the construction of the Orel–Riga and St Petersburg–Warsaw railways in the 1860s. In 1920, after suffering much damage as a front line city during World War I, it was given its current name. It prospered in the inter-war period but was again ravaged when it fell under Nazi control in World War II. Latvi won independence from the USSR in 1991 and the last Soviet troops left in 1993.

Modern City

With a large Russian population, the city is dominated by Soviet brutalist architecture. The collapse of the Soviet Union led to the decline of Daugavpils' transport manufacturing industries, and the city now has one of the highest unemployment rates in the country. It remains a vital road and rail junction, and vehicle repair depots still provide much employment. Other important industries include food processing, textile production and electrical instrument manufacture.

Places of Interest

The fortress is the town's leading attraction. There is a local arts and history museum, the house of the poet Janis Rainis, the Catholic church of Peter Pavil and the Orthodox church of Boris and Vienibas House, the centre of the city's cultural life. Dubrovin Park is popular while the Daugava dam, built in 1841 and stretching 6 km, is also of interest.

Davao, Philippines

Introduction

Davao, with a population of 1.147 m. (2000 census) is the largest city of the Philippines southern island, Mindanao and with an area of 244,000 hectares is the world's largest city in terms of land area. Situated at the mouth of the Davao River, the city serves as the agricultural and trading centre of Mindanao and encompasses nearly 50 ports in its sphere of influence. The city is known for its exotic fruits like pineapples, mangosteen, many species of banana and the odoriferous but highly sought after durian.

History

Davao was already home to a number of tribal communities, including Moros, when the Spaniards arrived. In 1847 led by Don Jose Oyanguren, a Spanish expedition established a Christian community in the mangrove swamps that is now Bolton riverside. Oyanguren defeated the local Moro chieftain, Datu Bago, and renamed the area Nueva Guipozcoa and became the regions first colonial governor.

Oyanguren's colony did not prosper and in 1900 American forces arrived in Mindanao. Transport and other communications were improved. A Japanese entrepreneur, Kichisaburo Ohta, was given permission to exploit vast territories that he transformed into abaca and coconut plantations. This enticed a wave of Japanese plantation workers in 1903 creating a Japan Kuo, or little Japan. The Japanese immigrants established large abaca plantations and developed commercial interests such as copra, timber, fishing and import-export trading. The province prospered.

President Elpidio Quirino formally inaugurated Davao as a city on 16 March 1937.

Modern City

Being a city within the heartland of Moro insurgency against the predominantly Catholic north has hindered economic growth in Davao. The Moro National Liberation Front's (MNLF) presence has held back tourism and foreign and Philippine business. During the 1980s the city was known as the 'murder city of the south.' After a determined effort to drive guerrillas from the city, modern Davao has regained a semblance of business confidence. It has timber and fishing industries and exports hemp and coffee.

Places of Interest

Mount Apo (grandfather of all), at 3,143 metres (10,311 ft) above sea level, is the tallest peak in the Philippines and is reached along the Tamayong Trail via the Calinan district. Lush vegetation and majestic waterfalls rate highly among its many attractions.

The Philippine Eagle Conservation and Nature Centre is located at the foot of Mount Apo. The Philippine Eagle, once known as the Monkey Eating Eagle, is the world's largest eagle. With a wing-span of approximately 2.5 metres, ii is found only in the east of the Philippines, in the Sierra Madre mountains of Luzon and heavily forested areas of Mindanao. The nature centre has been instrumental in saving the eagle from extinction.

San Pedro Cathedral, built in 1847, is Davao's oldest church. It is named after the patron saint of Davao and built by Don Jose Oyanguren.

Debrecen, Hungary

Introduction

Debrecen is Hungary's second largest city and the main town of the county of Hajdú-Bihar in the eastern part of the country. Long established as a trading centre, it was briefly national capital during World War II and is now an important site for industry and agriculture.

History

While there is evidence of Neolithic settlements in the area, Debrecen first appears in written records from 1235. On trade routes between Upper Hungary and Transylvania, and Poland and Western Europe, it was famed for its livestock fairs. From the 1530s it was an important centre of Calvanism and was later the seat of the Hungarian Reformed Church.

Under the tripartate rule of the Hapsburgs, the Turks and the Protestant princes of Transylvania, Debrecen was punitively taxed and suffered from dynastic rivalries in the second half of the 16th century. By the end of the following century the Hapsburgs had wrestled control of the town and designated it a Royal Free city. However, attempts at enforcing Germanization and Catholicism strained relations between the urban populace and the governing power. It was in Debrecen in April 1849 that Lajos Kossuth proclaimed Hungarian independence from the Hapsburgs. The uprising failed and Russian forces took the city.

Debrecen suffered severe damage during World War II, with half its buildings damaged or destroyed. During 1944 and 1945, with Nazi forces retreating westward and Soviet forces yet to arrive from the east, the city was the temporary seat of the Hungarian government. Under communist rule after the war, Debrecen consolidated its role as an industrial powerhouse.

Modern City

Debrecen's industrial base suffered with the collapse of communism in 1989. The economy has subsequently diversified. Important industries include pharmaceuticals, textiles, engineering and food processing. Agriculture is important in the surrounding area. There are several institutions of higher education.

Debrecen is on major road and rail networks. The airport receives domestic flights and flights from Austria, Russia, Ukraine and Israel. The nearest large international airport is Budapest-Ferihegy, though there are plans to build one in Debrecen.

Places of Interest

The city's main square is Kossuth Square. The Great Reformed Church is here, as well as a statue of Lajos Kossuth who declared Hungarian independence in the church. Other attractions include the Déri Museum and the Mihály Csokonai Theatre, the Reformed College and the forested Nagyerdő area. West of the city is the Hungarian Steppe, much of which is now a national park.

Delhi, India

Introduction

India's capital city, Delhi, stands on the west bank of the Yamuna river, midway between the Ganges and the Indus Valleys. The Union Territory of Delhi is bordered by the northern states of Uttar Pradesh and Haryana.

History

Delhi consists of the old and new Delhi. The origins of old Delhi are unclear. A thriving city called Indraprastha is mentioned in the Mahabharata, indicating a settlement as early as 1300 BC, yet the first evidence of Delhi as such came in the 1st century BC when Raja Dhilu established a city, naming it after himself.

In the 12th century AD the city became the capital of the Chauhans, making it Hinduism's most important centre in northern India. It then fell into Muslim hands when Qutab-ud-din Aibak took the city towards the end of the century. During the period of Muslim rule which followed, Delhi changed location six times. Its status as a capital city was also subject to change as various rulers moved their headquarters to other cities such as Agra and Fatehpur Sikri. The Mughal empire restored Delhi to its former importance when in 1638 emperor Shah Jahan began to construct what is now known as old Delhi, including the Red Fort and the Jama Masjid, one of India's largest mosques.

The British captured Delhi in 1803 when it was already an important trade centre. The population had grown to 150,000 by 1900. With growing social and economic problems in Kolkata, the British decided to move the capital to Delhi. New Delhi was founded in 1912 but construction, under two British architects, Sir Edwin Lutyens and Sir Herbert Baker, was not finished until 1931 when the city was officially declared India's capital. Delhi suffered further disruption during the partition of India in 1947, experiencing a massive increase in population and damage to property and buildings.

Modern City

The economic centre of the city lies in Old Delhi with government offices concentrated in New Delhi. The main employer in the region is the government. The city is an important trading centre, with several major banks and a stock exchange.

Delhi has strong transport links both internationally and domestically. Five national highways converge on the city; there is an important rail centre and the Indira Gandhi international airport. Traffic within the city is highly congested despite the recent construction of bypasses and the widening of roads. Much of the traffic consists of bullock carts, bicycles and old cars. In Oct. 2010 Delhi hosted the Commonwealth Games. In 2014 the WHO ranked Delhi as the most polluted city in the world. An estimated 25,000–50,000 residents die from illnesses related to air pollution in the city ever year.

Places of Interest

Delhi has several major tourist attractions including the Red Fort, the central Vista Park and the Jama Masjid, as well as parliament house (Sansad Bhavan) from the period of British colonial rule. Most of the city's financial and administrative offices are located in the central Vista Park, along with the presidential house and two secretariat buildings. The Raj Path runs through the park to India Gate, a war memorial to the unknown soldier that commemorates Indian soldiers who died in World War II.

As well as the culturally diverse architecture, New Delhi is also home to the National Museum of India. There are several centres of higher education including the University of Delhi (founded in 1922), Jawaharlal Nehru University (1969), and other institutions for medical, agricultural, and technological studies.

Denver, United States of America

Introduction

Denver is the capital and the largest city in the state of Colorado. Located on the western edge of the Great Plains near the Rocky Mountains on the South Platte River, Denver is nearly a mile above sea level, hence the 'mile high city'. A popular tourist destination, Denver is also Colorado's major economic and cultural centre.

History

Located in an area originally occupied by Cheyenne and Arapahoe Indians, Denver and Auraria were founded in 1858 after gold was found nearby and prospectors rushed to the area. Denver was named after James W. Denver, governor of Kansas, of which the settlement was then a part. The two settlements merged into the city of Denver in 1860.

When the gold seams quickly ran out many prospectors left the area but the city survived as a centre for the shipment of other mined goods. Colorado became a state in 1876 and Denver its designated capital 5 years later. The arrival of railroads and the discovery of silver in the late 1870s was the start of more than a decade-long boom. After the bottom fell out of the silver market, Denver maintained a low profile until World War II when many federal offices were moved to the city and armaments manufacturing thrived. After the war the suburbs grew substantially. Despite problems with air pollution and rising crime, Denver enjoyed a further renaissance in the 1990s when it gained a new airport, baseball stadium and light railway system.

Modern City

The city is served by Denver International Airport which opened in 1995. Three interstate highways pass through the city. There is an Amtrak train station and a Greyhound bus terminal. Skyline and RTD buses provide transport in the city and there is a light railway system.

Tourism and agriculture are the principal industries. The city serves the mining and ranching activities in the nearby Rocky Mountains and houses several military installations and nearly 250 federal offices. There are also several major communications and medical technology companies. Educational institutions include the University of Colorado at Denver, the University of Denver, Regis University, the University of Colorado Health Sciences Center and the Colorado School of Mines.

Places of Interest

Denver has more than 250 urban parks including City Park which houses the Denver Museum of Natural History. Other major cultural institutions include the Denver Art Museum, the Museum of Western Art and Gates Planetarium.

The Civic Center in the city centre houses the State Capitol, the Colorado State Museum and a public library. There is a zoo and botanical gardens and the Colorado History Museum, the Littleton Historical Museum and the Aurora history museum. Denver has resident opera, ballet and theatre companies and is also the base for the Colorado Symphony Orchestra.

Detroit, United States of America

Introduction

Located in southeastern Michigan, Detroit is the largest city in Michigan and the seat of Wayne county. The city occupies 143 sq. miles (370 km^2) and is connected to the upper and lower regions of the Great Lakes by the Detroit and Rouge Rivers, giving it strategic advantages that have helped it gain its status as one of the major industrial centres in the United States. Detroit is nicknamed the Motor City, in recognition of the key role it has played in the American automobile industry.

History

Fort Pontchartrain du Détroit was established in 1701 as a French trading post dealing in fur with the Chippewa Native Americans. In 1760 the British took control of the area. The Jay Treaty of 1794 led to a British withdrawal and the United States took control 2 years later. Detroit was incorporated as a city in 1802 and became the capital of the newly created Michigan Territory in 1805. A fire later the same year ravaged much of the city.

The British briefly regained control of Detroit in 1812, but it was returned to American control the following year. In 1818 the first steamboat run between Buffalo, New York and Detroit was established and the city soon became a distribution and processing centre for grain, flour and agricultural products. The Erie canal was completed in 1825 making the Great Lakes the largest inland waterway in the world and boosting Detroit's economic development. Michigan became a state in 1837 although the capital was moved from Detroit to Lansing in 1847. The building of a railroad linking Detroit with Chicago in 1852 confirmed its economic status and helped promote its iron and steel industries.

Detroit became a major centre for the automobile industry around the turn of the 20th century. Ransom E. Olds opened an automobile factory in 1897 and Henry Ford completed his assembly line by 1914. Ford's success transformed the city into the world's foremost producer of automobiles leading to a massive rise in the city's population as many migrants, particularly black people from the south, came in search of employment. During the First and Second World Wars Detroit was an important centre of armaments production.

After the war, the city's racial tensions often bubbled to the surface. Meanwhile, as the importance of water transportation faded, so the city's industries faltered. Many white people left the city centre for the suburbs and unemployment rose steeply. Race relations reached a low-point in 1967 when there was a week of race riots. The city's first black mayor took office in 1973 but social and economic problems continued throughout the 1980s as crime rose and the automobile industry struggled because of competition from Japan and Europe. However, the city fought back in the mid-1990s, leading to major improvements in its public services and infrastructure and a significant rise in investment.

Modern City

For all the problems it has suffered in the post-war period, Detroit remains one of the United States largest industrial centres. The city's economy is sensitive to market conditions in the automobile industry but has a firm manufacturing and shipping base. Apart from automobiles the city's main products are steel, chemicals and machinery.

The city is served by Detroit Wayne County Metropolitan Airport and has an extensive network of roads and highways. The city has Greyhound bus and Amtrak rail terminals. A People Mover, an elevated railway, and DOT buses are the major forms of transport in the city itself. The riverfront remains the heart of modern Detroit and houses the Renaissance Center, a complex of offices, hotels, theatres and shopping facilities. The city also houses the Medical Center, one of the United States' largest complexes of hospitals, clinics, and research laboratories. Detroit is home to Wayne State University, which includes Schools of Business, Law and Medicine.

Places of Interest

The Detroit Cultural Center houses several museums. The vast Detroit Institute of Art contains 100 galleries and includes, among others, 77 Matisses and 67 Picassos as well as work by Van Gogh and Rembrandt. Other major museums include the Museum of African-American History, the Detroit Historical Museum and, befitting the city's status as the birthplace of rhythm and blues, the Motown Museum.

Detroit's significant role in the history of automobiles is represented by the Henry Ford Museum and the Automotive Hall of Fame. Most of the city's arts venues are in the northwest sector of downtown Detroit, including the Detroit Opera House, the Music Hall Center for Performing Arts, the Fox Theatre and Orchestra Hall, which houses the Detroit Symphony Orchestra.

Dhaka, Bangladesh

Introduction

The capital of Bangladesh, Dhaka is situated in the south-central part of the country on the north bank of the Dhaleswari River, part of the Ganges delta. The city flourished during the 17th and early 18th centuries when it served as the Moghul capital of Bengal and with the creation of Bangladesh in 1971, it became the country's capital. The city's name was changed in 1982 from Dacca to Dhaka.

History

Little is known of the first inhabitants of what is today Dhaka though the surrounding region was home to two earlier Bengali capitals (Vikrampur and Sonargaon). The city's modern history began in 1608 when the Moghul Viceroys made it capital of Bengal. It remained capital until 1639 and again between 1660–1704. Its economy boomed as English, French and Dutch companies established themselves, trading the city's fine quality muslins and silks. Many of Dhaka's grandest buildings were constructed during this period, including Lalbagh Fort and the tomb of Pari Bibi, the wife of a Bengali governor. However, after the capital was moved to Murshidabad in 1704, Dhaka lost much of its prestige and the economy suffered.

The city came under British rule in 1765. But it was not until it became the provincial capital of Eastern Bengal and Assam in 1905 that it began to prosper again. Following Indian independence and the partition of the sub-continent in 1947, East Bengal joined Pakistan as East Pakistan while West Bengal joined India. In 1948 Muhammad Ali Jinnah, Pakistan's first Governor General, announced that Urdu would be Pakistan's state language. Bengalis, outraged at the attack on their mother tongue, Bangla, began a protest movement, the Bhasha Andolon (Language Movement). After the death of four protesters in Feb. 1952, Bangla was officially recognised.

In 1956 Dhaka was made capital of East Pakistan. However, Bengali nationalism thrived on widespread resentment at West Pakistan's economic exploitation of East Pakistan. In 1971 the political divide led to a war of independence with West Pakistan. After 9 months of fighting which caused much damage to the city, Bangladesh was created with Dhaka as its capital.

Modern City

Dhaka is one of the world's most populous cities. It sits in one of the most significant rice and jute producing areas and acts as the country's principal administrative and trade centre. Other important industries include: food processing, textiles, paper, chemicals and sugarcane.

Much of the city is low-lying and susceptible to seasonal flooding. Linked to this are the serious sanitation problems faced in areas outside the city. The slums, with a population of 2.4 m., are largely devoid of sanitation or health facilities. As a result, water borne illnesses are rife.

There is an international airport 12 miles north of the city and a major port at Narayanganj, 10 miles to the south. Other modes of transport within Dhaka include the inland waterways, cars, buses and over 300,000 rickshaws.

Places of Interest

There is a bustling Old Town with bazaars and mosques which incorporates the earlier Bengali capital of Vikrampur. In contrast, the modern quarter of Ramna in the north of the city is where most of the government buildings, universities and other important institutions are concentrated. There are over 700 mosques in Dhaka, among the most famous of which is the Star Mosque which dates from the Moghul period.

Dijon, France

Introduction

The principal city of Burgundy, Dijon is on the confluence of the Ouche and Suzon rivers in Eastern France. Once the seat of the powerful Dukes of Burgundy, the surrounding region is renowned for its fine wines.

History

In Celtic times Dijon was strategically placed on the trade route for tin. The area was conquered by Julius Caesar around 50 BC. By the end of the 5th century AD, a Germanic tribe, the Burgundii, settled and added the territory to their kingdom. Between the 5th–9th centuries, Dijon was the seat of the Bishops of Langres.

Dijon was fought over during the Carolingian wars. In the 10th century, a second kingdom was created and in 1015 Dijon was established as the capital by Robert I, Duke of Burgundy. Dijon prospered as an important market town, known for its wool, and vineyards surrounded the city. Medieval Dijon linked trade between the Mediterranean and Northern Europe. The Medieval trade in Eastern spices resulted in two *Dijonnais* specialities—mustard and *pain d'épices* (gingerbread).

The Dukes of Burgundy were at their zenith between 1342–1467, when Philip the Strong, John the Fearless and Philip the Good ruled. Burgundy became a separate and powerful kingdom. The territory included the majority of Belgium, Holland and Northeast France. At the time, Dijon had one of the most illustrious courts of Europe, attracting great artists and architects. In 1369 Philip the Strong married Marguerite of Flanders, and artists from the North were attracted to Dijon. During the Hundred Year War (14th–15th centuries) the Dukes warred with the Armagnacs (French) and sided with the English, to whom they delivered Joan of Arc. The Golden Age ended with the death of Charles the Unready and the kingdom was claimed by Louis XI. The king moved the parliament of Burgundy from Beaune to Dijon, which led to an increase in prosperity. In 1513 the inhabitants of Dijon resisted invasion by 30,000 Swiss and Germans. During the Wars of Religion (16th–17th centuries), despite being Catholic, Dijon suffered little under the protection of Philippe de Chabot, the governor of Burgundy.

Dijon's most prosperous era was in the 18th century when the city became a bishopric. The university was founded in 1722, the academy in 1740. Dijon's prosperity was interrupted by the Revolution (1789), although its subsequent decline only lasted until the arrival of the railway in 1851, when the city's prosperity returned. In 1870, despite strong resistance and the help of Garibaldi's volunteers, the Prussians took Dijon, although the city remained relatively unscathed during World War II. In 1956 Dijon was twinned with Stalingrad (Volgograd), becoming the first town in France to be twinned with a town from Eastern Europe.

Modern City

The capital of the Côte d'Or department, Dijon is an important industrial centre. Industries include automobile plants and engineering. Dijon and Burgundy are renowned for gastronomy and the Côte d'Or is one of France's major viticulture centres with the villages of Mersault, Nuits-Saint-Georges and Pommerol nearby.

Dijon is linked by road and rail to Paris, the northeast and southeast of France, Switzerland and Italy. The nearby airport offers domestic flights.

Places of Interest

The Musée des Beaux Arts, opened in 1783, houses the second richest collection of art in France, after Paris. The Salle des Gardes contains two sepulchres where Philip the Bold and John the Fearless are entombed. The Museum is housed in the Palais des Ducs, in the old town. The medieval building was renovated when the Dukes of Burgundy settled there in mid-14th century. It has a classical appearance with additions and restorations in the 17th and 18th centuries, although the 46 metre-high 15th century Tour de Philippe le Bon is still intact; as are the original kitchens, built in the mid-15th century. The one time palace now houses the town hall. The old town contains the Rue des Forges, the city's main road in the 18th century, with examples of

16th century half-timbered houses. The Burgundian Gothic Eglise Notre Dame, built between 1220–40, was the centre of municipal life until a town hall was created in 1500. The Cathedral St Bénigne, built in the 13th century, is on the site of a Romanesque basilica from the first half of the 6th century.

Dili, Timor-Leste

Introduction

Timor-Leste's capital is located on the north coast of the island on the Ombai Strait. Historically it is the chief port and commercial centre of Timor-Leste although much of the city was destroyed in the violence of the 1999 referendum.

History

Dili's importance as a centre for trade came with the arrival of the Portuguese in the 16th century.

After the Portuguese ceded control to Indonesia in 1975, Dili was invaded by Indonesian forces and in 1976 it was made Timor-Leste's capital. Dili remained central in the struggle between the East Timorese population and the Indonesian government. In Nov. 1991 Indonesian soldiers opened fire on unarmed members of a funeral procession making its way to Dili's Santa Cruz cemetery. Two hundred and seventy-one unarmed East Timorese were killed and 250 were reported missing in the aftermath.

Immediately after results of the UN-administered referendum in 1999 were declared, showing an overwhelming vote for increased autonomy, Indonesian forces once more invaded the capital. In the violence which followed more than half the homes in Dili were destroyed. The Indonesian government prevented humanitarian organizations from entering the city and most of the city's population fled to the surrounding hills.

Modern City

Main industries include coffee, oil and gas, fisheries and spices.

There is an international airport.

Places of Interest

Dili is set for a new chapter in its history following Timor-Leste's independence in May 2002.

Djibouti, Djibouti

Introduction

The port city of Djibouti, on the shore of an inlet in the Gulf of Aden, is the country's capital and home to two-thirds of its population.

History

The French began constructing the city in 1888 and made it capital of French Somaliland in 1892. Thanks to its rail connection to Addis Ababa it soon gained commercial importance as the main outlet for Ethiopian exports.

There was rioting in the city in 1967 after a referendum continued French rule in which opposition leaders and ethnic Somalis were excluded from voting.

Modern City

The port acts as the main transhipment point for neighbouring land-locked African countries. It is linked by rail with Addis Ababa in Ethiopia and has bus services to major towns and cities in the country.

The port's chief exports include coffee, hides and salt, while main industries are shipping and oil.

Places of Interest

Popular attractions are the central market, just south of the town centre, and the Aquarium Tropical de Djibouti which features marine wildlife from the Red Sea. There are boat trips to the nearby islands of Maskali and Moucha.

Dodoma, Tanzania

Introduction

Dodoma replaced Dar es Salaam as Tanzania's capital in 1974. It is located in the centre of the country.

History

Dodoma was originally a small settlement belonging to the Gogo tribe. As it was on a caravan route linking Lake Tanganyika and central Africa with the Indian Ocean, it soon developed as a trading centre. It was established as a city in 1907 by the Germans who laid the first rail connections. Between the First World War and 1961 when Tanzania gained independence, Dodoma was administered by the British, under whom it continued as an administrative centre.

In 1974 the Tanzanian government declared its intention to move the capital from Dar es Salaam to Dodoma. Although most government ministries and legislative buildings were soon moved, the government ran out of funds and was unable to complete the task.

Modern City

Dodoma is an important trade centre for peanuts, coffee, tobacco and sorghum. Other products include furniture, timber, processed food and soap. Nonetheless, it is now more important as a transportation and administrative centre than as a trade centre.

Dodoma has road, rail and air connections with Arusha, Dar es Salaam and Tanga.

Places of Interest

Dodoma is the only wine-producing region in the country.

Doha (Ad Dawhah), Qatar

Introduction

Approximately 60% of Qatar's population of 600,000 lives in Doha, the capital and largest city. It is situated on a bay, roughly halfway along the eastern coast of the Qatari peninsula. For long a small pearling and fishing settlement, Doha has been transformed by Qatar's oil-rich economy into a metropolitan city.

History

From the early 18th century Doha was known to Persian Gulf pirates for the protection afforded by its old port of Al Bida. In the mid-19th century, Qatar's first ruler from the Al Thani family (Sheikh Mohammed) took effective control of most of the peninsula and settled in Doha. In 1867 the town was destroyed in a war with neighbouring Bahrain. The Ottoman Turks subsequently maintained a garrison there until Qatar became a British protectorate in 1916, with Doha as the administrative centre. A downturn in the pearling industry in the early 20th century undermined the town's fragile economy. However, it expanded rapidly as oil exports, which began in 1949, brought new revenue sources to the national government.

Modern City

In 1971 Doha became the capital of the newly independent state of Qatar. It remains the country's commercial and cultural centre. Government departments, financial institutions, and the headquarters of major companies are all located there. It has a large, artificial deepwater port, completed in the 1970s, and serves as a major transhipment centre for cargo of the Gulf nations. The international airport is situated in the southeast of the city. Doha hosted a summit of the World Trade Organization in Nov. 2001.

Places of Interest

Qatar's principal cultural attractions are to be found in Doha. These include the Qatar National Museum, the National Library, the Ethnographic Museum and the restored Al-Kout Fort (and handicrafts centre), together with traditional souks and bazaars. There is a 7-km long Corniche or esplanade along the Doha bay, and a zoo.

Donetsk, Ukraine

Introduction

The capital of the Donetsk oblast, Donetsk is on the River Kalmius in the Donets Basin in the east of the country. It has long been an important centre of the Ukrainian mining and metallurgical industries.

History

At the heart of Ukraine's coal-mining region, the city was originally named Yuzovka after Welshman John Hughes who set up a steel mill to exploit coal in 1872. Donetsk was a purpose-built workers' settlement for the local factory. In 1924 it was renamed Stalino, reflecting the success of the Soviets in the revolution of 1917. In 1961 it became Donetsk.

Having suffered heavily during World War II Donetsk was redeveloped in the post-war era by the Soviets and its industrial capacity expanded.

In recent years miners have struck over poor working conditions, highlighted by two major accidents. An explosion in 1998 killed 63 miners and another explosion in May 1999 claimed 39 lives.

During the 2014 conflict between Ukraine and pro-Russian rebels, the city became a centre point for protests and violence. On 11 May 2014, the Donetsk and Luhansk *oblasts* held a referendum on independence from Ukraine. It was alleged that 90% of the population voted in favour of independence, and the self-proclaimed state of the Donetsk People's Republic was declared with Donetsk as its capital. Neither the referendum nor the DPR were recognized by any other state.

Modern City

Coal mining and metallurgy continue to be the mainstays of the economy. Also important are chemicals, textiles, food processing, heavy engineering and scientific research. There are a university and several institutions of higher education.

Donetsk lies on major road and rail routes and there is an airport.

Places of Interest

There is a concert hall and numerous theatres.

Douala, Cameroon

Introduction

Cameroon's most populous city, Douala is also the country's chief port, located on the Wouri River estuary, 24 km inland from the coast.

History

Originally comprising three villages, Akwa, Bell and Deïdo, Douala developed as a centre for the slave trade following the arrival of the Portuguese in 1472. After the efforts of English missionary.

Alfred Saker in 1845 a treaty was signed with Douala's chiefs, abolishing slavery. Saker became a national hero and is also credited with translating and publishing the bible in the national language.

In 1884 Douala became a German protectorate. The swampy areas surrounding the city were cleared for development and rail connections were put in place.

After the First World War Douala became part of French Cameroon.

Modern City

Douala's deep water port handles the bulk of Cameroon's overseas trade and has been adapted for the handling of timber, gasoline, bananas and bauxite.

The Wouri Bridge (built in 1955) connects Douala to Bonabéri and carries both rail and road connections. There are rail links to Kumba, Yaoundé and Ngaoundéré and road connections to all major towns and cities in Cameroon as well as an international airport.

Main industries include: textiles, palm-oil, soap and processed food. There is a branch of the University of Yaoundé as well as several vocational colleges.

Places of Interest

The city has a museum and a handicrafts centre.

Dresden, Germany

Introduction

Dresden is the capital city of Saxony. It was the third largest city in the former German Democratic Republic. Allied carpet-bombing raids in World War II virtually destroyed the city.

History

Dresden was originally known as Drezdzany, a Slavonic fishing village on the Elbe River that grew as two distinct settlements on opposite banks. A German colony was established on the south bank of the Elbe opposite a Slav settlement on the north bank. More recent settlements became known as Altstadt (Old Town) while the older Slav settlements, paradoxically, were known as Neustadt (New Town).

In the 11th century, Dresden was the power centre for Margrave Henry the Illustrious of Meissen. After his death it passed to the King of Bohemia. From the 15th century it became the residence of the Saxon Dukes and as such Dresden was the capital of an important Protestant territory and the centre of the most powerful German state after the Habsburg territories. It was during this period that the city underwent a period of redevelopment.

Dresden's golden era came under Elector Augustus the Strong who gathered around him artists, sculptors and architects who transformed the city into a centre of Baroque excellence, earning the tag 'The Florence of the North'.

Dresden was targeted during the Seven Years War (1756–63) when her rulers fled to Warsaw. Prussian troops occupied the city and there was widespread destruction. Another period of upheaval came with the Napoleonic wars. In a bloody battle before the gates of the city in Aug. 1813

Napoléon achieved one of his last victories (against 170,000 Austrians, Prussians and Russians under Prince Karl Philipp), before shifting his attention towards Leipzig and the Battle of the Nations.

Dresden, although stripped of her finery, became an important city during the 19th century. Railway connections and a port development on the Elbe attracted business. This coupled with a rich cultural life made Dresden a popular tourist destination. By the turn of the century it was the fourth largest city in the German Empire, with a population of more than half a million.

The city suffered greatly from deprivation and political upheaval in the aftermath of World War I. However towards the end of World War II it seemed that Dresden had been spared the wholesale destruction that had befallen Berlin. Then on the nights of 13 and 14 Feb. and 2 March and 17 April 1945, Dresden was destroyed by joint Anglo-American 'saturation' bombing raids. Between 35,000 and 135,000 people perished in the attacks. The reasons for targeting the city remain contested. In May 1945 Soviet troops occupied Dresden.

Reconstruction of Dresden began with the clearing of huge amounts of rubble. Then buildings of architectural, cultural or administrative importance were rebuilt. A policy of rejuvenation was continued under the socialist control of the German Democratic Republic. Sited in a valley, Dresden was the only major town in the former German Democratic Republic unable to receive any Western TV or radio broadcasts, giving rise to the nickname 'Valley of the Unknowing'.

Modern City

Since the peaceful democratic revolution and the reunification of Germany, Dresden has once again become an important regional capital and cultural centre. In 1998 Dresden received over 6.9 m. visitors.

Four bridges connect the northern and southern sections of the city. Dresden is linked by motorway to Berlin, Leipzig, Bavaria and Hessen and a further motorway to Prague is currently under construction. There is an international airport (Flughafen Dresden) outside the city centre. There are two railway stations (Hauptbahnhof on the southern side of the town and Dresden-Neustadt on the north) with connections to all major German and many European cities. There is also a suburban railway system.

In Aug. 2002 severe flooding hit the city, causing extensive damage and forcing 30,000 people to leave their homes.

Places of Interest

Among the city's most popular attractions are: the Albertinum, formerly the city's armoury, housing a sculpture collection, the New Masters Gallery, a coin collection and the Green Vault with a major collection of jewels and jewellery; the Zwinger, built in the early 18th century by Daniel Pöppelmann and the sculptor Balthasar Permoser in the Baroque style, housing the Old Masters Gallery, the Armoury Museum, the Porcelain Collection, the Zoological Museum and the Mathematical-Physical Salon; Katholische Hofkirche, the Cathedral of St Trinitatis, a Catholic cathedral in the Baroque style finished in 1754 by the Italian architect Gaetano Chiaveri. The crypt contains the remains of several Saxon kings.

The Royal Dresden Palace, the home and seat of government of the Saxon princes and kings from the 13th until the early part of the 20th century, suffered badly during the bombing campaigns of 1945 and restoration was only completed in 2013. In 2005 the Church of Our Lady was re-consecrated following a restoration project costing €180 m. It had been left ruined by the East German authorities as a symbol of the destruction of the Second World War. However, reconstruction began shortly after German reunification.

Dresden Zoo and Botanical Gardens are in Grosser Garten to the southeast of Altstadt.

Dubai City, United Arab Emirates

Introduction

Capital of the emirate of Dubai and second city of the UAE, Dubai City is considered the most vibrant city in the Gulf. Located on the coast in the northeast of the country, its prosperity is built on oil wealth. With its natural harbour, Dubai has long been an important commercial and trading centre and is increasingly promoted as a tourist destination.

History

Dubai Museum holds a collection of artefacts found in graves dating from the first millennium BC at nearby Al-Qusais. A caravan station dating from the 6th century AD has been excavated in the city suburb of Jumairah. Like neighbouring Abu Dhabi, the area came under Portuguese commercial domination in the early 16th century and then under British hegemony from the 18th. At that time the settlement at Dubai was a small port and fishing village inhabited by members of the Bani Yas tribe (who had also settled in Abu Dhabi). The Dubai and Abu Dhabi branches of the Bani Yas split in the first half of the 19th century, forming two dynastic lines from which the current ruling families (al-Maktoum and al-Nahyan) are descended.

Lacking the fertile hinterland of Abu Dhabi (with its oases of Liwa and Al-Ain), Dubai's inhabitants looked to the sea for a living based on fishing, pearling and maritime trade. At the turn of the 20th century Dubai was sufficiently prosperous to attract settlers from Iran and the Indian subcontinent. By around 1930 nearly a quarter of its population was foreign, and such cosmopolitan links helped to cement Dubai's reputation as the region's principal trading centre. Like the rest of the Gulf coast, it suffered from the decline of the pearling industry from the 1930s (owing to Japanese competition) and the general drop in trade in the Second World War. However, it maintained its position as the main entrepôt of the lower Gulf. Then in the 1960s oil was discovered in the emirate, prompting intensive infrastructure and industrial development.

Modern City

Having expanded along both banks of the Dubai Creek (a natural sea-water inlet which cuts through the centre of the city), Dubai's central business district is divided into two parts—Deira on the northern side and Bur Dubai to the south, linked by two bridges and a tunnel passing under the Creek. Beyond this core, the city extends to the emirate of Sharjah to the north, and spreads south and west along the Gulf through the districts of Satwa, Jumairah and Umm Suqeim. Further west lies the coastal industrial complex and free trade zone of Jebel Ali—a project conceived and directed by Sheikh Rashid bin Said al-Maktoum in the 1970s. In Jan. 2010 the world's tallest tower, the Burj Khalifa, opened in Dubai, standing 830 metres (2,722 ft) high.

Places of Interest

Dubai has sophisticated international transport links and offers some of the best conference and exhibition facilities in the Middle East, such as the Dubai International Congress Centre (which can accommodate 10,000 delegates) and Dubai World Trade Centre. There is also extensive hotel accommodation. Tourist attractions include the Bastakia district with its old waterfront wind tower houses, the Deira souk (market), the Dubai Museum and the Heritage and Diving Villages (recreating traditional lifestyles). The Emirates-sponsored Dubai World Cup, staged in March, is the richest single-day horseracing meeting in the world. Other notable events are the Dubai Air Show, Dubai Shopping Festival and Dubai Fashion Week.

Dublin, Ireland

Introduction

Dublin is the capital city of the Republic of Ireland and lies on the east coat, straddling the River Liffey. Its recorded history dates back to Viking times but for most of its existence it has fallen under British jurisdiction. A focus for the nationalist cause throughout the 19th and 20th centuries, it became capital of an independent Ireland in 1921. Since Ireland joined the European Community (EC) in 1973 Dublin's economy has grown and it is now a popular tourist destination, renowned for the vibrancy of its youthful population.

History

Celtic tribes inhabited the region for several centuries before Vikings made incursions in 795 AD. They established a settlement on the site of Dublin in 841, but the city's official foundation is put at 989 when Dubh Linn (*Dark Pool*) and Baile Átha Cliath (*Town of the Hurdle Ford*) merged. The Battle of Clontarf in 1014 signalled the end of Viking domination in the area, after which a series of Irish chiefs governed.

In 1169 Dublin was taken by Diarmait Mac Murchada, a local king, with the assistance of the Norman Earl of Pembroke, Richard de Clare (also called *Strongbow*). The Normans, pledging allegiance to Henry II, then occupied the city, so beginning English domination. In the 1170s Christ Church Cathedral was constructed and Dublin Castle and the city walls were erected early in the 13th century. Dublin's other cathedral, St Patrick's, appeared 50 years later.

Under the reign of Henry VIII (1509–47) and Elizabeth I (1558–1603) Dublin was the base from which to spread Protestantism and suppress Catholicism. Trinity College was established in 1592 on the site of a former monastery. After a Catholic rebellion failed in 1601 Dublin's population was swelled by new Protestant arrivals and in 1649 the forces of Oliver Cromwell arrived in Ireland. Dublin's already waning importance and prosperity declined further.

Dublin, now a bastion of Anglican Protestantism, became a refuge for Huguenots fleeing suppression on the continent. As a result the cloth trade flourished in the city and led to unprecedented levels of wealth. Rich traders were responsible for the rush of fine Georgian buildings for which the city is still famous. Dublin Castle was refurbished during this period, Phoenix Park laid out and Sackville Street (now O'Connel Street, the city's main thoroughfare) was constructed.

The British responded to the rising tide of nationalism that occurred in the late-17th century by passing the 1801 Act of Union. The Irish Parliament was dissolved and Dublin's golden age came to an end. Though not as badly affected as many parts of Ireland by the Great Famine of the 1840s, the city's economy nonetheless strained under the mass influx of rural labourers. As the 19th century progressed, the issue of home rule and English domination intensified and was centred on Dublin. The Easter Rising of 1916, a nationalist rebellion, was crushed by British troops and saw much structural damage to the city. It led to the Anglo-Irish Treaty of 1921, which provided for an Irish Free State (Excluding Ulster), with Dublin as capital.

A bloody civil war between those who accepted the treaty and those who refused to recognize Irish partition ensued. Many Dubliners perished and the city suffered further damage. Dublin led the way in establishing a functioning Irish state, but this emphasis on domestic issues led to the country's self-imposed exile from the international scene (it remained neutral during World War II). This allied with a struggling economy left Dublin inward looking and culturally stagnating.

Modern City

Dublin's outlook changed dramatically with Ireland's entry into the EC in 1973. It benefited from an inflow of capital and an economic revolution took hold. Light industry grew as did Dublin's success as a port. The city is home to several major brewers and distillers, most notably Guinness (the largest brewery in the world). Tourism also prospered and a cultural renaissance began, assisted by a youthful population, around half of whom are under 25. Dublin is a major centre for road, rail, sea and air transport and a bus service operates within the city.

Places of Interest

Popular tourist attractions include Trinity College (home to the 5th century Book of Kells), tours of the Guinness brewery and several whisky distilleries, the General Post Office (from where independence was declared after the 1916 uprising), the two cathedrals, Kilmainham Gaol and many other museums and galleries. O'Connell Street is Dublin's commercial centre, Grafton Street a tourist magnet and Temple Bar the bohemian quarter. The Dublin Writers' Museum reflecting the city's rich literary heritage–its former residents have included Jonathan Swift, Edmund Burke, Richard Sheridan, Oscar Wilde, James Joyce, George Bernard Shaw, William Butler Yeats, Samuel Beckett, Brendan Behan and Sean O'Casey.

Durban, South Africa

Introduction

Situated on the east coast Durban was originally known as Port Natal. It is the largest city in the KwaZulu Natal region of South Africa, the country's principal seaport and the busiest port on the continent.

History

Europeans first came to settle in 1824 under the leadership of Francis Farewell. However, Port Natal had long been a refuge for beleaguered seafarers and it is thought that Vasco da Gama anchored here in the fifteenth century. During the seventeenth century Dutch seafarers struck a deal with a local chief for a section of coastal land. The bay was blocked by a sandbar and by the time that the settlers made it across the sandbar in 1705 the chief had died and his son refused to honour his father's contract.

Finally, settlers from the Farewell Trading Company established a community. King Shaka of the Zulus allowed them to stay, convinced that these settlers posed no threat to the Zulu way of life. A fort was erected and the town of Durban, named after Sir Benjamin D'Urban, the Governor of the Cape Colony, was founded in 1835. Voortrekkers established their capital at Pietermaritzburg in 1837, turned southeast and, taking advantage of chaos caused by Zulu impies, claimed Durban for themselves. Despite sporadic attacks by both the Zulus and the British the Boers seized control of Durban at the Battle of Congella. The British retaliated by sending a frigate and recapturing the town. Within 2 years the British had secured and annexed all of Natal. Durban was created a city in 1935.

Modern City

Durban is home to the South African sugar. The city's major exports include sugar, grain, minerals and coal. Louis Botha airport is 15 km to the south. Durban railway station provides services to Johannesburg, Cape Town, Bloemfontein, Ladysmith, Kimberley and Pietermaritzburg, as well as numerous regional destinations. Local transport is by Mynah Buses which run from North and South Beaches into the city centre and adjoining suburbs.

Places of Interest

Durban's Local History Museum, in Durban's original court house, includes a reconstruction of the city's first white settler dwelling, a post office and an apothecary. Durban Art Gallery, established in 1892, is on Smith Street and houses a large collection of English, foreign and South African works. It houses beadwork, glass and carvings from Zulu culture as well as well known South African artists like Andrew Verster and Penny Siopis. The Natal Playhouse stages drama, avant-garde plays, opera, musicals and cabaret in five adjoining theatres.

Fitzsimons Snake Park holds venom-milking demonstrations; snakes include South African and exotic species. There is an aquarium in the heart of Durban's Golden Mile linked by an underground tunnel to the dolphinarium where daily seal and dolphin shows are held. Overlooking the Umgeni River, Umgeni River Bird Park ranks among the world's best. Many varieties of brightly coloured birds, both indigenous and exotic, inhabit walk-in aviaries set in picturesque gardens.

Dushanbe, Tajikistan

Introduction

Dushanbe, on the River Dushanbinka in the Hissar valley in the southwest of the country, is the former capital of Soviet Tajikistan. It is one of the region's most important transport and industrial hubs.

History

There is evidence of human habitation in the area dating back 7,000–9,000 years. The city originated from a village named after its weekly Monday market. The first written record of Dushanbe was in 1676, by which time it was long established as an important stopping-off point on silk trade routes. In 1875 it appears on a map as a fortress.

For a long period it was under the control of the Emir of Bukhara but in 1920 Emir Said Alimkhan was overthrown by the Soviets.

Dushanbe became a battleground as Enver Pasha led a Basmach armed rebellion to recapture the city from the Bolsheviks in 1922. Igrahim Bek also made the city his headquarters in his fight against the Bolsheviks but by 1923 Soviet control was firmly established. In 1929 it was renamed Stalinabad and designated capital of the Soviet Socialist Republic of Tajikistan. In the same year it was connected to the Trans-Caspian railway.

Under Soviet rule the city underwent rapid industrialization and was expanded to take in wide boulevards and public spaces. In 1961 it was given its current name. In 1979 the city was the base for the launch of the invasion into Afghanistan.

Modern City

Important industries include textiles, electrical manufacturing and consumer goods. The city has good road and rail links and there is an airport. Buses and trolleybuses run within the city. There is a university and several institutes of higher education.

Some areas are unsafe and visitors are warned to take advice from their embassy before travelling to the city. The Green Bazaar, the area around the airport and the residential area behind the Lakhuti Theatre are high risk districts.

Places of Interest

The city is divided into four administrative sectors. The suburb of Varsab was an elite recreational centre in Soviet times and is still regarded as the most attractive part of the city. There are many chaikhana, or teahouses, throughout the city. The major attractions are mostly on or around the Prosekt Rudaki. These include the main mosque, a nineteenth century synagogue and the opera house. There is a museum of ethnography while the Tajikistan Unified museum has exhibitions of history, natural history and art.

Düsseldorf, Germany

Introduction

Düsseldorf, 'the village on the Düssel', is the capital of Germany's North Rhine-Westphalia region and lies on the banks of the Rhine. It has long played an important role in European trade.

History

Neanderthal findings suggest the area around Düsseldorf has been inhabited for at least 52,000 years. It was first chartered by the Count of Berg in 1288 and became the capital of the duchy of Berg. This dynastic line ended with the assassination of Engelbert I in the following century.

The region succeeded to the Limburg and Jülich dynasties from the fourteenth century until the seventeenth century. It then became the capital of the Palatinate-Neuberg line. Düsseldorf suffered badly during the Thirty Years' War (1618–48) and during the War of the Spanish Succession (1701–14) but was restored by elector palatine Johann Willhelm II. Briefly under Napoleonic rule at the start of the nineteenth century, the town became part of Prussia in 1815.

A large portion of the city was reduced to ruins by some 200 air raids between 1942 and 1945. After the war many of the city's older buildings were restored.

Modern City

As a banking centre and home of the German fashion industry, Düsseldorf is one of Germany's most prosperous cities. It owes its historical prominence to the large Ruhr bituminous coalfield which allowed the area to develop as the centre of the most important industrial, mining and energy-generating area of Germany. Lohhausen Airport is 8 km north of the city. The main railway station is Hauptbahnhof and trains, trams, buses and U-Bahn all run within the city.

Places of Interest

Among Düsseldorf's finest galleries is the Kunstsammlung Nordrhein-Westfalen, which houses a display of twentieth century artists including Picasso, Matisse, Klee and Braque. Nearby is the Hochschule für bildende Künste (Academy of Art), housing several galleries. The building was designed by Hermann Riffart after the example of Italian renaissance buildings.

The Kunstmuseum includes a fine collection of Art Nouveau and Art Deco glass as well as Rubens' altarpiece of *The Assumption* and *Venus and Adonis*. The Schloß Jägerhof, which houses the Goethe Museum, was completed in 1772 as a residence for the local gamekeeper. It has been much renovated over the years after bombings and burnings.

The city is home to the Deutsche Oper am Rhein, which can house over 1,300 people. Also famous is the futuristic looking Düsseldorf Schauspielhaus theatre, built between 1968 and 1970 and nicknamed 'the cheese-box'.

Edinburgh (Dùn Èideaan), United Kingdom of Great Britain and Northern Ireland

Introduction

Edinburgh is the capital city of Scotland and seat of the new Scottish Parliament. It is situated to the south of the Firth of Forth and about 65 km northwest of the Scottish/English border at the River Tweed. Edinburgh is built on several hills and has two distinct sections: the medieval Old Town and the elegant Georgian New Town. Overlooking the city is Edinburgh Castle.

History

There is evidence to suggest that the area around Castle Rock (now the site of Edinburgh Castle) was inhabited by Celtic tribes as far back as 1500 BC. Many Iron Age hill forts were built during this period. The Roman invasion of Britain moved as far north as the Firth of Forth and it was there at the northernmost extremities of Roman occupation that the Antonine Wall was built to defend the empire from northern Barbarians. The Romans had a mutually respectful relationship with the Celtic Votadini tribe who had their capital at Traprain Law. By 500 AD the Votadini capital had moved north to the present site of Castle Rock, called Din Eidyin (Eidyin's Hill Fort). By 854 AD it had become Edwinesburgh (Edwine's Stronghold).

The town grew slowly throughout the latter part of the first millennium. In the late-eleventh century Malcolm III built his castle in Edinburgh (including a chapel for his wife, Margaret, which still stands). Malcolm's son, David I, founded Holyrood Abbey in 1128. Edinburgh Castle fell to the English forces of Edward I in 1296 but returned to Scottish hands in 1313. Nine years later the English raided Holyrood Abbey.

It was not until the fourteenth century that Edinburgh rose in political importance. In 1329 King Robert the Bruce gave Edinburgh a town charter. James I was crowned in Holyrood Abbey and most of his parliaments were held in the city. By the time of James III Edinburgh was known as the capital of Scotland. Under James IV the city developed as a seat of learning, culture and civil government, which in turn stimulated religious radicalism. John Knox, an exponent of this radicalism, was one of the most influential figures of the sixteenth century Reformation. In 1560 the Treaty of Edinburgh ended the 'old alliance' between Scotland and France.

From 1603 when James VI of Scotland (also James I of England) moved his court to England, Edinburgh was relegated to a political and cultural backwater. In 1707 the Act of Union between Scotland and England was signed and Edinburgh relinquished its rights as a capital to London. At first

Edinburgh did well out of the union and its economy stabilized and grew. Many new civic buildings were built and Edinburgh was at the centre of what was called the Scottish Enlightenment.

In the late eighteenth century Edinburgh New Town was designed by James Craig and Robert Adam in classical squares, terraces and crescents. Despite these improvements, Victorian and early Edwardian Edinburgh was much like other industrial cities found throughout Great Britain. Subject to an influx of workers from the surrounding countryside it was prone to epidemics, principally owing to the lack of proper sanitation.

Urban expansion throughout the twentieth century had caused serious harm to the city's outstanding architectural heritage but the establishment of the New Town Conservation Committee in the 1970s has ensured the city retains its aesthetic integrity.

Modern City

In modern times, Edinburgh has undergone cultural and political rejuvenation. Since 1947 the city has had an internationally renowned arts and theatre festival (running alongside an equally popular Fringe Festival). It is a major centre for electronics and engineering, commercial insurance and the professions. The nearby port of Leith remains a major trade centre. Edinburgh University has a reputation for its advanced research facilities.

Following a referendum held in 1997 the Scottish Parliament, which last assembled nearly 300 years ago, was re-established. On 1 July 1999 the Parliament, based in Edinburgh, was officially opened by the Queen. It has limited powers but will be able to make decisions on key issues such as education, taxation and health care. Tourism is a major earner (especially during the Festival).

Places of Interest

Popular attractions include: Edinburgh Castle; the Palace of Holyrood House (the Queen's official Scottish residence); the twelfth century St Giles' Cathedral; the Museum of Scotland; the National Gallery of Scotland; the Regimental Museum of the Royal Scots (Scotland's cavalry regiment); the Royal Museum (covering decorative arts, science, technology and geology); the Scottish National Gallery of Modern Art; the Scottish National Portrait Gallery. The Royal Mile is a grand thoroughfare running from the castle to Holyrood Palace and the city's other main street is Princes Street. The Edinburgh Military Tattoo is held each summer on the esplanade at the castle.

Associated with Edinburgh are Adam Smith (the eighteenth century economist), Alexander Graham Bell (inventor of the telephone), Sir Harry Lauder (a star of the music hall), Sean Connery (the actor) and several writers including James Boswell, Sir Walter Scott, Robert Louis Stevenson, Sir Arthur Conan Doyle and Muriel Spark.

Edmonton, Canada

Introduction

The capital of Alberta, Edmonton is situated on the North Saskatchewan River, in the centre of the province. The site attracted Native Canadian settlers for thousands of years before the arrival of the early fur traders in the eighteenth century. The first European to reach Alberta was the fur trader Anthony Henday, who explored the area in 1754–55, spending the winter with a tribe of Blackfoot Indians.

History

The city proper developed from Fort Edmonton, the Hudson's Bay Company's fur-trading post. This was established in 1795 at a site 20 miles downstream from the present city.

The Fort was abandoned in 1810 but another trading settlement developed on the site after 1864 and survived the Cree Indian Rebellion of 1885.

With the Hudson Bay Company's sale of its rights to the Dominion of Canada in 1870, Edmonton's growth accelerated. It became an important grain producer, encouraging many new settlers to move to the city. After the Yukon gold rush of 1897 they were joined by thousands of gold prospectors who arrived in the city having mistakenly followed newspaper promises of an 'All Canadian Route' to the gold fields that would avoid the dangerous Chilkoot Trail.

Edmonton continued to prosper as a centre for agricultural distribution with the arrival of the Canadian Pacific Railway at nearby Strathcona. In 1905 the Canadian Northern Railway reached the city, leading to its designation as the capital of the Province of Alberta.

To encourage settlement on a larger scale, the Canadian government launched a massive advertising campaign across Canada, the United States and Europe with the slogan 'COME SETTLE THE WEST!'. Cheap or even free land was offered as an incentive.

In 1912, Edmonton on the North side of the river and the town of Strathcona on the South amalgamated with a combined population of over 53,000. The High Level Bridge was completed in 1913, creating another link between the north and south sides of the city. The elegant Hotel Macdonald was completed in 1915.

Modern City

With the discovery of oil at Leduc (just south of the city) in 1947, Edmonton's industrial economy developed further. By the end of the year, there were 30 wells producing 3,500 barrels of oil a day. As further discoveries were made, natural gas also proved to be a valuable resource. Oil and agriculture continue to dominate the city's economy.

Places of Interest

Edmonton's main attractions are the West Edmonton Mall—one of the world's largest shopping centres—and Fort Edmonton Park, Canada's largest living history museum. The city's historic Old Strathcona district has recently been developed, with several museums, restaurants and bars opening up.

Esfahan, Iran

Introduction

Esfahan is the third largest city and the capital of the central province of the same name. An industrial centre, particularly for textiles, it also has some of the leading tourist attractions in Iran and is renowned for its architecture.

History

Having been invaded successively from the mid-seventh century by Arabs, Seljuk Turks (who made it the capital of their empire in the eleventh century) and Mongols (in the fourteenth century), Esfahan enjoyed a renaissance under the Safavid dynasty from the late 1500s. Abbas I made Esfahan the Persian capital, and under his patronage the city reached the peak of its commercial prosperity and architectural prominence in the early seventeenth century. It was badly damaged by Afghan invaders in the 1720s, and its population declined dramatically before recovering during the reign of Reza Khan (father of the last Shah of Iran) from 1925–41.

Modern City

Esfahan's agricultural hinterland produces cotton, grain and tobacco. The city's industries include traditional manufactures such as rugs, tiles and cotton fabrics, as well as steel making and oil refining. The university was established 1946.

Places of Interest

In the centre of the city lies a square, the Meidan Imam (a World Heritage Site), built in the early seventeenth century and one of the largest in the world. Other architectural attractions dating from the Safavid period include the Imam Mosque, Lotfallah Mosque, Ali Qapoo Palace, Chehel Sotoon Palace and Si-o-Se Pol Bridge (one of several old bridges that cross the Zayandeh River). The Vank Cathedral is the focal point of the Armenian Church in Iran. The Chahar Bagh Madrassa, a theological college, was built in the early eighteenth century. Esfahan has a Natural History Museum and Decorative Arts Museum.

Faisalabad, Pakistan

Introduction

Formerly known as Lyallpur, Faisalabad is in the northeast of Pakistan in the Punjab district. It is the third largest city in the country after Karachi and Lahore and is an important commercial centre for the region.

History

Founded in 1890 by Sir Charles James Lyall, the lieutenant governor of the Punjab (1887–92), after whom it was named, the city was laid out in the shape of the British flag. It served as the headquarters of the Lower Chenab colony before becoming a municipality in 1898. The Faisalabad district was constituted in 1904, carved from the neighbouring districts of Jhang Maghiana, Shekhupura, Multan and Sahiwal, on a plain between the Ravi and Chenab rivers. Originally desert land, irrigation from the Lower Chenab Canal turned the district into a fertile zone and made way for the harvesting of cotton and wheat, the two major crops grown in the region. During the 1930s industry came to the city with the establishment of the Lyallpur Cotton Mills.

Following the partition of the sub-continent in 1947, Faisalabad changed from a small town to a burgeoning city. Between 1947 and 1951 its population rose from 71,000 to 421,000. Population continued to grow after the Pakistani government promoted industrialization. Now the centre for textile production, the city is known as 'the Manchester of Pakistan'.

Modern City

The main industries are: chemical fertilizer, synthetic fibres, pharmaceuticals, tinned products, ghee (clarified butter), soap, textiles and textile machinery, bicycles, vegetable oil, hosiery, flour and sugar. The city is a wholesale centre for grain and cloth. There are a number of colleges affiliated to the University of the Punjab as well as to the West Pakistan Agricultural University. There are rail, road and air connections to Lahore and Multan and air connections to Lahore and Karachi.

Places of Interest

The central clock tower is now a main tourist attraction. From it, all eight segments of the city, containing the city's main bazaars and shopping precincts, are visible. There are several parks and recreational grounds.

Fès, Morocco

Introduction

A cultural, spiritual, intellectual and commercial centre and the oldest of the four imperial cities, Fès is to the north of Morocco, 160 km east of Rabat. Fès is divided into three areas, Fès el Bali (old town), Fès el Jedid (new town) and Ville Nouvelle (modern city). In 1981 the medina was designated a World Heritage Site. The town gave its name to the Fez, a brimless, cylindrical red felt hat with a tassel worn by some men in Muslim countries.

History

Fès was founded around 798 on the east bank of the Wadi Fès by Moulay Idriss I. His son, Moulay Idriss II, built on the west bank in 808 and the two parts were united in the eleventh century by the Almoravids. Over the next 80 years Fès became a major Islamic city. In 1250 Fès was conquered by the Merinids who made it their capital. Shortly after the new town (Fès el Jedid) was built with a Jewish quarter (Mellah) added in the fourteenth century. In the sixteenth century Fès was captured by the Saadians who made Marrakesh their capital. During the first half of the eighteenth century, under Moulay Abdallah, Fès once more became the capital with many mosques and medersas (schools for teaching the Koran). The Treaty of Fès in 1912 brought large parts of Morocco under a French protectorate and the capital moved to Rabat. The Ville Nouvelle was founded by General Lyautey in 1916 with much expansion taking place following WWII.

Modern City

The city's industrial quarter is found in the Ville Nouvelle, close to the railway station. Carpets, textiles, leather and traditional crafts are produced. There are also flour mills, oil-processing plants, tanneries and soap factories. The medina, which encompasses the oldest part of the city and the area built in the thirteenth and fourteenth centuries, is full of markets making and selling leather, pottery, perfume, jewellery and wrought iron ware. The commercial centre, known as the Kissaria, is the largest and oldest of all the medinas with much of its walls and gates still intact. The Qarawiyin Mosque, built in 859 AD, is the sight of one of the oldest universities and renowned as a centre of Islamic culture. The Sidi Mohammed ibn Abdellah University was founded in 1974. The city can be reached by train from Rabat, Marrakesh or Tangier. The international airport of Fès Sais is 15 km from the centre.

Places of Interest

The medina has most of the historic buildings as well as the markets. The ninth century Qarawiyn Mosque houses the tomb of its creator, Idriss II, but non-Muslims are not allowed entry. In Fès el Jedid is the Royal Palace and the Great Mosque, built in the thirteenth century by the Marinids. The Medersa Bou Inania is a theological college built in 1350. The Bartha Museum has collections of handicrafts from different regions of the country and the Arms Museum has a large collection of old fire arms and swords.

Florence (Firenze), Italy

Introduction

Florence is on the River Arno in the northcentral area of Italy. It is the capital of Tuscany and of the province of Firenze. The city is a major crossroads between Rome and northern Italy, and is notable for its cultural and artistic heritage.

History

Florence was founded in 59 BC as Florentia. By the third century AD it was provincial capital and commercial centre of the Roman Empire. With imperial decline, the city fell into the hands of the Ostrogoths, before being captured by the Byzantines and the Lombards. Prosperity was restored in the early eleventh century under the guidance of Countess Matilda of Tuscany.

Florence's economy continued to grow through the eleventh and twelfth centuries, but stability was threatened by an ongoing dispute between the Guelphs (Papal supporters who favoured the government of the mercantile classes) and the Ghibelines (Imperial supporters). The two factions favoured alternate modes of government for the city, and their opposition has to be set in a wider context of the dispute between the papacy and the Holy Roman Emperor as to whom should govern Christendom. The conflict was resolved in 1289 with the victory of the Guelph merchant families. At the end of the thirteenth century the new bourgeoisie regime introduced a constitution forbidding nobles and labourers alike from holding power. This was designed to ensure the continuation of mercantile control of the city and facilitated the emergence of a civil servant class vying for position in the Signoria (a government body dominated by the major trade guilds). The Guelphs in turn split into two factions, the Neri (blacks) and the Bianchi (whites). The latter was defeated and many of its members, including Dante Alighieri, were forced into exile.

Under mercantile leadership, Florence's system of government became increasingly democratic and the city became a commercial republic which prospered peacefully until 1348 when the Black Death halved its population of 90,000. Subsequent famine, economic collapse and rebellion further eroded Florence's power and splendour. The end of the fourteenth century witnessed the rise of three families, the Albizzi, the Ricci and the Medici, who had amassed substantial wealth derived from banking and commerce. The Medici gradually consolidated their power, becoming bankers to the papacy. Cosimo de' Medici patronized the arts and financed the building of the Medici

Palace, the church of San Lorenzo and the Monastery of St. Mark. Artists such as Donatello, Boccaccio, Ghiberti and Michelangelo were attracted to the city. Cosimo's legacy was perpetuated by his son, Piero, and his grandson, Lorenzo. When Lorenzo died in 1492, Charles VII of France invaded with the support of several Florentine noblemen. For a short while the city was subject to the puritanical leadership of the monk Girolamo Savonarola, but his ascetic rule was ended in 1498 when he was executed for heresy.

In 1512 the Medici returned to rule the city until 1527. Thereafter a power struggle between the papacy and the Emperor Charles V saw control of Florence passing from one ruler to another. In 1537, Charles made Cosimo de' Medici duke of Florence. Cosimo undertook the building of the Uffizzi, the renovation of the Palazzo Vecchio and the reconstruction of the Pitti Palace. He also took on the title of Cosimo I, Grand Duke of Tuscany, gaining control of many neighbouring territories, including the towns of Siena, Pisa and Arezzo. Despite these gains, Florentine influence within Europe was waning. The Medici dynasty ended with the death of Gian Gastone in 1737 when he city was taken over by Francis I of the House of Lorraine. In 1799 Florence became a part of the Napoleonic Empire but when Napoléon was defeated the Lorraines returned to rule until Leopold II abdicated in 1859 to make way for the unified kingdom of Italy under Victor Emmanuel. Florence was the provisional capital of the new kingdom from 1865–70.

The city's infrastructure suffered greatly during the twentieth century as a result of bombing in World War II and a disastrous flood in 1966. The latter brought forward the huge amount of work required to modernize the city and protect its treasures from decay. The process of restructuring and renovation continues today.

Modern City

Amerigo Vespucci airport is a 15-minute train journey from the main station and there are train services to Aeroporto Galileo Galilei at Pisa.

The Santa Maria Novella station is on Piazza Santa Maria Novella, opposite the church. Direct services operate from here to Bologna, Milan, Rome and Venice. The main bus station is alongside Santa Maria Novella.

Major highways connect Florence with Bologna and Milan in the north and Rome and Naples in the south. There are also motorways connecting the city to the west coast.

ATAF buses service the city centre.

Florence's major industries include the manufacture of rubber, chemicals, glassware, ceramics, wrought iron, shoes, jewellery and furniture. The city hosts several international fashion shows as well as an international antiques fair and numerous arts festivals.

Places of Interest

The redbrick duomo, created by Filippo Brunelleschi, is the third largest dome in the world. The interior of the Baptistry, thought to be the oldest building in the city, is decorated with mosaics of Dante's *Inferno* and the east doors feature Ghiberti's famous *Gates of Paradise*. The Museo dell'Opera di Santa Maria del Fiore is home to the Duomo's most important pieces, including a late Michelangelo *Pieta*.

The thirteenth century Palazzo Vecchio is the civic centre of Florence and its highly decorative state rooms contain some seminal examples of Mannerist art, the court style of Cosimo I.

The Franciscan Chiesa di Santa Croce is probably the city's most beautiful church. Monuments celebrate the achievements of Michaelangelo, Machiavelli, Ghiberti, Dante and Galileo.

The Ponte Vecchio is a world-famous bridge and the oldest in Florence. The bridge used to accommodate butchers and tanners but is now occupied by jewellers and tourist shops.

The Basilica di San Lorenzo and the Palazzo Medici, with interiors designed by Michelangelo, are testament to the power of the Medici dynasty.

The Palazzo Pitti is a fifteenth century palace housing six museums. There are fine collections of Titian and Rubens.

The Uffizi Gallery houses one of the world's most famous art collections, including incomparable examples of the works of Botticelli, da Vinci, Michelangelo, Raphael, Titian, Giotto, Caravaggio, Cimabue, Rubens and Rembrandt. There are also fine examples of Greek and Roman statuary.

The Bargello was previously a fortress, mansion and prison, and is now home to the Museo Nazionale which contains important works by Donatello and Michelangelo.

The Galleria del Accademia boasts impressive collections of painting and sculpture; the highlight is Michelangelo's *David*. His unfinished Slaves is also here.

Fongafale, Tuvalu

Introduction

Fongafale, the capital of Tuvalu, is the chief town of Funafuti Attol. It achieved capital status when Tuvalu won independence in 1978.

History

As part of the former Gilbert and Ellice Islands colony, Funafuti Atoll was used as a military base by the US from 1943. Two years after self government in 1974, Funafuti took over from Tarawa as the administrative centre.

Modern City

Fongafale is small and largely unspoilt with a modest tourist industry. There is a hotel, hospital and a small airport. Copra is the chief export.

Places of Interest

There are no famous tourist attractions. Most visitors come on official business but other visitors are attracted by the natural and unspoilt coastline.

Frankfurt am Main, Germany

Introduction

Frankfurt am Main, on the River Main, is the largest city of the *Land* of Hesse and was effectively national capital during the nineteenth century. It is now one of Germany's most important centres of industry and commerce, and home to the European Central Bank.

History

The name Frankfurt, which derives from 'ford or crossing of the Franks', probably originated around 500 AD but the first written mention of the city is to be found in the writings of Charlemagne's biographer, Einhard, in the late eighth century. However, there is also evidence of pre-Roman and Roman habitation.

It was in Frankfurt in 1152 that Frederick Barbarossa was elected ruler of Germany and in the thirteenth century the Hohenstaufen family built a new imperial castle to replace the original Pfalz (imperial castle). In the mid-fourteenth century the Golden Bull, which defined the constitutional structure of the Holy Roman Empire, assigned Frankfurt as the place of coronation for the emperors, a privilege it retained until 1806. Its stock exchange was established in 1585.

A Free City from the late-fourteenth century, in 1806, on the orders of Napoléon, Frankfurt became the administrative capital of the Confederation of the Rhine. Four years later it was the seat of government of the newly designated Grand Duchy of Frankfurt. Napoléon lost power in 1815, and Frankfurt temporarily reverted to free city status.

A year later the German Bundestag sat in Frankfurt, and continued to do so for the next 50 years. As such, it was effectively Germany's capital city. After the Seven Weeks War in 1866 between Prussia and Austria, Prussia annexed the city.

Germany unification brought with it rapid industrial and commercial expansion. Frankfurt further benefited from its position on Northern European trade routes. The construction of a canal network in the late nineteenth century increased its importance as an inland shipping port.

Frankfurt was badly hit by allied bombing in World War II and, although many key historical landmarks remain, many others have been restored and rebuilt. Its status as a financial centre has led to many impressive modern buildings.

Modern City

Frankfurt is a major centre for banking and trade fairs. It is the home of the European Central Bank. Its first organized trade fairs were held in the thirteenth century and today it hosts internationally important fairs for numerous industries including the motor, computer and book trades. Important manufactures include machinery, pharmaceuticals, chemicals, printing materials, leather goods and foodstuffs (including quality sausages-hence 'frankfurter'). The city's university is named after Goethe, one of Frankfurt's most famous residents.

The city's airport, Flughafen Rhein-Main, is one of Europe's busiest with the third highest passenger turnover after London Heathrow and Paris Charles de Gaulle and the second highest freight turnover after Paris Charles de Gaulle. The main station, the Hauptbahnhof, handles more trains than any other station in Germany. Frankfurt is linked to other German cities by Autobahnen (motorways) and local transport within the city is provided by the S-Bahn, U-Bahn, buses and Straßenbahn (trams).

Places of Interest

The Römerberg is the old central square of Frankfurt. Since the old town was almost entirely destroyed during World War II, most of the buildings that originally date from the fourteenth and fifteenth centuries have been sympathetically rebuilt or restored. Buildings here include the Haus zum Römer (the old Town Hall), and the Dom (Bartholomäuskirche), a Gothic church with a museum attached. The Paulskirche (St Paul's Church), opposite the Römerberg, served as the meeting place for Germany's first Democratic National Assembly after the 1848–49 revolution. Frankfurt has a zoo on the eastern side of town, famous for its rare species and giant aviary.

Museumsufer, a stretch of the south bank of the River Main between Eiserner Steg and the Friedensbrücke, is home to seven museums. Städelsches Kunstinstitut und Städtische Galerie is one of Germany's most important art collections. It includes works by masters of the Renaissance, numerous Old Masters, French impressionists, German Expressionists, cubists, surrealists and artists of the Bauhaus. It also houses collections of contemporary art and graphics.

Museum für Kunsthandwerk (Museum of Applied Arts), in a building by Richard Meier opened in 1985, contains art works dating as far back as the Neolithic period. Deutsches Filmmuseum (German Museum of Cinema) incorporates an exhibition of cinematic artefacts from the earliest days of motion pictures, as well as a cinema showing shorts and newsreels. Deutsches Architektur-Museum (German Architecture Museum) was designed by Oswald Mathias Ungers as part of a complex housing a villa of the Bismarck period. The museum has a collection of architects' plans, models and examples of European architecture.

Also popular is Goethe Haus, the birthplace of the writer Goethe, and the Museum für Post und Kommunikation (Museum of Post and Communications), which traces the history of German travel and communication with interactive video displays.

Freeport, The Bahamas

Introduction

Freeport is situated on Grand Bahama Island and is the second largest industrial city of the Bahamas. It is also the second most popular spot for visitors after Nassau. Encompassing an area of 596 km², the city is a free trade zone.

History

Until the mid-twentieth century the area was covered in pine forest, swamp and scrub land, although there was a lumber industry. In the late 1940s an American financier, Wallace Groves, bought the Pine Ridge lumber business. This proved to be the making of the city. In 1955 Groves' company, the Grand Bahama Port Authority, was granted 20,200 hectares of land to develop a free port and industrial centre.

Freeport's first major economic activity was as a ship-bunkering terminal exporting oil. In 1961 a cement plant was built. In 1963 Groves' negotiated

the development of Lucaya as a beachside tourist resort. In 1963 the first hotel opened as well as a casino. Further businesses included a chemical factory and a bottling company.

For two decades Freeport was firmly in control of the Grand Bahama Port Authority company (GBPA), which controlled all aspects of the business, including the port traffic. When the new Progressive Liberal Party government began a 'Bahamianisation' programme in the early 1970s, its major target was to bring the Port Authority under government control and to restrict the influence of the GBPA. Even so, in the 1990s Freeport's status as a free trade zone was extended until 2054.

Modern City

The man made port accommodates large vessels and the city has an international airport. Industries include oil refining, cement production and pharmaceuticals. Exports include agricultural produce and fish.

Places of Interest

Port Lucaya and marina area contains an International Bazaar designed to represent different countries. The Hydraflora Gardens contain an array of native plants.

Freetown, Sierra Leone

Introduction

Freetown is the capital, largest city and principal port of Sierra Leone. It lies on a peninsula on the south bank of the estuary of the Sierra Leone River. The port is a natural harbour on the Atlantic Ocean situated on the west coast of Africa. There is potential for development of the fine beaches but civil war and violent crime have deterred tourism and delayed building programmes.

History

The Portuguese explorer, Pedro da Sintra, named the wooded hills behind Freetown, Serra Leoa or Lion Mountains, in 1462. Two hundred years later the British, Dutch, French and Danish trading companies were vying with the Portuguese for control of coastal trade. Freetown was founded in 1787 by British abolitionists as a home for liberated slaves. The community was wiped out by disease and re-established in 1792 by the Sierra Leone Company with slaves from Nova Scotia that had fought for the British in the American War of Independence. Descendants of these slaves are known as Creoles. The peninsula was declared a British colony in 1808 with the interior being annexed in 1896. On 19 April 1961 Sierra Leone was granted independence. As the administrative capital and the centre of government, Freetown has suffered from the civil wars, corruption and violence that have dominated Sierra Leone's politics. Some of these governments profited from the lucrative trade in diamonds, but little filtered down to benefit the rest of the people. Hundreds of thousands were forced out of Freetown during the war.

Modern City

Lungi International Airport is located across the estuary from Freetown. The only link between the two is a limited ferry service. The national carrier is Sierra Leone National Airways with flights to Accra and Lagos. Many of the roads are in an extremely bad condition and plans for a 84 km narrow-gauge railway were abandoned in 1971. There is no passenger rail service. Credit cards are not accepted and medical services are poor. Major exports include bauxite, diamonds, gold, coffee and cocoa. Fourah Bay College (founded in 1827) and Njala University (1963) are constituent colleges of the University of Sierra Leone (1969). Fourah Bay became affiliated with Durham University in 1876. There is also a teachers' college, a technical institute and several government Christian and Muslim secondary schools. The Creole people are served by a number of periodicals.

Places of Interest

Much has been destroyed during the civil war. Several mosques and churches, built during the nineteenth century including Holy Trinity Church, have been destroyed by fire and have undergone renovation. The Anglican St George's

Cathedral dates from 1828. The State House and residence of the president was formerly known as Fort Thornton, built in 1796. The Sewa Grounds is an emporium selling African goods, traditional carvings, clothing, paintings, handbags and local arts and crafts. The National Museum of Sierra Leone houses wood and stone sculptures and a number of historical documents.

Gaborone, Botswana

Introduction

Gaborone is located midway along Botswana's southeastern border with South Africa. It is a modern city, but as recently as the early 1960s was little more than a village. It was chosen as the site for the newly independent nation's capital in 1966 because of its readily available water supply and its proximity to the cross-continental railway line.

History

The city was named after Chief Gaborone who led his tribe into the region in the 1880s. The country's diamond wealth was uncovered 5 years later, and Botswana went from being one of the poorest nations on earth to being one of Africa's few success stories. Gaborone's fortunes changed dramatically as well, the city becoming a major location for foreign investment. A monument to the source of its prosperity is found in the Orapa House. The building has specifically engineered floors to make the best use of daylight, without letting in direct sunlight, in order to assist the process of sorting and grading diamonds.

Modern City

Gaborone today is a major centre for commercial, shopping, banking and telecommunication facilities. It provides the headquarters for all government departments and private organizations operating within Botswana. There is an international airport on the outskirts of the city, and rail connections to Pretoria and Johannesburg in South Africa, Harare in Zimbabwe, and Windhoek in Namibia.

Places of Interest

The city's major attraction is The National Museum, located near the centre, which houses a collection of native arts and crafts as well as mounted wildlife. Historical evidence of the capital's past can be discovered at 'the Village' which, amongst other exhibits, allows visitors to examine the remains of a colonial fort. Just outside the city lies the Gaborone game reserve which contains kudu, rhino and zebra.

Gdańsk, Poland

Introduction

Gdańsk lies at the point where the Vistula River meets the Baltic Sea. Often a centre of European conflict, in 1938 Hitler demanded the annexation of the city. Poland's refusal, backed by England and France, provoked German aggression on 1 Sept. 1939 which triggered World War II. In 1980 the city's dockyards gave birth to the *Solidarity* movement.

History

There is evidence of a settlement at Gdańsk from around 2000 BC. Eastern Germanic tribes created settlements within the area throughout the first millennia BC. In the eighth century AD, the site of modern day Gdańsk became part of Pomerelia or Eastern Pomerania (a separate group of Polish peoples inhabiting the coastal regions) who retained control over the area until AD 1308. At this point, the city fell into the hands of the Teutonic Knights under whose control the city became known as Danzig (which remains the German name for the city). In 1466 power was returned to the

Poles following a war waged by King Casimir IV, who subsequently granted the city its autonomy as a reward for aid given during the 13 year campaign.

This freedom permitted the exploitation of Gdańsk's trade opportunities, the city developing as one of the most successful ports on the Baltic Sea. In 1754 it had the largest population of any Eastern European settlement and handled grain exports (of which Gdańsk held the country's monopoly) of more than 200,000 tonnes per annum. At the end of the eighteenth century, however, the city was caught up in the Napoleonic wars, which severely damaged the economy. In the aftermath Gdańsk was reduced to a province of West Prussia.

The signing of the post-World War I Treaty of Versailles in 1919 established Gdańsk as a free city, under the administrative jurisdiction of Poland, yet with its population and legislative assembly composed predominantly of Germans. Antagonism between Germany and Poland culminated in 1938 with Adolf Hitler's demand for the surrender of Gdańsk to the Third Reich. With the end of World War II the city returned to Poland. This led to the mass ethnic cleansing of Germans from the city and surrounding region.

Poland's government was modelled on Stalinist communism, yet within a decade there was the first of many pro-democracy riots. In 1970, the nation's increasing foreign debts and the collapse of Polish industry resulted in further riots in a number of Baltic seaports, including Gdańsk. Further strike action in 1980, centred on the city's shipyards, led to the creation of *Solidarity*, the first non-federal trade union to be established within a communist country. Soviet and Polish communist efforts to curb the popularity of Solidarity failed. In the open elections of 1989 only one of the 100 seats went to the communist party. Solidarity's leader, Lech Wałęsa, became president of Poland in 1990, remaining so until 1995.

Modern City

Gdańsk is home to Poland's largest maritime development, the Port Północny (North Port). With 18 km of quays it specialises in the handling of sulphur, coal, phosphorites, crude oil and pulp. However, bankruptcy hit the port in 1996 and a few years later it was acquired by a firm from the more prosperous neighbouring port of Glydnia. The city still remains one of the front-runners in Polish industry and, together with Glydnia, the two ports deal with the majority of Poland's import trade. Rail connections are extensive, with lines to Warsaw as well as other major European cities. The airport, 10 km to the west, is the second largest in Poland and has regular flights to Düsseldorf, Warsaw, Kraków and Berlin.

Places of Interest

Gdańsk was almost totally destroyed in World War II and subsequently underwent extensive restoration. The city is the former home of philosopher Arthur Schopenhauer and writer Günther Grass, and has a variety of theatres, galleries and museums. The Church of St Mary is one of the largest brick churches in the world, housing in one of its 30 chapels a 30 m high astronomical clock dating from the fifteenth century. The memorial to the Martyred Shipyard Workers with its three steel spires stands near the Lenin Shipyard. It was here in 1970 that 27 protesters were shot and where, a decade later, Lech Wałęsa founded Solidarity.

Geneva, Switzerland

Introduction

Geneva is situated near the French border in southwestern Switzerland at a confluence of Lake Geneva and the River Rhône. The city is home to over 200 international organisations.

History

Settlement in the area dates back to 3000 BC. The town was seized from its original Celtic inhabitants by the Romans in 58 BC, and was referred to as Genua by Julius Caesar. At this stage it was used as a military camp for Roman soldiers on their way into Gaul, but by AD 400 it had become a bishopric. The city was subject to frequent invasion by Germanic and Burgundian tribes, but was eventually incorporated into the Burgundian kingdom, serving as its capital from 443–534. Throughout the early feudal period

Geneva was an important hub for regional commerce and was ruled by the Genevese counts until their line died out at the beginning of the fifteenth century. The Dukes of Savoy then governed the city and its environs until 1533 when they were overthrown by a citizen's revolt. Savoy granted Geneva independence in 1536, when John Calvin visited the city for the first time. By 1541 Calvin had embarked on a programme of sweeping religious and social reforms and Geneva became a place of refuge for persecuted Protestants from all over Europe.

In 1602 Savoy attempted to recapture Geneva. The successful defence of the city is still celebrated. Geneva continued to thrive commercially, but the republican foundations for its government that had been established under Calvin was eroded by the increasing powers of Protestant nobles, many of whom were refugees from France or Italy. They systematically reduced the proportion of the Genevese population who could claim full rights as citizens. The consequence was to ferment social and political opposition to aristocratic rule and in 1792 the nobles were overthrown. Six years later Geneva was annexed by France. French rule lasted until 1814 when the canton opted to become a part of the Swiss Confederation. Having secured independence, the nobles grew in power once more, and 1846 working class revolt toppled the canton's conservative government. In 1860 the Savoyards accepted rule by France and a free zone was created for Geneva. Four years later a local businessman, Henri Dunant, set out the Geneva Convention, the first attempt to regulate the conduct of armed forces and protect prisoners of war. As a result the Red Cross was founded in the city, and Geneva's future role as a key player in all international affairs was assured. In 1919 the League of Nations based itself in the city, and after World War II the United Nations chose Geneva as its European headquarters. One consequence of its international role is that the city is reluctant to be involved in national affairs. Politics in Geneva continue to be focused on the canton rather than the nation.

Modern City

The Rhône and the lower lake basin bisect the city, and the city centre, comprising the major commercial streets and the historic Old Town, is located on the south bank. Also to the south are the university and the Plainpalais district. To the northeast is the heavily populated residential area of Eaux-Vives. The other suburbs and industrial sections lie in irregular belts around this central area. Geneva is an important transport hub and is served by several motorways, as well as by a high-speed railway system that provides a three-hour service to Paris. There is a large well-designed international airport 5 km to the northwest. Local transport consists of extensive bus, trolley and tram networks.

Geneva's enclosed geographical position has limited its scope as a manufacturing centre, but the chemical industry, which mainly produces perfumes and pharmaceuticals, is second only to that of Basle. Food processing and cigarette manufacturing are other important industries. The city is also one of the oldest banking centres on the continent.

Places of Interest

The Museum of Art and History, one of Geneva's premier cultural attractions, houses a vast and eclectic collection of paintings, sculpture and archaeology. The smaller Petit Palais contains an important collection of modern art. Other notable museums include the International Red Cross and Red Crescent Museum, the Museum of Old Musical Instruments and the Voltaire Museum. The historic city centre is dominated by the Cathedral St Pierre. One of Geneva's most famous landmarks is the Jet d'Eau (Water Jet), the official logo of the city's tourist office.

History

Genoa was founded in the fourth century BC and was a key Roman port. The city expanded rapidly into a powerful mercantile centre under the rule of several foreign powers. Genoa was occupied by the Franks in 774 and by the Saracens in the tenth century. A longstanding rivalry began with Venice, the other great Italian maritime power, over the control of the valuable Mediterranean trading routes.

At the beginning of the fourteenth century Genoa was a very prosperous city-state with colonies as far afield as the Black Sea. However its prosperity was marred by years of internal feuding between four powerful noble families (Fieschi, Grimaldi, Doria and Spinola) which culminated in an attempt to restore civic order through the election of a doge in 1339. The political problem was not resolved, and the city was captured by the French (1394) and the Milanese (1421). Genoa emerged from these occupations having lost a great deal of its wealth and control of its colonies in Sardinia and Corsica. The city's fortunes were restored in the sixteenth century by Admiral Andrea Doria who ushered in a new constitution that gave Genoa the status of a mercantile republic. Doria led the new republic into a military, political and artistic golden age that lasted well into the seventeenth century. Magnificent palaces were built, and artists like Rubens, Caravaggio and van Dyck worked in the city. The famous architect Galezeo Alessi designed and built many of the city's most important buildings.

In the eighteenth century, the decline in the importance of the Mediterranean as a trading route affected Genoa, but by the middle of the nineteenth century, under the leadership of Giuseppe Mazzini, Genoa was at the forefront of the campaign for the unification of Italy. A century later, at the end of World War II, the people of Genoa led the rise against the Germans and the Italian Fascists and liberated their own city before the arrival of the Allied troops. After a period of prosperity in the 1960s, port activity declined and with it the fortunes of the city. The port and the waterfront fell into disrepair and the city centre showed signs of neglect. In 1992, however, the Columbus Festival attracted huge investment and the new privatized port operations are handling increasingly large amounts of container business.

Modern City

Genoa is now Italy's chief port and handles passenger and freight traffic. It is the main source of the city's income. Shipbuilding is the major industry; other significant industries include petroleum, textiles, iron, steel, paper, sugar, cement and chemicals as well as the manufacture of electrical, railway, and marine equipment. The city is also a major centre for finance and commerce. Genoa is well served by roads and railways which connect it to major destinations in Italy, France and Switzerland. There is an international airport 6 km to the west of the city. Genoa was one of the European Capitals of Culture in 2004.

Places of Interest

Religious buildings include the Cattedrale di San Lorenzo, a twelfth century Gothic cathedral which allegedly once held the relics of St John the Baptist, the Ducal Palace and the Chiesa di San Matteo which houses the preserved sword of Andrea Doria. The Palazzo Doria Tursi, which functions as the town hall, contains some remnants of Christopher Columbus who was born in Genoa. The Palazzo Bianco and the Palazzo Rosso both house fine art collections, the former placing an emphasis on the works of Flemish and Dutch masters, and the latter boasting works by Van Dyck. The Museo d'Arte Orientale has one of Europe's most extensive collections of Eastern artwork.

Genoa, Italy

Introduction

Genoa is located in northwestern Italy about 120 km south of Milan on the Gulf of Genoa. The city has been an important Mediterranean seaport for centuries. It is the capital of Genova province and of the Liguria region and is the centre of the Italian Riviera.

Georgetown, Guyana

Introduction

On the east bank of the Demerara River where it flows into the Atlantic Ocean, Georgetown is the capital of Guyana, its main port and the country's only large city. Below sea level, Georgetown is protected by a sea wall.

History

The Guyanese coastline was originally marshy swampland covered in mangroves. The original inhabitants were the Warrau followed by the Caribs and Arawaks. The hostile terrain delayed the arrival of colonists. In the eighteenth century the area was reclaimed by the Dutch who built a system of drainage canals and a protective sea wall. Georgetown was founded by the British in 1781 and named after George III, although it was soon occupied by both the French and the Dutch, the latter naming it Stabroek. The town was built on a grid plan with tree lined avenues and buildings of local 'greenheart' wood. In 1784 the town was made the seat of government for the combined colonies of Essequibo and Demerara.

At the end of the Napoleonic Wars, the British purchased Guyana from the Dutch and in 1812 Stabroek became Georgetown. In 1837 the first town council met and 5 years later Georgetown was declared a city. The nearby sugar plantations were worked by African slaves until their liberation in 1838. Most ex-slaves refused to continue working the fields and created settlements in the inland bush. To resolve the labour crisis, the British used indentured labour from India. Between 1838–1917 around 250,000 Indians were brought to the country, most of whom remained. A smaller number of Portuguese and Chinese labourers were indentured in the nineteenth century giving Guyana a unique demographic mix.

In 1945 and 1951 Georgetown suffered widespread structural damage from two fires which destroyed many of the wooden buildings. The business quarter was subsequently rebuilt using concrete, although much of the centre and traditional buildings remain in wood. In 1970 British Guiana became the Republic of Guyana with Georgetown its capital.

Modern City

Guyana's principal port, Georgetown exports sugar, bauxite, rice and fruit. Industries include sugar refining and the manufacture of timber products, beer and drinks. The University of Guyana was established in 1963. The city is accessible by air at the nearby Timehri International Airport and by boat, although road connections are limited, serving only the coastline and a short distance inland. Many areas are only accessible by river.

Places of Interest

In the city centre many wooden colonial buildings still stand including the town hall (1888) and the high court. St Georges Cathedral, designed by Arthur Bloomfield, was built of wood in 1889 and is among the world's tallest wooden buildings. The oldest religious building in the city is the Neo-Gothic Scottish Presbyterian church. Museums include the National Museum displaying artefacts from Guyanese history, and an art collection specializing in Guyanese art housed in the nineteenth century Castellani House. In 1972 the indigenous Wai Wai used traditional methods to build a conical thatched building, the Umana Yana. Botanical gardens contain collections of orchids and palms.

Ghent, Belgium

Introduction

Ghent, the capital of the province of East Flanders, is situated on the junction of the Lys and Scheldt rivers in northwestern Belgium. It is the fourth largest city in Belgium, and its well-preserved medieval centre provides a reminder that it is also one of the oldest cities in the region.

History

Ghent is thought to have been settled in prehistoric times, but it was only during the Gallo-Roman era that the nucleus of a town appeared at the confluence of the rivers. During the eleventh and twelfth centuries Ghent's prosperity increased as it became a crucial trading centre, mainly because of its cloth industry. Its wealth meant it would frequently oppose its nominal rulers—during the Hundred Years War, for instance, the city supported Edward III of England, owing to its heavy reliance on English wool to

make cloth. In the fifteenth century Ghent was under the authority of the Dukes of Burgundy. In 1500 Charles V, Duke of Burgundy and future Holy Roman Emperor, was born in the city.

The rule of Charles and in particular his son Philip proved costly for Ghent. It became a prominent centre for dissent against Spanish rule, and in 1576 the Pacification of Ghent united the northern and southern provinces of the Lowlands in opposition to Spain. After the ensuing war, Ghent's cloth industry was left in ruins, unable to compete with English manufacturers. The city declined still further when its access to the sea was lost to the Dutch in the mid seventeenth century.

Ghent's fortunes began to revive when new industrial techniques were introduced to facilitate the production of cloth. The construction of the Ghent-Terneuzen Canal in 1827 restored the crucial route to the sea. As a result Ghent was able to reclaim its position as the capital of the Belgian textiles industry and also established itself as the second largest port in the country.

Modern City

Today Ghent's major exports are light machinery, paper and chemicals. Industry includes oil and chemical refining. It is also a major centre for banking and horticulture, hosting the famous flower show 'Les Floralies' every 5 years. Like all Belgian cities, Ghent has an efficient public transport network. To the southwest there is an international airport at St Denis-Westrem.

Places of Interest

Ghent's ancient medieval centre is extremely well preserved, and the Gothic cathedral of St Bavon, or Baaf, dates from the twelfth century. It also houses Van Eyck's celebrated altarpiece *The Adoration of the Lamb*. This artistic heritage is also evident within the city's many museums, most notable of which is the Museum of Fine Arts.

Glasgow (Glas Cu), United Kingdom of Great Britain and Northern Ireland

Introduction

Glasgow is the largest city in Scotland and the regional capital of Strathclyde. It is located on the River Clyde in the southwest of Scotland. Long reliant on commerce and heavy industry, the city underwent a renaissance during the 1980s and experienced large-scale regeneration.

History

There is archaeological evidence of a prehistoric settlement on the site of Glasgow and Stone Age canoes found near the River Clyde point to the existence of fishing communities. Towards the end of the first century AD the Romans had established a trading post on the site of the modern city. St Kentigern, better known as St Mungo ('Dear One') arrived in the area in the sixth century and founded a religious community. The church that St Mungo built was destroyed in the wars that swept the country in the years after his death. The cathedral that stands on the site of St Mungo's church dates from the twelfth century.

During the early twelfth century Glasgow became an episcopal see and was declared a royal burgh by William I in 1180. In 1300 at Bishop's Castle (now the site of the Royal Infirmary), William Wallace led 300 men to victory against an army of 1,000 English knights who had taken possession of the castle. The castle was the scene of further fighting during the sixteenth century when opposition forces clashed for the Scottish crown, then held by the infant Mary Queen of Scots. Glasgow University was founded in 1541.

Glasgow's location between the Scottish lowlands and highlands made it an accessible meeting place and ensured its importance as a trading centre. It was not, however, until the accession of James I of Scotland and VI of England as the first Stuart monarch of England and of Scotland in 1603 that Glasgow's growth accelerated significantly. After the 1707 Act of Union Glasgow was well positioned to take advantage of the growing trade with the West Indies and America. It became a prosperous town, trading in tobacco, rum and sugar, and the so-called Tobacco Lords built ostentatious mansions in the city.

The nineteenth century saw the dawning of Glasgow as a manufacturing centre. In 1812 Glaswegian Henry Bell was the first to fit a steam engine on to a boat. The Industrial Revolution brought coal mining, iron founding, chemical manufacturing and shipbuilding to Glasgow. The city saw a great influx of peasantry during the early years of the Industrial Revolution. This situation was compounded by the further influx of thousands of immigrants from Ireland, attempting to escape the effects of the potato famine. By 1848 deteriorating social conditions climaxed in 'Bread Riots'.

Many of those industries which had risen to prominence during the nineteenth century (notably shipbuilding) went into long-term decline after World War I. Important industries today include printing, food processing, tobacco, printing and chemicals. After World War II efforts were made to disperse the population of Glasgow's overcrowded areas into adjoining New Towns. However, this process hastened the inner urban decay already blighting the city.

Modern City

Glasgow experienced a cultural and financial renaissance during the 1980s and 1990s, attracting investors, tourists and students. It was the European City of Culture in 1990, the United Kingdom City of Architecture and Design in 1999 and has established itself as a major venue for international and national conferences.

Places of Interest

Among its most popular tourist attractions are: Glasgow Cathedral; the Botanic Gardens (including the Kibble Palace, built in 1873); the Art Gallery and Museum (housing exhibitions of art, history and science, fine arts, decorative arts, design and human and natural history); the Burrell Collection (with collections of European, Middle and Far Eastern fine and decorative art); the Gallery of Modern Art; the Museum of Transport; the People's Palace Museum (telling the story of Glasgow from 1175 to the present day).

Gothenburg, Sweden

Introduction

Gothenburg is in the southwest, on the estuary of the Göta river. It is Sweden's second largest city and Scandinavia's largest seaport. Besides being the capital of Västra Götaland, it is the commercial and industrial hub of southern Sweden.

History

Settlement in the area dates back to the stone age and the best preserved Viking ship in the world, the Äskekärrsskeppet, was found in the area in the 1930s. However, Gothenburg's story began in 1601 when King Charles IX allowed Holland to establish a colony to secure access to the Baltic. In 1611 the fledging colony was destroyed by the Danes. Charles' successor, Gustav II Adolf ordered the construction of a new city in 1621. The early inhabitants were mainly German and Dutch merchants and artisans. The Dutch were responsible for draining the surrounding marsh, and the city's development was largely financed by Dutch trade.

British commercial investment in the eighteenth century helped Gothenburg prosper and the city became a major centre for international trade, particularly for the import of goods from the far east. The foundation of the Swedish East India Company confirmed Gothenburg's importance which was further increased by the completion of the Göta canal in 1832. Gothenburg's shipyards were among the largest in Europe. In the twentieth century the city's maritime economy declined and when Volvo cars began production in 1927, vehicle manufacture became the major industry.

Modern City

By the end of the 1980s most of the large shipyards had closed down, and today only the Stena Lines ferry terminal and the fish harbour remain. The old shipyard Eriksbergsvarvet has been converted into a large exhibition- and conference centre known as Eriksbergshallen. Eriksberg is also the finishing point of the Tall Ships Race.

Significant exports include cars, ball bearings and paper. Volvo and Svenska Kullagerfabriken (the world's leading manufacturer of ball bearings) are the city's leading employers. Modern Gothenburg is the sport capital of the country. It hosts numerous large sporting events such as the Gothia Cup, the world's largest football tournament, with almost 30,000 young players. The arenas Ullevi and Scandinavium are located in the city centre and in addition to hosting sporting events, they are also popular venues for concerts. Rail and the Göta canal connect the city to the rest of the country. Nearby Landvetter airport provides international and domestic flights.

Places of Interest

The most successful attraction is the Liseberg amusement park, popular for its rides and rollercoasters and for staging big name concerts.

The Ostindiska House in the city centre is one of the country's largest museums of cultural history. Its permanent exhibitions feature the history of Gothenburg, shipping in Sweden and the Vikings. It houses the famous tenth century Äskekärr ship. The Museum of Art (Konstmuseet) has an excellent collection of late nineteenth century Nordic art, and also houses works by the old masters, including Rembrandt and Rubens. The maritime museum, Sjöfartshistoriska museet, was founded in 1913 by the Nautical Society of Gothenburg. Featuring exhibitions on shipping history, Gothenburg's harbour and shipyards, it has a notable collection of figureheads and an aquarium. The Opera House, Göteborgs Operan, is celebrated as a masterpiece of modern architecture.

Granada, Spain

Introduction

Granada is situated in the south of Spain on the northwest slope of the Sierra Navada Mountain. It is served by two rivers—the Genil to the south and the Darro to the east.

History

The history of Granada can be traced back to the fifth century BC when it was the site of an Iberian settlement originally called Elibyrge. It became part of the Roman Empire and was named Illiberis by both the Romans and the subsequent invaders, the Visigoths. The city gained importance when it was taken over by the Moors in the early twelfth century and was named Granada. It has been speculated that the name originates from the Spanish word for pomegranate *granada*, a fruit that grows in the area. Although this fruit now adorns the city's coat of arms, the name may in fact derive from the Moorish word *Karnattah* (or *Gharnatah*).

In 1238 the city became the capital of the Moorish kingdom of *Gharnatah*, which encompassed what is now Granada, Málaga and Almería. Foreign trade through the coastal city of Málaga and the silk industry created wealth. The site of the silk exchange was the Alcaicería, which is still there today, albeit not the original building. The successful Riconquista by the Catholic monarchs of Castile and Aragón, Ferdinand and Isabella, ended the Moorish reign in the fifteenth century. The city, the last Moorish stronghold, was captured on 2 Jan. 1492 when Spain became a united country. In 1492, the Jews were expelled and 10 years later any Moor unwilling to convert to Christianity was exiled. Even those who converted, the *Moriscos*, were eventually forced out a century later in the time of the Spanish Inquisition. Despite the racial intolerance, *Gitanos* (Spanish Gypsies) settled in Granada in the sixteenth century and are still present today. For centuries the *Gitanos* lived in *cuevas del Sacromonte*, caves dug into the Sacromonte hill, to the northeast of the Alhambra. Currently, more than half of Spain's *Gitanos* live in Andalucía and some still live in the *cuevas* workings as artisans.

A long period of decline caused partly by the loss of its enterprising Jewish and Moorish populations, continued until Granada became a popular tourist attraction in the nineteenth century. The successful cultivation of sugar beet in the Vega area to the west of Granada helped to boost the city's economy.

Granada was caught up in the Civil War. Captured by the Nationalists, the city witnessed mass killings. The target was anyone with leftwing or liberal sentiments. Among the 4,000 *Granadinos* who died was one of the leading Spanish literary figures of the twentieth century, the poet and playwright Federico García Lorca.

The twentieth century saw steady growth and development in Granada. The last few decades have brought increasing prosperity chiefly from tourism and intensive agriculture.

Modern City

Industries include textiles, sugar, brandy, soap, leather and tourism. Granada is host to an annual festival of dance and music in June and July. The University, founded in 1531, is to the west of central Granada.

Granada has national rail and road links and a domestic airport 17 km from the city.

Places of Interest

The city still contains remnants of the Moorish kingdom. Perhaps the most famous example is the castle of Alhambra, located on a hill to the east of Granada. The red stucco on its walls inspired its name, *al-hambra* or red in Arabic. Built between 1238–1358, the palace and a mixture of gardens and courts are combined with the citadel of Alcazaba. Directly northeast stands the Generalife (Garden of the architect), the royal summer palace.

Built on the site of the principal Moorish mosque, the Catedral de Santa María de la Encarnación, constructed between 1521 and 1714, is in the centre of Granada. Originally commissioned to the Gothic architect Enrique Egas, the Cathedral was eventually designed by the architect and sculptor Diego de Siloé in Renaissance style. The edifice was constructed around the capilla real, which was built by Egas between 1506–21 as a mausoleum for the Catholic Monarchs. Other historic churches include the sixteenth century Gothic Iglesia de Santo Domingo.

Directly west of the Alhambra is one of the oldest parts of the city, Albaicín, once the most heavily populated area in Moorish Granada. After the Riconquista, it was home to the Islamic population. Today, the area remains a maze of narrow, winding cobbled streets, containing remnants of the original architecture.

Granada's museums include a fine arts museum and La Casa de los Tiros which is devoted to the city's history. García Lorca's house is also open to visitors.

Graz, Austria

Introduction

Graz is situated in southeastern Austria on the Mur River. It is the second largest city and the capital of the federal state of Styria. The old town, marked by the centuries-long presence of the Habsburgs, is one of the best preserved in Central Europe. The city's universities, where famous intellectuals such as the astronomer Johannes Kepler have taught, have produced several Nobel Prize winners.

History

Graz was originally believed to occupy the site of a Roman settlement. It developed in the early twelfth century under the Styrian prince, Margrave Ottokar III of the Traungau family, who took control of the city and established it as his administrative centre. In 1192 the Frankish Babenberg dukes inherited Styria, making it a second residence after Vienna. After the demise of the Babenberg line, the city came under the control of King Bela IV of Hungary and later King Ottokar of Bohemia, before finally becoming the seat of the Leopold line of the Habsburgs in 1379. From 1480 the city was menaced by the plague and the threat of a Turkish invasion. During the fifteenth century it was a residence of the Holy Roman Emperors and was to become a centre of intellectual and political conflict as the Reformation swept across Europe in the sixteenth century. The Jesuit Karl-Franzens University was founded in 1585 under the auspices of Archduke Karl II of Inner Austria in an effort to recatholicize Styria.

The city was occupied by the French army in 1797, 1805 and 1809 during the Napoleonic Wars. By the terms of the peace treaty following the defeat of the Austrian troops in 1809 at Wagram, Graz's fortress was dismantled (only the clock tower, bell tower and some walls of the fortress remaining). The nineteenth century was a period of significant growth for the city. Following the Second World War, Graz was liberated by Soviet troops and then included in the British zone of occupied Austria until 1955.

Modern City

Graz is an important cultural centre, hosting annual musical events and festivals. It is the home of the University of Music and Performing Arts, which opened in 1963. Despite economic stagnation during the inter-war period and the devastation of the Second World War, the city today is prosperous. It has a broad industrial base and hosts Austria's two largest trade fairs—the Graz International Spring and Autumn Fairs. Graz was the European Capital of Culture in 2003.

Places of Interest

The core of the city retains its medieval and early modern flavour, while its outer reaches date from the nineteenth and twentieth centuries. The old town on the west bank of the river is dominated by the Schlossberg Park, a strongly fortified hill until 1809 when its defences were destroyed by the French. The park has an open-air theatre and a bell tower dating from 1588, and the clock tower—symbol of the city. Other attractions include the fifteenth century Gothic Church of St Aegidius (designated a cathedral in 1786) at Hauptplatz, and the Mausoleum of Emperor Ferdinand II, one of the best examples in Austria of Mannerism, the transitional style between Renaissance and Baroque. The Armoury (Landeszeughaus) at Herrengasse houses a collection of historical arms largely dating from the seventeenth century. The Renaissance-arcaded courtyard of the Styrian parliament (Landhaus) forms part of Austria's oldest museum, the Johanneum. The Schlossberg cave railway runs for 2 km and is the longest of its kind in Europe.

Guadalajara, Mexico

Introduction

Guadalajara is the second largest city in Mexico after Mexico City. The capital of the state of Jalisco, Guadalajara is situated to the west of the centre of Mexico at an altitude of 1,650 m with the Mexican high plateau and the Rio Grande de Santiago to its northeast. The surrounding region is covered by green and mountainous terrain.

History

In pre-Colombian times, the area that is now the State of Jalisco was inhabited by Huichol, Otomi, Nahua, Cora, Coyutec and Tepehua Indians until the arrival of the Conquistadors. The city was founded by Nuño Beltran de Guzmán, who named it after his hometown in Spain. Originally the capital of the state of New Galicia, also created by Guzmán, it was moved four times before it came to reside in its current location on 14 Feb. 1542. Infamously known as 'Bloody Guzmán', the Spaniard's ruthless colonization of the area eradicated nearly all the indigenous population and only a very small number survive today. As a consequence of this destruction of the Indian culture, Guadalajara evolved into a city dominated by Spanish influence, evident in the colonial architecture and wide, tree-lined avenues.

Although slow to expand due to its relative isolation, at the end of the eighteenth century the city began to develop and its population trebled over 40 years. Guadalajara evolved into an important centre for trade and agriculture specializing in wheat, cotton and wool. Gradually expanding and developing over the years with industrialization and improved transport networks, by the beginning of the twentieth century the city was the second largest in Mexico.

Guadalajara is also famous for its part in the abolition of slavery in Mexico. On 29 Nov. 1810 in the Palacio de Gobierno the revolutionary hero Miguel Hidalgo presented the edict against slavery that abolished the three century-long tradition. This led to Mexico becoming the first country to abolish the trade.

Modern City

A commercial and industrial centre of the western highland area, its industries include textiles, clothing and vehicle construction. Craftwork, especially glassware and pottery, still remains important. The city is an essential communications point, with road and rail networks between Mexico City and cities to the north as far as California, as well as across the Sierra Madre Occidental. The city has a large student population in two universities.

Originating from the southern part of the Jalisco state in the nineteenth century, the tradition of the Mariachis and their music is extremely important in Mexico and especially in Guadalajara where a yearly Mariachi festival takes place in Aug. and Sept.

Places of Interest

A good representation of pre-Colombian history can be found in Gudalajara's Central Regional Museum, which is itself an example of Baroque architecture. The nearby site of Iztépete, just outside the city, contains the remains of several ancient pyramids.

Guadalajara has a strong artistic heritage. It is the birthplace of the artist Gerardo Murillo, better known by his pseudonym Dr. Atl., the founder of modern Mexican muralism. Examples of his work can be seen in the Museo de Antropologia y História where both *Bathers* and *Lightening on the Waves* can be found. The city's other museums include the Museo Regional de Guadalajara. The Cathedral is a central focus of the city and another home to the city's art. It contains a painting by the seventeenth-century Spanish artist Bartolome Esteban Murillo, *The Assumption of the Virgin*.

Guangzhou, China

Introduction

Capital of Guangdong province, Guangzhou is the main industrial centre of south China. A thriving economic and trade centre, the city—still sometimes referred to by its old English name Canton—lies north of Hong Kong and about 145 km (90 miles) from the open sea. The tropical climate means that flowers are in bloom all year, giving Guangzhou its name 'City of Flowers'.

History

Guangzhou has been a gateway for trade with China for more than 1,700 years and it was the first port through which European merchants traded with the Chinese. The site has been occupied for more than 3,000 years. The city was the centre of a small state founded by the Shan people and was not finally absorbed into China until the second century AD. By the sixth century AD, the city was walled and had become an important centre of commerce, the home of Arab and Indian traders. Further growth and increasing prosperity in the eleventh century led to the construction of new walls to encompass a greatly expanded city.

Chinese explorers and traders sailed from Guangzhou in the twelfth and thirteenth centuries, opening up lucrative trade routes throughout Southeast Asia, and the Mongol invasion of northern China in the thirteenth century saw an influx of migrants from the north into the city. Guangzhou flourished under the Ming dynasty (1368–1644) and, because of the city's expansion, yet more walls had to be built. By the dawn of the sixteenth century the domination of Arab traders in the region had waned and the Portuguese arrived. In the next 100 years, Dutch and English merchants followed. The British East India Company made Guangzhou the centre of its operations in China at the end of the seventeenth century. More than a dozen 'factories'—trading posts established by different European countries—were built in the city's port.

Relations between the Chinese and the traders deteriorated early in the nineteenth century as the European and American traders found restrictions irksome. The Chinese, on their side, resented the illegal importation of opium by the foreigners via Guangzhou. In 1839 Chinese authorities destroyed a major haul of drugs imported by the British. In the resulting First Opium War (1839–42), Chinese forces were routed and Guangzhou only escaped destruction by paying what was effectively 'protection money' to the British. Under the terms of the Treaty of Nanjing (1842), Britain obtained free access to the port. France and the US gained similar trading concessions in Guangzhou 2 years later. Chinese resentment of these concessions—and of the use of

foreign flags for protection by pirates—led to the Second Opium War (1856–60). Franco-British forces briefly occupied Guangzhou in 1861.

Sun Yat-sen, the great nationalist leader, was a native of Guangzhou. He began his campaign to oust the Manchu dynasty in the city and led an uprising there in 1911. Although unsuccessful, the uprising was the spark that lit the national uprising against the imperial system later that year. Sun made Guangzhou the headquarters of his Kuomintang (Nationalist) Party, but after his death the city saw a power struggle between Communists and Nationalists. Guangzhou was occupied by the Japanese from 1938 to 1945 and, after the war, was under Nationalist control until the Communists took over in 1949.

Modern City

The city's industries include electric and electronic engineering (including household appliances and computers) as well as shipbuilding, machinery, textiles and many light industries. Foreign investment has been an important feature of the city's recent economic development. Guangzhou lies at the centre of a hub of road and railway routes and has an international airport. The 600-metre high Canton Tower, completed in 2010, is China's second tallest structure (after the Shanghai Tower) and the fifth tallest freestanding structure in the world. After Hong Kong, Guangzhou is China's principal centre for foreign trade.

Places of Interest

Yuexiu Park, which has several large artificial lakes, contains a fourteenth-century red-coloured pagoda that now holds the municipal museum. Other notable historic buildings are the Huaishen mosque, which dates from the sixth century and is thought to be the oldest in China, and the ornate Temple of the Six Banyan Trees. The China Export Commodities fair, held every spring and autumn, attracts many visitors.

Guatemala City, Guatemala

Introduction

Situated in a broad, elongated valley in the southern highlands at an altitude of 1,500 m, Guatemala City is the capital of Guatemala and the largest city in Central America.

History

Before the city was founded by colonists, the area was inhabited by the Maya. Until the eighteenth century Guatemala's capital was Antigua. A succession of natural disasters culminated in its destruction in 1773. Three years later Guatemala City was founded on a higher and safer site. The task of housing 30,000 migrants was further complicated by the country's economic difficulties which slowed development. Set out as a replica of Antigua, but with wider streets, many of the major buildings were not completed until the nineteenth century. After independence from colonial rule in 1821, Guatemala City was capital of the Confederation of Central America between 1823–39, when it became capital of Independent Guatemala.

At the beginning of the twentieth century, the population increased with the migration of Quezaltenango. At that time Guatemala's most important city, an earthquake had caused mass destruction. Guatemala City itself was susceptible to natural disasters, and earthquakes in 1917, 1918 and 1976 were particularly destructive. Six weeks of shocks in 1917 destroyed much of the city and its colonial heritage. It was rebuilt to the original plan.

Modern City

Guatemala City is the political, economic, cultural and industrial centre of Guatemala. The largest urban agglomeration in Central America, it is divided into 21 zones. Half of the country's industries and production centres are based here, including textiles, silverware, soap and food processing. The Universidad de San Carlos de Guatemala was founded in 1676. Guatemala City is linked nationally and internationally by road, rail and La Aurora airport. It is on the Inter American highway.

Places of Interest

Most of Guatemala City's colonial buildings have been destroyed by earthquakes, although some such as La Merced church have been rebuilt. Other religious buildings include the Neo-Classical cathedral built from 1783, and the Santo Domingo church. The Museo Nacional de Arqueología y Etnología contains rare Mayan artefacts, while the Museo Popol Vuh displays Mayan and Spanish colonial art. Twentieth century Guatemalan art can be viewed in the Museo Nacional de Arte Moderno while traditional indigenous textiles and weaving techniques are displayed in the Museo Ixchel del Traje Indígena. The nearby Mayan ruins Kaminal Juyú date from the early Classic period.

Guayaquil, Ecuador

Introduction

On the coastal lowlands at the mouth of the Guayas River, Guayaquil is the country's largest city and economic centre. The capital of the Guayas region, the city is Ecuador's main port.

History

Archaeological evidence points to the first permanent settlements in the region from around 3400 BC. In the mid-fifteenth century, despite strong resistance, the Incas invaded and colonized the area. Before the conquistadors arrived in the sixteenth century, the Manteño-Huancavilca peoples populated the lowlands. They dealt in gold, silver and copper and the area was an important trading centre.

In 1531 the conquistador Francisco Pizarro arrived in Ecuador and dispatched Sebastian de Belalcazar to conquer the lowland area. The indigenous population resisted the colonist's arrival in 1535 and uprisings ensued. Francisco de Orellana founded Guayaquil as Santiago de Guayaquil 2 years later to the west of the original settlement. Tradition has it that the name derives from the Huancavilca chieftain and his wife, Guayas and Quil, who killed themselves rather than surrender to the invader. The city was founded as the region's main port serving the interior and the Pacific coast. Locals' refusal to comply with Spanish demands led the colonists to employ African slaves and workers from the Quito area.

In the early nineteenth century Guayaquil was a strong centre of the independence movement. It was here in 1822 that Simón Bolívar met with his Peruvian counterpart José de San Martín to plan independence for the whole continent. Guayaquil was traditionally a liberal city in contrast to the conservative Quito. Following independence a number of conflicts broke out between the two regions. The political divide continued throughout the nineteenth century and into the twentieth. Guayaquil suffered various disasters, including pirate raids, plagues caused by poor sanitation and fires that destroyed the city's wooden infrastructure. An earthquake in 1942 resulted in extensive rebuilding.

Over the centuries, Guayaquil gradually developed as Ecuador's major commercial and economic area with its port as the focus. By the twenty-first century it handled nearly all Ecuador's imports and nearly half of its exports.

Modern City

A third larger than Quito, Guayaquil is Ecuador's economic capital and its centre of commerce. As the country's chief port, Guayaquil handles 50% of exports, such as fruit and coffee, and 90% of imports. Local industries include textiles, tanning, food processing and electrical equipment. Two universities, one founded in 1867 the other in 1962, are among the city's educational institutions. Guayaquil is served by an international airport 5 km north of the city, has rail links to Quito and road connections to the Pan-American Highway.

Places of Interest

Among the city's sites are the municipal museum, with modern art, ethnographic and archaeological displays, the San Francisco cathedral and church of Santo Domingo (1548). The Barrio de las Peñas retains a colonial feel with its traditional wooden buildings while the Parque del Centenario has heroic and historical monuments.

15 km west of the city lies an 8,650-acre nature reserve protecting 200 species of bird, jaguars and howler monkeys.

Haifa, Israel

Introduction

Israel's third largest city, Haifa is on the Mediterranean coast by Mount Carmel. The city is on three levels. The lower city is the commercial centre with a modern harbour, the middle level is an older residential sector and the top level has modern neighbourhoods overlooking the Mediterranean bay. The upper and the lower parts of the city are linked by Israel's only metro. Haifa is the world centre for the Baha'i faith and Israel's main port.

History

First mentioned in the Talmud (first to fourth century AD) as Sykaminos, the city was conquered in 1100 by the crusaders who named it Caiphas. Haifa took shape as a city in the seventeenth century. It was taken by Napoléon in 1799 and by the Egyptians in 1839, who surrendered it to Turkey in 1840. In 1918, British troops occupied the city. It became part of mandated Palestine, but in the 1948 Arab-Israeli War, the Jewish forces gained control from the Arabs. Haifa's deepwater port was opened in 1933 and expanded rapidly after Israel achieved statehood. Israel's oldest power plant (1934) is in Haifa and the city's petroleum refineries date from 1939.

Modern City

Industries include oil refining, chemicals, textiles, electrical equipment, shipbuilding, food processing, steel foundries and cement. There is a university (founded 1964) and an Institute of Technology (founded in 1912). The city has an airport.

Places of Interest

The Baha'i Shrine, with its Universal House of Justice, is the international governing body of the Baha'i religion. The remains of Said Ali Muhammad (one of the religion's founders) are buried inside the Shrine. The Stella Maris Church and Monastery of the Carmelite Order are centres of pilgrimage, as is Elijah's Cave. There is a Naval Museum and a Museum of Art. The National Maritime Museum covers 5,000 years of maritime history. The Reuben & Edith Hecht Museum's archaeological exhibits illustrate the theme 'The People of Israel in the Land of Israel'. A Sculpture Garden displays 22 bronze statues. Established in 1953 by Marcel Janco of the Dada movement, Ein Hod Artists' Village has become a centre for practicing artists from Israel and abroad.

Hamburg, Germany

Introduction

Hamburg, on the Elbe and Alster rivers, is Germany's largest and busiest port. It is the capital of Hamburg *Land*, in the north of Germany, and the country's second most populous city.

History

Founded in the ninth century, Hamburg was used by Archbishop Asinger as a base for crusades throughout Northern Europe. In the thirteenth century the town formed an alliance with Lübeck that became the basis of the Hanseatic League (an alliance of German trading towns in operation between the thirteenth and seventeenth centuries). Having gained the right to navigate the Elbe in 1189, it emerged as one of the League's leading lights. Except for a brief occupation by Napoléon in the early eighteenth century, Hamburg has never been subject to foreign rule.

Its geographical location at the confluence of several rivers made it a hub for Baltic trade while shipbuilding supported many other businesses. Hamburg is home to Germany's first stock exchange, founded in 1558, and the bank of Hamburg dates back to the early 1600s. Declared a Free Imperial City in 1618 Hamburg came to wield considerable power both locally and nationally. By the start of World War I, having recovered from a fire in the mid-nineteenth century that devoured a quarter of the city, Hamburg was one of the world's wealthiest cities, epitomised by the Hamburg-Amerika shipping line (then the largest in the world).

Although the city was bombed heavily in World War II, its wealth assisted in an extensive post-war rebuilding programme and most of the copper-roofed brick architecture was restored. Hamburg is a renowned centre of music with Felix Mendelssohn and Johannes Brahms both born in the city. Its opera house, Germany's oldest, saw the earliest performance of Händel's first opera.

Modern City

As well as shipbuilding and related industries, major industries include copper, machinery and publishing. There is an international airport, Fuhlsbüttel, north of the city. Of the four train stations (Hauptbahnhof, Dammtor, Altona and Harburg) the busiest is Hauptbahnhof. There are Autobahn links to major cities throughout central Europe while transport within the city includes the U-Bahn (underground), S-Bahn (surface trains) and buses.

Places of Interest

Among the city's best galleries is the Hamburger Kunsthalle (Fine Arts Museum), which has one of the largest art collections in Germany, incorporating works by artists as diverse as Master Bertram of Minden, Rembrandt, Manet, Monet and Warhol. The Museum für Kunst und Gewerbe (Museum of Decorative Arts) houses artefacts from ancient Egypt up to the present.

Außenalster, a stretch of water in the city centre, is popular for sightseeing pleasure cruises. Also popular is Hadag, the Hamburg docks, comprising 60 basins, and more than 68 km of quays. Several ships have been converted into museums and there is a large fish market on Sundays and public holidays.

Große Michaelskirche is an eighteenth century Baroque brick church. Built for the Lutheran sect to a design by the architect Sonnin, its tower (one of Hamburg's famous five and the only one you can climb) rises above the Elbe with a lantern turret in the form of a rotunda. Known as 'der Michel', it has become the city emblem. The Fernsehturm (Television Tower) has a revolving observation platform at 132 m, providing panoramic views of Hamburg. A new concert hall, the Elbphilharmonie, opened in Jan. 2017.

Hanoi, Vietnam

Introduction

Hanoi, meaning 'city located inside the arms of the river' is situated on the western bank of the Song Hong (Red River), 140 km. from the coast of the South China Sea at the Gulf of Tonkin. It is the capital city of the Socialist Republic of Vietnam.

History

The site of present Hanoi has seen habitation since prehistoric times. Historians believe that urban civilisation, at the bend of the To Lich River, can be traced to the seventh century. From here the city spread eastwards to meet the Song Hong, enveloping many lakes and waterways along the way.

By 1010 Emperor Ly Thai To, founding ruler of the Ly dynasty, had established the city as his capital renaming Dai La, as Hanoi was then known, as Thang Long (City of the Ascending Dragon). Thang Long remained a capital city until, in 1802, Emperor Gia Long, founding emperor of the Nguyen dynasty, moved his capital to Hué relegating the city to the status of a regional capital. Although the city had lost much of its political power it still retained its economic and cultural vibrancy. During the late Nguyen period the city became known as Dong Kinh. This name was corrupted by Europeans who called it Tonkin, (Eastern Capital) a name that came to be attributed to the entire region. In 1831 Emperor Tu Duc renamed the city Ha Noi.

On 20 Nov. 1873 the French imperial army, under the command of Francis Garnier, attacked Hanoi. This initial occupation was short lived, Garnier being killed by Chinese Black Flag bandits on 21 Dec. 1873. The subjugation of northern Vietnam had been halted and Paul-Louis-Félix Philastre, a French envoy, negotiated a French withdrawal from northern Vietnam in 1874. The treaty signed between the Hué court and the French resulted in the Vietnamese making concessions.

In 1882 a French colonial force of 250 men, under the leadership of Henri Rivière were sent to Hanoi. When Rivière was killed the French resolved to bring the entire Red River Delta under its control. In 1888 Emperor Dong Khanh surrendered the cities of Hanoi, Haiphong and Da Nang to the French. Under French occupation Hanoi became an important administrative centre and in 1902, the capital of the French Indo-Chinese Union.

In 1940 the Japanese occupied the Tonkin region to use it as a base to bring all of Indochina under their control. The Vichy French administration was permitted to remain in Hanoi.

In March 1945 the Japanese, as a precursor to withdrawal from Indochina, urged Emperor Bao Dai, a puppet king of French colonial rule, to proclaim Vietnamese independence. Bao Dai established his government at Hué.

In Aug. 1945, Ho Chi Minh and the Viet Minh (League for the Independence of Vietnam) seized power of Hanoi and on 2 Sept. 1945 proclaimed an independent Democratic Republic of Vietnam from Hanoi. The Viet Minh were, in turn, driven from the city by the returning French and it did not see the return of home rule until the French colonial forces decisive defeat at the battle of Dien Bien Phu (1954). Hanoi was now the capital city of the northern republic.

The Second Indo-Chinese or Vietnam War witnessed large-scale bombing of Hanoi by the United States.

Modern City

Modern Hanoi is a centre of industry and agriculture. Despite its disrupted and often violent history Hanoi still preserves many ancient architectural treasures including the Old Quarter and over 600 pagodas. There are several lakes in the city including Hoan Kiem Lake, West Lake, and Truc Bach Lake. The traditional handicrafts practised in Hanoi include bronze moulding, silver carving, lacquer and embroidery.

Places of Interest

Of historical interest in Hanoi is Ho Chi Minh's mausoleum and his stilt house which he occupied between 1958–69. The Old Quarter contains many market stalls as well as cafes and restaurants. Van Mie, or The Temple of Literature, is a shrine to Confucius. It is also notable for its traditional architecture. Hanoi's museums include a museum of fine arts and the Vietnamese Woman's Museum which was opened in 1995.

Hanover (Hannover), Germany

Introduction

Hanover is the capital of Lower Saxony in northwestern Germany. It is now most famous for hosting trade fairs and is known as the 'Exhibition City',

History

Hanover was founded in the 1100s on the south bank of the River Leine. In the Middle Ages it served as a gateway to the Rhine, Ruhr and Sarr river valleys. Churches and a city wall were built during the fourteenth century and the town acquired royal connections when the Duke of Calenberg moved his residence to Hanover in 1636.

In 1714 the kings of Hanover also became the kings of Britain and the two nations shared monarchs until the death of William IV in 1837. Following the Napoleonic Wars, the city became the capital of the kingdom of Hanover but was annexed by Prussia in 1866. The introduction of free trade promoted economic growth and by the twentieth century the population had grown to over 300,000.

During the Second World War the city was a target for strategic bombing and most of its historic centre was destroyed. In 1946 Hanover became part of the new state of Lower Saxony, with significant rebuilding in the post-war period leading to the emergence of a modern and highly industrialized city.

Modern City

Hanover's economy is dominated by the Messegelände, the main trade fairgrounds in the southeast of the city. It is one of the leading exhibition cities in the world, hosting more than 60 international and national exhibitions, including CeBIT (the world's biggest computer-related exhibition) and Hanover Messe, the world's biggest industrial fair. Continental AG, an auto and truck parts manufacturer, is one of the region's leading companies. The city's other manufactures include electrical equipment, chemicals and foodstuffs.

Hanover is one of the most important traffic junctions in northern Germany, with rail-, expressway- and air-links to Berlin. The city's central station, Hannover Hauptbahnhof, offers international and national connections, while Hanover/Langenhagen International Airport is 11 km north of the city centre.

Places of Interest

Most of the city's landmarks can be found in the Old Town. Historic buildings rebuilt and restored after the Second World War include the Old Town Hall, the Leibniz House, the Marktkirche and the Kreuzkirche. The New Town Hall includes four scale-models of the city and an observation deck. Among the most popular attractions are the Herrenhausen Gardens, a series of baroque gardens created in the seventeenth century, and Marienburg Castle, one of the most important neo-Gothic buildings in Germany.

Hanover has several notable galleries and museums. The Historical Museum traces the history of the city from its foundation to the present day, while the Sprengel Museum is considered one of the country's most important centres of modern art. Other museums include the Lower Saxony State Museum (the largest museum in Hanover) and the Kestnergesellschaft Museum, which hosts exhibitions from classical modernist to contemporary art.

Hanover also hosts the Schützenfest Hannover, the world's largest marksmen's festival, and Oktoberfest, the world's second largest Oktoberfest.

Harare, Zimbabwe

Introduction

Harare is in the northeast on an elevation of over 1,400 m. The city is the administrative, industrial and commercial hub of Zimbabwe.

History

Before British occupation in 1890 Harare was part of the domain of Chief Neherawa of Seki, and it is from him that the town takes its name. The British originally called the city Salisbury. It was used as a base for gold mining operations within the Zambezi valley. The gold never materialized, but the town remained an important centre of commerce and industry, attracting settlers who were looking for farmland. Racial segregation was a part of the town's life from the outset.

In 1923 Salisbury became the seat of colonial government in the region. Between 1953–63 it was the capital of the Federation of Northern Rhodesia, Southern Rhodesia and Nyasaland, and of Rhodesia during the period of the unilateral declaration of independence. Having gained independence, Zimbabwe retained Salisbury as its capital and renamed it Harare.

Modern City

Harare is the main distributive centre for tobacco. It is easily accessible by road, rail and air—the international airport is situated in nearby Kentucky. The centre is well planned with the downtown streets laid out in a grid, making it one of the less chaotic African cities.

Places of Interest

The National Art Gallery showcases a major collection of African art as well as the celebrated stone sculptures of Joram Nyanga and the work of a number of Shona sculptors. The picturesque Harare gardens and numerous other botanical gardens are located in and around the city. Just outside Harare, attractions include the ancient rock paintings of Dombawasha and the scenic Lake Chivero Recreational Park.

Havana (La Habana), Cuba

Introduction

Situated on the northwest coast of Cuba and traversed by the Almendares River, Havana is the capital of Cuba and the largest city in the Caribbean. A deep natural bay brought the city wealth and status. The city is the commercial, economic and industrial centre of Cuba. Since 1982 the old town has been a UNESCO world heritage site.

History

From the seventh century BC, the Siboney farmers and ceramic makers inhabited the area that is now Havana. They were followed by the Taíno. This small indigenous population was soon wiped out by colonists. The city was originally founded on the south coast of the island in 1514 by the Spanish colonist Diego Velásquez as San Cristóbal de la Habana, but the swampy location was soon abandoned for its present site in 1519. The natural harbour quickly became an important port and Havana developed into a base for the colonists on route between Spain and the New World. The strategic and commercial importance of the harbour soon brought Dutch, British and French invaders. At the end of the sixteenth century Cuba's governor moved to Havana from Santiago de Cuba, thus making it the capital.

The port's natural defences were fortified by a 10 m-high wall in the seventeenth century. Havana quickly grew in size and importance, becoming the principal trade centre in the Caribbean. Made rich by trading in sugar and African slaves, elaborate buildings, plazas and parks were created. Following a successful siege, British troops held the city for 6 months until Havana was restored to Spain through the 1763 Treaty of Paris which ended the 7 Years War.

Havana's prosperity attracted English, German and French immigrants who set up communities in the eighteenth century. By the nineteenth century the city rivalled New York and Buenos Aires in importance and had begun to expand beyond the city walls. In 1898 a ship exploding in Havana's harbour signalled the beginning of the Spanish/American war during which Cuba gained its independence. Havana was made capital of independent Cuba but it was occupied by American troops until 1902. The US had strong links with the island for the first half of the twentieth century and Havana was a favoured destination for US tourists until the arrival of Fidel Castro in 1959. The city's rich architecture was neglected over the following decades in favour of development away from the capital. The buildings became dilapidated until a renovation scheme was begun in the 1980s. In 1982 the city's old town was made a UNESCO heritage site. By the end of the twentieth century Havana had once again become a popular tourist destination.

Modern City

The centre of Cuba's commerce and economy, Havana is also the country's principal port with a substantial fishing industry. Principal industries include oil and sugar refining, textiles, rum, but especially cigars which are the country's principal export. Other Havana exports include coffee, sugar and cotton. The Universidad de la Habana was founded in 1728. The city is a rail and road terminus linking the rest of the island, and the José Martí International Airport is 25 km southwest of the centre.

Places of Interest

A network of old, narrow streets behind the port, Habana vieja, or the old town is the centre of commerce and nightlife and is rich in colonial architecture. The Plaza de la Catedral contains the Baroque Catedral de San Cristobal de la Habana, built between 1656–1724, and the Museo de Arte Colonial, built in 1720. The Plaza de Armas was once the seat of government and contains the former presidential palace, the Palacio de los Capitanes Generales, now the Museo de la Ciudad, dedicated to the city's history. The Plaza de la Revolución has statues of José Martí and Ernesto 'Che' Guevara, heroes of the Cuban Revolution. Ernest Hemmingway's room in the 1920s Hotel Ambos Mundos has been kept as it was when he wrote *For Whom the Bell Tolls*. One of the oldest of many tobacco factories, the Real Fabrica de Tabacos Partagas caters for visitors.

Helsinki, Finland

Introduction

Helsinki is in the south on a peninsula jutting into the Gulf of Finland. It is the capital as well as the economic and administrative centre of the country. It is the most northerly capital on the European continent. The city is noted for its natural harbours, waterways and parks.

History

Helsinki was founded in 1550 by King Gustav Vasa of Sweden as a Baltic trading post to rival Tallinn in Estonia. The new town was slow to develop and its original site on the mouth of the River Vantaa hindered its growth. In 1640 Helsinki was relocated to the Vironniemi headland, 5 km south and closer to the sea. The town prospered briefly after the move, but suffered during the eighteenth century. The expansion of Russia's military and commercial power, particularly after the foundation of nearby St Petersburg in 1703, caused the Finnish economy to stagnate. In addition a plague in 1710 wiped out much of Helsinki's population and made it vulnerable to attack. Russian troops razed the city in 1713 and occupied it until 1721. The city was captured again in 1742, but in 1748 the Swedes constructed the fortress of Suomenlinna on an outlying island, and this bastion greatly strengthened the city's defences.

The latter half of the eighteenth century was an era of prosperity for Helsinki. The city expanded its influence in the Baltic and enhanced its fleet of merchant ships. However, by 1808 the steady decline of Sweden as a superpower prompted the Russians to capture the city again and in 1809 Finland was ceded to Russia as an autonomous Grand Duchy. Three years later, Tsar Alexander I moved the capital from Turku to Helsinki. During the Russian invasion the city was razed, but after the country was annexed, Helsinki was rebuilt, largely under the auspices of the celebrated German architect, Carl Engel. By the end of the nineteenth century Helsinki was firmly established as the country's leading industrial city.

In Dec. 1917 Finland declared its independence and after a short but costly civil war, Helsinki was able to develop as the capital of an independent republic. The 1920s and 30s witnessed a boom in Helsinki's real estate and the construction of an Olympic stadium, although the city did not host the games until 1952 as a result of World War II. After the war emigration from the rural parts of Finland meant that Helsinki's population grew rapidly, and several suburbs were created to accommodate the influx of workers. During the 1960s and 70s the architectural designs of Alvar Aalto shaped the appearance of the modern city. In the 1980s Helsinki played a vital role as a base for the negotiations that ended the Cold War. Finland's entry into the EU marked another turning point in the city's history, and in 2000, in addition to celebrating its 450th anniversary, Helsinki was one of nine European cities of culture.

Modern City

The local economy is enhanced by the city's harbours and excellent road and rail connections to the interior of Finland and Russia. Although most exports pass through other ports on the Finnish coast, over half of the country's imports pass through the port of Helsinki, and the Wärtsilä shipyard is one of the most important in the world. Major industries include textiles, printing, clothing, glass and the processing of metal and food. Locally produced goods include the world famous Arabia porcelain.

The city has a thriving cultural life with several theatres, opera, ballet and numerous museums. The annual festival of Helsinki features performances of classical music by internationally renowned orchestras. The University of Helsinki is the second largest in Scandinavia.

In spite of its commercial and industrial significance there are no high rise buildings in the city and the centre is dominated by nineteenth century architecture lending it the atmosphere of a smaller town.

Places of Interest

The Ateneum, located in the city centre, is one of the foremost art galleries in Scandinavia. Its collection features works by nineteenth century Finnish artists. The City Museum's exhibits relate the history of Helsinki. The National museum is notable for its Finno-Ugric and Sami ethnological collection. A ferry connects Helsinki to Suomenlinna Island which is a UNESCO World Heritage Site. The island of Seurasaari has a large open-air museum recreating the rural Finland of the eighteenth and nineteenth centuries.

Ho Chi Minh City, Vietnam

Introduction

Hi Chi Minh City (formerly Saigon) is Vietnam's largest city and economic centre. The city is also South Vietnam's main port. Ho Chi Minh is by the Saigon River, north east of the Mekong delta.

History

In the Middle Ages, the city was a trade centre within Cambodia. During the seventeenth century it was taken over by the Chinese and Vietnamese, and became an administrative centre in 1699. The French settled the region in the eighteenth century, capturing Saigon in 1859. In 1862, the city became the capital of the French colony Cochinchina (including present day Laos, Cambodia, and Vietnam). Saigon was transformed into a metropolitan centre, and became the chief collecting point for the export of rice. In 1940, Saigon was occupied by the Japanese, who met resistance from the Viet Minh (communist forces) led by Nguyen Tat Thanh (also known as Ho Chi Minh). A declaration of independence in 1945 opened the First Indochina War against the French colonists. The war ended in 1954, with a peace agreement reached in Geneva. Vietnam was divided into north and south regions and Saigon became the capital of South Vietnam. During the Vietnam War (Second Indochina War), Saigon was the headquarters of the US military who backed the South against the communist North. In 1975, the city was captured by North Vietnamese troops, who changed its name to Ho Chi Minh City. During the 1980s and 1990s, Ho Chi Minh City experienced rapid economic growth, particularly in the manufacture of electronic products. The average income in Ho Chi Minh City is higher than in other parts of Vietnam.

Modern City

Ho Chi Minh City is Vietnam's centre for livestock and consumer goods. The city has an international airport (Tan Son Nhat International Airport). Buses run to Ho Chi Minh City from Laos and Cambodia, and also link the city to the rest of Vietnam. There is a university and a Stock Exchange.

Places of Interest

The Tet (Lunar New Year Festival) falls between 19 Jan. and 20 Feb. The Reunification Palace is an example of 1960s architecture, and is preserved as it was on the day of Vietnam's reunification. The building is used for official functions. Its basement contains a telecommunications room and a war room. The Giac Lam Pagoda is the city's oldest pagoda (place of worship), dating from 1744. The War Remnants Museum was formerly known as the Museum of Chinese and American War Crimes.

Hobart, Australia

Introduction

Hobart is Australia's second oldest city and the state capital of Tasmania. It nestles at the foot of Mount Wellington, a dormant volcano, in the southeast of the state, on the banks of the Derwent River. Less cosmopolitan than many of the other state capitals, its isolated situation has led to Hobart retaining much of its colonial character, which is reflected in its elegant Georgian and Victorian architecture.

History

The Aboriginal population of the Hobart region was largely killed off by the last quarter of the nineteenth century, victims of the white settlers and susceptibility to new diseases introduced with the colonists. George Bass, a British explorer, visited the area in 1798. By 1803 a settlement was established at Risdon Cove, around 8 km from Hobart's present site. It was founded by Lieutenant John Bowen on the orders of Philip Gidley King, the British governor of New South Wales who wanted to pre-empt any French attempts to colonize the island.

In 1804 the settlement, named Hobart Town after the earl of Buckinghamshire, was moved down the river. Its early population was a mix of convicts, sailors, free settlers and a few women and children. Though lacking natural resources, the town was located near a deep-water harbour that was unaffected by tidal changes. This enabled Hobart to become a trade hub and a centre for whalers and, until the 1830s, sealers who were active in the Bass Strait region. In the 1830s it also became a major ship-building town, though the industry died a slow death in the late nineteenth century with the decline in demand for wooden ships. The settlement was given city status in 1842 but retained its name Hobart Town until 1881.

Modern City

Cheap and plentiful hydro-electric power, exploited early in the last century, still provides the basis for a small industrial sector. Metal refining and chemical working are important as well as textile and cement manufacturing and food processing. There is also a large newsprint mill and a major confectionery complex owned by Cadbury-Schweppes. A significant population of traditional craftworkers, including wood carvers and potters, attract visitors but the key to the development of tourism in the city was the establishment of Australia's first legalized casino in Sandy Bay.

The deep-water port, which rivals Sydney, helps maintain Hobart's significance as a trading post and major exports include fruit, wool and wood. The city is at the centre of a major freight rail network and has good motorway and air links.

Places of Interest

Among the most important tourist attractions are the botanical gardens, Battery Point (the old port area which has retained much of its nineteenth century architecture including St George's Anglican Church) and Salamanca Place, an area dominated by the warehouses used during the colonial era and now converted into a modern cultural and commercial centre. This is also the arrival point for the winners of the Sydney to Hobart yacht race. Field Marshall Viscount Montgomery spent a number of his childhood years being educated in Hobart and the city is the birthplace of swashbuckling film star, Errol Flynn.

Hong Kong, China

Introduction

The skyline of Hong Kong is sometimes quoted as one of the wonders of the modern world. This bustling and prosperous community has grown in less than a century and a half from a collection of tiny fishing villages to become one of the world's major commercial and financial centres. After a century of British colonial rule, Hong Kong (Xianggang in Chinese) is now a Special Administrative Region of China, under a "one country, two systems" arrangement, which allows Hong Kong to maintain its capitalist system and a degree of autonomy for 50 years.

History

Rocky Hong Kong Island was settled by Cantonese in the first or second century BC. Little flat land and few resources meant that the island remained scantily populated. In 1821 British merchants arrived and used its fine, sheltered natural harbour as a base for the opium trade. After the First Opium War (1839–42) China was forced to cede the island to Britain. The adjoining southern section of the Kowloon Peninsula was ceded to Britain in 1860, after the Second Opium War. A further area of about 1000 km^2 (nearly 400 sq. miles) of countryside and islands, the New Territories, was leased from China for 99 years in 1898.

The colony flourished through trade and the population grew rapidly through immigration. The rural poor in neighbouring China and fugitives both sought refuge in the British colony. After the establishment of the republic in China (1911), nationalist feeling began to spread to Hong Kong. War between China and Japan in 1937 brought a further flood of refugees into the colony, which was itself occupied by the Japanese in 1941. But by the time Hong Kong fell, its population had been reduced by two-thirds as many Chinese residents fled back to China. British forces re-entered Hong Kong in 1945.

During the civil war between Communist and Nationalist forces in China many Chinese fled to Hong Kong. The colony continued to flourish as the principal trading link with China even after the Communists took over in 1949, but the (temporary) 1951 UN trade embargo on Communist China during the Korean War shook the colony. Hong Kong quickly diversified with industrialisation based on cheap labour. The industrial base developed in the 1950s, often relying on poor wages and working conditions. Labour unrest grew, culminating in riots and demonstrations in 1967.

Working conditions improved in the 1970s. High tech industries were established, the property and financial markets advanced and trade with China grew again. With the lease of the New Territories due to expire on 1 July 1997, concern grew about the future of Hong Kong. Sino-British negotiations began in 1982, with China laying claim to the entire colony. Agreement was reached in 1984 and, as a result, Hong Kong—the island, Kowloon and the New Territories—returned to China on 1 July 1997 as Special Administrative Region directly under the central government.

Modern City

Hong Kong has a GDP similar in size to that of Sweden. The metropolis has a free-trade policy that has made it one of the great centres of world trade, importing raw materials for its industries and finished goods for reexport. Hong Kong's industries include textiles, clothing, electrical and electronic goods, office machinery and photographic equipment. The new airport at Chek Lap Kok is a major centre of international air routes and the terminal is the world's largest enclosed space. The port handles about 175 m. tonnes of cargo a year and it is the world's busiest container port. An efficient rail and rapid-transit system provides public transport.

Places of Interest

Victoria Peak, known popularly as The Peak, 552 m (1811 ft) high, offers a panoramic view of Hong Kong and can be reached by an eight-minute tram ride. There are few historic buildings: visitors are instead drawn to outstanding modern architecture such as the 118-storey International Commerce Centre and the Bank of China Tower and the 88-storey Two International Finance Centre.

Many festivals provide attractions during the year including the Dragon Boat Festival and Chinese New Year. Hong Kong's annual Arts Festival is a major regional cultural event, while the Hong Kong International Film Festival (which dates from 1977) attracts Hollywood as well as Asian movies. Tourists are drawn by the shops and many leisure facilities including Ocean Park, one of the largest oceanariums in the world.

The harbour bustling with fishing boats, Chinese junks and floating restaurants is a popular attraction. Away from the city, the islands and the countryside are of interest. Lantau Island has ancient Chinese stilt houses, white sandy beaches and a 250-tonne Buddha.

Honiara, Solomon Islands

Introduction

Honiara, on the River Mataniko in the north of Guadalcanal island, is capital of the Solomon Islands.

History

Occupied by the Japanese in World War II, Guadalcanal was the scene of a bloody battle when US troops tried to re-take it in 1942. They eventually succeeded a year later. Honiara was developed from scratch after World War II around the sight of the US military base. It replaced Tulagi as capital city in 1952.

In 1999 and 2000 there was ethnic fighting in Honiari and the surrounding jungle.

Modern City

Honiara has a busy port and is 16 km from Henderson Airfield international airport. Pont Cruz is the city's transport hub. Major exports include wood, fish, coconut and gold.

Places of Interest

Tourist attractions include the Parliament building, the national museum, a botanical garden and Chinatown. Water Pump Village is not far from the city centre. Diving is a popular pastime and there are numerous World War II sightseeing tours.

Honolulu, United States of America

Introduction

The capital of Hawaii and the seat of Honolulu county is on a strip of land on the island of Oahu. Honolulu stretches from Makapuu Point in the east to Pearl Harbor in the west and is near to the Koolau mountains. Honolulu (from the Hawaiian for 'sheltered harbour') is the largest urban area and most important economic centre in Hawaii as well as an important Pacific port and tourist destination.

History

A Polynesian community was on the site of modern day Honolulu in AD 1100. The first European settlers were led by a British captain, William Brown, in 1794. The arrival of more Europeans and Americans in the early part of the nineteenth century saw Honolulu thrive as a trading centre. King Kamehameha's Hawaiian Royal Family made the city their main residence until the end of the monarchy in 1893. On 12 Aug. 1898 Honolulu and other sections of the Hawaiian Islands were formally annexed by the United States.

On 7 Dec. 1941, the Japanese launched a surprise attack on the naval base at Pearl Harbor, leading to the United States entering World War II. During the conflict Honolulu was a base for American troops in the Pacific. Hawaii entered the Union in 1959 after a plebiscite voted 17:1 in favour and Honolulu was made state capital.

Modern City

Industries include processed food (including canned pineapple), metal goods, clothing and building materials. Tourism is important with Waikiki beach at the heart of the hotel industry. Pearl Harbor Naval Base and Hickham Air Force Base are integral parts of the local economy.

The city is served by Honolulu International Airport and has a bus network with over 60 bus routes. The University of Hawaii at Manoa, Hawaii Pacific University and Chaminade University of Honolulu are all based in Honolulu.

Places of Interest

Diamond Head and the Punchbowl, two extinct volcanic craters, are both located in Honolulu. The latter is the site for the National Memorial Cemetery of the Pacific. The USS *Arizona* Memorial at Pearl Harbor and St Andrew's Cathedral commemorate those killed during the Japanese attack in 1941.

Bishop Museum contains collections of Polynesian art and artefacts. Other cultural institutions include the Honolulu Academy of Arts and the Alice Cooke Spaulding House. A theatre, exhibition hall and the city's symphony orchestra are located in the Neal S. Blaisdell Center. The Hawaii Maritime Center documents the city's seafaring past. The spacious plaza at King Street contains Iolani Palace, the home of the Hawaiian Royal Family until 1893, and the state capitol.

Houston, United States of America

Introduction

The largest city in Texas and the fourth biggest urban area in the United States, Houston is located in southeastern Texas and is the seat of Harris County. An important port, the city is linked by the Houston Ship Channel to the Intracoastal Waterway at Galveston and to the Gulf of Mexico. The command centre of the North American Space Agency (NASA) is located near Houston, which has led to it being nicknamed the 'space city'.

History

Houston was founded by brothers Augustus C. and John K. Allen in 1837 and named in honour of General Sam Houston, a hero in Texas' war of independence against Mexico. The brothers, who emigrated from New York, bought the plot of land on which the city was built after the original settlement in the area, Harrisburg, had been destroyed by the Mexicans. The Allens envisaged the new settlement becoming a 'great commercial emporium' and the capital of the Republic of Texas. However the Texan government was based in the town for just 2 years before moving to Austin in 1839.

Houston developed steadily into a port, with cotton shipping as its main industry. After a major flood and hurricane devastated Galveston in 1900, Houston became the state's major port. With a burgeoning real estate industry and excellent rail links the city was in a good position to exploit its strategic advantages when oil was discovered in 1901. Industrial expansion thereafter was rapid. A network of gas and oil pipelines was established as well as a striking series of skyscrapers along the Gulf Coastal Plain (which stands at an altitude of 12 m). However the prosperity wrought by the oil boom was not to the benefit of the whole city and downtown Houston was soon beset by poverty, particularly among the large numbers of African-Americans who migrated to the area from the rural south in the 1960s.

In 1961 the Johnson Space Center was built 22 miles from downtown Houston to act as the command base for flights made by American astronauts. By the beginning of the 1980s Houston was the third largest city in the United States but the end of the oil boom hit the city hard. Crime rates and traffic congestion rose rapidly while skyscraper building and infrastructure development slowed.

Modern City

Houston remains an important centre for oil, petrochemicals, natural gas and aerospace research. In terms of tonnage moved per year, the city is the third largest port in the United States. Continuing population increase has led to the expansion of the suburbs. The city houses the Texan Medical Center, where the first ever artificial heart transplant took place. The Medical Center is also the world's largest complex of specialist medical institutes and hospitals.

Houston is served by two airports; Houston International, which is 22 miles north of the city centre, and Hobby Airport, which is 7 miles southeast of downtown Houston and caters for domestic flights. The city has been a railway centre since the late nineteenth century and is on the Amtrak network. The city and its environs house several colleges and universities, including Rice University, the University of Houston and Texas Southern University. The medical center also houses the Baylor College of Medicine.

Places of Interest

The Museum District includes the Museum of Fine Arts, the Cullen Sculpture Garden and the private Menil collection of art. The city has resident theatre, ballet and opera companies as well as a professional symphony orchestra, housed in the Jesse H. Jones Hall for the Performing Arts (in Houston Civic Center), and the Wortham Theater Center. The Astrodomain, a major entertainment complex, contains the Astrodome, the world's first domed, air-conditioned stadium. The Astrodomain plays host to baseball matches, livestock shows, rodeos, other exhibitions and also contains an amusement park.

Sam Houston Historical Park and Market Square contain restored structures and some original buildings from the city's early history. Views of the modern skyline can be obtained from the observation floors of the Texaco Plaza and the Texas Commerce Tower. The Johnson Space Center and the San Jacinto Battleground State Historical Park (where the Texans defeated the Mexicans in 1836) are both located 20 miles south of the city.

Hyderabad, India

Introduction

The capital of Andhra Pradesh, Hyderabad is twinned with neighbouring city Secunderabad and is the country's fifth largest city.

History

Hyderabad was founded by the Muslim Qutb Shahi sultans of Golconda on the east bank of the River Musi in 1590. Intended to replace the town of Golconda as the capital of the empire, the old city had at its centre the Charminar, a prominent symbol of the status of the Qutb Shahi sultans. The town and surrounding region enjoyed nearly a century of peace and affluence until the downfall of the Qutb Shahi in 1685 when the Moghuls invaded. In 1713 the region was ruled by Asaf Jah who founded the Nizam dynasty of Hyderabad, a Muslim dynasty that was to successfully rule a Hindu community until 1948. Nizam Ali Kahn ruled independently until his death in 1748. It was then the turn of the British and the French to fight for the succession and in 1768, Nizam Ali Khan signed the Treaty of Masulipatam, agreeing to British demands. Territorial gains made by the Nizam were subsequently ceded to the British. In 1798 the Nizam accepted their protection, becoming the first Indian prince to do so.

The Nizam dynasty remained loyal to Britain throughout several wars, including the Indian mutiny of 1857–58. In return the British backed the Nizam dynasty though they retained the right to intervene if the actions of the Nizam threatened to undermine their position. With the partition of 1947, Hyderabad wanted to remain independent of India but despite calls for British intervention by the Nizam, India invaded the territory in 1948. In 1956 the state of Hyderabad was divided between surrounding regions, with the city of Hyderabad becoming the capital of Andar Pradesh.

In Aug. 2000 the city was hit by severe floods leaving 150 dead and forcing 500,000 from their homes.

Modern City

Today, Hyderabad's chief industries are the manufacture of transport equipment, textiles, pharmaceutical goods and cigarettes. The fastest growing industry is computer software. Known as the city of learning, Hyderabad has eight universities, including Osmania University (1918) and the agricultural university, Sindh (1947), 28 National Level Apex Research and Training Institutions, and several centres of excellence in areas such as defence research, chemical technology and molecular biology. This academic environment has produced an ideal climate for growth in the software sector with Microsoft further enhancing the city's standing by setting up one of its centres there in 1998.

Hyderabad's location makes it an important transport link between north and south. Its airport at Begumpet serves both domestic and international flights. Indian Airlines, NEPC and Jet Airways operate flights connecting Hyderabad with Delhi, Chennai, Kolkata and Mumbai. The city is also covered by an extensive rail network and is situated on the crossroads of national highways seven and nine, connecting it with most other major cities in India.

Places of Interest

There are several major tourist attractions in the city, the most important of which is the Charminar. The four pillared monument was built as a celebration of the end of a plague and contains one of the oldest mosques in Hyderabad. There are several theories as to what the Charminar was actually used for, ranging from a gateway to a school, to an elaborate water pump designed to get water to the higher reaches of the palace. The Ashtalakshmi Temple stands on the outskirts of the city and is one of few temples to have the Goddess Lakshmi represented in all eight of her forms. Golconda Fort, built in 1143 is a relic of the period before the city existed. Falaknuma Palace stands towards the south and commands a view of the entire city. Built in the late nineteenth century by Nawab Viqar-ul-Umara, the temple was built using marble imported from Italy. The Cyber Tower is an example of Hyderabad's position as a forerunner in software development. Not only does it act as a home for the city's information technology industry, but it also houses a major IT training institute.

Ibadan, Nigeria

Introduction

Ibadan is the second largest city in Nigeria and the capital city of Oyo state. It lies about 160 km from the Atlantic coast of Africa, in the southwest part of the country. More than 90% of Ibadan's population is Yoruban. The population is around 60% Muslim and 40% Christian.

History

The original Yoruba settlers are believed to have been fugitives from neighbouring villages. In 1829, the area was settled by the Ife, Ijebu and Oyo tribes who had emerged victorious from long-running tribal disputes. Ibadan came under the jurisdiction of the British government in 1893. A railway was opened 8 years later and the city prospered as a commercial centre.

Modern City

Ibadan has its old and new sections. The new town houses the business centre with modern amenities. There are hardly any heavy industries. The chief areas of commerce are handcrafts, corn milling, tobacco and beverage treatment, leatherwork, and services. Agriculture is in decline and farmers are mostly part-timers. Ibadan is well served by roads, rail and air as well as a regular bus service.

Places of Interest

The secretariat buildings, parliament, central bank and federal ministries are in the old part of Ibadan. The University of Ibadan (founded in 1962) and a technical institute are located in the city. Ibadan University was the *alma mater* of Nobel literature prize winner, Soyinka Wole. Other attractions include the palace of the Olubadan (the king) of Ibadan, the national archives, the university zoo, the Agodi Zoological Gardens, the International Institute of Tropical Agriculture and the Mbari Arts Centre. Several large markets are open every day.

Incheon, South Korea

Introduction

Incheon, a port on the Yellow Sea in the west of the country, is Korea's fourth largest city. The addition of a massive international airport has consolidated its role as a regional transport hub.

History

There is evidence of human habitation in the area during the Kochosun Period (2333 BC–108 BC). In the following centuries the city fell to numerous dynastic rulers who greatly expanded its borders. In the nineteenth century Incheon felt the repercussions of the Pyonginyango (when France invaded the country in 1866) and the Sinmiyangyo (a battle between the US navy and Korean troops in 1877). Treaties of friendship signed with the major Western powers during the 1880s boosted international trade and kickstarted the growth of Incheon Port, opened in 1883.

Incheon was named in 1949. The following year it was the scene of General MacArthur's landing during the Korean War.

Modern City

Incheon has a highly diversified economy. The service and transport industries are major employers. Also important are hi-tech and engineering manufactures, metallurgy and chemicals. Agriculture and mining are important in the surrounding area. There is a university.

Incheon is on major road and rail routes. Ferries run from the port and link up with the Trans-Mongolian railway. The international airport is on Yeongjong Island and has made the city one of the most important transport centres in Northeast Asia.

Places of Interest

The Jeondeungsa Buddhist temple is thought to be around 1,600 years old. The Dohobucheongsa (local magistrate's office) and Hyanggyo (Confucian school) give an insight into life under the Joseon dynasty which spanned the fourteenth to nineteenth centuries. Hwadojin Park was built as a fortress when the port was opened and now includes a major exhibition hall. Jayu Park is a Western-style green area with a memorial to the Incheon Landing. Other popular sites include Yeonan Harbour (with access to several nearby islands), China Town and the Wolmido Street of Culture.

Indianapolis, United States of America

Introduction

Indianapolis is the capital of Indiana, the word 'Polis' coming from the Greek word for city.

History

In 1821 the Indiana State Legislature approved a plan to build a new capital in the centre of the state's rich farming area. Indianapolis was designed by Alexander Ralston who based his plans on Pierre L'Enfant's designs for Washington, D.C.

Indianapolis became state capital in 1825 but grew slowly as the shallow White River restricted the quantity of raw materials that could be brought to the city to sustain industry. Growth accelerated after the arrival of a major road and rail links and in the Civil War, the city was a major training post for the Union Army. The discovery of gas fields in the 1890s was a further boost and by World War I Indianapolis had thriving automobile, metal work and agricultural industries. In 1909 the Indianapolis Motor Speedway was built by local businessmen Carl Fisher, James Allison, Frank Wheeler and Arthur Newby as a facility to test new cars. Two years later the inaugural Indianapolis 500-Mile Race was held at the arena.

Several labour unions established their headquarters in Indianapolis which in World War II was known as the 'Toolmaker to the Nation'. Manufacturing declined in the postwar years, until the merging of the city and county government structures in 1970 helped revitalize the city with an ambitious programme of public and private projects. Many of these projects were funded by the Lilly Endowment, an offshoot of the pharmaceutical company Eli Lilly which is still based in the city.

Modern City

The city is served by Indiana International Airport. Four interstate freeways and four federal highways link Indianapolis to the rest of the United States and there is an Amtrak train station and a Greyhound bus terminal. A Shuttle Express Van Service also operates in the city along with Skyline and RTD buses and a light railway system.

Manufacturing includes pharmaceuticals, electronic equipment, machinery, transportation equipment and metal products. The local, state and federal government are the city's biggest employers. Tourism, particularly linked to the Indianapolis 500 event, is also important to the city's economy.

Important higher educational institutions in Indianapolis include Butler University, Marian College, Purdue University at Indianapolis, the University of Indianapolis, Indiana University, the Christian Theological Seminary and Ivy Tech State College.

Places of Interest

The ten-block large area known as Mile Square is the historical heart of Indianapolis, housing the 87 m-tall Soldiers and Sailors Monument, which serves as the city's major landmark. Important cultural institutions include a medical history museum, The Children's Museum of Indianapolis, The Indianapolis Museum of Art and The Eiteljorg Museum of American Indians and Western Art. The restored house of former president Benjamin Harrison, who was from Indianapolis, is a popular visitor attraction.

The city has resident symphony orchestra, opera and ballet companies and a repertory theatre company. Indianapolis hosts several major track and field athletic events, and is often used for the United States Olympic and World Championship trials. The annual Indianapolis 500 Mile Race on the Memorial Day weekend is the world's largest annual single-day sporting event, attracting around 450,000 spectators to the Indianapolis Speedway Track. The Indianapolis Motor Speedway Hall of Fame Museum charts the history of the event.

Islamabad, Pakistan

Introduction

Pakistan's capital, Islamabad is a modern and spacious city, located against the backdrop of the Margalla hills.

History

In 1958 President Ayub Khan's government decided to build a new capital to replace Karachi. The aim was to offset the economic importance of Karachi and the political importance of Lahore but Karachi's humid climate and poor geographic location were also determining factors. A more central site was chosen at the northern end of the Potohar Plateau, noted for its agreeable climate and good water supply. A Greek firm of architects, Doxiadis Associates, proposed a triangular grid system with its apex leading towards the Margalla Hills. In 1961 construction began on the site that is now Islamabad.

The city was divided into eight zones including a diplomatic enclave, a commercial district, an industrial sector and an education sector. Initially the government found it hard to entice people to the new capital. Plots of land were sold at low prices by the Capital Development Authority and lower tax breaks were offered to make the city more appealing.

Modern City

The city is characterised by wide avenues, lined with trees. Population has risen, growing from 200,000 in 1981 to almost 800,000 in 1998. There is relatively little poverty. Traffic jams are rare and travelling across the city takes about 20 min. The pollution level is kept to a minimum. The city has an airport that caters for both international and domestic flights and is connected by road and rail to all the other major cities in Pakistan.

Institutes of higher education include, Quaid-e-Azam University (1965), Allama Iqbal Open University (1974) and the International Islamic University. Quaid-i-Azam university admits 550 students a year to its master programs and in 1998 its total enrolment stood at 2,650.

Places of Interest

The Shah Faisal Mosque, one of the largest mosques in the world, is located at the foot of the Margalla hills. The Daman-e-koh viewpoint is located on the hills themselves and offers views of the city's Presidential Palace and Legislative Assembly buildings.

Istanbul, Turkey

Introduction

Istanbul is situated in the northwest of the country at the junction of the Golden Horn (a river valley about 7 km long), the Bosphorus (a channel that connects the Mediterranean and the Black Sea) and the Sea of Marmara. The Golden Horn separates the old city of Stamboul from Beyoglu, the new city to the north.

History

The city's historical role as a capital of both the Islamic and Christian worlds belies surprisingly humble origins. It is thought to have been founded and named Byzantium by the Greek leader, Byzas, in 657 BC. Although ruled by a succession of Greek and Roman rulers, including Alexander the Great and Vespasian, the city remained insignificant until the third century AD when Constantine I, the first Roman emperor to adopt Christianity, chose it to be the 'New Rome', capital of the Roman empire. Constantine's decision led to the city trebling in population and to the construction of a number of churches and monuments that are now on the UNESCO world heritage list. The newly named Constantinople became one of the most powerful capitals in the world. It was by all accounts immensely wealthy and beautiful, and was to remain the first city of commerce until rivalled by the Italian maritime states.

Constantinople was at its peak in the sixth century under Justinian I. During his reign the monumental Aya Sofya was constructed. Its interior was for centuries the largest enclosed space in the world. However, the city's fortunes changed in 542 when a plague wiped out over half the population. Decline was to continue unabated for hundreds of years. In the twelfth and thirteenth centuries Constantinople was razed by successive crusading armies and marauding tribes. An era of recovery and stability finally began with the occupation of the Ottoman sultan Mehmed II in 1452. At the beginning of his rule Constantinople's population had fallen from an estimated 500,000 under Justinian to just 50,000. Gradually the city began to grow again, and its Christian monuments and buildings were made Islamic, with minarets installed around the Aya Sofya. The Ottoman dynasty restored the prestige of the city they named Istinpolin (which after several permutations became Istanbul). Under Süleyman II (1520–66) it promised once again to be the capital of the western world, but Charles V thwarted the sultan's imperial ambitions.

After Süleyman's rule the Ottoman empire and its capital began to lose influence. By the end of the nineteenth century Istanbul was the home of many foreign traders and troops, and this western influence culminated with the introduction of a railway and a regular water supply. In 1908 Istanbul was seized by the Young Turks who toppled the regime of Abdülhamid II. It was blockaded throughout World War I, and in 1918 it was placed under the combined authority of Britain, France and Italy. Subsequent occupation by Greece was ended by the Nationalists under Mustafa Kemal Atatürk, who chose Ankara as his new capital.

Modern City

Istanbul remains Turkey's first city and its largest port. It is the commercial and industrial hub, and produces and processes glass, textiles, flour, tobacco and cement, with income from tourism are increasing. It is served by road, rail and air, with Yesilköy Airport located 17 km to the west of the city. Buses and ferries provide transport within the city. In Oct. 2013 the Marmaray sea tunnel linking two continents and stretching over 76 km was opened across the Bosphorus Strait.

Places of Interest

The Topkapi Palace contains Ottoman relics, as well as an arms museum and an archaeological museum. The Museum of Turkish and Islamic Art has a world-renowned collection of artefacts, carpets and paintings. The Palais de la Culture is an important centre for theatre, ballet, opera and classical music. Istanbul was one of three cities named the 2010 European Capital of Culture by the European Union.

Izmir, Turkey

Introduction

Izmir is situated on the Aegean coast, at the head of the 50 km long Gulf of Izmir. It is the country's third city, the second-largest port, and also one of the oldest cities in the Mediterranean world.

History

The original site of Izmir, known then as Smyrna, was settled in the third millennium BC and is thought to have been contemporary with the first city of Troy. By 1500 BC it had become subject to the Hittite Empire. Greeks began to populate the region some 500 years later, and Smyrna is alluded to by the historian Herodotus. It is widely held that Homer may have lived in the city. Smyrna emerged as one of the most important and influential of the Ionian cities. This period of prosperity was brought to an end by the invasion of Lydia in 600 BC, when the thriving town was reduced to a village. It remained small and insignificant until the fourth century BC when a new city was built on the ancient site under the command of Alexander the Great. When Smyrna was occupied by Rome in the first century BC it was chosen as the centre of the Roman province of Asia.

Under the rule of the Byzantine emperors, Smyrna was made the capital of the naval province of Samos, and was a significant early Christian city. It became Islamic after the Seljuk conquest of the eleventh century, and was eventually incorporated into the Ottoman empire in 1415 under Sultan Mehmet Celebi. Despite suffering serious earthquakes in the seventeenth and eighteenth centuries Izmir retained its position as an important and prosperous port.

In May 1919 the port was occupied by Greek forces, and remained subject to Greek control for 3 years until it was liberated by Turkish troops led by Kemal Atatürk. During the course of this struggle the city was virtually destroyed by a fire. After World War II Izmir began to expand once again. It was selected as the command centre for NATO's land forces in southeast Europe. In 1955 the Aegean University was founded.

Modern City

The central commercial district of Izmir is called Konak, while to the south-west lie the primarily residential areas of Karantina and Güzelyali. On the north side are the recently expanded harbour and the industrial suburbs. Izmir has petrochemical and engineering works, and produces cement, food, cotton and woollen textiles. Its major exports include figs, cotton, vegetables and tobacco.

Places of Interest

The Culture Parks contain gardens, an amusement park and a zoo, all of which are popular with visitors. The Archaeological museum houses a notable collection of antiquities including famous statues of Poseidon and Demeter.

Jaffna, Sri Lanka

Introduction

Jaffna, one-time capital of Sri Lanka, is on flat, arid land on a peninsula at the northern-most tip of the island. It is connected to the mainland by a narrow strip of land known as Elephant's Pass. The city was once a major trading port, trading with southern India across the Palk strait as well as with nearby islands, yet its commercial importance has declined with the political turmoil of the past two decades. The name Jaffna derives from the Portuguese adaptation of the Tamil expression for 'port of the lyre'.

History

Jaffna is one of the oldest sites of habitation in lower south Asia. Before coming under Portuguese rule in 1619 and then under Dutch rule in 1658 the city was the capital of a Tamil kingdom. Links with the southern Indian state of Tamil Nadu are evident from this period and can be found in the city's architecture as well as in the customs and culture of the city's inhabitants. Under Tamil rule Jaffna existed as an autonomous region and, despite a brief period of Sinhalese rule in the fifteenth century under Parakramabahu VI, had firmly established itself in northern Ceylon by the fourteenth century thanks to a large influx of Tamil migrants. As the Sinhalese moved southwestwards, Jaffna and the northern, Tamil-occupied region was left as one side of an ethnic and linguistic divide. Brahmanic Hinduism travelled across the Palk strait from southern India and led to the building of Hindu temples and the establishment of Hindu institutions.

The Portuguese first tried to take Jaffna in 1560 although this expedition, as well as a subsequent invasion in 1591, were unsuccessful and it was not until 1619 that the kingdom and its capital were formally annexed to Portugal. The arrival of Catholic missionaries changed the architectural and religious complexion of the city (with many of Jaffna's nobility converting to Christianity) whilst a new language, Sri Lanka Portuguese Creole, developed from the social interaction between the two cultures.

The city was the last stronghold of the Portuguese and only surrendered to the Dutch forces after a three-month long siege. The Dutch were more successful than the Portuguese in establishing an effective economic system in Jaffna, utilizing the city's port in the lucrative trade of cinnamon and pearls in which they achieved a monopoly. Dutch law, which took a firm hold throughout the country, extended Jaffna's importance with the establishment of one of three major courts of justice in the city (with Colombo and Galle laying claim to the other two). The local, historical law of Jaffna retained political importance, however, and an attempt was made to codify it in 1707.

The arrival of the British in 1796 led to a further colonial period in Jaffna's history and to a large influx of Tamil labourers, brought in to work on the tea, coffee and coconut plantations. In 1948 Ceylon (the name which the British gave the island) gained independence. It was renamed as Sri Lanka in 1972. The disenfranchised Tamil population came under increasing pressure from successive Sinhalese governments. In 1976 the Liberation Tigers of Tamil Eelam (LTTE) was formed in response to the growing tensions in the northern and eastern parts of the island. In 1983 violence broke out between the Sri Lankan army and the LTTE. An Indian peacekeeping force, deployed in 1987, provided a short-lived respite which ended with their withdrawal in 1990. Jaffna then became the seat of a *de facto* LTTE state, complete with courts of justice and a police force. In Dec. 1995 the Sri Lankan army recaptured the city, forcing the LTTE into the jungle from where they continued to wage a guerrilla war. The take-over left much of the city in ruins and was preceded by a mass exodus of the city's inhabitants.

Modern City

With a diminished population and damage to property, the tourism industry has collapsed and travel to Jaffna is not recommended. This applies to the peninsula as a whole as well as the city. The population of Chavakachcheri, the second largest town in the Jaffna peninsula, has fallen from 20,000 to around 750 mainly army personnel. Jaffna Hospital, formerly one of Sri Lanka's best, lacks staff, medicine and equipment, and would be hard pressed to cope if tensions increase. Transport in and around Jaffna is poor. Recent attempts have been made to revive the damaged leather and fishing industries.

Places of Interest

Architectural remains from the Dutch period include a fort and a church. The fort, built in 1680 on top of earlier Portuguese fortifications, was besieged as recently as 1995 by Sri Lankan government forces after it had come under the control of the Tamil Tigers. There is an Archaeological Museum on Main St. which has remains of a Buddhist period in the peninsula's history.

Jakarta (Djakarta), Indonesia

Introduction

Jakarta is the capital of Indonesia and Southeast Asia's largest city. The city is located on the northern coast of West Java at the mouth and on the low alluvial plain of the Ciliwung River. It is a contrast of modern western architecture and traditional Indonesian culture. The rapid growth into a modern city and recent political turmoil reflect the economic and social development of Indonesia.

History

From the fourteenth century Jakarta was a small port of the Hindu Pajajaran Kingdom (thirteenth to sixteenth century), Sunda Kelapa. The Portuguese established themselves in the region to take advantage of the spice trade and were granted the right to build a fort. This port and the Portuguese fortress was captured on 27 June 1527 by the Islamic troops of Prince Fatahillah (Sunan Gunungjati) for the neighbouring Banten sultanate and renamed Jayakarta (Great Victory).

The next century was relatively peaceful as trade with Europeans grew but in 1618, after a skirmish between the British (backed by Jayakartians) and the Dutch Vereenigde Oost-Indishe Compagnie, the town was attacked and destroyed. It was rebuilt as the walled fortress capital of the Dutch East Indies, Batavia.

Dutch colonial rule in Indonesia brought prosperity to Batavia and many Indonesians and Chinese traders flocked to the city. By 1740, when it was evident that the walled city could no longer contain all its inhabitants; the Chinese were evicted. This prompted the massacre of 5,000 Chinese inhabitants by Dutch citizens.

During their colonial reign the Dutch brought non-Javanese slaves from other countries and built a series of canals. Subsequently an extensive system of urban railways was also developed linking Batavia with other cities on Java.

Batavia was the centre of Dutch trading and administrative activities for three centuries until, in March 1942, colonial forces surrendered to the invading Japanese army who reinstated the name of Jakarta in an attempt to win the sympathy of Indonesians. On 17 Aug. 1945, Indonesia's first president Sukarno proclaimed Indonesia independence. Sukano arrived in the city on 28 Dec. and established his government in the palace of the Dutch governor-general.

Modern City

In 1966 the city was declared a special metropolitan district with the status of a state or province.

Modern Indonesia is a sprawling metropolis that is no stranger to civil unrest. During the late 90s and into the new century thousands of protesters took to the streets to protest against political corruption. Many died and much property was destroyed in the resulting clashes between the armed forces and protestors. Indonesia's change of president on 23 July 2001 took place without the expected violence but the city remains volatile.

Jakarta exports rubber and tea and is a centre for railway engineering, tanning and saw-milling. The city's major manufactures include textiles and soap.

Places of Interest

The National Monument, or Monas as it is popularly called, was erected during the presidency of Sukarno. It represents the people's determination to achieve freedom and the crowning of their efforts in the Proclamation of Independence in Aug. 1945. The Monas is a 137-m tall marble obelisk, crowned with a flame coated with gold. The monument is open to the public and a lift carries visitors to the top for a commanding view of the city.

Sunda Kelapa, better known as Pasar Ikan (fish market) is located at the mouth of the Ciliwung River. It was formerly the harbour town of Sunda Kelapa where the Portuguese traded with the Hindu Kingdom of Pajajaran in the early sixteenth century.

Kasteel Batavia, the old fort and trading post of the Vereenigde Oost-Indishe Compagnie, can still be seen. Tall masted Bugis schooners from South Sulawesi anchor here.

Completed in 1627, the building that now houses the Jakarta Museum initially served as the Dutch East Indies Company's Town Hall. The Indonesian hero and renegade prince, Diponegoro, was said to have been imprisoned in its dungeon before his exile to South Sulawesi.

The Jakarta Museum provides a historical background with displays of maps and antiquities including furniture and porcelain used by the Dutch rulers of Batavia.

The Central Museum, established in 1778 by U.M.C. Rademacher and the Batavia Association of Arts and Sciences offers historical, archaeological and ethnographic artefacts and relics.

Jeddah, Saudi Arabia

Introduction

Jeddah is Saudi Arabia's second largest city, with a population of about 1.5 m. It is located on the Red Sea coast in the western province of Hejaz. The main port of the Kingdom, Jeddah has evolved into one of the Arab world's most important commercial centres. It is also the principal gateway into the country for Muslim pilgrims visiting the two holy mosques at Makkah and Madinah. The name Jeddah is thought to derive from the Arabic word meaning 'ancestor of women'. This theory is given credence by the location of what is traditionally believed to have been Eve's tomb within the city (a site since destroyed by the government).

History

Jeddah began as a small fishing settlement about 2,500 years ago. In AD 647 it was chosen by the caliph as the main port for the holy Islamic city of Makkah, and became known as Bilad al Kanasil, meaning City of Consulates. Having later fallen under Ottoman rule, the town was fortified in the sixteenth century by a stone wall, originally incorporating four gates. The town remained under Turkish sovereignty until the disintegration of the Ottoman Empire in the First World War. With the opening of the Suez Canal in 1869, Jeddah developed as one of the principal ports on the trade route between the Mediterranean and the Indian and Pacific Oceans. As it became more prosperous and cosmopolitan, European diplomatic delegations were established there. From 1916 Jeddah was part of the Kingdom of Hejaz, which was conquered by Abdulaziz in 1925. Following Saudi unification, its growth continued and in 1947 the city walls, as an obsolete obstacle to further expansion, were demolished.

Modern City

Jeddah has maintained its status as a major trading centre, although in recent years government ministries and foreign embassies have transferred to the capital, Riyadh. It is one of the principal ports in the Middle East, handling more than half of the Kingdom's sea traffic. The city has also been the focus since the mid-1970s of vast new commercial construction, financed by oil revenues. Having encompassed a land area of only 1 km^2 in 1947, it now covers 560 km^2, and its paved corniche along the Red Sea coastline stretches 80 km from north to south. The King Abdulaziz University was founded in 1967. The international airport is the busiest in the country for both passengers and freight. Its Hajj Terminal was built exclusively to accommodate some of the two million Muslim visitors who perform the pilgrimage annually. About 97% of pilgrims arriving by sea and 98% of those arriving by air pass through Jeddah. The city is also becoming an increasingly popular tourist destination in its own right. The Kingdom Tower, currently under construction and scheduled for completion in 2019, is set to be the world's tallest building. However, its final height has yet to be revealed.

Places of Interest

Jeddah's old city has examples of traditional houses built of coral limestone from the Red Sea and decorated with wooden facades. The Shorbatley House is among the best known. There is also a long-established souk or market. The main museums are the Museum of Archaeology and Ethnography, the Municipality Museum (in a restored traditional house) and the private Museum of Abdul Raouf Hassan Khalil. The Al-Shafee Mosque is one of the oldest in the city. The King Fahd Fountain by the coast is claimed to be the highest in the world.

Jerusalem, Israel

Introduction

The ancient city of Jerusalem, in the Judean mountains, is sacred to the three major monotheistic world religions of Judaism, Islam and Christianity and its history has been marked by political and religious turmoil. The seat of modern government, Israelis have designated it their capital. However, this is not recognized by the United Nations, as Arab East Jerusalem is part of the occupied territories captured in 1967.

History

Jerusalem was already the site of an important settlement by the fifteenth century BC. It was conquered by the Israelite King David about 1000 BC, who made it his capital. Solomon, David's successor, built the first great Temple which came to be recognised as the focal point of the Jewish faith. It was destroyed in 586 BC by the Babylonians as they sacked Jerusalem and exiled the Jewish population. When the Persians conquered Babylon in 537 BC, the Jews were allowed to return to Jerusalem and a second Temple was completed by around 515 BC. Persian rule gave way to the Hellenistic period from 332–167 BC and then to the Hasmonean (or Maccabee) dynasty. Roman control of Jerusalem, which began in 63 BC, witnessed the crucifixion of Jesus Christ in AD 33, the first revolt of the Jews from AD 66–70 resulting in the destruction of the second Temple, and the second revolt from AD 132–35 in which Jerusalem was razed and the Jews banished, creating a Diaspora. The Romans rebuilt the city as Aelia Capitolina, the basis of today's old city.

The legalization of Christianity in the Byzantine period from the early fourth century AD led to the building of churches at sites in Jerusalem linked to the life of Jesus, particularly the Church of the Holy Sepulchre. Briefly under Persian rule from 614, the city fell in 638 to the Muslims who, believing the prophet Muhammad to have ascended into heaven from there, built the Dome of the Rock (now the third most important religious shrine of Islam) on the Temple site. It was stormed by Crusaders in 1099 and retaken by Saladin in 1187. Egyptian Mameluke rule gave way in 1517 to Ottoman Turkish domination for the next four centuries. From the mid-nineteenth century Jerusalem became the destination for increasing numbers of Jewish immigrants, particularly from Russia.

Arab-Jewish antagonism in Palestine intensified from the 1930s, resulting in the 1948–49 war at the end of the British mandate. Jerusalem was divided between the Arab East, belonging to Jordan, and the Israeli West. Following the Six-day war in 1967 the Israeli government merged the two sectors, and in 1980 passed legislation declaring that a united Jerusalem was the capital of Israel. However this claim was rejected by virtually the entire international community.

Modern City

In addition to its religious significance, Jerusalem is the administrative heart of Israel, hosting the Knesset (Israeli parliament), the Supreme Court, government ministries and the Chief Rabbinate. It is also a centre of banking and finance, and has light industries such as diamond cutting and polishing and printing and publishing. The Hebrew University of Jerusalem, founded in 1918 and opened in 1925, is Israel's leading higher education institute with 23,000 students.

Places of Interest

The old walled city, divided into the Jewish, Muslim, Christian and Armenian quarters, holds the most sacred religious sites: the Islamic Al-Aqsa Mosque and Dome of the Rock; the Western (Wailing) Wall, all that remains of the second Temple and the holiest place of prayer for Jewish people; and the Christian Church of the Holy Sepulchre, thought to be where Jesus Christ was crucified, buried and resurrected. Other attractions include the Israel Museum, National Library, and Yad Vashem (the country's memorial to the victims of the Holocaust). The city is host to the annual Israel Festival of theatre, dance and music, the biennial Jerusalem International Book Fair, and other regular film, puppet theatre and choral music festivals.

Johannesburg, South Africa

Introduction

Johannesburg is South Africa's chief financial and industrial city. It is located in Gauteng Province about 65 km south of Pretoria, on the Highveld at 1,735 m above sea level.

History

Johannesburg thrived on the discovery of gold by Pieter Jacob Marais in the latter half of the nineteenth century. The city sits upon the Witwatersrand, a string of rocky ridges that have a large stratum of gold running through them. The locals call Johannesburg 'City of Gold'; Gauteng itself is a Sotho word meaning 'place of gold.' Earlier, the high plateau was inhabited by Boer farmers, grazing cattle and cultivating wheat and maize. The jobs and wealth the mines generated made Johannesburg the country's largest and most prosperous city. Much of that growth is on the city's outskirts, where the unemployed rural black population came in search of jobs and established townships. The most famous of these grew into Soweto, an acronym for 'South-Western Townships'.

The discovery of gold triggered a rush that saw miners travelling from as far away as Australia, Britain and the USA. The Transvaal, ill prepared for such an influx, sent Vice President Christiaan Johannes Joubert and Deputy Surveyor-General Johann Rissik to identify a city site. They are remembered in the name of the city they helped to found. Johannesburg grew fast and by the turn of the century had a population of over 100,000.

The British were keen to bring the Witwatersrand reef under their control. Backing disgruntled mine owners they turned a blind eye to the Jameson raid, an attempt to overthrow the Transvaal government. This did not succeed, but within 3 years the British had seized control of Transvaal and the Orange Free State.

In 1904, as part of a seemingly benevolent act to improve living conditions for black citizens, the black inhabitants of central Johannesburg were relocated to Klipspruit, 16 km away. Over the next two decades the white administration moved blacks, Indians and Chinese from the city into slums and shanties on the outskirts of the city. Deteriorating conditions for black workers spawned a new political movement and the rise of a militant African National Congress Youth League. Among its founding members was the young attorney, Nelson Mandela.

The 1948 general election was fought and won by the National Party, led by Daniel Malan, on a policy that became known as apartheid. During the next four decades millions of black South Africans were relocated to remote 'homelands'. The discontent that grew under the apartheid regime exploded on 16 June 1976 when the South African police opened fire on a student protest march in Soweto. The students were protesting against governmental legislation to make Afrikaans the language of instruction in black schools. Violent political protest continued until the white rulers were forced to negotiate an agreement that paved the way for South Africa's first fully democratic elections in 1994.

Modern City

Modern Johannesburg is a transport hub, and is well served by road, rail and air connections. Johannesburg International Airport, 20 km east of the city, is one of the largest on the continent. Bus services operate between the airport, the railway station in the city centre, and Rosebank, Sandton and Randburg at half-hour intervals. A municipal bus system provides transport within the city, and a separate bus company operates services to Soweto and Alexandra.

Places of Interest

The Market Theatre shows an eclectic mixture of traditional and contemporary theatre with comedy and dance. Johannesburg Zoo holds over 400 species of birds and animals set in an area of parkland and gardens. The South African Museum of Military History, at the eastern end of Johannesburg Zoo, has a large collection of military hardware from the various South African wars, including a vast array of weapons from the Boer War. Gold Reef City is a reconstruction of old-time Johannesburg; it has a Victorian fun fair, a trip down a mine shaft and tribal dancers. The Workers Museum illustrates the days of the gold rush and the plight of immigrant workers in the colony. Johannesburg Art Gallery exhibits an array of historical and contemporary South African art. The Gertrude Posel Gallery has a large collection of African tribal art including beadwork and masks.

Kabul (Kabol), Afghanistan

Introduction

Located in the north-east of Afghanistan, Kabul has existed for 3,500 years and has been the national capital since 1776. Its position in a valley between the Asmai and Sherdawaza mountain ranges, and its command of passes through the Hindu Kush mountains (notably the Khyber Pass), has ensured its strategic importance throughout the ages.

History

Kabul's long history has been punctuated by conflict. Used as a passageway by Alexander the Great during his Indian invasions of the fourth century BC, it had established itself as a regional seat of government by the eighth century AD. During the thirteenth century Genghis Khan wreaked devastation on the city and between 1504 and 1526 it served as capital of the Mogul Empire under Babur. It remained under Mogul influence until 1738 and Babur's garden and tomb can still be seen to the west of the city, at the foot of Sherdawaza.

During the nineteenth century, Kabul had a prominent role in the Anglo-Afghan Wars. In 1978, civil war overtook the city and a year later the Soviet Union invaded Afghanistan with a massive airlift of troops. The Soviet withdrawal in 1989 was the cue for the outbreak of destructive guerrilla warfare between rival Afghan groups. The Taliban imposed its Islamic-fundamentalist rule in 1996 but by then much of the population had moved out and large swathes of the city, including the University and the Dar ol-Aman Palace which housed the parliament and government departments, had suffered serious damage.

Much of Kabul was damaged in the campaign to overthrow the Taliban which followed the Sept. 11 terrorist attacks in the US and the Taliban's subsequent refusal to extradite chief suspect, Osama bin Laden. On 13 Nov. 2001 Kabul fell to the Afghan Northern Alliance, with the support of British and American troops. An Interim Administration took office in Kabul on 22 Dec. 2001 to oversee Afghanistan's transition to civilian government.

Modern City

Industries within the city include food-processing, rayon and wool milling, furniture-making, metal founding and marblework.

There is an international airport (Khwaja Rawash Airport). Bombed during the US campaign, the airport reopened in Jan. 2002. There are road connections to the ports on the Oxus and Amu Darya rivers.

With the setting up of the new government, commerce is reviving and Afghanistan's displaced population is beginning to return to the capital.

Places of Interest

Kabul University was once one of Asia's leading institution but it was damaged and lost many of its staff during the Taliban regime.

Kampala, Uganda

Introduction

Kampala is in southern Uganda to the north of Lake Victoria. It is the country's largest city as well as its administrative and commercial hub.

History

Originally a small settlement to the north of Mengo, the city is the former capital of what was once Buganda. Captain Frederick Lugard founded it as an outpost of the British East Africa Company in 1890. Kampala rapidly became the administrative headquarters of Uganda, but in 1905 the headquarters moved to Entebbe, and Kampala declined. When Uganda gained internal self-government in 1962 Kampala was proclaimed the national capital. The city suffered greatly under the rule of Idi Amin, and again in the 1980s when the struggle for control of the country was often violent. Since the 1990s the city has enjoyed substantial improvements in its economy and infrastructure.

Modern City

Kampala is constructed over seven hills and the city centre is on Nakasero hill. It accommodates international organizations, embassies, expensive hotels and government buildings. The rest of Kampala is divided into commercial, administrative, industrial and residential sections. While the city's industrial output is less significant than that of Jinja (60 km north of the capital) major exports include cotton, tobacco, sugar, tea and coffee. The city is also notable for the manufacture of metal goods. Kampala is very much the commercial heart of Uganda, and provides the headquarters for almost all the biggest national and international corporations. It is easily accessible by road, and there are regular rail services to Kenya. Boat services operate from Port Bell, 10 km to the east. Kampala's international airport is at Entebbe, 35 km southwest of the capital.

Places of Interest

The Uganda museum houses a notable collection of African musical instruments. The enclosure of the Kasubi royal tombs contains traditional buildings of the native Baganda people.

Kansas City, United States of America

Introduction

Kansas City is along the state border between Missouri and Kansas at the confluence of the Kansas and Missouri rivers. Kansas City, Kansas is predominantly a suburban residential area while Kansas City, Missouri is one of the most important distribution and market centres in the United States.

History

Kansas City was first settled by Europeans after the arrival of French fur traders in 1821. An important river port it was originally established as the Town of Kansas in 1850 and renamed Kansas City in 1889. The city acted as a staging point for gold prospectors heading west and was joined to St Louis by a railroad in 1865. The railroads helped the meat packing and distribution industry to establish itself in the city and Kansas grew rapidly at the beginning of the twentieth century, with the population doubling between 1910 and 1960. During the prohibition era Kansas City's controversial Mayor Prenderghast ensured that the city's jazz clubs could sell alcohol. In 1951 the Kansas River flooded, damaging the city's manufacturing industries and meat stockyards. By 1992 the last of the stockyards had closed but Kansas City's jazz scene and its many restaurants and theme parks remain popular with tourists.

Modern City

The city's main airport is located 25 miles from the downtown area and can be reached from the city centre by Shuttle Bus. There is a Metro Bus system, a Greyhound bus terminal and an Amtrak rail station. Kansas City's industries include food processing, metal production and transport equipment. Owing to its geographical location in the centre of the United States and excellent transport links, the city is a distribution and market centre for a variety of goods, including crops and livestock.

The city's institutions of higher education include the University of Missouri in Kansas City, Avila College, Rockhurst College and the Kansas City Art Institute (1885).

Places of Interest

The Nelson-Atkins Museum of Art includes a collection of Oriental art while the Black Archives of Mid-America houses a gallery of Afro-American art and sculpture. There is a Negro Leagues Baseball Museum and a jazz museum partly devoted to Charlie Parker, who was born in Kansas. Other cultural attractions include the Toy and Miniatures Museum and the Kansas City museum.

Kansas City Zoo and the tropical-themed water park Oceans of Fun are popular with visitors. The Harry S. Truman Sports Complex houses the Starlight Theater. Royal Stadium, where the Kansas City Royals baseball team is based, and Arrowhead Stadium, where the Kansas City Chiefs American football team play.

Karachi, Pakistan

Introduction

Karachi was the capital of Pakistan from the time of partition in 1947 until 1958 when it was moved to Islamabad. It has the highest population of any city in Pakistan with 9.2 m persons in 1998. Lying on the Arabian sea, northwest of the Indus delta, it is also Pakistan's busiest sea port, and handles all of the country's marine imports.

History

Karachi began as a small fishing village. In the eighteenth century, the khan of Kalat (the head of the city state of Kalat, founded in 1660 and now a part of Pakistan) moved to the settlement in search of a site with good sea port potential and natural defences. In 1795, the Talpura amirs took Karachi when the khan of Kalat removed his troops from the region, and built a permanent fort. The settlement quickly expanded and when the British arrived in 1839 it had already become a significant trading post. In 1842 the British annexed it, basing their army command headquarters there, and the small fishing village became one of the leading ports in the Indus Valley region.

With expansion came British investment and the introduction of a steam boat service in 1843 between Karachi and Multan. The port was then linked to the hinterland in 1878 when the Delhi-Punjab railway system was extended. Port facilities were improved constantly and after establishing a port trust to oversee administration, the east wharf was constructed, reaching completion in 1910. By 1914, as a result of Punjab's dominance in the grain market, Karachi had emerged as the largest port for exporting grain in the British Empire.

Continued growth led to further industrial development in areas such as manufacturing and by 1924 an airport had been constructed making Karachi the primary point of entry into India by air. In 1936, the city became the capital of the province of Sind. After the partition in 1947 and its new role as newly-formed Pakistan's capital, Karachi became an administrative and economic centre as well as an industrial one. By 1958 the city had become overcrowded due to the massive influx of refugees that had resulted from the partition. The government at the time decided that the capital should be moved to a more central location and Islamabad was subsequently constructed to fulfil the role. This took a great deal of pressure off the city as people began to move away to the new capital and nearby towns that had begun to establish themselves.

Modern City

Today the city of Karachi covers 591 km^2 and handles the entire sea-borne trade of Pakistan and Afghanistan. Its exports include grain, cotton, oilseeds, hides and wool and its manufactured goods include textiles, footwear, chemicals, plastics and electrical equipment. There are over 25 banks in the city with branches throughout Pakistan. There are over 20 general hospitals and several specialist ones for the treatment of such illnesses as tuberculosis and leprosy. The city has over 900 primary and secondary schools, half of which are privately run. The University of Karachi (established in 1957) is the city's principle institute of higher education and houses the city's largest library. It has over 20 graduate departments in arts and sciences and a school of graduate business administration as well as around 75 affiliated colleges providing a variety of courses.

Domestic and international transport links are excellent. The Karachi-Zahedan highway connects the city with Iran and the middle east. The Karachi-Peshawar highway links Karachi with the interior of Pakistan and the Karachi-Ormara runs along the coast. Pakistan's rail system is based in Karachi, connecting both the city with the interior and catering for commuter and passenger transportation within the city. The airport caters for both domestic and international flights.

Despite land and sea breezes, Karachi's extremely humid climate (varying from 58% in Oct. to 82% in Aug.) makes the dispersion of traffic fumes and disposal of industrial waste difficult. As a result, the city faces some pollution problems.

Places of Interest

Tourist attractions include the Quaid-I-Azam Mausoleum, a monument to Pakistan's founding father, Mohammed Ali Jinnah, and the Masjid-e-Tooba (Defence Mosque) which boasts a 65-m high white marble dome. Examples of Anglo-Indian architecture include Holy Trinity Cathedral and St Andrew's Church. Karachi has been criticized for its lack of open spaces and parks though Gandhi Gardens and the Fatima Jinnah gardens are popular attractions.

Kathmandu, Nepal

Introduction

Kathmandu, capital city of Nepal, is also called Katmandu or Kantipur. Originally known as Manju–Patan, its present name refers to Kastha–Mandap, a wooden temple built from a single tree in 1596. Situated in the country's central area in the lowland Valley of Nepal in the southern Himalayan mountains, Kathmandu sits 1,372 m (4,500 ft) above sea level at the confluence of the Vishnumati and Baghmati rivers. It is the country's largest city as well as being its economic, administrative and cultural centre. Historically a major tourist centre, Kathmandu had numerous historical monuments and shrines. However, many of these were severely damaged during the earthquake of April 2015.

History

Kathmandu was founded in 723 AD by the Licchavi King Gunakamadeva. The Newar people were the original inhabitants of the valley descending from the Mongols. Although Newari Buddhist colonies remain, Hinduism became the dominant religion especially with the arrival of the Malla Kings who ruled from the tenth to eighteenth centuries. Many temples and palaces were built during this period and Kathmandu was the centre of major trade routes through Nepal. In 1769 the Gurkhas, under King Prithvi Narayan Shah (descendant of the current dynasty), invaded, took power and unified Nepal making Kathmandu their capital. Following a war the Treaty of Kathmandu was signed in 1816 allowing territorial concessions to the British. Rule passed to the Ranas in 1846 who became hereditary prime ministers. The borders were closed although the Ranas made trips to Europe. In 1923 Nepal was granted independence. The divide between the rich and poor grew. A huge earthquake in 1934 destroyed many temples and palaces, killing thousands. Internal strife led to a coup in 1950, reinstating the Shah King Tribhuvan as ruler in 1951 when the borders were reopened. After a brief period of democracy political parties were banned and in 1962 the Panchayat system, a form of party–less government was incorporated. Executive power lay with the king. After years of uprisings, King Birendra agreed to legalise political parties and in 1990 a new constitution established a bi–cameral parliament. In 1991 the first democratic election was won by the NCP with the United Communist Party of Nepal (UCPN) forming the official opposition. Following accusations of corruption and economic mismanagement, the government was brought down by a vote of no confidence in 1994. A coalition government, with the UCPN at its head, was formed in 1994 but internal disputes led to its collapse in 1995. A right–wing coalition government was then formed led by the NCP. In 1997 the NCP lost a vote of no–confidence and a new coalition was formed under the National Democratic Party, NDP. In 1998 a minority government was formed by the NCP joined by the recently formed Communist Party of Nepal (Marxist–Leninist) CPN–ML and the Nepal Sadbhavana Pary (NSP). After further elections in 1999 a new government under the NCP was established. In June 2001 the king, queen and members of the royal family were shot dead by their son and heir, Crown Prince Diprendra, who then shot himself. The king's younger brother, Gyanendra, was crowned king. These events caused widespread rioting throughout the city. In April 2015 much of the city was devastated during an earthquake of 7.8 magnitude.

Modern City

The international Tribhuvan airport is to the east of the city. Other than from Bangkok, Dhaka or Frankfurt, visitors usually have to change planes, or even airlines, in India. Domestic airlines fly throughout the country; the most popular route is from Pokhara to Kathmandu. Bus services are inexpensive but crowded. Taxis are reasonably priced but it is advisable to negotiate the price in advance. The same is true of rickshaws.

Major industries within the town include tourism, clothing, handicrafts and cottage industries. The first surfaced road was built in 1956 and a major road construction programme was commenced in 1970. The Tribhuvan University was built in 1959. The Kaiser Library, located in the Ministry of Education, houses valuable, rare books and manuscripts. The city hosts many religious festivals. One of the most celebrated is the Maha Shivarati held every Feb. Thousands of Hindus gather to bathe, fast and visit the temple of Pashupatinath to worship Lord Shiva. Others include Gaijatra (the festival of the cow) in July to Aug. and the week-long Indrajatra (Aug. to Sept.), with cultural and religious events.

Places of Interest

Before the earthquake of April 2015, Kathmandu hosted many historical monuments, shrines and palaces, including the Kasthamandap temple built in 1596 (after which the city is named), Durbar Square (designated a World Heritage Site in 1979) and the Singha Durbar palace which housed the government's Secretariat. However, many of these were either severely damaged or destroyed during the strongest earthquake to hit Nepal since 1934.

Kaunas, Lithuania

Introduction

Kaunas, Lithuania's second city and its capital for part of the twentieth century, is on the confluence of the rivers Vilnya and Neman in the south of the country. Its status is based on its importance as a river port and trade centre.

History

Kaunas was settled in the fourth century and was used as a fortress from the tenth century. Owing to its strategic significance on Lithuania's western front, the town became a battleground as Teutonic knights fought Polish-Lithuanian troops and the city was sacked several times.

After the defeat of the knights in the early fifteenth century, Kaunas' river port flourished. As part of the Hanseatic League, shipbuilding and papermilling prospered. Having been ceded to Russia on the third partition of Poland at the end of the eighteenth century, the city was attacked by Napoleonic forces in 1812. It benefitted from rapid industrialization in the nineteenth century, especially after the opening of the railways.

With banning of the Lithuanian language, Kaunas (or Kovno in Russian) become a nationalist stronghold. It was the capital of independent Lithuania between 1919 and 1940, consolidating its position as a cultural and commercial centre. Occupied by the Germans in 1941, it suffered major structural damage during World War II and large numbers of citizens (especially Jews) were massacred or deported.

Under post-war Soviet rule, Kaunas underwent largescale rebuilding while retaining its strong nationalist identity. When, in the 1970s, a student burned himself to death in protest at Muscovite rule, there were nationalist riots. The city was prominent in the build-up to Lithuanian independence in 1991.

Modern City

The river port remains important to the local economy. Other major industries include metalwork, textiles and chemicals. There is a university and several institutes of higher education.

The city is served by road, river and rail links. Karmelava airport is 12 km from the city and Vilnius airport is 90 km away. Buses and trolley buses run within the city as well as a furnicular railway.

Places of Interest

Sights of interest in Kaunas include the cathedral of St Peter and St Paul, the ruins of the thirteenth century castle, the Jesuit church of St Xavier and the neo-Byzantine Church of St Michael the Archangel. The Resurrection Church, still under reconstruction, is regarded as a symbol of Lithuania's nationalist struggle. The baroque Pazaislis Monastery is just east of the city.

The Fascism and Jewish Genocide museum is housed in a nearby fort built during the Soviet era. There is also an open air museum, the Kaunas See Regional Park and several professional theatres.

Kharkiv (Kharkov), Ukraine

Introduction

An important trading and industrial centre, Kharkiv is in the north of the country around 40 km from the Russian border. Capital of Kharkiv oblast, it lies at the meeting point of the rivers Lopin, Kharkiv and Uda. Following widespread destruction during World War II it was rebuilt by the Soviets.

History

The city was first mentioned in 1655 when Cossacks settled on the banks of the river Kharkiv. An important fort and trading post on the Tatar frontier, it was among Ukraine's most prominent commercial cities in the seventeenth century. By the 1730s it was the administrative capital of the region and during the nineteenth century it expanded on the back of wealth generated by its coal and metal industries.

Following the Russian revolution it became capital of Soviet Ukraine from 1919 until Kiev succeeded it in 1934. The city underwent a cultural golden age in the early twentieth century, with the Vaplite writers association and the Berezil theatre at the forefront. However, Ukrainian nationalism was suppressed and Soviet culture came to dominate. The first wedding-cake style Soviet skyscraper was the House of State Industry in 1928.

Kharkiv was decimated during World War II. Under Nazi occupation from 1941–43 it witnessed fierce fighting. In the post-war period it was re-built along Soviet lines, incorporating wide avenues and brutalist architecture.

Modern City

Among the most important industries are engineering, chemicals, metalwork, machine tools, electrical goods and vehicle manufacturing, and food processing. Kharkiv has a university and numerous higher education and research institutions.

Kharkiv is Ukraine's largest railway junction and is on major road routes between Russia and Ukraine. There is an international airport and an underground railway.

Places of Interest

Among the buildings to survive World War II were the Pokrovsky Cathedral (dating from the seventeenth century), the Patriarchal Cathedral (built in the nineteenth century) and the bell tower built in tribute to Napoléon's defeat of 1812. There are several theatres and a planetarium. Also popular are the museums of history, natural history and fine arts as well as the Shevshenko Town Gardens, Gorky City Park, Forest Park and the city zoo.

Khartoum, Sudan

Introduction

The capital, transport, trade and administrative centre of Sudan. Also capital of Khartoum Province, the city lies in east central Sudan, south of the confluence of the Blue and White Nile Rivers. It is linked by bridges across the Blue Nile to Khartoum North and across the White Nile to Omdurman.

History

Khartoum was founded in 1821 by Muhammad Ali as an Egyptian military post to protect the British-supported Turko-Egyptian government of the Sudan. It grew into a thriving, garrisoned army town. During a revolt in 1884–85 against Anglo-Egyptian rule the town was attacked by Muhammad Ahmad, known as the Mahdi. Despite efforts by Major General Charles Gordon, then British Governor-General of the Sudan, the city was captured and Gordon and its inhabitants were massacred at the end of a ten-month siege. It was recaptured and rebuilt in 1898 by Lord Kitchener. It was the capital of Anglo-Egyptian Sudan from 1899–1956 when the city became the capital of the independent republic of Sudan. Civil wars have ensued with several coups and changes of government. Disease and starvation are rife throughout the country and Khartoum has not escaped.

Modern City

Much trade is derived from the river traffic on the Nile Rivers. Industries include textile and glass manufacturing, food processing and printing. A paved highway, completed in 1980, links Khartoum with Port Sudan. Railways connect the city with Egypt, Port Sudan and Al-Ubayyid. An oil pipeline was completed between the city and port in 1977. The national carrier, Sudan Airways, operates from the International Airport located near Khartoum. Photography in the city requires a permit. The University of Khartoum, founded in 1956, formerly the Gordon Memorial College, is noted for its African and Sudanese library. Nilayn University (1955) was formerly the Khartoum branch of Cairo University. Other libraries include the Flinders Petrie Library, named after the British Egyptologist, the Geological Research Library and the Sudan Medical Research Laboratories Library.

Places of Interest

The Sudan National Museum has collections of rare artifacts. There is also a Natural History Museum and an Ethnographical Museum. A collection of historical documents are housed in the National Records Office. There are two mosques, several cathedrals—Roman Catholic, Anglican and Coptic, as well as Greek and Maronite churches.

Khiva, Uzbekistan

Introduction

Khiva, in the south of the country on the River Amu Darya between the Karakum and Kyzylkum deserts, is one of Central Asia's best preserved cities. A major tourist destination, its centre is kept virtually as an open air museum.

History

According to popular legend, Khiva was founded by Shem, son of Noah. Archaeological finds confirm it existed in the sixth century. In the eighth century the town was an important trading post on the Silk Road and was sacked during the thirteenth century Mongol invasion. It became the capital of the Khivan Khanate in 1592 but was repeatedly sacked during tribal wars and an Iranian invasion.

In the seventeenth century it was developed as a centre of the slave trade, with at least a million people being sold. Diversifying into other trades during the late eighteenth and nineteenth centuries, it was ceded to Russia in 1873. Conquered by the Bolsheviks 1920, it served as capital of Khorezm Soviet People's Republic (1920–23) and the Khorezm Soviet Socialist Republic (1923–24). During the 1970s the authorities set about turning the city centre into a 'living museum'. It was recognized as a world heritage site by UNESCO in 1990.

Modern City

Khivans live and work outside the city walls in Dishan-Kala. Apart from tourism, the local economy relies on the textile industry (especially cotton and silk), carpet making and wood and metalworking.

Khiva is not easily accessible for visitors. The nearest airport is 28 km away in Urgench, but connecting buses and minibuses run regularly.

Places of Interest

The inner town, preserved by UNESCO, is called Itchan Kala. Leading tourist attractions include the Kukhna Ark Fortress (built in the seventeenth century), the Juma Mosque, the Tosh-Khovli Palace, the Pahlavon Mahmud Mausoleum and the Islom-Huja medressah and the Kalta Minor minaret.

Khudzand (Khojand), Tajikistan

Introduction

The administrative capital of the Khudzand region and Tajikistan's second city, Khudzand is on the River Syrdarya in the north of the country, at the entrance to the Fergana Valley.

History

Founded around 2,300 years ago by Alexander the Great as a fortress on ancient silk routes, the settlement marked the extent of his empire and was thus called Alexandria Eskhat (*Outermost Alexandria*). Plundered by Arabs in 711, the city nevertheless prospered and had many lavish palaces and mosques until it was razed to the ground in 1220 by Mongol forces under Genghis Khan.

Rebuilt on a more modest scale, in the early nineteenth century it was part of the Kokand khanate but was annexed by Russia in 1866. The Bolsheviks sacked the city in 1918, massacring many inhabitants to quell the Basmachi rebellion. Under the jurisdiction of Uzbekistan between 1924 and 1929, in 1929 it became part of the Tajik Soviet Socialist Republic (the rest of the Fergana Valley staying in the Uzbek Soviet Socialist Republic). In 1936 it was renamed Stalinabad, only reverting to its current name after independence in 1992.

Modern City

Among Tajikistan's richest areas, Khudzand remains important for silk production. Other major industries include textile and footwear manufacturing, food processing and tourism.

Places of Interest

The Panchshanbe Bazar is a vibrant market popular with visitors. Other attractions include a mosque, the mausoleum of Sheikh Massal ad-Din, a museum of history and a theatre.

Kigali, Rwanda

Introduction

Kigali is situated in the centre of Rwanda on the Ruganawa River. Before the civil war in 1994 it was a small but beautiful city. Much of it was subsequently destroyed, but restoration has been undertaken in recent years.

History

The city began its modern existence after 1895 as a trade post under German colonial rule. It emerged as the regional centre under the Belgian administration of 1919–62. Having gained independence from Belgium, it became capital of Rwanda in 1962.

Modern City

Kigali is spread over four hills. The industrial heartland is located in the southeast, and the city's exports include footwear, paint, varnish and tanned goods. It also has a number of radio-assembly warehouses. One of Rwanda's primary exports is tin, and many of the mining operations have their headquarters in Kigali. Kigali is connected by a number of roads, and the most reliable means of transport both to and from the city is by minibus. These can

be boarded at the Gare Routière. The buses run to a variety of destinations within Rwanda including Butare, Gitarama, Kibuye, Rusumo, Gatuna, Gisenyi and Ruhengeri. In Kanombe, about 12 km from the city centre, there is an international airport.

Places of Interest

There is a Muslim quarter near the city centre.

Kingston, Jamaica

Introduction

The capital of Jamaica, Kingston, is the largest city and main seaport. It lies on the fertile plains of Liguanea to the south-east of the island at the foot of the Blue Mountains. The harbour is the largest in the Caribbean and the seventh largest in the world. In 1872 Kingston succeeded Spanish Town as the island's capital and was founded by the British in 1693 to replace Port Royal which was destroyed by an earthquake in 1692. The partly submerged ruins of Port Royal can be seen at the entrance to the harbour.

History

Kingston has been repeatedly devastated by fires, floods, earthquakes and hurricanes. However by the eighteenth century around 3,000 brick houses had been built. Kingston's natural harbour brought trade and the naval wars brought ship building and industry. English immigrants arrived and sugar, cocoa, agricultural and forest industries expanded. As the plantations grew so did the slave industry and before its destruction Port Royal was one of the principal slave trading centres in the world. Kingston became notorious as a place of indulgence and when an act was passed in 1755 to make Kingston the capital, it was revoked by a new governor following anxious protests. Despite being beset by fires, earthquakes and epidemics, the city finally became the capital in 1872 only to be virtually wiped out by another earthquake in 1907. Headquarters House, once the seat of government built by Thomas Hibbert in 1755, is one of the few remaining houses of the period. It is now the headquarters of the Jamaica National Heritage Trust. Following the abolition of slavery in 1838, labour shortages caused a severe decline in the economy. Insurrections in 1865 led to Jamaica being made a Crown Colony and it was not until 1884 that representative government was partly restored. Sir Alexander Bustamante returned to the island from the USA in the 1930s. Recognizing the plight of the poor, Bustamante became their champion in confronting colonial power. In 1943 he formed the Jamaican Labour Party, became the country's first Premier in 1944 and its Prime Minister on independence in 1962. Kingston is the centre of Government which has seen rule by the JLP and the People's National Party. High levels of crime, violence and drug trafficking are major concerns. Until 2001 the highest court of appeal was the British Privy Council which had the power to commute the death penalty to a prison sentence. A number of Caribbean countries, including Jamaica, felt this undermined their authority and have replaced the Council with a Caribbean Court of Justice.

Modern City

Kingston's Norman Manley International Airport is situated on the Palisadoes peninsula about 30 min from the main business area in New Kingston. The original waterfront has been developed and shipping has moved to Newport West, adjacent to the extensive Kingston Industrial Estate. Much of Kingston is shanty town while New Kingston has benefited from modern planning with high rise buildings and spacious gardens. The hillside suburb of Beverley Hills has luxury homes. The Blue Mountains are the home of Jamaica's famous coffee. Goods manufactured in the city include textiles, petroleum and processed foods. Exports include coffee, rum, sugar molasses and bananas. The University of the West Indies, founded in 1948, is situated at Mona, 5 miles from Kingston.

Places of Interest

Kingston Parish Church was rebuilt following the earthquake of 1907. It has a memorial to Admiral Benbow by the sculptor, John Bacon. The clock tower was built as a memorial to those killed in WWI and its bell dates from 1715. The National Art Gallery on Ocean Boulevard has works by Jamaican artists. In the foyer is a statue of Bob Marley, the Jamaican reggae star, by the Jamaican sculptor Christopher Gonzalez. The Bob Marley Museum is in Hope Street, New Kingston. St Andrew Scots Kirk was founded by a group of Scottish merchants in 1813. It is noted for its music and choir, the St Andrews Singers. The Holy Trinity Cathedral replaced the church destroyed in 1907. Built in the Spanish Moorish style it has a dome and four minarets. National Heroes Park contains the graves and monuments of Alexander Bustamante, Norman Manley and Marcus Garvey. Kings House, the official residence of the Governor General and his wife, houses portraits by Sir Joshua Reynolds. Sovereign Centre is Jamaica's biggest and most Americanized shopping mall. Hope Botanical Gardens stretch for 100 acres at the foot of the Blue Mountains. It has a small zoo with birds and animals from all over the Caribbean and the Americas. In the Blue Mountains, the John Crow National Park offers trails and magnificent views across the plain.

Kingstown, St Vincent and the Grenadines

Introduction

The capital and chief port of St Vincent and the Grenadines, Kingstown is the country's main trade centre. It is located on the southwest coast of St Vincent island.

History

Kingstown was founded in 1722 by French settlers.

Modern City

The man-made deepwater harbour handles the island's overseas trade. Agriculture is the primary industry alongside fishing and tourism. Main exports include bananas and arrowroot.

There is a small international airport at Arnos Vale with flights to neighbouring islands in the Caribbean.

Places of Interest

The city is home to the West Indies' oldest botanical gardens, dating from 1763. Fort Charlotte, built by the British in 1806, stands 600 ft. above the bay, to the west of the city.

Kinshasa, Democratic Republic of the Congo

Introduction

Kinshasa is in the west on the south bank of the Congo just over 450 km from the Atlantic Ocean. It is one of the largest cities in sub-Saharan Africa. The city was originally formed from two villages, Nshasa and Ntamo (latterly called Kintamo).

History

The founder of Kinshasa was the explorer Sir Henry Stanley who forged an alliance with the ruler of Kintamo in 1877 and subsequently acquired a trading post there on a return visit in 1881. Out of deference to his patron, the Belgian king Léopold II, Stanley called the new post Léopoldville. The city became increasingly important after 1900 when it became the terminus for the crude oil trade. After the establishment of an air service from Stanleyville (now Kisangani), Léopoldville's prominence was assured. It was made the country's administrative headquarters in 1923. It finally became the

capital in 1960 following a series of insurgencies against colonial rule. It was renamed Kinshasa 6 years later.

Modern City

The city is divided into industrial, residential and commercial zones. To the north is the waterfront. The eastern part of the city forms the commercial hub, centring on the Boulevard du 30 Juin. To the west is the industrial heartland. It is situated close to the original site of Sir Henry Stanley's ivory trading post. Kinshasa's major industries include textiles, paper, beer, and food-processing, footwear, chemicals, woodwork, tyres and tobacco. East of the industrial zone is found the primarily administrative and residential district of Gombe which houses most of the city's wealthy citizens and expatriates. The poorer areas are mainly located in the east and west of Kinshasa.

Transport to and from the city is erratic. There is a rail and road connection to Matadi, and another road to Kikwit in the east. The Congo riverboat (Le Grand Pousseur) is the most reliable means of travelling from Kinshasa to Kisangani in the northeast. Ndjili International Airport is to the southeast of the capital. Within Kinshasa itself public transport consists of minibuses, taxis, buses and trucks which have been adapted to carry passengers and are known locally as fula-fula. Kinshasa is a vibrant but dangerous city. Many poor areas do not have regular supplies of electricity, running water or sanitation.

Places of Interest

The Académie des Beaux-Arts provides a taste of local artwork, and the Institut des Musées Nationaux houses a celebrated collection of ethnographic and archaeological exhibits. The city is one of the major centres of modern African music.

Klaipėda, Lithuania

Introduction

At the meeting point of the Courland Lagoon, River Neman and the Baltic, Klaipėda is Lithuania's key port.

History

A fishing village inhabited by ancient Balts, it was named Memel when German crusaders arrived in the thirteenth century. Lithuanian and Teutonic knights fought here. The castle was built by the Livonian Order in 1252 and occupied by the Teutonic knights in 1328. The Duchy of Prussia took over the town in 1525 and it was invaded and destroyed by Swedish forces in 1678.

Prussia re-took the city in 1701. Designated a city fortress in the middle of the century, it fell to Russian rule between 1757 and 1762. Capital for 1 year in 1808, in 1854 it was devastated by fire. This was the second time in its history, the city having been gutted in 1540. Memel became part of Germany in 1871, remaining so until World War I. The port thrived throughout the nineteenth century and rapid industrialization took hold.

Memel was returned to the Lithuanian Republic in 1923 and renamed Klaipėda in 1925. Annexed by Hitler in March 1939, it suffered significant damage during World War II. Soviets took the city in 1945, prompting an influx of Russian citizens who exploited the city's industrial potential. Lithuanian nationalism was increasingly evident from the 1960s. In 1991 Klaipėda became part of newly independent Lithuania.

Modern City

The economy relies on fishing, shipbuilding and related industries. Also important are textiles, paper and small-scale manufactures. There is a university.

Klaipėda is served by a bus and rail network as well as ferries. The nearest airport is Kaunas-Karmelava.

Places of Interest

Fire and war has destroyed most of the Old Town's original buildings. Remaining attractions include the Renaissance town hall, the churches of St John and Mary Queen of Peace, and a half-timbered Fachwerk building. The beaches of the Curonian Spit, a national park, attract a large number of tourists. There are museums of Lithuanian history and an art gallery.

Kobe, Japan

Introduction

Kobe is the capital of the Kobe prefecture, on Honshu island. Lying on the eastern side of the inland sea, it is one of Japan's most important commercial centres. In 1995, 4,500 people were killed and much of the city was destroyed in an earthquake.

History

In the eighth century Owada Anchorage (now called Wadamisaki Point) was established as a trading post and would develop over the centuries into Kobe's port. By the end of the thirteenth century the foundations of the modern urban area were in place, financed by trade with China and other Asian nations.

Under the Tokugawa Shogunate of the seventeenth century international trade was virtually ended, although the port continued to service domestic requirements. In 1868 international trade began again and 21 years later the City of Kobe was incorporated. Kobe flourished throughout the early part of the twentieth century but suffered badly during World War II when the population shrank. However, administratively conjoined with Osaka in the 1970s, it has subsequently prospered as part of Japan's second largest industrial zone, Keihanshin. Prone to typhoons, in 1995 Kobe was struck by an earthquake that lasted 20s, killed 4,500 people and devastated 100,000 buildings.

Modern City

Tertiary industries (including wholesaling, retailing and services) account for around three quarters of Kobe's economy today. Major heavy industries are shipbuilding, engineering and chemicals. It is also a famed centre of sake brewing. The main commercial area lies close to the harbour. There are two major railway stations (running *bullet* express trains), an airport and extensive port facilities. There are road connections with other major cities in the region. The Akashi Kaikyo Bridge, opened in the late 1990s, is the longest suspension bridge in the world.

Places of Interest

Motomachi is Kobe's main shopping street. There are two institutions of higher education, Kobe University and Hyogo University of Education. The Inland Sea National Park, nestled in the Rokko Mountains, can be accessed by road or cable car. Other attractions include Oji Zoo, the ancient burial tomb at Goshikizuka Kofun, several sake breweries and public parks. There is an annual municipal festival and a Luminarie, held each Dec. in remembrance of the earthquake victims.

Kolkata (Calcutta), India

Introduction

Kolkata (known as Calcutta until 2001) is India's second largest city and lies on the eastern bank of the Hooghly river, a subsidiary of the Ganges.

History

Kolkata was founded in 1690 by the East India Company after a peace treaty was signed between the company and the Mughal dynasty. The treaty paved the way for a factory to be built in the village of Sutanuti. Two other nearby villages, Kalikata and Govindapur, were then unified with Sutanuti, marking the beginning of modern Kolkata. A free trade agreement between the Mughal emperor, Farrukh-siyar, and the company in 1717 stimulated Kolkata's growth. In 1772 Kolkata became the capital of India.

In 1756 the town was captured by Siraj-ud-Dawlah, leader of the Nawab's of Murshidabad from Bengal. This led to the incident known as 'the Black Hole of Calcutta' in which 146 British soldiers were reportedly imprisoned for one night in a cell measuring 5.5 m. by 4.5 m. Only 23 soldiers survived the night. The British recaptured the town in 1757 and later defeated Siraj-ud-Dawlah, ensuring British control of the region.

Known as the 'city of palaces', Kolkata was divided into British and Indian districts. Although measures were taken to improve living conditions in the city between 1814–36, the low lying districts were devastated by cyclones towards the end of the century. The city is still divided between areas of great wealth and fine architecture, and areas of poverty with inadequate sewer systems, water supplies, and a huge homeless population.

Kolkata's position as a major financial trading post was damaged by the political and social upheavals brought about by the partition of Bengal in 1905. Although the split was later reversed, the troubles it created led the government to make Delhi the temporary capital of British India in 1912. Bengal was again partitioned in 1947 and Kolkata became the capital of West Bengal. But its reputation fell again as social tensions spilled over into rioting. The influx of refugees from East Pakistan (now Bangladesh) increased tensions further and the city continued its descent into turmoil as business began to leave the region in search of a more stable climate. The society neared breaking point in the 1960s and in the 1980s the government was forced to take action to improve conditions.

Modern City

Today the city is the world's largest producer of jute. It also supports textile, chemical, metal and paper industries. It has major transport links to the rest of India and beyond by road, rail and air, and is the most important trading port on the east coast of India. The integration of various communities and religions in Kolkata has left it culturally rich with Bengali, Hindi, Urdu and English spoken. There are several museums including the Indian Museum which is the oldest in India. There is a National Library and three universities. The University of Calcutta was founded by the British in 1857 and is now one of the largest teaching institutions in the world.

Places of Interest

Major tourist destinations are the Kali temple, the botanical garden (the largest of its kind in India) and the Victoria memorial. The city boasts some 30 museums and galleries including the Asiatic society (founded 1784), the Indian Museum (1814) and an academy of fine arts.

Among Kolkata's famous citizens are Mother Teresa (1910–97) and Rabindranath Tagore (1861–1941). Tagore became the first Asian Nobel laureate for literature in 1913 and was the composer of independent India's national anthem. Kolkata's most famous citizen, Mother Teresa, came to Bengal as a missionary. In 1948 she opened her order after the municipal authorities granted her the use of a hostel just outside the city. The hostel was devoted to giving the poor, sick, blind and dying of Kolkata a dignified place to live and die. She was beatified by the Roman Catholic Church in Oct. 2003.

Koror, Palau

Introduction

Koror, on Koror Island in the Caroline Islands, is Palau's capital city and main commercial and tourism centre.

History

Created by raised coral-limestone and volcanic rock, Koror passed from Spanish to German hands and was a bustling town under Japanese rule between 1921 and 1944. It suffered extensive damage during World War II, after which it came under UN jurisdiction and developed its commercial and tourist sectors. It has been capital of autonomous Palau since 1981. A new capital is being planned in Babelthuap, the larger island northeast of Koror.

Modern City

Major industries include Copra production and processing and tourism. Airai airport is close to the centre and a road connects Koror with Malakal Island, which has a major port.

Places of Interest

Leading attractions include the Belau national museum and the Micronesia Mariculture Demonstration Center on Malakal Island.

Košice, Slovakia

Introduction

Slovakia's second largest city, Košice has long been the southeastern administrative and cultural equivalent of the nation's western capital, Bratislava. It is now an important centre for trade and commerce as well as being the seat of the Constitutional Court of the Slovak Republic.

History

Although traces of settlements date back to the end of the Stone Age, the first written reference to Košice was in 1230. The city has the oldest coat of arms in Europe, received in 1369. It became a significant trade centre from the early fifteenth century. As part of Pentapolitana, an alliance of five eastern Slovak cities, the city profited from its geographical position near the Polish–Slovak frontier.

In the struggles for the Hungarian throne in the fifteenth century, Košice's municipal treasury financed expeditions against the Poles and the Hungarians under the leadership of Jan Jiskra. The military importance of the city increased as additions were made to its fortifications in the sixteenth and seventeenth centuries by Hungarian rulers eager to increase their defences in eastern Slovakia against the Turks. A Hungarian bishop, Benedict Kischdy, founded a Jesuit university in Košice in 1657 which was later to become a Royal Academy.

The nineteenth century saw further growth. In 1804 when Košice had its first bishop, the church of St Elizabeth was made a cathedral. The economy was boosted in 1870 after the construction of a railway station east of the town centre.

As the newly independent state of Czechoslovakia flourished after World War I there were prosperous times for Košice. Under Hungarian control throughout World War II, Košice came once more into the Czechoslovakian sphere in 1945 and was made the seat of the Slovak National Council. In the same year, the pro-Soviet 'Košice government' was formed. Although this was in operation for only 1 year, it orchestrated the 'Košice Program' which called for the violent repatriation of all resident Hungarians. It also began a process of economic centralization and state controlled education and industry which continued under communism.

Modern City

Along with chemicals, textiles, glass, minerals, and furniture, the region produces steel, Slovakia's main export industry. Previously a Slovakian company (VSZ Košice and eleziarne Podbrezová), the mammoth U. S. Steel Košice (affiliated to U. S. Steel) is one of the leading European steel manufacturers. Košice's train station was built in the late nineteenth century and provides services to major cities. The airport has regular flights to Bratislava, Prague and Vienna. In recent years the city has been home to an international television festival.

Places of Interest

The Cathedral of St Elizabeth is one of the few examples of high Gothic architecture to be found in Eastern Europe. Next to it is the Chapel of St Michael, the city's second oldest building. The city is home to the East Slovak Theatre, used by one of Slovakia's two professional ballet ensembles.

Kraków (Cracow), Poland

Introduction

Kraków, on the River Vistula, is Poland's third largest city and rivals Warsaw as a cultural centre. The national capital for 300 years until the early seventeenth century, it was briefly a free city within the Republic of Kraków in the nineteenth century. Though its population was decimated during the Nazi occupation, many of its oldest and most significant buildings were unscathed.

History

There is evidence of human habitation surrounding Kraków dating back 50,000 years. It was a major settlement for the Vistulanian tribe and the Great Moravian Empire between the sixth and tenth centuries. Around 1,000 the Polish king Bolesław I established the Kraków bishopric. Having suffered during Tatar incursions in the early part of the thirteenth century, Kraków achieved city status in 1257.

Wladyslaw I appointed Kraków capital of the recently re-united Polish state in the early fourteenth century. It blossomed culturally and economically. The town of Kazimierz was founded in 1335 and Casimir III established the academy of Kraków (now the Jagiellonian University) in 1364. The Jewish population was moved to Kazimierz in 1495 and by the end of the sixteenth century Kraków was in steep decline. After the Jagiellonian ancestral line ended, the city was devastated by fire in 1596 and Sigismund III transferred his court to Warsaw.

Kraków's stature was further diminished as a result of the Swedish occupation in the 1650s. Austrians took control of the city in 1776 before authority went to Russia. General Tadeusz Kosciuszko led an unsuccessful rebellion against Russia in 1794 and, in the third partition of Poland the following year, Kraków once again fell under Austrian jurisdiction.

From 1809–15 Kraków was part of the Duchy of Warsaw and from 1815 to 1846 it was part of the autonomous Kraków Republic. It then returned to Austro-Hungarian rule and experienced a period of growth that saw it regain prestige. The city came under Polish control when the Polish state was re-established in 1918. In Sept. 1939 the city fell to German invading forces. By 1940 plans were in place to establish the Auschwitz concentration camp and Birkenau death camp nearby. The city's population was terrorised throughout the war, with 55,000 Jews among the murder victims. Despite the elimination of huge swathes of the population, the city's structure largely survived as Wawel Castle was the base of the German governor. Soviet forces were quick to liberate the city in 1945.

Under communist rule Kraków's industrial base was greatly expanded but the area has become dangerously polluted. The city's workers' movement was influential in securing the overthrow of the communist regime in 1989.

Modern City

While retaining its industrial base, tourism has increased in importance in the post-communist era. In 2000 Kraków was a European City of Culture. Other important industries include metalwork (there are massive steel works in the purpose built Nova Huta area), chemicals, textiles and food processing.

Kraków is on several major rail routes with links to Warsaw, Vienna, Prague, Berlin and Budapest. Kraków-Balice (John Paul II) International Airport is 14 km from the city centre. Transport within the city includes buses and trams.

Places of Interest

Rynek Główny (the Main Square) dates from the thirteenth century and is among the largest and most impressive in Europe. It is home to the fourteenth century Sukiennice (Cloth Hall) and Town Hall Tower, the tenth century St Adalbert's church and the twin-towered St Mary's. The Royal Way leads to Wawel Castle, via the turreted Barbican and the Florian Gate, the only surviving part of the original city walls. The Jewish quarter, Kazmierz, gives an insight into Kraków's troubled history, and Auschwitz-Birkenau is within distance of the city.

Kuala Lumpur, Malaysia

Introduction

The legislative and commercial capital of Malaysia, Kuala Lumpur is the country's largest city. Situated centrally in Peninsular Malaysia, the city's growth during the second half of the twentieth century was remarkable, doubling in size within a generation. Ethnic Chinese form a large part of the city's population and dominate commerce. Ethnic Malays control the administration. In 2000 Putrajaya was named joint capital, although Kuala Lumpur is still the centre of administration as only the prime minister's office and two ministries have moved to the new capital.

History

The site of Kuala Lumpur was uninhabited until the 1850s, when the interior of the Malay state of Selangor was opened up by tin miners. In 1857 a group of Chinese miners navigated the Klang River to its shallow confluence with the Gombak River where they established a collection point for the tin found in major deposits to the east. The settlement was on the site of the present-day Kuala Lumpur suburb of Ampang. As local mining interests grew, so did a shanty town to serve the mines.

When a dispute over the succession to the throne of Selangor erupted into civil war, Britain stepped in to protect the Malay sultans, who were to be advised by a British resident. The first holder of this office in Selangor, Sir Frank Swettenham, arrived in Kuala Lumpur in 1882 which by then had replaced Klang as Selangor's capital.

Under Swettenham's guidance, the town, which had been largely destroyed by fire in 1880, was rebuilt in brick. When, in 1896, the Federation of Malay States was formed, Kuala Lumpur was named capital. Kuala Lumpur grew into a British colonial capital city.

During the first decades of the twentieth century the city's Chinese and Indian populations mushroomed. In 1941 the city was overrun by Japanese forces during their lightning invasion of the Malay Peninsula. After World War II (1939–45), the guerrilla movement against British rule, launched by the (ethnic Chinese) Malay Communist Party, had a dramatic effect upon the fortunes of the city. A series of strongly defended villages and other settlements was established around the edge of Kuala Lumpur to house people displaced by guerrilla activity elsewhere in Malaya. These settlements became, in time, suburbs of a rapidly expanding city.

When the Malay States gained independence in 1957 as the Federation of Malaya, Kuala Lumpur was named capital. In 1963, when Malaysia was formed from Malaya, Sabah, Sarawak and, briefly, Singapore, Kuala Lumpur became capital of the federation. Kuala Lumpur ceased to be part of Selangor state in 1974, when it was designated a federal territory. The 1980s and 1990s saw the transformation of the Malaysian capital into a modern city, symbolized by the Petronas Towers, the world's tallest office buildings at the time of opening in 1998, which dominate the city skyline. By the close of the twentieth century, the city's pollution, traffic problems and continuing urban sprawl gave rise to plans for a new capital Putrajaya on Kuala Lumpur's southern fringe.

Modern City

Kuala Lumpur is the principal cultural and political centre of Malaysia, despite the loss of some administrative functions to Putrajaya. It is the hub of Peninsular Malaysia's road and rail routes. Kuala Lumpur International Airport handles most of Malaysia's international flights, except some regional flights to other Asian states. The city has a rapid light transport rail system. As well as being an important banking and commercial centre, Kuala Lumpur is the most important industrial base in Malaysia. Sungai Besi is the principal industrial suburb and the Klang Valley downstream is the heart of Malaysia's modern high-tech industries. The Kuala Lumpur conurbation extends some miles down this valley to include Putrajaya. Major industries include food processing, engineering, tin smelting, rubber processing and, in the Klang Valley, textiles and electrical and electronic engineering.

Places of Interest

The 452-m (1,483-ft) Petronas Towers, designed by Argentine-born U.-S. architect Cesar Pelli, is one of the principal tourist attractions. Visitors are admitted to the sky-bridge that links the two towers on the 42nd floor. The Towers are in the modern office district known as the Golden Triangle. Nearby, the 421-m (1,381-ft) Menara Kuala Lumpur, or KL Tower, is another landmark. The viewing deck and revolving restaurant on this telecommunications tower are popular.

More traditional attractions include the huge Central Market and the colourful Chinatown with its temples and painted shop-houses. Two impressive Islamic structures lie south of the inner city: the Pusat Islam Malaysia (the Malaysian Islamic Centre) and the Masjid Negara, one of the largest mosques in South-East Asia. The Masjid Negara, which is set in gardens, has one large and 48 smaller domes and a minaret that rises from a pool. It is open to non-Muslims outside prayer times.

Merdeka Square is the centre of colonial Kuala Lumpur. Once a cricket ground, it is the square in which independence was proclaimed and is still the venue of parades and other ceremonies. Beside the square is the exclusive late Victorian Royal Selangor Club and the half-Moorish, half-Victorian domed Sultan Samad Building, which now houses the Supreme Court. At the confluence of the Klang and Gombak Rivers is the Masjid Jamek (Friday Mosque), a pink and cream-coloured building set among palm trees.

The Lake Gardens, west of the city centre, contain a deer park, orchid garden, butterfly farm, hibiscus garden and the National Monument. Other attractions include the National Museum, Parliament House, and the Islamic Arts Museum.

Kutaisi, Georgia

Introduction

Kutaisi is at the foot of the mountains bordering the Black Sea of west Georgia. A modern industrial centre, it is also one of the oldest cities in the region.

History

An important urban district by the sixth century BC, Kutaisi was the main city of Colchis and subsequently of Iberia, Abkhazia and Imeretia. The first documented mention of Kutaisi is in the third century BC, in a poem about Jason and the Argonauts, with Kutaisi described as the home of Medea.

When Georgia was united under Bagrat III in the tenth century AD, Kutaisi was made the administrative capital. Power changed hands on many occasions, with various Georgian dynasties, Mongols and Turks all holding the city at various times. It was razed by the Ottomans in 1510, suffered badly during the dynastic disputes of the mid-seventeenth century and had its castle and the twelfth century Bagrat cathedral destroyed by Turks in 1691.

Freed from Turkish rule in the late eighteenth century, in 1810 it came under Russian dominion and in 1846 was designated provincial capital. Soviets took control in 1921 and undertook a programme of industrial growth which still defines the character of the present-day city. During World War II it was a vital centre of armaments and vehicle manufacture.

Modern City

Major industries include vehicle, machine and clothing manufacturing and food processing. Roads offer the primary mode of access although there is an airport which operates domestic flights.

Places of Interest

Surrounded by mountains, most of Kutaisi's most popular sights are outside the town centre. These include the Motsameta monastery and the Gelati academy and monastery (build by David the Builder in the twelfth century). Further away is a nature reserve, Sataplia, and the ruins of the ancient city of Vani. The eleventh century cathedral is on a hill above the centre and there is a museum of history and ethnography.

Kuwait City, Kuwait

Introduction

Kuwait City, the capital, is situated in the east of the country on the southern shore of Kuwait Bay (which forms a natural harbour). Its name is derived from the Arabic word for 'fort'.

History

The origins of the city are usually put at around the early eighteenth century. About that time, elements of the Anaizah tribe (including the al-Sabahs, who were to become the ruling dynasty) migrated from the Arabian interior to the coast. The mainstays of the city's early economy were pearling, fishing and trade with the Indian sub-continent and east Africa. From that period it remained the only settlement of any consequence in terms of population in the territory. With the expansion of oil exploration and production from the 1930s and 1940s, Kuwait City and the surrounding area (now the populous suburbs of Hawalli, as-Salimiya, Jahra and Farwaniya) grew rapidly. The old city wall, built to keep marauding desert tribes out of the town, was demolished in 1957 to make way for further oil-driven development. In turn, the city became the commercial, financial and administrative engine of the country.

Modern City

The Iraqi invasion and occupation of Kuwait from Aug. 1990–Feb. 1991 resulted in extensive damage to the capital. Buildings and infrastructure suffered, and Iraqi forces systematically stripped all moveable assets from the city before their expulsion. However, the city has since been largely restored.

Places of Interest

The principal historical and architectural attractions and features are to be found in Kuwait City. These include the National Museum, Sadu House, National Assembly building, Sief Palace (the official seat of the Amir's court, the oldest parts of which date from the end of the nineteenth century) and Kuwait Stock Exchange. The Kuwait Towers opened in 1979 and have long been the country's main landmark. The largest of the three towers is 187 m in height. Their globe structures contain observation, restaurant and water storage facilities. The Al Hamra Tower is Kuwait's tallest building, at 414 m, and is also the world's tallest stone clad tower. The Great Mosque, built in 7 years, opened in 1986. The main prayer court can accommodate about 10,000 men at prayer time. It has an additional prayer court for women, which can hold nearly 1,000 worshippers.

Kyiv, Ukraine

Introduction

On the Dnieper River, Kyiv is the Ukrainian capital and its administrative, cultural and economic centre. As the powerful capital of Kievan Rus, as well as a religious and trade centre, the city was pivotal in Eastern Europe's history. Occupied by Lithuania, Poland, Germany and Russia, Kyiv was finally made capital of independent Ukraine in 1991.

History

Archaeological findings trace civilization in Kyiv back to the Stone Age. Between the sixth century and the third century BC the area was under the influence of first Scythia and then Sarmatia. The city was founded by prince Kyv of the Slavic Polyans tribe in 482. Four hundred years later the Varangian prince Oleg of Novgorod took Kyiv and made it the capital of Kievan Rus, the first unified state of the East Slavs, uniting Finnish and Slavic tribes. During the tenth century, trade was extended between the Baltic and Black Seas, shaping Kyiv's economy. The state, with Kyiv at its heart, gradually dominated Medieval Europe. Christianity was introduced in 988 leading to the construction of the Desyatynna Church, St Sophia's Cathedral (built from 1037) and, the religious and cultural centre of Kievan Rus, the Kyivan Caves Monastery (1051). By the early thirteenth century, Kyiv was one of Europe's largest cities.

Internecine struggles following the death of Yaroslav the Wise led to a break-up of the state principalities. In 1223 Genghis Khan's grandson, Batu Khan, invaded Kievan Rus and much of Kyiv was destroyed when the city was sacked by Mongols in 1240. The Lithuanian state took control of the city in 1362 and in 1484 Kyiv adopted the Magdeburg law of self-governance. Much reconstruction was undertaken during this period and the city was fortified against Tatar invasions, although it was burned during an attack in 1416 and in 1482 was plundered by the troops of Crimean khan Mengli Girai.

In 1569 Kyiv passed from Lithuanian to Polish control. In 1654 on the union of Ukraine and Russia the much diminished city was controlled by Moscow. By this time Moscow had long since eclipsed Kyiv in importance. Russian rule was consolidated, and Tsarist decrees suppressed the Ukrainian language and culture. Further misfortunes befell Kyiv when fires in 1718 and 1811 caused great damage, although the city did recover some of its commercial importance in the eighteenth century and was linked to Moscow by rail in the mid-nineteenth century.

Long a centre of suppressed nationalist sentiment, Kyiv was involved in the revolutionary events of 1905. Following the Bolshevik Revolution, Ukraine declared itself independent in 1918 with Kyiv its capital, but this was short-lived. After a Bolshevik invasion Kyiv was occupied in 1920 and its capital status transferred to Kharkiv until 1934. Despite increased industrial activity in the 1930s, the Soviets destroyed a large number of religious monuments. World War II, when Kyiv was under German occupation, spared little of what remained. Thousands were killed during this period including most of the city's Jewish population. In 1943 Russian troops expelled the Germans and Kyiv came once again under Soviet rule.

In the postwar period Kyiv became a centre for underground nationalist gatherings, many of which took the form of literary groups. Intellectuals and writers were executed in the city during the Stalinist purges. Much of the city was rebuilt and in the second half of the twentieth century industry developed. At the fall of Soviet Union, Kyiv became the capital of independent Ukraine.

Modern City

The political, economic and cultural centre of the Ukraine, Kyiv is also an important port. Its industries include engineering, metallurgy, chemicals and food processing. Kyiv's many educational institutions include Kiev's state university founded in 1833 and a polytechnic founded in 1898. The airport serves both domestic and international traffic. Rail links connect Kyiv to Moscow, Warsaw, Odessa and Kjarkiv while the city itself has a metro system. The Kyiv TV Tower, completed in 1973, is at 385 m the tallest lattice tower in the world.

Places of Interest

An abundance of Baroque and Byzantine architecture attest to Kyiv's rich history. The old town contains the eleventh century cathedral of St Sophia which has been turned into a museum for frescoes and tapestries. The Podil district is the old merchant's quarter and port. It contains the Baroque church of Mykola Prytysko built in 1631. Once the cultural heart of Kievan Rus, the Caves monastery contains the Baroque Dormition cathedral, churches and museums. The city's other museums include the Folk Architecture Museum and Rural Life, a grouping of traditional villages, and the Historical Treasures Museum.

Kyoto, Japan

Introduction

A leading cultural and industrial centre, Kyoto is in the southern Kyoto prefecture, 48 km northeast of Osaka, in the centre of Honshu island. The Japanese capital between 794 and 1868, Kyoto is now the centre of Buddhism and as such is a site of pilgrimage and tourism.

History

Archaeological evidence shows the area now Kyoto was inhabited during the Jomon (10,000–300 BC) and Yoyoi periods (300 BC–AD 300). Around the seventh century, the Hata clan migrated from China via Korea and settled the area. Around this time Koryuji, the first Buddhist temple, was built. Kyoto, first named Heiankyo ('city of peace and tranquillity'), was founded as the Japanese capital in 794, when natural disasters forced Emperor Kanmu to move his palace from nearby Nagaokakyo to Kyoto's wide valley. Flanked by the Kamo and Katsura rivers and surrounded by protective mountains, the city was built in the style of the capital of the Chinese Tang dynasty, Ch'ang-an (now Xian), around the imperial palace.

Kyoto was originally controlled by the powerful Fujiwara clan. At the time two Buddhist temples existed, Saiji and Toji (now the headquarters of the Shingon sect), but the construction of more temples inside the city limits was prohibited in an attempt to limit their power. Indeed, the growing influence of rich temples had prompted the imperial move to Nagaokakyo from the original capital of Heijokyo.

In 1177 Kyoto suffered a devastating fire which destroyed much of the city. Coupled with the decline of the Fujiwara leadership at this time, the country's new leaders Minamoto moved the capital to Kamakura in 1180. During this time, many Buddhist temples were established in the Kyoto area for the newly imported Zen sect. Over the next two centuries, these temples became cultural centres specializing in literature and arts. Kyoto was re-established as the capital during the Muromachi period (1338–1573) and under the control of the Ashikaga shoguns the palace became the imperial centre. Embroiled in a series of civil wars, Kyoto's superiority declined at the end of this period. The Ashikaga shogun's rule ended when the city was taken by the warlord Oda Nobunaga in 1568. His leadership, and that of his successor Toyotomi Hideyoshi, revitalized the city, although there was continuing conflict between the rulers and the Buddhist monks.

Hideyoshi invested much effort into the arts and as such benefited Kyoto. With the exception of a short period in the late nineteenth century, Edo (now Tokyo) succeeded Kyoto as capital in the early seventeenth century.

Unlike most Japanese cities, Kyoto suffered little bombing during World War II and still retains much of the original city structure, although modern edifices are springing up next to historic buildings. The expansion of suburban housing in the twentieth century and increased industrialization in the surrounding area meant Kyoto merged with the industrial cities of Osaka and Kobe. The three cities form part of the Keihanshin industrial zone, the second largest industrial agglomeration in Japan after the Tokyo–Yokohama metropolitan area.

Modern City

Traditionally the centre of silk weaving, Kyoto still produces fine garments for the entertainment industries. Artisans still practice traditional crafts for the large tourist industry. With many educational centres, Kyoto is one of the leading Japanese centres of learning. Established in 1897, Kyoto University is now Japan's second largest public university, while the Doshisha University was founded in 1873. Kyoto is connected to all major Japanese cities by bus and rail.

Places of Interest

Kyoto has many gardens and historic temples, some of which were entered onto the UNESCO world heritage list in 1994. Much of the extensive cultural heritage is preserved in the 1,660 Buddhist temples and numerous shrines which adorn the surrounding mountains. The Imperial Palace is one of three castles. Museums include the Kyoto Municipal Art Museum, the Municipal Commercial and Crafts Museum and the Kyoto National Museum founded in 1889.

La Coruña (A Coruña; Corunna; La Groyne), Spain

Introduction

Situated on the extreme northwest of the Spanish coast, the portal city of La Coruña is the capital of Galicia. Much of the trade between Spain and its South American colonies passed through La Coruña. Flanked by the Atlantic Ocean on both sides, the region has the heaviest rainfall in Spain.

History

The city's history possibly began with the Phoenicians. La Coruña was a port on the route of the Celtic tin trade on the way to Britain. The Romans arrived in the area in 60 BC and named the port Brigantium. It was later known as Ardobicum Corunium from which the city gets its current name. La Coruña was captured by the Moors in the eighth century, who controlled the area until the tenth century. The city was taken in 1002 with the defeat of the Arab leader Almanzar.

In 1386 John of Gaunt arrived with an army of 7,000 men to claim the crown of Castille in the name of his wife, Constanza, the daughter of Pedro the Cruel. It was from La Coruña that Felipe II embarked to England in order to marry Mary Tudor in 1554 and the Spanish Armada set sail on its way to invade England. Of the 130 ships that left on 26 July 1588, less than half returned to Spain. A year later, Sir Francis Drake, accompanied by Sir John Norris and an army of 7,000, sacked the town and destroyed much of the shipping.

La Coruña is the site of the grave of Sir John Moore, the Commander of the British forces during the Battle of Corunna in the Peninsular War. He is buried in the Jardín de San Carlos, situated in the old town. Moore was killed on 16 Jan. 1809; the British were forced to retreat from Valladolid to La Coruña, where Moore fended off a French attack but was mortally wounded in the process. The Irish poet Charles Wolfe commemorated Moore in his 1817 poem the *Burial of Sir John Moore*. Napoléon occupied the city of La Coruña for 6 months in 1809.

La Coruña is the birthplace of the novelist Emilia Condesa de Pardo Bazán. A fiction writer and essayist, she was made Professor of Romantic Literature at Universidad Central de Madrid in 1916. She was the first woman to be appointed to this role. The poet and novelist, Rosalía de Castro, was raised in La Coruña province. A nineteenth-century poet, she wrote in the Galician dialect. La Coruña was also the home to Picasso between 1891–95.

Modern City

La Coruña is the second most important fishing port in Spain. It is especially noted for sardines, and is the site of salting and canning. Its other major industries include petroleum, textiles, shipbuilding, glass and tobacco. The surrounding province is mainly agricultural and La Coruña exports onions and potatoes. La Coruña is accessible by sea, air, road and rail while a ferry service connects the city with the Canary Islands.

Places of Interest

The city's museums include a fine arts museum, a religious arts museum and the Museo de Arqueológia y Histórico. This building was originally a twelfth-century fort, which was used as a prison in the eighteenth century before being turned into a museum. Religious buildings include the twelfth century Iglesia de Santiago and the seventeenth century Iglesia de San Jorge.

The Romans built a 47-m lighthouse in 2 AD, the Torre de Hércules. It was later used as a fort and the lighthouse was restored in 1792.

La Paz, Bolivia

Introduction

Situated in the Andes in the northwest of Bolivia near the Peruvian boarder, La Paz lies along a deep 5 km-wide valley. The centre runs along the Choqueyapu River and the Cordillera Real Mountains form the city's backdrop. At an altitude of 3,600 m, La Paz is the world's highest capital. Although Sucre is the judicial capital of Bolivia, La Paz is the administrative, economic financial and commercial capital and is the seat of the country's government. The city has the largest population in Bolivia.

History

La Paz was founded on the site of the Inca settlement of Chuquiabo ('gold field') in 1548 by the Conquistador Alonso de Mendoza, chosen for the presence of gold in the Choqueyapu River. It was named Nuestra Señora de la Paz in celebration of the end of conflict in Peru between Conquistadors and Incas. Despite the short-lived gold interest, the location was an important commercial point on the trade route between Potosí, important for the presence of silver, and Lima, the main Spanish communication centre. Because of its key position La Paz became the political and commercial focal point of colonial life. Despite the high altitude, the altiplano plateau at 3,900 m offered climatic protection. The original settlement was created at Laja, now a small town southwest of the city, before being transferred shortly after to its current location. Restricted by the narrow valley, La Paz was not set out on the traditional colonial grid plan. The Plaza de los Españoles was built as the seat of government.

In 1781 an Aymaran uprising led by Tupac Katari laid siege to La Paz for 6 months, causing much structural damage. The siege ended when Katari was captured and executed. A second uprising lasting 2 months occurred in 1811. Between 1809–25 Bolivians fought for their independence. La Paz's local hero and revolutionary leader Pedro Domingo Murillo gave his name to the Plaza de los Españoles after he was hanged there during the conflict. After Independence La Paz was renamed La Paz de Ayacucho in honour of the site in Peru where José de Sucre successfully fought the final battle.

In 1898 La Paz became the official seat of the Bolivian government. Despite its importance, the city's population remained relatively small until the twentieth century when migrants from surrounding rural areas swelled the numbers. The expanding settlements climbed the canyon edges to the summit of the altiplano.

Modern City

La Paz is the economic, political, financial and commercial centre of Bolivia. Industries include flour milling, tanning and brewing while manufactures include textiles, chemicals and electrical appliances. The city also deals in the agricultural produce from the surrounding rural area. La Paz is connected to surrounding cities and countries by rail, road and air. The city's airport is located on the altiplano. Universities include the Universidad de San Andrés founded in 1830 and the Catholic University opened in 1966.

Places of Interest

The central Plaza de Murillo houses the presidential palace, known as the Palacio Quemado owing to the numerous fires it has suffered, and the cathedral which was built in 1835. Apart from the Iglesia de San Francisco (built 1549) and the Museo Casa Murillo dedicated to the independence hero, few colonial buildings survive. Housed in a former palace built in 1775, the Museo Nacional del Arte displays colonial works and Bolivian nineteenth and twentieth century art. Other museums of note include the Museo Tiwanaku, devoted to pre-Columbian culture from 500 BC–1200 AD, and the Museo de Metales Preciosos. One of the numerous indigenous markets, the Mercado de los Brugos (Witches' Market) sells traditional homeopathic remedies. Surrounding attractions include Lake Titicaca, the highest lake in the world, and the ruins of the 1,000 year old site of Tiahuanaco, from which artifacts are displayed in the Museo Nacional de Arqueología. The Andean peaks of Illimani and Illampú attract many climbers.

Lagos, Nigeria

Introduction

Nigeria's largest city and until Dec. 1991 the federal capital, Lagos retains many of the features of a centre of government. It extends over the islands of Lagos, Iddo, Ikoyi and Victoria.

History

Yoruba fishermen had settled on Lagos Island by the late fifteenth century. At this time Portuguese slave traders became active in the area, extending their activities until 1861 when the British took possession of Lagos. The city then came under the jurisdiction of various successive colonial administrations until 1914 when it became capital of the Colony and Protectorate of Nigeria. In 1960 it became the capital of independent Nigeria, and 7 years later the

capital of the newly-created provincial state of Lagos. Troubled by congestion and over-population, it was decided to move the federal capital in 1975.

Modern City

The city is concentrated on Lagos Island, in southwestern Nigeria, on the Bight of Benin. The mainly Yoruba population has become more heterogeneous as other Nigerians and West Africans have moved to the city. As one of Africa's most populous cities, Lagos has an inadequate infrastructure with most of the northwestern part (the original settlement) now a slum. Crime is a major concern.

The heart of the city lies on the southwestern shore of Lagos Island, the centre of commerce, finance, administration and education. The main industries are vehicle and radio assembly, food and beverage processing, metalworks, paints and soap. Textile, cosmetic and pharmaceutical manufacturing are also important. The traditional fishing industry survives. Street vendors crowd the city, taking advantage of traffic jams to find clients. There is an international airport and shipping terminals at Apapa and Tin Can Island.

Places of Interest

The southwest of Lagos Island is home to the national museum, whose treasures include traditional Benin Bronzes, sculptures and carvings. The University of Lagos and several major libraries are located in the city. Many government institutions remain in Lagos, with Victoria and Ikoyi Islands home to numerous embassies.

Lahore, Pakistan

Introduction

Lahore is the capital of the Punjab region and the second largest city in Pakistan. It lies in the northeast of the country on the Ravi river, very close to the Indian border.

History

The city's history has been a bloody one and though little is known about it prior to the Muslim period, Hindu legend states that the city was established by Loh, the son of Rama (a central Hindu deity). Between 1163–86, Lahore was the capital of the Turkish Ghaznavid dynasty, who ruled in northern India, Afghanistan and parts of Iran. In 1241, a Mongol army became the first of many to attack the city. It wasn't until Timur (Tamburlaine) of the Turkicized Barlas tribe, a Mongol sub-group, captured Lahore in 1398 that other Mongol armies stopped returning. Then in 1524, Babur, a founder of the Mughal dynasty and descendent of Gengis Khan took control. It was during the period of Mughal rule that Lahore grew wealthy and expanded. Between 1584–98 it was the Mughal emperor, Akbar's capital. Akbar built the massive Lahore fort and a red-brick wall that encompassed the city. During the rule of Shah Jahan (1628–58) the city enjoyed particular importance and often played host to royal visits. Lahore fort was extended and palaces, tombs and gardens were constructed.

After the death of the last great Mughal ruler, Aurangzeb, Lahore was fought over by Mughal rulers and Sikhs and later, in the mid eighteenth century, it became part of the Iranian empire. It later played an important role in the rise of the Sikh religion when it was captured by Ranjit Singh. During his rule, Lahore grew in stature as an important centre of government. This was not to last, however, and it declined significantly after Ranjit Singh's death in 1839. In 1846, a treaty signed with the Sikhs paved the way for the period of British rule that was to last until the partition of India in 1947. At this time, the once wealthy city of Lahore was in a state of neglect and ruin. This period led to regeneration in the city and after the partition, Lahore became the capital of the Indian region of West Punjab, and later, between 1955–70, the capital of West Pakistan.

Modern City

Main industries in Lahore include rubber, iron and steel production though textiles form the backbone of the city's industry. Lahore is also an important commercial and financial centre in Pakistan. The city is linked with other main cities in Pakistan by road as it is situated on the Karachi–Peshawar highway (1,740 km long) and by rail along the Karachi–Peshawar line. Lahore has an airport from which Pakistan International Airlines fly both domestic and international flights. International destinations include airports in Europe, East Asia, the Middle East, Africa and neighbouring Afghanistan.

The University of Punjab (1882) is located at Lahore and is Pakistan's oldest university. Its colleges were initially affiliated with the University of Calcutta but after the partition in 1947, it broke ties with its colleges on Indian soil. It now provides graduate and post-graduate training in law, commerce, medicine, dentistry, Islamic education and engineering. The Lahore University of Management Sciences (1985) and the University of Engineering and Technology (1961) are other centres for higher education located in the city.

Places of Interest

Though many of the old and historical buildings of Lahore have been lost through war, misrule and neglect, there are still buildings of notable architectural quality and historical value. Within the old city of Lahore there stands the mosque of Wazir Khan (1634) and Lahore fort which covers 14.5 ha. and remains a prominent example of Mughal architecture. The Badshahi mosque was built by Aurangzeb and is one of the largest mosques in the world. Another attraction is the Shalimar Gardens, constructed by Shah Jahan in 1642, which lie to the east of the city. Lahore archaeological museum (1894), is situated in Lahore park and contains many examples of the various dynasties to have occupied the city, including sculptures, paintings, jewellery, musical instruments, armour and clothing excavated from surrounding regions.

Larnaca (Larnaka), Cyprus

Introduction

Larnaca is the third largest city in Cyprus, located in the southeast on Larnaca Bay. Its modern name is thought to be a derivative of the ancient Greek word 'larnax', meaning sarcophagus, because of the discovery in the sixteenth century of many ancient tombs. Larnaca was the birthplace of the Greek philosopher Zenon, the founder of stoicism.

History

Larnaca was originally established as the city kingdom of Kition between the fourteenth and eleventh centuries BC by the Mycenaeans, who brought with them their Greek language, culture and religion. It developed as a major port, exporting copper mined in the Troodos mountains. Having subsequently come under Assyrian, Egyptian and Persian rule, the city prospered into Hellenistic times. Tradition has it that Lazarus, who was raised from the dead by Jesus Christ, brought Christianity to Kition and became its first bishop.

The city's vulnerability to earthquakes, floods and invaders led to a decline in the Middle Ages, although it remained a busy port under Ottoman rule from 1570. In the eighteenth and nineteenth centuries (during which time the toponym of Kition was abandoned and Larnaca adopted), it regained some of its former importance. It attracted foreign dignitaries, and some European states used it as a base for their consulates in preference to inland Nicosia, which was less accessible. During the British administration, Larnaca's influence waned again. Famagusta became the island's main seaport and other cities took greater advantage of the post-independence tourist boom. However, following the 1974 Turkish invasion, Larnaca became a focal point of the south's economic development. With the closure of the international airport at Nicosia, Larnaca's airfield was developed as the country's principal international airport. The commercial port was also upgraded for both freight and tourist traffic to compensate for the closure of Famagusta.

Modern City

Larnaca is well known for its lacework (a major export), silverware and pottery, and also for its elaborate celebrations at the festival of Kataklysmos (Festival of the Flood). There is a yacht marina and luxury hotel and apartment complexes along the 10-km seafront promenade. The island's oil refineries are located to

the north of the city. Larnaca hosts many nationalities, including Lebanese Christians who took refuge during that country's troubles in the 1980s.

Places of Interest

Larnaca Fort dates originally from the Frankish era and was renovated by the Ottomans in the early 1600s. The Church of Agios Lazaros was built in the ninth century over the tomb of St Lazarus. On the seafront promenade the Bust of Kimon commemorates the Athenian general who besieged Kition in 450 BC to free Cyprus from the Persians. City museums include the Pierides Museum Foundation and the Archaeological, Natural History and Byzantine Museums. The salt lake bordering the airport is the winter home of flamingos and other migratory birds. Near the lake is the Hala Sultan Tekkesi, one of Cyprus' most important Islamic pilgrimage sites. Further to the southwest is the Church of Panagia Angeloktisti ('built by the angels'), with mosaics dating from the sixth century. In the hills west of Larnaca, the Stavrovouni Monastery is the oldest in Cyprus.

Las Vegas, United States of America

Introduction

Las Vegas is the gambling capital of the United States of America and the self-styled 'entertainment capital of the world'. Covering an area of 136 sq. miles (352 km^2) in southern Nevada, Las Vegas is the seat of Clark county and is located in the middle of the Las Vegas valley, an area of desert surrounded by the Sierra Nevada and the Spring mountains. In the last 60 years Las Vegas has grown more rapidly than any other city in the United States, its population having multiplied 30 times since 1940.

History

The site occupied by modern day Las Vegas was originally settled by Native Americans who lived by fishing from the natural springs in the Las Vegas Valley. Spanish explorers found an oasis in the area in the 1820s and christened the area Las Vegas (literally 'the meadows'). Until the end of the nineteenth century the area was used as a stopping off point for traders travelling between Salt Lake City and Los Angeles.

In 1855 Mormon missionaries settled in the valley but their stay was short-lived and by 1900 the area's population was just 30. In 1905 the building of a railroad in the valley spurred a period of population growth. In 1909 the state of Nevada outlawed gambling but its relaxed laws on divorce proved attractive to many. The construction of the Boulder Dam began in 1931, bringing jobs as well as cheaper electricity and water to the city. The same year gambling was made legal and construction workers flocked to gamble in Las Vegas' new casinos.

The 1940s saw Las Vegas raised development. Casino and hotel complexes were established including the $7 m. Flamingo hotel built by gangster Bugsy Siegel. By the 1950s Las Vegas was the centre for live entertainment in the United States with performers such as Liberace and Frank Sinatra earning vast appearance fees. The arrival of the military provided a boost to the city's economy as several bases were established including the Las Vegas Aerial Gunnery School. Nuclear tests were held in the desert.

In 1967 the Nevada legislature broke the hold of organized crime on the gambling industry by passing a law allowing public corporations to own casinos. This led to a further boom in investment and expansion as new hotels catering for families and tourists sprang up, including the MGM Grand Hotel and Theme Park, which opened in 1993 and is the largest hotel in the world. Las Vegas' population grew by 83% in the 1990s, the fastest rate of growth in any metropolitan area in the United States.

Modern City

With nearly 30 m. visitors per year, Las Vegas' economy is largely reliant on tourism and is a popular convention venue. The military is also important to the economy with Nellis Air Force Base being the city's largest single employer. There are several other military bases near the city as well as a nuclear waste site at Yucca mountain. Las Vegas' rapid population growth has led to an employment boom in manufacturing and construction work, with the creation of new houses and hotels in turn leading to an increase in jobs in service industries.

Las Vegas is served by McCarran International Airport, which is located a mile from the Strip. CAT buses serve the whole city while the Las Vegas Strip Trolley is a streetcar service that operates along the Strip. There is a Greyhound bus terminal but no longer an Amtrak train station. However Amtrak does run a bus service that connects the Amtrak network to Los Angeles and Bakersfield in California.

The city's major institutes of higher education are the University of Nevada, Las Vegas, which was founded in 1957, and the Community College of Southern Nevada.

Places of Interest

As well as the huge number of casinos, Las Vegas has a multitude of outdoor and indoor shows, many featuring world famous entertainers. Annual events include the National Finals Rodeo and the Las Vegas Invitation Golf Tournament. Las Vegas is a popular destination for tours and conventions, including COMDEX, an annual computer show. The Las Vegas Motor Speedway opened in 1996.

In addition to gambling, there are many recreational opportunities. Red Rock Canyon National Conservation Area, Lake Mead National Recreation Area, the Hoover Dam and the Grand Canyon are accessible from the city.

Museums include the Liberace Museum (dedicated to the flamboyant twentieth-century Las Vegas performer), the Nevada State Museum and Historical Society, which features exhibits on Nevada's history from 12,000 BC to 1950, the Las Vegas Natural History Museum, with wildlife and dinosaur exhibits, and the Las Vegas Art Museum.

Lausanne, Switzerland

Introduction

Lausanne is located in the west, on the north shore of Lake Geneva. Built on the slopes of the Jorat heights, it is distinguished by many connecting tiers of buildings.

History

Settlement dates back to the Neolithic era, but Lausanne first came to prominence as a military camp used by the Romans from 15 BC onwards. The camp, named Lousonna, gradually expanded and flourished as a market town. The invasion of the Alemanni in AD 379 caused the inhabitants of Lousonna to abandon the original lakefront town and move to a better defended site which became the foundation for the old city of Lausanne. In 590 Bishop Marius transferred his bishopric to Lausanne. This served to enhance the city's commercial and religious significance. Pope Gregory X and Emperor Rudolf of Habsburg attended the consecration of Lausanne's cathedral in 1275.

By the beginning of the sixteenth century the citizens of Lausanne had become increasingly frustrated with the rule of the bishops. The arrival of one of Calvin's followers, Guillaume Farel, in 1529 prompted widespread social and religious unrest. An invasion by Berne in 1536 led to the destruction of most of the city's Catholic churches, and Lausanne's short-lived independence concluded with the imposition of Bernese rule. The university, founded 4 years later, became the first Francophone centre for Protestant theology. Berne's government continued until 1803 when Napoléon separated the Vaud canton from Berne and made Lausanne the new capital of Vaud. From this point the city began to develop, and by the beginning of the twentieth century it had become an important intellectual and cultural centre, attracting a large expatriate community, including many writers and artists.

Modern City

The old town and the cathedral are at the highest point of Lausanne, to the north. To the south, in the middle tier, is the city's transport hub and commercial zone, centred on Place St François. To the west of Place St François is the once derelict area of Flon that now accommodates numerous restaurants, bars and clubs. At the base of the city, by the waterfront, is the former fishing village of Ouchy. Lausanne serves as a junction for railway lines coming from Geneva, Fribourg, Berne and Vallorbe and is a stop on the route from Paris to Milan. There is a boat service operating on Lake Geneva.

Major industries include printing and food-processing as well as clothing, precision tools, metal and leather goods. Lausanne derives considerable revenue from tourism and hosting international conventions. The city has been the headquarters for the International Olympic Committee since 1915; it is also the home of the highest court in Switzerland, the Federal Tribunal.

Places of Interest

The twelfth century cathedral is one of the most popular cultural attractions, as is the Musée de l'Art Brut which houses a collection of eccentric, rough-hewn works created by artists many of whom were regarded as criminally insane. Other notable museums include the Museum of Fine Arts and the Olympic museum, which houses memorabilia from many of the games.

Leeds, United Kingdom of Great Britain and Northern Ireland

Introduction

Leeds is the UK's third largest metropolitan district and the leading city of West Yorkshire, in the north of England.

History

Leeds began life as an Anglo Saxon settlement on the northern bank of the River Aire. In the eighth century Leeds was mentioned by the Venerable Bede in his *Ecclesiastical History*, under the name Loidis (the likely origin of the name for residents of Leeds, Loiners). It was again mentioned in the Domesday Book in 1086, though now as Ledes.

The town grew as a local market and became a centre for cloth finishing for the West Yorkshire area. In 1207 a new town was founded by Maurice Paynel, the Lord of the Manor. By the sixteenth century Leeds had become one of the largest wool-manufacturing towns in England.

By the time of the Industrial Revolution Leeds was in a prime situation to take advantage of the improvements made in transportation, engineering and manufacturing. In 1699 the Aire and Calder Rivers were made navigable, linking Leeds with the Ouse, Humber and the sea. In 1816 the Leeds and Liverpool Canal was completed and in 1848 the railway made Leeds one of the leading locomotive industry centres. By 1840 the city population had grown to 150,000. Leeds earned city status in 1893.

The Yorkshire College of Science and the Medical School merged to form Leeds University in 1904 (Leeds Metropolitan University, the former polytechnic, achieved university status in 1993 as did Leeds Trinity University, the former Leeds Trinity University College, in 2012) and the city centre became a major financial and commercial area.

Modern City

Since the end of World War II Leeds has undergone extensive rebuilding. The city centre has been rebuilt and modern housing estates now stand where there used to be workers' slums. In 1993 Leeds was awarded the accolade of Environment City of the UK.

Modern Leeds is the commercial and retail hub of West Yorkshire. In St James' Hospital it has a world-renowned medical research centre. The city lies on major rail and motorway links and the Leeds-Bradford International Airport is located a few miles outside the city centre. It is an important provincial centre for theatre as well as a successful sporting city.

Places of Interest

Among the city's most popular tourist attractions are:

Lotherton Hall, ancestral home of the Gascoigne family, which hosts collections of furniture, ceramics, silver, paintings and textiles. The surrounding grounds are home to a wide range of wildlife. The gardens are set out in the Edwardian style.

Temple Newsam House, a Tudor–Jacobean Mansion, housing collections of decorative arts;

Kirkstall Abbey, built between 1152 and 1182 as the home to a community of Cistercian monks and lay brothers until dissolution by Henry VIII;

the City Art Gallery, founded in 1888, housing several collections, including significant French post-impressionist and British watercolour works as well as pieces by local artists;

the Henry Moore Institute, comprising former warehouses and a merchant's office and transformed into the headquarters of the Henry Moore Sculpture Trust in 1993;

Royal Amouries Museum, opened in 1996 in a custom-built building.

Leipzig, Germany

Introduction

Leipzig was the second largest city in the former German Democratic Republic and is located south-west of Berlin on the Leipzig basin (a flat plain in Western Saxony).

History

Leipzig started as a small Slav village near the confluence of the rivers Elster and Parthe. Its name is derived from 'Lipsk' which means 'the place where the lime trees grow'. Leipzig was first mentioned in 1015, in the chronicles of Bishop Thietmar von Merseburg. Leipzig has long been an important intellectual and cultural centre. The University of Leipzig was established in 1409. Among Leipzig's most famous residents are Richard Wagner (born here in 1813) and Felix Mendelssohn, and it also played a pivotal role in the career of Johann Sebastian Bach, who was organist and choirmaster of St Thomas' Church and City Musical Director. During the eighteenth century, the poet and novelist Johann Wolfgang Goethe studied at the university. Leipzig was also the first city in the world to produce a daily newspaper.

This cultural flowering was based on economic prosperity, brought about originally by trade in books and textiles. In addition, silver was discovered in the nearby 'Ore Mountains' in the sixteenth century. In 1813 Leipzig witnessed the victory of allied Austrian, Prussian, Russian, and Swedish troops over Napoleonic forces at the Battle of the Nations. Twenty-six years later, Leipzig was the terminus of Germany's first railway, which extended to Dresden.

The city was hit hard during World War II and much of its old architecture was lost to allied bombing. The reconstruction of the city was pursued under the communist government of East Germany. When citizens of the former German Democratic Republic began calling for a reunified Germany, Leipzig became one of the leading centres in the democratic revolution.

Modern City

Major industries include construction, chemicals and heavy manufactures. Its annual fair is important for East–West European trade.

The city's main airport is Flughafen Leipzig-Halle, 13 km northwest of Leipzig. The railway station, Hauptbahnhof, is the largest of its kind in the world and has links with all major cities in the country. There is also a smaller Bayerischer Bahnhof, predominantly for local journeys. Within the city, trams are easiest for getting around.

Places of Interest

The Battle of Leipzig/Battle of the Nations Monument is the memorial to the victory of the allies over Napoléon in Oct. 1813. Thomaskirche (St Thomas Church) was built in 1212. Johann Sebastian Bach was its cantor for the last 27 years of his life. His tomb has been in St Thomas' Church since 1950. Opposite the church is the Bach Museum, documenting the composer's life in Leipzig. The Opernhaus offers a mixture of modern and traditional productions, and the Neues Gewandhaus is home to Europe's oldest established orchestra, once led by Mendelssohn.

The Ägyptisches (Egyptian) Museum has one of Europe's leading collections of Egyptian artefacts and antiques. Meanwhile, the Grassi Museum Complex consists of three museums, including the Musikinstrumenten-

Museum, the Museum für Völkerkunde (Museum of Ethnology) and the Museum für Kunsthandwerk (Museum of Arts and Crafts).

Libreville, Gabon

Introduction

Libreville is Gabon's capital city.

History

The city was founded in 1849 by freed slaves around the site of a French fort. It was made capital of the French Congo in 1888 and capital of the Gabon territory of French Equatorial Africa in 1910. Before the development of Pointe-Noire in the Republic of Congo, it acted as the most important coastal port of western Africa.

In 1960 the city became capital of independent Gabon and in the following decade its population doubled. In 1990 and 1992 there was widespread rioting in protest to changes to the constitution and the electoral system.

Modern City

Main exports include timber, rubber and cocoa while main industries are palm-oil production and sawmilling. Although of less commercial importance than Port-Gentil, Libreville's port handles regional exports. There is a deepwater port at Owendo, 14.5 km to the south.

The city is served by an international airport (11 km north of the city) and road connections to most towns and cities in the country.

Places of Interest

The city is the educational centre for the country and is home to the Omar Bongo University, founded in 1970.

Liège, Belgium

Introduction

Liège is situated on the Meuse River in eastern Belgium. It is the capital of Liège province, as well as the most prominent Francophone community within Belgium.

History

Liège was known to the Romans, who called it Leodium, but according to legend it owes its origins to St Lambert, bishop of Maastricht who was murdered there in AD 705. St Hubert then decided to make Liège the capital of a new bishopric, and the city was to be ruled by bishop-princes for several centuries.

Notger was the first bishop to exercise secular as well as spiritual authority, and under his rule the city developed into a major intellectual centre. Since Liège was ruled over by a bishop-prince it rapidly assumed an identity independent of its powerful neighbours—Germany and France, and the city frequently had to defend its independence from their incursions. Liège was twice sacked by Charles the Bold during the fifteenth century, but after his death the city began to prosper again. However the relationship between the bishop-princes and their subjects became increasingly strained, and this left Liège vulnerable to foreign attack. The French bombarded the city in 1691 and it was captured by the English 11 years later during the war of the Spanish Succession. It was finally acquired by France in 1795, and was then ceded to the Netherlands, much to the chagrin of its citizens, in 1815. The Liègeois played a significant role in the Belgian revolution of 1830. Following Belgian independence the city gradually emerged as a major industrial centre.

Modern City

Liège remains prosperous today, largely due to the success of its industries which include steel, glass, arms and copper refining. There is an airport at Bierset, and the city is connected to a network of roads and railways. It is also an important river port.

Places of Interest

The Royal Conservatory of Music is home to the famous violin school founded by Eugène Ysäye, and the city has a renowned opera house as well as numerous theatres and concert halls. The importance of steel production and the manufacture of arms in the history of Liège are commemorated in the Arms Museum.

Liepāja, Latvia

Introduction

Liepāja, in the southwest of the country, was economically Latvia's second city for part of the twentieth century. A vital defence base under the Soviets, it has re-developed its commercial port facilities since Latvia gained independence.

History

The coastal town was founded by knights of the Livonian Order on the site of a fishing village. Granted town status by the Duke of Kurzeme in 1625, building of its port facilities started in 1697. In 1795 it fell under Russian control. Industrial development took off in the nineteenth century, with the expansion of the port and the coming of the railway. Towards the end of the nineteenth century the Russian authorities chose Liepāja to be the focus of their military activities in the region.

Between the two World Wars the city was second only to Riga in terms of economic importance but in 1967, having become the largest Soviet military base in the country, it was closed as a commercial port. Latvia won independence from the USSR in 1991 and Liepāja reopened as a commercial port the following year. The last Soviet military personnel left in 1994.

Modern City

The legacy of the Soviet military era left Liepāja with a poor infrastructure, bad housing and chronic pollution. There were high levels of unemployment and the city was made a special economic zone in a bid to rejuvenate the economy. The port has been redeveloped and the steel industry has flourished. Other major industries include food processing, textiles, and furniture and safety matches.

There are several institutes of higher education including a branch of Riga Technical University. As well as its port facilities, Liepāja is on major road, rail and air routes.

Places of Interest

The sandy beach is popular, but the sea is highly polluted. Attractions include the eighteenth century Holy Trinity Church, St. Joseph's cathedral and the museum of history and art.

Lille, France

Introduction

The ancient capital of French Flanders, Lille is situated on the canalized Deûle River, 14 km from the Belgian border. The capital of the Nord department in Nord-Pas-de Calais, Lille is a commercial and industrial centre and is one of France's largest conurbations.

History

Little is known of Lille's history before the eleventh century, although it originated as an island between the canals of the Deûle River. Thus, its name evolved from the Latin *insula* to the Old French *lisle*, island, which is also the name of the thread originally manufactured in Lille (e.g. lisle stockings). By the ninth century Lille had become the seat of the Count of Flanders and during the eleventh century was fortified by Count Baldwin IV. The town developed around the Palais Comtal and began to flourish. It was a strategic point on trade routes between northern Europe and southern France and Italy, and coupled with the fertility of the region, became the capital of Flanders. The wool trade attracted many international merchants.

Conquered by Philip II of France at the Battle of Bouvines in 1214, Lille was subsequently governed by Joanna of Flanders who founded the Hospice Comtesse in 1237. The building was restored in the seventeenth century and now houses a museum. In 1369, when Marguerite of Flanders married Philip the Bold, Duke of Burgundy, Flanders was incorporated into the Kingdom of Burgundy. In 1477, Lille, along with the rest of Flanders, came under Habsburg rule. The city was capital of the southern Netherlands in the sixteenth century.

In the seventeenth century Lille prospered economically and culturally. Louis XIV seized the city in 1667 and incorporated it into France. The Duke of Marlborough captured Lille in 1708, but only held the city for 5 years until the Treaty of Utrecht forced the English to cede Lille. Lille was made a departmental prefecture by Napoléon in 1803. The nineteenth-century industrial revolution brought prosperity and considerable expansion to the city. In 1864 the first rail link between Lille and Paris was built. Lille was occupied by the Germans in World Wars I and II, and suffered structural damage.

In 1982 Lille introduced the world's first automatic metro system. In 1997 the high speed Eurostar link between Lille and Brussels was opened. Consequently, the city is an increasingly important centre for business and tourism.

Modern City

Major industries include iron, steel, chemical plants and manufacturing. Traditionally, Lille is the most important centre of textiles in France. The city is a key transport crossing with rail connections to Paris, Brussels and London as well as an airport 8 km from the city centre. Lille hosts an annual international commercial fair. Lille has a large student population at two Universities and at various commercial and technical schools. The city was one of the European Capitals of Culture in 2004.

Places of Interest

The medieval streets of the old town have many restored houses and shops with elaborate ornamentation. Charles de Gaulle (1890–1970) is Lille's most famous son. There is a museum at his birthplace just north of Vieux Lille, the old district. Other museums in Lille include the Musée de l'Art Moderne—containing works by cubist and post-modern artists such as Braque, Picasso, Miro and Léger—and the Musée des Beaux-Arts. One of Lille's most famous landmarks is the seventeenth century Citadel. After the city was taken by Louis XIV, the town was expanded and the King commissioned the royal engineer Sébastien Leprestre de Vauban (1633–1707) to build the fortress. The pentagonal structure, which became a garrison, was built between 1667–70. The citadel is still a military base. The Vieille Bourse is found at the centre of Lille. The Flemish Renaissance-style buildings, built by Julien Vestré in 1652, encompass a courtyard once containing the stock exchange.

Lilongwe, Malaŵi

Introduction

Lilongwe is in south-central Malawi, and is the capital and second largest city in the country. It is the chief administrative centre, although its commercial and industrial importance is subordinate to that of Blantyre, the economic capital.

History

Lilongwe was founded in 1947 as an agricultural centre. In the 1960s the fertility of the surrounding countryside prompted Malawi's president,

Hastings Banda, to develop a new planned city that was to be an economic growth point for the area. Throughout the next decade government funding improved the new city's infrastructure and aided the development of transportation and agricultural. In 1975 the city was declared the national capital.

Modern City

The new city accommodates the government offices, embassies and main shopping malls. The old town lies to 5 km to the southwest and is dominated by the popular market. Lilongwe has rail connections to Zambia and southern Africa and an international airport. The city's industry is largely agricultural and there is an agricultural college. Major exports include tobacco.

Places of Interest

The Nature Sanctuary, situated between the old and new towns, has over 350 acres of indigenous woodland.

Lima, Peru

Introduction

Lima is in the centre of Peru on the coastal desert, to the west of the Andean foothills. Its port, Callao, is 13 km to the East. The Rímac River transverses the city.

History

The area around Lima has been inhabited since 4000 BC. Pre-Ceramic Age farmers and fishermen lived in Chilca (circa 4000 BC) and Asia (circa 2000 BC), just south of Lima. After being inhabited by the Wari around 800 AD, the area was settled by the Chancay people before coming under the rule of the Inca Empire.

Two years after they entered the Rímac Valley, Lima was colonized by Conquistadors led by Francisco Pizarro in 1535. Founded on 6 Jan., it was named Ciudad de los Reyes. Since the Inca capital Cuzco was too far from the coast, Lima was established as the capital of the new viceroyalty. Built from scratch, the city comprised low, solid buildings suitable for the earthquake-prone area. The city was the seat of the high court for all the viceroyalty and developed into a powerful capital. In 1551 the Universidad Nacional Mayor de San Marcos de Lima was founded, the oldest university in South America. The seat of the Inquisition for Spanish America was established in Lima in 1569. A thriving import-export trade developed with Spain.

Built in 1610 the Puente de Piedra spanning the Rímac, around which the city of Lima developed, was one of the first stone structures. Despite numerous earthquakes that in the seventeenth century (the worst being in 1746), the city continued to develop, although expansion was slow for the next two centuries.

Lima was a conservative city, loyal to its colonial tradition. Thus, Peru was the last mainland country to gain independence from Spain. After Independence (28 July 1821), much of the colonial architecture was destroyed including the city walls. Lima and its port were connected by the first railway built in Peru. In the War of the Pacific (1879–83) with Chile, Lima was taken on 17 Jan. 1881 when there was widespread destruction.

After Independence Lima remained a relatively small city until *Pueblos jóvenes*, or shantytowns, rapidly sprang up from the 1950s onwards. Former mansions were subdivided to house the influx of migrants. Poverty is wide spread and there is an absence of basic amenities in even the most established *pueblos jóvenes*.

Modern City

Lima is the dominant financial and industrial centre of Peru, manufacturing three fifths of Peru's industrial goods and controlling the majority of financial business. Principal industries include textiles, oil refining, automobile production and shipbuilding. One third of Peru's population is concentrated in Lima.

Traditional industries have recently been surpassed by smaller businesses, begun in the 1970s in an attempt to improve the economic situation of the poorest *Limeños*. In 1991 Lima was declared a UNESCO world heritage site

to preserve the few remaining historical buildings threatened by an ever-increasing population. Lima's Jorge Chavéz international airport is located at Callao. The Ferrocarril Central del Perú railway connects Lima to remote Andean highlands.

Places of Interest

The Cathedral is one of the few surviving examples of Colonial architecture. Although parts were destroyed in various earthquakes, reconstruction has followed original plans. Designed by the Spanish architect Francisco Becerra, construction began in 1598. The seventeenth-century Baroque church of San Francisco contains a library dating from the times of the Conquistadors. Lima's museums include the Museo de la Nación for Peruvian archaeology; the Museo de Oro del Perú, containing gold artefacts; and the Museo de Arte, which has displays spanning 400 years of Peruvian art. The Palacio de Gobierno also known as the Casa de Pizarro was the Conquistador's designated seat of government. The Plaza Bolívar contains a statue of Simón Bolívar built in 1851 by the Italian sculptor Adamo Tadolini.

Archaeological ruins around Lima are centred on Pachacamac, 30 km south of Lima. Dating from the early intermediate period (200 BC–600 AD), it was a ceremonial site of proto-Lima people, the Maramba, whose god was of the same name. It was then the site of Wari pilgrimage before being settled by the Incas who converted it into the Temple of the Sun. It was one of the largest pre-Colonial cities in Peru.

Limassol (Lemesos), Cyprus

Introduction

Limassol is the second largest city, located on the Bay of Akrotiri on the southern coastal plain. It is a major historical site, commercial centre, hub of the tourism and wine industries and the main port.

History

Limassol is situated between the two ancient city kingdoms of Amathus to the east and Kourion to the west. It came to prominence at the end of the Byzantine era when the English crusader king, Richard the Lionheart landed in 1191 and defeated the then ruler of Cyprus, Isaac of Komninos. Richard sold Cyprus to the Knights Templar, who established themselves in Limassol for the next two centuries until the city was ravaged by earthquakes and Genoese and Saracen attacks. Having declined under Ottoman rule, there was a partial recovery during the British administration when fruit and wine production and light industries such as shoemaking encouraged an influx of rural population. After the Turkish invasion of 1974, Limassol's development accelerated dramatically as it became the main cargo and passenger port in the south serving a growing tourist hinterland.

Modern City

Limassol harbour continues to expand to meet the demands of trade and passenger traffic. Ferry and cruise ship services operate to Greece, Israel, Egypt and a number of Greek islands. Wine and fruit are the main exports. The centre of the wine industry, the city hosts the annual summer Wine Festival. Britain maintains two military bases southwest of Limassol on the Akrotiri Peninsula.

Places of Interest

There are numerous archaeological and historic sites. Ancient Kourion, which became a permanent settlement under the Mycenaeans, is dominated by the Greco-Roman amphitheatre. The site also includes the House of Eustolios, a private residence dating from the fifth century with Christian-influenced and well-preserved mosaic floors; the Sanctuary of Apollo Hylates (God of the Woodland), dating from the eighth century; and the early Christian Basilica, thought to have been built in the fifth century. Limassol castle, erected in the fourteenth century on the site of an earlier Byzantine structure, houses the Medieval Museum. Other attractions include Kolossi Castle, which was occupied by the Knights of St John from the thirteenth century, the Archaeological Museum and Folk Art Museum.

Linz, Austria

Introduction

Located in the north of Austria, Linz is the capital of the federal state of Upper Austria. It is a major industrial centre and an important port on the River Danube lying between Vienna and Salzburg. For 12 years the composer Anton Bruckner, revered by some as 'God's Musician', was the organist at the city's Old Cathedral.

History

Linz dates back to the second century AD when it was a Roman fortress settlement called Lentia. Situated on trade routes, it had become a busy market town by the fifteenth century and was, for a time, the residence of the Emperor Frederick III and recognized as a regional capital. After Germany occupied Austria in 1938, large industrial plants were built in the southern part of the city.

Modern City

The historic centre has been restored with a large pedestrian zone and elegant residential housing. The main square has many different kinds of markets. A busy port, its most important industries are iron and steel, chemicals and textiles. For 3 weeks in Sept. the city dedicates its most prestigious music festival to Bruckner, presenting some of the world's most famous soloists and orchestras. Linz was one of two European Capitals of Culture for 2009.

Places of Interest

The old town centre on the south bank of the river features the Hauptplatz. This thirteenth century main square is dominated by the Trinity Column (Dreifaltigkeitssaule) which was sculpted in Salzburg marble in 1723 to mark the city's release from plague and war. Linz Castle, believed to originate from the eighth century, was once the residence of Friedrich III and now houses the Schlossmuseum. The seventeenth century Gothic Old Cathedral is where Bruckner first performed his D-minor Mass. The neo-Gothic New Cathedral was built in the nineteenth century and features Austria's second highest church spire (at 131 m) after St Stephen's in Vienna. On the north bank of the river the Neue Galerie displays nineteenth and twentieth century works by Austrian and German artists, including Gustav Klimt and Egon Schiele.

Lisbon, Portugal

Introduction

On the northern bank of the River Tagus on Portugal's southwest coast, Lisbon is surrounded by seven hills. A major port, the city lies where the Tagus widens to form the Mar de Palha (Sea of Straw), 15 km from the Atlantic Ocean. Known as the white city, Lisbon is the political, economic and cultural capital of Portugal.

History

The city's ancient name of Olisipo is thought to derive from the Phoenician *alis ubbo* (beautiful port). Phoenician merchants may have established a trading post on the hill of São Jorge around 1200 BC, although legend claims Ulysses founded Lisbon. The Romans settled the area in 205 BC and Julius Caesar created the municipium of Felicitas Julia. Lisbon developed into an important port. Following invasion by the Alani from the area northwest of the Black Sea and then the Germanic Suebi, in 457 AD the Visigoths conquered Lisbon. The Moors extended their power in the Iberian Peninsula to include Lisbon in 714. They resisted invasion by the Normans in 844 and by Alfonso VI of Castile and León in 1093 to rule the area unchallenged. King Alfonso Henriques of the newly independent Portugal united Norman, Flemish and English troops to finally expel the Moors in 1147.

At this time Lisbon's hillside nucleus had begun to extend towards the port area outside the city walls. Under Portuguese rule the royal palace replaced the Moorish Alcáçova on the São Jorge hill and it is believed that the mosque was the foundation for the Sé Patriarcal Cathedral. In 1256 Lisbon succeeded Coimbra as Portugal's capital. In 1290 the first university in Portugal was established in Lisbon, although it was transferred to Coimbra in 1537. In the fourteenth century land around the city was granted to Franciscans, Carmelites, Augustines and Trinitarians. The city itself comprised the central Baixa quarter, the Mouraria or Moorish quarter, and the Alfama, mainly inhabited by Christian and Jewish residents. During a war with Castile, King Ferdinand I built a 4 km defensive wall around the city (1373–75), with 77 towers and 38 gates to defend Lisbon from further invasion.

In 1415 the Portuguese age of discovery began and Lisbon grew in size, wealth and importance. Departing from Lisbon in 1493, Vasco de Gama's expedition to India opened the eastern trade route and ended Venetian commercial domination. The city's centre, including the royal residence, shifted to the port area of Ribeira. The city hummed with maritime trade attracting English, Netherlands, Flemish and French merchants. The British community grew in importance until the Cromwellian treaty in 1654 formalized trade by establishing the British Factory. A centre of trade, politics and community life, the Factory lasted until 1810. In 1498 the large Jewish community was expelled or forced to convert to Christianity. But even those who converted suffered in the 1506 pogrom and suffered under the Inquisition.

Maritime dominance in Africa, India and the Americas created vast wealth for Lisbon, a principle player in the slave trade. The height of Lisbon's prosperity came at the end of the seventeenth century, financed by Brazilian gold. But an earthquake on 1 Nov. 1755, followed by floods and then fire devastated the city. 30,000 people died and 9,000 buildings were destroyed, mainly in the Baixa. Lisbon was rebuilt to a neo-classical grid plan by a team of architects working under the prime minister Sebastião José de Carvalho, later the Marquês de Pombal.

Despite French and British occupation during the Peninsular War, civil war and violent civil unrest in the first half of the nineteenth century, Lisbon continued to expand and develop. This was aided by the arrival of the railway and an expansion and renovation of the harbour. In 1879 the Avenida de Liberdade was built. Tree-lined pavements with fountains bordered the six lane road. Following the assassination of King Carlos I in 1908 and the establishment of the First Republic in 1910, the capital's development was halted by a period of political instability. Lisbon provided shelter to over 200,000 refugees during World Wars I and II. Urban development regained impetus in the second half of the twentieth century. In 1966 the seventh longest suspension bridge in the world was built. The Ponte de 25 Abril spans the Tagus linking Lisbon with Almada. Lisbon hosted Expo 1998.

Modern City

By far the largest city in Portugal, 20% of the country's population live in Lisbon. Portugal's principal port and main industrial centre, Lisbon's key industries are chemicals, textiles, electronics and diamond cutting. It also has one of the world's largest cement plants. Major exports are wine, olive oil and cork. Lisbon's Portela airport is 10 km north of the city centre. The city has train links with Madrid and Paris. Internal travel is facilitated by a metro system and tram network as well as the funicular railways ascending the steep gradients to the bairro alto.

Places of Interest

The twelfth century cathedral is in the Alfama, the old town, characterized by its winding medieval streets. Overlooking this quarter is the Castelo de São Jorge. The castle's extensive grounds are enclosed by the original Moorish walls. Museums include the Gulbenkian with collections spanning all stages of eastern and western art, the Museu de Arte Antiga and the Museu Arqueológico do Carmo, housed in the shell of the destroyed Convento do Carmo church. The Teatro Nacional de Dona Maria stands on the site of the Inquisitional Palace, destroyed in the 1755 earthquake. The Mosteiro dos Jerónimos, a white tower built between 1512–21 to protect Lisbon's harbour, is in Belém near to the Torre de Belém. Both are examples of the Manueline architectural style. The castle at Sintra northwest of Lisbon, is where Byron began writing Childe Harold.

Liverpool, United Kingdom of Great Britain and Northern Ireland

Introduction

Liverpool is an industrial city and a major port in northwest England. It sits on the northeastern shore of the Mersey estuary and forms part of the greater metropolitan area of Merseyside. Merseyside consists of Knowsley, St Helens, Sefton, Wirral and the city of Liverpool.

History

King John issued a charter in 1207 for a town on the banks of the Mersey. He saw Liverpool as a convenient place to mount an attack on Ireland. The town grew slowly throughout the medieval period and for the first 400 years of its existence it consisted of seven small streets. However, in the late-sixteenth century it emerged as a port under the jurisdiction of Chester, before gaining recognition as a self-governing customs port in 1658.

During the seventeenth century it developed as the principal port linking Britain with Ireland and then as an important colonial port. Liverpool became a centre of the slave trade from West Africa, thriving as the need for cheap labour on the cotton plantations of North America increased. With the ending of both the slave trade in 1807, and the East India Company's monopoly on Indian trade, Liverpool was able to develop new trading patterns. A new dock system was built in 1824 which served until after World War II.

Liverpool's significance grew with the Industrial Revolution. As well as being a manufacturing city in its own right, it handled most of the goods coming from Manchester and the north-west of England. During the eighteenth century a series of docks were built on the Mersey and in 1830 the Manchester to Liverpool Railway was opened, the first of its kind in the world. Much of the city's population lived in poverty, a situation exacerbated by the Irish famine of the 1840s which created an influx of refugees. The population was also expanded by Chinese and black immigrant labour as well as by itinerant sailors. Liverpool suffered heavily in the 1930s economic slump and in World War II through Luftwaffe bombing.

Modern City

After the two world wars Liverpool fell into economic decline. However the city's contribution to the social, cultural and sporting prestige of the nation has remained a source of pride for the city. Liverpool produced The Beatles in the 1960s and is the home of the Royal Liverpool Philharmonic Orchestra. It has three universities: Liverpool University (founded in 1881), Liverpool John Moores and Liverpool Hope. The city's Aintree racecourse hosts the Grand National annually and it is also home to two of England's leading football teams, Liverpool and Everton. Large swathes of the city (including much of the old docklands) are now being re-generated and new businesses attracted. Liverpool was one of two European Capitals of Culture for 2008.

Places of Interest

Popular tourist attractions include:

Speke Hall, dating from 1490;
20 Forthlin Road, the former home of the McCartney family, where The Beatles met, rehearsed and wrote many of their earliest songs;
the Royal Liver Building, opened in 1911 and the first large scale building in the world to be made of reinforced concrete;
the Liverpool Cathedral Church of Christ, or Anglican Cathedral, the world's largest Anglican Church;
the Metropolitan Cathedral of Christ the King, or the Catholic Cathedral, originally designed by Sir Edwin Lutyens but completed in 1967 on the plans of Sir Frederick Gibberd;
the Liverpool Museum, the oldest of the national museums on Merseyside, hosting collections of archaeology, ethnology and the natural and physical sciences;
the Walker Art Gallery, home to collections of Dutch paintings from the fourteenth to the sixteenth centuries and works by major artists including Rembrandt, Rubens, Poussin, Monet and Degas;
the Mersey Maritime Museum detailing the maritime history of the city;

Lady Lever Art Gallery, founded by William Hesketh Lever in 1922, displaying 18th and nineteenth century British paintings;
the Tate Gallery Liverpool, opened in 1988 in a converted warehouse, hosting a collection of modern art.

Ljubljana, Slovenia

Introduction

The capital of Slovenia is Ljubljana, in the west of the country close to the confluence of the rivers Ljubljanica and Sava. Designated a capital in 1990, it is small compared to most other European capitals. Devastated by an earthquake in 1895, in which much of its finest Baroque architecture disappeared, it was rebuilt during the twentieth century. Many of its key buildings were designed or reconstructed by Slovenia's greatest architect, Jože Plečnik.

History

There is evidence of human habitation on the city site around 3000 BC but it was a base for Illyrian and Celtic tribes. Under Roman domination from the first to sixth centuries AD, a provincial capital called Emona was built. This was destroyed by Hun incursions during the fifth century. Recovery began with Slav colonization in the sixth century.

Ljubljana first appeared in written history in 1144 and by the thirteenth century it was the capital of the Carniola province. Coming under Habsburg jurisdiction in the first half of the fifteenth century, it suffered a devastating earthquake in 1511. The centre of the Slovenian Protestant reformation, the city continued to develop as a cultural and educational centre throughout the seventeenth and eighteenth centuries.

After Napoléon's victory over the Austrians at Wagram in 1809, he annexed the Illyrian Provinces (a region extending along the east coast of the Adriatic) and made Ljubljana its capital. In 1814 it reverted to Austria. The Vienna–Trieste railway in 1849 provided Ljubljana with new access routes to the rest of Europe. The city prospered until 1895 when another earthquake destroyed large parts of the city.

With the end of the Austro–Hungarian Empire after World War I Slovenia became part of the Kingdom of Serbs, Croats and Slovenes. Reconstruction of the city continued, principally under the guidance of the architect Jože Plečnik who took inspiration from classicism and mannerism. Among his many projects from the 1920s to the 1950s were the Three Bridges and the Shoemaker's Bridge, the National and University Library, the Market, St Michael's Church on the Marsh, the Church of St Francis, Ljubljana Stadium, the Cemetery, Tivoli Park and the restoration of Krizanke Monastery.

The Socialist Federal Republic of Yugoslavia succeeded the Kingdom of Serbs, Croats and Slovenes in the aftermath of World War II. The new country comprised six provinces, and Ljubljana once again had the status of provincial capital of Slovenia. Following the collapse of Yugoslavia's communist regime, Slovenia declared independence in June 1991, and Ljubljana became national capital.

Modern City

In addition to the main rail and bus stations there is an international airport, Brnik, 23 km from the city centre. The city's major industries include mechanical manufacturing, textiles and consumer goods.

An annual summer festival, from June to Sept. offers a wide choice of cultural events. Ljubljana University was founded in 1919, although there have been internationally recognized institutes of learning in the city since the mid-sixteenth century.

Places of Interest

Much of the city's remaining Baroque heritage is in the Old Quarter between the castle and the River Ljubljanica. Among the most popular attractions are the Town Hall, St Nicholas' Cathedral and its seminary, the Franciscan, Ursuline and Krizanke churches and the Fountain of Carniolan Rivers (created by Francisco Robba). Secular Baroque and Rococo architecture is exemplified by the Gruber Palace and Schweiger House. The later influence of Plečnik is evident in many of these buildings and in two of the city's greatest landmarks, the Three Bridges and the Shoemaker's Bridge. He was also responsible for much of the design of the popular Tivoli Park. There is a national library and several museums, including the national museum, national art gallery (with a fine collection of Slovenian impressionists) and a museum of modern art.

Łódź, Poland

Introduction

Łódź is Poland's second largest city and a major industrial centre. It rose to prominence only from the nineteenth century onwards. It fell under Nazi occupation within a week of Germany's invasion of Poland in 1939 and the urban population, particularly Jewish, was decimated by the end of the war. It re-established its industrial importance during the communist era.

History

Łódź first appears in written history in the early fourteenth century and was granted municipal status in 1423 by King Władysław Jagiełło. However, expansion was minimal and by the time the town fell under Prussian rule in 1793 it comprised only a few hundred people. Significant growth began in the early nineteenth century when customs restrictions between the Polish Kingdom and Russia were lifted and the textiles industry began to blossom.

By a government order in 1820 Łódź was designated a factory city and over the next decade the population swelled with immigrants from towns and villages throughout the region brought in to establish the textile industry in the area. Foremost among these early city patrons was Rajmund Rembielinski.

New technologies were introduced to promote the industry and the urban population virtually doubled every 10 years during the middle decades of the century, surpassing 300,000 by the end of the century. The city boundaries were suitably increased to cope with this period of urban growth. Workers' movements also established themselves and in 1892 the Łódź Rebellion, Poland's earliest general strike, occurred. There were further uprisings in the first decade of the twentieth century with many hundreds of people being injured or losing their lives.

The city fell under German control during World War I and lost over 40% of the population. This, accompanied by general economic downturn in the aftermath of the war and the loss of much of the Russian market, severely affected Łódź's continued development. Made provincial capital in 1922, by 1939 the city's population had recovered and stood at between 650–700,000.

Łódź fell to German forces in 1939 within a week of the Polish invasion. It was re-named Litzmannstadt and assigned to the newly-established Poznań District. In 1940 a Jewish ghetto was established and administered by Mordekchai Chaim Rumkowski. A Jewish elder, he encouraged the belief among the Jews that by becoming an efficient working unit for the Germans they would ensure their survival. However, his authoritarian leadership and ultimate failure to save the ghetto population has resulted in claims of collusion from some quarters.

Heinrich Himmler ordered the ghetto to be liquidated in June 1944 and of a population of over 300,000, less than 1,000 lived to see liberation. The city lost 120,000 non-Jews as well. Łódź's post-war recovery was further hampered by the destruction and theft of industrial machinery and raw materials by retreating German forces in 1945, although most of its buildings survived. Between 1945 and 1948 Łódź was the home of Poland's governing authorities.

Under communist rule Łódź was re-established as a major textiles and industrial centre. Growth continued chaotically in the pattern of its nineteenth century birth.

Modern City

Łódź Lublinek Airport provides domestic and international services and the city is on major rail (Warsaw–Wrocław) and road routes. The urban transport network includes buses and trams. Among the city's most important industries are chemicals, electrical engineering and textiles. It is also home to the Polish film industry.

Places of Interest

Piotrowska Street is the city's main thoroughfare. Poznański Palace is the grandiose former home of Jewish industrialist families in the late nineteenth and early twentieth centuries. St Joseph's Church is the city's oldest building, while the Jewish cemetery (with 180,000 gravestones and over 350,000 graves) is the largest in Europe. There is a history museum, a fine arts museum and a museum dedicated to film and cinematography.

Lomé, Togo

Introduction

The capital of Togo, Lomé, is on the Gulf of Guinea. The city is the centre for Togo's trade, culture, transport and administration. Prior to the country's political trouble, Lomé was one of West Africa's prime tourist centres. A lagoon divides the city between Togo and Ghana. Downtown includes the commercial and administrative area with hotels, a sport stadium and an industrial free trade zone. Uptown is chiefly a residential area, but has also two teaching hospitals, a university and an international airport.

History

In the twelfth century the Ewes moved into Togo from the Niger river valley. Portuguese traders arrived in the fifteenth century. In 1884, Togo became Germany's only self-supporting colony and in 1897, Lomé became the colonial capital. It was turned into a modern town with railways built between Lomé and the rest of the country. In 1968 the deepwater harbour was completed and the oil refinery was opened in 1978. In 1975, The Lomé Convention agreed trade concessions with EC countries for 46 African, Caribbean and Pacific Ocean states.

Modern City

Most of Togo's international trade goes through Lomé. Goods from Mali, Burkina Faso and Niger are shipped from the port. The capital's core exports are cacao, coffee, cotton and palm nuts. The city has processed food and textile industries. There is a university (founded in 1970). An international airport (Tokoin Airport) is outside Lomé. The Maison du Peuple (1972) is the headquarters for Togo's only political party.

Places of Interest

The National Museum has historical artefacts, pottery and woodcarvings. The Grand Marché is a three-storey market with modern goods and traditional African foods, arts and textiles. The Village Artisanal shows artists at work making batiks, wooden sculpture and leather goods. The Marché des Féticheurs has a collection of potions used in traditional medicine.

London, United Kingdom of Great Britain and Northern Ireland

Introduction

London is the capital city of the United Kingdom, located on the River Thames in the southeast of the country. Although there is evidence of settlements along the Thames long before the Roman occupation of Britain under Emperor Claudius, it was during the first century AD that Londinium was established as a hub of trade and commerce. It is now one of the world's most important commercial, financial and political centres as well as a major tourist destination.

History

By 60 AD the city was a major trading centre and by the year 200 had a population of 45,000 making it one of the largest provincial cities in the Western Empire. After the demise of the Roman Empire London's documented history is scarce until the Saxon settlements in the early fifth century AD when London re-emerged as an important trading centre. The first St Paul's Cathedral was built in 604 and after a brief lapse into paganism the city was Christian from 656, helping to restore links with the continent lost with the departure of the Romans.

During the eighth century the wars between the Saxons and the invading Danes reached London. King Alfred, realizing the strategic importance of the city, wrested it from the Vikings and established London as an important military and economic base to defeat the Danes. Soon after the Norman Conquest of Britain of 1066, William the Conqueror built the White Tower, eventually to become the Tower of London. The Norman Kings established Westminster as their official residence.

The modern city of London is believed to have grown as three distinct and individual conurbations—the City of London or 'Square Mile', the City of Westminster, and Southwark. London owes its prominence to its position on the Thames and its proximity to continental ports. Medieval London grew quickly and became one of the largest cities in Europe. It was an important trade centre for many Europeans and immigrants swelled the population.

In 1348 the Black Death hit London and over 10,000 Londoners were buried beyond the city walls at West Smithfield. Over the course of the sixteenth century London recovered and the city's population grew from 50,000 to 200,000 by 1600. However, during the seventeenth century London suffered several disasters including the Great Plague of 1664, an epidemic that lasted for 2 years. The death toll is estimated at 76,000. On 2 Sept. 1666 the Great Fire of London swept through the city's densely packed, timber-framed buildings. Much of London was destroyed, and 'the City' suffered particularly.

By the late eighteenth century London was the commercial and administrative centre of a burgeoning empire and the centre of world economy. During Queen Victoria's reign Great Britain built an empire that encompassed a quarter of the world. London itself was a sprawling metropolis, swallowing out-lying towns and villages. Major development began to combat the city's lack of infrastructure and its many health problems. The opening of the railways helped to ease congestion and communication and sanitation programmes were developed. The first police force, the Metropolitan Police, was established and the world's first underground railway was opened. A county council for the whole of the built-up area outside of the original City was established in 1888.

During World War I London suffered from aerial bombardment and during World War II it suffered large-scale damage and disruption in attacks by the Luftwaffe and Hitler's V1 and V2 rockets. Around 30,000 Londoners were killed and the cost to the architecture of London was massive. Whilst restoring the capital many Londoners moved away from the city centre and relocated in suburbs and in areas outside of London in the southeast.

After the Second World War the Port of London suffered substantial decline, with traders leaving their traditional home in London's Isle of Dogs for out-of-town ports such as Tilbury and Felixstowe. Similarly, much manufacturing and commercial business was attracted to less expensive sites elsewhere. As a result, despite extensive regeneration schemes, the inner suburbs suffered a decline from which they have only recently begun to recover.

On 7 July 2005 four bombs were detonated by Islamist extremists—three aboard London Underground trains and one aboard a bus. 52 people died and approximately 700 were injured.

Modern City

Modern London is a leading centre for financial and other services and for the arts. Its theatre is regarded among the best in the world. London is at the centre of the country's road network, has easy connections to several international airports (including Gatwick, Heathrow and Stansted) and is the fulcrum of the national rail system. Major railway stations include Charing Cross, Euston, King's Cross/St Pancras (St Pancras being the terminus for Eurostar services), Liverpool Street, London Bridge, Paddington, Victoria and Waterloo. Within the city there are extensive, though overstretched, bus and underground networks and the Docklands has its own light railway.

London hosted the 2012 Olympic Games (having previously done so in 1908 and 1948). Construction of London's newest skyscraper, 'The Shard', was completed in April 2012. Standing 309.6 m. tall, it is currently the tallest building in the European Union.

Places of Interest

Among London's most popular tourist attractions are: Buckingham Palace (the official residence of the Queen); the Tower of London (current home to the Crown Jewels, home to every Monarch from the eleventh–sixteenth century but also a former prison and scene of executions); the Houses of Parliament (the seat of parliament since the fourteenth century) and St Stephen's Tower (home of the Great Westminster Clock which holds the bell named Big Ben); Trafalgar Square (built in honour of Admiral Nelson after his victory at the Battle of Trafalgar in 1805); and the London Eye (a giant ferris wheel erected for the millennium).

Notable museums include: the British Museum (Britain's most popular museum, containing Prehistoric, Romano-British, Medieval, Renaissance, Modern and Oriental collections); the Natural History Museum; the Science Museum; the Museum of London; the Imperial War Museum. Major galleries include the National Gallery, the National Portrait Gallery, Tate Britain and the Tate Modern and the Victoria and Albert Museum.

Los Angeles, United States of America

Introduction

Los Angeles is the largest urban area and the second most populous city in the United States. Located in southwestern California, the city's western fringe is on the Pacific Ocean and to the east are the San Gabriel Mountains. The city covers an area of 503 miles^2 (1,302 km^2), while the Los Angeles-Long Beach metropolitan area covers 4,850 miles^2 (12,562 km^2). The seat of Los Angeles County, the city is popularly known as LA and is the centre of the US film and television industries as well as an important commercial, industrial and financial centre.

History

In 1781 a Spanish settlement called El Pueblo de la Reina de Los Angeles (the Town of the Queen of the Angels) was built on the site of LA. The area had previously been inhabited by around 200 Native Americans who had resettled after the Spanish established the nearby Mission San Garbil in 1771. The settlement came under Mexican control in 1821 and became a centre for cattle trading. Americans settled in the area throughout the early nineteenth century and by the 1840s Los Angeles was the largest settlement in Alta California.

After the Mexican-American War, the Treaty of Guadalupe Hidalgo (1848) gave control of the area to the United States. Two years later Los Angeles was incorporated as a city, although its population was only 1,500, and California was admitted to the Union. Growth was slow until the opening of the Santa Fe Railroad in 1876 and the Southern Pacific Railroad in 1885. The railways brought a massive increase in trading and many immigrants to the area and by 1890 Los Angeles' population had grown to 50,000. By the turn of the century it had risen to more than 100,000 and a decade later it had tripled to over 300,000. Water supply proved a major problem, although in 1913 a major project to pump water hundreds of miles away from Owens Valley was completed.

Aided by the opening of the Panama Canal in 1914 and the development of a harbour at San Pedro Bay, the city grew as a port. From the 1920s the discovery of oil and the rapid development in Los Angeles of the American film industry further enriched the city's diverse economy. After a period of economic depression, the Second World War provided a further boost to manufacturing while postwar service, electronics and aerospace industries thrived. The city was also firmly established as the heart of the US film, television and music industries.

Los Angeles had its problems in the 1990s. In April 1992, 58 people died in riots caused by the acquittal of four white policemen on charges of beating a black suspect. Two years later an earthquake struck, damaging or destroying thousands of buildings, causing 57 deaths and leading to the collapse of three freeways.

Modern City

The Los Angeles Metropolitan area employs 30% of California's workforce and accounts for more than 25% of its retail and wholesale sales. Manufacturing includes transportation equipment, agricultural and metal goods, petroleum and clothing. The city houses the headquarters of several major corporations and is a financial gateway between the United States and Asia. Los Angeles-Long Beach Port is also a leading centre for foreign trade. LA's status as the centre of the American entertainment industry attracts many multimedia companies.

The city has an extensive motorway system but little in the way of public transport. With one car for every two residents, the city's roads are congested and air pollution and smog are severe problems. European flights and some domestic ones fly to and from Los Angeles International Airport (popularly known as LAX) which is connected to the city by regular shuttle buses. There are several other airports in the LA area including Burbank, Long Beach, Ontario, Newport Beach and John Wayne Airport in Orange County. There is a 93-mile long Metro consisting of two rapid transit subway lines and four light railway lines. Buses are run by the LA County Metropolitan Transit Authority (MTA).

Los Angeles has several higher education institutions, including the Los Angeles campus of the University of California, the University of Southern California at Los Angeles and the Californian Institute of Technology.

Places of Interest

Sites of historical interest include the El Pueblo de Los Angeles Historic Monument and the city's oldest building, Avila Adobe. A new cultural attraction opened in 1997 when the Getty Center was unveiled at a cost of $1 bn. The complex, paid for by the legacy of the oil magnate John Paul Getty, houses historical and cultural exhibits, artwork and photography. The Los Angeles County Museum of Art has five museums and the largest collection of art in the city.

Exposition Park includes the California Science Center, the California Afro-American Museum and the Natural History Museum of Los Angeles County. The Music Pavilion hosts concerts by the Los Angeles Philharmonic Orchestra every winter. Other major performance venues include the Dorothy Chandler Pavilion, the Mark Taper Forum and the Ahmanson Theater. The Hollywood Bowl, a large outdoor amphitheatre, stages outdoor productions and events.

Luanda, Angola

Introduction

Located in northwestern Angola, Luanda is the country's largest city and the second busiest seaport.

History

Luanda was founded in 1576 by the Portuguese and was named São Paulo, a name it retained until Angola won its independence in 1975. The Cathedral of Luanda was built in 1583 and 12 years later the settlement was awarded city status by the Governor Manuel Cerveria Pereira, making it the first city to be founded by Europeans on the west coast of sub-Saharan Africa. For a while it was a major slave trading post, but when the slave trade declined during the first half of the nineteenth century its most successful exports were cotton, palm and giniguba oil, coffee, lime, leather and wax.

By the beginning of the twentieth century, newly developed road and rail networks established Luanda as an important centre for industry and commerce and the hub of a thriving colony. Owing to the rising price of coffee, the population increased rapidly after World War II.

Modern City

After liberation Luanda has suffered as a result of the emigration of many technically qualified people, the influx of rural migrants, urban fighting and a failing infrastructure. Today it is in the process of recovering from many years of domestic strife. To the east of the city lies the industrial heartland of Viana. The poor live in the more elevated part of Luanda, whereas the lower ground is occupied by the commercial zone. Today the city's major exports are coffee, cotton, diamonds, salt and iron. There is an oil refinery to the north of Luanda Bay.

Places of Interest

Amongst several sites of cultural significance and interest are the Museum of Anthropology, which houses a fine collection of native artwork, and the Slavery Museum.

Lucerne, Switzerland

Introduction

Lucerne is situated in the centre of Switzerland at a confluence of the Reuss River and Lake Lucerne. It is one of the largest and most important tourist resorts in the country.

History

Lucerne's origins are uncertain, but it is believed to have originated as a small fishing village. The city's name stems from a Benedictine monastery called St Luciaria founded in the area in the eighth century AD. Nothing is mentioned of Lucerne until 1178 when a lay order was established at the Kapelkirche (the present day St Peter's chapel). The city increased in size and significance when the St Gotthard Pass became a major trade route early in the thirteenth century. In 1291 Rudolf IV of Habsburg acquired the city, much to the chagrin of its citizens who had hoped for independence. In 1332 the city joined with the cantons of Uri, Schwyz and Unterwalden to oppose Austrian rule. They acquired their independence after defeating the Habsburg army at the battle of Sempach in 1386. Lucerne remained Catholic throughout the reformation, and in fact took on the leadership of the Catholic cantons. It was ruled by patrician families until 1798, when the arrival of Napoléon's armies precipitated the end of the regime. The city became the capital of the short-lived Helvetic Republic until 1803. After the downfall of Napoléon, Lucerne was a key player in the Sonderbund, an alliance of Catholic cantons opposed to the Protestant Confederation. The civil war that followed ended with a confederate victory, and Lucerne's association with the Sonderbund meant that it was rejected as a choice for capital of the new nation. A railway, completed in the mid nineteenth century, brought the earliest tourists to Lucerne. This development meant that by the turn of the century the city's population had more than tripled, and tourism had become the most important source of income.

Modern City

Lucerne's train station is on the south bank of the Reuss River, a short walk from the medieval centre. The old town and the city ramparts are on the north bank. Piltusstrasse runs southwest connecting the station and the older areas with the commercial district of modern Lucerne. There are a large number of boats, including several paddlesteamers, operating from the docks. Hourly trains connect the city to Geneva, Interlaken, Zürich, Lugano and Berne. The well-maintained N2 motorway allows drivers access to Lucerne. The city's economy is almost entirely dependent on tourism, and there is little industry or manufacturing.

Places of Interest

Popular attractions include Bertel Thorvaldsen's renowned Lion of Lucerne monument, the Glacier gardens which provide an insight into Lucerne's geological roots and the Kapellbrücke, an ancient bridge that was almost entirely destroyed by fire in the early 1990s only to be painstakingly reconstructed. The Transport museum houses a famous collection of travel-related memorabilia.

Lusaka, Zambia

Introduction

Lusaka is located in the south-central part of Zambia on a limestone plateau over 1,200 m. above sea level.

History

Lusaka's origins lie in the acquisition of the area just west of the present city by the British South Africa Company at the end of the nineteenth century. By 1924 the region had been taken over by the British Colonial Office. At this stage it was a sleepy agricultural centre, and although in the early 1930s it became the capital of what was then called Northern Rhodesia, it was not until the 1960s that it began to expand in population and size. It is now one of the fastest growing cities in central Africa.

The city was instrumental in securing Zambia's independence. It was here in 1948 that the Federation of African Societies established the Northern Rhodesian Congress. After the federation of Northern and Southern Rhodesia, Lusaka became a focal point for the anti-colonial activism and civil disobedience that culminated in an independent nation.

Modern City

Central Lusaka is a mixture of tradition and modernity, with rickety market stalls and high-rise towers nestling together. To the east lie government buildings, embassies and upmarket residencies. The West is poorer and far more crowded. The city has a mixed economy producing goods such as footwear, textiles and cement. It is also a major food-processing centre. The surrounding farmland is notable for corn, beef, dairy produce, hides and tobacco.

Lusaka is accessible by air, rail and bus. There is an international airport just outside the city, and since it lies on the junction of the Great North Road and the Great East Road it is possible to journey there by car from Malawi and Tanzania. There are rail connections to Livingstone, Ndola and across the border into Tanzania.

Places of Interest

Lusaka is not a tourist city, and has a relatively high rate of petty theft. It is, however, well served for museums and galleries. These include The Lusaka National Museum (which hosts exhibits dealing with subjects as diverse as witchcraft, ethnography, history and contemporary art) and the Henry Tayali Visual Arts Gallery which provides visitors with a taste of local art.

Luxembourg City, Luxembourg

Introduction

Luxembourg City, the capital of the Grand Duchy of Luxembourg, is in the south central part of the country at the confluence of the rivers Alzette and Pétrusse. It is the country's chief administrative and economic centre and is of growing international importance as the seat of the Court of Justice of the European Communities, the European Investment Bank, and, jointly with Strasbourg, of the European Parliament. It is also the headquarters of the European Coal and Steel Community. Bank accounts are strictly confidential and foreign nationals can earn interest tax–free. In 1994 the old town was added to the World Heritage List.

History

The site of a Roman settlement, the medieval fort was acquired in 943 AD by Count Siegfried of the Ardennes. For the next 400 years the castle was frequently attacked and rebuilt by Spaniards, French, Austrians and Dutch. The Grand Ducal Palace dates from 1572 and was originally built as the town hall. Following the Congress of Vienna in 1815, Luxembourg became a Grand Duchy, gained partial independence following the first Treaty of London but was ruled by the King of the Netherlands until gaining full independence in 1867. It was in 1890 that the former town hall became the home of the royal family. The city was occupied by the Germans during both world wars. In 1921 the country formed an economic union with Belgium and both joined with the Netherlands in 1948 to form the Benelux economic union. A founding member of the European Union, the European Court of Justice was established in the city to interpret the treaties established by the EU and to apply the laws made by the Council and Commission. The 'Summer in the City' Festival lasts from June to Sept. and encompasses major cultural events.

Modern City

The old city is surrounded by industrial and residential suburbs. Apart from being an international financial centre with over 250 institutions, Luxembourg's factories produce iron, steel, textiles, clothing, machinery, chemicals, processed food and beer. Findel Airport is located 6 miles northeast of the city. The city is served by a network of buses. Travel by rail has been made easier since the advent of Eurostar with connections from Brussels. The Luxembourg Music Conservatory was founded in 1909 and the University Centre of Luxembourg in 1969. The city was one of two European Capitals of Culture in 2007.

Places of Interest

The Fish Market in the heart of the old town is surrounded by seventeenth and eighteenth century buildings including the National Museum of History and Art. Following independence in 1867 much of the castle was dismantled but 7 miles of casements can be viewed from the Chemin de la Corniche on top of the old town wall. Since restoration work carried out in 1990 parts of the Ducal Palace have been opened to the public. Notre Dame Cathedral was built in the Gothic style by the Jesuits in 1623. Buried here are several royals including John the Blind, King of Bohemia and Count of Luxembourg from 1310–46. Also of interest are the Wenceslas Circular Walk in the Rham Plateau and an old town gate dating from 1590. The town quarter known as Grund has medieval houses lining the Alzette River. In the Kirchberg quarter is the eighteenth century Fort Thungen with its three circular towers.

Lviv (Lvov; Lwów; Lemberg), Ukraine

Introduction

Lviv is the main city of Lviv oblast in western Ukraine. Its importance on Baltic–Black Sea trade routes made it a victim of dynastic disputes over the centuries. It is now a major industrial and transport hub.

History

Galician King Danylo Halytsky established a fortress and named it in honour of his son Lev in the mid-thirteenth century. As the leading town of the Galicia region, Lev designated it his capital. Stormed and looted by the Poles under King Casimir in 1340, it was annexed to the Polish and Hungarian Kingdoms in 1349 and incorporated into Poland in 1387.

Briefly under the control of the Cossacks (1648) and the Swedes (1704), it came to Austria with the first partition of Poland in 1772. It underwent major urban expansion over the next century with the railway opening in the 1860s. Captured by Russia in the Great War, in 1918 Lviv became capital of the Western Ukrainian People's Republic until Poles re-took control the following year.

In 1939 it was occupied by the Red Army who again seized the city following a period of Nazi occupation during World War II. Ukrainian nationalist movements were put down by both regimes. The Ukrainian Greek-Catholic church was suppressed and many church leaders imprisoned, though it re-gained influence in the 1980s. In the late-1980s, as East European communism wained, Lviv was a hotbed of Ukrainian nationalism.

Modern City

Lviv relies on heavy industry, particularly vehicle manufacture. Other important industries include consumer goods, food processing and publishing. There are four universities.

The city is on several major motorway routes and nine railway routes. There is also an international airport.

Places of Interest

The Old Town is dominated by the architecturally diverse town square, ploschna Rynok. It includes the nineteenth century town hall, the Roman Catholic cathedral (built between 1370–1480 in the Gothic style), the

Armenian cathedral (dating from 1363) and Boyim chapel (from 1617). There is also a pharmaceutical museum. Just outside the city centre is the museum of popular architecture and life.

Lyons (Lyon), France

Introduction

The second largest conurbation in France and the third largest city, Lyons is the capital of the Rhône department in Southeast France. Situated on the confluence of the Rhône and Saône Rivers, Lyons is a major river port as well as an industrial and financial centre.

History

Lyons was founded by the Romans in 43 BC. The settlement on the Plateau Fourvière was named Lugdunum (hill of light or hill of crows). Under Augustus, Lugdunum was made the capital of the three Gauls—Aquitania, Belgica and Lugdunensis. As such, the town held an annual council and became the centre of the Roman road system. Lugdunum, along with Vienne, was the only Roman city to have two theatres, remains of which can be seen today.

Lugdunum's importance lasted three centuries. Despite attacks by Marcus Aurelius in 177 and Septimius Severus in 197, the second Century AD was the pinnacle of Lyons' classical development. In the same century Lyons converted to Christianity. Under Burgundian occupation, Lyons became a capital in 478. The city was taken by the Franks in 534. Despite being stripped of its capital status, Lyons remained an important religious centre and was the site of two Christian councils in 1245 and 1274. At the end of the first millennium, changes in language reduced Lugdunum into Lyon. In 1024 Lyons became the chief town in the kingdom of Provence. During the turbulent sixteenth century, Lyons remained relatively peaceful, owing to François I's patronage of the city.

In 1462 four annual fairs were inaugurated by Louis XIV. Lyons developed into an important trade centre, frequented by Italian merchant bankers. Prosperity increased further in the fifteenth century with the founding of Lyons' major industry, silk weaving. From the fifteenth–mid eighteenth centuries, Lyons was Europe's silk weaving capital. In the sixteenth century Lyons became a centre of printing with several hundred resident printers.

The Revolution (1789) caused a slump in the silk trade, and in 1793 Lyons, a Royalist stronghold, was besieged by the Montagnards. The attack destroyed many public buildings. The city prospered again with the introduction of the Jacquard loom, a steam powered method of weaving invented by Joseph-Marie Jacquard, a Lyons native, at the turn of the nineteenth century. This initiated Lyons' industrial and urban expansion of the nineteenth century. During this time, industrial unrest by the *Canuts*, or silk workers, unsettled the city. In one uprising of 1834, hundreds of workers were killed.

Lyons was occupied by the Germans in 1942 when the city was already the headquarters of the Resistance. The Resistance was helped in its efforts by the layout of the city centre, and especially the *Troubeles*. From the Latin *trans ambulare* (to walk across), these windy, narrow, maze-like streets, originally constructed to carry silk in all weathers, were ideal for avoiding pursuers. Some *Troubeles* in the old town date back to Roman times. It was at Lyons that Jean Moulin, the Resistance leader, was betrayed to the Germans in June 1943.

After a long period of stagnation, Lyons came into its own as one of France's leading business centres after 1950. In 1960 the Part-Dieu business district was created. In 1993 Lyons hosted the G7 summit.

Modern City

Lyons was traditionally famous for its silk production and now manufactures rayon and nylon. It is the headquarters of the leading bank Crédit Lyonnais and since 1989 has been the headquarters of Interpol. Lyons' industries include engineering, automobile production and pharmaceuticals. The city is an important centre of medical research.

Lyons has two railway stations and an international airport. The city is served by a metro system.

Places of Interest

The Presqu'Ile contains numerous monuments including the town hall and the Place des Terraux which houses the Musée des Beaux Arts. Vieux Lyons, Renaissance in style, is built around three churches. The oldest building in the district, the Cathédrale Saint Jean was built between twelfth–fifteenth centuries. Containing an astronomical clock and adorned with 280 medallions, it was the setting of Henri IV's marriage to Marie de Médicis; the Romanesque Eglise Saint Paul has an octagonal belfry and contains frescoes dating from 1480; and the nineteenth-century Eglise Saint Georges. Much of the old quarter was scheduled for demolition but instead, Lyons embarked on an imaginative scheme of renovation. Lyons is the hometown of the Lumière brothers and has a museum devoted to the nineteenth century pioneers of cinema.

Madrid, Spain

Introduction

Situated in the centre of Spain on a high plain by the river Manzanares, Madrid is the country's capital and the capital of the autonomous region of Madrid. The Puerta del Sol gate marks the epicentre of both Madrid and Spain from where all distances are measured.

History

Madrid was originally an insignificant Moorish town called Majrit, built around an alcázar (castle) situated on a plateau overlooking the river. Majrit was captured by the king of Castille and León, Alfonso VI, in 1083. The Moors continued to live in Madrid until the end of the Spanish Riconquista in 1492. Until then they were grouped together in the Moreria, an area that still holds this name. Although various monarchs passed through the city and a *cortes* was first summoned in Madrid in 1309, the town did not come into prominence until the sixteenth century. In 1561 Felipe II made Madrid the site of the *única corte* and the seat of government.

Madrid became the capital of Spain and the Spanish Empire. It was a surprising choice. Until this time the capital of the Castille and León Empire had been Valladolid, and the surrounding cities of Toledo and Segovia were much more important. But Felipe II chose Madrid because it was an uncontroversial choice. By contrast, Toledo was the centre of the Catholic Church in Spain. Apart from 5 years when Felipe III transferred the capital to Valladolid, Madrid has remained Spain's capital.

Madrid in the seventeenth century was home to Miguel de Cervantes (1547–1616), the author of the pioneering novel, Don Quixote; the dramatist and poet Lope de Vega (1562–1635); the latter's successor and *Madrileño* Pedro Calderón de la Barca (1600–81); and the painter Diego Velázquez (1599–1660).

During the War of Spanish Succession (1701–14), Madrid took the side of the Bourbons. Under their rule, the city grew rapidly. The most notable developments were during the rule of Carlos III, who was known as the 'mayor-king'. A serious effort was made to clean up Madrid. For his buildings Carlos used the Neoclassical architect, Juan de Villanueva (1739–1811), who had studied in Italy. His main achievement in Madrid was the Prado built between 1785–7. The architects Francisco Sabatini and Ventura Rodríguez were also engaged. Madrid's street lighting was improved and paving was introduced.

During the Peninsular War (1808–14), Madrid was in the hands of the French and Napoléon's brother Joseph Bonaparte occupied the palace. On 2 May 1808 the *Madrileños* rebelled against the French invaders. The uprising began around the Palacio Real and was concentrated at the Puerto del Sol where a statue now stands in memory, a bear and a bush, the city's emblem. This event is known as the beginning of the *Guerra de la Independencia*, as the Spaniards term the Peninsular War. The rebellion was unsuccessful but was praised by Fernando VII on his return from imprisonment in 1814. Wellington liberated Madrid in 1812.

The founder of the Partido Socialista Obrero Español, Pablo Iglesias (1850–1925), lived for most of his life in the capital. Madrid was a Republican stronghold during the Civil War. For 2 years it was under constant bombardment from Franco's Nationalists and suffered much damage.

The city was finally taken in March 1939. Madrid expanded under Franco who encouraged the suburban spread. During the 1950s and 60s vast urban development resulted in the destruction of some of Madrid's historical sites and buildings.

On 11 March 2004, Islamist extremists detonated ten explosives aboard four busy commuter trains during the morning rush hour. 191 people died and 2,050 were left injured.

Modern City

The city is the country's financial centre but Madrid's industry is second to Barcelona. Textiles, porcelain, glassware and leather goods are manufactured, also electrical and agricultural machinery and aircraft.

Madrid is connected nationally and internationally by air, rail and road. Domestic flights go from Madrid-Barajas Airport, while high speed trains link the capital to Seville, Malaga and Cadiz.

Places of Interest

One of the most important museums in the world, the Prado was originally intended by Carlos III as a museum of natural history. The world-famous art gallery was established there in 1818 by Ferdinand VII. It contains works by Spain's most important artists, including Velázquez and Goya. The latter's painting commemorating the *Madrileños'* uprising in the Peninsular War, *El Dos de Mayo* and *El Tres de Mayo*, hang here. The Prado includes works by the Dutch fifteenth century painter, Hieronymus Bosch, the Venetian high renaissance painter Titian Tiziano Vecellio and Titian's pupil, the Crete-born Domenikos Theotokopoulos, who was active in Spain and known as El Greco. Other museums include the modern art museum, the Museo Nacional Centro de Arte Reina Sofia, and the private fine arts museum, the Museo Thyssen-Bornemisza.

The Plaza Mayor was the site of many of Madrid's cultural and political events. It was the venue for royal festivities, plays, bullfights, festivals and executions. It was also the site of the trials of faith of the Inquisition—the *autos-de-fé*. Originally planned by Felipe II as a public meeting place, it was designed by Juan Gómez de Mora, an architect responsible for other civic buildings in the square's vicinity, and was built between 1617–19. It is surrounded by five-storey buildings and contains a statue of Felipe III, who ordered the square's construction. The last bullfight to be staged in the Plaza Mayor was in 1846 for the wedding of Isabella II to her cousin Francisco of Assisi.

The original Moorish alcázar was destroyed in an earthquake in 1466. The site became a medieval palace, which was extended by subsequent rulers. The palace was destroyed in a fire in 1734 and the construction of the Palacio Real was begun by Felipe V in 1738. The original architect was the Italian G.B. Sacchetti of Turin. It was completed in 1764. The adjoining Armería houses an impressive collection of armoury including the swords of the Conquistadors Hernán Cortés and Francisco Pizarro.

Mahajanga, Madagascar

Introduction

A historical centre and Madagascar's second port, Mahajanga is located in the most inaccessible western part of the island.

History

The eighteenth century Sakalava Empire originated in the area, and Mahajanga was made its capital. Sakalavan King Andriamandisoarivo chose it as a prime position for commercial exchange. Merchandise included slaves, weapons, precious stones, textiles and spices. The town was occupied by Arab explorers before coming under the control of French colonists in 1895.

Modern City

The economy relies on shipping and fishing and the cultivation of cotton, tobacco, corn, nuts and rice. The main industries are oil, textiles, sugar, cement and metallurgy. Baobabs forests, scattered islands, natural reserves and lakes and caves around a natural bay make it a major tourist resort. The city is accessible by air from Nosy Be and Antsiranana and by air and bus from the capital.

Places of Interest

The old town retains the architecture of the eighteenth century Arab occupation, and there are numerous mosques and churches. The three major markets are Tsaramandroso, Mahabibo and Bazar Be.

The town has several protected areas. The main reserves are Marotandrano, Ambohijanahary, Bemarivo, Kasijy and the Tampoketsa of Analamaitso. There are three natural reserves in the surrounding area, Namoroka, Ankarafantsika and the calcareous hills of Marovoay, although entry is restricted.

Majuro Atoll, Marshall Islands

Introduction

Majuro Atoll, in the Ratak Chain of islands, is the Marshall Islands' capital and its main port and commercial centre.

History

Having passed from Spanish to German hands, Majuro Atoll came under Japanese jurisdiction in 1914. It was captured by US forces in April 1944 and adapted into a base for aircraft carriers. Governed by the UN after the war, it became capital of the independent Marshall Islands in 1986. In 1997 and 1998 it suffered droughts after being hit by El Niño.

Modern City

Majuro Atoll is made up of around 60 islets, with the urban area concentrated on Delap, Uliga and Darrit. A single stretch of road connects the islets, making the atoll appear one long, thin island. There is an airport. The local economy relies on tourism, port-related activities and copra processing.

Places of Interest

Laura Village, to the west of the atoll, has retained a traditional rural character. The Alele museum has exhibits of early Marshallese life. The Majuro Peace Park is a war memorial constructed by the Japanese. The capitol building is among the most modernistic of the atolls buildings. Surrounded by virgin coral reef and waters filled with remnants from World War II, fishing and diving are popular pastimes.

Makkah (Mecca), Saudi Arabia

Introduction

The religious capital of Saudi Arabia, Makkah al-Mukarramah is located in the western province of Hejaz about 70 km inland from the Red Sea port of Jeddah. It is the birthplace of the Prophet Muhammad (AD 570–632), the founder of the Islamic faith, and is the most sacred of the Muslim holy cities. For fourteen centuries believers have been making the annual pilgrimage, or Hajj, to Makkah between the eighth and 13th days of the 12th month of the Islamic lunar calendar. The Hajj is one of the five 'pillars' or core religious duties of Islam. Around 2 m. pilgrims come to Makkah each year, some 1.3 m. of whom arrive from outside the Kingdom. The city is closed to non-Muslims.

History

Ancient Makkah was an oasis and staging post on the caravan routes linking the Mediterranean with Arabia, East Africa and south Asia. Mentioned (as Macoraba) by the Egyptian astronomer and geographer Ptolemy in the second century AD, it developed in Roman and Byzantine times into an important trading and religious centre. Muhammad and his followers (known as Muslims) took control of Makkah in AD 630. He had earlier declared himself a prophetic reformer, sent to restore the rites first established by the Hebrew patriarch Abraham which had been corrupted over centuries by pagan influences. He destroyed the city's pagan idols and declared it a centre of Muslim pilgrimage dedicated to the worship of Allah (God) alone. Muhammad died in AD 632, but the leaders who succeeded him (known as caliphs) continued to spread of the Islamic faith throughout and beyond the Arab world. In the sixteenth century Makkah came under Ottoman rule. It remained under Turkish sovereignty until the disintegration of the Ottoman Empire in the First World War. In 1924 the city was occupied by Abdulaziz Al-Saud, who subsequently made it the religious capital of the unified state of Saudi Arabia.

Modern City

Makkah is the seat of the Consultative Council (Majlis Al-Shura). The city's inhabitants make their living by providing accommodation for pilgrims and acting as guides and agents for services. During King Fahd's reign investment has gone into airport buildings, roads, water supplies and health provision. However, the influx of pilgrims has occasions caused safety problems in recent years, with congestion and fires leading to many deaths.

Places of Interest

The Sacred Mosque (Masjid Al-Haram), a vast structure ringed by seven minarets, is at the centre of Makkah. In the courtyard is the Ka'aba, a windowless, cube-shaped building in the direction of which Muslims face when they worship anywhere in the world. The Ka'aba contains the sacred Black Stone, which is believed to have been given to Abraham by the archangel Gabriel. The Mosque also houses the sacred Zamzam spring, associated by tradition with the biblical figures Hagar and Ishmael.

Malabo, Equatorial Guinea

Introduction

Malabo is the capital of Equatorial Guinea and home to most of the country's population. It is located on the north coast of Bioko island, on the rim of an inactive volcano.

History

The city was founded in 1827 as Port Clarence when the Spanish, who owned the island, allowed the British to use the site as a centre for their efforts to suppress the slave trade. It was renamed Santa Isabel in 1843 after Isabella II of Spain, becoming the capital of Spanish Guinea. In 1968 it was made capital of Equatorial Guinea and in 1973 was renamed Malabo. The population declined in 1969 after riots between the population on Bioko and mainland Rio Muna.

Modern City

The city is a centre for the country's trade and exports cocoa, copra, timber, fish and coffee.

There is an international airport.

Places of Interest

Reminders of the Spanish period include the Cathedral, located on the west side of the town in front of the Plaza de la Espania.

Malé, Maldives

Introduction

The capital of the Maldives, Malé lies in the centre of the 1,190 islands that make up the Maldivian archipelago. Surrounded by sea walls, Malé is 2 km by 1 km. Of the 199 inhabited islands, it is by far the most populous.

History

Little is known about Maldives' early history, though Malé has long been the seat of sultanates, royalty, governments and the social elite. From its early history, Malé was at the centre of lucrative trade routes. The islands were settled by merchant sailors, latterly those involved in the silk trade. Influenced by North African travellers, a twelfth-century king converted the Maldives from Buddhism to Islam, creating the first sultanates.

In the sixteenth century Portuguese sailors were permitted to build a fort on Malé. Wanting more control of the islands, a successful Portuguese invasion was mounted by Captain Andreas Andre. He controlled the islands until a local revolt expelled the Portuguese in 1573. The Maldives were under Dutch protection for a short period in the seventeenth century. Malabars from the Indian East Coast invaded the island and expelled the sultan in 1782. A short time later, Ghaazee Hassan Izzuddeen expelled the invaders. The Maldives became a British protectorate in 1887. Malé became the capital of the independent Maldives in 1965.

Modern City

Malé is the seat of government and major businesses. With around a third of the population, Malé is densely populated. The international airport is on the neighbouring island of Hululé, connected to Malé by *dhoanis*, or local boat.

Places of Interest

Built in 1656, Hukuru Miski is the oldest Maldivian mosque. It is decorated with stone carvings and has records of the islands' conversion to Islam. Tombs of national heroes and royalty are within its compounds. Capped with a gold dome, the Grand Friday Mosque is the islands' biggest mosque and Islamic centre.

The National Museum displays Maldivian culture and history including exhibitions of stone figures and pre-Islamic carvings.

Malmö, Sweden

Introduction

Malmö is in the southern province of Skåne. It is the country's third largest city and the commercial hub of southern Sweden. Malmö is linked to Copenhagen in Denmark via the Öresund Bridge, which was built in 2000. The city is famous for its numerous parks which provide a venue for summer festivals and other open-air events.

History

The name Malmö is a derivative of Malmhauger or 'sand heaps', and the original settlement was created by farmers and fisherman. The city itself was founded in 1275. For centuries afterwards the local economy survived by exporting salt herring to Catholic Europe. The city was occupied by the Danes and the German Hansa, but in 1658 it was formally ceded to Sweden. This was to prove detrimental to the city's prosperity since it was forced to surrender the trading privileges it had enjoyed under Danish rule. Its port was also dilapidated in the wake of successive conflicts. Population declined dramatically and only began to recover in the mid eighteenth century when a new harbour was constructed. The arrival of the railroad in the nineteenth century triggered an economic revival, and Malmö quickly established itself as a major centre for industry and transport.

Modern City

The completion of the Öresund link boosted Malmö's economic and political significance, and provided a valuable connection to the heart of Europe. An average of 1,102 lorries and 18,377 cars crossed the bridge every day in 2013. Today the city's major industries include food processing and shipbuilding and repair. Its port is one of the largest in Europe and handles large cargoes of imports and exports. Malmö is linked to Stockholm and Gothenburg by road and rail. There is an international airport 30 km to the east at Skurup. The city's most important cultural event is the Malmö Festival which takes place in Aug.

Places of Interest

Malmö's parks, Kungsparken, Slottsparken, Pildammsparken and Beijers Park are in the city centre. The central square, Malmö Stortorg, was the largest trading area of its kind in the sixteenth century. It is dominated by a statue of King Karl X Gustaf. The townhall dates from the same era. The fourteenth century church St Petri is a popular attraction and a notable example of the Baltic Gothic architectural style. The castle Malmöhus is Scandinavia's oldest remaining Renaissance castle. The art gallery is one of the largest centres for contemporary art in Europe. The Science & Technology/Maritime Museum deals with the history of industry and shipping in Skåne. It also features an interactive science centre. The Museum of Natural History has a large aquarium with tropical marine life. It provides information about rare wildlife in Scandinavia.

Managua, Nicaragua

Introduction

Situated on the western lowlands of Nicaragua, Managua is the country's capital and home to a third of the nation's population. Located on the southern coast of Lake Managua, the city is 45 km from the Pacific Ocean. At only 50 m. above sea level, Managua is Central America's hottest capital. The city is flanked by volcanoes limiting its expansion to the west.

History

What is now Managua was inhabited by Amerindians before the arrival of the Conquistadors in 1524. Evidence exists of pre-historic habitation more than 6,000 years ago. After colonization, Managua remained an inconsequential village between León and Granada. Soon after independence from Spanish rule, there was intense rivalry between León and Granada for the capital status. After Granada was destroyed by American mercenaries led by William Walker, Managua was chosen as compromise capital in 1857.

After destructive floods in 1876 and 1885 slowed development, progress was again halted by volcanic eruptions in 1932 and 1972. Nearly all the city centre was destroyed and has not been rebuilt. The few remaining buildings include the Hotel Intercontinental, the national theatre and the Government House and the National Palace. Managua's reconstruction was focused on urban development on the city's outskirts, especially towards the south. Foreign aid sent after the disaster was appropriated by the Somoza dictatorship. From the 1950s onwards, the capital's population expanded dramatically, growing 15-fold over the next 40 years. Many people came to the capital fleeing rural poverty and political violence. Half of Managua's inhabitants live in poverty (less than the national average) and many homes lack basic amenities such as water or sanitation.

Modern City

Industries include metallurgy, textiles and oil refining, although on a relatively low scale. The surrounding area is agricultural and produces mainly cotton, coffee and maize. The Cesar Augusto Sandino International Airport is situated 12 km east of Managua.

Murals and slogans, once an integral part of post-dictatorial Managua, are beginning to be painted over. Even the Plaza de la Revolución, with the tomb of the Sandinista leader Carlos Fonseca at its centre, has been renamed the Plaza de la República. Some of the destroyed city centre has been turned into parks. One new building in the area is the conference centre, el Centro de Convención Olof Palme, opened in the 1980s.

Places of Interest

The ruins of the Catedral Santo Domingo stand next to the Palacio Nacional in the Plaza de la República, a new version having been constructed away from the centre. Las Huellas de Acahualinca displays the footprints of humans and animals escaping an erupting volcano moulded into lava over 6,000 years ago. Other archaeological displays date from more recent Nicaraguan history (circa AD 400). Three other museums, El Museo de la Revolución, Julio Cortázar Museo de Arte Contemporanza and El Museo de Alfabetazzación are closed owing to financial cutbacks. On the shore of Lake Managua a theatre and statue are devoted to Nicaragua's most famous poet, Rubén Dario. Most markets were destroyed during the earthquake. The new Mercado Huembes specializes in crafts and ceramics. The Tiscapa Volcano (La Loma), next to the lake, offers a view of the city and the surrounding volcanoes. Managua has two major festivals, the Festival de Música y Juventud takes place in Feb. and the Fiestas Agostinas are celebrated in Aug. 23 km southeast of Managua in the Volcán Masaya National Park.

Manama, Bahrain

Introduction

Occupying the northeastern corner of the main island of the Bahrain archipelago, Manama is the capital, seat of government and commercial heart of the country. Based on oil wealth, the city has doubled in size since 1970.

History

There are references to Manama in Islamic manuscripts from the mid-fourteenth century. In 1521 it came under the rule of the Portuguese, exploring new trading routes in the Gulf region, before falling to the Persians in 1603. Subsequent Persian-Arab rivalry resulted eventually in Arab ascendancy in 1783 under Shaikh Ahmed bin Mohammed Al-Khalifa, whose dynasty still holds power in Bahrain today. From 1861 Bahrain became a British protectorate in all but name. Following the discovery of oil in 1932 Manama began to expand, becoming a free port in 1958. In 1971, it became the capital of the newly independent Bahrain.

Modern City

Traditional industries such as pearl fishing and boat building continue, but Manama is now a major oil centre, as well as the financial and commercial hub of the Gulf region. The northern edge of the city has undergone extensive redevelopment on reclaimed land, although many areas inland have changed little in the last 50 years. Manama is encircled by a ring of highways, linking it to the interior and to the causeways to Muharraq Island, the Sitra region and Saudi Arabia. Central Manama is about 10 km west of Bahrain International Airport.

Places of Interest

The chief cultural attractions are the National Museum, Al Fateh Islamic Centre and Grand Mosque, the Heritage Centre and Bait Al Qur'an. Other places of interest include the colourful Souk (marketplace), entry to which is guarded by a prominent building known as Bab Al Bahrain (literally 'Gateway to Bahrain'), which houses the Directorate of Tourism and Archaeology.

Manchester, United Kingdom of Great Britain and Northern Ireland

Introduction

Greater Manchester, once part of Lancashire, includes the city of Manchester, Salford, and the boroughs of Bolton, Bury, Oldham, Rochdale, Stockport, Tameside, Trafford and Wigan. Rising to prominence during the Industrial Revolution, Manchester is now an important commercial and media centre.

History

In AD 79 the Romans established a fort at the confluence of the rivers Irwell and Medlock and the town became a meeting place for seven Roman roads. In AD 919 the Saxon king Edward the Elder repaired what was left of the Roman fort to use as a defence against the invading Danes and there is a mention of a Parish church in the Domesday book in 1086. Medieval Manchester seemed destined to remain in the shadow of the larger town of Salford but in 1421 a college of priests was established. The church school that was founded in

1506 became the Manchester Grammar School in 1515. In the fourteenth century local weaving was stimulated by immigrant Flemish weavers. It was at this time that Manchester's reputation for woollen, linen and cotton goods was secured. By the sixteenth century Manchester had grown into a cloth trading market town.

The modern city of Manchester was born out of the industrial revolution. In the early eighteenth century Manchester was a market town with a population of 10,000. By the middle of the nineteenth century it had more than 30,000 inhabitants and soon engulfed its near neighbours such as Bolton, Salford, Eccles, Altrincham and Stockport.

In 1762 the first canal, built by James Brindley, was used to bring in coal and was extended to Liverpool to cope with increasing exports. By 1830 there were 99 cotton-spinning mills in Manchester and the first modern railway had been built between Manchester and Liverpool. As the industrial revolution progressed so Manchester developed its trade, diversifying into the building of steam engines, electrical machinery and armaments. In 1819 Manchester was the setting for the infamous Peterloo Massacre, when a gathering of 50,000 radicals in St Peter's Field was suppressed by the military. Eleven people were killed and around 400 were injured in an incident that led to widespread condemnation.

In 1853 Manchester received city status. During the nineteenth century Manchester was noted for political and intellectual debate and *The Manchester Guardian* (now *The Guardian*) was one of England's most important newspapers. Charles Hallé established his Hallé orchestra and subsequently assisted in founding the Royal Manchester College of Music in 1893. Friedrich Engels' 1845 book *The Condition of the Working Class in England* was rooted in his experiences in Manchester.

By 1911 Manchester had a population of 2 m. The pace of the industrial revolution slowed and the ability to buy cheaper textiles from abroad had a detrimental effect. It was left with many obsolete factories and dilapidated housing estates. The city was seriously damaged in German bombing raids of World War II.

Modern City

Despite Manchester's relative industrial decline in the twentieth century, it remains one of northern England's most important commercial and cultural centres. Banking and other services provide a large percentage of employment, though the suburbs of Greater Manchester also rely on a diverse range of manufacturing industries. Many of its slum areas were renovated in the late twentieth century. An IRA terrorist bomb in 1996, which injured more than 200 people and caused extensive damage to the city centre, resulted in a swathe of new building.

The city is well endowed with museums, galleries and theatres. The annual Hallé Concerts are world renowned and the city has produced a succession of influential pop bands during the 1980s and 1990s, including The Smiths, The Stone Roses and Oasis. Its night clubs were key to the emergence of dance music in Britain. Manchester has two famous football teams, United and City. The city hosted the Commonwealth Games in 2002. A new stadium was built, along with the Manchester Aquatics Centre. There is also an Olympic-standard cycling centre and Old Trafford is used for test cricket.

Manchester is well served by road and rail links, and the inner city has a tram system. There is an international airport around 15 km from the city centre. There are two universities; the University of Manchester (which merged with the University of Manchester Institute of Science and Technology in 2004) and Manchester Metropolitan. The University of Manchester was closely involved in the splitting of the atom and in the building of the first programmable computer.

Places of Interest

Notable attractions include: the fifteenth century Gothic Manchester Cathedral, overlooking the River Irwell and restored and extended in Victorian times; the Neo-Gothic Manchester Town Hall, designed by Alfred Waterhouse and completed in 1877. Situated in Albert Square, its Great Hall contains Ford Maddox Brown murals charting the city's history; the Royal Exchange, located in Saint Ann's Square, opened in 1809 and served as a market for cotton traders. Renovated after suffering damage in the 1996 IRA bombing, the Royal Exchange Theatre was re-opened in 2000; the Lowry, a futuristic centre housing two theatres and two art galleries, opened for the millennium. It is linked by footbridge to Trafford Wharfside, home to Manchester United Football Club and the Imperial War Museum North; the Central Library, a circular, bedomed, neo-classical building with a noted

reading room; Salford Museum and Art Gallery, including works by Salford's most famous artist L. S. Lowry; Castlefield Gallery is an artist-run contemporary art gallery; the City Art Galleries have collections of paintings, sculptures, ceramics and decorative arts, including an internationally famous collection of Pre-Raphaelite paintings.

Mandalay, Myanmar

Introduction

Mandalay, the former royal capital, is situated in central Myanmar on the Irrawaddy River. It is the country's second largest city and capital of Mandalay Division. It is the commercial and communications centre of northern and central Myanmar with trade links by rail, road, air and water. Mandalay is also the spiritual centre of Myanmar. The Mahamuni Pagoda, south of the city with its 12–foot Buddha is considered one of the country's most famous.

History

King Mindon, one of the last kings of the Konbaung Dynasty, built Mandalay between 1857 and 1859 as the capital of the independent Kingdom of Burma. The fortified city is in the shape of a square and it was named after Mandalay Hill at the northeast corner of the present city. King Mindon's palace, Myat Nan San Kyaw (Golden Palace), was built in the centre. The city was captured by the British in 1885 following a dispute between a British timber company and the Burmese government. Thereafter Mandalay (now called Ford Dufferin) became the British headquarters of Upper Burma. In 1935 the Government of Burma Act formally separated Burma from the Indian colony. During WWII the Japanese occupied Mandalay until it was recaptured by the British in 1945 under the command of General Sir William Slim. The city and palace were virtually destroyed. Burma was granted independence in 1948.

Modern City

Since there are no long haul flights into Myanmar, entry is via Southeast Asian connections. Leading industries include silk weaving, gold-leaf work, tea packing, jade cutting, brewing and distilling. Silverware, matches and woodcarvings are also produced. There is an Arts and Science University as well as a teacher training college. Further education includes agricultural, medical and technical institutions as well as a school of fine arts, music and drama. There is one modern hospital. The Zegyo bazaar is the largest market and lies to the west of the palace.

Places of Interest

The Golden Palace has been reconstructed and the Lion Throne, which survived the war, is exhibited at the national museum in Yangon. King Mindon built the Kuthodaw Pagoda in 1868 surrounding it with 729 marble slabs inscribed with the Tipitaka text (the three baskets of the Buddhist Pali canon). It is often referred to as the 'world's biggest book'. Kyauktawgi Pagoda (the pagoda of the great marble image), also built by King Mindon in 1865, stands at the foot of Mandalay Hill. It houses a large image of Buddha sculpted from a single block of Sagyin marble. The Mahamuni Pagoda was built in 1784 to house the Mahamuni Buddha brought by King Bodawapaya from Rakhine. It is the most revered pagoda in Mandalay and many gather each morning for the ritual washing of the Buddha's face. Other attractions include the Shwe In Bin Monastery, the Mandalay Museum and Library and the Silk Weaving Cottage Industry.

Manila, Philippines

Introduction

Located on the South-western side of Luzon island, on the eastern shore of Manila bay, Manila has been the principal city of the Philippines since the arrival of the Spanish Conquistadors in the sixteenth century. It is the largest metropolitan area in the Philippine archipelago and the second largest in Asia, after Jakarta. The Pasig River flows through the city and empties into Manila bay. 'Metropolitan Manila' (National Capital Region), consists of the cities Manila, Quezon City, Paranaque, Makati, Valenzuela, Pasig, Malabon, and Pasay.

History

In 1571 Miguel Lopez de Lagaspi sailed into a small but prosperous Muslim trading port, Maynilad. It was so called because a white-flowered mangrove plant (the nilad), which grew in abundance in the area ruled by Sultan Rajah Sulayman.

The 333-year colonization of the Philippines by the Spanish began with Legaspi's building of the 'distinguished and ever loyal city', a double walled stronghold, guarded at its entrance by Fort Santiago.

Manila became the Philippine capital under the colonisation of the Spanish and was the starting point for the catholicisation of the country under Andrés de Urdaneta, an Augustinian friar. Franciscan, Dominican, Jesuit, and other Augustinian missionaries followed, founding churches, schools and convents, many of which can still be seen.

The period between the Spanish arrival and their eventual departure wasn't particularly peaceful and included a Chinese invasion in 1574 and British occupation during the Seven-Years War (1756–63). The Philippines was ceded by the British under the terms of the Treaty of Paris (1763) along with Cuba, in exchange for the Florida Keys.

During the eighteenth and nineteenth centuries, with defeats in Europe and heavy losses at the hands of pirates, many Filipino's began to doubt the strength and heavenly mandate to rule of their European overlords. During the 1890s Manila became the centre of Philippine anti-Spanish sentiment. In 1892, Andrés Bonifacio formed the Katipunan, a secret, radical Filipino political association. The Katipunan movement frightened the Spanish and their supporters. The Spanish authorities arrested or exiled some 4,000 rebels. When, in 1896, the Spanish executed, by musketry, the Philippine author, poet, physician, and journalist, Jose Rizal, a year-long period of insurrection ensued.

Bonifacio was usurped and executed by Emilio Aguinaldo y Famy. Entering into an accord with the Spaniards, Aguinaldo agreed to exile in Hong Kong in exchange for 400,000 pesos.

Aguinaldo returned to Manila with Commodore George Dewey and the U.S. Asiatic Squadron. The United Sates declared war on Spain on 25 April 1898. The first action against the Spanish was the Battle of Manila Bay on 1 May. The US navy destroyed the Spanish fleet but lacked the force to take the city. Aguinaldo's Katipunan guerrillas maintained their operations until 15,000 US troops arrived at the end of July. The Spanish ceded the Philippines to the US for US$20m.

It seemed to many that Spanish signs had merely been replaced by new American ones. This new form of colonialism or 'tutelage' as the US called it was not tolerated by all and Filipino uprisings occurred for several years. Emilio Aguinaldo issued an order to guerrilla officers setting aside the days between 15 and 24 Sept. for a general offensive against the Americans. In 1901 a civil government was established with William Howard Taft as governor.

Upon the outbreak of World War II in the Pacific Manila made preparations for war. On 26 Dec. 1941, in an attempt to save it from a fate similar to Pear Harbour's, Manila was declared an 'open city' by General Douglas MacArthur, Commander of the newly-formed United States Armed Forces in the Far East (USAFEE). It is not certain if MacArthur's forces violated the terms of open city status or if Japan chose to ignore the decree, but on 27 Dec. Lt. Masaharu Homma, Commander-in-Chief of the Japanese Imperial Forces', attacked the city. General MacArthur had retreated to Bataan when, on 2 Jan. 1942, Japanese forces entered the city. Manila suffered relatively little but was razed to the ground during the US counter-offensive.

In 1946 President Harry Truman proclaimed the United States 'withdraws and surrenders all rights of possession, supervision, jurisdiction, control of sovereignty ... and ... recognises the independence of the Philippines.' Manila became the capital of the independent Republic of the Philippines under the leadership of Manuel A. Roxas. Manila was rebuilt with much aid from the US.

Despite a short move to nearby Quezon City, Manila has remained the hub of Philippine politics and education. In 1986, after the assassination of popular opposition leader, Benigno Aquino at Manila International Airport, and the corrupt election campaigning by President Ferdinand Marcos, over a million Filipinos gathered on the Epifanio de los Santos Avenue to stage their protest against the dictatorship of Marcos. This became known as the 'People Power' or 'EDSA' revolution.

Modern City

Manila today is not free of social unrest. During 2000–01 President Joseph Estrada was accused of corruption and embezzlement. On 20 Jan. 2001 pro-democracy demonstrators converged on EDSA for a second time and successfully ousted the incumbent president replacing him with his deputy, Mrs. Gloria Macapagal-Arroyo, daughter of former president Diosdado Macapagal. In July 2003 Ramon Cardenas, a former junior minister to ex-President Joseph Estrada, led a military uprising during which several hundred troops took possession of a shopping and residential complex in protest at alleged government corruption before withdrawing peacefully.

Places of Interest

Among Manila's leading attractions is the old walled Spanish town, home to most of the city's oldest churches and buildings. The Malate and Ermita area is the favoured destination for nightlife, with bars and restaurants in abundance.

Maputo, Mozambique

Introduction

Maputo is in the south of Mozambique and is the country's capital and chief port. The city was once regarded as an African tourist destination to rival Cape Town. However, over two decades of civil war has left much of Maputo's buildings in ruins.

History

At the end of the eighteenth century Maputo was a small settlement around a colonial fort. Its name is that of a Portuguese trader who explored the region in the sixteenth century. The town grew steadily and in 1887 it was declared a city. In 1895 a railroad connecting Maputo to Pretoria in South Africa was completed, and the city began to expand rapidly as a result. In 1907 it replaced the town of Mozambique as the capital of Portuguese East Africa. The city was at the centre of the country's lengthy campaign for independence from Portugal, and eventually was named the capital of Mozambique in 1975. The Portuguese population immediately abandoned the city leaving it without an administrative structure. Independence also entailed the severing of political ties with South Africa and a consequent decline in Maputo's tourist revenues. Stability and prosperity in the capital came under threat from the ruling Frelimo party's conflict with rebel political groups opposed to its Marxist-Leninist ideology. In Oct. 1992 Frelimo signed a peace accord with Renamo, the most prominent of the rebel groups, thus ending the civil war.

Modern City

Maputo is the country's administrative hub, and a major centre for communications and commerce. Its economy is heavily reliant on its port on Maputo Bay. Major exports include coal, cotton, sugar, chrome, ore, cement and hardwood. Industries include shipbuilding and repair, brewing, iron working and fish canning. The city is connected to South Africa, Swaziland and Zimbabwe by both road and rail. The University of Mozambique is based in Maputo.

Places of Interest

The original fort is still standing and is the oldest of Maputo's historic sites. The University houses a museum devoted to Mozambique's history. The National Art Museum showcases contemporary art.

Marrakesh, Morocco

Introduction

Second largest city in Morocco, situated in the northern foothills of the High Atlas Mountains, it is also one of the four imperial cities. The medina was designated a World Heritage Site in 1985.

History

Marrakesh was founded in 1062 by Youssef Ben Tachfine as the capital of the Almoravides, a Moorish people who came from North Africa to Spain in the eleventh and twelfth centuries. Under the Almoravides the town became an Islamic intellectual centre where many scholars and philosophers converged. Ancient ramparts and city gates are testament to the city's medieval preeminence. Invaded by the Almohads in 1147, Marrakesh then became their capital. The Almohads added to the grandeur erecting many fine buildings including the Koutoubia Mosque, considered one of the greatest works of North African architecture. During the rule of the Merinids in the thirteenth century, the city went into decline after they moved their capital to Fès but it revived under the Saadian occupation. In 1551 their leader, Mohammed Al Mahdi, made Marrakesh his capital. It was in this period that the famous El Badi Palace was built over 16 years and the city became an important Saharan trade centre. After French occupation in 1913, the modern part of the city was built.

Modern City

A cultural and tourist centre, Marrakesh is noted for its historic buildings, markets and festivals. The Place Djemaa el-Fna, a large square and once the main meeting place, lies at the heart of the old city. There are Jugglers, acrobats, storytellers and snake charmers. The Atlas Mountains offer winter sports and budget hotels provide cheap accommodation. Marrakesh is the rail terminus for other parts of Morocco and roads link the city with Casablanca, Rabat and the port of Safi. An international airport is about 5 km to the west. The new town, known as Gueliz, is flat, open and lined with orange and jacaranda trees. Famous for its fine leatherwork and carpets, local industries include tanning and handicrafts.

Places of Interest

The El Badi Palace, once the sixteenth century home of Sultan Ahmed El Mansour, was ransacked in the seventeenth century though its dungeons can still be explored. The National Festival of Moroccan Art takes place here every May or June. El Mansour also built the Saadian Tombs, a necropolis with over 160 tombs surrounded by palm trees and flowering shrubs. His collection of gold and marble ornaments can be found in the Dar Si Said Museum. The El Bahia Palace, built as a harem, has rooms that vary in size according to the importance of the wife or concubine. The Koutoubia Mosque, with its towering minaret built in the twelfth century, takes its name from the Arab word 'koutoub' meaning book. The Ali Ben Youssef Medersa, a well-preserved fourteenth century school for teaching the Koran, is the largest in North Africa.

Marseilles (Marseille), France

Introduction

The capital of the Bouches-de-Rhône region in the Midi, France's second city covers two thirds of the department. The largest commercial seaport in France, and the second in Europe after Rotterdam, Marseilles is situated on the Gulf of Lions at the mouth of River Rhône, and is flanked by limestone hills.

History

Marseilles was founded as Massalia by Greek seafarers from Phocaia in Asia Minor around 600 BC and is one of France's oldest cities. Its natural harbour was developed into an important trade centre and Massalia became powerful and prosperous, rivalling Carthage as a trade centre. The city supported the Romans in the Punic Wars but then switched to the defeated Pompey. Taken by Caesar in 49 BC, Marseilles was allowed to retain its independence but declined rapidly, decimated by disease and conflict and finally destroyed by the Moors in the ninth century.

Marseilles' revival began in the tenth century, under the Dukes of Provence. Marseilles was one of the principal embarkation points during the Crusades (eleventh to fourteenth centuries), when the town developed around the port. In 1481 Marseilles, along with Provence, was incorporated into France. An increasingly important trade centre as the gateway to the north and sub-Saharan Africa, the city was declared by Isabella I of Spain to be the centre of the world.

Marseilles sided with the Catholics in the Wars of Religion and rejected the Protestant Henri IV as king. The city also opposed Louis XIV, fearing a loss of its independence, but in 1660 the king put down a revolt and demolished the main gates of the city. Further opposition was deterred by the construction of two fortresses, Fort St Jean and Fort St Nicolas, by Louis Nicolas and Sébastien Leprestre de Vauban. Concurrently, Louis XIV began expanding and developing Marseilles. He ordered an expansion of the port in 1666 and declared it a free port in 1669.

In the seventeenth and eighteenth centuries the city prospered despite a devastating plague in 1720 that killed more than half the population. Marseilles' maritime commerce went from strength to strength and by the Revolution (1789) was trading with eastern Mediterranean countries, Russia and American colonies. During the French Revolution volunteers from Marseilles marched to Paris in July 1792 to the tune of *Chant de Guerre de l'Armée du Rhin* (1792), written in Strasbourg by Claude Rouget de Lisle. Hitherto unknown outside of Strasbourg, the song was called La Marseillaise, and was adopted as France's national anthem in 1795. Despite the volunteers' support, Marseilles suffered during the Revolution, especially during the violence of *La Terreur* (1793–94), when Marseilles became the city without a name. Maritime commerce suffered from the British trade blockade during the Napoleonic Wars (1792–1815).

After the French acquisition of Algeria in 1820, the zenith of Marseilles' maritime trading came with the opening of the Suez Canal in 1869. The harbour was consequently extended to accommodate large liners. Marseilles was a stronghold of the Resistance in World War II and an asylum for refugees. During the German occupation much of Marseilles' old port district was destroyed, especially the Panier quarter. The bombing revealed remains from the ancient city of Massalia, including a theatre, an aqueduct and a merchant ship. After the War, a mass urban development scheme was mounted. The bridge, blown up in 1944, was replaced by a tunnel. After the Algerian War (1954–62), many North Africans were attracted to Marseilles. Racial tension in the city was heightened by the Front National party.

Modern City

The city's major industries are ship repairing, oil-refining and metallurgy. Marseilles is famous for its long history of producing soap made with olive oil. Exports include olive oil, wine and sugar. The city has its own film studio founded in 1930 by the famous Provençal author and director, Marcel Pagnol—at that time, the only film studio outside Paris.

Marseilles is accessible by rail, road and air. The city's airport is 20 km northwest of the city. A metro system was opened in 1978.

Places of Interest

Marseilles is home to several museums including the Musée des Beaux-Arts. Housed in one of Marseilles' most attractive buildings, the museum has collections of French painting from sixteenth to nineteenth century, including Provençal works. The Musée des Docks displays the ancient remains of Massalia, discovered after World War II.

One of the few examples of Marseilles' distant past is the Abbaye Saint Victor. Erected on a third-century cemetery overlooking the old port, the abbey was founded in the fifth century. It became powerful during the eleventh and twelfth centuries. The church was rebuilt in the thirteenth century but no remains of the original monastery survive.

One of Marseilles' harbour islands, If, has the Château d'If containing the infamous dungeons immortalized in Alexandre Dumas' novels *The Count of Monte Cristo* and *The Man in the Iron Mask*.

Mary (Merv), Turkmenistan

Introduction

The administrative capital of Mary oblast on the River Morghab delta in the arid southeast of the country, Mary was initially called Merv after the nearby city, regarded as the oldest and best preserved oasis city on the Silk Road.

History

The original city of Merv was established between 7 BC and AD 300, with the exact date disputed. It's golden age was in the eleventh and twelfth centuries when it was the capital of the Seljuqs empire and a key post on the Silk Road. In 1221 it was destroyed by Toloi, the son of Genghis Khan, and was never to regain its former grandeur.

The modern city was founded by the Russians in 1884, 30 km from Merv but nonetheless given its name. In 1937 it was renamed Mary. It was subsequently developed as a transport hub and a base to exploit the surrounding Shatlyk gasfield.

Modern City

Mary is an important rail junction on the Turkmenbashy–Tashkent line and is well served by road and air. It is an important trade centre for wool, cotton, leather and grain. There are major sources of natural gas in the surrounding area. One of the other leading industries is plastics and there are various light industries.

Places of Interest

The chief attraction in Mary is the museum of history. Most tourists head for the remains of Merv, which include Sultan Sanjar's mausoleum (completed in 1140) and lesser ruins spanning the city's five major phases over several centuries.

Maseru, Lesotho

Introduction

Maseru, on the River Caledon close to the western border with South Africa, is Lesotho's capital and only major city.

History

Mshweshwe I, a Basotho chief, settled the town in the 1860s and in 1869 it was chosen by the British to be the administrative seat of Basutoland. Relieved of that title in 1871, it was again capital from 1884 until independence in 1966. It then became capital of independent Lesotho and since the 1970s has undergone a period of rapid expansion. In 1998 a fire destroyed much of the commercial centre, which has subsequently been rebuilt.

Modern City

A branch line links Maseru with the South African railway system, and most of Lesotho's main paved roads converge on the city. The airport, 40 km away from the centre, offers internal services as well as flights to South Africa. Buses run within the city.

There are some small manufacturing industries, such as rugs and soap. The University of Lesotho is based in Roma, not far from the city.

Places of Interest

Kingsway is the main thoroughfare through the city and was for a long time the country's only paved road. The Catholic Cathedral of Our Lady of Victories is among the city's most prominent sights. Just outside the city centre is the Papal Pavilion, built to commemorate a papal visit. There are several weaving centres popular with tourists while Lancer's Gap, the scene of a famous nineteenth century victory over British forces, offers unrivalled views of Maseru.

Mashhad, Iran

Introduction

Mashhad, in Khorasan province in the northeast, is Iran's second largest city. It is an important religious centre, sacred to Shia Muslims as the burial place and shrine of Ali ar-Rida, the eighth Imam. The city lies in a rich agricultural region, and local wool supplies form the basis of its carpet export trade.

History

Originally a small village known as Sanabad, Mashhad gained prominence from the early ninth century when Ali ar-Rida was reputedly poisoned and martyred there. His shrine became a site of Shia pilgrimage. The city was sacked, and the shrine badly damaged, by the Mongols in the thirteenth century, and again by Uzbek and Turkmen invaders in the sixteenth century. Prospering under the Safavid dynasty, it was restored by Abbas I, Shah of Persia, in the early seventeenth century, and was later briefly made the capital of the Persian empire by Nader Shah, who ruled from 1736–47. Although Mashhad became the commercial centre of Khorasan province during the nineteenth century, its major growth took place from the 1950s under the rule of Mohammad Reza Pahlavi.

Modern City

In addition to its religious significance, Mashhad is an industrial, commercial and transportation centre. The principal manufactures are carpets, textiles and processed foods. The university was founded in 1947. A rail link through Mashhad from Iran to Turkmenistan and the rest of Central Asia opened in 1996.

Places of Interest

The city's main attraction is the shrine of Ali ar-Rida and surrounding complex, which also includes the Goharshad Mosque, museums, libraries and theological schools. The grave of the caliph Harun ar-Rashid, who died around AD 809, is also in the shrine. The shrine itself is closed to non-Muslims. To the northwest of Mashhad lie the ruins of the ancient city of Tus.

Mbabane, Swaziland

Introduction

Situated at the northern end of the Ezulwini valley in the west of Swaziland, Mbabane is the country's capital and its largest town. It is named after Chief Mbabane Kunene. Despite its position as the commercial hub, most of the major cultural attractions and government buildings are located in the small royal town of Lobamba. Mbabane is primarily of financial importance.

History

The first settlement appeared towards the end of the nineteenth century as farmers began to inhabit the area near the royal cattle kraal. The British created the town in 1902, when they established an administrative headquarters for the newly colonized Swaziland. The following year Mbabane was declared the capital, but the town did not experience much growth until the development of a railway link to Mozambique in 1964. During the 1970s and 80s there was a construction boom, particularly in the residential and commercial sectors. In 1992 King Mswati III declared Mbabane a city.

Modern City

There are two small industrial parks on the city outskirts providing for publishing, plant assembly, motor mechanics and warehousing. There are rail and international air services operating from Matsapha, 30 km away. Local transport is provided by bus.

Places of Interest

The Indingilizi Gallery is an important centre for Swazi arts. The major attractions in the town are shopping malls, in particular the Swazi Plaza which also houses the local tourist office and Mbabane market, at the southern end of Allister Miller St.

Medan, Indonesia

Introduction

The capital of Sumatra, Medan (field), is the third largest city in Indonesia, a trading centre and an important harbour. It is by the Deli River in northeast Sumatra. The architecture is of solid Dutch buildings from the colonial era and ramshackle housing. Medan, once the centre of Sumatra's plantation-based economy, is now the island's centre of commerce and industry. Earthquakes and religious violence have hit the area and the situation remains unstable.

History

Around 10,000 years ago, Neolithic hunters settled in the areas around what is now Medan. In the eleventh century Arab, Chinese and Indian traders arrived. Kampung Medan (Medan Village) was founded around 1590s. The first inhabitants came from the Karo community. The village did not develop until 1862, when the Dutch settled and opened tobacco plantations. Deli wrapper leaf for cigars rapidly became world famous. It was also here where modern Indonesian oil industry began. International investments were bigger here than in other areas of Indonesia. Labourers were brought into Medan from China, India, Java and Madura. The population rose tenfold from 1880 to 1920. In 1915, Medan became the capital of North Sumatra Province. Among the first modern machine printed books, newspapers and magazines in Indonesia were published in Medan.

Modern City

Standards have fallen owing to economic turmoil. Industries include bricks, tile and machinery and exports include oil, rubber and palm oil. With a limited rail network, bus is the chief form of transport. There is an international airport (Polonia Airport). The city's two universities, The University of North Sumatra and The Islamic University of North Sumatra, were established in 1952.

Places of Interest

The sultan of Delis' palace, built by the Dutch in the nineteenth century, is the chief historical building. The Mosque, one of Indonesia's biggest, was built in 1906 in Moorish style. The ceremonial palace of the sultans of Deli, Istana Maimoon, was completed in 1888. Built in 1921, the Immanuel Protestant Church is an example of art-deco colonial architecture. Kampung Keling, the original centre of Medan's Indian community, has a temple (Sri Mariamman) built in 1884. There is a Military Museum displaying weapons used in the War of Independence and paintings showing struggles against the Dutch. The Museum of North Sumatra covers the region's culture and history. The Crocodile Farm, the largest in Indonesia, has regular performances of men fighting the animals.

Medellín, Colombia

Introduction

In the Aburrá Valley in the Cordillera Central, northwest Colombia, the industrial city of Medellín is the capital of the Antioquia region and the country's second largest city. It is on the tributary of River Cauca and flanked by the Porce River.

History

Little is known about the earliest inhabitants of the area, although the Quimbaya were resident in the region. The nearby Muisca people and the Taironas people of the Caribbean coast were the most powerful and sophisticated Pre-Columbian cultures and presented strong opposition to invading colonists. In Aug. 1541 the Conquistador Luis Tejelo defeated indigenous resistance and claimed the Aburrá Valley, but, sidetracked by the search for El Dorado, it wasn't until 1616 that the hamlet of San Lorenzo de Aburrá was founded. Having moved to its present site, in 1674 the town was established and named Villa de Nuestra Señora de la Candelaria de Medellín. It was named after a village in Extremadura. The town was centred around a local gold mining industry.

Because of the isolation and difficult terrain, Medellín remained cut off from the rest of Colombia and changed little over the subsequent years. In the nineteenth century Antioquia became a centre of coffee production and the only place in Colombia to grow the plant on small holds and not plantations. It became the regional capital in 1862 taking over from Santa Fe de Antioquia, 80 km northwest of Medellín. But it wasn't until the arrival of rail at the end of the nineteenth century that the city began to expand rapidly. The Ferrocarril de Antioquia connected the Cordillera Central with the Atlantic rail and boosted the lucrative coffee trade which became Colombia's chief export. The first textile mill opened in Medellín at the turn of the century and the city soon became the country's industrial centre. The city grew with the arrival of migrants attracted by work prospects. Cheap foreign competition affected the textile industry in the second half of the twentieth century and the void was filled with cocaine production which intensified from the 1970s. The illegal business reached its height in the 1980s with the Medellín cartel dominating the market. Medellín became Colombia's second largest city and shanty towns sprung up on the slopes around the city. The control of the Medellín cartel slipped when its leader Pablo Escobar was arrested in 1993, control transferring for 2 years to the Cali cartel, but cocaine production and distribution continued in Medellín.

Modern City

A highly industrialized city, Medellín is the national textile centre and one of the largest coffee production centres. It also has a large steel industry as well as food processing, chemical manufacturing and leather goods. Since the late 1970s Medellín has been infamous as a major centre of cocaine production and distribution and for the consequential violence. The city is accessible by road, rail and air. José María Córdoba international airport is 30 km southeast of Medellín. Since 1995 the city has had its own metro. The city's university was founded in 1822.

Places of Interest

The Basílica de la Candelaria church is one of the few remaining colonial buildings, as is the Veracruz church. Built between 1791–1802, the latter has a Baroque façade and triple bell chamber. The Basílica Metropolitana built in the early twentieth century, is said to be South America's largest brick building. Museums include the Museo de Antioquia with displays of works by the Colombian artist Fernando Botero, the Museo de Arte Moderno and the Museo Etnologico Miguel Angel Builes. The city's botanical gardens have an orchid display. Murals by Antioquian artist Pedro Nel Gómez inspired by Mexican muralism can be seen on various buildings. On the Cerro Nutibara hill, a replica of a typical Antioquian village has been recreated, the Pueblito Paisa.

Melbourne, Australia

Introduction

Situated at the apex of Port Phillip Bay in southeast Australia's Bass Strait, Melbourne is the country's second city after Sydney and capital of Victoria state. The city enjoys a temperate climate with the Dandenong ranges to the east and basalt plains to the west. Named in honour of the nineteenth century British prime minister, it served as the national capital until 1927 when it was succeeded by Canberra.

History

Europeans first made an appearance in 1802 when two naval captains, John Murray and Matthew Flinders, led separate expeditions to what is now Port Phillip Bay. The following year the bay was settled by a group of soldiers and convicts under Captain David Collins but, finding conditions hard, they soon left. John Batman secured a land deal with the local Aboriginals in 1835. However, his was a short stay and it was John Fawkner, arriving shortly afterwards, who built a settlement. It developed greatly during his long and prosperous life.

Melbourne was officially named in 1837 and 5 years later it received town status. It was planned on a rectangular grid by Robert Hoddle in 1840. City status was conferred after another 2 years and it became capital of the newly established state of Victoria in 1851. It was around this time that the city population began expanding rapidly on the back of a gold rush. However, as the white population doubled and then doubled again in little more than 3 years, the Aboriginal population fell. By 1860 there were only 2,000 Aborigines in the entire state.

Modern City

Melbourne is a key financial, communications and political centre. Other important industries include metal work, engineering, biotechnology, food processing and manufacturing, and the city's role as a port remains vital to Victoria's economy.

The city is well served by road, rail, sea and air and public transport includes an extensive tram network and a small underground rail system. Melbourne has traditionally been seen as sophisticated but also rather conservative. It is, however, extremely cosmopolitan, a result of the large number of immigrants who have come to the city since the time of the gold rush. Today over 100 nationalities are represented, with large populations of Cambodians, Chinese, Italians, Poles, Turks, Vietnamese and Yugoslavs, and one of the biggest Greek populations of any city in the world. Some 150 languages are spoken in the city.

Melbourne architecture is a mix of fine Victorian buildings alongside state of the art structures, like the 66-floor Rialto Towers, built in 1985. Federation Square, the redevelopment and construction of an entire 3.8 ha city block, was completed in Oct. 2002. It forms a link between the CBD and Yarra River over the Jolimont Rail Yards and has spurred the development of the north bank of the Yarra.

There are many distinguished museums, galleries and theatres, and the annual Melbourne International Arts Festival, first held in 1986, staged over 200 performances in 2001 at a cost of A\$16 m. Notable cultural figures who have resided in Melbourne include author Peter Carey, singer Nellie Melba, contemporary artists Howard Arkely and Jeffrey Smart and, more recently, Kylie Minogue. Sport also plays a major role in the lives of most Melburnians, with the city hosting international cricket, the Melbourne Cup, the Australian Tennis Open and numerous top-flight Australian Rules and rugby league teams. The city hosted the Commonwealth Games in 2006.

Places of Interest

The city's oldest building is the Mitre Tavern, constructed in 1837. Other sites of historical interest are the Old Gaol, where Ned Kelly was hanged in 1880, La Trobes' cottage, location of Victoria's first government, the restored ship Polly Woodside, originally built in 1885 and now the centrepiece of the Maritime Museum, and Captain Cook's cottage. The cottage was transported from Yorkshire and reassembled in Fitzroy Gardens in 1934.

Important museums include the Melbourne Museum, opened in 2000 by Museum Victoria, the State museum which has a collection of 16 m items. There are also museums dedicated to ancient Hellenic culture, immigration, gold, the Olympic Games, and Chinese Australian history. The State gallery, the National Gallery of Victoria, was founded in 1861 and is Australia's oldest public art gallery.

Popular attractions include Australia's oldest zoo, which houses 350 species and was founded in 1862, and the aquarium, which opened in 2000. The Crown Entertainment Complex and Victorian Arts Centre are major entertainment venues. The observation deck at Eureka Tower is the highest public vantage point in a building in the Southern Hemisphere, at 285 m.

Mexico City, Mexico

Introduction

The capital of Mexico, Mexico City is situated in the southern part of the high central plateau that is the Valley of Mexico. Surrounded by mountains, the city is built on the site of lakes that were filled in by the Aztecs to prevent flooding. Consequently there are problems of stability. There is no winter although the rainy season occurs between May and Sept.

History

Archaeological evidence points to habitation around a network of lakes 20,000 years ago. This became the metropolis of Teotihuacán, with around 200,000 inhabitants, 50 km northeast of Mexico City. Founded by the Aztecs as Mexico-Tenochtitlán in the fourteenth century, the settlement was a city of causeways and stone buildings built in the middle of a lake. When Hernán Cortés attacked Mexico-Tenochtitlán in 1521, the city covered around 13 km^2 of reclaimed land, equal to any European city of the time.

Having destroyed Tenochtitlán, Cortés built his own colonial city, incorporating the stones of the Aztec temples and palaces into the construction. This became the capital of the Viceroyalty of New Spain. The original site of Mexico City, for both the Aztecs and the Conquistadors, is now the historic centre at the heart of the city with the Plaza de la Constitución (more commonly known as the *Zócalo*) as its focus.

Despite the splendour and grandeur of Spanish buildings, the capital of the most powerful colonial empire of the time was a shadow of the Aztec's Tenochtitlán. War and disease decimated its population. It took until the early years of the twentieth century to attain the same population the Aztec capital had had in 1519. Even so, Mexico City became the most important centre of the New World and was Mexico's dominant social and commercial urban area. Consequently, it was a target for invaders and was captured by both the French and the USA during the nineteenth century. Mexico City became the country's capital when the country finally achieved independence in 1821. In 1917 President Carranza's new constitution established the city as the Republic's Federal Capital (The Distrito Federal), separate from the country's 31 states.

From 1930 onwards, coupled with increasing industrialization, Mexico City expanded rapidly in size and population. Much of the old city was destroyed. In 1985 the city suffered a major earthquake that killed more than 10,000 people and inflicted widespread damage on the city.

Modern City

Mexico City is the country's political, cultural, economic and financial centre and is highly industrial. Industries include construction, chemicals, plastics, cement, textiles and tourism. Currently the city produces a third of the country's industry and employs more than half of its industrial workforce. The surrounding region is mainly agricultural.

Millions of tourists visit the city every year, making tourism one of Mexico's major industries. Even so, pollution is a major problem. The pollutants become trapped in the bowl of the city by the surrounding mountains leaving permanent smog. A further problem is the number of people living in abject poverty in the city's numerous shantytowns or *ciudades perdidas*. There is a high disparity between the rich and poor, and a large contrast between the generally privileged minority population of European parentage and the poverty of many of the Indian population. A continuous migration from rural areas continues to swell the city's population, especially in the shantytowns. Crime is a problem.

Mexico City is accessible both nationally and internationally by air, rail and road. Much of the city is served by metro.

Places of Interest

The *Zócolo* square is the colonial heart of the city, and is the site of the Metropolitan Cathedral and the Palacio Nacional. Once the Viceroy's palace and residence of Hernán Cortés, the Palacio was built on the Aztec palace of Montezuma. Another important Aztec structure was the Templo Mayor. A centre of worship, the ruins of this double pyramid lie on the east side of the sixteenth century Metropolitan Cathedral, although much was used to build the cathedral itself. There is now a museum adjacent to the site. Mexico city's other museums include the National Anthropological Museum, the National Art Museum and the Diego Rivera Museum. The work of this famous muralist can be seen across the city, as can works by David Alfaro Siqueiros.

Miami, United States of America

Introduction

Miami is coextensive with Dade county and is one of the largest cities on the 'Gold Coast'. Located between the Florida Everglades and the Atlantic Ocean, Miami is a gateway between the United States and Latin America. With its favourable location, extensive beaches and subtropical climate, Miami is one of the world's most popular tourist destinations.

History

Originally inhabited by Native Americans, the site occupied by modern day Miami was first settled by Europeans in 1567 when the Spanish built a mission. In 1835 the US Army constructed a fort and Miami (meaning 'great water') was founded in 1870. It was incorporated as a city in 1896. The arrival of a railroad transformed the city's fortunes and saw the advent of the tourist trade. In the 1920s a property boom and the arrival of multinational companies were a further boost to prosperity although two hurricanes in 1926 and 1935 caused severe damage.

After World War II, Miami beach became a popular area for celebrities while large numbers of Cuban immigrants fleeing from Fidel Castro's regime also moved to the city, helping create a vibrant Hispanic community. Economically the city suffered in the 1960s and 70s, but the strengthening of links with Latin America and an increase in tourism saw Miami back on its feet by the 1980s. In 1992 Hurricane Andrew devastated the suburbs of Miami. At the time it was the costliest natural disaster in US history.

Modern City

More than half of Miami's economy relies on tourism. There are numerous hotels and leisure resorts, mainly around the Miami Beach area. In the last 20 years the economy has diversified with food processing, fishing, construction, printing and the manufacture of electronic equipment among the most important industries. Miami is also a trade and financial centre linking the United States and Latin America.

The city is served by Miami International Airport. Supershuttle minivans offer a 24-h transportation service and there are also Metrobus and Metro rail systems. There is a Greyhound bus terminal and a train station. Institutions of higher education in Miami include the University of Miami, Barry College, Florida Memorial College and the International Fine Arts College.

Places of Interest

The Art Deco District in Miami Beach has some of the best examples of Art Deco architecture in the United States. Major cultural institutions include the Museum of Science, the Bass Museum, the Wolfsonian Museum and the Historical Museum of Southern Florida. The Dade County Auditorium houses a resident symphony orchestra and a ballet company. Among the maritime attractions are the Miami Seaquarium and numerous water sports and beach recreation facilities.

Little Havana, a few miles west of downtown Miami, hosts a festival in March and has Cuban restaurants, shops and memorials. The Miami Dolphins American football team and the Florida Marlins baseball team are both based at the Sun Life Stadium (formerly known as the Joe Robbie Stadium).

Milan, Italy

Introduction

Milan is in northern Italy, and is situated in the Po river basin. The city is the capital of the region of Lombardy and of the province of Milan. It is the country's prosperous manufacturing and commercial heartland and is a leading European centre for finance.

History

Milan is believed to have been founded by Celtic tribes who settled along the Po River in the seventh century BC. The Romans occupied the town in 222 BC, naming it Mediolanum ('Middle of the Plain'). The town occupied a key position on the trade routes between Rome and North Western Europe and this ensured its growth and prosperity. Charlemagne chose Milan as the site to declare the freedom of Christians. Milan endured centuries of barbarian invasion, but by the eleventh century it was a bishopric and a free commune with autonomous government which had established itself as the leading city in Lombardy. Despite increasing prosperity, the city became embroiled in conflict with the neighbouring towns of Pavia, Como, Lodi and Cremona. The Holy Roman Emperor, Frederick I opted to exploit these rivalries in order to bring Milan under imperial control. His troops lay siege to the city for 9 months in 1162. Following its capture, there was widespread destruction. The city and its allies took revenge by forming the Lombard League that defeated the emperor's army at Legano in 1176.

In 1237 imperial forces inflicted another defeat on the city, and the loss of the battle of Cortenuova triggered a power struggle between two of the most powerful families in the city. The Torriani appealed to popular support whereas the Viscontis wanted power to reside with the aristocracy only. The Visconti faction triumphed at the Battle of Desio in 1277, and thus ensured their position as hereditary rulers of Milan for nearly 200 years. In 1450 the city was besieged by an army led by a renegade general, Francesco Sforza. Sforza's forces occupied Milan and Sforza himself took over the government of the city. Louis XII of France captured the Duchy in 1499, and the city remained under French control until 1513 when the Sforzas successfully recaptured it only to suffer a second French occupation 2 years later under Francis I. A decade of conflict was resolved in 1529 when a peace treaty formally ceded Milan to the Sforzas, however the premature death of the Duke in 1535 meant that the city fell under Spanish influence. This proved disastrous for Milan and its thriving economy stagnated. Spanish rule finally ended in 1706 and in 1713 Milan was passed to Austria under the Treaty of Utrecht. In 1797, Napoléon made Milan the capital of his Cisalpine Republic and, 5 years later, of the Italian republic. He chose the city to crown himself King of Italy in 1805. After a short-lived occupation by Austria, the troops of Vittorio Emanuele II and Napoléon III defeated the Austrian forces at the Battle of Magenta and in 1859 Milan was incorporated into the new unified Kingdom of Italy. The city was heavily bombed during World War II but was rebuilt and grew to become the economic and financial heart of modern Italy.

Modern City

Malpensa airport is 45 km from the centre of town and operates intercontinental flights. Linate airport is 7 km from the centre and handles domestic, European and intercontinental flights.

Most mainline trains arrive and depart from the Stazione Centrale. Intercity buses come into the Stazione Centrale. The Stazione Nord offers connections to Como, Erba and Varese.

Milan is also well served by road, there are connections to the south via the A1 motorway, to the east and west via the A4 and to the north via the A8/A9. Milan has a comprehensive Metro and bus system.

Milan's industries are predominantly mechanical and include the manufacture of motor vehicles, airplanes, motorcycles and electrical appliances. Other important industries include textiles, chemicals, paper and rubber. Milan is also the centre of Italy's publishing, advertising, design and fashion industries.

Milan hosted Expo 2015 under the theme 'Feeding the planet, Energy for life'.

Places of Interest

The white marble gothic Duomo is the third largest church in Europe. It was founded in 1386 by Gian Galezzo Visconti in the hope that the Virgin Mary would grant him a male heir. It took over 400 years to build. The façade is a mixture of Gothic and Baroque styles.

The Galleria Vittorio Emanuele is one of the earliest and most elegant shopping malls in the world. Built in 1877 by Giuseppe Mangoni, the Gallery's features include mosaic floors and a vast glass barrel vaulted roof.

The Pinacoteca di Brera is housed in a seventeenth century Palazzo di Brera and includes the largest and most important collection of works of the Venetian school outside Venice. Notable exhibits include the Monte Feltro altarpiece by Piero della Francesca, *The Meal at Emmaus* by Caravaggio, *Pietà* by Bellini and *The Dead Christ* by Mantegna.

The fifteenth century renaissance church of Santa Maria delle Grazie was built by the Dominicans and was finished by Bramante. The former refectory of the Monastery (Cenacolo Vinciano) houses Leonardo da Vinci's fresco of *The Last Supper*. The painting is permanently under restoration. The Museo Nazionale della Scienza e Tecnica has exhibits devoted to the exploration of Leonardo's inventions and his works of art.

The Teatro alla Scala is renowned as the world's most famous opera house. Verdi and Toscanini both conducted at La Scala and it was here that Maria Callas made her name. The theatre was built between 1776 and 1778 on the site of a church. The Museo del Teatro contains operatic memorabilia, including Verdi's top hat.

The Neo-classical Arco di Porta Ticinese (built 1801–14) leads to the Navigli district of Milan. The medieval canal system features footbridges designed by Leonardo da Vinci. Known as the Venice of Lombardy, this area of narrow pedestrian alleyways now has open-air markets and cafés.

Milwaukee, United States of America

Introduction

Milwaukee is on the Milwaukee River on the shore of Lake Michigan in the southeastern corner of Wisconsin. The largest city in the state, it is the seat of Milwaukee county and one of the leading industrial cities in the United States as well as a port. For many years Milwaukee was famous as the base of the American brewing industry.

History

Several Native American communities lived in the area now occupied by modern day Milwaukee, using the shore of Lake Michigan and the confluence of three local rivers as a meeting point. In the 1800s French fur traders settled in the area. By the nineteenth century the area had attracted the attention of land speculators. Milwaukee was incorporated as a city in 1846, taking its name from a Potawatomi Indian phrase meaning 'gathering place by water'. Wisconsin became a state 2 years later.

By 1850, German immigrants had established a dozen breweries and 225 bars in the city. Milwaukee became an important trading centre, shipping goods from farms in Wisconsin across the United States and to Europe. After the Civil War the growth of manufacturing brought more immigrants to the city, including many from Italy and Poland.

In the first half of the twentieth century, Milwaukee gained a reputation for efficient public services. Manufacturing grew during World War I, contracted during the depression but grew again in World War II. In the late 1960s the brewing industry began to decline, culminating in the closure of the Pabst brewery in 1996. Ambitious renewal projects got the city back on its feet. In 1982 the Grand Avenue Mall opened, acting as a catalyst for the

investment of over $1 bn. in redevelopment programmes, including the building of a new sports stadium and a convention centre.

Modern City

Despite the decline of the brewing industry one major brewer, Miller, is still based in the city. Milwaukee is an important marketing and distribution centre for Wisconsin's agricultural produce including grain, dairy products and fruit. Iron and steel industries are still strong although manufacturing's importance as a whole has fallen. Several major banks and insurance companies are based in the city and the service sector has expanded rapidly in recent years. As a port Milwaukee serves the Great Lakes and there is a deepwater canal.

Milwaukee is connected to Chicago via the Interstate 94 highway and is served by General Mitchell International Airport. There is an Amtrak rail station, a Greyhound bus terminal and an excellent public transport system. Educational institutions include the University of Wisconsin at Milwaukee, Concordia University of Wisconsin, Marquette University, the Milwaukee Institute of Art and Design and the Milwaukee School of Engineering.

Places of Interest

Major cultural attractions include the Milwaukee Art Museum, Charles Allis Art Museum, the Milwaukee Public Museum and Mitchell Park Conservatory while the Miller Brewery Company offers tours of its facility. Milwaukee has resident ballet and theatre companies as well as a symphony orchestra. Historical buildings include Saint Josaphat's Basilica where the dome is modelled on St Peter's in Rome. The Annunciation Greek Orthodox Church, designed by Frank Lloyd Wright, City Hall and Pabst Mansion are other architectural attractions.

Whitnall Park houses a nature centre and botanical gardens while the Mitchell Park Domes has examples of tropical plant life. Milwaukee County Zoo is another popular attraction. The city has major league baseball and basketball teams, although you have to travel 100 miles north to Green Bay to see Wisconsin's major league American football team, the Packers.

Minneapolis–St Paul, United States of America

Introduction

Minneapolis and St Paul are adjacent cities on opposite banks of the Mississippi River in Minnesota. Collectively they are known as the Twin Cities metropolitan region and they dominate the state's economic activities. St Paul, to the east, is the state capital of Minnesota and is built on seven hills while the terrain in Minneapolis is relatively flat.

History

The sites of modern-day Minneapolis and St Paul were originally inhabited by Sioux Indians. In 1819 a fort was built at the junction of the Minnesota and Mississippi rivers as a stopping off point for settlers heading west. In 1838 a French-Canadian trader Pierre Parrant became the first settler in the area occupied by modern-day St Paul, naming the settlement 'Pig's Eye' after his own nickname. The area was renamed St Paul after a nearby chapel in 1841. In 1849 St Paul was made the capital of Minnesota territory, a status it maintained when Minnesota entered the Union 9 years later.

In 1872, the merging of a fort with a Franciscan mission formed the new city of Minneapolis to the west of St Paul, its name being a hybrid of the Sioux word for water and the Greek word for city. The Twin Cities thrived with the arrival of a railroad. Minneapolis established itself as a centre for timber and flour production while St Paul developed livestock shipping and manufacturing industries. The flour industry in Minneapolis declined after World War I although it remained a major centre for the grain trade. In the latter half of the twentieth century both cities underwent substantial redevelopment programmes.

Modern City

The Twin Cities are served by Minneapolis-St Paul International Airport, approximately 10 miles south of both cities. The Amtrak rail station is midway between the two cities while the Metropolitan Council Transit Operations runs a bus service serving the entire Twin Cities area. Both cities have their own Greyhound bus terminals.

The Twin Cities are noted for their low crime rate and cleanliness. St Paul is the seat of Minnesota's state government. Industries include chemicals, processed food, electronic equipment, printed materials, petroleum and plastics. Major industries in Minneapolis include food processing, medical research, publishing, electrical equipment and transport machinery. Collectively the two cities are the base of around 30 of the 500 highest-ranked corporations in the United States.

Institutions of higher education in Minneapolis include Augsburg College, the Minneapolis College of Art and Design and the Twin Cities' campus of the University of Minnesota. Among others, St Paul contains Metropolitan State University, Hamline University, Concordia College-St Paul, the College of St Catherine and William Mitchell College of Law.

Places of Interest

Minneapolis has more high-rise buildings than St Paul, where the architecture is more traditional. The tallest structure is the IDS Center, which is formed of several glass-enclosed bridges, known as skyways. The Mall of America, the biggest shopping and entertainment complex in the United States, is 20 min away from both cities.

The Walker Art Center, the Frederick R. Weisman Museum, the Minneapolis Institute of Arts and the American Swedish Institute are among the most prominent cultural institutions in Minneapolis. The city also houses the historic Orpheum and Sate Theatres and has a resident orchestra and theatre company. The Hubert H. Humphrey Metrodome hosts the city's baseball and American football teams.

Minnesota's first-ever permanent structure, Fort Snelling, can be seen in St Paul. Other buildings of interest in the eastern half of the Twin Cities include the State Capitol and the City Hall. By the City Hall is a 36 ft. revolving sculpture by Carl Milles called Vision of Peace, created in the 1930s. St Paul's museums include the Science Museum of Minnesota, the Minnesota Museum of Art, the Minnesota Historical Society History Center and the Gibbs Farm Museum.

Minsk (Mansk), Belarus

Introduction

Minsk, lying on the Svisloch River, is the capital of Belarus and of the oblast of Minsk. Almost completely destroyed during World War II, it was rebuilt by the Soviets as a showpiece city. Belarus' most important industrial city and a major railway junction, it became capital of the newly independent state in 1991.

History

The first recorded mention of Minsk dates back to 1067 though it is believed that there was a settlement in place considerably earlier. Its early history was dominated by the dynastic wars between the houses of Kiev and Polacak and by 1101 it was the seat of a Principality. In 1116 the city came under Lithuanian control but was ravaged by Kievans 3 years later and again in 1129. Polacak reclaimed it in 1146 and formed a loose alliance with Lithuania over the ensuing decades. The city was effectively under Lithuanian control in the fourteenth century.

In the early sixteenth century the city came under attack from Muscovites and Tartars and in 1547 suffered major damage in a fire. Lithuania, in a weakened state, embarked on a political alliance with Poland in 1569 and Minsk was adopted as the operational centre in the wars against Ivan IV of Russia in 1563–79. Minsk prospered in the second half of the sixteenth century as numerous professional guilds emerged. Under Polish influence, the Orthodox religion lost out to closer ties with the Vatican, a situation that was to lead to religious strife.

Russia launched an attack on Lithuania and Belarus in 1652, taking Minsk 3 years later. A savage regime was imposed for all those not accepting Russian Orthodoxy and in 1657 a city rebellion was quashed. By the time the Russian forces were withdrawn in 1661, Minsk had been devastated and was beset by plague. A peace treaty, signed with Russia in 1667, allowed for the Russians to intervene under certain circumstances on behalf of the Orthodox population. Growth continued in the early part of the eighteenth century with the building of roads and canals and improved communications with neighbouring cities. Minsk suffered famines, plagues and, in 1737, a devastating fire. The Russians occupied the city in 1733, ostensibly in defence of the Orthodox minority, and in 1793 Minsk again fell to Russia.

In 1812, Napoléon and his troops took the city as they marched on Russia, but it fell back under Russian control when Napoléon retreated. There were severe typhus epidemics in 1848 and 1853. Two Catholic uprisings in the 1830s and 1860s were put down by the Russians, who imprisoned thousands and sent many more to Siberia. Russia failed to suppress Belorussian culture and history and, by the end of the nineteenth century, there was a growing tide of nationalism. A power struggle between the Nationalists and Russian Bolsheviks in 1917–19 culminated in the execution of hundreds of thousands of nationalists in the forests surrounding Minsk in the 1930s.

Nazi Germany destroyed the city in 1941. Virtually no buildings survived and the Jewish population, 40% of the total prior to German arrival, was decimated. The Soviets took control of Minsk once again towards the end of the war, carrying out a mass deportation of suspected Nazi collaborators and embarking on the rebuilding of the city. Modern Minsk is a well-planned city filled with avenues and parks and grand, if not always aesthetically pleasing, buildings. The city's population tripled in the 30 years up to 1989. When Belarus gained independence in 1991, Minsk was named the capital.

Modern City

Today Minsk is home to many cultural and educational institutions, and the few old buildings remaining, such as the Marlinsky Cathedral and the Bernadine Monastery, are being restored to their former glory. Industrially, machine manufacturing dominates although textiles are also important. It is served by two major airports, is at the centre of a number of major rail routes and has an underground system.

Places of Interest

Noteworthy architecture of the twentieth century includes the art deco Government House, the National Opera and Ballet and Academy of Sciences from the 1930s. The main thoroughfare is Praspekt Skarny, site of the Polish Catholic church. Other churches of interest are the baroque cathedral of St Dukhawski, the seventeenth century cathedral of St Peter and Paul and the nineteenth century Mary Magdeline church.

Mogadishu, Somalia

Introduction

Mogadishu is the largest city and capital of Somalia. The city is by the Indian Ocean, and is one of the country's major ports and commercial and financial centres. In Somalia's civil war (1990–94), the city was devastated but had to cope with a huge number of refugees. Large parts of the city are still in ruins.

History

Mogadishu was one of the first Arab settlements on the East African coast. The city was founded in the tenth century and by the twelfth century it had become a trade centre. During the sixteenth century it was governed by Portugal. In 1871, Mogadishu was taken over by the sultan of Zanzibar, who leased it to the Italians in 1892. The Italians bought the city in 1905. It was then the capital of Italian Somaliland until 1960. In World War II, Mogadishu was occupied by the British. Following Somalia's independence in 1960, the city remained the capital.

Modern City

Much of Mogadishu's manufacturing was destroyed in the civil war. Exports include bananas, skins and fish products. The capital has an international airport, and is linked by road with Ethiopia and Kenya, although there are few cars and buses within the city. Mogadishu has a university (founded 1954), and schools of Islamic law, industrial arts, public health and veterinary science.

Places of Interest

The National Museum is in Mogadishu's Garesa Palace, built by the sultan of Zanzibar in the late nineteenth century. The Mosque of Fakr ad-Din was built in 1269. There is a national park just outside Mogadishu.

Monaco, Monaco

Introduction

The city of Monaco is on top of a rocky promontory on the French Riviera. It is the capital and one of four districts of the Principality of Monaco. An old fortified town, it is the home of Prince Rainier III, Chief of State. Its ancient name is Monoecus.

History

From the sixth to the tenth century, Barbarians and Saracens occupied the territory. In 1191 Emperor Henry VI granted sovereignty of the country to the Genoese. In 1215 they settled on the rock and began building a fortress. This fortress of Monaco was seized in 1297 by François Grimaldi and his supporters. The Grimaldis allied themselves with France, except from 1524 to 1641 when they were under the protection of Spain. In 1731 Monaco passed into the female line. The heiress, Louise Hippolyte, married the Count of Torigni who took the name and arms of Grimaldi. In 1793 the royal family was dispossessed by the French Revolution, but with the fall of Napoléon in 1815 Monaco was placed under the protection of Sardinia by the Treaty of Vienna and the Grimaldis returned. In 1861 the country was again ceded to France and in 1865 a customs union was formed. The constitution of 1911 made provisions for an elected national council. This was dissolved in 1959 by Prince Rainier III after a dispute over budget and a national assembly was appointed in 1961. Following disagreements with France over tax rules a new constitution was promulgated in 1962. The national council was restored with the hereditary monarch as chief of state. In 1993 Monaco was admitted to the UN and in 1997 celebrated the 700th anniversary of the Grimaldi family.

Modern City

Tourism is of major importance. The nearest international airport is in Nice with Air Monaco providing a helicopter service to Fontvieille which takes 7 min. It is 20 min by train journey to La Condamine, the business district to the west of the bay. There are regular buses to the surrounding French countryside. Revenue comes from state-operated monopolies on tobacco and postage stamps, from franchises on radio, television and the casinos, and from taxes imposed since 1962. The town is the centre of the Monaco Grand Prix which takes place every May. In Jan. the Festival of Sainte-Dévote celebrates Monaco's religious traditions. A number of escalators, elevators and steps connect the district to the rest of the principality.

Places of Interest

The Prince's Palace was built in the thirteenth century. It is the home of Prince Rainier III but 15 rooms, including the Throne Room are open to the public. The changing of the guard takes place every day at 11.55 am. In the south wing, the Musée des Souvenirs Napoléoniens has personal items that belonged to the Emperor. There is also a collection of eighteenth and nineteenth century art. The Saint-Martin Gardens lead to the Museum of Oceanography, founded in 1910. It is considered one of the best aquariums in Europe and has a collection of the work of Jacques Cousteau. The nineteenth century Romanesque Byzantine cathedral, built in La Turbie white stone is found near the Place du Palais. It contains the remains of many former princes

and also, Grace Kelly, the American film actress and wife of Prince Rainier III who was killed in a car crash in 1982. Steps down the Rampe Major (ancient fortifications) lead to the port.

Monrovia, Liberia

Introduction

Liberia's capital, Monrovia, on Bushrod Island and Cape Mesurado is the country's chief Atlantic port. The civil war has destroyed much of the city. In 2001, the UN imposed an embargo on Liberia, banning trade. In Feb. 2002, President Taylor declared a state of emergency, to contain tension in the regions around Monrovia. In May 2002, the UN renewed its sanctions. Businesses and schools closed down following rebel attacks outside Monrovia. Travel to the capital is not recommended.

History

Monrovia (originally called Christopolis) was founded in 1822 by the American Colonization Society, as a settlement for freed American slaves. The city was named after the US President James Monroe. The population consists of descendants of settlers from North America who arrived 1830–71 and domestic migrants. In 1961, Monrovia hosted a conference serving to launch the Organization of African Unity. In 1989–92 there was a civil war. In 1996, violence erupted again and has since damaged the country and its capital.

Modern City

Monrovia is linked to Guinea and Sierra Leone through the Mano River Union. Prior to the UN embargo, core exports were iron ore, diamonds, rubber, timber and coffee. Industry is limited to food processing. The capital, a centre for higher education in Liberia, has a university (founded in 1851). The city's architecture is characterized by ruined shacks and colonial buildings in the style of the US southern states. There is an international airport (Robertsfield Airport).

In June 2003 the city witnessed fighting between government troops and forces from Liberians United for Reconciliation and Democracy (Lurd), leaving 300 civilians dead, 1,000 injured and 250,000 displaced before a ceasefire was called. International peacekeeping forces arrived in Aug. 2003.

Places of Interest

The Liberia National Cultural Centre includes artists from 16 ethnic Liberian groups. Fort Norris has a statue of Liberia's first president, Joseph Jenkins Roberts. Sapo National Park is just outside the capital. Among important buildings in Monrovia are the Capitol (founded in 1958), the Executive Mansion (founded 1964), The Temple of Justice and the City Hall, though many have been damaged in the wars. There is a National Museum.

Monterrey, Mexico

Introduction

Monterrey is the third largest city in Mexico. The capital of the northeastern state of Nuevo León, Monterrey is situated in a valley between mountain chains. At an altitude of 530 m on the eastern slope of the Sierra Madre Oriental, the city is surrounded by the Cerro de la Silla (1,740 m) and Cerro de las Mitras (2,380 m) mountain ranges. Embedded between these mountains, the city has been called a city 'de perfiles', or of silhouettes, and is situated in the flood plain of the Río Santa Catarina.

History

The history of the area began in 1579. Don Luis Carvajal y de la Cueva was ordered to discover, pacify and populate an area of approximately 200 leagues in the north of the new territory. This area would eventually contain

Monterrey. Maltreatment of the indigenous population resulted in an Indian rebellion that forced the surviving Spanish to retreat from the area. Years later Diego de Montemayor, along with a few colleagues, returned to the area and managed a more successful colonization. On 20 Sept. 1596, 34 people founded San Luis Rey de Francia, a town that would become Nuestra Señora de Monterrey. This site was within reach of accessible gold, silver, lead, copper and zinc. In 1823 the city became the capital of the state of Nuevo León.

Although the city developed into the industrial capital of Mexico, floods and continuing battles with the indigenous population thwarted immediate advances. Restricted access to Mexico City further prevented progress and in 1775 the population was only about 250.

Monterrey's industrial history began in 1854 with the opening of the first factory. Within a year 324 mills and factories had been set up. The city became an important centre for wool and cotton. Industry flourished in the area during the *Porfiriato*, the period of Porfirio Díaz's 35 years of absolute rule of Mexico at the end of the nineteenth century. Growth was further bolstered by investors from Europe and the USA, attracted by tax concessions, and the city's proximity to the USA. During the 1880s the city became the principal centre in Mexico for iron and steel works, aided in 1882 by the opening of rail connections to Texas and Loredo. Since 1921 Monterrey has had 10,000 registered businesses including pottery, textiles and breweries. The city's historical centre has been transformed by modern urban design. A 4 year project in the mid-1980s culminated in the Gran Plaza, a merger of two plazas into one long centre.

In 1985, 2,000 buildings in Monterrey were destroyed in an earthquake.

Modern City

An important industrial centre, Monterrey is home to some of Mexico's largest industrial groups, including the cement makers CEMEX and the industrial consortia Axa and Vitro. The city is also a centre of commerce and culture. Pollution is a problem as the high mountains trap the emissions of local industries. A major transport hub, Monterrey is linked to Mexico's major cities by air, rail and road.

Places of Interest

The surrounding industrial outskirts are contrasted by the historical city centre, although the town has few examples of architecture dating back to the colonial period. Many interesting sites are based in the central Gran Plaza, including the eighteenth century pale yellow cathedral which contrasts with the Faro de Comercio (Commerce Lighthouse), a symbol of Monterrey's commercial progress. The city's museums include the Mexican History Museum and the Contemporary Art Museum.

Montevideo, Uruguay

Introduction

Situated in a wide bay on the north bank of the River Plate across from Buenos Aires, Montevideo is the capital of Uruguay, the country's chief port and only large city.

History

The regions indigenous inhabitants were the Charrúa, a tribe of hunter-gatherers. The garrison town of San Felipe y Santiago de Montevideo was founded in 1726 by the Spanish governor of Buenos Aires, Bruno Mauricio de Zabala, as a defence post against Portuguese attack from Brazil. A citadel was erected with strong walls. Montevideo served for the navy and developed into an important port but remained subject to territorial disputes between Spanish Argentina and Portuguese Brazil. The surrounding area lacked in natural resources, but there was an abundance of wild cattle to exploit.

In the early nineteenth century an independence movement emerged led by José Artigas succeeded in taking Montevideo from the Spanish. When Artigas was forced into exile, the movement was continued by Juan Antonio Lavalleja until Uruguayan independence was established in 1828. Montevideo was made the capital. Continuing post-Independence conflict between Argentina and Brazil affected the city's progress, as did civil war between the

Blancos and Colorados (named after the white and red uniforms worn respectively). Between 1843–51 it was occupied by the Argentine dictator, Juan Manuel de Rosas.

Between 1880–90 the government was in the hands of an unpopular military dictatorship. Despite the regime's brutality, Montevideo developed and prospered as its population expanded. In the early twentieth century an influx of European immigrants, especially Italian, led to rapid urban development. A cycle of political tension and military dictatorships continued throughout the twentieth century. The city remains at the heart of the struggle to reform and democratize Uruguay.

Modern City

The commercial and financial centre of Uruguay, Montevideo is also an important port which handles most of the country's trade. Exports include meat and wool and the city has a substantial fishing industry. Manufactures include textiles and soap while meatpacking, tanning and flour milling make up the principal industries. The city is served by road, rail, sea and air links. The Universidad de la República was founded in 1849 while the Universidad del Trabajo del Uruguay was established in 1878 to provide vocational training. Montevideo is a popular summer resort.

Places of Interest

Few original colonial buildings remain, although the well preserved Ciudad Vieja, or old town, forms the heart of the city. Rebuilt at the turn of the nineteenth century, the Iglesia Matriz cathedral is the city's oldest building. Built between 1742–80, the original entrance to the fortress walls, the Puerta de la Ciudadela, still exists. The Museo del Gaucho y de la Moneda is devoted to the traditional gauchos, or cowboys, of the Pampas and the Museo (Joaquín) Torres García displays the abstract and cubist paintings of this *Montevideño* artist.

Montreal, Canada

Introduction

Canada's second largest city, and the second largest French-speaking city in the world after Paris, Montreal is as near to the European coast as to Vancouver. Regarded as one of North America's most appealing cities, Montreal has developed a vibrant cosmopolitan city life despite fluctuating tensions between the French and minority English-speaking communities. Two-thirds of the city's people are of French extraction with the rest a mix including groups of Eastern European, Italian, Chinese, Greek, Jewish, South American and West Indian origin.

History

Known as Hochelaga by the Huron Indians, the first European to visit the site of Montreal was French navigator and explorer Jacques Cartier, during his second voyage to the New World in 1535–36. Cartier was welcomed by the Indians on the slope of the mountain he named Mont Réal. Fifty years later Samuel de Champlain, the founder of Quebec city, became the second French arrival.

The city was founded by Paul de Chomedey in May 1642. Naming his settlement Ville-Marie, De Chomedey protected it from Indian attack by building a stockade. Granted its civic charter 2 years later, the city's first hospital was founded in 1644 followed by a girls school in 1653. Montreal's population reached 1,500 by 1672.

The city expanded rapidly in the first half of the eighteenth century when farming developed beyond the fortifications. Colonization was encouraged, with landowners leasing portions of property to farming families under the French seigniorial system.

Having surrendered to British forces in 1760, the city became part of the British North American Empire in 1763 along with the rest of New France. After a brief occupation by American revolutionary forces in 1775, the city returned to British control after the abortive US siege of Quebec in 1776.

Montreal and Quebec were linked with the appearance of the first Canadian steamship in 1809. From 1844–49 Montreal was Canada's capital, a distinction lost after a mob burned the Parliament building. In the mid-nineteenth century fires destroyed hundreds of buildings and in 1857 an economic slump causing widespread bankruptcies.

By 1900 the city's population had reached 270,000, with several surrounding towns and villages swallowed by the growing metropolis. In 1909 Montreal's famous ice-hockey team, the Canadiens, was founded. The team has gone on to win more world championships than any of its rivals.

Modern City

The Montreal Metropolitan Corporation was established in 1959. Development as a major North American city was consolidated in the 1960s, with a number of significant achievements. Work started on the city's underground system in 1962, with the Métro's construction overseen by engineers from Paris' own system. The Métro was completed 6 months before the opening of Expo 67. The exhibition was an internationally renowned success and leant its name to the city's first Major-League baseball team (the first such franchise outside of the US): the Montreal Expos.

Tensions between the French and English speaking populations have long been a fact of city life, with Montreal the driving force behind Quebecois separatism. Clashes between the two groups culminated in the terrorist campaign fronted by the Front de Liberation du Quebec in the 1960s; leading many English-speaking residents to desert the city for the Anglophone Toronto.

Despite a French-speaking majority, English is still the language of commerce and industry with most business leaders coming from old Montreal English-speaking families.

Places of Interest

Montreal has many cultural attractions. The historic Vieux-Montreal quarter of the city, with its gracious squares and the mammoth Basilique de Notre-Dame is in contrast to the typically North American offices and skyscrapers downtown.

The Place des Arts is the major arts complex with a series of concert halls and theatres. Nearby is the Place Desjardins, a striking modern building comprising many retail and business units.

The Jardin Botanique is second in international status only to Kew Gardens in London. Other landmarks include the Musée des Beaux Arts, the Olympic Stadium and Basilique de Notre-Dame. Both the city's International Jazz Festival in June and its Just Pour Rire (Just for Laughs) comedy festival are world renowned, attracting thousands of visitors every year.

Moroni, Comoros

Introduction

Moroni is the capital city of Comoros. It is a port city on Ngazidja, the largest island of the archipelago.

History

While the area around Moroni may have been settled earlier, its development began in the fifteenth century with the arrival of Shirazi royal clans from Persia. They dominated the island until French occupation in the nineteenth century. Moroni became Comoros' administrative capital in 1958, succeeding Dzaoudzi (on the island of Mayotte). It became capital of independent Comoros in 1975.

Modern City

Moroni houses the presidential residence and government ministries. The local economy is reliant upon port activities. Other important industries include food and drink processing and building materials.

There is an international airport, Iconi, and road links to other major towns on the island.

Places of Interest

The city has an old quarter, the medina, with narrow streets and buildings which reflect Moroni's Arab origins. The CNDRS (Centre National de Documentation et de Recherches Scientifiques) houses a museum, library and information centre. The museum's exhibits include ninth century pottery and ancient Korans. The Alliance Franco-Comorienne hosts cultural shows and theatrical performances. A new mosque with a capacity of 6,000 people was inaugurated in July 1998.

Moscow (Moskva), Russia

Introduction

Located on the Moskva river, Moscow is the capital of Russia. Its power was established during the middle ages by its location on important trade routes and its role as centre of the Russian Orthodox Church. After losing its status as national capital to St Petersburg in the eighteenth century, it was not until 1917 after the Bolshevik revolution that it was re-designated capital. The heart of one of the world's superpowers for most of the twentieth century, since 1991 Moscow has striven to re-establish itself as a modern, forward-looking metropolis.

History

Moscow's origins date back to 1147, when Prince Yury Dolgoruky of Suzdal settled and built a wooden fortress on Borovitsky Hill, the site of the present Kremlin. Moscow was captured and burned by the Mongols in the invasion of 1236–40. Well placed on trade routes across European Russia, the city's importance as a trading and artisan centre grew, overtaking the older centres of Suzdal and Vladimir.

Moscow's authority was enhanced by the transfer of the seat of the Russian Orthodox Church from Vladimir in 1326, making it the centre of Russian Orthodoxy. It claimed the title of the Third Rome after the fall of Constantinople in 1453. By the second half of the fifteenth century, Moscow's status as the capital of a unified Russian state was unchallenged. During the reign of Ivan III (the Great), the Kremlin was enlarged and fortified. In 1547 two fires destroyed much of the city and in 1571 the Crimean Tatars captured Moscow, razing everything but the Kremlin and killing most of the city's population.

At the beginning of the seventeenth century Moscow was occupied by Polish troops, but was liberated by Prince Dmitry Mikhaylovich Pozharsky, and a merchant, Kuzma Minin, in 1612. This paved the way for the arrival of the Romanov Dynasty in 1613. A relatively peaceful period was marked by uprisings and protests by the poor against the imposition of salt tax, which exacerbated their already poor living conditions.

The Slavonic-Greek-Latin Academy, Russia's first higher educational institution, was established in 1687. Russia's first newspaper was published in Moscow in 1703. In 1712 Peter transferred the capital to St Petersburg, halting the development of Moscow. However, industry picked up, and by the end of the eighteenth century there were about 300 factories in Moscow, more than half of them textile mills.

Napoléon invaded Russia in 1812. Troops and civilians alike were evacuated as the city was burned and looted. However, Russian resistance, food shortages and the prospect of winter drove French troops out. In 1813 a major rebuilding programme was launched. Industry developed throughout the nineteenth century and the population tripled. The Moscow stock exchange was established, railways opened between St Petersburg and Moscow and in 1861 the serfs were emancipated.

After the 1917 revolution Moscow regained its status as capital and by 1939 the population had reached over 4 m. The city was subject to bombardments and a siege by the Germans in 1941, but counterattack salvaged the capital. Moscow celebrated its 800th anniversary in 1947 and hosted the summer Olympic Games in 1980. In 1991 the city was at the centre of an attempted hard-line coup against Mikhail Gorbachev, the defeat of which heralded the end of Soviet communism and the rise of Boris Yeltsin.

Modern City

Since the collapse of communism, Moscow's economy has moved from a purely manufacturing and industrial base and is now more reliant on financial and service industries. It remains Russia's heavy industrial powerhouse, with engineering, metalwork, textiles, chemicals and food processing particularly important.

While consumer goods are far more readily available than during the Soviet era, high unemployment persists. Organized crime is widespread and the city has gained a reputation for violence. In addition, in the late 1990s it was the subject of several terrorist attacks, blamed on Chechnyan separatists. More recent attacks include the subway bombings in March 2010 by two female suicide bombers which killed 40 people and a further attack by a suicide bomber in Jan. 2011 at Moscow's main airport, Domodedovo, which killed 35 people.

Moscow is at the centre of Russia's road and rail networks. It is also a major port, with the river Moskva accessible to small shipping and the Moscow Canal open to large vessels. Public transport is provided by the grand metro system, buses, trolley buses and streetcars.

The Ostankino Tower, a television and radio tower completed in 1967, is at 540 m in height the tallest freestanding structure in Europe. The City of Capitals Moscow Tower, at 301.6 m in height, was the tallest building in Russia and Europe between its completion in 2009 and 2012 when the Shard in London surpassed it. The Mercury City Tower, also in Moscow, has been Europe's tallest building (at 338.8 m) since its completion in 2013.

Places of Interest

Moscow's most visited sights are the Kremlin and Red Square. The Kremlin embraces palaces and cathedrals, including the Cathedral of the Annunciation from 1484, the Terem Palace from 1635 and the Grand Kremlin Palace. The Kremlin walls are fortified with 20 different towers. Red Square is the site of the Lenin Mausoleum and the onion-domed St Basil's Cathedral (1552). Moscow has many other outstanding Orthodox churches and a wealth of icons.

Other popular sights include the Bolshoi Theatre (home of the world famous ballet), Pushkin Square and the Old Arbat, a street market that attracts artists and musicians. Of the Stalinist-era buildings, Moscow State University, with its wedding-cake style construction, is among the most famous. The State Pushkin Museum of Fine Arts and the State Tretyakov Gallery both have international reputations, as do the Moscow Art Theatre and the State Circus. Luzhniki Park was the main venue for the 1980 Olympics, while outside the city centre are Gorky Central Park of Culture and Moscow Zoo.

Mosul, Iraq

Introduction

Iraq's third largest city, Mosul lies on the west bank of the River Tigris in the northwest of the country, close to the ruined Assyrian city of Nineveh. It is about 400 km from Baghdad.

History

During the Abbasid dynasty from the eighth century, Mosul gained commercial importance as a staging post on the caravan trade route between India, Persia and the Mediterranean. Its chief export was cotton, the modern term 'muslin' having been derived originally from the name of the city. In the thirteenth century the city was sacked in the Mongol invasions, but revived under Ottoman rule after 1534 as the Turks made it an administrative and commercial centre for the surrounding region. Ottoman rule lasted until the First World War, the British taking control in 1918 until Iraq's independence in 1932.

Mosul was abandoned by the Iraqi army during the US-led invasion in 2003, allowing Kurdish troops to enter the city on 11 April. US troops quickly took control but failed to prevent the breakdown of order and widespread looting. An interim administration was elected in May to represent the Kurdish, Turkoman and Assyrian Christian minorities as well as the Arab majority.

The city was abandoned by the Iraqi army for a second time in June 2014 following attacks by the Sunni Islamist group known as Islamic State (IS). Approximately half a million citizens subsequently fled the city and the entire Christian population was expelled by the new militant administration.

Modern City

Prior to the IS occupation the economy of the city was based on agricultural produce and livestock, oil production and refining (with large oilfields to the east and north of the city), cement factories, textiles and tanneries. The airport, and most road and rail links to Baghdad, were destroyed in fighting between the army and IS. Built in 1967, the University of Mosul had been an IS stronghold between the summer of 2014 and early 2017. The Iraqi army seized it in Jan. 2017 and revealed that buildings and artefacts including rare manuscripts had been burnt.

Places of Interest

The city has been an important centre for historical and archaeological study but war has taken its toll. Mosul Museum contained many archaeological finds from the ancient sites of Nineveh and Nimrud but was looted during the 2003 US-led invasion and the 2014 occupation by IS. The Mosque of Nebi Yunis was reputed to be the site of the burial place of the Biblical Jonah before the building was demolished by IS. Mosul was also home to the twelfth century Great Mosque of Al-Nuri and to several ancient churches, reflecting the historical Christian presence in the city. However, all of these—including the Clock and Latin Church, the Chaldean Catholic Church of Al-Tahira (the oldest part of which was built in AD 300) and the Syrian Orthodox Church—were destroyed by IS. The ruins of Bash Tapia Castle, the only remaining part of Mosul's city wall, were also severely damaged by the jihadist group.

Mumbai (Bombay), India

Introduction

Bombay was officially renamed Mumbai in 1996. The city lies on the west coast of India and comprises seven islands brought together by landfills and breakwaters to form Bombay Island. The Arabian Sea flanks the west coast of the island while the city's harbour, the focus of most of India's international trade, lies on the east coast.

History

Though there is evidence of human presence in the greater Mumbai region during the Stone Age, it was the Kolis, a tribe of aboriginal fishermen, who first settled on the islands. At around 1000 BC the region became an important maritime trading post with Egypt and Persia. It was ruled by Asoka's empire in the third century BC, the Calukyas during the sixth to eighth centuries AD, and then by the Silahara chiefs between the ninth and the thirteenth centuries. The settlement of Mahikavati was founded on Bombay Island as a defence against raids by the Khalji dynasty of Hindustan.

Mumbai became part of the kingdom of Gujarat in 1348 when it was conquered by invading Muslim forces. The island was then ceded to the Portuguese in 1534 by the ruler of Gujarat after a failed attempt by the Europeans to conquer Mahikavati in 1507. In 1661 it became part of the British Empire when Charles II of England married the sister of the King of Portugal. In 1668, Britain rented the island to the British East India Company though at this time the region was neither as rich nor as powerful as its mainland rivals.

In 1853, the first railway in Asia was constructed between Mumbai and Thana. This, coupled with the arrival of steam ships and the construction of the first spinning and weaving mills in 1857, made Mumbai the largest cotton market in India. When The American Civil War (1861–65) interrupted cotton supplies to Britain, Mumbai became the chief supplier of cotton on the world market. Though the end of the civil war was to bring about the collapse of trade prices, the prosperity generated by the period of conflict established Mumbai as an important trading post. The Suez Canal was opened in 1869 leading to further expansion and prosperity, although such progress also led to the overcrowding and poverty that still plague the city today.

The importance of the city is underlined by the crucial role it has performed in Indian politics over the last 150 years. In 1885 it played host to the first meeting of the Indian National Congress. By 1942, it was at the centre of India's drive for independence with the 'Quit India' resolution, Mohandas Gandhi's campaign to bring about the end of British rule. The partition of India and Pakistan in 1947 left great rifts in the country and exacerbated tensions within Mumbai. Riots and terrorist activity between 1956 and 1960 led to the partition of the state into Gujarat and Maharashtra. Mumbai is now the capital of Maharashtra.

On 25 Aug. 2003, two bombs killed over 50 people and injured over 150. The attacks targeted a jewellery market and the Gateway of India monument. No organization claimed responsibility but officials suggested the involvement of Kashmiri militants. Prime Minister Atal Bihari Vajpayee led a march of Hindus through the city in remembrance of the victims from all communities. Calls were made for the resignation of the Maharashtra government for failing to prevent a string of terrorist attacks on the city. In a further attack more than 180 people were killed in seven blasts that hit the city's rail network on 11 July 2006. In Nov. 2008, Mumbai was hit by a series of bombing and shooting attacks that killed 174 people and wounded approximately 300. The attacks were believed to have been carried out by members of Lashkar-e-Taiba, a militant Islamist organization based in Pakistan.

Modern City

The inhabitants of Mumbai form a diverse society made up of many different religions, nationalities and cultures; this is reflected not only in the political troubles suffered by the region but also in terms of the education and cultural facilities it has to offer. The city plays host to many concerts and festivals and it is the home of India's film industry, dubbed 'Bollywood' after its American counterpart. The industry is the world's largest of its kind, turning out over 800 films a year.

As well as the film and the cotton-textile industries, commercial activity has expanded to cars, silk, chemicals and machinery. The huge influx of people has led to the growth of a 'twin city' on the mainland called Navi Mumbai (New Bombay). It is hoped that this will relieve some of the pressure on the urban areas of Mumbai. The city has transport links with every major city in India by road and rail. There are ferry services connecting it with mainland cities. Sahar airport, the busiest in the country, handles international flights. The city generates around 35% of the country's GNP and yet has some of the poorest slums in the world with approximately a third of its population living in conditions of extreme poverty and around half without running water.

Places of Interest

The Kamala Nehru park (known as the 'hanging gardens') gives a panoramic view of both the city and the popular Chaupati beach below. Within the city, the Victoria Gardens are home to a zoo and to the Victoria and Albert museum, whilst the Flora fountain, at the junction of Mahatma Gandhi road, Dadobhai Naoroji road and Veer Nariman road, is surrounded by some of the city's most attractive buildings, such as the university, the secretariat and the high court. One of the city's most famous monuments is the Gateway of India, built in 1911 to commemorate the arrival of George IV. Amongst a wide variety of museums and galleries of special interest are the Prince of Wales Museum of West India and the Jehangir gallery.

Munich (München), Germany

Introduction

Munich is the capital of Bavaria, in the south of Germany. On the River Isar, it is Germany's third most populous city after Berlin and Hamburg, and is a major industrial centre.

History

Founded in 1158 by Henry the Lion, in 1255 Munich became the residence of the Wittelsbach family who dominated urban affairs until the twentieth century. Under them the city was greatly enlarged, and areas that had been destroyed by the great fire of 1328 were rebuilt by Ludwig the Bavarian during the fourteenth century. By 1503 Munich was established as a wealthy trading centre with a population of 13,500. It was declared the capital of the duchy of Bavaria.

Continued outbreaks of plague decimated the population. Despite the Protestant reforms of Martin Luther that swept through Germany in the sixteenth century, Munich remained Catholic and Protestants were persecuted. During the 30 Years' War, Munich was invaded by Swedish troops and in 1632 surrendered to King Gustav Adolphus.

The city's freedom was bought from the Swedes but Munich then fell under Habsburg rule from 1705 to 1714. However, the eighteenth century saw Munich's Golden Age with an explosion of Baroque and Italianate architecture. During the nineteenth century, the city's prosperity continued when, under Napoléon's reorganization of Europe, Bavaria was elevated to the status of a Kingdom with Munich as its capital. The marriage of the Bavarian Crown Prince Ludwig I to the Saxon-Hildburghausen Princess Therese in 1810 was celebrated by a horse race that evolved into Oktoberfest (the famous annual Bavarian beer festival).

In 1818, Bavaria became the first German state with a written constitution. Under King Ludwig it expanded rapidly into a major cultural and artistic centre. Many of the city's most famous landmarks (including Königsplatz, Alte Pinakothek, Ludwigstrasse and the Königsbau and Festsaalbau sections of the Residenz) were built at this time. Ludwig I's grandson was the 'mad' King Ludwig who ruled from 1864–86. His obsessive programme of building castles and palaces throughout Bavaria depleted the city's coffers before he was declared mentally unfit to rule. He and his doctor were found drowned in Lake Starnberg.

His brother Otto's regent, Prince Luitpold, embarked on another programme of enlargement and expansion. By the turn of the twentieth century Munich had 500,000 inhabitants and was Germany's second city. After World War I, runaway inflation and political in-fighting provided Adolf Hitler with a natural home for his extreme politics. In the 1920s National Socialism was founded in Munich and its party headquarters established there.

The Munich Pact, under which the Czechoslovakian Sudetenland was ceded to Germany, was signed in the city in 1938 by Britain, France, Germany and Italy. The treaty marked the last chance of appeasing Hitler and its failure made war inevitable. Badly damaged during World War II, the city was largely rebuilt after 1945.

Modern City

Munich today is a thriving city with a strong local economy based on such industrial giants as BMW, Bayer pharmaceuticals and MAN (automotive and truck producers). Other important industries include processed food, beer and precision instruments. Franz-Josef Strauss Airport is the country's second most important air transport centre after Frankfurt. Munich is southern Germany's most important rail hub (the main station is Hauptbahnhof) and is on the route of several important Autobahnen (motorways). Within Munich there is an efficient zone-based transport system run by the MVV, which incorporates the S-Bahn (surface trains), U-Bahn (underground) and trams and buses.

Places of Interest

The square of Marienplatz, in the centre of the old town, is the heart of Munich. Located in the middle of the square is the Mariensäule (Mary Column), erected in 1590 to celebrate the removal of the Swedish forces. The Neues Rathaus (New Town Hall) is covered with gargoyles and statues and houses the famous Glockenspiel (carillon). The Altes Rathaus (Old Town Hall) was completely rebuilt after World War II. St Peterskirche was the city's first parish church in the eleventh century but the current gothic building was begun in the thirteenth century.

Other leading tourist attractions include:

The Residenz, the home of the Wittelsbachs, begun in 1385 and now home to the Residenz Museum (displaying treasures accumulated by the Wittelsbach family);
The Schatzkammer (Treasury), which houses a collection of jewels and precious objects from the tenth century onwards;
The Altes Residenztheater (Old Residence Theatre; also known as the Cuvilliés Theatre);
Schloß Nymphenburg, a large palace which houses several museums including the Marstallmuseum (housed in the former stables), the Nymphenburger Porzellan Sammlung Bäuml (a porcelain museum), Museum Mensch und Natur (a natural history museum), and Botanischer Garten (the Botanical Gardens);
Alte Pinakothek, Munich's most important art gallery containing works by Titian, Leonardo da Vinci, Raphael, Dürer, Rembrandt and Rubens;
The neighbouring Neue Pinakothek, which houses works from the eighteenth to the twentieth centuries by artists including Van Gogh, Klimt, Cézanne and Manet;
Deutsches Museum, the world's largest museum of science and technology;
BMW Museum, located behind the headquarters of the car manufacturer;
The Olympic Village, built for the 1972 games.

Muscat (Masqat), Oman

Introduction

Muscat is the capital city and main port. It is located in the north on the Gulf of Oman coast and, until 1970, lent its name to the official title of the country—Muscat and Oman. It is a long, linear city, its separate districts each having distinctive characters.

History

Archaeological evidence suggests human habitation in the Muscat area from the Stone Age. The earliest settlements date from the 3rd millennium BC. The tribes in the northern part of Oman were converted to Islam during the first generation of the Islamic era—the middle of the seventh century AD. In about 1507, Muscat and its hinterland came under Portuguese rule. The Portuguese realized the city's strategic importance in controlling the Persian Gulf and trade between the Arabian peninsula and Persia (Iran), and between Europe and India. They built forts and walled defences, but were ultimately unable to hold the town. In 1650 they were expelled by a revolt, after which Omani commercial power expanded throughout the Gulf and the Indian Ocean.

Civil war ravaged Oman in the first half of the eighteenth century, before Ahmad bin Said, founder of the present Al Said dynasty, gained power in 1749. In 1786 the capital was moved from the interior to Muscat. The heyday of the Omani empire was in the mid-nineteenth century under Sultan Said bin Sultan. He brought Dhofar under the Omani flag and extended Omani influence and control down the East African coast. When he died, his dominions were split in two. One son became the Sultan of Zanzibar, the other the Sultan of Muscat and Oman—an acknowledgement of the different interests of the coastal and interior regions of the country.

Modern City

Since the accession of Sultan Qaboos bin Said in 1970, and the targeted deployment of oil export revenues, Muscat has developed and expanded rapidly as the commercial, industrial and administrative heart of Oman. The old port of Muscat, Mutrah and Ruwi are at the core of the capital. The old port area, at the eastern end of the city and enclosed by a wall, contains the Sultan's palace, a harbour and fortress ruins. Mutrah, 3 km northwest of Muscat, includes the Sultanate's main deep-water seaport of Mina Qaboos, through which most of the country's international trade passes. With its corniche and souk, it is also a major attraction for visitors. Inland from Mutrah lies Ruwi, the modern financial and commercial district of the capital. Ruwi is host to the major international banks. Along the coast to the west are a number of new, mostly residential districts—Qurm, Shatti al-Qurm, Madinat as-Sultan Qaboos and Al-Khuwair. Modern highways link the city with other Omani centres and with the neighbouring United Arab Emirates.

Places of Interest

Muscat is rich in historic sites. The Portuguese forts of Jalali and Mirani, dating from the occupation, guard the sea entrance to the old port. Mutrah fort, also Portuguese, sits on a hill overlooking the present corniche. Another landmark is the Ruwi wall, the main gate of which has been restored. There are various museums, in particular the Natural History and Armed Forces Museums. The souk in Mutrah is considered one of the most interesting in the Gulf states.

N'Djaména, Chad

Introduction

Formerly Fort–Lamy, N'Djaména is the capital of Chad and the Chari–Baguirmi Prefecture. It is located on an alluvial plain on the Chari River near its confluence with the Logone River on the southwestern border next to Cameroon. The plain is flooded during the rainy season, July to Sept. It is the cultural, economic and administrative centre of Chad. The majority of the country's population live in N'Djaména and most of them are Muslim.

History

Fort-Lamy was established in 1900 by French forces on the site of the battle of Kousseri. The battle saw the defeat of the Sudanese warrior Rabih az-Zubayr, who had occupied lands east of Lake Chad. The name Fort-Lamy was chosen in recognition of a French colonial officer who died in the fighting.

The Kotoko settlement remained largely unchanged until Chad won independence in 1960. In 1973 it was re-named N'Djaména and from 1980–81 it was occupied by Libyan troops.

Modern City

Following a long period of civil war life is slowly returning to normal and N'Djaména is gaining its reputation as a friendly city. It lies at the centre of areas where cotton is grown, cattle raised and fish caught. An important market site, it has a refrigerated slaughterhouse with meat packing a major industry. There are also light–industry factories dealing in cigarettes, soap and beer. Roads are poor but paved and gravel–surfaced roads link the capital with Nigeria, The Sudan, the Central African Republic, Guélendeng, Sahr and Cameroon. Buses run to Sahr, the southern capital. There is no railway so the international airport at N'Djaména is vitally important. Cars may be hired. The University of Chad was established in 1971 and the National School of Administration in 1963. The National Institute of Human Sciences (1961) is affiliated to the National Museum (1963).

Places of Interest

The National Museum has collections of palaeontology and ethnography. The Great Mosque, built between 1974 and 1978 is the main focus in the city and serves the Muslim population. The cathedral was built by the French in colonial times. The historic quarter's daily market is a good place to buy Chadian rugs and jewellery.

Nagoya, Japan

Introduction

A port and industrial city on the Nobi Plain and the Ise Bay, central Japan, Nagoya is the capital of Aichi *ken*, or prefecture, Chubu region, Honshu island. It is served by the Kiso and Nagara Rivers.

History

The modern city of Nagoya was built around tomb mounds dating from the Kofun period (third–eighth centuries), and is surrounded by Shinto shrines. The city began as a castle town ordered by the first Tokugawa shogun, Ieyasu (1542–1616) for his son. Built as a defence against Osaka Castle's rival family, the Toyotomi, the castle replaced the original stronghold, Kiyosu, 8 km west. Affected by flooding, Kiyosu's inhabitants relocated to Nagoya. With increased industry and prosperity under the leadership of Tokugawa Muneharu (1730), Nagoya became the fourth largest domain after Edo (Tokyo), Osaka and Kyoto. It served as the base of the Owari, the largest branch of the Tokugawa family, until the end of the shogunate era in 1867.

In 1889 Nagoya became a city, and by 1921 it had incorporated 16 surrounding villages and towns. Its prosperity was aided by the opening of its port in 1907. In the early twentieth century it became the Japanese centre for aircraft construction and its industry increased during the Russo-Japanese War (1904) and World War I. During World War II, Nagoya suffered heavy bombardment which destroyed much of the city. It was redeveloped following the original city plan. After the war Nagoya developed rapidly expanding beyond the original city limits. Development of the port allowed for an increase in heavy industries and the economy benefited further from the opening of the *Tokaido Shinkansen* high speed railway in 1964. Since the 1960s Nagoya has swallowed up such surrounding towns as Toyota, becoming an industrial centre and one of Japan's largest cities.

Modern City

One of Japan's leading industrial centres, Nagoya specializes in aircraft and ammunition. Other industries include iron, steel and textiles. A network of canals serves the industrial areas. A high speed railway connects Nagoya to both Tokyo and Osaka, while the port and airport provide international travel. The city's two universities were founded in 1939 and 1950. Nagoya hosted Expo 2005, a world fair which took 'Nature's Wisdom' as its theme.

Places of Interest

The Atsuta shrine was founded around the second century to house the imperial sword *Kusanafi*. Rediscovered in 1880, the shrine was remodelled on the nearby Ise Shrine. Destroyed by fire during World War II, this Shinto shrine was rebuilt and has since received millions of pilgrims and staged many festivals. Built in 1612, Nagoya castle was a residence of the Tokugawa shogunate until 1869. Original adornment included two gilded dolphins on the roof. It was destroyed by bombardment during World War II, but was rebuilt in 1957. Some of the original lavish decoration survives. Opened in 1935, the Tokugawa Art Museum houses a large art collection amassed by the Tokugawa family. Displays include the twelfth century manuscript written by Murasaki Sikibu, the *Illustrated Tale of Genji*, and an extensive collection of Japanese swords. Among other museums is a fine art museum opened in 1999. Parkland includes the Higashiyama Botanical Gardens.

Nairobi, Kenya

Introduction

In the nineteenth century Nairobi was no more than a swampy tent city where the Masai grazed their livestock. It has since grown into one of the major African capitals with over 2 m. people. It is now the financial and administrative capital of Kenya.

History

Nairobi started out as a watering hole for the indigenous pastoral Masai people. They referred to the place as Uaso Nyirobi, the place of sweet waters. It was not until the late 1890s when the Mombasa–Uganda railway was built to bring trade and commerce to the interior regions of East Africa that the area became a railway mid-point. Settled by Indian labourers from Gujarat and the Punjab, the town succeeded Mombassa as the capital of British East Africa Protectorate in 1905. European highlands farming throughout the colonial period relied heavily on Nairobi.

On gaining independence in 1963, Kenya kept Nairobi as its capital. A period of rapid expansion followed which resulted in urbanization.

Modern City

Nairobi is a city of contrasts. As well as the business districts and expensive shopping centres, there are slums and high unemployment. As well as colourful, bustling markets there are sprawling middle-class suburbs. Nairobi is infamous for muggers notably round the Uhuru Park area. Nairobi is a religiously mixed city with many churches, mosques and temples. Nairobi has an international airport. It hosts the United Nations Environment Programme.

Places of Interest

The National Museum has displays of early human life in Africa. There are also other prehistoric relics and tribe crafts. The Snake Museum on Museum Road has live East African snakes on view.

The Nairobi National Park is 114 sq. km and has rhinos, hippos, lions and giraffes. The former home of Karen Blixen, author of *Out of Africa*, is at Langatta. The farmhouse was given to the Kenyan government and is now a museum with furniture and photographs of the Danish author.

Every neighbourhood in Nairobi has a market, but the best is said to be City Market on Muindi Mbingu Street. It is one of the largest markets in Africa.

Nantes, France

Introduction

The seventh largest city in France, Nantes is situated on the confluence of the Erdre and Loire Rivers in western France, and is the capital of the Loire-Atlantique department. 56 km from the Atlantic Ocean, the port is able to accommodate large vessels.

History

Nantes was originally the capital of the territory controlled by the Gallic tribe, the Namètes. Nantes was then occupied by the Romans and the city evolved into a trading centre. Nantes was fought over by the Normans and Bretons in the ninth and tenth centuries. After Norman occupation, the city was finally claimed by the Bretons in 937. Nantes was made the capital of Brittany by Peter I of Dreux, who was Count of Brittany between 1213–37 and Prince of the Capetian dynasty. Nantes was in direct competition with Rennes for the sovereignty of Brittany throughout the middle ages. One combatant was Gilles de Rais, Marshall of France who fought alongside Joan of Arc. Burned at the stake in Rennes in 1440, he was the inspiration for Charles Perrault's infamous Blue Beard, in his *Contes* of 1697. In 1560, the conflict was resolved by Francis II, who granted a communal constitution.

Nantes was firmly on the Catholic side during the Wars of Religion (1562–98). Henry IV entered the town in 1598 and there signed the Edict of Nantes, marking the end of the Wars. This decree secured the rights of the Protestant Huguenots, granting them freedom of conscience and civic and religious rights. The edict was unpopular with the Catholic Church and was revoked by Louis XIV in 1685 causing a large number of Huguenots to flee the area.

During the eighteenth century, Nantes became France's most important centre for the slave trade. This triangular trade with Africa and the West Indies provided great wealth for Nantes inhabitants. Sugar from the West Indies was used in the manufacture of fruit preserves and baked goods that are still in production today. This period of affluence prompted the construction of Baroque and Neo-classical buildings, including the Grand Théâtre and mansions on the Ile Feydeau. This riverside island, along with the Ile de la Glonette, was surrounded by canals that have since been filled in. The Revolution (1789) ended this period of prosperity. Not satisfied with the effectiveness of the guillotine, Jean-Baptiste Carrier, representing the Committee of Public Safety, implemented *noyades*. People were stripped, tied together and put in barges, which were sunk in the Loire River.

An urban renewal plan begun in 1920 was interrupted by the German occupation in World War II. Air raids between 1943–44 caused structural damage. After the war Nantes expanded and developed and has since become an important economic and industrial centre.

Modern City

Nantes' industries include shipbuilding, oil refining and engineering as well as food industries. The city is accessible by rail, sea and the Nantes-Atlantiques international airport. It also has a tram network. In 1961 a second University was founded, the first one, built in 1460, having been destroyed during the Revolution.

Places of Interest

Museums include the Musée des Beaux-Arts, the Musée Jules Verne and the Musée d'Histoire Naturelle. In 1466 the medieval castle was rebuilt by Francis II. The external medieval façade built in stone is contrasted with the luxury of the Renaissance-style interior. The king is buried in the Cathedral of St Pierre. The cathedral, begun in 1434 by Guillaume de Dommartin, was not completed until 1893. It was damaged in World War II and in a fire in 1972, but has since been restored. The tomb of Francis II and his wife was sculpted by the renowned fifteenth-century Gothic artist Michel Colombe. Completed in 1507, the marble sepulchre was commissioned by Francis' daughter, whose heart was temporarily entombed there.

Naples (Napoli), Italy

Introduction

Naples is situated in southwest Italy, in its own bay between the Gulf of Pozzuoli and the Gulf of Salerno. To the east of the city is the dormant volcano Vesuvius. Naples is the capital of the Campania region, and is an important centre of industry and commerce.

History

The city was founded around 600 BC by Phoenician traders and Athenian Greeks. They named the early settlement Neapolis (the new city). It rapidly prospered as a centre of Greek and Roman culture. Roman emperors favoured Naples as a winter residence. In AD 79 the eruption of Vesuvius destroyed the surrounding towns of Pompeii, Herculaneum and Stabiae.

In the eighth century Naples declared itself an independent republic and was self-governed until the twelfth century when a succession of noble families took over the city. The original Lombard rulers were replaced by the Normans, who were in turn overthrown by the Hohenstaufens in 1139. The Swabian dynasty of the Hohenstaufens, which lasted until 1266, ordered the construction of many new institutions including the University. The Angevins under Charles I, having taken Sicily, and defeated the last of the Hohenstaufens, made Naples the de facto capital of their territories. After a period of uprisings and civil disorder, Naples came under the rule of the Spanish house of Aragon. Alfonso V introduced new laws and a modern justice system to support them. He was also an enthusiastic patron of the arts and sciences.

In 1503 Naples and Sicily were absorbed into the Spanish Empire. From this point on a series of Spanish viceroys ruled the city in a highly autocratic fashion. Despite several popular uprisings, viceregal rule was only brought to an end by Austrian occupation in 1707. In 1734, under the leadership of the Spanish Bourbons, Naples was established as the capital of a large kingdom, consisting of itself, Sicily and much of the southern peninsula. This was a period of prosperity and much cultural activity.

From 1806–15 Naples was occupied by France, but after Napoléon's demise the Bourbons were reinstalled as the rulers of Naples. They retained power until 1860 by which time popular opposition to their complacence and despotism assisted Garibaldi's Italian unification movement in gaining control of the city. Naples was eventually rejected as a potential choice for the new nation's capital, and went into a decline which was compounded in the twentieth century when it was heavily bombed in World War II. The struggle to rebuild the badly damaged city is thought to have contributed to the post war boom in organized crime. The city suffered a major earthquake in 1980 and the close proximity of Vesuvius continues to threaten the city.

Modern City

The present municipal government has undertaken an ambitious restoration programme of the city's cultural treasures. This, combined with the success of an ongoing programme to reduce crime, has resulted in a dramatic increase in the city's tourist industry. Other important industries include food-processing, winemaking, textiles, petroleum refining, electronics and steel.

The city is served by regional, national and international trains and most of them arrive and depart from the Stazione Centrale. Intercontinental buses arrive and depart from the front of the Stazione Centrale. National and international air services operate from Capodichino Airport which is situated 5 km north of the city. Naples has a network of buses, trains, metro and funicular ATAN (city buses and trams). Ferries and hydrofoils serve Capri, Sorrento, Ischia, Procida, Forio, Casmicciola, Palermo, Cagliari, Milazzo and the Aeolian Islands.

Places of Interest

The national archaeological museum was created by Charles of Bourbon in the eighteenth century to display the collection of antiquities he had inherited from his mother, Elizabeth Farnese. The museum also houses the Borgia collection of Etruscan and Egyptian relics. The Farnese collection includes the famous Farnese Bull and remnants from Pompeii and Herculaneum.

The National Museum and Gallery of Capodimonte houses another celebrated Farnese family collection. The gallery features works by Titian, Goya, Botticelli, Caravaggio, Michelangelo, Masacchio and Lippi. The museum includes collections of arms, ivories, bronzes and porcelain (including over 3,000 pieces from the palace's own porcelain factory).

Following the course of an old Roman road, Decimanus Maximus, through the oldest part of Naples, Spaccanapoli refers to a maze of ancient streets with numerous churches, dilapidated palaces, small craft studios, cafés and shops. The three main streets are Vi Benedetto Croce, Via San Biagio dei Libri and Via Vicaria Vecchia. The streets trace the city's history from Graeco-Roman times to the present. The area is popular with tourists.

The Certosa di San Martino was built in the fourteenth century as a Carthusian Monastery and was subsequently rebuilt in the seventeenth century in Neapolitan Baroque now houses the Museo Nazionale di San Martino. The Baroque interior of the monastery's church contains works by Caracciolo, Guido Rein and Simon Vouet.

The royal palace was built at the beginning of the seventeenth century by Domenico Fontana. Its museum is housed within the royal apartments and has a large collection of Bourbon furnishings, tapestries, statues and paintings. The Palazzo Reale also houses the Biblioteca Nazionale, which contains more than 1.5 m. volumes.

The Teatro San Carlo is the largest and one of the most distinguished opera theatres in Italy.

Nassau, The Bahamas

Introduction

The capital of The Bahamas is on the northeast coast of New Providence Island. Only 39 km by 11, two thirds of Bahamians live on the island, mostly in Nassau. As a natural harbour, it has always played a key role in the islands' economy. It was renowned as a buccaneering town for a long period but today it is one of the world's most popular tourist destinations.

History

The islands of The Bahamas were originally inhabited by Lucayans, but disease and murder resulting from colonization wiped out the indigenous population. Nassau was first colonized in 1659 by a mix of Puritans, free blacks and slaves who had come from North America. It was originally called Charles Town and came into British possession in 1670. It was renamed Nassau in 1695 in honour of King William III of the house of Orange-Nassau. Nassau held a great attraction for pirates who took advantage of its location to lure ships into its shallow waters. The British, then at war with the Spanish, encouraged privateering (the government commissioning of private boats for war service). Countless Spanish galleons were ravaged and the Spanish retaliated by attacking the city, razing it with French help in 1703. The pirates responded by declaring an unofficial republic and installed Edward Teach, a feared pirate known as Blackbeard, as magistrate. However, piracy was largely driven out by 1718.

The city was already gaining a reputation as a popular health resort by 1740. It briefly fell into Spanish hands in 1782–83, before being re-taken by the British. 1788 saw the construction of Fort Charlotte, the largest fortification in the islands. During the American Civil War in the 1860s, Nassau profited by transporting cotton and equipment between the Confederates and the English. The city went through another economic boom in the 1920s when it became a major rum smuggling centre during the American prohibition, but it was soon drawing the greater part of its wealth from tourism. Edward VIII was among the city's devotees. Throughout the second half of the twentieth century, tourism continued to develop. In 1966 the natural harbour at Nassau was dredged to create Arawak Cay, capable of receiving large cruise ships. The first bridge to link Hog Island to Nassau was opened in 1967. Hog island was renamed Paradise Island in 1961 and was soon developed extensively as the central tourist area for Nassau. In 1973, in the year that Nassau became the capital of the newly independent Commonwealth of the Bahamas, the first Bahamasair plane landed in Nassau. In 1998 the second bridge connecting Paradise Island was opened.

Modern City

Today Nassau receives more than 1.25 m. tourists a year, attracted by its climate, beaches, aquatic life, nightclubs and casinos. There is an international airport not far from the city, as well as sea connections (Nassau is a centre for sea cruises) and transport links with the surrounding islands. Nassau is also a major offshore banking and finance hub. Major exports include salt, crawfish and pulpwood. The only institutions of tertiary education in the Bahamas are in Nassau. The College of the Bahamas was opened in 1974 offering associated degrees while the University of the West Indies Centre for Hotel and Tourism Management offers degrees.

Places of Interest

Colonial areas include parliament square which houses the government buildings. The Royal Victoria Gardens is 18 km of tropical flora. Built at the end of the eighteenth century, Fort Charlotte was intended to protect the harbour. The island's other forts are Fort Fincastle (1793) with its striking lighthouse, and Fort Montagu (1741). Museums include the Pirate Museum which attests to a violent legacy. The main trading centre is Bay Street with the Straw Market at its heart. Potters Cay is a small fish market frequented by locals. As with the out islands, New Providence is surrounded by coral reefs and offers scuba diving and fishing.

New Orleans, United States of America

Introduction

Hurricane Katrina devastated New Orleans in Aug. 2005. The storms claimed several hundred lives and destroyed vast swathes of the city, which fell victim to looting and lawlessness as discontent at the government's slow response grew. Rebuilding and repopulating the city is expected to take many years.

Located on the Mississippi River in southeastern Louisiana, about 112 miles (180 km) from the Gulf of Mexico and to the south of Lake Pontchartrain, New Orleans has historically been one of the most important ports and commercial centres in the United States. The city gave birth to Dixieland jazz and hosts an annual Mardi Gras festival. Its vibrant cultural heritage made it a popular international tourist destination.

History

The first European settler to visit the area occupied by modern day New Orleans was Frenchman René–Robert Cavelier in 1682. In 1718 another Frenchman Jean-Baptiste Le Moyne, the governor of Louisiana, established a settlement in the area and called it Nouvelle-Orléans in honour of the regent of France. In 1722 the town was made the capital of French Louisiana but it came under Spanish rule 41 years later allowing trade with Caribbean ports to flourish.

New Orleans returned briefly to French control but was sold on to the United States as one of the terms of the Louisiana Purchase in 1803 and was incorporated as a city 2 years later. In 1812 the city became the capital of Louisiana, although this status was transferred to Baton Rouge in 1849. Due to tensions between the Creoles (French-Spanish) and Americans the latter mainly settled in the Garden District and the Central Business District while the former lived on the other side of Canal Street in the French Quarter. The two groups united under future president Andrew Jackson to defeat the British in The Battle of New Orleans in 1815 but renewed conflict in the city between ethnic groups saw the city divided into three separate municipalities from 1836 until 1852.

In the first half of the nineteenth century, the steamboat boom on the Mississippi River transformed New Orleans into one of the busiest ports in the United States, with cotton and tobacco trading the mainstay of the city's economy. New Orleans' population grew rapidly and by 1840 it was the fourth largest city in the country.

At the beginning of the Civil War New Orleans was a Confederate stronghold but it was captured by the Union in April 1862 and the Mississippi trade routes were sealed off, to the detriment of the city's economy. The demise of the steamboat towards the end of the nineteenth century was another blow. However the draining of surrounding swampland enabled the city to expand in the early part of the twentieth century while the development

of commercial river barges and oil and petrochemical industries supported economic recovery.

After World War II several major regeneration programmes boosted the city as new bridges and overpasses were built and the French Quarter of the city was renovated. The development of the Mardi Gras festival into a major annual attraction and the city's reputation as the birthplace of jazz helped raise New Orleans' status as a popular tourist destination. The city gradually desegregated and elected its first black mayor in 1978. From the 1950s many residents left the inner city for the suburbs, leading to a fall in population and tax revenue while crime levels rose.

Much of New Orleans' infrastructure perished during Hurricane Katrina in 2005. Many businesses and much of the population subsequently left the city as preparations were made for rebuilding, expected to take many years.

Modern City

Prior to Hurricane Katrina, New Orleans had a diverse manufacturing base, with the major products being petroleum, grain, coal, cotton and foodstuffs. Dock facilities along the Mississippi River and the Gulf Intracoastal Waterway were key to the economy and helped maintain the city's status as one of the busiest ports in the United States. Every year more than 5,000 vessels docked at New Orleans and the city traded extensively with South and Central America.

New Orleans International Airport is 12 miles northwest of the city. Amtrak trains and Greyhound buses serve the Union Passenger Terminal while the Regional Transit Authority runs an extensive bus network within the city. There are also several streetcar services.

Among the city's institutes of higher education are Louisiana State University Medical Center, Tulane University, Loyola University, Xavier University of Louisiana, Dillard University, Southern University at New Orleans and the University of New Orleans.

Places of Interest

The French Quarter (Vieux Carré) was the most popular area of the city for tourists before Hurricane Katrina struck. At the centre of this section of New Orleans was Jackson Square, surrounded by the Saint Louis Cathedral, built in 1794 before being extensively remodelled in 1851. Canal Street separated the French Quarter from the Central Business District where the majority of the city's commercial operations were based including the New Orleans Convention Centre and Riverwalk, a large shopping complex.

The annual Mardi Gras festival is traditionally held during the week before Lent and features parades, balls and street dances. Other major festivals held annually included the Spring Fiesta and the New Orleans Jazz and Heritage Festival. Prominent cultural institutions include the Louisiana State Museum, the New Orleans Museum of Art and the Historic New Orleans Collection. Preservation Hall had regular jazz performances while the city also had an opera company and a philharmonic orchestra. The Louisiana Superdome ranks among the largest enclosed stadiums in the world.

New York, United States of America

Introduction

Located on the Eastern Atlantic coast of the United States at the mouth of the Hudson river, New York, affectionately referred to as the 'Big Apple', covers an area of 301 sq. miles. Home to 8,175,133 people in 2010, the city is made up of five boroughs: Staten Island and Manhattan are self-contained while Brooklyn and Queens are on the west of Long Island. The Bronx is the only borough with a land connection to the state mainland.

History

The earliest European explorations of the area now known as New York City are thought to have been made by the Florentine explorer Giovanni da Verrazano who landed on Staten Island in 1524. However the city began to take shape as a series of Dutch settlements. In 1624 a town named Fort Amsterdam (later renamed New Amsterdam) was established in Manhattan. Peter Minuit, who founded the town, was said to have bought the island for around $24 worth of goods.

The English seized the colony in 1664 when it was renamed New York after the Duke of York (later James II). From 1789–90 the city was briefly the US capital until the establishment of Washington, D.C. By 1810 New York had overtaken Philadelphia to become the most populous city in the United States. The opening of the Erie Canal in 1825, which linked the city to the Great Lakes, marked the beginning of the city's development as the nation's financial capital.

In 1898 a new charter was adopted and New York become a Metropolis of five boroughs known as Greater New York. This was achieved by incorporating Brooklyn, the Bronx, Queens and Staten Island into the city's structure. The Statue of Liberty, a gift from France in recognition of the friendship between the two countries, arrived in the United States in 1886. At the same time European immigrants were arriving in huge numbers. By 1930 New York was the most populous city in the world. While it can no longer lay claim to that crown it remains far and away the biggest metropolitan area in the United States.

In the twentieth century, New York's skyline was defined by a series of spectacular skyscrapers—mainly on Manhattan. This architectural trend began with the Flatiron building in 1902. Other equally striking structures followed, including the Chrysler Building (completed by 1930), the Empire State Building (1931) and the World Trade Centre (1970). The city's first subway was opened in 1904.

After World War II, a new wave of immigration began as many African Americans and Latin Americans arrived in New York, enhancing its reputation as a city of ethnic diversity. In 1996, the US Census bureau claimed that 11 of every 20 New York residents was an immigrant or the child of an immigrant and that 120 languages were spoken in New York schools.

On 11 Sept. 2001, New York City was devastated by a terrorist attack when two hijacked passenger aircraft, American Airlines flight 11 and United Airlines flight 175, were flown into the north and south towers of the World Trade Centre. The building collapsed with the loss of 2,753 lives. The World Trade Center ('Ground Zero') site is now home to the National September 11 Memorial & Museum. In Jan. 2011 the James Zadroga 9/11 Health and Compensation Act, providing health monitoring and financial aid to sick 9/11 workers, became law.

Modern City

A city with a high international profile, New York contains the headquarters of the United Nations and is an important centre for finance and business. The New York Mercantile Exchange is the world's largest physical commodities futures market. In the 1970s New York went perilously close to bankruptcy and in the aftermath of the Oct. 1987 stock market crash the city again faced serious financial problems.

The largest source of employment in the city is service industries such as insurance, finance, real estate, transport and construction. The major manufacturing industries are clothing and textiles, chemicals and electronic equipment. In recent years increasing automation has seen many jobs lost while rapidly increasing taxes and high crime rates have seen many companies leave the city.

New York elected its first black mayor in 1990 after David Dinkins was elected in Nov. 1989. In 1993 Dinkins was defeated by Rudy Giuliani, whose 'zero tolerance' policies on crime proved effective. Giuliani also won much praise for his conduct in the aftermath of the 11 Sept. 2001 attacks. He was succeeded by Michael Bloomberg, a lifelong Democrat who stood on the Republican ticket. Bloomberg was elected to a second term in 2005. In 2008 Bloomberg successfully campaigned to amend New York's mayoral rules which had previously prevented candidates from serving three consecutive terms. Consequently, he ran for a third term and won the election in Nov. 2009. He was succeeded by Bill de Blasio, the city's first Democratic mayor since Dinkins, in Jan. 2014.

New York is served by two international airports, John F. Kennedy in Queens and Newark in New Jersey. La Guardia, which is also in Queens, handles domestic arrivals. In 2008 the three airports serviced 107.0 m. passengers. The subway is open 24 h a day and handles 5.1 m. passengers on an average weekday (2009). There is also an extensive bus system. Port Authority Bus Terminal is a terminal for Greyhound buses while Penn Station is on the Amtrak rail network.

Among the city's institutes of higher education are Columbia University, Fordham University, New York University, The New School and the City University of New York.

Places of Interest

New York is a major cultural centre with a multi-billion dollar tourist industry. Total visitor spending from New York City tourism in 2009 was US$28.2 bn. In 2009, 45.6 m. tourists (37.0 m. domestic, 8.6 m. international) flocked to the city. The city's most iconic attraction is the Statue of Liberty, which is located in New York Harbour and can be reached by ferry. Just across the water from the Statue is Ellis Island, where a Museum of Immigration marks the fact that it was the first stop for many immigrants who entered the USA.

Manhattan contains the majority of the city's tourist attractions. The new One World Trade Center on the northwest corner of the World Trade Center site, Grand Central Subway Terminal, the headquarters of the United Nations, the Empire State Building, the Chrysler Building, the Flatiron Building, the Rockefeller Center and Times Square are among the most prominent landmarks. Also in Manhattan are the Cathedral of St. John the Divine, the world's largest gothic cathedral, and Macy's, the world's largest department store.

The Museum of Modern Art houses an extensive collection of nineteenth and twentieth century art while the Metropolitan Museum of Art contains over 3.5 m. works of art from all over the world. Central Park, located in the heart of Manhattan, is New York's largest public park, covering an area of 340 hectares.

Notable places of interest outside Manhattan include the New York Aquarium in Brooklyn, the Bronx Zoo and the Museum of the Moving Image in Queens.

Newcastle Upon Tyne, United Kingdom of Great Britain and Northern Ireland

Introduction

Newcastle is the principal city of the Tyne and Wear region in northern England. Formerly a major industrial centre, it suffered severe economic decline in the twentieth century. Boosted by the growth of the service sector in recent years, it is one of the most important cultural centres in the north of England.

History

Newcastle's history began with the Roman occupation of Britain. In the western suburbs of Newcastle upon Tyne was the site of a fort on Hadrian's Wall called Condercum. Closer to the modern day centre of the city there was a second fort, less impressive than Condercum but strategically important for guarding the Roman bridge across the river.

Robert Curthose, the eldest son of William the Conqueror, built a castle on the site of the Roman fort, which became known as *Newcastle*. The city was of military importance because of its location near the eastern border with Scotland and the town grew steadily within the medieval walls that enclosed the city from 1265.

Newcastle grew as a trading port and by the fourteenth century was accorded its own mayor and later made independent of Northumberland. As well as a centre for wool and cloth exports, the town was granted a coalmining charter in the thirteenth century. The Tyneside pits were among the first to be worked in England and for centuries Newcastle was a leading supplier of coals to London. By 1800 Newcastle was a first rank industrial and financial centre and gained a growing reputation for its glass and iron production.

Of all the industries on the Tyne the most important was shipbuilding. The shipyards along the Tyne were among the biggest and most productive in the world. The local availability of coal and iron ore in large quantities not only supplied raw materials for the shipyards but also for locomotive engineering, civil engineering and armament manufacture. In the industrial revolution, Newcastle upon Tyne was the home of many leading industrial pioneers, such as George Stephenson (steam transport), William Armstrong (hydro-electric pump), Sir Charles Algernon Parsons (inventor of the first steam turbine) and Joseph Swan (electric lighting).

Modern City

Modern Newcastle is noted for its vibrant nightlife and for its contribution to the national sporting life (it has successful football and rugby union sides and is a major athletics venue). The city is well-served by road, rail and sea and also has an international airport. Within the city there is a metro service.

By the turn of the twenty-first century shipbuilding had virtually disappeared from the region. Some heavy industry still exists but employment is provided principally by service industries. The University of Newcastle upon Tyne, formerly part of Durham University, was founded in 1937 and the Royal Grammar School, founded by Henry VIII, is among Britain's leading schools.

Places of Interest

Among Newcastle's most popular attractions are:

the Castle, built in 1080;
the Cathedral Church of St Nicholas;
the six bridges that span the Tyne, the most famous of which is The George V Bridge (Tyne Bridge) which opened in 1929 and served as a model for the Sydney Harbour Bridge. The Gateshead Millennium Bridge was opened in 2000, linking Newcastle Quayside with an arts and cultural complex at Gateshead Quays;
the Hancock Museum, the northeast's premier Natural Science Museum;
the Discovery Museum, the region's largest museum complex, including an exhibition of Newcastle's history from 1914 to the modern day;
the Corrymella Scott Gallery, specializing in twentieth century Scottish Art;
the Angel of the North, a controversial steel sculpture by Anthony Gormley situated on the site of a former coal mine.

Niamey, Niger

Introduction

Niamey, a river port on the river Niger in the southwest of the country, is capital of Niger and the Tillabéry department.

History

Originally inhabited by Maouri, Zerma and Fulani people, Niamey was a small village when the French occupied it in the late nineteenth century. In 1926 it was designated capital of the French colony of Niger and underwent a period of rapid expansion after World War II. In 1960 it became capital of independent Niger.

Modern City

A busy river port, Niamey lies at the junction of Niger's two main motorway's and has an international airport. The Kennedy Bridge links the two river banks, with the left bank being the more highly developed. Service industries provide most employment. Other industries include food and drink processing, building materials and pottery. NIamey is also a trading centre for locally farmed produce (especially nuts). There is a university.

Places of Interest

Leading attractions include the national museum, the Grande Mosqueé and the Grand Marché (redeveloped since burning down in the 1980s).

Nice, France

Introduction

A seaport and tourist resort, Nice is situated on the Côte d'Azur in Southeast France, 32 km from the Italian border. It is located in the Baie des Anges, an inlet of the Mediterranean Sea, and is surrounded by mountains. Nice is the capital of the Alpes-Maritimes region.

History

Nice was founded by the Phocaeans of Marseilles in 350 BC. Greek seafarers named the colony Nikaia after *nike* meaning victory. The colony was then conquered by the Romans in first century AD, who founded Cemenelum (Cimiez) in the northeast. Under the Romans, Nice developed into a trade centre. During the fourth century, the area suffered from raids from both the Counts of Provence and Savoy.

In the tenth century Nice was ruled by the Counts of Provence. In 1388 the inhabitants rejected the incoming Louis of Anjou, and allied themselves with the Count of Savoy, Amadeus VII (1360–91). During the seventeenth and eighteenth centuries, Nice was occupied at various times by the French, but the Counts of Savoy, by then the Kings of Sardinia, regained *Nizza*. From 1792–1814, Nice was annexed to France and served as a base for Napoléon's Italian campaigns. In 1860, Nice was incorporated into France at the Treaty of Turin. At this time, the city had a population of around 40,000.

In the nineteenth century, Nice's popularity as a tourist destination increased rapidly. It was a favoured destination of the English aristocracy and royalty. The first esplanade was built in 1770 and 7 years later Nice acquired its first casino. In 1822 the English community built the Promenade des Anglais. Originally a path along the shore, it is now a 4 km-long, tree-lined esplanade on the seafront. Many elaborate pastel-coloured mansions and hotels built at the turn of the twentieth century attest to the popularity of Nice as a resort for the rich and famous.

Racial disparity between rich and poor creates tension. Nice, along with many Côte d'Azur towns, is a bastion for the Front National (FN), which secures around 25% of votes in local elections. Between 1928–90 Nice was the preserve of the Médecin family. Jean Médecin held the position of mayor until 1966 when it was taken over by his son, Jacques. Graham Greene was among those who set out to prove the misappropriation of funds and culture of bribery that existed in Nice under *Médecinisme*. In 1990 Jacques Médecin escaped to Uruguay and was tried in 1992 for embezzlement. In 1994 an extradition order was enforced and he was imprisoned in Grenoble. He later returned to Uruguay where he died in 1998.

Modern City

The principal industry is tourism; others include food processing, perfume manufacture and olive oil distilleries. Since 1963 there has been a famous fruit and flower market in the old town. The University was opened in 1965 and an international arts school was founded in 1970. Nice hosts conferences at the Centre Universitaire Méditerranéen. Opened in 1933, the centre's first director was the poet and essayist Paul Valéry. In Dec. 2000 Nice hosted the EU summit. Nice is accessible by road, rail, air and sea.

Places of Interest

The city attracted many artists, including Henri Matisse. He died in the Hôtel Regina in Cimiez in 1954, a hotel built in 1896 to welcome Queen Victoria. The Musée Matisse is a Genoese Villa at Cimiez that houses many of his works, including *Blue Nude IV* and *Woman with Amphora*. The Promenade des Anglais runs from the new town in the west to the old town, where the Quai des Etats Unis continues to the harbour in the east. The Italianate old town is pedestrianized. Nice is rich in museums and art galleries, such as the Musée des Beaux-Arts and the Musée d'Art Moderne et d'Art Contemporain. The latter has Pop Art and New Realism exhibitions.

Nicosia (Lefkosia, Lefkoşa), Cyprus

Introduction

The capital and largest city of Cyprus since the twelfth century, Nicosia is situated on the Pedieos River almost in the centre of the island on the Messaoria Plain. It has been divided since 1974 into Greek and Turkish Cypriot sectors by the United Nations buffer zone known as the Green Line.

History

The city dates back to the Bronze Age and was originally known as Ledra. Its Greek name is thought by some to derive from Lefkos, the son of an Egyptian Ptolemy, who rebuilt the city in the third century BC. Others believe the name originated from the white poplar or lefki. Having grown extensively under Roman and Byzantine occupation, the city became a Frankish kingdom under the Lusignan dynasty from 1192 and then a Venetian dependency in 1489. The Venetians erected a circular wall between 1567 and 1570 to defend the city against Ottoman invaders. However, the Turks captured it in 1570 after a bitter siege. There were several revolts against Ottoman rule over the next three centuries, and Nicosia experienced little economic or cultural growth until the British assumed control of Cyprus from 1878.

Following independence in 1960, intercommunal violence between Greek and Turkish Cypriots brought about a de facto partition of Nicosia in 1963. The so-called Green Line was established by the British military, dividing the city into Greek and Turkish areas of control. The Turkish invasion of 1974 formalised this division. It has since remained in place under the jurisdiction of UN peacekeeping forces. The city airport, destroyed at the time of the invasion, has never been rebuilt.

Modern City

Although a divided city, Nicosia is the seat of government and administration. It is also a banking and commercial centre, with important textile, footwear and processed food industries. Cultural and historical attractions draw tourists to the city, particularly in the south. Each year in May the city hosts the International State Fair and the Nicosia Art Festival.

Places of Interest

The circular wall that surrounds the old city—in both the north and south—is a prime example of the Venetian period architecture. The walls are three miles in perimeter, with 11 bastions each bearing the name of an aristocratic family, together with three gates: the Paphos Gate to the south-west; Kyrenia (Girne) in the north and the Famagusta Gate in the east. Renovated in 1981, the Famagusta Gate is the best preserved of the original entrances and serves as a concert venue and exhibition hall.

Other attractions in the Greek Cypriot sector of the city include the Cyprus Museum; the Makarios Cultural Foundation, incorporating the European Art Gallery, Greek Independence War Gallery and Byzantine Art Museum; the Faneromeni Church; and the Bayrakytar and Omeriye Mosques. Places of interest in the Turkish Cypriot zone include the Büyük Hammam (Turkish baths); Cami Selimiye (or Selimye Mosque, the most prominent landmark in the north of the city); Cami Haydarpaşa (a Gothic structure); the Büyük Han and Kumarcilar Han (originally Turkish inns); and the Turkish Museum.

Nizhny Novgorod, Russia

Introduction

Nizhny Novgorod is in the west of the country on the confluence of the rivers Oka and Volga. It is Russia's fourth largest city, a major transport and industrial centre and the main city of the Volga administrative district.

History

Founded in 1221 by Grand Prince Yury Vsevolodovich, by 1350 Nizhny Novgorod was capital of its eponymous principality. Attacked by Tartar forces, it was absorbed into the Moscow principality towards the end of the century and was an important centre of Russian cultural and intellectual life. It was used as a base for attacks on Kazan, the Tartar capital, during the fifteenth and sixteenth centuries and, following Muscovite successes in the Volga region, prospered as a trade centre on East-West trade routes.

The city was a focus of the wars with Poland in the 'Time of Troubles' at the start of the seventeenth century, with local forces taking much credit in the defeat of Sigismund III. The arrival of the annual Makaryev trade fair in 1817, which went on to become the largest in the country, signalled a new period of prosperity. The last fair was held in 1917, the year of the Russian revolution.

From the nineteenth century onwards Nizhny Novgorod's principle industrial output was for the maritime and rail industries. The city produced vehicles, weapons and heavy manufactures in World Wars I and II, meeting Russia's needs when other industrial areas came under attack. From 1932 it was renamed Gorki, after the nineteenth century writer Maksim Gorki, who had lived there.

In the post-war era the city remained a major industrial centre, with one of Russia's largest car plants. Internationally, the city gained notoriety as the site of exile for the nuclear physicist and Nobel peace prize winner, Andrei Sakharov.

Modern City

Nizhny Novgorod is a major transport hub, and is well served by air, road, rail and river connections. The town lies on the Trans-Siberian railway with links to Moscow and St Petersburg. There is an international airport. Buses, overland trains and a subway run within the city.

Major industries include mechanical engineering and heavy manufacturing (including cars and sea and river vessels). There are also significant oil, chemicals and consumer goods sectors. The city has a university and several other institutes of higher education.

Places of Interest

The Kremlin dates from the sixteenth century, but is on the site of a much earlier wooden version. The Archangel Cathedral was built in the seventeenth century in recognition of the town's role during the 'Times of Trouble'. There is an art museum and a museum of history and architecture as well as several theatres.

Nouakchott, Mauritania

Introduction

Nouakchott, on a grassland plateau close to the west coast, was developed in the 1950s for the role of national capital.

History

Nouakchott was a small coastal village on important trade paths from Dakar until 1957, when it was selected as the site of the capital of soon-to-be independent Mauritania. A massive building programme commenced in 1958 and in 1960 it officially received its new status.

Mauritania had several territorial disputes with neighbouring countries during the 1970s and 1980s, and the city was attacked by Western Saharan forces in 1976. Decades of drought has seen the urban population swell with refugees from the surrounding areas and over-crowding is acute. Many of the suburbs consist of shanty towns.

Modern City

Administration provides much employment and there are several light industries, while handicrafts remain important. Reserves at nearby Akjoujt has made Nouakchott a major copper centre.

The city has an airport, good road connections and a deep-water port, built in the 1980s 8 km from the city. There is a university.

Nouakchott witnessed heavy fighting between rebel army factions and pro-government troops following an attempted coup against President Maaouya Ould Taya in June 2003.

Places of Interest

The Place de l'Indépendence is Nouakchott's focal point. Other major sights include the national museum, the national carpet office, the Moroccan Mosque and a mosque given by Saudi Arabia. There are popular markets in the city centre and in the Cinquième district. A short distance from the centre is the Port de Pêche, a traditional fishing area.

Novi Sad (Újvidék), Serbia

Introduction

Novi Sad, on the left bank of the Danube, is the capital city of Vojvodina and its commercial and cultural centre. In an area of long-standing military importance, the modern city was born in the late seventeenth century. It was under Ottoman and then Austro-Hungarian rule before coming under Yugoslav jurisdiction in the twentieth century.

History

Evidence of human habitation surrounding Novi Sad dates back 6,500 years. The Romans established a small settlement and later fortifications were built that developed into the Petrovaradin Fortress. The area fell to numerous invading forces before the Ottomans took control in 1526.

Austria wrested power from the Turks in the 1690s and set about re-building the Petrovaradin Fortress to reinforce the border with the Ottoman Empire. In 1748 Novi Sad, first mentioned in 1694 as a bridgehead adjacent to the fortress, was declared a free city. Developing as a trade centre, its cultural importance for Serbs likewise increased. In 1864 a major Serb institution, the Matica Srpska Arts and Culture Society, relocated to Novi Sad from Budapest, where it had been established 38 years earlier. The Serbian National Theatre was founded in 1861. The city was a home to socialism throughout the nineteenth century.

Following World War I the city was part of Yugoslavia. In World War II it was invaded by the Hungarian forces of Admiral Horthy, who annexed it in 1941, during which large numbers of Serbs and Jews were massacred. For its struggles during the war Novi Sad was awarded the Order of National Hero by President Tito in 1970.

In the aftermath of the war Novi Sad was designated capital of the Autonomous Province of Vojvodina and officially returned to the Yugoslav sphere of influence in 1947. It underwent much rebuilding in the communist era, consolidating its importance in the region. However, it suffered badly during the NATO bombing campaigns against Slobodan Milošević, with its power supplies cut off and many buildings, including its three famous bridges, destroyed.

Modern City

Among the chief industries are metal and chemical processing, agriculture, food processing, textiles, publishing and broadcasting. An important port, it links the Danube with the Bačka canal network. It is also on the Begrade–Budapest railway. The nearest airport is Belgrade.

Places of Interest

Renowned for its diverse ethnic make-up, Novi Sad has a rich cultural life. In addition to the university, the Serbian National Theatre and Matica Srpska are based here. The most famous tourist landmark is the well-preserved Petrovaradin Fortress, standing imposingly on a rock. The current construction was built largely between 1692 and 1780. It came under civil administration in 1950.

There are many churches, covering a wide spectrum of religious groups, with the Catholic Cathedral to St Mary among the most prominent. The Fruska Gora monasteries were built between the fifteenth and eighteenth centuries, of which 18 remain operational.

The Novi Sad museum complex includes an art gallery, underground military catacombs, parts of the fortress and a museum dedicated to the poet Jovan Jovanović Zmaj. The Musuem of Vojvodina complex is 30 km outside Novi Sad and includes collections of art, archaeology, ethnology and history. Its most famous treasures are two gold Roman helmets. There is an Institute for Nature Preservation, documenting the ecology of Vojvodina.

Novosibirsk, Russia

Introduction

Located on the banks of the Rivers Ob and Kamenka, Novosibirsk is the third largest city in Russia and the chief city of Western Siberia.

History

Novosibirsk was founded in 1893 during the construction of the Trans-Siberian Railway and quickly grew to be an important transit point for settlers moving further into Siberia.

It was named Novonikolayevsky to mark the accession of Tsar Nicholas II in 1895. Owing to the proximity of coalfields, industry developed quickly and the population grew from 7,800 in 1897 to 400,000 in 1937. In 1917 the Soviets seized power and during the subsequent civil war White Guards captured the city. A series of struggles over the territory led to a decline in the population as war and epidemics took their toll.

The city made some recovery with the start of Lenin's new economic policy in 1921. After the Bolsheviks formed the vast Siberian Region in 1925 it became an administrative centre and its name was changed to Novosibirsk, meaning New Siberia. During Stalin's push for industrialization Novosibirsk expanded to become an industrial centre.

Local industry burgeoned during the 5-year plans of the 1930s, and in World War II industrial plants from the European part of Russia were re-located there. In 1943 the Academy of Sciences opened its Siberian branch in Novosibirsk and in 1957 construction of the satellite town of Academgorodok incorporated 14 research institutes and a university. Building began on Novosibirsk's underground railway in 1979, with the first line opening in 1985.

Modern City

Novosibirsk is one of Russia's largest machine-building centres, with metallurgy, chemical and food processing among its most important industries. The city is an important rail hub. There are two airports providing services throughout Russia. Public transport within the city includes buses, trolley-buses and trams.

There is the Novosibirsk State University and several specialized institutes of higher education.

Places of Interest

The main thoroughfare is Krasny (Red) Prospect, a shopping street crossing the city from the Kamenka river to the airport. Novosibirsk has the largest railway station on the Trans-Siberian network. It also has one of Siberia's largest galleries, a zoo and a museum of regional studies. There is an active arts scene, with an opera house and several theatres.

Nuku'alofa, Tonga

Introduction

Nuku'alofa, in the north of Tongatapu (the main island of Tonga), is the capital and main harbour (surrounded by coral reef) of Tonga. Nuku'alofa translates as 'abode of love'.

History

Tongatapu joined the unified Kingdom of Tonga in 1845. Tonga was under Anglo–German and then English rule until 1970 when Nuku'alofa became capital of independent Tonga.

Modern City

Nuku'alofa has a deep-water port. Fua'amotu airport is 22 km from the city centre. The local economy relies upon tourism and the export of coconuts, copra, vanilla and bananas. Local crafts also bring in revenue and there is a small industries centre in the city outskirts. There is a branch of the University of the South Pacific on the island. Nuku'alofa has expanded into surrounding agricultural and wetlands in recent years to accommodate a swathe of shanty towns.

Places of Interest

The Royal Palace, built in 1867, is Nuku'alofa's most recognizable landmark though not open to the public, unlike the neighbouring park, Pangao Si'I. The nearby royal estate, Sia Ko Veiongo, was often plundered during 600 years of tribal conflict. The Royal Tombs contain the graves of all monarchs since 1893. The Basilica of St Anthony of Padua, the Centenary Chapel and St Mary's Cathedral are major attractions, as well as the War Memorial in the town centre and the National Centre with its collections of historical exhibits. Yellow Pier is a prime spot for diving, while the Talamahu and weekly flea markets are popular.

In the eastern part of Tongatapu is Ha'amonga'a Maui Trilithon, a 1,000 year old stone construction important in mystical beliefs. Nearby are the Pyramidal Stone Tombs, where many members of the ancient royal family are buried.

Odesa, Ukraine

Introduction

Capital of the Odeska *oblast*, Odesa is a major port on the Black Sea coast. Under Russian rule in the nineteenth century, it was the most important city after Moscow and St Petersburg.

History

Odesa was mentioned in 1415 as a Tatar settlement named Khadzhibei. As a port of strategic importance it was controlled by Lithuania–Poland and, from 1764, the Ottoman Turks. During the Russo-Turkish war of 1787–1791 Black Sea Cossacks took the settlement and renamed it Odesa in 1795. Using slave labour they rebuilt the port and town. From 1803–14 it was governed by the Duke of Richelieu, a French nobleman in exile. It grew as a key port (especially for grain) and benefitted from the introduction of the railways in the 1860s.

The Russian revolution of 1905 took in the *Potemkin* mutiny in Odesa, later depicted in Sergey Eisenstein's film, *Battleship Potemkin*. When Turkey blocked Allied access to the Dardanelles during World War I, the port of Odesa was closed and was subsequently attacked by Turkish forces. In the 1917 revolution the city changed hands several times before the Bosheviks prevailed. A famine hit the city in 1921–2 and it was besieged by Germans and Romanians in 1941. Capitulating after a long struggle, it served as capital of Transnistra under Romanian authority. Much of the fabric of the city was devastated during the occupation and an estimated 250,000 people (principally Jews) were murdered or deported. The Soviets liberated Odesa in April 1944 and during the Soviet era it remained a key port and ship-building centre.

Modern City

Ukraine's largest port, the local economy relies on fishing, whaling, ship-building and port-related activities. Engineering, chemicals, oil, food processing and consumer and heavy manufactures are also important.

Odesa has rail links with destinations throughout Ukraine, as well as Moldova and Romania, and there is an international airport. There is a university.

Places of Interest

Attractions include the catacombs, Prymorsky Bulvar (a seafront boulevard with parks and the steps featured in *Battleship Potemkin*), the classical Palace of Vorontsov, the Viennese-style Opera and Ballet theatre and the Pasazh shopping mall complete with Baroque sculptures. The cathedral of the Assumption, Pantelejmonovska church and Ilinsky cathedral are all popular. There are museums of archaeology, maritime history and literature. The Museum of Partisan Glory celebrates the resistance movement of World War II.

Oporto (Porto), Portugal

Introduction

Portugal's second city, Oporto (Porto) is on the northern bank of the Douro River 3 km from the Atlantic Ocean. In the north of the country, the hilly city rises up the Pena Ventosa from the steep rocky banks of the Douro. A port and industrial centre, Oporto was the capital of Portucale in medieval times.

History

The Phoenicians were attracted to Oporto as a stage on the ancient trade routes. The fifth century BC settlement of Cale on the south bank was conquered by the Romans in 300 BC. Castrum Novum was founded on the north bank of the Douro by the Alani tribe and taken by Visigoths in the sixth century AD. The Moors extended their empire to the area in 716, destroying the city in the process, but were driven out by the nobles of the northern region of Portucalense in 997. Oporto was made the capital of Portucale and remained so despite a Moorish attack in the eleventh century.

In June 1147 an English fleet en route for the Second Crusade stopped at Oporto and joined forces with the Portuguese to liberate Lisbon from Moorish rule. Oporto's connection with the English continued through the second millennium. Native to the city was Henry the Navigator, son of King João I and John of Gaunt's daughter Philippa of Lancaster, whose voyages of discovery took him around the Madeira Islands and the west coast of Africa. Strong trade links with the English began in the fourteenth century and the 1703 Methuen Treaty strengthened the trade in port wine. The treaty allowed for a reduced duty on port coming into Britain in return for lifting restrictions on the export of wool to Portugal. An English community was established in Oporto and the Feitoria Inglesa, or the English Factory, an association responsible for trade, was established in the early eighteenth century.

Between 1730–63 Oporto underwent a period of architectural development led by Italian architect Nicolau Nasoni. Despite turbulent politics and a cholera outbreak in the early nineteenth century, trade and commerce continued to develop. The arrival of the railway in the 1870s stimulated industrial expansion, and the city thrived throughout the twentieth century.

Modern City

Industries include chemicals, electronic equipment, tyres, textiles and soap. But Oporto's major export is port wine, and its major consumer is Britain. The Vila Nova de Gaia area on the south bank of the River Douro is the centre of port production and is home to *armazéns*, or port wine lodges. Other exports include cork, olive oil and fruit. The surrounding agricultural region produces cereals, olive and cork, oak trees and vegetables. Leixões, a manmade port to the north of Oporto, was built between 1892–1908. The Universidade do Porto was founded in 1911. The Pedras Rubras international airport is 13 km north of the city. Oporto began building a metro system in 1999, which was completed in 2002. The centre of Oporto was made a UNESCO heritage site in 1996, and the city became a European Capital of Culture in 2001.

Places of Interest

Port wine tasting and visits to production centres are available in many *armazéns* (wine lodges) in the Vila Nova de Gaia. The Torre dos Clérigos built in 1863 gives a view of the whole city. The twelfth century Romanesque Sé (cathedral) was reconstructed in the thirteenth century, but retains its original foundations. The adjoining gothic cloister added in the fourteenth century has a staircase built by Nasoni in the eighteenth century.

The fifteenth-century Gothic Igreja de São Francisco is decorated in an extravagant eighteenth century style adorned with gilded Rococo decorations. Adjacent to the church is Oporto's Bolsa, or stock exchange, a neo-classical building built between 1834–42. Oporto's museums included the Museu Nacional Soares dos Reis, named after the nineteenth century native sculptor António Soares dos Reis, which displays 18th and nineteenth century Portuguese art, glass and ceramic collections. Several churches contain small museums. Of the five bridges over the Douro, two are nineteenth century, including Alexandre-Gustave Eiffel's double tiered metal Maria Pia, and the Ponte Luís I, which towers 60 m. above the river.

Oran (Wahran), Algeria

Introduction

On the western Mediterranean coast of Algeria, dominated on one side by Mount Aidour, Oran is the country's second largest city and an important port.

History

Founded in 903 by Andalusian sailors, it was built on the prehistoric site of Ifri (meaning caves). The port flourished under the dynasty of the Zianides of Tlemcen and relations with Mediterranean countries were close. Between 1509–1792 the territory was intermittently occupied by the Spanish, although the arrival of the Ottomans in Algeria threatened their dominance. A destructive earthquake in 1790 compelled the Spanish to leave and the Ottomans took the city the following year. The city came under French colonial rule in 1831 and an artificial port was developed. The city was occupied briefly by Allied forces in 1942. Algeria secured its independence in 1962 after which many Europeans left the city.

Modern City

A principal port and industrial city, Oran's main industries are chemicals, textiles and food processing. Its university was founded in 1965 while a science and technological university opened 10 years later. The city is connected to Algiers and Morocco by rail and has an international airport nearby. Building is under way for a 32-station tram system, scheduled for completion during 2011.

Places of Interest

The citadel of Santa Cruz was built by the Turks while the Casbah or old city holds the vestiges of Spanish occupation. The Mosque was built in 1796 to commemorate the Spanish departure. Other religious buildings include the Sacre Coeur Cathedral (1913) and the Saint Louis Church (1679). Museums include the Musée Ahmed Zabana which exhibits art, natural history and archaeology. The French writer Albert Camus based his 1947 novel *La Peste* (The Plague) in Oran where he had been a teacher.

Osaka, Japan

Introduction

Osaka is the capital of the Osaka region. Situated along the delta of the Yodo River and centre of the Kinki region, it comprises of Osaka, Kyoto, Hyogo, Nara, Wakayama, Shiga and Mie, the city developed around the Great Castle constructed by Toyotomi Hideyoshi in 1583. It is one of the nation's busiest ports.

History

The history of Osaka dates from AD 300 when the city was known as Naniwa. The change of name occurred in the fourteenth century. In 1496 a fortress temple was built where the Great Castle of Osaka can be found today. The site was selected by Rennyo, a chief priest of the militant True Pure Land, a sect of Buddhism. The fortress was destroyed in a decade long siege with Nobunaga Oda in 1580. However, in 1583, Toyotomi Hideyoshi constructed the Great castle. Under Toyotomi Hideyoshi's rule, Osaka developed into a commercial district. The expansion of water transport contributed to Osaka's economic growth but the city went into decline after the death of Hideyoshi in 1598.

The excavation of canals under the direction of Edo (1603–1868) improved the transportation of rice and led to the way to Osaka becoming the 'kitchen of the nation'.

The Genroku period (1680–1710) favoured the performing arts such as Bunraku (Japanese puppet theatre) and kabuki, a style of theatre. Whilst Japan adopted the closed door policy to Westerners in the nineteenth century, the Japanese in Osaka studied the Dutch language and Western Science. Osaka then gained a reputation as the educational centre of Japan.

In 1889, the city was established as a modern municipality and further improvements were made to water supply, drainage and harbour construction.

Osaka remained prosperous until World War II. Trade links with China went out with the Communist Revolution and were not reinstated until the early 1970s. Recovery was slow as economic growth was concentrated in the Tokyo–Yokohama region.

Natural disasters slowed down growth. In Jan. 1995, a severe earthquake struck the Osaka–Kobe region causing major structural damage and great loss of life. The Hanshin expressway, the main road connecting Osaka and Kobe collapsed.

Modern City

Osaka is served by the bullet train and has an intricate subway system expanded in the 1980s. Many of the streets and expressways are one way, allowing for heavy commuting through the city each day. Located in Osaka Bay, Kansai International Airport opened in 1992 and is the world's largest 24 h airport on the sea. It can be reached by JR kanku special express train or Nankai Railways.

Chief industries are the production of machinery, electrical equipment, metals such as iron and steel, textiles, chemical and processed foods.

Places of Interest

Notable landmarks include the Shitennoji Buddhist temple and Temmangu, a Shinto shrine founded in 593 and 949 respectively.

Osaka is home to several universities: Osaka University (1931); Kansai University (1886) and Osaka City University (1949).

Osh, Kyrgyzstan

Introduction

Capital of the Osh region in southern Kyrgyzstan, Osh was once an important silk trading town. In recent years it has been at the centre of Uzbek–Kyrgyz tensions.

History

Archaeological finds suggest the area was inhabited 3,000 years ago. Appearing in written records of the ninth century, Osh was razed by Mongol invaders in the thirteenth century. Having been rebuilt, it was a major point on the Silk Road by the fifteenth century. In 1990 it witnessed violent disturbances between Uzbeks and Kyrgyzs.

Modern City

The city has old and new sections and is a terminus on the Osh–Khorugh road. Buses run in the area. Silk and cotton remain vital to the local economy, while food processing is also important. Cotton, tobacco and food crops are cultivated in the surrounding are.

Places of Interest

There is a museum, theatre, botanical garden and bazaar. Nearby is Suleiman mountain, a Muslim pilgrimage point, with mosques and a museum built into the mountain. Many travellers use Osh as a base from which to trek into the Pamir mountains.

Oslo, Norway

Introduction

On the southeast coast at the inlet of the Skagerrak at the head of the Oslo Fjord, Oslo is Norway's capital, largest city and chief port.

History

The first evidence of permanent habitation in the area are the remains of timber housing from around 1000, although the Oslo fjord had been inhabited since 800. During the Viking era the area developed as a trade and shipbuilding centre. King Harald III Hardraade (1047–66) founded Oslo around 1050 as a defence post against Danish attack on a plain to the east of the River Aker. The town grew up around a market place in an area rich in fir, lime, spruce and stone. The use of timber for dwellings left the town susceptible to fires, and in the early twelfth century stone began to be used for royal and ecclesiastic buildings. In 1299 Oslo was made Norway's capital. It was to remain so until 1536. It developed into a trading post for the Hanseatic League, a trading alliance of northern European towns. In 1397 Oslo and Norway came under Danish rule with the Union of Kalmar. In the mid-fourteenth century, Oslo's population was decimated by the Black Death and subsequent epidemics, and a century later the population had fallen by three quarters.

In 1624 Oslo was destroyed by fire. The regent, Christian IV (1577–1648), rebuilt the city further west and renamed it Christiania. Arkershus was reinforced and the new city was built around the castle. Wood for building was banned inside the city walls but timber housing outside was absorbed when the city expanded in 1794. In 1814 Christiania and Norway came under the control of Sweden. The city retained its new name until 1877 when it became Kristiania. Oslo developed rapidly in the nineteenth century, especially with industrial development from the middle of the century. The city limits were expanded in 1859 and 1878 and engulfed the surrounding towns. In 1866 it became a separate *fylke*, or county. In 1905 Kristiania became the capital of independent Norway, and 20 years later its name reverted to Oslo. During World War II Oslo was occupied by Germany.

Modern City

Oslo is Norway's industrial, financial and cultural centre. It also has a long heritage as an important shipping centre. The main exports are fish, paper, wood pulp and timber. Manufactures include electrical equipment, textiles and chemicals. Nearby Skøyen houses the Norwegian Trade Fair exhibition hall. Oslo is linked nationally and internationally by road, rail and air. It is home to the Norwegian Opera, the Norwegian Philharmonic and the National Theatre. Established in 1811, the Universitetet i Oslo houses the national library and a concert hall. Oslo is a centre of winter sports and hosts the Holmenkdlen ski jump competition. The city also hosts the annual Nobel Peace Prize.

Places of Interest

Oslo's cultural sites include the seventeenth century cathedral and the nineteenth century Royal Palace. The Vigelandsparken contains a large sculpture park, decorated with nearly 200 works by Norwegian sculptor Gustav Vigeland. Museums include the Nasjonalgalleriet, which displays nineteenth and twentieth century artists, including Matisse, Cézanne and Van Gogh. The Munch museum is dedicated to the Norwegian artist's life and works. A museum of Scandinavian contemporary art contains all aspects of postwar work. At Bygdøy a museum charts Viking history, including Thor Heyerdahl's Pacific expedition, and displays Viking ships, such as the *Fram* used by Fridtjof Nansen and Roald Amundsen.

Ostrava, Czech Republic

Introduction

Ostrava is the third largest city of the Czech Republic, close to the meeting point of the Czech, Slovakian and Polish borders. On the Ostravice River, it is a major industrial and mining centre.

History

There was a Slavic settlement in the area surrounding Ostrava from the eighth century. In 1267 Bishop Bruno of Olomouc established Ostrava as a fortified town. It fell briefly under Hussite occupation in 1428. A fire devastated the town centre in the mid-sixteenth century. During the 30 Years War Ostrava was twice occupied by Swedish forces (1621 and 1622) and once by Danish forces (1626). The coal reserves of the nearby Silesian coalfield were discovered in the 1760s.

The Rudolf Foundry, which later became the Vitkovice Ironworks, was established by the Austro-Hungarian empire in 1828. As part of Czechoslovakia in the inter-war period Ostrava suffered an economic downturn. It fell under Nazi rule during World War II and Hermann Göring established one of the Third Reich's largest munitions factories in the area. Liberated in April 1945, as part of communist Czechoslovakia the city's population expanded. Under Klement Gottwald the munitions factory was replaced by the Nova Hut (New Forge) steelworks, employing over 30,000 people.

Modern City

Among the city's most important industries are mining, metalwork, chemicals and vehicle manufacturing. Following the collapse of the communist regime in 1989, the coal industry went into serious decline. Banking and tertiary industries are making an impact. In 1997 the city was hit by major flooding in the Moravian region.

There is an international airport and the city is a road and rail hub. Public transport includes trams, buses and trolleybuses.

Places of Interest

Leading attractions include an observatory and planetarium, a geological pavilion, the Ostravar brewery, a zoo and the New City Hall viewing tower. St Wencelas Church dates from the thirteenth century and the Old Town Hall houses the city museum. The castle, from the thirteenth century, has been empty since the 1930s and is in bad repair. Restoration will be difficult as it sits on a hill which has sunk 15 metres owing to mine shaft subsidence.

Ottawa, Canada

Introduction

Ottawa lies on the confluence of the Ottawa, Gatineau and Rideau rivers. The Canadian government has invested heavily in making Ottawa a fitting national capital and despite popular criticism that it is dull, the city is favoured for its small-town atmosphere, order and grace.

History

The site of present-day Ottawa was first recorded by French explorer Samuel de Champlain in 1613. During the 1812 war between Britain and the United States, the Rideau river provided the British with a safe shipping route from the Ottawa River to Kingston, thus encouraging settlement. In 1826 the arrival of Lieutenant Colonel John By with the Royal Engineers to canalise the river led to further growth, of what then became known as Bytown.

Quarrels between Canada's other major cities in the mid-nineteenth century (Toronto, Quebec city, Montreal and Kingston) induced leaders to ask Queen Victoria to designate a capital for Canada. Inspired by some watercolours of the Gatineau Hills, Queen Victoria chose Bytown, rechristening it Ottawa in 1855. By the end of the century, the city was the fastest-growing metropolis in Eastern Canada. To acquire the dignity and grandeur fitting for capital status, Prime Minister William Mackenzie-King brought French architect Jacques Gréber to the city in 1937. Gréber beautified the city with a series of parks, avenues and tree-lined pathways.

Modern City

The Federal government remains the major employer, with numerous commercial and financial institutions, as well as embassies and trade associations, locating their headquarters in the city.

Ottawa has seen much change in recent years with Lebanese, Italian and Chinese communities adding to the cultural mix while historic districts, such as Byward Market have been renovated with the introduction of new restaurants and cafes.

Places of Interest

The city has the University of Ottawa, St Paul University and Carleton University. There is also the National Arts Centre, encompassing an opera house, two theatres, the National Library, the National Gallery of Canada and the National Museum of Science and Technology.

Ouagadougou, Burkina Faso

Introduction

Known locally as Ouaga, Ouagadougou is the capital of Burkina Faso. Situated in the middle of the country, it is the country's political and communications centre.

History

Ouagadougou was the capital of the Mossi kingdom of Wagadugu and the seat of its leader, the *Moro Naba*, or Ruler of the World. It was built around the Mossi palace of Mogho Naaba. The town came under French colonial rule at the end of the nineteenth century when the colony of Upper Volta was created. When the colony achieved independence in 1960, and later when it was renamed Burkina Faso in 1984, Ouagadougou remained its capital.

Modern City

Major industries include textiles, footwear and matches, while the surrounding agricultural region specializes in peanuts. The University of Ouagadougou was established in 1969. It has an international airport as well as being connected to the Côte d'Ivoire by rail and Niger by road. Biannually the city hosts the FESPACO Panafrican cinema festival, alternating with an international crafts show, the Salon international d'Artisanat Africain.

Places of Interest

Le Centre National de l'Artisanat promotes indigenous crafts, while the Musée National exhibits craftwork from different ethnic groups, including masks, jewellery, musical instruments and pottery.

Palermo, Italy

Introduction

Palermo is the capital, largest city, and chief port of Sicily. Located in the northwest of the island at the head of the Bay of Palermo and the foot of Monte Pellegrino, the city fronts the Conca d'Oro valley. Its strategic location has meant that it has been fought over for centuries.

History

Founded in the eighth century BC by the Phoenicians, Palermo became a Carthaginian base, and was subsequently seized by Rome in 254 BC. The Romans named it Panormus and the city suffered neglect under their rule. Its prosperity was restored in the sixth century when it became a part of the Byzantine Empire. From 831 to 1072 it was under the control of the Saracens. Palermo flourished under Arab rule, boosted by revenue from trade with North Africa. Much of the city's present character and architecture date from this period. The Normans occupied Palermo in 1072. Their ruler, Roger II, pronounced himself King of Sicily in 1130. His reign was the golden age for Palermo, and it was regarded as one of the most magnificent and cultured cities of twelfth century Europe. The kingdom was remarkable for the peaceful co-existence of Normans, Jews and Arabs.

The monarchy passed to the Hohenstaufens in 1194. The Holy Roman Emperor Frederick II established a court in Palermo, which was a renowned centre of culture. After Frederick's reign the city went into decline and was secured by the Angevin French in 1266. In 1282 French rule was overthrown by an uprising known as the Sicilian Vespers. By this stage Sicily's power was eclipsed by Naples and Palermo began to decline in power and influence. The island was then subject to Aragonese rule and subsequently became a part of Spain until it was captured by Garibaldi in 1860, and incorporated into unified Italy. In the years between the two world wars, Sicily became known as the power centre of the Mafia. Since World War II (during which Palermo suffered heavy bombing by the Allies) great efforts have been made to curb the Mafia's power and many trials have taken place of people accused of having dealings with the Mafia. Along with its political clean up, the city is tackling the restoration of its historic and architectural treasures.

Modern City

Palermo is a major producer of citrus fruits, fish and cereals and its industries include textiles, processed food, chemicals and shipbuilding. There are services running from the Stazione Centrale to destinations within Sicily as well as Intercity trains to Reggio Calabria, Naples and Rome. International and long distance buses arrive and depart from the Intercity bus station at Via Paolo Balsamo. Ferries arrive at and depart from Molo Vittorio Veneto off Via Francesco Crispi. There are services to Cagliari (Sardinia), Naples, Livorno, Genoa, the Aeolian Islands, Ustica, Malta and Tunisia.

Places of Interest

The Palazzo dei Normanni, or Palazzo Reale, is the seat of Sicily's regional government. The original ninth century Moorish fortress was extended by the Normans and restructured by the Hohenstaufens. The Chapel was built between 1130 and 1140 and is a superb example of Arab-Norman decoration and design. The Normans founded the Duomo, built in Sicilian-Norman style, at the end of the twelfth century. It houses the tombs of Emperor Frederick II and other rulers of Sicily from the houses of Hohenstaufen, Anjou and Aragon. Sicily has a lively tradition of puppet shows showcased in the Museo delle Marionette. The collection includes several puppets of Gaspare Canino—a celebrated nineteenth century puppet-maker as well as marionettes from all over the world. The Teatro Massimo theatre was constructed in the Neo-classical style between 1875 and 1897. It boasts the second largest indoor stage in Europe and the lavish interior has an opulent rotunda at its centre. The Regional Archaeological museum has one of best collections in the country of Etruscan artifacts.

Palikir, Micronesia

Introduction

Palikir, Micronesia's capital city, is in the Palikir Valley on Pohnpei, the largest island in the Federated States.

History

Palikir succeeded Kolonia as national capital in 1989. Kolonia remains the state capital of Pohnpei and the main commercial centre. However, all major government institutions have moved to Palikir.

Modern City

The chief employers are the government and the tourist industry. Fishing and agriculture is important in the surrounding region.

The airport (with links to Honolulu, Guam and other Micronesian airports) and most hotel accommodation is in Kolonia.

Places of Interest

Pohnpei's principal attraction is its natural environment, encompassing freshwater pools and waterfalls, a startling coastline and coral reefs, rainforest and the 700-year-old city of Nan Madol, known as the Venice of the Pacific. Diving, trekking and boat trips to nearby atolls are popular.

Panama City, Panama

Introduction

At the entrance to the Panama Canal in the Bay of Panama on the Pacific coast, Panama City is the country's capital and its industrial and trade centre.

History

Meaning 'many fish', Panama City was originally an indigenous fishing village. Panamá Viejo was founded by the conquistador Pedro Arias Dávila in 1519. It soon became a key point on the colonial trade route, receiving goods which were then sent on to Spain. In the sixteenth and seventeenth centuries the city was the target of pirate raids and outside attacks which caused a depreciation in trade and threatened its prosperity. An unsuccessful attack by Francis Drake in 1595 was followed by the decimation of the city in 1671 by the Welsh pirate Henry Morgan. Abandoning the old city, a new site 8 km southwest was settled by Alonso Mercado de Villacorta. In the eighteenth century the city suffered a decline in trade and several fires caused much destruction. Panama City was swallowed into the viceroyalty of New Granada (comprising Venezuela, Ecuador and Columbia) and eventually into independent Columbia.

A period of unrest characterized the nineteenth century, although the Californian gold rush and the arrival of an inter-oceanic railway restored Panama City's importance. Between 1879–89, a French team led by the creator of the Suez Canal, Ferdinand de Lesseps, invested 1 bn. francs in attempting to build a canal linking Panama City to the Caribbean Sea. Hampered by landslides and disease and the loss of many lives, the venture failed. The US also wanted to build a canal across the isthmus but negotiations with Columbia failed. When Panama fought for independence at the beginning of the twentieth century it was with US supported. In 1903 Panama City was made the capital of independent Panama. In the same year, the Hay-Bunau-Varilla Treaty was signed allowing the US sole control of the future canal and a 10 mile surrounding area called the Panama Canal Zone. The first ship sailed across the isthmus in 1914. Panama City prospered and developed. American communities sprung up around the area, including Panama City's port, Bilboa. Although within the US zone, Panama City remained Panamanian. In 1977 a treaty was signed by the US and Panama governments returning the area to Panamanian rule, although the US did not give up operational control of the area until 1999.

Modern City

As an important trade centre, the canal traffic is still the city's main source of income. Industries include the production of paper, clothing, plastics and chemicals. Universities include the Universidad de Panamá, founded in 1935 and the Universidad Santa Maria la Antigua opened in 1965. International flights arrive at the Tocumen airport, 27 km from the city centre. Other cities are connected by the Ferrocarril de Panamá rail road and the Transisthmian Highway.

Places of Interest

Much of Panama City's colonial heritage remains, including buildings which survived fires and invasion, and much is centred in the Casco Antiguo (old town). The Catedral San Francisco dates from 1673 while the 1798 Catedral Metropolitana is in the Plaza Catedral, originally the site of a Spanish jail.

Museums include the Museo Antropológico Reina Tomes de Araúz which tracks Panama's ethnography, the Museo de Arte Religioso Colonial with sixteenth to eighteenth century religious artefacts and the Museo de Arte Contemporaneo. The ruins of the original settlement are 8 km from the city centre.

Paramaribo, Suriname

Introduction

On the west bank of the Suriname River, Paramaribo is Suriname's capital and principal port. On the north Surinamese coast, the city is 15 km from the Atlantic Ocean.

History

Arawak and Carib tribes originally inhabited the area. Paramaribo was based on the indigenous village of Paramurubo, meaning 'Place of Parwa Blossoms'. French colonists established a trading post here in the early seventeenth century. The British captured the village in the mid-seventeenth century and extended the settlement, establishing sugar and tobacco plantations. Paramaribo was under British rule until a deal was made with the Dutch in 1667 by which the English took control of New Amsterdam (New York) in exchange for Suriname. Rapid expansion over the next 20 years led the Dutch colonist Abraham Crijnssen to name Paramaribo the territory capital. At the end of the seventeenth century under Governor Cornelis van Aerssen van Sommelsdijk, expansion continued and a canal system was built. Slaves and indentured labour brought over by the Dutch and British from India, China and Indonesia combined with the indigenous population and colonists to create a diverse ethnic mix still present today.

The city suffered from destructive fires in 1821 and 1832. When slavery was abolished in 1863, the city's population was swollen by the migration of free slaves from the rural plantations to the capital.

In the second half of the twentieth century, tourism and industry increased. When the county gained independence from The Netherlands in 1975, Paramaribo was retained as Suriname's capital.

Modern City

The chief port and administrative and economic centre, Paramaribo is home to two thirds of the country's population. Suriname's main export is bauxite, while other exports from Paramaribo include coffee, fruit and timber. Industries include cement and paint production. Domineestraat is the main commercial centre. The city is served by rail, road and two airports—the domestic Zorg-en-Hoop and the international Zanderij airport, 45 km south of the city. There are three flights a week to The Netherlands. Educational institutions founded in the 1960s include the Anton de Kom University of Suriname, the medical college and the agricultural research centre.

Places of Interest

Lined with tropical palms, Palamentuin Park is behind Onafhnkelijksplein (Unity Square), the site of Presidential Palace. Founded by the French in 1640, named Fort Willoughby under the British and rebuilt by the Dutch in the 18th, nearby Fort Zeelandia is Paramaribo's oldest monument. Pre-colonial artifacts are displayed in the Surinaams Museum while south of the city, the Brownsberg nature park has tropical rainforest.

Paris, France

Introduction

The capital of France since the tenth century, Paris is the country's cultural, commercial, financial and industrial centre. Situated on the Seine River in Northern France, Paris is one of Europe's most popular tourist destinations.

History

Paris originated as a fishing village on the Ile de la Cité, named after the Parisii, a Gallic tribe. In 52 BC the village was conquered by the Romans, who named it Lutetia. The town developed onto the Left Bank of the Seine. Paris was captured by the Franks under Clovis at the end of the fifth century, then came under Merovingian rule, although much of the control of the city was left to the Counts of Paris. It was one such, Hugh Capet, elected to the throne in 987, who made Paris into the national capital of the developing country now recognizable as France.

Medieval Paris flourished as a cultural and commercial centre. The creation of the University of Paris in 1200 marked the division of Paris into three parts—the Ile de la Cité, from whence the city has since developed in expanding concentric circles; the Right Bank, containing the commercial centre; and the Left Bank, the intellectual centre. In the mid-thirteenth century the Sorbonne was founded on the Left Bank.

The population was decimated by the Black Death (1348–49) and the Hundred Years War (1337–1453). Paris suffered during the struggle between the Armagnacs and the Burgundians (1407–35), and was occupied by the latter and by the English in 1418–35, before Charles VII restored Paris to French rule. The Pont Neuf (1577), the oldest bridge in Paris, was for 200 years the city's main street. During the Wars of Religion, Catholic Paris was the setting for the St Bartholomew's Day Massacre (24–25 Aug. 1572), when thousands of Huguenots were slaughtered. Instead of weakening the Protestants, the massacre only served to exacerbate the tensions and reignite the Wars of Religion. Parisians did not accept Henry IV (1589–1610) until he converted to Catholicism.

For 200 years Paris prospered. The renovation of the medieval Louvre castle was completed in 1674, although Louis XIV (1643–1715) transferred the Court to Versailles. This era ended with the Revolution. On 14 July 1789 the Bastille prison was stormed. In 1792 the monarchy was abolished and on 21 Jan. 1793 King Louis XVI was executed at the Place de la Révolution (now Place de la Concorde). The Committee of Public Safety brutally suppressed anyone suspected of Royalist sympathies. The Revolution was followed by Napoléon Bonaparte's rise to power and the industrialization of Paris. Napoléon I built the Arc de Triomphe on the Champs-Elysées to commemorate France's military victories. The eternal flame has marked the tomb of the Unknown Soldier since 1920.

The first railway was built in 1837. Rapid industrialization left many Parisians in squalid slums. The city saw revolutions in July 1830, when Charles X was dethroned, and in Feb. 1848, when Louis-Philippe—head of the July monarchy—was deposed. Napoléon III (1852–70) sought to improve Paris. Major urban planning and expansion began in 1855, enacted by Baron Georges Haussmann. These changes became the basis of modern Paris. Geometric boulevards replaced the medieval streets, modern sewers were installed and renovations made to many central buildings. One area to keep its traditional character was Montmartre. Built on the side of a steep hill, the Romans, who called this quarter Mons Mars, consecrated an altar to Mercury and a shrine to Mars. The steep narrow streets and alleyways of Montmartre became the centre of Bohemian life. 1871 saw another uprising. The Paris Commune resulted in the death of around 20,000 insurrectionists. Paris was occupied during the Franco-Prussian War of 1870–71, but German troops were halted before they reached Paris in World War I. Paris was occupied during World War II, although the city remained relatively unscathed.

Further urban developments in postwar France were coupled with social tensions. Housing shortages led to the building of HLMs (Habitation à Loyer Modéré; council flats), now an integral if unaesthetic part of the modern Parisian skyline. Modern cultural developments include the Pompidou Centre, opened in 1977. Under the presidency of François Mitterrand, projects included the building of the Bastille Opera House, the Louvre pyramid, La Villette science complex and L'Arche at La Défence.

Modern City

Paris is a major transportation hub—with two airports and seven main railway stations—and a cultural and intellectual centre of world status. Divided into 20 arrondissements, or districts, Paris is governed by a mayor. The city specializes in the production of luxury goods, including jewellery, haute couture and perfume. Major industries include vehicle production, metallurgy and chemicals, but its principal revenue is from tourism. The city is served by a metro system, and since 1994 Eurostar train services travel to Brussels and London. National rail serves all areas of France, while international rail services travel to Central and Eastern Europe and the Iberian Peninsula.

Places of Interest

The Ile de la Cité on the River Seine contains the Gothic Catédrale de Notre Dame de Paris (begun 1163). Originally the site of the Romans' altar to Jupiter, the cathedral witnessed Joan of Arc's trial for heresy in 1431. It was also the inspiration for Victor Hugo's novel *Notre Dame de Paris*. Features include two towers and two rose windows in purple stained glass. The Renaissance saw the renovation of the Louvre (1528). Built on the foundations of a medieval castle, it served as the Royal palace for hundreds of years, and is now an art gallery of international repute. Other museums include the Musée d'Orsay, the Musée Rodin, the Musée Picasso and the Pompidou Centre. Opened in 1977, the Pompidou Centre is a futuristic arts and culture centre with an externalized infrastructure with exposed piping and ventilation in primary colours.

The most frequented monuments include the Arc de Triomphe and the tomb of the unknown soldier, but without doubt the most famous is the Eiffel Tower. Designed by civil engineer Gustave Eiffel and built with 7,000 tonnes of wrought iron, the 300 m-high tower was completed for the International Exposition of 1889. The Père Lachaisse cemetery attracts visitors to the graves of Balzac, Proust, Chopin, Oscar Wilde and the 1960s singer Jim Morrison. The Palace of Versailles, formerly the official residence of the court of France, is also a popular tourist attraction.

Pärnu, Estonia

Introduction

Pärnu, on the River Pärnu on the Gulf of Riga, is among Estonia's most popular holiday resorts.

History

There is evidence of Stone Age human habitation in the area around Pärnu. It was first mentioned in written records in 1154 and by the middle of the next century it was an important trading village within the Hanseatic League. Livonian rule came to an end in 1561 after much bloodshed and destruction. Between 1562 and 1617 control of the city changed hands six times. In 1617 Swedish forces took control. In 1710 the plague-ridden town was ceded to Russia. The first rail connection in 1896 brought visitors to the beaches and mud baths and in 1925 the municipal authorities decided to develop the town as a modern resort.

Modern City

Pärnu is a major port and remains a popular beach and convalescence resort. Other important industries include food processing, wood-working and leather tanning. Pärnu is known as Estonia's 'Summer Capital' and is renowned for its nightlife.

Places of Interest

Sights include the medieval Red Tower, the baroque Elisabeth Church, and St. Catherine's Russian Orthodox church. There are also a number of examples of art nouveau and neo-classical buildings.

Perth, Australia

Introduction

Capital of Western Australia and home to 77% of the state's population, Perth lies on the banks of the Swan and Canning Rivers between the Indian Ocean and the Darling Ranges. It is served by the port of Fremantle ('Freo') which is 20 km away. Located far from any other Australian city, Perth is an important transport terminus. The discoveries of gold in the nineteenth century and of iron ore and nickel in the twentieth century made for a booming economy. The city's favourable climate and natural environment make it a popular tourist destination.

History

Nyoongar Aboriginals moved into the region 40,000 years ago but it was not until 1697 that Dutchman Willem de Vlamingh named the Swan River. By the 1820s there was a heavy British presence in Australia but much of the west coast remained unclaimed. Fearing French and American expansion, the British sent Captain James Stirling to choose a settlement site. The town was established 2 years later when Captain Sir Charles Fremantle landed in the area on 2 May 1829. Stirling named the settlement Perth on 12 Aug., in honour of the British secretary of state for the Colonies who came from Perth in Scotland.

Unlike many other Australian cities, Perth was originally inhabited by freemen. Its early years were blighted by financial hardship and a lack of human resources. To resolve this problem, convicts were sent from Britain from 1850 to be used as labour in the construction of public buildings. Queen Victoria declared Perth a city in 1856.

A gold rush in the 1890s in an area some 600 km to the east of Perth led to a rise in the city's fortunes and rapid population expansion. Further prosperity came with the re-development of the Fremantle Harbour at the turn of the twentieth century and with improvements in the Australian transport infrastructure, culminating in the opening of the Transcontinental Railway in Nov. 1917.

The city achieved further prosperity in the 1960s when it became a centre for iron ore and nickel mining. The appearance of many high-rise office towers altered the cityscape. In 1962 the city hosted the British Empire and Commonwealth Games. In the same year, Perth became known as the 'city of lights' because residents illuminated the city to greet astronaut John Glen on his Challenger flight. The 1980s saw Perth at the forefront of Western Australia's entrepreneurship, earning the state its nickname 'W.A. Inc.' which persisted until the 1987 stock market crash.

Modern City

Aside from port activities at Fremantle, where 22.5 m tonnes of cargo were processed in 2000–01, Perth's most important industries are metallurgy, food processing, oil, metal, rubber and printing. Publishing and printing account for half of all manufacturing and storage sector employees. The key sectors in the city centre are business and finance (66% of city employees), the civic sector (26%), and retail (13%). The city's biggest employer is the Royal Perth teaching hospital, which started life as a tent in 1829.

Perth is linked to other major Australian cities via a motorway network and by the Transcontinental Railway. It has an international airport 12 km from the city centre that handles around 430,000 passengers each month. Each year central Perth receives approximately 3 m. visitors. 30% of the city's population was born overseas. Many tourists and surfers are drawn by the Indian Ocean beaches, in particular those at Cottesloe, Scarborough and Trigg.

The University of Western Australia opened in 1913 to be followed in 1975 by Murdoch University, named after literature scholar Sir Walter Murdoch. The 1980s saw the opening of Edith Cowan University and the creation of Curtin University of Technology. A small Catholic University, Notre Dame, opened in Fremantle in 1990. Around half the workforce possess post-secondary or tertiary qualifications.

Major annual events include the Perth Royal Show, an agricultural festival and West Week, a commemoration of the state's foundation. The Perth Festival, established in 1953, is the oldest international arts festival in the Southern Hemisphere. Its 1,000 performances during Jan. and Feb. are attended by around 500,000 people annually and bring $A22.4 m. to the city's economy. An alternative arts festival is held simultaneously in the Northbridge district and the Artrage Festival takes place biennially in Oct.

Places of Interest

The city's oldest building is the Old Courthouse, now the Francis Burt Law Museum, dating from 1836/37. Other sites of historical interest include the old Gaol, originally opened in 1856, and Barracks Arch, the remains of the 1863 Pensioners' Guards Barracks. Perth Zoo opened in 1898; the Perth Mint was founded a year later. The Western Australian Museum, the state's largest museum, was established in 1891 and received 770,000 visitors in 2000–01. One of the country's best Aboriginal collections (some 40,000 objects, recordings and books) is held in the Berndt Museum of Anthropology at the University of Western Australia. Scitech Discovery Centre opened in 1988 and receives 325,000 visitors each year.

His Majesty's Theatre, built in 1904, is Australia's only surviving Edwardian theatre; other popular entertainment venues are the Regal Theatre, Perth Concert Hall, and Belvoir Amphitheatre. Key cultural facilities also include the Art Gallery of Western Australia, and the Perth Institute of Contemporary Art.

King's Park and botanic gardens, located on the edge of the CBD, opened in 1872 and contains the State War Memorial. Near Perth are the Yanchep and John Forrest National Parks, Penguin Island, and the Shoalwater Islands Marine Park. The Marine Park encompasses Seal Island, home to the world's rarest seal species, the Australian sea lion. The Aquarium of Western Australia, with about 400 species of marine life, received over 4.3 m. visitors from the aquarium's opening in 1988 up to 2004.

Philadelphia, United States of America

Introduction

The fifth largest city in the United States, Philadelphia is the nation's former capital and was the city where both the Declaration of Independence and the Constitution were written. Located in the southeastern corner of the eastern state of Pennsylvania, the city is roughly equidistant between New York City and Washington, D.C. and is located where the Schuylkill and Delaware rivers meet.

History

One of the most historic of all American cities, Philadelphia (which comes from the Greek words meaning 'city of brotherly love') was established by the English Quaker William Penn, who named the state of Pennsylvania in honour of his father. Previously the area had been explored by the Dutch and the Swedes and claimed by the British in the name of Charles II in 1664. Penn adopted the grid-like pattern for his new city that would become the staple of most American cities. He also warmly welcomed people of all ethnic and religious persuasions in what he called 'a holy experiment'. By the 1750s, Philadelphia was the second largest city in the British empire.

Penn's commitment to liberty of speech attracted many radicals, intellectuals and philosophers to Philadelphia which became known as the 'Athens of America'. The city's founding father even signed peace accords with local Native Americans. Penn's secretary James Logan founded one of America's first subscription libraries. Opened in 1731, the Library Company of Philadelphia is still in use today. In a similarly innovative vein, 1751 saw the first public hospital in America built in the city by Benjamin Franklin and Thomas Bond.

During the American War of Independence, Philadelphia was the nation's capital. The Declaration of Independence was drafted, written and read aloud in 1776, with the Constitution following in 1786. Nevertheless despite hosting these historic events, the city lost its status as the capital in 1800 after a compromise deal between Thomas Jefferson and Alexander Hamilton to create a new capital led to the building of Washington, D.C.

During the nineteenth century Philadelphia thrived as a manufacturing centre. Textiles and shipbuilding industries were joined by new industries, such as chemicals and food processing, in the early twentieth century.

Modern City

After World War II a decline in manufacturing saw significant pockets of the population move to the suburbs or to other states. This in turn led to a decline in the city's population and an increase in ethnic separation. Despite escalating social problems, the city has, in keeping with Penn's original vision, remained a symbol of diversity and tolerance in many ways—for example, it was the first American city to elect a black mayor.

Major redevelopment projects were undertaken from the 1950s onwards to reconstruct the downtown areas of Philadelphia, with special efforts being made in the lead up to the 1976 celebration of the United States' bicentenary. From 1987, height restrictions on buildings were also relaxed, allowing the city's first skyscrapers to be built.

Health care industries such as chemicals and pharmaceuticals are now the city's commercial mainstays, along with banking and publishing.

Among the city's institutes of higher education are the University of Pennsylvania, Temple University and Drexel University.

Places of Interest

Philadelphia remains a powerful draw for the cultural or historical tourist. The Philadelphia Museum of Art and the Rodin Museum are two particularly famed attractions. The city also contains Fairmount Park, the largest municipally owned landscaped park in the world, and the Philadelphia Zoo. Other popular sites include Independence Hall, where the Declaration of Independence was signed, and the iconic Liberty Bell.

Phnom Penh, Cambodia

Introduction

Phnom Penh is the capital city of Cambodia, situated at the confluence of the Tonlé Basǎk (Bassac), Tonlé Sap and Mekong rivers.

History

Penh, a wealthy Khmer woman, founded the city as a small Buddhist monastery in 1372. In 1434 King Chao Ponhea Yat chose the present site to succeed Angkor as the capital city, probably because of constant Siamese aggression and the final conquest of Angkor in 1431 and the Cambodian reluctance to submit to foreign overlords. Phnom Penh has never rivalled the glamour of Angkor and ruled for long periods over what wasn't a sovereign country but a satellite state of the Thais and Vietnamese.

On 17 April 1864 King Norodom accepted, on behalf of Cambodia, the status of French protectorate. He expected French protection to mean an end to incursions by the Thais and the Vietnamese but the French did little to stop the Thais temporarily annexing western parts of the country. During the 1870s the French colonial administration built a hotel, school, prison, barrack, bank, public works office, telegraph office, law court, a health services house and 300 concrete houses along the waterfront. These houses were sold to wealthy Chinese traders. In 1884 Cambodia's status was changed from that of protectorate to colony. By 1897 the city's population was 50,000 inhabitants but most of these were Chinese and Vietnamese traders.

In Sept. 1940, after Germany's invasion of France Japanese troops invaded Cambodia along with the rest of Indochina, meeting very little resistance. The Japanese instated a Vichy French Government in Phnom Penh.

The period between World War II and the Vietnam War was a relatively quiet and constructive one for Phnom Penh with the city population growing to 90,000 in 1970. Phnom Penh was witness to much building, including an International Olympic stadium and the Cambodia-Japan Friendship Bridge.

In 1969, with the encroachment of the Vietnam War into Cambodia, people in outlying villages fled to the relative safety of Phnom Penh to escape bombing, further swelling the population to 2 m. by 1975. In 1970, with Norodom Sihanouk in Moscow, Gen. Lon Nol staged a successful coup d'etat abolished the monarchy and declared Cambodia a republic. Sihanouk remained head of the Cambodian government in exile from Beijing, forming an alliance with patriotic forces including the Khmer Rouge.

The Khmer Rouge, a radical communist guerrilla movement, launched an offensive against the US sanctioned Lon Nol regime and within 5 years only Phnom Penh remained under the control of Lon Nol. On 17 April 1975 the Khmer Rouge rolled into Phnom Penh, executed large numbers of Cambodians associated with the Lon Nol regime and forcibly moved the inhabitants of the city to provincial labour camps. For nearly 4 years, during which time the Khmer Rouge, under the leadership of Pol Pot, enacted a brutal countrywide social experiment, Phnom Penh became a ghost town. It is estimated that more than a million Cambodians fell victim to the Khmer Rouge.

On 25 Dec. 1978 the Vietnamese army invaded Cambodia and quickly occupied the derelict Phnom Penh, installing a Vietnamese friendly government. Although this government was not internationally recognised it took until 1989 for a Cambodian coalition force to eject Vietnamese troops from Cambodia.

In 1991 King Norodom Sihanouk returned to Phnom Penh and a year later the United Nations Transitory Authority in Cambodia (UNTAC), led by Sihanouk, assumed control of the government form Phnom Penh.

In Nov. 2010, 347 people were killed and more than 500 injured in a human stampede during Phnom Penh's Khmer Water Festival celebrations. Prime Minister Hun Sen described the stampede as the biggest disaster the country had experienced since the mass killings of the Khmer Rouge regime.

Modern City

During the 1990s Phnom Penh received grant aid to repair and rebuild the city. Today Phnom Penh is the cultural, educational, and commercial centre of Cambodia; a bustling city covering an area over 41 km^2 and home to an estimated 10% of Cambodia's population.

Places of Interest

Phnom Penh has numerous *wats* (temple-monasteries), the most famous being Wat Ounalom, Wat Phnom and Wat Lang Ka. The Royal Palace was built on the site of the former citadel in 1866. The National Museum houses a large collection of Khmer art, dating from the sixth century to the present. The Silver Pagoda, within the Royal Palace, has a famous floor constructed from several thousand silver blocks and a seventeenth century Emerald Buddha. A genocide museum at Tuol Sleng and a mass grave at Choeung Ek pay tribute to those who suffered under the Khmer Rouge.

Phoenix, United States of America

Introduction

Phoenix is the eighth largest city in the United States and the largest in Arizona, as well as the state capital and the seat of Maricopa County. Located in the south of the state along Slat River in a valley surrounded by mountains, Phoenix is roughly equidistant between Los Angeles, California and El Paso, Texas and occupies an area of 420 sq. miles (1,088 km^2).

History

Native Americans (known as Hohokams) lived in the Salt River Valley where modern day Phoenix now stands as long ago as AD 1300 and developed the area's first irrigation canals. The area was re-settled in the 1860s after Jack Swilling visited the valley and discovered the irrigation system left by the Hohokams and founded his own irrigation company and village.

The name Phoenix was given to the new settlement in recognition of the fact that the new settlement had risen from the ashes of the previous Native American settlement. Phoenix became the seat of Arizona's territorial government in 1889 and the state capital in 1912 when Arizona attained statehood. The city's irrigation projects were fed by the Theodore Roosevelt dam, which was completed in 1911. The dam assured the city's water supply and enabled it to become a centre for industry and agriculture.

Modern City

Phoenix was famously described by writer Edward Abbey as 'the blob that is eating Arizona' as it has gradually expanded to fill the whole of the Salt River valley, and gobble up the towns of Mesa, Tempe and Scottsdale in the process. The population has also swelled rapidly, from around 100,000 in 1950 to nearly 1 m. in 1990.

The city is Arizona's major industrial, agricultural and financial centre. Among the most important industries are the manufacture of aerospace and electronic equipment, agricultural chemicals, air conditioning equipment, processed food and metal products. The irrigated land surrounding Phoenix produces many fruit and vegetable products and the city is a major distribution centre for these. Several military sites are located in and around the city including Luke Air Force Base.

Phoenix is served by Sky Harbor International Airport, which is located 3 miles to the east of the downtown area of the city. The city is no longer on the Amtrak train network, but has a local bus service (the Phoenix Transit System) and Greyhound buses terminate and leave from near the city's Civic Plaza.

Arizona State University is located nearby in Tempe.

Places of Interest

Visitor attractions include the Phoenix Museum of History, the Phoenix Art Museum and the Heard Museum, which is devoted to the history of Native Americans in Arizona. Papago Park, in the east of the city, contains Phoenix Zoo and a botanical garden. The most notable building is the State Capitol and Frank Lloyd Wright's architecture studio at Taliesin West. Every year Phoenix hosts the Arizona State Fair and the World Rodeo Championships.

Plovdiv, Bulgaria

Introduction

An important industrial and market town, Plovdiv, Bulgari's second city, is on the River Maritsa in the south-central part of the country.

History

Plovdiv was called Pulpudeva during the ancient Thracian period but was renamed Philippopolis when it was conquered by Philip II of Macedonia in the fourth century BC. In the middle of the first century AD it became a regional centre for Roman Thrace and was renamed Thrimonzium. From the late-fourth century it was ruled by Byzantium.

Huns over-ran the town in the fifth century and in the next century it was settled by Slavs. Khan Kroum successfully invaded in 815 but the city was incorporated into Bulgaria until Byzantine troops seized power in the early-tenth century. Having been plundered by Crusaders in the late twelfth century, Plovdiv was extensively rebuilt under Ivanko. In 1364 it was conquered by the Ottoman Turks who re-named it Filibe and again the city thrived commercially, although resentment grew at the cultural oppression.

From the middle of the nineteenth century the town became a focus for the Bulgarian national awakening. Following the Russo-Turkish War of 1877–78, Plovdiv was capital of Turkish Eastern Rumelia but 7 years later it was brought back into the Bulgarian state. The name Plovdiv was officially adopted in 1919. When a communist government took power after World War II, Plovdiv maintained close relations with Moscow but in 1989, shortly before the communist collapse, it was a focal point for pro-democracy demonstrations.

Modern City

Major industries include carpet-making, food processing, textiles, electrical goods manufacturing and metal working. The city is an important trade centre for the surrounding region which produces tobacco and food crops. Tourism is also important.

Plovdiv is well served by road and rail links and lies on the Belgrade–Sofia–Istanbul line. Kroumovo airport is a short distance from the city centre.

Places of Interest

The modern city extends over six hills but the ancient city centred on the Three Hills area, consisting of Nebet Tepe, Djambaz Tepe and Taxim Tepe. Nebet Tepe is an archaeological complex with remains from the prehistoric, Roman and Greek periods. Hissar Kapiya is the gateway of the Roman fortress constructed under the emperors Trajan and Marcus Aurelius while the Ancient Theatre, an amphitheatre that used to seat 7,000, is still used for musical and theatrical performances.

Other remains include medieval friezes and a giant watertank, Tsar Ivan Asen II's ruined fortress and the Bachkovo monastery. The Imaret and Djumaya mosques reflect the Ottoman phase. There are several old Christian churches including those of St Constance and Elena, St Marina, St Nedelia, St Petka and the Holy Virgin. Sahat Tepe is surmounted by one of the oldest clock towers in Eastern Europe. Other attractions include the City Garden (designed by Napoléon III's gardener) and the modern Rowing Canal sports and leisure area.

Plovdiv was one of two European Capitals of Culture for 2019, alongside Matera in Italy. The title attracts large European Union grants.

Plzeň (Pilsen), Czech Republic

Introduction

Plzeň is the Czech Republic's fourth largest city and the capital of Západočeský region. A Catholic stronghold during the Hussite wars of the fifteenth century, it is now principally an industrial city best known for its beer manufacture and the Skoda engineering works.

History

The site of modern Plzeň was established in 1295 by Wencelas II, at the centre of major Prague–Bavarian trade routes. Known as Nova Plzeň (New Plzeň), the new site was around 10 km from that of Old Plzeň, where a castle had been constructed in 976. The first brewery in the area was recorded in 1307.

The early Hussite movement found support from the town in the early fifteenth century, but was expelled in 1420. Despite being besieged three times by Hussite invaders (in 1427, 1431 and 1433–34), Plzeň remained resolutely Catholic. The period from 1550 to the seventeenth century was one of dynamic growth. The first Czech printed book, *Trojan Chronicle*, was published in Plzeň in 1468.

The town was devastated by fire in 1507, with two thirds of its buildings destroyed. It was the first of several fires to blight the town over the coming centuries, with the last major blaze occurring in 1835. In 1599 Emperor Rudolf II based himself in the city for a year in a bid to escape the Plague and made Plzeň the interim capital of the Holy Roman Empire. In 1618 the city fell to the Protestant forces of Count Arnost Manfeld. It also endured two outbreaks of the plague before the end of the century.

The city expanded again in the industrial revolution of the nineteenth century. The City Brewery was established in 1842 and was followed 17 years later by the Waldstein Engineering Works that would evolve into Skoda. Expansion continued throughout the century, although Plzeň was occupied by Prussian troops for 2 months during 1866.

Growth slowed during the twentieth century as a result of World War I and a general economic slump. The city came under fierce air attack during World War II, with over 6,500 houses destroyed and almost 1,000 people killed. It was liberated on 6 May 1945 by US forces led by General Patton. Under communist rule until 1989, Skoda became one of the leading suppliers of engineering and transport manufactures to the Eastern Bloc.

Modern City

Brewing and engineering dominate Plzeň's local economy, which has plentiful supplies of coal and iron ore. Textiles, paper and pottery are also important. Plzeň acts as a trade centre for the surrounding agricultural region.

Trams, buses and trolley buses run within the city. Plzeň is on an extensive rail network and its airport, a former military base, is undergoing a 10-year development plan that began in 2001. The University of West Bohemia was founded in Plzeň in 1949.

Plzeň was chosen by the EU to be one of the European Capitals of Culture for 2015, alongside Mons in Belgium.

Places of Interest

Plzeň's leading attraction is the Plzeňsky Prazdroj Brewery (City Brewery), home of Pilsner Urquell beer. The Skoda works has its own museum. St Bartholomew's Church dates from the thirteenth century while the sixteenth century town hall was created by the Renaissance architect, Giovanni de Statia. The Franciscan church and monastery have retained much of their Gothic heritage, while the Church of St Anna and St Ruzena Limanska is a fine example of Baroque design. The Grand Synagogue is among the largest synagogues in central Europe. The West Bohemia Museum has a collection covering the region's history from pre-historic times. Also open to the public is a network of multi-leveled cellars built between the thirteenth and nineteenth centuries.

Port Moresby, Papua New Guinea

Introduction

Port Moresby, on Port Moresby Harbour on the Gulf of Papua, is Papua New Guinea's capital and its main port.

History

The British sea captain John Moresby explored the area in 1873 and named the port after his father. It was claimed by the British 10 years later and served as an important Allied base during World War II. By this time New Guinea was an Australian-administered UN Trust Territory and Papua an Australian Overseas Territory. Port Moresby served as the administrative seat. Having been heavily developed, Port Moresby formed the National Capital District (established in 1974) and a year later it became capital of independent Papua New Guinea. There are proposals to transfer many of the capital's institutions to the suburb of Waigani.

Modern City

Port Moresby's port offers shipping services to Australia and other coastal ports. It has a good road infrastructure and the Jackson international airport is close to the city centre. Water comes from the nearby Laloki River but the city is prone to droughts.

Principal exports are copra, rubber and gold. Tourism is also an important revenue-earner. There is a university.

Places of Interest

Among the leading tourist attractions are the parliament building and the national museum and gallery. There is a bustling market at Gordons and a big shopping complex at Boroko. There are several unspoilt beaches nearby and Sinasi reef is popular with divers. A short distance from the city centre are the Rouna Falls and Varirata National Park.

Port of Spain, Trinidad and Tobago

Introduction

Port of Spain, the capital of Trinidad and Tobago, is one of the prime ports of the West Indies. The city is on Trinidad's west coast on the Gulf of Paria that separates the island from Venezuela. Port of Spain has a geometric pattern with squares and parks. Not dependent on tourism, the city has a diversified industry and is the financial capital of the Eastern Caribbean.

History

The town was first visited by Columbus in 1498. Originally a fishing village named Conquerabia by the native Indians, it was renamed Puerta de Espana (Port of Spain) by the Spaniards. In 1757 it replaced St Joseph as capital. By 1784 Port of Spain had become an important town with flourishing trade and commerce. In 1808, most of the town was destroyed by fire. The 1840s saw the liberation of African slaves on the island and their migration from the sugar plantations to the urban area. The city was the capital of the Federation of the West Indies from 1958–62.

Modern City

The chief airport of the Caribbean, Piarco International Airport, is east of the city. Educational institutions include Fatima College, St Mary's College and one of the campuses of the University of the West Indies. Petroleum products, rum and sugar are among the chief exports. Other exports include beer, margarine and oils, cigarettes, plastics and building materials. Port of Spain has sawmills, textile mills and citrus canneries. Angostura Bitters, known

worldwide, is produced only in Port of Spain. The capital is also famous for steel pan instruments and calypso music.

Places of Interest

Nineteenth century colonial buildings and hotels are geared towards business travellers. With its mix of ethnic groups the city has a diversified character. The centre of the old city, Woodward Square, is surrounded by Whitehall (the prime minister's office), the palace of the Roman Catholic archbishop, Knowsley House (government ministries' offices) and the Red House (neo-Renaissance building from 1906). There are Hindu temples and Muslim mosques in the city. Queen's Park Savannah, once part of a sugar plantation, is a public park with a race track. Next to it is the Magnificent Seven (a line of seven colonial buildings) including Stollmeyer's Castle, built to resemble a Scottish castle. Celebrations and festivals include the Carnival, the Hosay festival (Muslim religious festival) and the Hindu festival of Lights. Names of public places and streets reflect the city's links with various cultures, such as Lapeyrouse House, Calcutta Street and King George V Park.

Port-au-Prince, Haiti

Introduction

The capital of the West Indian republic of Haiti is in the southwest on the Gulf of Gonaïves. Haiti occupies the western third of the island of Hispaniola. Port-au-Prince is the chief port, commercial centre and seat of the Ouest department. The city has suffered from numerous civil wars, fires and earthquakes.

History

Nomadic hunter-gatherers occupied the territory around 2600 BC. The ancient Arawaks reached the island around 250 BC and by the fifteenth century several hundred thousand Taino and Ciboney Indians lived. Christopher Columbus landed in 1492. Realising the potential for gold mining he made the island a Spanish colony. Disease and cruelty killed off the Indian population and African slaves were imported. The French arrived in the sixteenth century and after much fighting the Spanish ceded the western end of the island to the French in 1731. In 1749 they founded the city of Port-au-Prince which they called L'Hôpital. In 1770 it replaced Cap Haïten the capital of Saint-Domingue becoming capital of the independent republic in 1804. In 1807 the port was opened to foreign commerce but the city continued to suffer from civil strife with frequent assassinations of heads of state. America occupied the country from 1915–34 and this was followed by a series of coups before Dr. Francois Duvalier (Papa Doc) came to power in 1957, followed by his son in 1971. Hurricane Georges caused more devastation in 1998. In Jan. 2010 the city was devastated by a 7.0 magnitude earthquake. Most of the central historic area of the city was destroyed. Numerous countries and voluntary organizations delivered aid as part of a worldwide relief effort.

Modern City

The white population and the mulattos live in the suburb of Pétionville in the hills to the southeast of the city. The black middle classes are concentrated around the capital with the poor living in squalor in the shanty urban areas. The harbour was modernised in the 1970s and 1980s to accommodate large container vessels. Exports include clothing, handicrafts and electronic goods. Most trade is with the USA. Textile, cottonseed oil, flour and sugar mills are located in or near the city and a stock-feeding station for cattle and horses was established in 1959. The Marché de Fer (Iron Market) is a nineteenth century French/African structure crammed with stalls. Tourism was once a principal source of foreign wealth, but numbers have dwindled. The 'quick' divorce laws however continue to attract visitors. Roads to Cap-Haïten, Les Cayes and Jacamel are paved but not kept in good repair. There are no railways but trucks and buses (taptaps) offer irregular and expensive services to the principal towns. Passenger-boats are limited. The international airport at Maïs Gâté, located 16 km (10 miles) to the north of the city, provides direct flights to the USA, Europe and other Caribbean nations. The State University of Haiti was established in 1920. The bicentenary was commemorated in 1949 by an international exposition.

Places of Interest

The Place du Champ-de-Mers, in the centre of the city, is the site of the National Palace (rebuilt in 1918), the army barracks and a statue of Jean-Jacques Dessalines, the black hero of the war of independence. Cathedrals in the city include the Cathédrale de Notre Dame and the Cathédrale de la Ste. Trinité (which has murals by some of the country's most important artists). The National Museum features King Christophe's suicide pistol and an anchor reputed to have come from Columbus' Santa Maria. The house of the local voodoo priest is in the city centre.

Portland, United States of America

Introduction

Known as the 'City of Roses', Portland is in northwestern Oregon and is the largest city in the state. The city is renowned for its setting in the Willamette Valley on the Willamette River with the Coast Range Mountains located to the west and the Cascade Range to the east. The seat of Multnomah County, Portland is an economic and business centre for the Pacific Northwest. It is also a major port.

History

Originally settled by Chinook Indians who fished and hunted around the Colombia and Willamette rivers, Portland was designed and constructed in 1845 by Asa Lovejoy and Francis Pettygrove. The duo tossed a coin to decide who got to name the new city and Pettygrove won, deciding on Portland, after his hometown of the same name in Maine.

In the nineteenth century, as a growing port and centre for the lumber trade, the city had a reputation for gambling, prostitution and opium dealing. Portland became more gentrified in the early part of the twentieth century after the arrival of a new railroad and the growth of the salmon fishing industry in the nearby Pacific. In 1905 the city hosted the Lewis and Clark Centennial Exposition, attracting more investment to the area. The advent of hydro-electric power from the Grand Coulee and Bonneville Dams in the 1930s and 40s helped create a boom for the developing aluminium smelting and shipbuilding industries.

After the war, competition from up-and-coming ports such as Seattle caused a slump until urban redevelopment projects were introduced in the 1970s to regenerate the downtown area. Portland's economy then successfully diversified into new, hi-tech industries while its reputation for positive environmental practices attracted residents to the city.

Modern City

The city is served by Portland International Airport, while the city's port has five marine terminals and a ship repair yard. Two interstate highways also serve Portland and there is a Greyhound bus terminal and an Amtrak railway station. The MAX light railway connects the city centre to the suburbs and the Tri-Met bus system provides transportation throughout the city.

Portland has a diverse economy with manufacturing and regional government among the city's largest employers. Nike is based there. Portland is also an important centre for the electronics industry with major corporations including Tektronix. Hi-tech computer and medical industries are also prominent.

Institutes of higher education include Portland State University, Reed College, Lewis and Clark College, the University of Portland, Concordia University (Oregon) and the Oregon Health Science University.

Places of Interest

The post-modern Portland Building, built in 1982, is a famous landmark. Cultural institutions include the Portland Art Museum, Oregon Museum of Science and Industry and the Oregon History Centre. The Portland Center for the Performing Arts has a symphony orchestra and opera and ballet companies.

Large parks include Forest Park while Washington Park has the Metro Washington Park Zoo, a forestry centre and the International Rose Test Gardens. The Rose Garden arena hosts the basketball games of the Portland Trail Blazers.

Port-Louis, Mauritius

Introduction

The capital of the Mauritius on the island of the same name, Port-Louis is the main port and commercial centre of the islands.

History

Port-Louis was founded by the French Governor Bertrand Mahé de Labourdonnais in 1735 as the colonial capital of Mauritius (then called Ile de France). Under French control, it was an important stop for French merchant ships travelling from Asia by the Cape of Good Hope. During the Napoleonic War (1800–15) it was occupied by British forces fighting for control of the surrounding area. Port-Louis suffered from the opening of the Suez Canal in 1869 as trade was diverted away from the area. It regained importance from 1967–75 when the canal was closed.

Modern City

Port-Louis is the seat of all governmental bodies and the base for most businesses. The main produce is sugar which accounts for a large proportion of exports leaving the deepwater harbour. The University of Mauritius was founded in 1965. The port is linked to the rest of the island by road.

Places of Interest

Several British and French colonial buildings remain including the eighteenth century government house and the Municipal Theatre built in 1822. The latter is used for Hindu weddings as well as local performances. Built on a central hill in 1838, the fortified citadel of Fort Adelaide affords a view over the city. Port-Louis has one Anglican and one Catholic cathedral, an art gallery and a natural history museum. The Champs de Mar race course was originally the site of French military parades.

Porto-Novo, Benin

Introduction

Though officially the capital, Porto-Novo is effectively the nation's second city after Cotonou. It lies on the coast above the Gulf of Guinea on a lagoon in the southeast of the country.

History

The city came into being during the late sixteenth and early seventeenth century, probably as a kingdom capital of the Adja people. It received its current name from the Portuguese who established trading posts later in the seventeenth century. Porto-Novo soon became a thriving slave trading centre, supplying the Americas and a small kingdom developed around the port.

Fearing British expansionism from their base in southern Nigeria, Porto-Novo permitted French intervention in 1863. It became capital of Dahomey (a province of French West Africa equating to modern Benin) in the early years of the twentieth century. Dahomey made a peaceful transition to independence in 1960 and Porto-Novo was declared the national capital.

Modern City

The city has road and rail connections with Cotonou, and is linked to Lagos by road. The mainstays of Porto-Novo's economy are exports of palm oil, cotton and kapok (tree fibres).

Places of Interest

Attractions include a large market, the Grand Marché d'Adjara, a Museum of Ethnography and a former Portuguese church that is now a mosque.

Poznań, Poland

Introduction

The former national capital and current capital of the Wielkopolska region, Poznań is situated in western Poland along the river Warta. Its location, resting on a line which runs from Paris to Moscow, has made it a historically successful trade centre.

History

In AD 966, Duke Mieszko I was baptised, bringing Poland as a nation into the realm of Western culture and religion. This event took place at Poznań, previously a minor fortified village, which subsequently became the episcopal see and capital of the country. Poznań was home to the first two Polish kings and to the nation's first cathedral, constructed in 968. Although the capital was moved to nearby Gniezno in 992, the city remained capital of the region and developed rapidly. In 1253 the town was given its charter. Growth increased steadily, reaching its highpoint during the Renaissance period following the departure of the Teutonic Knights from Prussia (1454).

The Second Partition of Poland (AD 1793) brought Poznań under Prussian control and began a process of Germanization which was to continue throughout the nineteenth century. Attempts to suppress the resident Poles demographically and culturally were enacted by Otto von Bismark in the 1870s, resulting in many of Poznań's citizens emigrating to America. Co-operative credit agreements made by Polish residents were effective in preventing total colonization, and after World War I Poznań was returned to Polish hands.

The onset of World War II and the German invasion of Poland brought destruction to the city and the mass murder or deportation of its inhabitants. After the war, the country fell under a strict communist regime which was increasingly challenged. On 28 June 1956, Poznań was the site for an important pro-democracy strike. The city's 50,000 industrial workers' demands for bread and freedom were initially rebuked with military action, resulting in 53 deaths. The action nevertheless persuaded the Polish United Worker's Party that significant changes had to be made, softening and ultimately ending the country's communist rule.

Modern City

Poznań's economy incorporates extensive foreign investment, with roughly 1,000 city-based companies benefiting from foreign participation. It is also, after Warsaw, Poland's second largest centre for banking. Since 1921, the city has been host to the Poznań International Fair, which organises over 30 specialized international trade-related events each year. Manufacturing forms a great part of the city's employment (the city has the lowest unemployment rate in the country), with main industries including metallurgy, the production of ship engines, railway cars, textiles, tele-transmission equipment and fertilizers. Poznań's Ławica airport handles domestic and international flights, whilst its railway system has excellent connections to Polish and other European destinations.

Places of Interest

The city is a leading cultural centre, with numerous educational institutions, several operatic and dance centres, and a number of theatres. It is also home to the country's oldest zoological garden. The cathedral, on an island on the river Warta, was the original seat of Mieszko's bishopric and stands near the Archdiocesan museum, which houses a fine collection of medieval through to modern art.

Prague (Praha), Czech Republic

Introduction

Prague lies on the River Vltava at the heart of Bohemia in the northeast of the country. It came into being with the foundation of Prague Castle as the main seat of the Premysl Dynasty in the 870s. The modern city is based around four historic towns (Hradčany, Mála Strana, Staré Mesto and Nové Mesto) merged by Emperor Joseph II in 1784, and the Jewish Quarter (Josefov).

History

Staré Mesto, the Old Town was first settled during the tenth century and is home to the Old Town Square. Charles IV, Bohemian king and Holy Roman Emperor, made Prague capital of Bohemia in the fourteenth century and it was to provide the setting for the wars between Jan Hus and the Catholic church in the early fifteenth century. In 1618 the Defenestration of Prague occurred when two Habsburg councillors were thrown from a window in Prague Castle. It was one of the triggers for the 30 Years' War which saw Czechs lose civil and property rights through enforced Catholicization and Germanization, and would impact on the nation for 300 years to come.

The twentieth century found Prague at the centre of great upheaval. In 1918, under the guidance of Tomáš Masaryk, it became the capital of the new Czechoslovakian state. During World War II it fell under Nazi control and, while many buildings went relatively unscathed, the intelligentsia and the Jewish population were effectively wiped out. Ironically, Terezin, Prague's concentration camp and ghetto, was shown to Red Cross observers in the early stages of the war as a model camp to appease Western fears. In 1946, a year after the city's liberation, the Communists came to power and the emergence of Klement Gottwald as president in 1948 ushered in decades of Soviet oppression. Alongside the removal of the Jewish population and the deportations of Germans and Hungarians after the war, Prague became one of Europe's most racially homogenous cities.

1968 saw the Prague Spring, when President Alexander Dubček approved liberalizing reforms against Soviet wishes in a search of 'socialism with a human face'. Soviet tanks rolled into the city in Aug. 1968 and put down the uprising, removed Dubcek and reinstalled totalitarian rule. Discontent grew in the ensuing years and on 17 Nov. 1989, in the face of a heavy handed police response, a series of protests spread around Wenceslas Square. Playwright and dissident Václav Havel led a group that negotiated the government's resignation on 3 Dec. The Velvet Revolution, so called because of its peaceful nature, had succeeded and Havel became president with Dubcek as speaker of the national assembly. Following the split of the Czech and Slovak states in 1993, Prague became capital of the Czech Republic.

Modern City

Principal industries include precision and heavy industry, food production, brewing, electronics, chemicals and tourism. Its history and architecture have made Prague a popular destination and it is well served by public transport. Today, while some of the economic reforms of Václav Klaus in the 1990s have not borne all their promised fruits, Prague remains relatively prosperous, especially when compared to the capitals of some East European neighbours.

In Aug. 2002 severe flooding hit the city, causing extensive damage and forcing 40,000 people to leave their homes.

Places of Interest

Prague's architecture encompasses 900 years of development, with fine examples of Romanesque, Gothic, Renaissance, Baroque, Art Nouveau and Cubist buildings set off by efficient post-war city planning. In addition, writers such as Franz Kafka, Rainer Maria Rilke, Jaroslav Hašek and Havel as well as composers like Smetana, Dvořák and Janáček have given Prague a rich cultural heritage.

Hradčany is the site of Prague Castle and the seat of Czech government. Adjoining it by the ornate Charles Bridge is Staré Mesto, the Old Town, which lies on the east bank of the Vltava. In the Old Town Square are the Gothic Tyn Church, the Town Hall, the Astronomical Clock and a statue to Jan Hus can be found. Mála Strana, or the Lesser Quarter, was founded in 1257 and today houses parks, gardens and many embassies. Nové Mesto, the New Town, was founded in 1348 and was the subject of nineteenth century sanitization, which explains its varied architecture. It is the commercial hub of the city and the site of Wenceslas Square, which is the city's most important district. Josefov, meanwhile, was a medieval Jewish ghetto and many of its synagogues are now museums. Together with the over-crowded cemetery, they are testament to Prague's Jewish heritage, as well as the persecution Jews suffered from the eleventh to the twentieth centuries.

Praia, Cabo Verde

Introduction

Praia is Cabo Verde's capital and its most populous city. It is located on the south shore of the island of São Tiago (Santiago).

History

Praia became the capital of Portuguese-controlled Cape Verde in 1770. It remained capital when the country gained independence in 1975.

Modern City

Praia's port is the commercial hub of the Cabo Verdean islands. It handles coffee, sugar cane and tropical fruit.
There is an international airport located west of the city.

Places of Interest

The island's beaches near the city are popular with tourists.

Pretoria, South Africa

Introduction

Pretoria is situated in the central northern part of the country, 60 km north of Johannesburg in Gauteng province. Known as Tshwane by the Sotho population, the city is South Africa's administrative capital. Its inhabitants refer to it as the Jacaranda City because it has such a large number of the celebrated trees. Pretoria holds a festival in Oct. each year when the Jacarandas blossom.

History

The city's history begins with the occupation of the surrounding fertile valley by Nguni-speaking black South African farmers. In the mid nineteenth century Andries Pretorius, a leader of the Voortrekkers, established a farm, Grootplaas, at the junction of the Apies and Crocodile rivers. In 1853 the Zuid-Afrikaansche Republiek (ZAR) which, under the leadership of Paul Kruger, had just secured its independence from Britain, needed a site for its new capital. Marthinus Pretorius established Pretoria on 16 Nov. 1855 and named it in honour of his father Andries Pretorius. At this time Pretoria was nothing more than a small rural backwater. Nonetheless the town remained the capital of the Transvaal until it became the administrative capital of the Union of South Africa in 1910. It was declared a city on 14 Oct. 1931 and in 1961 it became the administrative capital of the Republic of South Africa.

One of the world's biggest and most productive diamond mines was discovered 40 km east of Pretoria. This mine yielded the world's largest diamond, originally named the Cullinan but now known as the Star of Africa. The mining of diamonds brought much-needed revenue to the coffers of the ZAR in the wake of the costly Anglo-Boer Wars, and the city's economy is still heavily reliant on diamonds. Modern Pretoria is also home to Iscor (the South African iron and steel industry) as well as notable food-processing and engineering plants.

Modern City

Johannesburg International Airport serves Pretoria. There is an airport shuttle that runs between JIA and the city. The main bus station is on Church Square.

From here large numbers of buses service most parts of Pretoria, and local transport is also provided by numerous and inexpensive taxis. The main railway station is south of the city centre near the greyhound bus terminus. From here buses and trains connect to Johannesburg, Kimberley, Bloemfontein, Komatipoort, Nelspruit as well as Limpopo and Bulawayo.

Places of Interest

The Union Buildings to the northeast of the city centre are the home of the South African Government. Designed by Sir Herbert Baker, they were opened in 1913. The National Zoo, in an area of almost 70 ha, houses 140 mammal and 320 bird species; in the biggest inland sea-water aquarium there are over 300 fish species and in the reptile park there are over 90 reptile species as well as several amphibian and invertebrate species. The Voortrekker Monument is a massive granite monument set on Monument Hill and designed by Gerhard Moerdyk. Inside the monument is the Hall of Heroes, the four walls of which depict the history of the Great Trek in 1838. The State Theatre is a modern theatre with six auditoriums for opera, ballet and drama, as well as choral and symphony concerts. The Transvaal Museum of Natural History exhibits an enormous whale skeleton, as well as more traditional wildlife displays. The Austin Roberts Bird Hall, the most comprehensive in South Africa, contains a skeleton of the extinct Mauritian dodo. The Kruger House Museum celebrates the life of President Paul Kruger.

Priština, Serbia

Introduction

Priština is the capital of the province of Kosovo and Metohija. The Serbian capital until falling under Ottoman rule from the fourteenth to the early-twentieth century, relations between ethnic Serbs and Albanians have long been strained in the city. This culminated with Serbian 'ethnic cleansing' of the Albanian population during the Kosovan crisis of 1999. The city fabric was also badly hit by bombing.

History

There is evidence of human habitation in the region around Priština dating to the early Neolithic era. The city of Ulpiana, capital of the Illyrian province of Dardania, was established in the second century just southeast of modern Priština but was destroyed during the middle ages.

Priština was under Serbian rule until the Battle of Kosovo in 1389 when invading Ottoman forces defeated Prince Lazar and seized control. Over the next two centuries the city prospered as a centre of trade and mining centre (centred on the nearby Mount Kopaonik). From the seventeenth century onwards the city fought alongside Austria against the Turks, and was badly damaged as a result on several occasions.

By the nineteenth century one-fifth of the population was Serbian. An important regional centre for craft and trade fairs, it was twice devastated by fire (in 1859 and 1863). When the Ottoman Empire collapsed in 1912 Priština reverted to Serbian control. In the period between World Wars I and II, large numbers of Turks, Albanians and Muslims were removed from Kosovo and their land re-distributed to Serbs.

In the aftermath of World War II Priština was designated capital of Kosovo. The city underwent largescale re-development under communist Yugoslavia, with much of its Ottoman Eastern identity destroyed. Re-building went along traditional communist lines, with large new building complexes and wide boulevards.

When Serbia denied Kosovo its autonomy in 1989, many ethnic Albanians were removed from their jobs and political posts to be replaced by Serbs. After a decade of deteriorating Serb–Albanian relations, Serb forces began 'ethnically cleansing' the city in 1999, with a large proportion of the ethnic Albanian population displaced. The city was severely damaged during NATO bombing raids, which continued until a Serbian military withdrawal was agreed.

Modern City

Government in the city and Kosovo as a whole is in the hands of KFOR, the UN's peacekeeping force. The economy is based on mining, metallurgy, electrics, pharmaceuticals, food processing and textiles. Despite some growth, it continues to struggle as a result of the events of the 1990s.

There is an international airport and road and rail links to other major cities. There is a university (established in 1970), now recovering from neglect and harassment under the Belgrade regime and the effects of the 1999 conflict.

Places of Interest

The Gracanica Monastery dates from the first part of the fourteenth century and includes fine fresco work. The nearby Mausoleum of Sultan Murat was built in the mid-nineteenth century by Hurshid Pasha while the museum of Kosovo-Metohija has several departments exhibiting major artistic and archaeological finds.

Puebla, Mexico

Introduction

130 km south east of Mexico City, Puebla is the capital of the Puebla region and is fourth largest city in Mexico. The Atoyac River flows to the west of the city. The surrounding region is mountainous and bordered by the country's three largest peaks: Orizaba, Popocatépetl and Ixtaccihuatl.

History

The area that is now the state of Puebla was originally inhabited by Nahuatl-speaking Indians and is rich in archaeological sites. The city itself was founded in 1531 by Cuetlacoapa de Toribio as Puebla de los Angeles. It was heavily influenced by colonialism and had a high instance of Spanish architecture, still evident today. Puebla became famous for its tradition of glazed ceramics, which originated in the sixteenth century. With the decline of the ceramics trade, at the end of the seventeenth century Puebla thrived as a producer of cloth. On the trade route between the eastern seaport of Veracruz and Mexico City, Puebla was the second city of Mexico and one of the largest in the Spanish Empire.

In 1847, during the Mexican war, Puebla was occupied by the US. In May 1862, when Mexico was at war with France, the invaders were forced back at the Battle of Puebla by an army led by General Ignacio Zaragoza. In his memory the city's name was changed to Puebla de Zaragoza. The 5 May remains a national holiday in Mexico and an annual festival in Puebla. A second French attempt a year later was more successful and Puebla stayed under French rule until it was eventually reclaimed by Porfiro Díaz in 1867. The city of Puebla played an integral part in the Mexican Revolution. The anti-government activist, Aquiles Serdán Alatriste, was assassinated in his Puebla home in Nov. 1810, sparking off the revolution.

Religion played an important part in the city's history and Puebla has been called the 'City of Churches'. By 1630 the city had some 30 churches, all decorated by local artists. The city had the first public library in the Americas, opened in 1646.

Music flourished under colonial rule, although the upheavals of the nineteenth-century lead to a decline. The city suffered considerable structural damage in an earthquake of 1973.

Modern City

Local industries are textiles, ceramics (especially glazed tiles) and glass. The surrounding region is mainly agricultural, producing wheat, maize, tobacco and sugar. Its minerals are gold, silver and copper. There has been an increased industrialization from 1970 onwards, including the opening of a Volkswagen factory in 1970.

Puebla is connected to Mexico's major destinations by road, and to Guadalajara, Tijuana and Monterrey by a local airport 22 km away in Huejotzingo.

Places of Interest

Puebla is famous for its colonial architecture and the extensive decoration of these buildings. The eighteenth century *poblano*-style of architecture and sculpture originated in Puebla. (Puebla's inhabitants are called *Poblanos*.)

One of the most important buildings of Puebla is its cathedral containing work in onyx, gold and marble. The construction of the cathedral began in 1575 and was completed in the eighteenth century. Other religious buildings include the Iglesia de Santo Domingo with its lavishly decorated Capilla del Rosario.

The house of the revolutionary Auiles Serdán Alatriste is now the Regional Museum of the Mexican Revolution while the Museo Amparo specializes in Mesoamerican art.

Built in 1790 the Teatro Principal is one of the oldest theatres on the continent.

Putrajaya, Malaysia

Introduction

The new city of Putrajaya, 40 km south of Kuala Lumpur city centre, was declared administrative capital of Malaysia on 4 June 1999. The city is named for Tunku (Prince) Abdul Rahman Putra, the first premier of Malaysia; 'jaya' means 'success'.

History

The Malaysian government began the search for a suitable location for a new administrative capital in the 1980s. A site was found in 1993 and the project was launched in 1995, during an economic boom. Work started on the construction of an 'Intelligent City', in which administration would be electronically-based, and a twin city, called Cyberjaya. The twin cities were envisaged as part of a 50 km-long multimedia corridor.

In 1998–99 construction ground to a halt as economic boom gave way to economic crisis. However, in June 1999 Putrajaya became administrative capital and the staff of the prime minister's office transferred to their new headquarters. The vast majority of Malaysia's government ministries were relocated to Putrajaya by 2012. The project has been dismissed as grandiose by the Malaysian opposition, which has disputed the need for the new capital.

On 1 Feb. 2001 Putrajaya was removed from Selangor state and became Malaysia's third federal territory.

Modern City

Putrajaya is planned as a 'garden city' built around a 4.2 km ceremonial boulevard. Lakes have been created by damming rivers, and there are lush botanic gardens. There will be 15 neighbourhoods for a population of 330,000.

Places of Interest

Few major buildings have been completed. The Dataran Putra (Putra Grounds), a large park surrounding the central lake, is partly constructed. The Masjid Putra (Putra Mosque) is imposing, with a minaret that rises 116 m. The Seri Perdana (prime minister's official residence) has been completed and may be visited when there are no official functions.

Pyongyang, North Korea

Introduction

The capital of the People's Democratic Republic of Korea, Pyongyang, is reputedly the oldest city in Korea. However, there is very little to see from the city's historic past. Pyongyang was rebuilt after the Korean War (1950–53) with wide boulevards, parks and many large Stalinist-style monuments, most commemorating Kim Il Sung. Although more than 2 m. people live in Pyongyang, the visitor is struck by how empty and quiet the city is. There are very few cars, and even relatively few bicycles, no street traders, no bustling shops and no crowds. An eerie tidiness, maintained by armies of women with brooms, reinforces that impression that much of Pyongyang is deserted.

History

The site of Pyongyang has been inhabited for at least 4,000 years. According to legend, Tangun (the first Korean king, who may not have existed) had his capital in the region of modern Pyongyang. The city's recorded history can only be traced to 108 BC when a Chinese trading post was established near the Daedong River.

In AD 427, the date usually cited as the foundation of the city, Pyongyang became the capital of the kingdom of Koguryo. After 500, its walls were rebuilt and extended to enclose the present city centre. There were 16 city gates.

In the seventh century Pyongyang was taken by the Chinese. A revival in the city's fortunes did not occur until the tenth century when Pyongyang became the secondary capital of the Koryo dynasty of Korean kings. It flourished until the fourteenth century and became the second city in the land in size as well as in importance. Pyongyang was the target of invaders: the Japanese at the end of the sixteenth century and the Manchus at the beginning of the seventeenth century.

Pyongyang was one of the principal bases of European and other traders in the late nineteenth century. Protestant missionaries were established in the city, which soon had more Christians and more churches than any other city in the Far East. Banks and other financial interests flourished, but Pyongyang's prosperity was short-lived.

Pyongyang was fought over by the Chinese and the Japanese during the Sino-Japanese War of (1894–95). Both armies inflicted severe damage and, when the war was over, Pyongyang had been reduced to ruins and most of its inhabitants had fled. When the Japanese occupied the country in 1910, Pyongyang became a military base, a local seat of administration and, most importantly, an industrial city.

Pyongyang, and its industrial base, survived World War II (1939–45) and became the capital of a provisional Communist administration in 1946, and the official capital of the People's Democratic Republic of Korea when that state was proclaimed in 1948. But, again, war devastated the city. During the Korean War (1950–53) Pyongyang was repeatedly bombed by UN forces in the early stages of the war. In 1950 UN forces took the city, but it was retaken by Chinese troops and remained in Communist hands at the end of the war. The bombed city was rebuilt with the assistance of aid and planners from Communist China and the Soviet Union. The result was a harsh, but impressive, design based on grandiose thoroughfares and overpowering public monuments.

Modern City

Pyongyang is the principal cultural and political centre of North Korea and the country's main industrial centre. Despite its peripheral position within North Korea it has become the hub of road and rail routes. It has the country's only international airport, Sunan, but flights are infrequent. Pyongyang lacks the foreign financial institutions common in most capitals. Some industrial plants still use coal, which is mined nearby. Major industries include textiles (particularly cotton and wool goods) and food processing.

Places of Interest

One sight is compulsory for all foreign visitors—the huge statue of Kim Il Sung on the monumental square on top of Mansudae Hill. All visitors are brought by their official guide to lay flowers as a mark of respect to the founder of North Korea.

Also on the hilltop is the Museum of the Korean Revolution, from which there is a good view of the city and the Daedong River, which runs through its centre. On the eastern bank of the river rises the 170-m (558-ft) Tower of the Juche Idea (the national self-help philosophy expounded by Kim Il Sung). A lift journey to the top of the tower is rewarded by a view of the entire city and the fertile basin beyond. In the middle of the river are two fountains that spout water to a height of 150 m. (492 ft).

Many of the city sights are connected with Kim Il Sung. They include the Arch of Triumph, built where Kim rallied his supporters after the Japanese had quit Pyongyang in 1945. Near the arch is a large statue of a winged horse, the Chollima Statue, which commemorates the reconstruction of North Korea. The Monument to Victory in the Liberation War of the Fatherland (a massive group of North Korean soldiers) is also on the tourist itinerary.

In the suburb of Mangyeongdae is the supposed birthplace of Kim Il Sung. The thatched cottage, claimed to be his childhood home, has been carefully restored and contains some personal possessions. The Great Leader's body, embalmed, lies in the former Presidential Palace, but may not be viewed by foreigners except by invitation.

A few remains of historic Pyongyang can be seen including some stretches of the city wall and two of the 16 gates. Also worth a visit is the Central Botanical Garden, which has one hot house devoted to an orchid called kimilsungia and another to a begonia known as kimjongilia.

Quebec City, Canada

Introduction

French-speaking Quebec is located on the confluence of the St Lawrence and Saint-Charles rivers, to the north east of Montreal.

A UNESCO World Heritage Site since 1985, Vieux-Quebec is the only walled city in North America, part of a military inheritance which led to Winston Churchill to dub the city 'the Gibraltar of North America'.

History

It was at Quebec that Samuel de Champlain established the first permanent European settlement in Canada in 1608. It developed as a fur-trading post, although the site of the city was first visited by a European in 1535, when French explorer Jacques Cartier came across the Huron Indian village of Stadacona. To aid the defence of the settlement, it was moved to the clifftop in 1620 when the Fort St-Louis was built on the present site of the Château Frontenac, the gothic hotel which dominates the city.

Fighting continued between the British and French in North America throughout the seventeenth century with the British capturing Quebec in 1629 and holding the town until the Treaty of Saint-Germain-en-Laye (1632) when it was restored to French rule. The British made several further attempts to take the colony with the governor of Massachusetts, Sir William Phipps, leading a fleet to Quebec in 1690 before being beaten back by the town's governor, the Count de Frontenac. A British fleet foundered on the reefs of the St Lawrence River in 1711. The city finally fell to the British in 1759 when James Wolfe won a significant victory. The city had been under siege for 3 months but did not fall to Wolfe until his forces discovered an unguarded track, scaled the cliff of Cap Diamant and attacked the sleeping French forces from behind. Quebec was officially ceded to the British crown by the Treaty of Paris in 1763. An attack by the Americans in 1775, was repelled and the city was able to develop as a timber and shipbuilding centre.

Quebec became the provincial capital of Lower Canada in 1791 and was given its city charter in 1840. When the British North American colonies met in 1864 to plan the confederation of Canada, Quebec City was chosen as the seat of the conference.

Franklin D. Roosevelt and Winston Churchill twice met in Quebec City during the Second World War to plan the invasion of Europe. Quebec City became a symbol of French-Canadian culture and heritage in the 1960s.

Modern City

The capital of Quebec province, Quebec City's industries include textiles, publishing, tourism and ship building. It is also a major administrative and service centre. Laval University is one of its educational institutions. A port on the Lawrence River, Quebec City is served by Jean Lesage International Airport and bus and rail links.

Places of Interest

It contains many historic buildings including the Church of Notre-Dame des Victoires, built in 1688, the Ursuline monastery, the seminary, the Anglican cathedral and the Catholic basilica.

There are several museums including the Musée de la Civilisation, covering French-Canadian culture and society, and the Musée du Quebec, which contains a respected art collection.

Quito, Ecuador

Introduction

In an Andean basin just south of the equator on the slopes of the Pichincha volcano, Quito is the capital of Ecuador and of the Pichincha province. The political and cultural capital of the country, its old town was made a UNESCO heritage site in 1978.

History

Quito was originally inhabited by the Quitus. Between 1000–1487 the city was ruled by the Shyris, a mix of Quitus and lowland Cara Indians. After the town was invaded by the Incas in 1487, it became an important Inca city. All traces of Quito's pre-Colombian culture were eradicated when the warrior Tahuantinsuyo attacked and burned the city. In 1534 a new town laid out in the typical colonial grid plan was created by the conquistador Sebastián de Belalcázar. In 1563 Quito became the seat of government for the Real Audiencia de Quito, part of the Viceroyalty of Peru. Quito attracted many Jesuit, Franciscan and Augustinian missionaries who established strong religious communities. In the mid-sixteenth century, Franciscans founded an art school which inspired the decoration of numerous churches and cathedrals.

For over three centuries Quito remained a small isolated city, its Andean location providing little attraction for migrants. The first calls for Ecuadorian independence came in the second half of the eighteenth century. They were led by Quito-born physician and writer Eugenio de Santa Cruz y Espejo who voiced revolutionary ideas through satirical writings. After an uprising in Quito in 1809, a declaration making Ecuador the first self-governing region in the Americas was signed in the city's Monasterio de San Agustín. But this was short lived and the city was soon reclaimed. Independence eventually came in 1822 when Simon Bolivar's general, Venezuelan revolutionary hero Antonio José de Sucre, took Quito.

In 1908 the Guayaquil–Quito railway was built linking the capital with the country's second city and beginning an expansion to the north and south which continued throughout the twentieth century. By the end of the twentieth century, Guayaquil had overtaken Quito as Ecuador's economic centre, although the capital retained its political and cultural influence.

Modern City

Quito is Ecuador's second largest city and its main centre of textile production. Other industries include brewing, tanning and flour milling. The city's universities include the Universidad Central del Ecuador which was founded in 1586. Quito is linked with Peru and Colombia via the Pan-American Highway and its international airport is 10 km north of the centre.

Places of Interest

Quito's old town is rich in colonial architecture and full of historic churches and cathedrals decorated with wooden sculptures and paintings. With its Baroque altar and ceiling decorated in gold leaf, the Monasterio de San Francisco is the city's oldest colonial building dating from 1534. In the Plaza de la Independencia next to the presidential palace is the cathedral in which Sucre is buried. Quito's museums include the Casa de la Cultura Ecuatoriana, which displays a mix of traditional artefacts and contemporary art, the Museo Guayasamín, dedicated to the work of the indigenous painter Oswaldo Guayasamín, and the Museo de Arte y Historia, which shows 16th and seventeenth century colonial art. Sucre's Quito home is now a museum. 30 km southeast of Quito the Reserva Forestal de Pasochoa rain forest shelters a wide variety of birds and wildlife.

Rabat, Morocco

Introduction

Built on the coast of the Atlantic Ocean on the left bank of the Bou Regreg Estuary, Rabat is the capital of Morocco. It stands opposite Salé with which its history is closely linked. A city of trees and parks and one of Morocco's four imperial cities, Rabat has a mix of Arab and European architecture and culture.

History

The origins of the city date back to the seventh century. A Mauritanian trading post once stood in the southeast of the city. The area was first colonized by the Carthaginians, then by the Romans and in the tenth century, by the Berbers who were Muslims. Rabat was founded by the first Almohad ruler in the twelfth century as a garrison to fight the Spanish. The fort was later developed by Yacoub El Mansour who named the site Ribat E Fath meaning 'Victory Fortress'. From 1579–1603 a period of stability allowed the building of Rabat's fortified wall within which the modern city has developed. In 1609 Philip II of Spain expelled the Andalucian Moors from his Kingdom and many settled in Rabat and other parts of Morocco. The seventeenth century saw the rise of the 'Alawi Dynasty, in particular under the reign of Moulay Rachid who finished the building of the Casbah and the port in Rabat around 1666–69. In 1912 Rabat became the capital of the region that was now a French protectorate. The building of a new city was ordered under General Lyautey. Independence for Morocco was achieved in 1956 with Rabat remaining the nation's capital. In 1957 Morocco became a kingdom with the Sultan taking the title Mohammed V.

Modern City

With the silting up of the river, the port has lost importance but the city has a textile industry and manufactures building materials. Food, fish and fruit processing, handicrafts and tourism are also important. The Mohammed V International Airport is 30 km south of Casablanca which lies 92 km southwest of Rabat by road. A royal palace was built in the 1950s and the Mohammed V University in 1957. The railway station is in the centre of the modern city. Most of the administrative buildings and institutes including the National Conservatory of Music, Dance and Dramatic Arts are located on the southern outskirts.

Places of Interest

The most famous site is the Hassan Tower, the incomplete minaret of the great mosque begun by Yacoub El Mansour in the twelfth century. Behind its marble columns lies the Mohammed V Mausoleum. The Museum of the Oudayas, or Museum of Moroccan Arts, is situated in an opulent seventeenth century lodge built by Moulay Ismail and has collections of Moroccan carpets, musical instruments, jewellery in gold and silver with precious stones and pearls, and pottery from Rabat and Salé. The Archaeological Museum has bronzes dating from pre-Roman civilisations. The Postal Museum, founded in 1970, includes Morocco's first official stamp dated 12 May 1912. The Mohammed VI Modern and Contemporary Art Museum opened in 2014. It is Morocco's first major museum to be built since gaining independence from France in 1956.

Reykjavík, Iceland

Introduction

Reykjavík is Iceland's capital city, lying on Faxa Bay in the southwest of the country. Settled by Vikings, it is the focus of Icelandic life and is home to two thirds of the country's population. The world's most northerly-situated capital, it derives much of its energy from local geothermal springs.

History

The site of Reykjavík, according to the twelfth century Icelandic *Book of Settlements*, was settled in 874 by a Norwegian chieftain, Ingólfur Arnarson, who built a farm. He named it Reykjavík, which means 'smokey bay', because of the steam eminating from the natural hot springs.

The area, reliant principally on fishing, grew slowly over the ensuing centuries and it was not until the mid-eighteenth century that Reykjavík began to prosper as a trade centre. In 1786, with Iceland under the jurisdiction of Denmark, it became the seat of the Danish administrator and in 1843 it was chosen as the home of the Icelandic parliament (Alþingi).

In 1911 the University of Iceland was established in the city and in 1918 it became national capital, Iceland having been granted sovereign status. However, the county remained tied to Denmark until June 1944 when Reykjavík became capital of the newly independent nation. During World War II the city served as an important harbour for US ships crossing the Atlantic.

Modern City

A large percentage of the city's water and heating requirements have been met since the 1930s by the geothermal spring beneath the city. A side-effect of this is the ever-present aroma of hydrogen sulphide. Most urban construction is in concrete in a bid to counter earth tremors.

Fishing and fish related industries remain vital to the local economy. Other important industries include textiles, printing and metalwork. Tourism has become increasingly important in recent years. There is an international airport.

Places of Interest

Most of Reykjavík's leading attractions are to be found in the compact Old Town district, which nestles between Tjörnin (a small lake) and the harbour. Hallgrímskirkja (Church of Hallgrímur) is the city's tallest building and the second tallest in Greater Reykjavík after the Smáratorg Tower. Built between the 1940s and 1970s, it was designed to resemble basaltic lava.

The National Gallery houses a permanent collection of nineteenth and twentieth centuries works while the Reykjavík Art Museum hosts changing exhibitions of work by modern Icelandic and international artists. The National Museum, refurbished at the start of the twenty-first century, has a range of relics spanning 1,100 years. The national theatre and ballet are also based in the city.

On top of Öskjuhlíd Hill is Perlan (Pearl), a glass structure housing a restaurant built on hot water tanks. The Árbaer Open-Air Folk Museum, established on a farm first mentioned in the mid-fifteenth century, includes a turf church dating from 1842, and 27 homes.

Hot Pots (geothermal swimming pools) have controlled temperatures of up to 44°C (108°F), with the largest at *Laugardalslaug*. Tourists are also attracted to the phenomenon of the midnight sun, when it remains light until very late during the Summer.

Riga, Latvia

Introduction

At the Gulf of Riga on the River Daugava near the Baltic Sea, Riga is the capital of Latvia, its chief port and cultural and industrial centre. Originally inhabited by the ancient Livs tribe, Riga was under Swedish, Russian and Polish rule before spending much of the twentieth century under Soviet control (1940–91).

History

Riga is built on the site of a Liv (or Finno-Urgic) medieval fishing village used by amber traders crossing the Gulf of Riga. The settlement was founded in 1201 as a German fort by a Bremen bishop as a launch pad for crusades. At the same time, the Livonian Brothers of the Sword union was established. Allied to the Teutonic Knights, the fraternity used Riga as a base to conquer

Livonian tribes. More German settlers moved to the region, making Riga a stronghold of the German Baltic and a key trading post between Russia and the West. It became an archbishopric in 1253 and a member of the Hanseatic League in 1282, with the church, knights and merchants all struggling for power. Trade flourished and the town prospered over the next few centuries.

In 1561, Poland invaded the city. Riga was absorbed into the Commonwealth of Poland and Lithuania until Sweden wrested the city from the Poles in 1621. Riga became Sweden's second city but it was captured by the Russians in 1710. As the capital of Livonia (modern day northern Latvia and southern Estonia), Riga grew in size and importance throughout the eighteenth and nineteenth centuries. Russian communities moved in alongside the Germans and Latvians, and industry burgeoned, with the port thriving on the timber trade. With the emancipation of the serfs in 1861, many came to work and live in the city.

By World War I Riga was Russia's third city, but experienced much destruction during the German occupation. As capital of Independent Latvia (1918–40), Riga served as an observation point of Soviet activity for Western intelligence agents. In 1940 Soviet troops invaded Latvia and occupied Riga, deporting many Latvians to Siberia and northern Russia.

The Germans occupied the city for 3 years during World War II, inflicting structural damage and decimating the Jewish population. In 1944 the German army retreated under Soviet pressure, and Riga was incorporated into the USSR. More deportations ensued in the late 1940s as part of a Soviet agricultural collectivisation drive. An influx of Russians to the city filled the labour gap, while the USSR's Russification policy stifled the local culture. Under Soviet rule, the city became a leading manufacturing centre.

Following the collapse of the Soviet Union, in 1991 Riga once again became capital of Independent Latvia. In 2001 structural refurbishments and celebrations heralded Riga's 800th anniversary.

Modern City

Riga is the economic, industrial and cultural centre of Latvia. Industries include shipbuilding and engineering, metallurgy, textiles, chemicals and the production of diesel engines. The city's educational institutions include the university, established in 1919. Riga is connected by road and rail to major Eastern European cities, while an international airport is 8 km southwest of the city. The Riga Radio and TV Tower, completed in 1987, is at 368.5 m. in height the tallest structure in the European Union.

Riga was one of two European Capitals of Culture for 2014.

Places of Interest

Most of the major sights are situated in Old Riga, where the town's original nucleus was formed on the east bank of the Daugava River. Much of the original architecture survives including the Dome Cathedral, the Gothic St Peter's Church and the thirteenth century St Jacob's Church.

Riga castle, built for the Livonian knights in 1330, is now the presidential home. Museums include the Latvian Museum of Fine Art, showing local contemporary works by such artists as Janis Rozentâls and Karlis Padegs, and the Museum of Foreign Art accommodated in the Castle. Covering 100 hectares, the open air Ethnographic Museum preserves traditional Latvian village life.

80 km from Riga is the Baroque Rundale Palace. Designed by Bartomeleo Francesco Rastrella, the architect responsible for many of St. Petersburg's treasures, the palace was completed in 1768 and restored in the 1970s.

Rio de Janeiro, Brazil

Introduction

On Guanabara Bay on Brazil's southern Atlantic coast, Rio de Janeiro is the country's second largest city and its cultural heart. Rio de Janeiro was the capital of the Portuguese colony from 1716. In 1960 the capital status was transferred to the newly built, centrally located Brasília. An economic, financial and tourist centre, the city is the capital of the state of Rio de Janeiro.

History

The first mention of the city dates from the second Portuguese expedition to the New World in 1502, led by Gaspar de Lemos. Landing in Jan. and believing Guanabara bay to be the mouth of a river, he named the region Rio (river) de Janeiro (Jan.). The first settlers in the area arrived with Admiral Nicholas de Villegaignon in 1555 with the intention of establishing a colony of French Huguenots. The Portuguese governor Mem de Sá tried to expel the French but it was his nephew Estacio de Sá who finally forced the French to leave in the mid-1560s. Once in Portuguese hands, the city began to develop and by 1585 had a population of 3,850, of whom 750 were Portuguese and 100 African slaves.

Early economic activity centred on sugarcane plantations with labour provided by slaves from Africa and the indigenous population. The city began to grow rapidly following the discovery of gold in the nearby state of Minais Gerais at the end of the seventeenth century. Rio superseded the colonial capital Salvador in 1763 when the government moved to the city. The Portuguese built forts throughout Brazil including six in Rio but Rio suffered numerous attacks. The French made raids in 1710 and 1711 when Rene Duguay-Trouin, with a large fleet, held the city to ransom for 2 months before being expelled.

In 1808 during the Napoleonic wars the Portuguese royal family took refuge in Rio. The arrival of the court saw unprecedented artistic and cultural growth in the city. Following the return of the court to Europe, and the declaration of Brazilian independence in 1822, coffee overtook gold as the region's key product. In 1854 the first 'carnival march' heralded the popular annual Carnival.

With the proclamation of the Republic in 1889, Rio remained the capital of the country and underwent infrastructural improvements. By the end of the nineteenth century Rio had experienced a population explosion. The growth of industry encouraged major internal migration, particularly from the African ex-slaves who had been freed in 1888. This was coupled with large-scale European migration from Portugal, Italy and Germany. It led to a period of social disruption following a series of poor harvest. At the end of the nineteenth century the first *favela*, or shanty town, sprang up on the outskirts of the city, populated by returning ex-slaves who had been temporarily drafted into the army.

Following World War II there was a period of rapid modernization. These improvements coincided with a massive increase in population and rapid industrial growth. A vast oilfield was discovered in Rio state in 1974, leading to knock on benefits for the city. The influx of unskilled labour put new pressures on housing, resulting in more *favelas* on the outskirts of the city.

Modern City

Despite the loss of its capital status in 1960, Rio has remained the cultural capital of Brazil. It is the country's second largest city and an important, modern sea port. Its main exports are sugar and coffee. It is a major service industry centre. Industries include food processing, textiles and the manufacture of building materials, electrical equipment, chemicals and pharmaceuticals.

Many of Brazil's leading companies have their head offices in the city. Leisure and tourism are important to Rio's economy. It is unrivalled as the nation's liveliest city with its world famous beaches. However, a large part of the population, continue to live in shanty towns.

Rio de Janeiro has air, sea, rail and road links. The Galeão airport is for international flights while the Santos Dumont airport caters for domestic traffic. The city is served by a metro system.

Rio de Janeiro hosted the 2016 Olympic Games from 5–21 Aug.

Places of Interest

Among Rio's beaches most popular beaches are Copacabana and Ipanema. Landmarks include Pão de Açúcar ('Sugar Loaf') Mountain and Corcovado Mountain, on which stands the statue of Christ the Redeemer.

The Modernist Catedral Metropolitana in the heart of the city was completed in 1979 in a style reminiscent of ancient Mayan architecture. Among Rio's other religious buildings are the Mosteiro de São Bento and Nossa Senhora de Candelaria.

Rio's museums include the Museo Historico Nacional, opened in 1922, which has the largest collection of coins in Latin America. The Museu Nacional de Belas Artes (Fine Arts Museum) displays over 20,000 paintings and sculptures. The Museu de Arte Moderna (Modern Art Museum) opened in 1958.

Riyadh, Saudi Arabia

Introduction

Riyadh is the political capital of Saudi Arabia (Makkah being the religious capital). Located in Nejd in the central region of the Arabian peninsula, it is the seat of government and an important commercial, educational and cultural centre. The city extends for some 1,600 km^2 and has a population of over 3 m.

History

Situated at the confluence of several wadis (dry riverbeds) that channel underground water to the site, Riyadh has been a natural fertile area in an otherwise arid landscape since antiquity. In pre-Islamic times the settlement at the site was known as Hajar. Date groves and fruit orchards, irrigated by subterranean water and periodic rainfall, developed around the town, attracting traders from across the Arabian peninsula. Its modern name (derived from the Arabic word meaning garden) was first applied to those sections of the town where the groves and orchards predominated. In time the name came to refer to the whole settlement.

By the end of the eighteenth century Riyadh had become part of the first Saudi state. This was administered from Diriya by the Al-Saud family (forebears of the present ruling dynasty), who were followers of the puritanical Wahhabi Islamic sect. When Diriya fell under the control of the Ottoman Empire in 1818, the Al-Saud transferred their capital to Riyadh to the south. By 1824, the Al-Saud regained political control of central Arabia. A period of tribal warfare began in 1865 and resulted in the rival Al-Rashid family, with Ottoman support, extending its power over the Saudi state. The Al-Saud, under the leadership of Abdul Rahman, were forced into exile in 1891. However, Riyadh was recaptured in 1902 by Abdulaziz Ibn Abdul Rahman. This event marked the beginning of the formation of the modern state of Saudi Arabia. After establishing Riyadh as his headquarters, Abdulaziz proceeded over the next three decades to unite the different regions into one nation. In Sept. 1932, the country was named the Kingdom of Saudi Arabia and Riyadh became the capital of the new state. Where for centuries its main features and its size had remained largely unchanged, the city began to expand rapidly. At the start of the 1930s Riyadh had an estimated population of 30,000. Within three decades, the population reached 200,000, and 1.5 m. by 1988. Oil revenues financed a vast construction boom, and the city has increased in area from 8.5 km^2 in 1932 to its present 1,600 km^2.

Modern City

Riyadh is centre of government and diplomacy, ministries and foreign embassies having relocated from Jeddah since the early 1980s. Most embassies and offices of international organizations are in the Diplomatic Quarter in the northwest of the city. Riyadh is divided into 17 separately administered areas, known as branch municipalities. Two industrial zones have been established outside the city. The King Khalid international airport is the country's second busiest airport. There are two universities (the King Saud and the Imam Mohammed Ibn Saud Islamic Universities) and a number of specialized colleges, institutes and cultural centres. Riyadh was selected as the cultural capital of the Arab world for 2000. The King Fahd International Stadium can seat 80,000 sports spectators. Despite its commercial expansion, Riyadh has abundant public parks and open spaces making up about 4% of the city's area.

Riyadh was subject to a serious terrorist attack on 12 May 2003. Nine suicide bombers hit western targets including expatriate compounds. The headquarters of the Saudi Maintenance Company was also targeted. Al-Qaeda has been blamed by both the Saudi and US administrations. The attack came on the eve of a visit from US Secretary of State Colin Powell. Approximately 30 people died and 200 were injured.

Places of Interest

The old section of the city, known as the Qasr Al-Hokm district, has been rejuvenated as part of a multi-billion dollar project. Segments of the old city wall and other historic elements have been preserved and new building has incorporated traditional architectural elements. The complex houses the offices of the Riyadh Governate, conference halls, mosques, commercial buildings, shopping facilities and souks. Other notable features of the capital include the Masmakh Fortress (the recapture of which by Abdulaziz in 1902 heralded his future campaign of conquest); the Murabba Palace (built in 1946 by Abdulaziz as a home and seat of government); the National Museum; the King Saud University Museum; and the King Faisal Centre for Research and Islamic Studies. Riyadh Zoo is a popular leisure attraction. On the outskirts of the city there is one of the largest camel markets in the Middle East.

Rome, Italy

Introduction

The national capital, Rome is also the capital of Latium region and Rome Province. The city is located in central Italy and is built across seven hills on the banks of the Tiber River, 25 km from the Tyrrhenian Sea. Known as the Eternal City, Rome is one of the world's greatest cultural, religious and intellectual centres.

History

According to legend, Rome was founded in 753 BC by the twin descendants of Aeneas the Trojan, Romulus and Remus. There is evidence of settlement in the area dating back to the beginning of the 1st millennium BC. By the sixth century BC several Etruscan city-states were unified to form the kingdom of Rome.

The first Republic of Rome was declared in 509 BC. In 396 BC the city was largely destroyed by Gallic invaders, and only the Capitoline was retained. Reconstruction was swift, and in the third century the republic defeated Carthage, thus becoming the dominant power in the Mediterranean. In 44 BC, after the assassination of Julius Caesar, who did much to improve civic buildings and living conditions in the city, Augustus was declared Emperor. He strengthened Roman government and restored peace to the entire Roman basin. His reign was perceived as a golden age for the empire.

Rome's zenith was reached in the first and second centuries when the city's population was nearly 1 m. However it never managed to be economically self-sufficient and as a result went into a steady decline. The conversion of the Emperor Constantine in 314 gave Christians the freedom to practice their religion, previous to his rule Christianity had been prohibited. From this time onwards Rome has claimed supremacy in the Christian church and through nineteen centuries the Popes, the original bishops of Rome, have influenced religious and political thinking far beyond the Vatican City.

The emperor Justinian's efforts to restore Rome to its former glories following a series of invasions by the Vandals and Visigoths proved catastrophic. By the end of the sixth century, the population had dwindled to below 100,000. Partial restoration of the city's infrastructure came at the turn of the ninth century when Charlemagne was crowned holy Roman Emperor. From this time Rome's importance as the centre of the Christian world increased, and towards the end of the eleventh century it had grown wealthy on the profits of pilgrimages and religious donations. However the feuding of the city's nobility meant that for much of the thirteenth and fourteenth centuries the papacy was based in Avignon. It returned to Rome in 1377.

During the Renaissance the city briefly thrived, but a conflict between the papacy and the emperor Charles V culminated in the sack of Rome in 1527 and the destruction of many civic improvements. The counter-reformation witnessed the rebirth of the city, but Rome was never to have the resources of a trading empire like that of Venice, and once again it began to decline in prosperity, and corruption amongst its nobility grew. In 1798 Napoléon's troops captured Rome and it was briefly a republic free of papal rule. The papacy was reinstalled in 1814, and Pope Pius IX awarded the city a new liberal constitution, designed to improve its government. In 1861 Rome was incorporated into the unified kingdom of Italy, and in Oct. 1870 it became the new country's capital. Throughout the twentieth century Rome has earned revenue as a major tourist destination, and much of its recent history has been characterized by initiatives to restore and protect its wealth of archaeological and cultural treasures.

Modern City

Most flights arrive at Leonardo da Vinci Airport which is connected by train to the Termini station in central Rome. Some flights arrive at Ciampino Airport, which is linked by bus and subway to the centre. Most domestic, European and international rail services arrive and depart from the main Termini station. The city is connected to the north and south by the A1 motorway and to the west by the A24.

Urban transport is provided by bus and metro.

Rome is an important centre of commerce with varied industries, such as electronics, chemicals printing, publishing, food-processing engineering and filmmaking. A great deal of its income comes from tourism.

Places of Interest

Reflecting twelve centuries of Roman history, the Roman Forum acted as the political, religious and commercial centre of ancient Rome. The Forum is intersected by the Via Sacra, the oldest street in Rome.

The Palatine Hill rises above the Roman Forum and is the place where, according to legend, Romulus and Remus were discovered. The Farnesi Gardens, laid out in the sixteenth century on the site of Tiberius' palace, look out over the Forum and rest of Rome. The Imperial Forum sprawls across a site opposite the Roman Forum and contains the ruins of temples, basilicas and public squares constructed in the first and second centuries.

The Coliseum is a vast amphitheatre that was used as an arena for mock naval battles, gladiatorial contests and for fights to the death between men and wild animals. It was here that the Christians were fed to the lions.

The Capitoline Hill (Campidoglio) was the most sacred part of Ancient Rome and now serves as the seat of the City Government. The church of S. Pietro in Carcere marks the spot where St. Peter (the first Pope and Bishop of Rome) is thought to have been imprisoned by the Romans.

The Pantheon is a perfectly preserved ancient building which once served as a temple. Originally built by Agrippa in 27 BC and rebuilt by Hadrian (117–125 AD) it was converted into a church in the seventh century. The side chapels contain the tombs of the Kings of Italy and of the renaissance painter, Raphael. The Pantheon is situated in the historic Centro Storico.

The Piazza Navona was opened in 86 AD as a stadium hosting wrestling matches, javelin and discus throwing and chariot and foot races. It is now a pedestrianized space containing three fountains, including Bernini's master-piece, the *Fontana dei Quattro Fiumi* (Fountain of the Four Rivers), at the centre. Bernini completed the fountain in 1651.

The Baroque Palazzo Barberini was built for the Barberini family by the combined talents of Boromini, Bernini and Maderno in the seventeenth century. It now houses the Museo Nazionale d'Arte, which has a collection devoted to paintings from the eleventh–eighteenth centuries including works by Lippi, Tintoretto, Caravaggio, Raphael, Titian, Holbein, etc.

Just north of the Spanish Steps, the Villa Borghese was created by Scipione Borghese to celebrate his elevation to Cardinal. It features a park, a zoo and three notable art museums. The Galleria Borghese is housed in the Palazzo Borghese and contains collections of sculptures by Canova and Bernini and paintings by Raphael, Correggio, Titian and Caravaggio.

The Museo Nazionale Etrusco occupies the Villa Giulia and houses a collection of Etruscan artefacts.

The cathedral church of Rome, the Basilica di San Giovanni in Laterano is the oldest Christian Basilica in Rome. It was first begun by Constantine in 314 AD, rebuilt during the Baroque period by Borromini and altered again in the eighteenth century. The church has some important relics, including what are said to be the heads of Saints Peter and Paul.

The Lateran Palace was rebuilt in the sixteenth century and was the papal palace until the papal court returned from Avignon. The Scala Sancta is a vestige of the medieval palace and is said to be where Christ stood at his trial in the Palace of Pontius Pilate.

The famous Fontana di Trevi (Trevi Fountain) designed by Nicolo Salvi was commissioned by Pope Clement XIII in 1762 and depicts the ocean riding his chariot drawn by sea horses.

Roseau, Dominica

Introduction

Roseau, at the mouth of the River Roseau on the southwestern coast of Dominica, is the national capital and its main port.

History

The town was settled by the French in the mid-1700s. They called it Roseau after the French word for reeds, which grew in abundance. A subject of dispute between the French and English during the eighteenth century, it was devastated by two hurricanes and a massive fire during the late 1770s and early 1780s. In 1783, along with the rest of Dominica, the city was ceded to the British. Agriculture was a mainstay of the economy but Roseau also became the centre of a thriving slave trade in the early nineteenth century.

In 1978 Roseau became capital of independent Dominica but it was virtually destroyed by Hurricane David the following year. It has subsequently undergone major reconstruction and development.

Modern City

The local economy relies on the activities of the deep-water port. Leading exports include Vegetables, spices, limes and essential oils. Tourism is also important.

Canefield airport is 3 miles from the city centre and Melville Hall airport is 38 miles away. The port has ferry services and minibuses run within the city.

Places of Interest

Leading attractions include the parliament building, the Roman Catholic cathedral, the Anglican church of St George and the public library (built by Andrew Carnegie). The Old Market was the centre of the city's slave trade. There is a public market selling local produce and the Dominican museum has permanent exhibitions on the slave trade and Creole and Amerindian culture. Also popular are the botanic gardens and the nearby waterfalls at Trafalgar.

Rotterdam, Netherlands

Introduction

Rotterdam is situated on the New Meuse (Nieuwe Maas) River in the south of the Netherlands, just under 20 miles (30 km) from the North Sea, with the New Waterway canal connecting it to the coast.

History

The city entered the history books in 1283 when the land it was built on was reclaimed from the mouth of the Rotte river, and a fishing village was established. Rotterdam was chartered in 1328. Following the construction of a canal to the Schie, which was like the Rotte, a tributary of the New Meuse, the town became the major port of the region.

The seventeenth century was something of a golden age for the city, as it basked in the prosperity brought to the Netherlands via the newly discovered trade route to the Indies. Rotterdam's harbours and residential area underwent considerable expansion during this era, and as the eighteenth century dawned the city was second only to Amsterdam as a commercial and financial centre.

After the cessation of international trade during the French occupation of the Netherlands, Rotterdam began the process of re-establishing itself as a leading merchant city. In order to facilitate this process the New Waterway Canal was built. It was sufficiently large to carry ocean-going steamships, and was completed in 1872. After a series of further improvements, including the development of a rail connection with the southern Netherlands and the construction of a bridge across the Meuse, Rotterdam became the largest dredged harbour in the world.

Constant bombardment and German occupation during World War II brought chaos to the city and destroyed much of its port, and many of its older public buildings. The fifteenth century St Lawrence's church fell victim to Nazi artillery but was painstakingly restored after the war by the resilient locals. The rest of the city lay in ruins, but the result of this calamity was to inspire a new generation of Dutch architects to reinvent the centre. A completely different new inner city was planned and developed.

Modern City

Unlike many other attempts at post-war reconstruction, Rotterdam's spacious and modern centre has attracted widespread admiration from professionals and tourists. Despite this architectural change, the port remains the hub of Rotterdam's economy. It is the world's most important oil terminals; there are 5 major oil refineries located within its boundaries and the city's petrochemical industry is highly important to sustaining its success. Given the sheer volume of cargo that passes through it each year Rotterdam remains one of the busiest and largest harbours in the world. It is also well served by road and rail networks and there is an airport–Zestienhoven–to the northwest of the city. Rotterdam was made one of the European Capitals of Culture for 2001.

Places of Interest

Sites of cultural interest include the rebuilt St Lawrence's church with its statue of one of Rotterdam's most famous former inhabitants - Erasmus, De Doelen concert hall which is celebrated for the quality of its acoustics, and the Boymans-van Beuningen museum which houses a fine collection of Dutch and Flemish masterpieces. The Royal Rotterdam Zoological Garden Foundation is a renowned and popular zoo.

Rustavi, Georgia

Introduction

Rustavi, on the Kura river in southeast Georgia, is the largest city in the Kvemo Kartili region and the third largest in the country. Around 40 km. southeast of Tblisi, on the site of an ancient city, the modern town was developed by Soviet authorities in the second half of the twentieth century to be an industrial powerhouse.

History

The ancient town of Rustavi, home to the famous twelfth–thirteenth century poet Rustaveli, was destroyed by the Mongol Timur at the end of the fourteenth century. When iron ore was discovered in the vicinity in the 1940s, Stalin directed that the town should be developed to exploit it. An ironworks, steelworks, chemical plants and a major railway station on the Tbilisi-Baku line were erected. The city suffers severe pollution as a result of rapid industrialization.

Modern City

Poor infrastructure and high unemployment have led to high rates of crime and poverty. The chemical and metalworks are still the primary source of employment. The Rustavi TV company has had several run-ins with the government.

Places of Interest

The area west of the city produces wine and Rustavi vodka.

Saint-Louis, Senegal

Introduction

Saint-Louis, the third-largest town of Senegal, is just south of the border with Mauritania. The former capital city, it was subsumed in importance by Dakar from the second half of the nineteenth century. The city comprises an island and part of the Langue de Barberie peninsula, connected by the 500 m. long bridge, Pont Faidherbe.

History

Saint-Louis was founded in 1659 and was the capital of Mauritania–Senegal. Britain and France vied for dominance in the region, but it was under French jurisdiction in the mid-nineteenth century that Saint-Louis reached its commercial zenith as a trading and fishing centre.

The rise of Dakar from the 1860s reduced Saint-Louis' standing and, though Saint-Louis was made capital of French West Africa in 1893, it lost the position to Dakar in 1904.

Modern City

Saint-Louis is now a relatively minor town, dependent upon the fishing industry and its role as a transport hub.

Places of Interest

Pont Faidherbe was originally built for a location on the Danube but was shipped to Saint-Louis in 1897. The architecture of the island pays homage to the colonial era. The old governor's palace, a fort during the eighteenth century, is now a government building while the cathedral was built in the early nineteenth century. Other attractions include the Muslim cemetery, known for its numerous fishermen's graves, and the national park on the Langue de Barberie peninsula. The African quarter on the peninsula is the favoured area for nightlife. There is an annual jazz festival in May or June and occasional boat races.

Salt Lake City, United States of America

Introduction

Salt Lake City, the capital of Utah, is in the north of the state near to Great Salt Lake in the basin of Lake Bonneville. The major trade centre of Utah, the city is also known as the international headquarters of the Mormon Church and as the host city of the 2002 Winter Olympics.

History

Salt Lake City was built after Brigham Young, the leader of the Mormons (or Church of Jesus Christ of Latter-day Saints), arrived in the area with his followers in 1847. In 1849 the name Great Salt Lake City was adopted and the city became capital of the new territory of Utah in 1856. The city's name was shortened to Salt Lake City in 1868 and maintained its status as the capital when Utah was admitted to the Union in 1896. After 40 years of construction work the Mormon temple in the city was completed in 1893.

In the twentieth century the city thrived as its mining and manufacturing industries grew and it developed as a winter sports resort. In 2002 the city hosted the Winter Olympics.

Modern City

Salt Lake City International Airport is located 4 miles west of the downtown area. There is a Greyhound bus terminal and an Amtrak rail station and Gray Line runs bus tours of the city.

Lead, copper, silver, lead and zinc mining and processing operations near the city account for much of its economy. Other major products include metal goods, processed food, petroleum and textiles. Salt Lake City is also the seat of the University of Utah and Westminster College.

Places of Interest

Temple Square is the international headquarters of the Mormon Church and contains the 210 ft. high Temple (open only to confirmed Mormons), the Mormon Tabernacle and two visitor centres. The nearby Beehive House was built by Mormon leader Brigham Young in 1854 and now contains an exhibition on his life. Other Mormon visitor attractions include the Family History Library and the Museum of Church History and Art.

Utah State Capitol is located on a hill overlooking Temple Square. Other cultural institutions include the Hansen Planetarium and the Utah Museum of Fine Arts. Symphony Hall houses the Utah Symphony Orchestra while the Utah Jazz basketball team play at the Delta Center.

Salvador, Brazil

Introduction

Brazil's first capital, Salvador is the capital of the Bahia region in the northeast of the country. It remains one of Brazil's most important historical and cultural centres. The colonial centre was named a UNESCO world heritage site in 1985.

History

The explorer Amérigo Vespúcio discovered Salvador bay on All Saints' Day (1 Nov.) 1501. He thus named the area Baía de Todos os Santos (All Saints' Bay). The construction of the city was ordered by King Don João III, when a Portuguese fleet brought more than a thousand people in six ships to settle the area. The city proper was founded in 1549 as Brazil's colonial capital. Salvador was the main Atlantic port for ships travelling the *volta do mar*, or spice route to the East, and the surrounding region developed into an important region of sugar production and export.

In 1583 Salvador had a population 1,600 people. Its wealth attracted predators who made several attempts to take the city at the turn of the seventeenth century. The West Indian Company (backed by a variety of wealthy European investors) took the port in 1624, holding it until the Spanish expelled the invaders the following year.

In the early part of the eighteenth century gold and precious stones were discovered in central Brazil, bringing new wealth to the city. From this period date many of the city's most important buildings. In 1763 Salvador lost its capital status to Rio de Janeiro. But it retained some political power and was home to the Portuguese royal family during the Peninsular War (1808–14). In the war of independence, Salvador remained under Portuguese control until its liberation in 1823.

New immigrants began to arrive from the end of the nineteenth century, giving the city a rich multicultural background. The early twentieth century saw big changes particularly in the port over to the south of the city. But many of the historical sites to the north were preserved, and from 1967 restoration started. What survived of the historic centre of Salvador was declared a World Heritage Site in 1985.

From 1992, the government of Bahia began a large scale project for renewing Salvador's infrastructure and boosting its tourist industry. The ongoing Restoration Plan for the Historic Centre of Salvador was the largest programme of its kind ever mounted in Brazil. Hundreds of houses have been restored, and a number of important ruins reconstructed.

Modern City

A major port, Salvador's exports include sugar, cocoa and diamonds. Its principal industries are food and tobacco processing. Salvador is accessible by air, rail, road and sea. It has a funicular railway system and the 70-m. Lacerda Elevator linking the upper and lower cities. Educational institutions include the Universidade Federal da Bahia and the Universidade Católica do Salvador.

Places of Interest

There are many colonial sites. Religious buildings include the Igreja do Nosso Senhor do Bonfim, the Igreja Nossa Senhora do Rosário dos Pretos and the Catedral Basílica. Once a Jesuit church, the cathedral is decorated with Portuguese *azulejos*, or tile work. Built at the turn of the eighteenth century, the Baroque church of São Francis has carved woodwork decoration and a number of treasures such as Portuguese panels detailing the legend of the birth of Saint Francis.

Among Salvador's museums are the Museu de Arqueologia e Etnologia (Archaeology Museum), the Museu de Arte Sacra de Bahia (Religious Art

Museum) and the Museu da Cidade (City Museum). The Pelourinho, or Pelô, as it is known by the locals, is located in the historical centre of Salvador and contains some of the finest examples of colonial architecture in Latin America.

Salzburg, Austria

Introduction

Salzburg is situated on the border with Germany in the north central part of the country. It is the capital of the federal state of Salzburg and lies on the River Salzach. Extensively developed in the sixteenth and seventeenth centuries on the Italian model and boasting fine examples of Renaissance and Baroque architecture, it is now Austria's second most important tourist city.

History

Celts and Romans were in occupation before Salzburg was created a bishopric by St Rupert in the early eighth century. In 798 it was made an archbishopric, becoming one of the most significant in the Holy Roman Empire. It also gained wealth from the saltmines of the surrounding area. The Archbishops held power and wealth with Wolf Dietrich, who reigned from 1587–1612, among the most prominent. He employed architects and artists from Renaissance Italy to reconstruct the city and during his time Salzburg gained a new cathedral, the Residenzplatz (home to the archbishops) and a number of other grand public buildings.

Extensive rebuilding and extension continued under Dietrich's successors Markus Sittikus and Paris Lodron, who between them ruled until the middle of the seventeenth century. By this time Salzburg had its own university. For a long period Salzburg was in effect an independent city state but it fell under Habsburg rule in 1816 and 2 years later it was badly damaged by fire. The city escaped with little damage in the wars of the twentieth century and served as the base for US army personnel from 1945 until 1956.

Modern City

Salzburg has efficient road, rail and air links. Apart from tourism, other major industries include textiles, leather, brewing and metal work. It is also a major conference centre. Despite its reputation for austerity—Thomas Bernhard, a native writer, called the city "a fatal illness" because of its conservatism—Salzburg remains a major draw for visitors, tempted by its rich architecture and its alpine setting.

Places of Interest

Salzburg is overlooked by the Hohensalzburg Fortress, a grand construction built at the top of Mönchsberg (Monk's Hill) in 1077 and rebuilt and refined until the late seventeenth century. Existing as almost an independent town within Salzburg, it provided accommodation to the archbishops throughout the wars of the sixteenth and seventeenth centuries. It is the city's most visited tourist attraction. Other major attractions include the Natural History Museum and the nearby Hellbrunn Palace, built by Sitticus.

The Mozart industry thrives in the city. Mozart was born in Salzburg in Jan. 1756 and spent much of his life here. His image adorns tourist merchandise while his birthplace and a later residence are now open to visitors. It is his work that also forms the basis of the Salzburg Festival, a summer event that ranks among the world's finest musical festivals. Begun in 1920, it includes operas, plays and recitals with the emphasis firmly, though not exclusively, on Mozart. In 1999 it played to audiences of around 240,000, a figure some 100,000 greater than the city's population. Salzburg's reliance on its musical heritage continues with the burgeoning industry that has grown up around the film musical *The Sound of Music*, which was filmed at various local sites including St Peter's Abbey and the Mirabelle Gardens.

Samarkand (Samarqand), Uzbekistan

Introduction

Uzbekistan's second city, Samarkand is in the east of the country. One of the oldest cities in the region, it enjoyed a golden age in the fourteenth and fifteenth centuries. It remains an important industrial and trading town.

History

In the 3rd or 4th millennium BC the area was known as Afrosiab. By the fourth century there was a city called by the Greeks, Marakanda. The main city of Sogdiana and a strategic point on the Silk Road, it was seized by Alexander the Great around 329 BC. Called Sa-mo-quien by the Chinese, it became a melting pot of Western and Eastern cultures. Samarkand was invaded by Arabs in the early eighth century, who turned it into a centre of Islamic learning. It flourished commercially as part of the Umayyad empire and continued to do so under the Abbasids, Samanids, Seljuks and the shahs of Khwarazm.

In 1221 the city was destroyed by Genghis Khan but blossomed again under Timur, who seized power in 1370 and proclaimed Samarkand the capital of his empire. From there he launched a series of campaigns to vanquish the Golden Horde. His grandson Ulughbek ruled for 40 years, adding to the scientific element of Samarkand's infrastructure by opening a school of astronomy and founding the observatory in 1428. The Uzbek Shaybanids invaded in 1447 and helped build the foundations of Central Asia's economic and cultural stronghold. Much of the old town has remained intact since the fourteenth and fifteenth century. Samarkand eventually joining the khanate of Bukhara.

The city had declined by the eighteenth century and passed to Russia in 1868. Designated a provincial capital in 1887, it prospered again as improved transport links enabled trade to flourish. Between 1925 and 1930 it was capital of the Uzbek Soviet Socialist Republic, before being succeeded by Tashkent. Samarkand experienced another building boom under the Soviets.

Modern City

The local economy relies on agriculture, textiles (especially cotton and silk), tobacco and food processing, wine-making and vehicle and machine manufacturing. There is a university and several higher education institutions.

Samarkand is well served by road and rail links and there is an airport. Buses and trolley buses run within the city.

Places of Interest

The city's focal point is the Registan ('sandy place'), a collection of fourteenth and fifteenth century buildings. Bibi-Khanym mosque, which collapsed during an earthquake in 1897, is nonetheless a spectacular tribute to Timur's rule and is surrounded by a bazaar.

The Ulughbek madrasah was built in the early fifteenth century, the Sher Dor madrasah in the early 17th and the Tillya-Kari madrasah in the mid seventeenth century. The ancient city mausoleum Aksaray dates from the fifteenth century. Shahi-Zinda is an avenue of ornate tombs belonging to the families of Timur and Ulughbek, while Timur himself is believed to be buried in the Gur-Emir Mausoleum.

San Antonio, United States of America

Introduction

San Antonio is in south-central Texas on the San Antonio River and is the seat of Bexar county. One of the largest cities in the state, it has strong Mexican and Spanish influences. The city is known as the 'birthplace of the revolution', a reference to the famous Battle of the Alamo in 1836.

History

The area now known as San Antonio was inhabited by Coahuiltecan Indians before it was first settled by Spanish missionaries in 1691. In 1718 a Spanish military garrison was established and the area became a stopping point on the way to French trading posts in Louisiana. In 1731, a town was established near the Spanish Mission and the area was named San Antonio de Béjar.

San Antonio became the seat of the Spanish government in Texas. In 1821 Stephen F. Austin was granted a permit allowing 300 Anglo-American families to settle in the city. The Battle of the Alamo occurred in 1836 when a Mexican force led by Major General Santa Anna defeated a band of volunteer fighters at the Alamo fortress.

Towards the end of the nineteenth century large German communities settled in San Antonio and it became a major centre for the cattle and oil trades. In the 1920s, major floods killed 50 residents and caused the destruction of much of the downtown area. Regeneration was rapid, aided by the building of several military installations and bases in and around the city.

Modern City

San Antonio is only 150 miles from the Mexican border and the majority of its population are either Spanish-speaking or bilingual. In the surrounding region cattle, sheep and crop farming are crucial to the economy. The city is a major financial and manufacturing centre focused on aerospace equipment, chemicals and building materials. San Antonio is also a military centre with five major installations in or just outside the city.

There is an International Airport, a Greyhound bus terminal and an Amtrak train station. Educational institutions include the University of Texas at San Antonio, St. Mary's University, Trinity University, San Antonio College and Texas A&M University-San Antonio.

Places of Interest

The city's diverse cultural and historical heritage is well served by several major tourist attractions. The Institute of Texan Cultures and the Mexican Cultural Institute offer social and cultural histories of the area while popular historical sites include the Alamo fortress, five Franciscan missions, the Spanish Governor's Palace and La Villita, which is a reconstructed Spanish settlement area.

San Fernando Cathedral, built between 1731 and 1873, is the oldest cathedral in the United States. HemisFair Park, which is used for exhibitions and conventions, hosted the San Antonio World Fair in 1968. San Antonio River has been carefully landscaped and the River Walk is a focus for the city. The Fiesta San Antonio is held every April.

San Diego, United States of America

Introduction

Located in southern California near to the Mexican border, San Diego lies on the western coast of the United States along the Pacific Ocean. The seat of San Diego county, the city is an important port as well as a military and naval centre. The second largest city in California, San Diego's warm climate has helped it become a tourist centre as well as a popular retirement destination.

History

The area occupied by modern-day San Diego was first sighted by Europeans in 1542 and was originally named San Miguel. It was renamed San Diego de Alcalá de Henares in 1602. California's first military post and mission settlement were built in the area in 1769. Mexico assumed control of the area in 1834 and built a small town. The United States gained control in 1846 and in 1867 a new city called San Diego was designed by Alonzo E. Horton 3 miles south of the original military post.

Thanks to its agreeable climate and the building of the Sante Fe Railroad in 1884, San Diego grew rapidly from the 1880s onwards. Before World War II the major industry was aircraft construction. During the war San Diego's

natural deepwater harbour was used by the US Navy as its Pacific Command Center and it has retained its military importance ever since.

Modern City

The major industries are shipbuilding, electronic equipment and aerospace activities. San Diego Bay is the base for a large fishing fleet as well as an important port for the distribution of cotton. San Diego hosts the headquarters of the 11th US Naval District and also houses Army and Marine installations. San Diego county is an important area for fruit and vegetables and the city is the biggest outlet in southern California for farm produce.

The city's transport links to Arizona, New Mexico and the rest of southern California make it an important communications centre. Lindbergh Field Airport is located 2 miles from San Diego and the city centre has an Amtrak train depot and a Greyhound bus terminal. There is an integrated bus system while a tram system known as the San Diego Trolley is also in operation.

Universities include San Diego State University, the University of San Diego and the University of California at San Diego. The city also houses the Scripps Institution of Oceanography.

Places of Interest

Balboa Park is the centrepiece of the city's cultural life and contains 12 museums including the Timkin Museum of Art, the San Diego Museum of Art, the Natural History Museum and the Spanish Village Art Center. The world-renowned San Diego Zoo, which is home to many rare animals including Chinese pandas, is also located in Balboa Park.

Old Town San Diego has a historical park while the site of Presidio Hill, where the original Spanish military post and mission were located, now houses the Junípero Serra Museum. There are extensive sandy beaches, with Mission Beach and Pacific Beach among the most popular. Near Mission Bay is Sea World, the city's most popular tourist attraction, with its killer whales, dolphins and other marine life.

San Francisco, United States of America

Introduction

San Francisco is one of the most picturesque and liberal-minded of American cities. Occupying an area of 48 sq. miles and located on a series of steep hills, the city is the seat of San Francisco County and is located on the western coast of California at the entrance of one of the world's most famous natural harbours. To the north San Francisco is bordered by the Golden Gate strait, to the east it is bordered by San Francisco Bay and to the south is San Bruno mountain. The city's boundary also extends to the west to include the Farallon Islands which lie 32 miles into the Pacific Ocean.

History

The first settlements in the area now known as San Francisco were a series of villages populated by Native Americans known as Ohlone. By 1776 the Spanish, who had occupied much of the west coast of America, had established several missionary outposts, including the Mission Dolores, and named the area after Saint Francis of Assisi. Small towns were set up in an attempt to attract settlers and provide food for the mission.

The establishment of an independent Mexican state in 1821 ended the mission era. At this stage Montera was the only settlement of any note in the area, while San Francisco was known as Yerba Buena, a small town of around 500 inhabitants. The Mexican-American War of 1846 saw the US government gradually take control of the west coast. On Jan. 241,848, just 9 days after assuming formal control of the area, gold was discovered a few hundred miles east of San Francisco.

This discovery transformed the area. Over 100,000 people entered California in search of gold within 12 months of the discovery. The establishment of mines and the attendant trade that the gold rush brought to the area saw San Francisco develop from a tiny shantytown into a city of 35,000 inhabitants by 1853. An ever-increasing industrial base for the west coast, San Francisco's economy was boosted further by the discovery of silver ore in 1859. Soon the city had the most sophisticated mines in the country, a burgeoning stock exchange and was at the heart of the country's new transcontinental railroads.

By 1900, San Francisco was the ninth largest city in the United States. However 6 years later it was rocked by an earthquake which led to a huge fire throughout the city. Around 28,000 buildings were destroyed, 3,000 inhabitants killed and over half the city's population were left homeless by the event. The city was quickly rebuilt. Mayor James Rolph, who was elected in 1911, oversaw the building of a new Civic Center and City Hall and the opening of the Panama Canal and the Panama-Pacific International Exposition that promoted it acted as symbols of the city's recovery.

Landmarks such as the Golden Gate and Bay Bridges and the Coit Tower were built in the 1920s and 30s. During World War II, San Francisco was a major embarkation point for Pacific-based Allied troops and became a significant shipbuilding centre. After the war the city was eclipsed by Los Angeles as the main city of the west coast of the United States but thrived as a centre of alternative lifestyles and culture. The beat and Hippie movements of the 1950s and 60s had their roots in San Francisco and large gay communities were established and still exist in the city today.

Modern City

San Francisco's major industries are shipping and banking. The headquarters of the Federal Reserve Bank for the 12th district is in the city and several major companies such as Bechtel and Levi Strauss & Co. are also based in San Francisco. Nearly 90% of the population are employed in the service sector. The development of important high technology industries in the 'Silicon Valley' area to the south of San Francisco means that the city also features a wide array of multimedia companies.

The city is served by San Francisco International Airport, which handles both domestic and international flights. Amtrak trains stop across the bay in Richmond and there is a Greyhound bus terminal. Despite heavy traffic congestion and pollution, getting around the city by public transport is relatively straightforward thanks to a comprehensive and efficient system of trolleybuses, cable cars and buses which are run by the San Francisco Municipal Railway. The Bay Area Rapid Transit System (BART) is a light-rail system that connects San Francisco to the east bay while the CalTrain system runs from the city centre to the suburbs.

The largest university in the city is San Francisco State University, which is part of California State University. Other important institutions include the University of California at San Francisco (a medical school), City College of San Francisco, Golden Gate University and San Francisco Conservatory of Music.

Places of Interest

San Francisco is an important cultural centre with a large tourist industry. There are several important art galleries including the San Francisco Museum of Modern Art, the M.H. de Young Memorial Museum (which focuses on American art) and the California Palace of the Legion of Honor (which houses an important collection of European art). The Golden Gate Recreation Area contains four museums devoted to art and crafts from Mexican, African-American and other cultural backgrounds. The city's major park, Golden Gate Park, contains one of the largest museums of natural history in the world, the California Academy of Sciences, as well as large botanical gardens.

San Francisco has an opera company who perform at the War Memorial Opera House at the Civic Center as well as a resident ballet company and a symphony orchestra. There are several theatre companies including the American Conservatory Theater. Architecturally the city's most famed sight is the Golden Gate bridge. The bridge's orange towers are visible from virtually every hill in the city.

San José, Costa Rica

Introduction

In the province of the same name, San José is the capital of Costa Rica. Situated in the centre of the country on a high fertile plain, the city is at 1,160 m above sea level.

History

San José was founded in the early eighteenth century as a small village called Villa Nueva de la Boca del Monte del Valle de Abra. The capital of Costa Rica was the nearby city of Cartago, established in 1563. After independence in 1821, Costa Rica had four self-governed cities, Heredia, Alajuela and Cartago and San José. A move towards a centralized government led to friction—San José and Alajuela being more progressive than Cartago and Heredia. The resulting civil war in 1833 was fought on the Ochomogo Hills. With the San José troops victorious, the new capital became the centre of the coffee trade, the country's main industry in the nineteenth century.

San José expanded throughout the twentieth century. The city centre was developed on a grid pattern with numbered *calles* from north to south and numbered *avenidos* from east to west.

Modern City

The economic, industrial and cultural heart of Costa Rica, San José is the centre of the nation's coffee production. Industries include coffee and cocoa processing and textile production. A third of the Costa Rican population are resident in the San José province. The city is also home to numerous academic institutions including the Universidad de Costa Rica, established in 1940. The Juan Santa International Airport is at 15 km northwest of the city. San José's architecture is a mixture of Spanish colonial and modern North American. High industry and traffic congestion cause pollution.

Places of Interest

The style of the Teatro Nacional is based on the Paris Opéra. In the late nineteenth century a touring opera company refused to play in San José from lack of an appropriate venue. Thereafter, coffee barons and merchants financed the construction of the Teatro. Begun in 1890, it was inaugurated in 1897. It has sculptures created by the Italian artist Pietro Bulgarelli, overhead painted reliefs, a Renaissance façade and a grand staircase in the fashion of the Opéra. The Museo Nacional focusses on archaeology, pre-colonial art and Costa Rican history. The Museo de Jade houses jade figures created by the Chorotegas people who inhabited the Nicoya region from the fourteenth century. The Museo de Arte Costarricense displays works of Costa Rican artists from 1950. Several parks are found in San José, including the Parque de España and the Parque Nacional, the latter set in rain forest.

San Marino, San Marino

Introduction

Capital and country have the same name. The city, encircled by triple walls, is on the west side of Mount Titano. Roads and railways connect the city to other parts of Italy and the Adriatic coast. The landscape is agricultural.

History

According to tradition, the region was first inhabited in the fourth century by St Marinus and a group of Christians trying to escape prosecution. The country became independent in the twelfth century with San Marino as capital, and managed to remain independent thanks to its isolation and its mountain fortresses. In the nineteenth century, San Marino was a refuge for the revolutionary and promoter of Italian unification, Giuseppe Garibaldi.

Modern City

Tourism is the backbone of San Marino's economy. Around 3 m. tourists visit San Marino each year, although the capital has less than 5000 inhabitants. Many of the city's visitors are day-trippers from Italy. The economy is dependent on domestic enterprises owing to lack of mineral resources. Manufactures include building materials, textiles, ceramics, electronics and food products. Agricultural products are grains, fruit, cheese and olives. Another source of income is the sale of duty-free consumer goods and postage stamps. No cars are allowed in the city, but there are modern parking facilities outside the stone walls. The nearest international airport is in Rimini.

Places of Interest

Along the cliffs of Monte Titano are San Marino's three fortresses, la Rocca, la Cesta, and Montale, offering a panoramic view of the Adriatic coast. Museums include the Museum of Antique Weapons, the Wax Museum and the Vintage Car Museum. There is also a traditional crafts exhibition. In April, San Marino attracts visitors for The San Marino Grand Prix. In July the city celebrates Medieval Days with a week of processions, feasts and historic games. On 3 Sept. the Feast of the Foundation of the Republic is celebrated. There is a bust of Abraham Lincoln who, in 1861, became an honorary citizen of the republic. Notable buildings are the Gothic government house and the palace (reconstructed in 1894).

San Salvador, El Salvador

Introduction

Situated in the centre of the country, San Salvador is capital of El Salvador and of the San Salvador department. At the foot of the dormant San Salvador volcano, the city is on the Acelhuate River.

History

Around 3,000 BC the area was populated by Maya and other groups of Nahua peoples. In the eleventh century the Pipil built Cuscatlán as their capital. Their language was a variant of the Aztec language, Nahuatl. In 1535 the conquistador Pedro de Alvarado under the command of Hernando Cortés invaded. After defeating the Pipil, the Spanish founded San Salvador near Cuscatlán. Barely a year later the inhabitants were forced from the new settlement by a Pipil uprising. More conflict ensued and in 1528 San Salvador was moved to its present site. It became a city in 1546. El Salvador was under the captaincy general of Guatemala until independence from the Spanish in 1811. Thereafter San Salvador was the capital of the Federal Republic of Central America until it was made capital of El Salvador in 1841.

Built on a seismic fault, San Salvador's history is marked by devastating earthquakes. Particularly destructive were those of 1854, 1873 and 1986. Destruction caused by the 12-year civil war reached its climax in 1989 when the left wing rebels captured the city from government troops. The war prompted rural migration to the capital resulting in many shantytowns. Most recent damage to the city was caused by two powerful earthquakes in Jan. and Feb. 2001.

Modern City

San Salvador is the political, economic and commercial centre of El Salvador. Industries include coffee and other food processing, textiles and cigar and cigarette production. An international airport is 44 km south of the city. Regular bus services link the capital with other Central American capitals. The Colegio de la Asunción, now the Universidad Nacional, was founded in 1841. As a legacy of the war, crime is rampant in the city.

Places of Interest

San Salvador has no surviving colonial buildings and many modern buildings are damaged. The Catedral Metropolitana is a timeline of the city's natural disasters. First built in 1808 it was demolished by the 1873 and 1986 earthquakes and destroyed by fire in 1951. It was the site of the assassination of Archbishop Romero in 1980. The Museo Nacional displays Mayan artefacts including the Stela of Tazumal.

Sana'a, Yemen

Introduction

The capital and largest city of Yemen, Sana'a is located on a plateau 2,350 m. above sea level in the mountainous western region of the country, about 100 km from the Red Sea coast. It is one of Arabia's oldest settlements, supposedly founded according to folklore by Noah's son Shem in biblical times. Its name literally means `fortified place', the remains of the city walls dating back to the first century AD in pre-Islamic times.

History

By the fourth century AD Sana'a was an important centre and citadel in the kingdom of the Himyarites (which superseded the Sabaean kingdom around 115 BC) in southwest Arabia. Himyarite power came to an end in the early sixth century, and was followed by Abyssinian and then Persian rule until the advent of Islam in AD 628. Thereafter, Sana'a's fortunes reflected the fluctuating power of the Imams (kings and spiritual leaders) of the Zaidi sect—who built the theocratic political structure of Yemen that largely endured from 860 to 1962—and rival dynasties and conquerors. These included the Fatamid caliphs of Egypt, the Ayyubids and, from the early sixteenth century, the Ottoman Turks. The Ottoman Empire exercised nominal sovereignty until the end of the First World War (when Yemen became independent), although conflict with the Imams was frequent. Sana'a periodically lost its capital status to other cities over the centuries, most recently to Ta'iz from 1948–62 during the rule of Imam Ahmad. It then became the capital of the Yemen Arab Republic on that entity's establishment in 1962 following a military revolution, and of the unified Republic of Yemen in 1990.

Modern City

Since the political and military upheavals of the 1960s and early 1970s, Sana'a has expanded rapidly in area and population. However, the eastern section of the capital, comprising the old walled city, has not been affected by modern construction activity. Its architectural and archaeological significance has been recognized by its designation as a UNESCO World Heritage Site. Sana'a is the seat of government and administration. Economically, it is the commercial and marketing centre of an important fruit-growing region. There is an international airport about 20 km west of the city. Sana'a University was founded in 1970.

Places of Interest

The old walled city provides the principal attractions, with its squares (such as Maydan at-Tahrir), gates (notably Bab al-Yaman), numerous mosques (particularly the Al-Jami al-Kebir or Great Mosque, one of the oldest in the Muslim world) and the Souk al-Milh (central market). The National Museum is housed in Dar as-Sa'd or House of Good Luck, a former royal palace built in the 1930s.

Santiago, Chile

Introduction

At the centre of the country, Santiago is the capital of Chile and of Santiago province. Situated to the west of the Andean Cordillera mountain range in the north of the Chilean central valley, the city is traversed by the Mapocho River. Santiago is the country's centre for industry, commerce, finance and culture. Nearly a third of Chileans live in the capital.

History

Before the arrival of the conquistadors, the area around Santiago was inhabited by the Picunche who were ruled by the Incas from the fifteenth century. In villages in the Central Valley, were the Mapuche who were arable farmers. In 1541 the Spanish conquistador Pedro de Valdivia, founded Santiago del Nuevo Extremo (Santiago of the New Frontier). The Picunche offered little resistance and were put under Spanish rule. The Mapuche, however, attacked Santiago, nearly destroying the settlement in the process. For the next 2 years, the Spanish were restricted to a makeshift camp on the Santa María hill, until reinforcements arrived from Peru.

Under the control of the Viceroyalty of Peru, Santiago was secondary to other colonial cities and grew slowly. In the late sixteenth century the city consisted of only 200 houses. Susceptible to earthquakes, many of

Santiago's buildings were destroyed in a particularly violent tremor in May 1647. In the early nineteenth century, a system of *tajamares*, or dykes, drained the south bank of the Mapocho River allowing for construction. Santiago expanded and improved communications allowed for increased commerce with Valparaíso.

Following an 8 year war, independence from Spanish rule was achieved in 1818. Named Chile's capital, post-Independence Santiago prospered. Revolutionary hero Bernardo O'Higgins, who became the Supreme Director from 1818–22, was based in Santiago. During his reign O'Higgins effected structural improvements to the city including the transformation of a sheep track into the Alameda de las Delicias, a long tree-lined boulevard, still a focal point of Santiago. In the mid-nineteenth century Santiago was connected by rail to Valparaíso. In the second half of the twentieth century Santiago's population exploded. The large number of migrants led to the emergence of *callampas*, or shanty towns, on the outskirts of the city. Investment in low-cost housing in the 1960s partly alleviated the problem. By 1980 the city had expanded to the limit of the Cordillera Mountains and by the end of the twentieth century around a third of the country's population was living in the capital.

Modern City

Central Santiago is surrounded by 31 self-governed *comunas*, or districts, each with a mayor and its own municipal administration. Santiago is the centre of Chile's commercial activity, and houses around half the country's industry. Major industries include food processing, chemicals, metallurgy and textiles. The city is the financial hub of Chile and has its own stock exchange. The Aeropuerto Internacional Arturo Merino Benítez is 26 km west of central Santiago, serving international and domestic flights. A second airport to the southwest, Aeropuerto Los Cerrillos, handles domestic flights only. There is a metro system. Universities include the Universidad de San Felipe founded in 1758. Santiago suffers from a high level of pollution.

Places of Interest

On the central plaza, the mint, or Real Casa de la Moneda, was built in 1805. Designed by the Italian architect Joaquín Toesca y Ricci, La Moneda was the presidential palace after 1846. Toesca was also commissioned to restore Santiago's Catedral Metropolitana in 1778, the original having burnt down in 1769. Museums include the Museo de Santiago, dedicated to the city's history. The Museo Chileno de Arte Precolombino covers 4500 years of pre-colonial history and the Palacio de Bellas Artes houses collections of French, Italian and Chilean art. The Museo de la Solidaridad Salvador Allende houses works by artists in exile.

Santo Domingo, Dominican Republic

Introduction

Santo Domingo, the largest city, chief seaport and capital of the Dominican Republic, lies in the south of the country where the Ozama flows into the Caribbean. It is the industrial, commercial, administrative and financial centre of the country. The city is the oldest European settlement in the Western Hemisphere. The oldest part, known as the Colonial City, was declared a World Heritage Site by UNESCO in 1990.

History

Santo Domingo was founded in 1496 by Christopher Columbus' brother, Bartholomew, following Columbus' discovery of the island of Hispaniola in 1492. The western third of the island is now the Republic of Haiti and the remainder, the Dominican Republic. The original city was located on the left (east) bank of the Ozama River and was called Nueva Isabella in honour of Queen Isabella of Spain. Destroyed by a hurricane in 1502 it was rebuilt on its current location on the right bank. The city was sacked by Sir Francis Drake in 1586 but in 1655 another attack by the British was repelled. From 1795 to 1809 Santo Domingo was controlled by the French. With British help the French were forced to return the colony to Spain from which the Dominicans declared their independence in 1821. However in 1822 the Haitians invaded and ruled until 1844 when the Dominican Republic was founded with Santo

Domingo as its capital. Following annexation to Spain the city lost this status until 1865 when independence was restored. Between 1916–26 the country was under American military occupation. In 1936 the ruling dictator Rafael Trujillo changed the city's name Ciudad Trujillo, but it reverted back to Santo Domingo on Trujillo's assassination in 1961.

Modern City

In 1930 the harbour was greatly expanded. Leading industries, such as petrochemicals, plastics, metallurgy, refrigerators, cement, textiles and food processing are located in Santo Domingo. It is also a distribution outlet for sugar cane, beef and products of the region. A major network of roads connects the capital with the rest of the republic, however the only railway lines are to nearby sugar refineries. Las Americas International Airport lies 20 min to the east of the city with non-stop flights to cities in Europe and America. To reach other destinations internally, Air Santo Domingo operates daily domestic flights from Herrera to seven locations. Tourism is a major source of income. The historic 'Colonial City' is the most popular attraction. The waterfront thoroughfare, El Malecon, bustles with restaurants, cafés, high-rise hotels, office blocks and shops. There is a Carnival at the time of Independence Day on 27 Feb. Educational institutions include the oldest university in the Western Hemisphere, the Autonomous University of Santo Domingo founded in 1538.

Places of Interest

The first street ever built in the Americas is Calle de Las Damas. The restored sixteenth century palace of the Spanish Court, the Museum of the Royal Houses, stands close to the Alcázar de Colón (Castle of Columbus) built by Columbus' son Diego. The Cathedral Basilica Santa Maria La Menor dates from 1514 and was declared the first cathedral in the New World by Pope Paul III. To mark the 500th anniversary of Columbus' landing the Faro a Colón (Columbus Lighthouse) was erected to house his remains. The Plaza de la Cultura encompasses four museums including the Museum of Dominican Man.

São Paulo, Brazil

Introduction

Located 55 km from the Atlantic coast on the Tietê River, São Paulo is Brazil's largest city and the economic and industrial powerhouse of the nation. The city has developed into a cosmopolitan melting pot of nationalities and cultures in recent years and is estimated to be the third largest Italian city in the world, the largest Japanese city outside Japan, the third largest Lebanese city outside Lebanon, the largest Portuguese city outside Portugal and the largest Spanish city outside Spain.

History

The city was founded in 1554 by Jesuit priests José de Anchieta and Manoel de Nóbrega, who set up a mission by the Rio Tietê to convert the indigenous population, Tupi-Guarani. The town settlement attracted traders and adventurers looking for mineral wealth further inland. It became the seat of regional government in 1681.

Until the 1870s São Paulo was known as *cidade de barro* (mud city) as most of its buildings were built from clay and packed mud. The city grew slowly until the middle of the nineteenth century, when coffee growing expanded. As plantation owners moved in so the infrastructure grew, aided by plentiful hydro-electric power. By the end of the century the region had become the world's largest exporter of coffee. Related industrial growth and a population explosion soon followed.

Modern City

São Paulo is still Brazil's leading industrial centre, the largest city in South America and one of the largest cities in the world. It accounts for 33% of Brazil's total exports and 40% of its imports. Modern São Paulo numbers some 20,000 industrial plants of all types and around 2,000 banking agencies. Traditionally a centre of coffee production, in recent years the city has attracted foreign investment, particularly from German companies such as Volkswagen, Mercedes Benz, Audi and Siemens. Aside from the production of motorcars, São Paulo's industries include food processing, textiles, electrical equipment and heavy machinery.

São Paulo is served by the Aeroporto de Congonhas, the Aeroporto Internacional de São Paulo and the Aeroporto Viracopos. A shuttle service connects São Paulo to Rio de Janeiro. The city has road and rail connections as well as a metro system.

São Paulo's numerous education centres include a medical school and four universities. Waves of immigration have left the city with an extensive multi-cultural legacy.

Places of Interest

São Paulo's religious buildings include the Gothic Catedral da Sé. Begun in 1913, the cathedral took four decades to complete.

The Museu de Arte de São Paulo (Art Museum) houses one of Brazil's richest art collections. A new building designed by the architect Lina Bardi was inaugurated in 1968. It houses the most important European art collection in Latin America and contains works by Degas, Renoir, Modigliani and Bonnard amongst others. São Paulo's other museums include the Museu de Arte Modern (Modern Art Museum), founded in 1948, and the Museu de Arte Contemporânea (Contemporary Art Museum). Founded in 1963 the Museu de Arte Contemporânea houses a collection of more than 5,000 works, including oils, drawings, engravings, sculpture, paintings, ceramics and tapestry. It is the largest museum in Latin America specializing in twentieth century Western art. Museu Paulista, or the Museum of São Paulo, was built to commemorate Brazilian Independence and opened in 1895 as a natural science museum. Today it is a museum of history.

The city's monuments include the Memorial de America Latina, one of the largest cultural centres in Brazil. Designed by the Brasília architect Oscar Niemeyer, the memorial was built in 1989. The tree lined square, the Praça de República, is adjacent to the Edifício Itália, the city's second tallest building after Mirante do Vale.

São Tomé, São Tomé and Príncipe

Introduction

São Tomé, on the northeast coast of São Tomé Island, is the national capital and its most important port.

History

The Portuguese colonized São Tomé Island in the 1470s and established the town 30 years later. It became a bishopric in 1534. At first the sugar trade was the major revenue earner for the city but by the eighteenth century coffee and cocoa were more important. The labour-intensive work of the plantations meant that the city was at the centre of a thriving slave trade, which was not outlawed until 1875.

When independence seemed likely for the country there was a mass exodus of the city's Portuguese population. Many of these were the plantation owners and their absence seriously undermined the coffee and, more importantly, the cocoa industries. In 1975 São Tomé became capital of the Democratic Republic of São Tomé and Principé.

Modern City

The local economy relies on the port and its related activities. Major exports include cocoa, palm products, coffee and coconuts. Also important are fishing and tourism. A railway connects the city to the island interior and there is an international airport.

Places of Interest

The national museum is housed in the Fort São Sebastião. Other popular sites include the sixteenth century cathedral, the Augustinho Neto Manor House. The San Antonio Quarter is one of the city's best preserved districts.

Sapporo, Japan

Introduction

Sapporo, divided by the Ishikari river, is capital of the Hokkaido prefecture. Established in the last quarter of the nineteenth century, its early growth was facilitated by foreign advisors, notably the American Dr William Clark. Sapporo came to world attention in 1972 when it hosted the Winter Olympic Games.

History

There is evidence of seventh century habitation in Hokkaido (called Ezo until the nineteenth century). However, a trading post near the site of modern Sapporo was not founded until the early part of the nineteenth century.

In the mid-1850s Hokkaido came under the jurisdiction of the Tokugawa Shogunate and Sapporo experienced its first major population influx. In 1866 construction began on a canal that would prove vital for trade. Two years later Sapporo moved from Shogunate control to the Meiji emperor. At this point the agricultural economy developed a broader industrial base. Production of beer and dairy products were especially important. Growth continued under the guidance of the government's colonial office, which implemented a grid-based building scheme in 1871 and sought advice from Western experts on urban and industrial development.

Economic growth faltered in the early 1870s but recovered later in the decade when the population was boosted by immigrants from Honshu Island. In 1880 building started on the Sapporo–Otaru railroad and 6 years later the city was declared the prefecture's capital.

Industrial growth continued in the twentieth century, and Sapporo emerged unscathed from World War II. A development plan was formulated in 1950 to promote investment from Honshu and both the economy and the population boomed. In Feb. 1972 it played host to the Winter Olympics and in April of that year was designated an autonomous city.

Modern City

Food and drink processing are among the leading industries, along with publishing and sawmilling. The major port is Otaru. Sapporo is on a major rail network and Chitose airport provides domestic flights. The city has two universities, Hokkaido (founded by Dr Clark) and Hokkou Gakuen Kitami.

Places of Interest

Among Sapporo's leading landmarks are the Clock Tower (built in 1878) and the Hokkaido Government Building (1888). The 150-m tall TV Tower provides impressive views, as does nearby Mount Moiwa (accessible by cable car). The Okurayama Jump Hill was the focus of the 1972 Winter Olympics. There is an annual snow festival (featuring ice sculptures). Other attractions include the preserved frontier village in Napporo Forest Park, an art park with extensive exhibition spaces, the Hitsujigaoka Observation Hill (with a statue of Dr Clark), botanical gardens and the Moerenuma Park (designed by the sculptor Isamu Noguchi).

Sarajevo, Bosnia and Herzegovina

Introduction

Sarajevo is the capital of Bosnia and Herzegovina. Long ruled by the Ottoman Empire, its mixed population of Muslims, Christians and Jews lived in relative harmony for many centuries. Under Austro-Hungarian rule from the late nineteenth century, it became a hotbed of anti-Austrian sentiment. In 1914 Archduke Franz Ferdinand was assassinated in the city by a Serb nationalist, providing the catalyst for World War I. Sarajevo gained world recognition again in the 1990s when it suffered extensive damage in the bloody war with Yugoslavia.

History

There is evidence of Illyrian habitation in the region around Sarajevo. Afterwards Romans and then Goths settled in the area, and Slavs arrived in the seventh century. Sarajevo's importance increased as Bosnia established its independence over the ensuing centuries, and its expansion gathered new momentum when the region fell under the rule of the Ottomans in the fifteenth century. Settlements on opposing banks of the Miljacka River were linked by numerous new bridges, three of which are still in existence.

The population swelled with Muslims, adding to the mix of Orthodox and Catholic Christians and Shephardic Jews. Turkish Muslim culture inevitably dominated urban life but Sarajevo was noted for its ethnic and religious tolerance. It prospered economically although growth slowed in the seventeenth and eighteenth centuries. Savoyard forces attacked and razed the city in 1697.

The Ottomans declared Sarajevo administrative capital of Bosnia and Herzegovina in the mid-nineteenth century, a role it retained after 1878 when Austria-Hungary replaced the Ottomans. Despite general prosperity under the Hapsburgs, Sarajevo was central to the emergence of the national consciousness in the second half of the nineteenth century when the empire was widely unpopular. Events reached a climax on 28 June 1914 when Gavrilo Princip, a Serb nationalist, assassinated the Austrian Archduke Franz Ferdinand and his wife Sofia, who were visiting the city. Austrian–Serb relations collapsed and the knock-on effect in international relations led to World War I.

After the war, Sarajevo became part of the Kingdom of Serbs, Croats and Slovenes that soon evolved into Yugoslavia. Growth in the inter-war period was negligible and economic hardship widespread. During World War II it was a major centre of anti-Nazi resistance. From the mid-1950s the economy expanded, with major industries including food processing, brewing, tobacco, and furniture and automobile manufacturing. Sarajevo's international reputation was boosted in 1984 when it hosted the Winter Olympics.

Modern City

Disaster struck in the 1990s when communism collapsed in the Eastern Bloc and Yugoslavia fell apart. In 1992 Bosnia and Herzegovina declared independence and Yugoslav leader Slobodan Milošević responded by sending Serb forces into the country. A process of 'ethnic cleansing' began against Bosnian Muslims who were herded into Sarajevo from the surrounding countryside. The city witnessed fierce and bloody fighting as Serbs encircled the city in April 1992 and it suffered further damage during NATO airstrikes on Serb forces in 1995. The 1995 Dayton Peace Accord restored peace and ensured the withdrawal of Serb troops but not before more than 10,000 people had died and over 60,000 had been wounded.

Sarajevo is still in the process of recovering and rebuilding. It lies on major road and rail routes and its tourism sector is growing again.

Places of Interest

As well as a variety of museums and galleries, the city is home to two cathedrals, numerous mosques (including the Imperial Mosque, completed in the mid-fifteenth century) and a university.

Seattle, United States of America

Introduction

Seattle is the largest city in the state of Washington and one of the fastest growing in the United States. The seat of King county, Seattle is located on the west coast of Washington approximately 110 miles south of the Canadian border. The city is surrounded by mountains and located on a stretch of land between Lake Washington and Puget Sound. The Lake Washington Ship Canal runs through the centre of the city.

History

The area now occupied by modern day Seattle was first inhabited by Suquamish and Duwamish Native Americans. The first European settlers arrived at Akli Point in 1851. Washington Territory was created in 1853 and Seattle, incorporated as a city in 1865, was named after a Native American chief who had befriended the European settlers. The city's economy was dependent on its sawmill and in 1878 the residents built their own railroad to improve the city's trading status. The economy thrived as the log trade grew and, despite a devastating fire that destroyed much of the city, by 1891 Seattle had grown to over 40,000.

In 1897 the discovery of gold in the nearby Yukon River caused a boom as prospectors and miners moved into the city in large numbers. Between 1900 and 1920 the city's population tripled to more than 230,000. The Alaska-Yukon-Pacific Exposition in 1909 increased Seattle's international profile and highlighted its status as a major port on the Pacific rim. The completion of the Lake Washington Ship Canal brought more trade to the area and the First World War saw Seattle become an important ship and aircraft-building centre—with, in particular, the Boeing Company, founded at the turn of the century, providing jobs and prosperity. After a downturn during the 1930s Depression, the Second World War saw another industrial boom.

After the war, over 200,000 jobs were lost in the shipbuilding industry. Boeing remained crucial to the city's economy and the growth in the production of passenger jets and spacecraft in the 1950s and early 1960s helped the city back on to its feet. By 1956, one in two industrial workers in Seattle was employed by Boeing. However the aircraft manufacturer's fortunes plummeted in the 1970s and the decline of traditional fishing and sawmill industries saw Seattle's economic fortunes hit another downturn.

Seattle fought back in the 1990s as computer software, telecommunications and biotechnology companies based themselves in the city. In 1999 Seattle hosted the third ministerial conference of the World Trade Organisation (WTO) although the event was marred by clashes between police and anti-capitalist demonstrators.

Modern City

Seattle is a manufacturing and commercial centre with a diverse range of industries. Several corporations are based there including The Boeing Company, SAFECO Corporation, Alaska Airlines and Amazon.com. Computer giant Microsoft is also a major employer. There are still significant fishing and timber industries and the city is the nearest American port to Tokyo as well as the main link from the continental United States to Alaska, Asia and Siberia. The port houses 28 terminals and 30 steamship operators.

Seattle-Tacoma International Airport is 13 miles to the south of Seattle. There is a Greyhound bus terminal and an Amtrak station. The Metro Transit Bus system offers many free journeys within certain zones of the city and there is also an overhead monorail and regular ferries to Bainbridge Island and Bremerton. Plans are underway to link Seattle with Everett and Tacoma by a high-speed commuter rail link and a series of express buses.

Institutes of higher education in Seattle include the University of Washington, Seattle University, Seattle Pacific University, Pacific Lutheran University and the University of Puget Sound.

Places of Interest

The Seattle Center houses major attractions including the Pacific Science Center and Experience Music Project—an interactive museum devoted to popular music that opened in 2000. The Burke Museum of Natural History and Culture and the Henry Art Gallery are both on the campus of the University of Washington. Woodland Park Zoo is one of the finest zoos in the world and the Seattle Aquarium is on the waterfront.

Seattle has several theatre companies including the Seattle Repertory Theatre and the Intiman Theatre Company. There are also performance houses for music, drama, dance and opera, including the Seattle Centre Opera House and the Broadway Performance Hall. Cornish College of the Arts, founded in 1914, offers training courses for performers, writers and artists.

The city's baseball team, the Seattle Mariners, play at the new stadium at Safeco Field. The city's American football team, the Seattle Seahawks, moved into a new 67,000-seater stadium called Qwest Field in July 2002.

Seoul, South Korea

Introduction

The capital of South Korea, Seoul is also the country's biggest city. If the contiguous suburbs beyond the city boundary are included, Seoul houses 31% of South Korea's population. The city lies in the far north-west of the country, on the Han River some 37 miles (60 km) from the sea. Because much of Seoul was destroyed during the Korean War (1950–53), the city is largely modern.

History

The Han River basin was settled by the first century BC. The area was in the ancient Korean kingdom of Paekche, but was near the border of the other two kingdoms: Koguryo and Silla. In the eleventh century the king of Koguryo built a palace and a city near present-day Seoul.

In 1394, Yi Song-gye, the founder of the dynasty that ruled united Korea from 1302 until 1910, built a new capital for his kingdom. Seoul was the ideal site for a capital because it was at the centre of Korea, on a navigable river and with good natural defences. Known as Hanyang, the name was soon changed to Hansong, but the Korean capital was popularly known as Seoul.

City walls were constructed, and shrines, palaces and forts were built by the Yi dynasty over four centuries. The walls were rebuilt and extended in 1422. As the administrative centre of a highly centralized state, Seoul grew quickly. Within 50 years of its foundation, the city had more than 100,000 inhabitants. But the growth of Seoul was not continuous. In 1529 Japanese forces sacked the city, destroying much of the royal palace and the fortifications.

Seoul saw much reconstruction in the seventeenth and eighteenth centuries, but because the kingdom was so reclusive, with no trade or diplomatic relations with other countries, its growth was slow. By the turn of the twentieth century Seoul had fewer than 250,000 inhabitants. Development began anew in 1876 when Korea was obliged to open up to the outside world. Western commerce and diplomats arrived, but so did the Japanese who took over the country, deposing the Yi dynasty, in 1910.

Under Japanese rule the city was renamed Kyongsong but remained the administrative centre of the country. Most of the walls were demolished, streets were widened and paved and Western-style buildings constructed. Industrial suburbs developed. When Japanese rule ended in 1945, the city became the capital of an independent Korea and its name was officially changed to Seoul.

The city was near the border that divided a partitioned country into a Communist North and a pro-Western South. That proximity to the North cost Seoul dear when, in 1950, Communist forces swept in. The invasion and subsequent bombing devastated the city, which was in ruins when the Korean War ended in 1953. Since then, Seoul has more than doubled in area and population. A modern city has emerged with skyscrapers, wide highways and large satellite cities, some of which have more than 1 m inhabitants.

Modern City

Seoul is the principal cultural and political centre of South Korea and also the country's main industrial centre. The city has South Korea's main international airport (Kimp'o) and, despite being situated in a corner of the country, is a hub of road and rail routes. Seoul houses many foreign financial institutions as well as Korean banks and one of the world's dozen largest stock exchanges. Industries include textiles, chemicals and petro-chemicals, electrical and electronic engineering, and food processing. The regular street pattern of the ancient city focusing on the four major (surviving) gates, has been retained. Much development preceded the 1988 Seoul Olympic Games.

Places of Interest

Namsan Hill, the highest point in the city centre, is only 243 m (797 ft) high, but above it rises N Seoul Tower, at 480 m (1,574 ft). Below the tower lies Namsan Park, lined on one side by the remains of the city walls. The park, which can be reached by cable car, contains botanical gardens and a village of reassembled ancient Korean houses.

The former royal palaces are among Seoul's major tourist attractions. Changgyeonggung, the secondary palace, adjoins Jongmyo royal shrine, which contains memorials of all the Yi kings except two who were considered unworthy. The Changdeokgung palace and gardens are nearby.

The main palace, Gyeongbokgung, was largely destroyed during the Japanese occupation and the Korean War. A few buildings, including a towering pagoda, remain, but in 1995 wholesale reconstruction began. In the grounds of Gyeongbokgung is the National Folk Museum. Beside Gyeongbokgung is Cheongwadae, popularly known in English as The Blue House, the official residence of the President of South Korea.

Of the remaining city gates, fourteenth-century Namdaemun (South Gate) is the most impressive. The Daehanmun Gate is the site of a changing of the guard ceremony.

Seville (Sevilla), Spain

Introduction

The capital of Andalusia and the fourth largest city in Spain, Seville is an inland port on the Guadalquivir River located near the southern coast. It is 86 km from the Atlantic Ocean. The capital of succeeding Moorish kingdoms, Seville flourished as the main merchant city during Spain's golden age from 1492.

History

After the second Punic War, Seville was taken by the Romans who named it Hispalis. The town became the administrative centre of Hispania Ulterior. Later known as Baetica, the region covered what is now Andalusia. It was then conquered by the Silingi Vandals in early fifth century, by the Visigoths in 461 and by the Moors in 711 who named the town Ishbiliya.

Seville prospered under Moorish rule as a port on the only navigable river in Spain. It was made the capital of the Almoravid kingdom in 1091 and subsequently the Almohad capital in 1147. A large mosque was then constructed upon which the present cathedral stands. The city was reclaimed by the Spaniards in 1248 under Ferdinand III during the Riconquista. The king died there 4 years later. After a peaceful century when Christians, Muslims and Jews lived alongside each other, Seville became the most important town in Castille. But then Seville was chosen as the centre for the Spanish Inquisition. The Moors and the Jews were expelled in the fifteenth century and the Protestants in the sixteenth.

The city's golden age began with the discovery of the New World in 1492. Seville won a monopoly over the trade in 1503 based in La Casa de Contratacíon de las Indias (the trade house), and the city prospered and expanded dramatically. It became a centre of merchants and traders—*porto y puerta de Indias* (the port and the door to the Indies)—but also of artists and architects. The golden age of Sevillian art included Francisco Pacheco, Francisco de Herrera *el viejo* and his son Francisco de Herrera *el mozo*. Diego Velasquez was born in Seville, but was mainly active in Madrid and Italy.

Various natural disasters befell the city including a plague in 1649 that claimed half the population. Seville's prosperity suffered from direct competition with Cadíz—whose port proved easier access—and from the loss of Spain's colonies. Eventually Cadíz claimed the passing trade and La Casa de Contratacíon was transferred there in 1717. Seville declined in stature and suffered heavily in the Peninsular War (1808–14). Many artistic treasures were stolen by the French. At the end of the nineteenth century Seville's size was little more than it had been in 1248. At the same time, poor sanitation meant the city had the highest mortality rate in Europe.

Industrial development in the early twentieth century came to an abrupt halt with the arrival of the Civil War. Despite Republican resistance, the city fell very quickly to the Nationalists. This at least prevented damage to the city, a fate suffered by such cities as Valencia.

Throughout the second part of the twentieth century Seville expanded to become Spain's fourth largest city. Hope was raised with the election of the Sevillian president Felipe González in 1982 that Andalusia would benefit from a more decentralized system of government. In 1992 Seville was host to the Expo World Fair. It was an extravagant event, coinciding with the quincentennial anniversary of the discovery of the New World.

Modern City

The city's main exports are olives, fruit, wine and cork. Industries include textiles, machinery, chemicals, armaments and especially tourism.

12 km outside Seville, the San Pablo airport has both domestic and international flights. A high speed rail service arrives in Madrid in two and a half hours.

Places of Interest

The largest gothic church in the world, Seville's Cathedral was mainly constructed between 1402–1506. There are few traces of the original Mosque, although the cathedral's bell-tower (*La Giralda*) was built around the minaret. The cathedral contains a nineteenth-century statue of Christopher Columbus, originally erected in Havana but shipped to Spain when Cuba gained independence. The cathedral also contains works by the seventeenth-century Sevillian artist Bartolomé Esteban Murillo.

One of the most important examples of Moorish architecture is the Alcázar palace. Originally a fortress built in 913, the site was turned into a palace in the eleventh century and then a citadel by the Almohads. The only surviving structures from this time are part of the walls, the palace having been almost entirely rebuilt under Christian rule. After the Riconquista, the palace was used by Spanish monarchs for four centuries and much of Alcázar's reconstruction was carried out by Peter the Cruel in the fourteenth century.

Seville's museums include the museum of regional archaeology, a bull-fighting museum and the fine arts museum with displays of El Greco, Murillo and Velázquez.

Shanghai, China

Introduction

The largest city in China, Shanghai is also the country's principal port. The city is situated on the Huangpu River a few miles south of the mouth of the Chang Jiang Yangtze (Jiang Yangtze). The first Chinese port to be opened up to trade with the West, Shanghai grew to be China's main commercial centre. The municipality, which has provincial status, includes a large hinterland and 35% of the population within its boundaries is rural.

History

Shanghai's low-lying position in a delta region on the east coast of China is today one of its strengths. Historically, watery isolation held back its development. 1,000 years ago Shanghai was a small fishing village, but by the eleventh century the advantages of its natural deep-water anchorage had been recognised and Shanghai had become a port.

The town's growth was slow until locally-grown cotton spurred the development of a textile industry. After China was defeated in a war with Britain in 1842, the Chinese were obliged to virtually surrender Shanghai to Western control. The US, France and Britain were allocated areas of the city—so-called concessions—in which they developed trade, financial institutions and industries. In 1895 Japan obtained a similar concession. Shanghai rapidly became China's principal window on the world. By 1900, industry was flourishing, largely as a result of cheap local labour and foreign investment.

Foreign domination of the city came to be resented and in 1921 the Chinese Communist Party was founded in Shanghai. In 1925 there was an uprising of workers and students in the city which was not finally crushed by the then-ruling Nationalists until 1927. Shanghai was occupied by the Japanese from 1937 until 1945. During the civil war between Nationalists and Communists after the Second World War, Shanghai was controlled by the Nationalists and did not fall to the Communists until the final days of the conflict in 1949. Pollution problems in the 1950s and 1960s led to relocation of industries to the suburbs.

Modern City

Shanghai is both a sea and river port, served by a network of canals. The port has been greatly expanded in recent years and now handles around 190 m.

tonnes of cargo each year. The city is the centre of a rail network with routes converging from southern China. Shanghai has two airports: Lunghau now mainly handles domestic flights; the newer Hungchiao Airport is one of China's principal international airports. The city is China's largest foreign exchange trading centre and has major banking and insurance interests. Industries include steel, telecommunications, car production, electrical appliances, and chemicals and petro-chemicals, which are the basis of important plastic and synthetic fibre industries. Shanghai experienced a boom in construction in the 1990s, with over 3,000 high-rise buildings, causing the city to sink over a centimetre a year. In 1990 development began in the Pudong New Area, which includes a freeport, hi-tech, financial and industrial parks. The Shanghai World Financial Center, completed in 2008, is 492 m high, making it at the time China's tallest building (although since surpassed in height by a skyscraper and a television tower in Guangzhou and the Shanghai Tower). The Shanghai Tower became the city's tallest structure in 2014. It partly opened to the public in April 2016, and its sightseeing deck on the 118th floor officially opened in April 2017.

Places of Interest

Most attractions are in the Puxi area of the city, west of the Huangpu River. Shanghai's most famous tourist sight is the Bund, a stretch along the banks of the Huangpu lined with grand late nineteenth-century and early twentieth-century buildings in European style. The Bund is once again a financial centre. Today, the People's Square is the city centre. Dominated by a large fountain, the square's municipal buildings include the Shanghai Museum of Art and History, which has an important collection of bronzes and ceramics. Frenchtown, the old French Concession, is known for its restaurants, shopping streets and colonial tree-lined boulevards.

Among the most prominent modern landmarks of the city is the 468-m high Oriental Pearl TV Tower, the 15th tallest freestanding tower in the world. The tower comprises 11 spheres, which house sightseeing, catering, conference and hotel facilities, and is connected to the Bund by an underwater sightseeing tunnel.

The Yuyuan Garden dates from the sixteenth century. Bounded by a wall decorated with dragons, it includes pavilions and streams as well as the Grand Rockery constructed from some 2,000 tonnes of rocks.

Shiraz, Iran

Introduction

Shiraz is the capital of the southwestern province of Fars, in the Zagros mountains. Noted for its parks, gardens and religious architecture, the city is also a trading and transport centre, linked to the Persian Gulf seaport of Bushehr. The ruins of the ancient city of Persepolis, a World Heritage Site, are to the northeast.

History

Recorded during the Seleucid, Parthian and Sassanid periods (dating from the fourth century BC to the mid-seventh century AD), the city of Shiraz later became an important centre of the medieval Islamic world. It suffered Mongol invasions and occupations during the thirteenth and fourteenth centuries, and was sacked by Afghan invaders in the early eighteenth century. Significant restoration took place during the reign of Karim Khan Zand in 1750–79, much of which has survived despite several earthquakes.

Modern City

Shiraz is the commercial hub of the surrounding region, which produces grapes (for Shiraz wine), citrus fruit, cotton and rice. It is noted for silverware and traditional inlay work, rugs, brocades and other textiles. Cement and fertilizer are also important manufactures. The University of Shiraz was founded in 1954 and has over 12,000 students. There is an international airport.

Places of Interest

The citadel of Karim Khan Zand, with four circular towers, dominates the city centre. The Shohada (or Martyrs) Mosque is one of the largest and oldest in Iran. Other landmarks include the Vakil (or Regent's) Mosque, Shah Cheragh mausoleum, and the tombs of two Persian poets Hafez (c.1320–90) and Saadi (c.1220–90). The city hosts an annual arts festival.

Singapore City, Singapore

Introduction

Singapore City (lion city), the capital of the Republic of Singapore and one of the world's busiest free ports, is situated on the southern coast of the country. Though having few natural resources it a major centre for international trade, high-tech manufacturing and finance. The modern and colonial areas of the city face each other across the Singapore River.

History

Until the fourteenth century Singapore City was a fishing village in the Malay kingdom of Sri Vijaya when it became part of the Javanese Majapahit Empire. The country was claimed by the Malacca sultanate in fifteenth century, the Portuguese in the sixteenth and the Dutch in the seventeenth century. The modern city was founded in 1819 when Sir Thomas Stamford Raffles, the administrator of the British East India Company, recognized the potential for a port and established a trading base. In 1824 the entire island was ceded to the company by the Sultan of Jahore. The excellent location on the narrow passage between the Indian Ocean and the South China Sea was further enhanced by the opening of the Suez Canal in 1869. Large numbers of immigrants were attracted to the city, particularly from China and India. In 1921 Britain designated the island its principal naval base in East Asia, but in 1942 it was captured by the Japanese. The city was liberated by the British in 1945 and established as a separate Crown Colony from Malaya the following year. In 1955 responsibility for domestic policy passed to locally elected ministers and in 1959 Singapore became a self-governing state. 1963 saw the union of Singapore, Malaya, North Borneo (Sabah) and Sarawak as the confederation of Malaysia. In 1965 Singapore split from Malaysia and Singapore City was designated capital of the independent republic.

Modern City

Singapore City is the political and judicial centre of the Republic. With over 600 shipping lines, Keppel Harbour is one of the busiest in the world and the city is a major centre for oil refining and distribution. It is also a leading supplier of electronic components and one of Asia's most important financial centres with over 128 banks and 78 merchant banks. It was here that the UK-based Barings bank collapsed following corrupt dealings by the derivatives trader Nick Leeson in 1995. Tourism is a growing industry. Changi, one of the largest international airports in Asia, is located 20 min from the centre. It is served by over 63 airlines flying to 149 destinations. Car ownership is restricted but the Mass Transit System provides underground services between commercial and residential centres. A 26-km railway crosses the Johor strait and links with the Malaysian railway system. The National University of Singapore was established in 1905, the National Arts Council in 1991 and the National Heritage Board in 1993.

Places of Interest

Raffles Hotel, built in 1887, is famous for its literary associations. Chijmes, formerly a gothic cloistered convent, now has shops and leisure activities. The Old Parliament House, with its bronze elephant presented in 1871 by the King of Siam, was built as a colonial mansion in 1827. The Supreme Court was designed in the classical style in 1939 by an Italian architect. La Pau Sat, a Victorian cast-iron structure, was built as a wet market in 1894, located in the business centre it now sells local produce. Open to visitors on public holidays, the Istana was the official residence of the representative of the British Crown and is now the official residence of the president. The Kranjii Memorial and grounds were built as a tribute to the allied forces of WWII. Singapore's past presidents are buried here. Merlion Park is home to the national icon of a half-lion, half-fish statue created in 1972. The Asian Civilisations Museum houses Buddhist artifacts and imperial porcelain. Many temples and mosques are located along the Singapore River including the Tan Si Chong Su Temple built in 1876.

Skopje (Shkup; Skoplje; Usküb), Macedonia

Introduction

Skopje is the capital of the Republic of Macedonia and lies on the Vardar River in the north of the country. With a recorded history from the fourth century BC, the city has had many conquerors and has been devastated on numerous occasions by natural disaster. Only around 20% of Skopje remained standing after an earthquake in 1963.

History

Skopje, or Scupi as it was called in Latin, was settled by an Illyrian tribe, though whether it was the Peonis or Dardans is disputed. It subsequently came under Roman control and the Emperor Diocletian made it the capital of the Dardania region in the fourth century AD. The town was destroyed by an earthquake in 518 but was soon prospering again under the guidance of the Byzantine Emperor, Justinian. The name Skopje first came into use in 625 when Slavs stormed the city.

Skopje fell into Serbian hands for the first time in 1189 but in Jan. 1392, following their successful invasion of Macedonia, Turkey seized it and made it their provincial capital. The city became a major trade hub but went into decline after it was razed by Austrian forces in the late seventeenth century in a bid to eradicate cholera. There were numerous uprisings against the Turkish powers, the most serious of which was the seventeenth century Karposh uprising. None, however, were successful and it was not until 1913, during the Balkan Wars, that Turkish power was replaced by Serbian rule.

When the new Yugoslav state was born in 1918, Skopje was integrated. Nazi and then Bulgarian troops occupied the city during World War II but it was liberated in 1944. The following year it was declared the capital of the Republic of Macedonia. In 1963 the city was devastated by an earthquake that killed over 1,000 and left around 125,000 people homeless. Financial assistance poured in from around the world and most of the city was completely redesigned and rebuilt. It now has distinct industrial and residential areas along with a number of satellite zones. The Japanese civic planner, Kenzo Tanga, was among the most prominent of Skopje's designers.

Modern City

The city's major commercial region is on the Vardar's right bank. Industries include metal work, chemicals, electrical machinery, textiles and foodstuffs. It is also an important trade centre for local cotton, tobacco, meat and grain. Skopje Airport is Macedonia's largest and the city lies on the major road and rail routes between Belgrade and Athens.

Places of Interest

A number of ancient monuments and buildings still exist including the sixth century Kale Fortress, the large fifteenth century Turkish Daud Pasha Baths, the sixteenth century Kurshumli-An district and Clock Tower and the main bridge over the Vardar, originally constructed by the Romans and rebuilt by the Turks. Skopje is the birthplace of Agnes Gonxha Bojaxhiu, who would become better known as the Nobel Peace Prize-winner, Mother Teresa of Calcutta.

Sofia (Sofiya), Bulgaria

Introduction

Sofia is the capital of Bulgaria, situated in the west of the country in the Sofia Basin. Inhabited since the eight century BC, it was under Ottoman control from the late fourteenth until the late-nineteenth century.

History

The Thracian Serdi tribe were the first people to settle in the Sofia area. They gave way to the Romans in the late first century BC, who made the city provincial capital of Inner Dacia. The city prospered under Constantine I (AD 280–337), when Christianity became the Empire's chosen religion. From the end of the fourth century until the mid-fifth century, Sofia was a major centre of the Byzantine Empire but in AD 441 it was taken by Attila the Hun. It fell again under Byzantine influence, becoming particularly successful during the sixth century rule of Emperor Justinian. Bulgars took the city for the first time in 809, lost control to Byzantia in the early eleventh century but re-imposed their rule around 1185.

During the fourteenth century the city became known as Sofia, named after the fourth century basilica of St. Sofia that still stands today. The Ottomans seized Sofia in 1382, making it capital of the province of Rumelia and beginning their long period of domination. The Muslim influences of this time are still evident in such buildings as the fifteenth century Buyuk Mosque, which houses the National Archaeological Museum, and the Banay Bashi Mosque.

The Ottomans were ousted from Sofia in Jan. 1878 by Russian troops, following a 2-year war that accounted for 200,000 Russian casualties. On 3 April 1879 Sofia became the official capital of Bulgaria. Over the next half century the city's population increased some 15-fold. At the outbreak of World War II Bulgaria was aligned with the Axis powers, but Tsar Boris III's refusal to declare war on Russia antagonised Germany. Bulgaria was invaded and Sofia occupied until 1944 when Russian troops liberated the city.

Modern City

As capital of a Soviet satellite state, Sofia experienced rapid industrialization. Major industries include metal work, textiles, food processing, printing and engineering. Agriculture is important in the area surrounding the city. There are road, rail and air links and public transport within the city is provided by trams, buses and trolley buses, as well as cable lifts up to Vitosha in summer.

Places of Interest

The city landscape is dominated by the Alexander Nevski Memorial Church, completed in 1912 to commemorate the efforts of the Russian forces during the War of Liberation with the Turks. Other major landmarks include the Church of St Nicholas, the Central Synagogue and St Nedlia's Orthodox Church. There are many museums and galleries, and remnants of the Roman walls exist at various locations. Sofia has a reputation for its natural springs and the nearby Mt Vitosha provides high-quality skiing.

Split (Spalato), Croatia

Introduction

Split lies on the Adriatic coast and is the principal city of the Dalmatia region of Croatia. Originally centred around the palace of the Roman Emperor Diocletian, it suffered major damage from Allied and German attack during World War II. However, most of its historical districts were left undamaged and the well-preserved Roman and medieval buildings are now a popular tourist draw.

History

Emperor Diocleatian, infamous for his persecution of Christians, constructed a palace in the Bay of Aspalathos between AD 295–305 to serve as a retirement home. It consisted of two well-fortified sections: living quarters for troops and servants; and a complex incorporating residences for the emperor, an ornate courtyard and several temples and baths. In the early seventh century Avars and Slavs raided the nearby town of Salona and its residents fled to the palace, constructing new homes within the palace walls.

Split came under Byzantine rule although it briefly fell to Venice at the end of the tenth century and then to the Croatian king around 1070. In 1105 it became a free commune under the jurisdiction of the Hungarian-Croatian rulers and entered a phase of economic and cultural prosperity. Venice held the city between 1420 and 1797 and Split found itself regularly caught up in the disputes between Venice and Turkey, resulting in a period of relative decline.

The Venetians were supplanted by the Austro-Hungarians who set about expanding the city limits. Industrial growth followed and the harbour made Split an important trade hub. In addition its importance as an administrative centre increased. The French, under Napoléon, replaced Austria-Hungary and ruled between 1808–13, but Split returned to the Hapsburgs until 1918, when it became part of the new Yugoslavian state.

The city expanded again in the inter-war period and its population swelled. The harbour area was partially destroyed during World War II, but the area centred around the Roman palace escaped. The harbour was repaired during the communist era and new sections constructed. In 1992 the city left Yugoslavia when Croatia declared independence.

Modern City

Modern Split is an industrial powerhouse. Major industries include plastics, metal work, chemicals and port related activities. The region around the city is agricultural. Split has good rail and road connections, an international airport and ferry services to Italy and Greece.

Places of Interest

Tourist attractions are based around the old palace, partly a museum (with fine examples of Roman, medieval, Renaissance and Baroque art and architecture) but still the city's vibrant centre. The numerous museums and galleries include a permanent exhibition of the sculptures of Ivan Mestrovi.

Sri Jayawardenapura Kotte, Sri Lanka

Introduction

Sri Jayawardenapura Kotte, or Kotte, is the legislative, administrative and judicial capital of Sri Lanka, lying some 5 miles (8 km) southeast of Colombo, Sri Lanka's commercial capital.

History

Kotte was originally a kingdom under the suzerainty of the Sinhalese and the capital of Ceylon between 1415–1565. It flourished during the fifteenth century and with the rule of Parakramabahu VI (1412–67), the last native king to unite the whole of the country, it became Ceylon's capital. After the death of Parakramabahu VI the kingdoms of Jaffna and Kandy broke away from Kotte.

In 1505 a Portuguese fleet, commanded by Lourenço de Almeida, landed at Colombo. A warm reception from the king of Kotte, Vira Parakrama Bahu, encouraged them to establish formal ties with Ceylon and in 1518 they were given trading concessions. In 1521 the kingdom was split between the three sons of Vijayabahu, the then king of Kotte. Fraternal rivalry led to territorial disputes and to the oldest of the brothers, Bhuvanaika Bahu, who ruled from the city of Kotte itself, to seek Portuguese support. An agreement made between Bhuvanaika Bahu and the Portuguese in 1543 gave increased privileges and a tribute of cinnamon to the Portuguese in return for guaranteed protection for the Sinhalese ruler's grandson, Prince Dharmapala, who succeeded to the throne. The latter converted to Christianity in 1557 and became even more dependent than his grandfather on Portuguese assistance. With his conversion, the Sinhalese population turned against Dharmapala, and the once-fraternal struggle developed into a broader conflict between the Portuguese and the Sinhalese. The city's importance was undermined by this change in public feeling and the Portuguese centred themselves instead in nearby Colombo. In 1580 Dharmapala signed away his sovereignty to the Portuguese and upon his death in 1597 the Portuguese took control of Kotte.

Successive periods of Dutch (1658–1796) and British (1796–1900) rule saw a consolidation of power in Colombo and the decline of Kotte's importance. It regained stature once more after Sri Lanka gained its independence in 1948. Although Colombo was initially retained as the country's capital, it soon became apparent that expansion within the confines of the city was limited and the construction of administrative buildings would have to take place elsewhere. The areas of marshland surrounding Kotte, once serving as a valuable form of defence, offered the opportunity for urban expansion and in 1982 a National State Assembly building was opened on an island in reclaimed swampland in Lake Diyawanna Oya. From 1983 onwards government offices were transferred to Kotte. Almost all government ministries, aside from those related to trade and commerce which have remained in Colombo, have now been relocated.

Modern City

There is an international airport at Katunayake. The university of Sri Jayawardenapura, located in Gangodawila, on the outskirts of the city, caters for 7,000 students.

Places of Interest

Architectural remains from Kotte's rich history are few, as many of the ancient buildings have been built over in recent times. Tourists are not allowed to enter the parliamentary complex.

St George's, Grenada

Introduction

Grenada's capital, St George's, is on the south west coast of the island. The city is the country's main port with a natural harbour. Cocoa, bananas and nutmeg (Grenada is one of the world's leading producers) are exported. St George's is the chief charter-boat and yachting centre of the eastern Caribbean. The capital reaches from the harbour to the Carenage, a commercial and government. St George's is regarded as one of the most picturesque cities in the Caribbean, with its nineteenth century Creole houses roofed with red fishscale tiles.

History

Christopher Columbus sighted Grenada in 1948, but the city of St George's dates from a French settlement in 1650. The French and the English fought each other for control of the island throughout the seventeenth and eighteenth centuries, unit the British took Grenada in 1783. When the island gained independence within the Commonwealth in 1974, St George's remained its capital.

Modern City

The main industries are sugar and rum. Tourism is increasingly important. The nearest airport is Point Salines International Airport on Grenada's southwest coast, 3 miles outside the capital. There are no buses operating from the airport but there are rental cars and taxis. Visitors need to purchase a local driving license, available from the car rental companies. Most buses leave St George's from the Esplanade bus terminal. The city is also a port of call for cruise ships. St George's University is the country's only university. Granada's biggest festival is its Carnival, which takes place in St George's on the second weekend in Aug. The Carnival includes calypso and steel band competitions.

Places of Interest

The Grenada National Museum in the centre of St George's includes fragments of Amerindian pottery, an old rum still and a marble bathtub that used to belong to Empress Josephine of France. St George's Methodist Church, built in 1820, is the oldest church building. Overlooking the city are two forts, Fort George (built by the French in 1705) and Fort Frederick (completed by the British in 1791). The Mabuya Fishermen Museum has ships' wheels and shark jaws. Outside the capital there are several waterfalls including the Concord Falls and the Royal Mount Carmel Falls.

St John's, Antigua and Barbuda

Introduction

St John's is Antigua and Barbuda's capital and its only city. On Antigua's northwest coast, it is built around the islands largest natural harbour.

History

Before British colonialization in the seventeenth century, Arawak Indians inhabited the area. Architecturally, the modern tourist-oriented complexes are off-set by many well preserved buildings from the colonial era making St John's an interesting, if not entirely beautiful, city.

Modern City

The city is now split between areas of vigorous tourism-based commercialism and considerable poverty.

Places of Interest

St John's is dominated by the twin-steepled Georgian Cathedral that is now in its third incarnation, its antecedents having been devastated by earthquakes in 1683 and 1745. The current building was erected in 1845. Tourism centres around two main areas; Redcliffe Quay, originally a slave compound until the abolition of slavery in 1834; and Heritage Quay, which opened in 1988 and entices in cruise ship visitors with its promises of duty free shopping. Elsewhere, there are ample museums, bars, clubs and casinos. St John's is also the island's most significant port.

Lord Nelson's shadow looms over St John's as a result of his having spent two periods in the city. He served 3 years of his early career here and returned in 1805, shortly before the Battle of Trafalgar, while pursuing the French Admiral Villeneuve. The city's favourite son, though, is the cricketer Sir Viv Richards who has both a museum and a road dedicated to him.

St Louis, United States of America

Introduction

A large city in eastern Missouri, St Louis is to the south of the confluence of the Mississippi and Missouri rivers on a rolling plateau. At the heart of a large metropolitan area that includes ten counties in Missouri and Illinois, St Louis is a major business and commercial centre as well as the birthplace of T.S. Eliot and Chuck Berry.

History

Settlement of the site now occupied by St Louis began in 1764 with the arrival of French fur trader Pierre Laclede. A village was constructed in the area a year later and named St Louis after King Louis IX of France. The Spanish took control of the area in 1770 before it retuned to French hands and subsequently became part of the United Sates after the 1803 Louisiana Purchase.

The arrival of large numbers of immigrants from Germany and Ireland augmented the largely French population and St Louis became a crucial gateway for settlers and traders heading west on wagon trails. The arrival of steamboats and the railroads further boosted the city's commercial value and by the beginning of the twentieth century it was an important centre for manufacturing.

In 1904 St Louis hosted the Olympic Games and a World Fair. After World War II the city's economic influence waned and its population fell between 1950 and 1990. However the city's prosperity was boosted by a series of urban renewal projects. The striking Gateway Arch was completed in 1965 and other new buildings appeared in the ensuing years such as the Cervantes Convention Center and the Union Station mall.

Modern City

St Louis is a major transport centre. The city is served by Lambert-St Louis International Airport and there is an Amtrak rail station and a Greyhound bus terminal. The Bi-State Transit System runs a light railway and BSTS buses link the suburbs to the rest of the city. There are also excellent Interstate Highway links.

St Louis is one of the United States' leading inland ports, with links to the Mississippi, the Great Lakes, the Ohio River system and the Gulf of Mexico. The city has thriving warehouse and haulage industries and major manufactured products include chemicals, beer, petroleum, wood, metal, processed food and electrical equipment. Tourism and service industries are also important to the St Louis economy.

St Louis University, Webster University, Washington University, the University of Missouri-St Louis and Harris-Stowe State University are all based in the city.

Places of Interest

The Gateway Arch, designed by Eero Saarinen, is seen as the most potent landmark in modern St Louis. Located on the riverfront as part of the Jefferson National Expansion Memorial, it is a 630 ft-tall structure, symbolizing the city's status as the gateway to the west. The Arch has an observation deck. The nearby Museum of Westward Expansion charts the city's history while other landmarks include the Old Courthouse and the Old Cathedral of St Louis of France.

Notable cultural attractions include St Louis Science Center, St Louis History Museum and the St Louis Art Museum. The International Bowling Hall of Fame charts the history of ten-pin bowling from ancient Egypt to the modern day and the city has a resident symphony orchestra. The substantial theatre district includes the Fabulous Fox Theater while the St Louis Cardinals baseball team play at Busch Memorial Stadium. The city also has large botanical gardens and a zoo.

St Petersburg, Russia

Introduction

St Petersburg, on the River Neva, is Russia's second city after Moscow and was the national capital from 1712–1918. Created by Peter the Great to serve as a fitting capital and an entry to Europe, its location on the Gulf of Finland ensured its importance as a port and industrial centre. Having survived years under German siege during World War II, the city emerged as Moscow's rival for artistic and cultural excellence.

History

The region around the Gulf of Finland was settled by Russians in the eighth and ninth centuries. It came under the control of Novgorod but fell to Muscovite princes along with Novgorod in the fifteenth century. The Swedes annexed the area in 1617 but Peter I (the Great) wrested it back in the second Northern War. The founding date of St Petersburg is 1703, when Peter I laid the foundation stone for the Peter-Paul fortress. This marked the beginning of construction for Peter's new capital, designed to be a 'window on Europe'.

The re-location of the capital from Moscow to St Petersburg took place in 1712. The eighteenth century witnessed a melding of Russian and European culture as the nobility and merchant classes were drawn to the city. Secular literature and art flourished as St Petersburg spearheaded Russia's golden age of culture.

A range of architectural styles was employed in the creation of the new city. Italian architect Rastrelli was one of several designers of the colourful Russian Baroque style which can be seen in the Winter Palace and Smolny Convent. Catherine the Great preferred classicism, reflected in buildings such as the Pavlovsk Palace outside the city. This merged into a more individual Russian Empire style, monuments of which include the new Admiralty and the Kazan Cathedral.

Industry also thrived, with canals and a railway connection to Moscow feeding the city's commercial growth. Along with industry, the proletariat grew rapidly, but a poor city infrastructure failed to meet their needs, leading to squalor and discontent. Revolutionary ideas spread as did epidemics, and uprisings were not uncommon.

These factors along with Russia's defeat in the Russo-Japanese war sparked off a general strike in 1905. A march to the Winter Palace ended in 'Bloody Sunday', with troops firing on the protesters. Tsar Nicholas was forced to make concessions with the 'October Manifesto', establishing the Duma as a constitutional body and promising civil rights. At the onset of World War I, St Petersburg was renamed Petrograd. In Feb. 1917, rioting in the city led to the creation of a provisional government and Tsar Nicholas' abdication. Lenin returned from exile the same year to lead the October Revolution and declare a new government of the Soviets.

Marking a break from the tsarist past, the Bolsheviks moved the capital from Petrograd to Moscow in 1918. By 1920 less than a third of the population remained in the city, the rest having been driven out by revolution and civil war. After Lenin's death in 1924, the city was renamed Leningrad. In 1934 the assassination of Leningrad's party leader Sergei Kirov marked the beginning of Stalin's purges.

Hitler's army reached the outskirts of Leningrad soon after Germany's invasion of Russia on 22 June 1941. The city was shelled incessantly and besieged for 872 days, resulting in the deaths of over half a million civilians. Much of the infrastructure was destroyed. Reconstruction programmes started immediately after the war, and although Moscow was the heart of the USSR, Leningrad remained Russia's cultural centre, leading in art, popular music and literature.

In 1990 Anatoly Sobchak was elected mayor. Under his leadership the city has slowly opened up to foreign investment and free-market development. In 1991 Leningraders voted to restore the name of St Petersburg.

Modern City

St Petersburg has Russia's biggest port. Other important industries include engineering and chemicals processing, as well as light industry. There is a university with internationally renowned research facilities.

As well as being a vital port for vessels of all sizes, the city is an important road and rail hub. Transport within the city includes a metro system, buses, trams and trolleybuses.

Places of Interest

The main thoroughfare, Nevsky Prospekt, is home to many sights, including the tall-spired admiralty building and the gold domed Cathedral of St Isaac. The Winter Palace houses the Hermitage museum. The fortress of Peter and Paul is the city's oldest building and formerly served as a political prison. Among the baroque buildings of the early eighteenth century are the Alexander Nevsky monastery, built in 1710, and the Cathedral of Saint Peter and Saint Paul from 1733. Neoclassical buildings include the Academy of Arts (1772), the Marble Palace (1785) and the Taurida Palace (1788). St Petersburg's university was established in 1804 and there are many theatres (including the Kirov, home of the famous ballet), museums, scientific and medical institutes and libraries.

Stockholm, Sweden

Introduction

Stockholm is situated on an archipelago at a confluence of Lake Mälaren and Salt Bay. It is the capital, the largest city and the financial hub of the country. The city is spread across numerous islands centring on Gamla Stan (the historic old town).

History

The Mälaren region in which Stockholm is located has been the political heart of Sweden for centuries. The chieftain Birger Jarl ordered the construction of a fortified settlement in 1252. The settlement expanded rapidly as a result of trade with German city states, particularly in copper and iron. Within a century Stockholm was Sweden's largest community with formidable defences. By the mid fifteenth century it was the capital. The Danes invaded Stockholm in 1471 but were defeated at the Battle of Brunkeberg. The invasion triggered civic unrest, with several nobles and burghers defecting to the Danish side. A rebellion broke out in 1520 but following a 2-year siege was eventually quelled by the triumphant entry into the city of Gustav I Vasa. During Gustav's reign power was centred on the king who was more concerned with military expansion than with trade. The power of the Swedish empire in the seventeenth century revived Stockholm as an economic powerhouse, and the city finally began to develop beyond the medieval centre.

The end of the seventeenth century and the start of the 18th marked a turbulent period in the city's history. It suffered plague, famine and fire within a 20-year period. The population was decimated and many of the old wooden buildings were destroyed. When Stockholm was rebuilt it was in stone instead of timber. In the late eighteenth century the city became an important scientific and artistic centre. Stockholm's finest academies and cultural institutions date from this era. The early nineteenth century witnessed widespread rioting as a result of the monarchy's failure to implement social reforms but town planning and sanitation in the 1860s improved conditions. In 1912 the city hosted the Olympic games. The 1960s saw the development of new satellite towns and suburbs. A second construction boom in the 1980s caused property prices in Stockholm to rise dramatically.

Modern City

The major islands of Stads Island, Helgeands Island and Riddar Island form the city centre and are linked by bridges and overpasses. To the north lies the commercial and financial district of Norrmalm and the civic centre on Kungs Island. To the east is the cultural and recreational area of Djurgården. The devaluation of the krona in the early 1990s boosted Swedish tourism and led to an overhaul of the city's tourist facilities and the establishment of hundreds of new bars and restaurants.

Important industries include the manufacture of metals and machinery, printing, paper and chemicals. The port is the second largest in the country and handles both import and export freight. Leading educational establishments include the University of Stockholm, the Karolinska Medical Institute and the Royal Institute of Technology. The Royal theatre and opera house and the Stockholm Philharmonic are internationally renowned. Transport within the city is provided by metro, local trains and buses. Arlanda international airport is 42 km to the north. Road and rail link the city to the rest of Sweden and there are ferry services to Finland and the Baltic States.

Stockholm was named the first European Green Capital for 2010. Run by the European Commission, the award recognizes local efforts to improve the environment, the economy and the quality of life of growing urban populations.

Places of Interest

Gamla Stan is notable for its traditional architecture. Kungliga Slottet (the new royal palace) is the largest royal residence in the world and many apartments are open to the public. Skansen, the oldest open air museum in the world, was founded in 1891 to show the development of Swedish society. Haga Park has a tropical aviary and a museum with a permanent exhibition on royal pavilions and parks. On display in the Vasa museum is a seventeenth century warship, which sank on its maiden voyage but was subsequently recovered.

Strasbourg, France

Introduction

Strasbourg is in the Northeast of France on the confluence of the Ill and Rhine rivers. Alsace has its own language, Alsatian, a Germanic dialect that has survived attempts by both the French and Germans to impose their own languages.

History

Strasbourg originated as the Celtic fishing village of Argentorate before it became a Roman garrison under Nero Claudius Drusus in around 40 BC. By the second century BC the town had 20,000 inhabitants. In the fifth century it was occupied by the Franks who named it Strateburgum, or 'city of roads', due to its key position on the road between France and Germany. In 842 it was the site of the signing of the 'Serment de Strasbourg', the oldest written example of Old French. In medieval times the town prospered, reaching its zenith in the sixteenth century. Several leaders of the Reformation lived in Strasbourg, including Calvin between 1538–42 and Martin Bucer. An Alsatian by birth, Bucer moved to Strasbourg in 1523 following his excommunication for marrying a former nun. He became a leader of Protestantism in Strasbourg before moving to England in 1549. Although a Protestant stronghold, Strasbourg was not involved in the Thirty Years War (1618–48).

In 1681, weakened by the economic repercussions of wars, Strasbourg fell to Louis XIV. Allowing the city its autonomy within his kingdom, Strasbourg became the capital of the province of Alsace. The Treaty of Rijswijk ended the War of the Grand Alliance (1689–97). Louis XIV agreed to surrender his conquered territories, although he kept Alsace and Strasbourg. In April 1792, at the beginning of the war with Austria, the soldier and composer, Claude Rouget de Lisle, was commissioned to write a battle song. He composed the *Chant de Guerre de l'Armée du Rhin*. It achieved immediate popularity. Adopted by volunteers coming from Marseilles, it was sung as they entered Paris in July 1792. Thus was born *La Marseillaise*, adopted as the French national anthem in 1795.

Strasbourg kept its independent status until the Revolution (1789) when it was demoted to a borough capital, and the city was formally amalgamated with France. It remained part of France until the Franco-Prussian war. Following a 50-day siege, Strasbourg was annexed into the German Empire by the 1871 Treaty of Frankfurt, along with the rest of Alsace and the north of Lorraine.

At the end of World War I Strasbourg was returned to France. There was an attempt to reverse the German influence by banning German newspapers and abolishing church schools. Despite the presence of the Maginot Line, Strasbourg was occupied for a second time by the Germans between 1940–44. Under Nazi occupation, the inter-war years' efforts were reversed. Both the French and Alsatian languages were outlawed and German enforced. Strasbourg suffered heavy bombardment in 1944. Immediately after the War, the town was restored and a programme of urban development ensued. The old centre remained intact.

In 1949 the Council of Europe was set up in Strasbourg to promote European unity. In 1959 the European Court of Human Rights was opened in Strasbourg. Strasbourg's status as a European city was confirmed by the opening of the European Assembly in 1979.

Modern City

The capital of the Alsace region, Strasbourg's industries include oil and gas refining. A University town from 1566 and a cultural centre, Strasbourg is the seat of the European Parliament, the European Court of Human Rights and the Council of Europe. The city is linked to Paris, Germany and Luxembourg by rail and road. It also has an airport and a tram system.

Places of Interest

A network of canals, the area of La Petite France was designated a protected zone in 1974. Islands are linked by the Pont Couvert bridge. The area is an example of traditional Alsatian houses. In the centre of Strasbourg is the gothic Cathédrale de Notre Dame, the spire of which can be seen from any point in the city. Originally the site of a Roman temple, the early church was built in 496. In 1015 the cathedral was built, but was destroyed by fire. A second was begun at the end of the twelfth century. The West front, designed by Erwin von Steinbach in 1284, is embossed with statues. Ulrich von Ensigenk, the architect of the Ulm Cathedral, built the octagonal base of the spire in 1399. The cathedral houses stained glass windows from the twelfth to fourteenth centuries. Inside can be found the *horloge astronomique*, which chimes noon every day at 12.30. Rebuilt in the mid-nineteenth century, it was originally sixteenth century.

Strasbourg is home to the Musée des Beaux-Arts, the Musée Archéologique and the Musée d'Art Moderne et Contemporain. Built from glass and pink granite, the modern art museum was opened in 1998.

Stuttgart, Germany

Introduction

Stuttgart lies in the Neckar Valley and is the capital of Baden-Württemberg in the south of Germany. Since the nineteenth century it has been one of Germany's industrial powerhouses.

History

Stuttgart derives its names from a Stuotgarten (stud farm) established in AD 950 by Duke Liudolf of Swabia. By 1160 the area was emerging as a trade centre. The town flourished after becoming the residence of the Counts of Württemberg in the fourteenth century and won city status in 1321. In 1495 it became the capital of the Duchy of Württemberg and from 1805 was the capital of the Kingdom of Württemberg.

Stuttgart suffered badly during the Thirty Years' War (1618–48), losing half its population. To celebrate the end of a devastating famine in 1818, King Wilhelm I inaugurated the annual Cannstatter Volksfest (beer festival). In the nineteenth century the Industrial Revolution and, in 1871, the arrival of Gottlieb Daimler's automobile transformed Stuttgart into a key industrial centre. Having been decimated by Allied bombing raids in the Second World War, the city was largely rebuilt after 1945.

Modern City

Stuttgart is renowned for producing motor vehicles and electronic equipment. It is the headquarters of industrial giants including Mercedes-Benz, Porsche, Bosch, Hewlett Packard and IBM. Other important industries include research and development and publishing. Stuttgart is also a major banking hub, with the second largest stock exchange in Germany, and is one of Germany's centres for wine-production and brewing.

The city is linked by motorway to Munich and Singen and has an international airport (Flughafen Stuttgart). The main railway station is Stuttgart Hauptbahnhof. Local transport within the city is provided by the S-Bahn, U-Bahn, buses and Straßenbahn (trams). There is also an inland port.

Places of Interest

Schlossplatz (Royal Square) is the old central square of Stuttgart. Many of its surrounding buildings, dating from the fourteenth and fifteenth centuries, were damaged during the Second World War but have been sympathetically rebuilt or restored. Sites of historic interest around the square include the *Siftskirche* (a Gothic church), the *Altes Schloss* (a renaissance castle) and the *Königsbau* (the King's Building).

Stuttgart is home to a renowned city ballet, the State Opera and a Philharmonic Orchestra. Among its many fine museums is the Stuttgart State Gallery, which contains an extensive collection of fourteenth- to twentieth-century works by masters including Rembrandt, Monet, Renoir, Cézanne, Dalí, Matisse and Picasso.

Other leading tourist attractions include:

The Mercedes-Benz and Porsche Museums, located behind the headquarters of the car manufacturers;
The Wilhelma Gardens, created for King Wilhelm I in the middle of the nineteenth century as a Mauritian garden. They are the sole zoological-botanical gardens in Europe and home to over 8,000 animals encompassing a thousand species;
The 'Green U', a series of gardens and parks shaped in the form of a U;
Cannstatt Volksfest, the annual Stuttgart Beer Festival, and the second largest of its kind in the world;
The Fernsehturm Stuttgart, the world's first TV tower.

Sucre, Bolivia

Introduction

In an Andean valley in central Bolivia, Sucre is the country's judicial capital and the capital of the Chuquisaca department. The city is traversed by the River Cachimayo.

History

In pre-Columbian times, the region of Choque-Chaca (Silver Hill) was inhabited by the Charcas Indians. Pedro Anzures founded the town of La Plata there in 1538. In the mid-sixteenth century an *audencia*, or administrative area, was established by Gonzalo Pizarro with La Plata as its capital. This area incorporated most of Bolivia, Paraguay, southeast Peru, northern Chile and Argentina. It became an archbishopric in 1609 and 15 years later the Universidad de San Francisco Xavier was established. The town's name changed to Chuquisaca in 1776. By then it was the religious, educational, political and judicial centre of the country.

Chuquisaca was the heart of the independence movement from 1809. When independence from Spanish rule was granted in 1825 Bolivia was named after its liberator, Simón Bolívar. The city became the Bolivian capital in 1839 and the following year Chuquisaca was renamed Sucre after fellow Venezuelan revolutionary and the first president of Bolivia (1826–28), Antonio José de Sucre. Geographical isolation led to a challenge for capital status by the increasingly important city of La Paz. As a compromise to the resulting conflict, Sucre remained the national capital and judicial seat while La Paz became the country's political and administrative centre.

Modern City

Sucre is the judiciary seat of Bolivia. Aside from its capital status, agriculture is the main economic activity, although there is some oil refining and cement production. Since 1991 Sucre has been a UNESCO world heritage site. The national university, the Universidad de San Francisco Xavier, is one of Latin America's oldest dating from 1624. Sucre is connected by rail to Potosí and by road to surrounding towns.

Places of Interest

Sucre has preserved much of its colonial heritage. There's a seventeenth century cathedral, with a museum, the Mudejar style churches of San Miguel and San Fernando, and the Iglesia de la Recoleta which displays paintings from the sixteenth to twentieth centuries. The Casa de la Libertad documents the struggle for independence and is the place where the declaration was signed. Other museums include the Museo Textil Etnográfico (Ethnographic Textile Museum) which displays traditional weaving styles while Cal Orcko, 10 km north of Sucre, contains dinosaur prints and evidence of prehistoric plant and animal fossils.

Sukhumi, Georgia

Introduction

The Black Sea port of Sukhumi (Sukhum in Abkhaz) is the capital of the autonomous republic of Abkhazia. A once-popular tourist resort, it has been at the centre of a guerilla war since the early 1990s.

History

The earliest settlement, known as Dioscurias, was founded by the Greeks in the sixth century BC. Called Sebastopolis during the Roman and Byzantine periods, in the sixteenth to eighteenth centuries it was ruled by the Ottomans who named it Sukhum-Kale. It fell under Russian control in 1810.

In the civil war between Georgia and the secessionist Abkhazia in 1992–3, Sukhumi was seized by separatist Abkhazian forces. Up to 250,000 ethnic Georgians joined a mass exodus. The city is still in a state of post-war ruin.

Modern City

Industries include electrical manufacturing, food processing and wine-making. Sukhumi has a local airport, a port and road and rail links.

Places of Interest

A once popular tourist destination, the industry was badly affected by the violence of the 1990s. Travellers should seek advice. Among its attractions are the botanical gardens and sanatoriums with baths filled from sulphur springs.

Surabaya, Indonesia

Introduction

Surabaya is Indonesia's second largest city and its chief naval base. It is the capital and economic centre of the province Jawa Timur and is on the northeast coast of Java opposite Madura Island. The Mas River runs through the city centre.

History

There are records of Chinese trading vessels landing at Surabaya from the ninth century. Surabaya's foundation day is the 31 May 1293 when a local chief beat an army sent by Genghis Khan to occupy East Java, following which the city turned into a famous port. From 1743, Surabaya developed into a Dutch East India trading centre. In 1905, Surabaya was declared as a municipality and in 1926 it became the capital of East Java. In 1942–45, Surabaya was occupied by the Japanese and the city was heavily bombed.

Modern City

The port, Tanjungperak, is next to Indonesia's chief naval station, Ujung. Exports include sugar, coffee, cassava, spices, vegetable oils, teak, tobacco, rubber and petroleum products. There is also a fishing fleet. Industries include railways, petroleum refineries, metal production and shoe factories. The rail and road system links Surabaya to the western and eastern coasts of Java. There is an international airport at Tanjungperak. The university (Airlangga University), founded in 1954, has law, medicine and dental surgery faculties. There is also a naval college and the Tenth of November Institute of Technology.

Places of Interest

Pemuda Street is Surabaya's business, shopping and historical hub. The Grahadi, formerly the residence of the Dutch colonial governor, is still used as the official residence of the governor of East Java. The Kali Mas (River of Gold) is at the edge of the city. The Ampel Mosque, East Java's oldest, lies in the Kampung Arab (Kasbah Quarter), the heart of the old city. The Chinese temple Hok An Kong is three centuries old. Surabaya Zoo, one of the most complete in South East Asia, was founded by the Dutch in 1912 and has 500 species. There is a flower market (Kayun) and an ethnographic archaeological museum (Mpu Tantular Museum).

Suva, Fiji

Introduction

Suva, on the southeast edge of Viti Levu, is Fiji's capital city, chief port and tourist centre. It is surrounded by a deep water harbour and rainforest.

History

Founded by native Fijians, the first Europeans arrived in Suva in the 1860s. Fiji was ceded to Britain in the mid-1870s and Suva, with its strategically located port, was selected as colonial capital in 1882. The population was swelled by Indian immigrants brought in by the British to work on sugar plantations. Racial tensions became strained between the Europeans, Fijians and Indians.

Suva was an Allied air and naval base during World War II and in 1952 it won city status. In 1970 it became capital of newly independent Fiji. Racial tensions sporadically erupted, as in 2000 when businessman George Speight led an unsuccessful coup which attempted to exclude Indians from government.

Modern City

Suva's population is a mix of Fijian, Hindi and English. The port is a major staging post for trans-Pacific traffic. The city is well served by road and air connections, including Nadi international airport 200 km away. The economy relies on its free port activities and the tourist industry. Also important are soap and cigarette making, food processing and brewing. The University of the South Pacific was founded here in 1968.

Places of Interest

Pacific Harbour, a short distance from Suva's centre, is the focus of much tourist activity. Within the city, major attractions include: the Fiji Museum, with historical and ethnological collections; several churches, the best known of which is the Catholic Cathedral; Parliament and Government House (home of the president); the Suva Municipal Market (renowned for its fruit, vegetables and seafood); the tropical Thurston Gardens; and the traditional handicraft centre. Also popular is Orchid Island, close to the city centre, with a large array of indigenous flora and fauna.

Sydney, Australia

Introduction

Situated on the low hills surrounding Port Jackson on the southeast Australian coast, Sydney is widely regarded as Australia's first city. It is the capital of New South Wales and home to more than half the state's population. The city was named after Lord Thomas Townshend Sydney, an eighteenth-century politician.

History

The territory surrounding Sydney shows signs of habitation going back 50,000 years. At the time of European colonization, most of the land belonged to the Aboriginal Cadigal clan. Captain Arthur Phillip was the first Westerner to establish a settlement in the area, docking at Port Jackson in 1798. His original destination had been the nearby Botany Bay discovered by Captain James Cook 10 years earlier. Phillip, along with around 750 convicts and some military staff under his order, set up camp in a small inlet which he named Sydney Cove, now referred to as Darling Harbour.

Though blessed with a beautiful shoreline, the land was poor and the environment testing. The ensuing decades saw the settlement continue as a penal colony for British and Irish convicts, and for the first 15 years of its existence there was a grave threat from starvation. However, free settlers gradually moved into the area and it soon became an important trading centre. Throughout this period there was considerable friction between the free settlers, the convicts and the colonial governors, and also between the Britons and the Aboriginals. Unable to contend with the settlers' aggression or the new diseases the settlers brought with them (an outbreak of smallpox in 1789 killed half of Sydney's residents), the native population was severely reduced.

In the early nineteenth century the settlement lost its reputation as a lawless outpost and began to prosper through international trade. Under the guidance of Governor Lachlan Macquarie and assisted by the architect Francis Greenaway who found himself in the area after a fraud conviction, the city expanded and major public buildings and public spaces were laid out. This expansion accelerated in the latter half of the century when various infrastructures were put into place, including railway links. By 1900 the population had increased by almost 700% from the 60,000 who had lived there in 1850.

There has always been rivalry between Melbourne and Sydney. Just as Melbourne became a state capital, Sydney was declared capital of New South Wales on 1 Jan. 1901. Sydney's two greatest landmarks, the Harbour Bridge and the Jørn Utzel-designed Opera House, appeared in 1932 and 1973 respectively. There was a massive construction drive in the 1970s and recent projects include the Darling Harbour redevelopment and large scale renovations for the 2000 Olympics.

Modern City

Sydney and Melbourne are the nation's economic powerhouses. Sydney has important manufacturing and service industries and is a vital centre of commerce and finance as well as a major port. It is well served by road, rail, sea and air; public transport within the city is provided by buses, an underground, a monorail and ferries. The Metro Monorail opened to mark Australia's 1988 bicentenary; although contentious, it now handles 4 m. passengers annually. A new railway, the Metro Light Rail, began operations in 1997.

Sydney has the normal 'big city' problems of rising crime, pollution and lack of space, and away from the city centre's highrise skyline there is a suburban straggle. Unemployment is around 7%. However, the significant populations of Asian, Middle Eastern and Mediterranean origin (notably Vietnamese, Lebanese, Greek and Italian) give Sydney an international ambience. Over a third of the city's population were born overseas and more than 20 languages are in daily use.

Graduates account for 20% of the workforce. Major tertiary institutions are the University of Sydney, dating from 1850, the University of New South Wales, opened in 1949, Macquarie University (1964), the city's University of Technology (1987), and the University of Western Sydney (1989). Collectively, the institutions are home to some 152,000 students. The Australian Catholic University also has a campus in the city.

The arts are centred round the Opera House, which provides for numerous artistic disciplines in addition to opera. Notable cultural figures who have resided in Sydney include writers 'Banjo' Paterson (*Waltzing Matilda* lyricist) and Henry Lawson, artists Sir William Dobell and Russell Drysdale, and soprano Joan Sutherland. For many Sydneysiders much leisure time is spent in outdoor pursuits. The city is most famous for its beach and water sports, with areas such as Bondi and Palm Beach gaining a world reputation. While Sydney has developed many admirable characteristics, it is its natural setting that remains its defining feature.

High-profile events include the Film Festival, founded in 1954 at Sydney University and now screening some 150 films over 2 weeks in June. Since 1974 the festival has also toured 60 Australian towns. When the city hosted the Olympic Games in 2000, Australia fielded its largest Olympic team to date and won what was at the time its highest number of gold medals (since surpassed by the 17 gold medals won at the 2004 Athens Olympics).

Places of Interest

Sites of historical interest include the reportedly haunted Quarantine Station, built in 1832 and active until 1984, and the city's Observatory. Now an astronomical museum and planetarium, the Observatory was used from the mid-nineteenth century until 1982. The Rocks, Sydney's historic quarter, is located in the harbour on the site of the original colonial settlement, and the Royal Botanic Gardens, founded in 1816, are the oldest in Australia.

Important museums located in Sydney are the National Maritime Museum, Museum of Contemporary Art, and the Australian Museum, founded in 1827 but only opened to the public 30 years later. In 2002–03, the museum received 386,000 visitors at its main site. Other cultural attractions include the New South Wales Art Gallery, the country's largest gallery incorporating its only dedicated photography gallery.

Popular tourist destinations include Taronga Zoo, which opened in 1916 and receives 1.4 m. visitors each year, Wonderland Sydney, the largest theme and wildlife park in the Southern Hemisphere, the city Aquarium, and the shopping and entertainment facilities at Darling Harbour. Daring visitors can climb the harbour bridge.

Tabora, Tanzania

Introduction

Located in the central west region of Tanzania, Tabora (formerly Kazeh) is the capital of the Tabora region.

History

Tabora developed in the mid-nineteenth century as a centre for the Arab slave trade. At its height, some half a million caravans passed through the city each year. Control of the city went to the Nyamwezi tribe in 1876 before it came under German and then British rule. Since independence Tabora has retained importance as an agricultural centre.

Modern City

There is an airport for local flights and rail connections to Kigoma and Mwanza. Buses run to Dodoma but road connections are generally poor.

Main produces include vegetables, cotton, tobacco and cassava.

Places of Interest

The fort, or Boma, was built by the Germans and stands to the southeast, overlooking the city.

Kwihara museum, located 10 km from the town, contains artifacts belonging to the famous nineteenth century missionary and explorer, Dr Livingstone, who lived there briefly before making his last journey in 1872.

Taipei, China (Taiwan)

Introduction

The capital of Taiwan, Taipei has grown rapidly in the last half century. To its inhabitants, Taipei is the capital of a country—the Republic of China—but to most of the rest of the world it is the capital of a Chinese province. Yet despite the small, and declining, number of resident foreign diplomats, Taipei, with its government buildings and parliament, still feels like a capital city.

History

Taipei is a young city by Chinese standards. The site was originally a lake, fished by members of a native Taiwanese people, thought to have originated in the Pacific islands. In 1790 a farmer from the mainland established a farm in what is now central Taipei. Other Chinese followed and within a generation the former lake basin was well-populated by mainland Chinese. Several rival communities were founded by immigrants from different parts of the mainland. In 1853 rivalry turned to violence and one group fled a short distance north to establish a new community on the banks of the Tamsui River.

The new settlement on the riverbank became a market centre for the northern part of the island and developed trade. The river channelled development and the various small communities were soon merged in a growing city, Taipei. Four city walls, penetrated by five gates, were built. In 1886 Taiwan was given the status of a province of China and Taipei was designated provincial capital. This new role quickened the city's growth.

In 1895 Japan took Taiwan from China. Under Japanese rule the infrastructure of the city was developed and its status as the administrative and commercial centre of the island was enhanced. But Taipei suffered much damage at the end of World War II and when Chinese rule was restored to Taiwan in 1945 much of the city was in ruins. Reconstruction began. The new Chinese governor, Chen Yi, was perceived as corrupt and the Taiwanese quickly grew to resent Chinese administration. In 1947 anti-Chinese riots broke out in the city. The unrest was harshly put down and some 30,000 Taiwanese were killed. When the Communists took over on the mainland in 1949, the Nationalists (Kuomintang), under General Chiang Kai-shek (Chiang Chieh-shih) took refuge on Taiwan, making Taipei their capital.

Modern City

Taipei has grown rapidly as a capital and a major industrial centre, the seat of Taiwan's important textile and clothing industry. Other major industries include shipbuilding, electrical goods and machinery, consumer goods and motorcycles. Since the 1960s many high-rise buildings have been constructed and the city and its agglomeration now house one-fifth of the population of Taiwan. The city is a road and rail centre, and has an efficient rapid-transport system, an international airport (Chiang Kai-shek) and a smaller airport for domestic flights.

Places of Interest

As a young metropolis, which suffered great war damage in 1945, Taipei is a city of new buildings. Yet its principal attraction is the world's finest collection of Chinese antiquities, the National Palace Museum, whose contents were brought from Beijing by the Nationalists. Other attractions include the Botanical Gardens, the ornate 18th-century Lungshan Temple and the dominating Chiang Kai-shek Memorial, a marble-covered overpowering building that contains an exhibition to the life of the Nationalist leader. The 101-storey Taipei 101, formerly known as the Taipei World Financial Center, was the world's tallest skyscraper from 2004 until 2010 and is now the sixth tallest. It contains the world's fastest elevator. There are observation decks on the 89th and 91st floors.

Tallinn, Estonia

Introduction

Situated on the Gulf of Finland on Estonia's northern coast, Tallinn is the country capital and the chief port.

History

Tallinn was first mentioned in 1154 by the Arabian geographer al-Idrisi, who referred to the city as 'Kaleweny', although a settlement had been there for over a millennium. Under King Valdemar II, the Danes conquered the city in 1219. Valdemar built a fortress on the Toompea hill, which dominates the city and overlooks the harbour. The settlement around the foot of the hill created the Lower Town. The name Tallinn evolved from the Estonian for 'Danish fortification'. The city joined the Hanseatic League in 1285 and trade prospered. Over time the Lower Town expanded to the harbour while the Toompea fortification was encompassed by a wall. The harbour attracted Russian, Scandinavian and German merchants. Following a deal between the Danish occupiers and German crusaders, Teutonic knights acquired Tallinn in 1346, changing its name to Reval.

During the sixteenth century, Tallinn, along with other Baltic regions, fell victim to hostilities as neighbouring powers fought for control. Ivan the Terrible besieged Livonia in the mid-sixteenth century leading to the demise of the Teutonic Knights. During the ensuing Livonian War (1558–83), Sweden repelled the Russians and took control of Tallinn, occupying it for a century and a half. Eventually, in 1721 Russia's Peter the Great forced the Swedes out of Tallinn to begin a long Russian occupation.

The city's importance and prosperity was increased after a rail link to St Petersburg was opened in 1870 and Tallinn served the Russian empire as a major ice free port. The emancipation of the serfs the following year swelled the city's ethnic Estonian population, many of whom worked in the shipyards.

Russian rule ended in 1918, and the renamed Tallinn became the capital of independent Estonia. But the country's independence was shortlived and in 1940 Stalin's army occupied the city after which many Estonians were deported to Siberia. Between 1941–44 German troops captured the city. Few parts of Tallinn survived World War II unscathed, with Soviet bombing inflicting the most damage. The city once again found itself under Soviet control and more deportations ensued. The population was replaced by Russian migrants. Finally, in 1991 Tallinn once again became the capital of independent Estonia.

Modern City

Aside from the port's commercial activity, Tallinn has engineering and shipbuilding industries as well as cement, paper and textile production. Educational institutions include a technical university and a science academy. Tallinn has an international airport 2.5 km from the city centre and is 90 min from Helsinki by hydrofoil. Other ferries go to Stockholm. Rail services connect the city to other Baltic capitals.

Places of Interest

Although a largely modern city, much of Tallinn's medieval aspect survives in Vanalinn, the old town, and some of the city walls remain. A UNESCO heritage site since 1997, Vanalinn contains the Gothic town hall, built in the late fourteenth century, and the thirteenth century Holy Spirit Church.

Constructed in the early eighteenth century, Kadriog Palace was designed by Italian architect Niccolo Michetti for Peter I. Built in Baroque style on the city's original Danish fort, Toompea Castle now houses Estonia's riigikogu, or parliament. Museums include the Estonian Art Museum (KUMU) and a foreign art museum housed in the Kadriog Palace.

Tangier, Morocco

Introduction

Situated in a bay on the Strait of Gibraltar on the northern coast of Morocco, Tangier is 27 km from the southern tip of Spain and commands the western entrance to the Mediterranean. It has been ruled and occupied by the British, Spanish, Portuguese and the Arabs, and for over 40 years enjoyed status as an international city before being integrated with the rest of Morocco on independence in 1956.

History

A Phoenician trading post, the town became a Carthaginian settlement around 500 BC and then a Roman settlement called Tingis. After the destruction of Carthage it was affiliated with the Berber kingdom of Mauretania. It then became an autonomous state under Roman protection, eventually becoming a Roman colony in the third century during the reign of Diocletian, and ending as the capital of Mauretania Tingitana. For 300 years, from the fifth century onwards, it changed hands between the Vandals, the Byzantines and the Arabs. From the eighth to the fifteenth centuries it was occupied by Islamic dynasties and became an important Mediterranean port trading with Europe. In 1471 the Portuguese conquered the city who, along with the Spanish, ruled until 1662 when it was given to Charles II as part of the dowry of Catherine of Berganza. After an unsuccessful attempt by Moulay Ismail to seize the city in 1679, the British destroyed and abandoned it whereupon it fell into decline until the mid-nineteenth century when Europe adopted it as a diplomatic centre. At the Algeciras Conference in 1906, attended by the European powers, Tangier and a surrounding area were granted special status as an International Zone. The city was governed by an international commission with the Sultan as nominal ruler. In 1929 Spain was given police powers, taking total control during WWII from 1940–45 when it once more came under international authority until joining Morocco following that country's independence in 1956.

Modern City

With its close proximity to Spain and Gibralter, visitors can explore the city on a day-trip. Excellent road and rail connections with other major towns make it a good starting point for further touring. Otherwise Tangier is primarily a shipping centre with some building trade, fishing and a textile industry, mainly dealing in carpets. Rural activities include poultry farming and market gardening. The old town (medina), enclosed by fifteenth century ramparts, has the Grand Socco and the Petit Socco markets. The university was founded in 1971.

Places of Interest

The Museum of Moroccan Arts is located in the prince's apartments of the seventeenth century palace, Dar el Makhzen, once the governor's residence, in the Place de la Kasbah. The palace's kitchens now house the Museum of Antiquities. The Sidi Bouabid Mosque dominates the medina and the trees in the Mendoubia Gardens are 800 years old. The Forbes Museum has a collection of 115,000 toy soldiers that belonged to the American billionaire Malcolm Forbes. The American Legation Museum documents the history of the relationship between Morocco and the USA.

Tartu, Estonia

Introduction

Tartu, on the River Emajõgi, is Estonia's second city and is home to a university founded in 1632 by Gustavus II Adolphus of Sweden.

History

Estonian settlers erected a fortress, Tarbatu, on the city site around AD 600. In 1030 Yaroslav the Wise of Kyevan Rus seized control of the area and built a new fortress which he called Yuryev. Estonian forces reclaimed the area in 1061 but were later defeated by the Teutonic Knights, who called the town Dorpat. It joined the Hanseatic League in the 1280s.

In 1558, at the start of the Livonian war, Russian forces under Ivan the Terrible took the undefended town. Poland, Sweden and Denmark then joined the conflict. In 1582 Tartu was absorbed into the Polish–Lithuanian kingdom. It fell under Swedish control between 1600 and 1603, was under Polish jurisdiction from 1603 until 1625 and then became a Swedish possession. In 1632 Gustav II Adolphus of Sweden founded the university.

Russia briefly held Tartu from 1656–61 and in 1704 it was again seized by Russia, under the guidance of Peter I. Having sacked the city, he ordered the deportation of the German population. Three massive fires during the course of the eighteenth century (1708, 1763 and 1775) gutted virtually all Tartu's medieval buildings, and the city was rebuilt along Baroque and Classical lines.

In the second half of the nineteenth century Tartu was prominent in the Estonian National Revival. The university was at the centre of intellectual debate and the town hosted the first Estonian song festival, the first national theatre and a leading writers' association. Held by Soviet forces in 1919, in July 1941 it was invaded by German troops. It suffered much structural damage and up to 12,000 citizens were murdered during World War II. Re-occupied by the USSR in 1944, Tartu was prominent in Estonia's anti-Soviet nationalist movement during the 1980s.

Modern City

Important industries include food processing, textiles and the manufacturing of agricultural equipment and consumer goods. There are good road, rail and air links and buses run within the city.

Places of Interest

The university has an observatory, art collection, library and botanical gardens. The university has sporadically been in exile and is currently trying to recover many of its treasures from Voronezh, where it was situated in the early twentieth century. Other major sights include the town hall, the thirteenth century Gothic cathedral, the fourteenth century St John's church and several museums and galleries.

Tashkent (Toshkent), Uzbekistan

Introduction

Tashkent, on the Chirchik river in the foothills of the western Tien Shan mountains, is Uzbekistan's capital and the largest city in Central Asia.

History

Established in the first century AD, Tashkent had a succession of names including Chach, Chachkent, Shashkent and Binkent. Arabs seized control in the seventh century and the Turkish shahs of Khwarazm became the rulers in the twelfth century. Situated on the Silk Road between Samarkand and Beijing, the city prospered. In the thirteenth century it came under the Mongols led by Genghis Kahn and in the following century the Timurids

ruled. They were succeeded by the Shaybanids and, in 1809, the khans of Kokand.

Following the Russian invasion of 1865, the city was made the administrative centre of Turkestan. The Trans-Caspian railway linked it with Russia in 1889. Soviet rule was established in 1917 but when the Turkestan Autonomous Soviet Socialist Republic was divided 7 years later, Samarkand was made capital of Uzbekistan. Capital status was transferred back to Tashkent in 1930.

Most of Tashkent was destroyed in an earthquake in 1966, which left over 300,000 homeless. Soviet brutalist architecture replaced most of the infrastructure. After the collapse of the USSR it was confirmed as capital of independent Uzbekistan.

Modern City

At the centre of a rich cotton producing region, textile and related industries are vital to the urban economy. Also important are tobacco and food processing, chemicals, agricultural machinery and consumer goods.

A major transport hub, Tashkent is on the Trans-Caspian railway. There is a metro system within the city and a nearby international airport. There is a university and several institutes of higher education.

Places of Interest

Leading attractions include the Palace of Arts, the fifteenth century Barakkhan Madrasah theological school and numerous theatres, such as the Navoi Opera and Ballet. There are museums of fine arts and applied arts, and the large Chorsu bazaar is also a major attraction.

Tbilisi, Georgia

Introduction

Regarded as the hub city of the Caucasus, Tbilisi is national capital and home to a quarter of the Georgian population. The city is divided by the Mtkvari river, with the city centre located on the southern right bank. The name 'tbili' meaning 'warm' refers to the warm springs in and around the city.

History

There is evidence of settlements as early as Neolithic times and Roman records of the city date from the fourth century, when it was named 'Tphilado'. In the mid-fifth century it was designated capital of the Georgian empire. The city was invaded by the Persians in the sixth century and by Arabs in the seventh century.

In 1121, King David the Builder took over the city, making it the seat of a united Georgia. As his name suggests, he was responsible for reconstructing a land devastated by war. Among his achievements were the monastery and academy of Gelati.

The Turkmen were the next to ravage Tbilisi, followed by Mongols, Turks, Persians and Russians. A Persian incursion at the end of the eighteenth century saw the city ravaged by fire. Russia took control in 1801, developing Tbilisi's role as a regional centre by improving transport links with other cities. In 1921 it became the Georgian capital. Soviet rule left its mark in the form of Socialist Realist architecture. As Georgia approached independence, Tbilisi was the focus for political demonstrations.

Modern City

As Georgia's industrial powerhouse, major industries include engineering, heavy manufacturing, textiles and food and drink processing. There is a state and a technical university and the Georgian Academy of Sciences is based here.

Tbilisi is at the centre of extensive road and rail networks and there is an international airport. Within the city there is an underground system as well as bus, trolley bus, cable car and tram services.

Places of Interest

The old town has Georgian orthodox churches, a synagogue, an ancient temple, the Armenian cathedral and a mosque, illustrating the various influences on the city's culture and history. Other sights include the Narikala Fortress and Anchiskhati, the city's oldest church dating from the sixth century. The numerous thermal baths for which Tbilisi is famous mostly date from the seventeenth century although only six are now operational. The city's main artery, named after a national poet, is Rustavelis Gamziri. The Georgian Parliament, Rustaveli Theatre and Paliashvili Opera House are to be found here. Looking down on the city is the statue of The Mother of Georgia.

Tegucigalpa, Honduras

Introduction

On a high plain surrounded by mountains in the centre of the country, Tegucigalpa is the capital of Honduras and of the Francisco Morazán department. It is traversed by the Choluteca, the Guacerique and the San José Rivers.

History

Pre-Columbian Honduras was populated by Maya and Lenca peoples. Attracted by the abundance of silver, colonists founded Tegucigalpa as a mine in 1578. Originally known as Real de Minas de San Miguel de Tegucigalpa, the municipality of Tegucigalpa was created the following year. The name was taken from the Nuhuatl word for silver mountain. It quickly developed into the most important mining centre in Central America and the town expanded to accommodate increasing numbers of settlers.

Tegucigalpa developed gradually. In 1821 a bridge was built connecting the city to the settlement of Comayaguela. From 1537 until the late nineteenth century the Honduran capital and political centre was Comayague, a city to the northwest. Tegucigalpa became the capital in 1880. In the twentieth century, the city continued to grow, incorporating Comayaguela in 1938. New *barrios* were created, as were three additional bridges to Comayaguela. In the second half of the century a migration of the rural population to the capital led to shantytowns on the outskirts. From the 1970s improved transport connections allowed for more industry. In 1998 the city, and the entire country, was devastated by Hurricane Mitch. In 1999 torrential rains forced the Choluteca River to burst its banks, covering much of the capital in mud and causing widespread damage. Nationwide hurricane damage forced many living in rural areas to migrate to Tegucigalpa in search of food and employment. By the turn of the twenty-first century, much of the city's infrastructure had been restored.

Modern City

Tegucigalpa is the industrial centre of Honduras with food processing, brewing and distilling plants. Manufactures include textiles and chemicals while silver, zinc and lead are mined in the surrounding region. The capital is accessible by road and plane, although there is no rail network. The Toncatin International Airport is 7 km from the city, and bus services from Comayaguela link the capital to other cities and Central American capitals. The Inter-Oceanic Highway connects Tegucigalpa with the Pacific and Atlantic coasts.

Places of Interest

Many colonial buildings remain. The sixteenth century San Francisco church is the oldest church in the city. The San Miguel Cathedral was built between 1765–82 and contains a gold Baroque altar. Next to the cathedral, the Parque Central is the focal point of the city. Opened in 1996, the Galeria Nacional de Arte displays Mayan artefacts, silver work and contemporary art. Other museums include the Museo Antropología e Historia and an art museum housed in the old university, the Antiguo Paraninfo Universitaria. 21 km northeast of the city, the Parque Nacional la Tigra contains acres of cloud forest inhabited by ocelots, pumas and monkeys and abundant in orchids. 11 km away, the Valle de Angeles is a sixteenth century mining town restored to its original state. It is famous for its *artesanía*, or handicrafts.

Tehran, Iran

Introduction

Tehran is the capital and largest city, located in the north of Iran about 100 km from the Caspian Sea. The second most populous city in the Middle East after Cairo, Tehran is the commercial, administrative and cultural heart of the country. It underwent extensive modernization and industrialization in the twentieth century.

History

The old sector of Tehran, dating from the fourth century AD, was a suburb of the ancient Persian capital of Rey destroyed during the Mongol invasions of the thirteenth century. After the fall of Rey, many of its inhabitants settled in Tehran. Having been the occasional residence of the Safavid rulers in the seventeenth century, the city rose to prominence in the late eighteenth century after it was captured by the founder of the Qajar dynasty. It was the capital from 1788. In 1943 it was the site of the Tehran Conference of World War II Allied leaders. There was fierce fighting in Tehran preceding the overthrow of the Shah in the 1979 revolution, and the subsequent US embassy hostage drama was played out in the capital.

Modern City

Tehran's development accelerated under the Pahlavi dynasty from 1925, since when much of the city has been rebuilt. It is the seat of government and the industrial hub of the country. Local manufactures include textiles, cement, bricks and processed foods. The National Iranian Oil Company administers the nationalized oil and gas resources from the capital, and there is an oil refinery at Rey. The international airport (Mehrabad) is the busiest in the country. The construction of the Imam Khomeini International Airport is nearing completion. Higher education institutions include Tehran University (the oldest, founded in 1934), Amirkabir University of Technology, the Academy of Medical Sciences and Iran University of Science and Technology.

Places of Interest

Tehran is noted for its museums, in particular the National Museum of Iran, the Islamic Arts Museum, Reza Abbasi Museum, Glassware and Ceramics Museum, Museum of Contemporary Art, Carpet Museum, National Jewels Museum, Sa'adabad Palace, Niavaran Palace and Golestan Palace. Other landmark buildings are the Sepahsalar and Imam Khomeini Mosques and the Baharstan Palace (the seat of the Majlis). The shrine of Ayatollah Khomeini to the south of the city is a pilgrimage centre.

Tel Aviv, Israel

Introduction

Cosmopolitan Tel Aviv is a comparatively new city, founded by Zionist settlers and dating from 1909. Located on the Mediterranean coast, it incorporated the ancient neighbouring seaport of Jaffa in 1950. It is now Israel's main urban and business centre and also home to many of the country's main cultural attractions.

History

By the early twentieth century the Jewish quarter of the biblical town of Jaffa was seriously overcrowded. Zionist families moved out to build a European-style suburb, which by the mid-1920s numbered nearly 40,000 inhabitants. Its growth accelerated in the 1930s with the further waves of Jewish immigration from Nazi Germany, and it became the largest city in British-administered Palestine. This expansion continued after the creation of the state of Israel in 1948 and the subsequent incorporation of Jaffa.

Modern City

The commercial heart of Israel, Tel Aviv is home to banks, insurance companies, the stock exchange and around half of Israel's industrial enterprises. Most of the country's press and publishing concerns are based here and, with some 10 km of coastline, it is an important tourist centre. Ben-Gurion International Airport, Israel's busiest, lies to the south of the city. Tel Aviv University was inaugurated in 1956 and there are also several rabbinical institutes.

Places of Interest

Independence Hall is the site of the historic declaration that brought the state of Israel into being in 1948. The main museums are the Tel Aviv Museum of Art, Beit Hatefutsot (Diaspora Museum) and Eretz Israel Museum. Tel Aviv is the base of some of the country's major cultural attractions, such as the Israel Philharmonic Orchestra, New Israel Opera, and Habimah and Cameri Theatres. The Carmel Market in the Yemenite Quarter of the city is one of the largest open-air markets in the Middle East.

The Hague, Netherlands

Introduction

The Hague is situated in the south of the Netherlands, 6 km from the North Sea. Although Amsterdam is the nominal capital, The Hague is the country's administrative centre and the royal court and government offices are all located here.

History

The city began life in 1248 as a castle settlement built by Count William II in a woodland area known as Haghe or "hedge". Several buildings were gradually erected around the castle, amongst them the Knights' Hall in 1280. The Binnenhof ("Inner Courtyard") in The Hague's old quarter is now composed of these medieval constructions. In the mid fourteenth century the Hofvijver, an artificial lake, was dug just north of this central cluster, and it remains a popular feature of the modern city.

Over the course of the next two centuries The Hague developed its commercial power, and in 1559 William of Orange, stadtholder of the Netherlands, named the city as his capital. It was to become a major centre for opposition to imperial Spanish rule, and in 1585 the States General, the political opponents of Philip II, established themselves as the de facto government of the Dutch Republic, basing themselves in the Binnenhof.

During the seventeenth century The Hague was increasingly used as a base for diplomatic negotiation since the Dutch Republic had emerged as a powerful force in European affairs. When the French occupied the country at the end of the eighteenth century it became the capital once again, and following liberation in 1815 it alternated with Brussels as the place of congregation for the States General. The nineteenth century witnessed a considerable growth in the city's prosperity, mainly because of the mercantile success of the Dutch East India Company.

Following The Hague Peace Conferences held in 1899 and 1907 the city became a centre for international law, a pre-eminent position that it still holds today. Dutch central government returned to The Hague not long afterwards in 1913.

Modern City

The Hague today lacks the industrial clout of Amsterdam, there is little heavy industry to speak of, although ceramics, furniture, glass, and luxury items are produced here, and printing and publishing are prominent industries. The city's major role is as an administrative base for government and commerce.

Places of Interest

The area around the Binnenhof, which architecturally dates back to the fifteenth and eighteenth centuries, contains a number of significant landmarks including the Great Church of St Jacobs and the royal palace which is known locally as the Huis ten Bosch. The Binnenhof Courtyard itself is a popular destination for visitors, and near the historically important Knights' Hall lies the palatial Mauritshuis, the Royal Picture Gallery, which displays works by Rembrandt, Rubens, Vermeer, Van Dyck and other national artists. The Kröller-Müller Museum houses works by another Dutch favourite— Van Gogh.

Thessaloniki, Greece

Introduction

Thessaloniki, capital of the region of Macedonia, is situated in northeastern Greece at the head of a bay opening into the Thermaic Gulf. The city stretches over 12 km in a bowl formed by low hills. It is the second most populous city in the country and an important centre of commerce and industry, with a port matched only by that of Piraeus.

History

The city was founded in 316 BC, and named after the daughter of Kassandros, a general of Macedonia and father to Alexander the Great. It emerged as a strategically important military and commercial outpost of the Roman empire, conveniently located on the Via Egnatia that ran from the Adriatic coast to Byzantium. The Roman emperor Galerius chose it as the capital of the eastern empire. Under Byzantine rule it continued to prosper, and for centuries was second only to Constantinople as an economic, cultural and spiritual centre. After a series of attacks by Goths, Bulgarians, Epirots and Normans, the city was reincorporated into the restored Byzantine empire in 1246. However in 1423, following persistent assaults on the city by the Ottoman Turks, Thessaloniki sought protection by ceding itself to Venice. In 1430 it was captured by the sultan Murad II. The Turkish occupation was countered by strenuous efforts to preserve the Greek language. An influx of Jewish immigrants, fleeing Spanish persecution, served to abate the dramatic decline in population after the war with the Ottomans.

The city remained under Ottoman control until 1912 when it was captured by Greek troops in the First Balkan war. The following year the terms of the Treaty of Bucharest formally ceded Thessaloniki to Greece.

In 1917 devastating fire broke out destroying thousands of homes. The resulting housing crisis was made worse by the arrival of refugees from Asia minor who had been expelled by Atatürk's regime. The city had to be reconstructed and expanded to accommodate its enlarged population. It was built on a meticulously planned grid system, and is notable for its broad streets.

Modern City

The waterfront, which includes the main squares of Platia Elefterias and Platia Aristoteleous, spans the distance between the White Tower in the east and the port to the west. To the north lies a university campus and the site of the International Trade Fair which is held every year. Bordering the centre is the old Turkish quarter of Kastra, just within the surviving city walls. There are rail connections to and from Athens and into other Balkan countries. A regular coach service operates between Thessaloniki and Athens. There are connections by sea with the islands of Lemnos, Lesos and Chios, with seasonal connections to the Sporades, Cyclades and Dodecanese island groups. The airport lies 16 km outside the city and is served by a number of domestic and international carriers.

Thessaloniki's major exports are chrome, manganese and both unprocessed and processed agricultural goods. The busy industrial sector has several steel works, petrochemical plants and oil refineries, and produces alcoholic drinks, carpets, textiles, flour, soap and bricks.

Places of Interest

The Archaeological Museum is considered one of the best in Europe, and houses a collection of artefacts mainly excavated from the tomb of Philip II of Macedon. The White Tower museum contains an exhibition of the history and art of Byzantine Thessaloniki.

Thimphu, Bhutan

Introduction

Bhutan's capital and largest city nestles into the Himalayas on the banks of the Raidak River around 2,000 m above sea level in the west of the country. As with the rest of the country, it is largely unspoilt by influences from the outside world.

History

There is evidence of human habitation in the surrounding region dating back to 2000 BC. Its first appearance in documented history occurred in the second century AD, and Buddhism was established as the principal religion six centuries later. Thimphu was made the official seat of government in 1962, which used to coincide with wherever the monarch was residing at a particular time. The coronation of Jigme Wangchuk in 1974 gave rise to the first visit of foreign media in the country's history.

Modern City

Thimphu is served by an airstrip and is located on the main Indo-Bhutan National Highway. The economy is based upon agriculture, with an emphasis on rice. Tourism is carefully regulated.

Places of Interest

Perched above the town is Tashi Chho Dzong (Fortress of the Glorious Religion), built in 1772 but completely refurbished in 1961 to serve as the seat of Government and headquarters of the Central Monastic Body. The whole city underwent major renovation in this period, financed largely with Indian backing. There is a fine School of Arts and Crafts, a Memorial Chorten, a National Library, an Indigenous Hospital and a stadium dedicated to archery, the national sport. The city also provides access to remarkable mountain views and testing treks.

Tianjin, China

Introduction

The principal port of northern China, Tianjin stands where two rivers merge to flow as the Ho Hai 55 km (35 miles) to the Yellow Sea. Tianjin, which is sometimes known by its former English name, Tientsin, is a major route centre. Like Beijing, Shanghai and Chongqing, Tianjin is a municipality with provincial status. The city is the fifth largest urban area in China: more than 45% of the population of the municipality live in rural areas.

History

Tianjin lies in a marshy area that had few settlements until the twelfth century when the town of Chih-ku was founded where the Tzuya and Hai rivers come together. The town grew quickly as a port and market centre and by the fourteenth century had a flourishing salt industry. In 1368 the town became a garrison and was renamed Tienchin-wei (meaning Defence of the Heavenly Ford). Fortifications were built and Tianjin grew as the terminus of the Grand Canal.

By the seventeenth century Tianjin was the main commercial centre of northern China with trade channelled down the nearby Huang He (Yellow River), China's second longest navigable river. In the 1850s the Huang He shifted its course and the Grand Canal silted up. Tianjin lost its advantages.

During the Second Opium War (1856–60), China was forced to cede areas of the city to France and Britain for trading posts. In 1860, British and French forces shelled Tianjin, which was declared a free port at the peace of 1860. Resentment at foreign domination led to an uprising in Tianjin in 1870. One after another, after 1895, Japan, Germany, Russia, Austria, Italy and Belgium acquired concessions in Tianjin. Nationalist feelings in the city grew and violent demonstrations in 1900 led to the occupation of Tianjin by European forces and the demolition of the city walls.

Japanese forces occupied Tianjin in 1937 and remained in control until 1945. After World War II the city was in Nationalist hands until taken by the Communists in 1949.

Modern City

The port of Tianjin is the commercial gateway to Beijing. The navigation channel is being widened and deepened to take ships of up to 100,000 tonnes. The city is the focus of several rail routes and has large railway yards and rolling stock repair facilities. A network of inland waterways still brings goods to the port for export. Following the major Tangshan earthquake of 1976 parts of central Tianjin were reconstructed in the early 1980s. These new buildings contrast with European-style structures that dated from the early twentieth century and monumental Communist architecture from the 1950s. Tianjin concentrates on heavy industry including heavy machinery, mining equipment, iron and steel, and shipbuilding and repair. Chemicals and textiles are also important.

In Aug. 2015 a series of huge blasts hit the port area of Tianjin after a hazardous chemicals storage facility exploded. Over 100 people died and more than 700 were left injured.

Places of Interest

The city's principal attraction is the Fine Art Museum which has a major collection of historic Chinese paintings. One half of the area of Shuishang Park is lakes in which stand 13 islets crowned by pavilions and temples.

Tirana (Tiranë), Albania

Introduction

Albania's predominantly Muslim capital is situated 17 km east of the Adriatic coast on the Ishm River in central Albania. Positioned on a fertile plain, its surrounding area contains evidence of Neolithic inhabitants. A Roman fortress was present around AD 520, but the establishment of the modern city is generally put at around 1614 when the Turkish general, Barkinzade Süleyman Pasa, is reputed to have constructed a mosque, bakery and some baths.

History

During the eighteenth century the town began to grow as a trade centre and gained a reputation for its fabrics, leather, pottery and silverware. It was during this period that the Etehem Bay mosque, still preserved in the city's main Skanderbeg Square, was constructed. During the nineteenth century Tirana was the subject of feudal conflicts until the Toptani family gained control. Around this time several prominent figures of the Rilindja (the Albanian nationalist awakening) were active in the city and the nationalist Bashkimi (Unity) group was founded here in 1908.

The city underwent Serbian occupation for a time during the first Balkan War of 1912–13, but in 1920, following a decree by the provisional government at Lushnjë, Tirana became capital of Albania. However, at this stage it was still a relatively small town with an estimated population of 17,000. Zog I became Albanian President in 1925 and from 1928–39 he was King during which time, despite much resistance to his rule in Tirana, the city enjoyed a degree of calm. Throughout the 1930s a number of urbanization schemes were put into place, including the construction of Skanderbeg Square. However, Zog's close relationship with Mussolini's Italy was to backfire, and Tirana was occupied firstly by Italy and then Germany during World War II.

German forces were expelled in Nov. 1944 and the Communist Party, which had been established in Tirana 3 years earlier, entered the city and consolidated their power. In Nov. 1946 they declared Albania a communist People's Republic and, with Chinese and Soviet assistance in the 1950s, Tirana grew apace. Hydro-electric and thermal power plants were constructed and light industry, manufacturing and mining all prospered. However, Albania's relationship with the USSR was not easy and following Soviet intervention in Czechoslovakia in 1968, Albania withdrew from the Warsaw Pact. Its special relationship with China, though, lasted until 1978.

Modern City

By the late 1980s Tirana was Albania's industrial powerhouse and lay at the centre of President Ramiz Alia's liberalization programme. In 1992 the Communists were ousted from power and there followed a turbulent decade for Tirana as it witnessed increasing political instability and deteriorating relations with Serbia. Among its most important industries are metalwork, food processing, textiles and chemicals. It is on Albania's main rail network and has an international airport.

Places of Interest

There are numerous theatres, museums and concert halls as well as a National Institute of Folklore. The old city was torn down in the 1950s. Skanderbeg Square is Tirana's focal point and it is here that the Etehem Bay mosque stands side by side with the Soviet-built Palace of Culture.

Tiraspol, Moldova

Introduction

Located on the Dniester river in the east of the country, Tiraspol is an industrial centre surrounded by agricultural land. In recent years it has seen the rise of a Russian separatist movement.

History

There was an ancient Romanian village called Sucleia on the site of the modern city. Russian forces constructed a fortress here in 1792 during the Russo–Turkish wars and the town was founded 3 years later, marking the extremity of the Russian empire.

It was the capital of the Moldovian Autonomous Soviet Socialist Republic from 1929–40, and then of the Moldovian Soviet Socialist Republic. Occupied by Nazi forces in 1941, it was re-taken by Soviet troops in 1944.

Around 40% of the population is Russian, with ethnic Moldovans making up around 20%. Tensions rose between the two communities and an organized Russian separatist movement appeared during the 1980s. In 1991 Moldova gained independence and the separatists responded by declaring the region of Transdniestr a republic and Tiraspol its capital.

Modern City

Agriculture dominates the surrounding area but food processing, wine-making, textiles, furniture and electrical goods are important to the city.

International travellers are likely to fly into Chisinau. Tiraspol is well-served by road links and is on the main Odesa–Chisinau rail route.

Places of Interest

Tiraspol has few traditional tourists attractions but in many respects remains a model of a Soviet town.

Toamasina, Madagascar

Introduction

Known as Tamatave until 1979, Toamasina is Madagascar's biggest harbour and commercial centre. It is located in the east of the island.

History

The city was built around the port which served as a trading post for European merchants in the eighteenth century. Toamasina was taken by the Merina king Radama I in 1817 who expanded the port. After it was taken by French colonists in the late nineteenth century, they used the port as a base from which to conquer the interior. A battle between the Merina army and the French fleet was fought here. In 1927 Toamasina was decimated by a hurricane. Since rebuilt, it over the twentieth century Toamasina has developed into Madagascar's leading commercial centre.

Modern City

Toamasina is also a financial and commercial centre. Most foreign trade passes through the port. Main industries are food processing, especially rum production. Its principal exports are cloves, coffee, and vanilla. The Bazar Be market sells regional crafts including wickerwork. The city's university was founded in 1977. Toamasina is linked to the capital by rail.

Places of Interest

The university museum exhibits precious stones and regional crafts, and hosts exhibitions of archaeology and photographs. Music and theatre productions are held at the Palais des Enfants. These include traditional Betsimsaraka dancers, Hira Gasy Theatre Companies, groups of Salegy and Kwassa Kwassa (music and dance).

Tokyo, Japan

Introduction

Tokyo, Japan's capital, is in the Southern Kantō area bordered by the Saitama prefecture to the North, the Tamagawa River and Kanagawa river to the South, the Edogawa River and Chiba prefecture to the East and by the Yamanishi prefecture to the West. Tokyo has 23 administrative centres or 'ku'. The 23 ku system, adopted in 1949, is the basis of Tokyo's self government. The Greater Tokyo Metropolitan area consists of Saitama, Kanagawa and Chiba prefectures.

History

Tokyo was first a small village called Edo in the twelfth century. In 1457, a castle was built in Edo which was later taken by the first of the Tokugawa Shoguns, Ieyasu in 1590. Japan adopted and enforced the policy of national seclusion until the arrival of the US Commodore Matthew C. Perry to Tokyo Bay in 1854.

Tokyo has been the administrative centre of Japan since the early years of the seventeenth century but only became the official capital in 1868 under the Meiji Restoration when the Emperor Meiji moved the court from Kyoto, the former capital of Japan to Edo. Edo was then renamed Tokyo, literally meaning 'Eastern Capital'.

The Meiji era (1868–1912) brought about the rapid absorption of Western civilisation. Japan's first railway was opened between Tokyo and Yokohama in 1869 and the first rail connection between Shinsaibashi (Tokyo) and Yokohama was in operation by 1872. The postal system was established in 1871. In 1885, Hirobumi Ito became Japan's first prime minister and the cabinet system of government was adopted. The Great Kanto earthquake struck Tokyo in Sept. 1923 (see Natural Disasters) killing 140,000 people.

Five months after the Japanese attack on Pearl Harbour, Tokyo experienced its first air raid in April 18, 1942. 102 bomb attacks reduced the city to rubble between Nov. 1944 and Aug. 1945.

In 1964 the first Olympic Games in Asia were held in Tokyo. The Bullet Train (Shinkansen), connecting Tokyo and Osaka and the Shuto express way opened. Since 1964, Japan's bullet train has extended, as far as Hakata on the island of Kyushu (Tokaido-sanyo shinkansen) in the south west, Morioka (Tohoku shinkansen) in the north and Niigata (Joetsu shinkansen).

Economic growth in the 1960s was exemplified by the mass production of household electrical appliances. The 1970s saw the result of the environmental problems associated with rapid industrialisation such as water, noise and air pollution.

The oil shock of 1973 brought economic growth to a sudden halt. Land prices skyrocketed in the 1980s and Tokyo experienced the effects of the 'bubble economy' in 1986 with advanced technology stimulating rapid economic growth. In 1992 the bubble burst and Tokyo suffered. To revitalise the economy The 'Tokyo Vision 2000' plan was devised by the TMG to form the basis of the development of Tokyo in the twenty-first century.

Service industries such as retail, wholesale, insurance and finance make up 63% (1999) of Tokyo's economy. Primary industries such as fishing and agriculture are of marginal significance.

Modern City

Tokyo is one of the world's leading producers of technologically advanced products such as automobiles, electronic equipment and machines, metals, chemicals, textiles and processed foods.

Places of Interest

Main train stations in Tokyo include Tokyo Station which links the North and West of Japan by the high speed bullet train (Shinkansen); Shinjuku station connecting Tokyo with the west of Tokyo prefecture and the prefecture of Saitama to the north and Ueno station which provides links with the prefectures of Chiba and Ibaraki in the east. The Bullet train departing from Shinagawa station gets to Yokohama in just under 20 min.

Tokyo is home to the Japanese Emperor, who lives in the Imperial Palace, the original site of the Edo castle. There are more than 50 universities and colleges in the Tokyo region. Nihon University founded in 1889 and the University of Tokyo established 1887 are among the most prestigious. In 2011 the Tokyo Skytree (a broadcasting and observation tower) became Japan's tallest structure at 634 m. It is the world's second tallest structure after the Burj Khalifa in Dubai, United Arab Emirates.

Toronto, Canada

Introduction

Toronto is Canada's largest city and the fifth largest in North America.

The capital of Ontario, Toronto is the economic and cultural focus of English-speaking Canada.

What was once a largely Anglophone city has been swollen by immigration from across the globe and now offers a cosmopolitan mix of styles and cultures. The three most frequently spoken languages are English, Cantonese and Italian.

History

Situated on the northern shore of Lake Ontario, what is now Toronto was first inhabited by the Seneca and later Mississauga Indians. The name Toronto, taken from the Huron for "place of meeting", derives from one of three small forts built between 1720–50 by the French to defend their trade with the Indians against European competitors. After the defeat of the French in 1759, the settlement survived as a trading post.

Loyalist Americans came to the area after the US War of Independence, preferring British rule to that of the new Republic. Some 40,000 are believed to have settled around the Great Lakes and St Lawrence River. Settlement continued throughout the nineteenth century as large numbers of British immigrants sought new lives abroad.

In 1781 negotiations were opened by the Governor of Canada, Lord Dorchester, to purchase from the Indians a site for the new capital of Ontario. Around 250,000 acres were bought for 1,700.

In 1793 Colonel John Graves Simcoe, lieutenant governor of Upper Canada, chose a site for Toronto that was far enough away from the US border to make it easy to defend. Changing its name from Toronto to York, the city consisted of 12 cottages and a military garrison by 1795. The United States took advantage of the Napoleonic Wars to declare war on Britain and in 1813 US forces entered a practically defenceless York, occupying and pillaging it for 11 days before British forces were able to recapture it. The speaker's mace, taken during the occupation, was not returned to the city until 1934 and the city's Royal Standard is still held in the US Naval Academy in Annapolis, Maryland.

The city's population reached 9,000 by 1834 when its original name, Toronto, was restored. Three years later the former mayor William Lyon Mackenzie led a badly organized uprising. Although Mackenzie was forced to flee to America, his action led to the liberalising of the government of Upper Canada.

Fire in 1849 destroyed much of the downtown area, including St James' Cathedral. The arrival of the Grand Trunk and Great Western railways in the 1850s brought prosperity. The city industrialized quickly with the population growing from 45,000 in 1861 to 208,000 in 1901. Many of the city's finest buildings were constructed at this time including a new St James' Cathedral, St Lawrence Hall and University college. Badly hit by the Depression of the 1930s, Toronto was left with a shortage of public services, a problem compounded by the Second World War.

In 1954 the Council of Metropolitan Toronto was established to ease the municipal burden and solve the city's severe sewage and water problems. The council oversaw a series of urban improvements including the city's underground system, a new airport terminal and the construction of roads and expressways.

Modern City

Toronto became one of the fastest growing cities in North America, with an influx of European immigrants altering the cultural makeup. By 1961 less than half the population of the inner city were of British extraction. Immigration has continued with large numbers from the West Indies and Asia adding to the mix.

Places of Interest

Toronto is an important cultural centre with three theatres, a number of internationally renowned orchestras and musical groups and a series of museums and galleries, of which the Art Gallery of Ontario and the Royal Ontario Museum are the best known.

Amongst the city's celebrated sights is the CN Tower, the world's largest freestanding structure, which dominates the skyline.

Sport is an essential part of Toronto life with the city supporting the Maple Leafs ice hockey team and the Blue Jays, the only non-US baseball team to win the World Series. The Toronto Stock Exchange is one of the largest in North America by value of trading.

The Canadian National Exhibition was first launched in 1879 as the Toronto Industrial Exhibition and is reputed to be the world's largest annual exhibition.

Toulouse, France

Introduction

Situated on the Garonne River and the Canal du Midi, Toulouse is France's fourth city. It is the capital of Haute-Garonne and principal city of France's largest region, the Midi-Pyrénées.

History

Toulouse originated as a Celtic village populated by the Volcae Tectosages tribe. It was occupied by the Romans in the second and third centuries when it was called Tolosa. In 418 Toulouse came under the control of the Visigoths, who made the city their capital from 419–507. Toulouse was then incorporated into the Merovingian kingdom. Following the repulsion of the Saracens in 778, Toulouse flourished as the principal town in the Kingdom of Aquitaine (781–848).

Toulouse expanded during the eleventh century when the St Sernin church was on the route of the pilgrimage to Santiago de Compostela in Galicia. As Comte de Toulouse Raymond IV extended his territory as far as East Savoy. Raymond V successfully defended Toulouse from Henry II, who had acquired Aquitaine by his marriage to Eleanor in 1152. Toulouse's golden age was between 1189–1209. In 1190 the counts created the *Capitouls*, the seat of administration. The current town hall, built on the same site, retains the name of these first consuls. In 1229 the second university in France was established in Toulouse.

When at the turn of the thirteenth century, the ascetic Cathar Church split from the Catholic Church, the Pope reacted by excommunicating the Count of Toulouse and launching two crusades against the 'heretics'. The Cathars hid in Albi and other chateaux (thus gaining the name Albigensians), but were unable to escape King Philippe-Auguste's Catholic troops. In 1244, 200 Cathars were burned alive at the Château de Ségur. In 1215

St. Dominique founded Les Jacobins monastery as a refuge. It became the burial site of St Thomas Aquinas (1225–74). The end of the Albigensian Crusade saw the end of Toulouse's autonomy.

Once recovered from the turmoil of the Albigensian crisis, Toulouse flourished as the artistic and literary centre of medieval Europe. The College du Gai Savoir was founded in 1323 and literary societies blossomed. The city's prosperity was enhanced by the discovery of 'pastel', a woad plant that produced a pale blue dye. Pastel became extremely popular all over Europe and brought great fortune to Toulouse. Merchants built grand houses in Italian Renaissance style, using the now famous rose red brick. The prosperity was brought to an end in the sixteenth century when Portuguese merchants began importing indigo from India. In the sixteenth century Toulouse began its printing industry.

During the Wars of Religion, Toulouse supported the Catholics, a problematic choice, as the surrounding region was mainly Huguenot. The following two centuries were economically stagnant. On 10 April 1814 Toulouse was the setting for the final battle of the Peninsular War when the Duke of Wellington defeated Marshal Soult.

Toulouse benefited from the arrival of the railways in the nineteenth century. In 1919 the centre of aeronautics was established, strategically positioned away from Germany. In the 1920s, pilots flew the first planes from Toulouse across the Atlantic. Antoine de Saint-Exupéry found the themes for such novels as *Night Flight* (1931) as a pioneer of mail routes to North Africa and South America.

Modern City

Traditionally dependent on agriculture, Toulouse has become Europe's principal centre of aeronautics and aerospace, producing Concorde, Airbus and military hardware. Other industries range from chemicals to publishing. Toulouse has the largest student population outside Paris. The city is served by road, rail and air connections. The Blagnac airport is 10 km west of the city.

Places of Interest

Opened in June 1997, the Cité de l'Espace is a park devoted to Toulouse's space programmes. Built mid-fifteenth century, the Hôtel d'Assézat is now an art gallery with works by Matisse, Monet and Canaletto. The Musée des Augustins is housed in a fourteen–fifteenth century Gothic Augustinian monastery and displays art from the fifteenth–seventeenth centuries.

The basilica of the St Sernin church is the largest Romanesque church in Europe. The church was built between the eleventh and thirteenth centuries around a ninth century basilica, originally created to house the body of the city's first bishop, St Sernin. Other religious buildings include the Eglise Notre Dame de Taur.

Tripoli, Lebanon

Introduction

Tripoli lies on the Mediterranean coast in the northwest of the country about 65 km from Beirut. It is Lebanon's second largest city and port, an important commercial and industrial centre, and a beach resort.

History

Founded around 700 BC, Tripoli became the capital of the Phoenician triple federation of city states—Sidon, Tyre and Aradus—before coming under Seleucid and then Roman control. In AD 638 the city was taken by the Muslim Arabs. In the early twelfth century it was besieged and captured by Christian crusaders under Raymond of Saint-Gilles (who built the citadel overlooking the city). The crusaders were ousted by the Mameluks in 1289, and the city was destroyed in the process. For four centuries after 1516 Tripoli was under nominal Ottoman rule. It was incorporated into the state of Lebanon in 1920 under the French mandate. Having been occupied by the British and French in the Second World War, it then became part of the independent republic of Lebanon. With a predominantly Muslim population, Tripoli was a centre of rebellion against the Christian-dominated government in 1958 and again in the civil war of 1975–76.

Modern City

Tripoli comprises Al Mina (the port area) and the city proper, which contains the modern centre (Saahat at-Tall) as well as the old quarter dating from the Mameluk era of the fourteen–fifteenth centuries. The city's main industries are oil storage and refining, soap manufacturing, cotton goods, sponge fishing, and fruit and tobacco processing.

Places of Interest

Tripoli's principal historic landmarks are the Saint-Gilles citadel, the fifteenth century Lion Tower (built to protect the port), the Great Mosque (dating back to 1294) and the Teynal Mosque (to 1336).

Tripoli, Libya

Introduction

Tripoli is the capital, largest city and main seaport. It is in the northwest on the Mediterranean coast. Around a third of the country's estimated population of 5.6 m. live there.

History

Tripoli was one of several settlements along the North African coast established by the Phoenicians. Subsequent Carthaginian rule gave way to Roman dominance from 146 BC. The street plan of the old walled city was laid down in Roman period, during which time Tripoli (along with neighbouring Sabratha and Leptis—the other cities of Tripolitania) prospered. When the Roman empire fell into decline, the area was invaded first by the Vandals in AD 455 and then by the Byzantines in the sixth century. In AD 645 Tripoli was conquered by the Muslim Arabs. It remained under the control of a succession of Arab dynasties, except for a brief period of Norman supremacy from 1146–58, until the beginning of the sixteenth century when it was stormed by Spanish forces. In 1551 Tripoli was taken by the Turks. It remained a part of the Ottoman empire (and a haven for Mediterranean pirates in the eighteenth and early nineteenth centuries) until 1911 when it fell to Italian colonization. The city had begun to spread beyond the confines of the old walled city in the eighteenth century, and in these outer areas the Italians established new administrative quarters and official residences. Upon Italy's defeat in the Second World War, Tripoli was occupied by the British from 1943 until Libya's independence in 1951. Following the 1969 revolution the city expanded rapidly into sprawling suburbs. In April 1986 areas of the city were bombed by United States military aircraft in a reprisal raid for alleged Libyan terrorist activities. Anti-government protests in Tripoli during Feb. and March 2011 sparked a civil war that resulted in the deaths of hundreds of Libyans. In March the UN enforced a no-fly zone over the country and Tripoli came under air attack for the second time since 1986. After months of fighting the rebels seized control of the city, bringing an end to Col. Gaddafi's 42-year rule.

Modern City

A coastal oasis, Tripoli serves an agricultural area producing olives, fruit and vegetables. Textiles and fishing are important industries. It is the main centre for commerce and shipping, with an international airport and a coastal highway link to Benghazi (Libya's second city) and neighbouring Egypt. The city centre and most of the major commercial streets radiate from Green Square. The Al-Fateh University opened in 1973.

Places of Interest

The ancient walled city is dominated by a castle, dating from Roman times and extended by the Spanish and the Ottoman Turks. The adjoining Jamhiriya Museum has one of the finest collections of classical art in the Mediterranean area. The old quarter has a number of historic mosques—particularly the Ahmed Pasha Karamanli, An-Naqah (the oldest in Tripoli) and Gurgi Mosques—and the Roman Arch of Marcus Aurelius.

Trondheim, Norway

Introduction

Situated in the deeply indented Trondheim fjord in western Norway, Trondheim is the capital of the Sør Trøndelag *fylke*, or region, and is the country's third largest city. Among hills covered in pine forests, it is traversed by the Nid River. It is Norway's oldest city.

History

Following the death of King Haakon in 995, King Olaf Tryggvesson returned from exile in England. Two years later he founded Kaupangr on the mouth of the River Nid as his capital. A Christian convert, he built a church as well as a palace, and the town soon developed into a trading centre. In 1000 Olaf was killed at the battle of Svolder. In the same year, the Viking Leif Eriksson set sail from the village on a voyage across the Atlantic, via Greenland, landing at what is now Newfoundland. 16 years later Kaupangr was renamed Nidaros, meaning Nid River estuary. In 1030 King Olaf Haraldsson, another Christain king, was killed at the battle of Stiklestad. Olaf's body was brought back to Nidaros. The following year he was canonized and the town developed into a one of the major pilgrim centres of Medieval Europe. With expansion and the construction of new churches, Nidaros became Norway's capital and an important religious, cultural and educational centre. At the end of the eleventh century Christ Church was built by King Olaf Kyrre reputedly on Saint Olaf's burial site. With the establishment of a bishopric shortly after, Christ Church became a cathedral. In the mid-twelfth century Nidaros became an archbishopric which included Norway, Greenland, Iceland, the Hebrides, Shetland, the Orkneys and the Isle of Man.

The town's importance as a trading port waned when the Hanseatic League made Bergen its principal port, although it retained its religious importance. In 1380 it lost its capital status. In the sixteenth century Nidaros was renamed Trondhjem. The town's economy and political influence declined after the Reformation. In the eighteenth century, a small merchant aristocracy emerged.

Over the centuries, Trondheim suffered many fires, made worse by tightly packed wooden houses. After a particularly destructive fire in 1681 the town was rebuilt with wider streets. Two new forts were built. The cathedral did not escape from the city's fires and by the nineteenth century it was seriously dilapidated. A move to revive the country's heritage at this time led to the restoration of the cathedral, beginning in 1869.

With the arrival of rail in the mid-nineteenth century, Trondheim developed rapidly. The natural harbour was expanded and the city became an important centre of industry and education. In 1930 the city's name reverted to Nidaros, but strong public opinion forced the name to be changed back barely a year later, albeit with a slightly different spelling. It was occupied by Nazi forces in 1940 and as a strategically important naval base was bombed by the Allies. In the post-war period it underwent major reconstruction.

Modern City

Trondheim is an important seaport and fishing centre. Industries include food processing, shipbuilding and metallurgy. The city exports fish, wood pulp, timber and metals. Founded in 1968, the Norwegian University of Science and Technology is the country's second largest university. Trondheim is linked internationally by Trondheim Airport Værnes, nationally by rail and to the remote northern regions by ferry.

Places of Interest

Since 1814 the Gothic cathedral has been the site of the coronation of Norwegian monarchs. Originally a wooden chapel built in 1031 over Olaf's burial site, it became Christ Church when built in stone from 1070–90. Between the twelfth and fourteenth centuries the present cathedral was built. It has richly ornamented stone sculptures, although many of these are recent additions. The archbishop's castle, the Erkebispegården is adjacent to the cathedral. Museums include the Trøndela Folk Museum of local cultural history, the Museum of Natural History and Archaeology and the Art Gallery which displays Norwegian art from the nineteenth and twentieth centuries. Specializing in music history, the Ringve museum has a collection of instruments from around the world.

Tunis, Tunisia

Introduction

The capital and largest city in Tunisia situated 10 km (6 miles) inland from the Gulf of Tunis on the shores of a lake linked by a deep–water channel to the new port of La Goulette on the Mediterranean Sea. The old part of the city, the medina, was designated a World Heritage Site in 1979.

History

Founded by the Libyans, Tunis was surrendered to the Phoenicians around the ninth century BC. During the Third Punic War in 146 BC it was conquered by the Romans. The Arabs took control in the seventh century AD with Tunis becoming the capital under the Aghlabites from 894–905. The city prospered, especially under the rule of the Hafsid Dynasty (1230–1574). Between 1534–74 the town was attacked by a number of factions including the Turkish pirate, Barbarossa, the Austrians, and the Turks in 1574 who ruled until the French invaded in 1881. During the reign of the Husseinid Dynasty many palaces and mosques were built forming much of the area known as the medina. The French built the new town area between the medina and Tunis Lake. The city was occupied by the Germans for 6 months during WWII. Self–government was granted by the French in 1955 and the city became the national capital of Tunisia on gaining independence in 1956. In 1957 a republic was established and the monarchy abolished with the prime–minister, Habib Bourguiba becoming president. In 1975 the constitution was changed making Bourguiba President–for–life. Overthrown by a bloodless coup in 1987, the minister for the interior, Zine El Abidine Ben Ali, became president. A new constitution was promulgated in 1988. Ben Ali was re–elected in 1999. Democratic reforms were introduced but since 1999 political rights have been reduced and media censorship is common. The death of Bourguiba in 2000 has brought about widespread dissent against Ben Ali's strict regime.

Modern City

The Ville Nouvelle is the commercial part of Tunis. Centred around Avenue Habib Bourguiba it is lined with colonial French buildings with wrought–iron railings. After independence many of the streets were renamed. The centre is linked to the port, La Goulette, by a water channel, and by rail and road across a causeway through Lake Tunis. Chief exports include carpets, fruit, iron–ore and olives. Ferries run from the port to Europe. The International Airport of Tunis–Carthage is located northeast of the city. Tourists come to see the medina and its many mosques, palaces and markets. The Festival of Carthage held every July is another main attraction. The University of Tunis was founded in 1960.

Places of Interest

Before the arrival of the French the medina was the centre of Tunis. The Great Mosque Ez–Zitouna (the Olive Tree) is the largest and most venerable. Building commenced in 732 and finished in 864 with the minaret added in 1834. Its 184 columns surrounding the courtyard were brought from the ruins of Carthage. It was once the Islamic University. Close–by is the Souk el Attarine, a market specialising in perfume. Dar el Haddad is one of the oldest palaces built in the sixteenth century. Sidi Youssef Mosque, a seventeenth century Turkish mosque, was the first to have an octagonal minaret. The Mosque of the Kasbah was built during 1231–32. The Bibliotheque Nationale, built in 1813 as barracks by Hammouda Husseinid, is now the National Library. Dar Hussein, an Arab house decorated with colourful tiles and plaster lacework, is now the National Art and Archaeology Institute. The Bardo National Museum, to the west of the town, is of Spanish Moorish architecture and exhibits relics from every period of Tunisia's past, including a very fine collection of Roman mosaics.

Turin (Torino), Italy

Introduction

The city stands at the confluence of the Dora Riparia and the Po rivers in northwest Italy and is the crossroads of many important transalpine routes from France and Switzerland. It is the capital of the Piedmont region and the second largest industrial city in Italy (after Milan).

History

The city takes its name from the Taurini tribe, which inhabited the region during the first century and made the original settlement their capital. In the early fifth century, the town converted to Christianity and became a bishopric. One hundred years later, Turin was a Lombard duchy before becoming subject to Frankish rule. From the beginning of the eleventh century, Turin was connected to the house of Savoy, a dynasty that was to rule not only Piedmont and Savoy but also, from 1720, Sardinia. The power of the Savoys grew until in the eighteenth century. Turin reached its zenith during the reign of Charles Emmanuel II, when the court there emulated that of Louis XIV's Versailles in grandeur and influence. It was during this period that many of the most celebrated examples of Baroque architecture in the city were built.

The French invaded Turin in 1798, expelling Charles Emmanuel II, and after the fall of Napoléon the city endured occupation by Austria and Russia, before the restoration of rule by the House of Savoy in 1814. The new ruler Vittorio Emanuele I, was a supporter of the Risorgimento—the movement for the unification of Italy—and made his capital a political base for this struggle. After the success of the Franco-Piedmontese allied campaigns against the Austrians, Vittorio Emanuele II was proclaimed King of Italy. Turin became the seat of the Italian government and the new country's capital from 1861–65. The House of Savoy remained in power until the proclamation of the Italian Republic in 1946. Turin was the birthplace of Italian cinema, with Pietro Fosco shooting his silent film 'Cabiria' on the banks of the Po in 1914. Turin was heavily bombed throughout World War II.

Modern City

In the post-war years the city has become a major industrial centre and the focus for the Italian Trade Union movement. Turin's giants of industry, Olivetti, Fiat (founded by the powerful Agnelli family) and Lancia, have given rise to manufacturing industries such as tyre-making and coachbuilding (most famously Pinin Farina) and the city is renowned for its electromechanical expertise—the Politecnico at Turin University produces most of the motor industry's engineers. Other important industries include the manufacture of rubber, plastics, chemicals, chocolate, fortified wines and paper. As well as being a notable junction for road and rail, Turin also has an international airport.

Places of Interest

The fifteenth century Duomo di San Giovanni houses the famous Turin shroud in which, according to some, Christ's body was wrapped after the crucifixion. The Baroque Palazzo Carignano served as the first national parliament from 1861–64, it now contains the Museo Nazionale del Risorgimento Italiano, notable for its historic documents and political memorabilia of Italy in the nineteenth century. The Palazzo dell'Accademia delle Scienze houses an Egyptian museum with one of the world's finest collections of ancient Egyptian art. The armoury of the Palazzo Reale contains one of the best collections of medieval and renaissance arms and armour.

Ulaanbaatar, Mongolia

Introduction

Ulaanbaatar (also spelt Ulan Bator) is the capital and the largest city of the Republic of Mongolia. It is on the Tuul River at the foot of the mountain Bogdo Khan Uul which rises 3000 ft. above the capital. The city is dominated by communist style highrise apartment buildings. Ulaanbaatar is Mongolia's commercial, political, cultural and transportation centre. Accounting for 50% of Mongolia's industry production the city is 10 times the size of the country's second largest city. Ulaanbaatar has the country's only university, founded in 1942.

History

The city was founded in 1639 as a centre for Mongolian Lamaism by lord of the Khakha Tribe, Tusheey Khaan Gombodorj. The city was then called Urga. In 1706, it changed name to Ikh Khuree (Big Monastery). In the 1860s the town flourished as a commercial centre on the tea route between China and Russia. In 1911, Mongolia became independent from China and the city changed its name to Niislel Khureheh (Capital of Mongolia). During the Russian civil war, the city was the headquarters of the White Army of Baron von Ungern-Sternberg. In 1921 the city was occupied by Mongolian revolutionary troops, led by Damdiny Sühbaatar, and the Soviet Red Army. In 1924, the Mongolian People's Public was declared, and Mongolia became the world's second communist country. Niislel Khureheh became capital under the name Ulaanbaatar (Red Hero), and aid from the Soviet Government helped to develop the city. Mongolian communism remained fairly independent of Moscow until Stalin gained absolute power in the late 1920s. This led to Soviet totalitarianism with a particularly ruthless campaign against religion. In 1937, Stalinist purges destroyed many monasteries in Ulaanbaatar and monks were executed. As communism fell, the city grew rapidly in the early 1990s, thanks to the introduction of capitalism and privatization.

Modern City

Industries include woollen textiles, leather products, paper, cement, glassware and processed foods. The city is the centre point for Mongolia's road network and caravan routes. It has an international airport and is on the Trans-Siberian Rail Road linking China with Russia. It is illegal to cross into Mongolia by car or bus. Entry and exit visas are required by all nationalities. According to a World Health Organization report published in Sept. 2001 Ulaanbaatar is the second most polluted city in the world and the most polluted capital.

Places of Interest

The centre of Ulaanbaatar is the Sühbaatar Square which is flanked by the State Parliament House and the Palace of Culture (containing the Mongolian Art Gallery). The largest museum is the Museum of Natural History, which exhibits Mongolia's geography, flora and fauna and recent Mongolian history. The Zanabazar Museum of Fine Arts has paintings, carvings and sculptures, many by the artist and Buddhist, Zanabazar. It also shows rare religious items, such as cloth paintings and Buddhist statues. The Ulaanbaatar State Public Library has a collection of eleventh century Sanskrit manuscript. One of the monasteries that survived the Stalinist purges is the Gandantegchinlen Khiid (The Great Place of Joy), which has several temples decorated with gold and jewels. The Gandan monastery is the most important Lama shrine in Mongolia. The Winter Palace of Bogd Khaan (built between 1893 and 1903) was the residence of Mongolia's 8th Bogd Khaan (Living Buddha) and last king who died in 1924. In the grounds of the palace there are 6 temples containing gifts to the Bogd Khaan.

Vaduz, Liechtenstein

Introduction

Vaduz is on the River Rhine and is the small capital of the Principality of Liechtenstein. The town is the seat of the government and of parliament. Vaduz is a centre for tourism and agriculture and also has engineering industries. Owing to liberal taxation laws, the capital is an international finance centre and banks dominate the centre of Vaduz. It is home to the ruling Prince Hans-Adam II (among the richest men in the world), whose castle overlooks the town.

History

Vaduz was first mentioned in a document dated 1150. In 1342, it became the dominant town in the county of Vaduz. In 1719, the two counties Vaduz and Schellenberg united to create the Imperial Principality of Liechtenstein. The Royal Castle in Vaduz has belonged to the ruling family since 1712 but Francis Joseph II was the first to make it his permanent residence in 1938.

Modern City

The nearest airport is Kloten in Zürich (Switzerland). There is no railway service in Vaduz, but there are bus and taxi services. The city centre is open to pedestrians only. The success of the local industry and revenue from the many foreign companies has made Liechtenstein a wealthy country and the people of Vaduz enjoy one of the highest living standards in the world.

Places of Interest

Liechtenstein is famous for its stamps and in Vaduz there is the Postage Stamp Museum which contains 300 frames of stamps including rare examples dating from 1912. The State Art Collection (Staatliche Kunstsammlung) includes pictures acquired by the princes of Liechtenstein including works by Rubens. The Ski Museum shows 100 years of skiing history, and the National Museum (Landesmuseum) contains coins, weapons and folklore exhibits. The Royal Castle (Schloss Vaduz), which dates from the twelfth century, is not open to the public.

Valencia, Spain

Introduction

The country's third largest city, Valencia is on the eastern coast of Spain. Situated on the Guadalaviar estuary, the city links the Turia River with the Mediterranean Sea.

History

Valencia was originally the site of a Greek and Carthaginian settlement. It was founded by the Romans around 140 BC and rebuilt as the Roman colony of Valentia. It was then taken by the Visigoths in 413 and by the Moors in 714. When the Moorish kingdom was split into regions, Valencia became the capital of the Moorish territory of the same name in 1021. Under the Moors' rule, the city became important agriculturally and as a trading centre for silk, ceramics, leather and paper.

Valencia was taken by the Spanish in 1012, but was recaptured by the North African Almoravids in 1092. The Almoravids controlled the rest of Moorish Spain throughout the eleventh century. When the Spaniards returned it was with an army led by the Castillian nobleman, Rodrigo Díaz de Vivar, better known as El Cid (Arabic *as-sid*: 'lord'), who captured the city after 20 months of fighting. Independent under El Cid, Valencia was the only place in Moorish Spain not ruled by the Almoravids. He held the city until his death in 1099 but the Almoravids retook the city 3 years later. The oscillation between Moorish and Christian rule eventually ended in 1238 with the Riconquista, when Valencia was added to the kingdom of Aragón by Jaime I.

After the unification of Spain in 1479 under the Catholic monarchs, Isabella and Ferdinand, a peaceful Valencia grew and prospered. It became an important centre for arts and developed into the centre of the Valencian school of painting. Over the next two centuries the school included such artists as Juan Sariñena (1545–1619), who was Valencia's official artist at the end of the sixteenth century, and Francisco Ribalta (1565–1628). The city was the home to the first printing press in Spain, set up in 1474. In the fifteenth and sixteenth centuries Valencia became an increasingly important centre for trading and finance. The city's prosperity suffered as a result of the expulsion of the *Moriscos* (Moors who had converted to Christianity) during the Spanish inquisition.

During the Spanish Civil War Valencia was the seat of the Republican Government and was only taken by the Nationalists on 30 March 1939. Many buildings were destroyed during the crossfire, including many of the city's churches. It was in Valencia that the unsuccessful coup of 1981 was staged.

Modern City

Valencia's industries include orange growing and processing, rice and silk as well as shipbuilding, motor vehicles, textiles and metallurgy. The surrounding region of Valencia, of which the city is the capital, is made up of the provinces of Alicante, Castellón and Valencia. The University dates from about 1500.

The city has sea, road and national rail links. The international airport is 8 km from the city.

Places of Interest

To the east of the city centre is the oldest area, Barrio del Carmen. This is the site of the two surviving gates of the medieval city walls, destroyed in 1871 to make way for modernization. At the heart of the ancient city is the cathedral. Constructed between 1262–1482, it has examples of Baroque and Gothic style architecture. The adjoining museum claims to be the holder of the 'Holy Grail', used by Jesus at the Last Supper. There are also fine arts and history museums as well as the Museo de Bellas Artes which has collections of Valencian Impressionists, Goya, Velázquez and works of the Valencian School.

Valletta, Malta

Introduction

The capital and chief port of Malta, the walled city of Valletta lies on the north coast of the island on the Sceberras Peninsula with a harbour on each side. Formerly an important British naval base, the dockyards have been converted for commercial use. It is the administrative, commercial and cultural centre. The city was designated a World Heritage Site in 1980.

History

In 1530 the island of Malta was granted to the Knights of St John of Jerusalem. The Ottoman Turks were defeated by the Knights following an invasion in 1565. In gratitude Pope Pius V and King Philip of Spain gave the Knights financial aid and the services of the Italian military engineer, Francesco Laparelli. The building of the fortress town, named after their Grand Master, Jean Parisot de Valette, commenced in 1566 and was completed 15 years later. Valletta's streets were built on a grid pattern on the peninsula site of Mount Sceberras which provided two natural deep harbours, Marsamxett and Grand Harbour. Laparellis left in 1570, the year that Valletta became the Maltese capital, and work was completed by the Maltese architect, Geolamo Cassar. His buildings include the Cathedral of St John and the Magisterial Palace. Napoléon invaded in 1798 and following appeals to Britain, Nelson besieged Valletta in 1799, driving out the French. The 1814 Treaty of Paris cited Malta a British crown colony. It became an important naval base and suffered severe damage during WWII. George VI awarded the island the George Cross in 1942. In 1961 the island became internally self–governing and gained independence in 1964. Malta became a republic within the Commonwealth in 1974 with Valletta its capital. In 1979 Malta declined to renew its agreement to allow the naval forces of NATO and Britain to maintain bases in Valletta's harbours.

Modern City

Although there is little industry in Valletta its freeport is a large transit centre for Mediterranean shipping. Shipbuilding and repair are also important. Exports include clothing, textiles, machinery and food. Tourism is a major source of income. Malta International Airport is at Luqa, about 5 km southwest of Valletta with Air Malta the national carrier. In summer there is a ferry service between Malta, Sicily, and Genoa, Italy. The University of Malta was founded by Pope Clement VIII in 1592 and the National Malta Library was built in the late eighteenth century. The Manoel Theatre dates from 1731. The Carnival, a week long festival, takes place every year in Feb. Predominantly Roman Catholic, Holy Week brings a number of celebrations including the Good Friday pageant.

Places of Interest

The interior of St John's Cathedral, a baroque masterpiece, has carved stone walls and painted vaulted ceilings. It has two paintings by the Italian master, Caravaggio, and houses the remains of many European noblemen including the tomb of Jean Parisot de Valette. The Upper Barrakka Gardens offer fine views of the Grand Harbour and the Cottonera. The Auberge de Castille, once the palace of the Spanish and Portuguese, is now the office of the prime minister and is not open to the public. The Palace of the Grand Masters, the seat of the president and parliament, has tapestries and frescoes depicting the Great Siege.

Valletta was one of two European Capitals of Culture for 2018, alongside Leeuwarden in the Netherlands. The title attracts large European Union grants.

Valparaíso, Chile

Introduction

Situated on the pacific coast in central Chile, Valparaíso is the country's second largest city, its principal port and the capital of the Valparaíso province. Located in a wide bay naturally protected to the south, Vaparaíso is surrounded by 45 hills and cliffs. The city is susceptible to earthquakes, the most destructive occurring in 1906. Valparaíso merges with the resort city of Viña del Mar.

History

The area that is now Valparaíso was originally inhabited by the Changos, who were farmers and fishermen. In 1536 the *Santiaguillo*, captained by Juan de Saavedra and carrying provisions from Peru, anchored in the bay. In 1544 the settlement of Valparaíso was founded by the Conquistador, Pedro de Valdivia. Over the next two centuries the settlement remained small. It was not until 1791 that a *cabildo* (town council) was established. In 1802, Valparaíso was officially named a city but at the turn of the nineteenth century Valparaíso still had only 5,000 inhabitants.

After Chile's independence from Spanish rule in 1818, Valparaíso flourished. The British were among the main traders, and a large British community was established in the business district and in the Cerro Alegre and Cerro Concepción areas. During the Californian gold rush, trade with America flourished as Chilean wheat was exported from Valparaíso. In 1866 a Spanish naval fleet attacked Valparaíso, causing extensive structural damage. Nonetheless, by 1880 the population had expanded 20-fold. Valparaíso was also becoming the centre for Chile's banking industry.

In 1906 a major earthquake devastated Valparaíso, killing 4,000 people. From 1910 the city was the terminus for the trans-Andean railway, connecting the Pacific coast to Mendoza in Argentina (passenger traffic to Argentina ceased in 1979). The city suffered further with the opening of the Panama Canal in 1914. When merchant ships no longer had to go round Cape Horn, trade declined. Population growth in the second half of the twentieth century slowed. In contrast, the population of the affluent coastal resort of Viña del Mar increased, until the two cities merged into one conurbation. In 1990 the reopened National Congress was established in Valparaíso.

Modern City

Valparaíso is the traditional centre for the navy and for other Chilean maritime activity. Most of Chile's imports arrive here. An important industrial centre, principal industries include ship repairing, textiles, chemicals and the manufacture of vegetable oils. Valparaíso has been home to the National Congress since 1990. Universities include the Universidad de Valparaíso, founded in 1911, and the Universidad Católica de Valparaíso, established in 1928. The towering hill tops are connected to the city centre by 15 *acensores*, or funicular trains, built between 1883–1916. There is also an *acensor artilleria*, or cable car as well as many narrow, windy paths. Valparaíso is connected to domestic cities via the Aeropuerto de Torquemada. Valparaíso has a summertime festival celebrating national dance traditions, the Festival de la Cueca y Tonada Inédita.

Places of Interest

The traditional centre of Valparaíso is the Plaza Sotomayor. The Monumento a Los Héroes de Inquique is a mausoleum dedicated to naval heroes from the War of the Pacific (1879–84), including Arturo Prat who gave his name to the redeveloped port area, Muelle Prat. An extravagant post-modernist building was erected in 1991 to house the National Assembly. The Isla Negra, on a cliff between Valparaíso and the small town of Cartegena, was home to the Nobel prize winning poet Pablo Neruda and is now a museum. The house of another Chilean Nobel prize winning poet, and native *Porteña*, Gabriela Mistral, has also been turned into a museum. Other museums include the Museo Municipal de Bellas Artes housed in the Art Nouveau Palacio Baburizza. Built in 1916 by Arnaldo Barison y Renato Schiavon, the museum displays a collection of Chilean paintings and works of international artists from the nineteenth and twentieth centuries. 20 murals painted by renowned Chilean artists are displayed on old buildings in the Cerro Bellavista district. Based on the site of an original 1559 chapel, the Iglesia Matriz was constructed in 1842.

Vancouver, Canada

Introduction

Famed for its magnificent waterfront, Vancouver is located just to the North of the US border in the South West of British Columbia, between the Burrard Inlet and the Fraser River delta.

The city is the industrial, commercial and financial heart of British Columbia, connected to the United States and the rest of Canada by four railways and an international airport.

History

The city originated in the 1870s as a sawmilling settlement originally called Granville. It was incorporated as a city after becoming the terminus for the Canadian Pacific Railroad in 1886. Built to entice British Columbia to join newly independent Canada, the railway opened the way for Vancouver to become the country's eastern gateway. At the same time, the city was renamed in honour of Royal Navy Captain George Vancouver, who navigated the coast in 1792.

The prominence of the city's port was consolidated in 1891 when the 'Empress of India' became the first ocean liner to arrive in Vancouver from the Orient. The opening of the Panama Canal in 1915 made the export of grain and lumber from Vancouver to the American East coast and Europe economically feasible.

Vancouver was Canada's third largest city by the middle of the twentieth century.

Modern City

In recent years Vancouver has made much of its claim to be 'the gateway to the Far East'. This has led to large-scale immigration particularly from Hong Kong, Vietnam and Japan and has helped to create the city's bustling Chinatown.

Vancouver is the fastest growing city in Canada. Its population increased by 17% between 1987 and 1992, with a further 50% increase predicted for the next decade.

Vancouver is North America's third largest film and TV production centre after Los Angeles and New York. The city hosted the 2010 Winter Olympics.

Places of Interest

Vancouver's museums include the Maritime Museum, the Museum of Anthropology, the Vancouver Museum and a planetarium. A conservatory and botanical garden are in Queen Elizabeth Park, the city's highest point, while the 400 ha Stanley Park houses an aquarium with whales, dolphins and piranhas.

Venice, Italy

Introduction

Venice is the capital of the province of Venezia and the region of Veneto in northern Italy. It is one of the world's oldest and most popular tourist destinations and was the greatest seaport in Medieval Europe. The city is situated on the 118 islands of the Venetian Lagoon and is criss-crossed by more than 150 canals and 400 bridges.

History

The settlement was established in the fifth and sixth centuries after barbarian invasions from the north drove the inhabitants of the surrounding countryside onto the islands of the lagoon.

In 466 a council of 12 townships was elected to give the refugee settlements a semblance of order. By 726 the first Doge, Orso, was elected to rule over the lagoon townships. This election was an act of defiance towards the Byzantine empire which threatened to capture the region. Independence was asserted more clearly in 828 when the several citizens of the lagoon stole the remnants of St Mark from Alexandria. To house these relics, work began on the Basilica di San Marco.

The city grew as a significant trading port and began to eclipse the Byzantine Empire in importance. The Crusades at the end of the eleventh century allowed the Venetians to gain control of trade routes across the Mediterranean. The Venetian trading empire expanded across the Aegean islands, Peleponesia, Crete and part of Constantinople and Venice also controlled many coastal forts on the Greek mainland.

The expansion of Venetian trade and the aggressive tactics displayed by the city's traders encroached upon the trade of the Byzantine Empire and the emperor encouraged traders from Pisa and Genoa to compete. During the ensuing centuries Venice vied with Genoa for maritime supremacy. In 1380 the Venetians defeated the Genoans and subsequently turned their attention towards the mainland. They captured and colonized Veneto and much of Lombardia and Emilia-Romagna.

In the fifteenth century the Ottoman empire's expansion coupled with Venice's involvement in costly wars with other Italian city-states did much to harm the city's ports of trade. Within a century the Venetian Republic had lost all its ports in the Mediterranean, and had embarked upon a lengthy decline in power and prosperity.

The end of the Venetian republic came in 1797 when Napoléon handed Venice to the Austrians. The last doge was deposed in May that year. Venice became a part of Napoléon's Italian Kingdom in 1805. After his defeat Venice reverted once more to Austrian rule and was eventually incorporated into the unified kingdom of Italy in 1866.

Since this time there has been a constant struggle between those who want to modernize the city and those who wish to protect its treasures. In the postwar era the problem has been compounded by environmental factors, most notably those of flooding, subsidence and pollution. Since the severe floods of Nov. 1966 there have been genuine fears that the city could be lost forever, and several international initiatives have been launched to rescue Venice from the damaging effects of the environment.

Modern City

Aeroporto di Venezia Marco Polo is 10 km from Venice and 25 km from Treviso. The Stazione Santa Lucia is located alongside the Canal Grande in Cannaregio and is directly linked with Padova, Verona, Trieste and Bologna. The Venice Simplon-Orient Express travels across Europe to and from major city destinations such as London, Paris Florence, Rome and Prague.

The A4 connects the city to the west and east of the country, the A13 runs to Padova, the A4 approaches Venice from the south and the A27 comes from the north.

Vaporetti are Venice's answer to buses. Vaporetto 1 makes the journey from Piazzale Roma, up the Canal Grande to San Marco and then on to the Lido. Water Taxis are expensive but easily available. Gondolas are intrinsically and romantically linked with travel around Venice, but they are expensive.

Since the turn of the nineteenth century tourism has been of vital importance to the city's economy. Arthur Symons once remarked that 'A realist, in Venice would become a romantic, by mere faithfulness to what he saw before him' and this mythical, romantic aspect to the city has appealed to visitors from all over the world. The negative side of this profitable industry is that there is very little in the local economy that does not depend on tourists for revenue, and the city has dwindled in population for decades.

Other industries include glassworking, lacemaking, textiles and the manufacture of furniture.

Places of Interest

Piazza San Marco has been the focal point of Venetian administration for over a millennium. Basilica di San Marco, which dominates the eastern side of the Piazza, is the cathedral church of the city. It was commissioned by Doge Domenico Contarini in the eleventh century. The original basilica dates back to the ninth century.

The Palazzo Ducale was the residence of the Doges until the fall of the Venetian Republic in 1797. This Venetian-gothic palace houses paintings by artists such as Tintoretto and Paolo Veronese.

The Bell Tower of St. Mark is known as 'El paron de casa' (the lord of the house) and this massive structure dominates Piazza San Marco.

The Bridge of Sighs, which spans the Rio di Palazzo, was built in about 1600 by Antonio Contino. It is said that prisoners, crossing the bridge from the Palazzo Ducale on their way to the prison on the other side, would sigh at their last sight of the lagoon.

Titian's *Assumption* hangs above the altar in the church Santa Maria Gloriosa dei Frari where he is buried. Other works on show include the *Madonna di Ca' Pesaro* and a statue of *John the Baptist* by Donatello.

The baroque Santa Maria della Salute stands at the point where the Grand Canal opens into the San Marco Basin. Its construction was begun in the 1631 by Baldassare Longhena in honour of the Virgin Mary. The Festa della Salute takes place every year on 21 Nov. City workers lay a pontoon bridge over the Grand Canal from the San Marco district to the church. Venetians parade to pay tribute to the continued health of the city and the Virgin Mary.

The Gallerie dell'Accademia is the biggest Venetian museum and is housed in the former church of Santa Maria della Carità. Its collection contains works by Giovanni Bellini, Tintoretto, Paolo Veneziano, Titian and Paulo Veronese.

The extensive Peggy Guggenheim modern art Collection was bequeathed to the city in 1979 and includes works by Picasso, Kandinsky, Chagall, Klee, Mirò and Dali.

The Correr Museum is housed in the Palazzo Pesaro. It is a civic museum and houses many important Venetian exhibits.

The Libreria Sansoviniani is located at the west side of the Piazzetta di San Marco. It was designed by Jacopo Sansovino and built in the sixteenth century. Inside the Libreria Sansoviniani are the Libreria Marciana and the city's archaeological museum.

Victoria, Canada

Introduction

The capital of British Columbia, Victoria is located on the southeastern tip of Vancouver Island, overlooking the Juan de Fuca Strait. Renowned as a seaside city, Victoria's is known as 'the City of Gardens' for its proliferation of public spaces.

History

The site of the city was originally inhabited by Salish natives with the present city founded in 1843 as Fort Camosun, a fur-trading outpost for the Hudson Bay Company. It was later renamed Fort Victoria.

Native peoples from across the island, attracted by the trading opportunities, settled near the Fort and were soon joined by British pioneers.

The Imperial Government of the Crown Colony of Vancouver Island was established in 1849 and on March 11, 1850, Richard Blanshard assumed office as Governor of the Colony of Vancouver Island. British residents and a complement of sailors from HMS Driver were assembled in front of the fort to hear the newly-arrived Governor read the Royal Commission, appointing him the first Governor of the first Crown Colony to be established in British territory west of the Great Lakes.

In 1859 government buildings were constructed at James Bay, South Fort, and christened 'The Birdcages'. In continuous use for almost 40 years they were replaced in the 1890s by the present Parliament Buildings, completed late in 1897.

The city benefited from an influx of settlers after the goldrush of the 1860s, and has since developed into a major Pacific Rim port and naval dockyard. But, the city failed to develop as a major industrial centre after Vancouver took on the role of Canada's western rail terminus. Today, employment is dominated by the civil service, retirement services and the tourist trade.

The city maintains a distinctly British feel having been capital of the Vancouver Island colony since 1848 before becoming the administrative centre of British Columbia in 1868. Kipling spoke of the waterfront as 'Brighton Pavilion with the Himalayas for a backdrop'. Victoria has more British-born residents than anywhere else in Canada.

Modern City

Victoria is the local government administrative centre and is also a popular tourist resort. Its educational institutions include the Victoria University, founded in 1963. It is connected to mainland Canada and the US by ferry and air, and by rail and road to the rest of Vancouver Island.

Places of Interest

Notable sights include the British Columbia Provincial Museum, the Victorian Parliament Buildings (seat of the provincial legislative assembly) and the Empress Hotel, built in 1908 by the Canadian Pacific Railway.

Victoria, Seychelles

Introduction

The capital city of the Seychelles, Victoria is on Mahé island where much of the population reside. A small capital, it is the country's major port and only town.

History

Although previously inhabited by the indigenous population, Victoria was founded in 1772 by French colonists 2 years after they first settled the Seychelles. Spice plantations were developed to rival the Dutch monopoly in the Indian Ocean, and Victoria's port was developed to accommodate this trade. When the British took the Seychelles from the French at the end of the eighteenth century, Victoria came under British control. To commemorate the Seychelles becoming an independent crown colony in 1903, a replica of London's Vauxhall Bridge clock tower was built in the centre of Victoria. In 1971 the islands' tourist industry received a boost when the British financed the building of an international airport near Victoria.

Modern City

Victoria is the seat of the government and administrative bodies and a business and cultural centre. The Seychelles' leading port, the deep water harbour can accommodate several freights. The town's main exports include coconut oil and fish. International flights travel to Victoria several times a week while other settlements on Mahé Island can be accessed by road. An International Conferences Centre was opened in 1994.

Places of Interest

The town centre retains much of its colonial aspect, although recent developments have modernized much of the town. Religious buildings include a Cathedral, a Hindu temple, a mosque and the colonial Capuchin Friary. The century old Botanical Gardens contain the native coco de mer palm trees and an orchid garden, while the Jardin du Roi gardens has a collection of tropical plants, fruits and spices. The three intertwined wings of the Traw Zwazo (three birds) sculpture symbolize the inhabitants' Asian, African and European origins. Museums include the Natural History Museum which displays the skeleton of the extinct native crocodile and shells of the giant tortoise. The National Museum has a display on the history of spice cultivation while the Seychelles People's United Party Museum provides information on the country's political history.

Vienna (Wien), Austria

Introduction

Austria's capital lies on the Danube in the northeast of the country. For centuries its geographical position at the heart of Europe ensured its importance as an imperial centre and a political powerhouse. Today it remains a major centre and is home to numerous important international organizations.

History

There is evidence of Paleolithic inhabitation in the area and Illyrians and Celts were also present on the site of the city before the Romans took control of what was then known as Vindobona. The Romans were ousted by Bavarians during the fifth century, who in turn gave way to the Frankish Babenbergs during the twelfth century. It was during this period that the town took advantage of its location on the route of the crusaders and began to prosper as a trading post.

However, Vienna's greatest period was to be under the rule of the Habsburgs, who took the city in 1278. Habsburg influence, extending into the early part of the twentieth century, saw varying fortunes. Hungarian and Turkish not to mention imperial squabbles, religious upheaval and economic upheaval had to be contended with. During the sixteenth century Emperor Ferdinand I enforced a strict and oppressive regime in a bid to stamp out insurrection. Reformation fervour deprived Vienna of most of its Protestant population.

Habsburg Vienna established itself as a centre for thinkers and artists. The opening decades of the eighteenth century saw much growth, with the Baroque influence of the father and son architects Fischer von Erlach predominating. Maria Theresa's reign brought some stability to the city after the disruption of the Austrian Wars of Succession. She instigated a number of reforms that paved the way for the enlightened despotism of her humanist son Joseph II. He provided for freedom of religion, put in place economic and educational reforms and was renowned as one of the greatest artistic patrons. By the end of his reign, Vienna's economy was based on manufacturing rather than trade and the population had swelled massively.

Napoléon held Vienna twice during the first decade of the nineteenth century and all but bankrupted the city. However, the city continued to grow and the economy boomed during the 1860s. The Ringstrasse, the city's ringroad on which are located some of Vienna's finest buildings, opened in 1865, new parks were created and power and water supplies were greatly improved. But Habsburg rule was coming to an end and in 1918, in the aftermath of World War I, a new German-Austrian republic was born.

By the 1930s, the new regime was in serious trouble. As political militancy increased, Chancellor Engelbert Dollfuss decided autocratic rule was needed and dispensed with parliament. The scene was set for Adolf Hitler, German chancellor and former Austrian citizen, to declare the Anschluss, annexing Austria in direct contravention of the terms of the Treaty of Versailles. The city's Jewish population either escaped abroad or perished at the hands of the Nazis.

Following defeat in World War II, the badly damaged Vienna was split into zones of occupation, with the Soviets, the US, the British and French each having their own spheres of influence. Much of the city was redeveloped in the late 1940s, 50s and 60s and in 1955 the Allied Occupation ended. Under the Austrian State Treaty, Vienna was now capital of a neutral country.

Modern City

The economy is reliant on commerce, banking, industry and civil administration. Tourism is also important. Among the most important manufactures are machinery, chemicals and metal goods. Major international organizations resident in the city include the International Atomic Energy Agency, the United Nations Industrial Development Organization, and the Organization of Petroleum Exporting Countries.

Vienna has two major railway stations, South and West. There is an international airport, Schwechat, road links with other major Austrian cities, and river and canal links to the Balkans and Romania. Public transport in the city includes trams and an underground.

Places of Interest

Vienna has always been a popular destination for travellers, not least because of its cultural heritage. Musical giants including the Strauss family, Mozart, Beethoven, Verdi, Wagner, Mahler and Schönberg all have strong links to Vienna, as do the artists Egon Schielle, Oskar Kokoschka and Gustav Klimt and the writers Arthur Schnitzler and Karl Kraus. Freud developed many of his psychoanalytic ideas while resident here. There are numerous fine theatres and the grand Staatsoper (State Opera) has a worldwide reputation. Other tourist attractions include the Vienna Boys' Choir, the Spanish Riding School, St Stephen's Cathedral, the Imperial Hofburg Palace, the Schönbrum Summer Palace, St Stephen's Cathedral, Prater (a public park dominated by the big wheel that featured in *The Third Man*) and Kunst Haus Wien, an extraordinary house that pays tribute to the exotic architecture of Friedensreich Hundertwasser.

Vientiane (Vieng Chan), Laos

Introduction

The administrative Capital of the Lao People's Democratic, Vientiane is the only city of any size in Laos but with barely half a million inhabitants it is the second smallest capital city in Asia, next to Bandar Seri Begawan.

Vientiane is situated on a plain on a bend in the Mekong River, 217-km southeast of Luang Phrabang, the former Royal Capital of Laos.

The city is noted for its canals, houses built on stilts, and many pagodas.

History

Although founded in the thirteenth century Vientiane came to prominence in the seventeenth century as the capital of a kingdom of the same name. In 1609 Lang Xang fell prey to rival contenders for the throne. The ensuing struggles split the country into three rival kingdoms, Vientiane, Laouangphrabang (now Luang Phrabang), and Champasak.

Conflict with the neighbouring Burmese and Siamese involved Vientiane and Laouangphrabang in internecine struggles. Weakened, Vientiane became a vassal state of Siam in 1778. Vientiane's destruction came when the Siamese punished the Lao for insurgencies in 1827. Vientiane lay ruined and wholly forgotten for four decades until, in 1867, a French expedition led by Ernest Doudart de Lagrée and Francis Garnier stumbled across the ruins of the city. From 1899–1953, with the exception of the Japanese occupation of Indo-China in 1945 Vientiane was the seat of the French Governor and the French administrative capital.

Modern City

The City's central river port location in a country that relies heavily on river transportation and its position in an intensively rice-cultivated hinterland ensured that Vientiane was to become the major economic centre in Laos. Modern Vientiane is a relaxed and clean city. The city is home to Mahavithagnalay Heang Xath Lao, the National University of Laos.

Places of Interest

The most important national monument in Laos, Pha That Luang [Great Sacred Stupa] is situated atop a hill in Vientiane. This monument dates from 1599. It was built on the site of a much older That erected in the third century, allegedly to house a breastbone of the Bhudda.

Wat Si Saket, the oldest monastery in Vientiane, was built in 1824 by King Anouvong. A wall surrounding the main temple contains 10,000 representations of the Buddha. It is said that there are 10,000 Buddhas.

The morning market, which opens from 6 a.m. to 6 p.m. trades in a wide variety of goods from Laos including silk and cotton weavings.

Vila, Vanuatu

Introduction

Vila (also known as Port Vila), on Mele Bay on the southwest coast of the island of Éfaté, is capital of Vanuatu and a thriving port.

History

Run jointly by the French and English in the early part of the twentieth century, the US used Vila as a military base during World War II when they developed Havannah Harbour.

Modern City

Vila's population comprises Vanuatuans, Vietnamese, French and British. Vanuatu's administrative and cultural centre, the local economy relies on port and related industries, tourism and food processing. It exports locally produced sandalwood, coffee and copra. Bauerfield international airport is just outside the centre. Kumul Highway is the main road.

Places of Interest

Leading attractions include a cultural centre, the Constitution Building, a fish market and a covered market. There is a French Quarter and a Chinese Quarter. The Anabrou cemetery has ornately decorated Chinese and Vietnamese graves. Independence Park is where Anglo-French joint rule was announced. Nearby is one of the city's leading landmarks, the Post Office building.

Vilnius, Lithuania

Introduction

In the east of the country, surrounded by hills, the Lithuanian capital Vilnius lies 250 km from the Baltic Sea on the confluence of the Neris and Vilnia Rivers. Variously under Polish, Russian and German occupation, Vilnius became the capital of independent Lithuania in 1991.

History

Archaeological evidence suggests the area now Vilnius has been inhabited for three millennia (with a castle dating from the fifth century), although the official founding dates from the city's first mention in a 1323 missal written by Grand Duke Gediminas. The duke built a city around two castles, with fortifications to ward off forays by Teutonic and Livonian Knights. Soon, Vilnius replaced Kernave as Lithuania's capital. Over the next two centuries, Vilnius expanded and prospered becoming an important trade centre. The growth in industry led to a flurry of building, and Vilnius became one of the largest European cities. A city wall was constructed to defend against Tatar invasions.

In 1569 Lithuania merged with Poland. The city declined in stature but did become a centre of Lithuanian, Polish and, especially Jewish culture. In the seventeenth century Vilnius, along with Poland, embarked on a golden age.

In 1795, with the third partition of Poland, Vilnius was swallowed into the Russian empire. Polonized Lithuanian and Polish aristocrats took refuge in the city, contributing to a Polish national revival with the first newspapers appearing in the language. As an annexed region, Lithuanian nationalism grew over the nineteenth century. In 1812 Vilnius suffered heavy damage by Napoléon's troops, although the French were expelled less than a year later. This was followed by two uprisings against the Tsarist regime in 1831 and 1863. The failed insurrections resulted in the execution of revolutionary leaders. The rise of industrialization in the nineteenth century was aided by the arrival in 1860 of rail links to Warsaw and St Petersburg.

For much of the twentieth century Vilnius remained under occupation by German, Russian or Polish forces. Despite regaining independence in 1918,

2 years later it came under Polish control. After a brief spell under Soviet forces, in 1941 Vilnius was taken by Nazi troops before they were expelled by the Russian army 3 years later. During this time, 90% of Vilnius' large Jewish population was decimated. After World War II, the Russians deported much of the remaining Polish population as the city was made the capital of the Lithuanian Socialist Soviet Republic. Also deported were many ethnic Lithuanians who were replaced by Russian migrants. At the time of the Soviet Union's collapse, Vilnius had a difficult transition to independence. In 1991 demonstrators in the capital were brutally suppressed by Soviet troops with 12 people killed. Nonetheless, in the same year, Vilnius became the capital of independent Lithuania.

Modern City

Industries include electronics, metallurgy, textiles, and machinery and chemical production. Vilnius university was founded by Polish Jesuits in 1579. 10 km south of the city, an international airport serves many European cities, while Vilnius is linked by road and rail to Riga and Tallinn. Vilnius was one of two European Capitals of Culture for 2009.

Places of Interest

Tourist sights in Vilnius include Gedimino Tower on Gediminas Hill, which offers the best view of the city. Vilnius' fourteenth century cathedral features the seventeenth century Baroque chapel of St Casimir, named after Lithuania's patron saint. The Old Town is the site of the president's palace and the Gothic St Anne's church, the latter much admired by Napoléon. Lithuania's main Russian Orthodox church, the seventeenth century Church of the Holy Spirit, holds the preserved bodies of three fourteenth century martyrs.

Briefly Lithuania's capital in medieval times, Trakai is around 30 km west of Vilnius. A peninsula on three lakes, the national park, castle ruins and villages full of ancient wooden cottages make it a popular day trip. It is home to one of Lithuania's smallest ethnic communities, the Karaites. There is also an ethnography museum.

Vladivostok, Russia

Introduction

An important seaport and administrative centre of the Primorsky region, Vladivostok is in southeastern Russia, on the Pacific Ocean. For much of the twentieth century it was the home of the Pacific Fleet.

History

Vladivostok was founded in 1860 as a Russian military outpost, the name meaning 'Rule the East'. In 1872 the main Russian naval base on the Pacific was transferred to Vladivostok, prompting rapid expansion. Growth was further boosted when the Chinese Eastern Railway provided an improved rail connection to the rest of the Empire at the beginning of the twentieth century.

Vladivostok was a vital Pacific entry port for military supplies from the US during World War I. Following the 1917 Russian Revolution, Vladivostok was occupied by foreign troops until 1922.

The Pacific Fleet continued to be based in Vladivostok and was expanded after World War II. Considered to be militarily sensitive, Vladivostok was a closed city from the 1950s until 1990. Following the collapse of the Soviet regime it re-established itself as a commercial port, with imports from around the world but notably from the Far East.

Modern City

In addition to its port and related industries, other important industries include engineering, chemicals, fisheries and food processing. There is an airport and the city marks the eastern extremity of the Trans-Siberian Railway.

There are several academic institutions including the Far Eastern Scientific Centre and the Far Eastern State University.

Places of Interest

The city has several theatres and orchestras. There is a museum devoted to the Pacific Fleet and another to local history.

Warsaw (Warszawa), Poland

Introduction

Warsaw, on the River Vistula, is the capital of Poland. It has been destroyed and re-built many times in its 700 year history, when it has been ruled by Swede, Prussian, French, German and Russian overlords. The population was decimated during World War II and the city underwent massive reconstruction in the communist and post-communist eras.

History

There is evidence of human habitation in the area surrounding Warsaw from the tenth century. In the 1370s the Mazovian dukes built a fortress on the site and in 1413 it became the seat of the dukedom. The last duke died in 1526 and the city fell under the jurisdiction of the Polish king, who resided in Kraków.

The Polish parliament moved to Warsaw in 1569 and in 1573 it was designated the seat of royal elections. It achieved city status in 1596 when Kraków was devastated by fire. A period or rapid commercial and cultural expansion ensued although it fell back during the Swedish occupations of 1655–56 and 1702 and the Russian occupations of 1792 and 1794.

Following the partition of Poland, Warsaw came under Prussian rule in 1795. As a provincial outpost, Warsaw's status deteriorated. Taken by Napoléon in 1806, the city was named capital of the grand duchy of Warsaw in 1807. Five years later Warsaw hosted a diet that re-established Poland. In 1813 the city fell once more under Russian control. Two years later it was designated capital of the Kingdom of Poland, which in practice was subordinate to Russia.

At the end of World War I Warsaw became capital of the newly established Second Polish Republic. In 1939 Poland was invaded by German forces and Warsaw suffered a reign of terror for the duration of World War II. 500,000 Jews were forced to live in a walled ghetto. A failed uprising in 1942 resulted in a liquidation of the ghetto, with hundreds of thousands sent to concentration and death camps. After Resistance forces fought with the Germans for 2 months in 1944, virtually the whole of the urban population was deported and 85% of the city destroyed. By the time of Warsaw's liberation in Jan. 1945, the Jewish population numbered 200.

Under Soviet control after the war, the city was re-built. Many of its oldest buildings were re-constructed but other areas were filled with brutalist architecture. In 1955 the monumental Palace of Culture was built. After the overthrow of communism in 1989 Warsaw was confirmed as the capital of the Polish Republic.

Modern City

Warsaw-Okecie International Airport is 10 km from the city centre, with a domestic airport adjacent to it. The city is on a major rail network and lies on the Moscow–Berlin and Gdańsk–Ostrava routes. Public transport within the city includes buses, trams and metros.

Until World War II Warsaw had been religiously and ethnically diverse but now the vast majority of the population are Roman Catholic Poles. Leading industries include metalwork, mechanical engineering, vehicle manufacturing, textiles, food processing and medical supplies. The city is also an important trade centre for the surrounding agricultural region.

Places of Interest

Warsaw is home to a university and the Polish Academy of Sciences. Stare Miasto (the Old Town) originated in the thirteenth century and includes the Rynek Starego Miasta (Old Town Square), St John's Cathedral and remnants of the old fortifications. Nowe Miasto (the New Town) dates back to the fourteenth century and incorporates the royal palace (rebuilt in the 1970s) and the Royal Route which extends south to the Baroque palace and grounds of Wilanow.

Other popular attractions include the Palace of Culture and Lazienki Park, complete with the Chopin Monument which hosts the annual Chopin festival. Chopin's heart is kept in the Church of the Holy Cross, while the Carmelite Church is close to the monument to Adam Mickiewich. The National Philharmonic is resident and the National Museum houses the country's most important art collection. The Jewish Ghetto incorporates several monuments to those who suffered during World War II as well as the Jewish Historical Institute Gallery (on the grounds of the old Great Synagogue).

Washington, D.C., United States of America

Introduction

The capital of the United States and its seat of national government, Washington, D.C. is located at the head of the Potomac River on the East Coast of the United States. The city occupies an area of 68 sq. miles (177 km^2), although the Washington Standard Metropolitan Statistical Area (WSMSA), which also contains counties in the surrounding states of Maryland and Virginia, covers a far larger area.

History

Originally an area of marshland, early settlements came after English adventurer Captain John Smith's exploration in 1608. After the end of the American War of Independence in 1783 and the inauguration of George Washington as President in 1789, Secretary of State Thomas Jefferson and Secretary of the Treasury Alexander Hamilton agreed, in a compromise deal, that the national capital would be located on the East Coast. President Washington chose the location personally by carving a diamond of territory from the states of Virginia and Maryland. This set in motion the establishment of a permanent seat of government for the new nation, which was named Washington, D.C. (District of Columbia) in honour of the first President and in reference to 'Columbia', a poetic name for the US at the time.

Maverick French army engineer Pierre Charles L'Enfant was entrusted with the task of designing the city under the supervision of three presidentially appointed commissioners. In 1792 L'Enfant was dismissed after a series of bitter disputes with the commissioners and local landlords. However, his basic vision of a grid-patterned city with the President's mansion on a hilltop, as well as a generous endowment of parks, squares and circles, was ultimately achieved after decades of mismanagement and chaos.

Construction of the city began in 1793 yet it wasn't until 1800 that Congress transferred to Washington from their temporary home of Philadelphia and President John Adams took up residence in the White House, which was still not completed. Some measure of local government was established in 1802, including a mayor and an elected council. In 1814 British forces attacked the city, setting fire to several public buildings, including the White House, and forcing President James Madison to take temporary residence in the Octagon.

At this stage in its history, the city lacked any significant public amenities. Its evolution was hampered by the fact that the District of Colombia had been made a politically neutral state whose residents did not have the right to vote in presidential or congressional elections. Congress therefore took little interest in the city other than to lobby for the national capital to be moved to a more westerly location. In 1846 the section of the District of Colombia to the southwest of the Potomac was ceded back to Virginia, reducing the size of the District to approximately 69 sq. miles (179 km^2).

After the end of the American Civil War and the assassination of President Abraham Lincoln, a new structure of city administration was established by Congress in 1871. Under the aegis of administrator Alexander 'Boss' Shepherd an ambitious public works programme began to bring the city's urban infrastructure up to scratch. Proper sewage systems, street lighting and pavements were finally installed.

America's participation in World War I and President Franklin D. Roosevelt's introduction of the New Deal both served to swell the city's population as employment opportunities rapidly increased. The ethnic mix of the city was transformed during the 1950s when large-scale migration from the southern states saw the black population of the city increase from 35% to 54%. In 1954 Washington, D.C. became the first American city to introduce racial integration within schools and in 1964 its residents were, for the first time since 1800, permitted to vote in presidential elections.

On 11 Sept. 2001, along with New York City, Washington was the target of a major terrorist attack when hijacked American Airlines Flight 77 crashed into the Pentagon killing nearly 200 people on the ground and all 64 on board the plane.

Modern City

The main source of employment is government service, although real estate, communications, insurance and tourist industries are also essential to the city's prosperity. However two-thirds of Washington's workforce live outside the District of Columbia.

Despite its status as the seat of national government, the larger metropolitan city suffers from complex social, economic and political problems. In 1968 the assassination of civil rights leader Martin Luther King Jr. led to violent riots in several areas of the city. The majority of the residents in the city itself are black, and unemployment levels are higher than the national average.

Washington is served by three major airports, Dulles International, Baltimore-Washington International Thurgood Marshall Airport and Ronald Reagan Washington National Airport. There are major rail links with New York, Philadelphia and Boston. The city also has a Metro Subway and two commuter rail networks which stretch from the major monuments in the city centre to outlying residential areas.

Places of Interest

Washington is sometimes dubbed 'Paris on the Potomac', and is said to be the most 'European' of all American cities, a reputation that has helped to change the city's previously staid image as the seat of American officialdom and bureaucracy. The capital city is home to many of the nation's most important monuments, artefacts and museums. The Supreme Court and the Library of Congress are located on Capitol Hill, which is almost directly in the centre of the city.

The National Mall, which runs for 2 miles (3.2 km) from the Capitol (the seat of the Senate and the House of Representatives) to the Potomac River, includes the White House, the President's official residence, and monuments to Presidents Washington, Jefferson, Lincoln and Franklin D. Roosevelt. Also located on the Mall, under the auspices of the Smithsonian Institution, are the National Air and Space Museum, the National Museum of Natural History, the National Museum of American History, the National Museum of American Art and the National Zoo among other attractions. The new National Museum of African American History and Culture, which was opened in Sept. 2016, and the United States Holocaust Memorial Museum, are also housed on the National Mall.

The National Archives are on the north side of the Mall while the headquarters of the Federal Bureau of Investigations (FBI) are on Pennsylvania Avenue and Ford's Theatre, where Abraham Lincoln was assassinated by John Wilkes Booth, is located on Tenth St. Arlington National Cemetery, which includes the grave of John F. Kennedy and the Tomb of the Unknown Soldier, is located across the Potomac River outside of the metropolitan city.

Wellington, New Zealand

Introduction

Located on the southern tip of North Island, New Zealand's capital is between the Cook Strait and the Tararua foothills. The city, some 2 km in diameter, surrounds Port Nicholson, a deep water harbour, and Mount Victoria (196 m). It enjoys a temperate climate with mild, but often extremely windy, winters. In 2000, the city accounted for 38% of the population, and 57% of the region's GDP. The other centres in the region (with population and GDP percentages) are the Kapiti Coast District (10%; 5%) Lower Hutt (23%; 21%), Porirua (11%; 6%), Upper Hutt (9%; 5%), and Wairarapa (9%; 6%).

History

Maori people have lived in Wellington since around AD 900, when the peninsula was discovered by Kupe, a Polynesian explorer. It was first named Te Upoko o te Ika a Maui, the head of the fish (North Island) pulled to the ocean surface by the legendary Maui. The first tribe arrived some 200 years later, led by Tara, a second-generation Polynesian migrant. Tara found Wellington to be an ideal location for a new settlement: it was, he said, 'at the very nostrils of the island'. The area was renamed Te Whanganui-a-Tara, the Great Harbour of Tara.

European settlers from the New Zealand Company sailed into the Great Harbour on 20 Sept. 1839. When their first choice of settlement at the mouth of the River Hutt, slightly north of present day Wellington, was found to be unsuitable, a harbour on the west shore was selected. The settlement was named Wellington in 1840, in honour of Britain's Arthur Wellesley (1769–1852), the first Duke of Wellington. Company directors and ships from the period have also been commemorated in street and place names across the region. An annual regional holiday, on 22 Jan., marks the arrival of 150 Company settlers in 1840.

Wellington became a borough in 1842, a municipality in 1853, and a city in 1886. It attained capital status on 26 July 1865, when the seat of government was transferred from Auckland. Today, parliament's executive wing is situated in the Beehive, a striking modernist building. The old Government Building of 1876 is one of the largest wooden structures in the world.

Modern City

Reclamation around Lambton Harbour took place from the 1850s to the 1970s. By 1900, the original shoreline had disappeared. A harbour development programme, together with the quayside Te Papa museum, has rejuvenated the waterfront. It is now a busy cargo port, handling some 7.5 m. tonnes p.a., and a centre for recreation and entertainment. The bay is popular with windsurfers, yachters, and jet skiers. The city's Courtenay and Lambton Quarters focus on entertainment and mainstream retail, and the Cuba and Willis Quarters contain lifestyle shops and cafés.

The city has the top average household income in the country. In the year to March 2000, Wellington's GDP was NZ$7,581 m. Whereas the other centres in the region are driven largely by agriculture, community services, and forestry, Wellington City's economy is strongly orientated towards financial and business services. Current growth areas are construction, mining, and professional, scientific and technical services. The regional Chamber of Commerce was inaugurated in 1856 and has 1,400 members. There are some 13,500 business units, and 1.4 m. sq. metres of central office space. In June 1996, around 5,800 people were registered unemployed.

Wellington is connected to the rest of North Island by road and rail, and by ferries to South Island. The Tranz Metro rail network, popular with commuters, serves the Wellington region. The regional council's bus and train contracts during 1994–5 were valued at NZ$22.4 m. The city's airport is both an international portal with daily flights to Los Angeles and London, and the hub of internal aviation services. Lambton Harbour imports mostly coal, minerals, motor vehicles, and petroleum products; it exports dairy products, fruit, hides, meats, newsprint, and wool.

In 1995, around 22,000 offences were reported, mostly involving theft or fraud. In the same year, there were 647 road accident casualties, including seven fatalities.

Victoria University has some 12,000 students. Other key institutions are Massey University, and the Wellington College of Education. Together, these three account for 9% of the country's tertiary students. 23% of Wellington's workforce possess a university qualification. However, in 1994, the percentage of Maori leaving secondary school with no qualifications was 48%; for Europeans the figure was 15%.

Places of Interest

The city is celebrated for its lively festival scene. Festivals, from comedy to jazz, take place almost every other month, culminating in the biennial International New Zealand Arts Festival. Other events include the Incredibly Strange Film Festival. The largest venues in Wellington are the WestpacTrust Stadium (capacity 34,500), the Queens Wharf Events Centre (capacity 5,050), the Michael Fowler Centre (capacity 2,500), and the Town Hall (capacity 2,000). The last two buildings comprise the Wellington Conference Centre, which contains 17 venues in all. Notable refurbished venues are the Opera House, and the Westpac Trust St. James Theatre. The Wellington Regional Aquatic Centre houses New Zealand's only Olympic size pool.

Notable historical sites include Old St. Paul's, a timber Gothic church built in 1866; the Katherine Mansfield Memorial, the house in which the writer was born in 1888; and Wallaceville Blockhouse, a wooden structure dating from 1860, later used as a police station. The cast iron Pencarrow lighthouse, the country's first, was shipped from England in 1859. It is located at the harbour entrance opposite Wellington. A Heritage Building Inventory lists nearly 500 properties of historical value.

Windhoek, Namibia

Introduction

Windhoek is in the centre of Namibia, about 650 km north of the Orange river. The city's high altitude means that its immediate environment is not as arid as the rest of the country, and the surrounding hills protect it from dry desert winds. Windhoek is the commercial, industrial and administrative hub of Namibia.

History

Prior to colonization the settlement was known as Aie Gams by its tribal inhabitants, the Khoikhoin and Herero people. This name refers to the hot springs that permeate the region. In the mid nineteenth century Afrikaners entered Namibia and their leader, Jonker Afrikaner, named the city after his home in the Cape colony. German farmers settled in the region in the 1890s and greatly reduced the native population. In 1908 diamonds were discovered nearby and an influx of prospectors boosted the town's population. In 1915 Boer forces under the command of Louis Botha occupied Windhoek. Under Boer rule the city became segregated, and compounds were built for black labourers. Namibia was later subject to the apartheid regime in South Africa. Indeed apartheid was enforced more rigidly in southwest Africa than in cities such as Cape Town. The country declared its independence in 1990, and life in Windhoek changed dramatically.

Modern City

German colonial buildings and modern office blocks dominate the city centre. The surrounding area is primarily for grazing sheep. Major roads and railways connect Windhoek to South Africa and the port of Walvis Bay. An international airport also serves the city. The economy is tied to the fur trade and livestock farming.

Places of Interest

One of the city's more striking buildings is the Christuskirche, a Lutheran church that combines neo-Gothic and Art Nouveau architecture. There is a display of meteorites in Post Street shopping centre, collected after a nineteenth century meteor shower. The Alte Feste, which was once a colonial fort, now houses a collection of cultural and historical artefacts. It also has a display commemorating the country's independence. The Owela natural history museum gives an insight into traditional village life.

Winnipeg, Canada

Introduction

The capital city of Manitoba, Winnipeg accounts for two thirds of the population of the province. Situated at the confluence of the Red and Assiniboine rivers, the city lies 60 miles north of the US border.

The name Winnipeg derives from the Cree Indian words 'win-nipuy' meaning muddy water.

History

The city grew from a series of trading posts built on the site from the 1730s.

The first post, Fort-Rouge, was established in 1738 by the French voyageur Sieur de la Vérendrye. This was followed by Fort Gibraltar, built by the North West Company in 1804, and Fort Garry, built by the Hudson's Bay Company in 1821.

While the fur trade was developing, a Hudson's Bay Company stockholder, Lord Selkirk, secured a large area of land which was named 'Assiniboia'. Selkirk encouraged many of his own impoverished Scottish crofters to settle on his lands, an action which caused resentment among local traders, Métis, descendants of French-speaking fur traders and their Native wives.

In 1816, 20 colonists who were killed in a battle with the Métis at Seven Oaks included the Governor of Assiniboia. The British settlers took flight, but returned soon after to rebuild. In 1821, peace was secured when the two fur companies merged. The Red River settlement flourished until a flood in 1826 wiped out the colony, and the settlers were forced to rebuild once again.

The colony remained a wild and often lawless place for much of the nineteenth century with an economy dependent on agriculture and the Red River trading routes with Minnesota in the United States.

Winnipeg became a major grain market and distribution centre for Canada's Prairie Provinces with the arrival of the Canadian Pacific Railroad, Canada's first transcontinental railway.

With the creation of Canada in 1867, the Red River Colony passed from British to Canadian control, an event which offended the Métis population. Resistance was spearheaded by Louis Riel who lead the capture of the Hudson's Bay Company's Fort Garry, leading to the creation of a provincial government. A delegation was sent to Ottawa to negotiate terms for admission into the Dominion of Canada. However the execution of English settler Thomas Scott by the Métis led to the dispatch of a military force from Ottawa.

By the turn of the century the city's population had been swollen by the arrival of thousands of immigrants from the Ukraine, Germany and Poland. The population grew from 300 in 1870 to 136,035 by 1911. By the outbreak of World War I, Winnipeg had become the third largest city in Canada and the largest grain producing centre in North America.

Modern City

Disaster hit the city in 1950 when the Red River overflowed its banks leaving Winnipeg and its surrounding communities devastated. The 80,000 residents who had to be moved created the largest evacuation in Canadian history.

Winnipeg is one of Canada's largest industrial, financial and commercial centres, with significant flour milling, meat-packing and food processing industries.

Places of Interest

The city is the centre of cultural life in Manitoba being the home of the Royal Winnipeg Ballet, the Manitoba Theatre Centre and seat of the University of Manitoba. The Winnipeg Art Gallery has the world's largest collection of Inuit art.

Wrocław (Breslau), Poland

Introduction

Wrocław is capital of the eponymous province and Poland's fourth largest city. On the Oder River where it meets with several other rivers, and overlooked by the Sudety mountains, it was historically important for its position on European trade routes. Control of the city passed between numerous empires over the centuries and it had a strong Germanic flavour until the end of World War II. It is now a major industrial centre.

History

There is evidence of stone age settlers in the area surrounding Wrocław. By the tenth century the settlement was called Vratislava and incorporated

Ostrów Tumski (the Cathedral Island). As part of Silesia, Wrocław falls under the jurisdiction of the Polish ruler Mieszko I at the end of the tenth century, beginning a period of control by the Piast dynasty. In 1000 Bolesław the Brave established the Wrocław bishopric.

Invading German forces were comprehensively defeated at the battle of Psie Pole in 1109. 29 years later Wrocław was designated capital of Silesia and in 1139 a Benedictine monastery was established by devouts from throughout Europe. The city was razed in 1241 during Tatar incursions and was rebuilt around a large market square, in a similar style to modern Wrocław. In 1262 Wrocław achieved full city rights in accordance with the Magdeburg statutes and was, after Prague, the largest city in central Europe.

Rule by the Piast dynasty ended with the death of Henry VI in 1336 and rule was assumed by Bohemia. Increasingly important as a destination on trans-continental trade routes, Wrocław joined the Hanseatic League (a coalition of Germanic trading towns) in 1387. Civil unrest broke out in 1418 between the merchant class and an alliance of workers and the church and, in conjunction with the Hussite Wars that spilled into the area, the city's development stalled.

On the death of King Ludwig in 1526 Wrocław came under the control of Ferdinand and the Habsburg dynasty. The Thirty Years War (1618–48) had a detrimental effect on urban expansion but was recovering by the end of the seventeenth century. The mid-eighteenth century saw the city fall under Prussian rule and it was re-named Bresslau by Frederic II. Developed as a military rather than commercial centre, its status diminished and its German character developed.

Between 1806 and 1811 it was under Napoleonic rule and its walls were razed to allow further expansion. After the defeat of Napoléon it reverted to Prussian rule and in 1871 became part of the new German Reich, as its third largest city. By the 1930s of a population of 650,000 around 600,000 were ethnic Germans. Under Nazi rule the small Polish and Jewish populations were persecuted.

Absorbing displaced Germans during World War II, the population exceeded 1 m. and in Aug. 1944 Breslau was declared a closed fortress. Around 700,000 civilians were evacuated and forced to cope with the conditions of a harsh winter, leading to large-scale loss of life. Soviet forces besieged the city from Jan. to May 1945, by which time around 70% of the city (including hundreds of its historically most important buildings) had perished. By the terms of the agreement of the post-war Potsdam crisis Wrocław fell under Polish jurisdiction for the first time since 1336.

The remaining ethnic German population fled the city or were subsequently evacuated, to be replaced by ethnic Poles from the Ukraine, Yugoslavia, Lithuania and the rest of Poland. Under communist rule, re-building started quickly and continued in the following decades. As with other major Polish cities, Wrocław had an active anti-communist underground movement by the 1980s which played a role in the downfall of the authorities in 1989.

Modern City

Among the most important industries are engineering, food processing, metal working and electronics. There is an international airport, two major river ports, motorway links and two large railway stations. There is also a university, dating back to the sixteenth century.

Places of Interest

The town hall is an impressive example of Gothic architecture, while the Hala Targowa (Market Hall) dating from 1908 remains a thriving commercial centre. The Market Square, one of central Europe's biggest, dates to the thirteenth century though many of its buildings have been reconstructed. The university comprises the splendid seventeenth century Baroque Leopoldine Hall. The Szczytnicki park lies in the middle of the city. Among the most important churches are the cathedral of St John the Baptist and the church of St Elizabeth.

There is the national museum, with a large collection of Silesian and Polish art, and museums of archaeology, ethnography, city history and natural history. Also popular is the large painting, *The Panorama of Raclawice Battle*, and the well preserved Jewish cemetery. The Polish Laboratory Theatre, resident in the city, has a reputation for innovation.

Wrocław was chosen by the EU to be one of the European Capitals for Culture for 2016, alongside San Sebastián in Spain.

Yamoussoukro, Côte d'Ivoire

Introduction

The purpose built capital of the Côte d'Ivoire, Yamoussoukro is in the centre of the country. The birthplace of President Houphouët-Boigny (1960–93), the town replaced the coastal city Abidjan as capital in 1983.

History

Yamoussoukro originated as a small village in the Baoulé region. In 1960 the leader of the Parti Démocratique, Félix Houphouët-Boigny, became president of newly independent Côte d'Ivoire. With the government based there, Yamoussoukro served as the country's unofficial capital for the next 20 years. Houphouët-Boigny ordered large scale building including roads, hotels, educational institutions and the largest church in the world. Costing US$150 m. and built between 1986–89, the Basilica was styled on St Peters in Rome. Landscaping included the construction of manmade lakes and a planted forest. In 1983 Yamoussoukro replaced Abidjan as national capital.

Modern City

Yamoussoukro is the country's administrative and transportation centre although Abidjan remains largest city. The principal industries are perfume and fishing, while the National Institute of Higher Technical Training is among several educational institutions. The city is served by a domestic airport and is linked by road to Abidjan.

Places of Interest

With its 150 m dome, the Our Lady of Peace of Yamoussoukro Basilica, made from marble and precious wood, can hold 18,000. Also built from wood and marble is the Houphouët-Boigny Foundation, which has an adjoining gardens and a marble approach.

Yangon, Myanmar

Introduction

The capital and largest city of Myanmar, Yangon is situated on a low ridge on the eastern bank of the Yangon River, 34 km north of the Gulf of Martaban, Andaman Sea. Traditionally the country's leading political, industrial, and commercial centre, Yangon handles more than 80 percent of Myanmar's foreign trade. In Nov. 2005 the government moved much of its infrastructure to a new 'capital', Pyinmana, 600 km north of Yangon. One of the world's leading rice markets, Yangon's other principal exports are teak and metal ores. Major industries are state owned. Principal state-owned industries produce pharmaceuticals, soap, rubber, textiles, aluminium, and rolled iron and steel. Yangon is also the centre of national rail, river, road, and air transport.

History

In 1755, King Alaungpaya, founder of the Kon-Baung Dynasty, conquered Dagon and reunited the whole of Myanmar under his rule. Appreciating the town's strategic importance in subjugating lower Myanmar he renamed the town Yangon, 'end of strife'.

Yangon was taken by the British in 1824 during the first Anglo-Burmese War but returned to Burmese control in 1826. In 1851 the British annexed Yangon renaming it Rangoon and making it the capital of Lower Burma. In 1852 Lieutenant Fraser of the British Engineering Corps established the city-centre's cantonment set out as a system of blocks intersected by streets running north-south and east-west. Rangoon was the capital of British-ruled Burma from 1874 until March 1942 when the Japanese took control during World War II, assisted by the Burma Independence Army led by Aung San. Aung San served as minister of defence in Ba Maw's puppet government from 1943–45 but became sceptical of Japanese promises of Burmese independence and was further disillusioned by Japanese treatment of Burmese

forces. In March 1945, Major General Aung San switched his 10,000 strong Burma National Army to the allied cause.

Rangoon was liberated on 3 May 1945. Aung San became deputy chairman of Burma's Executive Council in 1946 making him, in effect, Prime Minister, but he still remained subject to the British governor's veto. In Jan 1947 Aung San travelled to London where, after meeting with British prime minister, Clement Attlee, he was promised Burma's independence within 1 year. Yangon has been the nation's capital since Burma became independent in 1948.

Modern City

Isolationist policies in the latter half of the twentieth century led to a decline in Yangon's political and economic importance. With the gradual opening up of the country to the outside commercial world, Yangon has enjoyed rapid growth but remains politically troubled with the struggle between pro-democracy supporters, led by Nobel Prize winner Aung San Suu Kyi, and the ruling socialist government.

Places of Interest

The most notable of Yangon's many pagoda's is the Shwe Dagon Pagoda, a Buddhist temple complex on a hill north of the cantonment. This brick stupa, thought to be approx. 2,500 years old is covered in gold. It's shining dome rises 100 m above the city and is said to contain relics of the Buddha.

The Sule Pagoda is situated in the centre of the city. Its Mon name, Kyaik Athok, translates as 'the pagoda where a sacred hair relic is enshrined': it is thought to contain a single hair of the Buddha.

The People's Park and People's Square occupies over 130 acres between the Shwedagon Pagoda and Pyithu Hluttaw (Parliament).

The National Museum, on Pansodan Street, exhibits the lion throne of King Thibaw, the last King of Myanmar, alongside royal regalia and many ancient artefacts.

The Martyr's Mausoleum, close to the Shwe Dagon Pagoda is a memorial to Aung San and his fellow cabinet members who were assassinated in 1947 after securing independence for Myanmar.

Yaoundé, Cameroon

Introduction

Yaoundé is the capital of Cameroon, the country's administrative, financial, and communications centre and the seat of the government. The city stands on seven hills between the Sanaga and Nyong rivers. Yaoundé is at the centre of a rich agricultural district with a varied industry.

History

Yaoundé was founded in 1888 by German traders (in ivory) when Cameroon was a German protectorate. In 1915, the city was occupied by Belgium and in 1922 Yaoundé was declared the capital of French Cameroon. It remained capital after the independence of the Republic of Cameroon in 1960. In 1963 an Association Convention between the EEC and 17 African states and Madagascar was signed in Yaoundé.

Modern City

Manufactures include cigarettes, lumber and clay and glass products. The city is a trade centre for sugar, coffee, cacao and rubber. Yaoundé is a highway junction and is Cameroon's main railroad. There is an international airport. The only rail connection into the country is from the Central African Republic. The University of Yaoundé, founded in 1962, has a school of journalism and a school of administration and law.

Places of Interest

Located near the foot of Mont Fébé overlooking the capital, the Benedictine Monastery's Musée d'Art Camerounais has a collection of Cameroonian art, including bowls, masks, and Bamoun bronze pipes. The mountain has been developed as a resort, with hotel, nightclub, casino and golf course. The

Musée d'Art Nègre exhibits Bamound pipes, Baoulé textiles from Côte D'Ivoire and Congolese-Zairian masks. The collection of the Yaoundé National Museum includes sculptures, paintings and remnants of prehistoric ages.

Yekaterinburg, Russia

Introduction

Yekaterinburg, on the River Isset beneath the Ural Mountains, is the administrative capital of the Ural federal district in west central Russia. It is an important industrial centre and was the scene of Tsar Nicholas II's execution.

History

The city was founded in 1672 when members of the Russian sect of Old Believers settled there, establishing an iron foundry and a fortress. The settlement was named Yekaterinburg after Catherine I in 1783. It became the administrative centre for the ironworks of the Urals region, and a station on the Great Siberian Highway.

Tsar Nicholas II and his family were executed in Yekaterinburg in July 1918. The city was renamed Sverdlovsk after the Bolshevik leader Yakov Sverdlov in 1924 but regained its original name following the collapse of communism.

Modern City

A major railway intersection, local buses and trams run within the city. Yekaterinburg is one of Russia's largest industrial centres, especially for heavy engineering, metallurgical, chemical and tyre industries.

It is home to the A.M. Gorky State University and the Urals division of the Academy of Science.

Places of Interest

Yekaterinburg has several notable buildings exemplifying Russian eighteenth and nineteenth century classicism. Among the city's most important churches are the Church of Alexander Nevsky and the Church of Ascension. There is a geological museum, a fine arts museum and a museums of writers, as well as numerous theatres and an orchestra.

Yerevan, Armenia

Introduction

Armenia's capital is situated on the Razdan River at 1,020 m above sea level. It is overlooked by the extinct volcanoes of Mt. Aragats and Mt. Azhdaak as well as Mt. Arafat. One of the oldest constantly populated areas in the world, its first historical mention dates back to 607 AD. However, an engraved stone slab discovered in the 1950s confirms that the first settlement, called Yerbuni Fortress, was in place by 783 BC.

History

Yerevan was established as a part of the Armenian kingdom by the sixth century BC and had soon become a major trade centre. However, its history has been dominated by conquest and over the ensuing centuries it was in the possession of the Romans, Parthians, Arabs, Mongols, Turks, Persians and Georgians. It came under Russian control in the early part of the nineteenth century. In 1915 it suffered, as did the rest of the country, during the Turkish genocide that saw an estimated 1.5 m. Armenians die nationwide. A memorial to these events is situated on the hills just outside the city. Yerevan was officially established as the Armenian capital 5 years later.

Modern City

Important industries in Yerevan include chemicals, aluminium smelting, machinery and machine tool manufacture and wine and brandy making. There are also important hydro-electric works nearby. Industrial growth saw Yerevan expand considerably throughout the twentieth century with the population growing by about 1.25 m. between 1914 and 2000.

Places of Interest

Many of the city's most important buildings are in the downtown area, with the traditional constructions of characteristic Armenian pink tufa stone in stark contrast to some of the more functional Soviet-era buildings. Republic Square (formerly Lenin Square) is the city's central hub while the mosque of Hasan Ali Khan (the Blue Mosque) is its most recognisable structure.

With a rich heritage to be explored, Yerevan has the reputation of being a more relaxed city than many of its former Soviet equivalents.

Yokohama, Japan

Introduction

Yokohama is on Southern Honshu Island 30 km (18.6 miles) from Tokyo. It is the capital of Kanagawa prefecture and the second largest city in Japan. The Keihan Industrial zone, the area between Yokohama and Tokyo, is the centre of Yokohama's manufacturing district.

History

In 1854, US Commodore Matthew C. Perry visited Yokohama when it was a small fishing village. The city began to flourish in 1859 with the opening of the port. When Japan opened its doors to foreigners, under the Meiji Restoration (1868–1912), Yokohama had an influx in traders.

Japan's first railroad, in 1872, linked Tokyo and Yokohama. The area surrounding the original Yokohama station (now Sakuragicho station) developed as a nucleus for foreign business. The city of Yokohama was formerly established in 1889.

Yokohama was almost entirely destroyed in the 1923 Great Kanto earthquake and subject to heavy bombardment in World War II. Since then, Yokohama's trade has flourished. Major industries include steel mills, oil refineries and chemical plants, which all play a major role in trade and industry in Japan. Other exports include electrical equipment, textiles and processed food.

Modern City

In 1989 Yokohama celebrated the 100th anniversary of the City Government and the 130th anniversary of the opening of the Port. Yokohama's success as Japan's trading port has led to further improvements. Daikoku Pier was completed in 1990 and the construction of Minami Honmoku Pier commenced the same year. The Yokohama Port International Cargo Center Co. Ltd. was established and the operation of the Yokohama Air Cargo Terminal (YAT) commenced in 1992. An international passenger port terminal opened in 1993. Tokyo's Haneda airport and Narita airport in the Chiba prefecture both serve Yokohama. West of Yokohama, Atsugi airport serves domestic airlines.

Places of Interest

The Landmark Tower is the fourth tallest structure in Japan and also has the world's second fastest elevator. Museums include the Yokohama Maritime Museum, Yokohama Museum of Art, Mitsubishi Minato Mirai Industrial Museum, the Silk Museum and Yokohama archive of History. Yokohama is home to Kanazawa library, established in 1275 and known for its collection of historical documents. There are two private and two public universities and many Shinto shrines and temples.

Zagreb, Croatia

Introduction

Zagreb, the capital of Croatia since 1557, is located on the banks of the River Sava in the north of the country. It survived relatively unscathed after the Yugoslav wars of the 1990s, although it suffered some bomb damage in 1995. Located on trade routes between the Balkans and the rest of Europe, it is Croatia's most important industrial centre and has a burgeoning tourist trade.

History

The Roman Catholic bishopric founded in the area around 1093 comprised two distinct sections: Kaptol, inhabited by clerics and centred around St Stephen's Cathedral; and Gradec, the commercial district, based around St Mark's Church and built into the Medvednica Hill. Mongols took the city in the mid-thirteenth century and it was around this time that Gradec was fortified. Kaptol was fortified in the sixteenth century and the two settlements were linked following a rash of new building during the nineteenth century.

Zagreb was at the centre of an ideological debate during the second half of the nineteenth century between advocates of a united Yugoslavia and supporters of Croatian nationalism. After World War I, Croatia gained autonomy from Austria-Hungary in a state comprising Slavonia and Dalmatia. It then joined the new Kingdom of Serbs, Croats and Slovenes that evolved into the Kingdom of Yugoslavia in 1929.

Zagreb became the capital of a Croatian republic between April 1941 and May 1945, although it was not independent. After the war Croatia re-integrated into Yugoslavia. When Franjo Tudjman unilaterally declared Croatia an independent state in 1991, Zagreb became national capital again.

Modern City

Zagreb's major industries include machinery, cement, clothing, printing, chemicals and food processing. It is a major road and rail hub and there is an international airport. In recent years Zagreb has developed its conference facilities and is a popular tourist destination.

Places of Interest

There are extensive parks in the city as well as many of Croatia's most important museums, galleries and cultural institutions. The Church of St Stephen was re-modelled at the end of the nineteenth century but its interior includes artwork from the thirteenth century. Other landmarks include the Baroque St Catherine's Church, the gothic Church of St Mark (with an exuberantly tiled roof), palaces, the university dating from the seventeenth century and an ornate cemetery at Mirogoj to the north of the city.

Zaragoza, Spain

Introduction

Capital of the northeastern region of Aragón, Zaragoza is situated on the Ebro River. A primary railway junction between Barcelona and Madrid, Zaragoza was originally a crossing point on a key waterway. Zaragoza was the capital of the kingdom of Aragón in the twelfth to fifteenth centuries.

History

The site of an ancient Celtiberian settlement, the area was taken by the Romans in the first century BC and colonized under Emperor Augustus. It was named Ceaseraugusta from which the modern name derives, via the Arabic *Saraqustah*. It developed into a prosperous colony with more than 25,000 inhabitants. One of the first Spanish towns to be Christianized, it was here that the synod of the Christian Church was held in 380 AD.

In the fifth century Zaragoza was taken by the Visigoths and then by the Moors in 714. Charlemagne attempted to conquer the city in 778 but was forced to withdraw to cope with a domestic rebellion. During the ninth to eleventh century Zaragoza was the centre of an independent dynasty, the Beni Kasim, a Visigoth family independent of both Moors and Franks. The Almoravids captured the city in 1110, but 8 years later it was taken by King Alfonso I of Aragón. Zaragoza entered a long period of peace and prosperity at the heart of the kingdom of Aragón, founded in 1035. Marriage ties united Aragón with Barcelona in 1137 and then in 1479 Ferdinand of Aragón married Isabella of Castille and León. United under these Catholic Monarchs, the kingdom was strong enough to recapture the Moorish holdings.

Zaragoza played a memorable role in the Peninsular War (1808–13). To the surprise of the French, the citizens of Zaragoza refused to concede. In 1808 Jorge Ibort, a peasant leader, rallied the citizens into an organized resistance. Under the command of the Aragónese general and nobleman, José de Rebolledo Palafox y Melci, they held out until about 50,000 inhabitants had died. A legendary figure emerged from the struggle. Maria Augustín was immortalized as 'The Maid of Saragossa' in Byron's poem *Childe Harold*. The French eventually captured the city in 1809.

At the end of the nineteenth century, Zaragoza's economy benefited from the introduction of sugar refining. Out of industrialization came militant trade unionism. In 1933 a revolutionary committee of workers began a general strike that lasted 57 days. Even so, at the beginning of the Civil War the Nationalist attack took the city by surprise and the unions had no time to organize themselves. The city fell to the Nationalists in 1936.

Modern City

Zaragoza's major industries include engineering, chemicals, flour, sugar refining and wine and paper production. The original site of Zaragoza is found to the east of the centre on the banks of the Ebro River. Most of the industry is situated in the surrounding outskirts.

The city is accessible by air, rail and road.

Places of Interest

In the old town can be found the Basílica de Nuestra Señora del Pilar, a marble pillar erected in the memory of the sighting of the Virgin Mary by St John. The pillar is surrounded by a baroque edifice containing a chapel, the Capilla Santa, upon which Goya worked. An Aragónese native, Goya was born in the small hamlet of Fuendetodos, just south of Zaragoza. The Copulo was painted by the Sevillian artist Diego Velázquez.

To the west of the old town is the Aljafería palace. An example of Moorish architecture, it was built in the mid-eleventh century at the height of the Beni Kasim reign. It has been a palace of Berber Sheikhs, the residence of the kings of Aragón, the seat of the Inquisition between 1485–1759 and, from 1987, the Aragónese *cortes* (parliament).

Zürich, Switzerland

Introduction

Zürich is in the north central part of Switzerland, bridging the Limmat River to the northwest of Lake Zürich. The largest city in the country, it is also its industrial and financial heart.

History

There is evidence of Bronze age settlement in the area. The Romans built a customs post on the bank of the Limmat in 58 BC which they named Turicum. After the fall of the Roman Empire the region was occupied by the Alamannii and the Franks, and its expansion slowed as a result. During the eleventh and twelfth centuries the city began to flourish, primarily because of a booming trade in textiles. In 1218 it became a free city under the Holy Roman Empire. In 1336 the burgomaster Rudolf Brun acknowledged the increasing importance of the trade guilds by granting them constitutional power and reducing the authority of the nobility. Brun also presided over the incorporation of Zürich into the Swiss Confederation.

Zürich was the first Swiss city to embrace the Protestant religion, after Huldrych Zwingli preached a series of sermons at the Grossmünster. Catholic persecution caused many Protestants from neighbouring countries to seek refuge in Zürich and the city's population expanded. The sixteenth century witnessed the zenith of the city's influence and prestige.

In the 1830s Zürich began to shift towards more liberal, democratic policies. The 1830 constitution, which allowed for the election of the legislative and the executive branches of government, also helped to boost the city's economy and industries. Swiss neutrality during World War I meant that once again Zürich was home to many political dissidents including James Joyce and Lenin. Neutrality also ensured that the city became a major centre for international banking and it remains the most important market in the world for gold and precious metals.

Modern City

Zürich is served by an international airport 12 km to the northeast. There are frequent international trains and bus services. Well maintained motorways feed into the city. Local transport is provided by trams, buses and S-bahn suburban trains. There are also boat services.

The once renowned textile industry has been replaced by a prominent heavy manufacturing industry, with machine production especially dominant. Though less dependent than Lucerne on revenue generated by tourism, Zürich maintains a thriving tourist trade, and like Geneva it is an important meeting point for international conventions.

Places of Interest

The Swiss National museum houses scientific, artistic and historical exhibits. The Museum of Fine Arts has a large and eclectic permanent collection of art through the ages.

POLITICAL, ECONOMIC AND SOCIAL COUNTRY FACTSHEETS

Afghanistan

Da Afganistan Islami Jomhoriyat—Jamhuri-ye Islami-ye Afganistan (Islamic Republic of Afghanistan)

Factsheet

Capital: Kabul
Population estimate, 2015: 32.53 m.
GNI per capita, 2014: (PPP$) 1,885
HDI/world rank, 2014: 0.465/171
Internet domain extension: .af

Civil Aviation

There is an international airport at Kabul (Khwaja Rawash Airport). The national carrier is Ariana Afghan Airlines, which in 2010 operated direct flights from Kabul to Amritsar, Baku, Delhi, Dubai, Dushanbe, Frankfurt, Islamabad, İstanbul, Jeddah, Kuwait, Mashad, Moscow, Riyadh, Tehran and Urumqi, as well as domestic services. In 2014 it carried 253,040 passengers, up from 226,266 in 2013. The UN sanctions imposed on 14 Nov. 1999 included the cutting off of Afghanistan's air links to the outside world. In Jan. 2002 Ariana Afghan Airlines resumed services and Kabul airport was reopened. The airport was heavily bombed during the US campaign and although it is now functioning with some civilian flights it is still being used extensively by the military authorities. Afghanistan's first private airline, Kam Air, was launched in Nov. 2003.

Climate

The climate is arid, with a big annual range of temperature and very little rain, apart from the period Jan. to April. Winters are very cold, with considerable snowfall, which may last the year round on mountain summits. Kabul, Jan. 27 °F (−2.8 °C), July 76 °F (24.4 °C). Annual rainfall 13″ (338 mm).

Constitution and Government

UN sanctions were imposed in 1999 but were withdrawn following the collapse of the Taliban regime. Following UN-sponsored talks in Bonn, Germany in Nov. 2001, on 22 Dec. 2001 power was handed over to an Afghan Interim Authority, designed to oversee the restructuring of the country until a second stage of government, the Transitional Authority, could be put into power. This second stage resulted from a *Loya Jirga* (Grand Council), which convened between 10–16 June 2002. The Loya Jirga established the Transitional Islamic State of Afghanistan. A constitutional commission was established, with UN assistance, to help the Constitutional Loya Jirga prepare a new constitution. A draft constitution was produced for public scrutiny in Nov. 2003 and was approved by Afghanistan's *Loya Jirga* on 4 Jan. 2004. The new constitution creates a strong presidential system, providing for a *President* and two *Vice-Presidents*, and a bicameral parliament. The constitution imposes a limit of two 5-year terms for a president. The lower house is the 249-member House of the People (*Wolesi Jirga*), directly elected for a 5-year term, and the upper house the 102-member House of Elders (*Meshrano Jirga*). The upper house is elected in three divisions. The provincial councils elect one third of its members for a 4-year term. The district councils elect the second third of the members for a 3-year term. The president appoints the remaining third for a 5-year term. At least one woman is elected to the *Wolesi Jirga* from each of the country's 32 regions, and half of the president's appointments to the *Meshrano Jirga* must be women. The constitution reserves 25% of the seats in the *Wolesi Jirga* for women. The president

appoints ministers, the attorney general and central bank governor with the approval of the *Wolesi Jirga*. Cabinet ministers must be university graduates. Presidential and parliamentary elections, the first in 25 years, were scheduled for June 2004 but were put back to Oct. 2004. The parliamentary elections were subsequently delayed again and were set to be held in April 2005, but were postponed a further time until Sept. 2005. In Dec. 2005 an elected parliament sat for the first time since 1973.

Currency

The *afghani* (AFN) was introduced in Oct. 2002 with one of the new notes worth 1,000 old *afghani* (AFA). The old *afghani* had been trading at around 46,000 to the US$.

Defence

In 2013 military expenditure totalled US$2,898 m. (US$93 per capita), representing 13.8% of GDP. Since the fall of the Taliban, Afghanistan has had an all-volunteer professional-army. The UN-mandated international force, ISAF, assisted the government in the maintenance of security throughout the country until its mandate expired at the end of 2014. It had been led by NATO since 2003. About 12,900 personnel have been retained to train, advise and assist the Afghan National Security Forces in the context of Operation Resolute Support.

Economy

In 2012 agriculture accounted for 25% of GDP, industry 21% and services 54%.

Labour

The labour force in 2013 was 7,983,000 (5,569,000 in 2003). 49.0% of the population aged 15–64 was economically active in 2013. In the same year 9.2% of the population was unemployed. Afghanistan had 86,000 people living in slavery according to the Walk Free Foundation's 2013 *Global Slavery Index*.

Press

Afghanistan had approximately 540 newspapers in 2008 including 16 paid-for dailies. The main dailies were *Hewad*, *Anis* and the English language publications *Daily Outlook Afghanistan* and *Kabul Times*.

Rail

Historically, Afghanistan has lacked its own railway system although two short stretches of railway extend inside the country from the Uzbek and Turkmen networks. In Feb. 2012 the first major Afghan-run railway opened to commercial traffic at a cost of US$170 m., covering 75 km from Hairatan, a town on the border with Uzbekistan, to Mazar i Sharif. It is hoped it will be integrated into a wider network being developed as part of a Central Asia Regional Economic Co-operation programme.

Religion

The predominant religion is Islam. According to a study by the Pew Research Center entitled *Mapping the Global Muslim Population*, around 84–89% of the population in 2009 were Sunni Muslims and 10–15% Shias. The Taliban provoked international censure in 2001 by forcing the minority population of Afghan Hindus and Sikhs to wear yellow identification badges.

Roads

There were 42,150 km of roads in 2006, of which 29.3% were paved. A large part of the road network is in a poor state of repair as a result of military action, but rebuilding is under way. In Jan. 2003 women regained the right to drive after a 10-year ban. 431,600 passenger cars (15 per 1,000 inhabitants in 2007) and 153,600 lorries and vans were in use in 2008.

Shipping

There are practically no navigable rivers. A port has been built at Qizil Qala on the Oxus and there are three river ports on the Amu Darya, linked by road to Kabul. The container port at Kheyrabad on the Amu Darya river has rail connections to Uzbekistan.

Social Statistics

Based on 2008 estimates: birth rate, 46.5 per 1,000 population; death rate, 19.6 per 1,000. Infant mortality (2010), 103 per 1,000 live births. Life expectancy at birth, 2013, was 62.2 years for women and 59.7 years for men. Fertility rate, 2008, 6.6 births per woman. In spite of the ongoing conflict in the country, Afghanistan has made significant progress in recent years in reducing maternal mortality. The number of deaths per 100,000 live births among mothers was reduced from 1,100 in 2000 to 400 in 2013.

Telecommunications

There were 23,424,000 mobile phone subscriptions in 2014 (748.8 per 1,000 inhabitants) and 102,000 landline telephone subscriptions (3.3 per 1,000 inhabitants). In 2014, 6.4% of the population were internet users. In March 2012 there were 257,000 Facebook users.

Territory and Population

Afghanistan is bounded in the north by Turkmenistan, Uzbekistan and Tajikistan, east by China, east and south by Pakistan and west by Iran. The area is 652,230 km^2 (251,830 sq. miles). The last census was in 1979. Estimate, 2010, 27.96 m.; density, 42.9 per km^2. In 2011, 22.9% of the population lived in urban areas. The country is divided into 34 regions (*velayat*). The capital, Kabul, had an estimated population of 2.94 m. in 2009. Main ethnic groups: Pashtuns, 38%; Tajiks, 25%; Hazaras, 19%; Uzbeks, 6%; others, 12%. The official languages are Pashto and Dari.

Tourism

Owing to the political situation the tourism industry has been negligible since 2001. It is estimated that around 3,000–4,000 tourists visit the country annually.

Albania

Republika e Shqipërisë (Republic of Albania)

Factsheet

Capital: Tirana
Population estimate, 2015: 2.90 m.
GNI per capita, 2014: (PPP$) 9,943
HDI/world rank, 2014: 0.733/85=
Internet domain extension: .al

Civil Aviation

The national carrier, Albanian Airlines, ceased operations in Nov. 2011. Subsequently Belle Air, a low-cost carrier founded in 2005, became the *de facto* national carrier, but it in turn ceased operations in Nov. 2013. It had international flights to a number of destinations in Europe as well as some charter flights. In 2006 scheduled airline traffic of Albania-based carriers flew 2 m. km, carrying 213,000 passengers (all on international flights). The main airport is Mother Teresa International Airport at Rinas, 25 km from Tirana, which handled 1,394,688 passengers in 2009.

Climate

Mediterranean-type, with rainfall mainly in winter, but thunderstorms are frequent and severe in the great heat of the plains in summer. Winters in the highlands can be severe, with much snow. Tirana, Jan. 44 °F (6.8 °C), July 75 °F (23.9 °C). Annual rainfall 54″ (1,353 mm). Shkodër, Jan. 39 °F (3.9 °C), July 77 °F (25 °C). Annual rainfall 57″ (1,425 mm).

Constitution and Government

A new constitution was adopted on 28 Nov. 1998. The supreme legislative body is the single-chamber *People's Assembly* of 140 deputies. As from April 2009 all members are elected through proportional representation, for 4-year terms. Where no candidate wins an absolute majority, a run-off election is held. The *President* is elected by parliament for a 5-year term.

Currency

The monetary unit is the *lek* (ALL), notionally of 100 *qindars*. In Sept. 1991 the lek (plural, *lekë* or leks) was pegged to the ecu at a rate of 30 leks = one ecu. In June 1992 it was devalued from 50 to 110 to US$1.

Defence

Since 1 Jan. 2010 Albania has had an all-volunteer professional army. In 2013 defence expenditure totalled US$182 m. (US$61 per capita), representing 1.4% of GDP.

Economy

In 2009 agriculture accounted for 20.4% of GDP (down from 29.1% in 2000), industry 19.4% (up from 19.0% in 2000) and services 60.2% (up from 51.9% in 2000).

Labour

The labour force in 2013 was 1,287,000 (1,322,000 in 2003). 62.9% of the population aged 15–64 was economically active in 2013. In the same year 16.0% of the population was unemployed. Albania had 11,000 people living in slavery according to the Walk Free Foundation's 2013 *Global Slavery Index*.

Press

In 2008 there were 28 paid-for dailies (combined circulation of 77,000) and 82 paid-for non-dailies. The leading newspaper in terms of circulation is *Shekulli*.

Rail

Total length in operation in 2012 was 399 km. Passenger-km travelled in 2012 came to 16 m. and freight tonne-km to 25 m.

Religion

At the 2011 census the declared religious adherence of the population included: Muslims (mainly Sunnis, but with a significant Bektashi Shia minority), 56.7%; Catholics, 10.0%; Orthodox, 6.7%. The remainder follow other religions or are atheists. The Roman Catholic Church has five dioceses in the country, including two archdioceses. The Autocephalous Orthodox Church of Albania is headed by Anastasios, Archbishop of Tirana, Durrës and All Albania (b. 1929).

Roads

In 2009 there were around 15,000 km of roads including 3,412 km of national or primary roads. There were 237,932 passenger cars in 2007, as well as 29,506 buses and coaches and 59,645 lorries and vans. There were 384 fatalities in road accidents in 2007.

Shipping

In Jan. 2009 there were 46 ships of 300 GT or over registered, totalling 61,000 GT. The main port is Durrës, with secondary ports being Vlorë, Sarandë and Shëngjin.

Social Statistics

2007: births, 33,163; deaths, 14,528. Rates in 2007 (per 1,000): births, 10.5; deaths, 4.6. Infant mortality, 2010, was 16 per 1,000 live births. Fertility rate (number of births per woman), 1.9 in 2008. Annual population growth rate, 2008–10, 0.4%. Life expectancy at birth, 2007, was 73.4 years for men and 79.8 years for women. Abortion was legalized in 1991.

Telecommunications

In 2010 there were 333,000 landline telephone subscriptions (equivalent to 103.9 per 1,000 inhabitants) and 2,692,000 mobile phone subscriptions (or 840.2 per 1,000 inhabitants). In 2009, 41.2% of the population were internet users. Fixed internet subscriptions totalled 105,000 in 2009 (32.9 per 1,000 inhabitants). In March 2012 Albania had 1.06 m. Facebook users.

Territory and Population

Albania is bounded in the north by Montenegro and Serbia, east by Macedonia, south by Greece and west by the Adriatic. The area is 28,703 km² (11,082 sq. miles). The population at the census of Oct. 2011 was 2,821,977 giving a density of 98.3 per km². Population estimate, Jan. 2015: 2,893,005. In 2011, 52.9% of the population lived in urban areas. The capital is Tirana (population in 2011, 418,495). The country is administratively divided into 12 prefectures, 36 districts, 308 communes and 65 municipalities. In most cases prefectures are named after their capitals. The one exception is Dibër, where the capital is Peshkopi. The vast majority of the population are Albanians, with small Greek, Roma, Aromanian and Macedonian minorities. The official language is Albanian.

Tourism

In 2012 there were a record 3,156,000 international tourist arrivals, excluding same-day visitors (up from 2,469,000 in 2011); tourism expenditure in 2012 totalled US$1,623 m.

Algeria

Jumhuriya al-Jazairiya ad-Dimuqratiya ash-Shabiya
(People's Democratic Republic of Algeria)

Factsheet
Capital: Algiers
Population estimate, 2015: 39.67 m.
GNI per capita, 2014: (PPP$) 13,054
HDI/world rank, 2014: 0.736/83
Internet domain extension: .dz

Civil Aviation

The main airport is Algiers International Airport (also known as Houari Boumedienne Airport), which opened a new terminal in July 2006 to allow for more international air traffic; some international services also use airports at Annaba, Constantine and Oran. The national carrier is the state-owned Air Algérie, which in 2013 carried 4,703,000 passengers (3,182,000 on international flights). In 2012 Houari Boumedienne Airport handled 5,404,971 passengers (3,824,009 on international flights) and 25,359 tonnes of freight.

Climate

Coastal areas have a warm temperate climate, with most rain in winter, which is mild, while summers are hot and dry. Inland, conditions become more arid beyond the Atlas Mountains. Algiers, Jan. 54 °F (12.2 °C), July 76 °F (24.4 °C). Annual rainfall 30″ (762 mm). Biskra, Jan. 52 °F (11.1 °C), July 93 °F (33.9 °C). Annual rainfall 6″ (158 mm). Oran, Jan. 54 °F (12.2 °C), July 76 °F (24.4 °C). Annual rainfall 15″ (376 mm).

Constitution and Government

A referendum was held on 28 Nov. 1996. The electorate was 16,434,527; turnout was 79.6%. The electorate approved by 85.8% of votes cast a new constitution which defines the fundamental components of the Algerian people as Islam, Arab identity and Berber identity. It was signed into law on 7 Dec. 1996. Political parties are permitted, but not if based on a separatist feature such as race, religion, sex, language or region. There is no limit to the number of presidential terms after parliament voted in favour of abolishing the two-term limit in Nov. 2008, allowing the current president, Abdelaziz Bouteflika, to run for a third term. The President appoints the prime minister and cabinet ministers. Parliament is bicameral: a 462-member *National People's Assembly* elected by direct universal suffrage using proportional representation (389 prior to the elections of May 2012), and a 144-member *Council of the Nation*, one-third nominated by the President and two-thirds indirectly elected by the 48 local authorities. The Council of the Nation debates bills passed by the National Assembly which become law if a three-quarters majority is in favour.

Currency

The unit of currency is the *Algerian dinar* (DZD) of 100 *centimes*.

Defence

Conscription is for 18 months (6 months basic training and 12 months civilian tasks). Military expenditure totalled US$9,957 m. in 2013, equivalent to US$261 per capita and representing 4.7% of GDP.

Economy

In 2009 petroleum and natural gas (excluding refined petroleum) accounted for 31.0% of GDP; transport, communications, trade, restaurants, finance, real estate and services, 25.1%; public administration and defence, 10.9%; public utilities and construction, 10.9%.

Labour

The labour force in 2013 was 12,088,000 (9,648,000 in 2003). 46.5% of the population aged 15–64 was economically active in 2013. In the same year 9.8% of the population was unemployed. Algeria had 71,000 people living in slavery according to the Walk Free Foundation's 2013 *Global Slavery Index*.

Press

Algeria had 65 paid-for daily newspapers in 2008 (including five sports dailies), with a combined average daily circulation of 2.16 m. There were also 226 non-dailies in 2008.

Rail

In 2011 there were 3,720 km of 1,432 mm route (254 km electrified) and 1,090 km of 1,055 mm gauge. The railways carried 6.9 m. tonnes of freight and 24.7 m. passengers in 2008.

Religion

The 1996 constitution made Islam the state religion, established a consultative *High Islamic Council*, and forbids practices 'contrary to Islamic morality'. In 2010 the population was 97.9% Muslim according to estimates by the Pew Research Center's Forum on Religion & Public Life, with 1.8% religiously unaffiliated and 0.2% Christian. The vast majority of citizens are Sunni Muslims. The Armed Islamic Group (GIA) vowed in 1994 to kill 'Jews, Christians and polytheists' in Algeria. Hundreds of foreign nationals, including priests and nuns, were killed during the 10-year long civil war. Signalling an increasing tolerance amongst the Muslim community, the Missionaries of Africa's house at Ghardaia Oasis was reopened in 2000.

Roads

There were, in 2008, 111,261 km of roads including 29,146 km of highways and main roads. There were 2,042,800 passenger cars (58 cars per 1,000 inhabitants in 2005) and 1,166,200 lorries and vans in use in 2006.

Shipping

In Jan. 2009 there were 39 ships of 300 GT or over registered, totalling 723,000 GT. Skikda, the leading port, handled 23,203,000 tonnes of cargo in 2008.

Social Statistics

2007 estimates: births, 783,000; deaths, 149,000; marriages, 325,000. Rates (2007 estimates): births, 23.0 per 1,000; deaths, 4.4 per 1,000. Infant mortality in 2010 was 31 per 1,000 live births. Expectation of life (2007), 73.6 years for females and 70.8 years for males. Annual population growth rate, 1998–2008, 1.5%. Fertility rate, 2008, 2.4 births per woman.

Telecommunications

In 2014 mobile phone subscribers numbered 37,113,130 (929.5 per 1,000 persons). In the same year there were 3,098,787 main (fixed) telephone lines. 18.1% of the population were internet users in 2014. In June 2012 there were 3.6 m. Facebook users. Government plans to privatize Algérie Télécom, the major state-owned telecommunications company, were rejected in Feb. 2009. Mobilis, a subsidiary of Algérie Télécom, is one of three mobile phone networks operating in the country. It has the second largest market share, behind Djezzy and ahead of Nedjma.

Territory and Population

Algeria is bounded in the west by Morocco and Western Sahara, southwest by Mauritania and Mali, southeast by Niger, east by Libya and Tunisia, and north by the Mediterranean Sea. It has an area of 2,381,741 km^2 (919,595 sq. miles) and is the largest country in Africa. Population (census 2008) 34,080,030 (16, 847,283 female); density, 14.3 per km^2. In 2011, 67.1% of the population lived in urban areas. 2.5 m. Algerians live in France. 86% of the population speak Arabic, 14% Berber; French is widely spoken. A law of Dec. 1996 made Arabic the sole official language, but in March 2002 Tamazight, the Berber language, was given official status and also made a national language. The capital is Algiers (2008 census population, 2,364,230). Other major towns (with 2008 census populations over 200,000): Oran, 803,329; Constantine, 448,028; Annaba, 342,703; Blida, 331,779; Batna, 289,504; Djelfa, 265,833; Sétif, 252,127; Sidi-bel-Abbès, 210,146; Biskra, 204,661.

Tourism

In 2010 there were a record 2,070,000 foreign visitors, up from 1,912,000 in 2009 and 1,772,000 in 2008.

Andorra

Principat d'Andorra (Principality of Andorra)

Factsheet

Capital: Andorra la Vella
Population estimate, 2015: 70,000
GNI per capita, 2014: (PPP$) 43,978
HDI/world rank, 2014: 0.845/34
Internet domain extension: .ad

Civil Aviation

The nearest airport is Seo de Urgel, over the border in Spain 12 km to the south of Andorra.

Climate

Escaldes-Engordany, Jan. 35.8 °F (2.1 °C), July 65.8 °F (18.8 °C). Annual rainfall 34.9″ (886 mm).

Constitution and Government

The joint heads of state are the co-princes-the President of the French Republic and the Bishop of Urgel. A new democratic constitution was approved by 74.2% of votes cast at a referendum on 14 March 1993. The electorate was 9,123; turnout was 75.7%. The new constitution, which came into force on 4 May 1993, makes the co-princes a single constitutional monarch and provides for a parliament, the unicameral *General Council of the Valleys*, with 28 members, two from each of the seven parishes and 14 elected by proportional representation from the single national constituency, for 4 years. In 1982 an *Executive Council* was appointed and legislative and executive powers were separated. The General Council elects the President of the Executive Council, who is the head of the government. There is a *Constitutional Court* of four members who hold office for 8-year terms, renewable once.

Currency

Since 1 Jan. 2002 Andorra has been using the euro (EUR).

Labour

Only 1% of the workforce is employed in agriculture, the rest in tourism, commerce, services and light industry. Manufacturing consists mainly of cigarettes, cigars and furniture.

Press

In 2008 there were three daily newspapers with a combined circulation of about 32,000. *Diari d'Andorra* and *El Periodic d'Andorra* are paid-for, while *Bondia* is free. *L'Esportiu*, a daily Catalan-language sports paper, is included in *Diari d'Andorra*. In the 2013 *World Press Freedom Index* compiled by Reporters Without Borders, Andorra was ranked fifth out of 179 countries.

Religion

The Roman Catholic is the established church, but the 1993 constitution guarantees religious liberty. In 2011 around 90% of the population were Catholics.

Roads

There were 76,616 motor vehicles in 2012 including 52,038 private cars and 13,154 motorcycles and mopeds. A total of 4,111,528 vehicles entered the country in 2012 (4,178,116 in 2011).

Social Statistics

Births in 2006 numbered 843 (10.4 per 1,000 inhabitants) and deaths 260 (3.2). Life expectancy (2006): males, 78 years; females, 85 years. Annual population growth rate, 2000–05, 3.5%. Fertility rate, 2008, 1.3 births per woman (one of the lowest rates in the world). Infant mortality in 2010 was three per 1,000 live births.

Telecommunications

In 2010 there were 38,171 landline telephone subscriptions, equivalent to 449.8 per 1,000 inhabitants. There were 65,500 mobile phone subscriptions in 2010 (771.8 per 1,000 inhabitants). Andorra had 785.3 internet users per 1,000 inhabitants in 2009. Fixed internet subscriptions totalled 32,000 in 2009 (382.6 per 1,000 inhabitants).

Territory and Population

The co-principality of Andorra is situated in the eastern Pyrenees on the French-Spanish border. The country is mountainous and has an average altitude of 1,996 m. Area, 464 km^2. In lieu of a census, a register of population is kept. The estimated population at 31 Dec. 2013 was 76,098; density, 164 per km^2. In 2010, 88% of the population lived in urban areas. The chief towns are Andorra la Vella, the capital (population, 22,546 in 2013) and Escaldes-Engordany (13,859); other towns are Encamp, Sant Julià de Lòria and La Massana. In 2010, 38.8% of the residential population were Andorran, 31.4% Spanish, 15.4% Portuguese and 6.0% French. Catalan is the official language, but Spanish and French are widely spoken.

Tourism

Tourism is the main industry, accounting for 80% of GDP. In 2010 there were 1,808,000 international tourist arrivals (excluding same-day visitors).

Angola

República de Angola (Republic of Angola)

Factsheet

Capital: Luanda
Population estimate, 2015: 25.02 m.
GNI per capita, 2014: (PPP$) 6,822
HDI/world rank, 2014: 0.532/149
Internet domain extension: .ao

Civil Aviation

There is an international airport at Luanda (Fourth of February). The national carrier is Linhas Aéreas de Angola (TAAG), which in 2013 carried 1,322,000 passengers (669,000 on domestic flights and 653,000 on international flights).

Climate

The climate is tropical, with low rainfall in the west but increasing inland. Temperatures are constant over the year and most rain falls in March and April. Luanda, Jan. 78 °F (25.6 °C), July 69 °F (20.6 °C). Annual rainfall 13″ (323 mm). Lobito, Jan. 77 °F (25 °C), July 68 °F (20 °C). Annual rainfall 14″ (353 mm).

Constitution and Government

Under the Constitution adopted at independence, the sole legal party was the MPLA. In Dec. 1990, however, the MPLA announced that the Constitution would be revised to permit opposition parties. The supreme organ of state is the 220-member *National Assembly*. For the 2008 elections 30% of seats were guaranteed for women. There is an executive *President*, elected for renewable terms of 5 years, who appoints a *Council of Ministers*. In Dec. 2002 Angola's ruling party and the UNITA party of former rebels agreed on a new constitution. The president would keep key powers, including the power to name and to remove the prime minister. The president will also appoint provincial governors, rather than letting voters elect them, but the governor must be from the party that received a majority of votes in that province. A draft constitution was submitted to the constitutional commission of the Angolan parliament for consideration in Jan. 2004. A new constitution was adopted on 21 Jan. 2010 and came into effect on 5 Feb. although the opposition party UNITA boycotted the vote. Direct presidential elections were abolished. Instead the party with the majority in parliament will choose the president. A two 5-year term limit was introduced although it did not take effect until after the parliamentary elections in Aug. 2012, allowing President dos Santos to remain in power until 2022. The president was also made responsible for judicial appointments while the office of prime minister was replaced by that of a vice-president to be appointed by the president.

Currency

The unit of currency is the *kwanza* (AOA), introduced in Dec. 1999, replacing the *readjusted kwanza* at a rate of 1 kwanza = 1 m. readjusted kwanzas.

Defence

Conscription is for 2 years. Defence expenditure totalled US$6,049 m. in 2013 (US$326 per capita), representing 4.8% of GDP.

Economy

In 2011 agriculture accounted for 9% of GDP, industry 62% and services 29%.

Labour

In 2010 the estimated economically active population numbered 8,533,000 (53% males), up from 6,238,000 in 2000. Angola had 17,000 people living in slavery according to the Walk Free Foundation's 2013 *Global Slavery Index*.

Press

The government-owned *Jornal de Angola* (circulation of 42,000) was the only daily newspaper in 2008. The *Diário da República* is the official gazette. There are 12 private weekly publications and four smaller regional weeklies.

Rail

Prior to the civil war there was in excess of 2,900 km of railway (predominantly 1,067 mm gauge track), but much of the network was damaged during the war. However, restoration and redevelopment of the network is now under way, notably the Benguela Railway, linking the port city of Lobito with Huambo in Angola's rich farmlands and neighbouring Democratic Republic of the Congo and Zambia.

Religion

A study by the Pew Research Center's Forum on Religion & Public Life estimated that there were 17.3 m. Christians in 2010 and 790,000 followers of folk religions. A further 980,000 people had no religious affiliation. Catholics account for around 65% of Christians and Protestants 35%. In Feb. 2016 there was one cardinal.

Roads

There were 51,429 km of roads in 2001 and 671,100 vehicles in use in 2007. Many roads remain mined as a result of the civil war; a programme of de-mining and rehabilitation is under way.

Shipping

There are ports at Luanda, Lobito and Namibe, and oil terminals at Malongo, Lobito and Soyo. In Jan. 2009 there were 28 ships of 300 GT or over registered, totalling 21,000 GT.

Social Statistics

Life expectancy at birth, 2013, 50.4 years for males and 53.4 years for females. 2008 births (estimates), 775,000; deaths, 306,000. Estimated birth rate in 2008 was 43 per 1,000 population; estimated death rate, 17. Annual population growth rate, 2000–08, 2.9%. Fertility rate, 2008, 5.8 births per woman; infant mortality, 2010, 98 per 1,000 live births.

Telecommunications

In 2010 there were 303,200 main (fixed) telephone lines but mobile phone subscribers numbered 8.91 m. There were 32.8 internet users per 1,000 inhabitants in 2009. Fixed internet subscriptions totalled 320,000 in 2009 (17.2 per 1,000 inhabitants). In June 2012 there were 433,000 Facebook users.

Territory and Population

Angola is bounded in the north by the Republic of the Congo, north and northeast by the Democratic Republic of the Congo, east by Zambia, south by Namibia and west by the Atlantic Ocean. The area is 1,246,700 km² (481,350 sq. miles) including the province of Cabinda, an exclave of territory separated by 30 km² of the Democratic Republic of the Congo's territory. Angola's first census in more than 40 years was held in May 2014; the provisional population was 24,383,301, giving a density of 19.6 per km². In 2010, 58.5% of the population were living in urban areas. Population figures are rough estimates because the civil war led to huge movements of population. The most important towns are Luanda, the capital (2012 population estimate, 5.85 m.), Huambo, Lobito, Benguela, Kuito, Lubango, Malanje and Namibe. The main ethnic groups are Umbundo (Ovimbundo), Kimbundo, Bakongo, Chokwe, Ganguela, Luvale and Kwanyama. Portuguese is the official language. Bantu and other African languages are also spoken.

Tourism

In 2012 there were a record 528,000 non-resident tourists (up from 91,000 in 2002 and 195,000 in 2007), bringing revenue of US$711 m.

Antigua and Barbuda

Factsheet

Capital: St John's
Population estimate, 2015: 92,000
GNI per capita, 2014: (PPP$) 20,070
HDI/world rank, 2014: 0·783/58
Internet domain extension: .ag

Civil Aviation

V. C. Bird International Airport is near St John's. A domestic flight links the airports on Antigua and Barbuda.

Climate

A tropical climate, but drier than most West Indies islands. The hot season is from May to Nov., when rainfall is greater. Mean annual rainfall is 40″ (1,000 mm).

Constitution and Government

H.M. Queen Elizabeth, as Head of State, is represented by a Governor-General appointed by her on the advice of the Prime Minister. There is a bicameral legislature, comprising a 17-member Senate appointed by the Governor-General and an 18-member House of Representatives (with 17 members elected by universal suffrage for a 5-year term plus the Speaker). The Governor-General appoints a Prime Minister and, on the latter's advice, other members of the Cabinet. Barbuda is administered by a nine-member directly-elected council.

Currency

The unit of currency is the *East Caribbean dollar* (XCD), issued by the Eastern Caribbean Central Bank.

Defence

The Antigua and Barbuda Defence Force (ABDF) numbers 170 and has four units: the Antigua and Barbuda Regiment, the Service and Support Unit, the Coast Guard and the Antigua and Barbuda Cadet Corps. There are 75 reserves. In 2013 defence expenditure totalled US$26 m. (US$286 per capita), representing 2.1% of GDP.

Economy

In 2009 agriculture accounted for 1.7% of GDP, industry 22.0% and services 76.3%.

Labour

In 2008, 38,500 people were in employment. The main areas of activity were: hotels and restaurants, 5,800; wholesale and retail trade, repair of motor vehicles, motorcycles and personal and household goods, 5,500; public administration and defence, and compulsory social security, 5,000. The hourly minimum wage was raised to EC$7.50 (US$2.78) in Jan. 2008.

Press

The main newspapers are *The Antigua Sun* and *The Daily Observer*, with a combined circulation of 9,000 in 2008.

Religion

In 2010 an estimated 93.0% of the population were Christians (mainly Protestants) and 3.6% folk religionists according to the Pew Research Center's Forum on Religion & Public Life.

Roads

In 2012 there were about 1,170 km of roads. 20,100 vehicles were in use in 2009, including 13,400 passenger cars and 5,300 commercial vehicles.

Shipping

The main port is St John's Harbour. In Jan. 2009 there were 1,166 ships of 300 GT or over registered, totalling 9,620,000 GT.

Social Statistics

Expectation of life, 2009: males, 73 years, females, 76. Annual population growth rate, 2010–15, 1.1%. 2007: births, 1,240; deaths, 504. Infant mortality in 2010 was 7 per 1,000 live births; fertility rate, 2008, 2.1 births per woman.

Telecommunications

There were 41,700 fixed telephone lines in 2010, or 470.5 per 1,000 inhabitants. Mobile phone subscribers numbered 163,900 in 2010. There were 742.0 internet users per 1,000 inhabitants in 2009. Fixed internet subscriptions totalled 15,600 in 2009 (177.7 per 1,000 inhabitants).

Territory and Population

Antigua and Barbuda comprises three islands of the Lesser Antilles situated in the eastern Caribbean with a total land area of 442 km² (171 sq. miles); it consists of Antigua (280 km²), Barbuda, 40 km to the north (161 km²) and uninhabited Redonda, 40 km to the southwest (1 km²). The population at the census of May 2011 was 85,567 (1,634 on Barbuda); density, 194 per km². In 2011, 30.4% of the population lived in urban areas. The chief town is St John's, the capital, on Antigua (22,219 inhabitants in 2011). Codrington (914 inhabitants in 2001) is the only settlement on Barbuda. English is the official language; local dialects are also spoken.

Tourism

Tourism is the main industry, contributing about 70% of GDP and 80% of foreign exchange earnings and related activities. In 2010 there were 229,943 tourist arrivals by air and 557,635 cruise passengers arrivals.

Argentina

República Argentina (Argentine Republic)

Factsheet

Capital: Buenos Aires
Population estimate, 2015: 43.42 m.
GNI per capita, 2013: (PPP$) 17,297
HDI/world rank, 2014: 0.836/40
Internet domain extension: .ar

Civil Aviation

The main airport is Ministro Pistarini International Airport—also known as Ezeiza International Airport—which serves Buenos Aires and handled 7,910,048 passengers in 2009 (7,461,727 passengers on international flights). The second busiest airport is Aeroparque Jorge Newbery, also serving Buenos Aires, which handled 6,449,344 passengers in 2009. It is much more important as a domestic airport, with only 524,934 passengers on international flights in 2009. The national carrier, Aerolíneas Argentinas, was privatized in 1990 but renationalized in Sept. 2008. In 2006 scheduled airline traffic of Argentinian-based carriers flew 101 m. km, carrying 6,636,000 passengers (1,818,000 on international flights).

Climate

The climate is warm temperate over the pampas, where rainfall occurs in all seasons, but diminishes towards the west. In the north and west, the climate is more arid, with high summer temperatures, while in the extreme south conditions are also dry, but much cooler. Buenos Aires, Jan. 74 °F (23.3 °C), July 50 °F (10 °C). Annual rainfall 37″ (950 mm). Bahía Blanca, Jan. 74 °F (23.3 °C), July 48 °F (8.9 °C). Annual rainfall 21″ (523 mm). Mendoza, Jan. 75 °F (23.9 °C), July 47 °F (8.3 °C). Annual rainfall 8″ (190 mm). Rosario, Jan. 76 °F (24.4 °C), July 51 °F (10.6 °C). Annual rainfall 35″ (869 mm). San Juan, Jan. 78 °F (25.6 °C), July 50 °F (10 °C). Annual rainfall 4″ (89 mm). San Miguel de Tucumán, Jan. 79 °F (26.1 °C), July 56 °F (13.3 °C). Annual rainfall 38″ (970 mm). Ushuaia, Jan. 50 °F (10 °C), July 34 °F (1.1 °C). Annual rainfall 19″ (475 mm).

Constitution and Government

On 10 April 1994 elections were held for a 230-member constituent assembly to reform the 1853 constitution. The Justicialist National Movement (Peronist) gained 39% of votes cast and the Radical Union 20%. On 22 Aug. 1994 this assembly unanimously adopted a new constitution. This reduces the presidential term of office from 6 to 4 years, but permits the President to stand for two terms. The President is no longer elected by an electoral college, but directly by universal suffrage. A presidential candidate is elected with more than 45% of votes cast, or 40% if at least 10% ahead of an opponent; otherwise there is a second round. The Constitution reduces the President's powers by instituting a *Chief of Cabinet*. The bicameral *National Congress* consists of a Senate and a Chamber of Deputies. The Senate comprises 72 members (one-third of the members elected every 2 years to 6-year terms). The Chamber of Deputies comprises 257 members (one-half of the members elected every 2 years to 4-year terms) directly elected by universal suffrage. Voting is compulsory for citizens aged 18–70 and—with effect from the mid-term elections of Oct. 2013—optional for those aged 16 and 17.

Currency

The monetary unit is the *peso* (ARS), which replaced the *austral* on 1 Jan. 1992 at a rate of one peso = 10,000 australs. For nearly a decade the peso was pegged at parity with the US dollar, but it was devalued by nearly 30% in Jan. 2002 and floated in Feb. 2002.

Defence

Conscription was abolished in 1994. In 2013 defence expenditure totalled US$5,104 m. (US$120 per capita), representing 1.0% of GDP (compared to over 8% in 1981).

Economy

Agriculture contributed 7.5% of GDP in 2009, industry 31.8% and services 60.7%. In Jan. 2006 the government repaid the country's entire US$9.57 bn. debt to the IMF ahead of schedule.

Labour

In 2012 the labour force in urban areas totalled 16.90 m., of which 15.66 m. were employed and 1.24 m. were unemployed. The urban unemployment rate was 7.3% in 2012. Argentina had 35,000 people living in slavery according to the Walk Free Foundation's 2013 *Global Slavery Index*.

Press

In 2014 there were 47 daily newspapers with a combined average daily circulation of 1.4 m. The main newspapers are *Clarín*, *La Nación* and *Diario Popular*.

Rail

Much of the 34,000 km state-owned network (on 1,000 mm, 1,435 mm and 1,676 mm gauges) was privatized in 1993–94. 30-year concessions were awarded to five freight operators; long-distance passenger services are run by contractors to the requirements of local authorities. Metro, light rail and suburban railway services are also operated by concessionaires. The rail company carrying the most passengers is Trenes de Buenos Aires (190 m. in 2008); Ferrosur Roca carries the most freight (5.1 m. tonnes in 2005–06). The metro and light rail network in Buenos Aires extended to 75 km in 2005. A light railway opened in Mendoza in 2012, with a total length of 12.5 km.

Religion

The Roman Catholic religion is supported by the State; according to estimates by the Pew Research Center's Forum on Religion & Public Life there were 31.02 m. Catholics in 2010. There were four cardinals in Feb. 2016. Jorge Mario Bergoglio was a cardinal from 2001 until March 2013, when he was selected to succeed Benedict XVI as Pope. The Pew Research Center estimates that in 2010 there were also 2.96 m. Protestants, 440,000 other

Christians (including Latter-day Saints/Mormons), 400,000 Muslims, 330,000 folk religionists and 200,000 Jews.

Roads

In 2012 there were 228,512 km of roads, of which 34.6% were paved. The four main roads constituting Argentina's portion of the Pan-American Highway were opened in 1942. Vehicles in use in 2007 totalled 12,399,900. In 2005, 3,443 people were killed in road accidents.

Shipping

In Jan. 2009 there were 59 ships of 300 GT or over registered, totalling 500,000 GT. The leading ports are Buenos Aires (which handled 12,745,000 tonnes of cargo in 2008) and Bahía Blanca (12,676,000 tonnes of cargo in 2008).

Social Statistics

2010 births, 756,176; deaths, 318,602. Rates, 2010 (per 1,000 population): birth, 18.7; death, 7.9. Infant mortality, 2010, 12 per 1,000 live births. Life expectancy at birth, 2013, 72.6 years for males and 79.9 years for females. Annual population growth rate, 2005–10, 0.9%; fertility rate, 2008, 2.2 births per woman. Argentina legalized same-sex marriage in July 2010.

Telecommunications

The telephone service Entel was privatized in 1990. The sell-off split Argentina into two monopolies, operated by Telefónica Internacional de España, and a holding controlled by France Télécom and Telecom Italia. In 2000 the industry was opened to unrestricted competition. In 2014 mobile phone subscribers numbered 66.4 m. (1,588·0 per 1,000 persons). In the same year there were 9.6 m. main (fixed) telephone lines. In 2014, 64.7% of the population were internet users. In June 2012 there were 19.0 m. Facebook users.

Territory and Population

The second largest country in South America, the Argentine Republic is bounded in the north by Bolivia, in the northeast by Paraguay, in the east by Brazil, Uruguay and the Atlantic Ocean, and the west by Chile. The republic consists of 23 provinces and one federal district. Argentina also claims territory in Antarctica. The area is 2,780,400 km² (excluding the claimed Antarctic territory) and the population at the 2010 census 40,117,096, giving a density of 14 per km². In 2011, 92.6% of the population were urban. The population of the main metropolitan areas in 2010 was: Buenos Aires, 13,588,171; Córdoba, 1,453,865; Rosario, 1,236,089; Mendoza, 937,154; Tucumán, 794,327; La Plata, 787,294. 97% speak the national language, Spanish, while 2% speak Italian and 1% other languages. The 2010 census population included 1,805,957 persons born outside Argentina (550,713 born in Paraguay, 345,272 in Bolivia, 191,147 in Chile, 157,514 in Peru and 147,499 in Italy).

Tourism

In 2009, 4,329,000 tourists visited Argentina (excluding same-day visitors), down from a record 4,700,000 in 2008 and 4,562,000 in 2007. Of the 4,329,000 tourists in 2009, 3,413,000 were from elsewhere in the Americas and 722,000 were from Europe.

Armenia

Hayastani Hanrapetoutiun (Republic of Armenia)

Factsheet

Capital: Yerevan
Population estimate, 2015: 3.02 m.
GNI per capita, 2014: (PPP$) 8,124
HDI/world rank, 2014: 0.733/85=
Internet domain extension: .am

Civil Aviation

There is an international airport at Yerevan (Zvartnots), which handled 1,443,557 passengers and 8,323 tonnes of freight in 2009. In April 2013 the Armenian flag carrier, Armavia, ceased operations. In 2010 there were direct flights from Yerevan to over 40 international destinations.

Climate

Summers are very dry and hot although nights can be cold. Winters are very cold, often with heavy snowfall. Yerevan, Jan. −9 °C, July 28 °C. Annual rainfall 318 mm.

Constitution and Government

The constitution was adopted by a nationwide referendum on 5 July 1995. The head of state is the *President*, directly elected for 5-year terms. Parliament is a 131-member *Azgayin Zhoghov* (National Assembly), with 90 deputies elected by party list and 41 chosen by direct election. The government is nominated by the President.

Currency

In Nov. 1993 a new currency unit, the *dram* (AMD) of 100 *lumma*, was introduced to replace the rouble.

Defence

There is conscription for 24 months. Total active forces numbered 48,834 in 2011, including 25,880 conscripts. Defence expenditure in 2013 totalled US$447 m. (US$150 per capita), representing 4.3% of GDP. There is a Russian military base in Armenia with 3,303 personnel in 2011.

Economy

In 2009 agriculture contributed 18.9% of GDP, industry 35.8% and services 45.3%.

Labour

The labour force in 2013 was 1,536,000 (1,452,000 in 2003). 67.3% of the population aged 15–64 was economically active in 2013. In the same year 16.2% of the population was unemployed. Armenia had 11,000 people living in slavery according to the Walk Free Foundation's 2013 *Global Slavery Index*.

Press

In 2008 there were 11 paid-for daily newspapers and 49 paid-for non-dailies with a combined circulation of 116,000.

Rail

Total length in 2010 was 826 km of 1,520 mm gauge. Passenger-km travelled in 2010 came to 50 m. and freight tonne-km to 346 m.

Religion

Armenia adopted Christianity in AD 301, thus becoming the first Christian nation in the world. The Armenian Apostolic Church is headed by its Catholicos (Karekin II, b. 1951) whose seat is at Echmiatsin, and who is head of all the Armenian (Gregorian) communities throughout the world. In 2013 it numbered 9 m. adherents, two-thirds of whom lived outside of Armenia. There is a second see located at Antelias in Lebanon—the Catholicos of Cilicia is Aram I (b. 1947). An estimated 87% of the population belonged to the Armenian Apostolic Church in 2010 according to the Pew Research Center's Forum on Religion & Public Life. The largest religious minority is Armenian Catholicism.

Roads

There were 7,515 km of road network in 2007, of which 89.8% were paved. In 2007 there were 289,800 passenger cars and 25,679 buses and coaches. There were 371 fatalities as a result of road accidents in 2007.

Social Statistics

2010 births, 44,825; deaths, 27,921; marriages, 17,984; divorces, 2,097. Rates, 2010 (per 1,000 population): birth, 13.8; death, 8.6; marriage, 5.5; divorce, 0.9. Infant mortality, 2010, 18 per 1,000 live births. Annual population growth rate, 2008–10, 0.2%. Life expectancy at birth, 2013, 71.3 years for men and 78.0 years for women; fertility rate, 2013, 1.7 births per woman.

Telecommunications

There were 589,900 fixed telephone lines in 2010 (190.8 per 1,000 inhabitants). Mobile phone subscribers numbered 3.87 m. in 2010. There were 153.0 internet users per 1,000 inhabitants in 2009. Fixed internet subscriptions totalled 96,000 in 2010 (31.1 per 1,000 inhabitants). In March 2012 there were 283,000 Facebook users.

Territory and Population

Armenia covers an area of 29,743 km^2 (11,484 sq. miles). It is bounded in the north by Georgia, in the east by Azerbaijan and in the south and west by Iran and Turkey. The 2011 census population was 3,018,854; population density, 101 per km^2. Armenians account for 97.9%, Kurds 1.3% and Russians 0.5%- in 1989, prior to the Nagorno Karabakh conflict, 2.6% of the population were Azeris. Approximately 64% lived in urban areas in 2009. There are an estimated 8 m. Armenians worldwide, mainly living in Russia, the USA and Georgia as well as in Armenia itself. The capital is Yerevan (estimated population of 1,068,300 in 2014). The official language is Armenian.

Tourism

In 2010 there were 684,000 international tourist arrivals (excluding same-day visitors), up from 575,000 in 2009.

Australia

Commonwealth of Australia

Factsheet

Capital: Canberra
Population estimate, 2015: 23.97 m.
GNI per capita, 2014: (PPP$) 42,261
HDI/world rank, 2014: 0.935/2
Internet domain extension: .au

Civil Aviation

Qantas Airways is Australia's principal international airline. A total of 54 international airlines operated scheduled air services to and from Australia in& 2014. There are 11 international airports, the main ones being Adelaide, Brisbane, Cairns, Darwin, Melbourne, Perth and Sydney. In 2014–15 passenger movements totalled a record 147,353,391 (an increase of 0.6% on the previous financial year); domestic and regional passenger numbers totalled 113,486,916 and international 33,866,475; international freight increased by 6.3% to a record 936,733 tonnes; international mail decreased by 0.3% to 40,395 tonnes. Sydney (Kingsford Smith) handled the most traffic (26.5%) in Australia in 2014–15 (39,021,357 passengers, of which 25,513,156 on domestic and regional flights), followed by Melbourne International (21.7%) and Brisbane (14.9%). Internal airlines (domestic and regional) carried 54.0 m. passengers in 2010. Domestic airlines were deregulated in Oct. 1990. In 2014–15 there were 192 certified and 135 registered aerodromes in Australia and its external territories. At 30 June 2015 there were 15,287 registered aircraft on the Australian Civil Aircraft Register including 2,125 helicopters and 386 balloons.

Climate

Over most of the continent, four seasons may be recognized. Spring is from Sept. to Nov., summer from Dec. to Feb., autumn from March to May and winter from June to Aug., but because of its great size there are climates that range from tropical monsoon to cool temperate, with large areas of desert as well. In northern Australia there are only two seasons, the wet one lasting from Nov. to March, but rainfall amounts diminish markedly from the coast to the interior. Central and southern Queensland are subtropical, north and central New South Wales are warm temperate, as are parts of Victoria, Western Australia and Tasmania, where most rain falls in winter. Canberra, Jan. 68 °F (20 °C), July 42 °F (5.6 °C). Annual rainfall 25″ (635 mm). Adelaide, Jan. 73 °F (22.8 °C), July 52 °F (11.1 °C). Annual rainfall 21″ (528 mm). Brisbane, Jan. 77 °F (25 °C), July 58 °F (14.4 °C). Annual rainfall 45″ (1153 mm). Darwin, Jan. 83 °F (28.3 °C), July 77 °F (25 °C). Annual rainfall 59″ (1,536 mm). Hobart, Jan. 62 °F (16.7 °C), July 46 °F (7.8 °C). Annual rainfall 23″ (584 mm). Melbourne, Jan. 67 °F (19.4 °C), July 49 °F (9.4 °C). Annual rainfall 26″ (659 mm). Perth, Jan. 74 °F (23.3 °C), July 55 °F (12.8 °C). Annual rainfall 35″ (873 mm). Sydney, Jan. 71 °F (21.7 °C), July 53 °F (11.7 °C). Annual rainfall 47″ (1,215 mm).

Constitution and Government

Under the Constitution legislative power is vested in a Federal Parliament, consisting of the Queen, represented by a Governor-General, a Senate and a House of Representatives. Under the terms of the constitution there must be a session of parliament at least once a year. *The Senate* (Upper House) comprises 76 Senators (12 for each State voting as one electorate and, as from Aug. 1974, two Senators respectively for the Australian Capital Territory and the Northern Territory). Senators representing the States are chosen for 6 years. The terms of Senators representing the Territories expire at the close of the day next preceding the polling day for the general elections of the House of Representatives. In general, the Senate is renewed to the extent of one-half every 3 years, but in case of disagreement with the House of Representatives, it, together with the House of Representatives, may be dissolved, and an entirely new Senate elected. Elections to the Senate are on the single transferable vote system; voters list candidates in order of preference. A candidate must reach a quota to be elected, otherwise the lowest-placed candidate drops out and his or her votes are transferred to other candidates. The *House of Representatives* (Lower House) consists, as nearly as practicable, of twice as many Members as there are Senators, the numbers chosen in the several States being in proportion to population as shown by the latest statistics, but not less than five for any original State. Executive power is vested in the *Governor-General*, advised by an Executive Council. The Governor-General presides over the Council, and its members hold office at his pleasure. The policy of a ministry is, in practice, determined by the Ministers of State meeting without the Governor-General under the chairmanship of the Prime Minister. This group is known as the *Cabinet*.

Currency

The currency unit, the Australian dollar (AUD), is divided into 100 *cents*.

Defence

2013 defence expenditure was US$25,967 m., amounting to US$1,166 per capita and representing 1.6% of GDP.

Economy

In 2013 agriculture contributed 2% of GDP, industry 27% and services 71%.

Labour

In 2010–11 the total labour force (persons aged 15 and over) numbered 11,993,800 (5,458,500 females). There were 11,386,900 employed persons in 2010–11 (45% females) with 3,372,300 in part-time employment (70% females). Average weekly wage, May 2011, $A1,304.70 (men, $A1,397.70; women, $A1,159.20). Average weekly hours worked by full-time employed person, 2008–09: 39.8 h. In 2010–11 part-time work accounted for 30% of all employment in Australia. Foreign-born workers made up 28.8% of the labour force in Aug. 2014, the highest share of any major industrialized nation. In 2010 there were 227 industrial disputes recorded, which accounted for 126,600 working days lost (196,500 in 2008). In these disputes 54,800 workers were involved. In 2010–11, 606,900 persons were unemployed, of whom 19% had been unemployed for more than 1 year. The unemployment rate in Dec. 2015 was 5.8% (down from 6.1% in 2014 as a whole). Australia had 3,000 people living in slavery according to the Walk Free Foundation's 2013 *Global Slavery Index*.

Press

There were 49 English daily metropolitan newspapers in 2013 (2 national, 10 metropolitan and 37 regional). There are also 10 metropolitan Sunday newspapers. The papers with the largest circulations in June 2013 were the

Sunday Telegraph (New South Wales), with an average of 541,749 per issue; the *Sunday Herald Sun* (Victoria), with an average of 485,943 per issue; and the Saturday edition of the *Herald Sun* (Victoria), with an average of 416,662 per issue. In 2013 there were two free dailies, *mX* (with three editions, published in Brisbane, Melbourne and Sydney) and *Manly Daily*.

Rail

In 2012 Australia had 33,299 route-km of open track of which 17,034 km were standard gauge (1,435 mm), 12,595 km were narrow gauge (1,067 mm), 3,281 km were narrow gauge (610 mm) and 389 km dual gauge; a total of 3,300 route-km were electrified. In 2009–10 a total of 815.3 m. tonnes of freight were carried; passengers carried totalled 755 m. urban (train and tram); 15 m. non-urban.

Religion

Under the Constitution the Commonwealth cannot make any law to establish any religion, to impose any religious observance or to prohibit the free exercise of any religion. The following percentages refer to those religions with the largest number of adherents at the census of 2011. Answering the census question on religious adherence was not obligatory, however. Christian, 61.1% of population (including: Catholic, 25.3%; Anglican, 17.1%; Uniting Church, 5.0%; Presbyterian and Reformed, 2.8%; Eastern Orthodox, 2.6%; Baptist, 1.6%; Lutheran, 1.2%; Pentecostal, 1.1%). Religions other than Christian, 7.2% (including: Buddhism, 2.5%; Islam, 2.2%; Hinduism, 1.3%; Judaism, 0.5%). Other religions, 0.8%; no religion, 22.3%; not stated and others, 8.6%. The Anglican Church of Australia first ordained women as priests in 1992. Women have been ordained as bishops since May 2008. In Feb. 2016 the Roman Catholic church had two cardinals.

Roads

At 30 June 2012 there were an estimated 900,083 km of roads (around 42.7% of which were sealed), including 51,847 km of highways. As at 31 Jan. 2011 registration totals were: 12,525,000 passenger vehicles, 2,531,000 light commercial vehicles, 547,000 trucks, 88,000 buses and 679,000 motorcycles. In 2014, 1,056 persons were killed in road accidents (less than half the 1989 total of 2,407).

Shipping

The chief ports are Brisbane, Dampier, Fremantle, Gladstone, Hay Point, Melbourne, Newcastle, Port Hedland, Port Kembla, Port Walcott, Sydney and Weipa. Port Hedland overtook Dampier as Australia's busiest port in 2008–09, handling 159,391,000 tonnes of cargo (158,382,000 tonnes loaded and 1,009,000 tonnes discharged) compared to 140,824,000 tonnes for Dampier (140,122,000 tonnes loaded and 702,000 tonnes discharged). Iron ore exports to China are the principal factor behind the rapid growth of Dampier and Port Hedland (both of which are in Western Australia) during the 2000s. In Jan. 2009 there were 98 ships of 300 GT or over registered, totalling 1,258,000 GT. Of the 98 vessels registered, 45 were passenger ships, 26 general cargo ships, 15 bulk carriers, seven oil tankers, four liquid gas tankers and there was one container ship.

Social Statistics

Life expectancy at birth, 2010–12, 79.9 years for males and 84.3 years for females. 2013 births 308,065; deaths, 147,678; marriages, 118,962; divorces, 47,638. In 2012 the median age for marrying was 31.4 years for males and 29.4 for females. Infant mortality, 2012, was 3.3 per 1,000 live births. Population growth rate in 2014, 1.4%; fertility rate, 2013, 1.9 births per woman. Suicide rates (per 100,000 population, 2009): 10.4 (men, 16.0; women, 4.9). In the Human Development Index, or HDI (measuring progress in countries in longevity, knowledge and standard of living), Australia was ranked second (behind Norway) in the 2014 rankings published in the annual Human Development Report.

Telecommunications

In 2013 there were 10,350,000 main (fixed) telephone lines, down from 10,709,000 in 2009. Mobile phone subscribers numbered 24,940,000 in 2013 (1068·4 per 1,000 persons). In 2013, 83.5% of the population aged 15 or over were internet users. The fixed broadband penetration rate in Dec. 2010 was 24.1 subscribers per 100 inhabitants. In Dec. 2011 there were 10.7 m. Facebook users (48% of the population).

Territory and Population

Australia, excluding external territories, covers a land area of 7,692,024 sq. km, extending from Cape York (10.41′ °S) in the north some 3,680 km to South East Cape, Tasmania (43.39′ °S), and from Cape Byron, New South Wales (153.39′ °E) in the east some 4,000 km west to Steep Point, Western Australia (113.9′ °E). External territories under the administration of Australia comprise the Ashmore and Cartier Islands, Australian Antarctic Territory, Christmas Island, the Cocos (Keeling) Islands, the Coral Sea Islands, the Heard and McDonald Islands and Norfolk Island. Population (2011 census) 21,507,717; density, 2.8 per sq. km. In 2010, 89.1% of the population lived in urban areas. The capital is Canberra, with a 2011 census population of 356,586. The median age of the 2011 census population was 37 years. Australians born overseas (census 2011), 5,294,200 (24.6%—the highest proportion anywhere in the industrialized world), of whom 1,101,100 (20.8%) were from the United Kingdom. Aboriginals have been included in population statistics only since 1967. At the 2011 census 548,370 people identified themselves as being of indigenous origin (2.5% of the total population). The national language is English. The Migration Act of Dec. 1989 sought to curb illegal entry and ensure that annual immigrant intakes were met but not exceeded. Provisions for temporary visitors to become permanent were restricted. In 2011–12, 84,183 people who were born overseas became Australian citizens.

Tourism

In 2011 the total number of overseas visitors for the year stood at 5.9 m. (a 0.2% decrease on the previous year). The top source countries for visitors in 2011 were New Zealand (1,172,700); UK (608,300); China (542,000); USA (456,200); Japan (332,700); and Singapore (318,500). Tourism is Australia's largest single earner of foreign exchange.

Austria

Republik Österreich (Austrian Republic)

Factsheet

Capital: Vienna
Population estimate, 2015: 8.55 m.
GNI per capita, 2014: (PPP$) 43,869
HDI/world rank, 2014: 0.885/23
Internet domain extension: .at

Civil Aviation

There are international airports at Vienna (Schwechat), Graz, Innsbruck, Klagenfurt, Linz and Salzburg. The national airline is Austrian Airlines, which was privatized after a takeover by Lufthansa in Sept. 2009. In April 2015 Tyrolean Airways merged into Austrian Airlines. In 2010, 65 other airlines had scheduled flights to and from Vienna. In 2011, 312,502 commercial aircraft and 25,704,655 passengers arrived and departed; 227,938 tonnes of freight and 13,551 tonnes of mail were handled. In 2011 Vienna handled 21,069,398 passengers and 218,835 tonnes of freight. Austrian Airlines carried 11,261,000 passengers in 2011.

Climate

The climate is temperate and from west to east in transition from marine to more continental. Depending on the elevation, the climate is also predominated by alpine influence. Winters are cold with snowfall. In the eastern parts summers are warm and dry. Vienna, Jan. 0.0 °C, July 20.2 °C. Annual rainfall 624 mm. Graz, Jan. −1.0 °C, July 19.4 °C. Annual rainfall 825 mm. Innsbruck, Jan. −1.7 °C, July 18.1 °C. Annual rainfall 885 mm. Salzburg, Jan. −0.9 °C, July 18.6 °C. Annual rainfall 1,174 mm.

Constitution and Government

The constitution of 1 Oct. 1920 was revised in 1929 and restored on 1 May 1945. Austria is a democratic federal republic comprising nine states (*Länder*), with a federal *President* (*Bundespräsident*) directly elected for

not more than two successive 6-year terms, and a bicameral National Assembly which comprises a National Council and a Federal Council. The National Council (*Nationalrat*) comprises 183 members directly elected for a 5-year term by proportional representation in a three-tier system by which seats are allocated at the level of 43 regional and nine state constituencies, and one federal constituency. Any party gaining 4% of votes cast nationally is represented in the National Council. In 2007 Austria's voting age was reduced to 16-the lowest for national elections in the EU. The Federal Council (*Bundesrat*) has 61 members appointed by the nine states for the duration of the individual State Assemblies' terms; the number of deputies for each state is proportional to that state's population. In March 2016 the ÖVP held 22 of the 61 seats, the SPÖ 20, the FPÖ 13, the Greens 4, Team Stronach 1 with one unattached member. The head of government is a *Federal Chancellor*, who is appointed by the President (usually the head of the party winning the most seats in National Council elections). The *Vice-Chancellor*, the *Federal Ministers* and the *State Secretaries* are appointed by the President at the Chancellor's recommendation.

Currency

On 1 Jan. 1999 the euro (EUR) became the legal currency in Austria at the irrevocable conversion rate of 13.7603 schillings to one euro. The euro, which consists of 100 cents, has been in circulation since 1 Jan. 2002. On the introduction of the euro there was a 'dual circulation' period before the schilling ceased to be legal tender on 28 Feb. 2002.

Defence

The Federal President is C.-in-C. of the armed forces. Conscription is for a 6-month period, with liability for at least another 30 days' reservist refresher training spread over 8–10 years. Conscientious objectors can instead choose to undertake 9 months' civilian service. Defence expenditure in 2013 totalled US$3,232 m. (US$393 per capita), representing 0.8% of GDP.

Economy

In 2012 agriculture accounted for 2% of GDP, industry 28% and services 70%.

Labour

The unemployment rate in Dec. 2015 was 5.8%. Of 3,421,755 employees in 2011 (annual average), 573,571 worked in the manufacturing and production of goods; 529,976 in public administration and defence, and compulsory social security; 518,188 in wholesale and retail trade, and the repair of motor vehicles; 233,994 in human health and social work; 184,548 in accommodation and food service activities. In 2011 there were an average of 73,800 job vacancies. There were no recorded strikes between 2005 and 2009. Austria has one of the lowest average retirement ages but reforms passed in 1997 now make it less attractive to retire before 60. Only 15% of men and 6% of women in the 60–65 age range work, although the legal retirement ages are 60 for women and 65 for men. Austria has one of the lowest average retirement ages but reforms passed in 1997 now make it less attractive to retire before 60. Only 15% of men and 6% of women in the 60–65 age range work, although the legal retirement ages are 60 for women and 65 for men.

Press

There were 18 daily newspapers and 273 non-daily newspapers in 2014. The most popular newspaper is the mass-market tabloid *Kronen Zeitung*, with an average daily circulation of 815,000 in 2014. In the 2011–12 *World Press Freedom Index* compiled by Reporters Without Borders, Austria ranked fifth out of 179 countries.

Rail

The Austrian Federal Railways (ÖBB) has been restructured and was split up into ten new companies, which became operational on 1 Jan. 2005. Length of route in 2011, 5,500 km, of which 3,763 km were electrified. There are also a number of private railways. In 2011, 244.0 m. passengers and 107.6 m. tonnes of freight were carried by Federal Railways. There is a metro and tramway in Vienna, and tramways in Gmunden, Graz, Innsbruck and Linz.

Religion

In 2012 there were 5.36 m. Roman Catholics (5.92 m. in 2001). There were an estimated 520,000 Muslims in 2009 (350,000 in 2001). Orthodox Christians number around 500,000 and Evangelical Lutherans 300,000. The Roman Catholic Church has two ecclesiastical provinces and seven suffragan dioceses. In Feb. 2016 there was one cardinal.

Roads

In 2007 the road network totalled 107,262 km (Autobahn, 1,677 km; highways, 10,408 km; secondary roads, 23,657 km). In 2007 passenger cars in use numbered 4,245,600, lorries and vans 372,600, buses and coaches 9,300, and motorcycles and mopeds 642,800. There were 691 fatalities in road accidents in 2007.

Shipping

The Danube is an important waterway. Goods traffic (in 1,000 tonnes): 12,084 in 2005; 11,782 in 2006; 12,107 in 2007; 11,209 in 2008 (including the Rhine-Main-Danube Canal). There were four vessels of 300 GT or over registered in Jan. 2009, totalling 14,000 GT.

Social Statistics

Statistics, 2014: live births, 81,722 (rate of 9.6 per 1,000 population); deaths, 78,252 (rate of 9.2 per 1,000 population); infant deaths, 249; marriages, 37,458; divorces, 16,647. In 2011 there were 1,286 suicides (rate of 15.3 per 100,000 population), of which 973 males and 313 females. Average annual population growth rate, 2007–11, 0.4%. Life expectancy at birth, 2011, 83.4 years for women and 78.1 years for men.

Telecommunications

Österreichische Industrie Holding AG, the Austrian investment and privatization agency, holds a 28.4% stake in Telekom Austria. In 2014 mobile phone subscribers numbered 12,952,600 (1,519.1 per 1,000 persons). In the same year there were 3,254,700 main (fixed) telephone lines. In 2014, 81.0% of the population were internet users. In March 2012 there were 2.8 m. Facebook users.

Territory and Population

Austria is bounded in the north by Germany and the Czech Republic, east by Slovakia and Hungary, south by Slovenia and Italy, and west by Switzerland and Liechtenstein. It has an area of 83,879 sq. km (32,386 sq. miles), including 1,444 sq. km (558 sq. miles) of inland waters. Population (2011) 8,401,940; density, 101.9 per sq. km. Population estimate, Jan. 2015: 8,584,926. Austria has now adopted a register-based method of calculating the population rather than a traditional census, and had a full register-based census in 2011 for the first time. Previous population censuses: (1923) 6.53 m., (1934) 6.76 m., (1951) 6.93 m., (1971) 7.49 m., (1981) 7.56 m., (1991) 7.96 m, (2001) 8.03 m. In 2011, 67.8% of the population lived in urban areas. The official language is German.

Tourism

In 2011, 13,359 hotels and boarding houses had a total of 594,357 beds available; in the same year 23,012,000 non-resident tourists stayed in holiday accommodation and international tourist spending came to €14.3 bn. Of 126,002,551 overnight stays in tourist accommodation in 2011, 35,296,997 were by Austrians and 47,389,531 by Germans.

Azerbaijan

Azarbaijchan Respublikasy (Republic of Azerbaijan)

Factsheet

Capital: Baku
Population estimate, 2015: 9.75 m.
GNI per capita, 2014: (PPP$) 16,428
HDI/world rank, 2014: 0.751/78
Internet domain extension: .az

Civil Aviation

There is an international airport at Baku. Azerbaijan Airlines, the national airline, had international flights in 2010 to Aktau, Ankara, Astrakhan, Dubai, İstanbul, London, Milan, Moscow, Paris, Rostov, St Petersburg, Tel Aviv and Urumqi. In 2005 scheduled airline traffic of Azerbaijan-based carriers flew 14.8 m. km, carrying 494,800 passengers.

Climate

The climate is almost tropical in summer and the winters slightly warmer than in regions north of the Caucasus. Cold spells do occur, however, both on the high mountains and in the enclosed valleys. There are nine climatic zones. Baku, Jan. −6 °C, July 25 °C. Annual rainfall 318 mm.

Constitution and Government

Parliament is the 125-member *Melli-Majlis*, with all seats elected from single-member districts. A constitutional referendum and parliamentary elections were held on 12 Nov. 1995. Turnout for the referendum was 86%. The new constitution was approved by 91.9% of votes cast. As a result of a referendum held on 24 Aug. 2002 a number of changes were made to the constitution, including the distribution of the *Melli-Majlis* seats—previously, 25 seats were distributed proportionally among political parties. The validity of the outcome of the referendum was questioned by international observers. In a referendum on 18 March 2009 a measure to abolish presidential term limits was approved, with 91.8% of votes cast in favour.

Currency

The *manat* (AZM) of 100 *gyapiks* replaced the *rouble* in Jan. 1994. It was in turn replaced in Jan. 2006 by the *new manat* (AZN), also of 100 *gyapiks*, at 1 new manat = 5,000 manats.

Defence

Conscription is for 18 months, or 12 in the case of university graduates. In 2013 defence spending reached US$3.3 bn., up from US$0.4 bn. a decade earlier. Defence expenditure in 2013 was equivalent to US$209 per capita and represented 2.6% of GDP.

Economy

In 2010 agriculture accounted for 5.8% of GDP, industry 64.7% and services 29.5%.

Labour

In 2009 the economically active workforce numbered 4,331,800. The main areas of activity were: agriculture, hunting and forestry, 1,562,400; wholesale and retail trade/repair of motor vehicles, motorcycles and personal and household goods, 661,500; education, 346,900; public administration and defence/social security, 277,200. The unemployment rate in 2009 was 6.0%. The average monthly salary in 2009 was 298 manats. Azerbaijan had 33,000 people living in slavery according to the Walk Free Foundation's 2013 *Global Slavery Index*.

Press

In 2008 Azerbaijan published 32 paid-for daily newspapers with a combined circulation of 120,000. The leading paid-for daily is *Yeni Müsavat*, with an average daily circulation of 25,000 in 2008.

Rail

Total length in 2011 was 2,079 km of 1,524 mm gauge (1,244 km electrified). Passenger-km travelled in 2011 came to 1,660 m. and freight tonne-km to 7.8 bn. There is a metro and tramway in Baku and a tramway in Sumgait.

Religion

Azerbaijan is a secular state. In 2010 Muslims (mostly Shia) accounted for an estimated 97% of the population according to the Pew Research Center's Forum on Religion & Public Life, the balance being mainly Russian Orthodox, Armenian Apostolic and Jewish.

Roads

There were 59,141 km of roads (6,928 km highways and main roads) in 2006. Passenger cars in use in 2006 totalled 548,979 (57 per 1,000 inhabitants in 2005). In addition, there were 9,916 lorries and vans, and 27,474 buses and coaches. There were 1,107 fatalities as a result of road accidents in 2007.

Shipping

In Jan. 2009 there were 97 ships of 300 GT or over registered, totalling 458,000 GT. Baku is the main port.

Social Statistics

In 2009: births, 152,139; deaths, 52,514; marriages, 78,072; divorces, 7,784. Rates, 2009 (per 1,000 population): births, 17.2; deaths, 5.9; infant mortality (2010, per 1,000 live births), 39. Life expectancy in 2013: 73.9 years for females and 67.6 years for males. Annual population growth rate, 2005–12, 1.3%; fertility rate, 2013, 1.9 children per woman.

Telecommunications

In 2011 there were 1,684,000 landline telephone subscriptions (180.9 per 1,000 inhabitants) and 10,120,000 mobile phone subscriptions (1,087.5 per 1,000 inhabitants). There were 274.0 internet users per 1,000 inhabitants in 2009. Fixed internet subscriptions totalled 871,000 in 2010 (94.8 per 1,000 inhabitants). In March 2012 there were 782,000 Facebook users.

Territory and Population

Azerbaijan is bounded in the west by Armenia, in the north by Georgia and the Russian Federation (Dagestan), in the east by the Caspian sea and in the south by Turkey and Iran. Its area is 86,600 km^2 (33,430 sq. miles), and it includes the Nakhichevan Autonomous Republic and the largely Armenian-inhabited Nagorno-Karabakh. The population at the 2009 census was 8,922,447 (50.5% females); density, 103 per km^2. In 2011, 52.1% of the population lived in urban areas. The population breaks down into 91.6% Azerbaijanis, 2.0% Lezgis, 1.3% Armenians and 1.3% Russians (2009 census). Chief cities (estimates of Jan. 2013): Baku, 1,200,300; Gandja 322,600; Sumgait 290,500. There are 66 districts and 13 cities. The official language is Azeri.

Tourism

In 2012 there were 2,484,000 non-resident visitors; spending by tourists totalled US$2,634 m. in 2012.

The Bahamas

Commonwealth of The Bahamas

Factsheet

Capital: Nassau
Population estimate, 2015: 388,000
GNI per capita, 2014: (PPP$) 21,336
HDI/world rank, 2014: 0.790/55
Internet domain extension: .bs

Civil Aviation

There are international airports at Nassau and Freeport (Grand Bahama Island). The national carrier is the state-owned Bahamasair. In 2006 scheduled airline traffic of Bahamas-based carriers flew 8 m. km, carrying 1,033,000 passengers (456,000 on international flights).

Climate

Winters are mild and summers pleasantly warm. Most rain falls in May, June, Sept. and Oct., and thunderstorms are frequent in summer. Rainfall amounts vary over the islands from 30″ (750 mm) to 60″ (1,500 mm). Nassau, Jan. 71 °F (21.7 °C), July 81 °F (27.2 °C). Annual rainfall 47″ (1,179 mm).

Constitution and Government

The Commonwealth of The Bahamas is a free and democratic sovereign state. Executive power rests with Her Majesty the Queen, who appoints a Governor-General to represent her, advised by a Cabinet whom he appoints. There is a bicameral legislature. The *Senate* comprises 16 members all appointed by the Governor-General for 5-year terms, nine on the advice of the Prime Minister, four on the advice of the Leader of the Opposition, and three after consultation with both of them. The *House of Assembly* consists of 38 members elected from single-member constituencies for a maximum term of 5 years.

Currency

The unit of currency is the *Bahamian dollar* (BSD) of 100 *cents*. American currency is generally accepted.

Defence

The Royal Bahamas Defence Force is a primarily maritime force tasked with naval patrols and protection duties in the extensive waters of the archipelago. Personnel in 2011 numbered 860. The base is at Coral Harbour on New Providence Island. In 2013 defence expenditure totalled US$64 m. (US$201 per capita), representing 0.8% of GDP.

Economy

Services contributed 78.9% to GDP in 2013, with industry accounting for 19.2% and agriculture 1.9%.

Labour

The labour force in 2013 was 220,000 (165,000 in 2003). 80.2% of the population aged 15–64 was economically active in 2013. In the same year 16.2% of the population was unemployed.

Press

There were four paid-for dailies in 2008.

Religion

In 2010 the population was an estimated 96% Christian (mainly Protestant) according to the Pew Research Center's Forum on Religion & Public Life. Most of the remainder of the population is religiously unaffiliated.

Roads

There are approximately 2,700 km of roads, of which about 60% are paved. In 2007 there were around 27,100 vehicles in use.

Shipping

In Jan. 2009 there were 1,240 ships of 300 GT or over registered, totalling 43.93 m. GT (representing 5.6% of the world total and a figure exceeded only by the fleets of Panama and Liberia). Of the 1,240 vessels registered, 439 were general cargo ships, 273 oil tankers, 225 bulk carriers, 146 passenger ships, 78 liquid gas tankers, 62 container ships and 17 chemical tankers.

Social Statistics

2008 estimated births, 5,600; deaths, 2,000. Rates, 2008 estimates (per 1,000 population): birth, 16.7; death, 6.0; infant mortality (per 1000 live births), 2010, 14. Expectation of life was 72.1 years for males and 78.2 years for females in 2013. Annual population growth rate, 2005–10, 1.8%; fertility rate, 2008, 2.0 children per woman.

Telecommunications

There were 129,300 fixed telephone lines in 2010 (377.1 per 1,000 inhabitants) and mobile phone subscribers numbered 428,400. There were 338.8 internet users per 1,000 inhabitants in 2009. Fixed internet subscriptions totalled 38,600 in 2009 (114.0 per 1,000 inhabitants). In June 2012 there were 164,000 Facebook users.

Territory and Population

The Commonwealth of The Bahamas consists of over 700 islands and inhabited cays off the southeast coast of Florida extending for about

260,000 sq. miles. Only 22 islands are inhabited. Land area, 5,382 sq. miles (13,939 km²). Total census population for 2010 was 351,461. In 2011, 84.3% of the population were urban. The capital is Nassau on New Providence Island (246,329 in 2010). Other large towns are Freeport (on Grand Bahama), West End (also on Grand Bahama) and Coopers Town (on Abaco). English is the official language. Creole is spoken among Haitian immigrants.

Tourism

Tourism is the most important industry, accounting for about 60% of GDP. In 2010 there were 1,370,028 overnight tourist arrivals by air and 3,803,122 cruise ship visitors, up from 1,327,007 and 3,255,780 respectively in 2009.

Bahrain

Al-Mamlaka Al-Bahrayn (Kingdom of Bahrain)

Factsheet

Capital: Manama
Population estimate, 2015: 1.38 m.
GNI per capita, 2013: (PPP$) 38,599
HDI/world rank, 2014: 0.824/45
Internet domain extension: .bh

Civil Aviation

The national carrier is Gulf Air, now fully owned by the government of Bahrain after the other three former partners, Qatar, Abu Dhabi and Oman, withdrew in 2002, 2006 and 2007 respectively. In 2010 Gulf Air flew to about 40 international destinations. In 2014 Bahrain International Airport handled 8.10 m. passengers (all on international flights) and 219,332 tonnes of freight. In 2012 scheduled airline traffic of Bahrain-based carriers flew 83.5 m. km; passenger-km totalled 14.4 bn. in the same year.

Climate

The climate is pleasantly warm between Dec. and March but from June to Sept. the conditions are very hot and humid. The period June to Nov. is virtually rainless. Bahrain, Jan. 66 °F (19 °C), July 97 °F (36 °C). Annual rainfall 5.2″ (130 mm).

Constitution and Government

The ruling family is the Al-Khalifa who have been in power since 1783. The constitution changing Bahrain from an Emirate to a Kingdom dates from 14 Feb. 2002. The new constitutional hereditary monarchy has a bicameral legislature, inaugurated on 14 Dec. 2002. National elections for a legislative body took place on 24 and 31 Oct. 2002 (the first since the National Assembly was adjourned 27 years earlier). One chamber (*Council of Representatives*) is a directly elected assembly while the second (upper) chamber, a *Shura* consultative council of experts, is appointed by the King. Both chambers have 40 members. All Bahraini citizens over the age of 21—men and women—are able to vote for the elected assembly. In the Oct. 2002 national elections women stood for office for the first time.

Currency

The unit of currency is the *Bahraini dinar* (BHD), divided into 1,000 *fils*.

Defence

The Crown Prince is C.-in-C. of the armed forces. An agreement with the USA in Oct. 1991 gave port facilities to the US Navy and provided for mutual manoeuvres. In 2013 defence expenditure totalled US$1,394 m. (up from US$943 m. in 2011), with spending per capita US$1,088. The 2013 expenditure represented 5.0% of GDP.

Economy

Finance and real estate accounted for 28.5% of GDP in 2009, crude petroleum and natural gas 23.1% and manufacturing 14.7%.

Labour

The labour force in 2013 was 750,000 (more than double the 358,000 in 2003). 71.8% of the population aged 15–64 was economically active in 2013. In the same year 3.7% of the population was unemployed.

Press

There were eight daily newspapers in 2008 with a combined average daily circulation of 155,000.

Religion

Islam is the state religion. According to the Pew Research Center's Forum on Religion & Public Life, in 2010 the population was an estimated 70.3% Muslim (of whom around two-thirds Shia and a third Sunni), with 14.5% Christian and 9.8% Hindu.

Roads

A 25-km causeway links Bahrain with Saudi Arabia. In 2008 there were 3,942 km of roads, including 475 km of main roads and 563 km of secondary roads. Bahrain has one of the densest road networks in the world. In 2008 there were 310,200 passenger cars in use (404 per 1,000 inhabitants in 2007). In 2007 there were 91 fatalities in road accidents.

Shipping

In Jan. 2009 there were 15 ships of 300 GT or over registered, totalling 338,000 GT. The port of Mina Sulman is a free transit and industrial area.

Social Statistics

Statistics, 2009: births, 17,841; deaths, 2,387. Rates (per 1,000 population) in 2009: birth, 15.1; death, 2.0. Infant mortality (per 1,000 live births), 9 (2010). Life expectancy at birth, 2007, was 74.2 years for men and 77.4 years for women. Annual population growth rate, 2005–12, 4.7%; fertility rate, 2008, 2.3 children per woman. In 2006 there were 4,714 marriages and 1,130 divorces.

Telecommunications

Bahrain's telecommunications industry was fully liberalized on 1 July 2004. In 2014 there were 2,328,994 mobile phone subscriptions (1,732.7 per 1,000 inhabitants) and 284,684 landline telephone subscriptions (equivalent to 211.8 per 1,000 inhabitants). 91.0% of the population were internet users in 2014. Fixed internet subscriptions totalled 287,572 in 2014 (213.9 per 1,000 inhabitants). In March 2012 there were 346,000 Facebook users.

Territory and Population

The Kingdom of Bahrain forms an archipelago of 36 low-lying islands in the Persian Gulf, between the Qatar peninsula and the mainland of Saudi Arabia. The total area is 720 km². Total census population in 2010 was 1,234,571 (males, 768,414; females, 466,157) of which 568,399 were Bahraini and 666,172 non-Bahraini. Among Bahrainis 50.5% of the population in 2010 were males but among non-Bahrainis 72.2% were males. The population density was 1,715 per km² in 2010. In 2011, 88.7% of the population were urban. There are five governorates: Capital, Central, Muharraq, Northern, Southern. Arabic is the official language. English is widely used in business.

Tourism

In 2012 there were 8,062,000 foreign visitors (up from 6,732,000 in 2011, but down from the record high of 11,952,000 in 2010 before the Arab Spring of early 2011 and the subsequent turmoil experienced by Bahrain).

Bangladesh

Gana Prajatantri Bangladesh (People's Republic of Bangladesh)

Factsheet

Capital: Dhaka
Population estimate, 2015: 161.00 m.
GNI per capita, 2014: (PPP$) 3,191
HDI/world rank, 2014: 0.570/142
Internet domain extension: .bd

Civil Aviation

There are international airports at Dhaka (Hazrat Shahjalal) and Chittagong, and eight domestic airports. Biman Bangladesh Airlines was state-owned until July 2007 when it became a public limited company. In 2009 Dhaka's Hazrat Shahjalal International Airport handled 4,254,427 passengers (3,657,449 on international flights) and 147,239 tonnes of freight. In 2012 scheduled airline traffic of Bangladesh-based carriers flew 67.9 m. km; passenger-km totalled 8.1 bn. in the same year.

Climate

A tropical monsoon climate with heat, extreme humidity and heavy rainfall in the monsoon season, from June to Oct. The short winter season (Nov.–Feb.) is mild and dry. Rainfall varies between 50″ (1,250 mm) in the west to 100″ (2,500 mm) in the southeast and up to 200″ (5,000 mm) in the northeast. Dhaka, Jan. 66 °F (19 °C), July 84 °F (28.9 °C). Annual rainfall 81″ (2,025 mm). Chittagong, Jan. 66 °F (19 °C), July 81 °F (27.2 °C). Annual rainfall 108″ (2,831 mm).

Constitution and Government

Bangladesh is a unitary republic. The Constitution came into force on 16 Dec. 1972 and provides for a parliamentary democracy. The head of state is the *President,* elected by parliament every 5 years, who appoints a *Vice-President*. A referendum of Sept. 1991 was in favour of abandoning the executive presidential system and opted for a parliamentary system. There is a *Council of Ministers* to assist the President. The President appoints ministers. A 2011 constitutional amendment provided for a single-chamber parliament of 350 members, 300 directly elected every 5 years and 50 reserved for women, elected by the 300 MPs based on proportional representation in parliament. There have been 16 amendments to the Constitution altogether.

Currency

The unit of currency is the *taka* (BDT) of 100 *poisha*, which was floated in 1976.

Defence

The supreme command of defence services is vested in the president. Defence expenditure in 2013 totalled US$1,652 m. (US$10 per capita), representing 1.2% of GDP.

Economy

In 2011 agriculture accounted for 18% of GDP, industry 28% and services 54%.

Labour

In 2010 the economically active workforce totalled 56,651,000 over the age of 15 years (39,477,000 males). The main areas of activity (in 1,000) were as follows: agriculture, forestry and fishing, 25,727; wholesale and retail trade, and repair of motor vehicles, motorcycles and personal and household goods, 7,557; manufacturing, 6,737; transportation and storage, 3,983; construction, 2,617. In 2010, 4.5% of the workforce aged 15 or over were unemployed. For the 5-year period 2007–12 the National Minimum Wage Board established the minimum monthly wage at Tk.1,500 (equivalent to US$19) for all economic sectors not covered by industry-specific wages. The Ministry of Labor raised the minimum wage in the garment industry from Tk.1,662 (US$21) per month to Tk.3,000 (US$37) per month in 2010, but this still ranks among the lowest of any country. Bangladesh had 0.34 m. people living in slavery according to the Walk Free Foundation's 2013 *Global Slavery Index*, the tenth highest total of any country.

Press

In 2008 there were 430 paid-for daily newspapers with a combined circulation of 1.5 m.

Rail

In 2005 there were 2,855 km of railways, comprising 660 km of 1,676 mm gauge, 1,830 km of metre gauge and 365 km of dual gauge. Passenger-km travelled in 2008 came to 402.4 m. and freight tonne-km to 952 m.

Religion

Islam is the state religion. According to the Pew Research Center's Forum on Religion & Public Life the population was 89.8% Muslim in 2010, with Hindus accounting for 9.1%.

Roads

In 2015 there were 3,813 km of national highways, 4,247 km of regional highways and 13,242 km of district roads plus secondary and rural roads. In 2007 there were 158,100 passenger cars, 168,600 vans and lorries, 31,600 buses and coaches, and 653,500 motorcycles and mopeds. There were 3,160 fatalities as a result of road accidents in 2006.

Shipping

In Jan. 2009 there were 197 ships of 300 GT or over registered, totalling 407,000 GT. The main port is Chittagong, which handled 27,026,000 tonnes of cargo in 2006 (3,090,000 tonnes loaded and 23,936,000 tonnes unloaded). There is also a seaport at Mongla. There are 8,000 km of navigable inland waterways.

Social Statistics

2008 estimated births, 3,429,000; deaths, 1,054,000. In 2008 the birth rate was an estimated 21.4 per 1,000 population; death rate, 6.6; infant mortality, 2010, 38 per 1,000 live births (down from 99 per 1,000 in 1990). Life expectancy at birth, 2013, 71.5 years for females and 69.9 years for males. Annual population growth rate, 2000–08, 1.6%; fertility rate, 2008, 2.3 births per woman (down from 4.4 in 1990).

Telecommunications

Mobile phone subscribers numbered 126,866,091 in 2014 (800.4 per 1,000 inhabitants). There were 974,181 main telephone lines in the same year. Fixed internet subscriptions totalled 3,093,171 in 2014 (19.5 per 1,000 inhabitants). In 2014, 9.6% of the population were internet users. In March 2012 there were 2.5 m. Facebook users.

Territory and Population

Bangladesh is bounded in the west and north by India, east by India and Myanmar and south by the Bay of Bengal. The area is 147,570 km² (56,977 sq. miles). In 1992 India granted a 999-year lease of the Tin Bigha corridor linking Bangladesh with its enclaves of Angarpota and Dahagram. The most recent census took place in March 2011; population, 144,043,697 (72,109,796 males), giving a density of 976 persons per sq. km. In 2011, 28.6% of the population lived in urban areas. The country is administratively divided into seven divisions, subdivided into 21 *anchal* and 64 *zila*. The populations of the chief cities (2011 census) were as follows: Dhaka, 7,033,075 (Metropolitan area, 11,086,309); Chittagong, 2,592,439; Khulna, 663,342; Narayanganj, 543,090; Sylhet, 479,837; Tongi, 476,350; Rajshahi, 449,756; Bogra, 350,397; Barisal, 328,278; Comilla, 326,386. The official language is Bengali.

Tourism

In 2010 there were 303,000 non-resident tourists, spending US$81 m.

Barbados

Factsheet

Capital: Bridgetown
Population estimate, 2015: 284,000
GNI per capita, 2014: (PPP$) 12,488
HDI/world rank, 2014: 0.785/57
Internet domain extension: .bb

Civil Aviation

Grantley Adams International Airport is 16 km from Bridgetown. In 2009 it handled 1,939,059 passengers (down from 2,165,125 in 2008) and 21,098 tonnes of freight (up from 19,479 in 2008).

Climate

An equable climate in winter, but the wet season, from June to Nov., is more humid. Rainfall varies from 50″ (1,250 mm) on the coast to 75″ (1,875 mm) in the higher interior. Bridgetown, Jan. 76 °F (24.4 °C), July 80 °F (26.7 °C). Annual rainfall 51″ (1,275 mm).

Constitution and Government

The head of state is the British sovereign, represented by an appointed Governor-General. The bicameral Parliament consists of a Senate and a House of Assembly. The *Senate* comprises 21 members appointed by the Governor-General, 12 being appointed on the advice of the Prime Minister, two on the advice of the Leader of the Opposition and seven at the Governor-General's discretion. The *House of Assembly* comprises 30 members elected every 5 years. In 1963 the voting age was reduced to 18. The *Privy Council* is appointed by the Governor-General after consultation with the Prime Minister. It consists of 12 members and the Governor-General as chairman. It advises the Governor-General in the exercise of the royal prerogative of mercy and in the exercise of his disciplinary powers over members of the public and police services.

Currency

The unit of currency is the *Barbados dollar* (BBD), usually written as BDS$, of 100 *cents*, which is pegged to the US dollar at BDS$2 = US$1.

Defence

The Barbados Defence Force has a strength of about 610. In 2013 defence expenditure totalled US$33 m. (US$115 per capita), representing 0.7% of GDP.

Economy

In 2009 agriculture accounted for 3% of GDP, industry 23% and services 74%.

Labour

The labour force in 2013 was 161,900 (up from 149,500 in 2003). 80.8% of the population aged 15–64 was economically active in 2013. In the same year 11.6% of the population was unemployed.

Press

In 2008 there were two daily newspapers, the *Barbados Advocate* (est. 1895) and the *Daily Nation* (est. 1973). The *Daily Nation* has an average daily circulation of 33,000; the *Barbados Advocate*, 15,000.

Religion

In 2010 there were an estimated 240,000 Protestants and 10,000 Roman Catholics according to the Pew Research Center's Forum on Religion & Public Life, with the remainder of the population being unaffiliated or following other religions.

Roads

Barbados has some 1,600 km of roads. In 2007 there were 103,500 passenger cars, 15,200 lorries and vans, and 630 buses and coaches. There were 38 deaths as a result of road accidents in 2007.

Shipping

There is a deep-water harbour at Bridgetown. In Jan. 2009 there were 91 ships of 300 GT or over registered, totalling 642,000 GT.

Social Statistics

In 2007: births registered, 3,537; deaths registered, 2,213; birth rate, 12.9 per 1,000 population; death rate, 8.1 per 1,000 population; infant mortality (2010), 17 per 1,000 live births. Expectation of life, 2007, males 74.0 years and females 79.7. Population growth rate, 2005, 0.3%; fertility rate, 2008, 1.5 children per woman.

Telecommunications

In 2011 there were 141,000 landline telephone subscriptions (equivalent to 513.5 per 1,000 inhabitants) and 348,000 mobile phone subscriptions (1,270·1 per 1,000 inhabitants). Fixed internet subscriptions totalled 61,000 in 2009 (223.5 per 1,000 inhabitants). In Dec. 2011 Barbados had 118,000 Facebook users.

Territory and Population

Barbados lies to the east of the Windward Islands. Area 430 km² (166 sq. miles). In 2010 the census population was 277,821; density, 646.1 per km². In 2011, 45.1% of the population were urban. Bridgetown is the principal city: population (including suburbs), 122,000 in 2011. The country is divided into 11 parishes. The official language is English.

Tourism

In 2010 there were 532,180 overnight tourist arrivals by air (of which 181,054 were from the United Kingdom) and 664,747 cruise ship visitors, up from 518,564 and 635,746 respectively in 2009.

Belarus

Respublika Belarus (Republic of Belarus)

Factsheet

Capital: Minsk
Population estimate, 2015: 9.50 m.
GNI per capita, 2014: (PPP$) 16,676
HDI/world rank, 2014: 0.798/50=
Internet domain extension: .by

Civil Aviation

The main airport is Minsk National Airport, which handled 2,593,559 passengers in 2014 and 19,900 tonnes of freight. The national carrier is Belavia, which in 2017 operated on domestic routes and also flew to more than 50 international destinations. In 2014 Belavia carried 1,973,000 passengers.

Climate

Moderately continental and humid with temperatures averaging 20 °F (−6 °C) in Jan. and 64 °F (18 °C) in July. Annual precipitation is 22–28″ (550–700 mm).

Constitution and Government

A new constitution was adopted on 15 March 1994. It provides for a *President* who must be a citizen of at least 35 years of age, have resided for 10 years in Belarus and whose candidacy must be supported by the signatures of 70 deputies or 100,000 electors. At a referendum held on 17 Oct. 2004, 86.2% of votes cast were in favour of the abolition of the two-term limit on the presidency. The vote was widely regarded as fraudulent. There is an 12-member *Constitutional Court*. The chief justice and five other judges are appointed by the president. Four referenda held on 14 May 1995 gave the president powers to dissolve parliament; work for closer economic integration with Russia; establish Russian as an official language of equal status with Belarusian; and introduce a new flag. At a further referendum of 24 Nov. 1996 turnout was 84%. 79% of votes cast were in favour of the creation of an upper house of parliament nominated by provincial governors and 70% in favour of extending the presidential term of office by 2 years to 5 years. The Supreme Soviet was dissolved and a 110-member lower *House of Representatives* established, whose members are directly elected by universal adult suffrage every 4 years. The upper chamber is the *Council of the Republic* (64 seats; 56 members elected by regional councils and eight members appointed by the president, all for 4-year terms). In practice, since 1996 the Belarusian parliament has only had a ceremonial function.

Currency

The *rouble* was retained under an agreement of Sept. 1993 and a treaty with Russia on monetary union of April 1994. Foreign currencies ceased to be legal tender in Oct. 1994. Only banknotes are issued-there are no coins in circulation. In Jan. 2000 the Belarusian rouble was revalued at 1 new rouble (BYR) = 1,000 old roubles (BYB).

Defence

Conscription is for 18 months, or 12 in the case of university and college graduates. A treaty with Russia of April 1993 co-ordinates their military activities. All nuclear weapons had been transferred to Russia by Dec. 1996. Total active armed forces in 2011 numbered 72,940. In addition there are Ministry of Interior paramilitary troops numbering 110,000. Defence expenditure in 2012 totalled US$552 m. (US$57 per capita), representing 1.0% of GDP.

Economy

Mining and manufacturing contributed 25.3% to GDP in 2009; followed by finance, public administration, defence and services, 22.0%; construction, 10.7%; and trade and hotels, 10.7%.

Labour

The labour force in 2013 was 4,482,700 (4,665,400 in 2003). 66.1% of the population aged 15–64 was economically active in 2013. In the same year 6.0% of the population was unemployed. Belarus had 11,000 people living in slavery according to the Walk Free Foundation's 2013 *Global Slavery Index*.

Press

In Jan. 2013 there were about 1,500 registered print media in Belarus, of which more than 1,100 were non-state media. The most widely read paper is *Sovetskaya Belarussiya*, with a daily circulation of about 400,000. There are also Belarusian editions of the Russian daily *Komsomolskaya Pravda* and weekly *Argumenty i Fakty*.

Rail

In 2013 there were 5,490 km of railways in use (1,520 mm gauge), of which 1,013 km were electrified. Passenger-km travelled in 2013 came to 9 bn. and freight tonne-km to 44 bn.

Religion

The Orthodox Church claims the most adherents. There is a Roman Catholic archdiocese of Minsk and Mahilyou, and three dioceses. According to a report published by the Ministry of Foreign Affairs in 2011 an estimated 58.9% of the population were believers. Of these, 82% were Orthodox, 12% Catholic and the remainder followers of other religions.

Roads

In 2013 there were 101,030 km of roads (87.0% paved), including 15,735 km of national roads. There were 2,670,567 passenger cars in use as of 1 Jan. 2014 (282 per 1,000 inhabitants). In 2013 public transport totalled 10,546 m. passenger-km and freight 25,603 m. tonne-km. There were 894 fatalities as a result of road accidents in 2013.

Social Statistics

2013 births, 118,463 (rate of 12.5 per 1,000 population); deaths, 125,872 (rate of 13.3 per 1,000 population); marriages, 87,127; divorces, 36,105. Annual population growth rate, 2005–12, −0.5%. Life expectancy at birth, 2013, was 64.2 years for men and 75.8 years for women. Infant mortality, 2010, four per 1,000 live births; fertility rate, 2013, 1.5 children per woman.

Telecommunications

In 2011 there were 4,208,000 landline telephone subscriptions (equivalent to 440.2 per 1,000 inhabitants) and 10,694,900 mobile phone subscriptions (or 1,118.8 per 1,000 inhabitants). In 2011, 39.6% of the population were internet users. In March 2012 there were 409,000 Facebook users.

Territory and Population

Belarus is situated along the western Dvina and Dnieper. It is bounded in the west by Poland, north by Latvia and Lithuania, east by Russia and south by Ukraine. The area is 207,600 km² (80,155 sq. miles). The capital is Minsk. Other important towns are Homel, Vitebsk, Mahilyou, Bobruisk, Hrodno and Brest. On 2 Nov. 1939 western Belorussia was incorporated with an area of over 108,000 km² and a population of 4.8 m. Census population, 2009, 9,503,807; density, 45.8 per km². Estimate, Jan. 2014: 9,468,154. In 2011, 75.2% of the population lived in urban areas. Major ethnic groups: 81.2% Belarusians, 11.4% Russians, 3.9% Poles, 2.4% Ukrainians. Belarus comprises six regions (Brest, Homel, Hrodno, Mahilyou, Minsk and Vitebsk) and one municipality (Minsk City). Belarusian and Russian are both official languages.

Tourism

In 2011 there were 115,700 foreign tourists on organized trips. Spending by tourists totalled US$747 m. in 2011.

Belgium

Royaume de Belgique Koninkrijk België (Kingdom of Belgium)

Factsheet

Capital: Brussels
Population estimate, 2015: 11.30 m.
GNI per capita, 2014: (PPP$) 41,187
HDI/world rank, 2014: 0.890/21
Internet domain extension: .be

Civil Aviation

The former national airline SABENA (*Société anonyme belge d'exploitation de la navigation aérienne*) was set up in 1923. However, in Nov. 2001 it filed for bankruptcy. Its successor, Delta Air Transport (DAT), a former SABENA subsidiary, was given a new identity in Feb. 2002 as SN Brussels Airlines. In Nov. 2006 SN Brussels Airlines merged with Virgin Express and since March 2007 has been trading under the name Brussels Airlines. The busiest airport is Brussels National Airport (Zaventem), which handled 18,710,388 passengers in 2008 and 658,743 tonnes of freight.

Climate

Cool temperate climate influenced by the sea, giving mild winters and cool summers. Brussels, Jan. 36 °F (2.2 °C), July 64 °F (17.8 °C). Annual rainfall 33″ (825 mm). Ostend, Jan. 38 °F (3.3 °C), July 62 °F (16.7 °C). Annual rainfall 31″ (775 mm).

Constitution and Government

Belgium is a constitutional, representative and hereditary monarchy. The legislative power is vested in the King, the federal parliament and the community and regional councils. The King convokes parliament after an election or the resignation of a government, and has the power to dissolve it in accordance with Article 46 of the Constitution. The reigning King is **Philippe**, who succeeded his father, Albert II, on 21 July 2013. The communities are three in number and based on language: Flemish, French and German. The regions also number three, and are based territorially: Flemish, Walloon and the Brussels-Capital Region. Since 1995 the federal parliament has consisted of a 150-member *Chamber of Representatives*, directly elected by obligatory universal suffrage from 20 constituencies on a proportional representation system for 4-year terms, and a Senate. Most senators were directly elected until reforms that came into effect for the 2014 elections. Since the elections held on 25 May 2014 the *Senate* comprises 60 members (previously 71), of whom 50 are appointed by and from Community and Regional parliaments (29 by the Flemish parliament; 10 by the parliament of the French Community; 8 by the Walloon parliament; 2 by the French-speaking group in the Brussels-Capital Region parliament; and 1 by the parliament of the German-speaking Community). These senators co-opt a further ten senators (six Dutch-speaking and four French-speaking). The state reform that introduced these changes also devolved an array of powers from federal government to the regions and language communities. The federal parliament's powers relate to constitutional reform, federal finance, foreign affairs, defence, justice, internal security, social security and some areas of public health. The Senate is essentially a revising chamber, though it may initiate certain legislation, and is equally competent with the Chamber of Representatives in matters concerning constitutional reform and the assent to international treaties.

Currency

On an. 1999 the euro (EUR) became the legal currency in Belgium at the irrevocable conversion rate of BEF40.3399 to EUR1. The euro, which consists of 100 cents, has been in circulation since 1 Jan. 2002. On the introduction of the euro there was a 'dual circulation' period before the Belgian franc ceased to be legal tender on 28 Feb. 2002.

Defence

Conscription was abolished in 1994 and the Armed Forces were restructured, with the aim of progressively reducing the size and making more use of civilian personnel. Since 1 Jan. 2002 they have been organized into one unified structure consisting of four main components: the Land Component (Army), Naval Component (Navy), Air Component (Air Force) and Medical Component. In 2013 defence expenditure totalled US$5,294 m. (US$507 per capita), representing 1.0% of GDP.

Economy

Services contributed 76% of GDP in 2012, with industry accounting for 23% and agriculture 1%.

Labour

In 2010 (Labour Force Survey), 60,686 persons worked in the primary sector (agriculture, fishing and mining), 1,049,239 in the secondary sector (industry and construction) and 3,298,598 in the tertiary sector (services). The unemployment rate was 7.9% in Dec. 2015 (down from 8.5% in 2014 as a whole). In French-speaking Wallonia the rate is more than double that in Dutch-speaking Flanders.

Press

In 2013 there were 25 daily newspapers (23 paid-for and two free) with a combined circulation of 1,520,000. There were 14 newspaper online editions in 2012 with 3,818,000 unique daily visitors.

Rail

The length of railway operated in 2005 was 3,696 km (electrified, 3,110 km). In 2008, 217 m. passengers and 55.5 m. tonnes of freight were carried.

Religion

The Constitution provides for freedom of religion. Traditionally, Roman Catholicism has been the majority religion but it has been in rapid decline—according to the Pew Research Center's Forum on Religion &

Public Life, an estimated 62% of the population in 2010 were Catholics, 29% religiously unaffiliated and 6% Muslim. There are nine Roman Catholic dioceses including the Archdiocese of Mechelen-Brussel. In Feb. 2016 there was one cardinal.

Roads

Length of roads, 2006: motorways, 1,763 km; national roads, 12,585 km; secondary roads, 1,349 km; local roads, 136,559 km. Belgium has one of the densest road networks in the world. In 2007 there were 5,006,300 passenger cars in use, 29,000 buses and coaches, 696,700 lorries and vans, and 371,500 motorcycles and mopeds. Road accidents caused 994 fatalities in both 2008 and 2009 (1,470 in 2000).

Shipping

In Jan. 2009 there were 81 ships of 300 GT or over registered, totalling 3.93 m. GT. Antwerp is Europe's second busiest port in terms of both total cargo handled and container traffic after Rotterdam. In 2008, 189,390,000 tonnes of cargo were handled at the port of Antwerp (84,371,000 tonnes loaded and 105,018,000 tonnes discharged), with total container throughput 8,663,000 TEUs (20-foot equivalent units). The length of navigable inland waterways was 1,516 km in 2008; 108.2 m. tonnes of freight were carried on inland waterways in 2009.

Social Statistics

In 2009 there were 127,297 births, 104,509 deaths, 43,303 marriages and 32,606 divorces. In 2010 Belgium received 19,941 asylum applications, equivalent to 1.9 per 1,000 inhabitants. Annual population growth rate, 2005–10, 0.7%. Life expectancy at birth, 2009, was 77.2 years for men and 82.4 years for women. 2009 birth rate (per 1,000 population): 11.8; death rate: 9.7. Infant mortality, 2008, 3.8 per 1,000 live births; fertility rate, 2013, 1.9 children per woman. In 2003 Belgium became the second country to legalize same-sex marriage.

Telecommunications

In 2014 mobile phone subscribers numbered 12,734,724 (1,142.7 per 1,000 persons). In the same year there were 4,532,475 main (fixed) telephone lines. 85.0% of the population were internet users in 2014. The fixed broadband penetration rate in 2014 was 359.9 subscribers per 1,000 inhabitants. In March 2012 there were 4.6 m. Facebook users.

Territory and Population

Belgium is bounded in the north by the Netherlands, northwest by the North Sea, west and south by France, and east by Germany and Luxembourg. Its area is 30,528 sq. km. Population (at 1 Jan. 2015), 11,209,044 (5,703,950 females); density, 367.2 per sq. km. The Belgian exclave of Baarle-Hertog in the Netherlands has an area of seven sq. km and a population (2010) of 2,504. There were 1,195,122 resident foreign nationals as at 1 Jan. 2013. In 2011, 97.4% of the population lived in urban areas. Dutch (Flemish) is spoken by the Flemish section of the population in the north, French by the Walloon south. The linguistic frontier passes south of the capital, Brussels, which is bilingual. Population of the regions on 1 Jan. 2012: Brussels-Capital Region, 1,138,854; Flemish Region, 6,350,765; Walloon Region, 3,546,329. The most populous towns, with population on 1 Jan. 2012: Brussels, 1,138,854; Antwerp, 502,604; Ghent, 248,242; Charleroi, 203,871; Liège, 195,576; Bruges, 117,170; Namur (Namen) 110,096; Leuven, 97,656; Mons, 93,072; Mechelen, 82,325.

Tourism

In 2014 there were 17,068,872 overnight stays by non-resident visitors, including 4,144,256 by visitors from the Netherlands and 2,449,842 by visitors from France. A total of 11,293,395 overnight stays were for leisure, holiday and recreation purposes, 3,554,876 for conferences, congresses and seminars and 2,220,601 for other business purposes.

Belize

Factsheet

Capital: Belmopan
Population estimate, 2015: 359,000
GNI per capita, 2014: (PPP$) 7,614
HDI/world rank, 2014: 0.715/101=
Internet domain extension: .bz

Civil Aviation

There is an international airport (Philip S. W. Goldson) in Belize City. The national carrier is Maya Island Air, which operates scheduled domestic services and charter flights to Guatemala and Honduras. In 2013 Philip S. W. Goldson International handled 542,833 passengers (449,291 in 2008).

Climate

A tropical climate with high rainfall and small annual range of temperature. The driest months are Feb. and March. Belize City, Jan. 74 °F (23.3 °C), July 81 °F (27.2 °C). Annual rainfall 76″ (1,890 mm).

Constitution and Government

The head of state is the British sovereign, represented by an appointed Governor-General. The Constitution, which came into force on 21 Sept. 1981, provided for a National Assembly, with a 5-year term, comprising a 32-member *House of Representatives* (31 elected by universal suffrage plus the Speaker), and a *Senate* consisting of 13 members, six appointed by the Governor-General on the advice of the Prime Minister, three on the advice of the Leader of the Opposition, one on the advice of the Belize Council of Churches and the Evangelical Association of Churches, one on the advice of the Belize Chamber of Commerce and Industry and the Belize Business Bureau and one on the advice of the National Trade Union Congress of Belize and the Civil Society Steering Committee plus the Senate President.

Currency

The unit of currency is the *Belize dollar* (BZD) of 100 *cents*. Since 1976 $B2 has been fixed at US$1.

Defence

The Belize Defence Force numbers around 1,050 (2011) with 700 reservists. There are three infantry battalions, three reserve companies, a support group and an air wing. In 2013 defence expenditure totalled US$18 m. (US$53 per capita), representing 1.1% of GDP.

Economy

In 2011 agriculture accounted for 13% of GDP, industry 23% and services 64%.

Labour

The labour force in 2013 was 149,600 (100,800 in 2003). 68.3% of the population aged 15–64 was economically active in 2013. In the same year 11.7% of the population was unemployed.

Press

There are no daily newspapers although there were eight non-dailies in 2008, the largest of which were *Belize Times*, *The Amandala Press* and *The Reporter*.

Religion

In 2010 there were an estimated 160,000 Roman Catholics and 110,000 Protestants according to the Pew Research Center's Forum on Religion & Public Life, with the remainder of the population being unaffiliated or following other religions.

Roads

In 2006 there were 575 km of main roads and 2,432 km of other roads. There were 40,000 passenger cars in use in 2006 and 14,800 trucks and vans. In 2006 there were 68 deaths as a result of road accidents.

Shipping

The main port is Belize City, with a modern deep-water port able to handle containerized shipping. There are also ports at Commerce Bight and Big Creek. In Jan. 2009 there were 246 ships of 300 GT or over registered, totalling 950,000 GT. Nine cargo shipping lines serve Belize, and there are coastal passenger services to the offshore islands and Guatemala.

Social Statistics

2009 births (est.), 8,000; deaths (est.), 1,000. In 2009 the estimated birth rate per 1,000 was 25 and the death rate 4; infant mortality in 2010 was 14 per 1,000 live births; there were 2,020 marriages in 2004. Life expectancy in 2013 was 70.9 years for males and 77.1 for females. Annual population growth rate, 2005–10, 2.5%; fertility rate, 2013, 2.7 children per woman.

Telecommunications

In 2011 there were 28,800 landline telephone subscriptions (equivalent to 90.7 per 1,000 inhabitants) and 203,100 mobile phone subscriptions (or 638.7 per 1,000 inhabitants). Fixed internet subscriptions totalled 9,400 in 2010 (30.1 per 1,000 inhabitants).

Territory and Population

Belize is bounded in the north by Mexico, west and south by Guatemala and east by the Caribbean. Fringing the coast there are three atolls and some 400 islets (cays) in the world's second longest barrier reef (140 miles), which was declared a world heritage site in 1996. Area, 22,965 km². Population at the 2010 census, 324,528; density, 14.1 per km². The capital is Belmopan (2010 census population, 13,931). In 2010, 45.0% of the population were urban.

Tourism

There were 716 hotels and 7,111 hotel rooms in 2011. In 2012 there were 917,869 visitors of which 277,135 stayed overnight and 640,734 arrived on cruise ships.

Benin

République du Bénin (Republic of Benin)

Factsheet

Capital: Porto-Novo
Population estimate, 2015: 10.88 m.
GNI per capita, 2014: (PPP$) 1,767
HDI/world rank, 2014: 0.480/166
Internet domain extension: .bj

Civil Aviation

The international airport is at Cotonou (Cadjehoun), which in 2012 handled 466,778 passengers (all on international flights) and 5,237 tonnes of freight. Westair Benin, the only operational airline based in the country, was founded in 2002. In 2010 there were direct flights to 17 destinations in Africa as well as Paris.

Climate

In coastal parts there is an equatorial climate, with a long rainy season from March to July and a short rainy season in Oct. and Nov. The dry season increases in length from the coast, with inland areas having rain only between May and Sept. Porto-Novo, Jan. 82 °F (27.8 °C), July 78 °F (25.6 °C). Annual rainfall 52″ (1,300 mm). Cotonou, Jan. 81 °F (27.2 °C), July 77 °F (25 °C). Annual rainfall 53″ (1,325 mm).

Constitution and Government

The Benin Party of Popular Revolution (PRPB) held a monopoly of power from 1977 to 1989. In Feb. 1990 a 'National Conference of the Active Forces of the Nation' proclaimed its sovereignty and appointed Nicéphore Soglo prime minister of a provisional government. At a referendum in Dec. 1990, 93.2% of votes cast were in favour of the new constitution, which introduced a presidential regime. The *President* is directly elected for renewable 5-year terms. Parliament is the unicameral *National Assembly* of 83 members elected by proportional representation for 4-year terms. A 30-member advisory *Social and Economic Council* was set up in 1994. There is a *Constitutional Court*.

Currency

The unit of currency is the *franc CFA* (XOF) with a parity of 655.957 francs CFA to one euro.

Defence

There is selective conscription for 18 months. Defence expenditure totalled US$86 m. in 2013 (US$9 per capita), representing 1.0% of GDP.

Economy

Agriculture and fisheries accounted for 32.7% of GDP in 2009; trade and restaurants, 17.1%; finance, 10.7%; public administration, defence and services, 10.1%.

Labour

The estimated labour force numbered 3,825,000 in 2010 (54% males), up from 3,212,000 in 2005. Approximately half of the economically active population is engaged in agriculture, fishing and forestry.

Press

In 2008 there were 38 daily newspapers with an average circulation of 50,000. The main newspapers are *Le Matinal*, *Les Echos du Jour* and the government-controlled *La Nation*.

Rail

In 2005 there were 438 km of metre-gauge railway. In 2007 railways carried 0.1 m. tonnes of freight.

Religion

In 2010 there were an estimated 4.7 m. Christians, 2.1 m. Muslims and 1.6 m. folk religionists according to the Pew Research Center's Forum on Religion & Public Life. A further 450,000 people had no religious affiliation. Catholics account for around 56% of Christians and Protestants 43%. Voodoo became an official religion in 1996.

Roads

Benin had some 15,700 km of roads in 2010, of which about 6,100 km were main roads. Passenger cars in use in 2007 totalled 149,300, buses and coaches 1,100, and lorries and vans 35,700.

Shipping

There is a port at Cotonou, which handled 6,307,000 tonnes of cargo in 2008 (714,000 tonnes loaded and 5,593,000 tonnes discharged).

Social Statistics

2006 (estimates) births, 303,000; deaths, 79,000. Rates, 2006 estimates (per 1,000 population): births, 38.7; deaths, 10.1. Infant mortality, 2010 (per 1,000 live births), 73. Expectation of life in 2007 was 59.8 years for males and 62.1 for females. Annual population growth rate, 2010–15, 2.8%. Fertility rate, 2008, 5.4 children per woman.

Telecommunications

Mobile phone subscribers numbered 10,562,647 in 2014 (996.5 per 1,000 persons). In the same year there were 195,662 main (fixed) telephone lines. 5.3% of the population were internet subscribers in 2014.

Territory and Population

Benin is bounded in the east by Nigeria, north by Niger and Burkina Faso, west by Togo and south by the Gulf of Guinea. The area is 114,763 km², and the population (2013 census) 10,008,749; density, 87.2 per km². In 2011, 42.5% of the population were urban. Cotonou, the capital, had a population of 679,012 in 2013; other major towns are Abomey-Calavi, Godomey, Parakou and Porto-Novo. The official language is French.

Tourism

In 2011 there were 209,000 non-resident tourists. Tourist spending totalled US$188 m. in 2011.

Bhutan

Druk-yul (Kingdom of Bhutan)

Factsheet
Capital: Thimphu
Population estimate, 2015: 775,000
GNI per capita, 2014: (PPP$) 7,176
HDI/world rank, 2014: 0.605/132
Internet domain extension: .bt

Civil Aviation

In 2010 Drukair flew from Paro to Bagdogra (in India), Bangkok, Delhi, Dhaka, Kathmandu and Kolkata. In 2012 scheduled airline traffic of Bhutan-based carriers flew 3.0 m. km; passenger-km totalled 307 m. in the same year.

Climate

The climate is largely controlled by altitude. The mountainous north is cold, with perpetual snow on the summits, but the centre has a more moderate climate, though winters are cold, with rainfall under 40″ (1,000 mm). In the south, the climate is humid sub-tropical and rainfall approaches 200″ (5,000 mm).

Constitution and Government

Bhutan's first formal constitution came into force on 18 July 2008, after a period of almost 7 years of planning. There is a bicameral parliament. The lower house is the *National Assembly* (with a maximum of 55 members but currently with 47, all elected) and the upper house the 25-member *National Council* (with 20 members elected and five appointed by the king). Executive power is vested in the *Council of Ministers*. The reigning King is Jigme Kesar Namgyel Wangchuck (b. 1980), who succeeded his father King Jigme Singye Wangchuck (abdicated 14 Dec. 2006). He was crowned on 6 Nov. 2008. With the introduction of democratic elections in 2007–08, the King's role became more ceremonial. Nonetheless, all leading political parties have affirmed their loyalty to the monarchy, which remains central to political life. In 1907 the Tongsa Penlop (the governor of the province of Tongsa in central Bhutan), Sir Ugyen Wangchuck, GCIE, KCSI, was elected as the first hereditary Maharaja of Bhutan. The Bhutanese title is Druk Gyalpo, and his successors are addressed as King of Bhutan. The stated goal is to increase Gross National Happiness.

Currency

The unit of currency is the *ngultrum* (BTN) of 100 *chetrum*, at parity with the Indian rupee.

Economy

Agriculture accounted for 18.7% of GDP in 2009, with industry accounting for 43.2% and services 38.1%.

Labour

The labour force in 2013 was 393,400 (273,300 in 2003). 74.8% of the population aged 15–64 was economically active in 2013. In the same year 2.9% of the population was unemployed.

Press

Until 2006 there was only one newspaper, the government-controlled *Kuensel*, which is published in English, Dzongkha and Nepali. Two private non-dailies were launched in 2006. The country's first daily paper, the English-language *Bhutan Today*, was launched in 2008 and had an average daily circulation of 18,000 that year. Although still published, it no longer appears daily.

Rail

Bhutan does not currently have a railway network but there are plans for a line funded by India that would link the town of Toribari with Hasimara in India.

Religion

The state religion of Bhutan is the Drukpa Kagyupa, a branch of Mahayana Buddhism. Around 23% of the population is Hindu according to the Pew Research Center's Forum on Religion & Public Life.

Roads

In 2006 there were about 4,153 km of roads, of which 1,577 km were highways. In 2007 there were 19,600 passenger cars, 180 buses and coaches, 5,400 lorries and vans, and 7,500 motorcycles and mopeds. There were 111 fatalities in road accidents in 2007.

Social Statistics

2008 (estimates) births, 14,800 (rate of 21.5 per 1,000 population); deaths, 4,900 (rate of 7.1 per 1,000 population). Life expectancy at birth, 2013, was 68.0 years for men and 68.7 years for women. Infant mortality, 2010, 44 per 1,000 live births. Annual population growth rate, 2000–08, 2.5%; fertility rate, 2008, 2.6 children per woman.

Telecommunications

There were 26,300 fixed telephone lines in 2010 (36.2 per 1,000 inhabitants). Mobile phone subscribers numbered 394,300 in 2010. There were 136.0 internet users per 1,000 inhabitants in 2010. Fixed internet subscriptions totalled 6,700 in 2009 (9.3 per 1,000 inhabitants).

Territory and Population

Bhutan is situated in the eastern Himalayas, bounded in the north by Tibet and on all other sides by India. Area 46,650 km^2 (18,012 sq. miles); 2005 census population, 672,425 (364,482 males), giving a density of 14 per km^2. The capital is Thimphu (2005 population, 79,185). The country is divided into 20 districts (*dzongkhag*). The official language is Dzongkha.

Tourism

Bhutan was not formally opened to foreign tourists until 1974, but tourism is now the largest source of foreign exchange. In 2009, 23,000 tourists visited Bhutan; revenue totalled US$32 m.

Bolivia

Estado Plurinacional de Bolivia (Plurinational State of Bolivia)

Factsheet

Capital: Sucre
Seat of government: La Paz
Population estimate, 2015: 10.73 m.

GNI per capita, 2014: (PPP$) 5,760
HDI/world rank, 2014: 0.662/119
Internet domain extension: .bo

Civil Aviation

The three international airports are La Paz (El Alto), Santa Cruz de la Sierra (Viru Viru) and Cochabamba (Jorge Wisterman). The main airline is Aerosur. In 2005 scheduled airline traffic of Bolivian-based carriers flew 17.1 m. km, carrying 1,396,400 passengers.

Climate

The varied geography produces different climates. The low-lying areas in the Amazon Basin are warm and damp throughout the year, with heavy rainfall from Nov. to March; the Altiplano is generally dry between May and Nov. with sunshine but cold nights in June and July, while the months from Dec. to March are the wettest. La Paz, Jan. 55.9 °F (13.3 °C), July 50.5 °F (10.3 °C). Annual rainfall 20.8″ (529 mm). Sucre, Jan. 58.5 °F (14.7 °C), July 52.7 °F (11.5 °C). Annual rainfall 20.1″ (510 mm).

Constitution and Government

Bolivia's first constitution was adopted on 19 Nov. 1826. The present constitution, the fifteenth, came into effect following its acceptance in a referendum on 25 Jan. 2009 and defined Bolivia as 'a United Social State of Plurinational Communitarian Law'. Under its terms, running to 411 articles, the majority indigenous population has been granted increased rights (including recognition of indigenous systems of justice), state control is extended over the exploitation of natural resources and regional autonomy is enhanced. The separation of church and state is recognized and land reforms in favour of indigenous populations enshrined. A new 'plurinational Legislative assembly', consisting of a 130-member *Chamber of Deputies* and a 36-member *Senate*, took office following elections in Dec. 2009. The constitution also allows for the president to serve a maximum of two consecutive terms. However, in April 2013 a constitutional tribunal ruled that President Morales could seek a third consecutive term as his first term had begun under the old constitution.

Currency

The unit of currency is the *boliviano* (BOB) of 100 *centavos*, which replaced the *peso* on 1 Jan. 1987 at a rate of one boliviano = 1 m. pesos.

Defence

In 2013 defence expenditure totalled US$373 m., with spending per capita US$36. The 2013 expenditure represented 1.3% of GDP.

Economy

In 2012 agriculture accounted for 13.0% of GDP, industry 38.7% and services 48.3%. Bolivia's 'shadow' (black market) economy is estimated to constitute approximately 63% of the country's official GDP, one of the highest percentages of any country in the world.

Labour

The labour force in 2013 was 5,025,100 (3,913,600 in 2003). 74.2% of the population aged 15–64 was economically active in 2013. In the same year 2.6% of the population was unemployed.

Press

There were 25 paid-for daily newspapers in 2008 with a combined circulation of 145,000. The top-selling daily is the tabloid *El Deber*, with an average daily circulation of 15,000 (30,000 on Sundays).

Rail

In 2007 the railway network totalled 2,866 km of metre gauge track. Passenger-km travelled in 2007 came to 313 m. and freight tonne-km in 2005 to 1,027 m.

Religion

The State is independent from religion. The Roman Catholic church was disestablished in 2009. It has four archdioceses, six dioceses, five apostolic vicariates and two territorial prelatures. In 2010 there were an estimated 7.9 m. Roman Catholics and 1.4 m. Protestants according to the Pew Research Center's Forum on Religion & Public Life, with most of the remainder of the population being unaffiliated.

Roads

The total length of the road system was 62,479 km in 2004, of which 14,336 km were national roads. Total passenger cars in use in 2007 numbered 174,900, lorries and vans 468,800, and buses and coaches 7,000. There were 1,073 road accident fatalities in 2007.

Shipping

Lake Titicaca and about 19,000 km of rivers are open to navigation. In Jan. 2009 there were 43 ships of 300 GT or over registered, totalling 78,000 GT.

Social Statistics

In 2008 births totalled an estimated 263,000 (birth rate of 27.1 per 1,000 population); deaths totalled an estimated 73,000 (rate, 7.5 per 1,000); infant mortality (2010), 42 per 1,000 live births, the highest in South America. Expectation of life (2013) was 65.1 years for men and 69.5 years for women. Annual population growth rate, 2000–08, 1.9%. Fertility rate, 2008, 3.5 children per woman (the highest in South America).

Telecommunications

In 2011 there were 879,800 landline telephone subscriptions (equivalent to 87.2 per 1,000 inhabitants) and 8,353,300 mobile phone subscriptions (or 828.0 per 1,000 inhabitants). Fixed internet subscriptions totalled 114,000 in 2010 (11.5 per 1,000 inhabitants). In June 2012 there were 1.6 m. Facebook users.

Territory and Population

Bolivia is a landlocked state bounded in the north and east by Brazil, south by Paraguay and Argentina, and west by Chile and Peru, with an area of some 1,098,581 km^2 (424,165 sq. miles). Population (2012 census): 10,059,856 (5,040,409 females); density, 9.2 per km^2. In 2011, 67.0% of the population lived in urban areas. Population (2012 census, in 1,000) of the principal towns: Santa Cruz de la Sierra, 1,442; El Alto, 847; La Paz, 759; Cochabamba, 632; Oruro, 265; Sucre, 239; Tarija, 180; Potosí, 176; Sacaba, 150. Spanish along with the Amerindian languages Quechua and Aymará are all official languages.

Tourism

In 2010 there were 807,000 international tourists (excluding same-day visitors); total revenue from tourism was US$379 m. in 2010.

Bosnia-Herzegovina

Republika Bosna i Hercegovina (Republic of Bosnia and Herzegovina)

Factsheet

Capital: Sarajevo
Population estimate, 2015: 3.81 m.
GNI per capita, 2014: (PPP$) 9,638
HDI/world rank, 2014: 0.733/85=
Internet domain extension: .ba

Civil Aviation

There are airports at Sarajevo (Butmir), Tuzla, Banja Luka and Mostar. In 2012 Sarajevo handled 580,058 passengers (all international) and 1,858 tonnes of freight.

Climate

The climate is generally continental with steady rainfall throughout the year, although in areas nearer the coast it is more Mediterranean.

Constitution and Government

On 31 May 1994 the National Assembly approved the creation of the Muslim Croat federation (the Federation of Bosnia and Herzegovina). The government structure was established in 1996 as follows: Heading the state is a three-member *Presidency* (one Croat, one Muslim, one Serb) with a rotating president. The Presidency is elected by direct universal suffrage, and is responsible for foreign affairs and the nomination of the prime minister. There is a two-chamber parliament: the *House of Representatives* (which meets in Sarajevo) comprises 42 directly elected deputies, two-thirds Croat and Muslim and one-third Serb; and the *House of Peoples* (which meets in Lukavica) comprises five Croat, five Muslim and five Serb delegates. Below the national level the country is divided into two self-governing entities along ethnic lines.

Currency

A new currency, the *konvertibilna marka* (BAM) consisting of 100 *pfennig*, was introduced in June 1998. Initially trading at a strict 1-to-1 against the Deutsche Mark, it is now pegged to the euro at a rate of 1.95583 convertible marks to the euro.

Defence

Defence expenditure in 2012 totalled US$231 m. (US$60 per capita), representing 1.4% of GDP.

Economy

In 2010 agriculture accounted for 7.6% of GDP, industry 28.0% and services 64.4%.

Labour

The active labour force totalled 1,157,940 in April 2010 (62% males). Unemployment in April 2010 was 27.2% (25.6% for men and 29.9% for women). Among 15–24 year olds it was 57.5%.

Press

There were seven paid-for daily newspapers in 2008 with a combined circulation of 75,000 and 46 paid-for non-dailies.

Rail

There were 1,017 km of railways in 2008 (771 km electrified). It is estimated that up to 80% of the rail network was destroyed in the civil war, and it was not until July 2001 that the first international services were resumed. There are two state-owned rail companies-the Railway of the Federation of Bosnia and Herzegovina (ŽFBH) and the Railway of the Serb Republic (ŽRS). In 2008 ŽFBH carried 528,000 passengers and 8.1 m. tonnes of freight while ŽRS carried 727,000 passengers and 5.0 m. tonnes of freight.

Religion

According to estimates by the Pew Research Center's Forum on Religion & Public Life, in 2010 the vast majority of the population was Christian (1.98 m., of which 1.44 m. Orthodox Christians and 0.54 m. Catholics) or Muslim (1.70 m., most of whom were Sunnis). In Feb. 2016 the Roman Catholic church had one cardinal.

Roads

In 2005 there were an estimated 22,419 km of roads (4,104 km main roads). Passenger cars numbered 473,076 in 2007 (123 per 1,000 inhabitants). There were 428 road accident fatalities in 2007.

Social Statistics

2010 births, 33,779; deaths, 34,633. Rates per 1,000, 2010: birth, 8.8; death, 9.0. Annual population growth rate, 2000–08, 0.3%. Life expectancy at birth, 2013, was 73.8 years for men and 78.9 years for women. Infant mortality,

2010, eight per 1,000 live births; fertility rate, 2013, 1.3 children per woman (the joint lowest rate in the world).

Telecommunications

In 2011 there were 955,900 landline telephone subscriptions (equivalent to 254.8 per 1,000 inhabitants) and 3,171,300 mobile phone subscriptions (or 845.2 per 1,000 inhabitants). In 2010, 52.0% of the population were internet users.

Territory and Population

The republic is bounded in the north and west by Croatia, in the east by Serbia and in the southeast by Montenegro. The capital is Sarajevo. It has a coastline of only 20 km with no harbours. Its area is 51,210 km^2, including 210 km^2 of inland waters. Provisional census population, 2013, 3,791,622; density, 74.0 per km^2. In 2011, 49.2% of the population lived in urban areas.

Tourism

In 2010, 365,000 non-resident tourists stayed in holiday accommodation (up from 311,000 in 2009 and 171,000 in 2000).

Botswana

Lefatshe la Botswana (Republic of Botswana)

Factsheet

Capital: Gaborone
Population estimate, 2015: 2.26 m.
GNI per capita, 2014: (PPP$) 16,646
HDI/world rank, 2014: 0.698/106
Internet domain extension: .bw

Civil Aviation

There are international airports at Gaborone (Sir Seretse Khama) and at Maun and six domestic airports. The national carrier is the state-owned Air Botswana, which in 2013 carried 265,000 passengers (173,000 on international flights). In 2012 Gaborone handled 403,372 passengers.

Climate

In winter, days are warm and nights cold, with occasional frosts. Summer heat is tempered by prevailing northeast winds. Rainfall comes mainly in summer, from Oct. to April, while the rest of the year is almost completely dry with very high sunshine amounts. Gaborone, Jan. 79 °F (26.1 °C), July 55 °F (12.8 °C). Annual rainfall varies from 650 mm in the north to 250 mm in the southeast. The country is prone to droughts.

Constitution and Government

The Constitution was adopted in March 1965 and became effective on 30 Sept. 1966. It provides for a republican form of government headed by the President with three main organs: the Legislature, the Executive and the Judiciary. The executive rests with the President who is responsible to the National Assembly. The President is elected for 5-year terms by the National Assembly. The *National Assembly* consists of 63 members, of which 57 are elected by universal suffrage, four are specially elected members and two, the President and the Speaker, are *ex officio*. There is also a *House of Chiefs* to advise the government.

Currency

The unit of currency is the *pula* (BWP) of 100 *thebe*.

Defence

In 2013 defence expenditure totalled US$438 m. (US$206 per capita), representing 2.4% of GDP.

Economy

Services accounted for 52.5% of GDP in 2010, industry 45.0% and agriculture 2.5%.

Labour

The labour force in 2013 was 1,128,700 (867,600 in 2003). 78.9% of the population aged 15–64 was economically active in 2013. In the same year 17.6% of the population was unemployed.

Press

The government-owned *Daily News* is distributed free (circulation, 2008: 65,000). There is one other daily, the independent *Mmegi* ('The Reporter'), and 14 non-dailies.

Rail

The main line from Mafeking in South Africa to Bulawayo in Zimbabwe traverses Botswana. The total length of the rail system was 888 km in 2005, including two branch lines. In 2006, 426,894 passengers and 1,712,607 tonnes of freight were carried.

Religion

Freedom of worship is guaranteed under the Constitution. In 2010 there were an estimated 1.32 m. Protestants and 120,000 Roman Catholics according to the Pew Research Center's Forum on Religion & Public Life, with most of the remainder of the population being unaffiliated or folk religionists.

Roads

In 2005 the total road network was estimated to be 25,798 km (32.6% paved). In Dec. 2008 there were 256,498 motor vehicles registered. There were 497 deaths in road accidents in 2007.

Social Statistics

2008 (estimates) births, 47,000; deaths, 23,000. Rates, 2008 estimates (per 1,000 population): births, 24.5; deaths, 12.1. Infant mortality, 2010 (per 1,000 live births), 36. Expectation of life in 2013 was 62.1 years for males and 66.8 for females. In 2013, 21.9% of all adults between 15 and 49 were infected with HIV. Annual population growth rate, 2000–08, 1.4%. Fertility rate, 2008, 2.9 children per woman.

Telecommunications

In 2011 there were 149,600 landline telephone subscriptions (equivalent to 73.7 per 1,000 inhabitants) and 2,900,300 mobile phone subscriptions (or 1,428.2 per 1,000 inhabitants). In 2011, 7.0% of the population were internet users. In June 2012 there were 224,000 Facebook users.

Territory and Population

Botswana is bounded in the west and north by Namibia, northeast by Zambia and Zimbabwe, and east and south by South Africa. The area is 581,730 km^2. 2011 census population, 2,024,904; density, 3.5 per km^2. In 2011, 61.8% of the population were urban. The main towns (2011 census population) are Gaborone, 231,592; Francistown, 98,961; Molepolole, 66,466; Maun, 60,263; Mogoditshane, 58,079; Serowe, 50,820; Selebi-Phikwe, 49,411; Kanye, 47,007; Mochudi, 44,815; Mahalapye, 43,289. The official languages are Setswana and English.

Tourism

There were 2,145,000 international tourists (excluding same-day visitors) in 2010, with tourism receipts totalling US$218 m.

Brazil

República Federativa do Brasil (Federative Republic of Brazil)

Factsheet

Capital: Brasília (Federal District)
Population estimate, 2015: 207.85 m.
GNI per capita, 2014: (PPP$) 15,175
HDI/world rank, 2014: 0.755/75
Internet domain extension: .br

Civil Aviation

There are major international airports at Rio de Janeiro-Galeão (Antonio Carlos Jobim International) and São Paulo (Guarulhos) and some international flights from Brasília, Porto Alegre, Recife and Salvador. The main airlines are LATAM (created in June 2012 when the Brazilian carrier TAM merged with LAN Airlines, Chile's largest airline) and Gol (a low-cost airline launched in 2001). Brazil's busiest airport is Guarulhos (São Paulo), which handled 18,795,596 passengers in 2007, followed by Congonhas (São Paulo) with 15,244,401 passengers (all on domestic flights) and Brasília International (Presidente Juscelino Kubitschek International Airport) with 11,119,872 passengers.

Climate

Because of its latitude, the climate is predominantly tropical, but factors such as altitude, prevailing winds and distance from the sea cause certain variations, though temperatures are not notably extreme. In tropical parts, winters are dry and summers wet, while in Amazonia conditions are constantly warm and humid. The northeast *sertão* is hot and arid, with frequent droughts. In the south and east, spring and autumn are sunny and warm, summers are hot, but winters can be cold when polar air-masses impinge. Brasília, Jan. 72 °F (22.3 °C), July 68 °F (19.8 °C). Annual rainfall 60″ (1,512 mm).

Constitution and Government

The present Constitution came into force on 5 Oct. 1988, the eighth since independence. The *President* and *Vice-President* are elected for a 4-year term. To be elected candidates must secure 50% plus one vote of all the valid votes, otherwise a second round of voting is held to elect the President between the two most voted candidates. A constitutional amendment of June 1997 authorizes the re-election of the President for one extra term of 4 years. *Congress* consists of an 81-member *Senate* (three Senators per federal unit plus three from the Federal District of Brasília) and a 513-member *Chamber of Deputies*. The Senate is directly elected (two-thirds of it and one-third of it elected for 8 years in rotation every 4 years). The Chamber of Deputies is elected by universal franchise for 4 years. There is a *Council of the Republic* which is convened only in national emergencies.

Currency

The unit of currency is the *real* (BRL) of 100 *centavos*, which was introduced on 1 July 1994 to replace the former *cruzeiro real* at a rate of 1 real (R$1) = 2,750 cruzeiros reais (CR$2,750).

Defence

Conscription is for nine to 12 months. In 2013 defence expenditure totalled US$34,730 m. (US$173 per capita), representing 1.4% of GDP. Brazil was responsible for 49% of South America's military spending in 2013.

Economy

Agriculture accounted for 6.1% of GDP in 2009, industry 25.4% and services 68.5%.

Labour

The labour force in 2013 was 108,384,600 (90,365,500 in 2003). 75.0% of the population aged 15–64 was economically active in 2013. A constitutional amendment of 1996 prohibits the employment of children under 14 years. There is a minimum monthly wage, which was increased from R$622 to R$678 with effect from 1 Jan. 2013. In Sept. 2013, 4.9% of the workforce was unemployed based on figures from six of Brazil's largest metropolitan areas (down from 10.9% in Sept. 2004 and 7.7% in Sept. 2009).

Press

There were 784 daily newspapers in 2014 with a combined circulation of 8,478,000. In the same year there were 123 newspapers with online editions. The daily newspapers with the highest circulation are *Folha de S. Paulo* and the tabloid *Super Notícia*. In the 2013 *World Press Freedom Index* compiled by Reporters Without Borders, Brazil was ranked 108th out of 179 countries.

Rail

Brazilian railways have largely been privatized: all six branches of the large RFFSA network are now under private management. The largest areas of the network are now run by América Latina Logística (12,883 km of metre gauge in 2007) and Ferrovia Centro-Atlântica (7,080 km of metre-gauge).

Religion

According to the Pew Research Center's Forum on Religion & Public Life the population was an estimated 88.9% Christian in 2010, with folk religionists accounting for 2.8% and a further 7.9% unaffiliated. Only the USA has more Christians, although Brazil has the most Catholics of any country (an estimated 133.7 m. in 2010). The Roman Catholic Church has 44 ecclesiastical provinces, each headed by an archbishop. These ecclesiastical provinces are in turn subdivided into 215 dioceses. The Archbishop of São Salvador da Bahia (Murilo Sebastião Ramos Krieger) is also the Primate of Brazil. In Feb. 2016 there were ten Roman Catholic cardinals.

Roads

In 2004 there were 1,751,868 km of roads, of which 93,071 km were highways, national and main roads. In 2007 there were 37,978,000 vehicles in use, including 30,283,000 passenger cars. In 2006, 407,685 persons were injured in road accidents and 35,155 were killed.

Shipping

Inland waterways, mostly rivers, are open to navigation over some 43,000 km. Tubarão and Itaqui are the leading ports. In 2008 Santos, the leading container port, handled 2.68 m. TEUs (twenty-foot equivalent units). In Jan. 2009 there were 166 ships of 300 GT or over registered, totalling 2.02 m. GT.

Social Statistics

The total number of registered live births in 2006 was 2,799,128 (rate of 15.4 per 1,000 population); deaths, 1,020,211 (5.6); marriages, 889,828 (4.9); divorces 162,244 (0.9). The average age at first marriage in 2006 was 28.3 years for men and 25.4 for women. Life expectancy in 2006 was 68.5 years for males and 76.1 for females. Annual population growth rate, 2000–05, 1.5%; infant mortality, 2010, 17 per 1,000 live births (down from 50 per 1,000 in 1990); fertility rate, 2006, 2.0 children per woman.

Telecommunications

The state-owned telephone system was privatized in 1998. There were 44,128,188 main (fixed) telephone lines in 2014. In the same year 57.6% of the population were internet users. In June 2012 Brazil had 51.2 m. Facebook users, the second highest total after the USA (26% of the population).

Territory and Population

Brazil is bounded in the east by the Atlantic and on its northern, western and southern borders by all the South American countries except Chile and Ecuador. The total area (including inland waters) is 8,514,877 km². It is the world's fifth largest country and occupies 47.8% of South America. 2010 census population: 190,755,799 (93,406,990 males and 97,348,809 females). Population density, 2010, 22.4 per km². Population of principal cities (2010 census): São Paulo, 11,152,344; Rio de Janeiro, 6,320,446; Salvador, 2,674,923; Brasília, 2,482,210; Fortaleza, 2,452,185; Belo Horizonte, 2,375,151; Manaus, 1,792,881; Curitiba, 1,751,907; Recife, 1,537,704; Porto Alegre, 1,409,351. The official language is Portuguese.

Tourism

In 2012, 5,677,000 tourists visited Brazil (up from 5,433,000 in 2011 and 3,785,000 in 2002). In 2011 the largest number of tourists came from elsewhere in the Americas (3,402,000); 1,663,000 European tourists visited the country, down from 1,938,000 in 2007. Receipts in 2012 totalled US$6.89 bn. (US$6.83 bn. in 2011).

Brunei

Negara Brunei Darussalam (State of Brunei Darussalam)

Factsheet

Capital: Bandar Seri Begawan
Population estimate, 2015: 423,000
GNI per capita, 2013: (PPP$) 70,883
HDI/world rank, 2014: 0.856/31
Internet domain extension: .bn

Civil Aviation

Brunei International Airport (Bandar Seri Begawan) handled 1,262,343 passengers (all international) in 2005. The national carrier is the state-owned Royal Brunei Airlines (RBA).

Climate

The climate is tropical marine, hot and moist, but nights are cool. Humidity is high and rainfall heavy, varying from 100″ (2,500 mm) on the coast to 200″ (5,000 mm) inland. There is no dry season. Bandar Seri Begawan, Jan. 80 °F (26.7 °C), July 82 °F (27.8 °C). Annual rainfall 131″ (3,275 mm).

Constitution and Government

The Sultan and Yang Di Pertuan of Brunei Darussalam is HM Sultan Haji Hassanal Bolkiah Mu'izzadin Waddaulah. On 29 Sept. 1959 the Sultan promulgated a constitution, but parts of it have been in abeyance since Dec. 1962 under emergency powers assumed by the Sultan. Since 1984 the Legislative Council (*Majlis Masyuarat Megeri*) has been effectively replaced by a Council of Cabinet Ministers appointed and presided over by the Sultan. The constitution was amended in Sept. 2004, allowing for the Legislative Council to be reconvened, but with no independent executive powers and its 21 members chosen by the Sultan.

Currency

The unit of currency is the *Brunei dollar* (BND) of 100 cents, which is at parity with the Singapore dollar (also legal tender).

Defence

In 2013 military expenditure totalled US$416 m. (US$1,002 per capita), representing 2.5% of GDP.

Economy

In 2012 industry contributed 71.1% to GDP, services 28.2% and agriculture 0.7%. The fall in oil prices in 1997–98 led to the setting up of an Economic Council to advise the Sultan on reforms. In 1998 an investigation was mounted into the Amedeo Corporation, Brunei's largest private company, run by Prince Jefri, the Sultan's brother. Amedeo collapsed with large debts.

Labour

The labour force in 2013 was 200,400 (167,200 in 2003). 67.4% of the population aged 15–64 was economically active in 2013. In the same year 3.8% of the population was unemployed.

Press

In 2008 there were three daily newspapers with an average circulation of 41,000. The *Borneo Bulletin* and the *Brunei Times* are English-language papers, while *Media Permata* is a Malay paper.

Religion

The official religion is Islam. In 2010, 75.1% of the population were Muslims (mostly Sunnis of Malay origin) according to estimates by the Pew Research Center's Forum on Religion & Public Life. There are also some Christians, Buddhists and folk religionists.

Roads

There were an estimated 3,560 km of roads in 2005; 77.2% of all roads were paved in 2005. The main road connects Bandar Seri Begawan with Kuala Belait and Seria. In 2007 there were 252,700 passenger cars in use (649 per 1,000 inhabitants—one of the highest rates in the world), 16,700 vans and lorries, 1,500 buses and coaches, and 12,200 motorcycles and mopeds. There were 38 fatalities in road accidents in 2005.

Shipping

Regular shipping services operate from Singapore, Hong Kong, Sarawak and Sabah to Bandar Seri Begawan, and there is a daily passenger ferry between Bandar Seri Begawan and Labuan. In 2005 merchant shipping totalled 2.4 m. GRT. In 2005 vessels totalling 1,066,381 NRT entered ports and vessels totalling 1,061,339 NRT cleared.

Social Statistics

2005 births, 6,933; deaths, 1,072. Rates, 2005: birth per 1,000 population, 18.7; death, 2.9. There were 2,018 marriages in 2005. Life expectancy in 2007: males, 74.9 years; females, 79.6. Annual population growth rate, 1995–2005, 2.5%. Infant mortality, 2010, six per 1,000 live births; fertility rate, 2005, 2.1 children per woman.

Telecommunications

There is a telephone network linking the main centres. Brunei had an estimated 412,900 mobile phone subscriptions in 2009 (or 1,033.0 per 1,000 inhabitants) and 80,500 fixed telephone lines. There were 787.8 internet users per 1,000 inhabitants in 2009. Fixed internet subscriptions totalled 100,000 in 2009 (255.6 per 1,000 inhabitants). In March 2012 there were 234,000 Facebook users.

Territory and Population

Brunei, on the coast of Borneo, is bounded in the northwest by the South China Sea and on all other sides by Sarawak (Malaysia), which splits it into two parts, the smaller portion forming the Temburong district. Area, 5,765 km² (2,226 sq. miles). Population (2011 census) 393,372 (203,144 males), giving a density of 68.2 per km². 76.1% of the population lived in urban areas. The four districts are Brunei/Muara (2011 census: 279,924), Belait (60,744), Tutong (43,852) and Temburong (8,852). The capital is Bandar Seri Begawan (estimate 2001: 27,285). The official language is Malay but English is in use.

Tourism

In 2010, 214,290 non-resident tourists (excluding same-day visitors) arrived by air—up from 157,474 in 2009 but down from 225,757 in 2008.

Bulgaria

Republika Bulgaria (Republic of Bulgaria)

Factsheet

Capital: Sofia
Population estimate, 2015: 7.15 m.
GNI per capita, 2014: (PPP$) 15,596
HDI/world rank, 2014: 0.782/59
Internet domain extension: .bg

Civil Aviation

There is an international airport at Sofia (Vrazhdebna), which handled 3,467,455 passengers (3,266,427 on international flights) and 16,246 tonnes of freight in 2012. The bankrupt former state-owned Balkan Bulgarian Airlines was replaced by Bulgaria Air (initially named Balkan Air Tour) in 2002 as the new national flag carrier.

Climate

The southern parts have a Mediterranean climate, with winters mild and moist and summers hot and dry, but further north the conditions become more Continental, with a larger range of temperature and greater amounts of rainfall in summer and early autumn. Sofia, Jan. 28 °F (−2.2 °C), July 69 °F (20.6 °C). Annual rainfall 25.4″ (635 mm).

Constitution and Government

A new constitution was adopted at Tarnovo on 12 July 1991. The *President* is directly elected for not more than two 5-year terms. Candidates for the presidency must be at least 40 years old and have lived for the last 5 years in Bulgaria. American-style primary elections were introduced in 1996; voting is open to all the electorate. The 240-member *National Assembly* is directly elected by proportional representation. The *President* nominates a candidate from the largest parliamentary party as *Prime Minister*.

Currency

The unit of currency is the *lev* (BGN) of 100 *stotinki*. In May 1996 the lev was devalued by 68%. A new *lev* was introduced on 5 July 1999, at 1 new *lev* = 1,000 old *leva*.

Defence

Since 1 Jan. 2008 Bulgaria has had an all-volunteer professional army. Following restructuring the total strength of the armed forces has been reduced from more than 68,000 in 2002 to less than 32,000 in 2011. Defence expenditure in 2013 totalled US$751 m. (US$108 per capita), representing 1.4% of GDP.

Economy

Transport, communications, trade and restaurants contributed 21.8% to GDP in 2011; followed by mining, public utilities and manufacturing, 21.2%; finance and real estate, 15.0%; public administration and defence, 10.8%; and services, 6.8%.

Labour

A total of 2,949,600 persons were in employment in 2011, with the leading areas of activity as follows: manufacturing, 601,600; wholesale and retail trade, and repair of motor vehicles and motorcycles, 538,400; construction, 225,300; public administration and defence, and compulsory social security, 225,300; agriculture, forestry and fishing, 200,500. The unemployment rate was 12.3% in June 2012, up from 11.3% in 2011 as a whole and 5.6% in 2008. The monthly minimum wage was raised from 270 leva to 290 leva in May 2012.

Press

In 2012 there were 57 daily newspapers with a combined daily circulation of 639,000. The two biggest circulation paid-for dailies are *Telegraph* (which was only launched in 2005) and *Trud*, the only title from the socialist era that survived after 1989. A total of 8,263 book titles were published in 2012, including 2,171 fiction titles for adults.

Rail

In 2011 there were 3,947 km of 1,435 mm gauge railway (2,862 km electrified) and 125 km of 760 mm gauge. Passenger-km travelled in 2011 came to 2.07 bn. and freight tonne-km to 3.17 bn.

Religion

'The traditional church of the Bulgarian people' (as it is officially described) is that of the Eastern Orthodox Church. It was disestablished under the 1947 constitution. In 1953 the Bulgarian Patriarchate was revived. The Patriarch is Neofit (enthroned Feb. 2013). The seat of the Patriarch is at Sofia. The Bulgarian Orthodox Church has 15 dioceses, of which 13 are in Bulgaria and two abroad-one covering the United States, Canada and Australia, and the other Central and Western Europe. According to the Pew Research Center's Forum on Religion & Public Life the Orthodox population numbered an estimated 6.22 m. in 2010. There were also 1.02 m. indigenous Muslims (Pomaks) in 2010 and 310,000 people who were religiously unaffiliated.

Roads

In 2005 Bulgaria had 40,231 km of roads, including 331 km of motorways and 2,961 km of main roads. In 2007 there were 1,971,500 passenger cars (257 per 1,000 inhabitants), 262,900 lorries and vans, 26,300 buses and coaches, and 78,900 motorcycles and mopeds. In 2005 public transport totalled 13.7 bn. passenger-km. In 2007, 9,827 persons were injured in road accidents and 1,006 were killed.

Shipping

In Jan. 2009 there were 86 ships of 300 GT or over registered, totalling 890,000 GT. Bourgas is a fishing and oil-port.

Social Statistics

2008: live births, 77,712; deaths, 110,523; marriages, 27,722; divorces, 14,104. Rates per 1,000 population, 2008: birth, 10.2; death, 14.5; marriage, 3.6; divorce, 1.9; infant mortality, 11 per 1,000 live births (2010). There were 37,272 reported abortions in 2006. In 2005 the most popular age range for marrying was 25–29 for males and 20–24 for females. Expectation of life in 2007 was 69.6 years among males and 76.7 years among females. The annual population growth rate for the period 2010–15 was −0.6%, giving Bulgaria one of the fastest declining populations of any country. Fertility rate, 2008, 1.4 children per woman.

Telecommunications

The Bulgarian Telecommunications Company was privatized in Jan. 2004. In 2011 there were 2,310,800 landline telephone subscriptions (equivalent to 310.3 per 1,000 inhabitants) and 10,475,100 mobile phone subscriptions (or 1,406.8 per 1,000 inhabitants). In 2011, 51.0% of the population were internet users. In March 2012 there were 2.4 m. Facebook users.

Territory and Population

The area of Bulgaria is 111,002 km^2 (42,858 sq. miles). It is bounded in the north by Romania, east by the Black Sea, south by Turkey and Greece, and west by Serbia and the Republic of Macedonia. The country is divided into 28 districts. The capital, Sofia, has district status. The population of Bulgaria at the census of 2011 was 7,364,570 (females, 3,777,999); population density 66.3 per km^2. Population of principal towns (2011 census): Sofia, 1,202,761; Plovdiv, 338,153; Varna, 334,870; Bourgas, 200,271; Rousse, 149,642; Stara Zagora, 138,272; Pleven, 106,954; Sliven, 91,620; Dobrich, 91,030. Bulgarian is the official language.

Tourism

There were 6,541,000 non-resident tourists in 2012 (5,151,000 in 2007). Earnings from tourism were US$4,202 m. in 2012.

Burkina Faso

République Démocratique du Burkina Faso (Democratic Republic of Burkina Faso)

Factsheet

Capital: Ouagadougou
Population estimate, 2015: 18.11 m.
GNI per capita, 2014: (PPP$) 1,591
HDI/world rank, 2014: 0.402/183
Internet domain extension: .bf

Civil Aviation

The international airports are Ouagadougou (which handled 485,815 passengers in 2012) and Bobo-Dioulasso. The national carrier is Air Burkina, which in 2010 flew to Abidjan, Accra, Bamako, Cotonou, Dakar, Douala, Libreville, Lomé, Marseille, N'Djaména, Niamey and Paris in addition to operating on domestic routes. In 2013 Air Burkina carried 129,000 passengers (122,000 on international flights).

Climate

A tropical climate with a wet season from May to Nov. and a dry season from Dec. to April. Rainfall decreases from south to north. Ouagadougou, Jan. 76 °F (24.4 °C), July 83 °F (28.3 °C). Annual rainfall 36″ (894 mm).

Constitution and Government

At a referendum in June 1991 a new constitution was approved; there is an executive presidency and a multi-party system. Parliament consists of the 127-member *National Assembly*, elected by universal suffrage. The *Chamber of Representatives*, a consultative body representing social, religious, professional and political organizations, was abolished in 2002.

Currency

The unit of currency is the *franc CFA* (XOF) with a parity of 655.957 francs CFA to one euro.

Defence

There are three military regions. Defence expenditure totalled US$153 m. in 2013 (US$9 per capita), representing 1.3% of GDP.

Economy

Agriculture contributed 31.8% of GDP in 2009; followed by public administration, defence and services, 15.6%; manufacturing, 11.1%; trade and hotels, 11.1%; and construction, 6.7%.

Labour

The labour force in 2013 was 7,695,400 (5,625,600 in 2003). 85.1% of the population aged 15–64 was economically active in 2013.

Press

There were five dailies (two government-owned) with a combined circulation of 36,000 in 2008. The leading newspaper in terms of circulation is *Le Pays*.

Rail

The railway from Abidjan in Côte d'Ivoire to Kaya (600 km of metre gauge within Burkina Faso) is operated by the mixed public-private company Sitarail, a concessionaire to both governments.

Religion

According to estimates by the Pew Research Center's Forum on Religion & Public Life, in 2010 the population was 61.6% Muslim (nearly all Sunnis) with 22.5% Christian (mainly Catholic) and 15.4% folk religionists. In Feb. 2016 the Roman Catholic church had one cardinal.

Roads

The road system comprised 92,495 km in 2004 (including 15,271 km of main roads). There were 97,100 passenger cars (seven per 1,000 inhabitants), 55,700 lorries and vans, and 356,400 motorcycles and mopeds in use in 2007.

Social Statistics

2008 births (estimates), 719,000; deaths, 198,000. Estimated birth rate in 2008 was 47.2 per 1,000 population; estimated death rate, 13.0. Burkina Faso has one of the youngest populations of any country, with 73% of the population under the age of 30% and 45% under 15. Annual population growth rate, 2000–08, 3.3%. Expectation of life at birth, 2013, 56.9 years for females and 55.7 for males. Infant mortality, 2010 (per 1,000 live births), 93. Fertility rate, 2008, 5.9 children per woman.

Telecommunications

In 2011 there were 141,500 landline telephone subscriptions (equivalent to 8.3 per 1,000 inhabitants) and 7,628,100 mobile phone subscriptions (or 452.7 per 1,000 inhabitants). Fixed internet subscriptions totalled 28,700 in 2010 (1.7 per 1,000 inhabitants). In June 2012 there were 116,000 Facebook users.

Territory and Population

Burkina Faso is bounded in the north and west by Mali, east by Niger and south by Benin, Togo, Ghana and Côte d'Ivoire. Area: 270,764 km^2; 2006 census population, 14,017,262, giving a density of 51.8 per km^2. In 2011 the population was 26.5% urban. The largest cities in 2006 were Ouagadougou, the capital (1,475,223), Bobo-Dioulasso (489,967), Koudougou (88,184), Banfora (75,917), Ouahigouya (73,153) and Pouytenga (60,618). French is the official language.

Tourism

In 2009, 269,000 foreign tourists stayed in hotels or similar accommodation.

Burundi

Republika y'Uburundi (Republic of Burundi)

Factsheet

Capital: Bujumbura
Population estimate, 2015: 11.18 m.
GNI per capita, 2014: (PPP$) 758
HDI/world rank, 2014: 0.400/184
Internet domain extension: .bi

Civil Aviation

There were direct flights to Dar es Salaam, Kigali, Mwanza and Nairobi in 2010. Air Burundi is the state-owned national airline, but it has not been operational since Sept. 2009. Bujumbura International airport handled 291,838 passengers and 3,054 tonnes of freight in 2012.

Climate

An equatorial climate, modified by altitude. The eastern plateau is generally cool, the easternmost savanna several degrees hotter. The wet seasons are from March to May and Sept. to Dec. Bujumbura, Jan. 73 °F (22.8 °C), July 73 °F (22.8 °C). Annual rainfall 33″ (825 mm).

Constitution and Government

The constitution of 1981 provided for a one-party state. In Jan. 1991 the government of President Maj. Pierre Buyoya, leader of the sole party, the Union for National Progress (UPRONA), proposed a new constitution which was approved by a referendum in March 1992 (with 89% of votes cast in favour), legalizing parties not based on ethnic group, region or religion and providing for presidential elections by direct universal suffrage.

On 28 Feb. 2005 citizens voted overwhelmingly to adopt a new constitution laying the foundations for the end of a 12-year civil war, with 92% of votes cast in favour of the constitution. Burundi has a bicameral legislature, consisting of the *National Assembly* of 121 members, with 100 members elected to serve 5-year terms and 21 co-opted members, and the *Senate* of 43 members (36 elected and seven appointed, including four former presidents).

Currency

The unit of currency is the *Burundi franc* (BIF) of 100 *centimes.*

Defence

Defence expenditure totalled US$64 m. in 2013 (US$6 per capita), representing 2.5% of GDP.

Economy

Agriculture contributed 33.3% to GDP in 2011; followed by public administration and defence, 21.7%; manufacturing, 13.6%; and transport and communications, 6.7%.

Labour

The labour force in 2013 was 4,799,400 (3,287,700 in 2003). 83.6% of the population aged 15–64 was economically active in 2013.

Press

There was one state-controlled daily newspaper (*Le Renouveau*) in 2008 with a circulation of 20,000.

Religion

According to estimates by the Pew Research Center's Forum on Religion & Public Life, in 2010 the population was 91.5% Christian with the remainder being folk religionists and Muslims. Around four-fifth of Christians are Catholics and the rest Protestants.

Roads

Burundi has some 12,300 km of roads. There were 15,500 passenger cars (two per 1,000 inhabitants) and 32,700 lorries and vans in use in 2007.

Shipping

There are lake services from Bujumbura to Kigoma (Tanzania) and Kalémie (Democratic Republic of the Congo). The main route for exports and imports is via Kigoma, and thence by rail to Dar es Salaam.

Social Statistics

2008 estimates: births, 278,000; deaths, 112,000. Rates, 2008 estimates (per 1,000 population): birth, 34.5; death, 13.9. Life expectancy at birth, 2013, was 52.2 years for men and 56.1 years for women. Infant mortality, 2010, 88 per 1,000 live births. Annual population growth rate, 2000–08, 2.8%; fertility rate, 2008, 4.6 children per woman.

Telecommunications

There were 32,600 fixed telephone lines in 2010 (3.9 per 1,000 inhabitants) and mobile phone subscribers numbered 1.15 m. There were 21.0 internet users per 1,000 inhabitants in 2010. Fixed internet subscriptions totalled 5,000 in 2009 (0.6 per 1,000 inhabitants).

Territory and Population

Burundi is bounded in the north by Rwanda, east and south by Tanzania and west by the Democratic Republic of the Congo, and has an area of 27,830 km^2 (10,745 sq. miles) including 2,150 km^2 of inland water (830 sq. miles). The population at the 2008 census was 8,053,574 (4,088,668 females); density, 314 per km^2. In 2011, 11.3% of the population lived in urban areas (the smallest proportion of any country in the world). There are 17 regions, all named after their chief towns. The capital, Bujumbura, had a population of 497,166 in 2008. There are four ethnic groups—Hutu (Bantu, forming 81% of the total); Tutsi (Nilotic, 16%); Lingala (2%);

Twa (pygmoids, 1%). The local language, Kirundi, and French are both official languages.

Tourism

There were 212,000 foreign tourists in 2009 (202,000 in 2008).

Cabo Verde

República de Cabo Verde (Republic of Cabo Verde)

Factsheet
Capital: Praia
Population estimate, 2015: 521,000
GNI per capita, 2014: (PPP$) 6,094
HDI/world rank, 2013: 0.646/122
Internet domain extension: .cv

Civil Aviation

Amilcar Cabral International Airport, at Espargos on Sal, is a major refuelling point on flights to Africa and Latin America. A new international airport, Praia International Airport, has been built at Praia on São Tiago, and was opened in 2005. Transportes Aéreos de Cabo Verde (TACV), the national carrier, provided services to most of the other islands in 2010, and internationally to Bissau, Boston, Dakar, Fortaleza, Las Palmas, Lisbon and Paris. In 2006 Amilcar Cabral International Airport handled 562,972 passengers and 1,415 tonnes of freight.

Climate

The climate is arid, with a cool dry season from Dec. to June and warm dry conditions for the rest of the year. Rainfall is sparse, rarely exceeding 5″ (127 mm) in the northern islands or 12″ (304 mm) in the southern ones. There are periodic severe droughts. Praia, Jan. 72 °F (22.2 °C), July 77 °F (25 °C). Annual rainfall 10″ (250 mm).

Constitution and Government

The Constitution was adopted in Sept. 1992 and was revised in 1995 and 1999. The *President* is elected for 5-year terms by universal suffrage. The 72-member *National Assembly* (*Assembleia Nacional*) is elected for 5-year terms.

Currency

The unit of currency is the *Cape Verde escudo* (CVE) of 100 *centavos*, which is pegged at 110.265 to the euro.

Defence

National service is by selective conscription. The President of the Republic is C.-in-C. of the armed forces. Defence expenditure totalled US$9 m. in 2013 (US$18 per capita), representing 0.5% of GDP.

Economy

Agriculture accounted for 8.9% of GDP in 2009, industry 19.7% and services 71.4%.

Labour

In 2010 the estimated economically active population was 221,000 (57% males).

Press

In 2008 there were 12 non-daily newspapers although no dailies. The most popular newspaper is the weekly *A Semana*.

Religion

According to the Pew Research Center's Forum on Religion & Public Life, in 2010 the population was an estimated 89.1% Christian with a further 9.1% being religiously unaffiliated and the remainder followers of other religions. Around 90% of Christians are Catholics.

Roads

There are approximately 1,400 km of roads. In 2007 there were 49,800 vehicles in use.

Shipping

The main ports are Mindelo and Praia. In Jan. 2009 there were 19 vessels of 300 GT or over registered, totalling 19,000 GT. There is a state-owned ferry service between the islands.

Social Statistics

2008 estimates: births, 12,000; deaths, 2,000. Rates, 2008 estimates (per 1,000 population): birth, 24.1; death, 5.0. Annual population growth rate, 2000–08, 1.6%. Annual emigration varies between 2,000 and 10,000. Life expectancy at birth, 2013, was 71.1 years for men and 78.8 years for women. Infant mortality, 2010, 29 per 1,000 live births; fertility rate, 2008, 2.7 children per woman.

Telecommunications

In 2011 there were 74,500 landline telephone subscriptions (equivalent to 148.8 per 1,000 inhabitants) and 396,400 mobile phone subscriptions (or 791.9 per 1,000 inhabitants). There were 296.7 internet users per 1,000 inhabitants in 2009. Fixed internet subscriptions totalled 12,900 in 2009 (26.3 per 1,000 inhabitants).

Territory and Population

Cabo Verde is situated in the Atlantic Ocean 620 km off west Africa and consists of ten islands (Boa Vista, Brava, Fogo, Maio, Sal, Santa Luzia, Santo Antão, São Nicolau, São Tiago and São Vicente) and five islets. The islands are divided into two groups, named Barlavento (windward) and Sotavento (leeward). The total area is 4,033 km^2 (1,557 sq. miles). The 2010 census population was 491,875 (248,282 female), giving a density of 122 per km^2. The main towns are Praia, the capital, on São Tiago (127,832, 2010 census population) and Mindelo on São Vicente (70,468, 2010 census population). It is estimated that around 71% of the population are of mixed African and European descent, with 28% African (mainly Fulani, Balanta and Mandyako) and 1% European. The official language is Portuguese; a creole (Crioulo) is in ordinary use.

Tourism

Tourism has experienced huge growth in the past few years. In 2009 there were 287,183 non-resident tourists staying at hotels and similar establishments, compared to 267,188 in 2007 and 197,844 in 2005.

Cambodia

Preah Reach Ana Pak Kampuchea (Kingdom of Cambodia)

Factsheet
Capital: Phnom Penh
Population estimate, 2015: 15.58 m.
GNI per capita, 2014: (PPP$) 2,949
HDI/world rank, 2014: 0.555/143=
Internet domain extension: .kh

Civil Aviation

Phnom Penh International Airport handled 1,587,986 passengers in 2009 and Siem Reap International Airport 1,255,166. The flag carrier is Cambodia Angkor Air (51% state-owned), which began services in 2009.

Climate

A tropical climate, with high temperatures all the year. Phnom Penh, Jan. 78 °F (25.6 °C), July 84 °F (28.9 °C). Annual rainfall 52″ (1,308 mm).

Constitution and Government

A parliamentary monarchy was re-established by the 1993 constitution. King Norodom Sihamoni (b. 14 May 1953; appointed 14 Oct. 2004 and sworn in on 29 Oct. 2004) was chosen in the first ever meeting of the nine-member Throne Council following the abdication of his father King Norodom Sihanouk (b. 31 Oct. 1922) on health grounds. Cambodia has a bicameral legislature. There is a 123-member *National Assembly*. Its members are elected by popular vote to serve 5-year terms. There is also a 61-member *Senate*, established in 1999.

Currency

The unit of currency is the *riel* (KHR) of 100 *sen*.

Defence

The King is C.-in-C. of the Royal Cambodian Armed Forces (RCAF). Conscription has not been implemented since 1993 although it is authorized. Defence expenditure in 2013 totalled US$394 m. (US$26 per capita), representing 2.5% of GDP.

Economy

Agriculture accounted for 36% of GDP in 2009, industry 23% and services 41%.

Labour

The labour force in 2013 was 8,446,300 (6,311,500 in 2003). 84.9% of the population aged 15–64 was economically active in 2013. In the same year 0.3% of the population was unemployed.

Press

There were 22 paid-for daily newspapers in 2008 with a combined circulation of 60,000, including the English-language *Cambodia Daily*.

Rail

All official rail services had been suspended by 2009 owing to the dilapidated state of the 600 km metre gauge network. However, a rehabilitation project began in 2006 and freight services were resumed in Oct. 2010 between Phnom Penh and Touk Meas. Some passenger services have been restored and plans are under way to build a 255 km extension to link the country to Vietnam.

Religion

The constitution of 1989 reinstated Buddhism as the state religion; it had an estimated 13.69 m. adherents in 2010 according to the Pew Research Center's Forum on Religion & Public Life. There are small Muslim, folk religionist and Protestant minorities.

Roads

There were 39,704 km of roads in 2009, of which 8.2% were paved. In 2005 there were 195,300 passenger cars in use plus 3,200 buses and coaches, 32,100 lorries and vans and 566,300 motorcycles and mopeds. There were 1,545 fatalities in road accidents in 2007.

Shipping

There is an ocean port at Kompong Som; the port of Phnom Penh can be reached by the Mekong (through Vietnam) by ships of between 3,000 and

4,000 tonnes. In Jan. 2009 there were 730 ships of 300 GT or over registered, totalling 1,966,000 GT.

Social Statistics

2008 estimated births, 360,000; deaths, 121,000. Rates, 2008 estimates (per 1,000 population): births, 24.7; deaths, 8.3. Infant mortality, 2010 (per 1,000 live births), 43. Expectation of life in 2013 was 69.1 years for males and 74.5 for females. Annual population growth rate, 2000–08, 1.7%. Fertility rate, 2008, 2.9 children per woman, down from 5.8 births per woman in 1990.

Telecommunications

Cambodia had 20,451,982 mobile phone subscribers in 2014 (1,327.3 for every 1,000 persons) but only 361,056 main (fixed) telephone lines (23.4 per 1,000 population). 9% of the population were internet users in 2014.

Territory and Population

Cambodia is bounded in the north by Laos and Thailand, west by Thailand, east by Vietnam and south by the Gulf of Thailand. It has an area of about 181,035 km² (69,898 sq. miles). Population, 13,395,682 (2008 census), of whom 6,879,628 were females; density, 74.0 per km². The capital, Phnom Penh, had a population of 1,242,992 in 2008. Other cities are Battambang and Siem Reap. Khmer is the official language.

Tourism

In 2010 there were 2,399,000 international tourist arrivals (excluding same-day visitors), up from 2,046,000 in 2009 and 2,001,000 in 2008.

Cameroon

République du Cameroun (Republic of Cameroon)

Factsheet

Capital: Yaoundé
Population estimate, 2015: 23.34 m.
GNI per capita, 2014: (PPP$) 2,803
HDI/world rank, 2014: 0.512/153
Internet domain extension: .cm

Civil Aviation

There are 45 airports including three international airports at Douala, Garoua and Yaoundé (Nsimalen). In 2011 Douala handled 746,092 passengers. In 2012 scheduled airline traffic of Cameroon-based carriers flew 2.7 m. km; passenger-km totalled 638 m. in the same year.

Climate

An equatorial climate, with high temperatures and plentiful rain, especially from March to June and Sept. to Nov. Further inland, rain occurs at all seasons. Yaoundé, Jan. 76 °F (24.4 °C), July 73 °F (22.8 °C). Annual rainfall 62″ (1,555 mm). Douala, Jan. 79 °F (26.1 °C), July 75 °F (23.9 °C). Annual rainfall 160″ (4,026 mm).

Constitution and Government

The constitution was approved by referendum on 20 May 1972 and became effective on 2 June; it was amended in Jan. 1996. It provides for a *President* as head of state and government. The President is directly elected for a 7-year term, and there is a *Council of Ministers* whose members must not be members of parliament. A constitutional bill removing a two-term presidential limit was adopted in April 2008. The *National Assembly*, elected by universal adult suffrage for 5 years, consists of 180 representatives. The 1996 amendment to the constitution established a 100-seat *Senate*, although elections to it were not held until April 2013.

Currency

The unit of currency is the *franc CFA* (XAF) with a parity of 655.957 francs CFA to one euro.

Defence

The President of the Republic is C.-in-C. of the armed forces. Defence expenditure totalled US$393 m. in 2013 (US$19 per capita), representing 1.4% of GDP.

Economy

In 2009 agriculture, fishing and forestry contributed 21.6% of GDP; followed by trade and hotels, 19.4%; manufacturing, 15.0%; mining, 7.3%; finance and real estate, 6.9%; services, 6.7%.

Labour

The total labour force numbered 8,906,000 in 2013. 70% of employed persons work in agriculture. Cameroon had 0.15 m. people living in slavery according to the Walk Free Foundation's 2013 Global Slavery Index.

Press

In 2008 there was one national government-owned daily newspaper with a circulation of 25,000, four privately-owned dailies and about 200 other privately owned-newspapers that appeared at irregular intervals.

Rail

Cameroon Railways (Camrail), 977 km in 2011, link Douala with Nkongsamba and Ngaoundéré, with branches from M'Banga to Kumba and Makak to M'Balmayo. In 2011 railways carried 1.5 m. passengers and 1.6 m. tonnes of freight.

Religion

In 2010 there were an estimated 7.6 m. Roman Catholics, 6.2 m. Protestants, 3.6 m. Muslims and 0.7 m. folk religionists according to the Pew Research Center's Forum on Religion & Public Life. A further 1.1 m. people had no religious affiliation. In Feb. 2016 there was one cardinal.

Roads

There were about 51,300 km of roads in 2004, of which 8.4% were paved. In 2005 there were 174,900 passenger cars, 56,200 lorries and vans, 15,600 buses and coaches, and 65,600 motorcycles and mopeds. In 2007 there were 990 deaths in road accidents.

Shipping

In Jan. 2009 there were four vessels of 300 GT or over registered, totalling 2,000 GT. The main port is Douala; other ports are Bota, Campo, Garoua (only navigable in the rainy season), Kribi and Limbo-Tiko.

Social Statistics

2008 estimates: births, 704,000; deaths, 271,000. Rates, 2008 estimates (per 1,000 population): birth, 36.9; death, 14.2. Annual population growth rate, 2000–08, 2.3%. Infant mortality, 2010, 84 per 1,000 live births. Life expectancy in 2013: males, 53.9 years; females, 56.2. Fertility rate, 2008, 4.6 children per woman.

Telecommunications

There were 496,500 fixed telephone lines in 2010 (25.3 per 1,000 inhabitants) and mobile phone subscribers numbered 8.16 m. In 2010 there were 40.0 internet users per 1,000 inhabitants. In the same year 1.9% of households had internet access at home. In June 2012 there were 494,000 Facebook users.

Territory and Population

Cameroon is bounded in the west by the Gulf of Guinea, northwest by Nigeria, east by Chad and the Central African Republic, and south by the Republic of the Congo, Gabon and Equatorial Guinea. The total area is

475,650 km^2 (land area, 466,050 km^2). At the 2005 census the population was 17,463,836 (50.6% female); Jan. 2010 estimate, 19,406,100, giving a density of 41.6 per km^2. The population is composed of Sudanic-speaking people in the north (Fulani, Sao and others) and Bantu-speaking groups, mainly Bamileke, Beti, Bulu, Tikar, Bassa and Duala, in the rest of the country. The official languages are French and English.

Tourism

In 2010 there were 573,000 non-resident visitors (498,000 in 2009). Receipts from tourism totalled US$171 m. in 2010.

Canada

Factsheet

Capital: Ottawa
Population estimate, 2015: 35.94 m.
GNI per capita, 2014: (PPP$) 42,155
HDI/world rank, 2014: 0.913/9=
Internet domain extension: .ca

Civil Aviation

Civil aviation is under the jurisdiction of the federal government. The technical and administrative aspects are supervised by Transport Canada, while the economic functions are assigned to the Canadian Transportation Agency. The busiest Canadian airport is Toronto Pearson International, which in 2012 handled 34,912,029 passengers (21,265,866 on international flights), ahead of Vancouver International, with 17,742,065 passengers (9,170,801 on domestic flights) and Montreal (Pierre Elliot Trudeau International), with 13,798,672 passengers (8,466,108 on international flights). Toronto is also the busiest airport for freight, handling 417,022 tonnes in 2012. Air Canada (privatized in 1989) is the largest full-service airline and largest provider of scheduled passenger services in the Canadian market, carrying 34.9 m. revenue passengers in 2012; it took over its main competitor, Canadian Airlines, in 2000. Other major Canadian airlines are Air Transat and WestJet.

Climate

The climate ranges from polar conditions in the north to cool temperate in the south, but with considerable differences between east coast, west coast and the interior, affecting temperatures, rainfall amounts and seasonal distribution. Winters are very severe over much of the country, but summers can be very hot inland.

Constitution and Government

In Nov. 1981 the Canadian government agreed on the provisions of an amended constitution, to the end that it should replace the British North America Act and that its future amendment should be the prerogative of Canada. These proposals were adopted by the Parliament of Canada and were enacted by the UK Parliament as the Canada Act of 1982. This was the final act of the UK Parliament in Canadian constitutional development. The Act gave to Canada the power to amend the Constitution according to procedures determined by the Constitutional Act 1982. The latter added to the Canadian Constitution a charter of Rights and Freedoms, and provisions which recognize the nation's multi-cultural heritage, affirm the existing rights of native peoples, confirm the principle of equalization of benefits among the provinces, and strengthen provincial ownership of natural resources. Under the Constitution legislative power is vested in Parliament, consisting of the Queen, represented by a Governor-General, a Senate and a House of Commons. The members of the *Senate* are appointed until age 75 by summons of the Governor-General under the Great Seal of Canada. Members appointed before 2 June 1965 may remain in office for life. The Senate consists of 105 senators. The *House of Commons*, currently of 338 members, is elected by a first-past-the-post system. In 1977 the Queen approved the transfer to the Governor-General of functions discharged by the Sovereign. The Governor-General is assisted by a *Privy Council* composed of Cabinet Ministers.

Currency

The unit of currency is the *Canadian dollar* (CAD) of 100 *cents*.

Defence

The armed forces have been unified since 1968 as the Canadian Armed Forces (usually referred to as the Canadian Forces). The three commands are the Canadian Army (known until Aug. 2011 as Land Force Command), the Royal Canadian Navy (Maritime Command until Aug. 2011) and the Royal Canadian Air Force (Air Command until Aug. 2011). In 2011 the active armed forces numbered 65,700; reserves, 33,950. In 2010 defence expenditure totalled US$20,240 m. (US$600 per capita), representing 1.3% of GDP.

Economy

Services accounted for 70.8% of GDP in 2010, industry 27.7% and agriculture 1.5%.

Labour

In 2015 the labour force was 19,278,000 (10,182,400 males; 9,095,600 females), of whom 17,946,600 (9,422,700 males; 8,523,900 females) were employed. The unemployment rate in 2015 was 6.9% (7.5% among men and 6.3% among women).

Press

In 2014 there were 95 daily papers with a total average circulation of 5.31 m.; *The Globe and Mail* had the largest circulation at 358,000 in 2014, followed by *Toronto Star* with 343,000. *Le Journal de Montréal* is the largest francophone daily with an average daily circulation in 2014 of 233,000.

Rail

Canada has two great trans-continental systems: the Canadian National Railway system (CN), a body privatized in 1995 that operates the largest network with 36,565 km of routes in 2009, and the Canadian Pacific Railway (CP), with 21,055 km in 2009. A government-funded organization, VIA Rail, operates passenger services in all regions of Canada; 4.6 m. passengers were carried in 2008. There are several regional railways, operating 10,203 km in 2009. There are metros in Montreal and Toronto, and tram/light rail systems in Calgary, Edmonton, Ottawa, Toronto and Vancouver.

Religion

Membership of main religious denominations according to 2011 National Household Survey data: Roman Catholic Church, 12,728,885; United Church of Canada, 2,007,610; Anglican Church of Canada, 1,631,845; Muslim, 1,053,945; Canadian Baptist Ministries, 635,840; Christian Orthodox, 550,690.

Roads

In 2007 there were 1,409,000 km of public roads, including 17,000 km of motorways, 86,000 km of main roads and 115,000 km of secondary roads. The National Highway System, spanning almost 25,000 km, includes the Trans-Canada Highway and other major east-west and north-south highways. Registered road motor vehicles totalled 21,387,132 in 2009; they comprised 19,876,990 passenger cars and light vehicles, 829,695 trucks and truck tractors (weighing at least 4,500 kg), 85,579 buses and 594,866 motorcycles and mopeds.

Shipping

In Jan. 2009 there were 171 ships of 300 GT or over registered, totalling 1.29 m. GT. Of the 171 vessels registered, 114 were passenger ships, 26 oil tankers, 18 general cargo ships, 9 bulk carriers, 2 chemical tankers and 2 container ships. In 2009 the total tonnage handled by Canadian ports was 409.1 m. tonnes (251.0 m. loaded and 158.1 m. unloaded). Canada's leading port in terms of cargo handled is Vancouver. The major canals are those of the St Lawrence Seaway. In 2010 total traffic on the Montreal-Lake Ontario (MLO) section of the seaway was 26,920,000 tonnes; on the Welland Canal section it was 29,180,000 tonnes. There were 3,925 vessel transits in 2010, generating $60.7 m. CDN in toll revenue.

Social Statistics

Average annual population growth rate, 2000–10, 1.1%. Live births, 2009–10, 383,585; deaths, 244,677. Birth rate, 2009–10 (per 1,000 population), 11.2; death rate, 7.2. Suicides, 2011, 3,728 (10.8 per 100,000 population). Life expectancy at birth, 2013, was 79.3 years for men and 83.6 years for women. Infant mortality, 2010, five per 1,000 live births; fertility rate, 2013, 1.7 children per woman. Canada legalized same-sex marriage in 2005.

Telecommunications

In 2013 there were 28,360,000 mobile phone subscriptions (806.1 per 1,000 persons). In the same year retail access lines numbered 16,921,000. A 2010 survey found that 78% of households had a mobile phone and 13% only had a mobile phone; 17% only had a landline. In 2012, 81.5% of households had internet access. The fixed broadband penetration rate in Dec. 2010 was 30.7 subscribers per 100 inhabitants. In Dec. 2011 there were 17.1 m. Facebook users (49% of the population).

Territory and Population

Canada is bounded in the northwest by the Beaufort Sea, north by the Arctic Ocean, northeast by Baffin Bay, east by the Davis Strait, Labrador Sea and Atlantic Ocean, south by the USA and west by the Pacific Ocean and USA (Alaska). The area is 9,984,670 sq. km, of which 891,163 sq. km are fresh water. 2011 census population, 33,476,688 (51.0% female), giving a density of 3.7 per sq. km. Figures for the 2011 census population according to ethnic origin (leading categories), were: Canadian, 10,563,805; English, 6,509,500; French origins, 5,077,215; Scottish, 4,714,970; Irish, 4,544,870; German, 3,203,330; Italian, 1,488,425; Chinese, 1,487,580; First Nations (North American Indian), 1,369,115; Ukrainian, 1,251,170. Populations of Census Metropolitan Areas (CMA) and Cities (proper), 2011 census: Toronto CMA 5,583,064, city proper 2,615,060; Montreal CMA 3,824,221, city proper 1,649,519; Vancouver CMA 2,313,328, city proper 603,502; Ottawa-Gatineau CMA 1,236,324, Ottawa city proper 883,391; Calgary CMA 1,214,839, city proper 1,096,833.

Tourism

In 2010 foreign visitors made 15,864,000 overnight trips to Canada of which 11,749,000 were made by Americans. The next biggest tourist markets are the UK, France, Germany, Japan and Australia. Tourism expenditure by staying visitors amounted to $11,902 m. CDN in 2010. In 2010, 617,300 were employed in tourism.

Central African Republic

République Centrafricaine

Factsheet
Capital: Bangui
Population estimate, 2015: 4.90 m.
GNI per capita, 2014: (PPP$) 581
HDI/world rank, 2014: 0.350/187
Internet domain extension: .cf

Civil Aviation

There is an international airport at M'Poko, near Bangui, which handled 124,940 passengers (91,854 on international flights) in 2012.

Climate

A tropical climate with little variation in temperature. The wet months are May, June, Oct. and Nov. Bangui, Jan. 31.9 °C, July 20.7 °C. Annual rainfall 1,289.3 mm. Ndele, Jan. 36.3 °C, July 30.5 °C. Annual rainfall 203.6 mm.

Constitution and Government

Under the Constitution adopted by a referendum on 21 Nov. 1986, the sole legal political party was the *Rassemblement Démocratique Centrafricain*. In Aug. 1992 the Constitution was revised to permit multi-party democracy. Further constitutional reforms followed a referendum in Dec. 1994, including the establishment of a *Constitutional Court*. Following the coup of March 2003 Gen. François Bozizé suspended the constitution and dissolved parliament. However, at a referendum on 5 Dec. 2004, 90.4% of voters approved the adoption of a new constitution; voter participation was 77.4%. The new constitution resembles the previous one but permits the *President* to serve not more than two terms of 5 years. The President appoints the *Prime Minister* and leads the *Council of Ministers*. There is a 105-member *National Assembly*, with members elected in single-member constituencies for a 5-year term. However, the constitution was suspended by Michel Djotodia after he seized power in March 2013.

Currency

The unit of currency is the *franc CFA* (XAF) with a parity of 655.957 francs CFA to one euro.

Defence

Defence expenditure totalled an estimated US$54 m. in 2011 (approximately US$11 per capita), representing around 2.5% of GDP.

Economy

Agriculture, fishing and forestry contributed 50.2% to GDP in 2011; followed by trade, hotels and restaurants, 12.4%; finance and real estate, 6.4%; manufacturing, 6.2%; transport and communications, 5.4%.

Labour

The labour force in 2013 was 2,236,000 (1,777,000 in 2003). 79.2% of the population aged 15–64 was economically active in 2013.

Press

In 2008 there were 30 newspapers, of which six were dailies with a circulation of 5,000.

Religion

In 2010 there were an estimated 2.67 m. Protestants, 1.26 m. Roman Catholics and 0.37 m. Muslims according to the Pew Research Center's Forum on Religion & Public Life.

Roads

There were 20,278 km of roads in 2010, including 5,044 km of highways or main roads. In 2007 there were 1,200 passenger cars, 58 lorries and vans, and 4,500 motorcycles and mopeds. There were 583 road accident deaths in 2007.

Shipping

Timber and barges are taken to Brazzaville (Republic of the Congo).

Social Statistics

2008 births (estimates), 154,000; deaths, 74,000. Estimated birth rate in 2008 was 35.4 per 1,000 population; estimated death rate, 17.0. Infant mortality, 2010 (per 1,000 live births), 106. Expectation of life in 2013 was 48.3 years for males and 52.1 for females. Annual population growth rate, 2000–08, 1.8%. Fertility rate, 2008, 4.8 children per woman.

Telecommunications

There were 12,000 fixed telephone lines in 2010 (2.7 per 1,000 inhabitants). Mobile phone subscribers numbered 1.02 m. in 2010. In 2008, 1.0% of the population were internet users. In June 2012 there were 144,000 Facebook users.

Territory and Population

The republic is bounded in the north by Chad, northeast by Sudan, east by South Sudan, south by the Democratic Republic of the Congo and the Republic of the Congo, and west by Cameroon. Area, 622,984 km^2

(240,534 sq. miles). The population at the 2003 census was 3,895,139, giving a density of 6 per km². The capital, Bangui, had a census population in 2003 of 622,771. Other main towns, with 2003 census populations, are Bimbo (124,176), Bebérati (76,918), Carnot (45,421), Bambari (41,356) and Bouar (40,353). There are a number of ethnic groups, the largest being Gbaya (34%), Banda (27%) and Mandja (21%). Sango and French are the official languages.

Tourism

In 2009, 52,000 non-resident tourists-excluding same-day visitors-arrived by air (up from 31,000 in 2008).

Chad

République du Tchad (Republic of Chad)

Factsheet

Capital: N'Djaména
Population estimate, 2015: 14.04 m.
GNI per capita, 2014: (PPP$) 2,085
HDI/world rank, 2014: 0.392/185
Internet domain extension: .td

Civil Aviation

There is an international airport at N'Djaména, from which there were direct flights in 2010 to Abidjan, Addis Ababa, Cotonou, Douala, Johannesburg, Ouagadougou, Paris and Tripoli. There were 5,286 aircraft movements in 2011.

Climate

A tropical climate, with adequate rainfall in the south, though Nov. to April are virtually rainless months. Further north, desert conditions prevail. N'Djaména, Jan. 75 °F (23.9 °C), July 82 °F (27.8 °C). Annual rainfall 30″ (744 mm).

Constitution and Government

After overthrowing the regime of Hissène Habré, Idriss Déby proclaimed himself *President* and was sworn in on 4 March 1991. At a referendum on 31 March 1996 a new constitution was approved by 63.5% of votes cast. It defines Chad as a unitary state. The head of state is the *President*, elected by universal suffrage. On 26 May 2004 the *National Assembly* passed an amendment scrapping the two-term limit on the presidency, replacing it with an age limit of 70. The amendment was approved by referendum in June 2005. The National Assembly has 188 members, elected for a 4-year term.

Currency

The unit of currency is the *franc CFA* (XAF) with a parity of 655.957 francs CFA to one euro.

Defence

There are seven military regions. Total armed forces personnel numbered 25,350 in 2011, including republican guards. Defence expenditure totalled an estimated US$202 m. in 2012 (approximately US$18 per capita), representing around 2% of GDP.

Economy

In 2011 mining contributed 29.7% to GDP; followed by trade and hotels, 17.9%; agriculture, 15.8%; finance and real estate, 12.3%; public administration and defence, 8.1%.

Labour

The labour force in 2013 was 4,874,000 (3,415,000 in 2003). 71.9% of the population aged 15–64 was economically active in 2013. In the same year 7.1% of the population was unemployed.

Press

There are no daily newspapers; there were five non-dailies in 2008, including the government-owned *Info-Tchad*. Combined circulation was 4,000.

Religion

The northern and central parts of the country are predominantly Muslim. There were an estimated 6.21 m. Muslims (both Sunnis and Shias) and 4.56 m. Christians (more Catholics than Protestants) in 2010 according to the Pew Research Center's Forum on Religion & Public Life. Most of the remainder of the population is religiously unaffiliated, with some followers of folk religions.

Roads

In 2006 there were around 40,000 km of roads. 18,900 passenger cars were in use in 2006, plus 3,300 buses and coaches, 35,400 lorries and vans, and 63,000 motorcycles and mopeds. In 2007 there were 840 deaths in road accidents.

Social Statistics

2008 estimates: births, 499,000; deaths, 182,000. Rates, 2008 estimates (per 1,000 population): births, 45.7; deaths, 16.7. Chad has one of the youngest populations of any country, with 73% of the population under the age of 30% and 45% under 15. Annual rate of growth, 2000–08, 3.3%. Expectation of life in 2013 was 50.3 years among males and 52.1 among females. Infant mortality, 2010 (per 1,000 live births), 99. Fertility rate, 2008, 6.2 children per woman.

Telecommunications

There were 51,200 fixed telephone lines in 2010 (4.6 per 1,000 inhabitants). Mobile phone subscribers numbered 2.61 m. in 2010. There were 17.0 internet users per 1,000 inhabitants in 2010. Fixed internet subscriptions totalled 4,600 in 2009 (0.4 per 1,000 inhabitants).

Territory and Population

Chad is bounded in the west by Cameroon, Nigeria and Niger, north by Libya, east by Sudan and south by the Central African Republic. Area, 1,284,000 km². The population at the 2009 census was 11,039,873. About half the population lives in the southernmost 20% of the country's territory. Whereas in the south of the country most people are settled, in the north, east and centre people are generally nomadic or semi-nomadic. The capital is N'Djaména with 951,458 inhabitants (2009 census), other large towns being (2009 census figures) Moundou (137,251), Abéché (97,963) and Sarh (97,224). Following administrative reforms of 2002 and 2008, Chad's 14 prefectures were divided into 22 regions, including the City of N'Djaména (which is a commune governed by a special statute). The official languages are French and Arabic, but more than 100 different languages and dialects are spoken.

Tourism

In 2009, 31,000 non-resident tourists (including 16,000 from Europe) stayed in hotels or similar accommodation.

Chile

República de Chile (Republic of Chile)

Factsheet

Capitals: Santiago (Administrative), Valparaíso (Legislative)
Population estimate, 2015: 17.95 m.

GNI per capita, 2014: (PPP$) 21,290
HDI/world rank, 2014: 0.832/42
Internet domain extension: .cl

Civil Aviation

There are international airports at Antofagasta, Arica, Easter Island (Isla de Pascua), Iquique, Puerto Montt, Punta Arenas and Santiago (Comodoro Arturo Merino Benítez). In 2012 Santiago handled 14,168,282 passengers (6,753,584 on international flights). The largest airline is LATAM, created in June 2012 when the Chilean carrier LAN Airlines (formerly LAN-Chile) merged with TAM, Brazil's largest airline.

Climate

With its enormous range of latitude and the influence of the Andean Cordillera, the climate of Chile is very complex, ranging from extreme aridity in the north, through a Mediterranean climate in Central Chile, where winters are wet and summers dry, to a cool temperate zone in the south, with rain at all seasons. In the extreme south, conditions are very wet and stormy. Santiago, Jan. 67 °F (19.5 °C), July 46 °F (8 °C). Annual rainfall 15″ (375 mm). Antofagasta, Jan. 69 °F (20.6 °C), July 57 °F (14 °C). Annual rainfall 0.5″ (12.7 mm). Valparaíso, Jan. 64 °F (17.8 °C), July 53 °F (11.7 °C). Annual rainfall 20″ (505 mm).

Constitution and Government

A new constitution was approved by 67.5% of the voters on 11 Sept. 1980 and came into force on 11 March 1981. The *President* is directly elected for a non-renewable 4-year term. Parliament consists of a 120-member *Chamber of Deputies* and a *Senate* of 38 members. In March 2006 the Senate became fully elected, by abolishing non-elected senators and eliminating life seats for former presidents. Senators are elected for an 8-year term. Santiago is the administrative capital of Chile, but since 11 March 1990 Valparaíso has been the legislative capital.

Currency

The unit of currency is the *Chilean peso* (CLP) of 100 *centavos*.

Defence

Conscription is compulsory when there are not enough voluntary recruits. Military service lasts for a maximum of 12 months in the Army and 22 months in the Air Force and the Navy. In 2013 defence expenditure totalled US$4,594 m. (US$267 per capita), representing 1.6% of GDP. In 1985 defence spending had accounted for 10% of GDP.

Economy

Agriculture accounted for 3.2% of GDP in 2010, industry 42.9% and services 53.9%.

Labour

The labour force in 2013 was 8,603,000 (6,372,000 in 2003). 67.4% of the population aged 15–64 was economically active in 2013. In Nov. 2015, 6.2% of the active population was unemployed (compared to 6.4% in 2014 as a whole).

Press

In 2012 there were 65 daily newspapers (60 paid-for and five free) and 42 non-dailies (39 paid-for and three free). The dailies had a combined average daily circulation of 689,000 in 2012.

Rail

The total length of railway lines was (2014) 5,529 km, about a fifth of which was electrified, of broad- and metre-gauge. The state railway (EFE) transported 11.3 m. passengers in 2005. Freight operations are in the hands of the semi-private companies Ferronor, Pacifico and the Antofagasta (Chili) and Bolivia Railway (973 km, metre-gauge) which links the port of Antofagasta with Bolivia and Argentina. Passenger-km travelled in 2008 came to 759 m. and freight tonne-km in 2006 to 3,660 m. There are metro systems in Santiago (46.2 km) and Valparaíso (42.5 km).

Religion

In 2010 there were an estimated 12.29 m. Roman Catholics, 2.66 m. Protestants and 0.35 m. other Christians according to the Pew Research Center's Forum on Religion & Public Life. A further 1.47 m. people had no religious affiliation and there were 0.26 m. folk religionists. The Roman Catholic Church has five ecclesiastical provinces, each headed by an archbishop. In Feb. 2016 there were three cardinals.

Roads

In 2004 there were 80,505 km of roads, but only 20.8% were hard-surfaced. There were 2,414 km of motorways and 16,785 km of main roads. In 2007 there were 1,701,036 passenger cars, 849,282 trucks and vans, 170,217 buses and coaches and 63,257 motorcycles and mopeds. In 2006 there were 2,280 road accident fatalities.

Shipping

In Jan. 2009 there were 89 ships of 300 GT or over registered, totalling 632,000 GT. The leading ports are Antofagasta, Arica, Iquique, Puerto Ventanas, San Antonio, Talcahuano/San Vicente and Valparaíso.

Social Statistics

2007 births, 240,569; deaths, 93,000; marriages, 57,792. Rates, 2007 (per 1,000 population): birth, 14.6; death, 5.6; marriage, 3.5. Divorce was only made legal in 2004; abortion remains illegal. Annual population growth rate, 2008–10, 0.9%. Infant mortality, 2010 (per 1,000 live births), 8. In 2009 the most popular age range for marrying was 25–29 for both males and females. Expectation of life at birth (2013): males, 77.1 years; females, 82.7 years. Chile has the highest life expectancy in South America. Fertility rate, 2008, 1.9 children per woman.

Telecommunications

In 2012 there were 3,281,000 main (fixed) telephone lines. In the same year mobile phone subscriptions numbered 23,941,000. There were an estimated 413.0 internet users per 1,000 inhabitants in 2009. In June 2012 there were 9.4 m. Facebook users.

Territory and Population

Chile is bounded in the north by Peru, east by Bolivia and Argentina, and south and west by the Pacific Ocean. The area is 756,096 km² (291,928 sq. miles) excluding the claimed Antarctic territory. Many islands to the west and south belong to Chile: the Islas Juan Fernández (147 km² with a population of 792 in 2012) lie about 600 km west of Valparaíso, and the volcanic Isla de Pascua (Easter Island or Rapa Nui, 164 km² with a population of 5,761 in 2012), lies about 3,000 km west-northwest of Valparaíso. Population estimate, July 2012: 17,444,799, of which 8,809,706 females and 8,635,093 males (density of 23.1 per km²). 89.2% of the population lived in urban areas in 2011.

Tourism

There were 3,069,792 non-resident overnight tourists in 2011 (2,766,007 in 2010). Tourist receipts were US$2,751 m. in 2011.

China

Zhonghua Renmin Gonghe Guo (People's Republic of China)

Factsheet

Capital: Beijing (Peking)
Population estimate, 2015: 1,376.05 m.
GNI per capita, 2014: (PPP$) 12,547
HDI/world rank, 2014: 0.727/90=
Internet domain extension: .cn

Civil Aviation

There are major international airports at Beijing (Capital), Guangzhou (Baiyun), Hong Kong (Chek Lap Kok) and Shanghai (Hongqiao and Pudong). In 2012 there were 180 civil airports for regular flights. The national and major airlines are state-owned. The leading Chinese airlines operating scheduled services in 2013 were China Southern Airlines (91.8 m. passengers), China Eastern Airlines (79.1 m.) and Air China (77.7 m.). Other Chinese airlines include Hainan Airlines, Shandong Airlines, Shanghai Airlines, Shenzhen Airlines, Sichuan Airlines and Xiamen Airlines. In 2013 the busiest airport was Beijing (Capital International), with 83.7 m. passengers.

Climate

Most of China has a temperate climate but, with such a large country, extending far inland and embracing a wide range of latitude as well as containing large areas at high altitude, many parts experience extremes of climate, especially in winter. Most rain falls during the summer, from May to Sept., though amounts decrease inland. Monthly average temperature and annual rainfall (2012) for Beijing (Peking): Jan. 25.5 °F (−3.6 °C), July 81.3 °F (27.4 °C); annual rainfall 28.9″ (733 mm).

Constitution and Government

On 21 Sept. 1949 the *Chinese People's Political Consultative Conference* met in Beijing, convened by the Chinese Communist Party. The Conference adopted a 'Common Programme' of 60 articles and the 'Organic Law of the Central People's Government' (31 articles). Both became the basis of the Constitution adopted on 20 Sept. 1954 by the 1st National People's Congress, the supreme legislative body. The Consultative Conference continued to exist after 1954 as an advisory body. The unicameral *National People's Congress* is the highest organ of state power. Usually meeting for one session a year, it can amend the constitution and nominally elects and has power to remove from office the highest officers of state. There are a maximum of 3,000 members of the Congress (and currently 2,949), who are elected to serve 5-year terms by municipal, regional and provincial people's congresses. The Congress elects a *Standing Committee* (which supervises the *State Council*) and the *President* (currently Xi Jinping; b. 1953) and *Vice-President* for a 5-year term. When not in session, Congress business is carried on by the Standing Committee. The State Council is the supreme executive organ and comprises the Prime Minister, Deputy Prime Ministers and State Councillors. The *Central Military Commission* is the highest state military organ.

Currency

The currency is called Renminbi (i.e. People's Currency). The unit of currency is the *yuan* (CNY) which is divided into ten *jiao*, the *jiao* being divided into ten *fen*.

Defence

The Chinese president is chairman of the State and Party's Military Commissions. China is divided into seven military regions. The military commander also commands the air, naval and civilian militia forces assigned to each region. China's armed forces, totalling nearly 3.0 m. in 2013 including the paramilitary People's Armed Police, are the largest of any country. Conscription is compulsory, but for organizational reasons, is selective: only some 10% of potential recruits are called up. Service is for 2 years. A military academy to train senior officers in modern warfare was established in 1985. Defence expenditure in 2013 was US$112,173 m. (equivalent to US$83 per capita). China's military spending during the 2000s more than trebled. The nuclear arsenal consisted of approximately 260 operational warheads in Jan. 2015 according to the Stockholm International Peace Research Institute.

Economy

In 2012 agriculture accounted for 10.1% of GDP, industry 45.3% and services 44.6%.

Labour

The employed population at the 1990 census was 647.2 m. (291.1 m. female). By 2012 it had risen to 767.0 m. (2.8 m. more than in 2011), of whom 396.0 m. worked in rural areas (9.0 m. fewer than in 2011) and 371.0 m. in urban areas (11.9 m. more than in 2011). In Dec. 2010 China's registered urban jobless was 4.1%, with 9.08 m. registered unemployed in the country's cities.

Press

China has two news agencies: Xinhua (New China) News Agency (the nation's official agency) and China News Service. In 2012 there were 1,918 newspapers and 9,867 magazines; 48,230 m. copies of newspapers and 3,350 m. copies of magazines were published. In 1980 there were fewer than 200 newspapers. The Communist Party newspaper is *Renmin Ribao* (People's Daily), which had a daily circulation of 2.9 m. in 2008. The most widely read newspaper is *Cankao Xiaoxi*, with a daily circulation of 3.1 m. in 2008. China has the second highest circulation of daily newspapers after India, with an estimated average daily total of 137.8 m. in 2014. As of Sept. 2014 it was also home to the world's two most visited online news sites: Xinhua News Agency (90.2 m. unique desktop users per month) and People's Daily Online (89.1 m.). In the 2013 *World Press Freedom Index* compiled by Reporters Without Borders, China ranked 173rd out of 179 countries.

Rail

In 2013 there were 103,000 km of railway. The high-speed network, at 11,028 km in Dec. 2013, is the longest in the world. The high-speed line linking Beijing and Guangzhou, which opened in Dec. 2012, is the longest in the world at 2,293 km. The railways carried 1.53 bn. passengers in 2009 and 3.22 bn. tonnes of freight. China's railways are the busiest in the world, carrying 24% of global rail traffic. There are metro systems in Beijing, Chengdu, Dalian, Guangzhou, Haerbin (where the first line opened in Sept. 2013), Hangzhou (where the first line opened in Nov. 2012), Kunming (where the first line opened in June 2012), Nanjing, Shanghai, Shenyang, Shenzhen, Suzhou (where the first line opened in April 2012), Tianjin, Wuhan and Xian.

Religion

The government accords legality to five religions only: Buddhism, Islam, Protestantism, Roman Catholicism and Taoism. A new quasi-religious movement, Falun Gong, was founded in 1992, but has since been banned by the authorities. The movement has claimed some 100 m. adherents, although the Chinese government has disputed this. According to estimates (by the state-approved Xinhua news agency, the Chinese Academy of Social Sciences and the State Administration for Religious Affairs) there were 100 m. Buddhists, 23 m. Christians and more than 21 m. Muslims in the country in 2009. Other official figures indicate that there are 5.3 m. Catholics, although unofficial estimates are much higher.

Roads

The total road length in 2012 was 4,237,500 km, including 96,200 km of expressways (of which there had not been any as recently as the mid-1980s); 31,885 m. tonnes of freight and 35,570 m. persons were transported by road that year. The number of civilian motor vehicles was 109.30 m. in 2012, including 89.43 m. passenger vehicles and 18.95 m. trucks (more than double the number in 2008, when there were 51.00 m. civilian vehicles overall including 38.39 m. passenger vehicles and 11.26 m. trucks). China is the world's fastest-growing car market. There were 204,196 traffic accidents in 2012, with 59,997 fatalities.

Shipping

In Jan. 2009 there were 2,495 ships of 300 GT or over registered, totalling 25.36 m. GT. Of the 2,495 vessels registered, 1,022 were general cargo ships, 482 bulk carriers, 476 oil tankers, 178 passenger ships, 174 container ships, 83 liquid gas tankers and 80 chemical tankers. Mainland China's busiest port in 2012 was Ningbo-Zhoushan (handling 744.0 m. tonnes of cargo), followed by Shanghai (637.4 m. tonnes), Tianjin (477.0 tonnes), Guangzhou (Canton) (435.2 m. tonnes) and Qingdao (406.9 m. tonnes). Shanghai became the world's busiest container port in 2010 and handled 32.5 m. TEUs (20-foot equivalent units) in 2012. Inland waterways totalled 125,000 km in 2012; 4,587.0 m. tonnes of freight and 257.5 m. passengers were carried.

Social Statistics

Births, 2012, 16,350,000; deaths, 9,660,000. 2012 birth rate (per 1,000 population), 12.1; death rate, 7.2. In 2005 the birth rate rose for the first time since 1987. There were 13,235,900 marriages and 3,103,800 divorces in

2012. Life expectancy at birth, 2010, was 72.4 years for men and 77.4 years for women. Infant mortality, 2010, 16 per 1,000 live births. Fertility rate, 2013, 1.7 births per woman (compared to over 6 in the mid-1960s). Annual population growth rate, 2000–10, 0.6%. According to the World Bank, the number of people living in poverty (less than US$1.25 a day) at purchasing power parity declined from 835 m. in 1981 to 156 m. in 2010.

Telecommunications

In 2013 mobile phone subscriptions numbered 1,229,113,000 (887.1 per 1,000 persons), making China the biggest market for mobile phones in the world. In 2013 there were 226,985,000 main (fixed) telephone lines, down from a peak of 367,786,000 in 2006. In 2012 an estimated 42.3% of the population were internet users. In March 2012 there were only 447,000 Facebook users in mainland China (less than 0.1% of the population).

Territory and Population

China is bounded in the north by Russia and Mongolia; east by North Korea, the Yellow Sea and the East China Sea, with Hong Kong and Macao as enclaves on the southeast coast; south by Vietnam, Laos, Myanmar, India, Bhutan and Nepal; west by India, Pakistan, Afghanistan, Tajikistan, Kyrgyzstan and Kazakhstan. The total area (including Taiwan, Hong Kong and Macao) is estimated at 9,572,900 sq. km (3,696,100 sq. miles). China's sixth national census was held on 1 Nov. 2010. The total population of the 31 provinces, autonomous regions and municipalities and of servicemen on the mainland was 1,339,724,852 (652,872,280 females, representing 48.73%); density, 140 per sq. km. China's population in 2010 represented 19% of the world's total population. Population of largest cities in 2010: Shanghai, 20.22 m.; Beijing (Peking), 16.45 m.; Shenzhen, 10.36 m.; Guangzhou (Canton), 9.70 m.; Tianjin, 9.29 m. A number of widely divergent varieties of Chinese are spoken. The official 'Modern Standard Chinese' is based on the dialect of North China. Mandarin in one form or another is spoken by 885 m. people in China, or around 70% of the population of mainland China. The Wu language and its dialects has some 77 m. native speakers and Cantonese 66 m. China has 56 ethnic groups. According to the 2010 census 1,225,932,641 people (91.51%) were of Han nationality and 113,792,211 (8.49%) were from national minorities.

Tourism

In 2012 tourist numbers totalled 57.7 m. The World Tourism Organization predicts that China will overtake France as the world's most visited destination by 2020. It was the third most visited destination in 2012 after France and the USA. Income from tourists in 2012 was US$50.0 bn., ranking it fourth behind the USA, Spain and France. Expenditure by Chinese travellers outside of mainland China for 2013 was US$128.6 bn., the most of any country. In 2011 both German and US travellers abroad had spent more than those from China.

Colombia

República de Colombia (Republic of Colombia)

Factsheet

Capital: Bogotá
Population estimate, 2015: 48.23 m.
GNI per capita, 2014: (PPP$) 12,040
HDI/world rank, 2014: 0.720/97=
Internet domain extension: .co

Civil Aviation

The main international airports at Barranquilla, Bogotá (Eldorado), Cali, Cartagena and Medellín. The main Colombian airline is Avianca. In 2005 scheduled traffic of Colombian-based carriers flew 132.5 m. km and carried 9,933,100 passengers. The busiest airport is Bogotá, which in 2014 handled 27,430,266 passengers (19,075,679 on domestic flights) and 636,657 tonnes of freight.

Climate

The climate includes equatorial and tropical conditions, according to situation and altitude. In tropical areas, the wettest months are March to May and Oct. to Nov. Bogotá, Jan. 58 °F (14.4 °C), July 57 °F (13.9 °C). Annual rainfall 42″ (1,052 mm). Barranquilla, Jan. 80 °F (26.7 °C), July 82 °F (27.8 °C). Annual rainfall 32″ (799 mm). Cali, Jan. 75 °F (23.9 °C), July 75 °F (23.9 °C). Annual rainfall 37″ (915 mm). Medellín, Jan. 71 °F (21.7 °C), July 72 °F (22.2 °C). Annual rainfall 64″ (1,606 mm).

Constitution and Government

Simultaneously with the presidential elections of May 1990, a referendum was held in which 7 m. votes were cast for the establishment of a special assembly to draft a new constitution. The Assembly produced a new constitution which came into force on 5 July 1991. The *President* is elected by direct vote. In Oct. 2005 the constitution was amended to allow a president to be re-elected for a second term. A vice-presidency was instituted in July 1991. The legislative power rests with a *Congress* of two houses, the *Senate*, of 102 members (including two elected from a special list set aside for American Indian communities), and the *House of Representatives*, of 166 members, both elected for 4 years by proportional representation.

Currency

The unit of currency is the *Colombian peso* (COP) of 100 *centavos.*

Defence

There is selective conscription for 12–24 months. In 2013 defence expenditure totalled US$7,016 m. (US$153 per capita), representing 1.8% of GDP.

Economy

In 2010 agriculture accounted for 7.1% of GDP, industry 36.3% and services 56.6%.

Labour

The economically active workforce in 2014 was 23.65 m., of which 21.50 m. were employed. The main areas of activity in 2014 were: commerce, restaurants and hotels (employing 5.86 m. persons); community, social and personal services (4.28 m.); and agriculture, hunting, forestry and fishing (3.50 m.). The unemployment rate was 9.1% in 2014 (9.6% in 2013).

Press

There were 57 daily newspapers in 2014 (53 paid-for and four free); daily circulation totalled 1.53 m. in 2009.

Rail

The National Railways (2,532 km of route, 914 mm gauge) went into liquidation in 1990. There are currently two concessions operating—Ferrocarril del Oeste and Red Férrea del Atlántico. Ferrocarril del Oeste carried 360,000 tonnes of freight in 2007 and Red Férrea del Atlántico 22 m. tonnes in 2006. Passenger services are very limited. Total length in 2007 was 1,663 km. A metro system operates in Medellín.

Religion

The main religion is Roman Catholicism (an estimated 38.1 m. adherents in 2010 according to the Pew Research Center's Forum on Religion & Public Life), with the Archbishop of Bogotá as Primate of Colombia. The Roman Catholic Church has 13 ecclesiastical provinces, subdivided into 13 archdioceses and 52 dioceses. In Feb. 2016 there were four cardinals. The Pew Research Center estimated that there were also 4.64 m. Protestants in 2010 and 3.05 m. people who were religiously unaffiliated.

Roads

Total length of roads was 164,278 km in 2006 (including 14,143 km of main roads). In 2005 there were 2,686,000 vehicles in use, including 1,607,000 passenger cars. There were 5,486 road accident fatalities in 2006.

Shipping

In Jan. 2009 there were 31 ships of 300 GT or over registered, totalling 46,000 GT. The chief port is Cartagena, which handled 25.6 m. tonnes of foreign cargo in 2008. The Magdalena River is subject to drought, and navigation is always impeded during the dry season, but it is an important artery of passenger and goods traffic. The river is navigable for 1,400 km; steamers ascend to La Dorada, 953 km from Barranquilla.

Social Statistics

2008 estimates: births, 918,000; deaths, 248,000. Rates, 2008 estimates (per 1,000 population): births, 20.4; deaths, 5.5. Annual population growth rate, 2000–08, 1.5%. Life expectancy at birth, 2013, was 70.4 years for men and 77.7 years for women. Infant mortality, 2010, 17 per 1,000 live births; fertility rate, 2008, 2.4 children per woman. Abortion is illegal.

Telecommunications

In 2012 there were 6,291,000 main (fixed) telephone lines. In the same year mobile phone subscriptions numbered 49,066,000 (1,028.5 per 1,000 persons). There were 3,313,000 fixed internet subscriptions in 2011 and 3,093,000 wireless broadband subscriptions. In June 2012 there were 16.8 m. Facebook users.

Territory and Population

Colombia is bounded in the north by the Caribbean Sea, northwest by Panama, west by the Pacific Ocean, southwest by Ecuador and Peru, northeast by Venezuela and southeast by Brazil. The estimated area is 1,141,748 km^2 (440,829 sq. miles). Population census (2005), 42,888,592; density, 37.6 per km^2. In 2011, 75.4% lived in urban areas. Population of Bogotá, the capital (census 2005): 6,824,510. The official language is Spanish.

Tourism

In 2009 there were 1,354,000 non-resident visitors (including 1,064,000 from elsewhere in the Americas and 258,000 from Europe), bringing revenue of US$2,609 m.

Comoros

Union des Comores (Union of the Comoros)

Factsheet
Capital: Moroni
Population estimate, 2015: 788,000
GNI per capita, 2014: (PPP$) 1,456
HDI/world rank, 2014: 0.503/159
Internet domain extension: .km

Civil Aviation

There is an international airport at Moroni (International Prince Said Ibrahim). In 2009 it handled 149,071 passengers (98,638 international) and 627 tonnes of freight.

Climate

There is a tropical climate, affected by Indian monsoon winds from the north, which gives a wet season from Nov. to April. Moroni, Jan. 81 °F (27.2 °C), July 75 °F (23.9 °C). Annual rainfall, 113" (2,825 mm).

Constitution and Government

At a referendum on 23 Dec. 2001, 77% of voters approved a new constitution that keeps the three islands as one country while granting each one greater autonomy. The *President of the Union* is Head of State. The presidency rotates every 4 years among the three main islands. There used to be a *Federal Assembly* comprised of 42 democratically elected officials and a 15-member *Senate* chosen by an electoral college, but these

were dissolved after the 1999 coup. A new 33-member *Federal Parliament* was established following the elections of April 2004. In 2004 there were 15 deputies selected by the individual islands' parliaments and 18 by universal suffrage but this was changed to nine selected by the individual islands' parliaments and 24 by universal suffrage for the 2009 elections.

Currency

The unit of currency is the *Comorian franc* (KMF) of 100 *centimes*.

Economy

Agriculture accounted for 46.3% of GDP in 2009, industry 12.1% and services 41.6%.

Labour

The estimated economically active population in 2010 was 342,000 (53% males).

Press

There has not been a daily newspaper since *Le Matin des Comores* ceased publication in 2006. *Le Canal*, which is published in Mayotte, is distributed in the Comoros. There were five non-dailies in 2008. *Al-Watwan* is published 4 days a week in French and 1 day a week in Arabic.

Religion

Islam is the official religion: 98% of the population are Muslims; there is a small Christian minority. Following the coup of April 1999 the federal government discouraged the practice of religions other than Islam, with Christians especially facing restrictions on worship.

Roads

In 2005 there were 849 km of roads.

Shipping

In Jan. 2009 there were 184 ships of 300 GT or over registered, totalling 625,000 GT.

Social Statistics

2008 births (estimates), 21,000; deaths, 4,000. Estimated birth rate in 2008 was 32.4 per 1,000 population; estimated death rate, 6.7. Annual population growth rate, 2000–08, 2.2%. Infant mortality, 63 per 1,000 live births (2010). Expectation of life in 2013 was 59.5 years among males and 62.3 among females. Fertility rate, 2008, 4.0 children per woman.

Telecommunications

In 2011 there were 23,600 landline telephone subscriptions (equivalent to 31.3 per 1,000 inhabitants) and 216,400 mobile phone subscriptions (or 287.1 per 1,000 inhabitants). Fixed internet subscriptions totalled 1,600 in 2009 (2.3 per 1,000 inhabitants).

Territory and Population

The Comoros consists of three islands in the Indian Ocean between the African mainland and Madagascar with a total area of 1,862 km^2 (719 sq. miles). The population at the 2003 census was 575,660 (285,590 males), giving a density of 309 per km^2. In 2011, 28.3% of the population were urban. Population of the chief towns (2003 census): Moroni, 40,050; Mutsamudu, 20,828; Fomboni, 12,881; Domoni, 10,073. The indigenous population are a mixture of Malagasy, African, Malay and Arab peoples; the vast majority speak Comorian, an Arabized dialect of Swahili and one of the three official languages, but a small proportion speak one of the other official languages, French and Arabic, or Makua (a Bantu language).

Tourism

In 2010 there were 15,000 international tourists, bringing revenue of US$35 m.

Congo, Democratic Republic of the

République Démocratique du Congo

Factsheet

Capital: Kinshasa
Population estimate, 2015: 77.27 m.
GNI per capita, 2014: (PPP$) 680
HDI/world rank, 2014: 0.433/176
Internet domain extension: .cd

Civil Aviation

There is an international airport at Kinshasa (Ndjili). Other major airports are at Lubumbashi (Luano), Bukavu, Goma and Kisangani. The main carrier is Hewa Bora Airways. In 2009 Kinshasa handled 672,347 passengers (385,923 international) and 67,544 tonnes of freight.

Climate

The climate is varied, the central region having an equatorial climate, with year-long high temperatures and rain at all seasons. Elsewhere, depending on position north or south of the Equator, there are well-marked wet and dry seasons. The mountains of the east and south have a temperate mountain climate, with the highest summits having considerable snowfall. Kinshasa, Jan. 79 °F (26.1 °C), July 73 °F (22.8 °C). Annual rainfall 45″ (1,125 mm). Kananga, Jan. 76 °F (24.4 °C), July 74 °F (23.3 °C). Annual rainfall 62″ (1,584 mm). Kisangani, Jan. 78 °F (25.6 °C), July 75 °F (23.9 °C). Annual rainfall 68″ (1,704 mm). Lubumbashi, Jan. 72 °F (22.2 °C), July 61 °F (16.1 °C). Annual rainfall 50″ (1,237 mm).

Constitution and Government

A new constitution was adopted by the transitional parliament on 16 May 2005. It limits the powers of the president, who may now serve a maximum of two 5-year terms and lowers the minimum age for presidential candidates from 35 to 30. It allows a greater degree of federalism and recognises as citizens all ethnic groups at the time of independence in 1960. It also called for presidential elections by June 2006. In a referendum held on 18–19 Dec. 2005, 83% of voters approved the constitution in the country's first free vote in 40 years. The constitution was promulgated on 18 Feb. 2006.

Currency

The unit of currency is the *Congolese franc* (CDF) which replaced the former *zaïre* in July 1998.

Defence

Following the overthrow of the Mobutu regime in May 1997, the former Zaïrean armed forces were in disarray. In June 2003 command of ground forces and naval forces were handed over to the RCD-Goma and MLC factions respectively as part of the power-sharing transitional government. Supreme command of the armed forces will remain in the hands of the former government faction. A UN mission, MONUSCO, has been in the Democratic Republic of the Congo since 1999 (under the name of MONUC until June 2010). With 19,784 uniformed personnel in June 2015 it is the largest UN peacekeeping force in the world. An additional UN Intervention Brigade numbering approximately 3,000 personnel has been in the eastern part of the country since 2013 to neutralize anti-government rebels. The first UN peacekeeping force to be given an offensive combat mandate, it is composed of troops from Malawi, South Africa and Tanzania. In Dec. 2013 it became the first UN mission to deploy drones (unmanned aerial vehicles) to gather information for military intelligence. Defence expenditure totalled US$416 m. in 2013 (US$6 per capita), representing 2.2% of GDP.

Economy

Agriculture accounted for 45.5% of GDP in 2011 (one of the highest percentages of any country), industry 22.0% and services 32.5%.

Labour

The estimated economically active population in 2010 was 25.77 m. (59% males), up from 21.79 m. in 2005. Agriculture employs around 65% of the total labour force. The Democratic Republic of the Congo had 0.46 m. people living in slavery according to the Walk Free Foundation's 2013 *Global Slavery Index*, the eighth highest total of any country.

Press

In 2008 there were 12 daily newspapers with a combined circulation of 50,000.

Rail

Total route length was 3,641 km on three gauges in 2011, of which 858 km was electrified. In 2008 the Office National des Transports carried 1.2 m. passengers and in 2011 the Société Nationale des Chemins de Fer du Congo (SNCC) carried 46,000 passengers. The SNCC carried 573,000 tonnes of freight in 2011.

Religion

According to estimates by the Pew Research Center's Forum on Religion & Public Life, in 2010 the population was 95.8% Christian with 1.5% Muslim and 1.8% religiously unaffiliated. Around half the Christians are Catholics and half are Protestants. In Feb. 2016 there was one Roman Catholic cardinal.

Roads

In 2005 there were 171,250 km of roads (1.3% paved). In 2007 there were around 312,000 vehicles in use.

Shipping

The River Congo and its tributaries are navigable to 300-tonne vessels for about 14,500 km.

Social Statistics

2008 estimates: births, 2,883,000; deaths, 1,090,000. Rates (2008 estimates, per 1,000 population); birth, 44.9; death, 17.0. Annual population growth rate, 2000–08, 2.9%. Infant mortality in 2010 was 112 per 1,000 live births (the second highest in the world after Sierra Leone). Expectation of life in 2013 was 48.2 years for men and 51.8 for females. Fertility rate, 2008, 6.0 children per woman.

Telecommunications

In 2009 the Democratic Republic of the Congo had just 42,300 main (fixed) telephone lines (0.7 for every 1,000 persons), but there were 9,459,000 mobile phone subscribers (147.3 for every 1,000 persons). The Democratic Republic of the Congo has among the highest ratios of mobile phone subscriptions to fixed telephone lines. In 2010, 0.7% of the population were internet users. In June 2012 there were 808,000 Facebook users.

Territory and Population

The Democratic Republic of the Congo, sometimes referred to as Congo (Kinshasa), is bounded in the north by the Central African Republic, northeast by South Sudan, east by Uganda, Rwanda, Burundi and Lake Tanganyika, south by Zambia, southwest by Angola and northwest by the Republic of the Congo. There is a 37-km stretch of coastline that gives access to the Atlantic Ocean, with the Angolan exclave of Cabinda to the immediate north, and Angola itself to the south. The area is 2,344,860 km² (905,360 sq. miles), including 77,810 km² (30,040 sq. miles) of inland waters. A census has not been held since 1984, when the population was 29,916,800. The United Nations gave an estimated population for 2012 of 70.29 m.; density, 31 per km². 35.9% of the population was urban in 2011. The country is administratively divided into ten provinces plus Kinshasa city. The capital is Kinshasa (2010 population estimate, 8,415,000). Other main cities (with 2010 population estimates) are: Lubumbashi (1,486,000); Mbuji-Mayi (1,433,000); Kananga (846,000); Kisangani (783,000). The population is Bantu, with minorities of Sudaneses (in the north), Nilotes (northeast), Pygmies and Hamites (in the east). French is the official language, but of more than 200 languages spoken, four are recognized as national languages: Kiswahili, Tshiluba, Kikongo and Lingala. Lingala has become the *lingua franca* after French.

Tourism

In 2010 there were 81,000 non-resident tourist arrivals by air.

Congo, Republic of the

République du Congo

Factsheet

Capital: Brazzaville
Population estimate, 2015: 4.62 m.
GNI per capita, 2014: (PPP$) 6,012
HDI/world rank, 2014: 0.591/136
Internet domain extension: .cg

Civil Aviation

The principal airports are at Brazzaville (Maya Maya) and Pointe-Noire. In 2012 Brazzaville handled 957,472 passengers (675,193 on domestic flights) and 26,418 tonnes of freight.

Climate

An equatorial climate, with moderate rainfall and a small range of temperature. There is a long dry season from May to Oct. in the southwest plateaux, but the Congo Basin in the northeast is more humid, with rainfall approaching 100″ (2,500 mm). Brazzaville, Jan. 78 °F (25.6 °C), July 73 °F (22.8 °C). Annual rainfall 59″ (1,473 mm).

Constitution and Government

A new constitution was approved in a referendum held in Jan. 2002. Under the new constitution the president's term of office is increased from 5 to 7 years. The constitution provides for a new two-chamber assembly consisting of a house of representatives and a senate. The president may also appoint and dismiss ministers. 84.3% of voters were in favour of the draft constitution and 11.3% against. Turnout was 78%, despite calls from opposition parties for a boycott. The new constitution came into force in Aug. 2002. There is a 139-seat *National Assembly*, with members elected for a 5-year term in single-seat constituencies, and a 72-seat *Senate*, with members elected for a 6-year term (one third of members every 2 years).

Currency

The unit of currency is the *franc CFA* (XAF) with a parity of 655.957 francs CFA to one euro.

Defence

In 2012 military expenditure totalled an estimated US$325 m. (approximately US$74 per capita), representing around 2.5% of GDP.

Economy

Agriculture produced 3.4% of GDP in 2011, industry 76.6% and services 20.0%.

Labour

In 2010 the estimated economically active population was 1,637,000 (56% males), up from 1,256,000 in 2000. More than 50% of the labour force in 2010 were engaged in agriculture. The Republic of the Congo had 31,000 people living in slavery according to the Walk Free Foundation's 2013 *Global Slavery Index*.

Press

In 2008 there were five daily newspapers with a combined circulation of 8,000.

Rail

A railway connects Brazzaville with Pointe-Noire via Loubomo and Bilinga, and a branch links Mont-Belo with Mbinda on the Gabon border. Total length in 2005 was 797 km (1,067 mm gauge). In 2006 passenger-km totalled 167 m. and freight tonne-km 264 m.

Religion

In 2010 there were an estimated 2.08 m. Protestants, 1.22 m. Roman Catholics, 0.18 m. other Christians and 0.11 m. folk religionists according to the Pew Research Center's Forum on Religion & Public Life. A further 0.36 m. people had no religious affiliation.

Roads

In 2004 there were 17,289 km of roads, of which 5.0% were surfaced. Passenger cars in use in 2007 numbered 56,000 (15 per 1,000 inhabitants). There were 214 deaths in road accidents in 2007.

Shipping

The only seaport is Pointe-Noire. There are some 5,000 km of navigable rivers, and river transport is an important service for timber and other freight as well as passengers.

Social Statistics

2008 estimates: births, 125,000; deaths, 46,000. Rates, 2008 estimates (per 1,000 population): births, 34.5; deaths, 12.9. Infant mortality, 2010 (per 1,000 live births), 61. Expectation of life in 2013 was 57.4 years for males and 60.2 for females. Annual population growth rate, 2000–08, 2.2%. Fertility rate, 2008, 4.4 children per woman.

Telecommunications

There were 9,800 fixed telephone lines in 2010 (2.4 per 1,000 inhabitants). Mobile phone subscribers numbered 3.80 m. in 2010. There were 56.0 internet users per 1,000 inhabitants in 2011.

Territory and Population

The Republic of the Congo, sometimes referred to as Congo (Brazzaville), is bounded by Cameroon and the Central African Republic in the north, the Democratic Republic of the Congo to the east and south, Angola and the Atlantic Ocean to the southwest and Gabon to the west, and covers 342,000 km². At the census of 2007 the population was 3,697,490 (1,876,133 females); density, 11 per km². In 2011, 62.5% of the population were urban. Census population of major cities in 2007: Brazzaville, the capital, 1,373,382; Pointe-Noire, 715,334; Loubomo (Dolisie), 83,798; N'Kayi, 71,620; Impfondo, 33,911; Ouesso, 28,179. Main ethnic groups are: Kongo (48%), Sangha (20%), Teke (17%) and M'Bochi (12%). French is the official language. Kongo languages are widely spoken. Monokutuba and Lingala serve as *lingua francas*.

Tourism

In 2009, 85,000 non-resident tourists stayed in hotels and similar accommodation (up from 63,000 in 2008 and 54,000 in 2007).

Costa Rica

República de Costa Rica (Republic of Costa Rica)

Factsheet

Capital: San José
Population estimate, 2015: 4.81 m.

GNI per capita, 2013: (PPP$) 13,413
HDI/world rank, 2014: 0.766/69=
Internet domain extension: .cr

Civil Aviation

There are international airports at San José (Juan Santamaria) and Liberia (Daniel Oduber Quirós). The national carrier is Líneas Aéreas Costarriquenses (LACSA). In 2012 scheduled airline traffic of Costa Rican-based carriers flew 23.2 m. km; passenger-km totalled 4.9 bn. in the same year. In 2012 San José handled 3,217,400 passengers (2,287,416 on international flights) and 80,157 tonnes of freight.

Climate

The climate is tropical, with a small range of temperature and abundant rain. The dry season is from Dec. to April. San José, Jan. 66 °F (18.9 °C), July 69 °F (20.6 °C). Annual rainfall 72″ (1,793 mm).

Constitution and Government

The Constitution was promulgated on 7 Nov. 1949. The legislative power is vested in a single-chamber *Legislative Assembly* of 57 deputies elected for 4 years. The *President* and two *Vice-Presidents* are elected for 4 years; the candidate receiving the largest vote, provided it is over 40% of the total, is declared elected, but a second ballot is required if no candidate gets 40% of the total. Since 2003 former presidents have been permitted to stand again. Elections are normally held on the first Sunday in Feb. The President may appoint and remove members of the cabinet.

Currency

The unit of currency is the *Costa Rican colón* (CRC) of 100 *céntimos.*

Defence

In 2013 defence expenditure totalled US$397 m. (US$84 per capita), representing 0.8% of GDP.

Economy

Agriculture accounted for 7.3% of GDP in 2009, industry 27.3% and services 65.4%.

Labour

In the third quarter of 2015 the economically active population numbered 2,273,300 of which 2,063,100 were employed. The main area of employment in the period July–Sept. 2015 was trade and repairs (373,600), followed by manufacturing (241,000) and agriculture, ranching and fisheries (239,800).

Press

There were six daily newspapers in 2011 with a combined circulation of 380,000, and 50 non-dailies. The most widely read daily is *La Teja* (which was only launched in 2006), followed by *La Nación* and *Diario Extra.*

Rail

The nationalized railway system (Incofer) was closed in 1995 following an earthquake in 1991. Freight services and some commuter services have now been resumed. In 2007 passenger-km totalled 872,000 and freight tonne-km 230,000.

Religion

Roman Catholicism is the state religion; it had an estimated 3.11 m. adherents in 2010 according to the Pew Research Center's Forum on Religion & Public Life. The Archbishop of Costa Rica has seven bishops at Alajuela, Cartago, Ciudad Quesada, Limón, Puntarenas, San Isidro de el General and Tilarán. The Pew Research Center estimated that there were also 1.06 m. Protestants in 2010. The remainder of the population are religiously unaffiliated or followers of other religions.

Roads

In 2007 there were 36,654 km of roads, including 7,640 km of main roads. On the Costa Rica section of the Inter-American Highway it is possible to drive to Panama during the dry season. The Pan-American Highway into Nicaragua is metalled for most of the way and a new highway between San José and Caldera opened in Jan. 2010. Passenger cars in use in 2007 numbered 525,400, buses and coaches 12,300, vans and lorries 139,600 and motorcycles and mopeds 100,100. There were 339 fatalities as a result of road accidents in 2007.

Shipping

The chief ports are Limón on the Atlantic and Caldera on the Pacific. In Jan. 2009 there were two ships of 300 GT or over registered, totalling 2,000 GT.

Social Statistics

Births, 2008: 75,187; deaths, 18,021. 2008 rates per 1,000 population: births, 16.9; deaths, 4.0. Annual population growth rate, 2005–10, 1.6%. Life expectancy at birth, 2013, was 77.8 years for men and 82.2 years for women. Infant mortality, 2008, 9.0 per 1,000 live births; fertility rate, 2008, 2.0 children per woman.

Telecommunications

In 2011 there were 1,490,600 landline telephone subscriptions (equivalent to 315.4 per 1,000 inhabitants) and 4,358,100 mobile phone subscriptions (or 922.0 per 1,000 inhabitants). There were 343.3 internet users per 1,000 inhabitants in 2009. Fixed internet subscriptions totalled 271,500 in 2009 (59.1 per 1,000 inhabitants). In Dec. 2011 there were 1.6 m. Facebook users.

Territory and Population

Costa Rica is bounded in the north by Nicaragua, east by the Caribbean, southeast by Panama, and south and west by the Pacific. The area is estimated at 51,100 km^2 (19,730 sq. miles). The population at the census of May 2011 was 4,301,712 (2,195,649 females); density, 84.2 per km^2. In 2011, 64.9% of the population were urban. There are seven provinces (with 2011 census population): Alajuela (848,146); Cartago (490,903); Guanacaste (326,953); Heredia (433,677); Limón (386,862); Puntarenas (410,929); San José (1,404,242). The largest cities are San José (estimated population of 1,330,000 in 2011), Heredia, Cartago and Alajuela. Main ethnic groups (2011): White or Mestizo 84%, Mulatto 7%, Amerindian 2%, Black or Afro-Caribbean 1%. Spanish is the official language.

Tourism

In 2009 there were 1,923,000 non-resident tourists (excluding same-day visitors), down from 2,089,000 in 2008.

Côte d'Ivoire

République de la Côte d'Ivoire (Republic of Côte d'Ivoire)

Factsheet

Capital: Yamoussoukro
Seat of government: Abidjan
Population estimate, 2015: 22.70 m.
GNI per capita, 2014: (PPP$) 3,171
HDI/world rank, 2014: 0.462/172
Internet domain extension: .ci

Civil Aviation

There is an international airport at Abidjan (Félix Houphouët-Boigny Airport), which in 2012 handled 961,643 passengers (842,927 on international flights) and 16,755 tonnes of freight. The national carrier is Air Côte d'Ivoire, which in 2015 operated domestic services and flew to 19 other African countries.

Climate

A tropical climate, affected by distance from the sea. In coastal areas, there are wet seasons from May to July and in Oct. and Nov., but in central areas the periods are March to May and July to Nov. In the north, there is one wet season from June to Oct. Abidjan, Jan. 81 °F (27.2 °C), July 75 °F (23.9 °C). Annual rainfall 84″ (2,100 mm). Bouaké, Jan. 81 °F (27.2 °C), July 77 °F (25 °C). Annual rainfall 48″ (1,200 mm).

Constitution and Government

The 1960 constitution was amended in 1971, 1975, 1980, 1985, 1986, 1990, 1998 and 2000. The sole legal party was the Democratic Party of Côte d'Ivoire, but opposition parties were legalized in 1990. There is a 255-member *National Assembly* elected by universal suffrage for a 5-year term. The *President* is also directly elected for a 5-year term (renewable). He appoints and leads a Council of Ministers. In Nov. 1990 the National Assembly voted that its Speaker should become President in the event of the latter's incapacity, and created the post of Prime Minister to be appointed by the President. Following the coup of Dec. 1999 a referendum was held on 23 July 2000 on the adoption of a new constitution, which set eligibility conditions for presidential candidates (the candidate and both his parents must be Ivorian), reduced the voting age from 21 to 18, and abolished the death penalty.

Currency

The unit of currency is the *franc CFA* (XOF) with a parity of 655.957 francs CFA to one euro.

Defence

Defence expenditure totalled US$751 m. in 2013 (US$34 per capita), representing 2.7% of GDP.

Economy

In 2011 agriculture contributed 29.1% to GDP; followed by finance and real estate, 13.2%; trade and restaurants, 13.2%; manufacturing, 11.9%; public administration and defence, 8.3%. Côte d'Ivoire's 'shadow' (black market) economy is estimated to constitute approximately 47% of the country's official GDP.

Labour

The labour force in 2013 was 8,298,000 (6,551,000 in 2003). 67.9% of the population aged 15–64 was economically active in 2013. Côte d'Ivoire had 0.16 m. people living in slavery according to the Walk Free Foundation's 2013 *Global Slavery Index.*

Press

In 2008 there were 23 paid-for daily newspapers with an estimated combined circulation of 200,000.

Rail

From Abidjan a metre-gauge railway runs to Ouangolodougou near the border with Burkina Faso (660 km), and thence through Burkina Faso to Ouagadougou and Kaya. Operation of the railway in both countries is franchised to the mixed public-private company Sitarail.

Religion

According to the Pew Research Center's Forum on Religion & Public Life, in 2010 the population was an estimated 44.1% Christian and 37.5% Muslim, with 10.2% folk religionists and 8.0% religiously unaffiliated. Around 51% of the Christians are Protestants and 48% Catholics. In Feb. 2016 there was one Roman Catholic cardinal.

Roads

In 2007 there were 81,996 km of roads, including 142 km of motorways. There were 314,165 passenger cars, 78,575 vans and trucks, 38,105 motorcycles and mopeds and 17,512 buses and coaches in use in 2007.

Shipping

The main port is Abidjan, which handled 22.1 m. tonnes of foreign cargo in 2008. In Jan. 2009 there were two ships of 300 GT or over registered, totalling 1,000 GT.

Social Statistics

2008 estimates: births, 720,000; deaths, 223,000. Rates (2008 estimates, per 1,000 population); birth, 35.0; death, 10.8. Expectation of life in 2013 was 50.0 years for males and 51.6 for females. Annual population growth rate, 2000–08, 2.2%. Infant mortality, 2010, 86 per 1,000 live births; fertility rate, 2008, 4.6 births per woman. 29% of the population are migrants.

Telecommunications

There were 223,200 fixed telephone lines in 2010 (11 per 1,000 inhabitants). Mobile phone subscribers numbered 14.91 m. in 2010. In 2011 an estimated 2% of the population were internet users.

Territory and Population

Côte d'Ivoire is bounded in the west by Liberia and Guinea, north by Mali and Burkina Faso, east by Ghana, and south by the Gulf of Guinea. It has an area of 322,463 km^2 (including 4,460 km^2 of inland water). A census was held in 2014 for the first time in 16 years. The population was 22,671,331 (51.7% male), giving a density of 71.3 per km^2. The population was 51.3% urban in 2011. The country is administratively divided into 12 districts and the two autonomous districts of Abidjan and Yamoussoukro. In 2014 the census population of Abidjan was 4,395,243. Other major towns are Bouaké, Daloa, Korhogo, San-Pédro and Yamoussoukro. There are about 60 ethnic groups, the principal ones being the Baoulé (23%), the Bété (18%) and the Sénoufo (15%). French is the official language.

Tourism

There were 252,000 non-resident visitors in 2010; spending by tourists in 2010 (excluding passenger transport) totalled US$213 m.

Croatia

Republika Hrvatska (Republic of Croatia)

Factsheet

Capital: Zagreb
Population estimate, 2015: 4.24 m.
GNI per capita, 2014: (PPP$) 19,409
HDI/world rank, 2014: 0.818/47
Internet domain extension: .hr

Civil Aviation

The biggest international airports are Zagreb (Pleso), Split and Dubrovnik. The national carrier is Croatia Airlines, which carried 1,952,000 passengers in 2012. Zagreb Airport handled 2,317,170 passengers in 2012 (1,896,129 on international flights) and 6,929 tonnes of freight, Dubrovnik 1,455,470 passengers (1,215,168 on international flights) and Split 1,393,649 passengers (1,211,067 on international flights).

Climate

Inland Croatia has a central European type of climate, with cold winters and hot summers, but the Adriatic coastal region experiences a Mediterranean climate with mild, moist winters and hot, brilliantly sunny summers with less than average rainfall. Average annual temperature and rainfall: Dubrovnik, 16.6 °C and 1,051 mm. Zadar, 15.6 °C and 963 mm. Rijeka, 14.3 °C and 1,809 mm. Zagreb, 12.4 °C and 1,000 mm. Osijek, 11.3 °C and 683 mm.

Constitution and Government

A new constitution was adopted on 22 Dec. 1990 and was revised in both 2000 and 2001. The *President* is elected for renewable 5-year terms. There is a unicameral Parliament (*Hrvatski Sabor*), consisting of 151 deputies; 140 members are elected from multi-seat constituencies for a 4-year term, eight seats are reserved for national minorities and three members representing Croatians abroad are chosen by proportional representation. The upper house, the *Chamber of Counties*, was abolished in 2001.

Currency

On 30 May 1994 the *kuna* (HRK; a name used in 1941–45) of 100 *lipa* replaced the Croatian dinar at one kuna = 1,000 dinars.

Defence

Conscription was abolished on 1 Jan. 2008. Defence expenditure in 2013 totalled US$813 m. (US$182 per capita), representing 1.4% of GDP.

Economy

Agriculture contributed 5% of GDP in 2010, industry 27% and services 68%.

Labour

In 2009 the labour force numbered 1,762,000 people of whom 1,498,800 were employed. In 2013 the unemployment rate was 17.7%, up from 15.8% in 2012; youth unemployment among 15 to 24-year-olds was 51.5% (44.1% in 2012). The main areas of activity in 2009 were manufacturing (employing 272,800 persons), wholesale and retail trade/repair of motor vehicles and motorcycles (243,300), construction (140,700) and public administration and defence/compulsory social security (113,500). Croatia had 15,000 people living in slavery according to the Walk Free Foundation's 2013 *Global Slavery Index*.

Press

In 2013 there were 13 daily newspapers. The papers with the highest circulation in 2013 were *24sata* (daily average of 108,000 copies and 1,176,000 unique monthly visitors in Dec. 2013 for its online edition), *Večerni list* and *Jutarnji list*.

Rail

There were 2,722 km of 1,435 mm gauge rail in 2009 (985 km electrified). In 2009 railways carried 74 m. passengers and 12 m. tonnes of freight.

Religion

At the census of 2011 the principal denominations were: Roman Catholic, 3,697,143; Orthodox, 190,143; Muslims, 62,977; no religion or atheist, 163,375; not stated, 93,018. In Feb. 2016 there was one cardinal.

Roads

There were 29,333 km of roads in 2010 (including 1,126 km of motorways and 6,929 km of highways, national and main roads). In 2010 there were 1,515,449 passenger cars, 4,877 buses and coaches, and 157,731 goods vehicles. 56 m. passengers and 75 m. tonnes of freight were carried by road transport in 2010. There were 426 deaths in road accidents in 2010.

Shipping

The main ports in 2010 (ports that had total traffic of goods greater than or equal to 1 m. tonnes) are Bakar (2.4 m. tonnes), Omišalj (5.9 m. tonnes), Ploče (4.5 m. tonnes), Raša (1.9 m. tonnes), Rijeka (2.0 m. tonnes) and Split (2.7 m. tonnes). Figures for 2010 show that 27.5 m. passengers and 24.3 m. tonnes of cargo were transported. In 2010 merchant shipping (passenger and cargo ships) totalled 1,625,210 GT, including liquid bulk carriers 554,805 GT.

Social Statistics

2012: births, 41,771 (9.8 per 1,000 population); deaths, 51,710 (12.1). 2011: marriages, 20,211 (4.6); divorces, 5,662 (1.3); suicides (2009), 790 (17.8 per 100,000). Infant mortality, 2010, five per 1,000 live births. Annual population growth rate, 2005–10, −0.2%. In 2010 the most popular age range for marrying was 25–29 for both males and females. Life expectancy at birth,

2011, was 73.8 years for males and 79.9 years for females. Fertility rate, 2013, 1.5 children per woman.

Telecommunications

There were 1.87 m. fixed telephone lines in 2010 (423.7 per 1,000 inhabitants). Mobile phone subscribers numbered 6.36 m. in 2010. There were 603.2 internet users per 1,000 inhabitants in 2010. Fixed internet subscriptions totalled 1.50 m. in 2009 (339.7 per 1,000 inhabitants). In March 2012 there were 1.5 m. Facebook users.

Territory and Population

Croatia is bounded in the north by Slovenia and Hungary, in the east by Serbia and Bosnia and Herzegovina and in the southeast by Montenegro. It includes the areas of Dalmatia, Istria and Slavonia, which no longer have administrative status. Its area is 56,542 km². 2011 census population, 4,284,889; population density, 75.8 per km². In 2011, 58.0% of the population lived in urban areas. Zagreb, the capital, had a 2011 population of 688,163. Other major towns (with 2011 census population): Split (167,121), Rijeka (128,384) and Osijek (84,104). The official language is Croatian.

Tourism

In 2010, 9.11 m. non-resident tourists stayed in holiday accommodation (up from 8.69 m. in 2009 and 7.74 m. in 2005).

Cuba

República de Cuba (Republic of Cuba)

Factsheet

Capital: Havana
Population estimate, 2015: 11.39 m.
GNI per capita, 2014: (PPP$) 7,301
HDI/world rank, 2014: 0.769/67=
Internet domain extension: .cu

Civil Aviation

There is an international airport at Havana (Jose Martí). The state airline Cubana operates all services internally, and in 2010 had international flights from Havana to Bogotá, Buenos Aires, Cancún, Caracas, Guatemala City, London, Madrid, Mexico City, Montreal, Moscow, Panama City, Paris, Rome, San José (Costa Rica), Santiago, Santo Domingo and Toronto. In 2012 scheduled airline traffic of Cuban-based carriers flew 15.6 m. km; passenger-km totalled 2.7 bn. in the same year. In 2009 Havana Jose Martí International handled 6,632,862 passengers and 27,339 tonnes of freight.

Climate

Situated in the sub-tropical zone, Cuba has a generally rainy climate, affected by the Gulf Stream and the N.E. Trades, although winters are comparatively dry after the heaviest rains in Sept. and Oct. Hurricanes are liable to occur between June and Nov. Havana, Jan. 72 °F (22.2 °C), July 82 °F (27.8 °C). Annual rainfall 48″ (1,224 mm).

Constitution and Government

A Communist Constitution came into force on 24 Feb. 1976. It was amended in July 1992 to permit direct parliamentary elections and in June 2002 to make the country's socialist system 'irrevocable'. Legislative power is vested in the *National Assembly of People's Power*, which meets twice a year and consists of 612 deputies elected for a 5-year term by universal suffrage. The National Assembly elects a 31-member *Council of State* as its permanent organ. The Council of State's President, who is head of state and of government, nominates and leads a Council of Ministers approved by the National Assembly.

Currency

There are two currencies in Cuba. The official currency ('*moneda nacional*') is the *Cuban peso* (CUP) of 100 *centavos*. The *Convertible peso* (CUC), introduced in 1994 (pegged since April 2005 at 1 Convertible peso = US$1.08), is the 'tourist' currency.

Defence

The National Defence Council is headed by the president of the republic. Conscription is for 2 years. In 2011 defence expenditure totalled US$96 m. (US$9 per capita).

Economy

Services accounted for 75% of GDP in 2009, industry 20% and agriculture 5%.

Labour

The labour force in 2013 was 5,360,000 (4,727,000 in 2003). 65.9% of the population aged 15–64 was economically active in 2013. In the same year 3.2% of the population was unemployed.

Press

There were (2008) four national daily newspapers and 15 regional and local dailies with a combined circulation of 1.8 m. The most widely read newspaper is the Communist Party's *Granma*.

Rail

There were 4,066 km of public railway (1,435 mm gauge) in 2005, of which 140 km was electrified. Passenger-km travelled in 2007 came to 1,285 m. and freight tonne-km to 783 m. In addition, the large sugar estates have 7,162 km of lines in total on 1,435 mm, 914 mm and 760 mm gauges.

Religion

Religious liberty was constitutionally guaranteed in 1992. According to the Pew Research Center's Forum on Religion & Public Life, in 2010 an estimated 51.7% of the population was Roman Catholic, 23.0% had no religious affiliation and 17.4% were folk religionists. In 1994 Cardinal Jaime Ortega (b. 1936) was nominated Primate by Pope John Paul II. The Roman Catholic Church has three ecclesiastical provinces, each headed by an archbishop. In Feb. 2016 there was one cardinal.

Roads

In 2007 there were 68,395 km of roads, of which 29,609 km were paved. Vehicles in use in 2008 included 236,881 passenger cars and 171,081 trucks and vans. There were 1,403 fatalities as a result of road accidents in 2008.

Shipping

There are 11 ports, the largest being Havana, Cienfuegos and Mariel. In Jan. 2009 there were 15 ships of 300 GT or over registered, totalling 32,000 GT.

Social Statistics

2008 births, 122,569; deaths, 86,357; marriages, 61,852; divorces, 35,882; suicides, 1,357. Rates, 2008 (per 1,000 population): birth, 10.9; death, 7.7; marriage, 5.5; divorce, 3.2; suicide, 12.1 per 100,000 population. Infant mortality rate, 2008, 4.7 per 1,000 live births. Annual population growth rate, 2005–10, 0.0%. Life expectancy, 2013: 77.3 years for males and 81.3 for females. The fertility rate in 2008 was 1.6 births per woman.

Telecommunications

In 2011 there were 1,193,400 landline telephone subscriptions (equivalent to 106.0 per 1,000 inhabitants) and 1,315,100 mobile phone subscriptions (or 116.9 per 1,000 inhabitants). In 2011, 23.2% of the population were internet users.

Territory and Population

The island of Cuba forms the largest and most westerly of the Greater Antilles group and lies 215 km (135 miles) south of the tip of Florida, USA. The area is 109,884 km², and comprises the island of Cuba (104,339 km²); the Isle of Youth (Isla de la Juventud, formerly the Isle of Pines; 2,419 km²); and some 1,600 small isles ('cays'; 3,126 km²). Census population (2012), 11,167,325, giving a density of 101.6 per km². In 2011, 75.2% of the population were urban. The capital city, Havana, had a census population in 2012 of 2,106,146. Other major cities (2012 census populations in 1,000): Santiago de Cuba (431), Camagüey (301), Holguín (288), Guantánamo (217), Santa Clara (212), Las Tunas, (163), Bayamo (157), Cienfuegos (147), Pinar del Río (140) and Matanzas (134). The official language is Spanish.

Tourism

Tourism is Cuba's largest foreign exchange earner. There were 2,716,317 foreign visitors in 2011 (2,429,809 in 2009 and 2,531,745 in 2010), of whom 1,002,318 were from Canada, 175,822 from the United Kingdom and 110,432 from Italy.

Cyprus

Kypriaki Dimokratia—Kibris Çumhuriyeti (Republic of Cyprus)

Factsheet

Capital: Nicosia
Population estimate, 2015: 1.17 m.
GNI per capita, 2014: (PPP$) 28,633
HDI/world rank, 2014: 0.850/32=
Internet domain extension: .cy

Civil Aviation

Nicosia airport has been closed since the Turkish invasion in 1974. It is situated in the UN controlled buffer zone. There are international airports at Larnaca (the main airport) and Paphos. In 2009, 7,068,080 passengers, 59,092 aircraft and 38,502 tonnes of commercial freight went through these airports. In 2009, 2,318,107 passengers arrived at the two airports on scheduled flights and 2,306,850 passengers departed.

Climate

The climate is Mediterranean, with very hot, dry summers and variable winters. Maximum temperatures may reach 112 °F (44.5 °C) in July and Aug., but minimum figures may fall to 22 °F (−5.5 °C) in the mountains in winter, when snow is experienced. Rainfall is generally between 10″ and 27″ (250 and 675 mm) and occurs mainly in the winter months, but it may reach 48″ (1,200 mm) in the Troodos mountains. Nicosia, Jan. 50 °F (10.0 °C), July 83 °F (28.3 °C). Annual rainfall 19.6″ (500 mm).

Constitution and Government

Under the 1960 constitution executive power is vested in a *President* elected for a 5-year term by universal suffrage, and exercised through a Council of Ministers appointed by him or her. The *House of Representatives* exercises legislative power. It is elected by universal suffrage for 5-year terms, and consists of 80 members, of whom 56 are elected by the Greek Cypriot and 24 by the Turkish Cypriot community. As from Dec. 1963 the Turkish Cypriot members have ceased to attend, and the 24 seats allocated to the Turkish Cypriot community are no longer contested. Voting is compulsory, and is by preferential vote in a proportional representation system with reallocation of votes at national level.

Currency

On 1 Jan. 2008 the euro (EUR) replaced the Cyprus pound (CYP) as the legal currency of Cyprus at the irrevocable conversion rate of £C0.585274 to one euro.

Defence

Conscription is for 24 months. In 2013 defence expenditure totalled US$460 m., with spending per capita US$398. The 2013 expenditure represented 2.1% of GDP. In 1998 the then president cancelled a US$450 m. contract with Russia for the deployment of S-300 anti-aircraft missiles on the island and negotiated to place them on Crete instead.

Labour

Out of an average of 381,300 people in employment in 2009, 71,800 were in wholesale and retail trade/repair of motor vehicles and motorcycles; 44,300 in construction; and 34,800 in manufacturing. The unemployment rate was 7.1% in Sept. 2010. There were a total of 1,211 working days lost to strike action in 2009, up from 1,034 in 2008 but down from 10,289 in 2007.

Press

In 2008 there were 22 paid-for dailies daily newspapers with a circulation of 103,000. The most widely read daily is *Phileleftheros*.

Religion

The Greek Cypriots are predominantly Greek Orthodox Christians, and almost all Turkish Cypriots are Muslims (mostly Sunnis of the Hanafi sect). There are also small groups of the Armenian Apostolic Church, Roman Catholics (Maronites and Latin Rite) and Protestants (mainly Anglicans).

Roads

In 2007 the total length of roads in the government-controlled area was 12,246 km, of which 64.0% were paved. In 2007 there were 410,936 passenger cars, 117,498 trucks and vans, 3,292 buses and coaches and 41,211 motorcycles and mopeds. There were 71 deaths as a result of road accidents in 2009.

Shipping

The two main ports are Limassol and Larnaca. In 2009, 3,915 ships of 22,897,408 net registered tons entered Cyprus ports carrying 7,859,269 tonnes of cargo from, to and via Cyprus. In Jan. 2009 there were 867 ships of 300 GT or over registered, totalling 20.03 m. GT. Among the 867 vessels registered were 286 bulk carriers, 216 general cargo ships and 192 container ships. The port in Famagusta has been closed to international traffic since the Turkish invasion in 1974.

Social Statistics

2009 births, 9,608; deaths, 5,182; marriages, 12,769; divorces, 1,738. Rates, 2009 (per 1,000 population): birth, 12.0; death, 6.5; marriage (residents of Cyprus only), 7.9; divorce, 2.2. Life expectancy at birth, 2013, was 77.9 years for males and 81.8 years for females. Population growth rate, 2009, 0.8%; infant mortality, 2009, 3.3 per 1,000 live births; fertility rate, 2013, 1.5 children per woman. In 2009 the average age of first marriage (residents of Cyprus only) was 29.5 years for men and 27.4 years for women.

Telecommunications

In 2011 there were 405,000 landline telephone subscriptions (equivalent to 362.7 per 1,000 inhabitants) and 1,090,900 mobile phone subscriptions (or 977.1 per 1,000 inhabitants). There were 529.9 internet users per 1,000 inhabitants in 2010. Fixed internet subscriptions totalled 190,900 in 2009 (175.1 per 1,000 inhabitants). In March 2012 there were 554,000 Facebook users. CYTA (short for Cyprus Telecommunications Authority) is the state-owned national telecommunications provider. It has developed an extensive submarine fiber optic cable network linking Cyprus with neighbouring countries such as Greece, Israel and Egypt and—by extension—with the rest of the world.

Territory and Population

The island lies in the Mediterranean, about 60 km off the south coast of Turkey and 90 km off the coast of Syria. Area, 9,251 km^2 (3,572 sq. miles). The Turkish-occupied area is 3,355 km^2. The 2011 census population (government-controlled area only) was 856,857. 70.3% of the population lived in urban areas in 2010. Principal towns with populations (2011 census): Nicosia (the capital), 239,277; Limassol, 180,201; Larnaca, 84,591; Paphos,

62,122. Nicosia is a divided city, with the UN-patrolled Green Line passing through it. Greek and Turkish are official languages. English is widely spoken.

Tourism

There were 2,173,000 international tourist arrivals in 2010 (excluding same-day visitors). Most tourists in 2010 were from the UK (45.8%), followed by Russia (10.3%), Germany (6.4%) and Greece (5.9%). Tourist spending in 2010 totalled US$2,371 m.

Czech Republic

Česká Republika

Factsheet
Capital: Prague
Population estimate, 2015: 10.54 m.
GNI per capita, 2014: (PPP$) 26,660
HDI/world rank, 2014: 0.870/28
Internet domain extension: .cz

Civil Aviation

There are international airports at Prague (Ruzyně), Ostrava (Mošnov) and Brno (Turany). The national carrier is Czech Airlines, 56.0% of which is owned by the state. In 2007 it flew 82.9 m. km and carried 5,492,200 passengers (5,379,500 on international flights). In 2007 Prague handled 12,436,254 passengers; there were a total of 174,662 take-offs and landings.

Climate

A humid continental climate, with warm summers and cold winters. Precipitation is generally greater in summer, with thunderstorms. Autumn, with dry clear weather, and spring, which is damp, are each of short duration. Prague, Jan. 29.5 °F (−1.5 °C), July 67 °F (19.4 °C). Annual rainfall 19.3″ (483 mm). Brno, Jan. 31 °F (−0.6 °C), July 67 °F (19.4 °C). Annual rainfall 21″ (525 mm).

Constitution and Government

The constitution of 1 Jan. 1993 provides for a parliament comprising a 200-member *Chamber of Deputies*, elected for 4-year terms by proportional representation, and an 81-member *Senate* elected for 6-year terms in single-member districts, 27 senators being elected every 2 years. The main function of the Senate is to scrutinize proposed legislation. Senators must be at least 40 years of age, and are elected on a first-past-the-post basis, with a run-off in constituencies where no candidate wins more than half the votes cast. For the House of Representatives there is a 5% threshold; votes for parties failing to surmount this are redistributed on the basis of results in each of the eight electoral districts. There is a *Constitutional Court* at Brno, whose 15 members are nominated by the President and approved by the Senate for 10-year terms. Following a constitutional amendment that took effect in Oct. 2012, the *President* of the Republic is directly elected for a 5-year term. Candidates standing for office must be 40 years of age. In the event of no candidate winning an absolute majority, a second round is held between the two most successful candidates. A president may not serve more than two consecutive 5-year terms.

Currency

The unit of currency is the *koruna* (CZK) or crown of 100 *haler*, introduced on 8 Feb. 1993 at parity with the former Czechoslovakian koruna.

Defence

Conscription ended in Dec. 2004 when the armed forces became all-volunteer. Defence expenditure in 2013 totalled US$2,179 m. (US$214 per capita), representing 1.1% of GDP.

Economy

Agriculture accounted for 2.7% of GDP in 2014, industry 38.0% and services 59.3%.

Labour

In the fourth quarter of 2010 the economically active population numbered 5,281,800; 1.28 m. persons worked in manufacturing; 589,400 in trade; 445,500 in construction; 338,300 in human health and social work activities; and 327,500 in public administration and defence. In Dec. 2015 the unemployment rate was 4.5%-the joint lowest in the European Union (down from 6.1% in 2014 as a whole). The average monthly gross wage was Kč. 23,004 in 2010. On 1 Aug. 2013 the minimum wage was increased from Kč. 8,000 a month to Kč. 8,500. The Czech Republic had 38,000 people living in slavery according to the Walk Free Foundation's 2013 *Global Slavery Index*.

Press

There were 81 daily newspapers in 2014 (79 paid-for and two free) with a combined average daily circulation of 1,209,000. In 2011 there were 417 non-dailies. The newspaper with the highest circulation is *Blesk* (daily average of 265,000 copies in 2014).

Rail

In 2011 Czech State Railways had a route length of 9,470 km (9,448 km on 1,435 mm gauge), of which 3,020 km were electrified. Passenger-km travelled in 2011 came to 6.64 bn. and freight tonne-km to 13.85 bn. There is a metro (44 km) and tram/light rail system (496 km) in Prague, and also tram/light rail networks in Brno, Liberec, Most, Olomouc, Ostrava and Plzeň.

Religion

According to estimates by the Pew Research Center's Forum on Religion & Public Life, 76.4% of the population was religiously unaffiliated in 2010-more than in any other country. Most of the remainder of the population are Christians (90% Catholics in 2010). Dominik Duka (b. 1943) was installed as Archbishop of Prague and Primate of Bohemia in April 2010. In Feb. 2016 the Roman Catholic church had two cardinals. The largest Protestant church is the Evangelical Church of Czech Brethren, which unites Calvinists and Lutherans and has about 115,000 members. In 2009 there were 25 registered churches and religious societies.

Roads

In 2007 there were 657 km of motorways, 6,191 km of highways and main roads, 48,736 km of secondary roads and 72,927 km of other roads, forming a total network of 128,511 km. Passenger cars in use in 2007 numbered 4,280,100 (414 per 1,000 inhabitants), and there were also 555,200 lorries and vans and 20,400 buses and coaches. Motorcycles and mopeds numbered 860,100. There were 832 deaths as a result of road accidents in 2009.

Shipping

In 2009, 804,000 tonnes of freight were carried by inland waterways.

Social Statistics

2009 births, 118,667; deaths, 107,421; marriages, 47,862; divorces, 29,133. Rates (per 1,000 population), 2009: birth, 11.3; death, 10.0; marriage, 4.6; divorce, 2.8. Life expectancy at birth, 2013, 74.6 years for males and 80.7 years for females. In 2009 the most popular age range for marrying was 30–34 for males and 25–29 for females. Annual population growth rate, 2005–10, 0.5%. Infant mortality, 2010, three per 1,000 live births; fertility rate, 2013, 1.6 children per woman.

Telecommunications

In 2013 there were 2,001,000 main (fixed) telephone lines. In the same year mobile phone subscriptions numbered 13,670,000 (1,277.3 per 1,000 persons). Český Telecom was sold to the Spanish telecommunications firm Telefónica in April 2005. It has since become Telefónica O2 Czech Republic. In 2013, 74.1% of the population aged 16–74 were internet users. In March 2012 there were 3.5 m. Facebook users.

Territory and Population

The Czech Republic is bounded in the west by Germany, north by Poland, east by Slovakia and south by Austria. Its area is 78,867 km^2 (30,451 sq. miles), including 1,620 km^2 (625 sq. miles) of inland waters. The population at the 2011 census was 10,436,560; density, 135.1 per km^2. In 2011, 73.6% of the population lived in urban areas. The census population of the principal towns in 2011 (in 1,000): Prague, 1,269; Brno, 386; Ostrava, 296; Pilsen, 170; Liberec, 103; Olomouc, 101; České Budějovice, 94; Hradec Králové, 94; Ústí nad Labem, 93; Pardubice, 91; Havířrov, 77; Zlín, 75; Kladno, 68; Most, 65; Opava, 58. At the 2001 census 90.4% of the population was Czech, 3.7% Moravian and 1.9% Slovak. The official language is Czech.

Tourism

In 2010, 6,334,000 non-resident tourists stayed in holiday accommodation. Of these, 1,350,000 were from Germany, 414,000 from Russia, 368,000 from the UK, 351,000 from Poland and 333,000 from Italy.

Denmark

Kongeriget Danmark (Kingdom of Denmark)

Factsheet

Capital: Copenhagen
Population estimate, 2015: 5.67 m.
GNI per capita, 2014: (PPP$) 44,025
HDI/world rank, 2014: 0.923/4
Internet domain extension: .dk

Civil Aviation

The main international airport is at Copenhagen (Kastrup), and there are also international flights from Aalborg, Aarhus, Billund and Esbjerg. The Scandinavian Airlines System (SAS) resulted from the 1950 merger of the three former Scandinavian airlines. It is now known as Scandinavian Airlines. On 1 Jan. 2009 Denmark had 1,122 aircraft with a capacity of 19,077 seats. Copenhagen (Kastrup) handled 9,848,000 departing passengers in 2009, Billund 1,151,000, Aalborg 561,000 and Aarhus 255,000.

Climate

The climate is much modified by marine influences and the effect of the Gulf Stream, to give winters that may be both cold or mild and often cloudy. Summers may be warm and sunny or chilly and rainy. Generally the east is drier than the west. Long periods of calm weather are exceptional and windy conditions are common. Copenhagen, Jan. 33 °F (0.5 °C), July 63 °F (17 °C). Annual rainfall 650 mm. Esbjerg, Jan. 33 °F (0.5 °C), July 61 °F (16 °C). Annual rainfall 800 mm. In general 10% of precipitation is snow.

Constitution and Government

The present constitution is founded upon the Basic Law of 5 June 1953. The legislative power lies with the Queen and the *Folketing* (parliament) jointly. The executive power is vested in the monarch, who exercises authority through the ministers. The reigning Queen is **Margrethe II**, b. 16 April 1940; married 10 June 1967 to Prince Henrik, b. Count de Monpezat. The Queen receives a tax-free annual sum from the state. This was 79 m. kroner in 2015. The judicial power is with the courts. The monarch must be a member of the Evangelical-Lutheran Church, the official Church of the State, and may not assume major international obligations without the consent of the Folketing. The Folketing consists of one chamber. All men and women of Danish nationality of more than 18 years of age and permanently resident in Denmark possess the franchise, and are eligible for election to the Folketing, which is at present composed of 179 members; 135 members are elected by the method of proportional representation in 17 constituencies. Besides its legislative functions, every 6 years it appoints judges who, together with the ordinary members of the Supreme Court, form the *Rigsret*, a tribunal which can alone try parliamentary impeachments.

Currency

The monetary unit is the *Danish krone* (DKK) of 100 øre.

Defence

Denmark has a compulsory military service with mobilization based on the constitution of 1849. This states that it is the duty of every fit man to contribute to the national defence. In 2013 defence expenditure totalled US$4,509 m. (US$812 per capita), representing 1.4% of GDP.

Economy

In 2010 agriculture accounted for 1.2% of GDP, industry 21.8% and services 77.0%. Denmark gave US$3.0 bn. in international aid in 2014, equivalent to 0.86% of GNI (making Denmark one of only five industrialized countries to meet the UN target of 0.7%).

Labour

The labour force in 2013 was 2,902,000 (2,874,000 in 2003). 78.0% of the population aged 15–64 was economically active in 2013. In 2013, 34.9% of those in employment worked in the public sector. In Dec. 2015 the unemployment rate was 6.0% (down from 6.5% in 2014 as a whole), compared to the European Union average of 9.0%. The youth unemployment rate in the fourth quarter of 2015 was 10.7% (19.9% for the European Union as a whole).

Press

In 2014 there were 31 daily newspapers with a combined circulation of 1.09 m. The newspaper with the largest average circulation in 2014 was *MetroXpress* (a free paper; 325,000 on weekdays).

Rail

In 2012 there were 2,131 km of state railways of 1,435 mm gauge (619 km electrified). In 2011, 219 m. passengers were carried. DB Schenker Rail Scandinavia A/S (formerly the Danish State Railways Freight Division) carried 7.1 m. tonnes of freight in 2012. There were also 959 km of private railways. A metro system was opened in Copenhagen in 2002.

Religion

There is complete religious liberty. The state church is the Evangelical-Lutheran to which 80.9% of the population belonged in 2010. There are ten dioceses, each with a Bishop. The Bishop together with the Chief Administrative Officer of the county make up the diocesan-governing body, responsible for all matters of ecclesiastical local finance and general administration. Bishops are appointed by the Crown after an election by the clergy and parish council members. Each diocese is divided into a number of deaneries (107 in the whole country), each with its own Dean and Deanery Committee, who have certain financial powers. 81% of church finance derives from a voluntary tax paid by members, at a rate between 0.4–1.5% of income depending upon location. A further 12% comes from state subsidiaries and 7% from other sources, such as church lands.

Roads

Denmark proper had (1 Jan. 2009) 1,128 km of motorways, 3,790 km of other state roads and 69,500 km of other commercial roads. Motor vehicles registered at 1 Jan. 2010 comprised 2,120,322 passenger cars, 32,300 trucks, 462,359 vans, 14,509 buses and 147,373 motorcycles. There were 5,250 casualties in road accidents in 2009, resulting in 303 fatalities.

Shipping

On 1 Jan. 2010 the merchant fleet consisted of 462 vessels (above 100 GT) totalling 10.7 m. GT. In 2009, 40 m. tonnes of cargo were unloaded and 29 m. tonnes were loaded in Danish ports; traffic by passenger ships and ferries is not included.

Social Statistics

Live births, 2009: 62,818; deaths, 54,872. 2009 rates per 1,000 population: birth, 11.4; death, 9.9. Births outside marriage: 2006, 46.4%; 2007, 46.1%; 2008, 46.2%; 2009, 46.5%. Average annual population growth rate, 2005–09, 0.5%. Suicide rate, 2006 (per 100,000 population) was 11.9 (men, 17.5; women, 6.4). Life expectancy at birth, 2008–09, was 76.5 years for males and 80.8 years for females. In 2007 the most popular age range for marrying was 30–34 for males and 25–29 for females. Denmark was the first country to legalize same-sex unions, in 1989. Infant mortality, 2009, 3.0 per 1,000 live births. Fertility rate, 2009, 1.8 births per woman.

Telecommunications

In 2009 there were 2,062,000 main (fixed) telephone lines. In the same year mobile phone subscribers numbered 7,424,000 (134.1 per 100 persons). In 2010, 86% of the population had access to the internet at home and 88% had access to a computer at home. Denmark has one of the highest fixed broadband penetration rates, at 37.7 subscribers per 100 inhabitants in Dec. 2010. In March 2012 there were 2.8 m. Facebook users.

Territory and Population

Denmark is bounded in the west by the North Sea, northwest and north by the Skagerrak and Kattegat straits (separating it from Norway and Sweden), and south by Germany. A 16-km long fixed link with Sweden was opened in July 2000 when the Øresund motorway and railway bridge between Copenhagen and Malmö was completed. In 2010 an estimated 86.7% of the population lived in urban areas. In 2010, 91.4% of the inhabitants were born in Denmark, including the Faroe Islands and Greenland. On 1 Jan. 2013 the population of the capital, Copenhagen (comprising Copenhagen, Frederiksberg and Gentofte municipalities), was 1,230,728; Aarhus, 256,018; Odense, 170,327; Aalborg, 106,916; Esbjerg, 71,491; Randers, 60,895; Kolding, 57,583; Horsens, 55,253; Vejle, 52,449. The official language is Danish.

Tourism

In 2009, 8,457,000 overnight tourists visited Denmark; foreign tourists spent some 35,482 m. kroner in the same year. Foreigners spent 11,164,000 nights in holiday cottages, 4,258,000 nights in hotels and 2,750,000 nights at camping sites in 2009.

Djibouti

Jumhouriyya Djibouti (Republic of Djibouti)

Factsheet

Capital: Djibouti
Population estimate, 2015: 888,000
GNI per capita, 2013: (PPP$) 3,109
HDI/world rank, 2014: 0.470/168
Internet domain extension: .dj

Civil Aviation

There is an international airport at Djibouti (Ambouli), 5 km south of Djibouti. The national carrier is Air Djibouti, which was resurrected in 2015 after having gone into liquidation in 2002. In 2016 it had flights to Addis Ababa, Berbera, Dire Dawa, Hargeisa and Mogadishu.

Climate

Conditions are hot throughout the year, with very little rain. Djibouti, Jan. 78 °F (25.6 °C), July 96 °F (35.6 °C). Annual rainfall 5″ (130 mm).

Constitution and Government

After a referendum at which turnout was 70%, a new constitution was approved on 4 Sept. 1992 by 96.63% of votes cast, which permits the existence of up to four political parties. Parties are required to maintain an ethnic balance in their membership. The *President* is directly elected for a renewable 6-year term. Parliament is a 65-member *National Assembly* elected for 5-year terms. In April 2010 the constitution was amended to allow the president to stand for a third consecutive term. It also provided for the creation of a *Senate*.

Currency

The currency is the *Djibouti franc* (DJF), notionally of 100 *centimes*.

Defence

France—Djibouti's former colonial ruler—maintains a naval base and forces numbering 1,900 as of Feb. 2014. Defence expenditure totalled an estimated US$10 m. in 2011 (approximately US$13 per capita), representing around 1% of GDP.

Economy

In 2010 transport and communications contributed 25.3% of GDP; followed by trade and hotels, 16.7%; finance and insurance, 12.9%; public administration and defence, 12.1%; and construction, 11.5%.

Labour

The labour force in 2013 was 300,000 (227,000 in 2003). Unemployment in 2012 was 48%.

Press

There are no daily newspapers; in 2008 the government-owned *La Nation* was published four times a week.

Rail

Traffic carried is mainly in transit to and from Ethiopia. A new line linking Ethiopia and Djibouti is currently being built by China Civil Engineering Construction Corporation. It is expected to become operational during 2016.

Religion

According to the Pew Research Center's Forum on Religion & Public Life, in 2010 the population was an estimated 96.9% Muslim (Sunnis) with a small Christian minority.

Roads

In 2011 there were an estimated 1,300 km of roads.

Shipping

Djibouti is a free port and container terminal. In 2008, 5.82 m. tonnes of cargo were handled (7.33 m. tonnes in 2007).

Social Statistics

2008 estimates: births, 24,100; deaths, 9,300. Rates (2008 estimates, per 1,000 population); birth, 28.4; death, 11.0. 2006: marriages, 3,059; divorces, 723. Annual population growth rate, 2000–08, 1.9%. Infant mortality, 2010, 73 per 1,000 live births. Expectation of life, 2007: 53.7 years for men, 56.5 for women. Fertility rate, 2008, 3.9 children per woman.

Telecommunications

There were 18,500 fixed telephone lines in 2010 (20.8 per 1,000 inhabitants). Mobile phone subscribers numbered 165,600 in 2010. There were an estimated 95 internet users per 1,000 inhabitants in 2013.

Territory and Population

Djibouti is in effect a city-state surrounded by a semi-desert hinterland. It is bounded in the northwest by Eritrea, northeast by the Gulf of Aden, southeast by Somalia and southwest by Ethiopia. The area is 23,200 km² (8,958 sq. miles). The population at the 2009 census was 818,159. In 2011, 76.3% of the population lived in urban areas. Around half the population in 2005 were Somali (Issa, Gadaboursi and Issaq), 35% Afar, with some Europeans (mainly French) and Arabs. There are five administrative regions, plus the city of Djibouti (areas in sq. km): Ali-Sabieh (2,200); Arta (1,800); Dikhil (7,200); Djibouti (200); Obock (4,700); Tadjourah (7,100). The capital is Djibouti (2009 population, 475,322). French and Arabic are official languages; Somali and Afar are also spoken.

Tourism

There were 56,000 foreign tourists staying at hotels and similar establishments in 2011; tourist spending (excluding passenger transport) totalled US$19 m.

Dominica

Commonwealth of Dominica

Factsheet

Capital: Roseau
Population estimate, 2015: 73,000
GNI per capita, 2014: (PPP$) 9,994
HDI/world rank, 2014: 0.724/94=
Internet domain extension: .dm

Civil Aviation

There are international airports at Melville Hall and Cane Field. In 2010 there were direct flights to Antigua, Barbados, Georgetown, Guadeloupe, Porlamar (Venezuela), Puerto Rico, St Lucia and St Vincent.

Climate

A tropical climate, with pleasant conditions between Dec. and March, but there is a rainy season from June to Oct., when hurricanes may occur. Rainfall is heavy, with coastal areas having 70″ (1,750 mm) but the mountains may have up to 225″ (6,250 mm). Roseau, Jan. 76 °F (24.2 °C), July 81 °F (27.2 °C). Annual rainfall 78″ (1,956 mm).

Constitution and Government

The head of state is the *President*, nominated by the *Prime Minister* and the Leader of the Opposition, and elected for a 5-year term (renewable once) by the House of Assembly. The *House of Assembly* has 32 members, of whom 21 members are elected and nine nominated by the President in addition to the Speaker and the Attorney General.

Currency

The *East Caribbean dollar* (XCD) and the US dollar are legal tender.

Economy

In 2009 agriculture accounted for 14% of GDP, industry 15% and services 71%.

Labour

Around 25% of the economically active population are engaged in agriculture, fishing and forestry. In 2006 the minimum wage was US$0.75 an hour. The unemployment rate in 2008–09 was 14.0%.

Press

In 2008 there were no daily newspapers but there were four weeklies-*The Chronicle, The Sun, The Times* and *The Tropical Star*.

Religion

In 2010 around 94% of the population were Christians according to the Pew Research Center's Forum on Religion & Public Life, of whom two-thirds were Catholics and a third Protestants.

Roads

In 2010 there were an estimated 905 km of roads, of which 82% were paved. Approximately 24,600 vehicles were registered in 2014.

Shipping

There are deep-water harbours at Roseau and Woodbridge Bay. Roseau has a cruise ship berth. In Jan. 2009 there were 60 ships of 300 GT or over registered (including 15 bulk carriers and nine oil tankers), totalling 936,000 GT.

Social Statistics

Births, 2006 estimates, 1,080 (rate of 14.9 per 1,000 population); deaths, 540 (rate of 7.5); marriages (2009), 250; divorces (2009), 85. Life expectancy, 2007: male, 72 years; female, 76 years. Annual population growth rate, 2000–08, −0.2%. Infant mortality rate, 2010, 11 per 1,000 live births. Fertility rate, 2008, 2.1 births per woman.

Telecommunications

There were 15,500 fixed telephone lines in 2010 (228.5 per 1,000 inhabitants). Mobile phone subscribers numbered 98,100 in 2010. There were 474.5 internet users per 1,000 inhabitants in 2010.

Territory and Population

Dominica is an island in the Windward group of the West Indies situated between Martinique and Guadeloupe. It has an area of 750 km^2 (290 sq. miles) and a provisional population at the 2011 census of 71,293. The population density in 2011 was 95.1 per km^2. In 2010, 67.2% of the population were urban. The chief town, Roseau, had 14,725 inhabitants (provisional) in 2011. The population is mainly of African and mixed origins, with small white and Asian minorities. There is a Carib settlement of about 500, almost entirely of mixed blood. The official language is English, although 90% of the population also speak a French Creole.

Tourism

In 2010 there were 76,517 overnight tourist arrivals by air, up from 74,924 in 2009 although down from 84,041 in 2006. There were 517,979 cruise ship visitors in 2010 (when there were 272 cruise ship calls), down from 532,352 in 2009 although up from 379,643 in 2006.

Dominican Republic

República Dominicana

Factsheet

Capital: Santo Domingo
Population estimate, 2015: 10.53 m.
GNI per capita, 2014: (PPP$) 11,883
HDI/world rank, 2014: 0.715/101=
Internet domain extension: .do

Civil Aviation

The main airports are at Puerto Plata, Punta Cana and Santo Domingo (Las Américas). In 2009 Punta Cana was the busiest airport, handling 4,077,596 passengers, followed by Santo Domingo (2,887,175 passengers) and Puerto Plata (1,096,267). The largest airline operating in the Dominican Republic is the American low-cost airline JetBlue.

Climate

A tropical maritime climate with most rain falling in the summer months. The rainy season extends from May to Nov. and amounts are greatest in the north and east. Hurricanes may occur from June to Nov. Santo Domingo, Jan. 75 °F (23.9 °C), July 81 °F (27.2 °C). Annual rainfall 56″ (1,400 mm).

Constitution and Government

A new constitution came into force on 26 Jan. 2010, replacing one from 1966. The new constitution's provisions included the establishment of a Constitutional Court, Council of the Judiciary and Supreme Electoral Court. It also provides for recourse to instruments of direct democracy, including referenda and plebiscites. It outlaws same-sex marriages and abortion and defines Dominican nationals as the children of Dominican parents. The *President*, who has executive power, is elected for 4 years by direct vote but is prohibited from serving consecutive terms. A second round of voting in a presidential election is authorized when no candidate secures an absolute majority in the first ballot. There is a bicameral legislature, the *Congress*, comprising a 32-member *Senate* (one member for each province and one for the National District of Santo Domingo) and a 183-member *Chamber of Deputies*, both elected for 4-year terms. Citizens are entitled to vote at the age of 18.

Currency

The unit of currency is the *peso* (DOP), written as RD$, of 100 *centavos*.

Defence

In 2013 defence expenditure totalled US$378 m. (US$37 per capita), representing 0.6% of GDP.

Economy

In 2009 agriculture accounted for 6.2% of GDP, industry 32.5% and services 61.3%.

Labour

The labour force in 2013 was 4,636,000 (3,804,000 in 2003). The unemployment rate in 2013 was 14.9% (14.7% in 2012). The Dominican Republic had 23,000 people living in slavery according to the Walk Free Foundation's 2013 *Global Slavery Index*.

Press

In 2008 there were ten dailies (eight paid-for and two free) with a combined circulation of 465,000.

Rail

The railway system has been closed down with the exception of 142 km line from Guayubin to the port of Pepillo, used primarily for the banana trade. There is a metro in Santo Domingo.

Religion

The religion of the state is Roman Catholicism; according to estimates by the Pew Research Center's Forum on Religion & Public Life there were 6.67 m. adherents in 2010 (just over two-thirds of the population). The Pew Research Center estimated that Protestants numbered 2.08 m. in 2010 and 1.08 m. people were religiously unaffiliated. In Feb. 2016 there was one cardinal.

Roads

In 2002 the road network covered an estimated 19,705 km, of which 51.2% were paved. In 2007 there were 602,700 passenger cars (62 per 1,000 inhabitants), 525,400 lorries and vans, and 64,200 buses and coaches. Motorcycles and mopeds numbered 1.04 m. In 2008 there were 1,648 fatal road accidents resulting in 1,846 deaths.

Shipping

The main ports are Santo Domingo, Puerto Plata, La Romana and Haina. In Jan. 2009 there were five ships of 300 GT or over registered, totalling 5,000 GT.

Social Statistics

2009 estimates: births, 216,000; deaths, 59,000. Rates, 2009 estimates (per 1,000 population): birth, 22; death, 6. Annual population growth rate, 2005–10, 1.4%. Life expectancy, 2013: male, 70.4 years; female, 76.7 years. Infant mortality, 2010, 22 per 1,000 live births. Fertility rate, 2013, 2.5 children per woman.

Telecommunications

In 2011 there were 1,044,200 landline telephone subscriptions (equivalent to 103.8 per 1,000 inhabitants) and 8,770,800 mobile phone subscriptions (or 872.2 per 1,000 inhabitants). In 2011, 35.5% of the population were internet users. In Dec. 2011 there were 2.5 m. Facebook users.

Territory and Population

The Dominican Republic occupies the eastern portion (about two-thirds) of the island of Hispaniola, the western division forming the Republic of Haiti. The area is 48,671 km² (18,792 sq. miles). Census population 2010, 9,445,281. In 2011 the population was 69.8% urban. Population of the main towns (2010 census, in 1,000): Santo Domingo, the capital, 2,582; Santiago de los Caballeros, 551; Los Alcarrizos, 245; La Romana, 225; San Pedro de Macorís, 185. The population is mainly composed of a mixed race of European (Spanish) and African blood. The official language is Spanish; about 0.18 m. persons speak a Haitian-French Creole.

Tourism

In 2010 there were 4,124,543 non-resident tourist arrivals by air, up from 3,992,303 in 2009 and 3,979,672 in 2008. There were 352,539 cruise ship visitors in 2010 (when there were 264 cruise ship calls), down from 496,728 in 2009 and 475,206 in 2008. The Dominican Republic had 66,968 hotel rooms in 2010.

Ecuador

República del Ecuador (Republic of Ecuador)

Factsheet

Capital: Quito
Population estimate, 2015: 16.14 m.
GNI per capita, 2014: (PPP$) 10,605
HDI/world rank, 2014: 0.732/88
Internet domain extension: .ec

Civil Aviation

The Ecuadorian flag carrier is Tame. There are international airports at Quito (Mariscal Sucre) and Guayaquil (José Joaquín de Olmedo). In 2009 Quito handled 4,746,292 passengers and 143,767 tonnes of freight, and Guayaquil handled 3,382,554 passengers and 55,605 tonnes of freight.

Climate

The climate varies from equatorial, through warm temperate to mountain conditions, according to altitude, which affects temperatures and rainfall. In coastal areas, the dry season is from May to Dec., but only from June to Sept. in mountainous parts, where temperatures may be 20 °F colder than on the coast. Quito, Jan. 59 °F (15 °C), July 58 °F (14.4 °C). Annual rainfall 44″ (1,115 mm). Guayaquil, Jan. 79 °F (26.1 °C), July 75 °F (23.9 °C). Annual rainfall 39″ (986 mm).

Constitution and Government

An executive *President* and a *Vice-President* are directly elected by universal suffrage. The president appoints and leads a *Council of Ministers*, and determines the number and functions of the ministries that comprise the executive branch. Legislative power is vested in a *National Assembly* of 137 members, popularly elected by province. One seat is reserved for overseas voters. A new constitution came into force on 20 Oct. 2008. It was drafted by a Constituent Assembly set up by President Correa in Nov. 2007 and was approved with 63.9% of the vote in a referendum on 28 Sept. 2008. It superseded the previous constitution that had been in place for 10 years. The 2008 constitution, which includes 444 articles, allows a president to run for two consecutive 4-year terms, dissolve parliament and call early elections, and set monetary policy. The *National Congress* was abolished and replaced by a new *National Assembly*.

Currency

The monetary unit is the US dollar.

Defence

Military service is selective, with a 1-year period of conscription. The country is divided into four military zones, with headquarters at Quito, Guayaquil, Cuenca and Pastaza. In 2012 defence expenditure totalled US$1,509 m. (US$99 per capita), representing 2.1% of GDP.

Economy

Agriculture accounted for 10.4% of GDP in 2011, industry 36.8% and services 52.8%.

Labour

The labour force in 2013 was 7,554,000 (6,095,000 in 2003). 71.6% of the population aged 15–64 was economically active in 2013. Ecuador had 44,000 people living in slavery according to the Walk Free Foundation's 2013 *Global Slavery Index*.

Press

There were 47 daily newspapers in 2008, with a circulation of 591,000.

Rail

The railway network, only 10% of which was operational in 2008, has since been repaired and rebuilt. In 2015 it had a total length of 517 km.

Religion

The state recognizes no religion and grants freedom of worship to all. In 2010, 94.1% of the population were Christians according to estimates by the Pew Research Center's Forum on Religion & Public Life. Most of the remainder of the population was religiously unaffiliated. Of the Christians, 89% were Catholics and 10% Protestants. In Feb. 2016 there was one Roman Catholic cardinal.

Roads

In 2007 there were 43,670 km of roads. There were 507,500 passenger cars in 2007 (38 per 1,000 inhabitants) and 323,500 lorries and vans. There were 1,848 fatalities in road accidents in 2007. In 1998 storms and floods on the coast, caused by El Niño, resulted in 2,000 km of roads being damaged or destroyed.

Shipping

Ecuador has three major seaports, of which Guayaquil is the most important, and six minor ones. In Jan. 2009 there were 60 ships of 300 GT or over registered, totalling 222,000 GT.

Social Statistics

2008 estimates: births, 280,000; deaths, 70,000. Rates, 2008 estimates (per 1,000 population): birth, 20.8; death, 5.2. Life expectancy at birth, 2013, was 73.7 years for males and 79.4 years for females. Annual population growth rate, 2000–08, 1.1%. Infant mortality, 2010, 18 per 1,000 live births; fertility rate, 2008, 2.6 children per woman. In 2009 the most popular age for marrying was 20–24 for both men and women.

Telecommunications

In 2011 there were 2,210,600 landline telephone subscriptions (equivalent to 150.7 per 1,000 inhabitants) and 15,332,700 mobile phone subscriptions (or 1,045.5 per 1,000 inhabitants). In 2011, 31.4% of the population were internet users. In June 2012 there were 4.7 m. Facebook users.

Territory and Population

Ecuador is bounded in the north by Colombia, in the east and south by Peru and in the west by the Pacific ocean. The total area of the country is 256,369 km², including the Galápagos Archipelago (8,010 km²), situated in the Pacific ocean about 960 km west of Ecuador, and comprising 13 islands and 19 islets. Census population in 2010, 14,483,449; density, 53 per km². In 2011, 67.6% lived in urban areas. The population is an amalgam of European, Amerindian and African origins. Some 41% of the population is Amerindian: Quechua, Shiwiar, Achuar and Zaparo. The official language is Spanish. Quechua and other languages are also spoken.

Tourism

Foreign visitors numbered 968,000 in 2009, of whom 735,000 were from elsewhere in the Americas and 197,000 from Europe.

Egypt

Jumhuriyat Misr al-Arabiya (Arab Republic of Egypt)

Factsheet

Capital: Cairo
Population estimate, 2015: 91.51 m.
GNI per capita, 2014: (PPP$) 10,512
HDI/world rank, 2014: 0.690/108
Internet domain extension: .eg

Civil Aviation

There are international airports at Cairo, Luxor, Borg El Arab (serving Alexandria), Hurghada and Sharm El-Sheikh. The national carrier is Egyptair, which in 2013 carried 8,513,000 passengers (7,020,000 on international flights). In 2012 Cairo handled 14,839,421 passengers (12,865,751 on international flights). Hurghada was the second busiest airport in 2012, with 7,134,032 passengers.

Climate

The climate is mainly dry, but there are winter rains along the Mediterranean coast. Elsewhere, rainfall is very low and erratic in its distribution. Winter temperatures are comfortable everywhere, but summer temperatures are very high, especially in the south. Cairo, Jan. 56 °F (13.3 °C), July 83 °F (28.3 °C). Annual rainfall 1.2″ (28 mm). Alexandria, Jan. 58 °F (14.4 °C), July 79 °F (26.1 °C). Annual rainfall 7″ (178 mm). Aswan, Jan. 62 °F (16.7 °C), July 92 °F (33.3 °C). Annual rainfall (trace). Giza, Jan. 55 °F (12.8 °C), July 78 °F (25.6 °C). Annual rainfall 16″ (389 mm). Ismailia, Jan. 56 °F (13.3 °C), July 84 °F (28.9 °C). Annual rainfall 1.5″ (37 mm). Luxor, Jan. 59 °F (15 °C), July 86 °F (30 °C). Annual rainfall (trace). Port Said, Jan. 58 °F (14.4 °C), July 78 °F (27.2 °C). Annual rainfall 3″ (76 mm).

Constitution and Government

Following the popular uprising that led to President Hosni Mubarak being deposed in Feb. 2011, a Provisional Constitution came into force to supersede the previous constitution dating from 1971. It in turn was replaced by a constitution passed into law by President Mohamed Morsi in Dec. 2012. However, he was deposed by the military in July 2013 and another new constitution was drafted by a 50-member constituent assembly. Under the terms of this revised constitution, the *President* may serve a maximum of two 4-year terms and may be impeached by parliament. The president, who must be at least 40 years old and an Egyptian citizen without a non-Egyptian parent or spouse, appoints the *Prime Minister* subject to parliamentary approval. The president also appoints the ministers of foreign affairs, the interior and justice. For two presidential terms (or 8 years) from the promulgation of the constitution, the military has the right to approve the appointment of the defence minister, who must be a military officer. Parliament consists of a single chamber, the *House of Representatives*, which has the right to call a referendum on early presidential elections with a two-thirds majority. Islam is the state religion and the principles of *Sharia* (Islamic law) are the main source of legislation. However, freedom of belief is guaranteed by the state, as is equality of the sexes.

Currency

The monetary unit is the *Egyptian pound* (EGP) of 100 *piastres*.

Defence

Conscription is selective, and for 12–36 months, depending on the level of education. Military expenditure totalled US$5,278 m. in 2013 (US$62 per capita), representing 2.0% of GDP.

Economy

In 2009 agriculture accounted for 13.7% of GDP, industry 37.3% and services 49.0%.

Labour

The labour force in 2013 was 28,974,000 (21,796,000 in 2003). 52.7% of the population aged 15–64 was economically active in 2013. In the same year 13.2% of the population was unemployed. Egypt had 69,000 people living in slavery according to the Walk Free Foundation's 2013 *Global Slavery Index*.

Press

In 2008 there were 18 dailies (17 paid-for and one free) with a total average circulation of 2.74 m. The leading dailies are *Al-Ahram* and *Al-Gomhuriya*.

Rail

In 2011 there were 5,195 km of state railways (1,435 mm gauge). Passenger-km travelled in 2011 came to 40.8 bn. and freight tonne-km in 2010 to 1.6 bn. There are tramway networks in Cairo, Heliopolis and Alexandria, and a metro (63 km) opened in Cairo in 1987.

Religion

Islam has constitutionally been the state religion since 1980. According to estimates by the Pew Research Center's Forum on Religion & Public Life, in 2010 there were 77.0 m. Muslims (94.9% of the population) and 4.1 m. Christians (5.1%). The vast majority of Muslims are Sunnis. Most Christians belong to the Coptic Orthodox Church of Alexandria but there are also some Protestants and Catholics. The Coptic Church is headed by a pope (Tawadros II, enthroned Nov. 2012). It has four metropolitan archbishops and four metropolitan bishops. In Feb. 2016 there was one cardinal in the Roman Catholic church.

Roads

In 2006 there were 99,672 km of roads, of which 81.0% were paved. Vehicles in use in 2006 (in 1,000): passenger cars, 2,372 (29 per 1,000 inhabitants in 2005); lorries and vans, 1,463; motorcycles and mopeds, 751; buses and coaches, 79. There were 12,295 fatalities as a result of road accidents in 2007.

Shipping

In Jan. 2009 there were 100 ships of 300 GT or over registered, totalling 923,000 GT. Of the 100 vessels registered, 39 were general cargo ships, 34 oil tankers, 11 bulk carriers, eight passenger ships, six chemical tankers and two container ships. The Egyptian-controlled fleet comprised 113 vessels of 1,000 GT or over in Jan. 2009, of which 59 were under the Egyptian flag and 54 under foreign flags. The leading ports are Adabeya, Alexandria, Damietta, Dekheila, Port Said and Sokhna.

Social Statistics

Births (est.), 2009, 2,217,000 (28.8 per 1,000 population); deaths, 477,000 (6.2). Annual population growth rate, 2005–10, 1.7%. In 2010, 73% of the population was under 40 years old. Life expectancy at birth, 2013, was 68.8 years for males and 73.6 years for females. Fertility rate, 2013, 2.8 births per woman; infant mortality, 2010, 19 per 1,000 live births. Egypt has made some of the best progress in recent years in reducing child mortality. The number of deaths per 1,000 live births among children under five was reduced from 86 in 1990 to 21 in 2012.

Telecommunications

In 2013 mobile phone subscriptions numbered 99,705,000 (1,215.1 per 1,000 persons) and there were 6,821,000 fixed telephone lines. In 2005 the Egyptian government sold 20% of its holding in Telecom Egypt. There were 25,553,000 wireless broadband subscriptions and 2,675,000 fixed broadband subscriptions in 2013. In June 2012 there were 11.3 m. Facebook users.

Territory and Population

Egypt is bounded in the east by Israel and Palestine, the Gulf of Aqaba and the Red Sea, south by Sudan, west by Libya and north by the Mediterranean. The total area is 1,009,450 km² (including 6,000 km² of inland water), but the cultivated and settled area, that is the Nile Valley, Delta and oases, covers only 35,000 km². A number of new desert cities are being developed to entice people away from the overcrowded Nile valley, where 99% of the population lives. The 2006 census population was 72,798,031; density 72.5 per km². Estimate, Jan. 2013: 83,667,047. In 2011, 43.5% of the population were urban. The capital, Cairo, had a census population in 2006 of 7,740,018. Other major cities, with populations at the 2006 census (in 1,000): Alexandria, 4,028; Giza, 3,022; Shubra Al Khayma, 1,026; Port Said, 571; Suez, 485. The official language is Arabic, although French and English are widely spoken.

Tourism

There were 9,845,056 tourists in 2011, down from a record 14,730,813 in 2010. Of 12,535,885 foreign visitors in 2009 the main countries of origin were: Russia (2,035,330); UK (1,346,724); Germany (1,202,339).

El Salvador

República de El Salvador (Republic of El Salvador)

Factsheet

Capital: San Salvador
Population estimate, 2015: 6.13 m.
GNI per capita, 2014: (PPP$) 7,349
HDI/world rank, 2014: 0.666/116
Internet domain extension: .sv

Civil Aviation

The main airport is Monseñor Óscar Arnulfo Romero International Airport (commonly known as Comalapa International Airport) in San Salvador. The national carrier is Taca International Airlines. It flies to various destinations in the USA, Mexico and all Central American countries. In 2012 scheduled airline traffic of El Salvador-based carriers flew 86.1 m. km; passenger-km totalled 5.6 bn. in the same year. In 2012 El Salvador International handled 2,113,740 passengers (2,051,636 on international flights) and 23,363 tonnes of freight.

Climate

Despite its proximity to the equator, the climate is warm rather than hot, and nights are cool inland. Light rains occur in the dry season from Nov. to April, while the rest of the year has heavy rains, especially on the coastal plain. San Salvador, Jan. 71 °F (21.7 °C), July 75 °F (23.9 °C). Annual rainfall 71″ (1,775 mm). San Miguel, Jan. 77 °F (25 °C), July 83 °F (28.3 °C). Annual rainfall 68″ (1,700 mm).

Constitution and Government

A new constitution was enacted in Dec. 1983. Executive power is vested in a *President* and *Vice-President* elected for a non-renewable term of 5 years. There is a *Legislative Assembly* of 84 members elected by universal suffrage and proportional representation: 64 locally and 20 nationally, for a term of 3 years.

Currency

The *dollar* (USD) replaced the *colón* as the legal currency of El Salvador in 2003.

Defence

There is selective conscription for 12 months. In 2013 defence expenditure totalled US$154 m. (US$25 per capita), representing 0.6% of GDP.

Economy

Agriculture accounted for 12.6% of GDP in 2010, industry 26.9% and services 60.5%.

Labour

The labour force in 2013 was 2,712,000 (2,333,000 in 2003). 65.5% of the population aged 15–64 was economically active in 2013. In the same year 5.9% of the population was unemployed. El Salvador had 10,000 people living in slavery according to the Walk Free Foundation's 2013 *Global Slavery Index*.

Press

In 2005 there were five daily newspapers with a combined circulation of 250,000.

Rail

There are 555 km of 914 mm gauge railway. The railway was closed from 2002–06 but a limited service resumed in 2007.

Religion

In 2010 there were an estimated 3.16 m. Roman Catholics (51% of the population) and 2.21 m. Protestants (36% of the population) according to the Pew Research Center's Forum on Religion & Public Life, with 680,000 people religiously unaffiliated. There is an archbishop in San Salvador and bishops at Chalatenango, San Miguel, San Vicente, Santa Ana, Santiago de María, Sonsonate and Zacatecoluca.

Roads

In 2011 there were 7,298 km of roads, 53.2% of which were paved. Vehicles in use in 2011: passenger cars, 331,200; trucks and vans, 275,000. There were 12,396 road accidents in 2009 resulting in 1,033 fatalities.

Shipping

The main ports are Acajutla (which handled 5.86 m. tonnes of cargo in 2008) and Cutuco.

Social Statistics

2008 births (est.), 112,000; deaths (est.), 32,000. Rates (2008, per 1,000 population): births (est.), 18.3; deaths (est.), 5.2. Life expectancy at birth in 2013 was 67.8 years for males and 77.1 years for females. Annual population growth rate, 2005–10, 0.5%. Infant mortality, 2010, 14 per 1,000 live births; fertility rate, 2008, 2.3 births per woman. Abortion is illegal.

Telecommunications

The telephone system has been privatized and is owned by two international telephone companies. In 2010 there were 1,000,900 landline telephone subscriptions (equivalent to 161.6 per 1,000 inhabitants) and 7,700,300 mobile phone subscriptions (or 1,243.4 per 1,000 inhabitants). In 2010, 15.9% of the population were internet users. In Dec. 2011 there were 1.3 m. Facebook users.

Territory and Population

El Salvador is bounded in the northwest by Guatemala, northeast and east by Honduras and south by the Pacific Ocean. The area (including 247 km² of inland lakes) is 21,040 km². Population (2007 census), 5,744,113 (female 53%), giving a population density of 273 per km². In 2007, 62.7% of the population were urban. Some 2.5 m. Salvadoreans live abroad, mainly in the USA. The republic is divided into 14 departments. The official language is Spanish.

Tourism

There were 1,091,000 non-resident tourists in 2009 (excluding same-day visitors), down from 1,385,000 in 2008.

Equatorial Guinea

República de Guinea Ecuatorial (Republic of Equatorial Guinea)

Factsheet

Capital: Malabo
Population estimate, 2015: 799,000
GNI per capita, 2014: (PPP$) 21,056
HDI/world rank, 2014: 0.587/138
Internet domain extension: .gq

Civil Aviation

There is an international airport at Malabo. There were international flights in 2010 to Addis Ababa, Casablanca, Douala, Frankfurt, Madrid, Nairobi and Paris. In 2009 Malabo handled 283,981 passengers.

Climate

The climate is equatorial, with alternate wet and dry seasons. In Rio Muni, the wet season lasts from Dec. to Feb.

Constitution and Government

A Constitution was approved in a plebiscite in Aug. 1982 by 95% of the votes cast and was amended in Jan. 1995. It provided for an 11-member Council of State, and for a 41-member House of Representatives of the People. The President presides over a Council of Ministers. On 12 Oct. 1987 a single new political party was formed as the *Partido Democrático de Guinea Ecuatorial.* A referendum on 17 Nov. 1991 approved the institution of multi-party democracy, and a law to this effect was passed in Jan. 1992. The electorate is restricted to citizens who have resided in Equatorial Guinea for at least 10 years. A parliament created as a result, the *Cámara de Representantes del Pueblo* (*House of People's Representatives*), has 100 seats, with members elected for a 5-year term by proportional representation in multi-member constituencies. In Nov. 2011 further constitutional amendments were approved by referendum. Official results indicated 97.7% support and turnout of 91.8%, although opposition parties alleged fraud. The amendments relaxed restrictions on the number of terms the *President* can serve and on the age of incumbents (previously set at between 40 and 75 years old), and provide for the creation of a *Senate.* The Senate has 75 members of whom 55 are elected and 15 appointed by the president, with five other *ex officio* members. A new position of *Vice President* was established, to be appointed by the President.

Currency

On 2 Jan. 1985 the country joined the Franc Zone and the *ekpwele* was replaced by the *franc CFA* (XAF) which now has a parity value of 655.957 francs CFA to one euro.

Defence

In 2011 defence expenditure totalled an estimated US$8 m. (around US$12 per capita).

Economy

Crude petroleum contributed 58.8% to GDP in 2009; followed by construction, 18.4%; manufacturing, 13.4%.

Labour

In 2010 the estimated economically active population was 270,000 (69% males). The wage-earning non-agricultural workforce is small.

Press

There are no daily newspapers, although there are a number of periodicals that are published at varying degrees of regularity.

Religion

According to the Pew Research Center's Forum on Religion & Public Life, an estimated 81% of the population in 2010 was Roman Catholic. There are also small Protestant and Muslim minorities.

Roads

In 2015 the road network covered an estimated 2,700 km, around two-thirds of which are paved.

Shipping

Bata is the main port, handling mainly timber. The other ports are Luba, formerly San Carlos, in Bioko, and Malabo, Evinayong and Mbini on the mainland. In Jan. 2009 there were seven ships of 300 GT or over registered, totalling 5,000 GT.

Social Statistics

2008 estimates: births, 25,000; deaths, 10,000. Rates (2008 estimates, per 1,000 population); birth, 38.0; death, 15.0. Life expectancy (2013): male, 51.7 years; female, 54.6. Annual population growth rate, 2000–08, 2.8%. Infant mortality, 2010, 81 per 1,000 live births; fertility rate, 2008, 5.3 births per woman.

Telecommunications

In 2010 there were 13,500 main (fixed) telephone lines. In the same year mobile phone subscribers numbered 399,000 (570.1 per 1,000 persons). There were 60.0 internet users per 1,000 inhabitants in 2010.

Territory and Population

The mainland part of Equatorial Guinea is bounded in the north by Cameroon, east and south by Gabon, and west by the Gulf of Guinea, in which lie the islands of Bioko (called Macías Nguema from 1973 to 1979 and before that Fernando Pó) and Annobón (called Pagalu from 1973 to 1979). The total area is 28,051 km^2 (10,831 sq. miles). Although the population at the last census in 2015 was provisionally given as 1,222,442, the United Nations does not consider this to be an accurate figure. In 2011, 39.9% of the population were urban. The seven provinces are grouped into two regions—Continental (C), chief town Bata; and Insular (I), chief town Malabo. In 2014 the capital, Malabo, had an estimated population of 145,000. The main ethnic group on the mainland is the Fang, which comprises 85% of the total population; there are several minority groups along the coast and adjacent islets. The official languages are French, Portuguese and Spanish.

Tourism

The tourist industry is undeveloped and the tourism infrastructure is almost non-existent.

Eritrea

Hagere Ertra (State of Eritrea)

Factsheet

Capital: Asmara
Population estimate, 2015: 5.23 m.
GNI per capita, 2014: (PPP$) 1,130
HDI/world rank, 2014: 0.391/186
Internet domain extension: .er

Civil Aviation

There is an international airport at Asmara (Yohannes IV Airport). In 2010 there were scheduled flights to Cairo, Dubai, Frankfurt, Jeddah, Khartoum, Milan, Nairobi, Rome and Sana'a. In 2012 Asmara handled 211,811 passengers (200,248 on international flights) and 2,705 tonnes of freight.

Climate

Massawa, Jan. 78 °F (25.6 °C), July 94 °F (34.4 °C). Annual rainfall 8″ (193 mm).

Constitution and Government

A referendum to approve independence was held on 23–25 April 1993. The electorate was 1,173,506. 99.8% of votes cast were in favour. The transitional government consists of the *President* and a 150-member *National Assembly*. It elects the President, who in turn appoints the *State Council* made up of 14 ministers and the governors of the ten provinces. The President chairs both the State Council and the National Assembly. Eritrea is a single-party state.

Currency

The *nakfa* (ERN) replaced the Ethiopian currency, the *birr*, in 1997.

Defence

Conscripts (both male and female) are subjected to 6 months military training and 12 months work on national reconstruction. It has since been reduced to 16 months. The total strength of all forces was estimated at 201,750 in 2011. Defence expenditure totalled an estimated US$78 m. in 2011 (approximately US$13 per capita and around 3% of GDP).

Economy

In 2010 public administration and defence contributed 27.7% to GDP; followed by trade and hotels, 19.1%; agriculture and fishing, 17.1%; and construction, 13.6%.

Labour

In 2010 the estimated labour force was 2,230,000 (55% males). Eritrea had 44,000 people living in slavery according to the Walk Free Foundation's 2013 *Global Slavery Index*.

Press

In 2008 there were three government newspapers, one published three times a week and the others once a week. In Sept. 2001 the government closed down the country's eight independent newspapers. In the 2013 *World Press Freedom Index*, compiled by Reporters Without Borders, Eritrea ranked 179th and last out of the 179 countries covered. A number of journalists have been jailed.

Rail

In 2000 the reconstruction of the 117 km Massawa-Asmara line reached Embatkala, thus opening up an 80 km stretch from Massawa on the coast. In 2003 the line was rebuilt right through to Asmara.

Religion

According to the Pew Research Center's Forum on Religion & Public Life, in 2010 the population was an estimated 63% Christian (mainly Eastern Orthodox but also Catholics, in the south) and 37% Muslim (mainly Sunnis, along the coast and in the north).

Roads

There are some 14,000 km of roads including a number of asphalted highways. In 2007 there were 6.4 passenger cars per 1,000 inhabitants. About 500 buses operate regular services.

Shipping

Massawa is the main port; Assab used to be the main port for imports to Ethiopia. Both were free ports for Ethiopia until the onset of hostilities. In Jan. 2009 there were five ships of 300 GT or over registered, totalling 12,000 GT.

Social Statistics

2008 births (estimates), 182,000; deaths, 42,000. Estimated birth rate in 2008 was 37.0 per 1,000 population; estimated death rate, 12.4. Annual population growth rate, 2000–08, 3.7%. Life expectancy at birth, 2013, was 60.5 years for males and 65.2 years for females. Infant mortality, 2010, 42 per 1,000 live births; fertility rate, 2008, 4.6 births per woman.

Telecommunications

In 2011 there were 58,000 landline telephone subscriptions (equivalent to 10.7 per 1,000 inhabitants) and 241,900 mobile phone subscriptions (or 44.7 per 1,000 inhabitants). In 2010, 5.4% of the population were internet users.

Territory and Population

Eritrea is bounded in the northeast by the Red Sea, southeast by Djibouti, south by Ethiopia and west by Sudan. Some 300 islands form the Dahlak Archipelago, most of them uninhabited. Its area is 117,600 km² (45,410 sq. miles), including 16,600 km² (6,410 sq. miles) of inland waters. There has not been a census since Eritrea became independent in 1993. United Nations population estimate, 2010, 4.69 m.; density, 46 per km². 22.1% of the population were urban in 2011. There are six regions: Anseba, Debub, Debubawi Keyih Bahri, Gash Barka, Maekel and Semenawi Keyih Bahri. The capital is Asmara (2014 estimated population, 775,000). Other large towns are Keren, Teseney and Mendefera. Arabic and Tigrinya are the official languages.

Tourism

There were 79,000 foreign visitors in 2009, up from 70,000 in 2008.

Estonia

Eesti Vabariik (Republic of Estonia)

Factsheet

Capital: Tallinn
Population estimate, 2015: 1.31 m.
GNI per capita, 2014: (PPP$) 25,214
HDI/world rank, 2014: 0.861/30
Internet domain extension: .ee

Civil Aviation

There is an international airport at Tallinn (Lennart Meri International Airport), which handled 2.0 m. passengers (99% on international flights) and over 19,400 tonnes of freight and mail in 2014. The national carrier Estonian Air ceased operations and declared bankruptcy in Dec. 2015. The airline was 97.3% state-owned; in 2014 it carried 553,147 passengers (96% on scheduled flights). Estonian Air operated year-round services in 2014 to Amsterdam, Brussels, Copenhagen, Kyiv, Moscow, Oslo, St Petersburg, Stockholm, Trondheim and Vilnius, plus a number of seasonal routes.

Climate

Because of its maritime location Estonia has a moderate climate, with cool summers and mild winters. Average daily temperatures in 2008: Jan. −1.5 °C; July 17.0 °C. Rainfall is heavy, 600–800 mm per year, and evaporation low.

Constitution and Government

A draft constitution drawn up by a constitutional assembly was approved by 91.1% of votes cast at a referendum on 28 June 1992. Turnout was 66.6%. The constitution came into effect on 3 July 1992. It defines Estonia as a 'democratic state guided by the rule of law, where universally recognized norms of international law are an inseparable part of the legal system.' It provides for a 101-member national assembly (*Riigikogu*) elected for 4-year terms. There are 12 electoral districts with eight to 12 mandates each. The head of state is the *President*, elected by the Riigikogu for 5-year terms.

Currency

On 1 Jan. 2011 the euro (EUR) replaced the *kroon* (EEK) as the legal currency of Estonia at the irrevocable conversion rate of 15.6466 krooni to one euro.

Defence

The President is the head of national defence. Conscription is 8–11 months for men and voluntary for women. Conscientious objectors may opt for 16 months civilian service instead. Defence expenditure in 2013 totalled US$480 m. (US$379 per capita), representing 2.0% of GDP. The Estonian Defence Forces (EDF) regular component is divided into the Army, the Air Force and the Navy.

Economy

Agriculture contributed 4% of GDP in 2012, industry 29% and services 67%.

Labour

The workforce in 2010 totalled 686,800, of whom 570,900 were employed. The average monthly gross wage in the fourth quarter of 2011 was €865. The unemployment rate in Nov. 2015 was 6.5% (down from 7.4% in 2014 as a whole). Retirement age was 63 years for men and 61 years for women in 2012 although the female retirement age has increased gradually since then and is now 63. From 2017 the retirement age for both sexes will be increased gradually to reach 65 years in 2026.

Press

In 2014 there were ten daily newspapers (combined circulation of 178,000) and 27 non-dailies (302,000). *The Baltic Times* is an English-language weekly covering news from Estonia, Latvia and Lithuania.

Rail

Length of railways in 2009 was 919 km (1,520 mm gauge), of which 131 km was electrified. In 2009, 4.9 m. passengers and 45.9 m. tonnes of freight were carried.

Religion

There is freedom of religion in Estonia and no state church, although the population was traditionally seen as Lutheran. The Estonian Orthodox Church owed allegiance to Constantinople until it was forcibly brought under Moscow's control in 1940; a synod of the free Estonian Orthodox Church was established in Stockholm. Returning from exile, it registered itself in 1993 as the Estonian Apostolic Orthodox Church. By an agreement in 1996 between the Moscow and Constantinople Orthodox Patriarchates, there are now two Orthodox jurisdictions in Estonia. According to the Pew Research Center's Forum on Religion & Public Life, an estimated 59.6% of the population in 2010 had no religious affiliation and 39.9% were Christian. There was also a small Muslim minority. Among Christians, 51% in 2010 were Lutherans and 45% Orthodox.

Roads

As of 1 Jan. 2009 there were 16,487 km of national roads (28.4% of the total Estonian road network of 58,034 km). In Dec. 2010 there were 552,684 registered passenger cars in use, plus 81,204 lorries, 4,167 buses and 19,671 motorcycles. There were 1,340 road accidents and 78 fatalities in 2010.

Shipping

There were 11 commercial ports and five ports offering international passenger services in 2009. Tallinn handled 31.6 m. tonnes of cargo traffic in 2009 (82% of total transport of freight through Estonian ports). In 2009, 7.26 m. passengers travelled through the port of Tallinn (more than 80% on the Tallinn-Helsinki route). In Jan. 2009 the Estonian-controlled fleet comprised 108 vessels of 1,000 GT or over, of which 87 were under foreign flags.

Social Statistics

2012 registered births, 14,056; deaths, 15,450. Rates (per 1,000 population): birth, 10.9; death, 12.0. There were 7,915 registered abortions in 2012, including 6,056 legally induced abortions. Expectation of life in 2011 was 71.4 years for males and 81.3 for females. The annual population growth rate in the period 2005–10 was −0.1%. The suicide rate was 18.1 per 100,000 population in 2008 (rate among males, 30.6). The rate has more than halved in 13 years, having been 40.1 per 100,000 in 1995. Infant mortality in 2010 was four per 1,000 births. In 2012 total fertility rate was 1.6 births per woman.

Telecommunications

In 2011 there were 470,500 landline telephone subscriptions (equivalent to 351.0 per 1,000 inhabitants) and 1,863,000 mobile phone subscriptions (or 1,389.8 per 1,000 inhabitants). In 2011, 76.5% of the population were internet users. In March 2012 there were 448,000 Facebook users. In 2000 the Estonian parliament voted to guarantee internet access to its citizens.

Territory and Population

Estonia is bounded in the west and north by the Baltic Sea, east by Russia and south by Latvia. There are 1,521 offshore islands, of which the largest are Saaremaa and Hiiumaa, but only 12 are permanently inhabited. Area, 45,227 km² (17,462 sq. miles). The census population in Dec. 2011 was 1,294,455 (693,929 females), giving a density of 27.6 per km². In 2010, 69.5% of the population lived in urban areas. Of the whole population, Estonians accounted for 68.7% in 2011, Russians 24.8% and Ukrainians 1.7%. The capital is Tallinn (2011 population, 393,222 or 31.5%). Other large towns are Tartu (97,600), Narva (58,663), Pärnu (39,728) and Kohtla-Järve (37,201). In 2011 there were 15 counties, 47 cities and 193 rural municipalities. The official language is Estonian.

Tourism

In 2011, 808,000 non-resident tourists and 918,000 Estonians stayed in holiday accommodation. Of the foreign tourists most were from Finland (841,000), followed by Russia (203,000), Germany (104,000), Sweden (86,000) and Latvia (85,000).

Ethiopia

Ye-Ityoppya Federalawi Dimokrasiyawi Ripeblik (Federal Democratic Republic of Ethiopia)

Factsheet

Capital: Addis Ababa
Population estimate, 2015: 99.39 m.
GNI per capita, 2014: (PPP$) 1,428
HDI/world rank, 2014: 0.442/174
Internet domain extension: .et

Civil Aviation

There are international airports at Addis Ababa (Bole) and Dire Dawa. The national carrier is the state-owned Ethiopian Airlines, which in 2013 served 79 international and 18 domestic destinations. In the same year it carried 5,594,000 passengers (4,916,000 on international flights). In 2012 Addis Ababa (Bole) handled 7,511,465 passengers and 153,395 tonnes of freight.

Climate

The wide range of latitude produces many climatic variations between the high, temperate plateaus and the hot, humid lowlands. The main rainy season lasts from June to Aug., with light rains from Feb. to April, but the country is very vulnerable to drought. Addis Ababa, Jan. 59 °F (15 °C), July 59 °F (15 °C). Annual rainfall 50″ (1,237 mm). Harar, Jan. 65 °F (18.3 °C), July 64 °F (17.8 °C). Annual rainfall 35″ (897 mm). Massawa, Jan. 78 °F (25.6 °C), July 94 °F (34.4 °C). Annual rainfall 8″ (193 mm).

Constitution and Government

A 548-member constituent assembly was elected on 5 June 1994; turnout was 55%. The EPRDF gained 484 seats. On 8 Dec. 1994 it unanimously adopted a new federal constitution which became effective on 22 Aug. 1995. It provided for the creation of a federation of nine regions based (except the capital and the southern region) on a predominant ethnic group. These regions have the right of secession after a referendum. The *President*, a largely ceremonial post, is elected for a 6-year term by both chambers of parliament (renewable once only). The lower house is the 547-member *House of People's Representatives*; the upper house the 153-member *House of the Federation*.

Currency

The *birr* (ETB), of 100 *cents*, is the unit of currency.

Defence

In 2013 defence expenditure totalled US$351 m. (US$4 per capita), representing 0.8% of GDP.

Economy

Agriculture accounted for 48.8% of GDP in 2012, industry 10.1% and services 41.1%.

Labour

The estimated labour force in 2010 was 41,310,000 (52% males), up from 28,996,000 in 2000. Coffee provides a livelihood to a quarter of the population. Ethiopia had 0.65 m. people living in slavery according to the Walk Free Foundation's 2013 *Global Slavery Index*, the fifth highest total of any country.

Press

In 2008 there were three paid-for daily newspapers with a combined circulation of 92,000 and 54 paid-for non-dailies. In the 2013 *World Press Freedom Index* compiled by Reporters Without Borders, Ethiopia was ranked 137th out of 179 countries.

Rail

The Ethiopian-Djibouti Railway has a length of 781 km (metre gauge), but much of the route is in need of renovation. There are still passenger services from Dire Dawa, Ethiopia's second largest city, to Djibouti. However, there have not been services between Addis Ababa and Dire Dawa for many years. A new line linking Ethiopia and Djibouti is currently being built by China Civil Engineering Construction Corporation. It is expected to become operational during 2016. Passenger-km travelled in 2005 came to 145 m. and freight tonne-km to 118 m.

Religion

According to estimates by the Pew Research Center's Forum on Religion & Public Life, 62.8% of the population in 2010 were Christians, 34.6% were Muslims and 2.6% folk religionists. Among the Christians, 69% in 2010 were Ethiopian Orthodox and 30% Protestants. The predominant church in the country is the Ethiopian Orthodox Tewahedo Church; the Head of all Archbishops and Patriarch of the Ethiopian Orthodox Tewahedo Church is Abune Mathias (enthroned 3 March 2013). In Feb. 2016 there was one cardinal in the Roman Catholic church.

Roads

There were 44,359 km of roads in 2007. Passenger cars in use in 2007 numbered 70,900 (one per 1,000 inhabitants) and there were also 149,000 lorries and vans, and 17,100 buses and coaches. In 2007 there were 2,517 deaths in road accidents.

Shipping

In Jan. 2009 there were nine ships of 300 GT or over registered, totalling 118,000 GT.

Social Statistics

Births, 2008 estimate, 3,086,000; deaths, 954,000. Rates per 1,000 population, 2008 estimates: births, 38.2; deaths, 11.8. Expectation of life at birth in 2013 was 62.0 years for males and 65.3 years for females. Annual population growth rate, 2000–08, 2.6%; infant mortality, 2010, 68 per 1,000 live births; fertility rate, 2008, 5.3 births per woman.

Telecommunications

The state-owned Ethio Telecom is the sole telecommunications service provider. There were 908,900 fixed telephone lines in 2010 (11.0 per 1,000 inhabitants). Mobile phone subscribers numbered 6.52 m. in 2010. There were 7.5 internet users per 1,000 inhabitants in 2010. Fixed internet subscriptions totalled 74,600 in 2009 (0.9 per 1,000 inhabitants). Ethiopia's internet penetration rate is one of the lowest in Africa. In June 2012 there were 599,000 Facebook users.

Territory and Population

Ethiopia is bounded in the northeast by Eritrea, east by Djibouti and Somalia, south by Kenya and west by South Sudan and Sudan. It has a total area of 1,127,127 km^2. The secession of Eritrea in 1993 left Ethiopia without a coastline. The 2007 census population was 73,750,932 (36,533,802 females); density, 65.4 per km^2. In 2007, 83.9% of the population lived in rural areas. Ethiopia has 11 administrative divisions-eight states (Afar, Amhara, Benshangul/Gumaz, Gambella, Oromia, the Peoples of the South, Somalia and Tigre) and three cities (Addis Ababa, Dire Dawa and Harar). The population of the capital, Addis Ababa, was 2,739,551 in 2007. Other large towns (2007 populations): Dire Dawa, 233,224; Nazret, 220,212; Mekele, 215,914; Gonder, 207,044. There are seven major ethnic groups (in % of total population in 2007): Oromo, 35%; Amhara, 27%; Somali, 6%; Tigrinya, 6%; Sidamo, 4%; Gurage, 3%; Welaita, 2%. The *de facto* official language is Amharic (which uses its own alphabet). Oromo is also widely spoken. In total there are around 80 local languages.

Tourism

In 2011 there were 523,000 international tourist arrivals (excluding same-day visitors), up from 330,000 in 2006; tourist spending (excluding passenger transport) totalled US$1,998 m. in 2011, up from US$639 m. in 2006.

Fiji

Matanitu Tugalala o Viti (Republic of Fiji)

Factsheet

Capital: Suva
Population estimate, 2015: 892,000
GNI per capita, 2014: (PPP$) 7,493
HDI/world rank, 2014: 0.727/90=
Internet domain extension: .fj

Civil Aviation

There are international airports at Nadi and Suva. The national carrier is Fiji Airways (51% government-owned). In 2013 it provided services to Australia, Hong Kong, New Zealand, USA and a number of Pacific island nations. In 2012 Nadi handled 1,856,667 passengers (1,602,216 on international flights).

Climate

A tropical climate, but oceanic influences prevent undue extremes of heat or humidity. The S. E. Trades blow from May to Nov., during which time nights are cool and rainfall amounts least. Suva, Jan. 80 °F (26.7 °C), July 73 °F (22.8 °C). Annual rainfall 117″ (2,974 mm).

Constitution and Government

Parliament was reopened in Oct. 2001, having been suspended following a coup in May 2000. In 2006 another coup brought Commodore Frank Bainimarama to power but on 9 April 2009 the court of appeal declared his government illegal and he stood down. The next day the president repealed the constitution and assumed all governing power. The court was disbanded and Bainimarama's government restored. In March 2012 he disbanded the Great Council of Chiefs, which had existed in name only since April 2007 when Bainimarama suspended its operations. It had previously been responsible for appointing the president and 14 members of the Senate. A new constitution received presidential assent on 6 Sept. 2013 and came into immediate effect. It was drawn up by the government itself after proposals from an independent Constitutional Committee were rejected. The new constitution established a single-chamber 50-seat *Parliament* as the country's supreme authority, elected every 4 years by proportional representation from a single national constituency. The voting age was reduced from 21 to 18. The executive authority of the State is vested in the *President*, who is appointed by Parliament. The presidential term of office is 3 years and may be renewed once.

Currency

The unit of currency is the *Fiji dollar* (FJD) of 100 *cents*.

Defence

In 2013 defence expenditure totalled US$58 m. (US$65 per capita), representing 1.4% of GDP.

Economy

Agriculture accounted for 13% of GDP in 2009, industry 18% and services 69%.

Labour

The labour force in 2013 was 345,000 (314,000 in 2003). 57.2% of the population aged 15–64 was economically active in 2013. In the same year 8.3% of the population was unemployed.

Press

In 2008 there were three national dailies with a combined circulation of 40,000.

Rail

Fiji Sugar Cane Corporation runs 600 mm gauge railways at four of its mills on Viti Levu and Vanua Levu, totalling 597 km.

Religion

In 2010 the population was 64.4% Christian according to estimates by the Pew Research Center's Forum on Religion & Public Life, with 27.9% Hindu and 6.3% Muslim. Among Christians, 84% in 2010 were Protestants and 15% Catholics.

Roads

The road network covers some 7,500 km. There were a total of 94,400 passenger cars and 48,000 lorries and vans in 2007. In 2006, 89 fatalities were caused by road accidents.

Shipping

The three main ports are Suva, Lautoka and Levuka. The gross registered tonnage of ocean-going shipping entering the ports in 2007 totalled 8,361,785 GRT including liquid bulk carriers of 2,530,718 GRT. A total of 694 foreign vessels called into Suva port in 2007, 348 into Lautoka and 93 into Levuka. The inter-island shipping fleet is made up of private and government vessels.

Social Statistics

2009 estimates: births, 19,000; deaths, 6,000. Rates, 2009 estimates (per 1,000 population): birth, 22; death, 7. Annual population growth rate, 2005–10, 0.9%. Life expectancy at birth in 2013 was 67.0 years for males and 73.0 years for females. Infant mortality, 2010, 15 per 1,000 live births; fertility rate, 2013, 2.6 births per woman.

Telecommunications

In 2013 there were 70,725 main (fixed) telephone lines and mobile phone subscriptions numbered 930,406 (105.6 per 100 persons). There were 148.2 internet users per 1,000 inhabitants in 2010. In 2009 there were 24.7 fixed broadband subscriptions per 1,000 inhabitants and 8.3 mobile broadband subscriptions per 1,000 inhabitants. In Dec. 2011 there were 163,000 Facebook users.

Territory and Population

Fiji comprises 332 islands and islets (about one-third are inhabited) lying between 15 and 22 S. lat. and 174 E. and 178 W. long. Total area, 18,333 km² (7,078 sq. miles). Total population (2007 census), 837,271 (females,

410,095); ethnic groups: Fijian, 475,739; Indian, 313,798; other Pacific islanders, 15,311; part-European/European, 13,724; Rotuman, 10,335; Chinese, 4,704; other, 3,660. Population density (2007), 45.7 per km²; 50.7% of the population lived in urban areas in 2007. The population of the capital, Suva (including Nasinu), was 173,137 at the 2007 census. Other large towns are Lautoka (52,220), Nausori (47,604) and Nadi (42,284). English, Fijian and Hindustani are all official languages.

Tourism

There were 542,000 foreign tourists in 2009 (excluding same-day visitors), down from 585,000 in 2008.

Finland

Suomen Tasavalta—Republiken Finland (Republic of Finland)

Factsheet
Capital: Helsinki
Population estimate, 2015: 5.50 m.
GNI per capita, 2014: (PPP$) 38,695
HDI/world rank, 2014: 0.883/24
Internet domain extension: .fi

Civil Aviation

The main international airport is at Helsinki (Vantaa), and there are also international airports at Turku, Tampere, Rovaniemi and Oulu. The national carrier is Finnair. Scheduled traffic of Finnish airlines covered 177 m. km in 2012. The number of passengers in 2012 was 10.6 m. and the number of passenger-km 24,953 m.; the air transport of freight and mail amounted to 711.7 m. tonne-km. Helsinki-Vantaa handled 12,611,187 passengers in 2009 (10,238,302 on international flights) and 122,107 tonnes of freight and mail. Oulu is the second busiest airport, handling 688,860 passengers in 2009, and Tampere-Pirkkala the third busiest, with 628,105 in 2009.

Climate

A quarter of Finland lies north of the Arctic Circle. The climate is severe in winter, which lasts about 6 months, but mean temperatures in the south and southwest are less harsh, 21 °F (−6 °C). In the north, mean temperatures may fall to 8.5 °F (−13 °C). Snow covers the ground for 3 months in the south and for over 6 months in the far north. Summers are short but quite warm, with occasional very hot days. Precipitation is light throughout the country, with one third falling as snow, the remainder mainly as rain in summer and autumn. Helsinki (Helsingfors), Jan. 30.2 °F (−1.0 °C), July 68.4 °F (20.2 °C). Annual rainfall 27.9″ (708.7 mm).

Constitution and Government

Finland is a republic governed by the constitution of 1 March 2000 (which replaced the previous constitution dating from 1919). Although the president used to choose who formed the government, under the new constitution it is the responsibility of parliament to select the prime minister. The government is in charge of domestic and EU affairs with the president responsible for foreign policy 'in co-operation with the government'. Parliament consists of one chamber (*Eduskunta*) of 200 members chosen by direct and proportional election by all citizens of 18 or over. The country is divided into 15 electoral districts, with a representation proportional to their population. Every citizen over the age of 18 is eligible for parliament, which is elected for 4 years, but can be dissolved sooner by the president. The *president* is elected for 6 years by direct popular vote. In the event of no candidate winning an absolute majority, a second round is held between the two most successful candidates.

Currency

On 1 Jan. 1999 the euro (EUR) became the legal currency in Finland at the irrevocable conversion rate of 5.94573 marks to one euro. The euro, which consists of 100 cents, has been in circulation since 1 Jan. 2002. On the introduction of the euro there was a 'dual circulation' period before the mark ceased to be legal tender on 28 Feb. 2002.

Defence

Conscript service is 6–12 months. Total strength of trained and equipped reserves is about 490,000 (to be 350,000). In 2013 defence expenditure totalled US$3,814 m. (US$724 per capita), representing 1.4% of GDP.

Economy

Agriculture accounted for 3.0% of GDP in 2013, industry 26.9% and services 70.1%.

Labour

In 2009 the labour force was 2,678,000 (51% males). Of this total, 71.5% of the economically active population worked in services (including 15.9% in trade and restaurants) and 15.4% in manufacturing. In Dec. 2015 unemployment was 9.5% (up from 8.7% in 2014 as a whole).

Press

Finland had 235 newspapers in 2014, of which 46 were dailies (45 paid-for and one free) and 189 non-dailies. The total circulation of all newspapers in 2014 was 2.2 m. In the same year Finland had 175 newspaper online editions. There were 2,471 registered periodicals in 2014. The bestselling newspapers in 2014 were *Helsingin Sanomat* (average daily circulation, 285,223 copies), *Ilta-Sanomat* (110,226) and *Aamulehti* (106,842). In 2014 a total of 10,352 book titles were published. In the 2013 *World Press Freedom Index* compiled by Reporters Without Borders, Finland was ranked first out of 179 countries.

Rail

In 2009 the total length of the line operated was 5,919 km (3,067 km electrified), all of it owned by the State. The gauge is 1,524 mm. In 2009, 67.6 m. passengers and 32.9 m. tonnes of freight were carried. There is a metro (21 km) and tram/light rail network (117 km) in Helsinki.

Religion

Liberty of conscience is guaranteed to members of all religions. National churches are the Lutheran National Church and the Greek Orthodox Church of Finland. The Lutheran Church is divided into nine dioceses (Turku being the archiepiscopal see) and some 460 parishes. The Greek Orthodox Church is divided into three bishoprics (Kuopio being the archiepiscopal see) and 27 parishes, in addition to which there are a monastery and a convent. Percentage of the total population at the end of 2009: Lutherans, 79.9; Greek Orthodox, 1.1; others, 1.3; not members of any religion, 17.7.

Roads

At 1 Jan. 2010 there were 78,161 km of public roads, of which 50,987 km were paved. At the end of 2009 there were 3,246,414 registered cars, 111,267 lorries, 332,645 vans and pick-ups, 13,017 buses and coaches and 12,821 special automobiles. Road accidents caused 279 fatalities in 2009.

Shipping

The total registered mercantile marine in 2009 was 644 vessels of 1,534,000 GRT. In 2009 the total number of vessels arriving in Finland from abroad was 30,238 and the goods discharged amounted to 45.1 m. tonnes. The goods loaded for export from Finnish ports amounted to 37.5 m. tonnes. The lakes, rivers and canals are navigable for about 9,747 km. Timber floating is still practised; in 2010 bundle floating was about 0.5 m. tonnes.

Social Statistics

Live births, 2009: 60,430; deaths, 49,883. In 2009 the rate per 1,000 population was: births, 11; deaths, 9; marriages, 6; infant deaths (per 1,000 live births), 2.6. Annual population growth rate, 1999–2009, 0.3%. In 2008 the suicide rate per 100,000 population was 30.7 among men and 8.5 among women, giving Finland one of the highest suicide rates in Europe. Life expectancy at birth, 2008, 76.3 years for males and 83.0 years for females. The most popular age range for marrying in 2008 was 25–29 for both males and females. Fertility rate, 2009, 1.9 births per woman.

Telecommunications

In 2012 mobile phone subscriptions numbered 9,320,000 (1,723.2 per 1,000 persons). In the same year there were 890,000 main (fixed) telephone lines. In Aug. 2010 around 99% of Finnish households owned at least one mobile phone. In 2013 there were 123.6 wireless broadband subscriptions per 100 inhabitants and 30.8 fixed broadband subscribers per 100. In March 2012 there were 2.1 m. Facebook users.

Territory and Population

Finland, a country of lakes and forests, is bounded in the northwest and north by Norway, east by Russia, south by the Baltic Sea and west by the Gulf of Bothnia and Sweden. At the most recent ten-yearly census on 31 Dec. 2010 the population was 5,375,276. The semi-autonomous province of the Åland Islands (Ahvenanmaa) occupies a special position as a demilitarized area and is 91% Swedish-speaking. Åland elects a 30-member parliament (*Lagting*), which in turn elects the provincial government (*Landskapsstyrelse*). It has a population of 28,354. The capital is Mariehamn (Maarianhamina). In 2009, 68.1% of the population lived in urban areas. Nearly one-fifth of the total population lives in the Helsinki metropolitan region. Finnish and Swedish are the official languages. Three Sami languages are spoken in Lapland.

Tourism

There were 2,220,267 foreign tourists in 2009; the income from tourism was €2,022 m. Major international tourist attractions include Uspensky Cathedral, Helsinki Cathedral and Suomenlinna (all in Helsinki). Helsinki's churches and Santa Park in Rovaniemi are particularly popular among foreigners, who account for the majority of their visitors.

France

République Française (French Republic)

Factsheet

Capital: Paris
Population estimate, 2015: 64.40 m
GNI per capita, 2014: (PPP$) 38,056
HDI/world rank, 2014: 0.888/22
Internet domain extension: .fr

Civil Aviation

The main international airports are at Paris (Charles de Gaulle), Paris (Orly), Nice-Côte d'Azur, Lyon (Satolas), Marseille-Provence, Beauvais-Tillé, Toulouse (Blagnac), Nantes (Atlantique), Bordeaux (Mérignac) and Lille (Lesquin). The national airline, Air France, was 54.4% state-owned but merged in Oct. 2003 with the Dutch carrier KLM to form Air France-KLM. In 2013 Air France-KLM carried 77.3 m. passengers and 1.3 m. tonnes of cargo on board its 552 aircraft. In 2012 Charles de Gaulle airport handled 61,611,934 passengers (56,201,242 on international flights) and 2,150,950 tonnes of freight.

Climate

The northwest has a moderate maritime climate, with small temperature range and abundant rainfall; inland, rainfall becomes more seasonal, with a summer maximum, and the annual range of temperature increases. Southern France has a Mediterranean climate, with mild moist winters and hot dry summers. Eastern France has a continental climate and a rainfall maximum in summer, with thunderstorms prevalent. Paris, Jan. 37 °F (3 °C), July 64 °F (18 °C). Annual rainfall 22.9″ (573 mm). Bordeaux, Jan. 41 °F (5 °C), July 68 °F (20 °C). Annual rainfall 31.4″ (786 mm). Lyon, Jan. 37 °F (3 °C), July 68 °F (20 °C). Annual rainfall 31.8″ (794 mm).

Constitution and Government

France is a decentralized republic, indivisible, secular, democratic and social; all citizens are equal before the law (Art. 1). National sovereignty resides with the people, who exercise it through their representatives and by referendums

(Art. 3). The head of state is the *President* (currently Emmanuel Macron, b. 1977 and assumed office in May 2017), who must be a French citizen, have attained the age of 18 years and be qualified to vote. The President sees that the Constitution is respected; ensures the regular functioning of the public authorities, as well as the continuity of the state; is the protector of national independence and territorial integrity (Art. 5). The President appoints (and dismisses) a Prime Minister and, on the latter's advice, appoints and dismisses the other members of the government (*Council of Ministers*) (Art. 8); presides over the Council of Ministers (Art. 9); may dissolve the National Assembly, after consultation with the Prime Minister and the Presidents of the two Houses (Art. 12); appoints to the civil and military offices of the state (Art. 13). Parliament consists of the National Assembly and the Senate. The *National Assembly* is elected by direct suffrage by the second ballot system (by which candidates winning 50% or more of the vote in their constituencies are elected, candidates winning less than 12.5% are eliminated and other candidates go on to a second round of voting); the Senate is elected by indirect suffrage (Art. 24). The *Constitutional Council* is composed of nine members whose term of office is 9 years (non-renewable), one-third every 3 years; three are appointed by the President of the Republic, three by the President of the National Assembly, three by the President of the Senate; in addition, former Presidents of the Republic are, by right, life members of the Constitutional Council (Art. 56). It oversees the fairness of the elections of the President (Art. 58) and Parliament (Art. 59), and of referendums (Art. 60), and acts as a guardian of the Constitution (Art. 61). The *Economic, Social and Environmental Council* advises on Government and Private Members' Bills (Art. 69). It comprises representatives of employers', workers' and farmers' organizations in each Department and Overseas Territory.

Currency

On 1 Jan. 1999 the euro (EUR) became the legal currency in France at the irrevocable conversion rate of 6.55957 francs to one euro. The euro, which consists of 100 cents, has been in circulation since 1 Jan. 2002. On the introduction of the euro there was a 'dual circulation' period before the franc ceased to be legal tender on 17 Feb. 2002.

Defence

The President of the Republic is the supreme head of defence policy and exercises command over the Armed Forces. He is the only person empowered to give the order to use nuclear weapons. He is assisted by the Council of Ministers, which studies defence problems, and by the Defence Council and the Restricted Defence Committee, which formulate directives. In 2013 defence expenditure totalled US$52,352 m. (equivalent to US$794 per capita). Defence spending as a proportion of GDP was 1.9% in 2013. The nuclear arsenal consisted of approximately 290 warheads in Jan. 2015 according to the Stockholm International Peace Research Institute.

Economy

Agriculture accounted for 1.7% of GDP in 2014, industry 19.4% and services 78.9%.

Labour

Of 30,031,000 people in employment in 2013. By sector, 74.5% worked in services (58.1% in 1980), 22.0% in industry and construction (33.1% in 1980) and 3.4% in agriculture (8.8% in 1980). Some 3.1 m. people work in the public sector at national and local level. The unemployment rate was 10.2% in Dec. 2015 (down slightly from 10.3% in both 2013 and 2014). The rate among the under 25s is more than double the overall national rate.

Press

There were 118 daily papers in 2014 (84 paid-for—of which 23 national—and 34 free). The leading dailies are: *Ouest-France* (average circulation, 732,000), *Le Figaro* (average circulation, 325,000), *Le Monde* (average circulation, 299,000), *Sud Ouest, La Voix du Nord, Le Parisien, L'Équipe* and *Le Dauphiné Libéré*. The *Journal du Dimanche* is the only national Sunday paper. In 2014 total average daily press circulation was 8.9 m. copies. The daily newspaper websites with the highest number of unique monthly visitors are *Le Figaro* (9,036 in Dec. 2014) and *Le Monde* (7,899 in Dec. 2014). A total of 72,139 book titles were published in 2012 (70,109 in 2011).

Rail

In 1938 all the independent railway companies were merged with the existing state railway system in a Société Nationale des Chemins de Fer Français (SNCF), which became a public industrial and commercial establishment in 1983. Legislation came into effect in 1997 which vested ownership of the railway infrastructure (track and signalling) in a newly established public corporation, the Réseau Ferré de France (RFF/French Rail Network). In 2010 the RFF-managed network totalled 29,473 km of track (15,424 km electrified). High-speed TGV lines link Paris to the southwest, southeast and east of France, and north from Paris and Lille to the Channel Tunnel (Eurostar).

Religion

A law of 1905 separated church and state. A survey conducted by the French Institute of Public Opinion in 2010 estimated that some 64% of the population was Roman Catholic, 28% non-religious/atheist, 3% Protestant and 5% belonged to other religions. In Feb. 2015 there were nine cardinals. The Catholic Church had 13,822 diocesan priests in 2011, down from 18,528 in 2001. There are generally estimated to be about 5 m.–6 m. Muslims in France. France has the third largest Jewish population, after Israel and the USA.

Roads

In 2007 there were 951,125 km of road, including 11,010 km of motorway and 9,115 km of highways and main roads. France has the longest road network in the EU. Around 90% of all freight is transported by road. In 2007 there were 30.70 m. passenger cars (498 per 1,000 inhabitants), 6.27 m. lorries and vans, and 83,000 buses and coaches. Road passenger traffic in 2007 totalled 775 bn. passenger-km. In 2007 there were 4,620 road deaths, down from 8,445 in 1997.

Shipping

In Jan. 2009 there were 232 ships of 300 GT or over registered, totalling 6,025,000 GT. Of the 232 vessels registered, 88 were passenger ships, 58 oil tankers, 43 general cargo ships, 26 container ships, 13 liquid gas tankers, three bulk carriers and there was one chemical tanker. The French-controlled fleet comprised 285 vessels of 1,000 GT or over in Jan. 2009, of which 164 were under foreign flags and 121 under the French flag. The chief ports are Marseille, Le Havre, Dunkerque, Calais and Saint-Nazaire. France has extensive inland waterways. Canals are administered by the public authority France Navigable Waterways (VNF). In 2006 there were approximately 8,800 km of navigable rivers and canals (the longest network in the EU), with a total traffic in 2009 of 68.0 m. tonnes.

Social Statistics

Births, 2013: 781,621; deaths, 558,408. Live birth rate (2011) was 12.5 per 1,000 population; death rate, 8.5; marriage rate, 3.7; divorce rate, 2.1. 52.9% of births in 2009 were outside marriage. In 2009 the average age at first marriage was 31.7 years for males and 29.8 years for females. Abortions were legalized in 1975; there were an estimated 209,300 in 2009. Life expectancy at birth, 2009, 77.7 years for males and 84.4 years for females. Annual population growth rate, 2005–10, 0.6%. In 2012 the suicide rate per 100,000 population was 15.1 (males, 24.9; females, 7.0). Infant mortality, 2010, three per 1,000 live births; fertility rate, 2013, 2.0 births per woman. In 2013 France received 60,234 asylum applications (35,404 in 2008), the third highest total after Germany and the USA. France legalized same-sex marriage in May 2013.

Telecommunications

France Télécom, the country's largest telecommunications operator, was founded in 1988 and rebranded as Orange on 1 July 2013. It is 13.45% state-owned. In 2013 there were 39.1 m. main (fixed) telephone lines. In 2012 mobile phone subscriptions numbered 62.3 m. (973.8 per 1,000 persons). The largest operators are Orange, with a 38% share of the market, and SFR, with a 30% share. There were 24.2 m. fixed internet subscriptions and 33.1 m. wireless broadband subscriptions in 2013. In March 2012 there were 23.5 m. Facebook users (37% of the population).

Territory and Population

France is bounded in the north by the English Channel (*La Manche*), northeast by Belgium and Luxembourg, east by Germany, Switzerland and Italy, south by the Mediterranean (with Monaco as a coastal enclave), southwest by Spain and Andorra, and west by the Atlantic Ocean. The total area of metropolitan France is 543,965 km^2. The population was 58,518,395 at the census of 1999 and 63,920,247 on 1 Jan. 2014 (density, 117.5 persons per km^2). In 2011, 85.9% of the population lived in urban areas. In 2004 there were 4.96 m. people of foreign extraction in France (8.1% of the population). There are 13 metropolitan regions, which are divided into 96 metropolitan *départements*. In 2015 these consisted of 36,529 communes. The official language is French.

Tourism

There were 83,633,000 foreign tourists in 2013; tourism receipts were US$56.7 bn. France is the most popular tourist destination in the world, and receipts from tourism in 2013 were exceeded only in the USA and Spain. In 2012, 83.4% of tourists were from elsewhere in Europe and 7.8% from the Americas. Most visitors come from Germany, the UK, Belgium/Luxembourg, Italy, the Netherlands and Switzerland. As at 1 Jan. 2014 there were 1,245,600 beds at 17,100 tourist hotels.

Gabon

République Gabonaise (Gabonese Republic)

Factsheet

Capital: Libreville
Population estimate, 2015: 1.73 m.
GNI per capita, 2014: (PPP$) 16,367
HDI/world rank, 2014: 0.684/110=
Internet domain extension: .ga

Civil Aviation

There are international airports at Libreville (Léon M'Ba Airport), Port-Gentil and Franceville (Masuku); scheduled internal services link these to a number of domestic airfields. Libreville, the main airport, handled 839,571 passengers and 18,268 tonnes of freight in 2012. In 2012 scheduled airline traffic of Gabonese-based carriers flew 2.6 m. km; passenger-km totalled 115 m. in the same year. Gabon Airlines was established in July 2006 as a successor to the bankrupt national carrier Air Gabon, but it ceased operations in 2011.

Climate

The climate is equatorial, with high temperatures and considerable rainfall. Mid-May to mid-Sept. is the long dry season, followed by a short rainy season, then a dry season again from mid-Dec. to mid-Feb., and finally a long rainy season once more. Libreville, Jan. 80 °F (26.7 °C), July 75 °F (23.9 °C). Annual rainfall 99″ (2,510 mm).

Constitution and Government

On 21 March 1997 the government presented to the Parliament legislation aimed at reforming the constitution in a number of key areas: notably, the bill mandated the creation of a Vice-President of the Republic, the extension of the presidential term of office from 5 to 7 years, and the transformation of the Senate into an Upper Chamber of Parliament. Gabon has a bicameral legislature, consisting of a 120-member *National Assembly* (with members elected by direct, popular vote to serve 5-year terms) and a 102-member *Senate* (elected for 6-year terms in single-seat constituencies by local and departmental councillors). In July 2003 Gabon's parliament approved an amendment to the constitution that allows the president to seek re-election indefinitely. The head of government is the *Prime Minister*, who appoints a Council of Ministers.

Currency

The unit of currency is the *franc CFA* (XAF) with a parity of 655.957 francs CFA to one euro.

Defence

In 2013 military expenditure totalled US$263 m. (US$161 per capita), representing 1.4% of GDP.

Economy

Agriculture accounted for 5% of GDP in 2009, industry 54% and services 41%. Gabon's 'shadow' (black market) economy is estimated to constitute approximately 47% of the country's official GDP.

Labour

The labour force in 2013 was 628,000 (472,000 in 2003). 62.5% of the population aged 15–64 was economically active in 2013. In the same year 20.3% of the population was unemployed. There is a 40-h working week. Gabon had 14,000 people living in slavery according to the Walk Free Foundation's 2013 *Global Slavery Index*.

Press

In 2008 there was one government-controlled daily newspaper (*L'Union*) with a circulation of 20,000.

Rail

The 669 km standard gauge Transgabonais railway runs from the port of Owendo to Franceville. Total length of railways, 2011, 810 km. In 2011 passenger-km travelled came to 118 m. and freight tonne-km to 2,417 m.

Religion

According to the Pew Research Center's Forum on Religion & Public Life, 76.5% of the population in 2010 was Christian and 11.2% Muslim, with 6.0% followers of folk religions; of the Christians, 69% were Catholics and 31% Protestants.

Roads

Gabon has some 10,000 km of roads. In 2010 there were about 195,000 registered vehicles. There were 252 deaths in road accidents in 2010.

Shipping

In Jan. 2009 there were 12 ships of 300 GT or over registered, totalling 6,000 GT. Owendo (near Libreville), Mayumba and Port-Gentil are the main ports. Rivers are an important means of inland transport.

Social Statistics

2008 estimates: births, 39,000; deaths, 14,000. Estimated rates, 2008 (per 1,000 population): births, 27.3; deaths, 9.7. Annual population growth rate, 2000–08, 2.0%. Expectation of life at birth, 2013, 62.4 years for males and 64.5 years for females. Infant mortality, 2010, 54 per 1,000 live births; fertility rate, 2008, 3.3 births per woman.

Telecommunications

In 2010 there were 30,400 landline telephone subscriptions (equivalent to 20.2 per 1,000 inhabitants) and 1,610,000 mobile phone subscriptions (or 1,069.4 per 1,000 inhabitants). Fixed internet subscriptions totalled 22,200 in 2010 (14.7 per 1,000 inhabitants).

Territory and Population

Gabon is bounded in the west by the Atlantic Ocean, north by Equatorial Guinea and Cameroon and east and south by the Republic of the Congo. The area covers 267,670 km^2, including 10,000 km^2 of inland waters. Its population at the 2013 census was reported as 1,811,079. United Nations estimate, 2013, 1.82 m.; density, 7 per sq. In 2011, 86.4% of the population were urban. The capital is Libreville (703,940 inhabitants, 2013 census), other large towns (2013 census) being Port-Gentil (136,462), Franceville (110,568), Owendo (79,300) and Oyem (60,685). French is the official language.

Tourism

358,000 non-resident tourists arrived at Libreville airport in 2008, up from 169,000 in 2001.

The Gambia

Republic of The Gambia

Factsheet
Capital: Banjul
Population estimate, 2015: 1.99 m.
GNI per capita, 2014: (PPP$) 1,507
HDI/world rank, 2014: 0.441/175
Internet domain extension: .gm

Civil Aviation

There is an international airport at Banjul (Yundum), which handled 313,173 passengers and 1,247 tonnes of freight in 2009. The then national carrier, Gambia International Airlines, ceased operations in 2007. A new national carrier, Gambia Bird, began scheduled services in Oct. 2012 but then suspended operations in Dec. 2014.

Climate

The climate is characterized by two very different seasons. The dry season lasts from Nov. to May, when precipitation is very light and humidity moderate. Days are warm but nights quite cool. The SW monsoon is likely to set in with spectacular storms and produces considerable rainfall from July to Oct., with increased humidity. Banjul, Jan. 73 °F (22.8 °C), July 80 °F (26.7 °C). Annual rainfall 52″ (1,295 mm).

Constitution and Government

The 1970 constitution provided for an executive *President* elected directly for renewable 5-year terms. The President appoints a *Vice-President* who is the government's chief minister. The single-chamber *National Assembly* has 53 members (48 elected by universal adult suffrage for a 5-year term and five appointed by the President). A referendum of 8 Aug. 1996 approved a new constitution by 70.4% of votes cast. It took effect in Jan. 1997 and thereby created the Second Republic. Under this, the ban on political parties imposed in July 1994 was lifted. Members of the ruling Military Council resigned from their military positions before joining the Alliance for Patriotic Reorientation and Construction (APRC).

Currency

The unit of currency is the *dalasi* (GMD), of 100 *butut.*

Defence

The Gambian National Army, 800 strong, has two infantry battalions, one engineer squadron and one company of presidential guards. The marine unit of the Army consisted in 2011 of approximately 70 personnel operating seven patrol boats. Defence expenditure totalled an estimated US$6 m. in 2011 (approximately US$4 per capita), representing around 0.5% of GDP.

Economy

Agriculture contributed 29.5% of GDP in 2010; followed by trade and hotels, 25.6%; finance and real estate, 12.7%; transport and communications, 10.7%; and public administration, defence and services, 6.1%.

Labour

The labour force in 2010 totalled 751,000 (52.1% males). Around 70% of the economically active population are engaged in agriculture. The Gambia had 14,000 people living in slavery according to the Walk Free Foundation's 2013 *Global Slavery Index.*

Press

In 2008 there were three daily newspapers—the *Daily Observer, The Point* and the government-owned *Gambia Daily.*

Religion

In 2010 an estimated 95.1% of the population was Muslim (mainly Sunnis) and 4.5% Christian according to the Pew Research Center's Forum on Religion & Public Life.

Roads

There were some 3,742 km of roads in 2004, of which 19.3% were paved. Number of vehicles (2007): 8,800 passenger cars; 2,600 lorries and vans.

Shipping

The chief port is Banjul. Ocean-going vessels can travel up the Gambia River as far as Kuntaur. In Jan. 2009 there were five ships of 300 GT or over registered, totalling 32,000 GT.

Social Statistics

2008 estimates: births, 61,000; deaths, 19,000. Estimated birth rate in 2008 was 36.8 per 1,000 population; estimated death rate, 11.3. Annual population growth rate, 2000–08, 3.0%. Expectation of life, 2013, was 57.5 years for males and 60.2 for females. Fertility rate, 2008, 5.1 births per woman; infant mortality, 2010, 57 per 1,000 live births. The Gambia has made some of the best progress in recent years in reducing child mortality. The number of deaths per 1,000 live births among children under five was reduced from around 153 in 1990 to approximately 106 in 2008.

Telecommunications

In 2010 there were 48,800 landline telephone subscriptions (equivalent to 28.2 per 1,000 inhabitants) and 1,478,300 mobile phone subscriptions (or 855.3 per 1,000 inhabitants). There were 92.0 internet users per 1,000 inhabitants in 2010.

Territory and Population

The Gambia takes its name from the River Gambia, and consists of a strip of territory never wider than 10 km on both banks. It is bounded in the west by the Atlantic Ocean and on all other sides by Senegal. The area is 10,690 km^2, including 2,077 km^2 of inland water. Census population, 2013 (provisional): 1,882,450, giving a density of 219 per km^2. In 2011, 58.9% of the population were urban. The largest ethnic group is the Mandingo, followed by the Wolofs, Fulas, Jolas and Sarahuley. The country is administratively divided into eight local government areas (LGAs). The official language is English.

Tourism

Tourism is The Gambia's biggest foreign exchange earner. In 2009 there were 142,000 non-resident charter tourists (excluding same-day visitors).

Georgia

Sakartvelos Respublika (Republic of Georgia)

Factsheet
Capital: Tbilisi
Population estimate, 2015: 4.00 m.
GNI per capita, 2014: (PPP$) 7,164
HDI/world rank, 2014: 0.754/76
Internet domain extension: .ge

Civil Aviation

The main airport is Tbilisi International Airport. The main Georgian carrier is Georgian Airways. In 2009 Tbilisi handled 702,596 passengers (714,976 in 2008) and 12,245 tonnes of freight.

Climate

The Georgian climate is extremely varied. The relatively small territory covers different climatic zones, ranging from humid sub-tropical zones to permanent snow and glaciers. In Tbilisi summer is hot: 25–35 °C. Nov. sees the beginning of the Georgian winter and the temperature in Tbilisi can drop to −8 °C; however, average temperature ranges from 2–6 °C.

Constitution and Government

A new constitution of 24 Aug. 1995 defines Georgia as a presidential republic with federal elements. The head of state is the *President*, elected by universal suffrage for not more than two 5-year terms. The 150-member *Supreme Council* is elected for 4-year terms, with 73 members elected in single-seat constituencies and 77 by proportional representation. There is a 5% threshold. Amendments limiting the power of the president in favour of the prime minister were passed in Oct. 2010 and came into force after Giorgi Margvelashvili was sworn in as president in Nov. 2013. The prime minister now has executive authority over domestic and foreign policy. The president remains head of state but no longer has the right to initiate laws, introduce a budget or hold an office in a political party.

Currency

The unit of currency is the *lari* (GEL) of 100 *tetri*, which replaced coupons at 1 lari = 1 m. coupons on 25 Sept. 1995.

Defence

The total strength of the Armed Forces consisted of 20,655 personnel in 2011. Conscription is currently for 15 months although a bill proposing a move to an all-professional army was registered with parliament in 2015. The UN peacekeeping mission (United Nations Observer Mission in Georgia, or UNOMIG, which was established in Aug. 1993) ended in June 2009 owing to a lack of consensus among Security Council members on mandate extension. Following the collapse of the USSR in 1991 Russia maintained two bases in Georgia with some 4,000 personnel. The last Russian troops left Georgia in Nov. 2007. However, several thousand soldiers returned in Aug. 2008 when Moscow responded to Georgia's military attack on separatist forces in South Ossetia. Despite a subsequent withdrawal, some forces remain as part of a 'buffer zone' around South Ossetia and Abkhazia. Georgia hopes to join NATO, although its bid to become a member is fiercely opposed by Russia. Defence expenditure in 2013 totalled US$389 m. (US$85 per capita), representing 2.3% of GDP.

Economy

Agriculture accounted for 9.2% of GDP in 2014, industry 24.4% and services 66.4%. Georgia's 'shadow' (black market) economy is estimated to constitute approximately 62% of the country's official GDP, one of the highest percentages of any country in the world.

Labour

The labour force in 2013 was 2,417,000 (2,259,000 in 2003). 69.3% of the population aged 15–64 was economically active in 2013. In the same year 14.6% of the population was unemployed. Georgia had 16,000 people living in slavery according to the Walk Free Foundation's 2013 *Global Slavery Index*.

Press

In 2008 there were ten dailies with a combined circulation of 45,000, as well as 73 other papers.

Rail

Total length in 2011 was 1,262 km (1,225 km of 1,524 mm gauge and 37 km of 900 mm gauge), (all electrified). In 2011 railways carried 20.1 m. tonnes of freight and 3.3 m. passengers. There is a metro system in Tbilisi.

Religion

The Georgian Orthodox Church has its own organization under Catholicos (Patriarch) Ilia II who is resident in Tbilisi. According to estimates by the Pew Research Center's Forum on Religion & Public Life, in 2010 there were 3.8 m. Orthodox and 500,000 Muslims (both Shias and Sunnis), plus small numbers of Catholics.

Roads

There were 20,329 km of roads in 2007 (94.1% hard-surfaced). Passenger cars in use in 2007 numbered 416,300, and there were also 51,500 lorries and vans and 42,800 buses and coaches. In 2007 there were 737 road deaths.

Shipping

In Jan. 2009 there were 199 ships of 300 GT or over registered, totalling 617,000 GT. The principal port is Poti, which handled 8.1 m. tonnes of cargo in 2008 (7.7 m. tonnes in 2007).

Social Statistics

Births, 2011, 58,014; deaths, 49,818. Rates, 2011: birth, 12.9 per 1,000 population; death, 11.1 per 1,000. Annual population growth rate, 2005–10, −0.4%. Life expectancy, 2013, 70.5 years for males and 77.8 years for females. Infant mortality, 2010, 20 per 1,000 live births; fertility rate, 2013, 1.8 births per woman.

Telecommunications

In 2011 there were 1,342,400 landline telephone subscriptions (equivalent to 310.1 per 1,000 inhabitants) and 4,430,600 mobile phone subscriptions (or 1,023.5 per 1,000 inhabitants). There were 269.0 internet users per 1,000 inhabitants in 2010. Fixed internet subscriptions totalled 176,500 in 2009 (40.4 per 1,000 inhabitants). In March 2012 there were 908,000 Facebook users.

Territory and Population

Georgia is bounded in the west by the Black Sea and south by Turkey, Armenia and Azerbaijan. Area, 69,700 km^2 (26,900 sq. miles). Its provisional census population in 2014 was 3,729,635 (excluding Abkhazia and South Ossetia); density (excluding Abkhazia and South Ossetia), 65.2 per km^2. 2014 population including estimates for Abkhazia and South Ossetia: 4,026,000. In 2012, 53.2% of the population lived in urban areas. The capital is Tbilisi (Jan. 2012 population estimate, 1.17 m.). Other principal towns (with Jan. 2012 population estimates in brackets): Kutaisi (196,800), Batumi (125,800), Rustavi (122,500). Georgians accounted for 86.8% of the 2014 census population; others included 6.3% Azerbaijanis, 4.5% Armenians and 0.7% Russians. Georgian is the official language. Armenian, Russian and Azeri are also spoken.

Tourism

Investment in tourism has increased substantially in recent years, and large numbers of hotels have been built. In 2010 there were 2,032,000 international visitors, up from 1,423,000 in 2009. Most visitors in 2010 were from Armenia (548,000), Turkey (536,000), Azerbaijan (498,000) and Russia (171,000).

Germany

Bundesrepublik Deutschland (Federal Republic of Germany)

Factsheet

Capital: Berlin
Seats of government: Berlin, Bonn
Population estimate, 2015: 80.69 m.
GNI per capita, 2014: (PPP$) 43,919
HDI/world rank, 2014: 0.916/6=
Internet domain extension: .de

Civil Aviation

Lufthansa, the largest carrier, was set up in 1953 and was originally 75% state-owned. The government sold its final shares in 1997. Other airlines include Air Berlin (Germany's second largest airline and Europe's third largest low-cost carrier), Condor, Eurowings, Germanwings and TUIfly. In 2012 the airlines of the Lufthansa Group carried 103 m. passengers (20 m. on long-haul flights); revenue passenger-km totalled 204.8 bn. In 2014 civil aviation had 768 aircraft over 20 tonnes and 790 helicopters. In 2014 there were 104.82 m. passenger arrivals and 104.32 m. departures. Main international airports: Berlin (Schönefeld), Berlin (Tegel), Bremen, Cologne-Bonn, Düsseldorf, Frankfurt am Main, Frankfurt (Hahn), Hamburg (Fuhlsbüttel), Hanover, Leipzig, Munich, Nuremberg and Stuttgart. In 2014 Frankfurt am Main handled 59.55 m. passengers and 2,164,000 tonnes of freight. It is the busiest airport in Europe in terms of freight handled.

Climate

Oceanic influences are only found in the northwest where winters are quite mild but stormy. Elsewhere a continental climate is general. To the east and south, winter temperatures are lower, with bright frosty weather and considerable snowfall. Summer temperatures are fairly uniform throughout. Berlin, Jan. 31 °F (−0.5 °C), July 66 °F (19 °C). Annual rainfall 22.5″ (563 mm).

Constitution and Government

The Basic Law (*Grundgesetz*) was approved by the parliaments of the participating *Bundesländer* and came into force on 23 May 1949. It is to remain in force until 'a constitution adopted by a free decision of the German people comes into being'. The Federal Republic is a democratic and social constitutional state on a parliamentary basis. The federation is constituted by the 16 *Bundesländer* (states). Executive power is vested in the *Bundesländer*, unless the Basic Law prescribes or permits otherwise. Federal law takes precedence over state law. Legislative power is vested in the *Bundestag* (Federal Assembly) and the *Bundesrat* (Federal Council). The Head of State is the Federal *President,* who is elected for a 5-year term by a *Federal Convention* specially convened for this purpose. No president may serve more than two terms. Executive power is vested in the Federal government, which consists of the Federal *Chancellor* (currently Angela Merkel, b. 1954 and assumed office in 2005), elected by the Bundestag on the proposal of the Federal President, and the Federal Ministers, who are appointed and dismissed by the Federal President upon the proposal of the Federal Chancellor. Federal laws are passed by the Bundestag and after their adoption submitted to the Bundesrat, which has a limited veto.

Currency

On 1 Jan. 1999 the euro (EUR) became the legal currency in Germany at the irrevocable conversion rate of 1.95583 DM (Deutsche Mark) to one euro. The euro, which consists of 100 cents, has been in circulation since 1 Jan. 2002. It was still possible to make cash transactions in German marks until 28 Feb. 2002, although formally the mark had ceased to be legal tender on 31 Dec. 2001.

Defence

Germany officially ended its compulsory military service on 1 July 2011. The total strength of the *Bundeswehr* (Federal Defence Forces of Germany) in Oct. 2012 was 195,893, including 7,132 in the vocational training service. In 2013 defence expenditure totalled US$44,201 m. (US$545 per capita), representing 1.2% of GDP.

Economy

Services accounted for 69.0% of GDP in 2014, industry 30.3% and agriculture 0.7%. Manufacturing's share of total GDP was 22.6%. In terms of total aid given, Germany was the third most generous country in the world in 2014 after the USA and the UK, donating US$16.6 bn. in international aid in the course of the year. This represented 0.42% of GNI (compared to the UN target of 0.7%).

Labour

Retirement age was traditionally 65 years, but is being raised gradually to 67 in a process that started at the beginning of 2012 and is to continue through to 2029. In 2012 the workforce was 43.88 m., of whom 41.57 m. were working and 2.32 m. (1.02 m. females) were unemployed. In 2014 the workforce was 44.67 m., of whom 42.58 m. were working and 2.09 m. (0.90 m. females) were unemployed. The standardized unemployment rate was 4.5% in Dec. 2015—the joint lowest in the European Union (down from 5.0% in 2014 as a whole and 5.2% in 2013). Unemployment in 2015 was at its lowest level since the reunification of Germany in 1990. Youth unemployment (under 25) is—at just 7.3% in Dec. 2014—the lowest in the European Union, helped by the fact that a quarter of employers provide formal apprenticeship schemes for young people. Long-term unemployment is particularly high, with 47.4% of the labour force in 2010 having been out of work for more than a year. In Jan. 2005 the number of people out of work reached 5 m., the highest total since the 1930s, although by Oct. 2010 it had fallen to below 3 m. as Germany made a strong recovery from the recession. A national minimum wage of €8.50 per hour was introduced for the first time in Jan. 2015.

Press

The daily press is mainly regional. The daily with the highest circulation is the tabloid *Bild* (2.22 m. copies per day in the fourth quarter of 2014, down from 3.03 m. in the fourth quarter of 2009). In 2014 the total circulation figures for the 349 German daily newspapers came to 16.3 m. The total circulation of daily newspapers in Germany is the highest in Europe. The leading daily newspaper websites are *Bild.de* (17.3 m. unique monthly visitors in Dec. 2014), *die Welt* (9.0 m.), *Süddeutsche.de* (5.8 m.) and *ZEIT ONLINE* (5.7 m.).

Rail

Legislation of 1993 provides for the eventual privatization of the railways, but the state-owned Deutsche Bahn still dominates the market. On 1 Jan. 1994 West German Bundesbahn and the former GDR Reichsbahn were amalgamated as the Deutsche Bahn, a joint-stock company in which track, long-distance passenger traffic, regional passenger traffic, goods traffic and railway stations/services are run as five separate administrative entities. These were intended after 3–5 years to become companies themselves, at first under a holding company, and ultimately independent. In 2013 the total length of railway track was 37,860 km (nearly all 1,435 mm gauge track). 2,613 m. passengers were carried in 2013 and 365.0 m. tonnes of freight in 2014. There are metros in Berlin (152 km), Hamburg (101 km), Munich (101 km) and Nuremberg (35 km), and tram/light rail networks in over 50 cities.

Religion

In 2013 there were 24,171,000 Roman Catholics in 11,085 parishes, 23,040,000 Protestants in 14,412 parishes; and in 2014, 100,437 Jews with 71 rabbis and 100 synagogues. The Federal Office for Migration and Refugees estimated in 2009 that there were between 3.8 m. and 4.3 m. Muslims resident in Germany, a number exceeded in the EU only in France. There are seven Roman Catholic archbishoprics (Bamberg, Berlin, Cologne, Freiburg, Hamburg, Munich and Freising, Paderborn) and 20 bishoprics. A concordat between Germany and the Holy See dates from 10 Sept. 1933. In April 2005 Cardinal Joseph Ratzinger, former archbishop of Munich and Freising, was elected Pope as Benedict XVI. In Feb. 2013 he became the first Pope to resign in 600 years, citing age and declining health as the reasons for his decision. There were ten cardinals in Feb. 2016. The Evangelical (Protestant) Church (EKD) consists of 22 member-churches comprising nine Lutheran Churches, 11 United-Lutheran-Reformed Churches and two Reformed Churches. The Free Evangelical Church (BFeG) has some 460 communities.

Roads

In 2014 the total length of the road network was 230,377 km, including 12,917 km of motorway *(Autobahn)*, 39,389 km of federal highways and 86,210 km of secondary roads. The motorway network is the largest in Europe. On 1 Jan. 2015 there were 53,715,600 motor vehicles, including: passenger cars, 44,403,100 (more than one car for every two persons); lorries, 2,701,300; buses, 77,500; motorcycles, 4,145,400. In 2013, 9,306 m. passengers were transported by scheduled road transport services. There were 302,435 accidents in 2014 resulting in injuries to passengers. Road casualties in 2014 totalled 392,912, with 389,535 injured and 3,377 killed. In 2014 there were 4.2 fatalities per 100,000 population.

Shipping

At 31 Dec. 2015 the mercantile marine comprised 351 ocean-going vessels of 10.30 m. GT. Sea-going ships in 2014 carried 300.1 m. tonnes of cargo. The busiest port, Hamburg, handled 126.0 m. tonnes of cargo in 2014, ranking it third in Europe behind Rotterdam and Antwerp. Hamburg is Europe's second busiest container port after Rotterdam. Navigable rivers and canals had a total length of 7,728 km in 2013. The inland waterways fleet on 31 Dec. 2014 included 842 motor freight vessels totalling 1.11 m. tonnes and 362 tankers of 689,341 tonnes. 228.5 m. tonnes of freight were transported in 2014.

Social Statistics

Live births, 2013: 682,069; deaths, 893,825. Rates (per 1,000 population), 2013: birth, 8.5; death, 11.1; marriage, 4.6; divorce, 2.1; infant mortality, 3.3 per 1,000 live births; stillborn rate, 3.7 per 1,000 live births. Life expectancy, 2013: men, 78.8 years; women, 83.4. Suicide rates, 2010, per 100,000 population, 12.3 (men, 18.6; women, 6.1). Annual population growth rate, 2001–11, −0.3%; fertility rate, 2013, 1.4 births per woman (one of the lowest rates in the world).

Telecommunications

Telecommunications were deregulated in 1989. On 1 Jan. 1995, three state-owned joint-stock companies were set up: Deutsche Telekom, Postdienst and Postbank. The partial privatization of Deutsche Telekom began in Nov. 1996; in 2013 the German government held only 14.5% of shares directly, and a further 17.4% indirectly through the government bank KfW. In 2010 there were 45.6 m. main (fixed) telephone lines, down from 54.8 m. in 2005. Mobile phone subscribers numbered 104.6 m. in 2010 (1,270.4 per 1,000 persons), up from 79.3 m. in 2005. T-Mobile and D2 Vodafone are the largest networks, with 36% and 32% of the market share respectively. Germany had 67.4 m. internet users in Dec. 2011. The fixed broadband penetration rate in Dec. 2010 was 31.9 subscribers per 100 inhabitants. In March 2012 there were 22.1 m. Facebook users (27% of the population).

Territory and Population

Germany is bounded in the north by Denmark and the North and Baltic Seas, east by Poland, east and southeast by the Czech Republic, southeast and south by Austria, south by Switzerland and west by France, Luxembourg, Belgium and the Netherlands. Area: 357,340 sq. km. Population estimate, 31 Dec. 2014: 81,197,537; density 227 per sq. km. Of the total population in 2014, 65,223,097 lived in the former Federal Republic of Germany (excluding West Berlin) and 15,974,440 in the six new states of the former German Democratic Republic (including 3,469,849 in Berlin). On 31 Dec. 2014 there were 8,152,968 resident foreigners, including 1,527,118 Turks, 674,152 Poles, 574,530 Italians, 355,343 Romanians, 328,564 Greeks and 263,347 Croats. In 2014 Germany received 202,834 asylum applications (of which 173,072 first time applications), up from 28,018 in 2008 although down from 438,191 in 1992. The Federation comprises 16 *Bundesländer* (states). The *Bundesländer* with the largest populations in Dec. 2013 (in 1,000) are: North Rhine-Westphalia, 17,572; Bavaria, 12,604; Baden-Württemberg, 10,631; Lower Saxony, 7,791; Hessen, 6,045.The capital is Berlin; the Federal German government moved from Bonn to Berlin in 1999. Populations of the largest cities in Dec. 2011 (in 1,000) are: Berlin, 3,502; Hamburg, 1,799; Munich/München, 1,378; Cologne/Köln, 1,017; Frankfurt am Main, 692. The official language is German.

Tourism

In 2014 there were 51,865 places of accommodation with 3,563,595 beds (including 13,270 hotels with 1,095,075 beds). 32,999,000 foreign visitors and 127,791,000 tourists resident in Germany spent a total of 424,062,000 nights in holiday accommodation. The most visited city is Berlin with 11,871,000 over-night visitors in 2014; Bavaria is the most visited *Bundesland* with 32,462,000 (6,594,000 visited Munich). In 2014 the Netherlands was the country of origin of the largest number of overnight visitors (4,238,000), ahead of Switzerland (2,778,000) and the UK (2,415,000). In 2014 tourism brought in €32.6 bn. Expenditure by German travellers in foreign countries for 2014 was €70.3 bn.

Ghana

Republic of Ghana

Factsheet

Capital: Accra
Population estimate, 2015: 27.41 m.
GNI per capita, 2014: (PPP$) 3,852
HDI/world rank, 2014: 0.579/140
Internet domain extension: .gh

Civil Aviation

There is an international airport at Accra (Kotoka), which handled 2,424,153 passengers (1,726,051 on international flights) in 2012. As well as domestic flights, in 2010 there were direct international services connecting Accra with more than 20 destinations.

Climate

The climate ranges from the equatorial type on the coast to savannah in the north and is typified by the existence of well-marked dry and wet seasons. Temperatures are relatively high throughout the year. The amount, duration and seasonal distribution of rain is very marked, from the south, with over 80″ (2,000 mm), to the north, with under 50″ (1,250 mm). In the extreme north, the wet season is from March to Aug., but further south it lasts until Oct. Near Kumasi, two wet seasons occur, in May and June and again in Oct., and this is repeated, with greater amounts, along the coast of Ghana. Accra, Jan. 80 °F (26.7 °C), July 77 °F (25 °C). Annual rainfall 29″ (724 mm).

Constitution and Government

After the coup of 31 Dec. 1981, supreme power was vested in the Provisional National Defence Council (PNDC), chaired by Flight-Lieut. Jerry John Rawlings. A new constitution was approved by 92.6% of votes cast at a referendum on 28 April 1992. The electorate was 8,255,690; turnout was 43.8%. The constitution sets up a presidential system on the US model, with a multi-party parliament and an independent judiciary. The *President* is elected by universal suffrage for a 4-year term renewable once. The unicameral *Parliament* has 275 members, elected for a 4-year term in single-seat constituencies.

Currency

The monetary unit is the *cedi* (GHS) of 100 *pesewas*. It was introduced in July 2007 and is equal to 10,000 old cedi (GHC).

Defence

Defence expenditure totalled US$306 m. in 2013 (US$12 per capita), representing 0.6% of GDP. Between 2012 and 2013 Ghana increased its defence spending by 129%, the largest rise of any country that year.

Economy

Agriculture accounted for 31.8% of GDP in 2009, industry 19.0% and services 49.2%.

Labour

In 2013 the number of economically active persons totalled 14.04 m. Females constituted 51.7% of the labour force in 2013. The unemployment rate was 5.2% in 2013. Ghana had 0.18 m. people living in slavery according to the Walk Free Foundation's 2013 *Global Slavery Index*.

Press

There were 12 paid-for daily newspapers in 2008 with a combined circulation of 210,000 plus 95 paid-for non-dailies.

Rail

Total length of railways in 2006 was 953 km of 1,067 mm gauge, all in the south of the country. In 2010 a US$6 bn. deal was signed with China National Machinery Import & Export Corp. to construct a railway linking Kumasi (the northernmost point of the existing network) with Paga in the north of the country on the border with Burkina Faso. In 2006 railways carried 1.6 m. tonnes of freight and 2.3 m. passengers.

Religion

In 2010 the population was 74.9% Christian according to estimates by the Pew Research Center's Forum on Religion & Public Life, with 15.8% Hindu and 4.9% folk religionist. Protestants constituted 81% of Christians in 2010 and Catholics 17%. In Feb. 2016 the Roman Catholic church had one cardinal.

Roads

In 2005 there were 57,614 km of roads, including 11,177 km of highways, main and national roads. About 14.9% of all roads are paved. A Road Sector Strategy and Programme to develop the road network ran from 1995 to 2000. There were 493,800 passenger cars in use in 2007, 158,400 lorries and vans, and 121,100 buses and coaches. Motorcycles and mopeds numbered 149,100.

Shipping

The chief ports are Tema and Takoradi. In 2008, 8.7 m. tonnes of cargo were handled at Tema and 4.0 m. tonnes at Takoradi. There is inland water transport on Lake Volta. In Jan. 2009 there were 14 ships of 300 GT or over registered, totalling 15,000 GT. The Volta, Ankobra and Tano rivers provide 168 km of navigable waterways for launches and lighters.

Social Statistics

2008 estimates: births, 756,000; deaths, 259,000. Rates, 2008 estimates (per 1,000 population): births, 32.4; deaths, 11.1. 2013 life expectancy, 60.2 years for men and 62.1 for women. Infant mortality, 50 per 1,000 live births (2010). Annual population growth rate, 2000–08, 2.2%; fertility rate, 2008, 4.0 births per woman.

Telecommunications

Ghana Telecom was privatized in 1996. There were 277,900 fixed telephone lines in 2010 (11.4 per 1,000 inhabitants). Mobile phone subscribers numbered 17.44 m. in 2010. There were 85.5 internet users per 1,000 inhabitants in 2010. Fixed internet subscriptions totalled 92,700 in 2009 (3.9 per 1,000 inhabitants). In June 2012 there were 1.3 m. Facebook users.

Territory and Population

Ghana is bounded west by Côte d'Ivoire, north by Burkina Faso, east by Togo and south by the Gulf of Guinea. The area is 238,533 km^2; the 2010 census population was 24,658,823 giving a density of 103.4 persons per km^2. In 2011, 52.2% of the population were urban. An estimated 3 m. Ghanaians lived abroad in 2006. Ghana is divided into ten regions. In 2010 the capital, Accra, had a population of 1,848,614. Other major cities are Kumasi, Tamale, Sekondi-Takoradi and Ashiaman. About 42% of the population are Akan. Other tribal groups include Moshi (23%), Ewe (10%) and Ga-Adangme (7%). About 75 languages are spoken; the official language is English.

Tourism

There were 931,000 non-resident tourists in 2010, spending US$706 m.

Greece

Elliniki Dimokratia (Hellenic Republic)

Factsheet
Capital: Athens
Population estimate, 2015: 10.96 m.
GNI per capita, 2014: (PPP$) 24,524
HDI/world rank, 2014: 0.865/29
Internet domain extension: .gr

Civil Aviation

There are international airports at Athens (Spata 'Eleftherios Venizelos') and Thessaloniki-Makedonia. The airport at Spata opened in 2001. The national carrier, Olympic Airlines, ceased operations in Sept. 2009 and Olympic Air, the new airline formed from its privatization, commenced flights that month. In Oct. 2013 Olympic Air was acquired by Aegean Airlines, the largest Greek airline in terms of the number of passengers carried. Apart from the international airports there are a further 25 provincial airports. 5.70 m. passengers were carried in 2005, of whom 2.90 m. were on domestic and 2.80 m. on international flights. Olympic Airlines operates routes from Athens to all

important cities of the country, Europe, the Middle East and USA. In 2006 Athens airport (Spata) handled 15,079,708 passengers (9,611,095 on international flights).

Climate

Coastal regions and the islands have typical Mediterranean conditions, with mild, rainy winters and hot, dry, sunny summers. Rainfall comes almost entirely in the winter months, though amounts vary widely according to position and relief. Continental conditions affect the northern mountainous areas, with severe winters, deep snow cover and heavy precipitation, but summers are hot. Athens, Jan. 48 °F (8.6 °C), July 82.5 °F (28.2 °C). Annual rainfall 16.6″ (414.3 mm).

Constitution and Government

Greece is a presidential parliamentary democracy. A new constitution was introduced in June 1975 and was amended in March 1986, April 2001 and May 2008. The 300-member *Chamber of Deputies* is elected for 4-year terms by proportional representation. There is a 3% threshold. Extra seats are awarded to the party which leads in an election. The Chamber of Deputies elects the head of state, the *President*, for a 5-year term.

Currency

In June 2000 EU leaders approved a recommendation for Greece to join the European single currency, the euro, and on 1 Jan. 2001 the euro (EUR) became the legal currency at the irrevocable conversion rate of 340.750 drachmas to 1 euro. The euro, which consists of 100 cents, has been in circulation since 1 Jan. 2002. On the introduction of the euro there was a 'dual circulation' period before the drachma ceased to be legal tender on 28 Feb. 2002.

Defence

Prior to 2001 conscription was generally: (Army) 18 months, (Navy) 21 months, (Air Force) 20 months. However, following a gradual shortening of military service, in 2015 conscription was 9 months for the Army and 12 months for the Navy and the Air Force. In 2013 defence expenditure totalled US$5,681 m., with spending per capita US$527. The 2013 expenditure represented 2.3% of GDP (the second highest percentage in the EU).

Economy

Agriculture accounted for 4% of GDP in 2012, industry 14% and services 82%.

Labour

The labour force in 2013 was 5,008,000 (4,935,000 in 2003). 68.1% of the population aged 15–64 was economically active in 2013. In the same year 27.2% of the population was unemployed. In 2014 there was a monthly minimum wage of €683.76, down from €876.62 in 2012. The 'official' retirement age is 67, although on average Greek men retire at 63 and women at 59. In 2013 only 36% of Greeks between the ages of 55 and 64 were in employment. Unemployment was 24.5% in Oct. 2015 (down from 26.6% in 2014 as a whole and 27.5% in 2013). Youth unemployment—those under 25—is particularly high, at 48.6% in Oct. 2015 (although it was 60.5% in Feb. 2013). Greece has the highest rate of self-employed people in the European Union, at 36.8% of total employment in 2012.

Press

There were 45 daily newspapers published in 2008 (41 paid-for and four free) with a combined daily circulation of 1,447,000. The papers with the highest circulation are the free *City Press* and *Metro*.

Rail

In 2011 the state network, Hellenic Railways (OSE), totalled 2,554 km, of which 1,782 km were of standard 1,435 mm gauge and 772 km were of narrow gauge (1,000 mm and 600 mm). Railways carried 3.2 m. tonnes of freight and 15.3 m. passengers in 2012. A 52-km long metro opened in Athens in 2000.

Religion

Greek Orthodoxy is the state religion. The primate of the Greek Orthodox Church is Archbishop Ieronymos II of Athens and All Greece (b. 1938). According to the Pew Research Center's Forum on Religion & Public Life, an estimated 88.3% of the population in 2010 was Orthodox. Muslims constituted 5.4% of the population in 2010 and people with no religious affiliation 6.2%. There are also small numbers of Protestants and Catholics.

Roads

There were 116,631 km of roads in 2005, including 868 km of motorway, 9,299 km of national roads and 30,864 km of secondary roads. Number of motor vehicles in 2005: 4,303,129 passenger cars (388 per 1,000 inhabitants), 1,186,483 trucks and vans, 1,124,172 motorcycles and 26,829 buses. There were 1,612 road deaths in 2007. With 14.4 deaths per 100,000 population in 2007, Greece has among the highest death rates in road accidents of any industrialized country.

Shipping

In Jan. 2009 there were 1,127 ships of 300 GT or over registered, totalling 37.14 m. GT. Of the 1,127 vessels registered, 412 were oil tankers, 260 bulk carriers, 252 passenger ships, 120 general cargo ships, 45 container ships, 26 chemical tankers and 12 liquid gas tankers. The Greek-controlled fleet comprised 3,094 vessels of 1,000 GT or over in Jan. 2009, of which 2,361 were under foreign flags and only 737 under the Greek flag. There is a canal (opened 9 Nov. 1893) across the Isthmus of Corinth (about 7 km). The principal port is Piraeus, which handled 10,477,000 tonnes of cargo in 2008 (4,463,000 tonnes loaded and 6,014,000 tonnes discharged).

Social Statistics

2009: 117,933 live births; 108,316 deaths; 59,212 marriages; 13,163 divorces (2008); 505 still births. 2009 rates: birth (per 1,000 population), 10.5; death, 9.6; marriage, 5.3; divorce, 1.2 (2008). Average annual population growth rate, 2005–10, 0.2%. In 2012 the suicide rate per 100,000 population was 3.8 (men, 6.3; women, 1.3). Expectation of life at birth, 2014, 78.0 years for males and 83.8 years for females. In 2005 the most popular age range for marrying was 25–29 for females and 30–34 for males. Infant mortality, 2009, 3.2 per 1,000 live births; fertility rate, 2005, 1.2 births per woman (one of the lowest rates in the world).

Telecommunications

In 2012 there were 5,461,000 main (fixed) telephone lines. In the same year mobile phone subscriptions numbered 13,360,000 (1,201.0 per 1,000 persons). In 2013, 59.8% of the population aged 16–74 were internet users. There were 19.9 fixed broadband subscribers per 100 inhabitants in Dec. 2010. In March 2012 there were 3.6 m. Facebook users.

Territory and Population

Greece is bounded in the north by Albania, the Former Yugoslav Republic of Macedonia (FYROM) and Bulgaria, east by Turkey and the Aegean Sea, south by the Mediterranean and west by the Ionian Sea. The total area is 131,958 km² (50,949 sq. miles), of which the islands account for 25,026 km² (9,663 sq. miles). The population was 10,815,197 according to the census of March 2011 (5,512,404 females and 5,302,703 males), giving a density of 82.0 per km². In 2011, 61.7% of the population lived in urban areas. This excludes the population of the Monastic Republic of Mount Athos (a self-governing community composed of 20 monasteries). As well as 9,903,268 Greek nationals, there were 199,101 citizens of other European Union countries in Greece in March 2011, plus 708,003 citizens of other countries and 4,825 stateless persons or people with no specified citizenship. The largest cities (2011 census populations) are Athens (the capital), 3,168,036 (including the municipalities of Piraeus, Peristeri and Kallithea); Thessaloniki, 806,396; Patras, 195,265; Heraklion, 157,452; Larissa, 144,651; Volos, 130,094; Acharnai, 100,723. The modern Greek language had two contesting literary standard forms, the archaizing *Katharevousa* ('purist'), and a version based on the spoken vernacular, 'Demotic'.

Tourism

Tourism is Greece's biggest industry, in 2011 accounting for 16.5% of GDP. In 2011 there were a record 16,427,000 foreign tourists (of which 10,698,000

from citizens of other European Union countries), up from 15,007,000 in 2010 and 14,915,000 in 2009. However, 2012 saw a decline with tourist arrivals falling to 15,518,000. There were 397,660 hotel rooms and 763,407 hotel beds in 2010 (358,721 rooms and 682,050 beds in 2005).

Grenada

Factsheet

Capital: St George's
Population estimate, 2015: 107,000
GNI per capita, 2014: (PPP$) 10,939
HDI/world rank, 2014: 0.750/79
Internet domain extension: .gd

Civil Aviation

The main airport is Maurice Bishop International Airport (MBIA), at St George's. Union Island and Carriacou have smaller airports. In 2010 there were direct flights from MBIA to Antigua, Barbados, Frankfurt, London, Miami, Porlamar (in Venezuela), Puerto Rico, St Vincent, Tobago, Toronto and Trinidad. MBIA handled 353,649 passengers in 2012 (293,933 on international flights) and 1,846 tonnes of freight.

Climate

The tropical climate is very agreeable in the dry season, from Jan. to May, when days are warm and nights quite cool, but in the wet season there is very little difference between day and night temperatures. On the coast, annual rainfall is about 60″ (1,500 mm) but it is as high as 150–200″ (3,750–5,000 mm) in the mountains. Average temperature, 27 °C.

Constitution and Government

The head of state is the British sovereign, represented by an appointed *Governor-General*. There is a bicameral legislature, consisting of a 13-member *Senate*, appointed by the Governor-General, and a 15-member *House of Representatives*, elected by universal suffrage.

Currency

The unit of currency is the *East Caribbean dollar* (XCD).

Defence

Modelled on the British system, the 730-strong police force includes an 80-member paramilitary unit and a 30-member coastguard.

Economy

Agriculture accounted for 5.2% of GDP in 2010, industry 17.1% and services 77.7%.

Labour

In 2008 the labour force numbered 47,600, of whom 35,700 persons were employed. Unemployment was 24.9% in 2008.

Press

In 2008 there were five weekly newspapers and several others that were published irregularly.

Religion

According to the Pew Research Center's Forum on Religion & Public Life, half of the population in 2010 was Catholic and half Protestant.

Roads

In 2001 there were 1,127 km of roads, of which 61.0% were hard-surfaced.

Shipping

The main port is at St George's; there are eight minor ports. In Jan. 2009 there were four ships of 300 GT or over registered, totalling 2,000 GT.

Social Statistics

Births, 2008 estimates, 2,000; deaths, 600. Rates per 1,000 population, 2008 estimates: birth, 19.4; death, 6.1. Life expectancy, 2013: 70.3 years for males; 75.3 years for females. Infant mortality, 2010, nine per 1,000 live births. Annual population growth rate, 2000–08, 0.3%; fertility rate, 2008, 2.3 births per woman.

Telecommunications

There were 28,400 fixed telephone lines in 2010 (271.5 per 1,000 inhabitants). Mobile phone subscribers numbered 121,900 in 2010. There were 334.6 internet users per 1,000 inhabitants in 2010. Fixed internet subscriptions totalled 10,900 in 2009 (104.8 per 1,000 inhabitants).

Territory and Population

Grenada is the most southerly island of the Windward Islands with an area of 344 km^2 (133 sq. miles); the state also includes the Southern Grenadine Islands to the north, chiefly Carriacou (58.3 km^2) and Petite Martinique. The total population at the 2011 census (provisional) was 103,328 (52,651 males); density, 300 per km^2. In 2011, 39.7% of the population were urban. The Borough of St George's, the capital, had 36,823 inhabitants in 2011 (provisional). 52% of the population is Black, 40% of mixed origins, 4% Indian and 1% White. The official language is English. A French-African patois is also spoken.

Tourism

In 2010 there were 106,156 non-resident tourist arrivals by air and 333,556 cruise passenger arrivals. There were 206 cruise ship calls in 2010.

Guatemala

República de Guatemala (Republic of Guatemala)

Factsheet

Capital: Guatemala City
Population estimate, 2015: 16.34 m.
GNI per capita, 2014: (PPP$) 6,929
HDI/world rank, 2014: 0.627/128
Internet domain extension: .gt

Civil Aviation

There are international airports at Guatemala City (La Aurora) and Flores. In 2013, 59,078 domestic flights and 40,505 international flights arrived at and departed from La Aurora; the international flights carried 2,107,670 passengers.

Climate

A tropical climate, with little variation in temperature and a well-marked wet season from May to Oct. Guatemala City, Jan. 63 °F (17.2 °C), July 69 °F (20.6 °C). Annual rainfall 53″ (1,316 mm).

Constitution and Government

A new constitution, drawn up by the Constituent Assembly elected on 1 July 1984, was promulgated in June 1985 and came into force on 14 Jan. 1986. In 1993, 43 amendments were adopted, reducing *inter alia* the President's term of office from 5 to 4 years. The President and Vice-President are elected by direct election (with a second round of voting if no candidate secures 50% of the first-round votes) for a non-renewable 4-year term. The unicameral *Congreso de la República* comprises 158 members, elected partly from constituencies and partly by proportional representation to serve 4-year terms.

Currency

The unit of currency is the *quetzal* (GTQ) of 100 *centavos*, established on 7 May 1925.

Defence

In 2013 defence expenditure totalled US$256 m. (US$18 per capita), representing 0.5% of GDP.

Economy

In 2011 agriculture accounted for 11.8% of GDP, industry 29.3% and services 58.9%.

Labour

The labour force in 2013 was 6,628,000 (4,595,000 in 2003). 69.7% of the population aged 15–64 was economically active in 2013. In the same year 3.0% of the population was unemployed. Guatemala had 13,000 people living in slavery according to the Walk Free Foundation's 2013 *Global Slavery Index*.

Press

In 2008 there were nine paid-for daily newspapers, the main ones being *Nuestro Diario* and *Prensa Libre*.

Rail

Ferrovías Guatemala (a subsidiary of Railroad Development Corporation, which secured a 50-year concession to upgrade Guatemala's decrepit rail network in 1997) operated 322 km of railway in 2007, with six locomotives carrying 40,000 tonnes of freight. However, after a contractual dispute with the government, the company suspended its operations in Sept. 2007 and no trains have run since then.

Religion

In 2010 there were an estimated 8.37 m. Roman Catholics, 5.13 m. Protestants and 0.20 m. other Christians according to the Pew Research Center's Forum on Religion & Public Life. A further 0.59 m. people had no religious affiliation.

Roads

In 2012 there were 16,293 km of roads, of which 44.6% were paved. Vehicles in use in 2007 numbered 1,558,100.

Shipping

The chief ports on the Atlantic coast are Puerto Barrios and Santo Tomás de Castilla: on the Pacific coast, Puerto Quetzal and Champerico. Santo Tomás de Castilla, Guatemala's busiest port, handled 4.7 m. tonnes of cargo in 2008.

Social Statistics

Births, 2006, 368,399; deaths, 69,756. 2006 rates per 1,000 population: birth, 28.4; death, 5.4. Life expectancy, 2007: male 66.7 years, female 73.7. Annual population growth rate, 2005–10, 2.5%. Infant mortality, 2010, 25 per 1,000 live births; fertility rate, 2008, 4.1 births per woman.

Telecommunications

The government own and operate the telecommunications services. There were 1.50 m. fixed telephone lines in 2010 (104.1 per 1,000 inhabitants). Mobile phone subscribers numbered 18.07 m. in 2010. There were 105.0 internet users per 1,000 inhabitants in 2010. In Dec. 2011 there were 1.7 m. Facebook users.

Territory and Population

Guatemala is bounded on the north and west by Mexico, south by the Pacific ocean and east by El Salvador, Honduras and Belize, and the area is 108,889 km^2 (42,042 sq. miles). In March 1936 Guatemala, El Salvador and Honduras agreed to accept the peak of Mount Montecristo as the common boundary point. The population at the last census, in 2002, was 11,237,196. The estimated population in 2012 was 15,073,400; density, 138 per km^2. In 2011, 49.9% of the population were urban. There are four recognized ethnic groups: Maya (the native people of the country); Ladino (people of mixed European and indigenous ancestry); Garifuna (a mix of African, Arawak and Carib); Xinca (also native people of the region but not descendants from the Maya). In 2012, 40% of the population identified themselves as indigenous. 51% speak Spanish, the official language of Guatemala, with the remainder speaking one or a combination of the 23 Indian dialects. In 2010 Guatemala City, the capital, had an estimated population of 2,584,000. Other major towns are Mixco, Villa Nueva, Quetzaltenango, Petapa and Escuintla.

Tourism

There were 1,876,000 non-resident visitors in 2010 (up from 1,777,000 in 2009 and 1,715,000 in 2008).

Guinea

République de Guinée (Republic of Guinea)

Factsheet

Capital: Conakry
Population estimate, 2015: 12.61 m.
GNI per capita, 2014: (PPP$) 1,096
HDI/world rank, 2014: 0.411/182
Internet domain extension: .gn

Civil Aviation

There is an international airport at Conakry (Gbessia). In 2010 there were scheduled flights to Abidjan, Bamako, Banjul, Bissau, Brussels, Casablanca, Dakar, Freetown, Monrovia, Nouakchott and Paris, as well as domestic services. In 2006 there were 103,200 air arrivals and 153,800 departures plus 9,600 passengers in transit. A total of 8.53 m. tonnes of air freight were handled in 2006.

Climate

A tropical climate, with high rainfall near the coast and constant heat, but conditions are a little cooler on the plateau. The wet season on the coast lasts from May to Nov., but only to Oct. inland. Conakry, Jan. 80 °F (26.7 °C), July 77 °F (25 °C). Annual rainfall 172″ (4,293 mm).

Constitution and Government

There is a 114-member *National Assembly*, 38 of whose members are elected on a first-past-the-post system, and the remainder from national lists by proportional representation. It was dissolved following the military coup of Dec. 2008, but reinstated after parliamentary elections held in Sept. 2013 (the first in 11 years). On 11 Nov. 2001 a referendum was held in which 98.4% of votes cast were in favour of President Conté remaining in office for a third term, requiring an amendment to the constitution (previously allowing a maximum two presidential terms). The referendum, which also increased the presidential mandate from 5 to 7 years, was boycotted by opposition parties.

Currency

The monetary unit is the *Guinean franc* (GNF).

Defence

There is selective conscription for 2 years. Defence expenditure totalled an estimated US$42 m. in 2011 (approximately US$4 per capita), representing around 1% of GDP.

Economy

Agriculture produced 16.9% of GDP in 2009, industry 31.0% and services 52.1%.

Labour

In 2010 the labour force was 4,092,000 (54.8% males). The agricultural sector employs 80% of the workforce. Guinea had 82,000 people living in slavery according to the Walk Free Foundation's 2013 *Global Slavery Index*.

Press

In 2008 there were two daily newspapers (circulation 25,000).

Rail

A railway connects Conakry with Kankan (662 km). A line 144 km long linking Conakry and Fria, where there is a bauxite mine and aluminium plant, opened in 1960 and a third line opened in 1973 links bauxite deposits at Sangaredi with Port Kamsar (134 km). There are two further railway used by the bauxite industry, running from Tougué to Dabola (130 km) and from Débéle to Conakry (102 km).

Religion

In 2010, 84.4% of the population was Muslim and 10.9% Christian according to estimates by the Pew Research Center's Forum on Religion & Public Life. Most Muslims in Guinea are Sunnis and most Christians are Catholics. In Feb. 2016 there was one cardinal in the Roman Catholic church.

Roads

In 2008 there were 6,758 km of roads, 35.4% of which were asphalted. In 2011 there were 299,200 vehicles in use.

Shipping

There are ports at Conakry and for bauxite exports at Kamsar (opened 1973). Merchant shipping totalled 1,000 GT in 2008.

Social Statistics

2008 estimates: births, 390,000; deaths, 108,000. Rates, 2008 estimates (per 1,000 population): births, 39.6; deaths, 11.0. infant mortality, 2010, 81 per 1,000 live births. Life expectancy, 2013, 55.3 years for males and 56.9 for females. Annual population growth rate, 2000–08, 2.0%; fertility rate, 2008, 5.4 births per woman.

Telecommunications

The Société guinéenne des télécommunications, which was privatized in 1995, became 100% state-owned again in 2008 after Telekom Malaysia sold its 60% stake in the company. The company ceased operations in 2013 after it filed for bankruptcy but there are plans for its relaunch during 2016. There were 18,000 fixed telephone lines in 2010 (1.8 per 1,000 inhabitants). Mobile phone subscribers numbered 3.49 m. in 2009. There were 9.6 internet users per 1,000 inhabitants in 2010.

Territory and Population

Guinea is bounded in the northwest by Guinea-Bissau and Senegal, northeast by Mali, southeast by Côte d'Ivoire, south by Liberia and Sierra Leone, and west by the Atlantic Ocean. The area is 245,860 km² (94,930 sq. miles), including 140 km² (50 sq. miles) of inland water. In 2014 the census population (provisional) was 10,628,972 (density 43.2 per km²). The capital is Conakry. In 2011, 35.9% of the population were urban. Guinea is divided into seven administrative regions and the governorate of Conakry (national capital). These are in turn divided into 34 administrative regions. The major divisions (with their areas in sq. km) are: Boké, 31,186; Conakry (special zone-national capital), 450; Faranah, 35,581; Kankan, 72,156; Kindia, 28,873; Labé, 22,869; Mamou, 17,074; Nzérékoré, 37,668. The main towns are Conakry (provisional census population, 2014, 1,667,864), Nzérékoré, Kankan, Kindia, Manéah and Siguiri. The ethnic composition is Fulani (38.6%), Malinké (or Mandingo, 23.2%), Susu (11.0%), Kissi (6.0%), Kpelle (4.6%) and others (16.6%). The official language is French.

Tourism

In 2012, 96,000 non-resident tourists arrived at Conakry airport.

Guinea-Bissau

Republica da Guiné-Bissau (Republic of Guinea-Bissau)

Factsheet

Capital: Bissau
Population estimate, 2015: 1.84 m.
GNI per capita, 2014: (PPP$) 1,362
HDI/world rank, 2014: 0.420/178
Internet domain extension: .gw

Civil Aviation

There is an international airport serving Bissau (Osvaldo Vieira). In 2010 there were scheduled flights to Conakry, Dakar, Lisbon and Praia.

Climate

The tropical climate has a wet season from June to Nov., when rains are abundant, but the hot, dry Harmattan wind blows from Dec. to May. Bissau, Jan. 76 °F (24.4 °C), July 80 °F (26.7 °C). Annual rainfall 78″ (1,950 mm).

Constitution and Government

A new constitution was promulgated on 16 May 1984 and has been amended five times since, most recently in 1996. The Revolutionary Council, established following the 1980 coup, was replaced by a 15-member Council of State, while in April 1984 a new National People's Assembly was elected comprising 150 representatives elected by and from the directly-elected regional councils for 5-year terms. The sole political movement was the *Partido Africano da Independência da Guiné e Cabo Verde* (PAIGC), but in Dec. 1990 a policy of 'integral multi-partyism' was announced, and in May 1991 the National Assembly voted unanimously to abolish the law making the PAIGC the sole party. The *President* is Head of State and Government and is elected for a 5-year term. The *National Assembly* now has a maximum of 102 members. In the wake of the coup of April 2012 the military junta suspended the constitution and dissolved parliament (although it was resumed in Nov. 2012), and defied international demands for the constitution's restoration.

Currency

In May 1997 Guinea-Bissau joined the French Franc Zone, and the *peso* was replaced by the franc CFA at 65 pesos = one franc CFA. The *franc CFA* (XOF) has a parity rate of 655.957 francs CFA to one euro.

Defence

There is selective conscription. In 2012 defence expenditure totalled US$26 m., with spending per capita US$16. The 2012 expenditure represented 2.9% of GDP.

Economy

In 2012 agriculture accounted for 38.7% of GDP; followed by commerce, 18.5%; food processing, 11.3%; public administration services, 7.9%; transport and telecommunications, 5.0%.

Labour

The labour force in 2010 was 648,000 (52.7% males). Guinea-Bissau had 12,000 people living in slavery according to the Walk Free Foundation's 2013 *Global Slavery Index*.

Press

There are no daily newspapers. In 2008 there were six non-daily papers, which had a combined weekly circulation of 10,000 copies.

Religion

In 2010 there were an estimated 680,000 Muslims, 470,000 followers of folk religions and 300,000 Christians according to the Pew Research Center's Forum on Religion & Public Life.

Roads

In 2009 there were about 4,400 km of roads, of which 10% were paved. In 2008 there were 42,200 passenger cars in use (27 per 1,000 inhabitants in 2007) and 9,300 lorries and vans.

Shipping

The main port is Bissau; minor ports are Bolama, Cacheu and Catió.

Social Statistics

2008 births (estimates), 65,000; deaths, 27,000. Estimated rates per 1,000 population, 2008: births, 41.2; deaths, 17.2. Annual population growth rate, 2000–08, 2.4%. Life expectancy, 2013: male, 52.8 years; female, 55.8. Infant mortality, 2010, 92 per 1,000 live births; fertility rate, 2008, 5.7 births per woman.

Telecommunications

There were an estimated 5,000 fixed telephone lines in 2010 (3.3 per 1,000 inhabitants) and 402,000 mobile phone subscriptions in 2011 (or 259.8 per 1,000 inhabitants). There were 24.5 internet users per 1,000 inhabitants in 2010. Fixed internet subscriptions totalled 699 in 2009 (0.5 per 1,000 inhabitants).

Territory and Population

Guinea-Bissau is bounded by Senegal in the north, the Atlantic Ocean in the west and by Guinea in the east and south. It includes the adjacent archipelago of Bijagós. Area, 36,125 km² (13,948 sq. miles). 2009 census population, 1,520,830 (783,196 females); density, 42.1 per km². In 2011, 30.2% of the population were urban. The largest ethnic group are the Balanta (nearly a third of the population), Fulani, Manjaco and Mandinga. Portuguese remains the official language, but Crioulo is spoken throughout the country.

Tourism

In 2007, 30,000 non-resident tourists arrived by air.

Guyana

Co-operative Republic of Guyana

Factsheet

Capital: Georgetown
Population estimate, 2015: 767,000
GNI per capita, 2014: (PPP$) 6,522
HDI/world rank, 2014: 0.636/124
Internet domain extension: .gy

Civil Aviation

There is an international airport at Georgetown (Timehri), which handled 438,532 passengers in 2009. In 2010 there were direct flights to Antigua, Barbados, Miami, New York, Port of Spain, St Kitts and the British Virgin Islands.

Climate

A tropical climate, with rainy seasons from April to July and Nov. to Jan. Humidity is high all the year but temperatures are moderated by sea-breezes. Rainfall increases from 90″ (2,280 mm) on the coast to 140″ (3,560 mm) in the forest zone. Georgetown, Jan. 79 °F (26.1 °C), July 81 °F (27.2 °C). Annual rainfall 87″ (2,175 mm).

Constitution and Government

A new constitution was promulgated in Oct. 1980. There is an *Executive Presidency* and a *National Assembly*. The president is elected by simple majority vote as the designated candidate of a party list in parliamentary elections; there are no term limits. The National Assembly has 69 members who serve 5-year terms (65 directly elected, plus three non-elected ministers and the Speaker).

Currency

The unit of currency is the *Guyana dollar* (GYD) of 100 *cents*.

Defence

In 2013 defence expenditure totalled US\$35 m. (US\$48 per capita), representing 1.2% of GDP. The army, navy and air force are combined in a 1,100-strong Guyana Defence Force.

Economy

In 2009 agriculture accounted for 24.0% of GDP, industry 30.9% and services 45.1%.

Labour

In 2010 the estimated economically active population was 342,000 (66% males).

Press

In 2008 there were three daily newspapers (the state-owned *Guyana Chronicle* and the privately-owned *Kaieteur News* and *Stabroek News*) with a combined average daily circulation of 32,000.

Rail

There is a government-owned railway in the North West District, while the Guyana Mining Enterprise operates a standard gauge railway of 133 km from Linden on the Demerara River to Ituni and Coomacka.

Religion

In 2010 the population was an estimated 66.0% Christian according to the Pew Research Center's Forum on Religion & Public Life, with Hindus constituting 24.9% and Muslims 6.4%.

Roads

There are approximately 4,000 km of roads. In 2008 there were 44,700 passenger cars in use, plus 28,100 lorries and vans, and 37,100 motorcycles and mopeds.

Shipping

The major port is Georgetown; there are two other ports. In Jan. 2009 there were 28 ships of 300 GT or over registered, totalling 25,000 GT. There are 217 nautical miles of river navigation. There are ferry services across the mouths of the Demerara, Berbice and Essequibo rivers.

Social Statistics

2009 estimates: births, 14,000; deaths, 5,000. Rates, 2009 estimates (per 1,000 population): birth, 18; death, 6. Life expectancy at birth in 2013: male 63.6 years and female 68.9 years. Annual population growth rate, 2005–10, 0.7%. Infant mortality, 2010, 25 per 1,000 live births; fertility rate, 2013, 2.5 births per woman.

Telecommunications

In 2011 there were 152,600 landline telephone subscriptions (equivalent to 201.8 per 1,000 inhabitants) and 518,800 mobile phone subscriptions (or 686.2 per 1,000 inhabitants). In 2010, 29.9% of the population were internet users. In March 2012 there were 124,000 Facebook users.

Territory and Population

Guyana is situated on the northeast coast of Latin America on the Atlantic Ocean, with Suriname on the east, Venezuela on the west and Brazil on the

south and west. Area, 214,999 km^2 (83,013 sq. miles). In 2012 the census population (provisional) was 747,884; density 3.5 per km^2. Guyana has the highest proportion of rural population in South America, with only 28.7% living in urban areas in 2011. Ethnic groups by origin: 49% Indian, 36% African, 7% mixed race, 7% Amerindian and 1% others. The capital is Georgetown (2012 provisional census population, 24,849; urban agglomeration, 118,363); other towns are Linden, New Amsterdam, Anna Regina and Corriverton.

Tourism

141,000 non-resident tourists arrived at Timehri airport in 2009 (130,000 in 2008).

Haiti

République d'Haïti (Republic of Haiti)

Factsheet

Capital: Port-au-Prince
Population estimate, 2015: 10.71 m.
GNI per capita, 2014: (PPP\$) 1,669
HDI/world rank, 2014: 0.483/163
Internet domain extension: .ht

Civil Aviation

There is an international airport at Port-au-Prince. Cap Haïtien also has scheduled flights to the Turks and Caicos Islands. In 2001 Port-au-Prince handled 913,022 passengers (771,656 on international flights) and 13,455 tonnes of freight.

Climate

A tropical climate, but the central mountains can cause semi-arid conditions in their lee. There are rainy seasons from April to June and Aug. to Nov. Hurricanes and severe thunderstorms can occur. The annual temperature range is small. Port-au-Prince, Jan. 77 °F (25 °C), July 84 °F (28.9 °C). Annual rainfall 53″ (1,321 mm).

Constitution and Government

A new constitution was signed off by President Martelly in June 2012, replacing one promulgated in 1987. The 2012 constitution had received parliamentary backing in May 2011 but was not written into law until after a year of legal wrangling. Among its provisions is the re-legalization of dual citizenship, which had been criminalized under the 1987 constitution. Haitians living abroad, who are responsible for remittances equivalent to 20% of GDP, have the right to own land in Haiti and to stand for political office (with the exceptions of the presidency, premiership, as a senator or a member of the Chamber of Deputies). The constitution also established a permanent constitutional court to mediate in disputes between parliament and the executive, as well as an electoral council to oversee free and fair elections. Women are required to hold at least 30% of government posts. There is a bicameral legislature (a 119-member *Chamber of Deputies* and a 30-member *Senate*) and an executive *President*, directly elected for a 5-year term.

Currency

The unit of currency is the *gourde* (HTG) of 100 *centimes*.

Defence

After the restoration of civilian rule in 1994 the armed forces and police were disbanded and an Interim Public Security Force formed, although this was later also dissolved. In 1995 a new police force-Police Nationale d'Haiti (PNH)-was recruited from former military personnel and others not implicated in human rights violations. The PNH currently has about 2,000 members. A UN peacekeeping force, MINUSTAH, has been in Haiti since 2004. Following the earthquake of Jan. 2010 the UN Security Council passed a resolution recommending an increase in overall force levels to support the immediate recovery, reconstruction and stability efforts in the country. As of June 2015 MINUSTAH consisted of 4,577 uniformed personnel. In the period 2002–12 annual defence expenditure is estimated to have averaged US$8 m.

Economy

Trade and restaurants contributed 26.9% to GDP in 2010–11; followed by agriculture and forestry, 23.8%; finance and real estate, 11.3%; and services, public administration and defence, 11.3%.

Labour

In 2010 the labour force was 4,161,000 (53.0% males). The unemployment rate in 2009 was around 70%. Haiti had 0.21 m. people living in slavery according to the Walk Free Foundation's 2013 *Global Slavery Index*.

Press

There were two paid-for daily newspapers in 2008 with a combined circulation of 23,000.

Religion

According to estimates by the Pew Research Center's Forum on Religion & Public Life, 86.9% of the population in 2010 was Christian and 10.6% had no religious affiliation; of the Christians, 65% were Catholics and 34% Protestants. The Roman Catholic Church comprises two ecclesiastical provinces, each headed by an archbishop. In Feb. 2016 there was one Roman Catholic cardinal. Voodoo was recognized as an official religion in 2003.

Roads

Total length of roads was estimated at 3,500 km in 2013, although most of the network was in a poor state of repair.

Shipping

Port-au-Prince and Cap Haïtien are the principal ports, and there are 12 minor ports. In Jan. 2009 there were three ships of 300 GT or over registered, totalling 2,000 GT.

Social Statistics

2009 estimates: births, 266,000; deaths, 89,000. Rates, 2009 estimates (per 1,000 population): birth, 27; death, 9. Annual population growth rate, 2005–10, 1.5%. Expectation of life at birth, 2013, 61.2 years for males and 65.0 years for females. Infant mortality, 2010, 70 per 1,000 live births; fertility rate, 2013, 3.1 births per woman.

Telecommunications

The state telecommunications agency is Teleco. There were 108,300 fixed telephone lines in 2009 (11 per 1,000 inhabitants). Mobile phone subscribers numbered 3.65 m. in 2009. There were 83.7 internet users per 1,000 inhabitants in 2010. Fixed internet subscriptions totalled 100,000 in 2007 (ten per 1,000 inhabitants). In Dec. 2011 there were 295,000 Facebook users.

Territory and Population

Haiti is bounded in the east by the Dominican Republic, to the north by the Atlantic and elsewhere by the Caribbean Sea. The area is 27,065 km² (10,450 sq. miles). The Île de la Gonâve, some 40 miles long, lies in the gulf of the same name. Among other islands is La Tortue, off the north peninsula. Census population, 2003, 8,373,750; density, 309 per km². On 1 July 2009 the official population estimate was 9,923,243. In 2011, 53.6% of the population were urban. The capital is Port-au-Prince (2009 estimated population, 875,978; urban agglomeration, 2,296,386); the other main cities are Gonaïves (228,725 in 2009) and Cap Haïtien (155,505). Most of the population is of African or mixed origin. The official languages are French and Créole. Créole is spoken by all Haitians; French by only a small minority.

Tourism

In 2009 there were 387,220 stopover tourists (including 268,224 from the USA); cruise passenger arrivals in 2009 numbered 439,055.

Honduras

República de Honduras (Republic of Honduras)

Factsheet

Capital: Tegucigalpa
Population estimate, 2015: 8.08 m.
GNI per capita, 2014: (PPP$) 3,938
HDI/world rank, 2014: 0.606/131
Internet domain extension: .hn

Civil Aviation

There are four international airports: San Pedro Sula (Ramón Villeda) and Tegucigalpa (Toncontín) are the main ones, plus Roatún and La Ceiba, with over 80 smaller airstrips in various parts of the country. In 2012 San Pedro Sula handled 769,516 passengers (700,892 on international flights) and 15,775 tonnes of freight, and Tegucigalpa handled 581,740 passengers (466,956 on international flights) and 3,674 tonnes of freight.

Climate

The climate is tropical, with a small annual range of temperature but with high rainfall. Upland areas have two wet seasons, from May to July and in Sept. and Oct. The Caribbean Coast has most rain in Dec. and Jan. and temperatures are generally higher than inland. Tegucigalpa, Jan. 66 °F (19 °C), July 74 °F (23.3 °C). Annual rainfall 64″ (1,621 mm).

Constitution and Government

The present Constitution came into force in 1982 and was amended in 1995. The *President* is elected for a single 4-year term. Members of the *National Congress* (total 128 seats) and municipal mayors are elected simultaneously on a proportional basis, according to combined votes cast for the Presidential candidate of their party. In March 2009 the then president, Manuel Zelaya, proposed a referendum to approve an assembly to revise the constitution. His opponents feared that he was seeking revisions to allow him to stand for re-election. A constitutional crisis culminated in a military coup and Zelaya's exile to Costa Rica.

Currency

The unit of currency is the *lempira* (HNL) of 100 *centavos*.

Defence

Conscription was abolished in 1995. In 2013 defence expenditure totalled US$177 m. (US$21 per capita), representing 0.9% of GDP.

Economy

Agriculture accounted for 11.9% of GDP in 2009, industry 26.8% and services 61.3%.

Labour

The labour force in 2013 was 3,275,000 (2,413,000 in 2003). 64.5% of the population aged 15–64 was economically active in 2013. In the same year 3.9% of the population was unemployed.

Press

Honduras had six national daily papers in 2008, with a combined circulation of 200,000.

Rail

The small government-run railway was built to serve the banana industry and is confined to the northern coastal region and does not reach Tegucigalpa. Much of the network is now out of service and in 2012 only 62 km of 914 mm gauge railway were operational.

Religion

In 2010 there were an estimated 3.82 m. Roman Catholics and 2.78 m. Protestants according to the Pew Research Center's Forum on Religion & Public Life, with a further 790,000 people not having any religious affiliation. In Feb. 2016 there was one cardinal.

Roads

Honduras is connected with Guatemala, El Salvador and Nicaragua by the Pan-American Highway. There are some 14,000 km of roads, of which about 21% are paved. In 2007 there were 487,700 passenger cars in use, 31,500 buses and coaches, 165,200 lorries and vans, and 94,400 motorcycles and mopeds.

Shipping

The largest port is Puerto Cortés on the Atlantic coast. There are also ports at Henecán (on the Pacific) and Puerto Castilla and Tela (northern coast). In Jan. 2009 there were 359 ships of 300 GT or over registered, totalling 489,000 GT. Honduras is a flag of convenience registry.

Social Statistics

2009 estimates: births, 201,000; deaths, 37,000. Rates, 2009 estimates (per 1,000 population): birth, 27; death, 5. 2013 life expectancy, 71.5 years for men and 76.2 for women. Annual population growth rate, 2005–10, 1.7%. Infant mortality, 2010, 20 per 1,000 live births; fertility rate, 2013, 3.0 births per woman. Abortion is illegal.

Telecommunications

In 2011 there were 609,200 landline telephone subscriptions (equivalent to 78.6 per 1,000 inhabitants) and 8,062,200 mobile phone subscriptions (or 1,039.7 per 1,000 inhabitants). There were 110.9 internet users per 1,000 inhabitants in 2010. Fixed internet subscriptions totalled 72,400 in 2009 (9.7 per 1,000 inhabitants). In Dec. 2011 there were 1.1 m. Facebook users.

Territory and Population

Honduras is bounded in the north by the Caribbean, east and southeast by Nicaragua, west by Guatemala, southwest by El Salvador and south by the Pacific Ocean. The area is 112,492 km^2 (43,433 sq. miles). In 2013 the census population was 8,303,771 (4,251,456 females), giving a density of 73.8 per km^2. In 2011, 52.2% of the population lived in urban areas. The chief cities and towns are (2009 estimated populations): Tegucigalpa, the capital (990,600), San Pedro Sula (646,300), Choloma (223,900), La Ceiba (172,900), El Progreso (122,000), Choluteca (91,000), Comayagua (78,300), Puerto Cortés (68,400), La Lima (67,100), Danlí (62,100). The official language is Spanish. The Spanish-speaking population is of mixed Spanish and Amerindian descent (87%), with 6% Amerindians.

Tourism

In 2009 there were 870,000 non-resident tourists, down from 899,000 in 2008 although up from 831,000 in 2007.

Hungary

Magyarország

Factsheet

Capital: Budapest
Population estimate, 2015: 9.86 m.
GNI per capita, 2014: (PPP$) 22,916
HDI/world rank, 2014: 0.828/44
Internet domain extension: .hu

Civil Aviation

Budapest airport (Ferihegy) handled 8,095,367 passengers in 2009 (all on international flights) and 54,355 tonnes of freight. Malév, the former national carrier, ceased operations in Feb. 2012. The largest Hungarian airline is now Wizz Air, which started flying in 2004 and is Central and Eastern Europe's largest low-cost carrier.

Climate

A humid continental climate, with warm summers and cold winters. Precipitation is generally greater in summer, with thunderstorms. Dry, clear weather is likely in autumn, but spring is damp and both seasons are of short duration. Budapest, Jan. 32 °F (0 °C), July 71 °F (21.5 °C). Annual rainfall 25″ (625 mm). Pécs, Jan. 30 °F (−0.7 °C), July 71 °F (21.5 °C). Annual rainfall 26.4″ (661 mm).

Constitution and Government

On 18 Oct. 1989 the National Assembly approved by an 88% majority a constitution which abolished the People's Republic, and established Hungary as an independent, democratic, law-based state. In April 2011 parliament passed proposals for a new constitution, known as the 'Easter constitution', by a vote of 263 to 44 (with one abstention). It came into force on 1 Jan. 2012. Two of the three main opposition parties refused to vote in protest at what critics claimed were attacks by the ruling Fidesz party on the rights of various minority groups, including those with mental illness, the gay and lesbian community, and pro-abortion bodies. The constitution's preamble emphasizes Hungary's Christian heritage while other clauses restrict the voting rights of those with 'limited mental ability'. It defines marriage as a union of a man and a woman, and stipulates that the life of a foetus should be protected from conception. The head of state is the *President*, who is elected for 5-year terms by the National Assembly. The single-chamber *National Assembly* currently has 199 members (386 prior to the elections of April 2014), made up of 106 elected in individual constituencies and 93 allocated by proportional representation from party lists (including minority-list seats). It is elected for 4-year terms.

Currency

A decree of 26 July 1946 instituted a new monetary unit, the *forint* (HUF) of 100 *fillér*. The forint was made fully convertible in Jan. 1991 and moves in a 15% band against the euro either side of a central rate of €1 = 282.4 forints.

Defence

The President of the Republic is C.-in-C. of the armed forces. Conscription was abolished in 2004. In 2013 defence expenditure totalled US$1,100 m. (US$111 per capita), representing 0.8% of GDP.

Economy

Agriculture accounted for 4.6% of GDP in 2013, industry 30.1% and services 65.3%.

Labour

In 2009 out of an economically active population of 4,202,600 there were 3,781,900 employed persons, of which 3,309,900 were employees. Among the employed persons in 2009, 64.2% worked in services, 31.2% in industry and construction, and 4.6% in agriculture. Average gross monthly wages of full-time employees in 2009: 199,837 forints. Minimum monthly wage, 2009, 71,500 forints (more than twice the 2000 level). There were a total of 6,474 working days lost to strike action in 2009, down from 25,004 in 2008. The unemployment rate was 6.3% in Nov. 2015 (down from 7.7% in 2014 as a whole). Long-term unemployment is particularly high, with 50.6% of the labour force in 2010 having been out of work for more than a year. The normal retirement age is 62 years 6 months but is increasing gradually to 65 for both men and women by 2022. Hungary had 36,000 people living in slavery according to the Walk Free Foundation's 2013 *Global Slavery Index*.

Press

In 2014 there were 31 daily newspapers with a combined circulation of 1,210,000. The most widely read newspapers are the free tabloid *Metropol* and the paid-for tabloid *Blikk*. A total of 12,841 book titles were published in 2009 in 36.02 m. copies.

Rail

In 2011 the rail network was 7,896 km in length; 115.6 m. passengers were carried that year. Rail Cargo Hungaria carried 29.1 m. tonnes of freight in 2012. There is a metro in Budapest (38.2 km), and tram/light rail networks in Budapest (332.0 km), Debrecen, Miskolc and Szeged.

Religion

According to the Pew Research Center's Forum on Religion & Public Life, an estimated 81.0% of the population in 2010 was Christian and 18.6% had no religious affiliation. Of the Christians, 73% in 2010 were Catholics and 26% Protestants. The Roman Catholic primate of Hungary is Péter Erdő, Archbishop of Esztergom-Budapest, installed in Jan. 2003. The Roman Catholic Church comprises four ecclesiastical provinces and nine suffragan dioceses. In Feb. 2016 the Roman Catholic church had one cardinal.

Roads

In 2007 there were 195,719 km of roads, including 1,157 km of motorways, 6,745 km of main roads and 23,280 km of secondary roads; 37.7% of roads were paved. Passenger cars numbered 3,012,200 in 2007; lorries and vans, 829,800; motorcycles and mopeds, 135,900; and buses and coaches, 17,900. In 2007 there were 20,635 road accidents with 1,232 fatalities.

Shipping

In 2008 there were 1,440 km of navigable waterways. In 2009 the Hungarian river fleet comprised 318 pushed or towed barges, 83 self-propelled barges and 80 other pushed or towed vessels. In 2009, 7.75 m. tonnes of cargo and 859,000 passengers were carried. The Hungarian Shipping Company (MAHART) has agencies at Amsterdam, Alexandria, Algiers, Beirut, Rijeka and Trieste. It has 23 ships and runs scheduled services between Budapest and Esztergom.

Social Statistics

2011: births, 88,049; deaths, 128,795; marriages, 35,812; divorces, 23,335. There were 2,422 suicides in 2011. Rates (per 1,000 population), 2011: birth, 8.8; death, 12.9; marriage, 3.6; divorce, 2.3. Population growth rate, 2009, −0.2%. The suicide rate, at 24.6 per 100,000 population in 2009, is one of the highest in the world (although it has fallen since the mid-1980s when it was over 44 per 100,000). Expectation of life at birth, 2011, 70.9 years for males and 78.2 years for females. Infant mortality, 2010, 5 per 1,000 live births. Fertility rate, 2011, 1.2 births per woman.

Telecommunications

In 2013 there were 2,978,000 main (fixed) telephone lines. In the same year mobile phone subscribers numbered 11,590,000 (1,164.3 per 1,000 persons). Matav, the privatized former national telephone company, still has more than 80% of the fixed line market. 72.6% of the population aged 16–74 were internet users in 2013. There were 19.6 fixed broadband subscribers per 100 inhabitants in Dec. 2010. In March 2012 there were 3.8 m. Facebook users.

Territory and Population

Hungary is bounded in the north by Slovakia, northeast by Ukraine, east by Romania, south by Croatia and Serbia, southwest by Slovenia and west by Austria. The peace treaty of 10 Feb. 1947 restored the frontiers as of 1 Jan. 1938. The area of Hungary is 93,030 km^2 (35,919 sq. miles), including 690 km^2 (266 sq. miles) of inland waters. At the census of 1 Oct. 2011 the population was 9,937,628 (52.5% females). 67.7% of the population was urban in Jan. 2008; population density, Oct. 2011, 108.1 per km^2. Hungary is divided into 19 counties (megyék) and the capital, Budapest, which has county status. The official language is Hungarian.

Tourism

In 2011, 3,822,000 non-resident tourists and 4,199,000 domestic tourists stayed in holiday accommodation (3,462,000 and 4,011,000 respectively in 2010). The main countries of origin of non-resident tourists in 2011 were: Germany (542,000), Austria (295,000), the UK (221,000) and Romania (216,000).

Iceland

Lyðveldið Ísland (Republic of Iceland)

Factsheet

Capital: Reykjavík
Population estimate, 2015: 329,000
GNI per capita, 2014: (PPP$) 35,182
HDI/world rank, 2014: 0.899/16
Internet domain extension: .is

Civil Aviation

Icelandair is the national carrier, serving 27 destinations in Europe and 16 in north America. In 2011 it carried 1.7 m. passengers. The second largest airline is the low-cost carrier WOW air. The main international airport is at Keflavík (Leifsstöd), with Reykjavík for flights to the Faroe Islands, Greenland and domestic services. Keflavík handled 2,112,014 passengers in 2011 (of which 412,440 transit passengers) and 36,628 tonnes of freight.

Climate

The climate is cool temperate oceanic and rather changeable, but mild for its latitude because of the Gulf Stream and prevailing S.W. winds. Precipitation is high in upland areas, mainly in the form of snow. Reykjavík, Jan. 31.1 °F (−0.5 °C), July 51.1 °F (10.6 °C). Annual rainfall, 2009: 28.1″ (713 mm).

Constitution and Government

The present constitution came into force on 17 June 1944 and has been amended four times since, most recently on 24 June 1999. The President is elected by direct, popular vote for a period of 4 years (no term limits). The *Alþingi* (parliament) is elected in accordance with the electoral law of 1999, which provides for an *Alþingi* of 63 members. The country is divided into a minimum of six and a maximum of seven constituencies. There are currently six constituencies: Northwest (10 seats); Northeast (10 seats); South (10); Southwest (11); Reykjavík north (11); and Reykjavík south (11).

Currency

The unit of currency is the *króna* (ISK) of 100 *aurar* (singular: *eyrir*).

Defence

Iceland possesses no armed forces. Under the North Atlantic Treaty, US forces were stationed for many years in Iceland as the Iceland Defence Force. In Sept. 2006 an agreement was signed between USA and Iceland, withdrawing all US forces from the island.

Economy

Agriculture accounted for 7.8% of GDP in 2012, industry 23.6% and services 68.6%.

Labour

In 2013 the labour force was 190,000 (170,000 in 2003). 84.4% of the population aged 15–64 was economically active in 2013. Iceland has a very high employment rate among older workers, with 55.3% of the population aged 65–69 in 2014 still working. The unemployment rate in Dec. 2015 was 3.6% (down from 5.0% in 2014 as a whole).

Press

In 2008 there were four daily newspapers (two paid-for and two free) and 20 non-daily newspapers. Combined circulation was 336,459 (of which dailies accounted for 278,154 and non-dailies 58,305). Iceland has the highest circulation rates of daily newspapers in the world, at 817 per 1,000 adult inhabitants in 2008. Iceland publishes more books per person than any other country in the world. In 2008, 1,637 volumes of books and booklets were published.

Religion

The national church, the Evangelical Lutheran, is endowed by the state. There is complete religious liberty. The affairs of the national church are under the superintendence of a bishop. In 2010, 251,487 persons (79.2% of the population) were members of it (93.2% in 1980). 16,497 persons (5.2%) belonged to Lutheran free churches. 39,310 persons (12.4%) belonged to other religious organizations and 10,336 persons (3.3%) did not belong to any religious community.

Roads

On 1 Jan. 2009 the length of the public roads (including roads in towns) was 12,888 km. Of these 7,829 km were main and secondary roads and 5,059 km were provincial roads. Total length of surfaced roads was 4,566 km. A ring road of 1,400 km runs just inland from much of the coast; about 80% of it is smooth-surfaced. Motor vehicles registered at the end of 2009 numbered 238,149, of which 207,226 were passenger cars (643 per 1,000 inhabitants) and 30,923 lorries and vans; there were also 9,420 motorcycles. There were 15 fatal road accidents in 2009 with 17 persons killed.

Shipping

On 1 Jan. 2008 the merchant fleet consisted of 52 vessels totalling 8,515 GT, including 49 passenger ships and ferries of 7,669 GT.

Social Statistics

Live births in 2009, 5,027; deaths, 2,002. 2009 rates per 1,000 population: births, 15.8; deaths, 6.3. 64.4% of births are to unmarried mothers, the highest percentage in Europe. Population growth rate, 2009, −0.5%. In 2009 the most popular age range for marrying was 30–34 for males and 25–29 for females. Life expectancy, 2009: males, 79.7 years; females, 83.3. Infant mortality, 2009, 2.4 per 1,000 live births (one of the lowest rates in the world); fertility rate, 2009, 2.2 births per woman. Iceland legalized same-sex marriage in July 2010.

Telecommunications

The number of telephone main lines was 168,023 in 2013; mobile phone subscribers, 356,264 (more than the population of Iceland and equivalent to 1,081 subscriptions per 1,000 population). In 2013, 96.6% of the population (the highest percentage in the world) were internet users. The fixed broadband penetration rate in Dec. 2010 was 33.7 subscribers per 100 inhabitants. In March 2012 there were 210,000 Facebook users.

Territory and Population

Iceland is an island in the North Atlantic, close to the Arctic Circle. Area, 102,819 km^2 (39,698 sq. miles). Of the population of 317,630 in 2010, 20,428 were domiciled in rural districts and 297,202 (93.6%) in towns and villages (of over 200 inhabitants). Population density (2010), 3.1 per km^2. The capital, Reykjavík, had on 1 Jan. 2013 a population of 118,918; main other towns were: Kópavogur, 31,719; Hafnarfjörður, 26,800; Akureyri, 17,963; Keflavík og Njarðvík, 14,153; Garðabær, 11,421. The official language is Icelandic.

Tourism

There were 459,252 visitors in 2010; revenue totalled 152,941 m. kr. Overnight stays in hotels and guest houses in 2009 numbered 1,939,667 (of which foreign travellers, 1,553,927; Icelanders, 385,740). Tourism accounts for 19.4% of foreign currency earnings.

India

Bharat (Republic of India)

Factsheet

Capital: New Delhi
Population estimate, 2015: 1,311.05 m.

GNI per capita, 2014: (PPP$) 5,497
HDI/world rank, 2014: 0.609/130
Internet domain extension: .in

Civil Aviation

The main international airports are at Chennai, Delhi (Indira Gandhi), Kolkata, Mumbai and Thiruvananthapuram, with some international flights from Ahmedabad, Amritsar, Bangalore, Calicut, Goa and Hyderabad. Air transport was nationalized in 1953 with the formation of two Air Corporations: Air India for long-distance international air services, and Indian Airlines for air services within India and to adjacent countries. Indian (as Indian Airlines became in 2005) merged into Air India in Feb. 2011. Both domestic and international air transport have been opened to private companies, the largest of which is Jet Airways. Two leading budget airlines, IndiGo and SpiceJet, now operate international as well as domestic services. All operational airports handled a total of 116.9 m. passengers (87.1 m. domestic and 29.8 m. international) in the year to 31 March 2008. Total aircraft movements reached 1.31 m. and freight volumes increased to over 1.7 m. tonnes. In 2007 Mumbai was the busiest airport, handling 25.2 m. passengers, followed by Delhi, with 23.3 m. passengers. Both airports were privatized in 2006, with extensive modernization.

Climate

India has a variety of climatic sub-divisions. In general, there are four seasons. The cool one lasts from Dec. to March, the hot season is in April and May, the rainy season is June to Sept., followed by a further dry season until Nov. Rainfall, however, varies considerably, from 4″ (100 mm) in the N.W. desert to over 400″ (10,000 mm) in parts of Assam.

Constitution and Government

The Constitution was passed by the Constituent Assembly on 26 Nov. 1949 and came into force on 26 Jan. 1950. It has since been amended 96 times. India is a republic and comprises a Union of 29 States and seven Union Territories. Each State is administered by a Governor appointed by the President for a term of 5 years while each Union Territory is administered by the President through a Lieut.-Governor or an administrator appointed by him. The head of the Union (head of state) is the *President* in whom all executive power is vested, to be exercised on the advice of ministers responsible to Parliament. The President, who must be an Indian citizen at least 35 years old and eligible for election to the House of the People, is elected by an electoral college of all the elected members of Parliament and of the state legislative assemblies, holds office for 5 years and is eligible for re-election. There is also a *Vice-President* who is *ex officio* chairman of the Council of States. There is a *Council of Ministers* to aid and advise the President; this comprises Ministers who are members of the Cabinet and Ministers of State and deputy ministers who are not. The *Prime Minister* is appointed by the President; other Ministers are appointed by the President on the Prime Minister's advice. Parliament consists of the President, the *Council of States* (*Rajya Sabha*) and the *House of the People* (*Lok Sabha*).

Currency

The unit of currency is the *Indian rupee* (INR) of 100 *paise*.

Defence

The Supreme Command of the Armed Forces is vested in the president. As well as armed forces of 1,325,000 personnel in 2011, there are 1,301,000 active paramilitary forces including 208,000 members of the Border Security Force based mainly in the troubled Jammu and Kashmir region. Military service is voluntary but, under the amended constitution, it is regarded as a fundamental duty of every citizen to perform National Service when called upon. Defence expenditure totalled US$36,297 m. in 2013 (US$30 per capita), representing 1.8% of GDP. According to the Stockholm International Peace Research Institute, India's nuclear arsenal was estimated to consist of 90–110 nuclear warheads in Jan. 2015.

Economy

Agriculture accounted for 18.0% of GDP in 2013 (down from 55% in 1950), industry 30.7% (up from 15% in 1950) and services 51.3% (up from 30% in 1950).

Labour

The labour force in 2013 was 487,882,000 (442,357,000 in 2003). 56.4% of the population aged 15–64 was economically active in 2013. In the same year 3.6% of the population was unemployed. India's working-age population is set to overtake that of China to become the world's largest around 2025. India had 13.96 m. people living in slavery according to the Walk Free Foundation's 2013 *Global Slavery Index*, the highest total of any country.

Press

There were 99,660 registered publications in March 2014 (up from 73,146 in March 2009), with a total circulation of 450.6 m. In 2011 there were 4,397 dailies with a total circulation of 175.70 m. (up from 162.35 m. in 2010). India's circulation of paid-for dailies overtook that of China in 2008 to become the highest of any country; in 2014 it totalled 264.3 m. Hindi papers have the highest number and circulation, followed by English and Urdu. The newspaper with the highest circulation is the *Dainik Bhaskar*, a Hindi-language paper (daily average of 3.6 m. copies in 2014 and a readership of 13.8 m.). The English-language paper with the highest circulation is *The Times of India*, with a daily average of 3.4 m. copies in 2014.

Rail

Indian railway system is government-owned (under the control of the Railway Board). There are 17 zones. The total length of the Indian railway network was 64,460 km in March 2011 (19,607 electrified), with the Northern zone having the longest network, at 6,968 km. There are metros in Bangalore (6.7 km), Chennai (19.7 km), Delhi (189.6 km) and Kolkata (25.5 km).

Religion

India is a secular state; any worship is permitted, but the state itself has no religion. The principal religions in 2011 were: Hindus, 966 m. (80% of the population); Muslims, 172 m. (14%); Christians, 28 m.; Sikhs, 21 m.; Buddhists, 8 m.; Jains, 4 m. In addition to having the largest Hindu population of any country, India has the third highest number of Muslims, after Indonesia and Pakistan. In Feb. 2016 the Roman Catholic church had five cardinals.

Roads

In March 2011 there were 3,790,342 km of roads of which 2,341,480 km were surfaced. Roads are divided into six main administrative classes, namely: national highways, state highways, other public works department (PWD) roads, *Panchayati Raj* roads, urban roads and project roads. In 2006 there were 11,526,000 passenger cars, 64,743,000 motorcycles and scooters, 992,000 buses and coaches, and 4,436,000 lorries and vans. In 2007 there were 476,219 road accidents resulting in 114,444 deaths.

Shipping

In Jan. 2009 there were 625 ships of 300 GT or over registered, totalling 8.57 m. GT. Of the 625 vessels registered, 301 were general cargo ships, 117 oil tankers, 108 bulk carriers, 51 passenger ships, 22 liquid gas tankers, 16 container ships and ten chemical tankers. The Indian-controlled fleet comprised 403 vessels of 1,000 GT or over in Jan. 2009, of which 347 were under the Indian flag and 56 under foreign flags. The busiest container port is Jawaharlal Nehru, which handled 3.9 m. 20-ft equivalent units (TEUs) in 2008. There are about 3,700 km of major rivers navigable by motorized craft, of which 2,000 km are used. Canals, 4,300 km, of which 900 km are navigable by motorized craft.

Social Statistics

Many births and deaths go unregistered. The Registrar General's data suggests a birth rate for 2009 of 22.5 per 1,000 population and a death rate of 7.3, which would indicate in a year approximately 27.2 m. births and 8.8 m. deaths. The growth rate is, however, slowing, and by 2010 had dropped to 1.4%, having been over 2% in 1991. Expectation of life at birth, 2013, 64.7 years for males and 68.3 years for females. In 2010, 50% of the population was aged under 25. Population growth rate, 2001–11, 17.64% (the lowest since 1941–51). Infant mortality, 2009, 50 per 1,000 live births; fertility rate, 2013, 2.5 births per woman. Child deaths (under the age of five) fell from 123 per 1,000 in 1990 to 64 per 1,000 in 2009.

Telecommunications

The telephone system is in the hands of the Telecommunications Department, except in Delhi and Mumbai, which are served by a public corporation. In 2010 there were 35.1 m. main (fixed) telephone lines. Mobile phone subscriptions numbered 752.2 m. in Dec. 2010 (623.9 per 1,000 persons), more than double the number just 2 years earlier and treble the number 3 years earlier. The number of fixed line subscribers has been gradually falling since 2005. India's largest mobile phone operator is Bharti Airtel, with a 22.8% market share in July 2014, ahead of Vodafone and Idea Cellular. An estimated 12.6% of the population were internet users in 2012. In March 2012 there were 45.0 m. Facebook users.

Territory and Population

India is bounded in the northwest by Pakistan, north by China (Tibet), Nepal and Bhutan, east by Myanmar, and southeast, south and southwest by the Indian Ocean. The far eastern states and territories are almost separated from the rest by Bangladesh. The area is 3,287,263 km^2 (land area, 2,973,190 km^2; water area, 314,073 km^2). A Sino-Indian agreement of 7 Sept. 1993 settled frontier disputes dating from the war of 1962. Population, 2011 census: 1,210,854,977. 51.5% of the population was male and 48.5% female. Density, 407.3 persons per km^2. There are also 20 m. Indians and ethnic Indians living abroad, notably in Malaysia, the USA, Saudi Arabia, the UK and South Africa. 68.8% of the population was rural in 2011. Goa is the most urban state, at 62.2% in 2011; and Himachal Pradesh the most rural, at 90.0% in 2011. By 2050 India is expected to have a population of 1.62 bn. It is projected to overtake China as the world's most populous country around 2022. Largest urban agglomerations (with 2011 census populations): Mumbai (Bombay), 18,394,912; Delhi, 16,349,831; Kolkata (Calcutta), 14,057,991; Chennai (Madras), 8,653,521; Bangalore, 8,520,435.

Tourism

In 2012 there were 6,578,000 non-resident overnight tourists (up from 6,309,000 in 2011 and 5,082,000 in 2007). Of the non-resident overnight tourists in 2011, 34% were from Europe, 21% from the Americas and 19% from East Asia and the Pacific. Tourist receipts amounted to US$18.3 bn. in 2012.

Indonesia

Republik Indonesia (Republic of Indonesia)

Factsheet

Capital: Jakarta
Population estimate, 2015: 257.56 m.
GNI per capita, 2014: (PPP$) 9,788
HDI/world rank, 2014: 0.684/110=
Internet domain extension: .id

Civil Aviation

Garuda Indonesia is the state-owned national flag carrier. Merpati Nusantara Airlines, their domestic subsidiary, suspended all services in Feb. 2014 due to cashflow issues. There are international airports at Jakarta (Sukarno-Hatta), Denpasar (on Bali), Medan (Sumatra), Pekanbaru (Sumatra), Ujung Pandang (Sulawesi), Manado (Sulawesi), Solo (Java) and Surabaya Juanda (Java). Jakarta is the busiest airport, in 2012 handling 57,772,762 passengers (42,660,093 domestic passengers, 11,286,687 on international passengers and 3,285,982 direct transit passengers) and 634,751 tonnes of freight. In 2012 scheduled airline traffic of Indonesia-based carriers flew 466.8 m. km; passenger-km totalled 82.9 bn. in the same year.

Climate

Conditions vary greatly over this spread of islands, but generally the climate is tropical monsoon, with a dry season from June to Sept. and a wet one from Oct. to April. Temperatures are high all the year and rainfall varies according to situation on lee or windward shores. Jakarta, Jan. 78 °F (25.6 °C), July 78 °F (25.6 °C). Annual rainfall 71″ (1,775 mm).

Constitution and Government

The constitution originally dates from Aug. 1945 and was in force until 1949; it was restored on 5 July 1959. The political system is based on *pancasila*, in which deliberations lead to a consensus. There is a 560-member *Dewan Perwakilan Rakyat* (House of People's Representatives), with members elected for a 5-year term by proportional representation in multi-member constituencies. An upper house, the *Dewan Perwakilan Daerah* (House of Regional Representatives), has 132 members elected by single non-transferable vote to serve 5-year terms. The two chambers together form the *Majelis Permusyawaratan Rakyat* (People's Consultative Assembly). The constitution was changed on 10 Aug. 2002 to allow for direct elections for the president and the vice-president. There is no limit to the number of presidential terms. Although predominantly a Muslim country, the constitution protects the religious beliefs of non-Muslims.

Currency

The monetary unit is the *rupiah* (IDR) notionally of 100 *sen*.

Defence

There is selective conscription for 2 years. In 2013 defence expenditure totalled US$8,366 m. (up from US$6,524 m. in 2012), with spending per capita US$33. The 2013 expenditure represented 0.9% of GDP.

Economy

Agriculture accounted for 15.3% of GDP in 2009, industry 47.7% and services 37.0%.

Labour

The labour force in 2013 numbered 122,125,000, up from 103,424,000 in 2003. 70.0% of the population aged 15–64 was economically active in 2013. Women constituted 38.0% of the workforce in 2013. In the same year 6.3% of the population was unemployed. Indonesia had 0.21 m. people living in slavery according to the Walk Free Foundation's 2013 *Global Slavery Index*.

Press

In 2014 there were a total of 653 newspapers (of which 431 were dailies and 222 non-dailies), with a total circulation of 10,994,000.

Rail

In 2005 the national railways totalled 6,482 km of 1,067 mm gauge, comprising 3,012 km on Java (of which 565 km electrified), 1,348 km on Sumatra and 2,122 km which was non-operational. Passenger-km travelled in 2008 came to 18.5 bn. and freight tonne-km to 5.5 bn.

Religion

Indonesia has six officially recognized religions: Islam, Catholicism, Protestantism, Buddhism, Hinduism and Confucianism. In 2010 there were an estimated 209.1 m. Muslims according to the Pew Research Center's Forum on Religion & Public Life (making Indonesia the country with the largest Muslim population). There were also 13.9 m. Protestants in 2010, 7.2 m. Catholics, 4.1 m. Hindus and 1.7 m. Buddhists. As a proportion of the total population in 2010, 87.2% were Muslims, 9.9% Christians, 1.7% Hindus and 0.7% Buddhists. In Feb. 2016 there was one cardinal.

Roads

In 2006 there were 324,150 km of classified roads (27,668 km of highways or main roads), of which 54% was surfaced. Motor vehicles, 2005: passenger cars, 5,494,034; buses and coaches, 1,184,918; trucks and vans, 2,920,828; motorcycles, 28,556,498. There were 11,451 fatalities in road accidents in 2005.

Shipping

There are 16 ports for ocean-going ships, the largest of which is Tanjung Priok, which serves the Jakarta area and has a container terminal. In 2007 cargo traffic at Tanjung Priok totalled 42.0 m. tonnes. The national shipping company Pelajaran Nasional Indonesia (PELNI) maintains inter-island

communications. In Jan. 2009 there were 1,856 ships of 300 GT or over registered, totalling 5.15 m. GT. Of the 1,856 vessels registered, 1,095 were general cargo ships, 261 oil tankers, 246 passenger ships, 92 bulk carriers, 85 container ships, 67 chemical tankers and ten liquid gas tankers.

Social Statistics

Estimated births, 2008, 4,222,000; deaths, 1,434,000. 2008 estimated birth rate, 18.6 per 1,000 population; death rate, 6.3. Life expectancy in 2013 was 68.8 years for men and 72.9 for women. Annual population growth rate, 2000–08, 1.3%. Infant mortality, 2010, 27 per 1,000 live births; fertility rate, 2008, 2.2 births per woman.

Telecommunications

In 2013 there were 30,723,000 main (fixed) telephone lines; in the same year mobile phone subscriptions numbered 313,227,000 (1,253.6 per 1,000 persons). The number of mobile phone subscriptions more than doubled between 2008 and 2013. 15.8% of the population were internet users in 2013, up from 6.9% in 2009. In March 2012 there were 43.5 m. Facebook users.

Territory and Population

Indonesia, with a land area of 1,910,931 km² (737,615 sq. miles), consists of 17,507 islands (6,000 of which are inhabited) extending about 3,200 miles east to west through three time-zones (East, Central and West Indonesian Standard time) and 1,250 miles north to south. The largest islands are Sumatra, Java, Kalimantan (Indonesian Borneo), Sulawesi (Celebes) and Papua, formerly West Papua (the western part of New Guinea). Population at the 2010 census was 237,641,326; density, 124.4 per km². Indonesia has the fourth largest population in the world, after China, India and the USA. In 2011, 44.6% of the population were urban. The capital, Jakarta, had an estimated population of 9.61 m. in 2010. Other major cities (2010 census population in 1 m.): Surabaya, 2.77; Bandung, 2.39; Bekasi, 2.33; Medan, 2.10; Tangerang, 1.80; Depok, 1.74; Semarang, 1.52. The principal ethnic groups are the Acehnese, Bataks and Minangkabaus in Sumatra, the Javanese and Sundanese in Java, the Madurese in Madura, the Balinese in Bali, the Sasaks in Lombok, the Menadonese, Minahasans, Torajas and Buginese in Sulawesi, the Dayaks in Kalimantan, the Irianese in Papua and the Ambonese in the Moluccas. There were an estimated 6.5 m. Chinese resident in 2005. Bahasa Indonesia (Indonesian) is the official language; Dutch is spoken as a colonial inheritance.

Tourism

In 2010 there were 7,003,000 international tourist arrivals (excluding same-day visitors), up from 6,324,000 in 2009 and 5,002,000 in 2005. The main countries of origin of non-resident tourists in 2010 were: Singapore (1,129,000), Malaysia (1,035,000), Australia (731,000) and China (422,000).

Iran

Jomhuri-e-Eslami-e-Iran (Islamic Republic of Iran)

Factsheet
Capital: Tehran
Population estimate, 2015: 79.11 m.
GNI per capita, 2014: (PPP$) 15,440
HDI/world rank, 2014: 0.766/69=
Internet domain extension: .ir

Civil Aviation

There are international airports at Tehran (Mehrabad), Shiraz and Bandar-e-Abbas. Tehran is the busiest airport, in 2014 handling 13,617,094 passengers. The Imam Khomeini International Airport, construction of which began in 1977 before being halted in 1979, was inaugurated in Feb. 2004. The first flight arrived at the airport in May 2004 but it was then shut down by Iran's Revolutionary Guard, citing breaches of security by the foreign operators. The state-owned IranAir is the flag-carrying airline. In 2012 scheduled airline traffic of Iranian-based carriers flew 105.4 m. km; passenger-km totalled 13.6 bn. in the same year.

Climate

Mainly a desert climate, but with more temperate conditions on the shores of the Caspian Sea. Seasonal range of temperature is considerable, as is rain (ranging from 2″ in the southeast to 78″ in the Caspian region). Winter is normally the rainy season for the whole country. Abadan, Jan. 54 °F (12.2 °C), July 97 °F (36.1 °C). Annual rainfall 8″ (204 mm). Tehran, Jan. 36 °F (2.2 °C), July 85 °F (29.4 °C). Annual rainfall 10″ (246 mm).

Constitution and Government

The Constitution of the Islamic Republic was approved by a national referendum in Dec. 1979. It was revised in 1989 to expand the powers of the presidency and eliminate the position of prime minister. It gives supreme authority to the *Spiritual Leader* (*wali faqih*), a position which was held by Ayatollah Khomeini until his death on 3 June 1989. Ayatollah Seyed Ali Khamenei was elected to succeed him on 4 June 1989. Following the death of the previous incumbent, Ayatollah Ali Khamenei was proclaimed the *Source of Knowledge (Marja e Taghlid)* at the head of all Shia Muslims in Dec. 1994. The 86-member *Assembly of Experts* was established in 1982. It is popularly elected every 8 years. Its mandate is to interpret the constitution and select the Spiritual Leader. Candidates for election are examined by the *Council of Guardians*. The *Islamic Consultative Assembly* has 290 members, elected for a 4-year term in single-seat constituencies. All candidates have to be approved by the 12-member *Council of Guardians*. The *President of the Republic* is popularly elected for not more than two 4-year terms plus a third non-consecutive term and is head of the executive; he appoints Ministers subject to approval by the *Islamic Consultative Assembly (Majlis)*. The president is Iran's second highest-ranking official. Legislative power is held by the *Islamic Consultative Assembly*, directly elected on a non-party basis for a 4-year term by all citizens aged 17 or over.

Currency

The unit of currency is the *rial* (IRR) of which 10 = 1 *toman*.

Defence

18 months' military service is compulsory (10 months in the case of university graduates). In 2013 defence spending totalled US$17,749 m., with spending per capita US$222. The 2013 expenditure represented 4.1% of GDP (down from 5.2% in 2012).

Economy

Agriculture accounted for 9.0% of GDP in 2013, industry 40.2% and services 50.8%. Manufacturing's share of total GDP was 11.7%.

Labour

The labour force numbered 26,643,000 in 2013, up from 22,262,000 in 2003. 47.2% of the population aged 15–64 was economically active in 2013. Women constituted 18.3% of the workforce in 2013. In the same year 12.9% of the population was unemployed. Iran had 65,000 people living in slavery according to the Walk Free Foundation's 2013 *Global Slavery Index*.

Press

In 2008 there were 183 paid-for daily newspapers and more than 3,300 non-dailies. Approximately 80% of the Iranian press is printed in Farsi; much of the remaining 20% is in English or Arabic. In the 2013 *World Press Freedom Index* compiled by Reporters Without Borders, Iran ranked 174th out of 179 countries.

Rail

The State Railways totalled 8,217 km in 2011, of which 148 km were electrified. The railways carried 28.6 m. passengers in 2011 and 33.1 m. tonnes of freight. An isolated 1,676 mm gauge line (94 km) in the southeast provides a link with Pakistan Railways.

Religion

The official religion is the Shia branch of Islam. In 2009 approximately 90–95% of the population were adherents according to the Pew Research Center's

Forum on Religion & Public Life, with most of the remainder of the population being Sunnis. However, adult attendance at Friday prayers is low compared to other Muslim countries, with some analysts putting the figure as only 2%, and Islam plays a smaller role in public life today than it did even in the mid-2000s.

Roads

In 2006 the total length of roads was 174,301 km, of which 1,429 km were motorways, 27,256 km main roads, 41,129 km secondary regional roads and 104,487 km other local roads. In 2007 there were 920,100 passenger cars; 862,600 motorcycles and mopeds; 179,700 vans and lorries; 4,900 buses and coaches. In 2006 there were 165,130 road accidents resulting in 6,380 deaths.

Shipping

In Jan. 2009 there were 202 ships of 300 GT or over registered, totalling 959,000 GT. Of the 202 vessels registered, 148 were general cargo ships, 18 bulk carriers, 12 oil tankers, 12 passenger ships, seven container ships, four chemical tankers and there was one liquid gas tanker. The Iranian-controlled fleet comprised 191 vessels of 1,000 GT or over in Jan. 2009, of which 126 were under foreign flags and 65 under the Iranian flag. The principal port is Bandar-e-Abbas, which handled 52,373,000 tonnes of cargo in 2008 (17,185,000 tonnes loaded and 35,161,000 tonnes discharged).

Social Statistics

2007–08 births, 1,286,716; deaths, 412,735. Rates (2007–08, per 1,000 population): birth, 18.1; death, 5.8. Expectation of life at birth, 2013, 76.1 years for females and 72.2 years for males. Infant mortality, 2010, 22 per 1,000 live births. Annual population growth rate, 2005–10, 1.1%; fertility rate, 2013, 1.9 births per woman. Iran has had one of the largest reductions in its fertility rate of any country in the world over the past quarter of a century, having had a rate of 4.8 births per woman in 1990. 2.3% of Iran's adult population are dependent on opiates-the second highest rate in world behind Afghanistan.

Telecommunications

In 2013 Iran had 29,689,000 main (fixed) telephone lines (383.3 per 1,000 population). In 2013 there were 4,351,202 fixed broadband subscriptions, more than double the number in 2011.

Territory and Population

Iran is bounded in the north by Armenia, Azerbaijan, the Caspian Sea and Turkmenistan, east by Afghanistan and Pakistan, south by the Gulf of Oman and the Persian Gulf, and west by Iraq and Turkey. It has an area of 1,648,195 km² (636,368 sq. miles) including 116,600 km² (45,020 sq. miles) of inland water, but a vast portion is desert. Population (2011 census): 75,149,669. Population density: 46 per km². The population was 71.3% urban in 2011. At the 2011 census the populations of the principal cities were: Tehran, 8,154,051; Mashhad, 2,749,374; Esfahan, 1,756,126; Karaj, 1,614,626; Tabriz, 1,494,908; Shiraz, 1,460,665; Ahvaz, 1,112,021; Qom, 1,074,036. The official language is Farsi or Persian.

Tourism

There were 3,354,000 non-resident visitors in 2011 (1,402,000 in 2001), spending US$2,574 m.

Iraq

Jumhouriya al 'Iraqia (Republic of Iraq)

Factsheet

Capital: Baghdad
Population estimate, 2015: 36.42 m.
GNI per capita, 2014: (PPP$) 14,003
HDI/world rank, 2014: 0.654/121
Internet domain extension: .iq

Civil Aviation

In 2000 there were international flights for the first time since the 1991 Gulf War, with air links being established between Iraq and Egypt, Jordan and Syria. Since 2003 the two international airports at Baghdad and Basra have undergone post-war reconstruction. Major domestic airports are at Mosul, Kirkuk and Irbil. In May 2010 the government dissolved the state airline, Iraqi Airways, owing to a legal dispute with Kuwait dating back to the Iraqi invasion in 1990. It began flying again in 2012 and now serves a number of destinations in Europe, the Middle East and Asia.

Climate

The climate is mainly arid, with limited and unreliable rainfall and a large annual range of temperature. Summers are very hot and winters are cold. Baghdad, Jan. 50 °F (10 °C), July 95 °F (35 °C). Annual rainfall 6″ (140 mm). Basra, Jan. 55 °F (12.8 °C), July 92 °F (33.3 °C). Annual rainfall 7″ (175 mm). Mosul, Jan. 44 °F (6.7 °C), July 90 °F (32.2 °C). Annual rainfall 15″ (384 mm).

Constitution and Government

Until the fall of Saddam Hussein, the highest state authority was the Revolutionary Command Council (RCC) but some legislative power was given to the 220-member *National Assembly*. The only legal political grouping was the National Progressive Front (founded 1973) comprising the Arab Socialist Renaissance (Ba'ath) Party and various Kurdish groups, but a law of Aug. 1991 legalized political parties provided they were not based on religion, race or ethnicity. In July 2003 a 25-man Iraqi-led governing council met in Baghdad for the first time since the US-led war in an important staging post towards full self-government. The temporary Coalition Provisional Authority was dissolved on 28 June 2004. Power was handed over to the interim Iraqi government which assumed full sovereign powers for governing Iraq. It became a transitional government after elections in Jan. 2005. The 275-member Transitional National Assembly approved a draft new constitution on 29 Aug. 2005. It was approved in a nationwide referendum held on 15 Oct., with 78.6% of votes cast in favour. The constitution states that Iraq is a democratic, federal, representative republic and a multi-ethnic, multi-religious and multi-sect country. Islam is the official religion of the state and a basic source of legislation. Elections were held in Dec. 2005 for the new 275-member *Council of Representatives*. In Dec. 2009 the number of seats was increased from 275 to 325 ahead of the March 2010 elections. In Nov. 2013 this was further increased to 328 ahead of the April 2014 elections.

Currency

From 15 Oct. 2003 a new national currency, the new *Iraqi dinar* (NID), was introduced to replace the existing currencies in circulation in the south and north of the country.

Defence

Following the downfall of Saddam Hussein, recruitment began in July 2003 for a new professional army run by the US military. Saddam Hussein's forces numbered 400,000 at their peak. In Nov. 2008 Iraq's parliament approved a plan that saw the last American troops leave the country in Dec. 2011. In 2013 military expenditure totalled US$16,897 m. (US$530 per capita), representing 7.2% of GDP.

Economy

In 2011 oil and gas accounted for about 60% of GDP.

Labour

In 2011 the labour force was 7.9 m. (72% of working age males and 13% of working age females). The state employs nearly two-thirds of the workforce. Unemployment was officially put at 12% in Feb. 2012. Iraq had 28,000 people living in slavery according to the Walk Free Foundation's 2013 *Global Slavery Index*.

Press

In 2008 several hundred daily and weekly publications appeared regularly, the most popular of which, *Al-Sabah* ('The Morning'), had an average circulation of 50,000.

Rail

In 2005 railways comprised 2,032 km of 1,435 mm gauge route. Passenger-km travelled in 2014 came to 99 m. and freight tonne-km to 249 m.

Religion

The constitution proclaims Islam the state religion, but also stipulates freedom of creed and religious practices. In 2010 the population was 99.0% Muslim according to the Pew Research Center's Forum on Religion & Public Life; there were also an estimated 270,000 Christians.

Roads

In 2012 there were 59,623 km of roads (up from 40,988 km in 2007). Vehicles in use in 2006 included 785,000 passenger cars and 1,345,000 lorries and vans. In 2005 there were 1,789 road accident deaths.

Shipping

In Jan. 2009 there were 18 ships of 300 GT or over registered, totalling 86,000 GT. A 565-km canal was opened in 1992 between Baghdad and the Persian Gulf for shipping, irrigation, the drainage of saline water and the reclamation of marsh land. Iraq has three oil tanker terminals at Basra, Khor Al-Amaya and Khor Al-Zubair. Its single deep-water port is at Umm Qasr.

Social Statistics

2008 estimates: births, 940,000; deaths, 177,000; marriages, 171,000. Birth and death rates, 2008 estimates (per 1,000 population): births, 31.2; deaths, 5.9. Life expectancy at birth, 2007, was 64.2 years for men and 71.8 years for women. Annual population growth rate, 2000–08, 2.5%. Infant mortality, 2008: 36 per 1,000 live births. Fertility rate, 2008: 4.1 births per woman. Estimated maternal mortality rate per 10,000 live births, 2005: 30.

Telecommunications

There were 1.72 m. fixed telephone lines in 2010 (55.6 per 1,000 inhabitants). In the same year mobile phone subscriptions numbered 23.26 m. (75.1 per 1,000 inhabitants). Mobile phones were banned during the Saddam Hussein era. Fixed internet subscriptions totalled just 270 in 2010. In March 2012 there were 1.6 m. Facebook users.

Territory and Population

Iraq is bounded in the north by Turkey, east by Iran, southeast by the Persian Gulf, south by Kuwait and Saudi Arabia, and west by Jordan and Syria. In April 1992 the UN Boundary Commission redefined Iraq's border with Kuwait, moving it slightly northwards in line with an agreement of 1932. Area, 434,128 km^2. Population, 1997 census, 22,046,244; density, 50.8 per km^2. 2009 estimate, 31,664,466, density 72.9 per km^2. In 2009, 69.0% of the population lived in urban areas. The most populous cities are Baghdad (the capital), with an estimated population of 6,150,000 in 2011, Mosul and Basra. Around 1.4 m. Iraqis protected and assisted by the Office of the United Nations High Commissioner for Refugees are displaced within the country. In 2014 Iraqis dropped to the ninth largest refugee group with just 377,700 living abroad (down from 1,873,500 in 2008), mainly in Syria and to a lesser extent Jordan. The population is approximately 80% Arab, 17% Kurdish (mainly in the north of the country) and 3% Turkmen, Assyrian, Chaldean or other. Shia Arabs (predominantly in the south of the country) constitute approximately 60% of the total population and Sunni Arabs (principally in the centre) 20%. The official language is Arabic.

Tourism

In 2010 there were 1,518,000 foreign tourists, up from 864,000 in 2008.

Ireland

Éire

Factsheet

Capital: Dublin
Population estimate, 2015: 4.69 m.
GNI per capita, 2014: (PPP$) 39,568
HDI/world rank, 2014: 0.916/6=
Internet domain extension: .ie

Civil Aviation

Aer Lingus and Ryanair are the two major airlines operating in Ireland. Aer Lingus was founded in 1936 as a State-owned enterprise. It was privatized in 2006 and was bought in 2015 by International Airlines Group (IAG), the owner of British Airways. In the year ended 31 March 2012 Ryanair carried 75.8 m. passengers (all on international flights); revenue passenger-km totalled 94.3 bn. In addition to Aer Lingus and Ryanair, there are 13 other independent air transport operators. Dublin, the busiest airport, is operated by the Dublin Airport Authority plc as is Cork, the second busiest; Shannon, the third busiest, used to be as well but has been a publicly owned commercial airport operated and run by the Shannon Airport Authority plc since the beginning of 2013. In 2012 Dublin handled 19.1 m. passengers (an increase of 1.9% on 2011) and 111,069 tonnes of freight and mail.

Climate

Influenced by the Gulf Stream, there is an equable climate with mild south-west winds, making temperatures almost uniform over the whole country. The coldest months are Jan. and Feb. (39–45 °F, 4–7 °C) and the warmest July and Aug. (57–61 °F, 14–16 °C). May and June are the sunniest months, averaging 5.5 to 6.5 h each day, but over 7 h in the extreme southeast. Rainfall is lowest along the eastern coastal strip. The central parts vary between 30–44″ (750-1,125 mm), and up to 60″ (1,500 mm) may be experienced in low-lying areas in the west. Dublin, Jan. 40 °F (4 °C), July 59 °F (15 °C). Annual rainfall 30″ (750 mm). Cork, Jan. 42 °F (5 °C), July 61 °F (16 °C). Annual rainfall 41″ (1,025 mm).

Constitution and Government

Ireland is a sovereign independent, democratic republic. Its parliament exercises jurisdiction in 26 of the 32 counties of the island of Ireland. On 14 June 1937 a new constitution was approved by Parliament and enacted by a plebiscite on 1 July 1937. This constitution came into operation on 29 Dec. 1937. Under it the name Ireland (Éire) was restored. The head of state is the *President*, whose role is largely ceremonial, but who has the power to refer proposed legislation which might infringe the Constitution to the Supreme Court. The *Oireachtas* or National Parliament consists of the President, a House of Representatives (*Dáil Éireann*) and a Senate (*Seanad Éireann*). The *Dáil*, consisting of 158 members, is elected by adult suffrage on the Single Transferable Vote system in constituencies of three, four or five members. A maximum period of 90 days is afforded to the Senate for the consideration or amendment of Bills sent to that House by the *Dáil*, but the Senate has no power to veto legislative proposals. No amendment of the Constitution can be effected except with the approval of the people given at a referendum.

Currency

On 1 Jan. 1999 the euro (EUR) became the legal currency in Ireland at the irrevocable conversion rate of 0.787564 Irish pounds to 1 euro. The euro, which consists of 100 cents, has been in circulation since 1 Jan. 2002. On the introduction of the euro there was a 'dual circulation' period before the Irish pound ceased to be legal tender on 9 Feb. 2002.

Defence

The total strength of the Permanent Defence Force in Dec. 2011 was 9,438 (including 565 women) and the total strength of the Reserve Defence Force was 5,220. In Dec. 2011, 529 Defence Forces personnel were involved in 11 peace-support missions throughout the world. Defence expenditure in 2011 totalled €926.83 m., representing 0.6% of GDP.

Economy

Agriculture accounted for 1.4% of GDP in 2013, industry 26.1% and services 72.5%.

Labour

The total labour force in 2008 was 2,239,600, of whom 126,700 were out of work. The unemployment rate in April and May 2001 was just 3.7%, down from 17.1% in Sept. 1985. However, it rose sharply as a consequence of the global economic crisis, peaking at 15.1% in Nov. 2011 and again in Feb. 2012. It has gradually fallen since then and in Dec. 2015 was 8.8%. Of those at work in 2008, 1,246,400 were employed in the services sector, 492,000 in the industrial sector and 113,800 in the agricultural sector. Employment rose by approximately 40% between 1998 and 2008. In 2001 there were only 69,400 unemployed people, down from 226,000 in 1987, although this figure has risen steadily back up since then and in 2009 exceeded the 1987 total, with 264,600 unemployed. Ireland, along with the UK and Sweden, decided to open its labour market to nationals of the new EU member states in May 2004. Poles in particular went to Ireland following the EU expansion and by 2011 were the largest ethnic minority ahead of UK nationals; there were 122,585 Polish citizens in Ireland at the time of the 2011 census. On 1 Feb. 2011 the minimum hourly wage was lowered to €7.65 from €8.65. The normal retirement age is 65 years.

Press

In 2014 there were nine dailies and seven Sunday newspapers (all in English) with a combined circulation of 1,202,000. There were 60 newspaper online editions in 2014.

Rail

The total length of railway open for traffic in 2009 was 1,919 km (52 km electrified), all 1,600 mm gauge. A massive investment in public transport infrastructure is taking place in Ireland. The second National Development Plan that ran from Jan. 2007 to Dec. 2013 allowed for €12.9 bn. to be invested in public transport, particularly in the Greater Dublin area.

Religion

According to the census of population taken in 2011 the principal religious professions were as follows: Roman Catholics, 3,861,335; Church of Ireland (including Protestants), 129,039; Muslims, 49,204; Orthodox, 45,223; Presbyterians, 24,600; Other stated religions, 136,126; Not stated or no religion, 342,725. In Feb. 2016 there were two cardinals.

Roads

On 31 Dec. 2012 there were 95,811 km of public roads, consisting of 5,515 km of National Primary Roads (including 1,187 km of motorway), 2,716 km of National Secondary Roads, 11,607 km of Regional Roads and 78,773 km of Local Roads. Number of licensed motor vehicles at 31 Dec. 2011: private cars, 1,887,810; public service vehicles, 33,405; goods vehicles, 320,966; agricultural and industrial vehicles, 71,677; motorcycles, 36,582; other vehicles, 74,716. In 2011 a total of 186 people were killed in road accidents.

Shipping

In Jan. 2009 there were 32 ships of 300 GT or over registered, totalling 122,000 GT. Total cargo traffic passing through the country's ports amounted to 41,880,000 tonnes in 2009 (down from 51,081,000 in 2008). Dublin handled 18.6 m. tonnes of cargo in 2009 and Cork 8.0 m. tonnes.

Social Statistics

Births, 2012, 71,674; deaths, 29,186. 2012 rates (per 1,000 population): birth, 15.6; death, 6.4. Annual population growth rate, 2005–10, 1.5%. Expectation of life at birth, 2011, 78.3 years for males and 82.8 years for females. In 2009 the suicide rate per 100,000 population was 11.8 (men, 19.0; women, 4.7).

Infant mortality in 2010, three per 1,000 live births; fertility rate (2013), 2.0 births per woman.

Telecommunications

The largest mobile telephone operators in terms of subscribers are Vodafone Ireland and O2 Ireland. In 2013 there were 4,755,000 mobile phone subscriptions (1,027.6 per 1,000 population) and 2,034,000 fixed telephone subscriptions. In 2013, 78.3% of the population aged 16–74 were internet users. The fixed broadband penetration rate stood at 21.1 subscribers per 100 inhabitants in Dec. 2010. In March 2012 there were 2.1 m. Facebook users.

Territory and Population

The Republic of Ireland lies in the Atlantic Ocean, separated from Great Britain by the Irish Sea to the east, and bounded in the northeast by Northern Ireland (UK). In 2011, 62.3% of the population lived in urban areas. The population at the 2011 census was 4,588,252 (2,315,553 females), giving a density of 67.0 persons per km². The census population in 2011 was the highest figure since 1861 when the census recorded a population of 4.40 m. The capital is Dublin (Baile Átha Cliath). Town populations, 2011: Greater Dublin, 1,110,627; Cork, 198,582; Limerick, 91,454; Galway, 76,778; Waterford, 51,519. The official languages are Irish (the national language) and English; according to the 2011 census, Irish is spoken by 1.77 m. persons in the Republic of Ireland aged 3 years and over (1.66 m. in 2006). It is a compulsory subject at school.

Tourism

Total number of overseas tourists in 2008 was 7,839,000 (a 2.2% fall from 2007). In 2008 earnings from all visits to Ireland, including cross-border visits, amounted to €4,781 m. 49% of visits in 2008 were from Great Britain. Irish residents made 7,877,000 visits abroad in 2008 (a 2.1% increase on 2007).

Israel

Medinat Israel (State of Israel)

Factsheet

Capital: Jerusalem
Population estimate, 2015: 8.06 m.
GNI per capita, 2014: (PPP$) 30,676
HDI/world rank, 2014: 0.894/18
Internet domain extension: .il

Civil Aviation

There are international airports at Tel Aviv (Ben Gurion), Eilat (J. Hozman), Haifa and Ovda. Tel Aviv is the busiest airport, in 2012 handling 13,133,992 passengers (12,400,479 on international flights) and 285,813 tonnes of freight. El Al is the flag carrier. In 2005 scheduled airline traffic of Israeli-based carriers flew 97.9 m. km and carried 4,382,200 passengers. In 2010 services were also provided by another Israeli airline, Arkia, and by around 50 international carriers.

Climate

From April to Oct., the summers are long and hot, and almost rainless. From Nov. to March, the weather is generally mild, though colder in hilly areas, and this is the wet season. Jerusalem, Jan. 12.8 °C, July 28.9 °C. Annual rainfall, 657 mm. Tel Aviv, Jan. 17.2 °C, July 30.2 °C. Annual rainfall, 803 mm.

Constitution and Government

Israel is an independent sovereign republic, established by proclamation on 14 May 1948. The *President* (head of state) is elected by the Knesset by secret ballot by a simple majority; his term of office is 7 years. He may only serve for one term. The Knesset, a one-chamber Parliament, consists of 120 members.

It is elected for a 4-year term by secret ballot and universal direct suffrage. Under the system of election introduced in 1996, electors vote once for a party and once for a candidate for Prime Minister. To be elected Prime Minister, a candidate must gain more than half the votes cast, and be elected to the Knesset. If there are more than two candidates and none gain half the vote, a second round is held 15 days later. The Prime Minister forms a cabinet (no fewer than eight members and no more than 18) with the approval of the Knesset.

Currency

The unit of currency is the *shekel* (ILS) of 100 *agorot*.

Defence

Conscription (for Jews and Druze only) is 3 years (usually 4 years for officers; 24 months for women). Israel is one of the few countries with female conscription. A law passed in March 2014 ended the wholesale army exemptions granted to ultra-Orthodox seminary students. It is set to be fully implemented in 2017 and will involve an annual enlistment quota. The Israel Defence Force is a unified force, in which army, navy and air force are subordinate to a single chief-of-staff. The Minister of Defence is *de facto* C.-in-C. Defence expenditure in 2013 totalled US$15,163 m., representing 6.0% of GDP (compared to 30% in the early 1970s). Expenditure per capita in 2013 was US$1,967, a figure exceeded only by Oman and Saudi Arabia. Israel has an undeclared nuclear weapons capability. Israel has an undeclared nuclear weapons capability. According to the Stockholm International Peace Research Institute, the nuclear arsenal was estimated to have about 80 warheads in Jan. 2015.

Economy

Services account for about 82% of GDP, industry 16% and agriculture 2%.

Labour

The economically active workforce was 2,270,500 in 2001 (1,236,200 males). The principal areas of activity were: manufacturing, mining and quarrying, 394,200; wholesale and retail trade/repair of motor vehicles, motorcycles and personal and household goods, 299,800; education, 283,700; and real estate, renting and business activities, 277,200. Unemployment was 5.2% in Dec. 2015.

Press

In 2012 there were 11 daily newspapers with an estimated combined circulation of 1.1 m. The most widely read paper is the free *Israel Hayom*.

Rail

There were 1,079 km of standard gauge line in 2011. 35.9 m. passengers and 6.2 m. tonnes of freight were carried in 2011. One of the smallest metro systems in the world (1,800 metres) was opened in Haifa in 1959. A tram system in Jerusalem opened in Aug. 2011.

Religion

Religious affairs are under the supervision of a special ministry, with departments for the Christian and Muslim communities. The religious affairs of each community remain under the full control of the ecclesiastical authorities concerned: in the case of the Jews, the Ashkenazi and Sephardi Chief Rabbis, in the case of the Christians, the heads of the various communities, and in the case of the Muslims, the Qadis. The Druze were officially recognized in 1957 as an autonomous religious community. According to the Pew Research Center's Forum on Religion & Public Life, in 2010 there were an estimated 5.6 m. Jews, 1.4 m. Muslims, 230,000 people with no religious affiliation and 150,000 Christians.

Roads

There were 17,870 km of paved roads in 2007, including 344 km of motorway. Motor vehicles in use in 2007 totalled 1,805,400 passenger cars, 362,200 lorries and vans, 94,800 motorcycles and mopeds, and 21,300 buses and coaches. There were 398 fatalities as a result of road accidents in 2007.

Shipping

Israel has three commercial ports-Haifa, Ashdod and Eilat. In Jan. 2009 there were 15 ships of 300 GT or over registered, totalling 428,000 GT.

Social Statistics

2008 births, 156,923; deaths, 39,484; marriages, 50,038; divorces, 13,488. 2008 crude birth rate per 1,000 population of Jewish population, 20.4; Non-Jewish: Muslims, 28.5; Christians, 16.5; Druzes, 21.0. Crude death rate per 1,000 (2008), Jewish, 6.2; Muslims, 2.5; Christians, 4.7; Druzes, 3.0. Infant mortality rate per 1,000 live births (2005–09), 4.0 (Jewish, 2.9; Muslims, 7.5; Christians, 2.3; Druzes, 5.2). Life expectancy, 2013, 79.9 years for males and 83.6 for females. Average annual population growth rate, 2005–10, 2.3%. Fertility rate, 2008, 2.8 births per woman. There were 16,892 immigrants in 2011, up from 13,699 in 2008 but down from 199,516 in 1990 and 176,100 in 1991 following the fall of communism in Eastern Europe and the break-up of the former Soviet Union.

Telecommunications

In 2011 there were 3.5 m. main (fixed) telephone lines. In the same year mobile phone subscribers numbered 9.2 m. (1,219.8 per 1,000 persons). There were 25.8 fixed broadband subscriptions per 100 inhabitants in 2009 and 62.5 mobile broadband subscriptions per 100 inhabitants. In 2009, 74.5% of households had a computer and 66.3% of households had internet access at home. In March 2012 there were 3.5 m. Facebook users.

Territory and Population

The area of Israel, including the Golan Heights (1,154 km^2) and East Jerusalem, is 22,072 km^2 (8,522 sq. miles), of which 21,643 km^2 (8,357 sq. miles) are land. The population in Dec. 2011 was 7.84 m. (5.91 m. Jews, 1.61 m. Arabs and 0.32 m. others), including East Jerusalem, the Golan Heights and Israeli settlers in the West Bank but excluding 200,000 foreign workers. Population density, 362 per km^2. In 2011, 91.9% of the population lived in urban areas. On 23 Jan. 1950 the Knesset proclaimed Jerusalem the capital of the State and on 14 Dec. 1981 extended Israeli law into the Golan Heights. Population of the main towns (Dec. 2011): Jerusalem, 804,400; Tel Aviv/Jaffa, 404,800; Haifa, 270,300; Rishon le-Ziyyon, 232,400; Ashdod, 212,300; Petach Tikva, 210,400. The official languages are Hebrew and Arabic.

Tourism

In 2011 there were 2,820,000 tourist arrivals (excluding same-day visitors), up from 2,803,000 in 2010 and 2,417,000 in 2000. The main countries of origin of non-resident tourists in 2011 were the USA (21%), followed by Russia (13%) and France (10%). 86% of all tourist arrivals in 2011 were by air and 14% were by land border crossings.

Italy

Repubblica Italiana (Italian Republic)

Factsheet

Capital: Rome
Population estimate, 2015: 59.80 m.
GNI per capita, 2014: (PPP$) 33,030
HDI/world rank, 2014: 0.873/27
Internet domain extension: .it

Civil Aviation

Alitalia commenced operations in Jan. 2009 as a privately-owned company (25%-owned by Air France-KLM), having taken over the name, landing rights and significant assets of the former national carrier (also Alitalia, which went bankrupt in 2008) and having merged with rival airline Air One. In 2013 the Alitalia group carried 23,993,486 passengers. In 2012 Rome (Fiumicino) airport handled 36,980,157 passengers (24,925,722 on

international flights) and 143,172 tonnes of freight. Milan Malpensa was the second busiest for passengers, handling 18,522,760 (14,773,460 on international flights), but the busiest for freight, with 414,318 tonnes.

Climate

The climate varies considerably with latitude. In the south, it is warm temperate, with little rain in the summer months, but the north is cool temperate with rainfall more evenly distributed over the year. Florence, Jan. 47.7 °F (8.7 °C), July 79.5 °F (26.4 °C). Annual rainfall 33″ (842 mm). Milan, Jan. 38.7 °F (3.7 °C), July 73.4 °F (23.0 °C). Annual rainfall 38″ (984 mm). Naples, Jan. 50.2 °F (10.1 °C), July 77.4 °F (25.2 °C). Annual rainfall 36″ (935 mm). Palermo, Jan. 52.5 °F (11.4 °C), July 78.4 °F (25.8 °C). Annual rainfall 35″ (897 mm). Rome, Jan. 53.4 °F (11.9 °C), July 76.3 °F (24.6 °C). Annual rainfall 31″ (793 mm). Venice, Jan. 43.3 °F (6.3 °C), July 70.9 °F (21.6 °C). Annual rainfall 32″ (830 mm).

Constitution and Government

The Constitution dates from 1948. Italy is 'a democratic republic founded on work'. Parliament consists of the *Chamber of Deputies* and the *Senate.* The Chamber is elected for 5 years by universal and direct suffrage and consists of 630 deputies. The Senate is elected for 5 years on a regional basis by electors over the age of 25, each Region having at least seven senators. The total number of senators is 322, of which 315 are directly elected. The *President* is elected in a joint session of Chamber and Senate, to which are added three delegates from each Regional Council (one from the Valle d'Aosta). The President can dissolve the chambers of parliament, except during the last 6 months of the presidential term. There is a *Constitutional Court* that consists of 15 appointed judges, five each by the President, Parliament (in joint session) and the highest law and administrative courts. The Court can decide on the constitutionality of laws and decrees, define the powers of the State and Regions, judge conflicts between the State and Regions and between the Regions, and try the President and Ministers.

Currency

On 1 Jan. 1999 the euro (EUR) became the legal currency in Italy at the irrevocable conversion rate of 1,936.27 lire to 1 euro. The euro, which consists of 100 cents, has been in circulation since 1 Jan. 2002. On the introduction of the euro there was a 'dual circulation' period before the lira ceased to be legal tender on 28 Feb. 2002.

Defence

Head of the armed forces is the Defence Chief of Staff. Conscription was abolished at the end of 2004 with the military becoming all-professional from 2005. In Aug. 1998 the government voted to allow women into the armed forces. In 2013 defence expenditure totalled US$25,229 m. (US$410 per capita), representing 1.2% of GDP.

Economy

Agriculture accounted for 2% of GDP, industry 24% and services 74% in 2012. Italy's 'shadow' (black market) economy is estimated to constitute approximately 17% of the country's official GDP.

Labour

The labour force in 2013 was 25,474,000 (24,007,000 in 2003). 63.9% of the population aged 15–64 was economically active in 2013. Of those in employment in 2013, 69.4% worked in services, 27.2% in industry and 3.4% in agriculture. Unemployment stood at 11.4% in Dec. 2015 (down from 12.7% in 2014 as a whole). In 2012 the pensionable retirement age was 62 for women employed in the private sector, 63 for self-employed women and 66 for men (both employed and self-employed) and women in the public sector. The pensionable retirement age for women not in the public sector is gradually increasing and will be 66 years by 2018. It is expected that the age will increase for both sexes to at least 67 in 2021. Italy had 8,000 people living in slavery according to the Walk Free Foundation's 2013 *Global Slavery Index.*

Press

In 2011 there were 97 paid-for dailies with a combined circulation of 4.3 m. copies and ten free dailies with a combined circulation of 1.7 m. copies.

Several of the papers are owned or supported by political parties. The church and various economic groups exert strong right of centre influence on editorial opinion. Most newspapers are regional but *Corriere della Sera* (which has the highest circulation of any Italian newspaper), *La Repubblica*, *Il Sole 24 Ore*, *La Gazzetta* and *La Stampa* are the most important of those papers that are nationally circulated. In 2011 there were 101 newspaper online editions.

Rail

The length of state-run railway (*Ferrovie dello Stato*) in 2011 was 16,726 km (11,925 km electrified). Italy's first section of high-speed railway opened in 1981; by 2009 the total length had reached 923 km. In 2011 the railways carried 522.9 m. passengers and 46.1 m. tonnes of freight. There are metros in Milan (76.0 km), Rome (38.0 km), Naples (29.8 km), Turin (9.6 km), Genoa (5.3 km) and Catania (3.8 km).

Religion

The treaty between the Holy See and Italy of 11 Feb. 1929, confirmed by article 7 of the Constitution of the republic, lays down that the Catholic Apostolic Roman Religion is the only religion of the State. Other creeds are permitted, provided they do not profess principles, or follow rites, contrary to public order or moral behaviour. The appointment of archbishops and of bishops is made by the Holy See; but the Holy See submits to the Italian government the name of the person to be appointed in order to obtain an assurance that the latter will not raise objections of a political nature. In Feb. 2016 there were 47 cardinals. According to the Pew Research Center's Forum on Religion & Public Life, in 2010 there were an estimated 50.3 m. Roman Catholics, 7.5 m. people with no religious affiliation, 2.2 m. Muslims, 800,000 Protestants and 500,000 other Christians.

Roads

Roads totalled 175,430 km in 2005, of which 6,542 km were motorways, 21,524 km were highways and main roads, and 147,364 km were regional and provincial roads. In 2005 there were 47,104,048 motor vehicles, including: passenger cars, 34,882,476 (594 per 1,000 inhabitants); buses and coaches, 96,477; vans and trucks, 3,982,001. There were 5,426 fatalities in road accidents in 2005.

Shipping

In Jan. 2009 there were 779 ships of 300 GT or over registered, totalling 13.32 m. GT. Of the 779 vessels registered, 280 were passenger ships, 212 oil tankers, 131 general cargo ships, 62 bulk carriers, 45 chemical tankers, 26 liquid gas tankers and 23 container ships. The Italian-controlled fleet comprised 745 vessels of 1,000 GT or over in Jan. 2009, of which 527 were under the Italian flag and 218 under foreign flags. The chief ports are Genoa (which handled 54,218,000 tonnes of cargo in 2008), Trieste (48,279,000 tonnes in 2008) and Taranto (43,271,000 tonnes in 2008). Gioia Tauro, the busiest container port, handled 3.5 m. 20-ft equivalent units (TEUs) in 2008.

Social Statistics

Vital statistics (and rates per 1,000 population), 2008: births, 576,659 (9.6); deaths, 585,126 (9.8). Marriages in 2007, 250,360 (4.2); divorces in 2006, 49,534 (0.8). Infant mortality rate, 2010 (up to 1 year of age): three per 1,000 live births. Expectation of life, 2007: females, 84.0 years; males, 78.1. In 2010, 20.3% of the population was over 65—one of the highest percentages in the world. Annual population growth rate, 2010–15, −0.1%; fertility rate, 2008, 1.4 births per woman. With only 17.7% of births being to unmarried mothers in 2007 (albeit up from 8.1% in 1995), Italy has one of the lowest rates of births out of marriage in Europe. In 2006 there were 3,701 suicides; 76.8% were men.

Telecommunications

There were 20,570,000 main (fixed) telephone lines in 2014. 62.0% of the population were internet users in 2014. There were 235.3 fixed broadband subscribers per 1,000 inhabitants in 2014. In March 2012 there were 20.9 m. Facebook users.

Territory and Population

Italy is bounded in the north by Switzerland and Austria, east by Slovenia and the Adriatic Sea, southeast by the Ionian Sea, south by the Mediterranean Sea, southwest by the Tyrrhenian Sea and Ligurian Sea and west by France. The area is 302,071 km^2. Population in 2011, 59,433,744 (30,688,237 females). Density: 197 per km^2. In 2011, 68.6% of the population lived in urban areas. Communes of more than 250,000 inhabitants, with population resident at the census of 9 Oct. 2011: Rome (Roma), 2,617,175; Milan (Milano), 1,242,123; Naples (Napoli), 962,003; Turin (Torino), 872,367; Palermo, 657,561; Genoa (Genova), 586,180; Bologna, 371,337; Florence (Firenze), 358,079; Bari, 315,933; Catania, 293,902; Venice (Venezia), 261,262; Verona, 252,520. The official and by far the most widely spoken language is Italian.

Tourism

In 2010, 43.6 m. international tourists visited Italy (43.2 m. in 2009); receipts from tourism in 2010 were US$38.8 bn. (US$40.2 bn. in 2009). Only France, the USA, China and Spain received more foreign tourists in 2010.

Jamaica

Factsheet

Capital: Kingston
Population estimate, 2015: 2.79 m.
GNI per capita, 2014: (PPP$) 7,415
HDI/world rank, 2014: 0.719/99
Internet domain extension: .jm

Civil Aviation

International airlines operate through the Norman Manley and Sangster airports at Palisadoes and Montego Bay. Sangster International is the busiest for passenger traffic, handling 3,378,000 passengers in 2006–07. Norman Manley airport is busier for freight, handling 16,136 tonnes of freight in 2006 but only 1,715,078 passengers.

Climate

A tropical climate but with considerable variation. High temperatures on the coast are usually mitigated by sea breezes, while upland areas enjoy cooler and less humid conditions. Rainfall is plentiful over most of Jamaica, being heaviest in May and from Aug. to Nov. The island lies in the hurricane zone. Kingston, Jan. 76 °F (24.4 °C), July 81 °F (27.2 °C). Annual rainfall 32″ (800 mm).

Constitution and Government

Under the constitution of Aug. 1962 the Crown is represented by a Governor-General appointed by the Crown on the advice of the Prime Minister. The Governor-General is assisted by a Privy Council of six appointed members. The Legislature comprises the *House of Representatives* and the *Senate*. Electors and elected must be Jamaican or Commonwealth citizens resident in Jamaica for at least 12 months before registration.

Currency

The unit of currency is the *Jamaican dollar* (JMD) of 100 *cents*.

Defence

In 2013 defence expenditure totalled US$129 m. (US$44 per capita), representing 0.8% of GDP.

Economy

In 2009 agriculture accounted for 6.2% of GDP, industry 22.1% and services 71.7%.

Labour

The labour force in 2013 was 1,291,000 (1,202,000 in 2003). 67.8% of the population aged 15–64 was economically active in 2013. In the same year 15.0% of the population was unemployed.

Press

In 2008 there were three daily newspapers with a combined circulation of 115,000.

Rail

Passenger traffic ceased in 1992, but restarted in 2011. However, it closed again in Aug. 2012 as a result of the service suffering heavy losses. Freight transport continues on a limited basis, mainly for carrying bauxite to docks.

Religion

Freedom of worship is guaranteed under the Constitution. The main Christian denominations are Anglican, Baptist, Roman Catholic, Methodist, Church of God, United Church in Jamaica and the Cayman Islands (Presbyterian-Congregational-Disciples of Christ), Moravian, Seventh-day Adventist, Pentecostal, Salvation Army and Quaker. Pocomania is a mixture of Christianity and African survivals. Non-Christians include Hindus, Jews, Muslims, Bahai followers and Rastafarians.

Roads

In 2007 the island had 22,121 km of roads, including 44 km of motorway and 4,922 km of main roads. In 2006 there were 373,700 passenger cars in use and 29,100 motorcycles and mopeds. There were 350 fatalities in traffic accidents in 2007.

Shipping

In Jan. 2009 there were 21 ships of 300 GT or over registered, totalling 229,000 GT. Kingston handled 16.3 m. tonnes of cargo in 2008 (down from 17.7 m. tonnes in 2007).

Social Statistics

Vital statistics (2006): births, 46,277 (17.4 per 1,000 population); deaths, 16,317 (6.1); marriages, 23,181 (8.7); divorces, 1,768 (0.7). There were 17,100 emigrants in 2006, mainly to the USA. Expectation of life at birth, 2007, 68.3 years for males and 75.1 years for females. Annual population growth rate, 2008–10, 0.3%; infant mortality, 2010, 20 per 1,000 live births; fertility rate, 2008, 2.4 births per woman.

Telecommunications

In 2011 there were 272,100 landline telephone subscriptions (equivalent to 98.9 per 1,000 inhabitants) and 2,974,700 mobile phone subscriptions (or 1,081.2 per 1,000 inhabitants). There were 261.0 internet users per 1,000 inhabitants in 2010. Fixed internet subscriptions totalled 114,600 in 2009 (42.0 per 1,000 inhabitants). In Dec. 2011 there were 684,000 Facebook users.

Territory and Population

Jamaica is an island in the Caribbean Sea about 150 km south of Cuba. The area is 10,991 km² (4,244 sq. miles). The population at the census of April 2011 was 2,697,983, distributed on the basis of the 13 parishes of the island. Chief towns (in 1,000), 2011: Kingston (metropolitan area), 585; Portmore, 182; Spanish Town, 147; Montego Bay, 110; May Pen, 62. In 2011, 52.1% of the population were urban. The population is about 92% of African ethnic origin. The official language is English. Patois, a combination of English and African languages, is widely spoken.

Tourism

In 2011 there were a record 1,951,752 non-resident overnight tourists and 1,125,481 cruise passenger arrivals (down from a peak of 1,336,994 in 2006).

Japan

Nihon (or Nippon) Koku (Land of the Rising Sun)

Factsheet

Capital: Tokyo
Population estimate, 2015: 126.57 m.
GNI per capita, 2014: (PPP$) 36,927
HDI/world rank, 2014: 0.891/20
Internet domain extension: .jp

Civil Aviation

The main international airports are at Fukuoka, Hiroshima, Kagoshima, Nagoya, Naha, Niigata, Osaka (Kansai International), Sapporo, Sendai and two serving Tokyo—at Narita (New Tokyo International) and Haneda (Tokyo International). The principal airlines are Japan Airlines International (JAL), formed when Japan Airlines and Japan Air System merged in 2001, and All Nippon Airways. In the financial year 2008 Japanese companies carried 92.89 m. passengers on domestic services and 16.43 m. passengers on international services. In 2007 Narita handled 35,478,146 passengers (mainly on international flights) and 2,254,421 tonnes of freight (making it the 7th busiest airport in the world for freight).

Climate

The islands of Japan lie in the temperate zone, northeast of the main monsoon region of southeast Asia. The climate is temperate with warm, humid summers and relatively mild winters except in the island of Hokkaido and northern parts of Honshu facing the Sea of Japan. There is a month's rainy season in June-July, but the best seasons are spring and autumn, although Sept. may bring typhoons. Tokyo, Jan. 5.8 °C, July 25.4 °C. Annual rainfall 1,467 mm. Hiroshima, Jan. 5.3 °C, July 26.9 °C. Annual rainfall 1,541 mm. Nagasaki, Jan. 6.8 °C, July 26.6 °C. Annual rainfall 1,960 mm. Osaka, Jan. 5.8 °C, July 27.2 °C. Annual rainfall 1,306 mm. Sapporo, Jan. –4.1 °C, July 20.5 °C. Annual rainfall 1,128 mm.

Constitution and Government

The Emperor is Akihito (b. 23 Dec. 1933), who succeeded his father, Hirohito on 7 Jan. 1989 (enthroned, 12 Nov. 1990); married 10 April 1959, to Michiko Shoda (b. 20 Oct. 1934). The 1947 constitution supersedes the Meiji constitution of 1889. In it the Japanese people pledge themselves to uphold the ideas of democracy and peace. The Emperor is the symbol of the unity of the people. Sovereign power rests with the people. The Emperor has no powers related to government. Fundamental human rights are guaranteed. Legislative power rests with the *Diet*, which consists of the *House of Deputies* (Shugi-in), elected by men and women over 20 years of age for a 4-year term, and an upper house, the *House of Councillors* (Sangi-in) of 242 members (96 elected by party list system with proportional representation according to the d'Hondt method and 146 from prefectural districts), one-half of its members being elected every 3 years. The number of members has been reduced in recent years. There had been 252 members until 2001 and 247 members from 2001 until elections of July 2004.

Currency

The unit of currency is the *yen* (JPY).

Defence

Japan has renounced war as a sovereign right and the threat or the use of force as a means of settling disputes with other nations. Its troops had not previously been able to serve abroad, but in 1992 the House of Representatives voted to allow up to 2,000 troops to take part in UN peacekeeping missions. A law of Nov. 1994 authorizes the Self-Defence Force to send aircraft abroad in rescue operations where Japanese citizens are involved. Following the attacks on New York and Washington of 11 Sept. 2001, legislation was passed allowing Japan's armed forces to take part in operations in the form of logistical support assisting the US-led war on terror. The legislation permits troops to take part in limited overseas operations but not to engage in combat. In May 2003 parliament passed a series of measures in response to North Korea's nuclear programme. Central government won increased control over the military which now has greater freedom to requisition civilian property in the event of attack. In Jan. 1991 Japan and the USA signed a renewal agreement under which Japan pays 40% of the costs of stationing US forces and 100% of the associated labour costs. US forces in Japan totalled 40,180 in 2011 (mostly marines and air force personnel). Total armed forces in 2011 numbered 247,750. Defence expenditure in 2013 totalled US$50,977 m. (US$401 per capita). In 2013 defence spending represented 1.0% of GDP.

Economy

In 2011 services accounted for 73% of GDP, industry 26% and agriculture 1%.

Labour

The labour force in 2013 was 65,559,000, down from 66,934,000 in 2003. 74.9% of the population aged 15–64 was economically active in 2013. Of those in employment in 2013, 69.1% worked in services, 25.8% in industry and 3.7% in agriculture. In that year 42.6% of the labour force was female. In Dec. 2015 unemployment stood at 3.3%, down from a record high of 5.7% in July 2009. The youth unemployment rate in 2013 was the lowest in the industrialized world, at just 6.9%. Long-term unemployment rose from 26.6% of the labour force between 16 and 64 having been out of work for more than a year in 2001 to 39.4% in 2011. The declining population means that the United Nations expects the working-age population in 2050 to be lower than it was in the 1950s. Retirement age is being raised progressively from 60 years to reach 65 by 2025. Japan had 80,000 people living in slavery according to the Walk Free Foundation's 2013 *Global Slavery Index*.

Press

In 2014 daily newspapers numbered 104 with aggregate circulation of 45.45 m. including four major English-language newspapers. The newspapers with the highest circulation are *Yomiuri Shimbun* (daily average of 9.2 m. copies in 2014) and *Asahi Shimbun* (daily average of 6.8 m. copies in 2014). They are also the two most widely read newspapers in the world. Japan has one of the highest circulation rates of daily newspapers in any country. In the 2013 *World Press Freedom Index* compiled by Reporters Without Borders, Japan was ranked 53rd out of 179 countries. In 2013, 82,589 new book titles were published.

Rail

The first railway was completed in 1872, between Tokyo and Yokohama (29 km). Most railways are of 1,067 mm gauge, but the high-speed 'shinkansen' lines are standard 1,435 mm gauge. In April 1987 the Japanese National Railways was reorganized into seven private companies, the Japanese Railways (JR) Group-six passenger companies and one freight company. Total length of railways in 2008–09 was 27,343 km, of which the JR had 19,987 km and other private railways 7,356 km. In 2008–09 the JR carried 8,984 m. passengers (other private, 13,992 m.) and 33 m. tonnes of freight (other private, 13 m.). An undersea tunnel linking Honshu with Hokkaido was opened to rail services in 1988.

Religion

State subsidies have ceased for all religions, and all religious teachings are forbidden in public schools. In Dec. 2012 Shintoism claimed 100.94 m. adherents, Buddhism 85.14 m.; these figures overlap. Christians numbered 1.91 m.

Roads

The total length of roads (including urban and other local roads) was 1,196,217 km at 1 April 2008. There were 54,736 km of national roads of which 49,756 km were paved. In 2006, 79.2% of all roads were paved. Motor vehicles, at 31 March 2010, numbered 78,693,000, including 40,419,000 passenger cars and 6,362,000 trucks. In 2007 there were 5,353,648 new vehicle registrations. In 2009 there were 4,914 road deaths (10,679 in 1995).

Shipping

In Jan. 2009 there were 2,524 ships of 300 GT or over registered, totalling 12.29 m. GT. Of the 2,524 vessels registered, 966 were general cargo ships, 499 oil tankers, 370 bulk carriers, 306 passenger ships, 249 chemical tankers, 162 liquid gas tankers and 22 container ships. The Japanese-controlled fleet is the largest in the world, comprising 3,674 vessels of 1,000 GT or over in Jan. 2009. Only 646 of the 3,474 vessels in Jan. 2009 were flying the Japanese flag. The busiest ports are Nagoya (218,130,000 freight tons handled in 2008), Chiba, Yokohama, Kitakyushu and Osaka.

Social Statistics

Births, 2007, 1,090,000; deaths, 1,108,000. Birth rate of Japanese nationals in present area in 2007, 8.6 per 1,000 population (1947: 34.3); death rate, 8.8. Marriage rate in 2007 (per 1,000 persons), 5.7; divorce rate, 2.0. In 2007 the mean age at first marriage was 30.1 for males and 28.3 for females. The infant mortality rate per 1,000 live births, 2 (2010), is one of the lowest in the world. In 2007 only 2.0% of births were outside marriage. Life expectancy at birth was 86.0 years for women and 79.0 years for men in 2007. Japan's life expectancy is the highest of any sovereign country. In 2012 the total fertility rate was 1.41 births per woman (compared to a low of 1.26 in 2005 but 1.91 in 1975 and 3.65 in 1950). There was a total of 33,093 suicides in 2007, a rate of 35.8 males per 100,000 and 13.7 females per 100,000. The rate among women is one of the highest in the world. A UNICEF report published in 2010 showed that 14.9% of children in Japan live in relative poverty (living in a household in which disposable income—when adjusted for family size and composition—is less than 50% of the national median income), compared to just 4.7% in Iceland.

Telecommunications

Telephone services have been operated by private companies (NTT and others) since 1985. In 2013 there were 1,176.3 mobile phone subscriptions per 1,000 inhabitants and 479.9 fixed telephone subscriptions per 1,000 population. In March 2012 there were 7.7 m. Facebook users (only 6% of the population).

Territory and Population

Japan consists of four major islands, Honshu, Hokkaido, Kyushu and Shikoku, and many small islands, with an area of 377,950 km². Census population of 1 Oct. 2010 (2005 census in brackets), 128,057,352 (127,767,994); of which males, 62,327,737 (62,348,977), females, 65,729,615 (65,419,017); population density (land area only), 351 per km² (351 per km²). In 2011, 67.0% of the population lived in urban areas. The official language is Japanese. Japan is divided into 43 prefectures, one metropolis (Tokyo), one territory (Hokkaido) and two urban prefectures (Kyoto and Osaka). The Tokyo conurbation, with a population in 2010 of 36.9 m., is the largest in the world, having overtaken New York around 1970. The leading cities, with population in 2010 (in 1,000), are: Tokyo, 8,946; Yokohama, 3,689; Osaka, 2,665; Nagoya, 2,264; Sapporo, 1,914; Kobe, 1,544.

Tourism

In 2012 there were 8,358,000 foreign visitors (up from 6,219,000 in 2011 although down from 8,611,000 in 2010). Of the foreign visitors in 2011, 77% were from elsewhere in East Asia and the Pacific, 12% from the Americas and 9% from Europe. Tourist receipts amounted to US$16.2 bn. in 2012.

Jordan

Al-Mamlaka Al-Urduniya Al-Hashemiyah (Hashemite Kingdom of Jordan)

Factsheet
Capital: Amman
Population estimate, 2015: 7.60 m.
GNI per capita, 2014: (PPP$) 11,365
HDI/world rank, 2014: 0.748/80
Internet domain extension: .jo

Civil Aviation

The Queen Alia International airport is at Zizya, 30 km south of Amman. There are also international flights from Amman's second airport. Queen Alia International handled 6,250,048 passengers in 2012 (6,190,911 on international flights) and 96,855 tonnes of freight. Royal Jordanian is the national carrier.

Climate

Predominantly a Mediterranean climate, with hot dry summers and cool wet winters, but in hilly parts summers are cooler and winters colder. Those areas below sea-level are very hot in summer and warm in winter. Eastern parts have a desert climate. Amman, Jan. 46 °F (7.5 °C), July 77 °F (24.9 °C). Annual rainfall 13.4″ (340.6 mm). Aqaba, Jan. 61 °F (16 °C), July 89 °F (31.5 °C). Annual rainfall 1.4″ (36.7 mm).

Constitution and Government

The Kingdom is a constitutional monarchy headed by H. M. King **Abdullah Bin Al Hussein** II, born 30 Jan. 1962, married H. M. Queen Rania (Rania Al-Yassin, b. 31 Aug. 1970) on 10 June 1993. He succeeded on the death of his father, H. M. King Hussein, on 7 Feb. 1999. The Constitution ratified on 8 Dec. 1952 provides that the Cabinet is responsible to Parliament. It was amended in 1954, 1958, 1960, 1973, 1974, 1976, 1984 and 2011. The legislature consists of a *Senate* of 60 members appointed by the King and a *House of Representatives* of 150 members (15 are reserved for women) elected by universal suffrage.

Currency

The unit of currency is the *Jordan dinar* (JOD), usually written as JD, of 1,000 *fils*, pegged to the US dollar since 1995 at a rate of one dinar = US$1.41.

Defence

Defence expenditure in 2013 totalled US$1,216 m. (US$188 per capita), representing 3.6% of GDP.

Economy

Services accounted for 65.5% of GDP in 2009, industry 31.6% and agriculture 2.9%.

Labour

The labour force in 2013 was 1,717,000 (1,294,000 in 2003). 43.6% of the population aged 15–64 was economically active in 2013. In the same year 12.6% of the population was unemployed. Jordan had 13,000 people living in slavery according to the Walk Free Foundation's 2013 *Global Slavery Index*.

Press

In 2008 there were seven paid-for daily newspapers with a combined circulation of 270,000 and 23 paid-for non-dailies.

Rail

The 1,050 mm gauge Hedjaz Jordan Railway (HJR) runs from the Syrian border to Amman. HJR controls 496 km of track but much of it is out of use.

Religion

According to the Pew Research Center's Forum on Religion & Public Life, in 2010 an estimated 97.2% of the population were Muslims (mainly Sunnis) and 2.2% Christians (mainly Orthodox).

Roads

Total length of roads, 2007, 7,768 km, of which 3,206 km were main roads. In 2007 there were 536,700 passenger cars (94 per 1,000 inhabitants), 2,800 motorcycles and mopeds, 17,200 coaches and buses, and 230,800 lorries and vans. There were 992 deaths in road accidents in 2007 (388 in 1992).

Shipping

In Jan. 2009 there were 21 ships of 300 GT or over registered, totalling 315,000 GT. The main port is Aqaba, which handled 17.3 m. tonnes of foreign cargo in 2008.

Social Statistics

Births (est.), 2008, 180,000; deaths, 20,000. Rates, 2008 per 1,000 population: birth (est.), 31; death (est.), 4. Annual population growth rate, 2008–10, 2.2%. Life expectancy at birth in 2013; 72.3 years for men, 75.6 for women. Infant mortality, 2010, 18 per 1,000 live births; fertility rate, 2008, 3.1 births per woman.

Telecommunications

In 2011 there were 465,400 landline telephone subscriptions (equivalent to 73.5 per 1,000 inhabitants) and 7,482,600 mobile phone subscriptions (or 1,182.0 per 1,000 inhabitants). In 2000 the government sold a 40% stake in Jordan Telecommunications Company (Jordan Telecom) to France Télécom. In 2006 France Télécom (rebranded as Orange in 2013) became the majority shareholder when it purchased a further 11% of Jordan Telecom from the government. Jordan Telecom's monopoly on fixed-line services ended on 1 Jan. 2005. In 2011, 34.9% of the population were internet users. In March 2012 there were 2.2 m. Facebook users.

Territory and Population

Jordan is bounded in the north by Syria, east by Iraq, southeast and south by Saudi Arabia and west by Israel. It has an outlet to an arm of the Red Sea at Aqaba. Its area is 89,342 km^2 (including 540 km^2 inland water). The 2004 census population was 5,103,639; Dec. 2012 estimate, 6,388,000, giving a density of 71.5 per km^2. In 2011, 78.6% of the population lived in urban areas. The largest towns, with 2004 census population, are: Amman, the capital, 1,036,330; Zarqa, 395,227; Irbid, 250,645. The official language is Arabic.

Tourism

In 2009 there were 3,789,000 non-resident tourists (excluding same-day visitors), up from 3,729,000 in 2008 and 3,431,000 in 2007.

Kazakhstan

Qazaqstan Respūblīkasy (Republic of Kazakhstan)

Factsheet

Capital: Astana
Population estimate, 2015: 17.63 m.
GNI per capita, 2014: (PPP$) 20,867
HDI/world rank, 2014: 0.788/56
Internet domain extension: .kz

Civil Aviation

The national carrier is Air Astana, which carried 3,770,000 passengers in 2014. There are international airports at Almaty and Astana.

Climate

The climate is generally fairly dry. Winters are cold but spring comes earlier in the south than in the far north. Almaty, Jan. −4 °C, July 24 °C. Annual rainfall 598 mm.

Constitution and Government

Relying on a judgement of the Constitutional Court that the 1994 parliamentary elections were invalid, President Nazarbayev dissolved parliament on 11 March 1995 and began to rule by decree. A referendum on the adoption of a new constitution was held on 30 Aug. 1995. The electorate was 8.8 m.; turnout was 80%. 89% of votes cast were in favour. The Constitution thus adopted allowed the President to rule by decree and to dissolve parliament if it holds a no-confidence vote or twice rejects his nominee for Prime Minister. It established a parliament consisting of a 39-member Senate (two selected by each of the elected assemblies of Kazakhstan's 16 principal administrative divisions plus seven appointed by the president); and a lower house (*Majlis*) of 77 (67 popularly elected by single mandate districts, with ten members elected by party-list vote). In June 2010 parliament approved an amendment to the constitution giving President Nazarbayev the title 'Leader of the Nation'.

Currency

The unit of currency is the *tenge* (KZT) of 100 *tiyn*, which was introduced on 15 Nov. 1993 at 1 tenge = 500 roubles.

Defence

Defence expenditure in 2013 totalled US$2,318 m. (US$131 per capita), representing 1.1% of GDP. There is currently conscription for 12 months, but Kazakhstan is set to switch to a fully professional army during 2016.

Economy

Agriculture accounted for 6.4% of GDP in 2009, industry 40.3% and services 53.3%.

Labour

The labour force in 2013 was 9,198,000 (7,756,000 in 2003). 78.6% of the population aged 15–64 was economically active in 2013. In the same year 5.2% of the population was unemployed. Kazakhstan had 47,000 people living in slavery according to the Walk Free Foundation's 2013 *Global Slavery Index*.

Press

There were 1,900 newspapers and magazines in 2008. The leading newspapers are the Kazakh-language *Egemen Kazakhstan* and the Russian-language *Kazakhstanskaya Pravda*.

Rail

In 2012 there were 14,319 km of 1,520 mm gauge railways. Passenger-km travelled in 2009 came to 14.9 bn. and freight tonne-km to 197.3 bn. The first section of a metro in Almaty, covering 8.6 km, opened in 2011. Eventually it is expected to reach 45 km in length.

Religion

In 2010 there were an estimated 11.3 m. Muslims according to the Pew Research Center's Forum on Religion & Public Life (70.4% of the population), with the main minorities being Orthodox Christians (3.4 m.), Catholics (380,000) and Protestants (310,000). A further 670,000 people had no religious affiliation.

Roads

In 2007 there were 93,123 km of roads, of which 23,507 were highways, main or national roads. Passenger cars in use in 2007 numbered 2,183,100, and there were also 359,200 lorries and vans, 83,400 buses and coaches, and 45,200 motorcycles and mopeds. There were 4,365 fatalities as a result of road accidents in 2007. With 28.2 deaths per 100,000 population in 2007, Kazakhstan has among the highest death rates in road accidents of any country.

Shipping

There is one large port, Aktau. In Jan. 2009 there were nine ships of 300 GT or over registered, totalling 33,000 GT.

Social Statistics

2007: births, 321,963; deaths, 158,297; marriages, 146,379; divorces, 36,107. Rates, 2007 (per 1,000 population): birth, 20.8; death, 10.2; marriage, 9.5; divorce, 2.3. Suicides in 2007 numbered 4,168 (rate of 26.9 per 100,000 population). Annual population growth rate, 2010–15, 1.6%. Expectation of life at birth, 2007, 59.1 years for males and 71.2 years for females. Infant mortality, 2010, 29 per 1,000 live births; fertility rate, 2008, 2.3 births per woman.

Telecommunications

There were 4.01 m. fixed telephone lines in 2010 (250.3 per 1,000 inhabitants). Mobile phone subscribers numbered 19.77 m. in 2010. There were 182.0 internet users per 1,000 inhabitants in 2009. Fixed internet subscriptions totalled 846,900 in 2010 (52.8 per 1,000 inhabitants). In March 2012 there were 452,000 Facebook users.

Territory and Population

Kazakhstan is bounded in the west by the Caspian Sea and Russia, in the north by Russia, in the east by China and in the south by Uzbekistan, Kyrgyzstan and Turkmenistan. The area is 2,724,900 km^2 (1,052,090 sq. miles). The population at the census of Feb. 2009 was 16,009,597 (density of 5.9 per km^2), of whom Kazakhs accounted for 63.1% and Russians 23.7%. Kazakhstan's administrative divisions consist of 14 provinces and three cities. In Dec. 1997 the capital was moved from Almaty to Aqmola, which was renamed Astana in May 1998 (the name of the province remained as Aqmola). Astana has a population of 613,006 (Feb. 2009 census). Other major cities, with Feb. 2009 populations: Almaty (1,365,632); Shymkent (603,499); Qaraghandy (459,778). The official languages are Kazakh and Russian; Russian is more widely spoken.

Tourism

In 2010 there were 3,393,000 non-resident tourists, up from 3,118,000 in 2009. There were 1,460 hotels in 2010.

Kenya

Jamhuri ya Kenya (Republic of Kenya)

Factsheet
Capital: Nairobi
Population estimate, 2015: 46.05 m.
GNI per capita, 2013: (PPP$) 2,762
HDI/world rank, 2014: 0.548/145=
Internet domain extension: .ke

Civil Aviation

There are international airports at Nairobi (Jomo Kenyatta International) and Mombasa (Moi International). The national carrier, Kenya Airways, is operated under a public-private partnership with the Kenyan government owning a 29.8% share and Dutch airline KLM 26.7%. In 2013 it carried 3,693,000 passengers (2,808,000 on international flights), serving 58 international and four domestic destinations. In 2010 Jomo Kenyatta International handled 5,484,771 passengers and Moi International 1,271,078.

Climate

The climate is tropical, with wet and dry seasons, but considerable differences in altitude make for varied conditions between the hot, coastal lowlands and the plateau, where temperatures are very much cooler. Heaviest rains occur in April and May, but in some parts there is a second wet season in Nov. and Dec. Nairobi, Jan. 65 °F (18.3 °C), July 60 °F (15.6 °C). Annual rainfall 39″ (958 mm). Mombasa, Jan. 81 °F (27.2 °C), July 76 °F (24.4 °C). Annual rainfall 47″ (1,201 mm).

Constitution and Government

A new constitution was approved in a referendum on 4 Aug. 2010 with 66.9% of votes cast in favour. Under its terms, the *President* and *Parliament* will have 5-year fixed terms. The president may not serve more than two terms. To be elected president, a candidate must secure at least 50% of votes cast, with at least a quarter coming from more than half of the county constituencies. The old 46 local government districts were restructured into 47 counties, with each county having a governor and a senator. Senators sit in a newly-created 68-member upper house, providing the country with a bicameral legislature following the elections of March 2013. The *National Assembly*, the lower house, is made up of 350 members following the election with 290 directly elected, 47 women, 12 nominated plus the Speaker (up from 224 previously, with 210 directly elected, 12 appointed plus the Speaker and the Attorney General). The *Senate* consists of 47 elected senators, 20 nominated senators plus the Speaker. Each county assembly must return at least one female MP. Parliament has the power to vet key appointments previously appointed by order of the president. The constitution also provides for a supreme court (the highest court in the land) backed by a court of appeals. Judges are subject to review by a judicial appointments panel.

Currency

The monetary unit is the *Kenya shilling* (KES) of 100 *cents*.

Defence

In 2013 defence expenditure totalled US$975 m. (US$22 per capita), representing 2.1% of GDP.

Economy

Agriculture contributed 22.6% of GDP in 2009, industry 15.3% and services 62.1%.

Labour

The labour force in 2013 was 16,969,000 (12,574,000 in 2003). 67.8% of the population aged 15–64 was economically active in 2013. In the same year 9.1% of the population was unemployed. Kenya had 37,000 people living in slavery according to the Walk Free Foundation's 2013 *Global Slavery Index*.

Press

In 2010 there were eight paid-for daily papers with a total average daily circulation of 310,000 plus 15 paid-for non-dailies. The most widely read paper is the English-language *Daily Nation*.

Rail

In 2006 there were 2,064 km of railways (metre gauge). Most of the network (1,918 km, including non-operational sections) is managed by Rift Valley Railways (Kenya) Ltd. In 2008–09, 4.4 m. passengers and 1.6 m. tonnes of freight were carried. The Magadi Railway Co. Ltd manages a 146 km stretch of line from Manzi to Konza to carry soda ash for export through Mombasa.

Religion

In 2010 there were 24.2 m. Protestants according to the Pew Research Center's Forum on Religion & Public Life, 9.0 m. Catholics, 3.9 m. Muslims and 0.7 m. folk religionists. A further 1.0 m. people did not have any religious affiliation. In Feb. 2016 there was one Roman Catholic cardinal.

Roads

In 2004 there were 63,265 km of roads (6,527 km of highways, national and main roads). There were, in 2007, 562,400 passenger cars in use, 210,900 vans and lorries, 180,800 motorcycles and mopeds, and 20,100 buses and coaches. There were 2,893 fatalities as a result of road accidents in 2007.

Shipping

The main port is Mombasa, which handled 16.4 m. tonnes of cargo in 2008; container traffic totalled 616,000 TEUs (twenty-foot equivalent units) in 2008. In Jan. 2009 there were six ships of 300 GT or over registered, totalling 6,000 GT.

Social Statistics

2008 births (estimates), 1,503,000; deaths, 451,000. Estimated birth rate in 2008 was 38.8 per 1,000 population; estimated death rate, 11.6. Annual population growth rate, 2000–08, 2.6%. Expectation of life at birth in 2007 was 53.2 years for males and 54.0 years for females. Infant mortality, 2010, 55 per 1,000 live births. Fertility rate, 2008, 4.9 births per woman. In 2005, 46% of Kenyans lived below the poverty line (down from 52% in 1997).

Telecommunications

Kenya had 283,500 landline telephone subscribers in 2011, or 6.8 per 1,000 persons. Since 1999 the government has been introducing measures to liberalize the telecommunications sector that have led to massive price reductions and improved services. In 2011 mobile phone subscribers numbered 26,980,800. The main mobile providers are Safaricom and Airtel Kenya. There were 209.8 internet users per 1,000 inhabitants in 2010. Fixed internet subscriptions totalled 8,300 in 2009 (0.2 per 1,000 inhabitants). In June 2012 there were 1.4 m. Facebook users.

Territory and Population

Kenya is bounded by South Sudan and Ethiopia in the north, Uganda in the west, Tanzania in the south and Somalia and the Indian Ocean in the east. The total area is 581,313 km². The 2009 census gave a population of 38,610,097 (19,417,639 females); density, 66 per km². In 2009, 70.2% of the population were rural. In 2006 more than 30,000 Somali refugees entered Kenya to escape the fighting that escalated in Somalia the course of the year. Kenya is divided into seven provinces and one national capital area (Nairobi; 2009 census population of 3,138,369). Other large towns (2009): Eldoret (252,061), Ruiru (236,961), Kikuyu (190,208), Thika (136,576). Most of Kenya's 38.61 m. people belong to 13 tribes. Swahili and English are both official languages, but people belonging to the different tribes have their own language as their mother tongue.

Tourism

In 2009 there were 1,392,000 non-resident tourists (down from a high of 1,686,000 in 2007). In 2009 receipts from tourism amounted to US$1,124 m., down from US$1,514 m. in 2007. Tourism is the country's leading source of hard currency.

Kiribati

Ribaberikin Kiribati (Republic of Kiribati)

Factsheet

Capital: Bairiki (Tarawa)
Population estimate, 2015: 112,000
GNI per capita, 2014: (PPP$) 2,434
HDI/world rank, 2014: 0.590/137
Internet domain extension: .ki

Civil Aviation

The national airline is the state-owned Air Kiribati. In 2010 there were scheduled services from Tarawa (Bonriki) to Fiji as well as domestic flights linking the main islands of Kiribati.

Climate

The Line Islands, Phoenix Islands and Banaba have a maritime equatorial climate, but the islands further north and south are tropical. Annual and daily ranges of temperature are small; mean annual rainfall ranges from 50″ (1,250 mm) near the equator to 120″ (3,000 mm) in the north. Typhoons are prevalent (Nov.-March) and there are occasional tornadoes. Tarawa, Jan. 83 °F (28.3 °C), July 82 °F (27.8 °C). Annual rainfall 79″ (1,977 mm).

Constitution and Government

Under the constitution founded on 12 July 1979 the republic has a unicameral legislature, the *House of Assembly* (Maneaba ni Maungatabu), comprising 46 members, 44 of whom are elected by popular vote, and two (the Attorney-General *ex officio* and a representative from the Banaban community) appointed for a 4-year term. The *President* is both Head of State and government. Presidential candidates are initially selected by members of parliament before facing a popular vote.

Currency

The currency in use is the Australian *dollar*.

Economy

Agriculture accounted for 26% of GDP in 2009, industry 8% and services 66%.

Labour

The economically active population classified as cash workers (not including village workers engaged in subsistence activities) totalled 13,133 in 2005. In 2005, 52.9% of cash workers were employed in public administration, 11.2% in transport and communication, 9.0% in retail trade, and 7.1% in agriculture and fishing. 6.1% of the labour force were unemployed in 2005; the unemployment rate in 2005 including village workers was 64.5%.

Press

In 2008 there were three newspapers with a combined circulation of 4,000.

Religion

In 2010 an estimated 50% of the population were Roman Catholics according to the Pew Research Center's Forum on Religion & Public Life and 40% Kiribati Protestants; there are also small numbers of Seventh-day Adventists, Latter-day Saints (Mormons) and Bahá'ís.

Roads

There are some 810 km of roads, of which about 130 km are sealed. There were 9,600 cars, 4,320 trucks and vans and 2,080 motorcycles in 2008.

Shipping

The main port is at Betio (Tarawa). Other ports of entry are Banaba, English Harbor and Kanton. There is also a small network of canals in the Line Islands. In Jan. 2009 there were 58 ships of 300 GT or over registered, totalling 245,000 GT.

Social Statistics

2005 estimates: births, 2,460; deaths, 810. Rates, 2005 estimates (per 1,000 population): births, 26.6; deaths, 8.7. Infant mortality rate (2010), 39 per 1,000 live births; life expectancy (2005), 61.0 years. Annual population growth rate, 2000–05, 1.8%; fertility rate, 2008, 3.1 births per woman.

Telecommunications

In 2011 there were 8,461 main (fixed) telephone lines and 13,788 mobile phone subscriptions. There were 90 internet users per 1,000 inhabitants in 2010.

Territory and Population

Kiribati (pronounced Kiribahss) consists of three groups of coral atolls and one isolated volcanic island, spread over a large expanse of the Central Pacific with a total land area of 811 km² (313 sq. miles). The capital is the island of Bairiki in Tarawa. The gradual rise in sea levels in recent years is slowly reducing the area of the islands. Most of the land is less than 3 m above sea level. Population, 2010 census, 103,058 (52,262 females); density, 127 per km². In 2011, 44.0% of the population lived in urban areas. Banaba, all 16 Gilbert Islands, Kanton (or Abariringa) in the Phoenix Islands and three atolls in the Line Islands (Teraina, Tabuaeran and Kiritimati—formerly Washington, Fanning and Christmas Islands respectively) are inhabited. The remaining 12 atolls have no permanent population; the seven Phoenix Islands comprise Birnie, Rawaki (formerly Phoenix), Enderbury, Manra (formerly Sydney), Orona (formerly Hull), McKean and Nikumaroro (formerly Gardner), while the others are Malden and Starbuck in the Central Line Islands, and Millennium Island (formerly Caroline), Flint and Vostok in the Southern Line Islands. The population is almost entirely Micronesian. English is the official language; I-Kiribati (Gilbertese) is also spoken.

Tourism

In 2011, 5,264 non-resident tourists-excluding same-day visitors-arrived by air at Tarawa and Kiritimati (the two most populous islands).

North Korea

Chosun Minchu-chui Inmin Konghwa-guk (Democratic People's Republic of Korea)

Factsheet
Capital: Pyongyang
Population estimate, 2015: 25.16 m.
GNI per capita, 2014: US$696
Internet domain extension: .kp

Civil Aviation

There is an international airport at Pyongyang (Sunan). There were flights in 2010 to Bangkok, Beijing, Shenyang and Vladivostok. The national carrier is Air Koryo.

Climate

There is a warm temperate climate, though winters can be very cold in the north. Rainfall is concentrated in the summer months. Pyongyang, Jan. 18 °F (−7.8 °C), July 75 °F (23.9 °C). Annual rainfall 37″ (916 mm).

Constitution and Government

North Korea adopted a new constitution in April 2009 that formalized *songun* or 'military first' politics as a guiding principle of state but dropped the word 'communism'. The Constitution provides for a 687-seat *Supreme People's Assembly* elected every 5 years by universal suffrage. Citizens of 17 years and over can vote and be elected. The government consists of the *Administration Council* directed by the Central People's Committee. In 1998, 4 years after the death of Kim Il-sung, the title of president was abolished. On the death of Kim Jong-il on 19 Dec. 2011 his son and designated successor, Kim Jong-un (b. 1983), assumed the role of 'supreme Leader'. About 3 m. people are affiliated with the ruling party, the Workers' Party of Korea. There are also the puppet religious Chongu and Korean Social Democratic Parties and various organizations combined in a Fatherland Front.

Currency

The monetary unit is the *won* (KPW) of 100 *chon*.

Defence

The Supreme Commander of the Armed Forces is Kim Jong-un. Military service is compulsory at the age of 16 for periods of 5–12 years in the Army, 5–10 years in the Navy and 3–4 years in the Air Force, followed by obligatory part-time service in the Pacification Corps to age 40. Total armed forces troops were estimated to number 1,106,000 in 2007, up from 840,000 in 1986 although down from 1,160,000 in 1997. Around 70% of the troops are located along or near the Demilitarized Zone between North and South Korea. Defence expenditure in 2012 totalled an estimated US$3.5 bn. in 2012, which is believed to equate to approximately 22% of GDP. North Korea was for many years suspected of having a secret nuclear-weapons programme, and perhaps enough material to build two warheads. In April 2009 North Korea was accused by South Korea and the UN of testing long-range nuclear missile technology. North Korea responded by walking out of international talks to wind up its nuclear programme. The following month Pyongyang claimed it had successfully completed underground nuclear tests. In June the UN imposed new sanctions, with Pyongyang stating its intent to weaponize plutonium supplies. A 'miniaturized' nuclear device was tested underground at the Punggye-ri test site in Feb. 2013, prompting new UN sanctions the following month.

Economy

Agriculture is estimated to account for approximately 25% of GDP, industry 60% and services 15%. In 2012 North Korea received approximately US$126 m. in foreign aid. North Korea was rated the joint most corrupt country in the world in a 2015 survey of 168 countries carried out by the anti-corruption organization *Transparency International*.

Labour

The labour force in 2013 was 15,206,000 (14,048,000 in 2003). 82.7% of the population aged 15–64 was economically active in 2013. In the same year 4.1% of the population was unemployed.

Press

There were three national daily newspapers and 12 regional dailies in 2008 with a combined circulation of 4.5 m. The party newspaper is *Nodong* (or *Rodong*) *Sinmun* (Workers' Daily News). In the 2013 *World Press Freedom Index* compiled by Reporters Without Borders, North Korea ranked 178th out of 179 countries.

Rail

Rail transport is provided by Korean State Railways. There is an extensive network of standard gauge lines totalling over 6,000 km and a network of 762 mm narrow gauge lines covering some 350 km. Main lines cover around 2,500 km. There is a metro and two tramways in Pyongyang. Two passenger trains crossed the border between North and South Korea on 17 May 2007 (one northbound and one southbound), completing the first cross-border journey in more than 50 years.

Religion

The state-sanctioned philosophy of *Juche* is the only government-recognized ideology, to the point of excluding all other religions. *Juche* means 'self-reliance' in Korean. Although the official North Korean line is that it is an atheistic philosophy, many observers maintain that is a religion. There are small numbers of Buddhists, Cheondoists and Christians. Persecution of Christians is considered to be more severe than in any other country.

Roads

There were 25,554 km of road in 2006. The first of two planned cross-border roads between the two Koreas opened in Feb. 2003.

Shipping

The leading ports are Chongjin, Wonsan and Hungnam. Pyongyang is connected to the port of Nampo by railway and river. In Jan. 2009 there were 223 ships of 300 GT or over registered, totalling 884,000 GT. The biggest navigable river is the Yalu, 698 km up to the Hyesan district.

Social Statistics

2008 estimated births, 327,000; deaths, 238,000. 2008 estimated birth rate, 13.7 per 1,000 population; death rate, 10.0. Annual population growth rate, 2000–08, 0.5%. Marriage is discouraged before the age of 32 for men and 29 for women. Life expectancy at birth, 2013, was 66.4 years for men and 73.4 years for women. Infant mortality, 2010, 26 per 1,000 live births; fertility rate, 2008, 1.9 births per woman.

Telecommunications

There were 1.18 m. main (fixed) telephone lines in 2013. A mobile phone service was introduced in Dec. 2008 4 years after a previous service had been shut down without explanation. In 2013 there were 2.42 m. subscribers (972 for every 10,000 inhabitants). It was only in 2013 that the number of mobile phone subscriptions surpassed the number of fixed telephone subscriptions.

Territory and Population

North Korea is bounded in the north by China, east by the Sea of Japan (East Sea of Korea), west by the Yellow Sea and south by South Korea, from which it is separated by a demilitarized zone of 1,262 km². Its area is 122,762 km². The census population in 2008 was 24,052,231; density 195.9 per km². In 2011, 60.3% of the population were urban. Pyongyang, the capital, had a 2008 census population of 2,581,076. Other large towns (census, 2008): Hamhung (703,610); Chongjin (614,892); Sinuiju (334,031). The official language is Korean.

Tourism

A 40-year ban on non-Communist tourists was lifted in 1986. In 2014 there were approximately 100,000 foreign tourists. On 19 Nov. 1998 North Korea received its first tourists from South Korea, on a cruise and tour organized by the South Korean firm Hyundai.

South Korea

Daehan Minguk (Republic of Korea)

Factsheet
Capital: Seoul
Population estimate, 2015: 50.29 m.
GNI per capita, 2014: (PPP$) 33,890
HDI/world rank, 2014: 0.898/17
Internet domain extension: .kr

Civil Aviation

There are six international airports in South Korea: at Seoul (Incheon), Busan (Gimhae), Daegu, Jeju, Yangyang and Cheongju. Incheon airport, 50 km to the west of Seoul and built on reclaimed land made up of four small islands, opened in March 2001 and is the largest airport in Asia. It replaced Gimpo Airport as Seoul's International Airport; Gimpo remains open for domestic flights and is the second busiest airport with 14.3 m. passengers in 2008. Incheon handled 30.0 m. passengers in 2008, while Jeju handled 12.4 m. and Busan 7.2 m. The national carrier is Korean Air, which in June 2009 operated flights to 101 cities in 39 countries.

Climate

The country experiences continental temperate conditions. Rainfall is concentrated in the period April to Sept. and ranges from 40″ (1,020 mm) to 60″ (1,520 mm). Busan, Jan. 36 °F (2.2 °C), July 76 °F (24.4 °C). Annual rainfall 56″ (1,407 mm). Seoul, Jan. 23 °F (−5 °C), July 77 °F (25 °C). Annual rainfall 50″ (1,250 mm).

Constitution and Government

The 1988 constitution provides for a *President*, directly elected for a single 5-year term, who appoints the members of the *State Council* and heads it, and for a *National Assembly* (*Gukhoe*), currently of 299 members, directly elected for 4 years (243 from constituencies and 56 from party lists in proportion to the overall vote). The current constitution created the Sixth Republic. The minimum voting age is 20.

Currency

The unit of currency is the *won* (KRW).

Defence

Peacetime operational control, which had been transferred to the United Nations Command (UNC) under a US general in July 1950 after the outbreak of the Korean War, was restored to South Korea on 1 Dec. 1994. In the event of a new crisis, operational control over the Korean armed forces will revert to the Combined Forces Command (CFC). Conscription is 21 months in the Army, 23 months in the Navy and 24 months in the Air Force. In Sept. 2007 it was announced that the length of conscription will be gradually reduced and that conscientious objectors will be allowed to choose community service in place of military service. In 2004 the USA and South Korea agreed to the redeployment of 12,500 US personnel in three phases that would continue until 2008. In April 2008 the number of troops had been reduced to 28,000 (mainly army and air force personnel) from 37,000 in 2002. The number of US troops in South Korea has remained unchanged since then. In 2013 defence expenditure totalled US$31,846 m. (US$651 per capita), representing 2.5% of GDP.

Economy

Agriculture accounted for 2.5% of GDP in 2013, industry 38.4% and services 59.3%.

Labour

In Sept. 2010 the population of working age was 40.68 m.; the economically active population was 24.91 m. (14.51 m. males and 10.40 m. females) including 16.44 m. persons employed in services, 5.85 m. in construction, manufacturing and mining, and 1.76 m. in agriculture, fisheries and forestry. 5.61 m. persons were self-employed in Sept. 2010. Unemployment was 3.5% in Dec. 2015—one of the lowest rates in the industrialized world. South Korea had 10,000 people living in slavery according to the Walk Free Foundation's 2013 *Global Slavery Index*.

Press

There were 324 daily newspapers in 2012. With 10.9 m. paid daily newspaper subscriptions in 2012, South Korea has the fifth highest newspaper circulation among developed countries. The most widely read dailies are *Chosun Ilbo* (average daily circulation of 1.8 m. per issue in 2013), *JoongAng Ilbo* (1.3 m. copies) and *Dong-A Ilbo* (907,000 copies). Newspaper online editions had 847,000 unique monthly visitors in 2010.

Rail

In 2009 Korail's system totalled 3,380 km of 1,435 mm gauge (including 240 km of high speed railways). In 2009 passenger-km travelled came to 31.3 bn. and freight tonne-km to 9.3 bn. In June 2000 it was agreed to start consultations to restore the railway from Seoul to Sinuiju, on the North Korean/Chinese border, by rebuilding a 12 km long stretch from Munsan, in South Korea, to Jangdan, on the South Korean/North Korean border, and an 8 km long stretch in North Korea. Two passenger trains crossed the border between North and South Korea on 17 May 2007 (one northbound and one southbound), completing the first cross-border journey in more than 50 years.

Religion

Traditionally, Koreans have lived under the influence of shamanism, Buddhism (introduced AD 372) and Confucianism, which was the official faith from 1392 to 1910. Catholic converts from China introduced Christianity in the eighteenth century, but a ban on Roman Catholicism was not lifted until 1882. The Anglican Church was introduced in 1890 and became an independent jurisdiction in 1993 under the Archbishop of Korea. According to the Pew Research Center's Forum on Religion & Public Life, in 2010 estimated affiliations of the main religions were: Buddhism, 11,050,000; Protestantism, 8,560,000; Roman Catholicism, 5,270,000. People with no religious affiliation numbered 22,350,000 in the same year, equivalent to 46.4% of the population. In Feb. 2016 there were two Roman Catholic cardinals.

Roads

In 2007 there were 102,061 km of roads, comprising 3,103 km of motorways, 14,225 km of highways and main roads and 84,733 km of secondary roads; 77.6% of roads (79,189 km) were paved. In 2006, 97,854 m. passenger-km were travelled by road and 12,545 m. tonne-km of freight were moved. In 2007 motor vehicles in use included 12,020,700 passenger cars, 4,189,000 vans and lorries, 182,100 buses and coaches, and 1,821,300 motorcycles and mopeds. In 2007 there were 6,166 fatalities as a result of road accidents (9,353 in 2000).

Shipping

In 2005 there were 52 ports (28 for international trade), including Busan, Incheon, Gunsan, Mokpo, Yeosu, Pohang, Donghae, Jeju, Masan, Ulsan, Daesan and Kwangyang. In Jan. 2009 there were 1,128 ships of 300 GT or over registered, totalling 13.41 m. GT. Of the 1,128 vessels registered, 350 were general cargo ships, 260 oil tankers, 242 bulk carriers, 81 container ships, 80 passenger ships, 67 chemical tankers and 48 liquid gas tankers. The busiest port is Busan, which was visited by 48,343 vessels of 354,350,000 GRT in 2005. Cargo handled in 2005 totalled 217,217,000 tonnes (112,103,000 tonnes loaded and 105,114,000 tonnes discharged).

Social Statistics

2008: births, 465,900; deaths, 246,100; marriages, 327,700; divorces, 116,500. Rates per 1,000 population in 2008: birth, 9.7; death, 5.1; marriage, 6.8; divorce, 2.4. In 2006 only 1.5% of births were outside marriage, one of the lowest rates in the world. South Korea has among the highest suicide rates of any country, at 36.6 per 100,000 inhabitants in 2012 (a rate of 49.9 among

males although only 23.4 among females). Expectation of life at birth, 2007, 82.4 years for females and 75.8 for males. Life expectancy had been 47 in 1955 and 62 in 1971. Infant mortality, 2010, four per 1,000 live births. The fertility rate in 2008 was 1.2 births per woman (the joint lowest rate in the world), down from 6.3 per woman in the period 1955–60. Annual population growth rate, 2005–10, 0.5%. In 2009 the average age of first marriage was 31.6 for men and 28.7 for women.. South Korea has one of the most rapidly ageing populations in the world, partly owing to an ever-decreasing birth rate. In 2009, 10.7% of the population were over 65, up from 2.9% in 1960. There were 16.92 m. households in 2009, with on average 2.8 members per household. According to the UN Human Development Report 2009, South Korea has an emigration rate of 3.1%; North America is the main destination, with 50.3% of South Korean migrants living there. Within South Korea, there are 551,200 foreign migrants, representing 1.2% of the total population.

Telecommunications

In 2014 mobile phone subscribers numbered 57,290,356 (1,157.1 per 1,000 persons). The largest operator, SK Telecom, has 49% of the market share for smartphone subscriptions, ahead of KT with 31%. There were 29,481,226 main (fixed) telephone lines in 2014. In 2014, 84.3% of the population were internet users. In March 2012 there were 6.4 m. Facebook users.

Territory and Population

South Korea is bounded in the north by the demilitarized zone (separating it from North Korea), east by the Sea of Japan (East Sea), south by the Korea Strait (separating it from Japan) and west by the Yellow Sea. The area is 99,461 km^2. The population at the census of 1 Nov. 2010 was 48,580,293; density, 488.4 per km^2 (one of the highest in the world). In 2011 the urban population was 83.3%. The official language is Korean. There are nine provinces (*do*) and seven metropolitan cities with provincial status. Cities with over 1,000,000 inhabitants (census 2010): Seoul, 9,794,304; Busan, 3,414,950; Incheon, 2,662,509; Daegu, 2,446,418; Daejeon,1,501,859; Gwangju, 1,475,745; Ulsan,1,082,567; Suwon, 1,071,913; Changwon, 1,058,021.

Tourism

A record 9,795,000 foreign nationals visited South Korea in 2011 (up from 8,798,000 in 2010 and 6,023,000 in 2005). The leading countries of origin of non-resident tourists in 2011 were: Japan (3,289,000), mainland China (2,220,000), the USA (662,000), Taiwan (428,000) and the Philippines (337,000). 12,694,000 South Koreans travelled abroad in 2011 (up from 12,488,000 in 2010 and 10,080,000 in 2005). In Nov. 1998 the first South Korean tourists to visit North Korea went on a cruise and tour organized by the South Korean firm Hyundai.

Kuwait

Dowlat al Kuwait (State of Kuwait)

Factsheet

Capital: Kuwait
Population estimate, 2015: 3.89 m.
GNI per capita, 2014: (PPP$) 83,961
HDI/world rank, 2014: 0.816/48
Internet domain extension: .kw

Civil Aviation

There is an international airport (Kuwait International). The national carrier is the state-owned Kuwait Airways. Kuwait's first low-cost airline, Jazeera Airways, began operations in Oct. 2005. In 2005 scheduled airline traffic of Kuwait-based carriers flew 50.7 m. km and carried 1,944,200 passengers. Kuwait International airport handled 8,967,413 passengers in 2012 and 184,784 tonnes of freight.

Climate

Kuwait has a dry, desert climate which is cool in winter but very hot and humid in summer. Rainfall is extremely light. Kuwait, Jan. 56 °F (13.5 °C), July 99 °F (36.6 °C). Annual rainfall 5″ (125 mm).

Constitution and Government

The ruler is HH Sheikh Sabah al-Ahmed al-Jaber al-Sabah, the 15th Amir of Kuwait, who succeeded on 29 Jan. 2006. *Crown Prince:* Sheikh Nawwaf al-Ahmed al-Sabah (b. 1937). The present constitution was approved and promulgated on 11 Nov. 1962. In 1990 the *National Council* was established, consisting of 50 elected members and 25 appointed by the Amir. It was replaced by a *National Assembly* or *Majlis al-Umma* in 1992, consisting at the time of 50 elected members. It now has 65 members, of whom 50 are elected. Women were eligible to stand for election and to vote in a council by-election held in April 2006 and in the full parliamentary election held in June 2006. Executive authority is vested in the *Council of Ministers*.

Currency

The unit of currency is the *Kuwaiti dinar* (KWD), usually written as KD, of 1,000 *fils*.

Defence

In Sept. 1991 the USA signed a 10-year agreement with Kuwait to store equipment, use ports and carry out joint training exercises. In March 2013, 15,000 US troops were stationed in Kuwait. Defence expenditure in 2013 totalled US$4,427 m. (US$1,642 per capita), representing 2.6% of GDP.

Economy

Agriculture accounted for 0.4% of GDP in 2014, industry 64.3% and services 35.3%.

Labour

The labour force in 2013 was 1,899,000 (1,051,000 in 2003). 70.1% of the population aged 15–64 was economically active in 2013. In the same year 3.2% of the population was unemployed. Approximately 80% of nationals work for the government, with around 95% of private jobs being filled by expatriates. In March 2013 the government announced its intention to reduce by a million the number of foreign workers over a period of 10 years.

Press

In 2008 there were 17 daily newspapers, with a combined circulation of 630,000. Formal press censorship was lifted in Jan. 1992.

Religion

In 2010 there were 2.0 m. Muslims according to estimates by the Pew Research Center's Forum on Religion & Public Life (of whom approximately two-thirds to three-quarters Sunnis and the rest Shias), plus 390,000 Christians and 230,000 Hindus.

Roads

There were 5,749 km of roads in 2004, 85% of which were paved. There were 750,600 passenger cars in use in 2007 (282 per 1,000 inhabitants), 573,200 lorries and vans, and 27,300 buses and coaches. In 2014 there were 99,047 road accidents involving injury with 461 fatalities.

Shipping

The port of Kuwait formerly served mainly as an entrepôt, but this function is declining in importance with the development of the oil industry. The largest oil terminal is at Mina Ahmadi. Three small oil ports lie to the south of Mina Ahmadi: Mina Shuaiba, Mina Abdullah and Mina al-Zor. In Jan. 2009 there were 52 ships of 300 GT or over registered (including 22 oil tankers), totalling 2.33 m. GT.

Social Statistics

Births, 2008, 54,571; deaths, 5,701. The birth rate in 2009 was 21.9 per 1,000 population and death rate 2.3 per 1,000 population (one of the lowest in the world). Expectation of life at birth, 2013, was 73.5 years for males and 75.5 years for females. Infant mortality, 2010, ten per 1,000 live births. Annual population growth rate, 2005–10, 5.3%. Fertility rate, 2008, 2.2 births per woman. Kuwait has had one of the largest reductions in its fertility rate of any country in the world over the past 30 years, having had a rate of 7.2 births per woman in 1975.

Telecommunications

In 2010 Kuwait had an estimated 566,000 landline telephone subscriptions (equivalent to 207 per 1,000 inhabitants) and 4.4 m. mobile phone subscriptions (or 1,608 per 1,000 inhabitants). In 2011, 74.2% of the population were internet users. In March 2012 there were 899,000 Facebook users.

Territory and Population

Kuwait is bounded in the east by the Persian Gulf, north and west by Iraq and south and southwest by Saudi Arabia, with an area of 17,818 km². In 1992–93 the UN Boundary Commission redefined Kuwait's border with Iraq, moving it slightly northwards in conformity with an agreement of 1932. The population at the 2011 census was 3,065,850; density, 172 per km². In 2011, 98.4% of the population were urban. In June 2014 the population was estimated at 4,039,445, of which 68.8% were non-Kuwaitis. The country is divided into six governorates: the capital (comprising Kuwait City, Kuwait's nine islands and territorial and shared territorial waters) (2011 census population, 326,513); Farwaniya (818,571); Hawalli (672,910); Ahmadi (588,068); Jahra (400,975); Mubarak al-Kabir (258,813). The capital city is Kuwait, with an estimated population in 2010 (metropolitan area) of 2,102,000. Other major cities are Hawalli, Qalib ash-Shuyukh and as-Salimiya. Over 78% speak Arabic, the official language. English is also used as a second language.

Tourism

There were 5,729,000 non-resident visitors in 2012 (up from 4,482,000 in 2007), bringing revenue of US$780 m.

Kyrgyzstan

Kyrgyz Respublikasy (Kyrgyz Republic)

Factsheet
Capital: Bishkek
Population estimate, 2015: 5.94 m.
GNI per capita, 2014: (PPP$) 3,044
HDI/world rank, 2014: 0.655/120
Internet domain extension: .kg

Civil Aviation

There is an international airport at Bishkek (Manas). The national carrier is Air Kyrgyzstan. In 2012 scheduled airline traffic of Kyrgyz-based carriers flew 5.0 m. km; passenger-km totalled 522.9 m. in the same year.

Climate

The climate varies from dry continental to polar in the high Tien-Shan, to sub-tropical in the southwest (Fergana Valley) and temperate in the northern foothills. Bishkek, Jan. 9 °F (−13 °C), July 70 °F (21 °C). Annual rainfall 14.8″ (375 mm).

Constitution and Government

A new constitution was adopted in June 2010 after it won overwhelming support in a referendum following the ousting of the incumbent president, Kurmanbek Bakiyev, in April 2010. Under the terms of the constitution, greater power is invested in parliament at the expense of the presidency. The president is allowed to serve a maximum of one 6-year term and cannot seek re-election, although the office does retain its power of veto and has the authority to appoint heads of various state institutions. The unicameral parliament (*Jogorku Kenesh*) is comprised of 120 seats, with no single party allowed to hold more than 65. Political parties cannot be constituted on religious or ethnic grounds and members of the armed forces, the judiciary and the police are banned from party membership.

Currency

On 10 May 1993 Kyrgyzstan introduced its own currency unit, the *som* (KGS), of 100 *tyiyn*, at a rate of 1 som = 200 roubles.

Defence

Conscription is for 12 months. Defence expenditure in 2013 totalled US$102 m. (US$18 per capita), representing 1.4% of GDP. The USA opened a military base in Kyrgyzstan in 2001 to aid the war in Afghanistan against the Taliban. The base was scheduled to close by the end of Aug. 2009 after an eviction notice was served on 20 Feb. 2009 giving the US military 180 days to vacate the site. However, on 23 June 2009 the Kyrgyz and US governments agreed a new deal that allowed a 1-year extension of the lease. The base closed when a further lease expired in June 2014. In Sept. 2003 Kyrgyzstan also agreed to allow Russia to open an air force base in the country.

Economy

Agriculture accounted for 21% of GDP in 2009, industry 27% and services 52%.

Labour

The labour force in 2013 was 2,677,000 (2,172,000 in 2003). 70.9% of the population aged 15–64 was economically active in 2013. In the same year 8.3% of the population was unemployed. Kyrgyzstan had 16,000 people living in slavery according to the Walk Free Foundation's 2013 *Global Slavery Index*.

Press

There were three national daily newspapers in 2008, with a combined circulation of 40,000.

Rail

In the north a railway runs from Lugovaya through Bishkek to Rybachi on Lake Issyk-Kul. Towns in the southern valleys are linked by short lines with the Ursatyevskaya-Andizhan railway in Uzbekistan. Total length of railway, 2011, 417 km. Passenger-km travelled in 2011 came to 83 m. and freight tonne-km to 798 m.

Religion

In 2010 there were an estimated 4.69 m. Muslims (mainly Sunnis) and 610,000 Christians (mainly Orthodox) according to the Pew Research Center's Forum on Religion & Public Life. There were 1,784 mosques, 359 Christian congregations, one synagogue and one Buddhist temple in 2008.

Roads

There were 34,000 km of roads in 2007. Passenger cars in use in 2007 numbered 229,700 (44 per 1,000 inhabitants). There were 1,252 road accident fatalities in 2007.

Social Statistics

2009 births, 135,494; deaths, 35,898; marriages (2006), 43,760. Rates, 2009 (per 1,000 population): birth, 26.4; death, 7.0; infant mortality (per 1,000 live births, 2010), 33. Life expectancy, 2007, 63.9 years for males and 71.4 for females. In 2003 the most popular age for marrying was 20–24 for females and 25–29 for males. Annual population growth rate, 2010–15, 1.6%; fertility rate, 2008, 2.5 births per woman.

Telecommunications

In 2010 there were 489,100 landline telephone subscriptions (equivalent to 91.7 per 1,000 inhabitants) and 5,275,500 mobile phone subscriptions (or 989.0 per 1,000 inhabitants). Fixed internet subscriptions totalled 68,900 in 2010 (12.9 per 1,000 inhabitants).

Territory and Population

Kyrgyzstan is situated on the Tien-Shan mountains and bordered in the east by China, west by Kazakhstan and Uzbekistan, north by Kazakhstan and south by Tajikistan. Area, 199,945 km² (77,199 sq. miles). Population (census 2009), 5,362,793 (51.3% females); density, 27 per km². In 2009, 65.9% of the population lived in rural areas. The republic comprises seven provinces (Batken, Djalal-Abad, Issyk-Kul, Naryn, Osh, Talas and Chu) plus the city of Bishkek, the capital (formerly Frunze; 2014 estimated population, 901,700). Other large towns (with 2014 estimates) are Osh (238,600), Djalal-Abad (96,600), Karakol (formerly Przhevalsk, 69,300), Tokmak (57,400), Uzgen (53,400), Balykchy (44,600) and Karabalta (42,200). The Kyrgyz are of Turkic origin and formed 69.2% of the population in 2008; the rest included Uzbeks (14.5%), Russians (8.7%) and Dungans (1.2%). The official languages are Kyrgyz and Russian.

Tourism

In 2010 there were 1,316,000 non-resident tourists, down from 2,147,000 in 2009. This was as a consequence of the political upheaval in April 2010 and the ethnic conflict that ensued.

Laos

Sathalanalath Pasathipatai Pasasonlao (Lao People's Democratic Republic)

Factsheet

Capital: Vientiane
Population estimate, 2015: 6.80 m.
GNI per capita, 2014: (PPP$) 4,680
HDI/world rank, 2014: 0.575/141
Internet domain extension: .la

Civil Aviation

There are three international airports at Vientiane (Wattay), Pakse and Luang Prabang. The national carrier is Lao Airlines, which in 2005 operated domestic services and international flights to Bangkok, Chiang Mai, Hanoi, Ho Chi Minh City, Kunming, Phnom Penh and Siem Reap (Cambodia). In 2006 scheduled airline traffic of Laos-based carriers flew 4 m. km, carrying 327,000 passengers (81,000 on international flights).

Climate

A tropical monsoon climate, with high temperatures throughout the year and very heavy rains from May to Oct. Vientiane, Jan. 70 °F (21.1 °C), July 81 °F (27.2 °C). Annual rainfall 69″ (1,715 mm).

Constitution and Government

In Aug. 1991 the National Assembly adopted a new constitution. The head of state is the President, elected by the National Assembly, which consists of 132 members (115 prior to the elections of April 2011). Under the constitution the People's Revolutionary Party of Laos (PPPL) remains the 'central nucleus' of the 'people's democracy'; other parties are not permitted. The PPPL's Politburo comprises 11 members, including Choummaly Sayasone (PPPL, *President*).

Currency

The unit of currency is the *kip* (LAK).

Defence

Military service is compulsory for a minimum of 18 months. Defence expenditure in 2013 totalled US$21 m. (US$3 per capita), representing 0.2% of GDP.

Economy

In 2009 agriculture accounted for 35.2% of GDP, industry 25.5% and services 39.3%.

Labour

The labour force in 2013 was 3,297,000 (2,569,000 in 2003). 80.6% of the population aged 15–64 was economically active in 2013. In the same year 1.3% of the population was unemployed. Laos had 50,000 people living in slavery according to the Walk Free Foundation's 2013 *Global Slavery Index*.

Press

In 2008 there were six paid-for national dailies with a combined circulation of 25,000.

Rail

A 3.5-km stretch of railway from Nongkhai, on the Thai bank of the Mekong River, across the Thai–Lao Friendship Bridge to Thanaleng in Laos was opened in 2009.

Religion

In 2010 there were an estimated 4.1 m. Buddhists and 1.9 m. folk religionists according to the Pew Research Center's Forum on Religion & Public Life. There is also a small Christian minority.

Roads

In 2006 there were 29,811 km of roads, of which 13.5% were paved. In 2007 there were 12,800 passenger cars (two per 1,000 inhabitants), 109,000 lorries and vans, 6,400 buses and coaches, and 506,500 motorcycles and mopeds. There were 5,198 traffic accidents with 608 fatalities in 2006. A bridge over the River Mekong, providing an important north-south link, was opened in 1994.

Shipping

The River Mekong and its tributaries are an important means of transport. In Jan. 2008 there were two ships of 300 GT or over registered, totalling 3,000 GT.

Social Statistics

2009 estimates: births, 141,000; deaths, 37,000. Rates, 2009 estimates (per 1,000 population): birth, 23; death, 6. Infant mortality (per 1,000 live births, 2010), 42. Life expectancy, 2013: 66.9 years for men and 69.7 for women. Annual population growth rate, 2005–10, 2.0%. Fertility rate, 2008, 3.5 births per woman.

Telecommunications

In 2011 there were 107,600 landline telephone subscriptions (equivalent to 17.1 per 1,000 inhabitants) and 5,480,900 mobile phone subscriptions (or 871.6 per 1,000 inhabitants). In 2011, 9.0% of the population were internet users. In March 2012 there were 156,000 Facebook users.

Territory and Population

Laos is a landlocked country of 236,800 km² (91,428 sq. miles) bordered on the north by China, the east by Vietnam, the south by Cambodia and the west by Thailand and Myanmar. Apart from the Mekong River plains along the border of Thailand, the country is mountainous, particularly in the north, and in places densely forested. The population (2005 census) was 5,621,982 (2,821,431 females); density, 24 per km². 2011 estimate: 6,385,057. In 2011, 34.3% of the population lived in urban areas. There are 16 provinces and one prefecture divided into 141 districts and one special region (*khetphiset*). The capital and largest town is Vientiane, with a population of (2005 estimate) 570,000. Other important towns are Savannakhet, Pakse, Xam Neua and Luang Prabang. The population is divided into three groups: about 67% Lao-Lum (Valley-Lao); 17% Lao-Theung (Lao of the mountain sides); and 7.4% Lao-Sung (Lao of the mountain tops), who comprise the Hmong and Yao (or Mien). Lao is the official language. French and English are spoken.

Tourism

There were 2,140,000 non-resident tourists in 2012 (up from 1,142,000 in 2007); revenue from tourism amounted to US$461 m.

Latvia

Latvijas Republika (Republic of Latvia)

Factsheet
Capital: Riga
Population estimate, 2015: 1.97 m.
GNI per capita, 2014: (PPP$) 22,281
HDI/world rank, 2014: 0.819/46
Internet domain extension: .lv

Civil Aviation

There is an international airport at Riga. A new national carrier, airBaltic, assumed control of Latavio and Baltic International Airlines in Aug. 1995 and began flying in Oct. 1995. It went on to become eastern Europe's first low-cost airline; in 2012 it carried 3.08 m. passengers and operated scheduled services to 55 destinations. It is 99.8% state-owned, with Transaero owning the remaining 0.2%. In 2010 Riga handled 4,663,692 passengers and 12,247 tonnes of freight.

Climate

Owing to the influence of maritime factors, the climate is relatively temperate but changeable. Average temperatures in Jan. range from −2.8 °C in the western coastal town of Liepāja to −6.6 °C in the inland town of Daugavpils. The average summer temperature is 20 °C.

Constitution and Government

The Declaration of the Renewal of the Independence of the Republic of Latvia dated 4 May 1990, and the 21 Aug. 1991 declaration re-establishing *de facto* independence, proclaimed the authority of the Constitution *(Satversme)*. The Constitution was fully re-instituted as of 6 July 1993, when the fifth Parliament *(Saeima)* was elected. The head of state in Latvia is the *President*, elected by parliament for a period of 4 years and for a maximum of two terms. The highest legislative body is the one-chamber parliament comprised of 100 deputies and elected in direct, proportional elections by citizens 18 years of age and over. Deputies serve for 4 years and parties must receive at least 5% of the national vote to gain seats in parliament. A seven-member *Constitutional Court* was established in 1996 with powers to invalidate legislation not in conformity with the constitution. Its members are appointed by parliament for 10-year terms. Executive power is held by the *Cabinet of Ministers*.

Currency

On 1 Jan. 2014 the euro (EUR) replaced the *lats* (LVL) as the legal currency of Latvia at the irrevocable conversion rate of 0.702804 lats to one euro.

Defence

The National Armed Forces (NAF) were created in 1994 and comprise the Land Forces, which are based on an infantry brigade and the National Guard, the Naval Forces, the Air Forces, the Logistic Command, the Training Doctrine Command and the National Defence Academy. Compulsory military service was abolished in Jan. 2007. In 2013 defence expenditure totalled US$300 m. (US$138 per capita), representing 1.0% of GDP.

Economy

Services accounted for 76.1% of GDP in 2009, industry 20.6% and agriculture 3.3%.

Labour

The total labour force (persons aged 15–74) in 2011 numbered 1,028,200. In 2011 there were 861,600 persons in employment in Latvia. The leading areas of activity were: wholesale and retail trade/repair of motor vehicles and motorcycles, 136,200; manufacturing, 114,400; education, 88,800. In 2011 women constituted 52% of the workforce. In 2011 there was a monthly minimum wage of 200 lats. Average gross monthly salary was 464 lats in 2011. The average gross monthly salary in the public sector in 2011 was 492 lats. The unemployment rate (persons aged 15–74) in the second quarter of 2012 was 16.1%, one of the highest rates in the EU.

Press

Latvia had 19 daily newspapers in 2008 (17 paid-for and two free) with a combined circulation of 370,000. The leading newspapers in terms of readership in 2008 were *Diena* and *Latvijas Avīze*, both of which are in Latvian, and the Russian-language *Vesti Segodnya*.

Rail

In 2014 there were 1,860 km of 1,520 mm gauge route (251 km electrified). In 2014, 57.0 m. tonnes of cargo and 19.2 m. passengers were carried by rail. The main groups of freight transported are oil and oil products, mineral fertilizers, ferrous metals and ferrous alloys.

Religion

In order to practise in public, religious organizations must be licensed by the Department of Religious Affairs attached to the Ministry of Justice. New sects are required to demonstrate loyalty to the state and its traditional religions over a 3-year period. According to estimates by the Pew Research Center's Forum on Religion & Public Life, 990,000 people (43.8% of the population) had no religious affiliation in 2010. There were some 450,000 Protestants in the same year, 430,000 Catholics and 370,000 Orthodox Christians. In Feb. 2016 the Roman Catholic church had one cardinal.

Roads

In 2014 there were 58,628 km of roads, including 20,150 km of state roads. Road passenger traffic in 2012 totalled 13,886 m. passenger-km; freight transport totalled 13,670 m. tonne-km in 2014. There were 3,728 road accidents in 2014 resulting in 212 deaths. Passenger cars in 2014 numbered 657,799 (331 per 1,000 inhabitants), in addition to which there were 83,205 lorries and tractors and 4,845 buses.

Shipping

There are two major ports. Riga handled 41.1 m. tonnes of cargo in 2014 and Ventspils 26.2 m. tonnes. There is a smaller port at Liepāja. A total of 65.1 m. tonnes were loaded at the three ports in 2014 and 9.1 m. tonnes unloaded. In Jan. 2009 there were 28 ships of 300 GT or over registered, totalling 240,000 GT.

Social Statistics

2010: births, 19,219 (rate of 8.6 per 1,000 population); deaths, 30,040 (13.4 per 1,000 population); marriages, 9,290 (4.1 per 1,000 population); divorces, 4,930 (2.2 per 1,000 population); infant mortality, 5.7 per 1,000 live births (2010). In 2007 life expectancy was 67.1 years for males but 77.1 years for females. In 2005 the most popular age range for marrying was 25–29 for males and 20–24 for females. The annual population growth rate in the period 2000–05 was −0.6%. Fertility rate, 2011, 1.2 births per woman (the joint lowest rate in the world). The suicide rate was 22.9 per 100,000 population in 2009 (rate among males, 40.0). In 2005 there were 1,886 immigrants and 2,450 emigrants.

Telecommunications

Telecommunications are conducted by companies in which the government has a 51% stake, under the aegis of the state controlled Lattelecom. There were 516,300 landline telephone subscriptions in 2011 (equivalent to 230.2 per 1,000 inhabitants) and 2,303,600 mobile phone subscriptions in 2009 (or 1,018.7 per 1,000 inhabitants). There were 684.2 internet users per 1,000 inhabitants in 2010. In 2009 there were 18.6 fixed broadband subscriptions per 100 inhabitants and 8.8 mobile broadband subscriptions per 100 inhabitants. In March 2012 there were 319,000 Facebook users.

Territory and Population

Latvia is situated in northeastern Europe. It is bordered by Estonia on the north and by Lithuania on the southwest, while on the east there is a frontier with the Russian Federation and to the southeast with Belarus. Territory, 64,559 km^2 (larger than Denmark, the Netherlands, Belgium and Switzerland), including 2,402 km^2 of inland waters. Population (2011 census), 2,070,371; density, 32.1 per km^2. The UN gives a projected population for 2015 of 2.03 m. In 2006, 68.0% of the population were urban. Major ethnic groups in 2006: Latvians 59.0%, Russians 28.5%, Belarusians 3.8%, Ukrainians 2.5%, Poles 2.4%, Lithuanians 1.4%, Jews 0.4%, Roma 0.4%, Germans 0.2%, Estonians 0.1%. There are 110 municipalities (*novadi*) and nine republican cities (*republikas pilsētas*). The capital is Riga (658,640, or nearly a third of the country's total population, at the 2011 census); other principal towns, with 2011 populations, are Daugavpils (93,312), Liepāja (76,731), Jelgava (59,511), Jurmala (50,840) and Ventspils (38,750). The official language is Latvian. Latgalian is also spoken.

Tourism

In 2010 there were 1,373,000 overnight non-resident tourists (1,323,000 in 2009). The main countries of origin of non-resident tourists in 2010 were Russia (189,000), Lithuania (182,000), Sweden (157,000) and Estonia (130,000).

Lebanon

Jumhouriya al-Lubnaniya (Republic of Lebanon)

Factsheet

Capital: Beirut
Population estimate, 2015: 5.85 m.
GNI per capita, 2014: (PPP$) 16,509
HDI/world rank, 2014: 0.769/67=
Internet domain extension: .lb

Civil Aviation

Beirut International Airport was served in 2010 by more than 40 airlines. It handled 5,960,414 passengers (5,913,225 on international flights) in 2012 and 84,911 tonnes of freight. The national airline is the state-owned Middle East Airlines. In 2012 scheduled airline traffic of Lebanese-based carriers flew 42.0 m. km; passenger-km totalled 4.1 bn. in the same year.

Climate

A Mediterranean climate with short, warm winters and long, hot and rainless summers, with high humidity in coastal areas. Rainfall is largely confined to the winter months and can be torrential, with snow on high ground. Beirut, Jan. 55 °F (13 °C), July 81 °F (27 °C). Annual rainfall 35.7″ (893 mm).

Constitution and Government

The first Constitution was established under the French Mandate on 23 May 1926. It has since been amended in 1927, 1929, 1943 (twice), 1947 and 1990. It is based on a separation of powers, with a President, a single-chamber *National Assembly* elected by universal suffrage at age 21 in 12 electoral constituencies, and an independent judiciary. The executive consists of the President and a Prime Minister and Cabinet appointed after consultation between the President and the National Assembly. On 21 Sept. 1990 President Haraoui established the Second Republic by signing constitutional amendments which had been negotiated at Taif (Saudi Arabia) in Oct. 1989. These institute an executive collegium between the President, Prime Minister and Speaker, and remove from the President the right to recall the Prime Minister, dissolve the Assembly and vote in the Council of Ministers.

Currency

The unit of currency is the *Lebanese pound* (LBP) of 100 *piastres*.

Defence

There were 14,000 Syrian troops in the country in early 2005, but in March 2005 Lebanon and Syria agreed that the troops would be redeployed to the Bekaa Valley in the east of the country. They were subsequently all withdrawn from Lebanon. The United Nations Interim Force in Lebanon (UNIFIL), created in 1978, had a strength of 1,990 in June 2006. Following the conflict between Israel and Lebanon of July–Aug. 2006 the Security Council established UNIFIL II, a more powerful peacekeeping force deployed to maintain the ceasefire, support the Lebanese armed forces and aid humanitarian efforts. In June 2015 UNIFIL II comprised 10,410 uniformed personnel from 37 countries. Conscription was reduced from 12 months to 6 in 2005, and was finally abolished in Feb. 2007. Defence expenditure in 2012 totalled US$1,735 m. (US$419 per capita), representing 4.2% of GDP.

Economy

Agriculture accounted for 5.9% of GDP in 2009, industry 23.4% and services 70.7%.

Labour

The economically active population in 2007 was 1,228,800 (921,600 males and 307,100 females), of whom 1,118,400 (842,400 males and 276,000 females) were in employment.

Press

In 2009 there were 14 paid-for daily newspapers with a combined circulation of 244,000 and two free dailies. The newspapers with the highest circulation are *An-Nahar* and *As-Safir*.

Rail

Railways are state-owned. There is 222 km of standard gauge track.

Religion

In 2010 an estimated 61.3% of the population were Muslims according to the Pew Research Center's Forum on Religion & Public Life (roughly similar numbers of Sunnis and Shias) and 38.3% Christians (mainly Catholics). In Feb. 2016 there were two cardinals.

Roads

There were 6,970 km of roads in 2005, including 170 km of motorway. Registered vehicles in 2011 numbered 1,525,738. In 2007 there were 4,281 road accidents resulting in 487 deaths.

Shipping

Beirut is the largest port, followed by Tripoli, Jounieh and Saida (Sidon). In Jan. 2009 there were 46 ships of 300 GT or over registered, totalling 140,000 GT.

Social Statistics

2008 estimates: births, 66,000; deaths, 29,000. Estimated rates, 2008 (per 1,000 population): births, 15.7; deaths, 7.0. Infant mortality was 19 per 1,000 live births in 2010; expectation of life (2013), 78.1 years for males and 82.3 for females. Annual population growth rate, 2000–08, 1.3%; fertility rate, 2008, 1.8 births per woman.

Telecommunications

In 2010 there were 887,800 landline telephone subscriptions (equivalent to 210.0 per 1,000 inhabitants) and 2,874,800 mobile phone subscriptions (or 680.0 per 1,000 inhabitants). In 2011, 52.0% of the population were internet users. In March 2012 there were 1.4 m. Facebook users.

Territory and Population

Lebanon is mountainous, bounded on the north and east by Syria, on the west by the Mediterranean and on the south by Israel. The area is 10,201 km^2 (3,939 sq. miles). The United Nations gave an estimated population for 2012 of 4.65 m.; density, 456 per km^2. In 2011, 87.4% of the population were urban. The principal towns, with estimated population (1998), are: Beirut (the

capital), 1.5 m.; Tripoli, 160,000; Zahlé, 45,000; Saida (Sidon), 38,000. The official language is Arabic.

Tourism

In 2009 there were 1,844,000 non-resident tourists (excluding Syrians, Palestinians, students and same-day visitors), up from 1,333,000 in 2008.

Lesotho

Muso oa Lesotho (Kingdom of Lesotho)

Factsheet
Capital: Maseru
Population estimate, 2015: 2.14 m.
GNI per capita, 2014: (PPP$) 3,306
HDI/world rank, 2014: 0.497/161
Internet domain extension: .ls

Civil Aviation

There are direct flights from Maseru's Moshoeshoe International Airport to Johannesburg. In 2004 it handled 37,162 passengers (36,045 on international flights).

Climate

A mild and temperate climate, with variable rainfall, but averaging 29″ (725 mm) a year over most of the country. The rain falls mainly in the summer months of Oct. to April, while the winters are dry and may produce heavy frosts in lowland areas and frequent snow in the highlands. Temperatures in the lowlands range from a maximum of 90 °F (32.2 °C) in summer to a minimum of 20 °F (−6.7 °C) in winter.

Constitution and Government

Lesotho is a constitutional monarchy with the King as Head of State. Following the death of his father, Moshoeshoe II, **Letsie III** succeeded to the throne in Jan. 1996. The 1993 constitution provided for a *National Assembly* comprising an elected 80-member lower house and a *Senate* of 22 principal chiefs and 11 members nominated by the King.

Currency

The unit of currency is the *loti* (plural *maloti*) (LSL) of 100 *lisente*, at par with the South African rand, which is legal tender. Total money supply in July 2005 was 1,659 m. maloti and foreign exchange reserves were US$539 m.

Defence

South African and Batswanan troops intervened after a mutiny by Lesotho's armed forces in Sept. 1998. The foreign forces were withdrawn in May 1999. The Royal Lesotho Defence Force has about 2,000 personnel. Defence expenditure totalled US$54 m. in 2013 (US$28 per capita), representing 2.1% of GDP.

Economy

In 2009 agriculture accounted for 7.7% of GDP, industry 32.9% and services 59.4%.

Labour

The labour force in June 2008 was 789,000 (54% males) of whom 609,000 were employed (including 247,000 in subsistence agriculture), giving an unemployment rate of 22.7%. Lesotho had 15,000 people living in slavery according to the Walk Free Foundation's 2013 *Global Slavery Index.*

Press

There were 14 non-daily newspapers and periodicals in 2008, but no dailies.

Rail

A branch line built by the South African Railways, one mile long, connects Maseru with the Bloemfontein–Natal line at Marseilles for transport of cargo.

Religion

A study by the Pew Research Center's Forum on Religion & Public Life estimated that there were 1.08 m. Protestants in 2010 and 999,000 Catholics, with most of the remainder of the population being religiously unaffiliated.

Roads

In 2009 the road network totalled about 6,550 km, of which around 1,220 km were paved. There were 75,000 motor vehicles in 2009 including 34,000 light vehicles, 21,000 medium vehicles and 13,000 minibuses. There were 402 deaths in 2007 as a result of road accidents.

Social Statistics

2008 estimated births, 59,000; deaths, 35,000. Rates, 2008 estimates: birth (per 1,000 population), 28.9; death, 16.9. Annual population growth rate, 2000–08, 1.0%. Life expectancy at birth in 2013 was 49.4 years. In 2011, 23.3% of all adults between 15 and 49 were infected with HIV. Infant mortality, 2012, 74 per 1,000 live births; fertility rate, 2008, 3.3 births per woman.

Telecommunications

In 2010 there were 38,600 landline telephone subscriptions (equivalent to 17.8 per 1,000 inhabitants) and 987,400 mobile phone subscriptions (or 454.8 per 1,000 inhabitants). There were 38.6 internet users per 1,000 inhabitants in 2010.

Territory and Population

Lesotho is an enclave within South Africa. The area is 30,355 km^2 (11,720 sq. miles). The census in 2006 showed a total population of 1,876,633 (963,835 females); density, 61.8 per km^2. There are ten districts, all named after their chief towns, except Berea (chief town, Teyateyaneng). In 2011 the capital, Maseru, had a population of 178,345. Other major towns (with 2011 estimated census population) are: Teyateyaneng, 61,578; Maputsoe, 48,243; Mafeteng, 30,602; Mohale's Hoek, 25,308. The official languages are Sesotho and English. The population is more than 98% Basotho. The rest is made up of Xhosas, approximately 3,000 expatriate Europeans and several hundred Asians.

Tourism

In 2010 there were a record 425,870 non-resident visitors, up from 343,743 in 2009 and 293,073 in 2008.

Liberia

Republic of Liberia

Factsheet

Capital: Monrovia
Population estimate, 2015: 4.50 m.
GNI per capita, 2014: (PPP$) 805
HDI/world rank, 2014: 0.430/177
Internet domain extension: .lr

Civil Aviation

There are two international airports (Roberts International and Sprigg Payne), both near Monrovia. In 2010 there were services to Abidjan, Accra, Addis Ababa, Banjul, Brussels, Casablanca, Conakry, Freetown, Lagos and Nairobi as well as internal flights.

Climate

An equatorial climate, with constant high temperatures and plentiful rainfall, although Jan. to May is drier than the rest of the year. Monrovia, Jan. 79 °F (26.1 °C), July 76 °F (24.4 °C). Annual rainfall 206″ (5,138 mm).

Constitution and Government

A constitution was approved by referendum in July 1984 and came into force on 6 Jan. 1986. Under it the *National Assembly* consisted of a 26-member *Senate* and a 64-member *House of Representatives*. For the elections of 2005 the number of seats in the Senate was increased to 30 and in 2010 a further nine seats were added to the House of Representatives, bringing the total to 73. The executive power of the state is vested in the *President*, who may serve up to two 6-year terms.

Currency

US currency is legal tender. There is a *Liberian dollar* (LRD), in theory at parity with the US dollar.

Defence

In June 2003 UN Secretary-General Kofi Annan called for an international peacekeeping force to restore peace after fighting broke out between government forces and Liberians United for Reconciliation and Democracy (LURD). An ECOWAS peacekeeping force of over 3,000 troops was deployed initially, but this has been replaced by the United Nations Mission in Liberia (UNMIL), totalling 5,934 uniformed personnel in June 2015. The Armed Forces of Liberia (AFL) were created in 2007 to replace the Liberian Army, which was demobilized in 1999. In 2009 there were approximately 2,100 troops. The AFL became operational in June 2013 when a Liberian platoon was deployed to Mali as part of the African-led International Support Mission in Mali (AFISMA). Defence expenditure totalled US$13 m. in 2011 (US$3 per capita), representing 0.8% of GDP.

Economy

Agriculture accounted for 39% of GDP in 2012, industry 16% and services 45%.

Labour

In 2010 the labour force was 1,374,000 (52.3% males). Liberia had 30,000 people living in slavery according to the Walk Free Foundation's 2013 *Global Slavery Index.*

Press

There were seven paid-for daily newspapers in 2008 with a combined circulation of 55,000, plus 24 paid-for non-dailies.

Rail

There is a total of 490 km single track. A 148-km freight line connects iron mines to Monrovia. There is a line from Bong to Monrovia (78 km). The railways were out of use for many years because of the civil wars but there is now some traffic, both freight and passenger. However, large sections of track have been dismantled.

Religion

In 2010 there were an estimated 3.4 m. Christians (mainly Protestants) and 480,000 Muslims (mainly Sunnis) according to the Pew Research Center's Forum on Religion & Public Life.

Roads

The road network totals around 10,000 km, much of it in extremely poor condition. In 2007 there were 7,400 passenger cars in use and 2,800 lorries and vans.

Shipping

There are ports at Buchanan, Greenville, Harper and Monrovia. Over 2,000 vessels enter Monrovia each year. The Liberian government requires only a modest registration fee and an almost nominal annual charge and maintains no control over the operation of ships flying the Liberian flag. In Jan. 2009 there were 2,203 ships of 300 GT or over registered, totalling 80.15 m. GT (a figure only exceeded by Panama's fleet). Of the 2,203 vessels registered, 741 were container ships, 669 oil tankers, 404 bulk carriers, 262 general cargo ships, 83 liquid gas tankers, 40 chemical tankers and four passenger ships.

Social Statistics

2008 births, estimate, 145,000; deaths, 40,000. 2008 rates (per 1,000 population), estimate: birth, 38.3; death, 10.5. Annual population growth rate, 2000–08, 3.7%. Life expectancy at birth (2013): 59.6 years for men and 61.5 years for women. Infant mortality in 2010 was at 74 per 1,000 live births. Fertility rate, 2008, 5.9 births per woman.

Telecommunications

In 2009 Liberia had just 2,200 main (fixed) telephone lines, but there were 1,058,000 mobile phone subscribers. No other country had such a high ratio of mobile phone subscriptions to fixed telephone lines in 2009. There were an estimated 5.1 internet users per 1,000 inhabitants in 2009.

Territory and Population

Liberia is bounded in the northwest by Sierra Leone, north by Guinea, east by Côte d'Ivoire and southwest by the Atlantic ocean. The total area is 97,036 km². At the last census, in 2008, the population was 3,476,608; density, 36 per km². In 2007, 59.5% of the population lived in urban areas. English is the official language spoken by 20% of the population. The rest belong in the main to three linguistic groups: Mande, West Atlantic and the Kwa. The population of Monrovia (the capital) was 970,824 in 2008 including its suburbs.

Libya

Dawlat Libya (State of Libya)

Factsheet

Capital: Tripoli
Population estimate, 2015: 6.28 m.
GNI per capita, 2014: (PPP$) 21,666
HDI/world rank, 2014: 0.724/94=
Internet domain extension: .ly

Civil Aviation

The UN ban on air traffic to and from Libya enforced since April 1992 was lifted in April 1999 following the handing over for trial of two suspected Lockerbie bombers. The national flag carrier, Libyan Airlines, was grounded in March 2011 as a result of the Libyan revolution but has now resumed operations. However, in Dec. 2014 all Libya-based carriers were added to the EU aviation safety blacklist, which either banned or restricted Libyan airlines from operating in the European Union.

Climate

The coastal region has a warm temperate climate, with mild wet winters and hot dry summers, although most of the country suffers from aridity. Tripoli, Jan. 52 °F (11.1 °C), July 81 °F (27.2 °C). Annual rainfall 16″ (400 mm). Benghazi, Jan. 56 °F (13.3 °C), July 77 °F (25 °C). Annual rainfall 11″ (267 mm).

Constitution and Government

Following the uprising in 2011 that culminated in the capture and killing of Libya's incumbent leader, Col. Gaddafi, the National Transitional Council (NTC)-formed in Feb. 2011-formally announced the country's 'liberation' in Oct. and appointed an executive committee to serve as the *de facto* interim government. A panel to draft a new constitution was elected in Feb. 2014. Once the new constitution has won approval by referendum, parliamentary elections are required to be held within 6 months. However, as of March 2015 the country was riven by civil unrest.

Currency

The unit of currency is the *Libyan dinar* (LYD) of 1,000 *millemes.*

Defence

Defence expenditure in 2013 was estimated US$4,771 m. (US$795 per capita), representing 5.0% of GDP. The former Libyan Army effectively ceased to exist as an organized force in 2011 as the civil war escalated. Much of the equipment was damaged or destroyed during the conflict.

Economy

Petroleum and natural gas contributed 71.6% to GDP in 2007; followed by public administration, defence and services, 6.9%; finance, insurance and real estate, 6.2%; and construction, 4.3%. Libya featured among the ten most corrupt countries in the world in a 2014 survey of 175 countries carried out by the anti-corruption organization *Transparency International.*

Labour

The labour force in 2010 was 2,379,000 (72.0% males). Libya had 18,000 people living in slavery according to the Walk Free Foundation's 2013 *Global Slavery Index.*

Press

In 2008 there were six daily newspapers with a combined circulation of 100,000.

Rail

Although there have not been any operational railways since 1965, some routes were under construction at the outbreak of the civil conflict in Feb. 2011. However, the projects were then abandoned. Talks were held in early 2013 between Chinese and Russian companies and the Libya Rail Implementation Authority when Libya was starting to show signs of a recovery but in early 2016 the projects were on hold again.

Religion

Islam is declared the State religion, but the right of others to practise their religion is provided for. In 2010 an estimated 96.6% of the population were Muslim (almost all Sunnis) according to the Pew Research Center's Forum on Religion & Public Life.

Roads

In 2010 the road network covered about 34,000 km. In 2007 there were 1,388,200 passenger cars in use (225 per 1,000 inhabitants), plus 310,500 lorries and vans. There were 2,301 deaths as a result of road accidents in 2009, which at 38.6 per 100,000 inhabitants gives Libya one of the highest traffic-related death rates in the world.

Shipping

In Jan. 2009 there were 28 ships of 300 GT or over registered, totalling 239,000 GT.

Social Statistics

Estimates, 2008: births, 147,000; deaths, 26,000. Estimated rates, 2008 (per 1,000 population): births, 23.3; deaths, 4.1. Life expectancy (2013), 73.5 years for men and 77.3 for women. Annual population growth rate, 2000–08, 2.0%; infant mortality, 2010, 13 per 1,000 live births; fertility rate, 2008, 2.7 births per woman.

Telecommunications

There were 1.23 m. fixed telephone lines in 2010 (193.3 per 1,000 inhabitants). Mobile phone subscribers numbered 9.53 m. in 2009. There were 108.0 internet users per 1,000 inhabitants in 2009. Fixed internet subscriptions totalled 772,500 in 2009 (123.3 per 1,000 inhabitants). In June 2012 there were 560,000 Facebook users.

Territory and Population

Libya is bounded in the north by the Mediterranean Sea, east by Egypt and Sudan, south by Chad and Niger and west by Algeria and Tunisia. The area is

1,759,540 km². The population at the 2006 census was 5,657,692; density, 3.2 per km². In 2011, 78.1% of the population lived in urban areas. The population is largely a mixture of Arab and Berber ethnicities. Libya is divided into 22 districts (*sha'biyat*). The two largest cities are Tripoli, the capital (with an estimated population of 1,095,000 in 2010), and Benghazi (estimated population of 678,000 in 2010). The official language is Arabic.

Tourism

In 2007 there were 106,000 non-resident visitors, down from 125,000 in 2006.

Liechtenstein

Fürstentum Liechtenstein (Principality of Liechtenstein)

Factsheet

Capital: Vaduz
Population estimate, 2015: 38,000
GNI per capita, 2014: (PPP$) 79,851
HDI/world rank, 2014: 0.908/13
Internet domain extension: .li

Climate

There is a distinct difference in climate between the higher mountains and the valleys. In summer the peaks can often be foggy while the valleys remain sunny and warm, while in winter the valleys can often be foggy and cold whilst the peaks remain sunny and comparatively warm. Vaduz, Jan. 0 °C, July 20 °C. Annual rainfall 1,090 mm.

Constitution and Government

Liechtenstein is a constitutional monarchy ruled by the princes of the House of Liechtenstein. The reigning Prince is **Hans-Adam II**, b. 14 Feb. 1945; he succeeded his father Prince Francis Joseph, 13 Nov. 1989 (he exercised the prerogatives to which the Sovereign is entitled from 26 Aug. 1984); married on 30 July 1967 to Countess Marie Kinsky von Wchinitz und Tettau. The monarchy is hereditary in the male line. The present constitution of 5 Oct. 1921 provided for a unicameral parliament (*Landtag*) of 15 members elected for 4 years, but this was amended to 25 members in 1988. Election is on the basis of proportional representation. The prince can call and dismiss the parliament, and following a referendum held on 16 March 2003, dismiss the government and veto bills. On parliamentary recommendation, he appoints the ministers. According to the constitution, the Government is a collegial body consisting of five ministers including the prime minister.

Currency

Swiss currency has been in use since 1920 and became legal tender in 1924.

Economy

Liechtenstein is one of the world's richest countries with a well diversified economy. Low taxes and bank secrecy laws have made Liechtenstein a successful financial centre.

Labour

The workforce was 32,435 in 2007, including employees commuting from abroad (16,242 in 2007). The farming population went down from 70% in 1930 to 1.1% in 2007. The rapid change-over has led to the immigration of foreign workers (Austrians, Germans, Italians, Swiss).

Press

In 2008 there were two daily newspapers (*Liechtensteiner Vaterland* and *Liechtensteiner Volksbatt*) with an estimated total circulation of 20,000.

Rail

The 10 km of main railway passing through the country is operated by Austrian Federal Railways.

Religion

Religious affiliation at the 2010 census: Roman Catholic, 75.9%; Protestant, 8.5%; Muslim, 5.4%; other religion, 2.2%; no religion, 5.4%; not stated, 2.6%.

Roads

There are 400 km of roads. Postal buses are the chief means of public transportation within the country and to Austria and Switzerland. There were 28,102 cars in 2013. There were 403 road accidents in 2012 (one fatal).

Social Statistics

In 2011 there were 395 births and 248 deaths (rates of 10.9 per 1,000 population and 6.8 respectively). The annual population growth rate was 0.7% over the period 2007–12.

Telecommunications

Liechtenstein had 18,559 main telephone lines in 2012 and 36,080 mobile phone subscriptions. In 2009 there were 751.9 fixed broadband subscriptions per 1,000 inhabitants and 452.2 mobile broadband subscriptions per 1,000 inhabitants.

Territory and Population

Liechtenstein is bounded on the east by Austria and the west by Switzerland. Total area 160 km² (61.8 sq. miles). The population (Dec. 2011) was 36,475 (18,433 females), including 12,144 resident foreigners, giving a density of 228 per km². The population of Liechtenstein is predominantly rural. Population of Schaan (2011), 5,853; Vaduz (2011), 5,236. The official language is German.

Tourism

In 2008, 77,957 overnight tourists visited Liechtenstein.

Lithuania

Lietuvos Respublika (Republic of Lithuania)

Factsheet

Capital: Vilnius
Population estimate, 2015: 2.88 m.
GNI per capita, 2014: (PPP$) 24,500
HDI/world rank, 2014: 0.839/37=
Internet domain extension: .lt

Civil Aviation

The main international airport is based in the capital, Vilnius. Other international airports are at Kaunas and Palanga. FlyLAL–Lithuanian Airlines, formerly Lithuania's largest airline, ceased operations in 2009. Air Lituanica, founded in 2013, was the national flag carrier until it ceased operations in May 2015. In 2015 a number of international airlines ran regular scheduled flights to Lithuania. Vilnius handled 1,308,065 passengers in 2009 and 4,336 tonnes of freight. Kaunas handled 456,698 passengers in 2009 and Palanga 105,195.

Climate

Vilnius, Jan. –2.8 °C, July 20.5 °C. Annual rainfall 520 mm. Klaipėda, Jan. –0.6 °C, July 19.4 °C. Annual rainfall 770 mm.

Constitution and Government

A referendum to approve a new constitution was held on 25 Oct. 1992. Parliament is the 141-member *Seimas*. Under a new electoral law passed in July 2000, 71 of the parliament's 141 members will defeat rivals for their seats if they receive the most votes in a single round of balloting. Previously they had to win 50% of the votes or face a run-off against the nearest competitor. The parliament's 70 other seats are distributed according to the proportional popularity of the political parties at the ballot box. The *Constitutional Court* is empowered to rule on whether proposed laws conflict with the constitution or existing legislation. It comprises nine judges who serve 9-year terms, one third rotating every 3 years.

Currency

On 1 Jan. 2015 the euro (EUR) replaced the *litas* (LTL) as the legal currency of Lithuania at the irrevocable conversion rate of 3.45280 litai to one euro. Total money supply was 13,884 m. litai in July 2005, foreign exchange reserves were US$3,411 m. and gold reserves 186,000 troy oz.

Defence

Conscription ended on 1 July 2009 but was reintroduced in 2015 in view of Russia's military intervention in Ukraine. Conscripts between the ages of 19–26 are subjected to 9 months of service. In 2013 defence expenditure totalled US$355 m. (US$101 per capita), representing 0.8% of GDP.

Economy

Agriculture accounted for 3.4% of GDP in 2009, industry 26.9% and services 69.7%.

Labour

In 2013 the number of employed persons was 1.3 m. (71.4% in private enterprises and 28.6% in the public sector). Employed population by activity (as a percentage): wholesale and retail trade, repair of motor vehicles and motorcycles, 17.6; manufacturing, 15.4; education, 9.7; construction, 7.7; transportation and storage, 7.3; human health and social work activities, 6.6; real estate activities, 1.2. Employment skills in 2013 included 41.0% with tertiary education and 55.0% with upper secondary and post-secondary non-tertiary education. There were a total of 3,080 working days lost to strike action in 2012 (31,601 in 2008; legal strikes did not take place in 2009–11 or in 2013). In 2013 average gross monthly earnings were 2,231.7 litai; legal minimum wage was 1,000 litai in 2013.

Press

In 2008 there were 327 newspapers (24 paid-for dailies, one free daily and 302 paid-for non-dailies). The papers with the highest circulation are the free *15 minučių* and the paid-for *Vakaro inios* and *Lietuvos rytas*.

Rail

In 2011 there were 1,767 km of railway track in operation in Lithuania. The majority of rail traffic was diesel propelled, although 122 km of track was electrified. In 2011, 4.7 m. passengers and 52.3 m. tonnes of freight were carried.

Religion

Under the Constitution, the state recognizes traditional Lutheran churches and religious organizations, as well as other churches and religious organizations if their teaching and rituals do not contradict the law. According to the Pew Research Center's Forum on Religion & Public Life, in 2010 there were an estimated 2.76 m. Catholics and 170,000 Orthodox Christians; a further 330,000 people had no religious affiliation. In Feb. 2016 there was one cardinal.

Roads

In 2007 there were 80,715 km of roads (including 309 km of motorways), of which 28.6% were paved. There were 1,587,900 passenger cars in use in 2007 (470 per 1,000 inhabitants), plus 14,000 buses and coaches, 14,500 lorries and vans, and 35,300 motorcycles and mopeds. There were 6,448 traffic accidents in 2007, with 740 fatalities.

Shipping

The ice-free port of Klaipėda plays a dominant role in the national economy and Baltic maritime traffic. It handled 29,880,000 tonnes of cargo in 2008 (22,218,000 tonnes loaded and 7,662,000 tonnes discharged); container traffic totalled 373,000 TEUs (twenty-foot equivalent units) in 2008. A 412 ha. site at the port is dedicated a Free Economic Zone, which offers attractive conditions to foreign investors. In Jan. 2009 there were 52 ships of 300 GT or over registered, totalling 348,000 GT. In Jan. 2009 the Lithuanian-controlled fleet comprised 64 vessels of 1,000 GT or over, of which 37 were under the Lithuanian flag and 27 under foreign flags.

Social Statistics

2009: births, 36,682; deaths, 42,032; marriages, 20,542; divorces, 9,270; infant deaths, 181. Rates (per 1,000 population): birth, 11.0; death, 12.6; marriage, 6.2; divorce, 2.8. The population started to decline in 1993, a trend which is set to continue. Annual population growth rate, 2010–15, −1.3%. In 2014, 8,809 live births were registered to unmarried mothers and there were 5,231 legally induced abortions. Life expectancy at birth in 2007 was 65.9 years for males and 77.7 years for females. In 2006 the most popular age range for marrying was 25–29 for males and 20–24 for females. Infant mortality, 2010, five per 1,000 live births; fertility rate, 2008, 1.3 births per woman (one of the lowest rates in the world). In 2014 there were 36,621 emigrants and 24,294 immigrants. Lithuania has one of the world's highest suicide rates, at 33.3 per 100,000 inhabitants in 2012 (a rate of 59.5 among males but only 10.9 among females). The male suicide rate is the highest in any country.

Telecommunications

A majority stake in Lithuanian Telecom (the only fixed telephone service provider) was sold to the Finnish and Swedish consortium SONERA in 1998 and by Jan. 2003 the telecommunications market was fully liberalized. In 2010 there were 733,700 landline telephone subscriptions (equivalent to 220.8 per 1,000 inhabitants) and 4,891,000 mobile phone subscriptions (or 1,471.6 per 1,000 inhabitants). There were 621.2 internet users per 1,000 inhabitants in 2010. Fixed internet subscriptions totalled 636,000 in 2009 (190.3 per 1,000 inhabitants). In March 2012 there were 983,000 Facebook users.

Territory and Population

Lithuania is bounded in the north by Latvia, east and south by Belarus, and west by Poland, the Russian enclave of Kaliningrad and the Baltic Sea. The total area is 65,300 km² (25,212 sq. miles), including 2,265 km² (875 sq. miles) of inland waters, and the population (2011 census) 3,043,429 (1,640,825 females); density, 48.3 per km². In 2011, 67.1% of the population lived in urban areas. Of the 2011 census population, Lithuanians accounted for 84.2%, Poles 6.6%, Russians 5.8% (9.4% in 1989), Belarusians 1.2% and Ukrainians 0.5%. There are ten counties (with capitals of the same name): Alytus; Kaunas; Klaipėda; Marijampolė; Panevėžys; Šiauliai; Tauragė; Telšiai; Utena; Vilnius. The capital is Vilnius (2011 census population, 535,631). Other large towns are Kaunas (315,933 in 2011), Klaipėda (162,360), Šiauliai (109,328) and Panevėžys (99,690). The official language is Lithuanian, but ethnic minorities have the right to official use of their language where they form a substantial part of the population.

Tourism

In 2010 accommodation establishments received 1,552,900 guests (up from 1,325,600 in 2005), of whom 840,400 were foreigners (681,500 in 2005). The leading countries of origin of non-resident overnight visitors in 2010 were: Poland (135,900), Russia (105,900), Germany (105,800) and Belarus (71,400). Lithuania had 908 accommodation establishments in 2010 with 50,087 beds, including 342 hotels with 23,137 beds.

Luxembourg

Grand-Duché de Luxembourg (Grand Duchy of Luxembourg)

Factsheet

Capital: Luxembourg
Population estimate, 2015: 567,000
GNI per capita, 2014: (PPP$) 58,711
HDI/world rank, 2014: 0.892/19
Internet domain extension: .lu

Civil Aviation

Findel is the airport for Luxembourg. 1,643,000 passengers and 856,450 tonnes of freight were handled in 2007. The national carrier is Luxair, in which the state has a 39.05% stake directly along with a further 21.81% indirectly through the Banque et Caisse d'Epargne de l'Etat (State and Savings Bank). Cargolux has developed into one of the major international freight carriers. In 2006 scheduled airline traffic of Luxembourg-based carriers flew 93 m. km, carrying 928,000 passengers (all on international flights).

Climate

In general the country resembles Belgium in its climate, with rain evenly distributed throughout the year. Average temperatures are Jan. 0.8 °C, July 17.5 °C. Annual rainfall 30.8″ (782.2 mm).

Constitution and Government

The Grand Duchy of Luxembourg is a constitutional monarchy. The reigning Grand Duke is **Henri**, b. 16 April 1955, son of the former Grand Duke Jean and Princess Joséphine-Charlotte of Belgium; succeeded 7 Oct. 2000 on the abdication of his father; married Maria Teresa Mestre 14 Feb. 1981. The separation of powers between the legislature and the executive is not very strong, resulting in much interaction between the two bodies. Only the judiciary is completely independent. The 12 cantons are divided into four electoral districts: the South, the East, the Centre and the North. Voters choose between party lists of candidates in multi-member constituencies. The parliament is the *Chamber of Deputies*, which consists of a maximum of 60 members elected for 5 years. There is a *Council of State* of 21 members appointed by the Sovereign.

Currency

On 1 Jan. 1999 the euro (EUR) became the legal currency in Luxembourg at the irrevocable conversion rate of 40.3399 Luxembourg francs to 1 euro. The euro, which consists of 100 cents, has been in circulation since 1 Jan. 2002. On the introduction of the euro there was a 'dual circulation' period before the Luxembourg franc ceased to be legal tender on 28 Feb. 2002. Euro banknotes in circulation on 1 Jan. 2002 had a total value of €5.6 bn.

Defence

There is a volunteer light infantry battalion of (2009) 900, of which only the career officers are professionals. In recent years Luxembourg soldiers and officers have been actively participating in peacekeeping missions, mainly in the former Yugoslavia. There is also a Gendarmerie of 600. In 2000 the Gendarmerie and the police force merged to form the Police Grand-Ducale. NATO maintains a squadron of E-3A *Sentries*. In 2013 defence expenditure totalled US$249 m. (US$484 per capita), representing 0.4% of GDP.

Economy

Services accounted for 86% of GDP in 2012 and industry 14%.

Labour

In 2004 the estimated total workforce was 301,000. The government fixes a legal minimum wage. Retirement is at 65. Employment creation was 3.2% in 2004–05. In Dec. 2014 the unemployment rate was 5.9%.

Press

There were eight paid-for daily newspapers in 2008 with an average circulation of 117,000 and two free dailies with an average circulation of 127,000; there were also 15 non-dailies. The German-language *Luxemburger Wort* has the highest circulation, with an average of 72,000 copies in 2008. In the 2013 *World Press Freedom Index* compiled by Reporters Without Borders, Luxembourg was ranked fourth out of 179 countries.

Rail

In 2011 there were 275 km of railway (standard gauge) of which 262 km were electrified; passenger-km totalled 349 m. in 2011.

Religion

According to the Pew Research Center's Forum on Religion & Public Life, an estimated 64.7% of the population in 2010 were Roman Catholics and 27.5% had no religious affiliation. There are small Protestant, Jewish, Greek Orthodox, Russian Orthodox and Muslim communities as well.

Roads

On 1 Jan. 2008 there were 2,894 km of roads of which 147 km were motorways. Motor vehicles registered at 1 Jan. 2008 numbered 394,917 including 321,520 passenger cars, 27,043 trucks, 1,455 coaches and 14,946 motorcycles. In 2009 there were 47 fatalities in road accidents.

Social Statistics

2010 rates per 1,000 population; birth, 11.6; death, 7.4; marriage, 3.5; divorce, 2.1. Nearly half of annual births are to foreigners. In 2008 the most popular age range for marrying was 30–34 for males and 25–29 for females. Life expectancy at birth in 2013 was 78.0 years for males and 83.0 years for females. Annual population growth rate, 2005–10, 2.1%. Infant mortality, 2010, two per 1,000 live births (one of the lowest rates in the world); fertility rate, 2008, 1.7 births per woman. In 2009 Luxembourg received 477 asylum applications.

Telecommunications

In 2013 there were 267,600 main (fixed) telephone subscriptions. Active mobile phone subscribers numbered 707,000 in 2008 (1,471.1 per 1,000 persons). There were an estimated 387,000 internet users in 2008. The fixed broadband penetration rate in Dec. 2010 was 33.5 subscribers per 100 inhabitants. In March 2012 there were 190,000 Facebook users.

Territory and Population

Luxembourg has an area of 2,586 km² (999 sq. miles) and is bounded on the west by Belgium, south by France and east by Germany. A census took place on 1 Feb. 2011; the population was 512,353 (including 220,522 foreigners); density, 198 per km². The percentage of foreigners living in Luxembourg has increased dramatically in recent years, from 26% in 1986 to 43% in 2011 (the highest percentage in the EU). In 2011, 85.4% of the population were urban. The capital, Luxembourg, has (Feb. 2011 census) 95,058 inhabitants; Esch-sur-Alzette, the centre of the mining district, 30,125; Differdange, 21,935; Dudelange, 18,781; Pétange, 16,085; Sanem, 14,470; Hésperange, 13,335. Lëtzebuergesch is spoken by most of the population, and since 1984 has been an official language with French and German.

Tourism

In 2010 there were 907,000 overnight tourists and 2,256,000 overnight stays; there were 7,751 hotel rooms in 2010. Tourists spent US$4,108 m. in 2010 (excluding passenger transport). Camping is widespread; there were 739,000 overnight stays at campsites in 2010.

Macedonia

Republika Makedonija (The Republic of Macedonia) (Former Yugoslav Republic of Macedonia)

Factsheet

Capital: Skopje
Population estimate, 2015: 2.08 m.
GNI per capita, 2014: (PPP$) 11,780
HDI/world rank, 2014: 0.747/81=
Internet domain extension: .mk

Civil Aviation

There are international airports at Skopje and Ohrid. A new Macedonia-based carrier, Aeromak, has been established to replace MAT Macedonian Airlines, the former flag carrier which ceased operations in 2009. In 2009 Skopje handled 602,298 passengers (658,366 in 2008) and 2,326 tonnes of freight. The much smaller airport at Ohrid handled 36,652 passengers in 2009 (44,413 in 2008).

Climate

Macedonia has a mixed Mediterranean-continental type climate, with cold moist winters and hot dry summers. Skopje, Jan. −0.4 °C, July 23.1 °C.

Constitution and Government

The *President* is directly elected for 5-year terms. Candidates must be citizens aged at least 40 years. The parliament is a 123-member single-chamber *Assembly (Sobranie)*, elected by universal suffrage for 4-year terms. There is a *Constitutional Court* whose members are elected by the assembly for non-renewable 8-year terms, and a *National Security Council* chaired by the President. Laws passed by the Assembly must be countersigned by the President, who may return them for reconsideration, but cannot veto them if they gain a two-thirds majority.

Currency

The national currency of Macedonia is the *denar* (MKD), of 100 *deni*.

Defence

The President is the C.-in-C. of the armed forces. Compulsory national military service was abolished in 2006. Defence expenditure in 2012 totalled US$129 m. (US$62 per capita), representing 1.3% of GDP.

Economy

Agriculture accounted for 11.3% of GDP in 2010, industry 27.8% and services 60.9%.

Labour

In April 2004 there were 522,995 employed persons, including: 116,300 in manufacturing; 87,608 in agriculture, hunting and forestry; 74,218 in wholesale and retail trade/repair of motor vehicles, motorcycles and personal and household goods; and 33,635 in education. The number of unemployed persons in 2004 was 309,286, giving an unemployment rate of 37.2%.

Press

There were 12 daily newspapers in 2008 with a circulation of 295,000 copies. *Dnevnik* is the most popular with a daily circulation of 50,000 copies in 2008.

Rail

In 2009 there were 699 km of railways (234 km electrified). 1.5 m. passengers and 2.9 m. tonnes of freight were transported in 2009. The former

Macedonian Railways was reorganized in 2007 with two new entities being created—Macedonian Railways Infrastructure (PE Makedonski eleznici Infrastructure, or M-I), which is responsible for the maintenance and operation of the infrastructure, and Macedonian Railways Transport (M Transport AD, or M-T), which is responsible for the operation of passenger and freight services.

Religion

Macedonia is traditionally Orthodox but the church is not established and there is freedom of religion. A study by the Pew Research Center's Forum on Religion & Public Life estimated that there were 1.33 m. Orthodox Christians in 2010 and 810,000 Muslims (mainly Sunni). In 1967 an autocephalous Orthodox church—the Macedonian Orthodox Church—split off from the Serbian Orthodox Church. Its head is the Archbishop of Ohrid and Macedonia, whose seat is at Skopje.

Roads

In 2007 there were 221 km of motorways, 690 km of other main roads, 3,774 km of regional roads and 9,155 km of local roads. There were 248,800 passenger cars in use in 2007, plus 2,300 buses and coaches, and 26,600 lorries and vans. In the same year there were 4,037 road accidents with 173 fatalities.

Social Statistics

In 2011: live births, 22,770; deaths, 19,465; marriages, 14,736; divorces, 1,753; infant deaths, 172. Rates (per 1,000 population): live births, 11.1; deaths, 9.5; marriages, 7.2; divorces, 0.9. Infant mortality, 2011 (per 1,000 live births), 7.6. Expectation of life at birth in 2007 was 71.7 years for males and 76.5 years for females. Annual population growth rate, 2005–10, 0.2%. In 2012 the most popular age range for marrying was 25–29 for males and 20–24 for females. Fertility rate, 2011, 1.6 births per woman.

Telecommunications

In 2011 there were 413,500 landline telephone subscriptions (equivalent to 200.3 per 1,000 inhabitants) and 2,257,100 mobile phone subscriptions (or 1,093.6 per 1,000 inhabitants). In 2011, 56.7% of the population were internet users. In 2002 the Hungarian firm Matav acquired a 51% stake in MakTel, the state monopoly telecommunications provider, in the most significant economic development in the country's history. The deal was worth €618.2 m. (US$568.4 m.) over 2 years. In March 2012 there were 880,000 Facebook users.

Territory and Population

Macedonia (referred to within the United Nations as the Former Yugoslav Republic of Macedonia) is bounded in the north by Serbia, in the east by Bulgaria, in the south by Greece and in the west by Albania. Its area is 25,713 km², including 490 km² of inland water. According to the 2002 census final results, the population on 1 Nov. 2002 was 2,022,547. A census scheduled for 2011 was deferred following ethnic disputes. The main ethnic group are Macedonians, followed by Albanians, with smaller numbers of Turks, Roma, Serbs and Bosniaks. Ethnic Albanians predominate on the western side of Macedonia. Population estimate, Dec. 2013, 2,065,769; density, 82 per km². Minorities are represented in the Council for Inter-Ethnic Relations. In 2011, 59.4% of the population lived in urban areas. Macedonia is divided into 84 municipalities. The major cities (with 2013 population estimates) are: Skopje, the capital, 497,900; Kumanovo, 72,800; Bitola, 72,400; Prilep, 65,400; Tetovo, 55,600. The official language is Macedonian, which uses the Cyrillic alphabet. Around 25% of the population speak Albanian.

Tourism

There were 261,696 foreign tourists in 2010, the highest total since 1991. The main countries of origin of non-resident tourists in 2010 were: Serbia (13.7%), Greece (10.3%), Turkey (7.7%) and Albania (6.5%).

Madagascar

Repoblikan'i Madagasikara (Republic of Madagascar)

Factsheet

Capital: Antananarivo
Population estimate, 2015: 24.24 m.
GNI per capita, 2014: (PPP$) 1,328
HDI/world rank, 2014: 0.510/154
Internet domain extension: .mg

Civil Aviation

There are international airports at Antananarivo (Ivato) and Mahajanga (Amborovy). The national carrier is Air Madagascar, which is 90.6% state-owned. In 2013 it carried 539,000 passengers (303,000 on domestic flights), serving six international and 22 domestic destinations. In 2012 Antananarivo handled 890,632 passengers (586,532 on international flights) and 22,276 tonnes of freight.

Climate

A tropical climate, but the mountains cause big variations in rainfall, which is very heavy in the east and very light in the west. Antananarivo, Jan. 70 °F (21.1 °C), July 59 °F (15 °C). Annual rainfall 54″ (1,350 mm). Toamasina, Jan. 80 °F (26.7 °C), July 70 °F (21.1 °C). Annual rainfall 128″ (3,256 mm).

Constitution and Government

A new constitution was promulgated on 10 Dec. 2010, having won 74.2% support at a referendum held in Nov. 2010. However, the referendum was boycotted by the three main opposition parties and turnout was 52.6%, with registered voters accounting for only about a third of the population. On the day of the vote there was an unsuccessful army mutiny against the rule of Rajoelina. The new constitution reduced the minimum age requirement for the presidency from 40 years to 35 (allowing the then 36-year old Rajoelina to stand in the next presidential election). It also demanded that presidential candidates should be resident in the country in the 6 months leading up to an election, which effectively ruled out Rajoelina's exiled predecessor, Marc Ravalomanana, from standing against him. Rajoelina's critics argued the constitution was designed to bolster the interim president's personal standing.

Currency

In July 2003 then President Marc Ravalomanana announced that the *Ariary* (MGA) would become the official currency, replacing the *Malagasy franc* (MGFr). The Ariary became legal tender on 1 Aug. 2003 at a rate of 1 *Ariary* = 5 *Malagasy francs.* The Ariary is subdivided into five *Iraimbilanja.* In July 2005 foreign exchange reserves were US$435 m. and total money supply was 1,324.0 bn. ariarys.

Defence

There is conscription (including civilian labour service) for 18 months. Defence expenditure totalled US$72 m. in 2013 (US$3 per capita), representing 0.7% of GDP.

Economy

In 2009 agriculture contributed 29.1% of GDP, industry 16.0% and services 54.9%.

Labour

The labour force in 2013 was 11,688,000 (8,182,000 in 2003). 89.7% of the population aged 15–64 was economically active in 2013. In the same year 3.6% of the population was unemployed. Madagascar had 19,000 people living in slavery according to the Walk Free Foundation's 2013 *Global Slavery Index.*

Press

In 2008 there were 13 daily newspapers with a total circulation of 115,000.

Rail

In 2005 there were 854 km of railways, all metre gauge. In 2005, 100,000 passengers and 300,000 tonnes of freight were transported.

Religion

In 2010 there were an estimated 8.11 m. Protestants and 7.26 m. Catholics according to the Pew Research Center's Forum on Religion & Public Life, with folk religionists numbering 900,000 and 1.4 m. people having no religious affiliation.

Roads

In 2012 there were 31,640 km of roads, 21.9% of which were paved. There were 146,300 passenger cars, 280,800 buses and coaches and 83,800 lorries and vans in 2008. 550 people died in road accidents in 2006.

Shipping

The main ports are Toamasina, Mahajanga, Antsiranana and Toliary. In Jan. 2009 there were 19 ships of 300 GT or over registered, totalling 18,000 GT.

Social Statistics

2008 estimates: births, 686,000; deaths, 176,000. Rates, 2008 estimates (per 1,000 population): births, 35.9; deaths, 9.2. Infant mortality, 2010 (per 1,000 live births), 43. Expectation of life in 2013 was 63.2 years for males and 66.2 for females. Annual population growth rate, 2000–08, 2.8%. Fertility rate, 2008, 4.7 births per woman.

Telecommunications

In 2011 there were 130,100 landline telephone subscriptions (equivalent to 6.5 per 1,000 inhabitants) and 8,159,600 mobile phone subscriptions (or 382.8 per 1,000 inhabitants). There were 17.0 internet users per 1,000 inhabitants in 2010. Fixed internet subscriptions totalled 8,300 in 2009 (0.4 per 1,000 inhabitants). In June 2012 there were 233,000 Facebook users.

Territory and Population

Madagascar is situated 400 km (250 miles) off the southeast coast of Africa, from which it is separated by the Mozambique channel. Its area is 587,041 km^2 (226,658 sq. miles), including 5,500 km^2 (2,120 sq. miles) of inland water. At the last census, in 1993, the population was 12,092,157 (50.45% female); density, 20.6 per km^2. The estimate for 2011 was 20,696,100; density, 35.6 per km^2. 69.8% of the population lived in rural areas in 2010. The indigenous population is of Malayo-Polynesian stock, divided into 18 ethnic groups of which the principal are Merina (24%) of the central plateau, the Betsimisaraka (13%) of the east coast and the Betsileo (11%) of the southern plateau. Foreign communities include Europeans (mainly French), Indians, Chinese, Comorians and Arabs. Malagasy, French and (since 2007) English are all official languages.

Tourism

In 2011, 225,005 non-resident tourists arrived by air (excluding same-day visitors), up from 196,052 in 2010 although down from the peak of 375,010 in 2008.

Malaŵi

Dziko la Malaŵi (Republic of Malaŵi)

Factsheet

Capital: Lilongwe
Population estimate, 2015: 17.22 m.

GNI per capita, 2014: (PPP$) 747
HDI/world rank, 2014: 0.445/173
Internet domain extension: .mw

Civil Aviation

The national carrier is Malawian Airlines, which is 49% owned by Ethiopian Airlines. It was founded in 2013 following the liquidation of the former flag carrier, Air Malawi. In 2012 scheduled airline traffic of Malaŵi-based carriers flew 3.7 m. km; passenger-km totalled 207.5 m. in the same year. The main international airports is Lilongwe (Lilongwe International Airport). The airport at Blantyre (Chileka) also has some international flights. Lilongwe handled 261,267 passengers in 2012 (198,620 on international flights) and 3,932 tonnes of freight.

Climate

The tropical climate is marked by a dry season from May to Oct. and a wet season for the remaining months. Rainfall amounts are variable, within the range of 29–100″ (725–2,500 mm), and maximum temperatures average 75–89 °F (24–32 °C), and minimum temperatures 58–67 °F (14.4–19.4 °C). Lilongwe, Jan. 73 °F (22.8 °C), July 60 °F (15.6 °C). Annual rainfall 36″ (900 mm). Blantyre, Jan. 75 °F (23.9 °C), July 63 °F (17.2 °C). Annual rainfall 45″ (1,125 mm). Zomba, Jan. 73 °F (22.8 °C), July 63 °F (17.2 °C). Annual rainfall 54″ (1,344 mm).

Constitution and Government

The *President* is also head of government. Malaŵi was a one-party state, but following a referendum on 14 June 1993, in which 63% of votes cast were in favour of reform, a new constitution was adopted on 17 May 1994 which ended Hastings Banda's life presidency and provided for the holding of multi-party elections. At these Bakili Muluzi was elected president with 47.2% of votes cast, beating President Banda and two other opponents. There is a *National Assembly* of 193 members, elected for 5-year terms in single-seat constituencies.

Currency

The unit of currency is the *kwacha* (MWK) of 100 *tambala*.

Defence

All services form part of the Army. Defence expenditure totalled US$25 m. in 2013 (US$2 per capita), representing 0.7% of GDP.

Economy

Agriculture accounted for 30% of GDP in 2010, industry 20% and services 50%.

Labour

The labour force in 2010 was 6,708,000 (51.5% female). Approximately 80% of the economically active population in 2010 were engaged in agriculture. Malaŵi had 0.11 m. people living in slavery according to the Walk Free Foundation's 2013 *Global Slavery Index*.

Press

There were two paid-for dailies and nine paid-for non-dailies in 2008. The two dailies are *The Nation* (average circulation of 15,000 copies daily in 2008); and *The Daily Times* (7,000 copies daily in 2008).

Rail

In 2005 Malaŵi Railways operated 797 km on 1,067 mm gauge, providing links to the Mozambican ports of Beira and Nacala. In 2009 passenger-km travelled came to 44 m. and freight tonne-km to 47 m.

Religion

According to estimates by the Pew Research Center's Forum on Religion & Public Life, in 2010 the population was 82.7% Christian (mainly Protestants) and 13.0% Muslim.

Roads

The road network consisted of 24,929 km in 2008, of which 16.3% were paved. There were 53,300 passenger cars and 59,800 vans and trucks in 2007.

Social Statistics

2008 estimates: births, 597,000; deaths, 182,000. Estimated rates, 2008 (per 1,000 population): births, 40.2; deaths, 12.3. Annual population growth rate, 2000–08, 2.8%. Expectation of life at birth in 2013 was 55.1 years for males and 55.4 for females. Infant mortality, 2010, 58 per 1,000 live births; fertility rate, 2008, 5.5 births per woman.

Telecommunications

In 2011 there were 173,500 landline telephone subscriptions (equivalent to 11.3 per 1,000 inhabitants) and 3,855,800 mobile phone subscriptions (or 250.7 per 1,000 inhabitants). In 2011, 3.3% of the population were internet users. In June 2012 there were 140,000 Facebook users.

Territory and Population

Malaŵi lies along the southern and western shores of Lake Malaŵi (the third largest lake in Africa), and is otherwise bounded in the north by Tanzania, south by Mozambique and west by Zambia. Area (including the inland water areas of Lake Malombe, Chilwa, Chiuta and the Malaŵi portion of Lake Malaŵi, which total 24,208 km²), 118,484 km² (45,747 sq. miles). Census population (2008), 13,077,160 (6,718,227 females); density, 138.7 per km². In 2011, 20.3% of the population were urban. Population of main towns (2008): Lilongwe, 674,448; Blantyre, 661,256; Mzuzu, 133,968; Zomba, 88,314. Population of the regions (2008): Northern, 1,708,930; Central, 5,510,195; Southern, 5,858,035. The official languages are Chichewa, spoken by over 58% of the population, and English.

Tourism

There were 755,031 non-resident tourists in 2009 (excluding same-day visitors), up from 742,457 in 2008.

Malaysia

Persekutuan Tanah Malaysia (Federation of Malaysia)

Factsheet

Capitals: Putrajaya (Administrative), Kuala Lumpur (Legislative and Financial)
Population estimate, 2015: 30.33 m.
GNI per capita, 2014: (PPP$) 22,762
HDI/world rank, 2014: 0.779/62
Internet domain extension: .my

Civil Aviation

There are a total of 19 airports of which five are international airports and 14 are domestic airports at which regular public air transport is operated. Malaysia Airlines, the national airline, is 52% state-owned, and operates domestic flights within Malaysia and international flights to nearly 40 different countries. A low-cost airline, AirAsia, began operations in Nov. 1996; its budget sister long-haul carrier, Air Asia X, started flying in Nov. 2007. In 2005 scheduled airline traffic of Malaysian-based carriers flew 282.7 m. km, carrying 23,026,000 passengers. In 2012 Kuala Lumpur handled 39,887,866 passengers (27,612,088 on international flights) and 702,226 tonnes of freight. Kota Kinabalu handled 5,848,135 passengers in 2012 and Penang 4,767,815.

Climate

Malaysia lies near the equator between latitudes 1° and 7° North and longitudes 100° and 119° East. Malaysia is subject to maritime influence and the interplay of wind systems which originate in the Indian Ocean and the South

China Sea. The year is generally divided into the South-East and the North-East Monsoon seasons. The average daily temperature throughout Malaysia varies from 21 °C to 32 °C. Humidity is high.

Constitution and Government

The Constitution of Malaysia is based on the Constitution of the former Federation of Malaya, but includes safeguards for the special interests of Sabah and Sarawak. It was amended in 1983. The Constitution provides for one of the Rulers of the Malay States to be elected from among themselves to be the *Yang di-Pertuan Agong* (Supreme Head of the Federation). He holds office for a period of 5 years. The Rulers also elect from among themselves a Deputy Supreme Head of State, also for a period of 5 years. In Feb. 1993 the Rulers accepted constitutional amendments abolishing their legal immunity.

Currency

The unit of currency is the Malaysian *ringgit* (RM) of 100 *sen*.

Defence

The Constitution provides for the Head of State to be the Supreme Commander of the Armed Forces who exercises his powers in accordance with the advice of the Cabinet. The Malaysian Armed Forces has participated in 25 UN peacekeeping missions in Africa, the Middle East, Indo-China and Europe. Since 2004 a lottery system has been in place to choose conscripts to serve 3 months of national service. In 2013 defence expenditure totalled US$5,000 m. (US$169 per capita), representing 1.5% of GDP.

Economy

In 2009 agriculture accounted for 9.5% of GDP, industry 43.8% and services 46.7%.

Labour

In 2001 the workforce was 9,892,000 (46.7% female in 2000), of whom 9,535,000 were employed (22.6% in manufacturing, 14.2% in agriculture, forestry and fishing, 10.5% in government services and 8.9% in construction). Unemployment was 3.8% in 2002. It is estimated that Malaysia has some 500,000 illegal workers. Malaysia had 25,000 people living in slavery according to the Walk Free Foundation's 2013 *Global Slavery Index*.

Press

In 2008 there were 50 daily newspapers (49 paid-for and one free) with a combined circulation of 4,750,000. The dailies with the highest circulation are the Malay-language *Mingguan Malaysia* and the Chinese-language *Sin Chew Daily*.

Rail

Length of route in 2011, 2,250 km, of which 350 km were electrified. The Malayan Railway carried 39.5 m. passengers and 5.4 m. tonnes of freight in 2010; the Sabah State Railway carried 594,000 passengers and 89,000 tonnes of freight in 2011. A railway from Kuala Lumpur to the international airport opened in 2002 and carried 3.9 m. passengers in 2009. There are two metro systems in Kuala Lumpur with a combined length of 56 km.

Religion

Malaysia has a multi-racial population divided between Islam, Buddhism, Taoism, Hinduism and Christianity. Under the Federal constitution, Islam is the official religion of Malaysia but there is freedom of worship. In 2001 there were an estimated 10.77 m. Muslims, 5.45 m. adherents of Chinese traditional religions, 1.88 m. Christians, 1.66 m. Hindus and 1.50 m. Buddhists.

Roads

Total road length in 2012 was 180,882 km, of which 78.1% were paved. In 2006 there were 7,024,000 passenger cars in use, 60,000 buses and coaches, 836,600 lorries and vans, and 7,458,100 motorcycles and mopeds. There were 6,287 deaths as a result of road accidents in 2006, which at 24.1 per 100,000 people ranks among the highest rates in the world.

Shipping

Port Kelang, the busiest port, handled 152,348,000 freight tons of cargo in 2008; container throughput in 2008 was 7,974,000 TEUs (twenty-foot equivalent units), making it Malaysia busiest container port. In Jan. 2009 there were 457 ships of 300 GT or over registered, totalling 6.43 m. GT. Of the 457 vessels registered, 189 were general cargo ships, 130 oil tankers, 45 container ships, 34 liquid gas tankers, 26 passenger ships, 20 chemical tankers and 13 bulk carriers. The Malaysian-controlled fleet comprised 307 vessels of 1,000 GT or over in Jan. 2009, of which 242 were under the Malaysian flag and 65 under foreign flags.

Social Statistics

2007 estimated births, 481,000; deaths, 120,000. 2007 rates (per 1,000 population): birth, 18.1; death, 4.5. Life expectancy, 2007: males, 71.9 years; females, 76.6 years. Annual population growth rate, 2000–08, 1.9%. Infant mortality, 2010, five per 1,000 live births; fertility rate, 2007, 2.3 births per woman. Today only 6% of Malaysians live below the poverty line, compared to 50% in the early 1970s.

Telecommunications

In 2013 there were 4,536,000 main (fixed) telephone lines. In the same year mobile phone subscribers numbered 42,996,000 (1,446.9 per 1,000 persons). 67.0% of the population were internet users in 2013. In March 2012 there were 12.4 m. Facebook users.

Territory and Population

The federal state of Malaysia comprises the 13 states and three federal territories of Peninsular Malaysia, bounded in the north by Thailand, and with the island of Singapore as an enclave on its southern tip; and, on the island of Borneo to the east, the state of Sabah (which includes the federal territory of the island of Labuan), and the state of Sarawak, with Brunei as an enclave, both bounded in the south by Indonesia and in the northwest and northeast by the South China and Sulu Seas. The area of Malaysia is 330,803 km^2 (127,724 sq. miles), and the 2010 census population 28,334,135; density, 85.7 per km^2. Malaysia's national waters cover 515,256 km^2. In 2011, 73.0% of the population lived in urban areas. Putrajaya, a planned new city described as an 'intelligent garden city', became the administrative capital of Malaysia in 1999 and was created a federal territory on 1 Feb. 2001. Bahasa Malaysia (Malay) is the official language of the country—50% of the population are Malays.

Tourism

In 2009, 23,646,000 international tourists visited Malaysia (up from 22,052,000 in 2008), making it the ninth most popular tourist destination; receipts from tourism in 2009 totalled US$15,772 m.

Maldives

Divehi Raajjeyge Jumhooriyyaa (Republic of the Maldives)

Factsheet
Capital: Malé
Population estimate, 2015: 364,000
GNI per capita, 2014: (PPP$) 12,328
HDI/world rank, 2014: 0.706/104
Internet domain extension: .mv

Civil Aviation

The former national carrier Air Maldives collapsed in April 2000 with final losses in excess of US$50 m. The national airline is now Maldivian, which was founded in 2000 and initially operated domestic flights only. It began to serve international destinations in Asia in 2008. In 2010 there were international flights from Malé International Airport (now officially known as Velana International Airport) to Bangalore, Bangkok, Bologna, Colombo, Doha,

Dubai, Düsseldorf, Frankfurt, Guangzhou, Kuala Lumpur, London, Milan, Moscow, Munich, Muscat, Paris, Rome, Singapore, Thiruvananthapuram and Zürich, as well as domestic services.

Climate

The islands are hot and humid, and affected by monsoons. Malé: average temperature 81 °F (27 °C), annual rainfall 59″ (1,500 mm).

Constitution and Government

The present constitution came into effect on 1 Jan. 1998. There is a Citizens' *Majlis* (Parliament) which consists of 77 members all of whom are directly elected for a term of 5 years. Political parties were not permitted until the introduction of a multiparty system in June 2005. In a referendum held on 18 Aug. 2007 voters supported the retention of a presidential system, with 62.0% of votes cast in favour and 38.0% for a switch to a parliamentary system. The President of the Republic is elected by the Citizens' Majlis.

Currency

The unit of currency is the *rufiyaa* (MVR) of 100 *laari*.

Defence

In 2008 military expenditure totalled US$43 m. (US$111 per capita), representing 3.4% of GDP.

Economy

Fisheries accounts for approximately 7% of GDP, industry 15% and services 78%.

Labour

In 2005 the economically active workforce totalled 99,000 of whom 96,000 were employed. More than two-thirds of the working population are engaged in tourism.

Press

In 2008 there were six paid-for daily newspapers and around 200 independent newspapers and periodicals in total.

Religion

The State religion is Islam—adherence to it is legally required of citizens.

Roads

In 2007 there were 3,060 passenger cars in use (10 per 1,000 inhabitants), 26,780 motorcycles and mopeds, 2,870 lorries and vans, and 74 buses and coaches.

Shipping

In Jan. 2009 there were 58 ships of 300 GT or over registered, totalling 130,000 GT.

Social Statistics

2006 births, 5,827; deaths, 1,084. Birth rate, 2006, per 1,000 population, 19.5; death rate, 3.6. Annual population growth rate, 2005–10, 1.8%. Life expectancy at birth in 2007 was 69.7 years for males and 72.7 years for females. Infant mortality, 2010, 14 per 1,000 live births; fertility rate, 2008, 2.0 births per woman. The Maldives has had the largest reduction in its fertility rate of any country in the world over the past quarter of a century, having had a rate of 6.1 births per woman in 1990. It has also made some of the best progress in recent years in reducing child mortality. The number of deaths per 1,000 live births among children under five was reduced from 94 in 1990 to 11 in 2012.

Telecommunications

There were 48,000 fixed telephone lines in 2010 (152.0 per 1,000 inhabitants). Mobile phone subscribers numbered 494,400 in 2010. There were 283.0 internet users per 1,000 inhabitants in 2010. Fixed internet subscriptions totalled 20,100 in 2009 (64.4 per 1,000 inhabitants). In March 2012 there were 120,000 Facebook users.

Territory and Population

The republic, some 650 km to the southwest of Sri Lanka, consists of 1,192 low-lying (the highest point is 2.4 m above sea-level) coral islands, grouped into 19 atolls and two cities. 199 are inhabited. Area 298 km² (115 sq. miles). In 2014 the preliminary census population was 341,256; density, 1,145.2 per km². In 2011, 41.3% of the population lived in urban areas. Capital, Malé (2014 provisional census population, 109,635). The official and spoken language is Divehi.

Tourism

Tourism is the major foreign currency earner. There were a record 791,917 tourist arrivals in 2010, spending US$714 m.

Mali

République du Mali (Republic of Mali)

Factsheet

Capital: Bamako
Population estimate, 2015: 17.60 m.
GNI per capita, 2014: (PPP$) 1,583
HDI/world rank, 2014: 0.419/179
Internet domain extension: .ml

Civil Aviation

There is an international airport at Bamako (Senou), which handled 533,054 passengers (446,793 on international flights) and 7,538 tonnes of freight in 2012. In 2010 Air Mali operated direct flights to Abidjan, Accra, Conakry, Cotonou, Dakar, Kinshasa, Libreville, Lomé, Luanda, Madrid, Marseille, Niamey, Nouakchott, Ouagadougou, Paris and Pointe-Noire. Air Mali ceased operations in Dec. 2012. There were also flights in 2010 with foreign airlines to Abidjan, Addis Ababa, Algiers, Brazzaville, Casablanca, Conakry, Cotonou, Dakar, Johannesburg, Libreville, Lomé, Nairobi, Niamey, Nouakchott, Ouagadougou, Paris, Tripoli (Libya) and Tunis.

Climate

A tropical climate, with adequate rain in the south and west, but conditions become increasingly arid towards the north and east. Bamako, Jan. 76 °F (24.4 °C), July 80 °F (26.7 °C). Annual rainfall 45″ (1,120 mm). Kayes, Jan. 76 °F (24.4 °C), July 93 °F (33.9 °C). Annual rainfall 29″ (725 mm). Tombouctou, Jan. 71 °F (21.7 °C), July 90 °F (32.2 °C). Annual rainfall 9″ (231 mm).

Constitution and Government

A national conference of 1,800 delegates agreed a draft constitution enshrining multi-party democracy in Aug. 1991, and this was approved by 99.76% of votes cast at a referendum in Jan. 1992. Turnout was 43%. The *President* is elected for not more than two terms of 5 years. There is a *National Assembly*, consisting of 147 deputies (formerly 116) plus 13 Malinese living abroad. A *Constitutional Court* was established in 1994. In May 2012 the rebel National Movement for the Liberation of Azawad (MNLA) and Ansar Dine, an Islamist militant group, declared Azawad—a region in the north covering over half of Mali's total land area—a breakaway Islamic state. The unilateral declaration went unrecognized by Bamako and the international community.

Currency

The unit of currency is the *franc CFA* (XOF), which replaced the Mali franc in 1984. It has a parity rate of 655.957 francs CFA to one euro.

Defence

There is selective conscription for 2 years. In 2013 military expenditure totalled US$301 m. (US$19 per capita), representing 2.6% of GDP.

Economy

Agriculture accounted for 39% of GDP in 2009, industry 21% and services 40%.

Labour

The labour force in 2013 was 5,748,000 (3,310,000 in 2003). 67.0% of the population aged 15–64 was economically active in 2013. In the same year 8.1% of the population was unemployed. Mali had 0.10 m. people living in slavery according to the Walk Free Foundation's 2013 *Global Slavery Index*.

Press

In 2008 there were 12 daily newspapers with an estimated combined circulation of 40,000.

Rail

Mali has a railway from Kayes to Koulikoro by way of Bamako, a continuation of the currently non-operational Dakar–Kayes line in Senegal; total length, 2005, 643 km (metre gauge). In 2005, 179,000 passengers and 1.7 m. tonnes of freight were transported.

Religion

The state is secular, but predominantly Sunni Muslim. According to the Pew Research Center's Forum on Religion & Public Life, an estimated 3.2% of the population in 2010 were Christians and 2.7% folk religionists.

Roads

There were 18,912 km of roads in 2005, of which 19.0% were paved. In 2007 there were 87,000 passenger cars (seven per 1,000 inhabitants), 26,800 lorries and vans, and 10,000 motorcycles and mopeds.

Shipping

For about 7 months in the year small steamboats operate a service from Koulikoro to Tombouctou and Gao, and from Bamako to Kouroussa.

Social Statistics

2008 estimates: births, 541,000; deaths, 200,000. Rates, 2008 estimates (per 1,000 population): births, 42.6; deaths, 15.7. Infant mortality, 2010 (per 1,000 live births), 99. Expectation of life in 2013 was 55.1 years for males and 54.9 for females. Mali was one of only two countries where the life expectancy at birth for males in 2013 was higher than for females (the other being Swaziland). Annual population growth rate, 2000–08, 2.4%; fertility rate, 2008, 6.5 children per woman.

Telecommunications

In 2013 there were 126,000 fixed telephone lines; mobile phone subscribers numbered 19,749,000 in the same year (129.1 per 100 persons). There were 27,677 fixed internet subscriptions in 2013. In June 2012 there were 141,000 Facebook users.

Territory and Population

Mali is bounded in the west by Senegal, northwest by Mauritania, northeast by Algeria, east by Niger and south by Burkina Faso, Côte d'Ivoire and Guinea. Its area is 1,248,574 km² (482,077 sq. miles) and it had a population of 14,528,662 at the 2009 census; density, 1.6 per km². In 2011, 36.6% of the population were urban. In 2009 the capital, Bamako, had a population of 1,809,000. The second largest town, Sikasso, had a population of 226,000 in 2009. The Bambara, Khassonké, Malinké and Soninké, all of which belong to the broader Mandé group, make up 50% of the population; the other leading groups are the Fula (17%), Voltaic (12%), Songhai (6%), and Tuareg and Moor (10%). The official language is French; Bambara is spoken by about 68% of the population.

Tourism

There were 169,000 non-resident tourists in 2010; tourist revenue totalled US$296 m. in the same year.

Malta

Repubblika ta' Malta (Republic of Malta)

Factsheet

Capital: Valletta
Population estimate, 2015: 419,000
GNI per capita, 2014: (PPP$) 27,930
HDI/world rank, 2014: 0.839/37=
Internet domain extension: .mt

Civil Aviation

The national carrier is Air Malta, which is 98% state-owned. In 2010 it carried 1.70 m. passengers and flew from Malta to nearly 40 destinations in other European countries. In 2012 there were 32,286 aircraft movements at Malta International Airport. A total of 3,658,972 passengers and 16,487 tonnes of cargo were handled.

Climate

The climate is Mediterranean, with hot, dry and sunny conditions in summer and very little rain from May to Aug. Rainfall is not excessive and falls mainly between Oct. and March. Average daily sunshine in winter is six hours and in summer over ten hours. Valletta, Jan. 12.8 °C (55 °F), July 25.6 °C (78 °F). Annual rainfall 578 mm (23″).

Constitution and Government

Malta is a parliamentary democracy. The constitution of 1964 provides for a *President*, a *House of Representatives* of members elected by universal suffrage and a Cabinet consisting of the Prime Minister and such number of Ministers as may be appointed. The Constitution makes provision for the protection of fundamental rights and freedom of the individual, and for freedom of conscience and religious worship, and guarantees the separation of executive, judicial and legislative powers. The House of Representatives currently has 70 members (65 directly elected). Malta uses the single transferable vote system.

Currency

On 1 Jan. 2008 the euro (EUR) replaced the Maltese lira (MTL) as the legal currency of Malta at the irrevocable conversion rate of Lm0.4293 to one euro.

Defence

The Armed Forces of Malta (AFM) are made up of a Headquarters and three Regiments. In 2011 they had a strength of 1,954 personnel. In 2013 defence expenditure totalled US$60 m. (US$145 per capita), representing 0.6% of GDP.

Economy

Services accounted for 65% of GDP in 2009, industry 32% and agriculture 3%.

Labour

The labour force in 2013 was 187,000 (162,000 in 2003). 63.4% of the population aged 15–64 was economically active in 2013. In the same year 6.5% of the population was unemployed. 30.5% of the labour force in 2013 had a secondary education as the highest level and 23.7% had a tertiary education.

Press

In 2008 there were two English paid-for dailies (*The Times* and *The Malta Independent*) and two Maltese dailies (*In-Nazzjon* and *L-Orizzont*). There were seven paid-for non-dailies and six Sunday newspapers (three in English and three in Maltese).

Religion

97% of the population belong to the Roman Catholic Church, which is established by law as the religion of the country, although full liberty of conscience and freedom of worship are guaranteed. In Feb. 2016 there was one cardinal.

Roads

In 2004 there were 3,096 km of roads, including 185 km of highways. 87.5% of roads are paved. Malta has one of the densest road networks in the world. Motor vehicles in use in 2007 included 203,900 passenger cars, 23,600 vans and lorries, 10,600 motorcycles and mopeds, and 690 buses and coaches. There were 1,209 casualties in traffic accidents in 2007, including 14 fatalities.

Shipping

There is a car ferry between Malta and Gozo. In Jan. 2009 there were 1,487 ships of 300 GT or over registered, totalling 31.65 m. GT; Malta's fleet was the sixth largest in terms of the number of ships and the eighth largest on the basis of gross tonnage. Of the 1,487 vessels registered, 498 were general cargo ships, 464 bulk carriers, 346 oil tankers, 78 container ships, 56 passenger ships, 24 liquid gas tankers and 21 chemical tankers.

Social Statistics

2009: births, 3,713; deaths, 3,221; marriages, 2,353; emigrants, 9,708 (1,771 Maltese); immigrants, 8,147 (1,190 returning Maltese). 2009 rates per 1,000 population: birth, 9.4; death, 7.8; marriage, 5.7. Abortion is illegal, as was divorce until Oct. 2011. Parliament voted in July 2011 to legalize divorce following a vote in favour of the reform by 52.7% to 47.3% in a referendum held in May. Until then Malta had been one of only three countries still to outlaw divorce (the others being the Philippines and the Vatican). In 2008 the most popular age range for marrying was 25–29 for both males and females. Life expectancy at birth in 2013: 77.5 years for males and 82.0 years for females. Annual population growth rate, 2005–10, 0.5%. Infant mortality in 2010: five per 1,000 live births; fertility rate, 2008, 1.3 births per woman.

Telecommunications

In 2013 there were 231,331 main (fixed) telephone lines; mobile phone subscribers numbered 556,652 in 2013 (129.8 per 100 persons). There were 135,758 fixed internet subscriptions in 2012 and 149,788 wireless broadband subscriptions. In March 2012 there were 192,000 Facebook users.

Territory and Population

The three Maltese islands and minor islets lie in the Mediterranean 93 km (at the nearest point) south of Sicily and 288 km east of Tunisia. The area of Malta is 246 km^2 (94.9 sq. miles); Gozo, 67 km^2 (25.9 sq. miles) and the virtually uninhabited Comino, 3 km^2 (1.1 sq. miles); total area, 316 km^2 (121.9 sq. miles). The census population in 2011 was 417,432 (Malta island, 386,057; Gozo and Comino, 31,375); density, 1,321 per km^2. In 2011, 94.8% of the population were urban. Chief town and port, Valletta, population 5,748 (2011 census). Other towns: Birkirkara, 21,749; Mosta, 19,750; St Paul's Bay, 16,395; Qormi, 16,394; Zabbar, 14,916. The constitution provides that the national language and language of the courts is Maltese, but both Maltese and English are official languages. Italian is also spoken.

Tourism

Tourism is a major component of the Maltese economy. In 2010 there were 1,336,000 staying foreign tourists, spending US$1,130 m.; 31% of tourists in 2010 were from the UK and 16% from Italy. Cruise passenger visits totalled 491,201 in 2010 (more than double the 2000 total of 170,782).

Marshall Islands

Republic of the Marshall Islands

Factsheet
Capital: Majuro
Population estimate, 2015: 53,000
GNI per capita, 2014: (PPP$) 4,674
Internet domain extension: .mh

Civil Aviation

There were two international airports and 30 airfields on 24 atolls and islands in 2004. The main airport is Majuro International. In 2017 there were flights to Guam, Honolulu, Kiribati, Micronesia and Nauru as well as domestic services. The national carrier is Air Marshall Islands.

Climate

Hot and humid, with wet season from May to Nov. The islands border the typhoon belt. Jaluit, Jan. 81 °F (27.2 °C), July 82 °F (27.8 °C). Annual rainfall 161″ (4,034 mm).

Constitution and Government

Under the constitution which came into force on 1 May 1979, the Marshall Islands form a republic with a *President* as head of state and government, who is elected for 4-year terms by the parliament. The parliament consists of a 33-member *House of Assembly* (Nitijela), directly elected by popular vote for 4-year terms. There is also a 12-member appointed *Council of Chiefs* (Iroij) which has a consultative and advisory capacity on matters affecting customary law and practice.

Currency

US currency is used.

Defence

The Compact of Free Association gives the USA responsibility for defence in return for US assistance. In 2003 the US lease of Kwajalein Atoll, a missile testing site, was extended by 50 years.

Economy

Agriculture accounts for approximately 15% of GDP, industry 13% and services 72%.

Labour

In 2004 the labour force was estimated at 17,342. Approximately 34% were unemployed in 2004. In 2007, 37% of employed people worked in the private sector. In the same year 35% of workers were employed in public administration, 18% in wholesale and retail trade, 12% in extra-territorial organizations and bodies and 8% in construction. Agriculture, hunting, forestry and fishing accounted for just 3%.

Press

There is a publication called *Micronitor* (The Marshall Islands Journal).

Religion

The population is mainly Protestant (primarily the United Church of Christ). Other Churches and denominations include Assemblies of God, Roman Catholics, Latter-day Saints (Mormons), Bukot Nan Jesus and Baptists.

Roads

There are paved roads on major islands (Majuro, Kwajalein); roads are otherwise stone-, coral- or laterite-surfaced. In 2004 there were 1,555 passenger cars and 159 trucks and buses.

Shipping

Majuro is the main port. In Jan. 2009 there were 1,125 ships of 300 GT or over registered, totalling 41.58 m. GT (a figure exceeded only by the fleets of Panama, Liberia and the Bahamas). Of the 1,125 vessels registered, 434 were oil tankers, 311 bulk carriers, 192 container ships, 110 general cargo ships, 56 liquid gas tankers, 15 chemical tankers and seven passenger ships. The ship's register of the Marshall Islands is a flag of convenience register.

Social Statistics

2006 births, estimate, 1,576; deaths, 318. 2006 rates per 1,000 population, estimates: birth, 30.3; death, 6.1. Infant mortality rate, 2010, 22 per 1,000 live births. Life expectancy, 2008: male, 68.9 years; female, 73.0. Annual population growth rate, 1998–2008, 1.6%; fertility rate, 2008, 3.7 births per woman.

Telecommunications

In 2014 there were 2,361 main (fixed) telephone lines. There is a US satellite communications system on Kwajalein and two Intelsat satellite earth stations (Pacific Ocean). The National Telecommunications Authority provides domestic and international services. Mobile phone subscribers numbered 15,500 in 2014. An estimated 11.7% of the population were internet users in 2013.

Territory and Population

The Marshall Islands lie in the North Pacific Ocean north of Kiribati and east of Micronesia, and consist of an archipelago of 31 coral atolls, five single islands and 1,152 islets strung out in two chains, eastern and western. Of these, 25 atolls and islands are inhabited. The land area is 181 km² (70 sq. miles). At the 2011 census the population was 53,158 (27,243 males); density, 294 per km². The capital is Mjauro (also known as Dalap-Uliga-Darrit) on Majuro Atoll (2011 population, 27,797) in the eastern chain. The largest atoll in the western chain is Kwajalein (2011 population, 11,408), containing the only other town, Ebeye. In 2011 the population was 72.1% urban. About 88% of the population are Marshallese, a Micronesian people. English is universally spoken and is the official language. Two major Marshallese dialects from the Malayo-Polynesian family and Japanese are also spoken.

Tourism

In 2011, 4,559 non-resident tourists (excluding same-day visitors) arrived by air. Tourism offers one of the best opportunities for economic growth.

Mauritania

Al-Jumhuriyah al-Islamiyah al-Muritaniyah (Islamic Republic of Mauritania)

Factsheet

Capital: Nouakchott
Population estimate, 2015: 4.07 m.
GNI per capita, 2014: (PPP$) 3,560
HDI/world rank, 2014: 0.506/156=
Internet domain extension: .mr

Civil Aviation

There are international airports at Nouakchott, Nouâdhibou and Néma. In 2012 scheduled airline traffic of Mauritania-based carriers flew 2.0 m. km; passenger-km totalled 160.8 m. in the same year. Mauritania Airlines International, founded in 2010, is the national flag carrier.

Climate

A tropical climate, but conditions are generally arid, even near the coast, where the only appreciable rains come in July to Sept. Nouakchott, Jan. 71 °F (21.7 °C), July 82 °F (27.8 °C). Annual rainfall 6″ (158 mm).

Constitution and Government

A referendum was held on 25 June 2006 to approve a new constitution. Turnout was 76.5%; 96.99% of votes cast were in favour. The constitution imposes a limit of two 5-year terms for a president, to be elected by popular vote. It also sets a maximum age of 75 for a president. There is a 56-member *Senate* (53 elected and three appointed) and a 146-member *National Assembly*. Following a coup d'état in Aug. 2008 a transitional government took power, headed by an 11-member High Council of State (all of whom came from the military). The junta retained the constitution and vowed to protect the country's democratic institutions. In April 2009 Gen. Mohamed Ould Abdel Aziz—the leader of the coup—stood down as head of government to run in the presidential elections of July 2009, which he won by a large margin.

Currency

The monetary unit is the *ouguiya* (MRO) which is divided into five *khoums*.

Defence

Conscription is authorized for 2 years. Defence expenditure in 2013 totalled US$145 m. (US$42 per capita), representing approximately 3% of GDP.

Economy

In 2010 agriculture accounted for 16.8% of GDP, industry 44.0% and services 39.2%.

Labour

In 2008 the economically active population was estimated at 1,353,000 (58% males). Of those in employment, 24.6% worked in commerce, 15.2% in administration, 14.9% in services and 10.5% in agriculture. The unemployment rate in 2008 was 31.2%. Slavery was only abolished in Mauritania in 1981, making it the last country where it was still being practised legally. Nonetheless, the practice remains widespread and there were 0.15 m. people living in slavery according to the Walk Free Foundation's 2013 *Global Slavery Index*.

Press

In 2008 there were four daily newspapers with a circulation of 9,000.

Rail

A 704-km railway links Zouérate with the port of Point-Central, 10 km south of Nouâdhibou, and is used primarily for iron ore exports. In 2008 it carried 11.1 m. tonnes of freight and 100,000 passengers.

Religion

Over 99% of Mauritanians are Sunni Muslim, mainly of the Qadiriyah sect.

Roads

There were about 11,066 km of roads in 2006, of which 26.8% were paved.

Shipping

The major ports are at Point-Central (for mineral exports), Nouakchott and Nouâdhibou.

Social Statistics

2008 estimates: births, 108,000; deaths, 33,000. 2008 rates, estimate (per 1,000 population): births, 33.6; deaths, 10.3. Expectation of life at birth in 2013 was 60.0 years for males and 63.1 for females. Annual population growth rate, 2000–08, 2.6%. Infant mortality, 2010, 75 per 1,000 live births; fertility rate, 2008, 4.5 births per woman.

Telecommunications

In 2013 there were 54,000 active fixed telephone subscriptions and 3,988,000 active mobile phone subscriptions (102.5 per 100 persons). In the same year an estimated 6.2% of the population were internet users.

Territory and Population

Mauritania is bounded west by the Atlantic Ocean, north by Western Sahara, northeast by Algeria, east and southeast by Mali, and south by Senegal. The total area is 1,030,700 km² (398,000 sq. miles) of which 47% is desert. The population at the 2013 census was 3,537,368; density, 3.4 per km². In 2011, 41.7% of the population lived in urban areas. Mauritania was traditionally a nomadic country but since independence in 1960 there has been rapid urbanization, primarily as a result of a series of droughts. It is estimated that around 40% of the population are Black Moors, 30% White Moors and 30% Black Africans of the Pulaar, Soninke and Wolof tribes. Arabic is the official language. French no longer has official status. Pulaar, Soninke and Wolof are national languages.

Tourism

There were 30,000 foreign tourists in 2000; spending by tourists totalled US$25 m.

Mauritius

Republic of Mauritius

Factsheet

Capital: Port Louis
Population estimate, 2015: 1.27 m.
GNI per capita, 2014: (PPP$) 17,470
HDI/world rank, 2014: 0.777/63
Internet domain extension: .mu

Civil Aviation

In 2012, 2,690,869 passengers were handled at Sir Seewoosagur Ramgoolam International Airport. The national carrier is Air Mauritius, which is partly state-owned. In 2013 it carried 1,318,000 passengers (1,196,000 on international flights).

Climate

The sub-tropical climate is humid. Most rain falls in the summer. Rainfall varies between 40″ (1,000 mm) on the coast to 200″ (5,000 mm) on the central plateau, though the west coast only has 35″ (875 mm). Mauritius lies in the cyclone belt, whose season runs from Nov. to April, but is seldom affected by intense storms. Port Louis, Jan. 73 °F (22.8 °C), July 81 °F (27.2 °C). Annual rainfall 40″ (1,000 mm).

Constitution and Government

The present constitution came into effect on 12 March 1968 and was amended on 12 March 1992. The head of state is the *President*, elected by a simple majority of members of the National Assembly. The role of *President* is largely a ceremonial one. The 69-seat *National Assembly* consists of 62 elected members (three each for the 20 constituencies of Mauritius and two for Rodrigues) and seven additional seats in order to ensure a fair and adequate representation of each community within the Assembly. The government is headed by the *Prime Minister* and a Council of Ministers. Elections are held every 5 years on the basis of universal adult suffrage.

Currency

The unit of currency is the *Mauritius rupee* (MUR) of 100 *cents*.

Defence

The Police Department is responsible for defence. Its strength was (2008) 8,000. In addition there is a special mobile paramilitary force of approximately 1,400, a Coast Guard of about 700 and a helicopter unit of about 100. Defence expenditure totalled US$83 m. in 2013 (US$63 per capita), representing 0.7% of GDP.

Economy

Agriculture accounted for 4.3% of GDP in 2009, industry 29.1% and services 66.6%.

Labour

In 2007 the labour force was estimated at 548,900. Manufacturing employed the largest proportion, with 30.8% of total employment; agriculture, forestry and fishing, 7.2%; wholesale and retail trade, 6.3%. In 2007 the unemployment rate was 8.5%.

Press

In 2008 there were four daily papers with a combined circulation of 110,000, plus 16 non-dailies.

Religion

In 2010 an estimated 56.4% of the population were Hindus according to the Pew Research Center's Forum on Religion & Public Life, with 25.3% Christians (mainly Catholics) and 16.7% Muslims.

Roads

In 2007 there were 75 km of motorway, 962 km of main roads and 991 km of secondary and other roads. In 2007 there were 144,400 passenger cars, 142,600 motorcycles and mopeds, 40,900 lorries and vans, and 4,000 buses and coaches. In 2007 there were 140 deaths as a result of road accidents.

Shipping

A free port was established at Port Louis in Sept. 1991. In 2008–09 Port Louis handled 6,295,000 tonnes of cargo. In Jan. 2009 there were three ships of 300 GT or over registered, totalling 13,000 GT.

Social Statistics

2007: births, 17,034 (rate of 13.5 per 1,000 population); deaths, 8,498 (6.7 per 1,000); marriages, 11,547 (9.2 per 1,000); divorces, 1,302 (1.0 per 1,000). In 2007 the suicide rate was 15.7 per 100,000 population among men and 4.7 per 100,000 among women. Population growth rate in 2007 was 0.65%. In 2007 the most popular age range for marrying was 25–29 for males and 20–24 for females. Life expectancy at birth in 2007 was 69.1 years for males and 75.8 for females. Infant mortality, 2010, 13 per 1,000 live births; fertility rate, 2007, 2.0 births per woman.

Telecommunications

In 2012 there were 349,100 main (fixed) telephone lines; mobile phone subscribers numbered 1,486,000 in 2012 (119.9 per 100 persons). In 2013, 39.0% of the population were internet users. In June 2012 there were 324,000 Facebook users.

Territory and Population

Mauritius, the main island, lies 800 km (500 miles) east of Madagascar. Rodrigues is 560 km (350 miles) east. The outer islands are Agalega and the St Brandon Group. Port Louis is the capital (128,851 inhabitants in 2010). Other towns: Beau Bassin-Rose Hill, 110,687; Vacoas-Phoenix, 106,404; Curepipe, 84,487; Quatre Bornes, 77,495. In 2010, 58.3% of the population were rural. The majority of the population are Indo-Mauritians (people of Indian descent). The Afro-Mauritians are the other major group, and there are also Sino-Mauritians (of Chinese origin) and Franco-Mauritians (descendants of French settlers). Mauritius has no indigenous population. The official language is English, although French is widely used. Creole and Bhojpuri are vernacular languages.

Tourism

In 2010 there were 934,827 visitors (including 605,401 from Europe and 226,207 from other African countries), bringing in US$1,227 m. in tourist revenue.

Mexico

Estados Unidos Mexicanos (United Mexican States)

Factsheet

Capital: Mexico City
Population estimate, 2015: 127.02 m.
GNI per capita, 2014: (PPP$) 16,056
HDI/world rank, 2014: 0.756/74
Internet domain extension: .mx

Civil Aviation

There is an international airport at Mexico City (Benito Juárez) and 55 other international and 29 national airports. Each of the larger states has a local airline which links it with main airports. The national carrier is Aeroméxico, which was privatized in 1988. In 2012 Mexico City handled 29,491,553 passengers (19,678,042 on domestic flights). Cancún was the second busiest airport for passengers in 2012, with 14,555,184 (9,855,771 on international flights). Guadalajara handled 7,448,214 passengers (4,966,411 on domestic flights).

Climate

Latitude and relief produce a variety of climates. Arid and semi-arid conditions are found in the north, with extreme temperatures, whereas in the south there is a humid tropical climate, with temperatures varying with altitude. Conditions on the shores of the Gulf of Mexico are very warm and humid. In general, the rainy season lasts from May to Nov. Mexico City, Jan. 55 °F (12.9 °C), July 61 °F (16.2°C). Annual rainfall 31″ (787.6 mm).

Constitution and Government

A new constitution was promulgated on 5 Feb. 1917 and has occasionally been amended. Mexico is a representative, democratic and federal republic, comprising 31 states and a federal district, each state being free and sovereign in all internal affairs, but united in a federation established according to the principles of the Fundamental Law. The head of state and supreme executive authority is the *President*, directly elected for a non-renewable 6-year term. The constitution was amended in April 2001, granting autonomy to 10 m. indigenous peoples. The amendment was opposed both by the National Congress of Indigenous Peoples and Zapatista rebels who claimed it would leave many indigenous people worse off. There is complete separation of legislative, executive and judicial powers (Art. 49). Legislative power is vested in a General Congress of two chambers, a *Chamber of Deputies* and a *Senate*.

Currency

The unit of currency is the *Mexican peso* (MXN) of 100 *centavos*. A new peso was introduced on 1 Jan. 1993: 1 new peso = 1,000 old pesos. The peso was devalued by 13.94% in Dec. 1994. Foreign exchange reserves were US$82,023 m. and gold reserves 288,000 troy oz in Sept. 2009.

Defence

Conscription is for 12 months. In 2013 defence expenditure totalled US$5,775 m. (US$50 per capita), representing 0.5% of GDP.

Economy

Agriculture accounted for 4.0% of GDP in 2009, industry 33.7% and services 62.3%.

Labour

In the period March–June 2001 the employed population totalled 39,004,300. The principal areas of activity were (in 1,000): wholesale and retail trade/repair of motor vehicles, motorcycles and personal and household goods, 8,839.2; manufacturing, 7,373.0; agriculture, hunting and forestry, 6,920.7; construction, 2,396.9; hotels and restaurants, 1,982.2; education, 1,971.6. Unemployment rate, Dec. 2014, 4.3%. The daily minimum wage for general workers at Jan. 2014 ranged from 63.77 new pesos to 67.29 new pesos. Mexico had 0.1 m. people living in slavery according to the Walk Free Foundation's 2013 *Global Slavery Index*.

Press

In 2008 there were 462 daily newspapers with a circulation of 4,590,000. The three leading dailies are *Esto* (average daily circulation of 320,000 in 2008), *La Prensa* (315,000) and *El Universal Gráfico* (300,000).

Rail

The National Railway, *Ferrocarriles Nacionales de México*, was split into four companies in 1995 as a preliminary to privatization. It ceased operations in 1999. The rail network comprises 26,717 km of 1,435 mm gauge. In 2010 railways carried 40.2 m. passengers and 104.6 m. tonnes of freight. There is a 202 km metro in Mexico City with 11 lines. There are light rail lines in Guadalajara (24 km) and Monterrey (32 km).

Religion

In 2010 there were an estimated 96.3 m. Roman Catholics according to the Pew Research Center's Forum on Religion & Public Life, giving Mexico the second largest Catholic population after Brazil. In Feb. 2016 there were five cardinals. The Church is separated from the State, and the constitution of 1917 provided strict regulation of this and all other religions. In 1991 Congress approved an amendment to the 1917 constitution permitting the recognition of churches by the state, the possession of property by churches and the enfranchisement of priests. Church buildings remain state property. There were also an estimated 9.4 m. Protestants and 2.0 m. other Christians in 2010. A further 5.3 m. people in 2010 were religiously unaffiliated.

Roads

The total road length in 2007 was 360,075 km, of which 6,565 km were motorways, 40,631 km other main roads, 73,874 km secondary roads and 239,005 km other roads. In 2005 there were 14,074,669 passenger cars, 7,111,172 trucks and vans and 264,726 buses and coaches. There were 5,398 fatalities as a result of road accidents in 2007.

Shipping

Mexico had 114 ports and terminals in 2007 (66 ocean navigation), of which the most important are Altamira, Progreso, Tampico, Tuxpan and Veracruz on the Gulf coast and Manzanillo on the Pacific coast. Mexico's busiest port is Manzanillo, which handled 22.11 m. tonnes of cargo in 2008 (7.74 m. tonnes loaded and 14.37 m. tonnes discharged). A law to privatize port operations was passed in 1993. In Jan. 2009 there were 81 ships of 300 GT or over registered, totalling 879,000 GT.

Social Statistics

Rates per 1,000 population, 2009: births, 18.0; deaths, 4.9. In 2006 the most popular age range for marrying was 20–24 for both males and females. Infant mortality was 14.7 per 1,000 live births in 2009. Life expectancy at birth in 2007 was 73.6 years for males and 78.5 years for females. Annual population growth rate, 2005–10, 1.8%. Fertility rate, 2008, 2.2 births per woman (less than half the number in the late 1970s). Much of the population still lives in poverty, with the gap between the modern north and the backward south constantly growing.

Telecommunications

Telmex (Teléfonos de México), a former state-run company privatized in 1991 and a wholly owned subsidiary of América Móvil, is the leading provider of fixed-line telephone services and broadband, with around 80% of the market. In 2011 there were 19,997,000 fixed telephone lines and 94,583,000 mobile phone subscribers (792.4 per 1,000 persons). The leading mobile phone operator is Telcel (part of América Móvil), which has about

70% of the market. In 2013 there were 13,539,000 fixed internet subscriptions and 16,865,000 wireless broadband subscriptions. In Dec. 2011 there were 31.0 m. Facebook users.

Territory and Population

Mexico is bounded in the north by the USA, west and south by the Pacific Ocean, southeast by Guatemala, Belize and the Caribbean Sea, and northeast by the Gulf of Mexico. It comprises 1,964,375 km^2 (758,464 sq. miles), including uninhabited islands (5,127 km^2) offshore. Population at recent censuses: 1970, 48,225,238; 1980, 66,846,833; 1990, 81,249,645; 2000, 97,483,412; 2005, 103,263,388; 2010, 112,336,538 (57,481,307 females). Population density, 57.2 per km^2 (2010). 78.1% of the population were urban in 2011. The *de facto* official language is Spanish, the mother tongue of over 93% of the population (2005), but there are some indigenous language groups (of which Náhuatl, Maya, Zapotec, Otomi and Mixtec are the most important) spoken by 6,011,202 persons over 5 years of age (census 2005). The populations (2010 census) of the largest cities (1,000,000 and more) were: Mexico City, 8,555,272; Ecatepcec de Morelos, 1,655,015; Guadalajara, 1,495,182; Heroica Puebla de Zaragoza, 1,434,062; Juárez, 1,321,004; Tijuana, 1,300,983; León de los Aldama, 1,238,962; Zapopan, 1,142,483; Monterrey, 1,135,512; Ciudad Nezahualcoyotl, 1,104,585.

Tourism

There were 21.45 m. non-resident tourists in 2009 (excluding same-day visitors), making Mexico the tenth most popular tourist destination; spending amounted to US$11,275 m. in 2009.

Micronesia

Federated States of Micronesia

Factsheet
Capital: Palikir
Population estimate, 2015: 104,000
GNI per capita, 2014: (PPP$) 3,432
HDI/world rank, 2014: 0.639/107
Internet domain extension: .fm

Civil Aviation

There are international airports on Pohnpei, Chuuk, Yap and Kosrae. There were 12 operational airports and airfields in total in 2012. Services are provided by United Airlines. In 2013 there were international flights to Guam, Honolulu, Manila, the Marshall Islands and Palau in addition to domestic services.

Climate

Tropical, with heavy year-round rainfall, especially in the eastern islands, and occasional typhoons (June–Dec.). Kolonia, Jan. 80 °F (26.7 °C), July 79 °F (26.1 °C). Annual rainfall 194″ (4,859 mm).

Constitution and Government

Under the Constitution founded on 10 May 1979, there is an executive presidency and a 14-member *National Congress*, comprising ten members elected for 2-year terms from single-member constituencies of similar electorates, and four members elected one from each State for a 4-year term by proportional representation. The *Federal President* and *Vice-President* first run for the Congress before they are elected by members of Congress for a 4-year term.

Currency

US currency is used.

Labour

In 2007 just over half the labour force were government employees. In 2007, 41.7% of employees worked in public administration, 21.1% in wholesale and retail trade and repairs and 7.0% in transport, storage and communications. Agriculture, hunting, forestry and fishing accounted for 1.7% of employees. The unemployment rate was 16.2% in 2010.

Religion

The population is predominantly Christian. Yap is mainly Roman Catholic; Protestantism is prevalent elsewhere.

Roads

In 2004 there were 240 km of roads (42 km paved).

Shipping

The main ports are Kolonia (Pohnpei), Colonia (Yap), Lepukos (Chuuk), Okat and Lelu (Kosrae). In Jan. 2009 there were 11 ships of 300 GT or over registered, totalling 9,000 GT.

Social Statistics

2009 estimates: births, 2,800; deaths, 700. Rates, 2009 estimates (per 1,000 population): birth, 25; death, 6. Infant mortality rate (2010), 34 per 1,000 live births. 2013 life expectancy, 68.0 years for men and 69.9 years for women. Population growth rate, 2005–10, –0.5%; fertility rate, 2008, 3.6 births per woman.

Telecommunications

There were an estimated 38,000 mobile phone subscriptions in 2009 (343.2 per 1,000 inhabitants) and 8,700 fixed telephone lines; in the same year there were an estimated 15,350 internet users.

Territory and Population

The Federated States lie in the North Pacific Ocean between 137° and 163° E, comprising 607 islands with a total land area of 701 km^2 (271 sq. miles). The 2010 census population was 102,843; density, 147 per km^2. In 2011, 22.8% of the population lived in urban areas. Kosrae consists of a single island. Its main town is Lelu (2,160 inhabitants in 2010). Pohnpei comprises a single island (covering 334 km^2) and eight scattered coral atolls. Kolonia (6,074 inhabitants in 2010) was the national capital until 1989. The new capital, Palikir (6,647 inhabitants in 2010), lies approximately 10 km southwest in the Palikir valley. Chuuk consists of 542 islets in a 7,190 km^2 reef-fringed lagoon (36,152 inhabitants in 2010); the state also includes coral atolls (12,502 inhabitants in 2010), the most important being the Mortlock Islands. English is used in schools and is the official language. Trukese, Pohnpeian, Yapese and Kosrean are also spoken.

Tourism

In 2012 there were 38,263 foreign visitors, up from 35,378 in 2011 although down from 44,738 in 2010.

Moldova

Republica Moldova (Republic of Moldova)

Factsheet
Capital: Chişinău
Population estimate, 2015: 4.08 m.
GNI per capita, 2014: (PPP$) 5,223
HDI/world rank, 2014: 0.693/107
Internet domain extension: .md

Civil Aviation

The main Moldovan-based airline is Air Moldova, which in 2013 carried 527,000 passengers. In 2010 it flew to Athens, Bucharest, Frankfurt, İstanbul, Larnaca, Lisbon, London, Madrid, Milan, Moscow, Paris, Prague, Rome, St Petersburg, Verona and Vienna. In 2012 the airport at Chişinău handled 1,220,496 passengers (almost all on international flights) and 2,766 tonnes of cargo.

Climate

The climate is temperate, with warm summers, crisp, sunny autumns and cold winters with snow. Chişinău, Jan. –7 °C, July 20 °C. Annual rainfall 677 mm.

Constitution and Government

A declaration of republican sovereignty was adopted in June 1990 and in Aug. 1991 the republic declared itself independent. A new constitution came into effect on 27 Aug. 1994, which defines Moldova as an 'independent, democratic and unitary state'. The 1994 constitution makes provision for the autonomy of Transnistria and the Gagauz (Gagauzi Yeri) region. Work began in July 2003 on the drafting of a new constitution to resolve the conflict between Moldova and Transnistria.

Currency

A new unit of currency, the *leu* (MDL), replaced the *rouble* in Nov. 1993.

Defence

Conscription is for 12 months (3 months for higher education graduates). In 2013 military expenditure totalled US$24 m. (US$7 per capita), representing 0.3% of GDP.

Economy

Agriculture accounted for 10.1% of GDP in 2009, industry 13.1% and services 76.8%.

Labour

In 2007 the labour force totalled 1,314,000. A total of 1,247,000 persons were in employment in 2007, including 409,000 engaged in agriculture, hunting, forestry and fisheries, 250,000 in public administration, education, heath and social work, 198,000 in wholesale and retail trade/hotels and restaurants and 128,000 in manufacturing. In 2007 the unemployment rate was 5.1%. Moldova had 33,000 people living in slavery according to the Walk Free Foundation's 2013 *Global Slavery Index*.

Press

In 2008 there were seven paid-for daily newspapers and 240 non-dailies. The dailies had a combined circulation of 303,000, with the most widely read being the Russian-language *Komsomolskaya Pravda v Moldove*.

Rail

Total length in 2011 was 1,146 km of 1,524 mm gauge. Passenger-km travelled in 2011 came to 363 m. and freight tonne-km to 1,172 m.

Religion

According to the Pew Research Center's Forum on Religion & Public Life, in 2010 the population was an estimated 95.5% Orthodox. There are two main Orthodox denominations. The larger Moldovan Orthodox Church is subordinate to the Russian Orthodox Church while the Bessarabian Orthodox Church is subordinate to the Romanian Orthodox Church.

Roads

There were 9,343 km of public roads in 2009 (94.3% hard surfaced). Registered passenger cars (including taxis) in 2008 numbered 366,351, there were 115,967 goods vehicles and 21,491 buses and minibuses. In 2005 there were 2,289 road accidents resulting in 391 deaths.

Shipping

In 2008, 0.11 m. passengers and 0,20 m. tonnes of freight were carried on inland waterways. In Jan. 2009 there were 63 ships of 300 GT or over registered, totalling 170,000 GT.

Social Statistics

2007: births, 37,973; deaths, 43,050. Rates, 2007 (per 1,000 population): births, 10.6; deaths, 12.0. In 2006 the most popular age at first marriage was 20–24 for both males and females. Life expectancy at birth in 2007 was 65.0 years for males and 72.6 years for females. Annual population growth rate, 2000–05, –0.2%. Infant mortality, 2010, 16 per 1,000 live births; fertility rate, 2008, 1.3 births per woman (one of the lowest rates in the world). In the period 2000–06, 48.5% of the population were classified as living below the national poverty line.

Telecommunications

There were 2,785,000 mobile phone subscriptions (772.8 per 1,000 inhabitants) in 2009 and 1,139,000 fixed telephone lines. In the same year there were 187,000 fixed broadband internet subscriptions and 80,000 mobile broadband subscriptions. In March 2012 there were 221,000 Facebook users.

Territory and Population

Moldova is bounded in the east and south by Ukraine and on the west by Romania. The area is 33,848 km² (13,067 sq. miles). At the last census, in 2004, the population was 3,938,679 (52.2% female). Population estimate, Jan. 2012: 4,077,000; density, 120 per km². In 2011, 47.7% of the population lived in urban areas. Ethnicity (2004): Moldovans accounted for 69.6%, Ukrainians 11.3%, Russians 9.3%, Gagauz 3.9%, Bulgarians 2.0%, Roma (Gypsy) 1.9% and others 2.0%. Apart from Chişinău, the capital (population estimate of 667,600 in 2012), major towns are Tiraspol (147,800 in 2012), Bălţi (144,300 in 2012) and Tighina (93,300 in 2012). The official Moldovan language (i.e. Romanian) was written in Cyrillic prior to the restoration of the Roman alphabet in 1989. It is spoken by 62% of the population; the use of other languages (Russian, Gagauz) is safeguarded by the Constitution.

Tourism

In 2010, 64,000 non-resident tourists stayed in holiday accommodation; 24% of tourists in 2010 were from Romania, 10% from Russia and 10% from Ukraine.

Monaco

Principauté de Monaco (Principality of Monaco)

Factsheet
Capital: Monaco
Population estimate, 2015: 38,000
GDP per capita, 2014: US$187,650
Internet domain extension: .mc

Civil Aviation

There are helicopter flights to Nice with Heli Air Monaco and Heli Inter. Helicopter movements (2004) at the Heliport of Monaco (Fontvieille), 37,521; the number of passengers carried was 112,379. The nearest airport is at Nice in France.

Climate

A Mediterranean climate, with mild moist winters and hot dry summers. Monaco, Jan. 50 °F (10 °C), July 74 °F (23.3 °C). Annual rainfall 30″ (758 mm).

Constitution and Government

On 17 Dec. 1962 a new constitution was promulgated which maintains the hereditary monarchy. The reigning Prince is **Albert II**, b. 14 March 1958, son of Prince Rainier III, 1923–2005, and Grace Kelly, 1929–1982; married Charlene Wittstock on 1 and 2 July 2011. Prince Albert succeeded his father Rainier III, who died on 6 April 2005. Executive power is exercised jointly by the Prince and a five-member *Council of government*, headed by a Minister of State (a French citizen). A 24-member *National Council* is elected for 5-year terms. The constitution can be modified only with the approval of the National Council. Laws of 1992, 2003 and 2005 permit Monegasque women to give their nationality to their children.

Currency

On 1 Jan. 1999 the euro (EUR) replaced the French franc as the legal currency in Monaco at the irrevocable conversion rate of 6.55957 French francs to one euro. The euro, which consists of 100 cents, has been in circulation since 1 Jan. 2002. On the introduction of the euro there was a 'dual circulation' period before the franc ceased to be legal tender on 17 Feb. 2002.

Labour

There were 49,610 persons employed in Jan. 2012. 45,442 worked in the private sector; 4,168 in the public sector. 32,401 French citizens worked in Monaco in 2012 (of which 29,778 in the private sector and 2,623 in the public sector).

Press

Monaco has no domestically-published daily newspaper. In 2008 there were two state weeklies: *Journal de Monaco* (published by the government) and *Monaco Hebdo*.

Rail

The 1.7 km of main line passing through the country are operated by the French National Railways (SNCF). In 2011, 5.45 m. people arrived at or departed from Monaco railway station.

Religion

Around three-quarters of the resident population are Roman Catholic. Much of the rest of the population does not have any religious affiliation. There is a Roman Catholic archbishop.

Roads

There were 77 km of roads in 2007. In 2004 there were 33,275 vehicles. Monaco has the densest network of roads of any country in the world. In 2004, 5,141,964 people travelled by bus.

Shipping

In 2004 there were 3,829 vessels registered, of which 12 were over 100 tonnes. 2,636 yachts put in to the port of Monaco and 1,193 at Fontvieille in 2004. 178 liners put in to port in Monaco; 10,581 people embarked, 10,195 disembarked and 104,202 were in transit.

Social Statistics

2008: births, 970; deaths, 545. 2005 marriages, 161; divorces, 69. Rates per 1,000 population, 2008: birth, 31.2; death, 17.5; marriage (2005), 5.0; divorce (2005), 2.1. Annual population growth rate, 1998–2008, 0.4%; fertility rate, 2008, 1.5 births per woman. Infant mortality per 1,000 live births (2010), 3.

Telecommunications

There were 46,850 fixed telephone lines in 2013 (1,238.4 per 1,000 inhabitants). Mobile phone subscriptions numbered 35,464 in 2013. An estimated 90.7% of the population were internet users in 2013.

Territory and Population

Monaco is bounded in the south by the Mediterranean and elsewhere by France (Department of Alpes Maritimes). The area is 1.97 km² (0.8 sq. miles), making it the second smallest sovereign country—only the Vatican City is smaller. The Principality is divided into four districts: Monaco-Ville, la

Condamine, Monte-Carlo and Fontvieille. Population (2008 census), 31,109; there were 6,687 Monegasques (22%), 8,785 French (28%) and 5,778 Italian (19%). In Dec. 2011 the population was estimated at 36,371. The population is 100% urban. The official language is French.

Tourism

In 2009, 264,540 foreign visitors (212,966 leisure and 51,574 business) spent a total of 778,451 nights in Monaco; the main visitors were French, followed by Italians and British. There were also 235,904 cruise ship passengers in 2009. There are three casinos run by the state, including the one at Monte Carlo.

Mongolia

Mongol Uls

Factsheet
Capital: Ulaanbaatar
Population estimate, 2015: 2.96 m.
GNI per capita, 2014: (PPP$) 10,729
HDI/world rank, 2014: 0.727/90=
Internet domain extension: .mn

Civil Aviation

MIAT Mongolian Airlines operates internal services, and in 2010 flew from Ulaanbaatar to Beijing, Berlin, Moscow, Seoul and Tokyo. In 2012 scheduled airline traffic of Mongolian-based carriers flew 7.4 m. km; passenger-km totalled 861.0 m. in the same year. In 2012 Ulaanbaatar handled 1,096,649 passengers and 6,143 tonnes of freight.

Climate

A very extreme climate, with 6 months of mean temperatures below freezing, but much higher temperatures occur for a month or two in summer. Rainfall is very low and limited to the months from mid-May to mid-Sept. Ulaanbaatar, Jan. –14 °F (–25.6 °C), July 61 °F (16.1 °C). Annual rainfall 8″ (208 mm).

Constitution and Government

The constitution of 12 Feb. 1992 abolished the 'People's Democracy', introduced democratic institutions and a market economy and guarantees freedom of speech. The *President* is directly elected for renewable 4-year terms. Since June 1992 the legislature has consisted of a single-chamber 76-seat parliament, the *Great Hural (Ulsyn Ich-Chural)*, which elects the Prime Minister.

Currency

The unit of currency is the *tugrik* (MNT) of 100 *möngö*.

Defence

Conscription is for 1 year for males aged 18–25 years. Defence expenditure in 2013 totalled US$133 m. (US$41 per capita), representing 1.1% of GDP.

Economy

In 2009 agriculture accounted for 19.6% of GDP, industry 33.0% and services 47.4%.

Labour

The labour force in 2013 was 1,302,000 (1,024,000 in 2003). 65.6% of the population aged 15–64 was economically active in 2013. In the same year 5.0% of the population was unemployed.

Press

In 2008 there were 15 paid-for daily newspapers with a combined circulation of 61,000 and 115 paid-for non-dailies with a circulation of 197,000. The leading paid-for dailies are *Udriin Sonin* (Daily News) and *Onoodor*.

Rail

The Trans-Mongolian Railway (1,815 km of 1,520 mm gauge in 2011) connects Ulaanbaatar with the Russian Federation and China. There are spur lines to Erdenet and to the coal mines at Baganuur, Nalayh and Sharyn Gol and the fluorspar mine at Bor-Öndör. A separate line connects Choybalsan in the east with Borzaya on the Trans-Siberian Railway. In 2011, 3.8 m. passengers and 18.4 m. tonnes of freight were carried.

Religion

Tibetan Buddhist Lamaism is the prevalent religion; the Dalai Lama is its spiritual head. In 2009 there were 457 registered places of worship; 239 of these were Buddhist, 161 Christian and 44 Muslim.

Roads

The total road network covers around 49,200 km, of which about 2,400 km are paved. There are 1,185 km of surfaced roads running around Ulaanbaatar, from Ulaanbaatar to Darhan, at points on the frontier with the Russian Federation and towards the south. Truck services run where there are no surfaced roads. Vehicles in use in 2007 included 110,200 passenger cars and 37,300 lorries and vans. In 2008 passenger transport totalled 1,215 m. passenger-km and freight 782 m. tonne-km. In 2007 there were 562 fatalities as a result of road accidents.

Shipping

There is a steamer service on the Selenge River and a tug and barge service on Hövsgöl Lake.

Social Statistics

Births, 2005, 45,326; deaths, 16,480. 2001 rates: birth, 17.8 per 1,000 population; death, 6.5 per 1,000; marriage, 5.9 per 1,000; divorce, 0.6 per 1,000. Annual population growth rate, 2000–05, 1.3%. Infant mortality rate, 2010, 26 per 1,000 live births. Expectation of life in 2007 was 63.0 years for males and 69.6 for females. Fertility rate, 2008, 2.0 births per woman. Mongolia has had one of the most impressive reductions in its fertility rate of any country in the world over the past quarter of a century, having had a rate of 4.2 births per woman in 1990.

Telecommunications

In 2013 there were 175,698 main (fixed) telephone lines; mobile phone subscribers numbered 3,526,000 in 2013 (124.2 per 100 persons). An estimated 17.7% of the population were internet users in 2013. In March 2012 there were 459,000 Facebook users.

Territory and Population

Mongolia is bounded in the north by the Russian Federation, and in the east and south and west by China. Area, 1,564,100 km^2 (603,900 sq. miles). Population (2010 census), 2,647,545. Density in 2010 was 1.7 per km^2, making Mongolia the most sparsely populated country in the world. In 2011, 62.5% of the population were urban. More Mongols live in China than in Mongolia (5.8 m. according to China's 2010 census). The population is predominantly made up of Mongolian peoples (78.8% Khalkh). There is a Turkic Kazakh minority (3.7% of the population) and 21 Mongol minorities. The official language is Khalkh Mongol, which uses a modified Cyrillic alphabet. The republic is administratively divided into 21 provinces (*aimag*) and the capital, Ulaanbaatar. The provinces are sub-divided into 334 districts or counties (*suums*).

Tourism

In 2011 there were 458,000 non-resident visitors to Mongolia; visitor numbers have doubled since 2003 and trebled since 2000.

Montenegro

Republika Crna Gora (Republic of Montenegro)

Factsheet

Capital: Podgorica
Population estimate, 2015: 626,000
GNI per capita, 2014: (PPP$) 14,558
HDI/world rank, 2014: 0.802/49
Internet domain extension: .me

Civil Aviation

The national carrier is Montenegro Airlines, which has flights to a number of cities throughout Europe. There are airports at Podgorica and Tivat, which handled 450,504 and 532,148 passengers in 2009 respectively.

Climate

Mostly a central European type of climate, with cold winters and hot summers. Podgorica, Jan. 2.8 °C, July 26.5 °C. Annual rainfall 1,499 mm.

Constitution and Government

The President is elected by direct vote to serve a 5-year term. There is an 81-member single-chamber *National Assembly*, elected through a party list proportional representation system to serve 4-year terms. The *Prime Minister* is nominated by the President and has to be approved by the National Assembly. Montenegro held a referendum on 21 May 2006 in which 55.5% voted for independence. The margin required for victory was 55.0%. Turnout was 86.6%.

Currency

On 2 Nov. 1999 the pro-Western government decided to make the Deutsche Mark legal tender alongside the dinar. Subsequently it was made the sole official currency, and consequently the euro (EUR) became the currency of Montenegro on 1 Jan. 2002.

Defence

The all-professional Military of Montenegro was formed from part of the Armed Forces of Serbia and Montenegro when the two countries became independent in 2006. Defence expenditure in 2013 totalled US$54 m. (US$82 per capita), representing 1.2% of GDP.

Economy

In 2009 agriculture accounted for 10.0% of GDP, industry 20.1% and services 69.9%.

Labour

In 2011 there were 163,082 people in employment, including 37,820 in wholesale and retail trade, repair of vehicles, personal and household goods; 19,195 in public administration and defence, and compulsory social security; 14,368 in manufacturing; 12,429 in accommodation and food service activities; 12,223 in education; 10,565 in health and social work; 9,188 in transport, storage and communications. Average gross monthly wages for 2011 were €722 and average net wages €484. Unemployment rate in 2011 was 19.7%.

Press

In 2008 there were four daily newspapers with a combined circulation of 46,000.

Rail

In 2009 there were 249 km of railway. 1.1 m. passengers and 2 m. tonnes of freight were carried in 2009.

Religion

The Serbian Orthodox Church is the official church in Montenegro. The Montenegrin church was banned in 1922, but in Oct. 1993 a breakaway Montenegrin church was set up under its own patriarch.

Roads

In 2013 there were 7,965 km of roads. Passenger-km in 2013 were 109 m.; tonne-km of freight carried, 67 m.

Shipping

In Jan. 2009 there were seven ships of 300 GT or over registered, totalling 13,000 GT.

Social Statistics

2008 live births, 8,258; deaths, 5,708; marriages, 3,445; divorces, 460. Life expectancy, 2013, 72.5 years for men and 77.2 years for women. Infant mortality per 1,000 births (2010), 7.

Telecommunications

There were 1,159,000 mobile phone subscriptions in 2011 and an estimated 171,000 landline telephone subscriptions. In 2012, 55.0% of households had internet access. In March 2012 there were 293,000 Facebook users.

Territory and Population

Montenegro is a mountainous country which opens to the Adriatic in the southwest. It is bounded in the west by Croatia, northwest by Bosnia and Herzegovina, in the northeast by Serbia and in the southeast by Albania. The capital is Podgorica (2011 census population, 150,977), although some capital functions have been transferred to Cetinje, the historic capital of the former kingdom of Montenegro. Its area is 13,812 km². Population at the 2011 census was 620,029; population density per sq. km, 44.9. The main ethnic groups in 2011 were: Montenegrins (44.98%); Serbs (28.73%); Bosniaks (8.65%); Albanians (4.91%). 61.5% of the population lived in urban areas in 2011. The official language is the Serbian language of the Iekavian dialect. The Roman and Cyrillic alphabets have equal status.

Tourism

In 2010 there were 1,087,794 non-resident overnight tourist arrivals. The main countries of origin were: Serbia (314,836); Russia (150,194); Bosnia and Herzegovina (103,025); France (42,099).

Morocco

Mamlaka al-Maghrebia (Kingdom of Morocco)

Factsheet
Capital: Rabat
Population estimate, 2015: 34.38 m.
GNI per capita, 2014: (PPP$) 6,850
HDI/world rank, 2014: 0.628/126=
Internet domain extension: .ma

Civil Aviation

The national carrier is Royal Air Maroc, which in 2013 carried 5,856,000 passengers (5,170,000 on international flights). The major international airport is Mohammed V at Casablanca; there are eight other airports. Casablanca handled 7,186,331 passengers in 2012 (6,551,781 on international flights) and 50,567 tonnes of freight. Marrakesh (Menara) handled 3,373,475 passengers in 2012 and Agadir (Al Massira) 1,384,931.

Climate

Morocco is dominated by the Mediterranean climate which is made temperate by the influence of the Atlantic Ocean in the northern and southern parts of the country. Central Morocco is continental while the south is desert. Rabat, Jan. 55 °F (12.9 °C), July 72 °F (22.2 °C). Annual rainfall 23″ (564 mm). Agadir, Jan. 57 °F (13.9 °C), July 72 °F (22.2 °C). Annual rainfall 9″ (224 mm). Casablanca, Jan. 54 °F (12.2 °C), July 72 °F (22.2 °C). Annual rainfall 16″ (404 mm). Marrakesh, Jan. 52 °F (11.1 °C), July 84 °F (28.9 °C). Annual rainfall 10″ (239 mm). Tangier, Jan. 53 °F (11.7 °C), July 72 °F (22.2 °C). Annual rainfall 36″ (897 mm).

Constitution and Government

The ruling King is **Mohammed VI**, born on 21 Aug. 1963, married to Salma Bennani on 21 March 2002; succeeded on 23 July 1999, on the death of his father Hassan II, who reigned 1961–99. The King holds supreme civil and religious authority, the latter in his capacity of Emir-el-Muminin or Commander of the Faithful. He resides usually at Rabat, but occasionally in one of the other traditional capitals, Fez (founded in 808), Marrakesh (founded in 1062), or at Skhirat. In Feb. and March 2011, Morocco experienced popular protests echoing those occurring in other North African states. In response King Mohammed established a commission to bring about 'comprehensive constitutional reform'. The new constitution came into effect on 29 July 2011, ahead of the parliamentary elections 4 months later. The Kingdom of Morocco is a constitutional monarchy. Parliament consists of a Chamber of Representatives composed of 395 deputies (up from 325 for the 2007 elections) directly elected for 5-year terms. A referendum on 13 Sept. 1996 established a second Chamber of Counsellors, composed of 270 members serving 9-year terms, of whom 162 are elected by local councils, 81 by chambers of commerce and 27 by trade unions.

Currency

The unit of currency is the *dirham* (MAD) of 100 *centimes*, introduced in 1959.

Defence

Compulsory national military service was abolished in 2006. Defence expenditure in 2013 totalled US$3,730 m. (US$114 per capita), representing 3.5% of GDP.

Economy

Agriculture accounted for 16.4% of GDP in 2009, industry 28.6% and services 55.0%.

Labour

Of 9,927,728 persons in employment in 2006, 43.3% were engaged in agriculture, fishing and forestry, 12.4% in commerce, 12.3% in industry (including handicrafts), 8.0% in construction and public works, 5.4% in general administration and public services, 4.0% in transport and communication and 14.5% in other services. The unemployment rate in 2006 was 9.7%. In Nov. 2006 the minimum hourly wage for non-agricultural workers was DH9.66. The minimum wage for agricultural workers is set at DH50 per day. Morocco had 51,000 people living in slavery according to the Walk Free Foundation's 2013 *Global Slavery Index*.

Press

In 2008 there were 33 paid-for daily newspapers. The leading dailies are the Arabic-language *Al-Massae, Assabah* and *Al-Ahdath al-Maghrebia* and the French-language *Le Matin du Sahara et du Maghreb*.

Rail

In 2010 there were 2,109 km of railways, of which 1,284 km were electrified. Passenger-km travelled in 2009 came to 4.19 bn. and freight tonne-km to 4.11 bn. In 2003 the construction of two 38 km-long rail tunnels under the Straits of Gibraltar was agreed with Spain although there are ongoing talks as to the project's feasibility.

Religion

Islam is the established state religion. 99% of the population are Sunni Muslims. There is also a small Catholic minority.

Roads

In 2007 there were 57,799 km of classified roads, including 813 km of motorways and 11,251 km of main roads. By 2010 the motorway network had been extended to 1,042 km. In 2007 freight transport totalled 697 m. tonne-km. In 2007 there were 1,644,500 passenger cars in use, 525,300 lorries and vans and 22,800 motorcycles and mopeds. There were 58,924 road accidents in 2007 (3,838 fatalities).

Shipping

The busiest ports are Casablanca (which handled 26,572,000 tonnes of foreign cargo in 2008), Mohammedia, Nador, Tanger Med and Tangier. In Jan. 2009 there were 37 ships of 300 GT or over registered, totalling 341,000 GT.

Social Statistics

2008 estimates: births, 645,000; deaths, 184,000. Estimated rates, 2008 (per 1,000 population): birth, 20.4; death, 5.8. Annual population growth rate, 2000–08, 1.2%. Life expectancy at birth in 2013 was 69.1 years for males and 72.7 years for females. Infant mortality, 2010, 30 per 1,000 live births; fertility rate, 2008, 2.4 births per woman.

Telecommunications

In 2013 there were 2,925,000 main (fixed) telephone lines; mobile phone subscribers numbered 42,424,000 in 2013 (128.5 per 100 persons). The main telecommunication company is Maroc Telecom, which was privatized in 2001. Maroc Telecom's principal competitor is Méditel. 56.0% of the population were internet users in 2013. In June 2012 there were 4.6 m. Facebook users.

Territory and Population

Morocco is bounded by Algeria to the east and southeast, Mauritania to the south, the Atlantic Ocean to the northwest and the Mediterranean to the north. Excluding the Western Saharan territory claimed and retrieved since 1976 by Morocco, the area is 458,730 km². The population at the 2004 census (including Western Sahara) was 29,891,708; density (including Western Sahara), 42.1 per km². At the 2004 census Western Sahara had an area of 252,120 km² and a population of about 356,000. The Moroccan superficie is 710,850 km². The population was 58.8% urban in 2011. Morocco has 16 states (*wilaya'at*) divided further into 71 prefectures and provincial units. The chief cities (with populations in 1,000, 2004) are as follows: Casablanca, 2,934; Rabat, 1,623; Fez, 947; Marrakesh, 823; Agadir, 679; Tangier, 670; Meknès, 536; Oujda, 401; Kénitra, 359; Tétouan, 321; Safi, 285; Mohammedia, 189; Khouribga, 166; Béni Mellal, 163. The official language are Arabic, spoken by 65% of the population, and Berber (since July 2011).

Tourism

In 2010 there were a record 9,288,000 non-resident tourists (excluding same-day visitors), up from 8,341,000 in 2009 and 8,209,000 in 2008.

Mozambique

República de Moçambique (Republic of Mozambique)

Factsheet

Capital: Maputo
Population estimate, 2015: 27.98 m.
GNI per capita, 2014: (PPP$) 1,123
HDI/world rank, 2014: 0.416/180
Internet domain extension: .mz

Civil Aviation

There are international airports at Maputo and Beira. The national carrier is the state-owned Linhas Aéreas de Moçambique (LAM), which in 2013 carried 684,000 passengers (462,000 on domestic flights). In the same year it served ten domestic and five international destinations. In 2012 Maputo handled 839,390 passengers (454,236 on international flights) and Beira 164,324 (105,467 on domestic flights).

Climate

A humid tropical climate, with a dry season from June to Sept. In general, temperatures and rainfall decrease from north to south. Maputo, Jan. 78 °F (25.6 °C), July 65 °F (18.3 °C). Annual rainfall 30″ (760 mm). Beira, Jan. 82 °F (27.8 °C), July 69 °F (20.6 °C). Annual rainfall 60″ (1,522 mm).

Constitution and Government

On 2 Nov. 1990 the People's Assembly unanimously voted in favour of a new constitution, which came into force on 30 Nov. This changed the name of the state to 'Republic of Mozambique', legalized opposition parties, provided for universal secret elections and introduced a bill of rights including the right to strike, press freedoms and *habeas corpus*. The head of state is the *President*, directly elected for a 5-year term. Parliament is a 250-member *Assembly of the Republic*, elected for a 5-year term by proportional representation.

Currency

The unit of currency is the *new metical* (MZN) of 100 *centavos*, which replaced the *metical* (MZM) in July 2006. The currency was revalued at a rate of 1 new metical = 1,000 meticais.

Defence

The President of the Republic is C.-in-C. of the armed forces. Defence expenditure totalled US$75 m. in 2013 (US$3 per capita), representing 0.5% of GDP. Conscription for both men and women is for 2 years.

Economy

Agriculture accounted for 31.5% of GDP in 2009, industry 23.6% and services 44.9%.

Labour

The economically active population in 2010 totalled an estimated 11,261,000 (52% females). In 2007, 75% of the employed workforce were engaged in agriculture, forestry and fisheries. The leading occupations in non-agricultural sectors were commerce and services. Mozambique had 0.17 m. people living in slavery according to the Walk Free Foundation's 2013 *Global Slavery Index*.

Press

There were two well-established daily newspapers in 2008 (*Notícias* and *Diário* in Maputo and Beira respectively) with a combined circulation of 13,000.

Rail

The railway system consists of three separate networks, with principal routes on 1,067 mm gauge radiating from the ports of Maputo, Beira and Nacala. Total length in 2009 was 3,116 km, mainly on 1,067 mm gauge with some 762 mm gauge lines, but only 1,929 km was operational. In 2009 passenger-km travelled on the Mozambique Ports and Railways network came to 164 m. and freight tonne-km to 2,078 m.

Religion

According to estimates by the Pew Research Center's Forum on Religion & Public Life, in 2010 the population was 56.7% Christian and 18.0% Muslim; 7.4% were folk religionists and 17.9% religiously unaffiliated. Of the Christians in 2010, an estimated 51% were Catholics and 48% Protestants. In Feb. 2016 there were two cardinals.

Roads

In 2008 there were 29,323 km of roads, of which 17.9% were paved. There were 290,600 vehicles in 2008. There were 5,438 road accidents in 2008, with 1,529 fatalities. The flooding of early 2000 washed away at least one fifth of the country's main road linking the north and the south.

Shipping

The principal ports are Maputo, Beira, Nacala and Quelimane. In Jan. 2009 there were six ships of 300 GT or over registered, totalling 5,000 GT.

Social Statistics

2008 estimates: births, 877,000; deaths, 357,000. Estimated rates per 1,000 population, 2008: births, 39.2; deaths, 15.9. Infant mortality per 1,000 live births, 2010, 92. Life expectancy at birth, 2013, was 49.3 years for males and 51.0 years for females. Annual population growth rate, 2000–08, 2.6%; fertility rate, 2008, 5.1 births per woman.

Telecommunications

There were 5,971,000 mobile phone subscribers in 2009 (260.8 per 1,000 inhabitants), up from just 51,000 in 2000. Fixed telephone lines numbered 82,400 in 2009, down from 87,400 in 2002. In 2009 there were 92,000 mobile broadband subscriptions and 12,500 fixed broadband internet subscriptions. There were 248,000 Facebook users in June 2012.

Territory and Population

Mozambique is bounded east by the Indian Ocean, south by South Africa, southwest by Swaziland, west by South Africa and Zimbabwe and north by Zambia, Malawi and Tanzania. It has an area of 799,380 km^2 (308,642 sq. miles) and a population, according to the 2007 census, of 20,252,223 (10,505,533 females), giving a density of 25.3 per km^2. In 2011, 39.2% of the population were urban. The capital is Maputo (2007 population, 1,094,628). Other large cities (with 2007 populations) are Matola (671,556), Nampula (471,717) and Beira (431,583). The main ethnolinguistic groups are the Makua/Lomwe (52% of the population), the Tsonga/Ronga (24%), the Nyanja/Sena (12%) and Shona (6%). Portuguese remains the official language, but vernaculars are widely spoken throughout the country. English is also widely spoken.

Tourism

Tourism is a potential growth area for the country. There were 3,110,000 non-resident visitors in 2009 (2,617,000 in 2008).

Myanmar

Pyidaunzu Thanmăda Myăma Nainngandaw (Republic of the Union of Myanmar)

Factsheet

Capitals: Naypyidaw/Pyinmana (Administrative and Legislative), Yangon/Rangoon (Commercial)
Population estimate, 2015: 53.90 m.
GNI per capita, 2014: (PPP$) 3,998
HDI/world rank, 2014: 0.536/148
Internet domain extension: .mm

Civil Aviation

The flag carrier is Myanmar National Airlines (Myanma Airways until 2014). The main airport is Yangon International Airport. In 2010 there were international flights to Bangkok, Beijing, Guangzhou, Hanoi, Kolkata, Kuala Lumpur, Kunming, Singapore and Taipei. In 2012 scheduled airline traffic of Myanmar-based carriers flew 1.0 m. km; passenger-km totalled 117.1 m. in the same year.

Climate

The climate is equatorial in coastal areas, changing to tropical monsoon over most of the interior, but humid temperate in the extreme north, where there is a more significant range of temperature and a dry season lasting from Nov. to April. In coastal parts, the dry season is shorter. Very heavy rains occur in the monsoon months May to Sept. Yangon, Jan. 77 °F (25 °C), July 80 °F (26.7 °C). Annual rainfall 104″ (2,616 mm). Sittwe, Jan. 70 °F (21.1 °C), July 81 °F (27.2 °C). Annual rainfall 206″ (5,154 mm). Mandalay, Jan. 68 °F (20 °C), July 85 °F (29.4 °C). Annual rainfall 33″ (828 mm).

Constitution and Government

In Nov. 1997 the country's ruling generals changed the name of the government to the *State Peace and Development Council* (SPDC). It nominally ceded power to an elected president in Feb. 2011 and was abolished a month later. In May 2008 an army-drafted constitution won 92.5% support in a referendum. The constitution specified that multi-party elections should be scheduled for 2010; 25% of parliamentary seats were automatically allocated to the military. It called for the creation of a National Defence and Security Council, dominated by military appointments, with the power to suspend the constitution under certain circumstances. It also laid out rules that would ban opposition leader Aung San Suu Kyi from holding public office. The constitution was formally adopted on 30 May 2008. The previous constitution, dating from 3 Jan. 1974, had been suspended since 1988. Amendments to the Political Party Registration law in Oct. 2011 now allow Aung San Suu Kyi to hold public office, although under the current constitution she is not eligible to stand in the presidential elections expected to take place in Oct. or Nov. 2015. The 440-member lower chamber, the House of Representatives (*Pythu Hluttaw*), has 330 elected seats with 110 appointed and the 224-member upper chamber, the House of Nationalities (*Amyotha Hluttaw*), has 168 elected seats with 56 appointed. Parliament convened in Jan. 2011 for the first time since 1988.

Currency

The unit of currency is the *kyat* (MMK) of 100 *pyas*.

Defence

The President of the Republic is C.-in-C. of the armed forces. Defence expenditure totalled US$75 m. in 2013 (US$3 per capita), representing 0.5% of GDP. Conscription for both men and women is for 2 years.

Economy

In 2009 agriculture accounted for 38.1% of GDP, industry 24.5% and services 37.4%.

Labour

The estimated labour force in 2013 was 31,670,000. Agriculture provides employment to two-thirds of the population. In 2001 there were 398,300 persons aged 18 years and over registered as unemployed. Myanmar had 0.38 m. people living in slavery according to the Walk Free Foundation's 2013 *Global Slavery Index*, the ninth highest total of any country.

Press

There were six daily newspapers in 2008, with a combined circulation of 420,000. In 2013 the publication of private daily papers was permitted for the first time in nearly 50 years.

Rail

In 2005 there were 4,809 km of route on metre gauge. Passenger-km travelled in 2006–07 came to 5,307 m. and freight tonne-km to 887 m.

Religion

In 2010 an estimated 80.1% of the population-mainly Bamars, Shans, Mons, Rakhines and some Kayins-were Buddhists according to the Pew Research Center's Forum on Religion & Public Life. The Pew Research Center estimated that a further 7.8% were Christians (mainly Protestants), 5.8% were folk religionists, 4.0% Muslims and 1.7% Hindus (the last two being mainly people of Indian origin). In Feb. 2016 the Roman Catholic church had one cardinal.

Roads

There were 27,000 km of roads in 2005, of which 11.9% were surfaced. In 2005 there were 194,411 passenger cars, 54,482 vans and lorries, 17,985 buses and coaches, and 640,313 motorcycles and mopeds. There were 1,638 deaths as a result of road accidents in 2007.

Shipping

There are nearly 100 km of navigable canals. The Irrawaddy is navigable up to Myitkyina, 1,450 km from the sea, and its tributary, the Chindwin, is navigable for 630 km. The Irrawaddy delta has approximately 3,000 km of navigable water. The Salween, the Attaran and the G'yne provide about 400 km of navigable waters around Moulmein. In Jan. 2009 merchant shipping totalled 140,000 GT (vessels of 300 GT and over). In 2006–07, 26.33 m. passengers and 4.28 m. tonnes of freight were carried on inland waterways. The ocean-going fleet of the state-owned Myanma Five Star Line in 2006–07 comprised 26 vessels; in addition there were eight chartered vessels. In 2006–07, 51,373 passengers and 10,954,800 tonnes of seaborne cargo were transported coastally and overseas. Myanmar's main port is Yangon, which handles about 90% of the country's imports and exports.

Social Statistics

2008 estimates: births, 1,020,000; deaths, 496,000. Estimated birth rate in 2008 was 21 per 1,000 population; estimated death rate, 10. Annual population growth rate, 2000–08, 0.8%. Life expectancy at birth, 2013, was 63.1 years for males and 67.2 years for females. Infant mortality, 2010, 50 per 1,000 live births; fertility rate, 2008, 2.3 births per woman.

Telecommunications

In 2011 there were 521,100 landline telephone subscriptions (equivalent to 10.8 per 1,000 inhabitants) and 1,243,600 mobile phone subscriptions (or 25.7 per 1,000 inhabitants). In 2011, 1.0% of the population were internet users. Following decades of military rule, Myanmar has one of Asia's lowest phone penetration rates.

Territory and Population

Myanmar is bounded in the east by China, Laos and Thailand, and west by the Indian Ocean, Bangladesh and India. Three parallel mountain ranges run from north to south; the Western Yama or Rakhine Yama, the Bagu Yama and the Shaun Plateau. The total area of the Union is 676,590 km^2 (261,230 sq. miles), including 23,070 km^2 (8,910 sq. miles) of inland water. In 2014 the census population (provisional) was 51,419,420; density, 78.7 per km^2. In 2011, 34.3% of the population lived in urban areas. The administrative capital is Naypyidaw (Pyinmana); its provisional census population was 1,158,367 in 2014. The largest city is Yangon (Rangoon), with a provisional population of 5,209,541 in 2014. Other leading towns are Mandalay (2014 provisional population of 1,225,133), Bago (Pegu), Hpa-an (Pha-an), Taunggyi, Monywa and Myitkyina.

Tourism

In 2011 there were 391,000 non-resident tourists (193,000 in 2008); spending by tourists totalled US$293 m. in 2011.

Namibia

Republic of Namibia

Factsheet
Capital: Windhoek
Population estimate, 2015: 2.46 m.
GNI per capita, 2014: (PPP$) 9,418
HDI/world rank, 2014: 0.628/126=
Internet domain extension: .na

Civil Aviation

The national carrier is the state-owned Air Namibia, which in 2013 carried 458,000 passengers (381,000 on international flights). In the same year it served six domestic and nine international destinations. In 2012 the major airport, Windhoek's Hosea Kutako International, handled 814,890 passengers (764,384 on international flights). Eros is used mainly for domestic flights.

Climate

The rainfall increases steadily from less than 50 mm in the west and southwest up to 600 mm in the Caprivi Strip. The main rainy season is from Jan. to March, with lesser showers from Sept. to Dec. Namibia is the driest African country south of the Sahara.

Constitution and Government

On 9 Feb. 1990 with a unanimous vote the Constituent Assembly approved the Constitution which stipulated a multi-party republic, an independent judiciary and an executive *President* who may serve a maximum of two 5-year terms. The constitution became effective on 12 March 1990 and was amended in 1999 to allow President Sam Nujoma to stand for a third term in office. The bicameral legislature consists of a 104-seat *National Assembly*, 96 members of which are elected for 5-year terms by proportional representation and up to eight appointed by the president by virtue of position or special expertise, and a 26-seat *National Council* consisting of two members from each Regional Council elected for 6-year terms.

Currency

The unit of currency is the *Namibia dollar* (NAD) of 100 *cents*, introduced on 14 Sept. 1993 and pegged to the South African rand. The rand is also legal tender at parity.

Defence

In 2013 defence expenditure totalled US$458 m. (US$210 per capita), representing 3.6% of GDP.

Economy

Agriculture accounted for 8.0% of GDP in 2010, industry 30.0% and services 62.0%.

Labour

Of 690,019 people in employment in 2013, 215,311 were engaged in agriculture, forestry and fishing; 79,391 in wholesale and retail trade; 57,668 in private households; 47,859 in construction; 41,797 in education; 36,767 in accommodation and food service activities; and 35,160 in administrative and support service activities. The unemployment rate in 2013 was 29.6%. Namibia had 16,000 people living in slavery according to the Walk Free Foundation's 2013 *Global Slavery Index*.

Press

There were four daily newspapers in 2008 with a combined circulation of 55,000.

Rail

The Namibia system connects with the main system of the South African railways at Ariamsvlei. The total length of the line inside Namibia was 2,628 km of 1,065 mm gauge in 2005.

Religion

According to estimates by the Pew Research Center's Forum on Religion & Public Life, in 2010 the population was 97.5% Christian (mainly Protestants) with 1.9% not having any religious affiliation.

Roads

In 2011 the road network covered 45,645 km. In 2008 there were 107,800 passenger cars in use and 117,400 lorries and vans. There were 368 deaths as a result of road accidents in 2007.

Shipping

Walvis Bay, the busiest port, handled 4,960,000 tonnes of cargo in 2007–08. There is a harbour at !Nami = Nüs (formerly Lüderitz) which handles mainly fishing vessels. Merchant shipping totalled 3,000 GT in Jan. 2009.

Social Statistics

Estimates, 2008: births, 59,000; deaths, 18,000. Estimated birth rate in 2008 was 27.6 per 1,000 population; estimated death rate, 8.6. Expectation of life, 2013: males, 61.7 years; females, 67.1. Annual population growth rate, 2000–08, 1.9%; infant mortality, 2010, 29 per 1,000 live births. The fertility rate dropped from 5.5 births per woman in 1994 to 3.4 births per woman in 2008.

Telecommunications

Telecom Namibia is the responsible corporation. In 2013 there were 183,000 main (fixed) telephone lines and 2,728,000 mobile phone subscribers (118.4 per 100 persons). An estimated 13.9% of the population were internet users in 2013. In June 2012 there were 172,000 Facebook users.

Territory and Population

Namibia is bounded in the north by Angola and Zambia, west by the Atlantic Ocean, south and southeast by South Africa and east by Botswana. The Caprivi Strip (Caprivi Region), about 300 km long, extends eastwards up to the Zambezi river, projecting into Zambia and Botswana and touching Zimbabwe. The area, including the Caprivi Strip and Walvis Bay, is 825,615 km^2. South Africa transferred Walvis Bay to Namibian jurisdiction on 1 March 1994. 2011 census population, 2,113,077 (1,091,165 females); density 2.6 per km^2. In 2011, 38.6% of the population were urban. The largest ethnic group is the Ovambo (about half the population), followed by the Kavango, Damara and Herero. Namibia is administratively divided into 14 regions. Towns with populations over 10,000 (2011): Windhoek, 325,858; Rundu, 63,431; Walvis Bay, 62,096; Swakopmund, 44,725; Oshakati, 36,541; Rehoboth, 28,843; Katima Mulilo, 28,362; Otjiwarongo, 28,249; Ondangwa, 22,822; Okahandja, 22,639; Keetmanshoop, 20,977; Ongwediva, 20,260; Helao Nafidi, 19,375; Tsumeb, 19,275; Gobabis, 19,101; Grootfontein, 16,632; Lüderitz (renamed !Nami≠Nüs in 2013), 12,537; Mariental, 12,478. English is the official language. Afrikaans and German are also spoken.

Tourism

In 2011 there were 1,027,000 non-resident tourists who spent US$645 m. Tourist numbers rose every year from 2003 to 2011.

Nauru

Ripublik Naoero (Republic of Nauru)

Factsheet
Population estimate, 2015: 10,000
GDP per capita, 2014: US$17,857
Internet domain extension: .nr

Civil Aviation

The only airport is Nauru International Airport. The national carrier, Nauru Airlines, is a wholly-owned government subsidiary. In 2017 it flew to Brisbane, Honiara, Majuro, Nadi, Pohnpei and Tarawa.

Climate

A tropical climate, tempered by sea breezes, but with a high and irregular rainfall, averaging 82″ (2,060 mm). Average temperature, Jan. 81 °F (27.2 °C), July 82 °F (27.8 °C). Annual rainfall 75″ (1,862 mm).

Constitution and Government

A Legislative Council was inaugurated on 31 Jan. 1966. The constitution was promulgated on 29 Jan. 1968 and was amended on 17 May 1968. A 19-member Parliament (18 prior to the June 2013 election) is elected on a 3-yearly basis.

Currency

The Australian dollar is in use.

Religion

In 2010 an estimated 79.0% of the population were Christians according to the Pew Research Center's Forum on Religion & Public Life, 8.1% folk religionists and 4.5% religiously unaffiliated.

Roads

There is a sealed road circling the island 19 km long, plus other roads running inland.

Shipping

Deep offshore moorings can accommodate medium-size vessels. Shipping coming to the island consists of vessels under charter to the phosphate industry or general purpose vessels bringing cargo by way of imports.

Social Statistics

2011 births, 370; deaths, 75. Infant deaths (2007), 12. Annual population growth rate, 1998–2008, 0.1%; fertility rate, 2008, 2.9 births per woman.

Telecommunications

There were 6,800 main telephone lines in operation in 2012.

Territory and Population

Nauru is a coral island surrounded by a reef situated 0.32′ S. lat. and 166° 56′ E. long. Area, 21.2 km^2 (8.2 sq. miles). At the 2011 census the population (provisional) totalled 10,084 (5,105 males). Population density, 476 per km^2. In 2011, 94% of the population were indigenous Nauruans. The *de facto* capital is Yaren.

Nepal

Sanghiya Loktantrik Ganatantra Nepal (Federal Democratic Republic of Nepal)

Factsheet
Capital: Kathmandu
Population estimate, 2015: 28.51 m.
GNI per capita, 2014: (PPP$) 2,311
HDI/world rank, 2014: 0.548/145=
Internet domain extension: .np

Civil Aviation

There is an international airport (Tribhuvan) at Kathmandu. The national carrier is the state-owned Nepal Airlines (formerly known as Royal Nepal Airlines). In 2012 Kathmandu handled 4,444,529 passengers (2,854,933 on international flights) and 13,198 tonnes of freight. In 2012 scheduled airline traffic of Nepali-based carriers flew 6.4 m. km; passenger-km totalled 608.1 m. in the same year.

Climate

Varies from cool summers and severe winters in the north to sub-tropical summers and mild winters in the south. The rainfall is high, with maximum amounts from June to Sept., but conditions are very dry from Nov. to Jan. Kathmandu, Jan. 10 °C, July, 25 °C. Average annual rainfall, 1,424 mm.

Constitution and Government

Following years of political turbulence an interim constitution was approved in Dec. 2006, effectively removing King Gyanendra as the head of the state. On 23 Dec. 2007 the interim government declared the establishment of the Federal Democratic Republic of Nepal, with the abolition of the monarchy approved by parliament 5 days later. This change entered into force on 28 May 2008 at the first meeting of a 601-member *Constituent Assembly* (with 240 seats filled on a first-past-the-post system, 335 filled through proportional representation and 26 nominated by the cabinet). The Constituent Assembly was charged with drafting a new constitution but failed to do so even though its deadline was extended several times. Elections to a new Constituent Assembly were held in Nov. 2013. The deadline for promulgation of a new constitution in Jan. 2015 was also missed owing to more delays in the drafting process.

Currency

The unit of currency is the *Nepalese rupee* (NPR) of 100 *paisas*. 50 *paisas* = 1 *mohur*.

Defence

The then King was formerly commander-in-chief of the armed forces, but he was stripped of the position in May 2006. The cabinet now has the power to appoint the army chief. Defence expenditure in 2013 totalled US$238 m. (US$8 per capita), representing 1.2% of GDP. As at 31 Jan. 2013, 4,462 personnel (including 3,677 troops) were deployed in UN peacekeeping operations.

Economy

Agriculture, forestry and fishing contributed 31.5% to GDP in 2009–10; followed by trade, restaurants and hotels, 14.7%; finance and real estate, 11.6%; and services, 11.1%.

Labour

The estimated labour force in 2008 totalled 12,032,000 (47% males). Nepal had 0.26 m. people living in slavery according to the Walk Free Foundation's 2013 *Global Slavery Index*.

Press

In 2008 there were 298 daily newspapers, including the official English-language *Rising Nepal*, 25 bi-weeklies, 1,442 weeklies and 273 fortnightlies. Press censorship was relaxed in 1991, but following the imposition of a state of emergency in 2005 the press was subjected to total censorship.

Rail

51 km (762 mm gauge) connected Jayanagar on the North Eastern Indian Railway with Janakpur and Bijalpura. It shut down in 2014 but is expected to reopen during 2018 after conversion to 1,676 mm gauge. Proposals for a 77-km long metro system in Kathmandu were submitted in 2012.

Religion

Nepal is a Hindu state. Hinduism was the religion of 80.7% of the people in 2010 according to estimates by the Pew Research Center's Forum on Religion & Public Life, with Buddhists comprising 10.3% and Muslims 4.6%. An estimated 3.7% of the population in 2010 were folk religionists. There is also a small Christian minority.

Roads

In 2006 there were 16,834 km of roads, of which 17% were paved.

Social Statistics

2008 estimates: births, 731,000; deaths, 185,000. Estimated rates per 1,000 population, 2008: births, 25.4; deaths, 6.4. Annual population growth rate, 2000–08, 2.1%. Expectation of life was 67.3 years for males and 69.6 years for females in 2013. Infant mortality, 2010, 41 per 1,000 live births; fertility rate, 2008, 2.9 births per woman.

Telecommunications

In Dec. 2011 there were 845,542 main (fixed) telephone lines in Nepal and mobile phone subscribers numbered 13,354,000 (49.2 per 100 persons). An estimated 13.3% of the population were internet users in 2013. In March 2012 there were 1.4 m. Facebook users.

Territory and Population

Nepal is bounded in the north by China (Tibet) and the east, south and west by India. Area 147,181 km²; 2011 census population, 26,494,504 (13,645,463 females); density 180.0 per km². In 2011, 19.2% of the population were urban. The country is divided into five developmental regions and 75 administrative districts. Capital, Kathmandu; population (2011) 1,003,285. Other towns include (2011 census population): Pokhara, 264,991; Lalitpur, 226,728; Biratnagar, 204,949; Bharatpur, 147,777. The indigenous people are of Tibetan origin with a considerable Hindu admixture. The Gurkha clan became predominant in 1559 and has given its name to men from all parts of Nepal. There are 18 ethnic groups, the largest being: Newars, Indians, Tibetans, Gurungs, Mogars, Tamangs, Bhotias, Rais, Limbus and Sherpas. The official language is Nepalese but there are 20 new languages divided into numerous dialects.

Tourism

In 2012 there were a record 803,000 non-resident tourists (up from 736,000 in 2010 and 527,000 in 2007). In 2011, 32% of tourists came from South Asia, 29% from Europe and 27% from East Asia and the Pacific. Tourist receipts amounted to US$379 m. in 2012.

Netherlands

Koninkrijk der Nederlanden (Kingdom of the Netherlands)

Factsheet

Capital: Amsterdam
Seat of government: The Hague
Population estimate, 2015: 16.93 m.
GNI per capita, 2014: (PPP$) 45,435
HDI/world rank, 2014: 0.922/5
Internet domain extension: .nl

Civil Aviation

There are international airports at Amsterdam (Schiphol), Rotterdam, Maastricht and Eindhoven. The Royal Dutch Airlines (KLM) was founded on 7 Oct. 1919. In Oct. 2003 it merged with Air France to form Air France-KLM, in which the French state owns a 15.7% stake. Airport passenger traffic reached 53.9 m. in 2011: Amsterdam handled 49.8 m. passengers, Eindhoven 2.6 m. and Rotterdam 1.1 m.

Climate

A cool temperate maritime climate, marked by mild winters and cool summers, but with occasional continental influences. Coastal temperatures vary from 37 °F (3 °C) in winter to 61 °F (16 °C) in summer, but inland the winters are slightly colder and the summers slightly warmer. Rainfall is least in the months Feb. to May, but inland there is a well-defined summer maximum in July and Aug. The Hague, Jan. 37 °F (2.7 °C), July 61 °F (16.3 °C). Annual rainfall 32.8″ (820 mm). Amsterdam, Jan. 36 °F (2.3 °C), July 62 °F (16.5 °C). Annual rainfall 34″ (850 mm). Rotterdam, Jan. 36.5 °F (2.6 °C), July 62 °F (16.6 °C). Annual rainfall 32″ (800 mm).

Constitution and Government

According to the Constitution (promulgated 1815; last revision, 2005), the Kingdom consists of the Netherlands and its overseas countries and territories. Their relations are regulated by the 'Statute' for the Kingdom, which came into force on 29 Dec. 1954 and was revised on 10 Oct. 2010. The Netherlands is a constitutional and hereditary monarchy. The royal succession is in the direct female or male line in order of birth. The reigning King is **Willem-Alexander**, succeeded to the crown on 30 April 2013, on the abdication of his mother. The monarch receives an allowance from the civil list. The central executive power of the State rests with the Crown, while the central legislative power is vested in the Crown and Parliament (the *States-General*), consisting of two Chambers. The upper *First Chamber* is composed of 75 members, elected by the members of the Provincial States. The 150-member *Second Chamber* is directly elected by proportional representation for 4-year terms. Members of the States-General must be Netherlands subjects of 18 years of age or over. The Hague is the seat of the Court, government and Parliament; Amsterdam is the capital. The *Council of State*, appointed by the Crown, is composed of a vice-president and not more than 28 members.

Currency

On 1 Jan. 1999 the euro (EUR) became the legal currency in the Netherlands at the irrevocable conversion rate of 2.20371 guilders to 1 euro. The euro, which consists of 100 cents, has been in circulation since 1 Jan. 2002. On the introduction of the euro there was a 'dual circulation' period before the guilder ceased to be legal tender on 28 Jan. 2002.

Defence

Conscription ended on 30 Aug. 1996. The total strength of the armed forces in 2011 was 37,368. Reserves: 3,189. In 2013 defence expenditure totalled US$10,350 m. (US$616 per capita), representing 1.3% of GDP.

Economy

Services accounted for 76% of GDP in 2012, industry 22% and agriculture 2%.

Labour

The total labour force (15–65 years) in 2011 was 7,811,000 persons (3,492,000 women) of whom 419,000 (195,000 women) unemployed. Of the 7,392,000 employed persons, 5,709,000 were in permanent employment, 606,000 were in flexible employment and 1,077,000 were self-employed. Nearly a third of all 15–65-year-old women were working between 20 and 35 h per week. By education level, the 2011 employed labour force included (in 1,000): primary education, 361; junior secondary education, 1,309; senior secondary education, 3,130; university education, 2,524 (bachelor, 1,639; masters or PhD, 885). The unemployment rate was 6.7% in Dec. 2014 (unchanged since 2013 as a whole but up from 5.3% in 2012).

Press

In 2008 there were 35 daily newspapers with a combined circulation of 5,309,000. The most widely read daily is *De Telegraaf*, with an average daily circulation of 670,000 copies in 2008. In the 2013 *World Press Freedom Index* compiled by Reporters Without Borders, the Netherlands was ranked second out of 179 countries.

Rail

All railways are run by the mixed company 'N.V. Nederlandse Spoorwegen'. Route length in 2011 was 3,013 km. Passenger-km travelled in 2009 came to 16.32 bn. Goods transported in 2010 totalled 36 m. tonnes. There is a metro (44 km) and tram/light rail network (154 km) in Amsterdam and in Rotterdam (76 km and 67 km). Tram/light rail networks operate in The Hague (128 km) and Utrecht (22 km). A tram link between Maastricht and Hasselt in Belgium is currently under construction; it is expected to open in 2017.

Religion

Population aged 12 years and over in 2009 was: Roman Catholics, 27%; Protestant Church in the Netherlands, 9%; Calvinist, 3%; other creeds, 10%; no religion, 44%. The Dutch Reformed Church merged with the Reformed Churches in the Netherlands and the Evangelical Lutheran Church in the Kingdom of the Netherlands in May 2004 to form the Protestant Church in the Netherlands—now the second largest church body in the country. The Roman Catholic Church has one archdiocese (of Utrecht) and six dioceses. In Feb. 2016 there were two Roman Catholic cardinals. The Old Catholic Church of the Netherlands has one Archbishop (of Utrecht), one Bishop (of Haarlem)

and 26 parishes. There were 1.0 m. Muslims in 2010 according to estimates by the Pew Research Center's Forum on Religion & Public Life; there were also small numbers of Hindus, Buddhists and Jews.

Roads

In 2008 the total length of the Netherlands road network was 136,135 km (including 2,637 km of motorways). Number of vehicles (2008): private cars, 7.39 m.; trucks and vans, 1.07 m.; motorcycles and mopeds, 1.37 m. There were 750 fatalities as a result of road accidents in 2008, equivalent to 4.6 fatalities per 100,000 population (one of the lowest death rates in road accidents of any industrialized country).

Shipping

In Jan. 2009 there were 810 ships of 300 GT or over registered, totalling 7,428,000 GT. Of the 810 vessels registered, 593 were general cargo ships, 83 container ships, 47 passenger ships, 43 oil tankers, 20 chemical tankers, 18 liquid gas tankers and six bulk carriers. The Dutch-controlled fleet comprised 578 vessels of 1,000 GT or over in Jan. 2009, of which 426 were under the Dutch flag and 152 under foreign flags. Total throughput at Rotterdam, the busiest port in the Netherlands and Europe and the third busiest in the world, was 386,957,000 tonnes in 2009 (down from a record 421,136,000 tonnes in 2008).

Social Statistics

Births, 2012: 175,959; deaths, 140,813. 2012 rates per 1,000 population: birth, 10.8; death, 8.4. Annual population growth rate, 2007–12, 0.5%. In 2009 the suicide rate per 100,000 population was 9.3 (men, 13.1; women, 5.5). In 2012 the average age for marrying was 37.0 years for males and 33.8 for females. Expectation of life, 2012, was 79.2 years for males and 82.9 for females. Infant mortality, 2012, 3.7 per 1,000 live births; fertility rate, 2012, 1.8 births per woman. Percentage of population by age in 2010: 0–14 years, 17.7%; 15–64, 67.0%; 65 and over, 15.3%. The Netherlands received 11,590 asylum applications in 2011, down from 13,333 in 2010. In 2001 the Netherlands became the first country to legalize same-sex marriage.

Telecommunications

In 2008 there were 7,317,000 main (fixed) telephone lines. In the same year mobile phone subscribers numbered 20,627,000 (1,248.0 per 1,000 persons). There were 14.3 m. internet users in 2008. The Netherlands has one of the highest fixed broadband penetration rates, at 38.1 subscribers per 100 inhabitants in Dec. 2010. In March 2012 there were 5.8 m. Facebook users.

Territory and Population

The Netherlands is bounded in the north and west by the North Sea, south by Belgium and east by Germany. The area is 41,543 km^2, of which 33,756 km^2 is land. Projects of sea-flood control and land reclamation (polders) by the construction of dams and drainage schemes have continued since 1920. More than a quarter of the country is below sea level. The population was 13,060,115 at the census of 1971 and 16,829,289 on 1 Jan. 2014. Population growth in 2013, 0.3%. Ongoing 'rolling' censuses have replaced the former decennial counts. In 2011, 83.3% of the population lived in urban areas. Urban agglomerations as at 1 Jan. 2010: Amsterdam, 1,053,413; Rotterdam, 996,183; The Hague, 633,201; Utrecht, 441,866; Eindhoven, 327,245; Leiden, 251,436; Dordrecht, 236,285; Tilburg, 227,614; Groningen, 205,814; Heerlen, 204,825; Haarlem, 197,660; Amersfoort, 173,674; Breda, 173,299; 's-Hertogenbosch, 165,007; Nijmegen, 162,963; Enschede, 157,052; Apeldoorn, 155,726; Arnhem, 148,513; Sittard-Geleen, 137,495; Zwolle, 119,030; Maastricht, 118,533; Leeuwarden, 94,073. Dutch is the official language. Frisian, spoken as a first language by 2.2% of the population, is also recognized as an official language in the northern province of Friesland.

Tourism

Tourism is a major sector of the economy. In 2011 international tourist spending totalled €10,400 m. A total of 11,299,000 non-resident tourists stayed in holiday accommodation in 2011 (up from 10,883,000 in 2010 and 9,921,000 in 2009).

New Zealand

Aotearoa

Factsheet

Capital: Wellington
Population estimate, 2015: 4.53 m.
GNI per capita, 2014: (PPP$) 32,689
HDI/world rank, 2014: 0.913/9=
Internet domain extension: .nz

Civil Aviation

There are international airports at Wellington, Auckland and Christchurch, with Auckland International being the main airport. The national carrier is Air New Zealand, which was privatized in 1989 but then renationalized in 2001, although in Nov. 2013 the government reduced its stake from 73% to 53%. There were 4,499 aircraft registered in Dec. 2011. In 2011 there were 1,019,685 domestic and international aircraft movements. A total of 21,852,000 passenger-km were flown in 2010 by New Zealand-based carriers on scheduled services.

Climate

Lying in the cool temperate zone, New Zealand enjoys very mild winters for its latitude owing to its oceanic situation, and only the extreme south has cold winters. The situation of the mountain chain produces much sharper climatic contrasts between east and west than in a north-south direction. The highest extreme temperature recorded in 2011 was 41.3 °C, at Timaru on 6 Feb., and the lowest −10.2 °C, at Manapouri on 26 July.

Constitution and Government

Definition was given to the status of New Zealand by the (Imperial) Statute of Westminster of Dec. 1931, which had received the antecedent approval of the New Zealand Parliament in July 1931. The Governor-General's assent was given to the Statute of Westminster Adoption Bill on 25 Nov. 1947. The powers, duties and responsibilities of the *Governor-General* and the *Executive Council* are set out in Royal Letters Patent and Instructions thereunder of 11 May 1917. In the execution of the powers vested in him the Governor-General must be guided by the advice of the Executive Council. Parliament is the *House of Representatives*, consisting of 121 members, elected by universal adult suffrage on the mixed-member-proportional system (MMP) for 3-year terms.

Currency

The monetary unit is the *New Zealand dollar* (NZD), of 100 *cents*.

Defence

The New Zealand Defence Force consists of three services: the Royal New Zealand Navy, the New Zealand Army and the Royal New Zealand Air Force. New Zealand forces serve abroad in Australia, Iraq and Singapore, and with UN peacekeeping missions. Defence expenditure in 2013 totalled US$2,715 m. (US$622 per capita), representing 1.5% of GDP.

Economy

Finance and real estate contributed 27.6% to GDP in 2008–09; followed by trade and hotels, 15.0%; manufacturing, 13.2%; services, 11.9%; transport and communications, 10.7%; and agriculture, forestry and mining, 7.2%. According to the anti-corruption organization *Transparency International*, New Zealand ranked equal first in a 2013 survey of the countries with the least corruption in business and government. It received 91 out of 100 in the annual index. New Zealand gave US$457 m. in international aid in 2013, equivalent to 0.26% of GNI (compared to the UN target of 0.7%).

Labour

There were 2,142,500 persons employed in the year ending Sept. 2007 (1,664,000 full-time and 478,500 part-time). The largest number of employed people worked in the education, health and community, and other services area (27.7%); followed by wholesale and retail trade, restaurants and hotels (22.4%); and finance and insurance, property and business services (14.7%). Average unemployment total for the year ending Sept. 2007 was 81,400. The unemployment rate in 2014 was 5.7%.

Press

In 2008 there were 22 paid-for daily newspapers with a combined circulation of 653,000. The *New Zealand Herald,* published in Auckland, had the largest daily circulation in 2008, with an average of 187,000 copies. Other major dailies are *The Dominion Post* and *The Press*, with circulations of 94,000 and 87,000 copies respectively. In 2008 there were also three Sunday newspapers. There were four paid-for non-dailies and 109 free non-dailies in 2007.

Rail

The national rail operator is Kiwi Rail. In 2008–09 KiwiRail rolling stock included 231 diesel, electric and shunting locomotives, 4,215 freight wagons, 50 passenger carriages and 16 non-passenger coaches. In 1994 a 24-h freight link was introduced between Auckland and Christchurch. In 2011, 4,128 km of 1,067 mm gauge railway was open for traffic (504 km electrified). In 2008–09 KiwiRail carried 4.0 m. tonnes of freight and 12.4 m. passengers. Total income in the financial year 2008–09 was NZ$636.6 m. and total expense NZ$573.3 m.

Religion

No direct state aid is given to any form of religion. According to the Pew Research Center's Forum on Religion & Public Life, in 2010 the population was an estimated 57.0% Christian with a further 36.6% being religiously unaffiliated and 2.1% Hindu. Of the Christians in 2010, an estimated 70% were Protestants and 25% Catholics. Anglicans are the largest denomination, with Roman Catholics second and Presbyterians third. For the Church of England the country is divided into seven dioceses, with a separate bishopric (Aotearoa) for the Maori. The Roman Catholic Church is divided into one Archdiocese (Wellington) and five suffragan dioceses. In Feb. 2016 there were two cardinals.

Roads

Total length of roads in 2007 was 93,748 km (65.4% paved), including 172 km of motorways. There were 10,893 km of highways, main or national roads. At 30 June 2008 motor vehicles licensed numbered 4,125,932, of which 2,788,938 were passenger cars and vans. In addition there were 577,684 trailers and caravans, 519,992 commercial vehicles, and 130,213 motorcycles and mopeds. In 2007 there were 422 deaths in road accidents.

Shipping

In Jan. 2009 there were 29 ships of 300 GT or over registered, totalling 150,000 GT. The busiest port is Tauranga, which handled a record 13,748,000 tonnes of cargo in 2009–10 (up from 13,458,000 tonnes in 2008–09).

Social Statistics

Live births in 2013: 58,717; deaths, 29,568. Birth rate, 2013, 13.1 per 1,000 population; death rate, 6.6 per 1,000 population; infant mortality rate, 4.4 per 1,000 live births. Annual population growth rate, 2011, 0.7%. In 2010 there were 522 suicides (380 males). Expectation of life, 2010–12: males, 79.3 years; females, 83.0. Fertility rate, 2013, 2.0 births per woman. New Zealand legalized same-sex marriage in Aug. 2013. In 2013 there were 88,235 permanent and long-term immigrants (84,402 in 2012) and 80,328 permanent and long-term emigrants (87,593 in 2012).

Telecommunications

The predominant telecommunications service provider is Spark New Zealand (or 'Spark'), known as Telecom New Zealand until Aug. 2014. Telecom New Zealand had been formed in 1987 and privatized in 1990. The largest mobile phone operators are Vodafone New Zealand and Spark. In 2013 there were 1,850,000 main (fixed) telephone lines. In the same year active mobile phone subscriptions numbered 4,766,000 (1,057.8 per 1,000 persons). An estimated 82.8% of the population were internet users in 2013. The fixed broadband penetration rate was 24.9 subscribers per 100 inhabitants in Dec. 2010. In Dec. 2011 there were 2.1 m. Facebook users.

Territory and Population

New Zealand lies southeast of Australia in the south Pacific, Wellington being 1,983 km from Sydney. There are two principal islands, the North and South Islands, besides Stewart Island, Chatham Islands and small outlying islands, as well as the territories overseas. New Zealand (i.e. North, South and Stewart Islands) extends over 1,750 km from north to south. Area, excluding territories overseas, 267,707 km^2. The main islands are: North Island, 114,154 km^2; South Island, 150,416 km^2; Stewart Island, 1,681 km^2; Chatham Islands, 963 km^2. The latest census took place on 5 March 2013. Of the 4,353,198 people counted, 4,242,048 were usually resident in the country and 111,150 were overseas visitors. In 2011, 86.2% of the population lived in urban areas. Density, 16 per km^2 (2013). English and Maori are the official languages.

Tourism

There were a record 2,617,930 tourists in the year to March 2012 of whom 1,168,316 were from Australia, 222,152 were from the UK, 184,056 were from the USA and 160,268 were from China. Tourism receipts totalled NZ$22,848 m. in 2010–11. Employment in tourism in 2010–11 totalled 188,100 (full-time equivalents), of whom 120,700 were directly employed in tourism and 67,400 indirectly.

Nicaragua

República de Nicaragua (Republic of Nicaragua)

Factsheet

Capital: Managua
Population estimate, 2015: 6.08 m.
GNI per capita, 2014: (PPP$) 4,457
HDI/world rank, 2014: 0.631/125
Internet domain extension: .ni

Civil Aviation

In 2013 airports in Nicaragua handled 1,206,172 passengers. The main airport, Augusto C. Sandino International Airport at Managua, handled 1,108,933 passengers in 2009 (of which 963,715 on international flights).

Climate

The climate is tropical, with a wet season from May to Jan. Temperatures vary with altitude. Managua, Jan. 81 °F (27 °C), July 81 °F (27 °C). Annual rainfall 38″ (976 mm).

Constitution and Government

A new constitution was promulgated on 9 Jan. 1987 and underwent reforms in 1995, 2000 and 2014. It provides for a unicameral 92-seat *National Assembly* comprising 90 members directly elected by proportional representation for a 5-year term, together with one seat for the previous president and one seat for the runner-up in the previous presidential election. Citizens are entitled to vote at the age of 16. The *President* and *Vice-President* are directly elected for a 5-year term commencing on 10 Jan. following their date of election. Amendments that came into force in Feb. 2014 ended restrictions on presidential re-election. Previously, the president could stand for a second term in office but not consecutively (although in Oct. 2009 the Supreme Court ruled in favour of a petition brought by President Daniel Ortega to remove the barrier against consecutive terms). Also abolished was the need for a minimum required vote to avoid a presidential run-off. Candidates leading after the first round of voting had previously required at least 40% of the vote (or 35% and a 5% margin over the second-placed candidate) to claim outright

victory. Other changes saw police and military figures permitted to serve in posts hitherto reserved for civilians, while the president was granted the power to issue decree-laws.

Currency

The monetary unit is the *córdoba* (NIO), of 100 *centavos*, which replaced the córdoba oro in 1991 at par.

Defence

In 2013 defence expenditure totalled US$85 m. (US$15 per capita), representing 0.8% of GDP.

Economy

In 2012 agriculture accounted for 20.0% of GDP, industry 26.7% and services 53.3%.

Labour

The workforce in 2001 was 1,900,400 (1,315,000 males). In 2001, 1,701,700 persons were in employment, of whom 739,000 were engaged in agriculture, hunting, forestry and fishing; 294,300 in community, social and personal services; 279,800 in wholesale and retail trade, and restaurants and hotels; and 131,600 in manufacturing. There were 159,500 unemployed in 2005, a rate of 7.2%.

Press

In 2008 there were seven paid-for daily newspapers in Nicaragua, with a total circulation of 175,000.

Religion

The prevailing form of religion is Roman Catholicism (3.38 m. adherents in 2010 according to estimates by the Pew Research Center's Forum on Religion & Public Life), but religious liberty is guaranteed by the Constitution. The Pew Research Center estimated that there were also 1.53 m. Protestants in 2010 and 730,000 people with no religious affiliation. In Feb. 2016 the Roman Catholic church had two cardinals.

Roads

Road length in 2007 was 20,333 km, of which 1,081 km were main roads. In 2007 there were 101,900 passenger cars (18 per 1,000 inhabitants), 7,700 buses and coaches, 179,900 lorries and vans and 61,200 motorcycles and mopeds. 522 fatalities were caused by road accidents in 2007.

Shipping

In Jan. 2009 there were two ships of 300 GT or over registered, totalling 1,000 GT. The Pacific ports are Corinto (the largest), San Juan del Sur and Puerto Sandino through which pass most of the external trade. The chief eastern ports are El Bluff (for Bluefields) and Puerto Cabezas. Construction of a Chinese-backed 278-km canal known as the Nicaragua Canal, linking the Atlantic and Pacific Oceans, began in Dec. 2014. The canal, which is set to be about four times the length of the Panama Canal, is expected to cost US$50 bn. and be completed in 2019.

Social Statistics

2008 estimates: births, 140,000; deaths, 27,000. Estimated rates (per 1,000 population), 2008: births, 24.6; deaths, 4.7. Annual population growth rate, 2000–08, 1.3%. 2013 life expectancy: male 71.8 years; female 77.9. Infant mortality, 2010, 23 per 1,000 live births; fertility rate, 2008, 2.7 births per woman. A law prohibiting abortion was passed in Nov. 2006.

Telecommunications

In 2011 there were 288,000 fixed telephone lines; mobile phone subscriptions numbered 4,824,000 in 2011 (81.7 per 100 persons). In 2011, 10.6% of the population were internet users. In Dec. 2011 there were 664,000 Facebook users.

Territory and Population

Nicaragua is bounded in the north by Honduras, east by the Caribbean, south by Costa Rica and west by the Pacific. Area, 131,812 km² (121,428 km² dry land). The coastline runs 450 km on the Atlantic and 305 km on the Pacific. The census population in May 2005 was 5,142,098 (density, 39.0 per km²). Estimate, June 2012: 6,071,000. 57.6% of the population were urban in 2011. 15 administrative departments and two autonomous regions are grouped in three zones. The capital is Managua with (2005 census population) 908,892 inhabitants. Other cities (2005 populations): León, 139,433; Chinandega, 95,614; Masaya, 92,598; Estelí, 90,294; Tipitapa, 85,948; Matagalpa, 80,228; Granada, 79,418; Ciudad Sandino, 72,501; Juigalpa, 42,763. The population is of Spanish and Amerindian origins with an admixture of Afro-Americans on the Caribbean coast. The majority of the population is mestizo (mixed Amerindian and white) and white. There are also Blacks and Amerindians. The official language is Spanish.

Tourism

In 2011 there were 1,060,000 non-resident tourists, spending US$378 m.

Niger

République du Niger (Republic of Niger)

Factsheet

Capital: Niamey
Population estimate, 2015: 19.90 m.
GNI per capita, 2014: (PPP$) 908
HDI/world rank, 2014: 0.348/188
Internet domain extension: .ne

Civil Aviation

There is an international airport at Niamey (Diori Hamani Airport), which handled 154,460 passengers in 2009 and 3,327 tonnes of freight. In 2010 there were international flights to Abidjan, Abuja, Accra, Algiers, Bamako, Casablanca, Cotonou, Dakar, Nouakchott, Ouagadougou, Paris and Tripoli as well as domestic flights; nine airlines flew to Niamey in 2010.

Climate

Precipitation determines the geographical division into a southern zone of agriculture, a central zone of pasturage and a desert-like northern zone. The country lacks water, with the exception of the southwestern districts, which are watered by the Niger and its tributaries, and the southern zone, where there are a number of wells. Niamey, 95 °F (35 °C). Annual rainfall varies from 22″ (560 mm) in the south to 7″ (180 mm) in the Sahara zone. The rainy season lasts from May until Sept., but there are periodic droughts.

Constitution and Government

Following a coup in Feb. 2010 a military junta suspended the constitution and dissolved the cabinet. In March 2010 the military leadership announced it had formed a transitional government and promised to return Niger to democracy. In Oct. 2010 a new constitution received 90.2% support in a referendum; turnout was 52.7%. Establishing Niger as a secular state, it reimposes a limit of two 5-year terms on the presidency (a provision abandoned in the constitution promulgated the previous year), prohibits members of the military from running for office and guarantees that the government will release data on national oil and mining revenues.

Currency

The unit of currency is the *franc CFA* (XOF) with a parity of 655.957 francs CFA to one euro.

Defence

Selective conscription for 2 years operates. Defence expenditure totalled US$70 m. in 2012 (US$4 per capita), representing 1.1% of GDP.

Economy

Agriculture, forestry and fishing contributed 43.3% of GDP in 2008; followed by trade and hotels, 13.8%; public administration and defence, 8.8%; and services, 8.8%.

Labour

The estimated economically active population in 2009 totalled 4,803,000 (68% males). Agriculture, fisheries and forestry remains the largest sector of employment. Niger had 0.12 m. people living in slavery according to the Walk Free Foundation's 2013 *Global Slavery Index*.

Press

In 2008 there was one government-owned daily newspaper and 45 private non-daily newspapers.

Religion

According to the Pew Research Center's Forum on Religion & Public Life, in 2010 the population was an estimated 98.4% Muslim (nearly all Sunnis). There are also small numbers of Protestants and people with no religious affiliation.

Roads

In 2007 there were 18,949 km of roads including 3,912 km of paved roads. Niamey and Zinder are the termini of two trans-Sahara motor routes; the Hoggar–Aïr–Zinder road extends to Kano and the Tanezrouft–Gao–Niamey road to Benin. A 648-km 'uranium road' runs from Arlit to Tahoua. There were, in 2005, 57,732 passenger cars, 11,261 vans, 2,613 buses and 1,035 lorries. In 2007 there were 676 road accidents resulting in 265 fatalities.

Shipping

Sea-going vessels can reach Niamey (300 km inside the country) between Sept. and March.

Social Statistics

Estimates, 2008: births, 787,000; deaths, 219,000. Estimated birth rate in 2008 was 53.5 per 1,000 population (the highest in the world); estimated death rate, 14.9. Niger has one of the youngest populations of any country, with 73% of the population under the age of 30 and 49% under 15. Infant mortality, 2010, 73 per 1,000 live births. Annual population growth rate, 2000–08, 3.6%. Expectation of life at birth, 2013, 58.3 years for males and 58.6 for females. Fertility rate, 2012, 7.6 children per woman (the highest anywhere in the world). A UNICEF report published in 2014 revealed that 77% of women aged 20–49 had been married or in union before the age of 18, the highest percentage of any country.

Telecommunications

There were 83,600 landline telephone subscriptions in 2010 (equivalent to 5.4 per 1,000 inhabitants) and 4,339,900 mobile phone subscriptions in 2011 (or 270.1 per 1,000 inhabitants). In 2011, 1.3% of the population were internet users.

Territory and Population

Niger is bounded in the north by Algeria and Libya, east by Chad, south by Nigeria, southwest by Benin and Burkina Faso, and west by Mali. Area, 1,186,408 km², with a population at the 2012 census of 17,138,707; density, 14.4 per km². In 2011, 17.2% of the population were urban. The country is divided into the capital, Niamey, an autonomous district, and seven departments. The population is composed chiefly of Hausa (53%), Djerma-Songhai (21%), Fulani (10%), Tuareg (10%) and Kanuri-Manga (4%). The official language is French. Hausa, Djerma and Fulani are national languages.

Tourism

In 2012 there were 94,000 non-resident tourists; spending by tourists totalled US$86 m. in 2011.

Nigeria

Federal Republic of Nigeria

Factsheet

Capital: Abuja
Population estimate, 2015: 182.20 m.
GNI per capita, 2014: (PPP$) 5,341
HDI/world rank, 2014: 0.514/152
Internet domain extension: .ng

Civil Aviation

Lagos (Murtala Muhammed) is the major airport, and there are also international airports at Abuja, Kano and Port Harcourt. After the former national carrier, Air Nigeria, ceased operations in 2012, the country's largest airline is now Arik Air. In 2012 Murtala Muhammed International Airport handled 7,186,595 passengers and 167,702 tonnes of freight.

Climate

Lying wholly within the tropics, temperatures everywhere are high. Rainfall varies greatly, but decreases from the coast to the interior. The main rains occur from April to Oct. Lagos, Jan. 81 °F (27.2 °C), July 78 °F (25.6 °C). Annual rainfall 72″ (1,836 mm). Ibadan, Jan. 80 °F (26.7 °C), July 76 °F (24.4 °C). Annual rainfall 45″ (1,120 mm). Kano, Jan. 70 °F (21.1 °C), July 79 °F (26.1 °C). Annual rainfall 35″ (869 mm). Port Harcourt, Jan. 79 °F (26 °C), July 77 °F (25 °C). Annual rainfall 100″ (2,497 mm).

Constitution and Government

The constitution was promulgated on 5 May 1999, and entered into force on 29 May. Nigeria is a federation, comprising 36 states and a federal capital territory. The constitution includes provisions for the creation of new states and for boundary adjustments of existing states. The legislative powers are vested in a *National Assembly*, comprising a *Senate* and a *House of Representatives*. The 109-member Senate consists of three senators from each state and one from the federal capital territory, who are elected for a term of 4 years. The House of Representatives comprises 360 members, representing constituencies of nearly equal population as far as possible, who are elected for a 4-year term. The *President* is elected for a term of 4 years and must receive not less than one-quarter of the votes cast at the federal capital territory. A president may not serve more than two consecutive 4-year terms. In 2006 Olusegun Obasanjo sought to alter the constitution to allow him to run for a third term, but he failed to win backing for the amendment.

Currency

The unit of currency is the *naira* (NGN) of 100 *kobo*.

Defence

In 2013 defence expenditure totalled US$2,143 m., equivalent to US$12 per capita and representing 0.8% of GDP.

Economy

Agriculture and fishing contributed 35.5% to GDP in 2009; followed by crude petroleum and mining, 28.5%; trade and hotels, 16.2%; and finance and real estate, 6.1%.

Labour

The labour force in 2013 was 54,199,000 (41,222,000 in 2003). 56.2% of the population aged 15–64 was economically active in 2013. In the same year 7.5% of the population was unemployed. Nigeria had 0.70 m. people living in slavery according to the Walk Free Foundation's 2013 *Global Slavery Index*, the fourth highest total of any country.

Press

In 2008 there were 28 paid-for daily newspapers with a combined circulation of 510,000 and 61 paid-for weeklies. The dailies with the highest circulation figures are *The Sun* and *ThisDay*.

Rail

In 2005 there were 3,505 route-km of track (1,067 mm gauge). There are plans to convert the entire network to 1,435 mm gauge. Passenger-km travelled in 2008 came to 773 m. and freight tonne-km to 41 m.

Religion

Muslims and Christians both constitute about 49% of the population; traditional animist beliefs are also widespread. Northern Nigeria is mainly Muslim; southern Nigeria is predominantly Christian and western Nigeria is evenly divided between Christians, Muslims and animists. Far more Nigerians consider their religion to be of prime importance rather than their nationality. In Feb. 2016 the Roman Catholic church had three cardinals.

Roads

The road network covered 193,200 km in 2004, including 15,688 km of main roads. In 2007 there were 4,560,000 passenger cars in use and 3,040,000 motorcycles and mopeds. There were 17,797 road accidents with 9,390 fatalities in 2007.

Shipping

In Jan. 2009 there were 107 ships of 300 GT or over registered, totalling 427,000 GT. The principal ports are Lagos and Port Harcourt. There is an extensive network of inland waterways.

Social Statistics

2008 estimates: births, 6,050,000; deaths, 2,420,000. Rates, 2008 estimates (per 1,000 population): births, 40; deaths, 16. Infant mortality, 2010, 88 (per 1,000 live births). Annual population growth rate, 2005–10, 2.7%. Life expectancy at birth, 2013, was 52.2 years for males and 52.8 years for females. Fertility rate, 2008, 5.3 children per woman.

Telecommunications

In 2010 there were 1,050,000 main (fixed) telephone lines. In the same year mobile phone subscribers numbered 87,298,000 (551.0 per 1,000 persons), up from 18,587,000 in 2005. Nigeria has now surpassed South Africa as the continent's largest mobile phone market. The largest mobile phone company is MTN Nigeria Communications. In 2012, 32.8% of the population were internet users. In June 2012 there were 5.1 m. Facebook users.

Territory and Population

Nigeria is bounded in the north by Niger, east by Chad and Cameroon, south by the Gulf of Guinea and west by Benin. It has an area of 923,768 km^2 (356,667 sq. miles). Census population, 2006, 140,431,790 (69,086,302 females); population density, 152.0 per km^2. Nigeria is Africa's most populous country. In 2011, 50.5% of the population were urban.

Tourism

In 2010 there were 1,555,000 international tourist arrivals, excluding same-day visitors (up from 1,414,000 in 2009); spending by tourists in 2010 totalled US$576 m.

Norway

Kongeriket Norge (Kingdom of Norway)

Factsheet

Capital: Oslo
Population estimate, 2015: 5.21 m.
GNI per capita, 2014: (PPP$) 64,992
HDI/world rank, 2014: 0.944/1
Internet domain extension: .no

Civil Aviation

The main international airports are at Oslo (Gardermoen), Bergen (Flesland), Stavanger (Sola), Sandefjord (Torp) and Moss (Rygge). Norway's largest airline is SAS Norge, a wholly-owned subsidiary of the Scandinavian Airlines System (SAS) Group. In 2010 Oslo (Gardermoen) handled 19,140,384 passengers (10,123,605 on international flights). Bergen is the second busiest airport for passenger traffic, with 5,189,714 passengers in 2010 (3,604,882 on domestic flights).

Climate

There is considerable variation in the climate because of the extent of latitude, the topography and the varying effectiveness of prevailing westerly winds and the Gulf Stream. Winters along the whole west coast are exceptionally mild but precipitation is considerable. Oslo, Jan. 24.3 °F (−4.3 °C), July 61.5 °F (16.4 °C). Annual rainfall 30.0″ (763 mm). Bergen, Jan. 34.3 °F (1.3 °C), July 57.7 °F (14.3 °C). Annual rainfall 88.6″ (2,250 mm). Trondheim, Jan. 26 °F (−3.5 °C), July 57 °F (14 °C). Annual rainfall 32.1″ (870 mm). Bergen has one of the highest rainfall figures of any European city. The sun never fully sets in the northern area of the country in the summer and even in the south the sun rises at around 3 a.m. and sets at around 11 p.m.

Constitution and Government

Norway is a constitutional and hereditary monarchy. The reigning King is **Harald V**, born 21 Feb. 1937, married on 29 Aug. 1968 to Sonja Haraldsen. He succeeded on the death of his father, King Olav V, on 21 Jan. 1991. The king and queen together receive an annual personal allowance of 10.8 m. kroner from the civil list, and the Crown Prince and Crown Princess together 9.0 m. kroner. The Constitution, voted by a constituent assembly on 17 May 1814 and modified at various times, vests the legislative power of the realm in the *Storting* (Parliament). The King has the command of the land, sea and air forces, and makes all appointments. The 169-member Storting (increased from 165 for the 2005 election) is directly elected by proportional representation. The country is divided into 19 districts, each electing from 4 to 15 representatives. The Storting, when assembled, divides itself by election into the *Lagting* and the *Odelsting*. The Storting elects five delegates, whose duty it is to revise the public accounts. The Lagting and the ordinary members of the Supreme Court of Justice (the *Høyesterett*) form a High Court of the Realm (the *Riksrett*) for the trial of ministers, members of the *Høyesterett* and members of the Storting. The impeachment before the *Riksrett* can only be decided by the Odelsting. The executive is represented by the King, who exercises his authority through the Cabinet. Cabinet ministers are entitled to be present in the Storting and to take part in the discussions, but without a vote.

Currency

The unit of currency is the *Norwegian krone* (NOK) of 100 *øre*.

Defence

In 2013 defence spending totalled US$7,523 m. (US$1,593 per capita), representing 1.4% of GDP. Expenditure per capita was the highest of any European country in 2013.

Economy

Services accounted for 57% of GDP in 2012, industry 42% and agriculture 1%.

Labour

The labour force averaged 2,602,000 in 2010 (1,224,000 females). The total number of employed persons in 2010 averaged 2,508,000 (1,187,000 females), of whom 1,835,000 were in full-time employment, 667,000 in part-time employment and 6,000 working unspecified hours. Distribution of employed persons by occupation in 2007 showed 492,700 in health and social work; 364,000 in trade; 300,200 in business services; 286,200 in manufacturing; 185,500 in education; 184,200 in construction; 167,300 in transport; 156,600 in public administration and defence; 78,800 in hotels and restaurants; 60,100 in agriculture. The unemployment rate in Nov. 2014 was 3.7% (one of the lowest in the industrialized world).

Press

There were 74 paid-for daily newspapers with a combined average net circulation of 2.19 m. in 2008, and in 2007 there were 151 non-dailies with a circulation of 623,000. Norway has among the highest circulation rates of daily newspapers in the world, at 580 per 1,000 adult inhabitants in 2007. In the 2013 *World Press Freedom Index* compiled by Reporters Without Borders, Norway was ranked third out of 179 countries. In 2007 a total of 7,074 book titles were published.

Rail

The length of state railways in 2010 was 4,169 km (2,566 km electrified). In 2009 passenger-km travelled came to 2,669 m. and freight tonne-km to 2,804 m. Sales and other operating income totalled 11,179 m. kroner in 2010. There is a metro (104 km) and a tram network (146 km) in Oslo.

Religion

There is freedom of religion, the Church of Norway (Evangelical Lutheran), however, being the national church. Its clergy are nominated by the King. Ecclesiastically Norway is divided into 11 dioceses, 100 deaneries and 1,298 parishes. About 80% of Norwegians belong to the Church of Norway (which had 3,848,841 members in 2009) and approximately 68% of infants were baptised in the Church in 2009. There were 431,287 members of registered and unregistered religious and philosophical communities outside the Church of Norway in 2009, subsidized by central government and local authorities, including 234,772 Christians and 92,744 Muslims. The Roman Catholics are under a Bishop at Oslo, and Prelates at Tromsø and Trondheim.

Roads

In Jan. 2011 the length of public roads (including roads in towns) totalled 93,509 km. Total road length in Jan. 2011 included: national roads, 10,496 km; provincial roads, 44,281 km; local roads, 38,732 km. Number of registered motor vehicles, 2010, included: 2,308,548 passenger cars (including station wagons and ambulances), 397,279 vans, 254,674 tractors and special purpose vehicles, 168,904 mopeds, 146,592 motorcycles, 81,330 goods vehicles (including lorries), 48,432 combined vehicles and 20,348 buses. In 2010, 9,130 injuries were sustained in road accidents, with 208 fatalities. Norway has one of the lowest death rates in road accidents of any industrialized country, at 4.3 deaths per 100,000 people in 2010.

Shipping

The Norwegian International Ship Register was set up in 1987. In 2010, 525 ships were registered (400 Norwegian) totalling 13,792,000 GT. 218 tankers accounted for 6,948,000 GT. There were also 882 vessels totalling 1,917,000 GT on the Norwegian Ordinary Register. These figures do not include fishing boats, tugs, salvage vessels, icebreakers and similar special types of vessels.

Social Statistics

2010 births, 61,442; deaths, 41,499. Rates per 1,000 population, 2010, birth, 12.6; death, 8.5; marriage, 4.8; divorce, 2.1. Average annual population growth rate, 2000–10, 0.86% (2010, 1.28%). In 2009 there were 573 suicides, giving a rate of 11.9 per 100,000 population (men, 17.3 per 100,000; women, 6.5). Expectation of life at birth, 2010, was 78.9 years for males and

83.2 years for females. Infant mortality, 2010, 2.8 per 1,000 live births; fertility rate, 2010, 1.95 births per woman. 55% of births are to unmarried mothers. In 2009 the average age at marriage was 37.3 years for males and 33.8 years for females (33.8 years and 31.0 years respectively for first marriages).

Telecommunications

At 31 Dec. 2010 there were 1,648,927 main (fixed) telephone lines and 5,648,673 mobile phone subscribers (1,148.0 per 1,000 persons). In 2013, 66.5% of the population aged 16–74 were internet users. In March 2012 there were 2.6 m. Facebook users. Since 2000 the government has been reducing its interest in Telenor, the country's largest telecommunications operator, and in March 2004 lowered its stake to 54.0%.

Territory and Population

Norway is bounded in the north by the Arctic Ocean, east by Russia, Finland and Sweden, south by the Skagerrak Straits and west by the Norwegian Sea. The total area of mainland Norway is 323,787 km², including 19,539 km² of fresh water. Total coastline, including fjords, 25,148 km. There are more than 50,000 islands along the coastline. Exposed mountain (either bare rock or thin vegetation) makes up over 70% of the country. 25% of the land area is woodland and 4% tilled land. Population (2001 census) was 4,520,947 (2,240,281 males; 2,280,666 females); population density per km², 14.8. Estimated population, 1 Jan. 2014, 5,109,056; population density, 16.8. With the exception of Iceland, Norway is the most sparsely populated country in Europe. The Arctic territories of Svalbard and Jan Mayen have an area of 61,397 km². Persons staying on Svalbard and Jan Mayen are registered as residents of their home Norwegian municipality. At Jan. 2011, 79.2% of the population lived in urban areas. Population of the principal urban settlements on 1 Jan. 2013: Oslo, 925,228; Bergen, 247,731; Stavanger/Sandnes, 203,771; Trondheim, 169,972; Drammen, 110,503; Fredrikstad/Sarpsborg, 106,758; Porsgrunn/Skien, 90,621; Kristiansand, 58,662. The official language is Norwegian, which has two versions: Bokmål (or Riksmål) and Nynorsk (or Landsmål).

Tourism

In 2007 there were 3,260,000 foreign holiday and leisure visitors (excluding same-day visitors) who stayed an average of 7.4 nights each, totalling 24,252,000 nights. The main countries of origin were Sweden (761,000), Germany (548,000), Denmark (431,000) and the UK (246,000). In 2010 there were 1,128 hotels and 782 camping sites. Spending by foreign tourists totalled 30.8 bn. kroner in 2007.

Oman

Saltanat 'Uman (Sultanate of Oman)

Factsheet

Capital: Muscat
Population estimate, 2015: 4.49 m.
GNI per capita, 2014: (PPP$) 34,858
HDI/world rank, 2014: 0.793/52=
Internet domain extension: .om

Civil Aviation

The national airline is Oman Air, which in 2007 had 15 aircraft and served 26 destinations. Oman formerly had a 50% share in Gulf Air with Bahrain, but withdrew in May 2007. In 2009 Seeb International Airport (Muscat) handled 4,556,502 passengers (3,983,413 international) and 64,418 tonnes of freight.

Climate

Oman has a desert climate, with exceptionally hot and humid months from April to Oct., when temperatures may reach 47 °C. Light monsoon rains fall in the south from June to Sept., with highest amounts in the western highland

region. Muscat, Jan. 28 °C, July 46 °C. Annual rainfall 101 mm. Salalah, Jan. 29 °C, July 32 °C. Annual rainfall 98 mm.

Constitution and Government

Oman is a hereditary absolute monarchy. The Sultan legislates by decree and appoints a Cabinet to assist him. The Basic Statute of the State was promulgated on 6 Nov. 1996. The present Sultan is **Qaboos bin Said Al Said** (b. Nov. 1940). He does not have any children and has not publicly named an heir or a designated successor. In 1991 a new consultative assembly, the *Majlis al-Shura*, replaced the former State Consultative Chamber. The Majlis consists of 84 elected members. It debates domestic issues, but has no legislative or veto powers. There is also an upper house, the *Majlis al-Dawla*, which consists of 83 appointed members; it too has advisory powers only. In Dec. 2002 the Sultan of Oman extended voting rights to all citizens over the age of 21.

Currency

The unit of currency is the *Rial Omani* (OMR). It is divided into 1,000 *baiza*.

Defence

Military expenditure in 2013 totalled US$9,246 m. (US$2,931 per capita), representing 11.7% of GDP.

Economy

Oil and natural gas (excluding petroleum products) contributed 41.0% to GDP in 2009; followed by manufacturing (including petroleum products) 10.3%; trade, restaurants and hotels, 10.2%; and finance and real estate, 9.9%.

Labour

In 2013 the labour force totalled 1,985,000 with the unemployment rate standing at 7.9%. Males constituted 85.9% of the workforce in 2013. In 2014 there were 232,980 persons in government service and 197,510 Omanis in the private sector. The employment of foreign labour is being discouraged following 'Omanization' regulations of 1994. More than a quarter of the total population are foreign workers. Following the unrest of early 2011 the private sector monthly minimum wage for national workers was increased in Feb. 2011 from RO 140 to RO 200. There is no minimum wage for foreign workers.

Press

In 2008 there were seven daily newspapers with a combined circulation of 239,000.

Religion

In 2010, 85.9% of the population were Muslims according to estimates by the Pew Research Center's Forum on Religion & Public Life. Most Omanis are Ibadhis, a distinct branch of Islam that is neither Sunni nor Shia. The Pew Research Center estimated that 6.5% of the population were Christians in 2010 and 5.5% Hindus.

Roads

A network of adequate graded roads links all the main sectors of population, and only a few mountain villages are not accessible by motor vehicles. In 2005 there were about 42,300 km of roads (16,500 km paved) including 953 km of dual carriageway. In 2007 there were 453,400 passenger cars in use (174 per 1,000 inhabitants), 113,300 vans and lorries, and 26,400 buses and coaches. In 2007 there were 8,816 road accidents and 798 deaths.

Shipping

In Mutrah a deep-water port (named Mina Qaboos) was completed in 1974. In 2008 it handled 6.3 m. tonnes of foreign cargo. In Jan. 2009 there were seven ships of 300 GT or over registered, totalling 17,000 GT.

Social Statistics

2008 estimates: births, 61,000; deaths, 8,000. Estimated rates, 2008 (per 1,000 population): births, 22.0; deaths, 2.7. Expectation of life at birth, 2013, was 74.8 years for males and 79.0 years for females. Average annual population growth rate, 2000–08, 1.8%. Fertility rate, 2008, 3.0 births per woman, down from 7.8 in 1988. Oman has achieved some of the most rapid advances ever recorded. Infant mortality declined from 200 per 1,000 live births in 1960 to eight per 1,000 live births in 2010, and as recently as 1970 life expectancy was just 40.

Telecommunications

In 2013 there were 351,000 main (fixed) telephone lines in Oman; mobile phone subscriptions numbered 5,617,000 in 2013 (1,546.5 per 1,000 persons). An estimated 60% of the population were internet users in 2012. In March 2012 there were 422,000 Facebook users.

Territory and Population

Situated at the southeast corner of the Arabian peninsula, Oman is bounded in the northeast by the Gulf of Oman and southeast by the Arabian Sea, southwest by Yemen and northwest by Saudi Arabia and the United Arab Emirates. There is an enclave at the northern tip of the Musandam Peninsula. The Sultanate of Oman occupies a total area of 309,500 km^2 and includes different terrains that vary from plain to highlands and mountains. Population at the census of Dec. 2010, 2,773,479 (1,612,411 males); density 9.0 per km^2. The population comprised 1,957,336 Omanis and 816,143 expatriates. In 2011, 73.3% of the population lived in urban areas. The census population of the capital, Muscat, in 2010 was 775,878. The official language is Arabic; English is in commercial use.

Tourism

Non-resident tourists staying at hotels and similar establishments numbered 1,276,000 in 2009 (down from 1,378,000 in 2008 although up from 1,182,000 in 2007).

Pakistan

Islami Jamhuriya e Pakistan (Islamic Republic of Pakistan)

Factsheet
Capital: Islamabad
Population estimate, 2015: 188.93 m.
GNI per capita, 2014: (PPP$) 4,866
HDI/world rank, 2014: 0.538/147
Internet domain extension: .pk

Civil Aviation

There are international airports at Karachi, Islamabad, Lahore, Peshawar and Quetta. The national carrier is the state-owned Pakistan International Airlines, or PIA. It operates scheduled services to 46 international and 24 domestic destinations. In 2006, 88,302,000 revenue-km were flown. The revenue passengers carried totalled 5.73 m. in 2006 and revenue tonne-km came to 1,801 m. Operating revenues of the corporation stood at Rs70,587 m. in 2006 and operating expenditure at Rs79,164 m.

Climate

A weak form of tropical monsoon climate occurs over much of the country, with arid conditions in the north and west, where the wet season is only from Dec. to March. Elsewhere, rain comes mainly in the summer. Summer temperatures are high everywhere, but winters can be cold in the mountainous north. Islamabad, Jan. 50 °F (10 °C), July 90 °F (32.2 °C). Annual rainfall 36″ (900 mm). Karachi, Jan. 61 °F (16.1 °C), July 86 °F (30 °C). Annual rainfall 8″ (196 mm). Lahore, Jan. 53 °F (11.7 °C), July 89 °F (31.7 °C). Annual rainfall 18″ (452 mm). Multan, Jan. 51 °F (10.6 °C), July 93 °F (33.9 °C). Annual rainfall 7″ (170 mm). Quetta, Jan. 38 °F (3.3 °C), July 80 °F (26.7 °C). Annual rainfall 10″ (239 mm).

Constitution and Government

Following the 1999 coup Gen. Musharraf announced that the Constitution was to be held 'in abeyance' and issued a 'Provisional Constitution Order

No. 1' in its place. In Aug. 2002 he unilaterally amended the constitution to grant himself the right to dissolve parliament. Gen. Pervez Musharraf, Chief of the Army Staff, assumed the responsibilities of the chief executive of the country following the removal of Prime Minister Nawaz Sharif on 12 Oct. 1999. He formed a National Security Council consisting of six members belonging to the armed forces and a number of civilians with expertise in various fields. A Federal Cabinet of Ministers was also installed working under the guidance of the National Security Council. Also formed was the National Reconstruction Bureau, a think tank providing institutional advice and input on economic, social and institutional matters. Following Musharraf's resignation in Aug. 2008, ousted Chief Justice Iftikhar Chaudry was reinstated in March 2009. The 2007 amendments to the constitution were subsequently revoked in July 2009 and in Aug. the Supreme Court ruled that Musharraf's actions had been illegal.

Currency

The monetary unit is the *Pakistan rupee* (PKR) of 100 *paisas*.

Defence

Defence expenditure in 2013 totalled US$5,890 m. (US$30 per capita), representing 2.5% of GDP. According to *Deadly Arsenals*, published by the Carnegie Endowment for International Peace, Pakistan has both chemical and biological weapon research programmes. The Stockholm International Peace Research Institute estimates that Pakistan possesses 100–120 nuclear warheads.

Economy

Agriculture accounted for 21.2% of GDP in 2010, industry 25.4% and services 53.4%.

Labour

Out of 45.29 m. economically active people in 2005, 37.81 m. were males. The rate of unemployment in 2005 was 6.8%. In 2005 a total of 17.18 m. persons were engaged in agriculture, forestry and fishing, 6.67 m. in manufacturing, 6.50 m. in community, social and personal services and 6.29 m. in wholesale and retail trade, restaurants and hotels. In 2001 there were four industrial disputes and 7,078 working days were lost. Pakistan had 2.13 m. people living in slavery according to the Walk Free Foundation's 2013 *Global Slavery Index*, the third highest total of any country.

Press

In 2007 there were 400 paid-for dailies and 1,200 paid-for non-daily periodicals. Average combined circulation of all dailies in 2007 was 9,935,000. The most popular daily papers in 2008 were *Jang*, with a circulation of 450,000, and *Express*, with a circulation of 375,000. The most widely read English-language paper is *Dawn*, with an average daily circulation of 225,000 copies in 2008.

Rail

In 2011 Pakistan Railways had a route length of 7,791 km (of which 293 km electrified) mainly on 1,676 mm gauge, with some metre gauge line. Passenger-km travelled in 2011 came to 20.6 bn. and freight tonne-km to 1.8 bn.

Religion

Pakistan was created as a Muslim state. Around 85–90% of Muslims are Sunni and 10–15% Shia according to estimates by the Pew Research Center's Forum on Religion & Public Life. Religious groups: Muslims, 93%; Christians, 2%; Hindus, Parsees, Buddhists, Qadianis and others. Pakistan has the second highest number of Muslims, after Indonesia. There is a Minorities Wing at the Religious Affairs Ministry to safeguard the constitutional rights of religious minorities.

Roads

In 2006 there were 260,420 km of roads, of which 65.4% were paved. There are ten motorways providing links between Pakistan's major cities. These include the M-1 from Islamabad to Peshawar, the M-2 from Islamabad to Lahore, the M-4 from Faisalabad to Multan and the M-9 from Karachi to Hyderabad. In 2007 there were 1,440,100 passenger cars in use, 187,100 vans and lorries, 170,400 buses and coaches and 2,684,300 motorcycles. There were 10,466 road accidents involving injury in 2007, with 5,465 fatalities. All traffic in Pakistan drives on the left. All cars must be insured and registered. Minimum age for driving: 18 years.

Shipping

In Jan. 2009 there were 16 ships of 300 GT or over registered, totalling 384,000 GT. The busiest port is Karachi. In 2008–09 cargo traffic totalled a record 38,732,000 tonnes (13,364,000 tonnes loaded and 25,368,000 tonnes discharged). In 2008–09, 2,386 vessels were handled at the port of Karachi. There are also ports at Port Qasim, which handled 25,023,000 tonnes in 2008–09, and Gwadar.

Social Statistics

Estimates, 2008: births, 5,324,000; deaths, 1,224,000. Estimated birth rate in 2008 was 30.1 per 1,000 population; estimated death rate, 6.9. Infant mortality (per 1,000 live births), 70 (2010). Formal registration of marriages and divorces has not been required since 1992. Expectation of life in 2013 was 65.7 years for men and 67.5 years for women. Annual population growth rate, 2000–08, 2.2%. Fertility rate, 2008, 4.0 births per woman.

Telecommunications

Telecommunications The telephone system is government-owned. In 2013 there were an estimated 6.4 m. main (fixed) telephone lines. In the same year mobile phone subscriptions numbered an estimated 127.7 m. An estimated 10.9% of the population were internet users in 2013. In March 2012 there were 6.4 m. Facebook users.

Territory and Population

Pakistan is bounded in the west by Iran, northwest by Afghanistan, north by China, east by India and south by the Arabian Sea. The area (excluding the disputed area of Kashmir) is 796,100 km^2 (307,380 sq. miles), including 25,220 km^2 (9,740 sq. miles) of inland water. 2011 provisional census population (excluding three districts of Balochistan, the agency of South Waziristan in the Federally Administered Tribal Areas, and the autonomous states Azad-Kashmir and Gilgit-Baltistan), 192,288,944. In 2011, 36.2% lived in urban areas. There were 1.6 m. refugees in 2012, mostly from Afghanistan, the highest number in any country and 17% of the global total. English, the official language, is used in business, higher education and in central government; Urdu is the national language and the *lingua franca*, although only spoken as a first language by about 8% of the population. Around 48% of the population speak Punjabi.

Tourism

In 2010 there were 906,800 non-resident tourists including 288,200 from the UK, 120,400 from the USA, 110,900 from Afghanistan, 46,200 from Canada and 43,700 from India. 54% of tourists in 2010 visited Punjab and 29% Sindh.

Palau

Beluu er a Belau (Republic of Palau)

Factsheet
Capital: Melekeok
Population estimate, 2015: 21,000
GNI per capita, 2014: (PPP$) 13,496
HDI/world rank, 2014: 0.780/60=
Internet domain extension: .pw

Civil Aviation

The main airport is on Koror (Roman Tmetuchl International Airport, near Airai). In 2010 there were scheduled flights to Guam, Manila, Seoul, Taipei and Yap (Micronesia). A new Palau-based carrier, Palau Airways, was founded in 2011 and launched scheduled passenger services between Koror and Taipei in May 2012, but it halted its operations in April 2013.

Climate

Palau has a pleasantly warm climate throughout the year with temperatures averaging 81 °F (27 °C). The heaviest rainfall is between July and Oct.

Constitution and Government

The Constitution was adopted on 2 April 1979 and took effect from 1 Jan. 1981. The Republic has a bicameral legislature, the *Olbiil Era Kelulau* (National Congress), comprising a 13-member *Senate* and a 16-member *House of Delegates* (one from each of the Republic's 16 states), both elected for a term of 4 years as are the *President* and *Vice-President*. Customary social roles and land and sea rights are allocated by a matriarchal 16-clan system.

Currency

US currency is used.

Labour

In 2005 the total labour force numbered 10,203 (6,214 males and 3,989 females), of whom 9,777 were employed (5,982 males and 3,795 females).

Press

There are three local newspapers—*Island Times*, *Tia Belau* and *Palau Horizon*—although none are published daily.

Religion

The majority of the population is Roman Catholic.

Roads

There were 146 km of roads in 2007 including the 85-km US-funded two-lane highway around Babelthuap, providing a link between the old capital of Koror and the new capital of Melekeok.

Shipping

There is a port at Malakal.

Social Statistics

2012 births, 268; deaths, 164. Rates, 2012 (per 1,000 population): births, 12.7; deaths, 7.8; infant mortality (2012), 12 per 1,000 live births. Annual population growth rate, 1998–2008, 1.0%. Expectation of life at birth, 2010: males, 61 years; females, 68. Fertility rate, 2008, 1.9 births per woman.

Telecommunications

In 2008 there were 7,400 main (fixed) telephone lines and 12,200 mobile phone subscribers.

Territory and Population

The archipelago lies in the western Pacific and has a total land area of 488 km^2 (188 sq. miles). It comprises 26 islands and over 300 islets. Only nine of the islands are inhabited, the largest being Babelthuap (396 km^2), but most inhabitants live on the small island of Koror (18 km^2) to the south. In Oct. 2006 the capital moved from Koror to Melekeok, a newly-built town in eastern Babelthuap. The total population of Palau at the time of the 2012 census was 17,501 (9,217 males and 8,284 females), giving a density of 35.9 per km^2. In 2005 approximately 73% of the population were Palauans and 16% Filipinos. In 2011, 84.3% of the population lived in urban areas. Some 6,000 Palauans live abroad. The local language is Palauan; both Palauan and English are official languages.

Tourism

Tourism is a major industry, particularly marine-based. There were 83,795 visitor arrivals in 2009 (down from a record 94,895 in 2004). Of the visitor arrivals in 2009, 68,329 were for tourist purposes. Visitors to Palau in 2009 included: 27,180 from Japan; 16,571 from the Republic of China; 13,193 from the Republic of Korea.

Panama

República de Panamá (Republic of Panama)

Factsheet

Capital: Panama City
Population estimate, 2015: 3.93 m.
GNI per capita, 2014: (PPP$) 18,192
HDI/world rank, 2014: 0.780/60=
Internet domain extension: .pa

Civil Aviation

There is an international airport at Panama City (Tocumén International). The national carrier is COPA, which flew to nearly 50 different destinations in 2010. In 2012 scheduled airline traffic of Panama-based carriers flew 134.8 m. km; passenger-km totalled 14.5 bn. in the same year. In 2005 Tocumén International handled 2,710,857 passengers and 100,063 tonnes of freight.

Climate

Panama has a tropical climate, unvaryingly with high temperatures and only a short dry season from Jan. to April. Rainfall amounts are much higher on the north side of the isthmus. Panama City, Jan. 79 °F (26.1 °C), July 81 °F (27.2 °C). Annual rainfall 70″ (1,770 mm). Colón, Jan. 80 °F (26.7 °C), July 80 °F (26.7 °C). Annual rainfall 127″ (3,175 mm). Balboa Heights, Jan. 80 °F (26.7 °C), July 81 °F (27.2 °C). Annual rainfall 70″ (1,759 mm). Cristóbal, Jan. 80 °F (26.7 °C), July 81 °F (27.2 °C). Annual rainfall 130″ (3,255 mm).

Constitution and Government

The 1972 constitution, as amended in 1978, 1983, 1994 and 2004, provides for a *President*, elected for 5 years, two *Vice-Presidents* and a 72-seat *Legislative Assembly* (since reduced to 71 seats) to be elected for 5-year terms by a direct vote. As a result of the amendment of 2004 there has only been one *Vice-President* since the election of May 2009. To remain registered, parties must have attained at least 50,000 votes at the last election. A referendum held on 15 Nov. 1992 rejected constitutional reforms by 64% of votes cast. Turnout was 40%. In a referendum on 30 Aug. 1998 voters rejected proposed changes to the constitution which would allow for a President to serve a second consecutive term.

Currency

The monetary unit is the *balboa* (PAB) of 100 *centésimos*, at parity with the US dollar. The only paper currency used is that of the USA. US coinage is also legal tender.

Defence

The armed forces were disbanded in 1990 and constitutionally abolished in 1994. Divided between both coasts, the National Maritime Service, a coast guard rather than a navy, numbered around 600 personnel in 2011. In addition there is a paramilitary police force of 11,000 and a paramilitary national air service of 400 with no combat capable aircraft. In 2013 defence expenditure totalled US$637 m. (US$179 per capita), representing 1.5% of GDP.

Economy

Agriculture accounted for 5.3% of GDP in 2010, industry 16.8% and services 77.9%.

Labour

The labour force in 2013 was 1,799,000 (1,414,000 in 2003). 69.9% of the population aged 15–64 was economically active in 2013. In the same year 4.1% of the population was unemployed.

Press

In 2008 there were seven dailies with a combined circulation of 233,000.

Rail

The 1,435 mm gauge Ferrocarril de Panama, which connects Ancón on the Pacific with Cristóbal on the Atlantic along the bank of the Panama Canal, is the principal railway. Traffic in 2004 amounted to 77,000 passengers and 700,000 tonnes of freight. The United Brands Company runs 376 km of railway, and the Chiriquí National Railroad 171 km.

Religion

80% of the population is Roman Catholic and 14% Protestant. The remainder of the population follow other religions (notably Islam). There is freedom of religious worship and separation of Church and State. Clergymen may teach in schools but may not hold public office. In Feb. 2016 there was one Roman Catholic cardinal.

Roads

In 2006 there were 13,365 km of roads, of which 34.1% were paved. The road from Panama City westward to the cities of David and Concepción and to the Costa Rican frontier, with several branches, is part of the Pan-American Highway. The Trans-Isthmian Highway connects Panama City and Colón. In 2007 there were 436,200 passenger cars, 174,500 lorries and vans and 20,100 buses and coaches. There were 425 road accident fatalities in 2007.

Shipping

Panama, a nation with a transcendental maritime career and a strategic geographic position, is the shipping world's preferred flag for ship registry. The Ship Registry System equally accepts vessels of local or international ownership, as long as they comply with all legal parameters. Ship owners also favour Panamanian registry because fees are low. The Panamanian merchant fleet is the largest in the world. In Jan. 2009 there were 6,842 ships of 300 GT or over registered, totalling 180.87 m. GT (representing 22.9% of the world total). Of the 6,842 vessels registered, 2,198 were bulk carriers, 2,174 general cargo ships, 1,078 oil tankers, 798 container ships, 221 chemical tankers, 201 liquid gas tankers and 172 passenger ships.

Social Statistics

2006 births, 65,764; deaths, 14,358; marriages, 10,747; divorces, 2,866. Birth rate, 2006 (per 1,000 population), 20.0; death rate, 4.4. Annual population growth rate, 2000–05, 2.5%. Expectation of life at birth, 2007, was 73.0 years for males and 78.2 years for females. In 2006 the most popular age range for marrying was 25–29 for both males and females. Infant mortality, 2010, 17 per 1,000 live births; fertility rate, 2006, 2.4 births per woman.

Telecommunications

Panama had 5,677,000 mobile phone subscriptions in 2009 (1,643.7 per 1,000 inhabitants) and 537,100 fixed telephone lines. There were 277.9 internet users per 1,000 inhabitants in 2009. In Dec. 2011 there were 896,000 Facebook users.

Territory and Population

Panama is bounded in the north by the Caribbean Sea, east by Colombia, south by the Pacific Ocean and west by Costa Rica. The area is 75,001 km². Population at the census of 2010 was 3,405,813 (1,693,229 females); density, 44.9 per km². The population was 75.5% urban in 2011. The largest towns (2010) are Panama City, the capital, on the Pacific coast (430,299) and its suburb San Miguelito (315,019). Other large towns are Las Cumbres, Tocumen, David, Arraiján and Colón. The population is a mix of African, American, Arab, Chinese, European and Indian immigrants. The official language is Spanish.

Tourism

In 2011 there were 1,473,000 non-resident tourists (1,324,000 in 2010); spending by tourists totalled US$2,925 m. in 2011 (US$2,552 m. in 2010).

Papua New Guinea

Factsheet

Capital: Port Moresby
Population estimate, 2015: 7.62 m.
GNI per capita, 2014: (PPP$) 2,463
HDI/world rank, 2014: 0.505/158
Internet domain extension: .pg

Civil Aviation

Jacksons International Airport is at Port Moresby. The state-owned national carrier is Air Niugini, which carried 1.5 m. passengers in 2013 (1.1 m. on domestic flights). In 2010 there were scheduled international flights to Brisbane, Cairns, Hong Kong, Honiara, Manila, Nadi, Singapore, Sydney and Tokyo.

Climate

There is a monsoon climate, with high temperatures and humidity the year round. Port Moresby is in a rain shadow and is not typical of the rest of Papua New Guinea. Jan. 82 °F (27.8 °C), July 78 °F (25.6 °C). Annual rainfall 40″ (1,011 mm).

Constitution and Government

The constitution took effect on 16 Sept. 1975. The head of state is the British sovereign, who is represented by a *Governor-General*, nominated by parliament for 6-year terms. A single legislative house, known as the *National Parliament*, is made up of 111 members: 89 district representatives and 22 provincial representatives (MPs). The members are elected by universal suffrage; elections are held every 5 years. All citizens over the age of 18 are eligible to vote and stand for election. Voting is by secret ballot and follows the limited preferential system. The *Prime Minister*, nominated by parliament and appointed by the Governor-General, selects ministers for the National Executive Council. The government cannot be subjected to a vote of no confidence in the first 18 months of office. The 20 provincial assemblies, comprising elected national MPs, appointed members and elected local government representatives, are headed by a Governor, normally the provincial representative in the National Parliament.

Currency

The unit of currency is the *Nepalese rupee* (NPR) of 100 *paisas*. 50 *paisas* = 1 *mohur*.

Defence

The Papua New Guinea Defence Force had a total estimated strength of 3,100 in 2011 consisting of land, maritime and air elements. The Land Element, the senior of the three services, had around 2,500 personnel in 2011. The Maritime Operations Element, with around 400 personnel in 2011, has four patrol boats and two landing craft. There is an Air Operations Element, 200 strong in 2011, but it does not possess any combat capable aircraft. Defence expenditure in 2013 totalled US$84 m. (US$13 per capita), representing 0.5% of GDP.

Economy

Agriculture, forestry and fishing contributed 34.8% to GDP in 2008; followed by mining and quarrying, 25.1%; construction, 10.4%; and public administration, defence and services, 8.4%.

Labour

In 2012 the economically active population numbered 3.19 m. persons. The rate of unemployment was 2.3%.

Press

In 2008 there were two daily newspapers (the *Papua New Guinea Post-Courier* and the *National*) and a number of weeklies and monthlies. The *Papua New Guinea Post-Courier* is the oldest (1969) and most widely read, with a daily circulation of 30,000 (2007).

Religion

The Constitution provides for freedom of religion. In 2010 there were an estimated 4.69 m. Protestants and 2.06 m. Catholics according to the Pew Research Center's Forum on Religion & Public Life.

Roads

The national road system comprises some 8,800 km and there are about 8,100 km of provincial roads, as well as district, local and other roads. However, much of the network is in poor condition. There were 38,200 passenger cars in use in 2007 and 11,300 lorries and vans.

Shipping

There are 12 entry and four other main ports served by five major shipping lines; the Papua New Guinea Shipping Corporation is state-owned. In Jan. 2009 there were 55 ships of 300 GT or over registered, totalling 44,000 GT.

Social Statistics

Estimates, 2008: births, 207,000; deaths, 52,000. Rates, 2008 estimates (per 1,000 population): births, 31.4; deaths, 7.9. Expectation of life at birth in 2013 was 60.4 years for males and 64.6 years for females. Annual population growth rate, 2000–08, 2.5%. Infant mortality, 2010, 47 per 1,000 live births; fertility rate, 2008, 4.1 births per woman.

Telecommunications

In 2009 there were 133.7 mobile phone subscriptions for every 1,000 inhabitants and 8.9 fixed telephone lines per 1,000 inhabitants. In the same year there were an estimated 18.6 internet users per 1,000 inhabitants. In 2004 the government rejected a bid by a South African joint venture to acquire a 51% stake in the state-owned telecommunications company Telikom PNG.

Territory and Population

Papua New Guinea extends from the equator to Cape Baganowa in the Louisiade Archipelago to 11.40′ S. lat. and from the border of West Irian to 160° E. long. with a total area of 462,840 km². According to the 2011 census the population was 7,275,324 (3,772,864 males); density, 15.7 per km². In 2011, 12.6% of the population lived in urban areas (the second lowest percentage in the world). In 2011 population of Port Moresby (National Capital District) was 364,125. Other main towns are Lae, Madang, Mount Hagen, Wewak, Goroka and Kimbe. Tok Pisin (or Pidgin, a creole of English), Hiri Motu and English are all official languages.

Tourism

In 2008 there were 114,000 non-resident tourists (excluding same-day visitors), up from 104,000 in 2007 and 78,000 in 2006.

Paraguay

República del Paraguay (Republic of Paraguay)

Factsheet

Capital: Asunción
Population estimate, 2015: 6.64 m.
GNI per capita, 2014: (PPP$) 7,643
HDI/world rank, 2014: 0.679/112
Internet domain extension: .py

Civil Aviation

There is an international airport at Asunción (Silvio Pettirossi). The main Paraguay-based carrier is TAM Airlines (formerly TAM Mercosur). In 2012 scheduled airline traffic of Paraguayan-based carriers flew 4.2 m. km;

passenger-km totalled 720.8 m. in the same year. In 2014 Asunción (Silvio Pettirossi) handled 915,425 passengers (840,459 on international flights) and 10,954 tonnes of freight.

Climate

A tropical climate, with abundant rainfall and only a short dry season from July to Sept., when temperatures are lowest. Asunción, Jbbb ggg jjjan. 81 °F (27 °C), July 64 °F (17.8 °C). Annual rainfall 53″ (1,316 mm).

Constitution and Government

On 18 June 1992 a Constituent Assembly approved a new constitution. The head of state is the *President,* elected for a non-renewable 5-year term. Parliament consists of an 80-member *Chamber of Deputies,* elected from departmental constituencies, and a 45-member *Senate,* elected from a single national constituency.

Currency

The unit of currency is the *guaraní* (PYG), notionally divided into 100 *céntimos.*

Defence

The army, navy and air forces are separate services under a single command. The President of the Republic is the active C.-in-C. Conscription is for 12 months (2 years in the navy). In 2013 defence expenditure totalled US$364 m. (US$55 per capita), representing 1.2% of GDP.

Economy

In 2012 agriculture accounted for 17.4% of GDP, industry 28.1% and services 54.5%.

Labour

The labour force in 2013 was 3,132,000 (2,485,000 in 2003). 73.4% of the population aged 15–64 was economically active in 2013. In the same year 5.0% of the population was unemployed. Paraguay had 20,000 people living in slavery according to the Walk Free Foundation's 2013 *Global Slavery Index.*

Press

In 2008 there were eight daily newspapers with a combined circulation of 135,000.

Rail

The President Carlos Antonio López (formerly Paraguay Central) Railway used to run from Asunción to Encarnación, on the Río Alto Paraná, with a length of 441 km (1,435 mm gauge), and connected with Argentine Railways over the Encarnación-Posadas bridge. However, most commercial operations ended in 1999.

Religion

Religious liberty was guaranteed by the 1967 constitution. Article 6 recognized Roman Catholicism as the official religion of the country. In 2010 there were 6.25 m. Christians (of which about 92% Catholics and 7% Protestants) according to estimates by the Pew Research Center's Forum on Religion & Public Life and 110,000 folk religionists.

Roads

In 2012 there were 30,401 km of roads, of which 17.0% were paved. Passenger cars numbered 240,700 in 2007, there were 248,100 lorries and vans, 12,800 buses and coaches, and 134,900 motorcycles and mopeds. There were 845 fatalities as a result of road accidents in 2007.

Shipping

Asunción, the chief port, is 1,500 km from the sea. In Jan. 2009 there were 32 ships of 300 GT or over registered, totalling 44,000 GT.

Social Statistics

2006 births, 112,659; deaths, 19,298. Rates, 2006 (per 1,000 population): birth, 18.7; death, 3.2. Annual population growth rate, 2000–05, 2.0%. Expectation of life, 2007: 69.6 years for males and 73.8 for females. Infant mortality, 2010, 21 per 1,000 live births; fertility rate, 2008, 3.0 births per woman.

Telecommunications

In 2013 there were 437,643 main (fixed) telephone lines; mobile phone subscribers numbered 7,053,000 in 2013 (103.7 per 100 persons). In the same year there were 115,772 fixed broadband subscriptions and 374 wireless broadband subscriptions. In March 2012 there were 1.0 m. Facebook users.

Territory and Population

Paraguay is bounded in the northwest by Bolivia, northeast and east by Brazil and southeast, south and southwest by Argentina. The area is 406,752 km^2 (157,042 sq. miles). The 2002 census population was 5,163,198. Although a census was held in 2012 only 76% of the population was covered. According to international standards, the population census of a country should have a coverage of at least 90% for it to be valid. Population estimate 2014: 6,657,000 (3,360,000 males), giving a density of 16 per km^2. In 2011, 62.1% lived in urban areas. In 2014 the capital, Asunción, had an estimated population of 2,307,000. Other major cities are Ciudad del Este, San Lorenzo and Luque. There are 17 departments and the capital city. The population is mixed Spanish and Guaraní Indian. There are 89,000 unassimilated Indians of other tribal origin, in the Chaco and the forests of eastern Paraguay. The official languages are Spanish and Guaraní: 24.8% of the population speak only Guaraní; 51.5% are bilingual (Spanish/Guaraní); and 7.6% speak only Spanish.

Tourism

In 2011 there were 524,000 foreign tourists, spending US$281 m.

Peru

República del Perú (Republic of Peru)

Factsheet

Capital: Lima
Population estimate, 2015: 31.38 m.
GNI per capita, 2014: (PPP$) 11,015
HDI/world rank, 2014: 0.734/84
Internet domain extension: .pe

Civil Aviation

There is an international airport at Lima (Jorge Chávez International). The main airline is the Chilean-owned Lan Perú. The main airline is LATAM Perú, which was founded in 1998 as LAN Perú. In 2012 scheduled airline traffic of Peruvian-based carriers flew 108.4 m. km; passenger-km totalled 13.1 bn. in the same year. In 2012 Jorge Chávez International handled 13,330,290 passengers (6,901,988 on international flights) and 293,675 tonnes of freight.

Climate

There is a very wide variety of climates, ranging from tropical in the east to desert in the west, with perpetual snow in the Andes. In coastal areas, temperatures vary very little, either daily or annually, though humidity and cloudiness show considerable variation, with highest humidity from May to Sept. Little rain is experienced in that period. In the Sierra, temperatures remain fairly constant over the year, but the daily range is considerable. There the dry season is from April to Nov. Desert conditions occur in the extreme south, where the climate is uniformly dry, with a few heavy showers falling between Jan. and March. Lima, Jan. 74 °F (23.3 °C), July 62 °F (16.7 °C). Annual rainfall 2″ (48 mm). Cusco, Jan. 56 °F (13.3 °C), July 50 °F (10 °C).

Annual rainfall 32″ (804 mm). El Niño is the annual warm Pacific current that develops along the coasts of Peru and Ecuador.

Constitution and Government

The 1980 constitution provided for a legislative *Congress* consisting of a *Senate* and a *Chamber of Deputies*, and an Executive formed of the President and a Council of Ministers appointed by him. Elections were to be every 5 years with the President and Congress elected, at the same time, by separate ballots. On 5 April 1992 President Fujimori suspended the 1980 constitution and dissolved Congress. A referendum was held on 31 Oct. 1993 to approve the twelfth constitution, including a provision for the president to serve a consecutive second term. 52.2% of votes cast were in favour. The constitution was promulgated on 29 Dec. 1993. In Aug. 1996 Congress voted for the eligibility of the President to serve a third consecutive term of office. Congress has 130 members, elected for a 5-year term by proportional representation. All citizens over the age of 18 are eligible to vote. Voting is compulsory.

Currency

The monetary unit is the *nuevo sol* (PEN), of 100 *céntimos*, which replaced the *inti* in 1991 at a rate of 1 m. intis = 1 nuevo sol.

Defence

Conscription was abolished in 1999. In 2013 defence expenditure totalled US$2,844 m. (US$95 per capita), representing 1.3% of GDP.

Economy

Agriculture produced 6.8% of GDP in 2010, industry 35.9% and services 57.3%.

Labour

The labour force in 2014 totalled 16,396,400 (56% males). In 2014, 37.3% of those in employment were engaged in services, 24.9% in agriculture, forestry and fisheries, and 18.0% in commerce. In the same year 3.7% of the workforce was unemployed, down from 5.3% in 2004. Peru had 82,000 people living in slavery according to the Walk Free Foundation's 2013 *Global Slavery Index*.

Press

In 2008 there were 89 paid-for daily newspapers, of which 23 were national and 66 regional and local. The leading dailies are *Libero* (with an average daily circulation in 2008 of 214,000), *Trome* (average daily circulation in 2008 of 213,000) and *El Comercio* (average daily circulation in 2008 of 199,000).

Rail

Total length (2008), 1,884 km on 1,435- and 914-mm gauges. Passenger-km travelled in 2005 came to 126 m. and freight tonne-km to 1,101 m. A mass transit system opened in Lima in 2003. Peru's first metro, also in Lima, opened in Jan. 2012.

Religion

Religious liberty exists, but the Roman Catholic religion is protected by the State, and since 1929 only Roman Catholic religious instruction is permitted in schools, state or private. In 2010 an estimated 95.5% of the population were Christians according to the Pew Research Center's Forum on Religion & Public Life, with 3.0% having no religious affiliation. Of the Christians, 85% were Catholics and 13% Protestants. In Feb. 2016 there was one cardinal.

Roads

In 2006 there were 78,986 km of roads, of which 13.9% were paved. In 2007 there were 917,100 passenger cars, 480,900 lorries and vans and 44,400 buses and coaches. There were 67,155 road accidents involving injury in 2006 with 3,481 fatalities.

Shipping

In 2004 there were 46 sea-going vessels and 651 lake and river craft. In Jan. 2009 there were nine ships of 300 GT or over registered, totalling 87,000

GT. Callao is the busiest port, handling 18,191,000 tonnes of cargo in 2008. There are also ports at Chimbote, Paita and Talara.

Social Statistics

2009 births (estimate), 604,000; 2009 deaths (estimate), 144,000. Rates per 1,000 population (2009): birth, 21; death, 5. Annual population growth rate, 2005–10, 1.1%; infant mortality, 2010, 15 per 1,000 live births. Life expectancy, 2013: males, 72.2 years; females, 77.6. Fertility rate, 2008, 2.6 births per woman.

Telecommunications

In 2010 there were 3,160,000 main (fixed) telephone lines; mobile phone subscriptions numbered 29,115,000 in 2010 (99.5 per 100 persons). In 2013, 39.2% of the population aged six and over were internet users. In March 2012 there were 8.2 m. Facebook users.

Territory and Population

Peru is bounded in the north by Ecuador and Colombia, east by Brazil and Bolivia, south by Chile and west by the Pacific Ocean. Area, 1,285,216 km^2 (including the area of the Peruvian part of Lake Titicaca). Census population, 2007, 27,412,157; density, 21.3 per km^2. In 2011 the population was 77.3% urban. The country is administratively divided into 25 regions and an autonomous province of Lima. The largest cities (with 2007 census populations) are: Lima, 8,472,935; Arequipa, 784,651; Trujillo, 682,834; Chiclayo, 524,442; Piura, 377,496; Iquitos, 370,962. In 1991 there were some 100,000 Peruvians of Japanese origin. Indigenous peoples account for 47% of the population. The official languages are Spanish (spoken by 83.9% of the population in 2007), Quechua (13.2%) and Aymara (1.8%).

Tourism

There were 2,846,000 non-resident tourists in 2012, up from 1,916,000 in 2007; tourist spending in 2012 totalled US$3,074 m., compared to US$2,007 m. in 2007.

Philippines

Republika ng Pilipinas (Republic of the Philippines)

Factsheet

Capital: Manila
Population estimate, 2015: 100.70 m.
GNI per capita, 2014: (PPP$) 7,915
HDI/world rank, 2014: 0.668/115
Internet domain extension: .ph

Civil Aviation

There are international airports at Manila (Ninoy Aquino) and Cebu (Mactan International). In Sept. 1998 the Asian economic crisis that had started more than a year earlier forced the closure of the national carrier, Philippine Airlines, after it had suffered huge losses. However, it has since resumed its operations both internally and externally. In 2005 scheduled airline traffic of Philippine-based carriers flew 28.4 m. km, carrying 6,610,400 passengers. In 2012 Manila handled 31,878,935 passengers (17,739,000 on domestic flights) and 460,135 tonnes of freight.

Climate

Some areas have an equatorial climate while others experience tropical monsoon conditions, with a wet season extending from June to Nov. Mean temperatures are high all year, with very little variation. Manila, Jan. 77 °F (25 °C), July 82 °F (27.8 °C). Annual rainfall 83.3″ (2,115.9 mm).

Constitution and Government

A new constitution was ratified by referendum in Feb. 1987 with the approval of 78.5% of voters. The head of state is the *President*, directly elected for a non-renewable 6-year term. Congress consists of a 24-member upper house, the *Senate* (elected for a 6-year term from 'at large' seats covering the country as a whole, half of them renewed every 3 years), and a *House of Representatives* of 291 members. In the *House of Representatives* 233 members are directly elected for a 3-year term and the rest are chosen from party and minority-group lists. A campaign led by the president at the time, Fidel Ramos, to amend the constitution to allow him to stand for a second term was voted down by the Senate by 23 to one in Dec. 1996.

Currency

The unit of currency is the *peso* (PHP) of 100 *centavos*.

Defence

An agreement of Dec. 1994 authorizes US naval vessels to be repaired in Philippine ports. The Philippines is a signatory of the South-East Asia Collective Defence Treaty. Defence expenditure in 2013 totalled US$2,205 m. (US$21 per capita), representing 0.8% of GDP.

Economy

Agriculture accounted for 12.3% of GDP in 2010, industry 32.6% and services 55.1%.

Labour

The labour force in 2013 was 42,923,000 (34,721,000 in 2003). 67.0% of the population aged 15–64 was economically active in 2013. The unemployment rate in Oct. 2013 was 6.5%. Philippines had 0.15 m. people living in slavery according to the Walk Free Foundation's 2013 *Global Slavery Index*.

Press

There were 28 daily newspapers in 2008, with a combined circulation of 3,870,000. The leading daily is *Remate*, with an average daily circulation of 620,000 in 2008.

Rail

In 2005 the National Railways totalled 419 km (1,067 mm gauge). In 2008 passenger-km totalled 16 m. There is a light metro railway in Manila.

Religion

In 2010 an estimated 92.6% of the population were Christians according to the Pew Research Center's Forum on Religion & Public Life, with 5.5% Muslims and 1.5% folk religionists. Of the Christians, 87% were Catholics and 12% Protestants. The Roman Catholic Church had four cardinals in Feb. 2016. There are 16 ecclesiastical provinces, each of which consists of an archdiocese and a number of suffragan dioceses and is overseen by an archbishop.

Roads

In 2013 roads totalled 216,612 km, including 32,227 km of national roads. In 2007 there were 937,600 passenger cars in use, 55,200 buses and coaches, 1,875,300 vans and lorries, and 2,647,500 motorcycles and mopeds. There were 6,240 road accidents involving injury in 2006 with 961 fatalities.

Shipping

The main ports are Cagayan de Oro, Cebu, Davao, Iloilo, Manila and Zamboanga. Manila, the leading port, handled 45,230,000 tonnes of cargo in 2008. In Jan. 2009 there were 838 ships of 300 GT or over registered, totalling 4,771,000 GT. Of the 838 vessels registered, 415 were general cargo ships, 168 passenger ships, 128 oil tankers, 83 bulk carriers, 21 chemical tankers, 15 liquid gas tankers and eight container ships.

Social Statistics

Births, 2007, 1,749,878; deaths, 2007, 441,956. Divorce is illegal. Birth rate per 1,000 population (2007), 19.7; death rate (2007), 5.1. Expectation of life at birth, 2007, was 69.4 years for males and 73.9 years for females. Annual population growth rate, 2000–05, 2.2%. Infant mortality, 2010, 23 per 1,000 live births; fertility rate, 2008, 3.1 births per woman. Abortion is illegal.

Telecommunications

In 2013 there were 3,149,000 main (fixed) telephone lines. In the same year mobile phone subscriptions numbered 102,824,000 (1,045.0 per 1,000 persons). An estimated 36.2% of the population were internet users in 2012. In March 2012 there were 27.7 m. Facebook users.

Territory and Population

The Philippines is situated between 21.25′ and 4.23′ N. lat. and between 116° and 127° E. long. It is composed of 7,100 islands and islets, 3,144 of which are named. Approximate land area, 300,076 km² (115,859 sq. miles). The largest islands (in km²) are Luzon (104,688), Mindanao (94,630), Samar (13,080), Negros (12,710), Palawan (11,785), Panay (11,515), Mindoro (9,735), Leyte (7,214), Cebu (4,422), Bohol (3,865) and Masbate (3,269). The census population in May 2010 was 92,337,852; density, 307.7 per km². In 2011, 49.1% of the population lived in urban areas. Population of Metro Manila in 2007, 11,553,427. Filipino (based on Tagalog) is spoken as a mother tongue by only 29.3%; among the 76 other indigenous languages spoken, Cebuano is spoken as a mother tongue by 23.3% and Ilocano by 9.3%. English, which along with Filipino is one of the official languages, is widely spoken.

Tourism

In 2012, 4,273,000 non-resident tourists brought revenue of US$4,963 m.

Poland

Rzeczpospolita Polska (Polish Republic)

Factsheet

Capital: Warsaw
Population estimate, 2015: 38.61 m.
GNI per capita, 2014: (PPP$) 23,177
HDI/world rank, 2014: 0.843/36
Internet domain extension: .pl

Civil Aviation

The main international airport is at Warsaw (Frederic Chopin), with some international flights from Kraków (John Paul II Balice International), Bydgoszcz, Gdansk, Katowice, Lódz, Poznan, Rzeszów, Szczecin and Wroclaw. The national carrier is LOT-Polish Airlines (99.8% state-owned). It flew 107.7 m. km in 2011, carrying 6,491,199 passengers (5,377,869 on international flights). In 2011 Warsaw handled 9,324,635 passengers (8,253,153 on international flights) and 60,625 tonnes of freight.

Climate

Climate is continental, marked by long and severe winters. Rainfall amounts are moderate, with a marked summer maximum. Warsaw, Jan. 24 °F (−4.3 °C), July 64 °F (17.9 °C). Annual rainfall 18.3″ (465 mm). Gdansk, Jan. 29 °F (−1.7 °C), July 63 °F (17.2 °C). Annual rainfall 22.0″ (559 mm). Kraków, Jan. 27 °F (−2.8 °C), July 67 °F (19.4 °C). Annual rainfall 28.7″ (729 mm). Poznan, Jan. 26 °F (−3.3 °C), July 64 °F (17.9 °C). Annual rainfall 21.0″ (534 mm). Szczecin, Jan. 27 °F (−3.0 °C), July 64 °F (17.7 °C). Annual rainfall 18.4″ (467 mm). Wroclaw, Jan. 24 °F (−4.3 °C), July 64 °F (17.9 °C). Annual rainfall 20.7″ (525 mm).

Constitution and Government

The present Constitution was passed by national referendum on 25 May 1997 and became effective on 17 Oct. 1997. The head of state is the *President*, who is directly elected for a 5-year term (renewable once). The President may appoint, but may not dismiss, cabinets. The authority of the republic is vested in the *Sejm* (Parliament of 460 members), elected by proportional representation for 4 years by all citizens over 18. There is a 5% threshold for parties and 8% for coalitions, but seats are reserved for representatives of ethnic minorities even if their vote falls below 5%. 69 of the Sejm seats are awarded from the national lists of parties polling more than 7% of the vote. The Sejm elects a *Council of State* and a *Council of Ministers*. There is also an elected 100-member upper house, the *Senate*. The President and the Senate each has a power of veto which only a two-thirds majority of the Sejm can override. The President does not, however, have a veto over the annual budget. The *Prime Minister* is chosen by the President with the approval of the Sejm. A *Political Council* consultative to the presidency consisting of representatives of all the major political tendencies was set up in Jan. 1991.

Currency

The currency unit is the *zloty* (PLN) of 100 *groszy*. A new zloty was introduced on 1 Jan. 1995 at 1 new zloty = 10,000 old zlotys.

Defence

Poland is divided into two military districts: Pomeranian (North) and Silesian (South). In 2013 defence expenditure totalled US$9,829 m. (US$256 per capita), representing 1.9% of GDP. Conscription ended on 1 Jan. 2010.

Economy

In 2011 trade, restaurants and hotels contributed 17.1% to GDP; followed by finance and real estate, 16.6%; manufacturing, 16.6%; services, 11.1%; construction, 6.2%; and transport and communications, 6.1%.

Labour

In 2008 a total of 14,037,000 persons were in employment. In Dec. 2008, 3,103,000 persons worked in industry, 2,269,000 in trade and repairs, 1,133,000 in property, renting and business activities, 1,039,000 in education, 840,000 in construction, 809,000 in transport, storage and communications, and 748,000 in health and social services. The unemployment rate increased steadily for several years peaking at 20.3% in the period Aug.–Oct. 2002 (more than double the EU average at the time). It has declined considerably since then, and in Dec. 2014 stood at 8.0%. Poland had 0.14 m. people living in slavery according to the Walk Free Foundation's 2013 *Global Slavery Index*.

Press

In 2011 there were 32 daily newspapers with a combined daily circulation of 3,108,400 (81 per 1,000 inhabitants). The most popular newspapers are *Fakt, Gazeta Wyborcza, Super Express* and *Rzeczpospolita*. 7,713 magazine titles were published in 2011 with a combined total of 1,437 m. copies. In 2011, 31,515 book titles were published.

Rail

In 2011 there were 19,725 km of railways in use managed by Polish State Railways (11,817 km electrified). Over 98% is standard 1,435 mm gauge with the rest broad gauge (1,520 mm). In 2011 railways carried 184.6 m. passengers and 140.5 m. tonnes of freight. Passenger-km travelled in 2011 came to 15.7 bn. and freight tonne-km to 37.2 bn. Some regional railways are operated by local authorities. An 11.1-km metro opened in Warsaw in 1995, extended by 2008 to 22.7 km. A second 32-km line is currently under construction. The initial 6.3 km of the line were opened in March 2015. The second phase of the project is due to be completed in 2019. There are also 14 tram/light rail networks with a total length of 930 km.

Religion

State relations are regulated by laws of 1989 which guarantee religious freedom, grant the Church radio and TV programmes and permit it to run schools, hospitals and old age homes. The Church has a university (Lublin) and seminaries. On 28 July 1993 the government signed a Concordat with the Vatican regulating mutual relations. The religious capital is Gniezno. Its archbishop, Henryk Muszynski (b. 1933) is the primate of Poland. Kazimierz Nycz was appointed archbishop of Warsaw on 1 April 2007. In Oct. 1978 Cardinal Karol Wojtyla, archbishop of Kraków, was elected Pope as John Paul II. In Feb. 2016 there were six cardinals.

Roads

The total length of public roads at the end of 2012 amounted to 412,000 km of which hard surface roads accounted for 68% and motorways amounted to 1,365 km. The total number of registered motor road vehicles and road tractors amounted to 24.9 m. as of 31 Dec. 2012, of which 18,744,000 passenger cars, 3,178,000 lorries, vans and road tractors, 99,900 buses, and 2,208 motorcycles and mopeds. In 2012 road transport totalled 20,012 m. passenger-km and freight 233,310 m. tonne-km. The number of persons killed in road accidents amounted to 3,577 in 2012, representing 9.3 deaths per 100,000 population. Poland has one of the highest death rates in road accidents in the European Union.

Shipping

The principal ports are Gdansk, Szczecin, Swinoujscie and Gdynia. The total volume of cargo traffic at all Polish seaports amounted to 58.8 m. tonnes in 2012, including 24.4 m. tonnes at Gdansk and 13.2 m. tonnes at Gdynia. The Polish maritime transport fleet carried 7.5 m. tonnes of cargo and 642,200 passengers in 2012. At the end of 2012 the Polish maritime fleet comprised 110 ships totalling 3,045,000 DWT. The total length of inland waterways at the end of 2012 was 3,659 km. In 2012 inland waterway transport totalled 24 m. passenger-km and 815 m. freight tonne-km.

Social Statistics

2010 (in 1,000): births, 415.0; deaths, 378.5; marriages, 228.3; divorces, 61.3; infant deaths, 2.1. Rates (per 1,000 population): birth, 10.8; death, 9.9; marriage, 6.0; divorce, 1.6; infant mortality (per 1,000 live births), 5.0. A law prohibiting abortion was passed in 1993, but an amendment of Aug. 1996 permits it in cases of hardship or difficult personal situation. The most popular age range for marrying in 2010 was 25-29 for both males and females. Expectation of life at birth, 2013, was 72.3 years for males and 80.5 years for females. In 2010 there were 17,360 emigrants (including 6,818 to Germany) and 15,246 immigrants. Number of suicides, 2008, 5,681; the suicide rate per 100,000 population was 26.4 among males and 4.1 among females in 2008. Population growth rate, 2010, 0.1%; fertility rate, 2008, 1.3 births per woman (one of the lowest rates in the world).

Telecommunications

In 2014 mobile phone subscribers numbered 56,905,306 (1,488.9 per 1,000 persons). In the same year there were 4,822,233 main (fixed) telephone lines. The privatization of Telekomunikacja Polska (TP SA), the former state telecom operator, was completed in 2001 with France Télécom (now Orange S.A.) purchasing a 49.8% stake in the company. This rose to 50.67% in June 2013. In April 2012 Telekomunikacja Polska was renamed Orange Polska in line with France Télécom's international branding. 66.6% of the population were internet users in 2014. In March 2012 there were 7.5 m. Facebook users.

Territory and Population

Poland is bounded in the north by the Baltic Sea and Russia, east by Lithuania, Belarus and Ukraine, south by the Czech Republic and Slovakia and west by Germany. Poland comprises an area of 312,685 km^2 (120,728 sq. miles). At the census of 31 March 2011 the population was 38,511,824, giving a density of 123.2 per km^2 In 2009, 61.0% of the population lived in urban areas. The country is divided into 16 regions or voivodships (*wojewodztwo*), created from the previous 49 on 1 Jan. 1999 following administrative reform. Population (in 1,000) of the largest towns and cities (2011 census): Warsaw (Warszawa), 1,700.6; Cracow (Kraków), 757.6; Lódz, 728.9; Wroclaw, 630.1; Poznan, 554.7; Gdansk, 460.3; Szczecin, 410.1; Bydgoszcz, 363.9; Lublin, 349.1; Katowice, 310.8; Bialystok, 294.0. The population is 96.7% Polish. Minorities at the 2011 census included 418,000 who stated that they were Silesians as a national-ethnic identification, 49,000 Germans, 37,000 Belarusians and 36,000 Ukrainians. There are an estimated 230,000 people in Poland of Kashubian ethnicity (direct descendants of an early Slavic tribe of Pomeranians). They generally declare Polish nationality and consider themselves both Poles and Kashubians. The official language is Polish.

Tourism

In 2011 there were 13,350,000 tourist arrivals, up from 12,470,000 in 2010 and 11,890,000 in 2009. The main countries of origin of non-resident tourists in 2011 were Germany (4,590,000), Ukraine (1,580,000), Belarus (1,220,000) and Lithuania (630,000).

Portugal

República Portuguesa (Republic of Portugal)

Factsheet

Capital: Lisbon
Population estimate, 2015: 10.35 m.
GNI per capita, 2014: (PPP$) 25,757
HDI/world rank, 2014: 0.830/43
Internet domain extension: .pt

Civil Aviation

There are international airports at Portela (Lisbon), Pedras Rubras (Porto), Faro (Algarve) and Funchal (Madeira). The national carrier is the state-owned TAP-Air Portugal, with some domestic and international flights being provided by Portugália. In 2006 scheduled airline traffic of Portuguese-based carriers flew 171 m. km, carrying 9,449,000 passengers (6,449,000 on international flights). In 2007 Lisbon handled 13,393,000 passengers (11,249,000 on international flights) and 82,645 tonnes of freight. Faro was the second busiest in terms of passenger traffic, with 5,471,000 passengers, and Porto was the second busiest for freight, with 31,991 tonnes.

Climate

Because of westerly winds and the effect of the Gulf Stream, the climate ranges from the cool, damp Atlantic type in the north to a warmer and drier Mediterranean type in the south. July and Aug. are virtually rainless everywhere. Inland areas in the north have greater temperature variation, with continental winds blowing from the interior. Lisbon, Jan. 52 °F (11 °C), July 72 °F (22 °C). Annual rainfall 27.4″ (686 mm). Porto, Jan. 48 °F (8.9 °C), July 67 °F (19.4 °C). Annual rainfall 46″ (1,151 mm).

Constitution and Government

Portugal is governed under the constitution of April 1976, amended in 1982, 1989, 1992, 1997, 2001, 2004 and 2005. The 1982 revision abolished the (military) Council of the Revolution and reduced the role of the President under it. Portugal is a sovereign, unitary republic. Executive power is vested in the *President*, directly elected for a 5-year term (for a maximum of two consecutive terms). Political parties may support a candidate in presidential elections but not actually field a candidate. The President appoints a Prime Minister and, upon the latter's nomination, other members of the Council of Ministers. The 230-member *National Assembly* is a unicameral legislature elected for 4-year terms by universal adult suffrage under a system of proportional representation. Women did not have the vote until 1976.

Currency

On 1 Jan. 1999 the euro (EUR) became the legal currency in Portugal at the irrevocable conversion rate of 200·482 escudos to 1 euro. The euro, which consists of 100 cents, has been in circulation since 1 Jan. 2002. On the introduction of the euro there was a 'dual circulation' period before the escudo ceased to be legal tender on 28 Feb. 2002.

Defence

Conscription was abolished in Nov. 2004. Portugal now has a purely professional army. In 2013 defence expenditure totalled US$2,773 m. (US$257 per capita), representing 1.3% of GDP.

Economy

Services accounted for about 76% of GDP in 2012, industry 22% and agriculture 2%.

Labour

The maximum working week was reduced from 44 h to 40 in 1997. A minimum wage is fixed by the government. In 2011 the minimum wage was €485 a month. Retirement is at 65 years for men and 62 for women. The labour force in 2013 was 5,397,000 (5,463,000 in 2003). In Dec. 2014 the unemployment rate was 13.4% (down from 16.5% in 2013 as a whole). Of those in employment in 2013, 68.5% worked in services, 24.9% in industry and 6.6% in agriculture. The immigrant population makes up 10% of the labour force.

Press

There were 24 daily papers in 2008 (of which 19 were paid-for and five free), with a combined circulation of 1,170,000. There were ten national dailies in 2008 and 14 regional and local dailies. The most widely read newspapers are *Correio da Manhã* and *Jornal de Notícias*.

Rail

In 2011 total railway length was 2,794 km. Passenger-km travelled in 2011 came to 3.75 bn. and freight tonne-km to 2.06 bn. There is a metro (19 km) and tramway (94 km) in Lisbon. New light rail systems were opened in Porto in 2002 and Almada in 2007.

Religion

There is freedom of worship, both in public and private, with the exception of creeds incompatible with morals and the life and physical integrity of the people. A study by the Pew Research Center's Forum on Religion & Public Life estimated that there were 10.01 m. Christians in 2010 (98% of which were Catholics) and 470,000 people with no religious affiliation. In Feb. 2016 there were three cardinals.

Roads

In 2005 there were 2,613 km of motorways, 5,883 km of national roads, 4,406 km of secondary roads and 63,900 km of other roads. In 2006 the number of vehicles registered included 5,234,500 passenger cars, 535,300 motorcycles and mopeds, 119,000 lorries and vans and 29,700 buses and coaches. In 2007 there were 854 deaths in road accidents.

Shipping

In 2007, 15,226 vessels of 151.82 m. tonnes entered all Portuguese ports; 367,391 passengers embarked and 368,095 disembarked during 2007. 21.17 m. tonnes of cargo were loaded in 2007 and 47.05 m. tonnes unloaded. In Jan. 2009 there were 154 ships of 300 GT or over registered, totalling 981,000 GT.

Social Statistics

2012: births, 89,841; deaths, 107,612; marriages, 34,423; divorces, 25,380. Rates per 1,000 population in 2012: birth, 8.5; death, 10.2; marriage, 3.3; divorce, 2.4. Annual population growth rate, 2005–10, 0.2%. Expectation of life at birth, 2013, was 76.9 years for males and 82.9 years for females. Infant mortality in 2010 was three per 1,000 live births, down from 77 per 1,000 live births in 1960, representing the greatest reduction in infant mortality rates in Europe over the past half century. Fertility rate, 2008, 1.4 births per woman.

Telecommunications

Portugal Telecom (PT) was formed from a merger of three state-owned utilities in 1994. It is now fully privatized. In 2013 there were 4,530,000 main (fixed) telephone lines. In the same year mobile phone subscribers numbered 11,991,000 excluding machine-to-machine subscriptions. 62.1% of the population aged 16–74 were internet users in 2013. There were 19.8 broadband subscribers per 100 inhabitants in Dec. 2010. In March 2012 there were 4.2 m. Facebook users.

Territory and Population

Mainland Portugal is bounded in the north and east by Spain and south and west by the Atlantic Ocean. The Atlantic archipelagoes of the Azores and of Madeira form autonomous but integral parts of the republic, which has a total area of 92,207 km². Population (2011 census), 10,562,178 (5,515,578 females). Mainland Portugal is divided into five regions. In 2011, 61.3% of the population lived in urban areas. The capital is Lisbon (Lisboa), with a population of 547,733 in 2011 (metropolitan area population, 2,821,876 in 2011). Other major cities are Porto, 237,591 in 2011 (metropolitan area population, 1,672,670 in 2011), Almada, Amadora, Braga, Funchal (in Madeira) and Vila Nova de Gaia. The official language is Portuguese.

The Azores islands lie in the mid-Atlantic Ocean, between 1,200 and 1,600 km west of Lisbon. They are divided into three widely separated groups with clear channels between, São Miguel (759 km^2) together with Santa Maria (97 km^2) being the most easterly; about 160 km northwest of them lies the central cluster of Terceira (382 km^2), Graciosa (62 km^2), São Jorge (246 km^2), Pico (446 km^2) and Faial (173 km^2); still another 240 km to the northwest are Flores (143 km^2) and Corvo (17 km^2), the latter being the most isolated and undeveloped of the islands.

Tourism

In 2010, 6,831,600 non-resident tourists stayed in holiday accommodation (6,478,700 in 2009) including: 1,375,800 from Spain; 1,111,200 from the UK; 728,800 from Germany; 574,800 from France. There were 2,011 hotel establishments with 279,506 beds in 2010.

Qatar

Dawlat Qatar (State of Qatar)

Factsheet

Capital: Doha
Population estimate, 2015: 2.24 m.
GNI per capita, 2014: (PPP$) 123,124
HDI/world rank, 2014: 0.850/32=
Internet domain extension: .qa

Civil Aviation

The flag carrier is Qatar Airways, which is state-owned and carried 18 m. passengers in 2012–13. Qatar's airport is Hamad International Airport, which opened in April 2014 to replace the old Doha International Airport (where passenger numbers had quadrupled between 2003 and 2013).

Climate

The climate is hot and humid. Doha, Jan. 62 °F (16.7 °C), July 98 °F (36.7 °C). Annual rainfall 2.5″ (62 mm).

Constitution and Government

Qatar is ruled by an *Amir*. HH Sheikh Tamim bin Hamad Al Thani (b. 1980) assumed power after his father, HH Sheikh Hamad bin Khalifa Al Thani, KCMG, abdicated on 25 June 2013. The heir apparent was Sheikh Hamad's third son, Sheikh Jasim bin Hamad Al Thani (b. 1978), but in Aug. 2003 he named his fourth son, Sheikh Tamim bin Hamad Al Thani, as heir apparent instead. Qatar's first written constitution was approved in June 2004 and came into force on 9 June 2005. It allows for a 45-member *Consultative Assembly* or *Majlis al-Shura*, with 30 members directly elected and 15 appointed by the Amir. A *Council of Ministers* is assisted by a 35-member nominated Advisory Council.

Currency

The unit of currency is the *Qatari riyal* (QAR) of 100 *dirhams*, introduced in 1973.

Defence

Defence expenditure in 2011 totalled an estimated US$3,476 m. (approximately US$1,880 per capita), representing around 2% of GDP.

Economy

Oil, natural gas and other mining contributed 51.7% to GDP in 2010; followed by finance and real estate, 13.4%; manufacturing (excluding oil- and natural gas-related manufacturing), 10.6%; and public administration and defence, 7.7%.

Labour

In 2011 the economically active population totalled 1,271,100. Males constituted 88% of the labour force in 2011; foreigners make up 94% of the workforce. Qatar has the lowest percentages of females in the workforce of any country.

Press

There are four Arabic language daily newspapers—*Al-Rayah*, *Al-Sharq*, *Al-Watan* and *Al-Arab*. *The Gulf Times*, *The Peninsula* and *Qatar Tribune* are English dailies. In 2008 the combined circulation was 115,000. *Qatar Chronicle*, launched in 2012, is an online news portal published on a daily basis in English and Arabic.

Religion

The population is predominantly Muslim, although there is a small Christian minority among expatriates.

Roads

In 2007 there were about 7,790 km of roads. Vehicles in use in 2007 totalled 605,700. In 2007 there were 199 fatalities as a result of road accidents.

Social Statistics

Births, 2008, 17,210; deaths, 1,942; marriages, 3,235; divorces, 939. 2008 rates per 1,000 population: births, 11.9; deaths, 1.3. Qatar's 2008 death rate was among the lowest in the world. Infant mortality, 2010 (per 1,000 live births), 7. Expectation of life in 2013 was 77.8 years for males and 79.5 for females. Annual population growth rate, 200–08, 9.1% (the highest in the world). Fertility rate, 2008, 2.4 births per woman.

Telecommunications

In 2013 there were an estimated 413,000 main (fixed) telephone lines; mobile phone subscribers numbered an estimated 3,310,000 in the same year. 69.3% of the population were internet users in 2012. In March 2012 there were 481,000 Facebook users.

Territory and Population

Qatar is a peninsula running north into the Persian Gulf. It is bounded in the south by Saudi Arabia. The territory includes a number of islands in the coastal waters of the peninsula, the most important of which is Halul, the storage and export terminal for the offshore oilfields. The area of Qatar is 11,571 km^2. Population at the census of April 2010, 1,699,435; density 146.9 per km^2. In 2011, 95.9% of the population lived in urban areas. The capital is Doha, which is the main port, and had a census population in 2010 of 521,283. Other towns are Dukhan (the centre of oil production), Umm Said (the oil terminal of Qatar), Ruwais, Wakra, Al Khour, Umm Salal Mohammad and Umm Bab. About 40% of the population are Arabs, 18% Indian, 18% Pakistani and 10% Iranian. Other nationalities make up the remaining 14%. Only about 10% of the population are Qatari citizens. The official language is Arabic.

Tourism

In 2008, 1,405,000 non-resident tourists stayed in hotels (964,000 in 2007).

Romania

România

Factsheet

Capital: Bucharest
Population estimate, 2015: 19.51 m.
GNI per capita, 2014: (PPP$) 18,108
HDI/world rank, 2014: 0.793/52=
Internet domain extension: .ro

Civil Aviation

Tarom (*Transporturi Aeriene Române*) is the 97.2% state-owned airline. In 2010 it provided domestic services and international flights to over 40 cities. The largest Romanian airline is Blue Air, a low-cost carrier founded in 2004. In 2016 it carried a record 3,590,129 passengers. Bucharest's main airport is Henri Coandă International Airport, generally known by its former official name of Bucharest Otopeni International Airport. A second Bucharest airport, Aurel Vlaicu International, used to be the country's second busiest airport but since early 2012 caters exclusively for business air traffic. Henri Coandă International handled 7,120,024 passengers in 2012 and 26,494 tonnes of freight.

Climate

A continental climate with an annual average temperature varying between 8 °C in the north and 11 °C in the south. Bucharest, Jan. 27 °F (−2.7 °C), July 74 °F (23.5 °C). Annual rainfall 23.1″ (579 mm). Constanţa, Jan. 31 °F (−0.6 °C), July 71 °F (21.7 °C). Annual rainfall 15″ (371 mm).

Constitution and Government

A new constitution was approved by a referendum on 18–19 Oct. 2003. Turnout was 55.7%, and 89.7% of votes cast were in favour. The Constitution, which replaces the previous one from 1991, defines Romania as a republic where the rule of law prevails in a social and democratic state. Private property rights and a market economy are guaranteed. The new pro-European constitution was aimed at helping Romania achieve EU membership. The head of state is the *President*, elected by direct vote for a maximum of two 5-year terms. The president is not allowed to be affiliated with any political party while in office. The President appoints the *Prime Minister*, who then has to be approved by a vote in parliament. The President is empowered to veto legislation unless it is upheld by a two-thirds parliamentary majority. The National Assembly consists of a 412-member *Chamber of Deputies* and a 176-member *Senate*; both are elected for 4-year terms from 43 constituencies through a proportional mixed member system. 18 seats in the Chamber of Deputies are reserved for ethnic minorities. There is a 3% threshold for admission to either house. Votes for parties not reaching this threshold are redistributed. There is a *Constitutional Court*.

Currency

The monetary unit has since 1 July 2005 been the *new leu*, pl. *new lei* (RON) notionally of 100 *bani*, which replaced the *leu* (ROL) at a rate of one new leu = 10,000 lei.

Defence

Compulsory national military service was abolished in 2006. In 2013 defence expenditure totalled US$2,475 m. (US$114 per capita), representing 1.3% of GDP.

Economy

In 2008 transport, communications, trade and hotels contributed 23.3% to GDP; followed by mining, quarrying, public utilities and manufacturing, 22.9%; public administration and services, 13.5%; and finance and real estate, 12.6%.

Labour

The labour force in 2006 totalled 10.04 m.; the employed population was 9.31 m. In the civilian labour force 29.7% worked in agriculture and 26.7% in manufacturing and construction. In 2006, 46% of the employed workforce were women. The standard retirement age is 65 years for men and 60 for women. A minimum monthly wage was set in 1993; it is 670 new lei for full-time adult employees from 1 Jan. 2011. The average gross monthly wage was 1,845 new lei in 2009. Unemployment was 7.2% in Jan. 2012 (7.3% in Jan. 2011). Romania had 24,000 people living in slavery according to the Walk Free Foundation's 2013 *Global Slavery Index*.

Press

In 2008 there were 80 daily papers (75 paid-for and five free) with a combined circulation of 1,634,000. The newspapers with the highest circulation in 2008 were *Libertatea*, *Click!* and *Cancan*.

Rail

Length of standard-gauge route in 2011 was 10,638 km, of which 4,031 km were electrified; there were 135 km of 1,524 mm gauge lines and four km of narrow-gauge. Freight carried in 2011, 54.8 m. tonnes; passengers, 53.5 m. There is a metro (62.4 km) and tram/light rail network (338 km) in Bucharest, and tramways in 13 other cities.

Religion

The government officially recognizes 17 religions (which receive various forms of state support); the predominant one is the Romanian Orthodox Church. It is autocephalous, but retains dogmatic unity with the Eastern Orthodox Church. Its *Patriarch* is Daniel (enthroned 30 Sept. 2007). There are six metropolitanates, made up of archdioceses and dioceses, with a total of 13,527 parishes. In Feb. 2016 there was one cardinal. Religious affiliation at the 2011 census included: Romanian Orthodox, 16,307,004 (about 81% of the population); Roman Catholic, 870,774; Protestant Reformed Church, 600,932; Pentecostal, 362,314; Greek Catholics, 150,593; Baptist, 112,850.

Roads

There were 81,693 km of roads in 2008, of which 281 km were motorways, 16,318 km main and national roads and 65,094 km secondary and other roads. Passenger cars in 2005 numbered 3,363,800 (156 per 1,000 inhabitants). In 2007 there were 2,712 fatalities as a result of road accidents.

Shipping

In Jan. 2009 there were 35 ships of 300 GT or over registered, totalling 150,000 GT. The Romanian-controlled fleet comprised 57 vessels of 1,000 GT or over in Jan. 2009, of which 11 were under the Romanian flag and 46 under foreign flags. The main ports are Constanţa and Constanţa South Agigea on the Black Sea and Galaţi, Brăila and Tulcea on the Danube. In 2009 the length of navigable inland waterways was around 1,730 km including 1,075 km on the Danube River.

Social Statistics

2010 (in 1,000): births, 212.2; deaths, 259.7; marriages, 115.8; divorces, 32.6. Rates, 2010 (per 1,000 population): live births, 9.9; deaths, 12.1; marriages, 5.4; divorces, 1.5. Infant mortality, 2010 (per 1,000 live births), 9.8. Expectation of life at birth, 2013, was 70.3 years for males and 77.5 years for females. In 2010 the most popular age range for marrying was 25–29 for males and 20–24 for females. Measures designed to raise the birth rate were abolished in 1990, and abortion and contraception legalized. The annual abortion rate, at approximately 41 per 1,000 women, ranks among the highest in the world. Population growth rate, 2010, −0.2%; fertility rate, 2008, 1.3 births per woman.

Telecommunications

In 2013 there were 4,720,000 main (fixed) telephone lines. In the same year mobile phone subscribers numbered 22,910,000. The telecommunications sector was fully liberalized on 1 Jan. 2003, ending the monopoly of the Greek-controlled operator Romtelecom (now Telekom Romania). In 2013, 49.8% of the population aged 16–74 were internet users. In March 2012 there were 4.2 m. Facebook users.

Territory and Population

Romania is bounded in the north by Ukraine, in the east by Moldova, Ukraine and the Black Sea, south by Bulgaria, southwest by Serbia and northwest by Hungary. The area is 238,391 km². Population (2011 census), 20,121,641; density, 84.4 per km². In 2011, 58.0% of the population lived in urban areas. Romania's population has been falling at such a steady rate since 1990 that its population at the time of the 2011 census was the same as that in the late 1970s. At the 2011 census the following ethnic minorities numbered over 25,000: Hungarians, 1,227,600 (mainly in Transylvania); Roma (Gypsies), 621,600; Ukrainians, 50,900; Germans, 36,000; Turks, 27,700. The actual number of Roma is estimated to be nearer 2 m. Romania has one of the largest Roma populations of any country. The official language is Romanian.

Tourism

In 2009, 1,275,600 non-resident tourists stayed in holiday accommodation (down from 1,465,900 in 2008) including: 181,100 from Germany; 141,600 from Italy; 100,300 from France; 76,900 from Hungary.

Russia

Rossiiskaya Federatsiya (Russian Federation)

Factsheet

Capital: Moscow
Population estimate, 2015: 143.46 m.
GNI per capita, 2014: (PPP$) 22,352
HDI/world rank, 2014: 0.798/50=
Internet domain extension: .ru

Civil Aviation

The main international airports are at Moscow (Domodedovo, Sheremetyevo and Vnukovo) and St Petersburg (Pulkovo). The national carrier is Aeroflot International Russian Airlines (51% state-owned), which carried 11.3 m. scheduled passengers in 2010. Rossiya, S7 Airlines, Transaero and UTair also operate internationally. In 2009 scheduled airline traffic of Russian-based carriers flew 836 m. km, carrying 34,403,000 passengers (11,992,000 on international flights). The three busiest airports all serve Moscow. Domodedovo is Russia's busiest airport in terms of passenger traffic (22,255,000 in 2010, a 19% increase on 2009).

Climate

Moscow, Jan. −9.4 °C, July 18.3 °C. Annual rainfall 630 mm. Arkhangelsk, Jan. −15 °C, July 13.9 °C. Annual rainfall 503 mm. St Petersburg, Jan. −8.3 °C, July 17.8 °C. Annual rainfall 488 mm. Vladivostok, Jan. −14.4 °C, July 18.3 °C. Annual rainfall 599 mm.

Constitution and Government

According to the 1993 constitution the Russian Federation is a 'democratic federal legally-based state with a republican form of government'. The Federation consists of 85 federal subjects (administrative units). This includes Crimea (a republic) and Sevastopol (a federal city), which acceded to Russia in March 2014. However, most of the international community still considers them to be officially part of Ukraine. The state is secular. The state itself is based upon a separation of powers and upon federal principles, including a Constitutional Court. A central role is accorded to the *President*, who defines the 'basic directions of domestic and foreign policy' and represents the state internationally. Parliament is known as the *Federal Assembly* (Federalnoe Sobranie). The 'representative and legislative organ of the Russian Federation', it consists of two chambers: the *Federation Council* (Sovet Federatsii) and the *State Duma* (Gosudarstvennaya Duma). The Federation Council considers all matters that apply to the Federation as a whole, including state boundaries, martial law, and the deployment of Russian forces elsewhere. The Duma approves nominations for Prime Minister, and adopts federal laws. A law was approved in June 2001 to reduce the proliferation of political parties (numbering some 200 in 2001). It took effect in July 2003. There is a 19-member *Constitutional Court*, whose functions under the 1993 constitution include making decisions on the constitutionality of federal laws, presidential and government decrees, and the constitutions and laws of the subjects of the Federation.

Currency

The unit of currency is the *rouble* (RUB), of 100 *kopeks*.

Defence

The President of the Republic is C.-in-C. of the armed forces. Conscription was reduced to 18 months for those drafted in 2007 and was further reduced to 1 year for those drafted from 1 Jan. 2008. A presidential decree of 1997 ordered a cut in the armed forces of 200,000 men, reducing them to an authorized strength of 1,004,000 in 1999. In 2011 active armed forces totalled 956,000, plus 474,000 personnel in paramilitary forces. There were estimated to be around 20 m. reserves (all armed forces) in 2011 of whom 2 m. had seen service within the previous 5 years. Defence expenditure totalled US$68,163 m. in 2013 (just over a tenth of that of the USA), equivalent to US$478 per capita and representing 3.1% of GDP. Russia was the world's third biggest military spender in 2013. Russia's strategic warhead count is now shrinking and stood at an estimated 1,780 in Jan. 2015 according to the Stockholm International Peace Research Institute. There are about a further 5,720 warheads held in reserve or scheduled to be dismantled, giving a total stockpile of around 7,500 warheads. Shortfalls in planned investments to replace current systems as they reach the end of their service lives means the number of strategic warheads will continue to decline. At the height of the Cold War each side possessed over 10,000 nuclear warheads.

Economy

Agriculture accounted for 4.0% of GDP in 2010, industry 35.4% and services 60.6%. The Ministry of Property Relations was established in 2000 with the mandate of overall federal policies on property issues and the management of state property, and in Dec. 2001 a new Federal Law on Privatization of State and Municipal Property was adopted. By that time a total of 129,811 enterprises had been sold. In 2010 only 30.9% of total employment was still in the public sector, down from 69.1% in 1992 and 37.8% in 2000.

Labour

In 2010 the economically active population numbered 75.45 m. (38.58 m. males and 36.87 m. females). Of those in employment in 2010, 18.1% worked in wholesale and retail trade/repair of motor vehicles, motorcycles and personal and household goods, 15.4% in manufacturing, 9.6% in agriculture and forestry, 8.8% in education, 7.9% in transport, 7.8% in construction and 7.0% in health and social work. The unemployment rate was 9.9% in May 2009—with 7.5 m. people unemployed using ILO methodology—down from 10.2% in April 2009 although up from 6.1% in Oct. 2008. Russia had 0.52 m. people living in slavery according to the Walk Free Foundation's 2013 *Global Slavery Index*, the sixth highest total of any country.

Press

In 2008 there were 533 daily newspapers. There were 27,510 non-daily newspapers in 2008. The most popular daily newspaper in 2008 was *Moskovsky Komsomolets*, with an average daily circulation of 750,000, followed by *Komsomolskaya Pravda*, with a circulation of 716,000. A presidential decree of 22 Dec. 1993 brought the press agencies ITAR-TASS and RIA-Novosti under state control. In 2008, 123,336 new or revised books were published, a figure exceeded only by China, the UK and the USA.

Rail

Length of railways in 2010 was 86,000 km, of which about half is electrified. In 2008, 1,295.6 m. passengers and 1,304.7 m. tonnes of freight were carried by rail; passenger-km travelled came to 176 bn. and freight tonne-km to 2,116 bn. There are metro services in Moscow (309 km), St Petersburg (105 km), Nizhny Novgorod (15 km), Novosibirsk (14 km), Samara (10 km), Ekaterinburg (9 km) and Kazan (7 km).

Religion

The Russian Orthodox Church is the largest religious association in the country. In early 2010 it had 160 dioceses with over 30,000 parishes, more than 200 bishops and 28,000 priests and about 790 monasteries. A survey conducted in 2012 by the Levada-Center (an independent, non-governmental polling and sociological research organization) estimated that some 74% of the population are Orthodox believers and 7% Muslims; 76% of Russians who described themselves as Orthodox believers were church-goers. There are still many Old Believers, whose schism from the Orthodox Church dates from the seventeenth century. The Russian Church is headed by the Patriarch of Moscow and All Rus' (Patriarch Kirill I—Metropolitan Kirill of Smolensk and Kaliningrad, b. 1946; elected Jan. 2009). Muslims represent the second largest religious community in Russia. In Feb. 2010 the Supreme Co-ordinating Council of Russian Muslims was established to be co-chaired by the heads of the three major organizations—Talgat Tadzhuddin of the Central Spiritual Board of Muslims, Rawil Gaynetdin of the Council of Muftis of Russia and Ismail Berdiyev of the Co-ordinating Muslim Council of the North Caucasus.

Roads

There were 933,000 km of roads in 2006, of which 80.9% were hard surfaced. In 2007, 78 bn. passenger-km were travelled by road. There were 29,249,000 passenger cars in use in 2007 plus 4,730,000 lorries and vans and 861,000 buses and coaches. In 2013 there were 27,000 road deaths.

Shipping

In Jan. 2009 there were 1,272 ships of 300 GT or over registered, totalling 4.90 m. GT. Of the 1,272 vessels registered, 857 were general cargo ships, 296 oil tankers, 58 bulk carriers, 24 chemical tankers, 24 passenger ships, 12 container ships and one liquid gas tanker. The Russian-controlled fleet comprised 1,418 vessels of 1,000 GT or over in Jan. 2009, of which 945 were under the Russian flag and 473 under foreign flags. In 2010, 16 m. passengers and 102 m. tonnes of freight were carried on 101,000 km of inland waterways. The busiest ports are Novorossiisk (which handled 81,633,000 tonnes in 2008), Primorsk (75,582,000 tonnes in 2008) and St Petersburg (59,945,000 tonnes in 2008).

Social Statistics

2008 births, 1,717,500; deaths, 2,081,000; marriages, 1,178,700; divorces, 703,400. Rates, 2008 (per 1,000 population): birth, 12.1; death, 14.7; marriage, 8.3; divorce, 5.0. At the beginning of the 1970s the death rate had been just 9.4 per 1,000 population. Death rates caused by alcohol abuse in 2009 were 77.0 males and 23.8 females per 100,000 population. Infant mortality, 2010 (per 1,000 live births), 9. There were 1,292,400 legal abortions in 2009. The annual abortion rate (34.2 per 1,000 women aged 15–49 in 2009) ranks among the highest in the world. The divorce rate is also among the highest in the world. The most popular age range for marrying in 2008 was 25–34 for males and 18–24 for females. Expectation of life at birth, 2012, was 64.6 years for males and 75.9 years for females. In 2012, 11% of Russians were living below the national poverty line. Annual population growth rate, 2000–10, −0.3%; fertility rate, 2008, 1.4 births per woman. The suicide rate in 2013 was 20 per 100,000 population, down from 39 per 100,000 in 2000.

Telecommunications

In 2013 there were 40,473,000 main (fixed) telephone lines. Active mobile phone subscriptions numbered 208,065,000 in 2012 (1,453.3 per 1,000 persons). There were 61.5 m. internet users in 2011. In March 2012 there were 5.2 m. Facebook users.

Territory and Population

Russia is bounded in the north by various seas (Barents, Kara, Laptev, East Siberian) which join the Arctic Ocean, and in which is a fringe of islands, some of them large. In the east Russia is separated from the USA (Alaska) by the Bering Strait; the Kamchatka peninsula separates the coastal Bering and Okhotsk Seas. Sakhalin Island, north of Japan, is Russian territory. Russia is bounded in the south by North Korea, China, Mongolia, Kazakhstan, the Caspian Sea, Azerbaijan, Georgia, the Black Sea and Ukraine, and in the west by Belarus, Latvia, Estonia, the Baltic Sea and Finland. Kaliningrad (the former East Prussia) is an exclave on the Baltic Sea between Lithuania and Poland in the west. Russia's area is 17,075,400 km^2 and it has nine time zones (11 until March 2010). The 2010 census population was 142,856,536 density, 8.4 per km^2 Ethnicity in 2010 showed 80.9% were Russians, 3.9% Tatars, 1.4% Ukrainians, 1.2% Bashkir, 1.0% Chechens and 1.0% Chuvash. In 2011, 73.2% of the population lived in urban areas. The two principal cities are Moscow (Moskva), the capital, with a 2010 census population of 11.50 m. and St Petersburg (formerly Leningrad), with 4.88 m. Other major cities (with 2010 populations) are: Novosibirsk (1.47 m.), Ekaterinburg (1.35 m.), Nizhny Novgorod (1.25 m.), Samara (1.16 m.) and Omsk (1.15 m.). In May 2000 President Putin signed a decree dividing Russia into seven federal districts (okrug), in the process creating a layer above the various federal subjects. The official federal language is Russian, although there are several other officially-recognized languages within individual administrative units.

Tourism

In 2011 arrivals of non-resident visitors—including Russians living abroad—totalled 24,932,000 (22,281,000 in 2010), of which 2,336,000 were tourists (2,134,000 in 2010). There were 7,866 hotels and similar establishments in 2011, with 537,000 beds.

Rwanda

Republika y'u Rwanda (Republic of Rwanda)

Factsheet

Capital: Kigali
Population estimate, 2015: 11.61 m.
GNI per capita, 2014: (PPP$) 1,458
HDI/world rank, 2014: 0.483/163=
Internet domain extension: .rw

Civil Aviation

There is an international airport at Kigali (Grégoire Kayibanda), which handled 458,807 passengers (382,766 on international flights) in 2012. A national carrier, Rwandair Express (since renamed RwandAir), began operations in 2003. In 2013 RwandAir served 16 destinations and carried 408,000 passengers (385,000 on international flights).

Climate

Despite the equatorial situation, there is a highland tropical climate. The wet seasons are from Oct. to Dec. and March to May. Highest rainfall occurs in the west, at around 70″ (1,770 mm), decreasing to 40–55″ (1,020–1,400 mm) in the central uplands and to 30″ (760 mm) in the north and east. Kigali, Jan. 67 °F (19.4 °C), July 70 °F (21.1 °C). Annual rainfall 40″ (1,000 mm).

Constitution and Government

Under the 1978 constitution the MRND was the sole political organization. A new constitution was promulgated in June 1991 permitting multi-party democracy. The Arusha Agreement of Aug. 1994 provided for a transitional 70-member National Assembly, which began functioning in Nov. 1994. The seats won by the MRNDD (formerly MRND) were taken over by other parties on the grounds that the MRNDD was culpable of genocide. A referendum was held on 26 May 2003 which approved a draft constitution by 93.4% (turnout was 87%). The new constitution, subsequently approved by the Supreme Court, provides for an 80-member *Chamber of Deputies* and a 26-member *Senate*, with the provision that no party may hold more than half of cabinet positions. 53 members of the Chamber of Deputies are directly elected, 24 women are elected by provincial councils, two members are elected by the National Youth Council and one is elected by a disabilities organization.

Currency

The unit of currency is the *Rwanda franc* (RWF) notionally of 100 *centimes*.

Defence

In 2013 defence expenditure totalled US$82 m. (US$7 per capita), representing 1.1% of GDP.

Economy

Agriculture accounted for 32.2% of GDP in 2010, industry 15.0% and services 52.8%.

Labour

In 2005–06 there were 4,377,000 employed persons, with 79% of the economically active population engaged in agriculture, fisheries and forestry. Rwanda had 80,000 people living in slavery according to the Walk Free Foundation's 2013 *Global Slavery Index*.

Press

The English-language *New Times* is published 6 days a week, with its sister publication the *Sunday Times* appearing on Sundays.

Religion

In 2010 an estimated 93.4% of the population was Christian according to the Pew Research Center's Forum on Religion & Public Life, with 3.6% having no religious affiliation. Of the Christians in 2010, an estimated 53% were Catholics and 46% Protestants. Before the civil war of the early 1990s there were nine Roman Catholic bishops and 370 priests. By the end of 1994, three bishops had been killed and three reached retiring age; 106 priests had been killed and 130 had sought refuge abroad.

Roads

Rwanda has some 14,000 km of roads. There are road links with Burundi, Uganda, Tanzania and the Democratic Republic of the Congo. In 2006 there were 4,130 motorcycles, 1,813 cars and jeeps, and 1,270 trucks and pick-ups. There were 308 road deaths in 2007.

Social Statistics

2008 estimates: births, 400,000; deaths, 141,000. Estimated birth rate in 2008 was 41 1 per 1,000 population; estimated death rate, 14 5. Annual population growth rate, 2005–10, 2.8%. Life expectancy at birth during the period 2005–10 was 61.1 years for females and 58 5 for males, up from 24.8 years for females and 21.4 years for males in 1990–95 (at the height of the civil war). Infant mortality, 2010, 44 per 1,000 live births; fertility rate, 2008, 5 4 births per woman.

Telecommunications

Rwanda had 45,338 fixed telephone lines in 2013 and 6,689,000 mobile phone subscriptions. An estimated 8.7% of the population were internet users in 2013. In June 2012 there were 144,000 Facebook users.

Territory and Population

Rwanda is bounded south by Burundi, west by the Democratic Republic of the Congo, north by Uganda and east by Tanzania. A mountainous state of 25,314 km^2 (9,774 sq. miles), its western third drains to Lake Kivu on the border with the Democratic Republic of the Congo and thence to the Congo river, while the rest is drained by the Kagera river into the Nile system. The population was 7,164,994 at the 1991 census, of whom over 90% were Hutu, 9% Tutsi and 1% Twa (pygmy). Following the genocide of 1994 ethnicity was not enumerated at the 2002 census, when the population was 8,128,553. Population at the 2012 census, 10,515,973; density, 415.4 per km^2. In 2011 the population was 19.2% urban. Since Jan. 2006 Rwanda has been reorganized into five provinces (*intara*) as follows (with 2012 census populations): Eastern (2,595,703), Northern (1,726,370), Southern (2,589,975), Western (2,471,239) and Kigali City (1,132,686). Among the reasons given for the change were the reduction of ethnic divisions and the suppression of reminders of the 1994 genocide. Kigali, the capital, had a population of 1,132,686 in 2012. Kinyarwanda, which is the language of the entire population, along with English and French are the official languages. In 2008 English replaced French as the language of instruction in schools. Swahili is spoken in the commercial centres.

Tourism

In 2012 there were 815,000 international tourist arrivals (excluding same-day visitors), up from 688,000 in 2011.

St Kitts and Nevis

Federation of St Kitts and Nevis

Factsheet

Capital: Basseterre
Population estimate, 2015: 56,000
GNI per capita, 2014: (PPP$) 20,805
HDI/world rank, 2014: 0.752/77
Internet domain extension: .kn

Civil Aviation

The main airport is the Robert Llewelyn Bradshaw International Airport (just over 3 km from Basseterre). In 2010 there were flights to Antigua, Atlanta, British Virgin Islands, Charlotte, London, Miami, Nevis (Newcastle), New York, Puerto Rico, Sint Maarten and the US Virgin Islands.

Climate

Temperature varies between 21.4–30.7 °C, with a sea breeze throughout the year and low humidity. Average annual rainfall is between 1,270 mm and 1,905 mm.

Constitution and Government

The British sovereign is the head of state, represented by a Governor-General. The 1983 constitution described the country as 'a sovereign democratic federal state'. It allowed for a unicameral Parliament consisting of 11 elected Members (eight from St Kitts and three from Nevis), three appointed Senators and one *ex officio* member. Nevis was given its own Island Assembly and the right to secession from St Kitts.

Currency

The *East Caribbean dollar* (XCD) (of 100 *cents*) is in use.

Economy

Agriculture accounted for 1.5% of GDP in 2009, industry 20.0% and services 78.5%.

Labour

Of 24,778 persons on St Kitts aged 15 or over in 2001, 17,044 were economically active of whom 16,171 were employed and 873 were unemployed. The country has a phenomenon of the working poor—the unemployment rate among the poor in 2001 was very low at 5.3% on St Kitts and 5.0% on Nevis.

Press

In 2008 there was one daily newspaper with a circulation of 2,000. There were also four non-dailies.

Rail

In 2005 there were 50 km of railway, formerly operated by the sugar industry but now used for tourist purposes.

Religion

According to the Pew Research Center's Forum on Religion & Public Life, an estimated 94.6% of the population were Christians in 2010 with 1.6% religiously unaffiliated. Anglicans are the largest denomination.

Roads

There are about 380 km of roads.

Shipping

There is a deep-water port at Bird Rock (Basseterre). In Jan. 2009 there were 200 ships of 300 GT or over registered, totalling 892,000 GT. Among the 200 vessels registered were 132 general cargo ships and 47 oil tankers. The government maintains a commercial motor boat service between the islands.

Social Statistics

Births, 2008, 709; deaths, 357. Rates, 2008 (per 1,000 population): births, 13,8; deaths, 7.0. Infant mortality, 2010 (per 1,000 live births), 7. Life expectancy in 2012 was 73.3 years. Annual population growth rate, 2000–08, 1.3%; fertility rate, 2008, 1.8 births per woman.

Telecommunications

In March 2013 there were an estimated 77,000 mobile phone subscriptions and an estimated 19,200 main (fixed) telephone lines. In 2010, 56.5% of households had internet access.

Territory and Population

The two islands of St Kitts and Nevis are situated at the northern end of the Leeward Islands in the eastern Caribbean. Nevis lies 3 km to the southeast of St Kitts. Population, 2001 census, 46,325. In 2011, 32.6% of the population were urban. In 2001, 92.4% of the population were of African origin. English is the official and spoken language.

Tourism

In 2008 there were 533,353 visitors in total including 400,916 cruise ship passengers and 127,705 staying visitors.

St Lucia

Factsheet

Capital: Castries
Population estimate, 2015: 185,000
GNI per capita, 2014: (PPP$) 9,765
HDI/world rank, 2014: 0.729/89
Internet domain extension: .lc

Civil Aviation

There are two international airports: Hewanorra International (near Vieux-Fort) and George F. L. Charles (near Castries). In 2009 Hewanorra handled 513,959 passengers (483,632 in 2008) and George F. L. Charles—which handles inter-Caribbean flights—309,132 passengers (358,313 in 2008).

Climate

The climate is tropical, with a dry season from Jan. to April. Most rain falls in Nov.–Dec.; annual amount varies from 60″ (1,500 mm) to 138″ (3,450 mm). The average annual temperature is about 80 °F (26.7 °C).

Constitution and Government

The head of state is the British sovereign, represented by an appointed Governor-General. There is a 18-seat *House of Assembly* (17 members elected for 5 years plus the speaker) and an 11-seat *Senate* appointed by the Governor-General.

Currency

The *East Caribbean dollar* (XCD) (of 100 *cents*) is in use. US dollars are also normally accepted.

Economy

In 2010 agriculture contributed 3.5% of GDP, industry 16.6% and services 79.9%.

Labour

In the period April–June 2004 the labour force totalled 78,210. The unemployment rate was 21.0% in 2004.

Press

There are no daily newspapers. In 2008 there were six paid-for non-daily newspapers: the thrice-weekly *The Voice* and *The Star*; and the weekly *The Mirror*, *The Crusader*, *The Vanguard* and *One Caribbean*.

Religion

According to estimates by the Pew Research Center's Forum on Religion & Public Life, 91.1% of the population in 2010 was Christian and 6.0% had no religious affiliation. In Feb. 2016 there was one cardinal.

Roads

The island has about 1,200 km of roads, mainly unpaved.

Shipping

There are two ports, Castries and Vieux Fort.

Social Statistics

2011: births, 2,009; deaths, 983. Rates, 2011 (per 1,000 population): births, 12.0; deaths, 5.9. Infant mortality, 2010 (per 1,000 live births), 14. Expectation of life in 2013 was 72.2 years for males and 77.5 for females. Annual population growth rate, 2005–10, 1.4%; fertility rate, 2008, 2.0 births per woman.

Telecommunications

In March 2013 there were an estimated 77,000 mobile phone subscriptions and an estimated 19,200 main (fixed) telephone lines. In 2010, 56.5% of households had internet access.

Territory and Population

St Lucia is an island of the Lesser Antilles in the eastern Caribbean between Martinique and St Vincent, with an area of 617 km² (238 sq. miles). Population (2010 census, provisional) 165,595; density, 268.4 per km². In 2011 the population was 28.1% urban. The official language is English, but 80% of the population speak a French Creole. In 2010, 85% of the population was African/Black, 11% were of mixed race and 2% of East Indian ethnic origin. The capital is Castries (population, 1999, 57,000).

Tourism

In 2010 there were 305,937 tourist arrivals by air, up from 278,491 in 2009. St Lucia received 670,043 cruise ship visitors in 2010 (when there were 380 cruise ship calls), down from 699,306 in 2009. There were 7,613 other same-day visitors in 2010.

St Vincent and the Grenadines

Factsheet

Capital: Kingstown
Population estimate, 2015: 109,000
GNI per capita, 2014: (PPP$) 9,937
HDI/world rank, 2014: 0.720/97=
Internet domain extension: .vc

Civil Aviation

Argyle International Airport on mainland St Vincent—the country's first international airport—was inaugurated in Feb. 2017. There are regional airports on Bequia, Canouan, Mustique and Union Island in the Grenadines.

Climate

The climate is tropical marine, with northeast trades predominating and rainfall ranging from 150″ (3,750 mm) a year in the mountains to 60″ (1,500 mm) on the southeast coast. The rainy season is from June to Dec., and temperatures are equable throughout the year.

Constitution and Government

The head of state is Queen Elizabeth II, represented by a Governor-General. Parliament is unicameral with a 23-member *House of Assembly* consisting of 15 members directly elected for a 5-year term from single-member constituencies, six senators appointed by the Governor-General (four on the advice of the Prime Minister and two on the advice of the Leader of the Opposition) and two *ex officio* members.

Currency

The currency in use is the *East Caribbean dollar* (XCD).

Economy

Agriculture accounted for 6.9% of GDP in 2009, industry 18.9% and services 74.2%.

Labour

The Department of Labour is charged with looking after the interest and welfare of all categories of workers, including providing advice and guidance to employers and employees and their organizations and enforcing the labour laws. In 2001 the total labour force was 43,779, of whom 34,521 (21,274 males and 13,247 females) were employed.

Press

In 2008 there was one daily newspaper, *The Herald*. There were also nine weekly papers.

Religion

In 2010 an estimated 88.7% of the population were Christians according to the Pew Research Center's Forum on Religion & Public Life and 3.4% Hindus, with a further 2.5% religiously unaffiliated.

Roads

There are more than 800 km of roads, around half of which are paved. Vehicles in use (2008): 9,250 passenger cars, 12,900 vans and lorries, and 1,220 motorcycles and mopeds.

Shipping

In Jan. 2009 there were 580 ships of 300 GT or over registered, totalling 5.10 m. GT. Among the 580 vessels registered were 413 general cargo ships, 80 bulk carriers and 31 passenger ships.

Social Statistics

Births, 2008 estimate, 1,900; deaths, 800. 2008 estimated rates (per 1,000 population): births, 17.6; deaths, 7.5. Infant mortality, 2010, 19 per 1,000 live births. Life expectancy, 2013, was 70.4 years for males and 74.7 years for females. Annual population growth rate, 2000–08, 0.1%; fertility rate, 2008, 2.1 births per woman.

Telecommunications

In 2013 there were 125,400 mobile phone subscriptions (1,146.3 for every 1,000 inhabitants) and 19,100 fixed telephone lines. In the same year an estimated 52.0% of the population were internet users.

Territory and Population

St Vincent is an island of the Lesser Antilles, situated in the eastern Caribbean between St Lucia and Grenada, from which latter it is separated by a chain of small islands known as the Grenadines. The total area of 389 km^2 (150 sq. miles) comprises the island of St Vincent itself (345 km^2) and those of the Grenadines attached to it, of which the largest are Bequia, Mustique, Canouan, Mayreau and Union. The population at the 2012 census was 109,991 (provisional), of whom 99,757 lived on St Vincent; density, 283 per km^2. In 2011, 49.8% of the population lived in urban areas. The capital, Kingstown, had 26,721 inhabitants in June 2012 (provisional, including suburbs). The population is mainly of Black (72.8% in 2001) and mixed (20.0%) origin, with small White, Asian and American minorities. English is the official language, although French patois is widely spoken.

Tourism

There were 72,478 tourist arrivals by air in 2010, down from 97,432 in 2006. Cruise passenger arrivals numbered 110,954 in 2010 and there were also 42,603 yacht passengers.

Samoa

O le Malo Tutoatasi o Samoa (Independent State of Samoa)

Factsheet

Capital: Apia
Population estimate, 2015: 193,000
GNI per capita, 2014: (PPP$) 5,327
HDI/world rank, 2014: 0.702/105
Internet domain extension: .ws

Civil Aviation

There is an international airport at Apia (Faleolo), which handled 321,973 passengers and 1,175 tonnes of freight in 2009. The national carrier is Virgin Samoa, known until 2011 as Polynesian Blue. In 2007 it operated domestic services and international flights to Auckland, Brisbane and Sydney.

Climate

A tropical marine climate, with cooler conditions from May to Nov. and a rainy season from Dec. to April. The rainfall is unevenly distributed, with south and east coasts having the greater quantities. Average annual rainfall is about 100″ (2,500 mm) in the drier areas. Apia, Jan. 80 °F (26.7 °C), July 78 °F (25.6 °C). Annual rainfall 112″ (2,800 mm).

Constitution and Government

HH Malietoa Tanumafili II, who was Head of State for life, died on 11 May 2007. The Head of State is henceforth elected by the Legislative Assembly and holds office for 5-year terms. The executive power is vested in the *Head of State*, who swears in the *Prime Minister* (who is elected by the Legislative Assembly) and, on the Prime Minister's advice, the Ministers to form the Cabinet. The Constitution also provides for a *Council of Deputies* of three members, of whom the chairman is the Deputy Head of State. The *Legislative Assembly* contains 49 members serving 5-year terms. 47 are elected exclusively by *matai* (customary family heads) and the other two by non-Samoans on separate electoral rolls.

Currency

The unit of currency is the *tala* (WST) of 100 *sene*.

Economy

Agriculture accounted for 9.7% of GDP in 2010, industry 28.1% and services 62.2%.

Labour

In 2001 the total labour force numbered 52,945 (36,739 males).

Press

There are two dailies, plus a weekly, a fortnightly and a monthly. The most widely read newspaper is the independent *Samoa Observer*.

Religion

According to the Pew Research Center's Forum on Religion & Public Life, an estimated 96.8% of the population were Christians in 2010 with 2.5% having no religious affiliation.

Roads

The road network covers around 1,150 km. In 2005 there were 5,920 passenger cars plus 4,600 lorries and vans in use.

Shipping

In Jan. 2009 there were four ships of 300 GT or over registered, totalling 9,000 GT.

Social Statistics

2006: births, 4,935; deaths, 728. Rates, 2006 (per 1,000 population): births, 27.3; deaths, 4.0. Expectation of life in 2007 was 68.4 years for males and 74.7 for females. Annual population growth rate, 2001–06, was 0.5%. Infant mortality, 2010, 17 per 1,000 live births; fertility rate, 2006, 4.2 births per woman.

Telecommunications

There are three radio communication stations at Apia. Radio telephone service connects Samoa with American Samoa, the Fiji Islands, New Zealand, Australia, Canada, USA and UK. In 2008 there were 28,800 main (fixed) telephone lines; mobile phone subscribers numbered 124,000 in 2008 (69.3 per 100 persons). There were 9,000 internet users in 2008.

Territory and Population

Samoa lies between 13° and 15° S. lat. and 171° and 173° W. long. It comprises the two large islands of Savai'i and Upolu, the small islands of Manono and Apolima, and several uninhabited islets lying off the coast. The total land area is 2,785 km² (1,075 sq. miles), of which 1,694 km² (654 sq. miles) are in Savai'i and 1,091 km² (421 sq. miles) in Upolu (including Manono and Apolima. The population was 187,820 at the 2011 census; density, 67 per km². The population at the 2011 census was 143,418 in Upolu (including Manono and Apolima) and 44,402 in Savai'i. The capital and chief port is Apia in Upolu (population 36,735 in 2011). In 2011, 20.1% of the population lived in urban areas. The official languages are Samoan and English.

Tourism

In 2008 there were 122,163 foreign tourists.

San Marino

Repubblica di San Marino (Republic of San Marino)

Factsheet

Capital: San Marino
Population estimate, 2015: 32,000
GDP per capita, 2014: US$58,393
Internet domain extension: .sm

Civil Aviation

The nearest airport is Rimini, 10 km to the east in Italy, which had scheduled flights in 2010 to Cologne-Bonn, Frankfurt, Hamburg, Karlsruhe, Liverpool, London Stansted, Luxembourg, Münster, Munich, Nuremberg, Stuttgart, Tirana and Vienna.

Climate

Temperate climate with cold, dry winters and warm summers.

Constitution and Government

The legislative power is vested in the *Great and General Council* of 60 members elected every 5 years by popular vote, two of whom are appointed every 6 months to act as *Captains Regent*, who are the heads of state. Executive power is exercised by the ten-member *Congress of State*, presided over by the Captains Regent. The *Council of Twelve*, also presided over by the Captains Regent, is appointed by the Great and General Council to perform administrative functions.

Currency

Since 1 Jan. 2002 San Marino has been using the euro (EUR). Italy has agreed that San Marino may mint a small part of the total Italian euro coin contingent with their own motifs.

Defence

Military service is not obligatory, but all citizens between the ages of 16 and 55 can be called upon to defend the State. They may also serve as volunteers in the Military Corps. There is a military Gendarmerie.

Labour

Out of 20,530 people in employment in 2006, 6,247 worked in manufacturing and 2,901 in wholesale and retail trade. In 2006 there were 473 registered unemployed persons.

Press

San Marino had four paid-for daily newspapers in 2008 (including one sports paper). There are also three dailies published in Italy that include pages on San Marino.

Religion

A 2010 study by the Pew Research Center's Forum on Religion & Public Life estimated that 91.6% of the population were Roman Catholics, with 7.2% religiously unaffiliated.

Social Statistics

Births registered in 2009, 306; deaths, 233; marriages, 238; divorces, 63. Birth rate, 2009 (per 1,000 population), 9.3; death rate, 6.9. Annual population growth rate, 2000–05, 2.7%; fertility rate, 2008, 1.5 births per woman; infant mortality rate, 2010, two per 1,000 live births (one of the lowest rates in the world).

Telecommunications

San Marino had 18,800 fixed telephone subscriptions in 2013 and 36,800 mobile phone subscriptions. In the same year an estimated 50.8% of the population were internet users.

Territory and Population

San Marino is a land-locked state in central Italy, 20 km from the Adriatic. Area is 61.19 km² (23.6 sq. miles) and the population (June 2012), 32,368; population density, 529.0 per km². At July 2010, 12,722 citizens lived abroad. In 2010, 94.1% of the population were urban. The capital, San Marino, has 4,236 inhabitants (June 2012); the largest town is Serravalle (10,540 in June 2012), an industrial centre in the north. The official language is Italian.

Tourism

In 2007, 2.16 m. tourists visited San Marino (1.47 m. Italians and 696,000 other foreigners).

São Tomé and Príncipe

República Democrática de São Tomé e Príncipe (Democratic Republic of São Tomé and Príncipe)

Factsheet

Capital: São Tomé
Population estimate, 2015: 190,000
GNI per capita, 2014: (PPP$) 2,918
HDI/world rank, 2014: 0.555/143=
Internet domain extension: .st

Civil Aviation

São Tomé airport had flights in 2010 to Cape Verde, Libreville, Lisbon, Luanda and Port-Gentil. In 2007 São Tomé handled 50,625 passengers. There is a light aircraft service to Príncipe.

Climate

The tropical climate is modified by altitude and the effect of the cool Benguela current. The wet season is generally from Oct. to May, but rainfall varies considerably, from 40″ (1,000 mm) in the hot and humid northeast to 150–200″ (3,800–5,000 mm) on the plateau. São Tomé, Jan. 79 °F (26.1 °C), July 75 °F (23.9 °C). Annual rainfall 38″ (951 mm).

Constitution and Government

The 1990 constitution was approved by 72% of votes at a referendum of March 1990 and became effective in Sept. 1990. It abolished the monopoly of the Movement for the Liberation of São Tomé e Príncipe (MLSTP). The *President* must be over 34 years old, and is elected by universal suffrage for one or two (maximum) 5-year terms. He or she is also head of government and appoints a Council of Ministers. The 55-member *National Assembly* is elected for 4 years. Since April 1995 Príncipe has enjoyed internal self-government, with a five-member regional government and an elected assembly.

Currency

The unit of currency is the *dobra* (STD) of 100 *centimos*.

Economy

In 2010 wholesale and retail trade, hotels and restaurants were estimated to have contributed 28% to GDP; followed by agriculture, forestry, fishing and hunting, 19%; transport, storage and communication, 15%; and construction, 10%.

Labour

In 2001 the economically active population was 52,150. The unemployment rate was 15.7% in 2001.

Press

In 2008 there was one daily newspaper. Two government-owned and six independent papers were also published irregularly.

Religion

In 2010 an estimated 82.2% of the population were Christians according to the Pew Research Center's Forum on Religion & Public Life, with 12.6% religiously unaffiliated. Of the Christians in 2010, an estimated 86% were Catholics and 14% Protestants.

Roads

There were 500 km of roads in 2009, 375 km of which were paved. Approximately 4,500 passenger cars, 2,183 motorcycles and over 1,800 trucks and vans were in use in 2008.

Shipping

São Tomé is the main port, but it lacks a deep water harbour. Neves handles oil imports and is the main fishing port. In Jan. 2009 there were 14 ships of 300 GT or over registered, totalling 19,000 GT.

Social Statistics

2006: births, 5,072; deaths, 1,111. Rates, 2006 (per 1,000 population): birth, 33.4; death, 7.3; infant mortality (2010), 53 per 1,000 live births. Expectation of life, 2006, 63.5 years for males and 68.5 years for females. Annual population growth rate, 2000–05, 1.9%; fertility rate, 2008, 3.8 births per woman.

Telecommunications

In 2013 there were 7,000 fixed telephone subscriptions; mobile phone subscriptions numbered 125,300 that year (64.9 per 100 persons). In 2013 an estimated 23.0% of the population were internet users.

Territory and Population

The republic, which lies about 200 km off the west coast of Gabon, in the Gulf of Guinea, comprises the main islands of São Tomé (845 km²) and Príncipe and several smaller islets including Pedras Tinhosas and Rolas. It has a total area of 1,001 km² (387 sq. miles). Population (census, 2012) 179,200; density, 179 per km². In 2011, 63.0% of the population were urban. The official language is Portuguese. Lungwa São Tomé, a Portuguese Creole, and Fang, a Bantu language, are the spoken languages.

Tourism

In 2011 there were 12,000 non-resident tourists.

Saudi Arabia

Al-Mamlaka al-Arabiya as-Saudiya (Kingdom of Saudi Arabia)

Factsheet

Capital: Riyadh
Population estimate, 2015: 31.54 m.
GNI per capita, 2014: (PPP$) 52,821
HDI/world rank, 2014: 0.837/39
Internet domain extension: .sa

Civil Aviation

The national carrier is the part-privatized Saudi Arabian Airlines, which in 2006 owned 139 aircraft and served 76 destinations. In 2005 scheduled airline traffic of Saudi-based carriers flew 117.1 m. km and carried 11,126,300 passengers. There are four major international airports, at Jeddah (King Abdulaziz), Dhahran, Riyadh (King Khaled) and Dammam (King Fahd). There are also 23 domestic airports. Jeddah handled 25,785,463 passengers in 2012 (17,547,530 on international flights) and 265,629 tonnes of freight in 2011. Riyadh was the second busiest airport in 2012, handling 17,690,764 passengers (8,720,576 on domestic flights) and 305,943 tonnes of freight.

Climate

A desert climate, with very little rain and none at all from June to Dec. The months May to Sept. are very hot and humid, but winter temperatures are quite pleasant. Riyadh, Jan. 58 °F (14.4 °C), July 108 °F (42 °C). Annual rainfall 4″ (100 mm). Jeddah, Jan. 73 °F (22.8 °C), July 87 °F (30.6 °C). Annual rainfall 3″ (81 mm).

Constitution and Government

The reigning King, **Salman bin Abdulaziz Al-Saud** (b. 1935), Custodian of the two Holy Mosques, succeeded in Jan. 2015, after King Abdullah's death. *Crown Prince:* Prince Mohammad bin Naif bin Abdulaziz Al-Saud (b. 1959). There is no formal constitution, but three royal decrees of 1 March 1992 established a Basic Law which defines the systems of central and municipal government, and set up a 60-man Consultative Council (*Majlis Al-Shura*) of royal nominees in Aug. 1993. Saudi Arabia is an absolute monarchy; executive power is discharged through a *Council of Ministers,* consisting of the King, Deputy Prime Minister, Second Deputy Prime Minister and Cabinet Ministers. The King has the post of *Prime Minister* and can veto any decision of the Council of Ministers within 30 days. In Oct. 2003 the government announced that municipal elections would be held in 2004 for the first time (although they were subsequently postponed until 2005), followed by city elections and partial elections to the *Majlis Al-Shura* in the following years. In March 2011 the government announced that the second municipal elections, previously scheduled for 2009, would be held on 22 Sept. 2011 (later delayed to 29 Sept.). Women were not eligible to vote, but they will be at the next elections set to take place during 2015.

Currency

The unit of currency is the *rial* (SAR) of 100 *halalah*.

Defence

In 2013 defence expenditure totalled US$59,560 m. (up from US$48,531 m. in 2011), with spending per capita US$2,211. The 2013 expenditure represented 8.0% of GDP. 5,000 US troops were stationed in Saudi Arabia after the 1991 Gulf War and were joined by a further 20,000 during the 2003 conflict. However, virtually all US troops have now been withdrawn. In March 2011 the Gulf Co-operation Council's Peninsula Shield Force, which is based in Saudi Arabia and whose mission is to protect the security of member states from any external aggression, consisted of approximately 40,000 troops.

Economy

Agriculture accounted for 2% of GDP in 2008, industry 70% and services 27%.

Labour

The labour force in the first half of 2015 totalled 11,912,200. In 2015 females constituted 15.8% of the labour force—one of the lowest percentages of females in the workforce of any country. In the first half of 2015, 15.7% of the employed population were engaged in public administration and defence/compulsory social security, 13.0% in construction, 12.5% in wholesale and retail trade/repair of motor vehicles, and 12.3% education. There are 9 m. foreign workers, including over 1 m. Egyptians and over 1 m. Indians. In the period Jan.–June 2015 unemployment was 5.7% overall but 11.6% for Saudis. Saudi Arabia had 58,000 people living in slavery according to the Walk Free Foundation's 2013 *Global Slavery Index*.

Press

In 2008 there were 16 daily newspapers with a combined circulation of 1,420,000. The most widely read newspapers are the Saudi-owned London-based *Asharq Al-Awsat* ('The Middle East'), *Al-Riyadh* and *Al-Watan*.

Rail

In 2012, 1,412 km of 1,435 mm gauge lines linked Riyadh and Dammam with stops at Hofuf and Abqaiq. The network is being extended, consisting of links to Jeddah, the Jordanian border, and Makkah and Madinah. The line under construction from Makkah to Madinah via Jeddah will be Saudi Arabia's first high-speed rail link. It is expected to open in late 2016 or early 2017. In 2008 railways carried 1.1 m. passengers and 4.6 m. tonnes of freight. The first line of a metro system in Makkah opened in 2010, covering 18.1 km.

Religion

According to the Pew Research Center's Forum on Religion & Public Life, in 2010 an estimated 78–83% of the total population were Sunni Muslims, 10–15% Shias, 4% Christians and 1% Hindus. The *Grand Mufti*, Sheikh Abdul Aziz bin Abdullah bin Mohammed Al-Sheikh, has cabinet rank. A special police force, the Mutaween, exists to enforce religious norms. The annual *Hajj*, the pilgrimage to Makkah, takes place from the 8th to the 13th day of Dhu al Hijjah, the last month of the Islamic year. It attracts more than 1.8 m. pilgrims annually.

Roads

In 2005 there was a total road network of 221,372 km (21.5% paved), including 3,891 km of motorway. A causeway links Saudi Arabia with Bahrain. Passenger cars in use in 2005 numbered 3,206,000 (415 per 1,000 inhabitants in 2004) and there were 1,127,900 lorries and vans. Women are not allowed to drive. In 2004–05 there were 293,281 road accidents resulting in 5,168 deaths.

Shipping

The ports of Dammam and Jubail are on the Persian Gulf and Jeddah, Yanbu and Jizan on the Red Sea. There is a deepwater oil terminal at Ras Tanura. In 2009 the major ports handled 142.3 m. tonnes of cargo (84.1 m. tonnes loaded and 58.2 m. tonnes discharged). In Jan. 2009 there were 83 ships of 300 GT or over registered (including 38 oil tankers, 18 general cargo ships and 14 passenger ships), totalling 1.25 m. GT.

Social Statistics

2008 estimates: births, 590,000; deaths, 92,000. Birth rate (2008 estimate) was 23.4 per 1,000 population; death rate, 3.6. 75% of the population is under the age of 30. Expectation of life at birth, 2013, was 73.9 years for males and 77.6 years for females. Annual population growth rate, 2000–08, 2.4%. Infant mortality, 2010, was 15 per 1,000 live births, down from 58 in the years 1980–85. Fertility rate, 2008, 3.1 births per woman.

Telecommunications

In 2013 there were 4.9 m. main (fixed) telephone lines. In the same year mobile phone subscriptions numbered 53.1 m. (1,842.0 per 1,000 persons). The government sold a 30% stake in Saudi Telecom Company (STC) in Dec. 2002. STC lost its monopoly in the mobile phone market in 2005 and in landline services in 2007. In 2013 an estimated 60.5% of the population were internet users. In March 2012 there were 5.1 m. Facebook users.

Territory and Population

Saudi Arabia, which occupies nearly 80% of the Arabian peninsula, is bounded in the west by the Red Sea, east by the Persian Gulf, Qatar and the United Arab Emirates, north by Jordan, Iraq and Kuwait and south by Yemen and Oman. The total area is 2,149,690 km^2 (829,995 sq. miles). Riyadh is the political, and Makkah (Mecca) the religious, capital. Population at the census of April 2010 (provisional), 27,136,977; density, 12.6 per km^2. Approximately 32% of the population are foreigners. In 2011, 82.3% of the population lived in urban areas. Principal cities (with 2010 provisional census populations in 1 m.): Riyadh, 5.19; Jeddah, 3.43; Makkah, 1.53; Madinah, 1.10; Dammam, 0.90; Hofuf, 0.66. The Neutral Zone (5,700 km^2, 3,560 sq. miles), jointly owned and administered by Kuwait and Saudi Arabia from 1922 to 1966, was partitioned between the two countries in 1966, but the exploitation of the oil and other natural resources continues to be shared. The official language is Arabic.

Tourism

There were 14,276,000 international tourists in 2012; spending by tourists in 2012 totalled US$8.4 bn.

Senegal

République du Sénégal (Republic of Senegal)

Factsheet
Capital: Dakar
Population estimate, 2015: 15.13 m.
GNI per capita, 2014: (PPP$) 2,188
HDI/world rank, 2014: 0.466/170
Internet domain extension: .sn

Civil Aviation

The international airport is at Dakar/Yoff (Léopold Sédar Senghor), which handled 1,882,242 passengers and 21,816 tonnes of freight in 2008. Air Sénégal International was 49% state-owned and 51% owned by Royal Air Maroc (RAM). Sénégal Airlines was launched as a replacement national carrier in Oct. 2009 although it is 64% privately-controlled. Flights, initially only within Africa, commenced in Jan. 2011.

Climate

A tropical climate with wet and dry seasons. The rains fall almost exclusively in the hot season, from June to Oct., with high humidity. Dakar, Jan. 72 °F (22.2 °C), July 82 °F (27.8 °C). Annual rainfall 22″ (541 mm).

Constitution and Government

A new constitution was approved by a referendum held on 7 Jan. 2001. The head of state is the *President*, elected by universal suffrage for not more than two 5-year terms (previously two 7-year terms). However, in Jan. 2012 the incumbent, Abdoulaye Wade won a court ruling allowing him to run for a third term on the grounds that the constitutional provision was not enacted until a year after his first term of office had begun. The *President* has the power to dissolve the National Assembly, without the agreement, as had been the case, of a two-thirds majority. The new constitution also abolished the upper house (the Senate), confirmed the status of the prime minister and for the first time gave women the right to own land. Senegal has a bicameral legislature. For the 150-member *National Assembly*, 90 members are elected by simple majority vote in single or multi-member constituencies for 5 years with 60 elected by a system of party-list proportional representation. The Senate was re-established in Jan. 2007 6 years after being dissolved. In Sept. 2012 parliament voted to abolish it after severe floods hit Senegal, with the money that would be saved going towards improving the country's flood defences and aid for flood victims.

Currency

The unit of currency is the *franc CFA* (XOF) with a parity of 655.957 francs CFA to one euro.

Defence

There is selective conscription for 2 years. Defence expenditure totalled US$231 m. in 2013 (US$17 per capita), representing 1.6% of GDP.

Economy

Agriculture accounted for 17% of GDP in 2012, industry 24% and services 59%.

Labour

The labour force in 2013 was 6,118,000 (4,484,000 in 2003). 78.0% of the population aged 15–64 was economically active in 2013. In the same year 10.3% of the population was unemployed. Senegal had 0.10 m. people living in slavery according to the Walk Free Foundation's 2013 *Global Slavery Index.*

Press

In 2008 there were 26 daily newspapers with a total average circulation of 123,000 copies and 30 non-dailies.

Rail

There were previously four railway lines but the total length of the track fell from 1,034 km (metre gauge) in 1986 to 645 km in 2005. There is also a suburban rail service linking Dakar and Rufisque, which carried 4.9 m. passengers in 2009. In 2009, 364,000 tonnes of freight were carried.

Religion

According to a study by the Pew Research Center's Forum on Religion & Public Life, in 2010 there were an estimated 11.98 m. Muslims (equivalent to 96.4% of the population). Most Muslims in Senegal are members of Sufi brotherhoods—Sufis are often described as being 'mystic' Sunnis. There were also an estimated 450,000 Christians in 2010, around 93% of whom were Catholics. There was one Roman Catholic cardinal in Feb. 2016.

Roads

The length of roads in 2006 was 14,805 km, of which 29.3% were paved. In 2008 there were 205,704 passenger cars, 56,795 trucks and vans and 15,982 coaches. There were 320 deaths as a result of road accidents in 2007.

Shipping

In Jan. 2009 there were three ships of 300 GT or over registered, totalling 5,000 GT. 10.6 m. tonnes of freight were handled in the port of Dakar in 2008. The Senegal River is closed to foreign flags. The Saloum River is navigable as far as Kaolack, the Casamance River as far as Ziguinchor.

Social Statistics

2005 estimates: births, 430,000; deaths, 132,000. Rates, 2005 estimates (per 1,000 population): births, 39.4; deaths, 12.1. Annual population growth rate, 2000–05, 2.8%; infant mortality, 2010, 50 per 1,000 live births. Life expectancy in 2007 was 53.9 years for men and 56.9 for women. Fertility rate, 2008, 5.0 births per woman. 51% of the population were living in poverty in 2005.

Telecommunications

In 2013 there were 343,700 main (fixed) telephone lines; mobile phone subscriptions numbered 13,134,000 that year (92.9 per 100 persons). In 2013 an estimated 20.9% of the population were internet users. In June 2012 there were 666,000 Facebook users.

Territory and Population

Senegal is bounded by Mauritania to the north and northeast, Mali to the east, Guinea and Guinea-Bissau to the south and the Atlantic to the west with The Gambia forming an enclave along that shore. A short section of the boundary with The Gambia is undefined. Area, 196,720 km^2, including 4,190 km^2 of inland water. Population (2013 census), 13,508,715 (50.1% female). Density, 70.2 per km^2. In 2011 the population was 42.7% urban. Dakar, the capital, had an estimated population in 2010 of 2,396,800. Other large cities (with 2010 population estimates) are: Touba Mosquée (620,500), Thiès (278,200), Mbour (199,400), Kaolack (193,400), Saint-Louis (180,900) and Rufisque (173,100). Ethnic groups are the Wolof (36% of the population), Fulani (16%), Serer (16%), Diola (9%), Tukulor (9%), Bambara (6%), Malinké (6%) and Sarakole (2%). The official language is French; Wolof is widely spoken.

Tourism

In 2011 there were 968,000 international tourist arrivals (excluding same-day visitors), up from 900,000 in 2010.

Serbia

Republika Srbija (Republic of Serbia)

Factsheet
Capital: Belgrade
Population estimate, 2015: 8.85 m.
GNI per capita, 2014: (PPP$) 12,190
HDI/world rank, 2014: 0.771/66
Internet domain extension: .rs

Civil Aviation

The national airline (and the former national carrier of Yugoslavia) is Air Serbia, known as Jat Airways until Oct. 2013. In Jan. 2010 it flew to 30 destinations in 23 countries. The main airport is Belgrade Nikola Tesla Airport, which handled 2,386,402 passengers and 7,690 tonnes of cargo in 2009.

Climate

Most parts have a central European type of climate, with cold winters and hot summers. Belgrade, Jan. 1.4 °C, July 23.0 °C. Annual rainfall 687 mm.

Constitution and Government

A new constitution was approved in a referendum held on 28–29 Oct. 2006, with 53.0% of the electorate (and 96.6% of those voting) supporting the proposed constitution. It declares the province of Kosovo and Metohija an integral part of Serbia and grants Vojvodina financial autonomy. Kosovo Albanians were not able to vote. Turnout was 54.9%. The *President* is elected by universal suffrage for not more than two 2-year terms. There is a 250-member single-chamber *National Assembly.*

Currency

The unit of currency of Serbia is the *dinar* (RSD) of 100 *paras.*

Defence

Conscription was abolished with effect from 1 Jan. 2011. In 2013 defence expenditure totalled US$681 m. (US$94 per capita), representing 1.6% of GDP.

Economy

Agriculture accounted for 9% of GDP in 2012, industry 30% and services 61%.

Labour

In April 2010 there were 2,412,106 workers employed (without Kosovo and Metohija), including 549,816 in agriculture, forestry and water management; 405,485 in manufacturing; 346,038 in wholesale and retail trade and repair; 170,146 in health and social work; 148,943 in education; and 142,514 in transport, storage and communications. In April 2010 there were 1,582,455 employees and 641,712 self-employed persons. Average annual salary in 2009 (without Kosovo and Metohija) was 31,733 dinars. Unemployment in April 2010 (without Kosovo and Metohija) was running at 19.2%. Serbia had 26,000 people living in slavery according to the Walk Free Foundation's 2013 *Global Slavery Index*.

Press

In 2008 there were 19 daily newspapers (18 paid-for and one free). The two largest newspapers are *Blic* (readership of 836,000 in 2008) and *Večernje novosti* (553,000).

Rail

Railways are operated by eleznice Srbije; total length of network in 2011 (excluding Kosovo and Metohija) was 3,809 km. In 2009, 8.4 m. passengers and 10.4 m. tonnes of freight were carried (without Kosovo and Metohija). In Sept. 2010 the state-owned railway companies of Serbia, Croatia and Slovenia announced the creation of a joint venture called Cargo 10 to improve the management of freight trains along the route known as Corridor 10 that passes through all three countries.

Religion

Serbia has been traditionally Orthodox. Muslims are found in the south as a result of the centuries-long Turkish occupation. The Serbian Orthodox Church with its seat in Belgrade has five metropolitanates (including one covering Australia and New Zealand), 34 eparchies (dioceses) and one autonomous archeparchy. Its *Patriarch* is Irinej (enthroned 23 Jan. 2010).

Roads

The length of roads in 2007 was 39,184 km, including 374 km of motorway and 5,133 km of main roads. In 2007 there were 1,476,600 passenger cars in use, 162,900 lorries and vans, 24,900 motorcycles and mopeds, and 8,900 buses and coaches. There were 962 deaths as a result of road accidents in 2007.

Social Statistics

In 2008 there were a total of 69,083 live births in Serbia (without Kosovo and Metohija), a rate of 9.4 per 1,000 inhabitants. There were 102,711 deaths (14.0 per 1,000) and 38,285 marriages (5.2 per 1,000). Population growth rate, 2005–10, –0.6%. Life expectancy in 2013 was 71.3 years for men and 76.9 for women. Infant mortality was 6 per 1,000 live births in 2010.

Telecommunications

There were 3,110,300 landline telephone subscriptions in 2010 (383.0 per 1,000 inhabitants) and 9,915,300 mobile phone subscriptions (1,220.8 per 1,000 inhabitants). An estimated 40.2% of households had a computer in 2010 and 51.5% of the population were internet users in 2013. In March 2012 there were 3.2 m. Facebook users.

Territory and Population

Serbia is bounded in the northwest by Croatia, in the north by Hungary, in the northeast by Romania, in the east by Bulgaria, in the south by Macedonia and in the west by Albania, Montenegro and Bosnia and Herzegovina. According to the constitution it includes the two provinces of Kosovo and Metohija in the south and Vojvodina in the north. With these Serbia's area is 88,361 km^2; without, 55,968 km^2. Population at the 2011 census was (with Vojvodina but without Kosovo and Metohija) 7,186,862; population density per km^2, 92.8. Population at the 2011 census without both Vojvodina and Kosovo and Metohija was 5,255,053. The population was 56.4% urban in 2011. The capital is Belgrade (2011 census population, 1,166,763). The official language is Serbian.

Tourism

In 2011, 764,000 non-resident tourists stayed in holiday accommodation (up from 682,000 in 2010 and 645,000 in 2009). There were 280 hotels in 2011, with 16,034 rooms and 25,841 beds.

Seychelles

Republic of Seychelles

Factsheet

Capital: Victoria
Population estimate, 2015: 96,000
GNI per capita, 2014: (PPP$) 23,300
HDI/world rank, 2014: 0.772/64
Internet domain extension: .sc

Civil Aviation

Seychelles International airport is on Mahé. In 2010 Air Seychelles flew on domestic routes and to Cape Town, Doha, Dubai, Frankfurt, Johannesburg, London, Mauritius, Milan, Nairobi, Paris, Réunion, Rome, Singapore and Zürich. In 2013 it carried 356,000 passengers (188,000 on international flights). Seychelles International handled 650,928 passengers (517,542 on international flights) in 2012 and 4,500 tonnes of freight.

Climate

Though close to the equator, the climate is tropical. The hot, wet season is from Dec. to May, when conditions are humid, but southeast trades bring cooler conditions from June to Nov. Temperatures are high throughout the year, but the islands lie outside the cyclone belt. Victoria, Jan. 80 °F (26.7 °C), July 78 °F (25.6 °C). Annual rainfall 95″ (2,287 mm).

Constitution and Government

Under the 1979 constitution the Seychelles People's Progressive Front (SPPF) was the sole legal Party. There is a unicameral People's Assembly consisting of 34 seats, of which 25 are directly elected and nine are allocated on a proportional basis, and an executive *President* directly elected for a 5-year term (with a maximum of three successive terms). A constitutional amendment of Dec. 1991 legalized other parties. A commission was elected in July 1992 to draft a new constitution. The electorate was some 50,000; turnout was 90%. The SPPF gained 14 seats on the commission, the Democratic Party, eight; the latter, however, eventually withdrew. At a referendum in Nov. 1992 the new draft constitution failed to obtain the necessary 60% approval votes. The commission was reconvened in Jan. 1993. At a further referendum on 18 June 1993 the constitution was approved by 73.6% of votes cast. The elections of 1993 were the first multiparty ones since 1974.

Currency

The unit of currency is the *Seychelles rupee* (SCR) divided into 100 *cents*.

Defence

The Seychelles People's Defence Force comprises all services. Personnel (2011) Army, 200; paramilitary national guard, 250; paramilitary coastguard, 200 including 80 marines. Defence expenditure totalled US$12 m. in 2013 (US$127 per capita), representing 1.0% of GDP.

Economy

Trade and hotels contributed 24.6% to GDP in 2008; followed by transport and communications, 16.7%; finance and real estate, 12.0%; public administration and defence, 9.7%; and manufacturing, 8.6%.

Labour

Some 76% of employed persons work in the services sector. In 2015, 9,093 people worked in accommodation and food service activities. In 2015, 33,344 were formally employed in the private sector, 9,317 in the public sector and 5,762 in the parastatal sector.

Press

In 2008 there was one daily newspaper (circulation of 3,000), as well as three weekly papers.

Rail

There are no railways in the Seychelles.

Religion

82% of the inhabitants are Roman Catholic, the remainder of the population being followers of other religions (mainly Anglicans, with some Seventh-day Adventists, Bahá'ís, Muslims, Hindus, Pentecostalists and Jehovah's Witnesses) or religiously unaffiliated.

Roads

In 2006 there were 502 km of roads, of which 96.0% were surfaced. There were 6,800 private cars in 2006 (80 per 1,000 inhabitants), 2,600 commercial vehicles, 300 taxis and 215 buses.

Shipping

The main port is Victoria, which is also a tuna-fishing and fuel and services supply centre. In Jan. 2009 there were 12 ships of 300 GT or over registered, totalling 165,000 GT. Sea freight (2006) comprised: imports, 534,000 tonnes; exports, 4,604,000 TEUs (twenty-foot equivalent units); transhipments (fish), 74,000 tonnes.

Social Statistics

2012 births, 1,645; deaths, 651. 2012 rates per 1,000 population, birth, 18.6; death, 7.4; infant mortality (2010), 12 per 1,000 births. Annual population growth rate, 2005–10, 0.9%. Life expectancy at birth in 2008 was estimated to be 68 years for males and 79 for females. Fertility rate, 2008, 1.9 births per woman.

Telecommunications

There were 110,700 mobile phone subscriptions (equivalent to 1,313.6 per 1,000 inhabitants) in Jan. 2010 and 26,100 fixed telephone lines. In 2013 an estimated 50.4% of the population were internet users.

Territory and Population

The Seychelles consist of 115 islands in the Indian Ocean, north of Madagascar, with a combined area of 455 km² (175 sq. miles) in two distinct groups and a 2010 census population of 90,945. The Granitic group of 40 islands cover 244 km² (94 sq. miles); the principal island is Mahé, with 160 km² (62 sq. miles) and 78,539 inhabitants (2010 census), the other inhabited islands of the group being Praslin, La Digue, Silhouette, Fregate, North and Denis, which together had 12,406 inhabitants in 2010. The Outer or Coralline group comprises 75 islands spread over a wide area of ocean between the Mahé group and Madagascar, with a total land area of 211 km² (81 sq. miles). Victoria, the chief town, had a census population of 26,450 in 2010. In 2011, 55.9% of the population were urban. The official languages are Creole, English and French but 91% of the population speak Creole.

Tourism

Tourism is the main foreign exchange earner. Visitor numbers were a record 208,034 in 2012, up from 194,753 in 2011.

Sierra Leone

Republic of Sierra Leone

Factsheet

Capital: Freetown
Population estimate, 2015: 6.45 m.
GNI per capita, 2014: (PPP$) 1,780
HDI/world rank, 2014: 0.413/181
Internet domain extension: .sl

Civil Aviation

Freetown Airport (Lungi) is the international airport. The national carrier is Leone Airways, operated by Arik Air (a Nigerian airline) under a joint venture agreement. In 2012 scheduled airline traffic of Sierra Leone-based carriers flew 2.6 m. km; passenger-km totalled 153.7 m. in the same year.

Climate

A tropical climate, with marked wet and dry seasons and high temperatures throughout the year. The rainy season lasts from about April to Nov., when humidity can be very high. Thunderstorms are common from April to June and in Sept. and Oct. Rainfall is particularly heavy in Freetown because of the effect of neighbouring relief. Freetown, Jan. 80 °F (26.7 °C), July 78 °F (25.6 °C). Annual rainfall 135″ (3,434 mm).

Constitution and Government

In a referendum in Sept. 1991 some 60% of the 2.5 m. electorate voted for the introduction of a new constitution instituting multi-party democracy. The constitution has been amended several times since. The president, who is both head of state and head of government, is elected by popular vote for not more than two terms of 5 years. There is a 124-seat *National Assembly* (112 members elected by popular vote and 12 filled by paramount chiefs). There is a *Supreme Council of State (SCS)* and a *Council of State Secretaries*.

Currency

The unit of currency is the *leone* (SLL) of 100 *cents*.

Defence

In 2013 military expenditure totalled US$14 m. (US$3 per capita), representing 0.3% of GDP.

Economy

Agriculture, forestry and fishing contributed 57.4% to GDP in 2010; followed by services, 10.1%; trade and hotels, 8.0%; and transport and communications, 6.6%.

Labour

The economically active workforce was 1,935,000 in 2004 (51% males). In 2004 around two-thirds of the economically active population were engaged in agriculture, fisheries, forestry and hunting. 68,250 persons were registered unemployed in 2004. Sierra Leone had 45,000 people living in slavery according to the Walk Free Foundation's 2013 *Global Slavery Index*.

Press

In 2008 there were ten paid-for dailies with an average circulation of 22,000, plus 40 non-dailies.

Religion

According to estimates by the Pew Research Center's Forum on Religion & Public Life, 78.0% of the population in 2010 were Muslims (mostly Sunnis) and 20.9% were Christians (mainly Protestants).

Roads

There were 11,300 km of roads in 2007 (8% paved). Much of the damage to the road network as a result of the civil war has now been repaired. In 2007 there were 16,400 passenger cars in use and 14,100 vans and lorries. There were 71 deaths as a result of road accidents in 2007.

Shipping

The port of Freetown has one of the largest natural harbours in the world. Iron ore is exported through Pepel, and there is a small port at Bonthe. In Jan. 2009 there were 248 ships of 300 GT or over registered, totalling 547,000 GT.

Social Statistics

2008 estimates: births, 224,000; deaths, 88,000. Estimated birth rate in 2008 was 40.3 per 1,000 population; estimated death rate, 15.8. Annual population growth rate, 2000–08, 3.4%. Expectation of life at birth in 2013 was 45.8 years for females and 45.3 years for males (giving Sierra Leone the lowest life expectancy for females, for males and overall). The World Health Organization's *World Health Statistics 2009* ranked Sierra Leone in last place in a 'healthy life expectancy' list, with an expected 35 years of healthy life for babies born in 2007. Infant mortality was 114 per 1,000 live births in 2010 (the highest in the world). Fertility rate, 2008, 5.2 births per woman.

Telecommunications

In 2009 Sierra Leone had an estimated 1,160,000 mobile phone subscriptions and 32,800 main (fixed) telephone lines. The country's telecommunications network was virtually destroyed during the civil war, but since then the sector has been one of Sierra Leone's main successes. In 2009 there were an estimated 2.6 internet users per 1,000 inhabitants.

Territory and Population

Sierra Leone is bounded on the northwest, north and northeast by Guinea, on the southeast by Liberia and on the southwest by the Atlantic Ocean. The area is 71,740 km^2 (27,699 sq. miles). Population (census 2004), 4,976,871; density, 69.4 per km^2. In 2011, 38.8% of the population were urban. The capital is Freetown, with a 2004 census population of 772,873. Sierra Leone is divided into three provinces and one area (Western Area, of which Freetown is the capital). The provinces are divided into districts as follows: Bo, Bonthe, Moyamba, Pujehun (Southern Province); Kailahun, Kenema, Kono (Eastern Province); Bombali, Kambia, Koinaduga, Port Loko, Toukolili (Northern Province). The principal peoples are the Mendes (26% of the total) in the south, the Temnes (25%) in the north and centre, the Konos, Fulanis, Bulloms, Korankos, Limbas and Kissis. English is the official language; a Creole (Krio) is spoken.

Tourism

Tourism is in the initial stages of development. In 2012 there were 60,000 non-resident tourist arrivals by air (32,000 in 2007).

Singapore

Republik Singapura (Republic of Singapore)

Factsheet
Population estimate, 2015: 5.60 m.
GNI per capita, 2014: (PPP$) 76,628
HDI/world rank, 2014: 0.912/11
Internet domain extension: .sg

Civil Aviation

As of Sept. 2010, Singapore Changi Airport was served by 96 airlines with more than 5,100 weekly flights to and from some 200 cities in 60 countries and territories worldwide. A total of 37,203,978 passengers and 1,633,791

tonnes of freight were handled in 2009. The national airline is Singapore Airlines, which carried 16,480,000 passengers in 2009–10.

Climate

The climate is equatorial, with relatively uniform temperature, abundant rainfall and high humidity. Rain falls throughout the year but tends to be heaviest from Nov. to Jan. Average daily temperature is 26.8 °C with a maximum daily average of 30.9 °C and a minimum daily average of 23.9 °C. Mean annual rainfall is 2,345 mm.

Constitution and Government

Singapore is a republic with a parliamentary system of government. The organs of state—the executive, the legislature and the judiciary—are provided for by a written constitution. The present constitution came into force on 3 June 1959 and was amended in 1965. The Head of State is the *President*. The administration of the government is vested in the Cabinet headed by the *Prime Minister*. The Prime Minister and the other Cabinet Members are appointed by the President from among the Members of Parliament (MPs). The Cabinet is collectively responsible to Parliament. *Parliament* is unicameral consisting of 87 elected members and three Non-Constituency MPs (NCMPs), elected by secret ballot from single-member and group representation constituencies, as well as nine Nominated Members of Parliament (NMPs) who are appointed for a term of two and a half years on the recommendation of a Special Select Committee of Parliament. A Presidential Council to consider and report on minorities' rights was established in 1970.

Currency

The unit of currency is the *Singapore dollar* (SGD) of 100 *cents*.

Defence

Compulsory military service in peacetime for all male citizens and permanent residents was introduced in 1967. The period of service is 24 months. In 2013 defence expenditure totalled US$9,864 m. (US$1,807 per capita—the highest of any Asian country), representing 3.4% of GDP.

Economy

Services accounted for 73% of GDP in 2012 and industry 27%.

Labour

In June 2004 Singapore's labour force comprised 2,183,300 people, of whom 2,066,900 were employed. The principal areas of employment in June 2004 were manufacturing (356,700 people), wholesale and retail trade (319,700), business services (254,000), transport, storage and communications (212,500) and hotels and restaurants (129,300). The unemployment rate averaged 3.4% throughout 2004 (4.0% in 2003). The average worker put in 46.3 h a week in 2004; average monthly earnings in 2004 were S$3,329.

Press

In 2008 there were 11 daily newspapers, with a total daily circulation of 1,725,000 copies. The most popular paid-for daily is *The Straits Times*, with an average daily circulation of 389,000 in 2008.

Rail

Woodlands Train Checkpoint is the southern terminus of the Malaysian Keretapi Tanah Melayu (KTM) rail network. A main line used to run on through Singapore but ceased operating in 2011. Branch lines serve the port of Singapore and the industrial estates at Jurong. The total rail length of the Mass Rapid Transit (SMRT) metro is 93.2 km. The 20 km North-East Line (operated by SBS Transit), the world's first fully automated heavy metro, became operational in 2003.

Religion

According to the 2010 census, 33.3% of the population were Buddhists, 18.3% Christians, 14.7% Muslims, 10.9% Taoists and 5.1% Hindus; 0.7% belonged to other religions and 17.0% had no religion.

Roads

In 2007 there were 3,297 km of public roads (100% asphalt-paved). Singapore has one of the densest road networks in the world. In 2007 there were 517,000 passenger cars, 14,500 buses and coaches, 151,000 vans and lorries, and 144,300 motorcycles and scooters.

Shipping

Singapore has a large container port, the world's second busiest in terms of containers handled and shipping tonnage in 2012, second only to Shanghai. The economy is dependent on shipping and entrepôt trade. A total of 134,883 vessels of 2.4 bn. gross tonnes (GT) entered Singapore during 2014. In 2014, 4,595 vessels with a total of 82.2 m. GT were registered in Singapore. The Singapore merchant fleet ranked fifth among the principal merchant fleets of the world in 2014. Total cargo handled in 2014 was 581.3 m. freight tons, and total container throughput was 33,869,300 TEUs (twenty-foot equivalent units). Singapore was ranked first in the World Economic Forum's *Global Competitiveness Report 2009–2010* for the quality of its port facilities.

Social Statistics

2013 births, 39,720; deaths, 18,938. Birth rate per 1,000 resident population, 2013, 9.3; death rate per 1,000 resident population, 4.6. Population growth rate in the year ended 30 June 2014, 1.3%; infant mortality, 2010, two per 1,000 live births (one of the lowest in the world); life expectancy, 2013, 79.8 years for males and 84.7 years for females. Fertility rate, 2008, 1.3 births per woman. In 2010 the most popular age range for marrying was 25–29 years for both males and females.

Telecommunications

In 2013 there were 1,967,000 main (fixed) telephone lines. In the same year mobile phone subscriptions numbered 8,438,000 (1,559.2 per 1,000 persons). In 1997 Singapore Telecom, one of the largest companies in Asia, lost its monopoly with the entry of a new mobile phone operator. Singapore had three mobile phone operators in 2009—SingTel Mobile (owned by Singapore Telecom), M1 and StarHub Mobile. In 2013 there were 1,493.3 mobile broadband subscriptions per 1,000 inhabitants and 260.3 fixed broadband subscriptions for every 1,000 inhabitants. In March 2012 there were 2.6 m. Facebook users.

Territory and Population

The Republic of Singapore consists of Singapore Island and some 63 smaller islands. Singapore Island is situated off the southern extremity of the Malay Peninsula, to which it is joined by a 1.1 km causeway carrying a road, railway and water pipeline across the Strait of Johor and by a 1.9 km bridge at Tuas, opened on 2 Jan. 1998. The Straits of Johor between the island and the mainland are 914 m wide. The island is 716.1 km^2 in area, including the offshore islands. Census of population (2010): Chinese residents 2,793,980 (74.1%), Malays 503,868 (13.4%), Indians 348,119 (9.2%) and others 125,754 (3.3%); resident population, 3,771,721. Estimated total population in June 2014 was 5,469,724. The population is 100% urban. Population density, 7,540 per km^2. Malay, Chinese (Mandarin), Tamil and English are the official languages; Malay is the national language and English is the language of administration.

Tourism

International visitor arrivals totalled 15.6 m. in 2013, up from 14.5 m. in 2012. Tourism receipts rose from S$23.1 bn. in 2012 to S$23.5 bn. in 2013. In Dec. 2013 there were 196 gazetted hotels, providing 47,113 rooms.

Slovakia

Slovenská Republika (Slovak Republic)

Factsheet
Capital: Bratislava
Population estimate, 2015: 5.43 m.

GNI per capita, 2014: (PPP$) 25,845
HDI/world rank, 2014: 0.844/35
Internet domain extension: .sk

Civil Aviation

The main international airport is at Bratislava (M. R. Stefánik), which handled 1,413,193 passengers in 2012 and 22,565 tonnes of freight. There are also some international flights from Košice. Slovak Airlines (formerly the Slovak flag carrier) ceased operations in Feb. 2007, as did Air Slovakia in March 2010. SkyEurope (central Europe's first low-cost airline), which operated domestic services and also flew to a number of destinations in Europe, ceased operations in Sept. 2009. Danube Wings, launched in 2008, ceased operations in Dec. 2013.

Climate

A humid continental climate, with warm summers and cold winters. Precipitation is generally greater in summer, with thunderstorms. Autumn, with dry, clear weather and spring, which is damp, are each of short duration. Bratislava, Jan. –0.7 °C. June 19.1 °C. Annual rainfall 649 mm.

Constitution and Government

The constitution became effective on 1 Jan. 1993, creating a parliamentary democracy with universal suffrage from the age of 18. Parliament is the unicameral *National Council*. It has 150 members elected by proportional representation to serve 4-year terms. The constitution was amended in Sept. 1998 to allow for the direct election of the *President*, who serves for a 5-year term. The President may serve a maximum of two consecutive terms. The Judicial Branch consists of a *Supreme Court*, whose judges are elected by the National Council, and a *Constitutional Court*, whose judges are appointed by the President from a group of nominees approved by the National Council. Citizenship belongs to all citizens of the former federal Slovak Republic; other residents of 5 years standing may apply for citizenship. Slovakia grants dual citizenship.

Currency

On 1 Jan. 2009 the euro (EUR) replaced the *Slovak koruna* (SKK) as the legal currency of Slovakia at the irrevocable conversion rate of 30.126 koruny to one euro.

Defence

Since 1 Jan. 2006 Slovakia has had an all-volunteer professional army. In 2013 defence spending totalled US$995 m. (US$181 per capita), representing 1.0% of GDP.

Economy

Agriculture accounted for 3% of GDP in 2008, industry 38% and services 59%.

Labour

Out of 2,351,400 people in employment in 2011, 568,000 were in manufacturing, 304,000 in wholesale and retail trade/repair of motor vehicles, motorcycles and personal and household goods, 243,700 in construction and 164,200 in education. The average monthly salary in 2011 was €855. Unemployment stood at 19.2% in 2001, but then fell to 16.2% in 2005 and still further to 9.6% in 2008. It rose again to 14.5% in 2010 and was 14.7% in Dec. 2012. Slovakia had 19,000 people living in slavery according to the Walk Free Foundation's 2013 *Global Slavery Index*.

Press

Slovakia had ten daily newspapers in 2008 (nine paid-for and one free) with a combined average daily circulation of 508,000.

Rail

In 2011 the length of railway routes was 3,624 km. Most of the network is 1,435 mm gauge with short sections on three other gauges. In 2011, 47.5 m. passengers were carried and 43.7 m. tonnes of freight. There are tram/light rail networks in Bratislava, Košice and Trenčianske Teplice.

Religion

A federal Czechoslovakian law of July 1991 provides the basis for church-state relations and guarantees the religious and civic rights of citizens and churches. Churches must register to become legal entities but operate independently of the state. In 2011, 62.0% of the population were Roman Catholic, 5.9% members of the Evangelical Church of the Augsburg Confession, 5.8% Greek Catholic and 1.8% Calvinist. In Feb. 2016 there was one cardinal.

Roads

In 2014 there were 54,801 km of roads, including 420 km of motorways. There were 1,949,055 passenger cars in use in 2014, plus 265,424 vans and lorries, 8,876 buses and coaches and 80,791 motorcycles and mopeds. In 2014 there were 13,307 road accidents resulting in 229 fatalities.

Shipping

In 2012 vessels registered by Slovak enterprises numbered 218. Transport of goods on inland waterways in 2012 totalled 8.2 m. tonnes, of which 5.3 m. tonnes were transit goods and 2.9 m. tonnes international.

Social Statistics

Births, 2007, 54,424; deaths, 53,856; marriages, 27,437; divorces, 12,174. Rates (per 1,000 population), 2007: birth, 10.1; death, 10.0; marriage, 5.1; divorce, 2.3. Expectation of life, 2006, was 70.4 years for males and 78.2 for females. In 2006 the most popular age range for marrying was 25–29 for both males and females. Annual population growth rate, 1996–2006, 0.3%. Infant mortality, 2010 (per 1,000 live births), 7. Fertility rate, 2006, 1.2 births per woman (one of the lowest rates in the world).

Telecommunications

In 2013 there were 6,208,000 mobile phone subscriptions (1,139.1 per 1,000 inhabitants) and 967,000 fixed telephone lines. In 2000 Deutsche Telekom bought a 51% stake in the state-owned Slovak Telekom, with the Slovakian government retaining 49% of shares in the company. In 2015 Deutsche Telekom acquired these shares, resulting in Slovak Telekom now being fully owned by Deutsche Telekom. In 2013 an estimated 77.9% of the population aged 16–74 were internet users. In March 2012 there were 1.9 m. Facebook users.

Territory and Population

Slovakia is bounded in the northwest by the Czech Republic, north by Poland, east by Ukraine, south by Hungary and southwest by Austria. Its area is 49,034 km² (18,932 sq. miles). Census population in 2011 was 5,397,036 (2,769,264 females and 2,627,772 males); density, 110.1 per km². In 2011, 54.9% of the population lived in urban areas. There are eight administrative regions (*Kraj*), one of which is the capital, Bratislava. The capital, Bratislava, had a population in 2011 of 411,228. The population of other principal towns (2011, in 1,000): Košice, 240; Prešov, 92; Žilina, 81; Banská Bystrica, 80; Nitra, 79; Trnava, 66; Martin, 57; Trenčín, 56. The population is 80.7% Slovak, 8.5% Hungarian, 2.0% Roma, 0.6% Czech and 0.6% Ruthenian, with some Germans, Moravians, Poles and Ukrainians. A law of Nov. 1995 makes Slovak the sole official language.

Tourism

In 2010, 1,327,000 non-resident tourists stayed in holiday accommodation (1,298,000 in 2009); there were 3,126 accommodation establishments in 2010 with 57,406 rooms and 147,492 beds.

Slovenia

Republika Slovenija (Republic of Slovenia)

Factsheet
Capital: Ljubljana
Population estimate, 2015: 2.07 m.

GNI per capita, 2014: (PPP$) 27,852
HDI/world rank, 2014: 0.880/25
Internet domain extension: .si

Civil Aviation

There is an international airport at Ljubljana (Brnik), which handled 1,433,855 passengers (all on international flights) and 14,333 tonnes of freight in 2009. The national carrier, Adria Airways, has flights to most major European cities and Tel Aviv. In 2006 scheduled airline traffic of Slovenia-based carriers flew 15 m. km, carrying 850,000 passengers.

Climate

Summers are warm, winters are cold with frequent snow. Ljubljana, Jan. −4 °C, July 22 °C. Annual rainfall 1,383 mm.

Constitution and Government

The constitution became effective on 23 Dec. 1991. Slovenia is a parliamentary democratic republic with an executive that consists of a directly-elected president and a prime minister, aided by a council of ministers. It has a bicameral parliament (*Skupščina Slovenije*), consisting of a 90-member *National Assembly* (*Dravni Zbor*), 88 members elected for 4 year terms by proportional representation with a 4% threshold and two members elected by ethnic minorities; and a 40-member, advisory *State Council* (*Dravni Svet*), elected for 5 year terms by interest groups and regions. It has veto powers over the National Assembly. Administratively the country is divided into 199 municipalities and 11 urban municipalities. The Judicial branch consists of a *Supreme Court*, whose judges are elected by the National Assembly, and a *Constitutional Court*, whose judges are elected for 9 year terms by the National Assembly and nominated by the president.

Currency

On 1 Jan. 2007 the euro (EUR) replaced the *tolar* (SLT) as the legal currency of Slovenia at the irrevocable conversion rate of 239.64 tolars to one euro.

Defence

Compulsory military service for 7 months ended in Sept. 2003. The army became fully professional in 2010 when the compulsory reserve was replaced by a new system of voluntary reserve service. In 2013 defence spending totalled US$474 m. (US$238 per capita), representing 1.0% of GDP.

Economy

Agriculture accounted for 2% of GDP in 2012, industry 32% and services 66%.

Labour

Registered labour force was 920,184 in 2012, with 110,183 registered unemployed. The unemployment rate in Dec. 2014 was 9.7% (compared to 10.1% in 2013 as a whole). In 2012 the average monthly gross wage per employee was €1,525.47.

Press

In 2008 there were eight daily newspapers with a combined circulation of 380,000 and 253 non-dailies. The most popular paid-for daily is *Slovenske novice*, with an average daily circulation in 2008 of 88,000.

Rail

There were 1,228 km of 1,435 mm gauge in 2008, of which 503 km were electrified. In 2008, 16.7 m. passengers and 17.3 m. tonnes of freight were carried. In Sept. 2010 the state-owned railway companies of Slovenia, Croatia and Serbia announced the creation of a joint venture called Cargo 10 to improve the management of freight trains along the route known as Corridor 10 that passes through all three countries.

Religion

A study by the Pew Research Center's Forum on Religion & Public Life estimated that 78.4% of the population in 2010 were Christians and 3.6% Muslims, with 18.0% having no religious affiliation. Of the Christians in 2010, 94% were Catholics. In Feb. 2016 there was one cardinal.

Roads

In 2012 there were 38,985 km of road including 676 km of motorways. There were in Dec. 2013: 1,063,795 passenger cars; 2,465 buses; 90,560 goods motor vehicles; and 92,986 motorcycles and mopeds. 533 m. passenger-km were travelled by road in 2012. There were 18,904 road traffic accidents with material damage in 2013 in which 125 persons were killed. In 2013 there were 6.1 road deaths per 100,000 population.

Shipping

A total of 5,433 vessels arrived at or departed from Slovenia's ports in 2008 (4,447 cargo-carrying vessels and 986 passenger ships), including 4,474 at Koper. Goods traffic totalled 16.6 m. tonnes in 2008 (Koper, 16.5 m. tonnes).

Social Statistics

Live births, 2008, 21,817; deaths, 18,308. Rates, 2008 (per 1,000 population): birth, 10.8; death, 9.1. Infant mortality, 2010: two per 1,000 live births (one of the lowest rates in the world). There were 529 suicides in 2006 (22.8 per 100,000 population). In 2011 the most popular age range for marrying was 25–29 years for females and 30–34 years for males. Expectation of life, 2007, was 74.4 years for males and 81.7 for females. Annual population growth rate, 2000–05, 0.1%. Fertility rate, 2008, 1.4 births per woman.

Telecommunications

In 2009 there were 2,100,000 mobile phone subscriptions (1,039.8 per 1,000 inhabitants) and 1,034,000 fixed telephone lines. The leading telecommunications operator is the state-owned Telekom Slovenije. In 2009 there were 577,000 mobile broadband subscriptions and 479,000 fixed broadband internet subscriptions. In March 2012 there were 671,000 Facebook users.

Territory and Population

Slovenia is bounded in the north by Austria, in the northeast by Hungary, in the southeast and south by Croatia and in the west by Italy. The length of coastline is 47 km. Its area is 20,273 km^2. In Jan. 2011 the population at the register-based census was 2,050,189 (1,035,626 females); density per km^2, 101.1. The capital is Ljubljana: 2011 census population, 272,220. Maribor (population of 95,171 in 2011) is the other major city. In 2011, 49.5% of the population lived in urban areas. The official language is Slovene.

Tourism

In 2010, 1,869,000 non-resident tourists stayed in holiday accommodation (1,824,000 in 2009) including: 412,000 from Italy; 202,000 from Austria; 194,000 from Germany; 103,000 from Croatia.

Solomon Islands

Factsheet

Capital: Honiara
Population estimate, 2015: 584,000
GNI per capita, 2014: (PPP$) 1,540
HDI/world rank, 2014: 0.506/156=
Internet domain extension: .sb

Civil Aviation

A new terminal has been opened at Henderson International Airport in Honiara. The national carrier is Solomon Airlines. In 2006 scheduled airline traffic of Solomon Islands-based carriers flew 3 m. km, carrying 101,000 passengers (32,000 on international flights).

Climate

An equatorial climate with only small seasonal variations. Southeast winds cause cooler conditions from April to Nov., but northwest winds for the rest of the year bring higher temperatures and greater rainfall, with annual totals ranging between 80″ (2,000 mm) and 120″ (3,000 mm).

Constitution and Government

The Solomon Islands are a constitutional monarchy with the British Sovereign (represented locally by a Governor-General, who must be a Solomon Island citizen) as Head of State. Legislative power is vested in the single-chamber *National Parliament* composed of 50 members, elected by universal adult suffrage for 4 years. Parliamentary democracy is based on a multi-party system. Executive authority is effectively held by the Cabinet, led by the Prime Minister. The *Governor-General* is appointed for up to 5 years, on the advice of Parliament, and acts in almost all matters on the advice of the Cabinet. The Prime Minister is elected by and from members of Parliament. Other Ministers are appointed by the Governor-General on the Prime Minister's recommendation, from members of Parliament. The Cabinet is responsible to Parliament. Emphasis is laid on the devolution of power to provincial governments, and traditional chiefs and leaders have a special role within the arrangement.

Currency

The *Solomon Island dollar* (SBD) of 100 *cents* was introduced in 1977.

Defence

The marine wing of the Royal Solomon Islands Police operates three patrol boats and a number of fast crafts for surveillance of fisheries and maritime boundaries.

Economy

Agriculture accounted for 39% of GDP in 2009, industry 6% and services 55%.

Labour

The estimated economically active population in 2010 was 123,000 (69% males), up from 105,000 in 2005.

Press

There are three main newspapers in circulation. *The Solomon Star* (circulation: 5,000) is daily and the *Solomon Express* and *The Island Sun* are weekly. The Government Information Service publishes a monthly issue of the *Solomon Nius* that exclusively disseminates news of government activities. Non-government organizations such as the Solomon Islands Development Trust (SIDT) also publish monthly papers on environmental issues.

Religion

According to estimates by the Pew Research Center's Forum on Religion & Public Life, 97.4% of the population in 2010 were Christians (mainly Protestants).

Roads

In 2010 there was estimated to be a total of 1,875 km of roads, of which 104 km were paved. The rest of the network is surfaced with gravel, coral or earth.

Shipping

There are international ports at Honiara, Yandina in the Russell Islands and Noro in New Georgia, Western Province. In Jan. 2009 there were three ships of 300 GT or over registered, totalling 2,000 GT.

Social Statistics

2008 estimates: births, 16,000; deaths, 3,000. Estimated birth rate in 2008 was 30.4 per 1,000 population; estimated death rate, 6.2. Life expectancy, 2013, 69.2 years for women and 66.3 for men. Annual population growth rate, 2000–08, 2.6%. Infant mortality, 2010, 23 per 1,000 live births; fertility rate, 2008, 3.9 births per woman.

Telecommunications

Telecommunications are operated by Solomon Telekom, a joint venture between the government of Solomon Islands and Cable & Wireless (UK). Telecommunications between Honiara and provincial centres are facilitated by modern satellite communication systems. In 2014 there were 7,500 main (fixed) telephone lines; mobile phone subscriptions numbered 376,700 (658 per 1,000 persons). In 2011 an estimated 6% of the population were internet users.

Territory and Population

The Solomon Islands lie within the area 5° to 12° 30′ S. lat. and 155° 30′ to 169° 45′ E. long. The group includes the main islands of Guadalcanal, Malaita, New Georgia, San Cristobal (now Makira), Santa Isabel and Choiseul. The land area is estimated at 28,370 km² (10,954 sq. miles). The larger islands are mountainous and forest clad, with flood-prone rivers of considerable energy potential. Guadalcanal has the largest land area and the greatest amount of flat coastal plain. Population at the census of Nov. 2009, 515,870 (251,415 females); density, 18.2 per km². In 2011, 18.9% of the population lived in urban areas. The islands are administratively divided into nine provinces plus a Capital Territory. The capital, Honiara, on Guadalcanal, is the largest urban area, with a population in 2009 of 64,602. 93% of the population are Melanesian; other ethnic groups include Polynesian, Micronesian, European and Chinese. English is the official language, and is spoken by 1–2% of the population. In all 120 indigenous languages are spoken; Melanesian languages are spoken by 85% of the population.

Tourism

Tourism in the Solomon Islands is still in a development stage. The emphasis is on establishing major hotels in the capital and provincial centres, to be supplemented by satellite eco-tourism projects in the rural areas. In 2011 there were 22,941 foreign tourists.

Somalia

Jamhuuriyadda Federaalka Soomaaliya (Federal Republic of Somalia)

Factsheet

Capital: Mogadishu
Population estimate, 2015: 10.79 m.
GDP per capita, 2014: US$131
Internet domain extension: .so

Civil Aviation

There are international airports at Mogadishu and Hargeisa. In 2010 there were flights to Aden, Djibouti, Dubai, Jeddah, Nairobi, Sharjah and Wajir in addition to internal services.

Climate

Much of the country is arid, although rainfall is more adequate towards the south. Temperatures are very high on the northern coasts. Mogadishu, Jan. 79 °F (26.1 °C), July 78 °F (25.6 °C). Annual rainfall 17″ (429 mm). Berbera, Jan. 76 °F (24.4 °C), July 97 °F (36.1 °C). Annual rainfall 2″ (51 mm).

Constitution and Government

A new constitution was promulgated on 1 Aug. 2012 after over 20 years of non-functioning government. It replaced the constitution of 1979 that itself had lost authority after the ousting of President Siyad Barre in 1991. The 2012 constitution was adopted by the National Constitutional Assembly with 96% backing from the 645 community leaders present at the vote (from a total of 825). The constitution includes a bill of rights enshrining the equality of all citizens regardless of clan or religion. Islam is the single recognized state religion, with Sharia law serving as the foundation of the legal system. The right to education up to the secondary level is guaranteed for all, while female circumcision and the deployment of children in armed conflict are proscribed. Provision is included for the establishment of a Truth and Reconciliation Commission and for the implementation of a federal system of government (although details of how power and resources are to be split remains to be decided). There is currently a unicameral parliament with 275 members but

there are plans for a 54-member senate. Parliament elects the *President*, who in turn appoints a *Prime Minister*.

Currency

The unit of currency is the *Somali shilling* (SOS) of 100 *cents*.

Defence

Following the 1991 revolution there were no national armed forces for many years. However, in 2013 a first national army division was reinstated in a major step towards reviving the Somali Armed Forces. The Somali National Army reportedly comprised an estimated 20,000 personnel in mid-2014.

Economy

Agriculture accounts for approximately 59% of GDP, industry 10% and services 31%.

Labour

The estimated economically active population in 2010 was 3,627,000 (59% males), up from 3,267,000 in 2005. Somalia had 73,000 people living in slavery according to the Walk Free Foundation's 2013 *Global Slavery Index*.

Press

The Somali press collapsed in 1991, with most of its facilities destroyed. Since 2000 several independent newspapers have emerged, including the daily *Wartire in Hargeisa* (Somaliland) and the weeklies *Yamayska* and *Bulsho* in Puntland. There were seven daily newspapers in 2008. Average daily circulation of newspapers in 2008 totalled 21,000. In the 2013 *World Press Freedom Index* compiled by Reporters Without Borders, Somalia was ranked 175th out of 179 countries.

Religion

The population is almost entirely Sunni Muslims.

Roads

Before the start of the Somali Civil War in the mid-1980s the network had a total length of more than 21,000 km. In 2006, 90% of the road network was considered to be in a poor or a very poor state of repair. As the country begins to recover after years of conflict main roads are being repaired in order to facilitate the movement of goods and people.

Shipping

The main ports are at Berbera, Bosaso, Kismayo, Marka and Mogadishu. In Jan. 2009 there were three ships of 300 GT or over registered, totalling 2,000 GT. Piracy off the coast of Somalia was intensifying for several years with 215 attacks in the waters off Somalia recorded in 2009, 219 in 2010 and 236 in 2011. In 2012 there were only 75 recorded attacks, largely thanks to more patrolling of the waters off East Africa by international navies. In 2013 this fell to 15 attacks, and in 2014 further to 11. There were 14 actual hijacks in 2012, down from 28 in 2011 and 49 in 2010. In 2013 there were then only two hijacks, with both ships being released within a day as a result of naval intervention, and in 2014 and 2015 there were none at all.

Social Statistics

Births, 2008 estimate, 394,000; deaths, 140,000. Rates, 2008 estimate (per 1,000 population): birth, 44.1; death, 15.7. Infant mortality, 2010, 108 per 1,000 live births. Annual population growth rate, 2000–08, 2.4%. Life expectancy at birth, 2013, was 53.4 years for men and 56.7 years for women. Fertility rate, 2008, 6.4 births per woman.

Telecommunications

Somalia had 70,000 fixed telephone lines in 2012 (6.9 per 1,000 persons); mobile phone subscriptions numbered 1.8 m. in 2011 (181.7 per 1,000 persons). In 2013 an estimated 1.5% of the population were internet users.

Territory and Population

Somalia is bounded north by the Gulf of Aden, east and south by the Indian ocean, and west by Kenya, Ethiopia and Djibouti. Total area 637,657 km²

(246,201 sq. miles). A census has not been held since 1987, when the population was 7,114,431. The United Nations gave an estimated population for 2012 of 9.80 m.; density, 15 per km². Population counting is complicated owing to large numbers of nomads and refugee movements as a result of famine and clan warfare. In 2011, 37.9% of the population were urban. The country is administratively divided into 18 regions. The capital is Mogadishu (2010 population estimate, 1,426,000). Other large towns are Baidoa, Bosaso, Gaalkacyo and Hargeisa. The official language is Somali. Arabic, English and Italian are widely spoken.

Tourism

Tourism was unknown for many years during the worst of the civil war, but visitor numbers have been increasing slowly as some sense of normality returns to the country. Somaliland's relative safety compared to the rest of Somalia has allowed a slightly more advanced tourism industry to develop there.

South Africa

Republic of South Africa

Factsheet

Capitals: Pretoria/Tshwane (Administrative), Cape Town (Legislative), Bloemfontein (Judicial)
Seat of parliament: Cape Town
Seats of government: Cape Town, Pretoria
Population estimate, 2015: 54.49 m.
GNI per capita, 2014: (PPP$) 12,122
HDI/world rank, 2014: 0.666/116=
Internet domain extension: .za

Civil Aviation

Responsibility for civil aviation safety and security lies with the South African Civil Aviation Authority (SACAA). The Airports Company South Africa (ACSA) owns and operates South Africa's principal airports. The main international airports are: Johannesburg, Cape Town, Durban, Bloemfontein, Port Elizabeth, Pilanesberg, Lanseria and Upington. The flag carrier South African Airways (SAA), along with Airlink, Comair, Interair and SA Express, operate scheduled international air services. In 2010–11 O. R. Tambo International Airport (formerly Johannesburg International) handled 18,643,145 passengers (9,732,250 on domestic flights), Cape Town handled 8,200,547 passengers (6,781,143 on domestic flights) and Durban (King Shaka) handled 4,873,571 passengers (4,672,960 on domestic flights). O. R. Tambo Airport is also the busiest airport for freight, handling 252,063 tonnes of cargo in 2009.

Climate

There is abundant sunshine and relatively low rainfall. The southwest has a Mediterranean climate, with rain mainly in winter, but most of the country has a summer maximum, although quantities show a decrease from east to west. Pretoria, Jan. 73.4 °F (23.0 °C), July 53.6 °F (12.0 °C). Annual rainfall 26.5″ (674 mm). Bloemfontein, Jan. 73.4 °F (23.0 °C), July 45.9 °F (7.7 °C). Annual rainfall 22″ (559 mm). Cape Town, Jan. 69.6 °F (20.9 °C), July 54.0 °F (12.2 °C). Annual rainfall 20.3″ (515 mm). Johannesburg, Jan. 68.2 °F (20.1 °C), July 50.7 °F (10.4 °C). Annual rainfall 28.1″ (713 mm).

Constitution and Government

An Interim *Constitution* came into effect on 27 April 1994 and was in force until 3 Feb. 1997. Under it, the National Assembly and Senate formed a Constitutional Assembly, which had the task of drafting a definitive constitution. This was signed into law in Dec. 1996 and took effect on 4 Feb. 1997. The 1996 constitution defines the powers of the President, Parliament (consisting of the National Assembly and the National Council of Provinces—NCOP), the national executive, the judiciary, public administration, the security services and the relationship between the three spheres of government. A *Constitutional Court*, consisting of a president, a deputy president

and nine other judges, was inaugurated in Feb. 1995. *Parliament* is the legislative authority and has the power to make laws for the country in accordance with the Constitution. It consists of the National Assembly and the NCOP. The *National Assembly* consists of no fewer than 350 and no more than 400 members directly elected for 5 years. The *National Council of Provinces* (NCOP) consists of 54 permanent members and 36 special delegates and aims to represent provincial interests in the national sphere of government.

Currency

The unit of currency is the *rand* (ZAR) of 100 *cents*.

Defence

The South African National Defence Force (SANDF) comprises four services, namely the SA Army, the SA Air Force, the SA Navy and the SA Military Health Service (SAMHS). In 2012 the SANDF consisted of 62,082 active members (excluding 12,382 civilian employees). SAMHS personnel totalled 9,159 (including around 1,115 reservists) in 2011. South Africa ended conscription in 1994. Defence expenditure totalled US$4,848 m. in 2013 (equivalent to US$100 per capita), and represented 1.3% of GDP. Defence expenditure in 1985 had represented 3.8% of GDP. In 2013 South Africa was responsible for 21% of Africa's total defence expenditure.

Economy

Agriculture accounted for 3.0% of GDP in 2009, industry 31.1% and services 65.8%.

Labour

The labour force in South Africa numbered 17.1 m. in the fourth quarter of 2009, of which 4.2 m. were unemployed. In the fourth quarter of 2009 the unemployment rate was 24.3%, up from 21.9% in the fourth quarter of 2008. The Unemployment Insurance Fund (UIF) provides benefits to workers who become unemployed. All employees who work for more than 24 h a month contribute to the Fund. In the year ending March 2009 there were 7.6 m. contributors (7.3 m. in 2008). In the same period the UIF paid benefits to 627,244 beneficiaries, a total amount of R3.8 bn. South Africa had 45,000 people living in slavery according to the Walk Free Foundation's 2013 *Global Slavery Index*.

Press

The major press groups are Independent Newspapers (Pty) Ltd, Media24 Ltd, CTP/Caxton Publishers and Printers Ltd, and Johnnic Publishing Ltd. Other important media players include Primedia, Nail (New Africa Investments Limited) and Kagiso Media. Nail has unbundled into a commercial company (New Africa Capital) and a media company (New Africa Media). In 2008 there were 22 paid-for dailies, 12 paid-for Sunday newspapers and 100 paid-for non-daily newspapers plus one free daily and 167 free non-dailies. Newspapers with the highest circulations (Jan.–March 2008): *Sunday Times* (504,193); *Daily Sun* (499,436); *Rapport* (301,827); *Soccer-Laduma* (292,701); *Sunday World* (203,460); *Sunday Sun* (202,524); *City Press* (201,790); *Sowetan* (145,173). *Beeld* is the largest Afrikaans daily (105,149) and *Isolezwe* the largest isiZulu daily (99,098).

Rail

The Passenger Rail Agency of South Africa (PRASA) was formed in March 2009 as an umbrella organization to oversee the day-to-day running of rail services in South Africa. PRASA operates Metrorail, offering commuter rail services in urban areas and transporting 1.7 m. passengers on weekdays to 478 stations over 2,400 km of track; and Shosholoza Meyl, providing regional and long-distance rail transport.

Religion

South Africa is a secular state and freedom of worship is guaranteed by the Constitution. According to estimates by the Pew Research Center's Forum on Religion & Public Life, 81.2% of the population in 2010 were Christians but 14.9% did not have any religious affiliation. There are small numbers of Hindus and Muslims. Among the Christians, 90% in 2010 were Protestants and 9% Catholics. In 1992 the Anglican Church of Southern Africa voted by 79% of votes cast for the ordination of women. In Feb. 2016 there was one cardinal.

Roads

In 2011 the South African road network comprised some 747,000 km of roads and streets. Toll roads cover around 3,120 km of the national network. South Africa has the longest road network in Africa. As at 31 Oct. 2010 there were 9,797,413 registered motor vehicles. In 2009 a total of 13,768 people were killed in traffic accidents (14,920 in 2007 and 13,875 in 2008).

Shipping

South African Maritime Safety Authority (SAMSA) was established on 1 April 1998 as the authority responsible for ensuring the safety of life at sea and the prevention of sea pollution from ships. Approximately 98% of South Africa's exports are conveyed by sea. The largest ports include the deep water ports of Richards Bay. Durban, Cape Town and Port Elizabeth provide large container terminals for deep-sea and coastal container traffic. The Port of Durban handles 2.5 m. containers per annum. East London, the only river port, has a multi-purpose terminal and dry dock facilities. During 2008–09 the seven major ports handled a total of 184,628,480 tonnes of cargo (Richards Bay, 82,621,766 tonnes; Saldanha, 50,282,909 tonnes; Durban, 40,118,656 tonnes). In Jan. 2009 there were four ships of 300 GT or over registered, totalling 32,000 GT.

Social Statistics

Births: total number of registered live births in 2010 was 1,294,694 (down from a high of 1,677,415 in 2003). Deaths: the number of registered deaths increased from 317,236 in 1997 to 613,198 in 2006, with AIDS as the factor underlying much of the increase. Since then the increasing use of antiretroviral drugs has caused the number of registered deaths to fall to 480,476 in 2012. In 2012, 17.9% of all adults between 15 and 64 were infected with HIV. Estimated population growth rate, 2011–12, 1.3%. Fertility rate, 2009, 2.5 births per woman. Life expectancy at birth in 2013 was 58.2 years for males and 62.1 for females. It had been 59 years for males and 66 for females in the early 1990s but fell in the late 1990s and in the early part of the twenty-first century as a consequence of the AIDS epidemic. It was just 50.2 years for males and 53.9 for females in 2005 but has now risen again thanks to the development and improved availability of medical treatments for HIV. Infant mortality, 2010, 41 per 1,000 live births.

Telecommunications

In 2013 there were 3.9 m. main (fixed) telephone lines. In the same year mobile phone subscriptions numbered 76.9 m. (1,456.4 per 1,000 persons). The largest mobile phone networks are Vodacom and MTN. In 2011, 88.9% of households had a mobile phone; landline telephone, 14.5%. A new 14,000-km submarine cable, the West Africa Cable System, became operational in May 2012, allowing South Africa to greatly increase the capacity of its mobile phone and internet networks. In 2013 an estimated 48.9% of the population were internet users. In June 2012 there were 5.0 m. Facebook users.

Territory and Population

South Africa is bounded in the north by Namibia, Botswana and Zimbabwe, northeast by Mozambique and Swaziland, east by the Indian Ocean, and south and west by the South Atlantic, with Lesotho forming an enclave. Area: 1,219,090 km². This area includes the uninhabited Prince Edward Island (41 km²) and Marion Island (388 km²), lying 1,900 km southeast of Cape Town. At the census of 2011 the population was 51,770,560 (26,581,769 females), consisting of: Black African, 41,000,938 (79.2% of total population); Coloured, 4,615,401 (8.9%); White, 4,586,838 (8.9%); Indian/Asian, 1,286,930 (2.5%). 62.2% of the population were urban in 2011. In 2010 cities with the largest populations were (estimate in 1,000): Johannesburg (Gauteng), 3,763; Cape Town (Western Cape), 3,492; Durban (KwaZulu-Natal), 2,954; Pretoria/Tshwane (Gauteng), 1,468; Vereeniging (Gauteng), 1,174; Port Elizabeth (Eastern Cape), 1,097. Ekurhuleni Metropolitan Municipality had an estimated population of 3,284,000 in 2010. There are 11 official languages. English is the sole language of command and instruction in the armed forces.

Tourism

In 2012 there were 9.19 m. international tourist arrivals (excluding same-day visitors), up from 8.34 m. in 2011. Most visitors in 2012 came from Zimbabwe, Lesotho, Mozambique, Swaziland and Botswana. International tourist receipts in 2012 totalled US$10.0 bn., up from US$9.5 bn. in 2011. The number of people employed directly in tourism rose to 598,000 in 2011 from 567,000 in 2010.

South Sudan

(Republic of South Sudan)

Factsheet

Capital: Juba
Population estimate, 2015: 12.34 m.
GNI per capita, 2014: (PPP) $2,332
HDI/world rank, 2014: 0.467/169
Internet domain extension: .ss

Civil Aviation

There is an international airport at Juba with connections to Addis Ababa, Cairo, Entebbe, Khartoum and Nairobi. Other major airports include those at Malakal, Rumbek and Wau. South Supreme Airlines operates both domestic and international flights.

Climate

South Sudan's climate is tropical with wet and dry seasons. The winter is relatively cool and dry while the rainy season usually takes place from April to Dec. with most rain falling in the summer months. Juba, Jan. 81 °F (27.3 °C), July 76 °F (24.5 °C). Annual rainfall 38″ (965 mm). Wau, Jan. 79 °F (25.9 °C), July 78 °F (25.3 °C). Annual rainfall 44″ (1,118 mm).

Constitution and Government

An interim constitution was ratified shortly before independence and came into force on 7 July 2011. Under the constitution the *President* is the Head of State, Head of Government and Commander-in-Chief of the armed forces and serves a four-year term. The National Legislature consists of two Houses: the *National Legislative Assembly*, comprising members of the former Southern Sudan Legislative Assembly and all South Sudanese who were members of the National Assembly of Sudan; and the *Council of States*, which consists of South Sudanese who had seats in the Council of States of Sudan plus 20 members appointed by the President. Members of both houses serve four-year terms.

Currency

The official unit of currency is the *South Sudan pound* (SSP) of 100 *piastres*, introduced on 18 July 2011.

Defence

On independence the former rebel Sudan People's Liberation Army changed its name to the South Sudan Armed Forces. In 2013 defence expenditure totalled US$714 m. (US$64 per capita), representing 5.3% of GDP.

Rail

Total length of railway is 248 km, running from the Sudanese border to Wau.

Religion

A large percentage of South Sudan's population are Christian—primarily Roman Catholic, Anglican and Presbyterian. There are also followers of African traditional animist religions as well as Muslims.

Roads

Only a small proportion of South Sudan's road network is paved, but in Sept. 2012 a 192-km highway linking Juba, the capital, with Nimule, on the Ugandan border, was inaugurated.

Territory and Population

South Sudan is bounded in the north by Sudan, east by Ethiopia, southeast by Kenya, south by Uganda, southwest by the Democratic Republic of the Congo and west by the Central African Republic. Its area is 644,329 km². In 2008 the census population was 8.26 m. (disputed). More than half (51%)

of the population is below the age of 18. 83% of the population is rural. The country is composed of ten states. The capital, Juba, had a population of 230,000 in 2008. Other major cities are Wau (118,000), Malakal (115,000), Yei (111,000) and Yambio (106,000). The official language is English.

Spain

Reino de España (Kingdom of Spain)

Factsheet

Capital: Madrid
Population estimate, 2015: 46.12 m.
GNI per capita, 2014: (PPP$) 32,045
HDI/world rank, 2014: 0.876/26
Internet domain extension: .es

Civil Aviation

Spain's 15 busiest airports by passenger traffic in 2013 were: Madrid (Barajas), Barcelona (El Prat), Palma de Mallorca, Málaga, Gran Canaria, Alicante, Tenerife (South), Ibiza, Lanzarote, Valencia, Fuerteventura, Bilbao, Seville, Tenerife (North) and Girona. A small airport in Seo de Urgel serves Andorra and is 12 km from the border. Madrid (Barajas) handled 39,735,618 passengers in 2013, Barcelona (El Prat) 35,216,828 and Palma de Mallorca 22,768,032. Madrid (Barajas) is the busiest airport by cargo traffic, handling 366,969 tonnes of freight and mail in 2013, ahead of Barcelona (El Prat) with 98,087 tonnes and Zaragoza with 71,565 tonnes. The former national carrier Iberia Airlines completed its privatization process in April 2001, when shares were listed for the first time on the stock exchange. In April 2010 it signed a deal with British Airways to merge and create a new company called International Airlines Group, which was founded in Jan. 2011. However, both carriers still operate under their own brands. Of other airlines, the largest are the low-cost carrier Vueling Airlines and Air Europa. Services are also provided by about 70 foreign airlines. In 2005 Iberia carried 27.4 m. passengers (12.0 m. on international flights); passenger-km totalled 49.0 bn.

Climate

Most of Spain has a form of Mediterranean climate with mild, moist winters and hot, dry summers, but the northern coastal region has a moist, equable climate, with rainfall well distributed throughout the year, mild winters and warm summers, and less sunshine than the rest of Spain. The south, in particular Andalusia, is dry and prone to drought. Madrid, Jan. 41 °F (5 °C), July 77 °F (25 °C). Annual rainfall 16.8″ (419 mm). Barcelona, Jan. 46 °F (8 °C), July 74 °F (23.5 °C). Annual rainfall 21″ (525 mm).

Constitution and Government

Following the death of General Franco in 1975 and the transition to a democracy, the first democratic elections were held on 15 June 1977. A new constitution was approved by referendum on 6 Dec. 1978, and came into force 29 Dec. 1978. It has been amended twice since, in 1992 and 2011. It established a parliamentary monarchy. The reigning king is **Felipe VI** (Don Felipe de Borbón y Grecia), born 30 Jan. 1968. The King receives an allowance, part of which is taxable, approved by parliament each year. For 2014 this is €7.8 m. There is no formal court; the (private) *Diputación de la Grandeza* represents the interests of the aristocracy. Legislative power is vested in the *Cortes Generales*, a bicameral parliament composed of the Congress of Deputies (lower house) and the Senate (upper house). The *Congress of Deputies* has not less than 300 nor more than 400 members (350 in the general election of 2011) elected in a proportional system under which electors choose between party lists of candidates in multi-member constituencies. The *Senate* has 264 members of whom 208 are elected by a majority system. The *Constitutional Court* is empowered to solve conflicts between the State and the Autonomous Communities; to determine if legislation passed by the Cortes is contrary to the Constitution; and to protect the constitutional rights of individuals violated by any authority. Its 12 members are appointed by the monarch.

Currency

On 1 Jan. 1999 the euro (EUR) became the legal currency in Spain at the irrevocable conversion rate of 166.386 pesetas to one euro. The euro, which consists of 100 cents, has been in circulation since 1 Jan. 2002. On the introduction of the euro there was a 'dual circulation' period before the peseta ceased to be legal tender on 28 Feb. 2002.

Defence

Conscription was abolished in 2001. In 2013 defence expenditure totalled US$11,593 m. (US$245 per capita), representing 0.8% of GDP.

Economy

Agriculture accounted for 2% of GDP in 2012, industry 24% and services 74%. Spain's 'shadow' (black market) economy is estimated to constitute approximately 22% of the country's official GDP. In 2013 Spain gave US$2.4 bn. in international aid, compared to US$4.2 bn. in 2011. This represented 0.17% of GNI (compared to the UN target of 0.7%).

Labour

Out of 18,973,200 people in employment in 2005, 3,113,000 worked in manufacturing; 2,886,800 in wholesale and retail trade/repair of motor vehicles, motorcycles and personal and household goods; 2,357,200 in construction; 1,678,400 in real estate, renting and business activities; 1,291,100 in hotels and restaurants; and 1,196,700 in public administration and defence/compulsory social security. Spain's unemployment rate reached nearly 25% in 1994 but then fell steadily, declining to 8.3% in 2007. In Dec. 2014 the rate stood at 23.7%, down from 26.3% for three consecutive months from Feb. to April 2013, giving Spain the second highest unemployment rate in the EU (just below that of Greece). Spain had 6,000 people living in slavery according to the Walk Free Foundation's 2013 *Global Slavery Index*.

Press

In 2008 there were 161 daily newspapers (140 paid-for and 21 free) with a total daily circulation of 8.21 m. copies. The main paid-for titles are: *El País* (average daily circulation 435,000), *El Mundo* (336,000) and *As* (234,000), along with the dedicated sports paper, *Marca* (315,000). The leading free papers, notably *20 Minutos*, *Que!* and *ADN*, now have wider circulations than the paid-for dailies. In 2009, 96,955 printed books were published.

Rail

The total length of the state railways in 2011 was 15,680 km, mostly broad (1,668-mm) gauge (9,488 km electrified). The state railway system was divided in two in 2005; Administrador de Infraestructuras Ferroviarias (ADIF) now manages the infrastructure and Renfe Operadora runs train operations. There is an ever-expanding high-speed standard-gauge (1,435-mm) network, totalling 3,100 km in 2013. Only China has a longer high-speed rail network. The first high-speed line, from Madrid to Seville, opened in 1992. It was extended northwards from Madrid initially to Lleida, with passenger services beginning in 2003, and further to Tarragona (2006), Barcelona (2008) and the border with France (2013).

Religion

There is no official religion. In 2010 Roman Catholicism was the religion of 75.2% of the population according to estimates by the Pew Research Center's Forum on Religion & Public Life. In Feb. 2016 there were 11 cardinals. There are 70 dioceses and archdioceses including the archdiocese of Toledo, where the Primate resides. The Pew Research Center estimated that 2.1% of the population were Muslims, 2.0% were Orthodox Christians and 19.0% did not have any religious affiliation. While Spain is not traditionally an Orthodox country, numbers began to grow in the early 1990s when there was an influx of migrant workers from Eastern Europe (particularly from Romania).

Roads

In 2007 the total length of roads was 667,064; the network included 13,014 km of motorways, 12,832 km of highways/national roads and

140,165 km of secondary roads. In 2015 road transport totalled 363,942 m. passenger-km; freight transport totalled 209,387 m. tonne-km in 2015. Number of passenger cars in use (2007), 21,760,200; lorries and vans, 5,140,600; buses and coaches, 61,000; motorcycles and mopeds, 2,311,300. In 2007, 3,823 persons were killed in road accidents (5,604 in 1997).

Shipping

In Jan. 2009 there were 184 ships of 300 GT or over registered, totalling 2.39 m. GT. Of the 184 vessels registered, 63 were passenger ships, 49 general cargo ships, 29 oil tankers, 20 container ships, 11 liquid gas tankers, nine bulk carriers and three chemical tankers. The Spanish-controlled fleet comprised 259 vessels of 1,000 GT or over in Jan. 2009, of which 128 were under the Spanish flag and 131 under foreign flags. The leading ports are Algeciras-La Linea (74,845,000 tonnes of cargo in 2008), Barcelona, Bilbao, Cartagena, Las Palmas de Gran Canaria, Santa Cruz de Tenerife, Tarragona and Valencia.

Social Statistics

2008 births, 518,967; deaths, 385,954. Rate per 1,000 population, 2008: births, 11.7; deaths, 8.7; marriages, 4.3; divorces, 2.5. In 2005 the most popular age range for marrying was 25–29 for both males and females. Annual population growth rate, 2000–05, 1.5%. Suicide rate (per 100,000 population), 2005: 7.8. Expectation of life, 2007, was 77.5 years for males and 84.0 for females. Infant mortality, 2010, four per 1,000 live births; fertility rate, 2008, 1.4 births per woman.

Telecommunications

In 2013 there were 19,384,000 main (fixed) telephone lines. In the same year mobile phone subscriptions numbered 50,159,000 (1,068.9 per 1,000 persons). That same year, an estimated 76.2% of the population were internet users. The fixed broadband penetration rate stood at 23.4 subscribers per 100 inhabitants in Dec. 2010. In March 2012 there were 15.7 m. Facebook users.

Territory and Population

Spain is bounded in the north by the Bay of Biscay, France and Andorra, east and south by the Mediterranean and the Straits of Gibraltar, southwest by the Atlantic and west by Portugal and the Atlantic. Continental Spain has an area of 493,491 km^2, and including the Balearic and Canary Islands and the towns of Ceuta and Melilla on the northern coast of Africa, 505,693 km^2 (195,249 sq. miles). Population (census, 2011), 46,815,916 (23,711,613 females). In 2011, 77.6% of the population lived in urban areas; population density in 2011 was 93 per km^2. At the last linguistic census (2011) Catalan (an official EU language since 1990) was spoken in Catalonia by 73.2% of people and understood by 95.1%. It is also spoken in Baleares, Valencian Community (where it is frequently called Valencian) and in parts of Aragón, a narrow strip close to the Catalonian and Valencian Community boundaries, and Murcia, to the south of the Valencian Community. Galician, a language very close to Portuguese, was understood in 2007 by 98.0% of people in Galicia aged 15 and over and spoken to a high or moderate standard by 89.4%; Basque by a significant and increasing minority in the Basque Country, and by a small minority in northwest Navarra. It is estimated that one-third of all Spaniards speaks one of the other three official languages as well as standard Castilian. In bilingual communities, both Castilian and the regional language are taught in schools and universities.

Tourism

In 2010 Spain was behind only France, the USA and China in the number of foreign visitor arrivals, and behind only the USA for tourism receipts. In 2010, 52.7 m. tourists visited Spain; receipts for 2010 amounted to US$52.5 bn. In 2008 most tourists were from the UK (27.6%), followed by Germany (17.6%), France (14.2%), Italy (5.9%) and the Netherlands (4.3%). Of 268,552,000 overnight stays at hotels and inns in 2008, 49,633,000 were in the Balearics, 49,400,000 in the Canary Islands and 44,172,000 in Andalusia; overnight stays by visitors from abroad numbered 155,364,000 and by residents of Spain 113,118,000.

Sri Lanka

Sri Lanka Prajathanthrika Samajavadi Janarajaya (Democratic Socialist Republic of Sri Lanka)

Factsheet

Capitals: Sri Jayawardenapura Kotte (Administrative and Legislative), Colombo (Commercial)
Population estimate, 2015: 20.72 m.
GNI per capita, 2014: (PPP$) 9,779
HDI/world rank, 2014: 0.757/73
Internet domain extension: .lk

Civil Aviation

There is an international airport at Colombo (Bandaranaike). The national carrier is SriLankan Airlines, which has been part-owned and managed by Emirates since 1998. Mihin Lanka, a low-cost airline fully owned and funded by the government, was launched in 2007. In 2006 SriLankan Airlines carried 2,900,068 passengers (all on international flights). Colombo handled 4,740,187 passengers and 169,038 tonnes of freight in 2006.

Climate

Sri Lanka, which has an equatorial climate, is affected by the North-east Monsoon (Dec. to Feb.), the South-west Monsoon (May to July) and two inter-monsoons (March to April and Aug. to Nov.). Rainfall is heaviest in the southwest highlands while the northwest and southeast are relatively dry. Colombo, Jan. 79.9 °F (26.6 °C), July 81.7 °F (27.6 °C). Annual rainfall 95.4″ (2,424 mm). Trincomalee, Jan. 78.8 °F (26 °C), July 86.2 °F (30.1 °C). Annual rainfall 62.2″ (1,580 mm). Kandy, Jan. 73.9 °F (23.3 °C), July 76.1 °F (24.5 °C). Annual rainfall 72.4″ (1,840 mm). Nuwara Eliya, Jan. 58.5 °F (14.7 °C), July 60.3 °F (15.7 °C). Annual rainfall 75″ (1,905 mm).

Constitution and Government

A new constitution for the Democratic Socialist Republic of Sri Lanka was promulgated on 7 Sept. 1978. The executive *President* is directly elected for a six-year term. Under the terms of an amendment introduced in Sept. 2010, the previous bar on a president serving more than two terms was removed. Parliament consists of one chamber, composed of 225 members (196 elected and 29 from the National List). Election is by proportional representation by universal suffrage at 18 years. The term of Parliament is six years. The Prime Minister and other Ministers, who must be members of Parliament, are appointed by the President.

Currency

The unit of currency is the *Sri Lankan rupee* (LKR) of 100 *cents*.

Defence

Defence expenditure totalled US$1,793 m. in 2013 (US$83 per capita), representing 2.8% of GDP.

Economy

Agriculture accounted for 12.8% of GDP in 2010, industry 29.4% and services 57.8%.

Labour

The labour force in 2013 was 8,451,000 (7,914,000 in 2003). 59.4% of the population aged 15–64 was economically active in 2013. In the same year

4.4% of the population was unemployed. Sri Lanka had 19,000 people living in slavery according to the Walk Free Foundation's 2013 *Global Slavery Index*.

Press

In 2008 there were 18 paid-for daily newspapers with a combined circulation of 588,000. The papers with the highest circulation are *Lankadeepa* and *Divaina*, and the English-language *Daily News*.

Rail

In 2007 there were 1,463 km of railway (1,676 mm gauge). Passenger-km travelled in 2007 came to 4.77 bn. and freight tonne-km to 135 m.

Religion

In 2012 the population was 70% Buddhist, 13% Hindu, 10% Muslim and 6% Roman Catholic. In Feb. 2016 there was one Roman Catholic cardinal.

Roads

In 2006 the road network totalled 91,907 km in length, including 11,716 km of national roads and 15,532 km of secondary roads. Number of motor vehicles, 2006, 2,269,575, comprising 338,608 passenger cars, 77,233 buses and coaches, 431,594 trucks and vans and 1,422,140 motorcycles and mopeds. There were 2,239 fatalities in road accidents in 2006.

Shipping

In Jan. 2009 there were 36 ships of 300 GT or over registered, totalling 143,000 GT. Colombo is a modern container port; Galle and Trincomalee are natural harbours. The first of three phases of a new port at Hambantota was inaugurated in Nov. 2010. On completion it is set to be Sri Lanka's largest port.

Social Statistics

Statistics for 2008: births, 373,575; deaths, 123,814. 2008 rates per 1,000 population: birth, 18.5; death, 6.1; infant mortality rate, 2010 (per 1,000 live births), 14. Life expectancy, 2013, 77.4 years for females and 71.2 for males. Annual population growth rate, 2005–10, 0.8%. Fertility rate, 2008, 2.3 births per woman. Sri Lanka has the third oldest population in Asia, after Japan and Singapore, thanks largely to relatively good health and a low fertility rate.

Telecommunications

In Dec. 2012 there were 3,449,000 main (fixed) telephone lines; mobile phone subscriptions numbered 20,315,000 in 2013 (95.5 per 100 persons). In 2013 an estimated 21.9% of the population were internet users. In March 2012 there were 1.2 m. Facebook users.

Territory and Population

Sri Lanka is an island in the Indian Ocean, south of the Indian peninsula from which it is separated by the Palk Strait. On 28 June 1974 the frontier between India and Sri Lanka in the Palk Strait was redefined, giving to Sri Lanka the island of Kachchativu. 2012 census population: 20,359,439. Population (in 1,000) according to ethnic group and nationality in 2012 included: 15,173.8 Sinhalese, 2,270.9 Sri Lanka Tamils, 1,869.8 Sri Lanka Moors, 842.3 Indian Tamils, 40.2 Malays, 37.1 Burghers. Of the population of 20,359,439 in 2012, 10,502,805 were females. Density, 310 per km². In 2011, 14.3% of the population lived in urban areas. Colombo (the largest city) had an estimated 673,000 inhabitants in 2007. Sinhala and Tamil are the official languages; English is in use.

Tourism

In 2010 there were a record 654,000 foreign tourists, bringing revenue of US$1,044 m. The previous best year for tourist arrivals was 2004, the year of the Asian tsunami.

Sudan

Jamhuryat es-Sudan (The Republic of The Sudan)

Factsheet
Capital: Khartoum
Population estimate, 2015: 40.25 m.
GNI per capita, 2014: (PPP$) 3,809
HDI/world rank, 2014: 0.479/167
Internet domain extension: .sd

Civil Aviation

There is an international airport at Khartoum, which handled 2,178,097 passengers and 59,299 tonnes of freight in 2009. The national carrier is the government-owned Sudan Airways, which operates domestic and international services. In 2006 scheduled airline traffic of Sudan-based carriers flew 9 m. km, carrying 563,000 passengers (365,000 on international flights).

Climate

Lying wholly within the tropics, the country has a continental climate and only the Red Sea coast experiences maritime influences. Temperatures are generally high for most of the year, with May and June the hottest months. On the Red Sea coast, most rain falls in winter. Khartoum, Jan. 64 °F (18.0 °C), July 89 °F (31.7 °C). Annual rainfall 6″ (157 mm). Annual rainfall 39″ (968 mm). Port Sudan, Jan. 74 °F (23.3 °C), July 94 °F (34.4 °C). Annual rainfall 4″ (94 mm). Wadi Halfa, Jan. 50 °F (10.0 °C), July 90 °F (32.2 °C). Annual rainfall 0.1″ (2.5 mm).

Constitution and Government

On 26 May 1998 President Omar Hassan Ahmed al-Bashir approved a new constitution. Notably this lifted the ban on opposition political parties, although the government continued to monitor and control criticism until the constitution came legally into effect. In accordance with the peace deal agreed in Dec. 2004 to bring an end to the civil war and signed in Jan. 2005 there is a lower house, the 354-seat *National Assembly* (reduced from 450 following the independence of South Sudan), with members appointed by decree by the president, and an upper house, the *Council of States*, consisting of a maximum of 32 members (reduced from 52), of whom 30 are indirectly elected. A new interim power-sharing constitution was adopted on 6 July 2005 giving the south some autonomy and allowing former rebels to take up seats in the country's government.

Currency

The unit of currency is the *Sudanese pound* (SDG) of 100 *piastres*, introduced in Jan. 2007 to replace the *Sudanese dinar* (SDD) at a rate of 1 Sudanese pound = 100 Sudanese dinars.

Defence

There is conscription for one to 2 years. Defence expenditure totalled US$1,516 m. in 2013 (US$43 per capita), representing 3.0% of GDP.

Economy

Agriculture accounted for 24.9% of GDP, industry 28.3% and services 46.8% in 2010.

Labour

The estimated total workforce in 2010 was 13,885,000 (70% males), up from 11,997,000 in 2005. Sudan had 0.26 m. people living in slavery according to the Walk Free Foundation's 2013 *Global Slavery Index*.

Press

In 2008 there were 29 paid-for daily newspapers with a combined circulation of 90,000. Opposition newspapers are permitted although they are vetted by an official censor.

Rail

Total length in 2005 was 4,578 km. In 2008 the railways carried 100,000 passengers and 1.1 m. tonnes of freight.

Religion

Islam is the state religion. A study by the Pew Research Center's Forum on Religion & Public Life estimated that there were 30.49 m. Muslims in 2010 (mostly Sunnis), 1.81 m. Christians and 950,000 followers of folk religions. A further 350,000 people had no religious affiliation. Catholics account for around 55% of Christians and Protestants 40%. In Feb. 2016 the Roman Catholic church had one cardinal.

Roads

The road network covers around 32,400 km. There were an estimated 768,000 passenger cars and 300,000 trucks and vans in 2007.

Shipping

Supplementing the railways are regular steamer services of the Sudan Railways. Port Sudan is the major seaport; Suakin port opened in 1991. In Jan. 2009 there were five ships of 300 GT or over registered, totalling 23,000 GT.

Social Statistics

2009 estimates: births, 1,402,000; deaths, 382,000. Rates, 2009 estimates (per 1,000 population): birth, 9; death, 33. Infant mortality, 2010 (per 1,000 live births), 66. Expectation of life in 2013 was 63.9 years for females and 60.3 for males. Annual population growth rate, 2005–10, 2.4%. Fertility rate, 2008, 4.2 births per woman.

Telecommunications

In 2013 there were 416,000 fixed telephone subscriptions; mobile phone subscriptions numbered 27,658,000 that year (728.5 per 1,000 persons). There were 34,200 fixed broadband subscriptions in 2012 and 10.2 m. wireless broadband subscriptions in 2013. 21.0% of the population aged 15 and over were internet users in 2012.

Territory and Population

Sudan is bounded in the north by Egypt, northeast by the Red Sea, east by Eritrea and Ethiopia, south by South Sudan, southwest by the Central African Republic, west by Chad and northwest by Libya. Its area is 1,881,000 km². In 2008—when present-day South Sudan was still part of Sudan—the census population was 39,154,490. In 2011, 40.8% of the population was urban. The country is administratively divided into 17 states. The capital, Khartoum, had a provisional census population of 1,410,858 in 2008. Other major cities, with 2008 provisional population, are Omdurman (1,849,659), Khartoum North (1,012,211), Nyala (492,984), Port Sudan (394,561), Al Obeid (345,126), Kassala (298,529), Wadi Medani (289,482) and Al Qadarif (269,395). The country is mainly populated by Arab and Nubian peoples. Arabic and English are both official languages.

Tourism

In 2011 there were 536,000 international tourist arrivals (excluding same-day visitors), spending a total of US$185 m.

Suriname

Republiek Suriname (Republic of Suriname)

Factsheet

Capital: Paramaribo
Population estimate, 2015: 543,000
GNI per capita, 2014: (PPP$) 15,617
HDI/world rank, 2014: 0.714/103
Internet domain extension: .sr

Civil Aviation

There are two international airports. The larger airport (Johan Adolf Pengel) is 45 km south of Paramaribo while the smaller Zog en Hoop is 5 km west of Paramaribo. The national carrier is Surinam Airways, which in 2010 had flights to Amsterdam, Aruba, Curaçao, Miami and Port of Spain. In 2012 scheduled airline traffic of Suriname-based carriers flew 1.9 m. km; passenger-km totalled 1.3 bn. in the same year.

Climate

The climate is equatorial, with uniformly high temperatures and rainfall. The temperature is an average of 27 °C throughout the year; there are two rainy seasons (May–July and Nov.–Jan.) and two dry seasons (Aug.–Oct. and Feb.–April). Paramaribo, Jan. 21 °C, July 32.4 °C. Average rainfall 182.3 mm.

Constitution and Government

The current constitution was ratified on 30 Sept. 1987. Parliament is a 51-member *National Assembly*. The head of state is the *President*, elected for a five-year term by a two-thirds majority by the National Assembly, or, failing that, by an electoral college, the United People's Assembly, enlarged by the inclusion of regional and local councillors, by a simple majority.

Currency

The unit of currency is the *Suriname dollar* (SRD) of 100 *cents*, introduced on 1 Jan. 2004 to replace the *Suriname guilder* (SRG) at a rate of one Suriname dollar = 1,000 Suriname guilders.

Defence

In 2011 defence expenditure totalled an estimated US$55 m. (approximately US$100 per capita), representing 1% of GDP.

Economy

In 2011 agriculture contributed 10% of GDP, industry 38% and services 52%.

Labour

Out of 156,705 people in employment in 2004, 27,995 were in public administration and defence; 25,012 in wholesale and retail trade; 14,031 in construction; 12,593 in agriculture, fishing, hunting and forestry; and 10,971 in manufacturing. In 2004 there were 16,425 unemployed persons, or 9.5% of the workforce.

Press

There were four daily newspapers in 2008 with a combined circulation of 55,000.

Rail

There are two single-track railways.

Religion

A study by the Pew Research Center's Forum on Religion & Public Life estimated that in 2010 there were 270,000 Christians (including 150,000 Roman Catholics and 110,000 Protestants), 100,000 Hindus, 80,000 Muslims and 30,000 folk religionists. People with no religious affiliation also numbered 30,000 in 2010.

Roads

The road network covers some 4,000 km. In 2006 there were 81,778 passenger cars, 25,745 trucks and vans, 3,029 buses and coaches and 40,889 motorcycles and mopeds. There were 69 fatalities in road accidents in 2004.

Shipping

In Jan. 2009 there were four ships of 300 GT or over registered, totalling 4,000 GT. In 2004 vessels totalling 1,518,000 NRT entered ports and vessels totalling 2,142,000 NRT cleared.

Social Statistics

2007: births, 9,769; deaths, 3,374. Rates per 1,000 population: birth rate, 19.2; death rate, 6.6. Expectation of life, 2007, was 65.3 years for males and 72.5 for females. Annual population growth rate, 2000–05, 1.5%. Infant mortality, 2010, 27 per 1,000 live births; fertility rate, 2008, 2.4 births per woman. Abortion is illegal.

Telecommunications

In 2013 there were 868,600 mobile phone subscriptions (1,610.7 per 1,000 inhabitants) and 84,900 fixed telephone lines. In the same year an estimated 37.4% of the population were internet users.

Territory and Population

Suriname is located on the northern coast of South America between 2–6° North latitude and 54–59° West longitude. It is bounded in the north by the Atlantic Ocean, east by French Guiana, west by Guyana, and south by Brazil. Area, 163,820 km². Census population, 2012, 541,638; density, 3.3 per km². The capital, Paramaribo, had (2012 census) 240,924 inhabitants. Suriname is divided into ten districts. Major ethnic groups in percentages of the population in 2004: Indo-Pakistani, 26%; Creole, 18%; Javanese, 15%; Bushnegroes (Blacks), 15%; Amerindian, 4%. 69.8% of the population lived in urban areas in 2011. The official language is Dutch. English is widely spoken next to Hindi, Javanese and Chinese as inter-group communication. A vernacular, called 'Sranan' or 'Surinamese', is used as a *lingua franca*.

Tourism

In 2010 there were 204,000 international tourist arrivals (excluding same-day visitors), spending a total of US$61 m.

Swaziland

Umbuso weSwatini (Kingdom of Swaziland)

Factsheet

Capitals: Mbabane (Administrative), Lobamba (Legislative)
Population estimate, 2015: 1.29 m.
GNI per capita, 2014: (PPP$) 5,542
HDI/world rank, 2014: 0.531/150
Internet domain extension: .sz

Civil Aviation

There is an international airport at Manzini (Matsapha). A new airport, King Mswati III International Airport—also at Manzini—was inaugurated in March 2014 and received its first flights in Oct. 2014. The national carrier is Swaziland Airlink, which had direct flights from Manzini to Johannesburg in 2012. The unrelated Airlink also operated on the same route in 2012.

Climate

A temperate climate with two seasons. Nov. to March is the wet season, when temperatures range from mild to hot, with frequent thunderstorms. The cool, dry season from May to Sept. is characterized by clear, bright sunny days. Mbabane, Jan. 68 °F (20 °C), July 54 °F (12.2 °C). Annual rainfall 56″ (1402 mm).

Constitution and Government

The reigning King is **Mswati III** (b. 1968; crowned 25 April 1986), who succeeded his father, King Sobhuza II (reigned 1921–82). The King rules in conjunction with the Queen Mother (his mother, or a senior wife). Critics of the King or his mother run the risk of arrest. Political parties are banned. A new constitution was signed into law on 26 July 2005 and came into force in Jan. 2006. There is a *House of Assembly* of 65 members, 55 of whom are elected each from one constituency (*inkhundla*) and ten appointed by the King; and a *House of Senators* of 30 members, ten of whom are elected by the

House of Assembly and 20 appointed by the King. Elections are held in two rounds, the second being a run-off between the five candidates who come first in each constituency. There is also a traditional *Swazi National Council* headed by the King and Queen Mother at which all Swazi men are entitled to be heard.

Currency

The unit of currency is the *lilangeni* (plural *emalangeni*) (SZL) of 100 *cents* but Swaziland remains in the Common Monetary Area and the South African rand is legal tender.

Economy

Agriculture accounted for 7.4% of GDP in 2010, industry 46.5% and services 46.1%.

Labour

The labour force in 2013 was 446,000 (349,000 in 2003). 58.9% of the population aged 15–64 was economically active in 2013. In the same year 22.3% of the population was unemployed.

Press

In 2008 there were two daily newspapers: *The Times of Swaziland* (English-language with a circulation of 22,000 in 2008), founded in 1897, and *The Swazi Observer* (English, 15,000).

Rail

In 2005 the system comprised 301 km of route (1,067 mm gauge). There are north and south connections to South Africa's rail system, and a link in the northeast with Mozambique and the port of Maputo. In 2009, 4 m. tonnes of freight were transported.

Religion

In 2010 the population was an estimated 88.1% Christian (mainly Protestant) according to the Pew Research Center's Forum on Religion & Public Life. Most of the remainder of the population is religiously unaffiliated.

Roads

The road network covers around 8,300 km. There were 52,200 passenger cars in use in 2007 plus 41,800 lorries and vans and 8,100 buses and coaches. There were 235 fatalities in road accidents in 2007.

Social Statistics

2008 estimates: births, 35,000; deaths, 18,000. Estimated rates, 2008 (per 1,000 population): births, 29.9; deaths, 15.6. As a result of the impact of AIDS, expectation of life declined sharply. It was 59 years in 1990–95, but by 2000–05 was down to 45.9 years for females and 45.6 years for males. However, it has now started to rise again and in 2013 was 48.3 years for females and 49.6 years for males. Swaziland was one of only two countries where life expectancy at birth for males in 2013 was higher than for females (the other being Mali). In 2011, 26.0% of all adults between 15 and 49 were infected with HIV-the highest rate in any country. In 2010, 23% of Swazi children were orphans. In Sept. 2001 King Mswati III told the teenage girls of the country to stop having sex for 5 years as part of the country's drive to reduce the spread of HIV. Annual population growth rate, 2000–08, 1.0%. Infant mortality, 2010, 55 per 1,000 live births; fertility rate, 2008, 3.5 births per woman.

Telecommunications

In 2013 there were an estimated 46,000 main (fixed) telephone lines; mobile phone subscriptions numbered 805,000 in 2012 (65.4 per 100 persons). In 2013 an estimated 24.7% of the population were internet users.

Territory and Population

Swaziland is bounded in the north, west and south by South Africa, and in the east by Mozambique. The area is 17,364 km² (6,704 sq. miles). Population (2007 census), 1,018,449 (537,021 females); density, 58.7 per km². In 2011, 21.3% of the population were urban. The country is divided into four regions: Hhohho, Lubombo, Manzini and Shiselweni. Main urban areas: Mbabane, the administrative capital (60,281 inhabitants in 2007); Manzini; Big Bend; Mhlume; Nhlangano. The population is 84% Swazi and 10% Zulu. The official languages are Swazi and English.

Tourism

In 2011 there were 1,328,000 non-resident visitor arrivals (including tourists and same-day visitors), down slightly from 1,343,000 in 2010.

Sweden

Konungariket Sverige (Kingdom of Sweden)

Factsheet
Capital: Stockholm
Population estimate, 2015: 9.78 m.
GNI per capita, 2014: (PPP$) 45,636
HDI/world rank, 2014: 0.907/14=
Internet domain extension: .se

Civil Aviation

The main international airports are at Stockholm (Arlanda), Gothenburg (Landvetter), Stockholm (Skavsta) and Malmö (Sturup). The principal carrier is Scandinavian Airlines System (SAS), which resulted from the 1950 merger of the three former Scandinavian airlines. In 2008 Stockholm (Arlanda) handled 18,136,165 passengers (13,281,466 on international flights) and 187,000 tonnes of freight. Gothenburg (Landvetter) was the second busiest airport, handling 4,303,722 passengers (3,158,822 on international flights) and 100,000 tonnes of freight. Malmö handled 1,882,428 passengers in 2006 (1,181,970 on domestic flights).

Climate

The north has severe winters, with snow lying for 4–7 months. Summers are fine but cool, with long daylight hours. Further south, winters are less cold, summers are warm and rainfall well distributed throughout the year, although slightly higher in the summer. Stockholm, Jan. –2.8 °C, July 17.2 °C. Annual rainfall 385 mm.

Constitution and Government

The reigning King is **Carl XVI Gustaf**, b. 30 April 1946, succeeded on the death of his grandfather Gustaf VI Adolf, 15 Sept. 1973, married 19 June 1976 to Silvia Renate Sommerlath, b. 23 Dec. 1943 (Queen of Sweden). Under the 1975 constitution Sweden is a representative and parliamentary democracy. The King is Head of State, but does not participate in government. Parliament is the single-chamber *Riksdag* of 349 members elected for a period of 4 years in direct, general elections. The manner of election to the *Riksdag* is proportional. A parliament, the *Sameting*, was instituted for the Sami (Lapps) in 1993.

Currency

The unit of currency is the *krona* (SEK), of 100 *öre*.

Defence

In 2013 defence expenditure totalled US$6,633 m., with spending per capita US$727. The 2013 expenditure represented 1.2% of GDP.

Economy

Services accounted for 72% of GDP in 2012, industry 27% and agriculture 1%.

Labour

In 2008 there were 4,898,000 persons in the labour force, of which 93.8% were employed. The main areas of employment were as follows: trade and communication (838,000); financial services and business activities (739,000); health and social work (721,000); manufacturing, mining, quarrying, electricity and water supply (689,000); education, research and development (537,000); personal services and cultural activities, and sanitation (397,000); construction (306,000); public administration (261,000); agriculture, forestry and fishing (101,000). The unemployment rate in Dec. 2014 was 7.6%; youth unemployment was 24.0% in the third quarter of 2012. In 2008, 69.6% of men and 63.8% of women were in employment. The average monthly salary in 2008 was 27,100 kr. (29,400 kr. for men and 24,700 kr. for women). In 2008 a total of 106,801 working days were lost through strikes, compared to 1,971 in 2006.

Press

In 2008 there were 168 daily newspapers with an average weekday net circulation of 3.7 m. The leading papers in terms of circulation in 2008 were the free *Metro*, with an average daily circulation of 634,000 copies; the Social Democratic *Aftonbladet*, with an average daily circulation of 378,000; the independent *Dagens Nyheter*, with an average daily circulation of 340,000; and the liberal tabloid *Expressen*, with an average daily circulation of 304,000. In 2008 a total of 26,182 book titles were published.

Rail

Total length of railways at 31 Dec. 2012 was 11,136 km (8,194 km electrified). In 2012, 193 m. passengers and 66 m. tonnes of freight were carried. There is a metro in Stockholm (110 km), and tram/light rail networks in Stockholm (8 km), Gothenburg (118 km) and Norrköping (13 km).

Religion

The Swedish Lutheran Church was disestablished in 2000. It is headed by Archbishop Antje Jackelén (b. 1955) and has its metropolitan see at Uppsala. In 2008 there were 13 bishoprics and 1,802 parishes. The clergy are chiefly supported from the parishes and the proceeds of the church lands. Around 70% of the population, equivalent to 6.6 m. people, belong to the Church of Sweden. Other denominations, in 2010: Pentecostal Movement, 82,769 members; The Mission Covenant Church of Sweden, 60,445; InterAct, 32,138; Salvation Army, 5,159 soldiers; The Baptist Union of Sweden, 17,441; Swedish Alliance Mission, 13,687. There were also 96,950 Roman Catholics (under a Bishop resident at Stockholm). The Orthodox and Oriental churches number around 120,000 members. Although there are no official statistics on the number of Muslims, their numbers were estimated at 450,000–500,000 in 2010. An estimated 20,000 Jews lived in Sweden in 2010.

Roads

In 2009 there were 215,597 km of roads open to the public of which 98,467 km were state-administered roads (main roads, 15,329 km; secondary roads, 83,138 km). There were also 1,855 km of motorway. 79% of all roads in 2005 were surfaced. Motor vehicles in 2008 included 4,279,000 passenger cars, 510,000 lorries, 13,000 buses and 489,000 motorcycles and mopeds. There were 1,015,997 Volvos, 434,757 Saabs, 343,060 Fords and 327,379 Volkswagens registered in 2006. Sweden has the lowest death rate in road accidents of any industrialized country, at 2.7 deaths per 100,000 people in 2013. 260 people were killed in traffic accidents in 2013.

Shipping

The mercantile marine consisted on 31 Dec. 2008 of 1,036 vessels of 4.53 m. GT. Cargo vessels entering Swedish ports in 2008 numbered 19,396 (125.74 m. GT) while there were 75,343 passenger ferries (1,011.83 m. GT). The number of cargo vessels leaving Swedish ports in 2008 totalled 19,389 (125.47 m. GT) and the number of passenger ferries leaving was 75,636 (1,015.82 m. GT). The busiest port is Gothenburg. In 2007 a total of 42.33 m. tonnes of goods were loaded and unloaded there (39.46 m. tonnes unloaded from and loaded to foreign ports). Other major ports are Brofjorden, Trelleborg, Malmö and Luleå.

Social Statistics

Live births, 2008, 109,301; deaths, 91,449. Rates, 2008, per 1,000 population: births, 11.9; deaths, 9.9; marriages, 5.4; divorces, 2.3. Sweden has one of the highest rate of births outside marriage in Europe, at 55% in 2008. In 2008 the average age at first marriage was 35.1 years for males and 32.5 years for females. Expectation of life in 2013: males, 79.7 years; females, 83.9. Annual population growth rate, 2005–10, 0.8%. Infant mortality, 2010, two per 1,000 live births (one of the lowest rates in the world). Fertility rate, 2008, 1.9 births per woman. Sweden legalized same-sex marriage in May 2009. In 2008 Sweden received 24,353 asylum applications, equivalent to 2.6 per 1,000 inhabitants.

Telecommunications

In 2012 there were 4,169,000 main (fixed) telephone lines. In the same year mobile phone subscriptions numbered 11,848,000 (1,254.7 per 1,000 persons). In 2013, 94.8% of the population aged 16–74 were internet users. In the same year there were 110.3 wireless broadband subscriptions per 100 inhabitants and 32.6 fixed broadband subscriptions per 100. In March 2012 there were 4.5 m. Facebook users.

Territory and Population

Sweden is bounded in the west and northwest by Norway, east by Finland and the Gulf of Bothnia, southeast by the Baltic Sea and southwest by the Kattegat. The area is 450,295 km^2, including water (96,000 lakes) totalling 39,960 km^2. At the last census, in 1990, the population was 8,587,353. Parliament decided in 1995 to change to a register-based method of calculating the population. The recorded population at 31 Dec. 2012 was 9,555,893; density 23 per km^2. In 2011, 84.8% of the population lived in urban areas. There are some 17,000 Sami (Lapps). A 16-km long fixed link with Denmark was opened in July 2000 when the Öresund motorway and railway bridge between Malmö and Copenhagen was completed. The *de facto* official language is Swedish.

Tourism

In 2013 Swedes stayed 22,557,815 nights in hotels in Sweden and 11,223,586 at campsites; and foreign visitors stayed 6,874,759 nights in hotels and 3,273,264 at campsites. The leading countries of residence of the foreign visitors in 2013 were Norway (2,961,772 nights in hotels and at campsites), Germany, Denmark and the United Kingdom.

Switzerland

Schweizerische Eidtgenossenschaft—Confédération Suisse—Confederazione Svizzera (Swiss Confederation)

Factsheet
Capital: Berne
Population estimate, 2015: 8.30 m.
GNI per capita, 2014: (PPP$) 56,431
HDI/world rank, 2014: 0.930/3
Internet domain extension: .ch

Civil Aviation

Switzerland owns seven airports with international scheduled and charter traffic: Basle (the binational Euroairport, which also serves Mulhouse in France), Berne (Belp), Geneva (Cointrin), Lugano (Agno), Sion, St Gallen (Altenrhein) and Zürich (Kloten). In 2013 these airports handled 45,501,533 passengers and 403,250 tonnes of freight and mail. Swissair, the former national carrier, faced collapse and grounded flights in Oct. 2001. In April 2002 a successor airline, Swiss International Air Lines (Swiss), took over as the national carrier. Services were also provided in 2013 by over 80 foreign airlines. Zürich is the busiest airport, handling 24,853,679 passengers in 2013 and 327,055 tonnes of freight. Geneva handled 14,328,107 passengers and 36,276 tonnes of freight in 2013. Together these two airports accounted for 86% of Swiss passenger traffic in 2013.

Climate

The climate is largely dictated by relief and altitude, and includes continental and mountain types. Summers are generally warm, with quite considerable rainfall; winters are fine, with clear, cold air. Berne, Jan. 32 °F (0 °C), July, 65 °F (18.5 °C). Annual rainfall 39.4″ (986 mm).

Constitution and Government

A new constitution was accepted on 18 April 1999 in a popular vote and came into effect on 1 Jan. 2000, replacing the constitution dating from 1874. Switzerland is a republic. The highest authority is vested in the electorate, i.e. all Swiss citizens over 18. The Swiss vote in more referendums—three or four a year—than any other nation. The Federal government is responsible for legislating matters of foreign relations, defence (within the framework of its powers), professional education and technical universities, protection of the environment, water, public works, road traffic, nuclear energy, foreign trade, social security, residence and domicile of foreigners, civil law, banking and insurance, monetary policy and economic development. The legislative authority is vested in a parliament of two chambers: the Council of States (*Ständerat/Conseil des États*) and the National Council (*Nationalrat/Conseil National*). The chief executive authority is deputed to the *Bundesrat*, or Federal Council, consisting of seven members, elected for four years by the *United Federal Assembly*, i.e. joint sessions of both chambers, such as to represent both the different geographical regions and language communities. The *President* of the Federal Council (called President of the Confederation) and the *Vice-President* are the first magistrates of the Confederation.

Currency

The unit of currency is the *Swiss franc* (CHF) of 100 *centimes* or *Rappen*.

Defence

There are fortifications in all entrances to the Alps and on the important passes crossing the Alps and the Jura. Large-scale destruction of bridges, tunnels and defiles are prepared for an emergency. Conscripts complete 18–21 weeks of basic training and then regular annual refresher training up to a set number of service days. In 2013 defence spending totalled US$5,038 m. (US$630 per capita), representing 0.8% of GDP.

Economy

In 2008 finance and insurance contributed 22.3% to GDP; followed by manufacturing, 19.0%; services, 14.1%; trade and restaurants, 13.6%; public administration and defence, 9.7%; and transport and communications, 7.3%.

Labour

In 2011 the total working population was 4,366,000, of whom 670,000 people were in manufacturing, 615,000 in trade and 566,000 in health. The unemployment rate in the third quarter of 2013 was 4.7%. In 2011, 85.4% of men and 73.3% of women between the ages of 15 and 64 were in employment. The percentage of men in employment is one of the highest among the major industrialized nations. The foreign labour force was 1,014,000 in 2011 (410,000 women). Of these 187,000 were German, 158,000 Italian, 143,000 Portuguese and 60,000 French. In 2011 approximately 698,000 EU citizens worked in Switzerland.

Press

There were 95 daily newspapers in 2008 (87 paid-for) and 101 paid-for non-daily papers; the combined circulation of paid-for papers was 2,650,000 in 2008. The average circulation of free dailies rose from 619,000 in 2004 to 1,886,000 in 2008.

Rail

In 2010 the length of the general traffic railways was 5,105 km. In 2013 Swiss and foreign railway companies carried 477 m. passengers and 65 m. tonnes of freight. In Oct. 2010 the final breakthrough of the world's longest rail tunnel took place–the 57-km long tunnel under the Gotthard mountain range in the Alps linking Erstfeld and Bodio. The tunnel was officially opened in June 2016. There are a number of tram/light rail networks, notably in Basle, Berne, Geneva, Lausanne, Neuchâtel and Zürich. There are many other railway networks, the most important of which are the BLS (436 km) and Rhaetian (384 km) networks. Switzerland was ranked first for rail infrastructure in the World Economic Forum's *Global Competitiveness Report 2009–2010*.

Religion

There is liberty of conscience and of creed. The leading religion confessions in 2010 were the Roman Catholic Church (38.6% of the population) and the Swiss Reformed Church (28.0%). Other Christians accounted for 5.5% of the population in 2010 and Muslims 4.5%, while 20.1% did not have any religious affiliation. In Feb. 2016 the Roman Catholic church had four cardinals with Swiss nationality.

Roads

In 2011 there were 71,452 km of roads, comprising 1,415 km of motorways, 18,411 km of highways and national roads and 51,638 km of secondary and local roads. Motor vehicles in 2011 (in 1,000): passenger cars, 4,163; motorcycles and mopeds, 834; vans and lorries, 349; buses and coaches, 16. Freight transported by road in 2010 totalled 17.1 bn. tonne-km. Switzerland has one of the lowest death rates in road accidents of any industrialized country, at 4.1 deaths per 100,000 people in 2011. Road accidents injured 23,242 people in 2011 and killed 320 (down from 954 in 1990).

Shipping

In 2010 there were 1,226 km of navigable waterways. 6.0 m. tonnes of freight were transported on the Rhine in 2014. A merchant marine was created in 1941, the place of registry of its vessels being Basle. In 2007 it totalled 581,683 GRT.

Social Statistics

2008 live births, 76,691; deaths, 61,233. Rates (2008, per 1,000 population): birth, 10.0; death, 8.0; marriage, 5.4; divorce, 2.6. In 2011 the most popular age range for marrying was 30–34 for males and 25–29 for females. Expectation of life, 2008: males, 79.7 years; females, 84.4. In 2007 the suicide rate per 100,000 population was 15.1 (males, 21.9; females, 9.1). Annual population growth rate, 2000–05, 0.7%. Infant mortality, 2008, four per 1,000 live births; fertility rate, 2008, 1.5 births per woman. In 2008 Switzerland received 16,606 asylum applications, up from 10,844 in 2007.

Telecommunications

In 2012 there were 4.7 m. main (fixed) telephone lines. In the same year mobile phone subscriptions numbered 10.6 m. (1,320.6 per 1,000 persons). In 2010, 80.7% of households had internet access. The fixed broadband penetration rate in 2013 was 42.5 subscriptions per 100 inhabitants. In March 2012 there were 2.7 m. Facebook users.

Territory and Population

Switzerland is bounded in the west and northwest by France, north by Germany, east by Austria and Liechtenstein and south by Italy. In 2011, 73.7% of the population lived in urban areas. In Dec. 2013 the population was estimated at 8,139,631. Population density in 2010 was 189 per km². German, French, Italian and Romansch (which is spoken mostly in Graubünden) are the official languages. German is spoken by the majority of inhabitants in 19 of the 26 cantons, French in Fribourg, Vaud, Valais, Neuchâtel, Jura and Geneva, and Italian in Ticino. In 2013, 64.5% of the population aged over 15 gave German as their main language, 22.6% French, 8.3% Italian and 0.5% Romansch. At the end of 2011 the five largest cities were Zürich (377,000); Geneva (188,200); Basle (164,500); Lausanne (129,400); Berne (125,700).

Tourism

Tourism is an important industry. In 2013 there were 8.97 m. non-resident tourists staying at hotels and similar establishments, bringing revenue of US$20,440 m. Overnight stays by tourists in hotels and health establishments totalled 35,624,000 in 2013 (19,735,000 by foreigners). The main countries of origin of foreign tourists were Germany (4,573,000 overnight stays in 2013), the UK (1,640,000) and the USA (1,585,000). 13.60 m. Swiss citizens travelled abroad in 2013.

Syria

Jumhuriya al-Arabya as-Suriya (Syrian Arab Republic)

Factsheet

Capital: Damascus
Population estimate, 2015: 18.50 m.
GNI per capita, 2014: (PPP$) 5,771
HDI/world rank, 2014: 0.594/134=
Internet domain extension: .sy

Civil Aviation

Damascus airport has ceased operations on several occasions amid fierce fighting since the outbreak of the civil war in 2011. No major international air carriers currently fly to Damascus.

Climate

The climate is Mediterranean in type, with mild wet winters and dry, hot summers, though there are variations in temperatures and rainfall between the coastal regions and the interior, which even includes desert conditions. The more mountainous parts are subject to snowfall. Damascus, Jan. 38.1 °F (3.4 °C), July 77.4 °F (25.2 °C). Annual rainfall 8.8″ (217 mm). Aleppo, Jan. 36.7 °F (2.6 °C), July 80.4 °F (26.9 °C). Annual rainfall 10.2″ (258 mm). Homs, Jan. 38.7 °F (3.7 °C), July 82.4 °F (28 °C). Annual rainfall 3.4″ (86.7 mm).

Constitution and Government

A new constitution was adopted on 27 Feb. 2012, after receiving 89.4% support in a referendum with a turnout of 57.4%. It replaced the previous constitution promulgated in 1973. Among the new constitution's provisions is the removal of a previous clause confirming the Arab Socialist Renaissance (*Ba'ath*) Party, in power since 1963, as the 'leading party in the State and society'. The constitution proceeds to outlaw parties established on a 'religious, sectarian, tribal [or] regional' basis. The *President* is limited to two 7 year terms, although this clause may not be retroactively applied, allowing the incumbent, President Bashar al-Assad, to remain in office for potentially four terms. At a referendum on 27 May 2007 Bashar al-Assad (b. 1965) was confirmed as *President* for a second term, receiving 97.6% of the vote. Presidential elections may be contested, though any candidate must be a Muslim. The description of Syria as a 'planned socialist economy' in the 1973 constitution has been replaced by an assertion that the economy 'shall be based on the principle of developing public and private economic activity through economic and social plans'. The amended constitution was widely perceived as an attempt by President al-Assad to appease the opposition movement that emerged during the 2011 Arab Spring and placate international opinion against him. Nonetheless, the referendum was boycotted by leading opposition groups and received little support from the international community. Legislative power is held by a 250-member People's Assembly (*Majlis al-Sha'ab*), renewed every 4 years in 15 multi-seat constituencies.

Currency

The monetary unit is the *Syrian pound* (SYP) of 100 *piastres*.

Defence

Military service is compulsory for a period of 18 months. Defence expenditure in 2010 totalled US$2,296 m. (US$103 per capita), representing 3.9% of GDP.

Economy

In 2009 manufacturing, mining and public utilities contributed 31.4% to GDP; followed by agriculture, 21.1%; trade, restaurants and hotels, 17.0%; transport and communications, 10.1%; and public administration, 9.8%.

Labour

In 2005 the labour force totalled 5,312,000. Unemployment was 11.5% in 2005. Syria had 19,000 people living in slavery according to the Walk Free Foundation's 2013 *Global Slavery Index*.

Press

In 2008 there were four national daily newspapers with a combined circulation of 130,000 plus five regional and local dailies. In the 2013 *World Press Freedom Index* compiled by Reporters Without Borders, Syria ranked 176th out of 179 countries.

Rail

In 2008 the Syrian Railways operated 1,801 km of 1,435 mm gauge; in 2005 the smaller Hedjaz-Syrian Railway operated 338 km of 1,050 mm gauge. Passenger-km travelled on the Syrian Railways in 2008 came to 1.1 bn. and freight tonne-km to 2.4 bn.; passenger-km travelled on the Hedjaz-Syrian Railway in 2005 came to 412,000 and freight tonne-km to 1.4 m.

Religion

According to the Pew Research Center's Forum on Religion & Public Life, in 2010 the population was an estimated 92.8% Muslim and 5.2% Christian. Most Muslims in 2010 were Sunnis but there were also significant numbers of Shias.

Roads

In 2006 there were 40,032 km of roads, including 1,103 km of motorways, 5,971 km of main roads and 31,849 km of secondary roads; 95.8% of roads were paved. There were in 2007 a total of 446,100 passenger cars in use (22 per 1,000 inhabitants), 50,800 buses and coaches and 528,300 vans and lorries. In 2007 there were 13,465 road accidents involving injury resulting in 2,818 deaths.

Shipping

In Jan. 2009 there were 102 ships of 300 GT or over registered, totalling 314,000 GT. The main port is Lattakia.

Social Statistics

2008 births, estimate, 594,000; deaths, 72,000. Rates, 2008 estimate (per 1,000 population): birth, 28.0; death, 3.4. Infant mortality, 2010 (per 1,000 live births), 14. Expectation of life, 2013, was 71.8 years for males and 77.8 for females. Annual population growth rate, 2000–08, 3.1%. Fertility rate, 2008, 3.2 births per woman.

Telecommunications

In 2014 there were 14,039,000 mobile phone subscriptions (638.6 per 1,000 inhabitants). Syria had 3,629,000 fixed telephone lines in 2014. In the same year 28.1% of the population were internet users.

Territory and Population

Syria is bounded by the Mediterranean and Lebanon in the west, by Israel and Jordan in the south, by Iraq in the east and by Turkey in the north. The census of 2004 gave a population of 17,921,000; density, 97 per km². Estimate, 2011, 21,377,000. An estimated 7.6 m. Syrians are displaced within the country as a consequence of the civil conflict that began in 2011. There were an estimated 149,000 refugees in Syria in 2015, down from 755,000 in 2011, with most having left in the wake of the civil war. In 2011, 56.2% of the population lived in urban areas. The capital is Damascus (Dimashq), with a 2004 population of 1,414,913. Other principal towns are Aleppo, Homs, Lattakia, Hamah, Raqqah, Deir Ez-Zor, Hasakah and Al-Kamishli. Arabic is the official language, spoken by 90% of the population.

Tourism

In 2010 there were a record 8,546,000 international tourist arrivals (excluding same-day visitors), spending a total of US$6.19 bn. Tourist numbers have, however, declined considerably since 2010 as a result of the civil war.

Tajikistan

Jumkhurii Tojikiston (Republic of Tajikistan)

Factsheet
Capital: Dushanbe
Population estimate, 2015: 8.48 m.
GNI per capita, 2014: (PPP$) 2,517
HDI/world rank, 20,134: 0.624/129
Internet domain extension: .tj

Civil Aviation

There are international airports at Dushanbe and Khujand. The national carrier is Tajik Air, which has flights to 11 international destinations as well as operating domestic services. In 2012 scheduled airline traffic of Tajik-based carriers flew 10.4 m. km; passenger-km totalled 2.9 bn. in the same year.

Climate

Considering its altitude, Tajikistan is a comparatively dry country. July to Sept. are particularly dry months. Winters are cold but spring comes earlier than farther north. Dushanbe, Jan. −10 °C, July 25 °C. Annual rainfall 375 mm.

Constitution and Government

In Nov. 1994 a new constitution was approved by a 90% favourable vote by the electorate, which enhanced the President's powers. The head of state is the *President*, elected by universal suffrage. When the 1994 constitution took effect the term of office was 5 years. However, an amendment to the Constitution prior to the 1999 election extended the presidential term to 7 years, although a president could only serve one term. A further referendum approved in June 2003 allowed President Rakhmonov (now Rakhmon) to serve two additional terms after the expiry of the one that he was serving at the time, in Nov. 2006, theoretically enabling him to remain in office until 2020. The Organization for Security and Co-operation in Europe and the USA expressed concerns at the result. Tajikistan has a bicameral legislature. The lower chamber is the 63-seat *Majlisi Namoyandagon* (*Assembly of Representatives*), with 41 members elected in single-seat constituencies and 22 by proportional representation for 5 year terms. The upper chamber is the 34-seat *Majlisi Milliy* (*National Assembly*), with 25 members chosen for 5 year terms by local deputies, eight appointed by the president and one seat reserved for the former president.

Currency

The unit of currency is the *somoni* (TJS) of 100 *dirams*, which replaced the Tajik rouble on 30 Oct. 2000 at 1 somoni = 1,000 Tajik roubles.

Defence

Conscription is compulsory for 2 years. In 2011 the active armed forces had a strength of 8,800. Paramilitary forces totalled 7,500 including 3,800 interior troops and 2,500 emergencies ministry troops. 5,000 Russian Army personnel were stationed in the country in 2011. Defence expenditure in 2013 totalled US$189 m. (US$24 per capita), representing 2.2% of GDP.

Economy

Agriculture accounted for 26.6% of GDP in 2012, industry 22.5% and services 50.9%.

Labour

The economically active force in 2005 totalled 2,154,000. The principal areas of activity were: agriculture, 1,424,000; education, 186,000; industry, 121,000. In 2005 the unemployment rate was 3.8%. Tajikistan had 24,000 people living in slavery according to the Walk Free Foundation's 2013 *Global Slavery Index*.

Press

Media freedom suffered during the civil war between 1992 and 1997 when around 60 journalists were killed and many others fled the country. *Imruz News*, the first daily newspaper since 1992, was launched in Aug. 2010.

Rail

Length of railways, 2011, 621 km. Passenger-km travelled in 2011 came to 32 m. and freight tonne-km in 2009 to 1.3 bn.

Religion

The Tajiks are predominantly Sunni Muslims (80%); Shia Muslims, 5%.

Roads

The road network covers an estimated 30,000 km, nearly all of which was built in the Soviet era. There were 357,869 registered vehicles in use in 2010 (297,341 cars, 37,395 heavy trucks, 14,653 buses, and 8,480 motorcycles and mopeds). In 2010 there were 411 fatalities as a result of road accidents.

Social Statistics

Estimates, 2008: births, 192,000; deaths, 44,000. Rates, 2008 estimate (per 1,000 population): births, 28.1; deaths, 6.4. Life expectancy, 2013, 64.1 years for men and 70.8 for women. Annual growth, 2000–08, 1.3%. Infant mortality, 2010, 52 per 1,000 live births; fertility rate, 2008, 3.4 births per woman.

Telecommunications

In 2013 there were an estimated 6,125,000 mobile phone subscriptions (1,168.9 per 1,000 inhabitants) and an estimated 602,000 fixed telephone lines. There were an estimated 9.6 internet users for every 100 inhabitants in 2013. The internet was banned under the former president, Saparmurad Niyazov, and has only been available since 2007.

Territory and Population

Tajikistan is bordered in the north and west by Uzbekistan and Kyrgyzstan, in the east by China and in the south by Afghanistan. Area, 143,100 km^2 (55,200 sq. miles). It includes two regions (Sughd and Khatlon), one autonomous region (Gorno-Badakhshan Autonomous Region), the city of Dushanbe and regions of republican subordination. 2010 census population, 7,564,502; density, 53 per km^2. 84.3% of the population in 2010 were Tajiks, 12.2% Uzbeks, 0.8% Kyrgyz and 0.5% Russians. In 2011 only 26.4% of the population lived in urban areas, making it the most rural of the former Soviet republics. The capital is Dushanbe (2010 population, 724,844). Other large towns are Khujand (formerly Leninabad), Kulyab (Kulob) and Kurgan-Tyube. The official language is Tajik, written in Arabic script until 1930 and after 1992 (the Roman alphabet was used 1930–40; the Cyrillic, 1940–92).

Tourism

There were 450,000 foreign visitors in 2008.

Tanzania

Jamhuri ya Muungano wa Tanzania (United Republic of Tanzania)

Factsheet

Capital: Dodoma
Population estimate, 2015: 53.47 m.
GNI per capita, 2014: (PPP$) 2,411
HDI/world rank, 2014: 0.521/151
Internet domain extension: .tz

Civil Aviation

There are three international airports: Dar es Salaam, Zanzibar and Kilimanjaro (Moshi/Arusha). Although Air Tanzania is the national carrier, Precision Air carries far more passengers (743,000 in 2013) and serves more destinations (ten in 2013). Dar es Salaam is the busiest airport, handling 2,088,282 passengers in 2012 (1,100,666 on international flights), followed by Zanzibar with 787,813 (388,231 on domestic flights).

Climate

The climate is very varied and is controlled largely by altitude and distance from the sea. There are three climatic zones: the hot and humid coast, the drier central plateau with seasonal variations of temperature, and the semi-temperate mountains. Dodoma, Jan. 75 °F (23.9 °C), July 67 °F (19.4 °C). Annual rainfall 23″ (572 mm). Dar es Salaam, Jan. 82 °F (27.8 °C), July 74 °F (23.3 °C). Annual rainfall 43″ (1,064 mm).

Constitution and Government

The current constitution dates from 25 April 1977 but underwent major revisions in Oct. 1984. The *President* is head of state, chairman of the party and commander-in-chief of the armed forces. The *Prime Minister* is also the leader of government business in the National Assembly. The 357-member *Bunge (National Assembly)* is composed of 239 constituency representatives, 102 appointed women, ten Union presidential nominees (five of whom must be women), five representatives of the Zanzibar House of Representatives (two women), and one *ex officio* member (the Attorney General). In Dec. 1979 a separate constitution for Zanzibar was approved. Although at present under the same Constitution as Tanzania, Zanzibar has, in fact, been ruled by decree since 1964. The formation of a government of national unity was approved by 66.4% of voters in a referendum in July 2010. Following elections on 21 Oct. 2010 the new government was inaugurated in Nov. 2010.

Currency

The monetary unit is the *Tanzanian shilling* (TZS) of 100 *cents*.

Defence

Defence expenditure totalled US$327 m. in 2013 (US$7 per capita), representing 1.0% of GDP.

Economy

Agriculture accounted for 28.8% of GDP in 2009, industry 24.3% and services 46.9%.

Press

In 2008 there were 14 dailies with a combined circulation of 125,000.

Rail

In 1977 the independent Tanzanian Railway Corporation was formed. The network totalled 2,707 km (metre-gauge) in 2005, excluding the joint Tanzania-Zambia (Tazara) railway's 961 km in Tanzania (1,067 mm gauge) operated by a separate administration. In 2008 the state railway carried 0.5 m. passengers and 0.5 m. tonnes of freight, and in 2005 the Tazara carried 0.9 m. passengers and 0.6 m. tonnes of freight.

Religion

In 2010 an estimated 61.4% of the population was Christian and 35.2% Muslim according to the Pew Research Center's Forum on Religion & Public Life. Of the Christians in 2010, an estimated 53% were Catholics and 46% Protestants. Most Muslims are Sunnis but there are significant Shia and Ahmadi minorities. In Feb. 2016 the Roman Catholic church had one cardinal.

Roads

In 2008 there were 87,524 km of roads, including 10,042 km of highways or national roads. Passenger cars in use in 2007 numbered 80,900; there were also 369,900 lorries and vans, 23,100 buses and coaches, and 52,000 motorcycles and mopeds.

Shipping

In Jan. 2009 there were 20 ships of 300 GT or over registered, totalling 31,000 GT. The main seaports are Dar es Salaam, Mtwara, Tanga and Zanzibar. There are also ports on the lakes.

Social Statistics

2008 estimates: births, 1,765,000; deaths, 482,000. Rates, 2008 estimates (per 1,000 population): births, 41.5; deaths, 11.4. Annual population growth rate, 2000–08, 2.7%. Life expectancy in 2013 was 60.2 years for men and 62.9 for women. 45% of the population was below 15 years old in 2008. Infant mortality, 2010, 50 per 1,000 live births; fertility rate, 2008, 5.6 births per woman.

Telecommunications

In 2013 there were 165,000 main (fixed) telephone lines; mobile phone subscriptions numbered 27,443,000 that year (557.2 per 1,000 persons). In 2013 an estimated 4.4% of the population were internet users. In June 2012 there were 518,000 Facebook users.

Territory and Population

Tanzania is bounded in the northeast by Kenya, north by Lake Victoria and Uganda, northwest by Rwanda and Burundi, west by Lake Tanganyika, southwest by Zambia and Malaŵi, and south by Mozambique. Total area 942,799 km^2 (364,881 sq. miles), including the offshore islands of Zanzibar (1,554 km^2) and Pemba (906 km^2) and inland water surfaces (59,050 km^2). 2012 census population, 44,928,923, giving a density of 50.8 per km^2. In 2011, 26.9% of the population lived in urban areas. The chief towns (2012 census populations) are Dar es Salaam, the chief port and former capital (4,364,541), Mwanza (706,453), Zanzibar (501,459), Arusha (416,442), Mbeya (385,279). Dodoma, the capital, had a population of 213,636 in 2012. The United Republic is divided into 30 administrative regions of which 25 are in mainland Tanzania, three in Zanzibar and two in Pemba. The official languages are Swahili (spoken as a mother tongue by only 8.8% of the population, but used as a *lingua franca* by 91%) and English.

Tourism

There were 15 national parks in Tanzania in 2008. In 2010 there were 754,000 international tourist arrivals (excluding same-day visitors), bringing revenue of US$1,255 m. Tourism is the country's second largest foreign exchange earner after agriculture.

Thailand

Prathet Thai (Kingdom of Thailand)

Factsheet

Capital: Bangkok
Population estimate, 2015: 67.96 m.
GNI per capita, 2014: (PPP$) 13,323
HDI/world rank, 2014: 0.726/93
Internet domain extension: .th

Civil Aviation

There are international airports at Bangkok (Suvarnabhumi), Chiang Mai, Phuket and Hat Yai. The national carrier, Thai Airways International, is 51.03% state-owned. In 2005 scheduled airline traffic of Thai-based carriers flew 213.8 m. km, carrying 21,507,900 passengers. Suvarnabhumi, which only opened in 2006, handled 53,002,328 passengers in 2012 (39,358,339 on international flights) and 1,345,490 tonnes of freight.

Climate

The climate is tropical, with high temperatures and humidity. Over most of the country, three seasons may be recognized. The rainy season is June to Oct., the cool season from Nov. to Feb. and the hot season is March to May. Rainfall is generally heaviest in the south and lightest in the northeast. Bangkok, Jan. 78 °F (25.6 °C), July 83 °F (28.3 °C). Annual rainfall 56″ (1,400 mm).

Constitution and Government

Bhumibol Adulyadej, who was born 5 Dec. 1927, died on 13 Oct. 2016, having reigned as king for 70 years and 126 days. His son and heir apparent, Crown Prince **Vajiralongkorn**, ascended to the throne on 1 Dec. as King Rama X. Following the coup of May 2014, the existing constitution was superseded on 22 July by an interim replacement drafted by the military junta and signed into law by the King without public consultation. The interim constitution recognizes the status of the junta—the National Council for Peace and Order (NCPO)—as Thailand's legitimate executive authority, whilst granting it powers to recommend appointments to a new committee drafting a permanent constitution. A new parliament, a *National Legislative Assembly* of 200 members appointed by the NCPO, was established to replace the previous 150-seat Senate and 500-seat House of Representatives.

Currency

The unit of currency is the *baht* (THB) of 100 *satang*.

Defence

Conscription is for 2 years; if there are not enough volunteers a conscription lottery is held to fill the quota. In 2013 defence expenditure totalled US$6,213 m. (US$92 per capita), representing 1.5% of GDP.

Economy

In 2008 manufacturing contributed 34.9% to GDP; followed by trade and hotels, 19.0%; agriculture, forestry and fishing, 11.6%; and services, 7.5%. Thailand's 'shadow' (black market) economy is estimated to constitute approximately 48% of the country's official GDP.

Labour

The labour force in 2013 was 39,873,000 (36,471,000 in 2003). 78.3% of the population aged 15–64 was economically active in 2013. In the same year 0.7% of the population was unemployed. There is no nationwide minimum wage but a minimum wage is set at different levels at the provincial level. It varied between 159 baht and 221 baht per day in July 2011. Thailand had 0.47 m. people living in slavery according to the Walk Free Foundation's 2013 *Global Slavery Index*, the seventh highest total of any country.

Press

In 2008 there were 46 daily newspapers (45 paid-for and one free), with a combined circulation of 7.4 m. The newspapers with the highest circulation figures are *Thai Rath*, *Daily News* and *Kom Chad Luek*.

Rail

The State Railway totalled 4,041 km in 2012. Passenger-km travelled in 2011 came to 7.5 bn.; freight tonne-km transported in 2011 totalled 2.5 bn. A metro ('Skytrain'), or elevated transit system, was opened in Bangkok in 1999. A second (underground) mass transit system in Bangkok, the Bangkok Subway, was opened in 2004.

Religion

According to the Pew Research Center's Forum on Religion & Public Life, 93.2% of the population in 2010 was Buddhist, 5.5% Muslim and 0.9% Christian. Only Cambodia has a higher percentage of Buddhists in its population, and only China has more Buddhists. Most Muslims are Sunnis and among Christians there are more Protestants than Catholics. In Feb. 2016 the Roman Catholic church had two cardinals.

Roads

In 2006 there were 180,053 km of roads, of which 450 km were motorways. Vehicles in use in 2006 included: 3.80 m. passenger cars, 4.99 m. lorries and vans and 15.67 m. motorcycles and mopeds.

Shipping

In Jan. 2009 there were 612 ships of 300 GT or over registered, totalling 2,738,000 GT. Of the 612 vessels registered, 209 were oil tankers, 205 general cargo ships, 72 liquid gas tankers, 52 bulk carriers, 26 chemical tankers, 26 passenger ships and 22 container ships. The busiest ports are Laem Chabang and Bangkok.

Social Statistics

2005–06 births, 705,639; deaths, 440,024; marriages (2005), 345,234; divorces (2005), 90,688. Rates (per 1,000 population, 2005–06): birth, 10.9; death, 6.8; marriage (2005), 5.2; divorce (2005), 1.4. Annual population growth rate, 2000–05, 1.0%. Expectation of life (2007): 65.4 years for men; 72.1 years for women. Infant mortality, 2010, 11 per 1,000 live births; fertility rate, 2008, 1.8 births per woman.

Telecommunications

In 2013 there were 6.1 m. main (fixed) telephone lines. In the same year mobile phone subscriptions numbered 93.8 m. (1,400.5 per 1,000 persons). In 2013 an estimated 28.9% of the population aged 6 years and over were internet users. In March 2012 there were 14.2 m. Facebook users.

Territory and Population

Thailand is bounded in the west by Myanmar, north and east by Laos and southeast by Cambodia. In the south it becomes a peninsula bounded in the west by the Indian Ocean, south by Malaysia and east by the Gulf of Thailand. The area is 513,120 km^2 (198,117 sq. miles). At the 2010 census the population was 65,479,453; density, 127.6 per km^2. In 2011, 34.4% of the population lived in urban areas. Thailand is divided into six regions, 76 provinces and Bangkok, the capital. Population of Bangkok (2010 estimate), 8,213,000. Other towns (2010 estimates): Samut Prakan (1,093,000), Udon Thani (399,000), Chonburi (371,000), Nonthaburi (368,000), Nakhon Ratchasima (305,000), Lampang (282,000), Hat Yai (269,000), Rayong (230,000). Thai is the official language, spoken by 53% of the population as their mother tongue. 27% speak Lao (mainly in the northeast), 12% Chinese (mainly in urban areas), 3.7% Malay (mainly in the south) and 2.7% Khmer (along the Cambodian border).

Tourism

In 2010 there were 15,936,000 tourist arrivals, up from 14,150,000 in 2009. Tourist numbers have doubled since 1998. The leading nationalities of tourists in 2010 were Malaysia (2,059,000), China (1,122,000), Japan (994,000) and the United Kingdom (811,000).

Timor Leste

República Democrática de Timor-Leste (Democratic Republic of East Timor)

Factsheet
Capital: Dili
Population estimate, 2015: 1.19 m.
GNI per capita, 2014: (PPP$) 5,363
HDI/world rank, 2014: 0.595/133
Internet domain extension: .tl

Civil Aviation

There is an international airport at Dili (Presidente Nicolau Lobato International Airport).

Climate

In the north there is an average annual temperature of over 24 °C (75 °F), weak precipitation—below 1,500 mm (59″) annually—and a dry period lasting 5 months. The mountainous zone, between the northern and southern

parts of the island, has high precipitation—above 1,500 mm (59″)—and a dry period of 4 months. The southern zone has precipitation reaching 2,000 mm (79″) and is permanently humid. The monsoon season extends from Nov. to May.

Constitution and Government

The constitution promulgated in 2002 created a unicameral system with a *National Parliament* with a minimum requirement of 52 directly-elected seats and a maximum of 65. For the first term after independence the parliament had 88 members but this was reduced after the June 2007 legislative elections. The *President* is directly elected for a period of 5 years and may not serve more than two terms.

Currency

The official currency is the US dollar.

Defence

The Timor-Leste Defence Force comprises an army and a small naval element. In 2013 the army had 1,250 personnel and the naval element around 80. Defence spending totalled US$67 m. in 2013 (US$57 per capita), representing 1.6% of GDP.

Labour

In 2010 unemployment was officially 9.8% of the labour force between 15 and 64.

Press

In 2007 there were three daily newspapers: *Suara Timor Lorosae*, *Timor Post* and *Jornal Nacional Diario*. There were also three non-dailies in 2007.

Religion

Over 90% of Timor-Leste's population are Roman Catholic, with Protestants, Muslims, Hindus and Buddhists accounting for the remainder.

Social Statistics

2008 estimates: births, 44,000; deaths, 9,500. Rates, 2008 estimates (per 1,000 population): births, 40.0; deaths, 8.7. Annual population growth rate in 2000–08, 3.7%. Fertility rate, 2008, 6.5 children per woman. In 2013 life expectancy at birth was 66.0 years for males and 69.1 years for females. From having the world's highest rate of infant mortality in the early 1980s, Timor-Leste's infant mortality rate dropped to 46 per 1,000 live births in 2010, although the figure varies widely between urban and rural areas.

Telecommunications

In 2010 there were 2,907 landline telephone subscriptions (2,334 in 2005) and 350,891 mobile phone subscriptions (33,072 in 2005).

Territory and Population

Timor-Leste (East Timor) has a total land area of 14,954 km^2 (5,774 sq. miles), consisting of the mainland (13,987 km^2), the enclave of Oecussi-Ambeno in West Timor (817 km^2), and the islands of Ataúro to the north (140 km^2) and Jaco to the east (10 km^2). The mainland area incorporates the eastern half of the island of Timor. Oecussi-Ambeno lies westwards, separated from the main portion of Timor-Leste by a distance of some 100 km. The island is bound to the south by the Timor Sea and lies approximately 500 km from the Australian coast. Population at the census of July 2010, 1,066,409 (544,198 males); density, 71 per km^2. The largest city is Dili, Timor-Leste's capital. In 2010 its population was 192,652. In 2011, 28.6% of the population were urban. The ethnic East Timorese form the majority of the population. Timor-Leste's constitution designates Portuguese and Tetum (an Austronesian language influenced by Portuguese) as the official languages, and English and Bahasa Indonesia as working languages.

Tourism

In 2009, 44,131 non-resident tourists—excluding same-day visitors—arrived by air (up from 35,999 in 2008 and 22,254 in 2007).

Togo

République Togolaise (Togolese Republic)

Factsheet

Capital: Lomé
Population estimate, 2015: 7.31 m.
GNI per capita, 2014: (PPP$) 1,228
HDI/world rank, 2014: 0.484/162
Internet domain extension: .tg

Civil Aviation

In 2010 ASKY Airlines (a pan-African airline with its hub in Lomé) flew from Lomé-Tokoin airport to Abidjan, Accra, Bamako, Banjul, Brazzaville, Cotonou, Dakar, Douala, Kinshasa, Lagos, Libreville and Ouagadougou. There were international flights in 2010 with other airlines to Abidjan, Accra, Addis Ababa, Bamako, Casablanca, Cotonou, Dakar, Libreville, Ouagadougou, Paris and Tripoli (Libya). In 2012 Tokoin handled 472,313 passengers (417,672 on international flights) and 7,256 tonnes of freight.

Climate

The tropical climate produces wet seasons from March to July and from Oct. to Nov. in the south. The north has one wet season, from April to July. The heaviest rainfall occurs in the mountains of the west, southwest and centre. Lomé, Jan. 81 °F (27.2 °C), July 76 °F (24.4 °C). Annual rainfall 35″ (875 mm).

Constitution and Government

A referendum on 27 Sept. 1992 approved a new constitution by 98.1% of votes cast. Under this the *President* and the *National Assembly* were directly elected for 5-year terms. Initially the president was allowed to be re-elected only once. However, on 30 Dec. 2002 parliament approved an amendment to the constitution lifting the restriction on the number of times that the president may be re-elected. The National Assembly has 91 seats and is elected for a 5-year term.

Currency

The unit of currency is the *franc CFA* (XOF) with a parity of 655.957 francs CFA to one euro.

Defence

There is selective conscription that lasts for 2 years. Defence expenditure totalled US$72 m. in 2013 (US$10 per capita), representing 1.8% of GDP.

Economy

Agriculture contributed 31% of GDP in 2011, industry 16% and services 53%.

Labour

In 2010 the estimated labour force was 3,059,000 (56% males), up from 2,182,000 in 2000. In Aug. 2008 the statutory monthly minimum wage was raised to 28,000 francs CFA. Togo had 49,000 people living in slavery according to the Walk Free Foundation's 2013 *Global Slavery Index*.

Press

There is one government-controlled daily newspaper, *Togo-Presse* (circulation of 5,000 in 2008).

Rail

There are four railways (metre gauge) connecting Lomé, with Aného (continuing to Cotonou in Benin), Kpalimé, Tabligbo and (via Atakpamé) Blitta; total length in 2005, 532 km. In 2005 the railways carried 1.1 m. tonnes of freight. There has been no passenger rail service since 1996.

Religion

A study by the Pew Research Center's Forum on Religion & Public Life estimated that there were 2.64 m. Christians in 2010, 2.15 m. folk religionists and 840,000 Muslims. A further 370,000 people had no religious affiliation. Of the Christians in 2010, an estimated 60% were Catholics and 39% Protestants.

Roads

There were 11,652 km of roads in 2007, including 3,067 km of highways or national roads. In 2007 there were 10,600 passenger cars in use, 2,200 lorries and vans and 34,200 motorcycles and mopeds.

Shipping

In Jan. 2009 there were 18 ships of 300 GT or over registered, totalling 33,000 GT.

Social Statistics

2008 estimates: births, 212,000; deaths, 53,000. Estimated rates, 2008 (per 1,000 population): births, 32.9; deaths, 8.2. Expectation of life (2013) was 55.6 years for males and 57.4 for females. Annual population growth rate, 2005–10, 2.6%. Infant mortality, 2010, 66 per 1,000 live births; fertility rate, 2008, 4.3 births per woman.

Telecommunications

In 2013 there were 62,500 main (fixed) telephone lines in Togo; mobile phone subscriptions numbered 4,263,000 that year (625.3 per 1,000 persons). In 2013 an estimated 4.5% of the population were internet users.

Territory and Population

Togo is bounded in the west by Ghana, north by Burkina Faso, east by Benin and south by the Gulf of Guinea. The area is 56,600 km². 2010 census population, 6,191,155 (3,182,060 females); density, 109 per km². In 2011, 44.1% of the population lived in urban areas. In 2010, 42% were below the age of 15. The capital is Lomé (2010 census population, 837,437), other towns being Sokodé (95,070), Kara (94,878), Kpalimé (75,084), Atakpamé (69,261), Dapaong (58,071) and Tsévié (54,474). There are 37 ethnic groups. The south is largely populated by Ewe-speaking peoples (forming 23% of the population), Watyi (10%) and other related groups, while the north is mainly inhabited by Hamitic groups speaking Kabre (14%), Tem (6%) and Gurma (3%). The official language is French but Ewe and Kabre are also taught in schools.

Tourism

In 2010 there were 202,000 international tourists staying at hotels and similar establishments; spending by tourists totalled US$66 m. in the same year.

Tonga

Pule'anga Fakatu'i 'o Tonga (Kingdom of Tonga)

Factsheet

Capital: Nuku'alofa
Population estimate, 2015: 106,000
GNI per capita, 2014: (PPP$) 5,069
HDI/world rank, 2014: 0.717/100
Internet domain extension: .to

Civil Aviation

There is an international airport at Nuku'alofa on Tongatapu. The national carrier was the state-owned Royal Tongan Airlines, but it ceased operations in May 2004 owing to financial difficulties. In 2009 Nuku'alofa (Fua'Amotu International) handled 222,612 passengers and 1,417 tonnes of freight.

Climate

Generally a healthy climate, although Jan. to March hot and humid, with temperatures of 90 °F (32.2 °C). Rainfall amounts are comparatively high, being greatest from Dec. to March. Nuku'alofa, Jan. 25.8 °C, July 21.3 °C. Annual rainfall 1,643 mm. Vava'u, Jan. 27.3 °C, July 23.4 °C. Annual rainfall 2,034 mm.

Constitution and Government

The reigning King is **Tupou VI** (**'Aho'eitu 'Unuaki'otonga Tuku'aho Tupou VI**), born 12 July 1959, succeeded on 18 March 2012 on the death of his brother, George Tupou V. The current Constitution is based on the one granted in 1875. It was last amended in 2003 to increase the constitutional powers of the King and restrict media freedom. There is a Privy Council, Cabinet, Legislative Assembly and Judiciary. The 28-member *Legislative Assembly* is composed of 17 elected representatives of the people, nine nobles elected by their peers and two *ex officio* members. Prior to the Nov. 2010 election there were 32 members, of which only nine were elected representatives of the people (plus the nine nobles elected by their peers and also 14 appointed ministers).

Currency

The unit of currency is the *pa'anga* (TOP) of 100 *seniti*.

Economy

In 2010 agriculture accounted for 19% of GDP, industry 20% and services 61%.

Press

There are no daily newspapers. There were three paid-for non-daily newspapers in 2008: the *Tonga Chronicle* (a government-owned weekly), the *Times of Tonga* and *Matangi Tonga*.

Religion

Christianity is the main religion, with the Free Wesleyan Church being the largest denomination. There are also significant numbers of Later-day Saints and Catholics as well as followers of other religions. In Feb. 2016 there was one Roman Catholic cardinal.

Roads

There are about 680 km of roads. Registered vehicles in 2010 numbered 5,806, including 4,411 cars and four-wheeled light vehicles, 1,285 heavy trucks and 62 motorized two- and three-wheelers.

Shipping

In Jan. 2009 there were 29 ships of 300 GT or over registered, totalling 62,000 GT. The main port is Nuku'alofa.

Social Statistics

Births, 2008 estimates, 2,900; deaths, 600; marriages (Tongatapu only), 892; divorces, 95. Expectation of life, 2013: males, 69.8 years; females, 75.7. Annual population growth rate, 2000–08, 0.6%. Infant mortality, 2010, 13 per 1,000 live births. Fertility rate, 2008, 4.0 births per woman.

Telecommunications

The operation of the National Telecommunication Network and Services is the responsibility of the Tonga Telecommunication Commission (TCC). In 2011 there were 30,000 main (fixed) telephone lines; mobile phone subscriptions numbered 55,000 that year (52.6 per 100 persons). In 2013 an estimated 35.0% of the population were internet users. Ucall mobile GSM digital has been in operation in Tonga since Dec. 2001.

Territory and Population

The Kingdom consists of some 169 islands and islets with a total area, including 30 km^2 of inland waters plus uninhabited islands, of 748 km^2 (289 sq. miles), and lies between 15° and 23° 30' S. lat and 173° and 177° W. long, its western boundary being the eastern boundary of the Fiji Islands. The islands are split up into the following groups (reading from north to

south): the Niuas, Vava'u, Ha'apai, Tongatapu and 'Eua. The three main groups, both from historical and administrative significance, are Tongatapu in the south, Ha'apai in the centre and Vava'u in the north. Census population (2011) 103,252; density, 138 per km^2. In 2011, 23.5% of the population lived in urban areas. The capital is Nuku'alofa on Tongatapu; population (2011), 36,045 (urban population, 24,229). There are five divisions comprising 23 districts. Both Tongan and English are recognized as official languages.

Tourism

There were 46,040 tourist arrivals by air in 2011. Tourism receipts in 2011 totalled US$32 m.

Trinidad and Tobago

Republic of Trinidad and Tobago

Factsheet

Capital: Port of Spain
Population estimate, 2015: 1.36 m.
GNI per capita, 2014: (PPP$) 26,090
HDI/world rank, 2014: 0.772/64=
Internet domain extension: .tt

Civil Aviation

There is an international airport at Port of Spain (Piarco) and in Tobago (A. N. R. Robinson International Airport). In 2012 Piarco handled 2,724,888 passengers (1,723,835 on international flights) and 53,935 tonnes of freight. The national carrier is Caribbean Airlines, which has flights to 11 international destinations as well as operating domestic services. In 2012 scheduled airline traffic of Trinidad and Tobago-based carriers flew 52.8 m. km; passenger-km totalled 9.2 bn. in the same year.

Climate

A tropical climate cooled by the northeast trade winds. The dry season runs from Jan. to June, with a wet season for the rest of the year. Temperatures are uniformly high the year round. Port of Spain, Jan. 76.3 °F (24.6 °C), July 79.2 °F (26.2 °C). Annual rainfall 1,870 mm.

Constitution and Government

The 1976 constitution provides for a bicameral legislature of a *Senate* and a *House of Representatives*, who elect the *President*, who is head of state. The *Senate* consists of 31 members, 16 being appointed by the President on the advice of the *Prime Minister*, six on the advice of the Leader of the Opposition and nine at the discretion of the President. The *House of Representatives* consists of 41 (39 for Trinidad and two for Tobago) elected members and a Speaker elected from within or outside the House. Executive power is vested in the Prime Minister, who is appointed by the President, and the Cabinet.

Currency

The unit of currency is the *Trinidad and Tobago dollar* (TTD) of 100 *cents*.

Defence

The Trinidad and Tobago Defence Force consists of the Trinidad and Tobago Regiment, the Coast Guard, the Air Guard and the Defence Force Reserves. Personnel in 2011 totalled around 4,100. In 2013 defence expenditure totalled US$400 m. (US$326 per capita), representing 1.5% of GDP.

Economy

Industry accounted for 57% of GDP in 2012, services 42% and agriculture 1%.

Labour

The labour force in 2013 was 685,000 (617,000 in 2003). 71.0% of the population aged 15–64 was economically active in 2013. In the same year 3.6% of the population was unemployed. 71.0% of the population aged 15–64 was economically active in 2013. The unemployment rate in the fourth quarter of 2005 was a record low 6.7%.

Press

There were three daily newspapers in 2008—*Trinidad and Tobago Express*, *Trinidad and Tobago Guardian* and *Trinidad and Tobago Newsday*—with a total circulation of 140,000. There were also nine paid-for non-dailies in 2008.

Religion

An estimated 65.9% of the population in 2010 were Christians (mainly Protestants), 22.7% Hindus and 5.5% Muslims according to the Pew Research Center's Forum on Religion & Public Life.

Roads

In 2010 there were 8,320 km of roads, of which 51.1% were paved. There were 468,255 vehicles in use in 2007.

Shipping

In Jan. 2009 there were 11 ships of 300 GT or over registered, totalling 29,000 GT. The largest port is Port of Spain. The other main harbour is Point Lisas. There is a deep-water harbour at Scarborough (Tobago). A ferry service links Port of Spain with Scarborough.

Social Statistics

2008 births, 19,888; deaths, 10,463. 2008 birth rate (per 1,000 population), 15.2; death rate, 8.0. Expectation of life, 2013, was 66.4 years for males and 73.6 for females. Annual population growth rate, 1998–2008, 0.4%. Infant mortality, 2010, 24 per 1,000 live births; fertility rate, 2008, 1.6 births per woman.

Telecommunications

International and domestic communications are provided by Telecommunications Services of Trinidad and Tobago (TSTT). In 2013 there were 291,300 main (fixed) telephone lines; mobile phone subscriptions numbered 1,944,000 that year (1,449.4 per 1,000 persons). In 2013 an estimated 63.8% of the population were internet users. In Dec. 2011 there were 441,000 Facebook users.

Territory and Population

The island of Trinidad is situated in the Caribbean Sea, about 12 km off the northeast coast of Venezuela; several islets, the largest being Chacachacare, Huevos, Monos and Gaspar Grande, lie in the Gulf of Paria which separates Trinidad from Venezuela. The smaller island of Tobago lies 30.7 km further to the northeast. Altogether, the islands cover 5,128 km^2 (1,980 sq. miles), of which Trinidad (including the islets) has 4,828 km^2 (1,864 sq. miles) and Tobago 300 km^2 (116 sq. miles). In 2011 the census population was 1,328,019 (Trinidad, 1,267,145; Tobago, 60,874); density, 259 per km^2. In 2011, 14.2% of the population lived in urban areas. Capital, Port of Spain (2011 census, 37,074); other important towns, Chaguanas (83,516), San Fernando (48,838), Arima (33,606) and Point Fortin (20,235). The main towns on Tobago are Scarborough and Plymouth. Distribution of population by ethnic group (2011): East Indian, 35.4%; African, 34.2%; mixed races, 22.8%; others, 7.6%. The official language is English.

Tourism

In 2008 there were 432,551 tourist arrivals by air (of which 187,515 were from the USA), down from 449,453 in 2007. There were a record 119,600 cruise passenger arrivals in 2009.

Tunisia

Jumhuriya at-Tunisiya (Republic of Tunisia)

Factsheet

Capital: Tunis
Population estimate, 2015: 11.25 m.
GNI per capita, 2014: (PPP$) 10,404
HDI/world rank, 2014: 0.721/96
Internet domain extension: .tn

Civil Aviation

The national carrier, Tunisair, is 64.9% state-owned and in 2013 carried 3,710,000 passengers. There are eight international airports. In 2012 Tunis-Carthage handled 5,249,411 passengers (4,903,506 on international flights) and 16,666 tonnes of freight. Enfidha-Hammamet, which opened in 2009, handled 2,087,122 passengers in 2012 and Djerba 1,969,043.

Climate

The climate ranges from warm temperate in the north, where winters are mild and wet and the summers hot and dry, to desert in the south. Tunis, Jan. 48 °F (8.9 °C), July 78″ (25.6 °C). Annual rainfall 16″ (400 mm). Bizerta, Jan. 52 °F (11.1 °C), July 77 °F (25 °C). Annual rainfall 25″ (622 mm). Sfax, Jan. 52 °F (11.1 °C), July 78 °F (25.6 °C). Annual rainfall 8″ (196 mm).

Constitution and Government

Following the revolution of Jan. 2011 and the ousting of President Zine El Abidine Ben Ali, elections were held in Oct. that year for a Constituent Assembly with a mandate to draft and approve a new constitution. On 26 Jan. 2014 parliament approved the new constitution, achieving the required majority of two-thirds support from the Assembly with 200 of 216 votes cast. The constitution states that elections are to be held every 5 years. While Islam is acknowledged as the state religion, there is no reference to Islamic law as a source of legislation. Freedom of worship is guaranteed, as are the equal rights of men and women before the law. Executive power is divided between the *Prime Minister* and the *President*.

Currency

The unit of currency is the *Tunisian dinar* (TND) of 1,000 *millimes*.

Defence

Selective conscription is for 1 year. Defence expenditure in 2013 totalled US$769 m. (US$71 per capita), representing 1.6% of GDP.

Economy

In 2011 services accounted for 59.8% of GDP, industry 31.3% and agriculture 8.9%.

Labour

The economically active population totalled 3,593,200 in 2007. Out of 3,085,100 in employment, 48.6% were engaged in commerce and services, 32.1% in industry, mining, energy and construction, and 19.3% in agriculture and fisheries. Unemployment was 16.7% in 2012, with the rate among graduates being particularly high at over 25%.

Press

In 2009 there were nine paid-for daily newspapers (four in Arabic and five in French).

Rail

In 2007 there were 2,165 km of railways on metre and 1,435 mm gauge track. Passenger-km travelled in 2007 came to 1,487 m. and freight tonne-km to 2,197 m. There is a tramway in Tunis (32 km).

Religion

The constitution recognizes Islam as the state religion. According to estimates by the Pew Research Center's Forum on Religion & Public Life, more than 99% of the population are Muslims (mostly Sunnis).

Roads

The road network covered 19,371 km in 2008, including 359 km of motorways and 4,738 km of national roads. In 2007 there were 746,700 passenger cars, 300,500 lorries and vans, 10,100 buses and coaches, and 5,300 motorcycles and mopeds. There were 10,681 road accidents in 2007 resulting in 1,497 fatalities.

Shipping

There are ports at Tunis, its outer port Tunis-Goulette, Sfax, Sousse and Bizerte, all of which are directly accessible to ocean-going vessels. The ports of La Skhirra and Gabès are used for the shipping of Algerian and Tunisian oil. In Jan. 2009 there were 17 ships of 300 GT or over registered, totalling 125,000 GT.

Social Statistics

2008 estimates: births, 183,000; deaths, 61,000; marriages (2005), 74,000. Rates (2008 estimates): birth, 18 per 1,000 population; death, 6. Annual population growth rate, 2000–05, 1.0%. In 2005 the most popular age range for marrying was 30–34 for males and 25–29 for females. Expectation of life, 2007, was 71.8 years for males and 76.0 for females. Infant mortality, 2010, 14 per 1,000 live births; fertility rate, 2008, 1.8 births per woman.

Telecommunications

In 2009 there were 9,797,000 mobile phone subscriptions (953.8 per 1,000 inhabitants) and 1,279,000 fixed telephone lines. There were 340.7 internet users for every 1,000 inhabitants in 2009. In June 2012 there were 3.1 m. Facebook users.

Territory and Population

Tunisia is bounded in the north and east by the Mediterranean Sea, west by Algeria and south by Libya. The area is 163,610 km², including 9,080 km² of inland waters. Provisional census population, 2014: 10,982,754, giving a density of 70.7 per km². In 2011, 67.7% of the population were urban. Tunis, the capital, had 747,240 inhabitants (provisional) at the 2014 census. Other main cities (2014 census in 1,000, provisional): Sfax, 280.7 (estimate); Sousse, 230.3 (estimate); Ettadhamen, 143.0; Kairouan, a holy city of the Muslims, 139.5; Bizerte, 138.6; Gabès, 130.0 (estimate); La Soukra, 129.7. The official language is Arabic but French is the main language in the media, commercial enterprise and government departments. Berber-speaking people form less than 1% of the population.

Tourism

In 2011 there were 4,782,000 international tourist arrivals, excluding same-day visitors (down from 6,902,000 in 2010 in the wake of the revolution of early 2011); spending by tourists in 2011 totalled US$1,914 m.

Turkey

Türkiye Cumhuriyeti (Republic of Turkey)

Factsheet
Capital: Ankara
Population estimate, 2015: 78.67 m.
GNI per capita, 2014: (PPP$) 18,677
HDI/world rank, 2014: 0.761/72
Internet domain extension: .tr

Civil Aviation

There are international airports at İstanbul (Atatürk and Sabiha Gökçen), Dalaman (Muğla), Ankara (Esenboga), İzmir (Adnan Menderes), Adana and Antalya. The national carrier is Turkish Airlines, which is 49.1% state-owned. In 2014 it carried 54,675,000 passengers (31,967,000 on international flights) and flew 106,787 m. revenue passenger-km. In 2009 İstanbul's Atatürk Airport handled 29,854,119 passengers (18,396,050 on international flights) and 381,174 tonnes of freight.

Climate

Coastal regions have a Mediterranean climate, with mild, moist winters and hot, dry summers. The interior plateau has more extreme conditions, with low and irregular rainfall, cold and snowy winters, and hot, almost rainless summers. Ankara, Jan. 32.5 °F (0.3 °C), July 73 °F (23 °C). Annual rainfall 14.7″ (367 mm). İstanbul, Jan. 41 °F (5 °C), July 73 °F (23 °C). Annual rainfall 28.9″ (723 mm). İzmir, Jan. 46 °F (8 °C), July 81 °F (27 °C). Annual rainfall 28″ (700 mm).

Constitution and Government

On 7 Nov. 1982 a new constitution was adopted, which has subsequently undergone several revisions. Following a referendum on 21 Oct. 2007, it was amended so that the *President* will be directly elected by the people, rather than by *Parliament*, as is currently the case. Furthermore, the President will be able to serve for up to two 5 year terms, rather than being limited to a single 7 year term. This reform came into force at the presidential election of Aug. 2014. Further amendments were introduced after acceptance in a referendum on 12 Sept. 2010. Under their terms, military officers accused of crimes against the state may be tried in civilian courts. Legal protection previously granted to participants in the 1980 coup was removed. Government workers are granted the right to collective bargaining and restrictions on striking were loosened. The *Constitutional Court* was expanded, with the president and parliament having a greater say in judicial appointments. The Presidency is not an executive position; the President may not be linked to a political party but can veto laws and official appointments. There is a 550-member Turkish Grand National Assembly, elected by universal suffrage (at 18 years and over) for 4 year terms by proportional representation.

Currency

The unit of currency is the Turkish *lira* (TRY) of 100 *kuruş*.

Defence

The President of the Republic is C.-in-C. of the armed forces. Conscription is 15 months for privates, 12 months for reserve officers and 6 months for privates who have completed a university degree. In 2013 defence expenditure totalled US$10,742 m., with spending per capita US$133. The 2013 expenditure represented 1.3% of GDP.

Economy

In 2009 finance and real estate contributed 22.0% to GDP; followed by manufacturing, 15.0%; transport and communications, 13.3%; and trade and hotels, 13.2%.

Labour

Out of 22,047,000 people in employment in 2005 (16,346,000 men), 6,493,000 were engaged in agriculture, hunting, forestry and fisheries, 4,083,000 in manufacturing, 3,610,000 in wholesale and retail trade/repair of motor vehicles, motorcycles and personal and household goods and 1,246,000 in public administration and defence/compulsory social security. The unemployment rate in Oct. 2014 was 10.6%. Turkey had 0.12 m. people living in slavery according to the Walk Free Foundation's 2013 *Global Slavery Index*.

Press

In 2008 there were 81 daily newspapers with a combined average daily circulation of 5.6 m. The best-selling newspapers are *Zaman* and *Posta*, with average daily circulations of 756,000 and 632,000 respectively. In the 2013 *World Press Freedom Index* compiled by Reporters Without Borders, Turkey ranked 154th out of 179 countries. In March 2011, 57 journalists were in prison—more than in any other country.

Rail

Total length of railway lines in 2011 was 9,642 km (1,435 mm gauge), of which 2,789 km were electrified. Turkey's first high-speed line was opened in 2009 between Ankara and Eskişehir. Passenger-km travelled in 2011 came to 5.82 bn. and freight tonne-km to 11.30 bn. There are metro systems operating in Adana, Ankara, Bursa, İstanbul and İzmir.

Religion

Islam ceased to be the official religion in 1928. The Constitution guarantees freedom of religion but forbids its political exploitation or any impairment of the secular character of the republic. In 2010 the population was an estimated 98.0% Muslim (around 85–90% Sunni and 10–15% Shia) according to the Pew Research Center's Forum on Religion & Public Life. There are small numbers of Orthodox Christians and other Christians.

Roads

In 2006 there were 427,099 km of roads, including 1,987 km of motorway. In 2007 road vehicles in use included 6,472,200 passenger cars, 2,619,700 lorries and vans, 561,700 buses and coaches and 2,003,500 motorcycles and mopeds. There were 5,002 fatalities from road accidents in 2007.

Shipping

In Jan. 2009 there were 912 ships of 300 GT or over registered, totalling 5.05 m. GT. Of the 912 vessels registered, 469 were general cargo ships, 148 passenger ships, 123 oil tankers, 100 bulk carriers, 37 container ships, 27 chemical tankers and eight liquid gas tankers. The Turkish-controlled fleet comprised 1,156 vessels of 1,000 GT or over in Jan. 2009, of which 520 were under the Turkish flag and 636 under foreign flags. In 2007 Turkish ports handled 288.1 m. tonnes of cargo (114.6 m. tonnes loaded and 173.5 m. tonnes unloaded), more than double the 140.2 m. tonnes handled in 2003.

Social Statistics

Births, 2009, 1,241,617; deaths, 367,971. 2009 birth rate per 1,000 population, 17.3; death rate, 5.1. 2009 marriages, 591,472 (rate of 8.2 per 1,000 population); divorces, 114,162 (rate of 1.6 per 1,000 population). Population growth rate, 2009, 1.3%. Expectation of life, 2013, was 71.8 years for males and 78.7 for females. Infant mortality, 2010, 12 per 1,000 live births, declining significantly from 66 per 1,000 live births in 1990. Fertility rate, 2008, 2.1 births per woman. In 2009 the most popular age for marrying was 25–29 for males and 20–24 for females.

Telecommunications

In 2013 there were 13,552,000 main (fixed) telephone lines. In the same year mobile phone subscriptions numbered 69,661,000 (929.6 per 1,000 persons). In Nov. 2005 the government sold a 55% stake in Türk Telecom to a consortium led by Saudi Arabia's Oger Telecom and Telecom Italia. The government's stake fell to 30% in May 2008 through a public offering. In 2013 an estimated 46.3% of the population aged 16–74 were internet users. In March 2012 there were 31.0 m. Facebook users.

Territory and Population

Turkey is bounded in the west by the Aegean Sea and Greece, north by Bulgaria and the Black Sea, east by Georgia, Armenia and Iran, and south by Iraq, Syria and the Mediterranean. The area (including lakes) is 783,562 km² (302,535 sq. miles). The last traditional census was in 2000. In 2007 an address-based population registration system was established to replace ten-yearly censuses. The population at the census of 31 Dec. 2012 using this method was 75,627,384, giving a density of 98.3 per km². In 2011, 70.1% of the population lived in urban areas. Turkish is the official language. Population of cities of over 1,000,000 inhabitants in 2012: İstanbul, 13,522,528; Ankara, 4,417,522; İzmir, 2,803,418; Bursa, 1,734,705; Adana, 1,628,725; Gaziantep, 1,421,359; Konya, 1,107,886.

Tourism

In 2009, 25.5 m. international tourists visited Turkey, making it the seventh most popular tourist destination; receipts from tourism in 2009 totalled US$21.3 bn.

Turkmenistan

Türkmenistan

Factsheet

Capital: Ashgabat
Population estimate, 2015: 5.37 m.
GNI per capita, 2014: (PPP$) 13,066
HDI/world rank, 2014: 0.688/109
Internet domain extension: .tm

Civil Aviation

Turkmenistan Airlines, founded in 1992, is the flag carrier. In 2005 scheduled airline traffic of Turkmenistan-based carriers flew 9.5 m. km, carrying 1,899,800 passengers.

Climate

The summers are warm to hot but the humidity is relatively low. The winters are cold but generally dry and sunny over most of the country. Ashgabat, Jan. −1 °C, July 25 °C. Annual rainfall 375 mm.

Constitution and Government

A new constitution was adopted on 26 Sept. 2008. It provided for a head of state who is elected by popular vote for a 5 year term and abolished the 2,500-member *Khalk Maslakhaty* (People's Council), formerly the highest representative body. The *Majlis* (Assembly), which now serves as the sole legislative body, was increased from 65 to 125 members. The constitution also allows for a multiparty system. At a referendum on 16 Jan. 1994, 99.99% of votes cast were in favour of prolonging President Niyazov's term of office to 2002. In 1999 the *Khalk Maslakhaty* declared him president for life.

Currency

The unit of currency is the *newmanat* (TMT) of 100 *tenge*, introduced on 1 Jan. 2009 to replace the *manat* (TMM) at a rate of 1 TMT = 5,000 TMM.

Defence

Conscription is compulsory for 2 years. Defence expenditure in 2012 totalled US$539 m. (US$107 per capita), representing 1.6% of GDP.

Economy

In 2008 agriculture accounted for 12.3% of GDP, industry 53.7% and services 34.0%.

Labour

The estimated labour force in 2010 totalled 2,509,000 (53% males), up from 1,826,000 in 2000. Turkmenistan had 15,000 people living in slavery according to the Walk Free Foundation' 2013 *Global Slavery Index.*

Press

In 2008 there were two daily newspapers with a combined average circulation of 56,000. Approval is required from the president's office before publication. In the 2013 *World Press Freedom Index* compiled by Reporters Without Borders, Turkmenistan ranked 177th out of 179 countries.

Rail

Length of railways in 2011, 3,115 km of 1,520 mm gauge. A rail link to Iran was opened in 1996. In 2008, 6.2 m. passengers and 25.4 m. tonnes of freight were carried.

Religion

In 2010 an estimated 93.0% of the population were Muslims (mainly Sunnis) according to the Pew Research Center's Forum on Religion & Public Life, with 6.4% Christians (mainly Orthodox).

Roads

The total road network covers around 14,000 km. In 2006 there were 650 fatalities as a result of road accidents.

Shipping

In Jan. 2009 there were ten ships of 300 GT or over registered, totalling 23,000 GT. The main port is Turkmenbashi, on the Caspian Sea.

Social Statistics

2008 estimates: births, 111,000; deaths, 39,000. Estimated rates, 2008 (per 1,000 population): births, 21.9; deaths, 7.7. Annual population growth rate, 2000–08, 1.4%. Life expectancy, 2013: 61.4 years for males and 69.8 for females. Infant mortality, 2010, 47 per 1,000 live births; fertility rate, 2008, 2.5 births per woman.

Telecommunications

In 2013 there were an estimated 6,125,000 mobile phone subscriptions (1,168.9 per 1,000 inhabitants) and an estimated 602,000 fixed telephone lines. There were an estimated 9.6 internet users for every 100 inhabitants in 2013. Internet usage was banned under the former president, Saparmurad Niyazov, and has only been available since 2007.

Territory and Population

Turkmenistan is bounded in the north by Kazakhstan, in the north and northeast by Uzbekistan, in the southeast by Afghanistan, in the southwest by Iran and in the west by the Caspian Sea. Area, 448,100 km^2 (186,400 sq. miles). The 1995 census population was 4,483,251; density 10.0 per km^2. Estimate, 2010, 5.04 m.; density, 11 per km^2. The vast majority of citizens are Turkmen, but there are some Russians and Uzbeks. A dual-citizenship treaty between Turkmenistan and Russia has been rescinded. In 2011, 50.0% of the population lived in rural areas. There are five administrative regions (*velayaty*): Ahal, Balkan, Dashoguz, Lebap and Mary, comprising 42 rural districts, 15 towns and 74 urban settlements. The capital is Ashgabat (formerly Ashkhabad; 2004 estimated population, 827,500); other large towns are Turkmenabat (formerly Chardzhou), Mary (Merv), Balkanabad (Nebit-Dag) and Dashoguz. The official language is Turkmen, spoken by 77% of the population; Uzbek is spoken by 9% and Russian by 7%.

Tourism

In 2005 there were 12,000 non-resident tourists.

Tuvalu

Factsheet

Capital: Fongafale
Population estimate, 2015: 10,000
GNI per capita, 2014: (PPP$) 5,278
Internet domain extension: .tv

Civil Aviation

In 2010 Air Pacific operated two flights a week from Funafuti International to Suva in the Fiji Islands.

Climate

A pleasant but monotonous climate with temperatures averaging 86 °F (30 °C), though trade winds from the east moderate conditions for much of the year. Rainfall ranges from 120" (3,000 mm) to over 160" (4,000 mm). Funafuti, Jan. 84 °F (28.9 °C), July 81 °F (27.2 °C). Annual rainfall 160" (4,003 mm). Although the islands are north of the recognized hurricane belt they were badly hit by hurricanes in the 1990s, raising fears for the long-term future of Tuvalu as the sea level continues to rise.

Constitution and Government

The Head of State is the British sovereign, represented by an appointed Governor-General. The Constitution provides for a Prime Minister and the cabinet ministers to be elected from among the 15 members of the *Fale I Fono* (*Parliament*).

Currency

The unit of currency is the Australian *dollar* although Tuvaluan coins up to $A1 are in local circulation.

Economy

Finance, real estate, public administration, defence and services accounted for 50.5% of GDP in 2008; agriculture and fishing, 18.2%; trade, hotels and restaurants, 13.9%; transport and communications, 12.2%.

Press

The Government Broadcasting and Information Division produces *Tuvalu Echoes*, a fortnightly publication, and *Te Lama*, a monthly religious publication.

Religion

The majority of the population are Protestants who are members of the Congregational Christian Church of Tuvalu (also known as the Church of Tuvalu). There are also small numbers of Roman Catholics, Seventh-day Adventists, Jehovah's Witnesses, Bahá'ís, Muslims and Latter-day Saints (Mormons).

Roads

In 2013 there were just 8 km of roads.

Shipping

Funafuti is the only port and a deep-water wharf was opened in 1980. In Jan. 2009 there were 96 ships of 300 GT or over registered, totalling 1.03 m. GT. Of the 96 vessels registered, 40 were oil tankers, 36 general cargo ships, nine chemical tankers, five bulk carriers, four passenger ships and two container ships. Tuvalu is a 'flag of convenience' country.

Social Statistics

2005 births (est.), 230; deaths (est.), 60. Infant mortality, 2010, 27 per 1,000 live births. Expectation of life, 2008: males, 64 years; females, 63. Annual population growth rate, 1998–2008, 0.5%; fertility rate, 2008, 3.2 births per woman.

Telecommunications

In 2013 there were approximately 1,450 main telephone lines in operation. There were an estimated 3,400 mobile phone subscriptions, and some 37.0% of the population used the internet that year.

Territory and Population

Tuvalu lies between 5. 30′ and 11° S. lat. and 176° and 180° E. long. and comprises Nanumea, Nanumaga, Niutao, Nui, Vaitupu, Nukufetau, Funafuti (administrative centre; 2012 census population, 5,879), Nukulaelae and Niulakita. Population (census 2012) 10,640, excluding an estimated 1,500 who were working abroad, mainly in Nauru and Kiribati. Area approximately 26 km^2 (10 sq. miles). Density, 2012, 409 per km^2. In 2011, 50.9% of the population lived in urban areas. The population is of a Polynesian race. The official languages are Tuvaluan and English.

Tourism

There were 1,232 visitor arrivals in 2011, down from a record 1,665 in 2008.

Uganda

Jamhuri ya Uganda (Republic of Uganda)

Factsheet
Capital: Kampala
Population estimate, 2015: 39.03 m.
GNI per capita, 2014: (PPP$) 1,613
HDI/world rank, 2014: 0.483/163=
Internet domain extension: .ug

Civil Aviation

There is an international airport at Entebbe, 40 km from Kampala. Air Uganda, formed in 2007, was the national airline until July 2014. It ceased operations when the issuer of its air operator's certificate, the Ugandan Civil Aviation Authority, failed an audit carried out by the International Civil Aviation Organization. In 2012 scheduled airline traffic of Uganda-based carriers flew 3.8 m. km; passenger-km totalled 444.9 m. in the same year. In 2012 Entebbe handled 1,342,134 passengers (1,238,466 on international flights) and 56,519 tonnes of freight.

Climate

Although in equatorial latitudes, the climate is more tropical because of its elevation, and is characterized by two distinct rainy seasons, March–May and Sept.–Nov. In comparison, June–Aug. and Dec.–Feb. are relatively dry. Temperatures vary little over the year. Kampala, Jan. 74 °F (23.3 °C), July 70 °F (21.1 °C). Annual rainfall 46.5″ (1,180 mm). Entebbe, Jan. 72 °F (22.2 °C), July 69 °F (20.6 °C). Annual rainfall 63.9″ (1,624 mm).

Constitution and Government

The *President* is head of state and head of government, and is elected for a five-year term by adult suffrage. In Aug. 2005 Parliament amended the constitution to allow an incumbent to hold office for more than two terms, thus enabling President Museveni to serve another term in office. Having lapsed in 1966, the kabakaship was revived as a ceremonial office in 1993. Ronald Muwenda Mutebi (b. 13 April 1955) was crowned Mutebi II, 36th Kabaka, on 31 July 1993. Until 1994 the national legislature was the 278-member National Resistance Council, but this was replaced by a 284-member *Constituent Assembly* in March 1994. A new constitution was adopted on 8 Oct. 1995 and the Constituent Assembly dissolved. Uganda's parliament is now the 386-member *National Assembly* (238 members elected by popular vote, 137 indirectly elected from special interest groups—including women and the army—and 11 *ex officio* members). A referendum on the return of multi-party democracy was held on 29 June 2000, but 88% of voters supported President Museveni's 'no-party' Movement system of government. Turnout was 51%. In Feb. 2003 President Museveni pledged to lift the ban on political parties. In a referendum held on 28 July 2005, 92.4% of voters backed the restoration of a multi-party political system, although the opposition called for a boycott.

Currency

The monetary unit is the *Uganda shilling* (UGX) notionally divided into 100 *cents*.

Defence

Defence expenditure in 2013 totalled US$342 m. (US$10 per capita), representing 1.6% of GDP.

Economy

In 2010 agriculture accounted for 24.2% of GDP, industry 25.5% and services 50.3%.

Labour

The labour force in 2013 was 14,589,000 (10,709,000 in 2003). 78.1% of the population aged 15–64 was economically active in 2013. In the same year 4.2% of the population was unemployed. Uganda had 0.25 m. people living in slavery according to the Walk Free Foundation's 2013 *Global Slavery Index*.

Press

There were five daily newspapers in 2008 with a combined average daily circulation of 110,000.

Rail

In 2005 the Uganda Railways network totalled 1,241 km (metre gauge). In 1996 passenger services were suspended and have not been reinstated in the meantime. Freight tonne-km in 2015 came to 189 m.

Religion

According to the Pew Research Center's Forum on Religion & Public Life the population was 86.7% Christian in 2010, with Muslims accounting for 9.1%. Of the Christians, 51% in 2010 were Protestants and 49% Catholics. In Feb. 2016 there was one Roman Catholic cardinal.

Roads

The road network totals around 140,000 km (4% paved). In 2014 Uganda had 20,544 km of national roads. There were 81,300 passenger cars in use in 2007, 79,300 lorries and vans, 40,500 buses and coaches, and 176,500 motorcycles and mopeds. In 2007 there were 17,428 road accidents resulting in 2,779 deaths.

Social Statistics

2008 estimates: births, 1,461,000; deaths, 401,000. Rates, 2008 estimates (per 1,000 population): births, 46.2; deaths, 12.7. Uganda has one of the youngest populations of any country, with 76% of the population under the age of 30 and 48% under 15. Uganda's life expectancy at birth in 2013 was 58.0 years for males and 60.4 years for females. Life expectancy declined dramatically until the late 1990s, largely owing to the huge number of people in the country with HIV. However, for both males and females expectation of life is now starting to rise again. Annual population growth rate, 2000–08, 3.2%. Infant mortality, 2010, 63 per 1,000 live births; fertility rate, 2008, 6.3 births per woman.

Telecommunications

In June 2013 there were 207,500 main (fixed) telephone lines; mobile phone subscriptions numbered 16,569,000 in June 2013 (44.1 per 100 persons). In 2013 an estimated 16.2% of the population were internet users. In June 2012 there were 415,000 Facebook users.

Territory and Population

Uganda is bounded in the north by South Sudan, in the east by Kenya, in the south by Tanzania and Rwanda, and the west by the Democratic Republic of the Congo. Total area 241,550 km², including 41,740 km² of inland waters. The 2014 provisional census population was 34,856,813 (16,935,456 males, 17,921,357 females); density, 174 per km². The largest city is Kampala, the capital (provisional census population of 1,516,210 in 2014). Other major towns are Kira, Mbarara, Mukono, Gulu, Nansana, Masaka and Kasese. In 2011, 13.5% of the population lived in urban areas. The country is administratively divided into one city and 111 districts, which are grouped in four geographical regions (which do not have administrative status). The official languages are English and (since 2005) Kiswahili. About 70% of the population speak Bantu languages; Nilotic languages are spoken in the north and east.

Tourism

In 2011 there were 1,151,000 international tourist arrivals (excluding day-visitors); spending by tourists totalled US$950 m.

Ukraine

Ukraina

Factsheet

Capital: Kyiv (formerly Kiev)
Population estimate, 2015: 44.82 m.
GNI per capita, 2014: (PPP$) 8,178
HDI/world rank, 2014: 0.747/81=
Internet domain extension: .ua

Civil Aviation

The main international airport is Kyiv (Boryspil), and there are international flights from seven other airports. There are two major Ukrainian carriers. In 2012 Kyiv handled 8,478,091 passengers (7,432,008 on international flights) and 38,642 tonnes of freight. In the same year Simferopol (under Russian control since the annexation of Crimea in 2014) handled 1,113,900 passengers and Odesa 907,600 passengers.

Climate

Temperate continental with a subtropical Mediterranean climate prevalent on the southern portions of the Crimean Peninsula. The average monthly temperature in winter ranges from 17.6 °F to 35.6 °F (−8 °C to 2 °C), while summer temperatures average 62.6 °F to 77 °F (17 °C to 25 °C). The Black Sea coast is subject to freezing, and no Ukrainian port is permanently ice-free. Precipitation generally decreases from north to south; it is greatest in the Carpathians where it exceeds more than 58.5″ (1,500 mm) per year, and least in the coastal lowlands of the Black Sea where it averages less than 11.7″ (300 mm) per year.

Constitution and Government

A new constitution was adopted on 28 June 1996. It defines Ukraine as a sovereign, democratic, unitary state governed by the rule of law and guaranteeing civil rights. The head of state is the *President*, elected directly by the people for a 5 year term. Parliament is the 450-member unicameral *Verkhovna Rada* (*Supreme Council*), elected for 4 year terms. There is an 18-member *Constitutional Court*, six members being appointed by the President, six by parliament and six by a panel of judges. Constitutional amendments may be initiated at the President's request to parliament, or by at least one-third of parliamentary deputies. The Communist Party was officially banned in the country in 1991, but was renamed the Socialist Party of Ukraine. Hard-line Communists protested against the ban, which was rescinded by the Supreme Council in May 1993.

Currency

The unit of currency is the *hryvnia* (UAH) of 100 *kopiykas*, which replaced karbovanets on 2 Sept. 1996 at 100,000 karbovanets = 1 hryvnia.

Defence

In 2011 the armed forces numbered 129,925 personnel, with 1 m. reserves. Conscription was abolished in Oct. 2013, with Ukraine hoping to develop an all-professional military. However, it was reintroduced on 1 May 2014 in response to the escalating conflict with the pro-Russian insurgency in eastern Ukraine. Military expenditure in 2013 totalled US$2,418 m. (US$54 per capita), representing 1.3% of GDP.

Economy

In 2010 agriculture accounted for 8.3% of GDP, industry 31.3% and services 60.4%.

Labour

In 2011 a total of 20,324,000 persons aged 15 to 70 were in employment. The principal areas of activity were (in 1,000): wholesale and retail trade, and restaurants and hotels, 4,865; agriculture, hunting, forestry and fishing, 3,394;

manufacturing, 3,353. In 2011 there were 1,733,000 unemployed and the level of unemployment was 7.9%. Ukraine had 0.11 m. people living in slavery according to the Walk Free Foundation's 2013 *Global Slavery Index*.

Press

In 2008 there were 56 daily newspapers with an average combined circulation of 4.5 m. The newspapers with the highest circulation figures are *Fakty i Kommentarii*, *Komsomolskaja Pravda v Ukraine* and *Segodnja*.

Rail

Total length was 22,302 km in 2009. Passenger-km travelled in 2009 came to 48.3 bn. and freight tonne-km to 196.2 bn. There are metros in Kyiv, Kharkiv, Kryvy Rih and Dnipropetrovsk.

Religion

According to the Pew Research Center's Forum on Religion & Public Life an estimated 83.8% of the population in 2010 were Christians (over 90% of which were Orthodox), with 14.7% religiously unaffiliated. The Pew Research Center's study estimated that there were 34.9 m. Orthodox Christians in 2010. The Orthodox Church is split into three factions. The largest is the Ukrainian Orthodox Church, Moscow Patriarchate. The hierarchy of the Roman Catholic Church was restored by the Pope John Paul II's confirmation of ten bishops in 1991. In Feb. 2016 there were two cardinals. The Ukrainian Greek Catholic Church is a Church of the Byzantine rite, which is in full communion with the Roman Church. Catholicism is strong in the western half of the country.

Roads

In 2007 there were 169,422 km of roads, including 20,497 km of national roads. There were 5,939,600 passenger cars in use in 2007 and 714,300 motorcycles and mopeds. There were 63,554 road accidents involving injury in 2007 (9,574 fatalities).

Shipping

In 2007, 2 m. passengers and 15 m. tonnes of freight were carried by inland waterways. In Jan. 2009 there were 224 ships of 300 GT or over registered, totalling 770,000 GT. The main seaports are Illichivsk, Izmail, Mariupol, Mykolaïv, Odesa and Yuzhny. Odesa is the leading port, in 2008 handling 34,562,000 tonnes of freight.

Social Statistics

2009 births, 512,525; deaths, 706,739; marriages, 318,198; divorces, 145,439. Rates (per 1,000 population), 2009: births, 11.1; deaths, 15.3. Annual population growth rate, 2000–05, −0.9%. Life expectancy, 2007: males, 62.7 years, females, 73.8. In 2006 the most popular age range for marrying was 20–24 for both males and females. Infant mortality, 2010, 11 per 1,000 live births; fertility rate, 2008, 1.3 births per woman (one of the lowest rates of any country).

Telecommunications

In 2009 there were 55,333,000 mobile phone subscriptions (1,210.6 per 1,000 inhabitants) and 13,026,000 fixed telephone lines. There were 2,649,000 fixed internet subscriptions in 2009 and 1,733,000 mobile broadband subscriptions. In March 2012 there were 1.7 m. Facebook users.

Territory and Population

Ukraine is bounded in the east by the Russian Federation, north by Belarus, west by Poland, Slovakia, Hungary, Romania and Moldova, and south by the Black Sea and Sea of Azov. Area, 603,628 km² (233,062 sq. miles). At the last census, in 2001, the census population was 48,457,102, of whom 26,015,758 were female; Jan. 2014 estimate, 45,426,249, giving a density of 75 per km². In 2001, 78% of the population were Ukrainians, 17% Russians and 5% others. Ukraine's population is projected to drop to 42.37 m. by 2025 (the same population as in the late 1950s). In 2011, 69.1% of the population lived in urban areas. As of 1 Jan. 2014 Ukraine was divided into 24 provinces, two municipalities (Kyiv and Sevastopol) and the Autonomous Republic of Crimea. In March 2014 Crimea was annexed by Russia in a move lacking international recognition. In May 2014 separatists in Donetsk and Luhansk provinces unilaterally declared independence but the

Ukrainian government and the wider international community have rejected the legitimacy of these declarations. The capital is Kyiv (estimated population 2,814,258 in Jan. 2012). The 1996 constitution made Ukrainian the sole official language. Russian (the language of 33% of the population), Romanian, Polish and Hungarian are also spoken.

Tourism

There were 23,013,000 non-resident tourists in 2012; total receipts were US$5,988 m.

United Arab Emirates

Imarat al-Arabiya al-Muttahida

Factsheet
Capital: Abu Dhabi
Population estimate, 2015: 9.16 m.
GNI per capita, 2014: (PPP$) 60,868
HDI/world rank, 2014: 0.835/41
Internet domain extension: .ae

Civil Aviation

Dubai is the busiest airport, handling 66,431,533 passengers and 2,435,567 tonnes of freight in 2013 (up from 37,441,440 passengers and 1,824,992 tonnes of freight in 2008). Dubai was the seventh busiest airport in the world overall and the second busiest for international passenger traffic in 2013. However, in 2014 it overtook London Heathrow as the world's busiest airport for international traffic. As recently as 2006 it did not even rank among the 30 busiest airports in the world. Dubai set up its own airline, Emirates, in 1985. In 2013–14 it flew 215,353 m. international scheduled passenger-km, the most of any airline; it carried 44.5 m. passengers in 2013–14. Etihad Airways, the national airline of the United Arab Emirates, began operations in Nov. 2003.

Climate

The country experiences desert conditions, with rainfall both limited and erratic. The period May to Sept. is generally rainless. Abu Dhabi, Jan. 65 °F (18.3 °C), July 95 °F (35.0 °C). Annual rainfall 3.5" (89 mm). Dubai, Jan. 66 °F (18.9 °C), July 94 °F (34.4 °C). Annual rainfall 3.7" (94 mm).

Constitution and Government

The Emirates is a federation, headed by a *Supreme Council of Rulers* which is composed of the seven rulers which elects from among its members a *President* and *Vice-President* for 5 year terms, and appoints a *Council of Ministers*. The Council of Ministers drafts legislation and a federal budget; its proposals are submitted to a *Federal National Council* of 40 appointed members which may propose amendments but has no executive power. It was announced in Dec. 2005 that 20 of the 40 members would in future be elected through councils for each of the seven Emirates. There is a *National Consultative Council* made up of citizens. The current constitution came into force on 2 Dec. 1971 and was made permanent in 1996.

Currency

The unit of currency is the *dirham* (AED) of 100 *fils*.

Defence

Conscription was introduced in June 2014, and required all male high-school graduates aged 18 to 30 to serve in the armed forces for 9 months. Those who have not completed secondary school serve for 2 years. In 2011 defence expenditure totalled US$9,320 m. (US$1,810 per capita), representing 2.7% of GDP.

Economy

Crude petroleum and natural gas accounted for 36.8% of GDP in 2008; trade and hotels, 17.4%; finance and real estate, 15.1%; construction, 7.4%.

Labour

Males constituted 85% of the economically active labour force in 2005 (one of the highest percentages of any country in the world). Foreign workers make up over 90% of the workforce in the private sector. A total of 2,660,000 persons were in employment in 2005, with the leading areas of activity as follows: community, social and personal services, 587,900; construction, 502,700; wholesale and retail trade, restaurants and hotels, 460,200; manufacturing, 292,600. In 2005 the unemployment rate was 1.9%. The United Arab Emirates had 19,000 people living in slavery according to the Walk Free Foundation's 2013 *Global Slavery Index*.

Press

In 2008 there were 13 daily newspapers (12 paid-for and one free) with a combined circulation of 943,000.

Rail

Etihad Rail, a rail network linking the seven Emirates, is under construction and is expected to become operational by 2018. Commercial operations on the first of three phases began in Dec. 2015.

Religion

Most inhabitants are Sunni Muslims, with a small Shia minority.

Roads

In 2008 there were 4,080 km of roads. There were 1,279,100 passenger cars (293 per 1,000 inhabitants), 48,200 buses and coaches and 39,400 lorries and vans in 2007.

Shipping

There are 15 commercial seaports, of which five major ports are on the Persian Gulf (Zayed in Abu Dhabi, Rashid and Jebel Ali in Dubai, Khalid in Sharjah, and Saqr in Ras al-Khaimah) and two on the Gulf of Oman: Fujairah and Khor Fakkan. Rashid and Fujairah are important container terminals. In Jan. 2009 there were 124 ships of 300 GT or over registered, totalling 913,000 GT.

Social Statistics

2008 births, 68,779; deaths, 9,775. 2008 birth rate (per 1,000 population), 14.4; death rate, 1.6; infant mortality rate (per 1,000 live births), 6 (2010). Life expectancy, 2013, 76.1 years for men and 78.2 years for women. Annual population growth rate, 1998–2008, 4.4%; fertility rate, 2008, 1.9 births per woman. The UAE has had one of the largest reductions in its fertility rate of any country in the world over the past quarter of a century, having had a rate of 4.4 births per woman in 1990.

Telecommunications

In 2013 there were 2.1 m. main (fixed) telephone lines. In the same year active mobile phone subscriptions numbered 16.1 m. (1,718.7 per 1,000 persons). In 2013 an estimated 88.0% of the population were internet users. In March 2012 there were 2.9 m. Facebook users.

Territory and Population

The Emirates are bounded in the north by the Persian Gulf, northeast by Oman, east by the Gulf of Oman and Oman, south and west by Saudi Arabia. Their area is approximately 83,600 km^2 (32,300 sq. miles), excluding over 100 offshore islands. The total population at the last census in 2005 was 4,106,427 (68.3% male); density, 49 per km^2. Estimate, 1 July 2008, 4,765,000. The United Nations population estimate for 2008 was 6,799,000. About one-tenth are nomads. In 2011, 84.4% of the population lived in urban areas. Approximately 80% of the population are foreigners, the highest percentage of any country. The population of the United Arab Emirates has trebled since 2000. Populations of the seven Emirates, 2010 estimates unless otherwise indicated (in 1,000): Abu Dhabi, 1,968; Ajman, 263; Dubai, 1,836; Fujairah, 164; Ras al-Khaimah, 231 (2008 estimate); Sharjah, 830;

Umm al Qaiwain, 53 (2008 estimate). The chief cities are Dubai (2012 estimated census population of 2,067,291), Abu Dhabi, the federal capital (estimated census population of 975,735 in 2012), Sharjah and Al Ain. In addition to being the most populous Emirate, Abu Dhabi is also the wealthiest, ahead of Dubai. The official language is Arabic; English is widely spoken.

Tourism

In 2005, 7,126,000 tourists stayed in hotels and similar accommodation; spending by tourists in 2005 totalled US$3.218 m.

United Kingdom

Factsheet

Capital: London
Population estimate, 2015: 64.72 m.
GNI per capita, 2014: (PPP$) 39,267
HDI/world rank, 2014: 0.907/14=
Internet domain extension: .uk

Civil Aviation

All UK airports handled a total of 251.7 m. passengers in 2015 (238.6 m. in 2014). London area airports (Heathrow, Gatwick, London City, Luton, Southend and Stansted) handled 155.3 m. passengers in 2015. Heathrow handled 75.0 m. passengers and 1.5 m. tonnes of freight in 2015. Heathrow was the world's third busiest airport for passenger traffic in 2013 and Europe's busiest. For many years more international passengers used Heathrow than any other airport in the world, but in 2014 it lost this status to Dubai.

Climate

The climate is cool temperate oceanic, with mild conditions and rainfall evenly distributed over the year, though the weather is very changeable because of cyclonic influences. In general, temperatures are higher in the west and lower in the east in winter and rather the reverse in summer. Rainfall amounts are greatest in the west, where most of the high ground occurs. London, Jan. 39 °F (3.9 °C), July 64 °F (17.8 °C). Annual rainfall 25″ (635 mm). Aberdeen, Jan. 38 °F (3.3 °C), July 57 °F (13.9 °C). Annual rainfall 32″ (813 mm). Belfast, Jan. 40 °F (4.5 °C), July 59 °F (15.0 °C). Annual rainfall 37.4″ (950 mm). Birmingham, Jan. 38 °F (3.3 °C), July 61 °F (16.1 °C). Annual rainfall 30″ (749 mm). Cardiff, Jan. 40 °F (4.4 °C), July 61 °F (16.1 °C). Annual rainfall 42.6″ (1,065 mm). Edinburgh, Jan. 38 °F (3.3 °C), July 58 °F (14.5 °C). Annual rainfall 27″ (686 mm). Glasgow, Jan. 39 °F (3.9 °C), July 59 °F (15.0 °C). Annual rainfall 38″ (965 mm). Manchester, Jan. 39 °F (3.9 °C), July 61 °F (16.1 °C). Annual rainfall 34.5″ (876 mm).

Constitution and Government

The reigning Queen, Head of the Commonwealth, is **Elizabeth II** Alexandra Mary, b. 21 April 1926, daughter of King George VI and Queen Elizabeth; married on 20 Nov. 1947 Lieut. Philip Mountbatten (formerly Prince Philip of Greece), created Duke of Edinburgh, Earl of Merioneth and Baron Greenwich on the same day and created Prince Philip, Duke of Edinburgh, 22 Feb. 1957; succeeded to the crown on the death of her father, on 6 Feb. 1952. The supreme legislative power is vested in Parliament, which consists of the Crown, the House of Lords and the House of Commons. The executive government is vested nominally in the Crown, but practically in a committee of Ministers, called the Cabinet, which is dependent on the support of a majority in the House of Commons. The head of the Cabinet is the *Prime Minister* (currently Theresa May, b. 1956 and assumed office in July 2016).

Currency

The unit of currency is the *pound sterling* (.; GBP) of 100 *pence* (p.).

Defence

In accordance with the 2016 Budget the planned defence budget for 2016–17 is 35.0 bn. (27.7 bn. resource budget). Defence spending in 2013 represented 2.4% of GDP, down from 5.2% in 1985. Per capita defence expenditure in 2013 totalled 551 (US$900). Total number of the UK forces services personnel at 1 Jan. 2015 was 194,600 (down from 199,600 on 1 Jan. 2014), of which 154,200 were UK regular forces. There were an estimated 30,000 volunteer reservists. The nuclear arsenal consisted of about 150 Trident submarine-launched ballistic missile warheads in Jan. 2015 according to the Stockholm International Peace Research Institute. In addition there were some 65 non-deployed weapons in the nuclear stockpile.

Economy

In 2013 services accounted for 78% of GDP, industry 21% and agriculture 1% (63%, 35% and 2% respectively in 1989). In 2014 the British economy was the fifth largest in the world. Imports of goods in 2014 totalled 419,104 m. and exports 295,432 m.

Labour

In 2009 the UK's total economically active population (i.e. all persons in employment plus the claimant unemployed) was (in 1,000) 31,374 (13,452 females), of whom 28,979 (12,542 females) were in employment, including 24,937 (12,280 females) as employees and 3,850 (1,103 females) as self-employed. In 1999 only 27,167,000 people had been in employment, representing an increase of 1,812,000 in 10 years. However, the recession of 2008–09 resulted in the number of employees in 2009 being the lowest since 2005. The number of jobless people was 1,685,000 in the period Nov. 2015–Jan. 2016 (down from both 1,713,000 in the 3 months from Aug.–Oct. 2015 and 2,335,000 in the period Nov. 2013–Jan. 2014). The unemployment rate on the International Labour Organization (ILO) definition, which includes all those who are looking for work whether or not claiming unemployment benefits, was 5.1% in the period Nov. 2015–Jan. 2016 (down from 5.7% for the same period the previous year). The UK had 4,000 people living in slavery according to the Walk Free Foundation's 2013 *Global Slavery Index.*

Press

In Feb. 2016 there were 11 national dailies with a combined average daily circulation of 6,538,217 and ten national Sunday newspapers (5,870,963). In Jan. 2014 there were also 114 morning, evening and Sunday regional newspapers and 929 weeklies (345 of these for free distribution).The most widely read daily is the tabloid *The Sun*, with an average daily circulation of 1,787,096 in Feb. 2016. The most widely read Sunday paper is *The Sun on Sunday*, with an average circulation of 1,412,453 in Feb. 2016.

Rail

The rail network comprises 15,754 route km (around a third electrified). Annual passenger-km were a record 59.2 bn. in 2013. There were a record 1.59 bn. passenger journeys in 2013–14 on franchised operated services (more than double the 735.1 m. of 1994–95). The amount of freight moved declined gradually over many years to 13.0 bn. tonne-km in 1994–95 but has generally since risen and totalled 22.7 bn. tonne-km in 2013–14, the highest total since the early 1970s. In 2013–14 a total of seven people (excluding trespassers) were fatally injured on the railways and nine people on level crossings (compared to 1,713 deaths in road accidents in 2013).

Religion

Religious affiliation figures for England and Wales according to the 2011 census was: Christian, 59.3% of the population; no religion, 25.1%; Muslim, 4.8%; Hindu, 1.5%; Sikh, 0.8%; Jewish, 0.5%; Buddhist, 0.4%; other religion, 0.4%; not stated, 7.2%.

Roads

In 2009 there were 394,428 km of public roads in Great Britain, classified as: motorways, 3,560 km; trunk roads, 8,596 km; other major roads, 38,173 km; minor roads, 344,099 km. In 2013 journeys by car, vans and taxis totalled 641 bn. passenger km (less than 60 bn. in the early 1950s). Even in the mid-1950s passenger km in cars, vans and taxis exceeded the annual total in 2013 by rail. Licensed motor vehicles in 2014 included 28,183,000 private cars,

1,067,000 mopeds, scooters and motorcycles, 109,000 buses and 3,890,000 other private and light goods vehicles.

Shipping

The UK-owned merchant fleet (trading vessels over 100 GT) in Dec. 2012 totalled 675 ships of 21.6 m. DWT and 20.4 m. GT. These included 109 fully cellular container vessels, 107 general cargo vessels, 92 bulk carriers and 56 oil tankers. The UK-owned and registered fleet totalled 331 ships of 6.8 m. DWT. There are approximately 3,500 miles (5,630 km) of navigable canals and river navigations in Great Britain. In July 2012 a new waterways charity, the Canal & River Trust (CRT), took over the management of the network of waterways in England and Wales from British Waterways. In Scotland the 137 miles (220 km) of inland waterways remain under the control of British Waterways (operating as Scottish Canals), which is a stand-alone public body of the Scottish government.

Social Statistics

UK statistics, 2014 (provisional): births, 776,352; deaths, 570,341; marriages (2012, provisional), 301,254; divorces (2013), 126,716. UK rates (per 1,000 population), 2014: birth, 12.0; death, 8.8; marriage (2012, provisional), 4.7; divorce (2013), 2.0. The number of births in the UK in 2012 was the highest since 1972; the number of deaths in 2011 (552,232) was the lowest since 1930. The divorce rate in 2013 was at its lowest since the early 1970s. In 1976, for the only time in the twentieth century, deaths in the UK (680,800) exceeded births (675,500). In 2012 cancer caused 166,000 deaths (29% of all deaths in the UK), making it the biggest killer, ahead of respiratory diseases at 80,000 (14%), and coronary heart disease at 74,000 (13%). UK life expectancy, 2008–10: males, 78.2 years; females, 82.3. The World Health Organization's *World Health Statistics 2014* put the UK in joint 19th place in a 'healthy life expectancy' list, with an expected 71 years of healthy life for babies born in 2012. Annual population growth rate, 2001–10, 0.6%. In 2011, 16.8% of the total population was over 65, up from 14.2% in 1971. In 2014 there were 6,122 suicides (4,652 of whom were men), giving a suicide rate of 10.8 per 100,000 population. Infant mortality, 2014, 3.9 per 1,000 live births. Fertility rate, 2014, 1.8 births per woman. Of the 776,352 live births in the UK in 2014, 47.6% were to unmarried women, up from 6% in 1961 and 20% in 1986. In 1999 for the first time there were more births to women in the 30–34 age group in the UK than in the 25–29 bracket. 63% of dependent children lived in married couple families in the UK in 2010 and 23% in single-parent families.

Telecommunications

In 2015 there were four main mobile networks—EE, O2, Vodafone and Three. BT (then British Telecom) was established in 1981 to take over the management of telecommunications from the Post Office. In 1984 it was privatized as British Telecommunications plc, changing its trading name from British Telecom to BT in 1991. For many years it was the only fixed line provider, but there are now a large number of other providers with increased choice for consumers and a wide range of packages and deals. In 2013 there were 82.7 m. mobile telephone subscriptions in the UK, up from 43.5 m. in 2000 and 1.1 m. in 1990. 15% of people lived in a mobile-only household in 2013. In 2012 each mobile subscriber sent on average 153 text messages per month. However, the volume of mobile originated calls fell by 1% year-on-year to 122 bn. minutes.

Territory and Population

The land area of the United Kingdom in 2011 was 242,509 km². Census population, 2011, 63,182,178 (32,154,035 females); density, 261 per km². England had a population of 53,012,456 in 2011, Scotland 5,295,403, Wales 3,063,456 and Northern Ireland 1,810,863. 79.8% of the population lived in urban areas in 2011. London had a 2011 population of 8,174,000. In 2011, 17.6% of the population of the UK were under the age of 15, 66.0% between 15 and 64 and 16.4% aged 65 and over. In 1911 only 5.3% of the population had been 65 and over. Total international migration estimates for 2014 were: immigration, 632,000 (551,000 non-British); emigration, 320,000 (182,000 non-British). The number of immigrants into the UK in 2014, at 632,000, was the highest on record for a calendar year. 2008 saw the record number of emigrants from the UK, at 427,000.

Tourism

In 2010 UK residents made 119.4 m. trips within the UK, passing 373.3 m. nights in accommodation and spending 20,835 m. Of these, 78.7 m. were holidaymakers. Visits from foreign tourists to the UK totalled 29.8 m. in 2010 (down from a record 32.8 m. in 2007). Spending was 16.9 bn. in 2010. In 2010 the UK ranked sixth for international tourism arrivals behind the USA, Spain, France, Italy and China. The main countries of origin for foreign visitors in 2010 were: France (3.6 m.), Germany (3.0 m.), USA (2.7 m.), Ireland (2.6 m.) and Spain (1.8 m.).

United States of America

Factsheet

Capital: Washington, D.C.
Population estimate, 2015: 321.77 m.
GNI per capita, 2014: (PPP$) 52,947
HDI/world rank, 2014: 0.915/8
Internet domain extension: .us

Civil Aviation

The busiest airport in 2011 was Atlanta (Hartsfield–Jackson), which handled 92,389,023 passengers. There were 23 airports with more than 10 m. enplanements in 2013. The leading airports in 2010 on the basis of aircraft departures completed were Atlanta Hartsfield–Jackson (465,000); Chicago O'Hare (426,600); Dallas/Fort Worth (315,100). In 2011 Delta Air Lines carried the most scheduled passengers of any airline in the world with 163,838,000, ahead of United Airlines, with 141,799,000, and the low-cost carrier Southwest Airlines, with 135,274,000. Delta Airlines carried the most international passengers of any US carrier in 2010, with 21,029,000 (ranking it eighth in the world for international passengers carried). In 2015 US flag carriers in scheduled service enplaned 798.4 m. revenue passengers.

Climate

Pacific Coast: the climate varies with latitude, distance from the sea and the effect of relief, ranging from polar conditions in North Alaska through cool to warm temperate climates further south. *Mountain States:* varied, with relief exerting the main control; very cold in the north in winter, with considerable snowfall. In the south, much higher temperatures and aridity produce desert conditions. *High Plains:* continental climate with a large annual range of temperature and moderate rainfall, mainly in summer, although unreliable. *Central Plains:* temperate continental climate, with hot summers and cold winters, except in the extreme south. Rainfall is plentiful and comes at all seasons, but there is a summer maximum in western parts. *Mid-West:* continental, with hot summers and cold winters. *Great Lakes:* continental, resembling that of the Central Plains, with hot summers but very cold winters because of the freezing of the lakes. *Appalachian Mountains:* the north is cool temperate with cold winters, the south warm temperate with milder winters. Precipitation is heavy, increasing to the south but evenly distributed over the year. *Gulf Coast:* conditions vary from warm temperate to subtropical, with plentiful rainfall, decreasing towards the west but evenly distributed over the year. *Atlantic Coast:* temperate maritime climate but with great differences in temperature according to latitude. Rainfall is ample at all seasons; snowfall in the north can be heavy. *New England:* cool temperate, with severe winters and warm summers. Precipitation is well distributed with a slight winter maximum. Snowfall is heavy in winter.

Constitution and Government

The form of government of the USA is based on the constitution adopted on 17 Sept. 1787 and effective from 4 March 1789. By the constitution the government of the nation is composed of three co-ordinate branches, the executive, the legislative and the judicial. The executive power is vested in a president (currently Donald Trump, b. 1946 and assumed office in Jan. 2017), who holds office for 4 years, and is elected, together with a vice-president chosen for the same term, by electors from each state, equal to the whole number of Senators and Representatives to which the state may be entitled in the Congress. The President must be a natural-born citizen, resident in the country for 14 years, and at least 35 years old. The presidential election is held every fourth (leap) year on the Tuesday after the first Monday in Nov. The legislative power is vested by the Constitution in a Congress, consisting of a Senate and House of Representatives. The 5th article of the constitution provides that Congress may, on a two-thirds vote of both houses, propose amendments to the constitution, or, on the application of the legislatures of two-thirds of all the states, call a convention for proposing amendments, which in either case shall be valid as part of the constitution when ratified by the legislatures of three-fourths of the several states, or by conventions in three-fourths thereof, whichever mode of ratification may be proposed by Congress. Ten amendments (called collectively 'the Bill of Rights') to the constitution were added 15 Dec. 1791. The most recent amendment, the 27th, dates from 7 May 1992 and provides that no law varying the compensation of Senators or Representatives shall take effect until an election has taken place.

Currency

The unit of currency is the *dollar* (USD) of 100 *cents*.

Defence

Defence expenditure in 2012 totalled $655,388 m. ($2,088 per capita). Defence spending in 2012 represented 4.2% of GDP (down from 37.8% in 1944, 14.2% in 1953, 9.4% in 1968 and 6.2% of GDP in 1986 although up from the post-war low of 3.0% in 1999). Although conscription is not currently in force the Military Selective Service Act requires all males between the ages of 18 and 26 to register for compulsory military service should the need arise. Active duty military personnel in Sept. 2011 numbered 1,468,364, of which 214,098 were women. The USA is the world's largest exporter of arms, with 31.1% of the global major weapons total over the period 2010–14. The USA's last nuclear test was in 1993. In May 2010 the Obama administration announced that the USA had a total of 5,113 active nuclear warheads, down from a peak of 31,225 in 1967. The number of strategic nuclear warheads (intercontinental ballistic missiles, submarine-launched ballistic missiles and bombers) in Jan. 2015 was approximately 1,900. There were also about 180 non-strategic warheads in Jan. 2015, making a total of around 2,080 deployed warheads. Estimates of the number of firearms in the country are around 310 m., equivalent to 99 firearms for every 100 people, making the USA the world's most heavily armed country.

Economy

Services accounted for 79% of GDP in 2011, industry 20% and agriculture 1%. *Per capita* personal income in 2014 was $46,049, more than double the 1994 total of US$22,538.

Labour

According to the Bureau of Labor Statistics there were 157.1 m. people in the civilian labour force in 2015 (83.6 m. men and 73.5 m. women). There were 26.3 m. foreign-born persons in the labour force in 2015, representing 16.7% of the total. The unemployment rate was 4.9% in Jan. 2016 (its lowest since Feb. 2008), down from 8.0% in Jan. 2013 and 9.8% in Jan. 2010. The USA had 60,000 people living in slavery according to the Walk Free Foundation's 2013 *Global Slavery Index*.

Press

In 2014 there were 1,355 daily newspapers with a combined daily circulation of 42.7 m., the fourth highest in the world behind India, China and Japan. There were 953 morning papers and 402 evening papers, plus 923 Sunday papers (circulation, 42.8 m.). Unlike China and India, where circulation is rising, in the USA it has fallen since 1985, when daily circulation was 62.8 m. The most widely read newspapers are *USA Today* (average daily circulation in 2014 of 4.1 m.), followed by the *Wall Street Journal* (2.3 m.) and *The New York Times* (2.1 m.). According to research carried out by the Pew Research Centre, in 2008 for the first time more Americans obtained national and international news from the internet than from newspapers. As of Sept. 2014 the USA's three most used online news sites were *The Huffington Post* (68.5 m. unique desktop users per month), CNN (67.7 m.) and *The New York Times* (41.6 m.). In the 2013 *World Press Freedom Index* compiled by Reporters Without Borders, the USA was ranked 32nd out of 179 countries. The number of books published in 2010 reached a record high of 3,092,740 (up from 561,580 in 2008), largely as a result of 2,776,260 self-published

books and print-on-demand works being produced that year. US publishers' net sales revenue rose from $26.5 bn. in 2008 to $27.1 bn. in 2009 and $27.9 bn. in 2010.

Rail

Freight service is provided by nine major independent railroad companies and several hundred smaller operators. In 2013 the operational Amtrak rail system measured 21,356 miles. Outside the major conurbations, there are almost no regular passenger services other than those of Amtrak, which carried 30.8 m. passengers in fiscal year 2013.

Religion

The leading religious bodies according to the *2010 U.S. Religion Census: Religious Congregations & Membership Study* and based on the number of adherents are (in 1,000): Catholic Church, 58,964; Southern Baptist Convention, 19,896; United Methodist Church, 9,861; Church of Jesus Christ of Latter-day Saints, 6,145; Evangelical Lutheran Church in America, 4,181; Assemblies of God, 2,945; Muslims, 2,600 (estimate); Presbyterian Church (USA), 2,452; Jews, 2,257 (estimate); Churches of Christ, 1,584. Based on the number of congregations the largest is the Southern Baptist Convention, with 50,816 in 2010.

Roads

On 31 Dec. 2012 the total public road mileage was 4,092,730 miles (urban, 1,113,018; rural, 2,979,711). Urban roads in 2012 included 16,910 miles of interstate highways, 11,469 miles of other freeways and expressways, and 791,832 miles of local roads. Rural roads in 2012 included 30,522 miles of interstate highways, 4,395 miles of other freeways and expressways, and 2,036,976 miles of local roads. State highway funds were $143,797 m. in 2009. Motor vehicles registered in 2012: 245,184,447, of which 111,289,906 automobiles, 764,509 buses and 133,130,032 trucks. There were 211,814,830 licensed drivers in 2012 and 8,429,988 motorcycle registrations. The average distance travelled by a motor vehicle in 2012 was 11,705 miles. There were 33,883 fatalities in road accidents in 2009 and 32,885 in 2010 (the lowest total since 1949).

Shipping

At the end of 2007 the cargo-carrying US-owned fleet comprised 40,250 vessels, of which 39,695 were US-flag vessels. There were 38,936 US-flag tugs and barges for domestic coastwise, Great Lakes and inland waterway trade, 523 US-flag offshore supply vessels (which service offshore oil exploration and production) and 236 US-flag ocean and Great Lakes self-propelled vessels (10,000 DWT or greater) for US coastwise and international trade (of which 55 tankers, 76 containerships, 37 roll-on/roll-off carriers, 61 dry bulk carriers and seven general cargo carriers). The busiest port is South Louisiana, which handled 212,581,000 tons of cargo in 2009.

Social Statistics

Live births in 2014 totalled 3,988,076 (a rate of 12.5 per 1,000 population) and deaths 2,626,418 (8.2 per 1,000). Population growth rate, 2003–13, 0.9%. Marriages in 2012 totalled 2,131,000. In 2011 the median age at first marriage was 29 for males and 26 for females. In 2014, 7% of Black men were married to a White woman and 4% of Black women were married to a White man. The number of births to unmarried women in 2009 was 1,693,658 (41% of all births), compared to 666,000 in 1980 and 1,726,566 in 2008. The rate of births to teenagers was 29.4 per 1,000 women in 2012 (the lowest in record). The number of babies born to women aged 15–19 was 305,420 in 2012, down from 409,802 in 2009 and the fewest reported since the end of the Second World War. In 2009, 27.3% of children lived in one-parent households—the highest proportion in the industrialized world. Infant mortality rates, per 1,000 live births: 29.2 in 1950; 12.9 in 1980; 6.0 in 2013. Fertility rate, 2013, 1.9 births per woman (the lowest since the late 1980s). There were a reported 1,058,000 abortions in 2011, down from a peak in 1990 of 1,608,600. Expectation of life, 1970: males, 67.1 years; females, 74.7 years. 2014: males, 76.4 years; females, 81.2 years.

Telecommunications

In 2012 there were 138.6 m. main telephone lines in operation (436.5 per 1,000 inhabitants), down from 182.9 m. in 2003. There were 304.8 m. cellphone subscriptions in 2012 (960.1 per 1,000 persons), up from

160.6 m. in 2003. The leading cellphone operators are Verizon Wireless (with more than 115 m. subscribers), AT&T Mobility, Sprint Nextel and T-Mobile. In 2013 an estimated 84.2% of the population were internet users. 75.6% of households had a computer in 2011, with 71.7% of households having internet access at home. In 2014 e-commerce amounted to $304.9 bn. In 2012 there were 89.8 wireless broadband subscriptions per 100 inhabitants and only 28.4 fixed broadband subscriptions per 100. In Dec. 2011 there were 157.4 m. Facebook users (about three times as many as any other country and 50% the total population of the USA).

Territory and Population

The United States is bounded in the north by Canada, east by the North Atlantic, south by the Gulf of Mexico and Mexico, and west by the North Pacific Ocean. The area of the 50 states of the USA plus the District of Columbia is 3,796,742 sq. miles (9,833,517 km^2), of which 3,531,905 sq. miles (9,147,593 km^2) are land and 264,837 sq. miles (685,924 km^2) are water (comprising Great Lakes, inland and coastal water). The 2010 census population of 308,745,538 represented an increase of 9.7% since 2000 (the smallest percentage increase between 10-yearly US censuses since the Second World War). Minorities accounted for 92% of the growth. There were 156,964,212 females at the 2010 census, or 50.8% of the total population. 2010 density, 33.8 per km^2 (87.4 per sq. mile). Urban population (persons living in places with at least 2,500 inhabitants) at the 2010 census was 249,253,271 (80.7%); rural, 59,492,267. New York is the USA's largest city, with a 2010 census population of 8,175,133, ahead of Los Angeles (3,792,621), Chicago (2,965,598), Houston (2,099,451) and Philadelphia (1,526,006). The total number of immigrants admitted from 1820 to 2012 was 78,493,018. The number of immigrants admitted for legal permanent residence in the United States in fiscal year 2012 was 1,031,631.

Tourism

In 2013 the USA received 69,995,000 foreign visitors (66,657,000 in 2012), of whom 23,407,000 were from Canada and 14,547,000 from Mexico. 18% of all tourists were from Europe. Only France received more tourists than the USA in 2013. In 2013 visitors to the USA spent $172.9 bn., giving the USA by far the highest annual revenue from tourists of any country (Spain, which received the second most, had $62.6 bn.). Expenditure by US travellers in foreign countries for 2013 was $104.1 bn., second only to spending by German travellers in foreign countries.

Uruguay

República Oriental del Uruguay (Oriental Republic of Uruguay)

Factsheet

Capital: Montevideo
Population estimate, 2015: 3.43 m.
GNI per capita, 2014: (PPP$) 19,283
HDI/world rank, 2014: 0.793/52=
Internet domain extension: .uy

Civil Aviation

The largest international airport is at Montevideo (Carrasco). There were direct international services in 2010 to Asunción, Barcelona, Buenos Aires, Córdoba (Argentina), Curitiba, Florianópolis, Iguazu Falls, Lima, Madrid, Miami, Panama City, Porto Alegre, Rio de Janeiro, San Salvador, Santiago and São Paulo. Since the demise of Pluna the largest Uruguayan airline is now BQB Líneas Aéreas. There were 11 international airports in 2014. Nine had paved runways, one was semi-paved and one unpaved. In 2010 airports in Uruguay handled 2,195,336 passengers, of which 2,011,601 were at Carrasco. 26,832 tonnes of freight passed through Carrasco in 2010. In 2012 scheduled airline traffic of Uruguayan-based carriers flew 34.5 m. km; passenger-km totalled 1.5 bn. in the same year.

Climate

A warm temperate climate, with mild winters and warm summers. The wettest months are March to June, but there is really no dry season. Montevideo, Jan. 72 °F (22.2 °C), July 50 °F (10 °C). Annual rainfall 38″ (950 mm).

Constitution and Government

The Constitution was adopted on 27 Nov. 1966 and became effective in Feb. 1967; it has been amended in 1989, 1994, 1996 and 2004. Congress consists of a *Senate* of 31 members and a *Chamber of Deputies* of 99 members, both elected by proportional representation for 5-year terms although in the case of the Senate only 30 members are elected with one seat reserved for the Vice-President. The electoral system provides that the successful presidential candidate be a member of the party which gains a parliamentary majority. Electors vote for deputies on a first-past-the-post system, and simultaneously vote for a presidential candidate of the same party. The winners of the second vote are credited with the number of votes obtained by their party in the parliamentary elections. Referendums may be called at the instigation of 10,000 signatories. Voting is compulsory.

Currency

The unit of currency is the *Uruguayan peso* (UYU), of 100 *centésimos*, which replaced the *nuevo peso* in March 1993 at 1 Uruguayan peso = 1,000 nuevos pesos.

Defence

Defence expenditure totalled US$445 m. in 2013 (US$134 per capita), representing 0.9% of GDP.

Economy

Finance and real estate contributed 18.7% to GDP in 2010; followed by trade and hotels, 14.4%; manufacturing, 13.1%; services, 10.7%.

Labour

In 1996 the retirement age was raised from 55 to 60 for women; it remains 60 for men. The labour force in 2005 totalled 1,269,300 (54% males). In 2001, 22.4% of the urban workforce was engaged in wholesale and retail trade/repair of motor vehicles, motorcycles and personal and household goods/hotels and restaurants; 15.5% in manufacturing/electricity, gas and water supply; 9.2% in private households with employed persons; and 9.1% in financial intermediation and real estate, renting and business activities. In 2001 the unemployment rate in urban areas was 15.3%.

Press

In 2008 there were 34 paid-for dailies with an average circulation of 145,000. The newspaper with the highest circulation is *El País*, which sold a daily average of 46,000 copies in 2008.

Rail

The total railway system open for traffic in 2005 was 1,508 km of 1,435 mm gauge. Passenger services, which had been abandoned in 1988, were resumed on a limited basis in 1993. In 2007 the railways carried 600,000 passengers and 1.4 m. tonnes of freight.

Religion

State and Church are separate, and there is complete religious liberty. According to estimates by the Pew Research Center's Forum on Religion & Public Life, in 2010 the population was 57.9% Christian (mainly Catholics) with 40.7% not having any religious affiliation. In Feb. 2016 there was one cardinal.

Roads

Uruguay has more than 75,000 km of roads, including 8,776 km of national roads in 2016. Passenger cars in 2007 numbered 553,200 (151 per 1,000 inhabitants in 2005). There were 150 fatalities as a result of road accidents in 2005.

Shipping

In Jan. 2009 there were 25 ships of 300 GT or over registered, totalling 53,000 GT. In 2004 vessels totalling 5,067,000 NRT entered ports and vessels totalling 22,262,000 NRT cleared.

Social Statistics

2009: births, 47,152; deaths, 32,179. Rates (per 1,000 population), 2009: birth, 14.1; death, 9.6. Annual population growth rate, 2005–10, 0.3%. Infant mortality, 2010 (per 1,000 live births), 9. Life expectancy in 2013 was 73.7 years among males and 80.6 years among females. Fertility rate, 2008, 2.1 births per woman. Uruguay legalized same-sex marriage in Aug. 2013. In Oct. 2012 it became the second Latin American country (after Cuba) to legalize abortion for all women.

Telecommunications

There were 5,268,000 mobile phone subscriptions in 2013 (1,546.2 per 1,000 inhabitants) and 1,048,000 fixed telephone lines in the same year. In 2013 Uruguay had 720,000 fixed broadband internet subscriptions and 1,552,000 mobile broadband subscriptions. In March 2012 there were 1.5 m. Facebook users.

Territory and Population

Uruguay is bounded on the northeast by Brazil, on the southeast by the Atlantic, on the south by the Río de la Plata and on the west by Argentina. The area is 176,215 km² (68,037 sq. miles), including 1,199 km² (463 sq. miles) of inland waters. The total population at the 2011 census was 3,286,314; density, 18.8 per km². In 2011 Montevideo (the capital) accounted for 39.7% of the total population. It had a population in 2011 of 1,304,687. Other major cities are Salto (population of 104,011 in 2011) and Ciudad de la Costa (95,176 in 2011). 92.6% of the population lived in urban areas in 2011. 13% of the population are over 65; 24% are under 15; 63% are between 15 and 64. The official language is Spanish.

Tourism

There were 2,857,000 international tourist arrivals—excluding same-day visitors—in 2011 (2,349,000 in 2010). Receipts from tourism in 2011 totalled US$2,203 m.

Uzbekistan

Uzbekiston Respublikasy (Republic of Uzbekistan)

Factsheet
Capital: Tashkent
Population estimate, 2015: 29.89 m.
GNI per capita, 2014: (PPP$) 5,567
HDI/world rank, 2014: 0.675/114
Internet domain extension: .uz

Civil Aviation

The main international airport is in Tashkent (Vostochny). The national carrier is the state-owned Uzbekistan Airways. In 2012 scheduled airline traffic of Uzbekistan-based carriers flew 44.0 m. km; passenger-km totalled 6.3 bn. in the same year. In 2009 Tashkent handled 1,940,985 passengers and 35,791 tonnes of freight.

Climate

The summers are warm to hot but the heat is made more bearable by the low humidity. The winters are cold but generally dry and sunny. Tashkent, Jan. −1 °C, July 25 °C. Annual rainfall 14.8″ (375 mm).

Constitution and Government

A new constitution was adopted on 8 Dec. 1992 stating that Uzbekistan is a pluralist democracy. The constitution restricts the president to standing for two 5 year terms. In Jan. 2002 a referendum was held at which 91% of the electorate voted in favour of extending the presidential term from five to 7 years. Voters were also in favour of changing from a single-chamber legislature to a bicameral parliament. Based on the constitution President Karimov's term of office that started in Jan. 2000 ended in Jan. 2007, but according to election law a vote must be held in Dec. of the year in which the president's term expires. Pro-Karimov legislators maintained that he was eligible to stand again in the Dec. 2007 elections as he had only served one 7 year term despite having been president since 1990. Uzbekistan switched to a bicameral legislature in Jan. 2005 with the establishment of the 100-member *Senate* (with 16 members appointed by the president and 84 elected from the ranks of regional, district and city legislative councils). The lower house is the 150-member *Oliy Majlis* (Supreme Assembly). 135 seats are elected by popular vote for 5 year terms and 15 are reserved for the Ecological Movement.

Currency

A coupon for a new unit of currency, the *soum* (UZS), was introduced alongside the rouble on 15 Nov. 1993. This was replaced by the *soum* proper at 1 soum = 1,000 coupons on 1 July 1994.

Defence

Conscription is for 12 months. Defence expenditure in 2010 totalled US$1,422 m. (US$51 per capita), representing 3.7% of GDP.

Economy

Agriculture accounted for 19.5% of GDP in 2010, industry 35.4% and services 45.1%.

Labour

In 2013 there were 12.52 m. employed persons of whom 81% worked in the non-state sector. Agriculture accounted for 34% of total employment in 2010. The unemployment rate was 4.9% in 2013. Average monthly salary in 2004 was 53,201 soums. A minimum wage of 6,530 soums a month was imposed on 1 Aug. 2004. Uzbekistan had 0.17 m. people living in slavery according to the Walk Free Foundation's 2013 *Global Slavery Index*.

Press

In 2008 there were four paid-for daily newspapers with a combined circulation of 30,000.

Rail

The total length of railway in 2011 was 4,258 km of 1,520 mm gauge (727 km electrified). In 2011, 16.0 m. passengers and 80.9 m. tonnes of freight were carried. There is a metro in Tashkent.

Religion

In 2010 an estimated 96.7% of the population were Muslims (mainly Sunnis) according to the Pew Research Center's Forum on Religion & Public Life, with 2.3% Christians.

Roads

Length of roads, 2005, was 84,400 km (85% paved).

Social Statistics

2009 births, 649,700; deaths, 130,700; marriages, 227,600; divorces, 17,200. Rates, 2009: birth (per 1,000 population), 23.3; death, 4.7; marriage, 10.0; divorce, 0.6. Life expectancy, 2013, 65.0 years for men and 71.7 for women. Annual population growth rate, 1998–2008, 1.2%. Infant mortality, 2010, 44 per 1,000 live births; fertility rate, 2008, 2.3 births per woman.

Telecommunications

In 2012 there were 1,980,000 main (fixed) telephone lines; mobile phone subscriptions numbered 20,274,000 in the same year (710.3 per 1,000 persons). In 2013 an estimated 38.2% of the population were internet users. In March 2012 there were 129,000 Facebook users.

Territory and Population

Uzbekistan is bordered in the north by Kazakhstan, in the east by Kyrgyzstan and Tajikistan, in the south by Afghanistan and in the west by Turkmenistan. Area, 447,400 km^2 (172,700 sq. miles), including 22,000 km^2 (8,500 sq. miles) of inland water. A census has not been held since 1989, when the population was 19,810,077. A 'mini-census' based on 10% of the population was conducted in April 2011 but there are no future plans for a full census. Estimate, Jan. 2014, 30,493,000; density, 72 per km^2. The vast majority of the population are Uzbeks, with small Tajik, Kazakh, Tatar and Russian minorities. In 2008, 63.3% of the population lived in rural areas. The capital is Tashkent (2009 population estimate, 2,220,700); other large towns are Namangan, Samarkand, Andizhan, Nukus, Bukhara, Karshi, Kokand, Ferghana, Margilan, Chirchik and Urgench. The Roman alphabet (in use 1929–40) was reintroduced in 1994. Arabic script was in use prior to 1929, and Cyrillic from 1940–94. The official language is Uzbek. Russian and Tajik are also spoken.

Tourism

There were 975,000 non-resident tourist arrivals in 2010 (1,215,000 in 2009), excluding same-day visitors.

Vanuatu

Ripablik blong Vanuatu (Republic of Vanuatu)

Factsheet

Capital: Port Vila
Population estimate, 2015: 265,000
GNI per capita, 2014: (PPP$) 2,803
HDI/world rank, 2014: 0.594/134=
Internet domain extension: .vu

Civil Aviation

There is an international airport at Bauerfield Port Vila. In 2010 the state-owned Air Vanuatu flew to Auckland, Brisbane, Honiara, Nadi, Nouméa and Sydney as well as providing services between different parts of Vanuatu. In 2012 scheduled airline traffic of Vanuatu-based carriers flew 20.6 m. km; passenger-km totalled 863.8 m. in the same year.

Climate

The climate is tropical, but moderated by oceanic influences and by trade winds from May to Oct. High humidity occasionally occurs and cyclones are possible. Rainfall ranges from 90″ (2,250 mm) in the south to 155″ (3,875 mm) in the north. Vila, Jan. 80 °F (26.7 °C), July 72 °F (22.2 °C). Annual rainfall 84″ (2,103 mm).

Constitution and Government

Legislative power resides in a 52-member unicameral Parliament elected for a term of 4 years. The *President* is elected for a 5 year term by an electoral college comprising Parliament and the presidents of the 11 regional councils. Executive power is vested in a Council of Ministers, responsible to Parliament, and appointed and led by a Prime Minister who is elected from and by Parliament. There is also a *Council of Chiefs,* comprising traditional tribal leaders, to advise on matters of custom.

Currency

The unit of currency is the *vatu* (VUV) with no minor unit.

Defence

Vanuatu does not have an army but there is a Vanuatu Police Force and a paramilitary Vanuatu Mobile Force.

Economy

In 2011 agriculture accounted for 25.2% of GDP, industry 10.7% and services 64.1%.

Press

In 2008 there was one daily newspaper (the *Vanuatu Daily Post*) with a circulation of 3,000.

Religion

In 2010 an estimated 93.3% of the population were Christians (mainly Protestants) and 4.1% folk religionists according to the Pew Research Center's Forum on Religion & Public Life.

Roads

There are approximately 1,100 km of largely unpaved roads, mostly on Efate Island and Espiritu Santo. There were around 15,500 vehicles in use in 2008.

Shipping

In Jan. 2009 there were 57 ships of 300 GT or over registered, totalling 1.41 m. GT. Vanuatu is a 'flag of convenience' country. The chief ports are Port Vila and Santo.

Social Statistics

2008 estimates: births, 7,100; deaths, 1,200. Rates, 2008 estimates (per 1,000 population): births, 30.2; deaths, 5.0. Annual population growth rate, 2000–08, 2.6%. Life expectancy, 2013, was 69.7 years for males and 73.8 years for females. Infant mortality, 2010, 12 per 1,000 live births; fertility rate, 2008, 4.0 births per woman.

Telecommunications

In 2012 there were 4,800 main (fixed) telephone lines; active mobile phone subscriptions numbered 146,000 in the same year (590.8 per 1,000 persons). In 2013 an estimated 11.3% of the population were internet users.

Territory and Population

Vanuatu comprises 83 islands (65 of which are inhabited), which lie roughly 800 km west of the Fiji Islands and 400 km northeast of New Caledonia. The estimated land area is 12,190 km^2 (4,706 sq. miles). The larger islands of the group are: (Espiritu) Santo, Malekula, Epi, Pentecost, Aoba, Maewo, Paama, Ambrym, Efate, Erromanga, Tanna and Aneityum. They also claim Matthew and Hunter islands. Population at the 2009 census, 234,023 giving a density of 19.2 per km^2. In 2009, 75.6% of the population lived in rural areas. Port Vila (the capital) had a 2009 census population of 44,040 and Luganville 13,167. 39% of the population is under 15 years of age, 55% between the ages of 15 and 59 and 6% 60 or over. The national language is Bislama (spoken by 57% of the population); English and French are also official languages; about 30,000 speak French.

Tourism

In 2011 there were a record 248,898 non-resident visitor arrivals (154,938 by cruise ship and 93,960 by air), up from 237,648 in 2010 and 225,452 in 2009.

Vatican City State

Stato della Citt del Vaticano

Factsheet
Population estimate, 2011: 800
Internet domain extension: .va

Civil Aviation

The Vatican launched a charter airline, Mistral Air, in Aug. 2007 to fly pilgrims to holy sites across the world.

Constitution and Government

Vatican City State is governed by a Commission appointed by the Pope. The reason for its existence is to provide an extra-territorial, independent base for the Holy See, the government of the Roman Catholic Church. The Pope (currently Pope Francis, b. 1936 and elected 13 March 2013) exercises sovereignty and has absolute legislative, executive and judicial powers. The judicial power is delegated to a tribunal in the first instance, to the Sacred Roman Rota in appeal and to the Supreme Tribunal of the Signature in final appeal. A new Fundamental Law was promulgated by Pope John Paul II on 26 Nov. 2000 and became effective on 22 Feb. 2001; this replaced the first Fundamental Law of 1929. The Pope is elected by the College of Cardinals, meeting in secret conclave. The election is by scrutiny and requires a two-thirds majority.

Currency

Since 1 Jan. 2002 the Vatican City has been using the euro (EUR). Italy has agreed that the Vatican City may mint a small part of the total Italian euro coin contingent with their own motifs.

Press

In 2008 there was one daily evening paper, *L'Osservatore Romano*.

Religion

As the Vicar of Christ and the Successor of St Peter, the Pope is held to be by divine right the centre of all Catholic unity and exercises universal governance over the Church. He is also the sovereign ruler of Vatican City State. He has for advisers the Sacred College of Cardinals, consisting in March 2016 of 215 cardinals from 72 countries (one created by Pope Paul VI, 96 created by Pope John Paul II, 79 created by Pope Benedict XVI and 39 created by Pope Francis), of whom 116 are cardinal electors—those under the age of 80 who may enter into conclave to elect a new Pope. Cardinals, addressed by the title of 'Eminence', are appointed by the Pope from senior ecclesiastics who are either the bishops of important Sees or the heads of departments at the Roman Curia. In addition to the College of Cardinals, there is a Synod of Bishops, created by Pope Paul VI and formally instituted on 15 Sept. 1965. This consists of the Patriarchs and certain Metropolitans of the Catholic Church of Oriental Rite, of elected representatives of the national episcopal conferences and religious orders of the world, of the cardinals in charge of the Roman Congregations and of other persons nominated by the Pope. The Synod meets in both general (global) and special (regional) assemblies.

Territory and Population

The area of the Vatican City is 44 ha. or 0.44 km^2 (108.7 acres or 0.17 sq. miles), making it the smallest independent country in the world. It includes the Piazza di San Pietro (St Peter's Square), which is to remain normally open to the public and subject to the powers of the Italian police. Vatican City had about 800 inhabitants in 2011. It has its own railway station (for freight only), postal facilities, coins and radio. Twelve buildings in and outside Rome enjoy extra-territorial rights, including the Basilicas of St John Lateran, St Mary Major and St Paul without the Walls, the Pope's summer villa at Castel Gandolfo and a further Vatican radio station on Italian soil. *Radio Vaticana* broadcasts an extensive service in 40 languages from the transmitters in Vatican City and in Italy. The Holy See and the Vatican are not synonymous—the Holy See, referring to the primacy of the Pope, is located in Vatican City. The *de facto* official language is Latin.

Venezuela

República Bolivariana de Venezuela (Bolivarian Republic of Venezuela)

Factsheet
Capital: Caracas
Population estimate, 2015: 31.11 m.
GNI per capita, 2014: (PPP$) 16,159
HDI/world rank, 2014: 0.762/71
Internet domain extension: .ve

Civil Aviation

The main international airport is at Caracas (Simon Bolívar), with some international flights from Maracaibo. The national carrier is Conviasa, founded in 2004 as the successor to Viasa, which had ceased operations in 1997. In 2005 scheduled airline traffic of Venezuela-based carriers flew 31.0 m. km, carrying 3,240,200 passengers.

Climate

The climate ranges from warm temperate to tropical. Temperatures vary little throughout the year and rainfall is plentiful. The dry season is from Dec. to April. The hottest months are July and Aug. Caracas, Jan. 65 °F (18.3 °C), July 69 °F (20.6 °C). Annual rainfall 32″ (833 mm). Ciudad Bolívar, Jan. 79 °F (26.1 °C), July 81 °F (27.2 °C). Annual rainfall 41″ (1,016 mm). Maracaibo, Jan. 81 °F (27.2 °C), July 85 °F (29.4 °C). Annual rainfall 23″ (577 mm).

Constitution and Government

The present constitution was approved in a referendum held on 15 Dec. 1999. Venezuela is a federal republic, comprising 23 states and one federal district, plus 235 islands and 75 islets and cays that constitute the federal dependencies. Executive power is vested in the *President*. The ministers, who together constitute the Council of Ministers, are appointed by the President and head various executive departments. 92% of votes cast in a referendum (the first in Venezuela's history) on 25 April 1999 were in favour of the plan to rewrite the constitution proposed by then President Hugo Chávez. As a result, on 25 July the public was to elect a constitutional assembly to write a new constitution, which was subsequently to be voted on in a national referendum. In Aug. 1999 the constitutional assembly declared a national state of emergency. It subsequently suspended the Supreme Court, turned the elected Congress into little more than a sub-committee, stripping it of all its powers, and assumed many of the responsibilities of government. In Dec. 1999 Chávez's plan to redraft the constitution was approved by over 70% of voters in a referendum. Consequently presidents were able to serve two consecutive 6 year-terms instead of terms of 5 years which could not be consecutive, the senate was abolished and greater powers were given to the state and the armed forces. Chávez effectively took over both the executive and the judiciary. In Aug. 2007 Chávez presented a set of constitutional reforms, including an end to presidential term limits. The proposals were rejected in a national referendum held on 2 Dec. 2007, with 49% of votes cast in favour of the amendments to the constitution and 51% against. However, a referendum on 15 Feb. 2009 to abolish presidential term limits (and those of various other elected officials including National Assembly deputies) was approved with 54% of votes cast in favour and 46% against. Since the senate was dissolved under the constitution adopted in Dec. 1999 Venezuela has become a unicameral legislature, the 165-seat *National Assembly*, with members being elected for 5 year terms.

Currency

The unit of currency is the *bolívar fuerte* (VEF) of 100 *céntimos*. It was introduced on 1 Jan. 2008, replacing the *bolívar* (VEB) at a rate of one bolívar fuerte = 1,000 bolívares.

Defence

There is a 30 month conscript service obligation. Defence expenditure totalled US$5,240 m. in 2013 (US$184 per capita), representing 1.5% of GDP.

Economy

In 2010 industry accounted for 52% of GDP, services 42% and agriculture 6%.

Labour

The labour force in 2013 was 14,050,000 (11,877,000 in 2003). 68.8% of the population aged 15–64 was economically active in 2013. In the same year 7.5% of the population was unemployed. Venezuela had 80,000 people living in slavery according to the Walk Free Foundation's 2013 *Global Slavery Index*.

Press

In 2008 there were 108 daily newspapers (106 paid-for and two free) with a circulation of 2.53 m.

Rail

The railway network comprises 742 km of 1,435 gauge track. Freight tonne-km in 2007 came to 81 m. In 2006 Venezuela's first inter-city passenger service in nearly 70 years was opened with the inauguration of a line from Caracas to Cúa. Several other new lines are planned or currently under construction. There are metros in Caracas, Los Teques, Maracaibo and Valencia.

Religion

In 2010 there were an estimated 22.50 m. Catholics and 2.92 m. Protestants according to the Pew Research Center's Forum on Religion & Public Life, with 2.90 m. people having no religious affiliation. The Roman Catholic Church has nine ecclesiastical provinces, each headed by an archbishop. There was one cardinal in Feb. 2016.

Roads

The road network covers approximately 96,000 km. There were 2,952,100 passenger cars in use in 2007 (107 per 1,000 inhabitants) plus 84,000 lorries and vans. There were 6,218 fatalities as a result of road accidents in 2006.

Shipping

In Jan. 2009 there were 82 ships of 300 GT or over registered, totalling 784,000 GT. La Guaira, Maracaibo, Puerto Cabello, Puerto Ordaz and Guanta are the chief ports. The principal navigable rivers are the Orinoco and its tributaries the Apure and Arauca.

Social Statistics

2008 births, 581,480; deaths, 124,062. 2008 birth rate per 1,000 population, 20.8; death rate, 4.4. Annual population growth rate, 2008–10, 1.6%. Life expectancy, 2013, was 71.7 years for males and 77.7 years for females. Infant mortality, 2010, 16 per 1,000 live births; fertility rate, 2008, 2.5 births per woman. In 2011 the most popular age for marrying was 25–29 for both men and women.

Telecommunications

In 2012 there were 7,649,000 main (fixed) telephone lines; mobile phone subscriptions numbered 30,569,000 in the same year (1,020.5 per 1,000 persons). In 2012, 49.1% of the population were internet users. In June 2012 there were 9.7 m. Facebook users.

Territory and Population

Venezuela is bounded to the north by the Caribbean with a 2,813 km coastline, east by the Atlantic and Guyana, south by Brazil, and southwest and west by Colombia. The area is 916,445 km^2 (353,839 sq. miles) including 72 islands in the Caribbean. Population at the 2011 census was 27,227,930 (13,678,178 females and 13,549,752 males); density, 29.7 per km^2. Venezuela has the highest percentage of urban population in South America, with 93.4% living in urban areas in 2010. The official language is Spanish. English is taught as a mandatory second language in high schools. Caracas, Venezuela's largest city, is the political, financial, commercial, communications and cultural centre of the country. Caracas, Venezuela's largest city, is the political, financial, commercial, communications and cultural centre of the country. Caracas had a population of 1,942,652 in 2011. Maracaibo, the nation's second largest city (2011 population of 1,898,770), is located near Venezuela's most important petroleum fields and richest agricultural areas. Other major cities are Valencia, Barquisimeto and Ciudad Guayana.

Tourism

In 2009 there were 615,000 non-resident tourists (excluding same-day visitors), down from 771,000 in 2007 and 745,000 in 2008. Of the 615,000 tourists in 2009, 340,000 were from elsewhere in the Americas and 241,000 were from Europe.

Vietnam

Cộng Hòa Xã Hội Chu Nghĩa Việt Nam (Socialist Republic of Vietnam)

Factsheet
Capital: Hanoi
Population estimate, 2015: 93.45 m.
GNI per capita, 2014: (PPP$) 5,092
HDI/world rank, 2014: 0.666/116=
Internet domain extension: .vn

Civil Aviation

There are international airports at Hanoi (Noi Bai) and Ho Chi Minh City (Tan Son Nhat) and 13 domestic airports. The national carrier is Vietnam Airlines. In 2005 scheduled airline traffic of Vietnam-based carriers flew 43.7 m. km, carrying 3,762,200 passengers. The busiest airport is Ho Chi Minh City, which in 2012 handled 17,538,353 passengers and had 131,710 aircraft movements. Hanoi handled 11,341,039 passengers and had 84,304 aircraft movements in 2012.

Climate

The humid monsoon climate gives tropical conditions in the south, with a rainy season from May to Oct., and sub-tropical conditions in the north, though real winter conditions can affect the north when polar air blows south over Asia. In general, there is little variation in temperatures over the year. Hanoi, Jan. 62 °F (16.7 °C), July 84 °F (28.9 °C). Annual rainfall 72″ (1,830 mm).

Constitution and Government

The National Assembly unanimously approved a new constitution on 15 April 1992. Under this the Communist Party retains a monopoly of power and the responsibility for guiding the state according to the tenets of Marxism-Leninism and Ho Chi Minh, but with certain curbs on its administrative functions. Vietnam is a one-party republic. The powers of the National Assembly are increased. The 500-member *National Assembly* is elected for 5 year terms. Candidates may be proposed by the Communist Party or the Fatherland Front (which groups various social organizations), or they may propose themselves as individual Independents. The Assembly convenes three times a year and appoints a prime minister and cabinet. It elects the *President*, the head of state. The latter heads a *State Council* which issues decrees when the National Assembly is not in session. The ultimate source of political power is the Communist Party of Vietnam, founded in 1930; it had 3.6 m. members in 2011.

Currency

The unit of currency is the *dong* (VND).

Defence

Conscription is for 18 months (army) or 3 years (air force and navy). For specialists it is also 3 years. In 2013 defence expenditure totalled US$3,800 m. (US$41 per capita), representing 2.4% of GDP.

Economy

Agriculture accounted for 20.6% of GDP in 2010, industry 41.1% and services 38.3%.

Labour

The labour force in 2013 was 53,444,000 (44,284,000 in 2003). 82.2% of the population aged 15–64 was economically active in 2013. In the same year 2.2% of the population was unemployed. Vietnam had 0.25 m. people living in slavery according to the Walk Free Foundation's 2013 *Global Slavery Index*.

Press

In 2008 there were 55 paid-for daily newspapers with a combined circulation of 2.8 m. The Communist Party controls all print media but some criticism of government policy is allowed.

Rail

There were 2,347 km of railways in 2011, mostly metre gauge. Rail links with China were reopened in Feb. 1996. In 2011, 12.0 m. passengers and 7.2 m. tonnes of freight were carried.

Religion

Taoism is the traditional religion but Buddhism is widespread. At the census of 2009 the principal denominations were: Buddhists, 6,802,318; Catholics, 5,677,086; Hoa Hao (a tradition based on Buddhism), 1,433,252; Cao Dai (a synthesis of Christianity, Buddhism and Confucianism), 807,915; Protestants, 734,168; no religion, 70,193,377. In Feb. 2016 there were two cardinals. The Roman Catholic Church has 26 dioceses, including three archdioceses.

Roads

There were 160,089 km of roads in 2007, of which 47.6% were paved. In 2007 there were 1,146,300 passenger cars in use and around 21.78 m. motorcycles and mopeds. There were 13,200 fatalities in road accidents in 2007.

Shipping

In Jan. 2009 there were 918 ships of 300 GT or over registered (including 769 general cargo ships and 76 oil tankers), totalling 2,683,000 GT. The major ports are Hai Phong, Ho Chi Minh City and Da Nang. There are regular services to Hong Kong, Singapore, Thailand, Cambodia and Japan. There are some 19,500 km of navigable waterways.

Social Statistics

2008 estimates: births, 1,494,000; deaths, 469,000. Estimated birth rate in 2008 was 17.2 per 1,000 population; estimated death rate, 5.4. Life expectancy, 2013, was 71.3 years for males and 80.5 years for females. Annual population growth rate, 2010–15, 1.1%. Infant mortality, 2010, 19 per 1,000 live births; fertility rate, 2008, 2.1 births per woman. Vietnam has had one of the largest reductions in its fertility rate of any country in the world in recent years, having had a rate of 5.8 births per woman in 1975. Sanctions are imposed on couples with more than two children. The rate at which Vietnam has reduced poverty, from 58% of the population in 1993 to 20% in 2004, is among the most dramatic of any country in the world.

Telecommunications

In 2011 there were 10,175,000 main (fixed) telephone lines; mobile phone subscriptions numbered 127,318,000 in the same year (1,416.0 per 1,000 persons). In 2011, 35.1% of the population were internet users. In June 2012 there were 9.7 m. Facebook users. In March 2012 there were 3.2 m. Facebook users.

Territory and Population

Vietnam is bounded in the west by Cambodia and Laos, north by China and east and south by the South China Sea. It has a total area of 331,212 km^2 and is divided into eight regions, 58 provinces and five municipalities (Can Tho, Da Nang, Hai Phong, Hanoi and Thanh Pho Ho Chi Minh). At the 2009 census the population was 85,846,997; density, 259 per km^2. 31.0% of the population live in urban areas (2011). Major cities (with 2009 populations): Ho Chi Minh City (5,880,615), Hanoi (2,316,772), Da Nang (770,911), Hai Phong (769,739), Can Tho (731,545). 86% of the population are Vietnamese (Kinh). There are also 53 minority groups thinly spread in the extensive mountainous regions. The largest minorities are: Tay, Thai, Muong, Khmer, Mong and Nung. The official language is Vietnamese. Chinese, French and Khmer are also spoken.

Tourism

There were a record 6,014,000 international visitors in 2011 (up from 5,050,000 in 2010). Tourist numbers have doubled since 2003. The main nationalities of tourists in 2010 were China (905,000), South Korea (496,000) and Japan (442,000).

Yemen

Jamhuriya al Yamaniya (Republic of Yemen)

Factsheet

Capitals: Sana'a (Legislative and Administrative), Aden (Commercial)
Population estimate, 2015: 26.83 m.
GNI per capita, 2014: (PPP$) 3,519
HDI/world rank, 2014: 0.498/160
Internet domain extension: .ye

Civil Aviation

There are international airports at Sana'a and Aden. In 2012 Sana'a handled 1,598,661 passengers (1,176,447 on international flights) and 18,119 tonnes of freight. The national carrier is Yemenia. In 2012 scheduled airline traffic of Yemen-based carriers flew 22.0 m. km; passenger-km totalled 3.7 bn. in the same year.

Climate

A desert climate, modified by relief. Sana'a, Jan. 57 °F (13.9 °C), July 71 °F (21.7 °C). Aden, Jan. 75 °F (24 °C), July 90 °F (32 °C). Annual rainfall 20″ (508 mm) in the north, but very low in coastal areas: 1.8″ (46 mm).

Constitution and Government

Parliament consists of a 301-member *Assembly of Representatives* (*Majlis al-Nuwaab*), previously elected for a 6 year term in single-seat constituencies, and a new people's transitional council created in Feb. 2015 when the *Assembly of Representatives* was briefly suspended in the wake of the Houthi rebel uprising. The *Assembly* was reinstated following UN-brokered talks between rival factions. The constitution was adopted in May 1991 but was drastically amended in 1994 following the civil war. After popular protests in 2011 unseated President Saleh, his successor, Abdo Rabu Mansour al-Hadi, was expected to oversee the drafting of a new constitution. However, Hadi was himself the subject of a coup in early 2015 during which the Houthi rebels established a rival administration. Houthi representatives had earlier refused to enter negotiations on ratification of a draft constitution submitted in Jan. 2015.

Currency

The unit of currency is the *riyal* (YER) of 100 *fils*. During the transitional period to north-south unification the northern *riyal* of 100 *fils* and the southern *dinar* of 1,000 *fils* co-existed.

Defence

Conscription is for 2 years. Defence expenditure in 2013 totalled US$1,812 m. (US$71 per capita), representing 4.7% of GDP. Estimates of the number of small arms in the country are around 12 m., equivalent to 61 firearms for every 100 people, making Yemen second only behind the USA as the world's most heavily armed country.

Economy

Trade, restaurants and hotels accounted for 21.5% of GDP in 2009; crude petroleum and natural gas, 18.5%; transport and communications, 13.1%; and agriculture, forestry and fishing, 12.1%.

Labour

The labour force in 2013 was 7,343,000 (4,824,000 in 2003). 50.4% of the population aged 15–64 was economically active in 2013. In the same year 17.7% of the population was unemployed. Yemen had 41,000 people living in slavery according to the Walk Free Foundation's 2013 *Global Slavery Index*.

Press

In 2008 there were five daily newspapers with a combined average daily circulation of 40,000.

Religion

More than 99% of the population in 2010 was Muslim (60–65% Sunnis and 35–40% Shias) according to the Pew Research Center's Forum on Religion & Public Life, with small Hindu and Christian minorities—an estimated 150,000 and 40,000 respectively.

Roads

There were 71,300 km of roads in 2005 (8.7% paved). In 2007 there were 777,700 vehicles in use.

Shipping

In Jan. 2009 there were seven ships of 300 GT or over registered, totalling 17,000 GT. There are ports at Aden, Mokha, Al-Hodeidah, Mukalla and Nashtoon.

Social Statistics

2009 estimates: births, 886,000; deaths, 163,000. Rates, 2009 estimates (per 1,000 population): birth, 38; death, 7. Yemen has one of the youngest populations of any country, with 75% of the population under the age of 30 and 44% under 15. Life expectancy, 2013, was 61.8 years for males and 64.5 years for females. Infant mortality, 2010, 57 per 1,000 live births. Annual population growth rate, 1998–2008, 2.9%; fertility rate, 2008, 5.2 births per woman.

Telecommunications

In 2012 there were 1,104,000 main (fixed) telephone lines; mobile phone subscriptions numbered 13,900,000 in the same year (582.8 per 1,000 persons). In 2013 an estimated 20.0% of the population were internet users. In March 2012 there were 437,000 Facebook users.

Territory and Population

Yemen is bounded in the north by Saudi Arabia, east by Oman, south by the Gulf of Aden and west by the Red Sea. The territory includes 112 islands including Kamaran (181 km^2) and Perim (300 km^2) in the Red Sea and Socotra (3,500 km^2) in the Gulf of Aden. At the last census, in 2004, the population was 19,685,161; density, 35 persons per km^2. In 2011, 32.4% of the population lived in urban areas. The population of the capital, Sana'a, was 1,707,531 in 2004. The commercial capital is the port of Aden, with a population of (2004) 588,938. Other important towns are Ta'iz, the port of Hodeida, Mukalla, Ibb and Abyan. The official language is Arabic.

Tourism

There were 829,000 international tourist arrivals—excluding same-day visitors—in 2011 (1,025,000 in 2010). Receipts from tourism in 2011 totalled US$783 m.

Zambia

Republic of Zambia

Factsheet

Capital: Lusaka
Population estimate, 2015: 16.21 m.
GNI per capita, 2014: (PPP$) 3,734
HDI/world rank, 2014: 0.586/139
Internet domain extension: .zm

Civil Aviation

The former flag carrier, Zambian Airways, operated internal flights and in 2007 flew to Dar es Salaam, Harare and Johannesburg as well as operating domestic services, but ceased flying in Jan. 2009. Lusaka is the principal international airport. In 2012 Lusaka International handled 925,077 passengers (684,548 on international flights) and 5,194 tonnes of freight. Scheduled airline traffic of Zambian-based carriers flew 1.8 m. km in 2012; passenger-km totalled 28.7 m. in the same year.

Climate

The climate is tropical, but has three seasons. The cool, dry one is from May to Aug., a hot dry one follows until Nov., when the wet season commences. Frosts may occur in some areas in the cool season. Lusaka, Jan. 70 °F (21.1 °C), July 61 °F (16.1 °C). Annual rainfall 33″ (836 mm). Livingstone, Jan. 75 °F (23.9 °C), July 61 °F (16.1 °C). Annual rainfall 27″ (673 mm). Ndola, Jan. 70 °F (21.1 °C), July 59 °F (15 °C). Annual rainfall 52″ (1,293 mm).

Constitution and Government

Zambia has a unicameral legislature. In 2009 the number of seats in the *National Assembly* was increased from 159 to 280 with effect from the 2011 elections, with 240 members elected for a five-year term in single-member constituencies, 30 members elected by proportional representation and ten members appointed by the president. Candidates for election as president must have both parents born in Zambia (this excludes ex-president Kaunda). The constitution was adopted on 24 Aug. 1991 and was amended in 1996, shortly before the parliamentary and presidential elections. The amendment restricts the president from serving more than two terms of office.

Currency

The unit of currency is the *kwacha* (ZMK) of 100 *ngwee*.

Defence

In 2013 defence expenditure totalled US$390 m. (US$27 per capita), representing 1.7% of GDP.

Economy

In 2011 agriculture accounted for 19.5% of GDP, industry 37.4% and services 43.1%.

Labour

The labour force totalled 3,165,200 in 2000 (59% males). 71.6% of the economically active population in 2000 were engaged in agriculture, 7.5% in community services and 6.8% in trade. Zambia had 96,000 people living in slavery according to the Walk Free Foundation's 2013 *Global Slavery Index*.

Press

In 2008 there were three paid-for daily papers, *The Post*, the *Times of Zambia* and the *Zambia Daily Mail*. *The Post* is privately-owned and the *Times of Zambia* and the *Zambia Daily Mail* state-owned.

Rail

In 2005 there were 1,271 km of the state-owned Zambia Railways (ZR) and 891 km of the Tanzania-Zambia (Tazara) Railway, both on 1,067 mm gauge. A 27-km stretch of railway linking Chipata in the east of the country with Mchinji in Malawi was opened in Aug. 2010. This links with the existing railway to Nacala, one of Mozambique's leading ports.

Religion

In 1993 the then president declared Zambia to be a Christian nation, but freedom of worship is a constitutional right. In 2010 there were an estimated 8.87 m. Protestants, 2.75 m. Catholics and 1.11 m. other Christians according to the Pew Research Center's Forum on Religion & Public Life.

Roads

There were, in 2001, 91,440 km of roads, including 4,222 km of highway. 131,100 passenger cars were in use in 2007 and there were 75,500 trucks and vans.

Social Statistics

Estimates, 2008: births, 541,000; deaths, 218,000. Estimated birth rate in 2008 was 42.9 per 1,000 population; estimated death rate, 17.3. Zambia's life expectancy at birth in 2013 was 56.3 years for males and 60.0 for females. Life expectancy was declining for many years, largely owing to the huge number of people in the country with HIV, although it has now begun to rise again slowly. In 2009, 13.5% of all adults between 15 and 49 were infected with HIV. Annual population growth rate, 2000–08, 2.3%. Infant mortality, 2010, 69 per 1,000 live births; fertility rate, 2008, 5.8 births per woman.

Telecommunications

In 2013 there were 116,000 main (fixed) telephone lines; mobile phone subscriptions numbered 10,396,000 in the same year (715.0 per 1,000 persons). In 2013 an estimated 15.4% of the population were internet users. In June 2012 there were 236,000 Facebook users.

Territory and Population

Zambia is bounded by the Democratic Republic of the Congo in the north, Tanzania in the northeast, Malawi in the east, Mozambique in the southeast, Zimbabwe and Namibia in the south, and by Angola in the west. The area is 752,612 km² (290,584 sq. miles). Population (2010 census), 13,092,666; population density, 17.4 per km². In 2011, 35.9% of the population were urban. The republic is divided into ten provinces. The capital is Lusaka, which had a census population in 2010 of 1,747,152. Other major towns (with 2010 census population in 1,000) are: Kitwe, 501; Ndola, 451; Kabwe, 202; Chingola, 185; Mufulira, 151; Livingstone 134; Luanshya, 130. The population consists of over 70 Bantu-speaking ethnic groups, with the main groups being the Bemba (18%), Tonga (10%), Nyanja (8%) and Lozi (6%). The official language is English.

Tourism

There were a record 906,000 international tourist arrivals—excluding same-day visitors—in 2011 (815,000 in 2010 and 710,000 in 2009). Receipts from tourism in 2011 totalled US$146 m.

Zimbabwe

Republic of Zimbabwe

Factsheet

Capital: Harare
Population estimate, 2015: 15.60 m.
GNI per capita, 2014: (PPP$) 1,615
HDI/world rank, 2014: 0.509/155
Internet domain extension: .zw

Civil Aviation

There are three international airports: Harare (the main airport), Bulawayo and Victoria Falls. Air Zimbabwe, the state-owned national carrier, ceased operations in Feb. 2012 but resumed flying on a limited basis in May. After the government took over Air Zimbabwe's debts it began flying on international routes again in Nov. 2012. In 2012 scheduled airline traffic of Zimbabwe-based carriers flew 9.1 m. km; passenger-km totalled 566.6 m. in the same year. In 2009 Harare handled 612,208 passengers (674,281 in 2008).

Climate

Though situated in the tropics, conditions are remarkably temperate throughout the year because of altitude, and an inland position keeps humidity low. The warmest weather occurs in the 3 months before the main rainy season, which starts in Nov. and lasts until March. The cool season is from mid-May to mid-Aug. and, though days are mild and sunny, nights are chilly. Harare, Jan. 69 °F (20.6 °C), July 57 °F (13.9 °C). Annual rainfall 33″ (828 mm). Bulawayo, Jan. 71 °F (21.7 °C), July 57 °F (13.9 °C). Annual rainfall 24″ (594 mm). Victoria Falls, Jan. 78 °F (25.6 °C), July 61 °F (16.1 °C). Annual rainfall 28″ (710 mm).

Constitution and Government

In May 2013 a new constitution was signed into law, replacing one that had been in force since 1980. In a referendum on 16 March 2013 it received 92.9% support and won the required two-thirds support in the House of Assembly and the Senate along with presidential approval 2 months later, having been supported by both ZANU-PF and the MDC. Under its terms, the executive *President* is limited to two 5 year terms (not to be implemented retrospectively, ensuring that the incumbent, Robert Mugabe, qualified for up to a further two terms despite having held office since 1980). The *House of Assembly* is elected by universal suffrage for 5 year terms and comprises 210 members elected by secret ballot in 210 constituencies plus, for the first two parliaments, 60 seats for women elected by proportional representation. The *Senate* is made up of 80 members (six each from ten provinces elected by proportional representation, 18 Chiefs and two representatives of disabled persons). The 2013 constitution also provided for a strengthened Bill of Rights, removed immunity for presidents once they have left office, strengthened the powers of the judiciary and established a National Peace and Reconciliation Commission.

Currency

The use of the Zimbabwean dollar as an official currency was effectively abandoned on 12 April 2009. Currencies such as the South African rand, the Botswana pula, the pound sterling and the US dollar are used instead. The Zimbabwean dollar was officially withdrawn from circulation in Sept. 2015. Until 12 April 2009 the unit of currency was the *Zimbabwe fourth dollar* (ZWL), introduced on 2 Feb. 2009, with 12 zeros being removed to make 1 trn. dollars (ZWR) equal to one new dollar. The *Zimbabwe third dollar* (ZWR) had replaced the *Zimbabwe second dollar* (ZWD) on 1 Aug. 2008, with a conversion rate of 1 revalued dollar = 10 bn. old dollars (ZWD).

Defence

In 2013 military expenditure totalled US$356 m. (US$27 per capita), representing 3.2% of GDP.

Economy

Agriculture accounted for 13% of GDP in 2012, industry 32% and services 55%. Zimbabwe's 'shadow' (black market) economy is estimated to constitute approximately 63% of the country's official GDP, one of the highest percentages of any country in the world.

Labour

The labour force in 2011 totalled 6,084,000 (52.4% females). Unemployment in March 2007 was around 80%. Zimbabwe had 94,000 people living in slavery according to the Walk Free Foundation's 2013 *Global Slavery Index*.

Press

In 2008 there were two daily newspapers, both controlled by the government, with a combined circulation of 28,000. In Jan. 2002 parliament passed an

Access to Information Bill restricting press freedom, making it an offence to report from Zimbabwe unless registered by a state-appointed commission. In Sept. 2003 the independent *Daily News* was shut down for contraventions of the new press law. Zimbabwe's High Court ordered the government to allow its reopening but the order was ignored.

Rail

In 2005 the National Railways of Zimbabwe had 2,759 km (1,067 mm gauge) of route ways (483 km electrified). In 2005 the railways carried 3 m. passengers and 6.1 m. tonnes of freight (including the Beitbridge-Bulawayo Railway).

Religion

A study by the Pew Research Center's Forum on Religion & Public Life estimated that in 2010 there were 10.93 m. Christians, 990,000 people with no religious affiliation, 480,000 folk religionists and 110,000 Muslims. Of the Christians in 2010, 85% were Protestants and 13% Catholics.

Roads

The road network covers some 97,000 km but much of it is in poor condition. Number of vehicles in use, 2007: passenger cars, 1,214,100; lorries and vans, 186,800; buses and coaches, 15,600; motorcycles and mopeds, 109,000. There were 1,037 road accident fatalities in 2006.

Shipping

Zimbabwe's outlets to the sea are Maputo and Beira in Mozambique, Dar es Salaam, Tanzania and the South African ports.

Social Statistics

2008 estimates: births, 373,000; deaths, 199,000. Rates (2008 estimates, per 1,000 population); birth, 29.9; death, 16.0. Annual population growth rate, 2000–08, 0.0%. Zimbabwe–s expectation of life at birth in 2013 was 608 years for females and 58.8 for males, up from an average of 42.9 years in 2003 thanks to a sharp decline in the HIV prevalence attributed mainly to changes in sexual behaviour and to some extent to effective preventive programmes. Overall life expectancy had reached 61.4 years in 1985 before Zimbabwe was affected by the HIV/AIDS epidemic. In 2009, 14.3% of all adults between 15 and 49 were infected with HIV. Infant mortality, 2010, 51 per 1,000 live births; fertility rate, 2008, 3.4 births per woman.

Telecommunications

In 2013 there were 304,000 main (fixed) telephone lines; mobile phone subscriptions numbered 13,633,000 in the same year (963.5 per 1,000 persons). In 2013 an estimated 18.5% of the population were internet users. In June 2012 there were 236,000 Facebook users.

Territory and Population

Zimbabwe is bounded in the north by Zambia, east by Mozambique, south by South Africa and west by Botswana and the Caprivi Strip of Namibia. The area is 390,757 km^2 (150,871 sq. miles). Population at the 2012 census, 13,061,239 (6,780,700 female); density, 33.4 per km^2. In 2011, 38.8% of the population were urban. There are eight provinces and two cities, Harare and Bulawayo, with provincial status. Harare, the capital, had a population in 2012 of 1,485,231. Other main cities (with 2012 census populations) were Bulawayo (653,337), Chitungwiza (356,840), Mutare (186,208) and Epworth (167,462). The population is approximately 98% African, 1% mixed and Asian and there are around 70,000 whites. The main ethno-linguistic groups are the Shona (71%), Ndebele (16%), Ndau (3%) and Nyanja (3%). Other smaller ones include Kalanga, Manyika, Tonga and Lozi. The official language is English.

Tourism

International visitors numbered 2,423,000 in 2011 (2,239,000 in 2010 and 2,017,000 in 2009). Receipts in 2011 totalled US$664 m.

CHRONOLOGIES

Chronology of Significant International Events (1999–2017)

2017

Chronology of Events for December 2017

Week Beginning 31 December 2017

In a cabinet reshuffle in Syria, Gen. Ali Abdullah Ayyoub was appointed minister of defence.

Peru's defence minister, Jorge Nieto, resigned and was replaced 6 days later by Jorge Kisic. Cayetana Aljovín was named foreign minister.

Ahmed Isse Awad became foreign minister and Mohamed Abdi Sabriye interior minister following a cabinet reshuffle in Somalia.

Dato Paduka Lim Jock Hoi of Brunei was sworn in as secretary-general of the Association of South East Asian Nations (ASEAN).

Week Beginning 24 December

In a cabinet reshuffle in Chad, Abdoulaye Sabre Fadoul was named finance minister and Mahamat Zène Chérif foreign minister.

In a run-off election for the presidency in Liberia, George Weah (Coalition for Democratic Change) won with 61.5% of the vote against 38.5% for Joseph Boakai (Unity Party). Turnout was 55.8%.

In Pakistan, Miftah Ismail was named adviser to the prime minister for finance, revenue and economic affairs.

Constantino Chiwenga and Kembo Mohadi were appointed vice presidents in Zimbabwe, with Chiwenga also responsible for the defence portfolio.

Mali's government resigned, with the president, Ibrahim Boubacar Keita, appointing Soumeylou Boubèye Maïga as prime minister in succession to Abdoulaye Idrissa Maïga. In the new cabinet Tieman Coulibaly was named foreign minister, while Tiéna Coulibaly and Boubou Cissé remained defence minister and finance minister respectively.

Week Beginning 17 December

Sebastián Piñera won Chile's presidential run-off, winning 54.6% of the vote against 45.4% for Alejandro Guillier. Six other candidates had participated in the first round of voting a month earlier. Turnout was 46.7% in the first round and 49.0% in the second.

'Akilisi Pohiva was re-elected as Tonga's prime minister, winning 14 parliamentary votes against 12 for Siaosi Sovaleni.

In a cabinet reshuffle, Peter Dutton was made Australia's home affairs minister.

In Vanuatu, a cabinet reshuffle saw Ralph Regenvanu become foreign minister and Andrew Napuat minister of internal affairs before the prime minister, Charlot Salwai, survived a parliamentary no-confidence vote by 37 votes to 13.

Peru's president Pedro Pablo Kuczynski narrowly survived an impeachment vote in parliament. Carlos Basombrío resigned as interior minister the following day, with Vicente Romero replacing him 5 days later.

Week Beginning 10 December

A cabinet reshuffle in Kuwait resulted in Sheikh Nasser Sabah al-Hamad al-Sabah's appointment as defence minister, with Nayef Falah al-Hajraf named as finance minister.

Following a cabinet reshuffle in Mozambique, José Condugua António Pacheco became foreign minister.

Jens Stoltenberg's tenure as Secretary General of NATO was extended to 30 September 2020.

© Springer Nature Limited 2019
Palgrave Macmillan (ed.), *The Statesman's Yearbook Companion*,
https://doi.org/10.1057/978-1-349-95839-9

The People's Party and the far-right Freedom Party announced that they would form a coalition in Austria, with Sebastian Kurz as chancellor, Mario Kunasek as minister of defence, Hartwig Löger as finance minister, Karin Kneissl as foreign minister and Herbert Kickl as interior minister.

Week Beginning 3 December

In The Gambia, Habib Saihou Drammeh was named interior minister.

In a cabinet reshuffle in Sierra Leone, Alfred Palo Conteh was appointed minister of defence, Kaifala Marah minister of foreign affairs and Ismael Sengu Koroma minister of internal affairs.

Ali Abdullah Saleh, Yemen's former president, was killed in the country's civil war.

Lebanon's prime minister, Saad Hariri, rescinded his earlier resignation.

Commins Aston Mewa became minister of home affairs in the Solomon Islands.

In the Czech Republic, Andrej Babiš assumed office as prime minister. His government, sworn in a week later, included Karla Slechtová as defence minister, Alena Schillerová as finance minister, Martin Stropnický as foreign minister and Lubomír Metnar as interior minister.

Alain Berset was elected president for 2018 by the Swiss parliament with effect from 1 January.

Following the second round of elections to Nepal's House of Representatives (12 days after the first round), the Communist Party of Nepal (Unified Marxist-Leninist) held 121 of the 275 seats, the Nepali Congress won 63, the Communist Party of Nepal (Maoist-Centre) 53, the Rastriya Janata Party Nepal 17 and the Federal Socialist Forum–Nepal 16. The five remaining seats were shared among other parties and independents.

Beata Szydło resigned as prime minister of Poland, despite surviving a parliamentary no-confidence vote. She was replaced by finance minister Mateusz Morawiecki, who announced a largely unchanged cabinet that secured a parliamentary vote of confidence 5 days later.

Chronology of Events for November 2017

Week Beginning 26 November 2017

In Honduras's presidential elections, incumbent Juan Orlando Hernández won 43.0% of the vote, Salvador Nasralla 41.4% and Luis Orlando Zelaya 14.7%. Turnout was 57.5%. In parliamentary elections held at the same time, the National Party won 61 of 128 seats, Liberty and Refoundation 30 and the Liberal Party 26.

Mohamed Mursal Osman was appointed defence minister in Somalia.

José Antonio Meade resigned as Mexico's finance minister, with José Antonio González Anaya replacing him.

In Uzbekistan, Jamshid Kuchkarov was named finance minister.

Bohuslav Sobotka's government resigned in the Czech Republic.

Week Beginning 19 November 2017

Christian Georges Diguimbaye was dismissed as Chad's finance minister, with Abdoulaye Sabre Fadoul replacing him in an acting capacity.

Prime minister Mihai Tudose survived a parliamentary no-confidence vote in Romania.

In Kyrgyzstan, Sooronbay Jeenbekov was sworn in as president.

Week Beginning 12 November 2017

In Equatorial Guinea's parliamentary elections, the Democratic Party of Equatorial Guinea and allied groups took 99 of the 100 seats in the House of People's Representatives and all 55 directly-elected seats in the Senate. Turnout was 84.0%.

Borut Pahor retained the presidency in Slovenia, claiming 53.1% of the vote against 46.9% for Marjan Šarec in a run-off. Turnout was 42.1%.

Following a cabinet reshuffle in Georgia, Mamuka Bakhtadze became finance minister and Giorgi Gakharia interior minister.

In Tonga's parliamentary elections, the Democratic Party won 14 of the 17 popularly elected seats, with independents taking the other three. Turnout was 67.0%.

Week Beginning 5 November 2017

In the Solomon Islands prime minister Manasseh Sogavare resigned after losing a parliamentary no-confidence vote by 27 to 23. He was replaced 9 days later by Rick Hou, who received 33 votes against 16 cast for rival candidate John Moffat Fugui. Hou announced a cabinet featuring Sogavare as finance minister and Milner Tozaka as foreign minister.

Emmerson Mnangagwa was removed from the office of the vice-presidency in Zimbabwe. However, he was sworn in as president 18 days later following the resignation of the incumbent, Robert Mugabe. Mugabe had been under intense pressure to step down after senior military figures intervened following Mnangagwa's initial removal from office. As president, Mnangagwa named Kembo Mohadi as defence minister, Patrick Chinamasa as finance minister, Lieut.-Gen. (retd) Sibusiso Moyo as foreign minister and Obert Mpofu as home affairs minister.

Mai Ahmad Fatty was dismissed as minister of the interior in The Gambia, with justice minister Abubacarr Tambadou taking over the portfolio.

In St Vincent and the Grenadines, Camillo Gonsalves became finance minister in a cabinet reshuffle.

Chronology of Events for October 2017

Week Beginning 29 October 2017

In Kuwait, Sheikh Jaber Mubarak al-Hamad al-Sabah's government resigned. Two days later, Sheikh Jaber was reappointed premier by the Amir.

Shinzo Abe was re-elected as prime minister for a further term by the Japanese parliament.

In the Solomon Islands, Moses Garu became home affairs minister.

Ignazio Cassis took office as Switzerland's foreign minister.

Sir Michael Fallon resigned as secretary of state for defence in the UK and was replaced by Gavin Williamson.

Katrín Jakobsdóttir of the Left–Green Movement was invited to form a government in Iceland.

Lebanese prime minister Saad Hariri resigned while out of the country, but subsequently agreed to delay his resignation on his return to the domestic scene.

Week Beginning 22 October 2017

In elections in Argentina, 127 of the 257 seats in the Chamber of Deputies that were not contested at the previous elections in October 2015 were at stake. Following the elections, Let's Change and its allies held 107 seats, the Citizen's Unity Front 67, the Justicialist Party 40, United for a New Alternative 21, the Socialist Left 4 and others 19.

In Japan's parliamentary elections, the coalition between the ruling Liberal Democratic Party and the Komeito party won 313 seats (with 49.7% of the single-seat constituency vote); the opposition Constitutional Democratic Party of Japan 55 seats (8.8%); Party of Hope 50 (20.6%); Japanese Communist Party 12 (9.0%); Nippon Ishin no Kai 11 (3.2%); and Social Democratic Party 2 (1.1%). Independents took 22 seats. Turnout was 53.7%.

In the first round of presidential elections in Slovenia, Borut Pahor (independent) won 47.2% of the vote against Marjan Šarec (Marjan Šarec List) 24.8% and Romana Tomc (Slovenian Democratic Party) 13.7%. There were six other candidates. Turnout in the first round was 44.2%. In the run-off 3 weeks later, Borut Pahor received 53.1% of votes cast against 46.9% for Marjan Šarec. Turnout was 42.1%.

In Germany, Peter Altmaier replaced Wolfgang Schäuble as finance minister on an interim basis.

Following a cabinet reshuffle in Malaŵi, Cecilia Chazama became minister of home affairs and internal security.

Eugen Sturza was appointed minister of defence in Moldova by the chairman of parliament, Andrian Candu, who was acting as interim president while Igor Dodon was suspended from the office for his opposition to the appointment.

The Chinese Communist Party re-elected Xi Jinping as its general secretary.

In Italy, Paolo Gentiloni's government survived five Senate confidence votes related to the adoption of a new electoral law.

Jacinda Ardern, New Zealand's prime minister-designate, named a cabinet including Ron Mark as defence minister, Grant Robertson as finance minister, Winston Peters as foreign minister and Tracey Martin as minister of internal affairs.

In Kenya's re-run presidential elections, incumbent Uhuru Kenyatta received 98.3% and Raila Odinga 1.0% of votes cast after Odinga had urged his supporters to boycott the poll. Turnout was 38.8%.

Simón Zerpa took office as finance minister in Venezuela.

In Spain, Catalonia's parliament voted by 70 votes to ten to declare an independent republic. The central government in Madrid responded by suspending the region's autonomy, dissolving its parliament and dismissing its government.

In Iceland's parliamentary election, the Independence Party won 16 of 63 seats with 25.2% of votes cast, the Left–Green Movement 11 (16.9%), the Progressive Party 8 (10.7%), the Social Democratic Alliance 7 (12.1%), the Centre Party 7 (10.9%), the Pirate Party 6 (9.2%), the People's Party 4 (6.9%) and the Reform Party 4 (6.7%). Turnout was 81.2%.

Week Beginning 15 October 2017

In Austria's parliamentary elections, the Austrian People's Party won 62 seats with 31.5% of the vote, the Social Democratic Party 52 (26.9%), the Freedom Party 51 (26.0%), the New Austria 10 (5.3%) and Peter Pilz List 8 (4.4%). Turnout was 80.0%. Five days later, Sebastian Kurz of the Austrian People's Party was invited by the president to form a government.

In the presidential election in Kyrgyzstan, former prime minister Sooronbay Jeenbekov won with 54.7% of the vote, ahead of Omurbek Babanov with 33.7% and Adakhan Madumarov with 6.5%. There were eight other candidates. Turnout was 55.9%.

Nepal's prime minister, Sher Bahadur Deuba, dismissed all his government ministers affiliated to the Communist Party of Nepal (Maoist Centre), taking over personal responsibility for the home and foreign affairs portfolios.

In a cabinet reshuffle in South Africa, Ayanda Dlodlo became home affairs minister.

Constança Urbano de Sousa resigned as Portugal's interior minister and was replaced by Eduardo Cabrita. Three days later the government of António Costa survived a no-confidence motion by 122 to 105 votes.

Frank Bakke-Jensen became minister of defence in Norway and Ine Marie Eriksen Søreide minister of foreign affairs following a cabinet reshuffle.

In elections to the Czech Republic's Chamber of Deputies, the Action of Dissatisfied Citizens gained 78 seats (29.6% of the vote), the Civic Democratic Party 25 (11.3%), the Czech Pirate Party 22 (10.8%) and Freedom and Direct Democracy 22 (10.6%). Five other parties and groupings took the remaining seats. Turnout was 60.8%.

Week Beginning 8 October 2017

In a cabinet reshuffle in Zimbabwe, Ignatius Chombo was named finance minister, Walter Mzembi foreign minister and Obert Mpofu home affairs minister.

In the first round of Liberia's presidential elections, George Weah (Coalition for Democratic Change) won 38.4% of the vote against 28.8% for Joseph Boakai (Unity Party). Three other candidates each polled less than 10%. Turnout was 75.2%. Three weeks later, the Supreme Court delayed a run-off scheduled for 7 November pending a legal challenge to the results of the first round.

In the Netherlands, prime minister Mark Rutte was asked to form a new administration following the elections in March. His government was sworn in 2 weeks later and included Ank Bijleveld as defence minister, Wopke Hoekstra as finance minister, Halbe Zijlstra as foreign minister and Kajsa Ollongren as interior minister.

Somalia's minister of defence, Abdirashid Abdullahi Mohamed, resigned.

Prime minister Mercedes Aráoz and her government won a confidence vote in Peru by 83 votes to 17.

Following a reshuffle in the Solomon Islands, John Maneniaru took over the finance portfolio. Manasseh Maelanga resigned as the minister of home affairs.

Week Beginning 1 October 2017

Matteo Fiorini of Repubblica Futura and Enrico Carattoni of the Democratic Socialist Left were sworn in as San Marino's Captains Regent.

In Canada, Julie Payette took office as governor-general.

Jalal Talabani, Iraq's president from 2005–07, died.

In the Netherlands, Jeanine Hennis-Plasschaert resigned as defence minister and was replaced the following day by Klaas Dijkhoff.

The Mongolian parliament confirmed Ukhnaagiin Khurelsukh as the new prime minister. He named a cabinet including Nyamaa Enkhbold as defence minister, Chimed Khurelbaatar as finance minister, Damdin Tsogtbaatar as foreign minister and Tsend Nyamdorj as home affairs minister.

Chronology of Events for September 2017

Week Beginning 24 September 2017
In Germany's parliamentary elections to the Bundestag, the Christian Democratic Union/Christian Social Union of Chancellor Angela Merkel won 246 seats with 32.9% of votes cast, the Social Democratic Party 153 (20.5%), Alternative for Germany 94 (12.6%), the Free Democratic Party 80 (10.7%), the Left Party 69 (9.2%) and Alliance '90/the Greens 67 (8.9%). Turnout was 76.2%.

João Lourenço was sworn in as Angola's president. Salviano de Jesus Sequeira was named minister of defence and Manuel Domingos Augusto minister of foreign affairs.

Week Beginning 17 September 2017
In Switzerland, Ignazio Cassis was selected to succeed Didier Burkhalter as minister of foreign affairs.

In New Zealand's parliamentary elections, the National Party won 56 seats with 44.4%, the Labour Party 46 (36.9%), New Zealand First 9 (7.2%), the Green Party 8 (6.3%) and ACT New Zealand 1 (0.5%). Turnout was 79.8%.

Week Beginning 10 September 2017
In Norway's parliamentary elections, the Norwegian Labour Party won 49 of 169 seats (27.4%), the Conservative Party 45 (25.0%), the Progress Party 27 (15.2%), the Centre Party 19 (10.3%) and the Socialist Left Party 11 (6.0%). Four other parties won less than ten seats each. Turnout was 78.2%.

In a cabinet reshuffle in the Central African Republic, Marie-Noëlle Koyara was named defence minister and Brig.-Gen. Henri Wanzet-Linguissara interior minister.

Mari Alkatiri was sworn in as Timor-Leste's prime minister. He named Agostinho Sequeira Somotxo as defence minister, Rui Augusto Gomes as finance minister and Aurélio Guterres as foreign minister.

Peru's Congress voted by 77 votes to 22 to dismiss the government of prime minister Fernando Zavala, who was replaced by Mercedes Aráoz 2 days later. Claudia Cooper was named finance minister.

Bjarni Benediktsson resigned as Iceland's prime minister but remained in office on an interim basis.

Week Beginning 3 September 2017
Nirmala Sitharaman was appointed defence minister in India.

In Taiwan, Lin Chuan resigned as prime minister and was replaced by Lai Ching-te.

A cabinet reshuffle in Uzbekistan saw Abdusalom Azizov appointed minister of defence and Pulat Bobojonov minister of interior.

Adrian Tutuianu resigned as Romania's defence minister. He was replaced a week later by Mihai-Viorel Fifor.

Senegal's prime minister Mohamed Dionne resigned but was reappointed by president Macky Sall a day later. Dionne named Sidiki Kaba as foreign minister and Aly Ngouille Ndiaye as interior minister.

Pohiva Tu'i'onetoa was confirmed as Tonga's finance minister, having been nominated the previous week.

Following a cabinet reshuffle in Tunisia, Abdelkarim Zbidi was sworn in as defence minister, Mohamed Ridha Chalghoum as finance minister and Lotfi Brahem as interior minister.

Ramush Haradinaj was invited to form a government in Kosovo by president Hashim Thaçi. He was sworn in along with his government 2 days later.

Mongolia's parliament voted to remove Jargaltulgyn Erdenebat from the premiership. He was replaced by Ukhnaagiin Khurelsukh the following month.

In Moldova, president Igor Dodon requested the resignation of acting defence minister Gheorghe Galbura. Eugen Sturza replaced him in late October, after his nomination was accepted by Dodon following several rejections.

Edi Rama was reappointed as prime minister in Albania, with his government securing a parliamentary vote of confidence 4 days later.

In Uruguay, Raúl Sendic resigned as vice-president and was succeeded 4 days later by Lucía Topolansky.

Chronology of Events for August 2017

Week Beginning 27 August 2017
Sandra Jovel was named Guatemala's foreign minister.

Chile's minister of finance, Rodrigo Valdés, resigned and was replaced by Nicolás Eyzaguirre.

J. Y. Pillay was sworn in as Singapore's acting president when Tony Tan's term ended. Pillay gave way to Halimah Yacob, who won the presidency uncontested 12 days later.

Week Beginning 20 August 2017
Noël Nelson Messone became foreign minister in Gabon.

Kyrgyzstan's prime minister, Sooronbay Jeenbekov, resigned in order to contest the presidential elections scheduled for October. He was replaced as premier a day later in an acting capacity by Mukhammetkaly Abulgaziyev, who gave way to Sapar Isakov later in the same week.

In Guinea, Mamadi Touré was appointed foreign minister.

João Lourenço of the Popular Movement for the Liberation of Angola (MPLA) became president as a result of Angola's parliamentary elections, in which the MPLA won 150 of 220 seats with 61.1% of the vote, the National Union for the Total Independence of Angola (UNITA) 51 seats (26.7%) and the Broad Convergence for the Salvation of Angola-Electoral Coalition (CASA-CE) 16 (9.4%). Turnout was 76.1%.

Henry Rabary Njaka became foreign minister in Madagascar.

King Tupou VI dissolved Tonga's parliament ahead of elections scheduled for November.

Week Beginning 13 August 2017
In Algeria, prime minister Abdelmadjid Tebboune was dismissed by president Abdelaziz Bouteflika, who nominated Ahmed Ouyahia to succeed to the premiership the following day.

Albania's finance minister, Helga Vukaj, and interior minister, Dritan Demiraj, were among leading figures in the government who resigned. A new government announced 10 days later included Olta Xhaçka as defence minister, Arben Ahmetaj as finance minister, Ditmir Bushati as foreign minister and Fatmir Xhafaj as interior minister.

Clément Mouamba, the Republic of the Congo's prime minister, resigned along with his government. Four days later he was asked by president Denis Sassou-Nguesso to form a new government, which was announced the following day with its key positions unchanged.

Tunisia's acting finance minister, Fadhel Abdelkefi, resigned.

Week Beginning 6 August 2017
Three days after being sworn in for a new term, Iran's president Hassan Rouhani nominated his cabinet, with Amir Hatami as minister of defence, Massoud Karbasian minister of finance, Mohammad Javad Zarif minister of foreign affairs and Abdolreza Rahmani Fazli minister of the interior.

Incumbent Uhuru Kenyatta claimed victory in Kenya's presidential election, with 54.3% of the vote against 44.7% for Raila Odinga. However, the result was annulled by the Supreme Court 3 weeks later with new elections scheduled to be held before the end of October.

President Jacob Zuma survived a no-confidence motion in South Africa by 198 votes to 177.

Sri Lanka's foreign minister, Ravi Karunanayake, resigned and was replaced by Tilak Marapana.

Chronology of Events for July 2017

Week Beginning 30 July 2017
After a second round of parliamentary elections in the Republic of the Congo, the Congolese Labour Party of president Denis Sassou-Nguesso won 96 out of 151 seats. No other party exceeded ten seats.

At parliamentary elections in Senegal, the United in Hope coalition backing President Macky Sall won 125 of the 165 seats in the National Assembly. The Manko Wattu Sénégal coalition backing former President Abdoulaye Wade claimed 19 seats and Manko Taxawu Sénégal seven seats, with 11 smaller parties taking three seats or fewer. Turnout was 54%.

Jorge Arreaza was appointed Venezuela's foreign minister.

In Rwanda's presidential elections, Paul Kagame was re-elected for a third 7-year term with 98.8% of the vote. Philippe Mpayimana, an independent candidate, and Frank Habineza of the Democratic Green Party won 0.7% and 0.5% respectively. Turnout was 98.2%.

Moses Garu was appointed minister of national security in the Solomon Islands.

Week Beginning 23 July 2017

Ilir Meta was sworn in as Albania's president.

Morgan Johansson was appointed Sweden's minister of home affairs.

In Japan, Tomomi Inada resigned as minister of defence. Fumio Kishida replaced her in an acting capacity before Itsunori Onodera took over the portfolio after a reshuffle the following week. At the same time Taro Kono became foreign minister and Seiko Noda minister of internal affairs.

Nawaz Sharif resigned as prime minister in Pakistan after the Supreme Court disqualified him from holding public office. He was replaced 3 days later by Shahid Khaqan Abbasi, who won 221 of 339 votes in a National Assembly vote against 47 for Syed Naveed Qamar and 33 for Sheikh Rashid Ahmad. Abbasi announced a cabinet including Khurram Dastgir Khan as defence minister, Muhammad Ishaq Dar as finance minister, Khawaja Muhammad Asif as foreign minister and Ahsan Iqbal as interior minister.

Week Beginning 16 July 2017

Maria Ubach was named Andorra's foreign minister.

In Bosnia and Herzegovina, Dragan Čović became chair of the rotating presidency.

Souef Mohamed El Amine was appointed foreign minister in Comoros.

In India's presidential election Ram Nath Kovind of the Bharatiya Janata Party was elected by federal and state legislators, claiming 65.7% of the vote against 34.3% for Meira Kumar.

Gervais Rakotoarimanana resigned as finance minister in Madagascar. Vonintsalama Andriambololona succeeded him the following day.

A cabinet reshuffle in Malawi saw Emmanuel Fabiano become foreign minister.

Following a cabinet reshuffle in Côte d'Ivoire, Hamed Bakayoko became minister of defence and Sidiki Diakité interior minister.

Nurettin Canikli was appointed minster of defence in Turkey.

In Timor-Leste's parliamentary elections, the Revolutionary Front for an Independent East Timor (FRETILIN) won 29.7% of votes cast and 23 seats, ahead of the National Congress for Timorese Reconstruction (CNRT) with 29.5% (22 seats). Three other parties won eight seats or fewer. Turnout was 76.7%.

Week Beginning 9 July 2017

Oscar Raúl Aguad Beily was named minister of defence in Argentina.

In Lesotho, Tsukutlane Au took office as minister of home affairs.

Song Young-moo became South Korea's minister of defence.

Week Beginning 2 July 2017

Tallis Obed Moses was elected president of Vanuatu by an electoral college after receiving 40 of 57 votes in the fourth round of voting. He defeated 15 other candidates.

France's prime minister, Édouard Philippe, won a parliamentary vote of confidence by 370 votes to 67 (with 129 abstentions).

Tuimaleali'ifano Va'aletoa Sualauvi II was unanimously elected head of state by Samoa's Legislative Assembly.

Khaltmaagiin Battulga of the Democratic Party became Mongolia's president after winning 55.2% of valid votes against Miyeegombyn Enkhbold (Mongolian People's Party) with 44.8%. Turnout was 60.7%. In the first round held the previous week, no candidate had managed an overall majority.

Kenya's minister of internal security, Joseph Nkaissery, died. Fred Matiang'i assumed the portfolio in an acting capacity.

In Papua New Guinea, the final round of voting in parliamentary elections that began 2 weeks earlier resulted in the People's National Congress of prime minister Peter O'Neill winning 27 of 111 seats, the National Alliance Party 14 and the Pangu Party 11. Four weeks later parliament re-elected O'Neill as prime minister. He announced a cabinet including Solan Mirisim as defence minister, James Marape as finance minister and Rimbink Pato as foreign minister.

Chronology of Events for June 2017

Week Beginning 25 June 2017

In parliamentary elections in Albania, the Socialist Party won 74 of the 140 seats with 48.3% of votes, the Democratic Party 43 (28.8%), the Socialist Movement for Integration 19 (14.3%), the Party for Justice, Integration and Unity 3 (4.8%) and the Social Democratic Party 1 (1.0%). Turnout was 46.8%.

Mario Alberto Guillén was appointed finance minister in Bolivia.

After the resignation of his government, Romanian prime minister Sorin Grindeanu left office after losing a confidence vote in parliament. The following week he was succeeded by Mihai Tudose who named Adrian Țuțuianu as defence minister and Ionuț Mișa as finance minister.

Tedros Adhanom Ghebreyesus, from Ethiopia, succeeded Margaret Chan as director-general of the World Health Organization.

Carrie Lam was sworn in as Hong Kong's chief executive.

Week Beginning 18 June 2017

In Serbia, president Aleksandar Vučić nominated Ana Brnabić as prime minister. Two weeks later she announced her government including Aleksandar Vulin as defence minister.

Helmut Kohl, the chancellor of Germany from 1982–98, died.

In Vanuatu, president Baldwin Lonsdale died. He was replaced in an acting capacity by Esmon Saimon.

France held the second round of parliamentary elections, a week after the first round. President Emmanuel Macron's La République en Marche! (previously En Marche!) and its Presidential Majority allies won 350 of 577 seats, giving Macron an absolute parliamentary majority. La République en Marche! took 308 seats, Les Républicains 113, the Democratic Movement 42 and the Socialist Party 29. Turnout was 48.7% in the first round and 42.6% in the second. The following day Macron reappointed Édouard Philippe as prime minister.

The government of Finnish prime minister Juha Sipilä won a parliamentary vote of confidence by 104 votes to 85.

After Peru's minister of finance, Alfredo Thorne, resigned, prime minister Fernando Zavala assumed the portfolio.

Prince Mohammed bin Salman bin Abdulaziz Al-Saud was named Saudi Arabia's crown prince, deputy prime minister and minister of defence, and Prince Abdulaziz bin Saud bin Naif became interior minister.

Samuel Moncada was appointed foreign minister in Venezuela.

Botswana's president from 1980–98, Sir Ketumile Masire, died.

Week Beginning 11 June 2017

In parliamentary elections in Kosovo, an alliance of parties led by the Democratic Party of Kosovo won 39 of 120 seats with 33.7% of the vote, Self-Determination 32 seats with 27.5%, a coalition of parties led by the Democratic League of Kosovo 29 with 25.5% and the Serb List 9 with 6.1%, with the remaining seats going to smaller parties. Turnout was 41.2%.

In Estonia, Jüri Luik was appointed defence minister and Toomas Tõniste finance minister.

Ireland's prime minister Enda Kenny resigned and was replaced the following day by Leo Varadkar. Varadkar named himself as defence minister, with Paschal Donohoe as finance minister and Simon Coveney as foreign minister.

The Spanish prime minister Mariano Rajoy survived a parliamentary vote of no confidence by 170 votes to 82.

Didier Burkhalter announced his resignation as Switzerland's foreign minister, although he would stay in office until the end of October.

Week Beginning 4 June 2017

Santiago Peña resigned as Paraguay's finance minister and was replaced by Lea Giménez a day later.

In Nepal, Sher Bahadur Deuba was elected prime minister in a parliamentary vote, with 388 for and 170 against. He appointed Gyanendra Bahadur Karki as finance minister, Krishna Bahadur Mahara as minister of foreign affairs and Janardan Sharma as minister of home affairs.

Davor Božinović was appointed as interior minister in Croatia. The following week foreign minister Davor Ivo Stier resigned, with Marija Pejčinović Burić succeeding him a week later.

At a snap parliamentary election in the UK, the Conservative Party won 318 of 650 seats with 42.4% of votes cast (down from 331 in 2015, signalling the party's loss of its parliamentary majority). The Labour Party won

262 seats (40.0%), the Scottish National Party 35 (3.0%), the Liberal Democrats 12 (7.4%), the Democratic Unionist Party 10 (0.9%), Sinn Féin 7 (0.7%), Plaid Cymru 4 (0.5%) and the Green Party 1 (1.6%); There was also one independent. Turnout was 68.7% (66.1% in 2015).

In a cabinet reshuffle in South Korea spanning several days, Song Young-moo was named minister of defence, Kim Dong-yeon finance minister and Kang Kyung-wha minister of foreign affairs.

Chronology of Events for May 2017

Week Beginning 28 May 2017
In Argentina, Susana Malcorra resigned as foreign minister and was replaced by Jorge Marcelo Faurie.

Panama's *de facto* ruler from 1983–89, Manuel Noriega, died.

Aleksandar Vučić resigned as prime minister in Serbia in order to assume the presidency. Ivica Dačić, who had been prime minister from 2012–14, took over the premiership in an acting capacity.

In Lesotho's parliamentary elections, the All Basotho Convention won 48 of 120 seats, Democratic Congress 30, Lesotho Congress for Democracy 11, Alliance for Democrats 9, Movement for Economic Change 6, Basotho National Party 5 and Popular Front for Democracy 3. Five other parties won a single seat each and three seats remained vacant. Turnout was 46.4%.

The ruling Labour Party (LP) won 37 seats with 55.0% of votes cast in Malta's general elections. The Nationalist Force (NF; an electoral alliance between the Nationalist Party and the Democratic Party) won 30 with 43.7%. Turnout was 92.1%. The following week Edward Scicluna was named finance minister, Carmelo Abela foreign minister and Michael Farrugia as home affairs minister.

Week Beginning 21 May 2017
The Albanian parliament approved a cabinet reshuffle, with Helga Vukaj appointed as finance minister and Dritan Demiraj as interior minister.

After a cabinet reshuffle in Sri Lanka, Mangala Samaraweera became finance minister and Ravi Karunanayake foreign minister.

Tedros Adhanom Ghebreyesus of Ethiopia was elected director-general of the World Health Organization.

President Abdelaziz Bouteflika appointed Abdelmadjid Tebboune as prime minister in Algeria. While Bouteflika retained responsibility for the defence portfolio, Abderrahmane Raouia was named finance minister and Abdelkader Messahel foreign minister.

Lenín Moreno was sworn in as president of Ecuador. Miguel Ángel Carvajal Aguirre became minister of defence, Carlos Alberto de la Torre Muñoz minister of economy, María Feranda Espinosa Garcés minister of foreign affairs and César Antonio Navas Vera minister of interior.

Pushpa Kamal Dahal announced his resignation as Nepal's prime minister.

Week Beginning 14 May 2017
Édouard Philippe was sworn in as prime minister of France. He named Jean-Yves Le Drian as foreign minister, Gérard Collomb as interior minister and Bruno Le Maire as economy and finance minister.

Macedonia's president Gjorgje Ivanov asked Zoran Zaev to form a government. Two weeks later Zaev named Radmila Sekerinska-Jankovska as defence minister, Dragan Tevdovski as finance minister, Nikola Dimitrov as foreign minister and Oliver Spasovski as interior minister.

In Armenia, Karen Karapetyan was reappointed as prime minister.

Bruno Tshibala was sworn in as prime minister in the Democratic Republic of the Congo.

In presidential elections in Iran, Hassan Rouhani was re-elected with 57.1% of the vote ahead of Ebrahim Raisi with 38.3%, Mostafa Mir-Salim with 1.2% and Mostafa Hashemitaba with 0.5%. Turnout was 73.1%.

Francisco Guterres was sworn in as Timor-Leste's president.

Week Beginning 7 May 2017
Moon Jae-in of the Democratic Party of Korea won South Korea's presidential elections with 41.1% of the vote, ahead of Hong Jun-pyo of the Liberty Korea Party (24.0%). There were 11 other candidates and turnout was 77.2%.

At parliamentary elections in The Bahamas, the Free National Movement (FNM) won 57.0% of votes cast and 35 out of 39 seats against the ruling Progressive Liberal Party (PLP) with 37.0% and 4 seats. Hubert Minnis was sworn in as prime minister the following day. K. Peter Turnquest was named finance minister and Darren Henfield foreign minister.

In the Philippines, Alan Peter Cayetano was appointed foreign secretary.

Patrick Pruaitch was sacked as Papua New Guinea's treasurer, with prime minister Peter O'Neill assuming the portfolio.

In Sudan, prime minister Bakri Hassan Saleh named Mohamed Osman Suleiman Rikabi as finance minister and Hamid Mannan as interior minister.

Mauno Koivisto, twice prime minister of Finland and president from 1982–94, died.

Chronology of Events for April 2017

Week Beginning 30 April 2017
In Tunisia, Lamia Zribi was replaced as finance minister by Fadhel Abdelkefi in an acting capacity.

Bulgarian prime minister Boyko Borisov announced his new cabinet, including Krasimir Karakachanov as defence minister, Vladislav Goranov as finance minister, Ekaterina Gecheva-Zaharieva as foreign minister and Valentin Radev as interior minister.

In Algeria's parliamentary elections, the Front de Libération Nationale/National Liberation Front won 164 of 462 seats; Rassemblement National Démocratique/National Rally for Democracy, 97; Mouvement de la Société pour la Paix/Movement of Society for Peace, 33; Rassemblement de l'Espoir de l'Algérie/Rally for Hope for Algeria, 19. Independents took 28 seats and the remainder went to minor parties. Turnout was 38.3%.

In the Czech Republic, Andrej Babis was dismissed as minister of finance and replaced 3 weeks later by Ivan Pilný.

Ely Ould Mohammed Vall, Mauritania's military head of state from 2005 to 2007, died.

Week Beginning 23 April 2017
In the first round of presidential elections in France, Emmanuel Macron, the candidate for En Marche!, secured 24.0% of the vote, ahead of Marine Le Pen of the National Front (21.3%), François Fillon of the Republicans (20.0%) and Jean-Luc Mélenchon of La France Insoumise (19.6%). There were seven other candidates. In a run-off held 2 weeks later, Macron was elected president with 66.1% of votes cast against 33.9% for Le Pen. Turnout was 74.6% in the second round (77.8% in the first round).

Afghanistan's defence minister, Abdullah Habibi, resigned, with Tariq Shah Bahrami succeeding him in an acting capacity.

Gerry Brownlee was appointed New Zealand's foreign minister, with Mark Mitchell named defence minister.

In Bulgaria, president Rumen Radev granted Boyko Borisov a mandate to form a government.

Andrej Plenković, Croatia's prime minister, dismissed Vlaho Orepić as minister of interior, with Robert Kopal taking over the portfolio in an acting capacity.

The Albanian parliament elected Ilir Meta of the Socialist Movement for Integration as president after three failed rounds of voting. He was chosen by 87 votes to 2.

Agim Nuhiu resigned as interior minister in Macedonia.

Montenegro's parliament voted in favour of membership of the North Atlantic Treaty Organization.

Week Beginning 16 April 2017
Voters in a national referendum in Turkey approved a new constitution giving president Recep Tayyip Erdoğan additional political powers and abolishing the post of prime minister.

Week Beginning 9 April 2017
Abdoulaye Idrissa Maïga, Mali's minister of defence, was appointed prime minister. Tiéna Coulibaly took over responsibility for the defence portfolio.

Week Beginning 2 April 2017
The Republican Party of Armenia (HHK) won 58 of 105 seats with 49.2% of votes cast in Armenia's parliamentary elections. The Tsarukyan Alliance took 31 seats (27.4%), Way Out Alliance 9 (7.8%) and Armenian Revolutionary Federation 7 (6.6%). Turnout was 60.9%.

Lenín Moreno won 51.2% of the vote to Guillermo Lasso's 48.8% in Ecuador's presidential run-off. Turnout was 83.0%.

In Serbia, Aleksandar Vučić of the Serbian Progressive Party was elected president with 56.0% of the vote against 16.6% for Saša Janković. There were nine other candidates. Turnout was 54.4%.

Ismael Sueno was dismissed as interior minister in the Philippines, with Catalino Cuy succeeding him 2 days later.

In Morocco, prime minister Saadeddine Othmani named Mohamed Boussaid as economy and finance minister, Nasser Bourita as minister of foreign affairs and Abdelouafi Laftit as minister of the interior.

In the Democratic Republic of the Congo, Samy Badibanga resigned as prime minister. President Joseph Kabila appointed Bruno Tshibala as premier the following day.

In The Gambia's parliamentary elections, the United Democratic Party won 31 of the 53 elected seats with 37.5% of votes cast. The Gambia Democratic Congress, the Alliance for Patriotic Reorientation and Construction and the National Reconciliation Party claimed 5 seats each. Turnout was 42.8%.

Chronology of Events for March 2017

Week Beginning 26 March 2017
In parliamentary elections in Bulgaria, Citizens for the European Development of Bulgaria won 95 of 240 seats with 33.5% of the vote. The Bulgarian Socialist Party won 80 seats (27.9%), United Patriots 27 (9.3%), the Movement for Rights and Freedoms 26 (9.2%) and Volya 12 (4.2%).

In Hong Kong, Carrie Lam was elected chief executive with 777 votes in the 1,194-member election committee. John Tsang won 365 votes and Woo Kwok-hing 21.

Benin's minister-delegate in charge of defence, Candide Azannaï, resigned.

María Dolores Agüero was appointed foreign minister in Honduras, having held the post in an acting capacity since April 2016.

British prime minister Theresa May activated Article 50, formally commencing the UK's withdrawal from the European Union.

Adrian Hasler won a further term as Liechtenstein's head of government, claiming 17 votes. He also retained the finance portfolio, while Aurelia Frick remained foreign minister and Dominique Gantenbein became interior minister.

Malusi Gigaba became finance minister and Hlengiwe Mkhize home affairs minister following a cabinet reshuffle in South Africa.

In Paraguay, Lorenzo Darío Lezcano replaced Tadeo Rojas as interior minister.

Vanessa D'Ambrosio of the Democratic Socialist Left and Mimma Zavoli of Civic 10 took office as Captains Regent of San Marino.

Week Beginning 19 March 2017
Frank-Walter Steinmeier took office as Germany's president.

In presidential polls in Timor-Leste, Francisco Guterres of FRETILIN won with 57.1% of the vote against 32.5% for António da Conceição of the Democratic Party. Turnout was 71.2%.

Bruno Le Roux resigned as interior minister in France, with Matthias Fekl replacing him the following day.

Week Beginning 12 March 2017
In a cabinet reshuffle in Albania, Fatmir Xhafaj was appointed interior minister.

Haiti's prime minister-designate, Jack Guy Lafontant, announced his cabinet nominations. These included Hervé Denis as defence minister, Jude Alix Patrick Salomon as finance minister, Antonio Rodrigue as foreign minister and Max Rudolph Saint-Albin as interior minister. They were sworn in a week later.

János Áder was returned as Hungary's president after winning a simple majority in a second round of voting in parliament against László Majtényi.

Moussa Faki was sworn in as chairman of the African Union's Commission.

Colombia's vice president Germán Vargas Lleras resigned and was succeeded the following week by Gen. Óscar Naranjo.

In Morocco, King Muhammad VI dismissed prime minister Abdelilah Benkirane after he failed to form a government following the elections of October 2016. The King then appointed Saadeddine Othmani as prime minister.

In parliamentary elections in the Netherlands, the People's Party for Freedom and Democracy won 33 of 150 seats (with 21.3% of the vote), the Party for Freedom 20 (13.1%), Christian Democratic Appeal 19 (12.4%), Democrats '66 19 (12.2%), Socialist Party 14 (9.1%), Green Left 14 (9.1%), Labour Party 9 (5.7%), Christian Union 5 (3.4%), Party for the Animals 5 (3.2%) and 50Plus 4 (3.1%). Turnout was 81.9%.

Week Beginning 5 March 2017
Tonga's finance minister 'Aisake Eke resigned and was replaced by Tevita Lavemaau, with Siaosi Sovaleni becoming minister of foreign affairs.

In parliamentary elections in Micronesia, all ten seats were taken by non-partisan candidates.

A parliamentary commission in the Philippines rejected the appointment of Perfecto Yasay, Jr. as foreign secretary. The following day President Rodrigo Duterte appointed Enrique Manalo to the post in an acting capacity.

Donald Tusk was re-elected president of the European Council by 27 votes to one.

South Korea's Constitutional Court upheld the parliamentary impeachment of President Park Geun-hye effected in December 2016.

Chronology of Events for February 2017

Week Beginning 26 February 2017
Prime minister 'Akilisi Pohiva survived a parliamentary no-confidence vote in Tonga by 14 votes to 10.

In Lesotho, prime minister Pakalitha Mosisili suffered defeat in a parliamentary no-confidence vote.

Hassan Ali Kheyre was sworn in as Somalia's prime minister.

In Sudan, Bakri Hassan Saleh was appointed prime minister, becoming the first person to hold the post since 1989.

Aloysio Nunes Ferreira Filho was named as Brazil's foreign minister.

At parliamentary elections in Northern Ireland, the Democratic Unionist Party won 28 seats (28.1% of first preference votes); Sinn Féin 27 (27.9%); the Social and Democratic Labour Party 12 (11.9%); the Ulster Unionist Party 10 (12.9%); the Alliance Party 8 (9.1%). Three smaller parties won two seats or fewer and an independent also won a seat. Turnout was 64.8%.

Haiti's former prime minister and president, René Préval, died.

Week Beginning 19 February 2017
Jean-Claude Bouda became Burkina Faso's defence minister following a cabinet reshuffle.

Brazil's foreign minister, José Serra, resigned and was replaced by Marcos Galvão in an acting capacity.

Dovrangeldy Bayramov was named as Turkmenistan's minister of national security.

Week Beginning 12 February 2017
Germany's 1,260-member Federal Convention elected Frank-Walter Steinmeier as president with 931 votes. Christoph Butterwegge received 128 votes and there were 103 abstentions.

Gurbanguly Berdymukhammedov was re-elected president of Turkmenistan, claiming 97.7% of the vote. Turnout was 97.3%.

Prime minister Enda Kenny's government in Ireland won a confidence vote in parliament by 57 votes to 52 (with 44 abstentions).

Week Beginning 5 February 2017
In Chad, Christine Georges Diguibaye was named finance minister and Hissein Brahim Taha foreign minister.

In parliamentary elections in Liechtenstein the Progressive Citizens' Party (FBP) won 9 seats (35.2% of votes cast); the Patriotic Union (VU), 8 (33.7% of votes); the Independents, 5 (18.4%); and the Free List (FL), 3 (12.6%). Turnout was 77.8%.

Jovenel Moïse was sworn in as president of Haiti. Two days later Enex Jean-Charles resigned as prime minister and was succeeded by Jack Guy Lafontant, who was sworn in 6 weeks later.

In Romania, Sorin Grindeanu's government survived a no-confidence vote by 161 parliamentary votes to 8.

Somalia's parliament elected Mohamed Abdullahi Mohamed president in a run-off poll. He claimed 184 votes against 97 for incumbent Hassan Sheikh Mohamud and 46 for Sharif Sheikh Ahmed. Hassan Sheikh Mohamud had led after the first round of voting.

Jeff Sessions was confirmed as the USA's attorney general.

Chronology of Events for January 2017

Week Beginning 29 January 2017

Guinea's president Alpha Condé was elected chairperson of the African Union.

Erfan al-Hiyali was appointed defence minister in Iraq and Qasim al-Araji interior minister.

In The Gambia, Ousainou Darboe was sworn in as foreign minister, Mai Ahmad Fatty as interior minister and Amadou Sanneh as finance minister.

In the USA, Rex Tillerson was sworn in as secretary of state.

Week Beginning 22 January 2017

Bulgarian president Rumen Radev was sworn in and named Ognyan Gerdzhikov as interim prime minister. The caretaker government, pending fresh elections scheduled for March, featured Stefan Yanev as defence minister, Kiril Ananiev finance minister, Radi Naidenov foreign minister and Plamen Ouzounov as interior minister.

In Bolivia, Fernando Huanacuni became foreign minister.

Alexander Van der Bellen was sworn in as Austrian president.

Chad's minister of finance Mbogo Ngabo Seli was dismissed.

Sigmar Gabriel was named Germany's foreign minister.

Week Beginning 15 January 2017

Ayman Safadi was named Jordan's foreign minister and Ghaleb Zu'bi interior minister.

In Nicaragua, Denis Moncada became foreign minister and María Amelia Coronel interior minister.

Tonga's prime minister 'Akilisi Pohiva assumed responsibility for the internal affairs portfolio.

In the USA, Donald Trump was inaugurated as president and Mike Pence vice-president along with James Mattis as defence secretary and John F. Kelly as homeland security secretary.

Against a backdrop of domestic and international pressure, Yahya Jammeh ceded the presidency of The Gambia following disputed elections to Adama Barrow, who named Fatoumata Tambajang as his vice-president.

Sir Anerood Jugnauth, prime minister of Mauritius, announced his resignation, with power passing to his son Pravind Jugnauth.

Week Beginning 8 January 2017

Hashemi Ali Akbar Rafsanjani, president of Iran from 1989 until 1997, died.

In Côte d'Ivoire, prime minister Daniel Kablan Duncan and his government resigned. A day later, Duncan was appointed vice president, with Amadou Gon Coulibaly as prime minister. Hamed Bakayoko was named interior minister, Adama Koné finance minister and Marcel Amon Tanoh foreign minister.

Julio César Gandarilla was appointed Cuba's interior minister following the death of Carlos Fernández Gondín.

Northern Ireland's deputy first minister, Martin McGuinness, resigned, forcing the stepping down of Arlene Foster as first minister and the scheduling of early assembly elections.

In Canada, Chrystia Freeland was named foreign minister.

Bjarni Benediktsson became Iceland's prime minister, with Benedikt Jóhannesson as finance minister and Guðlaugur Þór Þórðarson as foreign minister..

Week Beginning 1 January 2017

Romania's prime minister-designate Sorin Grindeanu named Gabriel-Beniamin Leş defence minister, Viorel Ştefan finance minister, Teodor-Viorel Meleşcanu foreign minister and Carmen Daniela Dan interior minister.

Luis Videgaray became Mexcio's foreign minister.

In Venezuela, Ramón Lobo was appointed finance minister and Tareck El Aissami executive vice-president.

Nana Akufo-Addo was sworn in as Ghana's president. He subsequently named Dominic Nitiwul defence minister, Ken Ofori-Atta finance minister, Shirley Ayorkor Botchway foreign minister and Ambrose Dery interior minister.

Portugal's former prime minister and president, Mário Soares, died.

2016

Chronology of Events for December 2016

Week Beginning 25 December 2016

In Argentina, president Mauricio Macri sacked Alfonso Prat Gay as minister of finance, creating two new replacement posts in the process. These were filled by Luis Caputo and Nicolás Dujovne.

Kairat Abdrakhmanov became Kazakhstan's foreign minister.

Week Beginning 18 December 2016

In parliamentary elections in Côte d'Ivoire, the Rally of Houphouëtists for Democracy and Peace won 167 of 255 seats, independents 76, the Union for Democracy and Peace in Côte d'Ivoire 6, the Ivorian Popular Front 3, and the Union for Côte d'Ivoire 3. Turnout was 34.1%.

Lebanon's new prime minister Saad al-Hariri announced his government, with Gebran Bassil as foreign minister, Nuhad Mashnouk interior minister, Yaacoub Sarraf as defence minister and Ali Hasan Khalil finance minister.

In the Democratic Republic of the Congo, Samy Badibanga was sworn in as prime minister and named Léonard She Okitundu as foreign minister, Emmanuel Ramazani Shadari as interior minister, Crispin Atama Tabe as defence minister and Henri Yav Mulang as finance minister.

Igor Dodon was sworn in as president in Moldova. A few days later he dismissed Anatolie Salaru as minister of defence.

Week Beginning 11 December 2016

In parliamentary elections in Macedonia, the ruling Internal Macedonian Revolutionary Organization-Democratic Party for Macedonian National Unity (VMRO-DPMNE) won 51 of 120 seats with 39.4% of votes cast. The Social Democratic Union of Macedonia (SDSM) took 49 (37.9%), the Democratic Union for Integration (DUI) 10, the Besa Movement 5, the 'Alliance for the Albanians' coalition 3 and the Democratic Party of Albanians 2. Turnout was 66.8%.

In parliamentary elections in Romania, the Social Democratic Party (PSD) took 154 seats (45.5% of the vote) in the lower house, the National Liberal Party (PNL) 69 (20.0%), the Save Romania Union (USR) 30 (8.9%), the Democratic Union of Hungarians in Romania (UDMR) 21 (6.2%), the Alliance of Liberals and Democrats (ALDE) 20 (5.6%) and the People's Movement Party (PMP) 18 (5.3%). Turnout was 39.5%.

Guinea-Bissau's prime minister, Umaro Sissoco Embaló, named his government, including Eduardo Costa Sanha as defence minister, João Aladje Mamadu Fadia finance minister, Jorge Malú foreign minister and Botche Candé interior minister.

Week Beginning 4 December 2016

At the repeat run-off for the presidency in Austria (following the Constitutional Court's rejection of the previous poll), Alexander Van der Bellen (independent but affiliated to the Greens) claimed 53.8% of the vote to defeat the far-right Freedom Party candidate, Norbert Hofer (with 46.2%). Turnout was 74.2%.

In Uzbekistan's presidential election, the acting president and incumbent prime minister Shavkat Mirziyoyev (Liberal Democratic Party) took 88.6% of the vote, against 3.7% for Khatamjon Ketmonov, 3.5% for Narimon Umarov and 2.4% for Sarvar Otamuradov. Turnout was 87.8%. Abdulla Aripov was subsequently appointed prime minister, with Batyr Khojayev as finance minister.

Manuel Valls resigned as France's prime minister in order to stand for the presidency. He was replaced by Bernard Cazeneuve, whose position as interior minister went to Bruno Le Roux.

Following the rejection in a referendum of constitutional reforms that he had championed, Italy's prime minister, Matteo Renzi, resigned. Paolo Gentiloni replaced him and the following week announced a government including Angelino Alfano as foreign minister and Marco Minniti as interior minister.

John Key resigned as prime minister of New Zealand, with Bill English succeeding him a week later. His cabinet included Steven Joyce as finance minister.

In presidential elections in Ghana, Nana Akufo-Addo of the New Patriotic Party (NPP) won 53.8% of the vote and incumbent John Dramani Mahama of the National Democratic Congress (NDC) 44.4%. Turnout was 68.6%. In parliamentary elections held simultaneously the NPP won 171 of 275 seats and the NDC 104.

In Switzerland, the United Federal Assembly elected Doris Leuthard president for 2017, with 188 votes out of 207, and Alain Berset vice-president.

In South Korea, parliament voted to impeach the president, Park Geun-hye, amid allegations of corruption. Premier Hwang Kyo-ahn took over the presidency in an acting capacity.

Sheikh Muhammad Khaled al-Hamad al-Sabah was named Kuwait's defence minister, with Sheikh Khaled al-Jarrah al-Sabah as interior minister.

Chronology of Events for November 2016

Week Beginning 27 November 2016

Denmark's prime minister, Lars Løkke Rasmussen, announced a new government with Simon Emil Ammitzbøll as interior minister, Claus Hjort Frederiksen as defence minister, Kristian Jensen as finance minister and Anders Samuelsen as foreign minister.

Duško Marković was approved by Montenegro's parliament as prime minister. His government included Predrag Bošković as defence minister, Srđan Darmanović as foreign minister, Melvudin Nuhodžić as interior minister and Darko Radunović as finance minister.

Mariano González resigned as Peru's minister of defence. He was succeeded by Jorge Nieto 10 days later.

Adama Barrow of Coalition 2016 won The Gambia's presidential elections, claiming 43.3% of votes cast against 39.6% for incumbent Yahya Jammeh (Alliance for Patriotic Reorientation and Construction) and 17.1% for Mamma Kandeh (Gambia Democratic Congress). Jammeh initially conceded defeat after 22 years in power but then announced that he no longer accepted the result.

Week Beginning 20 November 2016

In Haiti's presidential elections, Jovenel Moïse was elected with 55.6% of the vote, against Jude Célestin with 19.6%, Jean-Charles Moïse 11.0% and Maryse Narcisse 9.0%. There were 23 other candidates. Turnout was 21%.

In parliamentary elections in San Marino, the San Marino First coalition won 25 of 60 seats with 41.7% of the vote, the Adesso.sm coalition 20 seats with 31.4% and the Democracy in Motion 15 seats with 23.2%. Turnout was 59.7%. As a majority was not reached in the Great and General Council, a run-off was held on 4 Dec. 2016 in which Adesso.sm took 57.9% of the vote and 35 seats and San Marino First 42.0% and 16 seats. The remaining nine seats were allocated to the Democracy in Motion. Turnout in the run-off was 50.1%.

In a cabinet reshuffle in Georgia, Dimitry Kumsishvili was appointed finance minister.

The Lithuanian parliament approved Saulius Skvernelis, an independent affiliated to Lithuanian Peasant and Greens Union as the new prime minister. He announced a cabinet including Raimundas Karoblis as defence minister, Linas Antanas Linkevičius as foreign minister, Eimutis Misiūnas as interior minister and Vilius Šapoka as finance minister.

In Côte d'Ivoire, Marcel Amon Tanoh succeeded Albert Toikeusse Mabri as foreign minister.

The Colombian government and left-wing rebel group FARC signed a revised peace agreement, following rejection of an earlier deal in a referendum in October. The new deal received congressional approval the following week.

Fidel Castro—Cuba's former premier, first secretary of its Communist Party and president of the Council of State and the Council of Ministers—died.

In parliamentary elections in Kuwait, opposition candidates won 24 of 50 seats in the National Assembly. Turnout was around 70%.

Week Beginning 13 November 2016

In Bulgaria, Rumen Radev won the run-off for the presidency with 59.4% of the vote against 36.2% for Tsetska Tsacheva. Turnout was 50.4%. In the first round of voting, held a week earlier, Radev had claimed 25.4% of votes and Tsacheva 22.0% against 19 other candidates.

Igor Dodon was elected Moldova's president after taking 52.1% of the vote in a run-off against Maia Sandu.

Samy Badibanga was named prime minister in the Democratic Republic of the Congo following the resignation of Augustin Matata Ponyo.

Mladen Ivanić took over the rotating presidency in Bosnia and Herzegovina.

Week Beginning 6 November 2016

In Nicaragua's presidential election, incumbent José Daniel Ortega Saavedra of the Sandinista National Liberation Front (FSLN) won 72.4% of votes cast, defeating Maximino Rodriguez (15.0%) and four other candidates. In parliamentary elections held on the same day, the FSLN won 70 seats, the Constitutionalist Liberal Party 13, the Independent Liberal Party 2 and the Nicaraguan Liberal Alliance 2, with three other parties each taking one seat. Two other seats were reserved for 'special members'.

Xiao Jie became China's finance minister.

In the USA's presidential election, Republican candidate Donald Trump beat his Democrat opponent Hillary Clinton. Trump won 306 electoral college votes in states where he won the popular vote, while Clinton claimed 232. However, the final tally was 304 for Trump and 227 for Clinton as seven college electors chose to vote for candidates other than the two front-runners. After elections held on the same day for the House of Representatives and 34 of 100 seats in the Senate, the Republicans secured majorities in both houses.

Estonia's prime minister, Taavi Rõivas, resigned following a no-confidence vote in parliament. President Kersti Kaljulaid subsequently asked Jüri Ratas to form a government, which included Andres Anvelt as interior minister, Sven Mikser as foreign minister, Sven Sester as finance minister and Margus Tsahkna as defence minister.

President José Mário Vaz of Guinea-Bissau dismissed the government of Baciro Djá and appointed Umaro Sissoco Embaló as prime minister 9 days later.

Jacob Zuma, South Africa's president, survived a no-confidence motion in parliament.

After gaining parliamentary approval, Kyrgyzstan's new cabinet took office. It included Ulan Israilov as interior minister.

Afghanistan's parliament voted to dismiss foreign minister Salahuddin Rabbani.

Chronology of Events for October 2016

Week Beginning 30 October 2016

Following the second round of Georgia's parliamentary elections, held 3 weeks after the first round, the ruling Georgian Dream coalition claimed 115 of 150 seats. The United National Movement won 27 seats, the Alliance of Patriots of Georgia 6 seats and Industry Will Save Georgia-Our Fatherland 1 seat. Turnout was 51.6%.

After 46 attempts, Lebanon's parliament elected a new president. Michel Aoun was sworn in after two rounds of voting and asked Saad Hariri to form a government.

The Organisation of Islamic Cooperation's secretary-general, Iyad Madani, resigned.

Tadeo Rojas became Paraguay's interior minister.

Muhammad al-Jadaan replaced Ibrahim bin Abdulaziz Al-Assaf as Saudi Arabia's finance minister.

Mariano Rajoy was sworn in for a new term as Spain's prime minister. The following month he named Alfonso Dastis as foreign minister, María Dolores de Cospedal as defence minister, Juan Ignacio Zoido as interior minister and Cristóbal Montoro as finance minister.

In a cabinet reshuffle in Ethiopia, Workneh Gebeyehu was named foreign minister and Abraham Tekeste finance minister.

Incumbent president Tommy Remengesau won 51.3% of the vote against 48.7% for Surangel Whipps, Jr. (his brother-in-law) in Palau's presidential run-off.

In a cabinet reshuffle Panos Skourletis was sworn in as the Greek interior minister.

Week Beginning 23 October 2016

After two rounds of parliamentary elections in Lithuania, the Lithuanian Peasant and Greens Union won 54 of the 141 seats; Homeland Union-Lithuanian Christian Democrats 31; Social Democratic Party of Lithuania 17; and Liberal Movement 14. Six other parties won ten seats or fewer and four seats went to independents.

Kyrgyzstan's government, headed by Sooronbay Jeenbekov, resigned following the collapse of the ruling coalition.

Montenegro's prime minister, Milo Đjukanović, announced his resignation and left office five weeks later.

In parliamentary elections in Iceland, the Independence Party won 21 of the 63 seats (with 29.0% of votes cast), the Left-Green Movement

10 (15.9%), the Pirate Party 10 (14.5%), the Progressive Party 8, the Revival Party 7, Bright Future 4 and the Social Democratic Alliance 3. Turnout was 79.2%.

Week Beginning 16 October 2016

Montenegro held parliamentary elections in which the Democratic Party of Socialists of Montenegro won 36 of 81 seats (with 41.4% of votes cast), the Democratic Front 18 (20.3%), the Key Coalition 9 (11.1%), Democratic Montenegro 8 (10.0%) and the Social Democratic Party 4 (5.2%). Four smaller parties won two seats or fewer. Turnout was 73.3%.

Danny Faure was sworn in as president of the Seychelles. He also took responsibility for the foreign affairs and defence portfolios. Vincent Meriton was later sworn in as vice-president.

Urbino Botelho was named foreign minister in São Tomé and Príncipe, and Arlindo Ramos added defence to his existing interior affairs portfolio.

In Belize, prime minister Dean Barrow took over the home affairs portfolio.

The Croatian parliament gave its backing to the new government of Andrej Plenković. Davor Ivo Stier was appointed foreign minister and Damir Krstičević defence minister. Vlaho Orepić remained as interior minister and Zdravko Maric as finance minister.

Kalla Moutari became Niger's defence minister and Hassoumi Massoudou was named finance minister in a cabinet reshuffle.

Week Beginning 9 October 2016

In Estonia, Kersti Kaljulaid was sworn in as president, having received 81 votes in the 101-member parliament. Two previous rounds of voting by the electoral college had failed to produce a clear winner.

Thailand's King Bhumibol Adulyadej died. After a period with an interim regent he was succeeded by Crown Prince Vajiralongkorn 7 weeks later.

The United Nations General Assembly approved António Guterres as the organization's next secretary-general, taking office on 1 January 2017.

Khalifa al-Ghawi proclaimed the reinstatement of his Tripoli-based government in Libya.

In Malaysia, the sultan of Kelantan, Muhammad V, was elected as the nation's paramount ruler.

Penisimani Fifita was appointed Tonga's internal affairs minister.

Week Beginning 2 October 2016

In Cabo Verde's presidential elections, incumbent Jorge Carlos Fonseca defeated Albertino Graça with 74.1% of the vote. Turnout was 35.5%.

In a popular plebiscite, voters rejected a peace deal signed by the Colombian government and left-wing rebel group FARC the previous week that was intended to end 50 years of civil conflict. Under the terms of the deal, FARC agreed to disarm and transform itself into a legal political party in return for government development programmes in rural areas and lenient sentences for ex-guerrillas responsible for alleged atrocities committed during the war. However, 50.2% of the electorate voted against it. A few days later Juan Manuel Santos, the president of Colombia, was awarded the Nobel Peace Prize for his efforts to end the conflict.

A new cabinet was named in Gabon, including Massard Kabinda Makaga as defence minister, Pacôme Moubelet Boubeya as foreign affairs minister and Lambert Matha as interior minister.

Vigen Sargsyan was appointed Armenia's defence minister.

In Morocco's parliamentary elections, the Islamist Parti de la Justice et du Développement (PJD/Party of Justice and Development) took 125 of 395 seats; Parti Authenticité et Modernité (PAM/Authenticity and Modernity Party) 102; Parti de l'Indépendance/Istiqlal (PI/Independence Party) 46; Rassemblement National des Indépendants (RNI/National Rally of Independents) 37; Mouvement Populaire (MP/Popular Movement) 27; and Union Socialiste des Forces Populaires (USFP/Socialist Union of Popular Forces) 20. A further six parties each obtained fewer than 20 seats. Abdelilah Benkirane was reappointed as prime minister.

Chronology of Events for September 2016

Week Beginning 25 September 2016

Gabon's president Ali Bongo Ondimba appointed Emmanuel Issoze-Ngondet, the foreign minister, as prime minister in place of Daniel Ona Ondo.

Dame Patsy Reddy took office as New Zealand's governor-general.

In Poland, Mateusz Morawiecki was appointed finance minister.

Marino Riccardi of the Party of Socialists and Democrats and Fabio Berardi of the Sammarinese Christian Democratic Party were sworn in as San Marino's Captains Regent.

Week Beginning 18 September 2016

In Russia's parliamentary elections, the ruling United Russia party claimed 343 of 450 seats (54.2% of the vote), the Communist Party 42 (13.3%), the Liberal-Democratic Party 39 (13.1%) and A Just Russia 23 (6.2%). Turnout was 47.9%.

At parliamentary elections in Jordan, the Islamic Action Front and its allies claimed 15 of 130 seats with most other seats going to pro-monarchy loyalists. Turnout was 37%. Incumbent prime minister Hani Al-Mulki was subsequently asked to form a new government.

Mateja Vranicar Erman became Slovenia's finance minister after receiving parliamentary approval.

Week Beginning 11 September 2016

In Belarus's parliamentary elections, independent candidates supportive of president Alyaksandr Lukashenka claimed 94 of 110 seats and the Communist Party 8, with the remaining seats going to smaller parties. Domestic turnout was recorded at 54.4%.

At parliamentary polls in Croatia, the Croatian Democratic Union coalition won 61 of 151 seats, the People's Coalition (led by the Social Democratic Party) 54, the Bridge of Independent Lists 13 and the Only Option Coalition 8. Turnout was recorded at 52.6%.

Ahmat Jidoud replaced Saïdou Sidibé as Niger's finance minister in an acting capacity.

Zambia's president Edgar Lungu appointed Harry Kalaba as foreign minister, Felix Mutati as finance minister, Davies Chama as defence minister and Steven Kampyongo as home affairs minister.

Momodou Alieu Bah was appointed interior minister in The Gambia..

Week Beginning 4 September 2016

In Angola, Archer Mangueira replaced Armando Manuel as finance minister in a cabinet reshuffle.

In a cabinet reshuffle in Malaŵi, Grace Chiumia became minister of home affairs and internal security.

Following the resignation of Luis Videgaray, José Antonio Meade was appointed Mexico's finance minister.

Dragos Tudorache was sworn in as interior minister of Romania following the earlier resignation of Petre Tobă.

In Armenia, Karen Karapetyan became prime minister. He was nominated by the ruling Republican Party of Armenia following the resignation of Hovik Abrahamyan as premier. Karapetyan named Vardan Aramyan as finance minister.

Karim Massimov was dismissed as Kazakhstan's prime minister by president Nursultan Nazarbayev and replaced by Bakhytzhan Sagintayev. In a subsequent cabinet reshuffle, Saken Zhasuzakov became minister of defence.

In Uzbekistan, Shavkat Mirziyoyev, the prime minister since 2003, became interim president, replacing Nigmatilla Yuldashev.

Jürgen Ligi succeeded Marina Kaljurand as foreign minister in Estonia.

In Fiji, prime minister Frank Bainimarama assumed the foreign affairs portfolio from Ratu Inoke Kubuabola who became defence minister.

Parliamentary elections in the Seychelles saw the Linyon Demokratik Seselwa alliance win 19 seats with 49.6% of the vote and the People's Party 14 with 49.2%. President James Michel of the People's Party announced that he would leave office in October.

Chronology of Events for August 2016

Week Beginning 28 August 2016

Brazil's suspended president Dilma Rousseff was formally impeached by the Senate following accusations she had breached budgetary laws. Michel Temer, who had served as acting president since her suspension in May 2016, took over on a permanent basis for the rest of her term.

Fiji's defence minister Timoci Lesi Natuva resigned citing personal reasons. Prime minister Frank Bainimarama took over his responsibilities on an interim basis.

Lieut.-Gen. Sir Jeremiah Mateparae's term as governor-general of New Zealand came to an end.

Süleyman Soylu was sworn in as interior minister of Turkey following the resignation of Efkan Ala.

An interim government was appointed in Macedonia in order to oversee elections scheduled to be held in December. Oliver Spasovski was sworn in as interior minister, with other key portfolios remaining unchanged.

Uzbekistan's long-serving president Islam Karimov died aged 78, having reportedly suffered a stroke. With no successor in place the chairman of the Senate, Nigmatilla Yuldashev, took over the presidency on an acting basis.

In Mali, defence minister Tiéman Coulibaly was removed from office by president Ibrahim Boubacar Keïta, having been accused of failing to counter deadly attacks against the army. Abdoulaye Idrissa Maïga subsequently took over Coulibaly's portfolio.

Evaristo Carvalho was sworn in as president of São Tomé and Príncipe.

Week Beginning 21 August 2016
Khaled al-Obeidi was dismissed as minister of defence in Iraq following allegations of corruption and accusations that he had weakened the country's armed forces in their fight against Islamic State.

In Gabon, incumbent president Ali Bongo Ondimba was re-elected with 49.8% of votes cast against 48.2% for Jean Ping. There were eight other candidates. Violence broke out in the capital following the announcement of Bongo's victory.

A new government took office in Tunisia. Lamia Zribi's appointment as finance minister was the only change to a key portfolio.

Week Beginning 14 August 2016
A new government was appointed in Chad. Pahimi Padacké was reappointed prime minister by president Idriss Déby, leading a cabinet that included Mbogo Ngabo Seli as finance minister and Bacher Ali as territorial administration and local governance minister. Other key portfolios remained unchanged.

In Yemen, Muhammad Ali al-Houthi and the Revolutionary Committee, which had effectively been in power since Houthi fighters seized control of the presidential palace in January 2015, handed power to Saleh Ali al-Sammad and the Supreme Political Council.

Danilo Medina was sworn in for a second term as president of the Dominican Republic alongside a new cabinet that included Paulino Sem as defence minister and Carlos Amarante Baret as interior minister.

Week Beginning 7 August 2016
In São Tomé and Príncipe, Evaristo Carvalho was elected president after Manuel Pinto da Costa withdrew from the second round run-off claiming that the first round had been fraudulent.

A cabinet reshuffle took place in Serbia. Goran Knežević became economy minister, Nela Kuburović justice minister and Aleksandar Antić mining and energy minister. Key portfolios remained unchanged.

In Zambia, incumbent president Edgar Lungu was re-elected with 50.4% of the vote, beating Hakainde Hichilema with 47.6%. Seven other candidates received less than 1% of the vote each. Turnout was 56.5%.

Jorge Menéndez became defence minister of Uruguay, taking over from Eleuterio Fernández Huidobro who had died a week earlier.

Chronology of Events for July 2016

Week Beginning 31 July 2016
In Belize, the ministry of national security was split between the incumbent minister, John Saldivar, who became defence minister, and Godwin Hulse, who became minister of police and immigration.

Levan Izoria was sworn in as defence minister of Georgia following the resignation of Tinatin Khidasheli the previous week.

Guðni Jóhannesson's term as president of Iceland began. He took over from Ólafur Ragnar Grímsson, who had held the office for 20 years.

In a cabinet reshuffle in Togo, Sani Yaya was appointed minister of state and minister of economy and finance. Other key portfolios were unchanged.

Japanese prime minister Shinzo Abe reshuffled his cabinet. Tomomi Inada became defence minister, with other key positions remaining the same.

In Nepal, Pushpa Kamal Dahal was elected prime minister by 363 parliamentary votes to 210. His cabinet included Krishna Bahadur Mahara as finance minister and Bimalendra Nidhi as home minister.

Week Beginning 24 July 2016
Khadga Prasad Oli announced his resignation as prime minister of Nepal after the withdrawal of the Communist Party of Nepal (Maoist Centre) from the coalition government and the subsequent tabling of a no-confidence motion against his premiership. Puspha Kamal Dahal succeeded him 12 days later.

In South Sudan, first vice president Riek Machar was dismissed by president Salva Kiir Mayardit. Taban Deng Gai took over Machar's position, while Stephen Dhieu Dau was appointed finance minister 4 days later. Michael Tiangjiek Mut was also sworn in as interior minister 4 days after that.

The president of Vietnam, Tran Dai Quang, was re-elected by the National Assembly. Prime minister Nguyen Xuan Phuc was also re-elected a day later with key positions in his cabinet remaining the same.

A cabinet reshuffle took place in Indonesia. Sri Mulyani Indrawati became finance minister and Enggartiasto Lukita trade minister. Other key portfolios were unchanged.

Pedro Pablo Kuczynski, the winner of presidential elections that took place in April and June in Peru, took office. His new cabinet included Fernando Zavala as prime minister, Carlos Basombrío as interior minister, Mariano Gonzales as defence minister and Ricardo Luna as foreign minister.

Week Beginning 17 July 2016
Former prime minister Evaristo Carvalho won the first round of presidential elections in São Tomé and Príncipe with 49.9% of the vote against incumbent president Manuel Pinto da Costa who took 24.8% of votes. Three other candidates contested the poll. A second round run-off was scheduled to take place 3 weeks later.

In Papua New Guinea, prime minister Peter O'Neill survived a parliamentary vote of no confidence by 85 votes to 21.

Week Beginning 10 July 2016
Mohamed Asim became foreign minister of the Maldives after Dunya Maumoon had resigned 8 days earlier.

In Nauru, Baron Waqa was re-elected president by parliament.

Dušan Mramor resigned as finance minister of Slovenia and Alenka Smerkolj took over on an interim basis.

Theresa May was sworn in as prime minister of the United Kingdom, replacing David Cameron who had been a key figure on the losing side in the British referendum on whether to remain in the European Union. Cameron had earlier announced his intention to resign as premier after the election of a new Conservative Party leader. May emerged as the winning candidate in the leadership race that was also contested by prominent eurosceptics who had campaigned to leave the EU. She subsequently appointed Philip Hammond as chancellor of the exchequer, Boris Johnson as foreign secretary and Amber Rudd as home secretary.

Week Beginning 3 July 2016
A new government led by prime minister Imad Khamis was appointed in Syria. Maamoun Hamdan became finance minister, with other key portfolios unchanged.

Aqil al-Khazali was sworn in as interior minister of Iraq following the resignation of Salem al-Ghabban.

Jargaltulgyn Erdenebat was sworn in as prime minister of Mongolia. His cabinet, which included Badmaanyambuu Bat-Erdene as defence minister and Tsendiyn Munkh-Orgil as foreign minister, was appointed later in the month.

Chronology of Events for June 2016

Week Beginning 26 June 2016
Since no political party had secured a majority at the polls 6 months earlier and negotiations had failed to produce a coalition government, another election took place in Spain. The Popular Party (PP) won 137 seats; the Spanish Socialist Workers' Party (PSOE), 85; Podemos (including En Comú Podem, Compromís and En Marea), 71; and Citizens (Ciudadanos), 32. Five other smaller parties and coalitions took the remaining 25 seats. Again, no single party attained a parliamentary majority.

A cabinet reshuffle took place in Malaysia. Tan Sri Noh Omar was appointed as minister of urban wellbeing, housing and local government and Datuk Johari Abdul Ghani as second finance minister. Other key portfolios remained unchanged.

At parliamentary elections in Mongolia, the Mongolian People's Party won 65 of the 76 available seats, the Democratic Party 9 and the Mongolian People's Revolutionary Party 1. An independent also won a seat.

Rodrigo Duterte was sworn in as president of the Philippines.

Elvin Nimrod became foreign minister of Grenada.

Parliamentary elections took place in Australia. The ruling Liberal/National Coalition won 76 seats and 42.1% of the primary vote (of which Liberal Party, 45 and 28.6%; Liberal National Party of Queensland (LNP), 21 and 8.6%; and National Party of Australia (NP), 10 and 4.6%). The opposition Labor Party (ALP) won 69 seats with 34.7% of the primary vote; Australian Greens 1 (10.2%); Nick Xenophon Team 1 (1.8%); and Katter's Australian Party 1 (0.5%). Independents took two seats.

Week Beginning 19 June 2016

Abdullah Habibi was sworn in as defence minister of Afghanistan, replacing Mohammad Masoom Stanekzai who was appointed head of the country's intelligence agency.

Adolf Mwesige became defence minister following a cabinet reshuffle in Uganda, with Frank Tumwebaze becoming minister for information, ICT and communications and Jeje Odongo internal affairs minister. Additionally, first lady Janet Museveni became minister of education and sports. Other key portfolios remained unchanged.

In the Maldives, Ahmed Zuhoor was sworn in as home affairs minister and Abdulla Jihad became vice president. Jihad's former position as finance minister was assumed by Ahmed Munuwwar.

In Finland, prime minister Juha Sipilä reshuffled his cabinet. Paula Risikko became interior minister and Petteri Orpo finance minister. Other key portfolios were unaffected.

Francisco Pascual Obama Asue was sworn in as prime minister of Equatorial Guinea after president Teodoro Obiang Nguema Mbasogo dissolved the previous government of Vicente Ehate Tomi. Obama Asue headed a new government that included the president's son, Teodoro Nguema Obiang Mangue, as first vice president and Vicente Eya Olomo as defence minister.

A referendum on continued membership of the European Union took place in the United Kingdom. Following a controversial campaign, with divisive consequences for both the Conservative and Labour political parties, voters backed an exit from the Union with 51.9% for 'Leave' and 48.1% for 'Remain', triggering a complex process of withdrawal.

In presidential elections in Iceland, Guðni Jóhannesson won with 39.1% of the vote against Halla Tómasdóttir with 27.5%, Andri Snær Magnason with 14.0% and former prime minister and central bank governor Davíð Oddsson with 13.5%. There were five other candidates. Turnout was 75.7%.

Week Beginning 12 June 2016

Mwigulu Nchemba was sworn in as home affairs minister of Tanzania. His predecessor, Charles Kitwanga, had been sacked in May for allegedly entering parliament under the influence of alcohol.

In Macedonia, Kiril Minovski became finance minister, taking over from Zoran Stavreski who had resigned citing health reasons.

Croatian prime minister Tihomir Orešković lost a parliamentary vote of no confidence by 125 votes to 15.

Week Beginning 5 June 2016

In Peru, Pedro Pablo Kuczynski won the presidential run-off election with 50.1% of the vote against Keiko Fujimori with 49.9%.

Parliamentary elections took place in St Lucia. The United Workers' Party won 11 seats with 54.8% of votes cast against six for the Saint Lucia Labour Party. Allen Chastanet was sworn in as prime minister a day later while his cabinet, which included Hermangild Francis as minister of home affairs, justice and national security, was appointed the following week.

Mario Fernández took over from Jorge Burgos as interior minister of Chile.

In a cabinet reshuffle in Algeria, Noureddine Boutarfa became energy minister and Haji Baba Ammi finance minister.

Chronology of Events for May 2016

Week Beginning 29 May 2016

Avigdor Lieberman was appointed defence minister of Israel following the resignation of Moshe Ya'alon.

In Kyrgyzstan, Kashkar Dzhunushaliyev took over from as Melis Turganbaev as interior minister on an interim basis.

Hani Al-Mulki was sworn in as prime minister of Jordan. Al-Mulki also became defence minister and Salameh Hammad was appointed interior minister, with other key portfolios remaining unchanged.

Week Beginning 22 May 2016

In Austria, Alexander Van der Bellen, who ran as an independent candidate but was affiliated to the Greens, overcame a considerable first round deficit to win the presidential run-off election with 50.3% of the vote against Norbert Hofer of the Freedom Party with 49.7%. However, the Constitutional Court later annulled the result after the Freedom Party had challenged the outcome and announced that the election would be rerun.

Parliamentary elections took place in Cyprus. The ruling Democratic Rally won 18 of 56 available seats, followed by the Progressive Party of the Working People with 16 and the Democratic Party 9. Five other parties took the remaining 13 seats.

Ahmet Davutoğlu resigned as prime minister of Turkey amid conflict with president Recep Tayyip Erdoğan. Binali Yıldırım, an ally of the president and incumbent minister of transport, maritime affairs and communications, was subsequently sworn in as prime minister in a move that was widely acknowledged to have enhanced Erdoğan's political power.

In Vietnam, 500 members of parliament were elected.

Azali Assoumani was sworn in as president of the Comoros.

In Mauritius, Pravind Jugnauth, the son of prime minister Sir Anerood Jugnauth, was sworn in as finance minister.

Baciro Djá was sworn in as the new prime minister of Guinea-Bissau. The previous government had been dismissed earlier in the month by president José Mário Vaz following a political stand-off with former premier Carlos Correia. Djá was subsequently joined by new appointments including Eduardo Costa Sanhá as defence minister and Henrique Horta dos Santos as finance minister.

Week Beginning 15 May 2016

In Austria, Christian Kern was sworn in as chancellor, taking over from Werner Faymann who had resigned following his Social Democratic Party's poor showing at the presidential election held in April.

Ri Yong-ho was announced as North Korea's new foreign minister.

Domitien Ndihokubwayo was sworn in as Burundi's minister of finance, budget and development planning, replacing Tabu Abdallah Manirakiza who took up a position at the Economic Community of Central African States.

A cabinet reshuffle took place in Montenegro. Raško Konjević became finance minister and Goran Danilović interior minister.

Tsai Ing-wen of the Democratic Progressive Party was sworn in as president of Taiwan following her victory in the presidential elections 4 months earlier. The first woman ever to hold the position, she was joined by new premier Lin Chuan and a cabinet that included Lee Ta-wei as minister of foreign affairs and Feng Shih-kuan as minister of national defence.

Week Beginning 8 May 2016

Rodrigo Duterte won presidential elections in the Philippines with 39.0% of the vote against Mar Roxas with 23.4%, Grace Poe with 21.4% and two other candidates.

In Brazil, President Dilma Rousseff was formally removed from power for 180 days after the Senate voted in favour of impeaching her by 55 votes to 22. Vice president Michel Temer took over as acting president, and was joined by an interim cabinet that included Raul Jungmann as defence minister and José Serra as minister of foreign affairs.

Azali Assoumani was elected president of the Comoros in a partially-rerun second round with 41.4% of the vote against Mohamed Ali Soilihi with 39.7% and Mouigni Baraka with 18.9%. The rerun of polling, which had originally taken place in April, was as a result of violence and electoral irregularities.

In a cabinet reshuffle in Djibouti, Ali Hassan Bahdon became defence minister with other key portfolios remaining unchanged.

The French prime minister Manuel Valls and his government survived a parliamentary vote of no confidence, which generated only 246 votes of the 288 needed to remove the administration. The vote had been called by the Republicans amid widespread civil unrest over controversial labour reforms.

Week Beginning 1 May 2016

In the United Kingdom, national elections took place in Northern Ireland, Scotland and Wales. In Northern Ireland, the Democratic Unionist Party won with 38 of 108 seats, ahead of Sinn Féin with 28 and the Ulster Unionist Party with 16. Elections to the Scottish Parliament held the same day saw the

Scottish National Party win a third term in government with 63 of 129 seats, while the Conservative Party took 31 and the Labour Party 24. The Labour Party won Assembly elections in Wales, taking 29 of 60 seats against Plaid Cymru's 12, the Conservative Party's 11 and the UK Independence Party's 7.

In Ireland, Enda Kenny was re-elected prime minister by parliament 70 days after the general election that had yielded no clear winner. His new government included Paul Kehoe as defence minister with other key portfolios remaining unchanged.

Chronology of Events for April 2016

Week Beginning 24 April 2016
Norbert Hofer of the Freedom Party won the first round of presidential elections in Austria with 35.1% of the vote, ahead of Alexander Van der Bellen (independent but affiliated to the Greens) with 21.3%, Irmgard Griss (independent) 18.9%, Rudolf Hundstorfer (Social Democratic Party) 11.3%, Andreas Khol (Austrian People's Party) 11.1% and Richard Lugner (independent) 2.3%. A second round run-off between Hofer and Van der Bellen was scheduled to take place in May.

Incumbent president Teodoro Obiang Nguema Mbasogo of Equatorial Guinea was re-elected with 93.7% of the vote against six other candidates.

Parliamentary elections took place in Serbia. The coalition led by the Serbian Progressive Party won 131 seats, the Socialist Party of Serbia–United Serbia–Greens–Communist Party coalition, 29, the Serbian Radical Party 22, Enough is Enough 16 and the coalition led by the Democratic Party also 16. The remaining seats went to smaller parties.

A cabinet reshuffle took place in Colombia. Jorge Eduardo Londoño became justice minister and Clara López Obregón labour minister. However, there were no changes to key portfolios.

A new government was appointed by president Salva Kiir in South Sudan, including Alfred Lado Gore as interior minister and Deng Alor as foreign minister.

In the Republic of the Congo, president Denis Sassou-Nguesso revived the post of prime minister—which he had previously abolished in 2009—appointing Clément Mouamba to the position. Mouamba was joined by a new government that included Calixte Ganongo as finance minister.

Week Beginning 17 April 2016
In Brazil, the lower house of Congress began impeachment proceedings against president Dilma Rousseff, with 367 deputies voting in favour compared with 137 against. Rousseff, who was accused of misappropriating public funds to cover budget shortfalls, denied any wrongdoing.

Bounnhang Vorachit was elected president of Laos. His new cabinet included Somdy Douangdy as finance minister and Saleumxay Kommasith as foreign minister.

Egyptian prime minister Sherif Ismail won a parliamentary vote of confidence by 433 votes to 38.

In a cabinet reshuffle in Austria, Johanna Mikl-Leitner was replaced by Wolfgang Sobotka as interior minister. There were no other changes to key portfolios.

A new government was appointed in Cabo Verde. Led by prime minister Ulisses Correia e Silva, it included Paulo Costa Rocha as internal administration minister and Luís Filipe Tavares as minister of foreign affairs and defence.

Week Beginning 10 April 2016
In Chad, Idriss Déby was re-elected to a fifth term as president following elections in which he defeated 13 other candidates. Turnout was 76.1%.

In Peru, Keiko Fujimori, daughter of former president Alberto Fujimori, won the first round of presidential elections with 39.9% against Pedro Pablo Kuczynski with 21.0%, Verónika Mendoza 18.8%, Alfredo Barnechea 7.0% and former president Alan García of Alianza Popular 5.8%. There were five other candidates. A second round run-off was scheduled to take place between Keiko Fujimori and Pedro Pablo Kuczynski in June.

Sooronbay Jeenbekov was sworn in as prime minister of Kyrgyzstan, taking over from Temir Sariyev who had resigned amid allegations of corruption.

Parliamentary elections took place in South Korea. The Minjoo Party of Korea won 123 of 300 seats, the Saenuri Party 122, the People's Party 38 and the Justice Party 6. 11 seats went to independents.

Oliver Mahafaly Solonandrasana, who had been serving as interior minister, took office as prime minister of Madagascar. He took over from Jean

Ravelonarivo who resigned following disagreements with president Hery Rajaonarimampianina over development policy. Mahafaly was joined by a new government 2 days later.

Parliamentary elections took place in Syria. The ruling National Progressive Front (led by the Ba'ath Party) won 200 of 250 seats. Opposition parties boycotted the election. It was reported that over 140,000 refugees crossed the border from Lebanon to vote.

Volodymyr Groysman was sworn in as prime minister of Ukraine. He took over from Arseniy Yatsenyuk who had resigned amid plummeting approval ratings. The only key change to the government was to the finance portfolio, which was assigned to Olexandr Danylyuk.

Week Beginning 3 April 2016
A cabinet reshuffle took place in Cambodia. Foreign affairs minister Hor Nam Hong was replaced by Prak Sokhon, while Sun Chanthol took over from Tram Iv Tek as minister of public works and transport. Deputy prime minister Keat Chhon, who had first served in government during the 1960s, retired.

In Iceland, Sigmundur Davíð Gunnlaugsson resigned as prime minister following the release of the 'Panama Papers'—a set of leaked documents from Panamanian law firm Mossack Fonseca detailing client information for over 200,000 offshore companies—revealing that his family had secret investments in overseas accounts. Sigurður Ingi Jóhannsson, also of the Progressive Party, took over as prime minister 2 days later.

South African president Jacob Zuma survived a parliamentary impeachment vote by 233 votes to 143. The group of opposition MPs that tabled the motion claimed that Zuma had ignored an order to repay public funds spent on upgrading his private home.

Patrice Talon was sworn in as president of Benin. He was joined by a new government that included Aurélien Agbénonci as foreign affairs minister and Sacca Lafia as interior minister.

In a cabinet reshuffle in Malaŵi, Jappie Mhango became home affairs minister and Francis Kasaila foreign minister.

Incumbent president Ismail Omar Guelleh was re-elected to a fourth term at elections in Djibouti.

In a mini cabinet reshuffle in Afghanistan, Taj Mohammad Jahid was sworn in as interior minister. Other key portfolios remained unchanged.

Chronology of Events for March 2016

Week Beginning 27 March 2016
Enex Jean-Charles took office as prime minister of Haiti. An interim government was sworn in with a mandate to organize the delayed second round of presidential and parliamentary elections.

Faustin-Archange Touadéra was sworn is president of the Central African Republic following his election 6 weeks earlier.

Gian Nicola Berti and Massimo Andrea Ugolini were sworn in as Captains Regent of San Marino.

Tran Dai Quang was sworn in as president of Vietnam, taking over from Truong Tan Sang who had completed his 5-year term.

Week Beginning 20 March 2016
Patrice Talon won the run-off presidential election in Benin, taking 65.4% of the vote against Lional Zinsou with 34.6%; 31 other candidates had taken part in the first round held 2 weeks earlier. Having already served two terms, incumbent president Yayi was constitutionally barred from participating.

Parliamentary elections took place in Cabo Verde. The Movement for Democracy won 40 of the 68 elected seats, the African Party for the Independence of Cabo Verde 29, and the Democratic and Independent Cabo Verdean Union 3.

In presidential elections in the Republic of the Congo, incumbent president Denis Sassou-Nguesso won with 60.2% of the vote against Guy Brice Parfait Kolélas with 15.0% and Jean-Marie Michel Mokoko with 13.7%. Six other candidates won under 5% of the vote each.

The ruling Nur Otan (Light of the Fatherland) party won snap parliamentary elections in Kazakhstan, taking control of 84 of the 98 elected seats. The vote, which had been scheduled to be held in August, took place 5 months early following a presidential decree in response to the country's faltering economy. The Democratic Party of Kazakhstan Ak Zhol (Bright Path) and the Communist People's Party of Kazakhstan won seven seats each.

In Niger, incumbent president Mahamadou Issoufou won presidential elections in a second round run-off with 92.5% against former prime minister Hama Amadou with 7.5%. Opposition groups had boycotted the second round, resulting in Issoufou's overwhelming victory. Another former prime minister, Senyi Oumarou, and a former president, Mahamane Ousman, took part in the first round held earlier in the month.

In a cabinet reshuffle in Egypt, Amr al-Garhy was sworn in as finance minister and Hossam Abdel Reheem minister of justice.

In Lebanon, parliament failed to elect a president for the 37th time since a first attempt in April 2014 owing to the lack of a quorum.

South Sudan's foreign affairs minister Barnaba Marial Benjamin was dismissed by president Salva Kiir. Bashir Gbandi took over on an acting basis.

Week Beginning 13 March 2016

A cabinet reshuffle took place in Sierra Leone. Momodu Kargbo was appointed finance minister, Alfred Palo Conteh internal affairs minister and Momodu Allieu Pat-Sowe minister of trade and industry.

In Mauritius, finance minister Vishnu Lutchmeenaraidoo became foreign affairs minister with prime minister Sir Anerood Jugnauth taking over his old portfolio.

John B. King, Jr. was sworn in as education secretary of the United States, having served in the position on an interim basis for the previous 10 weeks.

A new government was appointed in Kiribati. It included Teuea Toatu as finance minister and Atarake Nataara as internal affairs minister.

In Myanmar, Htin Kyaw of the National League for Democracy was elected president by parliament with runners-up Myint Swe and Henry Van Thio becoming first and second vice presidents respectively. Widely regarded as a proxy for NLD leader Aung San Suu Kyi who was barred from becoming president, Htin Kyaw led a cabinet that was sworn in later in the month. It included Lieut.-Gen. Sein Win as defence minister and Kyaw Win as planning and finance minister. The post of state counsellor, similar to the position of prime minister, was created to allow Aung San Suu Kyi to effectively rule behind the scenes.

In Bosnia and Herzegovina, Bakir Izetbegović—a Bosniak—took over the 8-month rotating presidency chairmanship.

Week Beginning 6 March 2016

Jose Rene Almendras became acting foreign secretary of the Philippines, taking over from Albert del Rosario who had resigned for health reasons.

Taneti Maamau won presidential elections in Kiribati, defeating two other candidates with 60.0% of the vote. He was sworn in 2 days later.

Marcelo Rebelo de Sousa was sworn in as president of Portugal, having been elected by parliament 6 weeks earlier.

Chronology of Events for February 2016

Week Beginning 28 February 2016

South African president Jacob Zuma survived a vote of no confidence in parliament by 225 votes to 99.

Zoran Đorđević became defence minister of Serbia.

A cabinet reshuffle took place in Ecuador. Guillaume Long was appointed foreign minister and Ricardo Patiño defence minister.

In Jamaica, Andrew Holness was sworn in as prime minister following his Labour Party's success at elections a week earlier. He formed a new government that included Audley Shaw as finance minister and Kamina Johnson Smith as foreign minister.

The ruling Human Rights Protection Party won parliamentary elections in Samoa, gaining 44 of 49 seats against the Tautua Samoa Party with 3 and independent candidates with 2.

Direction–Social Democracy, Slovakia's ruling party, won 49 seats with 28.3% of votes cast at parliamentary elections ahead of Freedom and Solidarity with 21 seats, Ordinary People and Independent Personalities 19, the Slovak National Party 15, Kotleba–People's Party Our Slovakia 14, We Are Family 11, Most–Híd 11 and Network 10.

Week Beginning 21 February 2016

The first round of presidential elections took place in Comoros. Mohamed Ali Soilihi won 17.6% of the vote, Mouigni Baraka 15.1%, former president Azali Assoumani 15.0% and Fahmi Said Ibrahim 14.4%. There were 21 other candidates.

Parliamentary elections took place in Jamaica. The opposition Labour Party won narrowly, taking 32 of 63 seats to oust the People's National Party with 31.

Fritz Jean was sworn in as prime minister of Haiti.

Prosper Douglas Bani became interior minister of Ghana.

Closely-contested parliamentary elections took place in Ireland. The ruling Fine Gael won 50 seats with 25.5% of the vote against Fianna Fáil with 44 and 24.3% and Sinn Féin with 23 and 13.8%.

Week Beginning 14 February 2016

Owing to the delay of scheduled elections, Jocelerme Privert was sworn in as the interim president of Haiti following the conclusion of Michelle Martelly's term the previous week.

Faustin-Archange Touadéra won presidential elections in the Central African Republic, defeating Anicet-Georges Dologuélé in a second round run-off.

In Chad, Albert Pahimi Padacké took office as prime minister, taking over from Kalzeubé Pahimi Deubet who had resigned 2 days earlier. New cabinet members including Mahamat Allamine Bourma Treye as finance minister were subsequently appointed.

A minor cabinet reshuffle took place in Albania. Arben Ahmetaj became finance minister with other key portfolios remaining unchanged.

The prime minister of Ukraine, Arseniy Yatsenyuk, survived a vote of no confidence as the motion failed to gain the required majority of 226 votes. Opposition groups had accused Yatsenyuk of corruption and failing to effectively introduce reforms.

In Uganda, incumbent president Yoweri K. Museveni was re-elected, defeating Kizza Besigye and six other candidates.

In Bulgaria, Bokyo Borisov's government survived a vote of no confidence called by the opposition over the country's ailing healthcare sector by 130 votes to 80.

Week Beginning 7 February 2016

In a cabinet reshuffle in Mauritania, Isselkou Ould Izid Bih was sworn in as foreign affairs and co-operation minister.

Several new members were brought into the government of French president François Hollande. They included former prime minister Jean-Marc Ayrault as minister of foreign affairs and international development and Green party leader Emmanuelle Cosse as minister of housing and sustainable homes.

Māris Kučinskis was appointed prime minister of Latvia following the resignation of Laimdota Straujuma. Dana Reizniece-Ozola was appointed finance minister, while other key cabinet portfolios remained unchanged.

Riek Machar was reappointed first vice-president of South Sudan following his dismissal in July 2013. Machar, who had been accused by president Salva Kiir of leading a failed coup d'état, was reinstated to implement a national unity government.

In Vanuatu, Charlot Salwai was elected and sworn in as prime minister.

Fijian prime minister Josaia Voreqe Bainimarama survived a parliamentary vote of no confidence by 28 votes to 11.

Chronology of Events for January 2016

Week Beginning 31 January 2016

Chang San-cheng, who had already been serving in the role on an acting basis, was officially appointed prime minister of Taiwan.

In Monaco, Serge Telle was sworn in as minister of state, responsible for leading the government and its foreign policy.

Dušan Vujović became acting defence minister of Serbia, taking over from Bratislav Gašić who had been removed from office following sexist remarks made towards a journalist.

Week Beginning 24 January 2016

Presidential elections took place in Portugal. Having served two consecutive terms, incumbent president Aníbal Cavaco Silva was prohibited from running for a third. With 52.0% of the vote, Marcelo Rebelo de Sousa of the Social Democratic Party defeated closest rival António Sampaio da Nóvoa (ind.) with 22.9%. Turnout was 48.7%.

In Austria, a minor cabinet reshuffle took place. Hans Peter Doskozil was appointed defence minister with other key portfolios remaining unchanged.

In the Marshall Islands, newly-elected president Casten Nemra lost a parliamentary vote of no confidence by 21 votes to 12. Hilda Heine was elected president the following day, becoming the first female ever to hold the position.

In a move that merged a number of ministries, the Amir of Qatar reshuffled his cabinet. Sheikh Mohamed bin Abdulrahman Al Thani's appointment as foreign minister represented the biggest change within the government.

Week Beginning 17 January 2016

In a cabinet reshuffle in Ghana, Prosper Douglas Bani was appointed interior minister with other key portfolios remaining unchanged.

Following the failure of two candidates to form governments earlier in the month, Pavel Filip, who had been serving as minister of information technology and communications, was elected prime minister of Moldova by parliament. Included in his cabinet were Alexandru Jizdan as interior minister, Anatol Şalaru as defence minister and Andrei Galbur as foreign minister.

Tihomir Orešković was sworn in as prime minister of Croatia. Orešković, the first independent ever to hold the premiership, led a coalition cabinet comprising members of the Croatian Democratic Union and the Bridge of Independent Lists. It included Vlaho Orepić as interior minister, Miro Kovač as foreign minister and Josip Buljević as defence minister.

Parliamentary elections took place in Vanuatu. The Party of Our Land won six of 52 seats, as did the Union of Moderate Parties and the Ground and Justice Party; the National United Party and Iauko Group both won four seats; Reunification Movement for Change and Nagriamel Party both won three. A number of smaller parties each took one or two seats and eight went to independents.

Week Beginning 10 January 2016

Aryeh Deri was sworn in as interior minister of Israel, taking over from prime minister Binyamin Netanyahu who had held the post on an interim basis following the resignation of Silvan Shalom the previous month.

In the Marshall Islands, Casten Nemra took office as president. New cabinet appointments included Daisy Momotaro as internal affairs minister and Kessai H. Note as foreign minister.

Arlene Foster, who served in the position on an interim basis on two previous occasions, was elected first minister of Northern Ireland, officially taking over from Peter Robinson. Foster became the first female and youngest person to ever hold the post.

A cabinet reshuffle took place in Côte d'Ivoire following the government's resignation 6 days earlier.

Prime minister Daniel Kablan Duncan retained his position, along with the majority of ministers holding key portfolios, although Albert Toikeusse Mabri took over foreign affairs from Charles Koffi Diby.

In Guatemala, Jimmy Morales was sworn in following his victory in the presidential election run-off in Oct. 2015. He retained a number of key cabinet members, including defence minister Williams Mansilla Fernández and foreign minister Carlos Raúl Morales. New additions to the government included Julio Héctor Estrada as finance minister and Francisco Rivas Lara as interior minister.

Boubou Cissé was sworn in as finance minister as part of a minor cabinet reshuffle in Mali.

Presidential elections took place in Taiwan. The Democratic Progressive Party candidate, Tsai Ing-wen, won with 56.1% of the vote against Eric Chu of the ruling Nationalist Party (Kuomintang) with 31.1% and James Soong Chu-yu of the People First Party with 12.8%.

Week Beginning 3 January 2016

A new government was appointed in Guinea by president Alpha Condé. It included Malado Kaba as finance minister and Makalé Camara as foreign affairs minister.

Paul Kaba Thieba was appointed prime minister of Burkina Faso. His government, which included Simon Compaoré as interior minister and Alpha Barry as foreign minister, was sworn in 6 days later.

Henrique Tokpah was sworn in as internal affairs minister and Marjon Kamara as foreign affairs minister in a cabinet reshuffle that took place in Liberia.

Tunisian prime minister Habib Essid reshuffled his cabinet. Hédi Majdoub became interior minister and Khemaies Jhinaoui foreign minister, with other key portfolios remaining unchanged.

In a cabinet reshuffle in Venezuela, Aristóbulo Istúriz became vice president, replacing Jorge Arreaza who was appointed minister of higher education, science and technology. Additionally, Rodolfo Medina took over at the ministry of banking and finance.

2015

Chronology of Events for December 2015

Week Beginning 27 December 2015

Israeli prime minister Binyamin Netanyahu took over the interior portfolio following the departure of Silvan Shalom, who had resigned over sexual harassment allegations.

Roch Marc Christian Kaboré was sworn in as president of Burkina Faso following his victory at elections held a month earlier. He took over from acting president Michel Kafondo, who had led the transitional government since November 2014.

In Switzerland, Johann Schneider-Ammann was sworn in as president for 2016 alongside Doris Leuthard as vice president. They had been elected to their respective positions by the federal council 3 weeks earlier.

Week Beginning 20 December 2015

Parliamentary elections took place in Spain. The Popular Party (PP) won 123 of the 350 seats with 28.7% of votes cast; the Spanish Socialist Workers' Party (PSOE), 90 with 22.0%; Podemos (including En Comú Podem, Compromís and En Marea), 69 with 20.7%; Citizens (Ciudadanos), 40 with 13.9%; Republican Left of Catalonia (ERC–CAT SÍ), 9 with 2.4%; and Democracy and Freedom (DL), 8 with 2.3%. Four other parties shared the remaining 11 seats. Turnout was 73.2%.

In Brazil, Nelson Barbosa took over as finance minister from Joaquim Levy whose policies had been the subject of widespread congressional opposition.

A cabinet reshuffle took place in South Korea. Hong Yun-sik was sworn in as interior minister and Yoo Il-ho as finance minister. Other key portfolios remained unchanged.

Georgian prime minister Irakli Garibashvili unexpectedly resigned. Giorgi Kvirikashvili, also of the Georgian Dream party, took over a week later.

Mohamed Said Fofana resigned as prime minister of Guinea along with his cabinet. Mamady Youla took over 6 days later, heading up a new government that included Makalé Camara as foreign affairs minister and Malado Kaba as finance minister.

Week Beginning 13 December 2015

Pravin Gordhan was appointed finance minister of South Africa. Gordhan, who had previously served in the post between 2009 and 2014, succeeded David van Rooyen who was removed from office by president Jacob Zuma just 3 days after taking over from Nhlanhla Nene.

Parliamentary elections in Egypt concluded, with the Free Egyptians Party emerging as the largest faction with 65 seats. Held in two phases stretching over more than 6 weeks with run-off elections 2 weeks later, 351 seats went to independent candidates and 245 to party representatives.

Incumbent president James Michel won presidential elections in the Seychelles with 50.2% of the vote against Wavel Ramkalawan with 49.8% in a second round run-off. Four other candidates took part in the first round held earlier in the month.

Week Beginning 6 December 2015

Parliamentary elections took place in Venezuela. The opposition Unidad Democrática (Democratic Unity Roundtable, MUD) won 109 seats and the Partido Socialista Unido de Venezuela (United Socialist Party of Venezuela, PSUV) 55 with the remaining three seats reserved for indigenous peoples.

Latvian prime minister Laimdota Straujuma announced her resignation, citing a need for a newly energized government. She would retain the position until the appointment of a new candidate.

Mauricio Macri was sworn in as president of Argentina following his victory in the presidential election run-off held 3 weeks earlier, taking over from Cristina Fernández de Kirchner who had been constitutionally barred from running for a third consecutive term. Macri was joined by new vice-president Gabriela Michetti and a cabinet that included minister of foreign affairs Susana Mabel Malcorra and finance minister Alfonso Prat Gay.

The ruling Unity Labour Party won parliamentary elections in St Vincent and the Grenadines, taking eight of 15 seats against the New Democratic Party with seven. Incumbent prime minister Dr. Ralph E. Gonsalves retained his post with new additions to his cabinet including veteran politician Louis Straker as foreign affairs minister.

The majority of newly-elected Tanzanian president John Magufuli's cabinet ministers were sworn in. Included in the government were Charles

Kitwanga as minister of home affairs and Augustine Mahiga as minister of foreign affairs, with the finance portfolio remaining vacant until later in the month when Philip Mpango was appointed to the post. Other key positions remained unchanged from the previous administration.

Chronology of Events for November 2015

Week Beginning 29 November 2015

Roch Marc Christian Kaboré was elected president of Burkina Faso with 53.5% of votes cast, defeating Zéphirin Diabré with 29.7% and 12 other candidates. Turnout was 60.0%.

Week Beginning 22 November 2015

With 51.4% of the vote, Mauricio Macri of the Let's Change coalition won the Argentinian presidential elections in a second round run-off against Daniel Scioli of the Front for Victory who took 48.6%. Four other candidates contested the first round held 4 weeks earlier.

In Turkey, prime minister Ahmet Davutoğlu's government was sworn in. Many of the ministers in the cabinet had previous experience in their portfolios, including Efkan Ala as interior minister, Mevlüt Çavuşoğlu as foreign minister and Bekir Bozdağ as justice minister.

Havo Moli was sworn in as foreign minister of Vanuatu.

A new coalition government led by António Costa of the Socialist Party was appointed in Portugal. Taking over from the conservative administration of Pedro Passos Coelho that had been ousted 2 weeks earlier, the cabinet included Mário Centeno as finance minister and Augusto Santos Silva as foreign affairs minister.

Week Beginning 15 November 2015

In Poland, a new government led by Beata Szydło of the Law and Justice Party was sworn in. Appointments in this first non-coalition cabinet since 1989 included Mariusz Błaszczak as interior minister and Witold Waszczykowski as foreign affairs minister.

Following the resignation of Victor Ponta, a new government with Dacian Cioloş as prime minister was appointed in Romania. Petre Tobă became interior minister, Lazăr Comănescu foreign affairs minister and Anca Dana Dragu public finance minister.

Week Beginning 8 November 2015

Parliamentary elections took place in Croatia. The Patriotic Coalition led by the Croatian Democratic Union won 59 seats, the Croatia is Growing coalition led by the Social Democratic Party of Croatia 56 and independent candidates running under the 'Bridge of Independent Lists' platform 19, with the nine remaining seats going to smaller parties and coalitions.

In the first openly contested elections to take place in Myanmar since 1990, the National League for Democracy (NLD), led by Aung San Suu Kyi, won 255 of 330 elected seats. The ruling Union Solidarity and Development Party won 30 seats, the Arakan National Party 12 and the Shan Nationalities League for Democracy 12. A further 14 seats went to seven smaller parties and independent candidates, with seven vacant owing to insurgent activity. 110 seats were constitutionally reserved for the military. The results meant that the NLD had the parliamentary majority needed to elect its nominee to the presidency.

Omar Zuhair Malhas was sworn in as finance minister in Jordan following a minor cabinet reshuffle.

Adam Shareef Umar became defence minister of the Maldives.

In Paraguay, Diógenes Martínez took over from Bernardino Soto as defence minister.

The government of Portuguese prime minister Pedro Passos Coelho, which had only been appointed 3 weeks earlier, lost a parliamentary vote of no confidence by 123 votes to 107. The vote, backed by an alliance of left-wing parties, was tabled in response to austerity measures planned by Coelho.

In a cabinet reshuffle in Macedonia, two members of the left-wing opposition were appointed to ministerial posts following a political crisis that had stretched back to July. Oliver Spasovski became interior minister and Frosina Remenski labour and social affairs minister.

In Nigeria, new cabinet ministers were sworn in. Among the new appointments were foreign minister Geoffrey Onyeama, interior minister Abdulrahman Dambzau and finance minister Kemi Adeosun. Other key portfolios remained unchanged.

Jioji Konrote was elected president of Fiji following a parliamentary vote.

Week Beginning 1 November 2015

The ruling New Azerbaijan Party won parliamentary elections in Azerbaijan, taking 70 of 125 seats. Civil Solidarity won two seats, with the remaining seats going to smaller parties and independents.

In Nigeria, new cabinet ministers were sworn in. Among the new appointments were foreign minister Geoffrey Onyeama, interior minister Abdulrahman Dambzau and finance minister Kemi Adeosun. Other key portfolios remained unchanged.

Snap elections took place that were called by Turkish president Recep Tayyip Erdoğan following the breakdown of coalition negotiations after elections 5 months earlier. The ruling Justice and Development Party regained its parliamentary majority by winning 317 of the 550 seats with 49.5% of votes cast, against 134 seats and 25.3% for the Republican People's Party, 59 seats and 10.8% for the People's Democratic Party, and 40 seats and 11.9% for the Nationalist Movement Party. Incumbent prime minister Ahmet Davutoğlu was subsequently asked by the president to form a new government.

In parliamentary elections in Belize, the ruling United Democratic Party won 19 of 31 seats with 50.5% of votes cast and the People's United Party 12 with 47.8%. Turnout was 72.7%.

Justin Trudeau was sworn in as prime minister of Canada alongside his new Liberal cabinet, which included Bill Morneau as finance minister, Stéphane Dion as foreign minister and Harjit Sajjan as defence minister. Justin Trudeau became the first child of a previous premier, Pierre Trudeau, to hold the position.

Victor Ponta resigned as prime minister of Romania following public demonstrations over alleged government corruption triggered by a deadly fire in a Bucharest nightclub. Sorin Cîmpeanu took over on an interim basis.

In Kyrgyzstan, a new government led by incumbent prime minister Temir Sariyev was appointed with key portfolios remaining unchanged.

A cabinet reshuffle took place in Nepal. Bishnu Prasad Paudel became finance minister and Bhim Bahadur Rawal defence minister.

John Magufuli was sworn in as president of Tanzania alongside vice-president Samia Suluhu Hassan.

Chronology of Events for October 2015

Week Beginning 25 October 2015

The first round of presidential elections took place in Argentina, in which Daniel Scioli of the Front for Victory won 37.1% of the vote against Mauricio Macri of the Let's Change coalition with 34.2% and Sergio Massa of the United for a New Alternative coalition with 21.4%. There were three other candidates. Turnout was 80.9%. A second round run-off between Scioli and Macri was scheduled to take place 4 weeks later. Parliamentary elections were also held, in which 130 of the 257 congressional seats that were not contested at the previous elections 2 years earlier were at stake. Following the elections the Front for Victory lost its majority in the Chamber of Deputies, but kept control of the Senate.

Alassane Ouattara was re-elected president of Côte d'Ivoire with 83.7% of the vote against Affi N'Guessan with 9.3%. Turnout was 54.6% with campaigning and voting carried out relatively peacefully despite a boycott by the main opposition party, the Ivorian Popular Front.

Jimmy Morales won presidential elections in Guatemala, taking 67.4% of the vote against Sandra Torres with 32.6% in a second round run-off.

In Haiti, Jovenel Moïse won 32.8% of the vote in presidential elections against Jude Célestin with 25.3% and Moïse Jean-Charles with 14.3%. 50 other candidates participated. Since no candidate received a majority of the vote, a second round run-off between Moïse and Célestin was scheduled to take place 9 weeks later.

The Law and Justice Party (PiS) won parliamentary elections in Poland with 235 of 460 seats and 37.6% of the vote against the ruling Civic Platform with 138 seats and 24.1%, Kukiz' 15 (K'15) with 42 and 8.8%, Modern 28 and 7.5%, Polish People's Party (PSL) 16 and 5.1% and German Minority (MN) 1 and 0.2%. The PiS became the first party to achieve an absolute majority in a free election in Poland.

John Magufuli won presidential elections in Tanzania with 58.5% of the vote against Edward Lowassa with 40.0% and six other candidates.

Week Beginning 18 October 2015

Parliamentary elections took place in Switzerland. The Swiss People's Party/Centre Democratic Union won 65 of 200 seats in the National Council with 29.4% of the vote, against the Social Democratic Party of Switzerland with 43 and 18.8%, FDP. The Liberals 33 and 16.4%, the Christian Democratic

People's Party 27 and 11.6% and the Green Party 11 and 7.1%. Seven other parties took the remaining 21 seats and turnout was 48.4%.

The opposition Liberal Party led by Justin Trudeau won parliamentary elections in Canada taking 184 of 338 seats with 39.5% of the vote—an increase of 150 seats over the previous election, representing the largest ever gain by a party in Canadian electoral history. The Conservative Party came second with 99 seats and 31.9 of votes, followed by the New Democratic Party with 44 and 19.7%, the Bloc Québécois 10 and 4.7% and the Green Party 1 and 3.5% Turnout was 68.5%, up from 61.4% in 2011.

In the Solomon Islands, seven cabinet ministers including former prime minister Derek Sikua resigned from the government of Manasseh Sogavare citing concerns over his leadership style.

A cabinet reshuffle took place in Brunei. The sultan and prime minister, Haji Hassanal Bolkiah Mu'izzadin Waddaulah, took over the foreign affairs portfolio and Pehin Orang Kaya Seri Kerna Dato Seri Setia Awang Haji Abu Bakar bin Haji Apong was appointed home affairs minister. Other key posts remained unchanged.

Week Beginning 11 October 2015

Alyaksandr Lukashenka secured a fifth consecutive term in office by winning presidential elections in Belarus with 84.1% of the vote. Three other candidates contested the poll but, despite independent observers noting a slight improvement in electoral procedures over previous years, veteran opposition figures were still banned from taking part.

In Guinea, Alpha Condé was returned as president with 57.9% of the vote against Callou Dalein Diallo with 31.4% in only the second democratic elections to have ever taken place in the country. Outbreaks of violence were reported during the campaign phase of the election, and at least three people died in clashes between rival groups.

Jioji Konrote was elected president of Fiji through indirect voting.

Week Beginning 4 October 2015

Parliamentary elections took place in Kyrgyzstan. The Social Democratic Party of Kyrgyzstan won 38 of 120 seats followed by Ata-Zhurt (Fatherland) with 28, the Kyrgyzstan Party 18, Onuguu-Progress 13, Bir Bol 12 and Ata Meken 11. Turnout was 57.6%.

The Portugal Ahead alliance formed by the Social Democratic Party (PSD) and the CDS-People's Party (CDS-PP) won the country's parliamentary elections, taking 102 of 230 seats with 36.9% of the vote. The Socialist Party (PS) followed with 86 seats and 32.3% with five other alliances and parties winning the remaining seats. Turnout was 55.9%. Incumbent prime minister Pedro Passos Coelho was subsequently asked by president Aníbal Cavaco Silva to form a government.

A new government led by prime minister Hailemariam Desalegn was formed in Ethiopia. The cabinet included new finance minister Abdulaziz Mohammed but other key portfolios remained unchanged.

Greece's government led by prime minister Alexis Tsipras, which had taken office 2 weeks earlier, won a parliamentary vote of confidence by 155 votes to 144.

Chronology of Events for September 2015

Week Beginning 27 September 2015

Romanian prime minister Victor Ponta survived a parliamentary vote of no confidence, which only gained 207 of the required 275 votes needed to pass the motion.

In Denmark, Peter Christensen replaced Carl Holst as defence minister. Holst had stepped down after it emerged that he had accepted a large pay-off from his previous job as administrative chairman of the South Denmark (Syddanmark) region.

Lorella Stefanlli and Nicola Renzi were sworn in as Captains Regent of San Marino.

In Singapore, the new government was sworn in following elections earlier in the month. Prime minister Lee Hsien Loong's cabinet included Kasiviswanathan Shanmugam as home affairs minister, Vivian Balakrishnan as foreign minister and Heng Swee Keat as finance minister.

In Brazil, president Dilma Rousseff shuffled her cabinet in response to escalating costs associated with federal administration. Aldo Rebelo was sworn in as defence minister, Aloizio Mercadante as education minister and Marcelo Castro as health minister. All ministers were also required to accept a 10% pay cut.

Sushil Koirala resigned as prime minister of Nepal following the adoption of a new constitution.

Week Beginning 20 September 2015

Snap parliamentary elections took place in Greece following Alexis Tsipras' resignation from the premiership a month earlier. The Coalition of the Radical Left (Syriza) won 145 of 300 seats with 35.5% of the vote, ahead of New Democracy (ND) with 75 seats and 28.1%. Smaller parties and coalitions took the remaining 80 seats. As a result, Tsipras was able to renew his Syriza anti-austerity coalition government with the Independent Greeks.

In Finland, prime minister Juha Sipilä's three-party coalition government won a parliamentary vote of confidence by 104 votes to 60. Opposition parties had tabled the motion following proposed cuts to education.

A deal between the Colombian government and the leftist rebel group FARC was agreed in Havana, Cuba. President Juan Manuel Santos and rebel leader Rodrigo Londoño Echeverri (aka 'Timochenko') stated that the two sides had agreed on a number of terms, including amnesty for FARC members, aiming to end the conflict that had spanned over 50 years. The government also agreed to increased development of rural areas and future political inclusion of FARC members. A final accord between the two sides was expected to be signed by March 2016, with FARC agreeing to disarm within a subsequent 60-day period.

In a cabinet reshuffle in Mali, Sanogo Aminata Mallé was appointed justice minister and Col. Salif Traoré security minister.

Crispin Atama Tabe was sworn in as defence minister following a cabinet reshuffle in the Democratic Republic of the Congo. Other key portfolios remained unchanged.

Week Beginning 13 September 2015

The European migrant crisis reached its peak to date when Hungary received 5,809 refugees in a single day at its border fence and Germany temporarily suspended its Schengen Accord border obligations with Austria. Approximately 500,000 migrants—mostly from Syria, Iraq, Kosovo, Albania and Afghanistan—had arrived in the European Union since the beginning of 2015, with EU states struggling to agree on how to distribute the new arrivals fairly.

Hannes Hanso was sworn in as defence minister of Estonia.

In Australia, prime minister Tony Abbott was defeated by Malcolm Turnbull in a Liberal Party leadership ballot by 54 votes to 44. Turnbull took over from Abbott as party leader, and a day later was sworn in as the new premier. His cabinet retained many of the previous government's key ministers, with Marise Payne taking over the defence portfolio.

In Burkina Faso, president Michel Kafando and prime minister Isaac Zida were detained by members of the presidential guard loyal to ex-president Blaise Compaoré. However, a deal between the presidential guard and the regular army was agreed a week later and Kafando and Zida returned to power.

Carlos Correia was sworn in as prime minister of Guinea-Bissau, having served in the position on three previous occasions.

Week Beginning 6 September 2015

In the first round of presidential elections in Guatemala, Jimmy Morales of the Frente de Convergencia Nacional took 23.8% of the vote, Sandra Torres of the Unidad Nacional de la Esperanza 19.8% and Manuel Baldizón of the Libertad Democrática Renovada 19.6%. 11 other candidates received less than 7% of the vote each. Turnout was 71.1%. A run-off between Morales and Torres was scheduled to take place 7 weeks later.

A new government led by prime minister Baciro Djá was named in Guinea-Bissau. However, 2 days later the supreme court ruled that Djá's appointment in August was unconstitutional, stating that parliament had not been properly consulted. Djá immediately resigned as prime minister.

The People's National Movement won 23 of 41 seats at parliamentary elections in Trinidad and Tobago. PNM leader Keith Rowley was sworn in as prime minister 2 days later, taking over from Kamla Persad-Bissessar whose United National Congress took only 18 seats. Rowley's cabinet included Colm Imbert as finance minister and Dennis Moses as foreign minister.

In Hungary, István Simicskó took over from Csaba Hende as defence minister. Hende had resigned amid an influx of migrants illegally entering the country and delays in the construction of a 160-km (100-mile) fence between Hungary and Serbia.

In Northern Ireland, Peter Robinson temporarily stood aside as first minister after parties rejected a proposal to adjourn power-sharing institutions in the wake of allegations that the IRA had been involved in a recent murder in Belfast. Robinson stated that the continued existence of IRA structures 'pushed devolution to the brink' following Sinn Féin's denial that the organization still existed. He appointed Arlene Foster to serve again as acting first minister, having previously done so in 2010.

A cabinet reshuffle in Gabon, which aimed to create a unified government before the 2016 elections, included Pacôme Moubelet Boubeya as interior minister and Mathias Otounga Ossibadjouo as defence minister. However, a number of opposition members turned down positions in the cabinet.

Ardouin Zéphirin was appointed interior minister in a cabinet reshuffle in Haiti. Other key portfolios remained unchanged.

Parliamentary elections took place in Singapore. The ruling People's Action Party won 83 of 89 seats (with 69.9% of votes cast) and the Workers' Party took six seats (with 12.5%). Seven other parties failed to gain any seats.

Egypt's prime minister Ibrahim Mahlab resigned amid a corruption probe into another cabinet member and following widespread national criticism of his government's performance. Sherif Ismail, who had served as minister of petroleum and mineral resources since July 2013, was appointed prime minister a week later with key portfolios remaining unchanged.

The Ugandan internal affairs minister Aronda Nyakairima died of a heart attack while conducting official duties abroad.

Chronology of Events for August 2015

Week Beginning 30 August 2015
Giorgi Kvirikashvili was sworn in as foreign minister of Georgia, taking over from Tamar Beruchashvili.

Guatemalan president Otto Pérez Molina resigned after prosecutors presented evidence of his involvement in the same customs ring scandal that had prompted the resignation of alleged co-colluder and vice-president Roxana Baldetti in May. Vice-president Alejandro Maldonado Aguirre took over the presidency on an interim basis. Having been stripped of his immunity from prosecution by Congress, Molina was subsequently arrested and jailed.

Samuel Weymouth Tapley Seaton was sworn in as governor-general of St Kitts and Nevis. Seaton had been acting as governor-general since May when Sir Edmund Wickham Lawrence was removed from office by the new government.

A new cabinet comprised chiefly of members of the Sri Lanka Freedom Party and the United National Party was appointed in Sri Lanka. It included S. B. Nawinne as minister of internal affairs, north western development and cultural affairs and Mangala Samaraweera as minister of foreign affairs.

Week Beginning 23 August 2015
A cabinet reshuffle took place in Chad in response to deadly attacks in the capital by the Nigeria-based Islamist group Boko Haram. Ahmat Mahamat Bachir was appointed public security and immigration minister and Abdelkerim Seid Bauche minister of territorial administration.

In Burundi, Gaston Sindimwo was sworn in as first vice president and Joseph Butore as second vice president following president Pierre Nkurunziza's re-election in July. Pascal Barandagiye was named interior minister and Aimée Laurentine Kanyana justice minister in the new cabinet, with other key posts unchanged.

Mexican president Enrique Peña Nieto reshuffled his cabinet, with José Antonio Meade moving from the ministry of foreign affairs to the social development ministry—a move widely regarded as a precursor to a potential presidential bid by Meade in 2018. Claudia Ruiz Massieu took over the foreign affairs portfolio.

Week Beginning 16 August 2015
In Malaŵi, president Peter Mutharika reshuffled his cabinet following allegations of ministerial corruption. Jean Kalilani became minister of home affairs and internal security, taking over from Atupele Muluzi, who became minister of lands, housing and urban development.

The United National Front for Good Governance alliance led by the United National Party won parliamentary elections in Sri Lanka. Taking 106 of 225 seats, the UNFGG increased its share of seats by 46 but failed to gain a majority, with the United People's Freedom Alliance (led by the Sri Lanka Freedom Party) winning 95 seats. Four other alliances and parties took the remaining 24 seats.

Turkish prime minister Ahmet Davutoğlu returned his mandate to president Recep Tayyip Erdoğan after failing to find a coalition partner to form a government following the June election. At the request of the president, Davutoğlu subsequently formed an interim government to oversee snap elections scheduled to take place in November. Included in the cabinet were

Selami Altınok as interior minister and Feridun Hadi Sinirlioğlu as foreign affairs minister.

In the Netherlands, the government of prime minister Mark Rutte survived a vote of no confidence by 120 votes to 13. The motion was put forward by the Eurosceptic politician Geert Wilders over Rutte's backing of a proposed aid package for Greece, which reneged on a pre-election promise that no further assistance would be given to the debt-stricken country.

Alexis Tsipras resigned as prime minister of Greece and called for new elections, stating that 'Greeks would have to decide whether he had represented them courageously with the creditors' during the financial bailout talks with European Union institutions and the IMF. A week later, Vassiliki Thanou-Christophilou was appointed head of an interim government that included Antonis Manitakis as interior minister and Petros Molyviatis as foreign minister.

In a cabinet reshuffle in Thailand, Apisak Tantivorawong became finance minister and Don Pramudwinai foreign minister.

Week Beginning 9 August 2015
A cabinet reshuffle took place in the Republic of the Congo. Jean-Claude Gakosso became foreign minister with all other key portfolios remaining unchanged.

In Libya, the prime minister of the Tobruk-based government, Abdullah al-Thanay, announced his resignation on television after being blamed for the lack of amenities and security by members of the public. However, he withdrew his offer to resign the following week.

In Guinea-Bissau, the government of prime minister Domingos Simões Pereira was dismissed by president José Mário Vaz following a series of disagreements, notably over the allocation of aid money and the appointment of a new armed forces chief. Baciro Djá was sworn in as Pereira's replacement 8 days later.

The inauguration of a new government in Suriname included Ashwin Adhin as vice-president, Niermala Badrising as foreign minister, Ronni Benschop as defence minister, Gilmore Hoefdraad as finance minister and Mike Noersalim as home affairs minister.

Brig.-Gen. Williams Mansilla Fernández was appointed defence minister of Guatemala.

Week Beginning 2 August 2015
In Bhutan, Lyonpo Damcho Dorji was appointed foreign minister taking over from Rinzin Dorji.

Despite opposition from president Tsakhiagiin Elbegdorj, Mongolian prime minister Chimed Saikhanbileg dismissed all six Mongolian People's Party members from his cabinet following a parliamentary endorsement.

Andrzej Duda was sworn in as president of Poland following his victory at the elections in May. He took over from Bronisław Komorowski, whose 5-year term came to an end following a narrow defeat to Duda over two voting rounds.

Chronology of Events for July 2015

Week Beginning 26 July 2015
Valeriu Streleț of the Liberal Democratic Party became prime minister of Moldova following Chiril Gaburici's resignation in June. His new government included Anatol Şalaru as defence minister, Vladimir Cebotari as justice minister and Ruxanda Glavan as minister of health. Other key portfolios remained the same.

In Georgia, corrections minister Giorgi Mghebrishvili became interior minister. He took over from Vakhtang Gomelauri, who had been appointed head of the state's security agency.

Week Beginning 19 July 2015
A major cabinet reshuffle took place in Burkina Faso amid rising tensions between prime minister Isaac Zida and military officials. President Michel Kafondo took over the defence portfolio from the prime minister, in addition to the security portfolio held by Col. Auguste Denise Barry. Zida subsequently handed over the foreign affairs portfolio to Moussa Nebie.

In a cabinet reshuffle in the Central African Republic, Samuel Rangba was sworn in as foreign minister and Dominique Saïd Paguindji as public security minister.

The USA and Cuba reopened their respective embassies in Havana and Washington, D.C. 54 years after diplomatic ties were severed in 1961.

Relations had been normalized following months of secret negotiations between the two countries held in Canada and Vatican City State.

Presidential elections took place in Burundi. Incumbent president Pierre Nkurunziza won with 69.4% of the vote against his nearest rival, Agathon Rwasa, with 19.0%. Several opposition parties boycotted the election amid controversy over Nkurunziza's eligibility for a third term. However, their names (including Agathon Rwasa, who had called for a boycott) appeared on the ballot paper nonetheless. Turnout was 73.4%.

In the Maldives, vice president Mohamed Jameel Ahmed lost a parliamentary vote of no confidence by 78 votes to 2. He was replaced by Ahmed Adeeb.

Week Beginning 12 July 2015

The 'Joint Comprehensive Plan of Action' was signed between Iran and the five permanent members of the UN Security Council—China, France, Russia, the United Kingdom and the United States—plus Germany. The treaty, which had been subject to a number of delays and extensions since the adoption of its precursor (the 'Joint Plan of Action') in November 2013, lifted a number of US, EU and UN sanctions on Iran in return for a scaling down of the country's nuclear development activities.

Dési Bouterse was re-elected as president of Suriname. He ran unopposed.

In Estonia, Marina Kaljurand was sworn in as foreign minister, replacing Keit Pentus-Rosimannus who resigned at the start of the month.

In Bosnia and Herzegovina, Dragan Čović took over the 8-month rotating presidency chairmanship.

Week Beginning 5 July 2015

A referendum on whether to accept financial bailout conditions offered by the European Commission, the International Monetary Fund and the European Central Bank took place in Greece. 61.3% of voters rejected the terms of the deal that was described by prime minister Alexis Tsipras as 'humiliating'. Finance minister Yanis Varoufakis, who had clashed with EU leaders during the negotiations, resigned the following day and was replaced by Efkleidis Tsakalotos.

In a cabinet reshuffle in Zimbabwe, Ignatius Chombo was sworn in as home affairs minister. Other key portfolios remained unchanged.

A cabinet reshuffle took place in Laos, including Khammanh Sounvileuth taking over as interior affairs minister and Brig.-Gen. Somkeo Silavong as public security minister.

Raimonds Vejonis was sworn in as president of Latvia, becoming the EU's first head of state affiliated to a green party. Raimonds Bergmanis subsequently took over the defence portfolio recently vacated by Vejonis.

Gen. Pak Yong-sik was confirmed by the North Korean government as the country's new defence minister. His predecessor, Hyon Yong-chol, had allegedly been executed in April on insubordination charges.

Chronology of Events for June 2015

Week Beginning 28 June 2015

A new government was appointed in Denmark following elections held earlier in the month. Lars Løkke Rasmussen, who had previously served as prime minister from 2009–11, returned to the premiership, leading a Liberal government that included Kristian Jensen as foreign affairs minister and Claus Hjort Frederiksen as finance minister.

The ruling National Council for the Defence of Democracy–Forces for the Defence of Democracy (CNDD–FDD) won parliamentary elections in Burundi, taking 77 of 100 seats with 60.3% of the vote. Despite opposition parties officially boycotting elections they remained on the ballot and won 23 seats, of which the Hope for Burundians coalition took 21 with 11.2% and Union for National Progress 2 with 2.5%.

In Madagascar, prime minister Jean Ravelonarivo survived a parliamentary vote of no confidence, which received only 95 of the required 101 votes.

The Afghan parliament rejected Masoum Stanikzai's candidacy for the defence portfolio. Stanikzai, who had been acting as interim defence minister, was the second nominee to be rejected by parliament during Ashraf Ghani Ahmadzai's presidency.

Week Beginning 21 June 2015

Luis Carlos Villegas became defence minister of Colombia.

In Spain, Íñigo Méndez de Vigo y Montojo took over from José Ignacio Wert as minister of education, culture and sport.

Week Beginning 14 June 2015

The Palestinian Fatah–Hamas unity government led by prime minister Rami Hamdallah resigned following claims by president Mahmoud Abbas that it was unable to function in Gaza. Abbas subsequently asked Hamdallah to form a new government.

In Benin, a new government was sworn in. Lionel Zinsou was appointed prime minister, heading a cabinet that included new appointees Saliou Akadiri as foreign minister and Placide Azandé as interior minister. Other key portfolios remained unchanged.

Parliamentary elections took place in Denmark. The Social Democratic Party won 47 of 175 mainland seats with 26.3% of the vote, the Danish People's Party 37 with 21.1%, the Liberal Party 34 with 19.5%, the Unity List—the Red-Greens 14 with 7.8% and the Liberal Alliance 13 with 7.5%. Other parties won ten seats or fewer. Although the Social Democratic Party won the most seats, the Liberal Party-led 'Blue bloc' took 90 seats compared to 85 for the Social Democratic Party-led 'Red bloc'.

French prime minister Manuel Valls survived a parliamentary vote of no confidence, which gained only 198 of the required 289 votes. The vote was called by opposition parties denouncing Valls' decision to bypass parliament in pushing through a number of economic reforms using an obscure constitutional mechanism.

Hwang Kyo-ahn was sworn in as prime minister of South Korea following Lee Wan-koo's resignation in April.

Week Beginning 7 June 2015

Parliamentary elections took place in Turkey. The ruling Justice and Development Party (AKP) lost 53 seats compared to the elections of 2011, taking 258 of 550 seats with 40.9% of the vote. Opposition parties increased their presence in parliament with the Republican People's Party gaining 132 seats (25.0%), the Nationalist Movement Party 80 (16.3%) and the People's Democratic Party 80 (13.1%). The elections were marred by violence amid accusations of fraud and corruption, but were judged to be fair by European Parliament and OSCE observers.

In Vanuatu, the government of prime minister Joe Natuman lost a confidence vote in parliament by 27 votes to 25. The following day Sato Kilman took over as premier for the fourth time and appointed a new cabinet that included Hosea Nevu as minister of internal affairs and Serge Vohor as minister of foreign affairs.

Chiril Gaburici announced his resignation as prime minister of Moldova following allegations he had falsified his school diplomas. Natalia Gherman took over as interim prime minister later in the month.

Romanian prime minister Victor Ponta survived a parliamentary vote of no confidence, which gained only 194 of the required 278 votes.

Chronology of Events for May 2015

Week Beginning 31 May 2015

Raimonds Vējonis won presidential elections in Latvia after five rounds of parliamentary voting. Vējonis, who was the incumbent defence minister, defeated three other candidates.

Ameenah Gurib-Fakim was elected president of Mauritius.

In Sudan, Ibrahim Ghandour was sworn in as foreign minister.

Week Beginning 24 May 2015

Andrzej Duda won presidential elections in Poland, taking 51.5% of the vote against Bronisław Komorowski with 48.5% in a second round run-off.

Parliamentary elections took place in Suriname in which the National Democratic Party won 26 of 51 seats. The V7 coalition was second with 18 followed by A-Combination with 5. Two other parties won a seat each.

In Madagascar, president Hery Rajaonarimampianina lost a parliamentary vote of no confidence by 121 votes to 4. Opposition parties (holding a majority of seats in parliament) claimed that he had violated the constitution and parliamentary conventions since coming to power in January 2014. However, his attempted impeachment was later dismissed by the constitutional court in June.

A new coalition government led by Juha Sipilä of the Centre Party was appointed in Finland. It included Timo Soini as deputy prime minister and minister of foreign affairs, and Petteri Orpo as interior minister. Former prime minister Alexander Stubb—who had been replaced by Sipilä—joined the government as finance minister.

Week Beginning 17 May 2015

In Burundi, Alain Aimé Nyamitwe was sworn in as minister of external affairs and Emmanuel Ntahomvukiye as minister of national defence following a cabinet reshuffle.

Salamah Hammad was appointed interior minister of Jordan.

In Guatemala, Eunice Mendizábal became interior minister.

Week Beginning 10 May 2015

In a cabinet reshuffle in Chile, Jorge Burgos became interior minister, Rodrigo Valdés finance minister and José Antonio Gómez defence minister. Other key portfolios remained unchanged.

David Granger of A Partnership for National Unity (in coalition with the Alliance for Change) was elected president of Guyana, winning with 50.3% of the vote.

In Micronesia, Peter M. Christian was appointed president.

Macedonian prime minister Nikola Gruevski reshuffled his cabinet following protests in the capital against his government. Mitko Chavkov became interior minister while other key portfolios remained unchanged.

Andreja Katič was sworn in as defence minister of Slovenia, taking over from Janko Veber. Veber had been dismissed the previous month following allegations he had illegally utilized Slovenia's military intelligence to assess the privatization of the state's telecommunications service.

A cabinet reshuffle took place in Algeria. Noureddine Bedoui became interior minister and Abderrahmane Benkhalfa finance minister.

In Guatemala, Alejandro Maldonado was sworn in as vice president following the resignation of Roxana Baldetti the previous week amid a corruption scandal.

In Israel, prime minister Binyamin Netanyahu's new five-party coalition government was approved by the Knesset. Included in the cabinet were Silvan Shalom as deputy prime minister and interior minister, and Moshe Kahlon as finance minister. Netanyahu took on the foreign affairs portfolio himself.

Week Beginning 3 May 2015

Avigdor Lieberman resigned as foreign minister of Israel declaring that he would not join Binyamin Netanyahu's new government, which was being formed at the time.

Despite polls suggesting a very close result, the Conservative Party won an outright majority of 331 seats at general elections in the United Kingdom. The Labour Party won 232 seats, down from 258, and the Liberal Democrats lost 49 seats taking their total tally down to 8. However, the Scottish National Party made huge gains, increasing their share of seats at Westminster by 50 to 56 and becoming the third largest party. As a consequence, prime minister David Cameron was able to form a new all-Conservative administration, changes to which included Michael Gove as secretary of state for justice and Sajid Javid as secretary of state for business, innovation and skills. Conservative ministers holding key portfolios before the election retained their positions.

Chronology of Events for April 2015

Week Beginning 26 April 2015

Parliamentary elections took place in Benin. The Cauri Forces for an Emerging Benin–Amana Alliance supporting president Yayi Boni won, taking 33 of 83 seats, ahead of Union Makes the Nation with 13.

Nursultan Nazarbayev was again re-elected president of Kazakhstan, extending his mandate by another 5 years. He subsequently reappointed prime minister Karim Masimov alongside his government, which remained unchanged.

A cabinet reshuffle took place in the Comoros. Abdoulkarim Mohamed was appointed minister of external relations and Houmed M'saidie minister of the interior.

South Korean prime minister Lee Wan-koo, who had been implicated in a bribery scandal, had his resignation accepted by president Park Geun-hye. The premiership remained vacant following Lee's departure.

In Saudi Arabia, the second cabinet reshuffle since King Salman bin Abdulaziz Al-Saud's accession to the throne 3 months earlier took place. Salman's nephew and interior minister Prince Mohammad bin Naif bin Abdulaziz Al-Saud was designated as the new heir apparent to the throne, becoming deputy prime minister. Additionally, Adel bin Ahmed Al-Jubeir became foreign minister, taking over from Prince Saud Al-Faisal bin Abdulaziz Al-Saud who retired having held the position since 1975.

Temir Sariyev was sworn in as prime minister of Kyrgyzstan, succeeding Dzhoomart Otorbayev who had resigned a week earlier following government turmoil surrounding the country's financial crisis. Sariyev's cabinet included several new appointments, with Adylbek Kasymaliev becoming finance minister and Oleg Pankratov economy minister. Other key positions remained unchanged.

Week Beginning 19 April 2015

Parliamentary elections took place in Finland. The Centre Party (KESK) won 49 seats, the Finns Party (PS) 38, the National Coalition Party (KOK) 37, the Social Democratic Party (SDP) 34, the Green League (VIHR) 15, the Left Alliance (VAS) 12, the Swedish People's Party (SFP) 9 and the Christian Democrats (KD) 5. One representative from the province of Åland was also elected. Prime minister Alexander Stubb of the KOK resigned later that month to allow the formation of a new government that would be led by Juha Sipilä of KESK.

Almaz Baketayev was appointed acting finance minister of Kyrgyzstan following Olga Lavrova's resignation earlier in the month.

Loretta Lynch was sworn in as attorney general of the United States, making her the first African–American woman and second woman to hold the position.

Faure Gnassingbé was re-elected president of Togo, receiving 58.8% of the vote against Jean-Pierre Fabre with 32.5% and three other candidates. Turnout was 60.9%.

Week Beginning 12 April 2015

Omar Hassan Ahmed al-Bashir was re-elected to a fifth term as president of Sudan, emerging victorious in the first elections held since the secession of South Sudan in 2011. Bashir took 94.0% of the vote against 15 other candidates. However, several opposition parties had boycotted the elections citing the government's repressive measures against civil society and the media.

Miguel Engonga Obiang Eyang became finance and budget minister of Equatorial Guinea.

Week Beginning 5 April 2015

In Haiti, foreign minister Duly Brutus resigned and was subsequently replaced by Lener Renaud on an interim basis.

A new coalition government comprised of the Estonian Reform Party, the Social Democratic Party, and the Union of Pro Patria and Res Publica was approved by parliament in Estonia. Taavi Rõivas remained prime minister and key cabinet positions were retained by members of the previous government.

A cabinet reshuffle took place in Malawi. Atupele Muluzi became minister of home affairs and internal security while other key portfolios remained unchanged.

Enele Sopoaga was sworn in as prime minister of Tuvalu.

Chronology of Events for March 2015

Week Beginning 29 March 2015

In Nigeria, Muhammadu Buhari of the All Progressives Congress defeated incumbent Goodluck Jonathan of the People's Democratic Party in presidential elections held over 2 days. Buhari won with 54.0% of the vote against 45.0% for Jonathan, with a turnout of 43.7%.

Islam Karimov was re-elected president of Uzbekistan with 90.4% of the vote following elections that attracted widespread condemnation from the international community owing to the lack of genuine opposition.

Eugen Teodorovici became Romanian finance minister following Darius Valcov's resignation earlier in the month.

Peruvian prime minister Ana Jara was removed from office following a failed congressional vote of confidence, in which she received only 42 of 116 votes. Jara had been accused of failing to control Peru's intelligence agency, which had allegedly been illegally gathering information on opposition political figures, journalists and business leaders. She was succeeded as premier by Pedro Cateriano 3 days later.

In Bosnia and Herzegovina, parliament approved a new government led by prime minister Denis Zvizdić. Included in the new cabinet were Marina Pendeš as defence minister and Igor Crnadak as foreign minister.

In Libya, the pro-Islamist General National Congress parliament based in Tripoli dismissed Omar al-Hasi as its prime minister. He was succeeded by Khalifa al-Ghawi.

Andrea Belluzi and Roberto Venturini were sworn in as Captains Regent of San Marino.

Week Beginning 22 March 2015

Former prime minister of Singapore Lee Kuan Yew died.

In South Sudan, president Salva Kiir's mandate was extended for 3 years following a constitutional amendment that was approved by parliament.

Week Beginning 15 March 2015

Parliamentary elections took place in Israel. Despite pre-election polling suggesting a victory for the centre-left Zionist Union, the Likud party emerged victorious winning 30 of 120 seats with 23.4% of the vote. The Zionist Union obtained 24 seats with 18.7% of votes and the Joint Arab List 13 with 10.5%. Seven other parties contested the poll, in which turnout was 72.4%.

Pakalitha Mosisili was sworn in as prime minister of Lesotho.

Hage Geingob was sworn in as president of Namibia alongside his cabinet.

Week Beginning 8 March 2015

In Venezuela, the former head of the country's intelligence service (SEBIN), Gustavo González, was appointed interior minister.

Roumyana Bachvarova took over from Veselin Vuchkov as interior minister of Bulgaria.

Prokopis Pavlopoulos began his mandate as president of Greece following his election to the position the previous month. Backed by the coalition government, Pavlopoulos succeeded Karolos Papoulias, who had held the position since 2005.

Week Beginning 1 March 2015

Parliamentary elections took place in Andorra. The Democrats for Andorra (DA) won 15 seats with 37.0% of the vote and the Liberals of Andorra (PLA) won 8 with 27.7%. Two other alliances and parties took the remaining five seats. Turnout was 65.6%. Prime minister Antoni Martí of the DA retained his position when the new government was approved by parliament a month later.

The Nationalist Republican Alliance won parliamentary elections in El Salvador, gaining 32 of 84 seats. The Farabundo Martí National Liberation Front won 31 and the Grand National Alliance 11. The remaining seats went to smaller parties and candidates running jointly for two parties.

In parliamentary elections in Estonia, the Estonian Reform Party took 27.7% of the vote and won 30 seats, the Centre Party 24.8% and 27 and the Social Democratic Party 15.2% and 15. Three other parties won the remaining seats.

Matia Kasaija was sworn in as finance minister of Uganda.

In Uruguay, Tabaré Vázquez was sworn in as president alongside a new government following his victory at the election run-off held 3 months earlier. He took over from fellow Broad Front member José Mujica.

In a cabinet reshuffle that took place in Egypt, Magdy Abdel Ghafar took over as interior minister with over key portfolios remaining unchanged.

Sebahattin Öztürk was sworn in as interior minister of Turkey following the resignation of Efkan Ala 2 days earlier.

Chronology of Events for February 2015

Week Beginning 22 February 2015

Parliamentary elections concluded in the Comoros. Held over two rounds, the Union for the Development of the Comoros won 8 of the 24 popularly-elected seats and the Juwa Party 7. Four other parties and independents won a total of nine seats.

Kané Aïchatou Boulama was appointed foreign minister of Niger.

In parliamentary elections in Lesotho, Democratic Congress won 47 of 120 seats, All Basotho Convention 46 and Lesotho Congress for Democracy 12. The remaining 15 seats went to smaller parties and independents.

Week Beginning 15 February 2015

Parliamentary elections took place in St Kitts and Nevis. The People's Action Movement gained 4 seats, Labour Party 3, the Concerned Citizens' Movement 2, the Nevis Reformation Party 1 and the People's Labour Party 1. Timothy Harris was sworn in as prime minister 2 days later.

Rui Maria de Araújo was sworn in as prime minister of Timor-Leste following Xanana Gusmão's resignation 10 days earlier. Araújo was joined in the government by Longuinhos Monteiro as interior minister and Hernâni Coelho as foreign affairs and co-operation minister.

In South Korea, Lee Wan-koo of the Saenuri Party took over from Chung Hong-won as prime minister. Lee's appointment came almost 10 months after Chung had submitted his resignation in the wake of the Sewol ferry disaster, which left 304 people dead.

José Luis Pérez Guadalupe became interior minister of Peru.

Ashton Carter was sworn in as the US secretary of defence, taking over from Chuck Hagel.

Prokopis Pavlopoulos was elected president by the Greek parliament. Pavlopoulos, who had been nominated by the ruling Syriza–Independent Greeks coalition government, received 233 votes in the fourth round of voting against Nikos Alivizatos with 30.

Moldova's president Nicolae Timofti appointed Chiril Gaburici prime minister.

In France, the government of prime minister Manuel Valls survived a parliamentary vote of no confidence, with the motion receiving only 234 of a required 289 votes. The vote was called by opposition conservatives denouncing Valls' decision to bypass parliament in pushing through a number of economic reforms.

In Yemen, Abdo Rabu Mansour al-Hadi, who had submitted his resignation as president almost a month earlier, fled to the southern city of Aden. He quickly retracted his resignation and reasserted his mandate as president, despite rebel control over the capital and imposition of a transitional government.

Week Beginning 8 February 2015

In Canada, defence minister Robert Nicholson took over the foreign affairs portfolio vacated by John Baird, who had unexpectedly announced his resignation in order to pursue interests in the private sector. Jason Kenney was sworn in as defence minister alongside Nicholson.

A new cabinet under Omar Abdirashid Ali Sharmarke was approved by parliament in Somalia.

Denis Zvizdić became prime minister of Bosnia and Herzegovina. A Party of Democratic Action member of Bosniak ethnicity, he had been designated premier by the recently appointed presidency.

Greek prime minister Alexis Tsipras won a parliamentary vote of confidence by 162 votes to 137.

In Zambia, president Edgar Lungu finalized his government line-up, retaining many key members of the previous administration. Lungu, who had been minister of defence under president Michael Sata, continued in the position whilst Davies Mwila took over at the ministry of home affairs.

Week Beginning 1 February 2015

In a cabinet reshuffle that took place in the Seychelles, Charles Bastienne was appointed home affairs minister, Joel Morgan foreign affairs and transport minister, and Jean-Paul Adam finance minister.

A cabinet reshuffle took place in Trinidad and Tobago, with Carl Alfonso becoming national security minister.

A unity government led by new prime minister Habib Essid took office in Tunisia. The cabinet, which had undergone a number of revisions following opposition from parliament, included Mohamed Najem Gharsalli as interior minister and Slim Chaker as finance minister.

Chronology of Events for January 2015

Week Beginning 25 January 2015

Early parliamentary elections triggered by parliament's failure to elect a new president the previous month took place in Greece. The Coalition of the Radical Left (Syriza) won 149 of 300 seats with 36.3% of the vote, New Democracy (ND) 76 with 27.8% and Golden Dawn 17 with 6.3%. Four other parties took the remaining 58 seats. Turnout was 63.9%. Syriza leader Alexis Tsipras was sworn in as prime minister the next day, followed by his cabinet a day later.

In Georgia, Vakhtang Gomelauri replaced Alexander Chikaidze as interior minister.

In Afghanistan, nine members of the cabinet nominated by president Ashraf Ghani Ahmadzai were approved by parliament. They included Eklil Hakimi as finance minister, Salahuddin Rabbani as foreign minister and Nur ul-Haq Ulumi as interior minister. Their appointment came more than 3 months after the elections that brought Ghani to power, with the remaining ministerial candidates expected to be in position following parliament's 45-day recess.

The president of Zimbabwe, Robert Mugabe, was elected chairman of the African Union for 2015. He took over from Mauritanian president Mohamed Ould Abdel Aziz.

In Taiwan, Kao Kuang-chi was sworn in as defence minister taking over from Yen Ming.

Sergio Mattarella was elected president of Italy following the resignation of the aged Giorgio Napolitano earlier in the month. Mattarella, who was not associated with a political party, won with 665 votes in the fourth round of voting by lawmakers and regional representatives. He took over from Pietro Grasso, who had been acting president since Napolitano's resignation.

Week Beginning 18 January 2015

In the Maldives, president Abdulla Yameen replaced Mohamed Nazim with Moosa Ali Jaleel as defence and national security minister.

Swedish prime minister Stefan Löfven survived a parliamentary vote of no confidence, which gained only 45 of the required 175 votes.

Early presidential elections that were held following the death of incumbent president Michael Sata 12 weeks earlier took place in Zambia. Edgar Lungu of the ruling Patriotic Front won 48% of the vote, narrowly beating Hakainde Hichilema of the United Party for National Development with 46.7%. Nine other candidates received less than 1% of the vote each. Held over 2 days, turnout was only 32.4%. Lungu was sworn in later that week, and assembled a new government including Inonge Wina as vice president, Jorge Ledezma Cornejo as defence minister and Davies Mwila as home affairs minister.

In Yemen, president Abdo Rabu Mansour al-Hadi and prime minister Khaled Bahah offered their resignations after Houthi rebels took control of the capital. Despite parliament's rejection of their proposals, the government was subsequently overthrown by the rebels, with a transitional council led by Mohammed Ali al-Houthi installed 2 weeks later.

Evo Morales was sworn in to his third term as Bolivian president. A new cabinet, which was sworn in a day later, included Hugo Moldiz as interior minister and Jorge Ledesma as defence minister. Luis Arce Catacora and David Choquehuanca retained their respective positions as the ministers of finance and foreign affairs.

King Abdullah of Saudi Arabia died aged 90. He had suffered from poor health over the previous 5 years and had reportedly been diagnosed with terminal lung cancer. His half-brother Salman, the crown prince whom Abdullah had nominated as his successor, was confirmed as King the same day.

Week Beginning 11 January 2015

Kolinda Grabar-Kitarović was elected Croatia's first female president. Grabar-Kitarović won the second round run-off with 50.7% of the vote against incumbent president Ivo Josipović. Turnout for the second round was 59.1%—an increase of 12% compared to the first round in which two other candidates also took part.

In South Sudan, David Deng Athorbei replaced Aggrey Tisa Sabuni as minister of finance, commerce and economic planning.

A new government that included Ravi Karunanayake as finance minister and Mangala Samaraweera as foreign minister was appointed in Sri Lanka.

Filipe Nyusi of the FRELIMO party was sworn in as president of Mozambique following his victory at elections held 3 months earlier. Carlos Agostinho do Rosário (also of FRELIMO) became prime minister 2 days later, and led a new cabinet that included Jaime Basílio Monteiro as interior minister and Atanásio Salvador Ntumuke as defence minister.

A cabinet reshuffle took place in the Central African Republic. Aristide Sokambi took over the justice portfolio from Marie-Noëlle Koyara, who moved to the ministry of defence, and Abdallah-Kadre Assane became finance minister. Other key portfolios remained unchanged.

In Haiti, Evans Paul was sworn in as prime minister following his nomination by president Michel Martelly. Interior minister Ariel Henry and finance minister Wilson Laleau were among the cabinet's new appointees.

In a cabinet reshuffle in Mauritania, Moktar Ould Diay was appointed finance minister and Vatma Vall Mint Soueina foreign affairs and co-operation minister.

Jean Ravelonarivo became prime minister of Madagascar, replacing Roger Kolo who had resigned alongside his cabinet over criticism of the government's response to power outages earlier that week.

Week Beginning 4 January 2015

In Paraguay, Santiago Peña was sworn in as finance minister following the resignation of Germán Rojos.

Parliamentary elections concluded in Uzbekistan. Held over two rounds, the Liberal-Democratic Party won 52 of 150 seats, followed by the Uzbekistan National Revival Democratic Party with 36, the People's Democratic Party of Uzbekistan with 27 and the Justice Social Democratic Party with 20. A further 15 seats were reserved for the Ecological Movement. Opposition parties were banned from participating and all candidates were loyal to president Islam Karimov.

In the Gambia, a cabinet reshuffle took place following an alleged coup attempt against president Yahya Jammeh the previous month. Neneh Macdouall-Gaye took over as foreign affairs minister and Mama Fatima Singhateh as attorney general and justice minister. Other key portfolios remained unchanged.

Arturo Corrales was sworn in as foreign minister of Honduras, taking over from Mireya Agüero de Corrales who had resigned 9 weeks earlier.

Presidential elections in Sri Lanka were won by Maithripala Sirisena of the New Democratic Front, who took 51.3% of the vote, ahead of incumbent president Mahinda Rajapaksa of the United People's Freedom Alliance (made up of several parties including the Sri Lanka Freedom Party) with 47.6%. 17 other candidates took part in the elections and turnout stood at 81.5%. Rajapaksa was subsequently investigated over an alleged attempt to retain power illegally following the elections. Sirisena was sworn in as president a day later alongside Ranil Wickremesinghe, who returned as prime minister having twice previously served in the post.

Modibo Keïta was appointed to lead a new government in Mali following the resignation of prime minister Moussa Mara. Keïta, who was tasked with dealing with the separatist Islamist and Tuareg groups in the north of the country, was joined by a new cabinet that included Tiéman Hubert Coulibaly as defence minister and Mamadou Diarra as economy and finance minister.

2014

Chronology of Events for December 2014

Week Beginning 28 December 2014

The NATO-led mission to Afghanistan known as the International Security Assistance Force ended. Active since late 2001, the force had comprised 42 countries (including 14 non-NATO members) and had undertaken combat operations throughout Afghanistan. A small number of troops remained in the country in an advisory capacity to oversee training and to provide assistance to Afghan security forces.

Presidential elections entered their third and final round in Greece. Former European Commissioner Stavros Dimas of the New Democracy party, who was the sole candidate, failed to secure a required quorum of 180 parliamentary votes, triggering the dissolution of parliament and the scheduling of fresh elections for the following month in accordance with the constitution.

A new government led by 'Akilisi Pohiva was ratified by parliament in Tonga. In addition to his duties as prime minister, Pohiva took over the foreign affairs portfolio, with the cabinet including Sosefo Fe'ao Vakata as minister of internal affairs and 'Aisake Valu Eke as minister of finance and national planning.

In anticipation of parliamentary elections scheduled for the following month, Michalis Theocharidis, who had no affiliation to a political party, became interior minister of Greece. The appointment of a non-partisan figure to the position in order to oversee voting had a precedent at previous elections.

A new cabinet took office in Brazil following the elections 2 months earlier in which incumbent president Dilma Rousseff retained her mandate. Containing fewer Workers' Party members than Rousseff's previous administration, the new government included former ambassador to the USA Mauro Vieira as foreign minister, Joaquim Levy as finance minister and Jaques Wagner as defence minister.

In Switzerland, Simonetta Sommaruga was sworn in as president for 2015 and Johann Schneider-Ammann as vice president.

Week Beginning 21 December 2014

Australian prime minister Tony Abbott reshuffled his cabinet, with Kevin Andrews taking over from David Johnston as defence minister.

Klaus Iohannis was sworn in as president of Romania following his victory at the elections held the previous month.

Beji Caid Essebsi won presidential elections in Tunisia. Held over two rounds, 88-year-old Essebsi beat incumbent interim president Moncef Marzouki in a run-off, gaining 55.7% of the vote to 44.3% for Marzouki.

Construction of a new 278-km interoceanic canal began in Nicaragua. Expected to be operational by 2020 and projected to cost US$50 bn. to construct, its development was financed by a Hong Kong-based group led by Chinese CEO Wang Jing.

Omar Abdirashid Ali Sharmarke was sworn in as the new prime minister of Somalia following parliamentary approval. He replaced Abdiweli Sheikh Ahmed.

Former prime minister of Belgium Leo Tindemans died aged 92. A key figure in the promotion of an integrated Europe, Tindemans also founded and served as president of the European People's Party from 1976–85.

Delcy Rodríguez Gómez took over from Rafael Ramírez as foreign minister of Venezuela, with Ramírez appointed Venezuela's permanent representative to the United Nations.

In Belarus, Andrei Kobyakov was sworn in as prime minister, replacing outgoing premier Mikhail Myasnikovich.

Week Beginning 14 December 2014

Early elections called by prime minister Shinzo Abe were held in Japan. Abe's Liberal Democratic Party in alliance with the Komeito party won 326 of 475 seats, the Democratic Party of Japan 73, the Japan Innovation Party 41 and the Communist Party of Japan 21. Three other parties and independents shared 14 seats. At 52.6%, turnout was the lowest since the Second World War. Abe's government remained unchanged in its key portfolios with the exception of Gen Nakatani's appointment later in the month as minister of defence.

A mini cabinet reshuffle in Romania saw Darius-Bogdan Vâlcov replace Ioana Petrescu as finance minister. Other key portfolios remained unchanged.

Week Beginning 7 December 2014

A cabinet reshuffle took place in the Democratic Republic of the Congo. Evariste Boshab was appointed interior and security minister, and Aimé Ngoy Mukena defence and veterans' rehabilitation minister.

Dominica's ruling Dominica Labour Party won 15 of 21 seats at parliamentary elections, losing three seats to the United Workers Party who were now represented by six members in the House of Assembly. Prime minister Roosevelt Skerrit, in power since 2004, retained his position and a new government was subsequently sworn in.

Isa Mustafa of the Democratic League of Kosovo was appointed prime minister of Kosovo, leading a new coalition government with the rival Democratic Party of Kosovo.

In Malta, home affairs minister Manual Mallia was dismissed by prime minister Joseph Muscat following an inquiry into a shooting incident involving his private driver. Carmelo Alba took over Mallia's portfolio.

Manasseh Sogavare, who had twice previously served as prime minister of the Solomon Islands, was elected to a third term by parliament. His new coalition government was completed later in the month, and included Douglas Ete as deputy prime minister and home affairs minister, Snyder Rini as finance minister and Milner Tozaka as foreign affairs and external trade minister.

In Mauritius, the Alliance of the People/Alliance Lepep (consisting of the Militant Socialist Movement, the Mauritian Social Democrat Party and the Muvman Liberater) defeated the ruling Labour Party (who had formed an alliance with Mauritian Militant Movement), winning 51 of 62 seats. Prior to the election, the Labour Party had announced plans for constitutional amendments to split power between the prime minister and largely ceremonial president (who was also a member of the Labour Party). The new government led by Sir Anerood Jugnauth was appointed a week later.

In Zimbabwe, president Robert Mugabe dismissed vice president Joyce Mujuru and seven other senior and vice ministers. Mujuru, who was widely considered Mugabe's likely successor, had been accused by state media and Mugabe's confidants of plotting against the ageing president. Emmerson Mnangagwa and Phelekezela Mphoko were subsequently sworn in as vice presidents.

Laurent Lamothe resigned as prime minister of Haiti following demonstrations over the postponement of elections.

Chronology of Events for November 2014

Week Beginning 30 November 2014

Pro-European Union parties prevailed in parliamentary elections in Moldova. The Party of Socialists of the Republic of Moldova (which was contesting its first-ever election) won 25 seats with 20.5% of the vote, the Liberal Democratic Party of Moldova 23 with 20.2%, the Party of

Communists 21 with 17.5%, the Democratic Party of Moldova 19 with 15.8% and the Liberal Party 13 with 9.7%.

In Somalia, prime minister Abdiweli Sheikh Ahmed was ousted by parliament after losing a vote of no confidence by 153 votes to 80.

Ólöf Nordal took over from Hanna Birna Kristjánsdóttir as interior minister of Iceland.

In Switzerland, federal council elections saw Simonetta Sommaruga become president and Johann Schneider-Ammann vice president.

In Kenya, Joseph Nkaissery was appointed acting cabinet secretary for interior and co-ordination of national government, taking over from Joseph Ole Lenku who had been dismissed by president Kenyatta in response to the massacre of 36 quarry workers by the Islamist group al-Shabab. He was confirmed in the post 2 weeks later.

Israeli prime minister Benjamin Netanyahu dismissed finance minister Yair Lapid and justice minister Tzipi Livni in response to their purported opposition to government policies.

In a cabinet reshuffle in Grenada, Clarice Modeste became foreign minister, Yolande Bain-Horsford tourism and civil aviation minister and Nickolas Steele health and social security minister. Other key portfolios remained unchanged.

In Uruguay, Tabaré Vázquez of the Broad Front (FA) won the presidential election run-off with 56.6% of the vote against Luis Alberto Lacalle Pou of the National Party (PN) with 43.4%. Vázquez had also won the first round of polling, gaining 49.5% of the vote against Pou with 31.9% and five other candidates. In the elections to the General Assembly that were run concurrently, the FA won 50 seats, the PN 32, the Colorado Party 13, the Independent Party 3 and the Popular Assembly 1.

Week Beginning 23 November 2014

In parliamentary elections that concluded in Bahrain, independent candidates won 36 of 40 seats, with Sunni parties taking four seats. Despite a boycott by the largely Shia opposition, independent Shia candidates held 14 seats in the new parliament.

In Namibia, presidential and parliamentary elections were the first in Africa to utilize electronic or e-voting. Hage Geingob of the South West Africa People's Organization (SWAPO) was elected president with 86.7% of votes cast. In the parliamentary elections held the same day, SWAPO won 77 of 96 seats, with nine other parties taking the remaining 19 seats.

Arseniy Yatsenyuk was re-elected prime minister of Ukraine by parliament, gaining 341 of 450 votes in favour of his appointment. His new cabinet was subsequently confirmed, and included Natalia Yaresko as finance minister and Aivaras Abromavicius as economic development and trade minister.

In polling in Tonga for 17 elected representatives in the Legislative Assembly, the Democratic Party of the Friendly Islands won nine seats and independent candidates eight.

In Belarus, Maj.-Gen. Andrei Ravkov was sworn in as defence minister.

Brazilian president Dilma Rousseff appointed Joaquim Levy as finance minister, taking over from Guido Mantego—a veteran from the administration of the previous president Lula da Silva who had held the post for over 8 years.

Patrice Trovoada, who had served as prime minister of São Tomé e Príncipe on two previous occasions since 2008, returned to the premiership following his Independent Democratic Action party's success at the National Assembly elections held 6 weeks earlier.

Talks between Iran and the P5+1 countries comprising the USA, Russia, China, UK, France and Germany to limit Iran's disputed nuclear development programme failed to meet a deadline for a conclusive agreement. A new deadline of June 2015 was set.

Bogdan Aurescu became foreign minister of Romania.

Week Beginning 16 November 2014

Parliamentary elections took place in the Solomon Islands. The Democratic Alliance Party won 7 seats, United Democratic Party 5 and People's Alliance Party 3. Three other parties took one seat each, with independent candidates winning 32.

Anabela Rodrigues took office as interior minister of Portugal, succeeding Miguel Macedo who had resigned over alleged corruption.

Michel Kafando was sworn in as Burkina Faso's transitional president following the military-led coup staged nearly 3 weeks earlier. Lieut.-Col. Isaac Zida, who had assumed the country's leadership following the ousting of former president Blaise Compaoré, was appointed prime minister of a new government.

In a cabinet reshuffle in Estonia, Keit Pentus-Rosimannus became foreign minister following the departure of Urmas Paet who became a member of the European Parliament.

In Bosnia and Herzegovina, Mladen Ivanić took over the 8-month rotating presidency chairmanship.

Klaus Iohannis of the National Liberal Party won the Romanian presidential election run-off with by 54.4% of the vote against 45.6% for incumbent prime minister Victor Ponta. Ponta had won the first round held 2 weeks earlier with 40.4% of votes cast to 30.4% for Iohannis and 5.4% for former prime minister Călin Popescu-Tăriceanu, but lost momentum to Iohannis in the second round.

Week Beginning 9 November 2014
In Lithuania, Saulius Skvernelis became interior minister, taking over from Dailis Alfonsas Barakauskas who resigned amid allegations of corruption.

Tamar Beruchashvili was sworn in as foreign minister of Georgia following the earlier resignation of Maya Panjikidze.

A new government was appointed in Yemen. It was led by Khaled Bahah, the country's former permanent representative to the United Nations. The government was composed of a diverse group of parties and independent technocrats.

Week Beginning 2 November 2014
Archbishop Paul Gallagher of the United Kingdom became secretary for relations with states of the Vatican City.

A new government was appointed in Yemen. It was led by Khaled Bahah, the country's former permanent representative to the United Nations. The government was composed of a diverse group of parties and independent technocrats.

Bokyo Borisov, who had previously served as prime minister of Bulgaria from 2009–13, was reappointed to the post following elections held the previous month. Despite his GERB party winning the most seats in parliament, Borisov fell short of a majority and was forced to form a coalition government with the Reformist Bloc and Alternative for Bulgarian Revival. A new cabinet was sworn in alongside Borisov.

Vladimir Amaryn was sworn in as finance minister of Belarus, taking over from Andrei Kharkovets who had resigned in July.

Mongolian prime minister Norov Altankhuyag was ousted after losing a parliamentary vote of no confidence by 36 votes to 30. His government had faced pressure from opposition groups over a mounting economic crisis exacerbated by collapsing commodity prices. Altankhuyag was succeeded by his deputy Dendev Terbishdagva as acting prime minister. Chimed Saikhanbileg subsequently became prime minister.

In Israel, Gilad Edan of the Likud party replaced Gideon Sa'ar as interior minister.

Latvian prime minister Laimdota Straujuma's new government was approved by parliament and subsequently sworn in.

The Republican Party won its biggest majority in the House of Representatives in over 60 years and also regained control of the Senate at the United States mid-term elections. With only 36.4% of eligible voters participating, turnout was the lowest since 1942.

In Georgia, Mindia Janelidze took over from Irakli Alasania as defence minister.

A cabinet reshuffle took place in Greece. Nikos Dendias became defence minister and Konstantinos Skrekas minister of development and competitiveness. Other key portfolios remained unchanged.

Maris Lauri was appointed finance minister of Estonia.

Chronology of Events for October 2014

Week Beginning 26 October 2014
The first parliamentary elections since the adoption of a new constitution—which had created the unicameral Assembly of the Representatives of the People—took place in Tunisia. Call of Tunisia (Nidaa Tounes) won 85 seats, Ennahda 69, Free Patriotic Union 16, Popular Front 15 and Tunisian Aspiration 8. 11 other parties gained four seats or fewer and three independents were elected.

Parliamentary elections in Ukraine saw the Petro Poroshenko Bloc win 132 of the 423 contested seats, the People's Front 82, Self Reliance Party 33, Opposition Bloc 29, Radical Party of Oleh Lyashko 22, All-Ukrainian Union 'Fatherland' 19 and the Svoboda (Freedom) Party 6. Four other parties won one seat each and 96 seats went to independents. Despite overall voter

turnout standing at 52.4%, participation in districts affected by the ongoing conflict with Russia (namely Dontesk and Luhansk) was significantly lower.

The president of Zambia, Michael Sata, died aged 77 in the United Kingdom whilst receiving treatment for an undisclosed condition at a hospital in London. Vice-president Guy Scott took over the presidency on an interim basis the following day.

Blaise Compaoré resigned as president of Burkina Faso after violent public opposition erupted following the announcement that he would attempt to extend his 27-year rule. The military then staged a coup, installing Lieut.-Col. Isaac Zida as the leader of a transitional government.

In Italy, Paolo Gentiloni was appointed foreign minister, taking over from Federica Mogherini who became the European Commission's foreign policy chief.

The new European Commission led by the former prime minister of Luxembourg Jean-Claude Juncker was sworn in. The incoming executive included four former European prime ministers and two former deputy prime ministers, with its mandate extending to 2019.

Week Beginning 19 October 2014
Joko Widodo took office as president of Indonesia. His cabinet, sworn in a week later, included Ryamizard Ryacudu as defence minister and Retno Lestari Priansari Marsudi as minister of foreign affairs.

Former prime minister of Australia Gough Whitlam died aged 98.

A mini cabinet reshuffle took place in Guinea. Mahmoudou Cissé took over as minister of security and civil protection and Cheick Taliby Sylla as minister of energy and hydraulics.

In Kazakhstan, Imangali Tasmagambetov took over from former prime minister Serik Akhmetov as minister of defence. Akhmetov had resigned amid allegations that he had influenced an anti-corruption case involving a government official.

Elections to the National Assembly were conducted in Botswana. The ruling Botswana Democratic Party (BDP) gained 37 seats with 46.5% of the vote, the Umbrella for Democratic Change 17 with 30.0% and the Botswana Congress Party 3 with 20.4%. Ian Khama was sworn in to a second term as president later in the month.

Week Beginning 12 October 2014
Incumbent president of Bolivia Evo Morales of the Movement Towards Socialism was re-elected to a third term following general elections in which the composition of the Chamber of Deputies and Senate was also decided. Morales won with 61.0% of votes cast against 24.5% for Samuel Doria Medina (Democratic Unity) and three other candidates.

In general elections that took place in Bosnia and Herzegovina, Bakir Izetbegović (Muslim; Party of Democratic Action—SDA), Dragan Čović (Croat; Croatian Democratic Union—HDZ BiH) and Mladen Ivanić (Serb; Alliance for Change—PDP SDS) were elected to the Presidency. In parliamentary elections the SDA won 10 seats, the Alliance of Independent Social Democrats 6, the Serbian Democratic Party 5 and the Democratic Front 5. Eight other parties or groupings won four seats or fewer.

In São Tomé e Príncipe, the Independent Democratic Action party won parliamentary elections taking 33 of 55 seats. The Liberation Movement of São Tomé e Príncipe-Social Democratic Party won 16 seats, Democratic Convergence Party-Reflection Group 5 and Union for Democracy and Development 1.

Stepan Poltorak was sworn in as defence minister of Ukraine following the resignation of Valeriy Heletey.

Mozambique's former defence minister Filipe Nyusi of the FRELIMO party won the presidential election with 57.0% of the vote against Afonso Dhlakama (RENAMO) with 36.6% and Daviz Simango (Democratic Movement of Mozambique) with 6.4%. FRELIMO retained its parliamentary majority following elections to the Assembly held the same day.

In the Netherlands, Bert Koenders was sworn in as foreign minister.

In Iraq, Haider al-Abadi's government was finally completed with the appointment of Khaled al-Obeidi as defence minister and Mohammed Salem al-Ghabban as interior minister. The two positions had been vacant for over a month while parliament failed to agree on nominees for the posts.

Week Beginning 5 October 2014
Incumbent Dilma Rousseff won the first round of Brazil's presidential elections with 41.6% of votes cast against 33.5% for Aécio Neves and 21.3% for Marina Silva. In parliamentary elections, the 'With the Strength of the People' coalition of nine parties (including the Workers' Party of which Dilma Rousseff is a member) took 304 of 513 seats against 128 for the 'Change

Brazil' alliance and 53 for the 'United for Brazil' alliance. In the presidential election run-off 3 weeks later, Rousseff was re-elected to a second term with 51.6% of the vote against 48.4% for Neves.

Parliamentary elections took place in Bulgaria. Citizens for the European Development of Bulgaria (GERB) won 84 of 240 seats with 32.7% of the vote, beating the Bulgarian Socialist Party-led BSP–Left Bulgaria with 39 and 15.4% and the Movement for Rights and Freedoms with 38 and 14.8%. The remaining seats went to five other parties. Boyko Borisov of GERB, who had been prime minister from 2009–13, subsequently returned to the premiership and was sworn in a month later.

In New Zealand, a cabinet reshuffle took place following the National Party's victory at the parliamentary elections held 3 weeks earlier. Leader of the house Gerry Brownlee became defence minister, succeeding Jonathan Coleman, who took over as health and sport and recreation minister. In addition to remaining minister for broadcasting and communications, Amy Adams took on the justice and courts portfolio. Other key positions remained unchanged.

A new coalition government with Charles Michel of the French-speaking Reformist Movement as prime minister was formed in Belgium following months of negotiations between the four main centre-right parties. Each of the four parties were represented in the new cabinet, with Kris Peeters (Christian Democratic and Flemish), Jan Jambon (New Flemish Alliance), Alexander De Croo (Open Flemish Liberals and Democrats) and Didier Reynders (Reformist Movement) appointed deputy prime ministers.

Greek prime minister Antonis Samaras won a vote of confidence in parliament by 155 votes to 131.

Chronology of Events for September 2014

Week Beginning 28 September 2014

In parliamentary elections in Latvia, the Social Democratic Party 'Harmony' won 24 of the 100 seats with 23.0% of the votes cast, Unity won 23 with 21.9%, and the Union of Greens and Farmers (comprising Latvian Farmers' Union and Latvian Green Party) took 21 with 19.5%. Three smaller parties also obtained seats. Turnout was 58.9%.

Former president of Haiti Jean-Claude 'Baby Doc' Duvalier died aged 63.

Melis Turganbayev was appointed interior minister in Kyrgyzstan following the resignation of Abdylda Suranchiyev.'

Gian Franco Terenzi and Guerrino Zanotti were appointed Captains Regent of San Marino.

Former prime minister of Norway Jens Stoltenberg took office as the 13th secretary general of NATO, replacing the outgoing Anders Fogh Rasmussen who had held the position for over 5 years.

In Afghanistan, Ashraf Ghani Ahmadzai was sworn in as president. An ethnic Pashtun, he was joined by his electoral rival Abdullah Abdullah (of Tajik and Pashtun descent) as chief executive, and Abdul Rashid Dostum (an Uzbek) and Sarwar Danish (a Hazara) as vice presidents.

Week Beginning 21 September 2014

Péter Szijjártó replaced Tibor Navracsics as foreign minister of Hungary.

Baldwin Lonsdale was sworn in as president of Vanuatu following eight rounds of voting in the parliamentary electoral college to choose a new head of state. Lonsdale took over from parliamentary speaker Philip Boedoro, who had been acting president since Iolu Abil's mandated term came to an end 3 weeks earlier.

Ewa Kopacz of the Civic Platform party took over from Donald Tusk as prime minister of Poland. Tusk had resigned a week earlier in order to assume the presidency of the European Council in December. Kopacz's new cabinet included Tomasz Siemoniak as deputy prime minister and minister of defence and Grzegorz Schetyna as foreign affairs minister.

In Yemen, prime minister Mohammed Basindawa resigned in the wake of protests against alleged government corruption and the marginalization of the country's Shia community, which had started a month earlier. A deal to form a new government was subsequently signed between the protest movement and other political parties.

Week Beginning 14 September 2014

Parliamentary elections took place in Sweden. The opposition Social Democratic Labour Party won 113 of 349 seats with 31.0% of votes, beating the ruling Moderate Party with 84 and 23.3%, the far-right Sweden Democrats with 49 and 12.9% and the Green Party with 25 and 6.9%. Four other parties took the remaining seats. Two weeks later the Swedish parliament approved

new prime minister Stefan Löfven's centre-left coalition government, which included Peter Hultqvist as defence minister and former vice president of the European Commission Margot Wallström as foreign minister.

In the Dominican Republic, Andrés Navarro was sworn in as foreign minister, taking over from Carlos Morales Troncoso who had held the post for over 10 years.

French prime minister Manuel Valls won a vote of confidence in parliament by 269 votes to 244.

In Fiji, the first parliamentary elections to take place under the new constitution of 2013 saw the FijiFirst party win with 59.2% of the vote, gaining 32 of 50 seats. The Social Democratic Party won 15 seats with 28.2% and the National Federation Party three with 5.5%. Turnout was 83.3%. Incumbent prime minister Frank Bainimarama of the FijiFirst party remained in office, and new cabinet members including Timoci Lesi Natuva as defence minister were sworn in later in the month.

Carlos Raúl Morales was sworn in as foreign minister of Guatemala following the resignation of Fernando Carrera, who became the country's permanent UN representative.

Miro Cerar, whose party had won the parliamentary election held in July, took office as prime minister of Slovenia after the National Assembly voted in favour of his appointment by 57 votes to 11.

A cabinet reshuffle took place in Cabo Verde. Jorge Tolentino became foreign minister and Rui Semedo defence minister. Other key portfolios remained unchanged.

Incumbent health minister Ruhakana Rugunda was appointed prime minister of Uganda. He replaced Amama Mbabazi, who had been dismissed by president Yoweri Museveni.

In Scotland, over 3.6 m. people took part in a referendum on whether the country should become independent of the United Kingdom. Voters against independence won with 55.3% of the vote in a turnout of 84.6%. Alex Salmond, who had spearheaded calls for secession from the United Kingdom, subsequently announced his resignation as first minister and leader of the Scottish National Party.

In parliamentary elections in New Zealand, the ruling National Party—led by prime minister John Key—won 60 of the 121 seats with 47.0% of votes cast; the Labour Party took 32 with 25.1%; the Green Party 14 with 10.0%; New Zealand First 11 with 8.7%; the Maori Party 2 with 1.3%; ACT New Zealand 1 with 0.7%; and UnitedFuture 1 with 0.2%. Turnout was 77.0%. The National Party subsequently formed a minority government with the support of the Maori Party, ACT New Zealand and UnitedFuture.

Week Beginning 7 September 2014

Haider al-Abadi was sworn in as Iraq's new prime minister alongside his cabinet, which included Shia, Sunni, Kurdish and Christian ministers. Al-Abadi's nominations for the defence and interior portfolios were, however, rejected by parliament. Both positions remained vacant for over a month amid the escalating conflict with the Sunni extremist group Islamic State.

Former first minister of Northern Ireland Ian Paisley died at the age of 88.

Chronology of Events for August 2014

Week Beginning 31 August 2014

The first cabinet reshuffle of Japanese prime minister Shinzo Abe's second term in office took place. Sanae Takaichi was sworn in as minister of internal affairs and communications, Midori Matsushima as justice minister and Akinori Eto as defence minister. Taro Aso remained deputy prime minister and minister of finance alongside Fumio Kishida at the ministry of foreign affairs.

The cabinet of Yemen, led by prime minister Mohammed Basindawa, was dismissed by president Abdo Rabu Mansour al-Hadi in response to widespread social unrest directed at the government.

A cabinet reshuffle in Venezuela included Rafael Ramírez being appointed foreign minister. Other key positions remained unchanged.

Margrethe Vestager resigned as economy and interior minister of Denmark in order to take up a senior position at the European Commission. In a mini-cabinet reshuffle, taxation minister Morten Østergaard took on the departing minister's portfolios, with Benny Engelbrecht succeeding him.

Thailand's new government headed by Gen. Prayuth Chan-ocha was endorsed and sworn in by king Bhumibol Adulyadej. Chan-ocha had previously led an interim government comprised of senior military officials that had seized power from the caretaker cabinet of Yingluck Shinawatra. Members of the new government included Prawit Wongsuwan as deputy prime minister and minister of defence and Anupong Paochinda as interior minister. Active and retired military officers made up over a third of the new government.

Week Beginning 24 August 2014

Ahmet Davutoğlu became prime minister of Turkey, replacing Recep Tayyip Erdoğan who had been sworn in as president a day earlier. Davutoğlu's government subsequently won a vote of confidence by 306 parliamentary votes to 133.

In Peru, prime minister Ana Jara and her government won a congressional vote of confidence by 55 votes to 54.

A ceasefire was declared between the Israeli government and Palestinian militants ending a 7-week conflict in Gaza. Violence between the two sides had gradually escalated since the swearing in of a Hamas–Fatah unity government on 2 June. Israel, which designates Hamas as a terrorist organization, refused to acknowledge the new administration or proceed with peace talks that had been restarted by US Secretary of State John Kerry a year earlier. According to the United Nations, over 2,200 Palestinians (nearly two-thirds of whom were civilians) were killed during the Israeli ground and air campaign while 67 Israeli soldiers and six civilians died as the result of Palestinian gunfire and rocket attacks. The Israelis maintained that only around a third of Palestinian deaths were civilians and gave the total figure as nearer 2,100.

Michael Spindelegger resigned as vice chancellor and finance minister of Austria. Reinhold Mitterlehner was sworn in as vice chancellor and Hans Jörg Schelling as finance minister.

In a cabinet reshuffle in the Gambia, Bala Garba Jahumpa was appointed minister of foreign affairs and Basirou Mahoney justice minister with other significant positions staying the same.

In Libya, the General National Congress (which had acted as the country's legislative authority from July 2012, but was dissolved in June 2014 following elections) reconvened to elect Omar al-Hasi as its new leader. Its successor assembly, in place since the June elections and led by Abdullah al-Thanay, had previously relocated from the capital to Tobruk amid escalating violence between rival militias—armed groups with which both governments were loosely affiliated.

Manual Valls resigned as prime minister of France following a conflict with economy minister Arnaud Montebourg, who had criticized the government's austerity measures and financial policy. President François Hollande immediately asked Valls to form a new government, which included Emmanuel Macron as Montebourg's replacement. Other key portfolios remained unchanged.

Week Beginning 17 August 2014

Albert Reynolds, former prime minister of Ireland from 1992–94, died.

In Mauritania, Yahya Ould Hademine was sworn in as prime minister. Diallo Mamadou Bathia joined the new government as defence minister, with other key portfolios remaining unchanged.

A cabinet reshuffle took place in Benin. Théophile Yarou was appointed minister of defence, Komi Koutché finance minister and Simplice Dossou Codjo interior minister.

Week Beginning 10 August 2014

Turkey's first direct presidential elections took place. Legislation passed in 2012 meant that the head of state would be elected by the public, rather than members of parliament. Incumbent prime minister Recep Tayyip Erdoğan won in a single round of voting with 51.8% of votes, against Ekmeleddin Mehmet İhsanoğlu with 38.4% and Selahattin Demirtaş with 9.8%. Over 41 m. people voted and turnout was 74.1%.

Week Beginning 3 August 2014

United States president Barack Obama authorized airstrikes against the Sunni Islamist group known as the 'Islamic State in Iraq and the Levant' (also referred to as Islamic State, ISIL, ISIS or IS), which has gradually occupied large areas of territory in Iraq and Syria since April 2013. The self-proclaimed caliphate led by Ibrahim Awwad Ibrahim Ali al-Badri al-Samarrai—commonly known by his *nom de guerre* Abu Bakr al-Baghdadi—responded to the strikes by publishing videos depicting the beheading of a number of western journalists, starting with US reporter James Foley. Military aid was subsequently provided to the Iraqi government and Kurdish resistance forces by other countries including the United Kingdom, Germany, France, Canada and Australia.

André Nzapayéké announced his resignation as prime minister of the Central African Republic along with his cabinet. His resignation came as part of a peace treaty between the government and the Séléka rebel alliance, who had demanded the appointment of a Muslim prime minister chosen from among its membership. Mahamat Kamoun was subsequently sworn in as the country's first Muslim premier, but Séléka boycotted the government and threatened to withdraw from peace talks as Kamoun does not have any political affiliation.

In a cabinet reshuffle in Serbia, minister of economy Dušan Vujović additionally took on the finance portfolio. Željko Sertić was appointed economy minister later that month.

In Libya, Aguila Salah Issa was sworn in as president of the House of Representatives, which had convened in Tobruk rather than Tripoli, the capital, owing to rival militia violence. He became the country's new *de facto* head of state, taking over from Abu Bakr Baira who had served on a temporary basis for a single day following the establishment of a new parliament. Issa was elected indirectly to the position, defeating Baira in two rounds of parliamentary voting.

Chronology of Events for July 2014

Week Beginning 27 July 2014

Julián Castro was sworn in as secretary of housing and urban development in the USA. He replaced Shaun Donovan, who became director of the office of management and budget. Two days later Robert McDonald was sworn in as secretary of veterans' affairs.

Week Beginning 20 July 2014

In Peru, prime minister René Cornejo resigned after one of his advisers was implicated in a defamation scandal. Ana Jara was subsequently sworn in as premier.

The Bulgarian coalition government led by Plamen Oresharski resigned following widespread national opposition to its economic reforms and its failure in dealing with deadly floods that hit the country in June. An interim cabinet took office 2 weeks later, with Georgi Bliznashki taking over from Oresharski as premier.

Anastase Murekezi was sworn in as prime minister of Rwanda, replacing Pierre Habumuremyi.

In Iraq, Fuad Masum of the Patriotic Union of Kurdistan was elected president through indirect voting, becoming only the second ethnic Kurd to hold the post.

Reuven Rivlin was sworn in as president of Israel taking over from 91-year-old Shimon Peres, who at the conclusion of his term was the oldest head of state in the world.

In Ukraine, Arseniy Yatsenyuk submitted his resignation as prime minister, citing the dissolution of the parliamentary coalition and its failure to adopt important legislation amidst the ongoing conflict with pro-Russian rebels. Deputy prime minister Volodymyr Groisman was subsequently selected by the government as his replacement. However, Yatsenyuk's resignation was rejected by parliament a week later.

Week Beginning 13 July 2014

Parliamentary elections took place in Slovenia. The Party of Miro Cerar won 36 seats, the Slovenian Democratic Party 21, the Democratic Party of Pensioners of Slovenia 10 and the United Left and Social Democrats 6 each. Two other parties took the remaining nine seats. Turnout was 51.7%.

In the United Kingdom, the biggest cabinet reshuffle of prime minister David Cameron's term took place. Secretary of state for defence Phillip Hammond moved to foreign and commonwealth affairs replacing William Hague, whilst Michael Fallon took over defence. Nicky Morgan was sworn in as secretary of state for education, replacing Michael Gove who became parliamentary secretary to the treasury and government chief whip. Other key portfolios remained unchanged.

A cabinet reshuffle took place in Ghana. Defence minister Mark Woyongo was reassigned to the interior ministry, with ex-minister of the interior Benjamin Bewa-Nyog Kunbuor replacing him. Other key positions were unaffected.

Week Beginning 6 July 2014

Eduard Shevardnadze, president of the former Soviet Republic of Georgia from 1995–2003, died aged 86.

In Indonesia, Joko Widodo of the Indonesian Democratic Party–Struggle won presidential elections with 53.2% of the vote against Great Indonesia Movement Party candidate Prabowo Subianto with 46.8%.

Hussein al-Sharhristani was sworn in as acting foreign minister of Iraq following the resignation of Hoshyar Zebari. Zebari, an ethnic Kurd, was one of a number of Kurdish members of the government who disassociated themselves from the Nouri al-Maliki-led administration subsequent to disagreements on dealing with the ongoing sectarian crisis.

In a cabinet reshuffle in Ireland, Charlie Flanagan replaced Eamon Gilmore as minister of foreign affairs. Minister for agriculture, food and the marine Simon Coveney also took over the defence portfolio from prime minister Enda Kenny, who had led the ministry on a temporary basis following the resignation of Alan Shatter in March. Other key portfolios remained unchanged.

Dušan Vujović was appointed the acting finance minister of Serbia, replacing Lazar Krstić. Vujović subsequently took on the role on a permanent basis, with parliament confirming his appointment 3 weeks later.

Chronology of Events for June 2014

Week Beginning 29 June 2014

Juan Carlos Varela was sworn in as president of Panama alongside his new cabinet. Appointments included Isabel Saint Malo de Alvarado as vice-president and minister of foreign affairs, Dulcidio de la Guardia as minister of economy and finance, and Milton Henríquez as minister of the interior.

In Ukraine, Col.-Gen. Valeriy Heletey was sworn in as defence minister, replacing Michail Koval who had led the ministry on an interim basis.

In Senegal, Aminata Touré was dismissed as prime minister by president Macky Sall and replaced 2 days later by Mohamed Dionne.

Week Beginning 22 June 2014

In Malaŵi, the composition of recently installed president Peter Mutharika's government was finalized. Mutharika took on the defence portfolio, whilst new additions to the cabinet included George Chaponda as minister of foreign affairs for a second time, Goodall Gondwe as minister of finance, economic planning and development, and Paul Chibingu as minister of home affairs and internal security.

José Mário Vaz of the African Party for the Independence of Guinea and Cabo Verde (PAIGC) was sworn in as president of Guinea-Bissau. He subsequently appointed Domingos Simões Pereira, also of the PAIGC, as prime minister. Geraldo Martins was sworn in as economy and finance minister, Mário Lopes da Rosa as foreign, international co-operation and communities minister and Cadi Mané as defence minister.

A cabinet reshuffle took place in Peru. Gonzalo Gutiérrez, who had been serving as Peru's ambassador to China, was appointed foreign minister, whilst Daniel Urresti took over the interior portfolio.

Alexander Stubb of the National Coalition Party was appointed prime minister of Finland following the resignation of Jyrki Katainen, gaining 96 parliamentary votes with 76 against.

The government of Poland's prime minister Donald Tusk cabinet won a parliamentary vote of confidence by 237 votes to 203. The vote was called by opposition parties in light of a series of leaked tapes of senior government officials.

Col.-Gen. Esmat Abdel Rahman was appointed minister of the interior in a mini cabinet reshuffle in Sudan.

Jean-Claude Juncker, former prime minister of Luxembourg and candidate of the European People's Party grouping in the European Parliament, was nominated as president of the European Commission. For the first time in the Commission's history, European political parties were able to submit candidates for the position, with MEPs subsequently electing Juncker to the presidency in mid-July with 422 votes in favour and 250 against.

Week Beginning 15 June 2014

A presidential run-off election between incumbent Juan Manuel Santos of the Social Unity Party and Óscar Iván Zuluaga of the Democratic Center took place in Colombia. Santos was returned for a second term with 51.0% against Zuluaga with 45.0%. Three other candidates participated in the first round of voting in May.

Andrej Kiska was sworn in as president of Slovakia following his victory in elections held in March. Kiska replaced Ivan Gašparovič, who had held office for 10 years—the longest presidential term in Slovakia's history.

In Spain, Felipe VI ascended to the throne following the abdication of his father, Juan Carlos.

Macedonian prime minister Nikola Gruevski's new cabinet was approved by parliament following his re-election to a third term as premier in April.

Zoran Jolevski's appointment as defence minister was the only key change to the government.

In presidential elections held in Mauritania, incumbent Mohamed Ould Abdel Aziz was returned for a second term with 81.9% of the vote. Three other candidates took the remaining 18.1% of votes. Turnout was 56.5%. The National Forum for Democracy and Unity (a coalition of opposition parties) boycotted the elections citing biased and unfair electoral conditions.

Week Beginning 8 June 2014

Independent candidate Abdel Fattah al-Sisi was sworn in as president of Egypt. Al-Sisi, who had previously served as deputy prime minister and minister of defence, retained acting prime minister Ibrahim Mahlab, confirming him in the post. The new cabinet, which included Mahfouz Saber as minister of justice and Sameh Shoukry as foreign affairs minister, was sworn in later in the month.

In the USA, Sylvia Mathews Burwell was sworn in as secretary of health and human services following her confirmation by the senate. She replaced Kathleen Sebelius, who had held the post since 2009.

A cabinet reshuffle in Greece included Gikas Hardouvelis becoming finance minister and Argyris Ntinopoulos interior minister.

In Libya, the Supreme Court declared the earlier election of Ahmed Maiteeq as prime minister as unconstitutional. It ruled that Abdullah al-Thanay therefore remained prime minister.

Indirect presidential elections took place in Israel. Likud candidate Reuven Rivlin won 63 parliamentary nominations in a run-off against Meir Sheetrit of Hatnuah with 53.

A cabinet reshuffle took place in Yemen. Jamal Abdullah al-Salal was sworn in as minister of foreign affairs and Mohammad Mansour Zemam as minister of finance, while Ahmed Obaid Bin Daghr and Abdullah Mohsen al-Akwa'a both became deputy prime minister.

The Antigua and Barbuda Labour Party won the country's parliamentary elections with 56.4% of the vote, gaining 14 of 17 seats. The United Progressive Party took the remaining 3 seats with 41.6%. Turnout was 90.3%. Gaston Browne was sworn in as prime minister a day later.

The second round of presidential elections, intended to represent the first democratic transfer of power in the country's history, were held in Afghanistan. Mohammad Ashraf Ghani Ahmadzai (ind.) initially claimed victory with 56.4% of the vote ahead of Abdullah Abdullah (National Coalition) with 43.6%. However, there were widespread allegations of fraud and Abdullah refused to concede defeat. Six other candidates participated in the first round of voting, which took place in April. A massive security operation was launched by the government after the Taliban had pledged to disrupt the elections. Sporadic violence and a shortage of ballot papers were reported across the country after over 8.1 m. people turned out to vote.

Week Beginning 1 June 2014

Salvador Sánchez Cerén took office as president of El Salvador alongside new cabinet appointments that included Ramón Aristides Valencia as minister of the interior and Hugo Martínez as foreign affairs minister. Other key portfolios remained unchanged.

Telangana became the 29th state of India after the Andhra Pradesh Reorganisation Act was passed by parliament earlier in the year. Hyderabad was designated as the joint capital for Telangana and Andhra Pradesh for a period of 10 years, with Andhra Pradesh governor E. S. L. Narasimhan additionally assuming the governorship of Telangana.

A Palestinian unity government, containing both the West Bank-based Fatah and the Gaza-based Hamas, was sworn in. Fatah's Rami Hamdallah became prime minister.

In Laos, Maj.-Gen. Sengnouane Xayalath was sworn in as acting defence minister.

The first multi-candidate presidential elections to be held for over 40 years took place in Syria. Incumbent president Bashar al-Assad of the Ba'ath Party won 88.7% of the vote against Hassan al-Nouri (National Initiative for Administration and Change in Syria) with 4.3% and Maher Hajjar (ind.) with 3.2%. Turnout was 73.4%. The elections were condemned as a 'disgrace' and 'illegitimate' by the United States, United Kingdom and the Syrian rebel opposition engaged in armed struggle against the Ba'athist government.

In Finland, Antti Rinne became deputy prime minister and minister of finance, taking over both portfolios from Jutta Urpilainen.

A new cabinet was appointed in Hungary, following the victory of the alliance of Fidesz-Hungarian Civic Alliance and the Christian Democratic People's Party at the parliamentary elections 2 months earlier. Tibor Navracsics moved from the ministry of justice to the ministry of foreign affairs and trade, with László Trócsányi replacing him. New appointments included Miklós Seszták as minister of national development.

In Mauritius, Prime Minister Navin Ramgoolam took over the finance portfolio following the resignation of Xavier-Luc Duval.

Petro Poroshenko was sworn in as president of Ukraine, taking over from Oleksandr Turchynov who had been acting head of state since the ousting of Viktor Yanukovych earlier in the year. He subsequently nominated Pavlo Klimkin, who had previously served as the Ukrainian ambassador to Germany, as foreign minister. Klimkin was sworn in a day later.

Chronology of Events for May 2014

Week Beginning 25 May 2014

In Belgium's parliamentary elections, the New Flemish Alliance won 33 seats; the Socialist Party, 23; the Reformist Movement, 20; Christian Democratic and Flemish, 18; Open Flemish Liberals and Democrats, 14; Socialist Party Alternative, 13; the Humanist Democratic Centre, 9; Green, 6; Ecolo, 6; Flemish Interest, 3; the Workers' Party Coalition, 2; Francophone Democratic Federalists, 2; and the People's Party, 1. Turnout was 89.4%. For the first time, the Senate was not directly elected following reforms that came into force from 2014.

Elections to the European Parliament took place across EU member states. They were the eighth parliamentary elections since 1979, when candidates were first directly returned by universal suffrage. Eurosceptic parties made considerable gains throughout Europe, with the United Kingdom Independence Party, France's Front National and the Danish People's Party in Denmark all topping their respective country's polls. Parties that are members of the European People's Party parliamentary group won 221 of the 751 seats and of the Alliance of Socialists and Democrats 191. Turnout across the continent was an estimated 43.1%.

Presidential elections that were originally scheduled to take place in March 2015 were held in Ukraine. Moved forward following the Ukrainian revolution and subsequent ousting of Viktor Yanukovych from the presidency 3 months earlier, voting in a number of constituencies in the east of the country could not take place owing to pro-Russian civil unrest. Independent candidate Petro Poroshenko won 54.7% of the vote against 12.8% for former prime minister Yuliya Tymoshenko, 8.3% for Oleh Lyashko, 5.5% for Anatoliy Hrytsenko and 5.2% for Serhiy Tihipko. There were 16 other candidates. Turnout was 60.2%.

Incumbent president Dalia Grybauskaitė won the Lithuanian presidential run-off election with 57.9% of the vote against Zigmantas Balčytis with 40.1%. Turnout was 47.3%. Five other candidates participated in the first round of voting.

In Lebanon, parliament failed to elect a new president after outgoing incumbent Michel Suleiman's 6-year term came to an end. Since the Lebanese constitution prohibits successive presidential terms, prime minister Tammam Salam and his cabinet assumed the powers of the presidency on an interim basis.

In Mali, defence and veterans Affairs Minister Soumeylou Boubèye Maïga resigned following the defeat of the army by rebel groups in the northeastern region of the country. He was subsequently replaced by Ba N'daou.

In Egypt, former defence minister Abdel Fattah al-Sisi, who prompted the military overthrow of Mohamed Morsi in July 2013, won presidential elections with 96.9% of the vote, although the turnout was low at only 47.5%.

Palestinian president Mahmoud Abbas asked prime minister Rami Hamdallah to form a unity government composed of both Hamas and Fatah. It was the first unified government in Palestine since the territories became a UN non-member observer state in 2012, and was the result of a reconciliation deal signed by both Hamas and Fatah the previous month. Hamdallah's cabinet included Riyad al-Maliki as foreign affairs minister and Mamoun Abu Shahla as minister of labour. Israel refused to recognize the newly sworn-in government since it categorizes Hamas as a terrorist organization.

Sloan D. Gibson was sworn in as acting United States secretary of veterans affairs following the resignation of Eric Shinseki.

Week Beginning 18 May 2014

José Mário Vaz won 61.9% of the vote in the presidential run-off in Guinea-Bissau against Nuno Gomes Nabiam with 38.1%. Turnout for the first elections since the military coup of April 2012 was 78.2%.

Presidential elections took place in Malawi. Democratic Progressive Party candidate Peter Mutharika won with 36.4% of the vote, ahead of Lazarus Chakwera of the Malawi Congress Party with 27.8%, incumbent president Joyce Banda of the People's Party with 20.2% and Atupele Muluzi of the United Democratic Front with 13.7%. There were eight other candidates. Mutharika was sworn in later in the month.

Week Beginning 11 May 2014

Parliamentary elections ended in India. Held in nine phases over 5 weeks since early April, the elections were described as the biggest-ever exercise in democracy with over 550 m. valid votes counted. The Bharatiya Janata Party (BJP) led the National Democratic Alliance (NDA) to the largest parliamentary majority gained since the elections of 1984, winning 336 of 543 seats (of which the BJP took 282). The ruling United Progressive Alliance (UPA) won only 58 seats, with the Indian National Congress—the main party in the UPA—taking 44. The remaining seats went to smaller parties and independents. Later in the month BJP leader Narendra Modi was sworn in as prime minister alongside his cabinet, which included Rajnath Singh as minister of home affairs and Arun Jaitley as minister of finance, of corporate affairs and also defence.

In Vanuatu, the government of prime minister Moana Carcasses Kalosil lost a confidence vote in parliament by 35 votes to 11. Joe Natuman replaced Carcasses as premier, while Charlot Salwai became minister of internal affairs and Sato Kilman minister of foreign affairs.

The government of Finland survived a vote of no confidence that was rejected by parliament by 98 votes to 68.

In Laos, deputy prime minister and minister of defence Douangchai Phichit was killed in a plane crash.

Week Beginning 4 May 2014

Ahmed Maiteeq was sworn in as prime minister of Libya and asked by parliament to form a government. His cabinet, which included Milud Ahmed Khalifa Hamid as finance minister and al-Arif Saleh al-Khoja as interior minister, was appointed 3 weeks later. However, outgoing interim premier Abdullah al-Thanay refused to hand over power, questioning the legitimacy of Maiteeq's election.

Elections took place in Panama. Juan Carlos Varela of the Panameñista Party was elected president with 39.1% of the vote against José Domingo Arias (Democratic Change) with 31.4% and Juan Carlos Navarro (Revolutionary Democratic Party) with 28.1%. Four other candidates each took less than 1% of the vote. Turnout was 76.8%.

A new government was appointed in Algeria, with Abdelmalek Sellal returning as prime minister after standing down in March to run president Ahmed Bouteflika's successful campaign to win re-election. Key portfolios at the foreign affairs and interior ministries remained unchanged. However, new additions to the cabinet included Mohamed Djellab as minister of finance.

In Slovenia, prime minister Alenka Bratušek announced her resignation after losing the leadership of her Positive Slovenia party. She was expected to continue as premier until the appointment of a replacement.

A cabinet reshuffle took place in Croatia following the dismissal of the finance minister, Slavko Linić, by prime minister Zoran Milanović. It was alleged that Linić had illegally written off tax debts from a firm facing bankruptcy. Boris Lalovac took over as finance minister, while other key portfolios remained unchanged.

Sir Frank Kabui was re-elected to a second term as governor-general of the Solomon Islands. He defeated two other candidates in the fourth round of voting in which he achieved the required majority of 23 parliamentary votes.

Parliamentary elections took place in South Africa. The African National Congress won 249 of 400 seats and retained their majority in parliament (despite losing 16 seats). The Democratic Alliance gained 89 seats; Economic Freedom Fighters, 25; Inkatha Freedom Party, 10; National Freedom Party, 6; United Democratic Movement, 4; and Freedom Front Plus, 4. Six Smaller parties took the remaining 13 seats. South Africans living abroad were able to vote for the first time in the nation's history, following the electoral amendment act of Nov. 2013.

Yingluck Shinawatra was dismissed as prime minister of Thailand after the country's constitutional court convicted her of abuse of power and was replaced as premier by Niwattumrong Boonsongpaisan in a caretaker capacity. The charge related to the illegal transfer of the chief of national security to another post in 2011. Nine other ministers, including finance minister Kittirat Na-Ranong and foreign minister Surapong Towijakchaikul, were also removed from office following the investigation. Gen. Prayuth Chan-ocha was subsequently endorsed by King Bhumibol Adulyadej as acting prime minister, after the army chief led a military coup d'état against the caretaker government.

In Ireland, prime minister Enda Kenny took over the defence portfolio from Alan Shatter, who had also been in charge of the justice ministry. In a mini cabinet reshuffle, Frances Fitzgerald was sworn in as minister of justice and equality, with Charles Flanagan replacing her as the minister of children and youth affairs. Other key portfolios remained unchanged.

Luis Guillermo Solís was sworn in as president of Costa Rica after winning elections held the previous month. Helio Fallas became vice president and minister of finance, alongside new foreign affairs minister Manuel González Sanz and justice minister Cristina Ramírez Chavarría.

Chronology of Events for April 2014

Week Beginning 27 April 2014
In Macedonia, incumbent president Gjorgje Ivanov of the Internal Macedonian Revolutionary Organization-Democratic Party for Macedonian National Unity (VMRO-DPMNE) was re-elected to a second term after winning elections against Stevo Pendarovski of the Social Democratic Union of Macedonia (SDSM). In the run-off held on 27 April, Ivanov won with 55.3% against Pendarovski with 41.1%. Turnout was 54.4%. In May, the SDSM announced that it would boycott parliament after accusing Ivanov of electoral fraud.

A new government led by Aleksandar Vučić was appointed in Serbia following parliamentary elections in March. It included former prime minister Ivica Dačić as foreign minister, Nebojša Stefanović as interior minister and Bratislav Gašić as defence minister, whilst Lazar Krstić remained at the ministry of finance.

In South Korea, prime minister Chung Hong-won offered his resignation, taking responsibility for a ferry disaster that left over 300 people dead or missing. It was accepted in principle by president Park Geun-hye. However, he was expected to continue as premier until local elections scheduled to take place in June.

Week Beginning 20 April 2014
In Chad, Abderahim Bireme Hamid became minister of the interior and public security, taking over from Mahamat Yaya Oki Dagache.

A cabinet reshuffle in Angola saw João Manuel Gonçalves Lourenço appointed minister of defence. Other key portfolios remained unchanged.

An indirect presidential election was held in Lebanon, but no candidate reached the required two-thirds majority vote. A second round the following week and three further attempts in May all failed to produce a winner.

Week Beginning 13 April 2014
General elections took place in Guinea-Bissau. In the presidential elections, José Mário Vaz of the African Party for the Independence of Guinea and Cape Verde (PAIGC) took 40.9% of the vote ahead of Nuno Gomes Nabiam (ind.) with 24.8%, Paulo Gomes (ind.) 10.4% and Abel Incanda of the Party for Social Renewal (PRS) 7.0%. Nine other candidates also took part. A run-off between Vaz and Nabiam was scheduled to take place on 18 May. In parliamentary elections held on the same day, the PAIGC won 57 of 100 National Assembly seats and the PRS 41. Four seats went to smaller parties.

In Madagascar, Roger Kolo was sworn in as prime minister by President Hery Rajaonarimampianina. Kolo's government was confirmed 2 days later, and included Gen. Jean Olivier Dominique Rakotozafy as minister of defence, Arisoa Lala Razafitrimo as minister of foreign affairs and Olivier Mahafaly Solonanrasana as minister of the interior.

Samoan finance minister Faumuina Tiatia Liuga resigned amidst an investigation by the auditor general and a parliamentary select committee into alleged corruption at the Samoa Land Corporation. The finance portfolio was subsequently taken on by prime minister Tuila'epa Sailele Malielegaoi.

Abdelaziz Bouteflika was re-elected to a fourth term as president of Algeria in elections held on 18 April. He won 81.5% of votes cast, beating former prime minister Ali Benflis with 12.2%, Abdelaziz Belaid with 3.4% and three other candidates. Turnout was 51.7%. Abdelmalek Sellal, who had stepped down as prime minister to run Bouteflika's campaign, was subsequently reinstated as premier following the elections.

Week Beginning 6 April 2014
In Costa Rica, Luis Guillermo Solís of the Citizens' Action Party won the presidential election against National Liberation Party candidate Johnny Araya. Since neither Solís nor Araya achieved the 40% vote share required

for an outright victory in the first round, a run-off between the two candidates was scheduled to take place. However, Araya announced on 5 March 2014 that he would not contest the presidency after opinion polls suggested that Solís would win by a huge margin. Nonetheless, as Costa Rican law prohibits candidates from withdrawing their name from the ballot, a run-off was held on 6 April, with Luis Guillermo Solís winning 77.8% of the vote and Johnny Araya 22.2%.

Viktor Orbán was re-elected to a third term as prime minister of Hungary, after parliamentary elections saw the alliance of the Fidesz-Hungarian Civic Alliance and the Christian Democratic People's Party win 133 of 199 National Assembly seats.

The Libyan parliament confirmed Abdullah al-Thanay as prime minister. However, he resigned less than a week later after he and his family were attacked by gunmen. Ahmed Maiteeq was sworn in as his replacement in May.

Mamour Alieu Jagne was sworn in as foreign minister of the Gambia following a cabinet reshuffle. Other key portfolios remained unchanged.

Elections to the House of People's Representatives were held in Indonesia. The Indonesian Democratic Party-Struggle won 109 of 560 seats, the Party of Functional Groups (Golkar) 91, the Great Indonesia Movement Party (Gerindra) 73, the Democratic Party 61, the National Mandate Party 49, the National Awakening Party 47, the Prosperous Justice Party 40, the United Development Party 39, the Nasdem Party 35 and the People's Conscience Party 16.

Chronology of Events for March 2014

Week Beginning 30 March 2014
Jean-Marc Ayrault resigned as prime minister of France after the ruling Socialist Party suffered a major defeat in local elections. President François Hollande swore in Manuel Valls as his replacement the same day. A cabinet reshuffle also took place, with Michel Sapin replacing Pierre Moscovici at the ministry of finance and Bernard Cazeneuve taking on the interior portfolio that had been vacated by new prime minister Valls.

In San Marino, Luca Beccari of the Christian Democratic Party and Valeria Ciavatta of the Popular Alliance of Democrats were sworn in as Captains Regent.

A cabinet reshuffle took place in Haiti. Duly Brutus replaced Pierre-Richard Casimir as foreign affairs minister whilst Lener Renaud took over from Jean Rodolphe Joazile as minister of defence. Marie-Carmelle Jean-Marie returned to her post as the head of the ministry of finance, one year after resigning from the position.

Serik Akhmetov resigned as prime minister of Kazakhstan along with his government. The same day, former prime minister Karim Massimov returned to the post after being unanimously approved by parliament. He was joined in the new government by outgoing premier Akhmetov, who took over at the ministry of defence.

Tigran Sargsyan resigned as prime minister of Armenia. Parliament speaker Hovik Abrahamyan subsequently assumed the premiership.

In Malta, Marie-Louise Coleiro Preca was sworn in as president, having been nominated by parliament 3 days earlier.

Moussa Mara became prime minister of Mali following Oumar Tatam Ly's resignation.

Week Beginning 23 March 2014
Adolfo Suárez González, Spain's first democratically-elected prime minister following the dictatorship of Francisco Franco, died at the age of 81.

In Ukraine, Mikhail Koval was appointed acting defence minister after Ihor Tenyukh resigned from the post. Tenyukh had faced criticism over his failure to withdraw Ukrainian troops from Crimea after strategic points were overwhelmed by Russian forces.

Taavi Rõivas became the youngest premier in the European Union at the age of 34 after he was sworn in as the new prime minister of Estonia, replacing Andrus Ansip who had resigned earlier in the month. A new cabinet that included Hanno Pevkur as interior minister and Sven Mikser as minister of defence was appointed the same day.

Egyptian defence minister Abdel Fattah al-Sisi resigned from his post and announced his intention to run for president in elections that were scheduled to be held in May. Sedki Sobhi was sworn in as his replacement a day later.

Former Norwegian prime minister Jens Stoltenberg was designated as the next NATO Secretary General, replacing Anders Fogh Rasmussen whose term was set to expire in Sept. 2014.

In Slovakia, independent candidate Andrej Kiska won the presidential election run-off against incumbent prime minister Robert Fico of the Direction-Social Democracy party. Fico had won the first round of polling, gaining 28.0% of the vote against Kiska with 24.0% and 12 other candidates. However, Kiska reversed these results in the second round held 2 weeks later, winning 59.4% against 40.6% for Fico.

Week Beginning 16 March 2014

A Serbian Progressive Party-led coalition won parliamentary elections held in Serbia, gaining 158 of 250 seats and 48.4% of the vote. A coalition of the Socialist Party of Serbia, the Party of United Pensioners of Serbia and United Serbia won 44 seats with 13.5% of votes, the Democratic Party 19 with 6.0% and the New Democratic Party–Greens-led coalition 18 with 5.7%. The remaining 11 seats went to smaller parties and independent candidates.

A cabinet reshuffle took place in the Marshall Islands. Tony deBrum took over the foreign affairs portfolio and David Kabua the ministry of internal affairs. Other key positions remained unchanged. The following day the government survived a parliamentary vote of no-confidence by 17 votes to 13. Joe Oliver took over as Canada's finance minister from Jim Flaherty. Flaherty died less than a month later from natural causes.

In Kyrgyzstan, prime minister Zhantoro Satybaldiyev and his coalition government resigned. A day earlier the Ata-Meken party had withdrawn from the coalition, accusing Satybaldiyev of corruption. President Almazbek Atambayev subsequently swore in Dzhoomart Otorbayev as prime minister. He formed a new coalition government that included members from the Social Democratic Party of Kyrgyzstan, Ata-Meken and the Ar-Namys party.

The newly appointed Lebanese government won a parliamentary confidence vote by 96 votes to 5.

The accession of Crimea to the Russian Federation was ratified by both the lower and upper houses of parliament in Russia, creating the Republic of Crimea and the Federal City of Sevastopol. Russian president Vladimir Putin appointed Oleg Belaventsev as plenipotentiary representative to the newly-formed federal subjects of Russia.

In Thailand, parliamentary elections held the previous month were ruled invalid by the Constitutional Court after it emerged that voting did not take place on the same day across the country.

Parliamentary elections took place in the Maldives. The Progressive Coalition headed by the Progressive Party of Maldives won 33 of 85 seats, the Maldivian Democratic Party 26, Jumhooree Party 15, Maldives Development Alliance 5 and Adhaalath Party 1. Five seats went to independent candidates.

Week Beginning 9 March 2014

The Democratic Front for the Reunification of the Fatherland, headed by the Korean Workers' Party, won all 687 seats in North Korea's parliamentary elections.

In Bosnia and Herzegovina, Bakir Izetbegović took over the 8-month rotating presidency chairmanship.

In a cabinet reshuffle in Papua New Guinea, Don Polye was dismissed as treasury minister and replaced later in the month by Patrick Pruaitch. Pruaitch's portfolio at the ministry of forestry and climate change was taken over by Douglas Tomuriesa.

Michelle Bachelet was sworn in for her second term as president of Chile, followed by her new cabinet including Heraldo Muñoz as foreign minister and Alberto Arenas as minister of finance. Claudia Pascual, as minister of the national women's service, became the first minister representing the Communist Party of Chile to assume a cabinet position since 1973.

In Libya, prime minister Ali Zeidan was ousted by parliament after losing a vote of no confidence, which was held over the escape of a rogue North Korean oil tanker from a rebel-controlled port. He was subsequently replaced by defence minister Abdullah al-Thanay, who took over the premiership on an interim basis.

Abdelmalek Sellal resigned as prime minister of Algeria in order to run incumbent president Abdelaziz Bouteflika's campaign for re-election. Minister of energy and mines Youcef Yousfi was sworn in as acting prime minister.

Lien Thikeo was appointed finance minister of Laos.

Ahmad Tejan Kabbah, the former president of Sierra Leone who oversaw the end of the civil war that lasted from 1991–2002, died at the age of 82.

In Zambia, Harry Kalaba was appointed foreign minister.

Tasos Mitsopoulos was sworn in as defence minister of Cyprus. However, he died from natural causes 8 days later and Christoforos Fokaides took over the post.

In Mozambique, Agostinho Mondlane replaced Filipe Nyussi as minister of defence. The previous week Nyussi had been named as ruling party FRELIMO's candidate in the presidential elections scheduled to take place later in the year.

Week Beginning 2 March 2014

In Mozambique, Agostinho Mondlane replaced Filipe Nyussi as minister of defence. The previous week Nyussi had been named as ruling party FRELIMO's candidate in the presidential elections scheduled to take place later in the year.

A cabinet reshuffle took place in Yemen. Abdou Hussein al-Tarb took over as interior minister and Khaled Bahah as oil and mineral resources minister.

Chronology of Events for February 2014

Week Beginning 23 February 2014

In Estonia, prime minister Andrus Ansip announced his resignation from the post with effect from the following week in order to enable the appointment of a successor to lead his Reform Party in the 2015 elections. He had been the longest-serving prime minister in the European Union, having taken office in April 2005.

The prime minister of Egypt, Hazem al-Beblawi, resigned. Housing minister Ibrahim Mahlab was named as his successor by president Adly Mansour. He was sworn in a week later alongside a new cabinet including Hani Qadri Demian as finance minister. Other key portfolios remained unchanged.

In Peru, César Villanueva resigned as prime minister less than 4 months after being appointed to the post. René Cornejo—who had previously served as minister of housing, construction and sanitation—was appointed as his replacement.

In Taiwan, Chen Wei-zen replaced Lee Hong-yuan as minister of the interior.

Seven National Liberal Party (PNL) ministers resigned from the Romanian government following disagreements with the Democratic Liberals over the composition of the cabinet. Another PNL member, Daniel Chițoiu, had resigned as deputy prime minister and minister of finance earlier in the month. Subsequent changes to the cabinet included Constantin Nita's appointment as minister of economy and Ioana Petrescu as minister of finance.

In a cabinet reshuffle in Vanuatu, Paul Telukluk took over the internal affairs portfolio whilst Stephen Kalsakau became minister for climate change.

Week Beginning 16 February 2014

Martha Elena Ruiz Sevilla became the new defence minister of Nicaragua, taking over from Ruth Esperanza Tapia Roa.

Ukrainian president Viktor Yanukovych was impeached by parliament, with 328 of 449 MPs voting in favour of his removal from power. He had fled the capital before the vote took place, following escalating violence surrounding the 'Euromaidan' protests against closer trade and diplomatic ties with Russia. Oleksandr Turchynov of the Fatherland party was appointed interim president of Ukraine a day after the impeachment took place, and a new caretaker cabinet was sworn in 4 days later. As an ally of the ousted regime, Russia reacted by placing its armed forces on standby around military bases in Ukraine's autonomous republic of Crimea. It cited its obligation to protect resident Crimean ethnic Russians and its Black Sea naval fleet, which is stationed in the region.

Week Beginning 9 February 2014

Sushil Koirala was elected prime minister of Nepal after his party, the Nepali Congress, won 196 of 575 seats in constituent assembly elections held 3 months earlier. His cabinet was sworn in 2 weeks later.

Italian prime minister Enrico Letta resigned after his party, the Democratic Party (PD), voted in favour of installing a new government. PD secretary Matteo Renzi, who had led party criticism of Letta's performance, was subsequently asked to form a government by president Giorgio Napolitano. He was sworn in as prime minister later in the month, along with a new cabinet that included Roberta Pinotti as defence minister, Federica Mogherini as foreign minister and Pier Carlo Padoan as finance minister.

Tammam Salam became prime minister of Lebanon almost 11 months after Najib Mikati had announced his resignation from the post. He headed a new government that included members from both the Western-backed 14 March Alliance and the pro-Syria 8 March Alliance.

Week Beginning 2 February 2014

In the USA, Janet Yellen took office as chair of the board of governors of the Federal Reserve, becoming the first woman ever to hold the position.

In presidential elections held in Costa Rica, Citizens' Action Party candidate Luis Guillermo Solís won 30.6% of the vote against Johnny Araya of the National Liberation Party with 17.2% and 11 other candidates. Araya subsequently announced that he would not contest the scheduled run-off between the top two candidates after polls suggested that Solís would win by a substantial margin.

In El Salvador, Salvador Sánchez Cerén of the Farabundo Martí National Liberation Front won 48.9% of the vote in the first round of presidential elections against Norman Quijano of the Nationalist Republican Alliance, who took 39.0%, and three other candidates. A run-off between the leading two candidates took place 5 weeks later, with Cerén winning 50.1% of votes cast against 49.9% for Quijano. Although Quijano alleged that the poll was fraudulent and challenged the outcome, El Salvador's electoral court ruled the result as fair and confirmed Cerén as the winner.

In Mauritania, prime minister Moulaye Ould Mohamed Laghdaf and his cabinet resigned following parliamentary elections in late 2013. President Mohamed Ould Abdel Aziz asked him to form a new cabinet a day later.

A cabinet reshuffle took place in Denmark following the resignation of Socialist People's Party ministers over privatization of the state-owned energy company. Martin Lidegaard of the Social Liberal Party took over as foreign affairs minister but other key portfolios remained unchanged.

Chronology of Events for January 2014

Week Beginning 26 January 2014

The Tunisian Constituent Assembly approved a new constitution by 200 of 216 votes cast. A new caretaker government led by Mehdi Jomaa was also sworn in later that week.

Daniel Ona Ondo became prime minister of Gabon. His cabinet included new appointments Guy Bertrand Mapangou as interior minister and Ernest Mpouho as defence minister.

Juan Orlando Hernández was sworn in as president of Honduras.

In Ukraine, Mykola Azarov resigned as prime minister amid widespread protests over the government's pro-Russia stance. He was subsequently replaced by his first deputy, Serhiy Arbuzov, who was appointed to head the government on an interim basis.

A new government was appointed in the Czech Republic. Bohuslav Sobotka of the Czech Social Democratic Party took over the premiership from Jiří Rusnok, who had resigned from office 5 months earlier after losing a parliamentary vote of no confidence. The new cabinet included Lubomír Zaorálek as foreign minister, Martin Stropnický as defence minister and Milan Chovanec as interior minister.

A cabinet reshuffle in New Zealand saw Peter Dunne replacing Chris Tremain as internal affairs minister. Other key portfolios remained unchanged.

The government of Nauru survived a motion of no confidence, which was defeated by 11 votes to 7.

Fernando Núñez Fábrega resigned as foreign minister of Panama, with Francisco Álvarez de Soto subsequently replacing him.

Week Beginning 19 January 2014

Laimdota Straujuma was sworn in as prime minister of Latvia, becoming the first woman to serve as the country's head of government. New cabinet members were simultaneously appointed, including Vjačeslavs Dombrovskis (brother of departing prime minister Valdis Dombrovskis) as minister for economics.

In Romania, interior minister Radu Stroe resigned. He was succeeded by deputy prime minister Gabriel Oprea, who took on his portfolio on an interim basis.

Hery Rajaonarimampianina was sworn in as president of Madagascar, succeeding Andry Rajoelina.

Week Beginning 12 January 2014

In Guinea, prime minister Mohamed Said Fofana resigned along with his government. Three days later he was reinstated to the position by president Alpha Condé and asked to lead a reshuffled cabinet that included Mohamed Diaré as finance minister and Cheick Sako as justice minister.

In Venezuela, Rodolfo Marco Torres took over from Nelson Merentes as finance minister.

In Somalia, a new 25-member cabinet was sworn in. Ridwan Hirsi Mohamed became deputy prime minister and minister for religious affairs with Hussein Abdi Halane taking over the finance portfolio and Abdirahman Duale Beyle foreign affairs.

Week Beginning 5 January 2014

In a cabinet reshuffle in Kuwait, Anas al-Saleh was appointed finance minister, Ali Saleh al-Omair oil minister and minister of state for national assembly affairs, and Nayef Mohammed al-Ajmi minister of justice and Awqaf and Islamic affairs. Other key portfolios remained unchanged.

Lisiate 'Akolo was dismissed as finance minister of Tonga, with 'Aisake Valu Eke subsequently taking over the post.

In the Central African Republic, president Michel Djotodia and prime minister Nicolas Tiangaye resigned amid escalating sectarian violence. Catherine Samba-Panza was elected acting president and head of state by parliament 2 weeks later, becoming the first woman to hold the post in the nation's history.

Former prime minister of Israel Ariel Sharon died.

2013

Chronology of Events for December 2013

Week Beginning 29 December 2013

William Mgimwa, the finance minister of Tanzania, died. Saada Mkuya Salum, who was already serving in an acting capacity, was subsequently confirmed in the post.

Week Beginning 22 December 2013

Geoffrey Mwamba resigned as defence minister of Zambia. Edgar Lungu was named his successor with Ngosa Simbyakula taking over the home affairs portfolio from Lungu.

A cabinet reshuffle took place in Turkey following a corruption scandal. Emrullah İşler became a deputy prime minister replacing Bekir Bozdağ, who was appointed justice minister following Sadullah Ergin's resignation from the post.

In Afghanistan, Din Mohammad Mubarez Rashidi became counter-narcotics minister, Zarar Ahmad Moqbel Usmani foreign affairs minister and Mohammad Akbar Barakzai mines and petroleum minister.

Mario Bergara was sworn in as economy and finance minister of Uruguay following the resignation of Fernando Lorenzo from the post earlier in the month.

The internal affairs minister of Vanuatu, Patrick Crowby, died.

Week Beginning 15 December 2013

In Chile, centre-left former president Michelle Bachelet won a run-off presidential election for a second time with 62.2% of the vote against centre-right candidate Evelyn Matthei with 37.8%. Turnout was 42.0%—the lowest since Chile's return to democracy in 1990.

In Austria, chancellor Werner Faymann's new government was sworn in.

The US Senate confirmed Jeh Johnson as Secretary of Homeland Security by 78 votes to 16. He was sworn in 1 week later.

Angela Merkel was sworn in for a third term as chancellor of Germany, alongside her coalition cabinet.

Hery Rajaonarimampianina won 53.5% of the vote in the presidential run-off in Madagascar against Jean Louis Robinson with 46.5%. Turnout was 50.8%. Rajaonarimampianina was sworn in as president a month later.

In Tanzania, defence minister Shamsi Vuai Nahodha and home affairs minister Emmanuel Nchimbi were dismissed.

Abdiweli Sheikh Ahmed was sworn in as prime minister of Somalia following the resignation of Abdi Farah Shirdon, who had lost a parliamentary vote of no confidence by 184 votes to 65 3 weeks earlier.

Week Beginning 8 December 2013

In Denmark, Villy Søvndal resigned as foreign minister, citing health reasons. Holger K. Nielsen took over his portfolio.

Fernando Delfim da Silva resigned as foreign minister of Guinea-Bissau, followed by interior minister António Suka Ntchama a week later.

Adhamjon Ahmedbayev was appointed interior minister of Uzbekistan.

Week Beginning 1 December

In a major cabinet reshuffle in Sudan, Bakri Hassan Salih took over as first vice president, Hassabo Mohamed Abdul-Rahman as second vice president,

Abdel-Wahid Youssef Ibrahim as interior minister and Badr Al-Deen Mahmoud as finance minister.

Xavier Bettel was sworn in as prime minister of Luxembourg. He was joined by new cabinet appointments Étienne Schneider as deputy prime minister and minister of economy, internal security and defence, Pierre Gramegna as finance minister and Daniel Kersch as interior minister.

In Switzerland, federal council elections saw Didier Burkhalter elected president and Simonetta Sommaruga vice president. They were sworn in a month later.

Former president of South Africa Nelson Mandela died aged 95.

Chronology of Events for November 2013

Week Beginning 24 November 2013

In presidential elections in Honduras, Juan Orlando Hernández was elected president with 36.9% of the vote; Xiomara Castro received 28.8%, Mauricio Villeda 20.3% and Salvador Nasralla 13.4%. There were four other candidates.

An agreement between Iran and the P5+1 countries comprising the USA, Russia, China, UK, France and Germany to temporarily suspend Iran's uranium enrichment in return for the easing of international sanctions was signed in Geneva, Switzerland. Known as the 'Joint Plan of Action', it represented the first official accord between the USA and Iran for 34 years.

In a major cabinet reshuffle in Poland, Elżbieta Bieńkowska became the new deputy prime minister and infrastructure and development minister with Mateusz Szczurek taking over the finance ministry.

The collapse of a supermarket in Latvia that killed 54 people led to the resignation of prime minister Valdis Dombrovskis, who took political responsibility for the disaster.

The prime minister of Thailand, Yingluck Shinawatra, survived a vote of no confidence that was rejected in parliament by 297 votes to 134.

Week Beginning 17 November 2013

In Bangladesh, an interim cabinet was appointed in order to conduct parliamentary polls ahead of the elections in Jan. 2014.

Djimrangar Dadnadji resigned as prime minister of Chad following a proposed parliamentary motion of no confidence over the arbitrary arrest of government officials suspected of complicity with a coup plot. Kalzeubé Pahimi Deubet replaced Dadnadji as prime minister.

Week Beginning 10 November 2013

Greek prime minister Anthonis Samaras' cabinet survived a parliamentary motion of no confidence by 153 votes to 124.

Avigdor Lieberman was sworn in as foreign minister of Israel for the second time in 4 years.

Giorgi Margvelashvili was sworn in as the president of the former Soviet republic of Georgia. Prime minister Irakli Garibashvili and his cabinet took office 3 days later with Alexander Chikhaidze as interior minister. Other key portfolios remained unchanged.

Abdulla Yameen of the Progressive Party was elected president of the Maldives. He defeated incumbent Mohamed Nasheed of the Maldivian Democratic Party in the run-off with 51.4% of the vote against 48.6%. Yameen was sworn in the following day. Mohamed Jameel Ahmed became vice president and Dunya Maumoon foreign minister.

Week Beginning 3 November 2013

In Swaziland, a new cabinet was sworn in with Chief Mgwagwa Gamedze as minister of foreign affairs, Princess Tsandzile as minister of home affairs and Martin Dlamini as minister of finance.

Bakhyt Sultanov was appointed deputy prime minister and finance minister of Kazakhstan.

In Tajikistan, incumbent president Emomalii Rakhmon was re-elected for his fourth term with 83.1% of the vote against 5.0% for Ismail Talbakov. There were four other candidates. Two weeks later Rakhmon appointed Kokhir Rasulzoda prime minister. Sherali Mirzo was subsequently named defence minister and Sirodjiddin Aslov foreign affairs minister.

Typhoon Haiyan struck in Southeast Asia killing over 6,000 people, mostly in the Philippines.

Chronology of Events for October 2013

Week Beginning 27 October 2013

In parliamentary elections in Argentina, 127 of the 257 seats in the Chamber of Deputies were contested. Following the elections the Front for Victory and its allies held 132 seats (of which the Front for Victory itself had 111), the Radical Civic Union and its allies 54 (of which the Radical Civic Union itself had 40), the Renewal Front and its allies 19 (of which Renewal Front itself had 11), Republican Proposal and its allies 18 and the UNEN coalition 7. The remainder of the seats went to smaller parties.

Giorgi Margvelashvili of the Georgian Dream coalition won presidential elections in the former Soviet republic of Georgia with 62.1% of the vote against 21.7% for Davit Bakradze of the United National Movement and 10.2% for Nino Burjanadze of the Democratic Movement–United Georgia.

Zarar Ahmad Moqbel Usmani was appointed acting foreign minister of Afghanistan.

In Swaziland, King Mswati III reappointed Barnabas Sibusiso Dlamini as prime minister and named Chief Mgwagwa Gamedze foreign minister, Sibusiso Shongwe justice minister and Princess Tsandzile interior minister.

César Villanueva was sworn in as prime minister of Peru.

Week Beginning 20 October 2013

Following the resignation of prime minister Jean-Claude Juncker, early parliamentary elections took place in Luxembourg. The Christian Social Party won 23 seats with 33.7% of the vote, the Socialist Workers' Party 13 and 20.3%, and the Democratic Party 13 and 18.3%. Three other parties also won seats.

In Azerbaijan, following the dismissal of defence minister Safar Abiyev, Zakir Hasanov took over the portfolio.

In the Czech Republic's parliamentary elections, the Czech Social Democratic Party won 50 seats with 20.5% of the vote; the Action of Dissatisfied Citizens won 47 with 18.7%; the Communist Party of Bohemia and Moravia won 33 with 14.9%; the TOP 09 won 26 with 12.0%; and the Civic Democratic Party 16 with 7.7%. Two other parties also won seats.

Week Beginning 13 October 2013

Pietro Parolin took office as secretary of state of the Vatican City.

Erna Solberg was sworn in as prime minister of Norway. Siv Jensen became finance minister, Børge Brende foreign minister and Ine Marie Eriksen Søreide defence minister.

In a cabinet reshuffle in Chad, Abderahim Bireme Hamid was named interior minister and Bédoumra Kordjé finance minister.

Week Beginning 6 October 2013

The Ethiopian parliament unanimously elected Mulatu Teshome Wirtu as president.

In presidential elections in Azerbaijan, incumbent Ilham Aliyev was re-elected with 84.5% of the vote against 5.5% for Jamil Hasanli.

Suriname, president Dési Bouterse dismissed finance minister Adelien Wijnerman.

In Malaŵi, president Joyce Banda dissolved the government. Five days later she appointed a new cabinet with Maxwell Mkwezalamba as finance minister. Other key ministers were reinstated.

Salaheddine Mezouar was appointed foreign minister and Mohamed Hassad interior minister in a cabinet reshuffle in Morocco.

The Organization for the Prohibition of Chemical Weapons was awarded the Nobel Peace Prize for 'its extensive work to eliminate chemical weapons'.

Chronology of Events for September 2013

Week Beginning 29 September 2013

In parliamentary elections in Austria the Social Democratic Party (SPÖ) won 52 seats with 26.8% of votes cast; the Austrian People's Party (ÖVP), 47 with 24.0%; the Freedom Party (FPÖ), 40 with 20.5%. Three other parties also obtained seats. Turnout was 74.9%.

Charles Savarin was unanimously elected president of Dominica by the parliament. He was sworn in 2 days later.

Anna Maria Muccioli and Gian Carlo Capicchioni were sworn in as captains regent of San Marino.

Italian prime minister Enrico Letta and his cabinet won a vote of confidence in the Senate by 235 votes to 70.

Week Beginning 22 September 2013

In parliamentary elections in Germany, the Christian Democratic Union/Christian Social Union of Chancellor Angela Merkel (CDU/CSU) won 311 seats (five seats short of an absolute majority) with 41.5% of the vote; the Social Democratic Party (SPD) won 192 with 25.7%; the Left Party won 64 seats with 8.6%; the Greens (Grüne), 63 with 8.4%. The Free Democratic Party (FDP) did not reach the 5% threshold to enter parliament for the first time since 1949. Turnout was 71.5%.

Aun Porn Moniroth became economy and finance minister of Cambodia in a cabinet reshuffle.

Week Beginning 15 September 2013

Camillo Gonsalves became foreign minister of St Vincent and the Grenadines.

In a cabinet reshuffle in Mauritania, Mohamed Ould Mohamed Rare was appointed interior minister and Ahmed Ould Teguedi foreign minister.

In Togo, a new cabinet was announced with Robert Dussey as foreign minister; Damehane Yark remained security minister and Adji Otèth Ayassor finance minister. President Faure Gnassingbé had reappointed Kwesi Ahoomey-Zunu prime minister earlier in the month.

Week Beginning 8 September 2013

In parliamentary elections in Norway the ruling Norwegian Labour Party (DNA) won 55 out of 169 seats with 30.8% of the vote; the Conservative Party (H), 48 with 26.8%; and the Progress Party (FrP), 29 with 16.3%. Smaller parties won ten seats or fewer. The Labour Party lost power as a coalition of right-wing parties won more seats. Turnout was 78.2%.

Mamnoon Hussain was sworn in as president of Pakistan.

In Albania, the government of Edi Rama took office. Mimi Kodheli became defence minister, Ditmir Bushati foreign minister, Shkëlqim Cani finance minister and Saimir Tahiri interior minister.

In a cabinet reshuffle in Algeria, Ramtane Lamamra was appointed foreign minister and Tayeb Belaiz interior minister.

A new cabinet, consisting only of members of Robert Mugabe's ZANU-PF, took office in Zimbabwe with Sydney Sekeramayi as defence minister, Patrick Chinamasa as finance minister and Kembo Mohadi as home affairs minister. Simbarashe Mumbengegwi stayed on as foreign minister.

Mariyam Shakeela became acting foreign minister of the Maldives following the death of the previous minister Abdul Samad Abdulla.

In Nigeria, Viola Onwuliri was appointed acting foreign minister following the dismissal of Olugbenga Ashiru.

Week Beginning 1 September 2013

Omar Daudzai was appointed interior minister in a cabinet reshuffle in Afghanistan.

Roberto Carvalho de Azevêdo took office as director-general of the World Trade Organization.

In Senegal, President Macky Sall dismissed the entire government. A new cabinet was announced the following day with Aminata Touré as prime minister, Amadou Ba as finance minister and Abdoulaye Diallo as interior minister. Mankeur Ndiaye stayed on as foreign minister and Augustin Tine as armed forces minister.

Nebojša Rodić was appointed defence minister and Lazar Krstić finance minister in a cabinet reshuffle in Serbia.

In a cabinet reshuffle in Madagascar, Jacques-Ulrich Randriantiana became acting foreign minister and Lantoniaina Rasoloelison finance minister.

In Mali, Ibrahim Boubacar Keïta was sworn in as president. The following day Oumar Tatam Ly was appointed prime minister. His cabinet included Zahabi Ould Sidi Mohamed as foreign minister, Soumeylou Boubèye Maïga as defence minister and Bouaré Fily Sissoko as finance minister. Moussa Sinko Coulibaly stayed on as interior minister.

Aurelio Iragorri Valencia became interior minister of Colombia.

Gary Griffith was appointed national security minister of Trinidad and Tobago.

In the USA, Rand Beers became the acting secretary of homeland security following the resignation of Janet Napolitano.

In parliamentary elections in Australia, the opposition Liberal/National Coalition won 90 seats and 45.6% of the primary vote (of which the Liberal Party 58 and 32.0%) and the ruling Labor Party (ALP) won 55 seats with 33.4%. Eleven days later Tony Abbott's new cabinet was sworn in with Julie Bishop as foreign minister, David Johnston as defence minister and Mathias Cormann as finance minister.

Chronology of Events for August 2013

Week Beginning 25 August 2013

In the Maldives, Asim Ahmed became acting foreign minister following the death of Abdul Samad Abdulla.

Madagascar's foreign minister Pierrot Rajaonarivelo and finance minister Hery Rajaonarimampianina resigned to run in the upcoming presidential election.

In Togo, the government of Kwesi Ahoomey-Zunu resigned.

Luiz Alberto Figueiredo was appointed Brazil's foreign minister following the resignation of Antônio Patriota.

Week Beginning 18 August 2013

Michel Djotodia was sworn in as president of the Central African Republic, marking the intended start of an 18-month transition period leading to elections. Josué Binoua was named security minister in a cabinet reshuffle announced 4 days later.

Aziz Akhenouch was appointed acting finance minister of Morocco.

James Wani Igga was named vice president of South Sudan by president Salva Kiir.

Week Beginning 11 August 2013

In the second round of presidential elections in Mali, Ibrahim Boubacar Keïta was elected president with 77.6% of the vote. He defeated Soumaïla Cissé. Turnout was 51.5% in the first round and 45.8% in the second.

In the Czech Republic, the government of Jiří Rusnok resigned following a defeat (100 votes to 93) in a vote of no confidence in the Chamber of Deputies.

In a cabinet reshuffle in Niger, Hassoumi Massaoudou became interior minister, Karidjo Mahamadou defence minister and Marou Amadou justice minister.

In Zambia, following the dismissal of foreign minister Effron Lungu, Wylbur Simuusa took over his portfolio.

In Egypt, vice president Mohamed ElBaradei resigned.

Jaime Miranda became foreign minister of El Salvador.

Horacio Cartes was sworn in as president of Paraguay. His cabinet included Eladio Loizaga as foreign minister, Francisco de Vargas as interior minister, Bernardino Soto as defence minister and Germán Rojas as finance minister.

Week Beginning 4 August 2013

Hassan Rouhani was sworn in as president of Iran.

Kuwait's new cabinet took office with Sheikh Sabah Khaled al-Sabah al-Hamad as first deputy prime minister and foreign minister, Sheikh Mohammed Khaled al-Hamad al-Sabah as deputy prime minister and interior minister and Sheikh Khaled al-Jarrah al-Sabah as deputy prime minister and defence minister. Salem Abdulaziz al-Saud al-Sabah became finance minister.

Abdullah al-Thanay became defence minister of Libya. Two weeks later Sadiq Abdulkarim Abdulrahman was appointed acting interior minister following the resignation of Muhammad Khalifa al-Sheikh.

In Benin, President Yayi Boni dismissed the government. A new cabinet named 3 days later included Ali Yérima as defence minister and François Houéssou as interior minister. Nassirou Arifari Bako stayed on as foreign minister and Jonas Gbian as finance minister.

Nicolai Wammen was appointed defence minister in a cabinet reshuffle in Denmark.

Chronology of Events for July 2013

Week Beginning 28 July 2013

In parliamentary elections in Cambodia, the ruling Cambodian People's Party won 68 of the 123 seats with 48.8% of votes cast and the Cambodian National Rescue Party won 55 seats with 44.5% of the vote. The opposition rejected the result, claiming there were 'serious irregularities'.

Mamnoon Hussain was elected president in indirect elections in Pakistan with 432 votes against 77 for Wajihuddin Ahmed.

Presidential and parliamentary elections took place in Zimbabwe. In the presidential elections, incumbent Robert Mugabe was re-elected for his seventh term with 61.1% of the vote against 33.9% for Morgan Tsvangirai and 2.7% for Welshman Ncube. Tsvangirai accused Mugabe of fraud and rejected the result. Of the 210 seats contested in the House of Assembly the Zimbabwe African National Union-Patriotic Front (ZANU-PF) won 160 seats, against 49 for the Movement for Democratic Change-Tsvangirai (MDC-T). The remaining seat was won by an independent. Of the 60 available seats in the Senate, the ZANU-PF won 37 and the MDC-T 21. The Movement for Democratic Change-Ncube (MDC-N) won the two remaining seats.

In Tuvalu, the governor-general removed prime minister Willy Telavi from office and appointed Enele Sopoaga as the caretaker leader. A few days later Sopoaga was elected prime minister in a parliamentary ballot. His cabinet was subsequently sworn in with Vete Sakaio as deputy prime minister, Taukelina Finikaso as foreign minister, Maatia Toafa as finance minister and Namoliki Sualiki as home affairs minister.

Week Beginning 21 July 2013
In Afghanistan, interior minister Ghulam Mujtaba Patang was dismissed although he stayed on in a caretaker capacity.

South Sudan's president Salva Kiir dissolved the government. Over the following week he appointed a new cabinet with Barnaba Marial Benjamin as foreign minister, Kuol Manyang Juuk as defence minister, Aggrey Tisa Sabuni as finance minister and Aleu Ayeny Aleu as interior minister.

In parliamentary elections in Togo, the ruling Union for the Republic won 62 of 91 seats, the Save Togo Collective 19 seats and the Rainbow Alliance 6. Turnout was 46.9%.

Week Beginning 14 July 2013
In a government reshuffle in Canada, Peter MacKay became justice minister, Robert Nicholson defence minister and James Flaherty finance minister.

The US Senate approved Thomas Perez as secretary of labor. As a result, for the first time since Barack Obama's inauguration for his second term as president 6 months earlier he had a complete team of fully-fledged cabinet secretaries and no acting secretaries.

Week Beginning 7 July 2013
In Bosnia and Herzegovina, Željko Komšić took over the 8-month rotating presidency chairmanship.

In the Czech Republic, Jiří Rusnok's caretaker government was sworn in. Martin Pecina was appointed interior minister, former prime minister Jan Fischer finance minister and Jan Kohout minister for foreign affairs. Vlastimil Picek remained defence minister.

Kebba S. Touray became finance minister in a cabinet reshuffle in the Gambia.

Jean-Claude Juncker resigned as prime minister of Luxembourg following claims of several cases of misconduct by the country's security agency, which the prime minister oversees. He remained the head of a caretaker government.

The second round of parliamentary elections was held in Bhutan. The People's Democratic Party won 32 of the 47 seats with 54.9% of votes and the Bhutan Peace and Prosperity Party won 15 seats and 45.1% of the votes. Turnout was 55.3% in the first round and 66.2% in the second. Two weeks later Tshering Tobgay's cabinet was sworn in with Rinzin Dorji as foreign minister, Damcho Dorji as home minister and Namgay Dorji as finance minister.

In a government reshuffle in the Comoros, El-Anrif Said Hassane was appointed foreign minister, Abdou Ousenni justice minister and Houssen Hassan Ibrahim interior minister.

Chronology of Events for June 2013

Week Beginning 30 June 2013
Manuel López Ambrosio was appointed defence minister of Guatemala.

In a cabinet reshuffle in Thailand, prime minister Yingluck Shinawatra took on the defence portfolio.

Croatia became the 28th member of the European Union.

Albert II, the King of Belgium, announced his decision to abdicate on 21 July in favour of his son, Crown Prince Philippe.

Mohamed Morsi was ousted in a 'democratic coup' following mass protests by Egyptians who favoured a secular administration. The head of Egypt's Supreme Constitutional Court, Adly Mansour, was appointed interim president the following day. New elections were called, the constitution suspended and the parliament dissolved. Clashes between Morsi's opponents and loyalists demanding his reinstatement resulted in a wave of violence in major cities.

Carmen Meléndez was appointed defence minister of Venezuela.

Week Beginning 23 June 2013
In parliamentary elections in Albania, the Alliance for a European Albania won 83 of the 140 seats with 57.6% of votes cast and the Alliance for Employment, Prosperity and Integration won 57 with 39.5% of the votes. Turnout was 53.5%.

In a government reshuffle in Greece, Evangelos Venizelos became foreign minister, Dimitris Avramopoulos defence minister and Yiannis Michelakis interior minister.

In Libya, Nouri Abusahmain was elected interim head of state. Later that week, defence minister Mohammed Mahmoud al-Bargati was removed from office after widespread dissatisfaction with his responses to violence across the country.

Sheikh Hamad, the Amir of Qatar, abdicated in favour of his son, Crown Prince Sheikh Tamim bin Hamad Al Thani. Subsequently, Sheikh Tamim appointed a new government with Sheikh Abdullah bin Nasser bin Khalifa Al Thani as prime minister and interior minister. Khalid bin Mohamed Al Attiyah became foreign minister, Ali Sherif Al Emadi finance minister and Hamad bin Ali Al Attiyah minister of state for defence affairs.

Julia Gillard resigned as prime minister of Australia after being defeated by Kevin Rudd in the Labor Party leadership ballot. Rudd was sworn in as prime minister the following day. His cabinet included Stephen Smith as minister for defence, Bob Carr as minister for foreign affairs and Chris Bowen as treasurer.

In presidential elections in Mongolia, incumbent president Tsakhiagiin Elbegdorj was re-elected with 50.2% of the vote against 42.0% for Badmaanyambuugiin Bat-Erdene and 6.5% for Natsagiin Udval. Turnout was 98.7%.

Week Beginning 16 June 2013
In the Czech Republic, the government of Petr Nečas resigned. Jiří Rusnok was appointed prime minister a week later.

In South Sudan, finance minister Kosti Manibe Ngai was suspended from office following allegations of corruption. Marial Awou took over his portfolio.

Abdel Kader Konaté became minister of finance in a cabinet reshuffle in Mali.

Week Beginning 9 June 2013
In a cabinet reshuffle in the Central African Republic Nicolas Tiangaye was reappointed prime minister. Léonie Banga-Bothy became foreign minister and Christophe Bremaïdou finance minister; president Michel Djotodia retained the post of defence minister.

In presidential elections in Iran, Hassan Rouhani was elected president with 50.7% of the vote; Mohammad Baqer Qalibaf received 16.6% and Saeed Jalili 11.4%. There were three other candidates. Turnout was 72.2%.

Week Beginning 2 June 2013
Nawaz Sharif was sworn in as the prime minister of Pakistan. In the cabinet announced 2 days later Sharif took on the foreign minister portfolio while Muhammad Ishaq Dar became finance minister and Chaudhry Nisar Ali Khan interior minister.

A new cabinet took office in Guinea-Bissau with Fernando Delfim da Silva as foreign minister and Gino Mendes as finance minister.

In parliamentary elections in Nauru, Baron Waqa's supporters won 14 of the 19 seats. He was subsequently elected president by parliament, winning 13 votes to Roland Kun's five. In the cabinet announced 2 days later Waqa took on the foreign affairs portfolio while David Adeang became minister for finance and justice and Charmaine Scotty home affairs minister.

Chronology of Events for May 2013

Week Beginning 26 May 2013
In parliamentary elections in Equatorial Guinea, the ruling Democratic Party of Equatorial Guinea won all but one seat in both houses of the parliament. The remaining seat in both houses was obtained by the Convergence for Social Democracy.

In Libya, following the resignation of interior minister Ashur Shwayel, Mohammed Khalifa al-Sheikh took over his portfolio. Later in the week chairman of the General National Congress and de facto president Mohamed Magariaf resigned. He was succeeded on an acting basis by Giuma Attaiga.

Nauru's finance, justice and foreign affairs minister, Roland Kun, resigned.

In Moldova, Iurie Leancă's cabinet was sworn in. New appointments included Natalia Gherman as deputy premier and minister of foreign affairs and Tatiana Poting as deputy premier for social affairs. Other key portfolios remained unchanged.

Week Beginning 19 May 2013

In a cabinet reshuffle in Indonesia, Chatib Basri became finance minister.

Sigmundur Davíð Gunnlaugsson of the Progressive Party was sworn in as the prime minister of Iceland. His cabinet included Gunnar Bragi Sveinsson as foreign minister, Bjarni Benediktsson (the Independence Party leader) as finance minister and Hanna Birna Kristjánsdóttir as interior minister.

Gen. Aronda Nyakairima was appointed interior minister of Uganda.

In a cabinet reshuffle in Vietnam, Dinh Tien Dung became finance minister.

Week Beginning 12 May 2013

Jang Jong-nam was appointed armed forces minister of North Korea.

In Peru, following the resignation of foreign minister Rafael Roncagliolo, Eda Rivas took over his portfolio.

Week Beginning 5 May 2013

In parliamentary elections in Malaysia, the 13-party National Front coalition (Barisan Nasional) won 133 of 222 seats with 46.7% of the votes cast. The opposition People's Front coalition (Pakatan Rakyat) won 89 with 50.1%. Turnout was 84.8%. Ten days later a new cabinet was formed, with Ahmad Zahid Hamidi becoming home affairs minister and Hishammuddin Hussein defence minister.

Fayyad Abdel Moneim was appointed finance minister in a cabinet reshuffle in Egypt.

Cécile La Grenade was sworn in as governor-general of Grenada.

In a cabinet reshuffle in Armenia, David Sargsyan became finance minister.

Armando Manuel succeeded Carlos Alberto Lopes as Angola's finance minister.

In Vanuatu, following the dismissal of finance minister Willie Jimmy, Maki Simelum took over his portfolio.

In parliamentary elections in Pakistan, the Pakistan Muslim League-N (PML-N, led by ex-prime minister Nawaz Sharif) won 125 of the National Assembly's 272 elected seats with 32.7% of votes cast; the Pakistan People's Party (PPP, led by Bilawal Bhutto) won 31 seats with 15.0% of the vote; and the Pakistan Movement for Justice (PTI, led by Imran Khan) gained 28 seats with 16.8%. Turnout was 55.0%. The elections represented the first civilian transfer of power in Pakistan following the completion of a 5-year term by a democratically-elected government.

In parliamentary elections in Bulgaria, Citizens for the European Development of Bulgaria won 97 of 240 seats with 30.5% of the votes cast; the Bulgarian Socialist Party won 84 with 26.6%; the Movement for Rights and Freedoms won 36 with 11.3%; and the Attack coalition 23 with 7.3%. Turnout was 51.3%. Two weeks later the new prime minister, Plamen Oresharski, and his cabinet were sworn in. Kristian Vigenin became foreign minister, Angel Naydenov defence minister and Tsvetlin Yovchev interior minister.

Chronology of Events for April 2013

Week Beginning 28 April 2013

Having been asked to form a government 4 days earlier, Enrico Letta took office as the prime minister of Italy. His cabinet included Emma Bonino as foreign minister, Fabrizio Saccomanni as finance minister and Mario Mauro as defence minister.

Fausto Herrera became minister of finance in a cabinet reshuffle in Ecuador.

Willem-Alexander was invested as King of the Netherlands following the abdication of his mother, Queen (now Princess) Beatrix.

In a cabinet reshuffle in Honduras, Arturo Corrales was appointed security minister. Mireya Agüero took over his foreign affairs portfolio.

Week Beginning 21 April 2013

In presidential elections in Paraguay, Horacio Cartes was elected with 45.8% of the vote against 36.9% for Efraín Alegre. There were nine other candidates. Turnout was 68.6%.

In Trinidad and Tobago, following the resignation of national security minister Jack Warner, Emmanuel George took over his portfolio.

In a cabinet reshuffle in Nauru, Roland Kun was appointed minister for finance, justice and foreign affairs.

Abdul Hamid was elected president of Bangladesh.

Iurie Leancă was appointed acting prime minister of Moldova.

In parliamentary elections in Iceland, the Independence Party (SSF) won 19 of the 63 seats with 26.7% of the votes cast. The Progressive Party (FSF) also won 19 seats but with 24.4% of the vote. Four other parties obtained seats. Turnout was 81.4%.

Week Beginning 14 April 2013

A special presidential election was held in Venezuela following the death of president Hugo Chávez Frías. Nicolás Maduro was elected president with 50.7% of the vote against 49.1% for Henrique Capriles Radonski. There were five other candidates. Turnout was 78.7%. Five days later Maduro was sworn in and subsequently named his cabinet, including Jorge Arreaza as vice-president, Nelson Merentes as finance minister and Miguel Rodríguez Torres as interior and justice minister. Elías Jaua remained foreign minister and Diego Molero defence minister.

Hatta Rajasa became acting finance minister of Indonesia.

In a cabinet reshuffle in Nauru, Roland Kun was appointed minister for finance, justice and foreign affairs.

Giorgio Napolitano was re-elected president of Italy by an assembly of lawmakers and regional representatives, winning 738 votes to Stefano Rodotà's 217.

Week Beginning 7 April 2013

In presidential elections in Montenegro, incumbent president Filip Vujanović was re-elected for a third term with 51.2% of the vote against 48.8% for Miodrag Lekić. Turnout was 63.9%.

The former British prime minister Margaret Thatcher died, aged 87.

Wilson Laleau was appointed finance minister of Haiti following the resignation of Marie-Carmelle Jean-Marie.

Uhuru Kenyatta took office as the president of Kenya.

Sally Jewell was sworn in as the interior secretary of the USA.

In the Central African Republic, Michel Djotodia was elected interim president by the National Transitional Council.

Chronology of Events for March 2013

Week Beginning 31 March 2013

Abdoulkader Kamil Mohamed was sworn in as the prime minister of Djibouti. Hassan Darar Houffaneh was appointed defence minister and Hassan Omar Mohamed interior minister. Mahamoud Ali Youssouf remained foreign minister and Ilyas Moussa Dawaleh finance minister.

Pak Pong-ju was appointed prime minister of North Korea.

Antonella Mularoni and Denis Amici were inaugurated as captains regent of San Marino.

In Cyprus, following the resignation of finance minister Michalis Sarris, Charis Georgiadis took over his portfolio.

Aldo Bumçi was appointed foreign minister in a cabinet reshuffle in Albania.

Week Beginning 24 March 2013

Mir Hazar Khan Khoso was sworn in as caretaker prime minister of Pakistan. A week later Malik Habib was appointed interior minister.

In Italy, foreign minister Giulio Terzi resigned.

François Bozizé, the president of the Central African Republic, was forced to flee the country as the Séléka rebel coalition under the leadership of Michel Djotodia took control of the capital. Nicolas Tiangaye was reappointed prime minister and a transition government was subsequently named with Djotodia as defence minister, Charles Armel Doubane as foreign minister and Georges Bozanga as finance minister.

Adrian Hasler took office as the prime minister and finance minister of Liechtenstein. His cabinet included Thomas Zwiefelhofer as interior and justice minister with Aurelia Frick remaining foreign minister.

Week Beginning 17 March 2013

In South Korea, president Park Geun-hye appointed Yun Byung-se as foreign minister, Hwang Kyo-ahn as justice minister and Bahk Jae-wan as finance minister. The cabinet list was finalized a week later when Kim Kwan-jin was appointed defence minister.

Binyamin Netanyahu was sworn in for his third term as the prime minister of Israel. Netanyahu also took on the foreign affairs portfolio. Moshe Ya'alon became defence minister, Gideon Sa'ar interior minister and Yair Lapid finance minister.

Vlastimil Picek was appointed defence minister of Czech Republic.

Alenka Bratušek was sworn in as the prime minister of Slovenia. Her cabinet included Karl Erjavec as foreign minister, Roman Jakič as defence minister, Uroš Čufer as finance minister and Gregor Virant as interior minister.

In Lebanon, the government of Najib Mikati resigned but stayed on in a caretaker capacity.

Following the resignation of Sato Kilman, Moana Carcasses Kalosil became the new prime minister of Vanuatu. His cabinet included Edward Natapei as foreign minister, Willie Jimmy Tapangararua as finance minister and Patrick Crowby as interior minister.

Week Beginning 10 March 2013
Gerald Klug was appointed defence minister of Austria.

A caretaker government in Bulgaria took office with Marin Raykov as prime minister and minister of foreign affairs, Petya Purvanova as interior minister, Todor Tagarev as defence minister and Kalin Hristov as finance minister.

The papal conclave elected Cardinal Jorge Mario Bergoglio to the papacy. He became Pope Francis and was inaugurated a week later as the 266th Supreme Pontiff.

In Tunisia, Ali Larayedh was sworn in as caretaker prime minister. His cabinet took office the following day including Rachid Sabagh as defence minister and Lotfi Ben Jeddou as interior minister.

Abdul Hamid was appointed acting president of Bangladesh as incumbent Zillur Rahman underwent medical treatment abroad. Rahman died a week later in Singapore after a long illness.

Xi Jinping was elected president of China by the National People's Congress. Li Yuanchao became vice president and Li Keqiang premier.

Khil Raj Regmi took office as interim prime minister of Nepal. He subsequently named his cabinet with Shankar Koirala as finance minister; Madhav Prasad Ghimire took over the foreign affairs and interior portfolios.

Week Beginning 3 March 2013
The government of Grenada was sworn in with the finance, national security and home affairs portfolios assigned to prime minister Keith Mitchell. Elvin Nimrod was named deputy premier and Nickolas Steele foreign affairs minister.

In presidential elections in Kenya, Uhuru Kenyatta was elected with 50.1% of the vote against 43.3% for Raila Odinga. There were six other candidates. In parliamentary elections Uhuru Kenyatta's Jubilee alliance won 167 seats (of which The National Alliance won 89); Raila Odinga's Coalition for Reforms and Democracy alliance, 141 (of which the Orange Democratic Movement won 96); and Musalia Mudavadi's Amani coalition, 24 (of which the United Democratic Forum won 12). Five other parties also won seats.

In Belgium, following the resignation of finance minister Steven Vanackere, Koen Geens took over his portfolio.

Only non-partisans were elected in parliamentary elections in Micronesia.

Mihály Varga became the finance minister of Hungary.

Miloš Zeman was sworn in as the president of the Czech Republic.

John Brennan was sworn in as the director of the CIA.

Following the death of Hugo Chávez, Venezuela's vice president Nicolás Maduro took over as president. Jorge Arreaza was named vice president.

In parliamentary elections in Malta, the opposition Labour Party (MLP) won 39 of 69 seats with 54.8% of votes cast and the Nationalist Party (NP) won 30 with 43.3%.

Chronology of Events for February 2013

Week Beginning 24 February 2013
In the second round of presidential elections in Cyprus, Nicos Anastasiadies was elected with 57.5% of the vote against 42.5% for Stavros Malas. Anastasiadies and his all male cabinet were sworn in a week later.

In parliamentary elections in Italy, Pier Luigi Bersani's centre-left coalition won 345 of 630 seats in the Chamber of Deputies (including the Democratic Party with 297 seats), former prime minister Silvio Berlusconi's centre-right coalition 125 (including People of Liberty, 98), Beppe Grillo's Five Star Movement 109 and Prime Minister Mario Monti's coalition 47. In the Senate, Bersani's coalition won 123 of 315 seats (including the Democratic Party 113), Berlusconi's coalition 117 (including People of Liberty 98), the Five Star Movement 54 and Monti 19.

Park Geun-hye was sworn in as the president of South Korea.

In a cabinet reshuffle in Poland, Jan-Vincent Rostowski became deputy prime minister and finance minister. Bartlomiej Sienkiewicz was named interior minister.

Claver Gatete was named finance minister of Rwanda.

In Panama, following the resignation of Rómulo Roux, Fernando Núñez Fábrega took over as foreign minister.

In the USA, Charles 'Chuck' Hagel and Jacob 'Jack' Lew were sworn in as defence secretary and treasury secretary respectively.

In Zambia, Effron Lungu was appointed foreign minister following the dismissal of Given Lubinda.

Week Beginning 17 February 2013
In presidential elections in Ecuador, Rafael Vicente Correa Delgado was re-elected with 57.2% of the vote against 22.7% for Guillermo Lasso. There were six other candidates. In parliamentary elections, Alianza PAIS won 91 of 131 seats with 52.3% of the vote and Creating Opportunities 12 with 11.4%. Six other parties also won seats.

In presidential elections in Armenia, Serzh Sargsyan was re-elected with 58.6% of the vote. He defeated Raffi Hovannisian. Turnout was 60.1%. Protests over alleged electoral fraud followed.

Jiang Yi-huah took office as prime minister of Taiwan. His cabinet included Mao Chi-Kuo as deputy premier and Chang Chia-juch as economic affairs minister. Lin Yung-lo remained foreign minister.

In a cabinet reshuffle in Chad, Ali Mahamat Zene Ali Fadel became interior minister and Issa Ali Taher economy minister.

In parliamentary elections in Grenada, New National Party won all 15 seats taking 60.0% of the vote; the ruling National Democratic Congress failed to obtain any seats with 39.3%. Turnout was 85.0%. Keith Mitchell was sworn in as prime minister the following day.

In Pakistan, following the resignation of finance minister Abdul Hafeez Shaikh, Saleem Mandviwalla took over his portfolio.

In Tunisia, the government of prime minister Hamadi Jebali resigned after failing to reshape the government as a response to a political crisis. The crisis was sparked by the assassination of opposition leader Chokri Belaid earlier in the month.

In Bulgaria, the government of prime minister Boyko Borisov resigned following nationwide street protests against austerity measures and high electricity prices.

In parliamentary elections in Barbados, the ruling Democratic Labour Party won 16 of 30 seats with 51.3% of the vote and the Barbados Labour Party won 14 with 48.3%. A week later prime minister Freundel Stuart announced his cabinet with no change in key portfolios.

In parliamentary elections in Djibouti, the Union for a Presidential Majority won 43 of 65 seats with 61.5% of the vote; the Union for National Salvation won 21 seats with 35.6%; the Centre of Unified Democrats took one seat with 3.0%. Turnout was 69.2%. The opposition rejected the result and claimed that the vote was rigged.

Abdylda Suranchiyev was appointed interior minister of Kyrgyzstan.

Week Beginning 10 February 2013
In parliamentary elections in Monaco, Horizon Monaco won 20 of 24 seats with 50.3% of the vote; the Monegasque Union won 3 with 39.0%; and Renaissance won one seat with 10.7%. Turnout was 74.5%.

Pope Benedict XVI announced that he would resign at the end of the month, citing health reasons.

Anthony Carmona was elected president of Trinidad and Tobago.

Week Beginning 3 February 2013
In parliamentary elections in Liechtenstein, the Progressive Citizens' Party (FBP) won 10 of 25 seats with 40.0% of the vote; the Patriotic Union (VU) won 8 with 33.5%; the Independents won 4 with 15.3%; and the Free List (FL) won 3 with 11.1%. Turnout was 79.8%.

Reckya Madougou became minister of justice in a cabinet reshuffle in Benin.

In a cabinet reshuffle in St Kitts and Nevis, Dr. Earl Asim Martin was appointed deputy prime minister and Patrice Nisbett foreign minister.

Ismail Ismail was named finance minister in a cabinet reshuffle in Syria. Other key portfolios remained unchanged.

Chronology of Events for January 2013

Week Beginning 27 January 2013

President Morsi declared a 30-day state of emergency and curfew in three Suez Canal provinces hit hardest by a wave of violent protests sparked by the second anniversary of the Egyptian revolution.

Queen Beatrix of the Netherlands announced her abdication as of 30 April with her eldest son, Prince Willem-Alexander, becoming the country's first king since 1890.

In Slovenia, following the resignation of ministers of finance and justice, prime minister Janez Janša temporarily took over the finance portfolio and Zvonko Černač became the acting justice minister.

John Kerry succeeded Hillary Clinton as the United States Secretary of State.

Week Beginning 20 January 2013

Barack Obama was sworn in for his second term as the president of the United States.

In Chad, Djimrangar Dadnadji was appointed prime minister following the resignation of Emmanuel Nadingar. Subsequently a cabinet was announced including Atteib Habib Doutoum as finance minister and Abdoulaye Sabre Fadoul as justice minister.

In a cabinet reshuffle in Haiti, David Bazile was appointed interior minister.

In parliamentary elections in Israel, Likud Yisrael Beiteinu (an alliance of Likud and Yisrael Beiteinu) won 31 of 120 seats with 23.3% of the votes cast; the Yesh Atid won 19 with 14.3%; the Labour Party won 15 with 11.4%; the Jewish Home won 12 with 9.1%; and Shas won 11 with 8.8%. Turnout was 67.8%.

Muammer Güler was appointed interior minister in a cabinet reshuffle in Turkey.

In the second round of the Czech Republic's first ever direct presidential elections, Miloš Zeman was elected president with 54.8% of the vote to Karel Schwarzenberg's 45.2%. There had been nine candidates in the first round 2 weeks earlier. Turnout was 61.3% in the first round and 59.1% in the second.

Week Beginning 13 January 2013

Elías Jaua was named foreign minister of Venezuela.

Tommy Remengesau was sworn in as the president of Palau.

Nicolas Tiangaye took office as the prime minister of the Central African Republic. A new cabinet was announced 2 weeks later with Michel Djotodia Amnadroko as defence minister, Parfait-Anicet M'bay as foreign affairs minister and Enoch Derant Lakoué as economy minister.

Over 800 people were held hostage at a gas facility near In Amenas in Algeria. Following a siege lasting several days, Algerian special forces launched an attack on the site in order to free the hostages; the assault ending the crisis resulted in the death of around 80 people.

Week Beginning 6 January 2013

In a cabinet reshuffle in Egypt, Gen. Mohamed Ibrahim became interior minister and El-Morsi Hegazy finance minister.

John Atta Mills was sworn in as the president of Ghana.

In Guatemala, foreign minister Harold Caballeros resigned. A week later Fernando Carrera took over the portfolio.

Mohamed Abdulaziz was appointed acting foreign minister of Libya by prime minister Ali Zeidan.

2012

Chronology of Events for December 2012

Week Beginning 30 December 2012

Ueli Maurer took office as president of Switzerland.

The US Senate passed a last-minute deal averting the so-called fiscal cliff, a combination of dramatic spending cuts and tax increases mandated to come into effect in January 2013. The agreement involved delaying federal budget cuts for 2 months and returning to Bill Clinton-era tax rates for top earners of 39.6% for individuals earning US$400,000 and above and households earning US$450,000 and above.

In Burkina Faso, Luc Adolphe Tiao's government was sworn in. Dramane Yaméogo became justice minister; other key portfolios remained unchanged.

In a cabinet reshuffle in Sierra Leone, Joseph B. Dauda was named internal affairs minister, Samura Kamara foreign minister and Kaifala Marah finance minister.

Week Beginning 23 December 2012

In Ukraine, Mykola Azarov was reappointed as prime minister following his resignation a few weeks earlier. A new cabinet was appointed by president Viktor Yanukovych including Leonid Kozhara as foreign minister and Pavlo Lebedev as defence minister. Other key portfolios remained unchanged.

President Mohamed Morsy ratified the new constitution of Egypt. The constitution had been approved in the previous weeks by the Egyptian people in a two-stage referendum.

Week Beginning 16 December 2012

In parliamentary elections in Japan, the Liberal Democratic Party (LDP) won 294 of 480 seats with 43.0% of the single-seat constituency vote; the ruling Democratic Party (DPJ) 57 with 22.8%; and the Restoration Party (JRP) 54 with 11.6%. Turnout was 59.3%, the lowest since the Second World War. Two weeks later Shinzo Abe was elected prime minister for a second time. He formed a cabinet with Fumio Kishida as foreign minister, Itsunori Onodera as defence minister, Yoshitaka Shindo as internal affairs minister and Taro Aso as finance minister.

In presidential elections in South Korea, Park Geun-hye was elected president with 51.6% of the vote. Turnout was 75.8%.

Elyes Fakhfakh was appointed finance minister of Tunisia.

Italian Prime Minister Mario Monti resigned following the passage of the 2013 budget.

Week Beginning 9 December 2012

In parliamentary elections in Romania, the Social Liberal Union (USL) alliance won 273 of 412 seats with 58.6% of the vote in the Chamber of Deputies; the Right Romania Alliance won 56 with 16.5%; and the People's Party–Dan Diaconescu 47 with 14.0%. Turnout was 41.7%. Two weeks later Victor Ponta's cabinet was sworn in with Daniel Chițoiu as deputy prime minister and finance minister and Radu Stroe as interior minister. Mircea Dușa became defence minister while Titus Corlățean continued as foreign minister.

In São Tomé e Príncipe, following the dismissal of Patrice Trovoada's cabinet, Gabriel Arcanjo da Costa was appointed prime minister. Two days later a new government took office including Natália Pedro da Costa Umbelina Neto as foreign minister, Óscar Aguiar Sacramento e Sousa as interior and defence minister and Hélio Silva Vaz d'Almeida as finance minister.

In Estonia, following the resignation of justice minister Kristen Michal, Hanno Pevkur took over the portfolio.

In Mali, Diango Cissoko was appointed prime minister following the forced resignation of Cheick Modibo Diarra by the military. Subsequently a new cabinet was announced with no changes in key portfolios.

In a cabinet reshuffle in the Czech Republic, Karolina Peake was named defence minister. She was dismissed a week later and prime minister Petr Nečas provisionally took over the portfolio.

In Israel, Binyamin Netanyahu became the acting foreign minister following the resignation of Avigdor Lieberman.

Week Beginning 2 December 2012

In parliamentary elections in Burkina Faso, the Congress for Democracy and Progress won 70 of 127 seats; the Alliance for Democracy and Federation–African Democratic Rally 19; and the Union for Progress and Change 19. Turnout was 76.0%.

In Montenegro, Milo Đukanović's government was sworn in. Igor Lukšić became deputy prime minister and foreign minister, Radoje Žugić finance minister and Raško Konjević interior minister. Milica Pejanović continued as defence minister.

In the second round of presidential elections in Slovenia, Borut Pahor was elected president with 67.4% of the vote. He defeated incumbent Danilo Türk. Pahor was sworn in 3 weeks later.

In a major government reshuffle in Namibia, Hage Geingob was appointed prime minister, Netumbo Nandi-Ndaitwah foreign minister and Nahas Angula defence minister. Untoni Nujoma was named justice minister and Pendukeni Iivula-Iithana home affairs minister.

The government of San Marino was sworn in. Pasquale Valentini became foreign minister and Gian Carlo Venturini interior and defence minister.

In the presidential elections in Ghana, John Dramani Mahama of the National Democratic Congress (NDC) ensured victory in the first round with 50.7% of the vote. He defeated Nana Akufo-Addo of the New Patriotic Party (NPP), who received 47.7%. Turnout was 79.4%. In parliamentary elections held simultaneously, the NDC won 148 of 275 seats and the NPP 123. Turnout was 80.0%.

Chronology of Events for November 2012

Week Beginning 25 November 2012

Following the resignation of Ecuador's defence minister Miguel Carvajal, Maria Fernanda Espinosa was sworn in as his successor.

Francis Zammit Dimech was named foreign minister of Malta.

In a cabinet reshuffle in Ethiopia, Tedros Adhanom was appointed foreign minister.

In North Korea, Kim Kyok-sik replaced Kim Jong-gak as defence minister.

Palestine was granted 'non-member observer' status in the United Nations.

Enrique Peña Nieto took office as president of Mexico. His cabinet included José Antonio Meade as foreign minister, Miguel Ángel Osorio Chong as interior minister and Gen. Salvador Cienfuegos Zepeda as defence minister.

Week Beginning 18 November 2012

In Poland, the vice prime minister and minister of economy Waldemar Pawlak resigned. Two weeks later Janusz Piechocinski took over both posts.

Sato Kilman was re-elected prime minister of Vanuatu. He named Charlot Salwai finance minister and Toara Daniel Kalo internal affairs minister; Alfred Carlot remained foreign minister.

In Côte d'Ivoire, following the dismissal of Jeannot Ahoussou-Kouadio's government, Daniel Kablan Duncan was appointed prime minister. The cabinet subsequently named included Charles Koffi Diby as foreign minister, Hamed Bakayoko as interior minister and Paul Koffi Koffi as defence minister.

In a government reshuffle in Bosnia and Herzegovina, Zekerijah Osmić became defence minister.

Algirdas Butkevičius took office as the prime minister of Lithuania. The new cabinet was announced 2 weeks later with Linas Antanas Linkevičius as foreign minister, Rimantas Šadžius as finance minister, Dailis Alfonsas Barakauskas as interior minister and Juozas Bernatonis as justice minister.

Week Beginning 11 November 2012

In parliamentary elections in San Marino, the San Marino Common Good coalition won 35 of 60 seats with 50.7% of the vote; the Agreement for the Country coalition won 12 with 22.3%; the Active Citizenship coalition 9 with 16.1%; and the Network Civic Movement 4 with 6.3%. Turnout was 63.8%. A new cabinet was announced 2 weeks later with Pasquale Valentini as foreign minister, Giancarlo Venturini as interior minister and Claudio Felici as finance minister.

Xi Jinping was elected General Secretary of the Chinese Communist Party and consequently new president. Li Keqiang, Zhang Dejiang, Yu Zhengsheng, Liu Yunshan, Wang Qishan and Zhang Gaoli were also chosen as members of the country's principal decision making body, the Standing Committee of the Politburo.

In Somalia, Abdi Farah Shirdon's government was sworn in. Fowsiyo Yusuf Haji Adan became foreign minister, Abdihakim Mohamoud Haji defence minister, Mohamoud Hassan Suleiman finance minister and Abdikarim Hussein Guled interior minister.

Presidential and parliamentary elections were held in Sierra Leone. The incumbent president Ernest Bai Koroma was re-elected with 58.7% of the vote. In parliamentary elections, the All People's Congress won 67 of 124 seats with 53.7% of the vote and the Sierra Leone People's Party 42 with 38.3%; 12 seats were allocated for elected chiefs.

Week Beginning 4 November 2012

In a cabinet reshuffle in Chile, Rodrigo Hinzpeter was appointed defence minister and Andrés Chadwick interior minister.

In the Netherlands, Mark Rutte's new government was sworn in. Frans Timmermans became foreign minister, Jeanine Hennis-Plasschaert defence minister, Jeroen Dijsselbloem finance minister and Ronald Plasterk interior minister.

Prince Muhammad bin Nayef was appointed interior minister of Saudi Arabia by King Abdullah.

In the second round of presidential elections in Palau, Tommy Remengesau was elected president with 58.0% of the vote. He defeated incumbent leader Johnson Toribiong.

In Russia, following the dismissal of Anatoly Serdyukov, Sergey Shoigu was named defence minister.

Barack Obama was re-elected in the US presidential elections with 50.9% of the vote and 332 electoral college votes; the Republican candidate Mitt Romney received 47.3% of the vote and 206 electoral votes.

CIA director David Petraeus resigned.

In Bosnia and Herzegovina, Nebojša Radmanović took over the 8-month rotating presidency chairmanship.

Chronology of Events for October 2012

Week Beginning 28 October 2012

In Ukraine's parliamentary elections, the Party of Regions won 187 seats with 30.0% of the vote, Yuliya Tymoshenko's Fatherland 102 with 25.5%, Vitali Klitschko's Ukrainian Democratic Alliance for Reform 40 with 14.0%, Svoboda 38 with 10.4% and the Communist Party of Ukraine 32 with 13.2%. 51 seats were divided between various small parties and independent candidates. Turnout was 58.0%.

In a government reshuffle in Thailand, Phongthep Thepkanjana was appointed deputy prime minister, Surapong Towijakchaikul deputy prime minister and foreign minister and Charupong Ruangsuwan interior minister. Other key posts remained unchanged.

In a major cabinet reshuffle in Senegal, Mankeur Ndiaye was appointed foreign minister and Pathé Seck interior minister. Other key portfolios remained unchanged.

In Vanuatu's parliamentary elections, the Party of Our Land won 8 of 52 seats, the People's Progressive Party 6, the Union of Moderate Parties 5, the Ground and Justice Party 4, the National United Party 4 and the Iauko Group 3. Turnout was 63.2%.

In Libya, the government of Ali Zeidan took office. Senior ministers included Mohammed Mahmoud al-Bargati as defence minister, Alkilani al-Jazi as finance minister and Salah Bashir Margani as justice minister.

In a cabinet reshuffle in the Gambia, Susan Waffa Ogoo was appointed foreign minister.

Week Beginning 21 October 2012

In Bosnia and Herzegovina, the defence minister Muhamed Ibrahimović was dismissed.

In Georgia, Bidzina Ivanichvili's government was sworn in. Irakli Alasania was appointed deputy prime minister and defence minister, Nodar Khaduri finance minister, Maya Panjikidze foreign minister and Thea Tsulukiani justice minister.

In a major government reshuffle in India, Salman Khurshid was named foreign minister. Other key portfolios remained unchanged.

Week Beginning 14 October 2012

In the two rounds of Lithuania's parliamentary elections, the Social Democratic Party of Lithuania won 38 of the 141 seats, Homeland Union-Lithuanian Christian Democrats 33 and Labour Party 29. Turnout was 52.9%.

In Montenegro's parliamentary elections, the ruling Coalition for European Montenegro won 39 of 81 seats with 45.6% of the vote, the Democratic Front 20 with 22.8%, the Socialist People's Party 9 with 11.1% and Positive Montenegro 7 with 8.2%. Turnout was 72.8%.

Week Beginning 7 October 2012

In presidential elections in Venezuela, incumbent president Hugo Chávez was re-elected. He subsequently appointed Nicolás Maduro as vice president and Nestor Reverol as interior minister. Some weeks later Diego Molero was named defence minister.

In Mozambique, Alberto Vaquina was appointed prime minister following the dismissal of Aires Ali.

Abdullah Ensour was appointed prime minister of Jordan by King Abdullah II. The government was named the following day with Ensour also serving as defence minister; Awad Khlewait became interior minister, Suleiman Hafez remained finance minister and Nasser Judeh foreign minister.

The European Union was awarded the Nobel Peace Prize for 'promoting peace, democracy and human rights over six decades.'

Chronology of Events for September 2012

Week Beginning 30 September 2012
Angola's new government was sworn in including Manuel Vicente as vice president and Ângelo de Barros Veiga Tavares as new interior minister. Other key portfolios remained unchanged.

In parliamentary elections in Georgia, the opposition Georgian Dream coalition won 83 of the 150 seats, with the ruling United National Movement taking 67 seats. Turnout was 59.8%.

In a cabinet reshuffle in Japan, Koriki Jojima became finance minister, Shinji Tarutoko interior minister and Keishu Takana justice minister.

Denise Bronzetti and Teodoro Lonfernini took office as captains regent of San Marino.

In a cabinet reshuffle in Guinea, Kerfalla Yansané was appointed economy and finance minister and Lounceny Fall foreign minister.

Abdi Farah Shirdon was appointed prime minister of Somalia by president Hassan Sheikh Mohamud.

Week Beginning 23 September 2012
In parliamentary elections in Belarus, independent candidates won 104 of 109 seats, the Communist Party 3, the Agrarian Party 1 and the Republican Party of Labour and Justice 1. All the elected deputies were supporters of President Lukashenka as the two main opposition parties boycotted the election. Turnout was 74.2%.

In Kazakhstan, Serik Akhmetov was appointed prime minister following the resignation of Karim Masimov. Subsequently a cabinet was announced including Krymbek Kusherbayev as deputy prime minister and Yerlan Idrisov as foreign minister.

In a cabinet reshuffle in the Republic of the Congo, Charles Richard Mondjo was appointed defence minister and Raymond Zéphirin Mboulou interior minister.

In Thailand, deputy prime minister and interior minister Yongyuth Wichaidit resigned following allegations of corruption.

Week Beginning 16 September 2012
In Dominica, following the resignation of president Nicholas Liverpool, Eliud Williams was sworn in as his successor.

Following the resignation of Georgia's interior minister Bacho Akhlaia, Eka Zguladze took over the portfolio.

In Ethiopia, the acting prime minister Hailemariam Desalegn was sworn in as prime minister.

In a cabinet reshuffle in Norway, Espen Barth Eide was appointed foreign minister while Anne-Grete Strøm-Erichsen took over the defence portfolio.

Week Beginning 9 September 2012
Hassan Sheikh Mohamud was elected president of Somalia. He was sworn in a week later.

Mustafa Abu Shagur was elected prime minister of Libya, but was dismissed the following month after failing to form a government.

In the Netherlands' parliamentary elections, the People's Party for Freedom and Democracy won 41 of 150 seats with 26.6% of the vote, the Labour Party 38 with 24.8%, the Party for Freedom 15 with 10.1%, the Socialist Party 15 with 9.7%, the Christian Democratic Appeal 13 with 8.5%, the Democrats 66 12 with 7.9%, the Christian Union 5 with 3.2%, Green Left 4 with 2.3%, the Reformed Political Party 3 with 2.1%, the Party for the Animals 2 with 1.9% and 50+ 2 with 1.9%. Turnout was 74.3%.

In a cabinet reshuffle in Afghanistan, Bismallah Mohammadi became defence minister and Mujtaba Patang interior minister.

In a major cabinet reshuffle in Bangladesh, Mahiuddin Khan Alamgir was appointed interior minister. Other key portfolios remained unchanged, but there were a number of changes among more minor posts.

Week Beginning 2 September 2012
Abdelmalek Sellal was appointed prime minister of Algeria by president Abdelaziz Bouteflika. The government was named the following day with no changes in key portfolios.

Chronology of Events for August 2012

Week Beginning 26 August 2012
In a cabinet reshuffle in Myanmar, Lieut.-Gen. Wai Lwin became defence minister and U Win Shein finance minister.

Romanian president Traian Băsescu resumed office, following an attempted parliamentary impeachment.

In Angolan parliamentary elections, the Popular Movement for the Liberation of Angola (MPLA) gained 175 seats in the National Assembly with 71.8% of votes cast, National Union for the Total Independence of Angola (UNITA) 32 with 18.7%, Broad Convergence for the Salvation of Angola–Electoral Coalition (CASA–CE) 8 with 6.0%, Social Renewal Party 3 with 1.7% and the National Front for the Liberation of Angola 2 with 1.1%. Turnout was 62.8%.

In the Philippines, following the death of interior secretary Jesse Robredo, Manuel 'Mar' Roxas took over the portfolio.

In Kyrgyzstan, following the resignation of the government, the parliament approved the new government with Zhantoro Satybaldiyev as prime minister, Erlan Abdyldayev as foreign minister and Olga Lavrova as finance minister; Taalaibek Omuraliyev remained defence minister and Zarylbek Rysaliyev interior minister.

Week Beginning 19 August 2012
In Belarus, Vladimir Makei was appointed foreign minister following the dismissal of Syarhey Martynau.

A national unity government formed in Mali included Tieman Coulibaly as foreign minister. Other key portfolios remained unchanged.

Russia joined the World Trade Organization.

Mauricio Cárdenas was named finance minister of Colombia.

In a minor cabinet reshuffle in the Gambia, Mamadou Tangara became foreign minister.

Week Beginning 12 August 2012
In a cabinet reshuffle in Panama, Rómulo Roux was appointed foreign minister.

In Myanmar, following the resignation of vice president Tin Aung Myint Oo, Nyan Tun was sworn in as his successor.

Sam Kutesa was reinstated as Uganda's foreign minister after stepping down 10 months earlier following allegations of corruption.

Danilo Medina Sánchez was sworn in as president of the Dominican Republic. Carlos Morales Troncoso continued as foreign minister and José Ramón Fadul as interior minister; Adm. Sigfrido Pared Pérez became defence minister and Simón Lizardo finance minister.

Week Beginning 5 August 2012
Kwesi Bekoe Amissah-Arthur was sworn in as vice president of Ghana.

In a cabinet reshuffle in Haiti, Pierre Richard Casimir was appointed foreign minister and Ronsard Saint-Cyr interior minister.

Mircea Dușa became the Romanian interior minister following the resignation of Ioan Rus. Titus Corlățean was named foreign minister.

In Syria, prime minister Riyad Hijab defected and fled to Jordan. The Syrian regime released a statement saying Hijab had been dismissed but no official explanation was offered. Wael al-Halki was sworn in as his successor.

In Timor-Leste, a new cabinet took office with José Luís Guterres as foreign minister and Cirilo José Cristóvão as defence and security minister; Emília Pires remained finance minister.

Libya's newly formed national assembly elected former opposition leader Mohamed Magariaf as the country's interim president. Magariaf won 113 votes in the 200-member General National Congress, with his opponent Ali Zeidan receiving 85 votes.

Norov Altankhuyag took office as prime minister of Mongolia. A week later numerous cabinet members were approved, including Luvsanvandan Bold as foreign minister, Dashdemberel Bat-Erdene as defence minister and Chultem Ulaan as finance minister.

Chronology of Events for July 2012

Week Beginning 29 July 2012
In a cabinet reshuffle in India, Palaniappan Chidambaram was appointed finance minister, while Sushil Kumar Shinde succeeded him as home affairs minister.

In Honduras, following the resignation of finance minister Héctor Guillén, Wilfredo Cerrato was appointed his successor.

In Egypt, Hisham Qandil's government was sworn in. Moumtaz Saïd continued as finance minister while Mohammed Kamel Amr was appointed foreign minister, Field Marshal Mohamed Hussein Tantawi defence minister and Ahmed Gamal Eddin interior minister. Ten days after later Mahmoud Mekki was appointed vice president and Abdel Fattah al-Sisi became defence minister after Tantawi was ordered to retire.

Week Beginning 22 July 2012

In Peru, following the resignation of the government of Óscar Valdés, Juan Jiménez was sworn in as prime minister. His cabinet included Pedro Cateriano Bellido as defence minister and Wilfredo Pedraza as interior minister.

Bujar Nishani took office as the president of Albania.

In Egypt, Hisham Qandil was named prime minister by president Mohamed Morsy.

In Ghana, president John Atta Mills died. He was succeeded by vice president John Dramani Mahama. Kwesi Bekoe Amissah-Arthur was named vice president a week later.

In Pakistan, Rehman Malik was sworn in as interior minister.

The Serbian parliament voted in a government headed by prime minister Ivica Dačić. Dačić continued as interior minister while Ivan Mrkić was appointed foreign minister, Aleksandar Vučić defence minister and Mladan Dinkić finance minister.

In Tunisia, finance minister Houcine Dimassi resigned. The secretary of state for finance, Slim Besbes, took over the portfolio.

Week Beginning 15 July 2012

Francisco Álvarez de Soto became acting foreign minister of Panama with Roberto Henríquez becoming minister of the presidency.

Parliamentary elections were held in Papua New Guinea between 23 June and 17 July 2012. Prime minister Peter O'Neill's People's National Congress won 27 of 111 seats; the Triumph Heritage Empowerment Party 12; PNG Party 8; the National Alliance Party 7; the United Resources Party 7; the People's Party 6; the People's Progress Party 6; and the Social Democratic Party 3. A number of smaller parties each took one or two seats, with 16 going to independents.

In Syria, defence minister Gen. Dawoud Rajha was killed in a bomb attack. Gen. Fahad Jassim al-Freij was sworn in as his successor.

Pranab Mukherjee was sworn in as the president of India following his victory in the indirect presidential elections. Mukherjee gained 713,763 votes while his opponent won 315,987.

Rajkeswur Purryag was elected president of Mauritius and sworn in the following day.

Week Beginning 8 July 2012

In Italy, Vittorio Grilli replaced Mario Monti as economy and finance minister.

In Togo, the government of Gilbert Houngbo resigned. Kwesi Ahoomey-Zunu took office as prime minister 8 days later. The cabinet subsequently named included Col. Yark Damehane as security and civil protection minister. Other key portfolios remained unchanged.

Week Beginning 1 July 2012

In China, Leung Chun-ying took office as chief executive of Hong Kong.

In Kuwait, following the resignation of the government, the Emir reappointed Sheikh Jaber Mubarak al-Hamad al-Sabah as prime minister. The new cabinet was announced 2 weeks later with Nayef al-Hajraf as finance minister. Other key portfolios remained unchanged.

In presidential elections in Mexico, Enrique Peña Nieto of the Institutional Revolutionary Party (PRI) won 39.1% of the vote, Andrés Manuel López Obrador of the Party of the Democratic Revolution (PRD) 32.4% and Josefina Vázquez Mota of the National Action Party (PAN) 26.0%. Turnout was 63.1%.

In parliamentary elections in Senegal, the United in Hope coalition won 119 of 150 seats and the Senegalese Democratic Party 12. Turnout was 36.8%.

Jim Yong Kim took office as the president of the World Bank.

Following the resignation of Montenegro's foreign minister Milan Rocen, Nebojša Kaluđerović was appointed to the post.

In a cabinet reshuffle in Albania, Edmond Panariti was appointed foreign minister and Flamur Noka interior minister.

In Georgia, parliament confirmed the new cabinet of prime minister Vano Merabishvili, including Dimitri Shashkin as defence minister and Bacho Akhalaia as interior minister. Other key portfolios remained unchanged.

Yannis Stournaras was sworn in as finance minister of Greece.

In Libya's parliamentary elections, the National Forces Alliance won 39 of 80 seats allocated to registered parties and the Justice and Construction Party 17; 120 of the 200 members were elected as independents.

In parliamentary elections in Timor-Leste, the National Congress for Timorese Reconstruction won 36.7% of the vote and 30 of 65 seats, the Revolutionary Front for an Independent East Timor 29.9% and 25 seats, the Democratic Party 10.3% and 8 seats, and the Front for National Reconstruction of Timor-Leste–Change 3.1% and 2 seats. Turnout was 74.8%.

Chronology of Events for June 2012

Week Beginning 24 June 2012

Following the resignation of Pranab Mukherjee, India's prime minister Manmohan Singh took over the finance portfolio.

In Serbia, president Tomislav Nikolić asked Ivica Dačić to form a government.

In presidential elections in Iceland incumbent Ólafur Ragnar Grímsson won 52.8% of the vote, Thóra Arnórsdóttir 32.2% and Ari Trausti Guðmundsson 8.6%.

Week Beginning 17 June 2012

After two rounds of parliamentary elections in France, the Socialist Party along with its allies won with a total of 331 seats, providing the new government with an absolute parliamentary majority. The Socialist Party (PS) won 280 of the 577 available seats; the Union for a Popular Movement (UMP), 194; Miscellaneous Left (DVG), 22; Europe Ecology–the Greens (EELV), 17; Miscellaneous Right (DVD), 15; Radical Party of the Left (PRG), 12; the New Centre (NC), 12; the Left Front (FDG), 10; the Radical Party (PRV), 6; and others, 9. After resigning (a traditional procedure following French legislative elections) Jean-Marc Ayrault was reappointed prime minister with no changes in the key cabinet posts.

In a presidential run-off in Egypt, Mohamed Morsy won 51.7% of the vote and Ahmed Shafik 48.3%. The following week prime minister Kamal Ganzouri and his cabinet resigned. Morsy was sworn in as president 5 days later.

In parliamentary elections in Greece, New Democracy won 129 seats with 29.7% of the vote; Syriza (Coalition of the Radical Left), 71 (26.9%); Pasok (Panhellenic Socialist Movement), 33 (12.3%); Independent Greeks, 20 (7.5%); Golden Dawn, 18 (6.9%); Democratic Left, 17 (6.3%); and the Communist Party, 12 (4.5%). Antonis Samaras was sworn in as prime minister 3 days later. His cabinet included Dimitris Avramopoulos as foreign minister, Panos Panagiotopoulos as defence minister, Evripidis Stylianidis as interior minister and Vassilis Rapanos as finance minister. Owing to ill health Rapanos failed to take office and was replaced by Yannis Stournaras.

In the USA, commerce secretary John Bryson resigned. Rebecca M. Blank, who had previously taken over when Bryson took a medical leave of absence, continued as acting secretary.

In Nigeria, defence minister Bello Mohammed was dismissed.

In a cabinet reshuffle in Trinidad and Tobago, Winston Dookeran was appointed foreign minister, Larry Howai finance minister and Jack Warner national security minister.

Week Beginning 10 June 2012

In Kenya, interior minister George Saitoti was killed in a plane crash.

Nauru's president Sprent Dabwido appointed a new cabinet that included Kieren Keke as foreign minister and Roland Kun as finance minister.

Albania's parliament elected Bujar Nishani president in a fourth round after previous votes had failed to result in the required three-fifths majority.

In a cabinet reshuffle in South Africa, Nosiviwe Mapisa-Nqakula was appointed defence minister.

Prince Ahmed bin Abdulaziz Al-Saud was appointed Saudi Arabia's new interior minister after the death of Crown Prince Nayef.

Rubén Candia Amarilla was sworn in as Paraguay's new interior minister following the resignation of Carlos Filizzola. In an impeachment trial held 6 days later, the Senate voted to remove president Fernando Lugo by 39 votes to 4. Vice president Frederic Franco was sworn in as president. The new cabinet included Carmelo Caballero as interior minister, José Félix Fernández Estigarribia as foreign minister and María Liz Arnold as defence minister.

Week Beginning 3 June 2012

In a cabinet reshuffle in Japan, Satoshi Morimoto became defence minister.

In Pakistan, the Supreme Court suspended interior minister Rehman Malik's Senate membership. He was reappointed as adviser on interior affairs the following day. Two weeks later, the Supreme Court disqualified prime minister Yousaf Raza Gilani from office. President Asif Ali Zardari nominated Makhdoom Shahabuddin as prime minister but replaced him with Raja Pervez after a judge ordered Shahabuddin's arrest. Ashraf was elected in parliament with 211 votes. The interior portfolio was left vacant in the new cabinet. Other key portfolios remained unchanged.

In Malta, prime minister Lawrence Gonzi won a confidence vote in parliament by 35 votes to 34.

In Syria, Riyad Hijab was sworn in as prime minister. Key portfolios in the new cabinet, sworn in 3 weeks later, remained unchanged.

Tom Motsoahae Thabane was sworn in as Lesotho's prime minister, also taking the defence portfolio. Leketekete Ketso was appointed finance minister and Joang Molapo home affairs minister.

Chronology of Events for May 2012

Week Beginning 27 May 2012
In Barbados, Elliot Belgrave took office as governor-general.

Tigran Sargsyan was reappointed prime minister of Armenia with no changes in the main cabinet posts.

In the Central African Republic, finance minister Sylvain Ndoutingaï was replaced by Albert Besse.

Syed Naveed Qamar was appointed defence minister of Pakistan.

Week Beginning 20 May 2012
In presidential elections in the Dominican Republic, Danilo Medina Sánchez of the ruling Dominican Liberation Party won 51.2% of the votes and Hipólito Mejía of the Dominican Revolutionary Party 47.0%.

Taur Matan Ruak was sworn in as Timor-Leste's new president.

Following the resignation of Ignacio Milam Tang's government, Vincenté Ehaté Tomi was named Equatorial Guinea's new prime minister. Agapito Mba Mokuy was appointed foreign minister and Marcelino Owono Edu finance minister.

In the first round of presidential elections in Egypt, Mohamed Morsy (Freedom and Justice Party) came first with 24.8% of the vote, followed by Ahmed Shafik (ind.) with 23.7%, Hamdeen Sabahi (Dignity Party) 20.7%, Abdel Moneim Aboul Fotouh (ind.) 17.5% and Amr Moussa (ind.) 11.1%. There were eight other candidates.

In parliamentary elections in Lesotho, the Democratic Congress won 48 of 120 seats, All Basotho Convention 30 and Lesotho Congress for Democracy 26. Prime minister Pakalitha Mosisili resigned 4 days later.

Week Beginning 13 May 2012
In Estonia, Urmas Reinsalu was sworn in as defence minister after the resignation of Mart Laar.

Following the resignation of Peru's interior minister Daniel Lozada and defence minister Alberto Otárola, Wilver Calle was named interior minister and José Urquizo defence minister.

In Grenada, prime minister Tillman Thomas and his government defeated a no-confidence motion by 8 votes to 5. Two days later foreign minister Karl Hood resigned and the prime minister took over the portfolio.

In Slovakia, prime minister Robert Fico's government won a confidence vote in parliament winning 82 votes.

In Haiti, Laurent Lamothe's new cabinet took office. Jean Rodolphe Joazile became defence minister and Marie-Carmelle Jean Marie finance minister.

Week Beginning 6 May 2012
In parliamentary elections in Armenia, the Republican Party of Armenia won 69 of 131 seats with 44.1% of votes cast; Prosperous Armenia 36 with 30.2%; Armenian National Congress 7 with 7.1%; Armenian Revolutionary Federation 6 with 5.7%; and Rule of Law 6 with 5.5%. Tigran Sargsyan was reappointed prime minister 4 weeks later.

In the presidential run-off in France, François Hollande was elected president with 51.6% of votes cast against 48.4% for Nicolas Sarkozy. Hollande was sworn in 9 days later and named Jean-Marc Ayrault as prime minister. The government, sworn in the following day, included Laurent Fabius as foreign minister, Jean-Yves Le Drian as defence minister, Manuel Valls as interior minister and Pierre Moscovici as finance minister.

In parliamentary elections in Greece, New Democracy won 108 of 300 seats with 18.9% of votes cast; Coalition of the Radical Left 52 with 16.8%; Pasok (Panhellenic Socialist Movement) 41 with 13.2%; Independent Greeks, 33 with 10.6%; Communist Party 26 with 8.5%; Golden Dawn 21 with 7.0%; and Democratic Left 19 with 6.1%. The leaders of New

Democracy, Coalition of the Radical Left and Pasok were each unable to agree on terms for setting up a government. The president's efforts to form a national unity government also failed and new elections were scheduled for June. Panagiotis Pikrammenos was sworn in as interim prime minister, leading a government that included Petros Molyviatis as foreign minister, Frangoulis Frangos as defence minister, Antonios Manitakis as interior minister and Georgios Zanias as finance minister.

In presidential elections in Serbia, Boris Tadić gained 25.3% of the vote, followed by Tomislav Nikolić with 25.0%, Ivica Dačić with 14.2% and Vojislav Koštunica with 7.4%. There were eight other candidates. In the run-off held 2 weeks later, Nikolić won with 49.5% of the vote against 47.3% for Tadić. Nikolić took office as president at the end of May.

In parliamentary elections in the Bahamas, the Progressive Liberal Party won 48.6% of votes cast and 29 out of 38 seats against the ruling Free National Movement with 42.1% and 9 seats. The following day, Perry Christie was sworn in as prime minister and finance minister. Bernard Nottage was later sworn in as national security minister with Frederick Mitchell as foreign minister.

Vladimir Putin was inaugurated as Russia's president. He nominated Dmitry Medvedev as prime minister. The new government, named 3 weeks later, included Vladimir Kolokoltsev as interior minister. Other key portfolios remained unchanged.

In the Democratic Republic of the Congo, prime minister Augustin Matata Ponyo's government won an investiture vote in parliament (324–53).

In parliamentary elections in Algeria, the Front de Libération Nationale/National Liberation Front won 208 out of 462 seats; Rassemblement National Démocratique/National Rally for Democracy took 68 seats; the Green Algeria Alliance, 49; Front des Forces Socialistes/Front of Socialist Forces, 27; and Parti des Travailleurs/Workers' Party, 24. Independents gained 18 seats and the remainder went to minor parties.

János Áder took office as Hungary's president.

In Guinea-Bissau, Manuel Serifo Nhamadjo accepted nomination as transitional president for 1 year. Five days later, he named Rui Duarte Barros as prime minister. The new government, appointed the following week, included Faustino Fudut Imbali as foreign minister, Col. Celestino Carvalho as defence minister, Antonio Suca Intchama as interior minister and Abubacar Demba Dahaba as finance minister.

Chronology of Events for April 2012

Week Beginning 29 April 2012
In a cabinet reshuffle in Tanzania, Shamsi Vuai Nahodha was named defence minister, William Mgimwa finance minister and Emmanuel John Nchimbi home affairs minister.

In the second round of parliamentary elections in Iran, with 65 of the 290 seats being contested, President Mahmoud Ahmadinejad's opponents won 41 seats and his supporters 13. 11 seats went to independents.

Week Beginning 22 April 2012
In the first round of French presidential elections, François Hollande gained the largest number of votes (28.63% of those cast) against nine opponents. His nearest rivals were the incumbent president Nicolas Sarkozy, who came second with 27.18% of votes cast, and Marine Le Pen, with 17.90%.

In a cabinet reshuffle in Ecuador, Miguel Carvajal was appointed defence minister.

In the Netherlands, prime minister Mark Rutte's government resigned.

With the resignation of Awn Khasawneh as Jordan's prime minister, King Abdullah II designated Fayez Tarawneh to form a government. In the new cabinet sworn in the following week, Tarawneh also assumed the defence portfolio. Ghabib Al Zu'bi was appointed interior minister and Suleiman Al Hafez finance minister.

In the Czech Republic, prime minister Petr Nečas' government won a confidence vote in parliament (105–93).

In Romania, Mihai-Răzvan Ungureanu's government was defeated in a no-confidence vote which was supported by 235 of the 460 members of parliament. President Traian Băsescu designated Victor Ponta as prime minister. A week later parliament approved Ponta's government, which included Andrei Marga as foreign minister, Gen. Corneliu Dobrițoiu as defence minister, Ioan Rus as interior minister and Florin Georgescu as finance minister.

Week Beginning 15 April 2012

In the presidential run-off in Timor Leste, Taur Matan Ruak was elected president with 61.2% of the vote against 38.8% for Francisco Guterres.

In a cabinet reshuffle in the Gambia, Mambury Njie became foreign minister, Lamin Kaba Bajo interior minister and Abdou Kolley finance minister.

Jim Yong Kim was named president of the World Bank, to take office on 1 July.

Augustin Matata Ponyo was appointed prime minister of the Democratic Republic of the Congo. His government was named 10 days later and included Raymond Tshibanda as foreign minister and Alexandre Lubal Tamu as defence minister.

In Sweden, Karin Enström was appointed defence minister.

In a cabinet reshuffle in Tonga, Lisiate 'Aloveita 'Akolo was named finance minister.

Week Beginning 8 April 2012

In a cabinet reshuffle in Benin, president Yayi Boni took charge of the defence portfolio and Jonas Gbian was appointed finance minister.

In Haiti, the Senate endorsed the nomination of Laurent Lamothe as prime minister by 19 votes to three. Three weeks later, the Chamber of Deputies also approved Lamothe as prime minister with 62 votes to three against.

In North Korea, Kim Jong-gak was appointed defence minister. Kim Jong-un was elected First Secretary of the Workers' Party of Korea and was also named First Chairman of the National Defence Commission 2 days later.

In parliamentary elections in South Korea, the Saenuri Party won 152 out of 300 seats with 42.8% of votes cast; the Democratic United Party 127 with 36.5%; the Unified Progressive Party 13 with 10.3%; and the Liberty Forward Party 5 with 3.2%. Three seats went to independents.

Following the coup a month earlier in Mali, Dioncounda Traoré was sworn in as president. Cheick Modibo Diarra was subsequently appointed acting prime minister. The new government, announced a week later, included Sadio Lamine Sow as foreign minister, Col. Yamoussa Camara as defence minister, Col. Moussa Sinko Coulibaly as territorial administration (interior) minister and Tiéna Coulibaly as finance minister.

Guinea-Bissau's interim president Raimundo Pereira was deposed in a military coup and the presidential run-off was aborted. The following week, Manuel Serifo Nhamadjo was named transitional president but he refused the nomination.

In Lithuania, Artūras Melianas was appointed interior minister.

Week Beginning 1 April 2012

In San Marino, Maurizio Rattini and Italo Righi were sworn in as captains regent.

Fernando Herrero resigned as Costa Rica's finance minister. Two weeks later, Edgar Ayales was appointed to the post.

Following the resignation of Pál Schmitt, the president of the National Assembly, László Kövér, became Hungary's acting president. János Áder was elected president a month later by 262 votes to 40.

In a cabinet reshuffle in New Zealand, Chris Tremain was appointed internal affairs minister.

Jules Baillet became finance minister in a cabinet reshuffle in Niger.

In Senegal, Macky Sall was sworn in as president. Abdoul Mbaye was appointed prime minister and the new government included Alioune Badara Cissé as foreign minister, Augustin Tine as defence minister, Mbaye Ndiaye as interior minister and Amadou Kane as finance minister.

With the resignation of Boris Tadić, speaker of parliament Slavica Đukić Dejanović became Serbia's acting president.

In Slovakia, Robert Fico was appointed prime minister. His government included Miroslav Lajčák as foreign minister, Martin Glváč as defence minister, Robert Kaliňák as interior minister and Peter Kažimír as finance minister.

Following the death of Bingu wa Mutharika, Malaŵi's vice president Joyce Banda took over as president. A week later Khumbo Hastings Kachali was appointed vice president. The new cabinet included Ephraim Mganda Chiume as foreign minister, Ken Kandodo as defence minister and Uladi Mussa as home affairs minister.

Chronology of Events for March 2012

Week Beginning 25 March 2012

In a presidential run-off in Senegal, Macky Sall won 65.8% of the vote and incumbent Abdoulaye Wade 34.2%.

In a cabinet reshuffle in Kenya, Sam Ongeri was appointed foreign minister and Njeru Githae finance minister.

In parliamentary elections in the Gambia, the Alliance for Patriotic Reorientation and Construction won 43 seats, the National Reconciliation Party 1 and independents 4.

With the resignation of Sten Tolfors, infrastructure minister Catharina Elmsäter-Svärd took over Sweden's defence portfolio on an acting basis.

Following the resignation of Sir Anerood Jugnauth, vice president Monqiue Ohsan-Bellepeau became acting president of Mauritius.

Week Beginning 18 March 2012

In Germany, Joachim Gauck was elected Federal President by the Federal Convention with 991 votes, against 126 for Beate Klarsfeld and 108 abstentions.

In the first round of presidential elections in Guinea-Bissau former prime minister Carlos Gomes Júnior took 49.0% of votes cast, ahead of former president Mohamed Ialá Embaló with 23.4%, Manuel Serifo Nhamadjo with 15.7% and former interim president Henrique Roas with 5.4%.

Filippos Sachinidis was appointed Greece's finance minister after the resignation of Evangelos Venizelos.

Lithuania's interior minister Raimundas Palaitis resigned. Health minister Raimondas Šukys took over the portfolio on a temporary basis.

Mali's president Amadou Toumani Touré was ousted in a military coup, with Capt. Amadou Haya Sanogo proclaiming himself chairman of the National Committee for the Restoration of Democracy and State.

Week Beginning 11 March 2012

With the resignation of Côte d'Ivoire's prime minister Guillaume Soro, president Alassane Ouattara took over the defence portfolio and appointed Jeannot Ahoussou-Kouadio as prime minister.

In Montenegro, parliament elected Milica Pejanović Đurišić as defence minister.

In Cyprus, following the resignation of Kikis Kazamias as finance minister, a cabinet reshuffle led to Vassos Shiarly becoming finance minister and Eleni Mavrou interior minister.

Nicolae Timofti was elected Moldova's president with 62 votes in the 101-seat parliament, bringing an end to nearly 3 years of political deadlock.

Week Beginning 4 March 2012

In presidential elections in Russia, prime minister Vladimir Putin won 63.6% of the votes cast. Gennady Zyuganov took 17.2% of the vote, Mikhail Prokhorov 7.9%, Vladimir Zhirinovsky 6.2% and Sergey Mironov 3.9%. 'Procedural irregularities' were reported and the Communist Party of the Russian Federation refused to recognize the result.

In the Maldives, Abdul Samad Abdulla was appointed foreign minister and Abdulla Jihad finance minister.

Following the resignation of the Democratic Republic of the Congo's prime minister Adolphe Muzito, deputy prime minister Louis-Alphonse Koyagialo Ngbase te Gerengbo was named acting prime minister.

In parliamentary elections in Belize, the United Democratic Party won 17 of 31 seats with 50.4% of votes cast and the People's United Party 14 with 47.5%. Five days later the new cabinet was named with John Saldivar as defence minister.

In Bosnia and Herzegovina, Bakir Izetbegović took over the rotating presidency.

In parliamentary elections in Slovakia, Direction–Social Democracy won 83 seats with 44.4% of votes cast, ahead of the Christian Democratic Movement 8.8% (16 seats), Ordinary People and Independent Personalities 8.6% (16), Most–Híd 6.9% (13), the Slovak Democratic and Christian Union–Democratic Party 6.1% (11) and Freedom and Solidarity 5.9% (11).

Chronology of Events for February 2012

Week Beginning 26 February 2012

In presidential elections in Senegal, incumbent Abdoulaye Wade won 34.8% of the vote, ahead of former prime minister Macky Sall with 26.6%,

Moustapha Niasse with 13.2% and Ousmane Tanor Dieng with 11.3%. A run-off was scheduled for 18 March.

In Papua New Guinea, prime minister Peter O'Neill doubled as finance minister after sacking Don Polye.

In the Solomon Islands, national security minister Clay Forau replaced former foreign affairs minister Peter Shanel who had been sacked by the prime minister earlier in the month. David Tome was sworn in as national security minister 2 days later.

In Trinidad and Tobago, a parliamentary no-confidence motion against prime minister Kamla Persad-Bissessar was defeated by 29 votes to 11.

Week Beginning 19 February 2012

In presidential elections in Yemen, the sole candidate, vice president Abdo Rabu Mansour al-Hadi, won 99.8% of the vote.

Following the resignation of Australian foreign minister Kevin Rudd, trade minister Craig Emerson took over the portfolio on an interim basis.

In Haiti, prime minister Garry Conille resigned. Foreign minister Laurent Lamothe was designated prime minister a week later.

Week Beginning 12 February 2012

In presidential elections in Turkmenistan, incumbent Gurbanguly Berdymukhammedov was re-elected with 97.0% of the vote, against Yarmukhammet Orazgulyev with 1.2%.

In Gabon, prime minister Paul Biyoghé Mba resigned. Two weeks later, president Ali-Ben Bongo Ondimba appointed Raymond Ndong Sima as prime minister. The new government included Emmanuel Issozé Ngondet as foreign minister and Christiane Rose Ossoucah Raponda as budget minister. Rufin Pacôme Ondzounga remained defence minister and Jean François Ndongou interior minister.

In Honduras, Héctor Guillén became finance minister, replacing William Chong Wong, who resigned a day earlier.

In Kuwait, Sheikh Jaber Mubarak al-Hamad al-Sabah's new cabinet was announced with Sheikh Ahmad Khaled al-Sabah as defence minister. Other key ministries remained unchanged.

With the resignation of Christian Wulff, the president of the Bundesrat, Horst Seehofer, became Germany's acting president.

Week Beginning 5 February 2012

In a presidential run-off in Finland, Sauli Niinistö won 62.6% of the vote against 37.4% for Pekka Haavisto. Niinistö took office 3 weeks later.

In Romania, following the resignation of Emil Boc, justice minister Catalin Predoui was appointed interim prime minister. President Traian Băsescu then nominated Mihai-Răzvan Ungureanu as the new prime minister. Three days later, Ungureanu's cabinet, which included Bogdan Alexandru Drăgoi as finance minister and Gabriel Berca as interior minister, was sworn in.

Following the resignation of Mohamed Nasheed, vice president Mohamed Waheed Hassan Manik was sworn in as the president of the Maldives. He appointed Mohamed Nazim as defence minister and Mohamed Jameel Ahmed as home affairs minister. The following week, Mohamed Waheed Deen was nominated vice president.

In Burundi, Tabu Abdallah Manirakisa was appointed finance minister.

Ukraine's president, Viktor Yanukovych, sacked defence minister Mykhailo Yezhel replacing him with Dmytro Salamatin.

In Bosnia and Herzegovina, prime minister Vjekoslav Bevanda's government was confirmed in parliament by 26 votes to seven. It included Zlatko Lagumdžija as foreign minister, Muhamed Ibrahimović as defence minister and Nikola Špirić as finance minister.

In Guinea-Bissau, following the resignation of prime minister Carlos Gomes Júnior to stand as a presidential candidate, Maria Adiatú Djaló Nandingna was appointed acting prime minister.

In Slovenia, parliament confirmed and swore in prime minister Janez Janša's cabinet. It included Karl Erjavec as foreign minister, Aleš Hojs as defence minister, Janez Šušteršič as finance minister and Vinko Gorenak as interior minister.

Chronology of Events for January 2012

Week Beginning 29 January 2012

Yayi Boni, president of Benin, became the chairman of the African Union for 2012.

In parliamentary elections in Kuwait, 34 of the 50 available seats were won by opposition parties. The Sunni Islamic Bloc and the Popular Action Bloc both gained 13 seats, the Shias 7 and the Pro-government Sunnis 5. Three days later prime minister Sheikh Jaber Mubarak al-Hamad al-Sabah resigned but was asked to form a new cabinet the following day.

Week Beginning 22 January 2012

Rosen Plevneliev took office as Bulgaria's president.

In the first round of presidential elections in Finland, Sauli Niinistö of the National Coalition Party came first with 37.0% of the vote, followed by Pekka Haavisto (Green League) with 18.8%, Paavo Väyrynen (Centre Party) 17.5% and Timo Soini (True Finns) 9.4%.

In a cabinet reshuffle in Thailand, Sukumpol Suwanatat became defence minister and Kittirat Na Ranong finance minister.

Cristian Diaconescu was sworn in as Romania's foreign minister after the dismissal of Teodor Baconschi.

In a cabinet reshuffle in Ghana, interior minister Benjamin Kunbour was named justice minister with William Kwesi Aboah replacing him.

Following Uhuru Kenyatta's resignation, Njeru Githae was appointed Kenya's acting finance minister.

Week Beginning 15 January 2012

In parliamentary elections in Kazakhstan, president Nursultan Nazarbayev's Nur Otan (Light of the Fatherland) Party took 83 of the 98 seats with 81.0% of votes cast, the Democratic Party of Kazakhstan Ak Zhol (Bright Path) 8 with 7.5% and the Communist People's Party of Kazakhstan 7 with 7.2%. There were widespread allegations that the elections were fraudulent and failed to meet international standards.

Following Fedir Yaroshenko's resignation, Valeriy Khoroshkovsky became Ukraine's finance minister.

Week Beginning 8 January 2012

Following the death of Malam Bacai Sanhá, Raimundo Pereira became acting president of Guinea-Bissau.

After all six rounds of parliamentary elections in Egypt, the Democratic Alliance of Egypt won 235 of 498 elected seats (including 213 for the Freedom and Justice Party), taking 37.5% of the vote; the Islamist Bloc 123 seats (including 107 for the Al-Nour Party), taking 27.8%; the New Wafd Party 38 (9.2%); and the Egyptian Bloc 34 (8.9%).

Moldova's Constitutional Court ruled the Dec. presidential election invalid owing to violations of secret voting procedures.

In a cabinet reshuffle in Zambia, Given Lubinda was appointed foreign minister.

Naoki Tanaka was appointed Japan's defence minister in a cabinet reshuffle.

In presidential elections in Kiribati, Anote Tong was re-elected president with 42.2% of the vote, defeating Tetaua Taitai who took 35.0% and Rimeta Beniamina with 22.8%. The following week Tong and his cabinet were sworn in with Tong doubling as foreign minister, Teima Onorio as internal affairs minister and Tom Murdoch as finance minister.

Otto Pérez Molina, a former army general, was sworn in as Guatemala's president. His cabinet included Harold Caballeros as foreign minister, Col. Ulises Noé Anzueto as defence minister, Pavel Centeno as finance minister and Mauricio López Bonilla as interior minister.

In presidential elections in Taiwan, Ma Ying-jeou (Nationalist Party/ Kuomintang) won 51.6% of the vote and Tsai Ing-wen (Democratic Progressive Party) 45.6%. In elections to the Legislative Yuan held the same day, the Nationalist Party won 64 seats with 44.5% of votes cast; the Democratic Progressive Party, 40 seats (34.6%); the Taiwan Solidarity Union, 3 seats (9.0%); and the People First Party, 3 seats (5.5%).

Week Beginning 1 January 2012

In Switzerland, Eveline Widmer-Schlumpf was sworn in as president, Didier Burkhalter as foreign minister and Alain Berset as interior minister with Ueli Maurer remaining as defence minister.

In an indirect presidential election in the Marshall Islands, Christopher Loeak won with 21 votes against 11 for incumbent Jurelang Zedkaia. A week later Loeak and his cabinet took office, including Philip Muller as foreign minister, Dennis Momotaro as finance minister and Wilbur Heine as internal affairs minister.

In Morocco, prime minister Abdelilah Benkirane's cabinet was announced with Saad-Eddine El Othmani as foreign minister, Mohand Laenser as interior minister and Nizar Baraka as finance minister.

Ramazon Rahimov was appointed Tajikistan's interior minister.

In Bosnia and Herzegovina, Vjekoslav Bevanda was designated prime minister and, a week later, was confirmed by parliament by 31 votes to two.

Jamaica's new prime minister, Portia Simpson-Miller, was sworn in. Her cabinet included Arnold Nicholson as foreign minister and Peter Phillips as finance minister.

In Slovenia, Zoran Janković was designated prime minister. His appointment was rejected by parliament and 2 weeks later Janez Janša, a former prime minister, was nominated. Parliament endorsed him with 51 votes to 39.

2011

Chronology of Events for December 2011

Week Beginning 25 December 2011
In parliamentary elections in Jamaica, the opposition People's National Party took 42 of the 63 seats with 53.3% of votes cast and the Jamaica Labour Party 21 with 46.6%.

In a cabinet reshuffle in Iceland, Oddný Harðardóttir was appointed finance minister.

Week Beginning 18 December 2011
Following his election in the Spanish parliament by 187 votes to 149, Mariano Rajoy Brey was sworn in as prime minister. His cabinet included José Manuel García Margallo as foreign minister, Pedro Morenés Eulate as defence minister, Jorge Fernández Díaz as interior minister and Cristóbal Montoro Romero as finance minister.

In Kyrgyzstan, parliament elected Omurbek Babanov as prime minister with 113 votes for and two against. Akylbek Japarov became finance minister and Taalaibek Omuraliev was appointed defence minister.

Week Beginning 11 December 2011
A new government, including Pierre Moukoko Mbonjo as foreign minister and Alamine Ousmane Mey as finance minister, took office in Cameroon.

Following the resignation of Salomón Lerner, interior minister Óscar Valdés Dancuart was sworn in as Peru's new prime minister. His cabinet included Daniel Lozada as interior minister and Alberto Otárola as defence minister.

In New Zealand, prime minister John Key's new cabinet was sworn in with Jonathan Coleman as defence minister and Amy Adams as internal affairs minister. Murray McCully remained foreign minister and Bill English finance minister.

In Papua New Guinea, the Supreme Court ordered the reinstatement of Sir Michael Somare as prime minister after ruling the parliamentary declaration of a vacancy of prime minister 4 months earlier and subsequent election of Peter O'Neill illegal. Somare and a new cabinet were sworn in by the governor-general, Sir Michael Ogio. However, O'Neill refused to step down and his faction in parliament voted to suspend Ogio, making Jeffrey Nape acting governor-general. A few days later, Ogio was reinstated after announcing he had been wrong to swear in Somare's cabinet and instead backed O'Neill as legitimate prime minister.

Moncef Marzouki was sworn in as Tunisia's president having received 155 votes with three against in the Constituent Assembly. Hamadi Jebali formed a new government, which was approved by the Constituent Assembly 11 days later. Rafik Abdessalem was appointed foreign minister, Ali Laaridh interior minister and Houcine Dimassi finance minister.

In Malaysia, Tuanku Abdul Halim Muadzam Shah ibni Al-Marhum Sultan Badlishah took office as head of state.

At an election held in Switzerland's United Federal Assembly, Eveline Widmer-Schlumpf was elected president for 2012 and Ueli Maurer vice-president.

In Moldova, parliament was unable to elect a president with Marian Lupu winning 58 votes, three short of the 61 required.

In the Netherlands, Liesbeth Spies was appointed interior minister.

Anton Siluanov was appointed Russia's finance minister.

In parliamentary elections in Gabon, the Gabonese Democratic Party won 114 of 120 seats, the Rally for Gabon took three, and the Circle of Liberal Reformers, the Social Democratic Party and the Union for the New Republic one seat each.

In North Korea, president, supreme commander of the armed forces and chairman of the national defence commission, Kim Jong-il, died.

Week Beginning 4 December 2011
In parliamentary elections in Croatia, the Kukuriku coalition (comprising the Social Democratic Party, Croatian People's Party–Liberal Democrats, Istrian Democratic Assembly and Croatian Party of Pensioners) won 81 seats (40.0% of the vote), the ruling Croatian Democratic Union 47 (23.5%), the Croatian Labourists–Labour Party 6 (5.1%) and the Croatian Democratic Alliance of Slavonija and Baranja 6 (2.9%). A new cabinet with Zoran Milanović as prime minister, Vesna Pusić as foreign minister, Ante Kotromanović as defense minister, Ranko Ostojić as interior minister and Slavko Linić as finance minister was approved by parliament 3 weeks later.

In Kuwait, Sheikh Jaber Mubarak al-Hamad al-Sabah was sworn in as prime minister. His cabinet included Sheikh Ahmad Al-Humoud Al-Jaber Al-Sabah as interior and defence minister.

In Russia's parliamentary elections, United Russia won 238 seats with 49.5% of the vote, the Communist Party of the Russian Federation 92 seats with 19.2%, A Just Russia 64 with 13.2% and the Liberal Democratic Party 56 with 11.7%. There were reports of election fraud, leading to major protests.

In parliamentary elections in Slovenia, the Positive Slovenia party won 28 seats with 28.5% of votes cast, ahead of the Slovenian Democratic Party 26 with 26.2%, the Social Democrats 10 with 10.5% and Gregor Virant's Civic List 8 with 8.4%.

After 541 days without a government, a new administration took office in Belgium with Elio Di Rupo as prime minister, Didier Reynders as foreign minister, Steven Vanackere as finance minister and Jöelle Milquet as interior minister. Four days later the cabinet won a vote of confidence in the Chamber of Representatives (89–54).

St Lucia's new government headed by prime minister Kenny Anthony was sworn in, with Alva Baptiste as foreign minister and Victor Phillip La Corbiniere as home affairs and national security minister.

In Egypt, prime minister Kamal el-Ganzouri and his cabinet took office. Mohammed Ibrahim Youssef was appointed interior minister and Moumtaz Saïd finance minister.

Yemen's new prime minister, Mohammed Basindawa, and his cabinet were sworn in, including Abdelqader Qahtan as interior minister and Sakhr Ahmed Abbas as finance minister.

In Argentina, Juan Manuel Abal Medina was sworn in as cabinet chief and Hernán Lorenzino became economy minister.

Chronology of Events for November 2011

Week Beginning 27 November 2011
Mohammed Basindawa was appointed Yemen's prime minister.

In presidential elections in the Democratic Republic of the Congo, incumbent Joseph Kabila received 49.0% of votes cast and Étienne Tshisekedi 32.3%. Owing to a change in election laws, a potential run-off to be held in Feb. 2012 was shelved. Elections were held under difficult conditions, with incidents of violence. Tshisekedi rejected the result and declared himself president raising fears of civil unrest.

In Guyana's presidential election, Donald Ramotar of the People's Progressive Party/Civic (PPP/C) received 166,340 votes (48.6% of the vote), with David A. Granger of A Partnership for National Unity receiving 139,678 (40.8%) and Khemraj Ramjattan of Alliance for Change 35,333 (10.3%). The PPP/C won 32 seats in the parliamentary election, followed by A Partnership for National Unity 26 and Alliance for Change 7. Ramotar was sworn in as president. Key posts within the new cabinet remained unchanged.

In parliamentary elections in St Lucia, the opposition St Lucia Labour Party won 11 seats with 51% of votes cast against six for the United Workers' Party (47%). Kenny Anthony was sworn in as prime minister.

Following the resignation of Sheikh Nasser Muhammad al-Ahmad al-Sabah's government, Sheikh Jaber Mubarak al-Hamad al-Sabah was appointed prime minister of Kuwait.

Week Beginning 20 November 2011
In parliamentary elections in Spain, the Popular Party (PP) won 186 seats with 44.6% of votes cast, ahead of the Spanish Socialist Workers' Party (PSOE) with 110 and 28.7%, Convergence and Union (CiU; Catalan nationalists) with 16 and 4.2%, and the Communist-led United Left (IU) with 11 and 6.9%.

In Belgium, King Albert II rejected Elio Di Rupo's request to relieve him of the task of forming a Belgian government.

In Egypt, prime minister Essam Sharaf resigned. Three days later, Kamal el-Ganzouri was tasked with forming a new government.

José Atilio Benítez Parada was sworn in as El Salvador's new defence minister.

Róbert Ondrejscák became Slovakia's acting defence minister after the dismissal of Lubomír Galko. Five days later prime minister Iveta Radičová took over the portfolio.

In Tunisia, interim president Foued Mebazaa accepted prime minister Béji Caïd Essebsi's resignation.

In presidential elections in the Gambia, president Yahya Jammeh (Alliance for Patriotic Reorientation and Construction) was re-elected with 71.5% of the vote, against 17.4% for Ousainou Darboe (United Democratic Party) and 11.1% for Hamat Bah (ind.).

In Libya, prime minister Abdurrahim al-Keib's new government was sworn in with Ashur bin Khayyal as foreign minister, Osama Juili as defence minister, Hassan Zoglem as finance minister and Fawzi Abdelali as interior minister.

In parliamentary elections in Morocco, the opposition Islamist Parti de la Justice et du Développement (PJD/Party of Justice and Development) gained 107 seats of 395 seats, ahead of Parti de l'Indépendance/Istiqlal (PI/Independence Party) with 60, Rassemblement National des Indépendants (RNI/National Rally of Independents) with 52 and Parti Authenticité et Modernité (PAM/Authenticity and Modernity Party) with 47. Four days later, Abdelilah Benkirane was sworn in as prime minister.

In New Zealand's parliamentary elections, the ruling National Party won 60 seats with 48.0% of the vote, ahead of the Labour Party with 34 and 27.1%, the Green Party with 13 and 10.6%, and New Zealand First with 8 and 6.8%.

Week Beginning 13 November 2011

In Kyrgyzstan, Almazbek Atambayev resumed his duties as prime minister following his victory in the presidential election. He was sworn in as president just over 2 weeks later.

With the resignation of Danny Philip, Gordon Darcy Lilo was elected prime minister of the Solomon islands, defeating Milner Tozaka by 29 votes to 20. His new cabinet included Rick Hou as finance minister, Peter Shanel as foreign minister and Manasseh Maelanga as home affairs minister.

Following Silvio Berlusconi's resignation, Mario Monti, an economist, was sworn in as Italy's new prime minister. His cabinet included himself as economy and finance minister, Giulio Terzi Sant'Agata as foreign minister, Giampaolo Di Paola as defence minister and Anna Maria Cancellieri as interior minister. The new government won votes of confidence in the Senate (281–25) and in the Chamber of Deputies (556–61).

In Moldova, the scheduled presidential election was postponed after the registration deadline expired with no candidates.

In Poland, prime minister Donald Tusk formed a new government that included Jacek Cichoki as interior minister. Other key portfolios remained unchanged.

Week Beginning 6 November 2011

In Saudi Arabia, Prince Salman bin Abdulaziz Al-Saud was sworn in as defence minister.

In a presidential run-off in Guatemala, Otto Pérez Molina won 53.7% of the vote and Manuel Baldizón 46.3%.

In Nicaragua's presidential elections, incumbent José Daniel Ortega Saavedra of the Sandinista National Liberation Front (FSLN) was elected with 62.5% of votes cast, defeating Fabio Gadea Mantilla (31.0%) and Arnoldo Alemán (5.9%).

In a cabinet reshuffle in Burundi, Laurent Kavakure was appointed foreign minister and Gabriel Nizigama public security minister.

With Anatoliy Mohylyov's appointment as prime minister of Crimea, Vitaliy Zakharchenko became Ukraine's interior minister.

In a presidential run-off in Liberia, Winston Tubman called on his supporters to boycott the poll and Ellen Johnson-Sirleaf gained 90.7% of the vote.

Following the resignation of Marcus Stephen as Nauru's president, Frederick Pitcher was elected to the position, defeating Milton Dube by 9 votes to 8. However, the following week, parliament voted 9–8 to remove Pitcher and he was replaced by Sprent Dabwido. In the new cabinet Dabwido also assumed the posts of foreign and home affairs minister and David Adeang became finance minister.

Michael D. Higgins was sworn in as president of Ireland.

After the death of Francisco Blake Mora in a helicopter crash, Juan Marcos Gutiérrez became Mexico's acting interior minister. The following week Alejandro Poiré was sworn into the post on a permanent basis.

In a cabinet reshuffle in Norway, Espen Barth Eide became defence minister.

Lucas Papademos was sworn in as Greece's prime minister. His government included Stavros Dimas as foreign minister, Demitris Avramopoulos as defence minister and Tassos Yiannitsis as interior minister. Evangelos Venizelos remained finance minister. The following week, the new government won a confidence vote 255–38.

Chronology of Events for October 2011

Week Beginning 30 October 2011

In Kyrgyzstan's presidential elections, former prime minister Almazbek Atambayev won 63.2% of the vote, ahead of Adakhan Madumarov with 14.7% and Kamchybek Tashiyev with 14.3%. There were 13 other candidates.

Two weeks after Albert Camille Vital and his government resigned, Omer Beriziky took office as Madagascar's prime minister.

Week Beginning 23 October 2011

In Bulgaria, Rosen Plevneliev won the first round of presidential elections with 40.1% of votes cast, ahead of Ivailo Kalfin with 29.0%, Meglena Kuneva with 14.0%, Volen Siderov with 3.6% and Stefan Solakov with 2.5%. In the second round held a week later Plevneliev won 52.6% of the vote and Kalfin 47.4%.

Following the formal resignation of Bruce Golding, Andrew Holness was sworn in as Jamaica's prime minister. The full government, announced 2 days later, included Kenneth Baugh as foreign minister and Audley Shaw as finance minister. In addition to becoming prime minister, Holness took over the defence portfolio.

In Libya, Mahmoud Jibril stood down as interim prime minister. Ali Tarhouni replaced him until Abdurrahim al-Keib was elected de facto prime minister a week later.

In parliamentary elections in Switzerland, the Swiss People's Party/Centre Democratic Union took 26.6% of the vote (54 seats), the Social Democratic Party of Switzerland 18.7% (46), the FDP/The Liberals 15.1% (30), the Christian Democratic People's Party 12.3% (28), the Green Party 8.4% (15), the Green Liberal Party 5.4% (12), the Conservative Democratic Party of Switzerland 5.4% (9), Evangelical People's Party 2.0% (2) and the Ticino League 0.8% (2). The Christian Social Party and the Geneva Citizens' Movement won one seat each.

Following the resignation of Marouf al-Bakhit, King Abdullah appointed Awn Khasawneh as Jordan's new prime minister. In the new government Khasawneh also took on the defence portfolio. Umayya Touqan was appointed finance minister and Mohammad Al Raoud interior minister.

In Latvia, prime minister Valdis Dombrovskis formed a new government that included Edgars Rinkēvičs as foreign minister and Rihards Kozlovskis as interior minister.

In presidential elections in Ireland, Michael D. Higgins (Labour) won 39.6% of the first preference votes, Seán Gallagher (ind.) 28.5%, Martin McGuinness (Sinn Féin) 13.7%, Gay Mitchell (Fine Gael) 6.4%, David Norris (ind.) 6.2%, Dana Rosemary Scallon (ind.) 2.9% and Mary Davis (ind.) 2.7%. Higgins won in the final count, with 61.6% of votes against 38.4% for Gallagher.

Week Beginning 16 October 2011

In Kuwait, Ali Al-Rashed was appointed acting foreign minister after the resignation of Sheikh Muhammad al-Sabah al-Salim al-Sabah. Five days later, Sheikh Sabah al-Khaled al-Hamad al-Sabah was sworn into the post on a permanent basis.

In a cabinet reshuffle in Swaziland, Mtiti Fakudze was named foreign minister and Prince Gcokoma home affairs minister.

In Haiti, prime minister Garry Conille and his government were sworn in. The cabinet included Thierry Mayard-Paul as defence and interior minister, Laurent Lamothe as foreign minister and André Lemercier Georges as finance minister.

Former Libyan leader Muammar Gaddafi was found by National Transitional Council troops and killed.

In the USA, John Bryson was sworn in as commerce secretary.

Saudi Arabia's defence minister, Prince Sultan bin Abdul-Aziz Al Saud, died.

Week Beginning 9 October 2011

In presidential elections in Cameroon, incumbent Paul Biya was re-elected with 78.0% of the votes ahead of John Fru Ndi with 10.7% and Garga Haman Adji with 3.2%.

In Poland's parliamentary elections the ruling Civic Platform won 207 of 460 seats with 39.2% of the votes, ahead of the Law and Justice Party with 157 seats and 29.9%; the Palikot Movement won 40 seats with 10.0%; Polish Peasants' Party won 28 with 8.4%; the Democratic Left Alliance won 27 with 8.2%; German Minority won one seat with 0.2%.

Egyptian finance minister Hazem Beblawi's resignation was rejected by the Armed Forces Supreme Council.

In the first round of presidential elections in Liberia incumbent Ellen Johnson-Sirleaf of the Unity Party received 43.9% of the vote, followed by Winston Tubman of the Congress for Democratic Change with 32.7% and Prince Yormie Johnson of the National Union for Democratic Progress with 11.6%. There were 13 other candidates. With no candidate receiving an absolute majority a run off was scheduled for 8 Nov. 2011.

In Slovakia, prime minister Iveta Radičová's government was defeated in a confidence vote receiving only 55 out of the 76 votes needed. The government was reappointed 2 weeks later in a caretaker capacity, with limited powers.

Uganda's foreign minister, Sam Kutesa, resigned ahead of a corruption investigation. Internal Affairs minister Hilary Onek announced his intention to follow Kutesa's example.

In Italy, prime minister Silvio Berlusconi won a confidence vote in the Chamber of Deputies (316–301).

In the United Kingdom, Philip Hammond was appointed defence secretary following the resignation of Liam Fox.

Week Beginning 2 October 2011

In Denmark, Helle Thorning-Schmidt took office as prime minister. Her government included Nick Hækkerup as defence minister, Bjarne Corydon as finance minister, Villy Søvndal as foreign minister and Margrethe Vestager as interior minister.

Libya's prime minister Mahmoud Jibril announced a mostly unchanged cabinet including himself as foreign minister, Ali Tarhouni as finance minister, Jalal al-Dghaili as defence minister and Ahmed al-Dharat as interior minister.

In Panama, Frank de Lima took office as finance minister.

Pierre-Damien Habumuremyi was sworn in as Rwanda's new prime minister with no changes in the main cabinet posts.

Ellen Johnson Sirleaf (Liberia), Leymah Gbowee (Liberia) and Tawakkul Karman (Yemen) were jointly awarded the Nobel Peace Prize for their 'non-violent struggle for the safety of women and for women's rights to full participation in peace-building work'.

Chronology of Events for September 2011

Week Beginning 25 September 2011

Jamaica's prime minister, Bruce Golding, announced his resignation, effective in Nov.

Following the resignation of Bolivia's defence minister, María Cecilia Chacón, and interior minister, Sacha Llorenti Soliz, president Morales appointed Rubén Saavedra and Wilfredo Chávez defence and interior minister respectively.

With the resignation of Aleksey Kudrin, Anton Siluanov was appointed as Russia's acting finance minister.

In San Marino, Gabriele Gatti and Matteo Fiorini were sworn in as captains-regent.

In parliamentary elections in the Seychelles the ruling Seychelles People's Progressive Front won all 31 available seats with 88.6% of the vote. The Popular Democratic received 10.9% of the vote but failed to win any seats. The main opposition party, the Seychelles National Party, boycotted the election. 31.9% of the votes cast were spoiled.

Week Beginning 18 September 2011

In Slovenia, prime minister Borut Pahor's government was defeated in a confidence vote 51–36.

In presidential elections in Zambia, Michael Sata (Patriotic Front) won 42.0% of the vote, Rupiah Banda (Movement for Multi-Party Democracy) 35.4% and Hakainde Hichilema (United Party for National Development) 18.2%. Three days later, Sata was sworn in as president. His cabinet was

sworn in the following week with Guy Scott as vice president, Alexander Chikwanda as finance minister, Chishimba Kambwili as foreign minister, Geoffrey Mwamba as defence minister and Kennedy Sakeni as home affairs minister.

Following Almazbek Atambayev's decision to run for president, Omurbek Babanov became Kyrgyzstan's acting prime minister.

In parliamentary elections in the United Arab Emirates, 20 seats in the Federal National Council were elected by the population and the other 20 chosen by the rulers of the Emirates. One woman was among the 20 candidates elected.

Week Beginning 11 September 2011

In the first round of presidential elections in Guatemala, Otto Pérez Molina of the Partido Patriota won with 36.0% of the vote. Manuel Baldizón of the Libertad Democrática Renovada took 23.2% and Eduardo Suger of Compromiso, Renovación y Orden 16.4%. Seven other candidates received less than 10% of the vote. A run-off was scheduled for 6 Nov.

In Costa Rica, Enrique Castillo was sworn in as foreign minister.

Slovakia's prime minister, Iveta Radičová, won a parliamentary no-confidence vote 78–69.

In parliamentary elections in Denmark the Liberal Party won 47 seats, with 26.7% of mainland votes cast, the Social Democratic Party 44 with 24.8%, the Danish People's Party 22 with 12.3%, the Social Liberal Party 17 with 9.5%, the Socialist People's Party 16 with 9.2%, the Unity List—the Red-Greens 12 with 6.7%, the Liberal Alliance 9 with 5.0% and the Conservative Party 8 with 4.9% Although the Liberal Party won the most seats, the Social Democratic Party-led 'Red bloc' took 89 seats compared to 86 for the Liberal party-led 'Blue bloc'. The following day, prime minister Lars Løkke Rasmussen resigned and Helle Thorning-Schmidt was appointed to the post.

In Haiti, the Chamber of Deputies endorsed President Michel Martelly's third choice for prime minister, Garry Conille.

In Honduras, Arturo Corrales was sworn in as foreign minister.

In Latvia's parliamentary elections Harmony Centre won 31 seats with 28.4% of the votes cast; Zatlers' Reform Party 22 with 20.8%; Unity 20 seats with 18.8%; National Alliance 14 seats with 13.9%; and the Union of Greens and Farmers 13 with 12.2%.

Week Beginning 4 September 2011

In a cabinet reshuffle in Colombia, Juan Carlos Pinzón Bueno was appointed defence minister.

In Slovenia, justice minister Aleš Zalar also took on the interior portfolio in an acting capacity following the resignation of Katarina Kresal.

Malaŵi's president, Bingu wa Mutharika, announced a new cabinet, including Peter Mutharika as foreign minister, Ken Lipenga as finance minister and Aaron Sangala as home affairs minister. The defence ministry was abolished.

In Cape Verde, Jorge Carlos Fonseca took office as president.

Following the resignation of Ernesto Cordero to become a presidential candidate at the elections in July 2012, José Antonio Meade was appointed Mexico's finance minister.

Chronology of Events for August 2011

Week Beginning 28 August 2011

Following the resignation of Jhalanath Khanal 2 weeks earlier, Baburam Bhattarai of the Unified Communist Party of Nepal (Maoist) was elected prime minister by parliament with 340 votes. His only rival, Ram Chandra Poudel of the Nepali Congress, received 235 votes. Bhattarai's new cabinet included Bijay Kumar Gachhadar as home affairs minister and Narayan Kaji Shrestha as foreign minister.

In Estonia, Toomas Ilves was re-elected as president, winning 73 votes to Indrek Tarand's 25 in the 101-seat parliament.

In response to the dismissal of Panama's foreign minister Juan Carlos Varela, finance minister Alberto Vallarino resigned. Roberto Henríquez was appointed foreign minister.

Juan Carlos Pinzón Bueno was appointed Colombia's new defence minister following the resignation of Rodrigo Rivera.

Sir Jeremiah Mateparae was sworn in as New Zealand's governor-general.

With the resignation of Naoto Kan, Yoshihiko Noda was elected as Japan's new prime minister. His cabinet included Yasuo Ichikawa as defence minister, Koichiro Gemba as foreign minister, Jun Azumi as finance minister and Tatsuo Kawabata as internal affairs minister.

Following the death of Cuba's defence minister Gen. Julio Casas Regueiro, Gen. Leopoldo Cintra Frías was appointed his successor.

Manuel Pinto da Costa took office as São Tomé e Príncipe's new president.

Week Beginning 21 August 2011

In a cabinet reshuffle in Kenya, Moses Wetangula was reinstated as foreign minister after a 10-month suspension.

In South Sudan, a new cabinet included Nhial Deng Nhial as foreign minister, Kosti Manibe Ngai as finance minister, Gen. John Kong Nyuon as defence minister and Gen. Alison Manani Magaya as interior minister.

In presidential elections in Singapore, Tony Tan Keng Yam won 35.2% of the vote, Tan Cheng Bock 34.8%, Tan Jee Say 25.0% and Tan Kin Lian 4.9%. Tony Tan was sworn in as president the following week.

Week Beginning 14 August 2011

In Nigeria, Ngozi Okonjo-Iweala was sworn in as finance minister.

Malaŵi's president, Bingu wa Mutharika, dissolved his cabinet and took responsibility for all portfolios.

Week Beginning 7 August 2011

In a cabinet reshuffle in Mauritius, Xavier-Luc Duval was appointed finance minister.

In the first round of Cape Verde's presidential elections, Jorge Carlos Fonseca won 37.3% of the vote against Manuel Inocêncio Sousa with 32.0%, Aritsides Lima with 27.4% and Joaquim Jaime Monteiro with 2.0%. In the run-off held 2 weeks later, Fonseca won 54.5% of the vote and Sousa 45.5%.

Celso Amorim took over as Brazil's defence minister after the resignation of Nelson Jobim.

In Libya, the chairman of the rebel National Transitional Council, Mustafa Muhammad Abdul Jalil, dissolved the cabinet. Chairman of the Executive Board Mahmoud Jibril was asked to form a new one. Two weeks later, rebel forces seized control of Tripoli, effectively displacing the regime of Qadhafi.

Gen. Dawoud Rajha replaced Gen. Ali Habib as Syria's defence minister.

Thailand's new prime minister Yingluck Shinawatra took office. Her cabinet included Gen. Yuthasak Sasiprapha as defence minister, Surapong Towijakchaikul as foreign minister, Yongyuth Wichaidit as interior minister and Thirachai Phuvanatnaranubala as finance minister.

In a procedural move following the swearing in of Chad's president Idriss Déby for a new term, the cabinet resigned. Prime Minister Emmanuel Nadingar was asked to stay on. A week later his cabinet was announced with Christian Georges Diguimbaye as finance minister.

Chronology of Events for July 2011

Week Beginning 31 July 2011

In Nepal, Narayan Kaji Shrestha was sworn in as home affairs minister.

Following the resignation of US commerce secretary Gary Locke, Rebecca M. Blank became acting commerce secretary.

In Haiti, the senate rejected by 16 votes to nil president Michel Martelly's nomination of Bernard Gousse as prime minister.

After Poland's defence minister Bogdan Klich resigned, Tomasz Siemoniak was sworn in to the post.

Week Beginning 24 July 2011

In Vietnam, Truong Tan Sang was elected president by the National Assembly, receiving 487 of 496 votes. He nominated prime minister Nguyen Tan Dung for another term; he was re-elected with 470 votes.

In Mauritius, finance minister Pravind Jugnauth resigned.

Macedonia's new cabinet was approved with Nikola Poposki as foreign minister and Fatmir Besimi as defence minister.

In Peru, president Ollanta Humala Tasso's cabinet took office with Solomón Lerner Ghitis as prime minister, Miguel Castilla Rubio as finance minister, Rafael Roncagliolo Orbegozo as foreign minister, Daniel Mora Zevallos as defence minister and Óscar Valdés Dancuart as interior minister.

Week Beginning 17 July 2011

In presidential elections in São Tomé e Príncipe, former president Manuel Pinto da Costa (ind.) won 35.8% of the votes cast against former prime

ministers Evaristo Carvalho (Independent Democratic Action/ADI) with 21.8%, Maria das Neves (ind.) with 14.0% and Delfim Neves (Democratic Convergence Party-Reflection Group/Force for Change Democratic Movement-Liberal Party) with 13.9%. Six other candidates received less than 5% of votes cast. A run-off was scheduled for 7 August.

In Pakistan, Hina Rabbani Khar was appointed foreign minister.

Somalia's new prime minister Abdiweli Mohamed Ali announced his cabinet, including Mohamed Mohamoud Hajji as foreign minister, Hussein Arab Isse as defence minister, Abdisamad Moallim Mohamoud Sheikh Hassan as interior minister and Abdinasir Mohamed Abdulle as finance minister.

Following the resignation of Egypt's foreign minister Mohamed al-Orabi, Mohammed Kamel Amr was appointed to the post. Hazem Beblawi replaced Samir Radwan as finance minister.

In Belgium, King Albert II rejected Elio Di Rupo's request to relieve him of the task of forming a government.

77 people were killed following a bomb explosion in Oslo and a subsequent shooting spree at a youth summer camp on the Norwegian island of Utøya. The attacks were carried out by a Norwegian right-wing extremist, Anders Behring Breivik. He was arrested and charged with terrorism for both attacks.

Week Beginning 10 July 2011

Following the resignation of Spain's interior minister Alfredo Pérez Rubalcaba, Antonio Camacho was appointed to the post.

Željko Komšić took over Bosnia and Herzegovina's rotating presidency. Four days later parliament rejected the appointment of Slavo Kukić as prime minister.

In Cyprus, with the resignation of defence minister Costas Papacostas, agriculture minister Demetris Eliades also gained the defence portfolio. A week later foreign minister Markos Kyprianou resigned. At the request of the president, the cabinet resigned and in August a new one was announced with Erato Kozakou Marcoullis as foreign minister and Kikis Kazamias as finance minister.

A new cabinet was named in Nigeria with Olugbenga Ashiru as foreign minister, Bello H. Mohammed as defence minister and Abba Moro as interior minister.

Week Beginning 3 July 2011

In parliamentary elections in Thailand, the Pheu Thai Party won a majority with 265 seats out of 500 and 53.0% of the vote, ahead of the ruling Democratic Party with 159 seats (31.8%) and Bhumjaithai with 34 seats (6.8%).

Christine Lagarde took office as managing director of the International Monetary Fund.

In Turkey, the new cabinet of prime minister Recep Tayyip Erdoğan was announced with İdris Naim Şahin as interior minister and İsmet Yilmaz as defence minister. Ahmet Davutoğlu remained foreign minister and Mehmet Şimşek kept the finance portfolio.

In Lebanon, prime minister Najib Mikati's cabinet received a confidence vote (68–0) in the 128-seat parliament.

In Latvia, Andris Bērziņš took office as president.

In a cabinet reshuffle in Turkmenistan, Dovletgeldy Sadykov was appointed finance minister.

South Sudan became independent and Salva Kiir Mayardit took office as president. Two days later a caretaker government was sworn in including Deng Alor Kuol as foreign minister, Nhial Deng Nhial as defence minister, Gier Chuang Aluong as interior minister and David Deng Athorbei as finance minister.

Chronology of Events for June 2011

Week Beginning 26 June 2011

Mohammed El Orabi became Egypt's new foreign minister.

In a cabinet reshuffle in France, François Baroin was appointed finance minster.

Leon Panetta took office as the United States defence secretary following the retirement of Robert Gates.

In a cabinet reshuffle in Jordan, Mazen Saket became interior minister.

Week Beginning 19 June 2011

Finland's new government was sworn in with Jyrki Katainen as prime minister, Erkki Tuomioja as foreign minister, Stefan Wallin as defence minister, Päivi Räsänen as interior minister and Jutta Urpilainen as finance minister.

Italy's prime minister Silvio Berlusconi won a confidence vote in the Chamber of Deputies (317–293).

The United Nations General Assembly re-elected Ban Ki-moon as secretary-general.

Week Beginning 12 June 2011

In parliamentary elections in Turkey, the ruling Justice and Development Party (AKP) won 326 of the 550 seats with 49.9% of votes cast, against 135 seats (25.9%) for the Republican People's Party (CHP) and 53 seats (13.0%) for the Nationalist Movement Party. The remaining seats went to independents. There were 12 parties that failed to secure the 10% of votes needed to gain parliamentary representation.

In Lebanon, prime minister Najib Mikati's new government consisted of Adnan Mansour as foreign minister, Fayez Ghosn as defence minister, Marwan Charbel as interior minister and Mohammed Safadi as finance minister.

In Laos, the Seventh Legislature of the National Assembly re-elected Choummaly Sayasone as president and Thongsing Thammavong prime minister. In the new cabinet Khampane Philavong became interior minister and Phouphet Khamphounvong finance minister.

In Vanuatu, the December 2010 election of Sato Kilman as prime minister was invalidated by the Supreme Court and the government of Edward Natapei was reinstated pending new elections. Ten days later, parliament elected Kilman as prime minister, defeating Serge Vohor 29–23. In the new cabinet Alfred Carlot was appointed foreign minister, Moana Carcasses Kalosil finance minister and George Wells internal affairs minister.

In a cabinet reshuffle in Greece, Stavros Lambrinidis became foreign minister, Panos Beglitis defence minister, Haris Kastanidis interior minister and Evangelos Venizelos finance minister. Four days later the government won a parliamentary confidence vote 155–143.

Week Beginning 5 June 2011

In parliamentary elections in Macedonia, the ruling Internal Macedonian Revolutionary Organization-Democratic Party for Macedonian National Unity (VMRO-DPMNE) won 56 seats (39.2% of the vote), the Social Democratic Union of Macedonia (SDSM) 42 (32.8%), the Democratic Union for Integration (DUI) 15 (10.3%), the Democratic Party of Albanians (DPA) 8 (5.9%) and the National Democratic Revival (NDP) 2 (2.7%).

In the presidential runoff in Peru, Ollanta Humala Tasso won with 51.5% of the vote against 48.5% for Keiko Fujimori.

In Portugal's parliamentary elections the Social Democratic Party (PSD) won 108 seats (38.7% of votes cast); the ruling Socialist Party (PS), 74 (28.0%); the People's Party, 24 (11.7%); the Democratic Unity Coalition, 16 (7.9%); and the Left Bloc, 8 (5.2%). Pedro Passos Coelho was named prime minister. The new cabinet included Paulo Portas as foreign minister, José Pedro Aguiar Branco as defence minister, Miguel Macedo as interior minister and Vítor Gaspar as finance minister.

Papua New Guinea's acting prime minister dismissed foreign minister Don Polye and appointed Ano Pala as foreign minister and Patrick Pruaitch finance minister in a cabinet reshuffle. The Supreme Court ruled to suspend Pruaitch, who was scheduled to face a tribunal over misconduct charges. He refused to leave his post and was backed by the acting prime minister.

In Latvia, justice minister Aigars Štokenbergs became interior minister.

Somalia's interior minister Abdishakur Sheikh Hassan Farah was fatally wounded by a suicide bomber. Following the resignation of prime minister Mohamed Abdullahi Mohamed, Abdiweli Mohamed Ali became acting prime minister and was subsequently sworn in on a permanent basis.

Following the resignation of Suriname's finance minister Wonnie Boedhoe, foreign minister Winston Lackin became acting finance minister.

Chronology of Events for May 2011

Week Beginning 29 May 2011

In Benin, Pascal Irénée Koupaki became prime minister, Nassirou Arifari Bako foreign minister, Benoit Dégla interior minister and Adidjatou Mathys economy and finance minister.

Côte d'Ivoire's new government was announced with Daniel Kablan Duncan as foreign minister.

The Japanese prime minister, Naoto Kan, survived a no-confidence motion in the House of Representatives by 293 votes to 152.

The first ballot of Latvia's presidential elections proved inconclusive with Andris Bērziņš receiving 50 votes and incumbent Valdis Zatlers 43 in the 100-seat parliament. In a second round Bērziņš was elected with 53 votes against 41 for Zatlers.

Week Beginning 22 May 2011

In parliamentary elections in Cyprus the Democratic Rally won 20 seats (34.3% of the vote), the Progressive Party of Working People 19 (32.7%), the Democratic Party 9 (15.8%), the Socialist Party 5 (8.9%), the European Party 2 (3.9%) and the Ecological and Environmental Movement 1 (2.2%).

In Vietnam's parliamentary elections, 458 of 500 seats went to Communist Party nominees.

Edward Ssekandi was appointed vice president of Uganda and Amama Mbabazi prime minister. In the new cabinet Maria Kiwanuka became finance minister and Hilary Onek internal affairs minister.

Ikililou Dhoinine took office as the Comoros' president. His cabinet featured Mohamed Bakri Ben Abdoulfatah Charif as foreign minister, M'Madi Ali as defence minister, Hamada Abdallah as interior minister and Mohamed Ali Soilihi as finance minister.

Week Beginning 15 May 2011

In Belgium, King Albert II asked Elio Di Rupo to form a new government. It was the eighth attempt since the election 11 months earlier to break the political deadlock.

Following allegations of sexual assault, Dominique Strauss-Kahn resigned as managing director of the International Monetary Fund. John Lipsky was appointed acting managing director.

In presidential elections in the Seychelles, incumbent James Michel (People's Party) won 55.5% of the vote against Wavel Ramkalawan (Seychelles National Party) with 41.4%.

Week Beginning 8 May 2011

Kuwait's new cabinet was sworn in. Key portfolios remained unchanged.

Djibouti's prime minister, Dilleita Mohamed Dilleita, was asked to form a new cabinet after he and his cabinet resigned. The new cabinet consisted of Abdoulkader Kamil Mohamed as defence minister, Ilyas Moussa Dawaleh as finance minister and Hassan Darar Houffaneh as interior minister.

Antoni Martí Petit was elected head of Andorra's government, having received 21 votes in the 28-seat parliament. His cabinet included Gilbert Saboya as foreign minister, Marc Vila Amigó as interior minister and Jordi Cinca as finance minister.

In Micronesia, Congress re-elected Manny Mori as president. He was unopposed.

With the resignation of Alfredo Vera, José Serrano was sworn in as Ecuador's interior minister.

In Vanuatu, the Court of Appeal nullified the election of Serge Vohor as prime minister and reinstated the government of Sato Kilman. Kilman appointed Alfred Carlot as foreign minister and George Wells as internal affairs minister. Seven days later the Kilman government survived a vote of no confidence, defeated by 27 votes to 25.

Michel Martelly was sworn in as Haiti's new president. Following the resignation of Jean-Max Bellerive, Daniel Gérard Rouzier was nominated prime minister.

Week Beginning 1 May 2011

Al-Qaeda leader Osama bin Laden was shot and killed by US forces in Pakistan.

In parliamentary elections in Canada, the ruling Conservative Party won 167 seats (39.6% of the vote), the New Democratic Party 102 (30.6%), the Liberal Party 34 (18.9%), the Bloc Québécois 4 (6.0%) and the Green Party 1 (3.9%). In the only major cabinet change, John Baird became foreign minister.

In the United Kingdom, national elections were held in Scotland, Wales and Northern Ireland. In Scotland, the Scottish National Party won 69 parliamentary seats, the Labour Party 37, the Conservative Party 15 and the Liberal Democrats 5. In Wales, the Labour Party won 30 assembly seats, the Conservative Party 14, Plaid Cymru 11 and the Liberal Democrats 5. In Northern Ireland, the Democratic Unionist Party won 38 assembly seats, Sinn Féin 29, the Ulster Unionist Party 16, the Social Democratic and Labour Party

14 and the Alliance Party 8. The Traditional Unionist Vote and the Green Party received one seat each.

In a cabinet reshuffle in South Korea, Bahk Jae-wan was appointed finance minister.

In Singapore's parliamentary elections, the ruling People's Action Party won 81 of 87 seats. The Workers' Party took the remaining six seats. In a cabinet reshuffle, Kasiviswanathan Shanmugam was named foreign minister, Ng Eng Hen defence minister and Teo Chee Hean home affairs minister.

Chronology of Events for April 2011

Week Beginning 24 April 2011
After Vanuatu's prime minister Sato Kilman and his cabinet lost a parliamentary vote of no confidence, Serge Vohor was elected prime minister. His new cabinet featured Joe Natuman as foreign minister, Bakoa Kaltongga as finance minister and Patrick Crowby as internal affairs minister.

In Chad's presidential elections, Idriss Déby won re-election with 88.7% of the vote, against 6.0% for Albert Pahimi Padacké and 5.3% for Nadji Madou.

In parliamentary elections in Laos, 132 members of the National Assembly were elected.

Week Beginning 17 April 2011
At the elections for Finland's 200-member parliament, the National Coalition Party (KOK) won 44 seats with 20.4% of the votes cast, the Social Democratic Party (SDP) 42 with 19.1%, the True Finns 39 with 19.1%, the Centre Party (KESK) 35 with 15.8%, the Left Alliance (VAS) 14 with 8.1%, the Green League (VIHR) 10 with 7.3%, the Swedish People's Party (SFP) 9 with 4.3% and the Christian Democrats (KD) 6 with 4.0%. One representative from the province of Åland was also elected.

Central African Republic's prime minister, Faustin-Archange Touadéra, was reappointed by president François Bozizé. Sylvain Ndoutingaï was named finance minister, other key portfolios remaining unchanged.

Following the suspension of Emmanuel Iheanacho, labour minister Chukwuemeka Ngozichineke Wogu took over the post of interior minister in Nigeria.

In a cabinet reshuffle in the Czech Republic, Jan Kubice was appointed interior minister.

Week Beginning 10 April 2011
In Peru's first round of presidential elections Ollanta Humala Tasso of Gana Perú (Peru Wins) won 31.7% of the vote, followed by Keiko Fujimori of Fuerza 2011 (Force 2011) with 23.5%, Pedro Pablo Kuczynski of Alianza por el Gran Cambio (Alliance for the Great Change) with 18.5% and former president Alejandro Celestino Toledo Manrique of Perú Posible (Peru Possible) 15.6%. There were six other candidates.

In Côte d'Ivoire, rival president Laurent Gbagbo surrendered after a military assault on his residence in Abidjan. He was put under UN guard.

With the resignation of Josef Pröll, Maria Fekter was sworn in as Austria's finance minister. Johanna Mikl-Leitner took the position of interior minister.

Following the dissolution of prime minister Tertius Zongo's cabinet in Burkina Faso, Luc-Adolphe Tiao was appointed prime minister. The new government included Yipènè Djibril Bassolet as foreign minister.

In Nigeria's presidential elections, incumbent Goodluck Jonathan, the candidate for the ruling People's Democratic Party, won against 19 opponents with 58.9% of the votes cast. Muhammadu Buhari of the Congress for Progressive Change received 32.0%, and Nuhu Ribadou of Action Congress of Nigeria 5.4%.

Week Beginning 3 April 2011
In parliamentary elections in Andorra, the Democrats for Andorra (DA) won 20 seats (55.1% of the vote) and the Social Democratic Party (PS) 6 (34.8%). The Lauredian Union won 2 seats.

In Kazakhstan's presidential elections, Nursultan Nazarbayev was re-elected against three other candidates with 95.6% of votes cast. In a cabinet reshuffle, Yerzhan Kazykhanov was appointed foreign minister and Kalmukhanbet Kassymov interior minister.

Cissé Mariam Sidibe Kaïdama was appointed Mali's prime minister. Her cabinet included Soumeylou Boubèye Maïga as foreign minister and Lassine Bouaré as finance minister.

A new cabinet was formed in Syria by President Bashar al-Assad. Newly appointed prime minister Adel Safar announced its composition with Maj.-Gen. Mohammad Ibrahim al-Shaar interior minister and Mohammad al-Jililati finance minister.

Having been found guilty of official misconduct by a leadership tribunal in March, Papua New Guinea's prime minister Sir Michael Somare was suspended from office for 14 days. He chose not to return to office after this period, instead taking indefinite medical leave. Sam Abal became acting prime minister.

In Bolivia, María Cecilia Chacón became the country's first female defence minister.

A new government took office in Estonia with Mart Laar as defence minister and Ken-Marti Vaher interior minister.

Niger's new president, Mahamadou Issoufou, was sworn in, appointing Brigi Rafini as prime minister. The new government included Bazoum Mohamed as minister of state for foreign affairs and Abdou Labo as minister of state for interior.

In presidential elections in Djibouti, Ismail Omar Guelleh was re-elected with 80.6% of the vote. Mohamed Warsama Ragueh took 19.4%.

Chronology of Events for March 2011

Week Beginning 27 March 2011
After a first round of parliamentary elections in the Central African Republic in January, a second round was held. The National Convergence Kwa Na Kwa won 36 seats (giving a total of 61 of 105 seats), independents 18 (giving a total of 26), candidates of the presidential majority 11 (giving a total of 11) and an opposition party 1 (giving a total of 2).

In Tunisia, interior minister Farhat Rajhi resigned and was replaced by Habib Essid.

The president of Turkmenistan, Gurbanguly Berdymukhammedov, dismissed the minister for national security Charymurat Amanov and appointed defence minister Yaylim Berdiyev in his place. Begench Gundogdiyev was appointed defence minister.

Myanmar's State Peace and Development Council was dissolved. Thein Sein was sworn in as president along with a new cabinet including Maj.-Gen. Hla Min as defence minister, U Wunna Maung Lwin as foreign minister, Lieut.-Gen. Ko Ko as home affairs minister and Tin Naing Thein as finance minister.

In Kuwait, the government of Sheikh Nasser Muhammad Al-Ahmad Al-Sabah handed in its resignation. It was the sixth cabinet led by the prime minister to resign since his appointment in 2006.

Maria Luisa Berti and Filippo Tamagnini took office as San Marino's captains regent.

Week Beginning 20 March 2011
A new government took office in Cape Verde with Jorge Borges as foreign minister and Jorge Tolentino as defence minister.

Yemen's president Ali Abdullah Saleh dismissed his entire cabinet amid escalating protests demanding his resignation. However, the president asked ministers to remain in place until a new cabinet could be appointed.

In the Maldives, Ahmed Naseem was named foreign minister.

In a cabinet reshuffle in Mauritainia, Hamady Ould Hamady was appointed foreign minister and Ahmedou Ould Dey Ould Mohamed Radhi defence minister.

Following the resignation of Héctor Lacognata, Jorge Lara Castro was sworn in as Paraguay's new foreign minister.

Portuguese prime minister José Sócrates submitted his resignation after parliament rejected his government's austerity measures, but stayed on to head a caretaker administration pending new elections.

In Canada, prime minister Stephen Harper's government fell on a vote of no-confidence. An election was called for 2 May.

Week Beginning 13 March 2011
In Benin's presidential elections, incumbent Yayi Boni was re-elected with 53.2% of the vote, ahead of Adrien Houngbédji with 35.7% and Abdoulaye Bio-Tchané with 6.3%.

The presidential run-off in Niger saw Mahamadou Issoufou win with 57.9% of votes cast against Seyni Oumarou with 42.1%.

In a cabinet reshuffle in Serbia, Prime Minister Mirko Cvetković doubled as finance minister.

Romania's prime minister Emil Bloc survived a fifth no-confidence vote in less than a year.

In Peru, 4 months before the end of his term as prime minister, José Antonio Chang resigned to head up a university. Justice minister Rosario del Pilar Fernández Figueroa was sworn in as his successor.

In Thailand, the prime minister and nine other cabinet ministers, including the finance, interior and foreign ministers, all survived no-confidence motions by narrow margins after allegations of corruption, mismanagement and conflicts of interest.

Week Beginning 6 March 2011

After only a month in office, Egypt's prime minister, Ahmed Shafiq, resigned. Asked to form a new government, former transport minister Essam Sharaf appointed Nabil El-Arabi foreign minister and Mansour El Essaoui interior minister.

In parliamentary elections in Estonia, the Reform Party won 33 seats with 28.6% of the votes cast, the Centre Party 26 with 23.3%, the Pro Patria and Res Publica Union 23 with 20.5% and the Social Democratic Party 19 with 17.1%.

With the resignation of Seiji Maehara, Yukio Edano was named Japan's acting foreign minister. Two days later, Takeaki Matsumoto was sworn in as foreign minister.

In a cabinet reshuffle in Oman, Sayyid Hamoud bin Faisal Al Busaidi was appointed interior minister.

In Micronesia's parliamentary elections, only non-partisan candidates were elected to the 14 seats. Micronesia has no established political parties.

Ireland's new prime minister Enda Kenny and his cabinet were sworn in with Eamon Gilmore as deputy prime minister and foreign minister, Alan Shatter defence minister and Michael Noonan finance minister.

Following the resignation of Madagascan prime minister Albert Camille Vital and his government, Vital was asked to form a new cabinet. Yvette Sylla became foreign minister and Florent Rakotoarisoa interior minister.

Japan's most powerful earthquake since records began triggered a tsunami that struck the country's eastern coastline. Over 10,000 people died. The World Bank estimated the damage to cost between US$120 bn. and US$235 bn., equivalent to 4% of Japan's GDP. A state of emergency was declared after the tsunami caused severe damage at the Fukushima I and II power plants.

Chronology of Events for February 2011

Week Beginning 27 February 2011

In a cabinet reshuffle in France, Alain Juppé was appointed foreign minister, Gérard Longuet defence minister and Claude Guéant interior minister.

In Tunisia, prime minister Mohamed Ghannouchi resigned and was succeeded by Béji Caïd Essebsi.

With the resignation of Germany's defence minister Karl-Theodor zu Guttenberg, interior minister Thomas de Maizière was named his successor and Hans-Peter Friedrich took over the interior ministry.

In parliamentary elections in Samoa, the ruling Human Rights Protection Party (HRRP) won 36 of 49 seats, against 13 for the Tautua Samoa Party (TSP).

Week Beginning 20 February 2011

Libya's interior minister Abdel Fattah Younis resigned and called on the army to join the people's revolution. Masoud Abdel Hafiz was appointed interior minister in his place.

In Ireland's parliamentary election, the opposition Fine Gael gained 76 seats with 36.1% of first preference votes; Labour Party 37 with 19.4%; Fianna Fáil 20 with 17.4%; and Sinn Féin 14 with 9.9%.

Michael Ogio was sworn in as Papua New Guinea's governor-general.

Week Beginning 13 February 2011

In Chad's first parliamentary election since 2002, the ruling Patriotic Salvation Movement and its allies won 131 seats. The main opposition parties, the National Union for Democracy and Renewal and the Union for Renewal and Democracy, won ten and eight seats respectively.

Following the resignation of Ahmed Ouanaïes, after only 2 weeks in office, Mouldi Kefi was appointed Tunisia's new foreign minister.

With Alberto Rumulo taking indefinite leave of absence, Erlinda Basilio was named the Philippines' acting foreign minister. Six days later, Basilio was replaced by Albert del Rosario.

In Ugandan elections, president Museveni was re-elected by 68.4% of votes cast, leaving his main rival, Kizza Besigye, with 26.0%. There were six other candidates.

Week Beginning 6 February 2011

In parliamentary elections in Cape Verde, the ruling African Party for the Independence of Cape Verde (PAICV) won 37 seats with 50.9% of the votes cast, the Movement for Democracy (MPD) 33 with 41.9% and the Democratic and Independent Cape Verdean Union 2 with 4.9%.

Jordan's new cabinet was sworn in with prime minister Marouf al-Bakhit as defence minister and Hussein Mjalli as justice minister.

After weeks of protests and calls for the Egyptian president to step down, Hosni Mubarak announced his resignation. Control was handed to the Armed Forces Supreme Council headed by the defence minister Mohamed Hussein Tantawi.

Chronology of Events for January 2011

Week Beginning 30 January 2011

In Niger's first round of presidential elections, former prime minister Mahamadou Issoufou won 36.1% of the votes, Seyni Oumarou 23.2%, Hama Amadou 19.8% and Mahamane Ousmane 8.4%. There were six other candidates. A run-off is scheduled for 12 March. In parliamentary elections held the same day, the Nigerien Party for Democracy and Socialism (PNDS) won 39 seats; the National Movement for the Development of Society (MNSD), 26 and the Nigerien Democratic Movement for an African Federation (MODEN/FA), 23.

After 7 months of political gridlock in which no candidate could muster enough votes to become Nepal's prime minister, Jhalanath Khanal was elected by the Constituent Assembly, securing 368 of 557 votes. His nearest rivals, Ram Chandra Poudel and Bijay Kumar Gachhadar, received 122 votes and 67 votes respectively.

In Myanmar, parliament convened for the first time in 22 years. Prime minister Thein Sein was elected president, winning 408 of 659 votes. Tin Aung Myint Oo (171 votes) and Sai Mauk Kham (75 votes) became first and second vice president respectively.

Week Beginning 23 January 2011

In the Central African Republic's presidential elections incumbent president Gen. François Bozizé won 66.1% of the vote. His closest challenger, Ange-Félix Patassé, secured 20.1%. There were three other registered candidates.

In Iran, acting foreign minister Ali Akbar Salehi was confirmed in office.

In presidential elections in Portugal incumbent Aníbal Cavaco Silva won 52.9% of the vote, Manuel Alegre 19.8%, Fernando Nobre 14.1% and Francisco Lopes 7.1%. There were two other candidates.

Events in Tunisia sparked unrest and protests in Egypt. President Hosni Mubarak appointed Omar Suleiman vice-president and asked prime minister Ahmed Nazif and his cabinet to resign. A new cabinet under Ahmed Shafiq was sworn in with Mahmoud Wagdi as interior minister and Samir Radwan as finance minister. Other key posts remained unchanged.

In Kyrgyzstan, finance minister Chorobek Imashev resigned. Dinara Shaydieva was appointed acting finance minister.

Week Beginning 16 January 2011

Ireland's government was on the verge of collapse following the resignation of six cabinet members. Prime minister Brian Cowen called an election for March 2011 (subsequently brought forward to February).

Nguyen Phu Trong was elected secretary general of Vietnam's communist party.

Week Beginning 9 January 2011

In Sudan, a referendum on full independence for the South took place with 98.8% in favour of secession. Southern Sudan is scheduled to become an independent country on 9 July 2011.

Following the resignation of Burkina Faso's prime minister and his cabinet, Tertius Zongo returned as prime minister. The only cabinet change was the appointment of Auguste Denise Barry as security minister.

After more than a third of prime minister Saad Hariri's cabinet resigned, Lebanon's president Michel Suleiman asked Hizbollah-backed Najib Mikati to form a new cabinet.

Weeks of protests and unrest over unemployment, poverty and corruption resulted in the ousting of Tunisian president Zine El Abidine Ben Ali. Prime

Minister Mohamed Ghannouchi agreed to act as interim president but was subsequently succeeded by Foued Mebazaa, the President of the Chamber of Deputies.

In a cabinet reshuffle in Chile, Andrés Allamand was named defence minister.

A cabinet reshuffle in Gabon saw Rufin Pacôme Ondzounga appointed defence minister and Emmanuel Issozet Ngondet finance minister.

In Moldova, prime minister Vladimir Filat's cabinet was approved and its members sworn in.

Marco Piccinini was appointed Monaco's new finance minister.

Papua New Guinea's parliament elected Michael Ogio governor-general, defeating Sir Pato Kakaraya 65–23. Sir Michael Somare resumed the position of prime minister.

Week Beginning 2 January 2011

Tonga's new cabinet was sworn in with prime minister Tu'ivakano as foreign and defence minister and Sunia Fili as finance minister.

In Kuwait, a vote of no-confidence in prime minister Sheikh Nasser Muhammad Al-Ahmad Al-Sabah was defeated by 25 votes to 22.

2010

Chronology of Events for December 2010

Week Beginning 26 December 2010

In the second round of presidential elections in the Comoros Ikililou Dhoinine won 61.1% of the vote, Mohamed Said Fazul 32.7% and Abdou Djabir 6.2%.

In a cabinet reshuffle in Croatia, Davor Božinović was appointed defence minister and Martina Dalić finance minister.

In Moldova, Vladimir Filat announced the resignation of his government. Marian Lupu was elected speaker and acting president. The incumbent prime minister was reappointed as the head of government 4 days later.

In a cabinet reshuffle, Elyor Ganiyev became Uzbekistan's foreign minister.

In Brazil, Dilma Rousseff took office as president and Michel Temer as vice president. Antônio Patriota was named foreign minister.

Estonia became the 17th country to adopt the euro.

Micheline Calmy-Rey was sworn in as president of Switzerland.

Week Beginning 19 December 2010

In Belarus' presidential elections, Alyaksandr Lukashenka won with 79.7% of the vote. His closest challenger, Andrei Sannikov, secured 2.4%. There were eight other opponents. Following the resignation of Syarhey Sidorski and his cabinet, Mikhail Myasnikovich became prime minister.

Iraq's new cabinet was approved and sworn in with incumbent prime minister Nouri al-Maliki as acting defence and interior minister and with Rafi Hiyad al-Issawi appointed finance minister.

A vote of no-confidence in Romanian prime minister Emil Boc was rejected by 190 votes. Another vote of no-confidence held 3 days later was cancelled after a protester jumped off the Romanian parliament's 7-metre (23-ft) high balcony.

Alpha Condé was sworn in as president of Guinea. Prime minister Jean-Marie Doré's government subsequently resigned and Mohamed Said Fofana was appointed prime minister. Edward Gnakoi Lamah became foreign minister and Condé himself defence minister.

In Montenegro, Milo Đukanović, the longest serving leader in the Balkans, announced his resignation. He was replaced by Igor Lukšić. The new government included Milorad Katnić as finance minister.

In a vote in Tonga's parliament, Lord Tu'ivakano was elected prime minister with 14 votes against 12 for 'Akilisi Phoiva.

Following a vote of no-confidence in Tuvalu's prime minister Maatia Toafa, Willy Telavi was elected his successor, defeating Enele Sopoaga by eight votes to seven. Apisai Ielemia was appointed foreign minister and Lotoala Metia finance minister.

The results of the 2010 US census were released. They showed an increase in the population to 308,745,538, representing a rise of 9.7% since 2000—the lowest percentage increase between ten-yearly US censuses since the Second World War.

Laos' prime minister Bouasone Bouphavanh resigned citing 'family issues'. Political tensions were thought to be behind the surprise announcement. Thongsing Thammavong was elected as his successor.

Week Beginning 12 December 2010

In Iran, president Mahmoud Ahmadinejad dismissed foreign minister Manouchehr Mottaki and named Ali Akbar Salehi acting foreign minister.

Having to face a tribunal over misconduct allegations, Papua New Guinea's prime minister, Sir Michael Somare, stood down. Deputy prime minister Sam Abal became acting prime minister.

In St Vincent and the Grenadines' parliamentary elections, the ruling Unity Labour Party won eight of 15 seats and the New Democratic Party seven. The new cabinet was later sworn in with prime minister Ralph Gonsalves also becoming finance minister and Douglas Slater foreign minister.

Violence broke out in Rome after Italy's prime minister Silvio Berlusconi and his cabinet won confidence votes in the Senate (162–135) and the Chamber of Deputies (314–311).

With Nilda Garré's appointment to the newly created post of security minister, Arturo Puricelli became Argentina's defence minister.

In a cabinet reshuffle in Mauritania, Mamady Camara was named finance minister.

The parliament of Kyrgyzstan approved a new government. Almazbek Atambayev was appointed prime minister, Zarylbek Rysaliev interior minister and Chorobek Imashev finance minister.

Week Beginning 5 December 2010

In a cabinet reshuffle in Papua New Guinea, Sam Abal was appointed deputy prime minister and Don Polye foreign minister.

Chronology of Events for November 2010

Week Beginning 28 November 2010

European ministers reached an agreement over an €85 bn. bailout for Ireland. The EU contributed €45 bn. and the IMF €22.5 bn. The rescue package was designed to safeguard financial stability in the euro area.

The whistle-blowing website Wikileaks released a series of US embassy secret cables. Revelations included a proposal by Arab leaders for a US attack on Iran to prevent the development of its suspected nuclear weapons and Chinese support for the reunification of Korea.

In the second round of presidential elections in Côte d'Ivoire the Independent Electoral Commission declared that Alassane Ouattara had won with 54.1% of the vote, ousting ruling president Laurent Gbagbo who received 45.9%. Gbagbo contested the results and the Constitutional Council declared him the winner with 51.5% of the vote. The UN called on Gbagbo to step down amid fears of violent clashes between rival factions.

The National Democratic Party won 420 seats in the elections of the People's Assembly in Egypt. Independents took 69 with the remainder going to other parties.

In Haiti's presidential elections Mirlande Manigat won 31.4% of the vote, Jude Célestin 22.5% and Michel Martelly 21.8%. There were widespread claims of voting irregularities.

The ruling Party of Communists of the Republic of Moldova won 42 seats in Moldova's parliamentary elections, the Liberal Democratic Party of Moldova 32 seats, the Democratic Party 15 and the Liberal Party 12.

Prime minister Edward Natapei was ousted after losing a confidence motion by 30 votes to 15 in Vanuatu. Sato Kilman was sworn in as prime minister. George Wells was appointed foreign minister, Willie Lop internal affairs minister and Moana Kalosil Carcasses finance minister.

In Liberia, Toga McIntosh was appointed foreign minister.

Joseph Dauda was appointed foreign minister in a cabinet reshuffle in Sierra Leone.

Week Beginning 21 November 2010

George Rebelo Pinto Chicoty was appointed foreign minister in a cabinet reshuffle in Angola.

In Burkina Faso's presidential elections Blaise Compaoré was re-elected with 80.2% of votes cast, defeating six other candidates.

Following a South Korean artillery exercise, North Korean forces fired shells and rockets at Yeonpyeong Island killing four and wounding at least 18 South Koreans. Kim Kwan-jin was appointed new defence minister of South Korea following the resignation of Kim Tae-young.

In Tanzania, with the announcement of a new cabinet, Shamsi Vuai Nahodha was appointed home affairs minister.

At elections in Tonga the Democratic Party of the Friendly Islands won 12 seats and independent candidates the other five.

Week Beginning 14 November 2010

The Fiji Islands' deputy prime minister and defence minister, Ratu Epeli Ganilau, resigned following an alleged conflict with prime minister Voreqe Bainimarama over US-based water company, Fiji Water. He was replaced by Joketani Cokanasiga in an acting capacity.

In a cabinet reshuffle in Grenada, Karl Hood was appointed foreign minister.

Week Beginning 7 November 2010

In Azerbaijan's parliamentary elections the New Azerbaijan Party gained 72 seats, with independents and a number of smaller parties sharing the remaining 53 seats.

In the first round of presidential elections in the Comoros, Ikililou Dhoinine won 28.2% of the vote, Mohamed Said Fazul 22.9%, Abdou Djabir 9.9% and Bianrifi Tarmidhi 9.3%. There were six other candidates.

Alpha Condé won the second round of Guinea's presidential elections with 52.5% of the vote against 47.5% for Cellou Dalein Diallo.

In Myanmar's parliamentary elections, the ruling Union Solidarity and Development Party won 259 of 330 seats in the House of Representatives. Opposition leader Aung Sang Suu Kyi was subsequently released from house arrest. She had urged pro-democracy parties to boycott the elections.

In Jordan's parliamentary elections, 103 of the 120 seats in the Chamber of Deputies were won by independents loyal to the king. The Islamic Action Front boycotted the vote.

Nebojša Radmanović took over Bosnia and Herzegovina's rotating presidency.

In Iraq, Jalal Talabani was re-elected president in a second round of parliamentary voting with 195 of 325 votes. He reappointed Nouri al-Maliki prime minister.

Monqiue Ohsan-Bellepeau was elected by parliament as vice-president of Mauritius.

In a cabinet reshuffle in France, Michèle Alliot-Marie was named foreign minister and Alain Juppé defence minister.

Chronology of Events for October 2010

Week Beginning 31 October 2010

Incumbent president Laurent Gbagbo won 38.0% of the vote in the first round of Côte d'Ivoire's presidential elections, the first in 10 years. Alassane Ouattara took 32.1% and Henri Konan Bédié 25.2%.

In Tanzania's presidential elections, Jakaya Kikwete of Chama Cha Mapinduzi (Revolutionary State Party) was re-elected with 62.8% of the vote.

Prime minister Valdis Dombrovskis appointed a new government in Latvia. It included Artis Pabriks as deputy prime minister and defence minister, Ģirts Valdis Kristovskis as foreign minister and Andris Vilks as finance minister. Linda Mūrniece remained interior minister.

In Nauru, Marcus Stephen was re-elected president.

Seven rounds of voting in the space of a month failed to elect a prime minister in Nepal. This brought the total number of rounds to 16.

Mark Maipakai succeeded Sani Rambi as internal security minister in Papua New Guinea.

In Switzerland, Eveline Widmer-Schlumpf took office as finance minister.

Following Bahrain's parliamentary elections, the cabinet resigned and was subsequently reappointed with no changes in key portfolios.

The Democratic Party lost their majority in the House of Representatives following the US mid-term elections. They conceded 63 seats to the Republicans, the party's largest congressional-seat loss since 1948.

In Liberia, president Ellen Johnson-Sirleaf dismissed her cabinet and appointed acting ministers in their place. Othello Warrick became interim defence minister, Elfreda Tamba finance minister and Sylvester Grigsby foreign minister.

Week Beginning 24 October 2010

Kenya's foreign minister Moses Wetangula stood down over corruption allegations. Interior minister George Saitoti added foreign affairs to his portfolio.

A parliamentary no-confidence motion designed to topple the Romanian prime minister, Emil Boc, fell 18 votes short of succeeding.

In Croatia, prime minister Jadranka Kosor won a parliamentary vote of confidence by 79 votes to 62.

Week Beginning 17 October 2010

In Spain, Trinidad Jiménez was appointed foreign minister.

In Bahrain's parliamentary elections the Shia Al Wefaq party took 18 seats while the Sunni Al Asala and Al Menbar groupings won 3 and 2 seats respectively. Independents won 17.

Following the death of Barbados' prime minister David Thompson, Freundel Stuart was sworn in as his successor. Adriel Brathwaite replaced Stuart as minister of home affairs.

Week Beginning 10 October 2010

The Netherlands Antilles was dissolved. Curaçao and Sint Maarten became autonomous countries within the Kingdom of the Netherlands.

Mohamed Abdulahi Mohamed was appointed prime minister of Somalia.

Week Beginning 3 October 2010

In Bosnia and Herzegovina, Bakir Izetbegović (Muslim; Party of Democratic Action), Željko Komšić (Croat; Social Democratic Party) and Nebojša Radmanović (Serb; Alliance of Independent Social Democrats) were elected to the Presidency. In parliamentary elections the Social Democratic Party of Bosnia and Herzegovina won 8 seats, the Alliance of Independent Social Democrats 8, the Party of Democratic Action 7, the Union for a Better Future of BiH 4, the Serbian Democratic Party 4 and the Croatian Democratic Union of Bosnia and Herzegovina 3. Six other parties won one or two seats.

Dilma Rousseff won the first round of Brazil's presidential elections with 46.9% of votes cast against 32.6% for José Serra and 19.3% for Marina Silva. In parliamentary elections, the 'For Brazil to Keep on Changing' coalition of ten parties (including the Workers' Party of which Dilma Rousseff is a member) took 311 of 513 seats against 136 for the opposition 'Brazil Can Do More' alliance. In the presidential election run-off 4 weeks later, Rousseff won 56.1% of the vote against 43.9% for Serra.

Sebastião Martins was sworn in as Angola's interior minister.

In Ethiopia, Meles Zenawi was reappointed prime minister. His cabinet featured Hailemariam Desalegne as deputy prime minister and foreign minister while Siraj Fegeta remained defence minister and Sufyan Ahmad finance minister.

The Netherlands' new government took office, headed by prime minister Mark Rutte. Uri Rosenthal was appointed foreign minister, Hans Hillen defence minister, Piet Hein Donner interior minister and Jan Kees de Jager finance minister.

Chronology of Events for September 2010

Week Beginning 26 September 2010

In Venezuela's parliamentary elections, the Partido Socialista Unido de Venezuela (United Socialist Party of Venezuela) of President Chávez won 96 seats, the opposition Mesa de la Unidad Democrática (Coalition for Democratic Unity) 64 and Patria para Todos (Fatherland for All) 2. The remaining three seats were reserved for indigenous peoples.

Angola's interior minister Roberto Leal Ramos Monteiro was sacked after he was accused of illegally extraditing a Portuguese citizen from São Tomé e Príncipe.

Romania's interior minister Vasile Blaga resigned in protest at police strike action which he called illegal. Traian Igaş took over the portfolio.

Italian prime minister Silvio Berlusconi won a parliamentary vote of confidence by 342 votes to 275.

Christopher Sinckler was appointed finance minister in a cabinet reshuffle in Barbados.

David Johnston was sworn in as Canada's governor-general.

Kim Hwang-sik took office as prime minister of South Korea.

Giovanni Francesco Ugolini and Andrea Zafferani were sworn in as captains regent of San Marino.

In Latvia's parliamentary elections the Unity coalition won 33 seats, Harmony Centre 29, Union of Greens and Farmers 22, National Alliance 8 and For a Good Latvia 8.

Week Beginning 19 September 2010

In Swedish parliamentary elections the Swedish Social Democratic Labour Party won 112 seats, the New Moderates 107, the Green Party 25, the Liberal Party 24, the Centre Party 23, the far-right Sweden Democrats 20, the Christian Democratic Party 19 and the Left Party 19. Prime minister Fredrik Reinfeldt formed a new government with key posts unchanged.

The Somali prime minister Omar Abdirashid Ali Sharmake resigned after disagreeing with president Sheikh Sharif Sheikh Ahmed on changes to the constitution. Abdiwahid Ilmi Gonjeh succeeded him in an acting capacity.

Week Beginning 12 September 2010

Zarylbek Rysaliev took over the interior ministry in Kyrgyzstan.

In Peru, prime minister Javier Velásquez resigned to run for president. He was succeeded by José Antonio Chang Escobedo. A new cabinet was appointed which included Jaime Fernando Thorne León as defence minister, Pio Fernando Barrios Ipenza as interior minister and Ismael Benavides Ferreyros as economy and finance minister. José Antonio García Belaúnde was retained as foreign minister.

Incumbent Australian prime minister Julia Gillard was sworn in along with her cabinet following the election a month earlier. Kevin Rudd was appointed foreign minister, Stephen Smith defence minister and Penny Wong finance minister. The treasurer, Wayne Swan, and the home affairs minister, Brendan O'Coyle, retained their posts.

In a cabinet reshuffle in Albania, Edmond Haxhisanto was sworn in as foreign minister.

Mauritius' vice president Angidi Chettiar died following a period of ill health.

In South Korea, Kim Hwang-sik was nominated prime minister.

Maatia Toafa was elected prime minister of Tuvalu by eight parliamentary votes to seven following elections. His cabinet included Monise Laafai as finance minister and Enele Sopoaga as foreign minister.

A cabinet reshuffle in Japan resulted in Yoshihiro Katayama becoming interior minister and Seiji Maehara foreign minister.

Week Beginning 5 September 2010

In Spain, the Basque separatist group ETA declared a permanent ceasefire although the government refused to enter talks until ETA agreed to renounce all violence.

A sixth parliamentary vote to elect a prime minister in Nepal was inconclusive. By the end of Sept. three more votes had taken place without any candidate winning a majority.

A cabinet reshuffle in Greece resulted in Dimitris Droutasas becoming foreign minister.

Bécaye Diop was appointed defence minister and Ousmane Ngom interior minister in a cabinet reshuffle in Senegal.

Chronology of Events for August 2010

Week Beginning 29 August 2010

A cabinet reshuffle in Burundi saw Maj.-Gen. Pontien Gaciyubwenge become defence minister.

Botswana's defence minister Ramadeluka Seretse resigned in the wake of corruption investigations. Presidential affairs minister Lesego Motsumi took over the defence portfolio on an acting basis.

Gheorghe Ialomitianu became finance minister after a cabinet reshuffle in Romania.

South Korea's foreign minister Yu Myung-hwan resigned accused of nepotism.

Week Beginning 22 August 2010

Danny Philip took office as prime minister of the Solomon Islands. His cabinet included Manasseh Maelanga as deputy prime minister and interior minister, Peter Shanel as foreign minister and Gordon Darcy Lilo as finance minister.

Week Beginning 15 August 2010

In Australia's elections to the House of Representatives, the Australian Labor Party won 72 seats, the Liberal Party 44, the Liberal National Party of Queensland 21 and the National Party of Australia 6. The Australian Greens, the National Party of Western Australia and the Country Liberal Party took one seat each while independents claimed four. Despite the opposition Liberal/National coalition taking 73 seats in total, Labor remained in power as a minority government with the support of several independents.

Week Beginning 8 August 2010

In South Korea, president Lee Myung-bak named Kim Tae-ho prime minister designate. However, Tae-ho later withdrew his candidacy after accusations of financial misconduct.

Paul Kagame was re-elected Rwanda's president with 93.1% of the vote.

The Czech government defeated a no-confidence vote in parliament by 118 votes to 82.

Slovakia's prime minister Iveta Radičová won a parliamentary vote of confidence by 79 votes to 66.

In Suriname, former coup leader Dési Bouterse took office as president. His new government included Robert Ameerali as vice-president, Lamuré Latour as defence minister, Wonnie Boedhoe as finance minister, Winston Lackin as foreign minister and Soewarto Moestadja as interior minister.

Week Beginning 1 August 2010

In São Tomé e Príncipe's parliamentary elections, Independent Democratic Action won 26 seats, the Liberation Movement of São Tomé e Príncipe-Social Democratic Party 21, the Party of Democratic Convergence 7 and the Force for Change Democratic Movement 1. Patrice Trovoada was sworn in as prime minister and appointed Carlos Olímpio Stock defence minister, Américo d'Oliveira dos Ramos finance minister and Manuel Salvador dos Ramos foreign minister.

Nepal's parliament failed to elect a new prime minister in a third and, 4 days later, a fourth attempt.

In Italy, prime minister Silvio Berlusconi won a parliamentary vote of no-confidence by 299 votes to 229.

In parliamentary elections in the Solomon Islands, the Democratic Party won 14 seats, Our Party 4, SI Party for Rural Advancement 3, Direct Development Party 3, Reform and Democratic Party of the Solomon Islands 2, Independent Democratic Party 2, independents 17 and five parties won one seat each.

Hungary's new president Pál Schmitt took office.

Bronisław Komorowski was sworn in as president of Poland.

Swiss finance minister Hans-Rudolf Merz announced that he intended to step down in Oct.

Colombia's new president Juan Manuel Santos was sworn in. His cabinet included Rodrigo Rivera Salazar as defence minister, Juan Carlos Echeverry as finance minister and María Ángela Holguín Cuéllar as foreign minister.

Chronology of Events for July 2010

Week Beginning 25 July 2010

South Korea's prime minister Chung Un-chan announced his resignation after the government lost in local elections and attempts to revise plans to move nine ministries and four government agencies out of Seoul to Sejong City failed to win parliamentary approval.

Week Beginning 18 July 2010

In Suriname, former dictator Dési Bouterse was elected president by the National Assembly, claiming 36 out of 50 votes against 13 for Chandrikapersad Santokhi with one abstention.

In parliamentary elections in Burundi the National Council for the Defense of Democracy–Forces for the Defense of Democracy won 80 of 100 available seats, the Union for National Progress 16 and Sahwanya Frodebu-Nyakuri 4.

Political deadlock continued in Nepal after two failed attempts by parliament to elect a prime minister.

Week Beginning 11 July 2010

In the Czech Republic, Petr Nečas was sworn in as prime minister. He appointed Karel Schwarzenberg foreign minister, Alexandr Vondra defence minister, Miroslav Kalousek finance minister and Radek John interior minister.

Several ministers resigned in Kyrgyzstan to run in parliamentary elections scheduled for Oct. prompting a cabinet reshuffle. Chorobek Imashev succeeded Temir Sariyev as finance minister.

A cabinet reshuffle in Mexico resulted in José Francisco Blake Mora's appointment to head the interior ministry.

Following the dismissal of Benin's interior minister Armand Zinzindohoué for fraud, Martial Souton was appointed his successor.

Week Beginning 4 July 2010

In the second round run-off of Poland's presidential elections Bronisław Komorowski won 53.0% of the vote against 47.0% for Jarosław Kaczyński.

Kubatbek Baibolov was appointed interior minister of Kyrgyzstan.

In the Maldives, president Mohamed Nasheed reappointed the cabinet that had resigned after clashing with the opposition-dominated parliament.

Iveta Radičová was sworn in as prime minister of Slovakia. Her cabinet included Ľubomír Galko as defence minister, Daniel Lipšic as interior minister, Ivan Mikloš as finance minister and former prime minister Mikuláš Dzurinda as foreign minister.

Chronology of Events for June 2010

Week Beginning 27 June 2010
In the first round of presidential elections in Guinea, Cellou Dalein Diallo of the Union of Democratic Forces of Guinea won 39.7% of the vote against 20.7% for Alpha Condé of the Rally of the Guinean People and 15.6% for Sidya Touré of the Union of Republican Forces.

Pierre Nkurunziza was re-elected president of Burundi with 91.6% of votes cast after opposition leaders boycotted the poll, making him the sole candidate.

In Hungary, Pál Schmitt was elected president by the National Assembly by 263 votes to 59 for András Balogh.

The Maldives' cabinet resigned after a threat of a no-confidence vote by the opposition-dominated parliament.

The Philippines' new president, Benigno Aquino III, took office. His cabinet included Voltaire Gazmin as defence minister, Alberto Romulo as foreign minister and Cesar Purisima as finance minister.

In an effort to end the political deadlock with a hostile parliament, Nepal's prime minister Madhav Kumar Nepal resigned.

Christian Wulff was sworn in as the president of Germany following a parliamentary vote.

In Kyrgyzstan, acting president Roza Otunbayeva was sworn in.

A cabinet reshuffle in Somalia saw Yusuf Hassan Ibrahim become foreign minister, Abukar Abdi Osman defence minister and Hussein Abdi Halane finance minister.

Week Beginning 20 June 2010
Juan Manuel Santos won the second round of presidential elections in Colombia with 69.1% of the vote against 27.5% for Antanas Mockus Šivickas.

In the first round of Poland's presidential elections, Bronisław Komorowski of the Civic Platform took 41.5% of votes cast, Jarosław Kaczyński of the Law and Justice Party 36.5%, Grzegorz Napieralski of the Democratic Left Alliance 13.7% and Janusz Korwin-Mikke of the Liberty and Rule Party 2.5%.

A cabinet reshuffle in Zimbabwe resulted in Theresa Makone becoming joint home affairs minister alongside Kembo Mohadi.

Australian prime minister Kevin Rudd was succeeded by his deputy Julia Gillard after she launched a leadership challenge.

In the Czech Republic, prime minister Jan Fischer resigned having previously announced that he would hold office only until elections were held. Petr Nečas of the Civic Democratic Party succeeded him.

Papua New Guinea's parliament re-elected Sir Paulias Matane as governor-general.

Week Beginning 13 June 2010
In Belgium's parliamentary elections, the New Flemish Alliance won 27 seats, the Socialist Party 26, Reformist Movement 18, Christian Democratic and Flemish 17, Socialist Party Alternative 13, Open Flemish Liberals and Democrats 13, Flemish Interest 12, the Humanist Democratic Centre 9, Ecolo 8, Groen! 5, List Dedecker 1 and the Popular Party 1.

A new Sudanese cabinet included Ali Mahmood Abdul-Rasool as finance minister and Ali Ahmed Karti as foreign minister. Lieut.-Gen. Abdel Rahim Mohamed Hussein remained defence minister and Ibrahim Mahmoud Hamid interior minister.

Following the Argentine foreign minister Jorge Taiana's unexplained resignation, Héctor Timerman was appointed to head the ministry.

Finland's prime minister Matti Vanhanen resigned for health reasons. Mari Kiviniemi was sworn in as his successor.

In Nauru's parliamentary elections, prime minister Marcus Stephen's supporters won nine of 18.

Week Beginning 6 June 2010
Afghanistan's interior minister, Hanif Atmar, resigned following a terrorist attack on a peace council of national leaders in Kabul. He was succeeded by Gen. Besmillah Mohammadi.

Dr. Mamadou Tangara took over the foreign affairs ministry in a cabinet reshuffle in the Gambia.

In North Korea, Choe Yong-rim replaced Kim Yong-il as prime minister.

In a cabinet reshuffle in the Seychelles, Danny Faure was appointed vice-president, Jean-Paul Adam foreign minister and Joel Morgan home affairs minister.

In Slovakian parliamentary elections, the incumbent Direction–Social Democracy won 62 seats, the Slovak Democratic and Christian Union–Democratic Party 28, Freedom and Solidarity 22, the Christian Democratic Movement 15, Most–Híd 14 and the Slovak National Party 9.

Chronology of Events for May 2010

Week Beginning 30 May 2010
In the first round of Colombia's presidential elections, Juan Manuel Santos of the Social National Unity Party won 46.7% of votes cast, against 21.5% for Antanas Mockus Šivickas of the Green Party, 10.1% for Germán Vargas Lleras of the Radical Change Party, 9.1% for Gustavo Petro of Alternative Democratic Pole and 6.1% for Noemí Sanín of the Colombian Conservative Party.

The Sudanese president Omar Hassan Ahmed al-Bashir dissolved the government. Three ministers remained in office including defence minister Lieut.-Gen. Abdel Rahim Mohamed Hussein. Salva Kiir Mayardit and Ali Uthman Muhammad Taha were reappointed vice presidents.

Germany's president Horst Köhler resigned after suggesting that the country might need to resort to military action to protect its commercial interests. The president of the Bundesrat Jens Böhrnsen became acting president.

The finance minister of Papua New Guinea, Patrick Pruaitch, was suspended from office while he was investigated on charges of ministerial misconduct. The deputy prime minister Puka Temu added the finance ministry to his portfolio.

In a cabinet reshuffle in Belize, the ministry of national security was split into a defence ministry headed by Carlos Perdomo and a police and public security ministry headed by Douglas Singh.

The prime minister of Jamaica, Bruce Golding, survived a vote of no-confidence by 30 votes to 28.

Japan's prime minister Yukio Hatoyama resigned after the coalition government split over the decision to maintain a US military base on the island of Okinawa.

Thailand's prime minister Abhisit Vejjajiva won a parliamentary vote of confidence by 246 votes to 186.

Abdul Hafeez Sheikh was sworn in as Pakistan's finance minister.

Week Beginning 23 May 2010
In a cabinet reshuffle in Madagascar, Gen. André-Lucien Rakotoarimasy was named armed forces minister and a politician known simply as Jean, interior minister.

In Trinidad and Tobago's parliamentary elections the People's Partnership Coalition won 29 of 41 seats, against 12 seats for the ruling People's National Movement.

Kamla Persad-Bissessar was sworn in as prime minister. Dr. Surujrattan Rambachan was allocated the foreign affairs portfolio, John Sandy national security and Winston Dookeran finance.

The Mega Combination coalition won 23 of the available 51 seats in Suriname's parliamentary elections, the New Front for Democracy and Development 14, A-Combination 7, the People's Alliance 6 and the Party for Democracy and Development through Unity 1.

The Comoros' new interim government was sworn in with Fahmi Saïd Ibrahim as foreign minister, Ibrahima Houmadi Sidi as defence and interior minister, and Mohamed Bacar Dossar as finance minister.

Daho Ould Kablia was appointed Algeria's interior minister in a cabinet reshuffle.

In the Czech Republic's parliamentary elections, the Czech Social Democratic Party won 56 seats, the Civic Democratic Party won 53, Tradition Responsibility Prosperity 09 won 41, the Communist Party of Bohemia and Moravia won 26 and Public Affairs 24.

Hungary's new government headed by prime minister Viktor Orbán was sworn in with Csaba Hende as defence minister, György Matolcsy as economic development minister, János Martonyi as foreign minister and Sándor Pintér as interior minister.

Week Beginning 16 May 2010

In the Dominican Republic's parliamentary elections the Dominican Liberation Party (PLD) and its allies won 105 seats in the chamber of deputies, the Dominican Revolutionary Party and its allies 75 and the Social Christian Reformist Party (PRSC) 3.

The Somali prime minister Omar Abdirashid Ali Sharmarke lost a vote of confidence but refused to stand down.

In Kyrgyzstan, the head of the interim government Roza Otunbayeva became acting president.

Namadi Sambo took office as vice president of Nigeria.

Week Beginning 9 May 2010

In the Philippines' presidential election, Benigno 'Noynoy' Aquino III took 42.1% of the votes cast, ahead of Joseph Estrada with 26.3%, Manny Villar with 15.4% and Gilberto Teodoro with 11.3%. There were five other candidates. Lakas-Kampi-Christian Muslim Democrats claimed 104 seats in parliamentary elections, the Liberal Party coalition 45, Nationalist People's Coalition 31 and the Nacionalista Party coalition 26.

Estonia, Israel and Slovenia were invited to join the OECD.

Week Beginning 2 May 2010

Indonesia's finance minister Sri Mulyani Indrawati resigned after accepting a post at the World Bank. Agus Martowardojo was sworn in as new finance minister later in the month.

The ruling Alliance of the Future won Mauritius' parliamentary election taking 45 of 62 seats. The Alliance of the Heart won 20 seats, the Rodrigues Movement two, and the Mauritian Solidarity Front and the Organization of the People of Rodrigues one each.

Nigeria's president, Umaru Yar'Adua, died following a long period of ill health. He was succeeded by the acting president, Goodluck Jonathan.

Following presidential elections in Togo, prime minister Gilbert Houngbo's government resigned but Houngbo was reappointed the following day. Elliot Ohin was appointed foreign minister in a new cabinet formed later in the month while Adji Ayassor remained finance minister and Col. Atcha Titikpina security minister.

In the UK's parliamentary elections the Conservative Party won 306 seats with 36.1% of votes cast, the Labour Party 258 with 29.0% and the Liberal Democrats 57 with 23.0%. The Conservative Party and the Liberal Democrats formed a coalition with David Cameron as prime minister and Nick Clegg as deputy prime minister. The cabinet included George Osborne as chancellor of the exchequer, William Hague as foreign secretary and Theresa May as home secretary.

Chile became a full member of the OECD.

In Costa Rica, Laura Chinchilla took office as president. Her government included Anabel González Campabadal as foreign minister, José María Tijerino Pacheco as public security minister and Fernando Herrero Acosta as finance minister.

Chronology of Events for April 2010

Week Beginning 25 April 2010

After two rounds of parliamentary elections in Hungary, the alliance of Fidesz-Hungarian Civic Alliance and the Christian Democratic People's Party won 263 of 386 seats in the National Assembly, the Hungarian Socialist Party 59, Movement for a Better Hungary 47 and Politics Can Be Different 16. One independent was elected.

Heinz Fischer retained the Austrian presidency after winning 78.9% of the popular vote.

Aivis Ronis took office as Latvia's foreign minister.

Week Beginning 18 April 2010

Victor Yano took office as minister of state in Palau.

The United People's Freedom Alliance won 144 of 196 seats following the second round of voting in Sri Lanka's parliamentary elections. The United National Front won 60, the Tamil National Alliance 14 and the Democratic National Alliance 7. D. M. Jayaratne was sworn in as prime minister and

named G. L. Peiris foreign minister and John Seneviratne home affairs minister. President Mahinda Rajapaksa retained the finance and defence ministries.

In Ecuador, Patricio Rivera was appointed finance minister in a cabinet reshuffle.

The Belgian government collapsed following the withdrawal of the Open Vld party from the ruling coalition. Prime minister Yves Leterme's government remained in office in a caretaker capacity.

In snap parliamentary elections in Nauru, president Marcus Stephen's supporters won 9 of the 18 seats thus perpetuating a political stalemate.

Week Beginning 11 April 2010

Sir Arthur Foulkes took office as the Bahamas' governor-general.

In Panama, following the split of the justice and government ministry in a cabinet reshuffle, Roxana Méndez became interior minister and José Raúl Mulino public security minister.

In Sudanese presidential elections incumbent Omar Hassan Ahmed al-Bashir was re-elected with 68.2% of the vote.

Week Beginning 4 April 2010

A new cabinet was appointed in Nigeria by acting prime minister Goodluck Jonathan. It included Henry Odein Ajumogobia as foreign minister, Adetokunbo Kayode as defence minister and Emmanuel Iheanacho as internal affairs minister.

In Kyrgyzstan, president Kurmanbek Bakiyev fled the country following anti-government protests in which at least 80 people died. The opposition Social Democratic Party of Kyrgyzstan seized power and the former foreign minister, Roza Otunbayeva, was made head of the interim government. She appointed Temir Sariyev deputy prime minister and finance minister and Bolot Sherniyazov interior minister.

Madagascar's armed forces minister, Col. Noël Rakotonandrasana, was sacked by prime minister Col. Albert Camille Vital after he was implicated in a plot to mount a military coup. The prime minister took over the armed forces ministry.

The president of Poland, Lech Kaczyński, died in a fatal plane crash that killed 95 others including many of the country's most senior officials. The parliamentary speaker, Bronisław Komorowski, took over as acting president.

In Rwanda, Gen. James Kabarebe was appointed defence minister.

Chronology of Events for March 2010

Week Beginning 28 March 2010

Ahmed Ould Moualaye Ahmed took over Mauritania's finance ministry in a cabinet reshuffle.

In San Marino, Marco Conti and Glauco Sansovini were sworn in as captains-regent.

Week Beginning 21 March 2010

A new Namibian cabinet was sworn in that included Utoni Nujoma as foreign minister.

In Latvia, disagreements over economic policy caused the People's Party to withdraw from the coalition government. Four cabinet ministers resigned including the foreign minister, Māris Riekstiņš, although he agreed to remain in office until a replacement could be appointed.

Tony Killeen was appointed Ireland's defence minister.

Week Beginning 14 March 2010

Nigeria's acting president, Goodluck Jonathan, dissolved the cabinet. He subsequently named Adetokunbo Kayode defence minister, Olusegun Olutoyin Aganga finance minister, Henry Odein Ajumogobia foreign minister and Emmanuel Iheanacho interior minister.

Victor Yano succeeded Sandra Pierantozzi as Palau's secretary of state at the behest of President Toribiong.

Week Beginning 7 March 2010

The Iraqi National Movement coalition won 91 of 325 seats in Iraq's parliamentary elections, the State of Law Coalition 89, the National Iraqi Alliance 70, the Kurdistan List 43 and the Movement for Change 8.

In Chile, Sebastián Piñera took office as president. Alfredo Moreno was appointed foreign minister.

Chronology of Events for February 2010

Week Beginning 28 February 2010

The People's Democratic Party won Takjikistan's parliamentary elections, taking 54 of 63 seats.

Niger's post-coup transitional government was sworn in. It included Touré Aminatou as foreign minister, Gen. Mamadou Ousseini as defence minister, Cissé Ousmane as interior minister and Anou Badamassi as economy and finance minister.

José Alberto Mujica took office as president of Uruguay. His cabinet included Luis Almagro as foreign minister, Fernando Lorenzo as finance minister, Eduardo Bonomi as interior minister and Luis Rosadilla as defence minister.

The Ukrainian prime minister, Yuliya Tymoshenko, was ousted after losing a parliamentary vote of confidence. Oleksandr Turchynov succeeded her in an acting capacity.

In Côte d'Ivoire, Gervais Kacou was appointed foreign minister.

Faure Gnassingbé of the Rally for the Togolese People won Togo's presidential elections with 60.9% of the vote against 33.9% for his nearest rival, Jean-Pierre Fabre of the Union for the Forces of Change.

Chad's prime minister, Youssouf Saleh Abbas, resigned after cabinet ministers were implicated in an embezzlement scandal. He was succeeded by Emmanuel Nadingar. There were no changes to key ministries.

In Bosnia and Herzegovinia, Haris Silajdžić took over the rotating chairmanship of the presidency from Željko Komšić.

Week Beginning 21 February 2010

A major cabinet reshuffle in Denmark resulted in Lene Espersen becoming foreign minister, Gitte Lillelund Bech defence minister and Bertel Haarder interior and health minister.

Pakistan's finance minister Shaukat Tarin resigned citing personal reasons.

In Honduras, Marlon Pascua was sworn in as defence minister.

Week Beginning 14 February 2010

The cabinet of Guinea's new prime minister, Jean-Marie Doré, included Bakary Fofana as foreign minister, Kerfala Yansané as economy and finance minister and Gen. Mamadouba Toto Camara as security minister.

The president of Nauru, Marcus Stephen, defeated a parliamentary vote of no-confidence.

In Croatia, Ivo Josipović took office as president.

The Irish defence minister, Willie O'Dea, resigned after a defamation case concerning a political rival. Prime minister Brian Cowen took over the defence portfolio.

Following a military coup in Niger, power went to a new political organization called the Supreme Council for the Restoration of Democracy headed by Salou Djibo. Mahamadou Danda was appointed interim prime minister.

Adolphe Mulenda Bwana Sefu was appointed interior minister and Matata Mponyo Mapon finance minister in a cabinet reshuffle in the Democratic Republic of the Congo.

The Labour Party withdrew from the Dutch coalition government after disputes over the Netherlands' military presence in Afghanistan. Subsequently, prime minister Jan Peter Balkenende tendered the government's resignation. A caretaker government of the remaining coalition partners still headed by Balkenende with Jan Kees de Jager as finance minister and Hirsch Ballin as interior minister was to remain in office to serve until elections scheduled for June 2010.

Week Beginning 7 February 2010

Laura Chinchilla of the National Liberation Party (PLN) won Costa Rica's presidential elections with 46.8% of the vote against 25.2% for Ottón Solís of the Citizens' Action Party (PAC) and 20.8% for Otto Guevara of the Libertarian Movement (ML). In parliamentary elections, the PLN took 22 of 57 seats, the PAC 12, the ML 9, the Social Christian Unity Party 6 and the Accessibility Without Exclusion Party 4, with the remaining seats going to minor parties.

Following the January re-election of the Labour Party in St Kitts and Nevis, a new government was sworn in. Prime minister Denzil Douglas took on the finance portfolio while the foreign affairs and national security ministries went to deputy prime minister Sam Condor.

The second round of presidential elections in Ukraine saw Viktor Yanukovych retain his first round majority against Yuliya Tymoshenko. He won 49.0% of the vote against her 45.5% although Tymoshenko challenged the results.

Nigeria's vice president, Goodluck Jonathan, was confirmed as acting president by the senate, having assumed power in Jan. after president Umaru Yar'Adua was incapacitated by ill health.

Madagascar's vice prime minister and foreign minister, Ny Hasina Andriamanjato, resigned over disagreements with the interim president, Andry Rajoelina. He was succeeded as foreign minister by Hyppolite Ramaroson.

In Lithuania, Audronius Ažubalis was sworn in as foreign minister.

In a dispute over preparations for long-postponed elections in Côte d'Ivoire, president Laurent Gbagbo dissolved the cabinet and the Independent Electoral Commission. However, he immediately reappointed prime minister Guillaume Soro to form a new government. Michel Amani N'Guessan remained defence minister but Désiré Tagro took over as interior minister and Charles Diby Koffi as finance minister.

Chronology of Events for January 2010

Week Beginning 31 January 2010

In Greece, parliament re-elected president Karolos Papoulias by a large majority.

Angola's new constitution took effect replacing the office of prime minister with that of vice-president. Fernando Dias dos Santos became the country's first vice-president while Carlos Alberto Lopes took on the finance portfolio.

Week Beginning 24 January 2010

Bolivia's new cabinet included Rubén Saavedra Soto as defence minister and Sacha Sergio Llorenti as finance minister.

The vice-president and defence minister of Venezuela resigned citing personal reasons. Elías Jaua was appointed new vice-president and Carlos Mata defence minister.

In Libya, Mohamed Abdul Quasim al-Zwai replaced Imbarek Shamekh as secretary general of the General People's Congress.

Jean-Marie Doré took office as prime minister of Guinea.

In Sri Lanka's presidential elections, the incumbent president Mahinda Rajapaksa was re-elected with 57.9% of the vote ahead of Sarath Fonseka with 40.2%.

Porfirio Lobo Sosa took office as president of Honduras. His cabinet included Mario Canahuati as foreign minister, África Madrid as interior minister and William Chong Wong as finance minister.

Despite dismissal by parliamentary vote, Ukrainian interior minister Yuriy Lutsenko was reappointed to the ministry in an acting capacity by prime minister Yuliya Tymoshenko.

Week Beginning 17 January 2010

Bulgaria's defence minister, Nikolai Mladenov, took over the foreign affairs portfolio. Anyu Angelov replaced him as defence minister.

Following the resignation of Lithuania's foreign minister, Vygaudas Ušackas, over disagreements with president Dalia Grybauskaitė, Audronius Ažubalis was appointed to the ministry.

Week Beginning 10 January 2010

In the second round runoff of Croatia's presidential elections, Ivo Josipović received 60.3% of votes cast against 39.7% for Milan Bandić.

Following two rounds of parliamentary elections in Uzbekistan, the Liberal-Democratic Party won the majority of the seats with 53, the People's Democratic Party 32, the National Revival Democratic Party 31 and the Justice Social Democratic Party 19.

Ecuador's foreign minister, Fander Falconí, resigned after disagreements with president Rafael Correa over oil exploitation negotiations. He was replaced by Ricardo Patiño.

In Equatorial Guinea, prime minister Ignacio Milam Tang and his cabinet resigned in order to fulfil a legal requirement following the re-election of president Brig.-Gen. Teodoro Obiang Nguema Mbasogo in Dec. They were reappointed later on the same day with no changes in key cabinet positions.

A major cabinet reshuffle in Tunisia resulted in Kamel Morjane becoming foreign minister, Ridha Grira defence minister and Mohamed Ridha Chalghoum finance minister.

In Venezuela, Jorge Giordani was appointed to head the newly-merged finance and planning ministries.

Aires Bonifácio Ali took office as prime minister of Mozambique.

Week Beginning 3 January 2010

In Dominica, a new cabinet was sworn in with prime minister Roosevelt Skerrit as foreign and finance minister and Charles Savarin as national security minister.

Taib Cherkaoui became interior minister of Morocco following a cabinet reshuffle.

Japan's finance minister, Hirohisa Fujii, resigned owing to ill health and purported disagreements with Democratic Party leader Ichiro Ozawa. He was succeeded by Naoto Kan.

A cabinet reshuffle in São Tomé e Príncipe resulted in António Paquete becoming interior minister.

2009

Chronology of Events for December 2009

Week Beginning 27 December 2009

Ivo Josipović of the Social Democratic Party of Croatia won the majority of the vote in the first round of Croatia's presidential elections with 32.4%, followed by 14.8% for Milan Bandić (ind.), 12.0% for Andrija Hebrang (Croatian Democratic Union) and 11.3% for Nadan Vidošević (ind.).

Doris Leuthard was sworn in as president of Switzerland.

Herman Van Rompuy was sworn in as president of the European Union.

In Afghanistan, the majority of president Hamid Karzai's cabinet nominations were rejected by parliament. However, the defence, finance and interior portfolios remained unchanged and were accepted.

Week Beginning 20 December 2009

Peru's finance minister Luis Carranza resigned. He was succeeded by Mercedes Rosalba Aráoz Fernández.

Week Beginning 13 December 2009

In the first round of Chile's presidential election, Eduardo Frei Ruiz-Tagle of the Christian Democratic Party took 44.1% of the vote against 29.6% for Sebastián Piñera Echineque of National Renewal. There were two other candidates.

The ruling Dominica Labour Party won 18 of 21 elected seats in Dominica's parliamentary elections and three seats went to the United Workers Party.

In Madagascar, president Andry Rajoelina dismissed compromise prime minister Eugène Mangalaza. Acting prime minister Cécile Manorohanta was appointed his successor but shortly afterwards Rajoelina appointed Col. Albert Camille Vital in her place.

Week Beginning 6 December 2009

In Bolivia's presidential election Evo Morales Ayma (Movement Towards Socialism) won 64.1% of votes cast against 26.6% for Manfred Reyes Villa (Progress Plan for Bolivia). The Movement Towards Socialism claimed 88 of 130 seats in elections to the Chamber of Deputies, Progress Plan for Bolivia 37, the National Unity Front 3 and the Social Alliance 2.

The pro-presidential party and its allies won 20 of 24 elected seats in Comoros' parliamentary election while the opposition took four.

In the second round run-off in Romania's presidential election incumbent Traian Băsescu retained the presidency with 50.3% of the vote against 49.7% for Mircea Geoană. The opposition contested the results and accused Băsescu of ballot-rigging.

The 15th United Nations Climate Change Summit began in Copenhagen.

In the second round of Moldova's indirect presidential elections, Marian Lupu of the Liberal Democratic Party of Moldova failed to gain enough votes to secure the presidency.

Jordan's prime minister, Nader Dahabi, resigned along with his cabinet after King Abdullah dissolved parliament in late Nov. Samir Zaid al-Rifai succeeded Dahabi as prime minister and defence minister. He appointed Mohammad Abu Hammour finance minister.

Chronology of Events for November 2009

Week Beginning 29 November 2009

President Nguema Mbasogo was re-elected with 95.4% of votes cast in presidential elections in Equatorial Guinea. The opposition accused Mbasogo of electoral fraud.

Presidential and parliamentary elections took place in Honduras. Early results indicated that Porfirio Lobo Sosa of the National Party had won 56% of votes cast against 38% for Elvin Santos of the Liberal Party.

In Uruguay's presidential election runoff, José Alberto Mujica Cordano gained 54.8% of the vote to Luis Alberto Lacalle's 45.2%.

Switzerland's vice president and minister of economic affairs, Doris Leuthard, was elected president for 2010. Moritz Leuenberger was named vice president.

Yukiya Amano of Japan succeeded Dr. Mohamed ElBaradei as head of the International Atomic Energy Agency.

Louise Mushikiwabo was named foreign minister and John Rwangombwa finance minister in a cabinet reshuffle in Rwanda.

Yury Zhadobin was appointed defence minister of Belarus.

In Vanuatu, prime minister Edward Natapei retained his seat in parliament after the chief justice ruled that it was unconstitutional to exclude him for lack of attendance. Natapei subsequently survived a parliamentary no-confidence motion by 36 votes to 11.

Week Beginning 22 November 2009

In the first round of Romania's presidential elections, incumbent Traian Băsescu of the Democratic Liberal Party won 32.4% of the vote, followed by Mircea Geoană (Social Democratic Party) with 31.2%, Crin Antonescu (National Liberal Party) with 20.0% and Corneliu Vadim Tudor (Greater Romania Party) 5.6%.

In Belgium, Yves Leterme was nominated by King Albert to replace Herman Van Rompuy as prime minister after the latter was made president of the European Council. Steven Vanackere replaced Leterme as foreign minister but otherwise key cabinet positions remained unchanged.

Vanuatu's prime minister Edward Natapei lost his seat after he failed to attend parliament on three consecutive occasions. He launched a legal appeal against the ruling and was scheduled to remain in office until after the announcement of the court's decision in Dec.

Incumbent president Hifikepunye Pohamba of the South West Africa People's Organization won presidential elections in Namibia with 75.3% of votes cast. In parliamentary elections held on the same day the South West Africa People's Organization won 54 of 72 seats, Rally for Democracy and Progress 8 and the Democratic Turnhalle Alliance, National Unity Democratic Organization and United Democratic Front 2 each.

Week Beginning 15 November 2009

In a cabinet reshuffle in Vanuatu, Moana Carcasses Kalosil was appointed internal affairs minister.

The Belgian prime minister Herman Van Rompuy was named the first president of the European Council.

In Afghanistan, Hamid Karzai was sworn for a second term as president.

Week Beginning 8 November 2009

The Lebanese prime minister Saad Hariri and his cabinet took office. Ali al-Shami was appointed foreign minister and Raya Haffar finance minister while Elias Murr remained defence minister and Ziad Baroud interior minister.

Marian Lupu failed to win the majority in a parliamentary vote to become president of Moldova. A new election was scheduled to be held within 30 days.

In Haiti, Jean-Max Bellerive was sworn in as prime minister. His cabinet included Marie-Michèle Rey as foreign minister and Ronald Baudin as finance minister while Paul Antoine Bien-Aimé remained interior minister.

Gombojav Zandanshatar became foreign minister of Mongolia.

Eugène Mangalaza was sworn in as prime minister of Madagascar, having been appointed 5 weeks earlier.

Week Beginning 1 November 2009

A second round runoff between the incumbent president Hamid Karzai and Abdullah Abdullah in Afghanistan's presidential elections was cancelled after Abdullah pulled out having questioned the impartiality of the Afghani Independent Electoral Commission. Karzai was duely elected.

Jurelang Zedkaia was sworn in as president of the Marshall Islands.

In Romania, parliament failed to endorse Lucian Croitoru as prime minister. Liviu Negoiţă was nominated prime minister by president Băsescu.

The Fiji Islands' president, Ratu Epeli Nailatikau, was sworn in having served in an interim capacity since July.

Chronology of Events for October 2009

Week Beginning 25 October 2009

Presidential elections in Tunisia resulted in president Zine El Abidine Ben Ali being re-elected by 89.6% of votes cast. In the parliamentary elections the ruling RCD won 161 of 214 available National Assembly seats, ahead of the Movement of Social Democrats with 16 and the Popular Unity Party with 12.

In Uruguay's presidential election a runoff was scheduled to be held between José Alberto Mujica Cordano who received 48.0% of the vote and Luis Alberto Lacalle de Herrera who received 29.1%. In the General Assembly elections the Broad Front won 50 seats in the Chamber of Deputies (16 in the senate), the National Party 30 (9 in the senate), the Colorado Party 17 (5 in the senate) and the Independent Party 2.

The prime minister of Mongolia, Sanj Bayar, resigned because of health problems. He was succeeded by foreign affairs minister Sukhbaataryn Batbold.

Following a cabinet reshuffle in Guinea-Bissau, Aristides Ocante da Silva was appointed defence minister, Adelino Mano Quetá foreign minister and José Mário Vaz defence minister.

The US Department of Commerce announced that the economy was out of recession. Third quarter growth of 3.5% was revised down to 2.2% in Dec.

Week Beginning 18 October 2009

After Afghanistan's Independent Election Commission found that Hamid Karzai had not won a 50% majority as initially declared in August's presidential election, a second round runoff between Karzai and Abdullah Abdullah was announced.

In Kyrgyzstan, prime minister Igor Chudinov resigned along with his cabinet to make way for government reforms sought by president Kurmanbek Bakiyev. Daniyar Usenov succeeded Chudinov as prime minister.

The National Movement for the Development of Society dominated parliamentary elections in Niger, winning 76 seats against 15 for the Social Democratic Rally and 7 for the Rally for Democracy and Progress. Opposition parties boycotted the election.

Norway's new cabinet was sworn in following September's parliamentary elections with Grete Faremo as defence minister and Sigbjørn Johnsen as finance minister.

In Indonesia's new cabinet Marty Natalegawa was made foreign minister, Purnomo Yusgiantoro defence minister and Gamawan Fauzi home affairs minister.

After losing a parliamentary vote of no-confidence, the president of the Marshall Islands Litokwa Tomeing was succeeded by Ruben Zackhras on a temporary basis before speaker Jurelang Zedkaia was elected the new president by parliament.

German chancellor Angela Merkel's new cabinet comprised Guido Westerwelle as foreign minister, Karl-Theodor Freiherr zu Guttenberg as defence minister, Thomas de Maizière as interior minister and Wolfgang Schäuble as finance minister.

Week Beginning 11 October 2009

The government of Timor-Leste led by prime minister Xanana Gusmão survived a parliamentary vote of no-confidence by 38 votes to 25.

In Portugal, prime minister José Sócrates appointed a new cabinet including Augusto Santos Silva as defence minister.

Abdoulaye Baldé was appointed defence minister and Bécaye Diop interior minister following a cabinet reshuffle in Senegal.

In Botswana's parliamentary elections the ruling Botswana Democratic Party gained 45 seats, ahead of the Botswana National Front with 6 and the Botswana Congress Party with 4.

Ali Bongo Ondimba was sworn in as Gabon's president. In the new cabinet Paul Biyoghé-Mba remained prime minister while Angélique Ngoma was made defence minister.

Week Beginning 4 October 2009

In Greece's parliamentary elections the opposition Pasok won 160 seats, the ruling New Democracy 91, the Communist Party 21, the Popular Orthodox Rally 15 and the Coalition of the Radical Left 13. Georgios Papandreou was sworn in as prime minister and foreign minister and appointed Evangelos Venizelos defence minister, Yiannis Ragoussis interior minister and Georgios Papaconstantinou finance minister. The government won a parliamentary vote of confidence shortly afterwards.

Gold prices hit a record high at US$1,040 an ounce.

Eugène Mangalaza was designated prime minister of a unity government in Madagascar after months of political upheaval. However, power-sharing collapsed when former president Marc Ravalomanana refused to recognize president Andry Rajoelina and prime minister Monja Roindefo refused to stand down. Mangalaza's appointment was then suspended by the State Council. Cécile Manorohanta was made acting prime minister.

Poland's deputy prime minister and interior minister Grzegorz Schetyna and justice minister Andrzej Czuma resigned after they were implicated in a gambling scandal. Economy minister Waldemar Pawlak became deputy prime minister and Jerzy Miller interior minister.

US president Barack Obama was awarded the Nobel Peace Prize for his 'extraordinary efforts to strengthen international diplomacy and co-operation between peoples'.

Petro Poroshenko was appointed foreign minister in the Ukrainian cabinet, filling a post that had been vacant since March.

Turkey and Armenia signed an agreement to normalize ties and establish diplomatic relations.

Chronology of Events for September 2009

Week Beginning 27 September 2009

In Germany's Bundestag elections the Christian Democratic Union/Christian Social Union won 239 seats; the Social Democratic Party, 146; the Free Democratic Party, 93; the Left, 76; and the Greens, 68.

The ruling Socialist Party retained power in Portugal's legislative elections winning 96 seats; the Social Democratic Party won 78; the Popular Party, 21; the Left Bloc, 16; and the Communist Party/Green Party coalition, 15.

In Romania, prime minister Emil Boc dismissed interior minister Dan Nica who had suggested that forthcoming presidential elections would be marred by fraud. This prompted the resignation of Nica's fellow Social Democratic Party members, resulting in the collapse of the coalition government. Vasile Blaga was appointed acting interior minister and justice minister Cătălin Predoiu took over as acting foreign minister.

Canadian prime minister Stephen Harper's government survived a parliamentary vote of no-confidence by 144 votes to 117.

A no-confidence motion brought against the prime minister of Finland, Matti Vanhanen, was dismissed by 117 votes to 27.

Francesco Mussoni and Stefano Palmieri were sworn in as captains-regent of San Marino.

In a cabinet reshuffle in Senegal, foreign minister Cheikh Tidiane Gadio lost his post to Madické Niang.

The new Supreme Court came into existence in the United Kingdom, replacing the Appellate Committee of the House of Lords as the highest court in the country.

Week Beginning 20 September 2009

The prime minister of Niger, Seyni Oumarou, resigned to run in October's presidential election. He was replaced temporarily by interior minister Albadé Abouba before Ali Badjo Gamatié took over the post on a permanent basis.

Week Beginning 13 September 2009

In Norway's parliamentary elections the ruling Labour Party won 64 out of 169 seats ahead of the Progress Party with 41 and the Conservative Party with 30.

Following his re-election, president of the Republic of the Congo Denis Sassou-Nguesso abolished the post of prime minister and reshuffled his cabinet. Gilbert Ondongo was appointed finance minister and Charles Zacharie Bowao defence minister.

José Manuel Barroso was re-elected president of the European Commission by 382 votes to 219. There were 117 abstentions.

Yukio Hatoyama took office as prime minister of Japan. His cabinet included Katsuya Okada as foreign minister, Toshimi Kitazawa as defence minister, Hirohisa Fujii as finance minister and Kazuhiro Haraguchi as internal affairs minister.

In Switzerland, Didier Burkhalter was named interior minister.

Week Beginning 6 September 2009

Following criticism of his government's handling of the recent Typhoon Morakot, Taiwanese prime minister Liu Chao-shiuan announced his resignation and that of his cabinet. He was succeeded by Wu Den-yih. The new cabinet comprised Timothy Yang as foreign minister, Kao Hua-chu as defence minister and Jiang Yi-huah as interior minister.

Malam Bacai Sanhá took office as president of Guinea-Bissau.

In Madagascar's latest cabinet reshuffle, Hery Rajaonarimampianina was named finance and budget minister and Cécile Manorohanta interior minister.

Saad Hariri stood down as prime minister-designate of Lebanon after Hizbollah politicians rejected his choice of cabinet ministers. However, he was reappointed by parliamentary vote shortly afterwards.

Chronology of Events for August 2009

Week Beginning 30 August 2009

In Gabon, the late president's son Ali Bongo Ondimba won the presidential election with 41.7% of votes cast against 25.9% for Andre Mba Obame and 25.2% for Pierre Mamboundou.

Legislative elections in Japan resulted in the ruling Liberal Democratic Party being ousted after winning only 119 seats compared to the Democratic Party of Japan's 308.

In a cabinet reshuffle in Uruguay, Pedro Vaz was appointed foreign minister and Gonzalo Fernández defence minister.

Iolu Abil was elected president of Vanuatu in the third round of parliamentary voting.

Moldovan president Vladimir Voronin announced his resignation in the wake of the Communist Party defeat at legislative elections. He appointed Vitalie Pirlog as acting prime minister.

In Albania, a coalition government was formed between the Democratic Party and the Socialist Movement for Integration. Sali Berisha remained prime minister while Ilir Meta was named foreign minister.

Chung Un-chan was named prime minister of South Korea and Gen. Kim Tae-young defence minister in a cabinet reshuffle.

Week Beginning 23 August 2009

Moldova's cabinet headed by prime minister Zinaida Greceanîi resigned after Greceanîi declared she was unable to hold the posts of prime minister and member of parliament simultaneously following July's election.

Bacho Akhalaia was appointed defence minister of Georgia in a cabinet reshuffle.

Week Beginning 16 August 2009

In Vanuatu, after president Kalkot Mataskelekele Mauliliu reached the end of his term of office, speaker Maxime Carlot Korman became acting president.

Louis B. Susman took up his duties as United States ambassador to the UK.

Niger's cabinet resigned, allowing a constitutional amendment to be passed that extends president Mamadou Tandja's term by 3 years. The cabinet was reappointed with no changes.

Ali Ahmed Jama Jangali was appointed foreign minister and Abdallah Boss Ahmed defence minister following a cabinet reshuffle in Somalia.

In Iran, president Mahmoud Ahmadinejad named Ahmad Vahidi defence minister and Mostafa Mohammad Najjar interior minister in his new cabinet while Manouchehr Mottaki and Shamseddin Hosseini remained as foreign and economy and finance minister respectively.

In the first round of Afghanistan's presidential election, initial counts suggested that Hamid Karzai would be re-elected president with 54% of the vote compared to his closest rival Abdullah Abdullah's 28%. However, doubt as to the validity of the elections was widespread at home and abroad with all candidates accused of ballot-rigging.

Week Beginning 9 August 2009

Gabon's defence minister Ali Bongo Ondimba stood down to run for president. Jean-François Ndongou succeeded him.

Week Beginning 2 August 2009

Costa Rican finance minister Guillermo Zúñiga resigned to work on the National Liberation Party's presidential campaign. He was succeeded by Jenny Phillips.

Mohamed Ould Abdel Aziz took office as president of Mauritania. His cabinet appointments included Naha Mint Mouknass as foreign minister, Hamadi Ould Hamadi as defence minister, Mohamed Ould Boilil as interior minister and Kane Ousmane as finance minister. Moulaye Ould Mohamed Laghdaf remained prime minister.

Chronology of Events for July 2009

Week Beginning 26 July 2009

Malam Bacai Sanhá claimed victory in the second round of Guinea-Bissau's presidential elections, claiming 63.3% of the vote against 36.7% for Mohamed Ialá Embaló.

In the Fiji Islands, Ratu Josefa Iloilo stepped down as president. Vice president Ratu Epeli Nailatikau succeeded him on an interim basis.

In Moldova's parliamentary elections the ruling Party of Communists of the Republic of Moldova won 48 seats, the Liberal Democratic Party of Moldova 18, the Liberal Party 15, the Democratic Party 13 and the Party Alliance Our Moldova 7.

Former Danish prime minister Anders Fogh Rasmussen took office as secretary general of NATO.

Week Beginning 19 July 2009

Kyrgyzstan's incumbent president Kurmanbek Bakiyev was re-elected with 76.1% of the vote in presidential elections although the results were disputed by several opposition candidates.

Ratu Inoke Kubuabola was appointed foreign minister in the Fijian cabinet.

Week Beginning 12 July 2009

In elections in the Republic of the Congo, incumbent president Denis Sassou-Nguesso was re-elected with 78.6% of the vote.

Dalia Grybauskaitė took office as president of Lithuania.

Japan's prime minister Taro Aso defeated a parliamentary vote of no-confidence by 333 votes to 139. He later dissolved parliament in preparation for a general election to be held in August.

Former Polish prime minister Jerzy Buzek was elected president of the European Parliament.

In Gabon, Jean Eyeghe Ndong resigned as prime minister. Interim president Rose Francine Rogombé appointed Paul Biyoghé Mba his successor. There were no major changes in the new cabinet.

In a cabinet reshuffle in Belgium, Yves Leterme became foreign minister and Annemie Turtelboom interior minister.

Mohamed Ould Abdel Aziz, leader of the 2008 coup, won Mauritania's presidential election with 52.6% of the vote against 16.3% for Messaoud Ould Boulkheir and 13.7% for Ahmed Ould Daddah.

Week Beginning 5 July 2009

Citizens for the European Development of Bulgaria won 116 of 240 seats in Bulgaria's legislative elections followed by the Coalition for Bulgaria (headed by the Bulgarian Socialist Party) with 40 seats, the Movement for Rights and Freedoms with 38, the Attack coalition with 21, the Blue Coalition with 15 and Order, Law and Justice with 10.

Željko Komšić took over Bosnia and Herzegovina's rotating presidency.

In a cabinet reshuffle in Argentina, Aníbal Fernández was appointed chief of the cabinet and Amado Boudou minister of economy and public finance.

Ingrida Šimonytė was sworn in as finance minister of Lithuania.

In the Solomon Islands, Frank Kabui took office as governor-general.

Zambia's defence minister George Mpombo resigned on personal grounds. In a subsequent reshuffle, home affairs minister Kalombo Mwansa was appointed defence minister and Lameck Mangani home affairs minister.

Honduras' foreign minister Enrique Ortez Colindres was moved to the interior ministry after attracting criticism for his remarks about US president Barack Obama. He resigned shortly afterwards. Carlos López Contreras took over as foreign minister.

In Indonesia's presidential election, incumbent Susilo Bambang Yudhoyono won 60.8% of the vote against 26.8% for former president Megawati Sukarnoputri.

Peru's president Alan García appointed a new cabinet that included Ángel Javier Velásquez Quesquén as prime minister, Rafael Rey Rey as defence minister and Octavio Edilberto Salazar Miranda as interior minister.

Chronology of Events for June 2009

Week Beginning 28 June 2009

In the first round of Guinea-Bissau's presidential elections, Malam Bacai took 39.6% of votes cast, ahead of former president Kumba Ialá with 29.4%, former interim president Henrique Rosa with 24.2% and Iaya Djaló with 3.1%.

Philemon Yang took office as prime minister of Cameroon with Edgard Alain Mebe Ngo'o as defence minister in the new cabinet.

In Lithuania, finance minister Algirdas Šemeta stepped down to become a European Union commissioner.

Croatia's prime minister Ivo Sanader resigned. He was succeeded by Jadranka Kosor.

Ricardo Martinelli took office as president of Panama. His cabinet included Juan Carlos Varela Rodríguez as vice-president and foreign minister, José Raúl Mulino as minister of government and justice and Alberto Vallarino Clément as finance minister.

Week Beginning 21 June 2009

A cabinet reshuffle in France saw Brice Hortefeux become interior minister.

President Manuel Zelaya's attempt to seek re-election in Honduras led to the resignation of defence minister Edmundo Orellana. Shorty afterwards, the president was overthrown by the military and sent into exile in Costa Rica. Roberto Micheletti was named new president, appointing Adolfo Lionel Sevilla minister of defence, Gabriela Núñez finance minister and Enrique Ortez Colindres foreign minister.

In Mauritania, before ousted president Mohmed Ould Cheikh Abdallahi resigned officially, he appointed a new cabinet that included Yedali Ould Cheikh as defence minister, Mohamed Ould R'Zeyzim as interior minister and Sidi Ould Salem as finance minister.

Week Beginning 14 June 2009

The Solomon Islands' parliament elected Frank Kabui as governor-general.

Vanuatu's prime minister Edward Natapei defeated a parliamentary vote of no-confidence. He appointed Joe Natuman foreign minister in a subsequent cabinet reshuffle.

In Kazakhstan, the defence mnister Daniyal Akhmetov was sacked over corruption allegations. Adilbek Dzhaksybekov took over the ministry.

Following a major cabinet reshuffle in Malawi, Joyce Banda became vice-preisdent, Ken Kandodo finance minister, Etta Banda foreign minister and Aaron Sangala interior minister.

Tsakhiagiin Elbegdorj took office as prime minister of Mongolia.

Week Beginning 7 June 2009

In European Parliament elections the European People's Party took 265 of 736 seats, Progressive Alliance of Socialists and Democrats 184, Alliance of Liberals and Democrats for Europe 84, Greens/European Free Alliance 55, European Conservatives and Reformists 54, European United Left/Nordic Green Left 35, Europe of Freedom and Democracy 32 and non-attached members 27.

The anti-Syrian opposition won 71 of 128 seats in Lebanon's parliamentary elections while Hizbollah and its allies took 29 and the Free Patriotic Movement and its allies 28.

In Luxembourg, the Christian Social People's Party won 26 of 60 seats in parliamentary elections, the Socialist Workers' Party 13, the Democratic Party 9, the Greens 7, the Alternative Democratic Reform Party 4 and the Left 1.

Following the death of Gabon's president Omar Bongo Ondimba, Rose Francine Rogombé became interim president. Jean François Ndongou was appointed interior minister in a subsequent cabinet reshuffle.

Gambian finance minister Musa Gibril Balal Gaye was sacked. He was succeeded by Abdou Kolley.

Montenegro's new cabinet, featuring Ivan Brajović as interior minister and Branko Vujović as economy minister, was approved by parliament.

Idrissou Daouda was named finance minister of Benin.

Incumbent Iranian president Mahmoud Ahmadinejad gained 62.6% of the vote in presidential elections ahead of Mir-Hossein Mousavi with 33.8%. The official results were widely disputed, sparking opposition protests across the country.

In Japan, Kunio Hatoyama resigned as interior minister following a dispute with prime minister Aso. He was succeeded by Tsutomu Sato.

Chronology of Events for May 2009

Week Beginning 31 May 2009

Mauricio Funes took office as president of El Salvador. His cabinet included Hugo Martínez as foreign minister, David Munguía Payes as defence minister, Carlos Cáceres as finance minister and Humberto Centeno as interior minister.

In the Maldives, Mohamed Shihab became home minister.

The resignations of home secretary Jacqui Smith and defence secretary John Hutton prompted a cabinet reshuffle in the UK. Alan Johnson became home secretary and Bob Ainsworth defence secretary.

Jaume Bartemu was elected president of Andorra by parliament. His new government included Xavier Espot Miró as foreign minister, Pere López as finance minister and Víctor Naudi as interior minister.

Australia's defence minister Joel Fitzgibbon resigned amidst allegations of ministerial misconduct. In the ensuing cabinet reshuffle, John Faulkner was appointed defence minister and Brendan O'Connor home affairs minister.

In Nepal, Sujata Koirala was appointed home minister.

Ukraine's defence minister Yuriy Yekhanurov was voted out of office after losing a parliamentary vote by 363 votes to 18. Valeriy Ivashchenko became acting defence minister.

Week Beginning 24 May 2009

In Mongolia's presidential election Tsakhiagiin Elbegdorj of the Democratic Party won 51.2% of the vote compared to 47.4% for the incumbent Nambaryn Enkhbayar.

Having been nominated by parliament Madhav Kumar Nepal was sworn in as prime minister of Nepal. Bidya Bhandari was appointed defence minister and Surendra Pandey finance minister.

The interior minister of Turkmenistan, Orazgendy Amanmyradov, was dismissed for his reported failure to lower the country's crime rates and levels of corruption. Iskander Mulikov succeeded him.

Week Beginning 17 May 2009

Dalia Grybauskaitė won Lithuania's presidential election with 69.1% of the vote, ahead of Algirdas Butkevičius with 11.8%.

In Colombia, Juan Manuel Santos resigned as defence mnister. He was succeeded by the commander of the armed forces Gen. Freddy Padilla de León.

Incumbent Malawian president Bingu wa Mutharika won a second term in office after he gained 66.0% of the vote against 30.7% for John Tembo in presidential elections although Tembo contested the results. Mutharika's party also achieved success in parliamentary elections winning 114 of 193 seats. The remainder went to the Malawi Congress Party (26), the United Democratic Front (17) and independents (32).

Salam Fayyad was reappointed president of the Palestinian Authority by president Mahmoud Abbas. Hamas refused to recognize the new Fatah-dominated coalition government.

In Estonia, prime minister Andrus Ansip fired three Social Democratic ministers, including finance minister Ivari Padar and interior minister Jüri Pihl, following disputes over economic policy. Agriculture minister Helir-Valdor Seeder was temporarily given the finance portfolio and justice minister Rein Lang the interior portfolio before they were later transferred to Jürgen Ligi and to Marko Pomerants respectively.

Horst Köhler was re-elected federal president of Germany.

Week Beginning 10 May 2009

In Iceland, prime minister Jóhanna Sigurðardóttir's government was re-established with no key changes following parliamentary elections.

Gjorgje Ivanov was sworn in as president of Macedonia.

The Indian National Congress (INC) and its allies won 262 of 543 seats in India's parliamentary elections, with the INC claiming 206 seats. The National Democratic Alliance won 159, the Bharatiya Janata Party 116, the Third Front 79 and the Fourth Front 27. Manmohan Singh was reappointed prime minister while Pranab Mukherjee became finance minister and S. M. Krishna foreign minister. The defence and home affairs portfolios remained unchanged.

In Kuwait's parliamentary elections, independents claimed the majority of seats taking 21 out of 50, followed by Sunni Islamists with 13, Liberals (7), Shia Islamists (6) and the popular Bloc (3). Sheikh Nasser Muhammad Al-Ahmad Al-Sabah regained his position as prime minister and reappointed his former cabinet with no changes in key portfolios.

Week Beginning 3 May 2009

In Nepal, the summary dismissal of the head of the army by prime minister Pushpa Kamal Dahal led the ministers of the Communist Party of Nepal (Unified Marxist-Leninist) including home minister Bamdev Gautam to resign. President Ram Baran Yadav reinstated the army chief, in turn prompting the resignation of prime minister Pushpa Kamal Dahal.

Ricardo Martinelli emerged the victor in Panama's presidential elections with 60.3% of the vote against 37.3% for Balbina Herrera of the ruling Revolutionary Democratic Party.

Moldovan prime minister Zinaida Greceanîi's government resigned before the first meeting of the new parliament. The cabinet, reappointed with no changes to key positions, was scheduled to hold office only until snap parliamentary elections could be called.

In the Czech Republic, Jan Fischer took over as prime minister of a caretaker government that included Jan Kohout as deputy prime minister and foreign minister, Martin Barták as deputy prime minister and defence minister, Eduard Janota as finance minister and Martin Pecina as interior minister.

Peter Tom took over from James Tora as home minister of the Solomon Islands.

Jacob Zuma was elected president of South Africa by parliament. He appointed Lindiwe Sisulu defence minister, Pravin Gordhan finance minister, Nkosazana Dlamini-Zuma home minister and Maite Nkoana-Mashabane, international relations minister.

The Dhivehi Rayyithunge Party won 28 of 77 seats in the Maldives' parliamentary elections, the Maldivian Democratic Party 25, the People's Alliance seven, the Dhivehi Qaumee Party two and the Justice Party one with the remaining 13 seats going to independents.

Chronology of Events for April 2009

Week Beginning 26 April 2009

Following the Social Democratic Party's victory in Andorra's legislative elections with 14 of 28 seats, Jaume Bartumeu became president-delegate.

Incumbent Rafael Vicente Correa Delgado won 51.9% of the vote against 27.9% for Lucio Edwin Gutiérrez Borbúa in Ecuador's presidential elections.

Héctor Lacognata became foreign minister of Paraguay.

The UK's military mission in Iraq was ended.

The prime minister of Senegal Cheikh Hadjibou Soumaré resigned for personal reasons. He was succeeded by Souleymane Ndéné Ndiaye who made no major changes to the cabinet.

Tonga's prime minister Fred Sevele added foreign affairs and defence to his portfolio following a cabinet reshuffle.

In Turkey, Mehmet Şimşek was named finance minister, Ali Babacan economy minister and Ahmet Davutoğlu foreign minister in a major cabinet reshuffle.

Week Beginning 19 April 2009

The African National Congress won 264 seats in South Africa's presidential elections followed by the Democratic Alliance with 67, Congress of the People with 30 and Inkatha Freedom Party with 18.

Said Summar was named Syria's interior minister in a cabinet reshuffle.

In Iceland's parliamentary election the Social Democratic Alliance won 20 of the 63 seats, the Independence Party 16, the Left-Green Movement 14, the Progressive Party 9 and the Citizens' Movement 4.

Week Beginning 12 April 2009

In Hungary, a vote of no-confidence resulted in Ferenc Gyurcsány being replaced as prime minister by Gordon Bajnai. Péter Balázs was named foreign minister and Péter Oszkó finance minister.

Gen. Mohamed Ould Abdel Aziz resigned as head of state to run in upcoming presidential elections in Mauritania. Ba Mamadou Mbaré became interim head of state.

Week Beginning 5 April 2009

Lars Løkke Rasmussen succeeded Anders Fogh Rasmussen as prime minister of Denmark following the latter's appointment as NATO secretary general.

In Moldova's parliamentary elections, the ruling Party of Communists of the Republic of Moldova (PCRM) won 61 seats, the Liberal Party 15, the Liberal Democratic Party of Moldova 14 and the Party Alliance Our Moldova 11. Turnout was 59.5%.

Elena Salgado was appointed finance minister in a cabinet reshuffle in Spain.

Incumbent Abdelaziz Bouteflika dominated Algeria's presidential elections winning 90.2% of the vote to claim a third term of office.

The court of appeals in the Fiji Islands ruled that prime minister Frank Bainimarama's government was illegal, forcing him to stand down. However, president Ratu Josefa Iloilo disbanded the court and restored Bainimarama to power. Ratu Epeli Nailatikau was appointed vice president.

The Democratic Party won 148 of 560 seats in Indonesia's parliamentary elections, the Party of the Functional Groups (Golkar) 108, the Indonesian Democratic Party-Struggle 93, the Prosperous Justice Party 59, the National Mandate Party 42, the United Development Party 39, the Great Indonesia Movement Party 30, the National Awakening Party 26 and the People's Conscience Party 15.

Sanoussi Touré was appointed finance minister in a cabinet reshuffle in Mali.

Chronology of Events for March 2009

Week Beginning 29 March 2009

Montenegro's parliamentary elections were dominated by prime minister Milo Đukanović's Coalition for European Montenegro which won 48 of 81 seats. The Socialist People's Party won 16, the New Serb Democracy 8, the Movement for Change 5 and the four ethnic Albanian parties 1 each.

The new Israeli coalition government took office with prime minister Binyamin Netanyahu at its head. Avigdor Lieberman was appointed foreign minister, Eliyahu Yishai interior minister and Yuval Steinitz finance minister. Ehud Barak remained defence minister.

Albania and Croatia joined NATO.

In San Marino, Massimo Cenci and Oscar Mina took office as captains regent.

The Group of Twenty Finance Ministers and Central Bank Governors (G-20) Leaders' Summit on Financial Markets and the World Economy was held in London to draw up a global plan for recovery and reform.

Malaysia's prime minister Dato' Seri Abdullah bin Haji Ahmad Badawi resigned. He was succeeded by finance minister Dato' Sri Haji Mohd Najib bin Tun Haji Abdul Razak.

George Abela was approved unanimously and sworn in as president of Malta.

Week Beginning 22 March 2009

Gjorgje Ivanov (VMRO-DPMNE) won in the first round of Macedonia's presidential elections with 35.1% of the vote compared to 20.5% for Ljubomir Frčkoski (Social Democratic Union of Macedonia/SDSM). He went on to secure victory in the second round winning 63.1% against Frčkoski's 36.9%.

Czech prime minister Mirek Topolánek's government was defeated in a no-confidence vote prompting his resignation and that of his cabinet. A new government headed by Jan Fischer was scheduled to replace them on 9 May.

Klaus Tschütscher was sworn in as head of Liechtenstein's government. He also took the finance portfolio, while Aurelia Frick became foreign minister and Hugo Quaderer interior minister.

In Monaco, Sophie Thévenoux was appointed finance minister.

Week Beginning 15 March 2009

Mauricio Funes won El Salvador's presidential election with 51.3% of the vote against 48.7% for Rodrigo Ávila.

Ongoing tensions between the government and parliament of Kuwait resulted in prime minister Sheikh Nasser Muhammad Al-Ahmad Al-Sabah submitting his cabinet's resignation which was accepted by the Emir.

The French government led by prime minister François Fillon won a vote of confidence in the National Assembly.

After months of political dispute, Madagascar's president Marc Ravalomanana resigned and the army handed over executive power to opposition leader and self-proclaimed president of the newly-formed High Authority of Transition Andry Rajoelina. Both he and prime minister Monja Roindefo were sworn in later in the month. The cabinet included Benja Razafimahaleo as finance minister, Masimana Manantsoa as interior minister and Ny Hasina Andriamanjato as foreign minister.

In Sierra Leone, Samura Kamara was appointed finance minister.

Hungary's prime minister Ferenc Gyurcsány unexpectedly announced his resignation, describing himself as an obstacle to progress in the country.

In the first round of presidential elections in Slovakia, incumbent Ivan Gašparovič won 46.7% of the vote and Iveta Radičová 38.1%. Gašparovič was declared the winner following a runoff held on 4 April.

Week Beginning 8 March 2009
In parliamentary elections in North Korea 687 candidates were elected unopposed.

Syria opened a stock exchange in Damascus after 40 years without one.

Mamy Ranaivoniarivo resigned as defence minister of Madagascar following a confrontation with the army, which refused to support the government.

In parliamentary elections in Antigua and Barbuda, the ruling United Progressive Party won 9 of 17 seats, the Antigua Labour Party 7 and the Barbuda People's Movement 1. The new cabinet included Harold Lovell as finance minister and Errol Cort as national security minister. Prime minister Baldwin Spencer retained the foreign affairs portfolio.

Mariano Fernández was appointed foreign minister of Chile and Francisco Vidal Salinas defence minister in a cabinet reshuffle.

In Latvia the new government led by prime minister Valdis Dombrovskis took office following the resignation of Ivars Godmanis. The cabinet included Imants Viesturs Lieģis as defence minister, Linda Mūrniece as interior minister and Einars Repše as finance minister. Māris Riekstiņš remained foreign minister.

Week Beginning 1 March 2009
In a cabinet reshuffle in Cuba, Bruno Rodríguez Parrilla was appointed foreign minister and Lina Pedraza Rodríguez finance minister.

Guinea Bissau's president João Bernardo Vieira was assassinated by members of the army after its chief of staff was killed in a bomb attack the day before. The president of the National People's Assembly, Raimundo Pereira, was sworn in as interim president.

The Ukrainian foreign minister Volodymyr Ohryzko lost a vote of no-confidence in parliament. Volodymr Khandohiy became acting foreign minister.

Vice president Ramón Carrizález Rengifo was appointed acting defence minister in a cabinet reshuffle in Venezuela.

In Libya, Mussa Kussa was named foreign minister and Abdulhafid Mahmoud Zlitni finance minister in a government reshuffle. Mubarak Abdallah al-Shamikh became secretary of the General People's Congress.

Chronology of Events for February 2009

Week Beginning 22 February 2009
In Jordan, a cabinet reshuffle resulted in the appointment of Nasser Judeh as foreign minister and Nayef Qadi as interior minister.

Tony deBrum was sacked as foreign minister of the Marshall Islands after criticizing the president, Litokwa Tomeing.

Week Beginning 15 February 2009
In a cabinet reshuffle in Uganda, Syda Bbumba became finance minister and Kirunda Kivejinja interior minister.

Japan's finance minister Shoichi Nakagawa resigned following widespread condemnation of his conduct at a G7 meeting in Rome. The state minister in charge of economic and fiscal policy, Kaoru Yosano, was named his successor.

Remigio Hernani Meloni resigned as interior minister of Peru citing personal reasons. Mercedes Cabanillas took over as his replacement.

Despite winning a no-confidence motion earlier in the month, Latvian prime minister Ivars Godmanis resigned over protests at the government's handling of the economic crisis. Valdis Dombrovskis was named his successor.

Week Beginning 8 February 2009
In Liechtenstein's parliamentary elections the Patriotic Union won 47.6% of the vote, the Progressive Citizens' Party 43.5% and the Free List 8.9%. Otmar Hasler resigned as head of government and Klaus Tschütscher was named his successor.

Cabinet changes in Madagascar included Cécile Manorohanta stepping down as defence minister to be replaced by Mamy Ranaivoniarivo and Rabenja Sehenoarisoa taking over from Gervais Rakotonirina as interior minister.

Likud's leader Binyamin Netanyahu was asked to form a new government in Israel following parliamentary elections in which the Kadima party won 28 of 120 seats, Likud 27, Yisrael Beytenu 15, Labour 13, Shas 11 and United Torah Judaism 5.

Kim Yong-chun became armed forces minister of North Korea.

In Zimbabwe, Morgan Tsvangirai took office as prime minister. The new coalition cabinet included Emmerson Mnangagwa as defence minister, Tendai Biti as finance minister, and Kembo Mohadi and Giles Mutsekwa as joint home affairs ministers. Simbarashe Mumbengegwi remained foreign minister.

Zillur Rahman became president of Bangladesh having run uncontested for the post.

Ukraine's finance minister, Viktor Pynzenyk, resigned following a disagreement with prime minister Yuliya Tymoshenko.

In Somalia, Omar Abdirashid Ali Sharmarke became prime minister. His cabinet included Mohamed Abdullahi Omaar as foreign minister, Mohamed Abdi Gandhi as defence minister, Sharif Hassan Sheikh Adan as finance minister and Sheikh Abdulkadir Ali Omar as interior minister.

Week Beginning 1 February 2009
Jóhanna Sigurðardóttir was sworn in as prime minister of Iceland. Össur Skarphéðinsson became foreign minister and Steingrímur J. Sigfússon finance minister.

In Ukraine, prime minister Yuliya Tymoshenko's government narrowly defeated a no-confidence motion in parliament.

Kakha Baindurashvili became finance minister of Georgia.

Chronology of Events for January 2009

Week Beginning 25 January 2009
In Slovakia, Miroslav Lajčák became foreign minister.

Iceland's government, headed by prime minister Geir H. Haarde, resigned.

Susan Rice succeeded Zalmay Khalilzad as the USA's ambassador to the United Nations.

In a cabinet reshuffle in Burundi, Augustin Nsanze took over as foreign minister and Edouard Nduwimana as interior minister.

Abdurahim Qahorov was appointed interior minister of Tajikistan.

In Georgia, first vice prime minister and finance minister Nika Gilauri took over as prime minister following the resignation of Grigol Mgaloblishvili.

Sheikh Sharif Sheikh Ahmed was elected Somalia's president by parliament. He defeated Maslah Mohamed Siad in a run-off by 293 votes to 126.

Arístides Mejía became vice president of Honduras. He was succeeded as minister of defence by Ángel Edmundo Orellana Mercado who was in turn replaced as foreign minister by Patricia Isabel Rodas Baca.

Week Beginning 18 January 2009
President François Bozizé of the Central African Republic dissolved the government but reinstated prime minister Faustin-Archange Touadéra the next day. A new cabinet was formed including Gen. Antoine Gambi as foreign minister, Gen. Jules Bernard Ouandé as national security minister and Albert Bessé as finance minister.

The Farabundo Martí National Liberation Front won 42.6% of the vote in El Salvador's parliamentary elections, followed by the Nationalist Republican Alliance with 38.6% and the National Conciliation Party with 8.8%.

Yoon Jeung-hyun succeeded Kang Man-soo as finance minister of South Korea.

In Peru, Luis Carranza became finance minister for the second time in 3 years following the resignation of Luis Valdivieso.

Barack Obama took office as the 44th president of the USA with Joe Biden as his vice-president. The cabinet included Hillary Clinton as secretary of state, Timothy Geithner as secretary of the treasury and Robert Gates who remained defense secretary.

The deputy prime minister of Kenya, Uhuru Kenyatta, was additionally given the finance portfolio.

Week Beginning 11 January 2009
The prime minister of Kuwait, Sheikh Nasser Muhammad Al-Ahmad Al-Sabah, and his cabinet returned to government having resigned in November over corruption allegations. Key portfolios remained unchanged.

The governor-general of Jamaica Sir Kenneth Hall announced his resignation. Patrick Allen was named his successor.

In Kyrgyzstan, Marat Sultanov was appointed finance minister in a cabinet reshuffle. Ednan Karabayev was replaced by Kadyrbek Sarbaev as foreign minister.

Johnson Toribiong was sworn in as Palau's president.

Week Beginning 4 January 2009

In a cabinet reshuffle in Madagascar, Gervais Rakotonirina was appointed interior minister.

Sheikh Hasina Wajed was sworn in as prime minister and defence minister of Bangladesh. The new cabinet also included Abul Maal Abdul Muhit as finance minister, Dipu Moni as foreign minister and Sahara Khatun as interior minister.

In Ghana, John Atta Mills took office as president and named Alhaji Muhammed Mumuni foreign minister, J. H. Smith defence minister, Cletus Avoka interior minister and Kwabena Dufuor finance minister.

Ioannis Papathanasiou took over the finance portfolio in a cabinet reshuffle in Greece.

2008

Chronology of Events for December 2008

Week Beginning 28 December 2008

The Awami League dominated Bangladesh's parliamentary elections taking 230 of 299 seats.

Slovakia adopted the euro as its currency.

The Belgian government led by prime minister Herman Van Rompuy received a vote of confidence from parliament.

In Zimbabwe, Patrick Chinamasa was appointed acting finance minister after Samuel Mumbengegwi was dismissed from the post by president Robert Mugabe.

Week Beginning 21 December 2008

Following the death of Guinea's president Lansana Conté a military-led group, calling itself the National Council for Democracy and Development (CNDD), seized power. The head of the junta, Capt. Moussa Dadis Camara, was declared president and established a new government headed by Kabiné Komara as prime minister.

Mansur Muhtar was appointed finance minister of Nigeria.

In Guinea-Bissau, president João Bernardo Vieira appointed Carlos Gomes Júnior prime minister.

Israeli forces launched a wave of military attacks across Gaza in an effort to destroy Hamas targets.

Week Beginning 14 December 2008

Somalia's parliament passed a vote of confidence in the government after president Abdullahi Yusuf Ahmed dismissed prime minister Nur Hassan Hussein. His successor Muhammad Mahmud Guled stood down only a week after taking office, stating that his appointment was destabilizing the peace process. When the president resigned a few days later, the speaker of parliament, Sheikh Aden Madobe, became acting president.

The Democratic Party of Turkmenistan won the majority of parliamentary seats in the country's elections. Outside observers disputed claims by CIS officials that the elections were free and challenged the high turnout figures.

Shettima Mustapha was appointed defence minister of Nigeria in a cabinet reshuffle.

In Belgium, prime minister Yves Leterme's government resigned after accusations of attempts to manipulate the outcome of a court case surrounding the breakup of the country's largest bank, Fortis. Herman Van Rompuy replaced Leterme and appointed Guido De Padt interior minister, Pieter De Crem defence minister and Didier Reynders finance minister.

Week Beginning 7 December 2008

In Ghana's parliamentary election, the National Democratic Congress won 114 of 230 seats and the New Patriotic Party 107. In presidential elections, Nana Addo Dankwa Akufo-Addo (NPP) took 49.1% of the vote and John Atta Mills (NDC) 47.9%. In a second round Atta Mills took 50.2% of the vote to beat Akufo-Addo.

Romania's prime minister designate Theodor Stolojan gave way to Emil Boc. Boc appointed Cristian Diaconescu foreign minister, Mihai Stănişoară

defence minister, Gheorghe Pogea finance minister and Gabriel Oprea interior minister.

Hans-Rudolf Merz was elected president of Switzerland for 2009 and Doris Leuthard vice president. Ueli Maurer was appointed to the Federal Council as defence minister.

Fander Falconí became foreign minister of Ecuador after María Isabel Salvador resigned from the post.

Chronology of Events for November 2008

Week Beginning 30 November 2008

Following terrorist attacks in Mumbai India's home affairs minister Shivraj Patil resigned. Finance minister Palaniappan Chidambaram was appointed home affairs minister and prime minister Manmohan Singh took over the finance portfolio.

In Romania's parliamentary elections the Social Democratic Party-Conservative Party alliance won 33.1% of the vote for the lower house (114 of 334 seats) followed by the Democratic Liberal Party with 32.4% (115) and the National Liberal Party with 18.6% (65).

Werner Faymann took office as chancellor of Austria. He appointed Michael Spindelegger foreign minister and Josef Pröll finance minister, while Norbert Darabos remained defence minister and Maria Fekter interior minister.

In the wake of public protests and demonstrations, the Constitutional Court of Thailand ordered the dissolution of prime minister Somchai Wongsawat's People's Power Party and banned him from politics for 5 years. The first deputy prime minister, Chaovarat Chanweerakul, became acting prime minister.

In Lithuania, a new government was formed that included Vygaudas Ušackas as foreign minister, Rasa Juknevičienė as defence minister, Raimundas Palaitis as interior minister and Algirdas Šemeta as finance minister.

The Georgian prime minister Grigol Mgaloblishvili dismissed the foreign minister Eka Tkeshelashvili and the defence minister Davit Kezerashvili. They were succeeded by Grigol Vashadze as foreign minister and Batu Kutelia as acting defence minister.

Week Beginning 23 November 2008

In Kuwait, prime minister Sheikh Nasser Muhammad Al-Ahmad Al-Sabah and his cabinet resigned in protest at charges of corruption levelled against them by parliament.

Andrius Kubilius was appointed prime minister of Lithuania.

Vanuatu's prime minister Edward Natapei defeated a no-confidence motion in parliament by 26 votes to 24.

Carlyle Glean was sworn in as governor-general of Grenada.

Week Beginning 16 November 2008

The African Party for the Independence of Guinea and Cape Verde won Guinea-Bissau's parliamentary election taking 49.8% of the vote (67 of 100 seats). The Party for Social Renewal won 25.3% and 28 seats.

In Dominica, Vince Henderson was appointed foreign minister in a cabinet reshuffle.

A cabinet reshuffle in Barbados included the appointment of Maxine McClean as foreign minister.

Week Beginning 9 November 2008

A new cabinet headed by president Mohamed Nasheed was formed in the Maldives. Ahmed Shaheed was appointed foreign minister, Ameen Faisal defence minister, Qasim Ibrahim home affairs minister and Ali Hashim finance minister.

In San Marino's parliamentary elections the Pact for San Marino coalition won 54.2% of the vote and 35 of 60 seats while the Reforms and Freedom coalition won 45.8% of the vote and 25 seats. The new cabinet included Antonella Mularoni as foreign minister, Gabriele Gatti as finance minister and Valeria Ciavatta as interior minister.

The Swiss defence minister, Samuel Schmid, resigned.

Week Beginning 2 November 2008

Following September's parliamentary elections, Borut Pahor was appointed prime minister of Slovenia. His cabinet included Samuel Žbogar as foreign minister, Ljubica Jelušič as defence minister, Franc Križanič as finance minister and Katarina Kresal as interior minister.

Iran's interior minister Ali Kordan was forced out of office on a parliamentary vote of 188 votes to 45. He was succeeded by Sadeq Mahsuli.

Following the death of the interior minister of Mexico Juan Camilo Mouriño Terrazo in a plane crash, Fernando Francisco Gómez-Mont Urueta was appointed his successor.

Johnson Toribiong narrowly defeated vice president Elias Camsek Chin in Palau's presidential election, winning 51.1% of the vote to Camsek's 48.9%.

In the US presidential elections Barack Obama (Democrat) won 365 electoral college votes, on 52.9% of votes cast. John McCain (Republican) won 173 electoral college votes, on 45.7% of votes cast. Initial results showed that the Democrats also won control of both the House of Representatives and the Senate, in the former increasing their representation to 256 of 435 members (final figure 257) and in the latter to 56 of 100 members.

Nebojša Radmanović took over Bosnia and Herzegovina's rotating presidency.

The National Party won 45.5% of the vote and 59 of 122 seats in New Zealand's parliamentary elections, leaving the Labour Party with 33.8% and 43 seats. John Key was named prime minister and appointed Bill English deputy prime minister and finance minister, Murray McCully foreign minister and Wayne Mapp defence minister.

Chronology of Events for October 2008

Week Beginning 26 October 2008

The Georgian president, Mikheil Saakashvili, dismissed prime minister Lado Gurgenidze and appointed Grigol Mgaloblishvili his successor.

Lawrence Cannon was named foreign minister of Canada in a cabinet reshuffle.

Former Ethiopian minister for federal affairs Siraj Fegeta was appointed defence minister.

In Zambia's presidential elections, acting president Rupiah Banda won the majority of the vote with 40.1%, defeating his opponent Michael Sata who gained 38.1%. Banda's new cabinet included justice minister George Kunda as vice president, Kalombo Mwansa as interior minister and Situmbeko Musokotwane as finance minister.

Week Beginning 19 October 2008

Jean-Marie Ehouzou was appointed foreign minister of Benin in a cabinet reshuffle while Armand Zinzindohoué was made interior minister.

In the Czech Republic, prime minister Mirek Topolánek's government narrowly survived a no-confidence vote.

Week Beginning 12 October 2008

In Lithuania, the opposition Homeland Union-Lithuanian Christian Democrats took 44 of the 141 seats winning 19.7% of votes cast and the Social Democratic Party of Lithuania 26 with 11.7%.

In Canada's parliamentary elections, the ruling Conservative Party won most votes taking 143 seats, followed by the Liberal Party with 76 and the Bloc Québécois with 50.

Ilham Aliyev was re-elected president of Azerbaijan, winning 88.7% of the vote. He reappointed Artur Rasizade prime minister.

In Swaziland, Barnabus Sibusiso Dlamini was appointed prime minister. He named Lutfo Dlamini foreign minister and Mgwagwa Gamedze interior minister. Majozi Sithole remained finance minister.

Week Beginning 5 October 2008

In Croatia, interior minister Berislav Rončević and justice minister Ana Lovrin were dismissed. They were replaced by Tomislav Karamarko and Ivan Šimonović respectively.

In a cabinet reshuffle in Gabon, Paul Toungai became foreign minister and Blaise Louembé was appointed minister of finance.

Following poor results in the Malaysian parliamentary elections in March, prime minister Abdullah Ahmad Badawi announced his intention to stand down in March 2009.

Mohamed Nasheed was named Maumoon Abdul Gayoom's successor after winning the second round of presidential elections in the Maldives with 54.2% of the vote.

The prime minister of Peru, Jorge del Castillo, resigned along with his cabinet after public protests over illegal government involvement with private oil companies. President Alan García Pérez appointed Yehude Simon Munaro

to be the new prime minister, while Luis Valdivieso Montano was named finance minister and Remigio Hernani Meloni interior minister.

Adolphe Muzito was appointed prime minister of the Democratic Republic of the Congo. His new cabinet included Alexis Thambwe Mwamba as foreign minister, Charles Mwando Nsimba as defence minister and Célestin Mbuyu Kabanga as interior minister.

Chronology of Events for September 2008

Week Beginning 28 September 2008

The Social Democratic Party narrowly defeated the Austrian People's Party in Austria's parliamentary elections, winning 57 of 183 seats to 51 respectively.

In elections in Belarus, all 110 parliamentary seats were won by pro-government candidates sparking anti-governmental protests against electoral fraud in Minsk and claims from the OSCE that the elections were undemocratic.

Assunção dos Anjos was named foreign minister in Angola's new cabinet, while Kundy Paihama remained defence minister.

Ernesto Benedettini and Assunta Meloni took office as captains regent of San Marino.

In a cabinet reshuffle in the UK, John Hutton was appointed defence secretary.

Week Beginning 21 September 2008

Israeli prime minister Ehud Olmert resigned following allegations of corruption. Foreign affairs minister Tzipi Livni was given a remit to form a new coalition government within 42 days.

In Slovenia's parliamentary elections, the opposition party, the Social Democrats, beat the ruling Slovenian Democratic Party, winning 29 of 90 seats to the Slovenian Democratic Party's 28.

In South Africa, President Thabo Mbeki resigned along with several cabinet colleagues. Ivy Matsepe-Casaburri became acting president until Kgalema Motlanthe of the ANC was elected president a few days later. He won 269 of 360 votes, against 50 for his opponent, Joe Seremane.

Following a cabinet reshuffle in the Fiji Islands, prime minister Frank Bainimarama took over as acting foreign minister.

Antoine Gizenga tendered his resignation as prime minister of the Democratic Republic of the Congo. Former minister of the budget Adolphe Muzito was named his successor.

Week Beginning 14 September 2008

The coalition led by the Rwandan Patriotic Front won the majority of the vote in Rwanda's parliamentary elections with 78.8% (42 of 53 directly elected seats).

The US investment bank, Lehman Brothers Holdings, Inc., filed for bankruptcy. Barclays Plc acquired the bank's core US assets while Nomura Holdings, Inc. took over its interests in the Asia pacific region, Europe and the Middle East.

In Swaziland, the cabinet was dissolved and Bheki Dlamini became acting prime minister prior to elections in which all 55 of the parliamentary seats were won by independents.

Uruguay's economy and finance minister, Danilo Astori, resigned and was replaced by Álvaro García.

Sir Anerood Jugnauth was re-elected president of Mauritius for a second 5-year term.

A new government was appointed in Mongolia led by prime minister Sanj Bayar. Sukhbaataryn Batbold was named foreign minister and Luvsanvandan Bold defence minister.

Week Beginning 7 September 2008

Following severe losses in the US housing market, Fannie Mae (the Federal National Mortgage Association) and Freddie Mac (the Federal Home Loan Mortgage Corporation) were placed under the protection of the Federal Housing Finance Agency (FHFA) by the US federal government.

Venezuela's interior minister, Ramón Rodríguez Chacín, resigned and Tarek El Aissami became interior minister.

Thai prime minister, Samak Sundaravej, was forced to resign. He was succeeded by Somchai Wongsawat who also became defence minister in the new cabinet. Other appointments included Sompong Amornwiwat as foreign minister and Suchart Thadathamrongvech as finance minister while Kowit Wattana remained interior minister.

The Large Hadron Collider, the world's highest-energy particle accelerator built by the European Organization for Nuclear Research (CERN) and situated near Geneva, was switched on for the first time.

Arvin Boolell was named foreign minister of Mauritius.

Chronology of Events for August 2008

Week Beginning 31 August 2008
In Japan, prime minister Yasuo Fukuda announced his resignation.

In Vanuatu, parliamentary elections resulted in no clear majority though the Party of Our Land (Vanua'aku Pati) took the largest number of seats, winning 11 of 52.

Thailand's foreign minister Tej Bunnag resigned citing personal reasons, to be replaced by Saroj Chavanaviraj. Meanwhile, anti-government protests forced prime minister Samak Sundaravej to declare a state of emergency in Bangkok.

A cabinet reshuffle in Burkina Faso saw former health minister Alain Bédouma Yoda become minister of foreign affairs and regional co-operation while Lucien Marie Noël Bembamba was appointed minister of economy and finance.

In Togo, Komlan Mally resigned as prime minister. He was succeeded by Gilbert Houngbo whose new cabinet included Mally as minister of health and Koffi Esaw as foreign minister.

Parliamentary elections in Angola were dominated by the Popular Movement for the Liberation of Angola (MPLA), which won 81.6% of the vote and 191 of the 220 seats.

Asif Ali Zardari, husband of the late prime minister Benazir Bhutto and co-chair of the Pakistani People's Party, was elected president of Pakistan.

Week Beginning 24 August 2008
In Haiti, a new six-party coalition cabinet was announced to replace the interim government that came to power in 2004. Michèle Pierre-Louis was named prime minister and Alrich Nicolas became minister of foreign affairs while Paul Antoine Bien-Aimé remained interior minister.

The foreign minister of New Zealand and leader of the political party, New Zealand First, Winston Peters, was forced to stand down after the Serious Fraud Office began to investigate him on charges of corruption and misuse of party funds. Prime Minister Helen Clark became acting foreign minister.

Week Beginning 17 August 2008
Facing impeachment on charges of violation of the constitution and gross misconduct, Pervez Musharraf resigned as president of Pakistan. He was automatically replaced by the speaker of the Pakistani senate, Muhammed Mian Sumroo.

President Levy Mwanawasa of Zambia died following a stroke in June. Vice president Rupiah Banda, who had been acting president since June, succeeded him.

Week Beginning 10 August 2008
President Evo Morales of Bolivia survived a recall referendum, winning 67.4% of the vote.

Pushpka Kamal Dahal, chairman of the Communist Party of Nepal, was elected prime minister. His new cabinet comprised Bamdev Gautam as deputy prime minister, Baburam Bhattarai as finance minister, Upendra Yadav as foreign minister and Ram Bahadur Thapa as defence minister.

In Paraguay, Fernando Lugo was sworn in as president. Appointments to his cabinet included Alejandro Hamed as minister of foreign affairs, Luis Bareiro Spaini as minister of defence and Dionisio Borda as minister of finance.

Pedro Rafael Peña was appointed armed forces minister in the Dominican Republic.

Week Beginning 3 August 2008
In Guinea-Bissau, president João Bernando Vieira dissolved the National People's Assembly, removing Prime Minister Martinho Ndafa Kabi from power. He was replaced by Carlos Correia.

Gen. Mohamed Ould Abdel Aziz staged a military coup in Mauritania, ousting president Sidi Mohamed Ould Cheik Abdallahi. Aziz founded a new High Council of State which appointed Moulaye Ould Mohamed Laghdaf prime minister.

In the Solomon Islands, prime minister Derek Sikua's government won a no-confidence motion by 39 votes to 8.

Chronology of Events for July 2008

Week Beginning 27 July 2008
In Cambodia's parliamentary elections the Cambodian People's Party (KPK) won 90 seats with 58.1% of the vote and the party of government critic Sam Rainsy won 26 seats with 21.9%.

Japanese prime minister Yasuo Fukuda reshuffled his cabinet, promoting Taro Aso to the post of secretary general of the Liberal Democratic Party. Former secretary general Bunmei Ibuki became minister of finance. Yoshimasa Hayashi was appointed minister of defence.

The prime minister of Thailand, Samak Sundaravej, announced eleven changes to his cabinet, including the appointment of Kowit Wattana as minister of the interior and Chaiya Sasomsup as minister of commerce.

Week Beginning 20 July 2008
In India, prime minister Manmohan Singh's government survived a confidence vote in the House of the People (Lok Sabha) by the margin of 275 votes to 256. The crisis was precipitated by the withdrawal of support for the government by the Left Front in protest at the Indo-US nuclear deal.

In Macedonia, a new government was approved by 78 votes to none following a vote in parliament. The ballot was boycotted by the opposition. The only change to the key positions was the appointment of Zoran Konjanovski as minister of defence.

Week Beginning 13 July 2008
King Albert II of Belgium declined to accept the resignation of prime minister Yves Leterme.

Ram Baran Yadav of the Nepali Congress was elected president of Nepal after a second round run-off against Ram Raja Prasad Singh of the Communist Party of Nepal (Maoist). Paramanand Jha of the Madhesi People's Rights Forum was elected vice president.

Week Beginning 6 July 2008
Mirko Cvetković was sworn in as prime minister of Serbia. New appointments in his cabinet included Diana Dragutinović as minister of finance and Ivica Dačić as minister of the interior.

In Equatorial Guinea, Ignacio Milam Tang was appointed prime minister. He named Estanislao Don Malavo minister of finance and Salvador Ondo Nkumu minister of justice.

Tillman Thomas took office as prime minister of Grenada. He appointed Peter David as minister of foreign affairs and Nazim Burke as minister of finance.

After 18 months without an administration, Lebanon announced the formation of a national unity government. Prime minister Fouad Siniora retained his position under president Michel Suleiman. Of the 30 ministers, 16 were from Western-leaning parties, with 11 representing the opposition coalition, which includes Hizbollah.

Chronology of Events for June 2008

Week Beginning 29 June 2008
Mongolia's parliamentary elections saw the ruling Mongolian People's Revolutionary Party returned to power with 47 of the 76 available seats, followed by the Motherland Democracy coalition with 26 seats.

Amos Kimunya, Kenya's finance minister, resigned following allegations of corruption, which he denied.

The prime minister of Mauritania, Yahya Ould Ahmed El Waghef, named a new cabinet with Abdallahi Ould Ben Hmeida as foreign minister, Sidi Ould Tah as finance minister and Mohamed Ould R'Zeizim as interior minister.

The price of crude oil reached US$146.69 a barrel.

Week Beginning 22 June 2008
Rafael Branco took office as prime minister of São Tomé e Príncipe following a vote of no-confidence against his predecessor Patrice Trovoada.

Ahmed Ouyahia was appointed prime minister of Algeria for a third time.

Nepalese prime minister Girija Prasad Koirala resigned.

A cabinet reshuffle in Cape Verde saw the appointment of José Brito as foreign minister.

Guatemalan minister of the interior Vinicio Gómez was killed in a helicopter crash. Vice interior minister Édgar Hernández Umaña was also among the victims. Francisco Jiménez was appointed Gómez's successor.

Robert Mugabe won Zimbabwe's presidential runoff. The ballot was uncontested following the withdrawal of opposition leader Morgan Tsvangirai in the face of the nationwide violence and intimidation against his supporters.

Crude oil traded at a new high of US$142.99 a barrel.

Week Beginning 15 June 2008

Guinea's prime minister Ahmed Tidiane Souaré named Amadou Lamarana Bah foreign minister and Almamy Kabèlè Camara defence minister.

Alí Rodríguez Araque took office as finance minister of Venezuela.

Week Beginning 8 June 2008

Kwame Addo-Kufour was sworn in as interior minister of Ghana.

Irish voters rejected the amended Lisbon Treaty by 53.4% to 46.6% in a nationwide referendum. Ireland was the only EU country to put the treaty to a popular vote.

Week Beginning 1 June 2008

Macedonia's parliamentary elections were won by incumbent prime minister Nikola Gruevski's For A Better Macedonia coalition with 48.8% of the vote and 63 seats, ahead of the Sun-Coalition for Europe with 23.7% of the vote (27 seats).

Senator Barack Obama was confirmed as the Democratic nominee for November's US presidential election.

Steven Preston was unanimously elected secretary of housing and urban development by the US Senate.

The Northern Ireland Assembly elected Peter Robinson first minister following the retirement of Ian Paisley.

Chronology of Events for May 2008

Week Beginning 25 May 2008

Gen. Michel Suleiman was sworn in as president of Lebanon. He endorsed the proposal of the incumbent Fouad Siniora as prime minister by parliament. The new cabinet contained no changes in the key portfolios.

Haitian president René Préval nominated Robert Manuel as prime minister following the Senate's rejection of Ericq Pierre as Jacques-Édouard Alexis' successor.

By 560 votes to four, Nepal's Constituent Assembly declared a republic, thus ending the reign of King Gyanendra.

Week Beginning 18 May 2008

In Yemen, Rashad Al-Masri was appointed interior minister following a cabinet reshuffle.

Ma Ying-jeou took office as president of Taiwan. Vincent Siew took up the post of vice president and Liu Chao-shiuan became prime minister.

Parliamentary elections in Georgia were dominated by Mikheil Saakashvili's United National Movement which claimed 59.2% of the vote and 119 of the 150 available seats. The Joint Opposition, an alliance of rightist parties, gained 17.7% of the votes and 17 seats.

The price of crude oil reached US$135.14 a barrel, having more than doubled in value over the previous 12 months.

Canadian foreign minister Maxime Bernier resigned. He was replaced by David Emerson, whose role as minister for international trade was assumed by Michael Fortier.

Week Beginning 11 May 2008

The members of the Pakistan Muslim League-Nawaz resigned from the government. Their resignations were not accepted by prime minister Yousaf Raza Gilani.

In the Dominican Republic's presidential elections, incumbent Leonel Antonio Fernández of the Dominican Liberation Party secured a third term as president, his second in succession. He won 53.8% of the vote against 40.6% for Miguel Vargas of the Dominican Revolutionary Party and 4.6% for Amable Aristy Castro of the Social Christian Reformist Party.

Kuwait's parliamentary elections saw Sunni Islamists gain 21 of the 50 seats, Shia and Popular Action Bloc nine, Liberals seven and independents the remaining 13. Prime minister Sheikh Nasser Muhammad Al-Ahmad Al-Sabah formed a new government, with no change in the significant posts.

Week Beginning 4 May 2008

In an election boycotted by most opposition parties the ruling Democratic Party of Equatorial Guinea and the allied Democratic Opposition won 99 of the 100 available seats. The remaining seat was won by the Convergence for Social Democracy.

Eka Tkeshelashvili was appointed foreign minister of the former Soviet republic of Georgia.

Bertie Ahern tendered his resignation as prime minister of Ireland. The following day the Dáil confirmed Brian Cowen as his successor by a majority of 88 votes to 76. The new incumbent named Mary Coughlan deputy prime minister, Micheál Martin foreign minister and Brian Lenihan finance minister.

Mauritania's prime minister, Zein Ould Zeidane, resigned and was replaced by Yahya Ould Ahmed El Waghef. A new cabinet included Cheikh El Avia Ould Mohamed Khouna as foreign minister and Mohamed Yehdhih Ould Moctar El Hacen as interior minister.

In elections to Nepal's newly established Constituent Assembly the Communist Party of Napal (Maoist) won 220 of 601 available seats, ahead of the Nepali Congress Party, which gained 110 seats, and the Communist Party (Unified Marxist-Leninists) with 103. The Madhesi People's Rights Forum gained 52 seats.

Dmitry Medvedev was sworn in as president of Russia. He nominated his predecessor Vladimir Putin as prime minister, confirmed by the Duma by 392 votes to 56.

Silvio Berlusconi began his third spell as prime minister of Italy by announcing a cabinet including Roberto Maroni as interior minister and Franco Frattini as minister of foreign affairs. The government was approved by both the Chamber of Deputies (335 votes to 275) and the Senate (173 to 137).

Chronology of Events for April 2008

Week Beginning 27 April 2008

Haitian president René Préval designated Ericq Pierre to be the new prime minister following the Senate's vote of no-confidence against Jacques-Édouard Alexis.

Week Beginning 20 April 2008

In Paraguay, presidential elections were won by Fernando Lugo of the Patriotic Alliance for Change who was elected with 42.3% of the vote, followed by Bianca Ovelar of the National Republican Association-Colorado Party (ANR) with 31.8% and Lino Oviedo of the National Union of Ethical Citizens (UNACE) with 22.8%. In the concurrent parliamentary elections the ANR won 30 of the 80 seats in the Chamber of Deputies, ahead of the Authentic Radical Liberal Party (PLRA) with 27 and UNACE with 15.

Pro-democracy candidates won six of the nine available seats in Tonga's parliamentary elections.

Carlos Fernández was appointed economy minister of Argentina.

Week Beginning 13 April 2008

A cabinet reshuffle was announced in Bulgaria 10 days after the resignation of interior minister Rumen Petkov. He was replaced by Mikhail Mikov, while Nikolai Tsonev became defence minister.

Raila Odinga was sworn in as the new prime minister of Kenya, a post created as part of a power-sharing agreement with incumbent president Mwai Kibaki following the disputed elections held in Dec. 2007.

Silvio Berlusconi's People of Freedom alliance emerged victorious in Italy's parliamentary elections, gaining 46.8% of the vote and 344 of the 630 seats in the Chamber of Deputies. The Democratic Party alliance gained 246 seats (37.5% of the vote) and the Centre Union 36 (5.6%). The People of Freedom alliance also gained control of the Senate after taking 174 of 315 seats with 47.3% of the vote, ahead of the Democratic Party alliance (132 seats with 38.0% of the vote) and the Centre Union (3 seats; 5.7% of the vote).

Following the resignation of Adrian Cioroianu, Lazar Comanescu was sworn in as Romania's foreign minister.

President Idriss Déby of Chad dismissed prime minister Nourradine Delwa Kassiré Koumakoye and replaced him with Youssouf Saleh Abbas. A new cabinet was announced, with Moussa Faki as foreign minister and Abacar Mallah as finance minister.

Annamuhammet Gochiyev was named finance minister of Turkmenistan.

Week Beginning 6 April 2008

Incumbent Filip Vujanović was re-elected in Montenegro's presidential elections with 51.9% of the vote, defeating Andrija Mandić (19.5%) and Nebojša Medojević (16.6%).

Serzh Sargsyan was sworn in as president of Armenia, having previously served as prime minister. He named a cabinet headed by new prime minister Tigran Sargsyan, with Edvard Nalbandyan as foreign minister and Seyran Ohanyan as defence minister.

In Bhutan, Jigme Thinley was installed as prime minister. In his new cabinet he appointed Ugyen Tshering as foreign minister and Wangdi Norbu as finance minister.

Javier Ponce became Ecuador's defence minister following the resignation of Wellington Sandoval.

In elections to Nepal's newly established Constituent Assembly the Communist Party of Napal (Maoist) won 220 of 575 available seats, ahead of the Nepali Congress Party, which gained 110 seats, and the Communist Party (Unified Marxist-Leninists) with 103. The Madhesi People's Rights Forum gained 52 seats.

José Luis Rodríguez Zapatero was re-elected prime minister of Spain at the second attempt, having failed to gain an absolute majority in the first round of voting in the Congress of Deputies. A relative majority, of 169 votes to 158 with 23 abstentions, was sufficient in the second round to confirm his appointment.

Chronology of Events for March 2008

Week Beginning 30 March 2008

Kamalesh Sharma took office as secretary-general of the Commonwealth.

Seretse Khama Ian Khama was sworn in as president of Botswana following the retirement of Festus Mogae. He named Ramadeluka Seretse defence minister, Phandu Skelemani foreign minister and was succeeded as vice-president by Mompati Merafhe.

Prime minister of Ireland Bertie Ahern announced his resignation, to take effect in May.

Week Beginning 23 March 2008

In the first democratic elections to be held in the country, the Bhutan Peace and Prosperity party won 67.0% of the vote, followed by the People's Democratic Party with 33.0%.

Yousaf Raza Gilani was elected prime minister of Pakistan by 264 votes to 42 in the National Assembly. His cabinet installed Shah Mehmood Qureshi as foreign minister, Chaudhry Ahmed Mukhtar as defence minister and Muhammad Ishaq Dar as finance minister.

The parliament of Moldova approved the cabinet of new prime minister Zinaida Greceanîi. Mariana Durlesteanu became finance minister and Valentin Mejinschi interior minister.

Elections were held in Zimbabwe. The results of the presidential election between Robert Mugabe and Morgan Tsvangirai were disputed. The Zimbabwe Electoral Commission withheld results pending a recount in 23 constituencies, a decision upheld by the High Court. In elections to the House of Assembly the Movement for Democratic Change won 99 seats. Robert Mugabe's ZANU-PF party, with 97 seats, lost its parliamentary majority for the first time in the country's history. However, these results too were subject to a recount.

Week Beginning 16 March 2008

The price of oil reached a new record high of $111.80 per barrel.

After dismissing foreign minister Madan Dulloo, the prime minister of Mauritius, Navin Ramgoolam, took on the portfolio in an acting capacity.

A cabinet reshuffle in The Gambia saw Omar Touray appointed foreign minister.

Yves Leterme was sworn in as prime minister of Belgium.

'Otenifi Afu'alo Matoto was made Tongan finance minister.

Week Beginning 9 March 2008

The Spanish Socialist Workers' Party retained power after winning 43.6% of the vote (169 seats) in Spain's parliamentary elections, followed by the Popular Party with 40.1% (153). The remaining 28 seats were divided between fringe parties.

Oldemiro Balói replaced Alcinda Abreu as foreign minister of Mozambique.

After victory in the Mississippi primary, Barack Obama stretched his lead in the race to become the Democratic candidate for the US presidency. Requiring 2,025 delegates to secure the nomination, Obama led Hillary Clinton by 1,596 delegates to 1,484 with ten state contests remaining.

Eliot Spitzer announced his resignation as governor of New York following revelations about his personal life. His post was taken by lieutenant-governor David Paterson.

The price of gold reached $1,000 an ounce.

The National People's Congress of China re-elected president Hu Jintao for a second 5-year term.

Week Beginning 2 March 2008

In Russia's presidential elections Dmitry Medvedev, the candidate endorsed by outgoing president Vladimir Putin, won 70.3% of the votes cast. Gennady Zyuganov of the Communist Party of the Russian Federation won 17.7% followed by the Liberal Democratic Party's Vladimir Zhirinovsky with 9.3%.

Muftah Mohammed Kaiba was appointed secretary of the General People's Congress of Libya.

John McCain was confirmed as the Republican candidate for November's US presidential election following the withdrawal of his only remaining rival for the nomination, Mike Huckabee.

Haris Silajdžić took over Bosnia and Herzegovina's rotating presidency.

Parliamentary elections in Malaysia saw the reigning National Front coalition gain 140 seats with 50.3% of the vote. Opposition parties won the remaining 82 seats with 46.5% of the vote, and took control of five of the 13 state assemblies (the National Front had previously held every state but one). Prime minister Badawi's cabinet included Datuk Seri Dr. Rais Yatim as foreign minister and Datuk Hamid bin Syed Jaafar Albar as minister of internal security and home affairs.

Malta's National Party narrowly retained power after winning 49.3% of the vote (35 seats) in parliamentary elections ahead of the Labour Party with 48.8% (34 seats). Prime minister Lawrence Gonzi's new cabinet included Tonio Borg as foreign minister and Carmelo Mifsud Bonnici as minister of home affairs.

Prime minister of Serbia Vojislav Koštunica resigned after his government was divided on the issue of the European Union's support for Kosovo's secession.

Chronology of Events for February 2008

Week Beginning 24 February 2008

In Cuba, Fidel Castro stood down as president. The National Assembly elected his brother, Raúl, as his successor.

Milo Đukanović was elected prime minister of Montenegro.

Lee Myung-bak was sworn in as president of South Korea. Han Seung-soo was elected prime minister. The new president's cabinet included Yu Myung-hwan as foreign minister, Lee Sang-hee as defence minister and Kang Man-soo as finance minister.

Week Beginning 17 February 2008

Incumbent Tassos Papadopoulos was eliminated from Cyprus' presidential contest in the first round. In a runoff between the two remaining candidates, Dimitris Christofias gained 53.4% of the vote to defeat Ioannis Kasoulidis with 46.4%. After being sworn in, Christofias named a cabinet including Kostas Papakostas as defence minister and Neoklis Silikiotis as interior minister.

In Pakistan's parliamentary elections the Pakistan's People's Party won 121 of 331 seats, followed by the Pakistan Muslim League-Nawaz with 91 and the Pakistan Muslim League with 54.

Presidential elections in Armenia saw incumbent prime minister Serge Sargsyan gain 52.8% of the vote to defeat former president Levon Ter-Petrosyan (21.5%).

Week Beginning 10 February 2008

The Electoral College of Trinidad and Tobago confirmed the re-election of President George Maxwell Richards, who was the only candidate for the position.

A cabinet reshuffle in Uruguay saw Gonzalo Fernández appointed foreign minister and José Bayardi defence minister.

Mizengo Pinda was sworn in as prime minister of Tanzania following the resignation of Edward Lowassa. The new cabinet included Mustafa Mkuro as finance minister, Lawrence Masha as home affairs minister and Hussein Mwinyi as defence minister.

In the Czech Republic, incumbent Václav Klaus was re-elected president. After several inconclusive rounds he defeated Jan Svejnar in an all-parliamentary vote by 141 to 111.

Week Beginning 3 February 2008

In Monaco's parliamentary elections, the Union for Monaco won 21 of the 24 seats. The remainder were claimed by the Rally and Issues for Monaco.

In Serbia's presidential election run-off, incumbent Boris Tadić gained 51.2% of the vote to narrowly defeat Tomislav Nikolić (48.8%).

In the United States, the contest for the presidential nominations continued after 'Super Tuesday', the day on which the largest number of state primaries and caucuses were held, failed to produce a conclusive result. In the Democratic contest Barack Obama won 13 states (838 delegates) and Hillary Clinton nine (826). Republican John McCain won nine states (602 delegates) to all but secure his nomination.

The king of Thailand endorsed prime minister Samak Sundaravej's new cabinet, which named Surapong Suebwonglee finance minister, Noppadon Pattama foreign minister and Chalerm Yoobamrung interior minister.

The United Democratic Party won 56.6% of the vote (25 of 31 seats) in Belize's parliamentary elections, ahead of the People's United Party with 40.7% (six seats). Prime minister Dean Barrow's cabinet included Wilfred Elrington as foreign minister and Carlos Perdomo as minister of national security.

Tomé Vera Cruz announced his resignation as prime minister of São Tomé e Príncipe. He was succeeded by Patrice Trovoada.

The Union for the Presidential Majority won 94.1% of the vote and all 65 seats in Djibouti's parliamentary elections after they were boycotted by the opposition.

Chronology of Events for January 2008

Week Beginning 27 January 2008

Thailand's parliament elected Samak Sundaravej as prime minister. The following day his nomination was approved by the king.

Jaroslav Baška was appointed Slovakian defence minister following the resignation of František Kašický.

Prime minister Željko Šturanović of Montenegro resigned, citing health reasons.

Week Beginning 20 January 2008

Faustin-Archange Touadéra was appointed prime minister of the Central African Republic following the resignation of Élie Doté. His cabinet included Dieudonné Kombe Yaya as foreign minister.

Parliamentary elections took place in Cuba with candidates standing unopposed in all 614 available seats. Turnout was 95%.

Romano Prodi's government lost a confidence vote in the Italian Senate, prompting the prime minister's resignation. Franco Marini was asked to form an interim administration by President Napolitano.

Week Beginning 13 January 2008

Álvaro Colom Caballeros was sworn in as president of Guatemala. Rafael Espada took the post of vice president, Haraldo Rodas became minister of external relations and Vinicio Gómez interior minister.

Parliamentary elections in Barbados saw the opposition Democratic Labour Party claim 20 of the 30 seats, with the remaining ten seats won by the Barbados Labour Party. David Thompson was sworn in as prime minister. His cabinet included Christopher Sinckler as foreign minister and Freundel Stuart as home affairs minister.

Following the resignation of Francisco Laínez, Marisol Argueta de Barillas was appointed foreign minister of El Salvador.

Juan Camilo Mouriño Terrazo succeeded Francisco Ramírez Acuña as Mexican minister of the interior.

Moldumusa Kongantiev became Kyrgyzstan's interior minister.

Week Beginning 6 January 2008

Sheikh Khalifa bin Ahmed Al-Khalifa, the defence minister of Bahrain, was dismissed.

In the Marshall Islands, Litokwa Tomeing succeeded Kessai Note as president after defeating him in parliament by 18 votes to 15. His cabinet included Tony deBrum as foreign minister, Jack Ading as finance minister and Norman Matthew as minister for internal affairs.

Kenyan president Mwai Kibaki announced an incomplete cabinet, which included Kalonzo Musyoka as vice president and George Saitoti as interior minister.

Kosovo's parliament re-elected incumbent Fatmir Sedjiu president. On the same day, Hashim Thaçi was elected prime minister.

Croatian prime minister Ivo Sanader's new government was approved by parliament. It included Gordan Jandroković as foreign minister, Branko Vukelić as defense minister and Berislav Rončević as interior minister.

2007

Chronology of Events for December 2007

Week Beginning 30 December 2007

Cyprus and Malta adopted the euro.

Ramón Carrizales Rengifo was appointed new vice president of Venezuela. Rafael Isea was named finance minister and Ramón Rodríguez Chacín interior minister.

Chilean minister of the interior Belisario Velasco resigned. Felipe Harboe Bascuñán succeeded him on an interim basis.

Somalian prime minister Nur Hassan Hussein named Ali Ahmed Jama as foreign minister, Mohiyadin Muhammad Haji as defence minister and Muhammad Ali Hamoud as finance minister. The new cabinet was sworn in and won a confidence vote in parliament by 223 votes to five.

In presidential elections in Georgia, Mikheil Saakashvili won 53.5% of the vote, Levan Gachechiladze 25.7% and Badri Patarkatsishvili 7.1%.

The spot price of crude oil briefly hit $100 per barrel before declining steadily to settle at just above $90 at the end of January.

Week Beginning 23 December 2007

Igor Chudinov was elected prime minister of Kyrgyzstan. His cabinet included Tajikan Kalimbetova as finance minister, but other key positions were unchanged.

Former prime minister of Pakistan Benazir Bhutto was killed in a suicide attack after an election rally in Rawalpindi.

Incumbent Mwai Kibaki won Kenya's presidential elections with 46.4% of the vote, followed by Raila Odinga with 44.1%. The legitimacy of the result was disputed, and nationwide protests led to the death of some 1,000 people.

In Croatia, interior minister Ivica Kirin resigned. Ivica Buconjić became acting interior minister.

Week Beginning 16 December 2007

The prime ministerial candidacy of Yuliya Tymoshenko was approved by the Ukrainian parliament. Her cabinet, which included Volodymyr Ohryzko as foreign minister, Yuriy Yekhanurov as defence minister and Viktor Pynzenyk as finance minister, was confirmed later the same day.

Derek Sikua was elected prime minister of the Solomon Islands having defeated Patteson Oti in parliament by 32 votes to 15.

In parliamentary elections in Kyrgyzstan the Ak Zhol (Bright Path) party won 71 of 90 seats, the Social Democratic Party of Kyrgyzstan 11 and the Party of Communists of Kyrgyzstan 8.

In South Korea, Lee Myung-bak of the Grand National Party won the presidential elections with 48.7% of the vote, followed by Chung Dong-young of the United New Democratic Party (26.1%) and the independent Lee Hoi-chang (15.1%).

Danilo Türk was sworn in as president of Slovenia.

Week Beginning 9 December 2007

Cristina Fernández de Kirchner took office as president of Argentina. Julio Cobos was appointed vice president, Florencio Randazzo minister of the interior and Martín Lousteau economy minister.

The Swiss parliament elected Pascal Couchepin as president for 2008, with 197 of 210 votes, and Hans-Rudolf Merz as vice president (193 of 211).

In the Solomon Islands, prime minister Manasseh Sogavare's government was defeated in a no-confidence vote in parliament by 25 votes to 22.

Following the resignation of Latvian prime minister Aigars Kalvitis, parliament approved a government led by Ivars Godmanis. Vinets Veldre became defence minister, Mareks Segliņš interior minister and Atis Slakteris finance minister.

Week Beginning 2 December 2007

In Russia's parliamentary elections United Russia won 64.2% of the vote and 315 of 450 seats, the Communist Party 11.6% (57), the Liberal-Democratic Party 8.2% (40) and Fair Russia 7.8% (38).

Komlan Mally was appointed prime minister of Togo. His cabinet included Léopold Gnininvi as foreign minister.

In the Czech Republic, prime minister Mirek Topolánek's government narrowly survived a no-confidence vote.

The Mongolian parliament ratified prime minister Sanj Bayar's new cabinet, which included Sanjaasuren Oyun as foreign minister, Jamiyandorj Batkhuyag as defence minister and Chultem Ulaan as finance minister.

Chronology of Events for November 2007

Week Beginning 25 November 2007

Croatian parliamentary elections resulted in the Croatian Democratic Union winning 66 of 153 available seats, followed by the Social Democratic Party of Croatia with 56.

Mikheil Saakashvili resigned as president of Georgia to concentrate on his re-election campaign. Parliamentary speaker Nino Burjanadze became acting president.

In Kyrgyzstan, Almazbek Atambayev was dismissed as prime minister. He was replaced on a temporary basis by Iskenderbek Aidaraliev.

Rafael Correa, president of Ecuador, dismissed interior minister Gustavo Larrea. Fernando Bustamente became acting interior minister.

Tharman Shanmugaratnam was named finance minister of Singapore.

In Chad, Mahamat Nour Abdelkerim was dismissed from the post of defence minister.

Week Beginning 18 November 2007

Parliamentary elections were held in Jordan, resulting in independent candidates winning 104 of the 110 available seats and the Islamic Action Front taking the remaining six. Nader Dahabi became prime minister and defence minister, while Salah Bashir was appointed foreign minister.

In a cabinet reshuffle in São Tomé e Príncipe, Ovídio Pequeno became foreign minister and Arlindo Carvalho finance minister.

Nur Hassan Hussein was named prime minister of Somalia. He appointed Muhammad Ali Hamoud foreign minister, Ismail Ahmed Nur defence minister and Muhammad Yusuf Weyrah finance minister.

In Australian parliamentary elections, the Australian Labor Party took 83 of 150 seats with 43.4% of votes cast. The Liberal Party won 55 seats with 36.3% and the National Party 10 with 5.5%. Kevin Rudd was sworn in as prime minister with Stephen Smith as foreign minister, Joel Fitzgibbon as defence minister and Lindsay Tanner as finance minister.

Week Beginning 11 November 2007

In Slovenia's presidential election runoff, Danilo Türk gained 68.0% of the vote against Lozje Peterle with 32.0%.

Lithuanian interior minister Raimondas Sukys announced his resignation, to take effect in early December.

In parliamentary elections in Denmark the Liberals won 26.3% of the vote (46 of 175 seats) followed by the Social Democrats with 25.5% (45) and the Danish People's Party with 13.8% (25). Prime minister Anders Fogh Rasmussen's new cabinet included Lars Løkke Rasmussen as finance minister.

Prime minister Yawove Agboyobo of Togo resigned.

A new government was named in Burundi, with Venant Kamana as interior minister.

Georgian prime minister Zurab Nogaideli resigned. Parliament approved the nomination of Vladimer 'Lado' Gurgenidze as his successor, with a largely unchanged cabinet.

In Pakistan, Mohammadmian Soomro was sworn in as prime minister of an interim government. Inam ul-Haq became foreign minister, Salim Abbas Jilani defence minister and Salman Shah finance minister.

Week Beginning 4 November 2007

In Guatemala's presidential election runoff Álvaro Colom Caballeros won 52.8% of the vote and Otto Pérez Molina 47.2%.

In parliamentary elections in Trinidad and Tobago the ruling People's National Movement won 26 of 41 seats with 45.9% of the vote. The United National Congress Alliance won the remaining 15 seats with 29.7% of the vote.

The new cabinet included Paula Gopee-Scoon as foreign minister and Karen Nunez-Tesheira as finance minister.

The first vice president of Burundi, Martin Nduwimana, resigned. Parliament selected Yves Sahinguvu as his successor.

Latvian Prime Minister Aigars Kalvitis announced the imminent resignation of his government. In spite of this, parliament approved three new ministers, including Māris Riekstiņš as foreign minister.

Mongolian prime minister Miyeegombo Enkhbold resigned. Two weeks later parliament elected Sanj Bayar to succeed him.

The United States Senate confirmed Michael Mukasey as attorney general.

Chronology of Events for October 2007

Week Beginning 28 October 2007

In Somalia, prime minister Ali Muhammad Ghedi resigned. Salim Eliyow Ebrow became acting prime minister.

Oil prices reached US$93.53 per barrel.

In the USA, Edward T. Schafer was nominated as agriculture secretary.

Nikola Špirić resigned as prime minister of Bosnia and Herzegovina.

Week Beginning 21 October 2007

In Polish parliamentary elections Civic Platform won 209 of 460 seats with 41.5% of the vote, followed by the ruling Law and Justice Party with 166 and 32.1% and the Left and Democrats with 53 and 13.2%.

Parliamentary elections were held in Switzerland, resulting in the Swiss People's Party winning 62 of the 200 available seats with 29.0% of votes cast. The Social Democratic Party of Switzerland won 43 and 19.5%, the Free Democrat Party 31 and 15.6% and the Christian Democratic People's Party 31 and 14.6%..

In Kyrgyzstan, prime minister Almazbek Atambayev and his cabinet resigned.

In a cabinet reshuffle in Madagascar, Cécile Manorohanta became defence minister and Hajanirina Razafinjatovo finance minister.

Week Beginning 14 October 2007

In parliamentary elections held in Togo, the Togolese People's Assembly won 50 of the 81 available seats, gaining 32.7% of votes cast, followed by the Union of Forces for Change with 27 and 30.8%.

Recently appointed Moroccan prime minister, Abbas El Fassi, announced his cabinet, naming Taieb Fassi Fihri foreign minister and Salaheddine Mezouar finance minister.

Roosevelt Skerrit, the prime minister of Dominica, took over the post of foreign minister. Rayburn Blackmore became national security minister.

Deng Alor Kuol was named foreign minister of Sudan.

In presidential elections in Kiribati, incumbent Anote Tong was re-elected with 64.3% of the vote, defeating Nabuti Mwemwenikarawa. In a cabinet reshuffle Naatan Teewe was appointed finance minister.

Artis Pabriks resigned as foreign minister of Latvia.

Week Beginning 7 October 2007

In Sierra Leone, president Ernest Bai Koroma appointed Zainab Bangura foreign minister, David Carew finance minister and Dauda Kamara internal affairs minister.

Girma Wolde-Giyorgis was re-elected president of Ethiopia by parliament.

Soe Win, the prime minister of Myanmar, died in office. He was succeeded by Thein Sein.

Chronology of Events for September 2007

Week Beginning 30 September 2007

Parliamentary elections held in Ukraine resulted in the Party of Regions winning 175 of 450 seats with 34.4% of the vote, followed by the Yuliya Tymoshenko Bloc with 156 and 30.7% and Our Ukraine–People's Self Defence with 72 and 14.2%.

In San Marino, Mirko Tomassoni and Alberto Selva were appointed captains-regent.

Thai prime minister Surayud Chulanont took over the interior affairs portfolio.

Week Beginning 23 September 2007

In parliamentary elections in Madagascar, the I Love Madagascar party won 105 of the 127 available seats.

In Thailand the interior minister Aree Wong-araya resigned.

The prime minister of Mali, Ousmane Issoufi Maïga, resigned. He was succeeded by Modibo Sidibé.

Dominique Strauss-Kahn was selected as managing director of the International Monetary Fund.

Week Beginning 16 September 2007

Parliamentary elections in Greece resulted in New Democracy winning 152 of 300 contested seats. The Panhellenic Socialist Movement won 102, the Communist Party 22 and the Coalition of the Radical Left 14.

Oil prices reached a high of US$82.51 per barrel.

In the USA, agriculture secretary Michael Johanns resigned.

Week Beginning 9 September 2007

In parliamentary elections in Guatemala, the National Union of Hope won 48 of 158 seats, followed by the Grand National Alliance with 37 and the Patriotic Party with 30.

Japanese prime minister Shinzo Abe resigned. Parliament elected Yasuo Fukuda as his successor.

Vladimir Putin, the Russian president, replaced prime minister Mikhail Fradkov, appointing Viktor Zubkov in his place.

Crispin Grey-Johnson was appointed foreign minister of The Gambia.

Oil prices rose above US$80 for the first time, reaching US$80.20 per barrel.

Week Beginning 2 September 2007

In parliamentary elections in Jamaica, the Jamaica Labour Party won 33 of the available 60 seats and 50.1% of the vote, against the ruling People's National Party with 27 and 49.8%. Bruce Golding was sworn in as prime minister. His cabinet included Kenneth Baugh as foreign minister and Audley Shaw as finance minister.

Mikael Odenberg resigned as Swedish defence minister. He was succeeded by Sten Tolgfors.

In a cabinet reshuffle in Cameroon, Henri Ayissi Eyebe was named foreign minister and Lazare Essimi Menye finance minister.

Parliamentary elections were held in Morocco, resulting in the Independence Party winning 52 seats, followed by the Justice and Development Party with 46, the Popular Movement 41 and the National Rally of Independents 39. Abbas El Fassi was appointed prime minister.

In St Lucia, prime minister Sir John Compton died in office. He was succeeded by Stephenson King who also took the foreign, home affairs and finance portfolios.

In a presidential run-off in Sierra Leone, Ernest Bai Koroma gained 54.6% of votes cast, defeating Solomon Berewa with 45.4%. Koroma appointed Samuel Sam-Sumana as vice president.

Chronology of Events for August 2007

Week Beginning 26 August 2007

In a cabinet reshuffle in Japan, Nobutaka Machimura was named foreign minister, Masahiko Komura defence minister and Fukushiro Nukaga finance minister.

US attorney-general Alberto Gonzales announced his resignation, to take effect in mid-September.

In the third round of presidential elections in Turkey, Abdullah Gül of the ruling Justice and Development Party was elected by parliament, winning 339 of the 550 available votes. In a subsequent cabinet reshuffle, Ali Babacan was appointed foreign minister and Beşir Atalay interior minister.

Chinese finance minister Jin Renqing resigned; he was replaced by Xie Xuren.

In Ecuador, defence minister Escudero Durán resigned and was succeeded by Wellington Sandoval.

Week Beginning 19 August 2007

In Jordan, finance minister Ziad Fariz resigned.

Ahmed Shaheed, foreign minister of the Maldives, left his post; he was replaced by Abdullah Shahid.

In a cabinet reshuffle in Liberia, Olubanke King Akerele was named foreign minister.

Zambian president Levy Patrick Mwanawasa dismissed foreign minister Mundia Sikatana. He was succeeded by Kabinga Mpande.

In parliamentary elections held in Nauru, supporters of president Ludwig Scotty won 15 of the available 18 seats. Scotty was subsequently re-elected as president, defeating Marcus Stephen by 14 votes to 3.

Week Beginning 12 August 2007

In Papua New Guinea, prime minister Sir Michael Somare was re-elected by parliament, winning 86 votes against Sir Julius Chan with 21. His new cabinet included Bob Dadae as defence minister, Patrick Pruaitch as finance minister and Sam Abel as foreign minister.

In a cabinet reshuffle in Canada, Peter MacKay was named defence minister and Maxime Bernier foreign minister.

Parliamentary elections in Kazakhstan resulted in the ruling Light of the Fatherland Party winning all 98 elected seats with 88.1% of votes cast.

Week Beginning 5 August 2007

As a result of the second round of elections in the Republic of the Congo the ruling Congolese Labour Party and its allies held 125 of the 137 available seats.

In Timor-Leste, president José Ramos-Horta appointed Xanana Gusmão prime minister. Gusmão also took the defence portfolio, with Zacarias da Costa as foreign minister and Emília Pires as finance minister.

The Polish interior minister Janusz Kaczmarek was dismissed. He was replaced by Władysław Stasiak.

Hamid Ansari was elected vice president of India.

Parliamentary elections were held in Sierra Leone, resulting in the All People's Congress winning 59 seats, followed by the Sierra Leone People's Party with 43 and the People's Movement for Democratic Change with 10.

Chronology of Events for July 2007

Week Beginning 29 July 2007

In a cabinet reshuffle in Vanuatu, George Wells was appointed foreign minister.

Oil prices reached a record high of US$78.77 per barrel.

Week Beginning 22 July 2007

In two rounds of parliamentary elections held in Mali a coalition led by the Alliance for Democracy in Mali and the Union for the Republic and Democracy won 113 of the 147 available seats.

In parliamentary elections in Cameroon the ruling Cameroon People's Democratic Movement won 153 of the 180 available seats.

Parliamentary elections were held in Turkey, with the ruling Justice and Development Party winning 341 of 550 seats with 46.7% of votes cast, followed by the Republican People's Party with 112 and 20.8% and the Nationalist Movement Party with 70 and 14.3%.

In Brazil, Nelson Jobim replaced Waldir Pires as defence minister.

Lyonpo Khandu Wangchuck resigned as prime minister of Bhutan. He was succeeded by Lyonpo Kinzang Dorji. Finance minister Wangdi Norbu and interior minister Jigme Thinley also announced their resignations.

Nigerian president Umaru Yar'Adua's new cabinet included Ojo Maduekwe as foreign minister, Mahmud Yayale Ahmed as defence minister and Shamasudeen Usman as finance minister.

Week Beginning 15 July 2007

Shimon Peres took office as president of Israel.

In Moldova, Vitalie Vrabie was appointed defence minister by president Vladimir Voronin.

Jim Nicholson announced his resignation as US secretary of veterans' affairs.

Raymond Paul Ndougou was named interior minister of the Central African Republic.

After three unsuccessful attempts at securing the required majority, Bamir Topi was elected president by the Albanian parliament.

In presidential elections in India, Pratibha Patil won the support of 65.8% of the federal and state legislators eligible to vote, defeating Bhairon Singh Shekhawat who won 34.2%.

Week Beginning 8 July 2007

Valdis Zatlers took office as president of Latvia.

Jarosław Kaczyński, the prime minister of Poland, dismissed deputy prime minister Andrzej Lepper.

In Cyprus, the Communist Progressive Party of the Working People withdrew from the coalition government, with foreign minister Yiorgos Lillikas and interior minister Neoklis Sylikiotis resigning from the cabinet. They were replaced by Erato Kozakou-Marcoullis and Christos Patsalidis respectively.

In Ghana, Kwesi Osei-Adjei was named foreign minister.

Clotilde Nizigama was appointed finance minister of Burundi as part of a cabinet reshuffle.

In Micronesia, Lorin S. Robert became foreign minister and Finley S. Perman finance minister.

Parliamentary elections were held in Papua New Guinea, with the National Alliance Party taking 27 of the 109 available seats, the Papua New Guinea Party 8 and the People's Action Party 6.

Week Beginning 1 July 2007

Israeli finance minister Avraham Hirchson resigned. In a cabinet reshuffle, Roni Bar-On became finance minister and Meir Sheetrit interior minister.

Robert Zoellick took office as president of the World Bank.

Miroslav Lajčák was appointed UN high representative for Bosnia and Herzegovina, replacing Christian Schwarz-Schilling. Željko Komšić became president. He will serve for 8 months as part of a 4-year rotating presidency representing the three major ethnic groups.

In Japan, defence minister Fumio Kyuma resigned; he was succeeded by Yuriko Koike.

In a cabinet reshuffle in Laos, Somdy Duangdy replaced Chansy Phosikham as finance minister.

Gen. Gustavo Rangel Briceño was appointed defence minister of Venezuela.

Chronology of Events for June 2007

Week Beginning 24 June 2007

In the first round of parliamentary elections in the Republic of the Congo, the Congolese Labour Party won 23 seats, the Congolese Movement for Democracy and Integral Development 4 and the Action Movement for Renewal 3.

Tony Blair resigned as prime minister of the United Kingdom and was succeeded by Gordon Brown. His new cabinet included Alistair Darling as chancellor of the exchequer, David Miliband as foreign secretary and Jacqui Smith as home secretary.

Parliamentary elections in Timor-Leste resulted in the Revolutionary Front for an Independent East Timor (FRETILIN) winning 21 of the 65 available seats, the National Congress for Timorese Reconstruction 18, the Timorese Social Democratic Association–Social Democratic Party 11 and the Democratic Party 8.

Week Beginning 17 June 2007

In a cabinet reshuffle in Benin, Moussa Okanla was named foreign minister, Gen. Félix Hessou interior minister and Soulé Mana Lawani finance minister.

Tuiatua Tupua Tamasese Efi was sworn in as head of state in Samoa after being elected by the legislative assembly.

Week Beginning 10 June 2007

In parliamentary elections in Belgium the Christian Democratic and Flemish Party won 30 of the 150 seats, followed by the Reformist Movement with 23, the Socialist Party 20, the Open Flemish Liberals and Democrats 18 and Flemish Interest 17. Prime minister Guy Verhofstadt, the leader of the Open Flemish Liberals and Democrats, subsequently resigned.

Two rounds of parliamentary elections in France resulted in president Nicolas Sarkozy's Union for a Popular Movement winning 314 of 577 available seats with 46.4% of votes cast. The Socialist Party won 185 with 42.3%, the New Centre 22 with 2.1% and the French Communist Party 15 with 2.3%. Prime minister François Fillon reshuffled his cabinet, with Christine Lagarde replacing Jean-Louis Borloo as finance minister.

Moldovan president Vladimir Voronin dismissed defence minister Valeriu Pleşca. He was temporarily succeeded by Ion Corobceanu.

In Israel, Shimon Peres was elected by the Knesset to succeed Moshe Katsav as president, defeating Reuven Rivlin and Colette Avital.

After fighting between the Fatah and Hamas parties in the Palestinian-Administered Territories, president Mahmoud Abbas dismissed the government of prime minister Ismail Haniya and declared his intention to rule by presidential decree. Salam Fayyad was appointed prime minister but Haniya's Hamas government unofficially retained power in the Gaza Strip.

Israeli defence minister Amir Peretz resigned. He was replaced by Ehud Barak.

Week Beginning 3 June 2007

In Burkina Faso, prime minister Paramanga Ernest Yonli resigned. He was replaced by Tertius Zongo, who appointed Col. Djibril Yipene Bassolet foreign minister.

Seyni Oumarou was appointed prime minister of Niger. His cabinet included Djida Hamadou as defence minister.

In parliamentary elections in Senegal, Coalition 'Sopi' (led by the ruling Senegalese Democratic Party) won 131 of the 150 available seats, gaining 69.2% of the vote. Prime minister Macky Sall subsequently resigned, and was succeeded by Cheikh Hadjibou Soumaré.

The acting prime minister of St Lucia, Stephenson King, who was appointed after Sir John Compton suffered a stroke, took over the foreign affairs, home affairs and finance portfolios.

Chronology of Events for May 2007

Week Beginning 27 May 2007

Syrian president Bashar al-Assad won 97.6% of the vote in a referendum that confirmed him in office for another 7-year term.

In Monaco, Jean Pastorelli was named foreign minister.

Umaru Yar'Adua was sworn in as president of Nigeria.

Basile Ikouébé was appointed foreign minister in the Republic of the Congo.

In Latvia, Valdis Zatlers was elected president by parliament, defeating Aivars Endziņš by 58 votes to 39.

Algerian prime minister Abdelaziz Belkhadem and his government resigned. President Abdelaziz Bouteflika appointed a new government, with Belkhadem remaining prime minister, Mourad Medelci becoming foreign minister and Karim Djoudi becoming finance minister.

Week Beginning 20 May 2007

Parliamentary elections in Vietnam resulted in Communist Party members winning 450 of the 493 seats, with non-party independents taking the remaining 43.

In Belize, defence minister Cordel Hyde was dismissed by prime minister Said Musa.

In parliamentary elections in Ireland, Fianna Fáil won 78 seats with 42.0% of votes cast, followed by Fine Gael with 51 and 27.4%, the Labour Party 20 and 10.3%, the Green Party 6 and 4.5%, and Sinn Féin 4 and 7.1%.

Week Beginning 13 May 2007

In Serbia, prime minister Vojislav Koštunica announced his new cabinet, including Vuk Jeremić as foreign minister, Dragan Jočić as interior minister and Mirko Cvetković as finance minister.

Rimantas Šadžius was appointed finance minister in Lithuania.

In parliamentary elections in Algeria the ruling coalition won 249 of 389 seats (consisting of the National Liberation Front with 136, the National Rally for Democracy 61 and the Movement of the Society for Peace 52). The remaining seats went to minor parties and independents.

In a referendum held in Romania, 74.5% of voters supported the reinstatement of Traian Băsescu as president. He subsequently returned to office.

Week Beginning 6 May 2007

In parliamentary elections in Burkina Faso, the Congress for Democracy and Progress won 73 of the 111 available seats, followed by the Alliance for Democracy and the Federation-African Democratic Rally with 14 and the Union for the Republic with 5.

In Nicaragua, Ruth Tapia Roa became defence minister.

Abdülkadir Aksu, the Turkish interior minister, resigned. He was replaced by Osman Güneş.

The Northern Ireland assembly was restored after an agreement was reached between the Democratic Unionist Party and Sinn Féin. Ian Paisley was sworn in as first minister, with Martin McGuinness as deputy first minister.

Immanuel 'Manny' Mori was elected president of Micronesia. Alik L. Alik became vice president.

The Samoan head of state, Malietoa Tanumafili II, died in office.

In parliamentary elections in Armenia, the Republican Party of Armenia won 64 seats followed by Prosperous Armenia with 24, the Armenian Revolutionary Federation 16, Rule of Law Country 9 and the Heritage Party 6.

Gen. Baïlo Diallo was named defence minister of Guinea.

In Icelandic parliamentary elections, the Independence Party won 25 of the 63 seats with 36.6% of the vote. The Alliance won 18 with 26.8%, the Left-Green Alliance 9 with 14.3%, the Progressive Party 7 with 11.7% and the Liberal Party 4 with 7.3%.

Parliamentary elections in the Seychelles resulted in the Seychelles People's Progressive Front winning 23 of the available 34 seats (56.2% of votes cast), against 11 for the Seychelles National Party-Democratic Party (43.8%).

Chronology of Events for April 2007

Week Beginning 29 April 2007

In presidential elections in Mali, Amadou Toumani Touré was re-elected president with 71.2% of votes cast against Ibrahim Boubacar Keita with 19.2%. There were five other candidates.

Meritxell Mateu Pi was named foreign minister and Antoni Riberaygua Sasplugas interior and justice minister in a cabinet reshuffle in Andorra.

In parliamentary elections in The Bahamas, the Free National Movement won 23 out of the 41 available seats with 49.9% of the vote against the ruling Progressive Liberal Party with 18 seats and 47.0%. Hubert Ingraham was sworn in as prime minister and finance minister, with Brent Symonette as deputy prime minister and foreign affairs minister.

Nikos Symeonides, the defence minister of Cyprus, died in office. He was succeeded by Christodoulos Pashiardis.

In elections to the Scottish Parliament, the Scottish National Party won 47 seats, against Labour with 46, the Conservatives 17 and the Liberal Democrats 16. Alex Salmond, the leader of the SNP, was elected first minister.

In Welsh Assembly elections the Labour Party won 26 seats, followed by Plaid Cymru with 15, the Conservatives 12 and the Liberal Democrats 6. Labour subsequently formed a coalition government with Plaid Cymru, with Rhodri Morgan re-elected as first minister.

Week Beginning 22 April 2007

In the first round of presidential elections in France, Nicolas Sarkozy gained 31.2% of the vote. His nearest rivals were Ségolène Royal with 25.9%, François Bayrou with 18.6% and Jean-Marie Le Pen with 10.4%. In the second round Sarkozy won 53.1% against Royal with 46.9%.

Israeli finance minister Avraham Hirchson stood down for 3 months while police investigated allegations of corruption. Prime minister Ehud Olmert became acting finance minister.

In parliamentary elections in Syria, the ruling National Progressive Front, led by the Ba'ath Party, won 172 of the 250 available seats. Independents won the remaining 78 seats.

Zalmay Khalilzad became the US ambassador to the United Nations.

Besnik Mustafaj resigned as foreign minister of Albania. He was replaced by Lulzim Basha.

In China, Yang Jiechi was appointed foreign minister.

Week Beginning 15 April 2007

In Finland, parliament re-elected Matti Vanhanen as prime minister. Appointing a new cabinet he named Ilkka Kanerva foreign minister, Jyrki Katainen finance minister and Anne Holmlund interior minister.

In Eritrea, Osman Saleh became foreign minister.

Husayn Elabe Fahiye was appointed foreign minister of Somalia.

The Romanian parliament voted by 322 to 108 to suspend president Traian Băsescu. The president of the senate, Nicolae Văcăroiu, became interim president.

Sidi Mohamed Ould Cheikh Abdellahi was sworn in as president of Mauritania. Zein Ould Zeidane was appointed prime minister, heading a cabinet including Mohamed Saleck Ould Mohamed Lemine as foreign minister, Abderrahmane Ould Hamma Vezaz as economy and finance minister, and Yall Zekaria as interior minister.

In presidential elections in Nigeria, Umaru Yar'Adua won 70.0% of votes cast ahead of Muhammadu Buhari with 18.7% and Atiku Abubakar with 7.2%.

Week Beginning 8 April 2007

In the first round of presidential elections in Timor-Leste, Francisco Guterres of the ruling FRETILIN party won 27.9% of the vote, followed by José Ramos-Horta with 21.8% and Ferdinand de Araújo with 19.2%. In the subsequent run-off Ramos-Horta was elected with 69.3% of votes cast against Guterres with 30.7%.

Martinho Ndafa Kabi was appointed prime minister of Guinea-Bissau. His new government included Maria da Conceição Nobre Cabral as foreign minister, Marciano Silva Barbeiro as defence minister and Issuf Sanhá as finance minister.

In North Korea, prime minister Pak Pong-chu was dismissed. He was replaced by Kim Yong-il.

Week Beginning 1 April 2007

In Nepal, a new coalition government included representatives of the rebel Maoist party. Sahana Pradhan was named foreign minister.

Han Duck-soo was sworn in as prime minister of South Korea.

In a cabinet reshuffle in Romania, Adrian Cioroianu was named foreign minister, Varujan Vosganian finance minister and Teodor Meleşcanu defence minister.

In Qatar, foreign minister Sheikh Hamad bin Jasim bin Jabir Al Thani was named prime minister.

Defence minister Serzh Sargsyan was appointed prime minister of Armenia. His former role was filled by Mikael Arutyunyan.

In Côte d'Ivoire, Guillaume Soro was sworn in as prime minister. His cabinet included Charles Diby Koffi as finance minister and Michel Amani N'Guessan as defence minister.

Estonian prime minister Andrus Ansip announced a new cabinet with Jaak Aaviksoo as defence minister, Urmas Paet foreign minister and Ivari Padar finance minister.

In Yemen, president Ali Abdullah Saleh appointed a new government headed by Ali Mohammed Mujawar, with Noman Taha Al-Souhaybi as finance minister and Abubakr Al-Qirbi foreign minister.

Chronology of Events for March 2007

Week Beginning 25 March 2007

Andranik Markayan, the Armenian prime minister, died in office.

In France, Nicolas Sarkozy stood down as interior minister to concentrate on his presidential campaign. He was replaced by François Baroin.

Carlos Vielmann resigned as interior minister of Guatemala. He was succeeded by Adela de Torrebiarte.

In a cabinet reshuffle in Chile, José Goñi Carrasco became defence minister and Carlos Maldonado Curti justice minister.

In Côte d'Ivoire, president Laurent Gbagbo named Guillaume Soro as prime minister.

Almazbek Atambayev became prime minister of Kyrgyzstan after the resignation of Azim Isabekov.

In parliamentary elections in Benin, Cauri Forces for an Emerging Benin won 35 of the 83 available seats with 22.5% of the vote, followed by the Alliance for Dynamism and Democracy with 20 seats and 16.9% and the Democratic Renewal Party with 10 and 9.8%.

Week Beginning 18 March 2007

In parliamentary elections in Finland, the Centre Party won 51 of the 200 available seats with 23.1%, followed by the National Rally Party with 50 seats and 22.3%, the Social Democratic Party with 45 and 21.4%, and the Left Alliance with 17 and 8.8%.

Aristides Gomes, the prime minister of Guinea-Bissau, resigned after parliament passed a censure motion against him.

In Ukraine, Arseniy Yatseniuk became foreign minister.

In Comoros, Mohamed Ali Solihi became finance minister after a cabinet reshuffle.

Week Beginning 11 March 2007

In presidential elections in Mauritania, Sidi Mohamed Ould Cheikh Abdellahi won 24.8% of the vote, ahead of Ahmed Ould Daddah with 20.7% and Zein Ould Zeidane with 15.3%. In the subsequent run-off election Abdellahi won 52.9% against Daddah with 47.1%.

Bujar Nishani was named interior minister in a cabinet reshuffle in Albania.

In the Palestinian-Administered Territories, president Mahmoud Abbas and prime minister Ismail Haniya announced a new cabinet with Ziad Abu Amr as foreign minister, Hani al-Qawasmi as interior minister and Salam Fayyad as finance minister.

Week Beginning 4 March 2007
In Chad the new prime minister Delwa Kassiré Koumakoye appointed his cabinet, including Gen. Mahamat Nour Abdelkerim as defence minister.

In parliamentary elections in Estonia, the Reform Party of prime minister Andrus Ansip won 31 of the 101 available seats with 27.8% of the vote, followed by the Centre Party with 29 seats and 26.1% and the Union of Pro Patria and Res Publica with 19 and 17.9%.

South Korean prime minister Han Myung-sook resigned; he was succeeded by Han Duck-soo.

Parliamentary elections in Northern Ireland resulted in the Democratic Unionist Party winning 36 of the available 108 seats with 30.1% of the vote. Sinn Féin won 28 seats with 26.2%.

Chronology of Events for February 2007

Week Beginning 25 February 2007
In presidential elections in Senegal, the incumbent Abdoulaye Wade won 55.9% of the vote against Idrissa Seck with 14.9%, Ousmane Tanor Dieng with 13.6% and Moustapha Niasse with 5.9%.

After public protests, Eugène Camara was dismissed as prime minister of Guinea. He was succeeded by Lansana Kouyaté.

Sir Michael Somare, prime minister of Papua New Guinea, took on the post of minister of defence following the dismissal of Martin Aini.

Week Beginning 18 February 2007
Romano Prodi, the Italian prime minister, resigned after losing a vote on foreign policy. President Giorgio Napolitano refused Prodi's resignation and the prime minister subsequently won confidence votes in the Senate and Chamber of Deputies.

In the Netherlands, Prime Minister Jan Peter Balkenende named his new cabinet including Maxime Verhagen as foreign minister, Wouter Bos as finance minister and Eimert van Middelkoop as defence minister.

Pascal Yoadimnadji, prime minister of Chad, died in office. A week later, President Idriss Déby appointed Delwa Kassiré Koumakoye as prime minister.

Week Beginning 11 February 2007
In presidential elections in Turkmenistan, acting president Gurbanguly Berdymukhammedov won 89.2% of the vote against five opponents.

Russian defence minister Sergei Ivanov became first deputy prime minister. He was succeeded as defence minister by Anatoly Serdyukov.

In parliamentary elections in Lesotho the Lesotho Congress for Democracy won 61 of 120 seats, followed by the National Independent Party with 21 and the All Basotho Convention with 17.

Week Beginning 4 February 2007
Antoine Gizenga, the prime minister of the Democratic Republic of the Congo, announced his new cabinet including Antipas Mbusa Nyamwisi as foreign minister, Chikez Diemu defence minister and Athanase Matenda Kyelu finance minister.

The president of Burundi, Pierre Nkurunziza, dismissed the second vice-president, Marina Barampama. Gabriel Ntisezerana was appointed to the post.

In Bosnia-Herzegovina, the new government under Prime Minister Nikola Špirić took office. The cabinet included Sven Alkalaj as foreign minister, Dragan Vrankić finance minister and Marina Pendeš acting defence minister.

Eugène Camara was named prime minister of Guinea by President Lansana Conté.

Chronology of Events for January 2007

Week Beginning 28 January 2007
In Sri Lanka, Rohitha Bogollagama became foreign minister and Karu Jayasuriya home affairs minister.

Lorena Escudero took office as Ecuador's defence minister, replacing Guadalupe Larriva who had died in a helicopter crash.

Week Beginning 21 January 2007
In parliamentary elections in Serbia, the Serb Radical Party won 81 of the 250 available seats with 28.6% of the vote, followed by the Democratic Party

with 64 seats and 22.7% and the coalition led by the Democratic Party of Serbia with 47 seats and 16.5%.

In Israel, Knesset speaker Dalia Itzik became acting president for 3 months while president Moshe Katsav faced allegations of criminal offences.

In parliamentary elections in The Gambia, the ruling Alliance for Patriotic Reorientation and Construction won 42 of the available 48 seats with 59.8% of the vote, followed by the United Democratic Party with four seats and 21.9%.

Azim Isabekov was appointed prime minister of Kyrgyzstan.

Week Beginning 14 January 2007
In Ecuador, Rafael Correa was sworn in as president with Lenín Moreno as vice-president.

Madagascan president Marc Ravalomanana named the interior minister, Gen. Charles Rabemananjara, as prime minister.

Week Beginning 7 January 2007
Nikola Špirić was appointed prime minister of Bosnia-Herzegovina.

Daniyal Akhmetov, the prime minister of Kazakhstan, resigned and was replaced by Karim Massimov. Akhmetov became defence minister.

In the Czech Republic, President Václav Klaus appointed a new government headed by Mirek Topolánek, with Karel Schwarzenberg as foreign minister, Vlasta Parkanová defence minister and Miroslav Kalousek finance minister.

Daniel Ortega was sworn in as president of Nicaragua. Jaime Morales became vice-president.

Alfred Gusenbauer became chancellor of Austria. The new cabinet included Norbert Darabos as defence minister, Günther Platter as interior minister and Wilhelm Molterer as finance minister.

2006

Chronology of Events for December 2006

Week Beginning 31 December 2006
Bulgaria and Romania joined the European Union.

Ban Ki-moon took office as Secretary-General of the United Nations.

Hugo Chávez, president of Venezuela, appointed Jorge Rodríguez as his vice-president. Pedro Carreño became interior minister and Rodrigo Cabezas finance minister.

Dr. Margaret Chan took office as director-general of the World Health Organization.

In the Fiji Islands, the army commander Frank Bainimarama returned power to the president, Ratu Josefa Iloilo. Bainimarama was subsequently named interim prime minister.

Week Beginning 24 December 2006
In the Democratic Republic of the Congo, president Joseph Kabila named Antoine Gizenga prime minister.

Former Iraqi president Saddam Hussein was executed for war crimes.

Week Beginning 17 December 2006
In parliamentary elections in Gabon, the Democratic Party won 82 of 120 available seats, followed by the Gabonese People's Union with eight seats and the National Woodcutters' Rally with seven.

Robert M. Gates was sworn in as US defence secretary.

Saparmurad Niyazov, president of Turkmenistan, died in office. The deputy prime minister Gurbanguly Berdymukhammedov was named acting head of state.

Week Beginning 10 December 2006
Former Chilean dictator Augusto Pinochet died.

In parliamentary elections in St Lucia, the United Workers' Party won 11 of the available 17 seats with 51.4% of the vote, against the Labour Party's six seats and 48.2%. Sir John Compton became prime minister.

In Malaysia, Sultan Mizan Zainal Abidin became the new head of state.

In Switzerland, parliament elected Micheline Calmy-Rey as president for 2007. Pascal Couchepin was elected vice-president.

King Jigme Singye Wangchuck of Bhutan stepped down to be succeeded by his son, Crown Prince Jigme Khesar Namgyel Wangchuck.

Week Beginning 3 December 2006

In presidential elections in Madagascar, incumbent Marc Ravalomanana won 54.8% of the vote, followed by Jean Lahiniriko with 11.7% and Roland Ratsiraka with 10.1%.

In Venezuelan presidential elections, Hugo Chávez was re-elected with 62.9% of the vote.

After a military coup in the Fiji Islands, the army commander Commodore Frank Bainimarama appointed himself acting president. The government of Laisenia Qarase was dismissed, and Jona Senilagakali was appointed interim prime minister.

Chronology of Events for November 2006

Week Beginning 26 November 2006

In the presidential run-off in Ecuador, Rafael Correa won 56.7% of the vote against Álvaro Noboa with 43.3%.

Felipe Calderón was sworn in as president of Mexico. The new cabinet included Patricia Espinosa as foreign minister, Gen. Guillermo Galván Galván as defence minister and Francisco Ramírez Acuña as interior minister.

In Tajikistan, Khamrokhon Zaripov became foreign minister and Makhmadnazar Salikhov interior minister.

Vasyl Tsushko was appointed interior minister of Ukraine after parliament dismissed Yuriy Lutsenko.

In the second round of parliamentary elections in Bahrain, Al Wefaq won two more seats for a total of 18 (including an allied independent), Al Menbar three for a total of seven and Al Asala one for a total of five. The prime minister and key cabinet portfolios remained unchanged.

Week Beginning 19 November 2006

In parliamentary elections in the Netherlands, the Christian Democratic Appeal won 41 of the 150 available seats with 26.5% of the vote, followed by the Labour Party with 33 and 21.2% and the Socialist Party with 25 and 16.6%.

In the first round of elections in Bahrain, the Shia grouping Al Wefaq won 16 of the 40 available seats while the Sunni groupings Al Menbar and Al Asala won four seats each.

Week Beginning 12 November 2006

Milan Parivodić became co-ordinator of the finance ministry in Serbia following the resignation of Mlađan Dinkić.

In Papua New Guinea, prime minister Sir Michael Somare appointed Paul Tiensten foreign minister.

Week Beginning 5 November 2006

In presidential elections in Nicaragua, former president Daniel Ortega won 38.0% of the vote, followed by Eduardo Montealegre with 29.0% and José Rizo with 26.2%. In parliamentary elections the Sandinista National Liberation Front won 38 of the 90 available seats, followed by the Constitutional Liberal Party with 25, the Nicaraguan Liberal Alliance with 22 and the Sandinista Renewal Movement with 5.

Nebojša Radmanović was inaugurated as president of Bosnia-Herzegovina. He will serve for 8 months as part of a 4-year rotating presidency representing the three major ethnic groups.

In presidential elections in Tajikistan, incumbent Emomali Rakhmonov won 79.3% of the vote.

In US mid-term elections the Democrats won control of both houses, with 233 of 435 seats in the House of Representatives and 51 of 100 seats (including two aligned independents) in the Senate.

Robert M. Gates was nominated US defence secretary following the resignation of Donald Rumsfeld.

In Montenegro, the parliament approved Željko Šturanović as prime minister by a 44 to 26 vote. The new cabinet included Milan Roćen as foreign minister and Boro Vučinić as defence minister; Jusuf Kalamperović remained interior minister and Igor Lukšić remained finance minister.

Chronology of Events for October 2006

Week Beginning 29 October 2006

The International Confederation of Free Trade Unions and the World Confederation of Labour merged to form the International Trade Union Confederation.

In a cabinet reshuffle in South Korea, Song Min-soon became foreign minister and Kim Jang-soo defence minister.

Week Beginning 22 October 2006

In the first round of presidential elections in Bulgaria, incumbent Georgi Parvanov won 64.0% of the vote, followed by Volen Siderov with 21.5% and Nedelcho Beronov with 9.8%. In the second round Parvanov won 75.9% of votes cast against Siderov with 24.1%.

Yoon Kwang-ung resigned as defence minister of South Korea.

In a cabinet reshuffle in India, Pranab Mukherjee became foreign minister and A. K. Antony replaced him as defence minister.

Sorin Frunzăverde was named defence minister of Romania following the resignation of Teodor Atanasiu.

In a cabinet reshuffle in The Gambia, Bala Garba Jahumpa was appointed foreign minister.

Week Beginning 15 October 2006

In the first round of presidential elections in Ecuador, Álvaro Noboa won 26.8% of the vote, followed by Rafael Correa with 22.8% and Gilmar Gutiérrez with 17.4%. In parliamentary elections the National Action Institutional Renewal Party won 28 of the 100 available seats with 27.8% of the votes cast, followed by the Patriotic Society with 23 and 18.6%, the Social Christian Party with 13 and 15.2%, and the Democratic Left-Ethical Democratic Network with 13 and 10.7%.

The European Union accepted Romania and Bulgaria for membership as from Jan. 2007.

José Jouvín was sworn in as economy and finance minister of Ecuador following the resignation of Armando Rodas.

Week Beginning 8 October 2006

North Korea successfully tested its first nuclear weapon at an underground test site.

Toomas Hendrik Ilves took office as president of Estonia.

In Zambia, president Levy Mwanawasa named Rupiah Banda as vice-president. The new cabinet included Mundia Sikatana as foreign minister, George Mpombo as defence minister and Ronnie Shikapwasha as home affairs minister.

The Czech Republic's president, Václav Klaus, accepted the resignation of the government.

Week Beginning 1 October 2006

In parliamentary elections in Austria, the Social Democratic Party won 68 of the 183 available seats with 35.7% of votes cast, followed by the Austrian People's Party with 66 and 34.2%, and the Freedom Party with 21 seats and 11.2% of the votes.

In elections in Bosnia-Herzegovina the three presidential seats were won by Nebojša Radmanović for the Serb seat, Željko Komšić for the Croat seat and Haris Silajdžić for the Muslim seat.

In presidential elections in Brazil, incumbent Luiz Inácio Lula da Silva won 48.6% of the vote, followed by Geraldo Alckmin with 41.6% and Heloísa Helena with 6.9%. In parliamentary elections for the Chamber of Deputies, the Brazilian Democratic Movement Party won 89 of the 513 available seats with 14.6% of the vote, followed by the Workers' Party with 83 seats and 15.0%, the Brazilian Social Democracy Party with 65 and 13.6%, and the Liberal Front Party with 65 and 10.9%.

Surayud Chulanont was sworn in as interim prime minister of Thailand. The new government included Nit Piboonsongkram as foreign minister, Gen. Boonrawd Somtas as defence minister, Pridiyathorn Devakula as finance minister and Aree Wong-araya as interior minister.

Fredrik Reinfeldt was approved as Sweden's prime minister. The new government included Carl Bildt as foreign minister, Mikael Odenberg as defence minister and Anders Borg as finance minister.

In parliamentary elections in Latvia, the People's Party won 23 of the 100 available seats with 19.6% of votes cast, followed by the Union of Greens and Farmers with 18 and 16.7%, the New Era Party with 18 and 16.4%, and the Harmony Centre with 17 and 14.4%.

Chronology of Events for September 2006

Week Beginning 24 September 2006

Shinzo Abe was elected prime minister of Japan. The new government included Koji Omi as finance minister, Yoshihide Suga as internal affairs minister and Fumio Kyuma as minister of state for defence.

Arnold Piggott was sworn in as foreign minister of Trinidad and Tobago following the resignation of Knowlson Gift.

In presidential elections in Zambia, incumbent Levy Mwanawasa won 43.0% of the votes cast, followed by Michael Sata with 29.4% and Hakainde Hichilema with 25.3%. In parliamentary elections, the Movement for Multi-Party Democracy won 72 of the 150 available seats ahead of the Patriotic Front with 44 and the United Democratic Alliance with 27.

Week Beginning 17 September 2006
In parliamentary elections in Sweden, prime minister Göran Persson's Swedish Social Democratic Labour Party won 130 of the 349 available seats with 35.2% of votes cast, followed by the New Moderates with 97 and 26.1%, the Centre Party with 29 and 7.9%, and the Liberal Party with 28 and 7.5%. Persson subsequently resigned and Fredrik Reinfeldt was asked to form a coalition government.

A military coup overthrew the government of prime minister Thaksin Shinawatra in Thailand. Gen. Sonthi Boonyaratkalin became head of the Council for Democratic Reform.

In presidential elections in Yemen, incumbent Ali Abdullah Saleh was re-elected with 77.2% of the votes cast, ahead of Faisal Bin Shamlan with 21.8%.

Incumbent Yahya Jammeh won the presidential election in The Gambia with 67.3% of the votes cast, followed by Ousainou Darboe with 26.7% and Halifa Sallah with 6.0%.

Toomas Hendrik Ilves was elected president of Estonia by an electoral college with 174 votes of the 345 available, ahead of incumbent Arnold Rüütel with 162.

Week Beginning 10 September 2006
In parliamentary elections in Montenegro, prime minister Milo Đukanović's Coalition for European Montenegro won 41 of 81 seats with 48.6% of votes cast, followed by the Serbian List with 12 seats and 14.7%, the Socialist People's Party with 11 and 14.1%, and the Movement for Change Party with 11 and 13.1%.

The king of Tonga, Taufa'ahau Tupou IV, died in New Zealand and was succeeded by his son George Tupou V.

President Faure Gnassingbé named Yawovi Agboyibo the new prime minister of Togo.

Week Beginning 3 September 2006
In the Czech Republic, the new government of Mirek Topolánek included Alexandr Vondra as foreign minister, Jiří Šedivý as defence minister, Vlastimil Tlustý as finance minister and Ivan Langer as interior minister.

Foreign minister Lyonpo Khandu Wangchuck took office as prime minister of Bhutan.

Chronology of Events for August 2006

Week Beginning 27 August 2006
In presidential and parliamentary elections in Guyana, incumbent president Bharrat Jagdeo's People's Progressive Party/Civic party won 36 of the 65 available seats with 54.3% of votes cast, followed by the People's National Congress with 22 seats and 34.0%, and the Alliance for Change party with 5 and 8.3%. The new cabinet included Clement Rohee as home affairs minister and Ashni Kumar Singh as finance minister.

In a government reshuffle in Central African Republic, prime minister Élie Doté also became finance minister and Côme Zoumara became foreign minister.

Week Beginning 20 August 2006
In Paraguay, Rubén Ramírez Lezcano took office as foreign minister.

Week Beginning 13 August 2006
In Macedonia, the new government of Nikola Gruevski included Antonio Milososki as foreign minister, Lazar Elenovski as defence minister, Gordana Jankulovska as interior minister and Trajko Slavevski as finance minister.

Czech prime minister Jiří Paroubek's government resigned and Mirek Topolánek was designated his successor.

Week Beginning 6 August 2006
The Somali government was dissolved and prime minister Ali Muhammad Ghedi was asked to form a new administration. The new cabinet included Ismail Mahmud Hurre as foreign minister, Barre Aden Shire as defence minister and Hassan Muhammad Nur 'Shatigadud' as finance minister.

In Equatorial Guinea, Ricardo Mangue Obama Nfubea was named prime minister following the resignation of Miguel Abia Biteo Borico's government.

Chronology of Events for July 2006

Week Beginning 30 July 2006
In presidential elections in São Tomé e Príncipe, incumbent Fradique de Menezes won 60.6% of the vote ahead of former foreign minister Patrice Trovoada with 38.8%.

In the Seychelles' presidential elections, incumbent James Michel won 53.7% of the vote ahead of Wavel Ramkalawan with 45.7%.

Following intestinal surgery, Fidel Castro ceded power in Cuba to his brother Raúl.

In parliamentary elections in Tuvalu, seven of the 15 sitting members were returned and eight new members were elected. The parliament subsequently elected Apisai Ielemia as prime minister and foreign affairs minister. The new cabinet also included Lotoala Metia as finance minister and Willy Telavi as home affairs minister.

Ukrainian president Viktor Yushchenko nominated Viktor Yanukovich as prime minister. He was subsequently approved by parliament.

Week Beginning 23 July 2006
Gert Rosenthal was named Guatemala's foreign minister following the resignation of Jorge Briz Abularach.

A new cabinet in San Marino included Fiorenzo Stolfi as foreign minister, Stefano Macina as finance minister and Valeria Ciavatta as interior minister.

In Peru, Alan García was sworn in as president. The new government included Luis Giampietri as vice-president, Jorge del Castillo as prime minister, José Antonio García Belaúnde as foreign minister, Allan Wagner Tizón as defence minister and Luis Carranza as finance minister.

Week Beginning 16 July 2006
Juan Manuel Santos became Colombia's new defence minister.

Gen. Raúl Baduel was sworn in as defence minister of Venezuela.

Week Beginning 9 July 2006
In the USA, Henry M. Paulson was sworn in as treasury secretary.

María Consuelo Araújo was appointed foreign minister of Colombia.

In a cross-border raid by Hizbollah fighters based in southern Lebanon two Israeli soldiers were seized. After Israeli prime minister Ehud Olmert described the capture as 'an act of war' Israeli planes bombed Hizbollah positions while ground troops crossed into southern Lebanon. Fighting continued until a ceasefire was announced a month later.

Oil prices reached a record high of US$78.40 per barrel.

Week Beginning 2 July 2006
In presidential elections in Mexico, Felipe Calderón won 35.9% of the vote, followed by Andrés Manuel López Obrador with 35.3% and Roberto Madrazo with 22.3%.

In Lithuania, the parliament approved Gediminas Kirkilas as prime minister. The new cabinet included Petras Vaitiekûnas as foreign minister, Juozas Olekas as defence minister and Raimondas Šukys as interior minister.

Robert Fico took office as prime minister of Slovakia with a cabinet which included Ján Kubiš as foreign minister, František Kašický as defence minister and Ján Pociatek as finance minister.

In parliamentary elections in Macedonia, the Internal Macedonian Revolutionary Organization-Democratic Party for Macedonian National Unity won 45 of 120 seats with 32.5% of votes cast, followed by prime minister Vlado Buckovski's Social Democratic League of Macedonia with 32 and 23.3%, the Democratic Union for Integration with 17 and 12.2%, and the Democratic Party of Albanians with 11 and 7.5%.

Jarosław Kaczyński became prime minister of Poland following the resignation of Kazimierz Marcinkiewicz.

Chronology of Events for June 2006

Week Beginning 25 June 2006
Montenegro became the 192nd member state of the United Nations.

In Romania, Prime Minister Călin Popescu-Tăriceanu's government defeated a no-confidence motion in parliament by 235 votes to 145.

Portuguese foreign minister Diogo Freitas do Amaral was replaced by defence minister Luís Amado. Nuno Severiano Teixeira subsequently became defence minister.

Week Beginning 18 June 2006

In Poland, prime minister Kazimierz Marcinkiewicz dismissed finance minister Zyta Gilowska and appointed Pawel Wojciechowski as her successor.

Venezuelan president Hugo Chávez appointed Gen. Raúl Baduel as defence minister.

In Vietnam, president Tran Duc Luong and prime minister Phan Van Khai resigned. The National Assembly subsequently approved Nguyen Minh Triet as president and Nguyen Tan Dung as prime minister. The new cabinet included Pham Gia Khiem as foreign minister, Phung Quang Thanh as defence minister and Vu Van Ninh as finance minister.

Week Beginning 11 June 2006

Following the resignation of Iceland's prime minister, Halldór Ásgrímsson, foreign minister Geir H. Haarde was appointed as his replacement and Valgerður Sverrisdóttir became foreign minister.

In parliamentary elections in Slovakia, the Direction Party won 50 of 150 seats with 29.1% of the votes cast, ahead of prime minister Mikuláš Dzurinda's Slovak Democratic and Christian Union-Democratic Party with 31 and 18.4%, the Slovak National Party with 20 and 11.7%, and the Party of Hungarian Coalition with 20 and 11.7%.

Week Beginning 4 June 2006

In parliamentary elections in San Marino, the Christian Democratic Party won 21 of 60 seats with 32.9% of the votes cast, followed by the Party of Socialists and Democrats with 20 and 31.8%, the Popular Alliance with 7 and 12.1%, and the United Left with 5 and 8.7%.

Following a cabinet reshuffle in Cyprus, Yiorgos Lillikas became foreign minister and Phivos Klokkaris defence minister.

In Iraq, Gen. Abdul-Qader al-Mifraji became defence minister and Jawad Polani interior minister.

The National Assembly of Laos elected Choummaly Sayasone president and Boungnang Volachit vice-president. Bouasone Bouphavanh became prime minister and Thongloun Sisoulith foreign minister.

Chronology of Events for May 2006

Week Beginning 28 May 2006

In presidential elections in Colombia, incumbent Álvaro Uribe Vélez won 62.3% of the votes cast followed by Carlos Gaviria Díaz with 22.0% and Horacio Serpa with 11.8%.

Lithuanian prime minister Algirdas Brazauskas resigned.

In Nigeria, internal affairs minister Magaji Mohamed resigned and was replaced by foreign minister Oluyemi Adeniji. Finance minister Ngozi Okonjo-Iweala subsequently became foreign affairs minister and Nenadi Esther Usman finance minister.

A new cabinet was named in Hungary, including Kinga Göncz as foreign minister and Imre Szekeres as defence minister.

In parliamentary elections in the Czech Republic, the Civic Democratic Party won 81 of 200 seats with 35.4% of votes cast, ahead of the Social Democratic Party with 74 and 32.3%, the Communist Party of Bohemia and Moravia with 26 and 12.8% and the Christian Democratic Union-People's Party with 13 and 7.2%.

Montenegro declared its independence and was subsequently recognized by Serbia as an independent nation.

Week Beginning 21 May 2006

In parliamentary elections in Cyprus, the Communist Progressive Party of Working People won 18 of 59 seats with 31.2% of votes cast, followed by the Democratic Rally with 18 and 30.3%, the Democratic Party 11 with 17.9% and the Socialist Party 5 with 8.9%.

In a referendum in Montenegro 55.5% voted for independence from Serbia.

The Director-General of the World Health Organization, Dr. Lee Jong-wook, died.

Algerian prime minister Ahmed Ouyahia resigned and was replaced by Abdelaziz Belkhadem.

In the USA, Dirk Kempthorne was sworn in as interior secretary.

Week Beginning 14 May 2006

In parliamentary elections in the Dominican Republic, the Dominican Liberation Party alliance won 96 of 178 seats with 52.4% of votes cast, followed by the Dominican Revolutionary Party alliance with 60 and 21.9%, and the Social Christian Reformist Party alliance with 22 and 23.3%.

Nouri al-Maliki was sworn in as Iraq's prime minister with a cabinet in which he became acting interior minister, Salam al-Zobaie acting defence minister and Bayan Jabr finance minister. Hoshyar Zebari retained the post of foreign minister.

Week Beginning 7 May 2006

Óscar Arias Sánchez took office as president of Costa Rica, with Laura Chinchilla as vice-president. The new cabinet included Bruno Stagno Ugarte as foreign minister, Guillermo Zúñiga as finance minister and Fernando Berrocal as security minister.

Giorgio Napolitano was elected president of Italy in the fourth round of voting and subsequently asked Romano Prodi to form a government. Prodi's cabinet included Massimo D'Alema as foreign minister, Arturo Parisi as defence minister, Giuliano Amato as interior minister and Tommaso Padoa Schioppa as economy and finance minister.

In parliamentary elections in the Fiji Islands, prime minister Laisenia Qarase's United Fiji Party won 36 of 71 seats, ahead of the Fiji Labour Party with 31 and the United People's Party with 2.

Chronology of Events for April 2006

Week Beginning 30 April 2006

In parliamentary elections in Laos the ruling Lao People's Revolutionary Party won 113 of 115 seats with Independents taking the other two seats.

In presidential elections in Chad incumbent Idriss Déby won re-election with 64.7% of the vote, against Delwa Kassiré Koumakoye with 15.1% and Albert Pahimi Padacké with 7.1%.

In Israel, Prime Minister Ehud Olmert's new cabinet was sworn in with Amir Peretz as defence minister, Avraham Hirschson as finance minister and Roni Bar-On as interior minister.

In the Solomon Islands Manasseh Sogavare took office as prime minister. His cabinet included Patteson Oti as foreign minister, Bartholomew Ulufa'alu as finance minister and Bernard Ghiro as interior minister.

In a cabinet shuffle in the United Kingdom, Margaret Beckett became foreign secretary, John Reid home secretary and Des Browne defence secretary.

In parliamentary elections in Singapore, the People's Action Party won 82 of 84 available seats with 66.6% of the vote, followed by the Workers' Party and the Singapore Democratic Alliance with one seat each and 16.3% and 13.0% of the vote respectively.

Week Beginning 23 April 2006

The second round of parliamentary elections in Hungary resulted in the Socialist Party winning 186 of 386 seats with 48.2% of votes cast, followed by the Fidesz-Hungarian Civic Union with 164 and 42.5%, the Alliance of Free Democrats with 18 and 4.7%, and the Hungarian Democratic Forum (MDF) with 11 seats and 2.8%.

Jan Eliasson became Sweden's foreign minister.

King Gyanendra appointed Girija Prasad Koirala as prime minister of Nepal. The new cabinet included Khadka Prasad Sharma Oli as foreign minister, Dr. Ram Sharan Mahat as finance minister and Krishna Sitaula as interior minister.

Week Beginning 16 April 2006

In the first round of Comoros' presidential elections on Anjouan, Ahmed Abdallah Mohamed Sambi won 23.7% of the votes, Mohamed Djaanfari 13.1%, Ibrahim Halidi 10.4% and Caabi El-Yachroutu 9.6%. In the subsequent run-off Ahmed Abdallah Mohamed Sambi won 58.0% ahead of Ibrahim Halidi with 28.3%. The new cabinet included Ahmed Ben Saïd Djaffar as foreign minister, Hassani Hamadi as finance minister and Mohamed Abdoulwahabi as defence minister.

The Bulgarian government survived a vote of no-confidence by 166 votes to 61.

As a result of the second round of parliamentary elections in Haiti the Lespwa party held 23 of the 87 seats, followed by the Fusion Social and Democratic party with 17 and the Christian National Union with 12.

In São Tomé e Príncipe a new government was formed which included Tomé Soares da Vera Cruz as prime minister, Carlos Gustavo dos Anjos as foreign minister and Maria Tebus as finance minister. Óscar Sacramento e Sousa remained defence and interior minister.

Iraq's president, Jalal Talabani, was re-elected with Tariq al-Hashemi and Adil Abdel-Mahdi as vice-presidents. Nouri al-Maliki subsequently became prime minister.

Week Beginning 9 April 2006
In Peru's presidential elections Ollanta Humala Tasso won 30.6% of the votes, followed by Alan García Pérez with 24.3% and Lourdes Flores Nano with 23.8%. In the subsequent run-off election Alan García Pérez won 52.6% against Ollanta Humala Tasso with 47.4%. In the parliamentary elections the Union for Peru party won 45 of the 120 seats with 21.1% of the votes cast, followed by the Peruvian Aparista party with 36 seats and 20.6%, and the National Unity party with 17 and 15.3%.

In parliamentary elections in Italy, Romano Prodi's Union coalition won 348 seats in the Chamber of Deputies and 158 in the Senate, against Prime Minister Silvio Berlusconi's House of Freedoms Alliance with 281 and 156 seats respectively. Berlusconi subsequently resigned.

Week Beginning 2 April 2006
In parliamentary elections in Thailand the Thai Rak Thai Party (TRT) gained 460 seats. The election had been boycotted by the three opposition parties after prime minister Thaksin Shinawatra refused to sign a pledge to implement constitutional reforms. As a result Thaksin stepped down temporarily. The Constitutional Court subsequently ruled that the elections were invalid.

In the Solomon Islands' parliamentary elections the National Party won 4 seats, the Rural Advancement Party 4, the People's Alliance Party 3, the Democratic Party 3 and Independents 30. Deputy Prime Minister Synder Rini succeeded in gaining the support of enough independent members of parliament to form a government. After rioting in Honiara, Rini resigned shortly before a motion of no-confidence was scheduled and was succeeded by Manasseh Sogavare, a former prime minister.

Benin's new president, Yayi Boni, named Mariam Aladji Boni foreign minister, Issifou Kogui N'Douro defence minister, Pascal Koukpaki finance minister and Edgar Alia security minister.

Aigars Kalvītis, Latvia's prime minister, accepted the resignations of ministers from the New Era party including defence minister Linda Murniece. Atis Slakteris was subsequently appointed defence minister.

In a cabinet reshuffle in Spain, interior minister José Antonio Alonso replaced José Bono Martínez as defence minister. Alfredo Pérez Rubalcaba replaced Alonso as interior minister.

Chronology of Events for March 2006

Week Beginning 26 March 2006
In parliamentary elections in São Tomé e Príncipe, the Force for Change Democratic Movement (MDFM) won 23 seats with 37.2% of votes cast, ahead of the Liberation Movement of São Tomé e Príncipe (MLSTP) 19 (28.9%) and Independent Democratic Action (ADI) 12 (20.0%).

In Ukraine's parliamentary elections, the Party of Regions of Ukraine won 186 of 450 seats with 32.1% of votes cast, the Yuliya Tymoshenko Election Bloc 129 (22.3%), the Our Ukraine Party 81 (13.9%), the Socialist Party 33 (5.7%) and the Communist Party 21 (3.7%).

Kadima won 29 of 120 seats with 21.8% of votes cast in parliamentary elections in Israel, followed by Labour with 19 and 15.1%, Shas with 12 and 9.6% and Likud with 12 and 8.9%.

Jamaican prime minister Percival J. Patterson, who had earlier announced his retirement, was replaced by Portia Simpson-Miller.

Parliamentary elections in Samoa were won by the Human Rights Protection Party with 30 of 49 seats, followed by the Samoa Democratic United Party with 10.

Week Beginning 19 March 2006
In presidential elections in Belarus, incumbent Alyaksandr Lukashenka won 87.5% of the votes cast followed by Alyaksandr Milinkevich with 6.5% and Sergei Gaidukevich with 3.7%.

The Palestinian prime minister proposed a new cabinet with Mahmoud Zahar as foreign minister, Omar Abdel-Razeq finance minister and Said Siam interior minister. The cabinet was subsequently approved by parliament with 21 votes in favour and 4 against.

In Sweden, foreign minister Laila Freivalds resigned and was replaced temporarily by deputy prime minister Bosse Ringholm. Jan Eliasson was later appointed foreign minister.

In a cabinet reshuffle in Afghanistan, Rangin Dadfar Spanta became foreign minister while acting interior minister Zarar Ahmad Moqbel was confirmed in his job.

Najah al-Attar was appointed second vice-president in Syria.

Week Beginning 12 March 2006
In parliamentary elections in Colombia, the Colombian Liberal Party won 38 of 166 seats ahead of the Social National Unity Party with 30 and the Colombian Conservative Party with 29. In the elections to the Senate the Social National Unity Party won 20 seats, the Colombian Conservative Party 18 and the Colombian Liberal Party 17.

Han Duck-soo became acting prime minister of South Korea after Lee Hae-chan resigned. Han Myung-sook was subsequently nominated as prime minister.

Week Beginning 5 March 2006
In presidential elections in Benin, Yayi Boni won 35.6% of the votes cast followed by Adrien Houngbédji with 24.1%, Bruno Amoussou with 16.2% and Léhadi Vinagnon with 8.4%. In the subsequent run-off Boni won 74.5% against Houngbédji with 25.5%.

Al-Baghdadi Al-Mahmoudi became general secretary of the General People's Committee in Libya and Ahmad Mounsi finance minister.

Ratu Josefa Iloilo was reappointed president of Fiji by the Council of Chiefs and vice-president Ratu Joni Madraiwiwi was also reappointed.

In Portugal, Aníbal Cavaco Silva was sworn in as president.

US interior secretary Gale Norton resigned.

In Chile, Michelle Bachelet took office as president and appointed Alejandro Foxley foreign minister, Vivianne Blanlot defence minister, Andrés Zaldívar interior minister and Andrés Velasco finance minister.

Chronology of Events for February 2006

Week Beginning 26 February 2006
Sulejman Tihić became chairman of the Presidency in Bosnia-Herzegovina.

In a cabinet reshuffle in South Korea, Lee Yong-sup became the minister for government administration and home affairs.

Week Beginning 19 February 2006
Jean-Louis Schiltz became Luxembourg's defence minister in a cabinet reshuffle.

In a cabinet reshuffle in Swaziland, Moses Mathendele Dlamini became foreign minister.

In presidential elections in Uganda, incumbent Yoweri Museveni won 59.3% of the votes cast ahead of Kizza Besigye with 37.4%.

Week Beginning 12 February 2006
In presidential elections in Cape Verde, incumbent president Pedro Pires won 51.0% of the votes cast against former prime minister Carlos Veiga with 49.0%.

Fred Sevele was appointed acting prime minister in Tonga following the resignation of Prince Lavaka ata Ulukalala.

In a cabinet reshuffle in Greece, Dora Bakoyannis became foreign minister and Evangelos Meimarkis defence minister.

Week Beginning 5 February 2006
In presidential elections in Costa Rica, former president Óscar Arias Sánchez of the National Liberation Party won 40.5% of the votes cast followed by Ottón Solís of the Citizens' Action Party with 40.3% and Otto Guevara of the Libertarian Movement with 8.4%. In parliamentary elections the National Liberation Party won 25 of 57 seats, the Citizens' Action Party 18, the Libertarian Movement 6 and the Social Christian Unity Party 4.

Stephen Harper was sworn in as prime minister of Canada with his cabinet, which included Peter MacKay as foreign minister, Gordon O'Connor as defence minister and James Flaherty as finance minister.

In presidential elections in Haiti, former president René Préval won 51.2% of the votes cast followed by former president Leslie Manigat with 12.4% and Charles Henry Baker with 8.2%.

In Kuwait, the Amir HH Sheikh Sabah nominated his half-brother Sheikh Nawaf, the interior minister, as crown prince and appointed his half-nephew

Sheikh Nasser as prime minister. Defence minister Sheikh Jaber was subsequently given the interior portfolio and the parliament unanimously approved Nawaf as crown prince.

Chronology of Events for January 2006

Week Beginning 29 January 2006
In the USA, Ben Bernanke became the 14th chairman of the Federal Reserve Board.

David Mwiraria resigned as Kenya's finance minister and was subsequently replaced by Amos Kimunya.

Martin Fedor was appointed defence minister in Slovakia.

In Angola, interior minister Osvaldo Serra Van-Dúnem died.

Violence escalated around the world in the wake of the publication in a Danish newspaper of cartoons satirizing the Prophet Mohammed.

Week Beginning 22 January 2006
Evo Morales became Bolivian president and Álvaro García vice-president. The new cabinet included David Choquehuanca as foreign minister, Walker San Miguel as defence minister, Alicia Muñoz as interior minister and Luis Alberto Arce as finance minister.

In parliamentary elections in Cape Verde, the African Party for the Independence of Cape Verde won 41 of 72 available seats with 52.2% of the votes cast, followed by the Movement for Democracy with 29 and 44.0% and the Christian, Independent and Democratic Union with 2 and 2.6%.

Former prime minister Aníbal Cavaco Silva won 50.5% of the votes cast in the Portuguese presidential elections, ahead of Manuel Alegre with 20.7% and former president Mário Soares with 14.3%.

In parliamentary elections in Canada, the Conservative Party won 124 of 308 available seats with 36.3% of the vote, followed by the Liberal Party with 103 and 30.2%, the Bloc Québécois 51 with 10.5% and the New Democratic Party with 29 and 17.5%.

Change and Reform (Hamas) won 74 of 132 seats ahead of Fatah with 45 in parliamentary elections in the Palestinian-administered Territory.

In Honduras, Manuel Zelaya was sworn in as president, with Milton Jiménez as foreign minister, Arístides Mejía defence minister, Jorge Arturo Reina interior minister and Hugo Noé Pino finance minister.

Week Beginning 15 January 2006
In the presidential election run-off in Chile, Michelle Bachelet won 53.5% of the votes cast against Sebastián Piñera with 46.5%. Bachelet's new cabinet includes Alejandro Foxley as foreign minister, Vivianne Blanlot as defence minister and Andrés Zaldívar as interior minister.

Finland's incumbent president Tarja Halonen won 46.3% of votes cast in the presidential election, ahead of Sauli Niinistö with 24.1%, prime minister Matti Vanhanen with 18.6% and Heidi Hautala with 3.5%. In the subsequent run-off, Halonen won 51.8% and Niinistö 48.2%.

Shaikh Jaber al-Ahmed al-Jaber al-Sabah, the 13th Amir of Kuwait, died. Although initially replaced by the crown prince, prime minister Shaikh Sabah al-Ahmed al-Jaber al-Sabah subsequently took over as amir.

In Liberia, Ellen Johnson-Sirleaf was sworn in as president and announced a cabinet that included Brownie J. Samukai as defence minister, Antoinette M. Sayeh as finance minister and George Wallace as foreign minister.

Brendan Nelson was appointed Australian defence minister after Robert Hill resigned.

President Omar Bongo Ondimba of Gabon named Jean Eyeghe Ndong as prime minister. The new cabinet included Jean Ping as foreign minister, Paul Toungui as finance minister and Ali Bongo Ondimba as defence minister.

Week Beginning 8 January 2006
Benin's defence minister, Pierre Osho, resigned.

In Mongolia, ministers from the Mongolian People's Revolutionary Party, including foreign minister Tsendiin Munkh-Orgil, defence minister Tserenhuugiin Sharavdorj, and justice and internal affairs minister Batbold Sundui, resigned and ended the government of prime minister Tsakhiagiyn Elbegdorj. The parliament subsequently elected Miyeegombo Enkhbold as prime minister; his cabinet included Nyamaa Enkhbold as foreign minister, Mishigiin Sonompil as defence minister and Nadmidiin Bayartsaikhan as finance minister.

Tzipi Livni was appointed Israeli foreign minister following the resignation of Silvan Shalom.

Week Beginning 1 January 2006
Moritz Leuenberger took office as president of Switzerland.

In Israel, deputy prime minister Ehud Olmert became acting prime minister after Ariel Sharon suffered a second stroke and brain haemorrhaging.

Tanzanian president Jakaya Kikwete announced his cabinet which included Asha-Rose Migiro as foreign minister, Juma Kapuya as defence minister and Zakia Meghji as finance minister.

In the United Arab Emirates, vice-president and prime minister Sheikh Rashid bin Said al-Maktoum died and was replaced by his brother Sheikh Muhammad bin Rashid al-Maktoum.

2005

Chronology of Events for December 2005

Two Weeks Beginning 18 December 2005
In presidential elections in Bolivia, Evo Morales of the Movement Towards Socialism won 53.7% of the votes cast, ahead of former president Jorge Quiroga with 28.6% and Samuel Doria Medina with 7.8%. In parliamentary elections the Movement Towards Socialism won 72 of 130 available seats in the Chamber of Deputies, followed by Democratic and Social Power with 43 seats, the National Unity Front 8 and the Revolutionary Nationalist Movement 7.

In Uzbekistan, interior minister Zokirjon Almatov resigned and was replaced by Anvar Salikhbayev.

Justice minister Solvita Aboltina became acting defence minister for Latvia after the resignation of Einars Repše.

Week Beginning 11 December 2005
In presidential elections in Chile, Michelle Bachelet of the Concertación coalition won 45.9% of the votes cast followed by Sebastián Piñera with 25.4% and Joaquín Lavín with 23.2%. In elections to the chamber of deputies, the Concertación coalition won 65 of 120 available seats with 51.8% of the votes cast ahead of the Alliance for Chile coalition with 54 seats and 38.6%.

Foreign minister Jakaya Kikwete won 80.3% of the votes cast in Tanzania's presidential elections, ahead of Ibrahim Lipumba with 11.7% and Freeman Mbowe with 5.9%. In parliamentary elections, the CCM won 206 of 232 available seats, the Civic United Front 19 and the Party for Democracy and Progress 5. Edward Lowassa was subsequently named prime minister and sworn in.

Palestinian president Mahmoud Abbas appointed Nabil Shaath acting prime minister after the resignation of Ahmed Qureia.

Week Beginning 4 December 2005
In Côte d'Ivoire, presidents Thabo Mbeki of South Africa and Olusegun Obasanjo of Nigeria, acting as mediators, announced the nomination of Charles Konan Banny as prime minister for a transitional period. A new cabinet was subsequently announced which included Banny as finance minister, Youssouf Bakayoko as foreign minister, René Aphing Kouassi as defence minister and Joseph Dja Blé as interior minister.

In presidential elections in Kazakhstan, incumbent Nursultan Nazarbaev was re-elected with 91.2% of the votes cast ahead of Zharmakhan Tuyakbai with 6.6%.

In parliamentary elections Venezuelan president Hugo Chávez's Fifth Republic Movement won 114 of 167 available seats, with the remaining seats being won by his allies.

The National Democratic Party won 388 of 432 allocated seats in Egypt's parliamentary elections, followed by independents with 112 seats (including 88 affiliated to the Muslim Brotherhood) and the New Wafd Party 6.

In parliamentary elections in St Vincent and the Grenadines, prime minister Ralph Gonsalves' Unity Labour Party won 12 of 15 seats with 55.3% of the votes cast, ahead of the New Democratic Party with 3 seats and 44.7%. Gonsalves subsequently took over the national security ministry.

The Swiss parliament elected Moritz Leuenberger as president for 2006 in parliament with 159 votes of 225. Micheline Calmy-Rey was elected vice-president with 167 of 218 votes.

Chronology of Events for November 2005

Week Beginning 27 November 2005

In presidential elections in Gabon, incumbent Omar Bongo Ondimba won 79.2% of the votes cast followed by Pierre Mamboundou with 13.6% and Zacharie Myboto with 6.6%.

In presidential elections in Honduras, Manuel Zelaya won 49.9% of the votes cast ahead of Porfirio Lobo Salsa with 46.2%. In parliamentary elections, the Liberal Party won 62 of 128 available seats, the National Party won 55, the Democratic Unification Party 5, the Christian Democratic Party 4, and the Innovation and Unity Party-Social Democracy 2.

In a cabinet reshuffle in Argentina, Jorge Taiana became foreign minister, Nilda Garré defence minister and Felisa Miceli economy minister.

A motion of no-confidence in Canadian prime minister Paul Martin's government was passed in the House of Commons by 171 votes to 133.

Week Beginning 20 November 2005

In Germany, the Bundestag elected Angela Merkel chancellor by 397 votes to 202 with 12 abstentions. Her new cabinet included Frank-Walter Steinmeier as foreign minister, Franz Josef Jung as defence minister, Peer Steinbrück as finance minister and Wolfgang Schäuble as interior minister.

Jordanian prime minister Adnan Badran resigned and was replaced by Marouf al-Bakhit who also took on the role of defence minister. Bakhit's new cabinet included Abdul Ilah Khatib as foreign minister, Ziad Fariz as finance minister and Eid al-Fayez as interior minister.

Week Beginning 13 November 2005

In presidential elections in Burkina Faso, incumbent Blaise Compaoré was re-elected with 80.3% of the votes cast, ahead of Bénéwendé Stanislas Sankara with 4.9%.

In presidential elections in Sri Lanka, prime minister Mahinda Rajapakse was elected with 50.3% of the votes cast against Ranil Wickremesinghe with 48.4%. Rajapakse was subsequently sworn in and Ratnasiri Wickremanayake became prime minister. The new government included Rajapakse as defence and finance minister, and Mangala Samaraweera as foreign minister.

Kadyr Gulyamov was replaced as Uzbekistan's defence minister by Ruslan Mirzayev.

Week Beginning 6 November 2005

In parliamentary elections in Azerbaijan, the ruling New Azerbaijan Party won 58 of 125 available seats, independents won 40 and the Azadlig opposition bloc 8.

Indian foreign minister K. Natwar Singh resigned and his portfolio was taken over by prime minister Manmohan Singh.

In the presidential run-off in Liberia, Ellen Johnson-Sirleaf won 59.6% of the votes cast with George Weah receiving 40.4%.

In Poland, the government of prime minister Kazimierz Marcinkiewicz won a vote of confidence in the lower house by 272 votes to 187.

Chronology of Events for October 2005

Week Beginning 30 October 2005

In a cabinet reshuffle in Japan, Taro Aso was appointed foreign minister, Fukushiro Nukaga defence minister, Heizo Takenaka internal affairs and Sadakazu Tanigaki was retained as finance minister.

Week Beginning 23 October 2005

In parliamentary elections to the Chamber of Deputies in Argentina, the Front for Victory won 50 of 127 seats with 29.9% of the votes cast, followed by the Radical Civic Union with ten seats and 8.9%. The Front for Victory plus its allies took 69 seats and the Radical Civic Union plus its allies 19.

Lamin Kaba Bajo was appointed foreign minister in a cabinet reshuffle in The Gambia.

In Guinea-Bissau, president João Bernardo Vieira dismissed the government of prime minister Carlos Gomes Júnior. Aristides Gomes was subsequently sworn in as prime minister and appointed acting interior minister. A government was formed that included António Isaac Monteiro as foreign minister, Hélder Proença as defence minister and Vítor Mandinga as finance minister.

Week Beginning 16 October 2005

The new government of prime minister Jens Stoltenberg was formed in Norway. It included Jonas Gahr Støre as foreign minister, Anne-Grete Strøm-Erichsen as defence minister and Kristin Halvorsen as finance minister.

In Georgia, prime minister Zurab Noghaideli replaced foreign minister Salome Zurabishvili with Gela Bezhuashvili.

Prime minister Helen Clark's new government in New Zealand, included Winston Peters as foreign minister and Phil Goff as defence minister. Michael Cullen remained finance minister.

In Poland, prime minister Marek Belka resigned and Kazimierz Marcinkiewicz was asked to form a new government by president Aleksander Kwasniewski. Marcinkiewicz was subsequently sworn in with a cabinet that included Stefan Meller as foreign minister, Radosław Sikorski as defence minister and Teresa Lubińska as finance minister.

Week Beginning 9 October 2005

In the first round of presidential elections in Poland, Donald Tusk won 36.3% of the votes, followed by Lech Kaczyński with 33.1% and Andrzej Lepper 15.1%. In the subsequent second round run-off Kaczyński won 54.0% and Tusk 46.0%.

In Nicaragua, the National Assembly elected Alfredo Gómez vice-president by 83 votes to 0.

A new cabinet was appointed in Ethiopia with Kuma Demeksa becoming defence minister.

In presidential elections in Liberia, George Weah of the Congress for Democratic Change won 28.3% of the vote, followed by Ellen Johnson-Sirleaf of the Unity Party with 19.8% and Charles Brumskine of the Liberal Party 13.9%.

Week Beginning 2 October 2005

In Estonia, Jürgen Ligi was appointed defence minister.

President Svetozar Marović nominated Zoran Stanković as Serbia and Montenegro's new defence minister.

Chronology of Events for September 2005

Week Beginning 25 September 2005

In parliamentary elections in Poland, the Law and Justice Party won 155 of 460 seats with 27.0% of the votes cast, followed by the Citizen's Platform with 133 and 24.1%, and the Self-Defence of the Polish Republic with 56 and 11.4%.

Sheikh Khalid bin Ahmed Al-Khalifa was named foreign minister of Bahrain.

Estonian defence minister Jaak Jõerüüt resigned.

In Iceland, Davíð Oddsson resigned as foreign minister and was succeeded by Geir H. Haarde. Árni Mathiesen replaced Haarde as finance minister.

Week Beginning 18 September 2005

In parliamentary elections in Germany, the Christian Democratic Union/Christian Social Union won 226 of 614 seats with 35.2% of the votes cast, followed by the Social Democratic Party with 222 and 34.2%, and the Free Democratic Party with 61 and 9.8%.

In Sudan, a national unity government was formed with Dr. Lam Akol as foreign minister and Lieut.-Gen. Abdel Rahim Mohamed Hussein as defence minister. Al-Zobeir Ahmed Hassan remained finance minister.

Domenico Siniscalco, Italian economy and finance minister, resigned and was replaced by Giulio Tremonti.

Week Beginning 11 September 2005

In parliamentary elections in Japan, prime minister Junichiro Koizumi's Liberal Democratic Party won 296 of 480 seats with 38.2% of the votes cast, ahead of the Democratic Party with 113 and 31.0%, and the New Komeito Party with 31 and 13.3%.

In Norway's parliamentary elections the Labour Party won 61 of 169 seats with 32.7% of the votes cast, followed by the Progress Party with 38 and 22.1%, and the Conservative Party with 23 and 14.1%.

The Labour Party won 50 of 121 seats with 41.1% of the votes cast in New Zealand's parliamentary elections, ahead of the National Party with 48 and 39.1%, and the New Zealand First Party with 7 and 5.7%.

Week Beginning 4 September 2005

Bhutan's prime minister, Yeshey Zimba, was replaced by Sangay Ngedup.

In presidential elections in Egypt, incumbent Hosni Mubarak was re-elected with 88.6% of the votes, followed by Ayman Nour with 7.3% and Noaman Gomaa with 2.8%.

President Viktor Yushchenko of Ukraine dismissed prime minister Yuliya Tymoshenko, appointing her predecessor Yuriy Yekhanurov in her place. Yekhanurov was subsequently approved by parliament in a second vote.

In Serbia and Montenegro, defence minister Prvoslav Davinić resigned.

Chronology of Events for August 2005

Week Beginning 28 August 2005

In Cyprus, the finance minister, Makis Keravnos, resigned and was replaced by Michalakis Sarris.

Oil prices reached a record high of US$70.85 per barrel.

In Kyrgyzstan, the premiership of Feliks Kulov was confirmed in parliament by 55 votes to eight.

In Suriname, a new cabinet took office which included Lygia Kraag-Keteldijk as foreign minister, Ivan Fernald as defence minister and Humphrey Hildenberg reappointed as finance minister.

Albanian president Alfred Moisiu asked Sali Berisha to form a government. The cabinet included Besnik Mustafaj as foreign minister, Fatmir Mediu as defence minister and Ridvan Bode as finance minister. The administration was confirmed in parliament by 84 votes to 53.

Week Beginning 21 August 2005

Manasseh Nshuti was named Rwanda's new finance minister.

In a cabinet reshuffle in Romania, finance minister Ionut Popescu was replaced by Sebastian Vlădescu.

Week Beginning 14 August 2005

Kurmanbek Bakiyev was sworn in as president of Kyrgyzstan and named Feliks Kulov acting prime minister.

In Singapore, incumbent president S. R. Nathan was re-elected as the only candidate eligible.

A cabinet reshuffle in Tunisia saw Abdelwahab Abdallah appointed foreign minister and Kamel Morjane defence minister.

In presidential elections in Burundi, the legislature elected Pierre Nkurunziza by 151 votes to 9. His new cabinet included Martin Nduwimana and Alice Nzomukunda as first and second vice-presidents, Antoinette Batumubwira as foreign minister, Gen. Germain Niyoyankana as defence minister and Dieudonné Ngowembona as finance minister.

Solón Espinosa resigned as defence minister of Ecuador and was replaced by Oswaldo Jarrín.

Week Beginning 7 August 2005

In a cabinet reshuffle in Chad, Ahmad Allam-mi was appointed foreign minister, Bichara Issa Djadallah defence minister and Abbas Mahamat Tolli finance minister.

Benjamin Netanyahu resigned as Israel's finance minister and was replaced by Ehud Olmert.

In Bulgaria, Sergey Stanishev's new cabinet included Ivailo Kalfin as foreign minister, Vesselin Bliznakov as defence minister and Plamen Oresharski as finance minister.

Pedro Pablo Kuczynski became prime minister of Peru with Óscar Maúrtua de Romaña as foreign minister, Marciano Rengifo Ruiz as defence minister and Fernando Zavala as economy and finance minister. Kuczynski subsequently won a vote of confidence by 60 votes to six with 29 abstentions.

In Sri Lanka, foreign minister Lakshman Kadirgamar was assassinated and was replaced by Anura Bandaranaike.

Chronology of Events for July 2005

Week Beginning 31 July 2005

King Fahd, Saudi Arabia's ruler, died. He was succeeded by his brother-in-law, Abdullah.

Mahmoud Ahmadinejad was sworn in as president of Iran. His new cabinet included Manouchehr Mottaki as foreign minister, Mostafa Mohammad-Najjar as defence minister and Davoud Danesh-Jaafari as finance minister.

In Mauritania, a coup resulted in the overthrow of president Maaouya Ould Sid'Ahmed Taya while he was attending the funeral of King Fahd. A Military Council for Justice and Democracy was formed, led by Col. Ely Ould Mohamed Vall, after which the incumbent prime minister Sghaïr Ould M'Bareck and his government resigned. Subsequently Sidi Mohamed Ould Boubacar was appointed prime minister. His cabinet included Ahmed Ould Sid Hamed as foreign minister and Abdallahi Ould Souleymane Ould Cheikh Sidiya as finance minister.

In Suriname, The United People's Assembly re-elected Ronald Venetiaan president with 560 of the 879 available votes against Rabin Parmessar with 315.

Week Beginning 24 July 2005

In Guinea-Bissau's second round run-off for the presidency, João Bernado Vieira was elected president with 52.4% of the vote against 47.6% for Malam Bacai Sanhá.

In Bulgaria, the parliament approved Sergey Stanishev as chairman of the council of ministers (prime minister) by 120 votes to 119.

Week Beginning 17 July 2005

A new cabinet was named in Lebanon, including Fouad Siniora as prime minister, with Elias Murr as defence minister, Fawzi Salloukh as foreign minister and Jihad Azour as finance minister. The new government subsequently won a confidence vote by 92 to 14.

In Portugal, finance minister Luís Campos e Cunha resigned and was replaced by Fernando Teixeira dos Santos.

In Jordan, the cabinet of prime minister Adnan Badran won a confidence vote by 66 votes to 37.

Week Beginning 10 July 2005

In presidential elections in Kyrgyzstan, acting president Kurmanbek Bakiyev won 88.9% of the votes, followed by Bakir Tursunbai with only 3.8%.

In Croatia, the parliament approved the appointment of Ivica Kirin as interior minister.

In a cabinet reshuffle in the Maldives, Ahmed Shaheed replaced Fathullah Jameel as minister of foreign affairs and Ahmed Thasmeen Ali became minister of home affairs.

Week Beginning 3 July 2005

In parliamentary elections in Albania, the Democratic Party won 56 of the 140 available seats, the Socialist Party of Albania 42, the Republican Party 11 and the Social Democratic Party 7.

In parliamentary elections in Mauritius, the Social Alliance won 42 of 70 seats with 48.8% of the votes cast, ahead of the coalition of the Mauritian Socialist Movement and the Mauritian Militant Movement with 24 and 42.6%. In the new cabinet Navin Ramgoolam became prime minister as well as defence and interior minister, with Madan Dulloo as foreign minister and Rama Sithanen finance minister.

In Burundi, the National Council for the Defence of Democracy-Forces for the Defence of Democracy (CNDD-FDD) won 64 of the 118 available seats with 58.6% of the votes cast, ahead of the ruling Front for Democracy in Burundi (Frodebu) party with 30 and 21.7%, and the Party of Unity for National Progress (UPRONA) with 15 and 7.2%.

In a cabinet reshuffle in Comoros, Adou Mari Madi replaced M'Saidie Houmed as defence minister, Aboudou Soefou replaced Souef Mohamed Elamine as foreign minister and Oubeidi Mze Chei succeeded Ahamadi Abdoulbastoi as finance minister.

Mark Vaile succeeded John Anderson as deputy prime minister of Australia.

In Slovakia, prime minister Mikuláš Dzurinda survived a vote of no-confidence which was supported by only sixty votes from the 122 Members of Parliament present in the 150-seat legislature.

In co-ordinated attacks, four suicide bombers struck central London and detonated three bombs on underground trains and a fourth an hour later on a bus. 52 people were killed and a further 700 injured.

The leaders of the Group of Eight (G-8) countries met at a summit in Gleneagles, Scotland to discuss aid for developing countries. The leaders agreed to cancel the debt of the 18 poorest African countries and to increase aid by US$50 bn. by 2010.

Chronology of Events for June 2005

Week Beginning 26 June 2005

In Bosnia-Herzegovina, Ivo Miro Jović took over as presidency chairman.

The finance minister of the former Soviet republic of Georgia, Valery Chachelashvili, resigned and was replaced by Aleksi Aleksishvili. Irakli Chogovadze subsequently succeeded Alexishvili as economic development minister.

In Germany, chancellor Gerhard Schröder lost a vote of confidence by 296 votes to 151 with 148 abstentions.

Week Beginning 19 June 2005

In presidential elections in Guinea-Bissau, former acting president Malam Bacai Sanhá won 35.5% of the votes ahead of former president João Bernardo Vieira with 28.9% and Kumba Ialá with 25.0%.

In the fourth and final round of parliamentary elections in Lebanon, independent candidates won 12 of the 28 seats available in Northern Lebanon. The Future Tide Movement won 7 seats, the Lebanese Forces 4 and the Qornet Shehwan Grouping 3. Overall the Opposition Bloc won 72 of 128 seats, Hizbollah, Amal and their allies won 35, and the Free Patriotic Movement and their allies 21. President Emile Lahoud subsequently appointed Fouad Siniora prime minister.

In Mongolia, Nambaryn Enkhbayar was inaugurated as president.

In parliamentary elections in Bulgaria, the Coalition for Bulgaria won 82 of the 240 available seats with 31.1% of the votes cast, ahead of the National Movement Simeon II with 53 and 19.9%, and the Movement for Rights and Freedoms with 34 and 12.7%.

Week Beginning 12 June 2005

In Greece, the prime minister, Kostas Karamanlis, won a parliamentary vote of confidence by 165 votes to 120.

In the third round of parliamentary elections in Lebanon, Michel Aoun's Free Patriotic Movement won 15 of 58 seats in Mount Lebanon and the Bekaa Valley. The Progressive Socialist Party won 14 seats, the Zahleh Dignity and Bekaa Accord Bloc 6 and the Future Tide Movement 5. Hizbollah won 4 seats and its allies 3.

Célestin Gaombalet resigned and was replaced as prime minister of the Central African Republic by Élie Doté. The new cabinet included Jean-Paul Ngoupandé as foreign minister and Théodore Dabanga as finance minister. President Gen. François Bozizé remained defence minister and interior minister Michel Sallé was reappointed.

Dismissed by president Thabo Mbeki, South Africa's deputy prime minister, Jacob Zuma, was replaced by Phumzile Mlambo-Ngcuka.

In presidential elections in Iran, the former president Ali Akbar Hashemi Rafsanjani won 21.0% of the votes followed by Mahmoud Ahmadinejad with 19.5%, Mehdi Karroubi 17.3% and Mohammed Baqer Qalibaf 13.9%. A subsequent run-off resulted in Ahmadinejad being elected with 61.7% of the votes against Rafsanjani with 35.9%.

Week Beginning 5 June 2005

In the second round of parliamentary elections in Lebanon the Amal Movement won 6 of the 23 available seats in southern Lebanon and its allies the Resistance and Development Bloc 7. Hizbollah won 5 seats and its allies 1.

Bolivian president Carlos Mesa Gilbert resigned and was replaced by Eduardo Rodríguez. The new cabinet included Armando Loaiza as foreign minister and Gonzalo Méndez as defence minister.

In Hungary, László Sólyom was elected president by parliament in a third round of voting. Sólyom won with 185 votes against Katalin Szili with 182.

In Bosnia-Herzegovina, the resignation of the foreign minister Mladen Ivanić was finally accepted by Prime Minister Adnan Terzić 6 months after it was submitted. Ana Trišić-Babić was appointed acting foreign minster.

Edem Kodjo was named as prime minister of Togo. His new cabinet included Zarifou Ayéva as foreign minister, Kpatcha Gnassingbé as defence minister and Payadowa Boukpessi as finance minister.

Chronology of Events for May 2005

Week Beginning 29 May 2005

At referendums in France and the Netherlands voters rejected the proposed EU constitution.

In the first round of parliamentary elections in Lebanon, Saad El Hariri's Martyr Rarik Hariri List won all 19 seats in Beirut.

In France, the prime minister Jean-Pierre Raffarin resigned and Dominique de Villepin, the interior minister, was appointed his sucessor. De Villepin's new cabinet included Philippe Douste-Blazy as foreign minister and Nicolas Sarkozy interior minister. Michèle Alliot-Marie was reappointed defence minister. The new government survived a vote of confidence in the National Assembly by 363 votes to 178 (with four abstentions) and in the Senate by 174 votes to 126.

In Mexico, Carlos Abascal became interior minister after Santiago Creel Miranda resigned.

In São Tomé and Príncipe, the prime minister Damião Vaz de Almeida resigned and was subsequently replaced by Carmo Silveira, who also became finance minister in the new cabinet.

In Andorra, Albert Pintat's new government included Juli Minoves Triquell as foreign minister and Ferran Mirapeix Lucas as finance minister.

Week Beginning 22 May 2005

In a cabinet reshuffle in Djibouti, Mahamoud Ali Youssouf became foreign minister and Ali Farah Assoweh finance minister. Ougoureh Kifleh Ahmed was reappointed defence minister.

In presidential elections in Mongolia, Nambaryn Enkhbayar won 53.4% of the vote against Mendsaikhany Enkhsaikhan with 19.7%.

Hong Kong's acting chief executive Donald Tsang resigned. Financial Secretary Henry Tang became the acting chief executive.

In parliamentary elections in Suriname, the ruling New Front for Democracy coalition won 23 of the 51 available seats with 41.5% of the vote, ahead of the National Democratic Party, which won 15 seats with 22.8%.

Week Beginning 15 May 2005

In Canada, Paul Martin's government won a vote of confidence in the House of Commons by 153 votes to 152.

In a cabinet reshuffle in St Vincent and the Grenadines, Mike Browne replaced Louis Straker as minister of foreign affairs.

Week Beginning 8 May 2005

In the presidential run-off in the Central African Republic, incumbent Gen. François Bozizé won 64.7% of the vote against Martin Ziguélé who won 35.3%. Following the second round of National Assembly elections the National Convergence coalition had 42 seats (including the National Unity Party with 3 seats and the Movement for Democracy and Development with 2), ahead of the Liberation Movement of the Central African People with 11 and the Central African Democratic Rally with 8.

In Belgium, Guy Verhofstadt's government won a vote of confidence by 97 votes to 50.

Jiří Paroubek's coalition government won a confidence vote in the Czech Republic by 101 votes to 99.

Week Beginning 1 May 2005

In a cabinet reshuffle in Algeria, Mohammed Bedjaoui became foreign affairs minister and Mourad Medelci finance minister.

José Miguel Insulza was elected Secretary-General of the Organization of American States after winning 31 of 34 votes.

The new Iraqi government of Ibrahim al-Jaafari included Hoshyar Zebari as foreign affairs minister and Saadoun al-Duleimi as defence minister.

In Bosnia-Herzegovina, the House of Representatives appointed Ivo Miro Jović as the Croat member of the presidency.

In parliamentary elections in Dominica the ruling Dominica Labour Party won 12 of the 21 available seats with 52.1% of the votes cast, the United Workers Party won 8 and ind. 1. In the subsequent cabinet reshuffle Charles Savarin became minister of foreign affairs.

In parliamentary elections in the UK the Labour Party won 356 seats with 35.2% of votes cast; the Conservative Party 197 with 32.3%; the Liberal Democratic Party 62 with 22.1%; others 3. In Prime Minister Tony Blair's new cabinet John Reid was appointed defence secretary but the other leading posts remained unchanged.

Chronology of Events for April 2005

Week Beginning 24 April 2005

In parliamentary elections in Andorra the Liberal Party of Andorra won 14 seats (41.2% of the vote), the Social Democratic Party 12 and the Andorran Democratic Centre 2.

In presidential elections in Togo, Faure Gnassingbé of the Togolese People's Assembly won with 60.2% of the vote. Emmanuel Bob Akitani of the Union des Forces de Changement took 38.2%. Nicolas Lawson won 1.0% and Harry Olympio won 0.6%. Akitani disputed the results but the Constitutional Court later confirmed Gnassingbé as president.

Week Beginning 17 April 2005

In Ecuador, the congress voted unanimously to dismiss President Lucio Gutiérrez. He was replaced by Vice-President Alfredo Palacio whose new cabinet included Antonio Parra as minister of foreign relations, Aníbal Solón as defence minister and Rafael Correa as economy and finance minister.

Italian prime minister Silvio Berlusconi formed a new government but kept the key ministers unchanged. His government later survived a confidence vote in the Chamber of Deputies by 334 votes to 240 and in the Senate by 170 votes to 117.

In Liechtenstein, a new government was sworn retaining Otmar Hasler as its head but introducing Rita Kieber-Beck as foreign minister and Martin Meyer as interior minister.

Week Beginning 10 April 2005

The Estonian parliament approved Andrus Ansip's cabinet which included Urmas Paet as minister of foreign affairs, Jaak Jõerüüt as defence minister and Aivar Sõerd as finance minister.

After failing to form a new government Omar Karami resigned as prime minister of Lebanon and was replaced by Najib Mikati. The new cabinet included Elias Murr as deputy prime minister and defence minister.

In a cabinet reshuffle in Zimbabwe, Simbarashe Mumbengegwi replaced Stanislaus Mudenge as foreign minister.

Martinho Dafa Cabi replaced Daniel Gomes as defence minister in a cabinet reshuffle in Guinea-Bissau.

In Tonga, the defence minister 'Aloua Fetu'utolu Tupou died and was replaced by the foreign minister, Sonatane Tu'a Taumoepeau Tupou, in an acting capacity.

Week Beginning 3 April 2005

In presidential elections in Moldova, Vladimir Voronin was re-elected with 75 votes. His opponent Gheorghe Duca received one vote. Voronin re-appointed Vasile Tarlev prime minister.

In Austria, Wolfgang Schüssel's government survived a vote of no-confidence by 94 votes to 84.

In Jordan, the government of prime minister Faisal al-Fayez resigned and Adnan Badran was appointed prime minister. A new government was later sworn in with Badran doubling as defence minister, Farouq Al Qasrawi as minister of foreign affairs, Awni Yerfas as interior minister and Basem Awadallah as finance minister.

In Iraq, Jalal Talabani was elected president by the National Assembly with Sheikh Ghazi al-Yawer and Adil Abdel-Mahdi becoming vice-presidents. Ibrahim al-Jaafari was appointed prime minister.

Prince Rainier III of Monaco died and was succeeded by his son Albert II.

In Djibouti, president Ismail Omar Guelleh was re-elected with 100% of votes after opposition parties boycotted the elections.

Chronology of Events for March 2005

Week Beginning 27 March 2005

In Bosnia-Herzegovina, Dragan Čović was dismissed as the Croat member of the presidency by UN High Representative, Paddy Ashdown.

In the Czech Republic, members of the KDU-ČSL resigned from the cabinet. Prime Minister Stanislav Gross subsequently resigned and was replaced by Jiří Paroubek.

Paul Wolfowitz was approved as president of the World Bank.

In parliamentary elections in Zimbabwe, the Zimbabwe African National Union-Patriotic Front won 78 of the 150 seats with 58.8% of votes cast and the Movement for Democtartic Change won 41 seats with 37.5%.

Pope John Paul II died.

Week Beginning 20 March 2005

Estonian Prime Minister Juhan Parts resigned. President Arnold Rüütel subsequently asked Andrus Ansip to form a new government.

In Namibia, Hifikepunye Pohamba was sworn in as president and appointed Nahas Angula prime minister.

Week Beginning 13 March 2005

In the first round of presidential elections in the Central African Republic, incumbent president Gen. François Bozizé received 42.9% of the vote, ahead of former prime minister Martin Ziguélé (Liberation Movement of the Central African People) with 23.5% and former president André Kolingba (Democratic Rally of Central Africa) 16.4%.

Parliamentary elections in Liechtenstein were won by the Progressive Citizens' Party with 12 out of 25 seats and 48.7% of the vote, ahead of the Patriotic Union with 10 and 38.2% and the Free List with 3 and 13%.

In parliamentary elections in Tonga the Human Rights and Democracy Movement won seven out of nine seats with 38.9% of votes cast.

Week Beginning 6 March 2005

In parliamentary elections in Moldova the Party of Communists of the Republic of Moldova won 56 seats with 46.0% of votes cast, the Democratic Moldova bloc 34 with 28.5% and the Christian Democratic People's Party 11 with 9.1%.

Hong Kong's chief executive Tung Chee-hwa resigned. Chief Secretary for Administration Donald Tsang became the acting chief executive.

Karolos Papoulias was sworn in as president of Greece.

In Portugal, José Sócrates was sworn in as prime minister. The new cabinet included Diogo Freitas do Amaral as foreign minister and Luís Amado as defence minister.

Chronology of Events for February 2005

Week Beginning 27 February 2005

In the first round of parliamentary elections in Kyrgyzstan, 35 of the 75 seats were allocated, thereby triggering a second round. However, following protests the Supreme Court annulled the results and the Upper House of parliament named Kurmanbek Bakiyev acting prime minister and acting president. The new parliament later confirmed Bakiyev as interim prime minister and the Upper House was dissolved.

In the first round of legislative elections in Tajikistan the People's Democratic Party of Tajikistan won 49 of 63 seats ahead of the Communist Party with 4 and the Islamic Renaissance Party of Tajikistan with 2.

The Lebanese government, led by prime minister Omar Karami, resigned.

In Uruguay, Tabaré Vázquez was sworn in as president. Rodolfo Nin Novoa became vice president. The new cabinet included Reinaldo Gargano as foreign minister and Azucena Berruti as defence minister.

Week Beginning 20 February 2005

In parliamentary elections in Portugal the Socialist Party won 120 seats with 45.1% of votes cast, the Social Democratic Party 72 with 28.7% and the Communist Party/Green Party coalition 14 with 7.6%.

The UN High Commissioner for Refugees, Ruud Lubbers, resigned. His deputy Wendy Chamberlin took over as acting high commissioner.

Week Beginning 13 February 2005

In Croatia, Kolinda Grabar-Kitarović became foreign minister.

Lebanon's former prime minister Rafiq al-Hariri was killed in a bomb attack.

The Kyoto Protocol, aiming to reduce total greenhouse gas emissions of developed countries, came into force.

Michael Chertoff was confirmed as US Secretary of Homeland Security, thereby filling the last vacancy in President George W. Bush's second-term cabinet. Major changes from his first-term cabinet included Condoleeza Rice as Secretary of State and Alberto 'Al' Gonzales as Attorney General.

Week Beginning 6 February 2005

In parliamentary elections in Thailand the ruling Thai Rak Thai party won 376 of 500 seats, ahead of the Democrat Party with 97 and the Thai Nation with 25.

In parliamentary elections in Denmark, the ruling Liberal Party took 52 seats with 29.1% of the vote, against 47 seats for the Social Democrats and 24 seats for the Danish People's Party.

Estonian foreign minister Kristiina Ojuland was dismissed. Rein Lang was subsequently appointed her successor.

Karolos Papoulias was elected president of Greece, receiving 279 votes in the 300-member parliament.

Chronology of Events for January 2005

Week Beginning 30 January 2005

In parliamentary elections in Iraq the Shia-backed United Iraqi Alliance won 140 of 275 seats with 48.1% of the vote, ahead of the Kurdish Unity List with 75 seats and 25.7% and prime minister Iyad Allawi's Iraqi List with 40 and 13.8%.

King Gyanendra of Nepal dismissed the government of prime minister Sher Bahadur Deuba and assumed power.

Armando Guebuza was sworn in as president of Mozambique.

Chad's prime minister Moussa Faki resigned. He was succeeded by Pascal Yoadimnadji.

Zurab Zhvania, prime minister of the former Soviet republic of Georgia, died. Finance minister Zurab Nogaideli succeeded him as prime minister.

Ukraine's parliament approved Yuliya Tymoshenko as prime minister. The new cabinet included Borys Tarasyuk as foreign minister and Anatolii Hrytsenko as defence minister.

Togo's president Gnassingbe Eyadéma died. The military installed his son, Faure Eyadéma, as his successor.

Week Beginning 23 January 2005

Viktor Yushchenko was sworn in as president of Ukraine. He named Yuliya Tymoshenko acting prime minister.

In Taiwan, prime minister Yu Shyi-kun and his cabinet resigned. President Chen Shui-bian appointed Frank Hsieh his successor.

Week Beginning 16 January 2005

George W. Bush was sworn in for a second term as US president.

In parliamentary elections in the Maldives all candidates for the 42 seats ran officially as independents, but both the government and the opposition Maldives Democratic Party—which operates in self-imposed exile out of Sri Lanka—claimed victory.

Week Beginning 9 January 2005

In the election for president of the Palestinian Authority Mahmoud Abbas won with 62.5% of votes cast, ahead of Mustafa Barghouti with 19.5%.

The second round of parliamentary elections were held in Uzbekistan, resulting in the Liberal-Democratic Party holding 41 of the 120 seats, ahead of the People's Democratic Party with 28.

A new government was formed in Israel, including Shimon Peres as deputy prime minister.

In a cabinet reshuffle in Zambia, home affairs minister Ronnie Shikapwasha was moved to the post of foreign minister.

Sam Kutesa was appointed Uganda's foreign minister in a cabinet reshuffle.

Week Beginning 2 January 2005

In the first round of presidential elections in Croatia incumbent president Stipe Mesić received 49.4% of the vote, ahead of Jadranka Kosor with 20.5% and Boris Mikšić 17.9%. In the subsequent run-off Stipe Mesić won a second term with 65.9% of votes cast, against 34.1% for Jadranka Kosor.

A cabinet reshuffle in the Democratic Republic of the Congo included the appointment of Adolphe Onusumba as defence minister.

Polish foreign Minister Włodzimierz Cimoszewicz announced his resignation. Adam Rotfeld was named his successor.

Croatia's foreign minister Miomir Žužul resigned.

In a cabinet reshuffle in Antigua and Barbuda prime minister Baldwin Spencer also became minister of foreign affairs.

2004

Chronology of Events for December 2004

Week Beginning 26 December 2004

An earthquake under the Indian Ocean triggered off a tsunami that resulted in more than 290,000 deaths, notably in Indonesia—where 233,000 people lost their lives—Sri Lanka, India and Thailand.

In the repeat of the presidential run-off in Ukraine, Viktor Yushchenko received 52.0% of the vote and Viktor Yanukovich 44.2%.

In the first round of elections in Uzbekistan, criticized for electoral abuses, the Liberal-Democratic Party won 21 of 62 seats, ahead of the People's Democratic Party with 18 and the Fidokorlar National-Democratic Party

with 9. All parties taking part in the election were loyal to President Islam Karimov—opposition parties were barred from participating. The subsequent second round resulted in the Liberal-Democratic Party holding 41 of the 120 seats, followed by the People's Democratic Party with 33.

Samuel Schmid took office as president of Switzerland.

Week Beginning 19 December 2004

In parliamentary elections in Turkmenistan, all 50 seats were filled by supporters of President Saparmurad Niyazov and his Democratic Party, no other parties being allowed to stand.

In Afghanistan, President Hamid Karzai announced a new cabinet, including Abdul Rahim Wardak as the new defence minister. Abdullah Abdullah remained foreign minister.

Week Beginning 12 December 2004

In Romania's second round run-off for the presidency Traian Băsescu was elected president with 51.2% of the vote against 48.8% for Adrian Năstase.

A cabinet reshuffle in Georgia included the appointment of Interior Minister Irakli Okruashvili as the new defence minister.

In the UK, Home Secretary David Blunkett resigned. Charles Clarke was appointed his successor.

The European Union agreed to begin membership negotiations with Turkey in Oct. 2005.

Week Beginning 5 December 2004

In presidential elections in Ghana, incumbent John Agyekum Kufuor of the New Patriotic Party (NPP) won 53% of the vote with John Atta Mills of the National Democratic Congress (NDC) taking 44%. Parliamentary elections were won by the New Patriotic Party, with 129 of 230 seats.

President Paul Biya of Cameroon appointed a new government with Ephraïm Inoni as prime minister. Laurent Esso was named foreign minister.

The Swiss parliament elected Samuel Schmid as president for 2005.

Cellou Dalein Diallo was appointed prime minister of Guinea 8 months after his predecessor's resignation.

In Portugal, the government of Prime Minister Pedro Santana Lopes resigned.

In parliamentary elections in Taiwan the Democratic Progressive Party took 89 of 225 seats with 35.7% of the vote, against 79 seats and 32.8% for the Nationalist Party.

Vanuatu's Prime Minister Serge Vohor was removed from office following a no-confidence motion vote. Deputy Prime Minister Ham Lini was elected his successor.

Chronology of Events for November 2004

Week Beginning 28 November 2004

In presidential elections in Romania Prime Minister Adrian Năstase of the National Union received 40.9% of the vote, with Traian Băsescu of the Justice and Truth Alliance second with 33.9% and Corneliu Vadim Tudor of the Greater Romania Party third with 12.6%. As a result a second round run-off was required in which Traian Băsescu was elected president with 51.2% of the vote against 48.8% for Adrian Năstase. In parliamentary elections the National Union won 132 of 332 seats with 36.6% of the vote, ahead of the Justice and Truth Alliance with 112 (31.3%).

In the Fiji Islands, Vice President Ratu Jope Seniloli resigned.

Somalia's Prime Minister Ali Muhammad Ghedi named a cabinet including Abdullahi Sheikh Ismail as foreign minister and Abdirahman Mahmud Ali as defence minister.

The Slovenian parliament approved the cabinet of the new prime minister, Janez Janša.

Week Beginning 21 November 2004

In the second round of presidential elections in Ukraine, deemed by western observers to be flawed, protesters gathered in central Kyiv after the election commission indicated that Viktor Yanukovich had won. The official second round results gave victory to Yanukovich, with 49.5% of the vote, against 46.6% for Yushchenko. However, parliament passed a resolution declaring the poll invalid and the Supreme Court annulled the second round of the election. When it was held again Viktor Yushchenko received 52.0% of the vote and Viktor Yanukovich 44.2%.

Latvian President Vaira Vīķe-Freiberga nominated Aigars Kalvitis as prime minister. The cabinet subsequently formed included former prime minister Einars Repše as defence minister.

Week Beginning 14 November 2004

Macedonian Prime Minister Hari Kostov resigned.

In Vanuatu, Marcellino Pipite replaced Barak Sopé as foreign minister.

Presidential elections in Namibia were won by Hifikepunye Pohamba (South West Africa People's Organization/SWAPO) with 76.4% of votes cast, ahead of Ben Ulenga (Congress of Democrats) with 7.3%. In parliamentary elections SWAPO won 55 of the available 72 seats, with 75.1% of the vote.

In the first round of presidential elections in Niger incumbent Mamadou Tandja won 40.7% of the votes followed by former prime minister Mahamadou Issoufou with 24.6% and former president Mahamane Ousmane with 17.4%. As a result a second round between the two leading candidates was required, in which Mamadou Tandja won 65.5% of the vote and Mahamadou Issoufou 34.5%.

The European Parliament approved the new European Commission headed by José Manuel Durão Barroso.

In Italy, Deputy Prime Minister Gianfranco Fini was appointed foreign minister.

A cabinet reshuffle in Lesotho included the appointment of Monyane Moleleki as foreign minister.

Week Beginning 7 November 2004

Burundi's President Domitien Ndayizeye dismissed his Vice-President, Alphonse Marie Kadege, replacing him with Frédéric Ngenzebuhoro.

In Estonia, Defence Minister Margus Hanson resigned. He was succeeded by Jaak Jõerüüt.

A cabinet reshuffle in Tunisia included the appointment of Abdelbaki Hermassi as foreign minister and Hédi M'henni as defence minister.

President Yasser Arafat of the Palestinian Administered Territories died. Parliament Speaker Rauhi Fattouh succeeded him as acting president.

Chronology of Events for October 2004

Week Beginning 31 October 2004

In the first round of presidential elections in Ukraine reformist former prime minister Viktor Yushchenko won 39.9% of the vote, with incumbent Prime Minister Viktor Yanukovich in second place with 39.3%. Following the second round run-off, deemed by western observers to be flawed, protesters gathered in central Kyiv after the election commission indicated that Viktor Yanukovich had won. The official second round results gave victory to Yanukovich, with 49.5% of the vote, against 46.6% for Yushchenko. However, parliament declared the poll invalid and the Supreme Court annulled the second round of the election. When it was held again Viktor Yushchenko received 54.1% of the vote and Viktor Yanukovich 45.9%.

In presidential elections in Uruguay, Tabaré Vázquez (Progressive Encounter-Broad Front-New Majority) received 50.4% of the vote, beating Jorge Larrañaga (National Party) into second place with 34.3%. Elections to the Chamber of Deputies were won by the Progressive Encounter-Broad Front-New Majority with 53 seats, ahead of the National Party in second place with 34 seats and the Colorado Party third with 10 seats.

Ferenc Somogyi was sworn in as Hungary's new foreign minister.

In presidential elections in Palau, incumbent Tommy Remengesau won with 63.6% of votes cast against 36.3% for Polycarp Basilius.

President Sheikh Zayed bin Sultan al-Nahyan of the United Arab Emirates died. The Federal Council elected his oldest son, Sheikh Khalifa bin Zayed al-Nahyan, his successor.

In the US presidential elections incumbent George W. Bush (Republican) won 286 electoral college votes, receiving 51.04% of votes cast. John Kerry (Democrat) won 252 electoral college votes, receiving 48.01% of votes cast. The Republicans also kept control of both the House of Representatives and the Senate, in the former increasing their representation to 231 of 435 members and in the latter to 55 of 100 members.

Somalian President Abdullahi Yusuf Ahmed named Ali Muhammad Ghedi prime minister.

Week Beginning 24 October 2004

In a cabinet reshuffle in Jordan, Hani al-Mulki was appointed the new foreign minister.

In presidential elections in Tunisia, incumbent Zine El Abidine Ben Ali (Constitutional Democratic Assembly) was re-elected with 94.5% of the votes cast, ahead of Mohamed Bouchiha (Popular Unity Party) with 3.8% and two other candidates. In parliamentary elections, the Constitutional Democratic Assembly won 152 of 189 seats, the Movement of Democratic Socialists 14 and the Popular Unity Party 11.

In parliamentary elections in St Kitts and Nevis, the ruling Labour Party won 7 of 11 seats, ahead of the Concerned Citizens Movement with 2 seats.

Petrus Compton succeeded Julian Hunte as foreign minister of St Lucia.

In Bosnia-Herzegovina, Borislav Paravac took over as Presidency Chairman.

In Latvia, the government of Prime Minister Indulis Emsis resigned.

The European Union's new constitution was signed by leaders of the 25 member states.

Parliamentary elections in Botswana were won by the ruling Botswana Democratic Front, with 44 of 57 seats, ahead of the Botswana National Front with 12 seats.

Week Beginning 17 October 2004

In a referendum held in Belarus 86.2% of votes cast were in favour of the abolition of the two-term limit on the presidency. The vote was widely regarded as fraudulent. Likewise, parliamentary elections, which gave an overwhelming majority to the government, were said to be corrupt.

Gen. Khin Nyunt was replaced as prime minister of Myanmar by Lt. Gen. Soe Win.

Ursula Plassnik was named Austria's new foreign minister.

Susilo Bambang Yudhoyono was sworn in as president of Indonesia and Jusuf Kalla as Vice-President. Hassan Wirajuda remained foreign minister with Juwono Sudarsono being appointed the new defence minister.

Prime Minister Rafiq al-Hariri of Lebanon resigned. President Émile Lahoud named Omar Karami his successor. The newly-appointed government included Mahmoud Hammoud as foreign minister and Abdul Rahim Mrad as defence minister.

In Nauru, followers of President Ludwig Scotty won a majority in parliamentary elections. He was elected president unopposed.

Week Beginning 10 October 2004

In the first round of parliamentary elections in Lithuania the Labour Party won 23 of 75 seats, ahead of Prime Minister Algirdas Brazauskas' coalition 'For a Working Lithuania' with 19 and the Homeland Union with 11. The remaining 66 seats were allocated in the second round, which gave the Labour Party a total of 39 seats, 'Working for Lithuania' 31 and the Homeland Union 25.

Somalia's Transitional Federal Parliament chose a new president. Abdullahi Yusuf Ahmed was elected in a third round run-off with 189 votes, against 79 for Abdullahi Ahmed Addou. There were 26 candidates in total in the first round.

In presidential elections in Cameroon incumbent Paul Biya was re-elected with 75.2% of the votes ahead of John Fru Ndi with 17.1% and Adamou Ndam Njoya with 4.7%.

Maatia Toafa, Tuvalu's acting prime minister for the previous 6 weeks, was confirmed by parliament by eight votes to seven against Elisala Pita.

Gambian President Yahya Jammeh dismissed Foreign Minister Baboucarr-Blaise Jagne and appointed Sidi Moro Sanneh his successor.

Victor Gaiciuc, Moldova's defence minister, was dismissed.

Week Beginning 3 October 2004

In parliamentary elections in Slovenia the Slovenian Democratic Party won 29 seats with 29.1% of votes cast, with the ruling Liberal Democracy of Slovenia in second place, with 23 seats and 22.8% of the vote.

President Levy Mwanawasa of Zambia dismissed Vice-President Nevers Mumba and appointed Lupando Mwape as his successor.

King Norodom Sihanouk of Cambodia abdicated on health grounds.

In a cabinet reshuffle in Thailand, Gen. Samphan Boonyanand replaced Gen. Chetta Thanajaro as defence minister.

Wangari Maathai, a Kenyan environmentalist and human rights campaigner, was awarded the Nobel Peace Prize.

In Australia's general election the governing coalition was returned to power, with the Liberal Party taking 75 of 150 seats in the House of Representatives and its partner the National Party 12, while the opposition Labor Party won 60 seats and independents 3.

Afghanistan's first-ever presidential election was won by head of the transitional government Hamid Karzai, with 55.4% of votes cast, defeating Yunus Qanooni, with 16.3% of the vote, and 16 other candidates.

Chronology of Events for September 2004

Week Beginning 26 September 2004
In a cabinet reshuffle in Japan, Nobutaka Machimura was appointed foreign minister.

The Mongolian parliament approved a new cabinet including Tsendiin Munkh-Orgil as foreign minister and Badarchyn Erdenebat as defence minister.

In Chile a cabinet reshuffle saw Ignacio Walker Prieto become foreign minister and Jaime Ravinet defence minister.

Hungary's parliament endorsed Ferenc Gyurcsány as prime minister.

In a cabinet reshuffle in Ireland, Dermot Ahern replaced Brian Cowen as foreign minister with Cowen moving to finance while Willie O'Dea became defence minister. Irish President Mary McAleese was confirmed for a second term.

Week Beginning 19 September 2004
In the parliamentary elections in Kazakhstan, President Nursultan Nazarbaev's Otan (Fatherland) party won 33 seats in the 77-seat assembly, with the pro-presidential Aist (Agrarian and Industrial Union of Workers Block) second with 10 seats. Observers said that the election fell short of both national and international standards. A second round run-off was required in several constituencies where no single candidate won a majority.

In Indonesia, Susilo Bambang Yudhoyono won the presidential election run-off with 60.9% of the vote, defeating incumbent Megawati Sukarnoputri with 39.1%.

President Leonid Kuchma of Ukraine dismissed his defence minister Yevhen Marchuk, appointing his predecessor Oleksandr Kuzmuk in his place.

Brunei's parliament was reopened for the first time in 20 years.

Week Beginning 12 September 2004
In Tonga, 'Aloua Fetu'utolu Tupou was appointed to replace Prime Minister Prince Lavaka ata Ulukalala as defence minister.

Iceland's Prime Minister Davíð Oddsson swapped positions with Foreign Minister Halldór Ásgrímsson.

President Fradique de Menezes of São Tomé e Príncipe dismissed Prime Minister Maria das Neves and appointed Damião Vaz de Almeida as her successor.

A cabinet reshuffle in Myanmar included the appointment of Maj. Gen. Nyan Win as foreign minister.

Week Beginning 5 September 2004
The foreign ministers of India and Pakistan met in the first formal ministerial talks since the two countries nearly went to war following an attack on the Indian parliament in late 2001.

Chronology of Events for August 2004

Week Beginning 29 August 2004
In the Maldives, President Maumoon Abdul Gayoom gave up the defence ministry, appointing Ismail Shafeeu as his replacement.

Martín Torrijos took office as president of Panama, with Samuel Lewis Navarro becoming first vice president and foreign minister.

A group of hostage takers seized a school in Beslan, in the Russian republic of North Ossetia. A 3-day standoff ended with more than 350 people being killed, nearly half of them children.

Tongan Prime Minister Prince Lavaka ata Ulukalala relinquished the foreign ministry, to be replaced by Sonatane Tu'a Taumoepeau Tupou.

The Lebanese parliament voted to extend President Émile Lahoud's 6-year term by three further years.

Week Beginning 22 August 2004
Pakistan's Prime Minister Chaudhry Shujaat Hussain resigned to allow Finance Minister Shaukat Aziz to take over the post.

In Tuvalu, Prime Minister Saufatu Sopoanga's government was toppled in a vote of no-confidence. Deputy Prime Minister Maatia Toafa became acting prime minister.

Week Beginning 15 August 2004
In the Dominican Republic Leonel Fernández took office as president. Rafael Alburquerque was named vice-president, Carlos Morales Troncoso foreign minister and Sigfrido Pared Pérez defence minister.

In a cabinet reshuffle in Belize, Prime Minister Said Musa took on the defence and finance portfolios.

President Gloria Macapagal-Arroyo of the Philippines appointed Alberto Romulo foreign secretary and Avelino Cruz defence secretary in a cabinet reshuffle.

In Bhutan, Lyonpo Yeshey Zimba took office as prime minister.

Week Beginning 8 August 2004
Singapore's Prime Minister Goh Chok Tong stepped down; Lee Hsien Loong was sworn in as his successor.

In Vanuatu the Electoral College failed to elect a president. The college later reconvened for a second round, and several votes were again inconclusive before Kalkot Mataskelekele was elected with 49 votes against 7 for Willie David Saul.

Week Beginning 1 August 2004
Following the earlier resignation of the Czech prime minister, Vladimír Špidla, the cabinet of his successor, Stanislav Gross, was appointed. Cyril Svoboda remained foreign minister, with Karel Kühnl becoming defence minister.

Chronology of Events for July 2004

Week Beginning 25 July 2004
In South Korea, Yoon Kwang Ung was named defence minister.

Vanuatu's Parliament elected Josias Moli as speaker and thus as acting president. Serge Vohor was elected prime minister and Barak Sopé named foreign minister.

A new cabinet was named in Luxembourg. Jean Asselborn became foreign minister and Luc Frieden defence minister.

Week Beginning 18 July 2004
In Belgium a new government was formed, including Karel De Gucht as the new foreign minister.

A new cabinet was named in Canada, including Pierre Pettigrew as foreign minister and Bill Graham as defence minister.

Josep Borrell of Spain was elected president of the European Parliament.

Luxembourg's Foreign Minister Lydie Polfer resigned. Defence Minister Charles Goerens took on her post.

The Democratic Republic of the Congo's Foreign Minister Antoine Ghonda was dismissed and replaced by Raymond Ramazani Baya.

Emmanuel Nadingar was named Chad's new defence minister in a cabinet reshuffle.

Week Beginning 11 July 2004
In Lithuania Valdas Adamkus took office as president for a second time, having previously served from 1998 to 2003.

In Comoros a new government was formed, including Houmed Msaidie as defence minister. Soeuf Mohamed Elamine remained foreign minister.

A new cabinet was formed in Cambodia. Tea Banh and Nhek Bun Chhay were named as co-defence ministers. Hor Namhong remained foreign minister.

Latvian Foreign Minister Rihards Pīks resigned. Parliament subsequently elected Artis Pabriks as his successor.

Palestinian Prime Minister Ahmed Qureia resigned, but President Yasser Arafat rejected the resignation and Qureia agreed to stay on.

Week Beginning 4 July 2004
In Nepal a new cabinet was named, with Prime Minister Sher Bahadur Deuba retaining the foreign and defence portfolios.

Portuguese Prime Minister José Manuel Durão Barroso resigned in order to assume the presidency of the European Commission. President Jorge Sampaio asked Pedro Santana Lopes to form a government. The new government included António Monteiro as foreign minister, with Paulo Portas remaining defence minister.

The Slovene parliament voted to dismiss Foreign Minister Dimitrij Rupel. Ivo Vajgl was subsequently elected to replace him.

President Thomas Klestil of Austria died. Heinz Fischer was sworn in as his successor.

Parliamentary elections in Vanuatu were won by the National United Party, with 10 out of 52 seats, ahead of the Union of Moderate Parties, the Vanua'aku Pati and independents, all of which won 8 seats.

Egypt's Prime Minister Atef Ebeid resigned. Ahmed Nazif replaced him, and formed a new government including Ahmed Aboul Gheit as foreign minister. Mohamed Hussein Tantawi retained the defence ministry.

Chronology of Events for June 2004

Week Beginning 27 June 2004

The USA resumed formal diplomatic relations with Libya.

Elections were held in Canada. The ruling Liberal Party of Prime Minister Paul Martin won 135 seats (172 in 2000), the Conservative Party 99 (in 2000 the Conservative Alliance won 66 and the Progressive Conservatives 12), the Bloc Québécois 54 (38 in 2000) and the New Democratic Party 19. The Green Party polled 4.3% and took no seats. One independent was elected. Turn-out was a record low of 60.5%.

Saddam Hussein was handed over to Iraqi custody and was formally charged with crimes against humanity, war crimes and genocide, including the ethnic cleansing of Kurds in 1988.

Portuguese Prime Minister José Durão Barroso was selected as the successor to Romano Prodi, the president of the European Commission.

A Qatari court convicted two Russian intelligence officers of the murder in Feb. 2004 of Zelimkhan Yanderbiyev, president of Chechnya from April 1996–Feb. 1997.

The High Court of Israel ordered a change of route for the planned security barrier around Jerusalem to prevent hardship for Palestinians.

Chaudhry Shujaat Hussain took office as prime minister of Pakistan.

New Caledonia's Congress re-elected Marie-Noëlle Thémereau as president of the government.

The Cambodian People's Party of Prime Minister Hun Sen and FUNCINPEC, the royalist party of Prince Norodom Ranariddh, agreed to form a coalition government, together with the Sam Rainsy Party.

On the 7th anniversary of handover to China, over 200,000 marched in Hong Kong to call for greater democracy, including the right to elect their chief executive.

Lee Hai-chan was approved as prime minister by South Korea's National Assembly.

Elections were held to Mongolia's Great Hural (parliament). Preliminary results gave the ruling Revolutionary People's Party (MAKN) 36 seats, the Motherland Democracy Coalition (EOA) 34 seats and the Republican Party one seat. Three independents were elected. Two seats claimed by the EOA were contested, prompting a recast in those constituencies.

Milan Babic, the former president and prime minister of the self-declared Serb Republic of Krajina in Croatia, was sentenced to 13 years for the persecution and ethnic cleansing of Croats.

Vladimír Špidla resigned as prime minister of the Czech Republic.

The US government ordered the evacuation of its citizens from Bahrain, the location of the US Navy's Fifth Fleet, in response to the threat of terrorism.

Horst Köhler took office as federal president of Germany.

Presidential elections were concluded in Serbia. In the first round, on 13 June, Tomislav Nikolić, of the Serb Radical Party, took 30.4% of the vote, followed by Boris Tadić (Democratic Party) with 27.6%, Bogoljub Karić with 18.2% and Dragan Maršićanin (Democratic Party of Serbia) with 13.3%. In the run-off on 27 June Tadić took 53.7%, defeating Nicolić with 45.0%.

Week Beginning 20 June 2004

It was announced that President Gloria Macapagal-Arroyo had won the presidential elections held on 10 May 2004. She defeated Fernando Poe Jr. by approximately 1 m. votes. Poe contested the result.

A South Korean civilian translator was executed in Iraq after being kidnapped by a rebel group, Jamaat al-Tawhid wa'l-Jihad. The group, reputedly led by al-Qaeda member Abu Musab al-Zarqawi, had demanded the withdrawal of South Korean troops from Iraq. Rebel insurgents co-ordinated attacks on security forces in four locations in Iraq. 40 died in Mosul and at least 20 in Ba'qubah, Ar-Ramadi and Falluja. Eight British sailors were captured by Iranian forces on the Shatt al-Arab waterway that separates Iran and Iraq. Although threatened with prosecution, they were released after 3 days.

John G. Rowland, the Republican governor of the US state of Connecticut, resigned after admitting undeclared favours and gifts.

Marek Belka was confirmed by the Sejm as prime minister of Poland, winning a motion of confidence.

Nearly 50 were killed by Chechen rebels in the neighbouring Russian republic of Ingushetia. Two senior government officials died and the interior ministry in the capital Magas (formerly Nazran) was destroyed.

Elections were held in the Georgian Autonomous Republic of Adjaria. Georgian President Mikhail Saakashvili's Victorious Adjaria bloc won 72% of the vote and took all but two of the seats in the Adjarian legislature, the Supreme Council.

Nauru's President René Harris was ousted by a parliamentary motion of no-confidence. He was succeeded by his predecessor, Ludwig Scotty.

After the death of Abdul Aziz al-Muqrin, the leader of al-Qaeda in Saudi Arabia, the Saudi government offered an amnesty to armed rebels.

Over 70 died and over 80 were injured after a petrol tanker collided with buses near Noşratabad, southeastern Iran.

A presidential election was held in Iceland. Incumbent Ólafur Ragnar Grímsson was re-elected with 85.6% of the vote. Baldur Ágústsson won 12.3% and Ástþór Magnússon won 1.9%.

Week Beginning 13 June 2004

The leaders of the 25 European Union member states approved a constitutional treaty in Brussels. The constitution must be ratified by each country, by parliament or referendum.

The National Commission on Terrorist Attacks upon the United States discredited claims that the Iraqi government and al-Qaeda cooperated in the attacks of 9 Sept. 2001.

34 coca farmers were massacred in the Norte de Santander Department of Colombia by rebel soldiers. The government blamed FARC for the killings.

The Shia cleric Moqtada al-Sadr, holding to a truce with US forces, ordered militia men not from Najaf to leave the city.

Elections took place to Luxembourg's Chamber of Deputies. The Christian Social Party (CSV) won 24 seats, the Socialist Workers' Party (LSAP) 14, the Democratic Party (DP) 10, the Greens 7 and the Action Committee for Democracy and Pensions Justice (ADR) 7.

Oscar Temaru, of the pro-independence Union for Democracy, was elected president of French Polynesia with the support of two small parties and a defector from the former ruling party.

The US Senate approved Alan Greenspan's fifth term as chairman of the Federal Reserve.

Søren Jessen-Petersen was named as the special representative and head of the United Nations Interim Administration in Kosovo (UNMIK).

Ivan Gašparovič took office as president of Slovakia.

Nathaniel Waena was elected by parliament as governor-general of the Solomon Islands. He defeated Sir Peter Kenilorea and the incumbent, Sir John Lapli.

Week Beginning 6 June 2004

Elections were held to the European Parliament from 10–13 June. The European People's Party-European Democrats became the largest group with 262 seats. The Party of European Socialists totalled 199 seats. Overall turn-out was 45.5%. The highest turn-out was in Belgium (90.8%) and the lowest in Slovakia (16.7%).

The UN Security Council unanimously endorsed the new Iraqi interim government.

President Joseph Kabila of the Democratic Republic of the Congo announced the prevention of a coup in Kinshasa and the arrest of 12 rebel soldiers. Government troops regained control of Bukavu in Sud-Kivu.

New Caledonia's Congress elected Marie-Noëlle Thémereau as *president of the government* but the immediate resignation of three ministers brought down the government.

President Aleksander Kwaśniewski of Poland renominated Marek Belka as prime minister.

Venezuela's electoral commission announced that a recall referendum would be held on the presidency of Hugo Chávez.

The leaders of the Group of Eight (G8) countries met in Georgia, USA. Promoting democracy in the Middle East, expanding peace-keeping forces in Africa and extending debt relief were endorsed.

Prime Minister Cándido Muatetema Rivas and the government of Equatorial Guinea resigned.

Chronology of Events for May 2004

Week Beginning 30 May 2004

Former US President Ronald Reagan died. He was given a state presidential funeral and a day of national mourning.

Sheikh Ghazi al-Yawer was named as interim president of Iraq. Iyad Allawi took office as interim prime minister and an interim government was sworn in 1 month ahead of schedule.

King Gyanendra reappointed Sher Bahadu Deuba as prime minister of Nepal.

The United Nations took control of peacekeeping in Burundi and Haiti, replacing an African Union force and a US-led multinational force respectively.

Prime Minister Ariel Sharon of Israel dismissed two members of his cabinet for opposing his plans for withdrawal from the Gaza Strip.

Antonio Saca took office as president of El Salvador.

Etienne Ys was sworn in as prime minister of the Netherlands Antilles.

Fighting intensified in the Sud-Kivu region of the Democratic Republic of the Congo. A former RCD-Goma general, Jules Mutebusi, claimed control of the main town, Bukavu, on the border with Rwanda.

Hari Kostov was approved as prime minister by the Assembly of Macedonia (FYROM).

The government of Georgia deployed troops in the separatist region of South Ossetia, ostensibly to counter smuggling. President Mikhail Saakashvili rejected Russian criticism of the operation but did send envoys to negotiate with the South Ossetian authorities.

Saudi militants took 50 foreign nationals hostage in the eastern port city of Khobar. 19 foreigners and 3 Saudis died in the attack. Militants also attacked US troops in Riyadh and Taif, in western Saudi Arabia.

Week Beginning 23 May 2004

The island of Hispaniola, shared by Haiti and the Dominican Republic, suffered flooding after heavy rains. It was estimated that 2,000 lost their lives. Aid agencies were hampered by an earthquake.

Iyad Allawi was named as interim prime minister of Iraq.

A peace agreement was signed at Naivasha, Kenya between the Sudanese government and the Sudan People's Liberation Army (SPLA), which controls southern Sudan. The agreement settled the administration of several disputed areas in Central Sudan.

Prime Minister Go Kun of South Korea formally resigned, having offered his resignation on 14 May.

An appeal court in Chile stripped ex-president Gen. Augusto Pinochet of his immunity from prosecution for alleged human rights abuses in the 1970s and 1980s.

Horst Köhler, formerly managing director of the International Monetary Fund, was elected federal president of Germany by the Federal Convention.

Bingu wa Mutharika was sworn in as president of Malaŵi.

Elections were held to the Territorial Assembly of French Polynesia. The People's Front-Rally for the Republic, the party of President Gaston Flosse, won 28 seats and the Union for Democracy won 27 seats. New Star (Fetia Api) and the Nicole Bouteau List took one seat each.

The National Assembly of Chad approved a constitutional amendment scrapping the two-term limit on the presidency, thus allowing President Idriss Déby to stand for re-election in 2006. The opposition boycotted the vote and called a national strike in protest.

Harri Holkeri, the special representative and head of the United Nations Interim Administration in Kosovo (UNMIK), resigned.

Alan Huckle took office as governor of Anguilla.

Sir Paulias Matane was elected by parliament governor-general of Papua New Guinea. However, his inauguration was delayed by a legal challenge from Sir Pato Kakaraya, elected governor-general on 4 Dec. 2003 but later disqualified.

Week Beginning 16 May 2004

Sonia Gandhi declined the premiership of India, despite emotional appeals from her supporters. Manmohan Singh, of the Indian National Congress, became India's first Sikh prime minister, forming a coalition government with the Dravida Progressive Federation (DMK), the Rashtria Janata Dal, the Lok Jan Shakti Party, the Nationalist Congress Party, the Telangana Rashtra Samithi, the Pattali Makkal Katchi and the Jharkhand Mukti Morcha.

Ezzedine Salim, the president of the Iraqi Governing Council, was killed in a bomb attack in Baghdad.

In presidential elections in the Dominican Republic, ex-president Leonel Antonio Fernández Reyna of the Dominican Liberation Party (PLD) won 57.1% of the vote, incumbent Rafael Hipólito Mejía Domínguez of the Dominican Revolutionary Party (PRD) 33.6% and Eduardo Estrella of the Social Christian Reformist Party (PRSC) 8.8%.

Shaikh Hamad bin Isa Al-Khalifa, the king of Bahrain, sacked Interior Minister Shaikh Mohammed bin Khalifa for ordering a crackdown on a Shia demonstration against the US occupation of Iraq.

President Olusegun Obasanjo of Nigeria declared a state of emergency in Plateau State, suspending the governor, after hundreds of deaths in Christian-Muslim violence.

An American soldier, Jeremy Sivits, was convicted and jailed for abusing Iraqi prisoners in Abu Ghraib jail.

President Roh Moo-hyun of South Korea joined the Uri ('Our') Party, the majority party in the National Assembly.

Spain withdrew the last of its troops from Iraq.

In Malaŵi's parliamentary elections the Malaŵi Congress Party (MCP—formerly the only legal party) won 59 seats; the United Democratic Front (UDF), 49; and the Mgwirizano coalition, 27. Independents took 38 seats. At the concurrent presidential elections Bingu wa Mutharika (UDF) won with 35% of the vote, ahead of John Tembo (MCP) with 27%, and Gwanda Chakuamba (Mgwirizano) with 26%. Both losing candidates challenged the results and the fairness of the elections.

The government of Indonesia lifted martial law in the province of Aceh, imposing a lesser state of emergency.

Massachusetts became the first American state to allow same sex marriages.

Week Beginning 9 May 2004

The Kremlin-backed president of Chechnya, Akhmad Kadyrov, was assassinated in Dzhohar (Grozny) on the orders of Shamil Basayev, a rebel warlord and former prime minister. Prime Minister Sergey Abramov became acting president.

The fourth and final phase of parliamentary elections were held in India. The Indian National Congress (INC) and its allies gained 217 seats (with the INC winning 145 seats); the National Democratic Alliance gained 185 seats (with the Bharatiya Janata Party (BJP) winning 138 seats); the Left Front (LF) won 59 seats; Samajwadi Party (SP) 36; Bahujan Samaj Party (BSP) 19; Janata Dal (Secular) (JD(S)) 4; and the Rashtriya Lok Dal (RLD) 3. Prime Minister Atal Bihari Vajpayee of the BJP resigned, remaining in a caretaker capacity while the INC organized a new government. Sonia Gandhi was elected leader in the *Lok Sabha* of the INC.

Roh Moo-hyun was reinstated as president of South Korea by the Constitutional Court, which rejected Roh's parliamentary impeachment. Prime Minister Goh Kun offered his resignation but was persuaded by Roh to remain until a new cabinet could be formed.

Crude oil prices hit record highs in New York, at over US$41 a barrel.

Marek Belka, Poland's prime minister-designate, was rejected by the *Sejm*.

The USA imposed economic sanctions on Syria for its continued occupation of Lebanon and its weapons programme.

The Chadian army responded to incursions of Sudanese militia from Sudan's Darfur region and warned Sudan's government, which it claims supports the Arab militia's attacks on black Sudanese refugees in Chad.

In elections to the Territorial Congress of New Caledonia, the conservative Rassemblement-UMP and Our Future Together won 16 seats each, the National Liberation Front of the Socialist Kanaks (FLNKS) 8, the Caledonian Union 7 and the National Front 4.

Insurgents loyal to Moqtada al-Sadr, an influential Shia cleric, began fighting US troops in Najaf, Iraq.

Branko Crvenkovski took office as president of Macedonia (FYROM).

President Alfred Maseng was removed from office by Vanuatu's Supreme Court, declaring his election invalid because of a previous criminal conviction. Roger Abiut became acting president.

Carlos Gomes Júnior, of the African Party for the Independence of Guinea and Cape Verde (PAIGC), took office as prime minister of Guinea-Bissau.

Deborah Barnes Jones was sworn in as governor of Montserrat.

Presidential elections in the Philippines were won by President Gloria Macapagal-Arroyo won, although results were not released until 20 June.

Week Beginning 2 May 2004

Allegations surfaced of abuse of Iraqi prisoners by American and British troops. Although the pictures of British soldiers abusing Iraqis were revealed to be a hoax, several US servicemen and women were court-martialled.

Prime Minister Surya Bahadur Thapa of Nepal resigned.

The Adjarian leader, Aslan Abashidze, fled the country after a wave of demonstrations and negotiations with Igor Ivanov, the Russian Security Council secretary. Georgia's president, Mikhail Saakashvili, granted immunity to Abashidze and his family to ensure a peaceful transfer of power. Saakashvili imposed direct presidential rule, disbanding the Adjarian parliament until elections scheduled for June.

Nauru's government averted bankruptcy by obtaining a loan from Hiranandani Corp. Worldwide, an Indian property group, to pay off debts totalling US$172 m.

In Panama's presidential election, Martín Torrijos Espino of the Revolutionary Democratic Party (PRD) won 47.5% of the vote. Guillermo Endara Galimany (Solidaridad) won 30.6%, José Miguel Alemán (Arnulfista Party; PA) 17% and Ricardo Martinelli (Democratic Change; CD) 4.9%. In the concurrent Legislative Assembly elections, the PRD won 41 seats, the PA 17, Solidaridad 8, the Nationalist Republican Liberal Movement (Molirena) 3, CD 2, the People's Party 2, and the National Liberal Party 1.

Leszek Miller resigned as prime minister of Poland. President Aleksander Kwaśniewski designated Marek Belka, the finance minister, as Miller's successor.

A Libyan court sentenced a Palestinian doctor and five Bulgarian nurses to death for deliberately infecting hundreds of Libyan children with HIV and causing the death of 40 children in a Benghazi hospital. The Bulgarian government rejected the verdicts, blaming poor hygiene for the spread of the virus.

The UN issued an ultimatum to the Eritrean government, demanding cooperation for the UN Mission to Ethiopia and Eritrea (UNMEE). Eritrea had accused UNMEE staff and soldiers of several abuses.

The second round of elections to the Islamic Consultative Assembly were held. Conservatives won 40 of 57 seats, reformists 8 and independents 9.

Fredis Refunjol was sworn into office as governor of Aruba.

Chronology of Events for April 2004

Week Beginning 25 April 2004

US troops engaged Shia fighters in Najaf, Iraq, killing over 40 insurgents.

After the resignation of Prime Minister Ahmed Mohamed Ag Hamani, Ousmane Issoufi Maïga took office as prime minister of Mali.

Elections were held to the Federal Assembly of the Comoros. Supporters of the three regional presidents won 12 of the 18 elected seats; supporters of Federal President Azaly Assoumani won six. Holding a majority, the regional presidents appointed an additional five legislators each.

In the Austrian presidential election Heinz Fischer (SPÖ) won 52.4% of the vote against 47.6% for Foreign Secretary Benita Ferrero-Waldner (ÖVP).

Ezzedine Salim, of the Daawa Islamic Party, assumed the presidency of the Iraqi Governing Council.

The run-off for presidential elections were held in Macedonia (FYROM). Branko Crvenkovski (Social Democratic League of Macedonia), the incumbent prime minister, took 60.6% of the vote against Saško Kedev (Democratic Party for Macedonian National Unity) with 39.4%.

The National Assembly elections in Equatorial Guinea were boycotted by most opposition parties. The ruling Democratic Party of Equatorial Guinea (PDGE) won 68 of the 100 seats, its allies (the so-called 'democratic opposition') won 30 seats and the Convergence for Social Democracy won 2.

Guinea's Prime Minister François Lonseny Fall resigned.

The mayor of Ilave, Peru, was killed by protesters accusing him of embezzling funds. Interior Minister Fernando Rospigliosi Capurro was forced to resign after being censured by Congress. He was replaced with Javier Reategui Rossello.

Violent clashes between security forces and Islamic rebels in southern Thailand left over 90 dead.

Week Beginning 18 April 2004

Senegal's prime minister, Idrissa Seck, was sacked by President Abdoulaye Wade and replaced with Macky Sall.

Ratu Sir Kamisese Mara, the independence leader of the Fiji Islands, died. Six days of mourning were declared.

Thabo Mbeki was re-elected as president of South Africa by parliament.

Prime Minister José Luis Rodríguez Zapatero ordered the withdrawal of Spanish troops from Iraq.

Week Beginning 11 April 2004

José Luis Rodríguez Zapatero took office as prime minister of Spain.

Parliamentary elections were held in South Africa. The African National Congress (ANC) won 279 seats in the National Assembly with 69.7% of votes cast, the Democratic Alliance (DA) 50, the Inkatha Freedom Party (IFP) 28, the United Democratic Movement (UDM) 9, the New National Party (NNP) 7, the Independent Democrats 7, the African Christian Democratic Party 6, Freedom Front Plus 4, the United Christian-Democratic Party 3, the Pan African Congress of Azania 3, Minority Front 2 and the Azanian People's Organisation (AZAPO) 2.

Elections to the National Assembly were held in South Korea. Our Party (Uri Dang; UD) won 152 seats, the Grand National Party (HD) 121, the Democratic Labour Party (MDD) 10, the Millennium Democratic Party (SMD) 9 and the United Liberal Democrats (JMY) 4. National Alliance 21 won one seat and two seats went to non-partisans.

France-Albert René was succeeded as president of the Seychelles by Vice-President James Alix Michel. Joseph Belmont was appointed vice-president.

In presidential elections in Slovakia Ivan Gašparovič (Movement for Democracy) defeated former prime minister Vladimír Mečiar of the HZDS.

Alfred Maseng was elected president of Vanuatu by an electoral college in the fourth round of voting, receiving 40 votes against 16 for the government-backed candidate Kalkot Mataskelekele.

Osama bin Laden offered Europe a truce in return for the evacuation of European troops from Muslim countries.

Week Beginning 4 April 2004

Elections to Indonesia's House of People's Representatives were held. The Party of the Functional Groups (Golkar) won 128 seats, the Indonesian Democratic Party of Struggle (PDIP) 109, United Development Party (PPP) 58, Democrat Party (PD) 57, National Awakening Party (PKB) 52, National Mandate Party (PAN) 52, Prosperous Justice Party (PKS) 45, Reform Star Party (PBR) 13, Crescent Star Party (PBB) 11, and the National Democracy Unity Party (PDK) 5. Six parties won under five seats each.

In presidential elections the incumbent Abdelaziz Bouteflika (National Democratic Rally) won a second term of office, gaining 85.0% of the votes cast. Ali Benflis (National Liberation Front; FLN) won 6.4% and Abdallah Djaballah (el-Islah) won 5.0%. There were three other candidates.

Eddie Fenech Adami, prime minister of Malta from 1987–96 and 1998–March 2004, took office as president.

Rolandas Paksas, the president of Lithuania, was impeached by the Seimas.

Mahinda Rajapaksa took office as prime minister of Sri Lanka.

The prime minister of the Netherlands Antilles, Mirna Louisa-Godett, and her government resigned after losing the support of coalition partners.

Chronology of Events for March 2004

Week Beginning 28 March 2004

Parliamentary elections were held in Georgia. The National Movement—Democrats, led by President Mikhail Saakashvili, won 67.0% of the vote (135 of the 235 seats) and the Rightist Opposition won 7.6% (15 seats). No other party achieved the 7% necessary to win a seat. 75 seats were taken in single-seat constituencies in Nov. 2003 and ten seats represent Abkhazians.

A series of bomb attacks in the Uzbek cities of Tashkent and Bukhara killed around 50 people, including over 30 Islamic militants.

In Guinea-Bissau's parliamentary elections, the African Party for the Independence of Guinea and Cape Verde (PAIGC) won 33.9% of the vote (45 of 100 seats). The Party for Social Renewal (PRS) took 26.5% (35) and the United Social Democratic Party (PUSD) 17.6% (17). The Electoral Union (UE) took two seats and the United Popular Alliance (APU) 1.

27 members of Sudan's Islamist Popular Congress Party were arrested on charges of plotting a coup. The party leader, Hassan al-Turabi, was also arrested.

The main suspect of the Madrid train bombings, Sarhane ben Abdelmajid Fakhet, and three associates were killed in a police raid of a flat in a Madrid suburb.

Over 15 men were arrested in Kinshasa, accused of attempting to overthrow the government of the Democratic Republic of the Congo.

The Constitutional Court of Lithuania ruled that President Rolandas Paksas had breached the constitution, allowing for impeachment proceedings in parliament.

Massud Barzani, the leader of the Kurdistan Democratic Party, assumed the presidency of the Iraqi Governing Council.

Four American civilian contractors were killed and their bodies dismembered in Falluja, Iraq.

Taiwan's opposition challenged the results of the presidential elections of 20 March at the High Court.

In elections in Sri Lanka the United People's Freedom Alliance gained 105 seats, the United National Party 82, the Sri Lanka Tamil Government Party/Tamil National Alliance 22, the National Heritage Party 9 and the Sri Lanka Muslim Congress 5.

Elections were concluded to the General Councils of the French Overseas Departments (Guadeloupe, Martinique, French Guiana and Réunion). At the General Council elections in the Departmental Collectivity of Mayotte the Union pour un Mouvement Populaire won nine seats, the Mouvement Départementaliste Mahorais won six and the Mouvement Républicain et Citoyen won two. The Mouvement Populaire Mahorais and Diverse Gauche won one seat each.

Week Beginning 21 March 2004

The Israeli airforce killed Sheikh Ahmed Yassin, the spiritual leader of Hamas, in Gaza City with several of his entourage. Hamas named Abdel Aziz al-Rantissi as its new Gaza leader. An Algerian-sponsored UN Security Council resolution, which condemned Israel's actions, was vetoed by the USA.

Elections to Malaysia's *Dewan Rakyat* and 11 state assemblies were held. The 14-party National Front Coalition (Barisan Nasional) gained 198 seats, obtaining 64.4% of the votes cast (the predominant partner, the United Malays National Organization, won 109 seats). The Democratic Action Party won 12 seats, the Islamic Party of Malaysia (PAS) won seven seats and the People's Justice Party won one seat. The National Front Coalition also gained a majority in every state assembly except Kelantan, held by PAS, which lost Terengganu.

The Sudanese government rejected claims by the UN representative, Mukesh Kapila, that it was supporting ethnic cleansing in Sudan's western Darfur province.

Presidential elections in El Salvador were won by Antonio Saca (Nationalist Republican Alliance), who received 57.7% of votes cast. He defeated Schafik Hándal of the National Liberation Front, who received 35.7%.

Lawrence Gonzi replaced Fenech Adami as prime minister of Malta.

Vanuatu's parliamentary speaker, Roger Abiut, became acting president.

Elections to the House of Representatives of Antigua and Barbuda were won by the United Progressive Party (UPP), which took 12 of the 17 seats. The UPP defeated the ruling Antigua Labour Party (ALP), with 4 seats, ending over 40 years of ALP government. Baldwin Spencer replaced Lester Bird as prime minister.

Week Beginning 14 March 2004

Taiwan's president, Chen Shui-bian, and Vice-President Hsiu-lien Annette Lu were wounded by unknown assailants while electioneering. The following day Chen narrowly defeated Lien Chan of the Kuomintang in presidential elections. Lien refused to accept the result, calling for it to be annulled, and organized large demonstrations.

Vladimir Putin was re-elected in Russia's presidential elections, gaining 71.2% of the votes cast. The Communist Party's Nikolai Kharitonov came second with 13.7% of the vote.

Anneli Jäätteenmäki, Finland's former prime minister, was acquitted of procuring secret documents concerning her predecessor's attitude to the Iraq War. Jäätteenmäki was forced to leave office after 2 months in June 2003.

The Spanish Socialist Workers' Party (PSOE) won a surprise victory in parliamentary elections, taking 164 seats in the Congress of Deputies with 42.6% of votes cast. The ruling Popular Party (PP) of Prime Minister José Maria Aznar took 148 seats with 37.6%. Convergence and Union (Catalan nationalists) won 10 seats, the Catalan separatist Republican Left of Catalunya (ERC) 8 seats, the Basque Nationalist Party 7 seats, the Communist-led United Left Coalition 5 seats, the Canarian Coalition 3 seats and the Galician Nationalist Bloc 2 seats. The Aragonese Junta, the Basque Solidarity Party and Navarra Yes took one seat each.

Fighting between Albanian and Serbian communities in the Kosovan town of Mitrovica left over 30 dead and forced the withdrawal of UN staff.

Georgia's president, Mikhail Saakashvili, lifted economic sanctions, imposed on the autonomous republic of Adjaria after the Adjarian leader, Aslan Abashidze, barred Saakashvili from entering Adjaria.

Week Beginning 7 March 2004

Ten bombs exploded on morning commuter trains in Madrid, killing 191 and injuring over 1,800. The Abu Hafs al-Masri Brigades, linked to al-Qaeda, claimed responsibility. However, Spanish authorities suggested that the attacks were carried out by a Moroccan organization, the Islamic Combatant Group.

President Roh Moo-hyun was impeached by the South Korean parliament and suspended from office, pending review by the Constitutional Court.

Parliamentary elections were held in Greece. New Democracy won 165 seats, Pasok (Panhellenic Socialist Movement) 117, the Communist Party 12 and the Coalition of the Left and Progress 6 seats. Dr. Kostas Karamanlis took office as prime minister, heading a New Democracy Government.

An interim constitution was signed by the Iraqi Governing Council.

Gérard Latortue took office as prime minister of Haiti.

Indulis Emsis was sworn in as prime minister of Latvia, Europe's first Green premier.

Chronology of Events for February 2004

Week Beginning 29 February 2004

Bomb attacks on the Shia community in Baghdad and Karbala killed over 270 people during the festival of Yaum Ashura. US officials linked the attacks to Abu Musab al-Zarqawi, a Jordanian member of al-Qaeda.

Over 40 people died in a suicide attack on the Shia community in Quetta, Pakistan.

Jean-Bertrand Aristide, Haiti's president, fled the country after rebel forces took the second city, Cap-Haïtien. The chief justice, Boniface Alexandre, became provisional president. The UN Security Council voted unanimously to send emergency peacekeeping forces.

Muhammad Bahr al-Ulum, a senior Shia cleric, assumed the presidency of the Iraqi Governing Council.

Mikhail Fradkov, nominated by President Vladimir Putin, was accepted as prime minister by the Russian Duma.

Vojislav Koštunica, previously president of Yugoslavia, took office as prime minister of Serbia. Predrag Marković, elected parliamentary speaker, became acting president.

The French Senate approved a ban on headscarves and religious symbols in state schools.

The Democratic Party withdrew from the Côte d'Ivoire government, blaming the breakdown of the unity coalition on President Laurent Gbagbo.

Week Beginning 22 February 2004

An earthquake killed over 560 people in northeast Morocco.

Russia's President Vladimir Putin dismissed his government, including Prime Minister Mikhail Kasyanov.

The president of Macedonia (FYROM), Boris Trajkovski, was killed in a plane crash in Bosnia-Herzegovina.

François Lonseny Fall, Guinea's foreign minister, was appointed prime minister.

Sulejman Tihić, the Muslim leader of the Party of Democratic Action, became chairman of the Presidency of Bosnia-Herzegovina.

The British government was accused by a former international development minister of spying on the UN secretary-general, Kofi Annan.

Week Beginning 15 February 2004

India and Pakistan's foreign ministers met in Islamabad for formal talks, the first in 3 years. Pakistan's President Pervez Musharraf rejected nuclear weapons development to rival that of India.

Haiti's Prime Minister Yvon Neptune called for international military intervention, which was rejected by the US government.

In elections in Iran, conservatives took a majority of the seats, reducing the reformist supporters of President Mohammad Khatami by two thirds.

An explosion on a train carrying fuel and chemicals killed nearly 300 people near Neyshabur, northeast Iran.

The death of a 17-year-old Aboriginal boy sparked riots in Sydney after claims of police responsibility.

Zurab Zhvania took office as prime minister of Georgia at the head of a new government.

Mozambique's finance minister, Luísa Diogo, became prime minister.

Week Beginning 8 February 2004

The French National Assembly voted to ban religious symbols in state schools, including the Islamic headscarf.

President Chandrika Kumaratunga of Sri Lanka dissolved parliament ahead of early elections.

The European Commission gave its approval to the merger of Air France and KLM, the Dutch national carrier.

Yves Dassonville took office as prefect of Martinique.

Week Beginning 1 February 2004

Dr. Mohsen Abdul Hamid, the secretary-general of the Iraqi Islamic Party, assumed the presidency of the Iraqi Governing Council.

Over 240 pilgrims were crushed to death during the Hajj in Mina, Saudi Arabia.

Two suicide attacks killed over 100 people and injured over 200 in the northern Iraqi city of Irbil. The targets were the offices of the main Kurdish parties, the Kurdistan Democratic Party and the Patriotic Union of Kurdistan.

Over 100 representatives of Iran's *Majlis* resigned in protest against the disqualification of electoral candidates by the Council of Guardians.

Ariel Sharon, prime minister of Israel, declared his intention of withdrawing Jewish settlements, with the co-operation of the settlers, from the Gaza strip.

German Chancellor Gerhard Schröder resigned as chairman of the Social Democratic Party.

A bomb on the Moscow metro killed 39 and injured over 100 people. President Vladimir Putin blamed Chechen separatists for the attack.

Jóannes Eidesgaard took office as prime minister of the Faroe Islands.

Latvia's prime minister, Einars Repše, and his government resigned after the departure of the government's coalition partner, Latvia's First Party.

Chronology of Events for January 2004

Week Beginning 25 January 2004

Japan sent non-combat troops to Iraq despite the pacifist restrictions of the Japanese constitution.

The interim president, Hamid Karzai, signed Afghanistan's new constitution, ratified by the *loya jirga* (grand council).

Lord Hutton delivered his report into the death of the British weapons expert Dr. David Kelly. The report cleared the government of wrongdoing and criticized the British Broadcasting Corporation (BBC) for its reporting. The BBC's director-general, Greg Dyke, and chairman, Gavyn Davies, resigned.

Alain Juppé, prime minister of France from 1995–97, was convicted of involvement in a payments scandal while he was financial director of Paris' city hall. His suspended sentence barred him from holding office for 10 years.

Lithuania's Constitutional Court ruled that President Rolandas Paksas violated the constitution when granting a Russian businessman citizenship.

Talks in Nairobi, hosted by the Intergovernmental Authority on Development (IGAD), produced a charter for the creation of federal government and a new parliament in Somalia. The self-declared state of Somaliland was the only major Somali power not to be represented in the agreement.

Week Beginning 18 January 2004

The Shia community held the largest demonstrations in Iraq since the fall of the Ba'athist regime. Iraq's most senior Shia cleric, Ayatollah Ali al-Sistani, demanded direct elections instead of the caucus arrangements preferred by the American authorities.

Senator John Kerry won the Iowa Democrat caucus, putting the favourite, Vermont's Governor Howard Dean, in third place behind Senator John Edwards.

Elections were held to the Diet of the Faroe Islands. The Party for People's Government, who favour independence from Denmark, won eight seats. The Union Party, the Equality Party (Social Democrats) and the People's Party each won seven seats.

Week Beginning 11 January 2004

The Haitian parliament's mandate expired with the failure to hold scheduled elections. Violent demonstrations in Port-au-Prince were held against President Jean-Bertrand Aristide.

Iran's spiritual leader, Ayatollah Khamenei, averted the resignation of the government by encouraging the Council of Guardians to review its decisions on the candidacies for the 2004 elections. The Council had disqualified over 2,000 candidates including 83 current members of the Majlis.

Sri Lanka's president, Chandrika Bandaranaike Kumaratunga, extended her term of office by a year, claiming it from her shortened first term. Prime Minister Ranil Wickremasinghe condemned the move as illegal.

Óscar Berger Perdomo was sworn in as president of Guatemala.

Italy's Constitutional Court rejected new legislation that gave the prime minister, Silvio Berlusconi, immunity from prosecution.

Week Beginning 4 January 2004

Pierre Charles, prime minister of Dominica, died in office. He was succeeded by Roosevelt Skerrit.

Mikhail Saakashvili was elected president of Georgia with 96.3% of the vote.

Jaap de Hoop Scheffer took office as secretary-general of the North Atlantic Treaty Organization.

India and Pakistan's premiers, Atal Bihari Vajpayee and Pervez Musharraf, met for the first time in nearly 3 years at the Lahore meeting of the South Asian Association for Regional Co-operation (SAARC). The two leaders timetabled talks on Kashmir and the SAARC member states agreed to set up a free-trade area in 2006.

Rebel members of the government of Côte d'Ivoire rejoined the cabinet after a 3-month boycott, renewing hopes for the peace process.

The *Nitijela* (House of Assembly) of the Marshall Islands re-elected President Kessai Note.

2003

Chronology of Events for December 2003

Week Beginning 28 December 2003

In the second round of Guatemala's presidential elections Óscar Berger of the Grand National Alliance (GANA) won 54.1% of the vote, defeating Álvaro Colom of the National Union for Hope (UNE), who won 45.9%.

Elections were held to Serbia's National Assembly. The Serb Radical Party won 82 of the 250 seats, the Democratic Party of Serbia 53 seats, the Democratic Party 37 seats, G17 Plus 34 seats, the Serb Renewal Movement-New Serbia 23 seats and the Socialist Party of Serbia 22 seats.

Adnan Pachachi, a pre-Baathist minister and leader of the Iraqi Independent Democrats, assumed the presidency of the Iraqi Governing Council.

Joseph Deiss assumed the presidency of the Swiss Confederation.

Week Beginning 21 December 2003

An earthquake with a magnitude of 6.6 near Bam, southeastern Iran, killed over 26,000 people and injured over 30,000. The city of Bam was destroyed.

President Lansana Conté of Guinea was re-elected with 95.6% of the vote against 4.4% won by Mamadou Bhoye Barry of the Union for National Progress. Opposition parties boycotted the elections.

Week Beginning 14 December 2003

A new government was appointed in the Central African Republic by President François Bozizé, headed by Prime Minister Célestin Gaombalet. Ex-Prime Minister Abel Gouma was appointed vice-president.

Carlos Ferrero Costa took office as prime minister of Peru.

Parliamentary elections were held in the 'Turkish Republic of Northern Cyprus'. The Republican Turkish Party-United Forces won 19 of the 50 seats, the Party of National Unity 18 seats, the Democratic Party 7 seats and the Peace and Democracy Movement 6 seats.

Sergei Sidorsky was confirmed as prime minister of Belarus by the Chamber of Deputies.

Announcing the suspension of Libya's weapons of mass destruction programmes, including nuclear and chemical weapons, the Libyan leader, Col. al-Qadhafi, pledged full co-operation with the International Atomic Energy Agency.

Week Beginning 7 December 2003

Saddam Hussein, the deposed president of Iraq, was captured near Tikrit by US forces.

The Commonwealth extended the suspension of Zimbabwe and Pakistan at the Heads of Government Meeting in Abuja, Nigeria. Robert Mugabe, the president of Zimbabwe, responded by withdrawing his country from the Commonwealth.

Paul Martin took office as prime minister of Canada.

In elections to the Russian State Duma, the United Russia Party, which supports President Vladimir Putin, took 222 of the 450 seats. The Communist

Party won 53 seats, the Rodina Bloc 45 seats, the Liberal-Democratic Party 38 seats, Yabloko 4 seats and the Union of Right Forces 2 seats.

The US Pentagon announced that companies from countries that opposed the US-led invasion of Iraq would be barred from bidding for contracts in the reconstruction of Iraq.

Heydar Aliyev, who stepped down as president of Azerbaijan in Oct. 2003 to allow the election of his son, died in the USA.

President Islam Karimov of Uzbekistan appointed Shavkat Mirziyayev prime minister.

Beatriz Merino, prime minister of Peru, and her cabinet resigned in accordance with the wishes of President Alejandro Toledo.

Angola's President José Eduardo dos Santos was reelected president of the ruling Movimento Popular de Libertação de Angola (MPLA), making him the presidential candidate for elections in 2005. Dos Santos had previously ruled out standing for re-election.

Croatia's President Stipe Mesić announced that Ivo Sanader would be appointed prime minister.

President François Bozizé of the Central African Republic dismissed Prime Minister Abel Gouma and his government.

Chronology of Events for November 2003

Week Beginning 30 November 2003
President Pervez Musharraf of Pakistan proposed the withdrawal of Pakistani troops from Kashmir on the condition of India's military withdrawal from Indian-controlled Kashmir. The proposal came after an agreement by the two governments to restore direct air links.

Abdul Aziz al-Hakim, of the Supreme Council for the Islamic Revolution in Iraq (Sciri) and brother of the murdered Sciri leader, Ayatollah Mohammad Baqr al-Hakim, assumed the presidency of the Iraqi Governing Council.

A petition calling for a referendum on Hugo Chávez's presidency was received by the National Elections Council of Venezuela. Chávez denied that 3.6 m. signed the petition but the Organization of of American States supported the claim.

Sir Pato Kakaraya was elected by parliament as governor-general of Papua New Guinea.

Week Beginning 23 November 2003
Eduard Shevardnadze resigned as president of Georgia after 2 weeks of demonstrations in Tbilisi. The election results of 2 Nov. were cancelled after allegations of serious irregularities. Nino Burjanadze, parliamentary speaker, was installed as acting president.

Northern Ireland's delayed elections were held. The Democratic Unionist Party won 30 of the 108 seats in the legislature, the Ulster Unionists 27 seats, Sinn Féin 24 seats and the SDLP 18 seats.

The government of Myanmar released five leading members of the National League for Democracy (NLD), but its secretary general, Aung San Suu Kyi, remained under house arrest.

Parliamentary elections were held in Croatia. The nationalist Croatian Democratic Union, once led by Franjo Tudjman, won 66 of the 152 seats in the Sabor (Assembly), defeating Prime Minister Ivica Račan's Social Democrats.

A ceasefire was declared between India and Pakistan at the Line of Control, the de facto border in Kashmir.

Parliamentary elections in Grenada were won by Prime Minister Keith Mitchell's New National Party, which took 8 of the 15 seats. The National Democratic Congress won the other seven seats. Mitchell was sworn in for an unprecedented third term.

King Mswati III of Swaziland inaugurated a new government, with Themba Dlamini as prime minister.

Week Beginning 16 November 2003
A suicide bomb attack on the British Consulate in Istanbul was blamed on Turkish terrorists supported by al-Qaeda. Ten consulate staff were killed, including the consul general. A simultaneous attack hit the Turkish headquarters of HSBC, the British-based multinational bank. 28 people died in total.

US President George W. Bush was received on a state visit to the United Kingdom. The visit prompted anti-war demonstrations in London.

The South African government approved free anti-retroviral drugs to combat HIV/AIDS.

Serbia was unable to elect a president for the fourth time, failing to reach the required 50% turn-out to validate the election results.

The International Monetary Fund resumed its aid programme to Kenya in recognition of President Mwai Kibaki's anti-corruption drive. A US$250 m. 3-year loan was approved, opening the way for other international donors.

Week Beginning 9 November 2003
The headquarters of the Italian police in An-Nasiriyah, Iraq were attacked by suicide bombers, killing 18 Italians and 9 Iraqis. Italian Prime Minister Silvio Berlusconi pledged to maintain military and police personnel in Iraq.

The president of Serbia and Montenegro, Svetozar Marović, apologized in Sarajevo for atrocities committed during Yugoslavia's war against Bosnia-Herzegovina.

The Palestinian National Council approved the appointment of Ahmed Qureia as prime minister and his cabinet, ending a period of emergency administration. The Palestinian president, Yasser Arafat, retained control of Palestinian security forces.

In elections to the Japanese Diet, Prime Minister Junichiro Koizumi's Liberal Democratic Party (LDP) maintained its majority in the House of Deputies, the lower house, by negotiating a coalition with the New Komeito Party and the New Conservative Party. The main opposition, the Democratic Party of Japan, increased its seats by 40 to 177, compared to the LDP's 240.

In Guatemala's presidential elections Óscar Berger of the Grand National Alliance (GANA) won 36% of the vote, Álvaro Colom of the National Union for Hope (UNE) won 27%, and former military leader Efraín Ríos Montt of the Guatemalan Republican Front (FRG) won 18%. A second round between Berger and Colom was scheduled for Dec. 2003. In congressional elections GANA won 49 seats, FRG 42, UNE 33, and the National Advancement Party (PAN) 16.

Week Beginning 2 November 2003
President Chandrika Kumaratunga suspended the Sri Lankan parliament and sacked three senior ministers, assuming their portfolios. Declaring a state of emergency, she accused the prime minister, Ranil Wickremasinghe, of undermining national security with concessions to Tamil Tiger rebels.

A draft constitution, excluding sharia law, was released for public scrutiny in Afghanistan. It would replace the modified 1964 constitution of Afghanistan if approved by the Constitutional Loya Jirga (Grand Council) in Dec. 2003.

Parliamentary elections in Georgia provoked daily demonstrations in the capital, Tbilisi. Protestors, opposition leaders and international observers have claimed serious voting irregularities. Preliminary results gave President Eduard Shevardnadze's For a New Georgia Block a narrow lead.

Gene Robinson was consecrated Episcopalian bishop of New Hampshire. The appointment of the openly homosexual clergyman was condemned by the primate of the Nigerian Church, the largest Anglican community, and brought the Anglican Church closer to schism.

In Mauritania's presidential elections incumbent Maaouya Ould Taya won 66.7% of the vote, defeating Mohamed Khouna Ould Haidalla, a former president, who took 18.7%.

Chronology of Events for October 2003

Week Beginning 26 October 2003
Three suicide bomb attacks on police stations and a bomb at the headquarters of the International Committee of the Red Cross (ICRC) in Baghdad killed 35 people and wounded 230. The ICRC announced that it would maintain its operations in Iraq.

Ghana's government approved the US$1.48 bn. merger of Ashanti Goldmines and the South African AngloGold, to be called AngloGold Ashanti. Ashanti's governing board rejected a US$1.7 m. offer from Randgold Resources, a UK-based company.

Malaysia's prime minister, Dr. Mahathir Mohamad, stepped down after 22 years in office. His deputy, Abdullah Ahmed Badawi, succeeded him.

Jalal Talabani, the leader of the Patriotic Union of Kurdistan (PUK), assumed the presidency of the Iraqi Governing Council.

The Nigerian government agreed to hand over control of disputed territory near Lake Chad containing 70,000 inhabitants to Cameroon in accordance with a ruling from the International Court of Justice (ICJ) in Oct. 2002.

HSBC, the world's second largest bank, acquired the Bank of Bermuda for US$1.3 bn.

King Abdullah of Jordan inaugurated a new government, led by Prime Minister Faisal al-Fayez. The new cabinet included three women.

Week Beginning 19 October 2003

The US Senate voted with the House of Representatives to end the ban on US citizens travelling to Cuba. 59 senators voted against the wishes of the president, who pledged to veto the bill.

Mikhail Khodorkovsky, chief executive of Yukos, Russia's largest oil company, was arrested on charges of fraud.

Ukraine's Supreme Council declared its opposition to Russian construction of a causeway in the Kerch Strait, which began in Sept. Russian doubts concerning Ukraine's sovereignty of the island of Tuzla, off the eastern coast of the Crimean peninsula, angered the Ukrainian government, which ordered a build-up of military forces in the area.

The government of Iran agreed to cooperate with the International Atomic Energy Agency (IAEA) over Iran's nuclear programme and delivered documentation to the agency. Iran's spiritual leader, Ayatollah Khamenei, denied that the government desired nuclear weapons.

Vice-president Carlos Mesa Gilbert was sworn in as president of Bolivia after the resignation of Gonzalo Sánchez de Lozada on 17 Oct. Mesa announced a new cabinet consisting of independents and promised a referendum on the sale of Bolivia's natural gas to the USA.

In Switzerland's parliamentary elections the right-wing Swiss People's Party won 28% of the votes (55 seats), the Social Democratic Party 24% (52 seats), the Liberal-Democratic Party 16% (36 seats), the Christian Democratic People's Party 13% (28 seats) and the Greens 8% (13 seats). Turn-out was 46%.

Week Beginning 12 October 2003

The UN Security Council passed an amended resolution on the future of Iraq. The unanimous resolution supported the role of the US-led Coalition Provisional Authority but insisted on Iraqi sovereignty 'as soon as is practicable'.

China became the third nation to send a manned spacecraft into orbit.

Gyude Bryant was sworn in as chairman of the National Transitional Government of Liberia.

President Gonzalo Sánchez de Lozada of Bolivia agreed to hold a referendum on the export of natural gas to the US. Sánchez was under siege in the presidential palace as protesters marched on La Paz, closing major roads and the international airport.

Elections to the consultative House of Assembly were held in Swaziland. Among the elected members was Obed Dlamini, the head of the banned Ngwane National Liberation Congress and a former prime minister. The Swaziland Democratic Alliance boycotted the elections.

Shirin Ebadi, an Iranian human rights lawyer and former judge, was awarded the Nobel Peace Prize.

Japan pledged US$1.5 m. to Iraq for short-term reconstruction.

The parliamentary election of President Maumoon Abdul Gayoom of the Maldives was approved in a national referendum. Gayoom, the sole candidate in the referendum, received over 90% support. Turn-out was 77%.

In elections in Azerbaijan, former President Heydar Aliyev's son, Ilham Aliyev, won the presidency with 79.5% of the vote. Isa Gambar of the Musavat Party took 12.6%. Allegations of voting irregularities were widespread.

President Mwai Kibaki suspended 23 Kenyan judges and 82 magistrates while tribunals investigated allegations of corruption.

The government of Saudi Arabia announced that municipal elections would be held in 2004 for the first time.

Week Beginning 5 October 2003

Arnold Schwarzenegger was elected governor of California, winning 48.7% of the vote. Incumbent Governor Gray Davis became the second governor in US history to lose a recall vote.

Ahmed Qureia became prime minister of an emergency cabinet after the president of the Palestinian Authority, Yasser Arafat, declared a state of emergency.

A peace deal was signed by Burundi's president, Domitien Ndayizeye, and Pierre Nkurunziza, the leader of the Burundian rebel National Council for the Defence of Democracy—Forces for the Defence of Democracy (CNDD-FDD). The talks in Pretoria, mediated by South African President Thabo Mbeki, resulted in a power-sharing agreement.

The Turkish National Assembly approved sending up to 10,000 Turkish troops to Iraq.

Acting President Akhmad Kadyrov won the Russian-organized presidential election in Chechnya with 81% of the vote.

The member states of the Association of South East Asian Nations (ASEAN) agreed to implement a free trade area by 2020. The agreement was settled at the ASEAN meeting in Bali, Indonesia.

The Israeli airforce attacked a camp at Ein Saheb, southern Syria, which the Israeli government described as a Palestinian terrorist training camp.

Members of the Chagossian community lost their case in the British High Court for the right to compensation and to return to their islands, part of the British Indian Ocean Territory. The Chagos islands were evacuated between 1967 and 1973 in preparation for the US Diego Garcia military base.

Chronology of Events for September 2003

Week Beginning 28 September 2003

The National Liberation Front (FLN), the majority party in Algeria's parliament, withdrew its support from the government. The party accused President Abdelaziz Bouteflika of attempting to prevent the FLN leader, Ali Benflis, from seeking the presidency in the 2004 election.

The United Nations took control of peacekeeping forces in Liberia, including 3,500 West African troops previously under the authority of ECOWAS.

In elections to Oman's Majlis al-Shura, the consultative assembly, 506 non-partisan candidates stood for 83 seats. Only two women were elected.

In Rwanda's first democratic parliamentary elections since the 1994 genocide, President Paul Kagame's Rwandan Patriotic Front (RPF) won 73.78% of the vote. Turn-out was reported at 99.48% by the electoral commission.

Paul Bérenger replaced Sir Anerood Jugnauth as prime minister of Mauritius.

Air France announced a merger with the Dutch airline KLM to become the world's third largest airline in passenger numbers.

South Korea's president, Roh Moo-hyun, resigned from the Millennium Democratic Party of his predecessor, Kim Dae-jung.

Iyad Allawi, the leader of the Iraqi National Accord, assumed the presidency of the Iraqi Governing Council.

Henrique Rosa took office as interim president of Guinea-Bissau. Artur Sanhá was appointed prime minister to head a transitional government chosen by the National Transition Council, chaired by Gen. Veríssimo Correia Seabra, in consultation with the political parties.

Dr. Nicholas Liverpool took office as president of Dominica. Previous incumbent Vernon Shaw did not seek re-election by parliament.

Violent demonstrations took place in La Paz and across Bolivia, voicing opposition to plans to export natural gas.

Pope John Paul II appointed 31 cardinals, enlarging the consistory to 195 cardinals, 135 of which were under 80 years of age and thus entitled to vote for a successor to the papacy.

Week Beginning 21 September 2003

A security pact was agreed by the Sudanese government and the Sudan People's Liberation Movement (SPLM). Talks were held in Naivasha, Kenya between the Sudanese president, Lieut.-Gen. Omar Hassan al-Bashir, and the leader of the SPLM, John Garang.

Aung San Suu Kyi was permitted by Myanmar's government to return home, under house arrest, from prison after undergoing surgery.

The power-sharing government of Côte d'Ivoire formed in March 2003 collapsed. Former rebel factions withdrew and ended their involvement in the disarmament programme. Peace talks in rebel-controlled Bouaké failed to settle differences with President Laurent Gbagbo.

Kenyan President Mwai Kibaki appointed Moody Awori vice-president to replace Michael Wamalwa, who died on 23 Aug.

Accession to the European Union was approved in a referendum in Latvia. 67% voted to join in May 2004. Turn-out was 72.5%.

Grand Ayatollah Hossein-Ali Montazeri, a leading Iranian cleric, criticized the Iranian government's attitude towards the USA and its failure to reform. Montazeri called for the resumption of diplomatic relations with the US.

Week Beginning 14 September 2003

The government of Guinea-Bissau was overthrown by a military coup, led by Gen. Veríssimo Correia Seabra, who declared himself president. Correia Seabra stated that he would lead a transitional government of national unity until elections could be held.

The World Trade Summit in Cancún, Mexico ended in deadlock. The summit had focused on farming subsidies, foreign investment and competition. Demonstrations, including the suicide of the leader of South Korea's farming federation, highlighted the divisions between delegates from the West and from developing countries.

Adoption of the euro in Sweden was rejected in a referendum, which went ahead despite the murder of the foreign minister, Anna Lindh. 56% voted against the single European currency. Turn-out was 81%.

Zimbabwe's High Court ordered the government to allow the re-opening of Zimbabwe's only independent newspaper. The Daily News was shut down on 12 Sept. for contraventions of a new press law. The order was ignored.

A mass grave containing the bodies of around 500 Bosnians, mostly Muslims, was discovered near Zvornik in eastern Bosnia-Herzegovina. Officials claimed they were the victims of Bosnian Serb forces.

The Reserve Bank of Zimbabwe issued a new temporary currency to provide higher denominations made necessary by rampant inflation. The unprecedented 'bearer cheques' represented bank notes until expiry on 31 Jan. 2004.

The USA vetoed a UN Security Council resolution condemning Israel's threat to 'remove' Yasser Arafat, the president of the Palestinian Authority, possibly by assassination or deportation. The USA rejected the resolution on the grounds that it did not sufficiently criticize 'terrorism' committed by Palestinian militants.

A referendum in Estonia approved accession to the European Union. 66.9% supported joining. Turn-out was 63%.

Gen. Sultan Hashim Ahmed, the minister of defence under Saddam Hussein, surrendered to US forces in Mosul, northern Iraq.

Week Beginning 7 September 2003
The UN Security Council lifted sanctions against Libya. All members voted for the resolution except for the US and France, which abstained.

Burkina Faso's border with Côte d'Ivoire reopened. The border was closed in Sept. 2002 after the president of Côte d'Ivoire, Laurent Gbagbo, claimed Burkinabe interference in its civil war.

The government of Argentina agreed to a new 3-year aid plan with the International Monetary Fund (IMF). US$21 bn. of debt was to be refinanced in the wake of Argentina's US$3 bn. default on 10 Sept.

Syrian President Bashar Al-Assad appointed Mohammed Naji Al-Otari prime minister.

Chronology of Events for August 2003

Week Beginning 31 August 2003
Mahmoud Abbas resigned as the Palestinian prime minister.

Hong Kong's Chief Executive Tung Chee-hwa announced that the proposed anti-subversion bill would be shelved. He promised public consultation in framing future bills concerning security.

UN troops took over peacekeeping duties from a French-led force in the Democratic Republic of the Congo's northeastern Ituri province.

Ahmad Chalabi, the leader of the Iraqi National Congress, assumed the presidency of the Iraqi Governing Council.

The Libyan government agreed a compensation package with the French government for the families of 170 people killed in the bombing of a French airliner over Niger in 1989.

Week Beginning 24 August 2003
Ayatollah Mohammed Baqr al-Hakim, one of Iraq's most important Shia Muslim leaders, was killed in a car bomb attack in Najaf. Ayatollah al-Hakim, leader of the Supreme Council for the Islamic Revolution in Iraq, had returned in May after 20 years in exile in Iran. Around 100 other people also died in the bombing.

A US$6 bn. joint venture between BP and TNK, Russia's third largest oil company, was approved. BP took a 50% stake in TNK, making it the world's second largest oil company.

President Paul Kagame won 95% of the vote against two opponents in Rwanda's first democratic elections since the 1994 genocide. Turn-out was 80%.

Two bombs in Mumbai, India killed at least 48 people and injured over 150. The attacks targeted a jewellery market and the Gateway of India monument. No organization claimed responsibility.

Gen. Khin Nyunt was appointed prime minister of Myanmar. Senior Gen. Than Shwe remained as head of state.

The government of Peru signed a free trade agreement on selected products with MERCOSUR, making it an associate member of the South American trading group.

Talks began in Beijing between North Korea, the USA, Japan, China and Russia concerning North Korean nuclear capabilities and the state's demands for a non-aggression pact with the USA.

The Canadian government signed an agreement granting the Tlicho Nation, an indigenous aboriginal group, jurisdiction over 39,000 km^2 of land in the north of the country. Federal government retained responsibility for criminal law and the Northwest Territories government control over services.

The member states of the Southern African Development Community (SADC) signed a Mutual Defence Pact.

Week Beginning 17 August 2003
A peace deal was signed by the Liberian government and Liberia's rebel groups, LURD (Liberians United for Reconciliation and Democracy) and MODEL (Movement for Democracy in Liberia). Liberia's President Moses Blah agreed to step down by 14 Oct. to allow a chairman to assume control of a transitional government. Gyude Bryant, the leader of the Liberian Action Party, and Wesley Johnson were chosen chairman and vice-chairman. The agreement, signed in Ghana's capital, Accra, apportioned five ministries each to the existing government, LURD and MODEL. The remaining six ministries were allocated to civil society and the political parties.

The UN building in Baghdad was attacked by a truck bomb, killing at least 20 people including the UN special representative for Iraq, Sérgio Vieira de Mello.

US military forces in Iraq captured Gen. Ali Hassan al-Majid, known as "Chemical Ali". Al-Majid was reported killed in April during an attack on his residence in Al-Basrah by British forces but no body was discovered. Kurkish forces captured the former Iraqi vice-president, Taha Yassin Ramadan, in Mosul.

President Yoweri Museveni of Uganda travelled to Soroti in central Uganda to oversee military operations against the Lord's Resistance Army (LRA). He dared the rebels to abduct him in place of the children and civilians routinely taken by the LRA.

The remaining hostages taken in the Algerian Sahara by an Algerian Islamist group in Feb. 2003 were freed. The nine Germans, four Swiss and one Dutchman were released by the Salafist Group for Preaching and Combat, which is seeking an orthodox Islamist state in Algeria, after talks with the Malian government and Taureg negotiators.

Argentina's Congress voted for the abolition of amnesty laws that provided members of the military regime of 1976–83 with immunity from prosecution for alleged human rights abuses.

Week Beginning 10 August 2003
Charles Taylor resigned the presidency of Liberia, handing power to Vice-President Moses Blah until the installment of a new president. Taylor went into exile in Nigeria, accusing the US of forcing him from office. Nigerian ECOWAS peacekeeping troops took control of the port in Monrovia, the Liberian capital, from rebel forces. The troops were unable to contain civilians entering the city via the Mesurado River bridges, resulting in looting of food supplies. A medical and food supply ship, sent by the UN World Food Programme, arrived at the capital's port.

The Libyan government promised to set up a US$2.7 bn. fund for the families of the Lockerbie bombing victims.

President Levy Mwanawasa of Zambia survived a motion in parliament to impeach him for corruption and other violations of the constitution. He accused his opponents, led by ex-vice-president Enoch Kavindele, of political motivation in response to his anti-corruption drive.

Thai Defence Minister Thamarak Isarangura announced the capture of Riduan Isamuddin, known as Hambali, thought to be the director of operations of Jemaah Islamiah and a senior member of al-Qaeda. Hambali, accused of masterminding the Bali bombings of Oct. 2002 and the attack on the Marriott Hotel in Jakarta on 5 Aug. 2003, was captured in a joint CIA-Thai operation.

Idi Amin, the former president of Uganda, died in Jeddah, Saudi Arabia. Amin had been threatened with prosecution for human rights abuses if he returned to Uganda. President Yoweri Museveni vetoed the return of his body for burial.

Nicanor Duarte Frutos was sworn in as president of Paraguay, having been elected in April 2003.

A merger was approved in Russia between Yukos and Sibneft which created the fourth-largest oil producer in the world, with a market capitalization of US$36 bn.

NATO took over peacekeeping duties in Afghanistan from the German- and Dutch-led International Security Assistance Force. It was NATO's first operational commitment outside Europe.

Maj.-Gen. Michael Jeffery was sworn in as governor-general of Australia, replacing Peter Hollingworth, who resigned in May 2003.

The European Commission granted the UN World Food Programme US$28 m. to alleviate food shortages in Zimbabwe. It was estimated that over 3 m. Zimbabweans were in urgent need of food.

The US authorized the US$1 bn. sale by Israel to India of the Phalcon early warning airborne radar system. Pakistan had expressed concerns that the sale would detrimentally affect the region's nuclear balance.

President Gloria Macapagal-Arroyo of the Philippines lifted the state of rebellion imposed in response to a military uprising on 27 July. 300 soldiers were charged with involvement in the mutiny led by Ramon Cardenas, a former junior minister to ex-President Joseph Estrada.

Week Beginning 3 August 2003

The Jordanian Embassy in Baghdad was attacked by a lorry bomb, killing 11 Iraqis and injuring 50.

The Indonesian capital, Jakarta, was hit by a suicide terrorist attack which killed 10 people and injured 150. The target was the Marriott Hotel in central Jakarta. The fundamentalist group Jemaah Islamiah was blamed.

Amrozi bin Nurhasyim became the first man to be convicted of participation in the 2002 Bali bombings which killed over 200 people. He was sentenced to death but his lawyers launched an appeal.

Sheikh Hamad bin Khalifa Al Thani of Qatar replaced Sheikh Jassim Bin Hamad as crown prince with Jassim's younger brother, Tamim.

The UN adopted a resolution drafted by the US calling for the immediate deployment of an ECOWAS peacekeeping force for Liberia, to be replaced by a full UN force on 1 Oct. France, Germany and Mexico abstained from the UN vote in protest at a clause exempting US troops from the jurisdiction of the International Criminal Court.

Ilham Aliyev, son of President Heydar Aliyev of Azerbaijan, was chosen as prime minister by parliament. Under constitutional changes introduced in 2002 he is eligible to assume presidential powers should the president become too ill to govern.

Ludwig Scotty was replaced by René Harris as president of Nauru.

Chronology of Events for July 2003

Week Beginning 27 July 2003

Ibrahim Al-Jaafari, of the Shia Daawa movement, assumed the leadership of the Iraqi Governing Council.

A suicide bomber at a military hospital in the Russian republic of North Ossetia killed 50 people and injured 70. Chechen rebels were blamed for the attack.

The Malaita Eagle Force (MEF), one of the most important rebel groups in the Solomon Islands, announced it would surrender its arms to international peacekeeping forces on 15 Aug.

Ramon Cardenas, a former junior minister to ex-President Joseph Estrada of the Philippines, was arrested following a military uprising in Manila. Several hundred troops took possession of a shopping and residential complex but withdrew peacefully after accusing Gloria Arroyo's government of corruption.

President Marc Ravalomanana of Madagascar announced that the Ariary would become the official currency by 30 Nov. 2003, replacing the Malagasy franc which superseded the Ariary during the period of French colonial rule.

The government of Zimbabwe announced the 60-day withdrawal of the Z$500 note, the highest-value note in circulation. Citizens had been hoarding cash as inflation neared 400%.

The Israeli government promised to release 540 Palestinians, including members of militant organizations. Israeli checkpoints in Ramallah and Hebron were dismantled.

The UN adopted a resolution supporting the creation of Western Sahara as a semi-autonomous area within Morocco for a transitional period extending up to 5 years, at which point the region's population would hold a referendum offering full independence, autonomy or Moroccan integration.

The Cambodian People's Party of Prime Minister Hun Sen won 68 out of 122 seats with 47.5% of the vote in Cambodia's parliamentary elections.

The Turkish parliament passed reforms designed to reduce the influence of the military in national politics in a bid to prepare Turkey for eventual EU membership.

Week Beginning 20 July 2003

Over 1 m. people signed a petition for a recall ballot in California, USA to remove Governor Gray Davis from office, in light of California's budget deficit of US$38 bn.

Iranian Minister of Intelligence Ali Yunesi announced that the government was holding members of the al-Qaeda terrorist network, including several leading figures.

A 2,225-strong Australian-led peacekeeping force landed in the Solomon Islands in an attempt to reassert the rule of law amid widespread inter-ethnic conflict. The peacekeeping force includes troops from Fiji, New Zealand, Papua New Guinea and Tonga.

Saddam Hussein's sons, Uday and Qusay, were killed in a gun battle in Mosul.

President Fradique de Menezes of São Tomé and Príncipe re-entered the country following an internationally-brokered agreement with the leaders of the 16 July coup. Under the terms of the agreement the coup leaders, who claim they staged the coup to highlight government corruption and poor quality of life, were granted amnesty. De Menezes agreed to establish a new government of national unity.

A US congressional report on intelligence gathering in the build-up to the 11 Sept. terrorist attacks on New York and Washington criticized the CIA and FBI for breakdowns in communication but found no single piece of intelligence that could have prevented the attacks.

Bomb blasts in the Spanish resorts of Alicante and Benidorm injured 13 people. The Basque separatist organization ETA claimed responsibility, having announced a summer campaign targeting tourism, one of Spain's key industries.

The refusal of the government of Myanmar to release Aung San Suu Kyi raised the possibility of the country's expulsion from the Association of South East Asian Nations (ASEAN). The threat was made by Malaysia's prime minister, Dr. Mahathir Mohamad, who was instrumental in Myanmar's accession to ASEAN in 1997.

Week Beginning 13 July 2003

The four vice-presidents in the new transitional government of the Democratic Republic of the Congo were inaugurated in Kinshasa. Jean-Pierre Bemba (MLC), Abdoulaye Yerodia Ndombasi (former government minister), Arthur Z'ahidi Ngoma (political opposition) and Azarias Ruberwa (RCD-Goma) pledged to support the peace accord originally laid down in Lusaka in 1999.

The Fiji Islands' supreme court declared that the government must include members of the opposition. Prime Minister Laisenia Qarase had excluded from the government MPs from the Indian-dominated Labour party in contravention of the constitution.

Rebel soldiers of the Hutu-dominated Forces Nationales de Libération (FNL) attacked the Burundian capital, Bujumbura. President Domitien Ndayizeye criticized the partial evacuation of UN staff running the humanitarian aid programme.

Army officers, led by Major Fernando Pereira, staged a coup in São Tomé and Príncipe, holding hostage Prime Minister Maria des Neves and several other leading government figures. Despite the use of force, no casualties were reported. The president was in Nigeria at the time.

Hong Kong's Chief Executive Tung Chee-hwa declared his intention to stay in his post despite the resignations of two leading ministers following public protests against a government-backed anti-subversion bill. Critics of the bill claimed that Hong Kong's freedom of politics, religion and expression would be compromised.

A 25-man Iraqi-led governing council convened in Baghdad for the first time since the US-led war in an important staging post towards full self-government. The council was charged with appointing and dismissing ministers, deciding on policy and preparing for free elections, although the US administration retained a power of veto. Recruitment began for a new national army to replace Saddam Hussein's 400,000 strong force demobilized in May 2003.

Alan Greenspan, chairman of the US Federal Reserve, reported to Congress that the economy could 'be embarking on a period of extended growth', during which interest rates would remain low. The Office of Management and Budget predicted that the federal budget deficit for 2003 would be

US$455 bn., in large part because of expenditure on the war and its aftermath in Iraq.

A 1,070 km pipeline started pumping oil for export from Chad into Cameroon. The project, partly financed by the World Bank and Exxon Mobil, was expected to earn annual revenues of US$80 m. for Chad and US$20 m. for Cameroon.

The Cypriot parliament ratified accession to the European Union by a unanimous vote.

The former Kuwaiti foreign minister Sheikh Sabah al-Ahmed al-Sabah was appointed prime minister by his brother the emir, Sheikh Jaber al-Ahmed al-Jaber al-Sabah. It was the first time since independence that the premiership was not held by the heir to the throne.

Week Beginning 6 July 2003

US General Tommy Franks, who led US forces in Iraq in 2003, retired as Army Chief-of-Staff and was replaced by Lieut.-General John Abizaid.

Voters rejected plans to increase regional autonomy for Corsica by 50.98% to 49.02% in a referendum. Under the proposals, Corsica would have established a single regional assembly (streamlining three existing institutions) and would have won limited control over energy, transport and regional aid.

In Mexico's elections of 6 July to the Chamber of Deputies, the lower house of Congress, President Vicente Fox's National Action Party (PAN) won 153 seats, losing a quarter of its seats. The main opposition party, the Institutional Revolutionary Party (PRI), won 224 seats. 28 seats were won by other parties.

Liberian President Charles Taylor accepted an offer of asylum from Nigeria but insisted he will not leave the country until he could guarantee an orderly handover of power.

Mauritania's President Maaouya Ould Taya appointed Sghaïr Ould M'Bareck prime minister.

Myanmar's armed forces destroyed the Myanmese camps of the National Socialist Council of Nagaland (NSCN), which has campaigned for the creation of a greater Naga state from the existing Indian province of Nagaland.

Belarus' Prime Minister Gennady Novitsky was sacked by President Alyaksandr Lukashenka. The first deputy prime minister, Sergei Sidorsky, was appointed acting prime minister.

Chronology of Events for June 2003

Week Beginning 29 June 2003

The two main rebel groups in the Democratic Republic of The Congo, the Congolese Rally for Democracy (RCD-Goma) and the Congolese Liberation Movement (MLC), accepted the command of ground forces and naval forces respectively. The government maintained supreme command of the armed forces. The agreement allowed the inauguration of a new transitional power-sharing government.

Israel withdrew its troops from the main north-south highway in the Gaza Strip and from positions throughout northern Gaza. The move came after the three main Palestinian militant groups (Hamas, Islamic Jihad and Fatah) agreed to a ceasefire.

Côte d'Ivoire's President Laurent Gbagbo and rebel leaders announced the end of the civil war which followed an aborted coup attempt against Gbagbo in Sept. 2002.

Taiwan was removed from the WHO list of areas infected with Severe Acute Respiratory Syndrome. The announcement confirmed that the outbreak, first reported in Nov. 2002 and responsible for over 800 deaths, has been contained.

A summit of 16 South Pacific foreign ministers voted in support of deploying an international peacekeeping force in the Solomon Islands. The 2,000-strong force was expected to be led by Australia with support from seven other nations, including New Zealand and Papua New Guinea.

In Kuwait's parliamentary elections, government supporters and independents lost seats to Islamist candidates.

Peru's President Alejandro Toledo appointed Beatriz Merino as prime minister. Merino is the first woman to hold the position.

Nigeria was hit by a general strike in response to large petrol price increases. President Olusegun Obasanjo declared the strikes illegal and police used teargas to disperse protestors in Abuja and Lagos.

Anote Tong was elected president of Kiribati, defeating his brother, Harry Tong, by a narrow margin.

Week Beginning 22 June 2003

Indian Prime Minister Atal Bihari Vajpayee visited China to improve relations between the two countries. India conceded recognition of Tibet as an autonomous region of the People's Republic of China. Vajpayee promised to prevent 'anti-China political activities in India' by Tibetans.

Japan, Myanmar's largest donor, suspended aid to Myanmar in protest over the detention of Aung San Suu Kyi, the leader of the National League for Democracy.

Agricultural ministers agreed to an overhaul of the EU agricultural subsidies system, which currently costs €43 bn. a year. The move followed complaints from the US, Africa and Australia that the EU's agricultural policy was distorting the global market.

The US Federal Reserve cut interest rates by a quarter of a percentage point to 1%, its lowest level in 45 years.

Liberians United for Reconciliation and Democracy (Lurd), Liberia's largest rebel group, called a ceasefire in the battle with President Charles Taylor's troops for the capital, Monrovia. It was estimated that 300 civilians were killed, 1,000 injured and 250,000 displaced in 3 days of fighting following the collapse of an earlier ceasefire.

Finnish Defence Minister Matti Vanhanen was elected prime minister by parliament after the resignation of Anneli Jäätteenmäki. Jäätteenmäki was accused of lying to MPs over the use of confidential government files during her election campaign.

Peru's Prime Minister Luis Solari and his cabinet resigned when tax cut proposals were rejected by the congress.

The WHO lifted its final travel warning, to Beijing, on account of Severe Acute Respiratory Syndrome (SARS).

The Atomic Energy Organization of Iran promised increased cooperation with the International Atomic Energy Agency (IAEA) but refused to allow inspections of the Kalaye Electric Company in Tehran which, it claimed, was not part of its Russian-managed nuclear programme.

Blijana Plavšić, the ex-president of the Republika Srpska in Bosnia-Herzegovina was sentenced to 11 years for crimes against Bosnian Muslims and Croats by the International War Crimes Tribunal at the Hague.

The government of Serbia and Montenegro agreed to talks with the authorities in Kosovo. The talks, the first since 1999, were not expected to address Kosovan self-determination.

Bosnian Croat Dragan Čović replaced Bosnian Serb Borislav Paravac as chairman of Bosnia-Herzegovina's rotating presidency.

Chad's President Idriss Déby appointed Moussa Faki prime minister.

Week Beginning 15 June 2003

All 15 EU heads of state approved Jean-Claude Trichet, head of the Bank of France, as the European Central Bank's next president.

Saddam Hussein's presidential secretary, Abid Hamid al-Tikriti, was captured by US forces in Iraq.

Legislation was passed by the Turkish parliament ending restrictions on broadcasting and printing in Kurdish and other minority dialects and languages.

In Jordan's delayed parliamentary elections, candidates loyal to the king won 62 of the 110 seats. The Islamic Action Front won 18.

Chief Minister Ralph O'Neal's Virgin Islands Party was defeated in parliamentary elections in the British Virgin Islands by the National Democratic Party. Orlando Smith took office as chief minister.

Week Beginning 8 June 2003

Iranian students held anti-government demonstrations in Tehran and other cities for over a week. The demonstrations, publicly supported by US President George W. Bush, were organized by Iranian television stations based in the USA.

Demonstrations in Nepal calling for an all-party government and the recall of parliament spread across the country. They were sparked by the appointment of the royalist Surya Bahadur Thapa as prime minister.

Mauritania's President Maaouya Ould Taya announced the failure of an attempted coup against him. Nouakchott, the capital, witnessed heavy fighting between rebel army factions and pro-government troops.

French troops arrived in Bunia, in the northeast of the Democratic Republic of the Congo, as part of a UN-mandated peacekeeping force.

Polish application for membership of the EU won 77% approval in a national referendum..

The Chinese Three Gorges Reservoir reached sufficient depth to support hydroelectric generation and the resumption of passenger and cargo shipping on the River Yangtze.

Imangali Tasmagambetov, the prime minister of Kazakhstan, resigned. He was replaced by Daniyal Akhmetov.

Sri Lanka received assurances from the international community for aid worth US$4.5 bn. over the next 4 years on condition of continuing progress towards peace. Japan and the Asian Development Bank were the two biggest donors, offering US$1 bn. each.

Czech application for membership of the EU won 77% approval in a national referendum.

UK Chancellor Gordon Brown ruled out the UK's early entry to the eurozone.

France was hit by a third national strike in three weeks, involving the rail, air and electricity sectors, protesting against government plans to increase pension contributions, raise the retirement age and reduce benefits.

Week Beginning 1 June 2003

Myanmar's opposition leader, Aung San Suu Kyi, was put under 'protective custody' after clashes between her National League for Democracy and government forces.

Police detained Morgan Tsvangirai, leader of Zimbabwe's opposition Movement for Democratic Change (MDC). The MDC had called for a week of protests, banned by the high court, against the government of President Robert Mugabe.

The Group of Eight (comprising leaders from the world's seven largest industrial nations and Russia) met in France. As well as the international economy, discussions focused on global terrorism and weapons of mass destruction.

Gnassingbé Eyadéma won a further term of office in Togo's presidential elections.

Liberia's President Charles Taylor was indicted by a UN-backed court for war crimes in neighbouring Sierra Leone.

The EU agreed to send troops to the Democratic Republic of Congo, the first time it has sent independent forces outside of Europe.

The Saudi government pulled out of a US$15 bn. investment project with an ExxonMobil-led consortium to exploit the country's massive gas reserves.

The European Central Bank cut its key interest rate by half a percentage point to 2%, the lowest European base rate since World War II. The bank, traditionally committed to countering inflation, made the cut as deflation and recession threatened the eurozone.

Chronology of Events for May 2003

Week Beginning 25 May 2003

The European convention on the future of the EU published its draft proposals. The paper called for an elected president with a term of at least two and a half years, an elected foreign affairs minister and common foreign and security policies. Further proposals included the election of a president of the European Commission by the European Parliament, closer integration of judicial and social security systems and the establishment of a European public prosecutor's office. Romano Prodi, president of the European Commission, criticized the constitution for 'lacking vision'.

Iraq's interim administration suspended several pre-war contracts agreed between Saddam Hussein and oil companies from China and Russia.

Saif al-Adel, the third highest ranked member of al-Qaeda, was reportedly arrested in Iran. He was believed to have been involved in the bombings of foreign interests in Riyadh in May 2003.

A new plan was proposed for the future of Western Sahara by the UN Secretary-General Kofi Annan, suggesting a transitional period of self-government before a referendum on independence from Morocco.

The Israeli cabinet accepted the internationally-brokered Middle East 'road map to peace', although with 14 'reservations'. Prime Minister Ariel Sharon described the Israeli presence in the West Bank and Gaza Strip as an 'occupation'.

The establishment of a transitional power-sharing government in the Democratic Republic of Congo was postponed because of disagreements between the government and RCD-Goma, the leading rebel group, over the composition of the army.

Nepal's Prime Minister Lokendra Bahadur Chand resigned. Several opposition parties had rejected the legitimacy of his appointment by King Gyanendra in Oct. 2002.

Brazil's Democratic Movement joined the Workers' Party-dominated coalition government of President Luiz Inácio Lula da Silva.

A new Rwandan constitution won 93% backing in a national referendum. Under its terms no single party would be able to dominate government. Opponents of the government claimed that a ban on grassroots campaigning would make it more difficult to unseat the incumbent administration.

Pakistan announced a new high commissioner to India following Indian Prime Minister Atal Bihari Vajpayee's earlier promise to resume full diplomatic relations with Pakistan.

Toronto, Canada suffered a renewed outbreak of Severe Acute Respiratory Syndrome (SARS), a week after being designated SARS-free by the WHO.

Jan Peter Balkenende of the Christian Democrat Appeal was sworn in as prime minister of the Netherlands for a second term. He headed a coalition which included the People's Party for Freedom and Democracy, and Democrats '66.

Peter Hollingworth resigned as Australia's governor-general. Hollingworth had been the subject of allegations of a rape in the 1960s (the charges were later dropped) and had been censured for his failure to dismiss a paedophile member of the clergy when he was archbishop of Brisbane.

The Republican Party won 31 of 131 seats in Armenia's general elections. The Rule of Law Country Party won 19 seats, the Justice party 14, the Armenian Revolutionary Federation 11, National Unity 9, and United Labour Party 6. 56 members were elected in single seat constituencies.

The value of the euro against the US dollar surpassed its launch value of $1.1747 for the first time.

Week Beginning 18 May 2003

The UN security council passed a resolution on Iraq's future jointly proposed by the US, UK and Spain. 14 of the 15 members voted in favour while Syria failed to attend. Under its terms UN special representatives would be appointed to co-operate with the occupying forces to form a new government. The occupying forces would remain until an internationally-acceptable government was in place. The mandate of the UN weapons inspectors was to be 'revisited' and the UN oil-for-food programme would be phased out over 6 months. Iraq's international debts would be administered by multilateral organizations and oil revenues would be protected from creditors until 2007 except in the event of an ecological disaster. In return all UN sanctions were to be lifted immediately.

Fighting resumed in Indonesia's Aceh province after the collapse of peace talks between the Indonesian government and the Acehnese rebel group, the Free Aceh Movement. President Megawati Sukarnoputri ordered a major offensive and declared martial law in the province.

An earthquake in northern Algeria killed at least 1,100 people, injured 6,800 and displaced thousands more.

Dr. Jong-Wook Lee was chosen as director-general of the World Health Organization.

Floods in the south of Sri Lanka killed 250 people and displaced 150,000 more.

US President George W. Bush declared the Philippines a 'major non-Nato ally'.

Prime Minister Guy Verhofstadt's Flemish Liberal and Democratic Party won 25 seats in Belgium's parliamentary elections. The Socialist Party also took 25 seats, the Reformist Movement 24 seats, the Socialist Party Different-Spirit coalition 23, the Christian Democratic and Flemish Party 21 seats and the Flemish Block 18 seats. Four other parties won seats.

Week Beginning 11 May 2003

Paul Bremer, the newly-appointed US administrator of Iraq, arrived in the country.

Over 30 people were killed in a series of suicide bombings launched against Western interests in Riyadh, Saudi Arabia. The US claimed the al-Qaeda terrorist network was responsible.

Over 40 people were killed and over 100 injured in suicide attacks in Casablanca, Morocco. Western targets, including a restaurant and an embassy, were hit. Moroccan authorities blamed Assirat el Moustaqim, a radical Islamic group.

The trial began in Indonesia of Amrozi, the first man to be charged in connection with the terrorist bombing of a nightclub on Bali which killed over 200 people in Oct. 2002.

Membership of the EU, scheduled for 2004, received 91% support in a national referendum in Lithuania.

Filip Vujanović won the Montenegrin presidency, claiming around 65% of the vote against two opponents.

Joseph J. Urusemal was elected president of Micronesia.

Restrictions on Palestinian travel were relaxed in what was seen as a confidence-building gesture following the publication of the 'roadmap to peace'. The Israeli government later scaled off the Gaza Strip, blaming the threat of suicide bombings.

North Korea announced its withdrawal from a 1992 accord with South Korea to maintain the Korean peninsula as a nuclear weapon-free zone.

In response to the opening of the border between Greek- and Turkish-controlled Cyprus in April 2003, Prime Minister Reçep Tayyip Erdoğan of Turkey lifted the ban on Greek Cypriots entering the Republic of Turkey.

Japan's parliament passed a series of measures giving central government increased control over the military and greater freedom to requisition civilian property in the event of attack.

The US expelled 14 Cuban diplomats on suspicion of spying as relations between the two nations continued to decline.

Former president Carlos Menem, who had a narrow lead after a first round of elections, withdrew from Argentina's presidential run-off. He was expected to suffer a heavy defeat as opposition rallied behind his opponent, Néstor Kirchner.

Week Beginning 4 May 2003
Indian and Bangladeshi guards clashed along a disputed stretch of shared border. Government officials from both countries met in Dhaka in a bid to reduce tensions.

Algeria's President Abdelaziz Bouteflika dismissed Prime Minister Ali Benflis following a series of clashes. Ahmed Ouyahia replaced him.

Amram Mitzna, leader of Israel's Labour Party, resigned. He blamed criticism from within his own party following a poor showing at the general elections of Jan. 2003 and his subsequent refusal to join a coalition led by Ariel Sharon.

The Independence Party of incumbent Prime Minister Davíð Oddsson won 22 out of 63 seats in Iceland's general elections. The Social Alliance won 20 and the Progressive Party 12.

US Vice-President Dick Cheney accepted President George W. Bush's invitation to run on a joint ticket at the presidential elections of 2004.

Austria's Trade Union Confederation called a national strike in protest at proposed pension reforms which would raise retirement age to 65 and reduce benefits.

Argentina's deputy foreign minister, Martin Redrado, announced that the Argentinian and Brazilian governments were considering the introduction of a joint currency.

The US and Singapore signed a free trade agreement, the first such agreement to be signed between the US and an Asian country, invalidating tariffs worth an estimated US$33 bn. per annum.

Italian Prime Minister Silvio Berlusconi appeared on trial for allegedly bribing judges in the 1980s.

Chronology of Events for April 2003

Week Beginning 27 April 2003
President George W. Bush formally claimed victory in the 'Battle of Iraq'.

The 'roadmap to peace', produced by the UN, EU, US and Russia, to end the conflict between Israelis and Palestinians, was published. The document called for an immediate ceasefire, an end to the Israeli occupation of Palestinian towns, a clampdown on Palestinian militants and the dismantling of Israeli settlements built since 2001. It proposed the establishment of an independent, democratic Palestinian state as early as 2005.

India's Prime Minister Atal Bihari Vajpayee announced plans to resume full diplomatic relations with Pakistan and restore air links. Pakistan welcomed the initiative and responded with reciprocal proposals.

Liberia's President Charles Taylor and Côte d'Ivoire's President Laurent Gbagbo agreed to greater co-ordination of military patrols on their shared border in a bid to counter rebel incursions.

President Vladimir Putin announced plans to increase Russia's military presence in Tajikistan following intelligence reports of increased activity by the Taliban and the al-Qaeda terrorist network in neighbouring Afghanistan.

UK Prime Minister Tony Blair postponed elections to the Northern Irish Assembly until late-2003 at the earliest. He claimed that Irish Republican Army assurances that it would not do anything to undermine the peace process did not go far enough.

The Greek-Cypriot government announced it would allow citizens of the 'Turkish Republic of Northern Cyprus' cross-border access to healthcare and other state benefits. Greek-Cypriot authorities would also recognize official documentation issued by the 'TRNC'. The Turkish-Cypriot authorities opened the border crossing in central Nicosia to allow day-passage for both Greek and Turkish communities.

The US announced plans to recall almost all of its 10,000 troops from Saudi Arabia.

The ruling General People's Congress of President Abdullah Saleh won 238 of a possible 301 seats in Yemen's general elections.

Nicanor Duarte Frutos of the ruling Colorado Party won Paraguay's presidential election with 37.1% of the vote.

The Thai government reported that over 2,250 people were killed, 9,000 arrested and a further 36,000 reported to police in a 3-month-long national drugs crackdown. The interior ministry blamed the majority of deaths on gang-related fighting. The UN voiced concern at the crackdown.

Domitien Ndayizeze, a Hutu, was sworn in as Burundi's new president in accordance with the terms of a power-sharing agreement between Hutus and Tutsis.

In elections to the Scottish Parliament, Labour took 50 of 129 seats, the Scottish Nationalists won 27, Conservatives 18 and Liberal Democrats 17. In elections for the Welsh Assembly, Labour won 30 of 60 seats, Plaid Cymru 12, Conservatives 11, Liberal Democrats 6 and independents 1.

Nauru First won 3 seats in Nauru's general elections while independents took the remaining 15.

Week Beginning 20 April 2003
Jay Garner, the former US general selected by Washington to head the Office of Reconstruction and Humanitarian Assistance for Iraq and oversee the transition to an interim administration in Iraq, arrived in the country.

The Ugandan People's Defence Force (UPDF) removed its troops from the Ituri region of north-eastern Democratic Republic of Congo. They were to be replaced by a United Nations observer mission (MONUC).

Talks between the US and North Korea in Beijing ended acrimoniously after North Korea admitted possessing nuclear arms and the ability to expand its arsenal.

Peace talks between the Nepalese government and Maoist rebels began after a ceasefire was agreed in Jan. 2003.

Peace talks between Uganda's government and the Lord's Resistance Army (LRA) collapsed.

Thomas White, secretary of the US army, resigned following a long-running dispute with Secretary of Defence Donald Rumsfeld.

Zimbabwe was paralysed by a general strike which followed a 200% jump in fuel prices.

Former French President Valéry Giscard d'Estaing, chairman of the European Convention on the future of the European Union, called for a full-time EU president and the reduction of the number of EU Commissioners.

President Yasser Arafat and Prime Minister Mahmoud Abbas agreed on the composition of the Palestinian Authority government, having earlier clashed over several key posts.

Following a declaration of support from President George W. Bush, Alan Greenspan, the chairman of the US Federal Reserve, agreed to stay for a fifth term in office due to begin in mid-2004.

The International Criminal Court (ICC), based at The Hague, elected Argentinian Luis Moreno Ocampo as its first prosecutor by a unanimous vote.

Week Beginning 13 April 2003
The US threatened economic, diplomatic or other undefined sanctions against Syria, which it suggested was harbouring members of Saddam Hussein's regime and has been involved in the development of chemical weapons.

EU members signed a treaty of expansion in Athens which will see the number of member countries rise from 15 to 25 in 2004.

At Nigeria's presidential elections incumbent President Olusegun Obasanjo of the People's Democratic Party (PDP) claimed 61.9% of the vote to defeat 18 candidates.

Anneli Jäätteenmäki was chosen to lead Finland's coalition government, comprising her Centre Party, the Social Democrats and the Swedish People's Party.

Sierra Leone's Truth and Reconciliation Committee held its first public hearings on the long-running civil war which ended in 2002.

The Afghan transitional government applied for membership of the World Trade Organization.

Full sequencing of the human genome was completed 2 years ahead of schedule.

Week Beginning 6 April 2003

US forces won control of Baghdad, ending the regime of Saddam Hussein whose whereabouts were not known.

UN staff reported that almost 1,000 people have been killed in ethnic fighting in the Ituri region in the northeast of the Democratic Republic of Congo.

Air France and British Airways announced that Concorde, the world's first supersonic jet which began commercial service in 1976, would be permanently grounded from Oct. 2003.

Membership of the EU was approved with 84% support in a referendum in Hungary. Turn-out was 46%.

Parliamentary elections in Nigeria were won by the ruling People's Democratic Party (PDP), which claimed 213 of the 360 seats. Opposition groups and international observers were highly critical of the election process.

In Malta's general election the ruling Nationalists of Prime Minister Eddie Fenech Adami won 34 out of 65 seats and 51.7% of the vote.

Chronology of Events for March 2003

Week Beginning 30 March 2003

The US House of Representatives approved a package providing around US$80 bn. to finance the war in Iraq, provide aid for allies, combat terrorism and support US airlines.

Teburoro Tito, president of Kiribati, resigned after losing a no-confidence motion in parliament. The opposition motion won 21 out of the 40 available votes.

The National Commission on Terrorist Attacks in the United States held its first public hearing into the 11 Sept. attacks. The 10-member body, headed by New Jersey governor Tom Kean, sits in New York and was established in 2002 to investigate intelligence failings.

EU forces began peacekeeping duties in Macedonia, the first time the EU had undertaken such work without NATO or American assistance.

Malaŵi's President Bakili Muluzi, scheduled to leave office in 2004, dismissed his cabinet after a dispute over his choice of successor.

The World Health Organisation issued a global alert concerning Severe Acute Respiratory Syndrome (SARS), which was particularly virulent in Asia.

The Presidential Movement (comprising the Union for the Benin of the Future, the African Movement for Development and Progress, the Key Force 5 and smaller parties) won 52 of 83 seats in Benin's general elections. Rebirth of Benin won 15 and Democratic Renewal 11.

Pier Marino Menicucci of the Christian Democrats and Giovanni Giannoni of the Socialist Party were sworn in as captains-regent of San Marino.

Week Beginning 23 March 2003

Václav Klaus was elected president by the Czech parliament, beating Jan Sokol in a run-off. It was parliament's third attempt in 6 weeks to choose a successor to Václav Havel, whose term of office ended in early-Feb. 2003.

Fighting between members of the Ijaw ethnic group and the military in Warri in Nigeria's Delta state led to the shut-down of operations by the three major oil companies, Shell, Chevron, and TotalFinaElf. Production losses amounted to 40% of oil production (767,500 barrels a day) and cost US$56 m. in 3 days.

Membership of the EU and NATO was approved in a twin referendum in Slovenia. Accession to the EU won 89.6% support while NATO membership received 66% backing.

The UN agreed to reinstate Iraq's oil-for-food programme, which was halted at the outbreak of war. Several UN security council members, including Syria, France, Russia and China, emphasised that resumption of the programme did not signify UN backing for the US-led invasion.

Russia delayed ratifying a US-Russian strategic arms control treaty until the war in Iraq ended.

North Korea withdrew from border liaison negotiations with US officials and parliament increased its defence budget. Pyongyang had earlier claimed that joint military exercises between the US and South Korea, which coincided with the Iraqi invasion, were a sign that the US intended to launch strikes on the North's nuclear establishments. North Korea also accused Japan of a 'hostile act' after it launched two spy satellites.

India and Pakistan both held tests of short-range, nuclear-capable missiles.

Russia's President Vladimir Putin promised greater autonomy for Chechnya. The announcement followed a referendum in Chechnya in favour of a new constitution which would keep Chechnya within Russia but provide a new president and parliament for the republic. Moscow claimed there was 95% turn-out for the vote although no international observers were present. The referendum was opposed by rebel separatist groups.

Gen. François Bozizé appointed Abel Goumba as prime minister of a transitional government in Central African Republic.

Amnesty International reported that up to 500 people had been arrested after a recent general strike in Zimbabwe. Members of the opposition Movement for Democratic Change were especially targeted. The Commonwealth of Nations earlier extended Zimbabwe's suspension until at least Dec. 2003.

Week Beginning 16 March 2003

US and coalition forces launched attacks on Iraq after the expiration of US President George W. Bush's ultimatum demanding the exile of Saddam Hussein and his sons. The US, UK and Spain had earlier ended attempts to engineer the passage of a new resolution through the UN security council authorizing the use of force after France reiterated its intention to veto such a motion.

In Cuba Fidel Castro's government arrested political dissidents after US envoy James Cason met with opposition figures. The movement of diplomats within the county was restricted in a tit-for-tat move after the US imposed similar restrictions in Washington.

The UN announced that it would establish a Water Co-operation Facility in Paris to mediate in international water disputes.

Representatives of Côte d'Ivoire's leading rebel groups failed to attend the second cabinet meeting of Seydou Diarra's unity government.

In the Palestinian-Administered Territories Mahmoud Abbas accepted Yasser Arafat's invitation to fill the newly-created role of prime minister.

Following a national referendum, Crown Prince Hans-Adam II of Liechtenstein was granted the power to appoint and dismiss governments at will.

Maxwell Richards was sworn in as president of Trinidad and Tobago, having been elected by parliament in Feb. by 43 votes against 25 for the opposition candidate Ganace Ramdial.

The UN human rights commission met in Libya for its annual 6-week session.

The Cambodian government is to establish a special court in partnership with the UN to try leaders of the Khmer Rouge, the regime of Pol Pot held responsible for the deaths of between 1 m. and 2.5 m. people in the 1970s.

In El Salvador's parliamentary elections, the FMLN (National Liberation Front) gained 31 of a possible 84 seats in the Legislative Assembly. ARENA, the party of President Francisco Flores Pérez, won 27, the Party of National Conciliation 16, the Democratic United Centre 5 and the Christian Democrat Party 5.

In Finland's parliamentary elections, the Centre Party won 55 of the available 200 seats (24.7% of the vote). The Social Democrats of Prime Minister Paavo Lipponen won 53 seats (24.5%). The National Coalition Party claimed 40 seats (18.5%), the Left Alliance 19 (9.9%), the Greens 14 (8%), the Christian Democrats 7 (5.3%) and the Swedish People's Party 8 (4.6%).

The US launched a military operation in Afghanistan's Kandahar province in a hunt for members of the Taliban and the al-Qaeda terrorist network.

In Central African Republic Gen. François Bozizé seized power from Ange-Félix Patassé in a coup.

The US senate voted against plans to search for oil in Alaska's Arctic National Wildlife Reserve.

Week Beginning 9 March 2003

North Korea launched a short-range anti-ship missile in the direction of the Sea of Japan, the second such missile test in 2 weeks.

UN-brokered talks between the leaders of the Greek and Turkish sectors of Cyprus, Tassos Papadopoulos and Rauf Denktaş, failed with neither side accepting UN proposals for the island's reunification.

The Japanese government refused calls to extradite immediately Peru's former president Alberto Fujimori who fled Peru in 2000 amid a corruption scandal.

53.6% of voters in a referendum supported Malta joining the EU in 2004. Turnout was 91%.

Tayyip Erdogan, leader of the Justice and Development Party (AK), was appointed Turkey's prime minister. His party deputy, Abdullah Gül, stood down from the premiership after Erdogan won a parliamentary seat in a by-election. Erdogan led the AK to victory in the Nov. 2002 elections but was ineligible for the premiership owing to a 1998 conviction for breaking a now-defunct religious law.

The six-times president of Nauru Bernard Dowiyogo died aged 57 in Washington, D.C. after heart surgery. Derog Gioura was appointed acting president.

Serbian Prime Minister Zoran Djindjić was shot dead outside Belgrade's government offices. The government declared a state of emergency and blamed an organized crime gang for the killing.

The permanent war crimes tribunal's first 18 judges, comprising 11 men and seven women, have been sworn in at The Hague.

Svetozar Marović was chosen by parliament to be Serbia and Montenegro's first president.

Chilean President Ricardo Lagos refused economics minister Jorge Rodriguez's resignation after the executive vice president of Corfo, the state business development agency, was forced to resign and the head of Corfo's treasury department was charged with fraud.

Hu Jintao was sworn in as China's president, succeeding Jiang Zemin. Zeng Qinghong was named vice president and Wen Jiabao prime minister.

The US authorized US$250 m. of aid for Pakistan, ending the last of its sanctions against the country implemented in 1999 after General Musharraf seized power in a coup.

Russia announced it was to close its last three plutonium-producing plants.

Week Beginning 2 March 2003

Iraq began destroying its al-Samoud II weapons in accordance with weapons inspectors' demands. Hans Blix, head of the inspections team, welcomed the news, calling it 'a very significant piece of real disarmament.' Meanwhile, the US and UK treated the move with scepticism and began attacks on anti-aircraft missile launchers in the southern no-fly zone.

The Turkish parliament has refused to allow the US to deploy tens of thousands of troops on its territory in advance of any war with Iraq. The decision imperils US$30 bn. worth of aid and loans from the US as well as a US$16 bn. IMF loan.

Germany, Russia and France announced their intention to block any proposed UN resolution permitting war in Iraq. The move caused a rift in the UN security council, with the US, UK and Spain pushing for a new resolution.

The president of the Palestinian Administered Territories, Yasser Arafat, nominated the PLO's general secretary Mahmoud Abbas as the administration's first prime minister. Arafat had agreed in principle to create the position following negotiations with representatives of the EU, the UN and Russia in Ramallah in Feb.

The US imposed economic sanctions on 77 members of Zimbabwe's ruling administration, including President Robert Mugabe. The sanctions, which freeze bank accounts and other assets and forbid Americans from any financial dealings with the 77, follow similar measures implemented by the EU.

Svetozar Marović was elected by the Serbia and Montenegrin parliament to be the country's first president. Deputy chairman of the Democratic Party of Socialists, Marović won 65 of the available 126 votes to head a five-man council overseeing foreign affairs, finance, defence, economic relations and human rights.

The Philippines suffered its most serious terrorist attack for 2 years when a bomb exploded at Davao airport, leaving 21 dead.

Khalid Sheikh Mohammed, believed by the US to be a senior al-Qaeda official and one of the key planners behind the 11 Sept. attacks, was arrested in Pakistan after a joint US-Pakistani operation.

Harry Marshall, a leading figure in Nigeria's All People's Party (APP), was murdered in the build-up to presidential elections in April. APP chairman Don Etiebet blamed President Olusegun Obasanjo and his People's Democratic Party (PDP), although the PDP condemned the killing.

Cuba's leader since 1959, Fidel Castro was re-elected to another 5 year term as president winning 100% of the 609 parliamentary votes.

In Belize's parliamentary elections the People's United Party of Prime Minister Said Musa won 21 of the 29 seats in the National Assembly.

Poland's prime minister Leszek Miller dismissed the Peasant Party from his coalition government after it failed to back his plans for a tax levy to improve the country's road infrastructure.

In Estonia's parliamentary election the leftwing Centre Party and the newly formed opposition conservative party Res Publica took 28 of 101 seats with 25.4% and 24.6% of votes respectively. Incumbent prime minister Siim Kallas's Reform Party secured 19 seats with 17.7%.

In Syria's parliamentary elections, the ruling National Progressive Front (led by the Baa'th Party) won 167 of 250 seats and independents the remaining 83. Turn-out was 63%.

In the Armenian presidential run-off between the two leading candidates, Robert Kocharyan won 67.5% of the vote against 32.5% for Stepan Demirchyan. Observers claimed the elections failed to meet international standards for a democratic poll.

In Micronesia's elections, President Leo Falcam has lost his seat for the state of Pohnpei to Resio Moses. Vice President Redley Killion, who secured the seat for the state of Chuuk, is a possible successor to Falcam, although the former speaker Jack Fritz is out of contention having lost to Killion.

Chronology of Events for February 2003

Week Beginning 23 February 2003

Former Zambian president Frederick Chiluba was charged with 66 counts of corruption centred around abuse of office and misuse of public money. Chiluba, elected in the country's first free vote in 1991, had his immunity from prosecution lifted after President Levy Mwanawasa, who succeeded Chiluba in 2002, accused him of involvement in an illegal arms deal. Chiluba denied the allegations.

South Korean President Roh Moo-hyun appointed former mayor of Seoul, Goh Kun, as prime minister. He had previously served in the position from 1997–98.

Israeli prime minister Ariel Sharon secured the support of the Shinui Party and the National Religious Party, allowing him to form a government with an overall majority. Sharon has been trying to form a workable government since Likud's electoral victory in Jan. 2003.

Zimbabwe's President Robert Mugabe attended a summit of African heads of state in Paris at the invitation of President Jacques Chirac, despite renewed EU sanctions banning Mugabe from entering the EU. Several EU governments and Zimbabwe's opposition expressed dissatisfaction at the invitation.

Following a 2 month debilitating national strike in Venezuela, one of three strike organizers, Carlos Fernández was arrested by Disip, the Venezuelan secret police. The president of the leading business Fedecámaras, Fernández was charged with treason and criminal conspiracy.

Václav Klaus was elected president by the Czech parliament. Klaus, a former prime minister, beat Jan Sokol in a run-off. It was parliament's third attempt in 6 weeks to choose a successor to Václav Havel, who stood down in early Feb. 2003.

In Kiribati's presidential election Teburoro Tito of the Mwaneaaban te Mauri Party was re-elected with 50.4% of votes cast, ahead of Taberannang Timeon of Boutokanto Koaava (Pillars of Truth) with 48.4% and Bakeua Bakeua Tekita with 1.2%.

Week Beginning 16 February 2003

Armenia's presidential elections went to a second round as no candidate took 50%. Incumbent Robert Kocharian took 48.3% of the vote, Stepan Demirchyan 27.3%, and Artashes Geghamyan 16.9%. Turn-out was 61.2%.

In Cyprus's presidential elections Tassos Papadopoulos of the Democratic Party defeated incumbent Glafcos Clerides after the first round of voting. Papadopoulos claimed 51.5% of the vote, rendering a second round unnecessary.

Mounir Al Motassadeq, a Moroccan, became the first person to be convicted in connection with the 11 Sept. terrorist attacks on the US. He was charged with 3,066 counts of accessory to murder and with membership of a terrorist organization. He was sentenced to 15 years for providing logistical support to a terrorist cell based in Hamburg.

Week Beginning 9 February 2003

The IAEA reported North Korea to the UN Security Council for failing to comply with nuclear non-proliferation accords. Pyongyang responded by asserting its capability to attack US interests throughout the world if provoked. It also declared that it would consider UN-imposed sanctions as a declaration of war. Japan said it would use military force to repel any threat from North Korea while China urged the UN to support on-going negotiations with Pyongyang.

A bomb exploded in Colombia in the southwestern town of Neiva killing 17 people. A week earlier a bomb detonated outside a social club in Bogotá killing 33 people and injuring around 160. In reaction, 20,000 people attended a peace rally in the capital. Several government ministers blamed the attack on the leftwing guerrilla group Farc. Leaders from the Central American countries signed a declaration of support for Colombia. A state of emergency was announced in Aug. 2002.

British Petroleum (BP) announced a US\$6.75 bn. investment into the Russian oil industry, aiming to create a new company producing 1.2 m. barrels of crude oil per day.

The Bolivian government abandoned plans to raise income tax to 12.5% after popular protests in La Paz led to the deaths of around 30 people and injuries to 100 more when government forces clashed with protesters.

The Iranian government announced plans to enrich uranium as part of a non-aggressive nuclear power programme. The US and EU responded by requesting Iran submit to increased levels of international inspections.

Paraguay's President Luis González Macchi survived a Senate vote to impeach him for allegedly misspending 115.6 bn. guaranís (\$17 m.) of government money. Voting 22 to 18 against him, the motion failed to attain the two thirds of votes needed to oust him from power.

In a referendum in Switzerland 70.3% of voters have accepted to extend direct democracy giving the electorate more influence over international treaties and domestic legislation. Turn-out was 28%.

In Monaco's parliamentary elections the ruling National Democratic Union lost power, winning only 3 of 24 seats. 21 seats were won by the opposition Union for Monaco. Turn-out was 80%.

Montenegro's elections failed for the second time to produce a president as turn-out was 47.7%, below the required 50%. Filip Vujanović again took the majority of the votes with 81.5% ahead of Dragan Hajduković (7.1%) and Aleksandar Vasilijević (3.9%). As parliamentary speaker, Vujanović remained acting head of state.

The parliament of Trinidad and Tobago's elected Maxwell Richards as president by 43 votes to 25 for Ganace Ramdial. Richard's, who does not represent any political party, will replace Arthur Robinson.

Week Beginning 2 February 2003

The Yugoslavian parliament voted 110 to 38 in favour of replacing the Yugoslav federation with a new single entity called Serbia and Montenegro. The parliaments of both Serbia and Montenegro also accepted the plan.

For the second time in a month the Czech parliament failed to choose a new president when no candidate secured the requisite 50% support from parliament. Václav Klaus (Civic Democratic Party) took 45% of the vote against 26% for Jaroslava Moserova (Christian Democratic Party). Václav Havel stood down from the presidency.

A 2 month national strike in Venezuela called by the opposition of President Hugo Chávez abated with many businesses, banks and schools reopening.

Following a narrow victory in the 2002 German general elections, results from Diet elections showed a defeat for Gerhard Schröder's Social Democrats in the chancellor's traditional stronghold of Lower Saxony and in Hessen, while the opposition Christian Democratic Union (CDU) increased its standing in the Bundesrat. The results were considered a reaction to unpopular economic measures introduced by Schröder since his re-election, as well as his perceived failure to tackle effectively a depressed economy and labour market.

The US stationed 113,000 troops in the Gulf while the UK committed 43,000. Other countries to have sent military representation include Australia, whose prime minister John Howard received domestic criticism for supporting the US and sending 2,000 troops. The senate passed a symbolic vote of no-confidence by 33 votes to 31.

Chronology of Events for January 2003

Week Beginning 26 January

In a report to the Security Council, Hans Blix (head of the UN weapons inspection team) criticized Iraq's insufficient cooperation and said the investigations neither proved nor disproved that Iraq has a nuclear weapons programme. But he added that 1,000 tonnes of chemical agents and 8,500 litres of anthrax remained unaccounted for. In reply, the Iraqi ambassador to the UN reiterated Iraq would comply with further inspections. The US said neither report altered its view that Iraq has no intention of disarming, although China, France and Russia said the inspectors should be given more time.

Nine European countries—Britain, Spain, Denmark, Poland, Italy, Portugal, Slovakia, Hungary and the Czech Republic—called for Europe to unite behind the US.

The head of the IAEA Mohamed El Baradei said he did not believe Iraq is in material breach of Resolution 1441, which requires that Iraq disarm, provide full access to sensitive sites and disclose its weapons programmes.

The US space shuttle *Columbia* broke up on its return flight to NASA's Kennedy Space Center. The aircraft exploded when entering the earth's atmosphere over Texas killing all seven astronauts.

Prime Minister Ariel Sharon's rightwing Likud party, having campaigned on security and defence, won Israel's general elections. The party's standing in the 120-seat Knesset increased from 19 to 37 seats, while the main opposition party Avoda (Labour) lost four seats (23 to 19). The secular centrist party Shinui more than doubled its standing winning 15 seats to become the third largest party while ultra-orthodox Shas lost six seats (17 to 11). Ahead of the elections, all Palestinian territories were closed off following an incursion into Gaza City by the Israeli army in which 12 people were killed and more than 40 injured. Previously rockets had been fired from the area at the Israeli town of Sderot.

Richard Reid, a British citizen, has been sentenced to life imprisonment at a court in Boston for attempting to blow up a transatlantic flight on 22 Dec. 2001 using explosives packed in his shoes.

Côte d'Ivoire's President Laurent Gbagbo and representatives of the major political parties and two of the three main rebel groups agreed a peace deal to resolve a 4 month long conflict. Under its terms Gbagbo remains president but a prime minister, approved by 'consensus', will serve along side him until elections in 2005. Seydou Diarra was appointed prime minister. The deal sparked protests in Abidjan by tens of thousands of Gbagbo supporters.

There was fighting in Afghanistan between rebel forces and US and coalition troops near Spin Boldak, close to Afghanistan's southern border with Pakistan. The rebels were believed to be led by faction leader Gulbuddin Hekmatyar.

Week Beginning 19 January

Talks between Hans Blix, Mohamed El Baradei (head of the IAEA) and the Iraqi government resulted in the promise of increased co-operation from Baghdad. The ten-point agreement included Iraq appointing a team of munitions investigators and permitting private interviews between Blix's inspectors and Iraqi scientists.

The US boosted its presence in the Gulf region to over 150,000 military personnel while the UK stationed around 35,000 troops, considerably exceeding earlier estimates of the UK contribution. Both US and UK officials have suggested military action could be avoided if Saddam Hussein went into exile, possibly with the promise of immunity. Large-scale anti-war protests took place throughout the world.

Milan Milutinović, Serbia's former president, surrendered to the international war crimes tribunal in The Hague. President from 1997 until 2002, he was indicted in 1999 along with Slobodan Milošević for his role during the 1998–99 Kosovo war in the persecution, deportation and murder of ethnic Albanians.

In the Dutch elections the ruling Christian Democratic Appeal (CDA) won 44 seats, while the social democratic PvdA's standing rose from 23 seats in 2002 to 42. List Pim Fortuyn's (LPF) representation dropped from 26 to 8.

Libya was appointed host of the annual meeting of the UN Commission on Human Rights on 17 March-23 April 2003. Nominated by African members, Libya's appointment raised concern among human rights groups, and led the US to demand a vote. The ballot by commission members resulted in 33 favourable votes to three, with 17 abstentions.

In Cuba's parliamentary elections 609 candidates, including President Fidel Castro, stood unopposed for the 609 national assembly seats.

Week Beginning 12 January

Talks aimed at re-igniting the Israeli–Palestinian peace process opened in the UK, despite the Israeli government preventing Palestinian representatives from attending. Representatives from the UN, the EU, Jordan, Egypt, Russia and Saudi Arabia discussed a potential new constitution for the Palestinian Administered Territories.

After 4 months of fighting resulting from a failed coup in the Côte d'Ivoire in Sept. 2002, representatives of the government and rebel groups signed a ceasefire and met for peace talks in Paris.

A state of emergency was called after bush fires caused widespread chaos in the Australian capital, Canberra. The fires burned for several days, killing four people and forcing thousands more to leave their homes.

The former army colonel and leader of a short-lived coup Lucío Gutiérrez, was sworn in as Ecuador's president.

Tens of thousands of people protested in the Indian province of Manipur in response to talks between the national government and the National Socialist Council of Nagaland (NSCN), which has demanded a greater Naga state since 1954. The government and NSCN met in Delhi in early Jan. to hold the first joint talks in 37 years. Although the future of the Nagas remained unresolved, the declaration by Thuingaleng Muivah that 'the war is over' led to concern in Nagaland's neighbouring states of Manipur, Arunachal Pradesh and Assam.

Week Beginning 5 January 2003
In Lithuania's presidential run-off, Rolandas Paksas of the Lithuanian Liberal Union won an unexpected victory over incumbent Valdas Adamkus, gaining 54.9% of votes to 45.1%.

North Korea withdrew from the nuclear Non-Proliferation Treaty with immediate effect, although the government claimed it had no intention of producing nuclear weapons.

In Djibouti's parliamentary elections, the Union for a Presidential Majority, a coalition of RPP (People's Rally for Progress) and FRUD (Front for the Restoration of Unity and Democracy), won all 65 seats with 62.2% of votes cast, against 36.9% for the Union for a Democratic Alternative.

Relations between Pakistan and India were strained by reported comments by India's defence minister George Fernandes that Pakistan would be destroyed in the event of a nuclear war with India. His speech followed President Musharraf's assertion that in the event of conflict, India should expect a 'non conventional war,' although a spokesman for Pakistan denied this referred to a nuclear strike.

2002

Chronology of Events for December 2002

Week Beginning 29 December 2002
Turkey's President Ahmet Necdet Sezer agreed to constitutional changes which allow the previously banned Recep Tayyip Erdogan, leader of the governing Justice and Development Party, to stand for a parliamentary seat and thus become eligible for the premiership.

Pascal Couchepin was sworn in as Swiss president for a 12 month term.

Luiz Inácio Lula da Silva of the Workers' Party was sworn in as Brazilian president. 200,000 people took to the streets in Brasília to celebrate his inauguration.

The Togo national assembly amended the constitution to allow President Gnassingbé Eyadéma, in power since 1967, to stand for re-election in 2004.

Pakistan's Prime Minister Mir Zafarullah Khan Jamali won a mandatory national assembly confidence vote by 188 of a possible 342 votes.

Week Beginning 22 December 2002
In Montenegro, Acting President Filip Vujanović of the Democratic Party of Montenegrin Socialists defeated three opponents in the race for the presidency, claiming 86.3% of votes. However, the result was declared invalid because turn-out was under 50%.

In Kenya, Mwai Kibaki of the National Rainbow Coalition won a landslide victory in the presidential election, ousting the KANU party for the first time since Kenya won independence in 1963. Kibaki defeated the KANU candidate Uhuru Kenyatta by 62.2% of votes to 31.3%.

Week Beginning 15 December 2002
The government of the Democratic Republic of Congo and leading rebel forces reached a power-sharing agreement aimed at ending the 4 year war. Joseph Kabila will remain as president until elections scheduled for 2004 and all groups will have representation in the cabinet.

Incumbent President Gen. Teodoro Obiang Nguema Mbasogo won with 99.5% of the vote in Equatorial Guinea's presidential election. Opposition candidates withdrew within 2 h of the polls opening, alleging malpractice.

US President George W. Bush ordered ten anti-ballistic interceptor missiles to be ready for deployment by 2004. The order is the first stage in the implementation of the United States's 'Son of Star Wars' missile defence system.

At the ANC party conference, South African president Thabo Mbeki was re-elected party chairman for a 4 year term.

Bulgaria announced the closure by 2006 of four of its six Soviet-style nuclear reactors on the country's sole nuclear power plant in Kozloduy (dating from the 1970s). The two oldest will close by 2003.

I Love Madagascar, the party of President Marc Ravalomanana, dominated Madagascar's parliamentary elections, winning 103 of the 160 available seats. The National Unity coalition won 22 seats, 22 seats went to independents and the remaining seats were shared by minor parties.

Myanmese leader Senior Gen. Than Shwe and Khaleda Zia, prime minister of Bangladesh, signed accords on closer economic cooperation and improved road and shipping links. Ties between the two governments were strained in the early 1990s, when up to 250,000 Muslim Rohingya refugees entered Bangladesh from Myanmar.

Roh Moo-hyun, the candidate of the Millennium Democratic Party, won South Korea's presidential elections, with 48.9% of the vote against 46.6% for Lee Hoi Chang, candidate of the Grand National Party.

Turkey was given a start date of Dec. 2004 for EU accession talks.

Adnan Terzić was elected prime minister by the parliament of Bosnia-Herzegovina.

Week Beginning 8 December 2002
A ceasefire was signed by the Burundi government and the country's principal rebel movement, the Forces for the Defence of Democracy.

The Indonesian government and the separatist Free Aceh Movement signed an internationally brokered peace deal to end separatist violence. In exchange for disarmament, Aceh, a province on Sumatra, was granted autonomy and self government from 2004.

Serbia's presidential elections were again declared invalid after the third round owing to a turn-out lower than the legally-required 50%. Yugoslav president Vojislav Koštunica took around 58% of votes to Vojislav Seselj's 36% and Borislav Pelevic's 4%. Parliamentary Speaker Nataša Micic was nominated interim president from Jan. 2003.

The North Korean government announced plans to re-activate a nuclear plant, unused since 1994. Earlier in the week US and Spanish ships seized a cargo of scud missiles travelling from North Korea to Yemen, although the shipment was later allowed to continue to Yemen.

The Sri Lankan government and the LTTE (Tamil Tigers) signed a peace deal to end a 19 year long conflict. One of its conditions was Tamil regional autonomy.

Week Beginning 1 December 2002
A national strike was begun by opponents of Venezuelan president Hugo Chávez after the Supreme Court's overruled a presidential referendum called for Feb. 2003. The strike centred on the state-owned petrol company.

Six months after US President George W. Bush called for a 'provisional Palestinian state', Ariel Sharon responded with a plan to grant Palestine around 40% of the West Bank. This would have to be kept demilitarized and Israel would maintain control over all points of entry and exit and over airspace. Sharon did not put a timeframe to the plan, stating that negotiations would not begin until Palestinian violence ended and Yasser Arafat was removed from power. The Palestinian authorities declared the proposals 'unacceptable'.

In the run-off for the Slovenian presidency Prime Minister Janez Drnovšek won with 56.5% of votes cast against 43.5% for Barbara Brezigar. Anton Rop is to succeed Drnovšek as prime minister.

The Colombian paramilitary organization the AUC announced a unilateral ceasefire.

The US secretary of the treasury Paul O'Neill resigned. The businessman John Snow was nominated his successor.

Serbia and Montenegro agreed a constitutional charter which would replace the Yugoslav Republic with the Union of Serbia and Montenegro. The union, also comprising Kosovo, would share a common foreign and defence policy.

In Greenland's parliamentary elections Siumut (Social Democratic) won ten of 31 seats, Inuit Ataqatigiit (leftist) eight, Atássut (Liberal) seven and the Democrats five. Turn-out was 75%.

Chronology of Events for November 2002

Week Beginning 24 November 2002
In Austria's parliamentary elections, Chancellor Wolfgang Schüssel's People's Party took 42.3% of votes, the Social Democratic Party won 36.9%, while the far right People's Party took 10.2%.

In the second round of Ecuador's presidential elections, Lucio Gutiérrez, an ex-army head and instigator of a coup in 2000, beat populist businessman Alvaro Noboa with 54.3% of votes.

Sixteen people were killed by a bomb explosion at an Israeli-owned hotel in the coastal resort of Mombasa, while a failed missile attack targeted an aeroplane leaving the city for Tel Aviv.

Montenegro's president Milo Djukanović was appointed prime minister, while Prime Minister Filip Vujanović was made acting president.

A Swiss referendum on tightening the country's immigration laws to reduce the number of people seeking asylum was rejected by 50.1% of votes. Turn-out was 47%. The referendum had been proposed in 1999 by the Swiss People's Party.

Week Beginning 17 November 2002
UN weapons inspectors arrived in Iraq.

Fernando da Piedade Dias dos Santos was appointed prime minister of Angola.

Over 200 people were killed during rioting between Muslims and Christians in the northern Nigerian city of Kaduna. The violence was sparked by tension surrounding the hosting of an international beauty pageant in Abuja and a newspaper article considered offensive by Muslims.

NATO invited Romania, Bulgaria, Latvia, Estonia, Lithuania, Slovakia and Slovenia to join the alliance in 2004.

The EU, Japan and South Korea suspended fuel oil shipments to North Korea.

Mir Zafarullah Khan Jamali, leader of the pro-President Musharraf Pakistan Muslim League (Quaid-e-Azam), was elected Pakistan's prime minister with 172 of 328 parliamentary votes, ahead of Maulana Fazlur Rehman (86 votes).

Week Beginning 10 November 2002
In Turkey, the chairman of the Justice and Development Party, Abdullah Gül, was appointed prime minister.

Chechen president Aslan Maskhadov appointed Mikhail Babich as prime minister to replace Stanislav Ilyasov who resigned the previous week.

In Slovenia's presidential election, Janez Drnovšek, the Liberal Democrat nominee and favoured candidate of presidential incumbent Milan Kučan, polled 44.4% while his nearest rival, Barbara Brezigar, won 30.8%. Since no candidate secured the 50% needed for outright victory, a run-off was scheduled for 1 Dec. 2002.

Chinese President Jiang Zemin and Prime Minister Zhu Rongji announced their retirements. The current vice president Hu Jintao was announced as Jiang's successor.

Ukrainian Prime Minister Anatolii Kinakh was dismissed by President Leonid Kuchma and replaced with Viktor Yanukovich.

Week Beginning 3 November 2002
In US mid-term elections President George W. Bush's Republicans won control of the Senate, taking 51 of 100 seats, and consolidated their dominance in the House of Representatives with 227 of 435 seats. Bush is the first Republican president to make mid-term gains since President Roosevelt in 1934.

Senegal's president Abdoulaye Wade dismissed Prime Minister Madior Boye and all government. Idrissa Seck was appointed her successor. In early Oct. the transport minister Youssou Sakho and the armed forces minister Youba Sambou resigned following the death of around 1,000 people in the sinking of a state-operated ferry.

In Turkey's parliamentary elections the Justice and Development Party (AKP) won 363 of the 550 seats, against 178 seats for the Republican People's Party (CHP). Prime Minister Bülent Ecevit's Democratic Left Party took 1% of votes, failing to secure the 10% of votes needed for parliamentary representation. Ecevit subsequently resigned.

Despite surviving a confidence vote, Israeli Prime Minster Ariel Sharon called early elections for Jan. 2003.

Einars Repse was appointed Latvian prime minister.

In a referendum in Gibraltar, voters rejected shared sovereignty with Spain by 99%. Turn-out was 88%. Neither Spain nor Britain recognized the referendum.

Chronology of Events for October 2002

Week Beginning 27 October 2002
Israel's coalition government collapsed when all members of the Labour Party resigned following a dispute over budget proposals.

Luiz Inácio Lula da Silva of the Workers' Party won Brazil's presidential run-off taking 61% to 38% of votes won by the Social Democracy Party's José Serra.

The Czech Republic, Poland, Hungary, Estonia, Latvia, Lithuania, Cyprus, Malta, Slovenia and Slovakia were nominated to join the EU in 2004.

A Chechen politician, Ahmed Zakayev, was arrested in Copenhagen at Russia's request on suspicion of involvement in a siege of a Moscow theatre by Chechen rebels. The Danish authorities later released him.

Branko Crvenkovski became Macedonia's prime minister.

A new cabinet appointed by Palestinian Administered Territories President Yasser Arafat was approved by parliament by 56 votes to 18.

Mufti Mohammad Sayeed was appointed Chief Minister of Jammu and Kashmir.

The Ruling Togolese People's Assembly party of President Gnassingbé Eyadéma won 72 seats in the 81-seat national assembly, down from 79 seats in 1999.

The Somali government and rebel groups signed a ceasefire in Eldoret, Kenya.

Week Beginning 20 October 2002
Ireland voted to support EU expansion by 62.9% to 37.1%.

In Montenegro's parliamentary elections, President Milo Djukanović's pro-independence Democratic List for a European Montenegro won 39 out of 75 seats while the 'Together for Changes' coalition won 30.

A siege of a Moscow theatre, in which 800 people were held hostage by Chechen rebels for 3 days, ended when Russian troops stormed the building. An anaesthetic gas, used to combat the rebels, also killed over 100 hostages.

In the first round of Ecuador's presidential elections, populist businessman Alvaro Noboa took 17.5% of votes while Lucio Gutiérrez, an ex-army head and instigator of a coup in 2000, won 19%.

A year after a failed coup in 2001, rebel forces believed to be loyal to the former army chief François Bozizé attempted to depose Central African Republic president Ange-Félix Petassé.

The first national elections since Dec. 1973 were held in Bahrain. 21 out of 40 seats were won by secular candidates, with the remaining seats going to Sunni and Shia representatives.

Week Beginning 13 October 2002
Northern Ireland's power-sharing executive was dissolved for the fourth time in 3 years and rule of the province returned to London.

The centre right coalition government of Dutch prime minister Jan Peter Balkenende collapsed after discord within the List Pim Fortuyn party forced the resignation of deputy prime minister Eduard Bomhoff and economy minister Herman Heinsbroek, both of the LPF.

Iraqi leader Saddam Hussein took 100% of votes in a referendum to extend his rule for a further 7 years.

A project to install a new pumping station in Lebanon which will provide villages with 3.6 m. cu. metres of water per year from the Wazzani River was criticized by Israel as a misappropriation of common resources. After Lebanon, the Wazzani flows through Jordan and ultimately into the Sea of Galilee.

The run-off for the Serbian presidency between Yugoslavian President Vojislav Koštunica and Deputy Prime Minster Miroljub Labus was declared invalid after turn-out was less than the legally-required 50%.

Jamaica's People's National Party secured a fourth consecutive term of office winning 34 seats (down from 50 in 1997), while the Jamaica Labour Party (JLP) took 26 seats (up from 10 in 1997).

Myanmar's border with Thailand re-opened. The border was closed in May after Myanmar accused Thailand of assisting Myanmese rebels fighting with the Myanmese army along the border.

Week Beginning 6 October 2002
In Kashmir's elections the ruling pro-India National Conference won 28 of the 87 seats (57 in 1996); the Indian Congress Party won 20 (7 in 1996); the People's Democratic Party, 16; and the Bharatiya Janata Party, 1 (8 in 1996). There was ongoing violence and voter intimidation throughout the elections and turn-out was estimated at 46%.

A bomb explosion on the tourist island of Bali killed over 180 people including many foreign nationals.

Russia and Georgia agreed to joint patrols on their shared border. Russia had earlier accused Georgia of allowing Chechen rebels to operate in the area.

In Trinidad and Tobago's parliamentary election Prime Minister Patrick Manning's People's National Movement won 20 of 36 seats against 16 seats for the opposition United National Congress. Turn-out was 69.8%.

In Pakistan's general elections the pro-Musharraf Pakistan Muslim League (Quaid-e-Azam) took 77 of 272 seats, former prime minister Benazir Bhutto's Pakistan People's Party won 62, a coalition of six Islamic parties, Muttahida Majlis-e-Amal, won 52 and the Pakistan Muslim League (Nawaz Sharif) of exiled former prime minister Nawaz Sharif took 14 seats.

The International Court of Justice awarded Cameroon ownership of the disputed Bakassi Peninsula in the Gulf of Guinea, which had been claimed by Nigeria.

Nepal's King Gyanendra appointed Lokendra Bahadur Chand as prime minister.

Driss Jettou was appointed Moroccan prime minister by King Muhammad VI.

Chronology of Events for September 2002

Week Beginning 29 September 2002

The US House of Representatives granted President George Bush the right to use 'necessary and appropriate' force against Saddam Hussein. The US continued to demand details of Iraq's chemical, biological and nuclear weapons programmes before inspectors would be allowed to re-enter the country.

After a 10-day siege by the Israeli army, President Yasser Arafat left his destroyed muqata'a, or compound, in Ramallah. The Israeli incursion had attracted widespread international criticism and protests from Palestinians. Israel had accused Arafat of harbouring wanted militants in the compound.

A US envoy visited North Korea, one of the countries President George Bush labelled an 'axis of evil'.

The Dalai Lama, the exiled spiritual leader of Tibet, and the Chinese government made their first formal contact since 1993.

In the first round of Serbia's election, Yugoslavian president Vojislav Koštunica and Deputy Prime Minister Miroljub Labus beat the favoured candidate of former premier Slobodan Milošević, Vojislav Seselj, to go into the second round run off.

Swedish prime minister Göran Persson won a confidence vote 174 to 158.

Cuba hosted its largest trade fair to include the US since the imposition of a trade embargo in 1962.

In Latvia the New Era party gained victory, taking 26 out of a possible 100 seats. The For Human Rights in a United Latvia alliance came second, while Latvia's Way, the party of out-going prime minister Andris Berzins, polled less than 5%.

Nepal's King Gyanendra sacked Prime Minister Sher Bahadur Deuba, the first such dismissal since multi-party democracy was introduced in 1990.

In Bosnia-Herzegovina's parliamentary elections, the Party for Democratic Action won ten seats with 32.5% of the vote, against five seats for both the Croat Democratic Union and the Serb Democratic Party. Sulejman Tihić, Dragan Čović and Mirko Šarović were elected to the three-member rotating presidency.

Maria das Neves was appointed prime minister of São Tomé e Príncipe.

Week Beginning 22 September 2002

The president of São Tomé e Príncipe Fradique de Menezes dismissed Prime Minister Gabriel Costa's cabinet.

Gerhard Schröder's Social Democrat-Green coalition government retained power with a much reduced majority of nine seats in elections to the Bundestag. The Social Democrats and the Christian Democratic/Social Union, the party of Schröder's main rival Edmund Stoiber, tied with 38.5% of the vote. The strong showing of the Greens (8.6%) and the weak return for Stoiber's ally, the Free Democrats (7.4%), ensured a further term for Schröder.

Mathias Reichhold was appointed leader of Austria's Freedom Party. The Austrian parliament was dissolved in preparation for a general election.

In India a nationwide strike was called following a raid on a Hindu temple in Gujarat in which 27 people died. A Muslim militant organization was blamed for the attack.

In Morocco's parliamentary elections the Socialist USFP (Union Socialiste des Forces Populaires) reduced its standing from 57 seats to 50, but took two more seats than the second place conservative PI (Istiqlal/ Parti d'Indépendence). The moderate Islamic party PJD (Parti de la Justice et du Développement) increased its standing from 14 to 42 seats, while the RNI (Rassemblement National des Indépendants) won 41. Turnout was 51.6%.

Week Beginning 15 September 2002

The Social Democrats, led by incumbent Prime Minister Göran Persson, won the Swedish general election. The opposition Moderate Alliance Party, second with 15.2% of the vote, had their worst election result since 1973.

An offer by Iraq to allow UN Security Council weapon inspectors to return was viewed sceptically by the US.

Macedonian Prime Minister Ljubčo Georgievski's Internal Macedonian Revolutionary Organization-Democratic Party for Macedonian National Unity was defeated in a general election. The new government will be headed by the Social Democratic League.

The Japanese prime minister Junichiro Koizumi met North Korean leader Kim Jong-il to discuss the re-establishment of diplomatic ties between the two countries.

After 19 years of civil war, peace talks brokered by Norwegian negotiators began between the Sri Lankan government and Tamil rebels.

An attempted coup in Côte d'Ivoire failed, although fighting continued between the government and rebel troops. The country's former military leader and suspected coup instigator, Gen. Robert Guéï, was killed in the initial fighting.

In Slovakia's parliamentary elections former prime minister Vladimír Mečiar's Movement for a Democratic Slovakia (HZDS) won the largest share of the vote with 19.5%. The Slovak Democratic and Christian Union of prime ministerial incumbent Mikuláš Dzurinda came second with 15.1%. With HZDS having no political allies, Dzurinda will continue to lead a centre-right coalition.

Week Beginning 8 September 2002

Chancellor Wolfgang Schüssel's governing coalition, incorporating his Austrian People's Party and the Austrian Freedom Party, collapsed following the resignation of the Freedom Party's leader, Susanne Riess-Passer, as vice chancellor and those of her party colleagues, Karl-Heinz Grasser and Mathias Reichhold at the finance and transport ministries. The resignations followed internal party wrangling over proposed tax cuts.

Worldwide ceremonies were held to mark the first anniversary of the 11 Sept. terrorist attacks in the US.

The Palestinian Administered Territories parliament resigned, pre-empting a confidence vote.

In a speech to the UN, President George Bush urged that the Security Council should demand the immediate readmission of weapons inspectors to Iraq or military action would be 'unavoidable'. Bush accused Iraq of stockpiling weapons of mass destruction and of harbouring members of the al-Qaeda terrorist network.

Switzerland became the 190th member of the UN.

Cuba announced its intention to sign the Nuclear Non-Proliferation Treaty and to ratify the Treaty of Tlatelolco.

Kim Suk Soo was appointed South Korean prime minister.

Week Beginning 1 September 2002

North Korea prepared to receive the Japanese prime minister Junichiro Koizumi despite the absence of diplomatic ties.

In South Korea, Typhoon Rusa killed over 100 people and caused extensive damage to the road, rail and telecommunitions systems.

President Hamid Karzai survived an attempted assassination by a gunman in Kandahar. The attack happened just a few hours after ten people were killed and dozens injured by a car bomb in the capital, Kabul.

It was reported that Afghanistan was once again the largest cultivator of opium, ahead of Southeast Asia, producing an estimated 2,950 tonnes in 2002.

The sustainable development summit in Johannesburg ended with new targets agreed for improving sanitation and water around the world. Plans to support the growth of renewable energy were blocked by the US and the American secretary of state, Colin Powell, was heckled during his speech.

Gibraltar's government unilaterally declared it would hold a referendum in Nov. concerning proposals for shared sovereignty between the UK and Spain. The British government is not expected to recognize the result.

The Sri Lankan government lifted the ban on the Tamil Tigers in preparation for peace talks.

Uganda and the Democratic Republic of Congo signed a peace agreement to end a 4 year conflict.

As the sole candidate for Bangladesh's presidential elections, Iajuddin Ahmed was appointed president-elect.

Chronology of Events for August 2002

Week Beginning 25 August 2002
The Spanish judiciary imposed a 3 year suspension on the political wing of ETA, Herri Batasuna, as a reconvened parliament voted 295 to ten to ban the party after it failed to condemn the latest spate of terrorist attacks.

A 10-day World Development Summit opened in Johannesburg, 10 years after the first earth summit took place in Rio.

The former military ruler of the Central African Republic, Gen. André Kolingba, was sentenced to death in absentia for his involvement in an attempted coup in 2001.

The South Korean parliament vetoed President Kim Dae-jung's second successive candidate for prime minister, Chang Dae-Whan.

The Kenyan president Daniel T. arap Moi has sacked his vice president George Saitoti after 13 years in the position. This follows a dispute over who will succeed Moi, who is due to stand down at the end of 2002.

The Namibian president Sam Nujoma has replaced his prime minister Hage Geingob with Theo-Ben Gurirab. He also outlined plans outlined plans to confiscate 192 farms belonging to foreign absentee landlords.

North and South Korea agreed to begin the restoration of road and rail links between the two countries.

Week Beginning 18 August 2002
International condemnation followed the sentencing to death by stoning of a woman accused of adultery in Northern Nigeria.

Harry Wijnschenk replaced Mat Herben as leader of the Dutch party List Pim Fortuyn.

Week Beginning 11 August 2002
Widespread floods in Europe following torrential rain killed 60 people in Russia and caused severe damage in several cities including Prague and Dresden.

Colombian president Álvaro Uribe called a state of emergency following several days of violence which began on his inauguration.

After many Zimbabwean farm owners defied an expulsion deadline, President Robert Mugabe began to evict white farmers as part of his land distribution policy.

President Olusegun Obasanjo rejected Nigerian parliament's calls for his resignation.

Indonesia's constitution was changed to allow for a directly elected president and prime minister and an end the automatic allocation of seats to the military.

President Mohammad Khatami became the first Iranian leader to visit Afghanistan for 40 years.

Week Beginning 4 August 2002
The British foreign office representative Mike O'Brien became the first government minister since 1983 to visit Libya's leader Muammar Qadhafi.

Chang Dae-Whan was appointed South Korean prime minister. He replaced Chang Sang, whose appointment in July 2002 was vetoed by parliament.

The IMF allocated US$30 bn. to Brazil to help stave off economic crisis.

Amid continuing violence, the UN's demand for an Israeli withdrawal from Palestinian administered areas was rejected by President Sharon and the US government.

The Dutch party List Pim Fortuyn's leader Mat Herben resigned.

Bolivian congress elected Gonzalo Sánchez president with 84 votes to Evo Morales's 43.

A temporary US loan of $1.5 bn. allowed Uruguayan banks to reopen, a week after the government closed them in emergency economic measures. Uruguay later received a US$3.8 bn. IMF loan.

Chronology of Events for July 2002

Week Beginning 28 July 2002
The Rwandan president Paul Kagame and the Democratic Republic of Congo president Joseph Kabila signed a peace agreement to end a 4 year war.

Iraqi leader Saddam Hussein hinted he would allow the resumption of UN weapons inspection, but US foreign policy remained committed to changing the Iraqi regime.

Papua New Guinea's first post-independence leader, Sir Michael Somare, was re-elected prime minister when his National Alliance Party won 19 seats.

Incumbent prime minister Sir Mekere Morauta's People's Democratic Movement won 12 seats.

Saufatu Sopoanga defeated Amasone Kilei by eight votes to seven to become Tuvalu's prime minister.

Week Beginning 21 July 2002
Vietnam's national assembly reappointed President Tran Duc Luong and Prime Minister Phan Van Khai, both of the Communist party, to second terms.

The leader of the militant Palestinian group Hamas, Salah Shehada, was killed in an Israeli bomb strike on a Gaza City apartment block.

The Albanian prime minister Pandeli Majko resigned.

Dutch Prime Minister Jan Peter Balkenende, head of the Christian Democratic Alliance (CDA), took office at the head of a right of centre coalition.

After 19 years of civil war, a peace deal was signed between the Sudanese government and rebel forces, although some fighting continued.

In New Zealand elections, Prime Minister Helen Clark won a second term in office. Her Labour Party took 41.3% of votes while the opposition National Party recorded its worst result for 70 years with 20.3% of votes.

Week Beginning 14 July 2002
Prompted by the failing health of Prime Minister Bulent Ecevit, Turkey's coalition government was on the brink of collapse as many key ministers resigned. Ecevit attempted to halt the crisis by bringing forward elections from 2004 to Nov. 2002. Opposition parties called for the prime minister's resignation.

At the Bastille Day parade on the Champs Elysées, a lone gunman, later found to be an extreme far right militant, made a failed assassination attempt on the French president Jacques Chirac.

Following a March referendum, Switzerland formally applied to join the UN.

Avul Pakir Jainulabdeen Abdul Kalam was elected president by the Indian parliament outvoting Rival Likshmi Seghal by an overwhelming majority.

Paraguay's president Luis González Macchi called a state of emergency as the economic crisis deepened as a result of problems in neighbour Argentina.

Relations between Spain and Morocco were strained when Moroccan troops landed on the uninhabited island of Perejil 200 metres off the Moroccan coast. Morocco, a Spanish possession since 1668. Spanish troops retook the island, removing the six Moroccan soldiers and the Moroccan flag. Spanish foreign minister Ana Palacio agreed to withdraw troops on the condition Morocco did not reoccupy the island.

Week Beginning 7 July 2002
Chang Sang was appointed South Korea's first female prime minister.

The Italian parliament voted to allow the royal family to return from exile. In reaction to the family's support of Benito Mussolini during World War II, the 1948 constitution banned male members of the House of Savoy from Italy.

Chronology of Events for June 2002

Week Beginning 30 June 2002
An investigation was launched into a US air attack in the central Uruzgan province in which 48 members of a wedding party were killed and 117 wounded.

Vice chairman of the Afghan interim government and urban development minister, Haji Abdul Qadir was assassinated in Kabul by an unknown gunman.

Former Madagascan president Didier Ratsiraka went into exile in the Seychelles after several regions under his control were taken by troops loyal to President Marc Ravalomanana. Ratsiraka had refused to accept the result of the presidential elections.

The International Criminal Court, set up in The Hague to try war crimes and crimes against humanity, was established. The US provoked international criticism for requesting immunity. After threatening to withdraw peace keeping forces in Bosnia, it was granted a 12 month exemption.

Croatia's prime minister Ivica Racan resigned, citing differences within the five-party coalition government in part over the decision to hand over two suspected war criminals. He was reinstated 5 days later and survived a vote of confidence.

In Bolivia's presidential elections, leftwing candidate Evo Morales came a close second behind the liberal former president Gonzalo Sanchez de

Lozada winning 21% of votes to 22.5%. The narrow margin gives responsibility to congress to elect the president.

Week Beginning 23 June 2002
A naval battle in the Yellow Sea between North and South Korea killed four South Korean and around 30 North Korean sailors. The North Korean president blamed the US and South Korea for the attack. South Korean president Kim Dae-Jung suspended rice shipments to the north and demanded an apology.

In the second round of the Republic of Congo's general elections the Congolese Labour Party took the highest number of seats winning 43 of 137.

Israel called up 2,000 reservists to occupy five West Bank towns as part of a campaign to end suicide bombing.

The Albanian parliament elected Alfred Moisiu to suceed Rexhep Meidani as president.

The sacked prime minister of Togo, Agbeyome Messan Kodjo, was replaced by Koffi Sama.

US President George Bush laid out his proposals for the future of Israel and Palestine. He offered the Palestinians a 'provisional state' which could be up and running within 18 months, with a settlement over permanent borders agreed within 3 years. In return, Bush advocated an end to violence and the appointment of a new Palestinian Authority leadership.

Week Beginning 16 June 2002
In the second round of French general elections, the centre right coalition Union for the Presidential Majority, comprising President Jacques Chirac's Rally for the Republic and the Liberal Democracy party, took 33.7% of votes and gained 357 of 577 seats in the Assemblée Nationale. President Jacques Chirac confirmed Jean-Pierre Raffarin prime minister of a majority rightwing government. After its success in the first round presidential elections, the far right National Front Party failed to gain a single seat.

The Bangladeshi president A.Q.M. Badruddoza Chowdhury resigned. The speaker Jamiruddi Sircar was made acting president.

Week Beginning 9 June 2002
In Afghanistan's first post-Taliban elections, the Emergency Loya Jirga (Grand Council) elected the interim leader Hamid Karzai as president with a large majority.

In the Czech elections, the Social Democratic Party (CSSD) retained power with 30.2% of votes cast. The conservative Civic Democratic Party achieved 24.5%. CSSD leader Vladimír Špidla replaced Miloš Zeman as prime minister.

Chad's Prime Minister Nagoum Yamassoum resigned. He was replaced by Haroun Kabadi.

Week Beginning 2 June 2002
Celebrations marked the Golden Jubilee of Britain's Queen Elizabeth II's.

Tonga's King Taufa'ahau Tupou IV began legal action after his court jester, a Californian financial advisor, lost £18 m. in bad investments.

Chronology of Events for May 2002

Week Beginning 26 May 2002
In the first round of Colombia's presidential elections, the independent Alvaro Uribe Vélez won an outright victory. Uribe replaced Andrés Pastrana as president with 53.1% of votes to the Liberal Party's Horacio Serpa Uribe's 31.8%. The elections were clouded by violence from rightwing paramilitary group (AUC) and Marxist guerrillas (FARC). Combatting FARC activities in Colombia's continuing civil war was at the centre of Uribe's campaign.

In Algeria's parliamentary elections, the rejuvenated National Liberation Front, party of Prime Minister Ali Benflis, won 199 of 389 seats while President Abdelaziz Bouteflika's National Democratic Rally took 47. With terrorist activity in the run up to the elections, some opposition parties refused to take part. Turn out was 46.1%.

Péter Medgyessy replaced Viktor Orbán as Hungary's prime minister.

Week Beginning 19 May 2002
Timor-Leste became independent.

Mounting tension between India and Pakistan over the disputed border in Kashmir was further heightened by the assassination of the moderate Kashmiri separatist politician Abdul Ghani Lone.

In Vietnam's parliamentary elections Communist Party members won 447 of 498 seats. Turnout was 99.7%.

Fianna Fáil, the party of the Irish prime minister Bertie Ahern, won 81 of 166 seats in the general election, followed by Fine Gael with 31 seats.

In Kyrgyzstan, Prime Minister Kurmanbek Bakiyev resigned. His deputy prime minister Nikolai Tanayev was named acting prime minister.

Russian president Vladimir Putin and US president George Bush signed an anti-nuclear deal agreing to reduce their respective strategic nuclear warheads by two thirds over the next 10 years.

In Sierra Leone's presidential elections, Ahmed Tejan Kabbah was returned for a second 5 year term with 70.6% of votes. In Jan. Kabbah had declared the country's 10 year civil war at an end.

Week Beginning 12 May 2002
The siege in Bethlehem's Church of the Nativity, in which Palestinian militants and 200 civilians were trapped for over a month, culminated in the exile of 13 Palestinian militants to various European countries.

In a recount of the contested Madagascan elections, Marc Ravalomanana was declared president. Incumbent president Didier Ratsiraka rejected the result.

In the Dutch elections the rightwing List Pim Fortuyn, the party of the murdered politician Pim Fortuyn came second behind the Christian Democrats. The People's Party for Freedom and Democracy (VVD) and the Labour Party (PvdA) lost 14 seats and 22 seats respectively.

Sierra Leone president Ahmad Tejan Kabbah secured a third term in office taking 70.1% of votes to Ernest Koroma's 22.3%. Kabbah's Sierra Leone People's Party was also successful in parliamentary elections taking 83 of 112 seats. All People's Congress won 22.

In Mali's presidential elections second round run off, Amadou Toumani Touré beat Soumaïla Cissé by 64.4% of votes to 35.7%. Turnout was 30.2%.

Week Beginning 5 May 2002
The rightwing Dutch politician Pim Fortuyn was assassinated in The Hague by an animal rights activist. Leader of List Pim Fortuyn, which he had founded 3 months earlier on an anti-immigration platform, Fortuyn was shot dead 9 days before national elections.

In the second round of the French presidential elections Jacques Chirac won a second consecutive presidential term in a landslide victory, with 82.21% of votes cast against 17.79% for Jean-Marie Le Pen. Turn-out was 79.7%. Socialist leaders had urged their supporters to vote for Chirac to ensure defeat for Le Pen.

After 19 months under house arrest, Myanmar's pro-democracy opposition leader Aung San Suu Kyi was released by the military government.

In Burkina Faso's general elections, the ruling Congress for Democracy and Progress Party took 57 of 111 seats. The coalition of Alliance for Democracy and Federation and the African Democratic Party won 17 seats.

In conflict between rightwing paramilitary forces (AUC) and the FARC Marxist guerrilla rebels in the run up to Colombia's presidential elections, 117 civilians were killed when a FARC mortar landed on the church in the northwestern village of Bojaya.

After results of the April presidential elections were disputed, the Comoros Election Commission was dissolved. Its replacement, the Ratification Commission, declared Azali Assoumani president.

Chronology of Events for April 2002

Week Beginning 28 April 2002
After 2 months of violence between Muslims and Hindus in the northwestern Indian province of Gujarat in which 800 people died, the government minister Ram Vilas Raswan resigned in protest over the government's inability to restore order.

A referendum confirmed General Pervez Musharraf as Pakistani president, giving him a further 5 years rule. Opposition parties boycotted the vote.

The Palestinian leader Yasser Arafat was released after a 5 month blockade of his Ramallah headquarters. Prime Minister Ariel Sharon refused to cooperate with a UN fact finding mission to Jenin to investigate Israel's military offensive into the refugee camp.

In the Bahamian parliamentary elections the Progressive Liberal Party beat the ruling Free National Movement with 50.8% to 41.1%.

In Vanuatu's general elections the Union of Moderate Parties took 15 out of 52 seats, while the party of Prime Minister Edward Natapei, the Party of Our Land, took 14. Prime Minster Edward Natapei remained in office.

Week Beginning 21 April 2002

In the first round of French presidential elections Jacques Chirac for the Rally for the Republic's came first with 19.87% of votes, with the National Front leader Jean-Marie Le Pen coming a surprise second with 16.86%. Incumbent prime minister Lionel Jospin, who received 16.17%, resigned as leader of the Socialist Party. The result caused a series of anti-Le Pen protest rallies across France.

In the second round of voting in the Hungarian parliamentary elections, the Socialists lost their first-round lead over the ruling party Fidesz-MPP winning 188 seats out of 386 to 178.

After failing to receive backing for his plan to salvage the country's banks, Argentinian Economy Minister Jorge Remes Lenicov became the latest minister to resign from a government struggling to stabilize its depressed economy. He was replaced by Roberto Lavagna, the ambassador to the EU who became the sixth economic minister in a year.

In Chad's general elections the Patriotic Salvation Movement won a landslide victory winning 112 out of 155 seats. Turnout was 52.8%.

In Greece 14 British and Dutch plane spotters sentenced to 1–3 years imprisonment for recording information about Greek military planes while on holiday, launched an appeal.

Week Beginning 14 April 2002

Prime Minister Wim Kok and his entire administration resigned after admitting that Dutch peace keeping forces could have done more to prevent the massacre of 8,000 Bosnian Muslims at Srebrenica by Serb forces in 1995.

The deposed Afghani king Mohammed Zahir Shah returned to his native country from Rome after nearly 30 years in exile. He was accompanied by the interim leader Hamid Karzai.

In Timor-Leste's first democratic elections, former separatist guerrilla leader Xanana Gusmão (FRETILIN) won a landslide victory with 82.6% of votes cast against 17.3% for Xavier do Amaral, his only rival. Turnout was 86%.

A deal was brokered to end the power struggle between Madagascar's two self-professed leaders, Marc Ravalomanana and Didier Ratsiraka. Both men agreed to a vote recount to determine the outcome of the disputed elections of Dec. 2001. 25 people were killed in violent protests between opposing factions.

As President Vladimir Putin told the Russian parliament that the military campaign in Chechnya was over, two landmines exploded in Grozny killing 17 police.

Week Beginning 7 April 2002

Tensions between Israelis and Palestinians increased as suicide bomb attacks on Israeli cities were countered with Israeli tanks occupying eight Palestinian towns. As tanks surrounded the building housing Yasser Arafat, the Palestinian leader refused Ariel Sharon's offer of a safe exit in return for self-imposed exile.

An agreement brokered in March to create a single entity called Serbia and Montenegro was officially ratified by both governments. Thus the name of Yugoslavia was relegated to history.

Abel Pacheco of the Social Christian Unity Party won the Costa Rican presidential run off with 58% of votes to Rolando Araya's (National Liberation Party) 42%.

In Hungary's first round election results, the leading party Fidesz-MPP's 41.1% was beaten by the Socialist's 42.1%.

Following anti-government protests, Venezuelan president Hugo Chavez was forced to resign in a military coup led by the businessman Pedro Carmona Estanga. Western and Latin American governments (but not the US) condemned the coup, refusing to acknowledge the new government headed by Carmona. The following day protests by Chavez supporters led the new president to resign and Chavez was reinstated.

Chronology of Events for March 2002

Week Beginning 31 March 2002

Parliamentary elections in Ukraine were won by the Our Ukraine party of former prime minister Viktor Yushchenko, with 112 of the 450 seats and 23.6% of the vote, ahead of For United Ukraine with 102 seats and 11.8% and the Communist Party with 66 seats and 20.0%.

In Portugal, José Manuel Durão Barroso was sworn in as prime minister, with António Martins da Cruz becoming foreign minister and Paulo Portas defence minister.

In Angola a ceasefire between the government and UNITA rebels was finally signed after 27 years of civil war. The agreement came after the government offered an amnesty to former rebels.

Queen Elizabeth the Queen Mother died at the age of 101.

Week Beginning 24 March 2002

In São Tomé e Príncipe, President Fradique de Menezes named Gabriel Costa prime minister.

An earthquake struck Afghanistan's remote northern province of Baghlan, killing an estimated 2,000 people.

Week Beginning 17 March 2002

Parliamentary elections in Portugal were won by the Social Democratic Party with 102 seats and 40.1% of votes cast, ahead of the Socialist Party with 95 seats and 37.8% of the vote. President Jorge Sampaio subsequently asked the Social Democrat leader José Manuel Durão Barroso to form the new government.

In Mali Prime Minister Mande Sidibe resigned. He was replaced by Modibo Keita.

Week Beginning 10 March 2002

In presidential elections in the Republic of the Congo, incumbent Denis Sassou-Nguesso was re-elected, with 89.4% of the vote.

In presidential elections in Zimbabwe, incumbent Robert Mugabe was re-elected, receiving 56.2% of votes cast according to official figures, with 41.9% for Morgan Tsvangirai.

The UN Security Council endorsed the idea of a Palestinian state for the first time.

In Bosnia-Herzegovina, Dragan Mikerević was elected prime minister.

Week Beginning 3 March 2002

In Haiti, President Jean-Bertrand Aristide appointed Yvon Neptune as prime minister.

In a referendum in Switzerland on membership of the United Nations, 54.6% of votes cast were in favour of joining.

The Kosovo parliament elected Ibrahim Rugova as president. Bajram Rexhepi was appointed prime minister.

In Croatia a deal agreed between coalition leaders resulted in most of the ministers who had resigned a week earlier, including defence minister Jozo Radoš, remaining in the cabinet.

In Madagascar, the defence minister of the government of Didier Ratsiraka, Marcel Ranjeva, resigned.

Chronology of Events for Febraury 2002

Week Beginning 24 February 2002

All cabinet members of the Croatian Social Liberal Party, including defence minister Jozo Radoš, resigned from the government.

In Madagascar, Marc Ravalomanana named Jacques Sylla as his prime minister. Meanwhile the foreign minister of the government of Didier Ratsiraka, Lila Ratsifandrihamanana, resigned and was replaced by Azaly Ben Marofo.

National assembly elections took place in Laos, where the revolutionary People's Party of Laos is the only legal political party.

Hong Kong's chief executive, Tung Chee-hwa, won a second term in office unopposed.

Week Beginning 17 February 2002

George Speight, who led a coup in Fiji in 2000, was condemned to death for treason but had his sentence commuted to life imprisonment.

Marc Ravalomanana, who claimed to have won the presidential elections in Madagascar outright after officials said that a run-off with incumbent president Didier Ratsiraka was needed, declared himself president.

Jonas Savimbi, the leader of the UNITA rebels in Angola, was killed in fighting with government troops.

In Sri Lanka, the government and leaders of the Tamil Tiger rebels formally agreed to an internationally-monitored ceasefire to bring an end 20 years of conflict.

Week Beginning 10 February 2002

Bahrain became a monarchy with the amir, Hamad bin Isa Al-Khalifa, proclaiming himself king.

President Cassam Uteem of Mauritius resigned. Both vice-president Angidi Chettiar and Chief Justice Ariranga Pillay served in turn as acting presidents for short durations before parliament elected Karl Offmann as the new president.

In Somalia, Prime Minister Hassan Abshir Farah appointed a new cabinet, including Yousuf Hassan Ibrahim Dheeg as foreign minister and Gen. Abdulwahab Mohamed Husssein as defence minister.

Week Beginning 3 February 2002

Choi Sung Hong was appointed as the new foreign minister of South Korea.

In presidential elections in Costa Rica, Abel Pacheco of the ruling Social Christian Unity Party received 38.6% of the vote, ahead of Rolando Araya of the National Liberation Party with 31.0%, and Ottón Solís of the Citizens' Action Party with 26.2%. A run-off was to be held in April.

Chronology of Events for January 2002

Week Beginning 27 January 2002

Ricardo Maduro took office as president of Honduras. New cabinet appointments included Guillermo Pérez Arias as foreign minister and Federico Brevé Travieso as defence minister.

Kazakhstan's prime minister Kasymzhomart Tokayev resigned, and was replaced by Imangali Tasmagambetov. Tokayev was appointed foreign minister.

Albanian prime minister Ilir Meta resigned.

Japanese prime minister Junichiro Koizumi dismissed foreign minister Makiko Tanaka. He subsequently named Yoriko Kawaguchi as foreign minister.

Week Beginning 20 January 2002

Yu Shyi-kun was named as Taiwan's new prime minister. He appointed a cabinet included Eugene Chien as foreign minister and Tang Yian-min as defence minister.

Georgi Purvanov took office as the new president of Bulgaria.

In a referendum in the Republic of the Congo voters approved a new constitution that grants the president greater executive powers.

Week Beginning 13 January 2002

The Jordanian government resigned but King Abdullah asked Prime Minister Ali Abu al-Ragheb to form a new cabinet, which included Marwan al-Muasher as foreign minister.

In Canada, Bill Graham was named as new foreign minister, replacing John Manley, who became deputy prime minister.

The president of the Comoros, Azali Assoumani, announced his resignation. A transitional government was formed, headed by Prime Minister Hamada Madi, who also became interim president.

In Haiti, Prime Minister Jean-Marie Chérestal resigned.

A cabinet reshuffle in Peru included the appointment of Aurelio Loret de Mola as defence as successor to David Waisman.

Week Beginning 6 January 2002

In Chile, president Ricardo Lagos appointed Michelle Bachellet Jeria as Latin America's first ever woman defence minister.

Estonian prime minister Mart Laar resigned.

Enrique Bolaños took office as president of Nicaragua and named a new cabinet including Norman José Caldera Cardenal as the new foreign minister, while José Adán Guerra remained as defence minister.

2001

Chronology of Events for December 2001

Week Beginning 30 December 2001

A new common currency, the euro, was introduced in 12 European Union member countries.

Kaspar Villiger took over as the president of Switzerland for 2002.

Italian foreign minister Renato Ruggiero resigned. Prime Minister Silvio Berlusconi took over the post.

Week Beginning 23 December 2001

Following the second round of parliamentary elections in Gabon, the ruling Gabonese Democratic Party won 84 out of 120 seats.

In a referendum on a new constitution in the Comoros, approximately 75% of votes cast were in favour of the proposed constitution granting the three islands of Grande Comore, Anjouan and Mohéli greater autonomy within a new federation.

In presidential elections in Zambia, Levy Mwanawasa won under the first-past-the-post system with only 28.7% of the vote. On taking office as president he announced a new cabinet including himself as defence minister and Katele Kalumba as foreign minister.

Week Beginning 16 December 2001

Parliamentary elections in Chile were won by the Party for Democracy of President Ricardo Lagos, with 63 of 120 seats and 47.9% of the vote.

Portuguese prime minister António Guterres resigned.

Argentina's president Fernando de la Rúa resigned as the country verged on bankruptcy. There were three acting or interim presidents (Ramón Puerta, Adolfo Rodríguez Saá and Eduardo Camaño), in the space of 10 days, before Eduardo Duhalde was elected to the presidency until new elections in 2003.

Avtandil Djorbenadze was approved as Georgia's new minister of state, having been proposed by President Eduard Shevardnadze.

Week Beginning 9 December 2001

In parliamentary elections in Trinidad and Tobago, the ruling United National Congress and the opposition People's National Movement both won 18 seats.

China officially became a member of the World Trade Organization.

In Malaysia, the raja of Perlis, Syed Sirajuddin ibni al-Marhum Syed Putra Jamalullail, was elected the country's new Yang di-Pertuan Agong (king).

Twelve people were killed in a suicide attack on the Indian parliament in Delhi.

Koloa Talake became Tuvalu's new prime minister after the government of his predecessor, Faimalaga Luka, lost a vote of no-confidence.

Week Beginning 2 December 2001

At parliamentary elections in Saint Lucia prime minister Kenny Anthony's Saint Lucia Labour Party retained power, winning 14 of the 17 seats with 54.2% of the vote.

The American firm Enron, once one of the biggest energy companies in the world, was formally declared bankrupt with debts in excess of US$13 bn.

A new transitional government for Afghanistan was agreed on at a conference in Germany. Hamid Karzai was to be chairman, Abdullah Abdullah foreign minister and Mohammad Fahim defence minister.

Parliamentary elections in the Solomon Islands were won by the People's Alliance Party, with 20 out of 50 seats.

In Guinea-Bissau, president Kumba Ialá dismissed prime minister Faustino Imbali and subsequently appointed interior minister Alamara Nhassé as his replacement.

In Sri Lanka, parliamentary elections were won by the United National Party, with 47.6% of the vote and 109 of 225 seats. UNP leader Ranil Wickremasinghe was subsequently sworn in as prime minister and appointed a new cabinet including Tyronne Fernando as foreign minister and Tilak Marapone as defence minister.

Chronology of Events for November 2001

Week Beginning 25 November 2001

In Honduras, Ricardo Maduro of the opposition Nationalist Party won the presidential election, with 52.2% of votes cast. In the parliamentary election the Nationalist Party won 61 of the 128 seats, ahead of the ruling Liberal Party of Honduras, with 55.

Parliamentary elections in Taiwan were won by the ruling Democratic Progressive Party, with 87 of 225 seats and 36.6% of the vote.

Week Beginning 18 November 2001

Parliamentary elections in Denmark were won by the Liberal Party, with 56 out of 179 seats and 31.3% of the vote. The Liberal Party leader Anders Fogh Rasmussen became prime minister and appointed a cabinet including Per Stig Møller as foreign minister and Thor Pedersen as finance minister.

A cabinet reshuffle in Kenya included the appointment of Marsden Madoka as foreign minister.

Macedonia's foreign minister Ilinka Mitreva and defence minister Vlado Buckovski both resigned. They were replaced by Slobodan Casule and Vlado Popovski respectively.

The king of Malaysia, Sultan Salahuddin Abdul Aziz Shah, died. The sultan of Terengganu, Tuanku Mizan Zainal Abidin ibni al-Marhum Sultan Mahmud, became acting head of state and was subsequently sworn in as king.

Guinea-Bissau's foreign minister Antonieta Rosa Gomes was dismissed, with Malam Mané being appointed as his replacement on an interim basis.

Week Beginning 11 November 2001

In the Bulgarian presidential election Georgi Purvanov, the Bulgarian Socialist Party candidate, won 36.3% of the vote followed by incumbent Petur Stoyanov with 34.9%. Purvanov won the subsequent run-off, with 53.3% of votes cast.

In Somalia, Hassan Abshir Farah was appointed as the new prime minister.
Badruddoza Chowdhury was sworn in as Bangladesh's new president.

The Taliban rule over Afghanistan effectively ended when they evacuated the capital Kabul and forces of the opposition Northern Alliance entered the city.

German chancellor Gerhard Schröder won a confidence vote in the Bundestag.

Week Beginning 4 November 2001

Enrique Bolaños of the Constitutional Liberal Party won the presidential election in Nicaragua, ahead of former president Daniel Ortega Saavedra of the Sandinista National Liberation Front. The CLP also won the parliamentary election.

David Trimble was elected first minister of Northern Ireland 4 months after resigning from the post.

The first minister of Scotland, Henry McLeish, resigned and was subsequently replaced by Jack McConnell.

Parliamentary elections in Australia were won by John Howard's ruling coalition of the Liberal and National parties, with 81 of the 150 seats and 40.7% of votes cast.

Chronology of Events for October 2001

Week Beginning 28 October 2001

In Somalia, prime minister Ali Khalif Galaid's government was defeated in a no-confidence motion, as a result of which the deputy prime minister Osman Jama Ali became acting prime minister.

In a cabinet reshuffle in Papua New Guinea, John Waiko became foreign minister.

In Burundi, president Pierre Buyoya, a Tutsi, was sworn in to head a new power-sharing government, with Domitien Ndayizeye, a Hutu, as vice-president.

Eduard Shevardnadze, president of the former Soviet Republic of Georgia, dismissed his entire cabinet.

Week Beginning 21 October 2001

In a cabinet reshuffle in Jamaica, Keith Knight was named as the new foreign minister.

In Greece, a cabinet reshuffle included the appointment of Yannos Papantoniou as defence minister.

Ukrainian defence minister Oleksandr Kuzmuk resigned, almost 3 weeks after his country's troops had accidentally shot down a Russian airliner with a missile. He was subsequently replaced by Volodymyr Shkidchenko.

Singapore's governing People's Action Party won a further term in office by default, after the opposition failed to nominate enough candidates for the general election. However, the election did take place as scheduled, with the People's Action Party winning 82 of the 84 seats contested.

Week Beginning 14 October 2001

In parliamentary elections in Argentina one-half of each chamber's membership was renewed. As a result the Justicialist Party became the leading party in the Chamber of Deputies, with 116 seats, ahead of the Alliance of the Radical Union and Frepaso with 88.

George Fernandes became India's defence minister for the second time, 7 months after resigning from the post.

The president of the Gambia, Yahya Jammeh, was re-elected with 53% of the vote.

Mauritania's ruling Democratic and Socialist Republican Party won 54 seats in the first round of the parliamentary election. They won a further 10 seats in the second round to give them a total of 64 of the 81 seats in the National Assembly.

Week Beginning 7 October 2001

In response to the terror strikes on New York and Washington, the US and Britain launched sustained air attacks on Afghanistan.

In Ethiopia, parliament elected Girma Wolde-Giyorgis as president.

The Nobel Peace Prize was awarded to the United Nations and its Secretary-General Kofi Annan for 'their work for a better organized and more peaceful world'.

Chronology of Events for September 2001

Week Beginning 30 September 2001

A parliamentary election in Bangladesh was won by the opposition Bangladesh Jatiyatabadi Dal (Bangladesh Nationalist Party), with 179 of the 330 seats.

Swissair, the national airline of Switzerland, narrowly avoided bankruptcy thanks to a rescue package, under which two Swiss banks took majority ownership. Sabena, the national airline of Belgium, filed for bankruptcy.

Week Beginning 23 September 2001

In Poland, the coalition of the Democratic Left Alliance–Labour Union won a parliamentary election, with 216 of the 430 seats and 41.0% of the vote.

Saudi Arabia cut off diplomatic relations with the Taliban regime in Afghanistan.

Week Beginning 16 September 2001

Guilherme Posser da Costa, prime minister of São Tomé e Príncipe, was dismissed and subsequently replaced by Evaristo Carvalho. He appointed a new cabinet including Patrice Trovoada as foreign minister and Luis Maria as defence minister.

In Timor-Leste Mari Alkatiri was sworn in as chief minister, and a new cabinet announced including José Ramos-Horta as foreign minister.

A special government assembly elected Arnold Rüütel as the new president of Estonia.

The United Arab Emirates cut off diplomatic relations with the Taliban regime in Afghanistan. The Saudi dissident Osama bin Laden, who was sheltered by the Taliban, became the chief suspect for the attacks on New York and Washington.

Week Beginning 9 September 2001

In presidential elections in Belarus that were generally considered to be flawed, incumbent Alyaksandr Lukashenka won 75.6% of the vote.

In parliamentary elections in Norway, Prime Minister Jens Stoltenberg's Labour Party won only 43 of 165 seats. This was ahead of the Conservative Party with 38, but Labour had insufficient support to form a government. Subsequently Kjell Magne Bondevik of the Christian People's Party took office as prime minister. His government included Jan Petersen as foreign minister and Per-Kristian Foss as finance minister.

The heart of New York City was devastated after hijackers flew two aeroplanes into the World Trade Center. A plane also crashed into the Pentagon, in Washington, D.C. Both towers of the World Trade Center subsequently collapsed. A fourth hijacked plane crashed near the town of Shanksville, Pennsylvania.

A cabinet reshuffle in Albania included the appointment of Arta Dade as foreign minister and Pandeli Majko as defence minister.

In Niger, Aïchatou Mindaoudou became the new foreign minister.

Week Beginning 2 September 2001

In a presidential election in the Seychelles, France Albert René won a sixth term in office, taking 54.2% of the vote.

South Korea's parliament passed a no-confidence motion against the minister in charge of policy towards North Korea. In a cabinet reshuffle President Kim Dae-jung replaced minister of unification Lim Dong-won with Hong Soon-young, the former ambassador to China.

Nicolae Dudau was appointed as Moldova's new foreign minister.

Chronology of Events for August 2001

Week Beginning 26 August 2001

The Central African Republic's defence minister Jean-Jacques Démafouth was dismissed and arrested. Pierre Angoa was appointed as his replacement.

In Macedonia, NATO troops began collecting ethnic Albanian rebel weapons and ammunitions as part of a peace mission aimed at restoring stability in the country.

In the Gambia, foreign minister Mamadou Lamin Sedat Jobe resigned and was replaced by Baboucarr-Blaise Jagne.

Timor-Leste's first democratic elections were won by the Revolutionary Front for an Independent East Timor (Fretilin), with 57% of the vote and 55 out of 88 seats.

Week Beginning 19 August 2001
The reformist majority in Iran's parliament ratified President Khatami's nominees to his new cabinet in spite of earlier threats to reject them.

A week-long election began in Fiji. The Fiji United Party of interim prime minister Laisenia Qarase won 31 of the 70 seats, and formed a coalition with the Conservative Alliance.

Week Beginning 12 August 2001
In Macedonia, rival political leaders signed a NATO-inspired peace accord to stop a 6-month rebellion by minority ethnic Albanians.

Pakistani president Gen. Pervez Musharraf, who had seized power in a coup in 1999, announced that federal and provincial elections would be held in October 2002.

Week Beginning 5 August 2001
President Hugo Banzer Suárez of Bolivia stepped down for health reasons and was replaced by the vice president, Jorge Quiroga Ramírez. He named a new cabinet including Gustavo Fernández Saavedra as foreign minister and Gen. Óscar Guilarte as defence minister.

In Zimbabwe, a cabinet reshuffle included the appointment of Sydney Sekeramayi as defence minister.

The new Indonesian president Megawati Sukarnoputri announced her cabinet, including Hassan Wirajuda as foreign minister and Matori Abdul Jalil as defence minister.

Chronology of Events for July 2001

Week Beginning 29 July 2001
Fradique de Menezes won the presidential election in São Tomé e Príncipe.

In Japan, the Liberal Democratic Party of prime minister Junichiro Koizumi won 64 of the 121 seats up for election in the 247-member upper house.

Iraqi president Saddam Hussein appointed Naji Sabri as foreign minister.

Week Beginning 22 July 2001
In Indonesia, the national assembly impeached President Abdurahman Wahid and elected his deputy Megawati Sukarnoputri as the new president.

Yugoslavian president Vojislav Koštunica named finance minister Dragiša Pešić as the country's new prime minister.

A cabinet reshuffle in Uganda included the appointment of James Wapakhabulo as foreign minister and Amama Mbabazi as defence minister.

Nicolae Cernomaz, Moldova's foreign minister, was dismissed.

In Peru, Alejandro Toledo took office as president and named a new cabinet including Roberto Dañino as prime minister, Diego García Sayán as foreign minister and David Waisman as defence minister.

Week Beginning 15 July 2001
The Indian and Pakistani leaders, Atal Bihari Vajpayee and Pervez Musharraf, met in Delhi for the first summit meeting between India and Pakistan in over 2 years.

Bulgarian president Petar Stoyanov asked Simeon Sakskoburggotski (the former King Simeon II) to form a new government. His cabinet included Solomon Passy as foreign minister and Nikolai Svinarov as defence minister.

Bosnia-Herzegovina's foreign minister, Zlatko Lagumdžija, was elected the country's new prime minister.

Nepal's prime minister, Girija Prasad Koirala, resigned. Sher Bahadur Deuba was subsequently appointed as his replacement.

Week Beginning 8 July 2001
Four members of Croatia's cabinet resigned, including defence minister Jozo Radoš, after the government's decision to send two of its citizens to the international war crimes tribunal in The Hague.

Agum Gumelar became Indonesia's new defence minister in a cabinet reshuffle.

Burundi's political parties agreed to let President Pierre Buyoya, a Tutsi, lead a new 3-year transitional government for 18 months, with a Hutu as vice-president. For the second 18 months the roles would be reversed.

In the Solomon Islands, David Sitai was named as the new foreign minister.

Week Beginning 1 July 2001
Algirdas Brazauskas, a former president of Lithuania, became the country's new prime minister.

Former Argentinian president Carlos Menem was formally charged in connection with his alleged role in illegal arms deals.

Batyr Berdyev, Turkmenistan's foreign minister, was dismissed and was replaced by Rashid Meredov.

Chronology of Events for June 2001

Week Beginning 24 June 2001
The Albanian parliamentary election was won by the ruling Socialist Party, with 42.0% of the vote and 73 of 140 seats.

Kofi Annan was elected for a second term as the Secretary-General of the United Nations.

Slobodan Milošević was extradited to the Netherlands-based United Nations court to face charges of crimes against humanity.

Yugoslavian prime minister Zoran Žižic resigned.

Northern Ireland's first minister David Trimble resigned and was replaced by Sir Reg Empey.

Week Beginning 17 June 2001
Bulgaria's parliamentary elections were won by the National Movement Simeon II, led by former King Simeon II, with 42.7% of the vote and 120 of 240 seats.

Lithuania's prime minister Rolandas Paksas resigned, to be replaced on an interim basis by Eugenijus Gentvilas.

In Pakistan, President Mohammad Rafiq Tarar was removed and Chief Executive Gen. Pervez Musharraf had himself sworn in as president.

Božidar Matić, prime minister of Bosnia-Herzegovina, resigned.

Week Beginning 10 June 2001
Parliamentary elections in San Marino were won by the Christian Democratic Party, with 25 of 60 seats and 41.5% of the vote.

Silvio Berlusconi was sworn in as prime minister of Italy. His cabinet included Renato Ruggiero as foreign minister and Antonio Martino as defence minister.

In a cabinet reshuffle in Kenya, President Daniel arap Moi named Chris Obure as the new foreign minister.

Carlos Menem, former president of Argentina, was placed under house arrest in connection with alleged arms trafficking.

Week Beginning 3 June 2001
Gyanendra Bir Bikram Shah became Nepal's new king on the death of Crown Prince Dipendra.

The Labour Party won the British general election, taking 413 of the 659 seats with 42.1% of the vote. In his new cabinet Prime Minister Tony Blair appointed Jack Straw foreign secretary as successor to Robin Cook and David Blunkett home secretary as successor to Jack Straw.

The Iranian presidential election was won by incumbent Mohammad Khatami, who received 78.3% of votes cast.

Chronology of Events for May 2001

Week Beginning 27 May 2001
Parliamentary elections in Cyprus were won by the opposition Communist Progressive Party of the Working People, with 34.7% of the vote and 20 seats.

Anatolii Kinakh was appointed as the new prime minister of Ukraine.

King Birendra Bir Bikram Shah Deva of Nepal was shot and killed by his son, Crown Prince Dipendra, who also killed several other members of the royal family before shooting himself.

Week Beginning 20 May 2001
In presidential elections in Chad Idriss Déby was re-elected, with 67.4% of the vote.

In the Mongolian presidential election Natsagiin Bagabandi was re-elected, winning 57.9% of the vote.

Samuel Insanally was sworn in as Guyana's new foreign minister.

Derviş Eroğlu's administration in the 'Turkish Republic of Northern Cyprus' resigned.

The African Union came into existence following its ratification by the required two-thirds of Organization of African Unity (OAU) member states.

Week Beginning 13 May 2001

The Italian parliamentary election was won by Silvio Berlusconi's House of Liberties coalition, which took 368 of the 630 seats.

A national unity government was formed in Macedonia, including ethnic Albanians.

In Egypt Amr Mahmoud Moussa was replaced as foreign minister by Ahmed Maher.

In Papua New Guinea foreign Minister Bart Philemon was dismissed and was replaced by John Pundari.

Week Beginning 6 May 2001

In Zambia a cabinet reshuffle included the appointment of Joshua Simunyandi as defence minister.

New Zealand's prime minister, Helen Clark, announced the abolition of the country's air combat wing, consisting of 17 Skyhawk jets, stating that New Zealand was not directly threatened by any country.

Chronology of Events for April 2001

Week Beginning 29 April 2001

Parliamentary elections in Senegal were won by the Coalition 'Sopi', led by President Abdoulaye Wade's Senegalese Democratic Party.

The Macedonian defence minister, Ljuben Paunovski, resigned.

In the Czech Republic, Jaroslav Tvrdík replaced Vladimír Vetchý as defence minister.

Week Beginning 22 April 2001

In Vietnam, Nong Duc Manh became secretary general of the Politburo of the Communist Party of Vietnam.

Junichiro Koizumi became prime minister of Japan and appointed a new cabinet including Makiko Tanaka as foreign minister and Gen. Nakatani as director general of the defence agency.

The communist-dominated parliament in Ukraine dismissed the reformist prime minister Viktor Yushchenko and his government.

Week Beginning 15 April 2001

Mullah Mohammad Rabbani, second in command of the Taliban movement in Afghanistan and the prime minister, died.

Vasile Tarlev became prime minister of Moldova.

Week Beginning 8 April 2001

In presidential elections in Peru, Alejandro Toledo received 36.5% of the vote against 25.8% for former president Alan García Pérez. The parliamentary elections held on the same day were won by Toledo's Peru Possible party, with 26.3% of the vote and 41 seats out of 120. Toledo won a run-off for the presidency in June, with 53.1% of votes cast.

The Netherlands became the first country to legalize euthanasia.

Vanuatu's prime minister, Barak Sopé, was dismissed in a vote of no-confidence, and was replaced by Edward Natapei.

Week Beginning 1 April 2001

Former Yugoslav president Slobodan Milošević was arrested at his villa in Belgrade and taken to prison.

A US surveillance plane made an emergency landing on the Chinese island of Hainan after a collision with a Chinese fighter jet. The crew of 24 were released after 12 days, but the disassembled plane was not returned until July.

President Ange-Félix Patassé of the Central African Republic dismissed the prime minister, Anicet Georges Dologuélé, and named Martin Ziguélé as his replacement.

In Moldova, parliament elected Communist Party leader Vladimir Voronin as president.

President Joseph Kabila of the Democratic Republic of the Congo dismissed his entire cabinet in an attempt to improve management of the country's affairs.

Chronology of Events for March 2001

Week Beginning 25 March 2001

In a cabinet reshuffle in South Korea, Han Seung-soo was named foreign minister and Kim Dong-shin defence minister.

In Laos, finance minister Boungnang Vorachith was named prime minister; other changes included Gen. Douangchay Phichith becoming defence minister.

In Belarus, defence minister Alyaksandr Chumakau was dismissed and was replaced by his predecessor, Leanid Maltseu.

In Russia, Sergey Ivanov was named defence minister and Boris Gryzlov interior minister in a cabinet reshuffle.

Parliamentary elections in St Vincent and the Grenadines were won by the Unity Labour Party, with 12 out of 15 seats, against 3 for the ruling New Democratic Party.

Week Beginning 18 March 2001

Ukrainian president Leonid Kuchma, who had been facing growing opposition calls to resign, dismissed his interior minister, Yuri Kravchenko.

In Guyana, parliamentary elections were won by the ruling People's Progressive Party, with 52.6% of the vote. The presidential election held on the same day was won by incumbent president Bharrat Jagdeo of the People's Progressive Party, with 53.1% of votes cast.

The Argentinian economic minister, Ricardo López Murphy, resigned just 2 weeks after assuming the post. Domingo Cavallo was sworn in as his successor.

In Guinea-Bissau president Kumba Ialá dismissed the prime minister, Caetano N'Tchama, replacing him with the foreign minister, Faustino Fadut Imbali.

Week Beginning 11 March 2001

In the Ugandan presidential elections incumbent Yoweri Museveni won 69.3% of the vote and his main opponent, Kizza Besigye, 27.8%. Local non-governmental monitors described the elections as flawed.

In the Fiji Islands, following a court ruling that the post-coup government of prime minister Laisenia Qarase was illegal and that Mahendra Chaudhry was still legally the prime minister, President Ratu Iloilo dismissed Chaudhry and installed his nephew Ratu Tevita Momoedonu as prime minister, only to reappoint Qarase.

The Indian defence minister George Fernandes resigned, with foreign minister Jaswant Singh taking on the defence ministry in addition to retaining responsibility for the foreign ministry.

Week Beginning 4 March 2001

In Switzerland a referendum on whether to begin immediate talks on joining the European Union was rejected, with only 23.3% of voters in favour.

The president of Benin, Mathieu Kérékou, received 45.4% of votes cast in the presidential election against 3 other candidates including former president Nicéphore Soglo, who received 27.1%. President Kérékou won the run-off, with 84.1% of the vote against 15.9% for Bruno Amoussou after Nicéphore Soglo and the third-placed candidate withdrew claiming fraud.

Horacio Jaunarena was named as Argentina's new defence minister, replacing Ricardo López Murphy who took over the economy ministry.

Dileita Mohamed Dileita was appointed prime minister of Djibouti.

Ariel Sharon took office as prime minister of Israel. His cabinet included Shimon Peres as deputy prime minister and minister of foreign affairs, and Salah Tarif, the first ever Arab to serve in an Israeli government, as a minister without portfolio.

Chronology of Events for February 2001

Week Beginning 25 February 2001

In Moldova the parliamentary elections were won by the PCRM (Communists), with 71 seats out of 101 and 49.9% of votes cast, ahead of the centrist BEAB.

Moustapha Niasse was replaced as prime minister of Senegal by Madior Boye. She is Africa's only woman prime minister.

A cabinet reshuffle in Sierra Leone included the appointment of Ahmed Rahmadan Dumbuya as foreign minister.

Week Beginning 18 February 2001
The first elections took place in Yemen since the unification of North Yemen and South Yemen in 1990. In a referendum voters also approved proposals to extend the presidential term from 5 to 7 years and the term for MPs from 4 to 6 years.

The parliament of Bosnia-Herzegovina confirmed Božidar Matić, a Croat from the multi-ethnic Social Democrats, as prime minister.

In Tuvalu the parliament elected Faimalaga Luka as prime minister.

Week Beginning 11 February 2001
In presidential elections in Cape Verde former prime ministers Pedro Pires and Carlos Veiga qualified for a run-off, defeating two other candidates. Pires won the run-off by just 17 votes, receiving 49.43% of votes cast.

In parliamentary elections in Liechtenstein, the opposition Progressive Citizens' Party won 49.9% of the vote to take 13 of 25 seats, the ruling Fatherland Union 41.4% (11 seats) and the Free List 8.8% (1 seat). Otmar Hasler subsequently took office as prime minister.

A cabinet reshuffle in Kuwait included the appointment of Shaikh Jaber Mubarak al-Hamad al-Sabah as the new defence minister.

In Bahrain a referendum was held in which proposals for a new national charter were approved, leading to a freely-elected parliament from 2003 or 2004. Bahrain will also become a constitutional monarchy and have an independent judiciary.

Week Beginning 4 February 2001
In the Israeli prime ministerial elections the right-wing Likud leader Ariel Sharon received 62.5% of the votes cast against 37.4% for incumbent Ehud Barak.

Jean-Bertrand Aristide took office as the president of Haiti for the fourth time following elections in November 2000.

In the Philippines Teofisto Guingona was sworn in as vice president and foreign secretary.

Chronology of Events for January 2001

Week Beginning 28 January 2001
In Mauritania, Dah Ould Abdi was named foreign minister.

Abdelbaset Ali Mohmed al Megrahi, one of two Libyans accused of the Lockerbie bombing in 1988 which killed 270 passengers and civilians on the ground, was sentenced to life imprisonment after being found guilty of murder by a Scottish court sitting in the Netherlands.

José Maria Neves took office as prime minister of Cape Verde following elections earlier in January, with Manuel Inocencio Sousa becoming foreign minister.

In a cabinet reshuffle in Venezuela, foreign minister José Vicente Rangel became the first civilian defence minister for 70 years, with interior minister Luis Alfonso Dávila taking over as foreign minister.

Week Beginning 21 January 2001
Peter Reith was appointed as Australia's defence minister on the retirement of John Moore.

In Tunisia, a cabinet reshuffle included the appointment of Dali Jazi as defence minister.

In Serbia, Zoran Djindjić of the Democratic Opposition of Serbia became prime minister.

An earthquake devastated much of the state of Gujarat in India, killing some 30,000 people.

Week Beginning 14 January 2001
In the Portuguese presidential election, incumbent Jorge Sampãio won a second term in office.

President Laurent Kabila of the Democratic Republic of the Congo was assassinated, allegedly by one of his own bodyguards. President Kabila's son Joseph Kabila was named as interim president.

California, the wealthiest state in the USA, experienced rotating blackouts as the state faced a power shortage.

In the Philippines, vice-president Gloria Macapagal-Arroyo was sworn in as president after President Joseph Estrada was forced from office amid large-scale street protests.

George W. Bush was inaugurated as the 43rd president of the United States of America.

Week Beginning 7 January 2001
Voters in Senegal approved a new constitution that reduced the presidential term of office from 7 to 5 years, gave the president powers to dissolve the national assembly and gave women equal property rights with men.

Brazilian foreign minister Luiz Felipe Palmeira Lampreia resigned. Celso Lafer was appointed as his replacement.

The German health and agriculture ministers both resigned amid public alarm over government mishandling of the BSE crisis.

2000

Week Beginning 31 December 2000
Moritz Leuenberger took over as the president of Switzerland for 2001.

Greece joined the single European currency, the euro, as its 12th member.

In Thailand, the parliamentary elections were won by the Thai Rak Thai (Thais Love Thais) party of Thaksin Shinawatra, a successful businessman with little experience of politics.

Week Beginning 24 December 2000
John Kufuor won 57.4% of the vote in the run-off for the Ghanaian presidency.

Adina Bastidas was named as executive vice-president of Venezuela by president Hugo Chávez.

Adrian Năstase was sworn in as Romania's new prime minister.

Week Beginning 17 December 2000
Yugoslavia joined the International Monetary Fund, succeeding to the membership of the former Socialist Federal Republic of Yugoslavia, which had ceased to exist in 1992.

In Sudan, the incumbent president Omar Hassan Ahmad al-Bashir won 86.5% of the vote in presidential elections.

Parliamentary elections in Serbia were won by the Democratic Opposition of Serbia with 64.1% of the vote.

Week Beginning 10 December 2000
Ion Iliescu won Romania's presidential election to become the country's president for a second time, having previously been in office from 1989 to 1996.

President Laurent Gbagbo's Ivorian Popular Front won the parliamentary elections in Côte d'Ivoire.

Parliamentary elections in Trinidad and Tobago were won by the United National Congress, the party of prime minister Basdeo Panday.

The last functioning reactor at the nuclear power station at Chernobyl, Ukraine, was closed down. It had been the scene of the world's worst nuclear disaster 14 years earlier.

George W. Bush was confirmed as the new president of the USA. He named Colin Powell, former chairman of the US Joint Chiefs of Staff and Gulf War hero, as his Secretary of State.

Week Beginning 3 December 2000
In Ghana, John Agyekum Kufuor gained 48.4% of the vote in the presidential election against 44.8% for vice-president John Atta Mills. A run-off was set for 28 December.

President Joseph Estrada of the Philippines was impeached by his House of Representatives.

Ionatana Ionatana, the prime minister of Tuvalu, died. He was replaced on an interim basis by deputy prime minister Lagitupu Tuilimu.

Israeli prime minister Ehud Barak announced his resignation and called a general election to gauge his country's support for his policy towards Palestine.

Week Beginning 26 November 2000
Voluntary euthanasia was made legal in the Netherlands.

In Haiti, presidential elections were won by former president Jean-Bertrand Aristide, who received 91.7% of the vote.

Canada's general election was won comfortably by the ruling Liberal party. It gave prime minister Jean Chrétien his third successive majority government.

Vicente Fox took office as Mexican president.

Week Beginning 19 November 2000

European Union defence ministers announced a Rapid Reaction Force with a pool of 100,000 soldiers, sailors and airmen from which a maximum of 60,000 would be drawn for any single mission. The force is to be ready for deployment by 2003.

Peru's President, Alberto Fujimori, resigned. The president of the Congress, Valentín Paniagua, succeeded to the presidency after the 1st and 2nd vice-presidents resigned. Javier Pérez de Cuéllar, the former UN Secretary-General, was appointed prime minister.

Japan's prime minister Yoshiro Mori survived a vote of no-confidence in parliament.

Week Beginning 12 November 2000

Jharkhand became the third Indian state to be created in November. It was formerly part of Bihar.

In Egypt's general election the ruling National Democratic Party won 388 of 454 seats in parliament. The banned Muslim Brotherhood Party won 17 seats.

Yugoslavia re-established diplomatic relations with the USA, Britain, France and Germany.

Week Beginning 5 November 2000

In Malawi the entire cabinet was dismissed by President Bakili Muluzi amid a huge corruption scandal involving the alleged spending of millions of pounds of aid on limousines for government ministers.

In the closest US presidential election in memory, a recount was required in Florida where the gap between the candidates Al Gore and George W. Bush fell within the permitted margin of error.

The party led by Azerbaijan's president, Heidar Aliev, won the country's general election. However, foreign observers questioned the validity of the vote.

Paramanga Ernest Yonli became the prime minister of Burkina Faso.

In India, Uttaranchal, previously part of Uttar Pradesh, was declared a new state.

Week Beginning 29 October 2000

The president of Kyrgyzstan, Askar Akaev, was re-elected for a third 5-year term. Independent monitors questioned the validity of the vote.

The UN Security Council voted unanimously to allow Yugoslavia back in to the UN after 8 years.

A new state in India, Chhattisgarh, was created out of part of Madhya Pradesh.

The president of Tanzania, Benjamin Mkapa, was re-elected with 71.1% of the vote.

Week Beginning 22 October 2000

President Robert Guéï of Côte d'Ivoire was forced out of office by protesters. Laurent Gbagbo, his main opponent in the recent elections, claimed victory.

Kofi Annan, the UN's secretary-general, named Ruud Lubbers as the new UN High Commissioner for Refugees.

Vojislav Koštunica, Yugoslavia's recently elected president, persuaded supporters of former president Slobodan Milošević to form a power-sharing government until general elections in December.

Week Beginning 15 October 2000

The general election in Slovenia was won by the centre-left coalition, led by Janez Drnovšek.

In the general election in Belarus mostly non-partisans were elected. Observers claimed the elections failed to meet international standards for a democratic poll.

Mirko Marjanović, an ally of Slobodan Milošević, resigned as the Serbian prime minister.

Martin Raguz became prime minister of Bosnia-Herzegovina.

Week Beginning 8 October 2000

The president of Somalia appointed Ali Khalif Galaid as the country's new prime minister.

In the Polish presidential elections Aleksander Kwaśniewski was re-elected for another 5-year term with 54% of the vote.

Algirdas Brazauska's Social Democratic Party won Lithuania's general election, but Rolandas Paksas of the Liberal Union, who came second, formed a coalition government to become prime minister.

Week Beginning 1 October 2000

The prime minister of Taiwan, Tang Fei, resigned. He was replaced by Chang Chun-Hsiung.

In the run-up to the presidential election, a state of emergency was announced in Côte d'Ivoire.

In Dominica, prime minister Rosie Douglas died. Pierre Charles was sworn in as his successor. He also took over the foreign ministry.

After 13 years in power Slobodan Milošević was forced to hand over to Vojislav Koštunica. The former president had to concede after massive public protests in the Yugoslavian capital, Belgrade.

Week Beginning 24 September 2000

The Yugoslav presidential election was won by Vojislav Koštunica who claimed to have gained an outright majority of 54%. However, his opponent, Slobodan Milošević, refused to concede and announced a run-off for 8 October.

A French referendum to shorten the length of the presidential term from 7 to 5 years found 70% of voters in favour, although only 30% of the electorate turned out.

In a referendum Denmark voted narrowly against the adoption of the euro. 53.2% of voters were against.

Violent clashes broke out between Palestinians and Israeli police following a visit to the Temple Mount by Israeli opposition leader Ariel Sharon.

Week Beginning 17 September 2000

An attempted military coup, aimed at overthrowing the Côte d'Ivoire ruler, General Robert Guéï, ended in failure.

Alberto Fujimori effectively resigned the presidency of Peru after announcing his withdrawal from new elections.

The USA's Senate voted to normalize trade relations with China, paving the way for the country's entry into the World Trade Organization.

The Amsterdam, Brussels and Paris stock exchanges merged to form Euronext.

Week Beginning 10 September 2000

The general election in Mauritius was won by the opposition alliance leader and former prime minister, Sir Anerood Jugnauth.

In Ecuador the sucre was officially replaced by the US dollar as the legal currency.

The European Union lifted sanctions imposed on Austria following the admission as a coalition partner of the far-right Freedom Party, after an inspection of the country's human-rights record found no irregularities.

Week Beginning 3 September 2000

A former prime minister of Lebanon, Rafiq al-Hariri, won a second term in office in the country's parliamentary elections.

Conditions on human rights that would have to be met for Turkey to be allowed to join the EU were dismissed by Huseyin Kivrikoğlu, Turkey's chief of the general staff.

Tuvalu became the 189th member of the United Nations.

Week Beginning 27 August 2000

Togo's prime minister Koffi Eugene Adoboli resigned, and was replaced by Agbeyome Messan Kodjo.

Jean-Pierre Chevènement, France's interior minister, resigned in protest at talks with separatist terrorists in Corsica before they had disavowed violence. He was replaced by Daniel Vaillant.

Myanmar's military government was condemned by the UN for its treatment of opposition leader Aung San Suu Kyi after she was prevented from leaving the capital, Yangon, and then placed under house arrest.

Week Beginning 20 August 2000

The Algerian prime minister, Ahmed Benbitour, resigned and was replaced by Ali Benflis, a close adviser of the president.

Abdiqassim Salad Hassan was elected as Somalia's first civilian president for 10 years by the new transitional parliament.

The president of the Democratic Republic of Congo, Laurent Kabila, suspended the Lusaka peace accord in favour of a proposed summit with Uganda, Burundi and Rwanda.

Week Beginning 13 August 2000

Talks in Zambia to secure peace in the Democratic Republic of the Congo broke down after president Laurent Kabila rejected the offer of the deployment of a UN-peacekeeping force mediated by the former Botswanan president, Ketumile Masire.

Hipólito Mejía took office as the president of the Dominican Republic. Cabinet appointments included Hugo Tolentino Dipp as foreign minister.

Official results of the elections held in Haiti in May and July confirmed the overwhelming victory of the Fanmi Lavalas Party of former President Jean-Bertrand Aristide, despite accusations of vote-rigging.

Civilian casualties were caused during the bombing of anti-aircraft sites in northern and southern Iraq by British and American forces.

Week Beginning 6 August 2000

Sri Lankan prime minister Sirimavo Bandaranaike resigned, to be succeeded by Ratnasiri Wickremanayake.

Lebanese government troops were deployed along the border with Israel for the first time since the withdrawal of Israeli troops from the region 2 months earlier.

Chechen rebels were blamed for a bomb planted in a Moscow underpass, which killed 8 and wounded nearly 100.

One of Russia's nuclear submarines sank with over 100 men on board.

Week Beginning 30 July 2000

In presidential elections in Venezuela, Hugo Chávez was re-elected for a 6-year term by a large majority.

Shimon Peres, twice a former prime minister, lost the Israeli presidential race to Moshe Katzav.

Ronald Venetiaan was chosen by the National Assembly to be Suriname's next president.

Week Beginning 23 July 2000

The American trade embargo on Cuba, which had stood for 40 years, was amended to allow for the export of food and medicine and an easing of travel restrictions.

President Alberto Fujimori of Peru was sworn in for a third term, and Federico Salas was named as his prime minister.

Voters in Côte d'Ivoire approved a change to the constitution preventing anyone with a foreign parent from standing for election. This prevented the opposition leader, Alassane Ouattara, from standing for president.

Week Beginning 16 July 2000

Ratu Josefa Iloilo became President of the Fiji Islands.

United Nations' troops freed 233 UN-peacekeepers who had been held by Sierra Leonean rebels for 2 months.

A comprehensive peace agreement for Burundi, brokered by Nelson Mandela, fell through when one of the main Hutu militia groups boycotted the signing.

Week Beginning 9 July 2000

A referendum in Syria confirmed Bashar Assad as the new president, with 97.29% of the vote.

In Yugoslavia, constitutional amendments making it possible for president Slobodan Milošević to extend his term of office caused increased tension between Serbia and Montenegro.

Israeli president Ezer Weizman resigned and Avraham Burg became interim president.

US Secretary of Commerce William M. Daley resigned, and was replaced by Norman Y. Mineta.

Week Beginning 2 July 2000

Vicente Fox of the National Action Party won the Mexican presidential elections, ending 71 years of Institutional Revolutionary Party rule.

A referendum in Uganda to decide whether to bring back multi-party democracy resulted in just over 50% of the electorate voting to keep President Yoweri Museveni's one-party system.

Laisenia Qarase was sworn in as interim prime minister of the Fiji Islands by the country's military rulers.

The parliamentary election in Mongolia was won by the ruling Mongolian People's Revolutionary Party.

Week Beginning 25 June 2000

While Robert Mugabe's ZANU-PF party won Zimbabwe's parliamentary elections, his lead did not stretch to the two-thirds majority he needed to change the constitution.

Yoshiro Mori's Liberal Democratic Party lost its parliamentary majority in Japan's election, forcing the prime minister to rely on his coalition partners.

A 6-year-old Cuban boy, Elián González, returned to the island with his father after lengthy disputes with relatives in Miami who wanted the United States Supreme Court to prevent his departure.

Week Beginning 18 June 2000

Ethiopia and Eritrea signed a ceasefire accord bringing an end to their 2-year war.

Israel's coalition government was weakened when Meretz, the left-wing secular ally of Ehud Barak, resigned, allowing the ultra-orthodox Shas to withdraw their own resignation.

Ali Abu al-Ragheb became Jordan's prime minister and defence minister.

Week Beginning 11 June 2000

The prime minister of the Solomon Islands, Bartholomew Ulufa'alu, was taken hostage by rebels.

A summit between Kim Jong II, leader of North Korea, and Kim Dae Jung, president of South Korea, took place in Pyongyang. The summit aimed to ease tensions between the two countries, which are still officially at war with one another.

In Zimbabwe, Robert Mugabe threatened the seizure of British and foreign-owned mines.

Week Beginning 4 June 2000

The first summit meeting between President Bill Clinton and Vladimir Putin took place in Moscow. The leaders discussed further nuclear arms reductions and the American missile defence system.

Ferenc Mádl was elected president of Hungary by the National Assembly in the third round of voting.

Syria's ruler for three decades, Hafez Assad, died. His son, Bashar, was nominated as his successor.

Andrej Bajuk's right-wing government took office in Slovenia.

Week Beginning 28 May 2000

Alberto Fujimori was re-elected for a third term in Peru's presidential elections. The United States along with several Latin American countries expressed their doubts over the legitimacy of the vote.

Unionists agreed to return to office in the power-sharing executive in Northern Ireland following an IRA proposal to put its guns 'beyond use'.

Fiji was placed under martial law by its military chief, Frank Bainimarama.

Week Beginning 21 May 2000

Israel's 22-year occupation of southern Lebanon ended abruptly as an orderly withdrawal broke down after the surrender of the Israeli-run Lebanese militia.

China was given permanent trade status with the United States after the American House of Representatives voted in favour, by 237 to 197.

An attempted military coup in Paraguay failed after the United States and Brazil put pressure on the commanders of the armed forces.

Week Beginning 14 May 2000

Tens of thousands of protesters marched through Washington, D.C. to demand stricter gun control laws.

Hipólito Mejía of the Dominican Revolutionary Party claimed victory in the presidential election in the Dominican Republic.

In the Fiji Islands, prime minister Mahendra Chaudhry was taken hostage in the country's parliament in a coup attempt led by George Speight, a failed businessman.

South Korean prime minister Park Tae-joon resigned; finance minister Yi Hun-chae took over as acting prime minister.

Chen Shui-bian took office as president of Taiwan, and appointed Tang Fei of the opposition Kuomintang as prime minister.

Week Beginning 7 May 2000

Vladimir Putin was inaugurated as the president of Russia.

In Yugoslavia, the chairman of the Executive Council of Vojvodina, Boško Perošević, was assassinated.

Croatia was invited to join NATO's Partnership for Peace programme.

Week Beginning 30 April 2000

The trial of the 2 Libyans accused of sabotaging the passenger plane that exploded over Lockerbie, Scotland in 1988 began in the Netherlands.

Ahmed Necdet Sezer became President of Turkey after 3 rounds of voting in the country's parliament.

President Kabila of the Democratic Republic of the Congo signed a security guarantee allowing the United Nations to bring in 5,000 support troops and 500 military observers to monitor the unstable ceasefire in the country.

Hundreds of United Nations peacekeepers were trapped by rebel forces in Sierra Leone as the bitter civil war continued.

Week Beginning 23 April 2000

The Colombian government's chief negotiator in the peace talks with the Colombian Revolutionary Armed Forces (FARC) rebels resigned after disagreements over their proposed peace tax.

Giuliano Amato was sworn in as the Italian prime minister after the resignation of Massimo D'Alema.

A new Spanish cabinet was formed 6 weeks after the general election. Among other changes, José María Aznar appointed Mariano Rajoy as first deputy prime minister and Josep Piqué as foreign minister.

Week Beginning 16 April 2000

After the resignation of the Hutu president, the leader of the Rwandan Patriotic Front, Paul Kagame, was elected to the post by parliament.

Following the approval of the arms' control treaty with the USA aimed at reducing both countries' nuclear arsenals, Vladimir Putin visited London on his first official trip to the West since being elected Russia's president.

The success of the proposed summit with North Korea was placed in doubt after South Korea's ruling party failed to secure a majority in parliamentary elections.

Slovakia's former prime minister, Vladimír Mečiar, was arrested and charged with bribery.

Week Beginning 9 April 2000

The US stock market fell sharply as investors deserted high-tech shares.

The ruling Panhellenic Socialist Movement secured a narrow victory in the Greek general election.

Eduard Shevardnadze was re-elected president of Georgia.

The government in Slovenia faced collapse after a junior partner pulled out of the coalition.

Week Beginning 2 April 2000

Pakistan's former prime minister, Nawaz Sharif, was sentenced to life imprisonment for terrorism and hijacking.

Yoshiro Mori took over as Japan's prime minister after Keizo Obuchi collapsed with a stroke.

In Zimbabwe, President Mugabe's supporters occupied white-owned farms as part of a campaign to secure land redistribution.

Week Beginning 26 March 2000

Vladimir Putin, Russia's acting president, was confirmed in the job by popular vote. He won nearly 53% of the vote against his nearest rival, the Communist leader, Gennadiy Zyuganov, who won 29%.

A shake-up of the French government brought in Laurent Fabius as finance minister and Jack Lang in charge of education.

Saddam Hussein's elder son, Uday, was elected to Iraq's parliament after winning 99.9% of the vote in Baghdad consistency.

Oil prices fell when OPEC agreed to increase production by 1.5 m. bbls. a day.

Week Beginning 19 March 2000

President Bill Clinton called on India and Pakistan to settle their dispute over Kashmir.

Angela Merkel, a former physicist from East Germany, was elected Christian Democrat leader.

Week Beginning 12 March 2000

In the lead-up to the Taiwanese presidential elections China warned the island's voters not to support pro-independence candidates.

Spanish prime minister José María Aznar won an overall majority in the general election, ending his centre-right People's Party's reliance on the Catalan party for a working majority.

Chen Shui bian, leader of Taiwan's Democratic Progressive Party, was elected president, raising fears in China of an imminent declaration of indeprendence.

Week Beginning 5 March 2000

The Super Tuesday party primaries and caucuses in the United States saw convincing victories for Republican George W. Bush against Senator John McCain, and vice-president Al Gore against Bill Bradley. Bush beat McCain in every state save four. Meanwhile Gore won by such large margins that Bradley withdrew and declared his support for Gore's presidential campaign.

In Britain left-wing Labour MP Ken Livingstone announced he was running as an independent candidate in London's first Mayoral elections. The move came after Livingstone was denied his party's official nomination by a widely derided electoral college system.

Week Beginning 27 February 2000

A 6-year-old boy shot dead a 6-year-old girl in a Detroit classroom, thus becoming the youngest gun-killer in the history of the United States.

In Britain, Home Secretary Jack Straw concluded that Chilean General Augusto Pinochet was not well enough to stand trial and halted extradition proceedings. The General, who had spent 17 months in Britain, left for Chile.

Flood waters in Mozambique continued to raise and it was estimated that around one million people had lost their homes.

Jörg Haider, whose far-right Freedom Party had joined Austria's coalition government last month, resigned as party leader in an attempt to dampen international anger against Austria.

Week Beginning 20 February 2000

China threatened to invade Taiwan if it continued to delay discussions about reunification.

Protests by Nigerian Christians against the imposition of the sharia (Islamic law) in the city of Kaduna led to the deaths of over 100 people.

A tropical cyclone devastated Mozambique, a country already suffering from severe flooding. The UN said US$13 m. worth of aid and urgently required for those worst affected.

Week Beginning 13 February 2000

Wolfgang Schäuble, the leader of the German Christian Democratic Party, resigned after accepting responsibility for his handling of the party's financing scandal.

The British home secretary, Jack Straw, was ordered by the High Court to give copies of the medical report of General Pinochet to 4 European governments. Details of the report were then leaked to 2 Spanish newspapers revealing that the former Chilean dictator's extradition was prevented owing to brain damage and memory failure making him unfit to face trial.

Zimbabweans voted against President Mugabe's plans to redraft the constitution. Nearly 55% of voters said no to increasing his powers and allowing him the opportunity of 2 further 5-year-terms.

The Reformists won a convincing majority in Iran's Consultative Assembly elections. It was a personal triumph for President Khatami and his supporters and was hailed by the United States as 'an event of historic proportions'.

Week Beginning 6 February 2000

Yugoslavia's last president before its collapse in 1991 was elected Croatian president. He invited 300,000 Serb refugees to return to the country.

The Yugoslavian defence minister, Pavle Bulatovié, was assassinated.

British people arrested 19 people after the hijackers of an Afghan airliner gave themselves up at Stansted airport.

Israel bombed 3 transformers supplying power to Beirut. Tripoli and Ballbek in response to the killing of its soldiers in the Israeli occupied area of South Lebanon. Elsewhere an official report revealed that the Israeli security service tortured Palestinian suspects during the 1988–92 uprising.

Vodafone AirTouch succeeded in acquiring the German company Mannesmann, creating the world's biggest mobile phone group.

Week Beginning 30 January 2000
In the New Hampshire primary Senator John McCain recorded a significant victory over his main rival for the Republican presidential nomination. George W. Bush, winning by 18 points. Vice President Al Gore narrowly beat Bill Bradley in the Democratic vote.

Jörg Haider's far-right Austrian Freedom Party looked set to join a coalition government led by the mainstream conservative party. The other EU nations threatened to isolate Austria if the deal went ahead despite the fact that Haider himself be kept of government.

Chechen rebels related towards the mountains as Russian forces looked to be on the verge of capturing Grony.

Despite a disarmament agreement signed last year, UN monitors reportal containing looting, murder and mutilation by rebels in the north of Sierra Leone.

Week Beginning 23 January 2000
An ETA bomb in Madrid which killed an army officer signalled the end of the Basque separatist group's ceasefire. 1 m. people marched in protest at the renewed violence.

Ecuador's vice president, Gustavo Noboa was sworn in as president after his predecessor. Jamil Mahuad was overthrown in a bloodless military coup.

Week Beginning 16 January 2000
In the week that former German Chancellor Helmut Kohl resigned as honorary chairman of the Christian Democrats following ongoing investigations into party funding, the former British opposition leader and European Commissioner, Neil Kinnock, unveiled plans for sweeping institutional reforms to reduce EU nepotism and corruption.

Serbian paramilitary leader Zeljko Raznatovic, better known as Arkan, was shot dead in a Belgrade hotel.

Chile elected its first socialist president for 30 years when Ricardo Lagos beat his right wing presidential rival Joaquín Lavin in a closely fought contest.

Glaxo Wellcome and SmithKline Beecham merged to form the world's biggest drug company with a market capitalization of around $172 bn. Elsewhere Vodafone AiiTouch raised its bid for (lie German telecoms company Mannesmann to 155 bn. euros.

Week Beginning 9 January 2000
The British Home Office decided that the former Chilean dictator General Augusto Pinochet in Britain for medical treatment, was too ill to stand trial for human rights abuses. The decision meant it was unlikely that the General would be extradited to Spain.

Internet giant AOL (America Online) and media conglomerate Time Warner announced they were to merge. The combined company, valued at around $320 bn., was to be known as AOL Time Warner. It described itself as the first fully integrated media and communications company for the internet century.

Week Beginning 2 January 2000
The Russian assault on Grozny entered its 2nd week with fierce fighting in the east and south of the city. In response to the conflict Islamic militants attacked the Russian embassy in Beirut. Two people were killed.

In Croatia, a centre left alliance defeated the nationalist party, the HDZ, which had held power since the country gained independence from Yugoslavia in 1991.

1999

Week Beginning 26 December 1999
Although the world was getting ready to celebrate the new millennium, experts generally stated that it would only begin on 1 January 2001.

Russian President Boris Yeltsin resigned, appointing the prime minister, Vladimir Putin, as his acting successor.

A criminal investigation began against the former German chancellor Helmut Kohl on allegations concerning campaign financing.

The Indian government released 3 Islamic militants in exchange for the safe return of 155 hostages held on board a hijacked Indian Airways plane in Afghanistan.

France announced it was to continue its ban on British beef, forcing the European Commission to pursue legal action.

A self-confessed murderer won a landslide victory in Guatemala's 1st presidential election for 40 years. Alfonso Portillo saw his popularity soar after admitting he murdered two rival law professors in Mexico in 1982. He campaigned under the slogan 'A man who can defend his life can defend the life of citizens'.

Global Recession Chronology (2007–09)

Credit Crunch Chronology for September 2009

1st – India's exports fell at an annualized rate of 28% in July, its tenth consecutive monthly contraction.

2nd – The de facto government of Honduras received US$150 m. from the IMF to boost its dollar reserves.

2nd – The OECD predicted that the recession in Iceland, marked by a large contraction in domestic demand, would be deeper than in most developed economies.

3rd – The OECD forecast the UK to be the only G7 economy to stay in recession at the end of 2009, while the eurozone and the USA would record two quarters of growth.

4th – The G20 group of nations agreed to continue fiscal stimulus until the recovery from recession was assured.

5th – The IMF sanctioned US$510 m. to Zimbabwe, its first loan to the country in a decade, to replenish the economy's dwindling foreign currency reserves.

8th – The EBRD announced it would invest a record €8 bn. (US$11.6 bn.) in central and eastern Europe in the course of 2009.

8th – Estonia's GDP shrank at an annualized rate of 16.1% in the second quarter of 2009, its sixth consecutive quarterly contraction. Latvia contracted by 18.7% and Lithuania by 19.5% in the same period.

8th – The gold price climbed above $1,000 per ounce for the first time since Feb. on the back of a weakening dollar and lingering concerns over the sustainability of the world economy's recovery.

9th – The FTSE 100 broke through the 5,000-point barrier for the first time since Oct. 2008.

11th – Brazil emerged from recession after it grew by 1.9% between April and June following two successive quarters of contraction.

14th – The European Commission predicted that the eurozone would grow by 0.2% in the third quarter and 0.1% in the fourth quarter, but GDP for the year would fall overall by 4%.

15th – Consumer Price Index inflation in the UK measured 1.6% in Aug., its lowest level since Jan. 2005.

15th – US Federal Reserve chairman Ben Bernanke claimed recession in the US was 'very likely over' but the economy would remain weak for some time owing to unemployment.

16th – Unemployment in the UK rose by 210,000 in the 3 months to July to take the total to 2.47 m., its highest level since 1995.

17th – The UK Office for National Statistics reported flat sales volumes in August compared with July, confounding analyst expectations of a 0.2% rise.

18th – The UK's public sector net borrowing totalled a record £16.1 bn. in Aug., with government's overall debt standing at £804.8 bn., or 57.5% of GDP.

20th – A further two US banks were closed by the country's federal regulator, taking the total number of US banks failing in 2009 to 94. Irwin Union Bank and Trust and Irwin Union Bank were shut down after their parent firm, Irwin Financial, failed to meet a Federal Deposit Insurance Corporation demand to boost their capital.

21st – The pound fell to its lowest level against the euro for 5 months as concerns continued about the underlying health of the British economy.

22nd – The Asian Development Bank made an upward revision of its growth forecast for India and China in 2009, with India expected to grow by 6.0% (up from an earlier forecast of 5.0%) and China by 8.2% (up from 7.0%).

23rd – The US dollar fell to a 1-year low against the euro with traders switching to other currencies as signs of economic recovery emerged.

23rd – The World Bank announced it was to provide India with US$4.3 bn. to fund infrastructure projects and support companies needing credit.

24th – Loss-making carrier Japan Airlines asked for a government bailout following recently announced plans to cut 6,800 jobs.

26th – Speaking at the end of the 2-day G20 summit, US President Barack Obama said the world's leading nations had agreed 'tough new measures' to prevent another global financial crisis, including regulation relating to the amount of money banks hold in reserve and a cap on pay for bankers.

29th – The Office for National Statistics revised growth figures for the UK in the second quarter from −0.7% to −0.6%.

29th – Core consumer prices in Japan fell 2.4% in Aug. year-on-year, the fourth successive month of contraction.

30th – The IMF slashed its forecast for the amount of bad debt likely to be written off globally between 2007 and 2010 from US$4.0 trn. to US$3.4 trn.

In Oct. 2009 US manufacturers reported that global output was growing at its fastest rate for 5 years. On 29 Oct. the Department of Commerce announced that the US economy was out of recession, growing by an annualized 3.5% in the third quarter. However, rising unemployment was an ongoing concern, standing at 10.2% in Oct. 2009 (its highest rate since 1983). US president Barack Obama responded to the news of the emergence from recession with caution, commenting: 'We anticipate that we are going to continue to see some job losses in the weeks and months to come.'

By the end of the third quarter of 2009, of the G7 economies only the UK remained in recession, having contracted by 0.4% in the period July–Sept.

Credit Crunch Chronology for August 2009

3rd – Barclays announced a pre-tax profit of £2.98 bn. (US$5 bn.) for the first 6 months of the year with an 8% increase in revenue.

3rd – HSBC saw pre-tax profits halve to £2.98 bn. (US$5 bn.) for the first half of 2009 compared to the same period the previous year, following the write-off of US$13.9 bn. of bad debt in the USA, Europe and Asia.

3rd – World stock markets were boosted by brighter economic data–Standard and Poor's 500 index tipped beyond 1,000 for the first time since Nov. 2008, London's FTSE closed at its highest rate since Oct. 2008, the three major US indexes added over 1.25% by the end of trade after positive manufacturing survey results from July and European indexes also rose.

4th – UBS reported a loss of SFr1.4 bn. (US$1.32 bn.) in the second quarter, an improvement on the SFr2 bn. loss made in the previous quarter.

4th – UniCredito, Italy's largest bank, unveiled better-than-expected second quarter earnings of €490 m. (US$706 m.), 9.2% higher than the previous quarter.

5th – Société Générale announced a second quarter profit of €309 m. (US$445 m.), 52% lower than the same period 12 months earlier.

6th – The Bank of England injected a further £50 bn. into the UK economy as part of its quantitative easing programme, bringing its total spending to £175 bn.

6th – Commerzbank made a €763 m. (US$1.1 bn.) net loss in the second quarter, a small improvement on the €861 m. loss registered in the previous quarter.

7th – RBS reported a pre-tax profit of £15 m. for the first 6 months of the year.

7th – Italy's economy shrank by 0.5% in the second quarter, its fifth consecutive quarterly contraction but an improvement on the record 2.7% fall in Jan.–March.

7th – The IMF and Angola began talks on a loan to help the African country cope with the global economic slowdown.

12th – Dutch financial services group ING announced a €71 m. (US$100 m.) profit in the 3 months to the end of June, its first profit in three quarters.

12th – Commonwealth Bank of Australia, the country's second largest bank by market capitalization, posted net earnings of A$4.72 bn. (US$3.89 bn.), 1% lower than the previous year owing to higher bad debt charges and reduced wealth management unit income.

12th – The UK unemployment rate increased to 7.8% in the second quarter, its highest level since 1995.

13th – France and Germany both recorded second quarter growth figures of 0.3%, bringing a year-long recession to an end. However, the Eurozone contracted by 0.1%, its fifth consecutive quarterly fall in output.

14th – Colonial BancGroup, a property lender based in Montgomery, Alabama, became the largest bank in the USA to collapse in 2009.

14th – The Nigerian Central Bank injected N400 bn. (US$2.6 bn.) into five banks and sacked their managers, after the regulator claimed the banks were undercapitalized and posed a risk to the entire banking system.

14th – Hong Kong posted growth of 3.3% between April and June following four consecutive quarters of contraction. Singapore also announced its emergence from recession, with annualized growth of 20.7% in the second quarter of 2009.

14th – South Africa's central bank slashed its lending rate by a half-point to a 4-year low of 7%, its sixth cut since Dec. 2008.

17th – Japan's economy grew by 0.9% in the second quarter of 2009, ending a run of four consecutive quarters of negative growth.

18th – The South African economy contracted for the third quarter in a row as output fell at an annualized rate of 3% between April and June.

18th – The CPI measure of inflation in the UK remained at the same level of 1.8% in July, although economists had forecast a decline to 1.5%.

20th – The UK's public sector net borrowing totalled £8 bn. in July, the first July deficit for 13 years, as the government's overall debt reached its highest level since 1974 at 56.8% of GDP.

20th – Mexico's economy contracted by 10.3% in the second quarter owing to a decline in demand for exports and falling levels of tourism resulting from the outbreak of swine flu in April and May.

24th – Thailand posted growth of 2.3% in the second quarter of 2009 as it emerged out of recession.

26th – The Malaysian economy expanded by 4.8% in the second quarter of 2009 following two straight quarters of contraction.

27th – US GDP shrank at an annualized rate of 1% in the second quarter, lower than the 1.5% decline predicted by many economists, as aggressive government spending eased the pace of contraction.

27th – Crédit Agricole, France's largest retail bank, announced a higher-than-expected second quarter profit of €201 m. (US$286 m.).

28th – The Office for National Statistics (ONS) revised the rate of contraction in the UK economy for the second quarter to 0.7% from the original estimate of 0.8%.

28th – Unemployment in Japan hit a record high of 5.7% in July and consumer prices fell by 2.2% compared to a year earlier, its fastest recorded pace.

31st – The Eurozone's annual rate of inflation fell by 0.2%, its third consecutive monthly decline.

Credit Crunch Chronology for July 2009

1st – Japan's Shinsei Bank and Aozora Bank merged to create the country's sixth largest bank with assets of 18 trn. yen (US$186 bn.).

1st – Unemployment in Ireland reached 11.9% in June, its highest level since 1996.

1st – India's exports were down 29.2% in May from the same month the previous year, the economy's eighth consecutive fall in exports.

7th – Inflation in the Philippines fell to 1.5% in June, its lowest level in 22 years.

10th – US carmaker General Motors (GM), 61% owned by the US government, emerged from its bankruptcy protection after creating a 'new GM' made up of four key brands, including Cadillac.

13th – The US deficit moved above US$1 trn. for the first time in history.

14th – Inflation in the UK fell below the Bank of England's target rate of 2% for the first time since 2007. Lower food prices caused the Consumer Prices Index to drop to an annual rate of 1.8% in June, down from 2.2% in May.

14th – Singapore grew at an annualized rate of 20.4% in the second quarter, its first quarterly expansion in a year following a revised contraction of 12.7% from January to March.

14th – Goldman Sachs reported a net profit of US$3.44 bn. for the second quarter of the year, higher than analysts had forecast.

15th – UK unemployment increased by a record 281,000 to 2.38 m. in the 3 months to May, its highest level in over 10 years.

15th – Japan's central bank downgraded its economic forecast to a contraction of 3.4% from 3.1% for the 12 months to end-March 2010, but reiterated that the worst of the recession was over.

15th – Russia's economy contracted by 10.1% in the first half of 2009, its sharpest decline since the early 1990s.

16th – China's economy grew at an annualized rate of 7.9% in the second quarter, up from 6.1% between January and March, as the government upgraded the growth forecast to 8% for 2009 as a whole.

16th – JP Morgan Chase unveiled a second quarter profit of US$2.72 bn., an increase of 36% on the same period the previous year.

17th – Ghana secured a US$600 m. 3-year loan from the IMF and was given access to a further US$450 m. from the IMF through the special facility set up by the G20 summit to assist poor countries.

20th – Iceland announced a 270 bn. kr. (US$2.1 bn.) recapitalization plan for its banking system, issuing bonds to three new banks set up in 2008 following the collapse of the country's three main banks.

21st – UK government debt increased to £799 bn., or 56.6% of UK GDP, its highest level since records began in 1974.

22nd – The National Institute of Economic and Social Research (NIESR) predicted UK GDP to fall by 4.3% in 2009 and UK GDP per capita to remain below its pre-recession levels until March 2014.

22nd – Morgan Stanley reported a loss of US$159 bn. in the second quarter of 2009, compared to a US$698 m. profit for the same period the previous year.

23rd – Credit Suisse unveiled a 29% increase in second quarter net profits of 1.57 bn. Swiss francs (US$1.48 bn.).

23rd – The Asian Development Bank said growth in East Asia, excluding Japan, would double to 6% in 2010, compared to a 3% expansion in 2009.

23rd – The rate of decline of Japan's exports slowed in June, a sign that government stimulus spending around the world may be supporting demand. However, exports were still 35.7% lower than the same month the previous year.

24th – The IMF approved a 20-month Stand-By Arrangement for Sri Lanka worth US$2.6 bn. to support the country's economic reform package.

24th – The UK economy contracted by 0.8% in the second quarter of 2009, much lower than the 2.4% decline in the previous quarter but above analysts' 0.3% prediction.

24th – The South Korean economy grew by 2.3% from April to June, its fastest expansion in five-and-a-half years.

28th – Deutsche Bank unveiled a net profit of €1.09 bn. (US$1.56 bn.) for the second quarter of 2009, a 67% increase in profits compared to the same period the previous year.

28th – BBVA, Spain's second largest bank, reported a net profit of €1.56 bn. (US$2.23 bn.) for the second quarter thanks to higher income from loans.

31st – Mizuho Financial Group revealed a net loss of 4.4 bn. yen (US$46 m.) for the second quarter, its fourth consecutive quarterly loss.

31st – Japan's jobless rate increased by 830,000 in June to 3.48 m., its highest level in 6 years.

31st – Eurozone unemployment reached 9.4% (or 14.9 m. people) in June, its highest level in 10 years.

Credit Crunch Chronology for June 2009

1st – US car manufacturer General Motors filed for chapter 11 bankruptcy protection, the biggest failure of an industrial company in US history.

2nd – Switzerland officially entered recession after the economy contracted by 0.8% in the first 3 months of 2009, following a decline of 0.3% in the final quarter of 2008.

3rd – Australia recorded a 0.4% rise in GDP for the first quarter compared to the same period last year, bucking international trends.

3rd – Lloyds Banking Group announced plans to cut 530 jobs and close one site in the UK by the end of 2009.

4th – Industrial and Commercial Bank of China (ICBC), the world's second largest bank by market value, unveiled plans to buy 70% of Bank of East Asia's Canadian unit as part of a move to expand overseas.

4th – The Bank of England kept interest rates unchanged at 0.5% for the third month in a row.

8th – The OECD claimed the pace of decline among its 30 member countries was slowing—the composite leading indicators index (CLI) rose 0.5 point in April.

9th – Lloyds Banking Group announced it was to shut all 164 Cheltenham & Gloucester branches, putting 1,660 jobs at risk.

9th – UK unemployment rose by 244,000 to 2.22 m. in the first 3 months of the year according to the Office for National Statistics (ONS), the largest quarterly rise in the jobless rate since 1981.

9th – Official figures showed that exports in Germany were 4.8% lower in April than in March and 28.7% down on the previous year, the biggest annual fall since records began in 1950.

10th – The European Central Bank provided an emergency €3 bn. to the central bank in Sweden, whose banks dominate the Baltic region's financial sector.

10th – BP's annual statistical review indicated that global oil consumption fell by 0.6% in 2008, the first fall since 1993 and the largest drop since 1982.

10th – Ten of the largest US banks gained permission from the US Treasury to repay US$68 bn. in government bail-out money received through the Troubled Asset Relief Programme (TARP).

11th – Figures revealed that Chinese exports fell by a record 26.4% in May from the same month the previous year.

11th – Revised GDP growth figures showed Japan contracted by 3.8% in the first quarter of 2009, less than the original estimate of 4%.

15th – The Confederation of British Industry (CBI) predicted the UK economy would contract by 3.9% in 2009 before seeing a return to growth of 0.7% in 2010.

15th – The IMF revised its growth forecast for 2010 for the USA, claiming that the economy would now grow by 0.75% compared to its forecast of 0% earlier in the year.

16th – The Bank of Japan said that the economy was no longer deteriorating, a more positive assessment than the previous month when it had stated that the economy was continuing to worsen. Nonetheless, it maintained interest rates at 0.1%.

16th – China introduced an explicit 'Buy Chinese' policy as part of its economic stimulus programme, leading to fears of an increase in protectionism across the world.

17th – The US government announced a major reform of banking regulation to curb excessive risk-taking among big banks and to prevent future financial crises. President Obama described the reforms as 'the biggest shake-up of the US system of financial regulation since the 1930s'.

17th – The OECD revised its growth forecast for Italy, predicted the economy would grow by 0.4% in 2010 compared to a previously estimated contraction of 0.4%. However, it downgraded its forecast for 2009 from a 4.3% decline to 5.3%.

17th – The World Bank raised its GDP growth forecast for China to 7.2% in 2009 from a previously estimated 6.5%, citing the impact of a fiscal stimulus package.

18th – Official figures showed inflation in India had turned negative for the first time since 1977. Wholesale prices fell 1.61% in the year to 6 June.

22nd – The Japanese government looked set to provide up to 100 bn. yen (US$1 bn.) in state aid to Japan Airlines, the country's biggest airline, on condition that the organization's management improves.

24th – The OECD said the world economy was near the bottom of the worst recession in post-war history and predicted that the 30 most industrialized countries would shrink by 4.1% in 2009. UK output was predicted to contract by 4.3% in 2009 and experience zero-growth in 2010.

24th – The European Central Bank pumped €442.2 bn. (US$628 bn.) in 1-year loans into the eurozone's weakened banking system in an effort to unlock credit markets and revive the region's economies.

24th – Orders for new durable goods in the USA rose unexpectedly by 1.8% in May from the previous month, going against expectations of a drop of 0.9%.

25th – The IMF said that Ireland's economy would contract by 8.5% in 2009 and warned it would experience the worst recession in the developed world and struggle to bail out its banks.

26th – New Zealand suffered a fifth straight quarterly contraction after official figures showed the economy shrank by 2.7% in the first quarter of 2009.

26th – Consumer prices in Japan fell by 1.1% in May compared to the same month the previous year, its biggest fall since records began in 1970, fuelling fears of a new bout of deflation.

26th – Spain unveiled a €9 bn. (US$12.7 bn.) fund aimed at saving banks suffering during the downturn.

30th – Eurozone inflation turned negative for the first time since records began in 1991, with consumer prices 0.1% lower in June than 12 months earlier.

30th – Malaysia launched economic liberalization measures aimed at attracting foreign investments, including changes to its long-standing policy of giving preferential treatment to the country's ethnic Malay majority.

Credit Crunch Chronology for May 2009

1st – US carmaker Chrysler filed for chapter 11 bankruptcy protection after a group of hedge and investment funds refused to restructure the company's US$6.9 bn. debt.

1st – The Reserve Bank of New Zealand reduced interest rates by 50 basis points to a record low of 2.5%. The bank governor, Alan Bollard, said he expected rates to remain at the current (or lower) level until the latter part of 2010.

4th – The European Commission forecast that the EU economy would contract by 4% in 2009, more than twice the level predicted at the beginning of the year. It claimed unemployment would now reach 10.9% in 2010.

5th – Japan offered US$100 bn. of financial assistance to Asian economies affected by the global economic slowdown in a meeting of the finance ministers of the ten-member Association of South East Asian Nations.

5th – UBS confirmed it had made a SFr2 bn. (US$1.75 bn.) loss in the first quarter of 2009.

6th – Volkswagen and Porsche agreed to merge, relieving the sports carmaker of its debt burden.

7th – Barclays announced a pre-tax profit of £1.37 bn. (US$2.07 bn.) for the first 3 months of the year, up 15% from the previous year.

7th – Commerzbank agreed to relinquish the core of its commercial property lending business together with Eurohypo's role in public sector finance, in a deal with European competition authorities to compensate for €18.2 bn. (US$24.2 bn.) of state aid it received.

7th – The European Central Bank cut its main interest rate by a quarter point to a record low of 1% and also announced plans to purchase €60 bn. (US$80.4 bn.) of covered bonds, which are backed by mortgage or public sector loans.

7th – The Bank of England announced it would pump a further £50 bn. (US$75 bn.) into the UK economy in a substantial expansion of its programme of government bond purchases.

8th – The Royal Bank of Scotland reported a pre-tax loss of £44 m. for the first quarter of 2009, compared with a profit of £479 m. for the same period the previous year.

8th – Several US banks unveiled plans to raise cash a day after the US Treasury said that ten of America's 19 largest banks failed their stress tests and needed to raise a combined total of US$74.6 bn. Wells Fargo and Morgan Stanley planned to raise US$7.5 bn. and US$3.5 bn. respectively through share sales, while Bank of America planned to sell assets and raise capital to secure US$33.9 bn. it needed.

13th – Franco-Belgian bank Dexia, which had been bailed out by three economies the previous year, posted a first quarter profit of €251 m. (US$341 m.) compared to a loss of €3.3 bn. (US$4.5 bn.) in 2008.

13th – The German cabinet agreed a 'bad bank' scheme, in which banks would be able to swap their toxic debt for government-backed bonds in return for paying an annual fee.

14th – Spain suffered a fall in GDP of 1.8% in the first quarter of 2009, its largest contraction in 50 years, according to the National Statistics Institute.

14th – Crédit Agricole unveiled a net profit of €202 m. (US$275 m.) in the first quarter, a 77% fall from the same period the previous year, after more than doubling its loan-loss provisions to €1.1 bn.

15th – According to Eurostat economies that make up the eurozone contracted by 2.5% in the first quarter of 2009, a higher-than-forecast decline.

15th – The EBRD revealed plans to invest a record €7 bn. (US$9.4 bn.) in 2009 to tackle the slowdown through investments in infrastructure, energy, corporate and finance projects.

17th – Carmaker General Motors announced plans to close up to 1,100 dealerships in the USA as it battled to reduce costs and stave off bankruptcy.

19th – Inflation in the UK as measured by the Consumer Prices Index (CPI) slowed to 2.3% in April from 2.9% the previous month.

20th – Japan's GDP slid by 4% in the first quarter, its largest decline since records began in 1955.

20th – Venezuela experienced its slowest rate of growth in 5 years, with GDP growing by 0.3% in the first quarter of 2009 as the fall in oil prices took effect.

21st – The Office for National Statistics said public sector net borrowing in the UK rose to £8.46 bn. in April compared to £1.84 bn. in the same month the previous year. Concerned about its significant debt burden, Standard & Poor's downgraded the UK's credit rating from 'stable' to 'negative' for the first time since it began analyzing its public finances in 1978.

22nd – Private equity firms paid US$900 m. to rescue BankUnited, a Florida-based bank worth around US$13 bn. It had been closed by federal regulators in what was the biggest US bank failure of 2009 so far.

22nd – The US Treasury provided automotive financing group GMAC with a further US$7.5 bn. in state aid to help it stay in business and offer loans to potential Chrysler and GM car buyers.

22nd – UK output declined by an unrevised 1.9% in the first quarter of 2009, according to figures published by the Office for National Statistics.

26th – South Africa fell into recession for the first time since 1992 following an annualized contraction of 1.8% and 6.4% in the previous two quarters.

27th – Riksbank announced it was raising foreign currency to boost its US$22 bn. currency reserves, causing a sharp fall in the Swedish krona as the central bank warned the worst of the financial crisis may not be over.

29th – India's economy grew by 5.8% in the first quarter of 2009, higher than forecast but down from 8.6% in the same quarter the previous year.

Credit Crunch Chronology for April 2009

2nd – The G20 agreed to tackle the global financial crisis with fresh measures worth up to US$1.1 trn. Pledges included US$750 bn. made available to the IMF to help troubled economies and US$250 bn. to boost global trade.

6th – Japan unveiled its latest stimulus package worth ¥10 trn. (US$98.5 bn.), equivalent to 2% of GDP.

7th – The Reserve Bank of Australia reduced its benchmark rate by a quarter-point to 3%, its lowest level since 1960.

7th – RBS announced it would shed a further 9,000 jobs from its global operations over the next 2 years.

14th – Goldman Sachs reported a higher than expected pre-tax quarterly profit of US$1.8 bn. The bank would also place US$5 bn. worth of shares on the stock market in order to repay an emergency US$10 bn. loan provided by the US government in 2008.

14th – Poland's government approached the IMF to secure a US$20.5 bn. credit line to increase bank reserves and make Poland 'immune to the virus of the crisis and speculative attacks'.

14th – Fortis bank posted a loss of €20.6 bn. (US$27.5 bn.) for 2008 following writedowns on debt and a separation of the business.

15th – UBS unveiled a first quarter loss of SFr2 bn. (US$1.75 bn.) and announced it would cut 8,700 jobs by next year in an effort to reduce costs.

16th – China's growth rate slowed to 6.1% in the first quarter of 2009, its slowest pace since quarterly GDP data was first published in 1992. Growth was down from 6.8% in the previous quarter and 9% for the whole of 2008.

16th – Consumer prices in the USA fell by 0.4% over the year to March owing to weak energy and food prices, the first year-on-year drop since Aug. 1955.

16th – JP Morgan Chase reported a higher than expected first quarter profit of US$2.1 bn. compared with net income of US$2.4 bn. in the first quarter of 2008.

18th – The IMF formally agreed a US$47 bn. credit line for Mexico under its new fast track scheme to help developing nations cope with the global financial crisis.

21st – UK annual inflation as measured by the Retail Prices Index (RPI) was −0.4% in March (down from 0 in Feb.), the first negative figure since 1960.

21st – Sweden's central bank reduced its key interest rate by a half point to a record low of 0.5%.

22nd – UK chancellor Alistair Darling admitted the economy faced its worst year since the Second World War as he unveiled his latest Budget report. The annual budget deficit would rise sharply to £175 bn. over the next 2 years with total government debt to reach 79% of GDP by 2013.

22nd – The IMF said global output would contract by 1.3% in 2009, a 'substantial downward revision' of its Jan. forecasts when it predicted growth of 0.5%. The UK economy was now projected to shrink by 4.1% in 2009, while Germany was set to decline by 5.6% and Japan by 6.2%.

22nd – India's central bank slashed interest rates for the sixth time in 6 months, reducing its key repo lending rate by a quarter-point to 4.75%.

27th – National Australia Bank, Australia's largest lender, announced a 9.4% fall in cash earnings to A$2 bn. (US$1.4 bn.) for the Sept.–March period.

28th – Fears over a swine flu outbreak continued to have an impact on global shares – the FTSE100 closed down by 1.7%, markets in Paris and Frankfurt ended nearly 2% down, Japan's Nikkei index fell by 1.7% and Hong Kong's Hang Seng shed 1.4%.

28th – Lithuania's economy contracted by 12.6% in the first quarter of 2009 compared to the same period in 2008, the largest year-on-year fall in the EU since the start of the recession.

29th – USA output contracted at an annualized rate of 6.1% in the first quarter of the year, a higher-than-expected result. The contraction was led by a 30% decline in exports, its largest fall in 40 years.

Credit Crunch Chronology for March 2009

2nd – US insurance company AIG unveiled a US$61.7 bn. loss in the fourth quarter of 2008, the largest in US corporate history, and received an additional US$30 bn. as part of a revamped rescue package from the US government.

2nd – HSBC, Europe's largest bank, confirmed it was looking to raise £12.5 bn. (US$17.7 bn.) from shareholders through a rights issue after it revealed pre-tax profits for 2008 of US$9.3 bn., down 62% on the previous year.

3rd – Nationalized UK bank Northern Rock confirmed it made a loss of £1.4 bn. (US$2.0 bn.) in 2008.

3rd – Toyota Motors, the world's largest carmaker by sales, asked for up to US$2 bn. in Japanese government-backed aid.

4th – The Australian economy shrank by 0.5% in the fourth quarter of 2008.

4th – The World Bank signed a US$2 bn. contingency facility to Indonesia, the largest ever loan granted to an economy not classified as in crisis. Indonesia's central bank reduced its interest rate by 50 basis points to 7.75%.

5th – The Bank of England cut interest rates from 1% to 0.5%. The Bank also announced it was to create £75 bn. of new money, called quantitative easing.

9th – Iceland nationalized Straumur-Burdar's, the last of the big four banks to be taken into public ownership.

10th – Malaysia revealed a 60 bn. ringgit (US$16.3 bn.) stimulus package over a 2 year-period, amounting to 9% of GDP. The plan contained increased spending on infrastructure, guaranteed funds for businesses, equity investments to boost the stock market and tax breaks.

14th – The G20 group of rich and emerging nations pledged a 'sustained effort'. to restore global growth with low interest rates and increase funds to the IMF.

16th – Serbia opened talks with the IMF over an emergency loan worth up to €2 bn. (US$2.6 bn.).

18th – The Bank of Japan provided up to 1,000 bn. yen (US$10 bn.) in subordinated loans to its commercial banks.

18th – The US Federal Reserve pledged US$1.2 trn. to buy long-term government debt and mortgage-related debt.

18th – UniCredito, one of Italy's largest banks, sought €4 bn. in aid from Italian and Austrian sources.

19th – The US Treasury promised up to US$5 bn. to auto parts suppliers, guaranteeing payment for products shipped.

20th – The IMF revised its global forecast for 2009, with the world economy set to shrink by between 0.5% and 1%. The world's most developed economies were expected to experience the largest contractions in GDP.

23rd – The US announced a 'Public-Private Investment Programme' to buy up to US$1 trn. worth of toxic assets. The US Treasury committed between US$75 bn. and US$100 bn. to the programme, in addition to contributions from the private sector.

25th – The IMF, along with the World Bank, European Commission and other multilateral organizations, unveiled a €20 bn. (US$27.1 bn.) financial rescue package for Romania. The agreement stipulated Romania reduce its budget deficit to less than 3% of GDP by 2011.

25th – Italian bank Banca Popolare di Milano became the fourth bank in the country to seek funding from the government's €12 bn. bank aid scheme. The bank requested €500 m.

26th – Official statistics revealed that Ireland's economy shrank by 7.5% in the fourth quarter of 2008 compared to the same period the previous year, its largest contraction in decades. For the whole of 2008, the economy contracted by 2.3%, its first fall since 1983.

26th – The US economy contracted at an annualized rate of 6.3% in the fourth quarter of 2008, its fastest rate since 1982.

27th – The UK economy shrank by 1.6% in the last 3 months of 2008, its largest fall in GDP since 1980 and higher than the earlier 1.5% estimate.

29th – The German government pumped €60 m. (US$80 m.) into Hypo Real Estate in return for an 8.7% stake.

30th – The Spanish government, with the Bank of Spain, launched a €9 bn. (US$12 bn.) bailout of savings bank Caja Castilla La Mancha, the country's first bank rescue in the financial crisis.

31st – The World Bank predicted the global economy would contract by 1.7% in 2009, the first decline since the Second World War. The forecast claimed that the most developed economies would shrink by 3%, while world trade would fall by 6.8%.

Credit Crunch Chronology for February 2009

3rd – The Australian government announced a second stimulus package of $A42 bn. (US$26.5 bn.) to boost long-term growth, including one-off cash payments to low-income families and investment in infrastructure. The Reserve Bank of Australia reduced interest rates by 1% point to 3.25%, its lowest level in 45 years.

5th – The Bank of England slashed interest rates by a half-point to a record low of 1%.

5th – Deutsche Bank unveiled a fourth-quarter loss of €4.8 bn. (US$6.1 bn.) and a net loss for 2008 of €3.9 bn. (US$5 bn.)—its first yearly loss since being restructured after the Second World War—citing 'unprecedented' operating conditions and 'weaknesses in our business model'.

9th – Barclays announced a pre-tax profit of £6.1 bn. (US$9 bn.) for 2008, down 14% on profits for the previous year.

9th – The French government agreed to provide Renault and Peugeot-Citroën with €3 bn. (US$3.9 bn.) each in preferential loans in return for maintaining jobs and sites in France. Renault Trucks, owned by Volvo, was offered a loan of €500 m. (US$650 m.), suppliers €600 m. (US$780 m.) and the financing arms of the two carmakers loan guarantees of up to €2 bn. (US$2.6 bn.).

10th – Former bosses of RBS and HBOS, two of the UK's largest financial casualties, apologized 'profoundly and unreservedly' for their banks' failure during the UK Treasury Committee's inquiry into the banking crisis.

10th – UBS declared a Swiss corporate history record loss of SFr19.7 bn. (US$17 bn.) for 2008 after suffering a net loss of SFr8.1 bn. (US$7 bn.) in the fourth quarter, including SFr3.7 bn. (US$3.2 bn.) in exposure to toxic assets. The bank announced it would axe a further 2,000 jobs at its investment banking arm.

12th – The Bank of Korea reduced interest rates by 50 basis points to a record low 2%.

12th – The Irish government revised its rescue plans for Allied Irish Bank and the Bank of Ireland. Each bank was to receive €3.5 bn. (US$4.5 bn.) and would be expected to increase lending and reduce senior executives' pay while remaining in the private sector.

12th – The Spanish economy fell into recession for the first time in 15 years, having shrunk by 1% in the fourth quarter of 2008.

17th – US President Barack Obama signed his US$787 bn. economic stimulus plan after Congress approved the package.

18th – Taiwan fell into recession after its economy slumped by 8.4% in the fourth quarter. Taiwan's central bank reduced interest rates by a quarter-point to 1.25%.

19th – The Bank of Japan bought 1 trn. yen (US$10.7 bn.) in corporate bonds and maintained a near-zero interest rate.

26th – Royal Bank of Scotland unveiled a loss of €24.1 bn. (US$34.2 bn.), the largest annual loss in UK corporate history, stemming from a €16.2 bn. (US$23 bn.) writedown of assets mainly linked to its purchase of ABN Amro. The bank also announced it would put €325 bn. of toxic assets into a new government insurance scheme, while the government would inject a further €13 bn. to strengthen its balance sheet.

27th – The European Bank for Reconstruction and Development (EBRD), the European Investment Bank (EIB) and the World Bank announced a €24.5 bn. (US$31 bn.) joint rescue package for banking sectors in Central and Eastern Europe. The 2-year initiative would include equity and debt financing and policies to encourage lending, particularly to small and medium-sized firms.

Credit Crunch Chronology for January 2009

8th – The Bank of England reduced interest rates by a half-point to 1.5%, the lowest level since the bank was founded in 1694.

8th – Commerzbank received €10 bn. (US$13.7 bn.) of capital from the German government in return for a 25% stake following liquidity problems arising from its decision to purchase Dresdner Bank from insurance company Allianz.

8th – South Korea's central bank cut interest rates from 3% to a record low of 2.5%.

9th – Official figures showed that more jobs were lost in the USA in 2008 than in any year since the Second World War, with 2.6 m. axed. The jobless rate increased to 7.2% in Dec. 2008, its highest level in 16 years.

13th – China's exports fell by 2.8% in Dec. compared to the previous year, the largest decline in 10 years.

13th – German chancellor Angela Merkel unveiled an economic stimulus package worth €50 bn. (US$67 bn.), including public investments and tax relief.

14th – The UK government guaranteed up to €20 bn. of loans to small and medium-sized businesses.

14th – Shares in Europe and the USA fell sharply following the release of official figures showing a 2.7% fall in US retail sales in Dec. London's FTSE 100 closed down by over 5%, the main markets in France and Germany lost nearly 4.5% and the US Dow Jones index fell by 3%.

15th – The European Central Bank slashed interest rates by a half-point to 2%, its lowest level since Dec. 2005.

16th – The Irish government moved to nationalize Anglo Irish Bank.

16th – Reporting a fourth quarter loss of US$8.29 bn., Citigroup announced plans to split into two new firms, Citicorp and Citi Holdings.

16th – Bank of America received US$20 bn. of fresh US government aid and US$118 bn. worth of guarantees following losses incurred in its takeover of Merrill Lynch. Merrill Lynch posted a fourth-quarter loss of US$15.3 bn. while Bank of America lost US$1.7 bn. in the same period.

19th – Spain became the first triple-A rated nation to have its credit rating downgraded since Japan in 2001.

19th – Denmark offered up to 100 bn. kroner (US$17.6 bn.) in loans to help recapitalize its banks.

20th – The French government offered its ailing car industry up to €6 bn. (US$7.7 bn.) in aid.

23rd – The UK economy officially entered recession after figures showed a fourth-quarter fall in GDP of 1.5% following a 0.6% drop the previous quarter.

25th – The French government provided €5 bn. (US$6.5 bn.) in credit guarantees to help Airbus.

26th – Dutch banking and insurance group ING estimated fourth-quarter losses of €3.3 bn. (US$4.3 bn.), prompting it to seek state guarantees, replace its chief executive and shed 7,000 jobs.

28th – The IMF warned that world economic growth would fall to 0.5% in 2009, its lowest level since the Second World War, and projected the UK economy would shrink by 2.8%, the worst contraction among developed nations.

28th – The International Labour Organization claimed 51 m. jobs could be lost in 2009, pushing the world unemployment rate to 7.1% compared with 6.0% at the end of 2008.

28th – Canada's Conservative government unveiled a $40 bn. CDN (US$32 bn.) stimulus plan including tax cuts and infrastructure spending.

29th – New Zealand's central bank reduced interest rates by 1.5% to 3.5%.

Credit Crunch Chronology for December 2008

4th – French President Nicolas Sarkozy announced a €26 bn. (US$33 bn.) stimulus plan, including a €1 bn. loan to carmakers and €5 bn. of new public sector investments. The French government would offer companies €11.5 bn. worth of credits and tax breaks on investments for 2009.

4th – The Bank of England cut interest rates by 1% to 2% with business surveys suggesting that the downturn had gathered pace.

4th – The Reserve Bank of New Zealand reduced interest rates by a record 150 basis points to 5%.

4th – The European Central Bank reduced its main interest rate by 75 basis points to 2.5%, its largest ever cut.

4th – Sweden's central bank cut interest rates by a record 1.75% to 2%, while Denmark's central bank Nationalbank followed with a 75 basis point reduction to 4.25%.

9th – The Bank of Canada lowered its benchmark interest rate by 75 basis points to 1.5%, its lowest rate since 1958.

11th – The Bank of Korea reduced interest rates by a record 1% to 3%.

16th – The US Federal Reserve slashed interest rates from 1% to a range between 0% and 0.25%, its lowest recorded level.

19th – Japan's central bank cut interest rates from 0.3% to 0.1%, having projected that the economy would shrink by 0.8% in the current fiscal year and experience zero growth for the year ending March 2010.

19th – The US government pledged US$17.4 bn. of its US$700 bn. originally allocated for the financial sector to help ailing carmakers General Motors, Chrysler and Ford.

22nd – China cut interest rates by 27 basis points to 5.31%, its fifth reduction in 4 months.

30th – The US Treasury unveiled a US$6 bn. rescue package for GMAC, the car-loan arm of General Motors, aimed at encouraging GMAC to offer funding to potential vehicle buyers.

Credit Crunch Chronology for November 2008

4th – HBOS revealed writedowns for the 9 months up to Sept. at €5.2 bn., up from €2.7 bn. for the first half of the year.

5th – The Italian government offered up to €30 bn. (US$39 bn.) to recapitalize banks.

5th – Australia's central bank slashed interest rates by a higher-than-expected 75 basis points to 5.25%, the lowest level since March 2005.

6th – The IMF approved a US$16.4 bn. loan to Ukraine.

6th – The Bank of England reduced interest rates by 1.5% to 3%, the lowest level since 1955.

6th – The European Central Bank lowered interest rates by a half-point to 3.25%.

9th – The Chinese government announced a US$586 bn. stimulus package. The plan to relax credit conditions, cut taxes and invest in infrastructure and social projects over a 2-year period equated to 7% of the country's GDP.

11th – US electronics retailer Circuit City filed for chapter 11 bankruptcy protection. It became the largest US retailer to fall victim to the credit crisis.

11th – Swedish investment bank Carnegie was taken over by the Swedish government after its licence was revoked for failures in internal controls.

14th – The eurozone officially slipped into recession after figures showed the area shrunk by 0.2% for the second consecutive quarter.

20th – The IMF approved a US$2.1 bn. loan for Iceland in an attempt to 'restore confidence and stabilize the economy'.

23rd – The US government agreed a bailout of Citigroup, injecting US$20 bn. of capital in return for preference shares. The move included a guarantee of up to US$306 bn. of Citigroup's risky loans and securities.

24th – In his pre-Budget report, Chancellor Alistair Darling unveiled a fiscal stimulus plan. VAT was reduced to 15% from 17.5% and an extra £20 bn. was to be pumped into the economy, with government borrowing set to increase to record levels.

25th – The IMF approved a US$7.6 bn. loan to Pakistan.

25th – The US Federal Reserve pumped a further US$800 bn. into the economy, with US$600 bn. to buy up mortgage-backed securities and US$200 bn. to unfreeze the consumer credit market.

26th – The European Commission unveiled a €200 bn. (US$256 bn.) economic recovery plan.

Credit Crunch Chronology for October 2008

3rd – The US House of Representatives passed a US$700 bn. rescue package. The plan aimed to buy up bad debts of failing banks while guaranteeing deposit accounts up to US$250,000.

3rd – US bank Wells Fargo announced a buy-out of Wachovia for US$15.1 bn.

3rd – The UK government increased guarantees for bank deposits to £50,000, effective from 7 October 2008.

6th – Germany's finance ministry, together with private banks, agreed a €50 bn. (US$68 bn.) deal to save Hypo Real Estate.

6th – French bank BNP Paribas announced it had agreed to take control of Fortis' operations in Belgium and Luxembourg, together with its international banking franchises, for €14.5 bn. (US$19.7 bn.).

6th – The Iceland Stock Exchange temporarily suspended trading in six of the economy's largest financial firms. Banks agreed to sell off their foreign assets to help bolster the domestic banking sector.

7th – The Icelandic government took control of Landsbanki, the nation's second largest bank. Internet bank Icesave, owned by Landsbanki, suspended all deposits and withdrawals.

8th – The UK government announced a £400 bn. (US$692 bn.) package of reforms, including £50 bn. to the top eight financial institutions, an extra

£100 bn. available in short-term loans from the Bank of England and £250 bn. in loan guarantees to encourage banks to lend to each other.

8th – Six central banks—the US Federal Reserve, the Bank of England, the European Central Bank, the Bank of Canada, the Swiss National Bank and Sveriges Riksbank—co-ordinated an emergency interest rate cut of half a percentage point.

8th – The UK government announced that it planned to sue Iceland to recover deposits in Icesave, the failed Internet bank that had earlier stopped customers from withdrawing money.

9th – The IMF drew up emergency plans to make funds available to governments affected by the financial crisis.

10th – Japan's Nikkei stock average shed 881 points, or 9.62%, to fall to its lowest level since May 2003. Yamato Life Insurance became Japan's first major victim of the global financial crisis.

10th – Singapore officially fell into recession after the export-dependent economy experienced a fall in demand from US and European markets.

10th – The FTSE 100 closed down 8.85%, having lost 381.7 points, its worst fall since the crash of 1987, knocking £89.5 bn. off the value of the UK's largest companies.

11th – The G7 nations agreed a five-point plan to unfreeze credit markets, including adoption of Britain's proposal to part-nationalize banks.

13th – The UK government announced an injection of £37 bn. into Royal Bank of Scotland (RBS), Lloyds TSB and HBOS in return for a controlling share of each company.

13th – Germany and France led a co-ordinated plan to restore liquidity into their banking sectors in a move costing up to €2 trn. for the EU's 27 states.

13th – The Dow Jones Industrial Average gained 936 points or 11%, its highest 1-day gain and its largest percentage jump since 1933, following news of plans to increase bank liquidity.

14th – The US government revealed a US$250 bn. plan to part-nationalize several banks.

15th – Retail sales in the US in Sept. recorded their biggest decline in over 3 years as the Dow Jones index fell by 7.87%, its largest decline since 26 Oct. 1987.

15th – JP Morgan Chase announced a quarterly profit fall of 84%, while Wells Fargo suffered a 25% drop in earnings.

16th – The Swiss government injected US$60 bn. into UBS in return for a 9.3% stake and a boost in capital, while Credit Suisse turned down the offer of state aid but raised capital from private investors and a sovereign wealth fund.

16th – Citigroup posted its fourth consecutive quarterly loss with a shortfall of US$2.81 bn. for the third quarter, following over US$13 bn. of writedowns.

17th – French bank Caisse d'Epargne admitted a €600 m. (US$807 m.) derivatives trading loss triggered by 'extreme market volatility' during the week of 6 October.

19th – Dutch savings bank ING received a €10 bn. (US$13.4 bn.) capital injection from the Netherlands authorities in return for preference shares in the company. The Dutch government established a €20 bn. fund to support domestic banks as required.

19th – South Korea announced a rescue package worth US$130 bn. offering a state guarantee on banks' foreign debts and promising liquidity to firms.

20th – Sweden's government offered credit guarantees up to 1.5 trn. kroner (US$205 bn.), with 15 bn. kroner set aside in a bank stabilization fund.

22nd – US bank Wachovia reported a US$24 bn. loss for the third quarter, the biggest quarterly loss of any bank since the beginning of the credit crunch.

24th – Official data showed that the UK economy contracted for the first time in 16 years, with a fall in economic growth of 0.5% for the third quarter.

24th – The Danish central bank raised interest rates by a half-point to 5.5%.

29th – The US Federal Reserve slashed interest rates by a half-point to 1%, its lowest level since June 2004.

29th – The IMF, European Union and World Bank announced a rescue package for Hungary, pledging US$25.1 bn. to promote confidence in the country's financial markets and its currency.

30th – Deutsche Bank reported a large fall in profits following writedowns of €1.3 bn. in the third quarter.

30th – Japan unveiled a 27 trn. yen (US$270.6 bn.) stimulus package for small businesses and to provide emergency cash to families exposed to the credit crunch.

31st – The Bank of Japan cut interest rates, from 0.5% to 0.3%, for the first time in 7 years in response to the global financial crisis.

Credit Crunch Chronology for September 2008

5th – Fears over a global economic slowdown, combined with news that the US economy had shed 84,000 jobs the previous month, led to losses in global stock markets. London's FTSE 100 experienced its biggest weekly decline since July 2002, while markets in Paris, Frankfurt, Japan, Hong Kong, China, Australia and India all fell between 2% and 3%.

7th – US mortgage lenders Fannie Mae and Freddie Mac, who together accounted for nearly half of all outstanding mortgages in the USA, were taken into public ownership in one of the largest bail-outs in US history.

7th – In the UK, Nationwide Building Society took ownership of smaller rivals Derbyshire and Cheshire Building Societies.

10th – The European Commission predicted that the UK, Spain and Germany would fall into recession and eurozone growth would fall to 1.3% in 2008, 0.4% less than previous projections.

15th – US investment bank Lehman Brothers filed for chapter 11 bankruptcy protection after it was unable to find a buyer. It became the first major bank to collapse since the beginning of the credit crisis.

15th – The Bank of America bought out US bank Merrill Lynch for US$50 bn.

15th – Fears over the strength of the global financial system following the collapse of Lehman Brothers caused stock markets across the globe to tumble. The FTSE 100 Index fell by 212.5 points, wiping £50 bn. off the top 100 British companies, while the Dow Jones Industrial Average shed 504 points, its biggest fall since the 9/11 attacks.

16th – The US Federal Reserve launched an US$85 bn. rescue package for AIG, America's largest insurance company, to protect it from bankruptcy in return for an 80% public stake in the business.

17th – Lloyds TSB agreed to take over HBOS, Britain's largest mortgage lender, in a deal worth £12 bn. following a run on HBOS shares.

17th – UK bank Barclays bought Lehman Brothers' North American investment banking and trading unit for US$250 m., along with the company's New York HQ and two data centres for a further US$1.5 bn.

18th – The US Federal Reserve, together with the European Central Bank, the Bank of England, the Bank of Japan, the Bank of Canada and the Swiss National Bank, pumped US$180 bn. of extra liquidity into global money markets.

22nd – Japan's largest brokerage house Nomura Holdings Ltd acquired the Asian operations of Lehman Brothers, worth around US$230 m.

22nd – Wall Street banks Morgan Stanley and Goldman Sachs give up their status as investment banks to become lower risk, tightly regulated commercial banks.

23rd – Nomura Holdings acquired the European and Middle Eastern equities and investment banking operations of Lehman Brothers.

25th – US mortgage lender Washington Mutual collapsed. Its assets were sold to JP Morgan Chase for US$1.9 bn.

25th – Ireland became the first eurozone economy to fall into recession.

29th – European bank Fortis was partially nationalized following talks between the European Central Bank and the Netherlands, Belgium and Luxembourg. Each country agreed to put €11.2 bn. (US$16.1 bn.) into the bank.

29th – UK mortgage lender Bradford & Bingley was taken into public ownership, with the government taking control of the company's £50 bn. mortgages and loans, while its savings unit and branches were to be sold to Spain's Santander.

29th – US bank Wachovia agreed to a rescue takeover by Citigroup, absorbing US$42 bn. of the company's losses.

29th – The Icelandic government took a 75% stake in Glitner, Iceland's third largest bank, for €600 m. (US$860 m.).

29th – The German government injected €35 bn. (US$50.2 bn.) into Hypo Real Estate, the country's second largest commercial property lender.

29th – A US$700 bn. rescue package was rejected by the US House of Representatives. Wall Street stocks plummeted, with the Dow Jones Index shedding 778 points, its biggest ever 1-day fall. The FTSE 100 lost 269 points in one of its worst-ever trading days.

30th – European bank Dexia was bailed out, with the Belgian, French and Luxembourg governments injecting €6.4 bn. (US$9 bn.).

30th – The Irish government stepped in with €400 bn. (US$562.5 bn.) to guarantee all deposits, debts and bonds in six banks until September 2010.

30th – Japan's Nikkei 225 stock fell by 4.1% to register its lowest closing point since June 2005, while in Hong Kong the Hang Seng index ended the day down 2.4%.

Credit Crunch Chronology for August 2008

1st – UK mortgage lender Alliance & Leicester revealed a £209 m. hit on risky assets and higher funding costs as pre-tax profits for the first half of the year fell by 99% on the previous year.

1st – US mortgage lender IndyMac Bank filed for chapter 7 bankruptcy protection.

4th – HSBC announced a 28% decline in half-year profits to £5.1 bn.

5th – French bank Société Générale reported a 63% fall in second-quarter profits, after its investment banking division lost €1.2 bn. (US$1.9 bn.) from sub-prime related investments.

6th – US mortgage lender Freddie Mac announced a second quarter loss of US$822 m., its fourth successive loss, with credit-related expenses doubling to US$2.8 bn. and US$1 bn. lost on company writedowns on the value of sub-prime mortgages.

7th – Barclays revealed a 33% decline in first-half year profits together with further writedowns of £2.4 bn. from bad loans and other credit impairment charges.

8th – RBS announced the second largest loss in UK banking history, with a pre-tax loss of £692 m. for the first half of the year, resulting from £5.9 bn. of writedowns.

29th – UK mortgage lender Bradford & Bingley reported a loss of £26.7 m for the first 6 months of the year.

30th – Chancellor Alistair Darling warned that the UK economy faced its worst economic crisis in 60 years and claimed that the downturn would be more 'profound and long-lasting' than most people had imagined.

Credit Crunch Chronology for July 2008

8th – A quarterly survey of businesses by the British Chambers of Commerce (BCC) found that the UK faced a serious risk of recession.

10th – Share prices in the USA's two largest mortgage finance companies, Fannie Mae and Freddie Mac, plummeted by nearly 50% as investor anxiety grew over government intervention that would leave their stock worthless.

11th – The FTSE 100 fell deep into a bear market (a 20% fall from its market peak in June 2007) as blue-chip stocks reached their lowest level since 31 Oct. 2005.

13th – US mortgage lender IndyMac Bank, based in California, collapsed, becoming the second largest financial institution to fall in US history.

14th – The US government announced emergency measures to expand credit access to mortgage finance companies Fannie Mae and Freddie Mac, and allow the Treasury to buy shares in the companies.

30th – UK bank Lloyds TSB revealed £585 m. of writedowns as pre-tax profits fell by 70% in the first half of the year.

31st – Nationwide recorded an 8.1% fall in the value of houses, the biggest annual fall in UK house prices since their surveys began in 1991.

31st – Halifax Bank of Scotland (HBOS) announced that its first-half profits fell by 72% to £848 m. while bad debts rose by 36% to £1.31 bn.

Credit Crunch Chronology for June 2008

19th – Chicago-based firm Hedge Fund Research showed 170 funds had been forced into liquidation during the first quarter, while fewer funds were launched than at any time since 2000.

19th – Two former managers of US investment bank Bear Stearns were charged with fraud. It was alleged they had misled investors about the health of their hedge funds.

25th – Major new investors in Barclays, including the Qatar Investment Authority, invested £1.7 bn. (US$3.3 bn.) for a 7.7% share in the business.

Credit Crunch Chronology for May 2008

2nd – The US Federal Reserve, European Central Bank and Swiss National Bank expanded liquidity by injecting an extra US$82 bn. into the banking system.

12th – HSBC announced it had written off US$3.2 bn. in the first quarter as a result of the sub-prime crisis.

13th – UK bank Alliance & Leicester disclosed a £391 m. writedown in the first quarter.

14th – UK mortgage lender Bradford & Bingley launched an emergency £300 m. rights issue.

15th – Barclays revealed a further £1.7 bn. in writedowns.

22nd – Swiss bank UBS launched a SFr16 bn. (US$15.5 bn.) rights issue to cover its US$37 bn. writedowns.

Credit Crunch Chronology for April 2008

1st – UBS revealed a further US$19 bn. of asset writedowns on top of the US$18.4 bn. already lost in 2007. Chief executive Marcel Ospel resigned.

7th – UK mortgage lender Abbey withdrew 100% mortgage deals available to UK borrowers.

8th – The IMF warned potential losses from the global credit crunch could reach US$945 bn.

10th – The Bank of England cut interest rates by a quarter point to 5%.

14th – Wachovia, the fourth largest US bank, revealed a US$4.4 bn. writedown for the first quarter following a jump in foreclosures in California and Florida.

16th – JP Morgan Chase reported a US$5.1 bn. writedown for the first quarter against investments in mortgage-backed securities and its portfolio of homeloans.

17th – Merrill Lynch unveiled a loss of US$1.96 bn. in the first quarter.

18th – Citigroup posted its second consecutive quarterly loss, of US$5.1 bn., and announced it would cut 9,000 jobs after writing off US$15.1 bn. in toxic assets.

21st – The Bank of England unveiled a £50 bn. plan to aid the UK banks by allowing lenders to exchange potentially risky mortgage debts for government-backed bonds.

22nd – Royal Bank of Scotland (RBS), the UK's second largest bank, revealed pre-tax writedowns of £5.9 bn. and requested £12 bn. from shareholders to rebuild its capital base.

24th – Credit Suisse reported a quarterly loss of SFr2.5 bn. (US$2.1 bn.), its first loss in nearly five years, following asset writedowns of US$5.2 bn.

30th – Nationwide Building Society recorded the first annual fall in UK house prices for 10 years, with prices 1% lower in April than the previous year.

Credit Crunch Chronology for March 2008

3rd – HSBC, the UK's largest bank, unveiled total writedowns of US$17.2 bn., despite an annual profit increase of 10%.

5th – Credit Agricole, France's largest retail bank, announced a loss of €857 m. (US$1.3 bn.) in the fourth quarter, following a €3.3 bn. charge at its Calyon investment banking arm on losses related to the credit crisis.

6th – Peloton Partners, a London-based hedge fund, was forced to liquidate its £1 bn. ABS Master Fund after failing to meet interest payments on loans taken out to buy assets.

7th – Carlyle Capital Corporation, a US$22 bn. credit fund owned by US private equity firm Carlyle Group, collapsed.

7th – The former chief executives of Merrill Lynch, Citigroup and Countrywide Financial were questioned before a Congressional committee over their large salary and pay-off packages while their firms experienced heavy losses.

7th – The US Federal Reserve made available up to US$200 bn. of emergency financing in response to 'rapid deterioration' in the credit markets.

14th – US investment bank Bear Stearns received emergency funding from JP Morgan Chase with the US Federal Reserve's backing, following a collapse in confidence from its hedge fund clients.

16th – Bear Stearns was bought out by JP Morgan Chase for US$236 m or US$2 per share, a fraction of its previous value, backed by US$30 bn. in loans from the US Federal Reserve.

16th – The US Federal Reserve lowered its lending rate to financial institutions by a quarter of a point to 3.25% and created a new lending facility for large investment banks to secure short-term loans.

18th – Wall Street investment banks Goldman Sachs and Lehman Brothers reported a halving of profits in the first quarter of 2008. The results were better than expected, boosting shares in both firms.

31st – Henry Paulson, the US Treasury Secretary, announced a package of reforms designed to help the Federal Reserve tackle financial market turmoil and improve regulation of the financial system.

Credit Crunch Chronology for February 2008

6th – Wall Street had its worst share losses in over a year, while the UK's FTSE 100 fell by 2.6%.

7th – The Bank of England reduced interest rates from 5.5% to 5.25%.

10th – Finance ministers from the G7 group of industrialized nations warned of worldwide losses from the US mortgage crisis of up to US$400 bn.

13th – The Financial Services Agency, Japan's financial watchdog, said Japanese banks had lost a total of 600 bn. yen (US$5.6 bn.) from the US sub-prime mortgage crisis in the previous 12 months.

14th – UBS confirmed it had made a loss of SFr4.4 bn. (US$4 bn.) in 2007, following US$18.4 bn. of writedowns.

14th – Commerzbank, Germany's second largest bank, announced writedowns of €774 m. (US$1.1 bn.), despite record-year profits.

17th – UK Chancellor Alistair Darling confirmed mortgage lender Northern Rock would be brought into temporary public ownership

Credit Crunch Chronology for January 2008

9th – The World Bank forecast a 0.3% slowdown in global economic growth to 3.3% in 2008 but claimed growth in China and India would soften the impact.

9th – James Cayne, chief executive of US investment bank Bear Stearns, stepped down.

11th – Countrywide Financial, the USA's largest mortgage lender, was bought by the Bank of America for US$4 bn.

15th – Citigroup reported a US$9.8 bn. loss for the fourth quarter, the largest in its history. The bank also announced a capital injection of US$6.9 bn. from the Government of Singapore Investment Corporation (GIC). In total Citigroup and Merrill Lynch had received over US$21 bn. from foreign investors including Saudi Arabia and Kuwait.

21st – Stock markets across the world suffered their biggest losses since 11 Sept. 2001, triggered by fears of a looming recession in the USA.

22nd – The US Federal Reserve slashed interest rates by 0.75% to 3.5%, its largest cut in over 25 years.

28th – European bank Fortis warned that its losses connected to US sub-prime mortgage debt could be as much as €1 bn. (US$1.5 bn.).

30th – The US Federal Reserve cut interest rates by a further 50 basis points from 3.5% to 3.0%.

31st – MBIA, the world's largest bond insurer, revealed a US$2.3 bn. loss in the fourth quarter.

Credit Crunch Chronology for December 2007

4th – The Bank of Canada cut interest rates by a quarter of a percentage point from 4.5% to 4.25%.

6th – The Bank of England lowered interest rates, from 5.75% to 5.5%.

6th – The Royal Bank of Scotland warned investors it expected to write off £1.25 bn. as a result of exposure to the US sub-prime mortgage market.

6th – President Bush unveiled plans to freeze rates on sub-prime mortgages for the next 5 years.

10th – UBS revealed it had written off a further SFr11.2 bn. (US$10 bn.) against its US sub-prime mortgage exposure.

10th – France's second largest bank, Société Générale, moved to bailout its structured investment vehicle with a credit line of up to US$4.3 bn.

11th – The US Federal Reserve cut interest rates for the third time in 4 months, reducing them from 4.5% to 4.25%.

12th – Five central banks from the UK, Europe and USA launched a US$110 bn. joint cash injection targeting international interbank borrowing markets.

14th – Citigroup brought US$49 bn. worth of sub-prime debts to keep afloat seven high-risk structured investment vehicles.

17th – The US Federal Reserve made US$20 bn. available to major banks to ease interbank lending rates as the first part of a plan agreed by five central banks.

18th – The Bank of England released £10 bn. of funds to UK banks and financial institutions.

18th – The ECB injected €348.7 bn. (US$502 bn.) into banks to help ease credit fears over the Christmas period.

19th – US investment bank Morgan Stanley wrote down US$9.4 bn. in sub-prime losses. A cash injection of US$5 bn. (equating to 9.9% of the bank) was provided by China Investment Corporation (CIC).

Credit Crunch Chronology for November 2007

1st – Swiss bank Credit Suisse revealed a US$1 bn. writedown.

4th – Citigroup announced further writedowns of US$8–11 bn. Charles Prince resigned as chairman and chief executive.

7th – US investment bank Morgan Stanley forecast a loss of US$3.7 bn. against fourth-quarter revenues.

9th – Wachovia, the USA's fourth largest lender, unveiled losses of US$1.1 bn. for Oct. owing to the continued decline in value of its mortgage debt.

13th – The Bank of America revealed it would write off US$3 bn. of bad debts linked to the US sub-prime crisis during the last quarter of 2007 and

would inject a further US$600 m. into a structured investment vehicle with high exposure to sub-prime mortgages.

14th – HSBC, the world's second largest bank, claimed it was writing off US$38 m. of loans a day to struggling Americans and raising its sub-prime bad debt provision to US$3.4 bn.

14th – The Bank of England forecast a sharp slowdown in UK domestic growth in 2008 together with higher inflation.

15th – Barclays, the UK's third largest bank, announced a writedown of US$2.6 bn. on securities related to the US sub-prime mortgage market, having lost US$1.64 bn. in Oct. alone.

16th – Northern Rock's Adam Applegarth resigned as chief executive.

20th – Shares in Paragon, the UK's third largest buy-to-let mortgage lender, were suspended after falling in value by 50%. It warned shareholders it could face collapse if it could not raise an extra £250 m.

20th – Freddie Mac, the USA's second largest provider of mortgage financing, announced its largest quarterly loss so far after unveiling US$4.8 bn. of bad debts and writedowns.

27th – Citigroup agreed to sell shares in its company worth US$7.5 bn. to the Abu Dhabi Investment Authority, making it the largest shareholder with a stake of 4.9%.

Credit Crunch Chronology for October 2007

1st – Swiss bank UBS revealed a writedown of SFr4 bn. (US$3.4 bn.) on hedge fund losses and exposure to the sub-prime mortgage market. The group announced plans to shed 1,500 jobs.

5th – Investment bank Merrill Lynch revealed a third-quarter writedown of US$5.5 bn.

15th – Citigroup announced a total of US$6.5 bn. in writedowns.

24th – Merrill Lynch announced US$8.4 bn. of losses and writedowns. A quarterly loss of US$2.24 bn. was the largest in its history. Stan O'Neal, chief executive, resigned 6 days later.

31st – The US Federal Reserve reduced interest rates from 4.75% to 4.5%.

Credit Crunch Chronology for September 2007

6th – The US Federal Reserve added US$31.25 bn. to the US money markets and the ECB lent an extra €42.2 bn. to banks.

10th – Victoria Mortgages, owned by US private equity group Venturion Capital, was forced into administration, becoming the first UK casualty of the sub-prime crisis.

13th – The Bank of England provided emergency financial support to Northern Rock, the UK's fifth largest mortgage lender.

17th – UK Chancellor Alistair Darling guaranteed Northern Rock's savings accounts, following several days of a run on the bank's deposits.

18th – The US Federal Reserve cut interest rates by half a point from 5.25% to 4.75%.

20th – Goldman Sachs announced record profits after hedging that the value of mortgage bonds would fall, despite losing US$1.5 bn. from the sub-prime crisis.

26th – UK banks shunned the Bank of England's auction of £10 bn. worth of 3-month loans, an emergency funding facility introduced by Governor Mervyn King.

Credit Crunch Chronology for August 2007

1st – Shares in Australia's Macquarie Bank fell by more than 10% after a warning to investors that its two Fortress funds could lose more than $A300m. (US$256 m.).

1st – Bear Stearns halted redemptions in a third hedge fund, Asset-Backed Securities, following a rush of withdrawals.

1st – German bank IKB was bailed out by rival banks for €8 bn. after it was exposed to losses in the US sub-prime sector.

6th – American Home Mortgage Investment (AHM), the tenth biggest home loan lender in the USA, filed for chapter 11 bankruptcy protection.

9th – France's largest bank, BNP Paribas, suspended three of its funds exposed to the US sub-prime mortgage market.

9th – The European Central Bank (ECB) injected €94.8 bn. into the eurozone banking market to stabilize overnight interest rates. The Fed quickly followed the ECB by announcing that it would provide US$12 bn. of temporary reserves to the American banking system.

10th – Continuing turmoil in the markets forced action from the world's central banks. In total US$120 bn. of extra liquidity was pumped into financial markets.

10th – The FTSE 100 Index fell by 3.7%, its largest drop in 4 years.

13th – Investment bank Goldman Sachs injected US$3 bn. into its Global Equity Opportunities hedge fund.

16th – The USA's largest mortgage lender, Countrywide Financial, received an US$11.5 bn. lifeline from 40 of the world's largest banks.

17th – The US Federal Reserve cut its primary discount rate, the rate at which it lends money to banks, by half a point from 6.25% to 5.75%.

22nd – Countrywide Financial received a US$2 bn. capital injection from the Bank of America.

23rd – US and European banks, including the Bank of America, Citigroup, JP Morgan Chase and Germany's Deutsche Bank, borrowed US$2 bn. from the US Federal Reserve to improve credit access.

23rd – Lehman Brothers closed its sub-prime mortgage unit, BNC Mortgage, releasing 1,200 workers.

31st – President George W. Bush announced plans to help struggling sub-prime mortgage borrowers. Federal Reserve chairman Ben Bernanke pledged to take action to protect the wider economy from market turmoil.

Credit Crunch Chronology for July 2007

3rd – United Capital Asset Management, a Florida-based hedge fund, suspended investor redemptions following heavy losses in sub-prime bonds and derivatives.

11th – Braddock Financial, based in Denver, Colorado closed its US$300 m. Galena fund owing to sub-prime losses.

19th – Ben Bernanke, chairman of the Federal Reserve, warned that the sub-prime crisis in the USA could cost up to US$100 bn.

27th – Absolute Capital, an Australian hedge fund, temporarily suspended redemptions for two of its funds.

31st – After losing over 50% of its capital, Boston-based hedge fund, Sowood Capital Management, was bought by larger rival, Citadel.

Credit Crunch Chronology for June 2007

25th – Queen's Walk Investment announced a loss of €67.7 m. (US$91 m.) in the year ending 31 March, reflecting a decline in the value of its UK and US mortgage-linked securities holdings.

28th – Caliber Global Investment, a London-listed fund, announced it would wind down over 12 months following a £4.4 m. (US$8.8 m.) loss from sub-prime investments.

29th – US investment bank Bear Stearns replaced the chairman and chief executive of its asset management business in an effort to restore investor confidence following the collapse of two of its hedge funds invested in the sub-prime mortgage market.

Credit Crunch Chronology for May 2007

3rd – Dillon Read Capital Management, a hedge fund, was forced to shut down following a SFr150m. (US$123 m.) first-quarter loss on US sub-prime mortgage investments.

Credit Crunch Chronology for April 2007

2nd – New Century Financial, based in California and second only to HSBC in the US sub-prime mortgage market, filed for chapter 11 bankruptcy protection, making over 3,200 employees redundant.

Natural Disasters Chronology (2004–17)

2017

Natural Disasters Chronology for 2017

Dec. – Two consecutive tropical storms—Urduja and Tembin—hit the Philippines killing at least 320 people, displacing over 400,000 and affecting more than 2.3 m.

Nov. – Tropical Cyclone Ockhi, which struck southern India and Sri Lanka, killed 115 people and left around 61,000 homeless.

Nov. – Typhoon Damrey affected more than 4.3 m. people and caused some 110 deaths in Vietnam.

Nov. – A 7.3 magnitude earthquake hit the border region between Iran and Iraq, particularly the province of Kermanshah and governorate of Halabja, killing at least 530 people and injuring nearly 7,400 in both countries. Hundreds of villages and at least 70,000 people were affected. Several historic sites and buildings were also severely damaged.

Oct. – At least 44 people died and some 40,000 were displaced in California's deadliest ever wildfires.

Oct. – Flash flood triggered by heavy rainfalls left 68 people dead, 34 missing and 32 injured in Vietnam.

Sept. – The deadliest earthquake since 1985 hit central Mexico, claiming at least 338 lives and resulting in the destruction of dozens of buildings.

Sept. – Category 5 Hurricane Maria caused severe damage to buildings and infrastructure in a number of Caribbean islands, particularly Dominica, Guadeloupe, Haiti and Puerto Rico, and killed at least 21 people.

Sept. – An 8.1 magnitude earthquake that had its epicentre in the Gulf of Tehuantepec, near the coastal state of Chiapas, resulted in the death of 98 people. A total of 2.5 m. people were affected by the most powerful earthquake to hit Mexico in a century.

Sept. – Category 5 Hurricane Irma hit several Caribbean islands, as well as Florida, Georgia and South Carolina in the USA. At least 102 people were killed.

Aug.–Sept. – In the USA category 4 Hurricane Harvey brought heavy flooding in Houston, Texas, and its surrounding areas, killing at least 83 people.

Aug. – In Sierra Leone mudslides left 409 people dead, over 100 injured and more than 600 missing.

Aug. – Monsoon flooding and landslides in northern and eastern India, Nepal and Bangladesh left over 1,200 people dead and displaced millions.

July – Over 92,000 people were displaced by monsoon rains in Myanmar's Ayeyarwady, Bago, Magway and Sagaing regions and Mon state.

June–July – Floods triggered by heavy rainfall left 243 people dead or missing in various parts of China, particularly in the provinces of Guizhou, Hunan, Jiangxi and Sichuan and the Guangxi Zhuang autonomous region. A total of 21 m. people were affected.

June – In China over 100 people were missing or feared dead as a landslide engulfed a village in Sichuan province.

June – In Portugal forest fires killed 64 people and injured over 200 near the city of Coimbra.

June – Floods and mudslides in the southeast of Bangladesh resulted in the death of over 150 people. Thousands of homes were destroyed and around 1,300 families were displaced.

May – Over 200 people died and hundreds of thousands were displaced by the worst floods to hit Sri Lanka for 14 years.

April – Flooding and mudslides killed 254 people and injured hundreds in the Colombian city of Mocoa.

March – In Bangladesh more than 850,000 households were affected by the flooding of vast areas of croplands caused by heavy rains in Dhaka, Mymensingh and Sylhet divisions.

Feb. – At least 137 people were killed in avalanches in northern areas of Afghanistan and Pakistan, most notably in the Afghan provinces of Nurestan and Badakhshan.

Jan.–April – Flooding and mudslides in Peru claimed 113 lives and left more than 178,000 people homeless.

Jan. – A series of earthquakes centred on Italy's Abruzzo, Lazio, Marche and Umbria regions sparked an avalanche that engulfed a hotel in Abruzzo, resulting in a reported 29 deaths.

2016

Natural Disasters Chronology for 2016

Dec. – Flash flooding in Boma, Democratic Republic of the Congo, left at least 50 people dead and displaced some 10,000.

Dec. – Indonesia's Aceh province was hit by a 6.5-magnitude earthquake that killed over 100 people.

Nov. – An earthquake of 7.8 magnitude hit North Canterbury in New Zealand, with two deaths reported. It was the second most powerful shock recorded in the country's history.

Oct. – Hurricane Matthew killed over 1,600 people, mainly in Haiti. 47 people also died in the United States. It was the deadliest Atlantic hurricane since Hurricane Stan in 2005 and the costliest since Sandy in 2012, causing an estimated USD$8.2 bn. in damage.

Aug. – Flooding caused by Typhoon Lionrock killed over 130 people in North Korea and 22 in Japan.

Aug. – An earthquake of 6.2 magnitude struck central Italy, killing 296 people. Most of the casualities were in the town of Amatrice in the Lazio region, which also had over three-quarters of its buildings flattened.

July – Flooding along the Yangtze River killed up to 200 people in central and southern provinces of China.

June – At least 23 people were killed in the worst flash flooding in living memory in the US state of West Virginia.

June – Parts of northern Europe, particularly France and Germany, were hit by severe flooding, causing at least 20 deaths together with extensive damage.

June – Floods triggered by heavy rainfall across southern China killed at least 350 people. Additionally, a tornado that hit the eastern Jiangsu province killed a further 99, bringing the combined death toll to around 450.

May – Torrential rain caused a series of landslides and floods that killed at least 100 people in Sri Lanka. An estimated 500,000 people were forced to flee their homes.

May – A large wildfire caused the evacuation of 100,000 residents from the city of Fort McMurray and surrounding areas in Alberta province in Canada. Even though no deaths were directly attributed to the fire, it was estimated to have been one of the costliest natural disasters in Canadian history.

April – 34 people in Saudi Arabia and Yemen died following serve flooding.

April – A series of powerful earthquakes struck the Kyushu region of Japan, killing 49 people and injuring over 3,120. The two main earthquakes that struck 2 days apart caused widespread damage worth an estimated US$5.5–7.5 bn. to buildings and infrastructure in Kumamoto City.

April – In Ecuador, an earthquake of 7.8 magnitude killed over 670 people and injured at least 27,730. It was the largest to hit the country since 1979, with much of the damage occurring in the western Manabí province.

March–April – Floods and landslides caused by heavy rain in northwestern Pakistan resulted in at least 180 deaths. Over 1,000 homes were also damaged throughout the region.

Feb. – An earthquake in the south of Taiwan toppled buildings in the coastal city of Tainan, killing more than 100 people.

Feb. – One of the strongest cyclones ever recorded in the southern hemisphere hit Fiji, leaving a trail of destruction and killing at least 44 people.

2015

Natural Disasters Chronology for 2015

Dec. – A storm system across much of central and midwestern USA sparked tornadoes in Texas, flooding in Missouri and blizzards in New Mexico, and caused at least 43 deaths.

Dec. – Some 180,000 people were evacuated in Argentina, Brazil, Paraguay and Uruguay as a result of some of the worst floods to hit South America for 50 years, with six casualties reported. Paraguay was the hardest-hit country, with over 144,000 people forced to flee their homes.

Nov.–Dec. – Heavy flooding caused by annual monsoon rainfall hit the southern Indian States of Andhra Pradesh and Tamil Nadu and the Union Territory of Puducherry. Over 500 people were estimated to have died, with the Tamil Nadu capital Chennai suffering the most casualties and damage.

Oct. – A 7.5 magnitude earthquake in northeast Afghanistan killed over 230 people in Pakistan and at least 100 in Afghanistan. However, more deaths were expected to be reported in remote areas of the two countries that are largely cut off from communications.

Oct. – In the Philippines 54 people died and over 80 were injured when Typhoon Koppu made landfall in northern areas of the country. 2.7 m. people were affected by the severe weather and damage costs were estimated to be approximately US$200 m.

Oct. – Massive landslides in Guatemala killed at least 161 people near Guatemala City. Rescue efforts were hampered by further landslides and rising water levels.

Sept. – Over 1 m. people were evacuated from their homes in Chile following an earthquake of 8.3 magnitude that occurred 46 km offshore from the city of Illapel. Tsunami warnings were triggered and waves as tall as 4.5 m (15 ft) were observed. 13 people died and at least six were reported missing.

July–Aug. Over 110 people died and 1.6 m. were displaced by flooding caused by torrential rain in Myanmar. More than 393,000 ha. of crops were also destroyed in the worst floods to hit the country in decades.

July – In Pakistan, heavy monsoon rains and flooding killed more than 200 people (mainly in the Khyber Pakhtunkhwa and Punjab provinces) and affected over 1.3 m.

May–June – A heatwave struck India, leading to the highest recorded temperatures since 1995. The extreme heat prompted major power outages caused by increased air conditioning usage in some cities and killed in excess of 2,500 people.

April–May – An earthquake of 7.8 magnitude in Nepal killed at least 8,000 people, injured over 19,000 and left hundreds of thousands homeless. An avalanche triggered by the earthquake killed 22 people on Mount Everest, making it the worst disaster ever to strike the mountain. Additionally, much of the capital Kathmandu was devastated, leaving many culturally significant buildings such as the Kathmandu Durbar Square severely damaged. A 7.3 magnitude earthquake 2 weeks later brought the combined death toll for the two disasters to over 8,600.

April – Wildfires caused by extremely dry weather and suspected human carelessness killed at least 34 people in southern Siberia, Russia. The fires affected over 11,000 km^2 and caused damage estimated at US$140 bn.

March – Cyclone Pam struck Vanuatu, destroying much of the country's infrastructure and leaving 11 people dead.

Feb. – The worst avalanches to affect Afghanistan for three decades killed over 300 people in Panjshir Province. Caused by heavy snowstorms, the extreme weather slowed down rescue efforts.

Jan. – Floods caused in part by Cyclone Bansi and Tropical Storm Chedza killed over 400 people in southeast Africa with Malawi suffering most of the casualties. 230,000 people were displaced in Malawi and 160,000 in Mozambique.

2014

Natural Disasters Chronology for 2014

Dec. – 66 people died in the Philippines following flooding and landslides caused by Tropical Storm Jangmi.

Nov. – Flash floods caused by storms killed 36 people in Morocco. Rainfall was measured as the heaviest in decades, and at least 117,000 were affected in southern regions of the country.

Oct. – Avalanches caused by Cyclone Hudhud killed 43 trekkers and guides on the Annapurna and Dhaulagiri mountains in Nepal. It was described as the worst mountaineering-related disaster in Nepal's history.

Sept. – Mount Ontake in Japan erupted, killing 56 people—mainly hikers and climbers. The volcano, whose slopes are popular with tourists, was thought to have been inactive prior to the last significant eruption of 1979. It was the deadliest volcanic event in Japan since Mount Tokachi erupted in 1926, killing 144.

Sept. – At least 560 people in the Kashmir region of northern India and east Pakistan were killed and over 230,000 evacuated in the worst floods to have affected the area in over 100 years.

Aug. – A 6.5 magnitude earthquake struck Yunnan province in southwest China. 617 people died, whilst 112 were confirmed missing. Overall damage to the region was calculated at US$9.9 bn.

Aug. – Landslides caused by the heaviest recorded rainfall since 1976 killed 74 people in Hiroshima, Japan. Evacuation orders were issued to approximately 106,000 residents, and over 180 houses were damaged in the event.

May – Flooding in Serbia, Bosnia and Herzegovina, and Croatia caused by exceptionally heavy rainfall killed at least 50 people, and affected over 1.6 m. across the Balkans and Southeast Europe. The Bosnian government estimated that the cost of the damages could exceed that of the Balkan war.

May – A landslide in the Badakhshan province of Afghanistan left over 2,000 people dead. Approximately 300 houses were buried in the wake of a nearby collapsing mountain, with the high casualty rate thought to have been amplified by the disaster taking place on Afghanistan's rest day (many of the victims being at home rather than at work).

April – In Nepal, the deadliest landslide ever to hit Mount Everest killed 16 people and injured nine. All of the victims were Sherpas working on the mountain.

March – A major mudslide engulfed the small rural town of Oso in the US state of Washington, killing at least 42 people with more unaccounted for.

2013

Natural Disasters Chronology for 2013

Dec. 2013–Feb. 2014 – An extreme front of cold weather, thought to be have been caused by a polar vortex, killed 21 in the USA and affected over 200 m. people across North America and northern Mexico. It cost the US economy an estimated US$5 bn. through damage and business closures, with record low temperatures recorded in cities throughout the country.

Jan. – In Australia a heatwave with temperatures reaching a record 40.3 °C national average caused numerous bush fires across the country. In the worst hit state, Tasmania, more than 20,000 ha. were burnt out and over 100 people declared missing.

Feb. – A meteor with the blast equivalent of approximately 20 atomic bombs crashed in the Chelyabinsk region of Russia causing a shockwave that damaged 7,200 nearby buildings and injured more than 1,400 people. The Chelyabinsk meteor was the largest known natural object to have entered Earth's atmosphere since 1908.

April – A 7.0 magnitude earthquake in remote rural areas of China's Sichuan province killed 196 people and injured over 13,000. A total of 237,655 persons were displaced and over two million people affected.

May – A tornado killed 24, injured over 375 people and damaged or demolished 12,000 homes in the Oklahoma City area. The tornado, sustaining winds of more than 200 mph (322 km/h), was ranked as an EF-5, which is the most powerful type of twister on the enhanced Fujita scale.

May–June – Flooding in central Europe, primarily southeast Germany, Austria and the Czech Republic, killed 25 people and caused over US$19 bn. worth of damage.

June – Heavy monsoon rains triggered floods and landslides in the Indian state of Uttarakhand, killing over 1,000. A total of 100,000 people were evacuated from the affected area and over 3,000 people were declared missing.

Aug. – Heavy floods across Sudan killed up to 50 people and damaged or destroyed more than 110,000 households, affecting over 570,000 people in total. In South Sudan 45,000 people needed humanitarian assistance following flooding, with a total of 200,000 affected by the rising waters.

Sept. – A 7.7 magnitude earthquake in Pakistan's southwestern province of Balochistan killed 359 people and injured over 600. Around 300,000 people were affected. A second 6.8 magnitude earthquake struck days later, killing 22 people.

Oct. – A 7.2 magnitude earthquake in the Bohol island province of the Philippines killed 222 people and displaced over 348,000. The energy released by the earthquake, which was the deadliest in the country for 23 years, was estimated to have been equivalent to 32 Hiroshima atomic bomb explosions.

Nov. – Super Typhoon Haiyan, the equivalent of the highest category of hurricane, killed at least 6,200 people, left 4.3 m. displaced and caused catastrophic destruction in the central Philippines. A total of 13.3 m. people were affected by one of the most powerful storms ever to hit land.

2012

Natural Disasters Chronology for 2012

Jan. – Heavy snowfall in northern Japan resulted in the deaths of at least 56 people.

Feb. – More than 150 people died as a result of freezing weather in Ukraine. Nearly 4,000 others were hospitalized with hypothermia and frostbite. Cold weather deaths were also reported across eastern and central Europe.

26 Feb. – Tropical Storm Irina killed at least 65 people in Madagascar.

7 March – At least three avalanches struck northeastern Afghanistan, killing more than 50 people.

April – Severe drought in 13 Chinese provinces left 7.8 m. people and 4.6 m. livestock without adequate drinking water. Over 4 m. ha. of crop land was affected.

7 April – An avalanche engulfed a Pakistani army battalion headquarters near the Indian border, burying 139 soldiers and civilians. Despite rescue operations, no bodies were found.

May – Heavy rains in China triggered flooding and landslides, resulting in over 100 deaths. Economic losses were estimated at US$2.68 bn. with more than 143,000 houses damaged and 950,000 ha. of farm land affected.

June – Colorado experienced its worst fire season with a total of four deaths in 2012. The High Park Fire was the US state's second largest blaze on record, consuming 35,308 ha. and destroying 248 homes. The Waldo Canyon Fire burned through 6,222 ha. and forced 32,000 people from

their homes. Other wildfires took place across Utah, Wyoming, Montana, New Mexico, Arizona and California.

June – At least 70 people were killed and a further 200,000 stranded as a result of flash floods and landslides in Bangladesh.

June – Floods triggered by heavy rainfall left 50 people dead and 42 missing in China. More than 10.4 m. people were affected by downpours. Torrential rain damaged over 100,000 houses and 738,000 ha. of crops, resulting in direct economic losses worth US$1.62 bn.

July – Floods in India's northeastern state of Assam forced approximately 2 m. people to leave their homes. Over 100 people died in flood-related incidents, including landslides and drowning.

July – The worst storm in China for 60 years led to widespread flooding in Beijing. Around 80 people were killed and more than 65,000 people had to be evacuated.

July–Aug. – Floods in North Korea killed around 170 people, more than 212,000 lost their homes and some 65,000 ha. of cropland was submerged.

July–Sept – More than 1.5 m. people were affected by floods in 13 countries in West and Central Africa. Niger, Chad, Senegal and Nigeria together accounted for more than 90% of the hardest hit areas. The estimated number of deaths was 340.

Aug. – Two earthquakes of 6.4 and 6.3 magnitude in northwestern Iran killed 306 and injured more than 3,000 people. At least 12 villages were levelled and 425 others damaged.

Aug.–Sept. – Heavy to intense monsoon rains in Pakistan caused around 400 deaths, and affected 13,500 villages and over 400,000 ha. of crops across Punjab, Sindh and Balochistan. With around 300,000 people in relief camps, displacement and disease outbreaks were widespread. A total of 4.5 m. people were affected.

Oct. – Hurricane Sandy, the largest Atlantic hurricane in diameter on record (1,000 miles across) with the highest winds at 110 mph, ravaged the Greater Antilles, Bahamas and most of eastern North America killing over 180 people and causing approximately $50 bn. in damage. In the US around 450,000 people along more than 400 miles of coastline were evacuated and over 8.5 m. households left without power. A total of 60 m. people were affected.

Nov.–Dec. – Typhoon Bopha, the strongest tropical cyclone to hit the Philippines in 2012, struck the south of the country killing around 1,100 people and displacing almost 100,000. Over 200,000 houses were partially or completely destroyed, with overall damages estimated at approximately US$900 m. A total of 6.2 m. people were affected.

2011

Natural Disasters Chronology for 2011

Jan. – Flash floods and mudslides in the southeast of Brazil resulted in the deaths of over 800 people. The World Bank lent $485 m. to help with rebuilding and disaster prevention efforts.

26 Jan.–3 Feb. – Tropical Cyclone Yasi, which struck northern Queensland, caused US$3.6 bn. worth of damage.

Jan.– June – In China drinking supplies for more than 1 m. people were affected by drought. The Chinese government admitted that work on the Three Gorges reservoir project was partially responsible.

14 Feb. – The Bingiza Cyclone, which hit northern Madagascar, left 15,000 people homeless and destroyed 8,530 buildings.

22 Feb. – A 6.3 magnitude earthquake hit Christchurch, New Zealand's second largest city, resulting in the deaths of 182 people. The earthquake was expected to cost insurers US$12 bn.

11 March – Japan experienced widespread destruction after a 9.0 magnitude earthquake in the western Pacific Ocean triggered a tsunami that struck the country's eastern coastline. Over 10,000 people died in the disaster and the World Bank estimated the damage to cost between US$120 bn. and US$235 bn., equivalent to 4% of Japan's GDP. The tsunami also caused severe damage at the Fukushima I and II power plants. A state of emergency was declared and over 200,000 people were evacuated.

29 March – A 6.8 magnitude earthquake that had its epicenter in the east of Myanmar resulted in the deaths of 75 people.

April–May – The tornado season in the United States was the deadliest since 1936 with 552 deaths. From 25–28 April an outbreak across the Southern, Midwestern and Northeastern United States resulted in over 300 deaths and caused an estimated total damage of US$10 bn. 160 people died when a single tornado hit Joplin, Missouri in May. Costs to rebuild the city were an estimated US$3 bn.

29 May – In Arizona more than 538,000 acres (218,000 ha.) burned in a wildfire known as the Wallow Fire.

June–Aug. – 159 people died in floods and landslides in Nepal. 70 of the country's 75 districts were affected.

26–29 July – At least 69 people were killed in South Korea after Seoul and its surrounding areas experienced its heaviest rains in a century.

July – Heavy monsoon rains triggered some of the worst flooding in Thailand in terms of the amount of water and people affected. More than 3 m. people were affected with over 500 deaths. Thailand's finance minister estimated that the floods would cut economic growth by at least one percentage point.

July – East Africa experienced the worst drought in 60 years. The drought sparked a severe food crisis across Somalia, Ethiopia and Kenya that put 13.3 m. lives at risk. The United Nations declared famine in several regions of Somalia, the first time a famine had been declared by the UN in almost 30 years.

21–28 Aug. – In the first major hurricane of the United States' annual hurricane season, Hurricane Irene struck North Carolina and moved through the Mid-Atlantic and New England, causing 56 deaths and more than US$7.3 bn. worth of damage.

28 Aug. – Flooding in Ibadan, Nigeria resulted in the deaths of at least 100 people.

Aug.–Sept. – Torrential rains and swollen rivers in Pakistan affected 7.5 m. people and caused 361 deaths.

Sept. – Almost 250 people died in Cambodia's worst floods in over a decade. 17 of the country's 23 provinces were affected.

23 Oct. – A 7.2 magnitude earthquake in Turkey killed more than 600 people and injured over 2,500. The city of Van and the town of Erciş in the south eastern region of Turkey were the most heavily affected.

16–18 Dec. – Flash floods triggered by a tropical storm on the southern island of Mindanao in the Philippines resulted in over 1,000 deaths.

2010

Natural Disasters Chronology for 2010

4 Jan. – Around 70,000 people in the east and northeast of drought-ridden Kenya were affected by landslides and flooding caused by heavy rains attributed to the El Niño climate pattern. 30,000 required emergency aid relief.

12 Jan. – An earthquake measuring 7.0 in magnitude struck Haiti some 16 km (10 miles) west of the capital Port-au-Prince in the region's strongest quake since 1770. Some 3 m. people were affected (30% of the total population) with at least 217,000 killed (2% of the population), 300,000 wounded and 1.3 m. left homeless. The capital suffered extensive damage with an estimated 97,000 homes destroyed and 30,000 businesses lost. By mid-Feb. 75% of affected people still required shelter. Infrastructure damage severely hindered emergency relief efforts. The Acting Principal Deputy Special Representative of the Secretary-General for the United Nations Stabilization Mission in Haiti (MINUSTAH), Anthony Banbury, said that it was 'the most challenging disaster response that the United Nations has ever faced'.

8–9 Feb. – 200 people died after a series of avalanches occurred in the Salang Pass north of Kabul in Afghanistan.

27 Feb. – An earthquake measuring 8.8 struck the west coast of Chile moving the city of Concepción three metres to the west. Although the initial official death toll of 850 was revised downwards, over 500 lost their lives.

1 March – In eastern Uganda, 100 people died and many more were missing feared dead following a landslide caused by heavy rains. 300,000 people were displaced.

April – In Brazil, heavy rains in Rio de Janeiro caused flash flooding and hundreds of landslides. At least 256 people were killed.

14 April – The northwest Chinese province of Qinghai suffered a 6.9 magnitude earthquake. Officials put the death toll at 2,220 and over 12,000 people suffered injuries.

May – Devastating floods swept through 20 of Afghanistan's 34 provinces with the worst affected areas in the north, northeast and west of the country. Some 10,000 houses were damaged or destroyed and an estimated 25,300 people affected.

29 May – Tropical storm Agatha hit the Central America killing 165 people in Guatemala with other fatalities in El Salvador and Nicaragua. 70,000 people lost their homes.

June – Northeast Brazil was badly affected by flooding leaving some 27,000 people homeless. 50,000 people were displaced from their homes.

June–Aug. – Seasonal rains and heavy flooding in China left over 3,000 people dead and 1,000 missing. Damages totalled over US$51.4 bn. with three-quarters of the country's provinces affected and some 645,000 houses destroyed. 15.2 m. people were evacuated from their homes. Gansu province of northwest China was one of the worst affected areas with some 1,500 people killed in mudslides on 8 Aug.

July – Russia's worst heatwave since records began sparked wildfires in the west of the country. Deaths directly attributed to the heatwave were in excess of 55,000.

14 July – Over half a million people were affected and 102 killed after Typhoon Conson struck the island of Luzon in the Philippines.

July–Aug. – Flooding in Pakistan caused by monsoon rains left a fifth of the country under water. Over 20 m. people were affected, more than in the 2004 Asian tsunami and the recent Kashmiri and Haitian earthquakes combined. 1.89 m. houses were damaged or destroyed and fatalities exceeded 1,700. UN Secretary-General Ban Ki-moon said, "In the past I have visited the scenes of many natural disasters around the world, but nothing like this. The scale of this disaster is so large—so many people, in so many places, in so much need."

Aug. – Flash floods in the Ladakh region of Jammu and Kashmir in India left nearly 200 dead and 400 missing and damaged 80% of the region's infrastructure.

4 Oct – At least 145 people died in flash floods in the Papua province of Indonesia.

22 Oct – Around 71,000 people were left homeless in Myanmar after Cyclone Giri struck.

25 Oct. – A 7.7 magnitude earthquake off the coast of Sumatra, Indonesia triggered a tsunami. The Mentawai islands of North and South Pagai were particularly affected and ten villages were destroyed completely. Over 500 people were killed.

Oct.–Nov. – Mount Merapi's eruption killed 304 people in Indonesia. Over 200,000 people were evacuated.

Nov. – Colombia experienced widespread flooding. More than 1,000 have been killed and 3 m. have lost their homes or livelihoods as a result of continuing heavy rains.

3 Nov. – Heavy rains caused flooding in the Philippines, killing 14 people. The number affected totalled over 450,000.

4 Dec. – 203 people died in floods triggered by heavy rains in southern India. Tens of thousands of people sought refuge in government relief camps.

Dec.–Jan. – Unprecedented levels of flooding in Queensland, Australia resulted in the deaths of 20 people. More than 200,000 people were affected and the cost of floods was estimated at $A1 bn.

2009

Natural Disasters Chronology for 2009

Jan. – 285,000 people were left homeless in Mozambique after heavy rains in Malawi and Zambia caused severe floods.

Feb. – Northeast China suffered a drought that began in Nov. and affected some 9.73 m. ha. (24.04 m. acres) of cropland (29% severely). Nearly 4 m. people and 2 m. livestock faced drinking water shortages.

Feb. – Floods in Queensland, Australia following torrential rain affected over 1 m. km² (400,000 sq. miles) of land causing around US$70 m. worth of damage.

7 Feb.– 14 March – In Australia, 173 people died in the 'Black Saturday' Bush Fires in Victoria making them the most deadly in the country's history. Over 450,000 ha. (1.1 m. acres) were burnt, 2,000 homes destroyed and 500 people injured.

16 Feb. – 44,000 people, mainly in the department of Nariño in Colombia, were badly affected when intense rainfall caused the River Mira to flood.

March – Angola, Namibia and Zambia experienced their worst flooding in 40 years with the River Zambezi swollen to record levels. Around 400,000 people were affected and food stocks and road infrastructure were badly damaged.

6 April – L'Aquila, the capital of the Abruzzo region in central Italy, experienced a 6.2 magnitude earthquake that left 307 dead.

April–May – Torrential rain in Brazil caused the worst flooding and mudslides in over 20 years in its northeastern states. Around 270,000 people were made homeless.

25 May – Cyclone Aila, which hit India and Bangladesh affecting much of West Bengal, left 190 dead and over 7,000 injured. Some 323,000 acres of crops were damaged and 600,000 houses destroyed.

9 July – 300 people were injured and over 10,000 houses collapsed after an earthquake measuring 6.0 hit China's Yunnan province.

8 Aug. – Northern Taiwan was struck by Typhoon Morakot that left over 600 dead.

30 Sept. – A 7.6 magnitude earthquake off the coast of Sumatra in Indonesia killed more than 1,100 people and left 135,000 houses severely damaged.

Sept.–Oct. – The Philippines experienced its worst typhoon season in decades. Typhoon Parma and tropical storm Ketsana caused the most destruction leaving around 900 dead and affecting over 4.5 m. In an average year the Philippines is hit by 20 typhoons.

28 Oct. – Torrential rain causing flash floods in southwest Somalia forced over 15,000 people to flee their homes.

Nov. – In El Salvador, a national emergency was declared after 200 people lost their lives in mudslides and floods affecting the capital San Salvador and the central San Vicente province. Victims numbered around 75,000.

2008

Natural Disasters Chronology for 2008

Jan.–Feb. – Extreme winter temperatures across 21 of the 31 provincial divisions of China affected 77 m. people. Among the hardest hit were Anhui, Henan, Hubei, Hunan, Jiangsu, Shandong and the municipality of Shanghai. A total of 485,000 homes were destroyed in snow storms and an estimated 1.66 m. people displaced.

Feb. – In Afghanistan, temperatures fell to −30 °C (−22 °F) during their coldest winter on record. Blizzard conditions resulted in over 1,300 deaths and more than 700 homes were destroyed in avalanches.

2 May – Cyclone Nargis swept through the Irrawaddy Delta and southern Yangon in Myanmar leaving nearly 140,000 dead and many more missing. A total of 2.4 m. people were severely affected and around 42% of food stocks destroyed.

12 May – An earthquake struck China's southwestern Sichuan province, measuring 7.9 in magnitude. With an estimated death toll of 87,000, it was the deadliest Chinese earthquake since the 1976 Tangshan quake. On 6 Nov. the government announced a 1trn. yuan (US$146 bn.) 3-year reconstruction plan making the earthquake the most costly natural disaster in the country's history.

June–Aug. – California experienced its worst wildfires in decades when freak dry lightning storms sparked as many as 2,000 fires across the north of the state. 530,000 ha. (1.3 m. acres) and 2,219 structures were burned resulting in approximately US$2 bn. worth of damage.

June – 11 m. people were affected by floods in the US states of Illinois, Indiana, Iowa, Michigan, Minnesota, Missouri and Wisconsin. Damage costs were an estimated US$10 bn.

17–26 June – Typhoon Fengshen (Frank) struck the Philippines with winds of up to 160 km/h (100 mph) and heavy rain causing flash floods, storm surges and landslides. Over 550 people were reported dead on land and an estimated 2.4 m. were displaced. In addition 856 people lost their lives when the Princess of the Stars, a ferry going from Manila to Cebu, capsized and sank.

July – Several states of India, notably Maharashtra, Bihar and Andhra Pradesh, were affected by flooding caused by heavy monsoon rains. The death toll numbered over 2,400.

Aug.–Sept. – Hurricane Hanna swept across the Caribbean and the east coast of the USA. Haiti suffered the majority of the casualties with around 530 dead in floods brought on by torrential rain. Combined with the victims of the preceding Tropical Storm Fay and Hurricane Gustav in Aug. and the ensuing Hurricane Ike later in Sept., the country's hurricane death toll for 2008 totalled approximately 800. 60% of the food harvest was also destroyed. In the wake of the disaster, then prime minister Michèle Pierre-Louis said 'We cannot keep going on like this. We are going to disappear one day. There will not be 400, 500 or 1,000 deaths. There are going to be a million deaths.'

29 Oct. – The province of Balochistan in Pakistan was hit by an earthquake measuring 6.4 in magnitude some 60 km (40 miles) to the north of Quetta leaving more than 200 dead.

2007

Natural Disasters Chronology for 2007

Feb.–March – Bolivia experienced its worst flooding in 25 years, which was attributed to the El Niño effect. The northeastern department of Beni was almost entirely covered by water.

9–15 March – Madagascar was buffeted by winds up to 245 km/h (150 mph) when Cyclone Indlala struck. 150 people died and 188,300 lost their homes according to the national disaster management agency.

March – Freak flash floods brought on by torrential rain and fast-melting snow affected a third of Afghanistan's provinces. More than 80 people were thought to have been killed. Further flooding in June in the Panjshir and Kapisa regions left some 100 dead and destroyed much farmland and livestock.

16 July – An earthquake measuring 6.6 struck the Niigata and Nagano prefectures in central Japan. Although fatalities were minimal, more than 1,000 people were injured and it was estimated to be the costliest natural disaster of the year with damages amounting to US$12.5 bn.

July – In China, a tenth of the population (some 119 m. people) were affected by heavy rains. Deaths caused by floods and landslides totalled 700.

July – A heatwave across central and southern Europe brought record temperatures of 41.9 °C (107.4 °F) to Hungary where some 500 people died as a result.

July–Oct. – Floods across south Asia were described as 'the worst in living memory' by UNICEF. Around 112,000 houses were damaged or destroyed in the northern Indian states of Bihar and Uttar Pradesh and 270,000 people were displaced in Nepal. In east Asia at least 600 died in North Korea in Aug. and 100,000 were left homeless as a result of floods and landslides. Bangladesh, Pakistan and Vietnam were also badly affected.

15 Aug. – 519 people died as a result of an 8.0 magnitude earthquake that struck off the coast of Peru around 145 km (90 miles) south-southeast of Lima affecting the Ica Region and the Lima Province. Over 35,500 buildings were destroyed and the road infrastructure, including the Pan American Highway, badly damaged.

Oct.–Nov. – Following a week's heavy rain, the southeastern Mexican states of Chiapas and Tabasco experienced severe flooding that left up to 800,000 people homeless.

11–16 Nov. – Cyclone Sidr formed in the Bay of Bengal and struck Bangladesh. Official government figures suggested 3,363 died as a result of the storm but humanitarian organizations claimed that the death toll was higher. Coming at the end of the monsoon season, flooding was exacerbated and infrastructure badly affected. 1.5 m. houses and 1 m. ha. (2.5 m. acres) of crops were damaged and 4 m. trees destroyed.

2006

Natural Disasters Chronology for 2006

Jan.–Feb. – An anticyclone bringing extreme cold weather extended across central and eastern Europe. Some 750 Ukrainians died as a result of the cold according to the country's ministry of health.

17 Feb. – In Southern Leyte in the Philippines, the village of Guinsaugon was submerged by a mudslide caused by rains from Typhoon Chanchu. 1,126 people were killed and around 8,000 affected.

27 May – A 6.3 magnitude earthquake struck the region of Yogyakarta on the Indonesian island of Java killing some 6,000 people and leaving around 50,000 injured. An estimated 127,000 buildings were completely destroyed and 1.17 m. people were made homeless.

July – Tropical storm Bilis swept through China, Taiwan and the Philippines. The death toll mounted to 843, over 500 of which occurred in the Chinese province of Hunan. Damage costs amounted to 34.82 bn. yuan (US$4.3 bn.).

17 July – At least 600 people were killed when the southern coast of the Indonesian island of Java was hit by a tsunami caused by a 7.7 magnitude undersea earthquake.

July – More than 3,000 deaths were caused by a heatwave across western Europe.

14–15 July – The North Korean provinces of Kangwon, North Hwanghae, South Hamgyong and South Pyongan were severely affected by flooding caused by high winds and torrential rain. Country officials reported around 550 dead and 300 missing but aid agency reports suggested that the true figure could be in the tens of thousands.

July–Aug. – A heatwave across most of the USA and parts of southern Canada saw record temperatures in many states. There were an estimated 130 deaths in California alone but subsequent research suggested figures closer to 350–450. 2006 was the second hottest year in the USA since records began in 1895 and only marginally cooler than the record average temperature of 1998. South Dakota had its hottest temperature on record on 15 July when it reached 49 °C (120 °F) at Usta.

Aug. – Almost 500 people died after Typhoon Saomai struck Taiwan and the east coast of China.

Aug. – The Barmer district of drought-prone Rajasthan, India experienced devastating flash floods owing to southwestern monsoon rains. The worst in 200 years, the floods left 800,000 people without homes.

Aug.–Oct. – In Ethiopia, the rivers Omo, Awash and Blue Nile all experienced flash flooding as a result of unprecedented heavy seasonal rain. Over 700 people were killed and 240,000 displaced.

Nov.–Dec. – Typhoon Durian struck the Philippines triggering flooding and mudslides that claimed the lives of some 1,400 people.

2005

Natural Disasters Chronology for 2005

Jan.–Feb. – Nearly 500 people were killed after 3 weeks of heavy rain and snow fell across Pakistan with Balochistan, the North-West Frontier Province and the Federally Administered Tribal Areas suffering the brunt of the damage.

22 Feb. – An earthquake measuring 6.4 on the Richter scale hit the Kerman province of Iran near the city of Zarand. Four villages were completely destroyed and there were an estimated 600–700 fatalities.

28 March – In Indonesia, at least 900 people lost their lives when an 8.7 magnitude earthquake struck off the coast of the island of Nias, west of Sumatra.

July–Aug. – Heavy monsoon rains caused flooding and landslides in the Indian states of Goa and Maharashtra. The city of Mumbai was particularly badly affected—of the 1,094 recorded deaths, 447 occurred there.

Aug. – The US states of Louisiana, Mississippi and Alabama were hit by Hurricane Katrina, estimated to be costliest hurricane in US history and the third deadliest. 80% of New Orleans was flooded. The official death toll mounted to 1,836 with several hundred others missing. Damages totalled an estimated US$110 bn.

Aug.–Sept. – The eastern Chinese provinces of Anhui, Fujian, Henan, Hubei, Jiangxi, Shanghai Municipality and Zhejiang were severely affected by Typhoons Talim and Khanun. The former resulted in the evacuation of some 1.84 m. people according to the ministry of civil affairs, and some 102,000 houses were destroyed. The State Flood Control and Drought Relief headquarters reported that Typhoon Khanun had affected 5.5 m. people and 2.25 m. ha. (5.56 m. acres) of cropland.

Sept.–Oct. – 600,000 people were evacuated from the Vietnamese provinces of Thanh Hoa, Ninh Binh and Nam Dinh to escape Typhoon Damrey. 130,000 ha. (320,000 acres) of rice fields ready for harvest were submerged under water and 200,000 people faced food shortages. China and the Philippines were also affected.

1–5 Oct. – Flooding and mudslides in Central America caused by Hurricane Stan claimed over 2,000 lives. Southwestern Guatemala was one of the worst affected areas with whole villages swept away by mud, notably Panabaj near Lake Atitlán.

8 Oct. – An earthquake measuring 7.6 in magnitude struck northern Pakistan and Kashmir leaving millions homeless. Pakistan suffered the most fatalities with 73,300 people killed. In India the death toll came to 1,300.

20 Nov. – In Honduras, 30,000 people were left homeless in the wake of Tropical Storm Gamma and another 60,000 were affected.

2004

Natural Disasters Chronology for 2004

26 Dec.– An underwater earthquake measuring 9.3 in magnitude struck west of northern Sumatra triggering a tsunami. It was the second largest earthquake ever recorded. The damage and destruction affected at least 5 m. people and 1.8 m. people were left homeless. The estimated total death toll exceeded 225,000 with Indonesia (165,700 deaths), Sri Lanka (35,400), India (16,400) and Thailand (8,300) the worst afflicted countries. Bangladesh, Kenya, Malaysia, the Maldives, Myanmar, the Seychelles, Somalia, South Africa, Tanzania and Yemen also experienced casualties.

A Political and Economic Chronology of the Olympic Games (1894–2028)

A Political and Economic Chronology of the Olympic Games

The Games that took place in Rio de Janeiro in Aug. 2016 were the XXXI Olympiad. Nineteen countries have hosted the Summer Olympic Games, including the United States four times, the United Kingdom three times, and Australia, France, Germany and Greece twice each. Today there are 206 National Olympic Committees.

According to the Olympic Charter: 'The goal of Olympism is to place sport at the service of the harmonious development of man, with a view to promoting a peaceful society concerned with the preservation of human dignity'.

Overall Medals Table (1896–2016)[1]

	Nation	Gold	Silver	Bronze	Total
1.	USA	1,022	794	704	2,520
2.	USSR	395	319	296	1,010
3.	Great Britain	263	295	289	847
4.	France	212	241	260	713
5.	Germany	191	192	232	615
6.	Italy	206	175	191	572
7.	China	227	164	152	543
8.	Australia	147	163	187	497
9.	Sweden	145	170	179	494
10.	Hungary	175	147	169	491

[1]Russia's combined tally as an independent state, part of the USSR and part of the Commonwealth of Independent States stands at 591 gold, 500 silver and 489 bronze (a total of 1,580 medals), which would put it second in this list. Germany's tally, including medals gained as a unified state and by both East and West Germany, is 428 gold, 442 silver and 476 bronze (a total of 1,346 medals), which would put it behind Russia but ahead of the USSR.

Origins

The first Olympic Games were a quadrennial series of athletic contests held at Mount Olympus in Greece in honour of the god Zeus, with competitors hailing from numerous city states and kingdoms. Records suggest they were first held in 776 BC and ran until 393 AD, when the Christian Roman emperor, Theodosius, banned 'pagan' rituals. The Modern Games occur every 4 years to reflect the Greek tradition. The Olympiads were used as the basis of a date system (i.e. time was denoted by 'Olympiads' rather than, say, 'years'.

In the nineteenth century there were several localized competitions held in Greece (and also in London) under the banner of the Olympics. However, the idea of an international revival of the ancient competition came from a Frenchman, Pierre de Coubertin (Baron de Coubertin). Born into the aristocracy in 1863, de Coubertin studied history and education (including physical education). An avid classicist, he became convinced that organized sport contributed to 'moral and social strength' and in 1889 began devising a plan to bring back the Olympic Games. To this end he convened an international congress of athletes and sports enthusiasts to meet in Paris.

1894

The International Olympic Committee (IOC) was founded in Paris on 23 June by de Coubertin and consisted of 13 members from Argentina, Austria-Hungary, Bohemia (now in the Czech Republic), France, Great Britain, Greece, Italy, New Zealand, Norway-Sweden, Russia and the USA.

Coubertin argued that the Games would bring the nations of the world closer together. He said: 'The Olympic Games will be a potent, if indirect factor in securing universal peace'.

Athens was selected to host the first Games in 1896 and the IOC's Greek representative, Demetrios Vikelas, was appointed the Committee's first president to oversee preparations. Vikelas, a businessman and writer, had little sporting background of his own but came to Paris as the representative of the Pan Hellenic Gymnastic Club and convinced other committee members that the Games should be held first in Athens, rather than in Paris as de Coubertin had anticipated. He was elected president rather than Coubertin as the committee's regulations stipulated the president should come from the next host country.

1896
Games of the I Olympiad
Host city: Athens (Greece).

The Games ran from 6–15 April and attracted 380,000 visitors. 241 athletes (all male) from 14 nations competed in 43 events. Participating countries were Australia, Austria, Bulgaria, Chile, Denmark, France, Germany, Great Britain, Greece, Hungary, Italy, Sweden, Switzerland and the USA. Belgium and Russia withdrew for logistical reasons.

Athletes competed as individuals or as representatives of clubs rather than as internationals. James Connolly of the USA won the triple jump to become the first modern Olympic champion. A Greek runner, Spyridon Louis, won the marathon (which began in the city of Marathon) in the event most symbolically important to the host country.

Following the Games, Baron de Coubertin replaced Vikelas as IOC president.

Final Medals Table

Nation	Gold	Silver	Bronze	Total
Greece	10	17	19	46
USA	11	7	2	20
Germany	6	5	2	13

1900
Games of the II Olympiad
Host city: Paris (France).

The Games ran from 20 May–28 Oct. and attracted 110,000 visitors. 997 athletes (975 male and 22 female) from 24 nations competed in 95 events.

Contemporaneously, Paris hosted the Exposition Universelle, which attracted 50 m. visitors and had prompted major infrastructural developments including the construction of the Gare de Lyon, Gare d'Orsay, Grand Palais and the first Metro line. The Games were held as part of the Exposition but garnered little interest, with many competitors unaware that they were participating in the Olympics at all. Women made their debut in competition, with Madame Després, Madame Filleaul Brohy and Mademoiselle Ohnier (all French) becoming the first when they took part in the croquet (playing against male opponents).

In the final of the coxed rowing, the Dutch crew replaced their usual cox with a local boy to lessen the weight in their boat. The crew won the race but the identity of the boy, believed to be aged between 7 and 10 years old and thus the youngest ever Olympic champion, was not recorded.

Final Medals Table

Nation	Gold	Silver	Bronze	Total
France	28	44	36	108
USA	19	14	15	48
Great Britain	16	6	9	31

1904
Games of the III Olympiad
Host city: St Louis (USA).
Unsuccessful candidate city: Chicago.

The Games ran from 1 July–23 Nov. and attracted 134,000 visitors. 651 athletes (645 male and six female) from 12 nations competed in 91 events.

St Louis hosted the World's Fair alongside the Games but, as happened in Paris, the Games attracted much less interest than competing attractions. The Fair featured a Boer War exhibition that included members of the Tswana tribe. Two of them, Len Tau and Jan Mashiani, competed in the marathon to become the first African competitors in the Olympics.

Gold, silver and bronze medals were awarded for the first time. Previously, winners had received silver medals.

Final Medals Table

Nation	Gold	Silver	Bronze	Total
USA	78	82	79	239
Germany	4	4	5	13
Cuba	4	2	3	9

1906
Athens (Greece) hosted the Intercalated Games. Though organized in conjunction with the IOC they were not officially recognized as part of the Olympic cycle. It was hoped the Games would reinvigorate the Olympic movement, which had lost much of the momentum created by the 1896 Games at the subsequent Paris and St Louis Games. The Intercalated Games were to be held in Athens at the mid-way point between each Olympics. However, by 1910 Greece was undergoing political and economic upheaval and plans for the tournament were halted and never revived.

Final Medals Table

Nation	Gold	Silver	Bronze	Total
France	15	9	16	40
Greece	8	13	13	34
Great Britain	8	11	5	24

1908
Games of the IV Olympiad
Host city: London (United Kingdom).
Unsuccessful candidate cities: Berlin, Milan.

With Rome having pulled out of hosting the Games in 1906, London was chosen as the replacement. The Games ran from 27 April–31 Oct. and attracted 680,000 visitors. 2,008 athletes (1,971 male and 37 female) from 22 nations competed in 110 events.

The Games cost £15,200 and brought in a profit of £6,400. It was the first Olympics to have a purpose-built stadium, at White City.

Athletes competed for the first time as representatives of their nation, as opposed to as individuals or representatives of a club. Finland, then a Grand Duchy within the Russian Empire, was permitted by Moscow to send its own team as long as it appeared at the opening ceremony under the Russian flag. Several Finnish athletes registered their protest by refusing to march under any flag. Meanwhile, Australia and New Zealand competed as a joint Australasian team.

British and US officials clashed at several points over differing rule interpretations, most notably after the 400 m final. The British runner, Wyndham Halswelle, was adjudged to have been denied victory after being blocked by a US opponent. The race was ordered to be re-run but Halswelle's three American opponents all withdrew in protest at the ruling, leaving Halswelle to run the race on his own and become the only gold medallist to claim a title unopposed in Olympic history.

In the marathon, the Italian runner Dorando Pietri was leading as he entered the White City Stadium for the final lap of the race but, suffering from exhaustion, headed in the wrong direction. Officials went to his aid, guiding him over the finishing line in first place but he was subsequently disqualified for accepting assistance. The affair attracted worldwide attention.

Final Medals Table

Nation	Gold	Silver	Bronze	Total
Great Britain	56	51	38	145

(continued)

Nation	Gold	Silver	Bronze	Total
USA	23	12	12	47
Sweden	8	6	11	25

1912
Games of the V Olympiad
Host city: Stockholm (Sweden).

The Games ran from 5 May–22 July and attracted 327,000 visitors. 2,407 athletes (2,359 male and 48 female) from 28 nations competed in 102 events. For the first time, athletes from all five continents were represented. Construction of the Olympic Stadium cost 1.2 m. kr. and 444 accredited journalists covered the action.

The Games were considered exceptionally well run, making use of technical innovations including automatic timing devices, a public address system and photo finish technology. Jim Thorpe, a Native American competitor, won the pentathlon and decathlon but was later disqualified after it was discovered he had received payment to play baseball prior to the Games, in violation of Olympic rules. His titles and gold medals were posthumously returned to his family in 1982.

Final Medals Table

Nation	Gold	Silver	Bronze	Total
Sweden	24	24	17	65
USA	26	19	19	64
Great Britain	10	15	16	41

1916
Games of the VI Olympiad
Host city: Berlin (Germany).
Unsuccessful candidate cities: Alexandria (the first African city to put itself forward to host the Games), Amsterdam, Brussels, Budapest, Cleveland.

The Games, which were awarded to Germany in May 1912, were cancelled as a result of the First World War.

1920
Games of the VII Olympiad
Host city: Antwerp (Belgium).
Unsuccessful candidate cities: Amsterdam, Atlanta, Budapest, Cleveland, Havana, Lyon, Philadelphia.

The Games ran from 20 April–12 Sept. and attracted 362,000 visitors. 2,626 athletes (2,561 male and 65 female) from 29 nations competed in 154 events.

Budapest was scheduled to be the host but lost out after Hungary's involvement in the First World War. In 1919 Antwerp was selected as its replacement 'to honour the suffering that had been inflicted on the Belgian people during the war'. Austria, Bulgaria, Germany, Hungary and Turkey were not invited.

At the opening ceremony doves were released to symbolise peace. The Olympic flag, based on a design suggested by de Coubertin in 1913, was unveiled for the first time, consisting of five interlocking rings, representing the union of the five continents.

Final Medals Table[1]

Nation	Gold	Silver	Bronze	Total
USA	41	27	27	95
Sweden	19	20	24	63
Great Britain	15	16	13	44

[1]Belgium became the first host nation not to top the medals table.

1924
Games of the VIII Olympiad
Host city: Paris (France).
Unsuccessful candidate cities: Amsterdam, Barcelona, Los Angeles, Prague, Rome.

The Games ran from 4 May–27 July and attracted 626,000 visitors. 3,089 athletes (2,954 male and 135 female) from 44 nations competed in 126 events. Athletes were housed in a forerunner of the modern Olympic Village, in a complex of specially erected though basic wooden cabins. Events were broadcast live on radio for the first time.

The Games cost 10 m. francs and recorded a loss of around 4.5 m. francs. A thousand accredited journalists reported on events.

American William DeHart-Hubbard became the first black athlete to win an individual Olympic gold, taking the long jump title.

The first Winter Olympics were also held, at Chamonix in France.

Final Medals Table

Nation	Gold	Silver	Bronze	Total
USA	45	27	27	99
France	13	15	10	38
Finland	14	13	10	37

1925
Henri de Baillet-Latour from Belgium replaced Baron de Coubertin as president of the IOC. De Baillet-Latour, of aristocratic birth, had become the Belgian representative on the IOC in 1903 and a year later co-founded the Belgian Olympic Committee. He was a driving force behind Antwerp winning the 1920 Games and was credited with their successful execution despite severe financial constraints. As IOC president he pledged to keep the Games free from commercialism.

1928
Games of the IX Olympiad
Host city: Amsterdam (Netherlands).
Unsuccessful candidate city: Los Angeles.

The Games ran from 17 May–12 Aug. and attracted 666,000 visitors. 2,883 athletes (2,606 male and 277 female) from 46 nations competed in 109 events. The Games cost US$1.2 m. and broke even.

Women competed in track and field events and gymnastics for the first time.

Germany sent a team, having been invited to the Games for the first time since the end of the First World War.

A triple jumper, Mikio Oda, and a swimmer, Yoshiyuki Tsuruta, won gold medals for Japan, becoming the first Asian Olympic champions.

Final Medals Table

Nation	Gold	Silver	Bronze	Total
USA	22	18	16	56
Germany	11	9	19	39
Finland	18	8	9	25

1932
Games of the X Olympiad
Host city: Los Angeles (USA).

Los Angeles hosted the Games against the backdrop of the Great Depression. The Games ran from 30 July–14 Aug. and attracted 1.25 m. visitors. 1,332 athletes (1,206 male and 126 female) from 37 nations competed in 117 events. Participation rates were lower than at any Games since 1904 owing to the costs involved in sending athletes to the USA, a problem made worse by California's underdeveloped transport infrastructure. Despite this, the Games were the first to make a significant profit. Los Angeles provided a purpose-built Olympic Village that set the standard for future Games. Situated in the Baldwin Hills district of the city, it was exclusively for male athletes who were housed in several hundred buildings. Other amenities included banks, post offices, a hospital, fire station, amphitheatre, a hospital and a fire station. After the Games, the village was dismantled. Female competitors stayed in a hotel on Wilshire Boulevard.

Judy Guinness, a fencer representing Great Britain, surrendered a gold medal when she notified judges that they had missed two touches against her.

Final Medals Table

Nation	Gold	Silver	Bronze	Total
USA	44	36	30	110
Italy	12	12	12	36
Finland	5	8	12	25

1936
Games of the XI Olympiad
Host city: Berlin (Germany).
Unsuccessful candidate cities: Alexandria, Barcelona, Budapest, Buenos Aires, Cologne, Dublin, Frankfurt, Helsinki, Lausanne, Nuremberg, Rio de Janeiro, Rome.

The Games ran from 1–16 Aug. and attracted 3.77 m. visitors. 3,963 athletes (3,632 male and 331 female) from 49 nations competed in 129 events. Germany spent US$25 m. on facilities. The Games were televised live for the first time, reaching an audience of 160,000 Berliners viewing the action at 25 viewing rooms around the city. There were also 1,710 accredited journalists. The Olympic Village, based near Elstal (to the west of Berlin), was subsequently used to house German and later Soviet troops.

The German Chancellor, Adolf Hitler, intended the Games to be a celebration of the German nation and his Nazi ideology. Prior to the Games the American Olympic Committee had debated a boycott in protest at Germany's anti-Semitic policies but chose to attend.

The African-American athlete, Jesse Owens, won four gold medals (100 m, 200 m, long jump and 4 × 100 m relay) which were widely celebrated as a response to Hitler's theories of Aryan racial superiority.

On the first day of competition, Hitler shook hands with German medallists only. The IOC told him that he either shake the hands of all medallists or none at all. He opted for the latter, prompting allegations that he wanted to avoid contact with any Jewish or black champions. The international press widely reported that Hitler had snubbed Owens specifically after his achievements. However, Owens would later comment in relation to the USA's own segregationist policies of the time: 'Hitler didn't snub me—it was FDR [US President, Franklin Delano Roosevelt] who snubbed me. The president didn't even send me a telegram'.

Shortly after the Olympics, the chief of the Olympic village, Capt. Wolfgang Fürstner, committed suicide when he learned that he had been classified as Jewish and dismissed from military service.

The Spanish Popular Front government boycotted the Games and arranged a rival socialist People's Olympiad in Barcelona, which was cancelled on the outbreak of the Spanish Civil War.

Final Medals Table

Nation	Gold	Silver	Bronze	Total
Germany	38	31	32	101
USA	24	21	12	57
Italy	9	13	5	27

1940
Games of the XII Olympiad
Host city: Helsinki (Finland).

Tokyo was awarded the Games in 1936 but was stripped of them in 1939 following the outbreak of the Second Sino-Japanese War. Helsinki was selected to replace Tokyo but the Games were cancelled indefinitely after the Second World War began in 1939.

1942
Henri de Baillet-Latour died. His successor as IOC president was not appointed until 1946.

1944
Games of the XIII Olympiad
Host city: London (United Kingdom).
Unsuccessful candidate cities: Athens, Budapest, Detroit, Helsinki, Lausanne, Montreal, Rome.

Having been awarded to London in June 1939, the Games fell victim to the war.

1946
Sigfrid Edström of Sweden became IOC president. Born in 1870, Edström was an industrialist and a noted sprinter in his youth, before becoming increasingly involved in sports administration. A leading organizer of the 1912 Games, he also established the International Amateur Athletics Federation. He was instrumental in reviving the Olympic movement following the Second World War.

1948
Games of the XIV Olympiad
Host city: London (United Kingdom).

London was selected without election, having been unable to host the XIII Olympiad. Unsuccessful candidate cities: Baltimore, Lausanne, Los Angeles, Minneapolis, Philadelphia.

The Games ran from 29 July–14 Aug. and attracted 1.25 m. visitors. 4,104 athletes (3,714 male and 390 female) from 59 nations competed in 136 events. Putting on the Games cost £742,000. TV rights were sold for 1,000 guineas (US$3,000) and pictures were available to private viewers for the first time.

Impacted by shortages of food and resources, these came to be known as the Austerity Games. Several teams, including the USA, brought with them their own provisions since in Britain rationing was still in force. There was insufficient funding to build an Olympic Village so male competitors were housed in RAF bases while female competitors stayed in university accommodation. Nonetheless, the Games were considered a success and represented an opportunity for the UK to emerge from its wartime shadow. Neither Germany nor Japan was invited to compete while the USSR refused its invitation.

Alice Coachman of the USA won the women's high jump to become the first black female champion.

Marie Provazníková, the president of the Czechoslovakian gymnastics team, became the first person to defect during a Games following the communist takeover in her homeland.

The International Wheelchair Games was held to coincide with the main Games. For veterans of the Second World War who had suffered spinal injuries, the tournament was the forerunner of the Paralympics.

Final Medals Table

Nation	Gold	Silver	Bronze	Total
USA	38	27	19	84
Sweden	17	11	18	46
France	11	6	15	32

1952
Games of the XV Olympiad
Host city: Helsinki (Finland).
Unsuccessful candidate cities: Amsterdam, Chicago, Detroit, Los Angeles, Minneapolis, Philadelphia.

The Games ran from 19 July–3 Aug. and attracted 1.38 m. visitors. 4,955 athletes (4,436 male and 519 female) from 69 nations competed in 149 events. The Games cost 1,581 m. marks. There were 1,848 accredited journalists covering events.

Germany returned to the Games for the first time since 1936, with a team comprising athletes only from West Germany. A team from the USSR also competed for the first time (Russia having last sent a team in 1912). However, Eastern Bloc nations refused to share the Olympic Village and were accommodated separately. Israel also sent a team for the first time.

Teams from the People's Republic of China (PRC) and the Republic of China (ROC; Taiwan) were included by the IOC, although the ROC withdrew in protest at being registered as 'China (Formosa)'.

Avery Brundage (USA) was appointed president of the IOC after Sigrid Edström retired. Born in 1887, Brundage competed at the 1912 Olympics in the pentathlon and decathlon. He was elected president of the Amateur Athletic Union in 1928, the US Olympic Committee in 1929 and the International Amateur Athletic Federation in 1930. He was against boycotting the 1936 Berlin Games, opposing the US IOC representative, Ernest Lee Jahncke, on the issue. Jahncke was expelled from the IOC over his stance and Brundage, who had argued that athletes should not become involved in 'the present Jew–Nazi altercation', replaced him. As IOC president, Brundage was vehemently opposed to professionalism in sport and to what he perceived as the mixing of sport and politics.

Final Medals Table

Nation	Gold	Silver	Bronze	Total
USA	40	19	17	76
USSR	22	30	19	71
Hungary	16	10	16	42

1956

Games of the XVI Olympiad
Host city: Melbourne (Australia) plus Stockholm (Sweden).
Unsuccessful candidate cities: Buenos Aires, Chicago, Detroit, Los Angeles, Mexico City, Minneapolis, Philadelphia, San Francisco.

The first Games to be held in the Southern Hemisphere ran from 22 Nov.–8 Dec. and attracted 1.5 m. visitors. 3,314 athletes (2,938 male and 376 female) from 72 nations competed in 145 events. Because of Australia's strict quarantine regulations, equestrian events were held in Stockholm, attracting an additional 240,000 spectators. The Games cost approximately £A1.76 m. (US$1.97 m.)

In Oct./Nov. 1956 Soviet forces had invaded Hungary to put down a popular uprising against the ruling communist regime. As a protest against Moscow's intervention, the Netherlands, Spain and Switzerland boycotted the Games.

Hungary met the USSR in the water polo competition in what became known as the 'Blood in the Water' match after the highly-charged contest ended with a member of the Soviet team cutting an opponent with a punch. The game was abandoned early for fear of crowd trouble and Hungary was awarded the match, having been leading 4–0.

45 Hungarian athletes (around 40% of the team) applied for political asylum. They included the artistic gymnast Ágnes Keleti. She had won a gold, silver and two bronzes at Helsinki in 1952 and followed up the achievement by gaining four golds and two silvers in Melbourne.

Meanwhile, Egypt, Iraq and Lebanon boycotted the Games in protest at British, French and Israeli involvement in the Suez Crisis, which had resulted in military action at the end of Oct. The People's Republic of China withdrew after organizers registered the committees from both the PRC and ROC as the 'Chinese National Olympic Committee'. East and West Germany competed as the United Team of Germany.

Final Medals Table

Nation	Gold	Silver	Bronze	Total
USSR	37	29	32	98
USA	32	25	17	74
Australia	13	8	14	35

1958

The People's Republic of China resigned from the IOC.

1959

The IOC declared that the ROC could not call itself the 'Chinese National Olympic Committee' as it lacked jurisdiction on the Chinese mainland.

1960

Games of the XVII Olympiad
Host city: Rome (Italy).
Unsuccessful candidate cities: Brussels, Budapest, Detroit, Lausanne, Mexico City, Tokyo.

The Games ran from 25 Aug.–11 Sept. and attracted 1.44 m. visitors. 5,338 athletes (4,727 male and 611 female) from 83 nations competed in 150 events. The cost of hosting the Games was US$7.2 m. The Games were the first to have global television coverage and rights were sold for US$1.2 m. There were 2,194 accredited journalists.

Abebe Bikila of Ethiopia became the first black African to win a gold medal, triumphing in the marathon (running barefoot).

Danish cyclist Knud Jensen died from a drug overdose during a road race. He was found to have amphetamines, vasodilators and high levels of caffeine in his system, although his autopsy also pointed to the extreme heat on the day of the race as a contributing factor. The incident led to the introduction of drug testing at the Games from 1968.

The ROC competed as the 'Republic of China (Formosa)'.

The first official Paralympic Games were held.

Final Medals Table

Nation	Gold	Silver	Bronze	Total
USSR	43	29	31	103
USA	34	21	16	71
Germany	12	19	11	42

1964

Games of the XVIII Olympiad
Host city: Tokyo (Japan).
Unsuccessful candidate cities: Brussels, Detroit, Vienna.

The Games, the first to be held in Asia, ran from 10–24 Oct. and attracted 2.06 m. visitors. 5,151 athletes (4,473 male and 678 female) from 93 nations competed in 163 events. Japan spent US$1.9 bn. on organization and construction of facilities. Television rights were sold for US$1.6 m. (the Games were covered in colour for the first time) and there were 3,204 accredited journalists.

The apartheid regime of South Africa was not invited. The ROC competed as 'Taiwan' for the first time, although participants retained the 'ROC' designation on their kit. East and West Germany competed as the United Team of Germany for the last time. Indonesia and North Korea withdrew over the banning of teams that had competed at the rival Games of the New Emerging Forces, held in Indonesia in 1963.

András Törö, a Hungarian bronze medal-winning canoeist from the Rome Games, defected, becoming a US citizen in 1971. He would compete for his adopted country in two subsequent Games.

Computers were used to track results for the first time.

Final Medals Table

Nation	Gold	Silver	Bronze	Total
USSR	30	31	35	96
USA	36	26	28	90
Germany	10	22	18	50

1968

Games of the XIX Olympiad
Host city: Mexico City (Mexico).
Unsuccessful candidate cities: Buenos Aires, Detroit, Lyon.

The Games ran from 12–27 Oct. and attracted 3.79 m. visitors. 5,516 athletes (4,735 male and 781 female) from 112 nations competed in 172 events. The cost of the Games was US$150 m. Television rights were sold for US$9.75 m. and there were 2,249 accredited journalists.

The build-up to the Games was marred by the Tlatelolco Massacre on 2 Oct., in which government forces shot dead at least 44 anti-government protesters in Mexico City. The incident was the culmination of several months of student-led protests, similar to those then occurring in the USA and several European and South American countries. The Mexican president, Díaz Ordaz, had decreed a hard line against the students and sent armed troops to patrol the 2 Oct. demonstration in Mexico City's La Plaza de las Tres Culturas. A government investigation would later put the death toll at just four and blamed communist infiltrators for the violence. However, declassified papers subsequently suggested that government snipers had discreetly fired on troops to prompt retaliatory fire against the demonstrators.

At the Games, East and West Germany, divided by the Berlin Wall since 1961, sent separate teams for the first time.

Tommie Smith and John Carlos, two African-American sprinters, won gold and bronze medals respectively in the 200 m. On the podium at the medal ceremony they both gave gloved-fist 'Black Power' salutes with their heads bowed as the US anthem was played. The gesture in support of the US civil rights movement led to the two being banned from the US team, with IOC president Avery Brundage claiming that such political statements went against the Olympic ethos.

Czechoslovak gymnast Věra Čáslavská turned her head away on the podium during the playing of the Soviet anthem as a protest against Moscow's involvement in suppressing protests in Prague 2 months earlier.

Final Medals Table

Nation	Gold	Silver	Bronze	Total
USA	45	28	34	107
USSR	29	32	30	91
Hungary	10	10	12	32

1972
Games of the XX Olympiad
Host city: Munich (West Germany).
Unsuccessful candidate cities: Detroit, Madrid, Montreal. (Detroit's bid was its seventh unsuccessful attempt, a record equalled by Los Angeles in 1980, although Los Angeles had held the Games in 1932 and did so again in 1984.)

The Games ran from 26 Aug.–10 Sept. and attracted 3.31 m. visitors. 7,134 athletes (6,075 male and 1,059 female) from 121 nations competed in 195 events. The budget for the Games was approximately US$750 m. Television rights sold for US$17.6 m. There were 4,587 accredited journalists.

In the early hours of 5 Sept. eight members of a radical Palestinian group, Black September, broke into the Olympic compound and headed for the apartments housing Israeli athletes. They killed two of the Israeli team and took a further nine hostage, demanding the release of 234 prisoners in Israel and two in Germany.

The militants later demanded to be flown to Cairo in Egypt and were transferred by helicopter to Munich's Fürstenfeldbruck Airport. There the German authorities launched a rescue mission, during which the nine hostages were killed along with five members of Black September and a German police officer.

The Games were suspended. A memorial service was held on 6 Sept. at the Olympic Stadium. Despite pressure from, among others, Willi Daume, the president of the Munich organizing committee, the Games resumed at the behest of Avery Brundage and the Israeli authorities. Brundage also took the opportunity to attack the exclusion of Rhodesia from the Games 4 days prior to the opening ceremony after several African nations had questioned the legitimacy of the regime of Ian Smith, who had unilaterally declared independence from the UK in 1965.

After the Games, Lord Killanin of Dublin and Spittal (Ireland) became president of the IOC on Brundage's retirement. A writer, film producer and businessman, Killanin had become chief of Ireland's Olympic Council in 1950.

Final Medals Table

Nation	Gold	Silver	Bronze	Total
USSR	50	27	22	99
USA	33	31	30	94
East Germany	20	23	23	66

1976
Games of the XXI Olympiad
Host city: Montreal (Canada).
Unsuccessful candidate cities: Los Angeles, Moscow.

The Games ran from 17 July–1 Aug. and attracted 3.19 m. visitors. 6,084 athletes (4,824 male and 1,260 female) from 92 nations competed in 198 events. The cost of the Games was $1.42 bn. CDN, a debt the city did not pay off until 2006. This financial failure ensured that only Los Angeles bid for the 1984 Games. Television rights were sold for US$34.9 m. There were 3,223 accredited journalists.

There was a boycott by 29 African nations (led by Tanzania) prompted by the IOC's refusal to bar New Zealand from the Games after its national rugby union side had toured South Africa, which had been expelled from the IOC in 1970 having been excluded from the 1964 and 1968 Games.

The ROC was banned because of its insistence on using the 'Republic of China' name since Canada recognized the government of the PRC as the sole, legitimate government of China.

Clarence Hill won bronze in heavyweight boxing, making Bermuda the territory with the smallest population ever to win an Olympic medal.

Final Medals Table

Nation	Gold	Silver	Bronze	Total
USSR	49	41	35	125
USA	34	35	25	94
East Germany	40	25	25	90

1979
The IOC recognized the PRC as the sole, legal representative of China. The ROC became a provincial, as opposed to national, body under the title 'Chinese Taipei'.

1980
Games of the XXII Olympiad
Host city: Moscow (USSR).
Unsuccessful candidate city: Los Angeles.

The Games ran from 19 July–3 Aug. and attracted 5.27 m. visitors. 5,179 athletes (4,064 male and 1,115 female) from 80 nations competed in 203 events. The cost of hosting the Games was put at 862.7 m. roubles (US$1.3 bn.). TV rights were sold for US$88 m. and there were 7,629 accredited journalists.

Prior to the Games, Lord Killanin resigned as IOC president to be replaced by Juan Antonio Samaranch (Spain). Born in 1920, Samaranch was a businessman who filled various posts, including head of the National Olympic Committee and minister for sports, in the autocratic regime of Gen. Franco. In 1977 he became Spain's ambassador to the USSR. As IOC president he oversaw rapid commercial strengthening of the movement.

The USA led a boycott of the Games in protest at the Soviet invasion of Afghanistan the previous Dec. 62 countries refused to compete, though some claimed this was for financial reasons. Chinese Taipei boycotted over the IOC's declaration of the previous year. Zimbabwe (formerly Southern Rhodesia) appeared for the first time since the country was excluded in 1972.

A Polish pole-vaulter, Władysław Kozakiewicz, directed an obscene 'bras d'honneur' gesture at the partisan Russian crowd while competing, which was used as a symbol of Polish defiance against Soviet rule by the emerging Solidarity movement in Poland. Kozakiewicz, who won the gold medal, later defected to West Germany.

Final Medals Table

Nation	Gold	Silver	Bronze	Total
USSR	80	69	46	195
East Germany	47	37	42	126
Bulgaria	8	16	17	41

1984

Games of the XXIII Olympiad
Host city: Los Angeles (USA).
Unsuccessful candidate city: New York.

The Games ran from 28 July–12 Aug. and attracted 5.02 m. visitors. 6,829 athletes (5,263 male and 1,566 female) from 140 nations competed in 221 events. The Games were the first to be funded predominantly by private business and cost US$546 m., recording a profit of US$222.5 m. The hosts largely used existing facilities and attracted unprecedentedly extensive corporate sponsorship. Television rights were sold for US$286 m. and there were 3,837 accredited journalists. The opening ceremony was watched by 2.5 bn. television viewers.

Claiming fears over security, the USSR led a communist boycott that included Afghanistan, Albania, Angola, Bulgaria, Cuba, Czechoslovakia, East Germany, Ethiopia, Hungary, Laos, Mongolia, North Korea, Poland and Vietnam. However, alone of the Eastern Bloc nations, Romania did participate. Iran and Libya stayed away owing to tense relations with the US government. Chinese Taipei, however, competed under the IOC-imposed banner for the first time.

Nawal El Moutawakel of Morocco won the women's 400 m hurdles to become the first African female champion.

Final Medals Table

Nation	Gold	Silver	Bronze	Total
USA	83	61	30	174
West Germany	17	19	23	59
Romania	20	16	17	53

1986

The Olympic Charter was revised to eliminate any differentiation between 'amateur' and 'professional' athletes, after decades of debate over the definition of each term.

1988

Games of the XXIV Olympiad
Host city: Seoul (South Korea).
Unsuccessful candidate city: Nagoya.

The Games ran from 17 Sept.–2 Oct. and attracted 3.31 m. visitors. 8,391 athletes (6,197 male and 2,194 female) from 160 nations competed in 237 events. Hosting the Games cost US$847 m. Television rights were sold for US$398.7 m. and there were 10,360 accredited journalists.

North Korea boycotted the Games after being refused co-hosting rights. It was supported by Cuba, Ethiopia, Nicaragua and the Seychelles. In 1987, under the international spotlight, South Korea had approved a new democratic constitution, having been under military rule since 1980.

The Canadian Ben Johnson won the 100 m final in a world record time but failed a post-race doping test. He was stripped of his title and record, becoming the most high-profile athlete to be found guilty of taking performance-enhancing drugs in the Games' history.

Final Medals Table

Nation	Gold	Silver	Bronze	Total
USSR	55	31	46	132
East Germany	37	35	30	102
USA	36	31	27	94

1992

Games of the XXV Olympiad
Host city: Barcelona (Spain).
Unsuccessful candidate cities: Amsterdam, Belgrade, Birmingham, Brisbane, Paris.

The Games ran from 25 July–9 Aug. and attracted 3.03 m. visitors. 9,356 athletes (6,652 male and 2,704 female) from 169 nations competed in 257 events. Hosting the Games cost US$1.4 bn. Television rights were sold for US$636 m. and there were 12,831 accredited journalists.

It was the first time that all IOC nations (with the exception of Afghanistan) had participated since 1972. 12 former Soviet nations (including Russia) that had acceded to the Commonwealth of Independent States competed as the Unified Team. Germany sent its first unified team since 1964, although it fared less well in terms of medals than the East German team alone in 1988. South Africa participated for the first time since 1960, having abolished apartheid, and Yemen sent a team following the unification of North and South Yemen in 1990.

Civil war-torn Yugoslavia was banned from team sports but individual athletes were permitted to compete as 'independent Olympic participants'. The former Yugoslav constituent states of Bosnia and Herzegovina, Croatia and Slovenia sent independent teams for the first time.

Derartu Tulu of Ethiopia won the women's 10,000 m, becoming the first female, black African champion.

Final Medals Table

Nation	Gold	Silver	Bronze	Total
Unified Team	45	38	29	112
USA	37	34	37	108
Germany	33	21	28	82

1994

For the first time, the Winter Olympics were held at the mid-point between Summer Games. Lillehammer in Norway hosted.

1996

Games of the XXVI Olympiad
Host city: Atlanta (USA).
Unsuccessful candidate cities: Athens, Belgrade, Manchester, Melbourne, Toronto.

The Games ran from 19 July–9 Aug. and attracted 8.38 m. visitors. 10,318 athletes (6,806 male and 3,512 female) from 197 nations competed in 271 events. The cost was US$1.7 bn., with TV rights generating revenues of US$900 m. There were 19,161 accredited journalists. The Games received widespread media criticism for excessive commercialism. The first official Games website was uploaded, receiving 189 m. hits over the course of competition.

On 27 July a bomb exploded in the Centennial Olympic Park, killing one and injuring 111. Eric Rudolph was later convicted of the attack, along with several other bombings. His motive was never conclusively established.

Russia appeared independently for the first time since 1912.

Paea Wolfgramm won silver in the super heavyweight boxing, making Tonga the independent country with the smallest population ever to win an Olympic medal.

Final Medals Table

Nation	Gold	Silver	Bronze	Total
USA	44	32	25	101
Germany	20	18	27	65
Russia	26	21	16	63

1999

Ten members of the IOC were expelled and a further ten disciplined over allegations of corruption during the bidding process for the 2002 Winter Olympic Games, awarded to Salt Lake City.

2000

Games of the XXVII Olympiad
Host city: Sydney (Australia).
Unsuccessful candidate cities: Beijing, Berlin, İstanbul, Manchester.

The Games ran from 15 Sept.–1 Oct., with 6.7 m. spectator tickets sold. 10,651 athletes (6,582 male and 4,069 female) from 199 nations and territories competed in 300 events. Hosting the Games cost US$3.84 bn. Television rights (covering 3.6 bn. people) were sold for US$1.3 bn. and there were 16,033 accredited journalists. The official Games website received 11.3 bn. hits over the course of competition.

For the first time, athletes from the two Koreas paraded together at an opening ceremony, under a single banner representing the Korean peninsula. Timor-Leste sent a team that competed as individuals under the Olympic flag. The province had voted for independence from Indonesia in a referendum the previous year and became a sovereign state in 2002.

Final Medals Table

Nation	Gold	Silver	Bronze	Total
USA	37	24	32	93
Russia	32	28	29	89
China	28	16	14	58

2001

Jacques Rogge (Belgium) was elected president of the IOC after Juan Antonio Samaranch stepped down. Born in 1942, he was a world champion yachtsman who appeared in three Olympics between 1968 and 1976, and also represented his country at rugby union. An orthopaedic surgeon, he headed the National Olympic Committee from 1989–92 and the European Olympic Committee from 1989–2001. He left office in 2013, with his tenure having coincided with a relatively calm period for the movement.

2004

Games of the XXVIII Olympiad
Host city: Athens (Greece).
Unsuccessful candidate cities: Buenos Aires, Cape Town, Rome, Stockholm.

In 2000 the IOC expressed concern at the slow progress of preparations in Athens. By March 2004 there was growing concern that venues and infrastructure projects would not be completed before the Games started, with the Greek organizing committee announcing that a planned roof for the aquatics complex would no longer be built. The Olympic Stadium was finally opened in Aug. 2004, as were Athens' new tram and light railway services. By the time of the opening ceremony, all venues were completed and ready for use.

The Games ran from 13–29 Aug. and 3.6 m. spectator tickets were sold. 10,625 athletes (6,296 male and 4,329 female) from 201 nations and territories competed in 301 events. The cost of the Games was put at US$11.6 bn. Television rights (covering 3.9 bn. people) were sold for US$1.5 bn. and there were 21,500 accredited journalists.

Kiribati sent a team for the first time, having become independent in 1979. Despite ongoing domestic instability, the Iraqi football team reached the semi-final stage.

Final Medals Table

Nation	Gold	Silver	Bronze	Total
USA	36	39	26	101
Russia	28	26	36	90
China	32	17	14	63

2008

Games of the XXIX Olympiad
Host city: Beijing (China).
Unsuccessful candidate cities: İstanbul, Osaka, Paris, Toronto.

The Games ran from 8–24 Aug., with 65 m. spectator tickets sold. 10,942 athletes (6,305 male and 4,637 female) from 204 nations and territories competed in 302 events. The Games were the most expensive in history with costs of US$20 bn. They were estimated to have contributed 1% towards Chinese GDP growth in the period 2001–07. Television rights were sold for US$1.7 bn.

The pre-Games Olympic Torch Relay was marred by protests along several legs aimed at China's civil rights record and, in particular, its treatment of Tibet. Nonetheless, the Games were widely hailed as a spectacular success, confirming China's emergence as one of the world's leading economic powers.

Final Medals Table

Nation	Gold	Silver	Bronze	Total
USA	36	38	36	110
China	51	21	28	100
Russia	22	21	29	72

2012

Games of the XXX Olympiad
Host city: London (United Kingdom).
Unsuccessful candidate cities: Madrid, Moscow, New York City, Paris.

The Games ran from 25 July–12 Aug., with 8.8 m. spectator tickets available. 10,490 athletes from 204 nations and territories competed in 302 events. London was awarded the Games on 6 July 2005, having defeated the Paris bid after four rounds of voting. The London bid had put the cost of the Games (including a contingency fund) at £2.4 bn. In 2007 the government revised the figure to £8.1 bn. (including a £2 bn. contingency fund).

In March 2011 Iran made a formal complaint to the IOC that the 2012 Games' logo resembled the word 'Zion'. An Iranian boycott was briefly threatened.

The Games witnessed the first participation by females from Brunei (one woman), Qatar (four women) and Saudi Arabia (two women). For the first time in Olympic history all countries and territories participating sent at least one female competitor. The host nation won 29 gold medals, the third highest total (ahead of Russia, which won more medals in total) and Great Britain's best showing since the 1908 Games.

The Paralympics, held in conjunction with the Olympic Games in the same host city since 1960, ran from 29 Aug.–9 Sept. 2012. A record 164 countries and territories and over 4,200 competitors participated.

Final Medals Table

Nation	Gold	Silver	Bronze	Total
USA	46	28	29	103
China	38	29	21	88
Russia	22	23	32	77

2013

Thomas Bach (Germany) was elected president of the IOC after Jacques Rogge stepped down having served the maximum 12 years in the position.

2016

Games of the XXXI Olympiad
Host city: Rio de Janeiro (Brazil).
Unsuccessful candidate cities: Chicago, Madrid, Tokyo.

The Games, which were the first to be held in South America, ran from 5 Aug.–21 Aug., with 6.1 m. spectator tickets available. 11,544 athletes from 207 nations and territories competed in 306 events. Rio de Janeiro was awarded the Games on 2 Oct. 2009, having defeated the Madrid bid after three rounds of voting.

Concerns over security, health and safety—particularly with regard to the Zika virus epidemic—and the instability of the Brazilian government were expressed by participating nations and the IOC during the build up to the games. Further controversy regarding the emergence of Russia's alleged state-sponsored doping programme also marred the games, resulting with the disqualification of the country's entire Paralympic team.

For the first time ever, athletes who had been forced to flee their respective countries competed as the 'Refugee Olympic Team'. The games were also the first to feature Kosovo and South Sudan. Kuwait did not compete, having been handed a suspension by the IOC over government interference in the country's Olympic committee.

Final Medals Table

Nation	Gold	Silver	Bronze	Total
USA	46	37	38	121
China	26	18	26	70
Great Britain	27	23	17	67

2020

Games of the XXXII Olympiad
Host city: Tokyo (Japan).
Unsuccessful candidate cities: İstanbul, Madrid.

2024

Games of the XXXIII Olympiad
Host city: Paris (France).

2028

Games of the XXXIV Olympiad
Host city: Los Angeles (USA).

Sources

www.bbc.co.uk

Guttmann, A., The Olympics: A History of the Modern Games (University of Illinois Press, 2002)

Hampton, Janie, The Austerity Olympics: When the Games Came to London in 1948 (Aurum Press, 2008)

International Olympic Committee (www.olympic.org)

Jewish Virtual Library (www.jewishvirtuallibrary.org)

LA84 Foundation (www.la84foundation.org)

The LA Times

The New Palgrave Dictionary of Economics Online (www.dictionaryofeconomics.com)

The Nielsen Company

Olympic Games Museum (www.olympic-museum.de)

Public Broadcasting Service (www.pbs.org)

Senn, Alfred E., Power, Politics and the Olympic Games (Human Kinetics, 1999)

White, J., The Olympic Games Miscellany (Prion Books, 2008)

Zarnowski, C. Frank (Ph. D.), 'A Look at Olympic Costs' in Citius, Altius, Fortius (The International Society of Olympic Historians, 1992).

TOPICAL ESSAYS (2007–16)

In Search of the Peace Dividend

The sense of relief that greeted the end of the cold war was soon joined by an eager anticipation of the peace dividend, an economic rebate after years of massive military spending. In the event the relief was palpable but the economic impact was short-lived. While world military expenditure in 2004 was still 6% below the 1988 cold war peak, this has to be balanced against an average annual rate of increase over the past 6 years of 4.2% in real terms. In the 3 years to 2004, this figure bounced up to 6%.

The major contributor to the escalation is the US budget for the 'global war on terrorism', primarily for operations in Afghanistan and Iraq, although the latter had no demonstrable link to terrorism. The money has come largely from supplementary appropriations on top of the regular defence budget. In 2003–05, these amounted to $238 billion, more than the combined military spending in 2004 of the entire developing world, including China and the Middle East.

But developing countries have also increased their military spending, even more than official figures suggest, often to finance internecine warfare. Low national income and violent conflict seem to go together since eight out of ten of the world's poorest countries are suffering or have recently suffered from large-scale armed conflict.[1]

The costs are hard to pin down. Governments engaged in civil war tend to play down military expenditure, which, in any case, does not take account of spending by non-government forces, often financed from the sale of natural resources. Moreover, the cost of fighting is only part of the total cost of war. Also to be taken into account, though difficult to quantify, is the impact on economic growth both on the country at war and on neighbouring countries that have nothing to do with the conflict.

Put like this it might seem that a sustainable peace dividend will remain beyond our grasp. But though not immediately apparent, there are grounds for optimism. Knowledge is increasingly emerging about the root causes of civil conflict starting with political, economic and social inequalities, extreme poverty, economic stagnation, poor government services, high unemployment and environmental degradation.[2] While some strategists call for the adoption of 'co-operative imperialism' which implies active military intervention in the affairs of developing countries by major powers, others argue that a long-term remedy requires an integrated policy on security and development, including new types of economic aid programmes, debt cancellation, the removal of barriers to trade in goods and services from low income countries and the sharing of technological know-how, some of which could be financed through a reallocation of resources from military to civil means of promoting peace and security.

This debate overlaps with the war on terrorism. The first official US reaction to the events of September 11, 2001 was to boost military spending and to spend more on internal security with increases in police manpower, more sophisticated intelligence services and tighter border controls. While these moves addressed the symptoms of terrorism, governments are aware of the need to address also the causes of terrorism. The National Strategy for Combating Terrorism, adopted by the USA in February 2003, specifies long-term measures against the 'underlying conditions that promote the despair and the destructive visions of political change that lead people to embrace, rather than shun, terrorism'.

Yet the USA still gives priority to military expenditure of a sort that could only be justified if a continental war was in prospect. Furthermore, the war on terrorism has also had a strong domestic impact in the USA. The Patriot Act, introduced after the attacks of September 11, 2001, sliced into civil liberties with powers for law enforcement agencies to use wire taps, search warrants and other surveillance techniques, often under the cloak of secrecy. That these radical changes to the US legal system were introduced with little in the way of public debate or protest is a measure of the widespread fear in the USA of what terrorists might achieve if they get their hands on high-tech weapons. But little has been done to help towards eradicating the breeding grounds of violence.

European countries spend less on the military but also give emphasis to internal security with wider powers to the police to hold suspects without trial, seemingly unaware that they risk the erosion of civil liberties and the alienation of minority groups whose co-operation is crucial to the success of counterterrorism.

All the evidence suggests that there will be little progress towards lifting the threat of terrorism until resources are reallocated from military build-up and ever more onerous domestic security in the richer nations to helping poorer countries achieve social cohesion, political stability and economic development. Policies to these ends might even produce the elusive peace dividend.

This is the thinking behind the concept of 'global public goods', embraced by the United Nations Development Programme.[3] At the national level, public goods, such as health, education and defence, are paid for, not by the individual citizen but by community-wide taxes. Similarly, global public goods—measures to promote peace and security—should be raised above individual countries to become world concerns. This may seem an obvious point but it has failed to make the required impact on developed countries. In fact, net resource flows from member countries of the OECD to countries in need of aid fell from $264 billion in 1995 to $151 billion in 2002. A World Bank study estimates that another $40–60 billion a year in foreign aid is required to reach the UN's Millennium Development Goals by 2015.[4] Broader policies to provide for poor countries and fragile states would require substantially more resources.

How is the necessary money to be raised? Various forms of global taxes have been suggested. In the 1980s, the Brandt Commission put forward the idea of imposing taxes on international trade, notably the arms trade, for development purposes. Grants from private foundations and other non-government organizations have increased in recent years. At the time of writing, Bill Gates has backed a health foundation for the developing world to the tune of $29 billion. However, national governments are notoriously slow to get the point. The best laid plans are liable to be disrupted by short-sighted politicians in pursuit of votes. Yet in an increasingly interdependent world the international financing of peace and security on an unprededented scale is a matter of urgency. We should not wait for another terrorist outrage to spur action.

Elisabeth Sköns (Stockholm International Peace Research Institute)

---

[1]F. Stewart. Root causes of violent conflict in developing countries. *British Medical Journal*, vol. 324, 9 Feb. 2002; p. 342.

[2]F. Stewart and V. FitzGerald (eds.) *War and Underdevelopment, vol. 1, The Economic and Social Consequences of Conflict*, OUP, 2001. (See also the UN's High Level Panel Report: http://www.un.org/secureworld/).

[3]I. Kaul et al, *Providing Global Public Goods: Managing Globalization*. UN Development Programme, OUP, 2003.

[4]World Bank. The costs of attaining the Millennium Development Goals.

© Springer Nature Limited 2019
Palgrave Macmillan (ed.), *The Statesman's Yearbook Companion*,
https://doi.org/10.1057/978-1-349-95839-9

Two Cheers for Democracy

Barry Turner Charts the Uneven Course for a Political Ideal

It is one of the great ironies of contemporary politics that while the western powers proclaim the virtues of democracy to the rest of the world, they themselves seem to be losing faith in the legitimacy of popular governments.

Judged by election figures, political participation has never been lower. In the OECD countries levels of voting in national and local elections is down by about 70% on 30 years ago. Political parties as mass organizations are a distant memory. Long gone are the days when party membership was the strength of grass roots organization. Even those voters who do turn out on election days are reluctant to involve themselves in the mechanics of democracy. Young people in particular find no virtue in championing political heroes; too many have turned out to have had feet of clay. Of all social groups politicians command least respect. Derided in the media for apparent or real ineptitude they are like the dreamer of the recurring nightmare entering a public stage, floundering with lines that have no relationship to the rest of the action. Few now look to politicians for examples of altruistic service to the community. The assumption is that they are in the job for all they can get.

The questions then arise: does all this amount to democracy in crisis? Should we not look to our own faults before counselling developing countries on how to manage their affairs? Even if it is pitching it too strong to talk of crisis to describe the state we are in, there are good reasons for reassessing the western practice of democracy, the better to avoid a crisis while giving constructive support to those countries that aspire to accountable government.

The starting point is to decide what democracy really means to us. Whatever this is, it is certainly not the same as the meaning attached to democracy by earlier generations. For the ancient Athenians, who were the first to put a form of democracy into practice, it suggested a process by which citizens could debate and decide collectively on matters of general concern. This sounds close to a perfect democracy until it is realized that the citizens of Athens were a small, highly select group. Nobody thought to consult the slaves who did most of the hard work, or those who were resident but unable to claim citizenship by birth or that half of the population who happened to be women.

When, 2,000 years later, democracy re-entered the European imagination, elitism was still the guiding principle. Those with property were alone regarded as qualified to have a share in government. A rising mercantile and professional class sought not an ideal of common consent so much as the right for themselves to determine how their taxes should be spent. The few communities where democracy had real substance were small and self-sufficient such as in Iceland where the sturdy and often aggressive individualism of the early Vikings was contained by the sure knowledge that to survive in a part of the world where nature gave little away, there was a need to stick together. Assemblies of freemen to resolve disputes were topped up by the Althing which served as a legislator, a fair, a marriage mart and the focus for a summer festival. It was by a majority vote in the Althing that Christianity was adopted as Iceland's official religion.

More mainstream were the Puritan congregations that devolved from the Reformation. Denying the authority of the priesthood and proclaiming equality in the sight of God, their experience of self government in religious and social matters gave them a taste for democracy as we might begin to understand it. Rejecting force as a means of implementing decisions, the Puritans sought collective agreement by the 'fellowship of discussion', or what the Quakers called 'the sense of the meeting'. It was a short step from the theological stance to a belief that politics could be managed in the same way.

The issue was put to the test in the Putney Debates (1647–49) which took place during the English Civil War that overthrew the monarchy and led to the trial and execution of Charles I. It was here that the practicalities of government, of getting things done, came up against the idealism of denominational egalitarianism which looked to rule by consent. That everyone should agree to every law before it could be implemented was clearly a non-starter. No matter, the radical voices at the Putney Debates made a powerful case for the universal right to be heard. As Colonel Rainboro famously asserted, 'the poorest he that is in England hath a life to live as the richest he'. It followed that 'every man that is to live under a government ought first by his own consent put himself under that government'. And in a later passage from the

Debates, 'Every man born in England cannot, ought not, neither by the law of God nor the law of nature, to be exempted from the choice of those who are to make laws for him to live under and, for ought I know, to lose his life under'.

Rainboro's strict logic came up against the fear that the uneducated and property-less rabble would act irresponsibly to destroy the social fabric. At the same time there was a firm rejection of the creed professed by Charles I on the scaffold, that a distinction had to be drawn between those born to rule and the rest who were born to obey. The argument would be familiar today in countries groping towards some form of democracy.

A century on from the English Civil War, civil upheavals on both sides of the Atlantic restored democracy to the forefront of political discourse. The starting point was the independence of the American colonies. The newly created states began with a clear political slate on which to draw the framework for government at regional and at national level. Borrowing from the philosopher John Locke, the constitution makers stressed individual rights to life, liberty and the pursuit of happiness as the essential safeguard against government abuse of power. What emerged was a hands-off type of administration that suited the vigorous, self reliant society that was pioneering the new America.

The contrast with France in the wake of its own revolution could not have been greater. An established and independent nation sought to turn the political structure on its head by promoting the power of the people over the claims of aristocracy and monarchy to rule on their own terms. In February 1794, Maximilien Robespierre, the dominant figure of the Revolution who had a distinctly undemocratic way of dealing with those who disagreed with him, defined democracy as 'a state in which the sovereign people, guided by laws which are its own work, does by itself all it can do well, and by delegates all that it could not'. Since, for the most part, Athenian-style democracy was impractical for a country the size and social complexity of France, it was to representative government that Robespierre looked to express the general will. But having chosen their representatives, the people had to accept what was enacted in their name. In this way, the sovereignty of the nation took on an almost mystical power, a contrast indeed from the American model which supported a self-regulating society with little need of government.

The two ideals, though much adapted over 200 years, remain distinct and thus a source of confusion in any discussion of the function and organization of democracy. Following to varying degrees the example of France, other European countries tend to favour the state over the individual. In the US, the reverse holds good. European citizens expect their governments to do ever more to enhance their welfare and economic well being. Hence the social model that is derided in the US for its failure to acknowledge the virtue of rugged individualism. It is no coincidence that socialism thrived in Europe but failed even to establish a toe hold in the US.

On the face of it, there is no reason why the two styles of democracy should not continue to coexist, offering a choice to those nations that still have some way to catch up. The problem is that neither model is setting an example of unqualified success. As we saw earlier there are signs of disillusionment with democracy as a force for good government.

The reasons are not far to seek. Start with Europe. The distance between politicians and their electorates is widening. Those in power profess their enthusiasm for communicating with the populace but they do so in a hectoring, propagandist manner aimed more at manipulation than enlightenment. Sound bites have supplanted constructive debate. Rarely does a politician admit to error or even to lack of knowledge. Opposition, as defined by those under attack, is ill informed and counter proposals are seen as counter productive. Taking its cue, the media treats politics as a knockabout contest, a branch of the entertainment industry with not quite the pulling power of sport.

The gulf between government and people is nowhere better demonstrated than in the evolution of the European Union, a noble ideal that is foundering on the refusal of the administrative elite to accept the need for public accountability. Power is concentrated on an unelected Commission backed by a Council of Ministers who speak for their governments but who cannot be said to have any direct relationship with those for whom they legislate. Such accountability as there is centres on the European Parliament, a sad excuse for a popular forum which serves chiefly as a gravy train for politicians who have been unable to make the grade on their home ground.

Predictably, when there is a reluctant acknowledgement of the obligation to carry public opinion, the process can go horribly wrong. So it was with the referenda in France and the Netherlands on the proposed European constitution. That it was rejected decisively in both countries should not have come as a surprise. Next to no attempt was made to explain to voters what the constitution entailed or why it was thought to be necessary. The patronizing assumption that they had no need to worry their heads about such complicated matters produced the inevitable angry response. But even then, the European establishment was unwilling to accept the lesson. The first reaction from on high was that the referenda would have to be repeated because, first time, they had failed to produce the 'correct' result. The same tendency can be seen in national politics where each state is citing the complexity of modern life as the excuse to take more power to itself in the day-to-day management of public affairs. This has happened most obviously with the counter action against terrorism, now regarded as a self evident justification for lightly discarding civil rights.

Here the spotlight switches to the US, the country that traditionally governs with a light touch. For those of us who admire American democracy and the dynamic society it has created, it comes as a shock to find that the president can assume the power to imprison without trial anyone he decides is an 'enemy combatant' and wiretap ordinary Americans without a warrant. His defenders argue that the war on terrorism justifies extreme measures but it is precisely at times of national emergency that politicians, if they are to be effective, need to be sensitive to views of ordinary people. To ignore governmental checks and balances is to suggest a contempt for the electorate that must surely undermine the democratic process.

The irony is that President Bush has put great store by promoting democracy in those countries where terrorism thrives. Not surprisingly, many are confused by the messages coming from Washington. To the impartial observer it would seem that the American democracy is moving closer to the European concept of the state, with its attendant bureaucracy, demanding a loyalty that overrides minority or even majority concerns. This impression is strengthened by the role that money now plays in America in electing anyone to high office. The starting point for a Congressional seat is a fighting fund of up to $5 million. To aspire to the presidency increases the stakes a hundred-fold. The advantages this gives to the wealthy and well connected hardly needs to be spelt out.

There are those who look to the IT revolution to restore power to the people. In a world in which everyone can talk to everyone else, opinion can surely be mobilized as never before. An example was provided in the run-up to the last presidential election. When Howard Dean announced his bid for the Democratic nomination, he was a long odds outsider with just 432 signed up supporters and $1,100,000 in the bank. Within weeks he was a serious contender thanks to a campaign manager who used the Internet and mobile phones to win over 700,000 converts and raise $50 million, mostly from donations. Though Dean fell well short of his ultimate objective, it is a safe assumption that presidential campaigns will never be quite the same again.

There is comfort too in knowing that while the authority of elected assemblies is increasingly called into question, citizens of the old-established democracies are finding other ways of making their opinions count. The power of lobbies in the democratic system is still imperfectly understood. While, by clever manipulation of the media, pressure groups representing dubious causes can exercise an influence out of all proportion to their popular appeal, there is a profusion of voluntary organizations, including leading charities, which engage the interest and energy of those who might otherwise belong to political parties. In the UK, over 50% of the population is regularly engaged in clubs and other social groups, all of which have the potential for exercising political influence.

There is one other source of comfort for true democrats. This is in knowing that even if politicians are inclined to ignore basic liberties when they think they can get away with it, there are two safeguards built into the system—multiple political parties and open and free elections. Politicians who take too much upon themselves while ignoring those who put them in power, are liable, eventually, to meet their comeuppance. Electoral apathy can reverse dramatically if, as A. D. Lindsay argued in his classic study of *The Modern Democratic State,* the average voter 'feels his shoes pinching'. 'Only he, the ordinary man, can tell whether the shoes pinch and where; and without that knowledge the wisest statesman cannot make good laws.' The low turnout at recent elections in the US and in Europe suggests that for the moment the shoes are not pinching too hard.

But this can change. Meanwhile, it ill becomes those countries that are used to democracy in one form or another to assume that they are beyond improvement. Equally, we must acknowledge that democracy comes in all shapes and sizes and what may fit one country at any particular time may not necessarily suit all. Countries like Russia and China that are only now beginning the slow progression towards responsible government deserve understanding and support.

It is a truism to say that democracy is most valued where it is absent. Wherever there is dictatorship, aspirations to democracy are growing ever more vocal. The appeal lies not so much in what democracy can do as in its hope of ending the corruption and cruelty associated with unaccountable authority. Those of us who are lucky enough to live in relatively free societies must recognize the need to protect and nourish what we have, the better to support those who are trying to join the club.

Further Reading

John Dunn, *Setting the People Free. The Story of Democracy.* Atlantic, 2005
Robert Fatton and R. K. Famazani (eds.), *The Future of Liberal Democracy. Thomas Jefferson and the Contemporary World.* Palgrave, 2004
A. D. Lindsay, *The Modern Democratic State*, OUP, 1943
A. S. P. Woodhouse (ed.), *Puritanism and Liberty*, Dent, 1951

Looking Back

As China and India Make Their Impact on the World Economy, William Keegan Fears a Return to Protectionism

If last year our theme was that 'nationalism is back in fashion', the most marked development since then on the economic front has been something traditionally associated with nationalism: the rise of protectionist sentiment in some of the major economies, and with it a feeling of insecurity which leads nations to move away from the 'multilateralist' ideals of the post-Second World War period towards nationalist strategies, bilateral trade deals and economic decisions based on strategic considerations.

This is a far cry from the perhaps naive triumphalism that followed the fall of the Berlin Wall in 1989 and the collapse of the Soviet Union in 1991. Notwithstanding the 'irrational exuberance' (in former Federal Reserve chairman Alan Greenspan's famous phrase) that led to the Dot.Com boom, and its subsequent collapse, the 1990s and early years of the new millennium were characterized by a widely shared sense (on the part of both proponents and opponents) that neo-liberal economies had swept the board; that 'globalization' was the name of the game; and that economic interdependence and multilateral trading links were contributing to a more peaceful world.

In some ways the more extreme apostles for globalization were as optimistic as those, in an earlier phase of this phenomenon during the second half of the nineteenth century and early years of the twentieth, who convinced themselves that such global economic links would somehow provide nations with an economic incentive to eschew war. How wrong they were then, and how tempting of fate were those who took similar views during this more recent phase of globalization.

'Globalization' means many things to many people: essentially it has involved a proliferation of the links between different national economies formed by a growth in world trade at a far faster rate than the expansion of gross domestic product; and, in particular, a veritable boom in the size of overseas investment—foreign direct investment, or FDI as it is known by economists.

The importance of FDI is graphically illustrated by the official calculation that some 60% of China's exports and imports are accounted for by foreign-owned or foreign-controlled companies. Having turned inward for several centuries, China, under its Communist rulers, began to cultivate foreign capital and the expertise of foreign management during the closing decades of the twentieth century, in an attempt to 'catch up' with the 'capitalist' West, while persisting with one-party rule. After 1991 the Chinese rulers saw the chaos of 'Wild East' capitalism in the former Soviet Union, and were determined to exercise, when it came to encouraging the country's re-engagement with the rest of the world, a very Chinese form of 'economic liberalism'.

It is important to see China, and the much more democratic India, as re-engaging with the world economy after a long period of relative quiescence. Thus in 1820 China's share of world GDP had been some 33%, and India's 16%, compared with 24% for Western Europe and less than two percent for the United States. The nineteenth and the twentieth centuries saw the economic dominance first of Europe and then the United States.

By 1973 China's share of world GDP was 4.5% and India's 3%, against 26% for Western Europe and 22% for the United States.[5]

Between 1973 and 1998 China's share almost trebled (to 11.5%). India was slower off the mark—rising from a 3% share to a 5% share during that period; but by the time of the January 2006 meeting of the World Economic Forum in Davos, the surge in economic growth in both countries was one of the principal focuses of interest. By 2004 China had overtaken France and Italy in size of GDP, and in 2005, according to one reckoning, it was the turn of the UK to be overhauled. This meant that, although not a member of the Group of Eight countries (the US, Japan, Germany, France, the UK, Italy, Canada and Russia that attend the annual economic summits), China was now ranked fourth largest in the world economy, although in terms of GDP per capita it was still way down the list, with average income of US$1,500 per capita, compared with $40,000 for the US.

Economic analysts have been vying with one another in the production of forecasts of when China might eventually overtake the US in sheer size of the economy; and, of course, there has been much discussion of whether the entire Chinese growth phenomenon is sustainable, or whether there will be some kind of social implosion.

Whatever the outcome, the importance for the world economy has been that the 'outsourcing' of so much industrial production and assembly to Chinese 'cheap labour' has led to a revival of protectionist pressures in the West, most notably in the United States. One may also see the negative results of the referendums on the European Constitutional Treaty in France and the Netherlands in 2005 as in part reflecting 'fears for jobs' associated with the 'outsourcing' that has become a feature of globalization.

There is a paradox here, because when they go to the shops or buy (as happens increasingly) 'on line', members of the public benefit from the low prices resulting from intense competition in what economists like to call 'product markets', and in particular from the competition that comes from 'low wage' countries such as China. But the problem is that often this is perceived to be at the price of jobs at home. Economists can preach until the cows come home about the virtues of 'comparative advantage' (each country specializing in producing what it is especially good at, and at the most economic prices) but the victims who lose their jobs (and therefore have less to spend at Wal-Mart) are understandably less enthusiastic. In theory international trade is not a 'zero sum game'; in practice economic policymakers do not conduct policy in such an enlightened fashion that the 'losers' can easily find alternative jobs elsewhere, for all the politicians' talk of 're-skilling' and improving 'competitiveness'.

A closely related paradox has been the coincidence in recent years of a remarkable period of sustained economic expansion in the US and a marked rise in protectionist feeling in Congress. In France, during the 2005 referendum, unease about globalization and neo-liberal economics was manifested less in complaints about the Chinese threat than in fears of competition from the Polish plumber.

It is interesting, but perhaps not reassuring, that protectionist sentiment has been manifested both on a side of the Atlantic where unemployment was relatively high (Western Europe) and a side where, until the Federal Reserve embarked on a deliberate policy of monetary 'tightening', unemployment was relatively low.

The importance politicians, officials and economists attach to China was graphically illustrated when, in discussing the impact of the sharp rise in energy prices between 2002 and 2005, Mervyn King, the Governor of the Bank of England, preferred to couch the impact on the rest of the world in terms of a 'China shock' rather than, as economists have traditionally done, an 'energy shock'.

Thus a spectacular increase in demand for energy on the part of the Chinese and Indian economies had contributed to a doubling of the price of oil within 4 years. By past standards, notably the two 'oil shocks' of the 1970s, this could have been both 'inflationary', in prompting trade unions to press for higher wages in compensation for lost purchasing power, and 'deflationary', in that the diversion of purchasing power from domestically-produced goods to imported oil can have an adverse effect on demand and employment.

But the 'China shock' seemed to alter the equation: while the price of energy rose, there was little sign of inflation in the price of internationally traded goods; and the reduced power of the trade unions diminished their ability to secure compensatory increases in wages, and thus produce what economists call 'second round effects' (on inflation).

Here one can point to a significant difference between the experience of 'globalization' in the nineteenth and early twentieth centuries, and the more recent phenomenon. In the hey-day of the British Empire, Britain was 'the workshop of the world', and the Empire provided it with both a source of raw materials for its products and a market for those products. The modern phase of globalization, however, involves the production or assembly of those goods themselves in cheap locations all over the world, not least China.

Before the Thatcher Revolution and the revival of neo-liberal economics, with their emphasis on the importance of 'markets' and 'the consumer', there was a widespread feeling that governments in Europe tended to be cowed by 'producer groups'. When a factory was threatened with closure, it would be bailed out by government funds in order to preserve jobs. The neo-liberal counter-revolution was against such practices, and in favour of the letting ailing firms take their punishment in the market place. If consumers' preference had shifted, or if they wished to buy similar goods from cheaper sources, then the market was said to be 'working'. In the 1980s and the 1990s the bias of economic policy shifted away from interventionism and towards the interests of the consumer as opposed to the producer.

But, as regards the labour force, the consumer and the producer may be the same person. As noted above, 'losers' cannot always find employment elsewhere, as the economics textbooks glibly suggest.

One can see the dilemma in the 'China shock'. Multinational firms, the 'capitalists' of old, seek higher profits (or to restore falling profit margins in a more competitive world) by 'outsourcing' to, or producing in, 'cheap labour' locations such as China. The Western consumer takes advantage of what seem amazingly cheap prices. But he or she or their cousin may lose their job. It is this phenomenon that lies behind the growing protectionist pressure in the US Congress, and the reaction against 'neo-liberal economics' in the French referendum in May 2005.

But there is another aspect to the 'China shock', and that is the impact on the global energy balance. For, although the price of oil and gas had been rising for several years, it was in 2005–06 that the world became conscious once again of the possibility of a serious energy crisis.

During the golden years of economic prosperity that followed the reconstruction efforts after the Second World War, energy, in the words of one OECD economist 'was something we took for granted'. The quintupling of oil prices in the mid-1970s by the newly aggressive OPEC group was most certainly a shock, as was the second oil crisis in 1979. There were sporadic efforts at conservation and there was a search for new sources of supply. And despite a protracted false dawn, when the real price of oil seemed to have stabilized in the late 1980s and 1990s at a lower level than the crisis points of the 1970s, there was some conservation. As a result, the initial reaction to the rise in the price in recent years was that there was no need to panic, because energy consumption per unit of GDP was virtually half what it had been in the 1970s.

On the other hand, there was a lot more GDP, not least in China and India. By 2005–06 it had become clear that there was also a shortage of refining capacity. Despite President Carter's dictum in the late 1970s that the battle to cope with the energy crisis had become 'the moral equivalent of war', the US, for all its natural endowments of energy, was still dependent on supplies from the troubled Middle East. Indeed, somewhat ironically in view of the way things turned out, the desire to secure supplies of energy was undoubtedly one of the factors that prompted the joint US/UK invasion of Iraq in 2003.

By 2005 Britain, which had enjoyed the remarkable windfall of North Sea oil and gas from the 1970s, had once again become a net importer of oil. During the intervening period, with 'globalization' and privatization all the rage, the prevailing philosophy was that it did not really matter who owned the ultimate sources of energy supply, and Mrs. Thatcher had insouciantly made a virtue out of fighting the miners and running down indigenous sources of coal in favour of imports.

But with the revival of nationalism, and the doubling in the price of oil between 2002 and 2005, came a revival of concerns about security of energy supplies. These concerns were epitomized in the shocked reaction around the world to the brief period in January 2006 when the Russian energy company Gazprom cut off supplies of gas to Ukraine, with consequential effects on a number of Western European countries during what happened to be a particularly cold spell.

Although brief, and followed by protestations from President Putin and his colleagues that this was a special case to do with a prolonged political dispute between Russia and Ukraine, the episode concentrated minds on the issue of the security and reliability of energy supplies. In the UK, for instance,

---

[5] *The World Economy*, Angus Maddison, OECD, 2004

the controversial subject of nuclear power came back onto the agenda. Moreover, such were the alarmist forecasts about future pressures on resources of energy that the government appeared to be seeing nuclear energy not as an alternative to other sources, but as part of an approach in which no possible source of supply could be dismissed from the equation of future needs.

Meanwhile nineteenth century geo-politics seemed to have returned with a vengeance as China and India in their turn sought to establish secure sources of energy from regimes that met varying degrees of approval or disapproval from Washington, and complicated the US government's attempts to formulate an agreed United Nations policy towards Iran and its nuclear ambitions. In one particularly interesting episode, Congressional opposition prevented China from making a bid for a prominent US energy corporation.

On top of all these worries about security of energy supply and protectionist pressures associated with 'globalization' there was increasing concern about the medium to long-term implications of demand for energy for the future of the world as we know it. This promised to make the 'sustainability' of economic growth a key concern of governments and economics in the next few years.

Globalization

A Winning Formula with Too Many Losers?

The attractions of globalization have worn thin. Why should this be so? When it first came into popular currency, globalization was tied to the breaking down of trade barriers and the spread of democracy, thoroughly good things by all accounts since free trade boosts prosperity while democracy promotes individual choice, the antidote to oppression and exploitation. In the closing years of the twentieth century the success stories of globalization were all around us, from the collapse of the centralized economies of Eastern Europe to the entry of India and China into the world market. Over the past two decades of globalization, the proportion of the world's population in absolute poverty has dropped from 30% to 20%.[6]

And yet. The sheer pace of globalization has aroused hostility and not just from those who fear change of any sort. Unemployment, particularly amongst the unskilled in developed economies, has been blamed on the outsourcing of jobs to countries where labour is cheap. The twin themes of deprivation and exploitation have led to a regeneration of Marxist calamity merchants peddling fears of power-crazed moguls of the sort that populate James Bond movies. There is reaction too on the right. The US elections in November 2006 bolstered the protectionist tendency in Congress while in Europe politicians who proclaim the free market invariably temper their enthusiasm with promises to rein back on globalization. The image of capitalism out of control is reinforced by headline stories of overpaid business leaders who are ready to break or bend the law to their corporate advantage. Inevitably the cry goes up of democracy itself at risk from the anonymous men in suits who exercise power without responsibility.

As in every caricature there are particles of truth in all this. To return to basics, there can be no doubt that globalization is changing the pattern of employment with a movement of unskilled work from high cost to low cost economies. The losers are naturally aggrieved and see no reason why governments should not act to protect their livelihood. But the deadlock over the Doha round of world trade talks notwithstanding politicians know very well that there can be no return to old-style protectionism. To put up barriers against cheap imports would not only invite retaliation, which would further damage employment, but would also lead to price increases. At this point, consumer self-interest invariably wins out against sympathy for the unemployed.

There is always the option of state subsidies but like import duties these can invite counter measures and are also socially disruptive in that they favour certain groups who may not be seen as particularly deserving. As a last resort, appeals for protection of the home market are backed by protestations on behalf of low-paid workers in developing economies, portrayed as the

victims of capitalist exploitation. The alternative, of having no work at all, is rarely mentioned.

Can, therefore, nothing be done to boost employment in the advanced economies? It would help if the sights were raised on education and training. The demand for skilled workers outpaces supply in all the developed countries. But the greatest benefit would come from a change in knee-jerk thinking about employment. It is no coincidence that the USA has one of the best records in job creation. The American way of life demands a readiness to adapt—even if some sectors, such as the steel workers, cotton growers and farmers, seem to be able to claim special status. The contrast with Europe is with societies where the job for life, irrespective of the value of its output, takes on the force of natural law.

It is not only globalization that makes this position unsustainable in the long run. The pace of technological change is such that many jobs which now look to be reasonably secure will soon be overtaken by pushbutton machinery. There is an irony here. Of all the European economies, France and Germany come under attack for the rigidity of their labour laws. But the mere fact that employers are reluctant to take on additional staff if they are liable to be stuck with them for the duration has added to the attraction of labour-saving technology which can be changed at will. This helps to explain why French and German productivity is higher than that of Britain where the labour laws are flexible enough to allow for short-term hiring, one way of postponing capital investment.

The protectionist backlash against globalization gains strength when it shifts the focus from employment as such to the transworld firms that do the employing. Needing big business to underpin their economic strategy, politicians readily submit to pressure for special treatment ranging from tax breaks to state contracts on generous terms. The popular impression of major companies having it all their own way is reinforced by stories of dodgy dealings that go unpunished. Arrogance is displayed all too visibly when less than competent CEOs award themselves lavish salaries and benefits. The potential for shareholders to check excesses is rarely exercised. Profit comes before public responsibility.

The flip side of the argument tells us that, for the most part, global companies are giving their customers what they want. When they fail to do so, their profits and power fade away. A few years ago the price of a plane ticket was kept artificially high by the big five airlines. Then along came the no-frills independents to break the oligarchy and to send prices tumbling. Open competition is a wonderful corrective to vaunting commercial ambition. Of the 100 top companies listed in 1970, over half have shut down, largely as a result of failing to keep up with consumer demands.

Competition is the only sure way of putting the customer first, though evidence points to growing business awareness of social issues. In particular, environmental campaigns have had their effect on company behaviour. CEOs are well aware that an unfavourable image is liable to damage the bottom line.

The role of consumer democracy in raising the ethical standards of big business looks set to increase. Even as the power of mass labour loses out against the ability of companies to move their centres of operation to wherever they can achieve the best terms for hiring and firing, consumers have the potential for organizing powerful lobbies to influence policy on the treatment of employees as much as on standards of production.

Where does this leave democratically elected governments? Opponents of globalization make much of a supposed weakness of the nation state in its relations with the giant corporations. The argument turns on a correlation between company turnover and government tax revenue. Thus, Noreena Hertz is able to assert that '51 of the 100 biggest economies in the world are now corporations'.[7] But this is to compare like with unlike. What matters to a company is not so much turnover as profit, in other words turnover minus all the costs of production. Government income via taxation is not subject to the same condition. Whatever comes into a state exchequer is real in the sense that it can be spent in whatever way the government directs. A valid comparison demolishes Hertz's claim that corporations now rule the world. In fact, the financial resources available to a modestly sized country exceed the profits of all global companies combined.

Moreover, all governments, democratic or otherwise, possess powers that company executives cannot begin to contemplate. Where is the global business that can raise its own army or issue its own currency? When times are hard, it is to governments that business turns to for protection or for bailing it

---

[6] *Globalisation, Growth and Poverty*, World Bank, 2002

[7] Noreena Hertz, *The Silent Takeover: Global Capitalism and the Death of Democracy.* Heinemann, 2002

out of trouble. But if the balance is weighted so heavily in favour of the politicians why are they not more effective in forcing business to pay its fair share of tax? The short answer is that governments do just that. Allowing for a degree of tax avoidance, a feature of society since money let alone globalization was first thought of, the employees and shareholders of a global company pay tax of up to 50% or more on what they earn and consume. The taxpayer with a stake in Unilever, with more than 500 subsidiaries in over 90 countries, is treated no differently than the taxpayer who runs a small business from a back room.

Nothing is ever simple. The army of accountants and lawyers on the payroll of a global company exercise their combined talents on minimizing the tax that has to be paid on profits, invariably by registering the head office in one of the offshore tax havens or in one of the other financial centres of easy virtue where bankers ask few questions and answer even fewer. It is all desperately unfair though it has to be said that government revenue lost in this way is petty cash when set against the gains generated by economic growth.

But the question still hovers. With so many well publicized abuses of the system, should not governments take a more active role in policing the activities of global companies? The push for governments to be assertive is led by the Marxist tendency who are still hoping that sheer greed will eventually cause global companies to implode. Meanwhile, they argue, politicians should do all they can to frustrate commercial hegemony. The end product would be a return to the highly centralized, politically dominated economy. Given its track record of incompetence and corruption, few would welcome a revival of the model. But there are many who visualize a halfway house where the free market can be allowed to operate within politically determined boundaries.

For democrats who are so inclined, and they are to be found in every parliamentary assembly, the challenge is in knowing where to draw the line. It is one thing to assert, for example, that the state should impose minimum terms of employment but at what point does the bureaucratic passion for expanding the rule book conflict with commercial logic? A rational decision on whether to open or close a factory is more likely to be made on commercial rather than political (vote catching) grounds. It is a safe general rule that a heavy handed bureaucracy frustrates entrepreneurial initiative and is thus the enemy of prosperity.

There is a much stronger case to be made for politics as the safety net. Instead of trying to behave as business managers, they would better serve their electorates by easing the transition to globalization. High on the priority list would be a social wage for those displaced by economic change. In some European countries, notably in Scandinavia, generous welfare benefits are available to the jobless while they look for work. In Denmark, payments are as high as 80% of previous earnings. To deter the workshy, the social wage is linked to retraining schemes. The result is low unemployment combined with labour flexibility, a formula that less innovative governments claim is impossible to achieve.

A variation on the social wage theme is attracting support in the USA where government-sponsored wage insurance covers any worker over 50 who is forced into a lower paid job by the changing trade pattern. The government pays half the difference between the old and new wage for 2 years up to a maximum of $10,000. Germany and France have similar schemes and in France there are no age qualifications.

While looking after their own, the rich nations should spare some creative thoughts for the emerging economies. The undoubted benefits of globalization for countries like India and China which, for the first time in their history, can visualize the eradication of poverty, should not be allowed to mask the teething pains caused by their industrial revolutions. In a recently published exposé of the toy industry, we find that manufacturing for the American retail market (a $21 billion business) is concentrated on the Pearl River Delta in southern China. Three million workers in 8000 factories make 80% of all American toys. Working conditions are atrocious. Young women work 15-h shifts, 7 days a week.[8] Everybody agrees that they are entitled to a better life but the companies that exploit cheap labour are disinclined to push for minimum standards and an effective system of inspection. Here, globalization is the excuse for maximizing profits at the expense of human dignity. Free trade deserves better, sooner.

And then there are those countries still struggling towards the lower slopes of economic subsistence. Saddled with debt (and, yes, of course,

corruption comes into it but crippling debt is still crippling debt) much of Africa will remain in dire poverty until the imbalances of globalization are corrected. The World Bank calls for investments to remove bottlenecks in infrastructure, education and health. Above all, lowering trade barriers to allow for easier access of poor countries to global markets would boost incomes.[9] The philanthropist, George Soros, is among those who believe that a more radical policy is needed. Soros puts the case for the USA to take the lead with a Marshall Plan updated for the twenty-first century.[10] Bearing in mind that US non-defence foreign aid is just 0.1% of GDP as against 3% when the first Marshall Plan was launched in 1947, this is asking a lot. Nonetheless, such an imaginative project would do more to civilize globalization, not to mention combating ideological extremism and terrorism, than all the money spent on military hardware.

But why should the USA act alone? Quite apart from the commercial commonsense of creating prosperity (and markets) in what are now the poorest regions, charity cries out against a world in which more than a billion humans live on less than a dollar a day, 826 million suffer malnutrition and 10 million die each year for lack of basic health care.

Joseph Stiglitz, former chief economist of the World Bank and Nobel prize-winner, has called for a new global reserve currency financed by countries running trade surpluses. The resources created would be used to encourage development in the poorest countries and to create global public goods such as promoting public health and increasing literacy. In these enlightened times, some 770 million people round the world are unable to read or write.[11]

If the governments of the rich nations hold back from a massive redistribution of resources they could at least give closer attention to the environmental side effects of globalization. The World Bank identifies three global public goods—mitigating climate change, containing infectious diseases and preserving marine fisheries—that 'demonstrate the need for and benefits of international policy cooperation'. It would be a start.

Globalization offers the best chance for reducing world poverty. The prospects according to the World Bank are 'nothing short of astounding'. In the next quarter century the output of the global economy is set to rise from $35 trillion to $72 trillion. The number of people living in dire poverty could halve.[12] But if the scaremongers have their way it could so easily all go wrong. The need for bold, constructive politics has never been greater.

Barry Turner

In Defence of Scepticism

Of all the English words debased by overuse, 'expert' and 'expertise' are among the most frequently abused. Anyone who does anything, however mundane, with a modicum of skill, is said to be an expert. And along with the appellation goes the presumed right to instruct the rest of us on how to think and act.

An exaggeration? Then think only of the power of the fashion merchants and other arbiters of 'good taste', the marketing and public relations gurus, religious dogmatists, scientists with research grants to protect, futurologists, self-appointed moral censors, educationists (I mean those who pronounce on the practice of education), purveyors of psychobabble and, more influential than all the rest, the guardians of financial institutions who, in a crisis, are forever telling us not to panic, at least not until they have secured the safety net for their own investments.

The rot starts at the top with governments increasingly relying on 'expert' advisers whose qualifications and experience lend credence to 'I know' rather than 'I think'. Moreover, it is 'I know' within an ideological context. The public servant offering objective advice, some of which may be unpalatable, has been sidelined. This trend in state management is aimed at getting things

---

[8]Eric Clark, *The Real Toy Story*. Transworld Publishers, 2007

[9]*Global Economic Prospects. Managing the Next Wave of Globalization*. The World Bank, 2007

[10]George Soros, *On Globalization*. Public Affairs, 2002

[11]Joseph Stiglitz, *Making Globalisation Work*. Norton, 2006

[12]The World Bank, 2007

done with maximum agreement and minimum fuss. It is often said of politicians that they delight in the cut and thrust of open debate, that they ask nothing more than to elicit and then to implement the popular will. Not true. Most start with a clear idea of what they want to achieve. Their aim is to win the argument not to extend it. Hence the reliance on experts to deflect opposition and to reinforce the political message.

Policies that fail are excused and quickly forgotten in the rush of yet more experts to advise on how to do better next time. And we believe them. Why?

Largely it is because we live in a complex society driven by specialization. Since there is only so much we can absorb, the desire for predictability allows others to make decisions on our behalf. After all, those who know most must surely know best. But expertise does not sit well with argument or contradiction. Over broad acres of life, thinking for ourselves is becoming a rarity. Told in an authoritarian tone that black is white and two and two make five, we are liable to pause before disagreeing.

The voluntary surrender of independent judgement is evident in every society, however liberal its image. Rules and regulations proliferate while the pattern of life is ordered and constrained by those who wrap themselves in the mantle of expertise. In Britain, even those governments pledged to cut back on interference in day-to-day life have soon converted to dedicated meddling. It was in the time of Margaret Thatcher, paragon of the free market, that the phrase 'nanny state' was coined. Tony Blair was another who somehow managed to reconcile his professed love of freedom with the urge to control. His term in office added new laws at an average of 2,684 a year, up by a quarter on the preceding decade.

Experts with the heaviest clout trade on fear. Health hazards are an obvious example. Hardly a day passes without a warning from some government body that we are eating or drinking too much of the wrong thing. Success in identifying real dangers, such as the risk from smoking, is outweighed by the plethora of scare stories that turn out to be less than earth shattering. Not long ago it was a bird flu epidemic we all had to worry about. The current fad is for doomsday warnings of the effects of obesity. There is one simple rule for losing weight; eat less. But that doesn't stop the dietary experts, often in government employ, from giving out lengthy advice on adopting a healthier lifestyle. Evidence that many fat people are as they are because their bodies contain a higher than average number of fatty cells is studiously ignored. Instead the heavyweights are urged to spend their free time jogging round the park where the casual observer might conclude that they have more chance of dying from heart failure than of achieving a lower reading on the scales. The slim and disgustingly fit do not escape scot-free. They are given plenty of other spurious reasons for fearing for their lives.

Washington's obsession with terrorism has spawned a government-backed security industry that parades its 'expert' credentials to justify restrictions on civil liberties. In the wake of 9/11 over 20,000 specialist security firms were set up, dedicated to instilling fear of the unknown. One enterprising company does well by providing bullet-proof jackets for sniffer dogs. Yet where is the logic in devoting unlimited resources to combating terrorism when many more lives are lost from poverty and disease (arguably the root causes of terrorism) or, in the context of western affluence, road accidents and family shootouts? In the 5 years following 9/11 there were 100,000 murders in the US, the equivalent of a World Trade Center disaster every 2 months.

Another area of life which touches us all and where politically motivated expertise has run riot is education. Who can doubt that the system is failing us? Illiteracy levels remain stubbornly high while teenage standards of general knowledge and understanding of the world begs the question as to how students fill their time in 15 or more years of full-time learning.

The cause of failure can be traced to the 1960s when a justifiable reaction against rote learning produced a less justifiable bias against academic teaching. According to the experts, those who were quick to get out of the classroom and into the lecture hall where they could tell their former colleagues how to do their job, what to teach was less important than how to teach. Most of this new found expertise consisted of stating the obvious while avoiding the first essential, that to be a successful teacher you must know your subject. The result today is that we have teachers loaded with pedagogic qualifications but with a less than adequate grasp of the scholarship they are supposed to hand on.

Misguided policies have led us away from the cultural, moral and intellectual purposes of education to career-orientated learning. Yet beyond the central skills of reading, writing and numeracy, there is no evidence of an economic return on education. Quite the opposite, in fact. In a technological world, a workforce needs, above all, the ability to adapt to change. Rigid vocational training, which is what most youngsters get, puts up barriers to change. But politicians and their advisers are victims of their own spin. They

cannot bring themselves to believe Alison Wolf (*Does Education Matter?*) who shows convincingly that the more effort put into organizing education for economic ends, the higher the likelihood of waste and disappointment.

Never have we had so many qualifications, yet productivity continues to fall below forecasts. We are encouraged—maybe we encourage ourselves—to be over impressed by letters tagged on to a name. In industry, the advent of the MBA has done little to increase the supply of imaginative entrepreneurs though it has led to greater influence for 'expert' consultants.

The frailty of expertise shows up most blatantly in economics. One might think that examples of economic planning that have gone horribly and expensively wrong—from the short term rescue of clapped out industries to investing taxpayers' money in prestige projects like the supersonic airliner—would dent public confidence. Not a bit of it. Increasingly, we look to economists to reassure us that all is well in the best of all possible worlds.

In the spring of 2007, before the markets began to turn somersaults, Martin Wolf, writing in the *Financial Times*, warned against the chorus of expert optimism on the future of the world economy.

'The most obvious reason for taking today's euphoria with a barrel of salt is that nobody ever expects shocks. That is what makes them shocks. If I think back to the noteworthy events of my own adult lifetime, I observe that none of the big events was expected. The oil shocks of 1974 and 1979, the determination of Paul Volcker, then Federal Reserve chairman, to crush inflation in the early 1980s, the Mexican default of 1982, the stock market crash of 1987, Saddam Hussein's invasion of Kuwait in 1990, the collapse of the Soviet empire between 1989 and 1991, the 'tequila crisis' of 1994 and 1995, the Asian and Russian crises of 1997 and 1998 and, not least, September 11 2001 were, if not "unknown unknowns", at least "ignored unknowns".'

Wolf added, 'People who think they know what is going to happen next are fools', while Samuel Brittan, another commentator with a welcome sense of fallibility, observed that 'experts are never as likely to be wrong as when they speak with near unanimity'.

The economic model that takes account of all variables simply does not—cannot—exist. Yet assertions bordering on certainty are a large part of the daily diet of economic intelligence, much of it from government sources.

It is unfair to suggest that all spurious expertise is politically led. A roundup of past scare stories that turned out to be spurious or, at best, misleading, suggests that there are experts quite capable of making fools of themselves without the assistance of the state. We recall the Club of Rome warning 30 years ago that the depletion of the world's natural resources would bring economic disaster in the 1990s. It didn't happen. Then there were the threats of a population explosion. Now, apparently, we must worry about a population decline. Global warming is the latest big fear but in the 1960s we were told to prepare for a second ice age. Nuclear energy was once declared to be the biggest single threat to our survival. Today it is widely touted as environmentally friendly.

The argument here is not anti knowledge. The more people in and out of government who know their subjects the better. But it is perilous to award the experts, many of them self-proclaimed, the freedom to rule our lives. We should reawaken the spirit of the Enlightenment, defined by Immanuel Kant as 'man's emergence from his self-imposed immaturity'. He went on, 'Immaturity is the inability to use one's understanding without guidance from another. This immaturity is self-imposed when its cause lies not in lack of understanding, but in lack of resolve and courage to use it without guidance from another.' We can start by recovering our childlike curiosity. There is never any harm in asking 'Why?'. Scepticism is second nature to intelligence.

The Net is an encouragement to think for ourselves. At one level it can overwhelm by the sheer weight of information—much of it unreliable. But to any forceful argument, the Net can be relied upon to offer a counter argument. It is no longer an excuse to say, 'I didn't know' or 'I didn't know enough'. More, we should always be conscious of the telltale signs of expertise overlapping with dottiness or downright mania—the arrogance of the scientist who is always 'right', the mission rant of a preacher, the cosy 'trust me' assurance of the guru. Even those experts who come over as relatively sane cannot be one hundred per cent right. No one ever is. Including the present writer.

Barry Turner

References
Gordon Graham, *The Case Against the Democratic State.* Societas, 2002
Martin Wolf, *Financial Times.* 25.5.07
Samuel Brittan, *Financial Times.* 17.8.07
Jennifer Michael Hecht, *Doubt: A History.* HarperCollins, 2003
Alison Wolf, *Does Education Matter?* Penguin, 2002

The Way It Was, and Is

The old, old question is back on the agenda. Can history teach us anything? Do the experiences of the past provide lessons for the present and the future?

There are those who argue that history can be used, or abused, to support any action or inaction. There is always a justifying precedent or a lesson to be learned if you search hard enough in the archives. At best, history is a false friend. 'There has never been a time,' argues Tony Blair, 'when, except in the most general sense, a study of history provides so little instruction for our present day.' There speaks the true radical. Until Blair came along, his Labour party had been weighed down and made virtually impotent by a slavish regard for its Marxist-Socialist tradition. For Blair, history was a brake on fresh thinking, the knee-jerk antidote to change.

The counter view holds that to ignore history is to deny something that is fundamental to our understanding of ourselves and our place in the wider scheme of things. Recently, the debate has been hotting up.

The revival of interest has a lot to do with the invasion of Iraq and the overthrow of Saddam. In defending his action, the former US President was wont to call history to his aid by invoking Munich and the fatal consequences of trying to appease an evil dictator—Saddam portrayed as Hitler. This begs several questions. For a start, was stopping Hitler before he became a world menace really a practical proposition?

Received wisdom has it that World War Two could have been averted if the democracies had taken an early initiative instead of allowing Hitler to dictate the international agenda. Germany was certainly vulnerable in 1936 when, sending his troops into the demilitarized Rhineland, Hitler delivered the first heavyweight shock to the European security system. Propaganda magnified German military power. If Britain and France had acted decisively, the Nazi reign of terror might now be the stuff of horror fiction.

Instead we had appeasement, with the democracies all the while backing off as Hitler absorbed Austria and began the carve-up of Czechoslovakia. The culmination of this unedifying and, in the end, fruitless attempt at pacification was the false promise at Munich of 'peace in our time' and the indelibly humiliating spectacle of Neville Chamberlain, an elderly prime minister, a politician from another age, alighting from his aircraft waving a scrap of paper to demonstrate the Fuhrer's good faith.

When it all ended in *blitzkrieg* and a long bloody war, appeasement and Munich became the hate words of the political lexicon, to be deployed against anyone suspected of weakness in the face of a real or imagined enemy.

But this is to ignore the fact that in the mid-1930s there was virtually no public appetite in the western democracies for action against Germany, least of all among those who would have to do the fighting. Then again, suppose Anglo-French forces had confronted the Wehrmacht as it marched into the disputed territory of the Rhineland? Knowing what we know now, it is unlikely that Hitler would have been long deterred from his territorial ambitions. Unless, of course, the Allies had overthrown the Nazi dictatorship. But what then? There was no evidence of a friendly government in waiting and it is almost beyond credulity that France and Britain could have imposed direct rule.

Even if this had been achieved, opposition could have been expected from what we now call the international community. Had Britain and France stood up to Germany in the Rhineland, it is likely that they would have been seen as the aggressors, not least in the US where Roosevelt had been elected on an isolationist ticket. Joseph Kennedy, US ambassador to Britain, came out publicly in favour of Munich. There was a mark Hitler had to overstep before the democracies could achieve a unity of purpose. He did so with his invasion of Poland.

In vowing not to repeat the calamitous errors of the appeasers of Nazi Germany, President Bush was presumably relying on his audience knowing little of modern history. If they had been better informed they would surely have recognized, as Bush himself should have recognized, that Saddam, whatever his pretensions, was no Hitler. More than that, the odium heaped on Munich is largely wisdom after the event. Finally, there is nothing inherently wrong in politicians trying all ways to negotiate themselves out of trouble.

An undeserved knee-jerk condemnation has landed Munich with its sour reputation. But it is arguable that the years after Munich have provided more than enough evidence of the damage so called anti-appeasers can cause when they are too quick on the draw. Korea, Vietnam, Suez, and now Iraq spring to mind. As Winston Churchill reminded President Eisenhower, 'To jaw-jaw is always better than to war-war.'

In other words, the debate on Iraq could have done with more history, not less. As Johan Tosh points out (*Why History Matters*), to know more about the past is to illuminate the contours of the present, equipping us to make intelligent decisions. To take examples at random, a study of the antecedents of modern terrorism would suggest that for governments to imitate the methods of terrorists is no way to defeat the evil itself. Attacking poverty, ignorance and the other sources of violent dissent might produce more positive results.

Closer to home, every generation discovers youth crime while bemoaning the loss of the good old days when young people respected their elders and spoke only when spoken to. An illusion, of course, as even a brief reading of social history quickly reveals. The fears engendered by tumultuous youth have been replicated since the days of ancient Greece.

To connect with yet another current concern, dramatic ups and downs of the international economy seem always to come as a surprise to the latest generation of financial high flyers. They choose to believe, maybe for sanity's sake they have to believe, that they have the means to break the business cycle. Eventually, experience teaches them otherwise. The market turmoil of the past year has unquestionably been acerbated by the arrogance of those financial analysts who are so preoccupied with the neat rows of figures that show up on their computer screens that they ignore the social, economic and historical context in which we all have to operate. Belatedly, the central banks have realised that the risk models used by the commercial banks take a short term view of the past, often as little as 10 years. Yet, in the UK alone, a further look back into history would have shown fluctuations in gross domestic product four times greater than that of the past decade, that of unemployment five times greater, that of inflation seven times greater and that of earnings 12 times greater.

Ground-breaking economists from Adam Smith to Maynard Keynes may have lacked computer power but they did have an understanding of history that enabled them to give due weight to the human element in monetary and fiscal affairs. A positive side effect of the current recession could be second thoughts on the academic tendency to think of economics exclusively as a branch of mathematics.

But there is no virtue in rushing to the other extreme. History, by itself, is always fallible. That much is clear when historians take sides, falling out on the validity of the evidence, let alone on the interpretation of the evidence.

A totally objective history, the aspiration of Leopold von Ranke and his school, 'only to say how it really was', is a chimera. There is always room for argument. Historians who take to prediction are especially suspect. Leading the pack are the Marxists who must now be wondering how it all went so horribly wrong for them. The literary market can always find a place for the historian who is keen to tell us how it will be. Often they are right in theory but misguided in practice. One of the historical bestsellers of all time, Norman Angell's *The Great Illusion*, published in the build-up to World War One, argued convincingly that in the modern industrial state there can be no victors in war, everyone stands to lose. But then he went on to conclude that major conflicts were a thing of the past, an overestimate of political intelligence if ever there was one.

In our own era we have had most famously, the 'End of History' thesis attached to the collapse of the Soviet empire and the apparently conclusive, all embracing triumph of social democracy. For many obvious reasons, there is less confidence now that the western democracies are likely to have it all their own way. It is an unfailing rule that prophecies based on history are invariably negated by events beyond the range of reasonable expectation.

If the futurologist can give history a bad name, so too can certain types of popularizers who draw on the past to reinforce national prejudices and myths. The heritage industry with its emphasis on sanitized versions of life in wildly different circumstances to our own can mislead but is not necessarily harmful. More contentious is the deployment of selective evidence to support dubious claims of past injustices and to justify lasting antagonisms. Think of Northern Ireland, in itself a case study of historical misinformation.

At its best, history helps us to explore options by opening up questions. It is part of the search for truth, or at least the semblance of truth, for the real thing is almost certainly for ever elusive. The Greeks knew this since their word that became 'history' originally meant 'to inquire' and to choose wisely between conflicting accounts. As Ludmilla Jordanova shows (*History in Practice*), 'The study of the past is indeed inspiring and instructive but it is not a fount of clear unambiguous lessons or recipes. Rather it is an arena for contemplation and thought'. And, it may be added, a source of endless fascination for amateur and professional alike.

Barry Turner

References

John H. Arnold, *History: A Very Short Introduction*. OUP, 2000

Ludmilla Jordanova, *History in Practice*. Hodder Arnold, 2000

James J. Sheehan, *The Monopoly of Violence: Why Europeans Hate Going to War*. Faber, 2007

Johan Tosh, *Why History Matters*. Palgrave, 2008

Keeping Up with the News

Online Competition is Putting Newspapers at Risk—Should we Care?

Asked to lead a university seminar on careers in the media, a journalist friend spoke about his life in newspapers and the role of the press in a functioning democracy. He invited comments. Silence. To provoke discussion, he put a question. How many of you take a daily paper? No hands went up. Weekly? No hands went up. Now and then? A few, a very few hands were lifted. It dawned on my friend that instead of talking about the future of his industry he had instead given a history lesson.

That newspapers are in trouble no one can doubt. On both sides of the Atlantic they are either shutting down or cutting back on costs to a point where the value of the product risks being fatally undermined. We all know why this is happening. Online competition is taking away readers and advertisers, each accelerating the decline of the other. The question is, does it matter?

There are those who argue that newspapers, their owners and the journalists they employ, had it coming to them; that in their pursuit of the trivial and artificial, their dependence on a celebrity culture ('An individual emptiness gawped at by a collective emptiness . . . a manifestation of the cretinisation of our culture'.[13]) they are all culpable. It is surely no coincidence that journalists rival politicians for the lowest rank in public esteem.

There is, however, a strong counter argument, put succinctly by the philosopher A. C. Grayling who asserts that a free press 'although it always abuses its freedom in the hunt for profit, is necessary with all its warts, as one of the two essential estates of a free society, the other being an independent judiciary'.[14] For all the miles of column inches devoted to mindless, often degrading, ephemera, the press is the first line of defence against the political, doctrinal and commercial manipulators who try to work the system in defiance of the public interest. Television has its role but traditionally, the BBC excepted, it depends on the press for its lead as do the online bloggers and twitterers. Though opinion is unfettered it is diminished if not supported by serious and costly investigative journalism.

Cost. It always comes back to that economic imperative. Newspapers have not done themselves any favours by making much of their content available online free of charge. This apparently loony business model was based on the assumption that internet users would be so inspired as to rush out to buy the print version or become so hooked on the online service that, eventually, they would be happy to pay for access.

The strategy has foundered on the popular conception of the net as a benevolent information provider unencumbered by the profit motive. Specialist services such as those provided by the *Wall Street Journal* and the *Financial Times* can sustain a substantial price tag but general news, by definition short-lived and easily discarded, has yet to find a profitable niche.

As the mightiest media mogul of them all, Rupert Murdoch is characteristically robust, predicting that 'newspapers will reach new heights in the twenty first century'. The form of delivery may change but 'the potential audience for our content will multiply many times over. Our real business isn't printing on dead trees. It is giving our readers great journalism and great judgement'.[15]

No one would argue with that though there might be disagreement on what constitutes great journalism and great judgement. In a vigorous attack on the BBC for trying to dominate the market with 'state-sponsored news', James Murdoch, Rupert's heir apparent, claims that 'the ability to generate a profitable return is fundamental to media quality, plurality and independence'.[16]

But while the BBC has its faults, the denigration of public service broadcasting would be more convincing if the privately owned media was shown to be genuinely independent. Even if we have moved a long way from the dictum of Lord Beaverbrook, creator of the mass circulation Express group, who told a Royal Commission on the press that he owned newspapers not for profit but for disseminating political propaganda, it is still true that press freedom often translates into the freedom of newspaper owners to promote causes they hold most dear. Editorial judgement is only free within the parameters set by those who hold the purse strings. Readers know this. It is not surprising to find that public broadcasting has the higher trust rating.

Even if the BBC cuts back on activities that threaten open competition, it is not about to abandon its online ventures. Indeed, non-profit online services are set to increase as wealthy foundations, mostly in the US, are persuaded to back independent investigative reporting.

The success of free newspapers which account for 7% of global circulation, 8% in the US and 23% of circulation in Europe alone, suggests that advertisers are by no means convinced that only paying readers make the best customers.

That said, subscriptions, if they can be made to work, are unarguably the best guarantee of newspaper survival. In Japan, where 90% of newspapers are sold on monthly subscriptions with a guarantee of home delivery, circulations are holding up remarkably well. The challenge for the American and European press is to hold together on the need for subscriptions. It takes only one major paper to offer free journalism for a potentially devastating circulation war to break out. If this happens, and it is a distinct probability, the paying option will have to be made more enticing by newspapers creating their own distinctive websites. It will not be enough simply to reproduce hard print onscreen. There has to be more must-read content with more inside information on high value subjects.

Leading the way is the *New York Times* with a digital edition that is awash with videos, charts and specialist blogs, all calculated to entice the reader to sign on for the long term. The *NYT* will charge for full access to its website from 2011. But it is still to be seen whether this editorial profusion will generate sufficient income to support worldwide news gathering of the quality traditionally associated with America's top newspaper.

Meanwhile, the search is on for ways in which powerful brands (which is what newspapers with instantly recognizable names really are) can be used to generate revenue from add-on services and products. The Murdoch papers already have this well in hand with enterprises ranging from fantasy football associated with the tabloid *Sun* to a wine club promoted by the upmarket *Sunday Times*. The full potential of branding has still to be realized as the digital guru Chris Anderson points out; there might even be a case for reassessing free online access since 'companies ought to be able to make huge amounts of money around the thing being given away as Google gives away its search and email and makes its money on advertising'.[17] One possibility for Murdoch with his multimedia interests is to bundle print and television together in a one for all subscription. Equally, stand alone newspapers might forge strategic partnerships with parallel media.

Another option to be taken seriously, though up to now entirely foreign to the private enterprise instinct of the Anglo-American press barons, is state subsidy. Put baldly, the acceptance of government help would seem to place at risk the first requirement of a free press, that it should be immune to political interference. But no one is suggesting an all-embracing subsidy which shifts the balance of ownership.

In Sweden, financial support for the press is largely in the form of a grant-aided national system of early morning delivery. There are also easy term loans to encourage the updating of print technology. France has a novel scheme whereby eighteenth birthdays are marked by the gift of a newspaper subscription, compliments of the government. Press subsidies in one form or another are common in Austria, Norway and Spain where they are judged to be essential to the diversity of the press, particularly at regional and local level.

---

[13]Raymond Tallis, *The Times*. October 14th, 2009

[14]A. C. Grayling, *Liberty in the Age of Terror*. Bloomsbury, 2009

[15]Boyer Lectures. ABC Radio National. November 16th, 2008

---

[16]MacTaggart Lecture. Edinburgh International Television Festival. August 28th, 2009

[17]Chris Anderson, *Free: The Future of a Radical Price*. 2009

The formula is attracting interest in the US where Leonard Downie, a vice president and former executive editor of *The Washington Post*, has put his name to a report advocating a national fund for local news with money collected from a federal tax on telecom users, broadcast licensees and internet service providers. Grants would be made by independent local news fund councils for innovative reporting and support services.[18]

But whether by self help or state help, newspapers can only meet the online challenge by reinventing the ways they do business and the ways they serve their readers. The accountants' knee jerk solution to a deficit, to fire expensive front line journalists, is to accelerate the downward spiral—falling circulations following superficiality. Swamped by gossip served up as information, readers of hard print as much as those seduced by online, will need more guidance on finding a way through the maze of irrelevancy. That means hiring top rank journalists who combine inquiring minds with the ability to communicate clearly and persuasively. Such paragons do not come cheaply.

Time is short. Even if all that needs to be done is done, it may not be enough. Waiting in the wings are Google, Microsoft and the other internet giants who must see news gathering as one of the next big things in their business plans. The media revolution is only just beginning.

Barry Turner

What Hope for the Jobless?

Is there any return to full employment? Or will mass unemployment be ever with us? Barry Turner weighs up the options.

There are 15 million unemployed in America. And another 15 million without jobs in Europe. That's a lot of people. The raw figures are somehow more revealing and more terrifying than percentages which delude by their simplicity. A point up here, a point down there, what's the difference? Which is perhaps why unemployment is not yet the hot political issue it should be. Optimism, some might say, unnatural optimism, is the other reason. The assumption is of a rising demand for labour carried along in the wake of economic recovery.

It could happen but the evidence for national growth creating a healthy demand for labour is hard to find. Some job opportunities will appear but others are likely to be lost as technology takes up the slack. Plans for government-sponsored job creation in labour-intensive services such as education and care of the elderly conflict with the need to reduce national deficits. There are no prizes for guessing what will take priority.

One does not have to be a doomsday prophet to recognize that we may never return to the near full employment enjoyed by previous generations. This suggests we should start now to adapt to a culture which no longer has the day at the workplace as the very focus of being.

This is hardly a revolutionary thought. But ideas on advancing what in the 1930s was called the Leisure Society have rarely moved beyond think tank publications. Could it be that the work ethic is so fundamental that we can't bear to contemplate the alternative? To hear politicians talk, you would certainly believe so. Jobs for all is a slogan shared by all parties.

The complaint is not simply that the objective is almost certainly unachievable but that it is also unimaginative, a step back into the future.

There is something inherently ridiculous in the concept of work for work's sake. As Ralf Dahrendorf was fond of pointing out, we act as if our lives depend on work while at the same time doing all we can to reduce its burden. It would be a simple matter, for example, to multiply the jobs in road building by replacing mechanical diggers with picks and shovels. But who in their right mind would really want this to happen? There is no going back on the technological society, nor should we want to. The only alternative is to begin a serious reassessment of what life is, or should be, all about.

Theoretically, we all enjoy leisure. Those in work say they can't get enough of it. But when it does come in abundance, the hours prove hard to fill. Depression follows. This is why so many of those among the long-term unemployed, who have all the time in the world, find it impossible to organize their lives constructively. Or why some retired people who have hitherto led frenetic lives, fall into apathy and die early.

It would help to encourage a more positive attitude to leisure. This has to start with education which, in recent years, has become vocationally orientated, on the bullish assumption that qualifications make for job creation. Even if this is true, the emphasis on training for work, and work only, sharpens the distinction between those who have it and those who can't get it. For the latter, there is a consequent loss of identity, social status and self esteem.

A stronger cultural element in education would bring out talents that make for life satisfaction beyond the wage cheque—learning to play a musical instrument, say, or to paint or to climb a mountain. It is no coincidence that those blessed with a good rounded education seldom have any difficulty in filling every waking hour which is why schemes for voluntary redundancy often find the brightest and the best first in line.

If changes in education depend on a political initiative, so too do changes in work practices which must come if the gap between the have and have nots is to be narrowed. Increases in productivity should not simply be translated into wage increases for those who have work. Instead, the trend should be towards shorter working weeks, shorter working years and a shift in social values that allows for work sharing. To some extent this is already happening. Longer paid holidays and maternity leave, the introduction of paternity leave and sabbaticals are common to advanced companies. Time off for community service has great potential for stimulating voluntary activities that overlap work and leisure. Old-fashioned employers fear that work sharing is synonymous with idle hands. But there are many case histories where flexibility in the traditional work pattern has resulted in greater all-round satisfaction and higher output.

The tragedy of the current recession is that fear of unemployment and its consequences, at best a fall in living standards, at worst requisitioned homes, has made enlightened work practices harder to implement. When France introduced the thirty-five-hour week, the net result was for those in work to claim more overtime, the reverse of what was intended. Fear of unemployment was greater than the desire for leisure. That fear has intensified so that, for example, older people are hanging on to jobs that might otherwise go to their children, a tendency increased by a general lifting of the retirement age. We have entered what Tony Judt has called the 'age of insecurity' and it will take great political skill and imagination to get us out of it. Failure will be a society at war with itself, the ultimate paradox of the liberating power of technology.

Barry Turner, 2011

At the Outer Limits of Knowledge

We are defined by science. No matter if we are mystified by equations or never get to shake a test tube, we all function in a scientific framework that determines the way we think and act.

This is a recent phenomenon. For most of history the boundaries of Western inquiry and creativity have been set by religion. Without subscribing to the fable that science and religion are necessarily in conflict (many, if not most, of the great scientific discoveries have been set firmly in the Christian or, at least, the deistic tradition), it is nonetheless true that in matters of dispute, the clerics commanded the high ground.

The kick-start to a long process of change came with the Enlightenment when the brotherhood of sceptics—Voltaire, Hume, Kant among them—questioned the need for divine intercession of any kind, at any time. It was not long before the challenge was put to the test. The evolutionary theories that took hold of the nineteenth century imagination were deployed by Darwin's acolytes, though interestingly not by Darwin himself, as weapons against religious orthodoxy.

---

[18]*Financial Times*. October 21st, 2009

The contest was between two types of fundamentalism. On the religious side were those who refused to give up on the literal reading of the Bible. Opposite them, at the other extreme, were the disciples of reason and progress who proclaimed science as the new religion, the only source of knowledge and the deliverer of truth.

The middle ground was held by scientists who recognized the limits of their discipline and by believers who saw that scientific laws along with the dramatic advances in industry, technology and medicine did not preclude a Creator or militate against the value of Christianity as a cultural heritage and a way of life. But, as ever, common-sense argument was all but drowned out by the sound of dogmatic fury.

By the turn of the last century, the mechanical view of nature as promoted by T. H. Huxley, otherwise known as Darwin's bulldog, had extended beyond the basic tenets of evolution to encompass much that was distinctly unscientific. Tying their creed to 'the survival of the fittest', a sharper version of Darwin's 'competitive struggle for existence', Herbert Spencer and Ernst Haeckel gave the lead to a form of social Darwinism that was racist and militarist. It was but a short step from claiming that some humans are less fit than others to a conviction that inferior types are expendable and that only an elite deserve to live.

Marx brought his version of rational analysis to bear on politics and economics while Freud, on even shakier empirical evidence, claimed to have plumbed the deepest recesses of human consciousness. Both turned out to be horribly wrong on most of the essentials but such was the fervour, one is tempted to say the religious fervour, they engendered, their cause was taken up in other guises. New academic disciplines struggling for recognition adopted the scientific label as a sign of legitimacy.

So it was that the insights of the early psychologists and sociologists were sidelined by a passion for measurement which, trading on the obvious, had the supposed virtue of scientific validity. In economics, mathematics assumed the dominant role with policy based on increasingly elaborate macro models, noted for their predictive value of telling us what we ought to have done last week.

Giving up on the big questions, philosophy became entangled in the roots of human language where the minutiae of human intercourse could be dissected and analyzed to the point of impenetrable tedium. The extension of linguistic analysis to literature reduced criticism to a study of the particular use of words. Judgements as to what was 'good' or 'bad' were said to be irrelevant to 'structuralism' which 'like any science, made a virtue of impartiality ... and would as happily treat a children's nursery rhyme as Paradise Lost'. For visual art, the scientific trend was towards hard definition of what constituted works of art, with phrases like 'significant form' and the 'common core of emotional expression' attempting a precision that proved to be more controversial than any value judgement. Even in architecture, the subjective idea of beauty lost out to functionalism, a laudable concept of producing 'more beautiful things for everyday use' which deteriorated into a formulaic aim of achieving maximum efficiency at the lowest cost. Hence the concrete and metal configurations designed from the inside out. They were not much to look at but they did the job.

Inevitably, the scientific mindset carried over to general education where tests of mental agility, a key factor in scientific reasoning, were assumed to give an accurate reading on all facets of intelligence, including creativity. A parallel movement worked against those studies – art, music, the classics – that were not strictly practical. That an increasing share of the standard school curriculum was directly vocational was a response to those who asked, what point can there be to education if it cannot be measured in material benefits?

Recent years have brought a healthy reaction against some of the more dubious exercises in scientism. Linguistic analysis and structuralism have just about had their day. Economic models are no longer held to be inviolate (how could it be otherwise after the recent banking implosion?). Intelligence tests have proved, at best, to be an unreliable guide to ability or performance. Arguments on relative values in art, architecture and literature are back in fashion.

Yet no sooner is the stage cleared of the debris left by shoddy scientism than a new set is constructed for a reprise. This time it is the turn of the militant atheists who tie themselves to evolution as the incontrovertible truth. While this is not the place for theological debate, it is surely relevant to point out that the harsh, supercilious tone adopted by Richard Dawkins, Christopher Hitchens, Sam Harris et al., recalls an earlier generation of intellectual dogmatists: God is dead; science reigns; end of message.

'What is most repellent about the new atheism,' writes James Wood, 'is its intolerant certainty; it is always noon in Dawkins' world, and the sun of science and liberal positivism is shining brassily, casting no shadow.'

To which Marilynne Robinson has this to add:

The degree to which debunking is pursued as if it were an urgent crusade, at whatever cost to the wealth of insight into human nature that might come from attending to the record humankind has left, and without regard for the probative standard scholarship as well as science should answer to, may well be the most remarkable feature of the modern period in intellectual history.

A justifiable response to Dawkins peevish complaint that society has been brainwashed to excuse the failings of Christianity is that we have been brainwashed into expecting science to provide all the answers, that a scientific overlay is all that is needed to give veracity to dubious propositions. This is not to deny the huge advances made by science or the benefits mankind has accrued by way of painstaking research and brilliant insight by some of the finest minds of any generation. But that is a long way from claiming science to be all embracing.

The track record of the various branches of science is by no means uniform. As David Papineau points out, while post-1800 chemistry can claim a succession of triumphs, cosmology has done less well. Overall, 'if you look at post scientific theories, they all turn out to be wrong, so our present theories are probably wrong too'.

In the early part of the last century, Bertrand Russell dismissed the need for a Creator with the supposedly inarguable assertion that the world did not have a beginning in any ordinary sense of the word. 'The idea that things must have a beginning is really due to the poverty of our imagination.' Then, a few years later, after Edwin Hubble found that the universe is expanding, the steady state theory gave way to the Big Bang, an explanation for the origin of the universe that, as Marilynne Robinson reminds us, is closer to Genesis than Russell's extrapolation.

It was not long before we were introduced to quantum mechanics and geometrodynamics where the excitement of breaking new ground tended to obscure the fact that in this strange realm nothing is as it seems, where the very process of observation disrupts calculations. As noted by Brian Ellis:

Many space-time quantum physicists would be quite puzzled by the suggestion that the theories they accept and work with might literally be true, since they have no clear conception at all of the reality with which these theories might correspond.

If quantum theory leaves many unanswered, maybe unanswerable, questions, so too does evolution, at least in the blanket form touted by popular science. The imponderables start with the most fundamental of all questions, the origins of life. Images of creatures emerging from the primeval slime are the stuff of science fiction but remain unsupported by the fossil record. Claiming too much for evolution takes us into perilous territory.

Writing at around the time when Spencer was adding an extra dimension to evolution, William James was engaged on his classic *The Varieties of Religious Experience*. In his summing up he had this to say:

I believe that the claims of the sectarian scientist are, to say the least, premature. The universe ... [is] ... a more many-sided affair than any sect, even the scientific sect, allows for. What, in the end, are all our verifications but experiences that agree with more or less isolated systems of ideas ... that our minds have framed. But why in the name of common sense need we assume that only one such system of ideas can be true?

He concluded, 'The obvious outcome of our total experience is that the world can be handled according to many systems of ideas.'

Or as André Gide put it: 'Believe those who seek the truth, doubt those who find it.'

Barry Turner, 2011

References
Dennis Sewell, *The Political Gene*, p. 32
Rónán McDonald, *The Death of the Critic,* p. 117
James Wood, *The New Yorker*, 31.8.09
Marilynne Robinson, *Absence of Mind*, p. 29
David Papineau in *Philosophy Bites* ed. by David Edmonds and Nigel Warburton, p. 109
Brian Ellis in *The Philosophy of Science* ed. by David Papineau, p. 168
William James, *The Varieties of Religious Experience*, p. 89

Where Do We Get the Energy? The Nuclear Debate

The nuclear debate is at risk of overheating. It needs to cool off, argues Barry Turner.

'Nuclear' and 'crisis' go together. Any environmental setback catches the headlines but with the nuclear label attached it takes on mammoth proportions. It happened 25 years ago when the pride of Soviet nuclear technology at Chernobyl (now part of Ukraine) was ripped apart. It happened again when the recent earthquake and tsunami in Japan knocked out the nuclear plant at Fukushima. Led by vocal public opinion, which instinctively associates anything nuclear with wipe-out weaponry, governments across the globe have hastened to reassure voters that their policy is safety first. Of the 400 new stations planned worldwide, many are now on hold with cancellations a real possibility. Among the leading economies, Germany has announced a nuclear phase-out.

An overreaction? Energy experts who take global warming seriously certainly think so. Nuclear is free of carbon emissions while producing vastly more energy per unit than fossil fuel, a multiple of up to 2 million according to one assessment.[19] As clean options, solar and wind power have their cheerleaders but the wind comes and goes and the sun does not always shine.

Anyway, who is to say that nuclear power is inherently unsafe? In the first of the nuclear scares, at Three Mile Island in Pennsylvania in 1979, no lives were lost. There were 57 fatalities at Chernobyl and while the risk of cancer was increased for those closest to the radiation fallout, estimates for the number affected have fallen over the years from the high hundreds of thousands to the low tens. As for Fukushima, it is too early to be certain but so far there are no deaths or even serious health hazards directly attributable to the accident.

Contrast this with the human cost of exploiting fossil fuels, starting with the thousands who have died digging for coal or drilling for oil. The pollution caused by coal burning is a killer on a massive scale, not to mention the environmental problems it is building up for future generations. In 2009 alone, the world's electricity generators spewed out 9 billion tonnes of carbon dioxide.

Yet public concern at these hazards is muted or, at least, not evidenced in the marches, demonstrations and intense political lobbying associated with the nuclear industry.

Familiarisation is the key. We have grown up with coal and oil, forgetting, for example, that worldwide, there are over a million road deaths a year. But nuclear energy is new and, by definition, unpredictable. And while no energy fix is entirely without risks, one of those attached to nuclear is really scary.

The overlap with military technology was demonstrated as early as the mid-seventies when India tested a nuclear weapon design using plutonium separated out of its breeder reactor programme. The current worry is that the uranium enrichment plants in Iran will be used to produce nuclear weapon materials. Diplomatic nerves were stretched early in the year when it was reported that the Iranians were having problems in getting their first nuclear reactor to work. A shortage of home-produced expertise in operating a nuclear plant safely suggests that Iran may have a disaster in the making.

But a nuclear ban across Europe and America, even if it were feasible, will not call a halt to weapons proliferation or, for that matter, to the development of nuclear energy for entirely legitimate purposes. While the Fukushima accident created a backlash in some countries, notably Germany and in Japan itself, there was no move in China to hold back on the 77 reactors it has at various stages of construction or in Russia which has ten reactors in the making.

As might be expected from a country nuclear-dependent for 80% of its electricity, the reaction from France was measured, with commentators pointing out that the Japanese reactors survived the sixth most powerful earthquake ever recorded and that the crisis was caused by the loss of electric power from the grid and the failure of the backup diesel generators. No one doubts there are lessons to be learned. Strengthening the lines of defence will be a priority for the industry, which can expect to be more heavily regulated.

Though this will add cost it will be a long way short of making nuclear energy prohibitively expensive.

Meanwhile, fears of contamination from nuclear waste (a big issue in the US where a US$20 billion-investment in storing spent nuclear fuel in the Nevada mountains recently succumbed to political pressure for alternatives to be explored) will fade in the wake of new technology. Already, most of the nuclear waste in France is processed for reuse.

But whatever reassurances the industry can provide it is likely that expansion will be slower than predicted before the Japanese earthquake. Many governments will pause before they agree to commission new reactors. Sensitivity to voters' wishes—or prejudices—will be one factor. Of greater moment is the dawning realisation that alternative sources of energy are more readily accessible than was previously supposed. Far from running out, oil will soon be flowing more freely with vast reserves discovered off the coasts of Africa and Brazil. The latest oil sand projects in Canada now supply more oil to the United States than Saudi Arabia. Natural gas, cleaner and cheaper, looks set to take over from coal as a primary energy source. Supplies in the US are so plentiful as to hold out the prospect of a thriving export market. Other regions, including Europe, Asia and North Africa, are similarly favoured. Most significantly, the price of gas has fallen by half in the last 5 years, making the initial heavy investment in nuclear energy less appealing.

Nuclear energy will have its day but not yet. It could well turn out that Fukushima is less the reason than an excuse for applying the brakes.

Barry Turner, 2011

Openness. Not Always the Best Policy

How far can we trust politicians? The Wikileaks controversy shows that much of what we think of as democracy is conducted behind closed doors. But perhaps that is as it should be. Total freedom of information, argues Barry Turner, would make effective government impossible.

You don't have to be crooked to go into politics, but it helps. That is the typical voter talking. It is a view strengthened with every well publicized instance of chicanery in high places. But the real causes of cynicism go much deeper and have more to do with the way we manage our democracy than with individual transgressions.

As with so much else that is changing in the social fabric, the starting point for discussion is the power of modern communications. Instant news has revolutionized our perception of democracy. For public consumption, political issues are reduced to the lowest common denominator of understanding—or supposed understanding. Politicians are bombarded with deceptively simple questions which demand equally simple answers. But since every contention is multi-layered with subtleties, clear and straightforward responses are rare. Instead, politicians resort to prevarication or, when pressed, to meaningless waffle which in turn leads to the charge of duplicity. And duplicity is the close cousin of downright dishonesty.

The problem is aggravated by the constraints of party discipline which minimize the opportunities for politicians to speak freely. Even at local level, party loyalists are liable to react aggressively if the person they have elected to speak for them shows much independence of spirit. It was a tendency Edmund Burke warned against over 200 years ago when he told the electors of Bristol: 'Your representative owes you, not his industry only but his judgement, and he betrays instead of serving you if he sacrifices it to your opinion'. He was right. Democracy can only function effectively if politicians are allowed to do their job without for ever looking over their shoulder. Much of what happens in government simply does not lend itself to free and open discussion.

Every emergency throws up examples. In the latest recession when some countries faced a run on the banks, it would have taken recklessness bordering on insanity for politicians in power to express openly their nightmare fears. A bad situation could only have been made worse. Instead, all the talk was of recovery round the corner, even if fingers were crossed while the words were uttered. Dishonest? Up to a point. But to quote again the great Edmund Burke, if 'falsehood and delusion are allowed in no case whatsoever ... as an exercise of all the virtues, there is an economy of truth' which can be justified on practical grounds.

---

[19]John Hofmeister, *Why We Hate the Oil Companies*. Palgrave, 2010

The failure to recognize this fundamental fact (the very phrase 'economy of truth' when used some time ago by a senior British civil servant was judged to be a clear indication that the administration he represented could not be trusted in anything) inhibits political initiative and puts politicians in the way of slavishly following public opinion instead of leading it. So it is that the failure to abide by the letter to election pledges, even when unpredictable events demand a change of emphasis or direction, is judged to be dishonest whereas it could just as logically be evidence of responsible government.

Politicians make it worse for themselves by adopting a defensive strategy of obsessive secrecy on the principle of what the voters don't know, they won't question. The overlay is a bureaucratic failure to recognize any distinction between what is really important and the mere trivialities of routine administration. It would be healthier for democracy if more transparency was accompanied by a willingness among politicians to confess not to knowing all the answers and to accept, occasionally, that they could be wrong. They might also resolve to give short shrift to interviewers pressing for worthless sound bites on complex issues.

The new media is often credited with narrowing the gap between politicians and their electors. This is true to the extent that those in public service are besieged by appeals for support, help, justice, compensation or any of the other remedies for real or supposed grievances. A British politician, a senior minister in the present government, tells me that when he was first elected 40 years ago, he received at most a dozen letters a week. Now, he needs a full-time assistant just to keep track of his post.

Maybe that is as it should be. Electors have a right of access to their representatives. And they are entitled to a hearing. What they should not have is the prerogative to dictate which invariably gives power to unelected lobbyists for single-issue pressure groups.

What of politicians who really are dishonest? Voters should certainly be able to hold to account representatives who betray their trust. But longer term, the only sure way of reducing the number of dodgy characters in public life is to pay our politicians salaries that are sufficient to lift them above temptation. The recent scandal of British politicians abusing their expenses revealed a culture in which extravagant or, in some cases, outrageously venal claims were accepted on the nod as the only way of compensating for inadequate pay. As Burke might have said, it is another fundamental truth that if political standards fall short, it is the voters who must ultimately accept the blame.

Barry Turner, 2011

Spread a Little Happiness

What makes people happy? For many, the question is rhetorical. Happiness is an abstract concept shaped into something tangible by individual choice. What delights one person can drive another to distraction. That said, on the biggest concerns of life there must be some common ground. Most of us accept that a comfortable income brings greater happiness than poverty. Maybe there are other, less obvious, areas of consensus. Could it be that what divides us in terms of personal choice has been allowed to obfuscate the essentials of a happy state?

There are politicians who believe so. Some time before he became Britain's prime minister, David Cameron was arguing that simple economic indicators tell only half the story. His call for the 'big society', which he carried over into government, remains short on detail. But in so far as he is promoting a more active community spirit he is signalling a retraction of the rampant individualism that favours material prosperity over all other forms of human endeavour. In this Cameron is echoing the views of many other European leaders, notably President Sarkozy of France, who espouse 'quality of life'—how people relate to each other and to their surroundings—as the only valid means of assessing human happiness.

Devotees of unbridled capitalism are not impressed. They dismiss the quality of life argument as a defensive cover for the failure of Europe to match the energy, innovation and economic growth of the United States. There is some truth in this. Envy of American achievement is a powerful engine for anti-American sentiment. Yet beyond political point-scoring, inquisitive psychologists and economists who ask questions before propounding grand theories are finding evidence to suggest that while minimum standards are a prerequisite, happiness cannot simply be counted in possessions or judged by the size of a bank balance. Surveys conducted over half a century show that while, unsurprisingly, the rich are happier than the poor, affluent societies as a whole have not added much, if anything, to their happiness quota.

Part of the explanation is that happiness is relative. Many of the luxuries of yesteryear such as electronically equipped kitchens and cars that rarely break down are now taken for granted. But it may also be true that in becoming more individualistic and in giving way to rampant consumerism we have lost touch with values that tend towards a general happiness. Family relationships have declined (the unmarried account for over half the households in the US) despite evidence to suggest that married people are happier. Broken families put children at risk, leaving them emotionally isolated at a time when they most need support.

Widespread unemployment persists with little in the way of social programmes to combat the accompanying malaise and sense of failure. Mutual trust is at a premium and while mental illnesses are increasing at an alarming rate, their treatment is judged secondary to finding cures for physical ailments. Depression is now the most common cause of long-term sickness in the UK. Then again, though we are all richer than our forerunners of 50 or 100 years ago, the gap between the haves and the have-nots remains as great as ever while media preoccupation with the affairs of the wealthy prompts envy and resentment. And not just the media. Cheap and easy travel is a constant reminder of how other lives are apparently better or worse than our own. The poor are easily forgotten, it is the rich who leave the enduring impression. We aspire to the bigger home, car or television screen and we are unhappy when they remain out of reach. Add to all this a work pattern which makes a virtue of stress and we are left with the paradox that, for many, the pursuit of material comforts actually militates against quality of life.

As nobody in their right mind wants to do away with the fruits of prosperity, the solution must be to achieve a social balance, wealth creation without accompanying pain. In pursuit of this objective there is much to learn from the Nordic countries which are consistently among the highest scorers in the international happiness stakes. Not all the conditions that are said to favour general contentment can be easily replicated. Denmark, for example, is a small, homogenous society with a strong sense of national identity. Problems of conflicting cultures which beset other western countries are rare though the resistance of recent immigrants to doing things 'the Danish way' may portend a shock to the system. For now, however, the Danish social contract which puts a high value on mutual trust and consensus in politics and business has produced enormous benefits, not least an enviable living standard extending to decent housing for all, a generously funded health service and cheap, efficient public transport. Most critically, education is driven by a spirit of egalitarianism. Knowledge and qualifications are sought as much for advancing the public interest as for individual aggrandisement.

Critics hasten to point out that the Danes, as all Scandinavians, pay highly for their privileges with tax rates that are way above the international average. But the general feeling is that the money collected by the state is well spent. If other governments demand less, more goes in waste and incompetence. Even so, while the evidence points to a correlation between income equality favoured in Scandinavia and a culture of trust and respect as the basis for a healthier lifestyle, it is improbable, to put it mildly, that a political programme founded on these principles would find favour in countries that have, for generations, promoted individualism. At best, a broader view of national well-being will support more family friendly practices at work such as flexible hours and parental leave and encourage activities that promote community life.

More hopefully, the findings of positive psychology suggest that individualism might be made to serve the happiness of the greatest number with the simple realization that taking the initiative in caring for others by engaging in voluntary services brings its own reward in an enhanced sense of purpose and personal fulfilment.

'Produce any happy person,' writes Richard Layard, 'and you will find a project'. He added, 'Happiness comes from outside and within. The two are not in contradiction. The true pilgrim fights the evils of the world out there and cultivates the spirit within.'

Barry Turner, 2011

More Reading

Daniel Dorling, *Injustice. Why Social Inequality Persists* The Policy Press, 2011

Pascal Bruckner, *Perpetual Euphoria. On the Duty to be Happy* Princeton University Press, 2011

Michael Foley, *The Age of Absurdity. Why Modern Life Makes it Hard to be Happy* Simon & Schuster, 2010

Richard Layard, *Happiness: Lessons From a New Science* Penguin, 2011 (2nd revised ed)

Martin Seligman, *A New Understanding of Happiness and Well-Being and How to Achieve Them* Nicholas Brealey, 2011

Ivan Robertson and Cary Cooper, *Well-Being, Productivity and Happiness at Work* Palgrave Macmillan, 2011

The Future Balance of Economic Power

The Economic Confidence of the West has Taken a Battering in Recent Years While the East has Flourished. Is this how it will be for the Long Term?

Do we progress? The conviction that mankind is moving towards some sort of promised land gains popular currency when times are good. Some years ago a sample of college leavers was asked to grade the events in their lives to date and then to say how they saw the future. When their answers were transposed on to a graph, the early part showed a roller coaster of ups and downs while expectations were represented by a smooth rising curve. Needless to add, this was in the days of economic boom when higher education was a passport to a safe and well-paid career. If the experiment was repeated today, the prospects would not look so rosy.

Future? What Future?

The dark mood that weighs on much of the western hemisphere appears to float away over that part of the developing world embraced by the example of India and China. After generations of underachievement or no achievement at all, these countries are finding hidden strengths that have raised the competitive stakes in the global economy and are causing unease or downright fear among those who have had it so good for so long. When jobs are lost and incomes remain static or decline, there is always someone to blame.

But the highs and lows can both be overdone. If it is too soon to write off the West, by the same token the emerging superpowers may soon be in for a few knocks to their self-confidence. This is not to suggest a catastrophic reversal of their economic fortunes though clearly that is always a possibility. Rather, the headlong rush towards prosperity will engender social and political pressures that will upset the timetable.

The history of the industrial powers that had their start in the steam age provide a salutary warning. As the ruling oligarchies of Europe and America gave way to the class of wealthy entrepreneurs they had helped to create, so it will be in China. Can popular democracy be far behind? And what will that do for tightly managed economies?

As a functioning democracy, albeit with oligarchic tendencies, India might be said to enjoy a head start in accommodating rapid growth. But with millions still in abject poverty, one does not have to be a Marxist to anticipate disruptive, possibly violent, demands for a more equitable distribution of national wealth.

Then again, everywhere there are powerful underlying movements which weigh against unbridled expansionism. This certainly happened in the second half of the nineteenth century when Britain was at the peak of its commercial and imperialistic power. The industrial revolution, parallel in many ways to what is happening today in the once quiescent nations of the East, spurred a fierce reaction from the opponents of materialism, those who believed that the 'dark Satanic mills' brought nothing but misery and degradation. Incredible as it must now seem, the favoured

antidote to change was a cult of medievalism, the conviction popularized by some of the outstanding intellectuals and commentators of their day (including, incidentally, Thomas Carlyle, the originator of *The Statesman's Yearbook*) that everything was so much better in the thirteenth and fourteenth centuries. The image was of a social idyll, with benevolent rulers watching over the lower orders, who, snug and secure, were content to live their simple lives. The reality, of course, was hunger, violence, dirt and disease when, as Thomas Hobbes observed, lives were brutish and short.

Rival powers to Britain created their own legends to offset the pain of industrial expansion—for example, hundreds of Western movies have fixed the image of the sturdy independence of the New World settlers, beholden to no man and ready to overcome all obstacles in the pursuit of the American dream. The money men had no part to play in this drama, except as villains. We might expect the developed countries to have dispelled their fantasies about the 'good old days'. Yet in times of crisis there are many who gaze longingly in the rearview mirror. In the States, support for the Tea Party comes largely from disaffected voters who somehow imagine that the country can run itself perfectly well without the attention of politicians and bureaucrats. Similarly, in Europe, the far-right parties and the far right of the main parties trade on a populist agenda that would have them backtrack on a European union that has delivered peace and prosperity unprecedented in any single member country.

Fortunately, on both sides of the Atlantic the democracies are sufficiently resilient to combat narrow nationalism and bigotry. When voters are focused on choices that really matter, as in national elections, they can usually be relied upon to reject rule by the rednecks. Countries in transition have a long way to go before they reach this level of maturity. Which is why we should not visualize their progress as an uninterrupted upward curve. Who can doubt that there are countercultures, looking back to a supposed golden age, at work today in India and China? In Russia, there are even those who reflect fondly on the days of Stalin.

There are many other imponderables, more or less significant depending on how events unfold. One is the knowledge explosion which is louder in the US than anywhere else on earth. Whatever the next big breakthrough—something, say, on the scale of the internet—the balance of probability is that it will have its start in Silicon Valley. The point here is simply that economic advance is not a precise science. The rise of the East, if it continues, need not be accompanied by a decline of the West, even if the present omens suggest otherwise.

In countering the doom merchants we need to remind ourselves that while the Western model of mixed economy capitalism has its fault lines, notably the widening gap between the affluent and an underclass frustrated by its inability to realise its potential, there is no reason why, given time, imaginative politics cannot meet the challenges.

Do we progress? Yes, but only in fits and starts.

Barry Turner, 2012

The Battle for Berlin

Three years after the end of the war in which American and British air forces had all but obliterated German cities, Allied aircraft were once again circling Berlin. But this time they were carrying not bombs but food and fuel for a city under siege by Soviet forces. It was, quite simply, the most ambitious relief operation of its kind ever mounted.

Berlin was a divided city in a divided country in a divided Europe. It was not supposed to be like that. In the immediate post war, the Western allies—America, Britain and France—hoped to cooperate with the Soviet Union to make a lasting European peace. But between communism and democracy there were few meeting points. Holed up in the Kremlin, the ever distrustful Stalin saw himself surrounded by enemies. Above all, he feared a resurgent Germany fed by democratic and thus anti-Soviet doctrine.

So it was that the four-power occupation of Germany and of Berlin settled into an East-West split. The problem for Berlin was that it happened to be a hundred and twenty miles inside the Russian zone. In the euphoria of victory, the Western powers had assumed right of access to the German capital but the only firm guarantee specified three twenty-mile wide air corridors linking Berlin to Hamburg, Hanover and Frankfurt. For road, rail and canal, the Russians claimed absolute control. As one Eastern European country after another—Hungary, Romania, Bulgaria, Poland—fell to Soviet control, Stalin saw his chance of raising the stakes in Germany.

Supposing all the land routes to Berlin were cut off. By Stalin's calculations the Allies had only two options—a humiliating withdrawal or buying the right to stay in Berlin by accepting Soviet terms for the rest of Germany. It was almost inconceivable to Kremlin strategists that their former allies would resort to force. Stalin decided to test their resolve.

Without warning, all land routes to West Berlin were closed. For the two million citizens trapped in the city, there was enough food and fuel for just 27 days. General Lucius Clay, the US military governor in Germany, was all for calling Stalin's bluff. His request to Washington was for authority to reopen the road and rail routes with all traffic accompanied by armed escorts ready to shoot their way through. Clay's British counterpart, General Sir Brian Robertson, urged caution. 'If you send an armed convoy, it'll be war,' he warned Clay. But apart from caving in, what possible alternative could there be?

The answer was provided by a mid-ranking Royal Air Force officer, a veteran of the Allied invasion of German-occupied Europe. Air Commodore Rex Waite worked away at planning an airlift. No one asked him to take on what was thought to be an impossible job. It was just something he felt he could do, like a crossword puzzle. The result was a brilliant exercise in logistics.

He first identified eight air bases in West Germany for loading and two receiving airports in West Berlin—Gatow and Tempelhof, both of which would need radical upgrading to bear the extra traffic.

But the most daunting task was to plot a schedule that would allow convoys of aircraft to land safely, unload and take off with precision timing. He worked alone, jotting drawings and calculations in a tiny notebook with the stub of a pencil.

Waite took his plan to his sceptical superiors, who passed it up the line until it reached Clay. For want of other constructive ideas, the general took it seriously. On June 26, 1948, he ordered the US Air Force to begin a daily routine of flying 225 tons of provisions into Berlin.

Clay conceded that the venture 'may prove me to be the craziest man in the world'. As for the Russians, they had no doubt that it would fail, and revelled in the fact.

That it did not was down to ingenious ways of improving carrying capacity. Fresh bread contained a third of its own weight in water, so bags of flour were sent instead. Sacks and cardboard replaced tins and wooden boxes for packaging.

Goods such as newsprint and cigars were given priority as morale boosters. Under the same heading came a grand piano for the Berlin Philharmonic.

Pilots who saw hungry children gathered outside the perimeter fence started dropping tiny parachutes made of handkerchiefs loaded with bundles of chocolate and sweets as they made their final approach. As word spread of the warm gesture of the 'candy bombers', so the loyalty to the West of a whole new generation of West Berliners was cemented.

The Americans flew into Tempelhof, which had been Hitler's showpiece airport close to the city centre. The British used Gatow, but only after tar for the runway was purloined from a factory in the Russian sector, barrels of it rolled through the wire at night by sympathetic East Berliners.

When the call went out for steamrollers to finish the job, one well-wisher drove his from Leipzig, 100 miles away, past the secret police checkpoints along the way.

Air traffic control, a technology in its infancy, was a nightmare. At Gatow, it amounted to a single radio operated from a van parked beside the runway. Rigid rules were learned, from hard experience.

No plane was to be on the ground in Berlin for longer than 50 min. There was to be no stacking over the airport. With planes landing so closely together, it one missed its slot, there was no going round: it had to fly back to its home base and start again.

With overcrowded air corridors and frequent engine failure, inevitably there were accidents. On what was dubbed 'Black Friday', the weather suddenly turned hostile over Tempelhof. Low, dense cloud and blinding rain cut out the radar and 'everything went to hell'.

A massive American C-54 Skymaster carrying ten tons of supplies missed the runway and crashed. Flames from the wreckage brought the next arrival to an emergency stop, which blew its tyres. Meanwhile, banks of waiting aircraft were at increasing risk of collision.

For months on end, the British and American relief planes roared in, one after another in a constant stream, often landing only minutes apart. In one 24-h period, an astonishing 1,400 aircraft came into Berlin's two airports, one every single minute.

And the Soviets tried every tactic to stop them, short of shooting them down. They buzzed, they threatened, they tried to blind the pilots with bright spotlights.

But, for all the difficulties, supplies were getting through. By September, planes were delivering 4,600 tons a day, more than enough to meet minimum demands. Confidence that the Airlift was succeeding drowned out Soviet propaganda.

As winter approached, it became clear that everything now depended on the severity of the season ahead. It didn't look good when pea-souper fog grounded the planes for half of November. Then December was bitterly cold, putting an extra strain on the city's inhabitants.

Electricity and gas were restricted to four hours a day, and one hot meal a day was the best any ordinary family could hope for. Soap and clothing were scarce. Freedom came at a high price but most West Berliners were prepared to pay it.

In the end, a mild January came to the rescue. The planes were able to keep up their delivery schedules and the risk of a total shutdown of West Berlin's essential services vanished. Supplies were now coming in at an unprecedented 5,547 tons a day, and the Airlift organizers were confident of pushing that figure up by another 1,000 tons if they had to. The Soviets knew they were beaten. As early as mid-December, Stalin had ordered a toning down of triumphalist propaganda. On 12 May 1949, the blockade was finally lifted. It had been an extraordinary achievement.

Over eleven months, from June 1948 to May 1949, 2.3 m. tons of supplies were shifted on 277,500 flights. Average daily deliveries included 4,000 tons of coal, a bulk cargo never before associated with air carriers. That record day of nearly 1,400 aircraft—close on one a minute—landing and taking off in West Berlin created a traffic controller's nightmare at a time when computer technology was still in its infancy. But just about every statistic of the Airlift broke a record of some sort. For those who took part, the sense of achieving something remarkable was to stay with them for the rest of their lives.

But for the Airlift the whole of Germany might well have fallen under Soviet control. France and Italy, with powerful communist parties, could have followed. Eastern Europe was already in thrall to Moscow. The Airlift sent a message to Stalin. America and Britain would stand firm. Less than a year after the blockade was lifted, America abandoned the last vestiges of isolationism with the creation of NATO and a commitment to lead the defence of Europe. There was to be no retreat. The confrontation in Berlin was the first and arguably the decisive round in the Cold War.

Barry Turner, 2013

The Reeds at Runnymede

Magna Carta was 800 Years old in 2015. Barry Turner Explores its Origins and Explains how it came to be the Guiding Spirit for the British and American Constitutions.

I was brought up on Magna Carta. As a schoolboy in Bury St Edmunds, a rural market town of medieval origins, I learned that it was here, in January 1215, in the once great abbey, that the heads of England's noble families gathered to pledge mutual support in their opposition to the tyrannical rule of King John. The sequel, 6 months later, was at Runnymede, a riverside meadow between London and Windsor, where John put his seal to a pro-gramme of reform called the Charter of Liberties or, subsequently and more famously, Magna Carta.

My introduction to the 'greatest constitutional document of all times'[20] came in the aftermath of a world war against fascism. It made for an inspiring story of an earlier victory over despotism, one, that for young people, was given a lift by tales of Robin Hood and his band of outlaws who ran rings round King John and his villainous Sheriff of Nottingham.

But while it did not take long to discover that Robin Hood was the stuff of legend, the myths attached to Magna Carta had more staying power. Even now, with the status of near holy writ bestowed on the 'oldest liberty docu-ment' it can come as a surprise that John's reputation as a thuggish oppressor was overstated, that the barons were by no means united in their resistance to the monarchy and that liberty, as understood by the champions of Magna Carta, was narrowly confined.

Like all warrior kings, John could be treacherous and brutal. With a personality driven by jealousy and suspicion, he was not one to inspire loyalty. But his problems were not entirely of his own making. Inheriting the crown from his brother Richard Coeur de Lion, or Richard the Lionheart—names that remind us of the strong Anglo-French connection—John came to the throne at a time when England was beginning the long transition into a modern state. While Richard, the great Crusader, had put military prowess above all else, he had fought his battles abroad. In his absence, which accounted for most of his reign, the English countryside was at peace. Benefiting from technological advances, ranging from water power to windmills, the barons, ensconced in their great castles, needed to feel secure in managing their estates. It was a reverie that became increasingly remote once John had taken on the mantle of royalty. As he saw it, he had a divine right to rule as he thought fit. This included surrounding himself with a talented bureaucracy (John was, above all, an efficient administrator) to enforce his will and to swell the royal exchequer.

The king's tax-raising powers were many and various. They included 'scrutage', the money paid in lieu of military service, an inheritance tax on large estates and a sort of transfer fee on wealthy widows who remarried. Though underpinned by feudal custom, these charges were resented on several counts. For one thing, John enforced them more rigorously than any of his predecessors. His coterie of treasurers and bailiffs seemed to take malicious pleasure in bending established rules to maximise the royal income.

At the same time, the rate at which taxes were levied was liable to be raised arbitrarily. There was some justification for this since the increased flow and circulation of coinage had doubled or even trebled prices. But with the concept of inflation as yet unknown, the barons concluded that they were paying more merely to satisfy royal greed. The censure might have been lighter had not John spent lavishly on ill-fated adventures across the Channel. Pressure on him mounted after his attempts to regain family territory in northern France ended ingloriously in 1214 at the Battle of Bouvines when Brittany and Normandy were irretrievably lost to the French crown.

Recognising the discontent that was bubbling up around him, John conceded enough to give the impression of reform. But it was too little too late. To add to his troubles abroad, he was soon faced with rebellion at home. With more than their share of grievance, it was the northern barons who took the lead. But they failed in their attempts to create a united front. Challenging the King in the exercise of his hitherto undisputed right to have the last word was, for many powerful landowners, an offence against the natural order. In the incipient civil war the barons who were for or against John were evenly balanced while the majority kept well in the background. Playing on the strength of tradition, John might have faced down the crisis but for one critical factor, his failure to hold London, the strong point of any campaign to win the country.

Both sides moved cautiously towards a deal. Casting himself as medi-ator, Stephen Langton, Archbishop of Canterbury, delved into ancient documents to find some sort of precedent for restraining the royal prerog-ative. But how was it possible to limit some kingly powers without limiting all his powers? And who would act as the impartial judge of royal right and wrong?

For those of us who are distant observers of the scene, another question arises. Were the barons speaking for themselves alone or do we go along with the nineteenth-century historian, William Stubbs, that their demands 'were no selfish exaction of privilege' and that they had 'cut themselves loose from Normandy and Norman principles and reconciled themselves to the nobler position of leaders of their brother Englishmen'?

Phrases like 'community of the whole land' and 'consent of the kingdom' are not hard to find in Magna Carta. But it is surely inconceivable that the barons had in mind a nation in any modern sense, let alone a constitutional monarchy. Their idea of good government was oligarchic with king and nobility working more or less in harmony supported by those of sufficient wealth and social standing to be called freemen. Excluded were the unfree, the serfs or villeins who made a subsistence living in service to their lords. They comprised over half the population.

So it was that much of Magna Carta addressed specific grievances with financial concessions to the barons as the first consideration. For the rest, the clauses that had bearing on the relationship between the king and his subjects were cast in vague terms that made for easy adaptation over the centuries. Thus 'consent of the kingdom' without which 'no scrutage or aid shall be imposed' eventually took on a much wider signif-icance to the point where the American colonies, looking to independence from Britain, could cite Magna Carta in support of 'no taxation without representation'.

This was a concept beyond the wildest imaginings of the gathering at Runnymede who had no compunction in exercising autocratic judgement on the lower orders. The claim that the barons were championing the liberties of all men can only be sustained on the supposition that they were doing so without knowing it.

But if Magna Carta was not the birth certificate of freedom, it was, as Simon Schama argues, the 'death certificate of despotism'. Schama goes on to say that Magna Carta 'spelled out for the first time, and unequivocally ... that the law was not simply the will or whim of the king but was an independent power in its own right, and that kings could be brought to book for violating it'.[21]

The implications were not lost on John. Within weeks of the ceremony at Runnymede it was clear that he had no intention of holding to his part of the agreement. Claiming that his consent had been secured by force he appealed to the Pope, as supreme overlord, to intervene. Conscious of his own vulnerability, the Pontiff declared Magna Carta to be 'illegal and unjust'. For their part the barons enlisted as standard bearer Prince Louis of France, whose asset was a distant claim to the English throne. A lengthy civil war was in prospect when King John reputedly lost a large part of his worldly wealth in an ill-fated journey across The Wash in East Anglia and promptly succumbed to dysentery. His heir, a nine-year-old boy, was crowned Henry III in October 1215. No longer feeling under threat, the barons quickly rallied to the young king while Prince Louis, whose invasion force disembarked at Sandwich in Kent in May the following year, was soon sent packing.

While Henry was growing up under the tutelage of those who had stood against his father, Magna Carta gained authenticity. Supplemented in 1217 by a Forest Charter that gave freemen the right to turn forest land to commercial advantage so long as they did not cause damage to their neighbours, Magna Carta was amended slightly before it was reissued in 1225. It was this document that entered the statute books.

Curtailment of royal power was tightened in 1258 with the Provision of Oxford, which created a 15-member privy council, selected by the barons, to advise the king and to oversee his administration. A parliament was to be held three times a year. The battle between king and nobility had a long way to run but the principle of consent could no longer be ignored. In 1354 a statutory reference to the 'due process of law' was assumed to extend to all men, free or otherwise.

As the years passed, lawyers and political philosophers, keen to assert beyond challenge that England was governed by common laws to which even the highest in the land were subordinate, adopted Magna Carta as the cornerstone of a constitution. Critical to its evolvement was the work of Sir Edward Coke, the foremost jurist of Renaissance England. Stressing the freedom of the individual, Coke attempted to show that Magna Carta was 'the fountain of all the fundamental laws of the realm'. His selective interpretation led, in 1628, to the Petition of Right, an attempt to constrain

---

[20]Said by Lord Denning, (1899–1999) a leading member of the British judiciary

[21]Simon Schama, *A History of Britain;* p. 162

the king's power to impose taxes without Parliamentary approval or otherwise to behave as if the entire country was his to command. For his part, Charles I was content to make formal recognition of Magna Carta but resolutely rejected any attempt by Parliament to limit royal prerogatives. The upshot was civil war culminating in the execution of Charles in 1649.

But there was still some way to go before Parliament was recognized as the supreme legislative institution. This came with the Glorious Revolution of 1688 when the throne was occupied by the Protestant William of Orange and his wife Mary. Their accession was marked by a Bill of Rights containing 13 articles defining the limitations on the royal prerogative and confirming the rights of Parliament and of all citizens. In effect, the Bill was an updating of Magna Carta, with, for example, Parliament as guardian of the common law and the sole authority for levying taxes.

By then, Magna Carta was making its impact on America. Its first appearance across the Atlantic was in the royal charter supporting the settlement of Jamestown, Virginia in 1607. Drafted under the direction of Coke, the founding document declared that 'the persons which shall dwell within the colonies shall have all the Liberties as if they had been abiding and born within this our realm of England'. These or similar words appear in the inaugural charters of, among others, Connecticut, Maine, Maryland, Massachusetts and North Carolina where, in 1663, land was granted on the same terms as the 'Great Deed of Grant' of Virginia, known as the 'Great Charter' and as 'a species of Magna Carta'. The governor of the Commonwealth of Massachusetts consulted books of English law including Coke on Magna Carta 'to the end we may have better light for making and proceeding about laws'.

The suggestion is that whatever the popular conception of Magna Carta, the framers of the rule of law for the New World knew well enough that the instrument of government, acknowledged reluctantly by King John in 1215, was not in itself a blueprint for a new society. Rather, it was a basis on which a consensual form of government could be built.

So it was that the barons who met at Runnymede were mythologized into champions of popular sovereignty. This was the guiding principle for the framers of the American Constitution and the subsequent Bill of Rights, which guaranteed freedom of religion, assembly, speech and of the press.

The spirit of Magna Carta is as potent as ever. While, 800 years on, we celebrate Magna Carta, not for what it was but for what later generations made of it, Runnymede marks the origin of the two essential tenets of working democracy—the accountability of government to the people and liberty from arbitrary arrest and imprisonment.

But in celebratory mood, it is easy to be complacent. Politicians pay lip service to essential liberties but recent experience suggests that they have other priorities. In the name of security, democratic governments collect masses of data on their citizens who remain unaware of how much the authorities know about them or how the information might be used.

There is more than enough evidence to show that intelligence agencies should be hauled in before they inflict real damage on those they are paid to protect. It is still hard to believe that as part of the Bush war on terror, prisoners were held in Guantanamo Bay without trial and that torture was justified as 'enhanced interrogation'.

Then again, the impact of the commercial giants on legislation and executive decision-making raises questions of transparency and accountability. And we have hardly begun to understand the reach of online search engines. Google alone is the 'largest holder of information, both public and private, in world history'.[22] Could Google's dominance be a threat to civil liberties? Who can say? But its co-operation with the Chinese Government between 2005 and 2010 in censoring politically sensitive search words is hardly encouraging.

Facebook with over one billion users has built an enormous resource of data on individual profiles that could put ordinary privacy at risk. The fact that most of the information is freely given does nothing to reduce the risk of commercial or political abuse. By way of balance the web with its myriad links between protest groups has the potential for exposing infringements on civil liberties and for containing the political tendency to meddle in affairs that are best left to the private domain.

Maybe what is needed is a Magna Carta for the twenty-first century, an attempt, however imperfect, to reassert fundamental freedoms in the age of globalization of knowledge and of unprecedented concentrations of power. There are no easy answers. Nor were there any in 1215. But the barons made a start on finding solutions to what then must have seemed to be intractable problems. In this anniversary year, we would do well to follow their example.

Barry Turner, 2014

Falling Out Over Suez

60 years on from the Suez Crisis, Barry Turner reflects on an episode that tested Anglo–American relations.

The special relationship between the United States and Britain has had an uneven history. Its high point was in the early months of the Second World War when President Roosevelt responded to Prime Minister Churchill's appeal for aid by mobilizing the American economy as a life support for the British war effort. Less than 20 years on came the lowest point.

In 1956 Britain, France and Israel invaded Egypt. The ostensible justification was to protect the international status of the Suez Canal, a waterway of world significance not least for connecting Middle East oil to its European markets. Oil accounted for half the Canal's traffic and met two-thirds of Europe's demand.

In reality, the crisis was more about the threat to Anglo–French interests and to the very existence of Israel posed by President Nasser of Egypt, the prime exponent of Arab nationalism. A populist of formidable talent, Nasser was intent on eradicating what he called 'colonial' influence in his country. In July 1956 he declared the Suez Canal, for generations under Anglo–French management, to be nationalized. In one swift, dramatic move he had proved himself a leader who could defy two big powers.

They resolved to strike back. With good reason to fear Nasser's ascendancy, Israel joined an alliance that gave the excuse for a pre-emptive strike against a declared enemy.

In Washington, President Dwight Eisenhower watched the unfolding events with a growing sense of dismay and anger. To his advisers, Eisenhower spoke of his 'double-crossing allies' while in a sharp telephone conversation with Prime Minister Eden in London he skipped the usual preliminaries to get straight to the point. 'I can only assume that you are out of your mind' was his opening gambit. He spoke closer to the truth than he realized.

How did it get to this? At the heart of the crisis was the failure of European politicians to grasp that the days of Western imperialism were drawing rapidly to a close (Soviet imperialism was another matter) and that Europe itself had been marginalized in a Cold War that recognized only two world rivals—the USA and the USSR. With their history of empire building, the truth was particularly galling for France and Britain, both sensitive to whatever touched on their self-importance.

For almost a century, Britain had played a dominant role in Egyptian affairs. While the French had built the Suez Canal, it was the British who gave a much needed boost to Egyptian finances with the purchase of a 44% holding in the enterprise. That was in 1875. By then, the Canal had gained significance as the gateway to India, the jewel in Britain's imperial crown. After putting down nationalist rebels, British forces stayed on in Egypt to create a protectorate—in effect a British colony by another name.

French interest, however, remained strong. It was not simply that the Suez Canal Company was managed from Paris or even that Egypt was imbued with French language and culture. What really concerned the Quai d'Orsay was the possibility of unrest in Egypt spreading to French-controlled Algeria and Tunisia.

After the Great War, the American ideal of self-government for subject peoples came adrift in the Middle East where Arab princes took power under

---

[22]Peter Dahlgren, *The Political Web;* p. 57

the mandatory guidance of France and Britain. The setting of new boundaries, however neat and tidy on paper, was a recipe for tribal and ideological conflict. The biggest muddle of all was reserved for Palestine, selected by Britain as the setting for a Jewish homeland. From the first days of a British mandate, Palestine was marred by violence. Today we might ask: what has changed?

Egypt gained independence of a sort in 1923. While constitutional government was created, Britain held on to control of defence and security, rights that became all the more important in the build up to the Second World War when it was clear that Italy had designs on Egypt. Efforts to secure Egyptian loyalty led to the 1935 Anglo–Egyptian Treaty. The moving force was the young Anthony Eden, recently promoted to foreign secretary. Credited with a diplomatic triumph, he could not have guessed that the document he signed contained more than a hint of the finale to his political career. The period of entitlement of the British military to remain in the Canal Zone was to end in 1956.

As a loyal supporter of Winston Churchill in his opposition to the Hitler regime, Eden was highly regarded as foreign minister and as Churchill's closest colleague. Assumed by all to be the heir apparent, he followed Churchill as premier in 1955. But by then, though only in his fifties, he was a spent force. In poor health and given to violent mood changes, his political thinking was rooted in the past. Britain without her empire was beyond his imagination.

'The Empire', as he put it, 'is our life; without it we should be no more than an insignificant island off the coast of Europe.' His conviction was echoed in the Quai d'Orsay. France 'n'est rien sans les colonies.' Nasser played on these fears. Having come to power after a military overthrow of the Egyptian monarchy, he all but persuaded Washington that his political ambitions were in line with the best traditions of American democracy.

Britain and France were having none of that. The view from their side of the Atlantic was that Nasser was a Hitler in the making, a nationalist fanatic who planned a takeover of the entire Middle East while annihilating the recently created independent state of Israel.

Neither side had it right. Nasser was no democrat but his power to damage the Western alliance or to inflict pain on Israel was limited by territorial and political rivalries that were endemic to the Middle East. His mistake was to overplay his hand with Washington. Eisenhower favoured rational discussion over confrontation but he was no soft touch. When Nasser tried to hurry along an arms deal by threatening to transfer his allegiance to the Soviet Union, the warning sirens in Washington were loud and clear.

Relations between Egypt and the USA deteriorated further over the financing of the Aswan Dam. A worthy project to bring into cultivation two million acres of arid land came up against doubts that Egypt could guarantee a massive loan. When the USA pulled out of the deal, Nasser appealed to the Russians who were far more accommodating.

The fear of the Cold War spreading to the Middle East seemed to justify the stance of Britain and France. But US disillusionment with Nasser fell a long way short of securing Washington's willingness to bring armed pressure to bear. In the naïve belief that Eisenhower would be compelled to follow their lead, the two European powers pushed ahead with their scheme to bring down Nasser.

The nationalization of the Suez Canal was the spark in the tinderbox. With France as Israel's closest ally, a triple alliance took shape. The arch plotters were Eden and his opposite numbers in France and Israel—Guy Mollet and David Ben-Gurion.

To say that the plan was fantastical is to put it mildly. After a half-hearted attempt at conciliation, Israel was to attack Egypt; Britain and France would then intervene with an expeditionary force to separate the combatants and save the Canal. No account was taken of world opinion which, in the event, turned out to be almost uniformly hostile. Little account was taken of the United Nations; a fact even more remarkable given that Eden was one of its principal architects.

At 3.00 p.m. on 29 October 1956, the Israeli Air Force struck against Egyptian positions in Sinai. The next day, an ultimatum from France and Britain was addressed to the governments of Israel and Egypt. It called on them to stop hostilities, to withdraw their forces to a distance of ten miles from the Canal and to allow Anglo–French forces to occupy key positions.

The ultimatum, rejected by Egypt, set off a veritable hurricane of protest. It was led by the US Secretary of State, John Foster Dulles, who with a 'heavy heart' spoke before the UN General Assembly to discuss two of America's

oldest and closest allies. To add to his discomfort, the Soviet Union joined him in condemning the 'aggressors', a gesture of staggering hypocrisy in view of Moscow's decision to send troops to Hungary to bring into line the liberal reformers who had taken over the government.

The USSR continued to bluster with contrived outrage. Nikita Khrushchev, the new strong man in Moscow, threatened rocket attacks to 'curb aggression' against Egypt. However much Eisenhower was opposed to the Suez adventure, Soviet involvement was not to be tolerated. 'If those fellows start something', he told his advisers, 'we may have to hit 'em—if necessary, with everything in the bucket.'

That the Suez War was a gigantic mistake destined to end in disaster became apparent to the British political elite at an early stage of the campaign. At least six members of Eden's cabinet had severe doubts while the minister of defence, no less, came out openly against the use of force. He also recognized, along with others, that Eden—with his fragile temper and refusal to acknowledge reasoned argument that told against him—was close to a breakdown. Yet, there was only one resignation and that of a junior minister.

When eventually Anglo–French forces landed in Egypt, the conflict was short and sharp. An overwhelming majority in the UN in favour of an immediate ceasefire, together with an oil embargo against Britain and France, concentrated minds on finding an exit. But it was financial pressure from the USA that clinched the argument. Harold Macmillan, as finance minister in the Eden government, warned of fast disappearing gold reserves and threats from Washington to expose sterling to turmoil in the currency markets. A run on the pound was the last thing the precarious British economy needed.

Macmillan exaggerated. Britain's financial plight was nowhere near as serious as he made out. Moreover, the US was not about to disrupt the world economy to score a point against Britain. As the Tory leader who took over when Eden was forced to resign, the suspicion is that Macmillan engineered his own succession. A more probable explanation is that he was convinced the government was in an impossible position. It was largely on his urging that Eden accepted a ceasefire.

What else was learned from the Suez debacle or, perhaps, what was not learned? It was many years before Britain and France recognized that imperialism was a lost cause. Independence for British colonies came slowly and often painfully while France bucked the trend with fruitless efforts to bind her overseas possessions ever closer to the motherland. It was only after a savage and demoralizing war that Algeria was surrendered to nationalists. It needed the exceptional prestige and presence of Charles de Gaulle to effect the change.

De Gaulle was less easily persuaded that on the world stage the USA was the undisputed leader of the Western democracies. France withdrew from NATO as the first move towards creating an independent nuclear deterrent. By contrast, Macmillan, who had succeeded Eden as prime minister at the start of 1957, moved quickly to repair and strengthen Anglo–American relations. When he met with Eisenhower in March 1957, the President reported 'by far the most successful international meeting I have attended since the close of World War Two'. The special relationship was back on track.

In bowing to the White House, Britain accepted, though implicitly, that worldwide responsibilities could no longer be sustained on such a small economic base. A start was made on reducing the size of the military while making it fitter for a more limited purpose.

The biggest loser of the Suez War, though he was the last to realise it, was Abdul Nasser. After the ceasefire he proclaimed a great victory over the invaders. It was true that Egyptian control of the Canal was affirmed but that was a long way from concluding that the Egyptian armed forces had emerged from battle with much distinction. In reality they failed at almost every stage of the campaign, their few successes being more the result of luck than strategic judgment. The myth fostered by Nasser was that with advanced military technology, his forces were invincible. The bitter truth became apparent a decade later with the Egyptian defeat in the Six Day War. Soviet arms were to no avail. Israeli raids destroyed 286 of 340 Egyptian warplanes on the ground. The story went around of Marshal Zokharov, chief of the Soviet general staff, telephoning Nasser to let him know that his latest batch of aircraft was ready for delivery. 'Or would it save time if we just blew them up now?'

As the true story of the Suez War began to emerge from the archives, Anthony Eden was cast as the undisputed villain of the piece. The real indictment against Eden was not so much that he was devious or dishonest but rather he did not understand the country he was governing. Over 20 years of world travel in the grand style, cavorting with diplomats and politicians who themselves had outmoded, or at best second-hand, impressions of what Britain represented, had left him with an exaggerated view of his country's readiness or ability to fight for the values he held most dear. Eden had no feel for the better-educated and better-informed generation that was coming of age.

The rebellious spirit that was beginning to find its strength in the late fifties had its origins in America, where rising living standards and cash to spare had released teenagers from their parents' purse string and freed them from traditional authority. The new radicalism soon spread to Europe, where young people were besotted with American culture popularized by sound and screen. The gap between old and new was widening at the time of Suez. Eden and his friends, mostly of pre-war vintage, failed to connect with the young; few even bothered to try. To many of military age in 1956, the Suez episode was a throwback—evidence that their elders had lost their grip.

Barry Turner, 2015

What Future for Democracy?

Barry Turner Investigates Democracy's Role in the Modern World

Democracy is in poor health. Freedom House, a watchdog group which reports on political rights and civil liberties, calculates that of 195 countries assessed over the last 8 years, there has been a net decline in freedom. Democracy has languished in Bangladesh, Kenya, Thailand and Venezuela and would appear to be in terminal collapse in Russia and Turkey.

Expectations that the Arab Spring would spread democracy throughout the Middle East have been disappointed. Meanwhile, in the US and Europe where modern democracy was born and nurtured, there is widespread disillusionment with a system of government that is prone to inefficiency and to a none too subtle form of corruption which favours the wealth and power of a small minority.

If voting patterns are anything to go by, political participation is in sharp decline. According to the OECD, levels of voting in national and local elections are down 70% on 30 years ago. In several of what are dubbed 'advanced' countries there is a disturbing trend towards authoritarianism, a desire for a strong leader who will sort things out. Shades of the 1930s begin to close in.

And it has all happened so quickly. A mere quarter century ago, at the end of the Cold War, futurologists were as one in declaring that unrepresentative governments, of whatever political hue, had no future. What has gone wrong? Before venturing into muddy waters it would be as well to agree on what we mean by democracy. Commonly-held features can be identified—the right to vote in open and honestly managed elections, liberty of conscience, freedom of speech, universal education, minimum living standards, the protection of minority rights and the private ownership of property. But none of these are absolutes. Even the interpretation of something as apparently fundamental as freedom of speech fluctuates wildly between democracies. Similarly, across the range of democracies, the right to vote is more or less free depending upon the electoral system in place.

Throughout history there have been ebbs and flows in the direction and interpretation of democracy. The early Athenians were the first to practise a form of government by which citizens could debate and decide collectively on matters of general concern. The idea made no sense to Plato and Aristotle who argued that democracy, in handing power to the commonality, was a recipe for the destruction of the state. It was a contention that was to be echoed down the ages by the promoters of strong government led by a political

messiah, royal or otherwise. A more charitable view of the commonality was fed into the mainstream by Christianity. With each person judged to be spiritually equal in the sight of God, every individual was able to claim certain rights which a ruler was bound to respect.

Pre-eminent among the post-medieval philosophers, Thomas Hobbes attempted a rational foundation for the exercise of sovereign power by deducing that citizens willingly ceded some of their rights in return for protection. Their freedom was to do whatever they liked outside whatever was explicitly forbidden by law. With the advance towards a more structured society, elitism prevailed. The concept of private property was intrinsically linked to the state, and only by its mandate could it exist. However, in denying the authority of the Church, the Protestant Reformers experienced self-government in religious and social matters and got a taste for true democracy. During the English Civil War (1642–49), the Puritan Colonel Rainboro famously asserted, 'the poorest he that is in England hath a life to live as the richest he'. It followed that 'every man that is to live under a government ought first by his own consent put himself under that government'. In rejecting a distinction between those born to rule and the rest who were born to obey, he made an argument familiar today in countries groping towards some form of democracy.

A century on from the English Civil War, upheavals on both sides of the Atlantic restored democracy to the forefront of political discourse. In America, the newly created states began with a clean political slate on which to draw the framework for government at regional and national level. The constitution-makers stressed individual rights to life, liberty and the pursuit of happiness as the essential safeguard against government abuse of power. What emerged was a hands-off type of administration that suited the vigorous, self-reliant society that was pioneering the new America.

The contrast with France in the wake of its own revolution could not have been greater. Maximilien Robespierre, the dominant figure of the Revolution, defined democracy as 'a state in which the sovereign people, guided by laws which are its own work, does by itself all it can do well, and by delegates all that it could not'. In other words, having chosen their representatives, the people had to accept what was enacted in their name. The two ideals remain distinct and thus a source of confusion in any discussion of the function and organization of democracy. Following to varying degrees the example of France, other European countries tend to favour the state over the individual. In the US, the reverse holds good.

As depicted in popular history, the nineteenth to the early twentieth centuries was a people's march towards liberal democracy. But with the expansion of civil rights, the creation of political parties and wider participation in elections came counter-movements aimed at restraining democracy, driven by fear of rule by the mob. At its mildest the philosophy of restraint was expressed by Edmund Burke, who argued that once elected, representatives should be permitted to exercise independent judgment without pandering to popular opinion. But this was too subtle for uncompromising authoritarians who leaned on nationalism, with religious overtones, as the strongest antidote to democracy. When, as in Europe's revolutions of 1830 and 1848, regimes were overthrown, they were quickly succeeded by other authoritarian rulers.

At the same time, the resort to violent revolution proved the need for every ruler, of whatever persuasion and power, to be able to draw on a generous measure of popular support. If democracy has within it the assumption of government by consent, every government, however dictatorial, has within it an element of democracy. Nationalism, furthermore, can implode. This became clear after 1914 when hundreds of thousands of young patriots marched off to slaughter in northern France. Their sacrifice brought the old European order crashing down.

With the widening of the franchise, notably to women, the framework of modern Western democracy was put in place. But it was not secure. Two forces threatened to overwhelm democracy—fascism and communism. Each movement usurped the name of democracy for its own ends. Democracy's finest hours came in 1945 with the defeat of fascism and in 1989 with the collapse of Soviet communism. By 2000 the number of democracies had increased from 66 in 1987 to 121. The momentum of the freedom march was judged to be unstoppable. But we were wrong. Democracy has stalled and there is now a real threat of a roll-back. In the wide-ranging debate on what needs to be done to revitalize democracy, politicians are inclined to believe that once economic growth is back on track all will be well. It could happen. Anything *could* happen. But the emergence from recession should not fool us into believing that democracy is in the clear. The fault lines go much deeper. For one thing, our technology-driven industrial revolution destroys more jobs than it creates. Andrew McAfee of MIT's Sloan School of Management estimates that 50% of current jobs will eventually be automated out of existence. The almost inevitable scarcity of employment is the biggest single threat to democracy. When a rising generation feels itself economically and politically emasculated, it is liable to lash out at those held to be responsible, notably elected politicians who have failed to deliver on their promises. Riots in American inner cities and in the French suburbs are a disturbing pointer to the future.

Globalization has become a hate word for the disaffected. While the dismantling of international trade restrictions has reduced the number of people in absolute poverty, at the same time the gap between rich and poor countries has widened, as has the gap between rich and poor within each country. Inequality is on display for all to see in the games played by powerful interest groups who make no pretence of representing the general public. Cosy capitalism feeding on greed is apparent everywhere as powerful lobbies vie with each other for a bigger share of government favours and handouts. Leading companies are now so powerful as to be beyond government (i.e. democratic control) and can frustrate political mandates by relocating the hub of their activities to wherever the profit is greatest and interference minimal. The commercial world's big players no longer think of national boundaries as setting any limit on their activities.

Public cynicism at the way business succeeds in manipulating governments is diluted by party pledges to spend, spend, spend. But this has done nothing to improve the health of democracy. Quite the reverse. With the state taking on more and yet more responsibilities, the machinery of government has become dependent on an overweight bureaucracy that is remote from the lives of ordinary citizens. A safe generalization is that bureaucracy feeds on itself to become ever fatter.

Those in power profess their enthusiasm for communicating with the people but they do so in a hectoring, propagandist manner aimed more at manipulation than enlightenment. Taking its cue, the media treats politics as a knockabout contest, a branch of the entertainment industry with not quite the pulling power of sport. The gulf between government and people is nowhere better demonstrated than in the evolution of the European Union, a noble idea that is foundering on the refusal of the administrative elite to accept the need for public accountability.

There are those, an increasing number, who argue that democracy in the Western tradition is simply no longer workable. For inspiration they look to China and other vibrant Asian economies where authoritarianism is tempered by self-government in small things that can be decided without upsetting the system. Technocrats in political guise are able to plan long-term policies that are said to be too complex for the vagaries of democracy dependent on promises and bribes of popular election.

While conceding that in our interconnected world it makes sense to delegate decision-making to experts in such matters as global warming, safeguarding computer networks, cracking down on money laundering and combating terrorism, the all-embracing rule by technocrats throws up too many fears of the abuse of power. Scant regard for human rights and the arrogance of unelected officials suggest that the path of 'managed' capitalism is anything but smooth.

Instead of giving up on democracy, we should focus on making it work better for the twenty first century. A start could be made by recognizing that democracy creates many of its own problems by trying to do too much. The top heavy welfare state, unsustainable in the long run, spreads its favours too widely. If democracy is to be saved, the resources of the state must be redirected towards those of the greatest need. This means putting a brake on the hand-out of goodies to the relatively wealthy. In the US the housing subsidy to the richest fifth, by allowing mortgage interest to be tax deductible, is four times the amount spent on public housing for the poorest fifth.

Targeting the outcasts—the socially deprived who, under the present system, have little hope of breaking out of the poverty cycle—will greatly improve their life chances. But the challenge is not simply to raise standards to achieve greater equality of opportunity. Rather, we should be looking to creating a society which evens the balance between earning a living and the time allocated to family and to life enrichment.

One way of encouraging voters to play a more active role in determining how their country should be run is demonstrated in the direct democracy practised in Switzerland where 50,000 signatures on a petition, just over 1%

of the total of qualified voters, are enough to submit any new countrywide law to a vote of the whole people. With twice that number of signatures a proposal for a new law can be voted on, effectively sidelining parliament.

Critics argue that what suits a small, relatively uncomplicated society is less obviously attractive to a large, diverse country. A more serious objection has to do with framing referendum questions that can be clearly understood. Furthermore, the resort to a nationwide vote on sensitive issues can offend human rights. In Switzerland a 2009 poll banned the construction of minarets attached to mosques—even though the Swiss constitution protects freedom of religion. It is easy to imagine that an over-hasty resort to a referendum in the wake, say, of a terrorist atrocity could lead to a majority vote for the return of barbaric punishments. Abrupt changes in public mood are no guide to good government.

This is not to dismiss the value of referendums but merely to suggest that they must be judged in relation to other aspects of a working democracy. It is relevant to note that Switzerland has a long tradition of linking referenda to devolution. The delegation of power away from the centre is vital to the re-energizing of democracy. There are encouraging signs that national politicians are beginning to realize this. In Britain, until recently a highly centralized state, devolution to Scotland and Wales is being extended to clearly identifiable regions such as Greater Manchester. France is beginning to move the same way with a new regional structure that is close to German federalism, the favoured model for decentralization.

The only way forward for the EU as a whole is for more democracy, not less. Democracy may not always produce the 'right' results according to the mandarins but the alternative is a breakdown in the system and the collapse of what until now has been one of the more successful exercises in international co-operation. The policy of subsidiarity, so often discussed for the EU, so seldom practised, should now be implemented in full. More European legislation should be referred to national parliaments in draft form; each member state should be free to decide its own tax policies; the Council of Ministers should meet in public and the European Parliament should be given increased powers.

A foremost concern must be the role of money in democratic elections. Even if wealth alone is not a guarantee of electoral success, the fact that it is near impossible to aspire to high office without strong financial support is a denial of democratic rights. Those who donate expect to be rewarded. Clearly spending limits need to be imposed but the much favoured alternative of relying on state subsidy tends to benefit the established parties. The better solution is to put a strict upper limit on individual and company donations, monitored by an independent watchdog. One of the welcome side effects of this would be the encouragement of parties to broaden their support.

Despite the current tribulations, there is comfort for true democrats in knowing that while there are open and free elections, politicians who are ineffectual or who take too much upon themselves while ignoring those who put them in power are certain, eventually, to meet their comeuppance. In Italy, the voters dismissed an oligarchic prime minister who discovered that wealth and media power are not in themselves enough to secure re-election. Democracy in Nigeria triumphed in 2015 when the incumbent president was ejected in a largely peaceful election, an example to much of the rest of Africa where democracy is respected more in theory than in practice.

There is comfort too in knowing that while the authority of elected assemblies is increasingly called into question, citizens are finding other ways of making their opinions count. While, by clever manipulation of the media, pressure groups representing dubious causes can exercise an influence out of all proportion to their popular appeal, there is a profusion of voluntary organizations, including leading charities, which engage the interest and energy of those who might otherwise belong to political parties.

Consumers also have the potential to make their wishes known. Every company needs its market; a threat to withdraw the market by ceasing to buy a particular product concentrates minds wonderfully. The role of consumer democracy in restraining business pretensions should not be underrated. Meanwhile, the potential of the internet to stimulate democracy by disseminating information and by promoting dialogue has still to be tested. Though an increasing proportion of news and comment is appearing online in countries where the media is otherwise tightly controlled, the censors are already at work. Even in the older democracies the freedom of the internet and its ability to create dissent is being cited within political circles as justification for official secrecy. For democracy to thrive this, of all exclusions, is in urgent need of demolition. The model here is the Swedish constitution, which rules that legal justification is required before a public authority can refuse access to documents or information.

Above all, politicians need to remind voters of the virtue of freedom. Democracies are typically richer than non-democracies, are less likely to go to war and have a better record of fighting corruption. Democracy allows for the voice of the people to be heard. It is in the nature of democracy that it will always be a shifting concept, defined at any one time by a mix of high ideas and socio-economic practicalities. What may fit one country at a particular time may not necessarily suit all. But the fundamentals are clear enough.

Those of us who are lucky to live in relatively free societies must recognize the need to protect and nourish what we have, the better to support those who, sooner or later, will want to join the club.

Select Bibliography
Philip Coggan, *The Last Vote: The Threats to Western Democracy*, 2013 John Dunn, *Setting the People Free. The Story of Democracy*, 2005

Robert Fatton, Jr and R. K. Ramazani (eds.), *The Future of Liberal Democracy: Thomas Jefferson and the Contemporary World*, 2004
David Graeber, *The Utopia of Rules*, 2015
Jean Grugel, *Democratization, a Critical Introduction*, 2002
Andrew McAfee and Eric Brynjolfsson, *The Second Machine Age: Work, Progress and Prosperity in a Time of Brilliant Technologies*, 2014
John Micklethwait and Adrian Wooldridge, *The Fourth Revolution: The Global Race to Reinvent the State*, 2014
Larry Siedentop, *Inventing the Individual: The Origins of Western Liberalism*, 2014
Luigi Zingales, *A Capitalism for the People: Recapturing the Lost Genius of American Prosperity*, 2012

EDITED EXTRACTS OF PALGRAVE PUBLICATIONS

Under the Shadow of Defeat

Karine Varley's book *Under the Shadow of Defeat* is the first wide-ranging analysis of how memories of the Franco-Prussian War shaped French political culture and identities. Examining war remembrance as an emerging mass phenomenon in Europe, it sheds new light on the relationship between memories and the emergence of new concepts of the nation.

One Hundred and Forty Years Ago

Aftermath of the Franco-Prussian War

In the wake of military defeat, nations have a talent for reinventing themselves. The pain of transition from humiliation to self-respect can be softened by a thick layer of historical reinterpretation, a retelling of the story that minimizes blunders and builds on myth. By way of example, Germany after the Great War immediately springs to mind but in a revealing study of 1870–71, 'l'année terrible', when proud France was crushed by the upstart Prussia, Karine Varley (*Under the Shadow of Defeat. The War of 1870–71 in French* Memory) shows that a recognizable pattern of self justification and myth creation was well in place by the end of the nineteenth century.

It is one of the paradoxes of nineteenth-century France that while most of the country wanted to forget the Franco-Prussian War, it gave rise to one of the greatest waves of commemorative activity the nation had ever seen. Within only 7 years of the war ending, some 460 memorials had been erected while crowds of thousands faithfully honoured the anniversaries of the defeat. In 1899 one journalist complained that there were more German corpses in French paintings relating to the war than there had ever been lying on the battlefields.

If Bismarck had been looking for an occasion to launch war against France, France in turn had been looking to cut a rising Prussia down to size. Few in France doubted that the war would see a rapid French victory. Yet within a few days of the outbreak of war, French forces were forced onto the defensive, suffering heavy losses. By the end of the month, they had been pushed back to the two cities that were to symbolize the ruin of the Second Empire: Metz and Sedan. At Metz, Marshal Bazaine allowed his men to become encircled, only to surrender 2 months later along with 137,000 men of the Army of the Rhine. The battle at Sedan on 1 September was a disaster waiting to happen; encircled, exhausted and demoralized French forces faced an enemy twice as numerous. Physically drained by ill health, and having lost all hope of victory, Napoleon III surrendered 83,000 men, 6000 horses and himself.

News of the defeat at Sedan brought insurrection in Paris, the overthrow of the Second Empire and the proclamation of a republican Government of National Defence ready to consider peace but refusing to surrender one inch of French soil. With Bismarck continuing to demand Alsace-Lorraine, German forces began to march towards Paris to begin a siege that was to last until 26 January 1871. As food supplies in Paris ran out, the French government sued for an armistice.

The peace divided the country with some of the major cities, including Paris, calling for the war to continue. The government's decision to relocate to Versailles, rather than return to the capital, fuelled suspicions that reactionary rural elements were deliberately targeting republican and left-wing Paris. Socialists and left-wing extremists backed by radicalized guardsmen, artisans and workers rose up to proclaim a new Paris Commune. Clashes between forces supporting the Commune and the reconstituted army based at Versailles on 2 April marked the beginnings of the civil war which was to bring violent suppression and around a further 22,000 dead.

Had the fighting ended at Sedan it might have been written off as the collapse of the Second Empire, but because the war had resumed under the republican Government of National Defence, it became a defeat not only of the regime but of the nation as well. The defeat cast a dark shadow over France's political and cultural development. After the humiliation and anger came soul-searching and a widespread conviction that something must have been fundamentally rotten at the very core of the nation. It was a time when every political, cultural, religious and social group competed to offer their own panacea. The war dead lay at the heart of ideas on the regeneration of France. The post-1871 cult of the fallen placed unprecedented emphasis on the mass of common soldiers, invoking their patriotic self-sacrifice to lift and unify the nation after its collapse.

In the period between 1871 and 1873, when France was under occupation and still reeling from the suppression of the Paris Commune, a wave of memorial building spread across the nation, concentrated particularly in the areas directly affected by the war. After 1873 the state's burial of all fallen soldiers on French territory triggered bellicose nationalism and the construction of further monuments. Then the political fault lines shifted again. Revenge became secondary to tensions between radical and moderate republican memories of the war and expressions of Catholic patriotism. The early 1900s inaugurated a new phase in the construction of war memorials, inspired partly by the effects of the Dreyfus Affair, the nationalist revival and fears of the rise of socialist internationalism.

Between 1871 and 1914, military painting overshadowed impressionism for a public eager to consume images of patriotism and heroism. Reproductions in the illustrated press, postcards and prints furthered the dissemination of paintings relating to the war and the recovering army, at once responding to and fuelling a market for images of patriotism. Popular literature presented the war as a test of moral strength. As with military art, literature portrayed real and fictional tales of glory rather than the wider picture of collapse, transforming the war into an adventure story with *francs-tireurs* as the intrepid heroes. Spies, barbaric Germans and precociously patriotic children filled the pages of novels.

The republican consolidation of power ushered a wave of reforms designed to instil patriotism within the population. Maps of France were introduced into classrooms so that pupils would develop a sense of national belonging; they featured Alsace-Lorraine shaded in a different colour to Germany to sustain hopes that the annexation was only temporary. Gymnastics became compulsory in schools in 1880, while in July 1882 the government introduced school battalions to improve the physical fitness of the nation's future soldiers. Recreational gymnastics, rugby, rifle and military education societies sprang up across the nation, their members seeking to reverse the physical and skills deficiencies of French soldiers in 1870. Even the Tour de France, which began in 1903, perpetuated *revanchist* memories of the war. During the period 1906–11, the race crossed into Alsace-Lorraine, allowing spectators the opportunity to voice their feelings on the annexation as they lined the route singing the *Marseillaise*. Music hall performances often harked back to the war and to aspirations of *revanche*, with song sheets easily available to purchase from street vendors. There was no escape even on holiday. Tourists were encouraged to forego the pleasures of the seaside in favour of a fortifying trip to the battlefields of 1870–71.

For some historians, the military parade at Longchamps on 29 June 1871 symbolizes the magnitude of French delusions. The army marched for 4 h before crowds of around 9000. Newspapers reported the event as a tremendously uplifting boost for the nation, nothing less than the beginning of the national recovery. Coming a mere 6 months since the war had ended, at a time when eastern areas remained under German occupation, the parade appears somewhat premature, inaugurating a cult of the army that seemed bizarrely impervious to its recent collapse. Yet such interpretations result from separating memories of the war from memories of the Paris Commune. The army at Longchamps was thus not the army that had been routed by Germany, but rather the Army of Versailles that had successfully defeated the insurgency.

The Catholic Church articulated a very clear theological explanation for the recent misfortunes; it defined republican experiments as a betrayal of the

© Springer Nature Limited 2019
Palgrave Macmillan (ed.), *The Statesman's Yearbook Companion*,
https://doi.org/10.1057/978-1-349-95839-9

nation's divinely ordained mission as eldest daughter of the Church and an assault on the very heart of French national identity. Whereas republicans traced their vision of the nation back to the Revolution of 1789, Catholics traced theirs back to the fifth century. Thus not only was Catholicism the religion of the sovereign for over 1300 years, but it was a defining element in the creation of the nation as well. There was a widely held view that France had been divinely selected to perform God's will and that any deviation from this vocation would incur due punishment. Thus in the eyes of the Catholic Church, cataclysmic events such as wars and revolutions were not the products of shifting political and social forces but God's punishment for national infidelity.

If republican claims over the character of the nation were rooted in recent French history, republicans laid claim to a more deeply rooted concept of the nation. Having been called upon to defend the revolution in the call to arms of 1792, the French people were no longer subjects but citizens who had earned themselves a stake in the French nation. While the Catholic Church maintained that the cult of the dead provided confirmation of immortality, republicans held that immortality was achieved and sustained through the cult of the dead. They could not offer the reward of eternal life, so they offered eternal memory instead.

The most spectacular and striking aspects of the republican campaign were in the cultural sphere. The creation of Bastille Day as a national holiday in 1880 mobilized communities across the nation in an overt attempt to redefine France along republican lines. The celebration suggested that if storming the Bastille had brought political and social liberation, then moral and spiritual liberation could only be achieved once the 'clerical Bastille' had been demolished.

The construction of the Sacré-Coeur basilica at Montmartre was one of the most prominent manifestations of the rivalry between the Church and the republican state. Even during its construction, it represented an aggressive and unambiguous assault on republicanism that culminated most strikingly in the erection of a luminous cross on top of the scaffolding of the Sacré-Coeur on 14 July 1892. Visible across much of Paris, the basilica rivalled republican architectural symbols such as the Eiffel Tower, which was built for the centenary of the Revolution, and of course the Panthéon.

Every political, religious and social group hunted for scapegoats to exonerate themselves from responsibility for the defeat. A moderate republican interpretation of the war sought to constitute itself as the dominant memory; yet because its parameters were so narrow, excluding the experiences of the Second Empire and Paris Commune and insisting upon an entirely glorious image of the army, they were easily infringed by all those who sought to challenge this political vision of the nation.

The myths of the French resistance in the Second World War and their role in the restoration of national pride are now a familiar subject of enquiry; much less, however, is known of the representations of resistance and martyrdom that emerged with the Franco-Prussian War. The two concepts embody an idea of the nation as one of ideas not aggressive military might, and of the resilience, patriotism and intelligence of the people. In their democratic qualities, the concepts are implicitly republican, but in their glorification of suffering, they are also implicitly Christian. Notions of a racial and cultural German 'other' served further to reinforce this newly created self-image.

Reference

Varley, Karine, *Under the Shadow of Defeat. The War of 1870–71 in French Memory*. Palgrave Macmillan, 2008.

The Failure of Democratic Nation Building

Events in the Middle East have raised expectations for a democratic agenda. But as Albert Somit and Steven Peterson show in their book **The Failure of Democratic Nation Building**, recent experience of democracy building by the US suggests that these hopes may be misplaced.

Taking the oath of office for his second term, George W. Bush promised 'to seek and support the growth of democratic movements', declaring that democracy around the world 'is the urgent requirement of our nation's security'. He dreamed of transplanting Americanized democracy first in Iraq and then the greater Middle East. This new manifesto penetrated deep into the US military and civilian bureaucracies.

Announced in late 2005, a little-noticed Pentagon directive placed stability operations on a par with combat missions. In another shift toward a democracy-crusading agenda, the US Department of State unveiled the Office of the Coordinator for Reconstruction and Stabilization 'to help stabilize and reconstruct societies'. Nation building in broken countries became a State Department priority because the 'security challenges' are 'threatening vulnerable populations, their neighbors, our allies, and ourselves'.

In places as far afield as Liberia, Haiti, Ukraine, Kyrgyzstan, Lebanon and the Republic of Georgia, the United States advanced its agenda by ushering out despotic regimes or protesting authoritarian power grabs in fraudulent elections. One of the first tests for America's initiative came from the former American colony of Liberia which had endured more than a decade of misrule and barbarity in a multisided civil war. Fuelled by ethnically based rival rebel factions, the conflict engulfed the countryside until capped by an agreement in 1997. As part of the settlement, Charles Taylor, the biggest warlord, was engineered into the Liberian presidency by a dubious election. His ascension brought neither peace nor progress. Liberia soon slipped back into anarchy, as a smouldering second countryside civil war converged on Monrovia. By late summer 2003, the West African nation had become the archetypical failed state, chaotic and impoverished.

The US insisted on a cease-fire among the warring parties and the abdication and exile of President Taylor before deploying troops from a 2300 US Marine taskforce. Just 200 Marines actually disembarked on August 14, 2003 to supply logistical support to a larger contingent of Nigerian peacekeepers. The exercise represented a less than overwhelming display of US power. But it sufficed to change the regime and led to a democratic election well after the US armed forces departed.

Like Liberia, the Republic of Haiti shared a tortuous history with the United States. During its 19-year US military occupation in the early twentieth century, Haiti had been an American colony in all but name. The Caribbean nation captured more of Washington's attention in the 1990s when conditions became especially onerous on the island republic. President Clinton's displacement of the junta to return Jean-Bertrand Aristide to the presidency did not bring a happy ending. After winning a second term in a 2000 election, he incited mobs to intimidate and assassinate political opponents, politicized the police and robbed the government coffers.

The Bush administration cringed at that thought of a militarized intervention. It, nonetheless, grew apprehensive at the prospect of Haitian boat people washing up on Florida beaches. Washington intensified pressure on the defrocked slum priest to resign. On February 28, Aristide boarded a US military aircraft and made a dawn departure. The United States landed 200 Marines as the lead contingent of international peacekeepers from France, Chile and Canada before a UN force arrived in June. Compared to the violent regime changes of the Afghan and Iraqi dictatorships, Haiti was a velvet-gloved operation that many Bush officials favoured.

Libya, a terrorist-sponsoring rogue state, decided to come in from the cold on the heels of the US invasion of Iraq. Pressures on the Qaddafi regime had mounted as international sanctions stifled oil production. In December 2003, Libya agreed to give up its WMD, ratify the nuclear test ban treaty and open its arms sites to international inspection. The regime also renounced terrorism. In turn, Washington and the United Nations dropped their restrictions on Libyan commerce and travel. But the US refrained from pressing for democracy or even regime change. It swallowed its democracy promotion rhetoric because deposing Libya's authoritarian rule might play into the hands of Qaddafi's Islamic theocratic opponents. For American interests, it was a wisely pragmatic choice.

Elsewhere, America's diplomatic squeeze resulted in political changes that satisfied aspiring democratic populations within each of the countries but did not require a US occupation. On the Eurasian landmass, the three 'color revolutions' in Georgia, Ukraine and Kyrgyzstan offered positive outcomes for America's prudent non-military tack. As the Republic of Georgia approached its November 2, 2003 elections, the US government transferred its loyalties from President Eduard Shevardnadze, the defunct Soviet Union's last foreign minister, to the opposition. When the Columbia University-trained lawyer Mikheil Saakashvili disputed the election results as fraudulent, his followers took to the streets and seized the parliament building in the so-called Rose Revolution.

Though Russo-American tensions mounted over Georgia, Shevardnadze resigned the presidency and defused the powder keg. Rescheduled elections ran in January 2004, and the pro-Western reformer became president. He demanded the dismantling of Russian army bases, welcomed Western oil companies to construct a pipeline from Azerbaijan across Georgia to Turkey's seaports and joined other Black Sea states in training exercises with a US destroyer.

Another significant democratic transition occurred in Ukraine. In November 2004, the Bush administration refused to accept the result of a tainted election. 17 days and nights of demonstrations were sponsored by US and European governments.

The Orange Revolution that led to an election victory for the Western-leaning reformer Viktor Yushchenko in late 2004 owed its nurturing, not its birth, to $58 million spent by the United States in the two previous years to train democratic activists, conduct public opinion surveys, maintain a website and broadcast independent radio news.

In Kyrgyzstan, the United States joined with European governments to fund and tutor the democratic opposition. Washington alone pumped in $12 million to underwrite civil society centres, which trained pro-democracy cadres, disseminated materials and broadcast Kyrgyz-language programmes. It was small money shrewdly spent.

The Kyrgyz pro-democracy movement staged anti-regime rallies in what became known as the 'Lemon Revolution' that ousted the repressive President Askar Akayev. That a democratically mobilized population turned out its dictator in an Islamic country encouraged US officials to take heart in their promotion of representative government in Afghanistan, Iraq and elsewhere in the Middle East. But the real lesson was lost that the democracy arose from within the country, not from the imposition of a non-Muslim occupation army as in Iraq.

It was in Lebanon that Washington boasted of the first regional example of the 'demonstration effect'. The January 2005 elections in Iraq, according to this view, set off a 'Baghdad spring' that rippled across the Near East, particularly in Lebanon. Syrian military and intelligence units had occupied the Mediterranean country since 1976. Sceptics interpreted Syria's intervention as an attempt to restore Lebanon to Greater Syria as it had been under the Ottoman Empire.

When a bomb killed former prime minister Rafik Hariri, an opponent of Syria's presence, in mid-February 2005, his countrymen demanded a return of their sovereignty, genuine democracy and freedom from Syrian hegemony in what the international media dubbed the 'Cedar Revolution'.

Internationally isolated, Syria relented. Parliamentary elections followed delivering a majority of seats to an anti-Syrian coalition. Washington saw this as evidence that the Bush strategy was bearing fruit. But they ignored the fact that the Lebanese had elections and parliaments before the US-led invasion of Iraq. Moreover, only months later Lebanon stood at the brink of civil war as the Syrian- and Iranian-sponsored radical Shiite movement Hezbollah ('the Party of God') consolidated its political position as a player within the Lebanese government and then provoked conflict with Israel in July 2006.

Lebanon's largely passive ousting of Syrian rule marked a high point for the Bush White House's democracy campaign. At the American University in Cairo in June 2005, Condoleezza Rice delivered a direct political appeal to Egypt and Saudi Arabia, two of America's closest Arab allies, to hold genuine elections, empower women and tolerate free expression. Asserting that democracy does not lead to 'chaos or conflict', she added, 'Freedom and democracy are the only ideas powerful enough to overcome hatred and division and violence.' The secretary's claims went too far for democracy, however. It is not a panacea for all the world's violent and dysfunctional nations. Elections, referendums and elected officials in Iraq and Afghanistan delivered neither peace nor security to their electorates.

Democratic inroads irked Russia, which interpreted Washington's programme as a means to serve America's geopolitical priorities. Moscow pushed back by standing behind the dictatorial Aleksandr Lukashenko in his rigged re-election to the presidency of Belarus. The Kremlin also courted Kazakhstan and other former Soviet Republics in Central Asia with the aim of imposing a Cold War-style exclusion of the United States. Strikingly, it joined with China, a sometimes hostile neighbour, in forming the six-member Shanghai Cooperation Organization (SCO), a quasi-alliance. Along with Uzbekistan and Tajikistan, the seemingly pro-American governments in Kazakhstan and Kyrgyzstan also joined SCO, in which Beijing and Moscow promoted regional military cooperation and an 'energy club' that invited no membership from the United States. Washington's democratization, in short, created a Sino-Russian backlash. There were other ominous developments.

While the Middle East witnessed a big shake-up in its political dynamics, the downside was the realization that it enabled regimes hostile to US interests to come to power through the ballot box. Rather than bringing harmony to Turkey, a vital American regional ally, the autonomy of the Iraqi Kurds reinspired the Kurdish minority in Turkey to wage a fresh guerrilla war that in the 1980s had claimed 35,000 lives. In this case, democracy gave rebirth to territorial conflict. Elsewhere in the Middle East, the US-backed democracy push worked against American interests.

From Washington's perspective, Egypt's late 2005 election painted a worrisome picture. Its parliamentary contest produced substantial gains for the Muslim Brotherhood, a fivefold increase from its previous showing, despite officially organized harassment of its candidates. In neighbouring Gaza, there was another dramatic example of unintended consequences when, 5 months after Israel's disengagement from the territory, the parliamentary elections in January 2006 saw a democratically elected terrorist movement, Hamas, come to power. As a spin-off from the Muslim Brotherhood, Hamas' political victory was at the expense of the Palestinian Fatah, the chosen partner of Tel Aviv and Washington. Gazan militants fought each other and fired rockets into Israel.

In reaction to the rise of Shiite political forces in Iraq and Lebanon and to the electoral gains by Islamic fundamentalists in Egypt and Gaza, other Middle East states either slowed their reform process or cracked down on democracy. Qatar postponed parliamentary elections; Bahrain backtracked and imposed a constitution calling for a second appointed legislative house to curtail the elected house's power; Jordan placed democratization authority on the backburner; Yemen clamped down on the media; and Syria suppressed the political opposition.

Washington took note. Non-democratic stability and cooperation came back into vogue. Ilham Aliyev, Azerbaijan's corrupt and autocratic but friendly leader, was welcomed to the White House in spring 2006. The promise of honest elections in Kazakhstan turned sour. But neither state was punished by Washington, which understood their importance as Iran made a bid for nuclear arms and Russia reasserted its influence in the Caucasus and Central Asia. Moreover, Azerbaijan and Kazakhstan were oil exporters.

As a new 'great game' dawned between the United States, Russia and China for advantage in this crucial hydrocarbon zone, America had less latitude to advance democracy. Instead, it had to revert to its former policy of accommodating friendly dictators.

Meanwhile, the risk of a two-sided or even three-sided civil war loomed over Iraq despite the acknowledged success of two elections. The Middle East stood apart from other arenas by virtue of its religious-based civilization and unremitting hostility to colonialism, Western cultural penetration and non-Muslim occupying forces. Washington wrongly discounted these factors in Iraq as it clung for too long at the glimpses of voters going to the polls. An election in no way guaranteed an acceptable government strong enough to govern a deeply divided society.

Other threats emerged to confront America's stabilization goals. Chief among the immediate destabilizing powers is Iran, which oddly enough benefited most from America's removal of Saddam Hussein and the Taliban regime. Instead of showing gratitude, the Islamic Republic worsened America's Iraqi predicament by bolstering Shiite insurgents. Like the provocative North Korean nuclear test in October 2006, Iran's growing nuclear capability and frequent threats to Israel unsettled the Middle East.

As the world's fourth largest producer of oil, Iran presented a tough adversary. Its horde of petrodollars and its untapped crude reserves gave Tehran financial strength to resist international pressure and to fund proxy wars through terrorist-linked Hamas in Gaza and Hezbollah in Lebanon.

Another major destabilizing element radiating from the Middle East remains Al Qaeda and its clones. The loss of Afghanistan was a setback to these terrorist networks. But they have carved out safe havens in weak states such as Somalia, Sudan and the anarchic belts along the Afghanistan-Pakistan border. In Europe, they have taken advantage of immigrant enclaves and open societies to launch bombings as in Madrid and London. Along with the objective of destroying Israel and putting an Islamic regime in its place, they seek to overturn apostate governments in Muslim countries such as Egypt, Jordan, Saudi Arabia, Yemen, Pakistan and Bangladesh, whether through the ballot box or subversion. At this juncture, the Middle East and parts of South Asia look far less than secure, casting into doubt future US exertions to achieve friendly, harmonious governments through the spread of democracy.

Reference

Somit, Albert and Peterson, Steven A., *The Failure of Democratic Nation Building*. Palgrave Macmillan, 2010.

The Secret History of Democracy

Events in the Middle East have raised expectations for a democratic agenda. Benjamin Isakhan and Stephen Stockwell detect signs of an emerging democracy in their book *The Secret History of Democracy*.

The tendency of Western media to emphasize the daily atrocities of post-Saddam Iraq has obscured success stories of Iraq's fledgling democracy. Yet there is much evidence to suggest a return to a civic culture in Iraq, where the streets have become a locus for deliberation and debate.

Following the fall of the Ba'athist regime, a complex array of political, religious and ethno-sectarian factions formed political parties and civil society movements, many of which have written policy agendas, engaged in complex political alliances and debated key issues. They also sponsor their own media outlets which have been enthusiastically read by a people thirsty for uncensored news, even if it is partisan. This was particularly true in the lead up to the elections and referendum when citizens were provided with a rich assortment of information on key policies, politicians and parties.

The subsequent elections saw millions—young and old, Sunni and Shia, Kurd and Arab, Christian and Muslim—risk threats of violence to line the streets, patiently waiting to take part in the first truly democratic elections held in Iraq for many decades. It was the same for the January 2009 provincial elections which saw colourful campaign posters glued to walls all over the country while party volunteers handed out leaflets at security check-points. Other volunteers used more traditional tactics, such as going door-to-door, giving radio interviews or calling public assemblies where ordinary citizens were invited to grill candidates on their policies.

The story of democracy in Iraq begins immediately after the fall of Baghdad in April 2003, when the nation witnessed a series of spontaneous elections. In northern Kurdish cities such as Mosul, in majority Sunni Arab towns like Samarra, in prominent Shia Arab cities such as Hilla and Najaf and in the capital of Baghdad, religious leaders, tribal elders and secular professionals summoned town hall meetings where representatives were elected and plans were hatched for reconstruction projects, security operations and the return of basic infrastructure.

Such moves were initially supported by the occupying forces. But fearing that the people of Iraq would elect 'undesirables' such as military strongmen or political Islamists, the United States was quick to quell these drives towards democratization and to exert its own hegemony. Members of the Interim Iraqi Government were appointed by the head of the coalition authority and, at the end of June, all local and regional elections were stopped. Decisions made by local councils were revoked, and the mayors and governors who had been elected by their own constituents were replaced by hand-picked representatives. Not surprisingly, these moves met with opposition across Iraq and prompted some of the earliest protests of the post-Saddam era.

When the coalition attempted to install a puppet government in Baghdad, senior religious figures such as Grand Ayatollah Ali Al-Sistani were able to mobilize thousands of Iraqis to call for a general election prior to the drafting of the Iraqi constitution. Al-Sistani took the unprecedented step of issuing politically motivated *fatwas*, urging his clergymen into local politics and encouraging the faithful, including women, to vote in elections.

In mid-January 2004, more than 100,000 Shia marched through Baghdad, while a further 30,000 took to the streets of Basra. They called on the US occupation to conduct free and fair national elections.

However, if it was Al-Sistani who was to have the most impact over the political landscape during the first months of the occupation, it was the younger, more radical Moqtada Al-Sadr who was to gain both notoriety and political influence in the years that followed. This began when the coalition forced the closure of two publications produced by Al-Sadr, *Al-Hawza* (the name of a particular Shia seminary in Najaf where a number of leading clerics teach) and the quarterly journal *Al-Mada* (*The View*). Both advocated an Islamic republic for Iraq and featured vitriolic attacks on Israel and on the American-led occupation. Thousands of protestors gathered at the paper's office in central Baghdad vowing to avenge *Al-Hawza*'s closure. In a twist of irony, it was the forced closure of *Al-Hawza*, rather than anything printed in its pages that incited his Mahdi Army to violence.

Indeed, throughout 2004 Al-Sadr led several military uprisings against the occupation. These events helped to refine Al-Sadr's mastery of anti-occupation rhetoric and to distinguish him from Al-Sistani as a strong militant religious leader who had both the strength and the gall to take on the

United States. However, when his military campaign failed, Al-Sadr switched to (mostly) non-violent political struggle, with calls for tolerance, national unity and social inclusion, and the transformation of the Mahdi Army from militia to social welfare organization. On the second anniversary of the invasion of Iraq, Al-Sadr orchestrated massive protests in Baghdad. Thousands travelled from all over the nation to attend one of the largest political rallies in Iraqi history.

What was particularly interesting was that Al-Sadr ordered his followers to wave only Iraqi flags, and not flags of the Mahdi Army or of other Shia Arab organizations. This was a self-conscious attempt to move the protests beyond the level of a pro-Al-Sadr, Shia-backed movement, into more of a nationalist struggle against occupation, something which would appeal to Iraqis of all persuasions. In the event, a number of Sunni Arabs attended the Baghdad protests, as well as a small contingent of Iraqi Christians.

These anti-occupation protests have become an annual event. In addition, the followers of Al-Sadr have organized other demonstrations against the lack of basic infrastructure and public services such as electricity, fuel and potable water, against the high cost of ice and against the increasingly bleak employment market.

Following up on the strength of these protests, Al-Sadr has further demonstrated his political instincts and knowledge of democratic mechanisms. For example, in 2005, he instructed his followers to collect the signatures of one million Iraqis in a petition that asked the US and coalition troops to leave the country. More recently, he launched a nation-wide civil disobedience campaign in response to raids on the cleric's offices and to the arrest of members of his organization. In several key Baghdad neighbourhoods such as Mahmoudiya and Yusufiya, members of the Mahdi Army marched in a show of force, while in Abu Disher the streets were emptied and the stores and schools closed. Then, in October 2008, thousands of Iraqis took to the streets of Sadr City and in the south-eastern province of Missan to object to a new draft of the US-Iraqi Security pact, which would extend US troop presence until 2011. When the Iraqi government ignored the protests and signed the deal, Al-Sadr's followers reappeared in the streets.

The key reason why the Shia Arab protests have been so effective is the fact that they make up the majority of Iraq's population. The minorities in Iraq, such as the Sunni Arab (around 20%), the Kurds (around 20%) and the Iraqi Christians (around 3%), cannot command such impressively large demonstrations. Nonetheless, these minorities have also been able to utilize the power of the streets to air their concerns and advocate political change. For example, the Sunni Arab minority conducted general strikes in resistance to US blockades of Sunni cities. In Ramadi, the entire town shut down for 2 days as US troops launched a major offensive across the Sunni region. Sunni Arab protests were to gather increased momentum as members of the former ruling minority found themselves increasingly ostracized by the Shia Arab and Kurdish dominated central government. In 2005, Sunni Arab demonstrations were held in the towns of Hit, Ramadi, Samarra and Mosul to protest the new constitution which had been drawn up without their approval.

In addition, the Sunni-Arab population of northern cities such as Kirkuk and Mosul has frequently taken to the streets to protest what it sees as the Kurdish domination of Nineveh's regional administration. Most recently, 2008 saw the Sunni-Arab population of the Baghdad suburb of Adhamiyah protest against moves by Kurds to incorporate the oil province of Kirkuk into the autonomous Kurdish region.

At around the same time, the Kurds were conducting their own protests regarding Kirkuk. Thousands gathered in cities such as Sulaymanyah, Arbil, Kirkuk and Dohuk after the Iraqi Parliament passed a law that would see a power-sharing arrangement devised for Kurdistan's multi-ethnic cities. The Kurds have also rallied against the inequities they see across their own region. During March and August 2006, and more recently in August 2008, largely peaceful demonstrations broke into angry protest against the regional governor's failure to provide basic public services.

Caught in the political and sectarian cross-fire of post-Saddam Iraq, smaller ethno-religious minorities such as the Turkomans, the Faili Kurds (Shiite Kurds) and the Christian minority of Iraq (made up mostly of Syriac-speaking Assyrians and Chaldeans) are often forgotten alongside the three larger ethno-sectarian groups. While they have been the victims of violence and harassment, they have nonetheless been politically active, scoring minor successes in coalitions with the larger groups and with their own political protests. In 2008, hundreds of Iraqi Christians demonstrated across key towns in northern Iraq to express their indignation at not being able to elect their own representatives. They also called for autonomy in their ancestral homeland.

Iraq has also seen a variety of civil movements emerge that are not so much concerned with issues regarding ethno-religious rights, their resistance to occupation or their rejection of state policy, but the plight of normal Iraqi citizens—ordinary people who demand better working conditions, higher salaries, safer environments and better infrastructure. While many of these protests have occurred in specific ethno-religious areas and often organized by one ethno-religious group, their common element is the people's struggle for a more inclusive and equitable future. For example, the Iraqi people have repeatedly protested against corruption and nepotism in their local and national governments and called for the resignation of senior officials.

Women's rights have become a particular concern in post-Saddam Iraq. Iraqi women of all ethnicities and religious persuasions mounted protest campaigns after the invasion in 2003. Women's rights and social justice activists joined forces in a group known as 'Women's Will', which has organized a boycott of the US goods that have flooded the Iraqi market since the invasion. In June 2005 protests were organized by Islamic human and women's rights organizations in Mosul to press for the immediate release of all Iraqi women in US custody. So effective was this campaign that the United States was forced to release twenty-one Iraqi women who had been held as a bargaining chip against relatives suspected of resistance.

Iraq has also seen the emergence of powerful workers' movements. Iraqi doctors, nurses, taxi drivers, university staff, police, customs officers and emergency service personnel have repeatedly engaged in non-violent protests, strikes, sit-ins and walk-outs. They have done so to draw attention to poor working conditions, the pressures under which they work, unfair dismissals, ineffectual government regulation and the dangerous nature of their jobs. The nation's largest and most powerful independent union, the General Union of Oil Employees, later renamed the Iraqi Federation of Oil Unions (IFOU), began to flex its political muscles in May 2005 when it came out against the privatization of Iraq's oil industry.

In June 2005, around 15,000 workers conducted a peaceful 24-h strike, cutting oil exports from the south of Iraq. This was in support of demands made by Basra Governor Mohammad Al-Waili that a higher percentage of Basra's oil revenue be invested in infrastructure. The IFOU also demanded the removal of fifteen high-ranking Ba'ath loyalists in the Ministry of Oil as well as pay increases for the workers.

In May 2007, the IFOU threatened to strike again, but this was postponed when a meeting with Iraqi Prime Minister Nouri Al-Maliki resulted in efforts to find solutions acceptable to both sides. However, when the government failed to deliver on any of its promises, the oil workers went on strike across southern Iraq. A few days later, the Iraqi government responded by issuing arrest warrants for IFOU leaders. In the face of intimidation the union held firm, taking the further step of closing the main distribution pipelines, including supplies to Baghdad.

These indigenous, localized and highly coordinated movements reveal the strength of the Iraqi people's will towards democracy. When given the opportunity they are more than capable of utilizing democratic mechanisms independently of foreign interference. The movements also indicate the degree to which democratic practise and culture are familiar to the people of Iraq. The Iraqi people implicitly understand that, by taking to the streets, they force their government to take their opinions into account. Another important point is that the actions of key religious figures such as Al-Sistani and Al-Sadr contradict the common belief that Islam is incompatible with democracy. Similarly, the protests conducted by the Sunnis, the Kurds and the Christians reveal that Iraqi culture, in its many rich and divergent guises, is open to democracy.

The Iraqi protest movements have revealed the strength of feeling against the United States and its self-proclaimed status as a harbinger of democracy in the Middle East. That the United States was so determined to shut down the original grassroots democratic impetus is also revealing, in that it demonstrates the US administration's desire to exert its hegemony over the Iraqi people via an installed government rather than to foster and encourage genuine democratic reform. When the United States attempted to eschew democracy in favour of a puppet government, it was the power of the Iraqi people that put in motion a series of events that led to the formation of an Iraqi government elected by the people, in free and fair elections.

While the Iraqi citizenship's participation in, and engagement with, democratic mechanisms such as elections, an independent press and mass demonstrations do not themselves qualify Iraq as a robust and stable democracy, they are positive milestones towards this end. Specifically, a strong protest culture is not only crucial in re-establishing a participatory and engaged public life, but it can also help to abate the many conflicts across Iraq and thereby to aid the shift towards a free, egalitarian and democratic nation.

Reference

Isakhan, Benjamin and Stockwell, Stephen (eds.), *The Secret History of Democracy*. Palgrave Macmillan, 2011.

With Clearer Heads and Clearer Lenses, What Might We Learn?

Do Europeans have anything to teach their American cousins? Most certainly, argues Professor Leif Johan Eliasson of the University of Pennsylvania. In his book *America's Perceptions of Europe* he makes the case for a clearer appreciation of European achievements as a way of strengthening the US in meeting the challenges of globalization.

Americans are told from a young age that they live in the best country in the world, that others are envious and that they can do anything they want because they have all the best schools and technology. By the time youngsters begin high school, let alone college, they have joined their elders in believing that if someone somewhere else is producing a better car or TV, a more sophisticated phone or plane, or carrying out new life-saving surgery, they must in some way be cheating. The American labour unions promulgate their favourite mantra of being able to compete with anyone as long as the playing field is level, only thereafter to espouse a million excuses for other countries' superior productivity including dismal labour standards.

Meanwhile, pundits blame foreign governments' currency manipulation or industrial subsidies, while proclaiming lower American taxes as the solution to all ills. To crown the blame-game, ideological factions whose wealth and prosperity stems from the free flow of goods, services and ideas subscribe to that self-defeating folly called protectionism.

The truth is that most European countries, the northern ones in particular, have succeeded in part by emulating America's strengths, while, and this is crucial, avoiding its failings; by substituting rigorous curriculum for feel-good education standards and embracing globalization, openness and adaptability as the twenty-first-century way of life.

The quintessential American question—'what can we do to improve our competitiveness and prosperity?'—might be answered by following the European policy of lowering corporate taxes, removing the burden of health care costs (eight times more costly for an American automobile manufacturer such as Ford than for BMW, Fiat or Peugeot), while improving the delivery of social programmes. A tougher high school curriculum to prepare students for vocational training or college is also essential.

You are probably thinking there are thousands of bright, talented Bill Gates, Warren Buffets and brain surgeons-to-be across America, and you are correct. But young wizards' enthusiasm fade when not challenged, when prevailing norms reflect declining standards. American high school students score lower than half of their European peers on international student assessment tests in math, reading and particularly science (in Europe, Finland comes out top in all three categories). If this trend continues, well-paying jobs will be lost to more competitive environments. Half of science graduate students at American universities are now foreigners who are finding better paying jobs elsewhere, lending their talent to other markets. There are not enough American students interested in science to fill domestic gaps, and while Europe has similar problems, it is now more open to attracting skilled labour than America.

It is true that European start-ups struggle to find venture capital, face more business bureaucracy and have higher first-decade mortality rates than American firms. But university-business research hubs to improve innovation, research, business and competitiveness are popping up across Europe, with good results. Investments are flowing in and businesses are benefiting from more American-inspired, business-friendly bankruptcy laws. Regarding small business regulations, it is clear that Europe is emulating the United States to improve competitiveness.

Fiscal responsibility matters. Twelve European countries led by the Germans and Dutch and including economic 'bad boys' Italy and Greece save more of their earnings than do Americans, leaving them better able to weather downturns. This provides greater purchasing power without racking up debt and helps explain why although seemingly overtaxed and underpaid, they import lots from America. American exports bound for Europe rose 60% from 2003 to 2007, and it is not 60 cent rubber ducks in these shipments; rather, high-value goods such as transportation equipment, chemicals and computers topped the list!

Many European countries have lower annual deficits than the United States and also more realistic assumptions of economic growth over the next decade. Admittedly Latvia, Ireland, Greece, Portugal and Great Britain will suffer severe budget problems until at least 2014, but American states such as New Jersey, New York and California (with roughly the same combined population) also suffer humungous deficits, all in addition to the US federal debt. Both Americans and Europeans will have to endure tax increases and spending cuts; yet European citizens will still have health care and schooling for all citizens, while their American peers may not.

European trouble spots include Greece, a laggard in information society, financial liberalization and sustainable development, and Italy and Bulgaria, where corruption remains the major concern. Italy and Greece also have huge national debts and low birth rates, leaving the country of Parma ham and the cradle of democracy the closest we have to 'sclerotic' western European states. Then again, the states of Louisiana, Illinois and New Jersey can give the Europeans a run for their money.

In today's global economy, where nanosecond transactions zip across the globe, transatlantic interests overlap. The engine of much new and existing business depends in different ways on high-tech components and gadgets in nanoform, as in iPods, laptops or magnets in automobile manufacturing, wind turbines or solar cells. These all depend on access to rare-earth metals, 97% of which are in China. This means Europe and the United States may soon be exchanging dependency on Middle East oil for Chinese metals. This is an area where co-operation and joint pressure against an authoritarian-led monopoly that threatens to hamstring both economies is critically important. While China owns a quarter of US foreign-owned debt, Europe is less beholden to Chinese economic adventures.

Throughout Europe cell phones are cheap, ubiquitous and cutting-edge—the same applies to internet access. Estonia, Finland, Sweden and others have most government services online and available to all citizens. Though getting better, American federal, state and local governments could learn a thing or two about information access and web page organization from their European counterparts.

The costly patent system in Europe is nothing to envy. Years of business pleas to improve competitiveness has led to no more than an agreement to use a common language in applying for patents. A one-stop-shop to approve and enforce a European-wide patent would lower costs by half. Naturally, the entire European process applies to American firms operating in Europe, so they would benefit as well. Despite these problems, a third of global technology and electronics patents are European, proving that innovation is not lacking.

This extends to the environment. Norway has a 10-year project of catching carbon emissions from factories and sinking them into deep-sea depositories, soon to be expanded in Britain. Europe has extensive experience with cap-and-trade initiatives aimed at lowering greenhouse gas emissions. Twenty-seven American states in 2009, with more to follow, are involved in some form of regional trading scheme, so American and European experiences can be mutually beneficial in improving effectiveness, thereby setting global standards.

Europeans are convinced that welfare assistance helps stave off many social ills, and since European welfare systems were institutionalized before the continent became as racially diverse as the United States, and before the globalized economy took off, they are far less likely to be dismantled in the face of economic turbulence or massive immigration. During the 2008–09 recession, when more people needed help with housing, child care and education loans, no one was thrown out on the street or forced into bankruptcy because they needed a kidney but lacked insurance.

American unemployment in 2009 was higher than the European average, and roughly 25 million American citizens were using food stamps. It is worth pondering how the Danes and others combine a flexible, easy-hire-easy-fire job market—ranked as competitive as the American—with extensive social safety nets.

At the same time critics are wrong to dismiss the American welfare system as a mere skeleton, where individualism reigns supreme and inequality and poverty abound. US public assistance is far more extensive than commonly believed even among Americans. Combining private and public spending on social programmes, the United States is a 'middle of the pack' country, spending more than Spain, Finland or Austria, but less than Britain, France or Sweden.

International Issues

The strongest possible endorsement of globalization is found in northern and eastern Europe, in countries such as Sweden, Finland and the Czech Republic. Citizens in the five largest European countries and America are less welcoming to free trade, foreign investments and the internationalization of culture and other areas of life; this despite being the greatest recipients and providers or trade and business investments and having invented and driven the system for decades.

Americans' views of Europeans as less *willing* to fight are correct. Nation building and peacekeeping remain their forte, and Europe will never match US fighting power. But a transatlantic division of labour, even if unspoken, may be mutually beneficial. Economic reality prevents the United States from having the resources to fight every war. Cuts in new weapons and equipment over the coming decade make the case for multinational production lines and increased co-operation. Both conservatives and liberals have testified that success in war, including the fight against terrorism, requires a ratio of nine-to-one non-military to military means. Yet US commitments in the twenty-first century are just the opposite. This is where Europe's expertise compliments America's.

In 2004, I attended a debate between two four-star generals, one British, one American. The British general argued that experience in Northern Ireland, Bosnia and parts of Africa showed that confidence-building through community patrols and involvement was the only way to win the hearts and minds and sustain long-term peace. The American general countered that this was too dangerous, while adding that Americans should not be involved in nation-building. Interestingly, the successful 2008 'surge' strategy advocated and implemented by General Petraeus in Iraq, and subsequent American community involvement, has mimicked the British line.

Round and Round We Go

We see increased transatlantic harmonization of views and policies, from economics to finance, technology and international conflicts. Leaders on both sides of the pond are moving closer ideologically and responses in various surveys show similar trends. But public distortions continue, as was evident in the 2009 American debate on health care. Calling universal care socialist because it exists in a European country, disregarding all the facts, shows the enduring strength of prejudice.

Transatlantic efforts remain critical to political stability and economic growth across the world. Former German Foreign Minister Joschka Fischer's argument that 'Europe is weak and the US is blind', implying a Europe limited in its ability to back economic power with military force and an America ignorant of cultural forces and the benefits of diplomatic endeavours, is slowly being replaced with greater EU capabilities and a diversification of American foreign policy.

The narrowing of ideological and practical differences is clear in America's move toward the European model of a larger role for the state, visible in expanding American social assistance programmes and intervention in the economy. At the same time northern and continental European countries have adopted features of Anglo-Saxon capitalism (e.g., freer labour markets and lower business taxes). Furthermore, a 2009 survey revealed that more Americans support higher taxes on the wealthiest citizens than do French, Italian and British citizens. European and American citizens also share corresponding views on terrorism, global warming, energy, Islamic extremism and Iran's nuclear programme, even if Europe is less concerned about China's ascendancy.

Europeans and Americans have shared interests. In 2009, roughly 60% of Europeans held favourable views of Americans and the number of Americans wanting closer ties to Europe was roughly the same, while suspicion of China's intentions was rising on both sides of the Atlantic. For Americans it takes time adjusting to not being the sole superpower in all areas (economic, social and military). But America should welcome a strong, influential and competitive Europe that embraces many of the same values Americans hold dear, but which is also not afraid to assert its will and push its agenda in ways inherently conducive to capitalism, democracy and prosperity. In an ever more interdependent world, the potential for successful American foreign engagements can only increase when citizens' perspectives are not clouded by myths, misperceptions and distortions of our closest allies.

Reference

Eliasson, Leif Johan, *America's Perceptions of Europe.* Palgrave Macmillan, 2010.

Ireland's Boom and Bust

Few countries have been as dramatically transformed in recent years as Ireland. Ireland emerged as the fastest-growing country in Europe, however just a few years after celebrating their newly-won status among the world's richest societies, now saddled with a wounded, shrinking economy, soaring unemployment, and ruined public finances. In his book *When the Luck of the Irish Ran Out* David J. Lynch offers an insightful, character-driven narrative of how the Irish boom came to be and how it went bust.

For much of the twentieth century Ireland was the odd man out in Europe. While other countries rebuilt and modernised, Ireland stagnated. In the 1980s one-third of the population lived below the poverty line. Incredibly, fewer people held jobs in 1987 than had been working in 1926. Ireland was long on charm and short on almost everything that mattered to a modern economy: jobs, roads, telephone lines.

Making a phone call in Ireland required time, patience and a bit of luck. One-quarter of the country's telephone exchanges were creaky manual museum pieces; one dated to the nineteenth century. As late as 1984 calls routinely failed to connect or endlessly rang busy. And tens of thousands of Irish men and women could only dream of such frustrations. In Greater Dublin alone, the waiting list for a telephone held forty thousand names.

Still the telephone network was positively futuristic compared to the roads. Highways in modern Ireland were all but unknown. The lack of by-pass roads skirting town centers meant that motorists journeying between any two major cities—say, Dublin and Cork or Waterford and Galway—had to pick their way through interminable local traffic in dozens of small villages. To travel from a town in the midlands to the capital—a distance of perhaps 75 miles as the crow flies—consumed a soul-crushing 4 h.

And then, over the span of a decade, everything changed. A sclerotic economy, freed by bold policies and ample investment imported from the United States, roared into a growth miracle dubbed the Celtic Tiger. The culture, too, long dormant under the censorious hand of the Catholic Church, erupted in a fountain of creativity. Even the open wound of Northern Ireland healed, thanks to a peace midwived by American diplomats. Suddenly, the Irish, long on the periphery of global affairs, were at the center of everything. As 1989 dawned, growth was percolating at an annual rate of 5.6% versus almost nothing 3 years earlier. An August 1986 devaluation of the pound effectively cut the price of Irish goods on global markets, giving exporters a boost. Critically, interest rates were on the decline as well, making it easier for businesses to invest in new factories. But the job market remained becalmed: total employment in 1989 was no higher than it had been in 1974.

To create an adequate number of jobs, Ireland needed to attract the world's best companies to its shores. It was a mark of the pragmatism and utter absence of ideology at the heart of Irish politics that Fianna Fáil, architects of the failed protectionist "Little Ireland" model throughout the party's history, transformed itself into a fierce advocate of free trade.

By the late 1980s, foreign investment, especially from the United States, had brought manufacturers such as Fruit of the Loom, Bausch & Lomb and Digital Computers to Ireland. But the country remained a minor-league economic player. Then in October 1989, Intel, the US multinational, chose a 55-acre site on a former stud farm in Leixlip, about 15 miles west of Dublin, for its new plant. The Silicon Valley giant was drawn to Ireland by its well-educated, English-speaking workforce, low corporate taxes and generous state grants. The three-phase development promised 2600 total jobs. The decision gave Ireland a sort of globalization seal of approval, one that elevated a chronically ill economy into a place worth a second look.

A succession of tax-cutting budgets aimed at stimulating enterprise culminated with Fianna Fáil's election victory in 1997. The standard and top rates of personal tax fell, from 26% and 48% to 24% and 46%, respectively, as did corporate taxes, cut from 40% to 32%. Finance Minister Charles McCreevy made his biggest splash, however, by halving the capital gains tax from 40% to 20%. McCreevy slashed the gains levy over the objections of his department's senior professionals, who feared a plunge in revenue. Instead, the government's take soared: from IR£84 million in 1996 to IR £609·2 million by 2000.

Ireland's robust performance, meanwhile, was beginning to revive fears of inflation. As the country entered its fifth consecutive year of strong growth, there were signs that annual price increases would near 3%. The currencies of Ireland's trading partners, including the US dollar, had strengthened and a

tight labor market threatened to push wages up. In the first quarter of 1998, new home prices were up 25% from 1 year earlier. But Irish officials weren't overly concerned; the rising house prices, they said, could be explained by strong economic growth, favourable demographics—including the annual arrival of thousands of immigrants—and low interest rates. The government concentrated on growing employment while preparing for what it hoped would be an eventual 'soft land' for the hard-charging economy. The chief impediment was the white-hot housing market. In April 1999, the Central Bank sent a letter to all Irish credit institutions reminding them of the dangers of 'a lending policy that is excessively flexible'. Complicating the policy challenge, the Central Bank was about to lose one of the principal tools for managing an economy: control over its money supply. Ireland was proud to be among the first 11 countries that would participate in the planned single European currency.

Joining the euro meant surrendering to the planned European Central Bank (ECB) control over both the country's interest rates and the value of its currency. Moreover, the process of joining the euro would involve a massive jolt of adrenaline for the already supercharged Irish economy. To bring the Irish economy in line with Germany, Europe's dominant economy, interest rates needed to drop sharply.

The economy might be overheating, but at least it was finally producing jobs. By the end of 2000, the number of those working was 40% higher than it had been just 6 years earlier. But the economy was running above capacity. Unemployment was now 'significantly below' the level associated with stable prices. Sure enough, inflation in 2000 hit a disturbing 5.5%, more than double the eurozone average. Property prices also were getting out of hand. Where once the economy had grown thanks to exporting, it was now deriving three quarters of its forward momentum from domestic demand. That was a sign that the nature of the Irish boom was changing, shifting more toward consumption than production, and that the government needed to either raise taxes or cut spending to cool the economic engine.

The Irish boom was living on borrowed time. The bursting of the internet bubble, rising oil prices, and a synchronized slowdown in the United States, Japan, and Germany all combined to halve global growth, producing 'the sharpest slowdown in global economic activity in two decades'. As an extremely open economy dependent upon global trade, Ireland was especially hard hit. By the end of 2001, growth had 'effectively ceased'.

But the Irish were about to get some help from friends in America. To prevent the 9/11 upheaval from capsizing the US and global economies, the Federal Reserve slashed interest rates to 1% and kept them there. The decision of the ECB to lower rates from 4.75% in 2001 to barely 2% 2 years later, gave a massive financial stimulus to Ireland, at times making borrowed money effectively free.

The government poured fuel on the economic fire with its own free-spending ways. The number of workers on the public payroll jumped by 22% in just 4 years. By the late 1990s, public-sector pay was spiralling out of control. In 2000, the government introduced a process called 'benchmarking' which was intended to align compensation for government workers with prevailing rates for similar jobs in the private sector. In theory, the new pay system would be coupled with improvements in public-sector efficiency. In practice, the head of the major teachers' union gleefully compared the results to 'going to an ATM'. In mid-2002, the first report of the new pay-review board recommended salary increases of up to 25%.

Despite a nod to prudence, the 2002 budget was a veritable laundry list of giveaways: more generous old age pensions, fatter child benefits, a 20% increase in provisions for free electricity for qualifying households, and even a sharp cut in the betting tax. Along with those goodies came personal tax cuts worth US$568 million as well as reductions in corporate levies valued at US$311 million. In the event, government spending in 2002 would increase 6.3% after taking inflation into account, on top of an even more lavish 12.1% real increase the previous year. If this were prudence, it was hard to conceive of profligacy. At a time when prices were rising in Ireland at a pace more than twice the eurozone average, the government was stepping on the economic accelerator.

The economy grew by only 2.9% in 2002, its weakest performance in a decade, and what growth took place was predominantly in the construction and housing sectors. Easy money from the banks coupled with stimulative government policies encouraged limitless building. In 2002, for the first time in any 12-month period, Irish builders threw up more than 50,000 homes. In 2003, more than 62,000 were built, a record quickly surpassed the following year, when more than 72,000 arose. It was as if the engine of construction, once started, could not be stilled. Despite the supply increase, prices kept rising, too. They were up 14% in 2003 alone and had roughly tripled since

1996. The pace was insane, clearly speculative and unsustainable. And yet the building frenzy roared on. Buying and selling homes became a national obsession.

In February 2007, housing prices wobbled and then turned down for the first time in a decade. Once property prices started to slide, the Irish economy was like a running movie in reverse. Everything had grown with property. Just as it once had made sense to buy the house today because tomorrow's prices would be higher, now the smart move was to wait. Prices would only be cheaper next week, next month, or even next year. Once that essential truth took hold, Irish banks were doomed.

The Irish recession that began officially in mid-2008 was the steepest downturn in any advanced nation, far outpacing that of the United States. The Irish housing bubble was three times as big as that of the United States. Real house prices in the United States rose roughly 50% in the decade preceding 2006; in Ireland they rocketed 172%. So when the bubble popped—Irish house prices dropped by one-third from their February 2007 peak and kept sinking—the damage was commensurately greater. As if to prove the point, Ireland's output in the fourth quarter of 2009 was nearly 17% below its peak production in the same period 2 years earlier. (Over the same period, US quarterly output fell by about 7%.) The number of unemployed jumped quickly from 101,000 at the end of 2007 to more than 267,000 2 years later.

Not everything about the Celtic Tiger, however, was illusory. Much in Irish life genuinely has changed for the better. Outside of the People's Republic of China, in fact, few societies in the closing years of the twentieth century transformed themselves so quickly. The number of Irish people at work was almost 70% higher than it had been in 1984. Set against the long sweep of Irish history, that was no small achievement. The world's best companies, especially in the software and pharmaceuticals industries, now consider the island an important part of their global operations. Irish artists, musicians and poets remained able cultural ambassadors. The influence of the once-omnipotent Catholic Church has receded and, despite a handful of isolated killings involving dissident republicans, the North is at peace.

But if it is wrong to exaggerate the scale of retrenchment amid the global financial crisis that began in 2007, it is equally ill-advised to minimize either the blow that has been absorbed or the challenges that lie ahead. Ireland is not going back to the misery of the 1980s. Neither can it return to the easy affluence of the Celtic Tiger. Gone is the romance of *The Quiet Man* Ireland of old. Gone, too, is the high-octane, consumption-first ethos of the Tiger. Neither was sustainable. Neither was real. And good riddance to both. The current crisis may put an end to any notion of Irish exceptionalism, but with a little luck, it will leave Ireland on a sounder footing.

For those hoping for a Celtic revival, the greatest misfortune would be if the world economy rebounds so powerfully that Irish elites believe they can stick with business as usual. If the politicians and financiers aren't compelled by circumstances to adapt, they will not. The world has changed since the 1980s, with the collapse of the Berlin Wall and the rise of new competitors in Asia, eastern Europe and Latin America. The global bar is being set higher, and Ireland must adapt.

Reference

Lynch, David J., *When the Luck of the Irish Ran Out.* Palgrave Macmillan, 2010.

The Popular Image of North Africa and the Middle East

Will the popular image of North Africa and the Middle East change after the Arab Spring? Keith Dinnie examines the possibilities in his article for *Place Branding and Public Diplomacy* journal.

The recent dramatic upheavals in North Africa and the Middle East have gripped the world's attention in a way that has unmistakable echoes of the collapse of communism in 1989. What effect, if any, will these developments have on the reputation and image of the countries concerned?

Much will depend on whether real reform occurs or if the old regimes manage to hold onto power. Should the pro-democracy movement peter out,

with a return to authoritarian rule, then it is unlikely that there will be any positive change in each country's image. Real radical change is the basis of improvement in country image.

If democracy does take root in the region, then such a historic shift can be expected to lead to significant changes. Instead of being submerged by a somewhat negative 'Middle East region brand' effect, individual countries will begin to assert their own unique identity. Instead of being monopolized by the image of one political leader, countries will be able to project the full richness and diversity of their respective cultures, as Spain has done in the years following the end of the Franco dictatorship in 1975.

Spain's transition to democracy and its subsequent cultural renaissance paved the way for it to become one of the countries most often quoted as an example of a successful nation brand. If real political change materializes, there is no reason why the countries of North Africa and the Middle East should not now follow a similarly positive trajectory. The obvious caveat is that these countries must avoid the post-dictator, political vacuum chaos of Iraq.

There are no limits to the creativity with which nations can attempt to project their identity to the rest of the world. On the other hand, the range of uncontrollable image determinants is very wide. They range from word-of-mouth and national stereotypes to export brands and the behaviour of a country's citizens.

Unfortunately for most of the countries of North Africa and the Middle East, country image perceptions held by foreign audiences have been dominated and distorted by politics, whether projected by the personal image of a military dictator or a more diffuse regional image of extremism, terrorism and so on. All the other factors have been overshadowed, resulting in country images that are incomplete, inaccurate and grotesquely skewed in a negative direction.

For Egypt and Tunisia, the situation is redressed to some extent by their tourist industries. Indeed, it is unlikely that many foreigners who have visited Tunisia in the past 20 years are or were aware of the country's leadership and political regime.

Visiting a country as a tourist may provide only a superficial impression of a country, but at least it allows personal interaction with locals and the host culture. In the absence of a significant tourist industry, external perceptions of other Middle East or North African countries are mediated to an unhealthy extent by the international media. This phenomenon is exacerbated by the striking absence of alternative image-formation factors such as sports performances or export brands, image determinants that can play a hugely significant role in country image perceptions. The country image of New Zealand, for example, is powerfully amplified by the All Blacks rugby team, whereas the country image of Japan is tightly linked with globally successful corporate brands such as Sony, Toyota and Toshiba. However, most foreign audiences would struggle to associate anything comparable with the countries of North Africa and the Middle East.

The closed nature of one-party states tends to be reflected in a lack of support for the promotion of cultural activities. The countries of North Africa and the Middle East lack influential cultural organizations such as Germany's Goethe-Institut or the United Kingdom's British Council, both of which play an important role in downplaying those two nations' imperialistic past and in supporting a more cosmopolitan image. This type of soft power projection through public diplomacy has not as yet been embraced by most countries in North Africa and the Middle East. The opportunity to do so now beckons, provided that the revolutionary impulse towards more open societies does not fade away.

Reference

Dinnie, Keith, 'The impact on country image of the North Africa and Middle East uprisings' in *Place Branding and Public Diplomacy* (volume 7, Number 2), ed. by Simon Anholt. Palgrave Macmillan, 2011.

We Are All Diplomats Now

In his article *Wikileaks, public diplomacy 2.0 and the state of digital public diplomacy*, Nicholas J. Cull explores the all-embracing potential for digital public diplomacy.

It happened in November. The world was weary of war and crisis when he stole the headlines. He was charismatic. He was radical. He had a point to prove. He defied years of diplomatic convention and laid the secrets of great power diplomacy before the world. His revelations captured the headlines and shocked the establishment. In laying bare these secrets he proclaimed a new approach to international affairs and—implicitly—the arrival of a new power. Julian Assange? November 2010? No. That vignette describes events in the now distant autumn of 1917 and the actions of Leon Trotsky, then the newly appointed People's Commissar for International Affairs for the Bolshevik government of Russia.

In November 1917 Trotsky published a number of secret treaties which had been found in the archives of the Tsar in the aftermath of the Russian revolution. In a statement of 22 November 1917 Trotsky argued that: 'The abolition of secret diplomacy is the primary condition for an honest, popular, truly democratic foreign policy. The Soviet Government regards it as its duty to carry out such a policy.' The documents that Trotsky published revealed a sorry tale of the backroom deals in which belligerent powers of the entente (Russia, France and Great Britain) promised various concessions of territory to the neutral nations that they sought to draw into the Great War.

Diplomacy swiftly adjusted to compensate for Trotsky's gambit. On 8 January 1918 the US president Woodrow Wilson replied in kind. His 'fourteen points' on which he claimed an equitable peace could be based included 'open covenants openly arrived at'. Others tried to give the new regime a taste of its own medicine with revelations of collusion between the Bolsheviks and the Kaiser's Germany. In time the Soviet state learnt the value of secrecy in diplomacy and reinstated the traditional approach, reaching new heights of double dealing in the pact with Hitler of August 1939, but for a season it enjoyed the fruits of its defiance of convention. Trotsky's revelation was a symbol that the Bolshevik state represented something new in world affairs. It was public diplomacy by leak.

The analogy with 1917 is not wholly academic. The coming (or is it a springing?) of WikiLeaks is just as indicative of a 'game change' as Trotsky's gambit was 96 years ago. As then, while the information itself is important what is crucial is the context. In 1917 the leak required an earth-shattering revolution. In 2010 all it took to challenge the diplomatic order of the day was a single individual with a well-placed accomplice and a little technical know-how.

Now, technical know-how is at the heart of the revolution in communications technology. WikiLeaks not only required a flash drive and surreptitious data dump to acquire its trove of material, but also needed the facilities of an easily accessible worldwide web to make it instantaneously available. Technology has given one individual the communication power that was the monopoly of the nation state in the previous century.

In the wake of the Trotsky leak the great powers faced a prolonged struggle to reassert their legitimacy and did so in part by shifting to greater openness with institutions such as the League of Nations.

In the wake of WikiLeaks the powers of our own time will have to consider again the dangers of double dealing, and work to ensure that there is a minimal gap between what is claimed in public and what is practised in private. For all its regrettable corrosion of the principles of confidentiality on which so much diplomacy rests, the shadow of WikiLeaks may play the classic role once memorably claimed for an Australian opposition party and thereafter embraced by the investigative press: 'keep the bastards honest'.

The Foundation: Public Diplomacy 1.0

The web-based revolution in public diplomacy has been a long time coming. As far back as the late 1960s some public diplomats had been anticipating a golden age of communication made possible by a network of computers. In February 1968 America's chief public diplomat, the director of the United States Information Agency, Leonard Marks, predicted that a world information grid of linked computers would be 'a fundamental step toward lasting world peace . . . The culture of all lands must be circulated through the houses of nations as our technology permits.'

The dawn didn't really break until the mid 1990s when the Mosaic browser system made it possible for the personal computers which had spread in the 1980s to access data platforms in the rapidly growing worldwide web.

For public diplomats the implications of this were slow to sink in. Web technology where it was used was a platform for press releases and one-way top-down communication. The pride of US public diplomacy was its system for making Voice of America available online, initially in script form but eventually as an audio stream. Journals became available online (cheaper than print) and the so-called 'wireless file' anthology of 'useful' American news and views which had been sent to embassies since the early 1930s became a website.

Amazing as it sounds now, the terrorist attacks of 9/11 found a number of US embassies still without websites. Other players around the world were more canny, realizing the value of a well-managed online identity. Cyber-image and, by extension, cyber-diplomacy became a tool in the public diplomacy toolbox. What seems to have been largely missed was the shift of power inherent in the new technology. Governments focused on how swiftly they could do what they had always done. Militaries looked to occupy cyber-space as if it were simply the modern equivalent of the prized high ground of old. Treasuries looked to save money by going 'paperless'. But the new technology meant more than that. It was empowering the individual in a new way.

While the great powers continued (and continue) to broadcast their speeches, press releases and so forth into the ether and across the web, the audience was no longer as likely to listen. Part of the change was rooted in the sheer number of voices suddenly speaking online and the range of choices available. But as the number of websites proliferated it became possible to seek out a source closely matching one's own sense of identity, and even to develop an identity based on an online connection. Many different imagined communities emerged online built from shared interests. Some had the potential to supplant national identity. Online communities based around radical Islamism were a case in point.

This proliferation of communities had one massive implication for public diplomacy and that was in the area of credibility. Public diplomacy relies on being credible to an audience but in this new environment polls revealed that credibility now rested not with the traditional generators of information—governments and news organizations—but with whoever seemed to be 'someone like me'.

The Coming of Web 2.0

By 2004 it became clear that the internet was changing and that a new term was needed to describe the quantum leap from the old world of web-pages and email to that of social media and sites based on user-generated content. The English-speaking internet community seized on a term first coined in the specialized literature in 1999 which drew an analogy to the release of the new version of a program: a version 2.0 (two-point-oh). The term Web 2.0 was used fairly loosely to discuss the explosion of user-generated content online including blogs, the crowd-sourced encyclopaedia site Wikipedia (founded 2001) and social media sites including Facebook (launched 2004), file-sharing sites like Flikr (launched 2004) and YouTube (launched 2005). By the end of 2006 the new trend was sufficiently established for Time magazine to perceptively name 'YOU' as the person of the year—an honour whose previous recipients include a parade of American presidents and world statesmen.

As the web became a domain for user-generated content a variety of sectors coined varieties of the Web 2.0 formulation for their own use including Library 2.0, Medicine 2.0, Government 2.0 and even Porn 2.0. Public Diplomacy 2.0—a sub-set of Government 2.0—was a late entrant in the field and owed its genesis to James K. Glassman, an American journalist and commentator who served as Undersecretary of State for Public Diplomacy for the final half of 2008. Although Glassman had a relatively short tenure in Washington DC he was a great enthusiast for the new media. He spoke of a unique opportunity to engage world opinion as never before and challenged the US Department of State to embrace the new technology.

Other ministries around the world underwent similar awakenings. Some were early adopters. In the spring of 2007 the Maldives and Sweden opened the first 'embassies' (or cultural centres) in the 'virtual world' of Second Life (launched in 2003). Many more people read about it in the old newspapers than actually visited online but that hardly dimmed the public diplomacy objective. An energetic Israeli diplomat posted to New York City named David Saranga dealt with the unenviable task of selling his nation's offensive against Gaza in late 2008 by organizing a press conference on the social networking site Twitter (then just 2 years old). The herd thundered in behind them, but to what effect is still not clear.

The Face of Public Diplomacy 2.0

The essential challenge of the Web 2.0 world is that it enabled the preferred source of 'someone like me' to become the principal point of contact for all information. In this regard it is a return to a village environment where one's key interlocutors and sources were the hundred or so 'like you' who made up the village. Now each person could gather their personal 'village' of friends in cyberspace without regard for the limitations of geography.

This poses a problem for the public diplomacy agency seeking to utilize new media channels. As each individual's cyber domain becomes more tailored to their own tastes and settled into a comfortable niche, the intervention of an outsider will seem increasingly incongruous. Both the US Department of State and Department of Defense have digital engagement teams participating in online discussions and 'correcting' misunderstandings of their interlocutors. This may be counterproductive if the intervention is judged to be at odds with the identity of the site.

The scale of successes is difficult to gauge. The number of friends on an organization's Facebook page became the immediate measure rather than any consideration of whether real engagement was taking place as a result of the link.

More interesting was the use of YouTube. The Bureau of Educational and Cultural Affairs has launched a number of competitions for user-generated films including a contest for the best short film on the theme of 'Democracy is'. Young filmmakers from around the world took part and their films were seen and circulated online. Winners of the first year's competition included filmmakers from Iran and Nepal. The strategy was empowering voices who could be 'someone like me' and hence credible to the audiences that the US really needed to influence.

In a similar vein James Glassman launched a project to assist young international activists. He drew together a remarkable range of young people, the most famous being Oscar Morales who in the spring of 2008 had used Facebook to initiate what became an international wave of protests against the FARC guerrillas in Colombia. Their conference resulted in the creation of the Alliance of Youth Movements: a support structure for those seeking to use new technology to transform their world. Its activities include a website with clear instruction on how to set up a blog or social media campaign.

The most elaborate use of the new media was the creation of full blown joint projects in cyberspace. The State Department funded a remarkable collaboration between a school of architecture in California and one in Cairo during which the students worked together on joint projects. When they eventually met they already knew and trusted each other. It was an indication of what was possible. Yet there have been problems. They are clearest in the US official use of Twitter.

Twitter

Twitter swept to prominence in 2008. The micro-blogging site seemed to offer an ideal technology for engaging foreign audiences. Its 140 character format required the discipline of brevity but was—by design—short enough to be read on the sort of handheld devices that much of the developing world used to access the internet. The United States and many other public diplomacy actors hurried to be part of the Twitter-revolution.

The first problem that the US ran into was the question of exactly how its personnel would conduct themselves online. Would they establish a feed in a formal capacity and use it as a platform to post the links for press releases and statements or would they seek to use the site to present themselves to the world, as a way to humanize US foreign policy.

A notable public diplomat who took the second course was Colleen Graffey, the Deputy Assistant Secretary of State with responsibility for US public diplomacy in Europe, a political appointee with a reputation for stridency in such issues as defence of conditions at the Guantanamo Bay prison. Her Tweets, however, seemed trivial when set against the events happening in the world. An infelicitous message in which she mentioned purchasing a bathing suit in the midst of a meltdown in the Middle East drew particular scorn.

The new-media experts who joined the Obama administration's foreign policy operation ran into similar problems. Jared Cohen was criticized after he memorably Tweet-ed about a wonderful Frappachino in Syria in June 2010. The real problem with the explosion of State Department Twitter sites was not their personalization but their neglect of a key dimension of the platform.

The essence of Twitter is that it opens a space not only to speak in 140 character bursts but to listen in the same way also. The State Department has paid lots of attention to how many people are following its postings, but generally forgets to think about following anyone themselves. Those who were 'following' others—the new technology superstars Jared Cohen, Alec Ross and Katie Stanton—turn out to have been following each other, which is to say other people tweeting in the US new media community, rather than the wider world that they were supposed to be engaging online.

The fixation with 'broadcast mode' in US online diplomacy is a major faux pas. It is the equivalent of going into a party and shouting about one's self

and leaving: a behaviour which is intolerable even if one is buying all the drinks, which the United States no longer is.

The first duty of a public diplomat is to listen and the new media have an amazing ability to make that listening both easier and visible. Suppose one of the US embassy Twitter sites were to begin to survey the online environment and click to follow selected writers and sites in their assigned country. Each of those writers might then receive an email saying 'Ambassador X or US embassy Y is now following you on Twitter'. This could encourage writers to reciprocate and follow, raising the possibility that they would re-tweet an embassy message or two and pass them further along their network with the added boost of their local credibility. It would certainly create a lineup of go-to feeds to help the embassy understand its country, which would be easily taken up by others in the embassy and beyond. Their Twitter-roll could be passed on to anyone else who cared to scroll down and right click. Fortunately, there are some embassies which have realized the potential of Twitter as a tool of listening. The US embassy in New Delhi, for example, is actively following feeds in its region.

A Tweet—like any other piece of information—is welcome to the extent that it is actually of interest to its recipient. There is a great danger that a Twitter feed will become 'spam' if it has too much to say on subjects beyond the precise interest of the reader. It is a mistake to insist on one-size-fits-all in a made to measure world. Twitter offers the potential for an unlimited variety of feeds and rather than expecting various diplomats to become providers of wisdom on every subject under the sun, it makes more sense to use discreet feeds to distribute information on discreet issues which will be of relevance to an audience. 'Tweet the issue' should be the mantra of public diplomats.

As already noted the great strength of Web 2.0 is its ability to connect people to others like themselves. With this in mind it is not wholly surprising that the greatest strides in Web 2.0 at the State Department have been internal to the department. Closed sites provide a platform for tasks as diverse as accumulating and disseminating best practice, the construction of a 'diplopedia' wiki with background and policy discussion on particular countries, a mechanism called 'communities@state' to bring diplomats together around shared interests and online sounding boards to feedback to management on ways to improve conditions within the department. Richard Boly, director of the Department's office of e.diplomacy proudly revealed how online suggestions had yielded the brilliant insight that more people would cycle to work if there were showers located adjacent to the bike storage.

The Illusions of Public Diplomacy 2.0

The world of communications technology continues to evolve at an exponential rate. Science fact outstrips the science fiction of just a few years ago. At the edge of this vortex of innovation we find the practitioners of Public Diplomacy 2.0 in the foreign ministries of the world typically struggling to pull their risk-averse and information-protective agencies into the new era.

The achievements of Public Diplomacy 2.0 are notable and worthy of scrutiny but they must not be mistaken for offering some mechanism for mastery of the new environment. To think such would be to confuse a surfer with the wave he rides and to ignore the impact of the wave as it reshapes the shore.

The traditional diplomatic actors are attempting to get their message out and to engage with the world, but their competitors are doing precisely the same—often with the advantage of a local affinity—and the world is in flux, fragmenting and regrouping into new networks.

Secretary of State Clinton has argued that connectivity is an absolute good and pledged the United States to work to make the blessings of the information society as widely available as possible, but the voters of the United States will have to accept that the voices they empower will be diverse and will include some that are critical and even openly hostile.

Rules to Live By

How then should practitioners of public diplomacy—large and small—respond to this world of WikiLeaks and the wider Web 2.0 environment? The first step is to acknowledge the transformation of the world of which this winter's online shenanigans is just one example. Whether in Tunisia or in Tunbridge Wells individuals are inherently more powerful than they have been at any time in history, more especially as they connect across networks. This global and wired public cannot be ignored and communication aimed only at its leaders will necessarily fall short.

The new technology opens a frightening aspect of chaos—the response of the diplomatic establishment to WikiLeaks had all the hallmarks of panic—but it also offers the opportunity for a new kind of politics and a new kind of diplomacy.

The first step for communicators is to acknowledge that they cannot be all things to all people. The task of public diplomacy should evolve to one of partnering around issues with those who share the same objectives and empowering those who will be credible with their target audience. Some nations are recognizing that being seen to be of help in building a network can be a valuable act of public diplomacy in its own right; hence the Swiss government has established its chain of SwissNex offices at strategic locations around the world to connect innovators with one another.

In planning new technology ventures I would propose the following. Rule 1: Be relevant. Don't assume that what is important to you will matter to your audience: tweet the issue. Rule 2: Be cooperative. Look for partners and be ready to pass on messages from others and by the same token craft your messages so as to make them easy for others to pass them on. Rule 3: Know your audience. Understand the ways in which they use social media and be consistent with that culture as you would if you were physically entering a conversation. Understand the credibility that comes from being 'like' your online interlocutor. Rule 4: Be realistic. Public Diplomacy 2.0 can't make a bad policy good any more than its 1.0 variety could. The prime need is not to say the right thing but to actually be the right thing, especially in an era of growing transparency. Rule 5: Listen. Do not let the 1001 new ways to speak that you have discovered online keep you from exploring 1002 new ways to listen. In the old media or the new, public diplomacy begins with listening.

Reference

Cull, Nicholas J., 'Wikileaks, public diplomacy 2.0 and the state of digital public diplomacy' in *Place Branding and Public Diplomacy* (volume 7, Issue 1). Palgrave Macmillan, 2011.

The End of Isolation

In his article ***Pearl Harbor and public diplomacy: 70 years on***, Nicholas J. Cull explores the British influence on the US entry into World War II.

Last December marked the 70th anniversary of one of the great turning points in international diplomacy: the entry of the United States into the Second World War following the Japanese attack on Pearl Harbor on 7 December 1941. Major US public diplomacy initiatives followed, including the Voice of America and appointment of the first wave of cultural attachés at American embassies. However, the public diplomacy preceding this momentous event also deserves to be revisited: specifically, the subtle campaign undertaken by Britain to wean the United States away from its profound historical attachment to neutrality and to secure its participation in the war.

Re-examined through the lens of contemporary understanding of the importance of public diplomacy and 'soft power', the British campaign now seems like the moment that foreign policy through engagement with a foreign public came of age.

The story begins in 1939 with Britain in trouble. The country faced a war for its existence, knowing that its only hope for survival—let alone victory—lay in securing help from rigidly neutral America. Although the United States had rescued the British 20 years previously in the Great War, the chances of this happening again were slim. The Great War now seemed futile and morally ambiguous, and the United States was in no hurry to be hoodwinked once again. In the days following the outbreak of the new war in Europe, the British wisely rejected a heavy propaganda campaign in the United States. They needed to find some way other than an overt appeal to rally America to their cause. The activities deployed extended across five areas: listening, advocacy, cultural diplomacy, exchange diplomacy and international broadcasting.

Britain certainly listened to American public opinion during the run up to Pearl Harbor. The government not only paid keen attention to the Gallup and other polls, but it also established a substantial apparatus to survey the American print media. Britain also listened to a wider range of contacts within American society, working through regional information offices attached to the consular network. The steady supply of reports ensured that the British government dodged some of the pitfalls of American opinion and was able to craft its messages to America's willingness to help. Hence, months after the Cabinet acknowledged that Britain needed American belligerence to have any chance of surviving, Churchill was still promising the

US public that material aid was all that was needed. 'Give us the tools,' he pledged to the United States in January 1941, 'and we will finish the job.'

Although the British Ambassadors to Washington, Lord Lothian (architect of the strategy of gentle persuasion) and his successor Lord Halifax, spoke often in public, they avoided direct appeals for American aid. They knew that the best strategy was simply to make it possible for Americans to hear Britain's leaders appealing to their own people and trust the Americans to draw the appropriate conclusions. The American media obliged with thorough press coverage and domestic rebroadcast of speeches by the Prime Minister and the King and Queen. The best example of this was the relaying of Winston Churchill's 'Finest Hour' speech, which included plenty of passages aimed squarely at a 'New World' audience. American exhibition of British official documentary films aimed at boosting morale at home worked similarly well. The approach was spot on. Contemporary studies have shown that information that is overheard is given much greater credibility than a direct hard sell: hence the genre of American television commercials in which the point is made by a conversation between two authoritative characters—often doctors discussing a new medication.

Cultural diplomacy was already part of Britain's approach to the United States. There had been a spectacular British contribution to the New York World's Fair of 1939, with a pavilion that included a display of the Crown Jewels and the common anchor of the British and US legal systems, Magna Carta. All American schools received a facsimile and a translation in the mail. An art exhibit showcased Henry Moore and Graham Sutherland, while musical events included the premiere of a special work from Ralph Vaughan Williams (*Dives and Lazarus*). The 1940 season of the Fair included more art and a poem by T. S. Eliot (*The Defence of the Islands*).

But once the war was underway, one cultural forum surpassed all others: the British presence in Hollywood. Perhaps it was the excellence of British theatrical training that gave British actors such prominence in the American film industry during its first decade of sound. Ambassador Lothian urged the stars of the era—David Niven and C. Aubrey Smith among them—to stay in place, telling stories that showed Britain at its best. Two great British directors soon joined them in the California sun. Alexander Korda and Alfred Hitchcock both relocated to the United States and began telling pro-British stories. Korda's historical allegory, *That Hamilton Woman*, which told the story of Nelson's resistance to Napoleonic tyranny, and Hitchcock's anti-neutrality caper, *Foreign Correspondent*, both did their bit. The process was led by American demand, but Britain's Ministry of Information was happy to help show business allies along. Examples ranged from supplying authentic sound effects for a Broadway play about a theatre during the Blitz, Lesley Storm's *Heart of a City*, and script advice for MGM's *Mrs Miniver*, which went on to be one of the most successful films of the war.

The pre-war non-governmental Anglo-American exchange network transitioned into the leadership of the wartime work. The best example was the ambassador Lord Lothian, who as secretary to the Rhodes Trust had overseen the operation of the Rhodes scholarships in the inter-war period. The director of the Ministry of Information's American Department—Sir Frederick Whyte—had earlier headed the English Speaking Union. The network of Rhodes scholars provided a ready-made set of advocates for the British cause while the reciprocal Harkness scholars program, established in the 1920s to expose the best and brightest of the British Empire to the United States, furnished talented and informed Britons ready to interpret the United States for British audiences. They included the BBC's young American correspondent, Alistair Cooke.

International Broadcasting provided the final dimension. Here the British effort was split. First and foremost, the British understood that the most credible voice to Americans would always be American and thus worked to facilitate American coverage of events in Britain. Edward R. Murrow of CBS became a particular confidant of the government, but the entire American press corps had access to interviews and stories quite beyond anything available to British or Commonwealth reporters. Murrow was eventually allowed to commentate live on the London Blitz as though it was a sporting event—a privilege that brought the sounds of war directly into every American living room.

The second front was the direct broadcasting over the shortwave North American service of the BBC. Programming included talks by J. B. Priestley, whose Yorkshire accent belied the US stereotype of the British 'toff'. Learning that American women were more likely to be isolationist than men, the BBC sought to explain the war to a female audience through the medium of soap opera. *Frontline Family*—an everyday story of London life in the Blitz—became the first ever soap opera created by the BBC. It was rebroadcast in the United States by the Mutual network.

Britain's radio news strategy was important. Unlike the Germans, the British resolved to tell the truth even when the news was bad (and opened the processes like the calculation of losses during the Battle of Britain to American media scrutiny). The strategy paid off and honesty about the damage suffered during the Blitz built credibility so that in years ahead the good news would also be believed.

Britain's public diplomacy strategy required a substantial bureaucracy divided between the Ministry of Information in the United Kingdom and the specially created British Information Services in the United States. The British hit on some of the great staples of persuasive communication, not the least being understanding the 'soft power' of victimhood. The British realized that children have a special potency as guileless innocents caught in a war that could not be of their making. Images of suffering British children were widely shown—Cecil Beaton's photograph of the wounded child Ellen Dunne was a classic case—and the British persuaded NBC to carry a programme called *Children Calling Home*, in which children who had been evacuated to the United States spoke over a BBC relay to their families.

Today's communicators speak of the value of the social media and the power that comes from relationships with 'people like oneself'. Britain sought to mobilize a social network decades before its digital descendent. There was the British official in New York—Major Berkeley Ormerod—whose job was wandering around making new friends for Britain in the media and urging the old ones to keep in touch, or the genial Irishman Angus McDonnell who arranged small parties in Washington, D.C. to introduce the rather austere Ambassador Lord Halifax at his best.

More broadly, the British Ministry of Information urged ordinary Britons with American contacts to use their pen-pal relationships to help the British cause, sending out suggestions of useful themes to include in outbound mail. The British were able to create and facilitate networks around their cause—what would now be called civil society or non-governmental organizations—such as labour unions or the aid organization Bundles for Britain, which channelled the American volunteer spirit into the collection of clothes and blankets for shipping to Britain.

But perhaps the most interesting development was the bid to redefine the 'meaning' of Britain. Culture and values are a resource as real as military and economic leverage. The case of wartime Britain reminds us that the soft power audit for any country will include elements that attract and elements that repel. Britain's achievement was to accentuate the positive aspects of the British 'brand' and hit on a plausible story to minimize the drag of the negative.

The obstacles were formidable. The British were the bad guys in the epic of the American Revolution. Americans defined themselves in opposition to Britain; they were classless in opposition to British class-consciousness, Republican in opposition to British monarchy, anti-Imperial in opposition to British Imperialism.

There were positive images in the mix as well, especially the familiarity that flowed from the shared language and literature, but the intimacy could be a mixed blessing. America seemed to get angrier at British missteps than at those of other nations, and the British appeasement of Hitler in 1938 was seen as a massive misstep by many Americans.

Wartime Britain's achievement was to generate a different kind of relevance for the American imagination: a heroic image that gave America something to admire. The moment of transition was the battle for Dunkirk in May 1940. American reporters framed the story as a death and resurrection. The old classist Britain was said to have perished in the fires of the battle for France and a new Britain had emerged with a coalition government and a dynamic new Prime Minister. Americans could retain their cherished stereotypes as true of the past but overlay them with a portrait of the new Britain engaged in a people's war.

Of course, the shift of image would have meant little had not the British people delivered on the claims made about them by the American commentators. The spectacle of all classes working together in the face of the German blitz on London bore out the new narrative. The Americans repressed incidents that flew in the face of this narrative without being asked. There was no doubting the impact of the David and Goliath spectacle of Britain fighting on against the odds. Hitler had long since given the American people something to hate. Now the British people gave them something to love.

Historians seeking to trumpet the impact of the British campaign are denied an outright victory. It was the Japanese attack that finished the job and pitched the United States into war. Yet that pre-emptive attack is not wholly disconnected from the undeniable shift in US opinion during the years 1940 and 1941. As Britain's well considered approach moved American feeling and thereby allowed the sympathetic president Roosevelt to take

incremental steps to aid Britain—swapping destroyers for bases; granting lend-lease aid; escorting British convoys—US relations with the Axis powers deteriorated. In the summer of 1941, Roosevelt all but declared naval war on Germany with an order to shoot U-boats on sight, and the American public was in no mood to appease the Japanese in their attempts to secure their holdings in Asia. Resigned to American belligerence sooner or later, the Japanese opted to pre-empt matters and struck first. The rest is history.

All campaigns have their unintended consequences. Some of the positive notions of a new Britishness were swiftly disproved. In the autumn of 1942, Churchill made it clear that his Britain still hoped to retain its Empire and America's Anglophobia snapped back into play in some quarters. But other elements in the new British 'brand' endured. The BBC's reputation for truth-telling and balance endured to be built on in post-war broadcasting.

Less helpful was the durability of the idea that Britain had resisted the Blitz because of a specific quality of the British people. That idea implied that other people would behave differently under bombardment and inhibited the United States from learning what now seems to be the demonstrable fact: that all humans tend to work together under external bombardment, given a reasonably cohesive government structure around them.

The United States committed lives, material and political capital to the task of inflicting Blitz-style devastation on Germany, Japan and later North Vietnam, Iraq and the Belgrade of Slobodan Milosevic on the assumption that those country's citizens would somehow behave differently from Churchill's people and crumble under bombardment rather than rallying to their government.

Contemporary communicators can draw many lessons from Britain's campaign against US neutrality. The power of cultivating what would now be called 'the journalism of attachment' has seldom been clearer. The value of foregrounding the experience of children, of working with culture and empowering local partners became obvious, as did the resources that flowed from the pre-existing elite exchange programmes. No less significantly, the entire operation rested on an essential foundation of listening: investing substantial resources in close monitoring of what would now be called 'open sources' and especially the press. Yet the limits of public diplomacy and place branding are also apparent. Britain's messages had to be based on demonstrable facts for the shift of reputation to take effect: sage advice for any era.

Reference

Cull, Nicholas J., 'Pearl Harbor and public diplomacy: 70 years on' in *Place Branding and Public Diplomacy* (volume 8, Issue 1). Palgrave Macmillan, 2012.

Greek Crisis in Perspective: Origins, Effects and Ways-Out

Breaking the cycle: Nicos Christodoulakis explains the Greek economic descent and what the country must do to recover.

In the aftermath of the global financial crisis of 2008, several European countries were engulfed in a spiral of rising public deficits and explosive borrowing costs that eventually drove them out of markets and into bail-out agreements with the International Monetary Fund (IMF), the European Union (EU) and the European Central Bank (ECB). Greece was by far the most perilous case, with a double-digit fiscal deficit, an accelerating public debt which in GDP terms was twice the Eurozone average, and an external deficit near US$5000 per capita in 2008, one of the largest worldwide.

In the wake of an EU bailout and two elections the situation remains critical. Unemployment is rocketing, social unrest undermines the implementation of reforms and the fiscal front is not yet under control, despite extensive cuts in wages, salaries and pensions. The possibility of Greece exiting the Eurozone is widely anticipated.

Greece joined the European Union in 1980. Membership inspired confidence in political and institutional stability but fed uncertainties over the economy. After a long period of growth, Greece faced recession not only as a consequence of worldwide stagflation, but also because on its way to integration with the common market it had to dismantle its system of subsidies and tariffs. Soon after accession, many firms went out of business and unemployment rose for the first time in decades.

The government opted for fiscal expansion including underwriting ailing companies. The effect was predictable: a chronic haemorrhage of public funds without any supply-side improvements. Similarly, the expansion of demand simply led to more imports and higher prices. The external deficit approached 8% of GDP in 1985, a level at which several Latin American economies had collapsed. A stabilization programme in October 1985 involved a devaluation by 15%, a tough incomes policy and extensive cuts in public spending. The programme achieved a rise in revenues by beating tax-evasion practices and replacing less effective indirect taxes with the VAT system. Public debt was immediately stabilized, but the programme was opposed from within the government and was abandoned in 1988.

Despite looming deficits, in 1989 the coalition government decided to abolish prison sentences for tax arrears, which was taken as a signal of relaxed monitoring, thus effectively encouraging further evasion.

Another bizarre measure was to cut import duties for repatriates buying luxury cars, thus depriving the budget of badly needed revenues and leading to black-market abuses.

As a result, revenues collapsed and the country suffered a major fiscal crisis until a majority government elected in 1990 enacted a new stabilization programme.

Although Greece was a signatory of the Maastricht Treaty in 1991, it was far from obvious how or when the country could comply with the convergence criteria. Public deficits and inflation were at two-digit levels and there was great uncertainty about the viability of the managed exchange rate.

In May 1994, capital controls were lifted in compliance with European guidelines and this promoted fierce speculation. Interest rates rose sharply and the Central Bank of Greece exhausted most of its reserves to stave off speculation. This proved to be an incentive to join the European Monetary Union to ward off more attacks. Soon after the 'Convergence Program' set time limits to satisfy the Maastricht criteria and included a battery of reforms in the banking and the public sectors.

However, international markets continued to doubt exchange rate viability. With the advent of the Asian crisis in 1997 spreads rose dramatically and Greece finally chose to devalue in March 1998 by 12.5% and subsequently to enter the Exchange Rate Mechanism. The country was not ready to join the first round of Eurozone countries and was granted a transition to 1999 to comply with the convergence criteria.

After depreciation, credibility was enhanced by structural reforms and reduced state borrowing so that when the Russian crisis erupted in August 1998 the currency came under very little pressure. Public expenditure was kept below the peaks it had reached in the previous decade and was increasingly outpaced by the rising total revenues. Tax collection improved with the introduction of a scheme of minimum turnover on SMEs, eliminating a large number of tax allowances, by the imposition of a levy on valuable property and a reorganization of the auditing system. With the privatization of public companies, public debt fell to 93% of GDP in 1999. Although still higher than the 60% threshold required by the European Treaty, Greece was said to be on track 'to lean toward that level', a formula used by other countries to enter EMU.

Market reforms, introduced for the first time in 1986, aimed at modernizing the outmoded banking and financial system in compliance with European directives. A major reform in social security in 1992 curbed early retirement and excessively generous pension/income ratios.

Throughout the 1990s, reforms were aimed at restructuring public companies whose deficits had contributed to the fiscal crisis in 1989. State banks were privatized or merged, several outmoded organizations were closed down and initial public offerings (IPOs) provided capital and restructuring finance to several utilities. Other structural changes included the lifting of closed-shop practices in shipping, the entry of more players into the mobile telephone market and efforts to make the economic environment more conducive to entrepreneurship and employment.

After 2000, the reform process gradually slowed. Proceeds from privatization peaked in 1999, but subsequently remained low as a result of the contraction in capital markets after the dot.com bubble and the global recession in 2003.

An attempt in 2001 to reform the pension system led to social confrontation and was finally abandoned, to be replaced by a watered-down version a year later. Two other reforms followed in 2006 and 2010, but the social security system was still burdened by inequalities, inefficiencies and structural deficits.

Reform fatigue spread more widely after the Olympic Games in 2004. Since then, reforms have been concentrated on small-scale IPOs, with important exceptions being the sale of Greek Telecom and the privatization of the national air carrier.

Despite primary surpluses achieved throughout 1994–2002, public debt fell only slightly. There were three reasons. First, the government had to issue bonds to qualify for joining the Euro, a capital injection which led to an increase in public debt without affecting the deficit.

Second, after a military stand-off in the Aegean, Greece increased defence expenditure to well above 4% of GDP. In line with Eurostat rules, the burden was fully recorded in the debt statistics at the time of ordering, but only gradually in the current expenditure according to the actual delivery of equipment. This practice created a lag in the debt-deficit adjustment which was removed in 2004 when the government reverted to accounting at the date of ordering. Though a decision by Eurostat in 2006 made the delivery-based rule obligatory for all countries, Greece did not comply. The result was that deficits were augmented for 2000–04 and scaled back for 2005–06.

The third reason was the strong appreciation of the yen/euro exchange rate by more than 50% between 1999 and 2001, which increased Greek public debt on loans in the Japanese currency contracted during the 1994 crisis. To alleviate this, Greece entered a currency swap in 2001 by which the debt to GDP ratio was reduced by 1.4% in exchange for a rise in deficits by 0.15% of GDP in subsequent years, so that the overall fiscal position remained unchanged in present value terms. Although the transaction had no bearing on the statistics for 1999 on which EMU entry was assessed, critics mistook it as a ploy to circumvent a proper evaluation.

After the Eurozone became operational, hardly any attention was paid to current account imbalances of Greece or any other deficit country. It was only in the aftermath of the 2008 crisis that the European Union started emphasizing the adverse effects that external imbalances might have on the sustainability of the common currency.

The reason for this complacency was not merely that devaluations were ruled out by the common currency. A widespread view held that external imbalances were mostly demand-driven and, as such, they would sooner or later respond to fiscal adjustment. This proved to be misguided optimism.

The deterioration in the Greek current account accelerated after 2004 as domestic demand rose in the post-Olympics euphoria, inflation differentials with other Eurozone countries widened and the euro appreciated further. A similar erosion of competitiveness took place in *all* other European countries that are currently in bailout agreements (Ireland by 12% and Portugal by 8%) or considered to be at the risk of seeking one (Spain by 9% and Italy by 8%).

However, Greece was particularly vulnerable. Accelerating labour costs, the poor quality of the regulatory framework, corruption practices and weak government were all crucial in shaping productivity and competitiveness. These factors explain the poor performance of Greece in attracting foreign direct investment in spite of the substantial fall in interest rates and capital flows within the Eurozone. While FDI remained almost static, its composition changed with inflows directed to non-manufacturing sectors, notably to real estate. Investments in real estate boost aggregate demand, raise prices, cause the real exchange rate to appreciate and hinder competitiveness. These developments manifest a major failure of Greece—and for that matter of other Eurozone countries—to exploit the post-EMU capital flows in order to upgrade and expand production.

The fiscal decline started with the disappearance of primary surpluses after 2003 and culminated with rocketing public expenditure and the collapse of revenues in 2009. Revenues declined as a result of a major cut in corporate tax rate from 35% to 25% in 2005 and inattention to the collection of revenues.

It was becoming evident that stabilizing the economy was not a policy priority. Concerned over the rising deficits in 2007, the government sought a fresh mandate to redress public finances, but—despite securing a clear victory—no such action was taken. Only a few months before the global crisis erupted, the government claimed that the Greek economy was 'sufficiently fortressed' and would stay immune to international shocks. Even after 2008, the government hesitated to implement measures to stem fiscal deterioration or to expand public spending to fight off the prospect of recession. A compromise included a consumption stimulus at the end of the year, combined with a bank rescue plan of €5 billion and a pledge to raise extra revenues. The first two were quickly implemented, whilst the latter was forgotten.

Weakened by internal divisions, the government opted for a general election in October 2009 as a new opportunity to address the mounting economic problems. The fiscal consequences were stunning: total public expenditure was pumped up by more than 5 percentage points, exceeding 31% of GDP at the end of 2009. (In actual amount, it exceeded €62 billion, twice the size in 2003.) The rise was entirely owing to consumption, as public investment remained the same at 4.1% of GDP.

Total receipts in 2009 fell by another 4% of GDP as a result of widespread neglect in tax collection and emergency capitalization of Greek banks. The deficit was revised from an estimated 6.7% of GDP before the elections to 12.4% in October 2009, and finally widened to 15.4% of GDP by the end of the year.

Even then, the budget for 2010 included an *expansion* of public expenditure while *excluding* privatizations, rather than the other way around. Rating agencies downgraded the economy, sparking massive credit default swaps in international markets.

But instead of borrowing cheaply in the short term as a means of gaining time to redress the fiscal situation, the government continued to issue long maturities, despite the escalation of costs. This had dramatic consequences in the international markets where a Greek *liquidity problem*, having the cash to meet the next interest payments, became a *solvency problem*, a fear that Greece would never be able to repay its existing debt.

The borrowing capacity was further undermined when the ECB threatened to refuse collateral status for downgraded Greek bonds, fuelling fears that domestic liquidity would shrink and precipitating a capital flight from Greek banks. In early 2010, borrowing costs started to increase for both short- and long-term maturities, Greece had become a front page story worldwide and the countdown began. In April 2010 the government was financially exhausted and sought a bailout.

The global financial crisis in 2008 revealed that countries with sizeable current account deficits are vulnerable to international market pressures because they risk a 'sudden stoppage' of liquidity. As Krugman (2011) recently suggested, the crisis in the southern Eurozone countries had rather little to do with fiscal imbalances and rather more to do with the sudden shortage of capital inflows required to finance external deficits.

This explains why, immediately after the crisis, sovereign spreads peaked, mainly in economies with large external imbalances, such as Ireland, Spain, Portugal and the Baltic countries, which were under little or no pressure from fiscal deficits. It is worth noting that countries with substantially higher debt burdens, such as Belgium and Italy, experienced only a small increase in their borrowing costs at that time.

Since Greece had a dismal record on both deficits, its exposure to the credit stoppage soon became a debt crisis. The current account was in free-fall after 2006, when domestic credit expansion accelerated, disposable incomes were enhanced by tax cuts and capital inflows from the shipping sector peaked as a result of the global glut. The external deficit exceeded 14% of GDP in 2007 and 2008 but no warning was raised by any authority, domestic or European. In fact, the government acted pro-cyclically and decided to reduce surcharges on imported luxury vehicles, responding to the pleas of car dealers. This opened the way for the pre-electoral spree.

Two facts emerge. One is that in periods of recession counter-cyclical activism usually takes the form of increased consumption, not public investment, and this has detrimental effects on public and external deficits without contributing to higher growth. Another recurring characteristic is the propensity of governments to increase public spending and to tolerate lower revenues in elections years.

EU authorities were unprepared for the Greek problem and undertook action only when they recognized the risks it posed for the banking systems of other European states. A joint loan of €110 billion was finally agreed in May 2010 by the EU and the IMF to substitute for inaccessible market borrowing. The condition was that Greece was to follow a Memorandum of fiscal adjustments to stabilize the deficit and structural reforms to restore competitiveness and growth. In the event of success, Greece would be ready to tap markets in 2012 and then follow a path of lowering deficits and higher growth.

Faced with a deepening recession and a failure to produce fiscal surpluses sufficient to guarantee the sustainability of Greek debt, the European Union intervened twice to revise the terms of the Memorandum. In the first major intervention in July 2011, the amount of aid was increased by €130 billion and repayment extended over a longer period.

Crucially, the EU recognized the perils of recession and allowed Greece to withdraw a total amount of €17 billion from structural funds without applying the fiscal brake of national co-financing. The plan looked powerful, except for the typical implementation lags. The agreement was only voted through by all member-state parliaments in late September 2011 and the release of structural funds was approved by the European Parliament in late November. Participation in the Private Sector Involvement had reached only 70% of institutional holders amid speculation that post-agreement buyers of Greek debt from the heavily discounted secondary market were expecting a huge profit.

Thus, a new intervention looked inevitable and in October 2011 a revised restructuring was authorized, envisaging cuts of 50% of nominal bond value that would eventually reduce Greek debt by €100 billion. Greek debt was expected to be stabilized at 120% of GDP by year 2020. The agreement was hailed in Greece but euphoria turned sour when the government surprised everybody by seeking a referendum for its approval. In the ensuing furore, the decision was annulled, the prime minister resigned and a coalition was formed in November 2011 to implement debt restructuring and to negotiate terms for the new round of EU-IMF loans.

Routinely considered the habitual wrongdoer, especially when compared with the other countries (Ireland and Portugal) which are undergoing similar adjustment programmes, a Greek exit from the Eurozone started to attract attention both at home and abroad.

Although the complications and costs in the banking sector would be enormous, the exit of Greece could prove attractive to some European politicians who get angrier every time a new round of aid is discussed. However, they overlook the fact that a Greek exit would lead to an aggravation of the crisis. If the result was a two-tier model of Economic Governance, based on an inner core of surplus economies in the north and a weaker periphery in the south, competitiveness can only be restored by a so-called 'internal devaluation' of labour costs, thus perpetuating the gap that is already widening between the Eurozone countries.

For Greece, exit would trigger an economic catastrophe. As the entire Greek debt would remain in euros, the rapid depreciation of the new national currency will make its servicing unbearable and the next move will be a disorderly default. Isolation from international markets would drive away investors while the financial panic would drain domestic liquidity on a massive scale. The creditor countries of the EU would start demanding repayment of their aid loans, and this would soon deprive Greece of its claim on the EU cohesion funds. Tensions would produce further conflicts with EU agencies and the pressure to consider complete disengagement from the European Union would gain momentum.

The only option for Greece is to complete the fiscal adjustment and become reintegrated into the Eurozone as a normal partner. To gain credibility, Greece must achieve key fiscal targets quickly in order to be able to revise some of the pressing—although so far unattainable—schedules and ensure greater social approval. To ensure that there will be no spending spree in future elections, the best option for Greece is to adopt a constitutional amendment on debt and deficit ceilings, just as Spain did in September 2011, alleviating market pressures, at least for the time being.

Greece needs a fast-track policy for exiting the long recession. €17 billion could be routed immediately to support major infrastructural projects and private investment in export-oriented companies. The growth-bazooka should be followed by structural reforms and privatizations to attract private investment as market sentiment is restored. In addition, instilling growth will help to control the debt dynamics and reduce public deficits without ever-rising taxes.

The Greek economy has cumulatively shrunk by nearly 15% since 2008, social tensions are multiplying and the future of Greece in the Eurozone is in jeopardy. Some consider such an outcome as a due punishment for past excesses, while others see it as an escape from further unemployment and recession. Both are illusory. The only viable way out of the current crisis is to restore growth and to adopt a realistic plan for privatizations and reforms. The lesson of the past 2 years is that the deep recession will otherwise continue to hinder any exiting from the crisis. Greece, and perhaps other Eurozone countries, need a 'corridor of confidence', to use Keynes' famous phrase, in order to put things in order.

Nicos Christodoulakis is a professor at the Athens University of Economics and Business. He was the Greek Minister of the Economy and Finance between 2001 and 2004. During the Greek EU presidency in the first half of 2003 he was chair of the Euro group and the Economic and Financial Affairs Council (ECOFIN).

Reference

Blume, Lawrence E. and Durlauf, Steven N. (ed.), *The New Palgrave Dictionary of Economics (online edition)*. Palgrave Macmillan, 2013.

The Financial Crisis and Its Lessons

In his article *The financial crisis and the regulatory response: An interim assessment* Howard Davies asks if we have done enough to prevent history repeating itself.

There is nothing quite like a financial crisis to focus political minds on how we regulate our affairs. In times of economic calm, politicians are not much concerned with supervisory agencies. The subject bores them. There is far more interest in pork barrel spending Bills, or in going to war with a country without too many voters at home. Only when markets go into spasm, and the public authorities have to step in with their cheque books, do legislators bend their minds to the issues. At that point it becomes clear that 'something' must be done, and that 'something' is usually either a raft of legislation giving regulators new powers to secure the doors of all the empty stables, or structural reform, or a combination of the two.

How, then, should we judge the latest raft of reforms? We cannot answer this question without offering a view on how far regulation was at fault, and how significant regulatory failings were, in the run-up to the crisis. If 'human error' was at issue, then there is in principle no need to change the law or the institutional structures. Instead, we should change the people, and hope the new crew do better next time around.

Regulatory Failings Pre-1997

My view is that regulatory failings did play a part, but that those failings were by no means the only or the most significant factors. The crisis came about because global imbalances, combined with relatively loose monetary policy, created the conditions in which leverage expanded rapidly. The monetary authorities on both sides of the Atlantic focused attention on retail price inflation, and assumed that control of inflation was a sufficient condition to maintain financial stability. In that environment, the incentive structures within financial firms pushed them to take on greater risks. In some cases, senior management had a poor understanding of the risks they were taking on, blinded by the complexity of new and dangerous products. As a result, when asset prices began to fall, and a liquidity squeeze developed, a number of markets collapsed.

At that point it became clear that financial regulators had not been tough enough, particularly in their approach to capital reserving, to constrain risk-taking or to ensure that institutions were sufficiently robust to cope with a period of severe stress.

It is wholly unrealistic to expect regulation to be the front line defence against booms and busts. Monetary policy is a far more effective, though still imperfect, weapon in that fight. However, it is reasonable to expect regulators to act as speed bumps when the traffic is accelerating too rapidly. They did not perform that function.

Most regulators now accept that there was too little capital in the banking system, and especially that capital requirements in the trading books of the investment banks were far too light. The regime assumed the effectiveness of hedging strategies, which proved of little value as previous price relationships broke down. It also assumed continuous liquidity, an assumption that proved dramatically false in 2007. Regulators, as much as the banks, failed to identify the damage that could be done by a collapse of confidence in highly complex over-the-counter deals, which were extremely difficult to price, even in normal market conditions.

The failure of regulators to identify dangerous trends and to warn against them was shared with the boards of the international financial institutions. The IMF was particularly weak in that respect, proclaiming, until just before the crisis hit, its belief that risk transfer innovations had made the financial system more robust, and bank failures less likely. Although individual institutions warned against specific trends and imbalances—the Bank for International Settlements (BIS) can probably claim the best record in the pre-crisis years—no entity pulled the pieces of the jigsaw together.

Structural Weaknesses

These weaknesses point to some structural issues, two of which stand out. If we look at the pre-crisis global regulatory architecture, we see a spider's web of interlocking relationships—with the Financial Stability Forum, set up in the wake of the Asian financial crisis of the late 1990s, sitting awkwardly in the centre. But while the FSF included the heads of the international standard setters—the Basel Committee, International Organisation of Securities Commissions (IOSCO) and so on—it had no authority to tell them what to do or when to do it. Each of them operated to their own leisurely timetable, dictated by their reluctance to devote energy to international issues, rather than to domestic fire-fighting.

Thus, the Basel Committee spent over a decade producing the new capital rules known as Basel 2, even though serious flaws in the original Capital Accord had been identified. Draft after draft was produced, of ever greater complexity, but no one asked the big question of whether there was enough capital in the banking system overall. By the time the crisis hit, there was broad agreement on Basel 2, but the United States had not resolved to implement it, and various versions were in existence, many of them relying excessively on banks' own internal models to determine risk.

The second obvious flaw in the global architecture was the lack of representation of the developing world. The membership of the financial bodies was mainly G7-based, at a time when the centre of the world's economic gravity was shifting rapidly to the East. The Basel Committee provided perhaps the most egregious example. In 2006, 10 of its 13 members were from Europe, and the European Commission and the European Central Bank (ECB) also attended. The most recent addition to the Committee, 5 years earlier, had been Spain.

Important countries, notably China, were becoming reluctant to be 'price-takers', simply accepting standards set by others, on which they had not been consulted. That created the risk of uneven application of global standards.

There were structural flaws elsewhere, too. It was already clear that the EU was living uncomfortably in a halfway house. Since member states were reluctant to adopt common standards, most formal authority still rested with national regulators.

The weaknesses were soon revealed all too starkly. The Icelandic bank case was the first severe test. Iceland is not a full member of the European Union, but it is part of the European Economic Area (EEA). According to EU law, a bank authorised in any country of the EEA is entitled to take deposits in all other countries, without needing authorization from the host regulator. When they began to run short of funds to fuel their aggressive expansion, Icelandic banks chose to seek retail deposits in the United Kingdom and the Netherlands, by the simple expedient of offering deposit rates slightly higher than those of the competition. When the crisis hit, and the three big Icelandic banks were revealed to be seriously overextended, they were unable to refund those deposits, and the Icelandic central bank was too small to be able to help. Thus, British and Dutch taxpayers were the only effective source of compensation for depositors in a bank over which their own regulators had had no authority. They paid up to the tune of several billion pounds.

Europeans drew two opposing conclusions. Those inclined to favour greater European integration used the experience to argue that the system of mutual recognition, on which the single financial market was originally constructed, was no longer viable, and that a system of pan-European regulation was clearly needed. Sceptics took the opposite view, maintaining that the real lesson was the need for host regulators to have the power to reject incomers from elsewhere in the EEA. That would begin to dismantle the Single Financial Market. Hedging his bets somewhat, the Chairman of the FSA noted that the episode clearly showed that we needed either 'more Europe or less Europe', and that the status quo was not tenable.

The crisis also revealed structural problems or regulatory gaps in individual countries. The United States was an obvious case in point. Critics have pointed to the lack of regulation of the mortgage market, to the existence of a multiplicity of banking regulators creating scope for regulatory arbitrage, to dysfunctional disputes between the two securities regulators the SEC and Commodities and Futures Trading Commission (CFTC), and to the lack of a body charged with oversight of systemic risk. The Dodd-Frank Act has made headway in some of these areas, but it is too early to say how effective those changes will prove to be.

In the United Kingdom, an early challenge to the regulators was the failure of Northern Rock, an almost exclusively domestic mortgage bank. The authorities' initial response was hesitant and for the first time in 150 years there was a fully-fledged run on a bank, with queues of depositors outside branches trying to withdraw their funds. It was widely argued that the fault lay in the reforms carried out by the Labour government in the late 1990s, and especially in the removal of banking supervision from the Bank of England. There was a political dimension to this argument, of course, but it certainly did seem that the so-called Tripartite system, involving the Treasury, the Bank of England and the FSA, had worked poorly.

This catalogue of regulatory failure is depressingly long. In Germany tough questions have been asked about the oversight of regional banks. The Dutch Central Bank has been widely criticized for presiding over the almost total collapse of its banking system. However, I will limit myself to asking whether the reforms agreed so far are a sufficient response to the crisis.

Post-crisis Reforms

Global

If we begin with the structural changes, the first and most rapidly agreed change was the switch from the G7 to the G20 as the basis for membership of the key financial oversight bodies. It was so obvious that an adequate response to the crisis needed cooperation from the large surplus countries that the convening of a G20 summit by President Obama in December 2008 was accepted by all countries without demur. Changes in the membership of the FSF and the Basel Committee followed quickly, after the April 2009 summit.

There are those who argue that even this broader membership is inadequate. Joe Stiglitz and others have advocated a system built on more comprehensively global lines. However, it seems unlikely that further expansion will be agreed in the near future.

Will this broader membership contribute to making the financial system safer? It is hard to say. We do not know what the new countries want to achieve. So far, the signs are that China sees advantage in implementing tougher capital standards, and is committed to their enforcement. However, the Chinese are determined to exclude from the agenda discussion of currency misalignments and global imbalance. Thus, for now, I would view the expansion of membership as an overdue change, reflecting the new economic realities, but not one that will necessarily promote the coordination of macroeconomic policies which would help avoid a recurrence of the catastrophic events of 2007–2009.

Also at the London summit, the G20 agreed to strengthen the centre of the system, by renaming the FSF the Financial Stability Board (FSB). What's in a name? Not necessarily a great deal, but the G20 finance ministers look to the FSB to present progress reports on the reform agenda. That gives the Board some purchase on the standard-setters and others, and it is reasonable to believe that it has had an effect on the working practices of the Basel Committee, which produced a new capital regime, Basel 3, in little more than 10% of the time it took to gestate Basel 2.

However, the FSB remains an informal body. There is no treaty basis for its existence. Its chair is a part-timer. For 4 years, Mario Draghi was simultaneously Governor of the Bank of Italy. Its capacity for independent action is strictly limited. The commitment of some of its members, notably the United States, is doubtful.

The Council on Global Financial Regulation (CGFR), a group of former regulators, central bankers and academics (of which I am a member), has advocated reforms to strengthen the position of the FSB. Although the output of the FSB has been disappointing so far the weakness, in the opinion of the CGFR, is more the consequence of its uncertain status than of its structure. It remains the only body that includes representatives of all the agencies needed to coordinate effective action at global level. But the institutional backing is still lacking. One cannot therefore give this area of reform more than a modest grade so far.

We can be more optimistic about the changes under way as a result of the Basel Committee's supercharged work on Basel 3. They have produced a new framework, with far tougher requirements. Banks will in future be required to hold significantly larger capital reserves, and a larger proportion of those reserves must be in the form of tangible common equity.

The Committee has also proposed a new resolution regime, which aims to allow banks to be wound up without causing severe disruption to the wider economy. Systemic institutions must prepare 'living wills', or 'funeral plans'. However, the details remain sketchy and, as the Lehman case demonstrated, there remain many obstacles to a rational cross-border insolvency regime.

The framework also allows for a 'countercyclical buffer', an additional reserve, which might be varied depending on regulators' view of the state of the business cycle, or of potential misalignments of asset prices. In addition, for the largest banks, there is a kind of 'too big to fail' supplement.

These reforms will undoubtedly make the banking system safer. However, the behaviour of bank shares seems also to be telling us that they will markedly reduce its return on equity. That may be appropriate, as banks will in future look more like regulated utilities, with tight controls on capital and indeed on dividends.

But what of the impact on the cost of bank borrowing, and thereby on investment in the economy more generally, and on economic growth and job creation? On that crucial question, there is no consensus whatsoever. The Basel Committee has argued that the impact would be very modest indeed, and that growth would be less than half a per cent lower over 5 years. The OECD has estimated the impact at about twice that size. However, economists at the Institute of International Finance, the trade association for the biggest international banks, argue that growth will be fully 3% lower over 5 years. If they are right, this would prove to be a very costly reform indeed.

On the countercyclical question, while there is agreement on an additional capital buffer, we do not know how decisions on its implementation will be made. How do we assess when markets are out of line, or when credit growth is too rapid? It was the failure to react pre-emptively to credit expansion that contributed as much as anything to the bubble which burst so dramatically in 2007. And who is to assess the appropriate response? In principle, one can respond to excess credit growth by raising interest rates, or by lifting capital requirements by expanding the countercyclical buffer. However, the first response is the province of monetary policymakers, whereas the second is a matter for regulators. These may seem arcane arguments at a time when the Federal Reserve has promised to maintain short-term interest rates at close to zero for the foreseeable future, but 1 day the problem will arise again.

In principle, the FSB could take a view, but so far members have been reluctant to stray into that territory. In Europe, the European Systemic Risk Board, chaired by the President of the ECB, could do so, but interest rates remain the jealously guarded province of the ECB's Governing Council. In the United States, the new Financial Stability Oversight Council might opine, but once again control over interest rates lies elsewhere, with the Federal Open Market Committee. In the United Kingdom, there is a new Financial Policy Committee (FPC), sitting alongside the Bank of England's Monetary Policy Committee (MPC), but with very different membership and procedures. It is hard to escape the conclusion that these structural reforms have not resolved the problem. We will, as before, depend on the judgement of the individuals in positions of influence—some of them the same people as before.

European

In Europe it is difficult to be optimistic about the response to the 'more or less Europe' question. We are a long way short of a single European regulator, or even an optional federal regime for pan-European institutions, on the American model. We now have a European Banking Authority, a European Securities and Markets Authority (ESMA) and a European Insurance and Occupational Pensions Authority. But they are located in three different cities (London, Paris and Frankfurt), reflecting a purely political deal. That does not facilitate cross-authority coordination.

In addition, they are barely 'authorities' in the normal sense of the term. Their powers are quite limited. ESMA has direct authority over credit rating agencies, but with that exception these bodies operate through national authorities. They are charged with preparing, over time, a single European rule book, and they have the ability to arbitrate in the implementation of directives. However, we remain a long way from a federal system of regulation, and it is not even clear that the new arrangements would prevent a recurrence of the Icelandic bank problem.

This aspect of European integration has taken a back seat during 2011, as bigger issues relating to the future of the eurozone have come to the fore. Will the eurozone move towards a fiscal union, as many believed would be the inevitable consequence of the single currency? Will there be a eurozone finance ministry? Would that ministry issue eurozone bonds, guaranteed collectively by all governments? If these changes come to pass, and commentators increasingly see them as necessary to maintain the integrity of the euro itself, then the structure of financial regulation may come back onto the political agenda. My forecast would be that a genuinely pan-European system of regulation will eventually be set up, at least for major cross-border firms, and at least in the eurozone. That will pose an interesting challenge for the United Kingdom and other non-eurozone members. In the meantime, Europe has decided to lodge in yet another halfway house, although one slightly closer to the federal model.

Already we are seeing the drawbacks of yet another interim solution. In the summer of 2011, as the markets reacted badly to continued uncertainty about the recovery, and the weak fiscal positions of southern European countries, some countries wished to introduce short-selling bans and appealed to ESMA to organize a pan-European solution. ESMA was unable to do so, lacking the power to oblige any state to act against its own domestic preferences. Four countries wanted to go ahead with a ban: the rest did not.

Thus, that is what happened, and the four bans were themselves slightly but significantly different in form. That was not a positive omen for the future.

United Kingdom

The United Kingdom's reforms are still work in progress. In what is described as a 'new approach to financial regulation', the prudential functions of the FSA have been carved out into a new Prudential Regulatory Authority (PRA), which will be a wholly owned subsidiary of the Bank of England.

There is also a new Financial Conduct Authority, located in the Bank of England, and chaired by the Governor, whose role is to 'contribute to the Bank's financial stability objective by identifying, monitoring and taking action to remove or reduce systemic risks'. So there are now four entities likely to be involved in crisis management: the Treasury, the Bank of England, the PRA and the FCA, with the FPC sitting between them. The effectiveness of the arrangements will depend crucially on the skills and wisdom of the participants, rather than on the particular structure within which they work.

Conclusions

In the 4 years since the crisis erupted, much has been done to correct the regulatory flaws it revealed. For a time, it seemed that the political obstacles, which had bedevilled earlier attempts at reform, would be blown away. Thus, there was talk of a global body with genuine power to enforce regulations—a World Financial Authority.

Now, although the crisis is far from over, the grander ideas have disappeared from the agenda. Tentative moves to strengthen the central nervous system of global finance have been made, but they fall well short of a revolution. In the United States, there have been only modest structural changes, but a barely digestible wave of new legislation. In the EU, we have the 'form' of European-wide regulation in the three new authorities, but not the substance. In the UK, we have once again shuffled the regulatory pack, and put the Bank at the top of the pile, from which it had been dislodged a decade or so earlier. What goes around comes around.

So, has a good crisis been wasted? The wise commentator would say that it is too soon to tell. However, overall, it is hard to escape the conclusion that there has so far been less in the way of significant reform than meets the eye.

Reference

Davies, Howard, 'The financial crisis and the regulatory response: An interim assessment' in *International Journal of Disclosure and Governance (volume 9, Issue 3)*. Palgrave Macmillan, 2012.

The Reckoning

In his book *The Reckoning* Michael Moran explores the intricate nature of arguably the most important economic relationship in the world today.

The most important economic relationship in the world—that between the United States and China

—is widely regarded as a one-way street, benefiting China and undermining the United States. But this is a simplistic view. In fact, China's dependency on the American market and commercial innovations represents a huge vulnerability for Beijing as it makes its way toward the centre of the global stage. Along with its increasing dependence on imported energy, persistent internal unrest and a susceptibility to bouts of inflation, China's *pushmipullyu* relationship with America presents terrible dilemmas for Beijing's communist leadership.

In spite of the alarmist headlines, China's rise as an economic giant, and eventually a military and diplomatic competitor to American power, is taking place under terms that the United States can influence and even harness to its own advantage. But the United States, in the three decades since China opened its economy to capitalism and began its breakneck sprint toward world-power status, has failed to develop a coherent strategy to leverage these advantages—particularly in innovation, technology and intellectual creativity. Such a strategy would require Washington to invest heavily in its own economic and creative strengths, as well as adjust its military posture in the Pacific to accommodate Chinese interests without sparking conflict. It would also require Washington to insist on greater Chinese participation

in international diplomacy and peacekeeping, and prepare American allies in Asia for the realignment of power that looms ahead.

A deep freeze enveloped US–China ties after the 1989 Tiananmen Square massacre. Gradually, isolation gave way to a paternalistic approach as the United States offered 'rewards' like most-favoured-nation trade status or membership in the World Trade Organization (WTO) as incentives for China to continue opening its economy to competition. All of this made sense early on, when China's home market was largely closed to foreign products and foreign direct investment (FDI) was limited to joint ventures with state firms. However, the approach lost its effectiveness after China absorbed Hong Kong's dynamic banking sector and after increasing numbers of Chinese trained in US and other foreign universities returned to their homeland. Powered by the mix of long-term economic planning, first-class financial acumen and cheap credit, China's growth accelerated, and it became clear that its emergence as an economic giant would happen no matter what the West thought.

The exact shape of the 'new geopolitical order', however, remains unclear. Some view the United States and China as rival standard-bearers of competing ideologies—democratic market capitalism and repressive state capitalism—bound to clash in the twenty-first century just as fascism, communism and democracy did in the previous one. But clinging too fervently to this belief risks creating a self-fulfilling prophesy, particularly in a world where the balance of power in Asia and elsewhere is in transition, and where none of the old talking shops, from the United Nations to the Association of Southeast Asian Nations (ASEAN) to the Asia-Pacific Economic Cooperation (APEC), are ready to offer a credible forum for mediating disputes.

The issues that receive obsessive attention from each side—the undervalued Chinese currency, disputed territorial claims in the South China Sea and China's gradual modernization of its military—raise the risk of a sudden miscalculation that could have tragic global consequences. What's more, the black-and-white view of this relationship obscures the fact that the United States retains the upper hand militarily and economically.

Washington should be plotting a future based on the awesome strengths of American free society and economic productivity. Instead, it scapegoats China, its chief competitor, for striving to lift its population out of destitution. Since the 2008 financial crisis, the United States has acted like a football team that can only play defence. Case in point is the running dispute over China's currency, the renminibi (RMB), also known as the yuan. The People's Bank of China—the country's central bank—has kept the RMB low in order to maximize the competitiveness of Chinese products. The dispute pits those who think a strong RMB would make US manufactured goods more competitive globally against those who see it as a relatively small issue in a very complicated relationship.

The larger problem is not about exchange rates but 'global imbalances'—the fact that China's consumers save at enormous rates and consume little compared with the spend-crazy, credit-addicted West. Getting Chinese consumers engaged in the global economy would do far more to employ American workers than a readjustment of its currency rates. Rather than building a mountainous surplus based on export earnings that it ploughs into US Treasuries and other investments, China could be recirculating that money domestically and stimulating a consumer boom that would produce a positive effect for every major manufacturing power on earth.

Of course, there are enormous structural impediments to this readjustment—for instance, Chinese banks effectively operate as funnels, sucking up much of the savings in Chinese households and transferring them (via bank balance sheets) to the corporate-state sector, underwriting its investments in massive infrastructure and other projects, and keeping consumer spending weak. Reforms to this system, which barely figure in US-China joint communiqués, would mean that more Chinese-made products would stay in China, with fewer dumped cheaply into foreign markets.

But such subtleties are lost on American legislators. Rather than focusing on ways to maintain and extend the US lead in high-end manufacturing, US politicians have waged a doomed battle to protect manufacturing industries like textiles and furniture that stand no hope of supporting what the American workforce considers a decent life. As a result, Congress has pressured for an appreciation of the RMB to be the featured 'task' of recent US financial talks with the Chinese. Granted, the United States has also established an annual bilateral economic summit that attempts to broaden the conversation to such areas as energy and climate change, but with US jobless rates hovering near 9%, the pressure to scapegoat isn't letting up anytime soon. The 'all eggs in one basket' foolishness of this is clear, and the idea that China will relent given the potential cost to its fragile domestic stability seems unlikely.

Like all powers emerging from long periods of backwardness, China wants to make the most of its labour cost advantages while they last—something that giants of nineteenth-century American capitalism understood very well. The idea of fair play, which figures high in the rhetoric of contemporary American politicians, did not feature at all in the development of American capitalism's march to global dominance.

Imagine, now, a China run by a democratically elected government accountable to Chinese voters. Given the likelihood that an appreciation of the RMB would cause mass layoffs as foreign factories switch to other, even cheaper Asian producers like Bangladesh or Vietnam, any government claiming to act in the name of its citizens would resist outside pressure to allow the RMB to appreciate.

Meanwhile, neither the Chinese nor other foreign holders of US Treasuries are under any illusion about the ultimate aim of US policy: a covert devaluing of the US dollar, which would drastically reduce the value of the enormous investment China and other US creditors hold as their shares of the US national debt.

This lack of a 'grand strategy' in America's approach to China shows up in minor trade and commercial disputes. Recently, a bid by the Chinese telecommunications company Huawei Technologies to buy the American firm 3Leaf was dropped under pressure from the US Committee on Foreign Investment in the United States, a Cold War-era body founded to prevent sensitive technology from falling into Soviet bloc hands. In 2007, the same panel refused to allow Huawei to buy an Internet routing company, 3Com, which was ultimately purchased by US giant Hewlett-Packard instead.

There will be times when such actions make sense. Some of China's largest firms remain deeply entangled with the state and China's military. And not all of China's proposed investments rose to the level of political fights—China's Lenovo bought IBM's PC business in 2006, and the huge construction firm China State Construction Engineering Corporation is a major contractor on the reconstruction of the San Francisco Bay Bridge and has won contracts for work on New York City's subway and other large infrastructure projects.

But China's FDI in US corporations remains tiny—a paltry $791 million in 2009, compared with the over $43 billion invested in China by American firms that same year. With China's appetite for such investments likely to increase by up to eight times in the next decade, the United States would be foolish to continue warding off such money particularly given that these investments would help, over time, support US exporters and offset the enormous trade deficit the United States has been running with China for decades (amounting to $273 billion in China's favour in 2010).

China's great manufacturing complexes now dominate global markets across vast product lines, including appliances, consumer electronics and consumer durables like sporting goods, clothing, toys, furniture and textiles. Yet China lacks something that Trenton and its nineteenth-century peers had in spades: innovators. Even in 2010, the year China officially overtook Japan as the world's second largest economy, no Chinese brand could viably be called a household name in any Asian market, let alone in the wider world. Something is retarding China's transition from copycat manufacturer to innovative top dog. The kind of manufacturing that accounts for nearly all of China's export earnings relies on low-cost inputs, including labour, as opposed to the quality and technology that underpin an advanced economy's manufacturing sectors, notably in Japan, Germany and the United States. The combination of a nineteenth-century business model and a twenty-first-century pseudo-communist political repression does not foster a climate of original innovation.

The problem might be solved in the long term by investment in R&D and reforms to China's economic incentives and education system—indeed, Japan suffered from precisely these problems early on in its emergence from the depths of destruction after World War II into a postwar economic powerhouse. But economists also suspect that the centralized nature of China's government will prove a lasting hindrance, allowing the United States and other advanced economies to maintain their lead in high-tech goods for far longer than might otherwise be the case.

This underscores a deeper dilemma. China's brute strength in manufacturing is based on the simple, and possibly unsustainable, deal that the Communist Party made with its urban elites—it will keep incomes rising and leave the urban elites alone to make money as long as they keep their political aspirations to themselves. But as more and more Chinese in the vast, poor interior clamour for their own piece of the pie, wages will rise and demands for safety and environmental codes will erode competitiveness. When this happens and jobless workers get angry, the urban elites may renege on the deal for a greater say in their own government. Even then, the rural millions may not have much patience left.

China is by no means doomed to remain a smokestack power. Increasing investment in science, technology and other innovation sectors, currently about 1.5% of the GDP, puts China at the top of the table among emerging economies in terms of R&D spending, and fourth overall behind only the United States, Japan and Germany. But the country's mediocre higher educational system, demographic and political challenges and corruption suggest that this will be more of a Long March than a Great Leap Forward.

Take the problem of demography. China certainly cannot be described as suffering from a shortage of people, but it is suffering from an acute shortage of a certain generation of people, thanks to its enforcement of one-child population control policies since 1979. China has enjoyed a larger 'demographic dividend' (extra growth as a result of the high ratio of workers to dependents) than its neighbours. But the dividend is near to being cashed out. Between 2000 and 2010, the share of the population under 14—future providers for their parents—slumped from 23% to 17%. China now has too few young people, not too many. China has around eight people of working age for every person over 65. By 2050 it will have only 2.2. Japan, the oldest country in the world, now has 2.6. China is getting old before it has got rich.

The US figure, according to Census Bureau projections, is 3.7 workers per retiree—and the trend will go gently upward. Indeed, of the countries that will rank as the world's largest economies later in this century, only the United States, Brazil and Turkey have managed to avoid acute 'dependency ratio' problems. For the United States, a relatively high birth rate and a much more open approach to immigration have saved it from the worst of the crisis.

In 2011, the Boston Consulting Group (BCG) reported that, owing to a number of changing economic realities—including rising salaries and economic expectations among Chinese workers, new labour, environmental and safety regulations abroad, the higher price of energy affecting transportation costs, and the US market and the uncertainties of political risk in these places—the cost benefits of producing in Asia no longer automatically outweigh the risks. Indeed, the BCG report predicts a 'renaissance for U.-S. manufacturing' as labour costs in the United States and China converge around 2015. Anecdotally, the effects can already be seen in new plants created in the United States and in some instances in which plants set up abroad a generation ago to leverage lower labour costs have relocated back to America.

If the main factors in these decisions were labour costs and the weak dollar, the victories would be Pyrrhic. 'Inputs'—energy, transportation, raw materials and other production costs—will fluctuate. But the decisive advantages include innovative management and production techniques, savings on transportation costs, lower political risk and corruption, and the productivity and relatively high skill levels of the American workforce.

The US economy, with its potent, creative corporate sector; transparent bureaucracy; world-beating universities; and highly skilled labour force, does not have to bow down in surrender to China. It can compete and adjust to the arrival of China and to the billion-odd other middle-income workers being added to the global economy in other emerging-market countries by stretching its lead in high-end, knowledge-based commerce. The true danger for the United States does not lie in predatory Asian sweatshops. Instead, danger lies in bumbling, for political reasons, into an overtly hostile stance that puts the world's two most powerful nations on course for a war so terrible that no nation, regardless of its choice of economic or political models, would survive it.

Reference

Moran, Michael, *The Reckoning. Debt, Democracy, and the Future of American Power*. Palgrave Macmillan, 2012.

Corruption

Corruption in government and business is widespread. But the tide is turning. Nick Kochan and Robin Goodyear explain what is being done to enforce minimum standards in their book *Corruption*.

As a proportion of world trade, the value of bribes is phenomenal. The World Bank estimates that more than US$1trn. in bribes are paid each year, amounting to 3% of the world's economy.

High-profile cases involving major companies have turned the spotlight on the extent to which bribery distorts global markets and destroys communities. With campaigning groups voicing demands for greater transparency, the corporate world is under growing pressure to adopt anti-corruption practices.

Transparency International (TI) is the foremost activist group in the field. This non-governmental organization (NGO) has chapters in over 90 countries. Founded in Berlin in 1993 by Peter Eigen, a former regional director of the World Bank, TI campaigns to promote transparency in elections, public administration, procurement and business, while lobbying governments to bring about change. The organization also develops and distributes practical guidance to help businesses operate ethically.

Its biggest achievement so far has been to raise awareness in governments, business and the general population—in its own words, to 'challenge the inevitability of corruption'. TI is best known for its annual Corruption Perceptions Index, a worldwide survey that ranks countries according to the level of corruption in public life. TI also publishes a Bribe Payers Index and, since September 2010, a Global Corruption Barometer, the only worldwide public opinion survey on corruption. TI has been directly involved in international anti-corruption agreements; it played a major part in establishing the Organization for Economic Cooperation and Development (OECD)'s Anti-Bribery Convention and in drafting the United Nations Convention against Corruption and the African Union Convention on Preventing and Combating Corruption.

Also established in 1993, Global Witness (GW) is an NGO based in London and Washington, D.C. It is an environmental group concerned with detecting and exposing the corruption and social problems associated with the exploitation of natural resources. The group campaigns for financial transparency as a way to expose corrupt relationships.

According to GW, in 2008 exports of oil and minerals from Africa were worth roughly £242bn. (US$393bn.)—over ten times the value of exported farm products (£23bn./US$38bn.) and nearly nine times the value of international aid (£27bn./US$44bn.). If used constructively this wealth could lift millions of people out of poverty. However, the main benefits of resource extraction are diverted by political, military and business elites in producer countries, and oil, mining, timber and other companies overseas.

The growing importance of transparency in government and business is illustrated by Publish What You Pay, a global network of over 600 civil organizations that lobby for disclosure in the extractive industries. Transparency is also a principal concern for the Center for Public Integrity, an independent investigative organization whose mission is concerned with the interaction between private interests and government officials and its effect on public policy.

The internet has provided a new way for people to tell their stories of corrupt practices. Websites such as www.ipaidabribe.com expose corruption at the grassroots level while at the same time providing a forum for discussion on how best to counter demands for bribes. Public resentment of corruption is expressed through social initiatives such as Bribebusters in India, currently piloted by lawyer and entrepreneur Shaffi Mather. Individuals and companies can hire Bribebusters, for a fee, to act on their behalf. Mather is particularly keen to combat individual demands for bribes, such as street vendors paying officials or drivers stopped for traffic offences paying police officers: It might be a small amount that each individual has to pay, but . . . there are multiple studies that estimate the bribes paid in 18 common services such as electricity, water and civic services . . . are around $4.5 bn. And we're not talking about the big scams or scandals, these are just bribes paid by the common man in his daily life.

Local schemes are complemented by organizations representing global business such as the International Chamber of Commerce, which has adopted a programme to combat bribery.

Domestic Responses with International Implications

Two pieces of legislation with international implications are the 1977 US Foreign Corrupt Practices Act (FCPA) and the 2010 UK Bribery Act.

These laws are feared by businesses because of their extraterritorial jurisdiction and potential for aggressive interpretation. The US FCPA, for example, though restricted to US citizens and nationals or those whose principal place of business is within the United States, is expanding to bring in more corporates. The UK Bribery Act has, potentially, an even wider reach; a Serious Fraud Office official explained that, 'In practice, a company registered anywhere in the world and having a part of its business in the UK could be prosecuted for failing to prevent bribery on its behalf wherever in the world

that bribe is paid.' Though recent guidance has excluded foreign companies whose only business in the United Kingdom is a stock exchange listing from the reach of the Bribery Act, businesses are taking the Act seriously because it marks a trend in corruption legislation by introducing a new corporate responsibility. Previously, 'knowledge' (however narrowly or widely interpreted) had been a key component in determining corporate liability for bribery. Robert Amaee, former head of the Serious Fraud Office (SFO)'s anti-corruption team, explains how the UK Bribery Act changes the rules of the game:

> The new Act sweeps away this requirement and introduces a new corporate offence of failing to prevent bribery. This is a novel concept under English law and one which we are likely to see more of in the years to come. It makes a commercial organization criminally liable if one of its employees, agents or subsidiaries bribes another person, intending to obtain or retain business or an advantage in the conduct of business for the company.

Legal firm McDermott Will & Emery suggests that national legislation such as the UK Bribery Act will drive up standards in company policy. The Bribery Act's broad scope, harsh penalties and narrow defences may be seen as a harbinger of other minimum standards for businesses.

Transnational Initiatives

Fighting corruption is often on the agenda at summits, for example at the G8 and G20. The thrust of the argument is that corruption is a global evil and that countries need to coordinate their efforts. Links between terrorist financing and money laundering have accelerated transnational attempts to address a whole range of financial misconduct.

In the EU Procurement Directive of 31 March 2004, Article 45 regulates the supply of goods and services to government bodies by companies and individuals. The Directive requires EU member states, for the first time, to exclude companies and individuals convicted of corruption from being awarded public procurement contracts.

Governments in other regions have also pledged to crack down on bribery. Twenty-five countries have now adopted the 1996 Inter-American Convention Against Corruption, which criminalizes the paying or accepting of bribes by public officials. The Association of Southeast Asian Nations (ASEAN) is also taking increased interest in tackling corruption, particularly in relation to 'gifts' to public officials.

In Africa, the New Partnership for Africa's Development (NEPAD) has started to focus more closely on corruption and how it adversely affects poverty relief. The 29 countries that signed its memorandum of understanding are committed to 'just, honest, transparent, accountable and participatory government and probity in public life'. Recognition in African governments of the impact of corrupt politicians is illustrated by the transnational African Parliamentarians' Network Against Corruption (APNAC), which works to 'strengthen parliamentary capacity to fight corruption and promote good governance'. In Dec. 2001, the 15 members of the Economic Community of West African States (ECOWAS) signed the Protocol on the Fight against Corruption, which requires all signatories to criminalize the paying and receiving of bribes, and provides an international cooperation framework to improve mutual law enforcement and facilitate asset confiscation.

The OECD has been increasingly active on corruption and bribery, particularly since 1997 when an OECD Convention established 'legally binding standards to criminalize bribery of foreign public officials in international business transactions', along with monitoring and enforcement measures to make it effective. It is the first and only international anti-corruption agreement to focus on the 'supply side' of the bribery transaction. While it has no direct powers of enforcement, the 38 signatories to the Convention commit themselves to enforcing this expression of intent through domestic legislation.

The OECD Working Group on Bribery in International Business Transactions is responsible for monitoring the implementation and enforcement of the 1997 Convention, in addition to the more recent 'Recommendation for Further Combating Bribery of Foreign Public Officials in International Business Transactions' and other related instruments. The OECD's country reports detailing the current state of anti-bribery measures, and data collected from participating countries, are available on its website (www.oecd.org).

The OECD has also played a role in attempting to improve the anti-corruption regimes of specific geographic regions. To date, 28 countries have endorsed a joint plan by the Asian Development Bank/OECD

Anti-Corruption Initiative for Asia and the Pacific, which aims to set minimum standards and safeguards to prevent corruption and bribery.

The growing consensus that corruption is a threat to development is evident in other policy initiatives at the highest level. After Resolution 55/61 in 2000, the United Nations Convention Against Corruption entered into force in Dec. 2005 with 145 signatories, stressing the importance of the principles of prevention, criminalization, international cooperation and asset recovery in countering the threat of corruption.

The UN Global Compact

Corporate social responsibility (CSR) initiatives reveal commitment from major companies to combat corruption. However, not all the principles lauded by the United Nations have received equal attention. This is changing rapidly. The UN Global Compact, a strategic policy initiative comprising 5300 businesses and six UN agencies, describes itself as the 'world's largest corporate citizenship and sustainability initiative'. The network aims to place ten universal principles into business philosophy and everyday operation including 'action against corruption in all its forms'.

Business Attitudes to Bribery

Some Western companies dismiss corrupt practices as intrinsic to the culture of certain countries, especially in the developing world. Bribery is seen as a necessary evil or as an informal tax on operating in certain regions. Faced with deliberate stalling by corrupt officials or simply with inefficient public administrations, corporations might turn a blind eye to the activities of their agents or subsidiaries in an effort to speed up transactions.

Despite an increase in the number of companies striving to eliminate corruption, the necessary cultural shift has not yet occurred. Thus the consequences of the UK Bribery Act might come as a shock to many boards. For example, when the Financial Services Authority (FSA) investigated 17 wholesale insurance intermediaries operating in the London market it found that they have:

> approached this area of their business far too informally (especially higher-risk business) and that, at present, many firms would not be able to demonstrate that they have in place adequate procedures to prevent bribery.

FSA concerns are echoed by other research. Over a third of respondents to a TI survey in 2010 thought that City of London businesses perceive bribery as standard procedure in some environments, and a survey by a City law firm showed that 20% of City businesses had no policy in place to address corrupt practices. These findings are not unique to British companies. All businesses that operate in a competitive environment may have an interest in tacitly condoning bribery in pursuit of profit.

Cultural Attitudes to Bribery: It's Just How Things Are Done

Some forms of the Chinese concept of 'guanxi', defined as ongoing 'relationships between or among individuals creating obligations for the continued exchange of favours', are closely associated with bribery and corrupt public officials; in other countries, this may be known as 'blat', 'bakshish' or 'relationship marketing'. In light of the extraterritorial jurisdiction of the UK Bribery Act, much effort has gone into determining the extent to which 'one culture's favour is another's bribe'.

Despite Lord Woolf's dismissal of the claim that competitors benefit from robust anti-corruption procedures as a thin excuse 'made for not doing things that you know you should', there is evidence to suggest that (in the short term at least) it is not unfounded. It is estimated that from 1977 to 2004 American companies lost 400 major contracts because of bribes given by competitors to foreign government officials. From a superficial perspective, bribery can be perceived as a good thing by maintaining market dominance and increasing efficiency for a particular company. But there are strong reasons against turning a blind eye to corruption, however it is dressed up.

Research tends to focus on the economic consequences of bribery in the countries in which it is received, rather than on the consequences of being caught paying bribes. This is a serious omission, as it is clear that this impact can be grievous. The news that a firm or subsidiary is being prosecuted, or has been convicted of bribery, can damage the share price. In late 2010, shares in Panalpina dropped 4.1% on the news of its admission of guilt in a deferred prosecution agreement concerning the bribery of officials in at least seven countries. According to Sam Eastwood, a partner with lawyers Norton Rose:

As international anti-corruption policies impact increasingly on global companies and their dealings with other companies, a dynamic of 'corporates policing corporates' is beginning to emerge. In order to protect themselves from liability, commercial organizations are increasingly requesting details of the anti-corruption policies and procedures of the companies with which they enter into business. This means that commercial organizations are becoming increasingly concerned with compliance with the Bribery Act and other jurisdictions' anti-corruption legislation, even if those laws do not directly apply to them.

The 2010 UK Foreign Bribery Strategy states that the government will actively support 'transparent companies with robust anti-corruption procedures' in order to 'ensure that ethical business will not be undercut by unscrupulous competitors or disadvantaged in access to [government] support'. Demonstrating a robust bribery risk management strategy will surely become an essential component of all corporate bids for government contracts.

Disbarment for a period of years from tendering for future lucrative contracts can have serious consequences. The German construction company Lahmeyer International suffered severe losses after it was banned from tendering for 7 years for World Bank-funded projects after a conviction for bribery in South Africa. The World Bank's Sanctions Committee found that Lahmeyer engaged in corrupt activities by bribing the Lesotho Highlands Development Authority's Chief Executive.

While in some cases debarring is discretionary and might be avoided if promises to rectify the situation are made (for example, with World Bank contracts), in others (for example, under the European Union Procurement Directives), a purchasing body must exclude from tendering any company that has been convicted of corruption. The risk of mandatory disqualification from tenders is something boards need to take seriously.

Countries, as well as companies, that acquire a reputation for receiving bribes are also damaged. The developing country that is so stigmatized will jeopardize its eligibility to receive future aid payments. The Millennium Challenge Corporation only gives aid to those states that are judged to be implementing principles of good governance, which includes an evaluation of their control over corruption. The UK investigation into BAE's activities in Saudi Arabia and elsewhere damaged the country's reputation for transparency.

The reputation for corruption serves as a bar on any form of business activity. Individuals with a reputation for corruption will be excluded from the job market. They will also burn their bridges with influential public officials. Companies perceived as corrupt may be precluded from tendering for lucrative contracts. Developing nations' governments have particular reason to fear being deemed corrupt; a reputation as a country where bribery of public officials is encouraged or tolerated does nothing to help attract foreign direct investment and international aid.

Reference

Kochan, Nick and Goodyear, Robin, *Corruption: The New Corporate Challenge*. Palgrave Macmillan, 7

Us Before Me

Poverty is a global problem of enormous magnitude. In her latest book *Us Before Me*, Patricia Illingworth explores the scope of the problem and the role of the individual in overcoming it.

Poverty is a global problem of enormous magnitude. According to the World Bank, 1.4 billion people live on $1.25 or less a day. Over 1 billion people in developing countries have inadequate access to water and 2.6 billion lack basic sanitation. Not only is there extreme poverty worldwide, there is also vast inequality. The wealthiest 20% of the world's population control 76% of the world's goods while 80% have what remains.

There is global homelessness as well. There are over 26 million internally displaced persons living in about 52 countries across the globe. In addition, there are over 10 million refugees. In a world of plenty, we do not care enough about other people to provide for their basic needs, despite the existence of human rights to food, shelter and medicines.

Sometimes we don't help others because we think it is morally wrong to do so. Some people believe they shouldn't help because it is not their responsibility to help; it is the responsibility of another person. Or they may believe that people should take personal responsibility for their own misery. Some people, such as those with 'donor fatigue', are weary of helping. But very often people don't help others because they are indifferent to the suffering and misery of other people or are simply preoccupied with their own affairs. They don't care.

It would be wrong to suggest that people never help others. People are especially attentive to their families, friends and—sometimes—communities. In some jurisdictions, people are required by law to help those with whom they have a close relationship, such as a child or spouse. People come to the aid of others when there is a highly publicized disaster. But given the persistence of severe poverty, there is much more that people could and should do. People need to *care* more about others. Unfortunately, care and concern for others is not the kind of emotion one can produce at will, or upon command.

Caring behaviour seems to arise among people who interact with one another. To build concern for others, the norm of self-interest needs to be counteracted with a new norm that shifts the focus from 'me' to 'us'. As the normative world now stands—in the West, at least—liberty, autonomy, self-determination, privacy, self-interest and sovereignty come together to shield people from the harm they cause others, directly and through their institutions, making them morally complacent and indifferent.

Pro-social norms are needed to transform the current culture of self-interest and indifference to one committed to helping others. Helping others, whether it is shovelling an elderly neighbour's snow, donating money to Oxfam, inventing drugs for neglected diseases or working with AIDS patients in Africa, needs additional support from ethics. With a moral commitment to build social capital people may come to be more fully engaged in local and global communities. They may be less tempted to analyze their generosity in terms of self-interest, but might instead celebrate it as an example of their desire to help the less fortunate and build strong communities. Additionally, if the data of social psychology is accurate, they will probably also be happier.

People are drawn to those whom they perceive to be similar to themselves. People may feel safe with like people. Trust is strengthened when there are frequent face-to-face interactions. It is also not surprising that social capital flourishes in homogeneous communities. People gravitate to communities where there are like people. Proximity helps here. But surely with rapid transit and communication, it is now possible to encourage face-to-face interactions among people from many places.

The potential to forge a new 'global' identity may be aided by changing demographics. There is growing evidence that racial, national and cultural classifications are changing, and that a mixed race identity is far more common than in the past. In the United States, for example, the number of Americans who count themselves as mixed race is changing dramatically due to increased immigration and intermarriage over the last two decades. At present, one in seven marriages in the United States is either interracial or interethnic. Those with mixed backgrounds have a 'fluid sense of identity', and reject the idea that they must choose one racial identity over another.

Both international personal relationships and international business relationships create and depend on global social capital. Individuals have international friendships and family and may belong to international organizations. International business networks are widespread and growing. They include not only transnational enterprises but also contractual and commercial networks. Global governance organizations such as the United Nations, World Bank, International Monetary Fund, General Agreement on Tariffs and Trade, and World Trade Organization all create and rely on extensive global social capital, as do the countless number of NGOs that exist worldwide. Most of these networks involve face-to-face interactions but internet networks and email are often used to sustain social capital in transnational interactions.

Social capital's global dimension is enormously important. Today, more than at any other time in history, international relations have the potential for great benefit, especially for the most vulnerable people in the world.

With a Little Help from the Law

For the most part, laws that foster generalized reciprocity will be helpful in sustaining social capital. When law encourages people to act for the sake of others, it nurtures social capital. When it encourages them to act for people who may not reciprocate, it nurtures generalized reciprocity. When the law encourages inclusion rather than exclusion, integration rather than segregation, it creates the social structures necessary for social capital.

Because international law is based on negotiation, cooperation and consent, it relies on transnational social capital and constitutes an opportunity to create social capital. Nations must interact with one another in order to come to agreements. To this end, they build countless networks. The need for agreements, which will support treaties, creates networks and trust as different countries collaborate to find mutually agreeable arrangements. Negotiation involves the kind of give and take that creates trust.

This process of cooperation is strongest in multilateral agreements. Prior to the General Agreement on Tariffs and Trade, bilateral agreements, which invite power exchanges to win privileges, were dominant. They often lead to conflict among trading partners. In contrast, a multilateral approach, combined with Unconditional Most Favored Nation status, as adopted by the World Trade Organization, treats all trading partners alike and invites cooperation. In an ideal world, if we want to use global giving as a way to cultivate global social capital we would encourage people to build networks with people from other countries, perhaps cultivate a more expansive identity so that they see themselves as members of a wider world.

The more people travel, study, work and marry abroad, the more they are likely to want to contribute directly to distant countries and to control where their money goes. As they learn more about the world, experience some of the deprivations of the world as deprivations of *their* global community, their desire to give globally is likely to grow, and with that, social trust and global social capital.

It is difficult for human beings to watch people suffer. Shifting our moral focus to *us* brings people who were previously invisible, whether the distant poor or the local homeless, within our range of vision, making it easier to treat them morally. It is much harder to be indifferent to the suffering of those with whom we are connected than to those with whom we have no connection. A moral duty to promote social capital underscores the moral value of connection to others. Being mindful of the moral obligation to create global social capital will be an important step toward realizing our global obligations and creating global social justice.

Reference

Illingworth, Patricia, *Us Before Me. Ethics and Social Capital for Global Well-Being*. Basingstoke/New York Palgrave Macmillan, 2012.

The Iron Brand

Nicholas J. Cull assesses the impact of Margaret Thatcher as an international communicator.

Margaret Thatcher's tenure as Prime Minister was a milestone in the evolution of political communication in Britain. Unlike her predecessors, she was closely tutored to make the best of television. She worked closely with leading lights in the British advertising industry to develop a string of potent messages for the 1979 general election. Her press secretary was an essential member of her team. Her advisers believed in the necessity to control messages and this was never as clear as during the 1982 Falklands/Malvinas war when the British government was able to limit reporting and thereby establish a model of media control. The United States adopted the model for its operations in Grenada, Panama and the first Gulf War. Thatcher's government worked equally hard to control the news from Northern Ireland. Thatcher understood terrorism as a form of communication and (borrowing a metaphor from the Chief Rabbi of the day) spoke of the need to deny the terrorist the 'oxygen of publicity'. The policy involved heavy-handed treatment of the British media including a broadcasting ban on the transmission of the voices of terrorists on British airwaves. News organizations were obliged to hire actors to quote paramilitary spokesmen.

Thatcher was a powerful voice for Britain. Her famous tag of 'Iron Lady' was in itself a testament to her international impact, being generated by a Soviet military newspaper in January 1976 in response to a confrontational speech. She immediately embraced the soubriquet as a badge of honour. Her abrasive style was not always welcome, particularly in the European Union where she was inclined to lecture her opposite numbers. Yet she raised the profile of her country in world affairs. As Simon Anholt has put it she, like Churchill before her and Blair after her, 'paid the rent' on the UK's international profile. Margaret Thatcher was impossible to ignore. She certainly made an impact on the newly democratic countries of Eastern Europe. For them she was the voice of freedom, an essential element in the final phase of the West's ideological assault on the Communist Bloc. Her rhetorical legacy in the other great democratic battles of the era is less clear. South Americans recall her support for the Pinochet regime in Chile. South Africans remember her opposition to the application of sanctions against the Apartheid regime and jibes against the 'terrorists' of the African National Congress.

Her wider contribution to British public diplomacy is mixed. While Thatcher's American analogue, Ronald Reagan, ushered in something of a golden age in American public diplomacy—expanding the budget for international engagement, boosting exchanges, modernizing Voice of America and launching multiple initiatives to promote democracy—the same cannot be said of Thatcher. The Foreign Office launched its Chevening Scholarship programme on her watch (1983) but there were few other major initiatives. The Westminster Foundation for Democracy, which built on Thatcher's commitment to democratization around the world, did not appear until 1993. It was an era of soldiering on.

The British Council spent a decade scrambling for resources. The BBC World Service was sucked into the Thatcher government's cuts. The White House archives from the time of President Jimmy Carter include an appeal from the BBC via the US embassy in London for the US to beg the new Prime Minister Thatcher not to cut the World Service budget by 30%. There were some backward steps in the fields of dialogue and cultural exchange. The Thatcher period saw Britain's withdrawal from UNESCO in protest against alleged mismanagement. It was a low point in the UK's international cultural relations.

Thatcher's public diplomacy was strongest in her defiance of Soviet hegemony in Eastern Europe. Star turns included the BBC Russian service's DJ, Seva Novgorodtsev. Another notable campaign was directed at the United States to contest the negative publicity around the Northern Ireland conflict. Tactics included upgrading the press relations apparatus originally established in the Second World War to ensure that the major consulates across the USA had resident experts on Northern Ireland. These spokesmen were regularly rotated through visits to the province and were hence equipped with the authority of recent first-hand experience. In concert, the Thatcher government channeled a flood of material unrelated to Northern Ireland across the Atlantic—making excellent use of the new British Council office in Washington DC, royal visits and the blockbuster show 'Treasure Houses of Britain' which displayed masterpieces from British country houses. The effort succeeded in preventing Britain being branded by the troubles. In retrospect this was probably a mixed blessing. Britain might have done better to have listened to the international concern over the troubles rather than drowning it out. The day was to come when the UK had to negotiate with terrorists. Meanwhile, a further round of violence kept the issues alive.

While the Thatcher period did not revolutionize representation of Britain it is possible to see the Blair-era interest in Britain's image as an extension of the Thatcher era. The 'New' Labour Party with its fixation on the power and priority of image had learned much from Thatcher. Yet just as Thatcher played a part in shaping public diplomacy, public diplomacy was critical to the image of Margaret Thatcher.

At the beginning of her career Margaret Thatcher was, by her own account, profoundly shaped by public diplomacy: that of the United States. In 1967 she was a rising star of the Conservative opposition backbenches. Although getting noticed for her spirited forays into financial affairs she had no experience in international matters and displayed no urgency to acquire any. Her approach to conservatism was patriotic and parochial. At this point the public diplomacy team at the US embassy selected her for a six- week 'international visitor program' tour to meet US opinion leaders. Her visit included a meeting with White House adviser Walt Rostow and a visit to NASA's Mission Control in Houston. Looking back on the experience in 1995 she commented: 'the excitement which I felt has never really subsided. At each stopover I was met and accommodated by friendly, open, generous people who took me into their homes and lives and showed me their cities and townships with evident pride'. It was a personal revelation and began a personal journey of ideological convergence between her take on British conservatism and the reinvigorated American conservatism. Her view of America certainly stood in contrast to that of her predecessor as leader of the Conservative Party, the Europhile Edward Heath, who had been an Atlantic sceptic since his own first visit to the US as a student debater in

1938. The result was that when the American swing to the right reached the White House in the form of Ronald Reagan, its British equivalent was already in place and open to collaboration. It was a handsome payoff for a tiny investment back in 1967 and one which US diplomats have not been slow to trumpet in the years since.

What then is the bottom line? That Thatcher shaped and was shaped by public diplomacy is a testament to the significance of both. She made the image of Britain overseas as surely as last year's Diamond Jubilee or the London Olympics. Not everybody approves of Margaret Thatcher and there has been a fierce debate over her legacy. But this has served to remind the world that Britain remains a country in which people expect to have a say, however controversial. Britain's first woman prime minister would have approved.

Reference

Cull, Nicholas J., 'The Iron Brand: Margaret Thatcher and public diplomacy' in *Place Branding and Public Diplomacy* (volume 9, Issue 2). Palgrave Macmillan, 2013.

Opening Windows of Opportunity

Nicholas J. Cull assesses the Hillary Clinton effect on US Public Diplomacy.

American diplomacy is highly susceptible to changes in its leadership. Other Western states are not nearly so volatile. Whatever the quality of diplomats in the field, in the United States the scramble for resources from the legislature, the battle to be heard at the policy-making table and the ability to corral one's own bureaucracy or manage an ever-tricky inter-agency process rests on the personality at the top.

In the old days of the United States Information Agency (USIA)—the one–stop shop for American public diplomacy from 1953–1999—fortunes rose and fell with the choice of leader. The last golden age of that agency rested on Charles Z. Wick and more particularly, on his friendship with President Reagan. Equally, USIA's decline can be tracked to the leadership problems of his successors. In the years since USIA was taken into the Department of State, the leadership of American diplomacy has flowed from the Secretary of State and from whoever is Under Secretary for Public Diplomacy. Hence, the departure of any Secretary of State is a good moment to take stock. When that Secretary has the global public profile of Hillary Clinton the argument for so doing is overwhelming.

It is hard to underestimate the public diplomacy problems inherited by Hillary Clinton when she took office in 2009. The Bush administration's approach to foreign policy and most especially its war in Iraq had alienated much of the world. While the White House soon learned to pay attention to public diplomacy, US diplomats faced an uphill battle rebuilding an effective apparatus out of the mess left by the merger of the USIA with the State Department. A rapid turnover and long gaps between the appointment of Under Secretaries raised as many problems as the relative merits of those who served. The best of Bush's Under Secretaries—James K. Glassman—was in office for only 6 months. The Secretaries of State left their own stamp. Colin Powell led a charge to digitization, finally pushing old-school technophobes to embrace websites, email and personal data devices. Powell's successor, Condoleezza Rice, touted what she termed transformational diplomacy, which amounted to a deployment of resources away from Europe to the Middle East. Judging by the scant attention given to diplomacy in her memoirs the subject was hardly a preoccupation. Hillary Clinton could not afford any such luxury.

The international agenda for the Obama administration was set in the President's inaugural address in which he pledged to 'extend a hand' to enemy governments 'if you are willing to unclench your fist' and promised the people of the Muslim world to 'seek a new way forward, based on mutual interest and respect'. The departure of the Bush administration gave the image of the United States an immediate boost: the country bounced to the head of Anholt-GfK Nation Brand Index in one of the very few dramatic movements yet seen in that surprisingly stable run of data. Hillary Clinton's job was to maintain the momentum and to deliver on the President's pledge of outreach. She embarked on a frenetic round of overseas visits, including meetings with the ordinary people of America's target countries. Her celebrity profile gave her a head start but it was not always easy. She became the focus for popular indignation at aspects of US policy. In Pakistan in 2011 she bore the brunt of public anger over civilian deaths from drone strikes. But under her guidance the US image changed to that of a country prepared to, in the preferred terminology of the moment, 'engage' international opinion. Clinton became the public face of 'Smart Power', a concept that blended hard power (military and economic) with the soft power of American values and culture.

Clinton's key lieutenants were her Under Secretaries of State for Public Diplomacy: first the TV executive and campaign contributor, Judith McHale, and then the former journalist and veteran of the Bill Clinton National Security Council staff, Tara Sonenshine.[1] McHale's improved administrative structure created in 1999 built a solid foundation for the future practice of US public diplomacy. Her effectiveness, however, was disputed within the Department and few mourned her early departure. Sonenshine, who took office in early 2012, has worked to re-energize diplomacy in the field and has maintained an impressive speaking schedule to explain the important role that public diplomacy plays in US foreign policy.

While the Under Secretary's direct province is limited to the International Information Programs and Educational and Cultural Affairs, public diplomacy has to involve everyone in the Department and in the wider bureaucracy. Hillary Clinton's allies to this end included the Secretary of Defense for most of her tenure, Robert Gates. Since the end of the Cold War and more especially the attacks of 11 September 2001, the Department of Defense had become a central player in the projection of America's image. Gates saw the danger of this and went so far as to argue that resources be diverted away from his department to strengthen the State Department's diplomatic capacity, including its approach to public diplomacy. Within the wider bureaucracy Hillary Clinton built on the precedent established during the tenure of Undersecretary Karen Hughes (2005–07) to maintain the Department's civilian leadership in a number of important cross-government initiatives, including inter-agency counter-radicalization. This effort has evolved into a Center for Strategic Counterterrorism Communications (CSCC), located at State, which pools resources from State, Defense and CIA to push back against Islamic extremism over new media. Under the leadership of Ambassador Richard LeBaron, the SCSS wisely de-coupled its work from any attempt to sell the United States in order to focus on connecting the potential targets of radicalization with online materials that undermine extremist claims and keep open other political approaches.

Clinton's public diplomacy initiatives have highlighted gender and women's issues, with the creation of the post of Ambassador-at-Large for Global Women's Issues. In the days immediately before Secretary Clinton's departure from office this post and its associated supporting office became permanent. No less significant, Clinton gave close attention to partnerships with non-governmental and corporate sectors. The threads of this work were drawn together in the Global Partnership Initiative, led by a Special Representative for Global Partnerships, Kris Balderston. This unit built on Bush-era partnership activity, such as the President's Emergency Plan for AIDS Relief (PEPFAR). A global campaign for clean cooking stoves was among projects that made a real difference to millions of lives around the world. By 2012 the department had 800 partners including the Chinese and Indian governments. But while Clinton placed great emphasis on issues of gender and partnership it was a third area which would become most closely associated with her term in office: new technology.

From the outset Clinton emphasized what her innovation advisor Alec Ross touted as 'Twenty-First Century Statecraft'. This had two prongs. The first was a diplomatic emphasis on the need for open internet connectivity and free international exchange online. The second prong was an attempt to integrate new technology into the practice of diplomacy. Within the State Department initiatives which had been small-scale and experimental during the final months of the Bush era now became large-scale. Most embassies acquired Twitter feeds and the bureau of International Information Programs launched Facebook platforms dedicated to 'getting the message out'.

New technology can create communities of interest that transcend geographical space and challenge the primacy of states. Perhaps future generations will look back and see online public diplomacy not as 'Twenty-First Century Statecraft' but as *post-state craft*. But even now the State Department's digital outreach often misses the opportunities for a two-way flow of information. If the United States is to flourish in the digital realm it must allow its diplomats in the field to build on their main strength, which is to create open-ended relationships.

The final months of Hillary Clinton's tenure were overshadowed by the deaths of Ambassador Christopher Stephens and his team in Benghazi, Libya, in September 2012. In the overheated atmosphere of a Presidential election campaign the Benghazi killings became a political football. Secretary Clinton's ability to stay calm prevented the affair from taking off in quite the way the opposition hoped. But the Benghazi tragedy may raise demands to move America's diplomats back from forward positions like the Benghazi consulate to the relative safety of embassy compounds. This would undermine the public diplomacy success of the Hillary Clinton era.

Whatever the strengths of new technology and the value of a charismatic leader at the helm, public diplomacy will always rest on the work of Foreign Service Officers in the field working to build relationships across what Edward R. Murrow termed 'the last three feet' separating one individual from another. Hillary Clinton embodied this lesson and led the way by example.

Hillary Clinton's departure provoked the inevitable flurry of media speculation on whether she intends to run for president in 2016. Her contribution to the field of public diplomacy as Secretary of State augurs well. Plainly, were she to attain that office it would be no bad thing for America's conversation with the world on which so much of our shared wellbeing depends.

Reference

Cull, Nicholas J., 'The end of the Hillary Clinton era in US public diplomacy' in *Place Branding and Public Diplomacy* (volume 9, Issue 1). Palgrave Macmillan, 2013.

Branding the City

Gjoko Muratovski examines the role of architecture and integrated design in branding a city to conclude that originality is the key to establishing a distinctive identity.

For thousands of years, architecture has been used to promote the power of the state. One has only to think of ancient Greece and imperial Rome to bring examples to mind. Closer to our own time, Napoleon embarked on a reconstruction of medieval Paris, a cause taken up by Napoleon III and Baron Haussmann to build the 'capital of capitals' to glorify the French empire. To flaunt the power of the Third Reich, Hitler visualized—though failed to realize—a mighty Berlin to dwarf Paris, while in Italy Mussolini resolved to make Rome greater than the Rome of Augustus. Red Square in Moscow was adapted to accommodate the grand ceremonial of the May Day military parades. Likewise, in the United States, George Washington commissioned the French architect, Pierre Charles L'Enfant, to design Washington, D. C. as a model for American city planning and as a symbol of world power. Other more recent American attempts at architectural propaganda include the Lincoln Memorial, the Jefferson Monument and the Vietnam Veterans Memorial.

Every world-renowned city has benefited from the construction of landmark monuments including London (the Tower of London), Paris (the Eiffel Tower), New York (the Statue of Liberty) and Rio de Janeiro (Christ the Redeemer). Canberra and Brasilia, both planned twentieth-century cities, were artificially created around governing bodies and national institutions.

More recently, architectural propaganda has evolved into branding, acting as a billboard to convey its message by the choice of style, material, technology or historical reference. For example, the iconic works of Charles Rennie Mackintosh in Glasgow and Antoni Gaudi in Barcelona play a central role in marketing those cities. Urban centres that are defined by their rich architectural and cultural heritage are seen as unique, attractive and lively. They need good architecture and design to develop their aesthetic and innovative values

---

[1]Subsequent to the time of writing the White House announced that Under Secretary Tara Sonenshine would leave office in June 2013, apparently as part of an effort to open vacancies to reward contributors to the 2012 election campaign. The decision was not applauded by the public diplomacy community and is a sad testament to the degree to which the cost of US elections corrodes wider aspects of US statecraft.

and to meet business and public needs. Architecture can contribute to overall well-being and can function as a source of civic pride.

Cities continue to use architecture to promote their image. Frank Gehry's Guggenheim Museum in Bilbao is a prime example. While it does not function particularly well as an exhibition space it is an exceptionally effective marketing tool for Bilbao.

The 'Bilbao effect' inspired Dubai, Abu Dhabi and Qatar, all of which have ventured into hugely ambitious architectural projects to raise their profile from desert communities to urban oases. As oil revenues decline, they have turned towards real estate and tourism. Dubai has set a target of attracting 15 million visitors to some of the world's most ambitious architecture including the tallest skyscraper, the first luxury underwater hotel and an artificial archipelago of residential islands. With its aggressive pursuit of bigger and better, Dubai now rivals Las Vegas as the leading desert city.

The economically stronger Abu Dhabi has been quick to establish its own vision of the future. Over the next decade, it aims to become one of the greatest cultural centres in the Middle East. The 'latter-day Xanadu', as the *New York Times* dubs it, will boast four museums, a performing arts centre and 19 arts pavilions designed by the likes of Frank Gehry, Zaha Hadid, Tadao Ando and Jean Nouvel. The plans include franchises of the Guggenheim and Louvre as well as an arts institute created by Yale University.

With its bid for the 2022 World Cup, Qatar has unveiled its own extravagant urban aspirations. With the help of Foster & Partners (led by British architect Lord Norman Foster) and Albert Speer & Partners (the son of Hitler's chief architect), Qatar has vowed to build 12 carbon-neutral stadiums that can be disassembled and shipped to other locations. There is also a plan to build seven solar-powered satellite cities.

This is all hugely impressive but there are drawbacks. One strong possibility is that these copycat 'reimagining' strategies could defeat the whole purpose of branding. This has already been recognised in the use of overly similar logos, visuals and slogans. Now we see the same thing with architecture. Cities hire the same 'brand-name' architects who produce the same signature buildings. This, in turn, results in a uniform, amorphous city image with no distinctive sense of place. The renowned Dutch architect and theorist, Rem Koolhaas, who is himself part of the Middle East renaissance with his master plan for a Waterfront City in Dubai, fears that the growing use of high-end architecture as a promotional tool will reduce cities to homogeneous architectural theme parks.

If architecture is to promote cultural values that respect heterogeneity, it must align city marketing with social and economic realities. Architects and developers need to adopt innovative models that acknowledge and build on a firm cultural and social foundation.

Reference

Muratovski, Gjoko, 'The role of architecture and integrated design in city branding' in *Place Branding and Public Diplomacy* (volume 8, Issue 3). Palgrave Macmillan, 2012.

The Eurozone Crisis: A Tale of 'North' and 'South'

The North—South divide on the future of the euro is damaging the EU, says Ansgar Belke. In this article, he suggests a compromise by which the two sides might settle their differences to mutual advantage.

After the European summit of June 2012 decided to break the vicious circle between banks and sovereign states, it seemed that political leaders were at last ready to deal with the threat to the euro. But optimism was soon lost in the cacophony of rival interpretations about what had been agreed. Still, the leaders had identified the critical issue: weak banks and weak sovereign states are like two bad swimmers that are pulling each other under water.

But which one should be saved first? Advocates of the Southern view say we should start with the sovereign states, by throwing them the lifejacket of joint-issued debt. In effect, richer countries would guarantee at least part of the debt of weaker ones.

Representatives of the Northern opinion, especially Germany, reckon instead that it is better to start by saving the banks. This would be done through stronger central supervision and the mutualisation of some liabilities in the banking sector, for instance through a joint fund to wind up failing banks and provide a Europe-wide guarantee of bank deposits. In effect, depositors in solid banks would be guaranteeing the savings of those in more fragile ones.

The Southern view is held by countries including Greece, Italy, Portugal and Spain and, since François Hollande took office, France. The Northern approach is taken by Germany, Austria, Finland and the Netherlands and was taken, while Nicolas Sarkozy was president, by France. Both sides recognize the danger that debt mutualisation could bring moral hazard (when protective measures remove the incentive to curb risky behaviour) and higher costs for creditor countries. For the North there is no getting around these problems. For the South these risks can be removed, or at least mitigated, by a careful design of the system. For instance, the Eurozone could impose conditions on countries seeking the benefit of jointly issued debt.

The South considers the panic that can increase borrowing costs and push countries into insolvency as the main threat to the Eurozone. The North reckons that the principal menace stems from removing this market pressure too quickly, dampening the need to reform.

Both speak of the political backlash. For the South it is excessive austerity in debtor nations that should be resisted; for the North it is *excessive liabilities* in creditor states that can cause resentment.

In some ways, though, the two sides are not so far apart. The North concedes that it is necessary to have some mutualisation of debt, if only to recapitalize banks. The South accepts that debt mutualisation must be limited to avoid moral hazard.

The Southern View: Some Basics

The main argument of the South runs as follows: since the 1970s economists have warned that a budgetary union would be a necessity for a sustainable monetary union. But the founders of the Eurozone ignored this warning. It is now clear that they were mistaken and that the governments of the euro area member countries face a hard choice. Either they move to a budgetary union or they abandon the euro. A disintegration of the Eurozone would produce huge economic, social and political upheaval. If euro area governments want to avoid this they have to look for strategies that move us closer towards a budgetary union.

A budgetary union, such as that of the US states, appears to be far off. But perhaps there is a strategy of taking small steps that lead us in the right direction. The Southern argument starts with the basic insight that Eurozone governments issue debt in euros, which is a currency they cannot control. In contrast, standalone countries like the UK endow bondholders with a guarantee that the cash to pay them at maturity will always be available. The fact that governments of the Eurozone are unable to deliver such a guarantee makes them vulnerable to upsurges of distrust and fear in the bond markets. This can trigger liquidity crises that drive countries towards default, forcing them to apply austerity programmes that lead to recession and a collapse of weaker banks. This is not to say that countries that have overspent in the past do not have to apply austerity. It is rather that financial markets, when driven by panic, force austerity on these countries with an intensity that can trigger major social and political backlashes. The effects are there to see in Greece, Italy, Spain and Portugal.

Proponents of the Southern view argue that some form of *pooling of government* debt is necessary to overcome this failure. Thereby, the weakest in the union are shielded from the destructive upsurges of panic in the financial markets of a monetary union.

They acknowledge that those that profit from the creditworthiness of the strong countries may exploit this by failing to reduce debts and deficits. The second obstacle is that the strongest countries will pay a higher interest rate on their debts as they become jointly liable for the debts of governments with lower creditworthiness. Thus debt pooling must be designed in such a way as to overcome these obstacles.

Moderate proponents of the Southern view agree, apparently in line with the Merkel government in Germany, that *three principles* should be followed. First, debt pooling should be *partial*—that is, a significant part of the debt must remain the responsibility of the national governments, so as to give them an on-going incentive to reduce debts and deficits. Second, an *internal transfer mechanism* between the members of the pool must ensure that the less creditworthy countries compensate (at least partially) the more creditworthy ones. Third, a *tight control mechanism* on the progress of national governments in achieving sustainable debt levels must be an essential part of debt pooling.

The Northern view holds that the mutualisation of the Eurozone's debt to bring about the convergence of interest rates will not in the long-run tackle the root of the problem. Instead it has the potential to sow the seeds of an even larger crisis. This is what happened in the early years of the euro. A lack of discipline in countries such as Greece and Portugal was matched by the build-up of asset bubbles in other member countries, such as Spain and Ireland. Structural reforms were delayed, while wages outstripped productivity growth. The consequence was a huge loss of competitiveness at the periphery which cannot be resolved by the mutualisation of debt.

Debt mutualisation can take different forms. One is to mutualise new sovereign debt through Eurobonds. Another is to absorb part of the old debt, as advocated by the German Council of Economic Advisors, into a partly gold-backed European Redemption Fund. A third means is to activate the Eurozone's 'firewall' by using rescue funds (either the temporary European Financial Stability Facility or the permanent European Stability Mechanism) to buy sovereign bonds or to inject capital directly into distressed banks. Indeed, the ECB is already engaged in a hidden form of mutualisation—of risk if not (yet) of actual debt—through its programmes of sovereign bond purchases and its long-term refinancing operations for banks.

The view of the North is that almost all these are bound to fail, either for economic or political reasons, or both. Even financially strong countries cannot agree to open-ended commitments that could endanger their own financial stability or, given that they are the main guarantors, the stability of the bailout funds. Also the danger of moral hazard is ever-present.

Then again, any form of debt mutualisation involves an element of subsidy, which severely weakens fiscal discipline: the interest rate premium on bonds of fiscally weaker countries declines and the premium for stronger countries increases. Fiscally solid countries are punished and less solid ones, in turn, are rewarded for their lack of fiscal discipline and excess private and public consumption.

If yields are too low there is no incentive for private investors to buy sovereign bonds. The countries risk becoming decoupled from the capital markets permanently and the debt problems become increasingly structural.

This is true also for the ECB's bond-buying activities. The credit risk is rolled over from the bonds of the weaker countries to those of the stronger ones, and the ECB is made responsible for its liability. Over time, the ECB's measures might even be inflationary. Having the rescue funds buy bonds is little different, except that they lack the lending capacity to be credible. If they are given a banking licence, as demanded by France's President Hollande, it would be no different from having the ECB buy bonds directly.

What about the European Redemption Fund (ERP) from the Northern perspective? This type of fund could be of particular help to Italy, which could unload half of its debt. But its partners could not force Italy to tax its citizens to ensure that it pays back the dormant debt. And with the assumption of debt, the credit rating of Germany might drop, owing to the increase in the German interest burden. The pressure on Italy and Spain to consolidate their budgets sustainably would be reduced. Meanwhile, the problems of Greece, Ireland and Portugal would not be solved, since these countries are unlikely to qualify for the ERP.

In addition to moral hazard, there are political obstacles, which would be most acute in the case of Eurobonds. Germany demands political union before Eurobonds can be considered. But it is sometimes said that this is putting the cart before the horse: a political union cannot be created simply to justify Eurobonds. Advocates from the Merkel government, like Finance Minister Wolfgang Schäuble, say treaty changes and high-level political agreements would be sufficient to make sure that euro area member countries comply with all decisions taken at the euro area level. This became clear when Schäuble came up with a plan to bolster the power of the EU's economic and monetary affairs commissioner. Even Mario Draghi, President of the European Central Bank, has supported this German scheme to allow the EU to intervene in countries' budgets and propose changes before they are agreed in parliaments. But the experience with Greece's adjustment casts severe doubt on the practicality of such a proposal.

The differences between Eurozone members—on everything from respect for the rule of law to administrative capacity—are so great that political union is unlikely to work, at least in the next couple of years. It follows from the perspective of the North that the basis for Eurobonds is extremely thin.

According to the Northern or German view, the introduction of Eurobonds would in principle have to be backed by tight oversight of national fiscal and economic policies. But there is no true enforcement as long as the individual Eurozone members remain sovereign.

Intervening directly in the fiscal sovereignty of member states would require a functioning pan-European democratic legitimacy, but we are far from that. Voters in Southern countries can reject the strong conditionality demanded by Brussels at any time, while those of Northern countries can refuse to keep paying for the South. And either can choose to exit the Eurozone.

The emphasis on pushing through a fiscal union as a precondition for debt mutualisation means the debate, at least in Germany, has become a question of 'all or nothing': either deeper political union or *deep chaos*. This narrows the strategic options for the players and reinforces the North—South divide.

However, there is an alternative to cooperative fiscal federalism involving bailouts and debt mutualisation. This is competition-based fiscal federalism, of the sort successfully operating in the USA, Canada and Switzerland, among others. These countries have largely avoided serious and sustained public debt in their component states. Sub-federal entities faced with insolvency have the incentive to take early corrective action—without having to engage in centralized fiscal policy coordination. This seems to be a compromise between the Southern and Northern views.

To achieve this sort of federalism, it is necessary to separate the fate of the banks from that of the sovereign states. What is needed is not a fiscal union *in first instance*, but a banking union. It should be based on four elements: a European bank with far-reaching powers to intervene; reformed banking regulations with significantly higher equity capital standards; a banking resolution fund; and a European deposit insurance scheme.

A less comprehensive, more clearly delineated banking union should be more acceptable for the North than the Europeanization of fiscal policy as a whole. This is because it touches upon only a small fraction of the fiscal policy areas which have to be subordinated to central control in a fiscal union.

Obviously, a central resolution authority has to be endowed with the resources to wind up large cross-border banks. Where does the money for this come from? In the long run, the existence of a resolution authority goes along with a deposit insurance scheme for cross-border banks. This should—according to the German view—be funded partly by the banking industry.

With the banking system and the debt crisis thus disentangled, banking sector losses will no longer threaten to destroy the solvency of solid sovereign states such as Ireland and Spain. Eurobonds will then not be needed, and neither will the bailout of sovereign states. The debt of over-indebted states could be restructured, which means that the capital market could exert stronger discipline on borrowers.

There are two questions yet to be resolved. If the banking sector is really to be stabilized, a solution will surely have to deal with the devalued sovereign debt that some are holding. Would the banks not be better off holding at least some Eurobonds instead of, say, Greek or Spanish bonds? That said, Southern economists who advocate Eurobonds need to find a way of making them politically acceptable. And how much political union is feasible, or even desirable, just for the sake of a single currency that many never loved? Critically, where does the burden end up?

Reference

Blume, Lawrence E. and Durlauf, Steven N. (ed.), *The New Palgrave Dictionary of Economics (online edition)*. Palgrave Macmillan, 2013.

How China Became Capitalist

Ronald Coase and Ning Wang examine China's embrace of capitalism.

When Mao Zedong, founder of the People's Republic of China, died on 9 Sept. 1976, China was in the midst of a Cultural Revolution that was meant to rejuvenate socialism, ridding it of capitalist corruption and bureaucratic rigidity. Mao believed that China could shrug off poverty and jump on to the 'golden highway' to socialism if the Chinese people, united in thought and action, threw all their talents and energy behind the collective cause. Instead, Mao's deeply flawed ideology reduced enterprising people to lifeless cogs in the socialist machines.

So it was that China started its post-Mao journey with no roadmap and no destination in mind.

The need for reform was urgent but, unable to contemplate eradicating communism and starting afresh, the policy was to adjust the existing system while learning from different models of capitalism.

Once the Chinese people were freed from the shackle of ideology, they were able to catch up quickly. The setting up of Special Economic Zones and the inflow of foreign direct investment quickly pulled millions out of poverty and raised the living standards for a quarter of humanity. These remarkable outcomes have convinced other countries, including India and Vietnam, of the benevolence of the market and the folly of state planning.

Moreover, the Chinese market transformation has opened up new horizons for global capitalism. As a rising economic power, China is now contributing to the development of many countries in Central and Southeast Asia, Latin America and Africa, whose economies have been increasingly integrated with the Chinese market. The operation of a vibrant and distinctive market economy in China makes a compelling case that capitalism can take root and flourish in an ostensibly non-Western society. By breaking the West's monopoly on capitalism, China helps to globalize capitalism and fortifies the global market order by adding cultural diversity.

Drawing upon its rich and long traditions in commerce and private entrepreneurship, capitalism with Chinese characteristics will continue to strike out on its own way. But what exactly is capitalism with Chinese characteristics? Most commentators have focused on the visible hand of the Chinese government and the remaining monopoly power of the Chinese Communist Party as the defining features. While these are undeniably important, they do not hold the key to understanding capitalism in China.

First, the role of the Chinese state in the economy has become progressively less significant. Before the economic reforms, the Chinese people had little economic freedom and the state controlled every aspect of the economy, from production, to retail and even consumption. Today, private entrepreneurship is the primary driving force of the Chinese economy.

Second, the Chinese Communist Party today no longer identifies itself as a revolutionary vanguard. The 'mandate of heaven' has replaced communism; the party-state rests its legitimacy on effective governance and the improvement of living standards for the people.

There is a downside. While China's manufacturing sector now produces almost all types of consumer goods, Western consumers would be hard pressed to name any Chinese brands, even though their houses are full of products made in China. Short on innovation and lacking their own distinctive products, many Chinese firms depend on taking orders from overseas markets and selling them under foreign brand names. This does not bode well for an economy aiming to top the world. As late as 2009, the United States manufactured more goods (US\$1.7trn. in manufacturing value added) than China (US\$1.3trn.). After a decades-long decline in employment (fewer than 12 m. workers at the second quarter of 2010), the US manufacturing sector still enjoys a significant lead over China, where manufacturing employs over 100 m. Chinese workers. Moreover, given the large presence of foreign firms and joint ventures in China, the growth of domestic capacity in manufacturing in China is far less impressive than the name, the 'workshop of the world', might suggest.

The education system makes it all too clear that growth in quantity will not compensate for a lack of progress in quality. The fatal organizational flaw of Chinese universities is their lack of autonomy. The majority of Chinese universities remain under the strict control of the Ministry of Education. As a result, they have become more skilled in currying favour with the Ministry of Education than in offering innovative research and educational programmes.

Chinese law and politics have also suffered severely from the lack of an active market for ideas. Although Chinese economic performance has surpassed the wildest expectations, progress in political reform has been disappointing. China is in no way near the point where the constitutional rights of citizens are resolutely protected. The Chinese legal system is still far away from where it can 'guarantee the equality of all people before the people's laws and deny anyone the privilege of being above the law'.

Without a forum to express their views, people of critical thinking and independent thought the most valuable human assets in any society find themselves labelled political dissidents. In turn, political dissidents are often deemed to be 'anti-Party', or 'anti-socialism, a charge that can end careers, if not lives.

The lack of a market for ideas is responsible for the lack of innovation in science and technology, the Achilles' heel in China's growing manufacturing sector. The dearth of innovation and remaining state monopolies gravely reduce the range of investment opportunities that Chinese entrepreneurs find profitable.

The post-Mao Chinese economic reform in the past few decades has transformed the country's economy and society. At Mao's death in 1976, China was one of the poorest countries in the world, with a GDP per capita below US\$200. By 2010, China was the world's second largest economy, with a GDP per capita at more than US\$4000. Over the same time span, China's share of the global economy rose from below 2% to about 9%. Private entrepreneurship now thrives throughout the country and forms the backbone of the Chinese economy. With the world's largest population of internet and cell phone users and the largest car market, Chinese society is open, energetic, mobile and well informed, full of dynamism and aspiration.

But a vibrant market for ideas is an indispensable foundation for an open society and free economy. During the past decades of reform and opening up, the introduction of the market for goods has brought prosperity back to China and fortuitously led the country back to its own cultural roots. With the development of a market for ideas China will stand not only as a world manufacturing centre but as a lively source of creativity and innovation.

Reference

Coase, Ronald and Wang, Ning, *How China Became Capitalist.* Palgrave Macmillan, 2012.

From China with Love

For the Western democracies, the Chinese economic miracle is a mixed blessing. In his new book, ***Myths, Politicians and Money***, Bryan Gould puts up some warning signals.

In the West, of course, dominated as we are by the Anglo-American model of capitalism, a close relationship between government and the private sector is regarded as anathema. The Western view has been that the best thing government can do for industry is to 'get off our backs'. Government intervention is almost invariably seen as unhelpful; second-guessing an infallible market, it is said, will always produce worse results than if it had been left to itself.

There can hardly be a starker contrast than with the approach followed by the Chinese government. To explore that contrast, and to ask the obvious questions, is not to endorse or commend all the Chinese have done and are doing. But it is surely prudent to recognize that the Chinese have achieved an economic performance that is already world-beating and is likely to overwhelm us and that they have done so while pursuing a very different political and ideological approach from our own. No dispassionate observer, comparing the West's recent history and immediate prospects with those of China, could possibly say that we have nothing to learn from the Chinese.

So how have the Chinese done it? In many respects, there is no mystery. A government that has virtually guaranteed stability and continuity is able to take a long strategic view. A government that sees little need to curry favour with voters or with particular interest groups has been free to pursue a single-minded objective—the economic development of the country. A government that can take decisions irrespective of the civil or property rights of individual citizens has been able to plan solely in accordance with those economic goals.

They have used that freedom of decision and action to be quite ruthless, and have accordingly attracted severe criticism from trade partners. A case in point has been their policy on the foreign exchange value of their currency. The Chinese Renminbi is still not fully convertible and its value is accordingly established by the direction of the Chinese government. By pegging its value to the US dollar for a long period, they have been able to take advantage, in terms of the competitive pricing of their exports, of the fall in the dollar's value.

There can be little doubt that the renminbi is substantially undervalued and that this is a deliberate element in Chinese trade policy. The size and persistence of the Chinese trade surplus is incontrovertible evidence of that undervaluation. The situation is reminiscent of the German and Japanese trade surpluses before the Second World War, which Keynes and others correctly characterized as a powerful and aggressive assault on the economic power of the USA and the UK. Keynes was clear that the creditor countries were as much to blame as debtor countries for the trade imbalances that threatened world peace. The Chinese government has a well-developed strategic view regarding where the national economy can and should develop, and literally every economic actor in China is required to comply with that strategy.

The Chinese government takes full responsibility for macroeconomic policy. It determines monetary policy (principally interest rates) and controls exchange rates and capital flows in and out of the country. It relies greatly on fiscal policy, principally public spending levels and taxation, to control inflation and to target sustainable growth rates. It exercises close control over the banking system and directs it to create large volumes of credit which are then channelled into investment in new productive capacity.

This is all quite different from the attitude of Western governments. In line with the general antipathy to allowing or recognizing either the actuality or possibility that governments might be able to help strategically in identifying what is needed for economic success, macroeconomic policy is almost totally ignored in Western countries. What passes for macroeconomic policy is limited to delegating to unelected and therefore unaccountable bankers the responsibility for fixing interest rates as part of a narrowly focused emphasis on controlling inflation. Everything else is left to the market. But if the Chinese are to achieve the living standards they want, comparable with those in the West, they are going to need access to a much larger share of the world's resources than they currently command. The resources they need now and will need even more in the future if they are to achieve their goals are in most cases finite—minerals and agricultural land, to name but two examples.

The best time to achieve that access and guarantee it into the future is to buy it now, when assets in most Western economies are relatively cheap and when China itself is cash-rich. But Chinese leaders will calculate that it is not enough to sign trade deals or conclude contracts to buy the products they need. If their future development is to be guaranteed, they need control over and ownership of the means of production. In other words, China's goals can only be achieved at the expense of others. A greater share of the world's finite resources for China means a smaller share for others. Chinese outward foreign direct investment is rising fast, and will go on rising. Nearly 20% of the US$227bn. total Chinese outward FDI was made in 2009, all the more remarkable in view of the overall fall in global FDI in that year. It is targeted at industrial capacity—particularly high-tech capacity—in the USA.

It is even more obviously focused on mineral resources in Australia, where Chinese investment has increased dramatically. The Australians have become increasingly wary of such investment. For example, a Chinese bid to gain control of the world's largest deposit of rare earths was blocked in 2009 by the Australian Foreign Investment Review Board. Rare earths are an essential element in much modern electronic communications technology and China already controls 95% of the world's rare earth reserves.

And it extends beyond Australia (where Chinese purchases of Australian farms have risen tenfold) even to a small economy such as New Zealand, where Chinese interest in food production has risen significantly. Some Chinese efforts to buy up not just dairy products but also dairy farms and production processes in New Zealand have aroused public anxiety.

The purchase of the farms was just one element in a total process which would take dairy production off Chinese-owned farms to be processed in Chinese-owned factories in New Zealand and then transported directly to be marketed to Chinese consumers. The farms would remain physically in New Zealand, and some local labour would be employed; but, to all intents and purposes, that element of New Zealand's dairy production would have been integrated into the Chinese economy. The farms might as well have been re-located in Zhejiang province.

Some firms are set up specifically to obtain overseas contracts as a means of extending Chinese influence, particularly in developing countries. The telecommunications and IT giant Huawei, which has set itself the goal of becoming a world leader in the field, has made huge strides in that direction. It is headed by a former senior officer in the People's Liberation Army, and it is reasonable to assume that it has close links to the senior echelons of the Chinese government. Concerns in the USA and Australia are such that Huawei has been excluded from participation in sensitive contracts for fear that national security might be compromised.

Chinese firms are often able to offer favourable prices and financing arrangements because their commercial operations are in effect guaranteed by cheap funding, which, in turn, is guaranteed by a virtually inexhaustible government purse. Chinese firms are already by far the biggest international infrastructure contractors, with strongly entrenched dominant positions throughout Africa and in Eastern Europe in particular. The Chinese government is able to combine these contractual arrangements with claims to be a significant aid donor to poor countries, particularly in regions such as the South Pacific.

The West should understand that a bid for a strategic asset by a Chinese firm may not be just a matter of a private firm taking advantage of a commercial opportunity. It may be part of a much wider picture in which the firm and its bid are to be seen as elements in a government-directed strategy to secure national goals. The economies of other, smaller countries could in effect by absorbed into the greater Chinese economy and be directed from Beijing.

None of this means that we should regard Chinese development as unalloyed bad news. Our concern should be to make sensible and prudent responses in our own interests while encouraging the Chinese to develop in a direction of mutual benefit rather than conflict.

The signs in this regard are not entirely discouraging. By contrast with the experience of the Great Depression, when American protectionism helped to drive the world economy into reverse, the Chinese economy has remained —through the current recession—dynamic, open and increasingly market-driven.

Moreover, the Chinese have their own reasons for changing course, at least to some extent. The Chinese economy is at present seriously unbalanced. Odd though it may seem to Westerners accustomed to concerns about a damaging emphasis on consumption rather than exports, the Chinese have the opposite problem.

A Chinese refusal to allow an appreciation of their currency so that their extreme and unfair competitiveness is reduced is likely to present them with an inflationary problem, which will do the job for them. One way or another, we are likely to see a rebalancing of the Chinese economy, towards domestic consumption and away from exporting, over the coming years.

At the same time, the Chinese face a problem that is familiar in the West but takes a more virulent form in China. Western countries recognize that care for the elderly will become increasingly expensive in the future, as the elderly constitute a higher and higher proportion of the population; in China, that problem is greatly exacerbated by the impact of the 'one child per family' policy of recent decades. A smaller workforce in future years will have to shoulder the burden of looking after an increasingly long-lived older generation.

The future may not, in other words, be as clear cut as we assume, and we should not forget the example of Japan. I recall spending time in Japan in 1980, at a time when the Japanese economy looked very much like today's Chinese economy, albeit on a smaller scale. The air was thick with predictions that Japan would overtake the USA as the world's largest economy by the turn of the century. We now know that those predictions came to nought—and it may be that China, as it emerges from the rapid growth of its initial development phase, will also find the going increasingly tough. With Chinese wages and raw material costs rising fast, and major firms such as General Electric reviewing the comparative advantages of manufacturing in the USA rather than China, it may be that the era of easy growth for China will come to an end.

This suggests that we should concentrate on trying to ensure that China is drawn into global efforts to regulate the world economy, by reforming the international monetary system and dealing with trade imbalances, and to achieve environmentally sustainable development. We need to strike a balance between accepting China's legitimate claim to a fair share of the world's scarce natural resources and our right to manage our own affairs.

While China is the most successful and significant of the new Asian powerhouses, India, Korea, Taiwan, Singapore, and increasingly Malaysia, Indonesia and Thailand, have all begun a rapid transformation. In most cases, economic success has been achieved by building a powerful partnership between government and private enterprise—something that runs counter to most current Western opinion as to the best way to produce economic efficiency.

Brazil, Russia and South Africa are also making impressive progress, notwithstanding both actual and threatened global recession—and they, too, have depended less on finance from Western financial institutions, following Western prescriptions less slavishly than might have been expected 20 years ago. We can now see a number of regimes enjoying wide popular support for policies which give priority to sharing resources more equally, raising living standards for the poor, strengthening public services and defying the power of multinational corporations.

The successful pursuit of policies that are affronts to the basic tenets of neo-liberalism has done little to shift opinion among Western business and political leaders, who prefer to avert their gaze from the evidence before them. But the rise of successful economies and healthier societies which pay little attention to the supposed triumph of Western ideology is at the very least a profound shock to the Fukuyama prediction that history is now behind us.

Reference

Gould, Bryan, *Myths, Politicians and Money.* Palgrave Macmillan, 2013.

The Rich Get Richer and the Poor Get Poorer

In his widely acclaimed book, *Myths, Politicians and Money*, Bryan Gould mounts an attack on globalization and unfettered markets.

It is now widely accepted that inequality in both wealth and income—and, as a consequence, in power as well—has widened substantially in many Western countries over recent decades. This trend has been most marked in the English-speaking democracies—countries such as the USA, the UK and New Zealand. This has been a particularly surprising development in a country such as New Zealand, which recently was one of the most egalitarian countries in the world.

Nobel Prize-winning economist Joseph Stiglitz has highlighted the extent to which this trend has disfigured American society and handicapped US economic development. By 2007, he reports, the income of the top 0·1% of households in the USA was 200 times greater than the average of the bottom 90%. It took them just a day and a half to earn what it took a year for the bottom 90% to receive, while the wealthiest 1% also owned more than a third of American wealth. Between 2002 and 2007, 65% of the increase in national income had gone to that same top 1%. Worse, since the global financial crisis, the trend has intensified: 93% of the increased national income in 2010 went to—yes—the top 1%. The statistics look even more alarming as we dig into the detail. The six heirs to the Wal-Mart empire, for example, own wealth worth as much as is owned by the whole of the bottom 30%.

While the American figures are the most extreme, they are reflected in the experience of other Western countries. In the UK, Michael Meacher MP recently made a telling analysis of the annual *Sunday Times* Rich List for 2012. He found that the wealth of the 1000 richest people in Britain (just 0·003% of the adult population) had increased by £155bn. over the past 3 years. That increase alone would have allowed them to pay off the entire current UK budget deficit and still have about £30 billion left over.

These super-rich were mainly bankers, hedge fund managers and private equity operators—a group that had been largely responsible for the financial crash. Yet while ordinary people had borne the burden of paying increased taxes (largely through increases in indirect taxation) in order to deal with the consequences of the crash, the super-rich had paid no increased tax specifically directed at them. The wealth of this super-rich group now totals £414bn., about one-third of the UK's total GDP. If the increase in their wealth over the past 15 years had been taxed at a 28% rate on capital gains, about £88 billion would have been raised, enough to pay off 70% of the entire deficit.

Salaries for senior managers in most of the Western world have, of course, risen hugely over the last two or three decades, in line with the increased value apparently placed by the market on their services. All kinds of bonuses, share options and other benefits are paid (but often not taxed) as part of the remuneration packages of executives. The top ten highest paid CEOs in 2011 earned about 77% of their total realized compensation through stock option exercises and vested equity, while those who own and direct corporations, especially in the financial sector, have done even better.

In the USA the portion of national income going to the richest 1% of the population tripled from 8% in the 1970s to 24% in 2007—an amazing statistic of which most people, not least in the USA, seem unaware. In addition, that same 1% also holds around 40% of all wealth. As Professor James K. Galbraith has shown, contrary to the constantly-made assertion that increased inequality is the consequence of 'real factors', such as the increased value of technology as compared to labour, the true explanation is that the huge growth in the financial sectors of Western economies has made bankers rich, and—equally important—pumped up the value of assets such as stocks, bonds and real estate. This supports the point made by Joseph Stiglitz that the huge growth in wealth of the richest has not been earned in the ordinary sense but is rent income—that is, an income gained entirely by virtue of being already wealthy.

At the same time, the global financial crisis has been used as the chance, in many Western countries, to reinforce the drive to reduce real wages and to further reduce the share of national income that goes to wage-earners. The share of wages in the UK's national income, for example, has been on a downward trend for three decades. Since the global financial crisis, however, that trend has intensified. In the 2 years 2010 and 2011, real wages fell on average by 7%, a downward trend that was set to continue to at least 2016, if the Office of Budget Responsibility's forecast is accepted. The suspicion must be that this is, at least in part, the consequence of a direct attempt by government to engineer, under the cover of the crisis, a further fall in the share of the national cake going to earnings.

The proportion of the British workforce in low-paid work has almost doubled over the last two decades and now stands at more than a fifth. This decline is the result of a four-year-long freeze (meaning a real cut after inflation) on public sector pay, the straitened finances of voluntary sector organizations and charities—so that many home care staff and those working with the homeless are facing substantial pay cuts—pay freezes in parts of the private sector including distribution and manufacturing, and the failure to maintain the real value of the minimum wage.

These current trends reflect a long and unattractive history. In the Great Depression of the early 1930s, most developed economies followed the call made by the multimillionaire US treasury secretary Andrew Mellon, after the 1929 crash, to 'liquidate labour'. It is sad to see history repeating itself in this way, as the rich defend their interests and pile the burdens on to the poor. The tragedy is that, in most Western economies, cutting pay simply squeezes even more of the lifeblood out of economies already suffering from a severe shortage of demand. Falling real wages over the last 3 years are the key explanation for economies struggling to escape from recession.

And this is not all. The benefits on which many unemployed are forced to rely are reduced, at least in terms of their real value. Their rights, either in work or out of work, are also reduced. The services on which they depend for the delivery of education, health care and housing attract fewer resources in comparative terms and are increasingly made available on a user-pays basis. The esteem they enjoy in their own eyes and those of others diminishes. And all this, in the case of the American worker in particular, in the aftermath of the global financial crisis which meant that for many such people their jobs, retirement incomes and homes had all been jeopardized by the monumental errors made by their supposed betters.

Nor is the differential treatment of the rich and the poor in income terms the whole story; there are many other advantages delivered to the rich and powerful by the policies applied in most Western countries over recent decades. In particular, tax rates on high income have been substantially reduced and taxes on capital have also been brought down, while in some countries, such as New Zealand, wealth is completely untaxed.

The tax burden has also been increasingly switched away from progressive taxes on income (so that high income-earners have been relieved of part of the burden) and towards regressive indirect taxation. A higher proportion of taxes on consumption necessarily impacts more severely on the less well-off, who spend a higher proportion of their incomes on goods that they need for day-to-day consumption, while a smaller proportion will go to capital goods, savings and investments, which is where the better-off tend to put their disposable income.

One of the starkest and most dramatic illustrations of the gulf that has developed between the small minority of super-rich and ordinary people was some research released in 2012. James Henry, former chief economist at consultancy McKinsey and an expert on tax havens, detailed in a report called *The Price of Offshore Revisited* his latest estimates of the amount of money squirreled away in offshore tax havens by the super-rich.

The total is truly staggering. Henry showed that at least US$21trn.—perhaps up to US$32trn.—has leaked tax-free into secretive jurisdictions such as Switzerland and the Cayman Islands. This sum is the equivalent of more than the total GDP of the USA and Japan combined. The detailed analysis in the report suggests that it would be enough to pay off Third World debt many times over, or to finance the stimulus required worldwide to enable the global economy to recover from recession.

The tax advantages enjoyed by the rich are not just a matter of low rates and ease of avoidance; they also reflect the structure of taxation in most advanced countries. Remarkably little attention is paid to the fact that property—the form in which the wealthiest often accumulate their wealth—is largely immune from taxation. The real scandal is the fact that the owners of property worth millions of pounds pay a property-based tax, such as the council tax, at minimal rates, and escape any tax at all on the development value of the land they own.

A further startling instance of how thoroughly the taxation system has been suborned by those whose liability is or should be greatest has only recently come to light. As Polly Toynbee reported in February 2013, the House of Commons Select Committee on the Treasury took evidence from the major accountancy firms as to their involvement in advising the British government on tax arrangements which applied to firms looking to the selfsame accountancy firms for tax advice.

The case that particularly attracted the select committee's attention was that of the Patent Box. This is a scheme that offers tax relief on patents, designed to encourage companies to innovate, invest in R&D and entice foreign companies to relocate to the UK. The relief is available on any product, provided that some part of that product—perhaps a very small part—contains a patent; the relief is retrospective, and therefore covers old patents as well as new ones. The Treasury estimates that this one scheme for tax relief will cost £1.1bn. per year in lost corporation tax, roughly the annual cost of benefit fraud in the UK—yet it is benefit fraud that hogs the headlines.

Another device is deferred compensation. The way this works is simple: most taxpayers are expected to pay 35% of their income in taxes the year they earn it. But CEOs do not have to pay the tax until they claim the cash, which can be earning interest in the meantime. Depending on how the money is invested, CEOs can engineer a substantial profit. Thus Michael Duke, CEO of Wal-Mart, received US$17,028,615 tax free in 2011, roughly 774 times more than one of his employees would have been allowed to do under normal tax rules.

Yet these sums shrink into insignificance compared with the money that hedge fund managers make. Raymond Dalio, for example, was paid an astronomical US$3bn. in 2011, but paid just 15% in taxes because the money was considered capital gains, as opposed to the average citizen, who would be required to pay 25% (in income tax). The cost to the taxpayer of this instance in 2011 was US$450 m.

Inequality is largely a function of the 'free market'. As long as the outcomes are sanctioned by the market, there is thought to be no limit to the share that some are entitled to take at the expense of others. Growing inequality has, therefore, a momentum all of its own; we find that even in hard times the rich and powerful continue to make gains while the rest languish. It operates on a ratchet, impossible to turn back, constantly clicking forward.

Wealth of course entrenches and grows itself. The best chance of being seriously wealthy is to be born into a seriously wealthy family. Even in the supposed land of opportunity—indeed, especially in the USA—social mobility has largely ground to a halt. Well-off families now spend eleven times more than the working-class on children's 'enrichment activities', which are so important for psychological well-being and character building. It is not just educational advantage, in other words, that can be bought; life chances of all kinds, including social exclusivity, are scooped by the well-off.

As society becomes more unequal, the growing inequality intensifies and feeds upon itself. On the part of the wealthy there is less understanding of the plight of the poor and disadvantaged, and there is less willingness to accommodate their interests and meet their needs. If a necessary part of the justification for the inequality is that the wealthy deserve their advantage because it is a proper reward for superior virtue, then it must follow that the poor are undeserving. The myth of the 'feckless' poor is sedulously fostered and believed.

The free market in its current extreme form has had the effect of weakening social cohesion and in particular the family. Paradoxically, the family is often held up by the proponents of 'free-market' reforms as the epitome of what is valuable in society. Yet the rate of family breakdown has grown sharply in those countries where free markets are most firmly entrenched.

This in turn has led to the growth of an underclass with predictably antisocial attitudes. Incredibly, its emergence is seen by the rich as a consequence of welfarism rather than an inevitable reflection of widening poverty and social dislocation. They demand tougher penalties for crime and more jails are built—5 m. Americans are in prison at any one time. The peccadilloes of the wealthy are excused, even celebrated, while the frailties of the poor are condemned.

One obvious indicator is the differing treatment accorded to different kinds of people when they lose their employment. When ordinary people lose their jobs the pressure is on to make sure that they are forced back into the workforce as soon as possible. The value of unemployment benefit is carefully monitored to ensure that the unemployed are not too comfortable, and that even low wage rates are more advantageous than the benefit. Top executives, on the other hand, enjoy a rather different experience if it is decided to dispense with their services. Many will have negotiated contracts that provide for substantial golden handshakes. Even those whose performance has been abysmal and who are dismissed for incompetence will walk away with generous compensation. Nor does their lack of success or even proven incompetence disqualify them from rebounding into other highly paid jobs.

There is nothing efficient about an economy that amasses great wealth in just a few hands. The decisions the super-rich take as to how they spend their money are often irresponsible, and at best capricious. The most common use of wealth is not to create new productive capacity and new jobs but simply to earn a 'rent income'. Instead of spreading purchasing power across the whole of society, where it can irrigate every part of the economy, the concentration of wealth compresses it so that it can do little good.

What is economically efficient about keeping large numbers out of work, as Western countries are currently doing, so that their productive contribution is lost? What is economically efficient about cutting the real incomes of the low-paid so that their purchasing power is not available to stimulate the economy? What is economically efficient about cutting benefits so that the health and education of large numbers in Western workforces suffer?

And what chance do we have of achieving an efficient and productive economy if competence and merit are overlooked, while privilege determines who occupy positions of power and accordingly take the decisions that matter? How can it be efficient when the people who run our affairs have little idea of how the economy and society really work?

Reference

Gould, Bryan, *Myths, Politicians and Money*. Palgrave Macmillan, 2013.

Threatening to Devour

Greed is blamed for the malfunction of financial markets. But there is more to it than that, argue Amitava Krishna Dutt and Charles K. Wilber who see greed and dishonesty overlapping across the economic spectrum.

In the wake of the global financial crisis, President Obama declared that 'the days of reckless greed are over' adding, 'We will not go back to the days of unchecked excess [when] too many were motivated only by the appetite for quick kills and bloated bonuses.' In any discussion of the crisis, greed has figured as a major cause. But what do we mean by greed? A clear definition is hard to find. Taking as our framework the neoclassical concept of individuals in pursuit of maximum utility, greed may simply be the accumulation of goods and money in preference, say, to leisure time spent with others.

But greed is also used to describe behaviour that transgresses laws and regulations. This might include insider trading and falsifying accounts. The problem here is that it is not always clear when a law is broken. There are many grey areas that require interpretation. Another approach is to class as greedy behaviour that which offends what is normally regarded as permissible. Examples range from giving information known to be untrue to holding back knowledge to maximize reward without taking account of how this might affect others. There are certainly links here with the recent financial crisis. It was greed that led financiers to conceal what they knew in order to increase loans and sell assets. This in turn contributed to greater indebtedness and the instability of financial markets.

Greed also led to compensation systems—bonuses for short-term profits—which created incentives to engage in destabilizing behaviour, so that greed fed greed. Thirdly, greed led financial elites to pressure the government into relaxing and preventing financial regulations with the purpose of increasing their incomes, which made the financial system more vulnerable. Lastly, greed on the part of the rich had an important role in bringing about increases in overall income inequality in countries like the USA, prompting engagement in business practices that depressed wages and support of tax breaks for themselves. The result was stagnation of the real incomes of the majority which, combined with other factors, led to large increases in consumer debt. While this maintained consumption and aggregate demand in the short run, it proved to be unsustainable in the longer run as debt burdens grew and asset bubbles burst.

But doesn't greed always exist and, if so, can one argue that greed had a specific role in bringing about the crisis? Although there is no doubt that greed—in the sense of breaking social norms in the pursuit of personal aggrandizement—is present to some degree at all times and places, its role is likely to increase in some circumstances. Two major aspects of the current crisis are its financial source and its international scope. Changes in the structure of economies have increased the size of the financial sector compared to that of the non-financial or 'real' sectors in many countries, while enhanced communication technology and relaxed control have increased the importance of international financial transactions. As a result the financial sector is more fertile ground for the conduct of greedy behaviour. Because the financial sector deals in assets which are intangibles—rather than goods and services whose properties are more easily perceived by buyers and sellers—there is greater scope for obfuscation and prevarication.

Then again, that many market participants are working in isolation using computers instead of dealing face-to-face with people makes social restraints on greedy behaviour less effective. That financial actors often work in a closed environment makes it more likely that greedy behaviour will become infectious in organizational culture or in the culture of the financial community at large. Moreover, the fact that the amounts that are traded in a short time can be very large makes the effects of greedy behaviour more pernicious. Regarding international transactions, it is possible that interactions between people from different countries may mean that they are less constrained by the social norms that are shared within a country. All of these factors can explain why greedy behaviour increased during the run-up to the global crisis.

Along with factors which intensified greed, there were socioeconomic changes which altered social norms. In 1980 the elections of Ronald Reagan in the USA and Margaret Thatcher in the UK represented an alternative social consensus to the prevailing Keynesian welfare state—a return to less government and freer markets. The result has been the growth of ideology fixated on competition and success as the measure of a person's worth. Daily events are reminders of its sway, as reflected in the exaltation of sports and movie stars and Wall Street and corporate executives; the negative attitude of the business community toward welfare legislation; the downsizing of corporations in which the managers and stock holders get richer while the employees get fired; and the whole philosophy of success which measures the value of people by their income.

The promotion of financial success and self-interest was epitomized in the 1980s by the goal of newly minted Harvard MBAs to make US$1 m. a year before their thirtieth birthday. By 2000 it was hedge fund managers and derivatives traders.

Businesses close industrial plants, create unemployment, devastate whole communities and call it an efficient reallocation of resources. They, who have prospered from free market policies, caution that nothing can be done because natural economic forces are dictated by globalization and competition. The poor, the unemployed and the underemployed are the ones who bear the burden of this free market ethic.

Government social programmes established during the previous 60 years are attacked because they supposedly reduce incentives and thus productivity. It was argued that lower taxes and fewer regulations on business result in higher profits, encouraging corporations and wealthy individuals to save and invest. Eventually the benefits trickle down so that even those on the bottom will be better off. However, this rarely happens.

If one believes that the natural order of society is one in which the strong win their way to power over the ruin of the weak, one will find nothing fundamentally wrong with this. It is then an easy step to understand, if not condone, the greed-driven behaviour within the financial sector that crossed the line to unethical insider trading, excessive risk-taking and neglect of obligations when handling other people's money. Since the movers and shakers of the financial world were seen as the Masters of the Universe, it is clear how government regulators were easy to convince that all was well. And given everyone's acceptance of the economics profession's teaching that markets know best, there was little reason to question what appeared to be unending success. Thus, a social consensus led to an atrophy of the normal legal, institutional and social mechanisms which, in earlier times, might have countered ethical lapses.

A central question we need to ask is whether the financial sector—especially as large as it has become—is good for society as a whole and whether such large profits for financial activities are justified? There is no question that the availability of finance can have positive consequences in terms of increasing production and income, utility and happiness. But this does not address the question as to whether the activity of financing justifies the rewards when the effort involved is simply making finance available.

Moreover, the idea that financial activity invariably has good consequences is questionable, especially when the financial sector becomes very large in relation to the rest of the economy. Market failures can lead to inefficiency by making the entire economy more crisis prone. When asset prices tumble and credit freezes the real sector is adversely affected as investment, output and employment drop, and unemployment rises. Also, large increases in income and asset inequality increases the power of financial interests to affect legislators and push for policy changes which are intended to bring about further increases in their income.

The neglect of these issues has led to an uncritical acceptance of the growing size of the financial sector. As a result, economists failed to recognize the crisis and even supported policies which made the crisis more likely.

The reluctance to examine the ethics of the financial sector is reflected in the use of terms like the *efficient* market hypothesis, capital market *liberalization* and financial *liberalization*, words which suggest hidden values in apparently value-free terms. The removal of regulation on banks and the decision to deregulate markets for new securities including derivatives can be traced to this problem.

The bias that economists and policymakers have shown toward efficiency and growth has supported neoliberal policies at the cost of other goals such as fairness, equality and the reduction of poverty and vulnerability. This neoliberal approach has justified weakening labour unions and reduced government support for the poor and the unemployed. It also means that policymakers are most concerned with the problems of government debt, thereby reducing their ability to pursue expansionary fiscal policies to reduce unemployment. All of this is not just the consequence of failing to take ethical issues seriously. It is also related to the nature of rewards in the economic profession, and also to the power and influence of those who believe that they benefit from such policies.

Reference

Dutt, Amitava Krishna and Wilber, Charles K., *Economics and Ethics: An Introduction*. Palgrave Macmillan, 2010.

PALGRAVE TITLES PRESENTED BY THEIR AUTHORS

The Scottish Nation at Empire's End, Bryan S. Glass

The British Empire was the largest and most powerful territorial unit ever created. In every corner of the globe a traveller could find the Union Flag flying above government buildings. However, two world wars and the rise of indigenous nationalist movements throughout imperial territories severely weakened Britain and forced a rapid decolonization effort in the 20-year period after 1945. Britain lost its position as the world's pre-eminent super-power abroad as Scottish nationalism arose at home.

The rise of a powerful Scottish nationalism, which brought Britain face-to-face with an independence referendum on 18 September, is perhaps the most important legacy of the failed empire. The Scots had gained so much from the British Empire since the mid-eighteenth century that its loss in the 1960s rocked the Scottish psyche. If the empire was still an effective force in the world there would be no talk of independence. But despite the efforts of historians and politicians to convince us that there was a powerful British

identity forged in the late-eighteenth and early-nineteenth centuries that can still be relevant today, any such identity was based heavily on the shared experience of empire. When the empire and all of its attendant benefits spectacularly ended, so too did much of the Scottish enthusiasm for the British political state.

The empire, after all, was one of the most important components of modern-day Scotland and the identity of its people. From the Act of Union in 1707, Scotland's involvement in commerce, missionary activity, cultural dissemination, emigration, and political action could not be dissociated from British overseas endeavours. In fact, Scottish national pride was closely linked with the benefits bestowed on this small nation through its access to the empire. Before the mid-1960s, support for the Scottish National Party (SNP) at Westminster elections was almost non-existent. When the imperial component of their identity was undermined, voting records show that many Scots responded by turning to an independence-seeking nationalism.

By examining the opinions of Scots from numerous professional and personal backgrounds during the era of decolonization, we are able to understand how much the empire meant to them. With the empire, Britain offered Scotland opportunity, prestige, and power on a global scale. When this outlet closed it may well have ended Scottish interest in Britain, too, as this once-proud imperial nation looks to reinvent itself on the global stage.

Bryan S. Glass is a Senior Lecturer in Modern British and British Imperial History at Texas State University. In his first book, **The Scottish Nation at Empire's End***, Glass discusses how the rise and fall of the British Empire profoundly shaped the history of modern Scotland and the identity of its people.*

Political Parties and the Concept of Power, Danny Rye

Research on political organization is characterized by narrow, and usually behavioural or hierarchical, approaches to power. However, theoretical debates point to greater possibilities. We consider that power is concerned with agents; how these powers are constituted is as significant as the actions and behaviour of individuals. How are human goals formulated, articulated and obtained? We are also concerned with the positive capacities invested in individuals and collectives as much as the power some apparently possess over others.

A framework containing five 'modes' of power, accounting for its oper-ation on different organizational levels, is proposed. These are: Individualis-tic, Strategic, Bureaucratic, Constitutive and Disciplinary. They should not be understood as parts of a holistic concept, but as a heuristic tool which supports and guides an analysis of power centred on the experience of party life.

Individualistic power generally explicates the conflicts between individ-uals and the resources they employ (the attempts of a 'controversial' MP to secure patronage and a leadership struggle on a London Borough Council serve to illustrate).

Strategic Power, however, recognizes the context of these confrontations. Those positionally able to manipulate or reconfigure rules and processes can effectively exclude or silence opponents. Reforms made to policy-making and internal election procedures, and how informal authority gave way to formal internal policing, illuminate how decision-making structures affect opportunities to articulate goals or grievances.

Bureaucratic power emphasizes how the party's administrative needs often take precedence over other activity. It underlines an organizational logic of centralization that engenders an impersonal machine-like control

© Springer Nature Limited 2019
Palgrave Macmillan (ed.), *The Statesman's Yearbook Companion*,
https://doi.org/10.1057/978-1-349-95839-9

which structures the agents' possibilities for action. This is exemplified by central control over candidate selection, intra-party discipline and the experience of routine tasks like meetings and canvassing.

Constitutive power emphasizes the everyday practices and habits by which structures and patterns of relations are reinforced and reproduced, including the conduct of meetings, a nationally-centred and career-oriented culture of party 'activism', as well as how training techniques can embed new patterns of behaviour.

Finally, disciplinary power focuses on the 'technical' problems of political organization and how their solution engenders detailed control and surveillance. Examples of this could include the effects of campaign organization and of modern marketing techniques on candidates.

This diverse, eclectic approach undoubtedly generates potential epistemological and methodological difficulties. However, a flexible ontology is argued for, accounting for both structure and agency, and an understanding of power as a diverse heuristic tool.

As a case study, the transformation of the British Labour Party between 1985 and 1997 exemplifies party organizational change. The key forces at work in the party's transition from what was regarded as a party divided, chaotic and apparently destined for oblivion to 'New' Labour, a slick and disciplined electoral machine are explored. The reflections of senior party figures and activists, along with archive and biographical material, are employed to illuminate and elaborate the theory.

Danny Rye is Associate Lecturer in Politics and Policy at the Department of Politics, Birkbeck College, University of London, UK. In **Political Parties and the Concept of Power** *Rye investigates the nature of the forces that make members and representatives both loyal and beneficial to a contemporary political party and asks whether power is more complex and nuanced than is frequently assumed.*

The State of Russia: What Comes Next?, Maria Lipman and Nikolay Petrov

Following events in Ukraine in late 2013 and early 2014, the regime of Vladimir Putin made sweeping political choices that will determine the country's development for many years to come. Post-2014, we are presented with a very different Russia with a qualitatively different leader, different elites and different citizens.

The regime has become ever more authoritarian and personalized. Today Putin bears far greater resemblance to a monarch and his power is unchecked; he, his inner circle, and the structures accountable directly to him have gained additional authority. The balance of power among the political elites is now significantly tilted in favor of the security and law-enforcement agencies that continue to receive additional powers to control both businesses and the public at large.

Additionally, the once peaceful decision-making process has taken on a militaristic dynamic; power is now structured vertically, with Putin at the apex. Critical decisions such as the 2014 annexation of Crimea and recent countersanctions against western food imports are being made by a narrow group of individuals with little, if any, prior deliberation or consideration of possible consequences.

The ideological unobtrusiveness of the 2000s is being replaced by propagandist harshness and aggression, primarily directed at the west and its 'agents'. This new ideology—combining great-power aspirations, isolationism and quasi-traditionalism with the Soviet pattern of intolerance to dissent—has been instrumental in building a nationwide consensus based on the

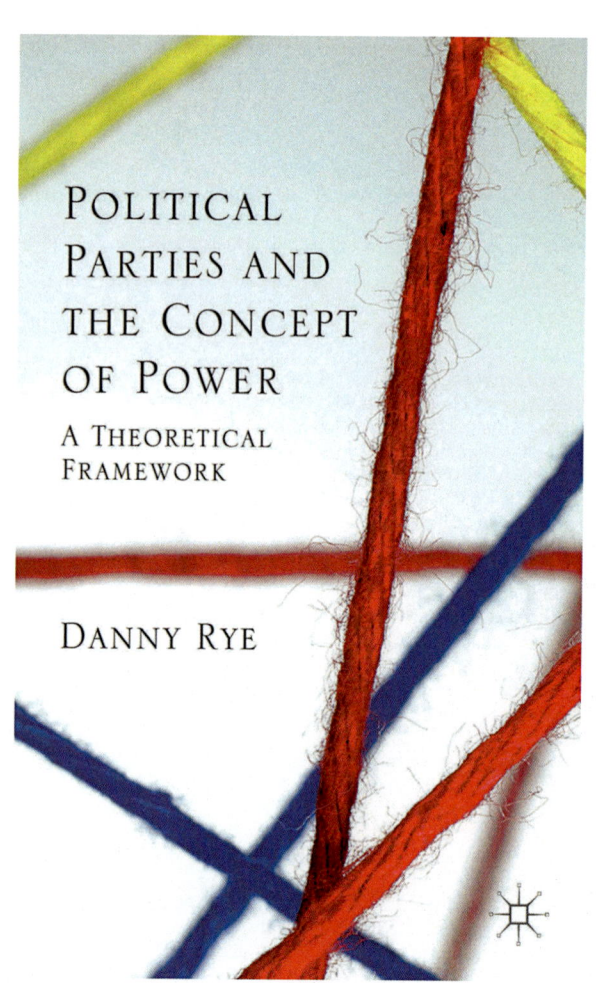

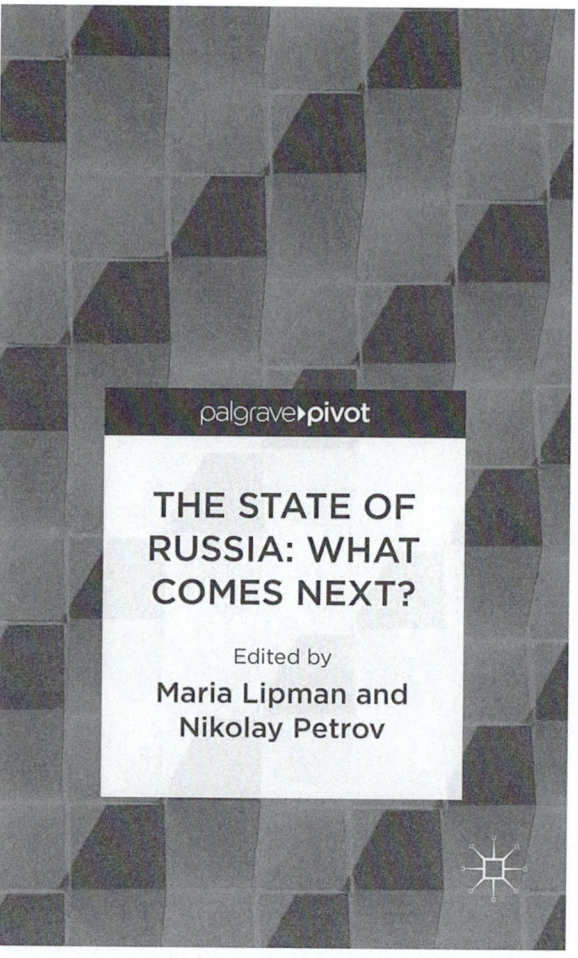

broadest possible support for the leader and his "besieged fortress" regime. The regime's ideology requires no doctrine, and the administration itself does not seek to deeply indoctrinate its subjects. It is however, concerned with discrediting ideas and values that may cast doubt on the supreme value of the state and the legitimacy of its leadership.

The transformation of 2014 did not just drastically narrow the range of possible developmental trajectories for Russia, but also set the country on a dead-end course of de-modernization that is dismantling the achievements of post-Soviet development. Furthermore, the weakening of the higher courts and expansion of extra-judicial persecution has undone years of efforts to strengthen judicial independence, humanize the justice system and raise public legal awareness. The virtual demolition of local governance deprives grass-roots democracy of its base and expels the public from civic life. The adverse effects on society are particularly strong as the Kremlin has steadily enhanced the paternalistic, conservative and xenophobic mindset. Repairing the damage and returning to the course of national modernization will be long and arduous.

Maria Lipman is an independent analyst. She has contributed to, and edited several volumes dealing with Russian politics and culture, and published a number of articles on the Russian media, politics and society.

Nikolay Petrov is Professor at Higher School of Economics, Moscow. He has been the author or editor of numerous publications dealing with analysis of Russia's political regime, post-Soviet transformation and socioeconomic and political development.

At a time when Russia's offensive foreign policy has caught the world unawares The State of Russia: What Comes Next offers a reassessment of the West's understanding of Russia and its president. Looking ahead to different possible scenarios of the Russian future, it analyses the current shifts in the Russian regime, traces the new trends in various spheres of Russian life, from the economy and foreign policy to the society and ideology, and projects them into the future.

*The State of Russia: What Comes Next? Published by **Palgrave Macmillan** June 2015.*

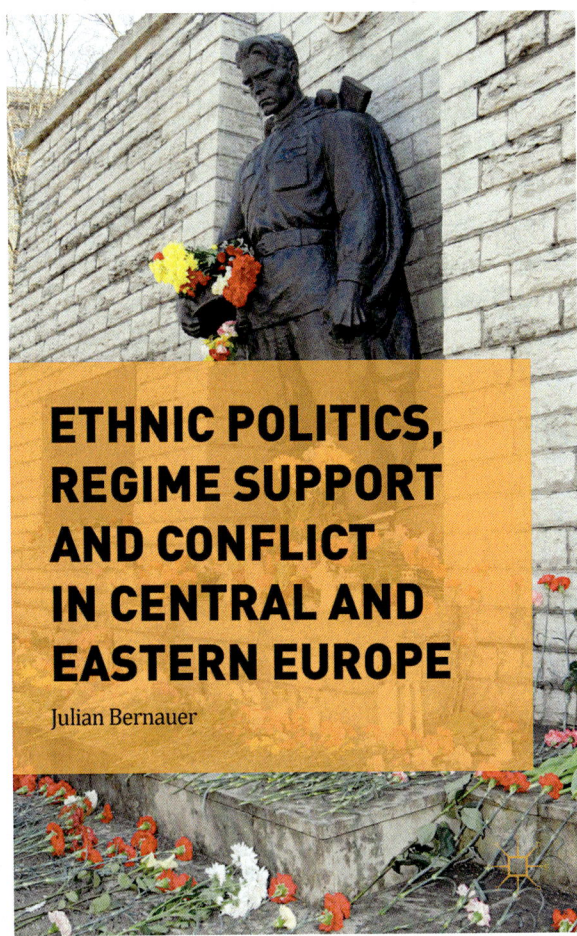

Ethnic Politics, Regime Support and Conflict in Central and Eastern Europe, Julian Bernauer

Ethnicity and ethnic parties have often been portrayed as threats to political stability. However, ethnicity's role in politics is far more diverse than indicated by serious incidents such as the 1990s Balkan Wars, peaked by the tragedy of the Srebrenica massacre in July 1995. As the continuing struggle for peace and democracy in countries such as Bosnia and Herzegovina or Kosovo demonstrates, deep ethnic divisions do not easily heal despite well-meaning political-institutional treatment. 'Consociational' arrangements, dictating the proportional representation of ethnic groups in government—such as the rotating presidency in Bosnia and Herzegovina shared between Bosniaks, Serbs and Croats—are only viable given sufficient popular and elite support.

But in less extreme settings, the political inclusion of ethnic minority groups has a more promising outlook. It can be argued that 'ethnic politics' is not entirely distinct from the ubiquitous 'party politics' model, in that the political modus operandi of minority group representatives certainly incorporates a desire to implement an agenda and to win office. Crucially however, opportunities and incentives to achieve these goals in a peaceful manner are needed. Hence, the organization of politics in heterogeneous societies does not necessarily need to aim at overcoming ethnicity, but rather should look to the descriptive representation of ethnic minority groups as a means to increase regime support and reduce conflict.

Examining up to 130 ethnic groups and their parties in central and eastern European democracies, we find some evidence that the factors influencing their electoral success, and indeed, the extent to which they are represented in parliament resemble many 'mainstream' parties'. Partisan-descriptive ethnic minority representation in central and eastern Europe has the potential to increase levels of satisfaction among members of respective minority groups and reduce protest by—arguably, and hopefully—allowing for political compromise. However, as an important qualifier, these patterns of regime support

are not observed for all individuals (for instance, women may not benefit as much from ethnically defined descriptive representation as men) and only participation in the executive branch of government appears to reduce protest activities such as demonstrations. The descriptive representation of ethnic minorities in politics hence demonstrates some potential for the successful integration of heterogeneous societies, but its role in ethnic conflict resolution surely remains context-dependent and controversial.

*Julian Bernauer is a Postdoctoral Researcher and Lecturer in Comparative Politics at the University of Berne. In his book, **Ethnic Politics, Regime Support and Conflict in Central and Eastern Europe** Bernauer analyses explanations for and consequences of the descriptive representation of ethnic minorities in central and eastern Europe via ethnic parties.*

Ethnic Politics, Regime Support and Conflict in Central and Eastern Europe. Published by Palgrave Macmillan Aug. 2015.

The Palgrave Encyclopedia of Imperialism and Anti-imperialism, Zak Cope

In today's world, devastating conflicts rage across the countries of the global South in the context of long drawn out economic stagnation and looming global recession. Many people around the world are now questioning whether the stated objectives of the richest and most powerful countries

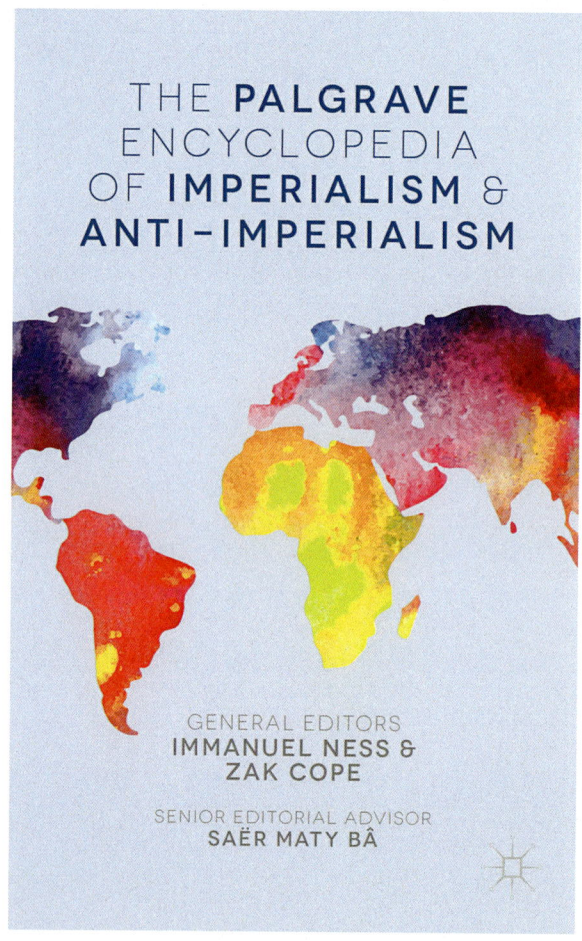

The *Palgrave Encyclopedia of Imperialism and Anti-Imperialism* is a brand new, two-volume publication that presents theoretical and historical accounts of imperialism and anti-imperialism from the beginnings of the capitalist world system in the sixteenth Century to the present day. Containing over 170 entries written by an international team of experts and scholars working in the field of imperialism and anti-imperialism, it provides in-depth studies of imperialism's roots, goals, tactics, and impact. The volume also covers the rich tradition of anti-imperialism, its intellectuals, leaders, theories and practices.

Dr Zak Cope obtained a PhD from the School of Politics, International Studies and Philosophy at Queen's University Belfast. He is the author of Dimensions of Prejudice: Towards a Political Economy of Bigotry (2008) and Divided World Divided Class: Global Political Economy and the Stratification of Labour under Capitalism (2012 and 2014).
    The Palgrave Encyclopedia of Imperialism and Anti-Imperialism. Published by **Palgrave Macmillan** Oct. 2015.

Hugo Chávez, Alí Primera and Venezuela: The Politics of Music in Latin America, Hazel Marsh

In February 1992, a Venezuelan colonel called Hugo Chávez, together with other officers from a movement that had formed within the military, led an unsuccessful coup attempt against the country's deeply unpopular government. Two years later, on the day he was released from prison having served time for his role in the failed coup, Colonel Chávez was asked by a journalist if he had a message for the people of Venezuela. 'Yes', he announced, 'Let them listen to Alí Primera's songs!' Within 5 years, having formed a new political organization and mounted a campaign rooted in these very songs, Hugo Chávez was elected president of Venezuela with 56% of the vote. He thus became the first head of state without links to the country's establishment parties in over 40 years.
    But who was Alí Primera, and why did Chávez link his political movement with his songs?
    Born in 1942, Alí Primera became Venezuela's best-known 'protest' singer. In his songs, Alí denounced the economic, cultural, political, racial and environmental impact of the oil industry on his country. His music was frequently prohibited, and his death in a car accident in 1985 was widely rumoured to have been ordered by state officials to silence a 'troublesome' voice. Popularly seen as a martyr who died fighting for the poor and the marginalized, Alí and his songs rapidly passed into the realm of myth, uniting Venezuelans in their denunciations of political corruption, increasing poverty levels and state oppression in the late 1980s and early 1990s.
    By urging Venezuelans to listen to Alí's songs, and by singing and quoting from these songs and honouring Alí's legacy, Chávez was able to connect his government with the masses on whose behalf Alí was seen to have struggled and suffered. But state institutionalization of Alí's legacy produced competing power struggles over who was best placed to legitimately interpret the songs 'correctly'. Official support for Alí's legacy endowed the songs with new significance; in the Chávez period, the songs created a space where political alternatives were not only imagined and shared, but also defended, challenged and resisted by Venezuelans actively redefining their relation to the state within a new social and political order.
    Hugo Chávez, Alí Primera and Venezuela: The Politics of Music in Latin America has important implications not only for scholars of popular music and Venezuelan political history, but also for readers seeking a better understanding of the dynamic ways in which Chávez was able to successfully identify himself so closely with the poor and marginalized masses in Venezuela, and they with him. In this book, which is part of the Palgrave series on the history of subcultures and popular music, Hazel Marsh elucidates the dynamic ways in which music and politics can intertwine in Latin America.

Hazel Marsh is a lecturer in the school of Politics, Philosophy, Language and Communication Studies, University of East Anglia. She has researched, and

involved—namely humanitarian interventionism and the responsibility to protect—are not simply cover stories for their pursuit of commercial, industrial, financial and military hegemony. In short, the word 'imperialism' is becoming more and more a part of the critical lexicon of those concerned with international affairs.
    We are now more than a century after the outbreak of the First World War, when economic crisis manifested by overproduction, falling rates of profit, and declining mass consumption led to conflict over preferential trade agreements, tariff barriers, trade routes, protected markets for investments and manufactures, and raw materials sources. The First and Second World Wars were at root based on a drive to colonialism by the leading capitalist powers as a means of securing protected markets. Each occurred in the context of the division of the entire world into core and peripheral capitalist nations within an economic world-system dominated by the financial and industrial monopolies of western Europe and its offshoots.
    An essay in the *Palgrave Encyclopedia Imperialism and Anti-Imperialism* on German imperialism and social imperialism between 1871 and 1933 discusses the struggle waged by German monopoly capital to secure against its competitors a dominant position in world markets by means of settler colonialism, the export of capital, unequal exchange, the imposition of economic dependency and, in some instances, the genocidal massacre of 'backward' peoples. It reveals the extent to which the socialist left in Germany did not seek to hinder the ascendance of German capital internationally but, on the contrary, acquiesced in it in so far as labour was thereby guaranteed rising wages and living standards. When, in the context of global depression, the German bourgeoisie turned to fascism as the program of a flailing capitalist elite which could not rule other than on an aggressive anti-labour and belligerently imperialist platform, the socialists failed to turn against their erstwhile allies. The essay thus elucidates many of the key problems facing the world today, pointing towards a solution based on genuine labour internationalism, and not the sectional interests of privileged classes and class fractions.

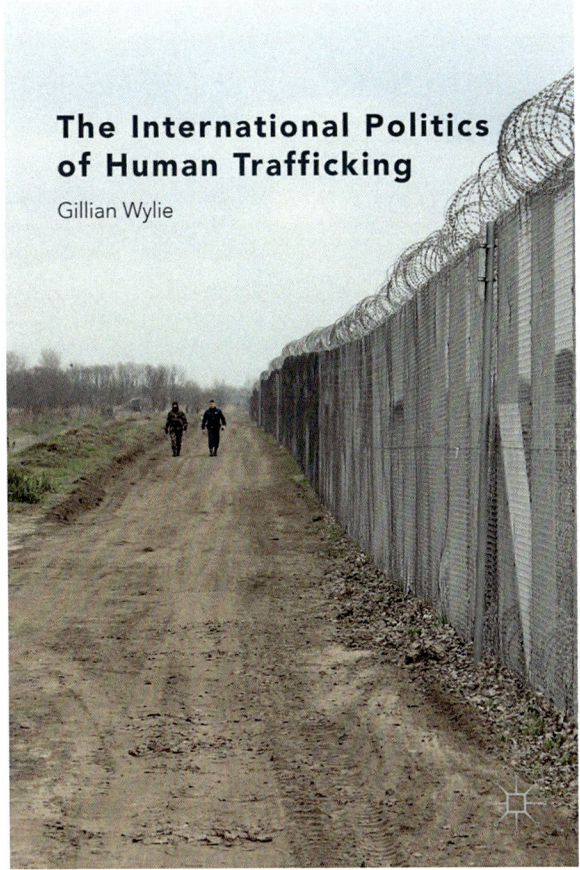

published on, popular music and the Mexican student movement, Venezuelan cultural policy in the Chávez period, resistance music in Oaxaca, Mexico, and representations of British Gypsies.

Hugo Chávez, Alí Primera and Venezuela: The Politics of Music in Latin America. Published by **Palgrave Macmillan** 2016.

The International Politics of Human Trafficking, Gillian Wylie

The 'migration crisis' of 2015–16 has cast European states into disarray, with members at odds over how to respond. Should refugee rights prevail? Will states agree to share the burden? Or is it imperative to stop people's movement in the name of national identity and security? In Europe's incoherent actions to date, elements of all these responses appear within each member and across the Union. Prominently however, responses which frame migrants as a security threat requiring exclusionary policies are on the rise. The Hungarian border fence, NATO operations in the Mediterranean and the EU–Turkey return deal being prime examples. Curiously, in seeking to legitimize this 'securitized' response to the migration crisis, frequent recourse is made to the language of combatting human trafficking. Hungarian Prime Minister Orban refers to the fence as a means to mete out 'punishment for human trafficking that will be so severe that it will be really deserved by those who do business with the life and fate of others' (NBC News, 2015). Similarly, NATO naval vessels patrol to 'crack down on human trafficking and criminal networks fuelling the migration crisis' (Deutsche Presse-Agentur, 2016). How has the concern to prevent human trafficking, borne for many out of the desire to protect the human rights of exploited people, become a means to justify the exclusion of migrants at Europe's borders?

This book seeks to answer this question by tracing the spectacular rise over the last 20 years of human trafficking as an international political issue. Before the 1990s interest in human trafficking was dormant but two decades later it is an international cause celebre. The anti-trafficking UN Palermo Protocol of 2000 spawned a host of new institutions, laws and policing regimes around the world. Simultaneously, new anti-trafficking law in the US gave the State Department a role in monitoring and judging all states responses to the issue. Nowadays anti-trafficking local and global civil society activism is rife and raucous, media depictions proliferate and even celebrities take up the cause. All of this despite the consensus that statistical claims about human trafficking are dubious.

The impetus behind all this activity can be traced to transnational advocacy work by radical feminists and faith-based organizations, particularly in relation to their concerns over sex trafficking in women and children. However, this book argues that the willingness of states to develop anti-trafficking frameworks stems only partially from moral concerns and essentially from their interests in enhancing border controls against the assumed threat of transnational organised crime and finding means to discipline the transnational mobility of people. Using the idea of a 'norm lifecycle', this book argues that the creation and shape of this new global architecture is rooted in the strange convergence of NGO advocacy with state's interests in seeking to manage the globalizing world.

Gillian Wylie is Assistant Professor of International Peace Studies in Trinity College Dublin. Her research and teaching interests span human trafficking and migration, international politics and gender issues as they relate to war and peace.

The International Politics of Human Trafficking. Published by **Palgrave Macmillan** 2016.

International Communism and the Cult of the Individual, Kevin Morgan

Communism was one of the defining political movements of the twentieth century. Viewed from different perspectives, it was at once a utopia, a system of government, an apparatus of terror and an international political movement stretching to almost every corner of the globe. It is also a movement hard to visualize without calling to mind the leaders who personified it. Marx, Lenin, Stalin, Mao—their images were ubiquitous and could be found on banners, posters, medals and on plinths in a thousand public squares. Communists themselves came to refer to this as the cult of the individual, or the cult of personality. The phrase has since come into general parlance and encapsulates the paradox of an age of mass politics that was crystallized in the figure of the leader.

It is said that no individual has had more books written about him than Stalin. Here was a cult that can be set alongside Hitler's or Mussolini's, and together they can tell us much about the cult of power in Europe's age of extremes. There were, however, some basic differences. Above all, what was distinctive about communism was its international character. Fascism was driven by nationalism, and its leader cults provided a symbolic centre around which states or nations mobilized. Communism, on the other hand, was a movement of such scope, cohesion and ambition internationally that it can only be likened to the world's great religions. It was not just that Lenin, Stalin and the others were found on banners the world over. Within each communist party there were also lower-level cults of the individuals who in each country incarnated the cause that communists stood for.

The fascination of a transnational study is that it therefore means exploring how common practices and ideals found expression in disparate historical circumstances. It takes us to the great symbolic centres of communist power, like Lenin's Red Square mausoleum in Russia and China's Tiananmen Square. But it also takes us to the Spanish civil war, the French resistance,

the gaols of Hitler and Mussolini, and to revolts against dictators in Latin America. As well as party leaders, it introduces us to the figures of the orator, the tribune, the martyr and the 'writer in arms'—and to the ways in which they were represented in film, on canvas, in poetry and musical tributes, and in the communists' predilection for hagiography (that is to say, unduly reverent biographical depictions). It is therefore also the story of Picasso, Brecht, Prokofiev and Neruda, as well as the political leaders whom they celebrated.

Lenin and Stalin may in many ways seem like figures from a bygone age. Nevertheless, in an era of Trump and Putin, it is difficult to see that the politics of personality have lost their relevance. At the same time, the commemoration of a figure like Nelson Mandela reminds us of the higher ideals that a particular individual may still come to symbolize. Exploring the communist politics of personality not only means seeking to unravel one of the truly intriguing phenomena of twentieth-century politics. It also confronts us with far more basic issues concerning the use and abuse of political power.

Kevin Morgan is Professor of Politics and Contemporary History at the University of Manchester, UK. He has published extensively on the history of the communist movement including the three volumes of his Bolshevism and the British Left (2006–13). He is a founding editor of the journal Twentieth Century Communism.
International Communism and the Cult of the Individual. Published by **Palgrave Macmillan** 2016.

The Russian Challenge to the European Security Environment, Roger Kanet

The most recent of a series of Palgrave publications on Russian foreign policy edited or coedited by Roger E. Kanet, *The Russian Challenge to the European Security Environment*, brings together a group of established scholars from Russia and the West. They trace the deterioration of East-West relations and Russia's growing challenge to the European security order in place for the past quarter century. Although the story that the authors tell of these changing relations varies somewhat, it generally departs from the dominant Western narrative in distributing the blame for the deterioration on both the West and Russia. During the 1990s, when Russia was attempting to adjust to its new and reduced post-Soviet status and seemed willing to join with the West, the Europe and the USA generally ignored Russia's interests and expanded their own involvement into what had been the Soviet sphere of domination. This expansionist approach culminated in the middle of the 2000s with the extension of both NATO and the EU into Central Europe and the Baltic region and with Western support for the 'colour revolutions' against Moscow's allies in Kyiv, Tbilisi, and Bishkek.

Although Russian policy toward the West had already begun to shift by the mid-1990s, it was not until Vladimir Putin became president and, most clearly, after the Bush Administration's largely unilateral invasion of Iraq and the challenge of the 'colour revolutions', that Moscow decided that the achievement of its objectives on the basis of cooperation with the West was impossible. The result has been a growing challenge to the dominant position of the West, both in Central and Eastern Europe and globally, as Russia has pursued the goal of reestablishing its position as the preeminent regional power and a top global actor.

The analyses that comprise the book begin with a focus on the growing Russian normative challenge to the existing Western-dominated world order and the fundamental incompatibility of emerging Russian policy objectives with those of the West. Russia has used both its dominant economic position in post-Soviet space and coercive diplomacy in its effort to thwart Western incursions into its 'sphere of influence' and to reestablish its position as the dominant regional power.

Russian interventions in both Ukraine and in Syria have been the most recent examples of the growing Russian–Western confrontation. The EU's Eastern neighbourhood policy challenged Russia's plans for a new Eurasia centered on Moscow and the latter moved to stop it. The result was Russian support for Russophone secessionists in Ukraine and Moscow's absorption of Ukrainian territory in Crimea—both policies widely supported by an increasingly nationalistic Russian population.

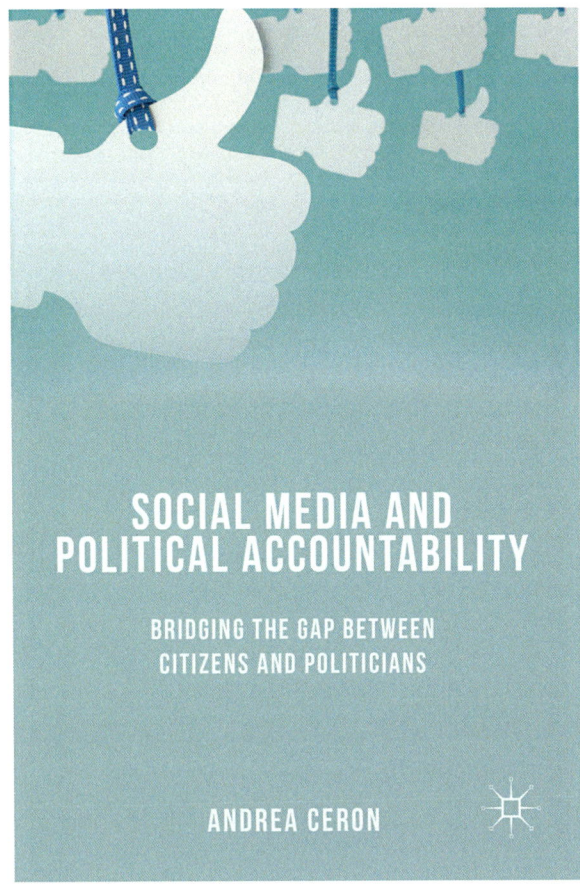

To briefly summarise, Russian relations with the West since the demise of the USSR began with a period of possible collaboration, but a period when the West took advantage of Moscow's weakness. This played to the advantage of nationalistic forces in Russia, headed by Vladimir Putin, who are committed to reestablishing Russia's greatness, regardless of the negative impact on relations with the West. The result is the confrontation that we witness today.

Roger E. Kanet is Professor of Political Science at the University of Miami. His most recent publications include a number of titles published by Palgrave Macmillan, including; Power, Politics and Confrontation in Eurasia: Foreign Policy in a Contested Area, 2015; Russia, Eurasian Integration and the New Geopolitics of Energy, 2015.

The Russian Challenge to the European Security Environment. Published by **Palgrave Macmillan** 2017.

Social Media and Political Accountability, Andrea Ceron

Verbal fights between supporters of rival parties often make us consider the Web as an environment that promotes negativity. Nor are politicians themselves exempt from 'gaffes' when they act impulsively, revealing their real feelings.

Indeed, social media can encourage such impulsive behaviour but it also represents an opportunity to foster transparency. As politicians start using social media to express their thoughts, they can be held accountable by their principals (that is to say, subjects from whom power is derived, such as voters, party activists, party leaders and interest groups), whether such preferences are sincere or expressed for purely strategic purposes. As a result, accountability and transparency can increase accordingly.

The purpose of my book, *Social Media and Political Accountability*, is to analyze a number of key episodes concerning the relationship between politics and social media in Italy. This is done by means of automated text analysis (whereby word frequencies across different texts are compared so as to extract the positions of various political actors) and supervised sentiment analysis (a method of opinion-mining from social media conversations by a mix of manual analysis and automated analysis deriving from machine learning). For instance, it investigates the endorsements made by centre-left politicians during their primary election of 2012, the effect of social media pressure on the selection of the Head of State in 2013 and the formation of the Letta and Renzi cabinets in 2013 and 2014, as well as several recent public policies.

The results highlight an overall lack of responsiveness toward the will of social media users when these are conceived as a stand-alone 'competing principal'. The behaviour of politicians seems barely affected by online pressure.

However, social media does play a role. Firstly, although politicians are not necessarily responsive toward the requests of their followers, by declaring online their political views politicians become exposed to citizens' control: social media users will underline and criticize any U-turn, as the analysis of the 'civil union bill' debate has demonstrated.

Secondly, social networking sites can help a party's leadership to control the behaviour of its MPs by requesting them to display public loyalty online and by checking which MP has expressed dissent, then punishing or rewarding them in light of their visible online behaviour.

The book's main finding is that analyzing politicians' tweets gives crucial information about the occurrence of party splits and about politicians' careers and the formation of governments. To cite just one example, the language adopted by Democratic Party politicians who eventually became ministers or junior ministers in the Renzi cabinet was significantly similar to the language used by the party's official Twitter account if compared to the language of politicians who did not get a career advancement.

Rather than restraining intraparty democracy, social networking sites therefore provide backbenchers with the opportunity to build their reputations, in terms of showing loyalty towards the leadership or expressing dissent to boost their popularity among rank-and-file members.

Summing up, even if social media are not becoming a new principal that politicians must satisfy, this does not imply that they are unable to bridge the gap between citizens and political elites. On the contrary, as long as social media increase politicians' incentives to respond to traditional principals, including party leaders, party activists and voters, they can contribute to making the gears of the political system more transparent. Likewise, by strengthening the chain of responsiveness that goes from voters to governments, social media can therefore reinforce the process of representative democracy.

Andrea Ceron is Assistant Professor at Università degli Studi di Milano, Italy, and co-founder of Voices from the Blogs Ltd, a University spin-off that analyzes social media. He has published articles in the British Journal of Political Science, European Journal of Political Research, Journal of Computer-Mediated Communication, New Media & Society, Information Sciences, and Party Politics.

Social Media and Political Accountability. Published by **Palgrave Macmillan** 2017.

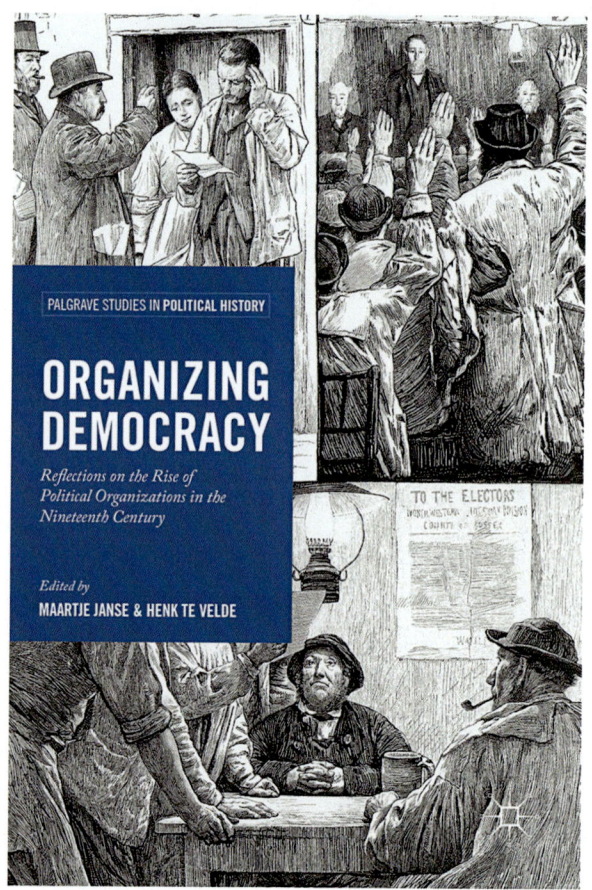

Organizing Democracy: Reflections on the Rise of Political Organizations in the Nineteenth Century, Maartje Janse and Henk te Velde

In *Organizing Democracy: Reflections on the Rise of Political Organizations in the Nineteenth Century* Maartje Janse and Henk te Velde bring together a group of scholars (most of them political historians) to reflect on a phenomenon that is too often taken for granted: political organizing.

The chapters of this book cover a wide range of case studies, from British petition campaigns to radical organizations in New York. Legal scholar Kevin Butterfield analyses the legal protection of membership rights in the early United States, while Nicolas Roussellier reappraises the 'failure' of political parties in Republican France. Together, the contributors explore the new types of political organization that emerged in Western Europe and the United States during the nineteenth century, from popular meetings to single-issue organizations and political parties.

The development of political organization has often been described as a movement towards democratic representation or political institutionalization. This book challenges the idea that the development of 'democracy' is a story of rise and progress at all. It is rather a story of continuous but never completely satisfying attempts at interpreting the rule of the people. Taking the perspective of nineteenth-century organizers as its point of departure, the authors show that contemporaries hardly distinguished between petitioning, meeting and association. The attraction of organizing was that it promised representation, accountability and popular participation. Only in the twentieth century did parties become reliable partners for the state in its ambitions to avert revolution, manage the unpredictable effects of universal suffrage, and reform society. This book analyzes the parties in their earliest stages, as just one type of civil society organization that did not differ much from other types. The promise of organization, and the experiments that resulted from it, deeply impacted modern politics.

This is the first volume of a new book series: Palgrave Studies in Political History—edited by Maartje Janse and Henk te Velde along with Hagen Schulz-Forberg (Aarhus)—which sets out to offer transnational accounts of new political history that connect institutional history with popular history.

Maartje Janse and Prof. Henk te Velde both lecture on Dutch history at Leiden University, Netherlands. Their most recent publications include books and articles such as: Passion and Reason: Modern Parliaments in the Low Countries, 2016; 'Holland as a little England'? British Anti-slavery Missionaries and Continental Abolitionist Movements in the Mid Nineteenth Century, 2015.

Organizing Democracy: Reflections on the Rise of Political Organizations in the Nineteenth Century. Published by **Palgrave Macmillan** 2017.

Varieties of Capitalism in Asia, David Hundt and Jitendra Uttam

The main claim of this book is that *the social origins of capitalism matter*. Previous studies of capitalism in Asia have paid little attention to contestation over the goals of capitalist development, and variation in the policies used to promote capitalism. This book, by contrast, maintains that 'social embeddedness' has been a precondition for the formation of strong and effective interventionist states in Asia. The most successful and stable capitalist economies have been typified by comparatively high degrees of social embeddedness, by which we simply mean that states are firmly rooted in society. Political leaders design economic policy so that it benefits more than just themselves, and to some degree they are accountable to society. The least successful and most unstable, meanwhile, have tended to have comparatively lower levels of embeddedness. These societies are the ones where leaders have generally sought to exploit their citizens, and the benefits of economic policy tend to be accumulated by a narrow segment of society.

A common challenge for Asian states has been to manage the transition away from agrarian-based economies to genuinely capitalistic systems. A key enabling mechanism in this is the embedding of capitalism in society. The broader the social base of capitalism, the better the system is likely to perform. Conversely, capitalist systems with narrow or shallow social bases run the risk of instability and weak legitimacy.

There is, however, substantial variety within Asian capitalism too. The book compares states that underwent broadly similar processes in similar periods of time, but with different results. Japan stands alone as the 'first generation' of Asian capitalism, having begun its concerted push for capitalist development soon after the Second World War. Japan has also been instrumental in spearheading industrialisation across the region. A series of carefully orchestrated structural shifts has resulted in Asia becoming the 'factory of the world'. Initially based on labour, then capital, and finally knowledge intensity, this system created regional 'followers' in the 1960s. Korea and Taiwan, and Singapore and Hong Kong, make up the 'second generation' of Asian capitalism. Malaysia, Thailand, India and China became the third generation in the 1970s and 1980s. Under pressure from domestic wage increases, Northeast Asian economies looked for opportunities to relocate their labour-intensive, mass-manufacturing industries to the second-tier producers in other parts of Asia. The meeting of Northeast Asia's capital, expertise and proven manufacturing technology on the one hand, and the readily available cheap labour in other Asian societies on the other, enabled a distinct model of capitalism to spread across the region.

Social embeddedness, this book shows, is essential to the survival of capitalism. A mass-participatory economy provides a higher degree of social embeddedness, which enables capitalism to flourish. Higher levels of participation have a positive impact on the size of markets and levels of investment. Corporate profits will increase if there is a bigger consuming class and a wider network of investors. In short, the experience of capitalism in Asia illustrates that leaders have a substantial interest in getting as many people as possible to buy into capitalism.

David Hundt is a Senior Lecturer in International Relations at Deakin University, in Melbourne, Australia. His most recent publications include articles such as: Public opinion, social cohesion and the politics of immigration in South Korea, 2016; Democracy, governance and political parties in India: an introduction, 2016; Neoliberalism, the developmental state and civil society in Korea, 2015.

Jitendra Uttam is an Assistant Professor in Korean Studies at India's Jawaharlal Nehru University in New Delhi. His recent publications include The Political Economy of Korea: Transition, Transformation and Turnaround, 2014.

INFOGRAPHICS COMMEMORATING SIGNIFICANT HISTORICAL ANNIVERSARIES

800th Anniversary of King John's Magna Carta

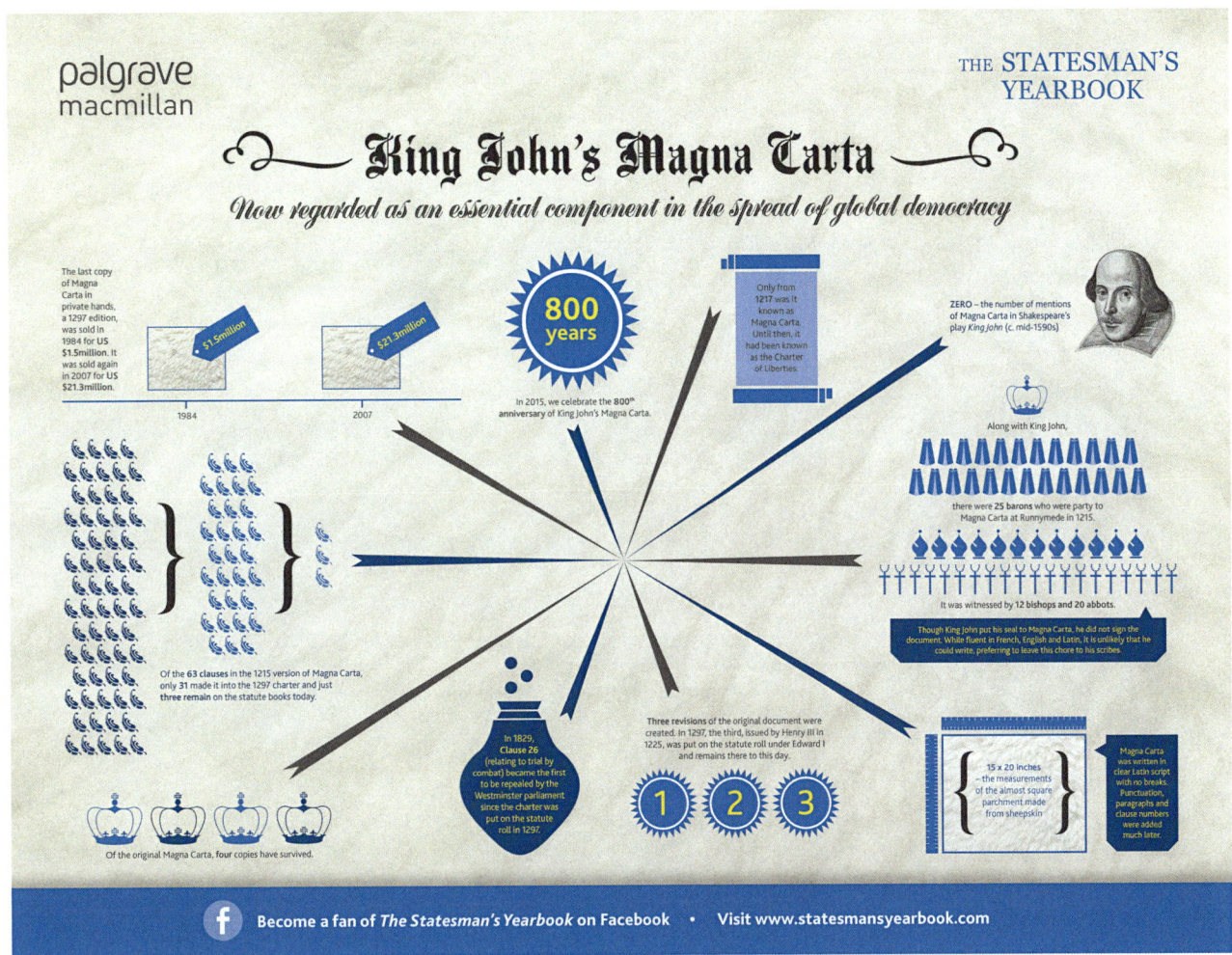

25 Years since the Fall of the Berlin Wall

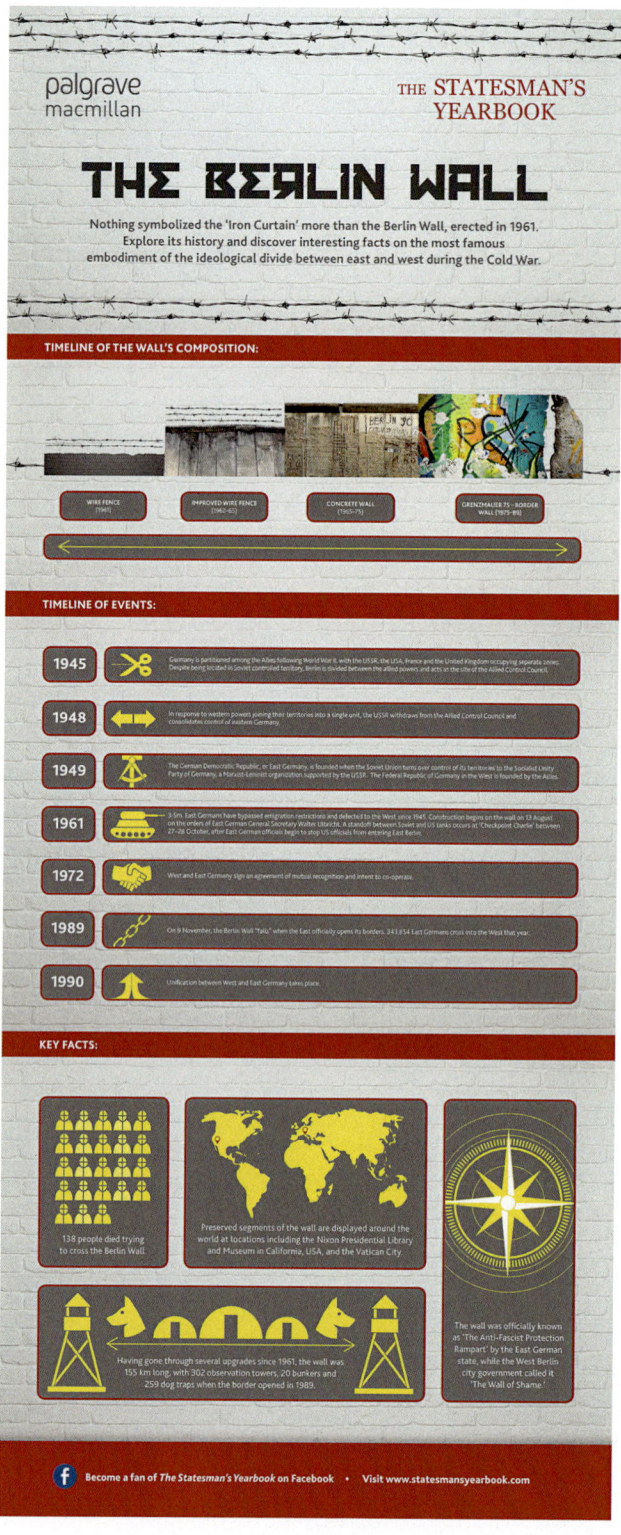

25 Years after the Release of Nelson Mandela from Prison

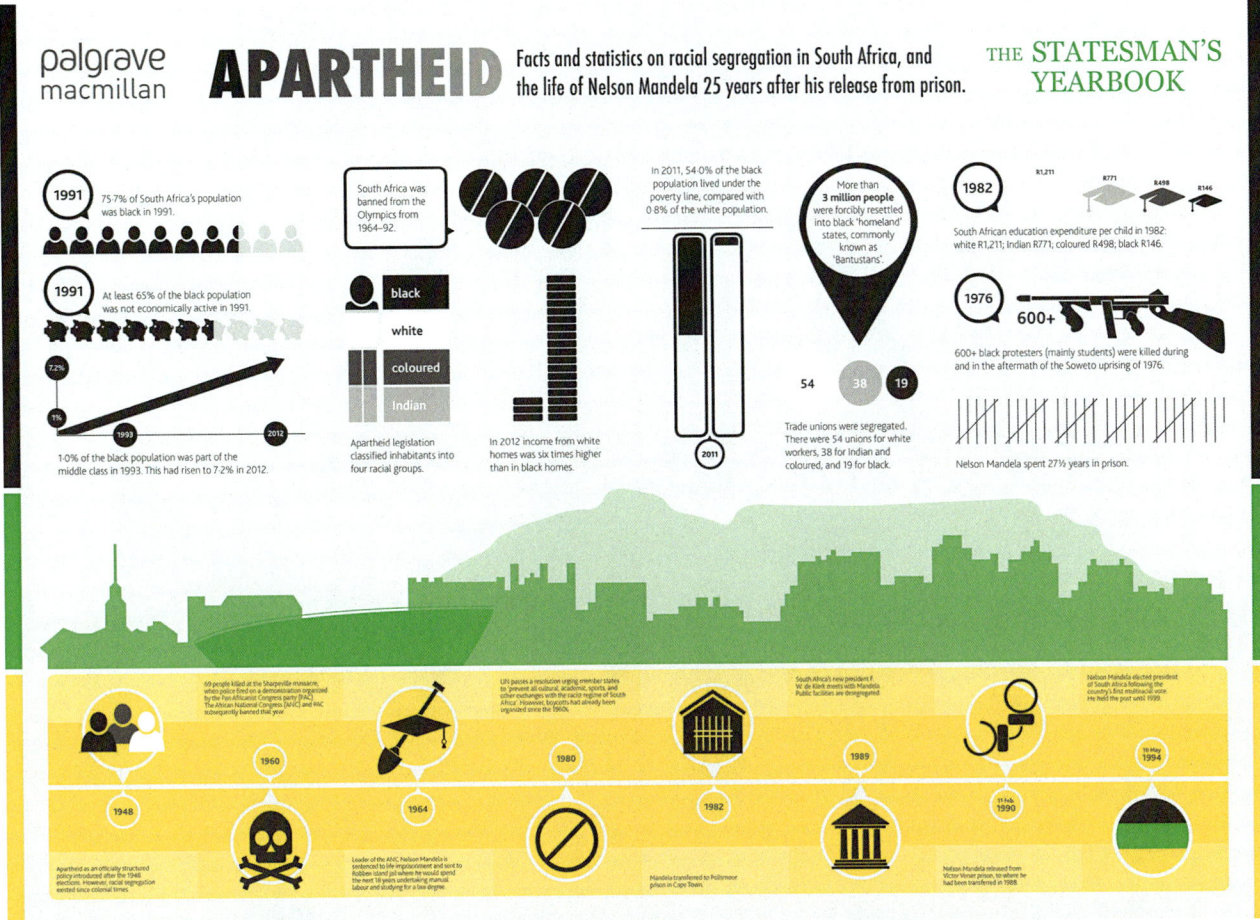

30 Years since the Sinking of the Rainbow Warrior

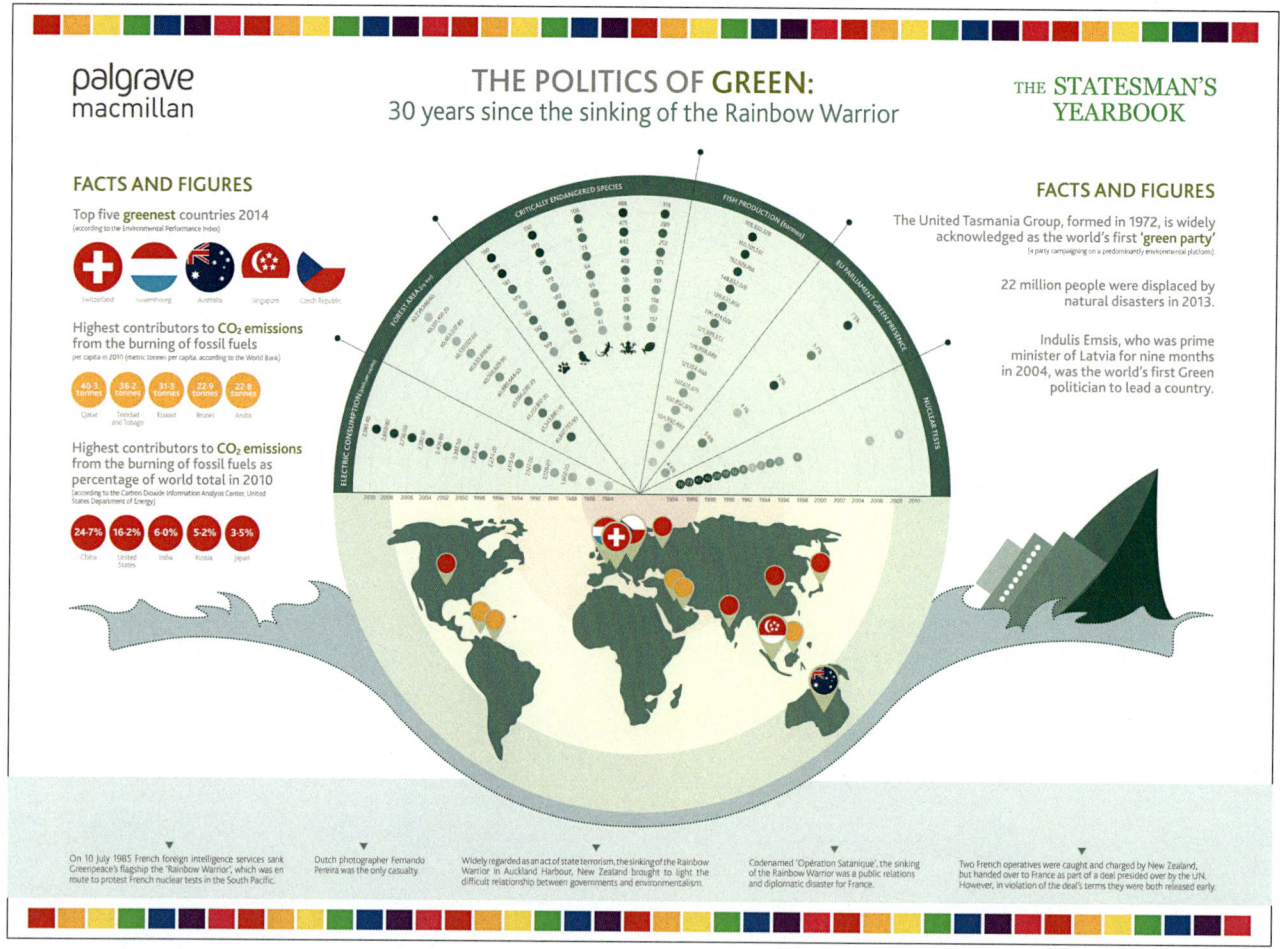

70 Years of the United Nations

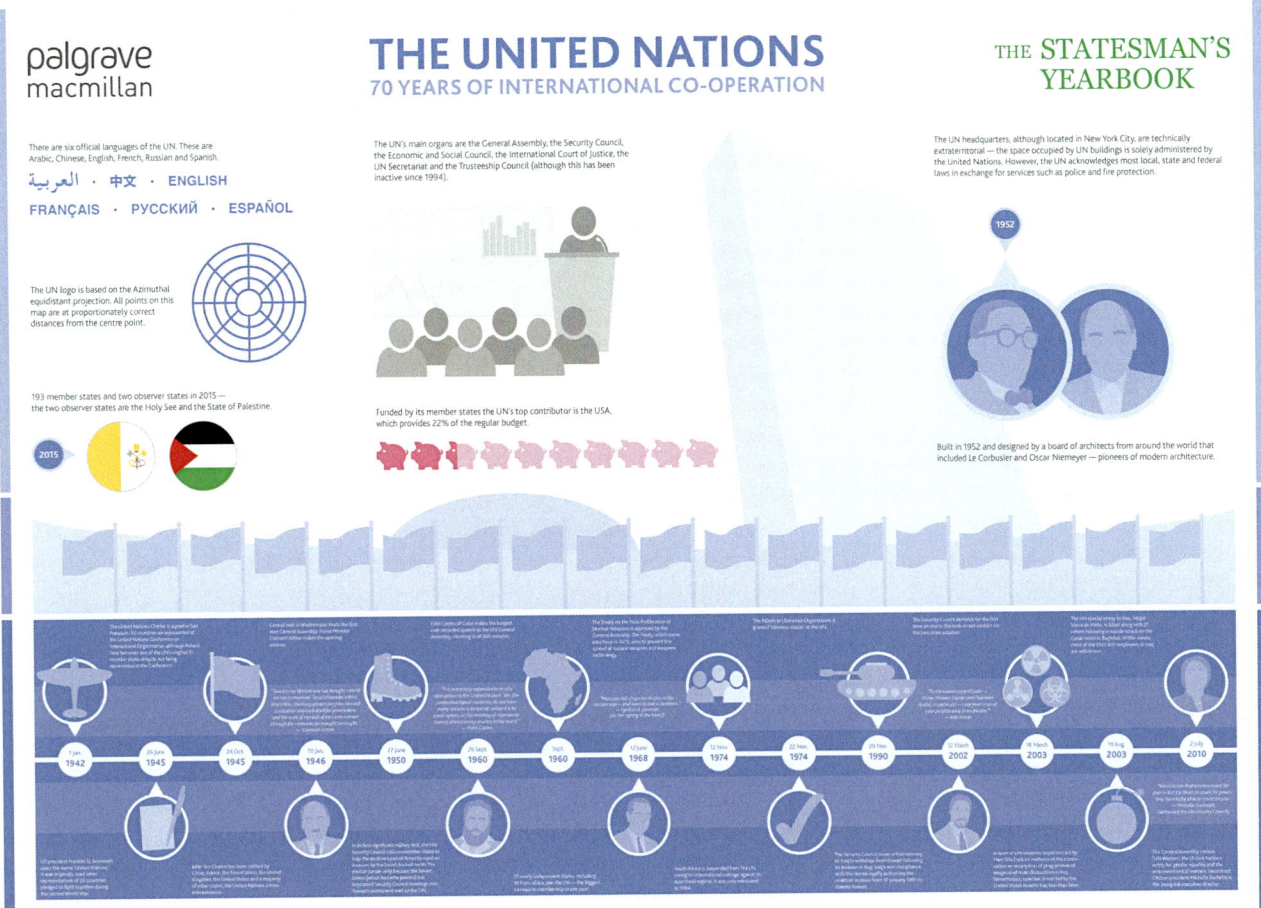

25 Years since the Gulf War

palgrave
macmillan

WAR AND COMMODITIES
25 YEARS SINCE THE GULF WAR

THE STATESMAN'S
YEARBOOK

In 2009 British chemist Sir David King predicted that wars in the future would be fought over natural resources, saying that 'Future historians might look back on our particular recent past and see the Iraq war as the first of the conflicts of this kind — the first of the resource wars'. On the 25th anniversary of the Gulf War, we look at the historical relationship between war and the earth's resources.

Top five countries by percentage share of total proved oil reserves:

Venezuela 17.5% | Saudi Arabia 15.7% | Canada 10.2% | Iran 9.3% | Iraq 8.8%

Percentage (%)

The Resource Curse
An economic theory and paradox that countries with an abundance of natural resources such as minerals and fuels tend to suffer more from poor economic growth than countries with fewer resources.

OIL

In 2014 about **46%** of the crude oil processed in US refineries was imported.

China's oil consumption growth accounted for about **43%** of global oil consumption growth in 2014.

THE COD WARS
1958–1976

A series of conflicts between Iceland and the United Kingdom (and to a lesser extent West Germany and Belgium) regarding fishing rights in the North Atlantic.
Three deaths are attributed to the conflicts with navies on both sides exchanging fire in waters surrounding Iceland.

THE TEA ACT
1773

When the British parliament tried to reduce the surplus of tea held by the then struggling British East India Company by granting the company tax-exempted rights to export the product directly to North America, colonists responded by boarding tea ships moored in Boston and dumping their shipments into the harbour. The act would have effectively undercut North American tea merchants and, as a consequence, galvanized existing anti-British attitudes in the colonies. The destruction of the tea in Boston is widely considered to be a key event of the burgeoning American Revolution.

CHACO WAR
1932–1935

The deadliest conflict fought in South America in the 20th century centred on a region called 'Chaco Boreal', thought to be rich in oil reserves. The war between Bolivia and Paraguay was sparked by rival oil companies—Royal Dutch Shell and Standard Oil—undertaking exploration on behalf of the two countries. Following the deaths of approximately 100,000 troops on both sides, Paraguay emerged as the victor, controlling most of the disputed territory by mid-1935. However, no commercially viable amounts of oil were discovered by Paraguay until 2012.

WORLD WAR I
1914–1918

One of World War One's often forgotten battles was fought by the navies of Germany and the United Kingdom off the coast of South America over 'caliche', a substance rich in sodium nitrate that is a key component of munitions. By 1911 Chile exported approximately 2.5m. tonnes per year, and as war broke out in Europe powers recognized the need to secure their interests in this natural resource. Following skirmishes in the South Atlantic, the United Kingdom successfully blockaded enemy shipments and German nitrate holdings were eliminated. However, Germany was able to successfully develop a method for synthetizing nitrates on an industrial scale, thus prolonging the war.

SUDAN/SOUTH SUDAN CONFLICT
2012

Less than a year after South Sudan gained independence in 2011 a conflict broke out with its neighbour, Sudan, over oil-rich border states. In response to a dispute over transit fees, Sudan closed the South's pipelines running through its territory with South Sudan reacting by occupying Sudan's largest oilfield near the town of Heglig. Fighting between the two countries resulted in casualties on both sides and a humanitarian crisis after civilians fled areas hit by conflict.

SUEZ CRISIS
1956

The Suez Canal, connecting the Mediterranean and Red Seas, allowed transportation for two-thirds of Western Europe's oil in 1955. Following the Egyptian revolution and Gamal Abdel Nasser's assumption of the presidency in 1956, the Canal was nationalized, having been jointly owned by British and French private investors. This, in part, led to the invasion of Egypt by Israel, the United Kingdom and France.
Approximately 2,000 troops on both sides were killed, with the crisis leading to the resignation of UK prime minister Anthony Eden and Egypt retaining control over the Canal.

WORLD WAR II OIL CAMPAIGN
1940–1945

The Allies identified German over-reliance on oil to fuel its campaigns in Europe, North Africa and Russia as a weakness even before the outbreak of war in 1939. Accordingly, RAF and USAAF bombers strategically attacked German refineries, with entire operations dedicated to knocking out vital oil infrastructure. 'Operation Tidal Wave', launched in Aug. 1943, attempted to destroy nine oil refineries in Romania but failed, losing 53 aircraft and 660 crewmen in a single day—the deadliest mission in US Air Force history.

TERRITORIAL DISPUTES IN SOUTH CHINA SEA
Ongoing

The area has recently been the subject of territorial disputes involving countries including China, Brunei, Malaysia, the Philippines and Vietnam over fishing rights and exploitation of unproven undersea oil and natural gas deposits. Claimant nations have, in the past, opened fire on fishing boats and allegedly regularly perform military drills in the area designed to simulate potential conflict over the region.

GULF WAR
1990–1991

The Iraqi invasion of Kuwait in 1990 was arguably largely fuelled by regional economic reliance on oil. Iraq had accused Kuwait of exceeding OPEC set quotas for oil production, which resulted in a depreciation of its value on the global market. Further accusations of Kuwait 'slant-drilling' within Iraqi borders (in addition to a range of other geopolitical tensions) led to the invasion of Kuwait by Iraq in Aug. 1990.
During the conflict, which was ended only after the intervention of coalition forces led by the United States, the Iraqi army set fire to 700 oil wells whilst in retreat from Kuwait and deliberately dumped approximately 400m. gallons of crude oil into the Persian Gulf in an apparent attempt to stop a potential landing by US Marines.

282 coalition deaths · 20,000–35,000 Iraqi deaths

80 Years since the Spanish Civil War

palgrave macmillan

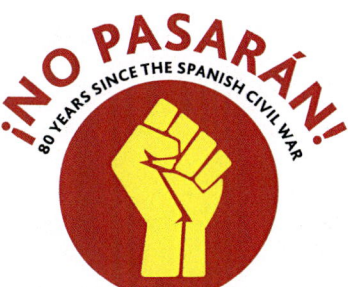

¡NO PASARÁN!
80 YEARS SINCE THE SPANISH CIVIL WAR

THE **STATESMAN'S** YEARBOOK

July 2016 marked the 80th anniversary of the start of the Spanish Civil War.

In the 1930s Spain found itself divided between left-wing Republicanism and right-wing Nationalism with the monarchy, landowners, clergy and the army at odds with the impoverished workers and peasants represented by the socialists and trade unions.

In 1936 armed conflict between these two sides broke out and would continue until 1939, resulting in the deaths of approximately 500,000 people and the establishment of a decades-long dictatorship.

Nationalists:
Comprised a number of political groups that supported the 1936 coup against the Republic, including rebel military units and the fascist 'Falange' party. They were directly supported by their right-wing ideological allies, Germany, Italy and Portugal, who sent troops and material to fight the left-wing Republicans.

Republicans:
Supporters of the Second Spanish Republic which was established in 1931. This included the Spanish Republican Army, the 'Popular Front' electoral alliance, and other socialist, communist and anarchist unions and groups. The Republicans were also supported by the Soviet Union, which provided material assistance, and Mexico, which contributed diplomatic aid.

International brigades:
The 'International Brigades' comprised foreign volunteers fighting for the Republicans. Amassed from many different countries, their ranks included the famous writers George Orwell and Ernest Hemingway. Other famous supporters included Willy Brandt, who later became the Chancellor of West Germany, and Paul Robeson, the American singer and actor.

An estimated **500,000** people died in the war

while **450,000** fled the country

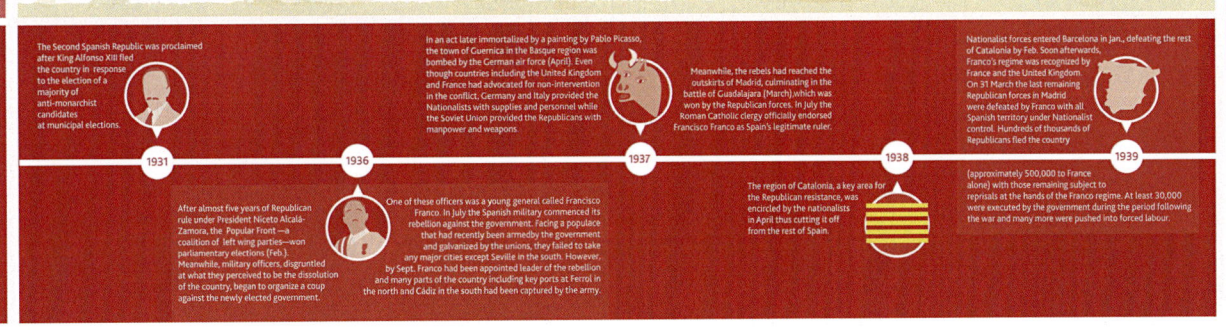

1931 — The Second Spanish Republic was proclaimed after King Alfonso XIII fled the country in response to the election of a majority of anti-monarchist candidates at municipal elections.

1936 — In an act later immortalized by a painting by Pablo Picasso, the town of Guernica in the Basque region was bombed by the German air force (April). Even though countries including the United Kingdom and France had advocated for non-intervention in the conflict, Germany and Italy provided the Nationalists with supplies and personnel while the Soviet Union provided the Republicans with manpower and weapons.

After almost five years of Republican rule under President Niceto Alcalá-Zamora, the 'Popular Front' — a coalition of left wing parties — won parliamentary elections (Feb.). Meanwhile, military officers, disgruntled at what they perceived to be the dissolution of the country, began to organize a coup against the newly elected government.

One of these officers was a young general called Francisco Franco. In July the Spanish military commenced its rebellion against the government. Facing a populace that had recently been armed by the government and galvanized by the unions, they failed to take any major cities except Seville in the south. However, by Sept. Franco had been appointed leader of the rebellion and many parts of the country including key ports at Ferrol in the north and Cádiz in the south had been captured by the army.

1937 — Meanwhile, the rebels had reached the outskirts of Madrid, culminating in the battle of Guadalajara (March), which was won by the Republican forces. In July the Roman Catholic clergy officially endorsed Francisco Franco as Spain's legitimate ruler.

1938 — The region of Catalonia, a key area for the Republican resistance, was encircled by the nationalists in April thus cutting it off from the rest of Spain.

1939 — Nationalist forces entered Barcelona in Jan., defeating the rest of Catalonia by Feb. Soon afterwards, Franco's regime was recognized by France and the United Kingdom. On 31 March the last remaining Republican forces in Madrid were defeated by Franco with all Spanish territory under Nationalist control. Hundreds of thousands of Republicans fled the country (approximately 500,000 to France alone) with those remaining subject to reprisals at the hands of the Franco regime. At least 30,000 were executed by the government during the period following the war and many more were pushed into forced labour.

The History of the United States Presidential Election

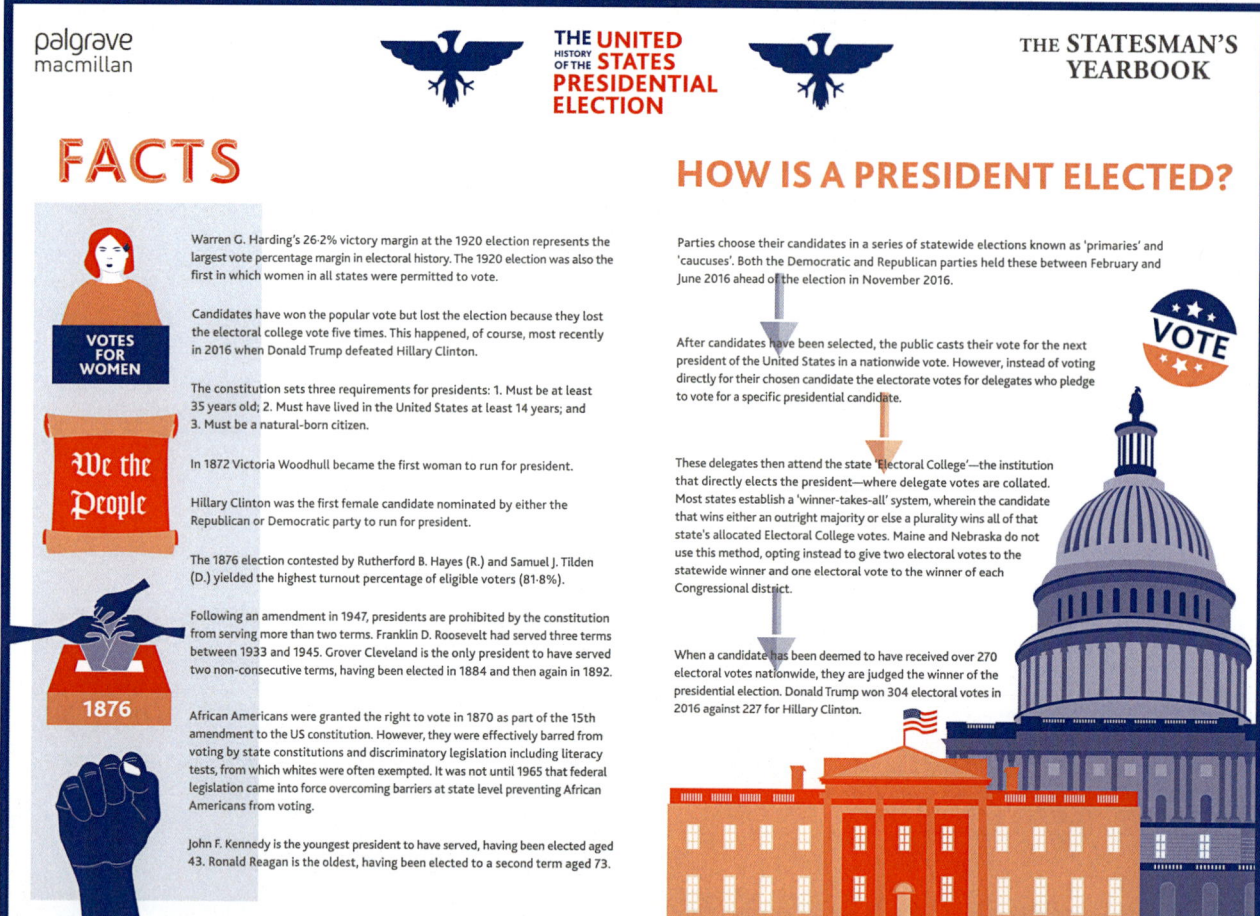

palgrave
macmillan

THE UNITED
HISTORY STATES
OF THE PRESIDENTIAL
ELECTION

THE STATESMAN'S
YEARBOOK

FACTS

VOTES FOR WOMEN

We the People

1876

Warren G. Harding's 26·2% victory margin at the 1920 election represents the largest vote percentage margin in electoral history. The 1920 election was also the first in which women in all states were permitted to vote.

Candidates have won the popular vote but lost the election because they lost the electoral college vote five times. This happened, of course, most recently in 2016 when Donald Trump defeated Hillary Clinton.

The constitution sets three requirements for presidents: 1. Must be at least 35 years old; 2. Must have lived in the United States at least 14 years; and 3. Must be a natural-born citizen.

In 1872 Victoria Woodhull became the first woman to run for president.

Hillary Clinton was the first female candidate nominated by either the Republican or Democratic party to run for president.

The 1876 election contested by Rutherford B. Hayes (R.) and Samuel J. Tilden (D.) yielded the highest turnout percentage of eligible voters (81·8%).

Following an amendment in 1947, presidents are prohibited by the constitution from serving more than two terms. Franklin D. Roosevelt had served three terms between 1933 and 1945. Grover Cleveland is the only president to have served two non-consecutive terms, having been elected in 1884 and then again in 1892.

African Americans were granted the right to vote in 1870 as part of the 15th amendment to the US constitution. However, they were effectively barred from voting by state constitutions and discriminatory legislation including literacy tests, from which whites were often exempted. It was not until 1965 that federal legislation came into force overcoming barriers at state level preventing African Americans from voting.

John F. Kennedy is the youngest president to have served, having been elected aged 43. Ronald Reagan is the oldest, having been elected to a second term aged 73.

HOW IS A PRESIDENT ELECTED?

VOTE

Parties choose their candidates in a series of statewide elections known as 'primaries' and 'caucuses'. Both the Democratic and Republican parties held these between February and June 2016 ahead of the election in November 2016.

After candidates have been selected, the public casts their vote for the next president of the United States in a nationwide vote. However, instead of voting directly for their chosen candidate the electorate votes for delegates who pledge to vote for a specific presidential candidate.

These delegates then attend the state 'Electoral College'—the institution that directly elects the president—where delegate votes are collated. Most states establish a 'winner-takes-all' system, wherein the candidate that wins either an outright majority or else a plurality wins all of that state's allocated Electoral College votes. Maine and Nebraska do not use this method, opting instead to give two electoral votes to the statewide winner and one electoral vote to the winner of each Congressional district.

When a candidate has been deemed to have received over 270 electoral votes nationwide, they are judged the winner of the presidential election. Donald Trump won 304 electoral votes in 2016 against 227 for Hillary Clinton.

100 Years since the Start of the Russian Revolution

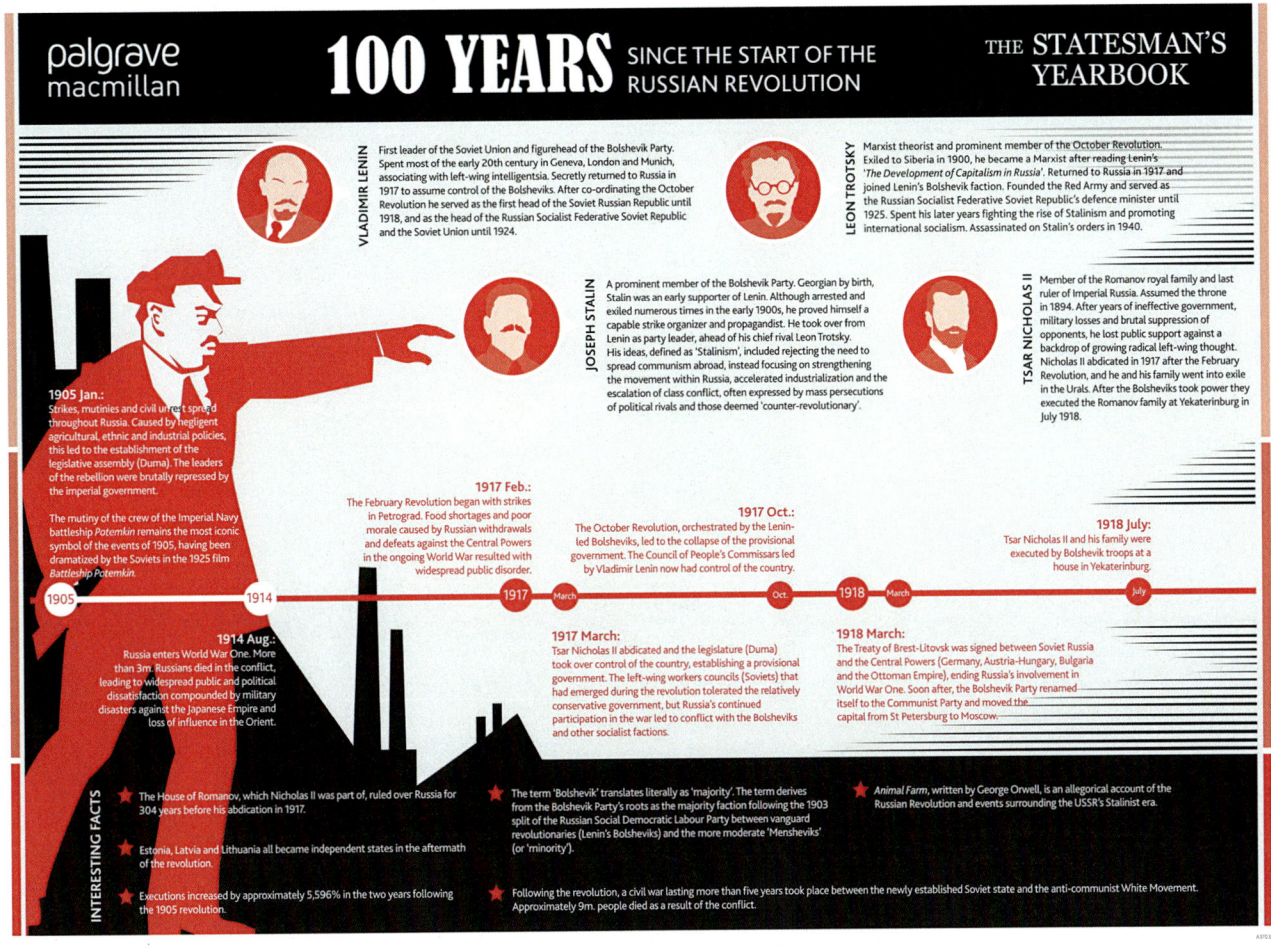

30 Years since Black Monday

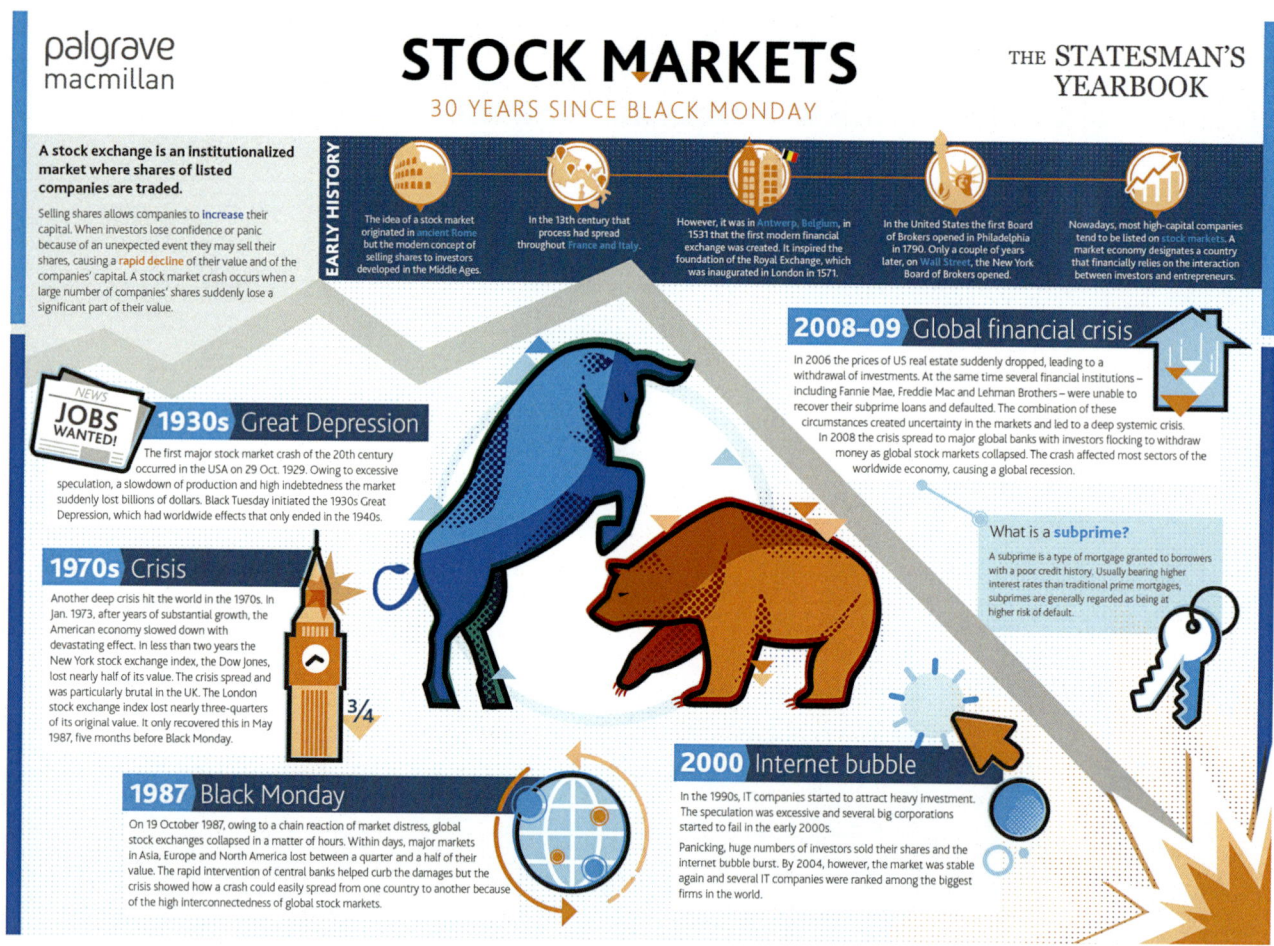

palgrave
macmillan

STOCK MARKETS
30 YEARS SINCE BLACK MONDAY

THE STATESMAN'S
YEARBOOK

A stock exchange is an institutionalized market where shares of listed companies are traded.

Selling shares allows companies to increase their capital. When investors lose confidence or panic because of an unexpected event they may sell their shares, causing a rapid decline of their value and of the companies' capital. A stock market crash occurs when a large number of companies' shares suddenly lose a significant part of their value.

EARLY HISTORY

The idea of a stock market originated in ancient Rome but the modern concept of selling shares to investors developed in the Middle Ages.

In the 13th century that process had spread throughout France and Italy.

However, it was in Antwerp, Belgium, in 1531 that the first modern financial exchange was created. It inspired the foundation of the Royal Exchange, which was inaugurated in London in 1571.

In the United States the first Board of Brokers opened in Philadelphia in 1790. Only a couple of years later, on Wall Street, the New York Board of Brokers opened.

Nowadays, most high-capital companies tend to be listed on stock markets. A market economy designates a country that financially relies on the interaction between investors and entrepreneurs.

2008–09 Global financial crisis

In 2006 the prices of US real estate suddenly dropped, leading to a withdrawal of investments. At the same time several financial institutions – including Fannie Mae, Freddie Mac and Lehman Brothers – were unable to recover their subprime loans and defaulted. The combination of these circumstances created uncertainty in the markets and led to a deep systemic crisis.
In 2008 the crisis spread to major global banks with investors flocking to withdraw money as global stock markets collapsed. The crash affected most sectors of the worldwide economy, causing a global recession.

JOBS WANTED!

1930s Great Depression

The first major stock market crash of the 20th century occurred in the USA on 29 Oct. 1929. Owing to excessive speculation, a slowdown of production and high indebtedness the market suddenly lost billions of dollars. Black Tuesday initiated the 1930s Great Depression, which had worldwide effects that only ended in the 1940s.

What is a subprime?

A subprime is a type of mortgage granted to borrowers with a poor credit history. Usually bearing higher interest rates than traditional prime mortgages, subprimes are generally regarded as being at higher risk of default.

1970s Crisis

Another deep crisis hit the world in the 1970s. In Jan. 1973, after years of substantial growth, the American economy slowed down with devastating effect. In less than two years the New York stock exchange index, the Dow Jones, lost nearly half of its value. The crisis spread and was particularly brutal in the UK. The London stock exchange index lost nearly three-quarters of its original value. It only recovered this in May 1987, five months before Black Monday.

3/4

2000 Internet bubble

In the 1990s, IT companies started to attract heavy investment. The speculation was excessive and several big corporations started to fail in the early 2000s.

Panicking, huge numbers of investors sold their shares and the internet bubble burst. By 2004, however, the market was stable again and several IT companies were ranked among the biggest firms in the world.

1987 Black Monday

On 19 October 1987, owing to a chain reaction of market distress, global stock exchanges collapsed in a matter of hours. Within days, major markets in Asia, Europe and North America lost between a quarter and a half of their value. The rapid intervention of central banks helped curb the damages but the crisis showed how a crash could easily spread from one country to another because of the high interconnectedness of global stock markets.

A Brief History of the Vietnam War, 50 Years after the Tet Offensive

THE STATESMAN'S YEARBOOK

THE VIETNAM WAR
50 YEARS SINCE THE TET OFFENSIVE

DIEN BIEN PHU

HANOI

The Tet Offensive is considered a turning point in the Vietnam War.

After years of guerrilla warfare, the North Vietnamese leaders switched to a conventional large scale strategy in an attempt to win the war. It consisted of a series of attacks by the National Liberation Front (also known as the **Viet Cong**) and the North Vietnamese Army across South Vietnam, including Saigon (now **Ho Chi Minh City**) and Hue.

The Offensive was launched in late January 1968 and was halted by the joint forces of the US Army and the Army of the Republic of Vietnam on 28 March of the same year, 50 years ago. The word 'Tet' comes from the name of the Vietnamese New Year celebrations.

The change of scale initiated by the Tet Offensive attracted the attention of the American public. From then on, opposition to the war (including from public figures) put pressure on successive White House administrations to end US involvement.

NORTH VIETNAM
SOUTH VIETNAM

Ho Chi Minh Trail
North Vietnam created this strategic route to move supplies and people into the South. It was considered **"one of the great achievements of military engineering of the 20th century."**

SAIGON
(now Ho Chi Minh City)

1945 THE ORIGINS OF THE WAR

When **World War II** came to an end in 1945, the French colonial administration in **Indochina** was weakened and disorganized. The **Viet Minh**, an armed nationalist movement created by **Ho Chi Minh** within the Indochinese Communist Party, took advantage of the post-war confusion to occupy the eastern coast of the Indochina peninsula and to proclaim the independence of the Democratic Republic of Vietnam (North Vietnam).

Despite the French efforts to regain control over the territory, the Viet Minh won a decisive battle at **Dien Bien Phu** in May 1954. Two months later the Geneva Conference established the partition of Indochina in four states: the Kingdom of Cambodia, the Kingdom of Laos, the communist-controlled Democratic Republic of Vietnam and the Republic of Vietnam (South Vietnam).

1955 THE AMERICAN INVOLVEMENT

In 1955 the Vietnamese communist party won several elections and the Viet Minh began a series of insurrections in the North and in the South. The previous year, the president of the USA **Dwight Eisenhower** (1953–61) formulated the '**domino theory**': at the peak of Cold War tensions the USA feared that if any country fell under the influence of communism, its neighbours would follow suit.

As there was no declaration of war, there is no clear date of the beginning of the Vietnam War. However, many Western historians consider that the conflict turned into a war on 1 November 1955, the day most American troops in Southeast Asia were ordered to relocate to Vietnam.

1975 FALL OF SAIGON AND REUNIFICATION OF VIETNAM

In the first hours of 30 April 1975 the North Vietnamese Army captured the southern capital, Saigon. American officials and thousands of civilians were promptly evacuated. By mid-morning South Vietnam had capitulated. Saigon was renamed **Ho Chi Minh City**. The **reunification** of the country as the Socialist Republic of Vietnam was achieved on 2 July 1976.

palgrave macmillan

5 **AMERICAN PRESIDENTS** HELD OFFICE DURING THE VIETNAM WAR:
- Dwight Eisenhower (1953–61)
- John F. Kennedy (1961–63)
- Lyndon Johnson (1963–69)
- Richard Nixon (1969–74)
- Gerald Ford (1974–77)

SEVERAL MASSACRES WERE PERPETRATED THROUGHOUT THE WAR
Notably the My Lai and the Phong Nhi and Phong Nhat massacres. Hundreds of thousands of civilians had to flee Vietnam. It is difficult to establish the human cost of the war and estimates vary greatly. However, it is thought somewhere between 1.2m. and 3.2m. people lost their lives during the conflict.